COLLEGE
FOOTBALL

ENCYCLOPEDIA

Cover design by Eric Baker Design Associates, Inc.

Book design and composition by Mada Design, Inc. / Stonesong Press.

Helmet illustrations by Carey Chiselbrook; renderings by Mike Johnson of Chapel Design & Marketing Ltd.

ISBN: 1-4013-3703-1

ESPN books are available for special promotions and premiums. For details contact Michael Rentas, Assistant Director, Inventory Operations, Hyperion, 77 West 66th Street, 11th floor, New York, New York 10023, or call 212-456-0133.

10 9 8 7 6 5 4 3 2

TABLE OF CONTENTS

HOW TO USE THIS BOOK

When we started this project three years ago, we knew only that there was no such thing as a college football encyclopedia. If you wanted to know who finished third in the voting for the 1968 Heisman Trophy, you had to troll the Internet. If you wished to confirm that Michigan was ranked sixth on Sept. 22, 1997, you hauled yourself to the local library for an afternoon of research. We wanted to have that information and more—much, much more—available at our fingertips. And so, we started combing through newspapers and media guides and bowl records. Before long, we had enlisted the brightest minds in the college football universe in our effort.

What you hold in your hands is the fruits of that labor, 1,632 pages of records and stats, polls and box scores, fight song lyrics and pep talk quotes, enough data to satisfy the needs of any college football fan. The information is broken up into five sections. The first—entitled **The Game**—is a collection of historical essays on hot-button topics such as

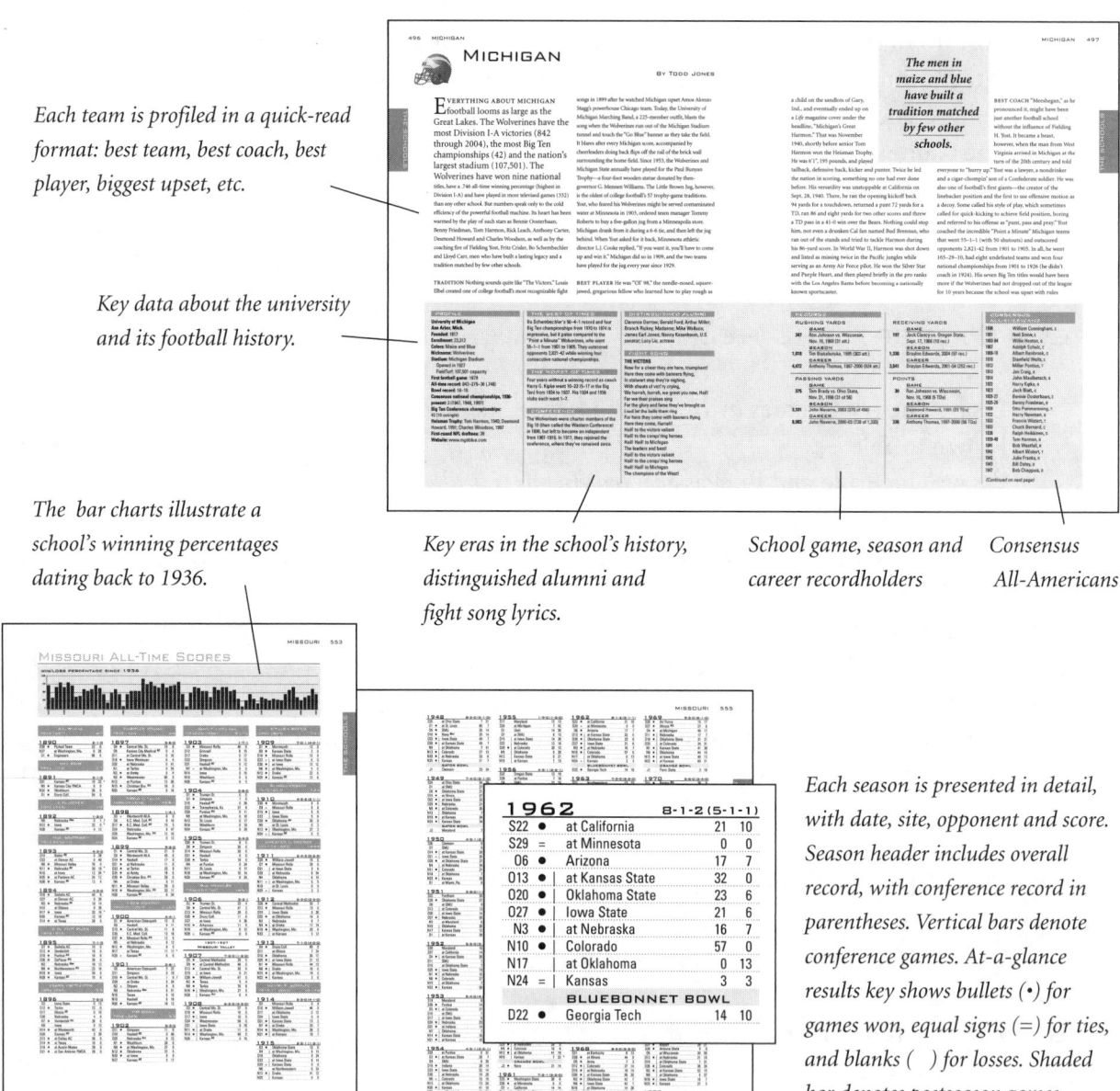

Each team is profiled in a quick-read format: best team, best coach, best player, biggest upset, etc.

Key data about the university and its football history.

The bar charts illustrate a school's winning percentages dating back to 1936.

Key eras in the school's history, distinguished alumni and fight song lyrics.

School game, season and career recordholders

Consensus All-Americans

Each season is presented in detail, with date, site, opponent and score. Season header includes overall record, with conference record in parentheses. Vertical bars denote conference games. At-a-glance results key shows bullets (•) for games won, equal signs (=) for ties, and blanks ( ) for losses. Shaded bar denotes postseason games.

the cult of the All-Powerful coach, the most low-down, dirty recruiting tricks and the timeless wisdom of *Rudy*. The second—**The Schools**—contains vital information on each of the 119 Division I-A programs, the Ivy League schools and the historically black colleges. The third—**The Annual Review**—delivers year-by-year snapshots for every season dating back to 1869, everything from Top 25 teams to leading rushers to Heisman Trophy vote counts. The fourth—**The Bowls**—offers summaries for every

significant postseason game ever played. And the fifth—**Postgame Wrap-Up**—serves up an all-you-can-eat menu of Top 11 lists from a distinguished panel of experts. We invite you to send us your own.

One other feature worth noting is the 16-page color insert chronicling the evolution of the helmets at 128 schools.

We have tried our best to assemble this information in a manner that is easy to read. Below you will find instructions on where to look for answers to your questions.

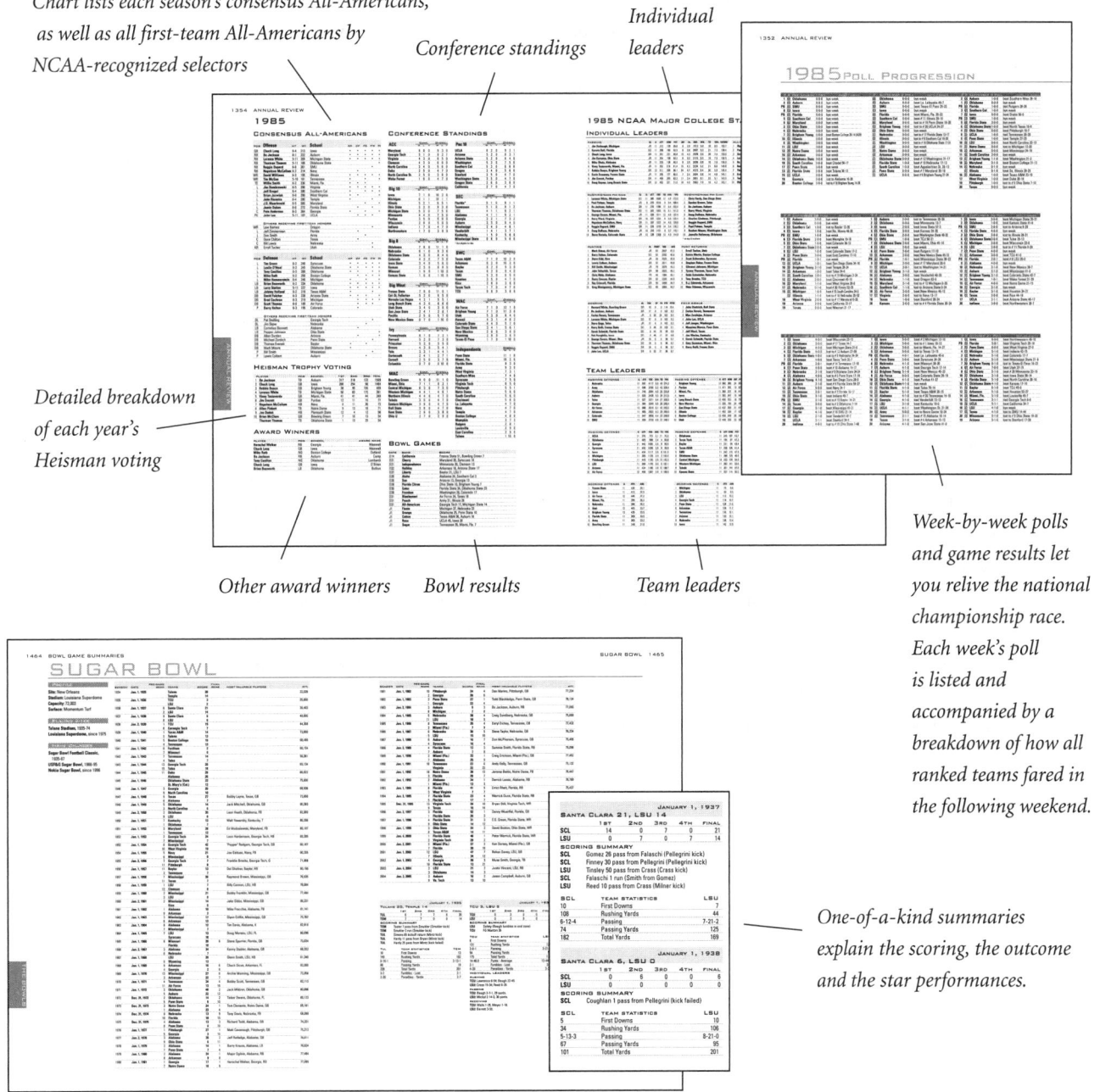

Chart lists each season's consensus All-Americans, as well as all first-team All-Americans by NCAA-recognized selectors

Conference standings

Individual leaders

Detailed breakdown of each year's Heisman voting

Other award winners

Bowl results

Team leaders

Week-by-week polls and game results let you relive the national championship race. Each week's poll is listed and accompanied by a breakdown of how all ranked teams fared in the following weekend.

One-of-a-kind summaries explain the scoring, the outcome and the star performances.

EDITOR'S NOTE

BY MICHAEL MacCAMBRIDGE

It has long been a given that baseball is the American team sport with the deepest roots and richest traditions. Yet on Nov. 6, 1869, when Princeton and Rutgers played the first intercollegiate football game, the National League of Professional Base Ball Clubs had yet to be formed. And the first Rose Bowl game, played between Michigan and Stanford on Jan. 1, 1902, predated the first World Series game by nearly two years.

If baseball became the national pastime in the subsequent decades, college football developed into something nearly as important—the most distinctive of American sporting passions.

For better or worse—and it's mostly the former—the convoluted structure and circumstances of college football remain unique even today. This book is an attempt to document that inimitable universe, in a manner more comprehensive than has ever been attempted before.

Inside this book you'll find:

• A series of vivid, memorable essays by some of the best writers in the business, covering nearly every major aspect of the sport's development.

• Capsule histories of every school in major college football, along with the seminal Ivy League and the nearly two dozen historically black colleges and universities that played such an important role in the development of the game in the middle of the 20th century. Each capsule history includes our expert writers' opinions on the best teams, coaches and players in the history of the school, as well as stories about their biggest and most memorable games, and details about each school's unique traditions and heritage. We also have extensive data for each school, ranging from the lyrics to each school's fight song to consensus All-Americans to individual record-holders to

the annual rushing, passing and receiving leaders going back, in most cases, several decades.

• All-time scores for each of the schools in the National Collegiate Athletic Association's Division I-A major college classification, plus the historically significant Ivy League schools. Those game results (more than 111,000 in all) include more than mere final scores. These sections are packed with information, including at-a-glance symbols to denote a win, loss or tie, and whether the contest was a conference game, and data including the date and site of the game.

• A thumbnail overview of every season in college football history, including consensus All-American teams and other award winners, conference standings and bowl results, and NCAA individual and team statistics. You'll find not just consensus All-American *selections*, but the first-team All-America *squads* for every selector recognized by the NCAA. There's plenty of other fascinating detail as well, including top-10 charts in team and individual statistical categories, from the NCAA, and the breakdown of voting (first, second and third place, plus the top 10 overall vote-getters) in the Heisman Trophy balloting, from the Downtown Athletic Club.

• A weekly review of every writers and coaches poll in college football history, along with the weekly results of every ranked team. These poll progression charts, an exclusive feature debuting in this book, provide the most detailed overview ever of each season's race for the mythical national championship.

They also offer a window to information that no one has compiled before. You may already know that only six consensus national champions (LSU, 1958; Minnesota, 1960; USC, 1962; Clemson, 1981; Brigham Young, 1984; Oklahoma, 2000) began the preseason unranked.

But I bet you didn't know that in the history of the AP poll, two teams have jumped from No. 8 to No. 1 in a single week. Wisconsin did it first, in the Sept. 29, 1952, poll, and Miami (Fla.) did it 36 years later in the Sept. 5, 1988, poll. (The Hurricanes were the only team to enjoy a larger jump from one poll to the next, going from No. 10 preseason to No. 1 in the first in-season poll of 1984, but there was a two-week gap there, during which Miami played two games.)

The biggest drop? Pittsburgh was ranked No. 1 in the Oct. 16 poll of 1939, then lost to Duquesne, 21-13, and dropped to No. 18.

There is much to be gleaned from this data, and we have just begun to do so. But as long as polls are instrumental in determining national champions, these charts will be a vital document chronicling each season's national championship race.

• A summary of scoring and/or statistics for every major college bowl game ever played. The spate of corporate sponsorship and name changes have robbed the bowl games of some of their purity, and the sheer volume of contests has somewhat diluted their significance, but their distinctive role in American sporting culture is hard to overstate. And here we present the most complete statistical record of more than a century of postseason showdowns. We've also added some texture to our histories of these games by including, for the first time anywhere, a complete list of where schools were ranked prior to and after each bowl game.

* * * *

There are books that address one or two of the above elements, but never before have all these different sources of information been contained, in such great detail, between two covers.

Getting that information there has been a labor of love.

One of the things that makes college football so absorbing is the myriad local and regional differences in the game. Those very same qualities have made the sport resistant to systematic documentation, especially during the sport's first century.

By contrast, the National Football League, with its rigorously documented record-keeping, has a catalog of every play in every game dating back for much of the league's history. In college football, though, there are several instances where two teams can't even agree on the final score of their own games, much less the statistics. We've tried to document those differences, ironing out the ones we can, and making note of those that remain matters of historical dispute.

There will be even more information and more detail in future editions. And we'd like your input. In a project this ambitious, there are bound to be mistakes. If you spot one, tell us and we'll correct it. Just go to www.espn.com and search with the keyword CFE. Then tell us what you found. We'll double-check it, then post your correction. That's not all. At the end of every season, we'll post updates on key stats, national leaders and the like.

We also hope you'll use the *Encyclopedia* link to contribute your own take on another innovation in this book, the Elevens section, where fans are asked to catalog their own lists of bests and personal favorites. Take a look at what some of the most respected experts in the game said in the back of the book, and then share your own choices with us. We'll print the best choices each week during the season at ESPN.com.

But for now, sit back and enjoy reveling in the rich texture of this sport. I'm sure there are some casual college football fans somewhere. But I haven't met any of them yet. This book is for you and all the rest of us—the true believers.

Fondling College Football

An Introduction

BY DAN JENKINS

COUNT ME AS ONE OF THOSE WITH A SINFUL LUST FOR college football. And yet I've never painted my face purple and white. Never worn a pig on my head. Never wheeled a two-ton smoker into a stadium parking lot and tried to barbecue a duplex. I've only occasionally contemplated whether life was more rewarding for a Cornhusker than it was for a Boilermaker, and rarely wondered what you'd get if you crossed a Hawkeye or a Buckeye with a Jayhawk or a Hokie. For that matter, what is a Hokie?

But I did marry a homecoming queen, which means I know as much about college football as the next person—as long as the next person is not Darrell Royal or Bear Bryant. What I mainly know is that college football is the most emotional, hysterical, colorful, musical, thunderous, riveting, dramatic, historical, suspenseful and meaningful game that was ever developed by mankind and Walter Camp for passionate Americans and shapely, adorable cheerleaders. College football is the sport where 80,000 people show up to watch a Poll Bowl, half of them wearing one color, half of them wearing another color. This is important, because 80,000 people wearing any color never filled a stadium to watch a math quiz.

It's also the sport in which the 40,000 fans of the winning team will shout, "We're No. 1!" for the next several years, and the 40,000 fans on the losing side will drown themselves in tears and whiskey.

But as somebody once said—it could have been Duffy Daugherty at Michigan State—"When you're playing for the national championship, it's not a matter of life and death. It's more important than that."

I'm particularly happy that the game was deemed important enough to urge Michael MacCambridge to dream up this crowd-pleasing book and go about the business of assembling, editing, scrubbing, and window-cleaning it. Michael is, of course, a college football junkie himself.

If you can't find whatever stat you're looking for in here, I suggest you run MacCambridge on a dive play

at Tommy Nobis and Dick Butkus, or send him on a crossing pattern over the middle between, say, Ronnie Lott and Jake Scott.

But without further adieu, let me list all the reasons why college football is the greatest game ever invented by mankind and Walter Camp for passionate Americans and shapely, adorable cheerleaders.

Not in any particular order, they are:

- Shapely, adorable cheerleaders.
- Fight songs. From "Wake up the echoes" to "Fight the team across the field" to "There is no place like Nebraska" to "Send the Yellow Jackets to a watery grave" to "We are the Aggies," and on into "Hail to the victors valiant, hail to the conquering heroes."
- College teams don't move, unlike NFL teams. The Crimson Tide, for example, has never left Tuscaloosa and relocated to Ann Arbor so the rich dwarf who owns the team can have more luxury boxes.
- The USC card section, one simmering Saturday afternoon in the LA Coliseum, spelling out, "FUCLA."
- Mr. Inside and Mr. Outside.
- The wire that Coach Earl "Red" Blaik received on Dec. 2, 1944, after the Black Knights of the Hudson had beaten Navy to complete a perfect season: "THE GREATEST OF ALL ARMY TEAMS. WE HAVE STOPPED THE WAR TO CELEBRATE YOUR MAGNIFICENT SUCCESS. MACARTHUR."
- Grantland Rice sitting in the press box of the Polo Grounds that day in 1924 and typing, "Outlined against a blue, gray October sky, the Four Horsemen rode again. In dramatic lore they are known as Famine, Pestilence, Destruction and Death. These are only aliases. Their real names are Stuhldreher, Miller, Crowley, and Layden. They formed the crest of the South Bend cyclone before which another fighting Army football team was swept over the precipice ... "
- The Michigan helmet.
- Bowl games before the contemptible BCS.
- In fact, bowl games before Poulan Weedeaters, which is to say before corporate sponsors.
- The glorious days when layouts of the All-America teams were plastered over the front pages of sport sections. Now, owing to misguided editors, you're lucky if you can find the All-America team on the agate page next to the bowling results.

• Granny, Damon, Ring, and all those ink-stained heroes of typewriter deadlines.

• Shapely, adorable collegiate showgirls.

• The words of Dr. George L. Cross, president of the University of Oklahoma, during the Sooners' 31-game wining streak from 1948 through 1950 (which is not to be confused with the Sooners' 47-game win streak from 1953 to 1957): "We want to build a university the football team can be proud of."

• "We'll fight 'em 'til hell freezes over, then fight 'em on the ice!" —TCU Coach Dutch Meyer just before his 1938 national champs, led by "Slingshot" Davey O'Brien, met Carnegie Tech in the Sugar Bowl.

• USC's John McKay saying before a No. 1 showdown with UCLA in 1967: "Remember this, guys. No matter what happens today, there are 800 million Chinese who don't give a damn."

• "The Seven Blocks of Granite." That would be your Lombardi and them at Fordham.

• "Little Boy Blue." That would be your Albie Booth at Yale.

• "The Baby-Face Assassin." That would be your Bill Corbus at Stanford.

• "The Noblest Trojan of Them All." Your Morley Drury at USC.

• Darrell Royal saying, "Talk about X's and O's all you want to, but most football games are won by angry people."

• Bear Bryant saying, "Offense wins games, defense wins titles."

• Bear giving credit to "good Mamas and Papas."

• Bum Phillips saying, "Bear can take his'n and beat your'n, or he can take your'n and beat his'n."

• Barry Switzer saying, "I want to call my book 'Have You Peed in a Bottle for the Trainer Today?' but the publisher won't let me."

• Frank Broyles saying, "Luck follows speed."

• "The Team of Destiny."

• Whoever the guy was who described Woody Hayes' offense as "three yards and a cloud of dust."

• Whoever said, "Chic Harley built Ohio Stadium as

> ## The Crimson Tide has never left Tuscaloosa and relocated in Ann Arbor to obtain more luxury boxes.

surely as God gave us concrete."

• Shapely, adorable showgirls.

• "The Blond Blizzard."

• "Undefeated, untied, unscored upon—and uninvited."

• "Kill, Bubba, kill!"

• "In Dodd we trust."

• "The Texas Aggie band has never lost a halftime."

• "A punt, a pass and a prayer."

• "A streak of fire, a breath of flame."

• "Old 98."

• Amos Alonzo Stagg.

• Touchdown Moses.

• "Tie one for the Gipper."

• The Stanford band.

• The Heisman Trophy.

***

Timeout. If the Heisman had started in 1889, for instance, the same year All-America teams originated, the winner undoubtedly would have been William Walter "Pudge" Heffelfinger, the Yale guard. He might have won the first three.

There could have been other multiple winners, such as T. Truxtun Hare at Penn, Charlie Daly, the brainy lad who made All-America quarterbacking both Harvard and Army; and certainly Willie Heston, the stud-muffin of Fielding H. "Hurry Up" Yost's point-a-minute teams at Michigan.

But having studied gridiron history as closely as I have the chicken fried steak, I will now choose all the deserving recipients from 1905, after Heston was gone, to 1935, the year Chicago's "One Man Gang," Jay Berwanger, received the first hunk of sculpture.

1905	Tom Shevlin, end, Yale
1906	Walter Eckersall, quarterback, Chicago
1907	Dwight "Tad" Jones, halfback, Yale
1908	George "Doc" Fenton, quarterback, LSU
1909	Ted Coy, fullback, Yale
1910	Earl Sprackling, quarterback, Brown
1911	Percy Wendell, halfback, Harvard
1912	Jim Thorpe, fullback, Carlisle
1913	Charley Brickley, halfback, Harvard
1914	Eddie Mahan, fullback, Harvard
1915	Charley Barrett, halfback, Cornell

1916	Elmer Oliphant, fullback, Army
1917	Joe Guyon, fullback, Georgia Tech
1918	Tom Davies, halfback, Pitt
1919	Chic Harley, halfback, Ohio State
1920	George Gipp, fullback, Notre Dame
1921	Bo McMillin, quarterback, Centre
1922	Brick Muller, end, California
1923	"Memphis Bill" Mallory, fullback, Yale
1924	Red Grange, halfback, Illinois
1925	Ernie Nevers, fullback, Stanford
1926	Benny Friedman, quarterback, Michigan
1927	Morley Drury, quarterback, USC
1928	Ken Strong, fullback, NYU
1929	Christian Keener "Red" Cagle, halfback, Army
1930	Marchy Schwartz, halfback, Notre Dame
1931	Gaius "Gus" Shaver, quarterback, USC
1932	Harry Newman, quarterback, Michigan
1933	Beattie Feathers, halfback, Tennessee
1934	Dixie Howell, halfback, Alabama

***

But back to the reasons why the greatest thing ever invented by mankind was the chicken fried steak—I mean, college football:

• Great names. Names that couldn't fail. Doak Walker, Johnny Lujack, Duke Slater, Slade Cutter, Bulldog Turner, Tuffy Leemans, Cliff Battles, Choo Choo Justice, Billy Cannon, Bruiser Kinard, Ace Parker, Fats Henry, Ducky Pond, Kyle Rote.

• And Crazy Legs Hirsch, Rags Matthews, Brud Holland, Tank McLaren, Tex Coulter, Buzz Buivid, Whizzer White, Pug Lund, Donn Moomaw, Joe Montana, Rocket Ismail, Nile Kinnick, Tarzan White, Bad News Cafego, John "Hurry" Cain, Clint Frank, Scrapiron Hammon, Bochey Koch, Ken Strong.

• Not to mention USC's social register: Grenville Lansdell Jr., Ambrose Schindler, Orville Mohler, Francis Tappaan, Marshall Duffield, Garrett Arbelbide, Irvine "Cotton" Warburton, Ford Palmer, Landon Exley, Raymond Sparling, Lindon Crow, Carson Palmer and Gordon Gray.

• As names go, it was a better world when coaches were named Pop, Jock, Tiny, Dutch, Rock, Tad, Stub, Biff, Buck, Slip, Clipper, Fritz, Greasy, Paddy, Buff, Zupp, Doc, Tuss, Chick, Bernie, Babe and Matty.

• All I know is, they then became Bud, Bear, Pappy, Biggie, Red, Woody, Shug, Bo, Bennie, Wally and Duffy.

• And just as suddenly they became Darrell, Frank, John, Bob, Joe, Ara, Vince, Barry, Tom, Steve and Bobby.

• As luck would have it, I happened to be in the press box the day Roger Valdiserri, Notre Dame's SID at the time, changed a name. When he said, "O. J. doesn't stand for Orange Juice, it stands for, 'Oh, Jesus, there he goes again!' "

• Moving right along with names, what were the odds on linemen Adolph "Tar" Schwammel of Oregon State and Frank "Zud" Schammel of Iowa both making All-America in 1933.

• "THIS STONE COMMEMORATES THE EXPLOIT OF WILLIAM WEBB ELLIS WHO WITH A FINE DISREGARD FOR THE RULES OF FOOTBALL AS PLAYED IN HIS TIME FIRST TOOK THE BALL IN HIS ARMS AND RAN WITH IT, THUS ORIGINATING … "

• Indian Jim Thorpe, Indian Joe Guyon, Indian Jack Jacobs.

• Bullet Bill Patterson of Baylor, Bullet Bill Osmanski of Holy Cross, Bullet Bill Dudley of Virginia.

• Game of the Week, Game of the Decade, Game of the Century.

• Tennessee's checkerboard end zone.

• The Big House.

• OU's Million Dollar Walk.

• Columbia's KF-79.

• Whose "dream backfield" is it, anyway? At Pitt it was Marshall Goldberg, Dick Cassiano, Johnny Chickerneo and Curly Stebbins. So, gentlemen, start your backfields.

• Around SMU, they'd shout Doak Walker, Kyle Rote, Paul Page and Dick McKissack.

• Army would recommend Glenn "Junior" Davis, Felix "Doc" Blanchard, Arnold Tucker and Tom "Shorty" McWilliams.

• Georgia Bulldogs might happily nominate Frankie Sinkwich, Charley Trippi, Lamar "Racehorse" Davis and Ken Keuper.

• Cal's Old Blues still boast of Vic Bottari, Sam Chapman, Johnny Meek and Dave Anderson.

• OU Sooners are quite fond of Billy Vessels, Eddie Crowder, Buddy Leake and Buck McPhail, but are equally enthralled by Tommy McDonald, Clendon Thomas, Billy Pricer and Jimmy Harris.

• Longhorn geezers fancy "Cowboy" Jack Crain, "Pistol" Pete Layden, Noble Doss and Vern Martin, all on the cover of *Life* one week in 1941.

• Nebraskans are still saluting Bob Devaney's No. 1 collectors, Johnny Rodgers, Jerry Tagge, Jeff Kinney and Bill Olds, but certain Huskers may well prefer Tom Osborne's Triplets—Turner Gill, Mike Rozier, Irving Fryar.

• Alabama has this legendary Rose Bowl quartet of Pooley Hubert, Johnny Mack Brown, Grant Gillis and Red Barnes, as well as the incomparable Rose Bowl quartet of Dixie Howell, Riley Smith, Jimmy Angelich and Joe Demyanovich.

• Notre Dame has scads of horsemen to brag about, from Harry Stuhldreher, Jim Crowley, Don Miller and Elmer Layden to Frank Carideo, Marchy Schwartz, Marty Brill and Moon Mullins to Johnny Lujack, Terry Brennan, Emil "Red" Sitko and Jim Mello.

• Thinking it's hard to top 1940's Battle of Dream Backfields, when Minnesota's George "Sonny" Franck, Bruce Smith, Bill Daley and Bob Sweiger won by a 7-6 eyelash over Michigan's Tom Harmon, Forest Evashevski, Bob Westfall and Paul Kromer.

• Gus Dorais to Knute Rockne. That started it. Then it wrought Benny Friedman to Bennie Oosterbaan, Dixie Howell to Don Hutson, "Slingin'" Sam Baugh to Walter Roach, Doyle Nave to Al Krueger, Gene Rossides to Bill Swiacki, "Sweet Bobby" Layne and Babe Parilli and "Dandy" Don Meredith to anybody with the same colored shirt, James Street to Cotton Speyrer, Jim Plunkett to Randy Vataha, Tom Clements to Dave Casper, Pat Haden to J. K. McKay, Steve Walsh to Michael Irvin and if you want to talk about Hail Marys, Doug Flutie to Gerry Phelan.

• Favorite bumper stickers. The one that said, "I'D RATHER BE ON PROBATION THAN LOSE TO BAYLOR." And the one in Alabama after the Tide's surprising '92 national title that read, "WE STILL HAVEN'T PLAYED ANYBODY." And the one that some creative SMU sorority sisters came up with before a big game against Texas in the early 1980s, which said, "OUR MAIDS WENT TO UT."

• Old oaken little brown tailgate jugs.

***

But now it's the day of a big game—huge—and I'm on hand to cover it. Strolling the campus two hours before the kickoff. Soaking up the atmosphere. I'm a campus collector. Never met one I didn't like.

I admire the quad, the drag, the fountain, the bell tower, the statues, the trees, the sweep of lawns. I wonder what it would have been like to go to school here.

Would I have ever made it to class without a shapely adorable to follow? Maybe I'd have just sat on this bench under these trees with enough cigarettes and coffee to get me through four years.

Now it's an hour before the game and I'm up on the outdoor photo deck of the press box. I want to watch the stadium fill up, see the bands march in, watch the teams warm up. Absorb it, smell it, breathe it, put on my own game face.

Then it's moments before the opening kickoff. Bands are blaring. Both sides of the stadium are fraught with nerves, noise, frenzy. The two teams are down on the sideline, totally pumped, hopping about.

Only seconds before the kickoff now. The starting lineups are on the field—poised, wired. The crowd is standing. The stadium shudders with a continuous roar.

The bell is about to ring for the opening round of a heavyweight championship fight. Gun's up for the Olympic 100. The Derby horses are in the gate at Churchill Downs. Sunday leaders at the Masters are heading for Amen Corner.

Yet here in this college football stadium, I'm enjoying my favorite moment in sports—and even though I'm safely enclosed in the cynical calm of the press box, I'm on my feet.

I might add that my ankles are taped.

THE GAME

There is a tendency, when you spend three years editing a college football encyclopedia, to focus on the acres of lore and overlook the fact that the game is a living thing, continually evolving from one year to the next. And so, this opening section sets out not only to review the sport's past, but also to reflect on the forces that are likely to shape its future.

In the following pages, you'll find:
- **Chuck Culpepper's** case for college football as the most American game.
- **Beano Cook's** list of the 10 most important days in the history of the sport. While it's true that Beano has been chronicling highlights like these for more than a half-century, he did not sit Forrest Gump-like in the Notre Dame locker room for Rockne's Gipper speech.
- As Tommy Lee Jones said upon surveying the train wreck in The Fugitive, "My, my, my, my, my... what... a... mess." Those words can just as easily summarize the sentiment in **Gene Wojciechowski's** essay on the 1984 Supreme Court decision that led to the birth of the BCS and the mountains of controversy that followed.
- **Andrew Bagnato** writes about the game's living legends—the coaches.
- **Bud Withers** ponders the history of recruiting and the ends to which a college will go to sign the next O.J. Simpson.
- **Vahe Gregorian** examines the state of sportsmanship and concludes that, in many significant ways, conduct on the field has never been better.
- **Joe Posnanski** fondly recalls the offense that once ruled the gridiron—the option.
- **Mark Wangrin** shows how integration forever changed the sport for the better.
- **Ed Krzemienski** takes a century-long trip to the movies, giving two thumbs up to the best college football films of all time.
- And three men used to getting the last word—**Chris Fowler, Lee Corso** and **Kirk Herbstreit** of *ESPN College GameDay*—join in a spirited discussion on where the game has been and where it's headed.

The Most American Game

136 Years—and Counting— of a National Treasure

BY CHUCK CULPEPPER

WE THE PEOPLE OF THE UNITED STATES, HELL-BENT ON building a more eccentric union, began behaving with a vivid weirdness Nov. 6, 1869, at 3 p.m. on a 120-by-75-yard field in central New Jersey.

There and then, Rutgers beat Princeton 6-4, whereupon Princeton sought redemption in a rematch to sustain functional respiration, whereupon Princeton beat Rutgers by 8-0 on Nov. 13, whereupon you'd think they'd have needed to play each other again, except they never did, and the teams finished the season with a certain imprecision as to who actually trumped who.

We were on our way.

Princeton and Rutgers faculty members insisted the newfangled college football—get this—interfered with studiousness. To describe people's fascination with the pugnacious game of 25-on-25 in which players in street clothes and suspenders chased a soccer-style round ball, barreled through a fence and toppled spectators that very first day, faculty wordsmiths summoned the most damning terminology.

They called it—get this—"overemphasis."

Eventually, through the years, 14 different "services" would opine that Princeton won that 1869 national championship, while three defiant stragglers would choose Rutgers, apparently having spotted a subtle nobleness in the Rutgers squad.

The most brutal of the six major team sports would become the oddest, as if we needed just one sport to remind us that life is often absurd—and often at its best when it is.

All manner of magnificent screwball behavior would flower across the next century, from Stanford students beheading a dummy dressed in Cal colors on a pristine day in 1899, Georgians blubbering over a ceremonial changing of a bulldog's collar, Auburn residents citing victories by

inexplicably hurling toilet paper into a cherished tree or a Texas bride-to-be dialing up the students selected to manage a longhorn steer's public appearances at football games. (She wanted to know if this steer, Bevo, could show up outside the church shortly after her vows. Her husband-to-be reportedly got teary.)

No other sport would flash kook credentials with such unapologetic abandon. No other sport would teem with loony concoctions called "bowls." No other would bustle for four months each fall before coming to no apparent resolution. No other would insist that your ranking this year depends partly on what you did last year and in previous years.

This sport would be built by peerlessly unusual men. It would post a litany of venerated games that ended in ties. Its participants would covet trophies that were—are—just plain weird. It would draw the (sometimes) intrusive interest of presidents of the United States.

This sport, grounded in the collision of human bodies and a craven need to beat the stuffing out of the citizens up the road, would become closely tethered to … religion.

BOWL GAMES

By 1902, with some 250 colleges playing football and more than 30,000 curious sorts showing up for certain games, Pasadena's Tournament of Roses people thought a football game might spruce up their festivities. One of coach Fielding H. Yost's scary "Point-a-Minute" Michigan teams led Stanford, 49-0, in that first (and almost last) Rose Bowl when Stanford sort of, well, quit with eight minutes left to play. Not impressed, the Tournament of Roses folk spent the next 14 years rummaging through life's spectacles, often ending up with races (chariots, ostriches and so on).

For a while after the Rose Bowl returned in 1916, the only other bowl of note was the Bacardi, occurring every so often in Havana. In the final Bacardi Bowl (1937), Villanova tied Auburn, 7-7, on your average, everyday blocked quick-kick for a touchdown.

Beginning in the 1930s, but especially after World War II, bowls rose and croaked. Phoenix had five editions of a Salad Bowl, which enabled people to leave the house saying, "I'm headed to the Salad Bowl."

Sponsors attached themselves, as in Shreveport's Poulan/Weedeater Independence Bowl. Houston alone has had, at various stages, an Oil Bowl, a Bluebonnet Bowl, an

Astro-Bluebonnet Bowl, a Galleryfurniture.com Bowl and a Houston Bowl (the current incarnation).

Orange, Cotton, Sugar, Sun, Gator, Peach, Liberty, the desert-come-lately Fiesta … bowls lived and breathed their own revered lives, and pretty soon your father could have his brilliant nuclear-engineer brain turned to dewy-eyed mush at the very pregame sight of the Virginia Tech band taking the Sugar Bowl field. You could see fans of Marshall University eating outdoors in a Holiday Inn parking lot in 18° weather hours before a Motor City Bowl in the general vicinity of Detroit. Or you could hear a coach (Nebraska's Tom Osborne) worry beforehand that halftime elephants might ruin the field.

Bowls sprouted as separate, tack-on addenda to the regular season, so their actual outcome could sometimes seem like … separate tack-on (and strangely irrelevant) addenda to the regular season. For instance, Oklahoma beat No. 1 Maryland, 7-0, in the 1954 Orange Bowl, for the ninth of Oklahoma's 47 consecutive victories under Charles Burnham "Bud" Wilkinson, but that did not alter the picture of the national title, already won by Maryland.

Why? Stop asking so many questions.

NO RESOLUTION

It's beautifully senseless that people didn't bother to fuse bowl games with national title considerations until the 1968 season. It's also beautifully senseless that a team's season rages week to week to week for three months, then suddenly breaks for up to six weeks before the ultimate game. It's also beautifully senseless to let chaos wash over your sport to create puzzles like 1978-79.

Two teams (Alabama, Southern California) battled it out for the top spot among teams winning their bowl games. One (USC) had routed the other (Alabama) in the other's sweet home (Alabama) during the season. But one conference (Alabama's) had a business deal with the Sugar Bowl. The other conference (USC's) had a business deal with the Rose Bowl. The team (Alabama) that wound up winning the bowl with the tougher opponent (Penn State) then won something called the Associated Press national championship, just ahead of the team (USC) that beat Alabama.

Beautifully senseless.

> *No other sport would flash kook credentials with such unapologetic abandon.*

PAST TENSE

It helps to do well this year, of course, but college football remains the only game in which it helps to have done well in preceding years, even in years so far back that the people who actually did well for you back then have actually, you know, died of natural causes. Last year matters, and not just in individual cases, as when O.J. Simpson's 64-yard run against UCLA in 1967 boosted him toward the 1968 Heisman Trophy.

Notre Dame went unbeaten in 1912, 1913 and 1919, but had a wee image compared with a reputed mastodon like Harvard which, having spent decades in fierce rows with 18-time titleist Yale and 15-time titleist Princeton, could claim national titles in 1912, 1913 and 1919.

Penn State spent years doing so-so or fair-to-middling or pretty good, so by the time it reached unbeaten years under Joe Paterno in 1968 and 1969, it lacked the cachet of national "champions" Ohio State and Texas. But in the early 1980s, it reached the top partly because people knew it from the 1960s.

This type of strangeness found a peak in the summer of 2004, when careful research uncovered a recognized but obscure Southern California national championship—from 1939. Those 1939 players who had managed to survive war, rock 'n roll and SUV emissions were feted at a halftime ceremony, the absurdity both manifest and lovely.

That championship, in turn, was discovered while USC carried another championship—shared in 2003 with Louisiana State—that bolstered it for 2004 in a perverse exercise called preseason polls. Preseason polls canvas voters as to how good they think teams might be come November and December. If people guessed you as No. 18 back when every team was 0–0, you might stall permanently behind somebody people thought of more highly at 0–0, but they might stall behind you next year if people thought more highly of you at 0–0 than of them at 0–0 at that time.

This may well fulfill a human need for some grand preposterousness to lighten the daily grind.

UNUSUAL MEN

Walter Camp, a Yale player and coach in the 19th century, gave the game the scrimmage line, the center snap, set plays and its first All-America teams. He participated on every rules commission through 1925, studied physical fitness, wrote

more than 30 books and 250 magazine articles (including advice for battling common colds) and wrote stories in New York and Philadelphia newspapers, albeit not covering himself. How did the father of our national exercise in sporting imprecision make his living? Up the ladder rungs to the chairmanship of the New Haven Clock Company.

Glenn Scobey "Pop" Warner, gave the game the huddle, the three-point stance, shoulder and thigh pads, numbered jerseys, the first spiral punt and spiral pass and the double-wing. He coached from 1895 through 1938 at Georgia, Cornell, Pitt, Stanford, Temple and, in the middle there, at somewhere even more noteworthy. His 1912 team at the Carlisle Indian School in Pennsylvania suddenly scored 505 points and went 12–1–1, led by one Jim Thorpe.

John Heisman, the namesake for the sport's paramount trophy, spearheaded the "hike" signal, the legalization of the forward pass and the concept of quarters rather than halves. He spent off-seasons as a Shakespearean actor and often infused musings from the Bard into his pregame talks. He also coached Georgia Tech's 222-0 win over Cumberland (Tenn.) on Oct. 7, 1916, a historic, thorough and thoroughly weird revenge for a 22-0 baseball drubbing of Tech by Cumberland in 1915.

TIES

Army and Navy tied 21-21 in a 1926 epic before more than 100,000 fans in Chicago. Army and Notre Dame tied 0-0 in a 1946 epic before more than 74,000 at Yankee Stadium. Michigan State and Notre Dame tied 10-10 as No. 2 and No. 1 in 1966. Harvard defeated heavily favored Yale (so concluded *The Harvard Crimson*) 29-29 in 1968. No. 1 Ohio State tied No. 4 Michigan 10-10 in a 1973 epic. Oregon and Oregon State tied in 1983 in a 0-0 poetry of difficulty (one of six 0-0 ties in their rivalry). And Florida State, trailing 31-3, scored a victory in a 31-31 tie against loathed neighbor Florida in 1994.

One of the ties in the preceding sequence, Ohio State-Michigan in 1973, wrought one of those special, unforgettable Sundays, the sort only college football can provide, when you sit around waiting for 10 athletic directors to vote on who gets to go to the Rose Bowl. You might be a child when this occurs, but you think it perfectly normal and explainable because all the adults around you think it perfectly normal and explainable. (Ohio State went to Pasadena that year, by a vote of 6-4.)

Ties used to play a big role in college football.

But after a century of debating which team "won" each game in this grand historical archive of ties, the people who run college football decided they didn't like ties anymore, and introduced overtime. Overtime has produced scores like Toledo 40, Nevada 37 in the first OT game (Las Vegas Bowl, 1995); Arkansas 58, Ole Miss 56 in seven overtimes (2001); Arkansas 71, Kentucky 63 in seven overtimes (2003); and Ohio State 31, Miami 24 in two overtimes in a stratospheric Fiesta Bowl (2002).

TROPHIES

After the deeply moving occasion when Stanford students beheaded that dummy with Cal colors, the ax they used became the Stanford Ax, swiped by Cal students in an ensuing brawl, then swiped back decades later. It used to travel to pep rallies in an armored car.

Yes.

Iowa and Minnesota play for a statuette of a pig, *Floyd of Rosedale*, a champion hog originally won by Minnesota's governor in a bet on the 1935 game. Floyd became the second-most-famous pig in his immediate family, after a brother who starred with Will Rogers in *State Fair*.

Yes.

And only in a nation so peculiar—occasionally to the point of tastelessness—could two teams from the Ohio heartland, Wittenberg and Ohio Wesleyan, play for years for a Native American skull unearthed during stadium construction. Mercifully, they discontinued the practice in 1989 and gave the skull a proper burial, which involved a Sioux medicine man.

Yes.

It's no surprise, then, that all this got started partly because Rutgers and Princeton students kept snatching a cannon from one another in the 1860s.

PRESIDENTIAL SEAL

Only college football has had a rough-and-ready president (Theodore Roosevelt) intercede in 1905, demanding modifications to ease bloodletting after a horde of deaths and major injuries in a sport that didn't even have helmets until two decades into its existence.

And only college football has had a markedly efficient president (Richard Nixon) poke his head into its championship decision process by helicoptering into the 1969 No. 1 Texas-vs.-No. 2 Arkansas colossus and absurdly presenting a national championship trophy to Texas thereafter.

And only college football has U.S. presidents visit a game (Army-Navy), then ceremonially switch sides at halftime as some sort of egalitarian ritual that would probably come off as extraterrestrial in many parts of the solar system.

RELIGION

According to Richard Harding Davis in *Harper's Weekly*, the perfect Princeton team of 1893 beat Yale, 6-0, then stood in the dressing room "naked and covered with mud and blood and perspiration," singing "Praise God From Whom All Blessings Flow."

Their religious experience would know a horde of echoes through the generations, from pregame prayers to Southern quarterbacks starting post-game interviews with *I'd like to thank my Lord and Savior Jesus Christ* to Notre Dame-Southern California in 1974. Ara Parseghian's Fighting Irish ran out to a 24-0 lead, but John McKay's Trojans came back to win 55-24. Afterward, Notre Dame president Father Theodore Hesburgh said to McKay, "That wasn't a very nice thing for a Catholic to do." McKay replied, "Father, that serves you right for hiring a Presbyterian" (Parseghian).

Only college football could bring about the sacrosanct mingling of the words "touchdown" and "Jesus," as happened with a mural in the heartland.

"You will come to no Christian end!" shouted a Rutgers professor, shaking an umbrella at the Rutgers and Princeton players that very first day, according to the Rutgers media guide.

Nobody heard him.

***

College football has doled out so many alien scenarios that, really, connoisseurs of quirks will never run out of raw material.

The ridiculous—Cal's Roy Riegels running the wrong way in the 1929 Rose Bowl, Stanford's band taking the field during Cal's kickoff return in 1982—gains acceptance as the sublime: People know Louisiana State has a geology department. Why? Because its Richter scale registered the roar emanating from a 7-6 win over Auburn in 1988. The renowned Oklahoma football team (est. 1895) is older than the renowned state of Oklahoma (est. 1907). Only in college football can a guy like SMU's Bobby Wilson score a diving, lunging touchdown to beat TCU in 1935, which allowed the team to snare a Rose Bowl berth with its $85,000 payout, and thus pay for stadium debts at his alma mater. Only in college football would a legendary coach, Earl "Red" Blaik of Army, receive postcards every day in 1946 from some Notre Dame entity titled The Society to Prevent Army's Third National Championship.

College football tells us we're odd, and then it tells us more than that.

We started in the East and moved gradually west, much like Amos Alonzo Stagg himself, who went from Springfield (Massachusetts) to win a national title at the University of Chicago in 1905—a huge 2-0 win over Yost's Michigan—and eventually to the University of the Pacific. People in the East don't much acknowledge the West Coast; it's as if they can't see over the Rockies. Maybe it's because games in the Pacific time zone often don't make the Sunday papers back East. Whatever, the resentment is particularly strong in the Pacific Northwest, which feels singularly omitted in life—and college football provides ample evidence. There was outrage in 2000 when a one-loss Florida State team got invited to the national title game, but one-loss Miami, which had beaten Florida State, didn't. In and around Seattle, the point was made, to mostly deaf ears back East, that the title game also overlooked one-loss Washington, which had beaten ... Miami.

We once had no television, so word of somebody's excellence took a few years to spread. Then we got television, giving us a true national village in which 50% of all sets turned on could tune in to Texas-Arkansas in 1969, or 55 million homes to the Nebraska-Oklahoma gem of 1971. And then we got cable television and satellite dishes, so we could watch nine games on a Saturday (and record another dozen) if we had no apparent life.

We have an intense American desire to be admired, and college football aches with it more than any game. Cal, too far west for much admiration, yearned for it until it crushed Ohio State in the 1921 Rose Bowl behind Harold "Brick" Muller. Alabama, too far south for much admiration, yearned for it until it changed the football world by beating Washington in the 1926 Rose Bowl behind Johnny Mack Brown. Carlisle, anonymous and seeking some due, upset Harvard, 18-15, on 11/11/11, behind Jim Thorpe. Small towns crow with pride when they become large, as when Memorial Stadium at Nebraska creates the state's third-largest "city" on Saturdays. Boise State got attention by building a blue field, but birds (thinking it water) crash-landed, prompting humanitarian adjustments. Oregon, perhaps feeling out of the center of things, sought attention by advertising a Heisman Trophy candidate with a billboard—3,000 miles away in Times Square.

We're very proud when we happen to come from the same place as somebody famous, which explains why you still can read Iowa obituaries from 2004 that mention acquaintance or friendship or teammate-hood with Nile Kinnick, Iowa's 1939 Heisman winner from Adel, still adored in the state long after his death in the Caribbean as a Navy pilot at 24.

We're a big country but also a bunch of little countries. Culturally, the Midwest has to play it conservative, what with

winter coming fast. The West can experiment; it's where people go to remake themselves. The South feels especially chesty when it's the best after a noted historical phase of being branded as inferior. Mini-countries form, congeal: Texas here, Oklahoma over there, Gators here, Seminoles over there, complete with healthy mutual loathing everywhere. At least on Saturdays.

We have a lot of money, which pays for big programs. But sometimes we're more creative when we don't have either. That's why any list of the most innovative coaches of all time will include John Gagliardi, the St. John's (Minn.) coach who has won more college football games than anyone else—without allowing tackling in practice. And Frosty Westering, who retired in 2003 with four national championships (one in NCAA Division III and three in NAIA Division II) from Pacific Lutheran in Tacoma, Wash., after coaching his players on the importance of singing—"When you're singing, there's a lifting of youself"—and of stopping practices to gaze at and appreciate Mount Rainier.

And we have a clear idea of what constitutes corruption—namely, that it's somebody else doing it, most of the time—but we can tolerate it and press on.

Maybe it's because on a fall Saturday in America, somebody's getting started around noon in crisp air in the East (you see the fans under blankets), and somebody in the Upper Midwest is trying to establish the running game, and in the South two sides get ready to take the wretched summer heat out on each other, with the West Coast set to throw it around in a few hours, if not into the night.

Maybe all that weekly possibility laced with all the glorious weirdness proves too much to resist. So as a college football coach might say before his bunch of young men attempts to flay the living innards out of another bunch of young men, God bless us.

Ten Days That Shook the Sport

Beano Cook's All-Time Best Moments

BY BEANO COOK

Polls, rankings and "top" lists—and controversy over who belongs where on which—have been woven into the fabric of college football since that inaugural autumn of 1869 when Rutgers bested Princeton, six goals to four. Princeton won the rematch ("The Game of the 19th Century") by a score of 8-0 later that season. And so the debate began. *Who do you think should have been invited to the White House by President Ulysses S. Grant? Who do you think deserved to be anointed the first national champion?* And so it has continued, for 136 years—and counting. What follows is one fan's personal top-10 list of the most important names, dates, moments and legends that make up the lore of college football. Perhaps you'll agree with all my selections. (Highly unlikely.) More likely you'll disagree with some of them. (Hey, this is college football.) For sure, you'll have your own favorites. Let the debate continue.

1. Nov. 10, 1928/Oct. 5, 1940: The "Win One for the Gipper" Speech

"I'm going to tell you something I've kept to myself for years. None of you ever knew George Gipp—it was long before your time. But you all know what a tradition he is at Notre Dame. And the last thing he said to me, 'Rock,' he said, 'sometime, when the team is up against it, and the breaks are beating the boys, tell them to go out there with all they got and win just one for the Gipper. I don't know where I'll be then, Rock,' he said, 'but I'll know about it ... and I'll be happy.'"

The speech, according to popular myth and *Knute Rockne, All American*, the 1940 Hollywood movie starring Pat O'Brien as Rockne and Ronald Reagan as the gifted yet doomed football star George Gipp, was given by the legendary Notre Dame coach in the locker room at Yankee Stadium before a 1928 game against heavily favored Army. Rockne's

undermanned charges, filled with renewed vigor and purpose, promptly went out and upended the undefeated Army Cadets, 12-6.

Or was it? Some people said no such thing happened, that Rockne never uttered a word about Gipp in the Irish locker room that cold, crisp, late-fall afternoon. Only one New York sportswriter, Notre Dame alum Francis Wallace of the New York *Daily News*, mentioned the Gipper speech in his account of the game. No Notre Dame player of that era ever stepped forward to verify the story—or debunk it. We'll probably never know just what happened in 1928. We do know that the world at large didn't learn about the story until Hollywood told it in 1940.

What we know about George Gipp is that he was a loner who shied away from attention and shunned photography. An inveterate gambler, party animal and pool shark who flaunted a flagrant disregard for most laws, school regulations and team rules, Gipp was nonetheless a hero to Notre Dame students and South Bend townsfolk alike, the star athlete who often passed on his gambling winnings to those needing money for tuition or train tickets. But he was also a thorn in the side of Notre Dame's administration and even his famed head coach. Gipp's behavior may even have contributed to his untimely death. Legend has it that after missing yet another curfew, Gipp was locked out of his campus residence, Washington Hall, by an overzealous priest, and forced to sleep outdoors on the frozen steps of the dorm. Shortly thereafter, he contracted the throat infection that killed him in December 1920.

Many college football stars (Princeton's Hobey Baker, Iowa's Nile Kinnick, Syracuse's Ernie Davis) have been cut down in the flower of their youth and lionized in death. But only the story of a young, dying Gipp—Notre Dame's first Walter Camp All-America selection—entreating his coach to win a game in his memory, survives in the minds of most college football fans.

And it is because of Rockne's speech.

2. Nov. 16, 1940: The Fifth-Down Game

Cornell, with a powerful offense averaging 30 points per game, a perfect 6–0 record and No. 2 ranking in the Associated Press poll—this is 1940, remember—is at Hanover, N.H., for its annual game with Dartmouth, then 3–4. The Big Red hasn't lost a game in nearly three seasons. But for almost four quarters, the spirited Indians, coached by

One fan's personal top-10 list of the most important dates in college football history.

the legendary Earl "Red" Blaik—who would leave Dartmouth after the season for West Point—bottle up the mighty Cornell offense. Late in the game, Dartmouth holds onto a precarious 3-0 lead when Cornell's offensive juggernaut finally awakens.

Cornell's ball, first and goal at the Dartmouth 6-yard line, less than a minute remaining on the clock: from this point, a series of events unfolds that will keep Cornell-Dartmouth in the headlines throughout the following week—and make it one of the great stories in college football history.

First down: Cornell fullback Mort Landsberg picks up three yards.

Second down: Cornell halfback Walt Scholl pushes the ball to the 1.

Third down: Landsberg, driving up the middle, nets only inches.

Fourth down: Cornell is flagged for delay of game. Referee Red Friesell spots the ball just beyond the 5-yard line. Nine seconds on the clock. Scholl, lining up at quarterback, lobs a pass into the end zone. Incomplete. Ball goes over to Dartmouth …

But wait. Linesman Joe McKenny signals Cornell's ball. Friesell, who's also lost count of the downs, concurs.

Fourth down—again: Scholl throws a touchdown pass. The extra point is good. Cornell 7, Dartmouth 3. Game over. Or was it?

The consensus view in the press box was that Cornell had used five downs to score. That was transmitted to the referee after the game. Both schools had filmed the contest, so the next evening Friesell watched the final sequence of plays and spotted his error. He contacted Asa Bushnell, commissioner of the Central Office for Eastern Intercollegiate Athletics. A stickler for rules, Bushnell advised Friesell that since the game was already entered into the official record books, the final score would stand.

When news of the error reached Cornell, president Edmund E. Day, athletic director Jim Lynah and coach Carl Snavely concluded that the honorable thing to do was to forfeit the game. Snavely sent a telegram to Blaik: *"I accept the final conclusion of the officials and without reservations concede the victory to Dartmouth, with hearty congratulations to you and the gallant Dartmouth team."*

Dartmouth athletic director W.H. McCarter responded immediately: *"Thank you for your wire. Dartmouth accepts the victory and your congratulations and salutes the Cornell team, the honorable and honored opponent of her longest football rivalry."*

Demoralized by the defeat, Cornell lost the following week to the Pennsylvania Quakers at Franklin Field and plummeted to a disappointing No. 15 finish in the final AP poll. But the gesture would be remembered and honored across the decades. (Especially after Colorado, en route to a national title in 1990, pointedly *didn't* concede a game it had won with a similar "fifth-down" victory over Missouri.) Today, if anybody followed Snavely and Day's honorable lead, especially with the multimillion dollar BCS pot of gold on the line, it's likely they'd be hung—not in effigy, but in person.

3. Nov. 20, 1982: The Play, California vs. Stanford

"Oh, my god! The most amazing, sensational, dramatic, heartrending, exciting, thrilling finish in the history of college football!"—California play-by-play announcer Joe Starkey of radio station KGO, from Memorial Stadium in Berkeley.

In the closing moments of the 1982 Big Game, as the Cal-Stanford rivalry is known in college football, John Elway—starting at his own 20-yard line and facing a 19-17 deficit—drove Stanford down the field. Elway converted a fourth-and-17 play during an improbable Cardinal drive that culminated in what looked to be a game-winning Mark Harmon field goal. Following the kick, joyous Stanford players swarmed the field. Just four seconds stood between a 20-19 lead becoming a 20-19 Cardinal win.

After clearing the Stanford team off the field and assessing the requisite 15-yard celebration penalty, the officials blew their whistles—and the ensuing four seconds—into college football history.

Stanford's squib kick was fielded by Cal defensive back Kevin Moen at the Bears' 43-yard line. Moen tossed the ball to Richard Rodgers, who lateraled it to freshman Dwight Garner. As three defenders swarmed Garner, he pitched the ball back to Rodgers. The Stanford band, believing the game to be over, left their seats and began to storm the end zone. Rodgers, stumbling to the Stanford 45, shoveled the ball to Cal receiver Mariet Ford. Out of nowhere came Moen, the play's catalyst, to catch a haphazard, over-the-shoulder lateral from Ford. In the process, Ford barreled into the three

remaining Stanford players and cleared a path for Moen, who then plowed into the Stanford band, now milling around dazedly in the end zone. The coup de grace was Moen's impromptu, celebratory spike on the head of Gary Tyrrell, a senior Stanford trombone player and engineering major.

The mood inside Memorial Stadium shifted immediately from the gloom of an expected loss to the euphoria of an inexplicable, improbable win. Cal fans and team members paraded around the field with the Axe, a symbolic trophy awarded to winners of the Big Game. Catatonic Cardinals fans stood motionless, unable to comprehend what they'd just witnessed. Stanford's coaching staff, on the other hand, protested loudly that the play should be ruled dead, that Garner's knee had touched the ground before his late toss to Rodgers. Motorists listening on their car radios to the madness engulfing Strawberry Canyon sat in intersections all over Northern California, unaware of successive green lights while waiting for the final decision. Some drove their cars into ditches.

Finally, the huddled and bewildered officials, led by referee Charles Moffett, issued their ruling. "The Play," as it would henceforth be known, stood.

Final score: Cal 25, Stanford 20.

Starkey, in the concluding remarks of his famous broadcast, said that "people years from now will say they were here today for what has to be, as of this moment, the greatest Big Game in history."

No argument here.

4. Dec. 7, 1963: The Birth of Instant Replay

Ask football fans if instant replay has its roots in the college or the professional game and most will go with the pros. But those who tuned in to the Army-Navy game on CBS on Dec. 7, 1963, know better.

When director Tony Verna, a Philadelphia native, returned to his hometown to direct the Army-Navy game that year, he arrived with a unique plan and a giant, 1,200-pound tape machine he had unplugged and transported from the CBS network control room (known as "Grand Central Station") in New York. Unbeknownst to all but a handful of CBS executives and his crew, Verna was going to attempt to give viewers an immediate second look at a play.

"Video replay" was Verna's unofficial name for the yet-to-be unveiled and considerably risky innovation. Risky because at that time the Army-Navy game was *the* showcase game in college football. In this pre-Super Bowl era, there was no grander stage in televised sports than the annual clash between the Cadets and Midshipmen. And in 1963,

the stakes were even higher. Millions of Americans would be tuning in to the high-profile military rivalry game because of the assassination of President John F. Kennedy 16 days earlier.

For Verna, the genesis for the idea came years before when, as a twentysomething wunderkind recently hired by CBS executive Tex Schramm, he worked on that network's telecasts of the 1960 Rome Olympics. The network aired the entire Olympics on tape delay—after the tape was flown across the Atlantic to New York. It was then that Verna learned videotape possesses two audio tracks. For his special replay, he would use one track for crowd noise, the other for a simple cue system that would help locate the correct spot on the tape. One solid, clean beep would indicate a team going into a huddle; two clean beeps would indicate a team breaking a huddle.

Several glitches occurred during his first attempts at fusing his taped technology with the game in progress. His monolithic tape machine was spitting out seven to nine seconds of video "hash," indecipherable, cluttered pictures, before locking into a clear shot of game action. Occasionally, his machine didn't work at all. Instead of football action, the monitor would reveal what was already on the tape, sometimes a scene from *I Love Lucy* or a Duz detergent commercial.

For three nervous quarters, Verna peered into his monitor and studied his two guinea pigs, Navy quarterback Roger Staubach and Army counterpart Rollie Stichweh. Verna had assigned one camera to follow only the two signal-callers, primarily because Staubach was so skilled with his ball-handling and fakes that most cameramen couldn't keep up with him. Although Staubach was the winner of the 1963 Heisman Trophy, it was Stichweh who made television history that day. Stichweh faked to an Army halfback before running into the end zone for a one-yard touchdown, Army's last in a 21-15 loss. The requisite beeps sounded in the production truck. Words passed through cables and into headsets. Seconds later, a clear image of Stichweh and the Army offense appeared on the monitor. Verna pulled the trigger and threw the picture on air.

"Here it comes," he warned play-by-play announcer Lindsey Nelson, to whom he had revealed his intentions only hours earlier, during the taxicab ride to Philadelphia's Municipal Stadium. Nelson didn't even have time to forewarn his audience that they would be witnessing television history. Most important, though, Stichweh "re-scampered" into the end zone and the very first instant replay went off without a technical hitch.

So as not to confuse viewers, Nelson alerted his audience to what they'd just seen: "This is not live! Ladies and gentlemen, Army did not score again!"

At the end of the game, praise for Verna came from far and near. "My boy," Schramm told Verna over the telephone, "what you have done here will have such far-reaching implications, we can't begin to imagine them today."

(In fact, during the early days of the innovation following the 1963 Army-Navy game, the phenomenon became so popular that viewers demanded to see it during practically every sporting event. Unfortunately, there weren't enough tape machines to go around.)

Schramm's words proved to be prophetic. In the ensuing decades, *instant replay*—Verna's not certain which of two announcers, Ray Scott or Pat Summerall, actually named his invention—became a cornerstone component of all sports telecasts.

And so it remains today.

5. Circa Early 1970s: The Army-Navy Postgame Show

The long, storied history of the Army-Navy rivalry has given us many of the game's great players, moments and legends. The names—Blaik, Blanchard, Beagle, Bellino, Cagle, Carpenter, Davis, Duden, Dawkins, Staubach, just to name a few—are synonymous with gridiron excellence. And the games, from the landmark clashes of the Roaring '20s to the thrilling finishes of the modern era, rank with college football's epic contests.

But in my opinion, the rivalry's most enduring legacy is not what has happened on the field during the series' 115-year history, but what transpires immediately *following the conclusion* of an Army-Navy game. That scene, for the uninitiated, is truly one of the most magical moments in college football. Unlike the scenes following other heated rivalry games, postgame scuffles at Army-Navy are rare. No trash-talking. No tasteless, teamwide celebration dances. No hurling of insults, profanities or bottles by fans. No tumbling goalposts.

When time expires, the winning team simply and purposefully moves en masse to the losing squad's side of the field and proceeds to sing that school's alma mater with its counterparts. The losing squad crosses the field and matches the gesture in front of the victor's cheering section. Win, lose or draw, it's a powerful moment that has sent chills throughout the Army Corps and the Navy Brigade, as well as the fans in attendance, for years.

No one, including old-timers, historians and officials associated with both schools, knows precisely when the tradition began. According to Navy football historian Jack Clary, it wasn't until sometime after the 1960s that the tradition, as known today, took its current form. But clearly, its roots go much deeper.

During the early years of World War II, gas rationing and travel restrictions prevented most fans and cheering squads from accompanying their teams to away games. As a result, for the 1942 Army-Navy game at Annapolis, some midshipmen were ordered by the Navy to sit in the visitor's section, and—take a deep breath here—cheer for Army. In 1943, Army earmarked a squad of Cadets to return the favor at West Point.

Imagine that taking place in the SEC.

The Army-Navy postgame show remains one of the classiest displays of respect in sports. And for good reason. When these players—especially the seniors playing in their last game—remove their helmets and sing each other's alma mater, it signifies the moment when they go from being rivals to being teammates on a much more important squad.

The tradition of the singing of the alma maters after the Army-Navy game is, in many ways, sportsmanship's last stand, a relic of a bygone era in sports when, to paraphrase legendary sportswriter Grantland Rice, it mattered not who won or lost, but how you played the game—and how you behaved when the final gun sounded.

6. Oct. 18, 1924 (Part I): The Original Ride of the Four Horsemen

Oct. 18, 1924, is the most sacred day in college football history because of two landmark games played on that date.

The story begins in the press box of the old Polo Grounds in New York, where Knute Rockne's Fighting Irish were leading Army 6-0 at halftime. In the press box, Grantland Rice of the *New York Herald Tribune* happened to overhear a conversation between a young Notre Dame press assistant named George Strickler and another New York writer. The writer commented on the skillful play of Notre Dame's backfield quartet—quarterback Harry Stuhldreher, halfbacks "Sleepy" Jim Crowley and Don Miller and fullback Elmer Layden—and Strickler remembered the Rudolph Valentino movie he'd recently seen, *The Four Horsemen of the Apocalypse*, a 1921 silent film that had been rereleased in 1924. The Fighting Irish backfield, Strickler said, was just like the Four Horsemen of the film.

Rice returned to his seat. Notre Dame went on to beat Army in an unremarkable game by the score of 13-7. And then the keys of Rice's typewriter clicked out the single most famous lead in the history of sports journalism:

Outlined against a blue-gray October sky the Four Horsemen rode again. In dramatic lore they are known as famine, pestilence, destruction and death. These are only aliases. Their real names are: Stuhldreher, Miller, Crowley and Layden. They formed the crest of the South Bend cyclone before which another fighting Army football team was swept over the precipice at the Polo Grounds yesterday afternoon as 55,000 spectators peered down on the bewildering panorama spread on the green plain below.

The Four Horsemen of Notre Dame became the most famous quartet of the 20th century—at least before the Beatles. Yet it wasn't until the following week that the famed moniker would become permanently embedded in the American sports vernacular. Strickler capitalized on his own idea by arranging for the four players to pose for a photograph on the backs of four large workhorses he had borrowed from a livery stable in South Bend. The wire services picked up the photo. And, after the Four Horsemen led Notre Dame to a 27-10 win over Stanford in the 1925 Rose Bowl and a perfect 10–0 record, they passed permanently into legend.

7. Oct. 18, 1924 (Part II): Red Grange Day

More than 800 miles from the Polo Grounds, across endless Midwestern grain fields in Champaign, Ill., another remarkable performance was taking place that autumn afternoon. On the field of the University of Illinois' newly dedicated Memorial Stadium, in a 39-14 Illini homecoming victory over the Michigan Wolverines, Harold "Red" Grange had the single greatest individual performance in college football history.

In the first 12 minutes, Grange ran for a total of 262 yards—and scored each of the first four times he touched the ball. On the opening kickoff, No. 77 caught the ball on the Illinois 5-yard line and never looked back. On his first offensive carry, he raced 67 yards for a touchdown. His next carry, he ran 56 yards for a touchdown. Touch No. 4 produced TD No. 4, a 44-yarder.

The first 12 minutes!

Grange then went to the bench … before the end of the first quarter. In the third quarter, he returned and ran 13 yards for his fifth touchdown. In the fourth quarter, he passed to Marion Leonard for his sixth score of the day. In 42 minutes of playing time, Grange gained a total of 402 yards on 21 rushing and kick-return carries, and also completed six passes for 64 yards.

"This man Red Grange of Illinois is three or four men and a horse rolled into one for football purposes," wrote sportswriter Damon Runyon. "He is Jack Dempsey, Babe

Ruth, Al Jolson, Paavo Nurmi and Man o' War. Put together, they spell Grange."

But it was Grantland Rice who pinned on Grange the immortal designation "Galloping Ghost." And that was *before* he saw Grange play. When Rice finally did see Grange live in action, he waxed poetic—literally—about the impact made by the greatest offensive halfback in college football history:

There are two shapes now moving
Two ghosts that drift and glide
And which of them to tackle
Each rival must decide.
They shift with special swiftness
Across the swarded range.
And one of them's a shadow,
And one of them is Grange.

8. Jan. 1, 1929: "Wrong Way" Riegels Runs to Destiny

The play unfolds so quickly, so unbelievably quickly, that Roy Riegels barely has time to react.

A fumble by Georgia Tech back "Stumpy" Thomason. A crazy bounce into the waiting arms of Riegels near the Yellow Jacket 36-yard line. The Cal center and captain-elect, although a solid player, is a relative unknown on the national college football scene. He feels himself get bumped, but when he regains his balance he does what any good defender would do: he turns toward the goal line, 64 yards distant, and runs. As hard and as fast as he can, Riegels runs over the green, sun-drenched expanse of turf. The cheers and the deafening noise from the massive Rose Bowl crowd ring like thunder in his ears. It's a glorious moment.

But soon it turns into something else.

Teammate Benny Lom, racing only a step or two behind, screams at Riegels to lateral him the ball. "Stop!" Lom yells frantically. "Stop! You're going the wrong way!" Thinking that Lom wants to shanghai his moment of glory, Riegels yells back, "Get away from me! This is my touchdown!"

Play-by-play announcer Graham McNamee can't believe his eyes. "What's the matter with me?" he shouts into his radio mike, relaying the moment to millions of listeners from Los Angeles to Long Island—at the time, the Rose Bowl is the only postseason bowl game in the country. "Am I crazy?"

Georgia Tech players on the sideline are incredulous. They start to jump up and down in surprise. Jackets coach Bill Alexander hushes them: "Let's see how far he can go." Riegels goes almost all the way. Finally, he tries to reverse himself, but by then the gleeful Yellow Jackets have caught up to him. He's swarmed at the Cal 1-yard line. Several plays

later, Cal is forced to punt. The punt is blocked by a surging Tech defense. Safety.

Despite a valiant effort in the second half that included a blocked punt from Riegels, the Bears couldn't counteract the effects of his wrong-way run. The safety from the botched fumble return would prove the difference in an 8-7 Georgia Tech victory.

"I started in the right direction but made a complete horseshoe turn after going four or five yards when I saw two players coming at me from the right," explained Riegels later. "In pivoting to get away, I completely lost my bearings. I wasn't out of my head at all. I hadn't been hurt. I just headed the wrong way."

The play immediately turned Riegels into a national celebrity. For several days he was the most famous athlete in the country. "Wrong Way" was forever etched into the collective American sports memory. Riegels received hundreds of bizarre gifts—upside down cakes, "Wrong Way" street signs, railroad tickets starting at the end of the line—but through it all, he remained a good sport. He even performed in a vaudeville show that made light of his claim to fame. Riegels' run also had a longstanding effect on the way the game was played: at the beginning of the 1929 season, the rules committee enacted legislation prohibiting a player from advancing a fumble that touches the ground. This rule, unofficially known as the Riegels Rule, wasn't rescinded until 1990.

In 1971, Georgia Tech's entire 1929 Rose Bowl team was honored by the school's athletic hall of fame. Riegels and Lom attended as special guests, where, to their surprise, they received similar tribute. Riegels, who returned for his senior season in 1929 and was named to several All-America teams, accepted the honor with the same wit and graciousness that had enabled him to weather the "Wrong Way" storm:

"Believe me, I feel I've earned this."

9. Oct. 10, 1936: Dotting the "i" in Ohio State

In Ohio State gridiron history, it wasn't exactly a red-letter day. The Buckeyes, under coach Francis "Close the Gates of Mercy" Schmidt (so nicknamed for his penchant for running up the score on inferior foes), didn't tally a single point in a 6-0 loss to Jock Sutherland's powerhouse Pittsburgh Panthers at Ohio Stadium.

Yet in college football history, that afternoon in the Old Horseshoe on the banks of the Olentangy River would be momentous. At halftime, a trumpet player in Ohio State's marching band, John Brungart, finished the very first "Script Ohio" formation by strutting to the top of the configuration

to symbolically dot the i in Ohio. Thus one of the great traditions in college football was born.

The formation was the brainchild of legendary Ohio State band director Eugene Weigel, who visualized the outline of "Script Ohio"—a large block "O" peeling off into a moving formation to give the impression that the band was literally writing on the field—after seeing a rotating sign above Times Square during a visit to New York City. He also gave credit to the airplane skywriting craze, which was popular at the time. Yet ironically, the first school marching band to spell out "Ohio" in script writing was that of the University of Michigan, during the 1932 Ohio State game, a goodwill gesture proffered by the visiting Wolverine band.

Weigel fine-tuned the formation in subsequent years into what it is today, the most famous and recognizable marching band movement in college football. During a rehearsal in the fall of 1937, Weigel shouted to Glen R. Johnson, a sousaphone player, "Hey, you! Switch places with the trumpet player in the dot." Weigel liked what he saw, and from that moment on only sousaphone players would anchor the formation's most-cherished spot.

To see the movement performed is like watching a Russian ballet. At exactly 16 measures from the end of "Le Regiment," a stirring military march, the drum major struts out toward the top of the i, with a sousaphone player high-stepping a few paces behind. The crowd, sensing the building emotion of the scene, begins to cheer wildly. According to the official Ohio State marching band description, the drum major halts and points to the hallowed spot of vacant turf and "the sousaphone player assumes the post of honor, doffs his or her hat and bows deeply to both sides of the stadium." Buckeye marching-band protocols restrict the dotting of the i to a sousaphone player who is at least a fourth-year band member. On very special occasions, though, nonband members, usually individuals very close to the school and the state of Ohio, receive this highest of honors. Among the select few nonsousaphonists who have dotted the i: Bob Hope and—of course—Woody Hayes.

10. (Tie) Jan. 2, 1922: The 12th Man Tradition

Texas A&M is perhaps the most tradition-rich school in all of college football. Reveille, the fine collie mascot of the Aggies, has few rivals save for Uga, the white bulldog who patrols between the hedges during games at the University of Georgia. Until 1999, the towering bonfire built by A&M students before the annual showdown with rival Texas was a sight to see. The ritual of kissing the nearest coed following an A&M touchdown is probably the tradition most envied by

male students at other schools. The fight song begins "Hullabaloo, Caneck! Caneck!"—whatever that means. And what other marching band regularly plays music from the soundtrack to *Patton*?

But for me, one tradition stands out among all others: the 12th Man.

The story of the 12th Man was born in Dallas, during the Dixie Classic—the forerunner of the Cotton Bowl—on Jan. 2, 1922. The Aggies, champions of the now-defunct Southwest Conference, were playing Centre College. It was a close, hard-fought contest, and A&M's limited reserves were wearing down. Dana X. Bible, a well-traveled coach who'd won at a number of schools in the early days of the game, remembered E. King Gill, an A&M basketball player who moonlighted on the football team. Gill had traveled from College Station with the team, but had not dressed. He'd been assigned by Bible to work up in the press box as a spotter for *Waco News-Tribune* sports editor Jinx Tucker. Gill was called down to the field, where he went beneath the crowded stands and donned the uniform of an injured Aggie player. Then he assumed his place on the Aggie sideline and in A&M football history. The Aggies won the game 22-14, but Gill's services were never needed. Gill later said, "I wish I could say that I went in and ran for the winning touchdown, but I did not. I simply stood by in case my team needed me."

Like those Texans who ventured from afar to help defend the Alamo, Gill's name became legendary at Texas A&M. In years after, the A&M cadet corps assumed the role of the 12th Man, remaining standing throughout games and keeping their characteristic yells at window-shattering levels. In the 1980s, coach Jackie Sherrill added to the tradition by creating an entire squad of 12th Men. Sherrill held open tryouts for regular students to join the squad as special-teams performers. R.C. Slocum altered the tradition slightly when he took over as head coach in 1989, choosing to place only one walk-on (who shared the cherished No. 12 with several other players) on the field for special-teams plays.

And Gill? He never played a down, but was honored by his alma mater in a manner only dreamed of by generations of great Aggie players ever since: with his very own lifesize statue on A&M's sprawling campus.

10. (Tie) Dec. 13, 1973: John Cappelletti's Heisman Trophy Acceptance Speech.

John Cappelletti had one of the greatest seasons in Penn State football history in 1973, rushing for 1,522 yards. In his two-year career in the Nittany Lion backfield—he played

defensive back in 1971—he logged a total of 2,639 yards and scored 29 touchdowns. After his stellar senior campaign, his name popped up on every award and All-America list. In December 1973, he was named one of five finalists for the highest honor in college football, the Heisman Trophy. No Penn State player had ever won the award.

When his name was announced, Cappelletti walked up to the dais and, with Vice President Gerald Ford standing next to him, Cappelletti broke into one of the most emotionally charged speeches in sports history, ranking up there with the Rockne's Gipper speech and Lou Gehrig's farewell address.

For several minutes, Cappelletti thanked everyone who had helped him in his journey to that night, including his parents and his high school and college coaches, Jack Gottshalk and Joe Paterno. Then he paused. His face streaked with tears and his powerful, athletic body overwhelmed by feeling, Cappelletti struggled to continue.

"The youngest member of my family, Joseph, is very ill," said Cappelletti, his voice cracking at the mention of his 11-year-old brother. "He has leukemia. If I can dedicate this trophy to him tonight, and give him a couple of days of happiness, this is worth everything. I think a lot of people think that I go through a lot on Saturday and during the week, as most athletes do, and you get your bumps and bruises and it is a terrific battle out there on the field. Only for me, it is on Saturday and it's only in the fall. For Joseph, it is all year round and it is a battle that is unending with him, and he puts up with much more than I'll ever put up with, and I think that this trophy is more his than mine because he has been a great inspiration to me."

Joey Cappelletti died in 1976. The story of the two brothers was made into a book and later, a television movie, *Something for Joey* (1977). After a brief NFL career, Cappelletti became a successful businessman in California, where he now lives with his wife and four children.

He concluded his speech that evening with another message of thanks: "I don't think I'll ever forget this night."

We won't either, John.

Postscript...

... And 42 More

You didn't really think I could stop with just *10* great days, did you? The lore of college football history consists of so many traditions, so many great moments, so many great individuals from so many schools, large and small, it would be criminal to restrict the sum to just a top-10 collection. So here, in no particular order, is my list of "Others Receiving Votes." Chances are, *you'll* want to move some of them up.

Get the Point. From the autumn foliage of the Hudson Valley to the Corps of Cadets parade on the Plain, from the echoes of "On, Brave Old Army Team" reverberating off the same stone barracks where Lee, Patton and MacArthur lived, to the game being played in its purest form at Michie Stadium, there is no greater college football experience than the third Saturday in October at West Point.

Roll ... Tide! If you can't get a dinner date with Sela Ward for ribs at Dreamland, check out the Bryant Museum, where the Bear's famed houndstooth hat is preserved for eternity. You won't be disappointed.

Death Valley, South Carolina. No visit to Clemson is complete without a cold beer at the Esso Club and a respectful touch of Frank Howard's Rock.

The Grove. Bring your appetite and a camera. Complete with champagne, silver candelabras and arguably the best spread of food in the SEC, the Grove at Ole Miss is one of the great tailgating destinations in all of college football.

Boolah, Boolah. The Yale "marching" band is undisciplined but lovable. Close your eyes and listen to the trumpets and horns blare (1913 alum) Cole Porter's "Bulldog!" while they stream out of the famed portals of the Yale Bowl.

Extra! Extra! The 1968 Harvard-Yale tie game was one of the greatest games in college football history, but the staff of the *Harvard Crimson* student newspaper deserves credit for the sport's most memorable headline: HARVARD BEATS YALE, 29-29.

Death, Taxes—and Lehigh-Lafayette. The game never has national-title or major-bowl implications, but the important thing to know is that it will be played just as it has been 140 times in the past 121 years, longer than any other continuous rivalry in college football history.

Orange Bowl. Sure, it's old and rickety, but for a big game there's nothing like the atmosphere at the old horseshoe in Little Havana.

Paging George P. Burdell. In 1927, a Georgia Tech student inaugurated what is possibly the longest-running practical joke in college football history by creating a mythical student named George P. Burdell. Tech students keep the tradition going by paging the nonexistent Mr. Burdell during Yellow Jacket football games, both home and away.

Winged Wolverine. The sight of that helmet—originally designed to help Wolverine quarterbacks locate friendly receivers—on a sun-splashed fall afternoon always gives me goose bumps.

Game of the Century. A new one's played every other season or so, but lucky people who saw the Nebraska-Oklahoma showdown on Thanksgiving Day 1971 can legitimately claim they witnessed the greatest college football game ever played. The No. 1 Cornhuskers, led by Jerry Tagge, Jeff Kinney and Rich Glover, edged Jack Mildren, Greg Pruitt and the rest of the No. 2 Sooners, 35-31. But the real winner that day was college football.

Wild Blue Yonder. Forget the pregame jet flyovers. The flight of Air Force's peregrine falcon mascot against a backdrop of snowcapped peaks of the Rampart Range steals the show in Colorado Springs.

The World's Largest Outdoor Cocktail Party. Bulldogs and Gators start arriving in Jacksonville, Fla., around Tuesday, and the party continues—in the parking lots, under the overpasses, anywhere and everywhere—well into Sunday. Oh, and the Georgia-Florida football game usually isn't half bad either.

Photo Op. Surrounded by majestic, towering pine trees, the University of North Carolina's Kenan Stadium is to college football what Augusta National is to golf—the most picturesque venue in the game.

Rock On. Slippery Rock University (formerly Slippery Rock State Teachers College) is located in Slippery Rock, Pa.

The school came to the attention of the nation in 1936, during a raging postseason debate about whether Minnesota or Pittsburgh deserved to be ranked No. 1 in the country. One sportswriter took a close look and decided, with impeccable logic, that neither did. After all, he argued, The Rock beat Westminster, which beat West Virginia Wesleyan, which beat Duquesne, which beat *Pittsburgh*, which beat Notre Dame, which beat Northwestern, which beat *Minnesota*. Slippery Rock's No. 1! The article was quickly reprinted all over the country. Since then, on fall Saturdays in major college stadiums and on radio and television shows across the nation (and on the Armed Forces Network overseas), public address announcers and radio-TV commentators will invariably include, at the end of a scoring update, the score of The Rock's game.

Cradle of Coaches. There must be something in the water in Oxford. Gridiron legends such as Paul Brown, Woody Hayes, Ara Parseghian, Weeb Ewbank and Jim Tressel all have cut their football teeth at Miami of Ohio.

Hail to the Chief. Even when Burt Reynolds is on campus, there's no more revered figure in Tallahassee on game day than Florida State's venerable Chief Osceola and his mottled mount, Renegade.

Georgia Conundrum. Pick one: 1) "How 'bout them dawgs!" 2) Between the Hedges. 3) Uga. Tough call. There's no wrong answer to this multiple-choice quiz in Athens.

Ernie Davis. It took 27 years for the first African-American to win the Heisman Trophy, which this great Syracuse running back did in 1961. Sadly, less than two years later Davis succumbed to leukemia.

White Tigers. When the LSU Tigers wear white during a home game under the lights in Baton Rouge, the visiting team can start its buses before kickoff. You'd have better luck invading Russia in the middle of winter.

Gold Pated. On Friday nights before a home game (Thursday evenings for road games), student volunteers at Notre Dame apply fresh coats of paint containing real gold dust to Irish helmets. An expensive tradition, but this is Notre Dame, after all.

Ball Coach's Visor. For many years, small tremors originating in Gainesville, Fla., could be felt as far south as Key West and as far north as Atlanta when Steve Spurrier would slam his visor into the turf at the famed "Swamp," a.k.a. Ben-Hill Griffin Stadium at Florida Field.

222-0. On Oct. 7, 1916, John Heisman's Georgia Tech Golden Tornado overwhelmed tiny Cumberland (Tenn.) College by the largest margin of victory in college football history. In the rout, Georgia Tech amassed an incredible 978 rushing yards and 32 touchdowns against the helpless Bulldogs, who, incidentally, suited up only 13 players. Of course, after Cumberland's semipro baseball team humiliated Tech 22-0 on the diamond in a game the previous spring, any betting man knew that Heisman was playing for keeps in Atlanta. Moral: take Tech— give the points.

What Is the Monon Bell? "I'll take Small-School College Football Traditions for $800, Alex." Answer: "It's a 300-pound railroad bell awarded to the winner of the Wabash Little Giants-DePauw Tigers rivalry game."

Walk the Walk. At Williams College, immediately following a homecoming win over archrival Amherst, the Ephs, still clad in their uniforms, march en masse up Spring Street in Williamstown, Mass., for cold refreshments and free haircuts at St. Pierre's Barber Shop.

Executive Privilege. When Calvin Coolidge was an Amherst student, he served as an assistant football coach and developed a series of plays that could be run in sequence without signals, a forerunner of the modern no-huddle offense. Never said much as president, either.

Keys to Victory. Before kickoffs at Washington State, Cougars fans rattle keys. Outside of Keith Jackson, the tradition is Pullman's greatest contribution to the game.

Gig 'Em, Aggies! According to Texas A&M lore, "The Aggie War Hymn," one of college football's most stirring fight songs, was written by Aggie alum J.J. "Pinky" Wilson while standing guard on the Rhine River during World War I.

Manila Bay … Midway … Coral Sea … Guadalcanal. The names of 44 famous battles in the history of the U.S. Navy and Marine Corps that ring the facade at Navy-Marine Corps Memorial Stadium in Annapolis constitute the toughest road schedule in history.

Old Oaken Bucket. Paul Bunyan's Axe and the Little Brown Jug have their supporters, but in my opinion those other Big Ten trophy games "pail" in comparison.

For Whom the Bell Tolls. In the University of Arizona's student union building hangs one of two ship's bells salvaged from the wreckage of the USS *Arizona* at Pearl Harbor. In honor of the 1,177 men killed that fateful December day, the bell tolls after Wildcat victories, except those over rival Arizona State and other in-state opponents.

Strawberry Canyon. In the modern era of escalating ticket prices, a free seat on the heights of scenic Strawberry Canyon outside of Cal's Memorial Stadium remains the best in college football.

Pig Sooie! Auburn's "War Eagle!" is full of passion, but Arkansas' battle cry is tops in the game.

All-Americans. The entire starting lineup from Montana State's 1941 squad perished in World War II.

Old Chicago. The Maroons claim one of the game's greatest coaches, Amos Alonzo Stagg; the first Heisman Trophy winner, Jay Berwanger; and the distinction of being the only Big Ten Conference team never to lose to Notre Dame.

The Price of Honor. The 1951 University of San Francisco Dons had a 9–0 record, college football's leading rusher and scorer in Ollie Matson, the nation's most intimidating defense—and a young SID named Pete Rozelle. Yet, because players refused to accept a bowl bid that would require them to leave their two black teammates at home, the small, cash-strapped school was forced to drop football. Forever.

Mood Swings. My Sundays in the fall are determined by how my alma mater, Pitt, does on Saturday. I'm sure it's the same with you.

Home Boys. What are the odds that one school—Texas Christian University—could give us three college football legends in Davey O'Brien, Slingin' Sammy Baugh *and* Dan Jenkins?

Way Down South. In 1899, tiny Sewanee (a.k.a. The University of the South) played five games in six days versus Tulane, Texas, Texas A&M, LSU and Mississippi. Sewanee went a perfect five-for-five, outscoring those foes 91-0.

Written in Stone. In college football, nicknames come and go. But thanks to defensive linemates Vince Lombardi, Alex Wojciechowicz, Nat Pierce, Ed Franco, John Druze, Leo Paquin and Al Bartbartsky, the legend of Fordham's Seven Blocks of Granite will never erode.

The Best Damn Band in the Land. From "Across the Field" and "Buckeye Battle Cry" to "Le Regiment," the selection of songs played by the Ohio State marching band is unsurpassed. Before I die, I want to do three things: listen to the OSU marching band play in the echo-filled rotunda under the entrance arches to Ohio Stadium, dot the i—and watch *Casablanca* one last time.

New Brunswick, N.J. The madness started here in 1869.

Judgment Call

How a Supreme Court Decision Led to the Birth of the BCS

By Gene Wojciechowski

THIS IS RICHARD NIXON'S DOING: THE BCS; CONFERENCE expansion; the neutering of Jan. 1 bowls; Notre Dame flying solo on NBC; more games on the plasma than you can shake a TiVo at.

All Nixon.

In 1970—and stay with me on this—our 37th president of the United States nominated a bow tie-wearing, bridge-playing Chicagoan to the U.S. Court of Appeals, Seventh Circuit. Five years later Nixon's appointee got a call from our next president, Gerald Ford, who succeeded RMN because of a little misunderstanding called Watergate. Anyway, Ford asked Judge Bow Tie to serve on the U.S. Supreme Court.

Nine years after that, the justice forever changed the business of college football. His name is John Paul Stevens, and on June 27, 1984, he essentially told the NCAA to stick a sock in its monopoly. Since then, the plate tectonics of the game have shifted and grinded so often that little remains of the previous college football epoch. It's like looking at your high school graduation photo 20 years later.

Justice Stevens didn't play much football, but he knew a thing or two, or three, about antitrust law. It's his specialty of sorts. So when the *NCAA* v. *Board of Regents of University of Oklahoma and Georgia Athletic Association* case made its way to the Supreme Court, Stevens was the guy to watch.

In short, OU and Georgia said the NCAA restrained free trade by artificially controlling the number of televised college football games. The NCAA said it did not. Did so. Did not.

Problem is, the NCAA got its shorts handed to it on the District Court level, then again on the Court of Appeals level. So it tried the Supreme Court, where it found Justice Stevens waving a forefinger at it like Dikembe Mutombo.

"Today we hold only that the record supports the District Court's conclusion that by curtailing output and blunting the ability of member institutions to respond to

consumer preference, the NCAA has restricted rather than enhanced the place of intercollegiate athletics in the Nation's life," wrote Stevens in the majority opinion. "Accordingly, the judgment of the Court of Appeals is affirmed."

In layman's terms, this is why you can now order up ESPN's GamePlan. "[The ruling] was sort of like the Berlin Wall," says Jim Delany, Big Ten commissioner and a former staff attorney for the North Carolina Justice Department. "I think it would have come down for other reasons. I think Oklahoma and Georgia expedited it."

"[It was] the definitive line of demarcation, without a doubt," says John Junker, executive director of the Fiesta Bowl. "It really brought the most powerful part of mass culture into our sport, which is television. And everything changed."

It changed because the NCAA was no longer the most powerful mom-and-pop shop on the block. Pre-1984 ruling: "What you basically did was sit around and wait for a fax to see who was going to be on [TV] that week, what two games," says Mark Womack, executive associate commissioner of the Southeastern Conference. Post-1984 ruling: "It created a five-, 10-fold interest in college football," says Junker.

If you tie a plumb line from *NCAA* v. *OU/Georgia* to this exact moment and snap the string just so, chances are it will leave a mark on just about every major college football business decision. Think biblical trickle-down effect (this begat that, which begat that, which begat that, etc.)

Back then the NCAA was an oligarchy when it came to providing "product" (as the TV network people call it) for the airwaves. If you were a college football fan, it was like eating at the school cafeteria: you took whatever was slopped on the plate. ABC and CBS—the two main broadcasting heavyweights for college football at the time—offered a brief and often predictable menu of choices for their national broadcasts: Alabama, Michigan, Notre Dame, USC, Oklahoma, Nebraska, Texas.

"It was a good package, but it probably kept college football from taking off," says Womack. "It kept it as a niche."

All that changed the nanosecond the Supreme Court cleared its throat. Deregulation meant freedom, which meant more of everything, especially college football broadcasts. Suddenly there were—gasp!—choices.

No longer bound by the NCAA's restrictions, conferences burst out of the building like fifth-graders on the last day of school. You mean we can make our own deals now? Suddenly every league commissioner worth his country club membership was looking at spreadsheets, ratings, the number of TV sets in their particular geographical region.

"I think it elevated the role of conferences," says former SEC commissioner Roy Kramer, one of the godfathers of the post-1984 era. "Conferences became the television entity."

Conference commissioners, says Kramer, became de facto marketing directors for their respective leagues, "whether you wanted to or not." Their influence began to extend into the networks, and slowly into the NCAA legislative process. The stronger your conference, the more clout you carried in your back pocket.

"I think [the 1984 ruling] changed the way people operated in the framework of the NCAA," Kramer says. "I expect to a degree, good or bad, it significantly drew the line in the sand between the major college programs who played football and those who did not play major college football, so to speak. The marketplace drove so many things."

History is about context, so remember the lay of the land in 1984. The four reigning bowls were the Rose, Orange, Sugar and Cotton, though the Fiesta was beginning to attract attention. Those were the days when the legendary Jim "Hoss" Brock, emissary extraordinaire from the Cotton Bowl, wore a groove line from Dallas to South Bend. If he could have extended a bowl invitation at the Irish's Blue-Gold spring game, he would have done it—and maybe he did. As it was, most of the elite teams were locked up for bowls long before regular season's end, either by wink-wink deals or by automatic berths. That's why the 1984 postseason lineup featured such bizarre matchups as No. 1 Brigham Young winning a national title vs. unranked Michigan in the Holiday Bowl, No. 5 Nebraska vs. No. 11 LSU in the Sugar and No. 8 Boston College vs. unranked Houston in the Cotton.

Meanwhile, the Big 12 was still the Big Eight. There was a Southwest Conference but no Conference USA, Big East (at least, not in football) or Mountain West. The Big Ten

Deregulation meant freedom, which meant more of everything, especially college football broadcasts.

actually had 10 members. The ACC had eight. The SEC had 10. Independents, such as Notre Dame, Penn State, Miami, Florida State, Pittsburgh, Boston College, Virginia Tech and Syracuse, still walked the earth.

With the NCAA out of the TV business, the College Football Association became a major player as a dealmaker. ABC still had the Big Ten and Pacific-10, but the CFA had most everyone else. Then along came another jolt of seismic activity.

In June 1990, Delany delivered to the Big Ten one of the great free agent signings: Joe Paterno and the Nittany Lions. It was a master move for all sorts of reasons. It added value to an already strong conference (which comes in handy during TV negotiation time) and it also gave the league a recruiting and TV foothold in the East.

Over the next two months, Kramer dropped his own little cluster bomb: the SEC would add Arkansas and South Carolina (becoming the first league with 12 teams and two divisions) and also add the first conference championship game at the end of the '92 regular season. Take that.

As Division I-A reconfiguration became the norm, so did the idea of a new world order. An ACC executive named Tom Mickle sat in a Greensboro, N.C., steakhouse and began jotting on a mustard-stained napkin. The scribble? Ideas for a revolutionary bowl format.

So much was happening so fast. In 1990, Notre Dame, the Hope diamond of independents, stunned college football's movers and shakers when it ditched the CFA and made its own exclusive deal with NBC, effective in 1991. The Big East officially formed in 1991, taking with it most of the important Eastern independents, including Miami. Turns out Notre Dame had conveniently failed to sign its agreement with the CFA, which, in essence, made the Irish free agents. And, oh, by the way, Kramer was bolting with his SEC, too, taking the 600-pound gorilla to CBS.

The final touch was Florida State's move in 1992 to the ACC. The independent, with the notable exception of Notre Dame, was all but extinct. The CFA would follow shortly thereafter.

Combine all these factors—conference expansion, the plucking of independents by the ACC, Big Ten and Big East

(footnote: had the Big East been an all-sports league, Penn State would have likely chosen it over the Big Ten), the Notre Dame-NBC smoochfest, the SEC's subsequent move to CBS, the backroom bowl negotiations—and the incubator was at a perfect setting for more change. Can you say The Bowl Coalition?

The Bowl Coalition, which lasted from 1992 to 1994, had its heart in the right place. It was developed to put a collar on the Hoss Brocks of the bowl world, increase interest in the college game, preserve the bowl structure, as well as create more attractive postseason matchups (translation: ka-ching, TV and attendance dollars). After all, Coalition supporters argued, there had been only eight No. 1 vs. No. 2 bowl games in the previous 29 years. The Big East, ACC, SEC, SWC, Big Eight and Notre Dame signed on, as did the Orange, Sugar, Fiesta, Cotton, Gator, John Hancock and Blockbuster bowls. The Pac-10 stuck its toe in the at-large pool by offering its No. 2 team.

The Coalition had its problems, but it did give America No. 1 Miami vs. No. 2 Alabama in the 1992 Sugar Bowl, No. 1 Florida State vs. No. 2 Nebraska in the 1993 Orange and No. 1 Nebraska vs. No. 3 Miami in the 1994 Orange. Then it morphed into The Bowl Alliance, which goosed things by eliminating conference tie-ins with the Sugar, Fiesta and Orange bowls. Presumably, that would help make it easier for league champions to play league champions, as well as increase the likelihood of a No. 1 vs. No. 2 game.

It worked, sort of. Top-ranked Nebraska played No. 2 Florida for the 1995 national title, but that was it for the premium pairing. As long as the Big Ten and Pac-10 were sending their champions exclusively to the Rose Bowl, there could be no true guarantee of a No. 1 vs. No. 2 title game.

This is where Delany, Kramer, Pac-10 commissioner Tom Hansen, then-ABC Sports executive Tony Petitti (now CBS Sports executive producer), the ACC's Gene Corrigan and, to a lesser extent, Big East commissioner Mike Tranghese and Big 8/12 commissioner Carl James began to shape what would soon become the Bowl Championship Series. In the end, ABC, using its juice from owning the Rose Bowl rights, gained control of the entire BCS telecast schedule. The Big Ten and Pac-10 gained entry into the national title game mix, but it cost the Rose Bowl its guaranteed tie-in with those two conference champions.

"The Rose Bowl tradition is probably the most important tradition, the most important external relationship the Big Ten has," says Delany. "There's a lot of pride, history, a lot of revenue, a lot of exposure tied into it. [But] if [the BCS] put together the 1-2 game, they very much had the

premier game. That's not to say the Rose Bowl wasn't important, but [the BCS] could put together that [title] game. And Penn State coming in … they wanted a bite at the apple."

Delany knew it was in his conference's best interests—and the Rose Bowl's—to take the BCS plunge. In retrospect, it seemed the most logical next step for college football, too.

Ta-da: No. 1 Tennessee vs. No. 2 FSU in the 1998 season, followed by No. 1 FSU vs. No. 2 Virginia Tech in 1999, then No. 1 Oklahoma vs. disputed No. 2 FSU in 2000, then No. 1 Miami vs. disputed No. 2 Nebraska in 2001, then No. 1 Miami vs. No. 2 Ohio State in 2002, then disputed No. 1 Oklahoma vs. No. 2 LSU in 2003, while AP No. 1 USC played in the Rose. And so on and so forth.

The disputes were the result of the BCS rankings, a mixture, depending on the year, of computer rankings, human polls, "quality wins," schedule strength, losses and quartile rank (you should have seen Kramer try to explain that to the assembled SEC media in 1998). Anyway, the thing was, and still is, more difficult to understand than Portuguese. "But from a business side, it's clearly an economic home run," says Tranghese of the BCS. "Even though our system has been mired in controversy, it allows the two best teams to come together. You could argue that the best football game played in the '90s was Ohio State-Miami. That could have never been played in the old system."

"We wanted to create interest, and beyond my greatest dreams it has done that," says Kramer. "A lot of that is because of the controversy. That's not all bad. We're not the NFL. If we have 200 young men holding up a finger with a [championship] ring on it, instead of 100 doing the same thing, that's not all bad."

True, but that doesn't mean there aren't other BCS facial tics. As the BCS grew stronger, the aura of Jan. 1 grew weaker. In fact, the last national championship game played between Nos. 1 and 2 on a Jan. 1 was the Miami-Ohio State game in 2003.

"I think it's the price of doing business," says Tranghese. "Personally, I think to a large degree we've given away Jan. 1 as our day. We're all guilty of it."

"Time will have to decide if that was the best way to do that or not," says Notre Dame associate athletics director John Heisler, who has been at the school since 1978. "I think we've lost something there."

The BCS was also responsible for creating the catfight between college football's haves (the BCS member conferences) and have-nots (the non-BCS members, like the

Mid-American and WAC). Congress, which apparently has nothing better to do with its time and taxpayer money, threw a small hissy fit. The non-BCS members threatened lawsuits until the torts came home.

A compromise was reached: a fifth BCS bowl was established, which will make it easier for a previously jilted non-BCS member to participate. In other words, they wanted access to the money and exposure. In the post-1984 era, it's almost always about the money.

All things considered, it is difficult to argue with college football's evolution and revolution. The NCAA maintained that increased television exposure might adversely affect live game-day attendance (at least, that's what it told the Supreme Court), but it hasn't worked out that way. Annual total attendance for all NCAA teams has increased most years since 1984.

"In our league the concern for years was, at what level is too much television? And when does it start to impact attendance in stadiums?" says the SEC's Womack. "But we haven't found that point yet. Everybody in our league has increased their stadium capacities during the past 10 years."

College football is many things, but no one will accuse of it of being Penn State-uniform dull. More like Oregon's bug-light yellow unis. Today, the Bowl Championship

Series and jerry-rigged No. 1 vs. No. 2 games, the next decade, a playoff? After all, 12-, eight- and four-team playoff models have been around longer than JoePa (well, maybe not that long), and the revenue potential is enticing. But college presidents, perhaps spooked by the 12-game schedule and influx of conference championship games, continue to resist lengthening the season. Conference commissioners aren't in a hurry to cede their power and paydays to an NCAA-run tournament. And you can bet the bowl directors aren't lobbying for a playoff system.

"It sounds easy on paper, but it's not nearly as easy when you get down to it," says Kramer, who readily admits the Alliance-Coalition-BCS was conceived in part as a preemptive strike against a playoff system. "I'm not convinced yet that a playoff would generate that much more [money]. I don't think it's the bonanza some people think it would be."

So what happens next? Who knows? This is the beauty of our times—nobody has a real clue, just as nobody could predict the future in the post-*NCAA* v. *OU/Georgia* age. The business of the game is as fluid as sweat. It is, as one BCS executive puts it, "a Byzantine empire … 1,000 different interests with 100 different masters."

Total Control

The Curious Cult of College Coaches

BY ANDREW BAGNATO

BO SCHEMBECHLER LOVED TO TELL THIS STORY: PRESIDENT Gerald Ford, a former Michigan center and co-captain, showed up at a Wolverines practice. Flanked by the Secret Service, Ford wandered onto the field. The team lined up in formation, but just before the snap the players realized that one of the president's bodyguards was standing in the path of the play. (It was a power run—what else?) Schembechler asked the agent to move. He wouldn't. The players glanced at Schembechler, who barked, "Run the guy over if you have to!" The ball was snapped and the agent barely lunged out of the way as the squad, winged helmets and all, thundered toward him. "Nothing," Schembechler wrote in his autobiography, "interferes with practice."

The anecdote is as instructive as it is amusing. College football coaches don't let anyone encroach on their turf—be it the president of the university or the president of the United States. On Saturday afternoons, the school president can walk through the packed grandstand without being recognized. Down on the field, his coach is escorted by state troopers. The coach is usually paid two or three times more than the president. And when was the last time anyone brought a life-size cutout of the Penn State president to a tailgate party outside Beaver Stadium?

It's no wonder college football coaches often believe they are larger than life. In many ways, they are. Some have been so big they required only one name: Woody. Bear. Ara. Bo.

"Football is a coach's medium, just as movies are a director's medium and fascism is a dictator's medium," wrote Jim Murray, the late *Los Angeles Times* Pulitzer Prize-winner. "I sometimes think the last stand of dictatorship in this world is the college football coach. His word is law, his rule is absolute, his power is unlimited."

Coaches are the perfect products of a game that inspires root-hog-or-die passion despite its sometimes-questionable ethics. College football is a colorful thread in the fabric of the nation, especially in the South and Midwest. In those places, college football coaches loom large.

Consider Bear Bryant, the legendary coach of the University of Alabama Crimson Tide. Alabama politicians courted Bryant, whose popularity transcended party lines. "Usually, Bryant was linked with church rather than state— 'The Bear walks on water,'" Alabaman Diane McWhorter wrote in a history of the Civil Rights era. "His televised postgame recap, *The Bear Bryant Show*, had become the City of Churches' strictest Sunday ritual." At a time when Alabamans struggled to come to grips with desegregation, Bryant's Tide was a source of statewide pride (except in Auburn precincts, where Bryant was loathed). Years after his death, a museum dedicated to Bryant attracts thousands of visitors to the Tuscaloosa campus.

To outsiders, coaches may appear to be distant figures. But players frequently develop an enduring emotional bond with their coach. Eight members of Bryant's 1982 Alabama team served as pallbearers at his funeral. Nine players on Eddie Robinson's last Grambling team were the sons of former Robinson players. "That [legacy] was the highest compliment for what we were trying to do at Grambling," Robinson, who retired with more victories than any college football coach in history, wrote in his autobiography.

Robinson often spoke about his role as a father figure to his players. Fans rarely see that side of a coach. But it doesn't stop the faithful from exalting them—the winners, at least. In 1988, after leading Notre Dame to its 11th, and last, national title, Lou Holtz was no longer viewed as a clipboard-toting quipster. He was now a business expert, despite having scant experience beyond football. Holtz wrote a best-selling business book, *Winning Every Day*, and by 2004, Holtz the coach/corporate guru was pulling in more than $40,000 per speaking engagement.

No matter what he does on Saturday, or to whom, Florida State coach Bobby Bowden often spends his Sunday mornings in the pulpit. "… And on the sixth day, he smote the Gators … " In Baton Rouge, Louisiana State fans sported Saint Nick T-shirts to herald the hiring of Nick Saban. Their adoration surpassed mortal understanding when he led the Bengal Tigers to a share of the 2003 national championship.

"We love our coaches because they are 'doers' and because the games they preside over transcend our routine day-to-day experiences, and because it is comforting to think of them as being, like movie stars and lead guitarists, 'bigger than life,'" wrote columnist Rick Telander, a former Northwestern cornerback.

Some have been so big they required only one name: Woody. Bear. Ara. Bo.

Coaches typically don't think of themselves as movie stars and lead guitarists (except former Washington coach Rick Neuheisel, who was known for playing a few licks at team parties). But they often see themselves as generals engaged in a critical, if bloodless, conflict. There are long ties between football and the military. "I learned a great many things in the Marines that helped me as a football coach," former Iowa coach Hayden Fry wrote in his autobiography. "The Marines train men hard and to do things the right way, just as a football team must train."

Former Notre Dame coach Frank Leahy served in the Navy. The University of Tennessee's cavernous stadium is named after General Robert Neyland, a former aide-de-camp to West Point superintendent Douglas MacArthur. After Neyland retired from the Army, the Volunteers hired him with a specific marching order: beat Vandy!

"Football is so similar to the military, and because they're so similar, a football program has to be run the same way," Colorado coach Gary Barnett once said. "You have to move large numbers of people and there has to be a high degree of order and control happening."

The coach's authority often seems as inviolable as that of an Army general. And like many generals, coaches often become swaddled in myth. Think of Patton with a playbook. No coach has enjoyed more mythic status than Knute Rockne. Having turned Notre Dame football into a standard-bearer for Catholic immigrants who couldn't find South Bend on a map, Rockne was already something of a celebrity when he perished in a plane crash in 1931. But he became ingrained in the national consciousness when a B-movie actor named Ronald Reagan played George Gipp in *Knute Rockne, All-American*. It didn't matter whether Gipp ever uttered that fabled deathbed request. Rockne's "Win One for the Gipper" pep talk quickly became part of American lore.

Rockne was the first college football coach to transcend the sport. But the spiritual father of the modern college football coach—the my-way-or-the-highway autocrat—is Amos Alonzo Stagg, who turned the University of Chicago into a national powerhouse at the turn of the century. School president William Rainey Harper hired Stagg to build a football team that would help Chicago earn the kind of recognition reserved for Ivy League institutions. Stagg did

that. But as the Maroons became more successful—they won seven titles in the conference now known as the Big Ten—Stagg began to assert his autonomy. "Stagg stubbornly refused to allow the athletic board to exercise control and, when it asked to examine the eligibility of players or showed any sign of asserting its authority, he complained vigorously to Harper," wrote John Sayle Watterson in *College Football*. "Through football, Stagg put Chicago in the limelight but often seemed more interested in his own reputation than in the institution that employed him."

The Maroons' fortunes had flagged by the time Stagg left the South Side in 1933. Fed up with the excesses of big-time football, the University of Chicago discontinued the sport in 1939 and dropped out of the Big Ten altogether in 1946. But the die had been cast for the modern college football coach—a dictator who jealously guarded the sanctity of his "program."

It wasn't long before all-powerful coaches such as Leahy at Notre Dame and Bud Wilkinson at Oklahoma began to dominate the sport. "Your head coach today has become an absolute dictator," William "Pudge" Heffelfinger, the first Walter Camp All-America in 1889, wrote in 1954.

Heffelfinger's description fits a score of latter-day coaches, including Michigan coach Lloyd Carr. Carr has been dubbed "Paranoid Lloyd" by beat writers covering the team because he's gone to such lengths to limit media access to one of the nation's most widely followed programs. Heffelfinger also would not have been surprised by Kansas State's Bill Snyder, who is renowned among peers for his almost obsessive attention to detail. During a team meal at the Wildcats' hotel, Snyder once complained to aides when the caterers provided butter in foil-wrapped packets. Snyder had wanted whipped butter because, he said later, it had less fat. "There are a lot of little things like that," Snyder said. "If you do pay attention to detail and the "little" things are important to you, you make them important to people in the program."

Football, by rule and by nature, breeds a need for control. Players line up in set formations before launching intricately planned attacks. Control is critical even after the whistle: a team may be penalized for "excessive celebration" if it parties too hard after scoring a touchdown. Ever watch a coach after his team hits pay dirt? He's the one grabbing

players and pulling them back to the bench. Never mind that 70,000 people in the stands are going bananas.

"You go through the history of great college coaches, and they have this history of being totally in control of everything," says Murray Sperber, a retired Indiana University sports historian.

The best coaches seem to exert the strictest control. Woody Hayes was a control freak. Lee Corso wasn't. Understand?

All this power can go to a man's head. At a time when many coaches in other sports have had to make concessions to professional leagues and adapt to changing social mores, college football coaches have mostly kept their fiefdoms intact. In basketball and baseball, the top prospects can go directly from the preps to the pros. Not in football. An NFL rule, upheld in a 2003 court challenge by former Ohio State tailback Maurice Clarett, bars players from entering the draft until they've been out of high school for three years. The rule gives college head coaches tremendous leverage over players. But they're facing other threats. They are being held increasingly responsible for their players' off-the-field conduct, not to mention their graduation rates—a concept foreign to Bryant and his peers. The old boys-will-be-boys attitude has been replaced by uncomfortable questions about who's minding the store. Part of this has to do with the broadening scope of the media in the Internet age. But coaches also believe the accountability is linked to the astronomical salaries they command. "Because of that, there's no question that people are less patient, less tolerant, and want to hold [coaches] more accountable when they make that much money," Oregon coach Mike Bellotti said.

This shift in attitude may pose the greatest challenge to the college coach's rule. Just ask Mike Price, fired by Alabama before he coached a single game. Price's sin? An off-season visit to a strip club after he had been warned by school officials about his public conduct. But while Price, who later latched on with Texas-El Paso, paid dearly for his actions, two other nationally publicized cases in the spring of 2004 showed that coaches have retained a good measure of invincibility.

At Ohio State, 14 Buckeye football players have been involved in at least 13 incidents since the school hired head coach Jim Tressel in 2001, an Associated Press search of court records revealed. Among the problems: assault, drunken driving, robbery and carrying a concealed weapon. To outsiders, the Buckeyes appeared to be running amok. Not to then-OSU athletic director Andy Geiger, who publicly absolved Tressel of any responsibility for his players' conduct. Think that had anything to do with the fact that Tressel led the Buckeyes to the 2002 national title?

"In my experience, if a coach is winning and they're making a lot of money [for the school], people have been more lenient," Texas coach Mack Brown said. "That's just the sort of society we live in."

Meanwhile, Colorado's Gary Barnett found himself embroiled in a controversy surrounding his program's recruiting practices. At least nine women, including former CU placekicker Katie Hnida, said they were sexually assaulted by Colorado football players or recruits. The first accusation surfaced in 1997, two years before Barnett's arrival in Boulder. The accusations provoked a public outcry, but Barnett was placed on administrative leave in February '04 only after making derogatory remarks about Hnida. The Boulder case drew the attention of Congress, which pressed the NCAA for tougher national recruiting rules. Recruiting is the lifeblood of college football and any effort to regulate it represents a serious challenge to the coaches' command.

From Miami to Seattle, coaches anxiously watched the CU situation unfold. Would the school hold Barnett responsible? And if so, would that signal an end to the hegemony coaches have enjoyed for a century?

They need not have worried. Although CU forced Barnett to adopt more stringent recruiting standards than his Big 12 rivals, he kept his job. Applause rippled through the packed campus news conference announcing Barnett's reinstatement. Elsewhere, Barnett's players openly celebrated. Score another victory for the dictators.

Rules Made, Rules Broken

A Brief, Colorful History of College Football Recruiting

BY BUD WITHERS

O N A JULY DAY IN 1948, LAVELL EDWARDS WAS OUTSIDE, irrigating his family's fruit and berry fields in Utah. A high school lineman of note, he was just two months from starting college, and because he had attended Orem High School near the Brigham Young University campus, that college would be BYU.

A younger brother summoned Edwards to the house. At the front door were two coaches from Utah State, who had seen Edwards' stout play in a high school all-star game and wondered: would he be interested in checking out the Aggies' campus?

"I drove myself to Logan," Edwards recalls. "I don't think they gave me any gas money."

At the last minute, Edwards decided to attend Utah State. His recruitment was typical of the day—devoid of five-star ratings, Internet message-board gossip and faux jerseys with his name on the back. A coach wouldn't know the makeup of his recruiting class until it walked onto campus.

"I got away from home," Edwards always said jokingly, "so I didn't have to milk those cows."

College football recruiting was more hit-and-miss back then, before there were summer camps, evaluation services and assistant coaches whose primary job it is not to allow a prospect in his assigned area to go undiscovered. In the first half of the 20th century, coaching staffs were no larger than half the size of today's. Recruiting was unscientific, air travel infrequent, and prospects usually attended colleges close to home.

Sitting upstairs in his home in Seattle's Capitol Hill district shortly before his death in 2003, 96-year-old Chuck Carroll recalled a career at the University of Washington that ended in his being named a consensus All-America halfback in 1928.

"It was just logical that I went to Washington," said Carroll, who grew up three miles from the UW campus. "But nobody asked me to come to Washington."

Today, the college coach who failed to put the squeeze on a player of Carroll's caliber would soon find himself applying for a job in telemarketing or peddling oranges on busy street corners. By contrast, many early-day prospects went unrecruited or misjudged—players like Harry Smith, a guard on a couple of Howard Jones' juggernauts of the late '30s at Southern California.

"I recruited Southern California for a long time, trying to convince them I was good enough," said Smith, who grew up in nearby Ontario. "I finally talked them into it."

Just don't confuse efficiency with innocence in the early years of college football recruiting. If the player-procurement process was spotty in the days before Tom Lemming began rating recruits in the late '70s, it was hardly less fraught with some of the issues that trouble college administrators and the National Collegiate Athletic Association in the 21st century. Those would include matters such as academic-athletic proportion and enforcement of rules designed to prevent the overzealous from stealing a competitive edge.

Soak in this cautionary passage: "The recruiting of American college athletes, be it active or passive, professional or nonprofessional, has reached the proportions of nationwide commerce. In spite of the efforts of not a few teachers and principals who have comprehended its dangers, its effect upon the character of the schoolboy has been profoundly deleterious.

"Its influence upon the nature and quality of American higher education has been no less noxious. The element that demoralizes is the subsidy, the monetary or material advantage that is used to attract the schoolboy athlete."

Sound like something that might have come out of the NCAA-mandated Presidents Commission of 1984, or the Knight Foundation Commission on Intercollegiate Athletics created in 1989? Actually, it's from "American College Athletics," prepared by the Carnegie Foundation for the Advancement of Teaching in 1929, decades before anyone had heard of hundred-dollar handshakes or bogus credit scandals.

That exhaustive treatise, generated from a study of 130 American colleges, reveals a fundamental truth about college recruiting: whether in the era of the Model T or the Cadillac Escalade, enforcement of the rules—by institution, by conference or, in the last half-century, by the NCAA—has been a contentious, ongoing struggle punctuated by ebb and flow both in rule-breaking and policing.

Comparing today's recruiting ills with those of a half-century ago, Wiles Hallock, a former commissioner of the

WAC and the Pac-8 (now the Pac-10), says, "Things really haven't changed very much since those days."

Nor were they grossly different in earlier decades. Released in the year of the great stock market crash, the Carnegie report addressed abuses that generations later would be considered startlingly de rigueur: jobs that overpaid athletes, financial breaks on room-and-board assessments, even the occasional sale of complimentary tickets at inflated values. If only a fraction of those practices were held out as enticements in recruiting, some renegade programs might have known the term "official letter of inquiry" during Prohibition.

Recruiting back then took a lot of different forms. Coaches did it, and so did academics, alumni and fraternity members. The most common practice was for universities to offer tuition aid, with the athlete then given a job to defray room-and-board costs.

Alumni often befriended recruits, some with more high-minded intentions than others. The case of Don Lund, who starred as a fullback at Michigan from 1942 to 1944, was typical. He grew up in Detroit as a fan of Michigan and the local pro teams. When a Wolverine alum from his neighborhood introduced himself, that cinched the deal. Lund, also recruited by Northwestern and Michigan State, worked at a lithographing company four years and played three sports.

Milt Vucinich, a fullback at Stanford from 1940 to 1942, tells a similar story. Alumni took him to San Francisco's Olympic Club for lunch and to football games at Stanford. Once in school, Vucinich made $15 a month handing out milk shake tokens at a local creamery, while many of his teammates waited tables at fraternities or sororities to pay for room and board.

Inevitably, some alumni lavished inducements on recruits, but in those days there was no national governance. One of the first attempts at enforcement came in the old Pacific Coast Conference, which installed Ed Atherton as commissioner to clean up the league. USC's Smith remembers Atherton's hands-on approach to enforcement in a one-on-one meeting the two had.

"He either thought I was real dumb or a hell of a liar," said Smith. "He asked, 'Did you ever get anything extra?' I said, 'No sir.' I was telling the truth. But there was a lot of stuff going on."

> ## The NCAA was called in because some conferences seemed powerless to police their own.

The end of World War II brought dramatic change to the landscape of college football. Universities were flooded with student veterans looking for a sports outlet. Jim Tatum, who had headed a Naval preflight team during the war, coached one of the developing powers of the game, Oklahoma. In one of the most aggressive recruiting campaigns in history, Tatum landed many discharged servicemen who had played at other colleges before the war. He also marked his one year at Oklahoma by taking advantage of sketchy NCAA rules to raid rival campuses, stage periodic tryouts, and assess as many as 600 would-be Sooners, including nine future All-Americas.

That sort of excess led two young men to open the NCAA office above a saloon in Kansas City in July 1952. Walter Byers, 30, was executive director and Wayne Duke, 23, was his assistant. Until then, the NCAA had been run on a part-time basis out of the Big Ten office.

The ignorance of the time is reflected in the NCAA manual, the object of so much scorn today. The first, published in 1954, was 31 pages.

Much of Byers' early NCAA tracked the pervasive point-shaving scandal in college basketball. In its first major infractions case, it shut down the Kentucky program for a year.

Football had its own primary source of friction, centering on the limits of scholarship aid. The so-called Sanity Code of 1948 provided for additional aid beyond tuition and fees if an athlete finished in the top 25% of his high school graduating class or kept a B average in college. Southern-led opposition defeated the measure at the 1950 NCAA convention, arguing that a full grant-in-aid system would eliminate illicit payments by alumni.

In 1956, the full scholarship became permissible. Alumni, nevertheless, seemed to need an outlet for their largess, so their abuse merely covered other expenses.

Byers' 1995 autobiography, *Unsportsmanlike Conduct: Exploiting College Athletes*, documents allegations against Kentucky and Texas A&M when Paul "Bear" Bryant was the coach. The NCAA went hard on an investigation of a new 1954 Oldsmobile driven by future Heisman Trophy-winner John David Crow, but couldn't prove wrongdoing. By the time Bryant had won six national titles at Alabama, his

immense legacy was secure, even as he winked at the innuendo.

"We never had to outbid anyone," Bryant once said. "We just met the competition."

Meanwhile, other factors focused the urgency of enforcement on the NCAA, as some conferences seemed powerless to police their own. When Vic Schmidt's regime investigated schools in the Pacific Coast Conference in the late '50s—the PCC would break up after violations and countercharges by several schools—Schmidt was forced out as commissioner. In the old, football-crazed Southwest Conference, commissioner Howard Grubbs exercised tight oversight of the league's programs despite pressure on him to butt out.

Intensifying the need for firm central control was the conference letter of intent, an exercise that annually preceded the national letter until the mid-'70s. Recruits, for instance, could sign a Big Eight Conference letter with Oklahoma and a Southwest letter with Texas before having to make a final declaration weeks later, while suitors sometimes were governed by different conference regulations. The one-on-one grudge matches magnified the intensity of recruiting battles and egged on benefactors with untoward intentions.

All the while, recruiting was going national. "The airplane changed recruiting," says former Big Eight commissioner Chuck Neinas. "When I was at Wisconsin [on the Badgers' broadcast team in the late 1950s], the rule of thumb was, we'd recruit within a six-hour drive of campus. Now Wisconsin recruits in Florida and Texas."

One of the programs in Neinas' Big Eight to prosper with out-of-state recruits was Nebraska, which won the 1971 national title with a quarterback from Wisconsin (Jerry Tagge), a defensive end from Ohio (Willie Harper) and a middle guard from New Jersey (Rich Glover).

Players like these belied a deadpan observation of their coach, Bob Devaney, about the urgency of attracting talent to a sparsely populated state like Nebraska.

"I don't expect to win enough games to be put on NCAA probation," Devaney quipped early in his tenure. "I just want to win enough to warrant an investigation."

The Huskers were hardly the only school with a vast sway in recruiting. Notre Dame has traditionally been a long-distance magnet, and programs like Michigan State established proficiency in unlikely places: the Spartans' dominating defense in 1966 was led by end Bubba Smith of Beaumont, Texas, and linebacker George Webster of Anderson, S.C. The year before that, 9 of 11 consensus

defensive All-Americas won those honors at schools outside of their home state.

By the early '70s, as David Berst began a 26-year tenure with the enforcement staff of the NCAA, the organization was hopelessly understaffed. When he arrived, there were two investigators and a supervisor.

"You needed more than that in Texas," laughs Darrell Royal, the longtime coach at Texas. "They had more on their plate than they could handle."

In fact, it might have taken two investigators just to make sure everything was straight with the recruitment in the late '60s of Jack Mildren of Abilene, Texas, a saga described in Dan Jenkins' book, *Saturday's America*. Mildren entertained overtures from Texas A&M, Texas Christian, Texas, Southern Methodist, Arkansas, Oklahoma, Notre Dame and UCLA.

Mildren not only was wooed on behalf of SMU by NFL owners such as Lamar Hunt of the Kansas City Chiefs and Clint Murchison of the Dallas Cowboys, he heard Ben Hogan discuss TCU over lunch in Fort Worth and picked up the phone one night to hear a pitch for Baylor coach John Bridgers from Johnny Unitas.

Finally, wrote Jenkins, Mildren chose Oklahoma "after two months, 27 official coaching visits, 500 letters, 100 telegrams and 150 long-distance calls."

It was in the '70s that the NCAA ramped up its enforcement staff dramatically—to five investigators by 1974 and to eight in 1976. Berst, NCAA director of enforcement from 1988 to 1998, said recently the staff is now at 18 investigators with five supervisors.

Perhaps the stepped-up scrutiny has something to do with the fact that the '70s is considered the era with the most crimes against college athletics. "The '70s were exactly that peak," says Berst. "There were some institutions that simply violated rules on every page of the manual."

And by then, there were a lot of pages. In 1974, 20 years after Byers and Duke turned out the first one, the manual had ballooned from 31 to 255 pages. A decade later, it was at 366, and would eventually top 500.

Oklahoma was tagged in 1973 for major recruiting violations on the watch of Chuck Fairbanks. Under Barry Switzer, the Sooners would repeat violations twice, most seriously in 1988.

Oklahoma State was late to the list of major violators, but jumped in with both feet. Starting with a 1978 case and including investigations concluded in 1980 and 1989, it ran up a total of five years' television and postseason bans and eight years of probation.

It was the Cowboys' Hart Lee Dykes, a wide receiver, who became one of the most infamous characters in NCAA lore. Dykes' testimony in the late '80s became crucial in incriminating four schools—Oklahoma State, Oklahoma, Texas A&M and Illinois—that committed major violations in recruiting him.

Still, there was no scofflaw quite like Southern Methodist. The Mustangs were whacked in 1974, 1976, 1981 and 1985. Then, when the '85 sanctions failed to clean up violations that included cash payments and cars, the NCAA pounded SMU with the "death penalty" in 1987, the only school in history to have its program suspended.

The NCAA's Byers recounted the SMU mind-set ingrained by coach Ron Meyer (1976-81) and sustained by Bobby Collins: "One of [Meyer's] recruiting techniques was to visit a prospect's high school and ask to confer in a private room with the player. Meyer would sit down and the youngster would sit down. Meyer would then pull out a plump money clip and peel off a hundred-dollar bill. He would get up, walk to a nearby bulletin board, pin up the C-note and announce, 'Young man, this is my calling card.'

"When their conversation was over, Meyer would put the bill back in his wallet. No NCAA violation there. The player understood that he would be contacted again in the near future."

Some at SMU would argue that it was only keeping up with the Joneses. Between 1985 and 1988, the NCAA socked seven of the nine Southwest Conference schools for major violations. One of those was Texas Christian, which made its only major football case in history a doozy. Seven players were found to be accepting cash, notably running back Kenneth Davis, who said he had received $32,000.

Why the spike in rule-breaking in the '70s, a trend that continued for at least a decade? The easy answer is that increased revenue, particularly from television, had piled on pressure to win. But Berst doesn't buy it.

"I don't think the money makes a difference at all," he says. "I believe people are motivated to get an advantage for all reasons, and [offenders] have some sort of character flaw. I think it has more to do with personal egos and weaknesses than it does the dollar."

Royal agrees, saying, "Some people, when they go into coaching, they choose whether they're going to abide by the rules or whether they're going to try to skip a few."

With the SMU example fresh, the number of NCAA major violators dropped during the 1990s. Neinas senses there were fewer "Trans-Am cars and slush funds." Perhaps, as Berst maintains, a stronger push by university presidents helped curb the lawlessness.

"We finally got circumstances where presidents were paying attention to their athletics programs," he says.

In the '70s, some 28 schools that endure today as Division I football-playing members were found guilty of major violations and 14 were struck from the postseason. In the '90s, 22 schools were sanctioned and only eight were slapped with bowl bans. Of the 14 denied postseason play in the '70s, 11 were banished for two years or more, compared to only three such miscreants in the '90s.

Not everyone agrees that it's all a function of the triumph of the lawful. Wayne Duke, who moved into that NCAA office more than a half-century ago, believes the NCAA has relaxed standards amid a national recognition that the abiding ethic is for schools and conferences to make money.

"I think they've become much more lenient," he says. "It's modern-day society. People don't stand up for rules. We forgive and forget."

Way back when, BYU must have done the same for LaVell Edwards, who in December 2004 was inducted into the College Football Hall of Fame. Twenty years after graduating from Utah State, he became coach at Brigham Young in 1972. He coached the Cougars to 257 victories over 29 seasons, winning the recruiting battles like the one BYU lost the day he walked off the family berry farm.

"How You Played the Game"

The Evolution of Sportsmanship in College Football

By Vahe Gregorian

JUST MINUTES AFTER UNDEFEATED, NO. 2-RANKED Cornell seemed to have beaten Dartmouth 7-3 in 1940 with a fourth-down touchdown pass on the last play of the game, referee Red Friesell was aghast at the realization that he had committed a "grave error" enabling the winning touchdown to transpire on what was actually a fifth-down play.

Upon confirming the fact a day later, Cornell athletic director James Lynah wired Dartmouth to say, "Cornell relinquishes claim to the victory." Cornell coach Carl Snavely also wrote Dartmouth, stating that "without reservation" he conceded the victory "with hearty congratulations to you, the gallant Dartmouth team."

It's worth noting, though, that Cornell president Edmund Ezra Day reportedly had urged the gesture as a sign of being "good sports" while holding the belief that Dartmouth would be "better sports" and not accept it. Still, it was a moment when the practices of those in collegiate football seemed to live up to the game's lofty ideals.

Flash-forward to 1990: Colorado defeats Missouri 33-31 … on a fifth-down play.

This time, thanks to television replays and postgame mayhem on the field in Columbia, Mo., the truth was evident within moments after the game. But when confronted about it afterward, Colorado coach Bill McCartney offered no gestures, or even words, of consolation or regret. Instead, he complained about the treacherous footing at Faurot Field: "If Missouri had outplayed us, and if the field conditions had been fair and an inadvertent mistake by an official had worked in our favor, I would call our squad and coaches together and discuss with them whether we should forfeit because we won unfairly. But I don't feel like we did."

Colorado went on to win the national title that season, for which McCartney reportedly received a bonus of more than $75,000. Years later, he would say he was "truly

remorseful" about the way the game had been won. And it's only fair to note that there was obvious confusion at play: the Buffaloes surely would not have spiked the ball to stop the clock on the true fourth down if they had not thought it to be third down as indicated by officials.

But the difference between McCartney's response and Cornell's 50 years before speaks eloquently to fundamental, widespread changes in societal standards of sportsmanship. It's easy to see the two events as a signal that winning by whatever means necessary had become the singular signature of sports in the late 20th century.

Yet those episodes better represented ideals of those generations than consistent practices of the times, better reflected extremes than the mainstream, better spoke to a premise than a promise.

Sportsmanship in the modern era of college football seems to be no more deplorable than it was a century ago —and in fact is in a position to thrive as never before in the wake of a new wave of legislation and awareness.

In recent years, the NCAA and conference commissioners have reasserted a degree of control over on-field misbehavior by players (and coaches), insisted on greater academic accountability and helped topple renegade empires (see the since-reinvented Oklahoma and Miami programs) whose criminality and vulgarity were notorious. Postgame handshakes, hugs and shared prayer circles suggest a level of fellowship and camaraderie among foes that may be unprecedented, even if it isn't universal.

Many of our perceptions are influenced by the warping mechanisms of today's saturation television and mass media coverage, the growth of sports talk-radio and Internet culture, and what Dan Doyle of the Institute for International Sport calls "the fallacy of the innocent past." Melded together, they leave us decrying the preposterous imagery we are inundated with as players gyrate in celebration dances, bark at opponents or play through the whistle instead of to the whistle—and they leave us yearning for yesteryear and the Golden Era of gentlemanly football.

An era that never existed, in college football or any other sport.

In the first decades of the 20th century, sportsmanship was held up as a Platonic ideal and hailed as part of the very fabric of the game, even though at the time the sport lacked order, structure and direction. "As to rules, we didn't violate any in those days," Michigan coach Fielding Yost said in the

early 1900s. "There weren't any."

Nevertheless, a clear social compact called for honorable play. It was considered proper to pursue sporting honor at least as much as anything else. The concept was articulated by no less than Knute Rockne: "Foul and dirty play is only an honest admission that your opponent is a better man than you." And it was famously endorsed by Grantland Rice:

For when the Great Scorer comes
To write against your name
He marks—not that you won or lost—
But how you played the game.

When Rice wrote those words in his 1923 poem, "Alumnus Football," they had resonance in a world still focused on college sports and espousing sportsmanship as a moral imperative.

And yet the demise of sportsmanship isn't as recent a phenomenon as some would suggest. It didn't commence with Clemson and South Carolina brawling in 2004, or with dozens of similarly ugly fights in the past few years alone.

Nor did it expire when Miami players arrived in Phoenix the week of the 1987 Fiesta Bowl wearing combat fatigues and stormed out of a steak fry with adversary Penn State, reportedly stoked by defender Jerome Brown's declaration, "Did the Japanese sit down and eat dinner with Pearl Harbor before they bombed it?" Or even when the Hurricanes strutted and trash-talked their way to more than 200 yards in penalties in the 1991 Cotton Bowl against Texas.

It didn't begin to crumble when Ohio State coach Woody Hayes socked Clemson linebacker Charlie Bauman in the 1978 Gator Bowl, or back in 1951, when Oklahoma A&M's Wilbanks Smith shattered the jaw of renowned Johnny Bright, a rare African-American playing at Lewis Field, with a forearm to the face well after the play had developed and he was out of it.

Sportsmanship didn't suddenly begin to disappear in the 1930s, when the University of Chicago dropped football because it had become too associated with professionalism. And it wasn't instigated by Georgia Tech abusing Cumberland 222-0 in 1916.

The decline of sportsmanship, in fact, began at the beginning.

American football traces its ancestry to rugby, believed

1940 marked a moment when the practices of those in college football lived up to the game's lofty ideals.

to have been spontaneously born in 1823 on a playing field in Rugby, England. Late in a soccer match, one William Webb Ellis simply picked up the ball and skedaddled away with it. Although some wonder if the tale is more folklore than fact, a plaque at the site acknowledges his act:

"This stone commemorates the exploit of William Webb Ellis who with a fine disregard for the rules of football, as played in his time, first took the ball in his arms and ran with it, thus originating the distinctive feature of the rugby game. AD 1823."

If American football wasn't inherently corrupt by extension of this original sin against sportsmanship, it managed to manufacture any number of transgressions against the spirit of fair play from day one.

Makeshift version that it was, the first collegiate game between Rutgers and Princeton in 1869 was (according to Rick Telander in his book, *The Hundred Yard Lie*) stained by the presence of at least one and perhaps up to four players who could have been ruled academically ineligible. And that was a trifle compared to the havoc that ruled the game into the early 20th century.

"The practice of dressing up the butcher's boy, the iron molder, the boiler maker, or even a bond salesman, in football clothing, which in those days concealed from partisan and opponent alike almost every distinguishing feature, was more than merely scandalous," said the 1929 Carnegie Report, a sweeping study of the state of college athletics. "The deception was so common and so amusing that at this distance it is almost impossible to appraise its viciousness."

Viciousness, though, was in a category of its own. Players routinely were known to gouge, punch, bite and kick opponents. "In all the games observed," said an 1884 report of the Harvard athletic committee, "the manifestation of gentlemanly spirit was lacking." According to Mark Bernstein's *Football: The Ivy League Origins of an American Obsession*, Harvard president Charles William Eliot was repulsed by the havoc and sadism he saw on the field and called football "more brutalizing than prizefighting, cockfighting or bullfighting."

By 1905, the appalling behavior had left the game's future in jeopardy. A number of schools already had outlawed football, and after nearly two dozen deaths at the

collegiate level that year President Theodore Roosevelt summoned the presidents of Harvard, Princeton and Yale to the White House and insisted they lead the way to making the game safer. Roosevelt didn't want to encourage "mollycoddles," but he also could no longer abide by the danger associated with the game: "I demand that football change its rules or be abolished. Brutality and foul play should receive the same summary punishment given to a man who cheats at cards. Change the game or forsake it!"

From this came the forward pass, the demise of so-called mass formations such as the flying wedge and an increase in the distance needed for a first down from five to 10 yards. From this also ultimately came the NCAA, which, like any governing body, was notoriously ineffective at legislating ethics—part of the reason that segregation, the most widespread and dehumanizing affront to sportsmanship, was permitted to rule the game until well into the second half of the century.

> *By 1905, the appalling behavior had left the game's future in jeopardy.*

As college football became a colossus on the American sporting landscape, the game offered what purists considered temptations that blurred the universities' academic mission. What the Carnegie report astutely grasped in 1929 is equally apt now: "No college boy training for a major team can have much time for thought or study … The college athlete, often a boy from a modest home, finds himself suddenly a most important man in the college life. He begins to live on a scale never before imagined. A special table is provided. Sports clothes and expensive trips are furnished him out of the athletic chest. He jumps at one bound to a plane of living of which he never before knew, all at the expense of some fund of which he knows little. When he drops back to a scale of living such as his own means can afford, the result is sometimes disastrous."

Afforded such stature and met with such demands outside the classroom, small wonder that principles of sportsmanship weren't always paramount on or off the field, even at the highest-minded of institutions. At West Point in 1951, for instance, 83 cadets were expelled for cribbing on exams. Nearly half of them were football players.

On the field, as elsewhere, poor sportsmanship seemed to become not only acceptable but even admirable in some circles. Attempts to hurt and intimidate other players, if not outwardly or publicly emphasized by coaches, were tacitly approved. The idea that the players had special privileges

was fostered from the moment recruiting began—and that was even when it was aboveboard.

By the 1960s, the only shame came in not doing all one could do to win, not all one could do within the rules, and it became a self-perpetuating process. "When a coach starts out, he sees what coaches do and he says, 'I'll do anything to win,'" the late Dan Devine, then at Notre Dame, told *Sports Illustrated* in 1978. "So he cheats. He teaches 'win at any cost.' When he's older, his career is in the balance. He says, 'I'll do anything to stay in.'"

As television became more and more of a presence in the 1960s and 1970s, so did an inclination to glorify those who stood out—and not always for their marvelous play alone. Showmanship became a permanent fixture, thanks to television's relentless presence and the rising notion of games as an extension of the entertainment business.

The University of Houston's Elmo Wright unofficially initiated "self-expression" as an integral part of college football with his end zone dancing in 1970; Florida State's "Neon" Deion Sanders and his successors ensured its permanent place in the game.

In the new era, many began to wonder what had become of sportsmanship. "Standing over an injured player and using profane language. Pointing to a beaten cornerback after catching a pass. Tactics intended to diminish or physically hurt players. Fifteen or 20 years ago," then-Stanford coach Bill Walsh said in 1978, "you could name one or two dirty players on a team. Now, there's continuous talking, insults and, before you know it, a clothesline from behind. Or a tackle on a player who is helpless, or when he doesn't expect to be hit."

By the late 1980s, Walsh's assessment looked like an understatement, its worst implications manifested in the form of the Miami Hurricanes, whose jaw-jacking and nasty behavior and dirty play defied any argument that what they were carrying out was legitimate self-expression. The 1995 rule change prohibiting excessive celebration came out of what then-rules committee chairman Vince Dooley called "the biggest problem facing college football today"—namely, unseemly on-field conduct. It was reinforced by a video called *College Football: A Celebration of Teamwork.* Here is an excerpt from the video's narration, which is cued to corresponding footage: "This player not only isolates himself from his teammates, but he also directs a machine-gun motion to the crowd. This is a

planned, excessive gesture that is not a display of spontaneous enthusiasm and has nothing to do with football … Dancing of any type is; by definition, choreographed and not spontaneous and not related in any way to the game of football."

Some observers at the time saw signs of racial prejudice in the legislation, asserting that the attempt to restrict on-field, postplay behavior stemmed from whites wanting to subdue blacks. The video prompted an exchange between Missouri defensive back Clayton Baker, an African-American, and then-coach Larry Smith, a Caucasian, that illustrates the divide in generations and cultures.

"Some of the things are unnecessary. But you can't take the emotion out of the game. That's the whole point of the game," said Baker. "Imagine if it was the first touchdown of your whole college career. You want to throw your hands up, because you'd be like, 'Thank God I finally got in here.' Instead, I'll have to tape my hands down. Or run like this, with my hands behind my back, until I get to the sideline. You have no choice."

Smith saw no middle ground, blaming the behavior on such forces as the World Wrestling Federation and the NFL. He told the team that players of his generation were just as intense but expressed their emotions toward the team, not toward the stands or cameras.

Baker's response? "When Coach Smith was playing, dude, they were lucky to be alive after the game. With those leather helmets? No face masks? They were like, 'Whew, that was one play I didn't get my nose broken.' If you did showboat then, someone just came along and gave you a forearm to the head. That's the way the game was played then."

Games, of course, are played differently now. Just as sportsmanship never thrived as we may perceive it did, neither is it dead and buried.

An outpouring of outrage over the 2004 Clemson-South Carolina brawl, amplified by the fact it came a day after the NBA's landmark brawl between the Detroit Pistons and Indiana Pacers, resulted in prompt denunciation and stringent policy changes by the two conferences involved. The schools policed themselves and their players: both were bowl eligible, but neither would accept an invitation in the wake of the incident.

In the same season, Oklahoma coach Bob Stoops lamented trying to punch in a late touchdown after the game had already been decided in the Sooners' 30-3 win over Nebraska. He was too consumed, he later said, with the need for a significant margin of victory to preserve the Sooners' No. 2 place in the polls and Bowl Championship Series rankings—an issue that will resurface periodically at least until college football adopts a playoff format. "Anyone who doesn't see the dilemma we're in is not being totally fair," Stoops told reporters. "We're in a bad

position right now. I made the wrong choice … I wish I chose sportsmanship over BCS points."

One need only visit the University of Nebraska on game day to witness a spectacle believed to be matchless in college football and perhaps any major sport. At game's end, hundreds of Cornhusker fans line the area between the visitors bench and the locker room and form a makeshift receiving line to applaud the other team. So startling is the sight that some first-time observers have mistaken it for mocking, particularly after a drubbing administered by one of the Nebraska juggernauts of the 1990s.

But the fact that Nebraska fans have done it even after rare defeats at home confirms that it isn't taunting. And University of Texas women's athletic director Chris Plonsky, who witnessed Nebraska fans chanting the name of Texas running back Ricky Williams during the Longhorns' 1998 upset of the Huskers, considers what she heard that day in Lincoln a "sacred" and "supreme" example of sportsmanship.

Perhaps the greatest effort to eradicate one aspect of poor sportsmanship came at the Division I-AA level in 2004 when the Gateway Football Conference enacted a policy requiring its teams to remove their helmets, cross the field and shake hands before each game. The rule was in response to a vicious 2002 postgame skirmish between Western Kentucky and Western Illinois that conference commissioner Patty Viverito said was "embarrassing on a monumental scale." This was something we felt we needed to do, Viverito told columnist Kathleen Nelson of the *St. Louis Post-Dispatch*. "Now that we've got it, we're darn proud of it. If a symbol can impact behavior positively, all the better."

Moreover, for all the downsides of overwhelming media scrutiny, there is this benefit for sportsmanship: a trend toward investigative reporting has helped rein in many of the brazen recruiting scams that ran virtually unchecked until the late 1970s.

Still, no one can say where sportsmanship goes from here. If a new emphasis on sportsmanship in college football seems to be blossoming, its sustained and successful execution is another matter—just as it was 100 years ago. But the cultivation of sportsmanship will always be a vital issue in college athletics and for our culture, for reasons that Yost articulated in a 1923 meeting of the American Football Coaches Association: "Democracy is based upon respect for opposition, respect for law, respect for authority and respect for government. Surely, the sportsmanship learned on the playground and athletic field is a vital stimulant to those ends, and for that reason, even if for no other, athletics and competitive games deserve an important place in our program of education."

Born to Run

A Reluctant Requiem for the Option Offense

BY JOE POSNANSKI

AT AN IOWA TRUCK STOP NEAR AMES, I HEARD THE DYING voice of the option. He was an older man wearing a John Deere baseball cap. That hardly distinguished him from anyone else in the joint. He had a red face and glasses, and he was eating the catfish noisily. When the waitress asked him what two side items he wanted, he said, "Corn and corn."

He was talking to a man across the booth, a man with a look of polite boredom on his face. The man had clearly heard this bit before.

"You'll see, schools will start running the option again," the corn-and-corn man said. "No doubt about it. The option *will* be back. The darned thing works."

This is how you know it's over. This is how you know that another piece of Americana has been swept into the dustbin of the obsolete, buried there under hula hoops and Rubik's cubes and leisure suits and hard contact lenses and cars with front-wheel drive. Through the years, in truck stops all across America, there've been men in John Deere caps (or Red Sox caps or "Buy American or Move to Japan" caps) muttering, "You'll see, big band music will be back," or "I don't care what anybody says about CDs, I'm keeping my records," or "Someday, baseball teams will start bunting again."

Now it's the option, once the quintessential play of college football, that leaves old men longing for the return of better days and leaves all of us to remember sunny Saturday afternoons when football players shouted "Hi Mom!" into the camera and television graphics covered the entire screen and men like Jack Mildren or Jeff Rutledge or Tommie Frazier ran the line and then, at the last possible moment, pitched the football to Greg Pruitt or Major Ogilvie or Ahman Green.

For 22 years, from 1969 (one year after Darrell Royal unveiled the wishbone and his own triple option) until 1990 (when Colorado played throwback with Darien Hagen and Eric Bienemy), the triple option was the offense of more national champions than any other.

The option in that era was more than an offense, certainly more than a play. It was a philosophy, a political movement, a revolt against modern art and disco and the NFL. And the forward pass. (This was a time when it was still called "the forward pass," so as not to confuse people.)

It was the play of your bigger-than-life coaches—Royal, Bear, Switzer, Osborne—who believed in their hearts that you didn't win football games by tricking the other team or, in the wimpy vocabulary of coaches today, "keeping the defense off-balance."

No, you won football games by running over the other guys.

"Nobody has the discipline or disciples of the playbook to run it anymore," says Barry Switzer. "It's a dinosaur." In his wild days at Oklahoma, Switzer brashly won three national titles by running the option over defenses. Now, though, even Switzer has turned into one of those disappointed men who lament the passing of the good old days and all the passing in these new confusing times.

"If people wanted to win," Switzer says, "they'd use the option."

***

Nobody really invented the option. The basic concept—run or pitch—goes back to rugby, which is essentially one continuous series of option plays. Still, there are at least 3,284 people who claim to have invented the option. Some believe it goes back to a higher source. An old high school coach I knew in a small town in Georgia would sometimes yell at his pass-loving quarterback, "If God intended for you to throw the ball, he wouldn't have invented the triple option."

Don Faurot probably gets the first bit of option credit for inventing the split-T offense in 1941 at Missouri. Like every coach in America, he looked hard at the newly designed T-formation, which Chicago Bears coach George Halas had just used to win the NFL Championship game 73-0. Faurot thought the T might be more effective if he split the offensive linemen, spread them apart. He thought this might give his quarterback more of a chance to run up and down the line. It was, in option football history, the discovery of fire.

"Most original and significant contribution to offensive football in the last 10 years," Oklahoma coach Bud Wilkinson said of the split-T. Faurot's Missouri used it to lead the nation in rushing in 1941 by running something fairly close to what would become the option. But it would be Wilkinson who fine-tuned the split-T, had his quarterback and running back run in tandem, and won four national championships in the 1950s including, at one point, 47 games in a row.

"It was the option, plain and simple," says Switzer, who played at Arkansas in those days, explaining the secret of

Oklahoma's success. But there were others who were tinkering with the option at the time. At a high school in Kentucky in the late 1950s, a coach named Homer Rice was experimenting with the idea of adding a fullback to the split-T, adding that famed third option. He and others liked to call the offense "Homer's triples," a nickname that hit the trash heap about 20 minutes after it was coined.

The option was a philosophy, a political movement, a revolt against modern art, disco and the NFL. And the forward pass.

"Nobody," says former option quarterback and U.S. congressman J.C. Watts, "could stop the option."

***

The beauty of the option is its simplicity. A quarterback has three distinct options: give the ball to the fullback; run the football; pitch the football. That's it. Later, coaches would try to add a fourth option, a passing option, but the forward pass and the option never did get along.

Around the same time, Bill Yeoman at the University of Houston grew tired of watching a linebacker blow up his offense, so he stuck a fullback in the middle of the play to take that linebacker out. He called the offense "the veer," a nickname with more staying power than Homer's triples, but it sill didn't earn him much credit when it came to the invention of the option.

No, the credit normally goes to a Texas assistant coach named Emory Bellard, who for years had this idea about having three backs standing behind the quarterback. He had seen Yeoman's offense and Rice's offense, but he wanted more. Finally, Darrell Royal told him to go ahead and figure out how to do it, and Bellard spent the summer in his backyard with his sons and a few stray former players, working on the offense that Houston sportswriter Mickey Herskowitz would dub "the wishbone."

After a bumpy start, the Texas wishbone would win 30 consecutive games, and the modern option was born. And, soon thereafter, the option would become America's offense.

Royal was always generous about sharing information with other coaches. He didn't care. In a world where coaches surround their practices with barbed wire fences, Royal kept his practices open, and coaches came from everywhere to learn about the option. Before long, the option would make its presence felt throughout the country, and become especially dominant in the Deep South and the Southwest. UCLA led the nation in rushing using the option under Pepper Rogers. Bear Bryant and Alabama went to the wishbone at Alabama. Georgia ran Vince Dooley's version of the veer. And, of course, the option play became religion in a couple of Midwestern states, Nebraska and Oklahoma. Those two schools stockpiled enough option quarterbacks and running backs to blow up college football dozens of times.

The quarterback, of course, is the key. He's the one who has to see if the middle linebacker is cheating to one side or another. (If he is, the quarterback simply gives the ball to the fullback, who blasts up the middle. This is what Nebraska did in the 1995 Orange Bowl, making a kid named Cory Schlesinger into a star and giving Tom Osborne his long-awaited national title.) The quarterback is the one who has to decide whether to run or pitch. (If that first defender is leaning the wrong way, a quarterback has to turn the ball upfield into the heart of the defense.) He's the one who has to get up from a ruthless hit even if he's pitched the ball ("If you want to defend the option," then-Miami coach Jimmy Johnson said, "you've got to hit the quarterback on every play").

Naturally, quarterbacks defined the play. Texas' James Street, the original option quarterback, ran the play with violence; every team that went up against Texas in 1969 understood that the option was aimed right for their throats. Much of the time, fullback Steve Worster would ram the ball up the middle. And, once the middle was softened up, Street would run down the line angrily with every intention of running over a defender. The Texas wishbone was coming to take your heart. The Longhorns didn't lose a game that year.

Oklahoma's Jack Mildren ran a different kind of option in 1971. He seemed to run leisurely, as if he was daring defenders to take their shots at him; you half expected him to wave at defenders and shout, "Na-na, na-na, you can't catch me!" At the last instant, just as he was getting clobbered by two defenders, he would pitch the ball to a little running back named Greg Pruitt, who that year was better than anyone in the world at making defenders miss. Since he usually had only one defender to

beat, Pruitt averaged an astounding 9.4 yards per rush that season, still an NCAA record for anyone who carried the ball 150 times or more.

Nebraska's Tommie Frazier so scared defenses with his own relentless running that defenders often ignored his wingman, a pretty fair running back named Ahman Green. That might have been the most unstoppable combination in the history of the option. In 1995, when Frazier was a senior and Green a freshman, the Cornhuskers averaged 52 points per game, 400 rushing yards per game; no opponent finished within two touchdowns of them all year. Then Nebraska destroyed Florida 62-24 in the Fiesta Bowl, a pounding so complete that Florida coach Steve Spurrier decided he had to go out and get himself a defensive coordinator who could, by God, stop the option. More on that choice later.

Oklahoma's Jamelle Holieway was probably the quickest option quarterback ever—defenses simply couldn't get to the corner fast enough to contain him. Alabama's Jeff Rutledge ran a picture-perfect option, always seeming to make precisely the right pitch or the right cut as Alabama's Bear Bryant won the 1978 national title in the twilight of his career.

In fact, every great option quarterback through the years—Tony Rice (Notre Dame), Dee Dowis (Air Force), Ray Goff (Georgia), Turner Gill and Eric Crouch (Nebraska), Nolan Cromwell (Kansas), Tracy Ham (Georgia Southern), Darian Hagan (Colorado)—inspires a different image.

Some ran fast, some took their time; some were magicians with their fake handoffs—constantly fooling ABC's announcer Keith Jackson—while others were unrelenting runners who would seem to be down but would then slip through for more yards.

That's the beauty of the option: it's all about the players.

The option is about a player's ability to make exactly the right decision at exactly the right time. Yep, it's all about the players. All about the quarterbacks.

Maybe that's why it's dying.

***

Everybody has a reason why nobody, save a military academy or two, runs the option these days. Some say the play simply doesn't work anymore: defensive players are too big and fast, the option is the horse-and-buggy of football; it has had its day.

Those people are just flat wrong.

"You couldn't defend it today," Switzer insists. When someone talks to him about defenses being bigger and faster, Switzer will start convulsing and muttering madly about

those Miami defenses of the 1980s that were plenty big and plenty fast and couldn't stop the option.

"Talent on defense has got nothing to do with it," Switzer says.

Al Saunders, the Kansas City Chiefs offensive coordinator who designed the NFL's top-scoring offense in 2002 and 2003, agrees with Switzer: "Oh, it still works. And it doesn't matter what level, either. I could run the option in the NFL and win with it. There is no doubt in my mind."

So what's the problem? Well, you could start off with Al Saunders' caveat: "Of course, you'd have to give me 15 quarterbacks, because I'd get one hurt every week."

Yes, quarterbacks do take a beating in the option. This seems to be reason No. 1 why the option has kicked the bucket: quarterbacks can't take the beating. See, it was one thing when linebackers and quarterbacks were more or less the same size, but these days 240-pound men running 4.6 40-yard dashes come plowing in and bash the quarterback on every play, whether he has the ball or not. It's hard to run the option with your quarterback on a stretcher.

Then there's Reason No. 1A: recruiting. Every kid these days wants to play the NFL-style offense, West Coast stuff, run-and-shoot stuff, five-receiver stuff. "It's all about the excitement of throwing the football," option master Turner Gill says. Try to a imagine big-time college coach walking into the home of a big-shot quarterback prospect, looking his Mama in the eyes, and saying, "Ma'am, you're son has a bright future, and we'd very much like him to run the option for us."

But the biggest reason the option has gone the way of the dodo can be summed up in two words: "Bob" and "Stoops." You see, the man who coaches Oklahoma these days was the man Steve Spurrier hired to be the defensive coordinator at Florida after Nebraska optioned all over the Gators in that 62-24 beating at the 1996 Fiesta Bowl. "Let's see how a team feels about running the option when their guy gets knocked out by an earhole shot," Stoops told *Sports Illustrated* when the magazine dared to suggest the option might be making a minicomeback. Teams didn't do much option running against Bob Stoops' Florida defense in 1996-98.

After that, Stoops went to Oklahoma, the Mecca of the option, and he had his quarterback throw. And throw. And throw. It should have been like Eminem rapping at Westminster Abbey—that is, something close to sacrilegious—except for one tiny detail: Oklahoma won. And then Oklahoma won some more. And then all those Oklahoma fans who had been raised on the option, who had sworn by the option, who had named their children after Steve Davis and Jack Mildren and J.C. Watts …

well, they dropped the option faster than you could say "Jamelle Holieway."

"I remember a game when Bob Stoops was coaching, and we weren't having much success running the ball," says J.C. Watts, the option quarterback who led Oklahoma to back-to-back Orange Bowl victories. "I heard the Sooner fans say, 'Quit trying to run it and just throw the damn ball.' How times have changed."

The option probably isn't coming back, despite the hopes of old men in Iowa truck stops. Sure, it still pops up now and again, an homage to days gone by, a wrinkle to shake up defenses, but its days of being a dominant offense are as distant as the days before Wal-Mart, when Mom and Pop stores ruled Main Street America.

The shame of it is that optionless football begins to look alike. There was a time when, on Saturday afternoons with leaves falling, you could turn to the television and, without thinking, say, "There's the Oklahoma option," or "There's the Alabama wishbone," and then you might look outside, on the front lawn, and see a kid running and then, at the last instant, pitching to the trailer. Nowadays, without the option on display, Saturdays and Sundays blend together. Nebraska runs the West Coast offense, no different than the Oakland Raiders.

Darrell Royal once said that a beautifully run option play is like music.

Well, the music has died.

And nobody pitches to the trailer anymore.

Delay of Game

The Gradual Arrival
of Integration
Revolutionized the Sport

BY MARK WANGRIN

Sam Cunningham was worried as he rode on the motor coach from the Birmingham airport to the Holiday Inn that September day in 1970. Worried about assignments. Worried about fumbling.

Heading to the hotel with the rest of his USC teammates, Cunningham looked at the houses flashing by his window, at the faces of the people on the porches. Black people, just like him. They watched the bus go by as if it were a procession of great dignitaries. If there was hope reflected in their eyes, he didn't notice it.

Some of his teammates knew where they were. This was Alabama, where seven years earlier the governor, George Wallace, had stood in the doorway in a vain attempt to prevent the integration of the state university. This was Birmingham, where the same year four young black girls were killed in the bombing of the Sixteenth Street Baptist Church. USC defensive lineman Tody Smith was a native of Orange, a city near the Gulf Coast of Texas and a stone's throw from Vidor, where a full 23 years later a federal court would be forced to order the desegregation of public housing. Tenants were harassed and a Ku Klux Klansman was accused of offering white children $50 bounties to beat up black children. Smith, teammates claimed, packed a handgun for the trip.

Cunningham, though, was a callow sophomore. This was his first college varsity game, and he wasn't about to ask questions or get involved in anything other than what it would take to beat Alabama the next night and to keep him from getting benched. "If the machine moved," he later said, "I moved with it." The machine was moving, and it was dragging the segregationist South with it.

One night later, on the evening of Sept. 12 at Legion Field, Cunningham carried only 12 times, but for 135 yards and two touchdowns, in a 42-21 rout of Alabama. An integrated Trojans team, with an all-black backfield, including tailback and Birmingham native Clarence Davis, ran by and through the all-white Crimson Tide.

After the game, Tide coach Paul "Bear" Bryant asked his USC counterpart, John McKay, if he could borrow the hard-running fullback. "Just for a minute," McKay said. "Not the whole season."

Bryant guided Cunningham over to the somber Tide locker room. There he looked at his team, gestured at Cunningham and said, "Gentlemen, this is what a football player looks like." One by one, Bryant's players lined up to shake Cunningham's hand.

At the time Cunningham felt only one emotion—embarrassment. He didn't want to be singled out like that, not to a bunch of players he and his teammates had just humbled. Growing up in an area of Santa Barbara, Calif., where blacks, whites, Hispanics and Asians mingled, he didn't know firsthand what racism was beyond an occasional snub here, an N-word there. Sure, he'd watched the nightly newscasts that showed Birmingham police chief Eugene "Bull" Connor turning police dogs and water cannons on civil rights protestors. He'd paid attention to the television and newspaper reports of the Montgomery bus boycott, and he'd been shaken by the assassination of Martin Luther King in Memphis two and a half years earlier. But he hadn't truly lived it.

Time has provided Cunningham and many others with perspective to suspect what motivated Bryant to schedule USC. Bryant had already integrated the Crimson Tide football team, having that spring signed a blur of a running back from Carroll High School in Ozark, Ala., named Wilbur Jackson, but freshmen weren't eligible to play on the varsity in 1970, so Jackson had to watch USC's epochal performance from the grandstands.

When the NCAA approved the addition of an 11th regular-season game, Bryant reportedly sought out USC for a home-and-home series with the purpose of introducing the new face of college football. The new face he was revealing was like Jackson's: swift, strong, talented—and black.

"Sam Cunningham did more to integrate Alabama in 60 minutes that night than Martin Luther King Jr. had accomplished in 20 years," Bryant assistant Jerry Claiborne said.

Cunningham felt as unworthy of that comparison as he did standing on the bench in the Alabama locker room after that game. "Nobody died, nobody went to jail," Cunningham responded. "It was just a contest of athletics that people believe in. Sometimes that's a neutral ground. I appreciate being compared with Dr. King, but that's a bit much."

What Cunningham and his USC teammates did that night was accelerate a long and contentious process toward critical mass. More than three-quarters of a century had passed since the first blacks had played football at predominantly white colleges, but now one of the staunchest bastions of resistance had at last fallen. It had taken more than time.

***

When the Supreme Court issued an interpretation in the landmark 1896 case *Plessy* v. *Ferguson* that the Equal Protection Clause of the Fourteenth Amendment did not mean equality of the races, much of the hard-fought progress scraped out during Reconstruction was lost. The phrase "separate but equal" to describe segregated facilities grew out of that decision. But the emphasis was more on the "separate" part, with most colleges ignoring the "equal." For the most part unwanted and unwelcome, black football players needed to be as strong-minded as they were strong-legged.

Integration started with skilled players like George Jewett, a medical student at Michigan in 1890; Frederick Douglas "Fritz" Pollard of Brown in 1915; and Paul Robeson of Rutgers, also in 1915. It continued with players such as Oze Simmons of Iowa, who was denied the team captaincy because of the color of his skin, and Jack Trice of Iowa State.

Trice died of injuries sustained during rough play when he tried to break up a three-man wedge against Minnesota in 1923. After Trice's death, a note he'd written on the eve of the game was found in his suit jacket: "My thoughts just before the first real college game of my life: the honor of my race, family and self is at stake. Everyone is expecting me to do big things. I will."

It's uncertain if Trice's injuries were the result of his being singled out because of his race. There was no uncertainty whatsoever in the case of All-America Drake halfback Johnny Bright, who, after handing off in a game against Oklahoma A&M in 1951, got his jaw broken with a right forearm from Aggies lineman Wilbanks Smith. Though irrefutable evidence of the cheap shot was captured in a series of Pulitzer Prize-winning shots by a

> ## "Sam Cunningham did more to integrate Alabama in 60 minutes that night than Martin Luther King Jr. accomplished in 20 years."

photographer for *The Des Moines Register* that were distributed nationwide over the Associated Press wires, the Missouri Valley Intercollegiate Athletic Association dismissed an official complaint by Drake. When the conference refused to discipline Smith or A&M, Drake withdrew in protest.

It wasn't until after World War II, in 1946, that pro football was integrated for the first time in 13 seasons, with Kenny Washington and Woody Strode joining the Los Angeles Rams in 1946, and future Hall of Famers Marion Motley and Bill Willis signing with the Cleveland Browns of the All-America Football Conference. In colleges after the war, schools outside the South began recruiting blacks in greater numbers, and players such as Jackie Robinson of UCLA, Buddy Young of Illinois and, later, Jim Brown of Syracuse forged successful, though often difficult, careers.

***

From well before the war, there was a tension between integrated and segregated schools. At first, many Northern schools refused to acquiesce to the demands of the Southern schools that they bench black players when the teams played. But as the schools looked to expand their national profiles, the sacrifice was more frequently made, both at home and on the road. In 1925 Northwestern agreed to sit Fred Moore against Tulane, and other schools picked up the trend. Maryland was willing to play Wilmeth Sidat-Singh of Syracuse when they thought he was a Hindu; the Terrapins refused when they learned he was an African-American.

In 1936, North Carolina scheduled a game against NYU at Yankee Stadium. North Carolina's president, Frank Porter Graham, quietly agreed to let NYU to play running back Ed Williams, and teams began honoring the practices of the host teams. Black players played in games hosted by Northern schools and sat when their schools played down south.

One of the earliest advances came in Dallas, when Penn State, which had two black players, accepted a bid to play Southern Methodist in the 1948 Cotton Bowl. Local merchants and politicians, fearing an economic loss if the

game turned into a confrontation, quickly desegregated a number of stores and hotels.

Dallas was the exception among Southern cities. In Miami, the state Board of Control, which then ran Florida's universities, adopted a formal policy in the late 1940s that banned public colleges from hosting games featuring integrated teams. At the same time in New Orleans, tickets for the Sugar Bowl bore the inscription, "This ticket is issued for a person of the Caucasian race."

For every step forward there were often two steps back. Two years after the landmark U.S. Supreme Court decision in *Brown* v. *Board of Education* desegregated public schools, Pittsburgh agreed to play Georgia Tech in the 1956 Sugar Bowl in New Orleans. Georgia's segregationist governor, Marvin Griffin, was critical of Georgia Tech for accepting the bowl bid because the Panthers played black fullback Bobby Grier, a stance that Tech president Blake R. Van Leer rejected. Griffin publicly ripped Tech's decision, sending a telegram to the university system's regents that proclaimed, "The South stands at Armageddon." Incensed, about 2,000 Tech students and local residents held a protest march in which they hanged Griffin in effigy. When it was finally settled on the field, Tech beat Pitt 7-0 in a game that hinged on a pass interference call against Grier at the Panthers' 1-yard line.

That Grier was allowed to play didn't go over well in the heart of the old Confederacy, and in the burgeoning spirit of Jim Crow laws, state legislators in Georgia and Louisiana introduced bills that would ban integrated sporting events in their states. In the summer of 1956, the Louisiana legislature approved such a bill, and governor Earl Long signed it into law. Wisconsin, led by a black quarterback, Sidney Willams, canceled a contract for home-and-home games with LSU in 1957 and 1958. Other teams, in football and basketball, followed suit. In 1958 a federal judge threw out the Louisiana law, a decision the U.S. Supreme Court upheld a year later.

Black enrollment at formerly all-white colleges in the South rose from 3,000 in 1960 to 24,000 by 1965 and 98,000 by 1970. With that rise in enrollment came a greater involvement from student groups, who worked to pressure the athletic departments from within. At Arkansas, a student group called Black Americans for Democracy was bent on integrating every on-campus activity. They drafted Hiram McBeth to try out for the football team in 1969. "It was a mission I was sent on," said McBeth, who successfully walked on but never played for the varsity. "I walked into the offices and said to the first white face I saw, 'I think I'd like to play football.'"

In rare instances, the head coach forced the issue. In 1956, Oklahoma coach Bud Wilkinson ignored criticism and signed halfback Prentice Gautt, who became the first African-American scholarship player at a Southern school. Gautt, who was occasionally asked by fellow students to shine their shoes and later earned a doctorate in psychology in part to better understand his experience, earned All-Big Eight honors in 1958 and 1959. "Initially there was a distance," Gautt said. "The guys on the team needed to see me play. They needed to see what kind of heart I had."

***

Morality and sentiment, though, couldn't be legislated or forced. The only place blacks were going to prove they belonged was on the field, starting with USC's decisive victory at Alabama. "It was on the field of competition, where sometimes people believe it more than anything else because they see it with their eyes and they have to believe it," Cunningham said. "It wasn't like a close game, where they could put any kind of asterisk on it. It was a decisive victory and people had to pay attention."

Across the South, coaches began recruiting African-American players, more for the sake of keeping up competitively than because of any social conscience. "We always went on a quick snap so if there was a sniper in the stands, he couldn't get a good shot at me," Southern Methodist's Jerry LeVias told a interviewer in *Rites of Autumn*, a 10-part ESPN series on the history of college football. "And if you would count the number of players in the huddle, you would count only 10, because I was in the middle of it." In 1966, LeVias became the first black to receive an athletic scholarship in the Southwest Conference, and his success convinced others to follow. Within four years, all of the other schools in the league had integrated programs. Texas' national title in 1969 was the last by an all-white team, though Julius Whittier was already on the freshman team.

"What I tell people all the time is that what we did that evening was simple compared with the athletes who came in and had to really go through what was once an all-white environment," Cunningham said. "We got on an airplane, we went to Birmingham, won a game, got on a plane and came back to California. Those players had to deal with things that didn't change over one football game."

As schools in the South began recruiting blacks, the ripple was felt across the country. Northern schools no longer could cherry pick the top talent from Southern states, as Michigan State did with Bubba Smith in Texas and

Minnesota did with Bobby Bell in North Carolina. Predominantly black colleges, which produced 20 first-round NFL draft picks from 1970 to 1978, lost their pipeline and produced only 12 first-rounders in the next 23 drafts. "The quality of black college football is not as good as it used to be in the 1970s, the 1960s and the 1950s," said veteran Florida A&M coach Billy Joe. "But if someone asked me if I would want to have integration or great football players, I'd rather have integration."

In 1970, only five faces on the 23-man consensus All-America team were black. By 1980, it was at 17. Since Ernie Davis of Syracuse won the Heisman Trophy in 1961, 24 of the next 38 winners have been African-Americans.

Coaching and administration have become the next frontier, and again, progress has been painfully slow. In 2004, 18 Division I-A coaches, including three blacks, were dismissed or resigned. Of their replacements only one, Tyrone Willingham, who was hired by Washington after getting fired after three seasons at Notre Dame, was African-American. Heading into the 2005 season the roster of blacks among the 119 major college coaches was easy to list: Willingham, UCLA's Karl Dorrell and Mississippi State's Sylvester Croom.

"Until people realize that we're all coaches, until people understand that we're all the same and stop dealing in black and white, that's just life; you deal with it," Miami defensive coordinator Randy Shannon told the *St. Petersburg Times* in January 2005. "What can be done? You can't make the president or athletic director or anybody hire you if they don't want to hire you."

Over the years, Cunningham grew apart from the USC program. After playing nine seasons with the New England Patriots, he concentrated on his marriage, raising his two daughters and his career as a landscape contractor. But in September 2003, at the invitation of coach Pete Carroll, Cunningham accompanied the team as it flew back to Alabama, this time for an early-season non-conference game at Auburn. He shared the sideline with the Trojans as they beat Auburn 23-0 on their way to the AP national title.

In a pregame speech to the team, Cunningham talked about the 1970 squad that beat Alabama but never mentioned the wider social ramifications of the game. "In 30 years they'll be just like me and the other players I played with," he said later. "They'll be part of the history. And you want to be part of the positive part of it, not the negative part of it. We want them to know we were just like them, to a point. What we did helped them and what they do helps us."

And he added: "I didn't have to strap on or put on anything. It was the easiest road trip I had in my life."

Certainly easier than the first one.

Saturday Matinees

College Football Goes to the Movies

By Ed Krzemienski

Two of America's favorite pastimes—college football and the movies—grew up together. In the mid-1890s, when both were infants, they experienced serious growing pains. Both grew up to become cornerstones of leisure in America. But what happened when the two first mixed? Specifically, how did the emerging Hollywood dream factory deal with the uniquely American incarnation of gladiatorial combat?

On one side sat a nascent motion picture industry. Although partially created and championed by the great American inventor Thomas Edison, visions of movie success looked as small as the images they provided. In fact, not long after the Lumière brothers presented moving photographic pictures to a paying audience in 1895, Louis Lumière remarked bleakly that "the cinema is an invention without a future."

On another side sat the equally problematic entertainment known as college football. Officially born with the soccer-style match between Rutgers and Princeton in 1869, college football had quickly become a focus of public concern. Two years before the Lumière brothers' debut, E.L. Godkin, founding editor of *The Nation*, wrote that colleges resembled "huge training grounds for young gladiators, around whom as many spectators roar as roared in the Flavian amphitheater." By the first decade of the 20th century, Godkin looked like a prophet: in the 1909 season alone, thirty college football players died and 216 were seriously injured.

Early on, Hollywood cast a critical eye on football, portraying the sport as stained by despondency and dishonesty. Three of Hollywood's initial forays into the world of college football carried with them overt messages of corruption on personal and institutional levels. Perhaps even more surprising than the cynicism in such early films is the fact that two of them were comedies.

In 1925, Pathé Studios released *The Freshman*, a film starring Harold Lloyd, one of the great physical comedians of the silent era. Lloyd plays Harold "Speedy" Lamb, a gentle young man who wants nothing more than to be popular at his new college. Fittingly, the school is introduced as "Tate University—a football stadium with a college attached." Using money that he saved from selling washing machines, Lamb wins over a large portion of his fellow classmates by footing the bill for their entertainment, but is told in no uncertain terms that he can never become the biggest man on campus unless he plays football. Accordingly, Speedy attempts to make the team. Accepted by the coach as a makeshift tackling dummy and full-time water boy, Speedy believes himself a full-fledged member of the team. That illusion is shattered on the day of the big game, versus Union State, when the coach refuses to put Lamb into the game despite a rash of injuries that has left the team on the verge of forfeiting the game. In true Hollywood style, and true to Lloyd's amazing physical comedic ability, Speedy enters the game and, after a few hilarious missteps, wins and becomes campus man No. 1.

Like the decade it bisected, *The Freshman* held an undertow of despondency beneath its waves of frolic. Tate University is an elitist community where only the rich are invited to play. Logically, then, Speedy Lamb buys his way into this community, but that leaves him just short of the top and broke. To catch the big man on campus, Chester A. "Chet" Trask, Speedy must become a football hero, and so he commences his pratfall to the top. But just what "top" does he achieve? At the risk of placing too much emphasis upon the "laugh so you don't cry" mentality, Speedy's "victory" is palpably melancholy. He gets the girl, but he already had her love long before he tried to win the love of his classmates. Moreover, she is not a campus belle, but the desk clerk at Speedy's boardinghouse. His success on the football field, as well, brings him adulation but only after humiliation. As he tried to do with his dwindling funds, Speedy purchases the love of his classmates with the winning touchdown, not with his own identity. The film's final scene, in which a clothed Speedy is doused by a shower, seems to indicate that he has been left, both figuratively and literally, "all wet."

All this may seem pretty heavy for a silent slapstick comedy from the "age of ballyhoo," but *The Freshman* revealed an accepted fact in American society of the 1920s: colleges were for the elite and college football was meant for the largest members of the elite.

The 1930s saw a new issue take hold of college football, illegal recruiting. With the release of a Carnegie Commission

Hollywood cast a critical eye on football, portraying a sport stained by dishonesty.

report in 1929, college football came under direct fire, as the report concluded that three-quarters of the 112 colleges studied were in violation of NCAA codes and the principles of amateurism. Such illegal recruiting practices existed from the earliest days of collegiate sport, when Harvard used an alumnus as its coxswain for its crew match with Yale in 1855, but the report seemed to indicate that college football was in a state of anarchy.

And who better to show the anarchy of college football than the Marx Brothers? Three years after the Carnegie Commission issued its report, the brothers went to college in *Horse Feathers*. Compared to this 1932 release, *The Freshman* looks like a veritable documentary.

Groucho stars as professor Quincy Adams Wagstaff, new president of Huxley College, who hopes to improve the school's football team, which has not won a game since 1888. Chico plays a bootlegger named Baravelli. Harpo is his partner, Pinky, the local dogcatcher and iceman. Introduced as the new president, Wagstaff sets up his agenda by singing, "Whatever it is, I'm against it." Then the madness really begins: Asked by a bum for money to get a cup of coffee, Pinky produces a cup and saucer of coffee from his pants pocket; asked to cut the cards at a speakeasy, Pinky produces a hatchet and does so. Baravelli calls the signals in the big game against Darwin as follows: "Humpty Dumpty sat on a wall/Professor Wagstaff gets the ball"; "Uno, due, tre, vendi/This-a time we go left endi"; and, before the final play of the game, "Hi diddle diddle/The cat and the fiddle/This time I think/We go through the middle." Pinky then rides a chariot across the goal line and sets several footballs down in the end zone to give Huxley a 31-12 victory.

For all of their silliness, though, the Marx Brothers were artful and incisive social critics. Taking on higher education fit into the overall catalogue of their satirical thrust. In *Horse Feathers*, Groucho identifies Huxley College's problem in no uncertain terms: "This college is a failure. The trouble is, we're neglecting football for education." To turn things around, he attempts to "recruit" a couple of professional players at the speakeasy, but is beaten to them by Darwin, an equally corrupt school, and Pinky and Baravelli serve as the Huxley ringers. The medium may have been Marxist anarchy, but the message that colleges were cheating to win

came through as loud as the audience's laughter.

Hollywood addressed the problems of college football without the comedic and musical baggage, as well. In 1937, Van Heflin starred in *Saturday's Heroes*, the motion picture industry's first full frontal attack on the commercialization of the college athletic department. Heflin plays Val Webster, a player who is dropped from the team for scalping tickets for some extra spending money. Webster becomes the assistant coach to the school's rival and helps beat his old team. More important than that ending, though, is the fact that *Saturday's Heroes* makes the case for open and frank subsidization of college football players. Needless to say, the topic of paying college players is not one that has gone away and, as college recruitment embraced more athletes with little or no independent financial means, the concept of paying collegiate athletes a stipend for their profitable services to their schools quickly became a topic of heightened concern.

The 1940s marked an abrupt shift in Hollywood's attitude toward football. The start of World War II and the first five years of the cold war meant that exposing even the most nefarious athletic department seemed a bit frivolous. Moreover, war, real and cold, was no time for anything smacking of anti-Americanism.

Even before the war began, Warner Bros. caught the patriotic wave in 1940 with a larger-than-life biography in the best wartime propaganda tradition. The studio that brought America epic biographies of Louis Pasteur and Émile Zola turned now to the legendary life of Knute Rockne. With Pat O'Brien in the title role and Ronald Reagan as George Gipp, director Lloyd Bacon's *Knute Rockne, All American* told the story of Notre Dame football as mythically as any Bible epic. In 1933, O'Brien had co-starred in *College Coach*, the story of a demanding but fictional head coach at the equally fictional Calvert College. Now he got the lead in a film about a real coach at a real college.

The story of Rockne's life is probably the best-known of any film on college football. Rockne creates the forward pass and the backfield in motion, the latter after watching the Rockettes. But what was most significant about Rockne's story was what it was *not*. It was not despondent or dishonest. Even when Rockne needs a star, he does not search

speakeasies or mention stipends for players. In fact, it seems Rockne never recruits at all. Rather, he simply allows fate to intervene in the form of George Gipp. Gipp's film entry into Notre Dame football could hardly be more syrupy. Reagan's Gipp happens across the field at just the moment Rockne is having problems with his kickers. Gipp kicks a couple of balls out of the stadium, but has no desire to play football since he is committed to baseball. Absurdly, Gipp wears a baseball glove—with street clothes—during the entire encounter. Of course, a player miraculously sent by God must return to Him with equal divinity. But not before imploring his coach to win one in memory of him— one, that is, for The Gipper.

> **Screen Plays, 1925-36**
> *The Freshman* (1925)
> *Salute* (1929)
> *The Forward Pass* (1929)
> *The New Halfback* (1929)
> *Eleven Men and a Girl*
>   Original title: *Maybe It's Love* (1930)
> *Touchdown* (1931)
> *Maker of Men* (1931)
> *Huddle* (1932)
> *Horse Feathers* (1932)
> *The All American* (1932)
> *College Humor* (1933)
> *College Coach* (1933)
> *The Band Plays On* (1934)
> *Hold 'Em Yale* (1935)
> *Fighting Youth* (1935)
> *Pigskin Parade* (1936)
> *Rose Bowl* (1936)

The real Rockne was, of course, more complex than the film presented. Murray Sperber's book *Shake Down the Thunder: The Creation of Notre Dame Football*, although just about as laudatory of Rockne as Hollywood was, dispelled some of the film's most overt myths. Rockne circumvented the school's academic standards for his players and engaged in high-priced recruiting. Gipp never graduated from high school, spent most of his time playing pool, earned money by gambling and ferrying copper miners to a local house of prostitution and skipped so many classes that Notre Dame expelled him. (The school reinstated Gipp at the urging of Rockne and when it became apparent that other schools, including Michigan and Army, sought his services.) The 1928 Army game looked nothing like it did in the film. Rockne's "Win one for The Gipper" speech is a highly fluid topic, sometimes occurring before the game and sometimes at halftime. Even the supposedly sacrosanct source of the Gipper story, Rockne's autobiography, was ghostwritten. In 1940, critics either hit the film as being overly sentimental and filled with mock heroics or damned it with the praise that it was "one of the best pictures for boys in years."

Whatever its misrepresentations, *Knute Rockne, All American* was the most significant sports film of its day. Sperber attributes the downfall of Notre Dame's head coach, Elmer Layden, to its 1940 release. The film, it seems, reminded viewers that whatever Layden was, he was no Rockne. In 1941, Frank Leahy replaced Layden.

The movie also introduced a form that became a template for sports films for the next six decades: the tragic biopic. The story in this form needed to be based on a real person who died tragically before achieving legendary status. Specifically, the subject went from rags, usually as an immigrant, to riches, generally in terms of celebrity and success if not money, to dust, by some heartbreaking disease or accident. In the sports oeuvre, Hollywood used the formula to its best early effect two years after *Knute Rockne, All American*—and, not coincidentally, with a much better actor—in *The Pride of the Yankees*, the life story of Lou Gehrig starring Gary Cooper.

There was, of course, fun and frolic as well in the Hollywood years surrounding World War II. And what better place than a college campus as a setting for tuneful cavorting? In 1936, Hollywood introduced a 14-year-old named Judy Garland (alongside Betty Grable and Jack Haley, who became a more famous Garland sidekick three years later as the Tinman in *The Wizard of Oz*) in *Pigskin Parade*. Because of a mistake in scheduling, Yale invites Texas State College instead of the University of Texas to play the Bulldogs in a charity football game. So as not to humiliate his new team, Texas State's coach searches for a star player. He appears in the form of Amos Dodd (Stuart Erwin), a muskmelon tosser by trade and barefoot footballer by film's end, who is smuggled into the student body on forged credentials. Amid dance interludes and musical numbers of the Yacht Club Boys (who set the mood by singing that they "would rather be in college"), Texas State humiliates Yale on a snow-covered field, led by its illegal recruit.

> **Screen Plays, 1937-49**
> *Life Begins in College* (1937)
> *Hold 'Em Navy* (1937)
> *Saturday's Heroes* (1937)
> *Navy Blue and Gold* (1937)
> *The Gladiator* (1938)
> *Touchdown Army* (1938)
> *Cowboy Quarterback* (1939)
> *$1000 a Touchdown* (1939)
> *Knute Rockne, All American* (1940)
> *The Quarterback* (1940)
> *Harmon of Michigan* (1941)
> *Rise and Shine* (1941)
> *The Male Animal* (1942)
> *The Iron Major* (1943)
> *The Spirit of West Point* (1947)
> *Good News* (1947)
> *Easy Living* (1949)

The wholesome concept included a continued interest in the holiest of holy rivalries, Army vs. Navy. Prior to the 1950s,

Hollywood produced five films that featured the Army-Navy game, including three (*Hold 'Em Navy, Navy Blue and Gold, Touchdown Army*) in less than a year (1937-38). In 1935, Cesar Romero starred in *Hold 'Em Yale*, a film based on Damon Runyon's short story of the same name. Both film and story dealt with a group of mugs accompanying a bratty heiress to the Harvard-Yale game and, in a prescient twist, with the problems inherent in tearing down goalposts. In 1941, a James Thurber short story became the source for *Rise and Shine*, a film about Boley Bolenciecwcz, a thinly veiled portrait of a former classmate of Thurber's at Ohio State. A year later, Henry Fonda and Olivia de Havilland starred in the screen adaptation of Thurber and Elliott Nugent's political football play, *The Male Animal*. Both play and film managed to combine the seemingly incongruous topics of a homecoming game and the Sacco-Vanzetti trial. And, in 1949, Irwin Shaw's short story "Education of the Heart" became the movie *Easy Living*.

Hollywood ended its brief détente of the 1940s, and when it returned to its part-time business of looking at college football through a trenchant lens, it did so with another interesting—and soon-to-be controversial— source. At the beginning of the 1950s, Millard Lampell was already best known as a collaborator with folk music legends Pete Seeger and Woody Guthrie. Lampell also wrote fiction, including a novel dealing with college football titled *The Hero*. Lampell and Sidney Buchman adapted the book for the 1951 film, *Saturday's Hero*. Starring John Derek, *Saturday's Hero* shared more than just a similar name with Van Heflin's 1937 movie. Derek stars as a naïve high school football star, Steve Novak. Attending college on an athletic scholarship, Novak hopes to get a genuine education while at school. What he encounters is a slave-driving coach, brutal teammates and a corrupt alumnus. In a complimentary review, *The New York Times* commented that the movie "makes college football look more vicious than organized

mugging and the white slave trade." Like its predecessor of a similar name, *Saturday's Hero* paints the picture of college corruption in broad strokes. All colleges, the film implies, cheat.

Even more interesting than the sweeping condemnation Lampell provided for *Saturday's Hero* was the one he came under a few years later. After initiating its investigation of communism in the motion picture industry with the blacklisting in 1947-48 of what became known as the Hollywood 10, the House Un-American Activities Committee gathered more than 300 additional names from 1951-54. Lampell's was among them. Lampell eventually re-emerged as a writer for television films. In 1966, while accepting an Emmy for his Hallmark television drama *Eagle in a Cage*, Lampell received an ovation when he said, "I think I ought to mention I was blacklisted for 10 years."

John Goldfarb, Please Come Home, released in 1965, was intended to be a comedy with the accoutrement of football, but Notre Dame didn't find it very funny. The movie told the story of Goldfarb, a U-2 pilot who crashes his plane in the imaginary Middle Eastern nation of Fawzia. In order to "come home," Goldfarb must coach the nation's football team against the Fighting Irish. Notre Dame agrees to play— and take a dive—in the game so that the United States can maintain a military base in Fawzia. Notre Dame sued 20th Century-Fox over the release of the film on the grounds that it "causes irreparable injury to the high prestige, reputation and goodwill of the University." Specifically, Notre Dame opposed scenes in which its boys are shown taking part in a burlesque harem feast the evening before the "big game." In December 1964, Judge Henry Clay Greenberg granted an injunction against the release of the film. By March 1965, the injunction had been lifted and the film was on the screen. Few deemed it worth the wait. *The New York Times* remarked that the release of the film was "a triumph for 20th Century-Fox … and the cause of free speech and the right to travesty. But the public ends up with a goose-egg laid by a turkey." Caught up in defending its name, Notre Dame gave the

---

Screen Plays, 1951-84
That's My Boy (1951)
Saturday's Hero (1951)
Bonzo Goes to College (1952)
The Rose Bowl Story (1952)
Trouble Along the Way (1953)
Football Now and Then (1953)
All-American (1953)
John Goldfarb,
  Please Come Home (1965)
Footsteps (1972)*
Return to Campus (1975)*
Something for Joey (1977)*
Grambling's White Tiger (1981)*
The Bear (1984)
* **Made-for-TV film**

Screen Plays, 1988-2002
Johnny Be Good (1988)
Everybody's All-American (1988)
Glory Days (1988)*
Triumph of the Heart:
  The Ricky Bell Story (1991)*
Necessary Roughness (1991)
Rudy (1993)
The Program (1993)
The Halfback of Notre Dame (1996)*
The Waterboy (1998)
Full Ride (2001)*
The Junction Boys (2002)*
* **Made-for-TV film**

> ### *The Top Five College Football Films of All Time*
> 1. The Freshman – *Hollywood never improved on its original*
> 2. Horse Feathers – *Anarchy, yes, but still more rational than the BCS*
> 3. The Program – *Take away the "romance" and this one's as accurate as anything on film*
> 4. Saturday's Hero – *A powerful indictment of college football*
> 5. Rudy – *Even if you hate Notre Dame*

movie far more attention than it warranted. As it was, people still stayed away in droves.

Possibly due to the legal flap with Notre Dame, but more likely because of the explosion of popularity for the NFL, Hollywood turned its attention away from the college gridiron and toward the professional version of the game. The 1970s saw a surge of professional football movies, including *Brian's Song* (1971), still regarded as one of the best made-for-TV productions ever; *Semi-Tough* (1977); *Heaven Can Wait* (1978); and, most significant of all, *North Dallas Forty* (1979).

The dearth of college football movies continued into the 1980s. *Grambling's White Tiger* (1981) was another true made-for-TV movie with the twist of a white quarterback, played by Bruce Jenner, trying to integrate into a predominantly black school. Except for Harry Belafonte's portrayal of Eddie Robinson, the film fails. Three years later, Gary Busey portrayed an even more legendary coach in *The Bear*. Somehow director Richard Sarafian manages to deaden the inherently interesting life story of Paul Bryant.

Hollywood returned to its dishonesty-despondency-tragedy approach to college football in the years wrapped around the start of the 1990s. Despondency came first, in 1988, with the screen adaptation of Frank Deford's novel, *Everybody's All-American*, which offered a star-studded interpretation of the quick rise and steady fall of Gavin Grey, and was widely interpreted as a veiled version of the life of 1959 Heisman Trophy winner Billy Cannon. Similar to Cannon, Grey leads LSU to its first national championship and enjoys a successful professional career. As it did with Cannon, Grey's malaise comes in retirement, where he longs to hear the cheers but is incapable of creating a replacement for the gridiron and truly becomes his nickname, the Grey Ghost.

The biggest problem with the film was not inaccuracy, but a new difficulty for the sports film—a bit too much accuracy. With sports pages peppered with stories of washed-up athletes scrounging for money, pathetically reliving their glory days, or both, watching the same thing happen in the course of a two-hour movie felt redundant.

In 1993, Hollywood released two films dealing with college football. Diametrically opposed in theme and spirit, *Rudy* and *The Program* encapsulate the motion picture industry's dual approach to presenting college football on film as well as any pair of movies ever will.

On the despondency-dishonesty side was *The Program*, a real sampler pack of a movie. Shown through a season at the fictitious Eastern State University, *The Program* offers a variety of realistic images. Although ESU plays a strange schedule, including teams from myriad conferences—Michigan and Iowa from the Big Ten, North Carolina from the ACC and Georgia Tech and Mississippi State from the SEC—its opponents are shown on-field with accurate uniforms and logos. The players, likewise, represent a rainbow coalition, including a trailer-trash quarterback and two divergent running backs, one semi-literate and another on the threshold of medical school. Both vie for the attention of another standard of college football: the recruiting date, in this case played by Halle Berry. Clemson used to call its dates the Bengal Babes and Maryland calls its the Black-Eyed Susans, but regardless of name, wooing a potential player for a weekend is the universal purpose of these coeds. Game day is accurately intense. Two players spit into each other's mouths to get fired up, and the coach, James Caan, calls for hits that induce "snot bubbles" from the opponent. A knee injury ends the season, and potentially the career, of the team's best defender; and the media scrutinizes the team's quarterback, a Heisman hopeful and an alcoholic.

The real purpose of *The Program*, though, is to look at corruption in college football. The coach's daughter takes an exam for her boyfriend, the backup quarterback. When the starter goes into rehab, the school allows the cheater to return. Alumni pay players, who accept the money without regret since they make so much for the school. One player uses steroids. He gains weight, muscle, intensity, a starting position and eventually a suspension from the coach after he assaults a woman at a party.

Most football experts, primarily former big-time college players, regard *The Program* as the most accurate representation of the intensity of a college football game. Jashon Sykes, a linebacker for the Denver Broncos and former

Colorado Buffalo, said, "Everything that you saw in that movie has either happened to me, I've experienced or I saw happen." In his review of *The Program*, Roger Ebert commented that by film's end, he was simultaneously rooting for Eastern State to win the final game and hoping it would do away with its football program.

On the sweeter side, there was *Rudy*. Director David Anspaugh was no stranger to Notre Dame or to underdog stories. Anspaugh was born a hundred miles or so from South Bend in Decatur, Ind., and, in 1980, served as associate producer on *Fighting Back*, a made-for-TV movie about Notre Dame alumnus and Vietnam veteran Rocky Bleier. Moreover, Anspaugh directed the highly successful basketball tale *Hoosiers*.

Rudy tells the true story of Daniel "Rudy" Ruettiger, an undersized, working-class kid—the third of 14, in fact—from Joliet, Ill., who dreams of one day playing for Notre Dame. Rudy, played by future hobbit Sean Astin, is neither smart enough—he suffers from a mild form of dyslexia—to get into the school nor good enough to make the team. Eventually, though, he transfers into Notre Dame from across the lake at Holy Cross Junior College as a 24-year-old sophomore and serves on the Fighting Irish practice team. Head coach Ara Parseghian (Jason Miller) notices Ruettiger and recognizes

heart when he sees it. With the support of groundskeeper Fortune (Charles S. Dutton), Rudy hangs around long enough to fulfill his dream of making it into the annals of Notre Dame football. He plays in the last moments of the last home game, tackles Georgia Tech's quarterback and is carried off the field by his teammates. He graduated in 1976 with a degree in sociology. Had it not been true, no one would have believed it. *Rudy* won an award at the 1994 *Heartland Film Festival*—held, fittingly, in Indiana—while others cringed at its mawkish sentimentality and worship of Notre Dame.

For eight decades, college football skipped across Hollywood like a flat rock over a very deep body of water. Despite the passage of time, the issues remained the same: campus heroes, getting the girl, winning the big game— almost always accompanied by illegal recruiting, cheating, career-ending injuries, the paying of players and the role of an athletic team as the focal point at an institution of higher learning. Indeed, the opening caption of Hollywood's earliest college football film, *The Freshman*, still rings absolutely true: "Do you remember those boyhood days when going to College was greater than going to Congress—when you'd rather be Right Tackle than President?"

After almost a century on celluloid, Hollywood's vision of college football remains unchanged.

Full-Contact Talking Drill

A Roundtable Discussion With the GameDay Crew

The ESPN College GameDay *crew—Chris Fowler, Lee Corso and Kirk Herbstreit—gathered at ESPN World Headquarters on a rare visit to Bristol for a freewheeling discussion moderated by ESPN College Football Encyclopedia editor Michael MacCambridge. Offscreen and on, the trio is an effortlessly collegial bunch. Fowler maintains his air of relaxed authority. Herbstreit is jovial and thoughtful. And Corso, ever the instigator, is by far the most demonstrative. They settled down to discuss their years together, the changes they've seen in college football and the most important issues facing the game today.*

THE SHOW

MacCAMBRIDGE: What do you guys remember about the first *GameDay* that was taped on a college campus?

FOWLER: It was November 1993, Notre Dame and Florida State, which I still think was the biggest regular-season game in college football in the last 15 or 20 years. No. 1 vs. No. 2. At Notre Dame. Late in the season. It was such an electric atmosphere because of Florida State quarterback Charlie Ward—the eventual Heisman Trophy winner—and the national championship implications.

We installed a set in the lobby of the Notre Dame Hall of Fame, surrounded by all the trophies. People were curious to see what was going on. They didn't understand the concept of a traveling pregame show.

But it's the game I remember.

CORSO: The rush we got from the people is what I remember. They saw us live. The adrenaline was flowing. It was like an actor doing a Broadway show.

FOWLER: The pep rally the night before was one of those vintage Notre Dame pep rallies, a real frenzy, and our set was right outside in the concourse. The pep rally was so incredible that a couple of guys on the set wanted to change their pick …

CORSO: Oh, I did.

FOWLER: … from Florida State to Notre Dame.

CORSO: That's right. There was no question in my mind. I said, "Jeez, Florida State's got to be a lot better than these guys if they're going to beat them after last night."

FOWLER: After Notre Dame won, I remember Lou Holtz coming out of his office, walking down the hall, and stepping right up onto our set—we were in the middle of a live segment. No introduction. Lee jumps up, gives him his microphone and his chair. And Holtz conducts this triumphant interview—and then goes out and loses to Boston College the next week.

MacCAMBRIDGE: Has there ever been a time when you were afraid that the fans were too unruly, that they were going to breech the perimeter and take over the set?

FOWLER: Hey, they did breech the perimeter. They didn't take over the set, but they could have. Michigan State vs. Michigan, East Lansing, 1999. We set up in the middle of a tailgating area, our set plopped down in the middle of this field. It wasn't even dawn when we arrived, but there was this crowd of people with their shirts off in freezing weather …

HERBSTREIT: Snowing!

FOWLER: A half-hour before the show, it was a frenzy. The crowd knocked down the chain-link fence around the set before the show. All kinds of objects, some of them funny, some of them dangerous, were flying through the air. Everything from radishes to coins to footballs to …

HERBSTREIT: Full beer cans!

FOWLER: … a full beer can almost decapitated Lee.

HERBSTREIT: A full can! It split Lee and me right in half, landed right in the set and exploded. We're live on TV! I've got to tell you, when you throw a full beer can from 50 yards as hard as you can throw it—if that hits Lee or me in the back of the head, it's medic!

CORSO: After that, we put a screen behind us.

FOWLER: It was a very, very good show. We were so alert, so afraid for our safety, that everybody was really focused. I remember coming off the set and the producer comes running out of the truck all excited. We were just happy to be alive.

PLAYOFF VS. BCS

MacCAMBRIDGE: What's the ideal way for college football to settle the national championship?

FOWLER: A playoff. It works in every other division in college football. It works in every other sport in college athletics. Division I-A football sticks out for being too entrenched in tradition to employ it.

Start small, just to check the impact. No dramatic, 16-team playoff. Set up some kind of a system for selecting

> ## *"Winning comes down to having an excellent defensive team, an excellent offensive line and excellent special teams. I don't care what offense you have."*

the teams, something like the selection committee in basketball, which does a pretty good job.

I would incorporate the current bowl system, keeping them involved in the process. But I would limit it to 11 regular-season games. If you have two teams playing 14 games, four teams playing 13 games, it's not a big deal.

Missed class time is such a nonfactor in this discussion compared to any other college sport. In baseball, for instance, they go on the road for a couple of weeks. Other athletes in other sports miss a lot more class than football players do.

Having said that, I don't think it will happen for a long time.

HERBSTREIT: I have mixed views. I think a playoff makes a lot of sense in terms of settling everything on the field and finding out who the true champion is. But part of me really appreciates the fact that we still have bowl games, and we still have teams that go 8–3 and then end their season on a positive note by going to a bowl game. They carry that into the next season.

So I think there's some value to having bowl games and not having all the emphasis on crowning a champion. If we leave the system the way it is now, we could just put another game at the end. How great would it have been to see Auburn play USC in 2005? Or LSU and USC the year before? And the year before that, Ohio State versus USC? The year before that, Miami and Oregon? It seems like there are always two teams still standing at the end under the current structure. So if we keep the system the way it is and add one game at the end, it would be fine with me.

CORSO: I would leave the system the way it is, but I would factor in strength of schedule. It isn't only how many games you win; it's also how many good teams you beat. And I'd cap margin of victory at 21 points. As a former coach, I can tell you the best way to tell how good your football team is, is to look at how many good teams you beat and how badly you beat them.

MacCAMBRIDGE: Margin of victory was in the formula earlier and was taken out. From your statement, it sounds like the BCS is going in the wrong direction.

CORSO: Absolutely. It's going back to the point where we argued all the time. I remember sitting there and saying, "You can't trust the coaches. You can't trust the newspaper people." We've got to do something else.

FOWLER: So they came up with a computer thing that nobody understands. That's what bothers people.

HERBSTREIT: Here's the thing that's really discouraging: the coaches and the media people who vote in the BCS polls don't—can't—watch most, much less all, of the games. They can't possibly be on top of what's going on in other conferences. They're too busy. The coaches may catch a highlight or two Saturday night, read the paper Sunday, talk to their SIDs and directors of football operations, and then vote for their Top 25.

They need to have a selection committee that actually watches five or six screens—every team, every game. Or at least a lot more than voters do now. So that, by the time they get done Saturday night, they've watched the Pac-10, the Big 12, the SEC, the Big Ten, the Big East and the ACC, and they know every team's strengths and weaknesses.

CORSO: To me, the AP writers probably have a better feel than the coaches, because the coaches have tunnel vision. They have to. They've got one opponent a week and one conference to conquer for 12 weeks. You talk to any coach who's in a premier program and he'll tell you, "I'm in the ACC. I can't tell you about the Big Ten. I don't know anything about the Big Ten."

FOWLER: It's tough to bash one poll versus another. They rarely differ much. One team might be ranked a couple of slots higher in one, but basically they're the same.

CORSO: So set up a committee of 16 or whatever—you know, former ADs, former coaches. They don't have a hidden agenda. They sit together in a room, eat pizza, watch games; and on Sunday night, after watching all the games and talking it over, they say, "Here's our Top 25." Eliminate the computers. Let a group of people who understand the game and have no axe to grind give you a Top 25.

MacCAMBRIDGE: What we saw in 2003 with Oklahoma vs. Kansas State was a team that was playing for nothing. You

heard before that game that even if they lost, Oklahoma was going to the national championship game. Do you think conference championship games are a good idea?

HERBSTREIT: If you're a Big 12 fan, how can you not want to see Oklahoma play Kansas State for the conference title? You talk to people in the Southeastern Conference, and their championship game is as big as any other, including the national championship. What's going to happen in Jacksonville in 2005-06 with the ACC, I think is great. It's great for us fans to be able to see those kinds of matchups.

But it's not fair that the Big 12 and the ACC and the SEC go through this and other conferences do not. I think every conference should have a championship game, or the concept should be eliminated.

FOWLER: Well, whether you like conference championship games or not, they're necessary in the big conferences, where you can't have a true round-robin tournament. You can't have an SEC or ACC or Big 12 champion without having a championship game. It's impossible. The schedules would never balance. You'd have nothing but controversy. You'd have three teams tied that didn't play each other, and you'd be deciding championships with goofy tiebreakers.

So you have to have a championship game. Whether it's fair or not in BCS terms is debatable. Some teams have been helped by playing the extra game in the BCS formula.

HERBSTREIT: A lot of times they're playing a team they've already beaten, and under the current system, they don't get any reward for that.

FOWLER: That's a problem. When you're LSU, and you beat Georgia twice, and it only costs you a quality win because Georgia drops down, that's a big problem.

HERBSTREIT: It's a huge problem.

FOWLER: You go into their backyard, and you beat them, and you get no reward in the BCS formula. In fact, you might be hurt by it.

HERBSTREIT: True, but you know what? I love conference championship games. As a college football fan, I think they're great.

EARLY EXITS

MacCAMBRIDGE: What about the fates of Maurice Clarett and Mike Williams? Will we continue to see this push from players wanting to enter the NFL draft early being tested in the courts?

HERBSTREIT: In 1996, Ron Dayne and Andy Katzenmoyer, both true freshmen, had outstanding years, and there was a lot of talk that they might push the envelope and come out. When

they decided not to, the feeling was that somewhere down the line it was going to happen. And once it did, who was going to stop them? They have that right. Eventually, they're going to take it to court and win. That's always been the feeling.

Then along comes Maurice Clarett. He wins the initial ruling from a judge, has a big smile on his face—and everybody's thinking, "Well, the dam just broke. All the top underclassmen are going to jump." Mike Williams gets caught up in it. Then the decision gets appealed. The collective bargaining agreement between the NFL Players Association and the NFL holds up. The NFL wins. Clarett loses.

My point is that somewhere out there the next guy in line has an agent telling him, "You don't need college. You're ready physically. You're ready emotionally. You're a top-five pick. Let's go." But now it's a lot easier for a coach or a parent to say, "Whoa, wait a second," because of the legal precedent. The key word is "now."

The NFL flexed its muscle. And to be honest, I think it's going to stop agents from having that choke hold on players, from trying to force them into the league too early. Some are ready. Some are not. But agents are always telling them they're ready.

CORSO: As long as there are agents and lawyers who want to push the envelope, there will be disgruntled athletes who want to come out sooner rather than later.

FOWLER: The athletes don't enjoy school very much. That's just a fact. There are plenty of players who would like to jump. They'd like to get paid right now. I think Lee's right. There will always be agents and lawyers urging them in that direction. The NFL has a sincere desire not to see the rule change, and they'll fight it. The NBA, on the other hand, is delighted to have a high schooler come into the league if it generates publicity. They're fine with that.

MacCAMBRIDGE: A lot of people I've talked to feel that this Clarett and Williams ruling was very important because they believe the early entries into the NBA have hurt not only the college game but also the pro game. If this case had gone the other way, would it have had a similarly negative impact on college football?

CORSO: No. In basketball, losing one guy affects the whole team. Losing Mike Williams or Maurice Clarett doesn't hurt USC or Ohio State as much as losing your top basketball player.

HERBSTREIT: Like at Syracuse, where Carmelo Anthony won the national championship, then left school early and went to the Nuggets.

FOWLER: But if some guys skip after freshman year, and some guys after sophomore year ... if that starts happening

in increasing numbers in college football, it would definitely hurt the sport.

HERBSTREIT: You see the difference in the summer basketball leagues, where NBA players are competing with high school kids. Naturally gifted athletes who are 17, 18, 19 years old kind of blend in with the NBA players physically.

Now go to an NFL camp and look at the bodies. Take Oklahoma's Adrian Peterson, the best running back to come into college football in a long time, and throw him into a scrimmage at an NFL camp. The difference between a high school player or a first-year freshman and those 25-year-old men? Night and day.

So I agree with Chris to an extent. If the courts rule the other way, you'd see a herd of underclassmen saying, "I'm ready to go! I'm ready to go!" But you'd see a lot of guys going out early and failing to make the cut. You'd see a lot of guys getting injured. You'd see promising careers burning out before they ever lit up. And 10, 15, 20 years down the road, you'd see people looking at the record and saying that's not the route to go in football.

You just can't do it in football.

RECRUITING WARS

MacCAMBRIDGE: Speaking of impressionable young players: in my opinion, as a fan, there's more focus on recruiting than ever before, and it's mainly because of the Internet. Does that have an impact on how players behave, how coaches behave?

FOWLER: Obviously, the Internet has affected every aspect of life. Information spreads across the country so quickly. So does misinformation. And rumors. And whispers about corruption and rules violations. A while ago, the main source of recruiting information was a handful of annual magazines. Today you have websites that are updated daily. One day: "So-and-so talked to the running backs coach at Tennessee." The next day: "That's off. Now he's visiting LSU."

There's a lot of garbage out there. If you have an appetite for it, you're never going to go hungry.

HERBSTREIT: If you're talking about the impact of the Internet on programs themselves, I don't think it affects them. Fans flock to the dot-coms, they get on the chat boards, and they throw stuff back and forth: "Yo, I saw Buster So-and-So at a football game, and he had a Nebraska hat on" … "Yo, two weeks earlier, I saw him wearing a Tennessee cap." And it just becomes fodder for those Internet sites, which I think are among the worst things going in the college football world. I wish there were some kind of virus we could send to all those chat rooms to implode them, because—

whatever their good intentions—they create more trouble for college football coaches and more trouble for programs.

The Internet as an information source? I call it a rumor mill.

The next thing you know, a coach has to go on a call-in show and field questions that start off, "Hey, I was just reading that you said this and that," and it sounds like the guy's talking about *USA Today*, *ESPN The Magazine* or something reputable, but he's really talking about some rumor some lunatic posted in some chat room.

I don't think it affects recruiting. But it must get pretty annoying to have to deal with a bunch of faceless morons who get off on instant messaging each other and spreading junk on chat rooms.

CORSO: What hurts coaches are the innuendoes, the rumors. You know, "Is this guy going here? Is that guy going there?" It hurts coaches when it comes to preparation. They've got to put up with that nuisance.

But I don't think the Internet affects coaches when it comes to actual selection of players. They've got a core group they're looking at. They know that group. That's the group they're recruiting.

THE COACHING LIFE

MacCAMBRIDGE: Speaking of coaching, over the past few years there have been a number of scandals involving coaches. We've seen problems in Colorado, Washington, Alabama. Is the abuse worse than it used to be? Or are we talking about greater visibility and scrutiny of coaches than ever before?

CORSO: It's visibility. When I had a problem with a kid in Bloomington, we would talk to the guy at the *Bloomington Herald-Times*. Now if an Indiana kid gets in trouble, the coach has to talk to everybody: ESPN, the Internet, *USA Today*. Like it or not, we used to be able to control the local press. Be nice to the guy, he'd be nice to you. You had time to deal with a problem. But now, the first time a guy gets in trouble his name is on the Internet, it's on ESPN and it's in *USA Today*.

FOWLER: It's tough to lump together all the off-the-field problems and make some general statement because the incidents are so different. What happened to Mike Price, what happened to Gary Barnett, they're not the same kinds of things. The only thing they have in common is that they involve very highly paid, highly visible, highly public figures. And whether you're in sports or politics or show business, if you're a well-known figure, you're subject to a different level of scrutiny these days. You're going to be tossed into the 24-hour news cycle. And there's a constant need for news to

be recycled, repackaged. I think that's been a factor in the coverage of the Colorado story, and it was a factor in the coverage of the Alabama and Washington stories, although they had shorter life spans.

Look, these guys make seven figures. They're on TV all the time. What they do with their private lives is now public fodder.

HERBSTREIT: We've seen coaches in big programs go from making $500,000 or so a year, which is a great living, to nearly $2 million. Consequently, coaches are held to higher expectations. It's like going to a Major League Baseball game. When your star player, who's making $12 million a year, strikes out with the bases loaded for the third straight time, what happens? He hears a lot of boos.

It's no different with coaches in today's big-time programs. The fans, they want 10 or 11 wins. "If you're making a million bucks, I need 10 or 11 wins. You make that kind of money, fine, I'm cool with it. As long as you get me my wins."

FOWLER: It's this endless churn. That's what you saw with Colorado. The elements of the case were not terribly dramatic. But there were revelations day after day. There were legal things that just kept this thing churning for months, and it fed the monsters of sports news and regular news.

CORSO: I had the first college-coach talk show in the country in 1969. Now there are talk shows everywhere, all the time, and they've all got airtime to fill.

HERBSTREIT: They're all trying to outdo one another.

MacCAMBRIDGE: Back to coaches for a minute. Despite all the good-faith efforts to increase diversity in the coaching ranks, college football seems to be dragging its heels. In the NFL in 2005, African-Americans hold six of the 32 head coaching jobs. Among the 119 Division 1-A schools in 2005, the number of African-American head coaches is three. What does this tell us, and what do you see happening in this area?

FOWLER: It's a big problem. A very sticky problem. Because you can't legislate a school's choice. You can't make a school pick a coach to create diversity. It's an embarrassment to the sport that such an imbalance exists when, on the field, the majority of the players are African-American.

I think everybody in the sport would like to see the situation improve. Guys like Sylvester Croom and Tyrone Willingham have to succeed to open the minds of the people who make the hires. I mean college presidents, trustees, chancellors—this isn't a very diverse group either. When they're making decisions on who is going to be the highest-paid employee in the state, they're not willing to take a chance.

HERBSTREIT: Everyone gets focused on why there aren't more minority head coaches. I suggest we look at the base of the pyramid. The graduate assistants. These guys line up a

hundred deep and say, "Can I be your GA? Can I be your GA?" with the hope of one day becoming an assistant coach, one day a coordinator.

More head coaches need to encourage minority athletes who don't make it to the NFL to stay involved with football at the GA level. "You didn't make it to the NFL. That's okay. This is a good way to go. You're a good player. You're a good leader."

If more minority players get into coaching at the ground level, then there will be a lot more minority candidates to choose from for coaching positions.

CORSO: One of the reasons there's such a small pool is because guys don't think there's anywhere to go. Now, when Sylvester Croom comes in, there are maybe 15 guys out there saying, "You know what? Maybe I could be a head coach in the SEC." But until he got there, why would you want to start at the bottom?

LAND VS. AIR

MacCAMBRIDGE: College football has traditionally featured more running than the pro game. But in the last few years we've seen an increase in passing. We've even seen a school like Nebraska install the West Coast offense. Does this spell the end of the option offense in major college football?

HERBSTREIT: There's a big misperception about the West Coast offense and the spread offense. Teams are still going to run the ball. And there are different forms of option plays. Maybe not the traditional down-the-line triple option. But in the shotgun they're doing a handoff …

CORSO: The wraparound handoff.

HERBSTREIT: And some teams are running the triple option off of the shotgun. The guy comes down, he keeps it and then he's pitching off to the next guy. So it gets away from what Lee and I and Chris would consider the good old-fashioned option of Jamelle Holloway. But it's still there. As long as defenses continue to play man coverage, which they're always going to do, it's a great play. Teams just have to have it in their package. I don't think you'll ever see the option eliminated in the college game.

FOWLER: As a change of pace, but not as a steady diet. Because it's very, very difficult to recruit quarterbacks for an option offense these days. Players with NFL aspirations don't want to play it. They think they'll be perceived as guys who don't throw well enough to be recruited as passers. But remember, today's short-passing games are achieving the same thing teams used to achieve with a "pure" running game. They're just doing it with different formations. They're getting four or five yards at a time. And they're eating up the clock. That's what the West Coast gives you: a ball-control offense with a

pass. You throw a screen, or you dump it off to the side or at the H-back or something. But it's not a wide-open offense.

CORSO: As I've said before, the essence of winning, in my mind, comes down to having an excellent defensive team, an excellent offensive line and excellent special teams. I don't care what offense you have.

HERBSTREIT: Trends come and go in college football. Strategies come and go. But Lee's dead on when it comes to defense. I don't care who you talk to, what era you look at, the teams that have the best chance at winning are the teams that have the best defense. Sometimes as analysts we overlook offensive line play. We get caught up in the quarterback and in who's got the fancy numbers. But still it comes down to blocking and tackling and the fundamentals of the game.

DEFENDING THE GAME

MacCAMBRIDGE: You guys see college football at its best every Saturday. But you're also close enough to see and hear about the other side—the abuses, the corruption, the things that aren't the way they should be. With a clear-eyed view of all that is right and all that is wrong in college football, how would you defend the game to its critics?

CORSO: I don't think you need to defend it. They've cleaned up the coaching profession 100% from when I was coaching. I mean the SMU situation was a real ballbuster. When that thing happened, everybody went, "Whoa, this is serious stuff!" From SMU on, they've cleaned up the profession when it comes to recruiting. Sure, there's some stuff out there. There are guys in any profession who go over the edge. That's why I used to say to my guys—and I know this sounds a little crazy—"When I get out of coaching, I want it to be better than when I got here. Now, behave yourself and do the right thing."

To me, college football is a great game and I don't have to defend it to those critics. They don't know what the hell they're talking about.

HERBSTREIT: The NCAA's stricter policing forces coaches to walk a fine line or pay the consequences. A couple of years ago, the SEC brought in a new commissioner, Mike Slive, whose principal assignment was to clean up the conference. His goal was to get everybody off probation, everybody doing things by the book, in three or four years.

Look, there are always going to be stories, and there are always going to be players who get into trouble, but I don't think college football has anything to be ashamed of. You

hear more about the bad things because good things aren't as much fun to talk about.

Until Saturday, when you watch the game.

There will be negatives here and there. But the positives are way in the majority.

FOWLER: College football is much cleaner than it used to be in terms of recruiting and academic scrutiny. People who think it used to be pure and clean are kidding themselves. Rules have been broken and trampled since the turn of the 20th century.

In this era, there's more scrutiny. More policing. And there's no doubt that it's cleaner.

The biggest threats to the integrity of college football are external to the programs. For instance, Ohio State quarterback Troy Smith was suspended for the Alamo Bowl at the end of the 2004 season and for the opening game of 2005 after admitting to receiving money from Buckeyes booster Robert Q. Baker, who'd played football for Jim Tressel's father at Baldwin-Wallace College.

Boosters are almost impossible to police. The same goes for agents, who are an increasing part of the mix. So there may be dangers that didn't exist to the magnitude that they do now. But if you love this sport, you have to live in denial to a certain degree. If you walk around thinking a college football roster is populated with student athletes who are there to get an education first, whose sole motivation is to go out and win for old State U.—well, you are just being naïve. We live in a different age. There's a lot more selfishness, a lot more individualism, a lot more people whose agenda is all about making a living in the sport. That aspect of college football, I think, has definitely changed for the worse. But there's not much you can do about it, because it's societal.

When all is said and done, you can still enjoy the positive aspects of the sport. You can appreciate the fact that players are learning a great lesson, getting a lot out of the college experience and their time on campus, whether it's one year or four years, 10 credits or 124, C's and D's or A's and B's. They're benefiting from being in a college environment. And the game is providing an opportunity for a hell of a lot of kids who wouldn't otherwise be able to get a college education.

The other side—the dark side—will always exist to a degree because college football is a sport and sports are a big business in America, and big business is about the bottom line.

You just have to focus on what is pure and simple about college football and not dwell on the dark side.

THE SCHOOLS

This section, the book's largest, contains historical essays and statistical data on every Division I-A program, as well as essays on the Ivy League schools, Grambling and 18 other historically black colleges and universities.

Here's what you should know about information that appears in these pages:

- **Enrollment.** Undergraduate enrollment only.
- **National Championships.** According to the NCAA's recognized list of consensus national champions since 1936 (the first year of the Associated Press poll).
- **Conference Championships.** Overall and outright titles in the conference to which the school currently belongs.
- **First-Round Draftees.** Updated through the 2005 NFL draft.
- **Consensus All-Americans.** As designated by the NCAA. Because the NCAA recognizes multiple lists, it's quite common for a player to receive first-team All-America honors from one or more selectors and not be acknowledged as a consensus All-American. For schools that have a history outside of Division I-A, we have included consensus All-Americans in other divisions as well.
- **All-Time Team.** Whenever a team recently selected by a respected authority was available, we included it.
- **Annual Leaders.** Due to recent changes in the NCAA's official record-keeping methodology, there is a great deal of disparity here. Prior to 2002, bowl game performances were not included in a school's rushing, passing and receiving statistics. Some schools have yet to revise their numbers. Others such as Colorado have resisted the change. Until all schools update their stats according to the NCAA model, records will skew to more recent performances, because today's players will be credited with stats from an extra game or two (in the case of conference championship games).
  Another complication: some schools identify as their receiving leader the player who gained the most yards in receptions, while others prefer the player who caught

the most passes. When two players caught the same number of passes, we've listed the player who gained the most yards.

- **All-Time Scores.** Compiled by BCS pollster Richard Billingsley, this section offers a bar chart for each school showing yearly winning percentage since 1936. (In calculating this percentage, a tie is treated as a half-win and a half-loss.) In the year-by-year summaries, the vertical lines beside opponents indicate a conference game. A bullet indicates a win, a blank indicates a loss, an equal sign indicates a tie. Conference affiliations are noted throughout. In the event of a change in conference name (PCAA to Big West) or size (Big 6 to Big 7 to Big 8), we have selected the most commonly used reference.

In the early years, forfeits were not uncommon, frequently because of difficult travel arrangements. There were, however, instances where schools did not agree on which opponent had forfeited. Since it's impossible to judge who did what 100 years after the fact, only the instances where *both* schools agreed are included.

American football evolved from rugby, and for over a decade shared many of its predecessor's characteristics. Not until Walter Camp, the father of American football, established a point value system and basic rules of play (1878-82) did the sport assume the basic form we love today. Only games that were played by American football rules resulting in American point values are listed in the encyclopedia.

Billingsley and the ESPN research staff went to heroic lengths to determine, once and for all, every disputed score involving Division I-A schools. The list was narrowed from over 900 contests to the current 420, mostly played before 1930. All games with disputed scores are footnoted, but we had to decide which outcome to record. If there was overwhelming evidence one way or another, through multiple reports or consensus, we selected the majority decision. Otherwise we granted the losing team the smallest margin of defeat.

AIR FORCE

BY DERRICK GOOLD

THE YOUNGEST OF THE THREE SERVICE academies, Air Force intended to compete with and eventually defeat both Army and Navy from the day it launched a football program in 1955. An impressive string of inventive coaches have helped to commandeer control of service academy football.

The Falcons won the Commander-in-Chief's Trophy in 16 of the first 31 years after it was instituted in 1972, including 13 of 16 entering 2005. Being innovative is essential to and is the basis of Air Force's success—especially given its strict admission requirements and unusual restrictions of the past, when linemen had to be small enough to fit in a cockpit. Air Force, which has finished in the Top 25 five times, initially leveled the playing field by rising above it with a free-flying passing attack. "Because we were Air Force, I thought it'd be a good idea to put it up in the air," said Ben Martin, a Navy grad now known as the father of Air Force football. Current coach Fisher DeBerry introduced the wishbone and has relied solely on the option. His quarterbacks have produced six of the 25 1,000-yard passing, 1,000-yard rushing seasons in Division I-A.

TRADITION Before every practice, the Falcons gather as a team and stand behind a thick blue line, on which that year's team motto is painted in white. In 2001, the motto was Champions Through Brotherhood; in 2000, Champions Every Day. The players cross the line together before practice—symbolically pledging to give all they've got that day. Each player is adopted by a flying squadron and sent a flight scarf bearing the squadron's patch. The scarves are hung in lockers during game days and worn on the belt during warmups to remind the Falcons of brothers and sisters abroad. The true spectacle of Air Force tradition comes just before games. The cadet wing marches onto the field in formation for the national anthem. Parachutists deliver the U.S. flag, the coin for the pregame toss and the game ball. And, for the finale, a flyby, which has included appearances by the Stealth fighter and Stealth bomber.

BEST PLAYER Defensive tackle Chad Hennings still holds the Academy's record for sacks and tackles for loss in a career and in a season. His consensus All-American senior season of 1987 included 24 of his 34 career sacks for a total loss of 182 yards. He also won the Outland Trophy that season as well as earning Academic All-America honors. Before winning three Super Bowls with Dallas, Hennings flew an A-10 tankbuster on escort missions in the Persian Gulf war in 1991.

PROFILE

U.S. Air Force Academy
Colorado Springs, Colo.
Founded: 1954
Enrollment: 4,157
Colors: Blue and Silver
Nickname: Falcons
Stadium: Falcon Stadium
   Opened in 1962
   Grass; 52,480 capacity
First football game: 1955
All-time record: 299–249–13 (.545)
Bowl record: 8–8–1
Outland Trophy: Chad Hennings, 1987
Website: www.airforcesports.com

THE BEST OF TIMES

Between 1982 and 1992, the Falcons went to nine bowl games, including four victories in seven trips with coach Fisher DeBerry.

THE WORST OF TIMES

After 1970, the Falcons didn't see a bowl game in the decade, and longtime coach Ben Martin was ushered out after four consecutive losing seasons (1974-77).

CONFERENCE

Air Force joined the Western Athletic Conference in 1980 and remained a member until 1998, winning one title outright (1998) and sharing two titles (1985, '95). Air Force was one of eight teams in 1999 to break from the WAC and create the Mountain West Conference.

DISTINGUISHED ALUMNI

Alonzo Babers, two-time Olympic track gold medalist; Susan Helms, first female astronaut to live on International Space Station; Paul Kaminski, directed development of Stealth technology; Gregg Popovich, NBA coach

FIGHT SONG

AIR FORCE SONG
Off we go into the wild blue yonder,
Climbing high into the sun;
Here they come zooming to meet our thunder,
At 'em boys, Give 'er the gun! (Give 'er the gun now!)
Down we dive, spouting our flame from under,
Off with one helluva roar!
We live in fame or go down in flame. Hey!
Nothing'll stop the U.S. Air Force!

Each player is adopted by a flying squadron and sent a flight scarf bearing the squadron's patch.

BEST COACH Five legendary coaches helped Air Force gain altitude in college football: Lawrence T. "Buck" Shaw (who beat out Vince Lombardi to become the Falcons' first varsity coach), Ben Martin, one-year coach Bill Parcells, Ken Hatfield and, most recently and most successfully, Fisher DeBerry. DeBerry rose to the head coach position for the 1984 season, continuing the option offense he had installed as a Falcons assistant three seasons earlier. Under DeBerry, the Falcons have won 14 Commander-in-Chief's Trophies, had 17 winning seasons, made a dozen bowl appearances and defeated Notre Dame three times. "Our first goal will always be to beat Army and Navy," said DeBerry, who has no military service but is the winningest coach in service academy history. "Our second goal will be to win [the conference]. The third goal is beating Notre Dame. And the fourth will be continuing to go to bowl games." DeBerry had a 161–94–1 record in his first 21 seasons.

BEST TEAM In 1985, DeBerry's second season as head coach, the Falcons led the NCAA with a dozen victories and signaled their assault on the Top 25 with a victory against Notre Dame in October, Air Force's fourth consecutive victory against the Irish. (Linebacker Terry Maki made a school-record 30 tackles in that game.) When Army came to Colorado Springs in early November, the Falcons were ranked No. 5 and were 9–0. They also boasted the best offense in the country (39.2 points per game); Army was unranked at 7–1 with the second-best offense (38.0 points per game). In the week leading up to the game, Air Force exchange students at West Point were spirited away in the middle of the night and pelted with food; on another day low-flying Air Force jets buzzed West Point. Air Force won 45-7. Quarterback Bart Weiss propelled the season en route to becoming the third player in NCAA history to pass (1,449) and rush (1,032) for more than 1,000 yards. The week after the Army win, the Falcons were ranked No. 4, the highest reached by the Academy, and were seeking the school's 14th consecutive victory when BYU upset them and spoiled a national title run.

BIGGEST GAME Air Force faced Army for the first time on Halloween night 1959, on the hallowed turf of Yankee Stadium. The Falcons tied the Cadets 13-13. Air Force—which didn't yet have a campus or home field and had had only one graduating class—tied the game with 10:27

RECORDS

RUSHING YARDS

	GAME
249	Dee Dowis vs. San Diego State, Sept. 2, 1989 (13 att.)
	SEASON
1,494	Beau Morgan, 1996 (225 att.)
	CAREER
3,612	Dee Dowis, 1986-89 (543 att.)

PASSING YARDS

	GAME
391	Bob Parker vs. Wyoming, Sept. 19, 1970 (29 of 46)
	SEASON
2,789	Bob Parker, 1970 (199 of 402)
	CAREER
4,789	Dave Ziebart, 1976-79 (424 of 879)

RECEIVING YARDS

	GAME
235	Ernie Jennings vs. Wyoming, Sept. 19, 1970 (8 rec.)
	SEASON
1,289	Ernie Jennings, 1970 (74 rec.)
	CAREER
2,392	Ernie Jennings, 1968-70 (148 rec.)

POINTS

	GAME
36	Dee Dowis vs. San Diego State, Sept. 2, 1989 (6 TDs)
	SEASON
132	Chance Harridge, 2002 (22 TDs)
	CAREER
252	Dee Dowis, 1986-89 (41 TDs, 3 two-pt. conv.); Beau Morgan, 1994-96 (42 TDs)

CONSENSUS ALL-AMERICANS

1958	Brock Strom	T
1970	Ernie Jennings	WR
1985	Scott Thomas	DB
1987	Chad Hennings	DL
1992	Carlton McDonald	DB

remaining. "The new kid on the block can't be ignored," said one Air Force coach. A year later, a thumping of Stanford would put Air Force on the map, but it was the tie with Army that showed how quickly the program was developing. Six years later, AFA defeated Army for the first time, at Soldier Field in Chicago.

BIGGEST UPSET Barefoot kicker Dallas Thompson actually hit two game-winners to upset No. 8 Notre Dame 20-17 in South Bend on Oct. 19, 1996. The unranked Falcons held the Irish to 67 yards rushing, sacking quarterback Ron Powlus three times and forcing him to fumble four times. The fourth came in overtime and set up Thompson's 22-yard chip. He nailed it, but a delay of game penalty forced him back five yards. Take 2. He pegged the 27-yarder just as smoothly for the Academy in its first overtime game.

STADIUM Built at a cost of $3.5 million in 1962, Falcon Stadium (capacity 52,480) is nestled into a natural bowl at the base of the Rampart Range in the Rocky Mountains—one of the more picturesque panoramas on Colorado's front range. Before Falcon Stadium, Air Force skipped around the state for home games. The Falcons played at Washburn Field and Penrose Stadium in Colorado Springs, Pueblo Stadium in Pueblo, the University of Colorado's Folsom Field in Boulder and the University of Denver's D.U. Stadium.

RIVAL Despite Air Force's recent dominance, its chief directive remains to defeat Navy and Army. Nine of the Academy's top 15 crowds have come for Army or Navy games, and six of those games drew more than 50,000 fans. The Commander-in-Chief's Trophy—all 170 pounds of it, with three sides to represent each of the academy's seals—arrives on Monday of the week before a service academy game and is placed in a strategic location so every player sees it four times a day. When the Falcons lost the trophy in 1996, the empty case was placed in the middle of the locker room. When an academy wins the trophy, the year is etched under that school's name. The senior class of the winning academy visits the White House for an official presentation from the trophy's namesake, the president of the United States. The Falcons' record against Army and Navy since 1984 was 34–8 through 2004.

TRAGEDY During Thanksgiving break in 1983, sophomore Brian Bullard and cadet Dianne Williams (a member of the varsity golf team) were caught in a snowstorm in Kansas.

The two died of carbon monoxide poisoning. Although Bullard was only in his first year on the varsity, The Bullard Award was created in his honor.

NICKNAME On Sept. 25, 1955, the first class to enter the Academy chose the falcon as the cadet wing's emblem because it captured its combat role. The school says the falcon embodies the qualities sought in Air Force cadets: "courage, intelligence, love of the wild sky, ferocity in attack, but gentle in repose—and discipline." No specific species of falcon was designated by the first class, so any falcon can serve as the Academy's mascot. However, the white-faced Arctic gyrfalcon has since been set as the official falcon of the Academy.

MASCOT In 1956, Mach 1 made his debut as the Academy's show falcon at games. Mach 1 remains the name of the falcon and Air Force's is one of just two performance mascots in the NCAA. The gyrfalcon is the show bird, while a prairie or peregrine falcon is used in the performance. A human mascot, The Bird, also attends games, arriving special delivery for each season's opener either by limousine, parachute, horseback or other showy means.

UNIFORMS The unmistakable blue lightning-bolt logo, with silver outline, has been on Air Force's helmet since the beginning and inspired the headgear worn by the NFL San Diego Chargers.

NUMBERS Nonflying cadets owe five years of active service after graduation. Pilots owe 10 after 10 months' undergraduate pilot training, and navigators owe six after nine months' training ... Kicker Dave Lawson hit a 60-yard field goal in 1974 and a 62-yarder in 1975 ... Quarterback Dee Dowis was 5'10", 153 pounds when he took a run at the Heisman Trophy in 1989. Dowis rushed for 1,286 yards and passed for 1,285. He had 18 total touchdowns that season, six in one game, and finished sixth in Heisman voting. He graduated with 3,612 career rushing yards, an NCAA record for quarterbacks at the time.

QUOTE "When the history of our administration is written, I will be credited with instituting a new permanent tradition. Every year I give the Commander-in-Chief's Trophy to the Air Force Academy." —Bill Clinton, presenting the CIC Trophy to Air Force for the seventh time during his presidency

AIR FORCE ALL-TIME SCORES

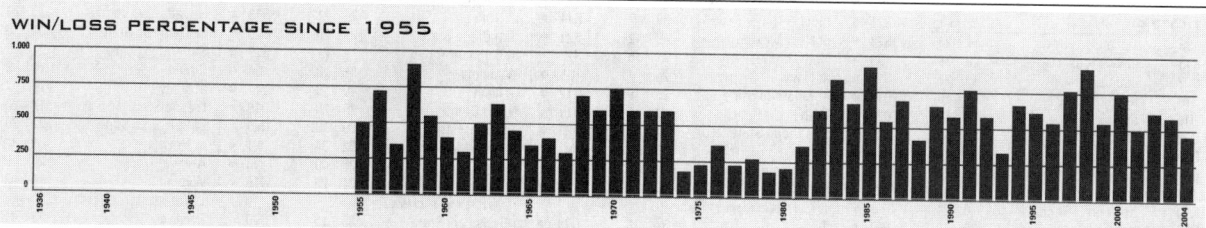

WIN/LOSS PERCENTAGE SINCE 1955

COL. ROBERT V. WHITLOW
1955 (.500)   4-4

1955   4-4-0
O8	●	Denver JV	34	18
O15	●	Colorado State JV	21	13
O22		Colorado JV *Pue*	0	32
O29		Kansas JV	0	33
N5		Utah JV	6	12
N12	●	Wyoming JV *Pue*	21	13
N19		at New Mexico JV	7	6
N26		Oklahoma JV	12	48

L.T. "BUCK" SHAW
1956-57 (.526)   9-8-2

1956   6-2-1
S29	●	at San Diego State	46	0
O6	●	at Colorado College	53	14
O13	●	Western	48	13
O20	●	Colorado Mines	49	6
O27	●	Ea. New Mexico	34	7
N3	●	No. Colorado	21	0
N10	=	at Whittier	14	14
N17		Idaho St. *Pue*	7	13
N24		Brigham Young	21	34

1957   3-6-1
S20		at UCLA	0	47
S28	●	Occidental	40	6
O5	●	Detroit	19	12
O11		at George Washington	0	20
O26		at Tulsa	7	12
N2	=	at Wyoming	7	7
N9		Denver	14	26
N16		at Utah	0	34
N23	●	New Mexico	31	0
N30		Colorado State	7	20

BEN MARTIN
1958-77 (.483)   96-103-9

1958   9-0-2
S26	●	at Detroit	37	6
O4	=	at Iowa	13	13
O11	●	Colorado State	36	6
O18	●	at Stanford	16	0
O25	●	Utah	16	14
N1	●	at Oklahoma State	33	29
N8	●	at Denver	10	7
N15	●	Wyoming	21	6
N22	●	at New Mexico	45	7
N29	●	at Colorado	20	14
		COTTON BOWL		
J1	=	TCU	0	0

1959   5-4-1
S26	●	at Wyoming	20	7
O3	●	at Trinity	27	6
O10	●	Idaho	21	0
O17		Oregon *Port*	3	20
O23	●	at UCLA	20	7
O31	=	Army *NYC*	13	13
N7		at Missouri	0	13
N14	●	Arizona *Bou*	22	15
N21		New Mexico *Den*	27	28
N28		at Colorado	7	15

1960   4-6-0
S24	●	Colorado State	32	8
O1	●	at Stanford	32	9
O8		Missouri *Den*	8	34
O15		Navy *Balt*	3	35
O22		at Wyoming	0	15
O29		George Washington	6	20
N5	●	Denver	36	6
N12		at UCLA	0	22
N26	●	at Colorado	16	6
D2		at Miami, Fla.	14	23

1961   3-7-0
S23		UCLA *Den*	6	19
S30		Kansas State	12	14
O7		at SMU	7	9
O14	●	at Cincinnati	8	6
O21		Maryland	0	21
O28		at New Mexico	6	21
N4	●	Colorado State	14	9
N11	●	at California	15	14
N18		at Baylor	7	31
D2		Colorado	12	29

1962   5-5-0
S22	●	Colorado State	34	0
S29		at Penn State	6	20
O6	●	at SMU	25	20
O13	●	at Arizona	20	6
O20		Oregon	20	35
O27		Miami, Fla.	3	21
N3	●	Wyoming	35	14
N10	●	at UCLA	17	11
N17		Baylor	3	10
N24		at Colorado	10	34

1963   7-4-0
S21	●	Washington	10	7
S28	●	Colorado State	69	0
O5		at SMU	0	10
O12	●	at Nebraska	17	13
O19		at Maryland	14	21
O26	●	Boston College	34	7
N2		Army *Chi*	10	14
N9	●	UCLA	48	21
N16	●	at New Mexico	30	8
D7	●	Colorado	17	14
		GATOR BOWL		
D28		North Carolina	0	35

1964   4-5-1
S19	●	at Washington	3	2
S26		at Michigan	7	24
O3	●	Colorado State	14	6
O10		Notre Dame	7	34
O17		Missouri	7	17
O24		at Boston College	7	13
O31	●	Arizona	7	0
N7	●	at UCLA	24	15
N14	=	Wyoming	7	7
N21		at Colorado	23	28

1965   3-6-1
S18		at Wyoming	14	31
S25		Nebraska	17	27
O2		Stanford	16	17
O9		California	7	24
O16	=	Oregon *Port*	18	18
O23	●	at Pacific	40	0
O30		UCLA	0	10
N6	●	Army *Chi*	14	3
N13	●	at Arizona	34	7
N20		Colorado	6	19

1966   4-6-0
S17		Wyoming	0	13
S24	●	at Washington	10	0
O1	●	Navy	15	7
O8	●	Hawaii	54	0
O15		Oregon	6	17
O22		Colorado State	21	41
O29		at UCLA	13	38
N5		at Stanford	6	21
N12	●	at North Carolina	20	14
N19		at Colorado	9	10

1967   2-6-2
S16	=	at Oklahoma State	0	0
S23		at Wyoming	10	37
S30		Washington	7	30
O7		at California	12	14
O14	●	North Carolina	10	8
O21	●	at Tulane	13	10
O28	=	Colorado State	17	17
N4		Army	7	10
N18		at Arizona	10	14
N25		Colorado	0	33

1968   7-3-0
S21	●	Florida *Tam*	20	23
S28	●	Wyoming	10	3
O5		at Stanford	13	24
O12	●	Navy *Chi*	26	20
O19	●	at Colorado State	31	0
O26	●	at Pittsburgh	27	14
N2	●	North Carolina	28	15
N9		Arizona	10	14
N16	●	Tulsa	28	8
N23	●	at Colorado	58	35

1969   6-4-0
S13	●	at SMU	26	22
S20		at Missouri	17	19
S27		Wyoming	25	27
O11	●	at North Carolina	20	10
O18	●	Oregon	60	13
O25	●	Colorado State	28	7
N1	●	at Army	13	6
N8	●	Utah State	38	13
N15		at Stanford	34	47
N22		at Notre Dame	6	13

1970   9-3-0
S12	●	Idaho	45	7
S19	●	at Wyoming	41	17
S26	●	Missouri *StL*	37	14
O3	●	Colorado State	37	22
O10	●	Tulane	24	3
O17	●	Navy *DC*	26	3
O24	●	Boston College	35	10
O31	●	at Arizona	23	20
N7		at Oregon	35	46
N14	●	Stanford	31	14
N21		Colorado	19	49
		SUGAR BOWL		
J1		Tennessee	13	34

1971   6-4-0
S18	●	Missouri	7	6
S25	●	Wyoming	23	19
O2		at Penn State	14	16
O9	●	SMU	30	0
O16	●	Army	20	7
O23	●	at Colorado State	17	12
O30		at Arizona State	28	44
N6		Oregon	14	23
N13	●	at Tulsa	17	7
N20		at Colorado	17	53

1972   6-4-0
S16	●	Wyoming	45	14
S23	●	Pittsburgh	41	13
S30	●	Davidson	68	6
O7	●	at Colorado State	52	13
O14	●	at Boston College	13	9
O21		Navy	17	21
O28	●	at Arizona State	39	31
N4		at Army	14	17
N11		Notre Dame	7	21
N18		Colorado	7	38

1973   6-4-0
S22	●	Oregon	24	17
S29	●	New Mexico	10	6
O6	●	Penn State	9	19
O13		at Colorado	17	38
O20	●	at Navy	6	42
O27	●	Davidson	41	19
N3	●	Army	43	10
N10	●	Rutgers	31	14
N17	●	at Arizona	27	26
N22		at Notre Dame	15	48

1974   2-9-0
S14	●	Idaho	37	0
S21		at Oregon	23	27
S28		at Wyoming	16	20
O5		Colorado	27	28
O12		Tulane	3	10
O19	●	Navy	19	16
O26		at Rutgers	3	20
N2		Brigham Young	10	12
N9		at Army	16	17
N16		Arizona	24	27
N23		at Notre Dame	0	38

1975   2-8-1
S13		Arkansas *LR*	0	35
S20		at Iowa State	12	17
S27	=	UCLA	20	20
O4		Navy *DC*	0	17
O11		at Brigham Young	14	28
O18		Notre Dame	30	31
O25		at Colorado State	10	47
N1	●	Army	33	3
N8	●	at Tulane	13	12
N15		California	14	31
N22		Wyoming	10	24

1976   4-7-0
S11	●	Pacific	36	3
S18		Iowa State	6	41
S25		at UCLA	7	40
O2		Kent State *Clev*	19	24
O9	●	Navy	13	3
O16		Colorado State	3	27
O23		Citadel	7	26
O30		at Army	7	24
N6	●	at Arizona State	31	30
N13		at Vanderbilt	10	34
N20	●	Wyoming	41	21

1977   2-8-1
S10	=	at Wyoming	0	0
S17		at California	14	24
S24	●	Pacific	15	13
O1		at Georgia Tech	3	30
O8		at Navy	7	10
O15		Arizona State	14	37
O22		at Baylor	7	38
O29		Boston College	14	36
N5		Army	6	31
N12	●	Vanderbilt	34	28
N19		at Notre Dame	0	49

BILL PARCELLS
1978 (.273)   3-8

1978   3-8-0
S9	●	at Texas-El Paso	34	25
S16	●	at Boston College	18	7
S23		Holy Cross	18	35
S30		at Kansas State	21	34
O7		Navy	8	37
O14		Colorado State	13	31
O21		Notre Dame	15	38
O28	●	Kent State	26	10
N4		at Army	14	28
N11		Georgia Tech	21	42
N18		at Vanderbilt	27	41

70 AIR FORCE

THE SCHOOLS

KEN HATFIELD
1979-83 (.449) 26-32-1

1979 2-9-0

S8		Tulsa	7	24
S15		at Wisconsin	0	38
S22		Illinois	19	27
S29		Kansas State	6	19
O6		at Navy	9	13
O13		Notre Dame	13	38
O20		at Oregon	9	17
O27		at Colorado State	6	20
N3	●	Army	28	7
N10		at Georgia Tech	0	21
N17	●	Vanderbilt	30	29

1980-1998 WAC

1980 2-9-1 (1-6-0)

S6	|	at Colorado State	9	21
S13	||	at Washington	7	50
S20	|	San Diego State	10	13
S27	=	at Illinois	20	20
O4		at Yale	16	17
O11	●	Navy	21	20
O18	||	at Tulane	7	28
N1	||	Boston College	0	23
N8		at Army	24	47
N15	● |	Wyoming	25	7
N22		at Notre Dame	10	24
N29	|	at Hawaii	12	20

1981 4-7-0 (2-5-0)

S12	|	at Brigham Young	21	45
S19	|	Wyoming	10	17
S26	|	at New Mexico	10	27
O3	● |	Colorado State	28	14
O10		at Navy	13	30
O17	||	Tulane	13	31
O24	●	at Oregon	20	10
O31	●	Army	7	3
N14		Notre Dame	7	35
N21	||	at Nevada-Las Vegas	21	24
N28	● |	San Diego State TOK	21	16

1982 8-5-0 (4-3-0)

S4		at Tulsa	17	35
S11	● |	San Diego State	44	32
S18		at Texas Tech	30	31
S25	● |	at Brigham Young	39	38
O2	|	New Mexico	37	49
O9	●	Navy	24	21
O16	|	Colorado State	11	21
O23	● |	at Texas-El Paso	35	7
O30	● |	Wyoming	44	34
N6	●	at Army	27	9
N20	●	Notre Dame	30	17
N27	|	at Hawaii	21	45
		HALL OF FAME CLASSIC		
D31	●	Vanderbilt	36	28

1983 10-2-0 (5-2-0)

S3	● |	at Colorado State	34	13
S10	●	Texas Tech	28	13
S17	|	at Wyoming	7	14
S24	|	Brigham Young	28	46
O8	●	at Navy	44	17
O15	● |	Texas-El Paso	37	25
O22	● |	Utah	33	31
O29	●	Army	41	20
N5	● |	Hawaii	45	10
N19	●	at Notre Dame	23	22
N26	● |	at San Diego State	38	7
		INDEPENDENCE BOWL		
D10	●	Mississippi	9	3

FISHER DeBERRY
1984-Present (.631) 161-94-1

1984 8-4-0 (4-3-0)

S1	● |	San Diego State	34	16
S8	●	No. Colorado	75	7
S15	|	at Wyoming	20	26
S22	|	at Utah	17	28
S29	● |	Colorado State	52	10
O6	●	Navy	29	22
O13	●	at Notre Dame	21	7
O20	|	Brigham Young	25	30
N3		at Army	12	24
N10	● |	at New Mexico	23	9
N24	● |	at Texas-El Paso	38	12
		INDEPENDENCE BOWL		
D15	●	Virginia Tech	23	7

1985 12-1-0 (7-1-0)

A31	● |	Texas-El Paso	48	6
S14	● |	at Wyoming	49	7
S21	●	Rice	59	17
S28	● |	at New Mexico	49	12
O5	●	Notre Dame	21	15
O12	●	at Navy	24	7
O19	● |	at Colorado State	35	19
O26	● |	Utah	37	15
N2	● |	San Diego State	31	10
N9	●	Army	45	7
N16	|	at Brigham Young	21	28
N23	● |	at Hawaii	27	20
		BLUEBONNET BOWL		
D31	●	Texas	24	16

1986 6-5-0 (5-2-0)

A30	● |	Hawaii	24	17
S6	● |	at Texas-El Paso	23	21
S20	|	Wyoming	17	23
S27	● |	Colorado State	24	7
O3	● |	at Utah	45	35
O11	●	Navy	40	6
O18		at Notre Dame	3	31
O25	● |	at San Diego State	22	10
N8		at Army	11	21
N22		at Rice	17	21
D6	|	Brigham Young	3	23

1987 9-4-0 (6-2-0)

S5	|	at Wyoming	13	27
S12	●	TCU	21	10
S19	● |	San Diego State	49	7
S26	● |	at Colorado State	27	19
O3	● |	Utah	48	27
O10	●	at Navy	23	13
O17		Notre Dame	14	35
O24	● |	Texas-El Paso	35	7
O31	|	at Brigham Young	13	24
N7	●	Army	27	10
N14	● |	at New Mexico	73	26
N21	● |	at Hawaii	34	31
		FREEDOM BOWL		
D30		Arizona State	28	33

1988 5-7-0 (3-5-0)

S3	● |	at Colorado State	29	23
S11	|	at San Diego State	36	39
S17	●	Northwestern	62	27
S24	|	Wyoming	45	48
O1	● |	New Mexico	63	14
O8	●	Navy	34	24
O15	● |	at Utah	56	49
O22		at Notre Dame	13	41
N5		at Army	15	28
N12	|	Brigham Young	31	49
N19	|	at Texas-El Paso	24	31
N26	|	at Hawaii	14	19

1989 8-4-1 (5-1-1)

S2	● |	San Diego State	52	36
S10	● |	Wyoming	45	7
S16	●	at Northwestern	48	31
S23	● |	Texas-El Paso	43	26
S30	● |	at Colorado State	46	21
O7	●	at Navy	35	7
O14		Notre Dame	27	41
O21		at TCU	9	27
N4	●	Army	29	3
N11	|	at Brigham Young	35	44
N25	● |	at Utah	42	38
D9	= |	at Hawaii	35	35
		LIBERTY BOWL		
D28		Mississippi	29	42

1990 7-5-0 (3-4-0)

S1	|	Colorado State	33	35
S8	● |	Hawaii	27	3
S15	●	Citadel	10	7
S22	|	at Wyoming	12	24
S29	|	at San Diego State	18	48
O6	●	Navy	24	7
O13		at Notre Dame	27	57
O27	● |	Utah	52	21
N3	|	Brigham Young	7	54
N10	●	at Army	15	3
N17	● |	at Texas-El Paso	14	13
		LIBERTY BOWL		
D27	●	Ohio State	23	11

1991 10-3-0 (6-2-0)

A31	●	Weber St.	48	31
S7	● |	at Colorado State	31	26
S14	● |	at Utah	24	21
S21	● |	San Diego State	21	20
S28	|	at Brigham Young	7	21
O5	● |	Wyoming	51	28
O12	●	at Navy	46	6
O19		Notre Dame	15	28
O26	● |	Texas-El Paso	20	13
N2	|	at New Mexico	32	34
N9	●	Army	25	0
N23	● |	at Hawaii	24	20
		LIBERTY BOWL		
D29	●	Mississippi State	38	15

1992 7-5-0 (4-4-0)

S5	●	Rice	30	21
S12	|	Hawaii	3	6
S19	● |	at Wyoming	42	28
S26	● |	New Mexico	33	32
O3	● |	at Texas-El Paso	28	22
O10	●	Navy	18	16
O17	|	Colorado State	28	32
O24	● |	at San Diego State	20	17
O31	|	Utah	13	20
N7	●	at Army	7	3
N14	|	Brigham Young	7	28
		LIBERTY BOWL		
D31		Mississippi	0	13

1993 4-8-0 (1-7-0)

S4	●	Indiana St.	63	21
S11	|	at Colorado State	5	8
S18	|	San Diego State	31	38
S25	|	at Brigham Young	3	30
O2	|	Wyoming	18	31
O9		at Navy	24	28
O16	|	at Fresno State	20	33
O23	●	Citadel	35	0
O30	● |	Texas-El Paso	31	10
N6	●	Army	25	6
N13	|	at Utah	24	41
N20	|	at Hawaii	17	45

1994 8-4-0 (6-2-0)

S3	|	Colorado State	21	34
S10	|	Brigham Young	21	45
S17		Northwestern	10	14
S24	● |	Texas-El Paso SA	47	7
O1	● |	at San Diego State	36	35
O8	●	Navy	43	21
O22	● |	Fresno State	42	7
O29	● |	at Wyoming	34	17
N5	●	at Army	10	6
N12	● |	Utah	40	33
N19		at Notre Dame	30	42
D3	● |	at Hawaii	37	24

1995 8-5-0 (6-2-0)

S2	● |	Brigham Young	38	12
S9	● |	Wyoming	34	10
S16	|	Colorado State	20	27
S23		at Northwestern	6	30
S30	● |	at New Mexico	27	24
O8	● |	Texas-El Paso	56	46
O14	●	at Navy	30	20
O21	|	at Utah	21	22
O28	● |	at Fresno State	31	20
N11	●	Army	38	20
N18		Notre Dame	14	44
N25	● |	at Hawaii	45	28
		COPPER BOWL		
D27		Texas Tech	41	55

1996 6-5 (5-3)

A31	● |	San Jose State	45	0
S7	● |	at Nevada-Las Vegas	65	17
S21	|	at Wyoming	19	22
S28	● |	Rice	45	17
O12		Navy	17	20
O19	●	at Notre Dame	20	17
O26	● |	Hawaii	34	7
N2	|	Colorado State	41	42
N9		at Army	7	23
N16	● |	at Fresno State	44	38
N28	|	at San Diego State	23	28

1997 10-3 (6-2)

A30	●	Idaho	14	10
S6	● |	at Rice	41	12
S13	● |	Nevada-Las Vegas	25	24
S20	● |	at Colorado State	24	0
S27	● |	San Diego State	24	18
O4	●	Citadel	17	3
O11	●	at Navy	10	7
O18	|	Fresno State	17	20
O25	|	at San Jose State	22	25
N1	● |	at Hawaii	34	27
N8	●	Army	24	0
N15	● |	Wyoming	14	3
		LAS VEGAS BOWL		
D20		Oregon	13	41

1998 12-1 (7-1)

S5	●	Wake Forest	42	0
S12	● |	at Nevada-Las Vegas	52	10
S17	● |	Colorado State	30	27
S26	|	at TCU	34	35
O3	● |	New Mexico	56	14
O10	●	Navy	49	7
O24	● |	at Tulsa	42	21
O31	● |	SMU	31	7
N7	●	at Army	35	7
N14	● |	at Wyoming	10	3
N21	● |	Rice	22	16
		WAC CHAMPIONSHIP		
D5	●	Brigham Young LV	20	13
		OAHU BOWL		
D25	●	Washington	45	25

1999-Present Mountain West

1999 6-5 (2-5)

S4	●	Villanova	37	13
S18	●	at Washington	31	21
S25	|	Wyoming	7	10
O2	● |	at San Diego State	23	22
O9	●	Navy RAJ	19	14
O16	|	Utah	15	21
O30	|	at Brigham Young	20	27
N6	●	Army	28	0
N13	● |	Nevada-Las Vegas	35	16
N20	|	at Colorado State	21	41
N27	|	at New Mexico	28	33

2000 9-3 (5-2)

S2	●	Cal St. Northridge	55	6
S9	● |	Brigham Young	31	23
S23	● |	at Utah	23	14
S30	|	at Nevada-Las Vegas	13	34
O7	●	Navy	27	13
O14	● |	at Wyoming	51	26
O21	|	New Mexico	23	29
O28		at Notre Dame	31	34
N4	●	at Army	41	27
N11	● |	Colorado State	44	40
N18	● |	San Diego State	45	24
		SILICON VALLEY CLASSIC		
D31	●	Fresno State	37	34

2001 6-6 (3-4)

S1		Oklahoma	3	44
S8	●	Tennessee Tech	42	0
S29	● |	at San Diego State	45	21
O6	●	Navy RAJ	24	18
O13	● |	Wyoming	24	13
O20	|	at Brigham Young	33	63
O27	|	at New Mexico	33	52
N3	●	Army	34	24
N8	|	at Colorado State	21	28
N17	|	Nevada-Las Vegas	10	34
N24		at Hawaii	30	52
D1	● |	Utah	38	37

2002 8-5 (4-3)

A31	●	Northwestern	52	3
S7	● |	New Mexico	38	31
S21	●	at California	23	21
S28	● |	at Utah	30	26
O5	●	Navy	48	7
O12	● |	Brigham Young	52	9
O19		Notre Dame	14	21
O26	|	at Wyoming	26	34
O31	|	Colorado State	12	31
N9	●	at Army	49	30
N16	● |	at Nevada-Las Vegas	49	32
N23	|	San Diego State	34	38
		SAN FRANCISCO BOWL		
D31		Virginia Tech	13	20

2003 7-5 (3-4)

A30	●	Wofford	49	0
S6	●	at Northwestern	22	21
S13	●	North Texas	34	21
S20	●|	Wyoming	35	29
S27	●|	at Brigham Young	24	10
O4		Navy[LAN]	25	28
O11	●|	Nevada-Las Vegas	24	7
O16	|	at Colorado State	20	30
N1	|	Utah	43	45
N8	●	Army	31	3
N15	|	at New Mexico	12	24
N22	|	at San Diego State	3	24

2004 5-6 (3-4)

S4		California	14	56
S11	●	Ea. Washington	42	20
S18	●|	at Nevada-Las Vegas	27	10
S25	|	at Utah	35	49
S30	|	Navy	21	24
O9	●	New Mexico	28	23
O23	|	Brigham Young	24	41
O30	|	at Wyoming	26	43
N6	●	at Army	31	22
N13	|	San Diego State	31	37
N20	●|	Colorado State	47	17

AIR FORCE ANNUAL STATISTICAL LEADERS

YR	RUSHING	YDS	ATT	AVG	PASSING	ATT	CMP	PCT	YDS	RECEIVING	REC	YDS	AVG
1956	Larry Thomson	788	138	5.7	Eddie Rosane	101	41	.41	648	Tom Jozwiak	13	260	20.0
1957	Phil Lane	350	90	3.9	John Kuenzel	125	55	.44	721	Tom Jozwiak	20	272	13.6
1958	Steve Galios	527	116	4.5	Rich Mayo	174	98	.56	1,019	Bob Brickey	25	281	11.2
1959	Monte Moorberg	408	95	4.3	Rich Mayo	211	110	.52	1,212	Mike Quinlan	29	373	12.9
1960	Mike Quinlan	583	93	6.3	Rich Mayo	238	108	.45	1,168	Mike Quinlan	17	146	8.6
1961	Terry Isaacson	468	118	4.0	Bob McNaughton	81	38	.47	415	Terry Isaacson	19	239	12.6
1962	Larry Tollstam	414	88	4.7	Terry Isaacson	120	52	.43	591	Dick Brown	17	236	13.9
1963	Terry Isaacson	801	162	4.9	Terry Isaacson	147	68	.46	946	Fritz Greenlee	15	323	21.5
1964	Steve Amdor	485	117	4.1	Tim Murphy	160	94	.59	1,154	Jim Greth	33	436	13.2
1965	Paul Stein	320	140	2.3	Paul Stein	225	114	.51	1,446	Bill Manning	25	251	10.0
1966	Mike Guth	394	90	4.4	Steve Turner	118	64	.54	776	Jim Schultz	33	525	15.9
1967	Dave Mumme	404	104	3.9	Gary Baxter	131	59	.45	555	Carl Janssen	18	259	14.4
1968	Curtis Martin	418	130	3.2	Gary Baxter	168	76	.45	1,036	Charlie Longnecker	45	622	13.8
1969	Jim DeOrio	493	124	4.0	Gary Baxter	273	127	.47	1,783	Ernie Jennings	51	729	14.3
1970	Brian Bream	1,276	294	4.3	Bob Parker	402	199	.50	2,789	Ernie Jennings	74	1,289	17.4
1971	Brian Bream	734	221	3.3	Rich Haynie	204	86	.42	1,335	Paul Bassa	31	513	16.5
1972	Joel Carlson	650	176	3.7	Rich Haynie	240	102	.43	1,570	Frank Murphy	31	539	17.4
1973	Chris Milodragovich	583	140	4.2	Rich Haynie	218	111	.51	1,378	Frank Murphy	30	415	13.8
1974	Ken Wood	708	203	3.5	Mike Worden	128	61	.48	798	Bob Farr	32	467	14.6
1975	Ken Wood	425	114	3.7	Mike Worden	214	99	.46	1,091	John Covington	26	213	8.2
1976	Ken Wood	497	123	4.0	Rob Shaw	198	98	.50	1,135	Paul Williams	45	684	15.2
1977	David Thomas	260	70	3.7	Dave Ziebart	298	140	.47	1,562	Steve Hoog	29	474	16.3
1978	Shelby Ball	720	173	4.2	Dave Ziebart	241	109	.45	1,350	Cormac Carney	57	870	15.3
1979	Shelby Ball	575	129	4.5	Dave Ziebart	223	118	.53	1,088	Mike Fortson	27	177	6.6
1980	Ted Sundquist	583	122	4.8	Scott Schafer	159	65	.41	944	Andy Bark	47	794	16.9
1981	John Kershner	685	120	5.7	Ed Antoine	97	42	.43	455	Mike Kirby	35	419	12.0
1982	John Kershner	1,056	226	4.7	Marty Louthan	152	76	.50	1,337	Mike Kirby	30	593	19.8
1983	John Kershner	934	166	5.6	Marty Louthan	116	62	.53	1,166	Mike Kirby	38	862	22.7
1984	Pat Evans	1,015	159	6.4	Bart Weiss	87	41	.47	668	Ken Carpenter	15	258	17.2
1985	Bart Weiss	1,032	180	5.7	Bart Weiss	141	80	.57	1,449	Ken Carpenter	42	869	20.7
1986	Pat Evans	777	191	4.1	Jim Tomallo	52	24	.46	474	Tyrone Jeffcoat	20	369	18.5
1987	Dee Dowis	1,315	194	6.8	Dee Dowis	112	45	.40	600	Tyler Barth	14	218	15.6
1988	Andy Smith	1,040	154	6.8	Dee Dowis	96	41	.43	870	Greg Cochran	12	243	20.3
1989	Dee Dowis	1,286	172	7.5	Dee Dowis	140	67	.48	1,285	Steve Senn	30	586	19.5
1990	Jason Jones	598	103	5.8	Jarvis Baker	24	8	.33	144	David Mott	8	102	12.8
1991	Rob Perez	1,157	233	5.0	Rob Perez	95	31	.33	732	Scott Hufford	8	334	41.8
1992	Jarvis Baker	550	190	2.9	Jarvis Baker	122	47	.39	705	Peter Wilkie	15	210	14.0
1993	Demond Cash	875	165	5.3	Demond Cash	78	30	.39	403	Richie Marsh	19	321	16.9
1994	Jake Campbell	689	110	6.3	Beau Morgan	89	41	.46	873	Jeremy Johnson	18	337	18.7
1995	Beau Morgan	1,285	229	5.6	Beau Morgan	169	90	.53	1,165	Jake Campbell	25	353	14.1
1996	Beau Morgan	1,494	225	6.6	Beau Morgan	180	95	.53	1,210	Marcus Alexander	23	382	16.6
1997	Spanky Gilliam	741	188	3.9	Blane Morgan	123	63	.51	975	Matt Farmer	23	380	16.5
1998	Spanky Gilliam	527	112	4.7	Blane Morgan	112	61	.55	1,144	Matt Farmer	35	650	18.6
1999	Mike Thiessen	827	160	5.2	Cale Bonds	80	44	.55	654	Matt Farmer	34	484	14.2
2000	Mike Thiessen	713	179	4.0	Mike Thiessen	195	112	.57	1,687	Ryan Fleming	52	930	17.9
2001	Keith Boyea	1,216	230	5.3	Keith Boyea	196	102	.52	1,253	Ryan Fleming	28	416	14.9
2002	Chance Harridge	1,229	252	4.9	Chance Harridge	144	64	.44	1,062	Adam Strecker	14	261	18.7
2003	Chance Harridge	914	180	5.1	Chance Harridge	161	80	.50	995	Alec Messerall	21	328	15.7
2004	Shaun Carney	596	159	3.7	Shaun Carney	149	91	.61	1,315	J.P. Waller	32	476	14.9

The NCAA began including postseason stats in 2002

AKRON

BY ED KRZEMIENSKI

AFTER SPENDING 40 YEARS AT THE small-college level, the Zips jumped to Division I-AA in 1980, then to Division I-A in 1987. Led by former Notre Dame coach Gerry Faust, Akron hit its peak in 1992 with a 7–3–1 record. Since then, Akron has sent nine players to the NFL. With a solid recruiting base and an annual schedule that typically includes multiple games against nationally ranked opponents, coach J.D. Brookhart, the student body and local fans have the right to be optimistic about the future of Zips football.

TRADITION Legend has it that in 1870, while on a search for a site for a proposed college, Akron industrialist John R. Buchtel lost a wagon wheel in a muddy bog at what is now the site of Kent State University. Buchtel returned to Akron and, along with the Ohio Universalist Convention, created Buchtel College, which in 1913 was renamed the University of Akron. Thirty-two years later, one of the original wagon wheels was discovered, and in 1946, the two schools began competing for the blue-and-gold Wagon Wheel in their annual game. Kent State won the initial meeting; the series was contested annually until 1954, but was not played again for 18 years. In 1972 when it resumed, 25,000 fans turned out at the Rubber Bowl for the rivalry's renewal.

BEST PLAYER Before he helped the Tampa Bay Buccaneers to a Super Bowl victory in January 2003, Dwight Smith led the nation with 10 interceptions, including two for touchdowns, as a cornerback for the Zips in 2000. The Bucs selected Smith, Akron's only consensus Division I-A All-America selection, in the third round of the NFL draft. In Super Bowl XXXVII, he returned two interceptions for touchdowns, helping the Bucs to a 48-21 win over the Oakland Raiders.

BEST COACH From 1973 to1985, Jim Dennison guided the Zips to 80 wins and nine winning seasons and oversaw the transition from Division II to 1-AA status in 1980. In 1976, after the 10–3 Zips ended the season second overall in Division II, the American Football Coaches Association named Dennison the College Division II Coach of the Year. Five years later, he had the Zips ranked in the 1-AA Top 10. Despite his success, in December 1985, Akron removed Dennison as coach (he was named an associate athletic director) and replaced him with the high-profile Faust.

BEST TEAM Gordon Larson's 1968 Zips won seven games and earned the school its first bowl berth. That Zips team packed quite an offensive wallop. Sophomore Jack Beidleman ran for 799 yards, classmate Dan Ruff caught 52 passes and accounted for more than 1,300 yards of total offense and senior quarterback Don Zwisler passed for 2,012 yards, fourth most in the nation. In the Grantland Rice Bowl, Zwisler and

---

PROFILE

University of Akron
Akron, Ohio
Founded: 1870
Enrollment: 19,242
Colors: Blue and Gold
Nickname: Zips
Stadium: Rubber Bowl
    Opened in 1940
    AstroPlay; 35,202 capacity
First football game: 1891
All-time record: 461–436–36 (.513)
Website: www.gozips.com

THE BEST OF TIMES

Before joining Division I, the Zips regularly appeared and won in the Division II playoffs. Akron finished No. 3 in the AP College Division poll in 1969. In 1976, Akron lost to Montana State in the Pioneer Bowl (the Division II title game).

THE WORST OF TIMES

From 1994 to 1998, the Zips endured five losing seasons, including two 2–9 marks and a 1–10 finish.

CONFERENCE

Akron became a member of the Mid-American Conference in 1992, and has remained there since. Prior to joining the MAC, the Zips played independently (1891-1914, 1937-42, 1966-77 and 1987-91), in the Ohio Athletic Conference (1915-36 and 1946-65), in the Mid-Continent Conference (1978-79) and in the Ohio Valley Conference (1980-86).

DISTINGUISHED ALUMNI

Dan Moldea, author; Jim Tressel, Ohio State football coach; George Wallace, comedian; Karen Ziemba, actress

FIGHT SONG

AKRON BLUE AND GOLD
We cheer the Akron Blue and Gold.
We cheer as the colors unfold,
We pledge anew, we're all for you,
As the team goes crashing through,
Fight! Fight!
We cheer the Akron warriors bold,
For a fight that's a sight to behold,
So we stand up, cheer and shout
For the Akron Blue and Gold.
Zzzip! Zip go the Zi—ips!
Zzzip! Zip go the Zi—ips!
Akron true Gold and Blue,
All for you and the Zi—ips too!

the Zips met their match against Louisiana Tech, losing 33-13. No shame for Akron, though, since Tech had a fair QB of its own—a junior named Terry Bradshaw.

BIGGEST GAME In the 1976 Pioneer Bowl, the Division II championship, Akron faced Montana State. The Zips were coming off an overtime upset of defending national champion Northern Michigan and carrying a 10–2 overall record. Trailing 17-0 in the third quarter, Akron cut the lead to 17-13, before finally succumbing to the Bobcats 24-13. Akron's runner-up finish in the Division II playoffs marked the best season in school history.

BIGGEST UPSET In 1894, John W. Heisman coached and quarterbacked Buchtel College (the forerunner to UA) to a victory in its only game of the year, a 12-6 win over Ohio State. Interestingly, Heisman did not technically work for the college.

HEARTBREAKER In order to gain a Division I-AA playoff berth, Akron needed a victory in the last game of the 1986 season over 1–9 Youngstown State and a loss by Ohio Valley Conference rival Murray State. With under a minute left in

> *The nickname was shortened to Zips when zippers became affiliated with fastening pants.*

the game, YSU threw a Hail Mary that two Akron defenders tipped into the hands of a prone Youngstown receiver. Then, with 27 seconds left, YSU cashed in with a touchdown pass to Lorenzo Davis. Akron's 40-39 loss, coupled with a Murray State win, scuttled the Zips' playoff hopes.

STADIUM In 1940, the University of Akron moved its home from Buchtel Field to the municipally owned Rubber Bowl, built in conjunction with the Civil Works Authority. In 1971, the school took over ownership of the Rubber Bowl and refurbished the stadium, adding lights and artificial turf. Located off-campus, and with a capacity of 35,202, the stadium trails only Ohio State's Ohio Stadium as the state's largest college football venue. The Cleveland Browns regularly played preseason games in the Rubber Bowl until 1973. In more than six decades playing at the Rubber Bowl, Akron has won 59% of its home games.

RIVAL The Zips consider Kent State their biggest rival, and the feeling is mutual. Though located just 10 miles apart, the schools' respective campuses appear vastly different, with Akron's urban milieu contrasting sharply with the bucolic, rural Kent State. However, that is the singular

RECORDS

RUSHING YARDS

	GAME	
295	James Black vs. Austin Peay, Nov. 19, 1983 (52 att.)	
	SEASON	
1,786	Mike Clark, 1986 (245 att.)	
	CAREER	
4,257	Mike Clark, 1984-86 (804 att.)	

PASSING YARDS

	GAME	
436	Charlie Frye vs. Miami (Ohio), Nov. 20, 2004 (26 of 43)	
	SEASON	
3,549	Charlie Frye, 2003 (273 of 421)	
	CAREER	
11,049	Charlie Frye, 2000-04 (913 of 1,436)	

RECEIVING YARDS

	GAME	
201	Willie Davis vs. Kent State, Sept. 1, 1984 (13 rec.)	
	SEASON	
1,041	Dan Ruff, 1968 (52 rec.)	
	CAREER	
2,577	Lavel Bailey, 1997-2000 (138 rec.)	

POINTS

	GAME	
30	Three tied; most recently by Bob Hendry vs. Eastern Michigan, Nov. 24, 2001 (5 TDs)	
	SEASON	
98	Jack Beidleman, 1969 (16 TDs, 1 two-pt. conv.)	
	CAREER	
266	Zac Derr, 1998-2001 (47 FGs, 125 PATs)	

CONSENSUS ALL-AMERICANS

1969	John Travis, OG
1971	Michael Hatch, DB
1976	Mark Van Horn, OG
1976-77	Steve Cockerham, LB
1980-81	Brad Reece, LB
1985	Wayne Grant, DL
1986	Mike Clark, RB
2000	Dwight Smith, DB

difference; the schools share identical colors and a similar student body. Inevitably, many of each team's players have competed against and beside each other in high school, adding even more familiarity to the rivalry. The Zips and Flashes first met in 1923 and played off and on until beginning their Wagon Wheel series in 1946, but the rivalry reached new heights in 1992, when Akron joined Kent State in the MAC. Akron leads the series 26–19–2.

NICKNAME In 1927, student Margaret Hamlin suggested that Akron take its nickname from a popular pair of rubber overshoes produced by the local B.F. Goodrich Company called Zippers. The school received permission from the company to use the name (today a company pays for advertising like that). Eventually the nickname was shortened to Zips when zippers came to be known for fastening pants and entered the lexicon. But as long as there are Golden Flashes up the road, Akron will not have the least-menacing nickname in northeast Ohio. Nevertheless, Zips stands out as one of the less frightening but unique names in the world of college football.

MASCOT While the original Zip was an overshoe, the Akron Zip is a kangaroo. Zippy, originally known as Mr. Zip, was born in 1953 when Dick Hansford, the UA Student Council adviser, got the idea for the mascot from a popular comic strip called "Kicky the Kangaroo." Despite a less-than-enthusiastic response from local newspapers, Mr. Zip debuted in 1955 and was upgraded a decade later to Zippy. Zippy now roams the sideline of the Rubber Bowl as a fluffy representation of a kangaroo in an Akron sweater and matching beanie.

UNIFORMS The official colors are metallic gold and Akron Blue, and the Zips' uniforms have always involved these colors. Akron's helmets, likewise, have always been some shade of gold (sometimes mustard); an A was added to the side of the helmet in 1966 and still remains. In 2001, the school added a red stripe to the helmets in support of the Fire Truck Fund, an effort to raise money to purchase a new fire truck for the New York City Fire Department after 9/11. A year later, the school unveiled a new logo that maintained the A, and incorporated what the school described as "a sleek, determined Kangaroo."

LORE After the 1892 season, Buchtel College students pleaded with the school's president, Reverend Orello Cone, to hire someone to coach the college's club teams. On Jan. 28, 1893, the school extended a one-year contract for a "gymnasium director" and "special teacher of gymnastics in baseball and football." The recipient of the lucrative contract that provided a $900 salary and a newly built baseball cage was John W. Heisman. After just one year, the faculty and board of trustees legislated Heisman's job out of existence. Alas, the University of Akron hasn't come close to a Heisman since.

QUOTE "It probably put five to 10 more years on my life. Akron's a tough job."—Gerry Faust, after his firing as Zips head coach after the 1994 season

AKRON ANNUAL STATISTICAL LEADERS

YR	RUSHING	YDS	ATT	AVG	PASSING	ATT	CMP	PCT	YDS	RECEIVING	REC	YDS	AVG
1990	Marcus Reliford	684	177	3.9	Jeff Sweitzer	186	87	.47	1,133	Bradford Jones	17	221	13.0
1991	Tyrone Nelson	769	142	5.4	Jeff Sweitzer	220	101	.46	1,599	Harold Robinson	37	779	21.1
1992	Marcel Weems	754	181	4.2	Marcel Weems	201	101	.50	1,383	Kenny Chapman	36	581	16.1
1993	Symeon Floyd	371	82	4.5	Marcel Weems	163	72	.44	1,157	Kenny Chapman	31	636	20.5
1994	DeShawn Brown	588	152	3.9	Brian Magrell	79	44	.56	548	DeShawn Brown	20	255	12.8
1995	Terrel Dixon	463	143	3.2	Mike Junko	148	78	.53	864	Eddie Alford	46	591	11.8
1996	Yasin Reeder	781	168	4.6	Mike Junko	125	60	.48	705	Devon Scott	30	399	13.3
1997	Greg Lomax	835	127	6.6	Greg Gromek	101	50	.50	715	Willie Spencer	43	521	12.1
1998	Greg Lomax	861	161	5.4	James Washington	300	148	.49	1,958	Lavel Bailey	41	558	13.6
1999	Brandon Payne	845	208	4.1	James Washington	240	131	.55	1,896	Lavel Bailey	42	941	22.4
2000	Brandon Payne	1,062	220	4.8	James Washington	283	143	.51	2,319	Lavel Bailey	44	876	19.9
2001	Bob Hendry	819	160	5.1	Charlie Frye	289	170	.59	2,053	Matt Cherry	48	630	13.1
2002	Bob Hendry	1,021	208	4.9	Charlie Frye	380	250	.66	2,824	Miquel Irvin	53	535	10.1
2003	Bob Hendry	981	231	4.2	Charlie Frye	421	273	.65	3,549	Matt Cherry	66	904	13.7
2004	Brett Biggs	871	185	4.7	Charlie Frye	346	220	.64	2,623	Domenik Hixon	66	882	13.4

Receiving leaders by receptions
The NCAA began including postseason stats in 2002

AKRON ALL-TIME SCORES

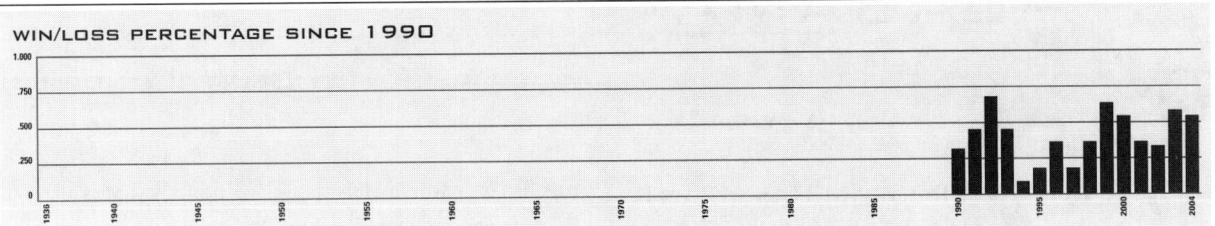

WIN/LOSS PERCENTAGE SINCE 1990

1990-1991
INDEPENDENT

GERRY FAUST
1986-94 (.449) 43-53-3

1990 3-7-1
S1	●	Illinois St.	17 7
S8	●	at Kent State	38 10
S15	=	Central Michigan	14 14
S22	●	Fullerton St.	48 17
S29		at Youngstown St.	23 28
O6		Western Michigan	20 24
O13		at Navy	13 17
O20		at Florida	0 59
O27		at Rutgers	17 20
N3		at Northern Illinois	28 31
N10		at Louisiana Tech	15 36

1991 5-6-0
S7		at Western Michigan	12 35
S14		Illinois St.	3 25
S21		at Central Michigan	29 31
S28	●	No. Arizona	49 14
O5		at East Carolina	20 56
O12	●	Youngstown St.	38 24
O19	●	Arkansas State	28 23
O26	●	Northern Illinois	17 7
N9		at Virginia Tech	24 42
N16		at Army	0 19
N23	●	at Temple	37 32

1992-Present
MAC

1992 7-3-1 (5-3-0)
S5	●	at Eastern Michigan	27 9
S12	●	Toledo	23 20
S19		at Western Michigan	20 24
O3	●	at Ohio U.	13 0
O10	●	at Kent State	16 20
O17	●	at Ball State	22 14
O24		Bowling Green	3 24
O31	●	Central Michigan	31 28
N7	●	Temple	29 15
N14	=	Youngstown St.	10 10
N21	●	at Cincinnati	24 22

1993 5-6-0 (4-4-0)
S2	●	at Central Michigan	23 13
S11	●	Kent State	42 7
S18	●	at Western Michigan	3 20
O2		at Army	14 35
O9	●	Miami, Ohio	31 13
O16		at Bowling Green	7 49
O23	●	at Temple	31 7
O30		at Ohio U.	13 21
N6	●	Eastern Michigan	19 7
N13		Ball State	9 31
N20		Youngstown St.	0 19

1994 1-10-0 (1-8-0)
S3		Temple	7 32
S10		Bowling Green	0 45
S17		at Kent State	16 32
S24		at Western Michigan	6 19
O8		at Miami, Ohio	14 50
O15		Central Michigan	0 47
O22		Toledo	25 48
O29		at Youngstown St.	7 41
N5		at Eastern Michigan	18 42
N12		at Ball State	28 38
N19	●	Ohio U.	24 10

LEE OWENS
1995-2003 (.396) 40-61

1995 2-9-0 (2-6-0)
S2		Eastern Michigan	29 49
S16		at Bowling Green	12 50
S23		at Kansas State	0 67
S30	●	Central Michigan	16 13
O7		at Western Michigan	3 7
O14		at Virginia Tech	27 77
O21		Ohio U.	23 29
O28	●	Kent State	14 6
N4		Youngstown St.	10 24
N11		at Toledo	7 41
N18		at Miami, Ohio	0 65

1996 4-7 (3-5)
A29		at Ohio U.	14 44
S7		Virginia Tech	18 21
S14		Toledo	10 27
S21		at Illinois	7 38
S28	●	Western Michigan	27 7
O5		at Kent State	17 32
O12		at Central Michigan	0 42
O19	●	Miami, Ohio	10 7
O26		at Northern Illinois	34 17
N2	●	Bowling Green	21 14
N9		at Eastern Michigan	17 20

1997 2-9 (2-7)
A30		at Nebraska	14 59
S13		at Miami, Ohio	20 49
S20		Bowling Green	28 31
S27		at LSU	0 56
O4	●	Central Michigan	53 14
O11		at Marshall	17 52
O18		at Eastern Michigan	0 45
O25		Ohio U.	17 21
N1		at Ball State	14 31
N8	●	Kent State	45 35
N15		at Toledo	10 42

1998 4-7 (3-6)
S5		Marshall	16 27
S12	●	Temple*Phil*	35 28
S26	●	Ball State	52 14
O3		at Pittsburgh	0 35
O10	●	at Kent State	45 16
O17		at Ohio U.	14 28
O24		Toledo	17 24
O31		at Central Michigan	27 28
N7		at Bowling Green	21 58
N14	●	Eastern Michigan	24 21
N21		Miami, Ohio	14 20

1999 7-4 (5-3)
S4		at Penn State	24 70
S11	●	at Buffalo	17 10
S18	●	at Temple	25 15
S25		at Eastern Michigan	17 38
O2	●	at Ball State	31 9
O9	●	Ohio U.	41 28
O16	●	Bowling Green	53 25
O23	●	at Navy	35 29
O30		Western Michigan	10 24
N6		at Miami, Ohio	23 32
N13	●	Kent State	37 34

2000 6-5 (5-3)
S2		at Virginia Tech	23 52
S9		at Central Michigan	7 17
S16	●	Central Florida	35 24
S23	●	at Ohio U.	23 20
S30	●	Miami, Ohio	37 20
O7	●	at Bowling Green	27 21
O14		Northern Illinois	35 52
O21		Connecticut	35 38
O28		Marshall	28 31
N11	●	Buffalo	49 14
N18	●	at Kent State	34 6

2001 4-7 (4-4)
A30	●	Ohio U.	31 29
S8		at Ohio State	14 28
S22		at Purdue	14 33
S29	●	Kent State	14 10
O6		at Western Michigan	14 31
O13		at Miami, Ohio	27 30
O20		Bowling Green	11 16
O27		at Marshall	33 50
N3		at Central Florida	17 57
N17	●	at Buffalo	41 14
N24	●	Eastern Michigan	65 62

2002 4-8 (3-5)
A31		at Iowa	21 57
S7		at Maryland	14 44
S14		Central Michigan	17 24
S21		at Virginia	29 48
S28		Miami, Ohio	31 48
O5		at Eastern Michigan	34 42
O12	●	Liberty	49 21
O26		at Central Florida	17 28
N2	●	Marshall	34 20
N9		at Ohio U.	10 27
N16	●	Buffalo	21 10
N23	●	at Kent State	48 10

2003 7-5 (5-3)
A28		Kent State	38 41
S6		at Wisconsin	31 48
S13	●	Eastern Michigan	24 17
S20	●	Howard	65 7
S27	●	at Buffalo	38 21
O4		at Miami, Ohio	20 45
O11	●	Cal Poly SLO	45 14
O18	●	Central Florida	38 24
O25		at Connecticut	37 38
N1		at Marshall	24 42
N8	●	at Central Michigan	40 28
N15	●	Ohio U.	35 28

J.D. BROOKHART
2004-Present (.545) 6-5

2004 6-5 (6-2)
S4		at Penn State	10 48
S11		Middle Tennessee	24 31
S18		at Virginia	0 51
S23	●	at Kent State	24 19
O2		at Northern Illinois	19 49
O9	●	Buffalo	44 21
O16	●	at Central Florida	26 21
O23	●	Ball State	35 23
N5	●	Marshall	31 28
N13	●	at Ohio U.	31 19
N20	●	Miami, Ohio	27 37

ALABAMA

BY GEOFFREY NORMAN

PERHAPS NO PROGRAM HAS MEANT as much to the identity, even the self-esteem, of its home state as Alabama. Certainly among the most distinguished traditions in the land, Alabama football's winning ways go back to a time when the state was, in just about all other regards, poor and backward. If the rest of the country in those times saw the face of Alabama in haunting portraits of hungry, down-trodden sharecroppers, the people of the state preferred to think of the boys in the red jerseys who crossed the country by train to win Rose Bowls. The Crimson Tide gave the Yellowhammer State something to be proud of at a time when pride was as precious—and scarce—as cash money.

TRADITION Alabama can claim all or part of 12 national championships and make a good argument that it was unfairly denied a couple of others. The Tide have won 21 Southeastern Conference championships and been to 52 bowl games, winning 29. More than 90 Alabama players have been named to various All-America teams, though none has ever won a Heisman—an anomaly that is also cause for pride. Football, after all, is a team sport, and the University of Alabama has produced great teams. A whole lot of them.

LANDMARK The Paul W. Bryant Museum, which houses 100 years of history and iconography, is conveniently located across the street (also named for Bryant) from the Coleman Coliseum athletic headquarters. It's a place where the faithful can gaze at photographs of the storied teams and various Bryant artifacts, including the famous hounds-tooth hat. The museum is also a treasure trove of archival material for scholars of the game.

BEST PLAYER You could spend an eon arguing this one. Strong cases could be made for Joe Namath, Johnny Mack Brown, Lee Roy Jordan, Ozzie Newsome, John Hannah, Cornelius Bennett, Derrick Thomas and Shaun Alexander. Bryant's favorite might have been quarterback Pat Trammell, leader of his first national championship team in 1961. ("He can't run and he can't throw," Bryant once said of Trammell. "All he can do is beat you.") But Don Hutson, one of the great receivers in the history of the game—college or pro—would probably get the most votes.

PROFILE

University of Alabama, Tuscaloosa
Tuscaloosa, Ala.
Founded: 1831
Enrollment: 15,888
Colors: Crimson and White
Nickname: Crimson Tide
Stadium: Bryant-Denny Stadium
   Opened in 1929
   Prescription Athletic Turf; 83,818 capacity
First football game: 1892
All-time record: 720–290–44 (.717)
Bowl record: 29–20–3
Consensus national championships, 1936-present: 7 (1961, 1964, 1965, 1973, 1978, 1979, 1992)
Southeastern Conference championships: 21 (16 outright)
Outland Trophy: Chris Samuels, 1999
First-round NFL draftees: 33
Website: www.rolltide.com/football

THE BEST OF TIMES

From a Dec. 7, 1963, win against Miami, Fla., all the way up to the 1968 Cotton Bowl loss to Texas A&M, the Crimson Tide went 40–3–2, the heart of a 1960s stretch that saw them win two national titles and play in five straight major bowl games.

THE WORST OF TIMES

The darkness before the dawn came in the J.B. Whitworth era at Alabama (1955-57) during which the Tide won just four games in three seasons, including three losses to Auburn by a combined score of 100-7. Solution: hire Paul "Bear" Bryant.

CONFERENCE

After 12 years in the Southern Conference, Alabama became a charter member of the SEC in 1933.

DISTINGUISHED ALUMNI

Mel Allen, baseball broadcaster; Hugo Black, Supreme Court justice; Harper Lee, author; Jim Nabors, actor; Sela Ward, actress

FIGHT SONG

YEA ALABAMA
Yea, Alabama! Drown 'em Tide!
Every 'Bama man's behind you,
Hit your stride.
Go teach the Bulldogs to behave,
Send the Yellow Jackets to a watery grave.
And if a man starts to weaken,
That's a shame!
For Bama's pluck and grit have
Writ her name in Crimson flame.
Fight on, fight on, fight on men!
Remember the Rose Bowl, we'll win then.
So roll on to victory,
Hit your stride,
You're Dixie's football pride,
Crimson Tide, Roll Tide, Roll Tide!!

Alabama was called the "Tusca-losers" before the 1926 Rose Bowl.

BEST COACH Bryant had some admirable predecessors at Alabama in Wallace Wade and Frank Thomas. But their accomplishments were eclipsed by Bryant's giant shadow. Bear returned to his alma mater in 1958 because, as he said, "Mama called." Coaching through 1982, Bryant won six national championships, 13 SEC titles and three coach of the year awards. His Bama teams went to 24 consecutive bowl games, compiling a 232–46–9 record. Impressive as the numbers are, they don't provide the full texture of Bryant's accomplishments. He won with the changing times, both football and societal. Bryant's first three national championship teams were all white; his last three were integrated. Bryant was not a leader in racial matters. But he was no bitter-ender, either, and when he saw the shape of things to come, he recruited and coached black players with the same old fervor. And he kept on winning. When he had a quarterback who could throw the ball—like Namath or Ken Stabler—he won with the passing game. When he had material for it, he converted to the wishbone. And, of course, his teams always played good defense. Bum Phillips said of Bryant and his ability to win with whatever material he had, "He can take his'n and beat your'n and then take your'n and beat his'n." Bryant himself put it most succinctly. "I ain't nothing," he once said, "but a winner."

BEST TEAM Among many contenders, the 1979 national title team probably deserves the nod by a small fraction. The team was trying to repeat and had to come back from a 17-7 hole against Tennessee. The Tide then beat LSU 3-0 and had to fight to get by Auburn 25-18. Alabama rolled over Arkansas 24-9 in the Sugar Bowl. And when the sums had been done and checked, Bama had scored 383 points while holding its foes to 67. This was the last Bryant team to win a national championship.

STORYBOOK SEASON Sweet as winning is, it's even sweeter beating those who consider themselves your betters, especially when nobody else believes in you. Alabama was fourth choice for the 1926 Rose Bowl after Dartmouth, Yale and Colgate had turned down the chance to play Washington. One Rose Bowl executive supposedly remarked, "I've never heard of Alabama as a football team and can't take a chance on mixing a lemon with a rose." Will Rogers referred to the Tide as "Tusca-

RECORDS

RUSHING YARDS

GAME
291   Shaun Alexander vs. LSU, Nov. 9, 1996 (20 att.)

SEASON
1,471   Bobby Humphrey, 1986 (236 att.)

CAREER
3,565   Shaun Alexander, 1996-99 (727 att.)

PASSING YARDS

GAME
484   Scott Hunter vs. Auburn, Nov. 29, 1969 (30 of 55)

SEASON
2,379   Gary Hollingsworth, 1989 (205 of 339)

CAREER
5,983   Andrew Zow, 1998-2001 (459 of 852)

RECEIVING YARDS

GAME
217   David Palmer vs. Vanderbilt, Sept. 11, 1993 (8 rec.)

SEASON
1,000   David Palmer, 1993 (61 rec.)

CAREER
2,070   Ozzie Newsome, 1974-77 (102 rec.)

POINTS

GAME
30   Santonio Beard vs. Mississippi, Oct. 19, 2002 (5 TDs); Shaun Alexander vs. BYU, Sept. 5, 1998 (5 TDs)

SEASON
144   Shaun Alexander, 1999 (24 TDs)

CAREER
345   Philip Doyle, 1987-90 (1 TD, 78 FGs, 105 PATs)

CONSENSUS ALL-AMERICANS

1930	Fred Sington	T
1934	Don Hutson	E
1934	Bill Lee	T
1934	Dixie Howell	B
1935	Riley Smith	B
1937	Leroy Monsky	G
1941	Holt Rast	E
1942	Joe Domnanovich	C
1945	Vaughn Mancha	C
1961	Billy Neighbors	T
1962	Lee Roy Jordan	C
1965	Paul Crane	C
1966	Ray Perkins	E
1966	Cecil Dowdy	T
1967	Dennis Homan	E
1967	Bobby Johns	DB
1971	Johnny Musso	B
1972	John Hannah	G
1973	Buddy Brown	G
1974	Woodrow Lowe	LB
1974-75	Leroy Cook	DL
1977	Ozzie Newsome	WR

(Continued on next page)

losers," and a Los Angeles sportswriter called them "Swamp Students." Alabama fell behind 12-0 and it looked like all the disparaging remarks were true, until the Tide came back on a touchdown reception by Brown—who later returned to California for a long career as a movie cowboy—and won the game 20-19. For Alabama fans, it was more than a victory. It was a validation.

BIGGEST GAME Of the many big games the Tide have played, perhaps the one with the most durable and resonant consequences was played in 1922, on the road against the University of Pennsylvania, a national power at that time. Grantland Rice wrote that the game would be a "breather" for Penn. The Tide won 9-7, the first time Alabama had gone up north and beat a football giant. After the game, a small white sign reading "Bama 9, Penn 7" appeared on a drugstore in downtown Tuscaloosa and remained there for more than 20 years.

BIGGEST UPSET The one that Alabama fans cherish most may be the 1966 Orange Bowl, in which the Tide beat Nebraska 39-28 to win the most improbable of Bryant's national championships. Going in, Alabama was ranked fourth in the nation behind three undefeated and untied teams. Alabama was 8–1–1, losing to Georgia 18-17 on a play that is disputed to this day and tying Tennessee when Stabler mistakenly threw the ball out-of-bounds to stop the clock on fourth down deep inside Vols territory with seconds remaining. On New Year's Day, Arkansas lost to LSU in the Cotton Bowl and Michigan State was knocked off by UCLA in the Rose. So at kickoff, there remained only one undefeated and untied team in the nation: Nebraska. To win at least one of the recognized national championships, the Tide merely had to go out and beat an undefeated team that outweighed Bryant's "little bitty boys" by about 20 pounds per man. On the first series, Alabama ran a tackle eligible. After scoring just before halftime, the Tide tried an onside kick, recovered the ball and went into the locker room ahead 24-7. At some point that night, while Ray Perkins was running wild with one of his many pass receptions, Bryant said to one of his assistants, "Isn't this just the damnedest football game

CONSENSUS ALL-AMERICANS (CONT.)		
1978	Marty Lyons,	DL
1979	Jim Bunch,	T
1980	E.J. Junior,	DL
1981	Tommy Wilcox,	DB
1982	Mike Pitts,	DL
1986	Cornelius Bennett,	LB
1988	Derrick Thomas,	LB
1989	Keith McCants,	LB
1990	Philip Doyle,	PK
1992	John Copeland,	DL
1992	Eric Curry,	DL
1993	David Palmer,	KR
1993	Antonio Langham,	DB
1996	Kevin Jackson,	DB
1999	Chris Samuels,	OL

you've ever seen?" Alabama won 39-28 and had its Associated Press national championship.

BEST GOAL-LINE STAND In the 1979 Sugar Bowl, second-ranked Alabama played No. 1 Penn State. Tough defense chararcterized the tight game, and late in the fourth quarter, with Alabama ahead 14-7, PSU recovered a fumble on the Tide 19. The Nittany Lions had their chance and mounted a drive. Then, on third and goal at the 1, Alabama held—barely. Penn State called for time and quarterback Chuck Fusina checked the distance. He looked toward the bench and spread his hands about 10 inches apart. "You got a foot to go," Marty Lyons told him. "You'd better pass." Fullback Mike Guman took a handoff and went up but not over. The impact popped the rivets in linebacker Barry Krauss' helmet. A stand for the ages.

BEST COMEBACK In 1960, Alabama was working its way back to glory. But it had been tied by Tulane and beaten by Tennessee when it traveled to Atlanta to play Georgia Tech, and fell behind 15-0 at the half. The Tide won on defense in those days, and this looked like too big a mountain to climb. Bryant came into the dressing room and, instead of breathing fire, slapped backs and grinned and said, "We've got 'em right where we want 'em." With Trammell injured, backup Bobby Skelton took Alabama on a touchdown drive that included four fourth-down plays. Still, the Tide were down by two with time running out. Skelton took the offense downfield again and every play was a white knuckler, the last a pass to the Tech 6. With three seconds left, the backup kicker put up a duck that hit the crossbar and limped over for a 16-15 win.

STADIUM Alabama plays in a stadium that opened as Denny Stadium in 1929 with a capacity of 12,000. The namesake, school president George Hutcheson "Mike" Denny, a man who believed in football and its value to the university, took an active interest—and might even be said to have meddled—in the football program. But none can deny his place in its success. With that success came stadium improvements and expansions. By 1966 it seated

60,000, and today holds almost 84,000. In 1975, something else was added—another name. This would be one Paul William Bryant, who played end on the team that beat Stanford in the 1935 Rose Bowl. He came back to Tuscaloosa a little more than a quarter of a century later, stayed another 25 years and became … well, immortal.

RIVAL Are you kidding? Auburn, man—the school Bryant once referred to as "that cow college on the other side of the state." Back in Bryant's playing days, Alabama did not play Auburn. The schools went some 41 years between games. The series was suspended in a dispute over per diem for the visiting team, among other things. After some pressure from legislators and other powers in the state, the schools agreed to schedule each other, and the respective student body presidents met to bury a symbolic hatchet. For years, the game was played at Legion Field in Birmingham and was called the Iron Bowl—a fitting moniker for the spirit and the hitting. The intensity of the play is matched by the passion of the fans, who include just about every living soul in the state of Alabama, not one of whom is neutral. Weddings and birthday parties are not scheduled in Alabama on the day of this game; you couldn't get anyone to come. Old friends, even family members, tend to stop speaking to one another if their loyalties clash. "I thought I understood something about rivalries," Bill Curry said after he had become the former head coach of Alabama. "But until I'd experienced Alabama-Auburn, I didn't

understand anything at all." Curry never beat Auburn, helping lead to his departure.

NICKNAME What exactly, the uninitiated might wonder, is a Crimson Tide and what does it have to do with football? The "Crimson" part is easy enough. The first Alabama team wore crimson-colored stockings, and this became the school's color. Sometime around the turn of the 20th century, some sportswriter started using a stanza—"The Thin Red Line"—from one of Rudyard Kipling's poems when referring to the Alabama team. Then, in a very wet game, another sportswriter turned the line of red moving inexorably down the field into a tide. Thus, the Crimson Tide and one of the more haunting cheers in all of football: Rooooooooooooooooooooooooooll, Tide!

MASCOT The improbable elephant is the result of the 1930 team, which was, by standards of the day, impressively large. According to one writer, when the Alabama team took the field for the second quarter against Mississippi, a fan shouted, "Hold your horses, the elephants are coming." That team went undefeated and stampeded Washington State in the Rose Bowl, 24-0, to win the national championship.

QUOTE "As long as they kick it off, there will be something of Coach Bryant in the game."

—Eddie Robinson, head coach, Grambling

ALL-CENTENNIAL TEAM

Fans selected the players prior to the 1992 season to commemorate the school's centennial season.

1958-82	Paul "Bear" Bryant, coach	
OFFENSE		
1928-30	Fred Sington,	OL
1944-47	Vaughn Mancha,	OL
1959-61	Billy Neighbors,	OL
1970-72	John Hannah,	OL
1977-79	Dwight Stephenson,	C
1974-77	Ozzie Newsome,	TE
1932-34	Don Hutson,	WR
1962-64	Joe Namath,	QB
1965-67	Kenny Stabler,	QB
1950-52	Bobby Marlow,	RB
1969-71	Johnny Musso,	RB
1985-88	Bobby Humphrey,	RB
1983-85	Van Tiffen,	PK
DEFENSE		
1973-76	Bob Baumhower,	DL
1975-78	Marty Lyons,	DL
1982-85	Jon Hand,	DT
1960-62	Lee Roy Jordan,	LB
1976-78	Barry Krauss,	LB
1983-86	Cornelius Bennett,	OLB
1985-88	Derrick Thomas,	OLB
1944-47	Harry Gilmer,	DB
1977-79	Don McNeal,	DB
1979-82	Jeremiah Castille,	DB
1979-82	Tommy Wilcox,	DB
1930-32	Johnny Cain,	P

ALABAMA ALL-TIME SCORES

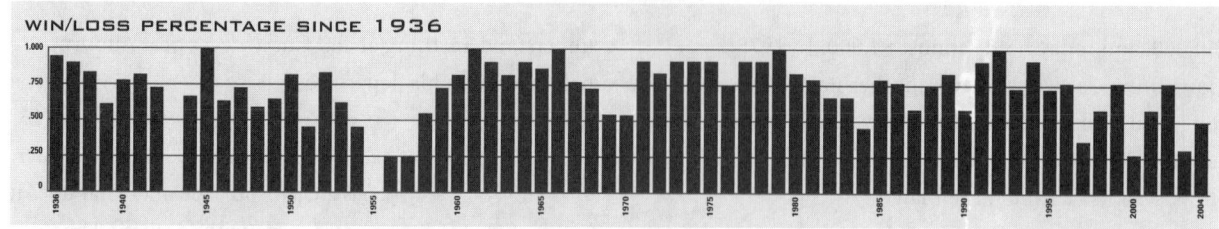

WIN/LOSS PERCENTAGE SINCE 1936

E.B. BEAUMONT
1892 (.500)   2-2

1892   2-2-0
N11 ●	B'ham HS *Birm*	56	0
N12 ●	B'ham HS *Birm*	4	5
D10 ●	B'ham HS *Birm*	14	0
F22	Auburn *Birm*	22	32

ELI ABBOTT
1893-95, 1902 (.350)   7-13

1893   0-4-0
O14	B'ham HS	0	4
N4	B'ham HS *Birm*	8	10
N11	Sewanee *Birm*	0	20
N30	Auburn *Mont*	16	40

1894   3-1-0
O27	at Mississippi	0	6
N3 ●	at Tulane	18	6
N15 ●	Sewanee *Birm*	24	4
N29 ●	Auburn *Mont*	18	0

1895   0-4-0
N2	Georgia *ColGa*	6	30
N16	at Tulane	0	22
N18	at LSU	6	12
N23	Auburn	0	48

OTTO WAGONHURST
1896 (.667)   2-1

1896   2-1-0
O24 ●	Birmingham HS	30	0
O31 ●	Sewanee	6	10
N14 ●	Mississippi State	20	0

ALLEN McCANTS
1897 (.000)   1-0

1897   1-0-0
N13 ●	Tuscaloosa AC	6	0

1898
NO TEAM

W.A. MARTIN
1899 (.750)   3-1

1899   3-1-0
O21 ●	Tuscaloosa AC	16	5
N11 ●	Montgomery AC	16	0
N24 ●	at Mississippi	7	5
N25	at New Orleans AC	0	21

M. GRIFFIN
1900 (.400)   2-3

1900   2-3-0
O21 ●	Taylor School	35	0
O26 ●	Mississippi	12	5
N3	Tulane	0	6
N17	Auburn *Mont*	5	53
N29	Clemson *Birm*	0	35

M.H. HARVEY
1901 (.600)   2-1-2

1901   2-1-2
O26 ●	Mississippi	41	0
N9 =	Georgia *Mont*	0	0
N15	Auburn	0	17
N26 ●	Mississippi State	45	0
N28 =	Tennessee *Birm*	6	6

ELI ABBOTT

1902   4-4-0
O10 ●	Birmingham HS	57	0
O13 ●	Marion Inst.	81	0
O18 ●	Auburn *Birm*	0	23
N1	Georgia *Birm*	0	5
N8 ●	Mississippi State	27	0
N19	Texas	0	10
N27 ●	Georgia Tech *Birm*	26	0
N29	LSU	0	11

W.B. BLOUNT
1903-04 (.588)   10-7

1903   3-4-0
O10	at Vanderbilt	0	30
O16	Mississippi State *ColMs*	0	11
O23 ●	Auburn *Mont*	18	6
N2 ●	Sewanee *Birm*	0	23
N9 ●	LSU	18	0
N14 ●	Cumberland	0	44
N26 ●	Tennessee *Birm*	24	0

1904   7-3-0
O3 ●	Florida U. Club	29	0
O8 ●	Clemson *Birm*	0	18
O15 ●	Mississippi State *ColMs*	6	0
O24 ●	Nashville	17	0
N5 ●	Georgia	16	5
N12 ●	Auburn *Birm*	5	29
N24 ●	Tennessee *Birm*	0	5
D2 ●	at LSU	11	0
D3 ●	at Tulane	6	0
D4 ●	at Pensacola AC	10	5

JACK LEAVENWORTH
1905 (.600)   6-4

1905   6-4-0
O3 ●	Maryville	17	0
O7 ●	at Vanderbilt	0	34
O14 ●	Mississippi State	34	0
O21 ●	at Georgia Tech	5	12
O25 ●	Clemson *Colu*	0	25
N4 ●	Georgia *Birm*	36	0
N9 ●	Centre	21	0
N18 ●	Auburn *Birm*	30	0
N23 ●	Sewanee *Birm*	6	42
N30 ●	Tennessee *Birm*	29	0

J.W.H. POLLARD
1906-09 (.783)   21-4-5

1906   5-1-0
O6 ●	Maryville	6	0
O13 ●	Samford	14	0
O20 ●	at Vanderbilt	0	78
N3 ●	at Mississippi State	16	4
N17 ●	Auburn *Birm*	10	0
N29 ●	Tennessee *Birm*	51	0

1907   5-1-2
O5 ●	Maryville	17	0
O12 ●	Mississippi *ColMs*	20	0
O21 ●	Sewanee	4	54
O25 =	Georgia *Mont*	0	0
N2 ●	Centre *Birm*	12	0
N16 ●	Auburn *Birm*	6	6
N23 ●	LSU *Mbl*	6	4
N28 ●	Tennessee *Birm*	5	0

1908   6-1-1
O3 ●	Wetumpka	27	0
O10 ●	at Samford	17	0
O17 ●	Cincinnati *Birm*	16	0
O24 ●	at Georgia Tech	6	11
O31 ●	U.T. Chattanooga	23	6
N14 ●	Georgia *Birm*	6	6
N20 ●	Haskell	9	8
N26 ●	Tennessee *Birm*	4	0

1909   5-1-2
O2 ●	Union	16	0
O9 ●	Samford	14	0
O16 ●	Clemson *Birm*	3	0
O23 =	Mississippi *JaM*	0	0
O30 ●	Georgia *Atl*	14	0
N13 ●	at Tennessee	10	0
N20 =	at Tulane	5	5
N25 ●	LSU *Birm*	6	12

GUY LOWMAN
1910 (.500)   4-4

1910   4-4-0
O1 ●	B'Ham South	25	0
O8 ●	Marion Inst.	26	0
O15 ●	Georgia *Birm*	0	22
O22 ●	Georgia Tech	0	36
N5 ●	Mississippi. *GrvMS*	0	16
N12 ●	Sewanee *Birm*	0	30
N19 ●	at Tulane	5	3
N24 ●	Wash. & Lee *Birm*	9	0

D.V. GRAVES
1911-14 (.625)   21-12-3

1911   5-2-2
S30 ●	Samford	24	0
O7 ●	at B'Ham South	47	5
O14 ●	Georgia *Birm*	3	11
O21 =	Mississippi State *ColMs*	6	6
O29 =	at Georgia Tech	0	0
N4 ●	at Marion Inst.	35	0
N18 ●	Tulane *Birm*	22	0
N25 ●	Sewanee *Birm*	0	3
N30 ●	Davidson *Birm*	16	6

1912   5-3-1
S28 ●	Marion Inst.	52	0
O5 ●	B'ham Southern	62	0
O12 ●	at Georgia Tech	3	20
O18 ●	Mississippi State *Abe*	0	7
O26 ●	Georgia *ColGa*	9	13
N2 ●	at Tulane	7	0
N9 ●	Mississippi	10	9
N16 ●	Sewanee *Birm*	6	6
N28 ●	Tennessee *Birm*	7	0

1913   6-3-0
S27 ●	Samford	27	0
O4 ●	B'ham Southern	81	0
O11 ●	Clemson	20	0
O18 ●	Georgia *Birm*	0	20
O25 ●	at Tulane	0	0
N1 ●	Mississippi Coll. *JaM*	21	3
N9 ●	Sewanee *Birm*	7	10
N14 ●	Tennessee	6	0
N27 ●	Mississippi State *Birm*	0	7

1914   5-4-0
O3 ●	Samford	13	0
O10 ●	B'Ham Southern	54	0
O17 ●	Georgia Tech *Birm*	13	0
O24 ●	at Tennessee	7	17
O31 ●	Tulane	58	0
N7 ●	Sewanee *Birm*	0	18
N13 ●	U.T. Chattanooga	63	0
N26 ●	Mississippi State *Birm*	0	9
D2 ●	Carlisle *Birm*	3	20

THOMAS KELLY
1915-17 (.700)   17-7-1

1915   6-2-0
O2 ●	Samford	44	0
O9 ●	B'ham Southern	67	0
O16 ●	Mississippi Coll.	40	0
O23 ●	Tulane	16	0
O30 ●	Sewanee *Birm*	23	10
N6 ●	at Georgia Tech	7	21
N13 ●	at Texas	0	20
N25 ●	Mississippi *Birm*	53	0

1909   5-1-2

1916   6-3-0
S30 ●	B'ham Southern	13	0
O7 ●	Southern	80	0
O14 ●	Mississippi Coll.	13	7
O21 ●	Florida *JacF*	16	0
O28 ●	Mississippi	27	0
N4 ●	Sewanee *Birm*	7	6
N11 ●	at Georgia Tech	0	13
N18 ●	at Tulane	0	33
N30 ●	Georgia *Birm*	0	3

1917   5-2-1
O3 ●	Ohio Am. Corp *Mont*	7	0
O12 ●	Marion Inst.	13	0
O20 ●	Mississippi Coll.	46	0
O27 ●	Mississippi	64	0
N3 =	Sewanee *Birm*	3	3
N10 ●	Vanderbilt *Birm*	2	7
N17 ●	at Kentucky	27	0
N29 ●	Camp Gordon *Birm*	6	19

1918
NO TEAM WWI

XEN SCOTT
1919-22 (.744)   29-9-3

1919   8-1-0
O4 ●	B'ham Southern	27	0
O11 ●	Mississippi	49	0
O18 ●	Samford	48	0
O24 ●	Marion Inst.	61	0
N1 ●	Sewanee *Birm*	40	0
N8 ●	at Vanderbilt	12	16
N15 ●	at LSU	23	0
N22 ●	Georgia *Atl*	6	0
N27 ●	Mississippi State *Birm*	14	6

1920   10-1-0
S25 ●	So. Military Acd.	59	0
O2 ●	Marion Inst.	49	0
O9 ●	B'ham Southern	45	0
O16 ●	Mississippi Coll.	57	0
O23 ●	Samford	33	0
O30 ●	Sewanee *Birm*	21	0
N6 ●	Vanderbilt *Birm*	14	7
N13 ●	LSU	21	0
N20 ●	Georgia *Atl*	14	21
N25 ●	Mississippi State *Birm*	24	7
N27 ●	at Case Coll.	40	0

1921-1932
SOUTHERN

1921   5-4-2 (0-1-1)
S24 ●	Samford	34	14
O1 ●	Spring Hill	27	7
O8 ●	Marion Inst.	55	0
O15 ●	Bryson Tenn.	95	0
O22 ●	Sewanee *Birm*	0	17
O29 =	LSU *NO*	7	7
N5 ●	Vanderbilt *Birm*	0	14
N11	Florida	2	9
N19 ●	Georgia *Atl*	0	22
N24	Mississippi State *Birm*	7	7
D3 ●	at Tulane	14	7

1922   6-3-1 (3-2-1)
S30 ●	Marion Inst.	110	0
O7 ●	Oglethorpe	41	0
O14	at Georgia Tech	7	33
O21 =	Sewanee *Birm*	7	7
O28 ●	at Texas	10	19
N4 ●	at Pennsylvania	9	7
N10 ●	LSU	47	3
N18 ●	at Kentucky	0	6
N25 ●	Georgia *Mont*	10	6
N30 ●	Mississippi State *Birm*	59	0

ALABAMA 81

THE SCHOOLS

WALLACE WADE
1923-30 (.812) 61-13-3

1923 7-2-1 (5-1-1)

S29	●	Union	12	0
O6	● |	Mississippi	56	0
O13		at Syracuse	0	23
O20	● |	Sewanee BIRM	7	0
O27	●	at Spring Hill	59	0
N3	= |	at Georgia Tech	0	0
N10	● |	Kentucky	16	8
N16	● |	LSU MONT	30	3
N24	● |	Georgia MONT	36	0
N29	|	Florida BIRM	6	16

1924 8-1-0 (5-0-0)

S27	●	Union	55	0
O4	●	at Furman	20	0
O11	●	Mississippi Coll.	55	0
O18	● |	Sewanee BIRM	14	0
O25	● |	at Georgia Tech	14	0
N1	● |	Mississippi MONT	61	0
N8	● |	Kentucky	42	7
N15		Centre BIRM	0	17
N27	● |	Georgia BIRM	33	0

1925 10-0-0 (7-0-0)

S26	●	Union	53	0
O2	●	B'ham Southern	50	7
O10	● |	at LSU	42	0
O17	● |	Sewanee BIRM	27	0
O24	● |	at Georgia Tech	7	0
O31	● |	Mississippi State	6	0
N7	● |	Kentucky BIRM	31	0
N14	● |	Florida MONT	34	0
N26	● |	Georgia BIRM	27	0
		ROSE BOWL		
J1	●	Washington	20	19

1926 9-0-1 (8-0-0)

S24	●	Millsaps	54	0
O2	● |	at Vanderbilt	19	7
O9	● |	Mississippi State MER	26	7
O16	● |	at Georgia Tech	21	0
O23	● |	Sewanee BIRM	2	0
O30	● |	LSU	24	0
N6	● |	Kentucky BIRM	14	0
N13	● |	Florida MONT	49	0
N25	● |	Georgia BIRM	33	6
		ROSE BOWL		
J1	=	Stanford	7	7

1927 5-4-1 (3-4-1)

S24	●	Millsaps	46	0
S30	●	So. Presb. U.	31	0
O8	= |	LSU BIRM	0	0
O15	|	at Georgia Tech	0	13
O22	● |	Sewanee BIRM	24	0
O29	● |	Mississippi State	13	7
N5	● |	Kentucky BIRM	21	6
N12	|	Florida MONT	6	13
N27	|	Georgia BIRM	6	20
D3	|	Vanderbilt BIRM	7	14

1928 6-3-0 (6-2-0)

O6	● |	Mississippi	27	0
O13	● |	at Mississippi State	46	0
O20	|	Tennessee	13	15
O27	● |	Sewanee BIRM	42	12
N3		at Wisconsin	0	15
N10	● |	Kentucky MONT	14	0
N17	|	at Georgia Tech	13	33
N29	● |	Georgia BIRM	19	0
D8	● |	LSU BIRM	13	0

1929 6-3-0 (4-3-0)

S28	●	Mississippi Coll.	55	0
O5	● |	Mississippi	22	7
O12	● |	U.T. Chattanooga	46	0
O19	|	at Tennessee	0	6
O26	● |	Sewanee BIRM	35	7
N2	|	at Vanderbilt	0	13
N9	● |	Kentucky MONT	24	13
N16	● |	at Georgia Tech	14	0
N28	|	Georgia BIRM	0	12

1930 10-0-0 (8-0-0)

S27	●	Samford	43	0
O4	● |	Mississippi	64	0
O11	● |	Sewanee BIRM	25	0
O18	● |	Tennessee	18	6
O25	● |	Vanderbilt BIRM	12	7
N1	● |	at Kentucky	19	0
N8	● |	at Florida	20	0
N15	● |	LSU MONT	33	0
N27	● |	Georgia BIRM	13	0
		ROSE BOWL		
J1	●	Washington State	24	0

FRANK THOMAS
1931-46 (.812) 115-24-7

1931 9-1-0 (7-1-0)

S26	●	Samford	42	0
O3	● |	Mississippi	55	6
O10	● |	Mississippi State MER	53	0
O17	|	at Tennessee	0	25
O24	● |	Sewanee BIRM	33	0
O31	● |	Kentucky	9	7
N7	● |	Florida BIRM	41	0
N14	●	Clemson MONT	74	7
N26	● |	at Vanderbilt	14	6
D2	●	at U.T. Chattanooga	39	0

1932 8-2-0 (5-2-0)

S24	●	Southwestern	45	6
O1	● |	Mississippi State MONT	53	0
O8	●	at George Washington	28	6
O15	|	Tennessee BIRM	3	7
O22	● |	Mississippi	24	13
O29	● |	at Kentucky	12	7
N5	● |	Virginia Tech	9	6
N12	|	at Georgia Tech	0	6
N24	● |	Vanderbilt BIRM	20	0
D5	●	Saint Mary's-Cal SF	6	0

1933-PRESENT
SEC

1933 7-1-1 (5-0-1)

S30	●	Oglethorpe	34	0
O7	= |	Mississippi BIRM	0	0
O14	● |	Mississippi State	18	0
O21	● |	at Tennessee	12	6
O28		Fordham NYC	0	2
N4	● |	Kentucky BIRM	20	0
N11	●	Virginia Tech	27	0
N18	● |	at Georgia Tech	12	9
N30	● |	at Vanderbilt	7	0

1934 10-0-0 (7-0-0)

S29	●	Samford	24	0
O5	● |	Sewanee MONT	35	6
O13	● |	Mississippi State	41	0
O20	● |	Tennessee BIRM	13	6
O27	● |	Georgia BIRM	26	6
N3	● |	at Kentucky	34	14
N10	●	Clemson	40	0
N17	● |	at Georgia Tech	40	0
N29	● |	Vanderbilt BIRM	34	0
		ROSE BOWL		
J1	●	Stanford	29	13

1935 6-2-1 (4-2-0)

S28	=	Samford	7	7
O5	●	at George Washington	39	0
O12	|	Mississippi State	7	20
O19	● |	at Tennessee	25	0
O26	● |	at Georgia	17	7
N2	● |	Kentucky BIRM	13	0
N9	●	Clemson	33	0
N16	● |	Georgia Tech BIRM	38	7
N28	|	at Vanderbilt	6	14

1936 8-0-1 (5-0-1)

S26	●	Samford	34	0
O3	●	Clemson	32	0
O10	● |	Mississippi State	7	0
O17	= |	Tennessee BIRM	0	0
O24	●	at Loyola-New Orleans	13	6
O31	● |	at Kentucky	14	0
N7	● |	Tulane BIRM	34	7
N14	● |	at Georgia Tech	20	16
N25	● |	Vanderbilt BIRM	14	6

1937 9-1-0 (6-0-0)

S25	●	Samford	41	0
O2	● |	Sewanee BIRM	65	0
O9	●	South Carolina	20	0
O16	● |	at Tennessee	14	7
O23	●	at George Washington	19	0
O30	● |	Kentucky	41	0
N6	● |	at Tulane	9	6
N13	● |	Georgia Tech BIRM	7	0
N25	● |	at Vanderbilt	9	7
		ROSE BOWL		
J1		California	0	13

1938 7-1-1 (4-1-1)

S24	●	at Southern Cal	19	7
O1	●	Samford	34	0
O8	●	North Carolina St.	14	0
O15	|	Tennessee BIRM	0	13
O22	● |	Sewanee	32	0
O29	● |	at Kentucky	26	6
N5	● |	Tulane BIRM	3	0
N12	= |	at Georgia Tech	14	14
N24	● |	Vanderbilt. BIRM	7	0

1939 5-3-1 (2-3-1)

S30	●	Samford	21	0
O7	●	Fordham NYC	7	6
O14	●	Mercer	20	0
O21	|	at Tennessee	0	21
O28	● |	Mississippi State	7	0
N4	= |	Kentucky BIRM	7	7
N11	|	at Tulane	0	13
N18	|	Georgia Tech BIRM	0	6
N30	● |	at Vanderbilt	39	0

1940 7-2-0 (4-2-0)

S27	●	at Spring Hill	26	0
O5	●	Mercer	20	0
O12	●	Samford	31	0
O19	|	Tennessee BIRM	12	27
N2	● |	at Kentucky	25	0
N9	● |	Tulane BIRM	13	6
N16	● |	at Georgia Tech	14	13
N23	● |	Vanderbilt BIRM	25	21
N30	|	Mississippi State	0	13

1941 9-2-0 (5-2-0)

S27	●	La. Lafayette	47	6
O4	|	Mississippi State	0	14
O11	●	at Samford	61	0
O18	● |	at Tennessee	9	2
O25	● |	Georgia BIRM	27	14
N1	● |	Kentucky	30	0
N8	● |	at Tulane	19	14
N15	● |	Georgia Tech BIRM	20	0
N22	|	at Vanderbilt	0	7
N29	●	at Miami, Fla.	21	7
		COTTON BOWL		
J1	●	Texas A&M	29	21

1942 8-3-0 (4-2-0)

S25	●	La. Lafayette MONT	54	0
O3	● |	Mississippi State	21	6
O10	●	Pensacola NAS MBL	27	0
O17	● |	Tennessee BIRM	8	0
O24	● |	at Kentucky	14	0
O31	|	Georgia ATL	10	21
N7	●	South Carolina	29	0
N14		at Georgia Tech	0	7
N21	● |	Vanderbilt BIRM	27	7
N28		Georgia Pre-Flight	19	35
		ORANGE BOWL		
J1	●	Boston College	37	21

1943
NO TEAM WWII

1944 5-2-2 (3-1-2)

S30	= |	at LSU	27	27
O7	●	at Samford	63	7
O14	●	Millsaps	55	0
O21	= |	at Tennessee	0	0
O27	● |	Kentucky MONT	41	0
N4	|	Georgia BIRM	7	14
N11	● |	Mississippi MBL	34	6
N18	● |	Mississippi State	19	0
		SUGAR BOWL		
J1		Duke	26	29

1945 10-0-0 (6-0-0)

S29	●	at Keesler AFB	21	0
O6	● |	at LSU	26	7
O13	●	South Carolina COLGA	55	0
O20	● |	Tennessee BIRM	25	7
O27	● |	Georgia BIRM	28	14
N3	● |	Kentucky LOU	60	19
N17	● |	at Vanderbilt	71	0
N24	●	Pensacola NAS	55	6
D1	● |	Mississippi State	55	13
		ROSE BOWL		
J1	●	Southern Cal	34	14

1946 7-4-0 (4-3-0)

S20	●	Furman BIRM	26	7
S28	● |	at Tulane	7	6
O5	●	at South Carolina	14	6
O12	●	La. Lafayette	54	0
O19	|	at Tennessee	0	12
O26	● |	Kentucky MONT	21	7
N2	|	at Georgia	0	14
N9	|	at LSU	21	31
N16	● |	Vanderbilt BIRM	12	7
N23		at Boston College	7	13
N30	● |	Mississippi State	24	7

HAROLD "RED" DREW
1947-54 (.646) 54-28-7

1947 8-3-0 (5-2-0)

S20	●	Southern Miss BIRM	34	7
S27	|	at Tulane	20	21
O4	|	at Vanderbilt	7	14
O11	●	Duquesne	26	0
O18	● |	Tennessee BIRM	10	0
O25	● |	at Georgia	17	7
N1	● |	at Kentucky	13	0
N15	● |	Georgia Tech BIRM	14	7
N22	● |	LSU	41	12
N29	●	at Miami, Fla.	21	6
		SUGAR BOWL		
J1		Texas	7	27

1948 6-4-1 (4-4-1)

S25	|	at Tulane	14	21
O2	= |	Vanderbilt MBL	14	14
O8	●	Duquesne	48	6
O16	|	at Tennessee	6	21
O23	● |	at Mississippi State	10	7
O30	|	Georgia BIRM	0	35
N6	●	Southern Miss	27	0
N13	● |	at Georgia Tech	14	12
N20	|	at LSU	6	26
N27	● |	Florida	34	28
D4	● |	Auburn BIRM	55	0

1949 6-3-1 (4-3-1)

S24	|	Tulane MBL	14	28
O1	|	at Vanderbilt	7	14
O7	●	Duquesne	48	8
O15	= |	Tennessee BIRM	7	7
O22	● |	Mississippi State	35	6
O29	● |	at Georgia	14	7
N12	● |	Georgia Tech BIRM	20	7
N19	●	Southern Miss	34	26
N26	● |	at Florida	35	13
D3	|	Auburn BIRM	13	14

1950 9-2-0 (6-2-0)

S23	●	U.T. Chattanooga BIRM	27	0
S30	● |	at Tulane	26	14
O7	|	Vanderbilt MBL	22	27
O13	●	Furman	34	6
O21	|	at Tennessee	9	14
O28	● |	Mississippi	14	7
N4	● |	Georgia BIRM	14	7
N11	●	Southern Miss	53	0
N18	● |	at Georgia Tech	54	19
N25	● |	Florida JACF	41	13
D2	● |	Auburn BIRM	34	0

1951 5-6-0 (3-5-0)

S21	●	Delta St. MONT	89	0
S29	|	LSU MBL	7	13
O6	|	at Vanderbilt	20	22
O12		Villanova	18	41
O20	|	Tennessee BIRM	13	27
O27	● |	at Mississippi State	7	0
N3	● |	at Georgia	16	14
N10	●	Southern Miss	40	7
N17	|	Georgia Tech BIRM	7	27
N24	|	Florida	21	30
D2	● |	Auburn BIRM	25	7

1952 10-2-0 (4-2-0)

S19	●	Southern Miss MONT	20	6
S27	● |	at LSU	21	20
O3	●	at Miami, Fla.	21	7
O11	●	Virginia Tech	33	0
O18	|	at Tennessee	0	20
O25	● |	Mississippi State	42	19
N1	● |	Georgia BIRM	34	19
N8	●	U.T. Chattanooga	42	28
N15	|	at Georgia Tech	3	7
N22	●	Maryland MBL	27	7
N29	● |	Auburn BIRM	21	0
		ORANGE BOWL		
J1	●	Syracuse	61	6

1953 6-3-3 (4-0-3)

S18		Southern Miss MONT	19	25
S26	= |	LSU MBL	7	7
O3	● |	at Vanderbilt	21	12
O10	●	Tulsa	41	13
O17	= |	Tennessee BIRM	0	0
O24	= |	Mississippi State	7	7
O31	● |	at Georgia	33	12
N7	●	U.T. Chattanooga	21	14
N14	● |	Georgia Tech BIRM	13	6
N21		at Maryland	0	21
N28	● |	Auburn BIRM	10	7
		COTTON BOWL		
J1		Rice	6	28

82 ALABAMA

THE SCHOOLS

1954 4-5-2 (3-3-2)

S17			Southern Miss *Mont*	2	7
S25	●	|	at LSU	12	0
O2	●	|	Vanderbilt *Mbl*	28	14
O9	●		Tulsa	40	0
O16	●	|	at Tennessee	27	0
O23		|	Mississippi State	7	12
O30	=	|	Georgia *Birm*	0	0
N6	=	|	at Tulane	0	0
N13		|	at Georgia Tech	0	20
N19			at Miami, Fla.	7	23
N27		|	Auburn *Birm*	0	28

J.B. WHITWORTH
1955-57 (.167) 4-24-2

1955 0-10-0 (0-7-0)

S24			at Rice	0	20
O1		|	at Vanderbilt	6	21
O8			TCU	0	21
O15		|	Tennessee *Birm*	0	20
O22		|	Mississippi State	7	26
O29		|	at Georgia	14	35
N5		|	Tulane *Mbl*	7	27
N12		|	Georgia Tech *Birm*	2	26
N18			at Miami, Fla.	12	34
N26		|	Auburn *Birm*	0	26

1956 2-7-1 (2-5-0)

S22			at Rice	13	20
O6		|	Vanderbilt *Mbl*	7	32
O13			TCU	6	23
O20		|	at Tennessee	0	24
O27	●	|	Mississippi State	13	12
N3		|	Georgia *Birm*	13	16
N10	●	|	at Tulane	13	7
N17		|	at Georgia Tech	0	27
N24	=		Southern Miss	13	13
D1		|	Auburn *Birm*	7	34

1957 2-7-1 (1-6-1)

S28		|	at LSU	0	28
O5	=	|	at Vanderbilt	6	6
O12			at TCU	0	28
O19		|	Tennessee *Birm*	0	14
O26		|	Mississippi State	13	25
N2	●	|	at Georgia	14	13
N9		|	Tulane *Mbl*	0	7
N16		|	Georgia Tech *Birm*	7	10
N23	●		Southern Miss	29	2
N30		|	Auburn *Birm*	0	40

PAUL "BEAR" BRYANT
1958-82 (.824) 232-46-9

1958 5-4-1 (3-4-1)

S27		|	LSU *Mbl*	3	13
O4	=	|	Vanderbilt *Birm*	0	0
O11	●		Furman	29	6
O18		|	at Tennessee	7	14
O25	●	|	at Mississippi State	9	7
N1	●	|	Georgia	12	0
N7		|	at Tulane	7	13
N15	●	|	at Georgia Tech	17	8
N22	●		Memphis	14	0
N29		|	Auburn *Birm*	8	14

1959 7-2-2 (4-1-2)

S19		|	at Georgia	3	17
S26	●		at Houston	3	0
O3	=	|	at Vanderbilt	7	7
O10	●		U.T. Chattanooga	13	0
O17	=	|	Tennessee *Birm*	7	7
O31	●	|	Mississippi State	10	0
N7	●	|	Tulane *Mbl*	19	7
N14	●	|	Georgia Tech *Birm*	9	7
N21	●		Memphis	14	7
N28	●	|	Auburn *Birm*	10	0
			LIBERTY BOWL		
D19			Penn State	0	7

1960 8-1-2 (5-1-1)

S17	●	|	Georgia *Birm*	21	6
S24	=	|	at Tulane	6	6
O1	●	|	Vanderbilt *Birm*	21	0
O15		|	at Tennessee	7	20
O22	●		Houston	14	0
O29	●	|	at Mississippi State	7	0
N5	●		Furman	51	0
N12	●	|	at Georgia Tech	16	15
N19	●		Tampa	34	6
N26	●	|	Auburn *Birm*	3	0
			BLUEBONNET BOWL		
D17	=		Texas	3	3

1961 11-0-0 (7-0-0)

S23	●	|	at Georgia	32	6
S30	●	|	Tulane *Mbl*	9	0
O7	●	|	at Vanderbilt	35	6
O14	●		North Carolina St.	26	7
O21	●	|	Tennessee *Birm*	34	3
O28	●		at Houston	17	0
N4	●	|	Mississippi State	24	0
N11	●		Richmond	66	0
N18	●	|	Georgia Tech *Birm*	10	0
D2	●	|	Auburn *Birm*	34	0
			SUGAR BOWL		
J1	●		Arkansas	10	3

1962 10-1-0 (6-1-0)

S22	●	|	Georgia *Birm*	35	0
S28	●	|	at Tulane	44	6
O6	●	|	Vanderbilt *Birm*	17	7
O13	●		Houston	14	3
O20	●	|	at Tennessee	27	7
O27	●		Tulsa	35	6
N3	●	|	at Mississippi State	20	0
N10	●		Miami, Fla.	36	3
N17		|	at Georgia Tech	6	7
D1	●	|	Auburn *Birm*	38	0
			ORANGE BOWL		
J1	●		Oklahoma	17	0

1963 9-2-0 (6-2-0)

S21	●	|	at Georgia	32	7
S28	●	|	Tulane *Mbl*	28	0
O5	●	|	at Vanderbilt	21	6
O12		|	Florida	6	10
O19	●	|	Tennessee *Birm*	35	0
O26	●		Houston	21	13
N2	●	|	Mississippi State	20	19
N16	●	|	Georgia Tech *Birm*	27	11
N30		|	Auburn *Birm*	8	10
D7	●		at Miami, Fla.	17	12
			SUGAR BOWL		
J1	●		Mississippi	12	7

1964 10-1-0 (8-0-0)

S19	●	|	Georgia	31	3
S26	●	|	Tulane *Mbl*	36	6
O3	●	|	Vanderbilt *Birm*	24	0
O10	●		North Carolina St.	21	0
O17	●	|	at Tennessee	19	8
O24	●	|	Florida	17	14
O31	●	|	Mississippi State *JaM*	23	6
N7	●	|	LSU *Birm*	17	9
N14	●		at Georgia Tech	24	7
N26	●	|	Auburn *Birm*	21	14
			ORANGE BOWL		
J1			Texas	17	21

1965 9-1-1 (6-1-1)

S18		|	at Georgia	17	18
S25	●	|	Tulane *Mbl*	27	0
O2	●	|	Mississippi *Birm*	17	16
O9	●	|	at Vanderbilt	22	7
O16	=	|	Tennessee *Birm*	7	7
O23	●		Florida State	21	0
O30	●	|	Mississippi State *JaM*	10	7
N6	●	|	at LSU	31	7
N13	●		South Carolina	35	14
N27	●	|	Auburn *Birm*	30	3
			ORANGE BOWL		
J1	●		Nebraska	39	28

1966 11-0-0 (6-0-0)

S24	●		Louisiana Tech *Birm*	34	0
O1	●	|	Mississippi *JaM*	17	7
O8	●		Clemson	26	0
O15	●	|	at Tennessee	11	10
O22	●	|	Vanderbilt *Birm*	42	6
O29	●	|	Mississippi State	27	14
N5	●	|	LSU *Birm*	21	0
N12	●		South Carolina	24	0
N26	●		Southern Miss *Mbl*	34	0
D3	●	|	Auburn *Birm*	31	0
			SUGAR BOWL		
J2	●		Nebraska	34	7

1967 8-2-1 (5-1-0)

S23	=		Florida State *Birm*	37	37
S30	●		Southern Miss *Mbl*	25	3
O7	●	|	Mississippi *Birm*	21	7
O14	●	|	at Vanderbilt	35	21
O21		|	Tennessee *Birm*	13	24
O28	●		at Clemson	13	10
N4	●	|	Mississippi State	13	0
N11	●	|	at LSU	7	6
N18	●		South Carolina	17	0
D2	●	|	Auburn *Birm*	7	3
			COTTON BOWL		
J1			Texas A&M	16	20

1968 8-3-0 (4-2-0)

S21	●		Virginia Tech *Birm*	14	7
S28	●		Southern Miss *Mbl*	17	14
O5		|	Mississippi *JaM*	8	10
O12	●	|	Vanderbilt	31	7
O19		|	at Tennessee	9	10
O26	●		Clemson	21	14
N2	●	|	Mississippi State	20	13
N9	●	|	LSU *Birm*	16	7
N16	●		at Miami, Fla.	14	6
N30	●	|	Auburn *Birm*	24	16
			GATOR BOWL		
D28			Missouri	10	35

1969 6-5-0 (2-4-0)

S20	●		at Virginia Tech	17	13
S27	●		Southern Miss	63	14
O4	●	|	Mississippi *Birm*	33	32
O11		|	at Vanderbilt	10	14
O18		|	Tennessee *Birm*	14	41
O25	●		at Clemson	38	13
N1	●	|	Mississippi State *JaM*	23	19
N8		|	at LSU	15	20
N15	●		Miami, Fla.	42	6
N29		|	Auburn *Birm*	26	49
			LIBERTY BOWL		
D13			Colorado	33	47

1970 6-5-1 (3-4-0)

S12			Southern Cal *Birm*	21	42
S19	●		Virginia Tech *Birm*	51	18
S26	●	|	Florida	46	15
O3		|	Mississippi *JaM*	23	48
O10	●	|	Vanderbilt	35	11
O17		|	at Tennessee	0	24
O24	●		at Houston	30	21
O31	●	|	Mississippi State	35	6
N7		|	LSU *Birm*	9	14
N14	●		at Miami, Fla.	32	8
N28		|	Auburn *Birm*	28	33
			BLUEBONNET BOWL		
D31	=		Oklahoma	24	24

1971 11-1-0 (7-0-0)

S10	●		at Southern Cal	17	10
S18	●		Southern Miss	42	6
S25	●	|	at Florida	38	0
O2	●	|	Mississippi *Birm*	40	6
O9	●	|	at Vanderbilt	42	0
O16	●	|	Tennessee *Birm*	32	15
O23	●		Houston	34	20
O30	●	|	Mississippi State *JaM*	41	10
N6	●	|	at LSU	14	7
N13	●		Miami, Fla.	31	3
N27	●	|	Auburn *Birm*	31	7
			ORANGE BOWL		
J1			Nebraska	6	38

1972 10-2-0 (7-1-0)

S9	●		Duke *Birm*	35	12
S23	●	|	Kentucky *Birm*	35	0
S30	●	|	Vanderbilt	48	21
O7	●	|	at Georgia	25	7
O14	●	|	Florida	24	7
O21	●	|	at Tennessee	17	10
O28	●		Southern Miss *Birm*	48	11
N4	●	|	Mississippi State	58	14
N11	●	|	LSU *Birm*	35	21
N18	●		Virginia Tech	52	13
D2		|	Auburn *Birm*	16	17
			COTTON BOWL		
J1			Texas	13	17

1973 11-1-0 (8-0-0)

S15	●	|	California *Birm*	66	0
S22	●	|	at Kentucky	28	14
S29	●	|	at Vanderbilt	44	0
O6	●	|	Georgia	28	14
O13	●	|	at Florida	35	14
O20	●	|	Tennessee *Birm*	42	21
O27	●		Virginia Tech	77	6
N3	●	|	Mississippi State *JaM*	35	0
N17	●		Miami, Fla.	43	13
N22	●	|	at LSU	21	7
D1	●	|	Auburn *Birm*	35	0
			SUGAR BOWL		
D31			Notre Dame	23	24

1974 11-1-0 (6-0-0)

S14	●		at Maryland	21	16
S21	●		Southern Miss *Birm*	52	0
S28	●	|	Vanderbilt	23	10
O5	●	|	Mississippi *JaM*	35	21
O12	●		Florida State	8	7
O19	●	|	at Tennessee	28	6
O26	●		TCU *Birm*	41	3
N2	●	|	Mississippi State	35	0
N9	●	|	LSU *Birm*	30	0
N16	●		at Miami, Fla.	28	7
N29	●	|	Auburn *Birm*	17	13
			ORANGE BOWL		
J1			Notre Dame	11	13

1975 11-1-0 (6-0-0)

S8			Missouri *Birm*	7	20
S20	●		Clemson	56	0
S27	●	|	at Vanderbilt	40	7
O4	●	|	Mississippi *Birm*	32	6
O11	●		Washington	52	0
O18	●	|	Tennessee *Birm*	30	7
O25	●		TCU *Birm*	45	0
N1	●	|	Mississippi State *JaM*	21	10
N8	●	|	at LSU	23	10
N15	●		Southern Miss	27	6
N29	●	|	Auburn *Birm*	28	0
			SUGAR BOWL		
D31	●		Penn State	13	6

1976 9-3-0 (5-2-0)

S11		|	Mississippi *JaM*	7	10
S18	●		SMU *Birm*	56	3
S25	●	|	Vanderbilt	42	14
O2		|	at Georgia	0	21
O9	●		Southern Miss *Birm*	24	8
O16	●	|	at Tennessee	20	13
O23	●		Louisville	24	3
O30	●	|	Mississippi State	34	17
N6	●	|	LSU *Birm*	28	17
N13			at Notre Dame	18	21
N27	●	|	Auburn *Birm*	38	7
			LIBERTY BOWL		
D20	●		UCLA	36	6

1977 11-1-0 (7-0-0)

S10	●	|	Mississippi *Birm*	34	13
S17			at Nebraska	24	31
S24	●	|	at Vanderbilt	24	12
O1	●	|	Georgia	18	10
O8	●		at Southern Cal	21	20
O15	●	|	Tennessee *Birm*	24	10
O22	●		Louisville	55	6
O29	●	|	Mississippi State *JaM*	37	7
N5	●	|	at LSU	24	3
N12	●		Miami, Fla.	36	0
N26	●	|	Auburn *Birm*	48	21
			SUGAR BOWL		
J2	●		Ohio State	35	6

1978 11-1-0 (6-0-0)

S2	●		Nebraska *Birm*	20	3
S16	●		at Missouri	38	20
S23			Southern Cal *Birm*	14	24
S30	●	|	Vanderbilt	51	28
O7	●		at Washington	20	17
O14	●	|	Florida	23	12
O21	●	|	at Tennessee	30	17
O28	●		Virginia Tech	35	0
N4	●	|	Mississippi State *Birm*	35	14
N11	●	|	LSU *Birm*	31	10
D2	●	|	Auburn *Birm*	34	16
			SUGAR BOWL		
J1	●		Penn State	14	7

1979 12-0-0 (6-0-0)

S8	●		at Georgia Tech	30	6
S22	●		Baylor	45	0
S29	●	|	at Vanderbilt	66	3
O6	●		Wichita St.	38	0
O13	●	|	at Florida	40	0
O20	●	|	Tennessee *Birm*	27	17
O27	●		Virginia Tech	31	7
N3	●	|	Mississippi State	24	7
N10	●	|	at LSU	3	0
N17	●		Miami, Fla.	30	0
D1	●	|	Auburn *Birm*	25	18
			SUGAR BOWL		
J1	●		Arkansas	24	9

1980 10-2-0 (5-1-0)

S6	●	Georgia Tech *Birm*	26	3
S20	●	Mississippi *JaM*	59	35
S27	● │	Vanderbilt	41	0
O3	● │	Kentucky *Birm*	45	0
O11	●	Rutgers *ERut*	17	13
O18	● │	at Tennessee	27	0
O25	●	Southern Miss	42	7
N1	│	Mississippi State *JaM*	3	6
N8	● │	LSU	28	7
N15		Notre Dame *Birm*	0	7
N29	● │	Auburn *Birm*	34	18
		COTTON BOWL		
J1	●	Baylor	30	2

1981 9-2-1 (6-0-0)

S5	● │	LSU	24	7
S12		Georgia Tech *Birm*	21	24
S19	● │	at Kentucky	19	10
S26	● │	at Vanderbilt	28	7
O3	●	Mississippi	38	7
O10	=	Southern Miss *Birm*	13	13
O17	● │	Tennessee *Birm*	38	19
O24	●	Rutgers	31	7
O31	● │	Mississippi State	13	10
N14	●	at Penn State	31	16
N28	● │	Auburn *Birm*	28	17
		COTTON BOWL		
J1		Texas	12	14

1982 8-4-0 (3-3-0)

S11	●	at Georgia Tech	45	7
S18	● │	Mississippi *JaM*	42	14
S25	● │	Vanderbilt	24	21
O2	●	Arkansas State *Birm*	34	7
O9	●	Penn State *Birm*	42	21
O16	│	at Tennessee	28	35
O23	●	Cincinnati	21	3
O30	● │	Mississippi State *JaM*	20	12
N6	│	LSU *Birm*	10	20
N13		Southern Miss	29	38
N27	│	Auburn *Birm*	22	23
		LIBERTY BOWL		
D29	●	Illinois	21	15

RAY PERKINS
1983-86 (.677) 32-15-1

1983 8-4-0 (4-2-0)

S10	●	Georgia Tech *Birm*	20	7
S17	● │	Mississippi	40	0
S24	● │	at Vanderbilt	44	24
O1	●	Memphis	44	13
O8		at Penn State	28	34
O15	│	Tennessee *Birm*	34	41
O29	● │	Mississippi State	35	18
N5	● │	at LSU	32	26
N12	●	Southern Miss *Birm*	28	16
N25		Boston College *Fox*	13	20
D3	│	Auburn *Birm*	20	23
		SUN BOWL		
D24	●	SMU	28	7

1984 5-6-0 (2-4-0)

S8		Boston College *Birm*	31	38
S15		at Georgia Tech	6	16
S22	●	La. Lafayette	37	14
S29	│	Vanderbilt	21	30
O6	│	Georgia *Birm*	14	24
O13	●	Penn State	6	0
O20	│	at Tennessee	27	28
N3	● │	Mississippi State *JaM*	24	20
N10	│	LSU *Birm*	14	16
N17	●	at Cincinnati	29	7
D1	● │	Auburn *Birm*	17	15

1985 9-2-1 (4-1-1)

S2	● │	at Georgia	20	16
S14	●	Texas A&M *Birm*	23	10
S21	●	Cincinnati	45	10
S28	● │	at Vanderbilt	40	20
O12		at Penn State	17	19
O19	│	Tennessee *Birm*	14	16
O26	●	at Memphis	28	9
N2	● │	Mississippi State	44	28
N9	= │	at LSU	14	14
N16	●	Southern Miss	24	13
N30	● │	Auburn *Birm*	25	23
		ALOHA BOWL		
D28	●	Southern Cal	24	3

1986 10-3-0 (4-2-0)

A27	●	Ohio State *ERut*	16	10
S6	● │	Vanderbilt	42	10
S13	●	Southern Miss *Birm*	31	17
S20	● │	at Florida	21	7
O4	●	Notre Dame *Birm*	28	10
O11	●	Memphis	37	0
O18	● │	at Tennessee	56	28
O25		Penn State	3	23
N1	● │	at Mississippi State	38	3
N8	│	LSU *Birm*	10	14
N15	●	Temple	24	14
N29	│	Auburn *Birm*	17	21
		SUN BOWL		
D25	●	Washington	28	6

BILL CURRY
1987-89 (.722) 26-10

1987 7-5-0 (4-2-0)

S5	●	Southern Miss *Birm*	38	6
S12	●	at Penn State	24	13
S19	│	Florida *Birm*	14	23
S26	● │	at Vanderbilt	30	23
O3	●	La. Lafayette *Birm*	38	10
O10		at Memphis	10	13
O17	● │	Tennessee *Birm*	41	22
O31	● │	Mississippi State *Birm*	21	18
N7	● │	at LSU	22	10
N14		at Notre Dame	6	37
N27	│	Auburn *Birm*	0	10
		HALL OF FAME BOWL		
J2		Michigan	24	28

1988 9-3-0 (4-3-0)

S10	●	at Temple	37	0
S24	● │	Vanderbilt	44	10
O1	● │	at Kentucky	31	27
O8	│	Mississippi	12	22
O15	● │	at Tennessee	28	20
O22	●	Penn State *Birm*	8	3
O29	● │	at Mississippi State	53	34
N5	│	LSU	18	19
N12	●	La. Lafayette *Birm*	17	0
N25	│	Auburn *Birm*	10	15
D1	●	at Texas A&M	30	10
		SUN BOWL		
D24	●	Army	29	28

1989 10-2-0 (6-1-0)

S16	●	Memphis *Birm*	35	7
S23	● │	Kentucky	15	3
S30	● │	at Vanderbilt	20	14
O7	● │	Mississippi *JaM*	62	27
O14	●	La. Lafayette	24	17
O21	● │	Tennessee *Birm*	47	30
O28	●	at Penn State	17	16
N4	● │	Mississippi State *Birm*	23	10
N11	● │	at LSU	32	16
N18	●	Southern Miss	37	14
D2	│	at Auburn	20	30
		SUGAR BOWL		
J1		Miami, Fla.	25	33

GENE STALLINGS
1990-96 (.810) 70-16-1

1990 7-5-0 (5-2-0)

S8		Southern Miss *Birm*	24	27
S15	│	Florida	13	17
S22	│	at Georgia	16	17
S29	● │	Vanderbilt	59	28
O6	●	at La. Lafayette	25	6
O20	● │	at Tennessee	9	6
O27		Penn State	0	9
N3	● │	at Mississippi State	22	0
N10	● │	LSU	24	3
N17	●	Cincinnati *Birm*	45	7
D1	● │	Auburn *Birm*	16	7
		FIESTA BOWL		
J1		Louisville	7	34

1991 11-1-0 (6-1-0)

S7	●	Temple *Birm*	41	3
S14	│	at Florida	0	35
S21	● │	Georgia	10	0
S28	● │	at Vanderbilt	48	17
O5	●	U.T. Chattanooga *Birm*	53	7
O12	●	Tulane	62	0
O19	● │	Tennessee *Birm*	24	19
N2	● │	Mississippi State	13	7
N9	● │	at LSU	20	17
N16	●	at Memphis	10	7
N30	● │	Auburn *Birm*	13	6
		BLOCKBUSTER BOWL		
D28	●	Colorado	30	25

1992 13-0-0 (8-0-0)

S5	● │	Vanderbilt	25	8
S12	●	Southern Miss *Birm*	17	10
S19	● │	Arkansas *LR*	38	11
S26	●	Louisiana Tech *Birm*	13	0
O3	● │	South Carolina	48	7
O10	●	at Tulane	37	0
O17	● │	at Tennessee	17	10
O24	● │	Mississippi	31	10
N7	● │	at LSU	31	11
N14	● │	at Mississippi State	30	21
N26	● │	Auburn *Birm*	17	0
		SEC CHAMPIONSHIP GAME		
D5	●	Florida *Birm*	28	21
		SUGAR BOWL		
J1	●	Miami, Fla.	34	13

1993 9-3-1 (5-2-1)

S4	●	Tulane *Birm*	31	17 †
S11	● │	at Vanderbilt	17	6 †
S18	● │	Arkansas	43	3 †
S25	●	Louisiana Tech *Birm*	56	3 †
O2	● │	at South Carolina	17	6 †
O16	= │	Tennessee *Birm*	17	17 †
O23	● │	at Mississippi	19	14 †
O30	●	Southern Miss	40	0 †
N6	│	LSU	13	17
N13	● │	Mississippi State	36	25 †
N20	│	at Auburn	14	22
		SEC CHAMPIONSHIP GAME		
D4		Florida *Birm*	13	28
		GATOR BOWL		
D31	●	North Carolina	24	10

1994 12-1-0 (8-0-0)

S3	●	U.T. Chattanooga *Birm*	42	13
S10	● │	Vanderbilt	17	7
S17	● │	at Arkansas	13	6
S24	●	Tulane *Birm*	20	10
O1	● │	Georgia *Birm*	29	28
O8	●	Southern Miss	14	6
O15	● │	at Tennessee	17	13
O22	● │	Mississippi	21	10
N5	● │	at LSU	35	17
N12	● │	at Mississippi State	29	25
N19	● │	Auburn *Birm*	21	14
		SEC CHAMPIONSHIP GAME		
D3		Florida *Atl*	23	24
		CITRUS BOWL		
J2	●	Ohio State	24	17

1995 8-3-0 (5-3-0)

S2	● │	at Vanderbilt	33	25
S9	●	Southern Miss *Birm*	24	20
S16	│	Arkansas	19	20
S30	● │	at Georgia	31	0
O7	●	North Carolina St.	27	11
O14	│	Tennessee *Birm*	14	41
O21	● │	at Mississippi	23	9
O28	●	North Texas	38	19
N4	● │	LSU	10	3
N11	● │	Mississippi State	14	9
N18	│	at Auburn	27	31

1996 10-3 (6-2)

A31	●	Bowling Green *Birm*	21	7
S7	●	Southern Miss *Birm*	20	10
S14	● │	Vanderbilt	36	26
S21	● │	Arkansas *LR*	17	7
O5	● │	Kentucky	35	7
O12	●	at North Carolina St.	24	19
O19	● │	Mississippi	37	0
O26	│	at Tennessee	13	20
N9	● │	at LSU	26	0
N16	│	at Mississippi State	16	17
N23	● │	Auburn *Birm*	24	23
		SEC CHAMPIONSHIP GAME		
D7		Florida *Atl*	30	45
		OUTBACK BOWL		
J1	●	Michigan	17	14

MIKE DUBOSE
1997-2000 (.511) 24-23

1997 4-7 (2-6)

A30	●	Houston *Birm*	42	17
S11	● │	at Vanderbilt	20	0
S20	│	Arkansas	16	17
S27	●	Southern Miss *Birm*	27	13
O4	│	at Kentucky	34	40
O18	│	Tennessee *Birm*	21	38
O25	● │	at Mississippi	29	20
N1		Louisiana Tech	20	26
N8	│	LSU	0	27
N15	│	Mississippi State	20	32
N22	│	at Auburn	17	18

1998 7-5 (4-4)

S5	●	Brigham Young	38	31
S12	● │	Vanderbilt *Birm*	32	7
S26	│	at Arkansas	6	42
O3	│	Florida	10	16
O10	● │	Mississippi	20	17
O17	●	East Carolina	23	22
O24	│	at Tennessee	18	35
O31	●	Southern Miss	30	20
N7	● │	at LSU	22	16
N14	│	at Mississippi State	14	26
N21	● │	Auburn *Birm*	31	17
		MUSIC CITY BOWL		
D29		Virginia Tech	7	38

1999 10-3 (7-1)

S4	● │	at Vanderbilt	28	17
S11	●	Houston *Birm*	37	10
S18		Louisiana Tech *Birm*	28	29
S25	● │	Arkansas	35	28
O2	● │	at Florida	40	39
O16	● │	at Mississippi	30	24
O23	│	Tennessee	7	21
O30	●	Southern Miss	35	14
N6	● │	LSU	23	17
N13	● │	Mississippi State	19	7
N20	● │	at Auburn	28	17
		SEC CHAMPIONSHIP GAME		
D4	●	Florida *Atl*	34	7
		ORANGE BOWL		
J1		Michigan	34	35

2000 3-8 (3-5)

S2		at UCLA	24	35
S9	● │	Vanderbilt *Birm*	28	10
S16		Southern Miss *Birm*	0	21
S23	│	at Arkansas	21	28
S30	● │	South Carolina	27	17
O14	● │	Mississippi	45	7
O21	│	at Tennessee	10	20
O28		Central Florida	38	40
N4	│	at LSU	28	30
N11	│	at Mississippi State	7	29
N18	│	Auburn	0	9

DENNIS FRANCHIONE
2001-02 (.680) 17-8

2001 7-5 (4-4)

S1		UCLA	17	20
S8	● │	at Vanderbilt	12	9
S22	● │	Arkansas	31	10
S29	│	at South Carolina	36	37
O6	●	Texas-El Paso *Birm*	56	7
O13	│	at Mississippi	24	27
O20	│	Tennessee	24	35
N3	│	LSU	21	35
N10	● │	Mississippi State	24	17
N17	● │	at Auburn	31	7
N29	●	Southern Miss *Birm*	28	15
		INDEPENDENCE BOWL		
D27	●	Iowa State	14	13

2002 10-3 (6-2)

A31	●	Middle Tennessee *Birm*	39	34
S7		at Oklahoma	27	37
S14	●	North Texas	33	7
S21	●	Southern Miss	20	7
S28	● │	at Arkansas	30	12
O5	│	Georgia	25	27
O19	● │	Mississippi	42	7
O26	● │	at Tennessee	34	14
N2	● │	at Vanderbilt	30	8
N9	● │	Mississippi State	28	14
N16	● │	at LSU	31	0
N23	│	Auburn	7	17
N30	●	at Hawaii	21	16

MIKE SHULA
2003-Present (.400) 10-15

2003 4-9 (2-6)

A30	●	South Florida *Birm*	40	17
S6		Oklahoma	13	20
S13	● │	Kentucky	27	17
S20		Northern Illinois	16	19
S27	│	Arkansas	31	34
O4	│	at Georgia	23	37
O11	●	Southern Miss	17	3
O18	│	at Mississippi	28	43
O25	│	Tennessee	43	51
N8	● │	at Mississippi State	38	0
N15	│	LSU	3	27
N22	│	at Auburn	23	28
N29		at Hawaii	29	37

2004   6-6 (3-5)

S4	●	Utah State	48	17
S11	● |	Mississippi	28	7
S18	●	Western Carolina	52	0
S25	|	at Arkansas	10	27
O2	|	South Carolina	3	20
O9	● |	at Kentucky	45	17
O16	●	Southern Miss	27	3
O23	|	at Tennessee	13	17
N6	● |	Mississippi State	30	14
N13	|	at LSU	10	26
N20	|	Auburn	13	21
MUSIC CITY BOWL				
D31		Minnesota	16	20

Neutral Site key: *NO* New Orleans, LA / *Lou* Louisville, KY / *JacF* Jacksonville, FL / *ERut* East Rutherford, NJ / *Birm* Birmingham, AL / *Fox* Foxboro, MA / *LR* Little Rock, AR / *GrnMS* Greenville, MS / *Mont* Montgomery, AL / *Abe* Aberdeen, MS / *Mer* Meridian, MS / *SF* San Francisco, CA / *NYC* New York, NY / *ColGa* Columbus, GA / *ColMs* Columbus, MS / *Colu* Columbia, SC / *Mob* Mobile, AL / *Atl* Atlanta, GA / *JaM* Jackson, MS
ƒ Forfeit † Game Later Forfeited # Disputed Victor * Disputed Score ‖ Designated Conference Game |2 Counted Twice in Conference Standings

ALABAMA ANNUAL STATISTICAL LEADERS

YR	RUSHING	YDS	ATT	AVG	PASSING	ATT	CMP	PCT	YDS	RECEIVING	REC	YDS	AVG
1937	Charley Holm	607	117	5.2	Joe Kilgrow	57	20	.35	302		NA	NA	NA
1938	Herky Mosley	465	78	6.0	Herky Mosley	63	28	.44	334		NA	NA	NA
1939	Paul Spencer	514	100	5.1	Herky Mosley	36	15	.42	172		NA	NA	NA
1940	Paul Spencer	503	104	4.8	Jimmy Nelson	43	21	.49	231	Holt Rast	8	110	13.8
1941	Jimmy Nelson	361	109	3.3	Jimmy Nelson	54	25	.46	394	Holt Rast	13	207	15.9
1942	Russ Craft	417	68	6.1	Russ Mosley	48	24	.50	352	Sam Sharp	13	240	18.5
1943		NA	NA	NA		NA	NA	NA	NA		NA	NA	NA
1944	Harry Gilmer	405	72	5.6	Harry Gilmer	66	32	.49	418	Hugh Morrow	10	107	10.7
1945	Lowell Tew	715	88	8.1	Harry Gilmer	88	57	.65	905	Rebel Steiner	18	315	17.5
1946	Harry Gilmer	497	133	3.7	Harry Gilmer	160	69	.43	930	Ted Cook	24	377	15.7
1947	Lowell Tew	571	107	5.3	Harry Gilmer	93	57	.61	610	Rebel Steiner	23	295	12.8
1948	Ed Salem	288	77	3.7	Ed Salem	110	52	.47	597	Bob Hood	7	150	21.4
1949	Tom Calvin	339	88	3.9	Ed Salem	75	40	.53	558	Al Lary	17	315	18.5
1950	Bobby Marlow	882	118	7.5	Ed Salem	86	44	.51	879	Al Lary	35	756	21.6
1951	Bobby Marlow	728	114	6.4	Clell Hobson	114	66	.58	847	Ken MacAfee	14	287	20.5
1952	Bobby Marlow	950	176	5.4	Clell Hobson	63	33	.52	336	Corky Tharp	10	115	11.5
1953	Corky Tharp	607	111	5.5	Bart Starr	119	59	.50	870	Bud Willis	11	191	17.4
1954	Corky Tharp	641	139	4.6	Albert Elmore	74	39	.53	499	Bobby Luna	16	304	19.0
1955	Clay Walls	164	49	3.3	Bart Starr	96	55	.57	587	Noojin Walker	14	154	11.0
1956	Don Comstock	316	76	4.2	Bobby Smith	40	16	.40	356	Charlie Gray	7	108	15.4
1957	Jim Loftin	477	106	4.5	Bobby Smith	83	32	.39	377	Willie Beck	9	126	14.0
1958	Bobby Jackson	472	143	3.3	Bobby Jackson	58	29	.50	408	Marlin Dyess	12	204	17.0
1959	Pat Trammell	525	156	3.4	Pat Trammell	49	21	.43	293	Marlin Dyess	10	149	14.9
1960	Pat Trammell	315	76	4.1	Robert Skelton	94	43	.46	575	Butch Wilson	13	204	15.7
1961	Mike Fracchia	652	130	5.0	Pat Trammell	133	75	.56	1,035	Richard Williamson	11	206	18.7
1962	Eddie Versprille	373	76	4.9	Joe Namath	146	76	.52	1,192	Richard Williamson	24	492	20.5
1963	Benny Nelson	612	97	6.3	Joe Namath	128	63	.49	765	Jimmy Dill	19	316	16.6
1964	Steve Bowman	536	106	5.1	Joe Namath	100	64	.64	757	David Ray	19	271	14.3
1965	Steve Bowman	770	153	5.0	Steve Sloan	160	97	.61	1,453	Tommy Tolleson	32	374	11.7
1966	Kenny Stabler	397	93	4.3	Kenny Stabler	114	74	.65	956	Ray Perkins	33	490	14.8
1967	Ed Morgan	388	103	3.8	Kenny Stabler	178	103	.58	1,214	Dennis Homan	54	820	15.2
1968	Ed Morgan	450	134	3.4	Scott Hunter	227	122	.54	1,471	George Ranager	31	499	16.1
1969	Johnny Musso	516	157	3.3	Scott Hunter	266	157	.59	2,188	David Bailey	56	781	13.9
1970	Johnny Musso	1,137	226	5.0	Scott Hunter	179	103	.58	1,240	David Bailey	55	790	14.4
1971	Johnny Musso	1,088	191	5.7	Terry Davis	66	42	.64	452	David Bailey	21	286	13.6
1972	Steve Bisceglia	603	125	4.8	Terry Davis	94	50	.53	777	Wayne Wheeler	30	573	19.1
1973	Wilbur Jackson	752	95	7.9	Gary Rutledge	57	33	.58	897	Wayne Wheeler	19	530	27.9
1974	Calvin Culliver	708	116	6.1	Richard Todd	67	36	.54	656	Ozzie Newsome	20	374	18.7
1975	Johnny Davis	820	123	6.7	Richard Todd	89	47	.53	661	Ozzie Newsome	21	363	17.3
1976	Johnny Davis	668	119	5.6	Jeff Rutledge	109	62	.57	979	Ozzie Newsome	25	529	21.2
1977	Johnny Davis	931	182	5.1	Jeff Rutledge	107	64	.60	1,207	Ozzie Newsome	36	804	22.3
1978	Tony Nathan	770	111	6.9	Jeff Rutledge	140	73	.52	1,078	Keith Pugh	20	446	22.3
1979	Steadman Shealy	791	152	5.2	Steadman Shealy	81	45	.56	717	Keith Pugh	25	433	17.3
1980	Billy Jackson	606	111	5.5	Don Jacobs	76	32	.42	531	Bart Kraut	16	218	13.6
1981	Ricky Moore	347	79	4.4	Walter Lewis	66	30	.46	633	Joey Jones	12	373	31.1
1982	Ricky Moore	600	111	5.4	Walter Lewis	164	102	.62	1,515	Joey Jones	25	502	20.1
1983	Ricky Moore	947	166	5.7	Walter Lewis	256	144	.56	1,991	Joey Jones	31	468	15.1
1984	Paul Carruth	782	163	4.8	Vince Sutton	135	60	.44	662	Greg Richardson	22	357	16.2
1985	Gene Jelks	588	93	6.3	Mike Shula	229	138	.60	2,009	Albert Bell	37	648	17.5
1986	Bobby Humphrey	1,471	236	6.2	Mike Shula	235	127	.54	1,486	Albert Bell	26	315	12.1
1987	Bobby Humphrey	1,255	238	5.3	Jeff Dunn	87	36	.41	484	Clay Whitehurst	18	278	15.4
1988	Murry Hill	778	136	5.7	David Smith	223	135	.61	1,592	Greg Payne	33	442	13.4
1989	Siran Stacy	1,079	216	5.0	Gary Hollingsworth	339	205	.61	2,379	Lamonde Russell	51	622	12.2
1990	Chris Anderson	492	106	4.6	Gary Hollingsworth	282	140	.50	1,463	Lamonde Russell	28	306	10.9
1991	Siran Stacy	966	200	4.8	Danny Woodson	101	64	.63	882	David Palmer	17	314	18.5
1992	Derrick Lassic	905	178	5.1	Jay Barker	243	132	.54	1,614	David Palmer	24	297	12.4
1993	Sherman Williams	738	168	4.4	Jay Barker	171	98	.57	1,524	David Palmer	61	1,000	16.4
1994	Sherman Williams	1,341	291	4.6	Jay Barker	226	139	.62	1,996	Curtis Brown	39	639	16.4
1995	Dennis Riddle	969	236	4.1	Brian Burgdorf	162	96	.59	1,200	Curtis Brown	43	557	13.0
1996	Dennis Riddle	1,079	242	4.5	Freddie Kitchens	302	152	.50	2,124	Michael Vaughn	39	702	18.0
1997	Curtis Alexander	729	155	4.7	Freddie Kitchens	237	121	.51	1,545	Quincy Jackson	28	472	16.9
1998	Shaun Alexander	1,178	258	4.6	Andrew Zow	256	143	.56	1,169	Quincy Jackson	48	621	12.9
1999	Shaun Alexander	1,383	302	4.6	Andrew Zow	264	148	.56	1,799	Freddie Milons	65	733	11.3
2000	Ahmaad Galloway	659	137	4.8	Andrew Zow	249	120	.48	1,561	Antonio Carter	45	586	13.0
2001	Ahmaad Galloway	881	174	5.1	Tyler Watts	172	94	.55	1,325	Freddie Milons	36	626	17.4
2002	Shaud Williams	921	130	7.1	Tyler Watts	181	112	.62	1,414	Triandos Luke	41	482	11.8
2003	Shaud Williams	1,367	280	4.9	Brodie Croyle	341	182	.53	2,303	Zach Fletcher	21	498	23.7
2004	Kenneth Darby	1,062	219	4.8	Spencer Pennington	152	82	.54	974	Tyrone Prothro	25	347	13.9

The NCAA began including postseason stats in 2002

ARIZONA

BY BUD WITHERS

THE SOUTHERNMOST MEMBER OF the Pac 10 Conference is also the league's most prominent anomaly. While the rest of the conference is known for its dizzying pass attacks and as a regular exporter of quarterbacks to the NFL, Arizona has played more of a traditional Midwestern brand of football. Its leading career passer, Tom Tunnicliffe, threw more interceptions than touchdown passes. The Wildcats have been more closely identified with a strong running attack and stout defense, not always to the satisfaction of a fan base that largely grew up someplace else and has adopted Arizona as a second team. Wildcats fans of all stripes rue the fact that their team has never played in the Rose Bowl.

TRADITION The winner of the Arizona-Arizona State game receives the Territorial Cup—the oldest rivalry trophy in the United States, dating back to 1899. In the finest tradition of college football trophies, it has been through the wringer; it was lost for a number of years before someone stumbled across it in the basement of a church that was about to be demolished. Meanwhile, beginning in 1938, the winner of the Arizona-New Mexico game was awarded the Kit Carson rifle, a trophy that was retired in 1997 because of its affront to Native Americans. Finally,

freshman students annually whitewash a 160-foot-high, 70-foot-wide "A" on 2,885-foot Sentinel Peak, west of Tucson.

BEST PLAYER Arizona probably didn't know what it was getting when a 17-year-old youngster migrated west to Tucson from Petersburg, Va., in 1980. By the time linebacker Ricky Hunley was finished in 1983, he had been in on a startling 566 tackles, was named All-Pac-10 three times and earned conference co-Defensive Player of the Year honors in 1983—enough to become Arizona's first and only player in the College Football Hall of Fame.

BEST COACH Other coaches had more victories—J.F. "Pop" McKale went 80–32–6 in the early years, and Dick Tomey won 95 games over 14 seasons—but Larry Smith had a more daunting assignment. When he was hired in 1980, the Wildcats were facing NCAA probation; they had been in the Pac-10 just two seasons and were an unknown quantity; and they had lost 13 of 15 in the series with hated Arizona State. Mostly with hard-nosed defense, Smith surmounted all three challenges, going 48–28–3 and beating ASU his last five seasons. Shortly after he coached Arizona's first bowl victory in 1986, Smith was hired at USC. He cleaned out his offices overnight without informing the players of his departure.

BEST TEAM In 1998, the Wildcats went 12–1, capping their best year with a 23-20 win over Nebraska in the

---

PROFILE

University of Arizona
Tucson, Ariz.
Founded: 1885
Enrollment: 28,482
Colors: Cardinal and Navy
Nickname: Wildcats
Stadium: Arizona Stadium
  Opened in 1929
  Grass; 56,002 capacity
First football game: 1899
All-time record: 522–378–33 (.577)
Bowl record: 5–7–1
Pac-10 Conference championships:
1 (shared)
Outland Trophy: Rob Waldrop, 1993
First-round NFL draftees: 7
Website: www.arizonaathletics.com

THE BEST OF TIMES

In its first period of sustained success since it joined the Pac-10 in 1978, Arizona went 31–13–2 in a four-year stretch from 1983 to 1986 under head coach Larry Smith.

THE WORST OF TIMES

A year after a near-mutiny over the style of head coach John Mackovic, the Wildcats had an early-season fortnight in 2003 against LSU, Oregon and Purdue in which they were outscored 166-30. Mackovic was fired in late September.

CONFERENCE

After time in the Border Conference (1931-60) and the Western Athletic Conference (1962-77), Arizona joined the Pac-10 along with Arizona State in 1978.

DISTINGUISHED ALUMNI

Joan Ganz Cooney, Children's Television Workshop founder; Greg Kinnear, actor; Geraldo Rivera, TV journalist; Richard Scobee, astronaut; Garry Shandling, actor/comedian; Morris Udall, U.S. congressman

FIGHT SONG

BEAR DOWN ARIZONA
Bear down, Arizona
Bear down, Red and Blue
Bear down, Arizona
Hit 'em hard, let 'em know who's who;
Bear down, Arizona
Bear down, Red and Blue
Go, go, Wildcats, go;
Arizona, bear down!

Holiday Bowl to earn a No. 4 ranking. Quarterback Keith Smith, who shared duties with Ortege Jenkins, had a school-record 174.2 pass efficiency rating. Running back Trung Canidate had an astonishing facility for the big play, scoring 10 of his 11 rushing touchdowns from 37 yards or longer. On defense, linebacker Marcus Bell excelled, as did cornerback Chris McAlister, who also won the Mosi Tatupu Award as the nation's top special-teams player. Even at 12–1, Arizona lost the Rose Bowl bid on a tiebreaker with UCLA.

BIGGEST GAME In the early 1990s, Tomey assembled defenses that were dubbed Desert Swarm in homage to the U.S. Desert Storm offensive in the Gulf War of 1991. Never was the defense so overwhelming on a national stage as in the 1994 Fiesta Bowl. A $5^1/_2$-point underdog, Arizona suffocated Miami 29-0, holding the 10th-ranked Hurricanes to a net offense of 182 yards and not allowing them inside the Arizona 40. It wasn't one of Miami's great teams, but the Canes were amply stocked with good athletes, making for a shocking end to the program's 168-game scoring streak. Said Miami coach Dennis Erickson, "They just kicked the living tar out of us."

BIGGEST UPSET When Arizona ventured to the Los Angeles Coliseum in 1981, USC tailback Marcus Allen was

Wildcats fans rue the fact their team has never played in the Rose Bowl.

headed toward a 2,427-yard season and a Heisman Trophy, and the No. 1-ranked Trojans were three-touchdown favorites over an Arizona team that would finish 6–5. Allen got his yards, finishing with 211 on 26 carries, but Arizona weathered an early 10-0 deficit and got close on two field goals by Brett Weber. Tunnicliffe flipped a 13-yard touchdown pass to Vance Johnson in the third quarter, and a defense led by Hunley and John Pace held the Trojans to 13 first downs and 297 total yards in a 13-10 upset. Said USC coach John Robinson, "We were outplayed and outcoached."

HEARTBREAKER Arizona has found some exasperating ways of keeping itself from the Rose Bowl, none more painful than against California on Nov. 13, 1993, when the Wildcats could have taken an undisputed league lead over USC and UCLA. After a 20-0 Arizona halftime lead melted to 20-17 with four minutes left, the Wildcats tried to run out the clock. Wide receiver Terry Vaughn was flagged for a personal foul for tossing the ball to an official, who, looking the other way, thought Vaughn was showing him up. That forced Arizona to try to throw for a first down, and Dan White's pass was tipped to Cal safety Eric Zomalt, who sped 35 yards for the winning score in a 24-20 game.

RECORDS

RUSHING YARDS

	GAME
288	Trung Canidate vs. Arizona State, Nov. 27, 1998 (18 att.)
	SEASON
1,602	Trung Canidate, 1999 (253 att.)
	CAREER
3,824	Trung Canidate, 1996-99 (604 att.)

PASSING YARDS

	GAME
492	Jason Johnson vs. California, Nov. 16, 2002 (31 of 45)
	SEASON
3,327	Jason Johnson, 2002 (239 of 410)
	CAREER
7,618	Tom Tunnicliffe, 1980-83 (574 of 1,069)

RECEIVING YARDS

	GAME
283	Jeremy McDaniel vs. California, Nov. 2, 1996 (14 rec.)
	SEASON
1,422	Dennis Northcutt, 1999 (88 rec.)
	CAREER
3,351	Bobby Wade, 1999-2002 (230 rec.)

POINTS

	GAME
32	Art Luppino vs. New Mexico State, Sept. 18, 1954 (5 TDs, 2 PATs)
	SEASON
166	Art Luppino, 1954 (24 TDs, 22 PATs)
	CAREER
360	Max Zendejas, 1982-85 (79 FGs, 123 PATs)

CONSENSUS ALL-AMERICANS

1941	Henry Stanton, E
1982-83	Ricky Hunley, LB
1987	Chuck Cecil, DB
1990	Darryll Lewis, DB
1992-93	Rob Waldrop, DL
1994	Steve McLaughlin, PK
1994	Tony Bouie, DB
1994-95	Tedy Bruschi, DL
1998	Chris McAlister, DB
1999	Dennis Northcutt, ALL-PURPOSE

BEST COMEBACK In his 14 seasons (1987-2000), Tomey sometimes motivated in unconventional ways. For instance, he was known to gather his team in a large circle just before kickoff and direct pairs of players to engage in fierce one-on-one hitting. In 1993, after his team fell behind Stanford 17-0 in the second quarter, he called a timeout and staged a verbal shakedown with his team encircling him. Arizona roared back to tie it, and with the score 24-24 in the waning moments, the Wildcats' Akil Jackson caused a fumble by Stanford quarterback Steve Stenstrom, setting up Steve McLaughlin's 27-yard field goal as time expired for a 27-24 victory.

WILDEST FINISH It was not only the most unforgettable climax to an Arizona game, but one of the most indelible in college history, when serendipity and sheer athleticism met at the west end of Washington's Husky Stadium in 1998. Down 28-24 with 2:52 left, Arizona took over at its 20. Quarterback Ortege Jenkins marshaled the Wildcats to the Washington 9 with 12 seconds remaining. No timeouts were left when Jenkins rolled to the right, broke back to the middle of the field and, at the 2, encountered three Washington defenders converging to make a game-ending stop. But as they crouched to tackle him, Jenkins made college football's most memorable somersault, going airborne and landing in the end zone to give the Wildcats a 31-28 victory. "I wasn't even looking at them, not really," Jenkins said. "I was just thinking, 'End zone, get in the end zone.'"

STADIUM Built in 1928 with a mere 7,000 seats, Arizona Stadium has undergone six expansions to its current capacity of 56,000. Gray and foreboding, it's not an edifice that reeks of character.

RIVAL In 1885, the Arizona Territorial Legislature placed a land-grant college in Tucson, while 120 miles north, Tempe got a teacher's college known as Tempe Normal. It was the start of an often-uneasy coexistence. The Arizona-Arizona State series has been punctuated by long stretches of dominance of one team over the other, with the mutual disdain spurred on by acts such as the time in 1937 when an Arizona State graduate wooed three prize freshman

recruits off the Arizona campus so he could enroll them in Tempe. Each school features a white "A" on a mountain outside its campus, which is the target of prank-minded painters from the rival school.

QUIRK For almost four decades, Art Luppino held the UA career rushing record, and for nearly as long, bitterness about his playing days. The Cactus Comet suffered an improperly treated concussion in 1954 and, two years later, a knee injury that went undiagnosed. In between, he was branded a malingerer by embattled coach Warren Woodson, who benched Luppino for a game in 1955, a year when Luppino led the nation in rushing. Luppino offered to quit, was forced to apologize to his teammates and, subsequently, carried ill feelings until reconciling with his old school in the early 1990s.

NICKNAME Bill Henry, a columnist for the *Los Angeles Times*, covered the Arizona-Occidental game in Southern California in 1914, writing, "The Arizona men showed the fight of wildcats." That was good enough for the Arizona student body, which quickly voted to adopt the name.

MASCOT Arizona's caged, live wildcat mascot gave way several decades ago to a student feline couple known as Wilbur and Wilma the Wildcat. Under signed agreement, they never reveal their identities until appearing at their final game, when they step out of a box with their headgear removed.

UNIFORMS At home, the Wildcats wear navy-blue jerseys, white pants with red piping and blue-and-white knee-length socks. Road jerseys are white with blue numerals. Helmets are white with red-and-blue striping and a red-and-blue block "A" on each side.

QUOTE "Tell them … tell the team to bear down … " —Last words of John Byrd "Button" Salmon, student-body president and quarterback, who died in a hospital shortly after a 1926 auto accident. The message, relayed to the Arizona football team by coach and athletic director J.F. "Pop" McKale, became the school slogan

ARIZONA ANNUAL STATISTICAL LEADERS

YR	RUSHING	YDS	ATT	AVG	PASSING	ATT	CMP	PCT	YDS	RECEIVING	REC	YDS	AVG
1958	Warren Livingston	187	63	3.0	Ralph Hunsaker	191	106	.55	1,129	Dave Hibbert	61	606	9.9
1959	Warren Livingston	380	57	6.7	Eddie Wilson	76	31	.41	476	Willie Peete	10	173	17.3
1960	Bobby Thompson	732	92	8.0	Eddie Wilson	116	62	.53	1,020	Joe Hernandez	24	440	18.3
1961	Bobby Thompson	752	103	7.3	Eddie Wilson	154	79	.51	1,294	Joe Hernandez	27	423	15.7
1962	Tom Kosser	415	64	6.5	Eddie Bricker	45	18	.40	313	Ken Cook	11	187	17.0
1963	Jim Oliver	214	49	4.4	Bill Brechler	82	34	.41	550	Floyd Hudlow	13	167	12.8
1964	Floyd Hudlow	402	73	5.5	Lou White	67	25	.37	419	Rickie Harris	28	391	14.0
1965	Brad Hubbert	526	133	4.0	Phil Albert	123	58	.47	559	Tim Plodinec	20	191	9.6
1966	Brad Hubbert	501	115	4.4	Mark Reed	365	193	.53	2,368	Jim Greth	76	1,003	13.2
1967	David Barajas	337	87	3.9	Bruce Lee	137	57	.42	635	Wally Scott	15	243	16.2
1968	Nokise Fuimaono	579	156	3.7	Mark Driscoll	152	62	.41	927	Ron Gardin	48	892	18.6
1969	Ron Gardin	759	188	4.0	Brian Linstrom	258	119	.46	1,598	Hal Arnason	30	489	16.3
1970	Willie Lewis	665	163	4.1	Brian Linstrom	141	59	.42	884	Hal Arnason	35	569	16.3
1971	Bob McCall	525	134	3.9	Bill Demory	199	91	.46	1,384	Charlie McKee	43	854	19.9
1972	Bob McCall	1,148	228	5.0	Bill Demory	174	76	.44	1,175	Barry Dean	22	414	18.8
1973	Jim Upchurch	1,184	210	5.6	Bruce Hill	216	104	.48	1,529	Theo Bell	47	790	16.8
1974	Jim Upchurch	1,004	216	4.6	Bruce Hill	249	133	.53	1,814	Theo Bell	53	700	13.2
1975	Dave Randolph	657	141	4.7	Bruce Hill	215	102	.47	1,747	Scott Piper	45	718	16.0
1976	Derriak Anderson	506	114	4.4	Marc Lunsford	132	70	.53	1,284	Keith Hartwig	54	1,134	21.0
1977	Derriak Anderson	568	122	4.7	Marc Lunsford	166	71	.43	1,344	Harry Holt	24	423	17.6
1978	Hubert Oliver	866	198	4.4	Jim Krohn	151	79	.52	996	Ron Beyer	21	296	14.1
1979	Hubert Oliver	1,021	197	5.2	Jim Krohn	175	93	.53	1,094	Tim Holmes	24	319	13.3
1980	Hubert Oliver	655	146	4.5	Tom Tunnicliffe	173	96	.55	1,204	Tim Holmes	33	545	16.5
1981	Vance Johnson	654	123	5.3	Tom Tunnicliffe	217	117	.54	1,420	Mark Keel	27	343	12.7
1982	Vance Johnson	443	111	4.0	Tom Tunnicliffe	328	176	.54	2,520	Brad Anderson	44	870	19.8
1983	Chris Brewer	586	114	5.1	Tom Tunnicliffe	351	185	.53	2,474	Jay Dobyns	50	694	13.9
1984	David Adams	750	188	4.0	Alfred Jenkins	312	156	.50	2,202	Jon Horton	45	880	19.6
1985	David Adams	511	138	3.7	Alfred Jenkins	278	150	.54	1,767	Jon Horton	43	685	15.9
1986	David Adams	1,175	238	4.9	Alfred Jenkins	232	118	.51	1,573	Derek Hill	32	523	16.3
1987	Ron Veal	566	161	3.5	Ron Veal	153	75	.49	1,239	Derek Hill	45	798	17.7
1988	Alonzo Washington	651	113	5.8	Ron Veal	105	40	.38	669	Derek Hill	25	508	20.3
1989	David Eldridge	788	143	5.5	Ron Veal	117	46	.39	517	Reggie McGill	11	170	15.5
1990	Art Greathouse	482	104	4.6	George Malauulu	101	46	.46	726	Terry Vaughn	22	431	19.6
1991	Billy Johnson	682	116	5.9	George Malauulu	99	52	.53	674	Terry Vaughn	21	270	12.9
1992	Ontiwaun Carter	739	195	3.8	George Malauulu	198	97	.49	1,210	Troy Dickey	28	395	14.1
1993	Ontiwaun Carter	837	178	4.7	Dan White	207	103	.50	1,410	Terry Vaughn	36	474	13.2
1994	Ontiwaun Carter	1,163	268	4.3	Dan White	296	169	.57	2,181	Richard Dice	56	969	17.3
1995	Gary Taylor	714	177	4.0	Dan White	297	150	.51	1,855	Rodney Williams	46	587	12.8
1996	Gary Taylor	564	120	4.7	Keith Smith	193	117	.61	1,450	Jeremy McDaniel	31	607	19.6
1997	Trung Canidate	804	138	5.8	Ortege Jenkins	235	115	.49	1,669	Dennis Northcutt	58	767	13.2
1998	Trung Canidate	1,220	167	7.3	Keith Smith	165	113	.68	1,732	Dennis Northcutt	63	922	14.6
1999	Trung Canidate	1,602	253	6.3	Keith Smith	228	131	.57	1,903	Dennis Northcutt	88	1,422	16.2
2000	Clarence Farmer	666	138	4.8	Ortege Jenkins	261	123	.47	1,647	Bobby Wade	45	626	13.9
2001	Clarence Farmer	1,229	209	5.9	Jason Johnson	298	169	.57	2,347	Bobby Wade	62	882	14.2
2002	Mike Bell	341	106	3.2	Jason Johnson	410	239	.58	3,327	Bobby Wade	93	1,389	14.9
2003	Mike Bell	920	168	5.5	Kris Heavner	237	121	.51	1,501	Biren Ealy	42	577	13.7
2004	Mike Bell	950	204	4.7	Richard Kovalcheck	136	67	.49	880	Syndric Steptoe	30	446	14.9

Receiving leaders by receptions
The NCAA began including postseason stats in 2002

ARIZONA ALL-TIME SCORES

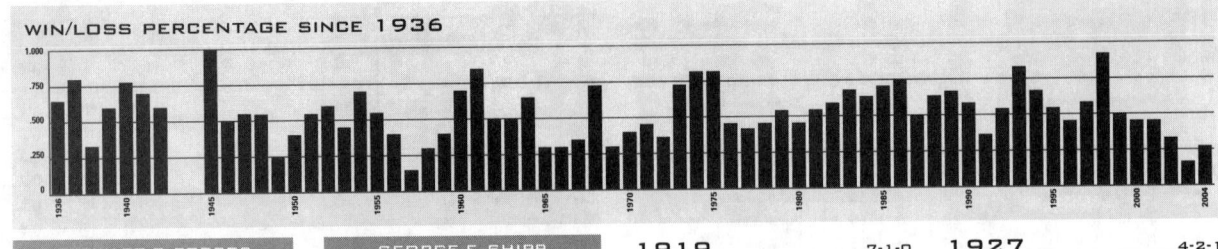

WIN/LOSS PERCENTAGE SINCE 1936

STEWART F. FORBES
1899 (.500)   1-1-1

1899   1-1-1
U	=	Tucson Town	0	0
U		Arizona State	2	11
U	●	Tucson	22	5

WILLIAM SKINNER
1900-01 (.778)   7-2

1900   3-1-0
U	●	Tucson Indians.	34	0
U	●	City of Tucson	45	0
U	●	Tucson Indians.	52	0
U		at Phoenix Indians	0	6

1901   4-1-0
U	●	Tucson Indians.	22	0
U	●	Tucson Indians.	47	6
U	●	Tucson Indians.	40	0
U		at Phoenix Indians Sch.	0	13
U	●	Phoenix Indians Sch.	6	0

LESLIE GILLETT
1902 (1.000)   5-0

1902   5-0-0
U	●	Tucson Indians. Sch.	17	0
U	●	Tucson Indians. Sch.	43	0
U	●	Fort Grant	28	0
U	●	Arizona State	12	0
U	●	Fort Huachuca NAC	34	0

ORIN A. KATES
1903-04 (.750)   5-1-2

1903   2-0-0
U	●	Tucson Indiansian Sch.	28	0
U	●	Tucson Indiansian Sch.	21	10

1904   3-1-2
U	=	Tucson Indiansian Sch	0	0
U	●	Tucson Indiansian Sch	6	5
U		at Phoenix H.S.	0	37
U	●	Tucson Indiansian Sch	26	0
U	●	Arizona I.S.	28	0
U	=	at Tombstone	6	6

WILLIAM M. RUTHRAUF
1905 (.667)   4-2

1905   4-2-0
U	●	at Phoenix Indians Sch.	34	0
U	●	Tucson Indians. Sch.	6	0
U	●	Tucson Indians. Sch.	22	0
U	●	Tombstone	17	0
U		Pomona	5	41
U		Loyola Marymount	0	55

1906-1907
NO TEAM

H.B. GALBREATH
1908-09 (.889)   8-1

1908   5-0-0
U	●	Tucson Indians.	27	0
U	●	Tucson Indians.	43	0
U	●	Tucson AC	36	0
U	●	Tucson Indians.	20	0
N26	●	at New Mexico	10	6 *

1909   3-1-0
U	●	Fort Huachuca	33	0
U	●	at New Mexico State	6	0
U	●	Prescott H.S.	21	0
N13		New Mexico	11	23

GEORGE F. SHIPP
1910-11 (.850)   8-1-1

1910   5-0-0
U	●	Tucson H.S.	21	0
U	●	El Paso Military	29	0
U	●	New Mexico State	18	2
U	●	at Tucson H.S.	18	6
N24	●	New Mexico	1	0 f

1911   3-1-1
U		at New Mexico State	0	3
U		at El Paso Military	5	0
U	=	Tucson H.S.	0	0
U	●	at Tucson H.S.	5	0
N30	●	at New Mexico	6	0

RAY L. QUIGLEY
1912 (.667)   2-1

1912   2-1-0
U	●	Tucson H.S	19	0
U	●	at New Mexico State	7	21 *
N30	●	at New Mexico	22	9 *

F.A. KING
1913 (.500)   2-2

1913   2-2-0
U	●	at New Mexico State	6	12
U	●	Phoenix Indians	13	0
U		Occidental	0	27
N21	●	at New Mexico	7	3

J.F. "POP" McKALE
1914-30 (.703)   80-32-6

1914   4-1-0
U	●	Douglas YMCA	21	0
U	●	Arizona State	34	0
U		at Occidental	0	14
U	●	at New Mexico State	10	0
U	●	Pomona	7	6

1915   5-3-0
O2	●	at Douglas YMCA	14	0
U	●	Arizona State	7	0
U	●	at Pomona	7	3
U	●	Phoenix Indians Sch.	56	0
U	●	22nd Infantry	49	0
U		at New Mexico State	0	3
U		at W. New Mexico	0	6
U		Whittier	0	22

1916   5-3-0
U	●	at Douglas YMCA	16	0
U	●	22nd Infantry	29	0
U		at Whittier	10	26
N4	●	Texas-El Paso	41	0
U	●	Phoenix Indians	55	0
U	●	New Mexico State	73	0
N30	●	at Rice	16	47 *
D9		Southern Cal PHO	7	20

1917   3-2-0
O20	●	at Southern Cal	6	31
U	●	at New Mexico State	26	7
U	●	U.S. Fld. Artillery	41	0
U		Camp Harry Jones	0	3
U	●	at Whittier	45	0

1918
NO TEAM WWI

1919   7-1-0
U	●	Arizona State	59	0
U	●	Phoenix Indians	60	0
U	●	Soldiers	20	0
U	●	at New Mexico State	33	0
U	●	Whittier	1	0 f
U		Pamona	7	19
N24	●	Texas-El Paso	46	0
U	●	Occidental	27	0

1920   6-1-0
U	●	Phoenix Indians	51	20
U	●	Camp Harry Jones	167	0
O30	●	at Texas-El Paso	60	7
U	●	New Mexico State	41	0
U		at Pomona	0	31
N20	●	New Mexico	28	7
U	●	Redlands	34	0

1921   7-2-0
U	●	Bisbee Legion	84	13
O15	●	Phoenix Indians	75	0
O22		at Texas A&M	13	17
O29	●	Texas-El Paso	74	0
N5	●	at New Mexico State	31	0
N19	●	at New Mexico	24	0
N24	●	N. M. Military	110	0
U	●	Whittier	7	0

CHRISTMAS BOWL
D26		Centre	0	38

1922   6-3-0
S30	●	at Texas-El Paso	18	0
U	●	Phoenix Indians	19	0
O14		at Southern Cal	0	15
U		at Santa Clara	7	8
N4	●	New Mexico State	21	7
U	●	Saint Mary's-Cal.	20	3
N18	●	New Mexico	10	0
N25		at Rice	7	14
D9	●	Utah State PHO	7	6

1923   5-3-0
O6	●	Phoenix Indians	48	0
O13	●	Phoenix JC	19	13
O20	●	Texas-El Paso	12	7
O27		at Saint Mary's-Cal.	20	22
N3	●	at New Mexico	14	7
N10	●	UC Davis PHO	7	9
N17		at Southern Cal	6	69
N29	●	Santa Clara	20	0

1924   2-4-0
O11		at Southern Cal	0	29
O18		at Utah	7	32
O25	●	New Mexico State	7	0
N1		at Nevada	14	23
N11		New Mexico	0	3
N27	●	at UC Davis	12	6

1925   3-3-1
O10	●	Arizona State	13	3
O16		Utah	0	9
O24		at Southern Cal	0	56
O31	●	New Mexico State	33	0
N7	●	at New Mexico	24	0
N14		at Texas	0	20
N26	=	Nevada	0	0

1926   5-1-1
O9	●	Phoenix JC	54	0
O16	●	Arizona State	35	0
O23	●	at New Mexico State	7	0
O30	●	Whittier	16	6
N6	●	New Mexico	21	0
N13	●	Occidental LA	7	9
N27	=	Colorado State	3	3

1927   4-2-1
O1	=	Occidental	14	14
O6	●	at Texas-El Paso	19	6
O22	●	E. Arizona JC	65	0
O29	●	New Mexico State	33	6
N5		at New Mexico	6	7
N19	●	UCLA	16	13
N24	●	Whittier	12	13

1928   5-1-2
S29	=	at UCLA	7	7
O13	●	Pomona	13	6
O20	●	at Arizona State	39	0
O27	●	at Texas-El Paso	12	6
N3	=	New Mexico	6	6
N10	●	at Southern Cal	7	78
N17	●	New Mexico State	40	0
N29	●	Whittier	28	7

1929   7-1-0
S27	●	Occidental PAS	16	7
O12	●	Cal Tech	35	0
O19	●	at Texas-El Paso	19	0
O26	●	New Mexico State	28	0
N2	●	Arizona State	26	0
N9		Pomona PHO	12	15
N23	●	at New Mexico	6	0
N28	●	Whittier	40	0

1930   6-1-1
O3	●	Cal Tech PAS	26	12
O11		at Rice	0	21
O18	●	Arizona State	6	0
O25	●	Occidental PHO	21	0
N1	●	Pomona	20	0
N8	=	at Texas-El Paso	0	0
N15	●	New Mexico	33	0
N29	●	Colorado State	16	0

1931-1960
BORDER

FRED A. ENKE
1931 (.389)   3-5-1

1931   3-5-1 (1-1-1)
S26		San Diego State	0	8
O3	●	Pomona	19	0
O10		at Oklahoma State	0	31
O23		Rice	0	32
O31		at Arizona State	6	19
N7		No. Arizona	19	12
N14	=	at New Mexico	7	7
N21	●	DePaul	14	13
N26		Colorado	7	27

A.W. "GUS" FARWICK
1932 (.444)   4-5

1932   4-5-0 (3-2-0)
S24	●	Occidental PAS	19	0
O1		Loyola Marymount	6	33
O8	●	New Mexico State	12	7
O14		at Texas Tech	0	21
O22	●	Arizona State	20	6
O29		No. Arizona PHO	6	7
N11	●	New Mexico	13	6
N19		at San Diego State	0	13
N26		Oklahoma State	6	13

G.A. "TEX" OLIVER
1933-37 (.723)   32-11-4

1933   5-3-0 (3-2-0)
S30	●	Occidental	18 0
O7		at Loyola Marymount	13 14
O14		Texas Tech	0 7
O27	●	at New Mexico State	6 0
N4	●	No. Arizona	24 0
N11		at New Mexico	0 7
N18	●	at Arizona State	26 7
N25	●	Whittier	26 0

1934   7-2-1 (2-1-1)
S29	●	San Diego State	7 0
O6	●	at Colorado State	7 3
O13		at Whittier	14 7
O20		Loyola Marymount	0 6
O26	=	New Mexico State	0 0
N3	●	New Mexico	14 6 *
N10	●	at Oklahoma City	26 6
N17	●	Arizona State	32 6
N29		Texas Tech	7 13 *
D7	●	Pacific Pho	31 7

1935   7-2-0 (4-0-0)
S28	●	Arizona State	26 0
O5	●	at Centenary	7 14
O12	●	Whittier	45 0
O19		at Loyola Marymount	6 13
O26	●	New Mexico State	9 6
N2	●	Oklahoma City	27 0
N11	●	at Texas Tech	7 6
N23	●	at New Mexico	38 6
N30	●	Drake	53 0

1936   5-2-3 (3-0-1)
S25	●	Brigham Young	32 6
O3		at Utah	6 14
O10	●	at Arizona State	18 0
O17	=	Centenary	13 13
O24	●	New Mexico State	28 7
O31	●	at Kansas	0 0
N7	●	New Mexico	28 0
N21	●	at Michigan State	0 7
N28	●	Wyoming Pho	58 0
D5	=	Texas Tech	7 7

1937   8-2-0 (3-1-0)
O2	●	Arizona State	20 6
O9	●	Oklahoma State	22 13
O16		at Texas Tech	0 20
O23		Centenary	13 18
O30	●	New Mexico State	27 12
N6		at Loyola Marymount	13 6
N13		at New Mexico	23 0
N20	●	Kansas	9 7
N27		Colorado State	47 0
D4	●	Oregon	20 6

ORIAN M. LANDRETH
1938 (.333)   3-6

1938   3-6-0 (0-3-0)
O1		at SMU	7 29
O8		New Mexico State	6 7
O15		Santa Clara Pho	0 27
O22	●	at Loyola Marymount	14 12
O29		New Mexico	7 20
N5	●	at Centenary	7 6
N12		Texas-El Paso	14 26
N19	●	Marquette	20 12
N26		Montana	0 7

MILES W. CASTEEL
1939-48 (.633)   46-26-3

1939   6-4-0 (1-2-0)
S23	●	Pomona	21 0
S30		at Minnesota	0 62
O14	●	New Mexico State	20 3
O21	●	Loyola Marymount Pho	25 7
O28		at Marquette	6 13
N4	●	Centenary	7 0
N11		at Texas-El Paso	6 14
N18	●	Pacific	12 7
N25		at New Mexico	6 7
N30	●	Montana	6 0

1940   7-2-0 (3-1-0)
S28	●	No. Arizona	41 0
O5	●	New Mexico State	41 0
O12		at Utah	0 24
O19	●	Centenary	29 0
O26	●	Oklahoma State	24 0
N2	●	at Texas-El Paso	20 13
N9	●	at Loyola Marymount	20 13
N23		New Mexico	12 13
N30	●	Marquette	17 14

1941   7-3-0 (5-0-0)
S27		at Notre Dame	7 38
O4	●	New Mexico State	47 0
O11	●	Reno	26 7
O18		at New Mexico	31 6
O25	●	at Arizona State	20 7
N1	●	Texas-El Paso	33 14
N8	●	No. Arizona	41 0
N22		at Oklahoma State	14 41
N29		Kansas State	28 21
D6		Utah	6 12

1942   6-4-0 (4-1-0)
S26	●	New Mexico State	53 0
O3		at Utah	14 0
O10	●	at Arizona State	23 0
O17	●	Oklahoma State	20 6
O24		at Marquette	0 39
N7	●	New Mexico	14 13
N14		Hardin-Simmons	26 34
N21	●	at Texas-El Paso	19 7 *
N26		Texas Tech	7 13
D5		Second Air Force	13 27

1943-1944
NO TEAM WWII

1945   5-0-0 (1-0-0)
S29	●	No. Arizona	52 6
O20	●	at San Diego State	46 0
O27	●	William Field	30 0
N3	●	Cal Tech	37 6
N17	●	San Diego State	28 0

1946   4-4-2 (2-2-1)
S28	●	Arizona State	67 0
O5		at Utah	7 14
O12	●	Texas-El Paso	27 13
O19	●	Pacific	47 13
O26		at Marquette	0 20
N2		Hardin-Simmons	8 19
N9	=	Santa Clara	21 21
N16		at New Mexico	13 13
N23		Texas Tech	0 16
N30	●	Kansas State	28 7

1947   5-4-1 (3-2-0)
S27	●	Wyoming	27 7
O4	●	Montana	40 7
O11		at Hardin-Simmons	7 35
O18	●	at Texas-El Paso	14 13
O25	●	New Mexico	22 12
N8		at Texas Tech	28 41
N15	●	at Arizona State	26 13
N22		Marquette	21 39
N29		Kansas	28 54
D6	=	Utah	20 20

1948   6-5-0 (3-2-0)
S25	●	San Diego State	14 6
O2		at Utah	14 47
O9	●	Hardin-Simmons	20 14
O16		at Michigan State	7 61
O23		Texas Tech	0 31
O30	●	Arizona State	33 21
N6	●	at New Mexico	14 6
N13	●	Texas-El Paso	14 25
N20	●	Iowa State	14 7
N27	●	Marquette Pho	24 14
		SALAD BOWL	
J1		Drake	13 14

ROBERT E. WINSLOW
1949-51 (.403)   12-18-1

1949   2-7-1 (2-4-0)
S24		New Mexico State	40 7
O1	=	Utah	12 12
O8		at Hardin-Simmons	0 35
O15		Texas-El Paso	0 28
O22		at Texas Tech	7 27
O29		at Denver	6 20
N5	●	New Mexico	46 14
N12		at Arizona State	7 34
N19		Michigan State	0 75
N26		Kansas	0 46

1950   4-6-0 (2-3-0)
S23		Western Texas	26 34
S30		at Utah	14 27
O7	●	Hardin-Simmons	32 28
O14		at Texas-El Paso	13 14
O21		at Colorad	25 28
O28		Denver	19 14
N4		at New Mexico	38 0
N11		Arizona State	13 47
N18		Texas Tech	7 39
N25	●	Iowa State	27 26

1951   6-5-0 (4-2-0)
S15	●	New Mexico State	67 13
S22		Utah	7 27
S29		at Oregon	21 39
O6	●	West Texas State	28 13
O13	●	Texas-El Paso	19 15
O27		at Texas Tech	0 41
N3	●	New Mexico	32 20
N10		at Arizona State	14 61
N17	●	Idaho	13 6
N24		at Hardin-Simmons	13 14
D21	●	at Hawaii	32 21

WARREN WOODSON
1952-56 (.540)   26-22-2

1952   6-4-0 (3-2-0)
S20	●	Hawaii	57 7
S27	●	New Mexico State	62 12
O4	●	at Utah	27 0
O11		Colorado	19 34
O18		at Marquette	7 37
O25	●	Hardin-Simmons	13 12
N1	●	at New Mexico	13 7
N8		Arizona State	18 20
N15	●	at Texas-El Paso	55 7
N22		Texas Tech	14 19

1953   4-5-1 (3-2-0)
S19		Utah	7 28
S26		at Colorado	14 20
O3	●	New Mexico State	46 7
O10	●	New Mexico	20 0
O17		Marquette	0 14
O31	●	West Texas State	39 6
N7		at Texas Tech	27 52
N14		Texas-El Paso	20 28
N21	=	Kansas State	26 26
N28	●	at Arizona State	35 0

1954   7-3-0 (3-2-0)
S18	●	New Mexico State	58 0
S25	●	at Utah	54 20
O9		Colorado	18 40
O16	●	Idaho	35 13
O23	●	at New Mexico	41 7
O30	●	West Texas State	48 12
N6		Texas Tech	14 28
N13		at Texas-El Paso	21 41
N20	●	Arizona State	54 14
N27	●	Wyoming	42 40

1955   5-4-1 (1-2-1)
S17	●	Colorado State	20 7
S24		at Colorado	0 14
O1	●	Idaho	47 14
O8	=	West Texas State	20 20
O15		Texas-El Paso	0 29
O22		Oregon	27 46
N5		at Texas Tech	7 27
N12	●	Montana	29 0
N19	●	New Mexico	27 6
N26		at Arizona State	7 6

1956   4-6-0 (1-2-0)
S15	●	Montana Pho	27 12
S22		Wyoming	20 26
S29	●	South Dakota State	60 0
O6		Utah State	7 12
O13		at Texas-El Paso	6 28
O20	●	at New Mexico	26 12
O27		Texas Tech	20 13
N3	●	West Texas State	20 13
N17		Arizona State	0 20
N24		Colorado	7 38

EDWARD A. DOHERTY
1957-58 (.225)   4-15-1

1957   1-8-1 (0-4-0)
S21		Brigham Young	14 14
S28		at Missouri	13 35
O12		at Colorado	14 34
O19		New Mexico	0 27
O26		Texas Tech	6 28
N2		West Texas State	20 21
N9		Hardin-Simmons	20 28
N16		Texas-El Paso	14 51
N23	●	Marquette	17 14
N30		at Arizona State	7 47

1958   3-7-0 (2-1-0)
S20	●	Utah State	7 6
S27		Iowa State	0 14
O4		at Tulsa	0 34
O11		Colorado	12 65
O18		at New Mexico	13 33
O25		Idaho	16 24
N1	●	West Texas State	15 8
N8		at Texas Tech	6 33
N15	●	at Texas-El Paso	14 12
N22		Arizona State	0 47

JIM LaRUE
1959-66 (.525)   41-37-2

1959   4-6-0 (2-1-0)
S19		Brigham Young	14 18
S26		at West Texas State	7 6
O3	●	Idaho	16 14
O17		New Mexico	7 28
O24		Colorado	0 18
O31		at Utah	6 54
N7	●	Texas Tech	30 26
N14		Air Force Bou	15 22
N21	●	Texas-El Paso	14 10
N28		at Arizona State	9 15

1960   7-3-0 (3-0-0)
S24		Utah	3 13
O1	●	Wyoming	21 19
O8		at Colorado	16 35
O15		Tulsa	16 17
O22	●	at New Mexico	26 14
O29	●	West Texas State	21 14
N5	●	Idaho	32 3
N12	●	at Texas-El Paso	28 14
N19	●	Kansas State	35 16
N26	●	Arizona State	35 7

1961
INDEPENDENT

1961   8-1-1
S23	●	Colorado State	28 6
S30	=	at Nebraska	14 14
O7	●	Hardin-Simmons	53 7
O14	=	Oregon Port	15 6
O21	●	New Mexico	22 21
O28		at West Texas State	23 27
N4	●	Wyoming	20 15
N11	●	Idaho Boi	43 7
N18	●	Texas-El Paso	48 15
N25	●	at Arizona State	22 13

1962-1977
WAC

1962   5-5-0 (2-2-0)
S22	●	Brigham Young	27 21
S29		at New Mexico	25 35
O6		at Missouri	7 17
O13		Air Force	6 20
O20		at Wyoming	8 31
O27	●	West Texas State	8 3
N3		Idaho	12 14
N10	●	Kansas State	14 13
N17	●	at Texas-El Paso	7 0
N24	●	Arizona State	20 17

1963   5-5-0 (2-2-0)*
S21		Utah State	0 42
S28		Brigham Young	33 7
O5		Washington State Spo	2 7
O12		Texas-El Paso	13 7
O19		Oregon	12 28
O26	●	at West Texas State	6 3
N2	●	Wyoming	15 7
N9	●	Idaho	34 7
N30		at Arizona State	6 35
D7		New Mexico	15 22

92 ARIZONA

THE SCHOOLS

1964 6-3-1 (3-1-0)

S26	● |	Brigham Young	39	6
O3	●	Washington State	28	12
O10	|	at New Mexico	7	10
O17		at Oregon	0	21
O23	● |	Wyoming	15	7
O31		at Air Force	0	7
N7	●	Idaho	14	7
N14	●	at Texas-El Paso	14	0
N21	=	Iowa State	0	0
N28	● |	Arizona State	30	6

1965 3-7-0 (1-4-0)

S18	● |	at Utah	16	9
S25	●	at Kansas	23	15
O2	|	at Wyoming	0	19
O9	|	New Mexico	2	24
O16		Washington State Spo	3	21
O23		San Jose State	7	13
N6	●	Texas-El Paso	10	3
N13		Air Force	7	34
N20	|	Brigham Young	3	20
N27	|	at Arizona State	6	14

1966 3-7-0 (1-4-0)

S17		at Iowa	20	31
S24		Kansas	13	35
O1	|	at Wyoming	6	36
O8	● |	at New Mexico	36	15
O22	|	Utah	19	24
O29	|	Brigham Young	14	16
N5		Oregon State Port	12	31
N12	●	Washington State	28	18
N19	●	Iowa State	27	24
N26	|	Arizona State	17	20

DARRELL MUDRA
1967-68 (.548) 11-9-1

1967 3-6-1 (1-4-0)

S16	|	Wyoming	17	36
S30	●	at Ohio State	14	7
O7		at Missouri	3	17
O14	=	Texas-El Paso	9	9
O21	|	Utah	29	33
O28		Indiana	7	42
N4	● |	New Mexico	48	13
N11	|	at Brigham Young	14	17
N18	●	Air Force	14	10
N25	|	at Arizona State	7	47

1968 8-3-0 (5-1-0)

S21	●	at Iowa State	21	12
S28	● |	at New Mexico	19	8
O5	● |	Texas-El Paso	25	0
O19	● |	Brigham Young	19	3
O26		at Indiana	13	16
N2	●	Washington State	28	14
N9	●	at Air Force	14	10
N16	● |	at Utah	16	15
N23	● |	Wyoming	14	7
N30	|	Arizona State	7	30
		SUN BOWL		
D28		Auburn	10	34

ROBERT W. WEBER
1969-72 (.381) 16-26

1969 3-7-0 (3-3-0)

S20	|	at Wyoming	7	23
S27		Kansas State	27	42
O4		at Iowa	19	31
O11		Houston	17	34
O18	● |	Texas El Pas	26	10
O25	● |	New Mexico	52	28
N1	|	at Brigham Young	21	31
N8		at Syracuse	0	23
N15	● |	Utah	17	16
N29	|	at Arizona State	24	38

1970 4-6-0 (2-4-0)

S19		at Michigan	9	20
S26	●	San Jose State	30	29
O3	●	Iowa	17	10
O10	● |	Brigham Young	24	17
O24	|	at Utah	0	24
O31		Air Force	20	23
N7	|	at New Mexico	7	35
N14	|	at Texas-El Paso	17	33
N21	● |	Wyoming	38	12
D5	|	Arizona State	6	10

1971 5-6-0 (3-3-0)

S18	●	Washington State Spo	39	28
S25	● |	at Texas-El Paso	14	6
O2		Texas Tech	10	13
O9	|	at Wyoming	3	14
O16		UCLA	12	28
O23	● |	Utah	14	3
O30	|	New Mexico	28	34
N6	●	Oregon State	34	22
N13	● |	at Brigham Young	27	14
N20		at San Diego State	10	39
N27	|	at Arizona State	0	31

1972 4-7-0 (4-3-0)

S9	● |	Colorado State	17	0
S16		at Oregon	7	34
S23		Washington State	6	28
O7		at UCLA	31	42
O14	● |	at New Mexico	27	15
O21		at Texas Tech	10	35
O28	● |	Texas-El Paso	45	22
N4	|	at Utah	27	28
N11	● |	Brigham Young	21	7
N18	|	Wyoming	14	22
N25	|	Arizona State	21	38

JAMES C. YOUNG
1973-76 (.705) 31-13

1973 8-3-0 (6-1-0)

S8	● |	at Colorado State	31	0
S15	● |	at Wyoming	21	7
S22	●	Indiana	26	10
O6	●	at Iowa	23	20
O13	● |	New Mexico	22	14
O20		Texas Tech	17	31
O27	● |	Utah	42	21
N3	● |	at Texas-El Paso	35	18
N10	● |	at Brigham Young	24	10
N17		Air Force	26	27
N25	|	at Arizona State	19	55

1974 9-2-0 (6-1-0)

S14	●	San Diego State	17	10
S21	●	at Indiana	35	20
S28	● |	at New Mexico	15	10
O5	● |	Texas-El Paso	42	13
O12	● |	at Utah	41	8
O19		at Texas Tech	8	17
O26	|	Brigham Young	13	37
N9	● |	Colorado State	34	21
N16	●	at Air Force	27	24
N23	● |	Wyoming	21	14
N30	● |	Arizona State	10	0

1975 9-2-0 (5-2-0)

S20	●	Pacific	16	0
S27	● |	at Wyoming	14	0
O4	●	Northwestern	41	6
O11	● |	at Texas-El Paso	36	0
O18	● |	Texas Tech	32	28
O25	|	New Mexico	34	44
N1	● |	at Brigham Young	36	20
N8	●	at San Diego State	31	24
N15	● |	at Colorado State	31	9
N22	● |	Utah	38	14
N29	|	at Arizona State	21	24

1976 5-6-0 (3-4-0)

S11	●	Auburn	31	19
S18		at UCLA	9	37
S25	|	Brigham Young	16	23
O2	●	at Northwestern	27	15
O9	● |	Texas-El Paso	63	12
O23		at Texas Tech	27	52
O30	● |	at Utah	38	35
N6	|	Wyoming	24	26
N13	● |	Colorado State	23	6
N20	|	at New Mexico	15	21
N27	|	Arizona State	10	27

TONY MASON
1977-79 (.471) 16-18-1

1977 5-7-0 (3-4-0)

S10		at Auburn	10	21
S17		San Diego State	14	21
S24	●	at Iowa	41	7
O1	|	at Wyoming	12	13
O8		Texas Tech	26	32
O22	● |	Utah	45	17
O29	|	at Brigham Young	14	34
N5	|	Colorado State	14	35
N12	● |	New Mexico	15	13
N19	● |	at Texas-El Paso	41	24
N26	|	at Arizona State	7	23
D3	●	at Hawaii	17	10

1978-PRESENT
PAC 10

1978 5-6-0 (3-4-0)

S9	●	Kansas State	31	0
S16	● |	Oregon State	21	7
S23		at Texas Tech	26	41
S30	●	Iowa	23	3
O7		at Michigan	17	21
O14	|	California	20	33
O27	|	at UCLA	14	24
N4	|	at Washington	21	31
N11	● |	at Oregon	24	3
N18	● |	Washington State	31	24
N25	|	Arizona State	17	18

1979 6-5-1 (4-3-0)

S1	●	Colorado State	33	17
S8	● |	Washington State Spo	22	7
S15	|	California	7	10
S22	=	Texas Tech	14	14
S29	●	San Jose State	38	18
O13	● |	Oregon	24	13
O20	|	Stanford	10	30
N3	|	at Southern Cal	7	34
N10		at San Diego State	10	42
N17	● |	Oregon State	42	18
N24	● |	at Arizona State	27	24
		FIESTA BOWL		
D25		Pittsburgh	10	16

LARRY SMITH
1980-86 (.627) 48-28-3

1980 5-6-0 (3-4-0)

S20		Colorado State	13	15
S27	● |	at California	31	24
O4	●	at Iowa	5	3
O11	|	Southern Cal	10	27
O18	|	Washington State	14	38
O25		Notre Dame	3	20
N1	● |	UCLA	23	17
N8	|	at Washington	22	45
N15	●	Pacific	63	35
N22	● |	at Oregon State	24	7
N29	|	Arizona State	7	44

1981 6-5-0 (4-4-0)

S12	|	UCLA	18	35
S19	|	California	13	14
S26	●	Fullerton State	37	16
O3	● |	Stanford	17	13
O10	● |	at Southern Cal	13	10
O17	● |	at Oregon	18	14
O24	|	Washington State	19	34
O31	●	Texas-El Paso	48	15
N14	● |	at Oregon State	40	7
N21		Fresno State	17	23
N28	|	at Arizona State	13	24

1982 6-4-1 (4-3-1)

S11	● |	Oregon State	38	12
S18	|	Washington	13	23
S25		Iowa	14	17
O9	= |	at UCLA	24	24
O16	●	at Notre Dame	16	13
O23	●	Pacific	55	7
O30	● |	at Washington State	34	17
N6	● |	at Stanford	41	27
N13	|	Southern Cal	41	48
N20	|	at Oregon	7	13
N27	● |	Arizona State	28	18

1983 7-3-1 (4-3-1)

S3	● |	Oregon State	50	6
S10	●	Utah	38	0
S17	● |	at Washington State	45	6
S24	●	Fullerton State	37	10
O1	= |	at California	33	33
O8	●	Colorado State	52	21
O15	|	Oregon	10	19
O22	|	at Stanford	22	31
N5	|	Washington	22	23
N12	● |	UCLA	27	24
N26	● |	at Arizona State	17	15

1984 7-4-0 (5-2-0)

S1		Fresno State	22	27
S8	● |	California	23	13
S15	● |	Oregon State Spo	27	8
S22		at LSU	26	27
S29	●	Long Beach State	31	24
O6	● |	Oregon	28	14
O20	|	at Southern Cal	14	17
O27	|	at Washington	12	28
N3	●	Utah State	45	10
N10	● |	Stanford	28	14
N24	● |	Arizona State	16	10

1985 8-3-1 (5-2-0)

S7	●	Toledo	23	10
S14	● |	Washington State	12	7
S21	● |	at California	23	17
S28		Colorado	13	14
O5	●	SMU	28	6
O19	●	San Jose State	41	0
O26	|	at Stanford	17	28
N2	● |	at Oregon State	27	6
N9	|	UCLA	19	24
N16	● |	Oregon	20	8
N23	● |	at Arizona State	16	13
		SUN BOWL		
D28	=	Georgia	13	13

1986 9-3-0 (5-3-0)

S6	●	Houston	37	3
S13	●	Colorado State	37	10
S20	● |	at Oregon	41	17
S27	●	at Colorado	24	21
O11	|	at UCLA	25	32
O18	● |	Oregon State	23	12
O25	● |	California	33	16
N1	|	Southern Cal	13	20
N8	● |	at Washington State	31	6
N22	● |	Arizona State	34	17
N30	|	Stanford Tok	24	29
		ALOHA BOWL		
D27	●	North Carolina	30	21

DICK TOMEY
1987-2000 (.595) 95-64-4

1987 4-4-3 (2-3-3)

S12		Iowa	14	15
S19	●	New Mexico	20	9
S26	|	at UCLA	24	34
O3	●	Bowling Green	45	7
O10	= |	at California	23	23
O17	● |	Oregon State	31	17
O24	|	at Washington State	28	45
O31	● |	at Stanford	23	13
N7	= |	Washington	21	21
N14	|	at Southern Cal	10	12
N28	= |	at Arizona State	24	24

1988 7-4-0 (5-3-0)

S3	● |	at Oregon State	24	13
S10	●	Texas Tech	35	19
S17		at Oklahoma	10	28
S24	●	Ea. Michigan	55	0
O1	|	Southern Cal	15	38
O15	● |	Washington State	45	28
O22	|	UCLA	3	24
O29	|	California	7	10
N5	● |	at Washington	16	13
N12	● |	Oregon	41	27
N26	● |	Arizona State	28	18

1989 8-4-0 (5-3-0)

S2	● |	Stanford	19	3
S9		at Texas Tech	14	24
S16	●	Oklahoma	6	3
S23	● |	Washington	20	17
S30	|	at Oregon	10	16
O14	● |	UCLA	42	7
O21	● |	at Washington State	23	21
O28	●	Pacific	38	14
N4	|	at California	28	29
N11	|	Southern Cal	3	24
N25	● |	at Arizona State	28	10
		COPPER BOWL		
D31	●	North Carolina State	17	10

1990 7-5-0 (5-4-0)

S8	●	Illinois	28	16
S15	●	at New Mexico	25	10
S22	● |	Oregon	22	17
S29	|	California	25	30
O6	● |	at UCLA	28	21
O13	|	at Oregon State	21	35
O20	● |	at Southern Cal	35	26
O27	● |	Washington State	42	34
N3	|	at Washington	10	54
N10		Stanford	10	23
N24	● |	Arizona State	21	17
		ALOHA BOWL		
D25		Syracuse	0	28

1991   4-7-0 (3-5-0)

S7		at Ohio State	14	38
S14	●	Stanford	28	23
S21		California	21	23
S28	●	Long Beach St	45	21
O5		at Washington	0	54
O12		at UCLA	14	54
O26		Miami, Fla.	9	36
N2	●	Oregon State	45	21
N9		at Washington St	27	40
N16	●	Southern Cal	31	14
N23		at Arizona State	14	37

1992   6-5-1 (4-3-1)

S5	●	Utah State	49	3
S12		Washington State	20	23
S19	=	at Oregon State	14	14
S26		at Miami, Fla.	7	8
O3	●	UCLA	23	3
O17	●	at Stanford	21	6
O24	●	at California	24	17
O31	●	New Mexico St	30	0
N7	●	Washington	16	3
N14		at Southern Cal	7	14
N21		Arizona State	6	7
		SUN BOWL		
D31		Baylor	15	20

1993   10-2-0 (6-2-0)

S4	●	Texas-El Paso	24	6
S11	●	Pacific	16	13
S18	●	at Illinois	16	14
S25		at Oregon State	33	0
O2	●	Southern Cal	38	7
O16	●	Stanford	27	24
O23	●	Washington State	9	6
O30		at UCLA	17	37
N6	●	Oregon	31	10
N13		at California	20	24
N26	●	at Arizona State	34	20
		FIESTA BOWL		
J1	●	Miami, Fla.	29	0

1994   8-4-0 (6-2-0)

S1	●	at Georgia Tech	19	14
S10	●	New Mexico State	44	0
S24	●	at Stanford	34	10
O1	●	Oregon State	30	10
O8		Colorado State	16	21
O15	●	at Washington State	10	7
O22	●	UCLA	34	24
O29		at Oregon	9	10
N5	●	California	13	6
N12		at Southern Cal	28	45
N25	●	Arizona State	28	27
		FREEDOM BOWL		
D27		Utah	13	16

1995   6-5-0 (4-4-0)

S2	●	Pacific	41	9
S7	●	Georgia Tech	20	19
S16		at Illinois	7	9
S23		Southern Cal	10	31
S30	●	California	20	15
O14		at UCLA	10	17
O21		Washington	17	31
O28	●	at Washington State	24	14
N4	●	at Oregon State	14	9
N11		Oregon	13	17
N24	●	at Arizona State	31	28

1996   5-6 (3-5)

A31	●	Texas-El Paso	23	3
S7		at Iowa	20	21
S14	●	Illinois	41	0
S21		at Washington	17	31
O5	●	Washington State	34	26
O12		at Southern Cal	7	14
O26	●	Oregon State	33	7
N2		at California	55	56
N9		at Oregon	31	49
N16	●	UCLA	35	17
N23		Arizona State	14	56

1997   7-5 (4-4)

S4		at Oregon	9	16
S13	●	UAB	24	10
S20		at Ohio State	20	28
S27		at UCLA	27	0
O4	●	San Diego State	31	28
O11	●	Stanford	28	22
O18		Washington	28	58
O25		at Washington State	34	35
N8	●	Oregon State	27	7
N15	●	California	41	38
N28	●	at Arizona State	28	16
		INSIGHT.COM BOWL		
D27	●	New Mexico	20	14

1998   12-1 (7-1)

S3		at Hawaii	27	6
S12	●	at Stanford	31	14
S19	●	Iowa	35	11
S24	●	at San Diego State	35	16
O3	●	at Washington	31	28
O10		UCLA	28	52
O17	●	at Oregon State	28	7
O24	●	La. Monroe	45	7
O31	●	Oregon	38	3
N7	●	Washington State	41	7
N14	●	at California	27	23
N27	●	Arizona State	50	42
		HOLIDAY BOWL		
D30	●	Nebraska	23	20

1999   6-6 (3-5)

A28		at Penn State	7	41
S5	●	at TCU	35	31
S11		Middle Tennessee	34	19
S18		Stanford	22	50
S25	●	at Washington State	30	24
O9	●	Southern Cal	31	24
O16	●	Texas-El Paso	34	21
O23		Oregon	41	44
O30	●	at UCLA	33	7
N6		Washington	25	33
N13		at Oregon State	20	28
N27		at Arizona State	27	42

2000   5-6 (3-5)

S2	●	at Utah	17	3
S9		Ohio State	17	27
S16	●	San Diego State	17	3
S30	●	at Stanford	27	3
O7	●	at Southern Cal	31	15
O14	●	Washington State	53	47
O21		at Oregon	10	14
O28		UCLA	24	27
N4		at Washington	32	35
N11		Oregon State	9	33
N24		Arizona State	17	30

2001   5-6 (2-6)

A30	●	at San Diego State	23	10
S8	●	Idaho	36	29
S22	●	Nevada-Las Vegas	38	21
S29		Washington State	21	48
O6		Oregon	28	63
O13		at Oregon State	3	38
O20		at Washington	28	31
O27		Southern Cal	34	41
N3	●	at California	38	24
N10		Stanford	37	51
N23	●	at Arizona State	34	21

2002   4-8 (1-7)

A31	●	No. Arizona	37	3
S14	●	Utah	23	17
S21		at Wisconsin	10	31
S28	●	North Texas	14	9
O5		Oregon	14	31
O12		at Washington	28	32
O19		at Stanford	6	16
O26		Washington State	13	21
N2		at Oregon State	3	38
N9		UCLA	7	37
N16	●	at California	52	41
N29		Arizona State	20	34

2003   2-10 (1-7)

A30	●	Texas-El Paso	42	7
S6		LSU	13	59
S13		Oregon	10	48
S20		at Purdue	7	59
S27		TCU	10	13
O4		at Washington State	7	30
O11		UCLA	21	24
O25		at California	14	42
N1		at Oregon State	23	52
N8	●	Washington	27	22
N15		Southern Cal	0	45
N28		at Arizona State	7	28

2004   3-8 (2-6)

S4	●	No. Arizona	21	3
S11		Utah	6	23
S18		Wisconsin	7	9
S25		Washington State	19	20
O9		at UCLA	17	37
O16		at Oregon	14	28
O23		California	0	38
O30		Oregon State	14	28
N6	●	at Washington	23	13
N13		at Southern Cal	9	49
N26	●	Arizona State	34	27

Neutral Site key: **Tok** Tokyo, Japan / **LA** Los Angeles, CA / **Pas** Pasadena, CA / **Nac** Naco, AZ / **Pho** Phoenix, AZ / **Bou** Boulder, CO / **Port** Portland, OR / **Boi** Boise, ID / **Spo** Spokane, WA
ƒ forfeit   † Game Later Forfieted   # Disputed Victor   * Disputed Score || Designated Conference Game |2 Counted Twice in Conference Standings

ARIZONA STATE

BY BUD WITHERS

IT'S BEEN KNOWN AS TEMPE NORMAL and Arizona State Teachers College. It's been a college and a university, and it's played in four different conferences. Like the growth of the area that surrounds it, Arizona State football has a feel of explosiveness to it. Through much of a history that includes night games back to 1930 because of the searing afternoon heat, it has featured mercurial offensive attacks that light up the desert. The Sun Devils' entertainment value has generally been high in a region in which many people have migrated from cold-weather climates and adopted ASU as a second team. Perhaps not surprisingly, then, fan support has tended to run hot and cold for ASU with the proliferation of pro sports in the area in the late 20th century.

TRADITION Nobody has a more exotic locale for preseason practice than ASU, which annually packs up for Camp Tontozona, a university-owned recreation area about 100 miles northeast of campus on the border of the Tonto National Forest near the town of Payson. It's roughly 30°

cooler there than in the notorious Valley of the Sun, where August temperatures can top 110°. The annual road trip there began in 1960.

BEST PLAYER No Sun Devil in history meant more to his team than a swashbuckling, tackle-shaking Idahoan named Jake "The Snake" Plummer, a quarterback whose contribution was greater than his 8,827 passing yards—which are second on ASU's career list. With magnetism and leadership, Plummer placed third in Heisman Trophy voting in 1996 and helped carry ASU to the brink of the national championship. Others deserve mention, however. A quarter-century earlier, in ASU's pre-Pac-10 days, Danny White (1971-73) had the most successful three-year run of any Sun Devils quarterback, and no Arizona State teams were more electric. Twelve times in his three years, the Sun Devils scored more than 50 points, and the 1972 club set a school record for points with 562. ASU went 32–4 on White's watch, which included a senior year in which he set a then-ASU season record for passing yards with 2,878. In terms of pure positional excellence, a case can also be made for Terrell Suggs, a high school running back from nearby Chandler who became the most feared defensive end in the college game by 2002. Suggs set an NCAA season record for sacks (24), amassed 31.5 tackles for loss and won the

---

Arizona State University
Tempe, Ariz.
Founded: 1885
Enrollment: 38,627
Colors: Maroon and Gold
Nickname: Sun Devils
Stadium: Sun Devil Stadium
    Opened in 1958
    Grass; 73,379 capacity
First football game: 1897
All-time record: 516–314–24 (.618)
Bowl record: 11–9–1
Pac-10 Conference championships: 2
First-round NFL draftees: 25
Website: www.thesundevils.com

Coming from behind with an eight-point fourth quarter, Arizona State edged Nebraska 17-14 in the 1975 Fiesta Bowl, capping a 12–0 season. That climaxed a wildly successful nine-year run in which ASU went 86–15.

The Sun Devils spent 1981 and 1982 on probation for a variety of NCAA violations, including extra benefits and lack of institutional control. ASU forfeited victories in 1979 and served a two-year television and one-year bowl ban.

After spending time in the Border Conference (1931-61) and the Western Athletic Conference (1962-77), Arizona State joined the Pac-10 along with Arizona in 1978.

Barry Bonds; Reggie Jackson; Phil Mickelson; Stephen Knott, managing partner, Knott's Berry Farm; David Spade, actor; Carolyn Grace James, soprano, Metropolitian Opera, New York; Al Michaels

ASU FIGHT SONG
Fight, Devils down the field
Fight with your might and don't ever yield
Long may our colors outshine all others
Echo from the buttes, give 'em hell, Devils!
Cheer, cheer for A-S-U
Fight for the old Maroon
For it's hail! Hail! The gang's all here
And it's onward to victory!
Where the bold saguaros
Raise their arms on high
Praying for strength for brave tomorrows
From the western sky
Where eternal mountains
Kneel at sunset's gate
Here we hail thee, alma mater
Arizona State!

The Sun Devils have traditionally featured mercurial offensive attacks that light up desert nights.

Lombardi Trophy with his devastating quickness on the edge.

BEST COACH When Dan Devine was wooed away by Missouri in 1957, his intention was to take his offensive line coach, Frank Kush, with him. But the Sun Devils tapped the hard-bitten, 28-year-old son of a Pennsylvania coal miner, and Arizona State never would be the same. Kush learned to win as a collegian; as a 5'9", 175-pound All-America guard at Michigan State, his teams went 26–1 in his three seasons. Devine hired him in 1955 to ASU, and that's the last place Kush coached college football. With 176 victories in 22 seasons, he is probably the most compelling figure in Arizona sports history. He had a driving—some would say brutal—style, but no ASU opponent ever was better conditioned, mentally or physically, than the Sun Devils. With a combination of that toughness, conditioning and Kush's affinity for speed, the Sun Devils were often dominating during his tenure, winning 67 and losing only 10 from 1967 to 1973. They also graduated from the Border Conference to the Western Athletic Conference to the Pac-10 during Kush's time. A former Sun Devil recruited on a football scholarship but better known for his baseball exploits applauded Kush's style in his enshrinement speech into the Baseball Hall of Fame. Said Reggie Jackson, "He was as tough as Charlie Finley and George Steinbrenner rolled into one."

Kush's demise as a coach came in midseason 1979, in a fashion perhaps befitting his reign. Kush had been sued by a former ASU punter, Kevin Rutledge, who claimed that the coach struck him on the sideline after a bad kick, and in the stormy aftermath, Kush was fired. He went on to coach professionally in Canada and with the NFL's Baltimore Colts. It is a measure of the passionate feelings Kush's ouster stirred that it wasn't until 1996 that ASU held Frank Kush Day and dedicated the field at Sun Devil Stadium in his name. He returned as special assistant to the athletic director in 2000 and then moved up to director of football development.

BEST TEAM Coach Bruce Snyder used to say that he ruined a pair of dress shoes in the snow recruiting Plummer in Boise, but Snyder was reimbursed many times over. Led by the slender quarterback, plus standout offensive linemen Grey Ruegamer and Juan Roque, wide receiver Keith Poole

RECORDS

RUSHING YARDS
GAME
250 Ben Malone vs. Oregon State, Oct. 27, 1973 (24 att.)
SEASON
1,565 Woody Green, 1972 (234 att.)
CAREER
4,188 Woody Green, 1971-73 (675 att.)

PASSING YARDS
GAME
536 Andrew Walter vs. Oregon, Oct. 19, 2002 (31 of 53)
SEASON
3,877 Andrew Walter, 2002 (274 of 483)
CAREER
10,617 Andrew Walter, 2001-04 (777 of 1,416)

RECEIVING YARDS
GAME
277 Ron Fair vs. Washington State, Oct. 28, 1989 (19 rec.)
SEASON
1,405 Shaun McDonald, 2002 (87 rec.)
CAREER
2,993 John Jefferson, 1974-77 (188 rec.)

POINTS
GAME
30 Three players; most recently by Ben Malone vs. Oregon State, Oct. 27, 1973 (5 TDs)
SEASON
136 Wilford White, 1950 (22 TDs)
CAREER
380 Luis Zendejas, 1981-84 (81 FGs, 137 PATs)

CONSENSUS ALL-AMERICANS

1972-73	Woody Green, HB
1977	John Jefferson, WR
1978	Al Harris, DL
1981-82	Mike Richardson, DB
1982	Vernon Maxwell, DL
1983	Luis Zendejas, PK
1984-85	David Fulcher, DB
1986	Danny Villa, OL
1987	Randall McDaniel, OL
1996	Juan Roque, OL
1996	Derrick Rodgers, DL
2002	Terrell Suggs, DL

and linebackers Derrick Rodgers and Pat Tillman, ASU put together a magical season in 1996 that appeared destined to end in a national championship. ASU earned a shot at the title with 11 straight victories, including harrowing wins over Washington, USC and UCLA.

The Pac-10 title brought ASU a Rose Bowl matchup against 10–1 Ohio State, coached by John Cooper, the man who had led ASU to its first Rose Bowl victory 10 years earlier. Sacked six times in the game, Plummer nevertheless darted 11 yards through a tough Buckeyes defense for the touchdown that gave his team a 17-14 lead with 1:40 left. But Ohio State drove 65 yards for the winning score with only 19 seconds remaining, aided by two penalties against ASU defensive backs. With a victory, the Sun Devils (11–1) surely would have been named national champions; there were no other major unbeaten teams left.

BIGGEST GAME It came in 1975, at a time when most of college football still scoffed at the Sun Devils' inflated accomplishments in the WAC. Led by cornerback Mike Haynes, linebacker Larry Gordon and wide receiver John Jefferson, ASU methodically munched up 11 straight opponents and earned a berth in the hometown Fiesta Bowl against Nebraska. The Huskers had a 14-6 third-quarter lead and knocked quarterback Dennis Sproul out of the game, but backup Fred Mortensen threw a 10-yard fourth-quarter TD pass to Jefferson, followed by a two-point conversion to Larry Mucker. The coach's son, Danny Kush, then kicked a 29-yard field goal with 4:50 left to win it for the Sun Devils, who earned a No. 2 ranking, their highest ever. *The Sporting News* went one better, naming the Sun Devils its No. 1 team.

BIGGEST UPSET Riding a 26-game winning streak, two-time defending national champion Nebraska journeyed to Tempe a 24-point favorite in 1996, a year after the ground-bound Cornhuskers had laid 77 points on Arizona State in Lincoln. Playing a safety near the line of scrimmage to stifle the Huskers' running game, the Sun Devils shocked Nebraska, recording a 19-0 shutout. The oddity of the night: the ASU defense recorded three safeties.

BEST COMEBACK Statistically, the Devils' largest comeback resulted in a 39-28 victory over San Diego State in 2002 after ASU trailed 22-0. But their most meaningful one was in 1996, when they rallied from a 28-7 first-half deficit at UCLA to a 42-34 victory that kept them undefeated after six games. The Sun Devils trailed 28-14 at halftime and were still behind

34-21 in the fourth quarter, but scored the last 21 points of the game. A 16-yard "throwback" pass from tailback J.R. Redmond to Plummer, plus the conversion kick, gave ASU the lead for good, 35-34. Plummer had the distinction of passing, running and receiving for touchdowns.

HEARTBREAKER Arizona State entered the 1998 season ranked eighth and full of hope that it might realize the national championship that had so narrowly eluded it two years before. As 18th-ranked Washington stared at a fourth-and-17 predicament on its own 37, trailing 38-35 inside the final minute, the Sun Devils seemed poised to stay in contention for that promise. But the Huskies' Brock Huard connected with tight end Reggie Davis, who got behind the ASU secondary for a 63-yard score with 28 seconds left, and ASU went down to a crushing 42-38 defeat. It didn't soothe the Sun Devils that Huard called it "destiny" and attributed it to God's will. ASU never seemed to recover, going on to a 5–6 season.

WILDEST FINISH The only tie in Arizona-Arizona State history came in bizarre fashion in 1987, after the Sun Devils seemingly had a 24-21 victory ensured on an interception with 1:21 left. Moments later, punter Mike Schuh muffed a snap at the ASU 38, then illegally tried to boot the ball out-of-bounds. Gaining a combined 25 yards on the play, Arizona took over and tied it 24-24 on Gary Coston's 30-yard field goal with two seconds left.

STADIUM Erected in 1958, Sun Devil Stadium had an original capacity of 30,000. Three renovations bumped it to its current capacity of 73,379. As home of the Fiesta Bowl, the facility has hosted two Bowl Championship Series title games, and the Bermuda grass surface gets high marks from both college and pro players. Since 1988, the Arizona Cardinals have also called Sun Devil Stadium home while they await construction of their own home field.

RIVAL While there is always passion to beat schools from Los Angeles, where many Sun Devils grew up, public enemy No. 1 is Arizona. For most of last century, it wasn't a fair fight. In nine games covering a span of 32 years until 1931, Arizona State didn't put up so much as a touchdown against Arizona. After winning in 1931, ASU went 18 years before another victory over the Wildcats. Arizona's 67-0 triumph in 1946—widest in the series—is credited with causing ASU to establish its Sun Angel Foundation booster group to upgrade the program.

NICKNAME The 1946 makeover included a nickname change from Bulldogs to Sun Devils, ratified by a landslide student vote.

MASCOT An alumnus of the school who worked for Walt Disney did the design for free. The demon is brought to life by Sparky, a student in a maroon-and-gold costume wielding a pitchfork.

UNIFORMS At home, the Sun Devils wear maroon jerseys and gold pants; on the road, white jerseys and white pants. Helmets for both occasions are gold with a maroon stripe down the middle and the school's Sparky logo on both sides.

WEIRDNESS Perhaps nobody has ever served a one-game NCAA suspension for stranger reasons than Sun Devils tailback J.R. Redmond in 1999. Redmond used the cell phone of a part-time athletic department employee at ASU, who then informed him that the call would violate NCAA rules unless he married her, which he did. Eventually, after athletic officials investigated, the employee resigned and Redmond was forced to pay to charity $418 in phone bills and $173 for the plane fare to his Las Vegas honeymoon. To no one's surprise, the couple quickly divorced.

QUOTE "I treat my players all the same: terrible."
—Frank Kush, on his equal-opportunity meanness

ARIZONA STATE ANNUAL STATISTICAL LEADERS

YR	RUSHING	YDS	ATT	AVG	PASSING	ATT	CMP	PCT	YDS	RECEIVING	REC	YDS	AVG
1957	Leon Burton	1,126	117	9.6	John Hangartner	100	61	.61	1,203	Clancy Osborne	20	351	17.6
1958	Leon Burton	642	108	5.9	John Hangartner	121	67	.55	1,208	Karl Kiefer	22	324	14.7
1959	Nolan Jones	689	143	4.8	Frank Urban	73	40	.55	536	Bob Rembert	15	232	15.5
1960	Nolan Jones	582	107	5.4	Ron Cosner	56	25	.45	422	Bob Rembert	11	178	16.2
1961	Nolan Jones	411	85	4.8	Joe Zuger	133	67	.50	879	Roger Locke	14	222	15.9
1962	Tony Lorick	704	105	6.7	John Jacobs	136	77	.57	1,263	Dale Keller	20	358	17.9
1963	Tony Lorick	805	105	7.7	John Torok	79	41	.52	600	Jerry Smith	42	618	14.7
1964	Gene Foster	311	82	3.8	John Torok	251	139	.55	2,356	Ben Hawkins	42	718	17.1
1965	Travis Williams	523	130	4.0	John Goodman	175	96	.55	1,165	Ben Hawkins	36	504	14.0
1966	Travis Williams	551	137	4.0	John Goodman	168	90	.54	1,259	Ken Dyer	29	496	17.1
1967	Max Anderson	1,188	191	6.2	Ed Roseborough	205	95	.46	1,494	Ken Dyer	39	654	16.8
1968	Art Malone	1,431	235	6.1	Joe Spagnola	104	57	.55	917	Fair Hooker	42	665	15.8
1969	Dave Buchanan	908	143	6.3	Joe Spagnola	205	92	.45	1,488	Calvin Demery	45	816	18.1
1970	Bob Thomas	1,024	187	5.5	Joe Spagnola	265	141	.53	2,146	J.D. Hill	61	1,009	16.5
1971	Woody Green	1,310	232	5.6	Danny White	195	101	.52	1,643	Calvin Demery	43	641	14.9
1972	Woody Green	1,565	234	6.7	Danny White	242	126	.52	2,196	Steve Holden	42	911	21.7
1973	Woody Green	1,313	209	6.3	Danny White	284	160	.56	2,878	Greg Hudson	62	974	15.7
1974	Freddie Williams	1,299	249	5.2	Dennis Sproul	199	96	.48	1,438	John Jefferson	30	423	14.1
1975	Freddie Williams	1,427	266	5.4	Fred Mortensen	115	60	.52	1,068	John Jefferson	52	921	17.7
1976	Freddie Williams	516	102	5.1	Dennis Sproul	243	111	.46	1,751	John Jefferson	48	681	14.2
1977	Mike Harris	794	183	4.3	Dennis Sproul	267	136	.51	2,003	John Jefferson	58	968	16.7
1978	Mark Malone	757	164	4.6	Mark Malone	236	106	.45	1,573	Chris DeFrance	33	680	20.6
1979	Robert Weathers	556	105	5.3	Mark Malone	289	148	.51	1,886	John Mistler	36	498	13.8
1980	Willie Gittens	759	138	5.5	Mike Pagel	334	184	.55	2,025	John Mistler	53	573	10.8
1981	Gerald Riggs	891	148	6.0	Mike Pagel	321	171	.53	2,484	Bernard Henry	39	647	16.6
1982	Darryl Clack	606	111	5.5	Todd Hons	336	185	.55	2,338	Doug Allen	30	424	14.1
1983	Darryl Clack	932	184	5.1	Todd Hons	324	199	.61	2,394	Don Kern	49	502	10.2
1984	Darryl Clack	1,052	208	5.1	Jeff Van Raaphorst	262	155	.59	2,062	Doug Allen	46	892	19.4
1985	Mike Crawford	787	191	4.1	Jeff Van Raaphorst	337	188	.56	2,367	Aaron Cox	43	855	19.9
1986	Darryl Harris	1,042	228	4.6	Jeff Van Raaphorst	269	160	.59	2,181	Aaron Cox	35	695	19.9
1987	Darryl Harris	948	202	4.7	Daniel Ford	257	128	.50	1,756	Aaron Cox	42	870	20.7
1988	Bruce Perkins	446	118	3.8	Daniel Ford	165	85	.52	1,166	Ryan McReynolds	28	271	9.7
1989	David Winsley	470	119	3.9	Paul Justin	314	183	.58	2,591	Ron Fair	64	1,082	16.9
1990	Leonard Russell	810	174	4.7	Paul Justin	253	131	.52	1,876	Eric Guliford	48	837	17.4
1991	George Montgomery	475	113	4.2	Bret Powers	234	127	.54	1,500	Eric Guliford	55	801	14.6
1992	Jerone Davidson	734	183	4.0	Grady Benton	225	149	.66	1,707	Eric Guliford	44	506	11.5
1993	Mario Bates	1,111	246	4.5	Jake Plummer	199	102	.51	1,650	Johnny Thomas	34	574	16.9
1994	Chris Hopkins	680	169	4.0	Jake Plummer	294	159	.54	2,179	Clyde McCoy	47	682	14.5
1995	Chris Hopkins	646	130	5.0	Jake Plummer	301	173	.57	2,222	Keith Poole	55	1,036	18.8
1996	Terry Battle	1,077	178	6.1	Jake Plummer	348	198	.57	2,776	Keith Poole	47	867	18.4
1997	Michael Martin	1,031	188	5.5	Ryan Kealy	297	162	.55	2,137	Lenzie Jackson	55	777	14.1
1998	J.R. Redmond	883	166	5.3	Ryan Kealy	261	150	.57	2,161	Lenzie Jackson	41	568	13.9
1999	J.R. Redmond	1,174	241	4.9	Ryan Kealy	267	148	.55	1,976	Todd Heap	55	832	15.1
2000	Tom Pace	720	180	4.0	Jeff Krohn	254	125	.49	1,751	Todd Heap	48	644	13.4
2001	Delvon Flowers	1,041	188	5.5	Jeff Krohn	213	115	.54	1,942	Shaun McDonald	47	1,104	23.5
2002	Cornell Canidate	493	130	3.8	Andrew Walter	483	274	.57	3,877	Shaun McDonald	87	1,405	16.1
2003	Loren Wade	773	136	5.7	Andrew Walter	421	221	.52	3,044	Derek Hagan	66	1,076	16.3
2004	Hakim Hill	566	122	4.6	Andrew Walter	426	244	.57	3,150	Derek Hagan	83	1,248	15.0

All statistics include postseason

ARIZONA STATE ALL-TIME SCORES

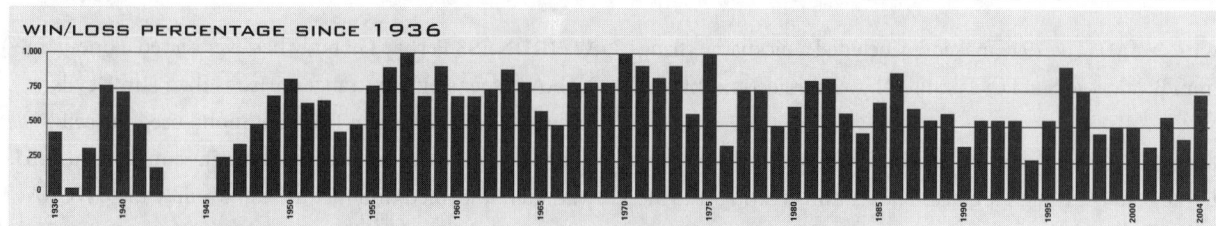

WIN/LOSS PERCENTAGE SINCE 1936

THE SCHOOLS

FRED IRISH
1897-1906 (.600)   12-8

1897   0-1-0
U	Phoenix Indians	20	38

1898
NO TEAM

1899   3-0-0
U	●	Phoenix Indians	6	0
U	●	at Phoenix H.S.	6	0
U	●	at Arizona	11	2

1900   1-1-0
U	Phoenix H.S.	0	5
U ●	at Phoenix H.S.	5	0

1901
NO TEAM

1902   2-1-0
U	Phoenix H.S.	39	0
U	Phoenix Indians	34	0
U	at Arizona	0	12

1903   2-0-0
U	●	at Phoenix H.S.	18	0
U	●	Phoenix Indians	15	0

1904   4-0-0
U	●	Phoenix H.S.	15	0
U	●	Phoenix Indians	24	0
U	●	at Phoenix Indians	30	0
U	●	Phoenix Indians	47	0

1905   0-3-0
U	Phoenix Indians	8	17
U	Phoenix H.S.	0	5
U	Tempe H.S.	0	6

1906   0-2-0
U	Phoenix Indians	6	17
U	Tempe H.S.	0	5

1907-1913
NO TEAM

GEORGE SCHAEFFER
1914-16 (.467)   7-8

1914   4-3-0
U	●	Tempe H.S.	12	6
U	●	Glendale H.S.	72	0
U		at Arizona	0	34
U		at Phoenix H.S.	9	13
U		Phoenix Indians	6	24
U	●	Phoenix Indians	34	7
U	●	at Prescott H.S.	10	7

1915   3-2-0
U		at Arizona	0	7
U	●	Phoenix H.S.	14	7
U	●	Phoenix Indian Alums	32	0
U	●	at No. Arizona	72	3
U		Phoenix Indians	7	19

1916   0-3-0
U	Phoenix Indians Alums	7	25
U	at No. Arizona	6	20
U	at Prescott H.S.	0	6

1917-1918
NO TEAM WWI

GEORGE COOPER
1919 (.000)   0-2

1919   0-2-0
U	at Arizona	0	59
U	at Phoenix H.S.	3	45

1920-1921
NO TEAM

ERNEST WILLS
1922 (.125)   0-3-1

1922   0-3-1
U		Mesa H.S.	6	13
U	=	Phoenix H.S.	13	13
U		Phoenix Coll.	0	12
U		at Phoenix Coll.	12	36

AARON McCREARY
1923-29 (.587)   25-17-4

1923   4-2-0
U		Phoenix H.S.	0	19
U	●	at Phoenix Indians	47	0
U	●	at Indians 2nd Team	61	6
U		at Phoenix Coll.	2	57
U	●	Phoenix Indians	18	14
U	●	at Mesa H.S.	24	6

1924   6-1-1
U	●	at Phoenix H.S.	24	0
U	●	at Phoenix Indians	13	10
U	●	Phoenix Coll.	34	0
U	●	No. Arizona	20	16
U	●	Phoenix Coll.	30	6
U	●	at Arizona JV	23	13
U		Phoenix Coll.Alums	3	27
U	=	Sherman Indians	13	13

1925   6-2-0
U	●	Sacaton Indians	55	0
O10		at Arizona	3	13
U	●	at Phoenix	32	0
U	●	at No. Arizona	3	0
U	●	at Arizona JV	20	6
U	●	at Phoenix Indians	11	7
N26		at Texas-El Paso	12	21	*
U	●	at Phoenix H.S.	18	6

1926   4-1-1
U	●	at Sacaton Indians	35	0
O16		at Arizona	0	35
U	●	Phoenix Coll.	28	7
U	●	Gila JC	20	0
N13	●	No. Arizona	14	0
U	=	Phoenix Indians	0	0

1927   2-3-1
O8		at Loyola, Marymount	3	25
O22		at No. Arizona	0	19
O29	●	at Gila JC	14	0
N12		at Phoenix Indians	0	6
N19	●	Phoenix Coll	46	0
N24	=	at Texas-El Paso	0	0

1928   3-2-1
O13	●	Gila JC	57	0
U	=	at Texas-El Paso	0	0
O20		at Arizona	0	39
N3	●	Phoenix Indians	19	6
N10		at New Mexico	6	27
N17	●	at Phoenix Coll.	51	0

1929   0-6-0
O5	at Texas-El Paso	7	31
O19	Arizona JV	0	7
O26	at No. Arizona	0	31
N2	at Arizona	0	26
N16	No. Arizona	0	27
U	Loyola, Marymount	6	21

TED SHIPKEY
1930-32 (.542)   12-10-2

1930   3-5-1
S27	●	Gila JC	39	0
O4		at Texas-El Paso	6	19
O18		at Arizona	0	6
O25		at New Mexico State	0	7
N1		at Sacramento JC	0	49
N8		at No. Arizona	0	0
N15	●	Arizona JV	39	6
N22	●	Fullerton JC	21	0
N27		at No. Arizona	6	7

1931-1961
BORDER

1931   6-2-0 (3-1-0)
S26	●	Sacaton Indians	66	0
O3		at Texas-El Paso	13	27	*
O17		New Mexico State	25	7
O24	●	at No. Arizona	20	6
O31	●	Arizona	19	6
N7		at Fresno State	7	0
N14		No. Arizona	7	13
N21	●	Arizona All Stars	13	7

1932   3-3-1 (2-2-1)
O8		Whittier	0	26
O15	=	at No. Arizona	6	6
O22		at Arizona	6	20
N5		at New Mexico State	7	6
N12	●	Texas-El Paso	15	14
N19		No. Arizona	6	20
D3		New Mexico	40	0	*

RUDY LAVIK
1933-37 (.345)   13-26-3

1933   3-5-0 (2-3-0)
S30		at Whittier	0	27
O7		at San Diego Marines	0	26
O21	●	at New Mexico	26	13
O28		at No. Arizona	0	13
N4	●	Fresno State	21	7
N11	●	New Mexico State	19	7
N18		Arizona	7	26
N25		No. Arizona	0	6

1934   4-3-1 (2-2-1)
S29	●	Cal Tech	25	7
O6		at Loyola Marymount	0	43
O20		New Mexico	12	18
O27	●	at No. Arizona	21	0
N3	●	No. Arizona	6	0
N10	=	at New Mexico State	7	7
N17		at Arizona	6	32
N29	●	at San Diego State	14	6

1935   2-5-1 (2-3-1)
S28		at Arizona	0	26
O5		Loyola Marymount	3	7
O19		at New Mexico State	6	7
O26	●	No. Arizona	6	0
N2		at New Mexico	0	13
N9	●	at Texas-El Paso	14	0
N16	=	No. Arizona	0	0
N23		Brigham Young	0	13

1936   4-5-0 (2-4-0)
S26		at Whittier	12	0
O3	●	Cal Tech	26	0
O10		Arizona	0	18
O24		at No. Arizona	0	19
O31	●	New Mexico	7	6
N7		New Mexico State	6	20
N14		at Texas-El Paso	19	0
N21		No. Arizona	7	13
N26		at San Jose State	6	33

1937   0-8-1 (0-5-0)
O2		at Arizona	6	20
O9		at Santa Barbra	7	27
O16		at San Diego	0	7
O23		No. Arizona	0	7
O30		at New Mexico	7	15
N6	=	Whittier	6	6
N11		Texas-El Paso	0	19
N20		San Jose State	6	25
N25		at New Mexico State	0	14

DIXIE HOWELL
1938-41 (.595)   23-15-4

1938   3-6-0 (0-4-0)
S19		San Jose State	7	18
S30		at New Mexico	0	21
O8	●	Cal Poly SLO	13	0
O15		at No. Arizona	13	19
O22		New Mexico State	12	14
O29	●	Santa Barbra	10	0
N12		Hardin-Simmons	7	12
N19		at Texas-El Paso	6	14
N24	●	at Whittier	21	0

1939   8-2-1 (4-0-0)
S21	●	at San Diego State	20	0
S30	●	West Texas State	19	0
O7	●	Cal Poly SLO	35	0
O14	●	Whittier	28	0
O20	●	at New Mexico State	7	0
O28	●	Texas-El Paso	27	7
N4		at Hardin-Simmons	7	19
N11	●	No. Arizona	41	6
N18	●	New Mexico	28	6
N25		at San Diego Marines	0	18
SUN BOWL
J1	=	Catholic U.	0	0

1940   7-2-2 (3-0-1)
S21	●	Cal Tech	21	13
S28	●	at West Texas State	19	13
O5		at Hardin-Simmons	0	17
O11	●	at New Mexico	13	6
O19	●	New Mexico State	42	0
O26	=	at Texas-El Paso	0	0
N2	●	at No. Arizona	12	0
N9		Gonzaga	7	7
N16	●	No. Colorado	41	0
N23	●	North Dakota	30	12
SUN BOWL
J1		Western Reserve	13	26

1941   5-5-1 (2-4-1)
S20	●	at Gonzaga	6	0
S27		Texas A&I	7	35
O4		West Texas State	7	13
O11	=	New Mexico	0	0
O18		at New Mexico State	19	14
O25		Arizona	7	20
N1	●	at No. Colorado	6	0
N8		Texas-El Paso	0	28
N15	●	No. Arizona	33	0
N22	●	at Fresno State	26	7
N29		Hardin-Simmons	0	20

HILMAN WALKER
1942 (.200)   2-8

1942   2-8-0 (2-5-0)
S26		at San Francisco	6	54
O3		at West Texas State	0	28
O10		Arizona	0	23
O17	●	New Mexico State	20	0
O24		at Hardin-Simmons	0	21
O31		Santa Ana AFB	0	40
N14		at Texas-El Paso	6	40
N21		Albuquerque Field	0	13
N28		at New Mexico	7	35
D5	●	at No. Arizona	14	2

1943-1945
NO TEAM WWII

STEVE COUTCHIE
1946 (.273)   2-7-2

1946   2-7-2 (1-4-1)
S21	=	Williams AFB	6	6
S28		at Arizona	0	67
O5	•	Pepperdine	13	12
O12		at Nevada	2	74
O19		Portland	0	13
O26	•	at Hardin-Simmons	6	46
N2	•	at New Mexico State	14	7
N9		Texas-El Paso	20	34
N16	•	No. Arizona	13	13
N23	•	West Texas State	0	7
N28		at Wichita State	19	34

ED DOHERTY
1947-50 (.595)   25-17

1947   4-7-0 (3-4-0)
S20	•	Cal Poly SLO	33	6
S27	•	at New Mexico	25	12
O4		Abilene Christian	7	13
O11		at Pepperdine	6	27
O18	•	No. Arizona	31	7
N1	•	New Mexico State	33	12
N8		at Texas-El Paso	0	21
N15	•	Arizona	13	26
N22	•	at West Texas State	7	35
N29		Nevada	13	33
D6	•	Hardin-Simmons	0	42

1948   5-5-0 (3-2-0)
S25	•	Western State	23	0
O2	•	Pepperdine	33	7
O9		at Utah State	17	22
O23	•	No. Arizona	40	0
O30		at Arizona	21	33
N5	•	at New Mexico State	52	7
N13		at Loyola Marymount	12	16
N20		at Hardin-Simmons	25	63
N26		Brigham Young	25	27
D14	•	New Mexico	28	17

1949   7-3-0 (4-1-0)
S24	•	at Pepperdine	33	13
O1		at Hardin-Simmons	13	34
O8	•	No. Arizona	62	6
O15	•	Brigham Young	49	21
O29	•	at New Mexico	28	19
N5	•	New Mexico State	68	32
N12	•	Arizona	34	7
N19	•	Loyola Marymount	7	27
D3	•	Utah State	27	12
SALAD BOWL				
J1		Xavier	21	33

1950   9-2-0 (4-1-0)
S23	•	at Brigham Young	41	13
S30	•	New Mexico	41	6 *
O7	•	No. Arizona	63	0
O14	•	at Hardin-Simmons	14	41
O21	•	Utah State	28	0
O28	•	New Mexico State	49	0
N4	•	San Diego State	31	13
N11	•	at Arizona	47	13
N18	•	Colorado State	21	13
N25	•	Idaho	48	21
SALAD BOWL				
J1		Miami, Ohio	21	34

LARRY SIEMERING
1951 (.650)   6-3-1

1951   6-3-1 (4-1-0)
S22	•	at Utah State	33	27
S29	•	at Arkansas	13	30
O6	•	Wayne State	50	6
O13	•	Hardin-Simmons	14	39
O20	=	at San Diego State	27	27
O27	•	New Mexico State	46	0
N3	•	West Texas State	34	0
N10	•	Arizona	61	14
N17	•	at Texas-El Paso	23	13
N24		Wyoming	7	20

CLYDE SMITH
1952-54 (.534)   15-13-1

1952   6-3-0 (4-0-0)
S20	•	at Hardin-Simmons	26	7
S27	•	Colorado State	40	14
O4		San Jose State	14	21
O18	•	West Texas State	48	14
O25		Houston	0	6
N8	•	at Arizona	20	18
N15		San Diego Navy	13	35
N22	•	Texas-El Paso	39	0
N29		Brigham Young	47	6

1953   4-5-1 (1-3-0)
S19		San Diego Navy	14	19
S26	•	at North Texas	14	0
O3		Texas-El Paso	27	28
O10	•	at San Jose State	35	20
O17	•	West Texas State	39	20
O24		at Houston	20	24
N7		Hardin-Simmons	20	27
N14	•	Brigham Young	26	18
N21	=	Midwestern State	12	12
N28		Arizona	0	35

1954   5-5-0 (3-1-0)
S18	•	Hawaii	28	14
S24	•	at Brigham Young	28	19
O2	•	Texas-El Paso	34	27
O9		San Jose State	12	19
O16		at Midwestern State	7	14
O23	•	West Texas State	21	14
O30	•	at Hardin-Simmons	14	13
N6		Cincinnati	7	34
N13		North Texas	13	20
N20		at Arizona	14	54

DAN DEVINE
1955-57 (.887)   27-3-1

1955   8-2-1 (4-1-0)
S17	=	at Wichita State	20	20
S24	•	Midwestern State	28	7
O1	•	San Diego Navy	42	0
O8		at San Jose State	20	27
O15	•	at San Diego State	46	0
O29	•	Hardin-Simmons	69	14
N5	•	West Texas State	27	7
N12	•	at Texas-El Paso	20	13
N19	•	New Mexico State	26	6
N26		Arizona	6	7
D3	•	at Hawaii	39	6

1956   9-1-0 (3-1-0)
S22	•	Wichita State	37	9
S29	•	North Texas	27	7
O6	•	at New Mexico State	28	7
O13	•	at Idaho	41	0
O20	•	at Hardin-Simmons	26	13
O27	•	San Jose State	47	13
N3	•	San Diego State	61	0
N10	•	Texas-El Paso	0	28
N17	•	at Arizona	20	0
N24	•	Pacific	19	6

1957   10-0-0 (4-0-0)
S21	•	at Wichita State	28	0
S28	•	Idaho	19	7
O5	•	at San Jose State	44	6
O12	•	Hardin-Simmons	35	26
O26	•	at San Diego State	66	0
N2	•	New Mexico State	21	0
N9	•	at Texas-El Paso	43	7
N16	•	Montana State	53	13
N23	•	Pacific	41	0
N30		Arizona	47	7

FRANK KUSH
1958-79 (.764)   176-54-1

1958   7-3-0 (4-1-0)
S20	•	Hawaii	47	6
S27		at Pacific	16	34
O4	•	West Texas State	16	13
O11		Hardin-Simmons	6	14
O18		San Jose State	20	21
O25		at Detroit	27	6
N1		New Mexico State	23	19
N8	•	Texas-El Paso	27	0
N22	•	at Arizona	47	0
N29	•	Marquette	42	18

1959   10-1-0 (5-0-0)
S19	•	West Texas State	43	22
S26	•	Utah State	34	12
O3		Montana State	31	14
O17	•	at Colorado State	24	9
O24		at San Jose State	15	24
O31	•	New Mexico State	35	31
N7	•	at Texas-El Paso	20	7
N14		Brigham Young	27	9
N21	•	Hardin-Simmons	14	8
N28	•	Arizona	15	9
D4	•	at Hawaii	14	6

1960   7-3-0 (3-2-0)
S17	•	Colorado State	39	0
S24		at West Texas State	14	3
O1	•	Washington State	24	21
O8	•	at Hardin-Simmons	28	0
O15	•	at Brigham Young	31	0
O22		San Jose State	7	12
O29	•	New Mexico State	24	27
N5	•	Texas-El Paso	24	0
N12	•	North Carolina St.	25	22
N26		at Arizona	7	35

1961   7-3-0 (3-0-0)
S23	•	Wichita State	21	7
S30	•	at Colorado State	14	6
O7		Utah	26	28
O14	•	at West Texas State	28	11
O21	•	Oregon State	24	23
O28	•	Hardin-Simmons	47	0
N4	•	at San Jose State	26	32
N11	•	at Texas-El Paso	48	28
N18	•	Detroit	40	6
N25	•	Arizona	13	22

1962-1977
WAC

1962   7-2-1 (1-1-0)
S22	•	at Wichita State	21	10
S29	•	Colorado State	35	0
O6	=	Washington State	24	24
O13	•	West Texas State	14	15
O20	•	San Jose State	44	8
O27	•	Texas-El Paso	35	7
N3	•	Utah State	34	15
N10	•	Utah	35	7
N17	•	New Mexico State	45	20
N24		at Arizona	17	20

1963   8-1-0 (3-0-0)
S21	•	Wichita State	13	33
S28	•	New Mexico State	14	13
O5	•	at Colorado State	50	7
O12	•	West Texas State	24	16
O19	•	at Texas El Paso	27	0
N2	•	Utah	30	22
N9	•	at San Jose State	21	19
N16	•	Wyomin	35	6
N30	•	Arizona	35	6

1964   8-2-0 (0-2-0)
S19	•	Utah State	24	8
S26	•	at West Texas State	34	8
O3	•	Wichita State	24	18
O10	•	Texas-El Paso	42	13
O24		at Utah	3	16
O31	•	Colorado State	34	6
N7	•	Kansas State	21	10
N14	•	San Jose State	28	16
N21	•	Idaho	14	0
N28		at Arizona	6	30

1965   6-4-0 (3-1-0)
S18		Brigham Young	6	24
S25		Utah State	0	13
O2		at West Texas State	14	22
O9	•	Wichita State	8	6
O16		at San Jose State	14	21
O23	•	New Mexico	27	14
O30	•	at Texas-El Paso	28	20
N13	•	Washington State	7	6
N20	•	Wyoming	14	10
N27	•	Arizona	14	6

1966   5-5-0 (3-2-0)
S17	•	Texas-El Paso	30	26
S24	•	at Wyoming	6	23
O1		West Texas State	20	21
O9		at Washington State	15	24
O14	•	at Brigham Young	10	7
O22		Oregon State	17	18
N5		Utah	6	21
N12	•	Oregon	14	10
N19	•	New Mexico	28	7
N26	•	at Arizona	20	17

1967   8-2-0 (4-1-0)
S16	•	San Jose State	27	16
S23		Oregon State	21	27
S30	•	at Wisconsin	42	16
O7		Texas-El Paso	33	32
O14	•	at New Mexico	56	23
O21	•	Washington State Spo	31	20
O28		Wyoming	13	15
N4	•	at Utah	49	32
N18		Brigham Young	31	22
N25	•	Arizona	47	7

1968   8-2-0 (5-1-0)
S21	•	Wisconsin	55	7
S28	•	Texas-El Paso	31	19
O5		at Wyoming	13	27
O12	•	Washington State	41	14
O19		Oregon State Port	9	28
N2	•	New Mexico	63	28
N9	•	Utah	59	21
N16	•	at Brigham Young	47	12
N23	•	San Jose State	66	0
N30		at Arizona	30	7

1969   8-2-0 (6-1-0)
S20	•	Minnesota	48	26
S27		Oregon State	7	30
O4	•	Brigham Young	23	7
O11		at Utah	23	24
O18	•	at San Jose State	45	11
N1	•	Wyoming	30	14
N8	•	at New Mexico	48	17
N15	•	at Texas-El Paso	42	19
N22	•	Colorado State	79	7
N29	•	Arizona	38	24

1970   11-0-0 (7-0-0)
S19	•	Colorado State	38	9
S26	•	Kansas State	35	13
O3		at Wyoming	52	3
O10	•	Washington State	37	30
O17	•	at Brigham Young	27	3
O24	•	at Texas-El Paso	42	13
N7	•	San Jose State	46	10
N14	•	Utah	37	14
N21	•	New Mexico	33	21
D5	•	at Arizona	10	6
PEACH BOWL				
D30	•	North Carolina	48	26

1971   11-1-0 (7-0-0)
S18	•	Houston	18	17
S25	•	at Utah	41	21
O2	•	Texas-El Paso	24	7
O9	•	at Colorado State	42	0
O16		Oregon State Port	18	24
O23	•	at New Mexico	60	28
O30	•	Air Force	44	28
N6	•	Brigham Young	38	13
N13	•	Wyoming	52	19
N20	•	at San Jose State	49	6
N27	•	Arizona	31	0
FIESTA BOWL				
D27	•	Florida State	45	38

1972   10-2-0 (5-1-0)
S16	•	at Houston	33	28
S23	•	Kansas State	56	14
S30	•	at Wyoming	43	45
O7	•	Oregon State	38	7
O14	•	Utah	59	48
O21	•	at Brigham Young	49	17
O28	•	Air Force	31	39
N4	•	at Texas-El Paso	55	14
N11	•	New Mexico	60	7
N18	•	San Jose State	51	21
N25	•	at Arizona	38	21
FIESTA BOWL				
D23	•	Missouri	49	35

1973   11-1-0 (6-1-0)
S15	•	at Oregon	26	20
S22	•	Washington State	20	9
S29	•	Colorado State	67	14
O6	•	at New Mexico	67	24
O13	•	San Jose State	28	3
O20	•	Brigham Young	52	12
O27	•	Oregon State Port	44	14
N3		at Utah	31	36
N10	•	Wyoming	47	0
N17	•	at Texas-El Paso	54	13
N25	•	Arizona	55	19
FIESTA BOWL				
D21	•	Pittsburgh	28	7

1974 — 7-5-0 (4-3-0)

S7	●		Houston	30	9
S21	●		TCU	37	7
S28			at Missouri	0	9
O5	●	|	at Wyoming	16	10
O19	●	|	Utah	32	0
O26	●	|	New Mexico	41	7
N2		|	Texas-El Paso	27	31
N9		|	at Brigham Young	18	21
N16			North Carolina St.	14	35
N23	●	|	Colorado State	26	21
N30		|	at Arizona	0	10
D7	●		at Hawaii	26	3

1975 — 12-0-0 (7-0-0)

S13	●		Washington	35	12
S20	●		at TCU	33	10
S27	●	|	Brigham Young	20	0
O4	●		Idaho	29	3
O11	●	|	at New Mexico	16	10
O18	●	|	at Colorado State	33	3
O25	●	|	Texas-El Paso	24	6
N1	●	|	at Utah	40	14
N8	●	|	Wyoming	21	20
N15	●		Pacific	55	14
N29	●	|	Arizona	24	21
			FIESTA BOWL		
D26	●		Nebraska	17	14

1976 — 4-7-0 (4-3-0)

S9			UCLA	10	28
S25			California	22	31
O2		|	at Wyoming	10	13
O9			Cincinnati	0	14
O16	●	|	at Texas-El Paso	23	6
O23	●	|	New Mexico	31	15
O30		|	at Brigham Young	21	43
N6			Air Force	30	31
N13		|	Utah	28	31
N20	●	|	Colorado State	21	19
N27	●	|	at Arizona	27	10

1977 — 9-3-0 (6-1-0)

S17	●		Northwestern	35	3
S24	●		Oregon State	33	31
O1			Missouri	0	15
O8	●	|	at New Mexico	45	24
O15	●		at Air Force	37	14
O22	●	|	Texas-El Paso	66	3
O29	●	|	at Utah	47	19
N5	●	|	Wyoming	45	0
N12	●	|	Brigham Young	24	13
N19		|	at Colorado State	14	25
N26	●	|	Arizona	23	7
			FIESTA BOWL		
D25			Penn State	30	42

1978-PRESENT
PAC 10

1978 — 9-3-0 (4-3-0)

S9	●		Pacific	42	7
S16	●		Brigham Young	24	17
S23		|	Washington State *Spo*	26	51
S30	●		Texas-El Paso	27	0
O7	●		at Northwestern	56	14
O14	●	|	Southern Cal	20	7
O28		|	at Washington	7	41
N4	●	|	California	35	21
N11		|	Stanford	14	21
N18	●	|	at Oregon State	44	22
N25	●	|	at Arizona	18	17
			GARDEN STATE BOWL		
D16	●		Rutgers	34	18

BOB OWENS
1979 (.429) 3-4

1979 — 6-6-0 (3-4-0)

S8		|	California	9	17
S15			Florida State *Tam*	3	31
S22	●		Toledo	49	0
S29	●	|	at Oregon State	45	0
O13	●	|	Washington	12	7 †
O20	●	|	Washington State	28	17
O27	●		Utah State	28	14
N3		|	Stanford	21	28
N10		|	at UCLA	28	31
N17	●		at West Virginia	42	7
N24		|	Arizona	24	27
D1			at Hawaii	17	29

DARRYL ROGERS
1980-84 (.670) 37-18-1

1980 — 7-4-0 (5-3-0)

S13	●		Houston	29	13
S20	●	|	Oregon State	42	14
S27			at Ohio State	21	38
O4		|	at Southern Cal	21	23
O11	●	|	Washington State	27	21
O25	●	|	Pacific	37	9
N1		|	at Washington	0	25
N8	●	|	California	34	6
N15		|	UCLA	14	23
N22	●	|	Oregon	42	37
N29	●	|	at Arizona	44	7

1981 — 9-2-0 (5-2-0)

S12	●		Utah	52	0
S19	●		Wichita State	33	21
S26		|	at Washington State	21	24
O3	●	|	at Washington	26	7
O10	●	|	Oregon	24	0
O17	●	|	California	45	17
O24	●	|	at Stanford	62	36
O31	●		San Jose State	31	24
N14		|	at UCLA	24	34
N21	●		Colorado State	52	7
N28	●	|	Arizona	24	13

1982 — 10-2-0 (5-2-0)

S4	●	|	at Oregon	34	3
S11	●		Utah	23	10
S18	●		at Houston	24	10
S25	●	|	at California	15	0
O2	●		Kansas State	30	7
O9	●	|	Stanford	21	17
O16	●		Texas-El Paso	37	6
O30	●	|	Southern Cal	17	10
N6	●	|	Oregon State	30	16
N13		|	Washington	13	17
N27		|	at Arizona	18	28
			FIESTA BOWL		
J1	●		Oklahoma	32	21

1983 — 6-4-1 (3-3-1)

S10	●		Utah State	39	12
S17	=	|	at UCLA	26	26
S24	●		Wichita State	44	14
O1	●	|	Stanford	29	11
O15	●	|	at Southern Cal	34	14
O22		|	Washington State	21	31
O29			Florida State	26	29
N5		|	at California	24	26
N12	●	|	Oregon State	38	3
N19	●		San Jose State	24	17
N26		|	Arizona	15	17

1984 — 5-6-0 (3-4-0)

S8			Oklahoma State	3	45
S15	●		San Jose State	48	0
S22		|	Southern Cal	3	6
S29	●	|	at Stanford	28	10
O6		|	California	14	19
O20	●	|	Oregon State	45	10
O27		|	UCLA	13	21
N3			Florida State	44	52
N10	●	|	at Oregon	44	10
N17	●		Colorado State	45	14
N24		|	at Arizona	10	16

JOHN COOPER
1985-87 (.722) 25-9-2

1985 — 8-4-0 (5-2-0)

S14			at Michigan State	3	12
S21	●		Pacific	27	0
S28	●	|	Southern Cal	24	0
O5		|	at UCLA	17	40
O12	●		Utah	34	27
O19	●		Utah State	42	10
O26	●	|	at Washington State	21	16
N2	●	|	at California	30	8
N9	●	|	Washington	36	7
N16	●	|	Stanford	21	14
N23		|	Arizona	13	16
			HOLIDAY BOWL		
D22			Arkansas	17	18

1986 — 10-1-1 (5-1-1)

S13	●		Michigan State	20	17
S20	●		SMU	30	0
S27	=	|	Washington State	21	21
O4	●	|	at UCLA	16	9
O11	●	|	at Oregon	37	17
O18	●	|	at Southern Cal	29	20
O25	●		Utah	52	7
N1	●	|	Washington	34	21
N8	●	|	California	49	0
N15	●		Wichita State	52	6
N22		|	at Arizona	17	34
			ROSE BOWL		
J1	●		Michigan	22	15

1987 — 7-4-1 (3-3-1)

S12	●		at Illinois	21	7
S19	●		Pacific	31	12
S26			Nebraska	28	35
O3	●		Texas-El Paso	35	16
O10		|	at Washington	14	27
O17	●	|	Washington State	38	7
O24	●	|	at Oregon State	30	21
O31		|	UCLA	23	31
N7	●	|	Oregon	37	17
N14		|	at California	20	38
N28	=	|	Arizona	24	24
			FREEDOM BOWL		
D30	●		Air Force	33	28

LARRY MARMIE
1988-91 (.511) 22-21-1

1988 — 6-5-0 (3-4-0)

S10	●		Illinois	21	16
S17	●		Colorado State	28	17
S24			at Nebraska	16	47
O1	●		Lamar	24	13
O8		|	Washington	0	10
O15		|	at Stanford	3	24
O22	●	|	at Washington State	31	28
O29	●	|	at Oregon	21	20
N5	●	|	Oregon State	30	24
N12		|	Southern Cal	0	50
N26		|	at Arizona	18	28

1989 — 6-4-1 (3-3-1)

S9	●		Kansas State	31	0
S16	●		San Jose State	28	21
S23			Houston	7	36
S30	●		Missouri	19	3
O7		|	at UCLA	14	33
O14	=	|	at Oregon State	17	17
O21		|	Oregon	7	27
O28	●	|	Washington State	44	39
N4	●	|	at Washington	34	32
N11	●	|	Stanford	30	22
N25		|	Arizona	10	28

1990 — 4-7-0 (2-5-0)

S8	●		Baylor	34	13
S15	●		Colorado State	31	20
S29			at Missouri	9	30
O6		|	Washington	14	42
O13		|	California	24	31
O20		|	at Oregon	7	27
O27		|	Southern Cal	6	13
N3	●	|	Oregon State	34	9
N10	●	|	at Washington State	51	26
N24		|	at Arizona	17	21
D2			Houston *Tok*	45	62

1991 — 6-5-0 (4-4-0)

S14	●		at Oklahoma State	30	3
S21	●	|	at Southern Cal	32	25
S28			Nebraska	9	18
O5	●		Utah	21	15
O12	●	|	at Oregon State	24	7
O19		|	Washington State	3	17
O26		|	UCLA	16	21
N2		|	at Washington	16	44
N9	●	|	Oregon	24	21
N16		|	at California	6	25
N23	●	|	Arizona	37	14

BRUCE SNYDER
1992-2000 (.563) 58-45

1992 — 6-5-0 (4-4-0)

S5		|	Washington	7	31
S19	●		Louisville	19	0
S26			at Nebraska	24	45
O3		|	at Oregon	20	30
O10	●		Pacific	39	5
O17	●	|	Oregon State	40	13
O24	●	|	at UCLA	20	0
O31		|	Southern Cal	13	23
N7		|	at Washington State	18	20
N14	●	|	California	28	12
N21	●	|	at Arizona	7	6

1993 — 6-5-0 (4-4-0)

S4	●		Utah	38	0
S18			at Louisville	17	35
S25	●		Oklahoma State	12	10
O2		|	at Oregon State	14	30
O9		|	at Washington State	25	44
O16		|	Oregon	36	45
O23	●	|	at Stanford	38	30
O30	●	|	Washington	32	17
N6	●	|	California	41	0
N13	●	|	at UCLA	9	3
N26		|	Arizona	20	34

1994 — 3-8-0 (2-6-0)

S3	●	|	Oregon State	22	16
S10			Miami, Fla.	10	47
S17			Louisville	22	25
S24		|	at California	21	25
O8	●	|	Stanford	36	35
O15		|	at Washington	14	35
O22		|	Washington State	21	28
O29	●		at Brigham Young	36	15
N5		|	at Oregon	10	34
N12		|	UCLA	23	59
N25		|	at Arizona	27	28

1995 — 6-5-0 (4-4-0)

A2		|	at Washington	20	23
S9	●		Texas-El Paso	45	20
A16			at Nebraska	28	77
S23	●	|	Oregon State	20	11
A30		|	at Southern Cal	0	31
O7		|	Stanford	28	30
O14	●		Brigham Young	29	21
A28	●	|	at Oregon	35	24
N4	●	|	UCLA	37	33
A11	●	|	at California	38	29
N24		|	Arizona	28	31

1996 — 11-1 (8-0)

S7	●	|	Washington	45	42
S14	●		North Texas	52	7
S21	●		Nebraska	19	0
S28	●	|	Oregon	48	27
O5	●		Boise State	56	7
O12	●	|	at UCLA	42	34
O19	●	|	Southern Cal	48	35
O26	●	|	at Stanford	41	9
N2	●	|	at Oregon State	29	14
N9	●	|	California	35	7
N23	●	|	at Arizona	56	14
			ROSE BOWL		
J1			Ohio State	17	20

1997 — 9-3 (6-2)

A30	●		New Mexico State	41	10
S13	●		at Miami, Fla.	23	12
S20			Brigham Young	10	13
S27	●	|	at Oregon State	13	10
O4		|	at Washington	14	26
O11	●	|	Southern Cal	35	7
O18	●	|	at Stanford	31	14
N1	●	|	Washington State	44	31
N8	●	|	at California	28	21
N15	●	|	Oregon	52	31
N28		|	Arizona	16	28
			SUN BOWL		
D31	●		Iowa	17	7

1998 — 5-6 (4-4)

S5		|	Washington	38	42
S12			at Brigham Young	6	26
S19	●		North Texas	34	15
S26	●	|	Oregon State	24	3
O3		|	at Southern Cal	24	35
O10			Notre Dame	9	28
O22	●	|	Stanford	44	38
O31	●	|	at Washington State	38	28
N7	●	|	California	55	22
N14		|	at Oregon	19	51
N27		|	at Arizona	42	50

1999
6-6   (5-3)

Date		Opponent		
S6	●	Texas Tech	31	13
S18		New Mexico State	7	35
S25	|	at California	23	24
O2	● |	UCLA	28	27
O9		at Notre Dame	17	48
O16	● |	at Washington	28	7
O23	● |	Washington State	33	21
O30	● |	at Oregon	17	20
N6	● |	at Southern Cal	26	16
N13	|	Stanford	30	50
N27	● |	Arizona	42	27

ALOHA BOWL

D25		Wake Forest	3	23

2000
6-6   (3-5)

Date		Opponent		
A31	●	at San Diego State	10	7
S16	●	Colorado State	13	10
S23	●	Utah State	44	20
S30		at UCLA	31	38
O7	|	California	30	10
O14	|	Washington	15	21
O21	● |	at Washington State	23	20
O28	|	Oregon	55	56
N4	|	Southern Cal	38	44
N11	|	at Stanford	7	29
N24	● |	at Arizona	30	17

ALOHA BOWL

D25		Boston College	17	31

DIRK KOETTER		
2001-Present (.531)		26-23

2001
4-7   (1-7)

Date		Opponent		
S8	●	San Diego State	38	7
S22	|	at Stanford	28	51
S29	●	San Jose State	53	15
O6	●	La. Lafayette	63	27
O13	|	at Southern Cal	17	48
O20	● |	Oregon State	41	24
O27	|	Washington	31	33
N3	|	at Oregon	24	42
N10	|	Washington State	16	28
N23	|	Arizona	21	34
D1	|	at UCLA	42	52

2002
8-6   (5-3)

Date		Opponent		
A24		at Nebraska	10	48
A29	●	Ea. Washington	38	2
S7	●	Central Florida	46	13
S14	●	at San Diego State	39	28
S28	● |	Stanford	65	24
O5		North Carolina	35	38
O12	● |	Oregon State	13	9
O19	● |	at Oregon	45	42
O26	● |	Washington	27	16
N2	|	at Washington State	22	44
N9	|	California	38	55
N16	|	at Southern Cal	13	34
N29	● |	at Arizona	34	20

HOLIDAY BOWL

D27		Kansas State	27	34

2003
5-7   (2-6)

Date		Opponent		
S6	●	No. Arizona	34	14
S13	●	Utah State	26	16
S20		at Iowa	2	21
S27	|	at Oregon State	17	45
O4	|	Southern Cal	17	37
O11	● |	Oregon	59	14
O18	●	at North Carolina	33	31
O25	|	at UCLA	13	20
N1	|	California	23	51
N8	|	at Stanford	27	38
N15	|	at Washington State	19	34
N29	● |	Arizona	28	7

2004
9-3   (5-3)

Date		Opponent		
S2	●	Texas-El Paso	41	9
S11	●	at Northwestern	30	21
S18	●	Iowa	44	7
S25	● |	Oregon State	27	14
O2	● |	at Oregon	28	13
O16	|	at Southern Cal	7	45
O23	● |	UCLA	48	42
O30	|	at California	0	27
N6	● |	Stanford	34	31
N13	● |	Washington State	45	28
N26	|	at Arizona	27	34

SUN BOWL

D31	●	Purdue	27	23

ARKANSAS

BY GEOFFREY NORMAN

A RKANSAS IS A RELATIVE NEWCOMER to the SEC. But when the Razorbacks joined the conference in 1992, they brought plenty to the party. This was a team that had been playing football since 1894, had won a national championship and many conference titles and had been part of some of the classic games in college football history. That includes the 1969 showdown that capped the sport's centennial season and lived up to its Game of the Century billing. Fans all over the country—including presidents of the United States—took an interest in those old Red River Shootout classics. And when Lou Holtz came to Fayetteville and took the Razorbacks to the big bowl games, Arkansas fans were relieved to find that the good times hadn't ended with state legend Frank Broyles' retirement as head coach. Some people miss the old Texas-Arkansas rivalry, but the cross-border wars with new conference foe LSU fill the void nicely, and the Razorbacks, under coach Houston Nutt, have showed signs of potency once more. The conference may be different, but the football—and the state's passion for it—remains unchanged.

TRADITION Nobody's sure exactly when it started; the 1920s is the best guess. Whenever the roots were planted, they remained after a group of Arkansas fans got an improbable cheer going that has carried down through the years and become one of the classic war cries in all of college football. Right up there with Alabama's "Roll Tide" is the "Hog Call," and it is simplicity itself, guaranteed to raise the hair on the back of the neck of any Arkansas fan.

Wooooo, Pig! Sooie!

Wooooo, Pig! Sooie!

Woooooooo, Pig! Sooie! Razorbacks!

There is, of course, a correct way to call the Hogs. Novices are advised to practice. You begin with both arms raised high and wave your fingers as the volume rises on the word "Wooooooo." The arms come down in a pumping motion on the word "Pig," then are extended again, vigorously, on the word "Sooie."

Done right, it is a thing of beauty.

BEST PLAYER Among the most graceful players to ever stride on a field, the six-foot, 180-pound Lance Alworth led the 1961 Razorbacks in rushing (110 carries for 516 yards), receiving (18 catches for 320 yards), punt returns (28 for 336 yards) and kickoff returns (13 for 300 yards). He was, in short, the offense. Alworth had an 11-year

THE BEST OF TIMES

Frank Broyles' Razorbacks ran wild in 1964 and 1965. A season-ending win over Texas Tech in 1963 launched Arkansas on a 22-game winning streak that ended with a 10-7 Cotton Bowl loss to hated LSU on New Year's Day 1966. In between, the Hogs won back-to-back Southwest Conference titles and the 1964 national championship. The 1964 Hogs racked up an astounding five consecutive shutout victories.

THE WORST OF TIMES

From 1948 to 1953, Arkansas stumbled to a 22–38 record and went just 10–26 in the SWC. The lone highlight of the period: a 16-14 win over Texas in 1951 that was the Razorbacks' first victory over the Longhorns in Fayetteville.

CONFERENCE

A charter member of the Southwest Conference in 1915, the Razorbacks remained in the SWC through 1991, before joining the SEC, one of the moves that marked a new era of conference fluidity in the college ranks.

DISTINGUISHED ALUMNI

J. William Fulbright; Jerry Jones; Pat Summerall; S. Robson Walton, Wal-Mart chairman; Lucinda Williams, country singer

FIGHT SONG

ARKANSAS FIGHT SONG
Hit that line, Hit that line, Keep on going,
Move that ball right down the field.
Give a cheer, Rah! Rah!
Never fear, Rah! Rah!
Arkansas will never yield.
On your toes Razorbacks to the finish.
Carry on with all your might.
For it's A-R-K-A-N-S-A-S for Arkansas,
Fight, Fight, Fi-i-ight.

career as a professional with the San Diego Chargers (where he would pick up his immortal nickname, Bambi) and the Dallas Cowboys, and later became the first American Football League player inducted into the Pro Football Hall of Fame.

> *Hugo Bezdek said they played "like a wild band of razorback hogs." It stuck.*

compiling a 144–58–5 record before retiring to devote himself exclusively to his duties as athletic director. In 1964, his 11–0 team won Arkansas' only national title, awarded by both the Football Writers Association and the Helms Foundation, whose votes came following the bowls. Good thing he got a second chance to make a first impression.

BEST COACH When Bowden Wyatt left the Razorbacks after the 1954 season for Tennessee, a young assistant from Baylor lobbied for the job. Arkansas turned him down in favor of a more experienced in-house man, Jack Mitchell. Three years later, Mitchell was out and Arkansas called on the man whom it had spurned before and now had a year of head coaching experience at Missouri. But Frank Broyles lost his first six at the Razorbacks helm in 1958, and many fans wished the school had taken a second pass on him. Then a win over Texas A&M turned things around as the Razorbacks won out that season. The next year, they went 9–2, tied for the Southwest Conference championship and ended Georgia Tech's eight-game winning streak in a 14-7 victory in the Gator Bowl.

Broyles kept winning and kept taking Arkansas to bowl games—10 altogether, nine of them on New Year's Day—

BEST TEAM The 1964 team is notable, of course, for its unblemished record. When all the bowl games had been played and all the dust had settled, the Razorbacks were the only undefeated team in the land. The AP and UPI had named Alabama national champions before the bowls, but then the Tide lost the Orange to Texas, a team Arkansas downed by a point in October. The Razorbacks came from behind in the Cotton Bowl to beat Nebraska 10-7 and distinguish themselves.

That 1964 squad has more than its spotless record to boast about. Four men associated with the team went on to coach college national championship teams: Broyles, of course; his assistant and former Arkansas player and team captain Barry Switzer; assistant Johnny Majors; and one of the players on that team, Jimmy Johnson. Johnson and Switzer went on

RECORDS

RUSHING YARDS
GAME 271 Dickey Morton vs. Baylor, Oct. 13, 1973 (28 att.)
SEASON 1,387 Madre Hill, 1995 (307 att.)
CAREER 3,570 Ben Cowins, 1975-78 (635 att.)

PASSING YARDS
GAME 387 Clint Stoerner vs. LSU, Nov. 28, 1997 (18 of 38)
SEASON 2,629 Clint Stoerner, 1998 (167 of 312)
CAREER 7,422 Clint Stoerner, 1996-99 (528 of 1,023)

RECEIVING YARDS
GAME 204 Mike Reppond vs. Rice, Nov. 6, 1971 (12 rec.)
SEASON 1,004 Anthony Lucas, 1998 (43 rec.)
CAREER 2,879 Anthony Lucas, 1995-99 (137 rec.)

POINTS
GAME 36 Madre Hill vs. South Carolina, Sept. 9, 1995 (6 TDs)
SEASON 120 Bill Burnett, 1969 (20 TDs)
CAREER 294 Bill Burnett, 1968-70 (49 TDs)

CONSENSUS ALL-AMERICANS
1948	Clyde Scott, B
1954	Bud Brooks, G
1965	Glen Ray Hines, T
1965-66	Loyd Phillips, DT
1968	Jim Barnes, G
1969	Rodney Brand, C
1970	Dick Bumpas, DT
1977	Leotis Harris, G
1977	Steve Little, K/P
1979	Greg Kolenda, T
1981-82	Billy Ray Smith Jr., DL
1982	Steve Korte, OL
1988	Kendall Trainor, PK
1988	Wayne Martin, DL
1989	Jim Mabry, OL
2002-03	Shawn Andrews, OL

to glory as coaches at both the college and the professional levels. The two Arkansas products are the only coaches in history to have won a college national championship and a Super Bowl. They both won the NFL's big prize with the Dallas Cowboys, whose owner, Jerry Jones, also played for the 1964 Razorbacks. This, plainly, was a team with some football magic.

BIGGEST GAME On the way to that undefeated season in 1964, Arkansas had to get past the defending national champion Texas Longhorns, who had not lost a regular-season game in four years. The game was a battle for the conference title, possibly the national championship, and that intangible thing that goes with any great rivalry—call it "pride."

The Longhorns missed an early field goal before the game became one of defense and punting. Midway through the second quarter, Texas punter Ernie Koy kicked 47 yards to the Arkansas 19, where Ken Hatfield took the ball and started toward the sideline. A wall of Razorbacks cleared the way until only Koy could stop him. Two Arkansas blockers made sure he didn't, and the Razorbacks went on to a narrow 14-13 victory and the perfect season.

BIGGEST UPSET Even before Lou Holtz suspended his two top running backs and best receiver just prior to the 1978 Orange Bowl, the Razorbacks were decided underdogs to the Oklahoma Sooners, contenders for a national title. Holtz was in his first year as head coach at Arkansas, and it was his burden to be the man who followed a legend—Frank Broyles. Before the season, experts picked his team to finish fifth in the Southwest Conference. The Razorbacks surprised everyone—except, perhaps, themselves and their coach— by losing only one game. Still, on paper Arkansas appeared overmatched by Oklahoma, especially after the suspensions.

Texas, which was responsible for Arkansas' lone defeat,

ALL-CENTENNIAL TEAM	
Chosen in 1994 by a committee of former players, sportswriters and sports information directors as well as fans.	
OFFENSE	
1952-54	Bud Brooks, OL
1963-65	Glen Ray Hines, OL
1973-76	R.C. Thielemann, OL
1974-77	Leotis Harris, OL
1981-82	Steve Korte, OL
1985-88	Freddie Childress, OL
1927-29	Wear Schoonover, WR
1963-65	Bobby Crockett, WR
1968-70	Chuck Dicus, WR
1970-72	Jim Benton, WR
1968-70	Bill Montgomery, QB
1970-72	Joe Ferguson, QB
1987-90	Quinn Grovey, QB
1946-49	Leon Campbell, RB
1946-48	Clyde Scott, RB
1957-59	Jim Mooty, RB
1959-61	Lance Alworth, RB
1987-89	Barry Foster, RB
1951-53	Lamar McHan, QB
1949-51	Pat Summerall, K/P
1974-77	Steve Little, K/P
1979-80	Steve Cox, P
DEFENSE	
1949-51	Dave Hanner, DL
1949-51	Fred Williams, DL
1954-56	Billy Ray Smith Sr., DL
1964-66	Loyd Phillips, DL
1975-78	Dan Hampton, DL
1979-82	Billy Ray Smith Jr., DL
1985-88	Wayne Martin, DL
1958-60	Wayne Harris, LB
1962-64	Ronnie Caveness, LB
1967-69	Cliff Powell, LB
1973-76	Dennis Winston, LB
1943-46	Alton Baldwin, DB
1960-62	Billy Moore, DB
1962-64	Ken Hatfield, DB
1964-66	Martine Bercher, DB
1985-88	Steve Atwater, DB

had lost its bowl game earlier in the day. If Oklahoma could beat the Razorbacks, it would be No. 1. But the Sooners couldn't stop reserve tailback Roland Sales, who ran for 205 yards and picked up another 52 yards receiving. The Razorbacks won—no, dominated—31-6.

HEARTBREAKER It was called the Big Shootout, and president Richard Nixon and evangelist Billy Graham were among the sellout crowd in Fayetteville. Millions of others were glued to their televisions on Dec. 6, 1969, as No. 1 Texas and No. 2 Arkansas played a game that didn't disappoint the hypesters. Going into the fourth quarter, the Razorbacks held a 14-0 lead. But James Street ran for a 42-yard touchdown and Texas scored its first two-point conversion of the season. Then, with four minutes left on fourth and three, Texas did something it never did—pass. The 44-yard completion set up the winning score and broke many Razorback hearts forever.

BEST GOAL-LINE STAND The 1947 Cotton Bowl was an entire game's worth of goal-line stands. The Razorbacks faced LSU on a 20° day and held the Tigers—and their illustrious quarterback, Y.A. Tittle—five times inside the 10 in the first half. With the game still scoreless, Arkansas stopped LSU on the 1 with time running out in the third quarter. The Tigers missed a field goal attempt. Then, as the game ended, LSU once more knocked on the door. But the Razorbacks held on their own 1 yet again, freezing the scoreless tie in the snow.

BEST COMEBACK The Razorbacks were down 17-7 to 18th-ranked LSU in the fourth quarter of a contest that would settle the 2002 SEC Western Division title. With 34 seconds left, Arkansas trailed by six with the ball on its 19 and no timeouts. Three plays took the Razorbacks all

the way down the field and into the end zone to tie the game. Understandably ebullient, the Arkansas players celebrated excessively and were penalized 15 yards on the extra point. Still, this was the Razorbacks' day. The kick was true and Arkansas made the SEC championship game for the second time since joining the conference.

STADIUM The first game at Donald W. Reynolds Razorback Stadium saw Arkansas defeat Oklahoma A&M 27-7 on Sept. 24, 1938. The stadium was a vast improvement over the old 300-seat facility built on a piece of land known as The Hill, and it's seen a number of improvements over the years. Its most recent and thorough renovation and expansion came before the 2001 season. The $110 million project raised the capacity from 51,000 to 72,000 and also added a number of suites.

RIVAL Texas and Arkansas first played each other in 1894. The always-fierce rivalry became incandescent during the 1960s, when the schools routinely played for conference and even national championships. This was the era of the one-point heartbreaker: Texas going down 14-13 in 1964; Arkansas losing what some called the Game of the Century, 15-14, in 1969. The schools, however, stopped playing every year when Arkansas left the Southwest Conference for the SEC.

Since there is no in-state foe, another school from a bordering state assumed archrival status—LSU. The two schools have actually gotten after each other for a long time and, as is typical of rivals, they like to spoil each others' seasons. The Razorbacks upset the Tigers in a scoreless tie in the 1947 Cotton Bowl and LSU ended a 22-game Razorbacks winning streak in the same bowl in 1966. LSU and Arkansas first played each other in 1901 and have met in six different cities and four different states. In 1996, with the game having attained full rivalry status, the Golden Boot trophy was introduced as spoils for the victors. The Boot is in the shape of the two states, is molded from 24-karat gold and is valued at $10,000. It stands four feet tall and weighs almost 200 pounds.

NICKNAME In 1909, the Arkansas Cardinals—as they were then known—went 7–0, scoring 186 points while allowing only 18. After a particularly satisfying win over LSU, Arkansas coach Hugo Bezdek told fans that his boys had

played "like a wild band of razorback hogs." In Arkansas, everyone knew exactly what he meant. And the name stuck.

MASCOT There are both costumed and live razorbacks at Arkansas games. The live animals are not true razorbacks, which exist today only in remote parts of Australia. But the Russian boar comes close enough, and a specimen whose name is Tusk I owns the honor. He lives on a farm near Fayetteville when he isn't attending games. In the past, some of his predecessors have lived up to the razorback legend for orneriness. One was known to have killed a coyote, a 450-pound domestic pig and seven rattlesnakes.

UNIFORMS The colors have been cardinal red and white for as long as Arkansas has been playing football. In fact, before they became the Razorbacks, Arkansas football teams were the Cardinals. The distinctive helmets with fierce and elegant Razorbacks logos date to 1964 and the famous undefeated, untied team.

WEIRDNESS Arkansas has played in two games that went into seven overtimes … and won both of them, on the road. The first was in 2001, when the Razorbacks beat Mississippi 58-56 in Oxford. Then, in 2003, the Razorbacks beat Kentucky in Lexington by a score that seems more likely to have come in a basketball game, 71-63.

LORE It is known as the Powder River Play, and it led to an upset of fifth-ranked Ole Miss on Oct. 23, 1954. Bowden Wyatt's squad, known affectionately as the 25 Little Pigs, was locked in a scoreless tie with the Rebels with some six minutes left when running quarterback Buddy Benson took the snap and began what looked like a sweep. Preston Carpenter slipped past the Ole Miss secondary and took a 33-yard pass from Benson and ran another 33 for a 66-yard touchdown that was the only score of the day. Wyatt had brought the play with him from Wyoming, where the famously deceptive Powder River runs a mile wide and six inches deep.

QUOTE "After all, he's on a four-year scholarship and I'm sitting here with a one-year contract." —Frank Broyles, explaining his reluctance to send in plays to his quarterback

> *Arkansas has played two games that went into seven overtimes … and won both.*

ARKANSAS ANNUAL STATISTICAL LEADERS

YR	RUSHING	YDS	ATT	AVG	PASSING	ATT	CMP	PCT	YDS	RECEIVING	REC	YDS	AVG
1945	John Hoffman	587	139	4.2	Bud Canada	69	24	.35	272	John Hoffman	11	196	17.8
1946	Ken Holland	397	112	3.5	Aubrey Fowler	40	18	.45	320	Clyde Scott	11	183	16.6
1947	Clyde Scott	659	152	4.3	Ken Holland	46	25	.54	360	Ross Pritchard	15	266	17.7
1948	Clyde Scott	670	95	7.1	Gordon Long	56	32	.57	449	Ross Pritchard	17	311	18.3
1949	Geno Mazzanti	757	123	6.2	Don Logue	79	31	.39	374	Pat Summerall	17	298	17.5
1950	Buddy Rogers	476	118	4.0	Jim Rinehart	139	59	.42	756	Bill Jurney	22	335	15.2
1951	Lamar McHan	433	127	3.4	Lamar McHan	135	53	.39	724	Pat Summerall	24	358	14.9
1952	Buddy Sutton	448	100	4.5	Lamar McHan	136	55	.40	743	Lewis Carpenter	19	335	17.6
1953	Lamar McHan	409	143	2.9	Lamar McHan	150	78	.52	1,107	Floyd Sagely	30	542	18.1
1954	Henry Moore	670	153	4.4	George Walker	85	45	.53	603	Preston Carpenter	21	234	11.1
1955	Henry Moore	701	134	5.2	George Walker	47	22	.47	347	Preston Carpenter	11	155	14.1
1956	Gerald Nesbitt	663	129	5.1	Don Christian	53	18	.34	260	Ronnie Underwood	7	154	22.0
1957	Gerald Nesbitt	624	145	4.3	George Walker	63	35	.56	587	Billy Kyser	10	179	17.9
1958	Jim Mooty	395	71	5.6	James Monroe	96	41	.43	512	Charlie Barnes	15	175	11.7
1959	Jim Mooty	519	93	5.6	James Monroe	30	19	.63	202	Steve Butler	9	107	11.9
1960	Lance Alworth	375	106	3.5	George McKinney	90	39	.43	728	Jimmy Collier	17	356	20.9
1961	Lance Alworth	516	110	4.7	George McKinney	68	32	.47	426	Lance Alworth	18	320	17.8
1962	Billy Moore	585	131	4.5	Billy Moore	91	51	.56	673	Jerry Lamb	23	378	16.4
1963	Jim Lindsey	444	130	3.4	Bill Gray	79	34	.43	483	Jerry Lamb	16	240	15.0
1964	Jack Brasuell	542	173	3.1	Fred Marshall	94	50	.53	656	Jim Lindsey	24	331	13.8
1965	Bobby Burnett	947	232	4.1	Jon Brittenum	149	75	.50	1,103	Bobby Crockett	30	487	16.2
1966	David Dickey	447	115	3.9	Jon Brittenum	143	76	.53	1,103	Tommy Burnett	29	401	13.8
1967	Russell Cody	383	95	4.0	Ronny South	142	84	.59	1,159	Max Peacock	30	468	15.6
1968	Bill Burnett	859	207	4.1	Bill Montgomery	234	134	.57	1,595	Max Peacock	39	497	12.7
1969	Bill Burnett	900	209	4.3	Bill Montgomery	173	93	.54	1,333	Chuck Dicus	42	688	16.4
1970	Bill Burnett	445	110	4.0	Bill Montgomery	195	110	.56	1,662	Chuck Dicus	38	577	15.2
1971	Dickey Morton	831	127	6.5	Joe Ferguson	271	160	.59	2,203	Mike Reppond	56	986	17.6
1972	Dickey Morton	1,188	242	4.9	Joe Ferguson	254	119	.47	1,484	Mike Reppond	36	475	13.2
1973	Dickey Morton	1,298	226	5.7	Mike Kirkland	151	75	.50	990	Jack Ettinger	28	411	14.7
1974	Ike Forte	974	187	5.2	Scott Bull	32	14	.44	238	Freddie Douglas	15	332	22.1
1975	Ike Forte	983	174	5.6	Scott Bull	71	33	.46	570	Freddie Douglas	13	232	17.8
1976	Ben Cowins	1,162	183	6.3	Ron Calcagni	57	17	.30	366	Charles Clay	7	174	24.9
1977	Ben Cowins	1,192	220	5.4	Ron Calcagni	137	73	.53	1,147	Donnie Bobo	22	454	20.6
1978	Ben Cowins	1,006	188	5.4	Ron Calcagni	103	62	.60	807	Robert Farrell	13	229	17.6
1979	Roland Sales	625	138	4.5	Kevin Scanlon	139	92	.66	1,212	Gary Stiggers	23	221	9.6
1980	James Tolbert	571	140	4.1	Tom Jones	166	93	.56	1,161	Gary Anderson	23	153	6.7
1981	Gary Anderson	616	121	5.1	Brad Taylor	99	53	.54	726	Gary Anderson	26	263	10.1
1982	Daryl Bowles	619	155	4.0	Brad Taylor	141	59	.42	1,073	Gary Anderson	26	486	18.7
1983	Derek Thomas	432	117	3.7	Brad Taylor	257	139	.54	1,837	Mark Mistler	33	401	12.2
1984	Marshall Foreman	804	183	4.4	Brad Taylor	147	82	.56	1,166	James Shibest	51	907	17.8
1985	James Rouse	550	99	5.6	Mark Calcagni	47	27	.57	561	James Shibest	20	446	22.3
1986	Greg Thomas	461	141	3.3	Greg Thomas	109	67	.61	1,032	James Shibest	22	473	21.5
1987	James Rouse	1,004	182	5.5	Quinn Grovey	62	38	.61	495	Derek Russell	16	297	18.6
1988	Barry Foster	660	132	5.0	Quinn Grovey	98	62	.63	966	Tim Horton	16	319	19.9
1989	James Rouse	895	163	5.5	Quinn Grovey	132	72	.55	1,149	Tim Horton	23	454	19.7
1990	E.D. Jackson	596	155	3.8	Quinn Grovey	235	120	.51	1,886	Derek Russell	43	897	20.9
1991	E.D. Jackson	641	143	4.5	Jason Allen	102	48	.47	603	Ron Dickerson	25	372	14.9
1992	E.D. Jackson	466	118	3.9	Barry Lunney Jr.	189	91	.48	1,015	Kirk Botkin	33	257	7.8
1993	Oscar Malone	555	89	6.2	Barry Lunney Jr.	202	104	.51	1,241	J.J. Meadors	28	429	15.3
1994	Oscar Malone	597	99	6.0	Barry Lunney Jr.	183	101	.55	1,345	J.J. Meadors	43	613	14.3
1995	Madre Hill	1,387	307	4.5	Barry Lunney Jr.	292	180	.62	2,181	Anthony Eubanks	43	596	13.9
1996	Oscar Malone	814	197	4.1	Pete Burks	224	115	.51	1,390	Anthony Eubanks	51	809	15.9
1997	Rod Stinson	413	111	3.7	Clint Stoerner	357	173	.48	2,347	Anthony Eubanks	51	870	17.1
1998	Chrys Chukwuma	870	149	5.8	Clint Stoerner	312	167	.54	2,629	Michael Williams	44	560	12.7
1999	Cedric Cobbs	668	116	5.8	Clint Stoerner	317	177	.56	2,293	Anthony Lucas	37	822	22.2
2000	Fred Talley	768	137	5.6	Robby Hampton	261	145	.56	1,548	Boo Williams	52	739	14.2
2001	Fred Talley	774	164	4.7	Zak Clark	179	88	.49	1,000	George Wilson	40	568	14.2
2002	Fred Talley	1,119	197	5.7	Matt Jones	234	122	.52	1,592	George Wilson	49	626	12.8
2003	Cedric Cobbs	1,320	227	5.8	Matt Jones	230	132	.57	1,917	George Wilson	50	900	18.0
2004	Matt Jones	622	83	7.5	Matt Jones	264	151	.57	2,073	Steven Harris	37	617	16.7

Receiving leaders by receptions
The NCAA began including postseason stats in 2002

ARKANSAS ALL-TIME SCORES

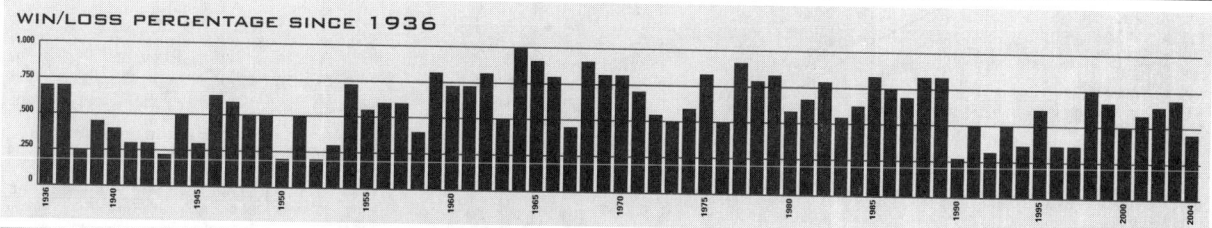

WIN/LOSS PERCENTAGE SINCE 1936

JOHN C. FUTRALL
1894-96 (.714)   5-2

1894   2-1-0
O13	●	Fort Smith HS	42 0
O27	●	at Fort Smith HS	38 0
N29		at Texas	0 54

1895   1-0-0
O12	●	Fort Smith HS	30 0

1896   2-1-0
O3	●	Fort Smith HS	10 0
O10	●	at Fort Smith HS	6 2
O24		at Drury Coll.	0 34

B.N. WILSON
1897-98 (.750)   4-1-1

1897   2-0-1
N6	●	Fort Smith HS	12 0
N20	=	at Drury Coll.	6 6
N25	●	at Ouachita College	24 0

1898   2-1-0
O22	●	Drury Coll.	17 0
N5	●	at Drury Coll.	12 6
N19		at FortScott HS	8 36

COLBERT SEARLES
1899-1900 (.667)   5-2-2

1899   3-1-1
O14	●	Drury Coll.	10 0
O28	●	Tulsa	11 0
N3	=	Tulsa *Mus*	0 0
N4		Oklahoma *Sha*	5 11
N18	●	Joplin HS	11 10

1900   2-1-1
O27	●	Webb City HS	15 0
N3	=	at Joplin HS	6 6
N10	●	Pierce C.C.	10 0
N24		at Drury Coll.	5 17

CHARLES THOMAS
1901-02 (.529)   9-8

1901   3-5-0
O12	●	Pierce C.C.	0 5
O19	●	Drury Coll.	22 0
O26		Fort Scott HS	6 17
N2		at Little Rock HS	0 5
N9	●	Tulsa	48 0
N16		K.C. Medics	6 10
N22		at LSU	0 15
N23		at Louisiana Tech	16 0

1902   6-3-0
O4	●	at Neosho HS	6 0
O11	●	at Kingfisher Coll.	15 6
O22		at Oklahoma	0 28
O28	●	Tulsa *Mus*	33 0
N1	●	Tahlequah S.	50 0
N8		at S.W. Missouri	5 15
N10		at Pierce C.C.	2 24
N17	●	Fort Scott HS	16 0
N27	●	Missouri Rolla	11 0

D.A. McDANIEL
1903 (.429)   3-4

1903   3-4-0
O10	●	S.W. Missouri	5 10
O16		at Missouri M.	6 17
O17	●	at Drury Coll.	10 6
O30		at Texas	0 15
O31		at Texas A&M	0 6
N7	●	FortSmith HS	17 9
N21	●	Oklahoma	12 0

A.D. BROWN
1904-05 (.400)   6-9

1904   4-3-0
O15		Drury Coll.	0 12
O22	●	Fort Scott HS	22 0
N4		at Dallas Med.	0 5
N5		at Baylor	6 17
N12		Wichita St.	12 6
N19		at Fort Smith	11 5
N26		Missouri Rolla	11 10

1905   2-6-0
O7		Kansas	0 6
O14		at Washington, Mo.	0 6
O16		at Drury Coll.	0 12
O26	●	Chilocco	6 0
O31		Texas	0 4
N12		Transylvania, Ky	0 6
N17		at Missouri Rolla	0 16
N30	●	KC Medics	26 0

F.C. LONGMAN
1906-07 (.406)   5-8-3

1906   2-4-2
S29		Chilocco	0 6
O8	=	Drury Coll.	0 0
O13		at Kansas	5 37
O30		at Texas	0 11
N6	●	S.E. Missouri St. *Hot*	12 0
N10		at Missouri	0 11
N24	●	at Tulane	22 0
N29	=	at LSU	6 6

1907   3-4-1
O5	=	Haskell	0 0
O12	●	Drury Coll.	23 0
O19		at Drury Coll.	17 6
O26		at St. Louis	6 42
O30		Texas	6 26
N6		at LSU	12 17
N18		Tennessee *Mem*	2 14
N23	●	Missouri Rolla	7 5

HUGO BEZDEK
1908-12 (.686)   29-13-1

1908   5-4-0
O3	●	Haskell	6 0
O10	●	Mississippi	33 0
O17		at St. Louis	0 24
O24	●	Henderson St.	51 0
O31		at Oklahoma	5 27
N7		at Texas	0 21
N14	●	Pittsburg St.	42 12
N21	●	Ouachita	73 0
N26		LSU *LR*	4 36

1909   7-0-0
O2	●	Henderson St.	24 0
O9	●	at Drury Coll.	12 6
O16	●	Wichita St.	23 6
O23	●	Oklahoma	21 6 *
O30	●	at Ouachita	56 0
N13	●	LSU *Mem*	16 0
N25	●	Washington, Mo. *LR*	34 0

1910   7-1-0
O1	●	Drury Coll.	33 0
O9	●	Henderson St.	63 0
O15		Kansas State	0 5
O22	●	Texas SW	13 12
O29	●	Texas A&M	5 0
N5	●	at Washington, Mo.	50 0
N15	●	Missouri Rolla	6 2
N24	●	LSU *LR*	51 0

1911   6-2-1
S30	●	S.W. Missouri St.	100 0
O7	●	Drury Coll.	65 0
O14	●	Hendrix College	45 0
O28		at Texas	0 12
N4	=	at Southwestern	0 0
N11	●	Missouri Rolla *Jop*	44 3
N18		Kansas State *KC*	0 3
N25		at Washington, Mo.	3 0
N30		LSU *LR*	11 0

1912   4-6-0
S28	●	Henderson St.	39 6
O5	●	Hendrix College	52 0
O12		Oklahoma State	7 13
O18		Texas A&M *Dal*	0 27
O26		at Baylor	0 6 *
N2	●	Southwestern	25 0
N9		at Wisconsin	7 64
N16		LSU *LR*	6 7
N23	●	at Washington, Mo.	13 7
N28		at Texas	0 48

E.T. PICKERING
1913-14 (.556)   10-8

1913   7-2-0
O3	●	Henderson St.	3 0
O11	●	Hendrix	26 0
O18	●	Oklahoma State	3 0
O25	●	Baylor	34 0
N1	●	Austin Coll. *FrS*	26 7
N8		LSU *Shre*	7 12
N15		Mississippi *LR*	10 21
N17	●	at Ouachita	14 3
N27	●	at Tulane	14 0

1914   3-6-0
O3	●	Hendrix	13 7
O10		Ouachita	9 15
O17	●	St. Louis	26 0
O24		Missouri Rolla	0 44
O31		at Oklahoma State	0 46
N7	●	LSU *Shre*	20 12
N14		Mississippi *LR*	7 13
N21		Oklahoma *OxC*	7 35
N28		at Drury Coll.	7 28

1915-1991
SWC

T.T. McCONNELL
1915-16 (.567)   8-6-1

1915   4-2-1 (1-1-0)
O2	●	Hendrix	41 0
O9	●	Ouachita	13 9
O23		Oklahoma State *FrS*	14 9
O30	=	at St. Louis	0 0
N5	●	LSU *Shre*	7 13
N14		Oklahoma	0 24
N20	●	Missouri Rolla	46 0

1916   4-4-0 (0-2-0)
S30	●	Pittsburg St.	34 20
O7	●	Hendrix	58 0
O14	●	Oklahoma Mines	82 0
O21	●	Missouri Rolla	60 0
N5		LSU *Shre*	7 17
N14		at Texas	0 52
N23		Oklahoma *FrS*	13 14
N30		Mississippi State *Mem*	7 20

NORMAN PAINE
1917-18 (.708)   8-3-1

1917   5-1-1 (0-1-1)
O6	●	Central Mo. St.	34 0
O13	●	Hendrix	19 0
O20	●	Missouri Rolla	32 0
O27	●	Tulsa	19 7
N3	●	LSU *Shre*	14 0
N17	=	Oklahoma *FrS*	0 0
N29		at Texas	0 20

1918   3-2-0 (0-1-0)
S28		Camp Pike	0 6
O5	●	Missouri Rolla	6 0
O19		at Oklahoma	0 103
O26	●	Tulsa	23 6
N2		at S.W. Missouri St.	12 6

J.B. CRAIG
1919 (.429)   3-4

1919   3-4-0 (1-2-0)
O11	●	Hendrix	7 0
O18	●	Missouri Rolla	20 0
O25		LSU *Shre*	0 20
N1		Tulsa	7 63
N8		at Texas	7 35
N15	●	Oklahoma	7 6
N27		at Rice	7 40

G.W. McLAREN
1920-21 (.594)   8-5-3

1920   3-2-2 (2-0-1)
O9	=	Hendrix	0 0
O16		TCU	2 19
O22	●	at SMU	6 0
O30	●	Missouri Rolla	14 0
N6		LSU *Shre*	0 3
N13	●	at Phillips	20 0
N25		at Rice	0 0

1921   5-3-1 (2-1-0)
O1	●	Hendrix	28 0
O8	●	Drury Coll.	40 0
O15	●	Ouachita *LR*	28 0
O22		Oklahoma State	0 7
O29	●	SMU *FrS*	14 0
N5		LSU *Shre*	7 10
N12	=	at Phillips	0 0
N19		Baylor	13 12
N24		at TCU	14 19

FRANCIS SCHMIDT
1922-28 (.654)   41-21-3

1922   4-5-0 (1-3-0)
S30	●	Hendrix	39 0
O7	●	Drury Coll.	22 0
O14	●	Ouachita *LR*	7 13
O21		at Baylor	13 60
O28	●	LSU *Shre*	40 6
N4		Tulsa	6 13
N11		at Rice	7 31
N18	●	SMU	9 0
N30		Oklahoma State *FrS*	0 13

1923   6-2-1 (2-2-0)
S29	●	Central Ark.	32 0
O6	●	Drury Coll.	26 0
O13	●	Rice *LR*	23 0
O20		Baylor	0 14
O27	●	LSU *Shre*	26 13
N3	=	Ouachita	0 0
N10		at SMU	6 13
N24	●	Phillips *Mus*	32 0
D1	●	Oklahoma State *FrS*	13 0

1924 7-2-1 (1-2-1)

S27	●	N.E. Oklahoma	54	6
O4	●	S.W. Missouri St.	47	0
O11	●	Hendrix	34	3
O18	|	at Baylor	0	13
O25	●	Mississippi LR	20	0
N1	●	LSU Shre	10	7
N8	= |	SMU	14	14
N15	●	Phillips FtS	28	6
N21	|	at Oklahoma State	0	20
N27	● |	TCU	20	0

1925 4-4-1 (2-2-1)

O3		at Iowa	0	25 *
O10		Oklahoma Baptist	0	6
O17	|	at Rice	9	13
O24	●	Phillips	45	0
O31	● ||	LSU Shre	12	0
N7	= |	at SMU	0	0
N14	|	at TCU	0	3
N21	● ||	Oklahoma State	9	7
N28	●	at Tulsa	20	7

1926 5-5-0 (2-2-0)

S26	●	Central Ark.	60	0
O2	● ||	Mississippi	21	6
O9		at Oklahoma	6	13
O16	●	Hendrix LR	14	7
O23	● ||	Centenary	33	6
O30		at Kansas State	7	16
N6	||	LSU Shre	0	14
N12	|	TCU	7	10
N19	●	at Oklahoma State	24	2
N25		at Tulsa	7	14

1927 8-1-0 (3-1-0)

O1	●	Ozark Coll.	32	0
O8	● |	Baylor	13	6
O15	|	at Texas A&M	6	40
O22	●	Missouri Rolla	34	0
O29	● ||	LSU Shre	28	0
N5	● |	at TCU	10	3
N12	●	Oklahoma State	33	20
N19	●	Austin Coll.	42	0
N26	●	Hendrix LR	20	7

1928 7-2-0 (3-1-0)

S29		at Mississippi	0	25
O6	●	Coll. Of Ozarks	21	0
O13	● |	Baylor Tex	14	0
O20	|	at Texas	7	20
O29	● |	Texas A&M	27	12
N3	● ||	LSU Shre	7	0
N17	●	Missouri Rolla	45	6
N24	●	Oklahoma Baptist	57	0
N29	●	Southwestern Mem	73	0

FRED THOMSEN 1929-41 (.480) 56-61-10

1929 7-2-0 (3-2-0)

S28	●	Ozark Coll.	37	0
O5	●	Henderson St.	30	7
O12	|	Texas	0	27
O19	|	at Baylor	20	31
O26	● |	at Texas A&M	14	13
N2	● ||	LSU Shre	32	0
N9	●	E. Central Oklahoma	52	7
N16	●	Centenary	13	2
N28	● ||	at Oklahoma State	32	6

1930 3-6-0 (2-2-0)

S27	●	Ozark Coll.	27	0
O4		at Tulsa	6	26
O11	|	at TCU	0	40
O18	● |	Rice	7	6
O25	● |	Texas A&M LR	13	0
N1		LSU Shre	12	27
N8		Oklahoma State	0	26
N15	|	Baylor	7	22
N27		at Centenary	6	7

1931 3-5-1 (0-4-0)

S26	●	Ozark Coll.	13	6
O3	●	Hendrix	19	0
O10	|	SMU	6	42
O17	|	at Baylor	7	19
O24		LSU Shre	6	13
O31	|	TCU	0	7
N7	=	at Chicago	13	13
N21	|	at Rice	12	26
N26	●	at Centenary	6	0

1932 1-6-2 (1-4-0)

S24	=	Hendrix	0	0
O1		Missouri Rolla	19	20
O8	|	at TCU	12	34
O15	● |	Baylor LR	20	6
O22		LSU Shre	0	14
N5	|	Rice	7	12
N12	|	at SMU	7	13
N18	|	Texas	0	34
N26	=	at Centenary	0	0

1933 7-3-1 (4-1-0)

S23	●	Ozark Coll.	40	0
S30	●	Oklahoma Baptist	42	7
O7	● |	TCU	13	0
O14	● |	Baylor LR	19	7
O21		LSU Shre	0	20
O28	● |	SMU	3	0
N11	|	at Rice	6	7
N18	●	Hendrix	63	0
N24	● |	at Texas	20	6
N30		at Tulsa	0	7
		DIXIE CLASSIC		
J1	=	Centenary	7	7

1934 4-4-2 (2-3-1)

S29	●	Ozark Coll.	13	0
O6	● |	at TCU	24	10
O13	● |	Baylor LR	6	0
O20		LSU Shre	0	16
O27	●	Missouri Rolla	20	0
N3	= |	at Texas A&M	7	7
N10	|	Rice	0	7
N17	|	at SMU	6	10
N23	|	Texas	12	19
N29	=	at Tulsa	7	7

1935 5-5-0 (2-4-0)

S28	●	Pittsburgh St.	12	0
O5	|	TCU	7	13
O12	|	at Baylor	6	13
O19		LSU Shre	7	13
O26	●	Ozark Coll.	51	6
N2	● |	Texas A&M LR	14	7
N9	|	at Rice	7	20
N16	|	SMU	6	17
N22	● |	at Texas	28	13
N28	●	at Tulsa	14	7

1936 7-3-0 (5-1-0)

S26	●	Pittsburg St.	53	0
O3	|	at TCU	14	18
O10	● |	Baylor	14	10
O16		at George Washington	6	13
O24		LSU Shre	7	19
O31	● |	at Texas A&M	18	0
N7	● |	Rice	20	14
N14	● |	at SMU	17	0
N26	●	at Tulsa	23	13
D3	● |	Texas LR	6	0

1937 6-2-2 (3-2-1)

S25	●	Central Oklahoma	25	0
O2	= |	TCU	7	7
O9	|	at Baylor	14	20
O16	● |	at Texas	21	10
O23	● |	SMU FtS	13	0
O30	● |	Texas A&M	26	13
N6	|	at Rice	20	26
N13	●	Mississippi Mem	32	6
N20	=	George Washington LR	0	0
N25	●	at Tulsa	28	7

1938 2-7-1 (1-5-0)

S24	●	Oklahoma State	27	7
O1	|	at TCU	14	21
O8	|	Baylor	6	9
O15	● |	Texas LR	42	6
O22		Santa Clara SF	6	21
O29	|	at Texas A&M	7	13
N5	|	Rice	0	3
N12	|	at SMU	6	19
N16		Mississippi Mem	14	20
N24	=	at Tulsa	6	6

1939 4-5-1 (2-3-1)

S23	●	East Central Oklahoma	32	6
S30		Mississippi State Mem	0	19
O7	● |	TCU	14	13
O14	|	at Baylor	7	19
O21	|	at Texas	13	14
O28		Villanova Phil	0	7
N4	|	Texas A&M	0	27
N11	= |	at Rice	12	12
N17	● |	SMU LR	14	0
N30	●	at Tulsa	23	0

1940 4-6-0 (1-5-0)

S28	●	East Central Oklahoma	38	0
O5	|	at TCU	0	20
O12	● |	Baylor	12	6
O19	|	Texas LR	0	21
O26	●	Mississippi Mem	21	20
N2	|	at Texas A&M	0	17
N9	|	Rice	7	14
N16	|	at SMU	0	28
N21		Fordham NYC	7	27
N28	●	at Tulsa	27	21

1941 3-7-0 (0-6-0)

S27	●	E. Cent. Okla.	56	0
O4	|	TCU	0	9
O11	|	at Baylor	7	20
O18	|	at Texas	14	48
O25	●	at Detroit	9	6
N1	|	Texas A&M LR	0	7
N8	|	at Rice	12	21
N15	|	SMU	7	14
N22		Mississippi Mem	0	18
N27	●	at Tulsa	13	6

GEORGE COLE 1942 (.300) 3-7

1942 3-7-0 (0-6-0)

S26	●	Wichita St.	27	0
O3	|	at TCU	6	13
O10	|	Baylor	7	20
O17	|	Texas LR	6	47
O24	●	Mississippi Mem	7	6
O31	|	at Texas A&M	0	41
N7	|	Rice	9	40
N14	|	at SMU	6	14
N21	●	at Detroit	14	7
N26		at Tulsa	7	40

JOHN TOMLIN 1943 (.222) 2-7

1943 2-7-0 (1-4-0)

S25	●	Missouri Rolla	59	0
O2	|	TCU LR	0	13
O9		Mont Navy	12	20
O16	|	at Texas	0	34
O30	|	Texas A&M	0	13
N6	|	at Rice	7	20
N13	● |	SMU SA	14	12
N19		Oklahoma State FtS	13	19
N25		at Tulsa	0	61

GLEN ROSE 1944-45 (.405) 8-12-1

1944 5-5-1 (2-2-1)

S23	●	Missouri StL	7	6
S29		Oklahoma State OkC	0	19
O7	= |	at TCU	6	6
O14		Norman NAS	7	27
O21	|	Texas LR	0	19
O28	●	Mississippi Mem	26	18
N4	● |	at Texas A&M	7	6
N11	● |	Rice	12	7
N18	|	at SMU	12	20
N23		at Tulsa	2	33
D2	●	Arkansas State	41	0

1945 3-7-0 (1-5-0)

S22	●	at Barksdale Field	12	6
S29		Oklahoma State	14	19
O6	● |	TCU	27	14
O13	|	at Baylor	13	23
O20	|	Texas LR	7	34
O27	●	Mississippi Mem	19	0
N3	|	Texas A&M	0	34
N10	|	at Rice	7	26
N17	|	at SMU	0	21
N23		at Tulsa	13	45

JOHN BARNHILL 1946-49 (.560) 22-17-3

1946 6-3-2 (5-1-0)

S21	●	N.W. Louisiana St.	21	14
S28	=	at Oklahoma State	21	21
O5	● |	at TCU	34	14
O12	● |	Baylor	13	0
O19	|	at Texas	0	20
O26		Mississippi Mem	7	9
N2	● |	at Texas A&M	7	0
N9	● |	Rice LR	7	0
N16	● |	SMU	13	0
N28		at Tulsa	13	14
		COTTON BOWL		
J1	=	LSU	0	0

1947 6-4-1 (1-4-1)

S20	●	N.W. Louisiana St.	64	0
S27	●	North Texas LR	12	0
O4	● |	TCU	6	0
O11	|	at Baylor	9	17
O18	|	Texas Mem	6	21
O25	●	Mississippi Mem	19	14
N1	= |	Texas A&M	21	21
N8	|	at Rice	0	26
N15	|	at SMU	6	14
N27	●	at Tulsa	27	13
		DIXIE BOWL		
J1	●	William & Mary	21	19

1948 5-5-0 (2-4-0)

S18	●	Abilene Christian LR	40	6
S25	●	East Texas St.	46	7
O2	● |	at TCU	27	14
O9	|	Baylor	7	23
O16	|	at Texas	6	14
O30	● |	at Texas A&M	28	6
N6	|	Rice LR	6	25
N13	|	SMU	12	14
N20	●	Tulsa LR	55	18
N27		William & Mary LR	0	19

1949 5-5-0 (2-4-0)

S24	●	North Texas LR	33	19
O1	● |	TCU	27	7
O8	|	at Baylor	13	35
O15	|	Texas LR	14	27
O22	●	at Vanderbilt	7	6
O29	● |	Texas A&M	27	6
N5	|	at Rice	0	14
N12	|	at SMU	6	34
N19		William & Mary LR	0	20
N26	●	Tulsa	40	7

OTIS DOUGLAS 1950-52 (.300) 9-21

1950 2-8-0 (1-5-0)

S23		Oklahoma State LR	7	12
S30	●	North Texas	50	6
O7	|	at TCU	6	13
O14	● |	Baylor	27	6
O21	|	at Texas	14	19
O28		Vanderbilt LR	13	14
N4	|	at Texas A&M	13	42
N11	|	Rice	6	9
N18	|	SMU LR	7	14
N23		at Tulsa	13	28

1951 5-5-0 (2-4-0)

S22	●	at Oklahoma State	42	7
S29	●	Arizona State	30	13
O6	|	TCU LR	7	17
O13	|	at Baylor	7	9
O20	● |	Texas	16	14
O27		Santa Clara LR	12	21
N3	● |	Texas A&M	33	21
N10	|	at Rice	0	6
N17	|	at SMU	7	47
N24	●	Tulsa LR	24	7

1952 2-8-0 (1-5-0)

S20	●	Oklahoma State LR	22	20
S27		Houston	7	17
O4	|	at TCU	7	13
O11	● |	Baylor LR	20	17
O18	|	at Texas	7	44
O25		Mississippi LR	7	34
N1	|	at Texas A&M	12	31
N8	|	Rice	33	35
N15	|	SMU	17	27
N22		at Tulsa	34	44

BOWDEN WYATT 1953-54 (.524) 11-10

1953 3-7-0 (2-4-0)

S26		Oklahoma State LR	6	7
O3	● |	TCU	13	6
O10	|	at Baylor	7	14
O17	|	Texas	7	16
O24		Mississippi Mem	0	28
O31	● |	Texas A&M LR	41	14
N7	|	at Rice	0	47
N14	|	at SMU	7	13
N21		LSU LR	8	9
N28	●	Tulsa	27	7

1954 8-3-0 (5-1-0)
S25 ● Tulsa 41 0
O2 ● | at TCU 20 13
O9 ● | Baylor 21 20
O16 ● | at Texas 20 7
O23 ● Mississippi LR 6 0
O30 ● | at Texas A&M 14 7
N6 ● | Rice LR 28 15
N13 | SMU 14 21
N20 LSU Shre 6 7
N27 ● at Houston 19 0
COTTON BOWL
J1 Georgia Tech 6 14

JACK MITCHELL
1955-57 (.583) 17-12-1

1955 5-4-1 (3-2-1)
S17 ● Tulsa 21 6
S24 ● Oklahoma State LR 21 0
O1 | TCU 0 26
O8 | at Baylor 20 25
O15 ● | Texas LR 27 20
O22 at Mississippi 7 17
O29 = | Texas A&M 7 7
N5 ● | at Rice 10 0
N12 ● | at SMU 6 0
N19 LSU LR 7 13

1956 6-4-0 (3-3-0)
S22 ● Hardin-Simmons 21 6
S29 ● Oklahoma State LR 19 7
O6 | at TCU 6 41
O13 | Baylor 7 14
O20 ● | at Texas 32 14
O27 ● Mississippi LR 14 0
N3 | at Texas A&M 0 27
N10 ● | Rice 27 12
N17 ● | SMU LR 27 13
N24 LSU Shre 7 21

1957 6-4-0 (2-4-0)
S21 ● Oklahoma State LR 12 0
S28 ● Tulsa 41 14
O5 ● | TCU LR 20 7
O12 ● | at Baylor 20 17
O19 | Texas 0 17
O26 ● Mississippi Mem 12 6
N2 | Texas A&M 6 7
N9 | at Rice 7 13
N16 | at SMU 22 27
N23 ● Texas Tech LR 47 26

FRANK BROYLES
1958-76 (.708) 144-58-5

1958 4-6-0 (2-4-0)
S20 | Baylor LR 0 12
S27 Tulsa 14 27
O4 | at TCU 7 12
O11 | Rice 0 24
O18 | at Texas 6 24
O25 Mississippi LR 12 14
N1 ● | at Texas A&M 21 8
N8 ● Hardin-Simmons LR 60 15
N15 ● | SMU 13 6
N22 ● at Texas Tech 14 8

1959 9-2-0 (5-1-0)
S19 ● Tulsa 28 0
S26 ● Oklahoma State LR 13 7
O3 ● | TCU 3 0
O10 ● | at Baylor 23 7
O17 | Texas LR 12 13
O24 Mississippi Mem 0 28
O31 ● | Texas A&M 12 7
N7 ● | at Rice 14 10
N14 ● | at SMU 17 14
N21 ● Texas Tech LR 27 8
GATOR BOWL
J2 ● Georgia Tech 14 7

1960 8-3-0 (6-1-0)
S17 ● Oklahoma State LR 9 0
S24 ● Tulsa 48 7
O1 ● | at TCU 7 0
O8 | Baylor 14 28
O15 ● | at Texas 24 23
O22 Mississippi LR 7 10
O29 ● | at Texas A&M 7 3
N5 ● | Rice LR 3 0
N12 ● | SMU 26 3
N19 ● | at Texas Tech 34 6
COTTON BOWL
J2 Duke 6 7

1961 8-3-0 (6-1-0)
S23 Mississippi J&M 0 16
S30 ● Tulsa 6 0
O7 ● | TCU LR 28 3
O14 ● | at Baylor 23 13
O21 | Texas 7 33
O28 ● Northwestern St. LR 42 7
N4 ● | Texas A&M 15 8
N11 ● | at Rice 10 0
N18 ● | at SMU 21 7
N25 ● | Texas Tech LR 28 0
SUGAR BOWL
J1 Alabama 3 10

1962 9-2-0 (6-1-0)
S22 ● Oklahoma State LR 34 7
S29 ● Tulsa 42 14
O6 ● | at TCU 42 14
O13 ● | Baylor 28 21
O20 | at Texas 3 7
O27 ● Hardin-Simmons LR 49 7
N3 ● | at Texas A&M 17 7
N10 ● | Rice 28 14
N17 ● | SMU LR 9 7
N24 ● | at Texas Tech 34 0
SUGAR BOWL
J1 Mississippi 13 17

1963 5-5-0 (3-4-0)
S21 ● Oklahoma State LR 21 0
S28 Missouri LR 6 7
O5 ● | TCU 18 3
O12 | at Baylor 10 14
O19 | Texas LR 13 17
O26 ● Tulsa 56 7
N2 ● | Texas A&M LR 21 7
N9 | at Rice 0 7
N16 | at SMU 7 14
N23 ● | Texas Tech 27 20

1964 11-0-0 (7-0-0)
S19 ● Oklahoma State LR 14 10
S26 ● Tulsa 31 22
O3 ● | at TCU 29 6
O10 ● | Baylor LR 17 6
O17 ● | at Texas 14 13
O24 ● Wichita St. LR 17 0
O31 ● | at Texas A&M 17 0
N7 ● | Rice 21 0
N14 ● | SMU 44 0
N21 ● | at Texas Tech 17 0
COTTON BOWL
J1 ● Nebraska 10 7

1965 10-1-0 (7-0-0)
S18 ● Oklahoma State LR 28 14
S25 ● Tulsa 20 12
O2 ● | TCU LR 28 0
O9 ● | at Baylor 38 7
O16 ● | Texas 27 24
O23 ● North Texas LR 55 20
O30 ● | Texas A&M LR 31 0
N6 ● | at Rice 31 0
N13 ● | at SMU 24 3
N20 ● | Texas Tech 42 24
COTTON BOWL
J1 LSU 7 14

1966 8-2-0 (5-2-0)
S17 ● Oklahoma State LR 14 10
S24 ● Tulsa 27 8
O1 ● | at TCU 21 0
O8 | Baylor 0 7
O15 ● | at Texas 12 7
O22 ● Wichita St. LR 41 0
O29 ● | at Texas A&M 34 0
N5 ● | Rice LR 31 20
N12 ● | SMU 22 0
N19 | at Texas Tech 16 21

1967 4-5-1 (3-3-1)
S23 Oklahoma State LR 6 7
S30 Tulsa 12 14
O7 ● | TCU 26 0
O14 = | at Baylor 10 10
O21 | Texas LR 12 21
O28 ● Kansas State LR 28 7
N4 | Texas A&M 21 33
N11 ● | at Rice 23 9
N18 ● | at SMU 35 17
N25 | Texas Tech LR 27 31

1968 10-1-0 (6-1-0)
S21 ● Oklahoma State LR 32 15
S28 ● Tulsa 56 13
O5 ● | at TCU 17 7
O12 ● | Baylor 35 19
O19 | at Texas 29 39
O26 ● North Texas LR 17 15
N2 ● | at Texas A&M 25 22
N9 ● | Rice 46 21
N16 ● | SMU LR 35 29
N23 ● | at Texas Tech 42 7
SUGAR BOWL
J1 ● Georgia 16 2

1969 9-2-0 (6-1-0)
S20 ● Oklahoma State LR 39 0
S27 ● Tulsa 55 0
O4 ● | TCU LR 24 6
O11 ● | at Baylor 21 7
O25 ● Wichita St. LR 52 14
N1 ● | Texas A&M 35 13
N8 ● | at Rice 30 6
N15 ● | at SMU 28 15
N27 ● | Texas Tech LR 33 0
D6 | Texas 14 15
SUGAR BOWL
J1 Mississippi 22 27

1970 9-2-0 (6-1-0)
S12 Stanford LR 28 34
S19 ● Oklahoma State LR 23 7
S26 ● Tulsa 49 7
O3 ● | at TCU 49 14
O10 ● | Baylor LR 41 7
O24 ● Wichita St. LR 62 0
O31 ● | at Texas A&M 45 6
N7 ● | Rice 38 14
N14 ● | SMU 36 3
N21 ● | at Texas Tech 24 10
D5 | at Texas 7 42

1971 8-3-1 (5-1-1)
S11 ● California LR 51 20
S18 ● Oklahoma State LR 31 10
S25 Tulsa 20 21
O2 ● | TCU 49 15
O9 ● | at Baylor 35 7
O16 ● | Texas LR 31 7
O23 ● North Texas 60 21
O30 | Texas A&M LR 9 17
N6 = | at Rice 24 24
N13 ● | at SMU 18 13
N20 ● | Texas Tech 15 0
LIBERTY BOWL
D20 Tennessee 13 14

1972 6-5-0 (3-4-0)
S9 Southern Cal LR 10 31
S23 ● Oklahoma State LR 24 23
S30 ● Tulsa 21 20
O7 ● | at TCU 27 13
O14 ● | Baylor 31 20
O21 | at Texas 15 35
O28 ● North Texas LR 42 16
N4 | at Texas A&M 7 10
N11 | Rice LR 20 23
N18 | SMU 7 22
N25 ● | at Texas Tech 24 14

1973 5-5-1 (3-3-1)
S15 at Southern Cal 0 17
S22 Oklahoma State LR 6 38
S29 ● Iowa State 21 19
O6 ● | TCU LR 13 5
O13 ● | at Baylor 13 7
O20 | Texas 6 34
O27 ● Tulsa LR 20 6
N3 ● | Texas A&M 14 10
N10 | at Rice 7 17
N17 = | at SMU 7 7
N24 | Texas Tech LR 17 24

1974 6-4-1 (3-3-1)
S14 ● Southern Cal LR 22 7
S21 Oklahoma State LR 7 26
S28 ● Tulsa 60 0
O5 ● | TCU 49 0
O12 | Baylor 17 21
O19 | at Texas 7 38
O26 ● Colorado State LR 43 9
N2 | at Texas A&M 10 20
N9 ● | Rice 25 6
N16 = | SMU LR 24 24
N23 ● | at Texas Tech 21 13

1975 10-2-0 (6-1-0)
S13 ● Air Force LR 35 0
S20 at Oklahoma State 13 20
S27 ● Tulsa 31 15
O4 ● | TCU LR 19 8
O11 ● | at Baylor 41 3
O18 | Texas 18 24
O25 ● Utah State LR 31 0
N8 ● | at Rice 20 16
N15 ● | at SMU 35 7
N22 ● | Texas Tech 31 14
D6 ● | Texas A&M LR 31 6
COTTON BOWL
J1 ● Georgia 31 10

1976 5-5-1 (3-4-1)
S11 ● Utah State LR 33 16
S18 ● Oklahoma State LR 16 10
S25 Tulsa 3 9
O2 ● | TCU 46 14
O23 | at Houston 14 7
O30 ● | Rice 41 16
N6 = | at Baylor 7 7
N13 | Texas A&M LR 10 31
N20 | SMU Shre 31 35
N27 | Texas Tech LR 7 30
D4 | at Texas 12 29

LOU HOLTZ
1977-83 (.735) 60-21-2

1977 11-1-0 (7-1-0)
S10 ● New Mexico St. LR 53 10
S17 ● Oklahoma State LR 28 6
S24 ● Tulsa 37 3
O1 ● | at TCU 42 6
O15 | Texas 9 13
O22 ● | Houston LR 34 0
O29 ● | at Rice 30 7
N5 ● | Baylor LR 35 9
N12 ● | at Texas A&M 26 20
N19 ● | SMU 47 7
N26 ● | at Texas Tech 17 14
ORANGE BOWL
J2 ● Oklahoma 31 6

1978 9-2-1 (6-2-0)
S16 ● Vanderbilt LR 48 17
S23 ● at Oklahoma State 19 7
S30 ● Tulsa 21 13
O7 ● | TCU LR 42 3
O21 | at Texas 21 28
O28 | at Houston 9 20
N4 ● | Rice 37 7
N11 ● | at Baylor 27 14
N18 ● | Texas A&M LR 26 7
N25 ● | at SMU 27 14
D2 ● | Texas Tech 49 7
FIESTA BOWL
D25 = UCLA 10 10

1979 10-2-0 (7-1-0)
S15 ● Colorado State LR 36 3
S22 ● Oklahoma State LR 27 7
S29 ● Tulsa 33 8
O6 ● | at TCU 16 13
O13 ● | at Texas Tech 20 6
O20 ● | Texas LR 17 14
O27 | Houston 10 13
N3 ● | at Rice 34 7
N10 ● | Baylor 29 20
N17 ● | at Texas A&M 22 10
N24 ● | SMU LR 31 7
SUGAR BOWL
J1 Alabama 9 24

1980 7-5-0 (3-5-0)
S1 | at Texas 17 23
S20 ● Oklahoma State LR 33 20
S27 ● Tulsa 13 10
O4 ● | TCU 44 7
O11 ● Wichita St. LR 27 7
O25 | at Houston 17 24
N1 | Rice LR 16 17
N8 | at Baylor 15 42
N15 ● | Texas A&M 27 24
N22 | at SMU 7 31
N29 ● | Texas Tech LR 22 16
HALL OF FAME CLASSIC
D27 ● Tulane 34 15

1981 8-4-0 (5-3-0)

S12	●		Tulsa	14	10
S19	●		Northwestern LR	38	7
S26	●		Mississippi JaM	27	13
O3		|	at TCU	24	28
O10	●	|	at Texas Tech	26	14
O17	●	|	Texas	42	11
O24		|	Houston LR	17	20
O31	●	|	at Rice	41	7
N7	●	|	Baylor LR	41	39
N14	●	|	at Texas A&M	10	7
N21		|	SMU	18	32
			GATOR BOWL		
D28			North Carolina	27	31

1982 9-2-1 (5-2-1)

S11	●		Tulsa	38	0
S18	●		Navy LR	29	17
S25	●		Mississippi LR	14	12
O2	●	|	TCU LR	35	0
O9	●	|	Texas Tech	21	3
O23	●	|	at Houston	38	3
O30	●	|	Rice	24	6
N6		|	at Baylor	17	24
N13	●	|	Texas A&M LR	35	0
N20	=	|	at SMU	17	17
D4		|	at Texas	7	33
			BLUEBONNET BOWL		
D31	●		Florida	28	24

1983 6-5-0 (4-4-0)

S10	●		Tulsa	17	14
S17	●		New Mexico LR	17	0
S24			Mississippi JaM	10	13
O1	●	|	at TCU	38	21
O15		|	Texas LR	3	31
O22	●	|	Houston	24	3
O29	●	|	Rice LR	35	0
N5		|	Baylor	21	24
N12		|	at Texas A&M	23	36
N19		|	SMU LR	0	17
N26	●	|	at Texas Tech	16	13

KEN HATFIELD
1984-89 (.753) 55-17-1

1984 7-4-1 (5-3-0)

S15	=		Mississippi LR	14	14
S22	●		Tulsa	18	9
S29	●		Navy LR	33	10
O6		|	TCU	31	32
O13	●	|	Texas Tech LR	24	0
O20		|	at Texas	18	24
O27	●	|	at Houston	17	3
N3	●	|	Rice LR	28	6
N10	●	|	at Baylor	14	9
N17	●	|	Texas A&M	28	0
N24		|	at SMU	28	31
			LIBERTY BOWL		
D27			Auburn	15	21

1985 10-2-0 (6-2-0)

S14	●		Mississippi JaM	24	19
S21	●		Tulsa LR	24	0
S28	●		New Mexico St. LR	45	13
O5	●	|	at TCU	41	0
O12	●	|	at Texas Tech	30	7
O19		|	Texas	13	15
O26	●	|	Houston LR	57	27
N2	●	|	at Rice	30	15
N9	●	|	Baylor LR	20	14
N16		|	at Texas A&M	6	10
N23	●	|	SMU	15	9
			HOLIDAY BOWL		
D22	●		Arizona State	18	17

1986 9-3-0 (6-2-0)

S13	●		Mississippi LR	21	0
S20	●		Tulsa	34	17
S27	●		New Mexico St. LR	42	11
O4	●	|	TCU	34	17
O11		|	Texas Tech	7	17
O18	●	|	at Texas	21	14
O25	●	|	at Houston	30	13
N1	●	|	Rice	45	14
N8		|	at Baylor	14	29
N15	●	|	Texas A&M LR	14	10
N22	●	|	at SMU	41	0
			ORANGE BOWL		
J1			Oklahoma	8	42

1987 9-4-0 (5-2-0)

S12	●		Mississippi JaM	31	10
S19	●		Tulsa	30	15
S26			Miami, Fla. LR	7	51
O3	●	|	at TCU	20	10
O10	●	|	at Texas Tech	31	0
O17		|	Texas LR	14	16
O24	●	|	Houston	21	17
O31	●	|	at Rice	38	14
N7	●	|	Baylor	10	7
N14		|	at Texas A&M	0	14
N28	●		New Mexico LR	43	25
D5	●		at Hawaii	38	20
			LIBERTY BOWL		
D29			Georgia	17	20

1988 10-2-0 (7-0-0)

S3	●		Pacific LR	63	14
S10	●		Tulsa	30	26
S17	●		Mississippi LR	21	13
O1	●	|	TCU	53	10
O8	●	|	Texas Tech LR	31	10
O15	●	|	at Texas	27	24
O22	●	|	at Houston	26	21
O29	●	|	Rice LR	21	14
N5	●	|	at Baylor	33	3
N12	●	|	Texas A&M	25	20
N26			at Miami, Fla.	16	18
			COTTON BOWL		
J2			UCLA	3	17

1989 10-2-0 (7-1-0)

S16	●		Tulsa	26	7
S23	●		Mississippi JaM	24	17
S30	●		Texas-El Paso LR	39	7
O7	●	|	at TCU LR	41	19
O14	●	|	at Texas Tech	45	13
O21		|	Texas	20	24
O28	●	|	Houston LR	45	39
N4	●	|	at Rice	38	17
N11	●	|	Baylor	19	10
N24	●	|	at Texas A&M	23	22
D2	●	|	SMU LR	38	24
			COTTON BOWL		
J1			Tennessee	27	31

JACK CROWE
1990-92 (.375) 9-15

1990 3-8-0 (1-7-0)

S15	●		Tulsa	28	3
S22			Mississippi LR	17	21
S29	●		Colorado State LR	31	20
O6		|	TCU LR	26	54
O13		|	Texas Tech	44	49
O20		|	at Texas	17	49
O27		|	at Houston	28	62
N3		|	Rice LR	11	19
N10		|	at Baylor	3	34
N17		|	Texas A&M	16	20
N24	●	|	at SMU	42	29

1991 6-6-0 (5-3-0)

A31			Miami, Fla. LR	3	31
S7	●	|	SMU LR	17	6
S21	●		La. Lafayette	9	7
S28			Mississippi JaM	17	24
O5	●	|	at TCU	22	21
O12	●	|	Houston	29	17
O19	●	|	Texas LR	14	13
N2		|	Baylor	5	9
N9		|	at Texas Tech	21	38
N16		|	at Texas A&M	3	13
N23	●	|	Rice LR	20	0
			INDEPENDENCE BOWL		
D29			Georgia	15	24

1992-PRESENT
SEC

JOE KINES
1992 (.350) 3-6-1

1992 3-7-1 (3-4-1)

S5			Citadel	3	10
S12	●	|	at South Carolina	45	7
S19		|	Alabama LR	11	38
S26			at Memphis	6	22
O3		|	Georgia	3	27
O10	●	|	at Tennessee	25	24
O17		|	Mississippi LR	3	17
O31	=	|	at Auburn	24	24
N7		|	at Mississippi State	3	10
N21			SMU LR	19	24
N27	●	|	LSU	30	6

DANNY FORD
1993-97 (.447) 25-31-1

1993 5-5-1 (3-4-1)

S4	●		at SMU	10	6
S11	●	|	South Carolina	18	17
S18		|	at Alabama	3	43 †
S25			Memphis LR	0	6
O2	●	|	at Georgia	20	10
O9		|	Tennessee LR	14	28
O16		|	Mississippi JaM	0	19
O30		|	Auburn	21	31
N6	=	|	Mississippi State LR	13	13
N13	●		Tulsa	24	11
N27	●	|	at LSU	42	24

1994 4-7-0 (2-6-0)

S3	●		SMU LR	34	14
S10		|	at South Carolina	0	14
S17		|	Alabama	6	13
S24			at Memphis	15	16
O1	●	|	Vanderbilt LR	42	6
O8		|	at Tennessee	21	38
O15	●	|	Mississippi	31	7
O29		|	at Auburn	14	31
N5		|	at Mississippi State	7	17
N12	●		Northern Illinois	30	27
N26		|	LSU LR	12	30

1995 8-5-0 (6-2-0)

S2			at SMU	14	17
S9	●	|	South Carolina	51	21
S16	●	|	at Alabama	20	19
S23	●	|	Memphis LR	27	20
S30	●	|	at Vanderbilt	35	7
O7		|	Tennessee	31	49
O14	●	|	Mississippi Mem	13	6
O28	●	|	Auburn LR	30	28
N4	●	|	Mississippi State LR	26	21
N11	●		La. Lafayette	24	13
N18		|	at LSU	0	28
			SEC CHAMPIONSHIP GAME		
D2			Florida Atl	3	34
			CARQUEST BOWL		
D30			North Carolina	10	20

1996 4-7 (2-6)

S7			SMU	10	23
S21		|	Alabama LR	7	17
S28	●		La. Monroe LR	38	21
O5		|	Florida	7	42
O12	●		Louisiana Tech LR	38	21
O19		|	at South Carolina	17	23
N2		|	at Auburn	7	28
N9	●	|	Mississippi	13	7
N16		|	at Tennessee	14	55
N23	●	|	at Mississippi State	16	13
N29		|	LSU LR	7	17

1997 4-7 (2-6)

S6	●		La. Monroe	28	16
S13			SMU Shre	9	31
S20	●	|	at Alabama	17	16
S27	●		Louisiana Tech LR	17	13
O4		|	at Florida	7	56
O18		|	South Carolina LR	13	39
O25		|	Auburn	21	26
N6		|	at Mississippi	9	19
N15		|	Tennessee LR	22	30
N22	●	|	Mississippi State	17	7
N28		|	at LSU	21	31

HOUSTON NUTT
1998-PRESENT (.616) 53-33

1998 9-3 (6-2)

S5	●		La. Lafayette	38	17
S19	●		SMU LR	44	17
S26	●	|	Alabama	42	6
O3	●	|	Kentucky LR	27	20
O10	●	|	at Memphis	23	9
O17	●	|	at South Carolina	41	28
O31	●	|	at Auburn	24	21
N7	●	|	Mississippi	34	0
N14		|	at Tennessee	24	28
N21		|	at Mississippi State	21	22
N27	●	|	LSU LR	41	14
			CITRUS BOWL		
J1			Michigan	31	45

1999 8-4 (4-4)

S4	●		at SMU	26	0
S18	●		La. Monroe LR	44	6
S25		|	at Alabama	28	35
O2		|	at Kentucky	20	31
O9	●		Middle Tennessee	58	6
O16	●	|	South Carolina LR	48	14
O30	●	|	Auburn	34	10
N6		|	at Mississippi	16	38
N13	●	|	Tennessee	28	24
N20	●	|	Mississippi State LR	14	9
N26		|	at LSU	10	35
			COTTON BOWL		
J1	●		Texas	27	6

2000 6-6 (3-5)

S2	●		S.W. Missouri St. LR	38	0
S16	●		Boise State LR	38	31
S23	●	|	Alabama	28	21
S30		|	Georgia	7	38
O7	●		La. Monroe	52	6
O14		|	at South Carolina	7	27
O28		|	at Auburn	19	21
N4		|	Mississippi	24	38
N11		|	at Tennessee	20	63
N18	●	|	at Mississippi State	17	10
N24	●	|	LSU LR	14	3
			LAS VEGAS BOWL		
D21			Nevada-Las Vegas	14	31

2001 7-5 (4-4)

A30	●		Nevada-Las Vegas LR	14	10
S8		|	Tennessee	3	13
S22		|	at Alabama	10	31
S29		|	at Georgia	23	34
O6	●		Weber St.	42	19
O13	●	|	South Carolina LR	10	7
O27	●	|	Auburn	42	17
N3	●	|	at Mississippi	58	56
N10	●		Central Florida	27	20
N17	●	|	Mississippi State	24	21
N23		|	at LSU	38	41
			COTTON BOWL		
J1			Oklahoma	3	10

2002 9-5 (5-3)

S7	●		Boise State	41	14
S14	●		South Florida LR	42	3
S28		|	Alabama	12	30
O5		|	at Tennessee	38	41
O12	●	|	at Auburn	38	17
O19		|	Kentucky	17	29
O26	●	|	Mississippi	48	28
N2	●	|	Troy State LR	23	0
N9	●	|	at South Carolina	23	0
N16	●	|	La. Lafayette	24	17
N23	●	|	at Mississippi State	26	19
N29	●	|	LSU LR	21	20
			SEC CHAMPIONSHIP GAME		
D7			Georgia Atl	3	30
			MUSIC CITY BOWL		
D30			Minnesota	14	29

2003 9-4 (4-4)

S6	●		Tulsa	45	13
S13	●		at Texas	38	28
S20	●		North Texas LR	31	7
S27	●	|	at Alabama	34	31
O11		|	Auburn	3	10
O18		|	Florida	28	33
O25		|	at Mississippi	7	19
N1	●	|	at Kentucky	71	63
N6	●	|	South Carolina N2	28	6
N15	●	|	New Mexico State	48	20
N22	●	|	Mississippi State	52	6
N29		|	at LSU	24	55
			INDEPENDENCE BOWL		
D31	●		Missouri	27	14

2004 5-6 (3-5)

S4	●		New Mexico State	63	13
S11			Texas	20	22
S18	●		La. Monroe LR	49	20
S25	●	|	Alabama	27	10
O2		|	at Florida	30	45
O16		|	at Auburn	20	38
O23		|	Georgia	14	20
N6		|	at South Carolina	32	35
N13	●	|	Mississippi	35	3
N20	●	|	at Mississippi State	24	21
N26		|	LSU LR	14	43

Neutral Site key: *StL* St. Louis, MO / *OkC* Oklahoma City, OK / *Dal* Dallas, TX / *Shre* Shreveport, LA / *JaM* Jackson, MS / *LR* Little Rock, AR / *Atl* Atlanta, GA / *Mus* Muskogee, OK / *Tex* Texarkana, TX / *SF* San Francisco, CA / *Phil* Philadelphia, PA / *Jop* Joplin, MO / *Hot* Hot Springs, AR / *KC* Kansas City, MO / *Mem* Memphis, TN / *FtS* Fort Smith, AR / *Sha* Shawnee, OK / *Mus* Muskogee, OK / *NYC* New York, NY / *SA* San Antonio, TX

f **Forfeit** † **Game Later Forfieted** # **Disputed Victor** * **Disputed Score** || **Designated Conference Game** |2 **Counted Twice in Conference Standings**

ARKANSAS STATE

BY RYAN HOCKENSMITH

O N THE WEST SIDE OF INDIAN Stadium, fans get a taste of Arkansas State football history every Saturday. That's where the school has designed the Ring of Honor, a small area where plaques commemorate 11 legends of the football program. It's a small commemoration for a small football program that's done some pretty big things. Among the inductees: players Bill Bergey and Maurice Carthon, and coaches Larry Lacewell and Bennie Ellender.

The program has bounced back and forth between Division I-A and I-AA. First, Bill Davidson brought his program up to I-A in 1975 and promptly went 11–0. In 1982, Lacewell, who went on to fame as the Dallas Cowboys director of scouting, oversaw a move back to I-AA. The Indians proceeded to qualify for the I-AA playoffs four times and decided to move back to the big-school ranks in 1992, where they have played ever since.

TRADITION For 24 hours before every homecoming game, the team's true freshmen, from redshirts to starters, along with managers and trainers, take turns banging an enormous war drum nestled in the heart of campus. Team members rotate all night, and the relentless drumming signifies the season's most important home game. "It can be heard for quite a distance," says former coach and Ring of Honor inductee Bill Templeton. "It's loud enough that many of those banging the drum end up hearing it for a week or so afterward."

BEST PLAYER Linebacker Bill Bergey finished his four-year career with 436 tackles (11.8 per game), and he holds the Indians' record for single-season tackles with 196. In 1969 the Cincinnati Bengals selected Bergey in the second round, the highest selection in Arkansas State history. Bergey went on to a stellar NFL career that included one Super Bowl appearance and nearly 1,200 tackles during seven seasons with the Philadelphia Eagles.

BEST COACH When popular eight-year coach Bennie Ellender left for Tulane after the 1970 season, his replacement, Bill Davidson, wanted to put his own stamp on the team. So he altered Ellender's very successful I-formation option offense by splitting the backs. Davidson admitted that he mostly just wanted to set himself apart from Ellender. It took some time, though. Davidson went a pedestrian 21–18–1 in his first four seasons, but he persevered. The team moved into Indian Stadium after his third season, with a move to Division I-A coming in 1975. Davidson juggled the pressures magnificently, and Arkansas State debuted with the big boys in big fashion. The Indians

PROFILE

Arkansas State University
Jonesboro, Ark.
Founded: 1909
Enrollment: 9,289
Colors: Scarlet and Black
Nickname: Indians
Stadium: Indian Stadium
    Opened in 1974
    Grass; 30,708 capacity
First football game: 1911
All-time record: 385–410–37 (.485)
Website: www.asuindians.com

THE BEST OF TIMES

From 1969 to 1975, Arkansas State went 51–19–2, highlighted by 11–0 seasons in 1970 and 1975. During this time, the Indians won two Pecan Bowls (1969-70) and made the move to Division I in 1975 the best way imaginable.

THE WORST OF TIMES

From 1992 to 2001, Arkansas State hit a rut. The Indians went just 28–82–1 with nine losing seasons, going through three head coaches; including Ray Perkins' disastrous 1992 season of four shutout losses and a 37–7 rivalry defeat to Memphis State, which degenerated into a vicious fourth-quarter brawl.

CONFERENCE

Arkansas State joined the Sun Belt Conference in 2001. It was previously affiliated with the Big West (1993-95, 1999-2000) and the Southland (1964-86) conferences.

DISTINGUISHED ALUMNI

Arthur Agee, subject of *Hoop Dreams*; James Pardew, U.S. ambassador to Bulgaria

FIGHT SONG

ARKANSAS STATE LOYALTY SONG
On, on, on to victory,
Brave team, you're second to none,
Let's make the game history,
Along with the others you've won,
Fight, fight, fight with all your might,
So that the world may see that I-N-D-I-A-N-S
means victory!

finished 11–0 that season, and Davidson managed winning seasons two of the next three years.

BEST TEAM Before that 1975 season, Davidson decided to reemphasize a smash-mouth option attack on offense. He moved David Hines from the secondary and put him at quarterback. The gamble paid dividends. Hines was the Southland Conference's offensive Player of the Year, and the Indians never trailed en route to their undefeated record. Arkansas State dominated opponents, winning by an average of 24.9 points. Around the school, the story goes that the Tangerine Bowl narrowed its list of possible opponents for unbeaten MAC champion Miami (Ohio) to undefeated Arkansas State and 7–4 South Carolina, before selecting the more established Gamecocks.

BIGGEST GAME Arkansas State eased into Division I-A in 1975, opening the season with wins over D2 schools Northwestern Louisiana, Idaho and McNeese State by a combined score of 89-13. The Indians' fourth game, against a Memphis State team that had just clubbed No. 7 Auburn, figured to break the spell. But ASU's three-touchdown underdogs outscored Memphis 13-0 in the fourth quarter, to

> *Each season, coach Larry Lacewell would pick a lineman for a big responsibility: running the fumblerooskie.*

win 29-10 and provide an enormous confidence boost to what proved to be the program's best team.

BIGGEST UPSET In 1981, Tulsa and Arkansas State were heading in opposite directions before their season finale against each other. The Golden Hurricane had won six straight games to get to 7–3 and into position for a bowl trip. Arkansas State was months away from dropping to Division I-AA, and the Indians had lost three of their last five, including a 3-2 home loss to Tennessee-Chattanooga and a 32-0 road rout to Louisiana Tech the week before. But the Indians built a 10-0 lead behind effective wishbone quarterback Tim Langford, who rushed for 111 yards on only 12 carries. On the last play of the half, Langford, who'd thrown only 63 passes in 11 games, heaved a bomb toward freshman split end Byron Dunnick, who pulled in the pass for a 57-yard touchdown. Arkansas State went on to win 31-7, giving Tulsa its worst loss of the season.

HEARTBREAKER For months after the 2000 season opener, Arkansas State coach Joe Hollis lay awake at night, pondering a monumental road win that slipped away from his Indians against North Carolina State. Arkansas State led 24-21 with less than three minutes left. Not only that,

RECORDS

RUSHING

	GAME
259	Dennis Bolden vs. McNeese State, Sept. 20, 1975 (26 att.)
	SEASON
1,390	Danny Smith, 2002 (254 att.)
	CAREER
3,959	Richie Woit, 1950-53 (772 att.)

PASSING

	GAME
403	Cleo Lemon vs. New Mexico State, Oct. 3, 1998 (25 of 49)
	SEASON
2,721	Cleo Lemon, 1998 (183 of 387)
	CAREER
7,706	Cleo Lemon, 1997-2000 (551 of 1,128)

RECEIVING

	GAME
284	Lennie Johnson vs. Southwest Missouri State, Nov. 8, 1997 (7 rec.)
	SEASON
1,002	Robert Kilow, 2000 (72 rec.)
	CAREER
2,730	Lennie Johnson, 1995-98 (156 rec.)

POINTS

	GAME
42	Steve Burks vs. Abilene Christian, Sept. 8, 1973 (7 TDs); Clifton Keller vs. C. Arkansas, Nov. 2, 1917 (7 TDs)
	SEASON
126	Richie Woit, 1951 (21 TDs)
	CAREER
342	Richie Woit, 1950-53 (57 TDs)

CONSENSUS ALL-AMERICANS

1953	Richie Woit, B
1964-65	Dan Summers, OG
1968	Bill Bergey, LB
1969	Dan Buckley, C
1969	Clovis Swinney, DT
1970	Bill Phillips, OG
1970-71	Calvin Harrell, RB
1971	Dennis Meyer, DB
1971	Wayne Dorton, OG
1973	Doug Lowrey, OG
1984-85	Carter Crawford, DL
1986	Randy Barnhill, OG
1987	Jim Wiseman, C
1987	Charlie Fredrick, DT

but the Indians had a first-and-goal at the N.C. State 2-yard line. Then the wheels came off. The Wolfpack held on four straight rushing attempts and then marched down the field for a tying field goal. Two overtimes later, another Arkansas State turnover gave NC State a 38-31 victory. The Indians never recovered from the loss and finished 1–10.

STADIUM With a move to Division I-A locked up for the following season, Arkansas State had no choice in 1974 but to upgrade from Kays Stadium, where the Indians had played for more than five decades. The school spent $2.5 million to construct Indian Stadium. It opened with a capacity of 16,343, eventually expanding to hold 30,708.

RIVAL After years of random acts of rivalry-related vandalism on their campuses, officials from Arkansas State and Memphis State agreed in 1955 to make their series the Paint Bucket Bowl. The winner received a paint bucket with paint and brushes and was given free rein over a certain spot on the loser's campus. Memphis State won both Paint Bucket games before the series was temporarily discontinued in 1957. But the rivalry lives on, as evidenced by the 1992 fourth-quarter melee that had three players from each team ejected and fans buzzing for years afterward about the closely contested series.

NICKNAME It took a few decades, but Arkansas State eventually pinned down a team name that stuck. As the only agricultural school in Eastern Arkansas, ASU first used Aggies as its team name in 1911. Aggies changed to Gorillas in 1925, but that nickname flopped. The school adopted Warriors in 1930 and changed to Indians a year later. That name has stuck for more than 70 years.

MASCOT With the approval of Arkansas Native American groups, the school has held tryouts every spring since 1996 to find its three-person mascot team, named the Indian Family. Candidates are graded on interviews, horsemanship, appearance, attitude, school activities and academics. One winner then becomes Chief Big Track, who's joined by an unnamed princess and unnamed brave. Chief Big Track is outfitted in an authentic war shirt, which features a hand-stitched and beaded Cherokee design, and wears a headdress made by Native Americans.

UNIFORMS Since the beginning of football at Arkansas State, the school's logo and uniforms have remained much the same. In one form or another, helmets and uniforms have featured the school colors, scarlet and black, often with a logo of an Indian on the helmet. "We've never had anything really flashy," Templeton says. "No stripes, no flashy colors—just good work clothes."

LORE At the beginning of each of Larry Lacewell's 11 seasons as the Indians' head coach, he'd pick out his fastest lineman and drop a big responsibility on the big man: that player would be in charge of running Lacewell's favorite trick play, a guard-around play commonly known as the fumblerooskie. Lacewell ran the play a handful of times each season and scored two touchdowns off it, none bigger than Kenneth Nelson's 30-yard rumble in a 1987 Division I-AA playoff game. With the clock ticking below three minutes and Arkansas State trailing Jackson State 24-21, Lacewell's team called the play in the huddle, without his input. It worked. Nelson scored, the Indians added another TD a minute later and Arkansas State won 35-32. Lacewell is still regarded as one of the inventors of the guard-around.

QUOTE "I will … "—Coach Steve Roberts' program slogan, universally accepted by current players and alumni as a form of accountability to the player and the team

THE SCHOOLS

ARKANSAS STATE ANNUAL STATISTICAL LEADERS

YR	RUSHING	YDS	ATT	AVG	PASSING	ATT	CMP	PCT	YDS	RECEIVING	REC	YDS	AVG
1950	Richie Woit	759	149	5.1		NA	NA	NA	NA		NA	NA	NA
1951	Richie Woit	1,125	227	5.0	Billy Sommers	43	20	.47	261	John Koldus	20	488	24.4
1952	Richie Woit	1,250	207	6.0	Billy Sommers	67	38	.57	610		NA	NA	NA
1953	Richie Woit	825	189	4.4	Bobby Spann	51	18	.35	334	Ronnie Allen	18	265	14.7
1954	Bill Templeton	232	50	4.6	Tommy Spiers	49	30	.61	368	Dan Spensieri	12	225	18.8
1955	Don Riggs	498	67	7.4	Tommy Spiers	98	44	.46	519	Jim Turley	10	132	13.2
1956	Eddie Romeo	701	111	6.3	Tommy Spiers	76	32	.42	396	Bob Gray	13	179	13.8
1957	Eddie Romeo	425	82	5.2	Bill Caldwell	65	28	.43	501	Howard Cissell	10	138	13.8
1958	Bill Nalley	248	50	5.0	Bill Caldwell	62	27	.44	388	Don Riggs	17	242	14.2
1959	Bill Caldwell	322	84	3.8	Bill Caldwell	132	62	.47	959	Alfred Bentley	28	554	19.8
1960	John Coffey	294	62	4.7	Jim McMurray	77	30	.39	344	Alfred Bentley	19	305	16.1
1961	Sammy Weir	345	85	4.1	Jim McMurray	70	30	.43	331	Gilbert Arnold	11	108	9.8
1962	Dick Martillo	629	119	5.2	Sammy Weir	75	30	.40	370	Hassel McCain	10	133	13.3
1963	Harold Wallin	281	72	3.9	Gary Everett	82	46	.56	692	Bill Pagano	12	198	16.5
1964	Eddie Rickus	394	85	4.6	Gary Everett	81	35	.43	454	Bill Pagano	14	210	15.0
1965	Terry Gwin	534	110	4.9	Tim Keane	67	27	.40	326	Gerald Jumper	12	139	11.6
1966	Terry Gwin	607	135	4.5	Tim Keane	158	70	.44	1,015	Gerald Jumper	32	511	16.0
1967	Frank McGuigan	488	129	3.8	Cecil LaGrone	145	70	.48	900	Gerald Jumper	47	727	15.5
1968	Frank McGuigan	1,220	269	4.5	James Hamilton	216	82	.38	1,238	Joe Waleszonia	29	507	17.5
1969	Calvin Harrell	824	205	4.1	James Hamilton	184	79	.43	1,172	Steve Lockhart	30	482	15.1
1970	Calvin Harrell	1,131	232	4.8	James Hamilton	200	96	.48	1,622	Chet Douthit	43	955	22.2
1971	Calvin Harrell	961	216	4.4	James Hamilton	199	81	.41	1,351	Steve Lockhart	27	382	14.1
1972	Stan Winfrey	869	168	5.2	James Flynn	66	21	.32	459	Steve Burks	9	170	18.9
1973	David Mitchell	968	191	5.1	Steve Burks	73	32	.44	407	Jaime Klipsch	12	178	14.8
1974	Willie Harris	654	150	4.4	James Flynn	89	39	.44	425	Jaime Klipsch	16	217	13.6
1975	Dennis Bolden	1,191	186	6.4	David Hines	70	26	.37	395	Orna Middlebrook	11	169	15.4
1976	Leroy Harris	1,046	150	7.0	Bucky Lane	62	28	.45	551	Orna Middlebrook	13	215	16.5
1977	Joe Griffin	635	115	5.5	Kennon Taylor	190	92	.48	1,404	Dikki Dyson	40	710	17.8
1978	Larry Lawrence	1,039	254	4.1	Kennon Taylor	182	78	.43	1,087	Jerome Miller	24	473	19.7
1979	Anthony Williams	789	173	4.6	Gene Bradley	198	91	.46	1,091	Anthony Williams	22	123	5.6
1980	Erven Beasley	433	84	5.2	Tim Langford	71	27	.38	281	Lee Charles Wright	9	95	10.6
1981	Maurice Carthon	678	153	4.4	Tim Langford	63	31	.49	345	Maurice Carthon	12	99	8.3
1982	Maurice Carthon	682	144	4.7	Tim Langford	80	39	.49	534	Waddell Kelly	12	170	14.2
1983	Dwayne Pittman	744	151	4.9	Tim Langford	166	90	.54	1,156	Judious Lewis	30	595	19.8
1984	Rickey Jemison	888	177	5.0	Dwane Brown	148	59	.40	748	Judious Lewis	23	323	14.0
1985	Rickey Jemison	918	175	5.3	Dwane Brown	152	72	.47	1,205	Cazzy Francis	32	667	20.8
1986	Rickey Jemison	1,002	224	4.5	Dwane Brown	120	58	.48	862	Cazzy Francis	21	400	19.1
1987	Richard Kimble	533	146	3.7	Dwane Brown	96	46	.48	665	Fred Barnett	32	608	19.0
1988	Earl Easley	861	196	4.4	Roy Johnson	50	23	.46	348	Fred Barnett	12	141	11.8
1989	Richard Kimble	977	225	4.3	Roy Johnson	122	61	.50	941	Fred Barnett	38	643	16.9
1990	Larry Harris	490	90	5.5	Roy Johnson	245	101	.41	1,561	Blake Denison	24	349	14.5
1991	Roy Johnson	782	170	4.6	Roy Johnson	263	120	.46	1,747	Kendricke Bullard	29	508	17.5
1992	Jerrold Seymore	395	103	3.8	Tom Sears	176	95	.54	1,159	Kendricke Bullard	22	325	14.8
1993	Marquis Williams	1,060	250	4.2	Johnny Covington	184	94	.51	1,069	Derrick Austin	22	309	14.1
1994	Corey Walker	630	175	3.6	Johnny Covington	185	85	.46	830	Derrick Austin	27	347	12.9
1995	Corey Walker	1,013	212	4.8	Johnny Covington	370	194	.52	2,127	Corey Walker	42	411	9.8
1996	Lamont Zachery	846	114	7.4	Jeremie Watkins	208	118	.57	1,481	Lennie Johnson	47	796	16.9
1997	Lamont Zachery	386	97	4.0	Cleo Lemon	205	90	.44	1,452	Lennie Johnson	46	852	18.7
1998	Lamont Zachery	558	122	4.6	Cleo Lemon	387	183	.46	2,721	Lennie Johnson	55	901	16.4
1999	Lamont Zachery	846	172	4.9	Cleo Lemon	230	105	.46	1,569	Robert Kilow	57	783	13.7
2000	Jonathan Adams	1,002	202	5.0	Cleo Lemon	306	173	.57	1,964	Robert Kilow	72	1,002	13.9
2001	Jonathan Adams	1,004	235	4.3	Elliot Jacobs	102	43	.42	586	Alvin Powell	36	507	14.1
2002	Danny Smith	1,390	254	5.5	Elliot Jacobs	258	136	.53	1,751	James Hickenbotham	27	468	17.3
2003	Shermar Bracey	530	112	4.7	Elliot Jacobs	273	145	.53	1,537	Mike Cox	35	477	13.6
2004	Antonio Warren	1,036	195	5.3	Nick Noce	315	164	.52	2,115	Chuck Walker	38	589	15.5

Receiving leaders by receptions
All statistics include postseason

ARKANSAS STATE ALL-TIME SCORES

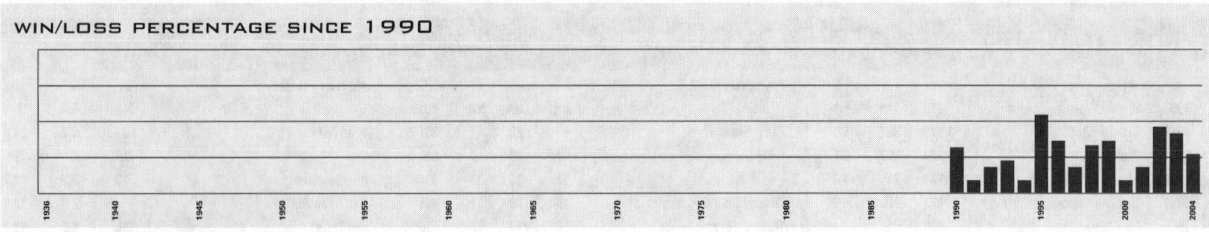

WIN/LOSS PERCENTAGE SINCE 1990

AL KINCAID	
1990-91 (.205)	4-17-1

1990-1992
INDEPENDENT

1990			3-7-1	
S1	=	at Memphis	24	24
S8	●	La. Monroe	23	18
S15		at Wyoming	27	34
S22		at Louisiana Tech	7	40
S29		at So. Illinois	20	17
O6	●	Northwestern St.	16	8
O13		at Northern Illinois	0	35
O20		at Mississippi	13	42
N2		at North Texas	26	35
N10		La. Lafayette	16	17
N17		at Toledo	28	43

1991			1-10-0	
A31		at Colorado State	24	38
S7		Northwestern St.	3	28
S14		at Northern Illinois	21	22
S21		at Memphis	21	31
S28		Louisiana Tech	10	42
O5		Central Florida	20	31
O12		at LSU	14	70
O19		at Akron	23	28
O26		SW. Missouri St.	20	37
N9	●	Troy State	20	17
N16		La. Lafayette	13	17

RAY PERKINS	
1992 (.182)	2-9

1992			2-9-0	
S5		at Toledo	0	49
S12		at Oklahoma	0	61
S19		Northern Illinois	0	31
S26	●	So. Illinois	42	38
O3		Northwestern St.	18	24
O10		Troy State	7	41
O17		at Memphis	7	37
O24		at Mississippi State	6	56
O31		at Louisiana Tech	0	23
N14		at East Carolina	18	35
N21	●	at La. Lafayette	20	7

1993-1995
BIG WEST

JOHN BOBO	
1993-96 (.307)	13-30-1

1993			2-8-1 (1-5-0)	
S4		at Florida	6	44
S11		New Mexico State	19	22
S18		at Northern Illinois	7	23
S25	●	So. Illinois	27	6
O2		at Louisiana Tech	3	17
O9		at Memphis	3	45
O16		La. Lafayette	3	19
O23	=	at Mississippi State	15	15
N6		La. Monroe	10	42
N13		at Pacific	6	20
N20	●	Nevada	23	21

1994			1-10-0 (0-6-0)	
S3		at Virginia Tech	7	34
S10		at Nevada	0	18
S17	●	So. Illinois	41	14
S24		at New Mexico State	17	24
O1		at Mississippi State	3	49
O8		at La. Lafayette	0	26
O15		at Memphis	6	15
O22		Pacific	16	30
N5		Northern Illinois	16	38
N12		at Colorado State	3	48
N19		Louisiana Tech	14	20

1995			6-5-0 (3-3-0)	
S2	●	Utah State	21	17
S9		at Nevada-Las Vegas	23	28
S16	●	So. Illinois	14	9
S23		at Louisiana Tech	25	28
S30		at Minnesota	7	55
O7		La. Lafayette	9	33
O14		at Texas Tech	25	63
O28		Jacksonville St.	37	6
N4	●	San Jose State	21	7
N11	●	at Northern Illinois	28	21
N18	●	Miss. Valley St.	55	3

1996-1998
INDEPENDENT

1996			4-7	
A31		at Brigham Young	9	58
S7	●	Austin Peay	24	0
S14		at UAB	17	42
S21		Northern Illinois	30	31
O5	●	Central Arkansas	17	7
O12		at La. Lafayette	31	42
O19		S.E. Missouri St.	38	9
O26		at Mississippi	21	38
N2		at East Carolina	16	34
N9	●	Louisiana Tech*LR*	55	38
N16		at Nevada	14	66

JOE HOLLIS	
1997-2001 (.232)	13-43

1997			2-9	
A30		at Georgia	7	38
S13	●	Central Arkansas	36	35
S20		So. Utah	24	34
S27		at Virginia Tech	0	50
O4		La. Lafayette	38	41
O11		at Memphis	9	38
O18		at Louisiana Tech	14	42
O25		at New Mexico State	20	34
N1		at Miami, Fla.	10	42
N8	●	SW. Missouri St.	35	27
N22		UAB	7	13

1998			4-8	
S5		at Minnesota	14	17
S12		at LSU	6	42
S19		SW. Missouri St.	28	24
S26	●	at Hawaii	20	0
O3	●	New Mexico State	34	31
O10		Idaho	14	52
O17		at La. Lafayette	19	21
O24		at Mississippi	17	30
O31		at Memphis	19	35
N7		Louisiana Tech	21	69
N14	●	La. Monroe	17	13
N21		Cincinnati	7	51

1999-2000
BIG WEST

1999			4-7 (2-3)	
S4		at Illinois	3	41
S11		at Mississippi	14	38
S18		at Memphis	26	31
S25		TCU	21	24
O2	●	Sam Houston St.	45	20
O9		at Utah State	14	20
O16		Idaho	24	30
O23	●	at North Texas	14	10
O30	●	La. Lafayette	31	27
N6		at Boise State	10	63
N13	●	Nevada	44	28

2000			1-10 (1-4)	
S2		at North Carolina St.	31	38
S9		at Oklahoma	7	45
S16		Memphis	17	19
S23		at TCU	3	52
S30		Richmond	27	30
O7		at Mississippi	10	35
O14		at Idaho	25	42
O21		New Mexico State	29	35
O28		at Utah State	31	44
N4		Boise State	14	42
N11	●	North Texas	53	28

2001-PRESENT
SUN BELT

2001			2-9 (2-4)	
S1		at Georgia	17	45
S8		at Baylor	3	24
S22		Jacksonville St.	28	31
O6		Mississippi	17	35
O13	●	La. Lafayette	26	20
O20		at North Texas	0	45
O27	●	Idaho	34	31
N3		at Middle Tennessee	6	54
N10		at New Mexico State	17	28
N17		La. Monroe	7	16
N22		Nicholls St.	22	28

STEVE ROBERTS	
2002-PRESENT (.389)	14-22

2002			6-7 (3-3)	
A25		at Virginia Tech	7	63
A30		San Jose State	14	33
S7	●	Tulsa	21	19
S14		at Illinois	7	59
S21	●	at La. Monroe	33	21
S28	●	Tennessee-Martin	30	10
O5	●	Middle Tennessee	13	7
O12		at Mississippi	17	52
O19		North Texas	10	13
O26		New Mexico State	21	26
N2	●	So. Utah	38	16
N9		at La. Lafayette	10	13
N16	●	at Idaho	38	29

2003			5-7 (3-3)	
A30		at Texas A&M	11	26
S6	●	Tenn. Martin	63	6
S13	●	S.E. Missouri St.	21	3
S20		at Tulsa	7	54
S27		at Memphis	16	38
O4	●	La. Monroe *LR*	44	41
O11		at Mississippi	0	55
O25		at Utah State	0	49
N1	●	at New Mexico State	28	24
N8	●	Idaho	24	23
N15		at North Texas	14	58
N20		Middle Tennessee	14	24

2004			3-8 (3-4)	
S4		at Missouri	20	52
S11		at LSU	3	53
S18		Memphis	35	47
S25	●	at La. Monroe	28	21
O2		at Mississippi	21	28
O9		at Middle Tennessee	17	45
O16	●	Troy State	13	9
O23		at La. Lafayette	24	27
N6		Idaho *Pull*	31	45
N11	●	Utah State	16	7
N18		North Texas	7	31

ARMY

BY KEVIN GLEASON

THE GLORY DAYS OF ARMY FOOTBALL can be summed up by a 17-word telegram wired to West Point following the Cadets' perfect 1944 season: "The greatest of all Army teams—STOP—We have stopped the war to celebrate your magnificent success. MacArthur." Just about all historical references to Army football lead to the 1940s, when the Cadets and their multitalented tandem of Glenn Davis and Felix "Doc" Blanchard helped bring three national titles to the banks of the Hudson.

The guiding force was a former Dartmouth coach named Earl Henry "Red" Blaik, who took over following a 1–7–1 finish in 1940 and brought home a 5–3–1 record his first season. Two years later, the Cadets signed Davis, a halfback out of LaVerne, Calif. Blanchard followed a year later in 1944 and won the Heisman Trophy in 1945. Davis won the Heisman in 1946 as Army won its third straight national championship and posted a three-season record of 27–0–1.

There were other good Army teams, even another Heisman winner—Pete Dawkins in 1958—but there probably will never be another period of grid dominance at West Point.

The team has been known as the Black Knights since 1999, introducing updated logos to complement the nickname change, but Army continues to search for an identity. The Academy ended a forgettable experiment by leaving Conference USA (where it posted a 9–41 record) following the 2004 season and returning to independent status. Army was overmatched from the start—smaller and slower and plainly less talented than other C-USA schools, many with far looser academic requirements.

TRADITION This is an institution—"school" seems trivial in describing Army—so doused in tradition that crossing Thayer Gate is like entering into a wonderful time warp. Home games follow the cadets' parade on The Plain and march into Michie Stadium. Skydivers deliver the game ball while shooting for 50-yard line landings. Cannons go off following each score as cadets, who stand the entire game, spill from the stands to perform push-ups—one for each of Army's points. Most touching, though, is when the last second ticks off and fans draw to a sudden silence as players face the Corps of Cadets and sing the alma mater. If the eyes don't well up then, bring the hankie to Army-Navy, where at the conclusion, the teams bunch to face their respective corps for the singing. For some, it's a moment when the realization hits hard: in mere months, some of these players will be risking their lives for a greater good.

PROFILE

U.S. Military Academy
West Point, N.Y.
Founded: 1802
Enrollment: 4,209
Colors: Black, Gold and Gray
Nickname: Black Knights
Stadium: Michie Stadium/Blaik Field
   Opened in 1924
   AstroPlay: 38,115 capacity
First football game: 1890
All-time record: 624–415–51 (.596)
Bowl record: 2–2
Consensus national championships, 1936-present: 3 (1944, 1945, 1946)
Heisman Trophy: Doc Blanchard, 1945; Glenn Davis, 1946; Pete Dawkins, 1958
Outland Trophy: Joe Steffy, 1947
First-round NFL draftees: 3
Website: www.goarmysports.com

THE BEST OF TIMES

Army went 27–0–1 from 1944 to 1946, winning consensus national titles in all three seasons.

THE WORST OF TIMES

We are experiencing them. The Black Knights took a five-year record of 7–51 into the 2005 season.

CONFERENCE

Army was an independent its first 108 years of football before debuting in Conference USA during the 1998 season. Having won seven of its first 34 conference games, Army announced in July 2003 its decision to leave C-USA and resume independence following the 2004 season. The Academy reasoned that it would have greater scheduling flexibility as an independent, but didn't rule out joining another conference.

DISTINGUISHED ALUMNI

Dwight Eisenhower; Ulysses S. Grant; Alexander Haig; Robert E. Lee; Douglas MacArthur; George Patton; Norman Schwarzkopf

FIGHT SONG

THE ARMY TEAM'S THE PRIDE AND DREAM
Of every heart in gray.
The Army line you'll ever find
A terror in the fray;
And When the Team is fighting
for the Black and Gray and Gold,
We're always near with song and cheer
And this is the tale we're told:
The Army team
Rah Rah Rah (Boom)
On, brave old Army team,
On to the fray:
Fight on to victory,
For that's the fearless Army way.

> *In mere months, some of these players will risk their lives for a greater good.*

BEST PLAYER In a three-way race among Davis, Blanchard and Dawkins, Davis emerges in a photo finish. As a sophomore at the Academy, he led the nation with 120 points while averaging 11.5 yards per carry. Davis, known as "Mr. Outside" for his adeptness around the edge, earned several national honors before winning the Heisman Trophy in his senior year. He finished his career with 2,957 rushing yards, 59 touchdowns and an average of 8.26 yards per carry, still an NCAA record. "Anybody who ever saw Davis carry the football," Blaik said in his book, *You Have to Pay the Price*, "must realize there could not have been a greater, more dangerous running back in the history of the game." Blanchard, known as "Mr. Inside," put his own signature on Army football, becoming the Academy's first Heisman winner in 1945. He also won the Sullivan Award that year to become the first football player chosen as the outstanding amateur athlete in America. A three-time All-America, Blanchard wound up with 1,666 yards rushing and 38 touchdowns.

BEST COACH Shortly into his tenure as superintendent, Brigadier General Robert L. Eichelberger decided Army's selection of graduate officers for coaching positions had become outdated. He called upon Blaik, a former Army assistant who had accepted the head coaching position at Dartmouth in 1934. Blaik's spectacular success in the 1940s gave no hint of the scandal that would rock his program in 1951. First, Navy ruined Army's chance at an unbeaten season with a 14-2 upset on the last day of the 1950 schedule. Months later, 90 cadets, including 37 football players, were dismissed from the Academy for cheating. Among those kicked out was Bobby Blaik, who had lettered as quarterback for his dad in the 1949 and 1950 seasons. Red Blaik was talked out of resigning by General Douglas MacArthur, who told him, "Earl, you must stay on. Don't leave under fire." Blaik rebuilt the program and took Army to an 8–0–1 season in 1958 that was highlighted by Dawkins' Heisman Trophy and split end Bill Carpenter, who would receive plays by hand signals 15 yards wide of the line of scrimmage rather than join teammates in the huddle. Blaik retired following the season. He went 121–33–10 from 1941 to 1958 and remains the winningest coach in school history. He received input from Sid Gillman, who served as line coach in 1948, and Vince Lombardi, who handled the backs for Blaik from 1949 to 1953. In all, 15 of Blaik's assistants went on to become head coaches. Blaik was twice a national Coach of the Year

RECORDS

RUSHING YARDS

	GAME	
269	Michael Wallace vs. Louisville, Oct. 7, 1999 (19 att.)	
	SEASON	
1,338	Mike Mayweather, 1990 (274 att.)	
	CAREER	
4,299	Mike Mayweather, 1987-90 (853 att.)	

PASSING YARDS

	GAME	
385	Leamon Hall vs. North Carolina, Sept. 25, 1976 (28 of 55)	
	SEASON	
2,234	Zac Dahman, 2003 (230 of 436)	
	CAREER	
5,502	Leamon Hall, 1974-77 (426 of 878)	

RECEIVING YARDS

	GAME	
186	Mike Fahnestock vs. Lehigh, Oct. 11, 1980 (7 rec.)	
	SEASON	
937	Mike Fahnestock, 1980 (47 rec.)	
	CAREER	
2,279	Clennie Brundidge, 1975-78 (147 rec.)	

POINTS

	GAME	
45	Elmer Oliphant vs. Villanova, Oct. 28, 1916	
	SEASON	
125	Elmer Oliphant, 1917	
	CAREER	
354	Glenn Davis, 1943-46 (59 TDs)	

CONSENSUS ALL-AMERICANS

1898	Charles Romeyn, B
1900	William Smith, E
1901	Charles Daly, B
1901-02	Paul Bunker, T/B
1902	Robert Boyers, C
1904	Arthur Tipton, C
1904-05	Henry Torney, B
1907	William Erwin, G
1911	Leland Devore, T
1913	Louis Merillat, E
1914	John McEwan, C
1916-17	Elmer Oliphant, B
1922	Edgar Garbisch, C
1926	Bud Sprague, T
1927-29	Red Cagle, B
1932	Milt Summerfelt, G
1943	Casimir Myslinski, C
1944-46	Doc Blanchard, B
1944-46	Glenn Davis, B
1945	Tex Coulter, T

(Continued on next page)

and was enshrined in the National Football Foundation Hall of Fame in 1964.

BEST TEAM Both the 1944 and 1945 national champions went 9–0, but the '44 team gets the edge for allowing just 35 points all season; the '45 team allowed a whopping 46. The '44 squad averaged 56 points per game and had four shutouts. Six first-team All-Americas led Army to a level of dominance not seen before, or after, in college football. Once asked what the best game he saw his team play was, Blaik replied, "That's easy. It was a Wednesday afternoon in October when they scrimmaged each other." Most talk of the 1944 team centers on Davis and Blanchard, but they were just two of the stars. The Cadets were so deep they used two offensive units: the Lombardo team, quarterbacked by Tom Lombardo and consisting mostly of freshmen, and the Kenna team, led by senior quarterback Doug Kenna, who started before yielding to Lombardo's unit in the second quarter. When the Cadets clinched their 9–0 season with a 23-7 win over Navy, Blaik told the team, "Seldom in a lifetime's experience is one permitted the complete satisfaction of being part of a perfect performance. To the coaches, the 23-7 is enough."

BIGGEST GAME Notre Dame and Army ranked 1-2 in the nation in 1946 before they played to a scoreless tie at Yankee Stadium. Six times Army moved inside the Irish 30, six times Army was stopped. Notre Dame got past midfield just three times. The tie snapped Army's 25-game winning streak and ultimately left some dispute as to the national champion. Army won its final two games to finish 9–0–1. Notre Dame finished No. 1 in the Associated Press poll and seven other rankings. Army was No. 1 in two other rankings, and three others had the teams co-champions. But Army advertises itself as 1946 national champion.

BIGGEST UPSET One week after opening the 1972 season with a 77-7 loss to Nebraska at Michie Stadium, Army won at Texas A&M 24-14 as a 30-point underdog.

STADIUM Only 15 Division I-A stadiums are older than Michie Stadium, named in honor of Dennis Mahan Michie and unveiled in 1924. In 1890, Michie, a cadet, accepted a challenge from Navy students to play a football game. He

organized a team that lost to Navy 24-0. The field was dedicated to the legendary Blaik in 1999, but even though "Blaik Field" is stenciled into parts of the artificial surface, it is and probably forever will be known as Michie Stadium.

CONSENSUS ALL-AMERICANS (CONT.)		
1945	John Green,	G
1946	Hank Foldberg,	E
1947	Joe Steffy,	G
1949	Arnold Galiffa,	B
1950	Dan Foldberg,	E
1957	Bob Anderson,	B
1958	Pete Dawkins,	B
1959	Bill Carpenter,	E

HEARTBREAKER As they say at Army, any loss to Navy is a heartbreaker. But a non-Navy game produced perhaps the most heartbreaking loss in the past 20 years. Army trailed national title contender Notre Dame 28-7 in their 1995 game before unleashing a wild comeback. Army cut it to 28-27 with 39 seconds left when coach Bob Sutton eschewed the extra point and an almost certain tie—the overtime format had not yet been adapted—to go for the two-point conversion and the win. Tight end Ron Leshinski caught a pass on a quick out, but as he turned one yard from the goal line, he was brought down by Irish defensive back Ivory Covington.

RIVAL Other rivalries decide rankings and championships, but Army-Navy continues as one of the finest rivalries in all of sports. Records really don't matter when they play, as television ratings have proved, in part because fans can expect a rugged competition that's often decided late. Through 2004, the series was tied 49-49-7. The two schools also delight in stealing each other's mascots.

NICKNAME A New York sportswriter first gave Army the Black Knights nickname during the 1930s or '40s. But the teams were known as the Cadets until 1999, when the athletic department went to Black Knights as a primary nickname. Cadets remains an acceptable moniker.

MASCOT Mules have served as the Army mascot since 1899. The most recent mascot is Raider, who has been with the team for more than 16 years and assumed the veteran role following the retirements of Trooper and Traveler in September 2002.

UNIFORMS The uniforms have stayed the same for the most part through the years. Four numbers, though, haven't been issued in recent years: 12, 24, 35 and 41. Nos. 24, 35 and 41 belonged to Heisman Trophy winners Dawkins, Blanchard and Davis. No. 12 symbolizes Army's 12th man, the Corps of Cadets. The uniforms include black-and-white jerseys, gold pants and gold helmets.

The cadet colors of black, gold and gray signify the components of gunpowder: charcoal, saltpeter (potassium nitrate) and sulfur.

QUOTE "I want an officer for a secret and dangerous mission. I want a West Point football player." —General George C. Marshall, chief of staff, U.S. Army, World War II

THE SCHOOLS

ARMY ANNUAL STATISTICAL LEADERS

YR	RUSHING	YDS	ATT	AVG	PASSING	ATT	CMP	PCT	YDS	RECEIVING	REC	YDS	AVG
1940	Hank Mazur	338	92	3.7	Jere Maupin	45	21	.47			NA	NA	NA
1941	Ralph Hill	346	82	4.2	Hank Mazur	53	20	.38	368		NA	NA	NA
1942		NA	NA	NA		NA	NA	NA	NA		NA	NA	NA
1943	Glenn Davis	634	95	6.7	Glenn Davis	49	21	.43	394		NA	NA	NA
1944	Glenn Davis	667	58	11.5	Tom Lombardo	47	27	.57	444	Glenn Davis	13	221	17.0
1945	Glenn Davis	944	82	11.0	Dick Walterhouse	29	18	.62		George Poole	10	135	13.5
1946	Glenn Davis	712	123	5.8	Arnold Tucker	76	42	.53	619	Glenn Davis	20	348	17.4
1947	Elwyn Rowan	750	123	6.1	Arnold Galiffa	49	22	.45	295	John Trent	9	NA	NA
1948	Gil Stephenson	887	153	5.8	Arnold Galiffa	95	44	.46	701	Dan Foldberg	15	NA	NA
1949	Gil Stephenson	592	134	4.4	Arnold Galiffa	97	50	.52	887	Dan Foldberg	20	308	15.4
1950	Alfred Pollard	638	87	7.3	Bob Blaik	98	42	.43	618	Dan Foldberg	22	304	13.8
1951	Tommy Bell	328	96	3.4	Frederic Meyers	57	21	.37	324	Lowell Sisson	15	199	13.3
1952	Freddie Attaya	684	120	5.7	Pete Vann	121	53	.44	788	Lowell Sisson	21	290	13.8
1953	Gerald Lodge	571	131	4.4	Pete Vann	113	63	.56	884	Lowell Sisson	16	217	13.6
1954	Tommy Bell	1,020	96	10.7	Pete Vann	99	48	.49	1,102	Don Holleder	17	495	29.1
1955	Pat Uebel	546	109	5.0	Don Holleder	65	22	.34	409	Art Johnson	9	203	22.6
1956	Bob Kyasky	707	129	5.5	Dave Bourland	50	21	.42	396	Art Johnson	11	211	19.2
1957	Bob Anderson	983	153	6.4	Dave Bourland	69	34	.49	509	Bill Graf	16	193	12.1
1958	Bob Anderson	564	126	4.5	Joe Caldwell	120	54	.45	1,097	Bill Carpenter	22	453	20.6
1959	Bob Anderson	340	76	4.5	Joe Caldwell	188	105	.56	1,343	Bill Carpenter	43	591	13.7
1960	Al Rushatz	648	162	4.0	Frank Blanda	164	92	.56	1,119	George Kirschenbauer	25	273	10.9
1961	Al Rushatz	556	127	4.4	Dick Eckert	105	56	.53	649	Tom Culver	20	305	15.3
1962	John Seymour	539	107	5.0	Cammy Lewis	85	34	.40	494	John Seymour	7	58	8.3
1963	Ken Waldrop	559	137	4.1	Rollie Stichweh	94	46	.49	464	Sam Champi	13	146	11.2
1964	Rollie Stichweh	655	129	5.1	Rollie Stichweh	119	66	.56	816	Sam Champi	25	347	13.9
1965	Sonny Stowers	822	204	4.1	Curt Cook	116	41	.35	463	Terry Young	17	184	10.8
1966	Charlie Jarvis	450	89	5.1	Steve Lindell	157	80	.51	1,035	Terry Young	37	539	14.6
1967	Charlie Jarvis	774	144	5.4	Steve Lindell	144	73	.51	843	Terry Young	41	516	12.6
1968	Charlie Jarvis	1,110	208	5.3	Steve Lindell	160	75	.47	1,043	Gary Steele	27	496	18.4
1969	Lynn Moore	983	187	5.3	Bernie Wall	132	66	.50	814	Joe Albano	30	394	13.1
1970	Ray Ritacco	417	123	3.4	Bernie Wall	183	85	.46	970	Joe Albano	54	669	12.4
1971	Ray Ritacco	427	118	3.6	Kingsley Fink	157	68	.43	799	John Simar	26	282	10.8
1972	Bob Hines	844	202	4.2	Kingsley Fink	194	88	.45	1,139	Jim Ward	32	393	12.3
1973	Willie Thigpen	268	74	3.6	Kingsley Fink	237	101	.43	1,141	Jim Ward	35	431	12.3
1974	Brad Dodrill	558	126	4.4	Scott Gillogly	75	30	.40	466	Jeff Jancek	13	188	14.5
1975	Tony Pyne	544	129	4.2	Leamon Hall	218	93	.43	1,107	Howie Williams	37	417	11.3
1976	Tony Pyne	438	109	4.0	Leamon Hall	344	162	.47	2,174	Clennie Brundidge	47	657	14.0
1977	Greg King	961	177	5.4	Leamon Hall	265	151	.57	1,944	Clennie Brundidge	51	842	16.5
1978	Jimmy Hill	678	166	4.1	Earle Mulrane	222	103	.46	1,419	Clennie Brundidge	44	726	16.5
1979	Jimmy Hill	441	118	3.7	Earle Mulrane	160	63	.39	656	Mike Fahnestock	19	283	14.9
1980	Gerald Walker	917	186	4.9	Jerryl Bennett	166	77	.46	1,065	Mike Fahnestock	47	937	19.9
1981	Gerald Walker	1,053	240	4.4	Jerryl Bennett	127	59	.47	582	Gerald Walker	24	158	6.6
1982	Andre Cuerington	487	132	3.7	Rich Laughlin	122	53	.43	632	Elton Akins	21	391	18.6
1983	Elton Akins	713	191	3.7	Rob Healy	142	71	.50	913	Scott Spellmon	34	501	14.7
1984	Doug Black	1,148	264	4.3	Nate Sassaman	56	28	.50	364	Benny White	17	241	14.2
1985	Doug Black	950	197	4.8	Rob Healy	47	27	.57	421	Benny White	13	213	16.4
1986	Tory Crawford	1,078	245	4.4	Tory Crawford	98	48	.49	816	Benny White	18	317	17.6
1987	Mike Mayweather	762	149	5.1	Tory Crawford	66	28	.42	566	Sean Jordan	13	292	22.5
1988	Mike Mayweather	1,022	191	5.4	Bryan McWilliams	31	13	.42	255	Sean Jordan	12	289	24.1
1989	Mike Mayweather	1,177	239	4.9	Bryan McWilliams	49	22	.45	460	Sean Jordan	9	220	24.4
1990	Mike Mayweather	1,338	274	4.9	Willie McMillian	34	15	.44	455	Myreon Williams	13	434	33.4
1991	Myreon Williams	924	186	5.0	Myreon Williams	47	14	.30	267	Monte Tomasino	5	122	24.4
1992	Steve Weber	750	175	4.3	Rick Roper	97	55	.57	708	Paul Andrzejewski	27	307	11.4
1993	Akili King	883	150	5.9	Rick Roper	92	55	.60	733	Leon Gantt	21	207	9.9
1994	Joe Ross	721	158	4.6	Ronnie McAda	99	51	.52	618	Ron Thomas	23	241	10.5
1995	John Conroy	809	182	4.4	Ronnie McAda	111	56	.51	761	Ron Leshinski	15	210	14.0
1996	Joe Hewitt	839	141	6.0	Ronnie McAda	87	55	.63	954	Ron Leshinski	17	259	15.2
1997	Johnny Goff	698	173	4.0	Johnny Goff	86	27	.31	384	Brad Miller	8	90	11.3
1998	Bobby Williams	783	127	6.2	Johnny Goff	69	30	.44	431	Grady Jett	14	180	12.9
1999	Michael Wallace	894	163	5.5	Joe Gerena	105	42	.40	661	Grady Jett	21	357	17.0
2000	Michael Wallace	1,157	192	6.0	Joe Gerena	151	72	.48	779	Omari Thompson	40	451	11.3
2001	C.J. Young	556	158	3.5	Chad Jenkins	286	156	.55	1,773	Clint Dodson	42	463	11.0
2002	Carlton Jones	611	161	3.8	Zac Dahman	184	89	.48	1,039	William White	30	384	12.8
2003	Carlton Jones	632	194	3.3	Zac Dahman	436	230	.53	2,234	Aaron Alexander	64	861	13.5
2004	Carlton Jones	1,269	209	6.1	Zac Dahman	265	145	.55	1,767	Aaron Alexander	37	505	13.5

Receiving leaders by receptions
The NCAA began including postseason stats in 2002

ARMY ALL-TIME SCORES

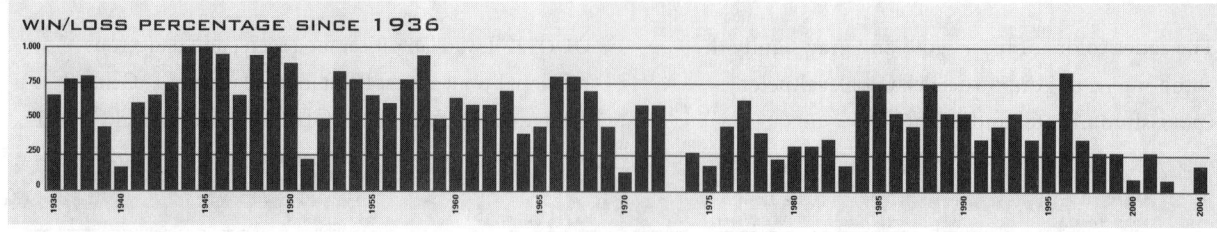

WIN/LOSS PERCENTAGE SINCE 1936

DENNIS MICHIE
1890, '92 (.583)   3-2-1

1890   0-1-0
N29	Navy	0	24

HARRY WILLIAMS
1891 (.750)   4-1-1

1891   4-1-1
O24 •	Fordham	10	6
O31 =	Princeton AC	12	12
N7 •	Stevens	14	12
N14 •	Rutgers	6	27
N21 •	Schuylkill	6	0
N28 •	at Navy	32	16

DENNIS MICHIE

1892   3-1-1
O8 =	Wesleyan	6	6
O22 •	Stevens	42	0
O29 •	Trinity	24	0
N19 •	Princeton AC	14	0
N26 •	Navy	4	12

LAURIE BLISS
1893 (.444)   4-5

1893   4-5-0
S30 •	Volunteers N.Y.	4	6
O7 •	Lafayette	36	0
O14 •	Lehigh	0	18
O21 •	Amherst	12	4
O28 •	Yale	0	28
N4 •	Union	6	0
N11 •	Trinity	18	11
N18 •	Princeton	4	36
D2 •	at Navy	4	6

HARMON GRAVES
1894-95 (.667)   8-4

1894   3-2-0
O6 •	Amherst	18	0
O13 •	Brown	8	10
O20 •	MIT	42	0
O27 •	Yale	5	12
N3 •	Union	30	0

1895   5-2-0
O5 •	Trinity	50	0
O12 •	Harvard	0	4
O19 •	Tufts	35	0
O26 •	Dartmouth	6	0
N2 •	Yale	8	28
N16 •	Union	16	0
N23 •	Brown *NWB*	26	0

GEORGE DYER
1896 (.583)   3-2-1

1896   3-2-1
O3 •	Tufts	27	0
O17 •	Princeton	0	11
O24 •	Union	44	0
O31 •	Yale	2	16
N7 •	Wesleyan	12	12
N21 •	Brown	8	6

HERMAN KOEHLER
1897-1900 (.632)   20-11-3

1897   6-1-1
O2 •	Trinity	38	6
O9 •	Wesleyan	12	9
O16 •	at Harvard	0	10
O23 •	Tufts	30	0
O30 =	at Yale	6	6
N6 •	Lehigh	48	6
N13 •	Stevens	18	4
N20 •	Brown	42	0

1898   3-2-1
O1 •	Tufts	40	0
O8 •	Wesleyan	27	8
O15 •	Harvard	0	28
O22 •	Lehigh	18	0
O29 •	Yale	0	10
N5 =	Princeton	5	5

1899   4-5-0
O2 •	Tufts	22	0
O7 •	Penn State	0	6
O14 •	Harvard	0	18
O21 •	Princeton	0	23
O28 •	Dartmouth	6	2
N4 •	Yale	0	24
N11 •	Columbia	0	16
N18 •	Syracuse	12	6
D2 •	Navy *PHIL*	17	5

1900   7-3-1
S29 •	Tufts	5	0
O6 =	Penn State	0	0
O13 •	Trinity	28	0
O17 •	De LaSalle	11	0
O20 •	Harvard	0	29
O27 •	Williams	6	0
N3 •	Yale	0	18
N7 •	Rutgers	23	0
N10 •	Hamilton	11	0
N17 •	Bucknell	18	10
D1 •	Navy *PHIL*	7	11

LEON KROMER
1901 (.750)   5-1-2

1901   5-1-2
O5 •	Franklin & Marshall	20	0
O12 •	Trinity	17	0
O19 •	Harvard	0	6
O26 •	Williams	15	0
N2 =	Yale	5	5
N9 =	Princeton	6	6
N23 •	Pennsylvania	24	0
N30 •	Navy *PHIL*	11	5

DENNIS NOLAN
1902 (.813)   6-1-1

1902   6-1-1
O4 •	Tufts	5	0
O11 •	Dickinson	11	0
O18 •	Harvard	6	14
O25 •	Williams	28	0
N1 =	Yale	6	6
N8 •	Union	56	0
N15 •	at Syracuse	46	0
N29 •	Navy *PHIL*	22	8

EDWARD KING
1903 (.722)   6-2-1

1903   6-2-1
S26 =	Colgate	0	0
O3 •	Tufts	17	0
O10 •	Dickinson	12	0
O17 •	Harvard	0	5
O24 •	Yale	5	17
O31 •	Vermont	32	0
N7 •	Manhattan	48	0
N14 •	Chicago	10	6
N28 •	Navy *PHIL*	40	5

ROBERT BOYERS
1904-05 (.639)   11-6-1

1904   7-2-0
O1 •	Tufts	12	0
O8 •	Dickinson	18	0
O15 •	Harvard	0	4
O22 •	Yale	11	6
O29 •	Williams	16	0
N5 •	Princeton	6	12
N12 •	NYU	41	0
N19 •	at Syracuse	21	5
N26 •	Navy *PHIL*	11	0

1905   4-4-1
S30 •	Tufts	18	0
O7 •	Colgate	18	6
O14 •	Virginia Tech	6	16
O21 •	Harvard	0	6
O28 •	at Yale	0	20
N11 •	Carlisle	5	6
N18 •	Trinity	34	0
N25 •	Syracuse	17	0
D2 •	Navy *PHI*	6	6

HENRY SMITHER
1906, '07 (.750)   7-2-1

ERNEST GRAVES
1906, '12 (.469)   7-8-1

1906   3-5-1
S29 •	Tufts	12	0
O6 •	Trinity	24	0
O13 •	Colgate	0	0
O20 •	Williams	17	0
O27 •	Harvard	0	5
N3 •	Yale	6	10
N10 •	Princeton	0	8
N24 •	Syracuse	0	4
D1 •	Navy *PHIL*	0	10

HENRY SMITHER

1907   6-2-1
O5 •	Franklin & Marshall	23	0
O12 •	Trinity	12	0
O19 =	Yale	0	0
O26 •	Rochester	30	0
N2 •	Colgate	6	0
N9 •	Cornell	10	14
N16 •	Tufts	21	0
N23 •	at Syracuse	23	4
N30 •	Navy *PHIL*	0	6

HARRY NELLY
1908-10 (.727)   15-5-2

1908   6-1-2
O3 •	Tufts	5	0
O10 •	Trinity	33	0
O17 •	Yale	0	6
O24 •	Colgate	6	0
O31 •	Princeton	0	0
N7 •	Springfield	6	5
N14 =	Wash. & Jeff.	6	6
N21 •	Villanova	25	0
N28 •	Navy *PHIL*	6	4

1909   3-2-0
O2 •	Tufts	22	0
O9 •	Trinity	17	6
O16 •	Yale	0	17
O23 •	Lehigh	18	0
O30 •	Harvard	0	9

1910   6-2-0
O8 •	Tufts	24	0
O15 •	Yale	9	3
O22 •	Lehigh	28	0
O29 •	Harvard	0	6
N5 •	Springfield	5	0
N12 •	Villanova	13	0
N19 •	Trinity	17	0
N26 •	Navy *PHIL*	0	3

JOSEPH BEACHAM
1911 (.813)   6-1-1

1911   6-1-1
O7 •	Vermont	12	0
O14 •	Rutgers	18	0
O21 •	Yale	6	0
O28 •	Lehigh	20	0
N4 =	Georgetown	0	0
N11 •	Bucknell	20	2
N18 •	Colgate	12	6
N24 •	Navy *PHIL*	0	3

ERNEST GRAVES

1912   5-3-0
O5 •	Stevens	27	0
O12 •	Rutgers	19	0
O19 •	Yale	0	6
O26 •	Colgate	18	7
N9 •	Carlisle	6	27
N16 •	Tufts	15	6
N23 •	Syracuse	23	7
N30 •	Navy *PHIL*	0	6

CHARLES DALY
1913-16, '19-22 (.804) 58-13-3

1913   8-1-0
O4 •	Stevens	34	0
O11 •	Rutgers	29	0
O18 •	Colgate	7	6
O25 •	Tufts	2	0
N1 •	Notre Dame	13	35
N8 •	Albright	77	0
N15 •	Villanova	55	0
N22 •	Springfield	14	7
N29 •	Navy *NYC*	22	9

1914   9-0-0
O3 •	Stevens	49	0
O10 •	Rutgers	13	0
O17 •	Colgate	21	7
O24 •	Holy Cross	14	0
O31 •	Villanova	41	0
N7 •	Notre Dame	20	7
N14 •	Maine	28	0
N21 •	Springfield	13	6
N28 •	Navy *PHIL*	20	0

1915   5-3-1
O2 =	Holy Cross	14	14
O9 •	Gettysburg	22	0
O16 •	Colgate	0	13
O23 •	Georgetown	10	0
O30 •	Villanova	13	16
N6 •	Notre Dame	0	7
N13 •	Maine	24	0
N20 •	Springfield	17	7
N27 •	Navy *NYC*	14	0

1916   9-0-0
S30 •	Lebanon Valley	3	0
O7 •	Wash. & Lee	14	7
O14 •	Holy Cross	17	0
O21 •	Trinity	53	0
O28 •	Villanova	69	7
N4 •	Notre Dame	30	10
N11 •	Maine	17	3
N18 •	Springfield	17	2
N25 •	Navy *NYC*	15	7

GEOFFREY KEYES — 1917 (.875) — 7-1

1917 — 7-1-0
O6	•	Carnegie Tech	28	0
O13	•	VMI	34	0
O20	•	Tufts	26	3
O27	•	Villanova	21	7
N3	•	Notre Dame	2	7
N10	•	Carlisle	28	0
N17	•	Lebanon Valley	50	0
N24	•	Boston College	13	7

HUGH MITCHELL — 1918 (1.000) — 1-0

1918 — 1-0-0
S28	•	Mitchell Field	20	0

CHARLES DALY

1919 — 6-3-0
S27	•	Middlebury	14	0
O4	•	Holy Cross	9	0
O11	•	Syracuse	3	7
O18	•	Maine	6	0
O25	•	Boston College	13	0
N1	•	Tufts	24	13
N8	•	Notre Dame	9	12
N15	•	Villanova	62	0
N29	•	Navy NYC	0	6

1920 — 7-2-0
O2	•	Union	35	0
O2	•	Marshall	38	0 *
O9	•	Middlebury	29	0
O16	•	Springfield	26	7
O23	•	Tufts	28	6
O30	•	Notre Dame	17	27
N6	•	Lebanon Valley	53	0
N13	•	Bowdoin	90	0
N27	•	Navy NYC	0	7

1921 — 6-4-0
O1	•	Springfield	28	6
O1	•	New Hampshire	7	10
O8	•	Middlebury	19	0
O8	•	Lebanon Valley	33	0
O15	•	Wabash	21	0
O22	•	Yale	7	14
O29	•	Susquehanna	53	0
N5	•	Notre Dame	0	28
N12	•	Villanova	49	0
N26	•	Navy NYC	0	7

1922 — 8-0-2
S30	•	Springfield	35	0
S30	•	Lebanon Valley	12	0
O7	•	Kansas	13	0
O14	•	Auburn	19	6
O21	•	New Hampshire	33	0
O28	=	Yale	7	7
N4	•	St. Bonaventure	53	0
N11	•	Notre Dame	0	0
N18	•	Bates	39	0
N25	•	Navy PHIL	17	14

JOHN McEWAN — 1923-25 (.750) — 18-5-3

1923 — 6-2-1
S29	•	Tennessee	41	0
O6	•	Florida	20	0
O13		Notre Dame BKLN	0	13
O20	•	Auburn	28	6
O27	•	Lebanon Valley	74	0
N3		at Yale	10	31
N10	•	Arkansas State	44	0
N17	•	Bethany	20	6
N24	=	Navy NYC	0	0

1924 — 5-1-2
O4	•	St. Louis	17	0
O11	•	Detroit	20	0
O18	•	Notre Dame NYC	7	13
O25	•	Boston U.	20	0
N1	=	at Yale	7	7
N8	•	Florida	14	7
N15	=	Columbia	14	14
N29	•	Navy BALT	12	0

1925 — 7-2-0
O3	•	Detroit	31	6
O10	•	Knox	26	7
O17	•	Notre Dame BNX	27	0
O24	•	St. Louis	19	0
O31		at Yale	7	28
N7	•	Davis & Elkins	14	6
N14	•	Columbia NYC	7	21
N21	•	Ursinus	44	0
N28	•	Navy NYC	10	3

BIFF JONES — 1926-29 (.775) — 30-8-2

1926 — 7-1-1
O2	•	Detroit	21	0
O9	•	Davis & Elkins	21	7
O16	•	Syracuse	27	21
O23	•	Boston U.	41	0
O30		at Yale	33	0
N6	•	Franklin & Marshall	55	0
N13	•	Notre Dame BNX	0	7
N20	•	Ursinus	21	15
N27	=	Navy CHI	21	21

1927 — 9-1-0
S24	•	Boston U.	13	0
O1	•	Detroit	6	0
O8	•	Marquette	21	12
O15	•	Davis & Elkins	27	6
O22		at Yale	6	10
O29	•	Bucknell	34	0
N5	•	Franklin & Marshall	45	0
N12	•	Notre Dame BNX	18	0
N19	•	Ursinus	13	0
N26	•	Navy NYC	14	9

1928 — 8-2-0
S29	•	Boston U.	35	0
O6	•	SMU	14	13
O13	•	Providence	44	0
O20		at Harvard	15	0
O27	•	at Yale	18	6
N3	•	De Pauw	38	12
N10	•	Notre Dame BNX	6	12
N17	•	Carleton	32	7
N24	•	Nebraska	13	3
D1	•	Stanford BNX	0	26

1929 — 6-4-1
S28	•	Boston U.	26	0
O5	•	Gettysburg	33	7
O12	•	Davidson	23	7
O19	=	at Harvard	20	20
O26		at Yale	13	21
N2	•	South Dakota	33	6
N9	•	at Illinois	7	17
N16	•	Dickinson	89	7
N23	•	Ohio Wesleyan	19	6
N30	•	Notre Dame BNX	0	7
D28	•	at Stanford	13	34

RALPH SASSE — 1930-32 (.813) — 25-5-2

1930 — 9-1-1
S27	•	Boston U.	39	0
O4	•	Furman	54	0
O11	•	Swarthmore	39	0
O18	•	Harvard	6	0
O25	=	Yale	7	7
N1	•	North Dakota	33	6
N8	•	Illinois BNX	13	0
N15	•	Ky. Wesleyan	47	2
N22	•	Ursinus	18	0
N29	•	Notre Dame CHI	6	7
D13	•	Navy BNX	6	0

1931 — 8-2-1
S26	•	Ohio Northern	60	0
O3	•	Knox	67	6
O10	•	Michigan State	20	7
O17	•	Harvard	13	14
O24	=	at Yale	6	6
O31	•	Colorado College	27	0
N7	•	LSU	20	0
N14	•	at Pittsburgh	0	26
N21	•	Ursinus	54	6
N28	•	Notre Dame BNX	12	0
D12	•	Navy BNX	17	7

1932 — 8-2-0
O1	•	Furman	13	0
O8	•	Carleton	57	0
O15	•	Pittsburgh	13	18
O22	•	Yale	20	0
O29	•	William & Mary	33	0
N5	•	Harvard	46	0
N12	•	North Dakota St.	52	0
N19	•	W.V. Wesleyan	7	0
N26	•	Notre Dame BNX	0	21
D3	•	Navy PHIL	20	0

GAR DAVIDSON — 1933-37 (.755) — 35-11-1

1933 — 9-1-0
S30	•	Mercer	19	6
O7	•	VMI	32	0
O14	•	Delaware	52	0
O21	•	Illinois CLEV	6	0
O28	•	at Yale	21	0
N4	•	Coe	34	0
N11	•	at Harvard	27	0
N18	•	Penn Military	12	0
N25	•	Navy PHIL	12	7
D2	•	Notre Dame BNX	12	13

1934 — 7-3-0
S29	•	Washburn	19	0
O6	•	Davidson	41	0
O13	•	Drake	48	0
O20	•	Southern U.	20	0
O27	•	at Yale	20	12
N3		at Illinois	0	7
N10	•	at Harvard	27	6
N17	•	Citadel	34	0
N24	•	Notre Dame BNX	6	12
D1	•	Navy PHIL	0	3

1935 — 6-2-1
O5	•	William & Mary	14	0
O12	•	Gettysburg	54	0
O19	•	Harvard	13	0
O26	•	at Yale	14	8
N2	•	Mississippi State	7	13
N9	•	at Pittsburgh	6	29
N16	=	Notre Dame BNX	6	6
N23	•	Vermont	34	0
N30	•	Navy PHIL	28	6

1936 — 6-3-0
O3	•	Wash. & Lee	28	0
O10	•	Columbia BNX	27	16
O17	•	at Harvard	32	0
O24	•	Springfield	33	0
O31	•	Colgate	7	14
N7	•	Muhlenburg	54	7
N14	•	Notre Dame BNX	6	20
N21	•	Hobart	51	7
N28	•	Navy PHIL	0	7

1937 — 7-2-0
O2	•	Clemson	21	6
O9	•	Columbia	21	18
O16	•	at Yale	7	15
O23	•	Washington, Mo.	47	7
O30	•	VMI	20	7
N6	•	at Harvard	7	6
N13	•	Notre Dame	0	7
N20	•	St. John's	47	6
N27	•	Navy PHIL	6	0

WILLIAM WOOD — 1938-40 (.482) — 12-13-3

1938 — 8-2-0
S24	•	Wichita St.	32	0
O1	•	Virginia Tech	39	0
O8	•	Columbia	18	20
O15	•	at Harvard	20	17
O22	•	Boston U.	40	0
O29	•	Notre Dame BNX	7	19
N5	•	Franklin & Marshall	20	12
N12	•	U.T. Chattanooga	34	13
N19	•	at Princeton	19	7
N26	•	Navy PHIL	14	7

1939 — 3-4-2
S30	•	Furman	16	7
O7	•	Centre	9	6
O14	=	at Columbia	6	6
O21	•	at Yale	15	20
O28	•	Ursinus	46	13
N4	•	Notre Dame BNX	0	14
N11		at Harvard	0	15
N18	=	Penn State	14	14
D2	•	Navy PHIL	0	10

1940 — 1-7-1
O5	•	Williams	20	19
O12	•	Cornell	0	45
O19	=	at Harvard	6	6
O26	•	Lafayette	0	19
N2	•	Notre Dame BNX	0	7
N9	•	Brown	9	13
N16	•	at Pennsylvania	0	48
N23	•	at Princeton	19	26
N30	•	Navy PHIL	0	14

EARL BLAIK — 1941-58 (.768) — 121-33-10

1941 — 5-3-1
O4	•	Citadel	19	6
O11	•	VMI	27	20
O18	•	at Yale	20	7
O25	•	Columbia	13	0
N1	=	Notre Dame BNX	0	0
N8	•	at Harvard	6	20
N15	•	at Pennsylvania	7	14
N22	•	West Virginia	7	6
N29	•	Navy PHIL	6	14

1942 — 6-3-0
O3	•	Lafayette	14	0
O10	•	Cornell	28	8
O17	•	at Columbia	34	6
O24	•	at Harvard	14	0
O31	•	at Pennsylvania	0	19
N7	•	Notre Dame BNX	0	13
N14	•	Virginia Tech	19	7
N21	•	Princeton BNX	40	7
N28	•	at Navy	0	14

1943 — 7-2-1
S25	•	Villanova	27	0
O2	•	Colgate	42	0
O9	•	Temple	51	0
O16	•	at Columbia	52	0
O23	•	at Yale	39	7
O30	=	at Pennsylvania	13	13
N6	•	Notre Dame BNX	0	26
N13	•	Sampson USN	16	7
N20	•	Brown	59	0
N27	•	Navy	0	13

1944 — 9-0-0
S30	•	North Carolina	46	0
O7	•	Brown	59	7
O14	•	Pittsburgh	69	7
O21	•	Coast Guard	76	0
O28	•	Duke NYC	27	7
N4	•	Villanova	83	0
N11	•	Notre Dame BNX	59	0
N18	•	at Pennsylvania	62	7
D2	•	Navy BALT	23	7

1945 — 9-0-0
S29	•	Louisville AAF	32	0
O6	•	Wake Forest	54	0
O13	•	Michigan BNX	28	7
O20	•	Melville R.I.	55	13
O27	•	Duke NYC	48	13
N3	•	Villanova	54	0
N10	•	Notre Dame BNX	48	0
N17	•	at Pennsylvania	61	0
D1	•	Navy PHIL	32	13

1946 — 9-0-1
S21	•	Villanova	35	0
S28	•	Oklahoma	21	7
O5	•	Cornell	46	21
O12	•	at Michigan	20	13
O19	•	Columbia	48	14
O26	•	Duke NYC	19	0
N2	•	West Virginia	19	0
N9	•	Notre Dame BNX	0	0
N16	•	at Pennsylvania	34	7
N30	•	Navy PHIL	21	18

1947 — 5-2-2
S27	•	Villanova	13	0
O4	•	Colorado	47	0
O11	=	Illinois BNX	0	0
O18	•	Virginia Tech	40	0
O25	•	at Columbia	20	21
N1	•	Wash. & Lee	65	13
N8	•	at Notre Dame	7	27
N15	=	at Pennsylvania	7	7
N29	•	Navy PHIL	21	0

THE SCHOOLS

1948 — 8-0-1

S25	●	Villanova	28	0
O2	●	Lafayette	54	7
O9	●	at Illinois	26	21
O16	●	Harvard	20	7
O23	●	at Cornell	27	6
O30	●	Virginia Tech	49	7
N6	●	Stanford *Bnx*	43	0
N13	●	at Pennsylvania	26	20
N27	=	Navy *Phil*	21	21

1949 — 9-0-0

S24	●	Davidson	47	7
O1	●	Penn State	42	7
O8	●	at Michigan	21	7
O15	●	at Harvard	54	14
O22	●	Columbia	63	6
O29	●	VMI	40	14
N5	●	Fordham	35	0
N12	●	at Pennsylvania	14	13
N26	●	Navy *Phil*	38	0

1950 — 8-1-0

S30	●	Colgate	28	0
O7	●	Penn State	41	7
O14	●	Michigan *Bnx*	27	6
O21	●	at Harvard	49	0
O28	●	at Columbia	34	0
N4	●	at Pennsylvania	28	13
N11	●	New Mexico	51	0
N18	●	at Stanford	7	0
D2		Navy *Phil*	2	14

1951 — 2-7-0

S29		Villanova	7	21
O6		at Northwestern	14	20
O13		Dartmouth	14	28
O20		at Harvard	21	22
O27	●	Columbia	14	9
N3		Southern Cal *Bnx*	6	28
N10	●	Citadel	27	6
N17		at Pennsylvania	6	7
D1		Navy *Phil*	7	42

1952 — 4-4-1

S27	●	South Carolina	28	7
O4		at Southern Cal	0	22
O11	●	Dartmouth	37	7
O18		Pittsburgh	14	22
O25	=	at Columbia	14	14
N1	●	VMI	42	14
N8		at Georgia Tech	6	45
N15	●	at Pennsylvania	14	13
N29		Navy *Phil*	0	7

1953 — 7-1-1

S26	●	Furman	41	0
O3		at Northwestern	20	33
O10	●	Dartmouth	27	0
O17	●	Duke *NYC*	14	13
O24	●	Columbia	40	7
O31	=	at Tulane	0	0
N7	●	North Carolina St.	27	7
N14	●	at Pennsylvania	21	14
N28	●	Navy *Phil*	20	7

1954 — 7-2-0

S25		South Carolina	20	34
O2	●	at Michigan	26	7
O9	●	Dartmouth	60	0
O16	●	at Duke	28	14
O23	●	at Columbia	67	12
O30	●	Virginia	21	20
N6	●	at Yale	48	7
N13	●	at Pennsylvania	35	0
N27		Navy *Phil*	20	27

1955 — 6-3-0

S24	●	Furman	81	0
O1	●	Penn State	35	6
O8		at Michigan	2	26
O15		Syracuse	0	13
O22	●	Columbia	45	0
O29	●	Colgate	27	7
N5		at Yale	12	14
N12	●	at Pennsylvania	40	0
N26	●	Navy *Phil*	14	6

1956 — 5-3-1

S29	●	VMI	32	12
O6	●	Penn State	14	7
O13		at Michigan	14	48
O20		at Syracuse	0	7
O27	●	at Columbia	60	0
N3	●	Colgate	55	46
N10	●	William & Mary	34	6
N17		at Pittsburgh	7	20
D1	=	Navy *Phil*	7	7

1957 — 7-2-0

S28	●	Nebraska	42	0
O5	●	at Penn State	27	13
O12		Notre Dame *Phil*	21	23
O19	●	Pittsburgh	29	13
O26	●	at Virginia	20	12
N2	●	Colgate	53	7
N9	●	Utah	39	33
N16	●	Tulane	20	14
N30		Navy *Phil*	0	14

1958 — 8-0-1

S27	●	South Carolina	45	8
O4	●	Penn State	26	0
O11	●	at Notre Dame	14	2
O18	●	Virginia	35	6
O25	=	at Pittsburgh	14	14
N1	●	Colgate	68	6
N8	●	at Rice	14	7
N15	●	Villanova	26	0
N29	●	Navy *Phil*	22	6

DALE HALL
1959-61 (.586) 16-11-2

1959 — 4-4-1

S26	●	Boston College	44	8
O3		at Illinois	14	20
O10		Penn State	11	17
O17	●	at Duke	21	6
O24	●	Colorado State	25	6
O31	=	Air Force *Bnx*	13	13
N7	●	Villanova	14	0
N14		at Oklahoma	20	28
N28		Navy *Phil*	12	43

1960 — 6-3-1

S17	●	Buffalo	37	0
S24	●	Boston College	20	7
O1	●	at California	28	10
O8		Penn State	16	27
O15		at Nebraska	9	14
O22	●	Villanova	54	0
O29	●	Miami, Ohio	30	7
N5	●	Syracuse *Bnx*	9	6
N12	=	at Pittsburgh	7	7
N26		Navy *Phil*	12	17

1961 — 6-4-0

S23	●	Richmond	24	6
S30	●	Boston U.	31	7
O7		at Michigan	8	38
O14	●	at Penn State	10	6
O21	●	Idaho	51	7
O28		West Virginia	3	7
N4	●	Detroit	34	7
N11	●	William & Mary	48	13
N18		Oklahoma *Bnx*	8	14
D1		Navy *Phil*	7	13

PAUL DIETZEL
1962-65 (.538) 21-18-1

1962 — 6-4-0

S22	●	Wake Forest	40	14
S29	●	Syracuse *NYC*	9	2
O6		at Michigan	7	17
O13	●	Penn State	9	6
O20	●	Virginia Tech	20	12
O27	●	at George Washington	14	0
N3	●	at Boston U.	26	0
N10		Oklahoma State	7	12
N17		Pittsburgh *Bnx*	6	7
D1		Navy *Phil*	14	34

1963 — 7-3-0

S21	●	Boston U.	30	0
S28	●	Cincinnati	22	0
O5		at Minnesota	8	24
O12	●	at Penn State	10	7
O19	●	Wake Forest	47	0
O26	●	Washington State	23	0
N2	●	Air Force *Chi*	14	10
N9	●	Utah	8	7
N16		at Pittsburgh	0	28
D7		Navy *Phil*	15	21

1964 — 4-6-0

S19	●	Citadel	34	0
S26	●	Boston College	19	13
O3		at Texas	6	17
O10		Penn State	2	6
O17		at Virginia	14	35
O24		Duke	0	6
O31	●	Iowa State	9	7
N7		Syracuse *Bnx*	15	27
N14		Pittsburgh	8	24
N28	●	Navy *Phil*	11	8

1965 — 4-5-1

S18		at Tennessee	0	21
S25	●	VMI	21	7
O2	●	Boston College	10	0
O9		Notre Dame *Flu*	0	17
O16	●	Rutgers	23	6
O23		at Stanford	14	31
O30		Colgate	28	29
N6		Air Force *Chi*	3	14
N13	●	Wyoming	13	0
N27	=	Navy *Phil*	7	7

TOM CAHILL
1966-73 (.506) 40-39-2

1966 — 8-2-0

S17	●	Kansas State	21	6
S24	●	Holy Cross	14	0
O1	●	Penn State	11	0
O8		at Notre Dame	0	35
O15	●	at Rutgers	14	9
O22	●	Pittsburgh	28	0
O29		Tennessee *Mem*	7	38
N5	●	George Washington	20	7
N12	●	at California	6	3
N26	●	Navy *Phil*	20	7

1967 — 8-2-0

S23	●	Virginia	26	7
S30	●	Boston College	21	10
O7		Duke	7	10
O13	●	at SMU	24	6
O21	●	Rutgers	14	3
O28	●	Stanford	24	20
N4	●	at Air Force	10	7
N11	●	Utah	22	0
N18	●	at Pittsburgh	21	12
D2		Navy *Phil*	14	19

1968 — 7-3-0

S21	●	Citadel	34	14
S28		Vanderbilt	13	17
O5		at Missouri	3	7
O12	●	California	10	7
O19	●	at Rutgers	24	0
O26	●	Duke	57	25
N2		at Penn State	24	28
N9	●	Boston College	58	25
N16	●	at Pittsburgh	26	0
N30	●	Navy *Phil*	21	14

1969 — 4-5-1

S20	●	New Mexico	31	14
S27	●	at Vanderbilt	16	6
O4		Texas A&M	13	20
O11		Notre Dame *Bnx*	0	45
O18		Utah State	7	23
O25	●	Boston College	38	7
N1		Air Force	6	13
N8	=	at Oregon	17	17
N15		Pittsburgh	6	15
N29	●	Navy *Phil*	27	0

1970 — 1-9-1

S12	●	Holy Cross	26	0
S19		Baylor	7	10
S26		at Nebraska	0	28
O3		at Tennessee	3	48
O10		at Notre Dame	10	51
O17		at Virginia	20	21
O24		Penn State	14	38
O31		at Boston College	13	21
N7		Syracuse	29	31
N14	=	Oregon	22	22
N28		Navy *Phil*	7	11

1971 — 6-4-0

S18		Stanford	3	38
S25	●	at Georgia Tech	16	13
O2	●	Missouri	22	6
O9		at Penn State	0	42
O16		at Air Force	7	20
O23	●	Virginia	14	9
O29		at Miami, Fla.	13	24
N6	●	Rutgers	30	17
N13	●	Pittsburgh	17	14
N27	●	Navy *Phil*	24	23

1972 — 6-4-0

S23		Nebraska	7	77
S30	●	at Texas A&M	24	14
O7	●	Lehigh	26	21
O14		Penn State	0	45
O21	●	at Rutgers	35	28
O28		Miami, Fla.	7	28
N4	●	Air Force	17	14
N11		at Syracuse	6	27
N18	●	Holy Cross	15	13
D2	●	Navy *Phil*	23	15

1973 — 0-10-0

S22		Tennessee	18	37
S29		California	6	51
O6		at Georgia Tech	10	14
O13		at Penn State	3	54
O20		Notre Dame	3	62
O27		Holy Cross	10	17
N3		at Air Force	10	43
N10		Miami, Fla.	7	19
N17		Pittsburgh	0	34
D1		Navy *Phil*	0	51

HOMER SMITH
1974-78 (.391) 21-33-1

1974 — 3-8-0

S14	●	Lafayette	14	7
S21		Tulane	14	31
S28		at California	14	27
O5		Penn State	14	21
O12		at Duke	14	33
O19		at Notre Dame	0	48
O26	●	Holy Cross	13	10
N2		Vanderbilt	14	38
N9	●	Air Force	17	16
N16		at North Carolina	42	56
N30		Navy *Phil*	0	19

1975 — 2-9-0

S13	●	Holy Cross	44	7
S20	●	Lehigh	54	32
S27		Villanova	0	10
O4		at Stanford	14	67
O11		Duke	10	21
O18		Pittsburgh	20	52
O25		at Penn State	0	31
N1		at Air Force	3	33
N8		Boston College	0	31
N15		at Vanderbilt	14	23
N29		Navy *Phil*	6	30

1976 — 5-6-0

S11	●	Lafayette	16	6
S18	●	Holy Cross	26	24
S25		North Carolina	32	34
O2	●	Stanford	21	20
O9		at Penn State	16	38
O16		at Tulane	10	23
O23		Boston College	10	27
O30	●	Air Force	24	7
N6		at Pittsburgh	7	37
N13	●	Colgate	29	13
N27		Navy *Phil*	10	38

1977 — 7-4-0

S10	●	Massachusetts	34	10
S17	●	VMI	27	14
S24		at Boston College	28	49
O1		Colorado	0	31
O8	●	Villanova	34	32
O15		Notre Dame *ERut*	0	24
O22	●	Lafayette	42	6
O29	●	Holy Cross	48	7
N5	●	at Air Force	31	6
N12		Pittsburgh *ERut*	26	52
N26	●	Navy *Phil*	17	14

1978 — 4-6-1

S16	●	Lafayette	24	14
S23		Virginia	17	21
S30	=	Washington State	21	21
O7		at Tennessee	13	31
O14		Holy Cross	0	31
O21		at Florida	7	31
O28	●	Colgate	28	3
N4	●	Air Force	28	14
N11	●	Boston College	29	26
N18		at Pittsburgh	17	35
D2		Navy *Phil*	0	28

LOU SABAN
1979 (.227) 2-8-1

1979 — 2-8-1

S15	●	Connecticut	26	10
S22	●	at Stanford	17	13
S29		North Carolina	3	41
O6	=	Duke	17	17
O13		at Penn State	3	24
O20		Baylor	0	55
O27		Boston College	16	29
N3		at Air Force	7	28
N10		Rutgers *ERut*	0	20
N17		Pittsburgh	0	40
D1		Navy *Phil*	7	31

ED CAVANAUGH
1980-82 (.333)   10-21-2

1980   3-7-1
S13	●	Holy Cross	28 7
S20	●	California	26 19
S27		at Washington State	18 31
O4		Harvard	10 15
O11	=	Lehigh	24 24
O18		at Notre Dame	3 30
O25		at Boston College	14 30
N1		Rutgers	21 37
N8	●	Air Force	47 24
N15		Pittsburgh	7 45
N29		Navy *Phil*	6 33

1981   3-7-1
S12		at Missouri	10 24
S19		VMI	7 14
S26	●	Brown	23 17
O3	●	at Harvard	27 13
O10		Rutgers	0 17
O17	●	Princeton	34 0
O24		Boston College	6 41
O31		at Air Force	3 7
N7		Holy Cross	13 28
N14		at Pittsburgh	0 48
N28	=	Navy *Phil*	3 3

1982   4-7-0
S11		at Missouri	10 23
S18	●	Lafayette	26 20
S25		at North Carolina	8 62
O2	●	Harvard	17 13
O9		Rutgers *ERut*	3 24
O16	●	at Princeton	20 14
O23		Boston College	17 32
O30	●	Columbia	41 8
N6		Air Force	9 27
N13		Pittsburgh	6 24
D4	●	Navy *Phil*	7 24

JIM YOUNG
1983-90 (.566)   51-39-1

1983   2-9-0
S10	●	Colgate	13 15
S17		at Louisville	7 31
S24	●	Dartmouth	13 12
O1		at Harvard	21 24
O8	●	Rutgers	20 12
O15		Notre Dame *ERut*	0 42
O22		Lehigh	12 13
O29		at Air Force	20 41
N5		Boston College	14 34
N12		at Pittsburgh	7 38
N25		Navy *Pas*	13 42

1984   8-3-1
S15	●	Colgate	41 15
S22	=	at Tennessee	24 24
S29	●	Duke	13 9
O6	●	Harvard	33 11
O13	●	Rutgers *ERut*	7 14
O20	●	Pennsylvania	48 13
O27		at Syracuse	16 27
N3	●	Air Force	24 12
N10		at Boston College	31 45
N17	●	Montana *Tok*	45 31
D1	●	Navy *Phil*	28 11
		CHERRY BOWL	
D22	●	Michigan State	10 6

1985   9-3-0
S14	●	Western Michigan	48 6
S21	●	Rutgers	20 16
S28	●	at Pennsylvania	41 3
O5	●	Yale	59 16
O12	●	Boston College	45 14
O19		at Notre Dame	10 24
O26	●	Colgate	45 43
N2	●	Holy Cross	34 12
N9		at Air Force	7 45
N16	●	Memphis	49 7
D7		Navy *Phil*	7 17
		PEACH BOWL	
D31	●	Illinois	31 29

1986   6-5-0
S13	●	Syracuse	33 28
S20		at Northwestern	18 25
S27		Wake Forest	14 49
O4	●	at Yale	41 24
O11	●	at Tennessee	25 21
O18		Holy Cross	14 17
O25		Rutgers *ERut*	7 35
N1		Boston College	20 27
N8	●	Air Force	21 11
N15	●	Lafayette	56 48
D6	●	Navy *Phil*	27 7

1987   5-6-0
S12		Holy Cross	24 34
S19	●	at Kansas State	41 14
S26	●	Citadel	48 6
O3		Wake Forest	13 17
O10		at Boston College	24 29
O17	●	Colgate	20 22
O24	●	Rutgers	14 27
O31	●	Temple	17 7
N7		at Air Force	10 27
N14	●	Lafayette	49 37
D5	●	Navy *Phil*	17 3

1988   9-3-0
S10	●	Holy Cross	23 3
S17		at Washington	17 31
S24	●	Northwestern	23 7
O1	●	Bucknell	58 10
O8	●	at Yale	33 18
O15	●	Lafayette	24 17
O22	●	Rutgers *ERut*	34 24
N5	●	Air Force	28 15
N12	●	Vanderbilt	24 19
N19		Boston College *Dub*	24 38
D3	●	Navy *Phil*	20 15
		SUN BOWL	
D24		Alabama	28 29

1989   6-5-0
S16		at Syracuse	7 10
S23	●	Wake Forest	14 10
S30	●	Harvard	56 28
O7		at Duke	29 35
O14	●	Holy Cross	45 9
O21	●	Lafayette	34 20
O28	●	Rutgers	35 14
N4		at Air Force	3 29
N11		Boston College	17 24
N18	●	Colgate	59 14
D9		Navy *ERut*	17 19

1990   6-5-0
S15	●	Holy Cross	24 7
S22	●	VMI	41 17
S29		at Wake Forest	14 52
O6		Duke	16 17
O13		at Boston College	20 41
O20	●	Lafayette	56 0
O27		Syracuse	14 26
N3	●	Rutgers	35 31
N10		Air Force	3 15
N17	●	at Vanderbilt	42 38
D8	●	Navy *Phil*	30 20

BOB SUTTON
1991-99 (.445)   44-55-1

1991   4-7-0
S14	●	Colgate	51 22
S21	●	North Carolina	12 20
S28	●	Harvard	21 20
O5	●	Rutgers *ERut*	12 14
O12	●	Citadel	14 20
O19	●	at Louisville	37 12
O26	●	Boston College	17 28
N2	●	Vanderbilt	10 41
N9	●	at Air Force	0 25
N16	●	Akron	19 0
D7		Navy *Phil*	3 24

1992   5-6-0
S12	●	Holy Cross	17 7
S19		at North Carolina	9 22
S26	●	Citadel	14 15
O10	●	Lafayette	38 36
O17	●	Rutgers *ERut*	10 45
O24		at Wake Forest	7 23
O31	●	Eastern Michigan	57 17
N7		Air Force	3 7
N14	●	No. Illinois	21 14
N21	●	Boston College	24 41
D5	●	Navy *Phil*	25 24

1993   6-5-0
S11	●	Colgate	30 0
S18	●	at Duke	21 42
S25	●	VMI	31 9
O2	●	Akron	35 14
O9	●	at Temple	56 21
O16	●	Rutgers	38 45
O23		at Boston College	14 41
O30	●	Western Michigan	7 20
N6		at Air Force	6 25
N13	●	Lafayette	35 12
D4	●	Navy *ERut*	16 14

1994   4-7-0
S10	●	Holy Cross	49 3
S15		at Duke	7 43
S24	●	Temple	20 23
O1		at Wake Fores	27 33
O8	●	Rutgers *ERut*	14 16
O15	●	Louisville	30 29
O22	●	Citadel	25 24
O29		Boston College	3 30
N5		Air Force	6 10
N12		Boston U.	12 21
D3	●	Navy *Phil*	22 20

1995   5-5-1
S9	●	Lehigh	42 9
S16		Duke	21 23
S23		at Washington	13 21
S30	=	Rice	21 21
O14		Notre Dame *ERut*	27 28
O21	●	at Boston College	49 7
O28	●	Colgate	56 14
N4		East Carolina	25 31
N11		at Air Force	20 38
N18	●	Bucknell	37 6
D2	●	Navy *Phil*	14 13

1996   10-2
S14	●	Ohio U.	37 20
S21	●	Duke	35 17
S28	●	North Texas *Irv*	27 10
O5	●	Yale	39 13
O12	●	Rutgers *ERut*	42 21
O19	●	Tulane	34 10
O26	●	at Miami, Ohio	27 7
N2	●	Lafayette	41 21
N9	●	Air Force	23 7
N16		at Syracuse	17 42
D7	●	Navy *Phil*	28 24
		INDEPENDENCE BOWL	
D31		Auburn	29 32

1997   4-7
S6		Marshall	25 35
S13	●	Lafayette	41 14
S20	●	at Duke	17 20
S27	●	Miami, Ohio	14 38
O4	●	at Tulane	0 41
O18	●	Rutgers	37 35
O25	●	Colgate	35 27
N8	●	at Air Force	0 24
N15	●	North Texas	25 14
N22		at Boston College	20 24
D6	●	Navy *ERut*	7 39

1998-2004
C-USA

1998   3-8   (2-4)
S12		Miami, Ohio	13 14
S19	●	Cincinnati	37 20
S26		at Rutgers	15 27
O3		at East Carolina	25 30
O10	●	at Houston	38 28
O17		Southern Miss	13 37
O24		at Notre Dame	17 20
N7		Air Force	7 35
N14		Tulane	35 49
N21		at Louisville	23 35
D5		Navy *Phil*	34 30

1999   3-8   (1-5)
S11		Wake Forest	15 34
S18		at Tulane	28 48
S25	●	Ball State	41 21
O2		East Carolina	14 33
O7	●	Louisville	59 52
O16		at Southern Miss	0 24
O23	●	New Mexico State	35 18
N6		at Air Force	0 28
N13		at Memphis	10 14
N20		Houston	14 26
D4		Navy *Phil*	9 19

TODD BERRY
2000-03 (.125)   5-35

2000   1-10   (1-6)
S4		at Cincinnati	17 23
S9		Boston College	17 55
S16		at Houston	30 31
S23	●	Memphis	16 26
O7		at New Mexico State	23 42
O14		at East Carolina	21 42
O21	●	Tulane	21 17
N4		Air Force	27 41
N11		at Louisville	17 38
N18		UAB	7 27
D2		Navy *Balt*	28 30

2001   3-8   (2-5)
S8		Cincinnati	21 24
S22		at UAB	3 55
S29		at Boston College	10 31
O6	●	Houston	28 14
O13		East Carolina	26 49
O20		at TCU	20 38
O27	●	Tulane	42 35
N3		at Air Force	24 34
N10		Buffalo	19 26
N17		at Memphis	10 42
D1		Navy *Phil*	26 17

2002   1-11   (1-7)
S7		Holy Cross	21 30
S14		at Rutgers	0 44
S21		Louisville	14 45
S28		Southern Miss	6 27
O5		at East Carolina	24 59
O12		TCU	27 46
O19		at Houston	42 56
O26		UAB	26 29
N9		Air Force	30 49
N16	●	at Tulane	14 10
N23		at Memphis	10 38
D7		Navy *ERut*	12 58

JOHN MUMFORD
2003 (.000)   0-7

2003   0-13   (0-8)
S6		Connecticut	21 48
S13		Rutgers	21 36
S20		Tulane	33 50
S27		South Florida	0 28
O4		at TCU	0 27
O11		at Louisville	10 34
O18		East Carolina	32 38
O25		at Cincinnati	29 33
N1		at UAB	9 24
N8		at Air Force	3 31
N15		Houston	14 34
N22		at Hawaii	28 59
D6		Navy *Phil*	6 34

BOBBY ROSS
2004-PRESENT (.182)   2-9

2004   2-9   (2-6)
S11		Louisville	21 52
S18		at Houston	21 35
S25		at Connecticut	3 40
O2		TCU	17 21
O9	●	Cincinnati	48 29
O16	●	at South Florida	42 35
O30		at East Carolina	28 38
N6		Air Force	22 31
N13		at Tulane	31 45
N20		UAB	14 20
D4		Navy *Phil*	13 42

AUBURN

BY GEOFFREY NORMAN

To outsiders, Auburn was long considered the redheaded stepchild of football in Alabama. There was the colossus up in Tuscaloosa, and then there was the other school, over in "the loveliest village on the Plains." Auburn had plenty of good years and great teams and All-America players, and when the two schools started playing each other in 1948 after a long hiatus, Auburn beat Alabama in the first game of what became perhaps college football's bitterest rivalry. But even the most devout Auburn fan and believer still felt resentment over being considered a second-class citizen when it came to football. This all changed on Dec. 2, 1989, when Auburn played Alabama at home for the first time. The days of no respect were in the rearview and steadily growing smaller.

In truth, Auburn has been one of the elite programs in the nation since 1957. That was the year the 10–0 Tigers were AP national champions but could not go to a bowl because of recruiting violations. Since then they have been, arguably, the best program in the nation not to have won a national championship. They've finished in the Top 10 13 times since, with a record of 364–169–11, gone to 26 bowl games, produced two Heisman Trophy winners and enjoyed a pair of undefeated seasons. But just as when the Tigers ran the table but were shut out of the national title game in 2004, the grand prize has remained out of reach.

TRADITION At the intersection of College Street and Magnolia Avenue in the town of Auburn is a drugstore—Toomer's—that serves what some say is the best lemonade in the land. John Heisman supposedly stopped in for a glass now and then, which is an interesting historical datum. But to the Auburn faithful, what resonates about Toomer's Corner is the image of the trees, parking meters, signs and everything else in the vicinity draped in garlands of toilet paper. This occurs after any big win, and if the victory is big enough, the place looks like a blizzard has passed through this small section of Alabama. Rolling Toomer's Corner, then, is the peculiarly Auburn tradition.

Another tradition, which is less proprietary, dates to the 1960s. This is the Tiger Walk, which began modestly enough, with a few fans lining up on Donahue Drive (named for "Iron" Mike Donahue, a former head coach) and applauding the players on their way to the stadium. The gathering grew in size and enthusiasm but achieved a permanent boost on the day of Auburn's first home game against Alabama in 1989. Hyperbole aside, the Tiger Walk has become a key ritual in any Auburn football weekend.

PROFILE

Auburn University
Auburn, Ala.
Founded: 1856
Enrollment: 18,896
Colors: Navy Blue and Burnt Orange
Nickname: Tigers
Stadium: Jordan-Hare Stadium
   Opened in 1939
   Grass; 87,451 capacity
First football game: 1892
All-time record: 644–381–48 (.623)
Bowl record: 17–12–2
Consensus national championships, 1936-present: 1 (1957)
Southeastern Conference championships: 6 (4 outright)
Heisman Trophy: Pat Sullivan, 1971; Bo Jackson, 1985
Outland Trophy: Zeke Smith, 1958; Tracy Rocker, 1988
First-round NFL draftees: 24
Website: www.auburntigers.com/football

THE BEST OF TIMES

Early in the Shug Jordan era, from 1954 to 1958, Auburn went 42–8–2 and beat archrival Alabama five straight times.

THE WORST OF TIMES

The team floundered coming out of World War II, winning just five games from 1947 to 1950. Help was on the way: Jordan was hired in 1951.

CONFERENCE

After 12 years in the Southern Conference, Auburn became a charter member of the SEC in 1933.

DISTINGUISHED ALUMNI

Charles Barkley; Rowdy Gaines, Olympic swimmer/commentator; Fob James, Alabama governor; Anne Rivers Siddons, author; Frank Thomas, baseball player

FIGHT SONG

WAR EAGLE!
War ... Eagle, fly down the field.
Ever to conquer, never to yield.
War ... Eagle, fearless and true.
Fight on, you orange and blue.
Go! Go! Go!
On to vict'ry, strike up the band.
Give 'em hell, give 'em hell;
Stand up and yell, Hey!
War ... Eagle win for Auburn,
Power of Dixie Land!

Thousands now participate two hours before kickoff.

> *Shug Jordan asked of Bear Bryant, "Just don't tell Auburn fans I helped you back up."*

BEST PLAYER Auburn has produced two Heisman winners: quarterback Pat Sullivan and running back Bo Jackson. The final voting would probably come down to a contest between these two, though there might be a few nostalgic holdouts for Red Phillips, who played end on and captained the 1957 national title team.

Both Sullivan and Jackson are remembered with profound fondness at Auburn. Sullivan to Terry Beasley was a magical passing combination, and Bo Jackson ran over an Alabama team—among others—like nobody before or since. If you had to pick one, it would probably be Jackson, based on what he did after he left Auburn. On the gridiron, the baseball diamond and in a dozen television ad campaigns, Bo knew how to get it done.

BEST COACH Though John Heisman once coached Auburn, he is not even in the running. On heart, the vote would undeniably go to Ralph "Shug" Jordan, who was both a great coach and a gentleman. The affable and unpretentious Jordan labored for 25 years in the shadow cast by Bear Bryant across the state. Still, Jordan's teams won 175 games along with the 1957 national championship. Impressive as that record is, Auburn people loved the man for his character more than the victories. To them, he was—and is—the soul of Auburn football.

However, a few unsentimental votes would undoubtedly be cast for Pat Dye, the guy who followed the guy who followed Jordan. Dye was a hardnosed, fundamental football coach who won 99 games and four SEC championships in 12 years at Auburn.

BEST TEAM Jordan's undefeated 1957 team gave up 28 points, only seven of which were scored by SEC opponents. In 10 regular-season games, the nearly impregnable defense shut out six teams, including rivals Georgia and Alabama. The 6-0 win over Georgia was highlighted by back-to-back goal-line stands. The Alabama game was the last of the season for this team, since recruiting violations prevented the Tigers from going to a bowl. This made the 40-0 victory over the Tide even sweeter than the No. 1 ranking in the AP poll. This team probably remains first in the hearts of Auburn fans, though the 13–0 2004 team comes close. The 2004 Tigers beat four Top 10 teams along the way and watched two other undefeateds play for the BCS championship. Auburn finished second in both polls.

RECORDS

RUSHING YARDS

GAME

307	Curtis Kuykendall vs. Miami, Fla., Nov. 24, 1944 (33 att.)

SEASON

1,786	Bo Jackson, 1985 (278 att.)

CAREER

4,303	Bo Jackson, 1982-85 (650 att.)

PASSING YARDS

GAME

416	Ben Leard vs. Georgia, Nov. 13, 1999 (24 of 32)

SEASON

3,277	Dameyune Craig, 1997 (216 of 403)

CAREER

8,016	Stan White, 1990-93 (659 of 1,231)

RECEIVING YARDS

GAME

263	Alexander Wright vs. Pacific, Sept. 9, 1989 (5 rec.)

SEASON

1,068	Ronney Daniels, 1999 (56 rec.)

CAREER

2,507	Terry Beasley, 1969-71 (141 rec.)

POINTS

GAME

36	Carnell Williams vs. Mississippi State, Oct. 18, 2003 (6 TDs)

SEASON

102	Bo Jackson, 1985; Stephen Davis, 1995; Carnell Williams, 2003 (17 TDs)

CAREER

276	Carnell Williams, 2001-04 (46 TDs)

CONSENSUS ALL-AMERICANS

1932	Jimmy Hitchcock, B
1957	Jimmy Phillips, E
1958	Zeke Smith, G
1960	Ken Rice, T
1964	Tucker Frederickson, B
1969	Buddy McClinton, DB
1970	Larry Willingham, DB
1971	Pat Sullivan, QB
1971	Terry Beasley, WR
1974	Ken Bernich, LB
1983, 1985	Bo Jackson, RB
1984	Gregg Carr, LB
1986	Ben Tamburello, C
1986	Brent Fullwood, RB
1987-88	Tracy Rocker, DL
1987	Aundray Bruce, LB
1990	Ed King, OL
1990	David Rocker, DL
1993	Wayne Gandy, OL
1993	Terry Daniel, P
1994	Brian Robinson, DB
2001	Damon Duval, PK
2004	Carlos Rogers, DB

STORYBOOK SEASON The 1993 team was on probation for violations of NCAA rules. No television. No bowl game. The college football equivalent of exile to Siberia. Still, Terry Bowden's team went 11–0. This incredible run included a victory over No. 4 Florida and an especially satisfying win against defending national champion Alabama.

BIGGEST GAME Dec. 2, 1989, Alabama at Auburn. According to Auburn AD David Housel, "The single most emotional day in Auburn history [was] when Alabama came to town to play on our turf." The Tiger Walk drew perhaps 10 times its usual crowd to greet the players coming into the stadium. "Donahue Drive was so crowded that the players had to walk single file, pushing their way through the people," said Housel. "There were at least 20,000 people out there. It was as though the Children of Israel had been freed from Pharaoh. Or the Berlin Wall had come down."

Alabama came in 10–0 and ranked No. 2 nationally, but Auburn won the game 30-20. It provided plenty of redemption for Dye, whose success following the Jordan legend helped increase the pressure on Alabama to agree to a home-and-home series. When Dye was hired in 1981, Auburn was in the midst of a bad streak against the Tide that would run to nine losses. Asked how long he thought it would take for Auburn to beat Alabama, Dye answered, "Sixty minutes."

BIGGEST UPSET In 1942, Georgia had Charley Trippi and Frank Sinkwich and Auburn didn't have a chance. But an Auburn assistant named Jordan discovered something: Trippi tipped off plays in the way he lined up before the snaps. Auburn used the knowledge to win 27-13—Georgia's only loss of the season.

WILDEST FINISH On Sept. 17, 1994, Auburn was down 23-9 to LSU going into the fourth quarter, and things looked bleak. Then, safety Ken Alvis intercepted a pass and

ALL-CENTURY TEAM	
In 1992, Auburn fans selected this team to commemorate the school's centennial season.	
1951-75	Ralph "Shug" Jordan, coach
OFFENSE	
1934-36	Walter Gilbert, OL
1958-60	Ken Rice, OL
1982-85	Steve Wallace, OL
1983-86	Ben Tamburello, OL
1988-90	Ed King, OL
1969-71	Terry Beasley, WR
1985-88	Lawyer Tillman, WR
1969-71	Pat Sullivan, QB
1976-79	Joe Cribbs, RB
1977-80	James Brooks, RB
1982-85	Bo Jackson, RB
1980-83	Al Del Greco, K
DEFENSE	
1957-59	Roger Duane "Zeke" Smith, DL
1979-83	Donnie Humphrey, DL
1985-88	Tracy Rocker, DL
1955-57	Jimmy "Red" Phillips, DE
1984-87	Aundray Bruce, DE
1957-59	Jackie Burkett, LB
1967-69	Mike Kolen, LB
1981-84	Gregg Carr, LB
1962-64	Tucker Frederickson, DB
1972-74	Mike Fuller, DB
1984-87	Kevin Porter, DB
1982-85	Lewis Colbert, P

returned it 42 yards for a touchdown. This was the first of five Auburn interceptions in that quarter, with two more of them taken to the end zone. Final score: 30-26, Auburn.

BEST COMEBACK Oh, there have been many stirring comebacks in the history of Auburn football. But none of them is a patch on what happened at Legion Field in Birmingham in December 1972. Alabama was undefeated, ranked second in the nation and thinking national championship. Auburn had lost only one game but was a decided underdog, which looked valid with less than six minutes left and Alabama leading 16-3.

Then, Bill Newton broke through and blocked an Alabama punt. The ball bounced into the hands of David Langner, who ran it in for a touchdown to make it 16-10.

Alabama took the kickoff but couldn't move and was forced to punt again. And again, Newton came clean and blocked it. Again, the ball bounced into Langner's hands and, again, he ran it in. The score was now 17-16 and will remain that forever. People who do not remember the score, however, do remember the words that you heard and saw on bumper stickers for years afterward: "Punt, Bama, Punt."

STADIUM Jordan-Hare Stadium has the eighth-largest seating capacity, at 87,000-plus, among on-campus college football stadiums. This is a point of pride with Auburn people. who for years could not get notable opponents to come to town because the village and the stadium were both too small to accommodate their fans and their pride.

So Auburn played many of its home games in Mobile, Montgomery and Birmingham. No more. The stadium has grown through a series of additions that began in 1949. The name was then changed from Auburn Stadium to Cliff Hare Stadium, after Clifford Leroy Hare, a member of the first Auburn football team, head of the old Southern Conference and chairman of Auburn's Faculty

Athletic Committee. The bifurcated name dates to 1973, when the stadium became the first anywhere to be named for an active head coach, in this case, Ralph "Shug" Jordan, perhaps the most beloved figure in all of Auburn football history. During Jordan's tenure, another 40,000 seats were added to the stadium. The playing surface is, and always has been, natural. As David Housel says with some asperity, "This is an ag school. If we couldn't grow grass, we'd be out of business."

RIVAL There are rivalries, and there are rivalries. The rivalry between Auburn and Alabama is, perhaps, more intense than any in the country. The key joke about the rivalry that made the rounds in the 1970s had Shug Jordan and Bear Bryant fishing together, when Bryant wondered aloud if he could walk on water like all the Bama fans said. Bryant stepped out onto the water and sank instantly. As he swam to the side of the boat and reached up to Jordan for assistance, Bryant said, "Shug, promise me you won't tell the Alabama fans I can't walk on water." And Jordan said, "All right, Bear. Just as long as you promise not to tell the Auburn fans I helped you back up."

Auburn's oldest rivalry, however, is not with Alabama, but Georgia. The Auburn-Georgia game brought football to the deep South in 1892, and the game has been played continuously—except for three war years—since 1898. It's the nation's seventh-oldest football rivalry.

DISPUTE Legion Field, 1967, and the opponent was—surprise—Alabama. The game was played in the mud and Auburn was ahead late, 3-0. Since nobody could move, the lead looked reasonably secure until Ken Stabler went on a long, twisting run that left players from both teams sprawled all over the field. At least two of them—both from Auburn—were there because of illegal blocks. In fact, one of the Tigers wasn't blocked at all, according to Auburn eyewitnesses. He was tackled.

Still, no flags. The touchdown counted. Alabama won the game 7-3.

It was one of those episodes on the "neutral" Legion Field site that fired Auburn's determination to play the game at home when they were the home team. So perhaps some good came of this play after all.

NICKNAME This gets complicated. Auburn's nickname is the Tigers. It is the only official nickname, though Auburn has often been called the War Eagles and Plainsmen.

The Plainsmen moniker is derived from Oliver Goldsmith's poem "The Deserted Village." The line goes: "Sweet Auburn, loveliest village of the plain … " People appropriated the line to describe the town in Alabama that was the home of what was officially Alabama Polytechnic Institute and later became Auburn University. One thing led to another and some sportswriters, looking for a little elegant variation, took to calling the Tigers the Plainsmen.

> *Tigers is the school nickname; War Eagle is the Auburn battle cry.*

"War Eagle" is the Auburn battle cry, equivalent to "Roll Tide" at Alabama. There are no "war eagles." The cry is singular and it does not refer to the players but to a legend involving a wounded Confederate soldier who found himself left for dead with nothing for company but an injured baby eagle. The soldier lived and recovered with the eagle. The man went on to teach at Auburn. At the first Georgia-Auburn game, in 1892, the eagle was among the spectators and, when Auburn scored, it took off and soared over the field. The Auburn fans saw this and began to shout, "War Eagle."

MASCOT It can be verified that Auburn won that War Eagle game 10-0. Other parts of the story are, no doubt, apocryphal in many elements. But the war cry has endured, and there is a golden eagle that appears at every Auburn game. That the bird, War Eagle VI, is also called Tiger does account for some of the confusion.

UNIFORMS The overlapping AU, on Auburn helmets since 1966, gives the team one of the most instantly recognizable looks in college football. The rest of the uniform has remained simple and largely unchanged through the years: blue jerseys at home, white on the road. Auburn has worn orange jerseys several times in the last half-century. Three jersey numbers have been retired: Bo Jackson's 34, Pat Sullivan's 7 and the 88 of Terry Beasley, Sullivan's favorite target.

QUOTE "College football is meant to be played on campus and on grass." — Ralph "Shug" Jordan

THE SCHOOLS

AUBURN ANNUAL STATISTICAL LEADERS

YR	RUSHING	YDS	ATT	AVG	PASSING	ATT	CMP	PCT	YDS	RECEIVING	REC	YDS	AVG
1947	Billy Ball	157	44	3.6	Travis Tidwell	94	43	.46	571	John Liptak	12	126	10.5
1948	Russell Inman	227	97	2.3	Travis Tidwell	56	25	.45	476	Erskinc Russell	10	198	19.8
1949	Charlie Langner	405	111	3.6	Travis Tidwell	105	49	.47	811	Erskinc Russell	25	454	18.2
1950	Jim McGowen	225	57	3.9	William Tucker	92	41	.45	414	Fred Duart	20	250	12.5
1951	Homer Williams	721	148	4.9	Allan Parks	149	67	.45	839	Lee Hayley	33	306	9.3
1952	Charles Hataway	433	114	3.8	Dudley Spence	135	68	.50	833	Lee Hayley	24	395	16.5
1953	Fob James	482	73	6.6	Bobby Freeman	85	42	.49	603	Jim Pyburn	25	379	15.2
1954	Joe Childress	836	148	5.6	Bobby Freeman	96	54	.56	865	Jim Pyburn	28	460	16.4
1955	Fob James	879	123	7.1	Howell Tubbs	49	28	.57	471	Jimmy Phillips	14	272	19.4
1956	Tommy Lorino	692	82	8.4	Howell Tubbs	61	34	.56	514	Jimmy Phillips	23	383	16.7
1957	Tommy Lorino	443	78	5.7	Lloyd Nix	60	33	.55	542	Jimmy Phillips	15	357	23.8
1958	Tommy Lorino	349	67	5.2	Lloyd Nix	98	49	.50	682	Geral Wilson	16	207	12.9
1959	Bobby Hunt	552	98	5.6	Bobby Hunt	36	15	.42	234	Leo Sexton	8	75	9.4
1960	Ed Dyas	451	89	5.1	Bryant Harvard	59	36	.61	493	Joe Leichtnam	10	131	13.1
1961	Larry Rawson	448	121	3.7	Bobby Hunt	119	55	.46	737	Dave Edwards	25	372	14.9
1962	Jimmy Sidle	398	61	6.5	Mailon Kent	121	59	.49	748	Howard Simpson	24	301	12.5
1963	Jimmy Sidle	1,006	185	5.4	Jimmy Sidle	136	53	.39	706	George Rose	15	202	13.5
1964	Tucker Frederickson	571	129	4.4	Joseph Campbell	53	30	.57	422	Tucker Fredrickson	14	101	7.2
1965	Tom Bryan	561	133	4.2	Alex Bowden	127	59	.46	941	Freddie Hyatt	21	368	17.5
1966	Richard Plagge	420	110	3.8	Larry Blakeney	95	45	.47	491	Freddie Hyatt	33	475	14.4
1967	Al Giffin	392	121	3.2	Loran Carter	178	86	.48	1,307	Freddie Hyatt	34	553	16.3
1968	Dwight Hurston	349	110	3.2	Loran Carter	248	112	.45	1,487	Tim Christian	47	623	13.3
1969	Mickey Zofko	565	119	4.7	Pat Sullivan	257	123	.48	1,686	Terry Beasley	34	610	17.9
1970	Wallace Clark	422	86	4.9	Pat Sullivan	281	167	.59	2,586	Terry Beasley	52	1,051	20.2
1971	Tommy Lowry	499	87	5.7	Pat Sullivan	281	162	.58	2,012	Terry Beasley	55	846	15.4
1972	Terry Henley	499	87	5.7	Randy Walls	97	46	.47	736	Sandy Cannon	11	191	17.4
1973	Secdrick McIntyre	315	64	4.9	Wade Whatley	53	29	.55	340	Rett Davis	12	112	9.3
1974	Secdrick McIntyre	839	170	4.9	Phil Gargis	81	35	.43	518	Thomas Gossom	20	294	14.7
1975	Phil Gargis	658	162	4.1	Phil Gargis	94	37	.39	400	Jeff Gilligan	23	421	18.3
1976	Phil Gargis	534	142	3.8	Phil Gargis	166	80	.48	1,118	Chris Vacarella	15	353	23.5
1977	Joe Cribbs	872	161	5.4	John Crane	108	43	.40	679	Byron Franklin	13	389	29.9
1978	Joe Cribbs	1,205	253	4.8	Charlie Trotman	111	53	.48	760	Rusty Byrd	14	220	15.7
1979	James Brooks	1,208	163	7.4	Charlie Trotman	131	58	.44	875	Byron Franklin	19	373	19.6
1980	James Brooks	1,314	261	5.0	Joe Sullivan	118	64	.54	772	Byron Franklin	32	598	18.7
1981	Lionel James	561	111	5.1	Joe Sullivan	65	28	.43	370	Chris Woods	13	213	16.4
1982	Bo Jackson	829	127	6.5	Randy Campbell	158	81	.51	1,061	Chris Woods	21	406	19.3
1983	Bo Jackson	1,213	158	7.7	Randy Campbell	142	78	.55	873	Ed West	16	189	11.8
1984	Brent Fullwood	628	117	5.4	Pat Washington	171	77	.45	1,202	Freddy Weygand	32	796	24.9
1985	Bo Jackson	1,786	278	6.4	Pat Washington	142	78	.55	873	Freddy Weygand	19	367	19.3
1986	Brent Fullwood	1,391	167	8.3	Jeff Burger	222	126	.57	1,671	Lawyer Tillman	35	730	20.9
1987	Stacy Danley	468	94	5.0	Jeff Burger	267	178	.67	2,066	Duke Donaldson	43	398	9.3
1988	Stacy Danley	877	179	4.9	Reggie Slack	279	168	.60	2,230	Freddy Weygand	38	577	15.2
1989	James Joseph	817	172	4.8	Reggie Slack	252	148	.59	1,996	Alexander Wright	30	714	23.8
1990	Stacy Danley	430	103	4.2	Stan White	338	180	.53	2,242	Greg Taylor	46	650	14.1
1991	Joe Frazier	651	140	4.7	Stan White	317	158	.50	1,927	Fred Baxter	28	391	14.0
1992	James Bostic	819	186	4.4	Stan White	305	157	.51	1,790	Orlando Parker	31	438	14.1
1993	James Bostic	1,205	199	6.1	Stan White	271	164	.61	2,057	Frank Sanders	48	842	17.5
1994	Stephen Davis	1,263	221	5.7	Patrick Nix	299	169	.57	2,206	Frank Sanders	58	910	15.7
1995	Stephen Davis	1,068	180	5.9	Patrick Nix	331	201	.61	2,574	Willie Gosha	58	668	11.5
1996	Rusty Williams	439	80	5.5	Dameyune Craig	310	169	.55	2,296	Karsten Bailey	45	592	13.2
1997	Rusty Williams	277	77	3.6	Dameyune Craig	403	216	.54	3,277	Karsten Bailey	53	840	15.8
1998	Michael Burks	483	152	3.2	Gabe Gross	197	88	.45	1,222	Karsten Bailey	43	651	15.1
1999	Heath Evans	357	93	3.8	Ben Leard	157	111	.71	1,423	Ronney Daniels	56	1,068	19.1
2000	Rudi Johnson	1,567	324	4.8	Ben Leard	319	193	.61	2,158	Ronney Daniels	34	378	11.1
2001	Carnell Williams	614	120	5.1	Daniel Cobb	158	89	.56	1,165	Tim Carter	35	570	16.3
2002	Ronnie Brown	1,008	175	5.8	Jason Campbell	149	94	.63	1,215	Marcel Willis	31	417	13.5
2003	Carnell Williams	1,307	241	5.4	Jason Campbell	293	181	.62	2,267	Jeris McIntyre	41	621	15.1
2004	Carnell Williams	1,165	239	4.9	Jason Campbell	270	188	.70	2,700	Courtney Taylor	43	737	17.1

Receiving leaders by receptions
The NCAA began including postseason stats in 2002

AUBURN ALL-TIME SCORES

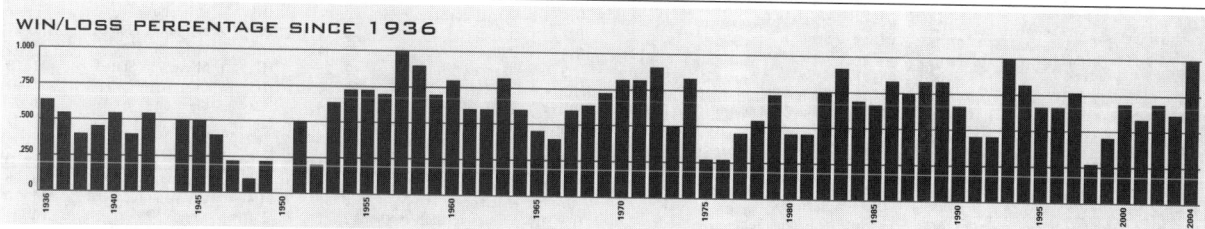

WIN/LOSS PERCENTAGE SINCE 1936

DR. GEORGE PETRIE
1892 (.500)   2-2

D.M. BALLIET
1892 (1.000)   1-0

1892   3-2-0
F20	•	Georgia *Atl*	10	0
N22		Duke *Atl*	6	34
N23		North Carolina *Atl*	0	64
N25	•	Georgia Tech *Atl*	26	0
F22	•	Alabama *Birm*	32	22

G.H. HARVEY
1893 (.750)   2-0-2

1893   2-0-2
N6	•	Vanderbilt *Mont*	30	10
N18	=	Sewanee *Atl*	14	14
N30	•	Alabama *Mont*	40	16
D7	=	Georgia Tech *Atl*	0	0

F.M. HALL
1894 (.250)   1-3

1894   1-3-0
N4		Vanderbilt *Mont*	4	20
N17	•	Georgia Tech *Atl*	94	0
N24		Georgia *Atl*	8	10
N29		Alabama *Mont*	0	18

JOHN HEISMAN
1895-99 (.722)   12-4-2

1895   2-1-0
N9		at Vanderbilt	6	9
N23		at Alabama	48	0
N28	•	Georgia *Atl*	16	6

1896   3-1-0
O6	•	at Mercer	46	0
N7		Georgia Tech	45	0
N8	•	Sewanee *Mont*	38	6
N26		Georgia *Atl*	6	12

1897   2-0-1
O23	•	at Mercer	26	0
O29	•	at Nashville	14	4
O30	=	at Sewanee	0	0

1898   2-1-0
N5	•	Georgia Tech	29	6
N15		North Carolina	0	24 *
N24	•	Georgia *Atl*	18	17

1899   3-1-1
O14	•	Georgia Tech	63	0
O21	•	Montgomery	41	0
O28	•	Clemson	34	0
N18	=	Georgia *Atl*	0	0
N30		Sewanee *Mont*	10	11

BILLY WATKINS
1900-01 (.650)   6-3-1

1900   4-0-0
O22	•	Nashville	28	0
N10	•	Tennessee *Birm*	23	0
N17	•	Alabama *Mont*	53	5
N29	•	Georgia *Atl*	44	0

1901   2-3-1
O19		Nashville *Birm*	5	23
N4		North Carolina	0	10
N8		Vanderbilt *Mont*	0	41 *
N15		at Alabama	17	0
N20		at LSU	28	0
N28	=	Georgia *Atl*	0	0

R.S. KENT
1902 (.500)   2-2-1

MIKE HARVEY
1902 (.000)   0-2

1902   2-4-1
O11	•	at Georgia Tech	18	6
O18	•	Alabama *Birm*	23	0
O25	=	at Tulane	0	0
O27		at LSU	0	5
N6		Sewanee *Birm*	0	6
N15		Clemson	0	16
N27		Georgia *Atl*	5	12

BILLY BATES
1903 (.571)   4-3

1903   4-3-0
O3	•	Montgomery AC	26	0
O17	•	Samford	58	0
O23		Alabama *Mont*	6	18
O31		Sewanee *Mont*	0	47
N11	•	LSU	12	0
N14	•	at Georgia Tech	10	5
N26		Georgia *Atl*	13	22

MIKE DONAHUE
1904-06, '08-22 (.730)   99-35-5

1904   5-0-0
O15	•	at Clemson	5	0
O22	•	Nashville *Birm*	10	0
O29	•	Georgia Tech	12	0
N12	•	Alabama *Birm*	29	5
N24	•	Georgia *Mac*	17	6 *

1905   2-4-0
O20		Davidson *Birm*	0	6
O27	•	Mississippi State *ColMs*	18	0
N4		at Vanderbilt	0	54
N11		Clemson	0	6 *
N18		Alabama *Birm*	0	30
N30	•	Georgia *Mac*	20	0 *

1906   1-5-1
O8	=	Maryville	0	0
O13	•	Gordon	15	0
O26	•	Sewanee *Birm*	5	10
N3		at Georgia Tech	0	11
N10		at Clemson	4	6
N17		Alabama *Birm*	0	10
N29		Georgia *Mac*	0	4

W.S. KIENHOLZ
1907 (.722)   6-2-1

1907   6-2-1
O5	•	Samford	23	0
O7	•	Maryville	29	0
O12	•	Gordon	34	0
O19		Sewanee *Birm*	6	12
O26	•	at Georgia Tech	12	6
N2	•	Clemson	12	0
N9	•	Mercer	63	0
N16	=	Alabama *Birm*	6	6
N28		Georgia *Mac*	0	6

MIKE DONAHUE

1908   6-1-0
O3	•	at Samford	18	0
O10	•	Gordon	42	0
O17	•	at Mercer	23	0
O24	•	Sewanee *Birm*	6	0
O31		LSU	2	10
N7	•	at Georgia Tech	44	0
N26	•	Georgia *Mont*	23	0

1909   5-2-0
O2	•	Samford *Mont*	11	0
O9	•	Gordon	46	0
O16	•	at Mercer	23	5
O23		at Vanderbilt	0	17
N6	•	at Georgia Tech	9	0 *
N13		Sewanee *Birm*	11	12
N25	•	Georgia *Mont*	17	5 *

1910   6-1-0
O8	•	Mississippi State	6	0
O15	•	at Samford	78	0
O22	•	Clemson	17	0
O29		at Texas	0	9
N5	•	at Georgia Tech	16	0
N12	•	Tulane *Gul*	33	0
N24	•	Georgia *Sav*	26	0

1911   4-2-1
O7	•	Mercer	29	0
O14	•	at Clemson	20	0 *
O21		Texas A&M *Dal*	0	16
O28	•	Mississippi State *Birm*	11	5
N4	•	at Georgia Tech	11	6
N17		at Texas	5	18
N29	=	Georgia *Sav*	0	0

1912   6-1-1
O5	•	Mercer *ColGa*	56	0
O12	•	Florida	27	13
O19	•	Clemson	27	6
O26	•	Mississippi State *Birm*	7	0
N2	•	at Georgia Tech	27	7
N9	•	LSU *Mbl*	7	0
N23	=	Vanderbilt *Birm*	7	7
N28		at Georgia	6	12

1913   8-0-0
O4	•	Mercer	53	0
O11	•	Florida	55	0
O18	•	at Clemson	20	0
O25	•	Mississippi State *Birm*	34	0
N1	•	LSU *Mbl*	7	0
N8	•	at Georgia Tech	20	0
N15	•	Vanderbilt *Birm*	14	6
N22	•	Georgia *Atl*	21	7

1914   8-0-1
S26	•	Marion	39	0
O3	•	N. Ala. AC	60	0
O10	•	Florida *JacF*	20	0
O17	•	Clemson	28	0
O24	•	Mississippi State *Birm*	19	0
N7	•	at Georgia Tech	14	0
N14	•	Vanderbilt *Birm*	6	0
N21	=	Georgia *Atl*	0	0
D5	•	Carlisle *Atl*	7	0

1915   6-2-0
O1	•	Marion *Sel*	78	0
O9	•	Florida	7	0
O16	•	Clemson *And*	14	0
O23	•	Mississippi State *Birm*	26	0
O30	•	at Georgia	12	0
N6	•	Mercer	45	0
N13		Vanderbilt *Birm*	0	17
N25		at Georgia Tech	0	7

1916   6-2-0
O7	•	at Samford	35	0
O14	•	Mercer	92	0
O20	•	Clemson	28	0
O28	•	Mississippi State *Birm*	7	3
N4	•	Georgia *ColGa*	3	0
N11	•	Florida *JacF*	20	0
N18		Vanderbilt *Birm*	9	20
N30		at Georgia Tech	7	33

1917   6-2-1
O6	•	Samford	53	0
O13	•	Camp Sheridan *Mont*	13	0
O19	•	at Clemson	7	0
O27	•	Mississippi State *Birm*	13	6
N3	•	Florida	68	0
N10		Davidson *Atl*	7	21
N17	•	at Vanderbilt	31	7
N24	=	Ohio State *Mont*	0	0
N29		at Georgia Tech	7	68

1918   2-5-0
O19	•	Oglethorpe	58	0
O26		Camp Griffin	0	26
N3	•	at Marion	20	7
N9		Camp Gordon *ColGa*	6	14
N16		Vanderbilt *Birm*	0	21
N28		at Georgia Tech	0	41
D7		Camp Sheridan *Mont*	0	7

1919   8-1-0
S27	•	Marion	37	0
O4	•	at Samford	19	6
O12	•	Camp Gordon	25	13
O17	•	Clemson	7	0
O25		at Vanderbilt	6	7
N1	•	Georgia *ColGa*	7	0
N8	•	at Spring Hill	10	0
N15	•	Mississippi State *Birm*	7	0
N27	•	at Georgia Tech	14	7

1920   7-2-0
S23	•	Marion	27	0
O2	•	Samford	88	0
O9	•	Fort Benning	14	2
O15	•	at Clemson	21	0
O23	•	Vanderbilt *Birm*	56	6
O30		Georgia *ColGa*	0	7
N6	•	B'ham Southern *Mont*	49	0
N13	•	Wash. & Lee *Birm*	77	0
N25		at Georgia Tech	0	34

1921-1932
SOUTHERN

1921   5-3-0 (1-2-0)
O1	•	at Samford	35	3
O8	•	Spring Hill *Mont*	44	0
O14	|	Clemson	56	0
O22	•	Fort Benning	14	7
O29	|	Georgia *ColGa*	0	7
N5	•	at Tulane	14	0
N12	|	Centre *Birm*	0	21
N24	|	at Georgia Tech	0	14

1922   8-2-0 (2-1-0)
S23	•	Marion	61	0
S30	•	at Samford	72	0
O7	•	Spring Hill *Mont*	19	6
O14		at Army	6	19
O21	•	Mercer	50	6
O28	•	Fort Benning	30	0
N4	|	Georgia *ColGa*	7	3
N11	•	Tulane *Mont*	19	0
N18	•	Centre *Birm*	6	0
N30	|	at Georgia Tech	6	14

BOOZER PITTS
1923-24, '27 (.417)   7-11-6

1923   3-3-3 (0-1-3)
S29	=	at Clemson	0	0
O6	•	B'ham Southern *Mont*	20	0
O13	•	Samford	30	0
O20		at Army	6	28
O27	•	Fort Benning	34	0
N3	|	Georgia *ColGa*	0	7
N10	|	Tulane *Mont*	6	6
N17		Centre *Birm*	0	17
N29	=	|	at Georgia Tech	0	0

1924   4-4-1 (2-4-1)

S27	●	at B'ham Southern	7	0
O4	●	Clemson	13	0
O11	=	Virginia Tech *Rich*	0	0
O18	●	Samford	17	0
O25	●	LSU *Birm*	3	0
N1		at Vanderbilt	0	13
N8		Tulane *Mont*	6	14
N15		Georgia *ColGa*	0	6
N27		at Georgia Tech	0	7

DAVE MOREY
1925-27 (.500)   10-10-1

1925   5-3-1 (3-2-1)

S26	●	at B'ham Southern	25	6
O3	●	at Clemson	13	6
O10	●	Virginia Tech	19	0
O17		Texas *Dal*	0	33
O24	●	Samford	7	6
O31		Tulane *Mont*	0	13
N7		Georgia *ColGa*	0	34
N14	●	Vanderbilt *Birm*	10	9
N26	=	at Georgia Tech	7	7

1926   5-4-0 (3-3-0)

S25	●	U.T. Chattanooga	15	6
O2	●	Clemson	47	0
O9	●	at Samford	33	14
O16	●	LSU *Mont*	0	10
O23	●	at Tulane	2	0
O30	●	Sewanee *Mont*	9	0
N6		Georgia *ColGa*	6	16	*
N13		Marquette *Birm*	3	19
N25		at Georgia Tech	7	20

BOOZER PITTS

1927   0-7-2 (0-6-1)

S24		Stetson	0	6
O1		at Clemson	0	3
O8		Florida	6	33
O15		LSU *Mont*	0	9
O22		Georgia *ColGa*	3	33	*
O29	=	at Samford	9	9
N5	=	at Tulane	6	6
N12		Mississippi State *Birm*	6	7
N24		at Georgia Tech	0	18

GEORGE BOHLER
1928-29 (.214)   3-11

1928   1-8-0 (0-7-0)

S28		B'ham Southern *Mont*	0	6
O6		Clemson	0	6
O13		at Florida	0	27
O20		Mississippi *Birm*	0	19
O27	●	Samford	25	6
N3		Georgia *ColGa*	0	13
N10		at Tulane	12	13
N17		Mississippi State *Birm*	0	13
N29		at Georgia Tech	0	51

JOHN FLOYD
1929 (.000)   0-4

1929   2-7-0 (0-7-0)

S27		B'ham Southern *Mont*	7	0
O5		at Clemson	7	26
O11		Florida *Mont*	0	19
O19		Vanderbilt *Birm*	2	41
O26	●	Samford	6	0
N2		at Tennessee	0	27
N9		at Tulane	0	52
N16		at Georgia	0	24
N28		at Georgia Tech	6	19

CHET WYNNE
1930-33 (.590)   22-15-2

1930   3-7-0 (1-6-0)

S26		B'ham Southern *Mont*	0	7
O4	●	Spring Hill	13	0
O11		Florida *JacF*	0	7
O18		at Georgia Tech	12	14
O25		Georgia *ColGa*	7	39
N1	●	Wofford	38	6
N8		at Tulane	0	21
N15		Mississippi State *Birm*	6	7
N22		at Vanderbilt	0	27
N27	●	South Carolina *ColGa*	25	7

1931   5-3-1 (3-3-0)

S25	●	B'ham Southern *Mont*	24	6
O10	=	at Wisconsin	7	7
O17	●	at Georgia Tech	13	0
O24		Florida *JacF*	12	13
O31	●	Spring Hill	27	7
N7		Tulane *Mont*	0	27
N14	●	Sewanee *Birm*	12	0
N21		Georgia *ColGa*	6	12
N26	●	South Carolina *Mont*	13	6

1932   9-0-1 (6-0-1)

S23	●	B'ham Southern *Mont*	61	0
O1	●	Erskine	77	0
O8	●	Duke *Birm*	18	7
O15	●	at Georgia Tech	6	0
O22	●	at Tulane	19	7
O29	●	Mississippi *Mont*	14	7
N5	●	Samford *Mont*	25	0
N12	●	Florida *Mont*	21	6
N19	●	Georgia *ColGa*	14	7
D3	=	South Carolina *Birm*	20	20

1933- PRESENT
SEC

1933   5-5-0 (2-2-0)

S22	●	B'ham Southern *Mont*	20	7
S29	●	at Samford	19	0
O14		at Georgia Tech	6	16
O21		at George Washington	6	19
O28	●	at Tulane	13	7
N4		at Duke	7	13
N11	●	Oglethorpe	27	6
N18	●	Georgia *ColGa*	14	6
N25		at Florida	7	14
D2		South Carolina *Birm*	14	16

JACK MEAGHER
1934-42 (.558)   48-37-10

1934   2-8-0 (1-6-0)

S21		B'ham Southern *Mont*	0	7
S29	●	Oglethorpe	15	0
O6		at Tulane	0	13
O13		at LSU	6	20
O20		at Vanderbilt	6	7
O27		at Kentucky	0	9
N3		Duke *Birm*	6	13
N10	●	at Georgia Tech	18	6
N17		Florida *Mont*	7	14
N24		Georgia *ColGa*	0	18

1935   8-2-0 (5-2-0)

S27	●	B'ham Southern *Mont*	25	7
O5	●	at Tulane	10	0
O12		Tennessee *Birm*	6	13
O19	●	Kentucky *Mont*	23	0
O25	●	at Duke	7	0
N2		at LSU	0	6
N9	●	at Georgia Tech	33	7
N16	●	Oglethorpe	51	0
N23	●	Georgia *ColGa*	19	7
N30	●	Florida *Mia*	27	6

1936   7-2-2 (4-1-1)

S25	●	B'ham Southern *Mont*	45	0
O3	=	at Tulane	0	0
O10	=	at Tennessee	6	6
O17	●	at Detroit	6	0
O24	●	Georgia *ColGa*	20	13
O30		Santa Clara *SF*	0	12
N7	●	at Georgia Tech	13	12
N14	●	LSU *Birm*	6	19
N21	●	Loyola-New Orleans	44	0
N28	●	Florida *Birm*	13	0

BACARDI BOWL

J1		Villanova	7	7

1937   6-2-3 (4-1-2)

S24	●	B'ham Southern *Mont*	19	0
O2	=	at Tulane	0	0
O9	=	Villanova *Phil*	0	0
O16	●	Mississippi State *Birm*	33	7
O23	●	at Georgia Tech	21	0
O30		at Rice	7	13
N6	●	Tennessee *Birm*	20	7
N13		at LSU	7	9
N20	=	Georgia *ColGa*	0	0
N27	●	Florida *JacF*	14	0

ORANGE BOWL

J1	●	Michigan State	6	0

1938   4-5-1 (3-3-1)

S23	●	B'ham Southern *Mont*	14	0
O1	=	at Tulane	0	0
O8		at Tennessee	0	7
O14	●	Mississippi State *Mont*	20	6
O22		at Georgia Tech	6	7
O29		at Rice	0	14
N5		Villanova *Phil*	12	25
N12	●	LSU *Birm*	28	6
N19	●	Georgia *ColGa*	23	14
N26		Florida *JacF*	7	9

1939   5-5-1 (3-3-1)

S29	●	B'ham Southern *Mont*	6	0
O7		at Tulane	0	12
O14	●	Mississippi State *Birm*	7	0
O21		Manhattan *NYC*	0	7
O28		at Georgia Tech	6	7
N4		at Boston College	7	13
N11	●	Villanova *Birm*	10	9
N18	●	at LSU	21	7
N25		Georgia *ColGa*	7	0
N30		Florida	7	7
D9		at Tennessee	0	7

1940   6-4-1 (3-2-1)

S27	●	Samford *Mont*	27	13
O5	●	at Tulane	20	14
O12	●	Mississippi State *Birm*	7	7
O19		at SMU	13	20
O26	●	at Georgia Tech	16	7
N2		Georgia *ColGa*	13	14
N9	●	Clemson	21	7
N16		LSU *Birm*	13	21
N23		at Boston College	7	33
N30	●	Florida *ColGa*	20	7
D7	●	Villanova *Mont*	13	10

1941   4-5-1 (0-4-1)

S26	●	Samford *Mont*	13	0
O4		at Tulane	0	32
O11	●	Louisiana Tech	34	0
O18		SMU *Birm*	7	20
O25		at Georgia Tech	14	28
N1		Georgia *ColGa*	0	7
N8		Mississippi State *Birm*	7	14
N15	=	LSU	7	7
N22	●	Villanova *Phil*	13	0
N29		Clemson	28	7

1942   6-4-1 (3-3-0)

S18	●	U.T. Chattanooga	20	7
S26		Georgia Tech *Mont*	0	15
O3	●	at Tulane	27	13
O10		at Florida	0	6
O17	=	at Georgetown	6	6
O23	●	Villanova *Mont*	14	6
O31		Mississippi State *Birm*	0	6
N7		Georgia Pre-Flight *ColGa*	14	41
N14	●	LSU *Birm*	25	7
N21	●	Georgia *ColGa*	27	13
N28	●	Clemson	41	13

1943)
NO TEAM WWII

CARL VOYLES
1944-47 (.405)   15-22

1944   4-4-0 (0-4-0)

S29	●	Samford *Mont*	32	0
O7	●	Fort Benning	7	0
O14		Georgia Tech	0	27
O21		Tulane	13	16
N4	●	Presbyterian	57	0
N11		Mississippi State *Birm*	21	26
N18		Georgia *ColGa*	13	49
N24	●	Miami, Fla.	38	19

1945   5-5-0 (2-3-0)

S21	●	Samford *Mont*	38	0
S28		at Maxwell Field	0	7
O6		Mississippi State *Birm*	0	20
O20	●	at Tulane	20	14
O27		at Georgia Tech	7	20
N3		Florida	19	0
N10	●	La. Lafayette	52	0
N17		Georgia *ColGa*	0	35
N24		Louisiana Tech	29	0
N30		at Miami, Fla.	7	33

1946   4-6-0 (1-5-0)

S27	●	Southern Miss *Mont*	13	12
O5	●	Furman	26	6
O12	●	St. Louis *Birm*	27	7
O19		at Tulane	0	32
O26		at Georgia Tech	6	27
N2		Vanderbilt *Mont*	0	19
N9		Mississippi State *Birm*	0	33
N16		Georgia *ColGa*	0	41
N23		Clemson *Mont*	13	21
N30		at Florida	47	12

1947   2-7-0 (1-5-0)

S27		Southern Miss *Mont*	13	19
O4	●	Louisiana Tech	14	0
O11	●	Florida *Mont*	20	14
O18		at Georgia Tech	7	27
O25		at Tulane	0	40
N1		at Vanderbilt	0	28
N8		Mississippi State *Birm*	0	14
N15		Georgia *ColGa*	6	28
N22		at Clemson	18	34

EARL BROWN
1948-50 (.172)   3-22-4

1948   1-8-1 (0-7-0)

S24	●	Southern Miss *Mont*	20	14
O2	=	Louisiana Tech	13	13
O9		Florida *Tam*	9	16
O16		at Georgia Tech	0	27
O23		at Tulane	6	21
O29		Vanderbilt *Mont*	0	47
N6		Mississippi State *Birm*	0	20
N13		Georgia *ColGa*	14	42
N27		Clemson *Mbl*	6	7
D4		Alabama *Birm*	0	55

1949   2-4-3 (2-4-2)

S23		Mississippi *Mont*	7	40
O8	=	Florida *Mbl*	14	14
O15		at Georgia Tech	21	35
O22		at Tulane	6	14
O29		at Vanderbilt	7	26
N5	●	Mississippi State	25	6
N19	=	Georgia *ColGa*	20	20
N26	=	Clemson *Mbl*	20	20
D3	●	Alabama *Birm*	14	13

1950   0-10-0 (0-7-0)

S22		Wofford *Mont*	14	19
S30		at Vanderbilt	0	41
O7		S.E. Louisana	0	6
O14		at Florida	7	27
O21		at Georgia Tech	0	20
O28		Tulane	0	28
N4		at Mississippi State	0	27
N18		Georgia *ColGa*	10	12
N25		Clemson	0	41
D2		Alabama *Birm*	0	34

RALPH "SHUG" JORDAN
1951-75 (.674)   175-83-7

1951   5-5-0 (3-4-0)

S29	●	Vanderbilt	24	14
O5	●	Wofford *Mont*	30	14
O13	●	Florida	14	13
O20		at Georgia Tech	7	27
O27	●	at Tulane	21	0
N3	●	Louisiana Coll.	49	0
N10		Mississippi *Mbl*	14	39
N17		Georgia *ColGa*	14	46
N24		at Clemson	0	34
D2		Alabama *Birm*	7	25

1952   2-8-0 (0-7-0)

S27		Maryland *Birm*	7	13
O4		Mississippi *Mem*	7	20
O11	●	Wofford	54	7
O18		at Georgia Tech	0	33
O25		Tulane *Mbl*	6	21
N1		at Florida	21	31
N8		Mississippi State	34	49
N15		Georgia *ColGa*	7	13
N22	●	Clemson	3	0
N29		Alabama *Birm*	0	21

1953 7-3-1 (4-2-1)

S25	●	Stetson *Mont*	47	0
O3	● |	Mississippi	13	0
O10	= |	at Mississippi State	21	21
O17	|	at Georgia Tech	6	36
O24	● |	Tulane *Mbl*	34	7
O31	● |	Florida	16	7
N6	●	at Miami, Fla.	29	20
N14	● |	Georgia *ColGa*	39	18
N21	●	at Clemson	45	19
N28	|	Alabama *Birm*	7	10
		GATOR BOWL		
J1		Texas Tech	13	35

1954 8-3-0 (3-3-0)

S25	●	U.T. Chattanooga	45	0
O2	|	at Florida	13	19
O9	|	at Kentucky	14	21
O16	|	at Georgia Tech	7	14
O23	●	Florida State	33	0
O30	● |	Tulane *Mbl*	27	0
N6	●	Miami, Fla. *Birm*	14	13
N13	● |	Georgia *ColGa*	35	0
N20	●	Clemson	27	6
N27	● |	Alabama *Birm*	28	0
		GATOR BOWL		
D31	●	Baylor	33	13

1955 8-2-1 (5-1-1)

S24	●	U.T. Chattanooga	15	6
O1	● |	Florida	13	0
O8	= |	Kentucky *Birm*	14	14
O15	● |	at Georgia Tech	14	12
O22	●	Furman	52	0
O29	|	at Tulane	13	27
N5	● |	Mississippi State	27	26
N12	● |	Georgia *ColGa*	16	13
N19	●	Clemson *Mbl*	21	0
N26	● |	Alabama *Birm*	26	0
		GATOR BOWL		
D31		Vanderbilt	13	25

1956 7-3-0 (4-3-0)

S29	|	Tennessee *Birm*	7	35
O6	●	Furman	41	0
O13	● |	at Kentucky	13	0
O20	|	at Georgia Tech	7	28
O27	●	Houston	12	0
N3	|	at Florida	0	20
N10	● |	Mississippi State	27	20
N17	● |	Georgia *ColGa*	20	0
N24	●	Florida State	13	7
D1	● |	Alabama *Birm*	34	7

1957 10-0-0 (7-0-0)

S28	● |	at Tennessee	7	0
O5	●	U.T. Chattanooga	40	7
O12	● |	Kentucky	6	0
O19	● |	at Georgia Tech	3	0
O26	●	at Houston	48	7
N2	● |	Florida	13	0
N9	● |	Mississippi State *Birm*	15	7
N16	● |	Georgia *ColGa*	6	0
N23	●	at Florida State	29	7
N30	● |	Alabama *Birm*	40	0

1958 9-0-1 (6-0-1)

S27	● |	Tennessee *Birm*	13	0
O4	●	U.T. Chattanooga	30	8
O11	● |	at Kentucky	8	0
O18	= |	at Georgia Tech	7	7
O25	●	Maryland	20	7
N1	● |	at Florida	6	5
N8	● |	Mississippi State	33	14
N15	● |	Georgia *ColGa*	21	6
N22	●	Wake Forest	21	7
N29	● |	Alabama *Birm*	14	8

1959 7-3-0 (4-3-0)

S26	|	at Tennessee	0	3
O3	●	Hardin-Simmons	35	12
O10	● |	Kentucky	33	0
O17	● |	at Georgia Tech	7	6
O23	●	at Miami, Fla.	21	6
O31	● |	Florida	6	0
N7	● |	Mississippi State *Birm*	31	0
N14	|	at Georgia	13	14
N21	●	Southern Miss	28	7
N28	|	Alabama *Birm*	0	10

1960 8-2-0 (5-2-0)

S24	|	Tennessee *Birm*	3	10
O1	● |	at Kentucky	10	7
O8	●	U.T. Chattanooga	10	0
O15	● |	Georgia Tech *Birm*	9	7
O22	●	Miami, Fla.	20	7
O29	● |	at Florida	10	7
N5	● |	Mississippi State	27	12
N12	● |	Georgia	9	6
N19	●	Florida State	57	21
N26	|	Alabama *Birm*	0	3

1961 6-4-0 (3-4-0)

S30	● |	at Tennessee	24	21
O7	|	Kentucky	12	14
O14	●	U.T. Chattanooga	35	7
O21	|	at Georgia Tech	6	7
O28	●	Clemson	24	14
N4	●	Wake Forest	21	7
N11	|	Mississippi State *Birm*	10	11
N18	● |	at Georgia	10	7
N25	● |	Florida	32	15
D2	|	Alabama *Birm*	0	34

1962 6-3-1 (4-3-0)

S29	● |	Tennessee *Birm*	22	21
O6	● |	at Kentucky	16	6
O13	●	U.T. Chattanooga	54	6
O20	● |	Georgia Tech *Birm*	17	14
O27	●	at Clemson	17	14
N3	|	at Florida	3	22
N10	● |	Mississippi State	9	3
N17	|	Georgia	21	30
N24	=	Florida State	14	14
D1	|	Alabama *Birm*	0	38

1963 9-2-0 (6-1-0)

S21	●	at Houston	21	14
S28	● |	at Tennessee	23	19
O5	● |	Kentucky	14	13
O12	●	U.T. Chattanooga	28	0
O19	● |	at Georgia Tech	29	21
N2	● |	Florida	19	0
N9	|	Mississippi State *Jam*	10	13
N16	● |	at Georgia	14	0
N23	●	Florida State	21	15
N30	● |	Alabama *Birm*	10	8
		ORANGE BOWL		
J1		Nebraska	7	13

1964 6-4-0 (3-3-0)

S19	●	Houston	30	0
S26	● |	Tennessee *Birm*	3	0
O3	|	Kentucky *Birm*	0	20
O10	●	U.T. Chattanooga	33	12
O17		Georgia Tech *Birm*	3	7
O24	●	Southern Miss	14	7
O31	|	at Florida	0	14
N7	● |	Mississippi State	12	3
N14	● |	Georgia	14	7
N26	|	Alabama *Birm*	14	21

1965 5-5-1 (4-1-1)

S18		Baylor	8	14
S25	= |	at Tennessee	13	13
O2	● |	Kentucky	23	18
O9	●	U.T. Chattanooga	30	7
O16		at Georgia Tech	14	23
O23		Southern Miss	0	3
O30	● |	Florida	28	17
N6	● |	Mississippi State *Birm*	25	18
N13	● |	at Georgia	21	19
N27	|	Alabama *Birm*	3	30
		LIBERTY BOWL		
D18		Mississippi	7	13

1966 4-6-0 (1-5-0)

S17	●	U.T. Chattanooga	20	6
S24	|	Tennessee *Birm*	0	28
O1	|	at Kentucky	7	17
O8	●	Wake Forest	14	6
O15		Georgia Tech *Birm*	3	17
O22	●	TCU	7	6
O29	|	at Florida	27	30
N5	● |	Mississippi State *Jam*	13	0
N12	|	Georgia	13	21
D3	|	Alabama *Birm*	0	31

1967 6-4-0 (3-3-0)

S23	●	U.T. Chattanooga	40	6
S30	|	at Tennessee	13	27
O7	● |	Kentucky	48	7
O14	●	Clemson	43	21
O21	●	at Georgia Tech	28	10
O27		at Miami, Fla.	0	7
N4	● |	Florida	26	21
N11	● |	Mississippi State	36	0
N18	|	at Georgia	0	17
D2	|	Alabama *Birm*	3	7

1968 7-4-0 (4-2-0)

S21		SMU	28	37
S28	● |	Mississippi State *Jam*	26	0
O5	● |	at Kentucky	26	7
O12	●	at Clemson	21	10
O19		Georgia Tech *Birm*	20	21
O26	●	Miami, Fla.	31	6
N2	● |	at Florida	24	13
N9	● |	Tennessee *Birm*	28	14
N16	|	Georgia	3	17
N30	|	Alabama *Birm*	16	24
		SUN BOWL		
D28	●	Arizona	34	10

1969 8-3-0 (5-2-0)

S20	●	Wake Forest	57	0
S27	|	at Tennessee	19	45
O4	● |	Kentucky	44	3
O11	●	Clemson	51	0
O18	●	at Georgia Tech	17	14
O25	|	at LSU	20	21
N1	● |	Florida	38	12
N8	● |	Mississippi State	52	13
N15	● |	at Georgia	16	3
N29	● |	Alabama *Birm*	49	26
		BLUEBONNET BOWL		
D31		Houston	7	36

1970 9-2-0 (5-2-0)

S19	●	Southern Miss	33	14
S26	● |	Tennessee *Birm*	36	23
O3	● |	at Kentucky	33	15
O10	●	at Clemson	44	0
O17	●	Georgia Tech	31	7
O24	|	LSU	9	17
O31	● |	at Florida	63	14
N7	● |	Mississippi State *Birm*	56	0
N14	|	Georgia	17	31
N28	● |	Alabama *Birm*	33	28
		GATOR BOWL		
J2	●	Mississippi	35	28

1971 9-2-0 (5-1-0)

S18	●	U.T. Chattanooga	60	7
S25	● |	at Tennessee	10	9
O2	● |	Kentucky	38	6
O9	●	Southern Miss	27	14
O16	●	at Georgia Tech	31	14
O23	●	Clemson	35	13
O30	● |	Florida	40	7
N6	● |	Mississippi State	30	21
N13	● |	at Georgia	35	20
N27	|	Alabama *Birm*	7	31
		SUGAR BOWL		
J1		Oklahoma	22	40

1972 10-1-0 (6-1-0)

S9	● |	Mississippi State *Jam*	14	3
S23	●	U.T. Chattanooga	14	7
S30	● |	Tennessee *Birm*	10	6
O7	● |	Mississippi *Jam*	19	13
O14	|	at LSU	7	35
O21	●	Georgia Tech	24	14
O28	●	Florida State	27	14
N4	● |	at Florida	26	20
N18	● |	Georgia	27	10
D2	● |	Alabama *Birm*	17	16
		GATOR BOWL		
D30	●	Colorado	24	3

1973 6-6-0 (2-5-0)

S15	●	Oregon State *Birm*	18	9
S22	●	U.T. Chattanooga	31	0
S29	|	at Tennessee	0	21
O6	● |	Mississippi	14	7
O13	|	LSU	6	20
O20	●	at Georgia Tech	24	10
O27	●	Houston	7	0
N3	|	Florida	8	12
N10	● |	Mississippi State	31	17
N17	|	at Georgia	14	28
D1	|	Alabama *Birm*	0	35
		SUN BOWL		
D29		Missouri	17	34

1974 10-2-0 (4-2-0)

S14	●	Louisville *Birm*	16	3
S21	●	U.T. Chattanooga	52	0
S28	● |	Tennessee	21	0
O4	●	at Miami, Fla.	3	0
O12	● |	Kentucky	31	13
O19	●	Georgia Tech	31	22
O26	●	Florida State	38	6
N2	|	at Florida	14	25
N9	● |	Mississippi State *Jam*	24	20
N16	● |	Georgia	17	13
N29	|	Alabama *Birm*	13	17
		GATOR BOWL		
D30	●	Texas	27	3

1975 3-6-2 (1-4-1)

S13		Memphis	20	31	
S20	=	at Baylor	10	10	
S27	|	at Tennessee	17	21	
O4		Virginia Tech	16	23	
O11	● |	at Kentucky	15	9	
O18	●	at Georgia Tech	31	27	
O25	●	at Florida State	17	14	
N1	|	Florida	14	31	†
N8	= |	Mississippi State	21	21	
N15	|	at Georgia	13	28	
N29	|	Alabama *Birm*	0	28	

DOUG BARFIELD
1976-80 (.500) 27-27-1

1976 3-8-0 (2-4-0)

S11		at Arizona	19	31	
S18		Baylor	14	15	
S25	● |	Tennessee *Birm*	38	28	
O2	● |	Mississippi *Jam*	10	0	
O9		at Memphis	27	28	
O16		Georgia Tech	10	28	
O23	●	Florida State	31	19	
O30	|	at Florida	19	24	†
N6	|	Mississippi State *Jam*	19	28	
N13	|	Georgia	0	28	
N27	|	Alabama *Birm*	7	38	

1977 5-6-0 (4-2-0)

S10	●	Arizona	21	10	
S17		Southern Miss	13	24	
S24	● |	at Tennessee	14	12	
O1	● |	Mississippi	21	15	
O8		North Carolina St.	15	17	
O15		at Georgia Tech	21	38	
O22		at Florida State	3	24	
O29	● |	Florida	29	14	†
N5	|	Mississippi State	13	27	
N12	● |	at Georgia	33	14	
N26	|	Alabama *Birm*	21	48	

1978 6-4-1 (3-2-1)

S16	●	at Kansas State	45	32
S23	●	at Virginia Tech	18	7
S30	● |	Tennessee *Birm*	29	10
O7		Miami, Fla.	15	17
O14	● |	at Vanderbilt	49	7
O21		Georgia Tech	10	24
O28	●	Wake Forest	21	7
N4	|	at Florida	7	31
N11	● |	at Mississippi State	6	0
N18	= |	Georgia	22	22
D2	|	Alabama *Birm*	16	34

1979 8-3-0 (4-2-0)

S15	●	Kansas State	26	18
S22	●	Southern Miss	31	9
S29	|	at Tennessee	17	35
O6	●	North Carolina St.	44	31
O13	● |	Vanderbilt	52	35
O20	●	at Georgia Tech	38	14
O27		at Wake Forest	38	42
N3	● |	Florida	19	13
N10	● |	Mississippi State	14	3
N17	● |	at Georgia	33	13
D1	|	Alabama *Birm*	18	25

1980 5-6-0 (0-6-0)

S13	●	at TCU	10	7
S20	●	Duke	35	28
S27	|	Tennessee	0	42
O4	●	Richmond	55	16
O11	|	at LSU	17	21
O18	●	Georgia Tech	17	14
O25	|	Mississippi State *Jam*	21	24
N1	|	at Florida	10	21
N8	●	Southern Miss	31	0
N15	|	Georgia	21	31
N29	|	Alabama *Birm*	18	34

PAT DYE
1981-92 (.711) 99-39-4

1981 5-6-0 (2-4-0)

S5	●	TCU	24	16
S19		Wake Forest	21	24
S26	|	at Tennessee	7	10
O3		at Nebraska	3	17
O10	● |	LSU	19	7
O17	●	at Georgia Tech	31	7
O24	|	Mississippi State	17	21
O31	● |	Florida	14	12
N7	●	North Texas	20	0
N14	|	at Georgia	13	24
N28	|	Alabama *Birm*	17	28

THE SCHOOLS

1982 — 9-3-0 (4-2-0)

S11	•	Wake Forest	28	10
S18	•	Southern Miss	21	19
S25	•	Tennessee	24	14
O2		Nebraska	7	41
O9	•	Kentucky	18	3
O16	•	Georgia Tech	24	0
O23	•	at Mississippi State	35	17
O30		at Florida	17	19
N6	•	Rutgers	30	7
N13		Georgia	14	19
N27	•	Alabama *Birm*	23	22
TANGERINE BOWL				
D18	•	Boston College	33	26

1983 — 11-1-0 (6-0-0)

S10	•	Southern Miss	24	3
S17	•	Texas	7	20
S24	•	at Tennessee	37	14
O1	•	Florida State	27	24
O8	•	at Kentucky	49	21
O15	•	at Georgia Tech	31	13
O22	•	Mississippi State	28	13
O29	•	Florida	28	21
N5	•	Maryland	35	23
N12	•	at Georgia	13	7
D3	•	Alabama *Birm*	23	20
SUGAR BOWL				
J2	•	Michigan	9	7

1984 — 9-4-0 (4-2-0)

A27	•	Miami, Fla. *ERut*	18	20
S15	•	Texas	27	35
S22	•	Southern Miss	35	12
S29	•	Tennessee	29	10
O6	•	at Mississippi	17	13
O13	•	at Florida State	42	41
O20	•	Georgia Tech	48	34
O27	•	at Mississippi State	24	21
N3		at Florida	3	24
N10	•	Cincinnati	60	0
N17	•	Georgia	21	12
D1	•	Alabama *Birm*	15	17
LIBERTY BOWL				
D27	•	Arkansas	21	15

1985 — 8-4-0 (3-3-0)

S7	•	La. Lafayette	49	7
S14	•	Southern Miss	29	18
S28	•	at Tennessee	20	38
O5	•	Mississippi	41	0
O12	•	Florida State	59	27
O19	•	at Georgia Tech	17	14
O26	•	Mississippi State	21	9
N2		Florida	10	14
N9	•	East Carolina	35	10
N16	•	at Georgia	24	10
N30	•	Alabama *Birm*	23	25
COTTON BOWL				
J1		Texas A&M	16	36

1986 — 10-2-0 (4-2-0)

S6	•	U.T. Chattanooga	42	14
S20	•	East Carolina	45	0
S27	•	Tennessee	34	8
O4	•	Western Carolina	55	6
O11	•	at Vanderbilt	31	9
O18	•	Georgia Tech	31	10
O25	•	at Mississippi State	35	6
N1		at Florida	17	18
N8	•	Cincinnati	52	7
N15		Georgia	16	20
N29	•	Alabama *Birm*	21	17
CITRUS BOWL				
J1	•	Southern Cal	16	7

1987 — 9-1-2 (5-0-1)

S5	•	Texas	31	3
S12	•	Kansas	49	0
S26	=	at Tennessee	20	20
O3	•	at North Carolina	20	10
O10	•	Vanderbilt	48	15
O17	•	at Georgia Tech	20	10
O24	•	Mississippi State	38	7
O31	•	Florida	29	6
N7		Florida State	6	34
N14	•	at Georgia	27	11
N27	•	Alabama *Birm*	10	0
SUGAR BOWL				
J1	=	Syracuse	16	16

1988 — 10-2-0 (6-1-0)

S10	•	Kentucky	20	10
S17	•	Kansas	56	7
S24	•	Tennessee	38	6
O1	•	North Carolina	47	21
O8	•	at LSU	6	7
O15	•	Akron	42	0
O22	•	Mississippi State	33	0
O29	•	at Florida	16	0
N5		Southern Miss	38	8
N12	•	Georgia	20	10
N25	•	Alabama *Birm*	15	10
SUGAR BOWL				
J2		Florida State	7	13

1989 — 10-2-0 (6-1-0)

S9	•	Pacific	55	0
S16	•	Southern Miss	24	3
S30	•	at Tennessee	14	21
O7	•	at Kentucky	24	12
O14	•	LSU	10	6
O21	•	at Florida State	14	22
O28	•	Mississippi State	14	0
N4	•	Florida	10	7
N11	•	Louisiana Tech	38	23
N18	•	at Georgia	20	3
D2	•	Alabama	30	20
HALL OF FAME BOWL				
J1	•	Ohio State	31	14

1990 — 8-3-1 (4-2-1)

S8	•	Fullerton St.	38	17
S15	•	Mississippi *JAM*	24	10
S29	=	Tennessee	26	26
O6	•	Louisiana Tech	16	14
O13	•	Vanderbilt	56	6
O20	•	Florida State	20	17
O27	•	at Mississippi State	17	16
N3		at Florida	7	48
N10	•	Southern Miss	12	13
N17	•	Georgia	33	10
D1	•	Alabama *Birm*	7	16
PEACH BOWL				
D29	•	Indiana	27	23

1991 — 5-6-0 (2-5-0)

A31	•	Georgia Southern	32	17
S14	•	Mississippi	23	13
S21	•	Texas	14	10
S28		Tennessee	21	30
O5		Southern Miss	9	10
O12	•	Vanderbilt	24	22
O26		Mississippi State	17	24
N2		Florida	10	31
N9	•	La. Lafayette	50	7
N16		Georgia	27	37
N30		Alabama *Birm*	6	13

1992 — 5-5-1 (2-5-1)

S5	•	at Mississippi	21	45
S12	•	Samford	55	0
S19	•	LSU	30	28
S26	•	Southern Miss	16	8
O3	•	Vanderbilt	31	7
O10	•	at Mississippi State	7	14
O17		at Florida	9	24
O24	•	La. Lafayette	25	24
O31	=	Arkansas	24	24
N14		Georgia	10	14
N26	•	Alabama *Birm*	0	17

1993 — 11-0-0 (8-0-0)

S2	•	Mississippi	16	12
S11	•	Samford	35	7
S18	•	at LSU	34	10
S25	•	Southern Miss	35	24
O2	•	at Vanderbilt	14	10
O9	•	Mississippi State	31	17
O16	•	Florida	38	35
O30	•	at Arkansas	31	21
N6	•	New Mexico St.	55	14
N13	•	at Georgia	42	28
N20	•	Alabama	22	14

1994 — 9-1-1 (6-1-1)

S3	•	at Mississippi	22	17
S10	•	La. Monroe	44	12
S17	•	LSU	30	26
S24	•	E. Tennessee St.	38	0
S29	•	Kentucky	41	14
O8	•	at Mississippi State	42	18
O15	•	at Florida	36	33
O29	•	Arkansas	31	14
N5	•	East Carolina	38	21
N12	=	Georgia	23	23
N19		Alabama *Birm*	14	21

1995 — 8-4-0 (5-3-0)

S2	•	Mississippi	46	13
S9	•	U.T. Chattanooga	76	10
S16	•	LSU	6	12
S30	•	at Kentucky	42	21
O7	•	Mississippi State	48	20
O14	•	Florida	38	49
O21	•	Western Michigan	34	13
O28		Arkansas *LR*	28	30
N4	•	La. Monroe	38	14
N11	•	at Georgia	37	31
N18	•	Alabama	31	27
HALL OF FAME BOWL				
J1	•	Penn State	14	43

1996 — 8-4 (4-4)

A31	•	UAB	29	0
S7	•	Fresno State	62	0
S14	•	at Mississippi	45	28
S21	•	LSU	15	19
O5	•	South Carolina	28	24
O12	•	at Mississippi State	49	15
O19	•	at Florida	10	51
N2	•	Arkansas	28	7
N9	•	La. Monroe	28	24
N16	•	Georgia	49	56
N23	•	Alabama	23	24
INDEPENDENCE BOWL				
D31	•	Army	32	29

1997 — 10-3 (6-2)

S4	•	at Virginia	28	17
S13	•	Mississippi	19	9
S20	•	at LSU	31	28
S27	•	Central Florida	41	14
O4	•	at South Carolina	23	6
O11	•	Louisiana Tech	49	13
O18	•	Florida	10	24
O25	•	at Arkansas	26	21
N1		Mississippi State	0	0
N15	•	at Georgia	45	34
N22	•	Alabama	18	17
SEC CHAMPIONSHIP GAME				
D6		Tennessee *Atl*	29	30
PEACH BOWL				
J2	•	Clemson	21	17

1998 — 3-8 (1-7)

S3		Virginia	0	19
S12	•	at Mississippi	17	0
S19	•	LSU	19	31
O3		Tennessee	9	17
O10	•	at Mississippi State	21	38
O17		at Florida	3	24
O24	•	Louisiana Tech	32	17
O31		Arkansas	21	24
N7	•	Central Florida	10	6
N14		Georgia	17	28
N21	•	Alabama *Birm*	17	31

1999 — 5-6 (2-6)

S4	•	Appalachian St.	22	15
S11	•	Idaho	30	23
S18	•	at LSU	41	7
S25	•	Mississippi	17	24
O2		at Tennessee	0	24
O9	•	Mississippi State	16	18
O16	•	Florida	14	32
O30	•	at Arkansas	10	34
N6		Central Florida	28	10
N13	•	at Georgia	38	21
N20		Alabama	17	28

2000 — 9-4 (6-2)

A31	•	Wyoming	35	21
S9	•	at Mississippi	35	27
S16	•	LSU	34	17
S23	•	Northern Illinois	31	14
S30	•	Vanderbilt	33	0
O7		at Mississippi State	10	17
O14		at Florida	7	38
O21	•	Louisiana Tech	38	28
O28	•	Arkansas	21	19
N11	•	Georgia	29	26
N18	•	at Alabama	9	0
SEC CHAMPIONSHIP GAME				
D2		Florida *Atl*	6	28
CITRUS BOWL				
J1		Michigan	28	31

2001 — 7-5 (5-3)

S1	•	Ball State	30	0
S8	•	Mississippi	27	21
S22		at Syracuse	14	31
S29	•	at Vanderbilt	24	21
O6	•	Mississippi State	16	14
O13	•	Florida	23	20
O20	•	Louisiana Tech	48	41
O27	•	at Arkansas	17	42
N10	•	at Georgia	24	17
N17		Alabama	7	31
D1	•	at LSU	14	27
PEACH BOWL				
D31		North Carolina	10	16

2002 — 9-4 (5-3)

S2	•	at Southern Cal	17	24
S7	•	Western Carolina	56	0
S14	•	Vanderbilt	31	6
S19	•	at Mississippi State	42	14
S28	•	Syracuse	37	34
O12	•	Arkansas	17	38
O19	•	at Florida	23	30
O26	•	LSU	31	7
N2	•	at Mississippi	31	24
N9	•	La. Monroe	52	14
N16		Georgia	21	24
N23	•	at Alabama	17	7
CAPITAL ONE BOWL				
J1	•	Penn State	13	9

2003 — 8-5 (5-3)

A30	•	Southern Cal	0	23
S6	•	at Georgia Tech	3	17
S13	•	at Vanderbilt	45	7
S27	•	Western Kentucky	48	3
O4	•	Tennessee	28	21
O11	•	at Arkansas	10	3
O18	•	Mississippi State	45	13
O25	•	at LSU	7	31
N1	•	La. Monroe	73	7
N8	•	Mississippi	20	24
N15	•	at Georgia	7	26
N22	•	Alabama	28	23
MUSIC CITY BOWL				
D31	•	Wisconsin	28	14

2004 — 13-0 (8-0)

S4	•	La. Monroe	31	0
S11	•	at Mississippi State	43	14
S18	•	LSU	10	9
S25	•	Citadel	33	3
O2	•	at Tennessee	34	10
O9	•	Louisiana Tech	52	7
O16	•	Arkansas	38	20
O23	•	Kentucky	42	10
O30	•	at Mississippi	35	14
N13	•	Georgia	24	6
N20	•	at Alabama	21	13
SEC CHAMPIONSHIP GAME				
D4	•	Tennessee *Atl*	38	28
SUGAR BOWL				
J3	•	Virginia Tech	16	13

BALL STATE

BY ED KRZEMIENSKI

IN 1918, FIVE BROTHERS, INDUSTRIAL-ISTS from Muncie, purchased the campus and buildings of the town's private normal school, renamed it after themselves and gave it to the state of Indiana. Whether George, Lucius, Frank, Edmund and William paid much attention to athletics is difficult to say, but with a last name like Ball, it's nice to think that they did. But while Ball State has the most overtly athletic name in its state, football recruiting remains a challenge. The better players attend Indiana, Purdue or Notre Dame; the best athletes play basketball. But in the Mid-American Conference, Ball State has more than held its own, winning the league title five times since joining in 1975. Hoping to continue its winning ways, the school hired Brady Hoke as its new head coach before the start of the 2003 season.

TRADITION Perhaps because the state is so generally enamored of basketball, Ball State has few staid football traditions. The team wears T-shirts and touches a sign—both sporting the motto "One at a Time"—before going onto the field, but there are no trophy games, nor even a truly heated rivalry. What the team does have, though, is the tradition of playing competitively in the MAC and sending many of its players to the NFL, including Tim Brown (1960-68),

Shafer Suggs, (1976-80), Bernie Parmalee (1991-2000) and Blaine Bishop (1993-2002).

BEST PLAYER From 1999 to 2002, Marcus Merriweather ran for more than 4,000 yards as a Cardinal. Entering his senior season, Merriweather needed 1,099 yards to become Ball State's career leading rusher. He eclipsed Parmalee's record with a 214-yard performance in the Cardinals' ninth game, against Western Michigan. Merriweather continued to add to his total, rushing for more than 1,600 yards in his record-setting season. All told, Merriweather holds the school rushing records for yards (career and single-season), attempts (career and single-season), 100-yard games and career touchdown runs.

BEST COACH John Magnabosco holds the Ball State coaching records for total games, victories and tenure. From 1935 to 1952, with 1943 off for the war, Magnabosco led the Cardinals to nine winning seasons, 68 total victories and a .586 winning percentage. In 1949, Magnabosco's squad went undefeated, a first in school history. A charter member of the Ball State Hall of Fame (begun in 1976), Magnabosco also lends his name to the football team's annual MVP award.

BEST TEAM In 1978, Dwight Wallace took over as head coach of a Ball State team on a roll. In the previous three years, under coach Dave McClain, who left for a Big Ten job at Wisconsin, the Cardinals had put together an overall

PROFILE

Ball State University
Muncie, Ind.
Founded: 1918
Enrollment: 16,134
Colors: Cardinal and White
Nickname: Cardinals
Stadium: Ball State Stadium
    Opened in 1967
    Grass; 22,500 capacity
First football game: 1924
All-time record: 372–331–32 (.528)
Bowl record: 0–3
Mid-American Conference championships:
5 (outright)
Website: www.ballstatesports.com

THE BEST OF TIMES

From 1989 to 1996, the Cardinals had only one losing season with three MAC championships and three bowl appearances.

THE WORST OF TIMES

Two years after winning the 1996 MAC championship, the team began a 6–27 three-year slide, including a winless 1999 season and a streak of 21 consecutive losses.

CONFERENCE

Ball State became a member of the Mid-American Conference in 1973, began competition in 1975 and has remained in the MAC since. The Cardinals were previously affiliated with the Conference of Midwestern Universities (1968-72), the Indiana Collegiate Conference (1950-68) and the Indiana Intercollegiate Conference (1922-50).

DISTINGUISHED ALUMNI

David Letterman; Daniel Baldwin, actor; Jim Davis, creator of *Garfield*; John Schnatter, founder of Papa John's pizza; Bonzi Wells, NBA player

FIGHT SONG

FIGHT, TEAM, FIGHT
Fight, team, fight for Ball State;
We must win this game.
Onward, now you Cardinals,
Bring glory to your name!
Rah! Rah! Rah!
Here's to both your colors—
Cardinal and white,
Praying for a victory—
So, FIGHT! FIGHT! FIGHT!

record of 26–7–0. The 1978 squad outdid them. The offense was led by quarterback Dave Wilson, who passed for more than 1,000 yards, and running back Archie Currin, who tallied another 735 yards on the ground. But this Cardinals team was defined by its stifling defense, spearheaded by MAC Defensive Player of the Year and future Kansas City Chief Ken Kremer. They dominated their opponents, shutting out four teams and never allowing more than 17 points in the 10-win season. Supporting Kremer on defense were five other All-MAC selections: Larry Williams, Al Rzepka, Bill Pindras, Bill Stahl and perhaps the most aptly named defensive tackle in college football history, Rush Brown. Finishing 10–1 (with a nonconference loss to Louisiana Tech), the Cardinals won the MAC and received some votes in the final AP poll, but did not receive a bowl invite. The MAC also named Wallace Coach of the Year.

BIGGEST GAME Bill Lynch's 1996 team started the season with two quick losses to Kansas and Miami (Ohio) and the chances for turning things around looked pretty slim. Traveling to Minnesota to take on a Big Ten foe that one year earlier had routed the Cardinals 31-7 meant a likely 0–3 start.

> *As might be expected, Ball State's original nickname, Hoosieroons, was not especially popular around campus.*

That much, in fact, was true. Minnesota defeated Ball State 26-23, but the Cardinals' performance that day turned the season around. Ball State senior punter Brad Maynard kicked five times for a 52.6-yard average, an accomplishment that made him MAC Defensive Player of the Week and helped the Cardinals to a late lead, but with 15 seconds left, the Gophers won on an 18-yard touchdown pass. It may seem strange for a three-point loss to stand as the biggest game in a school's history, but hanging with Minnesota launched Ball State into one of the greatest comeback seasons in MAC history. Beginning with Central Florida and ending with Toledo, Ball State ran off eight consecutive victories to capture its fifth league title before losing an 18-15 heart-breaker to Nevada in the Las Vegas Bowl. Never one to let the scoreboard stand in the way of recognizing a great team performance, Lynch said after the Minnesota game: "We did things to put ourselves in position to win. All we preach to them is to play hard with great effort; that's how you're supposed to play the game."

BIGGEST UPSET In 1997, the Cardinals looked dismal after seven games. Their only victory came against Division I-AA James Madison, and the season seemed

RECORDS

RUSHING YARDS

	GAME
260	Earl Taylor vs. Eastern Michigan, Nov. 20, 1976 (34 att.)
	SEASON
1,618	Marcus Merriweather, 2002 (332 att.)
	CAREER
4,002	Marcus Merriweather, 1999-2002 (851 att.)

PASSING YARDS

	GAME
469	Mike Neu vs. Toledo, Oct. 9, 1993 (28 of 40)
	SEASON
2,377	Neil Britt, 1983 (206 of 348)
	CAREER
6,271	Mike Neu, 1990-93 (580 of 970)

RECEIVING YARDS

	GAME
297	Brian Oliver vs. Toledo, Oct. 9, 1993 (12 rec.)
	SEASON
1,399	Dante Ridgeway, 2004 (105 rec.)
	CAREER
3,030	Dante Ridgeway, 2002-04 (238 rec.)

POINTS

	GAME
25	Tim Brown vs. Illinois State, Sept. 20, 1958
	SEASON
114	Mark Bornholdt, 1979 (19 TDs)
	CAREER
279	Kenny Stucker, 1988-91 (93 PATs, 62 FGs)

CONSENSUS ALL-AMERICANS

1967	Oscar Lubke, OT
1968	Amos Van Pelt, HB
1972	Douglas Bell, C
1973	Terry Schmidt, DB
1995-96	Brad Maynard, P

completely lost. Ball State stormed back, though, and won its final four games, including a 35-3 rout over No. 18 Toledo in the season finale.

HEARTBREAKER For the next-to-last game of the 2001 season, Ball State traveled to Northern Illinois needing a victory to clinch the MAC West division and the right to play Marshall for the conference championship. With three minutes left in the game, the Cardinals held a 29-26 lead until Huskies quarterback Chris Finlen ran one in from 13 yards out, giving the game to Northern Illinois 33-29. Ball State, Northern Illinois and Toledo ended in a first-place tie for the West. The tiebreaker sent Toledo, a team Ball State had earlier defeated, to the MAC championship game.

STADIUM In 1967, the Cardinals moved into Ball State Stadium and have played there ever since. After several upgrades in the 1990s and another at the outset of the new millennium, the stadium reached its current capacity of 22,500. In 1997, the school topped the 100,000 mark in total home attendance for the only time in its history. The school added permanent lights prior to the 2004 season opener. A student journalist recently suggested nicknaming the stadium The Nest.

RIVAL Ball State considers Miami (Ohio) its greatest rival, but Miami probably has more enmity for Cincinnati. Ball State and Miami first met in 1931, but did not play each other consistently until Ball State joined the MAC in 1975, and Ball State trails the series 8-15-1. In 1976, the Cardinals ended Miami's three-year, 16-game MAC winning streak when they beat the Redskins 23-6 on Sept. 18.

NICKNAME As might be expected, Ball State's original nickname, Hoosieroons, was not especially popular around campus. With growing discontent from administrators, coaches and students, the school newspaper, *The Easterner*, sponsored a contest to select a new name in 1927. On the line was $5 in gold and the school's reputation. Professor Paul Billy Williams, a loyal fan of the St. Louis Cardinals baseball team, expressed his admiration for the logo on Rogers Hornsby's sweatshirt and submitted the name. After a

student vote on the issue, Ball State became the Cardinals and Williams collected the prize. In 1989, another nationwide contest was held, this time to update the caricature of a running cardinal that served as the school logo. Inflation drove the prize to $2,000, and alumnus William Villarreal collected it for his drawing of a cardinal that displayed, in his words, "an attitude of strength, challenge and intelligence."

MASCOT Charlie Cardinal has served as the official mascot for Ball State since 1969. Originally, students representing Charlie wore a papier-mâché, feathered, smiling head. Since then, Charlie's outfit has grown into a giant cardinal with a fiercer visage and an altogether fluffier composition.

UNIFORMS Perhaps not surprisingly, the school's colors are cardinal red and white. At home, the team sports red jerseys with white numbers and red pants, both without stripes. On the road, the players don all-white outfits with red numbers. In 1971, having employed a red helmet design for much of the previous 25 years, Ball State switched to a white helmet with a red cardinal logo inspired by the St. Louis (now Arizona) Cardinals.

NUMBERS Maynard holds just about every punting record in Ball State history. For his career, he punted 242 times for 10,702 yards (including two 500-yard games) for a 44.2-yard average. As a professional, Maynard set a Super Bowl record with 11 punts for the New York Giants in 2001.

LORE From the home office in Muncie, tonight's Top Ten list: top 10 *Garfield* complaints. It is doubtful that Ball State football will produce a player or event to match the national recognition of the Top Ten list or Garfield the cat, creations of Ball State alumni David Letterman and Jim Davis, respectively. But then again, it's doubtful any football program could.

QUOTE "I want you to stand in front of a mirror and recite, 'I am a fighting Cardinal, the fiercest robin-size bird in all the world.'"—David Letterman, referring to his alma mater on a 2000 episode of *The Late Show With David Letterman*

BALL STATE ANNUAL STATISTICAL LEADERS

YR	RUSHING	YDS	ATT	AVG	PASSING	ATT	CMP	PCT	YDS	RECEIVING	REC	YDS	AVG
1957	Tim Brown	419	42	10.0	Ed Corazzi	92	39	.42	884	Nat Pittman	10	255	25.5
1958	Tim Brown	551	112	4.9	Ed Corazzi	56	29	.52	557	Tim Brown	10	213	21.3
1959	Dave Hooten	285	76	3.8	Ed Corazzi	78	37	.47	527	Nat Pittman	13	247	19.0
1960	Joe Robinson	324	79	4.1	Phil Sullivan	90	35	.39	495	Roger Zabik	8	109	13.6
1961	Joe Burvan	278	54	5.1	Phil Sullivan	69	20	.29	269	Larry Hamell	9	145	16.1
1962	John Walker	631	110	5.7	Terry Bonta	27	13	.48	163	John Walker	6	90	15.0
1963	Merv Rettenmund	635	83	7.7	Marv Rettenmund	29	12	.41	190	Larry Hamell	9	146	16.2
1964	Jim Todd	672	98	6.9	Frank Houk	47	28	.60	283	Jim Todd	11	111	10.1
1965	Jim Todd	850	128	6.6	Frank Houk	62	30	.48	563	Steve Demuth	8	203	25.3
1966	Amos VanPelt	744	150	5.0	Frank Houk	138	74	.54	1,122	Tim Hostrawser	18	282	15.6
1967	Amos VanPelt	894	148	6.0	Doc Heath	74	31	.42	467	Tim Hostrawser	7	125	17.9
1968	Amos VanPelt	571	144	4.0	Willard Rice	209	124	.59	1,592	Ed Alley	38	528	13.9
1969	Dave Means	468	128	3.7	Willard Rice	223	117	.53	1,408	Phil Faris	27	431	16.0
1970	Dave Means	510	116	4.4	Phil Donahue	164	63	.38	868	Willie Lenzy	31	470	15.2
1971	Tony Schmid	666	129	5.2	Phil Donahue	97	39	.40	605	Vic Comparetto	20	381	19.1
1972	Tony Schmid	661	126	5.2	Phil Donahue	188	91	.48	1,481	Kevin Canfield	41	588	14.3
1973	Tony Schmid	673	152	4.4	Rick Scott	115	65	.57	858	Kevin Canfield	38	534	14.1
1974	Dave Blake	1,125	263	4.3	Rick Scott	88	45	.51	816	Rick Clark	33	643	19.5
1975	Earl Taylor	901	178	5.1	Art Yaroch	121	50	.41	720	Mike Andress	23	480	20.9
1976	Earl Taylor	1,017	203	5.0	Art Yaroch	157	78	.50	1,088	Rick Morrison	36	420	11.7
1977	George Jenkins	1,070	208	5.1	Dave Wilson	177	115	.65	1,589	Rick Morrison	59	908	15.4
1978	Archie Currin	735	161	4.6	Dave Wilson	143	75	.52	1,037	Tim Clary	26	362	13.9
1979	Mark Warlaumont	713	140	5.1	Dave Wilson	160	87	.54	1,452	Tim Clary	30	468	15.6
1980	Ken Currin	548	134	4.1	Mark O'Connell	295	175	.59	1,921	Stevie Nelson	38	487	12.8
1981	Terry Lymon	633	130	4.9	Doug Freed	256	137	.54	1,517	Stevie Nelson	37	635	17.2
1982	Terry Lymon	635	134	4.7	Doug Freed	182	85	.47	989	Stevie Nelson	25	265	10.6
1983	Terry Lymon	517	96	5.4	Neil Britt	348	206	.59	2,377	Mike Leuck	67	667	10.0
1984	Burt Austin	551	144	3.8	Neil Britt	189	107	.57	1,205	Mike Leuck	48	410	8.5
1985	Carlton Campbell	747	204	3.7	Wade Kosakowski	242	140	.58	1,614	Deon Chester	45	617	13.7
1986	Carlton Campbell	688	167	4.1	Wade Kosakowski	212	137	.65	1,459	Ricky George	55	569	10.3
1987	Bernie Parmalee	1,064	215	4.9	Wade Kosakowski	237	130	.55	1,477	Deon Chester	50	838	16.8
1988	Mark Stevens	774	185	4.2	David Riley	263	168	.64	1,886	Eugene Riley	41	457	11.1
1989	Bernie Parmalee	672	181	3.7	David Riley	256	149	.58	1,929	Sean Jones	30	518	17.3
1990	Bernie Parmalee	1,010	240	4.2	Mike Neu	180	91	.51	1,004	Bernie Parmalee	30	185	6.2
1991	Corey Croom	1,053	291	3.6	Mike Neu	225	141	.63	1,491	Mike LeSure	49	629	12.8
1992	Corey Croom	1,157	301	3.8	Mike Neu	282	162	.57	1,628	Brian Oliver	37	423	11.4
1993	Tony Nibbs	777	172	4.5	Mike Neu	283	186	.66	2,148	Brian Oliver	62	1,010	16.3
1994	Tony Nibbs	1,210	221	5.5	Brent Baldwin	188	100	.53	1,342	Juan Gorman	49	662	13.5
1995	Michael Blair	819	218	3.8	Brent Baldwin	202	119	.59	1,192	Ed Abernathy	31	288	9.3
1996	Michael Blair	680	147	4.6	Brent Baldwin	205	121	.59	1,703	Ed Abernathy	29	425	14.7
1997	LeAndre Moore	884	173	5.1	Jake Josetti	217	106	.49	1,569	Adrian Reese	30	526	17.5
1998	LeAndre Moore	909	217	4.2	Clay Walters	172	88	.51	969	Adrian Reese	27	341	12.6
1999	Nick Dunbar	590	163	3.6	Brian Conn	257	150	.58	1,525	Adrian Reese	58	664	11.4
2000	Marcus Merriweather	1,004	225	4.5	Talmadge Hill	212	130	.61	1,455	Sean Schembra	40	484	12.1
2001	Marcus Merriweather	1,244	268	4.6	Talmadge Hill	301	159	.53	1,953	Billy Lynch	40	419	10.5
2002	Marcus Merriweather	1,618	332	4.9	Andy Roesch	202	113	.56	1,341	Dante Ridgeway	44	556	12.6
2003	Scott Blair	640	137	4.4	Talmadge Hill	253	154	.61	1,691	Dante Ridgeway	89	1,075	12.1
2004	Adell Givens	963	202	4.8	Cole Stinson	179	91	.51	1,101	Dante Ridgeway	105	1,399	13.3

Receiving leaders by receptions
The NCAA began including postseason stats in 2002

Ball State All-Time Scores

WIN/LOSS PERCENTAGE SINCE 1936

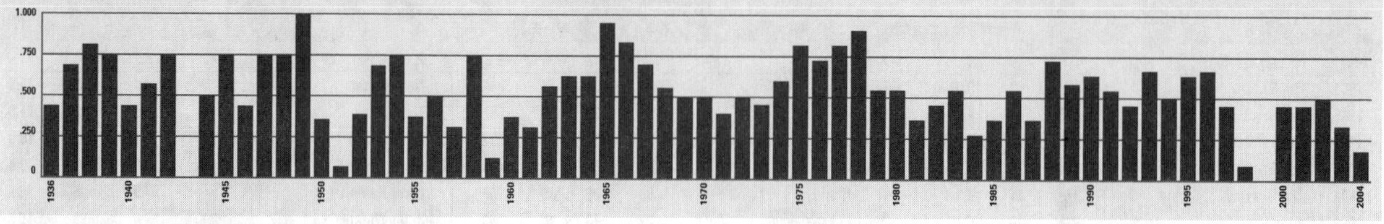

PAUL (BILLY) WILLIAMS
1924-25, '29 (.188) 3-13

1924 1-3-0

O18		at Indiana State	0	47
O31		at Indianapolis	2	13
N7	•	Central Normal	9	6
N22		at Earlham	0	21

1925 2-5-0

O2		at Wabash	0	67
O16		at Central Normal	0	12
O20		Indianapolis	0	6
O30	•	at Manchester	13	7
N6		Indiana State	7	20
N13	•	Merom	32	0
N20		Earlham	6	20

NORMAN WANN
1926-27 (.733) 10-3-2

1926 5-1-1

O2		at Wabash	0	46
O15	•	Indianapolis	35	0
O20	•	Manchester	19	3
O29	=	Central Normal	0	0
N6	•	at Oakland City	54	7
N13	•	Hanover	13	0
N30	•	at Earlham	6	0

1927 5-2-1

S24		at Butler	12	46
O7	•	Franklin	13	0
O14		Central Normal	0	18
O22	=	at Indianapolis	12	12
O29	•	Oakland City	32	7
N5	•	Cedarville	43	0
N12	•	at Hanover	12	6
N19	•	Defiance	27	19

PAUL B. PARKER
1928 (.571) 3-2-2

1928 3-2-2

S29	•	Concordia	52	0
O6	=	at Franklin	6	6
O13	=	Indianapolis	6	6
O27	•	Central Normal	12	7
N3		at Butler	6	12
N10	•	Hanover	6	0
N17		at DePauw	0	19

PAUL (BILLY) WILLIAMS

1929 0-5-0

S28		Indianapolis	0	7
O5		at Western Kentucky	0	13
O12		Franklin	6	12
O18		at Central Normal	12	14
N16		at DePauw	6	46

LAWRENCE McPHEE
1930-34 (.397) 15-23-1

1930 6-1-0

S27	•	Valparaiso	14	0
O11	•	Oakland City	34	6
O17	•	at Central Normal	21	0
O24	•	at Wabash	14	12
N1		at Manchester	7	13
N8	•	at Franklin	20	0
N15	•	Indianapolis	20	7

1931 2-6-0

S25	•	Central Normal	12	0
O3		at Miami, Ohio	6	47 *
O9		at Butler	0	34
O17		at Wabash	0	21
O23		Manchester	6	14
O31	•	Earlham	22	6
N6		at Indiana State	7	13
N14		Franklin	12	26

1932 4-4-0

S23		at Butler	12	13
O1	•	at Earlham	26	12
O7	•	Central Normal	18	0
O14	•	Oakland City	34	12
O22		at Franklin	0	13
O29		at Manchester	0	20
N5		Valparaiso	0	20
N12	•	Indiana State	12	0

1933 1-6-1

S29		at Butler	2	19
O7		at DePauw	0	9
O13	•	Central Normal	6	0
O20		Valparaiso	0	20
O28		Manchester	0	7
N4		at Indiana State	6	9
N11	=	Franklin	6	6
N18		at Hanover	0	20

1934 2-6-0

S28		Butler	4	13
O5	•	at Central Normal	20	0
O13		DePauw	0	13
O18		at Franklin	0	6
O27		at Valparaiso	13	30
N3		at Manchester	0	13
N10	•	Indiana State	15	6
N17		Hanover	6	19

JOHN MAGNABOSCO
1935-52 (.586) 68-46-14

1935 3-4-1

S28	•	Franklin	7	0
O4	•	Central Normal	13	0
O12		Valparaiso	6	20
O19		at DePauw	7	14
O26	•	Oakland City	25	0
N2		at Indiana State	6	12
N9	=	Manchester	0	0
N16		at Hanover	13	20

1936 3-4-1

S26		at Eastern Michigan	0	6
O3		Central Normal	6	25
O10	•	at Franklin	12	0
O17		Indiana State	0	3
O24	•	Oakland City	40	0
O31	=	DePauw	0	0
N7		at Manchester	13	21
N14	•	Hanover	7	0

1937 5-2-1

S25		Eastern Michigan	6	13
O2	•	Oakland City	52	0
O9	•	Central Normal	26	0
O16		at DePauw	0	13
O23	•	at Hanover	12	0
O30	•	Manchester	26	6
N6	•	at Indiana State	7	0
N13	=	Franklin	6	6

1938 6-1-1

S24		at Butler	6	12
O1	•	at Central Normal	26	0
O8	•	Indiana State	13	9
O15	•	at Manchester	20	14
O22	=	St. Joseph's	13	13
O29	•	at Valparaiso	13	0
N5	•	Hanover	19	0
N12	•	Earlham	21	0

1939 6-2-0

S23		at Butler	0	16
S30	•	Grand Rapids	27	6
O7	•	St. Joseph's	6	0
O21	•	at Indiana State	29	6
O27		at Central Michigan	0	7
N4	•	at Earlham	14	13
N11	•	Valparaiso	16	7
N18	•	Manchester	20	14

1940 3-4-1

S21	=	at Miami, Ohio	0	0
S28	•	DeSales	12	0
O5		Central Michigan	0	7
O19		at Manchester	6	7
O26	•	at Valparaiso	26	0
N2	•	Central Normal	27	2
N9		at Butler	0	26
N16		Indiana State	7	27

1941 3-2-2

O4	=	at Northern Illinois	6	6
O10		at Butler	6	13
O18		Central Michigan	6	7
O25	•	at Valparaiso	40	0
N1	=	Manchester	0	0
N8	•	Central Normal	33	0
N15	•	at Indiana State	7	0

1942 6-2-0

S19	•	Franklin	38	0
S26	•	Central Normal	34	0
O10		Bowling Green	14	26
O17	•	at Northern Illinois	14	0
O24		at Central Michigan	13	19
O31	•	at Manchester	28	6
N7	•	Valparaiso	21	0
N14	•	Indiana State	16	7

1943

NO TEAM

1944 2-2-0

O14		Central Normal	6	13
O21	•	Franklin	19	6
N4		at Central Normal	6	25
N11	•	Earlham	27	7

1945 4-1-1

S29	•	Central Normal	28	6
O6	•	Franklin	29	6
O13	=	at Wabash	0	0
O20		Valparaiso	6	7
O27	•	at Earlham	40	6
N3	•	Butler	16	2

1946 3-4-1

S28	•	Central Normal	27	6
O5		at Bowling Green	0	13 *
O12		Wabash	0	6
O19	•	at Valparaiso	20	6
O26		at Butler	6	20
N2	•	Manchester	41	6
N9	=	Eastern Michigan	7	7
N16		at Indiana State	0	3

1947 5-1-2

S27	=	at Butler	6	6
O4	•	Eastern Illinois	21	13
O11	•	Valparaiso	18	14
O18	=	St. Joseph's	6	6
O23	•	at Anderson	9	0
N1	•	at Manchester	19	0
N6		at Eastern Michigan	7	14
N15	•	Indiana State	14	0

1948 6-2-0

S25		at St. Joseph's	0	33
O2		at Eastern Illinois	0	12
O9	•	Huntington	53	0
O16	•	Eastern Michigan	23	14
O23	•	Anderson	14	7
O30	•	at Valparaiso	20	0
N6	•	Manchester	35	0
N13	•	at Indiana State	10	7

1949 8-0-0

S24	•	St. Joseph's	28	14
O1	•	at DePauw	33	13
O8	•	Anderson	35	0
O15	•	at Eastern Michigan	33	2
O29	•	Valparaiso	16	6
N5	•	at Manchester	50	7
N12	•	Indiana State	34	6
N19	•	Eastern Illinois	47	13

1950 2-4-1

S23		at Eastern Illinois	6	35
O7	•	DePauw	27	13
O14		Butler	7	33
O21		Eastern Michigan	0	13
O28		at Valparaiso	7	21
N4	=	at St. Joseph's	7	7
N11	•	Indiana State	27	7

1951 0-6-1

S22		Evansville	21	35
S29		at Wabash	19	34
O6		at DePauw	7	14
O13		at Butler	14	20
O20	=	Indiana State	0	0
O26		Valparaiso	12	34
N3		St. Joseph's	21	39

1952 3-5-1

S20	=	at Hanover	7	7
S27		at Eastern Michigan	14	26
O4		DePauw	25	40
O11		Butler	6	28
O18	•	at Indiana State	33	0
O25		at Valparaiso	13	14
N1	•	at St. Joseph's	21	6
N8		Wabash	19	39
N15	•	at Evansville	26	7

GEORGE SERDULA
1953-55 (.604) 14-9-1

1953 5-2-1

S19	=	Hanover	13	13
S26	•	Millikin	19	13
O3	•	at DePauw	28	7
O10		at Butler	7	25
O17	•	Indiana State	33	6
O22		Valparaiso UNK	7	27
O31	•	at St. Joseph's	14	6
N7	•	Evansville	42	28

1954 6-2-0

S18	•	at Hanover	40	6
S25	•	at Millikin	27	7
O2	•	DePauw	40	14
O9	•	Butler	26	13
O16		at Indiana State	13	14
O23		at Valparaiso	21	46
O30	•	St. Joseph's	26	6
N6	•	at Evansville	25	7

1955 3-5-0

S17	•	Hanover	39	0
S24	•	Indiana, (Pa.)	13	7
O1		at DePauw	6	19
O8		at Butler	13	20
O15	•	Indiana State	19	6
O22		Valparaiso	7	26
O29		at St. Joseph's	0	28
N5		Evansville	0	38

JIM FREEMAN
1956-61 (.396) 18-28-2

1956 — 4-4-0

S15	●	Hanover	12	7
S22	●	at Indiana, (Pa.)	26	0
O6	●	DePauw	19	6
O13		Butler	12	28
O20	●	at Indiana State	28	14
O27		at Valparaiso	12	49
N3		St. Joseph's	0	66
N10		at Evansville	7	33

1957 — 2-5-1

S14		at Hanover	6	34
S21		Illinois State	12	14
S28	=	Valparaiso	26	26
O12	●	at Evansville	27	13
O19		DePauw	14	40
O26		at Butler	7	27
N2		St. Joseph's	7	55
N9	●	at Indiana State	20	0

1958 — 6-2-0

S20	●	at Illinois State	31	14
S27		at Valparaiso	0	6
O4	●	Wooster	14	6
O11	●	Evansville	35	16
O18	●	at DePauw	20	6
O25	●	Butler	14	7
N1		at St. Joseph's	0	6
N8	●	Indiana State	26	8

1959 — 1-7-0

S19		Illinois State	6	22
S26		Valparaiso	6	24
O3		at Eastern Illinois	8	14
O10		at Evansville	0	10
O17	●	DePauw	30	24
O24		at Butler	0	27
O31		St. Joseph's	8	22
N7		at Indiana State	8	29

1960 — 3-5-0

S17		at Illinois State	3	7
S24		Valparaiso UNK	8	10
O1	●	Eastern Illinois	14	6
O8		Evansville	7	10
O15	●	at DePauw	24	20
O22		Butler	0	27
O29	●	at St. Joseph's	23	7
N5		Indiana State	23	26

1961 — 2-5-1

S23	=	Eastern Michigan	0	0
S30		at Butler	6	48
O7		DePauw	8	10
O14	●	at St. Joseph's	8	0
O21		Indiana State	0	41
O28		at Valparaiso	20	28
N4	●	Evansville	6	3
N11		at Ohio Northern	20	49

RAY LOUTHEN
1962-67 (.726) 37-13-3

1962 — 4-3-1

S21	●	at Eastern Michigan	14	0
S29	=	Butler	28	28
O6		at DePauw	6	7
O13	●	St. Joseph's	15	0
O20		at Indiana State	0	22
O27		Valparaiso	6	21
N3	●	at Evansville	27	7
N10	●	Bradley	42	22

1963 — 5-3-0

S21	●	Eastern Michigan	22	6
S28		at Butler	0	13
O5	●	DePauw	15	6
O12	●	at St. Joseph's	23	0
O19	●	Indiana State	15	7
O26		at Valparaiso	40	48
N2	●	Evansville	27	7
N9		at Bradley	14	28

1964 — 5-3-0

S19	●	Slippery Rock	26	7
S26	●	Butler	8	14
O3	●	at DePauw	23	20
O10	●	St. Joseph's	38	7
O17		at Indiana State	0	17
O24		Valparaiso	22	33
O31	●	at Evansville	23	16
N7		Akron	15	25

1965 — 9-0-1

S18	●	Indiana, (Pa.)	26	14
S25	●	at Valparaiso	14	6
O2	●	Evansville	42	13
O9	●	at Akron	16	14
O16	●	at DePauw	51	29
O23	●	Butler	22	7
O30	●	at Indiana State	52	15
N6	●	St. Joseph's	42	19
N13	●	Southern Illinois	30	19
		GRANTLAND RICE BOWL		
D11	=	Tennessee State UNK	14	14

1966 — 7-1-1

S17	●	at Indiana, (Pa.)	20	7
S24	●	Valparaiso	20	7
O1	=	at Evansville	21	21
O8		Northern Illinois	24	38
O15	●	DePauw	30	15
O22	●	at Butler	17	14
O29	●	Indiana State	31	20
N5	●	at St. Joseph's	29	16
N12	●	at Southern Illinois	15	14

1967 — 7-3-0

S16	●	Central Missouri	41	7
S23	●	at Valparaiso	39	7
S30	●	Evansville	31	10
O7		at Northern Illinois	14	28
O14	●	at DePauw	7	3
O21	●	Butler	65	7
O28	●	at Indiana State	26	24
N4		St. Joseph's	2	7
N11	●	Southern Illinois	24	6
		GRANTLAND RICE BOWL		
D9		Eastern Kentucky UNK	13	27

WAVE MYERS
1968-70 (.517) 15-14

1968 — 5-4-0

S14		Northern Illinois	20	40
S21		at Bowling Green	8	62
S28	●	Valparaiso	26	11
O5	●	at Evansville	26	3
O12		Eastern Michigan	7	43
O19	●	DePauw	17	12
O26	●	at Butler	24	21
N2		Indiana State	14	20
N9	●	at St. Joseph's	47	6

1969 — 5-5-0

S13	●	Buffalo	10	7
S20		Eastern Kentucky	0	13
S27	●	Butler	36	7
O4		at Akron	9	49
O11		Indiana State	0	26
O18	●	at Evansville	38	0
O25		at Northern Illinois	13	17
N1	●	Middle Tennessee	14	12
N8		at Southern Illinois	27	48
N15	●	Eastern Michigan	31	22

1970 — 5-5-0

S12	●	at Buffalo	14	7
S19		Eastern Kentucky	12	13
S26	●	at Butler	26	13
O3		Akron	0	31
O10	●	at Indiana State	28	26
O17	●	Evansville	21	14
O24		Northern Illinois	14	31
O31		at Middle Tennessee	7	14
N7	●	Southern Illinois	24	17
N14		at Eastern Michigan	0	60

DAVE McCLAIN
1971-77 (.642) 46-25-3

1971 — 4-5-1

S11	●	Central Michigan	9	6
S18		Western Michigan	0	9
S25	●	Butler	27	0
O2		at Akron	7	10
O9	●	Indiana State	20	17
O16		at Southern Illinois	8	33
O23	=	at Northern Illinois	10	10
O30		at Middle Tennessee	7	28
N6	●	Wittenberg	28	21
N13		at Western Illinois	20	21

1972 — 5-4-1

S16	●	Central Michigan	30	12
S23	●	at Butler	50	41
S30	=	Akron	21	21
O7	●	at Indiana State	21	10
O14	●	Dayton	28	7
O21		at Southern Illinois	7	13
O28	●	Middle Tennessee	24	0
N4		Western Illinois	17	21
N11		at Western Michigan	14	31
N18		at Illinois State	23	24

1973 — 5-5-1

S8		at Eastern Michigan	14	17
S15		at Central Michigan	7	14
S22	●	Butler	52	14
S29	●	at Akron	16	14
O6	●	Indiana State	18	17
O13		at Dayton	12	13
O20		at Northern Illinois	17	45
O27	●	Middle Tennessee	34	3
N3	=	Southern Illinois	16	16
N10		at Western Michigan	13	30
N17	●	Illinois State	27	18

1974 — 6-4-0

S14		Central Michigan	17	24
S21	●	at Butler	45	0
S28		Akron	21	26
O5		at Indiana State	22	31
O12	●	Richmond	38	23
O19	●	Youngstown State	21	14
O26		at Eastern Michigan	9	17
N2	●	at Middle Tennessee	43	14
N9	●	Northern Illinois	31	21
N16	●	at Illinois State	18	7

1975-PRESENT
MAC

1975 — 9-2-0 (4-2-0)

S6	●	Eastern Michigan	24	14
S13	● |	Toledo	38	28
S20	|	at Ohio U.	0	10
S27	|	at Miami, Ohio	28	35
O4	●	Indiana State	20	16
O11	●	at Richmond	25	14
O18	● |	Central Michigan	16	13
O25	● |	at Northern Illinois	3	0
N1	● |	at Bowling Green	27	20
N8	●	at Akron	17	14
N15	●	Illinois State	46	7

1976 — 8-3-0 (4-1-0)

S11	●	Louisiana Tech	41	28
S18	● |	at Miami, Ohio	23	6
S25	● |	at Toledo	27	14
O2	●	at Dayton	20	13
O9		at Illinois State	7	10
O16		Akron	0	3
O23	●	Appalachian State	20	7
O30	● |	at Northern Illinois	33	7
N6	●	Indiana State	24	9
N13	|	Western Michigan	10	24
N20	● |	at Eastern Michigan	52	3

1977 — 9-2-0 (5-1-0)

S10	● |	at Toledo	43	3
S17		at Villanova	16	38
S24	|	at Kent State	12	13
O1	● |	Central Michigan	28	12
O8	● |	Illinois State	27	16
O15	● |	Northern Illinois	31	6
O22	●	Cal Poly Pomona	66	10
O29	●	at Appalachian State	38	7
N5	●	at Indiana State	42	18
N12	● |	at Western Michigan	29	25
N19	● |	Eastern Michigan	45	21

DWIGHT WALLACE
1978-84 (.519) 40-37

1978 — 10-1-0 (8-0-0)

S9	● |	Miami, Ohio	38	14
S16	● |	Kent State	27	3
S23	● |	Toledo	20	0
S30	● |	at Central Michigan	27	0
O7	●	Indiana St.	7	0
O14		at Louisiana Tech	7	17
O21	●	at Illinois St.	14	7
O28	● |	at Eastern Michigan	21	0
N4	● |	at Bowling Green	39	14
N11	● |	Western Michigan	20	14
N18	● |	at Northern Illinois	31	13

1979 — 6-5-0 (4-4-0)

S8	|	at Miami, Ohio	3	27
S15	|	at Toledo	14	31
S22	● |	at Kent State	35	10
S29	●	S.E. La.	17	7
O6		at Indiana St.	13	18
O13	●	Illinois St.	42	14
O20	|	Central Michigan	30	31
O27	● |	Bowling Green	38	23
N3	● |	Eastern Michigan	28	10
N10	|	at Western Michigan	10	20
N17	● |	Northern Illinois	42	0

1980 — 6-5-0 (5-4-0)

S6	|	at Central Michigan	17	21
S13	● |	at Northern Illinois	18	17
S20	● |	Toledo	27	7
S27	|	Miami, Ohio	9	42
O4		at McNeese State	7	24
O18	● |	Eastern Michigan	26	0
O25	|	Western Michigan	15	17
N1	|	at Bowling Green	21	24
N8	● |	Kent State	34	7
N15	● |	Ohio U.	37	18
N22	●	Indiana St.	28	21

1981 — 4-7-0 (2-6-0)

S12	●	McNeese State	24	21
S19	|	at Toledo	0	40
S26	|	at Ohio U.	27	30
O3	● |	Northern Illinois	23	0
O10		at Indiana St.	7	31
O17	|	Kent State	7	17
O24	|	at Western Michigan	3	14
O31	● |	Eastern Michigan	35	13
N7	|	Bowling Green	10	14
N14	|	Central Michigan	7	28
N21	●	at Illinois St.	14	10

1982 — 5-6-0 (4-4-0)

S11	|	Toledo	14	31
S18		at Wichita St.	20	33
S25		Indiana St.	0	17
O2	● |	at Northern Illinois	14	7
O9	|	Ohio U.	7	34
O16	● |	at Kent State	21	3
O23	● |	Western Michigan	13	6
O30	● |	at Eastern Michigan	16	7
N6	|	at Bowling Green	7	28
N13	|	at Central Michigan	13	24
N20	●	Illinois St.	52	17

1983 — 6-5-0 (4-4-0)

S3	●	Rhode Island	42	26
S10	●	Wichita St.	25	21
S17	● |	at Ohio U.	31	14
S24	|	at Toledo	7	43
O1	|	Northern Illinois	14	27
O8		at Indiana St.	14	35
O15	● |	at Kent State	17	13
O22	● |	at Western Michigan	24	20
O29	● |	Eastern Michigan	33	20
N5	|	at Bowling Green	30	45
N12	|	Central Michigan	10	38

1984 — 3-8-0 (3-5-0)

S1		at Massachusetts	10	26
S8	|	Toledo	2	20
S15	|	Ohio U.	17	31
S22		at Washington State	14	16
S29	● |	at Northern Illinois	15	14
O6		Indiana St. IND	6	34
O13	|	Kent State	10	15
O20	● |	Western Michigan	23	20
O27	● |	at Eastern Michigan	17	10
N3	|	Bowling Green	13	38
N10	|	at Central Michigan	7	51

PAUL SCHUDEL
1985-94 (.554) 60-48-4

1985 — 4-7-0 (3-6-0)

S7	|	Bowling Green	6	31
S14	|	Miami, Ohio	13	17
S21		at Purdue	18	37
S28	● |	at Toledo	23	19
O5	● |	Northern Illinois	29	0
O12	● |	at Ohio U.	36	23
O19	|	at Kent State	16	45
O26	|	at Western Michigan	0	34
N2	|	Eastern Michigan	24	27
N9	●	Indiana St. IND	29	27
N16	|	Central Michigan	9	23

1986 — 6-5-0 (4-4-0)

A30	●	at Northern Illinois	20	10
S6	|	at Miami, Ohio	7	45
S13		at Purdue	3	20
S27	● |	Toledo	27	10
O4	●	Indiana St. IND	16	3
O11	● |	Ohio U.	30	9
O18	● |	Kent State	26	17
O25	● |	Western Michigan	24	10
N1	|	at Eastern Michigan	7	14
N8	|	at Bowling Green	17	20
N15	|	at Central Michigan	22	43

1987 — 4-7-0 (3-5-0)

Date		Opponent		
S12		at Toledo	17	21
S19		Bowling Green	0	24
S26		at Wisconsin	13	30
O3		at Miami, Ohio	20	30
O10	●	Kent State	24	23
O17		at Eastern Michigan	28	35
O24	●	Central Michigan	13	3
O31	●	Northern Illinois	42	17
N7		at Western Michigan	16	31
N14	●	Ohio U.	30	17
N21		Indiana St. IND	23	24

1988 — 8-3-0 (5-3-0)

Date		Opponent		
S3		Toledo	13	3
S10	●	at Bowling Green	34	10
S17	●	Massachusetts	44	17
O1	●	Miami, Ohio	45	14
O8	●	at Kent State	31	20
O15		Eastern Michigan	12	16
O22	●	at Central Michigan	27	20
O29	●	at Northern Illinois	18	17
N5		Western Michigan	13	16
N12	●	at Ohio U.	25	27
N17	●	Indiana St. IND	24	10

1989 — 7-3-2 (6-1-1)

Date		Opponent		
S2		at West Virginia	10	35
S9	=	at Rutgers	31	31
S16	●	at Bowling Green	28	3
S23		at Toledo	22	29
S30	●	Miami, Ohio	37	9
O7	●	at Kent State	23	21
O14	●	Western Michigan	14	13
O21	●	Indiana St. IND	34	27
O26	=	Central Michigan	13	13
N4	●	Eastern Michigan	23	17
N11	●	at Ohio U.	33	14

CALIFORNIA BOWL

D9		Fresno State FRE	6	27

1990 — 7-4-0 (5-3-0)

Date		Opponent		
S8	●	at Illinois St.	13	3
S15		at Wisconsin	7	24
S22		Toledo	16	28
S29	●	Bowling Green	16	6
O6		at Miami, Ohio	10	24
O13	●	Kent State	31	0
O20		at Western Michigan	13	14
O27	●	Indiana St.	42	0
N3	●	at Central Michigan	13	3
N10	●	at Eastern Michigan	20	13
N17	●	Ohio U.	23	6

1991 — 6-5-0 (4-4-0)

Date		Opponent		
A31		at Miami, Ohio	7	15
S7	●	at Navy	33	10
S14		at TCU	16	22
S21	●	Kent State	28	27
S28	●	at Indiana St.	14	10
O5		Western Michigan	16	25
O12	●	at Eastern Michigan	10	8
O26		at Central Michigan	3	10
N2	●	Ohio U.	10	6
N9	●	at Toledo	9	3
N16		Bowling Green	13	14

1992 — 5-6-0 (5-4-0)

Date		Opponent		
S5		at Clemson	10	24
S12		at Kansas	10	62
S19	●	at Kent State	10	6
S26	●	Miami, Ohio	19	9
O3		at Western Michigan	14	21
O10	●	Eastern Michigan	31	7
O17		Akron	14	22
O24	●	Central Michigan	24	23
O31	●	at Ohio U.	24	21
N7		Toledo	9	10
N14		at Bowling Green	6	38

1993 — 8-3-1 (7-0-1)

Date		Opponent		
S4		at Syracuse	12	35
S11	●	Illinois St.	45	30
S18	●	at Ohio U.	24	16
O2	●	at Central Michigan	20	17
O9	●	Toledo	31	30
O16		at Cincinnati	12	44
O23	=	Bowling Green	26	26
O30	●	at Eastern Michigan	18	13
N6	●	Miami, Ohio	21	0
N13	●	at Akron	31	9
N20	●	Kent State	28	3

LAS VEGAS BOWL

D17		Utah State LV	33	42

1994 — 5-5-1 (5-3-1)

Date		Opponent		
S3		at West Virginia	14	16
S17		at Purdue	21	49
S24	●	Ohio U.	21	14
O1	●	Central Michigan	31	28
O8	=	at Toledo	24	24
O15	●	Western Michigan	16	13
O22		at Bowling Green	36	59
O29		Eastern Michigan	20	41
N5		at Miami, Ohio	21	24
N12	●	Akron	38	28
N19	●	at Kent State	34	0

BILL LYNCH
1995-2002 (.411) 37-53

1995 — 7-4-0 (6-2-0)

Date		Opponent		
A31	●	at Miami, Ohio	17	15
S9	●	Western Illinois	20	7
S16	●	at Minnesota	7	31
S23	●	Western Michigan	10	0
S30	●	at Purdue	13	35
O7		at Toledo	14	17
O14	●	Bowling Green	30	10
O21	●	Eastern Michigan	35	40
O28	●	at Ohio U.	6	3
N4	●	at Kent State	28	13
N11	●	Central Michigan	24	16

1996 — 8-4 (7-1)

Date		Opponent		
A29		at Kansas	10	35
S7	●	Miami, Ohio	6	16
S14		at Minnesota	23	26
S21	●	Central Florida	31	10
O5	●	at Western Michigan	28	5
O12	●	Ohio U.	30	27
O19	●	at Bowling Green	16	11
O26	●	at Central Michigan	24	17
N2	●	at Eastern Michigan	39	25
N9	●	Kent State	50	6
N16	●	Toledo	24	14

LAS VEGAS BOWL

D19		Nevada LV	15	18

1997 — 5-6 (4-4)

Date		Opponent		
A30		at Miami, Ohio	10	27
S6	●	James Madison	24	6
S13		at Indiana	6	33
S20		at Purdue	14	28
S27		Marshall	16	42
O4		at Western Michigan	13	21
O11		at Eastern Michigan	32	38
O18	●	Central Michigan	37	34
O25	●	at Northern Illinois	21	14
N1	●	Akron	31	14
N8	●	Toledo	35	3

1998 — 1-10 (1-7)

Date		Opponent		
S5		at South Carolina	20	38
S12		Eastern Michigan	7	13
S19		at Iowa State	0	38
S26		at Akron	14	52
O3	●	Northern Illinois	18	13
O10		at Toledo	6	27
O17		Miami, Ohio	17	28
O24		at Marshall	10	42
N7		Western Michigan	23	24
N14		at Central Florida	14	37
N21		at Central Michigan	21	31

1999 — 0-11 (0-8)

Date		Opponent		
S4		at Indiana	9	21
S11		at Wisconsin	10	50
S18		Toledo	10	23
S25		at Army	21	41
O2		Akron	9	31
O9		at Northern Illinois	17	37
O23		at Western Michigan	0	28
O30		Ohio U.	25	37
N6		at Eastern Michigan	21	31
N13		at Bowling Green	14	35
N20		Central Michigan	21	27

2000 — 5-6 (4-3)

Date		Opponent		
S2		at Florida	19	40
S9		Western Ill.	14	24
S16		at Kansas State	0	76
S30		Northern Illinois	14	43
O7	●	at Miami, Ohio	15	10
O14	●	Eastern Michigan	33	14
O21	●	at Buffalo	44	35
O28	●	at Central Michigan	38	34
N4		Western Michigan	3	42
N11		at Toledo	3	31
N18	●	Connecticut	29	0

2001 — 5-6 (4-3)

Date		Opponent		
S1		at Auburn	0	30
S8		at Kentucky	20	28
S22		No. Iowa	39	42
S29		Miami, Ohio	20	28
O13	●	at Eastern Michigan	35	14
O20	●	Toledo	24	20
O27	●	at Connecticut	10	5
N3	●	Central Michigan	38	34
N10		Kent State	18	31
N17	●	at Northern Illinois	29	33
N24	●	at Western Michigan	35	31

2002 — 6-6 (4-4)

Date		Opponent		
S7		at Missouri	6	41
S14	●	Indiana St.	23	21
S21		at Clemson	7	30
S28	●	at Connecticut	24	21
O5		Northern Illinois	29	41
O12		at Toledo	17	37
O19	●	Eastern Michigan	42	17
O26		at Bowling Green	20	38
N2	●	Western Michigan	17	7
N16	●	at Central Michigan	38	21
N23	●	Buffalo	41	21
N30		at Marshall	14	38

BRADY HOKE
2003-PRESENT (.261) 6-17

2003 — 4-8 (3-5)

Date		Opponent		
A28	●	Indiana State	31	7
S6		Missouri	7	35
S13		at Pittsburgh	21	42
S20	●	Central Michigan	27	14
S27		at Boston College	29	53
O4	●	at Kent State	34	17
O18		Miami, Ohio	3	49
O25	●	Toledo	38	14
N1		at Northern Illinois	23	48
N8		at Western Michigan	20	28
N15		at Eastern Michigan	14	38
N22		Bowling Green	14	41

2004 — 2-9 (2-6)

Date		Opponent		
S2		Boston College	11	19
S11		at Purdue	7	59
S18		at Missouri	0	48
S25	●	Western Michigan	41	14
O2		at Toledo	14	52
O9		Eastern Michigan	24	31
O16		at Bowling Green	13	51
O23		at Akron	23	35
O30		Northern Illinois	31	38
N13	●	Central Florida	21	17
N20		at Central Michigan	40	41

Neutral Site key: FRE Fresno, CA / IND Indianapolis, IN / LV Las Vegas, NV / UNK Unknown, Unknown
ƒ Forfeit † Game Later Forfeited # Disputed Victor * Disputed Score ‖ Designated Conference Game |2 Counted Twice in Conference Standings

BAYLOR

BY MARK WANGRIN

THEY KNOW ENNUI IN WACO. FEARS of low expectations, coupled with low achievement, have rendered the only private school in the Big 12 a mere afterthought in discussions of the Big 12, except when the topic is about what in the world the Bears are doing there.

But there was a time ...

"There was no real hullabaloo when we won the title back in '24," said Sam Coates, who played on the second of the Bears' three conference championship teams in the 1920s. "After we beat Rice, we had dinner in Houston and Mr. [coach Frank] Bridges went duck hunting in Louisiana. We came home, and there was no celebration ... no big thing. Everybody acted like, in those days, they expected us to win it."

They would learn.

TRADITION In 1960, Baylor's yell leaders introduced the "Sic 'Em Bears" yell and the Bear Claw hand signal, made by slightly curving all five fingers. The yell and gesture became popular during coach Grant Teaff's tenure, and the claw is held up during the playing of the school song, "That Good Old Baylor Line." The Baylor Line is a freshman spirit organization that forms a line on the field before the start of each half to welcome the team onto the field.

BEST PLAYER Mike Singletary didn't have great size or speed, but the biggest obstacle he had to overcome in being a football standout was his Pentecostal minister father, who strictly forbade football. But the youngest of 10 children sneaked out of the house with his brothers to play. He chose Baylor because of Teaff and the school's Christian foundation, and developed a reputation as a fearless hitter. During his Bears career he broke 16 helmets, convincing the Baylor equipment manager to always carry two extra helmets to all games. The 1980 Lombardi Award finalist and two-time All-America made a staggering 662 career tackles, including 33 in one game against Arkansas. A second-round pick of the Chicago Bears in 1981, the six-foot, 230-pounder joined the line of great Chicago middle linebackers and was named to the Pro Football Hall of Fame in 1998.

BEST COACH Teaff wasn't Baylor's first choice to replace Bill Beall in 1972. Or the second. Or the third. But the 38-year-old former Angelo State and McMurry coach turned out to be the best choice $25,000 a year could buy. "All we expect you to do is make a few first downs," Teaff said a school official told him when he was hired. "And if you can get the plays off in under 25 seconds, that'd be great." Taking over a Baylor program that had won only three games over the previous three years, Teaff ignored cynics who called Baylor Grant's Tomb and talk that the

---

PROFILE

Baylor University
Waco, Texas
Founded: 1845
Enrollment: 10,606
Colors: Green and Gold
Nickname: Bears
Stadium: Floyd Casey Stadium
   Opened in 1950
   Prestige Turf; 50,000 capacity
First football game: 1899
All-time record: 505–491–43 (.507)
Bowl record: 8–8
First-round NFL draftees: 14
Website: www.baylorbears.com

THE BEST OF TIMES

Under coach Frank Bridges, the Bears went 32–13–4 from 1920 to 1924 and won Southwest Conference titles in 1922 and 1924. It would be 50 years before the Bears would win another one.

THE WORST OF TIMES

The Bears' decision to join the Big 12 in 1996 began a massive slide that saw them win only six league games in the first nine seasons of play. From 1998 to 2002, the Bears lost 29 consecutive Big 12 games.

CONFERENCE

Baylor and fellow Southwest Conference schools Texas, Texas Tech and Texas A&M joined with the Big Eight to form the Big 12 beginning in fall 1996. In 1915, Baylor was a charter member of the Southwest Conference.

DISTINGUISHED ALUMNI

Carroll Dawson, GM, Houston Rockets; Thomas Harris, author; Michael Johnson, four-time Olympic gold medalist; Drayton McLane Jr., owner, Houston Astros; Ann Richards, Texas governor

FIGHT SONG

BAYLOR FIGHT SONG
Bear down you Bears of old Baylor U
We're all for you, GO BEARS!
We're gonna show dear old Baylor spirit through and through
We're gonna fight them with all our might you Bruins bold
And win all our victories for the Green and Gold.
B-A-Y-L-O-R, Baylor Bears Fight.

Bears should leave the Southwest Conference, winning the SWC title in 1974. In 21 seasons, he won two conference titles, went 128–105–6, earned six league Coach of the Year honors and took the Bears to eight bowl games. Teaff, who became executive director of the American Football Coaches Association shortly after retiring as Baylor athletic director in the mid-1990s, was inducted into the College Football Hall of Fame in 2001.

> *When Grant Teaff was hired, he was told: "All we expect you to do is make a few first downs. And if you can get the plays off in under 25 seconds, that'd be great."*

Orange Bowl, where they lost 17-14 to Georgia Tech.

BIGGEST GAME In August 1974, a group of cynical sportswriters were grilling Teaff on how long the Bears could stay in the Southwest Conference before conceding they were out of their league. "I believe private schools, and Baylor in particular, will compete in the Southwest Conference," he said. If that seemed like cockeyed optimism at

BEST TEAM The early 1950s were known as the Golden Era at Baylor, a span that coincided with the tenure of coach George Sauer. Behind quarterback Larry Isbell, who was known as Laughing Larry because he would hold the ball up and laugh at opponents after carrying out a fake, the Bears had a prolific offense. The receiving duo of Stan Williams and Harold Riley and the running of fullback Richard Parma were complemented by the defensive skills of linebacker Gale Galloway, guard Bill Athey and tackle Ken Casner. In 1951, the Bears went 8–2–1 and only an upset loss to TCU denied them the Southwest Conference title. Still, they finished the season ranked ninth in the nation and earned a bid to their first major bowl, the

the time, it was even more ridiculous when Texas took a 24-7 halftime lead in Waco on Nov. 9. Cold, wet conditions—and the UT domination—inspired many of the 43,100 fans to head to their cars. Those who tuned in the game on the radio and heard Johnny Greene block a Longhorn punt came back. So did the Bears. Baylor scored 27 unanswered points to take their first win over UT in 18 years, 34-24. "As sick as I am, I told them that if we can't win the conference I hope Baylor does," UT coach Darrell Royal said. "They've waited a long time." The scoreboard was left on, and a steady procession of cars crawled past all night so fans could savor the score. Dr. Herbert H. Reynolds, then a university vice president

RECORDS

RUSHING YARDS

GAME

210   Jerod Douglas vs. Texas, Nov. 24, 1994 (20 att.)

SEASON

1,187   Walter Abercrombie, 1980 (229 att.)

CAREER

3,665   Walter Abercrombie, 1978-81 (732 att.)

PASSING YARDS

GAME

387   Buddy Humphrey vs. Rice, Nov. 29, 1958 (22 of 38)

SEASON

2,284   Cody Carlson, 1986 (157 of 287)

CAREER

5,995   J.J. Joe, 1990-93 (347 of 665)

RECEIVING YARDS

GAME

197   Gerald McNeil vs. Arkansas, Nov. 7, 1981 (10 rec.)

SEASON

1,140   Reggie Newhouse, 2002 (75 rec.)

CAREER

2,651   Gerald McNeil, 1980-83 (163 rec.)

POINTS

GAME

36   Jonathan Golden vs. Samford, Sept. 7, 2002 (6 TDs)

SEASON

119   Wesley Bradshaw, 1921 (14 TDs, 17 PATs, 6 FGs)

CAREER

220   Alfred Anderson, 1980-83 (36 TDs, 2 two-pt. conv.)

CONSENSUS ALL-AMERICANS

1930	Barton Koch	G
1956	Bill Glass	G
1963-64	Lawrence Elkins	E/B
1976	Gary Green	DB
1979-80	Mike Singletary	LB
1986	Thomas Everett	DB
1991	Santana Dotson	DL

and dean of facilities, and three other administrators camped out in the glow of the scoreboard, stirring at midnight for a rendition of "That Good Old Baylor Line." The victory gave Baylor its first winning season in 11 years and propelled the Bears to their first SWC title in 50 years. It also inspired a popular bumper sticker that read simply, "I believe."

BIGGEST UPSET Perhaps it's indicative of Baylor's modest accomplishments that the greatest upset in school history might be a 7-7 tie. In 1941, Texas was unbeaten and unchallenged, having earned the No. 1 ranking and the cover of *Life* magazine by not allowing an opponent within four touchdowns in the first six games of the season. Baylor was coming off three straight losses, including a 48-0 embarrassment at the hands of Texas A&M. But a last-second touchdown pass from backup tailback Kit Kittrell to a diving Bill Coleman tied the game. UT dropped to No. 2 and was upset by TCU the next week.

HEARTBREAKER No. 20 Baylor was up 17-0 on Texas A&M at Kyle Field in 1986 and a league title and trip to the Cotton Bowl were within reach. But then Aggies quarterback Kevin Murray, still stung by his role in the Bears' 20-15 victory the season before, got hot. "Last year I let the team down and Aggies all over the world down," said Murray, who threw three touchdowns and ran for another in the 11th-ranked Aggies' 31-30 win. "Murray just did miraculous things," said Teaff.

WILDEST FINISH After losing his 1999 opener to Boston College when kicker Kyle Atteberry missed a PAT in overtime, first-year coach Kevin Steele was looking to create an attitude in the closing seconds of the Bears' next game, against UNLV on Sept. 11. He got more than he bargained for. With less than 20 seconds to play, Baylor had a three-point lead and the ball at the Rebels' 8-yard line. Instead of having quarterback Jermaine Alfred take a knee and run out

the clock, Steele wanted to show his players the need to stay aggressive and called a running play. But UNLV cornerback Andre Hilliard slapped the ball out of Darrell Bush's hands at the 1 and UNLV's Kevin Thomas returned it for the game-winning touchdown in a 27-24 UNLV win. "To tell you the truth, I thought it was over with," UNLV tailback Jeremi Rudolph said. "I thought they were going to take a knee. Instead, they tried to run it down our throat and run the score up, but that's what you get for not running out the clock." Said a stunned Steele afterward, "I have an explanation, but it doesn't hold water. We talked about creating an attitude and getting after people. We were simply trying to create an attitude. It's one of those one-in-a-million things, the most unbelievable thing I've ever seen. It will go down in history as one of the most unbelievable why-did-he-do-its?"

STADIUM The Bears had played at a variety of venues, from Carroll Field to the Cotton Palace to Waco Stadium, before school officials decided to build a stadium of their own after World War II. Bond sales raised $1.5 million and the 50,000-seat Baylor Stadium opened on Sept. 30, 1950, with a 34-7 victory over Houston. Renamed in 1989 after longtime Baylor trustee Carl Casey and his wife donated $5 million to a renovation project in the name of his father, Floyd Casey, the stadium has undergone a series of face-lifts. The most significant came in 1999, when a new press box that included luxury suites was erected on the west side.

RIVAL Bears fans like nothing better than to beat Texas and Texas A&M, but that sentiment isn't shared. Both the Longhorns and Aggies have dominated the series, though Baylor has had its day. Twice since 1978, Baylor has upset UT when the Longhorns were in the Top 10. But the Bears have saved most of their venom for the Aggies. In 1926, fans from both schools brawled and an A&M student was killed when hit by a flying chair. Incensed, members of the

ALL-TIME TEAM

Selected by Texas Football *magazine in 1995.*

OFFENSE

1952-54	Jim Ray Smith, OT
1973-75	Mike Hughes, OT
1979, '81-83	Mark Adickes, OT
1978-80	Frank Ditta, OL
1973-74	Aubrey Schulz, C
1949-51	Stan Williams, E
1962-64	Lawrence Elkins, E
1980-83	Gerald McNeil, WR
1950-51	Larry Isbell, QB
1954-56	Del Shofner, HB
1959-61	Ronnie Bull, RB
1978-81	Walter Abercrombie, RB
1973-75	Bubba Hicks, PK
1945-48	George Sims, KR

DEFENSE

1970-72	Roger Goree, DE
1947-48	Buddy Tinsley, DT
1965-67	Greg Pipes, DT
1950-52	Bill Joe Athey, DG
1954-56	Bill Glass, DG
1949-51	Gale Galloway, LB
1977-80	Mike Singletary, LB
1986-89	James Francis, LB
1978-81	Vann McElroy, DB
1983-86	Thomas Everett, DB
1986-89	Robert Blackmon, DB
1968-70	Ed Marsh, P

Aggies Corps of Cadets loaded a cannon on a flatbed railroad car and headed off toward Waco with the intent of shelling the Baylor campus. Tipped off to the plan, Texas Rangers slowed the Aggie advance by felling a tree across the railroad tracks, giving the cadets time to reassess their mission. A&M hadn't lost in its last 18 games against the Bears until Oct. 30, 2004, when a gambling Guy Morriss followed the Bears' touchdown in the second possession of the first overtime by going for two. Shawn Bell hit Dominique Ziegler for the successful conversion and the Bears won 35-34 over the No. 16 Aggies.

DUBIOUS DISTINCTION Whenever talk of Big 12 expansion comes up, so does talk of dropping Baylor, the only private school in the conference. Included with fellow Southwest Conference refugees Texas, Texas A&M and Texas Tech only because of the political clout of then-Texas governor Ann Richards, Baylor Class of 1954, the Bears have struggled to be competitive, winning league titles only in nonrevenue sports. After Baylor was hit by a scandal in its basketball program in the summer 2003, including the murder of a player allegedly at the hands of a teammate and a subsequent cover-up of improper payments to players engineered by then-head coach Dave Bliss, Richards called for "a serious housecleaning" in August 2003. She wasn't specific on which heads would roll, but said, "I don't think it's reasonable or wise to leap to a conclusion. But it's a sad time for Baylor."

TRAGEDY Redshirt freshman offensive lineman John Karkoska had just earned a spot in the starting lineup when he collapsed while jogging a lap during practice on Sept. 13, 1990. Karkoska was taken to Hillcrest Baptist Medical Center with a high body temperature and elevated heart rate, where he remained in critical condition for nine days. Minutes before the Bears kicked off against Sam Houston State on Sept. 22, Karkoska died of kidney and liver failure. "John is gone but his spirit and memory will live with all who knew him or were touched by his exemplary life," said Teaff, who restored the Fighting Bear Award, given annually to the most tenacious Bears player, and named it after Karkoska.

NICKNAME In 1914, student Doyle Thrailkill of San Antonio won the $5 gold piece promised by former student George Baines Rosborough for suggesting Bears as the team's official name over such candidates as Buffaloes, Frogs, Antelopes and Ferrets.

MASCOT Three years after Bears was selected as the school nickname, soldiers stationed at Camp MacArthur outside Waco donated a live bear. That started a succession of bruins that were taught various carnival antics, including the ability to drink a bottle of Dr Pepper, which had been invented in Waco by a pharmacist. The most famous of the mascots was Joe College. An enterprising young man, Bill Boyd, bought the bear from a bankrupt zoo at the Cotton Palace in Waco and offered it to Baylor president Pat Neff, saying he'd care for the bear in exchange for full tuition. Neff agreed. In 1974, the student body voted to name all the live mascots Judge in honor of the school's namesake, Judge R.E.B. Baylor.

UNIFORMS Baylor has worn a combination of green and gold over the years, including knockoff uniforms of Green Bay when the Lombardi Packers were at their zenith. But when Teaff became coach he ditched the look in favor of kelly green jerseys and white pants. The Bears have worn metallic gold helmets through most of their history, with the exception of 1969 to 1971. But after winning only three games in those three seasons, the Bears switched back. The interlocking BU logo first appeared in 1969 and has remained since with slight variations. Early in the 1992 season, the logo was absent because the school had switched helmet manufacturers and the new shells required repainting every week, making the placement of decals difficult. But a fan and alumni protest succeeded in forcing the return of the logo by midseason.

QUIRK In 1923, Baylor played Arkansas in a heavy rain. Coach Frank D. Bridges, known as a trickster, took advantage of the poor visibility to play 12 men on defense the entire game. The officials never noticed and the Bears won 14-0. "Bridges had small and aggressive ball clubs," said Potts Anderson, an All-SWC guard. "He'd probably rather fool you than beat you."

LORE Texas came into Waco in 1978 needing a victory over the 2–8 Bears to sew up the Southwest Conference title. Teaff delivered one of the most famous pregame speeches in college football history. He set the stage two days before the game by telling his players an old joke: two Eskimos were ice fishing and one was catching everything, the other nothing. When the empty-handed fisherman demanded an explanation, the successful angler took a worm out of his mouth. "You have to keep the worms warm," he said. Just as his team was set to take the field on

Saturday, Teaff delivered the punch line. "The game is yours, but there's one thing I'll do for you; I'll keep the worms warm," he said, popping a juicy five-inch night crawler into his mouth. The Bears stormed out of the locker room and dismantled the four-touchdown favorite Longhorns 38-14. "It was so foreign to anything I'd ever done, it gave them a shock," Teaff said. "It was a big, fun thing that relaxed them. They went out giggling." Teaff later said he waited until the players were out of sight and then spit the worm into a trash can.

QUOTE "I believe."—Baylor's slogan under Grant Teaff in 1974, a truncated version of his answer to critics who asked how Baylor could compete in the SWC

BAYLOR ANNUAL STATISTICAL LEADERS

YR	RUSHING	YDS	ATT	AVG	PASSING	ATT	CMP	PCT	YDS	RECEIVING	REC	YDS	AVG
1945	Sammy Pierce	537	102	5.3		NA	NA	NA	NA	Joe Joiner	21	319	15.2
1946	Jerry Mangum	320	72	4.4		NA	NA	NA	NA		NA	NA	NA
1947	Lyle Blackwood	378	68	5.6	Jack Price	127	52	.41	569	J.D. Ison	11	167	15.2
1948	Ben Hall	251	80	3.1	Adrian Burk	121	62	.51	596	Jasper Flanakin	20	269	13.5
1949	Jerry Mangum	328	95	3.5	Adrian Burk	191	110	.58	1,428	J.D. Ison	42	457	10.9
1950	James Jeffrey	569	123	4.6	Larry Isbell	186	91	.49	1,220	Harold Riley	35	539	15.4
1951	Jerry Coody	570	125	4.6	Larry Isbell	214	105	.49	1,430	Stanley Williams	37	598	16.2
1952	L.G. Dupre	453	80	5.7	Cotton Davidson	156	53	.34	779	Charles Smith	21	370	17.6
1953	L.G. Dupre	593	134	4.4	Cotton Davidson	156	74	.47	1,092	Wayne Hopkins	21	351	16.7
1954	Del Shofner	545	88	6.2	Billy Hooper	107	56	.52	818	Henry Gremminger	18	323	17.9
1955	Reuben Saage	380	87	4.4	Bobby Jones	65	29	.45	439	Henry Gremminger	15	181	12.1
1956	Del Shofner	449	70	6.4	Doyle Traylor	27	15	.56	209	Del Shofner	14	249	17.8
1957	Larry Hickman	612	145	4.2	Doyle Traylor	88	43	.49	482	Earl Miller	16	249	15.6
1958	Larry Hickman	670	151	4.4	Buddy Humphrey	195	112	.57	1,316	Gerry Moore	31	357	11.5
1959	Ronnie Bull	459	91	5.0	Ron Stanley	145	83	.57	800	Ronnie Bull	20	183	9.2
1960	Ronnie Bull	454	113	4.0	Ron Stanley	134	75	.56	1,151	Ronnie Goodwin	25	407	16.3
1961	Ronnie Bull	411	91	4.5	Robert Ply	86	39	.45	468	Ronnie Bull	19	199	10.5
1962	Tom Daives	230	57	4.0	Don Trull	229	125	.55	1,627	Ronnie Goodwin	25	414	16.6
1963	Dalton Hoffman	458	98	4.7	Don Trull	308	174	.56	2,157	Lawrence Elkins	70	873	12.5
1964	Tom Davies	401	94	4.3	Terry Southall	225	118	.52	1,623	Lawrence Elkins	50	851	17.0
1965	Richard Defee	429	86	5.0	Kenny Stockdale	177	89	.50	978	Harlan Lane	56	643	11.5
1966	Richard Defee	332	80	4.2	Terry Southall	337	173	.51	1,986	Tommy Smith	41	483	11.8
1967	Charles Wilson	553	124	4.5	Alvin Flynn	144	62	.43	924	George Cheshire	39	475	12.2
1968	Pinkie Palmer	818	222	3.7	Steve Stuart	216	95	.44	1,320	Jerry Smith	40	509	12.7
1969	Randy Cooper	364	93	3.9	Steve Stuart	112	48	.43	535	Jerry Smith	31	373	12.0
1970	Matthew Williams	711	208	3.4	Si Southall	160	56	.35	905	Derek Davis	48	780	16.3
1971	Matthew Williams	469	131	3.6	Si Southall	104	21	.20	348	Mike Chandler	10	182	18.2
1972	Gary Lacy	669	168	4.0	Neal Jeffrey	171	89	.52	1,030	Charles Dancer	34	463	13.6
1973	Gary Lacy	666	146	4.6	Neal Jeffrey	251	132	.53	1,897	Charles Dancer	53	927	17.5
1974	Steve Beaird	1,104	267	4.1	Neal Jeffrey	181	100	.55	1,414	Phillip Kent	24	406	16.9
1975	Cleveland Franklin	1,112	200	5.6	Mark Jackson	151	70	.46	1,021	Ricky Thompson	27	425	15.7
1976	Gary Blair	857	225	3.8	Mark Jackson	211	105	.50	1,132	Tommy Davidson	45	559	12.4
1977	Greg Hawthorne	670	132	5.1	Steve Smith	91	46	.51	484	Tommy Davidson	34	419	12.3
1978	Walter Abercrombie	661	114	5.8	Steve Smith	213	101	.47	1,387	Robert Holt	18	393	21.8
1979	Walter Abercrombie	886	171	5.2	Mike Brannan	90	31	.34	604	Robert Mitchell	10	192	19.2
1980	Walter Abercrombie	1,187	229	5.2	Jay Jeffrey	162	72	.44	1,096	Robert Holt	29	464	16.0
1981	Walter Abercrombie	931	218	4.3	Jay Jeffrey	198	111	.56	1,643	Gerald McNeil	44	744	16.9
1982	Alfred Anderson	837	201	4.2	Mike Brannan	204	100	.49	1,459	Gerald McNeil	52	822	15.8
1983	Alfred Anderson	1,046	231	4.5	Cody Carlson	180	98	.54	1,617	Gerald McNeil	62	1,034	16.7
1984	Ron Francis	558	127	4.4	Tom Muecke	213	97	.46	1,402	Glenn Pruitt	32	586	18.3
1985	Derrick McAdoo	369	76	4.9	Tom Muecke	156	86	.55	1,448	Matt Clark	29	540	18.6
1986	Jeffrey Murray	459	106	4.3	Cody Carlson	287	157	.55	2,284	Matt Clark	23	418	18.2
1987	Charles Perry	494	156	3.2	Brad Goebel	305	158	.52	2,178	Charles Perry	25	242	9.7
1988	Eldwin Raphel	543	118	4.6	Brad Goebel	237	117	.49	1,524	Bobby Jack Goforth	23	380	16.5
1989	Eldwin Raphel	708	172	4.1	Brad Goebel	175	95	.54	1,255	Jeff Murray	37	321	8.7
1990	Eldwin Raphel	546	123	4.4	J.J. Joe	73	43	.59	714	Greg Anderson	24	288	12.0
1991	David Mims	852	148	5.8	J.J. Joe	206	109	.53	1,853	Melvin Bonner	34	836	24.6
1992	David Mims	518	80	6.5	J.J. Joe	189	88	.47	1,765	Melvin Bonner	39	818	21.0
1993	Brandell Jackson	899	171	5.3	J.J. Joe	197	107	.54	1,663	Marvin Callies	22	435	19.8
1994	Kalief Muhammad	529	97	5.5	Jeff Watson	201	102	.51	1,615	Ben Bronson	33	571	17.3
1995	Jerod Douglas	1,114	211	5.3	Jeff Watson	214	113	.53	1,508	Kalief Muhammad	37	542	14.6
1996	Jerod Douglas	667	117	5.7	Jermaine Alfred	184	90	.49	1,148	Kalief Muhammad	39	479	12.3
1997	Darrell Bush	693	103	6.7	Jeff Watson	260	143	.55	1,550	Derrius Thompson	32	420	13.1
1998	Darrell Bush	357	105	3.4	Jermaine Alfred	188	97	.52	1,268	Morris Anderson	37	639	17.3
1999	Darrell Bush	682	162	4.2	Jermaine Alfred	228	111	.49	1,230	Andra Fuller	26	308	11.8
2000	Darrell Bush	517	133	3.9	Guy Tomcheck	144	53	.37	602	Reggie Newhouse	40	629	15.7
2001	Anthony Krieg	252	70	3.6	Greg Cicero	255	129	.51	1,239	Reggie Newhouse	61	706	11.6
2002	Rashad Armstrong	647	159	4.1	Aaron Karas	251	150	.60	1,792	Reggie Newhouse	75	1,140	15.2
2003	Rashad Armstrong	1,074	258	4.2	Aaron Karas	239	135	.56	1,481	Robert Quiroga	42	490	11.7
2004	Paul Mosley	582	127	4.6	Dane King	222	131	.59	1,370	Marques Roberts	40	570	14.3

Receiving leaders by receptions
The NCAA began including postseason stats in 2002

BAYLOR ALL-TIME SCORES

WIN/LOSS PERCENTAGE SINCE 1936

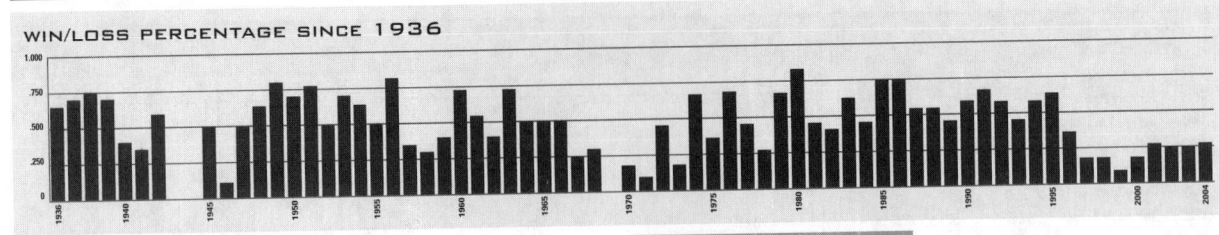

R.H. HAMILTON 1899-1900 (.786) — 5-1-1

1899 — 2-1-1
U	•	Toby's B.C.	20	0
U		Texas A&M	0	33
U	•	Toby's B.C.	6	0
U	=	TCU	0	0

1900 — 3-0-0
U	•	at Austin Coll.	11	6
U	•	Trinity	17	0
U	•	Weatherford Coll.	16	0

W.J. RITCHIE 1901 (.625) — 5-3

1901 — 5-3-0
U	•	St. Edwards	23	0	
U	•	Texas A&M *DAL*	17	6	
O26		Oklahoma	6	17	*
O29		Texas	0	23	
N5		at Texas A&M	0	6	
N23	•	TCU	36	0	*
U	•	Texas A&M	46	0	*
U	•	Texas A&M	42	9	*

J.C. EWING 1902 (.444) — 3-4-2

1902 — 3-4-2
S27		Trinity *DAL*	5	17
O10		Texas A&M *DAL*	6	11
O14		at Texas A&M	0	22
O18	=	Deaf School	6	6
O27		Trinity *WAX*	0	33
N1	•	TCU	0	0
N22	•	TCU	6	0
N27	•	St. Edwards	28	0
D1	•	TCU	20	0

R.N. WATTS 1903 (.563) — 4-3-1

1903 — 4-3-1
O3	•	TCU *Unk*	12	0	
O10	•	Fort Worth	23	0	
O17	=	Texas A&M *SA*	0	0	
O24		Texas *SA*	0	48	
O31	•	TCU *Unk*	5	0	
N7		at Texas A&M	0	16	*
N14	•	at Deaf School	6	0	
N21		at Texas A&M	0	5	

SOL METZGER 1904 (.313) — 2-5-1

1904 — 2-5-1
O1	=	TCU *Unk*	0	0
O8		Trinity	0	22
O15		Texas A&M	0	5
O29		TCU *Unk*	17	0
N5	•	Arkansas	17	6
N12		at Texas A&M	0	10
N19		at Texas	0	58
N24		TCU	0	5

ARCHIE WEBB 1905 (.143) — 1-6

1905 — 1-6-0
S23		TCU *Unk*	0	16
S30		Trinity *WAX*	5	22
O14		Texas A&M	0	42
O21		at Texas	0	39
O28	•	TCU *Unk*	10	6
N11		TCU *Unk*	0	17
N18		at Texas A&M	5	17

1906
NO TEAM

LUTHER BURLESON 1907 (.563) — 4-3-1

1907 — 4-3-1
O5	=	TCU	6	6
O12	•	Trinity	4	0
O19	•	Deaf School	33	0
O26		TCU	10	11
N2	•	Fort Worth *DAL*	11	5
N9		at Texas	11	27
N23	•	TCU	16	8
N30		at LSU	0	48

E.J. MILLS 1908-09 (.500) — 8-8

1908 — 3-5-0
O3		TCU *Unk*	0	15
O10	•	at Texas A&M	6	5
O17		at Texas	5	27
O24		TCU *Unk*	6	10
N7		at Tulane	2	10
N10		at LSU	0	89
N21	•	Tulane	6	0
N26	•	TCU *Unk*	23	8

1909 — 5-3-0
O9	•	S.W. Tex. St.	55	0
O16	•	Trinity	17	6
O20	•	Haskell	12	0
O23		TCU	0	9
O30	•	Texas A&M	6	9
N13		TCU	0	11
N20	•	at Hardin Simmons	16	3
N25	•	TCU	6	3

RALPH GLAZE 1910-12 (.540) — 12-10-3

1910 — 6-1-1
O8	=	at Daniel Baker	0	0	
O15	•	Austin Coll.	31	0	
O18	•	Haskell	52	3	
O22	•	TCU	52	0	
O29	•	Fort Worth Poly	39	0	
N5		Texas	0	1	f
N19	•	at TCU	10	3	
D3	•	Southwestern	27	5	

1911 — 3-4-2
S30	•	Fort Worth Poly	0	0
O7	•	Austin Coll.	0	9
O14	•	at Texas	0	11
O24		LSU	0	6
O28	•	TCU	12	0
N4	•	Winchester	63	0
N11	•	at Southwestern	5	5
N18	•	at Texas A&M	11	22
N25	•	Trinity	12	0

1912 — 3-5-0
O5		Austin Coll.	6	8	
O12	•	Fort Worth Poly	12	6	
O19		at TCU	0	22	
O26	•	Arkansas	6	0	*
N4		Texas	7	19	
N9		Southwestern	6	13	
N16	•	Trinity	41	0	
N28		Texas A&M *DAL*	0	53	

NORMAN PAYNE 1913 (.450) — 3-4-3

1913 — 3-4-3
S27	•	Howard Payne	15	6
O4	•	Texas St.	9	7
O11	=	Fort Worth Poly	0	0
O16		at Texas	0	77
O23		at LSU	0	50
O25		at Arkansas	0	34
O30	=	Trinity *WAX*	6	6
N15	•	Daniel Baker	6	0
N22		at Texas A&M	14	14
N27		Southwestern	7	14

G.P. "BUBS" MOSLEY 1914-19 (.615) — 30-18-4

1914 — 3-5-2
S26	=	Austin Coll.	0	0
O3	•	Howard Payne	9	0
O10		Texas	0	57
O17		Trinity	0	7
O24		at Oklahoma State	0	60
O31	=	Trinity	0	0
N7	•	TCU	28	14
N14	•	Daniel Baker	14	0
N20		at Rice	13	14
N26		Southwestern	6	7

1915-1995 SWC

1915 — 7-1-0 (3-0-0)
O2	•	Howard Payne	3	0
O8	•	at Rice	26	0
O16	•	Trinity *DAL*	49	0
O23	•	at Southwestern	10	0
N8		Sewanee	3	16
N13	•	Oklahoma State	12	6
N20	•	Daniel Baker	34	0
N25	•	TCU	51	0

1916 — 9-1-0 (3-1-0)
S30	•	Texas St.	76	0
O7	•	SMU	61	0
O14	•	Trinity	37	0
O21	•	at Howard Payne	47	0
O28	•	at Texas	7	3
N4	|	Southwestern	0	0
N11	|	Texas A&M	0	3
N18	•	at Oklahoma State	10	7
N25	•	Austin Coll.	26	0
N30	•	at TCU	32	14

1917 — 6-2-1 (2-1-0)
O6	•	Howard Payne	17	0
O13	•	Trinity *DAL*	55	0
O20	|	Oklahoma State	17	0
O27	•	Hardin Simmons	103	0
N3	|	Texas	3	0
N10	|	Texas A&M	0	7
N17	•	at SMU	0	0
N24	•	Southwestern	26	0
N29		at TCU	0	34

1918 — 0-6-0 (0-2-0)
O19		Mc Arthur Field	6	7
O26		Barron Field	0	26
N2	|	Texas A&M	0	19
N9	|	at SMU	0	14
N16		Southwestern	6	14
N28		TCU	7	12

1919 — 5-3-1 (0-3-1)
O4	•	Rusk	61	0
O11	•	Rice	0	8
O18	•	Austin Coll.	17	12
O25	|	Texas	13	29
N1	•	Southwestern	20	0
N15	|	Texas A&M	0	10
N18	•	Sewanee	21	7
N22	|	SMU	7	7
N27	•	at TCU	7	0

FRANK BRIDGES 1920-25 (.644) — 35-18-6

1920 — 4-4-1 (1-2-1)
S25	•	Austin Coll.	9	0
O2	|	at Rice	0	28
O9	•	Trinity	20	6
O16	•	Oklahoma State	7	0
O30		Southwestern	0	7
N6	•	Texas A&M	0	24
N13		TCU	9	21
N20	•	Howard Payne	20	3
N27	=	at SMU	0	0

1921 — 8-3-0 (2-2-0)
S24	•	Tarleton St.	35	0
O1	•	at Austin Coll.	17	13
O8	• |	Rice	17	14
O15		Boston College *DAL*	7	23
O22	•	Phillips	34	6
O29	•	Southwestern	16	0
N5	|	Texas A&M	3	14
N12	•	Hardin Simmons	21	0
N19	•	at Arkansas	12	13
N26	• |	SMU	28	0
D3	•	Mississippi Coll. *DAL*	24	0

1922 — 8-3-0 (5-0-0)
S30	•	North Texas	55	0
O7	•	Hardin Simmons	42	0
O14	• |	at Rice	31	0
O21	• |	Arkansas	60	13
O28	•	Mississippi Coll.	40	7
N4	• |	Texas A&M	13	7
N11		at Boston College	0	33
N18	• |	at Oklahoma State	10	0
N30	• |	at SMU	24	0
D9		Haskell	20	21
D9		Phillips	0	47

1923 — 5-1-2 (1-1-2)
S29	•	Hardin Simmons	14	0
O6	•	North Texas	33	7
O13	•	Howard Payne	20	6
O20	• |	at Arkansas	14	0
O27	• |	Ouachita	16	3
N3	=	Texas A&M	0	0
N10	|	Texas	7	7
N29	|	at SMU	0	16

1924 — 7-2-1 (4-0-1)
S27	•	Hardin Simmons	10	6
O4	•	North Texas	30	0
O11	•	Central Oklahoma *DAL*	6	13
O18	• |	Arkansas	13	0
O25	•	Austin Coll.	3	7
N1	• |	Texas A&M	15	7
N8	• |	at Texas	28	10
N15	= |	at SMU	7	7
N22	•	St. Edwards	30	7
N27	• |	at Rice	17	9

1925 — 3-5-2 (0-3-2)

S26			at Notre Dame	0	41	
O3	●		North Texas	20	6	
O10	=	|	TCU *DAL*	7	7	
O17			Trinity	3	10	
O24	●		Howard Payne	20	4	
O31		|	Texas A&M	0	13	
N7		|	at Texas	3	13	
N14		|	at SMU	6	7	
N21	●		St. Edwards	13	7	
N28	=	|	at Rice	7	7	

MORLEY JENNINGS
1926-40 (.577) 83-60-6

1926 — 6-3-1 (3-1-1)

S25	●		Southwestern	7	0	
O2			Loyola, La.	10	13	
O9	=	|	TCU *DAL*	7	7	
O16	●		Trinity	14	0	
O23	●		Howard Payne	23	7	
O30	●	|	Texas A&M	20	9	
N6	●	|	Texas	10	7	
N13		|	at SMU	3	31	
N20			St. Edwards	0	12	
N25	●	|	Rice	9	7	

1927 — 2-7-0 (0-5-0)

O1			Southwestern	6	19	
O8		|	at Arkansas	6	13	
O15	●		Trinity *WAX*	20	12	
O22	●		St. Edwards	12	6	
O29		|	TCU	0	14	
N5		|	at Texas	12	13	
N12		|	at SMU	0	34	
N24		|	at Rice	12	19	
D3			Centenary	6	9	

1928 — 8-2-0 (3-2-0)

S22	●		S.F. Austin	31	0	
S29	●		North Texas	45	0	*
O6	●		Trinity	33	0	
O13		|	Arkansas *TEX*	0	14	
O20	●		at Centenary	28	7	
O27	●		St. Edwards	48	7	
N3	●	|	at TCU	7	6	
N10		|	Texas	0	6	
N17	●	|	SMU	2	0	
N29	●	|	at Rice	25	14	

1929 — 7-3-1 (2-2-1)

S21	●		S.F. Austin	88	0	
S28	●		North Texas	32	0	
O5	●		Trinity	43	0	
O12	●		St. Edwards	19	0	
O19	●	|	Arkansas	31	20	
O26			at Centenary	12	27	
N2	●		Texas Tech	34	0	
N9	=	|	at Texas	0	0	
N16		|	at SMU	6	25	
N23		|	TCU	7	34	
N30	●	|	at Rice	19	0	

1930 — 6-3-1 (3-1-1)

S27	●		North Texas	33	0	
O4			at Purdue	7	20	
O11	●		Trinity	54	0	
O18	=	|	SMU	14	14	
O25			at Centenary	2	7	
N1	●		at Oklahoma Baptist	31	0	
N8		|	Texas	0	14	
N15	●	|	at Arkansas	22	7	
N22	●	|	at TCU	35	14	
N29	●	|	Rice	7	4	*

1931 — 3-6-0 (1-5-0)

O3	●		St. Edwards	23	0	
O10			at Centenary	13	24	
O17	●	|	Arkansas	19	7	
O24		|	at Texas A&M	7	33	
O31	●		Texas Tech	32	0	
N7		|	at Texas	0	25	
N14		|	at SMU	0	6	
N21		|	TCU	6	19	
N28		|	at Rice	0	20	

1932 — 3-5-1 (1-4-1)

O1	●		St. Edwards	32	0	
O8	●		at Loyola, La.	18	0	
O15		|	Arkansas *LR*	6	20	
O22	=	|	Texas A&M	0	0	
O29		|	at TCU	0	27	
N5		|	Texas	0	19	
N11			at Texas Tech	2	14	
N19	●	|	SMU	19	0	
N26		|	Rice	0	12	

1933 — 6-4-0 (4-2-0)

S30	●		St. Edwards	20	6	
O7			at Centenary	0	19	
O14		|	Arkansas *LR*	7	19	
O21	●		Hardin Simmons	21	0	
O28		|	at Texas A&M	7	14	
N4	●	|	TCU	7	0	
N12	●	|	at Texas	3	0	
N17			at Texas Tech	0	13	
N25	●	|	at SMU	13	7	
D2	●	|	Rice	7	6	

1934 — 3-7-0 (1-5-0)

S29	●		St. Edwards	33	0	
O5			at Texas Tech	7	14	
O13		|	Arkansas *LR*	0	6	
O20	●		at Hardin Simmons	13	6	
O27		|	Texas A&M	7	10	
N3		|	at TCU	12	34	
N10		|	at Texas	6	25	
N17			at Centenary	0	7	
N24	●	|	SMU	13	6	
D1		|	Rice	0	32	

1935 — 8-3-0 (3-3-0)

S21	●		Southwestern	39	0	
S28	●		Hardin Simmons	14	0	
O5	●		Texas A&I	6	0	
O12	●	|	Arkansas	13	6	
O19	●		at Oklahoma City	2	0	
O26	●	|	at Texas A&M	14	6	
N2		|	TCU	0	28	
N9		|	Texas	6	25	
N16	●		at Centenary	20	0	
N23		|	at SMU	0	10	
N30	●	|	at Rice	6	0	*

1936 — 6-3-1 (3-2-1)

S26	●		Hardin Simmons	13	0	
O3			Centenary *TYL*	0	10	
O10		|	at Arkansas	10	14	
O17	●	|	at Texas	21	18	
O24	=	|	Texas A&M	0	0	
O31		|	at TCU	0	28	
N7	●		Oklahoma City	48	6	
N14	●		at Oklahoma State	13	0	
N21	●	|	SMU	13	7	
N28	●	|	at Rice	10	7	

1937 — 7-3-0 (3-3-0)

S25	●		Southwestern	39	2	
O2	●		at Oklahoma City	33	0	
O9	●	|	Arkansas	20	14	
O16	●		at Centenary	20	0	
O23	●	|	at Texas A&M	13	0	
O30	●	|	TCU	6	0	
N6		|	Texas	6	9	
N13		|	at SMU	7	13	
N20	●		Loyola Marymount *BEAU*	27	13	
N27		|	at Rice	7	13	

1938 — 7-2-1 (3-2-1)

S24	●		Southwestern	33	0	
O1	●		Oklahoma State *WIFL*	20	6	
O8	●	|	at Arkansas	9	6	
O22	=	|	Texas A&M	6	6	
O29		|	at TCU	7	39	
N5	●	|	at Texas	14	3	
N12	●		at Loyola Marymount	35	2	
N19		|	SMU	6	21	
N26	●	|	at Rice	21	6	*
D3	●		Centenary	14	0	

1939 — 7-3-0 (4-2-0)

S30	●		Southwestern	34	0	
O7	●		at Oklahoma State	13	0	
O14	●	|	Arkansas	19	7	
O21			at Nebraska	0	20	
O28		|	at Texas A&M	0	20	
N4	●	|	TCU	27	0	
N11	●	|	Texas	20	0	
N18	●		at Centenary	13	6	
N25		|	at SMU	0	21	
D2	●	|	at Rice	10	7	

1940 — 4-6-0 (0-6-0)

S28	●		North Texas	27	20	
O5	●		at Denver	14	7	
O12		|	at Arkansas	6	12	
O19	●		Villanova *SA*	7	0	
O26		|	Texas A&M	7	14	
N2		|	at TCU	12	14	
N9		|	at Texas	0	13	
N16	●		Tulsa	20	6	
N23		|	SMU	4	7	
N30		|	at Rice	12	21	

FRANK KIMBROUGH
1941-46 (.402) 15-23-3

1941 — 3-6-1 (1-4-1)

S27	●		Hardin Simmons	20	0	
O4	●		at Denver	14	0	
O11	●	|	Arkansas	20	7	
O18			Villanova *PHIL*	6	14	
O25		|	at Texas A&M	0	48	
N1		|	TCU	12	23	
N8	=	|	Texas	7	7	
N15			at Tulsa	13	20	
N22		|	at SMU	0	14	
N29		|	at Rice	14	28	

1942 — 6-4-1 (3-2-1)

S19	●		Blackland AAF	68	0	
S26			Hardin Simmons	6	13	
O3	●		Oklahoma State *OKC*	18	12	
O10	●	|	at Arkansas	20	7	
O17	●		at Texas Tech	14	7	
O24	●	|	Texas A&M	6	0	
O31	●	|	at TCU	10	7	
N7		|	at Texas	0	20	
N14			at Tulsa	0	24	
N20	=	|	SMU	6	6	
N28		|	Rice	0	20	

1943-1944

NO TEAM WWII

1945 — 5-5-1 (2-4-0)

S15	●		Blackland AAF	40	0	
S22	●		West Texas St.	32	0	
S29		|	TCU	6	7	
O13	●	|	Arkansas	23	13	
O20	=		at Texas Tech	7	7	
O27		|	at Texas A&M	13	19	
N3	●		Southwestern	19	0	
N10		|	at Texas	14	21	
N17			Tulsa	7	26	
N24		|	at SMU	0	34	
D1	●	|	at Rice	17	14	

1946 — 1-8-0 (0-6-0)

S21	●		Southwestern	21	7	
S28		|	at TCU	16	19	
O12		|	at Arkansas	0	13	
O19			at Texas Tech	6	13	*
O26		|	Texas A&M	0	17	
N9		|	Texas	7	22	
N16			at Tulsa	0	17	
N23		|	SMU	0	35	
N30		|	at Rice	6	38	

BOB WOODRUFF
1947-49 (.645) 19-10-2

1947 — 5-5-0 (1-5-0)

S20	●		S.F. Austin	34	0	
S26	●		at Miami, Fla.	18	7	
O11	●	|	Arkansas	17	9	
O18	●		at Texas Tech	32	6	
O25		|	at Texas A&M	0	24	
N1		|	TCU	7	14	
N8		|	at Texas	7	28	
N15	●		at Tulsa	7	6	
N22		|	SMU	0	10	
N29		|	at Rice	6	34	

1948 — 6-3-2 (3-2-1)

S25	●		Tulsa	42	19	
O2	=		Mississippi State *MEM*	7	7	
O9	●	|	at Arkansas	23	7	
O16	●		Texas Tech	13	0	
O23	●	|	Texas A&M	20	14	
O30	●	|	at TCU	6	3	
N6		|	Texas	10	13	
N13			at Tulane	13	35	
N20		|	at SMU	6	13	
N27	=	|	Rice	7	7	
			DIXIE BOWL			
J1	●		Wake Forest	20	7	

1949 — 8-2-0 (4-2-0)

S24	●		South Carolina	20	6	
O1	●		at Mississippi State	14	6	
O8	●	|	Arkansas	35	13	
O15	●		at Texas Tech	28	7	
O22	●	|	at Texas A&M	21	0	
O29	●	|	TCU	40	14	
N5		|	at Texas	0	20	
N12	●		Wyoming	32	13	*
N19	●	|	at SMU	35	26	
N26		|	at Rice	7	21	

GEORGE SAUER
1950-55 (.637) 38-21-3

1950 — 7-3-0 (4-2-0)

S23			at Wyoming	0	7	
S30	●		Houston	34	7	
O7	●		Mississippi State *SHRE*	14	7	
O14		|	at Arkansas	6	27	
O21	●		Texas Tech	26	12	
O28	●	|	Texas A&M	27	20	
N4	●	|	at TCU	20	14	
N11		|	Texas	20	27	
N25	●	|	at SMU	3	0	
D2	●	|	Rice	33	7	

1951 — 8-2-1 (4-1-1)

S22	●		at Houston	19	0	
O6	●		at Tulane	27	14	
O13	●	|	Arkansas	9	7	
O20	●		Texas Tech	40	20	
O27	=	|	at Texas A&M	21	21	
N3		|	TCU	7	20	
N10	●	|	at Texas	18	6	
N17	●		Wake Forest	42	0	
N24	●	|	SMU	14	13	
D1	●	|	at Rice	34	13	
			ORANGE BOWL			
J1			Georgia Tech	14	17	

1952 — 4-4-2 (1-3-2)

S20	●		Wake Forest	17	14	
O4	●		Washington State	31	7	
O11		|	Arkansas *LR*	17	20	
O18	●		at Texas Tech	21	10	
O25	●	|	Texas A&M	21	20	
N1	=	|	at TCU	20	20	
N8		|	Texas	33	35	
N15			at Houston	6	28	
N22	=	|	at SMU	7	7	
N29		|	Rice	14	20	

1953 — 7-3-0 (4-2-0)

S19	●		at California	25	0	
O2	●		at Miami, Fla.	21	13	
O10	●	|	Arkansas	14	7	
O17	●		Vanderbilt	47	6	
O24	●	|	at Texas A&M	14	13	
O31	●	|	TCU	25	7	
N7		|	at Texas	20	21	
N14			Houston	7	37	
N21	●	|	SMU	27	21	
N28		|	at Rice	19	41	

1954 — 7-4-0 (4-2-0)

S18	●		Houston	53	13	
S25	●		at Vanderbilt	25	19	
O1			at Miami, Fla.	13	19	
O9		|	at Arkansas	20	21	
O16	●		Washington	34	7	
O23	●	|	Texas A&M	20	7	
O30	●	|	at TCU	12	7	
N6	●	|	Texas	13	7	
N20	●	|	at SMU	33	21	
N27		|	Rice	14	20	
			GATOR BOWL			
D31			Auburn	13	33	

1955 — 5-5-0 (2-4-0)

S17	●		Hardin Simmons	35	7	
S24	●		Villanova *PHIL*	19	2	
O1			Maryland	6	20	
O8	●	|	Arkansas	25	20	
O15	●		at Washington	13	7	
O22		|	at Texas A&M	7	19	
O29		|	TCU	6	28	
N5		|	at Texas	20	21	
N19		|	SMU	0	12	
N26	●	|	at Rice	15	7	

SAM BOYD
1956-58 (.500) 15-15-1

1956 — 9-2-0 (4-2-0)

S22	●		at California	7	6	
S29	●		Texas Tech	27	0	
O6	●		at Maryland	14	0	
O13	●	|	at Arkansas	14	7	
O27		|	Texas A&M	13	19	
N3		|	at TCU	6	7	
N10	●	|	Texas	10	7	
N17	●		at Nebraska	26	7	
N24	●	|	at SMU	26	0	
D1	●	|	Rice	46	13	
			SUGAR BOWL			
J1	●		Tennessee	13	7	

THE SCHOOLS

1957 — 3-6-1 (0-5-1)

Date		Opponent		
S21	●	Villanova	7	0
S28	●	Houston	14	6
O5		at Miami, Fla.	7	13
O12		Arkansas	17	20
O19	●	at Texas Tech	15	12
O26		at Texas A&M	0	14
N2		TCU	6	19
N9	=	at Texas	7	7
N23		SMU	7	14
N30		at Rice	0	20

1958 — 3-7-0 (1-5-0)

S20	●	Arkansas *LR*	12	0
S27	●	Hardin Simmons	14	7
O4		Miami, Fla.	8	14
O11		at Duke	7	12
O18	●	at Texas Tech	26	7
O25		Texas A&M	27	33
N1		at TCU	0	22
N8		Texas	15	20
N22		at SMU	29	33
N29		Rice	21	33

JOHN D. BRIDGERS
1959-68 (.481)   49-53-1

1959 — 4-6-0 (2-4-0)

S26	●	at Colorado	15	7
O3		LSU *SHRE*	0	22
O10		Arkansas	7	23
O17	●	Texas Tech	14	7
O24	●	Texas A&M	13	0
O31		TCU	0	14
N7		at Texas	12	13
N14		at Southern Cal	8	17
N21		SMU	14	30
N28	●	at Rice	23	21

1960 — 8-3-0 (5-2-0)

S24	●	Colorado	26	0
O1		at LSU	7	3
O8	●	at Arkansas	28	14
O15	●	at Texas Tech	14	7
O22	●	Texas A&M	14	0
O29		at TCU	6	14
N5		Texas	7	12
N12	●	Southern Cal	35	14
N19	●	at SMU	20	7
N26	●	Rice	12	7

GATOR BOWL
| D31 | ● | Florida | 12 | 13 |

1961 — 6-5-0 (2-5-0)

S23	●	Wake Forest	31	0
S30	●	at Pittsburgh	16	13
O14		Arkansas	13	23
O21		at Texas Tech	17	19
O28		at Texas A&M	0	23
N4	●	TCU	28	14
N11	●	at Texas	7	33
N18	●	Air Force	31	7
N25	●	SMU	31	6
D2		at Rice	14	26

GOTHAM BOWL
| D9 | ● | Utah State | 24 | 9 |

1962 — 4-6-0 (3-4-0)

S22		at Houston	0	19
S29		Pittsburgh	14	24
O13		at Arkansas	21	28
O20	●	Texas Tech	28	6
O27		Texas A&M	3	6
N3		at TCU	26	28
N10		Texas	12	27
N17	●	at Air Force	10	3
N24	●	at SMU	17	13
D1	●	Rice	28	15

1963 — 8-3-0 (6-1-0)

S28	●	Houston	27	0
O3		Oregon State *PORT*	15	22
O12	●	Arkansas	14	10
O19	●	at Texas Tech	21	17
O26	●	at Texas A&M	34	7
N2	●	TCU	32	13
N9		at Texas	0	7
N16		Kentucky	7	19
N30	●	at Rice	21	12
D7	●	SMU	20	6

BLUEBONNET BOWL
| D21 | ● | LSU | 14 | 7 |

1964 — 5-5-0 (4-3-0)

S24		at Washington	14	35
O3		Oregon State	6	13
O10		Arkansas *LR*	6	17
O17	●	Texas Tech	28	0
O24	●	Texas A&M	20	16
O31		at TCU	14	17
N7		Texas	14	20
N14	●	at Kentucky	17	15
N21	●	at SMU	16	13
N28	●	Rice	27	20

1965 — 5-5-0 (3-4-0)

S18	●	at Auburn	14	8
S25		Washington	17	14
O2		at Florida State	7	9
O9		Arkansas	7	38
O23	●	at Texas A&M	31	0
O30		TCU	7	10
N6		at Texas	14	35
N13		Texas Tech	22	34
N20	●	SMU	20	10
N27	●	at Rice	17	13

1966 — 5-5-0 (3-4-0)

S10	●	Syracuse	35	12
S24		Colorado	7	13
O1	●	Washington State *SPO*	20	14
O8	●	at Arkansas	7	0
O22	●	Texas A&M	13	17
O29		at TCU	0	6
N5		Texas	14	26
N12	●	at Texas Tech	29	14
N19		at SMU	22	24
N26	●	Rice	21	14

1967 — 1-8-1 (0-6-1)

S16		at Colorado	7	27
S23		at Syracuse	0	7
O7	●	Washington State	10	7
O14	=	Arkansas	10	10
O28	●	at Texas A&M	3	21
N4		TCU	7	29
N11		at Texas	0	24
N18		at Texas Tech	29	31
N25		SMU	10	16
D2		at Rice	25	27

1968 — 3-7-0 (3-4-0)

S21		at Indiana	36	40
S28		at Michigan State	10	28
O5		at LSU	16	48
O12		at Arkansas	19	35
O26	●	Texas A&M	10	9
N2		at TCU	14	47
N9		Texas	26	47
N16	●	Texas Tech	42	28
N23		at SMU	17	33
N30		Rice	16	7

BILL BEALL
1969-71 (.097)   3-28

1969 — 0-10-0 (0-7-0)

S20		Kansas State	15	45
S27		at Georgia Tech	10	17
O4		at LSU	8	63
O11		Arkansas	7	21
O25		at Texas A&M	0	24
N1		TCU	14	31
N8		at Texas	14	56
N15		at Texas Tech	7	41
N22		SMU	6	12
N29		at Rice	6	34

1970 — 2-9-0 (1-6-0)

S11		Missouri *StL*	0	38
S19	●	at Army	10	7
S26		Pittsburgh	10	15
O3		at LSU	10	31
O10		Arkansas *LR*	7	41
O24	●	Texas A&M	29	24
O31		at TCU	17	24
N7		Texas	14	21
N14		Texas Tech	3	7
N21		at SMU	10	23
N28		Rice	23	28

1971 — 1-9-0 (0-7-0)

S18		at Kansas	0	22
S25	●	Indiana	10	0
O1		at Miami, Fla.	15	41
O9		Arkansas	7	35
O23		at Texas A&M	9	10
O30		TCU	27	34
N6		at Texas	0	24
N13		at Texas Tech	0	27
N20		SMU	6	20
N27		at Rice	0	23

GRANT TEAFF
1972-92 (.548)   128-105-6

1972 — 5-6-0 (3-4-0)

S16		at Georgia	14	24
S23		at Missouri	27	0
O7	●	Miami, Fla.	10	3
O14		at Arkansas	20	31
O21		at Oklahoma State	7	20
O28	●	Texas A&M	15	13
N4		at TCU	42	9
N11		Texas	3	17
N18		Texas Tech	7	13
N25		at SMU	7	12
D2	●	Rice	28	14

1973 — 2-9-0 (0-7-0)

S15		Oklahoma	14	42
S22		at Pittsburgh	20	14
S29		at Colorado	28	52
O6	●	Florida State	21	14
O13		Arkansas	7	13
O27		at Texas A&M	22	28
N3		TCU	28	34
N10		at Texas	6	42
N17		at Texas Tech	24	55
N24		SMU	22	38
D1		at Rice	0	27

1974 — 8-4-0 (6-1-0)

S14		at Oklahoma	11	28
S21		at Missouri	21	28
S28	●	Oklahoma State	31	14
O5		at Florida State	21	17
O12	●	at Arkansas	21	17
O26		Texas A&M	0	20
N2		at TCU	21	7
N9	●	Texas	34	24
N16	●	Texas Tech	17	10
N23	●	at SMU	31	14
N30	●	Rice	24	3

COTTON BOWL
| J1 | | Penn State | 20 | 41 |

1975 — 3-6-2 (2-5-0)

S6	●	Mississippi	20	10
S20	=	Auburn	10	10
S27	=	at Michigan	14	14
O4		at South Carolina	13	24
O11		Arkansas	3	41
O25		at Texas A&M	10	19
N1	●	TCU	24	6
N8		at Texas	21	37
N15		at Texas Tech	10	33
N22		SMU	31	34
N29	●	at Rice	25	7

1976 — 7-3-1 (4-3-1)

S11		Houston	5	23
S18		at Auburn	15	14
S25		at Illinois	34	19
O2		South Carolina	18	17
O9	●	SMU	27	20
O16		at Texas A&M	0	24
N6	=	Arkansas	7	7
N13	●	at Rice	38	6
N20	●	Texas	20	10
N27	●	at TCU	24	19
D4	●	at Texas Tech	21	24

1977 — 5-6-0 (3-5-0)

S10		Texas Tech	7	17
S17	●	Kentucky	21	6
S24		at Nebraska	10	31
O1		at Houston	24	28
O8	●	SMU	9	6
O15		Texas A&M	31	38
O22	●	Air Force	38	7
N5		Arkansas *LR*	9	35
N12	●	Rice	24	14
N19		at Texas	7	29
N26	●	TCU	48	9

1978 — 3-8-0 (3-5-0)

S16		at Georgia	14	16
S23		at Kentucky	21	25
S30		at Ohio St.	28	34
O7		Houston	18	20
O14		SMU	21	28
O21	●	at Texas A&M	24	6
O28	●	at TCU	28	21
N4		at Texas Tech	9	27
N11		Arkansas	14	27
N18		at Rice	10	24
N25	●	Texas	38	14

1979 — 8-4-0 (5-3-0)

S8	●	Lamar	20	7
S15	●	Texas A&M	17	7
S22		at Alabama	0	45
S29	●	Texas Tech	27	17
O6		at Houston	10	13
O13	●	at SMU	24	21
O20	●	at Army	55	0
O27	●	TCU	16	3
N10		at Arkansas	20	29
N17	●	Rice	45	14
N24		at Texas	0	13

PEACH BOWL
| D31 | ● | Clemson | 24 | 18 |

1980 — 10-2-0 (8-0-0)

S13	●	at Lamar	42	7
S20	●	West Texas St.	43	15
S27	●	at Texas Tech	11	3
O4	●	Houston	24	12
O11	●	SMU	32	28
O18	●	at Texas A&M	46	7
O25	●	at TCU	21	6
N1	●	San Jose State	22	30
N8	●	Arkansas	42	15
N15	●	at Rice	16	6
N22	●	Texas	16	0

COTTON BOWL
| J1 | | Alabama | 2 | 30 |

1981 — 5-6-0 (3-5-0)

S5		Lamar	17	18
S12	●	Bowling Green	38	0
S19	●	at Louisiana Tech	28	13
S26	●	Texas Tech	28	15
O3		at Houston	3	24
O10		at SMU	20	17
O17	●	Texas A&M	19	17
O24	●	TCU	34	21
N7		Arkansas *LR*	39	41
N14		Rice	14	17
N21		at Texas	12	34

1982 — 4-6-1 (3-4-1)

S4	●	North Texas	21	17
S11		at Ohio St.	14	21
S25	●	at Texas Tech	24	23
O2		Houston	21	21
O9		SMU	19	22
O16		at Texas A&M	23	28
O23		at TCU	14	38
O30		at Tulane	15	30
N6	●	Arkansas	24	17
N13	●	at Rice	35	13
N20	·	Texas	23	31

1983 — 7-4-1 (4-3-1)

S10	●	Brigham Young	40	36
S17		at Texas El Paso	20	6
S24	●	Texas Tech	11	26
O1		at Houston	42	21
O8		at SMU	26	42
O15	=	Texas A&M	13	13
O22	●	TCU	56	21
O29		Tulane	24	18
N5	●	at Arkansas	24	21
N12	●	Rice	48	14
N19		at Texas	21	24

BLUEBONNET BOWL
| D31 | ● | Oklahoma State | 14 | 24 |

1984 — 5-6-0 (4-4-0)

S8		at Brigham Young	13	47
S22		at Oklahoma	15	34
S29	●	at Texas Tech	18	9
O6		Houston	17	24
O13		SMU	20	24
O20	●	at Texas A&M	20	16
O27	●	at TCU	28	38
N3	●	New Mexico	38	2
N10		Arkansas	9	14
N17	●	at Rice	46	14
N24		Texas	24	10

1985 — 9-3-0 (6-2-0)

S7	●	Wyoming	39	18
S14		at Georgia	14	17
S21		at Southern Cal	20	13
S28	●	Texas Tech	31	0
O5	●	at Houston	24	21
O12	●	at SMU	21	14
O19	●	Texas A&M	20	15
O26	●	TCU	45	0
N9	●	Arkansas *LR*	14	30
N16	●	Rice	34	10
N23		at Texas	10	17

LIBERTY BOWL
| D27 | ● | LSU | 21 | 7 |

1986 — 9-3-0 (6-2-0)

Date		Opponent		
S6	●	at Wyoming	31	28
S13	●	Louisiana Tech	38	7
S20		Southern Cal	14	17
S27	●	at Texas Tech	45	14
O4	●	Houston	27	13
O11		SMU	21	27
O18		at Texas A&M	30	31
O25	●	at TCU	28	17
N8	●	Arkansas	29	14
N15	●	at Rice	23	17
N22	●	Texas	18	13
BLUEBONNET BOWL				
D31	●	Colorado	21	9

1987 — 6-5-0 (3-4-0)

Date		Opponent		
S5	●	Louisiana Tech	13	3
S12		at Missouri	18	23
S19	●	at Nevada-Las Vegas	21	14
S26	●	Texas Tech	36	22
O3	●	at Houston	30	18
O10	●	Texas St.	36	15
O17		Texas A&M	10	34
O24		TCU	0	24
N7		at Arkansas	7	10
N14		Rice	34	31
N21		at Texas	16	34

1988 — 6-5-0 (2-5-0)

Date		Opponent		
S3	●	Nevada-Las Vegas	27	3
S10	●	at Kansas	27	14
S17	●	at Iowa St.	35	0
S24		at Texas Tech	6	36
O1		Houston	24	27
O8	●	S. W. Texas St.	45	7
O15		at Texas A&M	14	28
O22		at TCU	14	24
N5		Arkansas	3	33
N12	●	at Rice	20	10
N19	●	Texas	17	14

1989 — 5-6-0 (4-4-0)

Date		Opponent		
S9		at Oklahoma	7	33
S16		at Georgia	3	15
S23	●	Kansas	46	3
S30		Texas Tech	29	15
O7		at Houston	10	66
O14	●	at SMU	49	3
O21		Texas A&M	11	14
O28	●	TCU	27	9
N11		at Arkansas	10	19
N18		Rice	3	6
N25	●	at Texas	50	7

1990 — 6-4-1 (5-2-1)

Date		Opponent		
S1		at Nebraska	0	13
S8		at Arizona State	13	34
S22	●	Sam Houston St.	13	9
S29	●	at Texas Tech	21	15
O6		Houston	15	31
O13	●	SMU	52	17
O20	=	at Texas A&M	20	20
O27	●	at TCU	27	21
N10	●	Arkansas	34	3
N17	●	at Rice	17	16
N24		Texas	13	23

1991 — 8-4-0 (5-3-0)

Date		Opponent		
S7	●	Texas El Paso	27	7
S14	●	at Colorado	16	14
S21	●	Missouri	47	21
S28	●	at SMU	45	7
O5	●	at Houston	38	21
O12		Rice	17	20
O19		Texas A&M	12	34
O26	●	TCU	26	9
N2		at Arkansas	9	5
N16		Texas Tech	24	31
N23	●	at Texas	21	11
COPPER BOWL				
D31		Indiana	0	24

1992 — 7-5-0 (4-3-0)

Date		Opponent		
S5		Louisiana Tech	9	10
S12		Colorado	38	57
S19	●	Utah State	45	10
S26		at Texas Tech	17	36
O3	●	SMU	49	7
O10	●	at TCU	41	20
O17	●	Houston	29	23
O24		at Texas A&M	13	19
N7	●	Georgia Tech	31	27
N14		at Rice	31	34
N21	●	Texas	21	20
SUN BOWL				
D31	●	Arizona	20	15

CHUCK REEDY
1993-96 (.511)   23-22

1993 — 5-6-0 (3-4-0)

Date		Opponent		
S4		Fresno State	42	39
S11		at Colorado	21	45
S18	●	at Utah State	28	24
S25		Texas Tech	28	26
O2		at Houston	3	24
O9	●	at SMU	31	12
O16		Texas A&M	17	34
O23		TCU	13	38
N6		at Georgia Tech	27	37
N13	●	Rice	38	14
N20		at Texas	17	38

1994 — 7-5-0 (4-3-0)

Date		Opponent		
S3	●	Louisiana Tech	44	3
S10	●	at San Jose State	54	20
S17	●	Oklahoma State	14	10
S24		at Southern Cal	27	37
O1	●	at TCU	42	18
O8	●	SMU	44	10
O15		at Texas A&M	21	41
O22		at Texas Tech	7	38
O29	●	Houston	52	13
N12	●	at Rice	19	14
N24		Texas	35	63
ALAMO BOWL				
D31		Washington State	3	10

1995 — 7-4-0 (5-2-0)

Date		Opponent		
S2	●	at Tulsa	37	5
S16		Mississippi State	21	30
S23	●	at North Carolina St	14	0
S30	●	Texas Tech	9	7
O14	●	at Houston	47	7
O21		Texas A&M	9	24
O28	●	TCU	27	24
N4		at Miami, Fla.	14	35
N11	●	at SMU	48	7
N18	●	Rice	34	6
N23		at Texas	13	21

1996-PRESENT
BIG 12

1996 — 4-7 (1-7)

Date		Opponent		
S7	●	Louisiana Tech *Shre*	24	16
S14	●	at Louisville	14	13
S21	●	Oregon State	42	10
O5		at Texas Tech	24	45
O12		at Nebraska	0	49
O19		Oklahoma	24	28
O26	●	Iowa St.	49	21
N2		at Texas	23	28
N9		Texas A&M	7	24
N16		Missouri	42	49
N23		at Oklahoma State	17	37

DAVE ROBERTS
1997-98 (.182)   4-18

1997 — 2-9 (1-7)

Date		Opponent		
A30		Miami, Fla.	14	45
S6	●	at Fresno State	37	35
S20		at Michigan	3	38
O4		Texas Tech	14	35
O11		Nebraska	21	49
O18		at Oklahoma	23	24
O25		at Iowa St.	17	24
N1	●	Texas	23	21
N8		at Texas A&M	10	38
N15		at Missouri	24	42
N22		Oklahoma State	14	24

1998 — 2-9 (1-7)

Date		Opponent		
S12		at Oregon State	17	27
S19	●	North Carolina St.	33	30
S26		at Colorado	16	18
O3		at Texas Tech	29	31
O10	●	Kansas	31	24
O17		Texas A&M	14	35
O24		at Texas	20	30
O31		at Notre Dame	3	27
N7		Kansas State	6	49
N14		Oklahoma	16	28
N21		at Oklahoma State	10	24

KEVIN STEELE
1999-2002 (.200)   9-36

1999 — 1-10 (0-8)

Date		Opponent		
S4		at Boston College	29	30
S11		Nevada-Las Vegas	24	27
S18		at Oklahoma	10	41
S25		Texas	0	62
O2	●	North Texas	23	10
O9		at Texas A&M	13	45
O23		Texas Tech	7	35
O30		at Kansas State	7	48
N6		at Kansas	10	45
N13		Colorado	0	37
N20		Oklahoma State	14	34

2000 — 2-9 (0-8)

Date		Opponent		
A31	●	at North Texas	20	7
S16		Minnesota	9	34
S23	●	South Florida	28	13
S30		Iowa St.	17	31
O7		at Texas Tech	0	28
O14		Texas A&M	0	24
O21		at Nebraska	0	59
O28		at Texas	14	48
N4		Oklahoma	7	56
N11		Missouri	22	47
N18		at Oklahoma State	22	50

2001 — 3-8 (0-8)

Date		Opponent		
S8	●	Arkansas State	24	3
S22	●	New Mexico	16	13
S29		at Iowa St.	0	41
O6		at Texas A&M	10	16
O13		Nebraska	7	48
O20		at Oklahoma	17	33
O27		Texas Tech	19	63
N3		Texas	10	49
N10		at Missouri	24	41
N17		Oklahoma State	22	38
N24	●	So. Illinois	56	12

2002 — 3-9 (1-7)

Date		Opponent		
A31		at California	22	70
S7	●	Samford	50	12
S14		at New Mexico	0	23
S21	●	Tulsa	37	25
O5	●	Kansas	35	32
O12		Texas A&M	0	41
O19		at Colorado	0	34
O26		Kansas State	10	44
N2		at Texas Tech	11	62
N9		at Texas	0	41
N16		Oklahoma	9	49
N23		at Oklahoma State	28	63

GUY MORRISS
2003-PRESENT (.261)   6-17

2003 — 3-9 (1-7)

Date		Opponent		
A30		UAB	19	24
S6		at North Texas	14	52
S13	●	SMU	10	7
S20	●	Sam Houston St.	27	6
O4	●	Colorado	42	30
O11		at Texas A&M	10	73
O18		at Kansas	21	28
O25		Texas	0	56
N1		at Kansas State	10	38
N8		Texas Tech	14	62
N15		at Oklahoma	3	41
N22		Oklahoma State	21	38

2004 — 3-8 (1-7)

Date		Opponent		
S4		at UAB	14	56
S11	●	Texas St.	24	17
S25	●	North Texas	37	14
O2		at Texas	14	44
O9		Missouri	10	30
O16		at Nebraska	27	59
O23		Iowa State	25	26
O30	●	Texas A&M	35	34
N6		at Texas Tech	17	42
N13		at Oklahoma State	21	49
N20		Oklahoma	0	35

Neutral Site key: **Unk** Unknown, Unknown / **LR** Little Rock, AR / **Port** Portland, OR / **Spo** Spokane, WA / **StL** St. Louis, MO / **Dal** Dallas, TX / **Tex** Texarkana, TX / **Tyl** Tyler, TX / **Beau** Beaumont, TX / **WiFl** Wichita Falls, TX / **Wax** Waxahachie, TX / **SA** San Antonio, TX / **Phil** Philadelphia, PA / **OkC** Oklahoma City, Ok / **Mem** Memphis, TN / **Shre** Shreveport, LA
ƒ Forfeit † Game Later Forfieted # Disputed Victor * Disputed Score || Designated Conference Game |2 Counted Twice in Conference Standings

BOISE STATE

BY DAVE REARDON

THE MOST ISOLATED CITY IN THE continental United States is home to a mid-major's eye-popping incursion into college football's ruling power elite. (At least for the moment.) Before its heartbreaking loss to Louisville at the 2004 Liberty Bowl, Boise State possessed the nation's longest winning streak: 22 games. Not too shabby for a team that's only been in Division I-A since 1996.

TRADITION Now listen up: Do not believe the urban myth about birds crash-landing on the 50-yard line thinking it's a lake. Once considered a gimmick—okay, it was a gimmick—the blue turf at Bronco Stadium has become a trademark. Every now and then there's a movement to switch to green, but the idea always gets shot down. The current AstroPlay surface is the third blue field the stadium has sported; the first was installed in 1986. Boise State is the only college with a blue football field and, unless the rules are changed, it will remain the only one, because the NCAA has banned new fields in hues other than green.

BEST PLAYER Randy Trautman walked on at Boise State—and ended up in the College Football Hall of Fame. The defensive tackle from Caldwell, Idaho, led the Broncos to the Division I-AA national championship in 1980, and finished his career in 1981 with 285 tackles, including 29 for loss. The Broncos went 37–11 in his four years. He was drafted in the ninth round by the Washington Redskins, and ended up playing for Calgary in the CFL before returning to Boise, where he now works as a contractor.

BEST COACH Dan Hawkins led the Broncos to a 44–7 record in his first four years, and signed a $2.6 million contract extension at the end of the 2004 season designed to keep him in Boise through 2010. With his no-name players deftly executing a combination of fundamental plays and occasional trickery—including fake fumbles—Boise State has led the nation in offense twice under Hawkins and won three WAC championships. Hawkins' career has historically been about doing more with less; accordingly, he's comfortable in Boise's small-school environment. After serving as an assistant at Cal-Davis (his alma mater), his stops included College of the Siskiyous, Sonoma State and Willamette before he landed as an assistant at Boise State in 1998. He's earned loyalty from assistant coaches, and players love him because he finds ways to get hardworking third-and-fourth-stringers involved.

PROFILE

Boise State University
Boise, Idaho
Founded in 1932
Enrollment: 16,666
Colors: Blue and Orange
Nickname: Broncos
Stadium: Bronco Stadium
    Opened in 1970
    Blue AstroPlay; 30,000 capacity
First football game: 1933
All-time record: 296–136–2 (.684)
Bowl record: 4–1
Western Athletic Conference championships: 3 (outright)
Website: www.broncosports.com

THE BEST OF TIMES

It didn't take long for Boise State to begin dominating the WAC. After narrowly missing the league championship in 2001, their first year in the league, the Broncos went unbeaten in conference play from 2002 to 2004, while going 36-3 overall under coach Dan Hawkins. BSU was ranked 16th in the final 2003 AP poll and 12th in 2004.

THE WORST OF TIMES

Boise State has had only five losing seasons since its start as a four-year institution in 1968. The worst was a 2–10 mark (1–4 in the Big West) in 1996 under coaches Tom Mason and Pokey Allen. An eight-game losing streak included a 56-7 embarrassment at Arizona State.

CONFERENCE

Boise State has been a member of the WAC since 2001. BSU was independent in 1968-69, a member of the Big Sky Conference from 1970 to 1995 and a Big West school from 1996 to 2000.

DISTINGUISHED ALUMNI

Chris Childs, NBA player; Michael Hoffman, movie/TV director and producer; Dee Pickett, world champion cowboy

FIGHT SONG

THE BOISE STATE FIGHT SONG
Fight Broncos, celebrate the orange and blue,
Boise, we'll stand up and cheer for B-S-U!!!
Fight for distinction and our alma mater,
Bravely defending B-S-U!
Fight on courageously for Boise State!
Success and honor make her great (B-S-U)!
Boise's proud tradition, heads up competition,
Glory for B-S-U
Go orange! Go big blue!
Fight! Fight! B-S-U!!!

Don't believe the urban myth about birds crash-landing on the 50-yard line thinking it's a lake.

BEST TEAM The Broncos went into 2004 with an 11-game winning streak, but just three returning starters on offense and more question marks than usual. The heart of the team, three-time all-league quarterback Ryan Dinwiddie, was among those who had moved on. But sophomore Jared Zabransky proved to be more than adequate as a replacement, leading the Broncos to 493 yards per game, fourth in the nation. BSU won all 11 regular-season games, running its winning streak to a nation's-best 22, claiming a third WAC championship in a row and climbing to No. 10 in the AP poll. The magical run ended with a 44-40 loss to Louisville on New Year's Eve in the Liberty Bowl—a game matching the country's two most prolific offenses—and Boise State finished 12th in the national rankings.

BIGGEST GAME When Boise State beat Oregon State 53-34 on Sept. 10, 2004, it marked the Broncos' first victory over a Pac-10 school. Zabransky passed for three touchdowns and ran for a fourth as BSU avenged its only loss of 2003 (when the Beavers beat them 26-24 to snap the Broncos' 13-game winning streak).

BIGGEST UPSET In 2001, the Broncos showed that the WAC was not a one-team league, knocking off eighth-ranked Fresno State 35-30 on ESPN. Unheralded Dinwiddie outplayed Bulldogs star David Carr, passing for 297 yards and four touchdowns. Fresno had a chance late in the game, but Carr fumbled when he was sacked on fourth down at Boise's 5 with less than a minute left. The Broncos, under first-year coach Dan Hawkins, snapped the Bulldogs' 18-game home winning streak.

HEARTBREAKER The 1990 Broncos were 10–3 when they went to Reno for the Division I-AA quarterfinals. Nevada led through most of the second half, but Boise State tied it late to send the game into overtime. The Broncos missed a field goal in the first OT that might have won the game, then ultimately lost in the third extra session.

STADIUM Bronco Stadium seats just 30,000, but at the end of the 2004 season BSU was awaiting the results of a feasibility study for adding up to 10,000 new seats, as well as club seating and an improved press box. The current stadium, which

RECORDS

RUSHING YARDS

GAME
261 — Cedric Minter vs. Northern Michigan, Sept. 23, 1978 (25 att.)

SEASON
1,611 — Brock Forsey, 2002 (295 att.)

CAREER
4,475 — Cedric Minter, 1977-80 (752 att.)

PASSING YARDS

GAME
532 — Ryan Dinwiddie vs. Louisiana Tech, Oct. 4, 2003 (40 of 60)

SEASON
4,356 — Ryan Dinwiddie, 2003 (276 of 446)

CAREER
9,819 — Ryan Dinwiddie, 2000-03 (662 of 992)

RECEIVING YARDS

GAME
255 — Tim Gilligan vs. Louisiana Tech, Oct. 4, 2003 (16 rec.)

SEASON
1,192 — Tim Gilligan, 2003 (67 rec.)

CAREER
2,751 — Ryan Ikebe, 1993-96 (162 rec.)

POINTS

GAME
24 — Most recently, Brock Forsey, five times in 2002 season (4 TDs); 10 other times by six players

SEASON
192 — Brock Forsey, 2002 (32 TDs)

CAREER
408 — Brock Forsey, 1999-2002 (68 TDs)

CONSENSUS ALL-AMERICANS

1972	Al Marshall, OE
1973	Don Hutt, WR
1974	Jim McMillan, QB
1975	John Smith, FL
1977	Chris Malmgren, DT
1977	Terry Hutt, WR
1977	Harold Cotton, OT
1979	Joe Aliotti, QB
1979	Doug Scott, DT
1980-81	Randy Trautman, DT
1981	Rick Woods, S
1982	John Rade, LB
1982, 1984	Carl Keever, LB
1985	Marcus Koch, DE
1987	Tom DeWitz, OG
1987	Pete Kwiatkowski, DE
1990	Erik Helgeson, DE
1991	Frank Robinson, CB
1992	Michael Dodd, PK
1994	Joe O'Brien, DE
1994	Rashid Gayle, CB

replaced a smaller facility with the same name, opened in 1970 with 14,500 seats. There have been two expansions since. The program has come a long way since 1940, when the team (then Boise Junior College) played games at a 1,000-seat facility with wooden bleachers. For games attracting bigger crowds, bleachers were borrowed from Boise High School.

RIVAL The Governor's Cup, awarded to the winner of the annual Boise State-Idaho game, hasn't left the Broncos' grasp in six years, and the Vandals don't appear to be getting any closer. The 2004 outcome was 65-7, the biggest blowout in a series that dates back to 1971. Idaho, however, still leads the series 17-16-1 (through 2004).

NICKNAME In the early 1930s, when Boise Junior College was established, ranches surrounded the town and horses were still a very common means of transportation. Broncos was the logical choice.

MASCOT Buster Bronco recently got a $1,500 costume makeover. He appears at events with the cheerleaders, dancing and signing autographs. Buster is joined at games by a real horse that is trotted around the field after every Boise State touchdown.

UNIFORMS Boise State's uniforms are similar in appearance to the Denver Broncos': blue jerseys with orange piping, and blue helmets with a fierce horse's-head logo.

QUOTE "If we had knelt on the ball at the end of the game, wouldn't that have been the end of the game? Yeah, it would have been. But Gandhi didn't take a knee. Martin Luther King didn't take a knee. Thomas Edison didn't take a knee, and I sure as hell am not going to take a knee."—Dan Hawkins, after the 2003 game in which Boise State, leading Tulsa 20-14, went for another touchdown instead of running out the clock, winding up with a 27-20 win

BOISE STATE ANNUAL STATISTICAL LEADERS

YR	RUSHING	YDS	ATT	AVG	PASSING	ATT	CMP	PCT	YDS	RECEIVING	REC	YDS	AVG
1996	Reggie Etheridge	811	206	3.9	Tony Hilde	338	170	.50	2,473	Ryan Ikebe	61	959	15.7
1997	Gavin Reed	459	130	3.5	Nate Sparks	155	74	.48	1,157	Rodney Smith	64	917	14.3
1998	Eron Hurley	1,142	223	5.1	Bart Hendricks	279	150	.54	1,799	Rodney Smith	53	772	14.6
1999	Davy Malaythong	577	148	3.9	Bart Hendricks	351	203	.58	2,746	Jeb Putzier	39	514	13.2
2000	Brock Forsey	914	197	4.6	Bart Hendricks	347	210	.61	3,364	Lou Fanucchi	40	796	19.9
2001	Brock Forsey	1,207	246	4.9	Ryan Dinwiddie	322	201	.62	3,043	Jay Swillie	48	673	14.0
2002	Brock Forsey	1,611	295	5.5	Ryan Dinwiddie	205	134	.65	2,283	Billy Wingfield	62	1,138	18.4
2003	David Mikell	1,142	242	4.7	Ryan Dinwiddie	446	276	.62	4,356	Tim Gilligan	67	1,192	17.8
2004	Lee Marks	968	189	5.1	Jared Zabransky	327	206	.63	2,927	T.J. Acree	55	947	17.2

Receiving leaders by receptions
The NCAA began including postseason stats in 2002

BOISE STATE ALL-TIME SCORES

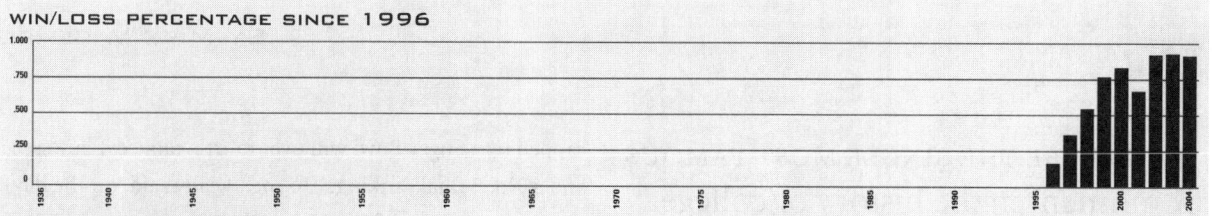

WIN/LOSS PERCENTAGE SINCE 1996

POKEY ALLEN		
1993-96 (.615)		24-15

TOM MASON		
1996 (.100)		1-9

1996-2000 BIG WEST

1996 2-10 (1-4)

A31		Central Michigan	21 42
S7	●	Portland St.	33 22
S14		Ea. Washington	21 27
S21		at Hawaii	14 20
S28		Northwestern St.	16 20
O5		at Arizona State	7 56
O12	|	at Nevada	28 66
O19	|	Utah State	14 39
N2		at Fresno State	7 41
N9	|	North Texas	27 30
N16	● |	at New Mexico State	33 32
N23	|	Idaho	19 64

HOUSTON NUTT		
1997 (.364)		4-7

1997 4-7 (3-2)

A30		Cal St. Northridge	23 63 †
S6		at Wisconsin	24 28
S13		at Central Michigan	26 44
S20	●	Weber St.	24 7
S27		at Washington State	0 58
O11	● |	New Mexico State	52 10
O18	● |	at North Texas	17 14
O25		Louisiana Tech	27 31
N1	|	at Utah State	20 24
N8	|	Nevada	42 56
N22	● |	at Idaho	30 23

DIRK KOETTER		
1998-2000 (.722)		26-10

1998 6-5 (2-3)

S5	●	Cal St. Northridge	26 13
S12		Washington State	21 33
S19	●	Portland St.	42 24
S26	●	at Utah	31 28
O3		at Louisiana Tech	28 63
O10	|	North Texas	13 21
O17	●	Weber St.	24 13
O24	● |	Utah State	30 16
O31	|	at Nevada	24 52
N7	● |	at New Mexico State	55 51
N21	|	Idaho	35 36

1999 10-3 (5-1)

S4		at UCLA	7 38
S11	●	So. Utah	35 27
S18		at Hawaii	19 34
S25	●	New Mexico	20 9
O2	●	Utah	26 20
O9	●	Ea. Washington	41 7
O16	|	at North Texas	10 17
O23	● |	Nevada	52 17
O30	● |	at Utah State	33 27
N6	● |	Arkansas State	63 10
N13	● |	New Mexico State	45 26
N20	● |	Idaho *Pull*	45 14
		HUMANITARIAN BOWL	
D30	●	Louisville	34 31

2000 10-2 (5-0)

S2	●	at New Mexico	31 14
S9	●	No. Iowa	42 17
S16		Arkansas *LR*	31 38
S23	●	at Central Michigan	47 10
O7		at Washington State	35 42
O14	●	Ea. Washington	41 23
O21	● |	North Texas	59 0
O28	● |	at New Mexico State	34 31
N4	● |	at Arkansas State	42 14
N11	● |	Utah State	66 38
N18	● |	Idaho	66 24
		HUMANITARIAN BOWL	
D28	●	Texas-El Paso	38 23

2001-PRESENT WAC

DAN HAWKINS		
2001-Present (.863)		44-7

2001 8-4 (6-2)

S1		at South Carolina	13 32
S8		Washington State	20 41
S22	● |	Texas-El Paso	42 17
S29	●	Idaho *Pull*	45 13
O6		at Rice	14 45
O13	● |	Tulsa	41 10
O19	● |	at Fresno State	35 30
O27	● |	Nevada	49 7
N3	|	at Louisiana Tech	42 48
N10	● |	at Hawaii	28 21
N17	● |	San Jose State	56 6
N24	●	Central Michigan	26 10

2002 12-1 (8-0)

A31	●	Idaho	38 21
S7		at Arkansas	14 41
S14	●	at Wyoming	35 13
S28	●	Utah State	63 38
O5	● |	Hawaii	58 31
O12	● |	at Tulsa	52 24
O19	● |	Fresno State	67 21
O26	● |	at San Jose State	45 8
N2	● |	at Texas-El Paso	58 3
N9	● |	Rice	49 7
N16	● |	Louisiana Tech	36 10
N23	● |	at Nevada	44 7
		HUMANITARIAN BOWL	
D31	●	Iowa State	34 16

2003 13-1 (8-0)

S6	●	Idaho St.	62 0
S13	●	at Idaho	24 10
S20		at Oregon State	24 26
S27	●	Wyoming	33 17
O4	● |	at Louisiana Tech	43 37
O11	● |	Tulsa	27 20
O18	● |	at SMU	45 3
O25	● |	San Jose State	77 14
O31	● |	at Brigham Young	50 12
N15	● |	Texas-El Paso	51 21
N21	● |	at Fresno State	31 17
N29	● |	Nevada	56 3
D6	● |	at Hawaii	45 28
		FORT WORTH BOWL	
D23	●	TCU	34 31

2004 11-1 (8-0)

S4	●	Idaho	65 7
S10	●	Oregon State	53 34
S18	● |	at Texas-El Paso	47 31
S25	● |	Brigham Young	28 27
O2	● |	SMU	38 20
O16	● |	at Tulsa	45 42
O23	● |	Fresno State	33 16
O30	● |	Hawaii	69 3
N13	● |	at San Jose State	56 49
N20	● |	Louisiana Tech	55 14
N27	● |	at Nevada	58 21
		LIBERTY BOWL	
D31		Louisville	40 44

BOSTON COLLEGE

BY MIKE VACCARO

IT MAY BE THE SINGLE MOST FAMOUS moment in the history of college football; it has surely been replayed more than any other contender. It was Nov. 23, 1984, and the Boston College Eagles were trailing the Miami Hurricanes 45-41, with time for only one more play. And Doug Flutie made that play. Weeks away from winning the Heisman Trophy, Flutie scrambled out of the pocket, reared back and threw a 48-yard prayer that Gerard Phelan somehow answered in the Miami end zone. It was the signature moment of Flutie's grand career and easily the play that defines Boston College in the minds of most college football fans. "Some plays will live forever," Flutie would say 15 years later. "And some plays, it seems, have a shelf life even longer than that."

BC's football history does extend beyond that one play, however. It is one of only two Catholic colleges (along with Notre Dame) that still plays Division I-A football, and the Eagles boast a tradition that BC's Jesuits cherish. In fact, before he went on to broader fame at that "other" Catholic school, Frank Leahy led the Eagles to an 11–0 record in 1940,

capped by a Sugar Bowl win over fourth-ranked Tennessee, and a No. 5 final ranking. "To me," Leahy said, on the day the Eagles returned from New Orleans to greet 100,000 supporters in downtown Boston, "this is the best football program in the world." A legion of Eagles fans would second that emotion.

TRADITION Game day at Boston College prominently features one of the largest and most popular musical acts in all of New England—the BC Marching Band, known as the Screaming Eagles. BC's troupe of musicians, color guard and twirlers warms up with the traditional pregame march across campus, followed by a concert at Commander Shea Field, where fans gather to tailgate. Then the band proceeds into Alumni Stadium, where it serves as a virtual co-star to the football team all afternoon. The highlight of each week is the halftime performance, which has ranged through the years from the Beatles to Bach, from *West Side Story* to *Phantom of the Opera*.

BEST PLAYER He was too small. That's what all the recruiters said. Syracuse recruited Doug Flutie and wanted to make him a defensive back, which would be like asking Beethoven to play rhythm guitar. Holy Cross wanted to do the

---

> ## "I didn't think there was any way they could throw one behind us," Jimmy Johnson would say. But Flutie did.

same thing. Only Boston College and newly hired coach Jack Bicknell agreed to let the standout from Natick High School try to play quarterback. "Maybe your instinct tells you he's too small," Bicknell would say a few years later, "but once you saw him play quarterback, you couldn't imagine how anyone in their right mind would want him to do anything else." Bicknell's faith was well-founded. All Flutie did in four years on The Heights was go 30–11–1 as a starter and single-handedly revitalize Boston College football. Overnight, BC became the hottest football story in the nation, and by the time he delivered a resounding 45-28 win over Houston in the 1985 Cotton Bowl in his final game, wrapping up a 10–2 season and a No. 5 national ranking, Flutie had amassed 10,579 career passing yards and 67 touchdowns. It was said Flutie had been worth millions of dollars to BC by his mere presence in the lineup. "What that kid does," Joe Paterno said after watching Flutie throw for 380 yards in a 27-17 BC win over Penn State in 1983, "is make people happy to watch football." The 1984 Heisman was just icing on the cake. At BC, they always knew Flutie could do no wrong.

BEST COACH BC has been blessed with an array of solid coaches through the years, from Mike Holovak (49–29–3 from 1951 to 1959) to Joe Yukica (68–37 from 1968 to 1977); from Tom Coughlin (21–13–1 from 1991 to 1993) to Bicknell (59–55–1, including a 40–19 mark from 1982 to 1986). But it's hard to argue with the two amazing years Leahy gave BC in 1939 and 1940. Across those two seasons, BC went 20–2, losing only to Florida (7-0) at Fenway Park and Clemson (6-3) in the Cotton Bowl. Within three weeks of punctuating his perfect 1940 season by beating Tennessee in the Sugar Bowl, Leahy was off to South Bend, where he would build a Rockne-size legend of his own at Notre Dame.

BEST TEAM It wasn't only Flutie, though he got most of the attention. BC also had future Outland Trophy recipient Mike Ruth anchoring its offensive line, and Flutie's favorite receiver, Phelan, was as good as any flanker in America in 1984. Mostly, though, the Eagles had flair, guts and an innate ability to find a way to win games. That character

RECORDS

RUSHING YARDS

GAME	
253	Phil Bennett vs. Temple, Sept. 23, 1972 (36 att.)
SEASON	
1,726	Mike Cloud, 1998 (308 att.)
CAREER	
3,725	Derrick Knight, 2000-03 (708 att.)

PASSING YARDS

GAME	
520	Doug Flutie vs. Penn State, Oct. 30, 1982 (26 of 44)
SEASON	
3,454	Doug Flutie, 1984 (233 of 386)
CAREER	
10,579	Doug Flutie, 1981-84 (677 of 1,271)

RECEIVING YARDS

GAME	
229	Scott Nizolek vs. Penn State, Oct. 30, 1982 (11 rec.)
SEASON	
1,149	Brian Brennan, 1983 (66 rec.)
CAREER	
2,388	Pete Mitchell, 1991-94 (190 rec.)

POINTS

GAME	
34	Ed Petela vs. Holy Cross, Nov. 26, 1949 (4 TDs, 10 PATs)
SEASON	
134	Keith Barnette, 1974 (22 TDs, 1 two-pt. conv.)
CAREER	
262	Brian Lowe, 1986-89 (57 FGs, 91 PATs)

CONSENSUS ALL-AMERICANS

1920	Luke Urban, E
1940	Gene Goodreault, E
1942	Mike Holovak, B
1984	Doug Flutie, QB
1984	Tony Thurman, DB
1985	Mike Ruth, DL
1994	Pete Mitchell, TE
1998	Mike Cloud, RB
2001	William Green, RB

first showed up in a 38-31 win in Week 2 at ninth-ranked Alabama, and it only deepened as the season went on, despite two heart-sickening defeats, both on the road, the first a 21-20 loss to West Virginia that effectively ended the Eagles' national championship dreams, the second a 37-30 shootout at Penn State. Nevertheless, sparked by the unforgettable 47-45 victory over Miami and a 45-28 win over Houston in the Cotton Bowl, the Eagles finished with a No. 5 ranking, tied for the school's highest season-ending result.

BIGGEST GAME The final play is the one that everyone remembers, but what's been lost to the haze of history is just how special BC's 1984 victory over Miami really was. Miami was the defending national champion and entered the game ranked 12th. BC, at 8–2, was ranked 10th, and trying to qualify for a New Year's Day bowl game. The two future Big East rivals went at each other right from the start, with BC jumping to a quick 14-0 lead before Miami, led by sophomore Bernie Kosar, stormed back to tie it up. From there, it was a back-and-forth offensive circus, with Flutie completing 34 of 46 passes for 472 yards and three TDs, and Kosar countering with 25 of 38 for 447 yards and two scores. "We knew," Flutie would say later, "it would all come down to who got the ball last." That turned out to be BC, with all of 28 seconds left, trailing 45-41. Three plays took the Eagles from their own 20 to the Canes' 48. And then … "I didn't think there was any way in the world they could throw one behind us and we wouldn't knock it down," Miami's first-year coach, Jimmy Johnson, would say. But Flutie did, right into the arms of Phelan, right into history and an endless spool of ESPN Classic reruns.

BIGGEST UPSET In 1992, Notre Dame stomped the Eagles in South Bend, 54-7. That made what happened Nov. 20, 1993, all the more shocking. The previous week, Notre Dame had stunned top-ranked Florida State, which allowed the Irish to assume the top spot in both polls. Maybe that's what enabled BC to jump all over them that day at Notre Dame Stadium, seizing a 38-17 lead early in the fourth quarter behind a career day from Glenn Foley, who would finish with 315 passing yards. But Notre Dame, playing its season finale and hoping to lock up the inside track to another national championship, stormed back, scoring 22 points in 10 minutes, capped by a four-yard pass from Kevin McDougal to Lake Dawson on fourth down, with only 1:09 left in the game. That gave Foley one last chance, and he grabbed it, driving the Eagles to within striking

range. And when David Gordon booted a 41-yarder straight through the uprights as time expired, BC had a 41-39 thriller in its pocket and Notre Dame was left to ponder what had gone wrong. "I told the players after the game, the greatest single reason for remorse in this world is lost opportunities," Irish coach Lou Holtz said later. "That applies to football, and that applies to life."

STADIUM Boston College's on-campus facility has been called Alumni Stadium ever since a simple, basic structure was built near the current middle campus in 1915. In 1957, the school opened a brand-new Alumni Stadium that seated 26,000 fans. Lights were added in 1971, and three expansions have brought the facility to its current capacity of 44,500. Before the stadium grew to sufficient size, the Eagles had played some home games at the former Foxboro Stadium, and in the 1930s and 1940s they often played important games at Fenway Park and Braves Field.

RIVAL The first warning shot came in 1941, when Notre Dame lured Leahy home a few weeks after the high-water mark in BC's history. Boston College and Notre Dame wouldn't meet until 1975, when they faced off in a nationally televised Monday night matchup won by the Fighting Irish, 17-3. Eight years later they would meet again, in the Liberty Bowl, with the Irish claiming a 19-18 victory. The rivalry wouldn't really gain momentum until 1992, when the only two Catholic colleges still playing Division I-A football began to play each other every year, and it reached an apex with BC's 41-39 toppling of No. 1-ranked Notre Dame in 1993. From that moment through 2004, BC was 7–5 against the Fighting Irish, highlighted by another kneecapping of a Notre Dame team with national title aspirations, on Nov. 2, 2002. The Irish entered the game as winners of the first eight games of the brief Tyrone Willingham era and were ranked fourth, but the Eagles dominated them, 14-7, in front of 80,935, the biggest crowd to ever see a game at Notre Dame Stadium. "Our players took that attendance figure as a sign that Boston College has arrived," BC coach Tom O'Brien said afterward. No one in New England or South Bend was eager to disagree.

NICKNAME The Eagle was born in 1920, when Rev. Edward McLaughlin, angered at a Boston newspaper cartoon depicting BC's track team as a cat licking clean a plate of its rivals, wrote an impassioned letter to The Heights, BC's student newspaper. "It is important

that we adopt a mascot to preside at our powwows and triumphant feats," the priest wrote. "And why not the Eagle, symbolic of majesty, power and freedom? Its natural habitat is the high places. Surely the Heights is made to order for such a selection." And so it was.

MASCOT The national attention that followed Father McLaughlin's letter brought gifts of two live mascots, one each from Texas and New Mexico, but neither stayed very long—one escaped and the other broke its beak trying. For the next 40 years, the official mascot was a stuffed and mounted golden eagle, which was kept in the school's athletic office. In 1961, the school acquired a 10-pound baby eagle and dubbed her Margo, a combination of maroon and gold, the school colors. For five years, the bird traveled between the Franklin Park Zoo and football stadiums all over the East, before succumbing to a viral infection before the Navy game in 1966. Thereafter, hastened by a new respect for the eagle's status as an endangered species, BC opted to go with a costumed person rather than the genuine article.

UNIFORMS A committee of students led by T.J. Hurley (Class of 1885), who also composed BC's fight song and alma mater, was appointed in the mid-1880s to select school colors. After considering the hues of rival Jesuit schools such as Holy Cross (purple), Fordham (maroon) and Georgetown (blue and gray), the committee selected two of the Papal colors, maroon and gold. As soon as the student body supported the recommendation, those became the colors of choice for all BC sports teams, and remain so today.

QUOTE "I'd like to think that my story is the kind of story that makes kids believe they can really be whatever they want to be, that it isn't just the stuff of fairy tales. And I'd like to think that kids will always look at Boston College as the kind of school where you can make those dreams come true." — Doug Flutie

BOSTON COLLEGE ANNUAL STATISTICAL LEADERS

YR	RUSHING	YDS	ATT	AVG	PASSING	ATT	CMP	PCT	YDS	RECEIVING	REC	YDS	AVG
1965	Brendan McCarthy	901	189	4.8	Ed Foley	120	57	.48	979	Charlie Smith	18	315	17.5
1966	Brendan McCarthy	585	139	4.2	Joe Marzetti	126	36	.29	549	Jim Kavanagh	17	282	16.6
1967	Brendan McCarthy	574	152	3.8	Joe Divito	159	69	.43	964	Barry Gallup	30	433	14.4
1968	Dave Bennett	804	156	5.2	Frank Harris	186	106	.57	1,398	Barry Gallup	46	735	16.0
1969	Fred Willis	610	128	4.8	Frank Harris	228	121	.53	1,562	Jim Catone	28	281	10.0
1970	Fred Willis	1,007	223	4.5	Frank Harris	241	139	.58	1,595	John Bonistalli	35	455	13.0
1971	Tom Bougus	1,058	199	5.3	Ray Rippman	192	88	.46	1,214	Ed Rideout	27	430	15.9
1972	Mike Esposito	930	182	5.1	Gary Marangi	248	117	.47	1,381	Mel Briggs	42	620	14.8
1973	Mike Esposito	1,289	254	5.1	Gary Marangi	169	102	.60	1,114	Dave Zumbach	41	509	12.4
1974	Keith Barnette	1,097	233	4.7	Mike Kruczek	151	104	.69	1,275	Dave Zumbach	43	557	13.0
1975	Keith Barnette	958	199	4.8	Mike Kruczek	164	107	.65	1,132	Mike Godbolt	30	354	11.8
1976	Glen Capriola	1,003	240	4.2	Ken Smith	119	59	.50	800	Dave Zumbach	24	354	14.8
1977	Dan Conway	613	137	4.5	Ken Smith	257	149	.58	2,073	Mike Godbolt	34	711	20.9
1978	Anthony Brown	748	162	4.6	Jay Palazola	152	71	.47	926	Paul McCarty	36	531	14.8
1979	Dan Conway	856	196	4.4	Jay Palazola	144	55	.38	747	Rob Rikard	24	603	25.1
1980	Shelby Gamble	702	181	3.9	John Loughery	225	94	.42	1,519	Tim Sherwin	29	371	12.8
1981	Leo Smith	403	88	4.6	Doug Flutie	192	105	.55	1,652	Brian Brennan	37	726	19.6
1982	Troy Stradford	606	109	5.6	Doug Flutie	348	162	.47	2,749	Scott Nizolek	39	658	16.9
1983	Troy Stradford	810	145	5.6	Doug Flutie	345	177	.51	2,724	Brian Brennan	66	1,149	17.4
1984	Troy Stradford	666	146	4.6	Doug Flutie	386	233	.60	3,454	Gerard Phelan	64	971	15.2
1985	Ken Bell	583	150	3.9	Shawn Halloran	423	234	.55	2,935	Kelvin Martin	49	958	19.6
1986	Troy Stradford	1,188	218	5.4	Shawn Halloran	258	159	.62	2,090	Kelvin Martin	41	545	13.3
1987	Jim Bell	1,015	213	4.8	Mike Power	233	133	.57	2,071	Darren Flutie	48	786	16.4
1988	Mike Sanders	424	81	5.2	Mark Kamphaus	158	100	.63	1,323	Tom Waddle	70	902	12.9
1989	Mike Sanders	707	153	4.6	Willie Hicks	148	70	.47	1,219	Mark Chmura	47	522	11.1
1990	Mike Sanders	317	88	3.6	Glenn Foley	349	182	.52	2,189	Mark Chmura	47	560	11.9
1991	Darnell Campbell	654	128	5.1	Glenn Foley	298	153	.51	2,222	Mark Chmura	43	587	13.7
1992	Chuckie Dukes	1,387	238	5.8	Glenn Foley	265	146	.55	2,231	Pete Mitchell	40	555	13.9
1993	Darnell Campbell	1,078	221	4.9	Glenn Foley	363	222	.61	3,397	Pete Mitchell	66	818	12.4
1994	David Green	1,018	199	5.1	Mark Hartsell	257	159	.62	1,864	Pete Mitchell	55	617	11.2
1995	Mike Cloud	626	102	6.1	Mark Hartsell	349	189	.54	1,888	Steve Everson	42	557	13.3
1996	Omari Walker	1,199	261	4.6	Matt Hasselbeck	330	171	.52	1,990	Dennis Harding	42	444	10.6
1997	Mike Cloud	886	136	6.5	Matt Hasselbeck	305	188	.62	2,239	Dennis Harding	29	432	14.9
1998	Mike Cloud	1,726	308	5.6	Scott Mutryn	286	171	.60	2,218	Anthony DiCosmo	47	804	17.1
1999	Cedric Washington	1,122	222	5.1	Tim Hasselbeck	260	145	.56	1,940	Dedrick Dewalt	38	604	15.9
2000	William Green	1,164	187	6.2	Tim Hasselbeck	229	124	.54	1,810	Dedrick Dewalt	38	676	17.8
2001	William Green	1,559	265	5.9	Brian St. Pierre	279	149	.53	2,016	Dedrick Dewalt	37	539	14.6
2002	Derrick Knight	1,432	259	5.5	Brian St. Pierre	407	237	.58	2,983	Keith Hemmings	41	559	13.6
2003	Derrick Knight	1,721	321	5.4	Quinton Porter	250	140	.56	1,764	Grant Adams	46	720	15.7
2004	Andre Callendar	637	138	4.6	Paul Peterson	355	221	.62	2,594	Grant Adams	52	745	14.3

Receiving leaders by receptions
All statistics include postseason

BOSTON COLLEGE ALL-TIME SCORES

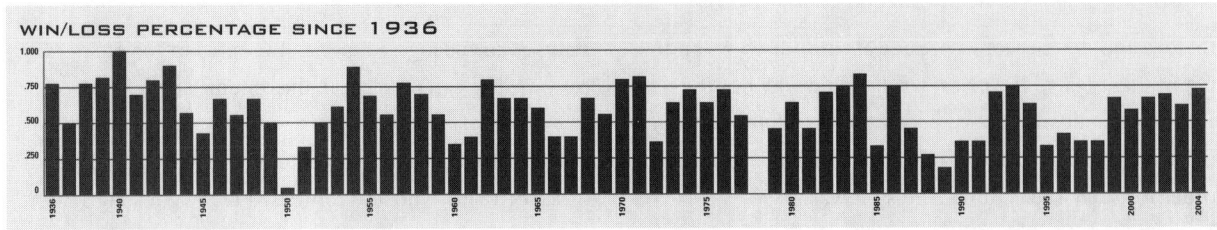

WIN/LOSS PERCENTAGE SINCE 1936

JOSEPH DRUM
1893 (.500)   3-3

1893   3-3-0

U	●	St. John's *Unk*	4	0
O4		MIT	0	6
U		Newton Independent *Unk*	0	10
U	●	Somerville H.S *Unk*	10	6
U		West Roxbury H. S. *Unk*	0	6
U	●	Boston U. *Unk*	10	6

WILLIAM NAGLE
1894 (.143)   1-6

1894   1-6-0

U		St. Anslems *Unk*	0	22
U		Andover *Unk*	0	32
U		St. Anslems *Unk*	0	10
U	●	Marlboro AC *Unk*	16	0
U		Whitman AC *Unk*	0	6
U		Brockton YMCA *Unk*	4	12
U		Boston U. *Unk*	0	28

JOSEPH LAWLESS
1895 (.375)   2-4-2

1895   2-4-2

O2		Andover *Unk*	0	22
O5		Campello *Unk*	10	28
O8		Tufts *Unk*	0	28
U	=	Hyde Park *Unk*	6	6
U	=	Whittman AC *Unk*	0	0
N9	●	Fitchburg *Unk*	6	0
U	●	Marlboro *Unk*	14	0
N28		Boston U. *Unk*	0	2

FRANK CARNEY
1896 (.714)   5-2

1896   5-2-0

O10		at Campello	0	24
U	●	Andover *Unk*	14	6
U	●	Exeter *Unk*	8	0
U		Tufts *Unk*	8	22
N14	●	at Holy Cross	6	2
N26	●	Boston U. *Unk*	10	0
N27		Holy Cross *Unk*	8	6 #

JOHN DUNLOP
1897-99, 1901 (.500) 16-16-2

1897   4-3-0

U	●	Campello *Unk*	14	4
O6		Tufts	0	12
O23		at Holy Cross	4	10
U	●	Whittman HS *Unk*	14	4
U	●	Harvard Law *Unk*	6	0
U		Exeter *Unk*	4	10
N25	●	Holy Cross *Bos*	12	0

1898   2-5-1

U		Exeter *Unk*	0	18
U		Newton AA *Unk*	0	5
O22		at Tufts	5	6
O26		Brown	0	6
U	●	Campello *Unk*	6	0
N5	=	at Holy Cross	0	0
N5		MIT	0	6
N24	●	Holy Cross *Bos*	11	0

1899   8-1-1

U	●	Exeter *Unk*	2	0
U	=	Bates *Unk*	0	0
O14	●	at MIT	24	0
U	●	Newton AA *Unk*	6	0
U	●	Andover *Unk*	6	0
U	●	New Hampshire AC *Unk*	6	0
O28	●	at Amherst	18	0
U	●	All College *Unk*	6	0
N18		at Brown	0	18
N30	●	Holy Cross	17	0

1900
NO TEAM

1901
1901   2-7-0

S28		at Brown	0	12
O9		at Dartmouth	0	45
O12		Bates	0	6
O19	●	Exeter	11	0
O26	●	New Hampshire	17	0
N9		Tufts	0	12
N16		at Holy Cross	0	11
N23		at Andover	0	11
N28		at Massachusetts	0	11

ARTHUR WHITE
1902 (.000)   0-9

1902   0-9-0

S20		Tufts	0	6
S27		Wesleyan	6	16
O4		Massachusetts	0	30
O18		at Bates	5	17
O25		Andover	0	24
N1		New Hampshire	6	10
N8		at Exeter	0	29
N15		at Tufts	0	26
N22		Holy Cross	0	22

1903-1907
NO TEAM

JOE REILLY / JOE KENNEY
1908 (.375)   2-4-2

1908   2-4-2

U		Bridgewater *Unk*	10	12
O17	=	St. Anselm *Unk*	0	0
U		Dean Academy *Unk*	0	18
O31		at New Hampshire	0	18
U	=	Connecticut *Unk*	0	0
U	●	Coll. Of Osteopathy *Unk*	9	0
N14	●	St. Anselm *Unk*	11	0
N26		Alumni *Unk*	0	6

CHARLES McCARTHY
1909 (.438)   3-4-1

1909   3-4-1

U		St. Alphon *Unk*	0	6
U		Andover *Unk*	0	10
O16		at Rhodes Island	0	9
O23		at New Hampshire	6	11
U	●	Coll. Of Osteopathy. *Unk*	35	0
N6	=	St. Anselm *Unk*	6	6
U	●	Connecticut *Unk*	17	0
N20	●	St. Anselm *Unk*	7	0

JIM HART
1910 (.167)   0-4-2

1910   0-4-2

O1		at New Hampshire	0	11
U		Andover *Unk*	0	11
U	=	Cushing Acad. *Unk*	5	5
O29		Holy Cross	3	34
U		at Dean Acad. *Unk*	8	12
U	=	Connecticut *Unk*	0	0

JOSEPH COURTNEY
1911 (.000)   0-7

1911   0-7-0

S23		Holy Cross	5	13
O14		at Colby	0	18
O21		at New Hampshire	0	12
U		Cushing Coll. *Unk*	0	17
U		Dean Acad. *Unk*	0	6
N11		Rhode Island	0	25
N30		St. Anselm	3	6

WILLIAM JOY
1912-13 (.467)   6-7-2

1912   2-4-1

U		Fordham *Unk*	0	14
O12		at Massachusetts	0	42
U		Colby *Unk*	0	55
U	=	Cushing *Unk*	6	6
U		Dean Acad. *Unk*	7	40
U	●	Connecticut *Unk*	13	0
N28	●	at St. Anselm	7	0

1913   4-3-1

S20		at Maine	0	6
O4		Springfield	6	27
O11		at Holy Cross	0	13
O18	●	at St. Anselm	19	0
N1	●	Worcester Tech	40	0
N8	=	at Fordham	27	27
N15	●	Rhode Island	27	0
N22	●	Connecticut	47	0

STEPHEN MAHONEY
1914-15 (.500)   8-8

1914   5-4-0

O3		at Maine	6	27
O10	●	at Rhode Island	21	0
O17		Bowdoin	0	20
O24	●	at New Hampshire	20	3
O31	●	Norwich	28	6
N7	●	St. Anselm	27	0
N14		at Holy Cross	0	10
N21		at Fordham	3	14
N26	●	Catholic U.	14	0

1915   3-4-0

O9		at Bowdoin	0	14
O16		at Maine	0	14
O23		at Tufts	0	26
O30		Holy Cross	0	9
N6	●	Fordham	3	0
N13		at Connecticut	7	6
N26	●	Norwich	35	0

CHARLES BRICKLEY
1916-17 (.750)   12-4

1916   6-2-0

S23		Neponset Wanderers	16	0
S30		at Dartmouth	6	32
O12	●	New Hampshire	19	0
O21		at Tufts	0	13
O28	●	at Trinity	21	7
N4	●	Rhode Island	39	0
N18	●	Worcester Tech	49	0
D2	●	Holy Cross *Bos*	17	14

1917   6-2-0

S29	●	Norwich	26	0
O6	●	Naval Reserves	40	0
O12	●	Tufts	20	0
O20		at Brown	2	7
N3	●	Rhode Island	48	0
N10	●	Holy Cross *Bos*	34	6
N17	●	Middlebury	31	6
N24		at Army	7	13

FRANK MORRISSEY
1918 (.714)   5-2

1918   5-2-0

O26	●	Camp Devens	13	0
N2	●	Norwich	6	0
N9	●	Camp Bumpkin	38	7
N16		Fordham *Bos*	0	14
N23		at Harvard	6	14
N30	●	Tufts	54	0
D7	●	Minneola Aviators	25	0

FRANK CAVANAUGH
1919-26 (.754)   48-14-5

1919   5-3-0

S27	●	U.S.S. Utah	22	0
O4		at Harvard	0	17
O11	●	Middlebury	25	0
O18	●	at Yale	5	3
O25		at Army	0	13
N8		Rutgers	7	13
N15	●	Holy Cross *Bos*	9	7
N29	●	Georgetown	10	9

1920   8-0-0

O9	●	Fordham	20	0
O16	●	at Yale	21	13
O30	●	at Springfield	12	0
N6	●	Boston U.	34	0
N13	●	Tufts	17	0
N20	●	Marietta	13	3
N27	●	at Georgetown	30	0
D2	●	Holy Cross *Bos*	14	0

1921   4-3-1

O1	●	Boston U.	13	0
O8	●	Providence	25	0
O15	●	Baylor *Dal*	23	7
O22		Detroit	0	28
O29	=	at Fordham	0	0
N5	●	Marietta	14	0
N19	●	at Georgetown	10	14
N26	●	Holy Cross *Bos*	0	41

1922   6-2-0

O7	●	Boston U.	20	6
O14	●	Fordham *Bos*	27	0
O21	●	at Detroit	8	10
O28		Lafayette	0	19
N4	●	Villanova	15	3
N11	●	Baylor	33	0
N18	●	Canisius	13	7
N25	=	Georgetown	0	0
D2	●	Holy Cross *Bos*	17	13

1923   7-1-1

S29	●	Providence	28	0
O12	●	Fordham *Bos*	20	0
O20	●	Canisius	21	0
O27		Marquette	6	7
N3	●	Georgetown	21	0
N10	●	Centenary	14	0
N17	●	Villanova	41	0
N24	=	Vermont	0	0
D1	●	Holy Cross *Bos*	16	7

1924   6-3-0

S27	●	Providence	47	0
O13	●	Fordham *Bos*	28	0
O18		at Syracuse	0	10
O25	●	Allegheny	13	0
N1	●	Haskell	34	7
N8	●	Marquette	34	7
N15	●	Centenary *Bos*	9	10
N22	●	Vermont	33	7
N29	●	Holy Cross *Bos*	0	33

1925   6-2-0

O3	●	Catholic U.	6	0
O12	●	Haskell	7	6
O17	●	Boston U.	54	7
O24	●	Allegheny	14	7
O31	●	Providence	51	0
N7	●	West Virginia *Bos*	0	21
N14	●	Wesleyan	6	7
N28	●	Holy Cross *Bos*	16	6

1926 — 6-0-2

O2	●	Catholic U.	28	0
O12	●	Fordham *Bos*	27	0
O23	●	at St. Louis	61	0
O30	●	W. V. Wesleyan	27	6
N6	●	Villanova	19	7
N13	=	Haskell	21	21
N20	●	Gettysburg	39	0
N27	=	Holy Cross *Bos*	0	0

D. LEO DALEY
1927 (.500) 4-4

1927 — 4-4-0

O1		Duke	9	25
O12		Geneva	0	13
O22	●	W. V. Wesleyan	33	0
O29	●	at Fordham	27	7
N5		Villanova *Bos*	7	13
N12		Georgetown	0	47
N19	●	at Connecticut	19	0
N29	●	Holy Cross *Bos*	6	0

JOE McKENNEY
1928-34 (.700) 44-18-3

1928 — 9-0-0

S29	●	Catholic U.	38	6
O6	●	at Navy	6	0
O12	●	Duke	19	0
O27	●	Boston U.	27	7
N3	●	Manhattan	60	6
N12	●	Fordham	19	7
N17	●	Canisius	24	0
N24	●	Connecticut St.	51	13
D1	●	Holy Cross *Bos*	19	0

1929 — 7-2-1

S23	●	Catholic U.	13	6
O5	●	Maine	42	0
O12	=	Villanova *Bos*	7	7
O19	●	at Dayton	23	7
O26	●	Canisius	40	6
N2	●	Duke	20	12
N9		Fordham	6	7
N16		at Marquette	6	20
N23	●	Boston U.	33	0
N30	●	Holy Cross *Bos*	12	0

1930 — 5-5-0

S27	●	Catholic U.	54	7
O6	●	Quantico Marines	13	7
O13		Fordham	0	3
O18		at Villanova	0	7
O25	●	Dayton	15	6
N1		Marquette	0	6
N8		Georgetown	19	20
N14	●	at Loyola-Chicago	19	0
N22	●	Boston U.	47	0
N29		Holy Cross *Bos*	0	7

1931 — 6-4-0

S26	●	Catholic U.	26	7
O3	●	Dayton *Bos*	13	0
O12		Fordham	0	20
O17		Villanova	6	12
O24		Marquette	0	7
O31	●	Georgetown	20	2
N7	●	at Western Maryland	19	13
N14	●	Centre	7	0
N21	●	Boston U.	18	6
N26		Holy Cross *Bos*	6	7

1932 — 4-2-2

O1	●	Loyola-Maryland	14	0
O12	●	Centre	6	0
O22		at Marquette	0	13
O29	●	Fordham	3	0
N5		Villanova	9	20
N11	=	Western Maryland	20	20
N19	●	Boston U.	21	6
N26	=	Holy Cross	0	0

1933 — 8-1-0

S30	●	St. Anselms	22	0
O7	●	Loyola-Chicago	37	0
O12	●	Centre	6	0
O21		at Fordham	6	32
O28	●	Boston U.	25	0
N4	●	Georgetown	39	0
N11	●	Villanova	9	0
N18	●	Western Maryland	12	9
D2	●	Holy Cross *Bos*	13	9

1934 — 5-4-0

S29	●	St. Anselm	18	6
O6	●	at Springfield	14	0
O13		Fordham	0	6
O20		at Western Maryland	0	40
O27		Providence	7	13
N3	●	Villanova	6	0
N12	●	Centre	7	0
N17	●	Boston U.	10	0
D1		Holy Cross *Bos*	2	7

DINNEY McNAMARA
1935 (.750) 3-1

HARRY DOWNES
1935 (.600) 3-2

1935 — 6-3-0

S28	●	St. Anselm	13	2
O5		at Fordham	0	19
O19	●	Michigan State	18	6
O26	●	New Hampshire	19	6
N2	●	Providence	20	6
N9		Western Maryland	6	12
N16	●	Springfield	39	0
N23	●	Boston U.	25	6
N30		Holy Cross *Bos*	6	20

GIL DOBIE
1936-38 (.685) 16-6-5

1936 — 6-1-2

O3	●	Northeastern	26	6
O12		Temple	0	14
O17	●	at New Hampshire	12	0
O24	●	Providence	26	0
O31	=	Michigan State	13	13
N7	●	North Carolina St.	7	3
N14	●	Western Maryland	12	7
N21	=	Boston U.	0	0
N28	●	at Holy Cross *Bos*	13	12

1937 — 4-4-1

S25	●	Northeastern	35	2
O2	●	Kansas State	21	7
O12	=	Temple	0	0
O23		Detroit	0	14
O30		North Carolina St.	7	12
N6	●	at Western Maryland	27	0
N13	●	Kentucky	13	0
N20		Boston U. *Bos*	6	13
N27		Holy Cross *Bos*	0	20

1938 — 6-1-2

S24	●	Canasius	63	12
S30	●	Northeastern	13	0
O12	●	Detroit	9	6
O21	=	at Temple	26	26
O29	●	Florida	33	0
N5	●	Indiana	14	0
N11	●	Boston U.	21	14
N19	=	St. Anselm	0	0
N26		Holy Cross *Bos*	7	29

FRANK LEAHY
1939-40 (.909) 20-2

1939 — 9-2-0

S30	●	Lebanon Valley	45	0
O6	●	St. Josephs	20	6
O12		Florida	0	7
O21	●	Temple	19	0
O28	●	St. Anselm	28	0
N4	●	Auburn	13	7
N11	●	at Detroit	20	13
N18	●	Boston U. *Bos*	19	0
N25	●	Kansas State	38	7
D2	●	Holy Cross	14	0
		COTTON BOWL		
J1		Clemson	3	6

1940 — 11-0-0

S21	●	Centre	40	0
S28	●	at Tulane	27	7
O12	●	Temple	33	20
O19	●	Idaho	60	0
O26	●	St. Anselm *Bos*	55	0
N2	●	Manhattan	25	0
N9	●	Boston U. *Bos*	21	0
N16	●	Georgetown	19	18
N23	●	Auburn	33	7
N30	●	Holy Cross	7	0
		SUGAR BOWL		
J1	●	Tennessee	19	13

DENNY MYERS
1941-42, '46-50 (.561) 35-27-4

1941 — 7-3-0

S20	●	St. Anselm	78	0
S27		at Tulane	7	21
O11		Clemson	13	26
O18	●	Manhattan	26	13
O25	●	Georgetown	14	6
N1	●	Temple	31	0
N8	●	Wake Forest	26	6
N15		Tennessee	7	14
N22	●	Boston U.	19	7
N29	●	Holy Cross *Bos*	14	13

1942 — 8-2-0

O3	●	West Virginia	33	0
O10	●	Clemson	14	7
O17	●	N.C. Pre-Flight	7	6
O25	●	Wake Forest	27	0
O31	●	Georgetown	47	0
N7	●	Temple	28	0
N14	●	Fordham	56	6
N21	●	Boston U. *Bos*	37	0
N28		Holy Cross *Bos*	12	55
		ORANGE BOWL		
J1		Alabama	21	37

MOODY SARNO
1943-45 (.605) 11-7-1

1943 — 4-0-1

O16	●	B.C. Army Training *Unk*	7	0
O23	●	Camp Hingham *Unk*	42	6
O30	●	Brooklyn *Unk*	37	6
N6	●	Rome Air Field *Unk*	64	0
N13	=	at Harvard	6	6

1944 — 4-3-0

O7		at Harvard	0	13
O13	●	CCNY	33	0
O20	●	NYU *Bos*	41	13
O28	●	Syracuse	19	12
N4		Melville PT	0	45
N12	●	Brooklyn	24	21
N26		Holy Cross *Bos*	14	30

1945 — 3-4-0

S29	●	Squantum NAS	13	0
O6		at Brown	6	51
O12	●	NYU *Bos*	28	0
O27		Merchant Marines *Bos*	20	33
N10		Villanova *Phil*	0	41
N17	●	Scranton	12	0
N25		Holy Cross *Bos*	0	46

DENNY MYERS

1946 — 6-3-0

S27		Wake Forest	6	12
O5	●	at Michigan State	34	20
O12	●	Merchant Marines *Bos*	56	7
O25	●	Villanova	14	12
N2	●	NYU *NYC*	72	6
N9	●	Georgetown	20	13
N16		Tennessee	13	33
N23	●	Alabama	13	7
N30		Holy Cross *Bos*	6	13

1947 — 5-4-0

S26	●	Clemson	32	22
O10	●	Kansas State	49	13
O17		LSU	13	14
O24	●	Villanova	6	0
N1	●	Georgetown	27	6
N8		Wake Forest	13	14
N15		at Tennessee	13	38
N22	●	Saint Mary's-Cal	25	7
N29		Holy Cross *Bos*	6	20

1948 — 5-2-2

S24	●	Wake Forest	26	9
O1	●	at Georgetown	13	6
O9	=	St. Bonaventure	7	7
O15	●	Villanova	20	13
O23		Mississippi *Mem*	13	32
O29		Clemson	19	26
N13	=	William & Mary	14	14
N20	●	Saint Mary's-Cal	19	7
N27	●	Holy Cross *Bos*	21	20

1949 — 4-4-1

S23		Oklahoma	0	46
S30	●	Wake Forest	13	7
O8		at Penn State	14	32
O14	=	Mississippi	25	25
O21		Georgetown	7	10
O28		Villanova	14	28
N5	●	at Clemson	40	27
N12	●	Fordham *Bos*	20	12
N26	●	Holy Cross *Bos*	76	0

1950 — 0-9-1

S22	=	Wake Forest	7	7
S30		at Oklahoma	0	28
O7		at Mississippi	0	54
O13		Fordham *Bos*	6	26
O20		Georgetown	10	20
O27		Georgia	7	19
N4		Penn State	13	20
N11		Clemson	14	35
N18		Villanova	7	29
D2		Holy Cross *Bos*	14	32

MIKE HOLOVAK
1951-59 (.623) 49-29-3

1951 — 3-6-0

S21		Wake Forest	6	20
O5		Mississippi *Mem*	7	34
O12		Fordham	19	35
O19		Detroit	13	19
O27		at Georgia	28	35
N2	●	Richmond	21	7
N10		at Clemson	2	21
N17	●	Villanova	20	13
D1	●	Holy Cross *Bos*	19	14

1952 — 4-4-1

S26	●	Richmond	14	7
O4	=	Wake Forest *W-S*	7	7
O10	●	Drake	20	14
O17		Villanova	7	28
O24	●	Fordham	14	13
O31		Clemson	0	13
N7	●	at Detroit	23	20
N15		Xavier	0	6
N28		Holy Cross *Bos*	7	21

1953 — 5-3-1

S26	=	Clemson	14	14
O3		at LSU	6	42
O11		Villanova	7	15
O16	●	Fordham *NYC*	20	13
O25	●	at Xavier	31	14
O31		Richmond	0	14
N7	●	Wake Forest	20	7
N15	●	Detroit	33	20
N28	●	Holy Cross *Bos*	6	0

1954 — 8-1-0

S25	●	at Detroit	12	7
O2	●	at Temple	12	9
O9	●	VMI	44	0
O16	●	at Fordham	21	7
O23	●	Springfield	42	6
O31		Xavier	14	19
N5	●	at Marquette	13	7
N13	●	Boston U.	7	6
N27	●	Holy Cross *Bos*	31	13

1955 — 5-2-1

S24	●	Brandeis	27	0
O8	●	Villanova	28	14
O15	●	Detroit	23	0
O21	=	Marquette	13	13
O29		at Xavier	12	19
N4		at Miami, Fla.	7	14
N12	●	at Boston U.	40	12
N26	●	Holy Cross *Bos*	26	7

1956 — 5-4-0

O5		at Miami, Fla.	6	27
O13	●	at Marquette	26	19
O20	●	at Rutgers	32	0
O28		at Detroit	7	12
N2	●	Villanova	7	6
N10		Quantico Marines	6	20
N18	●	Boston U.	13	0
N24	●	Brandeis	52	0
D6		Holy Cross *Bos*	0	7

THE SCHOOLS

1957 (7-2-0)

S21		Navy	6 46
S28	•	Florida State	20 7
O5	•	Quantico Marines	13 7
O12	•	Dayton	41 14
O19	•	Villanova	12 9
O26	•	at Detroit	20 16
N9	•	at Boston U.	27 2
N16	•	Marquette	19 14
N30	•	at Holy Cross	0 14

1958 (7-3-0)

S20	•	Scranton	48 0
S27	•	at Syracuse	14 24
O4	•	Villanova	19 21
O18	•	at Marquette	21 13
O25	•	Miami, Fla.	6 2
N1	•	Pacific	25 12
N8	•	Detroit	40 0
N15	•	Boston U.	18 13
N22	•	at Clemson	12 34
D6	•	Holy Cross	26 8

1959 (5-4-0)

S19	•	Navy	8 24
S26	•	at Army	8 44
O10	•	Villanova	39 6
O17	•	Dartmouth	35 12
O25	•	Marquette	16 0
O30	•	at Detroit	21 9
N7	•	Pittsburgh	14 22
N14	•	at Boston U.	7 26
N29	•	at Holy Cross	14 0

ERNIE HEFFERLE 1960-61 (.375)   7-12-1

1960 (3-6-1)

S17	•	Navy	7 22
S24	•	at Army	7 20
O8	•	at Marquette	12 13
O15	•	Detroit	17 19
O22	=	VMI	14 14
O28	•	at Miami, Fla.	7 10
N5	•	at Villanova	20 6
N12	•	Boston U.	23 14
N19	•	Clemson	25 14
N26	•	Holy Cross	12 16

1961 (4-6-0)

S23	•	Cincinnati	23 0
S30	•	at Northwestern	0 45
O7	•	at Houston	0 21
O13	•	at Detroit	3 20
O21	•	Villanova	22 6
N4	•	Iowa State	14 10
N11	•	at Texas Tech	6 14
N18	•	at Boston U.	10 7
N25	•	Syracuse	13 28
D2	•	at Holy Cross	26 38

JIM MILLER 1962-67 (.586)   34-24

1962 (8-2-0)

S22	•	Detroit	27 0
S29	•	at Villanova	28 13
O6	•	VMI	18 0
O13	•	at Syracuse	0 12
O20	•	Navy	6 26
O27	•	Houston	14 0
N3	•	at Vanderbilt	27 22
N10	•	Texas Tech	42 13
N17	•	Boston U.	41 25
D1	•	Holy Cross	48 12

1963 (6-3-0)

S21	•	at Syracuse	21 32
S28	•	Wichita St.	22 16
O4	•	at Detroit	20 12
O12	•	Villanova	34 0
O26	•	at Air Force	7 34
N2	•	Vanderbilt	19 6
N9	•	Buffalo	15 0
N16	•	Virginia	30 21
N30	•	at Holy Cross	0 9

1964 (6-3-0)

S19	•	Syracuse	21 14
S26	•	at Army	13 19
O10	•	at Tennessee	14 16
O17	•	Cincinnati	10 0
O24	•	Air Force	13 7
N7	•	at Villanova	8 7
N13	•	at Miami, Fla.	6 30
N21	•	Detroit	17 9
N28	•	Holy Cross	10 8

1965 (6-4-0)

S18	•	Buffalo	18 6
S25	•	Villanova	28 0
O2	•	at Army	0 10
O9	•	Penn State	0 17
O23	•	Richmond	38 7
O30	•	VMI	41 12
N5	•	at Miami, Fla.	6 27
N13	•	William & Mary	30 17
N20	•	at Syracuse	13 21
N27	•	at Holy Cross	35 0

1966 (4-6-0)

S17	•	at Navy	7 27
S24	•	Ohio U.	14 23
O1	•	VMI	14 0
O8	•	at Penn State	21 30
O15	•	Syracuse	0 30
O22	•	Buffalo	22 21
N5	•	William & Mary	15 13
N12	•	at Villanova	0 19
N19	•	at Massachusetts	14 7
N26	•	Holy Cross	26 32

1967 (4-6-0)

S23	•	at Villanova	27 24
S30	•	at Army	10 21
O14	•	Penn State	28 50
O21	•	Buffalo	14 26
O28	•	Maine	56 0
N4	•	at Cincinnati	21 27
N11	•	VMI	13 26
N18	•	Syracuse	20 32
N25	•	Massachusetts	25 0
D2	•	at Holy Cross	13 6

JOE YUKICA 1968-77 (.648)   68-37

1968 (6-3-0)

S28	•	at Navy	49 15
O5	•	Buffalo	31 12
O12	•	Villanova	28 15
O19	•	at Tulane	14 28
O26	•	Penn State	0 29
N9	•	at Army	25 58
N16	•	VMI	45 13
N23	•	at Massachusetts	21 6
N30	•	Holy Cross	40 20

1969 (5-4-0)

S27	•	Navy	21 14
O4	•	Tulane	28 24
O18	•	Villanova	6 24
O25	•	at Army	7 38
N1	•	at Penn State	16 38
N8	•	Buffalo	21 35
N15	•	VMI	49 32
N22	•	Massachusetts	35 30
N29	•	at Syracuse	35 10

1970 (8-2-0)

S19	•	at Villanova	28 21
S26	•	at Navy	28 14
O3	•	VMI	56 3
O10	•	Penn State	3 28
O24	•	at Air Force	10 35
O31	•	Army	21 13
N7	•	Buffalo	65 12
N14	•	at Pittsburgh	21 6
N21	•	at Massachusetts	21 10
N28	•	Holy Cross	54 0

1971 (9-2-0)

S11	•	at West Virginia	14 45
S18	•	at Temple	17 3
S25	•	Navy	49 6
O2	•	at Richmond	24 0
O9	•	Villanova	23 7
O16	•	at Texas Tech	6 14
O23	•	Pittsburgh	40 22
N6	•	at Syracuse	10 3
N13	•	Northern Illinois	20 10
N20	•	Massachusetts	35 0
N27	•	Holy Cross Fox	21 7

1972 (4-7-0)

S16	•	Tulane	0 10
S23	•	Temple	49 27
S30	•	at Navy	20 27
O7	•	at Villanova	21 20
O14	•	Air Force	9 13
O21	•	at Pittsburgh	20 35
N4	•	Syracuse	37 0
N11	•	at Georgia Tech	10 42
N18	•	Penn State	26 45
N25	•	at Massachusetts	7 28
D2	•	Holy Cross	41 11

1973 (7-4-0)

S15	•	Temple	45 0
S22	•	at Tulane	16 21
S29	•	at Texas A&M	32 24
O6	•	Navy	44 7
O12	•	at Miami, Fla.	10 15
O20	•	Pittsburgh	14 28
O27	•	Villanova	11 7
N10	•	at West Virginia	25 13
N17	•	at Syracuse	13 24
N24	•	Massachusetts	59 14
D1	•	at Holy Cross	42 21

1974 (8-3-0)

S14	•	Texas	19 42
S28	•	at Temple	7 34
O5	•	at Navy	37 0
O12	•	William & Mary	31 16
O19	•	at Pittsburgh	11 35
O26	•	at Villanova	55 7
N2	•	West Virginia	35 3
N9	•	Tulane	27 3
N16	•	Syracuse	45 0
N23	•	at Massachusetts	70 8
N30	•	Holy Cross	38 6

1975 (7-4-0)

S15	•	Notre Dame Fox	3 17
S20	•	at Temple	27 9
S27	•	at West Virginia	18 35
O4	•	Villanova	41 12
O11	•	Tulane	7 17
O18	•	Navy	17 3
O25	•	at Syracuse	14 22
N1	•	Miami, Fla.	21 7
N8	•	at Army	31 0
N22	•	Massachusetts	24 14
N29	•	at Holy Cross	24 10

1976 (8-3-0)

S11	•	Texas	14 13
S25	•	at Tulane	27 3
O2	•	at Navy	17 13
O9		Florida State	9 28
O16	•	West Virginia	14 3
O23	•	at Army	27 10
O30	•	at Villanova	3 22
N6	•	at Miami, Fla.	6 13
N13	•	Syracuse	28 14
N20	•	at Massachusetts	35 0
N27	•	Holy Cross	59 6

1977 (6-5-0)

S10	•	at Texas	0 44
S17	•	at Tennessee	18 24
S24	•	Army	49 28
O1	•	Pittsburgh	7 45
O8	•	Tulane	30 28
O15	•	at West Virginia	28 24
O22	•	Villanova	17 0
O29	•	at Air Force	36 14
N12	•	at Syracuse	3 20
N19	•	Massachusetts	34 7
N26	•	at Holy Cross	20 35

ED CHLEBEK 1978-80 (.364)   12-21

1978 (0-11-0)

S16	•	Air Force	7 18
S23	•	Texas A&M	2 37
S30	•	Navy	8 19
O7	•	Pittsburgh	15 32
O14	•	at Tulane	3 9
N4	•	at Villanova	16 28
N11	•	at Army	26 29
N18	•	Syracuse	23 37
N25	•	at Massachusetts	0 27
D2	•	Holy Cross	29 30
D10	•	Temple Tok	24 28

1979 (5-6-0)

S15	•	Tennessee	16 28
S22	•	Villanova	34 7
S29	•	at Stanford	14 33
O6	•	at Pittsburgh	7 28
O13	•	West Virginia	18 20
O20	•	at Miami, Fla.	8 19
O27	•	at Army	29 16
N3	•	Tulane	8 43
N17	•	Syracuse Ith	27 10
N24	•	Massachusettes	41 3
D1	•	at Holy Cross	13 10

1980 (7-4-0)

S13	•	at Pittsburgh	6 14
S20	•	Stanford	30 13
S27	•	at Villanova	9 20
O4	•	at Navy	0 21
O11	•	Yale	27 9
O18	•	at Florida State	7 41
O25	•	Army	30 14
N1	•	at Air Force	23 0
N15	•	Syracuse	27 16
N22	•	at Massachusettes	13 12
N29	•	Holy Cross	27 26

JACK BICKNELL 1981-90 (.517)   59-55-1

1981 (5-6-0)

S19	•	Texas A&M	13 12
S26	•	at North Carolina	14 56
O3	•	West Virginia	10 38
O10	•	at Penn State	7 38
O17	•	Navy	10 25
O24	•	at Army	41 6
O31	•	Pittsburgh	24 29
N7	•	Massachusetts	52 22
N14	•	at Syracuse	17 27
N21	•	Rutgers	27 21
N28	•	at Holy Cross	28 24

1982 (8-3-1)

S4	•	at Texas A&M	38 16
S18	=	at Clemson	17 17
S25	•	at Navy	31 0
O2	•	Temple	17 7
O9	•	at West Virginia	13 20
O16	•	Rutgers	14 13
O23	•	at Army	32 17
O30	•	Penn State	17 52
N6	•	at Massachusetts	34 21
N13	•	Syracuse	20 13
N20	•	Holy Cross	35 10

TANGERINE BOWL

D18	•	Auburn	26 33

1983 (9-3-0)

S3	•	Morgan St.	45 12
S10	•	Clemson	31 16
S17	•	Rutgers ERut	42 22
S24	•	West Virginia	17 27
O1	•	at Temple	18 15
O8	•	at Yale	42 7
O29	•	Penn State Fox	27 17
N5	•	at Army	34 14
N12	•	at Syracuse	10 21
N19	•	Holy Cross Fox	47 7
N26	•	Alabama Fox	20 13

LIBERTY BOWL

D29	•	Notre Dame	18 19

1984 (10-2-0)

S1	•	Western Carolina	44 24
S8	•	Alabama Birm	38 31
S22	•	North Carolina	52 20
O13	•	Temple	24 10
O20	•	at West Virginia	20 21
O27	•	Rutgers	35 23
N3	•	at Penn State	30 37
N10	•	Army	45 31
N17	•	Syracuse Fox	24 16
N23	•	at Miami, Fla.	47 45
D1	•	at Holy Cross	45 10

COTTON BOWL

J1	•	Houston	45 28

1985 (4-8-0)

A29	•	Brigham Young ERut	14 28
S7	•	Temple	28 25
S14	•	Maryland Fox	13 31
S21	•	at Pittsburgh	29 22
S28	•	Miami, Fla. Fox	10 45
O5	•	Rutgers	20 10
O12	•	at Army	14 45
O19	•	West Virginia	6 13
O26	•	at Cincinnati	17 24
N2	•	at Penn State	12 16
N16	•	at Syracuse	21 41
N23	•	Holy Cross	38 7

1986 — 9-3-0

Date		Opponent		
S6		Rutgers	9	11
S13	●	California	21	15
S20		Penn State *Fox*	14	26
O4		at SMU	29	31
O11	●	at Maryland	30	25
O18	●	Louisville	41	7
O25	●	at West Virginia	19	10
N1	●	at Army	27	20
N8	●	at Temple	38	29
N15	●	Syracuse	27	9
N22	●	at Holy Cross	56	26
HALL OF FAME BOWL				
D23	●	Georgia	27	24

1987 — 5-6-0

Date		Opponent		
S5	●	TCU	38	20
S12	●	Temple	28	7
S19		at Southern Cal	17	23
S26		Penn State *Fox*	17	27
O3	●	at Pittsburgh	13	10
O10	●	Army	29	24
O17	●	at Rutgers	24	38
O24	●	West Virginia	16	37
O31	●	Tennessee	20	18
N7		at Notre Dame	25	32
N14		at Syracuse	17	45

1988 — 3-8-0

Date		Opponent		
S1		Southern Cal	7	34
S10	●	Cincinnati	41	7
S17		at Penn State	20	23
S24		at TCU	17	31
O1	●	Pittsburgh	34	31
O15	●	Rutgers	6	17
O22		at West Virginia	19	59
N5		at Tennessee	7	10
N12	●	Syracuse	20	45
N19	●	Army *Dub*	38	24
N26		at Temple	28	45

1989 — 2-9-0

Date		Opponent		
S9	●	Pittsburgh	10	29
S16	●	Rutgers *ERut*	7	9
S23		at Penn State	3	7
S30		at Ohio State	29	34
O14	●	Temple	35	14
O21	●	Navy	24	27
O28	●	West Virginia	30	44
N4		at Syracuse	11	23
N11	●	at Army	24	17
N18	●	Louisville	22	36
N25		at Georgia Tech	12	13

1990 — 4-7-0

Date		Opponent		
S8		at Pittsburgh	6	29
S15		Ohio State	10	31
S29	●	at Navy	28	17
O6	●	Rutgers	19	14
O13	●	Army	41	20
O20		Penn State	21	40
O27	●	at West Virginia	27	14
N3		Syracuse	6	35
N10		at Louisville	10	17
N17		at Miami, Fla.	12	42
N24		Temple	10	29

1991-2004 BIG EAST

TOM COUGHLIN
1991-93 (.614) 21-13-1

1991 — 4-7-0 (2-4-0)

Date		Opponent		
A31		at Rutgers	13	20
S7		Michigan	13	35
S14		Georgia Tech	14	30
S28		at Penn State	21	28
O12	●	Louisville	33	3
O19		West Virginia	24	31
O26	●	at Army	28	17
N2	●	Pittsburgh	38	12
N9	●	at Temple	33	13
N16		at Syracuse	16	38
N23		Miami, Fla.	14	19

1992 — 8-3-1 (2-1-1)

Date		Opponent		
S5	●	Rutgers	37	20
S12	●	Northwestern	49	0
S19	●	Navy	28	0
S26	●	Michigan State	14	0
O3	=	at West Virginia	24	24
O17	●	at Penn State	35	32
O24	●	at Tulane	17	13
O31	●	Temple	45	6
N7		at Notre Dame	7	54
N14		Syracuse	10	27
N21	●	at Army	41	24
HALL OF FAME BOWL				
J1		Tennessee	23	38

1993 — 9-3-0 (5-2-0)

Date		Opponent		
S4		Miami, Fla.	7	23
S18		at Northwestern	21	22
S25	●	Temple	66	14
O2		at Syracuse	33	29
O9		Rutgers *ERut*	31	21
O23		Army	41	14
O30	●	Tulane	42	14
N6	●	Virginia Tech	48	34
N13		at Pittsburgh		330
N20	●	at Notre Dame	41	39
N27		West Virginia	14	17
CARQUEST BOWL				
J1		Virginia	31	13

DAN HENNING
1994-96 (.458) 16-19-1

1994 — 7-4-1 (3-3-1)

Date		Opponent		
S3		at Michigan	26	34
S17		Virginia Tech	7	12
S24	●	at Pittsburgh	21	9
O8	●	Notre Dame	30	11
O15	●	Temple	45	28
O22	=	Rutgers	7	7
O29	●	at Army	30	3
N3		at Louisville	35	14
N12	●	Syracuse	31	0
N19		at West Virginia	20	21
N26		at Miami, Fla.	7	23
ALOHA BOWL				
D25	●	Kansas State	12	7

1995 — 4-8-0 (4-3-0)

Date		Opponent		
A27		Ohio State *ERut*	6	38
S7	●	at Virginia Tech	20	14
S16		Michigan	13	23
S30		at Michigan State	21	25
O7	●	Pittsburgh	17	0
O14	●	West Virginia	19	31
O21		Army	7	49
O28	●	at Notre Dame	10	20
N4	●	at Temple	10	9
N11		Miami, Fla.	14	17
N18	●	at Syracuse	29	58
N24	●	at Rutgers	41	38

1996 — 5-7 (2-5)

Date		Opponent		
A31	●	at Hawaii	24	21
S14		Virginia Tech	7	45
S21		at Michigan	14	20
S28	●	Navy	43	38
O5		at West Virginia	17	34
O12	●	at Cincinnati	24	17
O19	●	Rutgers	37	13
O26		Syracuse	17	45
O31		at Pittsburgh	13	20
N9		Notre Dame	21	48
N16	●	Temple	21	20
N23		at Miami, Fla.	26	43

TOM O'BRIEN
1997-Present (.594) 57-39

1997 — 4-7 (3-4)

Date		Opponent		
S6		at Temple	21	28
S13	●	West Virginia	31	24
S20	●	at Rutgers	35	21
S27		Cincinnati	6	24
O4		Georgia Tech	14	42
O11	●	at Virginia Tech	7	17
O18		Miami, Fla.	44	45
O25		at Notre Dame	20	52
N1	●	Pittsburgh	22	21
N8		at Syracuse	13	20
N22	●	Army	24	20

1998 — 4-7 (3-4)

Date		Opponent		
S5	●	at Georgia Tech	41	31
S12	●	Rutgers	41	14
S19	●	Temple	31	7
S26		at Louisville	28	52
O8		Virginia Tech	0	17
O17		Syracuse	25	42
O24		Navy	31	32
O31		at Miami, Fla.	17	35
N7		Notre Dame	26	31
N14	●	at Pittsburgh	23	15
N21		at West Virginia	10	35

1999 — 8-4 (4-3-0)

Date		Opponent		
S4	●	Baylor	30	29
S18	●	at Navy	14	10
S25	●	at Rutgers	27	7
O2	●	Northeastern	33	22
O9		at Temple	14	24
O16	●	Pittsburgh	20	16
O23		Miami, Fla.	28	31
O30	●	at Syracuse	24	23
N13		West Virginia	34	17
N20	●	at Notre Dame	31	29
N26		at Virginia Tech	14	38
INSIGHT.COM BOWL				
D31		Colorado	28	62

2000 — 7-5 (3-4)

Date		Opponent		
S2		at West Virginia	14	34
S9		at Army	55	17
S23		Navy	48	7
S30		Virginia Tech	34	48
O7	●	Connecticut	55	3
O14	●	Syracuse	20	13
O21		at Pittsburgh	26	42
O28	●	Rutgers	42	13
N4	●	Temple	31	3
N11		at Notre Dame	16	28
N25		at Miami, Fla.	6	52
ALOHA BOWL				
D25	●	Arizona State	31	17

2001 — 8-4 (4-3)

Date		Opponent		
S1	●	West Virginia	34	10
S8	●	at Stanford	22	38
S22	●	at Navy	38	21
S29	●	Army	31	10
O6	●	Temple	23	10
O13		at Virginia Tech	20	34
O20	●	Pittsburgh	45	7
O27	●	Notre Dame	21	17
N10		Miami, Fla.	7	18
N17	●	at Rutgers	38	7
N24		at Syracuse	28	39
MUSIC CITY BOWL				
D28	●	Georgia	20	16

2002 — 9-4 (3-4)

Date		Opponent		
A31	●	Connecticut	24	16
S7	●	Stanford	34	27
S21		at Miami, Fla.	6	38
S28	●	Central Michigan	43	0
O10		Virginia Tech	23	28
O19	●	Navy	46	21
O26		at Pittsburgh	16	19
N2		at Notre Dame	14	7
N9		West Virginia	14	24
N16	●	Syracuse	41	20
N23	●	at Temple	36	14
N30	●	Rutgers	44	14
MOTOR CITY BOWL				
D26	●	Toledo	51	25

2003 — 8-5 (3-4)

Date		Opponent		
A30		Wake Forest	28	32
S6	●	at Penn State	27	14
S13	●	at Connecticut	24	14
S20	●	Miami, Fla.	14	33
S27	●	Ball State	53	29
O11	●	at Temple	38	13
O18	●	at Syracuse	14	39
O25	●	Notre Dame	27	25
N1		Pittsburgh	13	24
N8		West Virginia	28	35
N15	●	at Rutgers	35	25
N22	●	at Virginia Tech	34	27
SAN FRANCISCO BOWL				
D31	●	Colorado State	35	21

2004 — 9-3 (4-2)

Date		Opponent		
S2	●	at Ball State	19	11
S11	●	Penn State	21	7
S17	●	Connecticut	27	7
S25	●	at Wake Forest	14	17
O2	●	Massachusetts	29	7
O16	●	at Pittsburgh	17	20
O23	●	at Notre Dame	24	23
N6	●	Rutgers	21	10
N13	●	at West Virginia	36	17
N20	●	at Temple	34	17
N27		Syracuse	17	43
CONTINENTAL TIRE BOWL				
D30	●	North Carolina	37	24

THE SCHOOLS

BOWLING GREEN

BY ED KRZEMIENSKI

WITH A NAME EVOCATIVE OF A proper English estate, Bowling Green competes with Slippery Rock for most picturesque moniker in college football. But don't be fooled: the Falcons are no strangers to winning. Coach Doyt Perry introduced the concept in the 1950s, Bob Gibson and Don Nehlen extended the winning ways through the mid-1970s, Denny Stolz regained the touch in the first half of the 1980s and Gary Blackney did the same at the beginning of the 1990s. Seventeen times in the years since 1948 the Falcons have enjoyed seasons with two or fewer losses.

Such a strong gridiron history can be both scepter and burden. After six straight sub-.500 seasons, Bowling Green hired Urban Meyer as head coach in 2001. That seemed to do the trick as the Falcons rebounded from a 2–9 season to go 8–3, Division I-A's top turnaround that year. Meyer left for Utah after the 2002 season, but his successor, Gregg Brandon, kept the team "bowling" in each of his first two years.

At Bowling Green, that's just living up to expectations.

TRADITION Bowling Green plays two award games. The Anniversary Award goes to the winner of the game between the Falcons and Kent State. Begun in 1985, the game commemorates the schools' shared founding date (1910). Nothing, though, compares to the Peace Pipe Award that goes to the winner of the Bowling Green-Toledo game. The game originated on the basketball court during the 1947-48 season and was later picked up on the football field in 1980. After the original Peace Pipe—a six-foot-long wooden pipe—disappeared, a new trophy was created with a smaller version of the pipe.

BEST PLAYER Brian McClure began his career as Bowling Green's quarterback in the third game of his freshman season in 1982. Despite missing the last two regular-season games, McClure threw for more than 1,300 yards and was named MAC Freshman of the Year. But the best was still to come. In his sophomore season, McClure passed for 3,264 yards and was named MAC Offensive Player of the Year, the first of three consecutive times he copped that award. McClure led the Falcons to an 11–0 regular season in his senior year before losing his final collegiate start in the California Bowl. Overall, McClure

PROFILE

Bowling Green State University
Bowling Green, Ohio
Founded: 1910
Enrollment: 17,300
Colors: Orange and Brown
Nickname: Falcons
Stadium: Doyt L. Perry Stadium
     Opened in 1966
     Grass; 28,599 capacity
First football game: 1919
All-time record: 459–298–52 (.600)
Bowl record: 4–3
Mid-American Conference championships:
10 (9 outright)
First-round NFL draftees: 1
Website: www.bgsufalcons.com

THE BEST OF TIMES

During the Doyt Perry era (1955-64), the Falcons had a 77–11–5 record, along with five MAC championships.

THE WORST OF TIMES

Moe Ankney inherited an 11–1 team in 1986. After five straight losing seasons, Ankney was replaced by Gary Blackney, whose first-year record in 1991 was … 11–1.

CONFERENCE

Bowling Green joined the MAC in 1952 and has played there ever since. The Falcons also played in the Northwestern Ohio Intercollegiate Athletic Association from 1921 to 1931, in the Ohio Athletic Conference from 1933 to 1941 and as an independent from 1919 to 1920, in 1932 and from 1942 to 1951.

DISTINGUISHED ALUMNI

Tim Conway, comedian; Scott Hamilton, Olympic champion figure skater; Orel Hershiser, baseball player; Arnold Rampersad, author; Eva Marie Saint, Academy Award-winning actress; Nate Thurmond, Basketball Hall of Famer

FIGHT SONG

FORWARD FALCONS
(Played after a score)

Forward Falcons!
Forward Falcons!
Fight for victory,
Show our spirit,
Make them fear it,
Fight for ol' B-G.
Forward Falcons!
Forward Falcons!
Make the contest keen,
Hold up the fame
Of our mighty name
And win for Bowling Green!

AY ZIGGY ZOOMBA
(Played after a win)

Ay Ziggy Zoomba Zoomba Zoomba
Ay Ziggy Zoomba Zoomba Ze
Ay Ziggy Zoomba Zoomba Zoomba
Ay Ziggy Zoomba Zoomba Zi
Roll along, you B-G warriors
Roll along, and win for B-G-S-U.

> *Doyt Perry is not only the greatest football coach from Bowling Green, but also the most renowned person affiliated with the school's athletic program.*

led the Falcons to a 30–12 record, took them to two bowl games and set virtually all the Bowling Green passing records and five NCAA marks. He threw for more than 300 yards in a game 12 times and, perhaps most impressive, became only the second collegiate quarterback, after Doug Flutie, to pass for more than 10,000 yards in his career, finishing with 10,280.

BEST COACH Perry stands as not only the greatest football coach from Bowling Green, but also as the most renowned person ever affiliated with the school's athletic program. Three decades after lettering nine times in three sports from 1929 to 1931, Perry returned to Bowling Green to coach his alma mater. For the next 10 years, he led the football team to a 77–11-5 record that included two undefeated and five one-loss seasons, five MAC titles and a National College Division championship in 1959. Perry's .855 overall winning percentage ranks fifth on the

all-time NCAA list. In 1964, Perry became Bowling Green's athletic director. In 1988, the National Football Foundation ushered Perry into the College Football Hall of Fame, making him, to date, the only full-time MAC representative as a coach to receive this honor.

BEST TEAM The 1959 Falcons went 9–0, outscored their opponents 274-83 and won the mythical College Division championship. Perry's team ended its perfect season with a 13-9 thriller at Ohio University. Besides the season-ending game, the 1959 Falcons won by an average score of 33-9. How they scored that many points is a mystery, considering that Bob Colburn led the team with 788 yards passing, Chuck Comer led with 361 yards rushing and Bernie Casey paced Falcons receivers with 18 receptions. Along with Colburn and Casey, end Ron Blackledge and tackle Bob Zimpfer made the year's All-MAC team.

RECORDS

RUSHING YARDS

GAME		
225	Darryl Story vs. Ball State, Nov. 5, 1983 (37 att.)	
SEASON		
1,444	Fred Durig, 1951 (214 att.)	
CAREER		
3,423	Dave Preston, 1973-76 (830 att.)	

PASSING YARDS

GAME	
479	Brian McClure vs. Ohio U., Nov. 23, 1985 (31 of 49)
SEASON	
4,002	Omar Jacobs, 2004 (309 of 462)
CAREER	
10,280	Brian McClure, 1982-85 (900 of 1,427)

RECEIVING YARDS

GAME	
215	Robert Redd vs. Marshall, Sept. 29, 2001 (9 rec.)
SEASON	
1,138	Cole Magner, 2003 (99 rec.)
CAREER	
2,726	Robert Redd, 1998-2002 (211 rec.)

POINTS

GAME	
30	Dave Preston vs. Dayton, Sept. 21, 1974 (5 TDs)
SEASON	
134	Josh Harris, 2002 (22 TDs, 1 two-pt. conv.)
CAREER	
284	Josh Harris, 2000-03 (47 TDs, 1 two-pt. conv.)

CONSENSUS ALL-AMERICANS

1959	Bob Zimpfer, T
1982	Andre Young, DL

BIGGEST GAME First-year head coach Blackney took his 10–1 Falcons to the 1991 California Bowl against Fresno State. In the same bowl game six years earlier, the Bulldogs had humiliated Bowling Green 51-7. Few gave the double-digit-underdog Falcons much of a chance. Led by quarterback Erik White, who hooked up with receiver Mark Szlachcic a California Bowl-record 11 times, the Falcons stunned Fresno State and won their first bowl game, 28-21. A year later in the Las Vegas Bowl, Bowling Green repeated the achievement when it upset Nevada. Ironically, the Falcons' only 1991 loss came in a 24-17 thriller against West Virginia, coached by former Falcons player and head coach Don Nehlen.

BIGGEST UPSET Most teams in the MAC would probably dread a trip to West Lafayette, Ind., to open Purdue's season. Bowling Green seems to relish it. In 1972, the Falcons upset Purdue 17-14 and in 2003 they beat the Boilermakers 27-6. On both occasions, Purdue was ranked in the Top 20.

HEARTBREAKER Powered by freshman phenom Brian McClure, Bowling Green played Fresno State in the 1982 California Bowl. With McClure passing for 246 yards and Chip Otten running for 136, the Falcons led the Bulldogs 28-7 at the beginning of the fourth quarter. But in the final quarter, Fresno State stormed back. With 11 seconds left, the Bulldogs scored their third touchdown of the period, added the extra point and snatched away a 29-28 victory.

STADIUM In 1966, Bowling Green replaced 43-year-old University Stadium with a new venue bearing a familiar name: Doyt L. Perry Stadium. The official capacity today is 28,599. Tell that to the more than 33,000 fans who packed the stadium for Bowling Green's annual game against Toledo in 1983.

RIVAL Bowling Green and Toledo first met in 1919 and haven't missed an annual game since 1948. On the line is the Peace Pipe Award, a counterpoint to the Nike-Ajax missile Toledo traditionally aims at the Bowling Green 50-yard line. Bowling Green leads the series 36-29-4 (through 2004). Seven of the top eight attendance records for Perry Stadium are for games against Toledo.

NICKNAME Until 1927, Bowling Green teams were called the Normals. After reading an article on falconry, alum Ivan "Doc" Lake suggested the team use Falcons as its nickname. Lake suggested the name because, as he reported in the *Bowling Green Sentinel-Tribune*, where he was a writer, falcons "often attacked birds two or three times their size." Also, the practical Lake noted, the name fit well into headlines.

MASCOT Frieda and Freddie Falcon, two giant, furry, earthbound falcons, serve as the official mascots of Bowling Green. Freddie was born in 1950 and finally got a date in 1966. Winners of the contest to embody the pair remain anonymous until the final home basketball and hockey game, when each is "beheaded" in front of the student body.

UNIFORMS The official colors at Bowling Green have been brown and burnt orange since 1914. In that year, Leon L. Winslow, a faculty member, got the idea of the combination from a woman's hat at a Toledo trolley station. Uniforms have tended toward the orange side of the combination with brown highlights. Currently jerseys are orange with white numbers; helmets are orange with the profile of a white falcon outlined in brown.

LORE Although Bowling Green will never be mistaken for a service academy, the school has an interesting relationship with the military on the football field. During World War II, the Falcons added several military-oriented schools to their schedule. In the three middle war years, the team played Miami Naval, Grosse Isle Navy, Patterson Field and Bunker Hill Navy in addition to its regularly scheduled foes. Two decades later, during the Vietnam War, Bowling Green reprised its patriotism and played the Quantico Marines. The Falcons have a 4–2 record versus the military.

QUOTE "Ay Ziggy Zoomba Zoomba Zoomba!"
—A loose translation of a Zulu war chant that Air Force bombardier Gilbert Fox brought back to Bowling Green after World War II and that still serves as the school's unofficial fight song

BOWLING GREEN ANNUAL STATISTICAL LEADERS

YR	RUSHING	YDS	ATT	AVG	PASSING	ATT	CMP	PCT	YDS	RECEIVING	REC	YDS	AVG
1947	Jack Woodland	536	102	5.3	Ennis Walker	83	31	.37	476	Max Minnich	12	224	18.7
1948	Jack Woodland	522	108	4.8	Max Minnich	38	19	.50	405	Robert Schnelker	14	243	17.4
1949	Jack Woodland	694	133	5.2	Rod Lash	79	29	.37	599	Robert Schnelker	20	434	21.7
1950	Richard Pont	627	111	5.6	Rex Simonds	79	23	.29	319	Doug Mooney	8	36	4.5
1951	Fred Durig	1,444	214	6.7	Rex Simonds	95	36	.38	506	Jim Ladd	16	236	14.8
1952	Fred Durig	858	181	4.7	Bill Lyons	134	71	.53	915	Jim Ladd	43	632	14.7
1953	Bill Bradshaw	236	110	2.1	Bill Bradshaw	126	48	.38	865	Jim Ladd	31	473	15.3
1954	John Ladd	266	81	3.3	Bill Bradshaw	53	21	.40	414	Jack Hecker	12	274	22.8
1955	Carlos Jackson	505	86	5.9	Jim Bryan	64	45	.70	770	Jack Hecker	29	556	19.2
1956	Vic DeOrio	816	149	5.5	Don Nehlen	49	26	.53	362	Ray Reese	12	183	15.3
1957	Bob Ramlow	492	108	4.6	Don Nehlen	70	36	.51	499	Ray Reese	12	185	15.4
1958	Bob Ramlow	779	140	5.6	Bob Colburn	87	46	.53	685	Bernie Casey	16	310	19.4
1959	Chuck Comer	361	53	6.8	Bob Colburn	111	60	.54	788	Bernie Casey	18	264	14.7
1960	Don Lisbon	605	99	6.1	Jim Potts	71	44	.62	662	Clarence Mason	14	191	13.6
1961	Russ Hepner	637	137	4.6	Jim Potts	91	47	.52	712	Russ Hepner	14	187	13.4
1962	Don Lisbon	481	94	5.1	Tony Ruggiero	60	29	.48	393	Jay Cunningham	13	259	19.9
1963	Jay Cunningham	539	128	4.2	Jerry Ward	127	59	.47	858	Tom Sims	12	177	14.8
1964	Stew Williams	609	109	5.6	Jerry Ward	114	57	.50	726	Jay Cunningham	14	174	12.4
1965	Stew Williams	616	145	4.3	Dwight Wallace	66	34	.52	425	Dave Cranmer	16	180	11.3
1966	Dave Cranmer	374	81	4.6	P.J. Nyitray	79	38	.48	431	Eddie Jones	40	525	13.1
1967	Bob Zimpfer	538	128	4.2	P.J. Nyitray	164	73	.45	846	Eddie Jones	30	374	12.5
1968	Fred Mathews	733	207	3.6	P.J. Nyitray	144	78	.54	898	Eddie Jones	49	716	14.6
1969	Issac Wright	344	96	3.5	Vern Wireman	281	147	.52	1,666	Bob Zimpfer	48	785	16.3
1970	Julius Livas	279	109	2.6	Vern Wireman	174	60	.35	622	Bill Pittman	21	235	11.2
1971	Paul Miles	1,185	274	4.3	Reid Lamport	154	71	.46	1,006	Rick Newman	25	443	17.7
1972	Paul Miles	1,024	243	4.2	Reid Lamport	89	28	.32	430	Roger Wallace	16	242	15.1
1973	Paul Miles	1,030	250	4.1	Reid Lamport	161	70	.44	1,084	Roger Wallace	37	587	15.9
1974	Dave Preston	1,414	324	4.4	Mark Miller	134	67	.50	725	John Boles	25	291	11.6
1975	Dan Saleet	1,114	194	5.7	Mark Miller	187	98	.52	1,252	Dave Dudley	25	338	13.5
1976	Dave Preston	989	248	4.0	Mark Miller	245	126	.51	1,839	Jeff Groth	33	598	18.1
1977	Dan Saleet	572	137	4.2	Mark Miller	285	164	.58	2,103	Jeff Groth	39	693	17.8
1978	Dave Windatt	608	118	5.2	Mike Wright	259	134	.52	1,852	Jeff Groth	56	874	15.6
1979	Kevin Folkes	696	163	4.3	Mike Wright	210	104	.50	1,148	Dan Shetler	37	502	13.6
1980	Bryant Jones	806	174	4.6	Greg Taylor	77	43	.56	562	Dan Shetler	20	310	15.5
1981	Bryant Jones	1,051	253	4.2	Dayne Palsgrove	153	79	.52	732	Shawn Potts	31	391	12.6
1982	Chip Otten	673	157	4.3	Brian McClure	176	113	.64	1,391	Shawn Potts	50	841	16.8
1983	Darryl Story	724	166	4.3	Brian McClure	466	298	.64	3,264	Mark Dowdell	70	679	9.7
1984	Bernard White	1,036	247	4.2	Brian McClure	414	263	.64	2,951	Bernard White	56	400	7.1
1985	Bernard White	949	221	4.3	Brian McClure	371	226	.61	2,674	Stan Hunter	55	761	13.8
1986	Jeff Davis	825	180	4.3	Rich Dackin	194	114	.59	1,197	Gerald Bayless	34	300	8.8
1987	Shawn Daniels	423	121	3.5	Rich Dackin	330	189	.57	2,211	Reggie Thornton	47	698	14.9
1988	Mike McGee	538	146	3.5	Eric Smith	184	104	.57	1,306	Reggie Thornton	41	589	14.4
1989	LeRoy Smith	564	161	3.5	Rich Dackin	394	215	.55	2,679	Ronald Heard	51	916	18.0
1990	George Johnson	449	104	4.1	Erik White	262	127	.49	1,386	Mark Szlachcic	46	582	12.7
1991	LeRoy Smith	937	271	3.3	Erik White	323	185	.57	2,204	Mark Szlachcic	65	943	14.5
1992	Zeb Jackson	792	169	4.3	Erik White	344	195	.57	2,380	Mark Szlachcic	62	834	13.5
1993	Zeb Jackson	1,016	237	4.0	Ryan Henry	325	169	.49	2,242	Rameir Martin	56	876	15.6
1994	Keylan Cates	803	184	4.4	Ryan Henry	293	174	.59	2,368	Ronnie Redd	48	831	17.3
1995	Keylan Cates	910	220	3.9	Ryan Henry	177	90	.51	938	Eric Starks	32	433	13.5
1996	Courtney Davis	767	229	3.3	Bob Niemet	191	83	.44	1,129	Damron Hamilton	29	465	16.0
1997	Robbie Hollis	492	151	3.3	Bob Niemet	256	133	.52	1,723	Damron Hamilton	52	777	14.9
1998	Godfrey Lewis	753	163	4.6	Bob Niemet	144	68	.47	949	Kurt Gerling	34	656	19.3
1999	Joe Alls	592	117	5.1	Ricky Schneider	181	95	.53	1,121	Kurt Gerling	53	775	14.5
2000	John Gibson	514	155	3.3	Andy Sahm	244	123	.50	1,490	David Bautista	69	915	13.3
2001	Josh Harris	614	126	4.9	Andy Sahm	198	122	.62	1,326	Robert Redd	72	884	12.3
2002	Joe Alls	801	122	6.6	Josh Harris	353	198	.56	2,425	Robert Redd	83	973	11.7
2003	P.J. Pope	1,005	191	5.3	Josh Harris	494	325	.66	3,813	Cole Magner	99	1,138	11.5
2004	P.J. Pope	1,098	178	6.2	Omar Jacobs	462	309	.67	4,002	Cole Magner	77	746	9.7

Receiving leaders by receptions
All statistics include postseason

THE SCHOOLS

BOWLING GREEN ALL-TIME SCORES

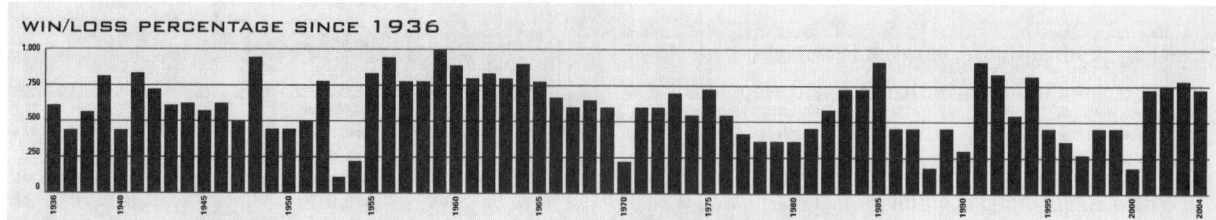

WIN/LOSS PERCENTAGE SINCE 1936

JOHN STITT
1919 (.000)   0-3

1919   0-3-0
O3		Toledo	0	6
O18		at Defiance	0	12
O23		Eastern Michigan	0	10

WALTER JEAN
1920 (.200)   1-4

1920   1-4-0
O5		at Findlay	6	10
O12		at Eastern Michigan	0	45	*
O16		Heidelberg	0	14
O23		Defiance	28	46
N6	●	at Kent State	7	0

EARL KRIEGER
1921 (.700)   3-1-1

1921   3-1-1
O1	=	Kent State	0	0
O7	●	at Defiance	7	0
O15	●	Findlay	151	0
O21		at Ashland	0	27
O29	●	at Toledo	20	7

ALLEN SNYDER
1922 (.643)   4-2-1

1922   4-2-1
S30		at Ohio Northern	0	27
O7		Adrian	0	7
O14	●	at Findlay	26	0
O19	●	Defiance	22	0
O28	●	at Huntington	38	6
N4	=	Toledo	6	6
N11	●	at Kent State	6	0

R.B. McCANDLESS
1923 (.375)   3-5

1923   3-5-0
S29		Ohio Northern	0	46
O6		at Heidelberg	12	3
O13	●	Bluffton	13	0
O19	●	Findlay	26	3
O27		at Toledo	0	27
N3		at Defiance	7	17
N10	●	Ashland	10	0
N24		at Baldwin-Wallace	0	25

WARREN STELLER
1924-34 (.619)   40-21-19

1924   3-4-0
O11		at Capital	0	19
O18	●	at Ashland	13	6
O25		at Toledo	7	12
O31		at Central Michigan	0	21
N8		Defiance	0	15
N15	●	at Bluffton	6	0
N24	●	Cedarville	34	0

1925   3-1-3
O3	=	at Otterbein	0	0
O10		Eastern Michigan	0	14
O16	=	Capital	0	0
O24	=	at Findlay	0	0
O31	●	at Defiance	2	0
N7	●	Bluffton	6	0
N20	●	Ashland	26	14

1926   4-3-1
S25		at Dayton	0	41
O2	●	at Bluffton	14	0
O9	●	Cedarville	25	0
O23		Findlay	6	7
O30	●	Central Michigan	13	0
N6	●	Defiance	30	7
N11		at Capital	0	15
N20	=	at Detroit CC	0	0

1927   5-1-1
S24	=	at Otterbein	0	0
O1	●	Ohio Northern	6	2
O15	●	at Kent State	13	0
O22	●	Detroit CC	6	0
O29	●	at Findlay	6	0
N11	●	at Defiance	15	0
N19		Bluffton	6	12

1928   5-0-2
S29	●	at Ohio Northern	7	0
O13	●	at Bluffton	6	0
O20	●	Toledo	14	0
N3	=	Defiance	12	12
N10	●	at Detroit CC	20	0
N19	●	Findlay	19	0
N26	=	Kent State	6	6

1929   4-2-1
S28		Baldwin-Wallace	0	18
O11		at Eastern Michigan	7	34
O18	●	Findlay	23	0
O26	●	at Toledo	0	0
N2	●	at Defiance	6	0
N9	●	Bluffton	15	0
N16	●	Detroit CC	25	2

1930   6-0-2
S27	●	Hope	19	0
O4	●	at Baldwin-Wallace	7	6
O11	●	at Bluffton	13	6
O18	●	Defiance	13	6
O25	=	at Findlay	6	6
N1	=	Toledo	0	0
N8	●	Albion	30	7
N15	●	at Detroit CC	19	7

1931   3-1-4
S26	=	at Baldwin-Wallace	0	0
O3	●	Mt. Union	6	0
O10	=	at Western Reserve	0	0
O17	●	Detroit CC	13	0
O24	=	Bluffton	0	0
O31		at Defiance	0	15
N7	=	Findlay	6	6
N14	●	Central Michigan	6	0

1932   3-3-1
S24		Baldwin-Wallace	0	24
O1	●	at Mt. Union	7	6
O14		at Bluffton	0	14
O22	●	Defiance	14	7
O29	=	at Hiram	0	0
N5	●	Toledo	12	6
N12		Ohio Northern	0	20

1933   2-3-2
S30		Mt. Union	6	7
O7	●	Bluffton	19	0
O14		at Baldwin-Wallace	6	58
O21		at Ohio Northern	6	0
O28		at Toledo	7	25
N4	=	Capital	0	0
N10	=	Hiram	0	0

1934   2-3-2
S29		at Mt. Union	0	12
O6	●	Otterbein	20	7
O13	=	Kent State	0	0
O20		at Hiram	3	13
O27	●	at Capital	13	0
N3		Toledo	0	22
N10	=	Ohio Northern	0	0

HARRY OCKERMAN
1935-40 (.510)   20-19-9

1935   1-6-0
O5		Capital	0	12
O12		Baldwin-Wallace	0	41
O19		at Ohio Northern	0	54
O26		at Kent State	0	45
N1		at Toledo	0	63
N9		Marietta	0	31
N16	●	Hiram	25	0

1936   4-2-3
S26		at Western Reserve	0	40
O3	=	at Capital	7	7
O10	●	Eastern Michigan	6	0
O17	●	at Wittenberg	13	0
O24		Kent State	0	6
O31	●	at Hiram	13	0
N7	●	at Ashland	20	0
N14	=	Ohio Northern	7	7
N20	=	Heidelberg	0	0

1937   3-4-1
S25	●	Hiram	12	0
O2		at Baldwin-Wallace	0	21
O9		at Eastern Michigan	0	25
O16	●	Capital	12	0
O23		Ohio Northern	7	9
O30	=	at Kent State	13	13
N6		Wittenberg	0	12
N11	●	at Heidelberg	12	0

1938   3-2-3
S24	=	at Capital	0	0
S30		at John Carroll	0	20
O8	●	Ashland	50	0
O15	●	Wittenberg	7	0
O22	=	at Ohio Northern	0	0
O29	=	Eastern Michigan	7	7
N5		Kent State	3	7
N12	●	at Hiram	28	7

1939   6-1-1
S30	●	Bluffton	35	0
O7	●	Wayne	9	0
O14		Capital	6	7
O21	●	Otterbein	26	6
O28	●	at Wittenberg	19	13
N4	●	at Kent State	34	0
N11	=	at Findlay	7	7
N18	●	at Eastern Michigan	23	13

1940   3-4-1
O5		Wittenberg	0	14
O11	●	at Findlay	14	7
O19	●	Eastern Michigan	15	0
O26	=	at Capital	7	7
N2		Kent State	0	13
N9	●	at Wooster	26	14
N16		at Eastern Kentucky	0	48
N21		at Wayne	0	19

ROBERT WHITTAKER
1941-54 (.565)   66-50-7

1941   7-1-1
S27	=	Wooster	14	14
O3		at Akron	0	8
O11	●	at Miami, Ohio	9	0
O18	●	at Eastern Michigan	20	6
O25	●	Heidelberg	39	6
N1	●	at Kent State	12	6
N8	●	at Wittenberg	13	0
N15	●	Findlay	47	0
N20	●	Wayne	19	0

1942   6-2-1
S26	●	Miami Naval	39	0
O3		at Ohio Wesleyan	14	15
O10	●	at Ball State	26	14
O17	●	at Wayne	20	6
O24	●	Miami, Ohio	7	6
O31		Kent State	0	7
N7	●	Wittenberg	10	0
N13	=	at Findlay	0	0
N21	●	Grosse Isle Navy	19	7

1943   5-3-1
S18	●	Ohio Wesleyan	18	7
S25	●	at Xavier	40	0
O2	●	Central Michigan	36	0
O9	●	Patterson Field	36	0
O16		Bunker Hill Navy	12	13
O23	=	at Baldwin-Wallace	7	7
O30	●	Alma	24	0
N6		at Miami, Ohio	6	45
N13		at Ohio Wesleyan	20	32

1944   5-3-0
S1	●	at Central Michigan	20	19
S9		Miami, Ohio	7	28
S16	●	at Ohio Wesleyan	13	6
S23		Baldwin-Wallace	6	13
S30	●	Alma	19	6
O7	●	Ohio Wesleyan	41	0
O14	●	at Case	20	18
O21		at Bunker Hill Navy	7	27

1945   4-3-0
A31	●	at Alma	15	0
S7	●	Central Michigan	19	6
S14		at Baldwin-Wallace	13	14
S22		at Miami, Ohio	0	26
S29	●	at Ohio U.	6	0
O6		at Oberlin	0	28
O13	●	Case	26	7

1946   5-3-0
S28		at Central Michigan	0	7
O5	●	Ball State	13	0	*
O12		Miami, Ohio	0	6
O19	●	at Kent State	13	0
O25	●	at Canisius	13	7
N2	●	Oberlin	14	0
N9		at St. Bonaventure	9	13
N16	●	Xavier	33	6

1947   5-5-0
S20		at Xavier	0	2
S27	●	Central Michigan	20	19
O4		at Dayton	13	20
O11		at Miami, Ohio	19	33
O18	●	Ohio U.	2	0
O25	●	Kent State	21	18
N1	●	Findlay	26	9
N8		at St. Bonaventure	14	21
N15	●	Northern Iowa	19	7
N22		at William & Mary	0	20

1948   8-0-1
S25	●	at Ohio U.	13	7
O2	●	at Central Michigan	13	12
O9	●	at Toledo	21	6
O16	●	Morris-Harvey	48	6
O23	●	Baldwin-Wallace	33	28
O30	●	at Findlay	28	7
N6	●	at Kent State	23	14
N13	●	Morningside	38	7
N20	=	John Carroll	13	13

1949   4-5-0
S24	●	Rider	47	14
O1	●	Central Michigan	20	0
O8		at Toledo	19	20
O15		at Morris-Harvey	0	21
O22		at Baldwin-Wallace	21	34
O28		at John Carroll	24	38
N5	●	Kent State	27	6
N12	●	at Mt. Union	35	7
N19		Eastern Kentucky	13	21

1950 — 3-4-2

S23	=	at Rider	0	0
S30		Miami, Ohio	6	54
O7	●	Bradley	20	14
O14		at Central Michigan	0	12
O21	=	Baldwin-Wallace	34	34
O28	●	at Toledo	39	14
N4		at Kent State	6	19
N11	●	Youngstown	22	7
N18		at Eastern Kentucky	7	34

1951 — 4-4-1

S22	●	Ohio Wesleyan	23	13
S29		at Miami, Ohio	7	46
O6		Mt. Union	13	26
O13		at Ohio U.	7	28
O20	●	at Baldwin-Wallace	27	20
O27		Toledo	6	12
N3	=	Kent State	27	27
N10	●	at Youngstown	20	0
N17	●	at Bradley	20	6

1952-PRESENT
MAC

1952 — 7-2-0 (2-2-0)

S20	●	Central Michigan	20	7
S27	|	Miami, Ohio	7	42
O4	●	at Ohio Wesleyan	45	0
O11	●	at Bradley	21	14
O18	●	Baldwin-Wallace	27	19
O25	● |	at Toledo	29	19
N1	● |	at Kent State	44	21
N8	●	Youngstown	50	0
N15	|	Ohio U.	14	33

1953 — 1-8-0 (0-4-0)

S18		at Youngstown	7	20
S26	|	at Miami, Ohio	0	47
O3		at Temple	0	27
O10	●	Bradley	39	13
O17		at Baldwin-Wallace	27	35
O24	|	Toledo	19	20
O31	|	Kent State	7	41
N7		Heidelberg	6	27
N14	|	at Ohio U.	14	22

1954 — 2-7-0 (0-6-0)

S18	●	at Dayton	18	0
S25	|	Miami, Ohio	7	46
O2		Waynesburg	7	12
O9	|	at Western Michigan	15	20
O16	●	Baldwin-Wallace	13	0
O23	|	at Toledo	7	38
O30	|	at Kent State	25	28
N6	|	Marshall	19	26
N13	|	Ohio U.	14	26

DOYT PERRY
1955-64 (.855) 77-11-5

1955 — 7-1-1 (4-1-1)

S17	●	Defiance	40	0
S23	= |	at Kent State	6	6
O1	● |	Western Michigan	35	0
O8	●	John Carroll	30	0
O15	●	at Baldwin-Wallace	34	14
O22	● |	Toledo	39	0
O29	● |	at Marshall	27	26
N5	|	at Miami, Ohio	0	7
N12	● |	at Ohio U.	13	0

1956 — 8-0-1 (5-0-1)

S15	●	Defiance	73	0
S22	● |	Kent State	17	0
S29	● |	at Western Michigan	27	13
O6	●	at Drake	46	7
O13	●	at Baldwin-Wallace	32	21
O20	● |	at Toledo	34	12
O27	● |	Marshall	34	12
N3	= |	Miami, Ohio	7	7
N10	● |	Ohio U.	41	27

1957 — 6-1-2 (3-1-2)

S21	●	Baldwin-Wallace	60	7
S28	●	at Xavier	16	0
O5	●	at Delaware	7	0
O12	= |	Western Michigan	14	14
O19	● |	Toledo	29	0
O26	● |	at Kent State	13	7
N2	|	Miami, Ohio	7	13
N9	= |	at Ohio U.	7	7
N16	● |	at Marshall	14	7

1958 — 7-2-0 (4-2-0)

S20	●	at Wichita State	20	14
S27	●	Lockbourne AFB	27	6
O4	●	at Dayton	25	0
O11	● |	at Western Michigan	40	6
O18	● |	at Toledo	31	16
O25	|	Kent State	7	8
N1	|	at Miami, Ohio	14	28
N8	● |	Ohio U.	33	6
N15	● |	Marshall	21	7

1959 — 9-0-0 (6-0-0)

S26	● |	at Marshall	51	7
O3	●	Dayton	14	0
O10	● |	Western Michigan	34	0
O17	● |	Toledo	51	21
O24	● |	at Kent State	25	8
O31	● |	Miami, Ohio	33	16
N7	●	at Southern Illinois	23	14
N14	●	Delaware	30	8
N21	● |	at Ohio U.	13	9

1960 — 8-1-0 (5-1-0)

S24	● |	Marshall	14	7
O1	● |	at Miami, Ohio	21	12
O8	● |	at Western Michigan	14	13
O15	● |	at Toledo	14	3
O22	● |	Kent State	28	0
O29	●	Cal Poly SLO	50	6
N5	●	Southern Illinois	27	6
N12	|	Ohio U.	7	14
N19	●	at Texas-El Paso	21	0

1961 — 8-2-0 (5-1-0)

S23	● |	at Marshall	40	0
S30	●	Dayton	28	11
O7	● |	Western Michigan	21	0
O14	● |	Toledo	17	6
O21	● |	at Kent State	21	6
O28	|	Miami, Ohio	6	7
N4	●	West Texas State	28	6
N11	● |	at Ohio U.	7	6
N18	●	at Southern Illinois	20	0
N23		Fresno State	6	36

1962 — 7-1-1 (5-0-1)

S22	● |	Marshall	48	6
S29	●	at Dayton	14	7
O6	● |	at Western Michigan	10	6
O13	● |	at Toledo	28	13
O20	● |	Kent State	45	6
O27	= |	at Miami, Ohio	24	24
N3		at West Texas State	7	23
N10	● |	Ohio U.	7	6
N17	●	Southern Illinois	21	0

1963 — 8-2-0 (4-2-0)

S21	●	Detroit	27	14
S28	●	at Southern Illinois	31	6
O5	●	Dayton	28	0
O12	● |	Western Michigan	16	7
O19	● |	Toledo	22	20
O26	● |	at Kent State	18	3
N2	|	Miami, Ohio	12	21
N9	● |	at Marshall	21	14
N16	|	at Ohio U.	0	16
N23	●	Xavier	26	15

1964 — 9-1-0 (5-1-0)

S19	●	Southern Illinois	35	12
S26	●	at North Texas	21	7
O3	●	Dayton	35	0
O10	● |	at Western Michigan	28	8
O17	● |	at Toledo	31	14
O24	● |	Kent State	41	0
O31	● |	at Miami, Ohio	21	18
N6	● |	Marshall	28	0
N14	|	Ohio U.	0	21
N21	●	at Xavier	35	7

BOB GIBSON
1965-67 (.679) 19-9

1965 — 7-2-0 (5-1-0)

S18	●	Cal St. LA	21	0
S25		at West Texas State	0	34
O2	●	at Dayton	9	0
O9	● |	Western Michigan	21	17
O16	● |	Toledo	21	14
O23	● |	at Kent State	7	6
O30	|	Miami, Ohio	7	23
N6	● |	at Marshall	20	7
N13	● |	at Ohio U.	17	7

1966 — 6-3-0 (4-2-0)

S17		at Tampa	13	20
S24	●	Dayton	13	0
O8	|	at Western Michigan	14	16
O15	● |	at Toledo	14	13
O22	|	Kent State	12	35
O29	● |	at Miami, Ohio	17	14
N5	● |	Marshall	14	6
N12	● |	Ohio U.	28	0
N19	●	at Temple	62	20

1967 — 6-4-0 (2-4-0)

S23	●	Quantico Marines	29	0
S30	●	at Dayton	7	0
O7	|	Western Michigan	6	10
O14	|	Toledo	0	33
O21	● |	at Kent State	7	6
O28	|	Miami, Ohio	7	9
N4	● |	at Marshall	9	7
N11	|	at Ohio U.	7	31
N18	●	Northern Illinois	17	7
N25	●	at Cal St. LA	42	27

DON NEHLEN
1968-76 (.598) 53-35-4

1968 — 6-3-1 (3-2-1)

S21	●	Ball State	62	8
S28	●	Dayton	20	14
O5	● |	at Western Michigan	17	10
O12	= |	at Toledo	0	0
O19	● |	Kent State	30	7
O26	|	at Miami, Ohio	7	31
N2	● |	Marshall	54	28
N9	|	Ohio U.	27	28
N16		at Northern Illinois	6	7
N23	●	at Xavier	44	14

1969 — 6-4-0 (4-1-0)

S20		Utah State	6	14
S27	●	at Dayton	27	7
O4	● |	Western Michigan	21	10
O11	|	Toledo	26	27
O18	● |	at Kent State	7	0
O25	● |	Miami, Ohio	3	0
N1		at Marshall	16	21
N8	● |	at Ohio U.	23	16
N15		at West Texas St.	12	28
N22	●	Northern Illinois	38	23

1970 — 2-6-1 (1-4-0)

S19		at Utah State	14	33
S26	=	Dayton	14	14
O3	|	at Western Michigan	3	23
O10	|	at Toledo	0	20
O17	● |	Kent State	44	0
O24	|	at Miami, Ohio	3	7
O31	●	Marshall	26	24
N7	|	Ohio U.	7	34
N14		West Texas State	7	23

1971 — 6-4-0 (4-1-0)

S18	● |	at Ohio U.	20	19
S25	●	East Carolina	47	21
O2	● |	Western Michigan	23	6
O9	|	Toledo	7	24
O16	● |	at Kent State	46	33
O23	● |	Miami, Ohio	33	7
O30		at Marshall	10	12
N6	●	at Texas Arlington	34	17
N13		Xavier	27	42
N20		at Dayton	16	26

1972 — 6-3-1 (3-1-1)

S16	●	at Purdue	17	14
S23	● |	at Miami, Ohio	16	7
S30	= |	at Western Michigan	13	13
O7	● |	at Toledo	19	8
O14	|	Kent State	10	14
O21		at San Diego State	19	35
O28	●	Marshall	46	7
N4	● |	Ohio U.	17	0
N11	●	Dayton	17	0
N18		at Tampa	22	29

1973 — 7-3-0 (2-3-0)

S15	●	at Syracuse	41	14
S22	●	at Dayton	31	16
S29	● |	Western Michigan	31	20
O6	● |	Toledo	49	35
O13	|	at Kent State	7	21
O20	|	Miami, Ohio	8	31
O27	●	at Marshall	24	21
N3	|	at Ohio U.	23	24
N10	●	Eastern Michigan	31	7
N17	●	Northern Illinois	21	20

1974 — 6-4-1 (2-3-0)

S14		at East Carolina	6	24
S21	●	Dayton	41	21
S28	● |	at Western Michigan	21	13
O5	|	at Toledo	19	24
O12	● |	Kent State	26	10
O19	|	at Miami, Ohio	10	34
O26	●	Marshall	28	3
N2	|	Ohio U.	22	33
N9	●	Arkansas State	17	0
N16	●	at Southern Miss	38	20
N23	=	at San Diego State	21	21

1975 — 8-3-0 (4-2-0)

S13	●	at Brigham Young	23	21
S20	●	Southern Miss	16	14
S27	●	at Dayton	21	14
O4	● |	Western Michigan	28	0
O11	● |	Toledo	34	17
O18	● |	Kent State CLEV	35	9
O25	|	Miami, Ohio	17	20
N1	|	Ball State	20	27
N8	● |	at Ohio U.	19	17
N15	●	at Southern Illinois	48	6
N22		at Texas Arlington	17	21

1976 — 6-5-0 (4-3-0)

S11	●	at Syracuse	22	7
S18	● |	Eastern Michigan	53	12
S25		San Diego State	15	27
O2	● |	at Western Michigan	31	28
O9	● |	at Toledo	29	28
O16	● |	Kent State	17	13
O23	|	at Miami, Ohio	7	9
O30	|	Central Michigan	28	38
N6	|	Ohio U.	26	31
N13	●	Southern Illinois	35	7
N20		at U.T. Chattanooga	29	49

DENNY STOLZ
1977-85 (.554) 56-45-1

1977 — 5-7-0 (4-3-0)

S10	●	at Grand Valley St.	17	6
S17	|	at Eastern Michigan	6	16
S24		Iowa State	21	35
O1	● |	Western Michigan	34	14
O8	● |	Toledo	21	13
O15	● |	at Kent State	14	10
O22	|	Miami, Ohio	13	33
O29	|	at Central Michigan	28	35
N5		U.T. Chattanooga	33	37
N12	● |	at Ohio U.	39	27
N19		at Hawaii	21	41
N26		at Long Beach St.	28	29

1978 — 4-7-0 (3-5-0)

S9		at Villanova	28	35
S16	● |	at Eastern Michigan	43	6
S23	●	Grand Valley St.	49	3
S30	|	at Western Michigan	20	24
O7	● |	at Toledo	45	27
O14	● |	Kent State	28	20
O21	|	at Miami, Ohio	7	18
O28	|	Central Michigan	7	38
N4	|	Ball State	14	39
N11		at Southern Miss	21	38
N18	|	Ohio U.	15	19

1979 — 4-7-0 (3-5-0)

S8	● |	Eastern Michigan	32	6
S15		at Iowa State	10	38
S22	|	Central Michigan	0	24
S29	● |	at Western Michigan	15	3
O6	|	Toledo	17	23
O13	● |	at Kent State	28	17
O20	|	Miami, Ohio	3	21
O27	|	at Ball State	23	38
N3		at Kentucky	14	20
N10	●	Southern Miss	31	27
N17	|	at Ohio U.	21	48

1980 — 4-7-0 (4-4-0)

S6		at Richmond	17	20
S13	|	Eastern Michigan	16	18
S20		Long Beach St.	21	23
S27		at Kentucky	20	21
O4	● |	at Western Michigan	17	14
O11	● |	at Toledo	17	6
O18	● |	Kent State	24	3
O25	|	at Miami, Ohio	3	7
N1	● |	Ball State	24	21
N8	|	at Central Michigan	10	32
N22	|	Ohio U.	20	21

THE SCHOOLS

1981 5-5-1 (5-3-1)
S12		at Baylor	0	38
S19		at Ohio U.	21	23
S26		at Michigan State	7	10
O3		Western Michigan	7	21
O10	=	Miami, Ohio	7	7
O17	•	at Northern Illinois	17	10
O24	•	Toledo	38	0
O31	•	Kent State	13	7
N7	•	at Ball State	14	10
N14	•	at Eastern Michigan	28	0
N21		Central Michigan	3	6

1982 7-5-0 (7-2-0)
S4	•	Ohio U.	40	0
S18	•	at Central Michigan	34	30
O2	•	Western Michigan	7	3
O9		at Miami, Ohio	12	17
O16	•	Northern Illinois	20	18
O23		at Toledo	10	24
O30	•	at Kent State	41	7
N6	•	Ball State	28	7
N13	•	Eastern Michigan	24	7
N20		at Long Beach St.	7	24
N25		at North Carolina	14	33
CALIFORNIA BOWL				
D18		Fresno State	28	29

1983 8-3-0 (7-2-0)
S10		at Fresno State	35	27
S17		at Brigham Young	28	63
S24	•	Miami, Ohio	17	14
O1	•	at Eastern Michigan	26	21
O8		Toledo	3	6
O15	•	at Western Michigan	23	20
O22		at Northern Illinois	23	24
O29	•	Central Michigan	15	14
N5	•	Ball State	45	30
N12	•	at Ohio U.	24	20
N19	•	Kent State	38	3

1984 8-3-0 (7-2-0)
S8	•	Richmond	55	28
S15	•	at Oklahoma State	14	31
S22	•	at Miami, Ohio	41	10
S29	•	Eastern Michigan	35	27
O6		at Toledo	6	17
O13	•	Western Michigan	34	7
O20	•	Northern Illinois	28	6
O27	•	at Central Michigan	21	42
N3	•	at Ball State	38	13
N10	•	Ohio U.	28	7
N17	•	at Kent State	27	10

1985 11-1-0 (9-0-0)
S7	•	at Ball State	31	6
S14	•	at Kentucky	30	26
S21	•	Miami, Ohio	28	24
S28	•	Akron	27	22
O5	•	at Western Michigan	48	7
O12	•	at Eastern Michigan	42	24
O19	•	Central Michigan	23	18
O26	•	Kent State	26	14
N2	•	at Northern Illinois	34	14
N16	•	Toledo	21	0
N23	•	at Ohio U.	38	17
CALIFORNIA BOWL				
D14		Fresno State	7	51

MOE ANKNEY
1986-90 (.398) 20-31-3

1986 5-6-0 (5-3-0)
S6	•	Ohio U.	21	16
S13		at Minnesota	7	31
S20		at Central Michigan	10	20
S27		at Miami, Ohio	7	24
O4	•	Western Michigan	17	3
O11	•	Eastern Michigan	24	10
O18		at Washington	0	48
O25	•	at Kent State	31	15
N1		Northern Illinois	8	16
N8		Ball State	20	17
N15		at Toledo	3	22

1987 5-6-0 (5-3-0)
S5		at Penn State	19	45
S12		Youngstown St.	17	20
S19	•	at Ball State	24	0
S26		Western Michigan	27	34
O3		at Arizona	7	45
O10	•	at Ohio U.	28	7
O17	•	Toledo	20	6
O31	•	at Miami, Ohio	7	17
N7	•	Kent State	30	20
N14	•	at Eastern Michigan	18	38
N21	•	Central Michigan	18	17

1988 2-8-1 (1-6-1)
S3		at West Virginia	14	62
S10		Ball State	10	34
S17		at TCU	12	49
S24		at Toledo	5	34
O1		at Western Michigan	10	37
O8	•	Ohio U.	42	0
O15		at Central Michigan	3	21
O22	•	Youngstown St.	20	16
O29	=	Miami, Ohio	21	21
N5		at Kent State	19	31
N12		Eastern Michigan	3	28

1989 5-6-0 (5-3-0)
S9		at East Carolina	6	41
S16		Ball State	3	28
S23	•	Central Michigan	24	20
S30		Akron	24	38
O7	•	at Ohio U.	31	28
O14	•	Toledo	27	23
O21		at Eastern Michigan	13	21
O28		at Miami, Ohio	13	17
N4	•	Kent State	51	28
N11	•	at Western Michigan	31	30
N18		at Tulsa	10	45

1990 3-5-2 (2-4-2)
S2	•	at Cincinnati	34	20
S8		at Virginia Tech	7	21
S22		at Central Michigan	0	17
S29		at Ball State	6	16
O6	=	Ohio U.	10	10
O13		at Toledo	13	19
O20	•	Eastern Michigan	25	15
O27	•	Miami, Ohio	10	10
N3	•	at Kent State	20	16
N10		Western Michigan	13	19

GARY BLACKNEY
1991-2000 (.545) 60-50-2

1991 11-1-0 (8-0-0)
A31	•	Eastern Michigan	17	6
S7		at West Virginia	17	24
S21	•	Cincinnati	20	16
S28	•	at Navy	22	19
O5	•	Central Michigan	17	10
O12	•	at Ohio U.	45	14
O19	•	at Toledo	24	21
O26	•	at Western Michigan	23	10
N2	•	at Miami, Ohio	17	7
N9	•	Kent State	35	7
N16	•	at Ball State	14	13
CALIFORNIA BOWL				
D14		Fresno State	28	21

1992 10-2-0 (8-0-0)
S3	•	Western Michigan	29	19
S12		at Ohio State	6	17
S19		at Wisconsin	18	39
S26	•	East Carolina	44	34
O3		at Central Michigan	17	14
O10	•	Ohio U.	31	14
O17	•	at Toledo	10	9
O24	•	at Akron	24	3
O31	•	Miami, Ohio	44	24
N7	•	at Kent State	28	22
N14	•	Ball State	38	6
LAS VEGAS BOWL				
D18	•	Nevada	35	34

1993 6-3-2 (5-1-2)
S4		at Virginia Tech	16	33
S11		Cincinnati	21	7
S25		at Navy	20	27
O2	•	Toledo	17	10
O9	•	at Ohio U.	20	0
O16	•	Akron	49	7
O23	=	at Ball State	26	26
O30	•	at Miami, Ohio	30	25
N6	•	Kent State	40	7
N13	•	at Central Michigan	15	17
N20	•	Western Michigan	14	14

1994 9-2-0 (7-1-0)
S1		at North Carolina St.	15	20
S10	•	at Akron	45	0
S17	•	Navy	59	21
S24	•	at Eastern Michigan	30	13
O1	•	at Cincinnati	38	0
O8	•	Ohio U.	32	0
O15	•	at Toledo	31	16
O22	•	Ball State	59	36
O29	•	Miami, Ohio	27	16
N5	•	at Kent State	22	16
N12		Central Michigan	33	36

1995 5-6-0 (3-5-0)
A31		Louisiana Tech	21	28
S9	•	at Missouri	17	10
S16	•	Akron	50	12
S23	•	at Central Michigan	16	22
S30	•	at Temple	37	31
O7		Miami, Ohio	0	21
O14	•	at Ball State	10	30
O21		Toledo	16	35
O28	•	at Western Michigan	0	17
N4	•	Ohio U.	33	7
N11	•	at Kent State	26	15

1996 4-7 (3-5)
A31		Alabama *Birm*	7	21
S14	•	Temple	20	16
S21	•	at Miami, Ohio	14	10
S28	•	Central Michigan	31	27
O5		at Toledo	16	24
O12	•	Kent State	31	24
O19		Ball State	11	16
O26		at Ohio U.	0	38
N2		at Akron	14	21
N9		Western Michigan	13	16
N16		at Central Florida	19	27

1997 3-8 (3-5)
A30		at Louisiana Tech	23	30
S6	•	Miami, Ohio	28	21
S13		at Ohio State	13	44
S20	•	at Akron	31	28
S27		at Kansas State	0	58
O4	•	Northern Illinois	35	10
O11	•	Western Michigan	21	34
O18		at Ohio U.	0	24
O25		Toledo	20	35
N1		at Kent State	20	29
N8		at Marshall	0	28

1998 5-6 (5-3)
S5		at Missouri	0	37
S12		at Penn State	3	48
S26		Central Florida	31	38
O3	•	Ohio U.	35	7
O10		at Miami, Ohio	12	24
O17		at Toledo	16	24
O24	•	Kent State	42	21
O31		Marshall	34	13
N7	•	Akron	58	21
N14		at Western Michigan	27	56
N21	•	at Northern Illinois	34	23

1999 5-6 (3-5)
S4		at Pittsburgh	10	30
S11	•	Tennessee Tech	40	15
S18		at Marshall	16	35
S25		at Kent State	27	41
O2	•	Toledo	34	23
O9		Miami, Ohio	31	45
O16		at Akron	25	55
O23		at Ohio U.	14	17
O30	•	Central Michigan	31	7
N13	•	Ball State	35	14
N20	•	at Central Florida	33	30

2000 2-9 (2-6)
S2		at Michigan	7	42
S9		Pittsburgh	16	34
S16		at Temple	14	31
S23	•	at Buffalo	17	20
S30	•	at Kent State	18	11
O7		Akron	21	27
O14		at Miami, Ohio	10	24
O21	•	Eastern Michigan	20	6
N4		Marshall	13	20
N11		Ohio U.	21	23
N22		at Toledo	17	51

URBAN MEYER
2001-02 (.739) 17-6

2001 8-3 (5-3)
S1	•	at Missouri	20	13
S8	•	Buffalo	35	0
S22	•	Temple	42	23
S29	•	at Marshall	31	37
O6	•	Kent State	24	17
O13	•	at Western Michigan	28	37
O20	•	at Akron	16	11
N3	•	Miami, Ohio	21	24
N10	•	at Ohio U.	17	0
N17	•	at Northwestern	43	42
N23	•	Toledo	56	21

2002 9-3 (6-2)
A29	•	Tennessee Tech	41	7
S14	•	Missouri	51	28
S21	•	at Kansas	39	16
O5	•	Ohio U.	72	21
O12	•	at Central Michigan	45	35
O19	•	Western Michigan	48	45
O26	•	Ball State	38	20
N2	•	at Kent State	45	14
N9	•	at Northern Illinois	17	26
N16	•	at South Florida	7	29
N23	•	Eastern Michigan	63	21
N30	•	at Toledo	24	42

GREGG BRANDON
2003-Present (.769) 20-6

2003 11-3 (7-1)
A28	•	Eastern Kentucky	63	13
S6	•	at Purdue	27	26
S13	•	Liberty	62	3
S20	•	at Ohio State	17	24
O4	•	Central Michigan	23	3
O11	•	at Western Michigan	32	21
O18	•	at Eastern Michigan	33	20
O25	•	Northern Illinois	34	18
N4	•	at Miami, Ohio	10	33
N15	•	Kent State	42	33
N22	•	at Ball State	41	14
N29	•	Toledo	31	23
MAC CHAMPIONSHIP GAME				
D4		Miami, Ohio	27	49
MOTOR CITY BOWL				
D26	•	Northwestern	28	24

2004 9-3 (6-2)
S4		at Oklahoma	24	40
S11	•	S.E. Missouri St.	49	10
S24	•	at Northern Illinois	17	34
O2	•	at Temple	70	16
O9	•	at Central Michigan	38	14
O16		Ball State	51	13
O23	•	at Ohio U.	41	16
O30	•	Eastern Michigan	41	20
N6	•	Western Michigan	52	0
N13	•	Marshall	56	35
N23	•	at Toledo	41	49
GMAC BOWL				
D22	•	Memphis	52	35

BRIGHAM YOUNG

BY STU DURANDO

Everything about Brigham Young football is divided into two eras: pre-LaVell Edwards and the modern times that have been marked by the arrival of the program's savior. By turning BYU into a quarterback factory and instituting an all-out passing attack, Edwards converted a program that won 173 games in its first 47 seasons into a national power, including a national championship in 1984. Following the occasional success of coach Ott Romney from 1928 to 1936, the program was a disaster until winning its first conference championship in the Western Athletic Conference in 1965. From 1922 to 1971, the Cougars were shut out 72 times. Under Edwards, who arrived in 1972, they averaged 32 points in 361 games and suffered only one shutout. The program has produced 1990 Heisman Trophy winner Ty Detmer and two Outland Trophy winners—Jason Buck in 1986 and Mohammed Elewonibi in 1989. Since Edwards' arrival, BYU has become known for producing record-setting quarterbacks who riddle defenses for ridiculous numbers. The school's affiliation with the Church of Jesus Christ of Latter-day Saints was partly responsible for the football program's early struggles. The school has lost an abundance of potential players over the years as male students have embarked on two-year missions for the church. Before 1972, players who went on missions were usually not welcomed back to the team, but Edwards changed that, leading to an increased source of talent for the Cougars.

TRADITION The victory bell is rung by fans after every home win. It is a duplicate of a bell donated to the school by the church in 1875 that was used to begin and dismiss classes before being destroyed in a fire in 1884. Since its reintroduction in 1912, the bell has suffered through other near catastrophes: it was beaten and cracked by students in 1949, stolen in 1958, and it fell from its perch during a dedication in 1973. The Old Wagon Wheel is specific to the BYU-Utah State rivalry and is awarded to the winner of the annual meeting. One short-lived practice was the tossing of tortillas at home games. Packages of the flimsy discs have since been banned from the stadium.

PROFILE

Brigham Young University
Provo, Utah
Founded: 1875
Enrollment: 29,932
Colors: Dark Blue, White and Tan
Nickname: Cougars
Stadium: LaVell Edwards Stadium
    Opened in 1964
    FieldTurf; 64,045 capacity
First football game: 1922
All-time record: 456–359–26 (.558)
Bowl record: 7–15–1
Consensus national championships, 1936-present: 1 (1984)
Mountain West Conference championships: 2 (1 outright)
Heisman Trophy: Ty Detmer, 1990
Outland Trophy: Jason Buck, 1986; Mohammed Elewonibi, 1989
First-round NFL draftees: 8
Website: www.byucougars.com

THE BEST OF TIMES

LaVell Edwards' reign as coach produced 29 years of prosperity. But the best run during his tenure came from 1976 to 1985 when the Cougars went 104–21, won 10 conference championships and captured a national title in 1984 with a 13–0 mark.

THE WORST OF TIMES

BYU fans are accustomed to their teams amassing a lot of points, but from 1953 to 1963 the Cougars were shut out 18 times as they stumbled to a 31–75–4 record. They beat rival Utah only once during the 11-year stretch and went through four coaches.

CONFERENCE

BYU began its fifth conference affiliation since 1922, when the Cougars joined the Mountain West in 1999. The move came after a 37-year relationship with the WAC. Previous conferences included the Skyline (1948-61), Mountain States (1938-47) and Rocky Mountain (1922-37).

DISTINGUISHED ALUMNI

Brian Billick, NFL head coach; Paul Boyer, Nobel Prize winner in chemistry; Stephen Covey, author; Orrin Hatch, U.S. senator; Johnny Miller, golfer; Andy Reid, NFL head coach

FIGHT SONG

THE COUGAR SONG
Rise all loyal Cougars
And hurl your challenge to the foe.
We will fight, day or night,
Rain or snow.
Loyal, strong and true,
Wear the White and Blue.
While we sing, get set to spring.
Come on Cougars, it's up to you. Oh!
(Chorus)
Rise and Shout, the Cougars are out
Along the trail to fame and glory.
Rise and shout, our cheers will ring out
As you unfold your victr'y story.
On we go, to vanquish the foe
For Alma Mater's sons and daughters.
As we join in song,
In praise of you, our faith is strong.
We'll raise our colors high in the blue
And cheer our Cougars of BYU.

BYU has become known for producing record-setting quarterbacks who riddle defenses for ridiculous numbers.

BEST PLAYER Although Ty Detmer didn't reach the professional heights of BYU quarterbacks such as Jim McMahon and Steve Young, no one can match his college résumé. The six-foot, 175-pound 1990 Heisman Trophy winner set 62 NCAA records and was a consensus All-America in 1990 and 1991. Detmer led the nation in passing in 1990 and total offense in 1991. En route to the Heisman, Detmer passed for 5,188 yards and 41 touchdowns as a junior in 1990. He finished third in the voting the following year. Detmer was a picture of consistency for three seasons, finishing first or second nationally in quarterback efficiency from 1989 to 1991.

BEST COACH The recounting of BYU's "modern" football history in its media guide starts with 1972, the year Edwards became coach and began to alter the path of the program. The 1984 national coach of the year was a stoic sideline figure who was known to delegate X's and O's. And contrary to his dour appearance, he forged tight relationships with coaches and players. He was coaching at Granite High School in Salt Lake City when he was offered an assistant coaching job at BYU in 1962. When Edwards became head coach, he kick-started the offense and proceeded to win 257 games, 20 Western Athletic Conference titles and one national championship in 29 seasons. The Cougars played in 22 bowl games under Edwards, whose only losing season came in 1973. He ranks sixth all time in career victories.

BEST TEAM Even when undefeated, BYU's ascent in the rankings has always been slower than that of other national powers. But on Nov. 17, 1984, the Cougars reached No. 1 with a 24-14 win at Utah. They followed with a win over Utah State and another over Michigan in the Holiday Bowl to secure their first national title with a 13–0 record. BYU was criticized for its schedule but was

RECORDS

RUSHING YARDS

	GAME
272	Eldon Fortie vs. George Washington, Sept. 29, 1962 (20 att.)

	SEASON
1,582	Luke Staley, 2001 (196 att.)

	CAREER
2,970	Jamal Willis, 1991-94 (584 att.)

PASSING YARDS

	GAME
619	John Walsh vs. Utah State, Oct. 30, 1993 (27 of 44)

	SEASON
5,188	Ty Detmer, 1990 (361 of 562)

	CAREER
15,031	Ty Detmer, 1988-91 (958 of 1,530)

RECEIVING YARDS

	GAME
263	Jay Miller vs. New Mexico, Nov. 3, 1973 (22 rec.)

	SEASON
1,241	Andy Boyce, 1990 (79 rec.)

	CAREER
3,065	Eric Drage, 1990-93 (162 rec.)

POINTS

	GAME
30	Luke Staley vs. Colorado State, Nov. 1, 2001, vs. Utah State, Oct. 5, 2001; Ronney Jenkins vs. San Jose State, Oct. 24, 1998; Eric Lane vs. Utah State, Oct. 13, 1979 (5 TDs)

	SEASON
170	Luke Staley, 2001 (28 TDs; 1 two-pt. conv.)

	CAREER
290	Luke Staley, 1999-2001 (48 TDs, 1 two-pt. conv.)

CONSENSUS ALL-AMERICANS

1979	Marc Wilson, QB
1980	Nick Eyre, OT
1981	Jim McMahon, QB
1982-83	Gordon Hudson, TE
1983	Steve Young, QB
1986	Jason Buck, DT
1989	Mohammed Elewonibi, OG
1990	Chris Smith, TE
1990-91	Ty Detmer, QB
2001	Luke Staley, RB

able to go undefeated by pulling out five games that were decided by a touchdown or less. Although the Cougars finished atop both polls, 22 Associated Press voters and six voters in the coaches' poll gave their first-place votes to either Washington (11–1) or Florida (9–1–1). As winner of the WAC, BYU was locked into finishing the season in the Holiday Bowl, where it met 6–5 Michigan.

BIGGEST GAME With the national title at stake on Dec. 21, 1984, quarterback Robbie Bosco was forced to the sideline with an injured knee in the first quarter of the Holiday Bowl. Bo Schembechler's grind-it-out Wolverines opened a 17-10 lead in the fourth quarter. But Bosco, who had returned in the second, led an 80-yard drive to tie the game with 10:51 left, and later connected with running back Kelly Smith for a game-winning 13-yard touchdown pass with 1:23 remaining. Linebacker Marvin Allen then clinched the national title with an interception. "You're the greatest BYU team that's ever been," Edwards told his players afterward.

BIGGEST UPSET The Cougars posted their first win over a No. 1-ranked team when Miami visited Provo on Sept. 8, 1990. Quarterback Ty Detmer led the 28-21 win, which sparked his Heisman candidacy. He directed the winning drive, completing it with a touchdown pass to Mike Salido and a two-point conversion pass. The Cougars held the Hurricanes scoreless for the final 26:48 in front of 66,235 fans, the second-largest crowd for a game in Provo.

STADIUM After BYU played in pastures, city parks and 5,000-seat Cougar Stadium, the school moved to a new stadium by the same name in 1964. It was renamed LaVell Edwards Stadium in 2000 before the coach's final home game. The initial capacity of 28,812 was quickly increased to 35,000 and in 1982 was boosted to 65,000. The project involved adding stands in both end zones, lowering the field by eight feet and removing the

ALL-20TH ANNIVERSARY	
The best players from the 1984-2004 era were chosen by Utah Valley Magazine *on the anniversary of BYU's national championship.*	
OFFENSE	
1988-89	Mohammed Elewonibi, G
1991-94	Evan Pilgrim, G
1995-96	Larry Moore, OL
1996-98	John Tait, OL
1979-80, 1983-84	Trevor Matich, C
1987-90	Chris Smith, TE
1982, 1984-86	Mark Bellini, WR
1990-93	Eric Drage, WR
1988-91	Ty Detmer, QB
1999-2001	Luke Staley, RB
1991-94	Jamal Willis, HB
1997-2000	Owen Pochman, PK
1980-85	Vai Sikahema, KR
DEFENSE	
1991-94	Randy Brock, DE
1998-2001	Ryan Denney, DE
1983-86	Shawn Knight, DT
1985-86	Jason Buck, DT
1982-85	Leon White, LB
1983-85	Kurt Gouveia, LB
1993, 1997-99	Rob Morris, LB
1981-84	Kyle Morrell, DB
1987-88	Rodney Rice, DB
1989-92	Derwin Gray, DB
1981-84	Lee Johnson, P

track, which had been used for the 1967 and 1975 NCAA championships.

BEST COMEBACK With Craig James and Eric Dickerson amassing 335 rushing yards for SMU, the Mustangs coasted to a 45-25 lead with 4:07 remaining in the 1980 Holiday Bowl. But quarterback Jim McMahon led a drive that cut the deficit to 45-32 before BYU recovered an onside kick, which was followed by a touchdown run by Scott Phillips. Another onside kick failed, but SMU was unable to move the ball and had to punt. A revived BYU squad blocked the punt and recovered on the SMU 41 with 13 seconds left. McMahon threw two incomplete passes before tight end Clay Brown pulled in the game-tying TD pass with no time left amid a crowd of SMU defenders. Kurt Gunther added the winning extra point.

RIVAL BYU's annual meeting with Utah wasn't much of a rivalry in the early years, as the Cougars failed to score in 11 of their first 16 games and didn't win until 1942. Utah won 34 of the first 40 meetings. But the Cougars eventually made amends for their early woes in the Holy War. After Edwards' arrival in 1972, BYU went 22–7 against Utah, including a last-minute rally in his final game as coach. Utah won the first meeting between the schools as ranked opponents in 1994, when BYU was No. 20 and the Utes No. 21. Utah emerged on top 34-31 in a game that featured four fourth-quarter lead changes. In 2003, Utah handed BYU its first shutout since 1975 with a 3-0 win.

NICKNAME The credit for selecting the school nickname goes to coach E.L. Roberts, who suggested teams be called Cougars because he used the word frequently to describe his athletes when talking to the media. Roberts coached football from 1919 to 1921, before BYU began playing collegiate competition. The birth of the nickname is Oct. 1, 1923.

MASCOT There was no substitute for the real thing, so after the school's nickname was chosen in 1923, a female cougar

and her two cubs were donated to the program. Live animals prowled the sideline through the late 1940s. They made their home on the south side of campus, but in 1929 they got loose, killing two dogs and stalking nearby livestock. They were captured, but after the incident BYU decided to borrow live mascots. In 1953, the school took a safer route, putting an end to the use of live animals and opting instead for students to dress up in a Cosmo the Cougar costume.

UNIFORMS After more than 30 years in which they sported a white helmet with a large capital "Y" set in a blue oval, the Cougars received a Nike makeover in 1999 and were mocked for their new look. The school unveiled new colors, including a darker shade of blue, but it was the new uniforms that generated the most attention due to a fat side-panel stripe that made the players look like they were wearing a bib. The following year, the bib look, which was only on home uniforms, was eliminated. And the entire design was scrapped in 2005, when BYU announced it would return to its classic, "old-style" uniforms and helmet design, while maintaining a slightly darker blue than what was used in LaVell Edwards' glory days. "This is the new look of BYU football," said new coach Bronco Mendenhall. "This is how people know BYU. Once you have a symbol that reflects greatness, it should not be changed. Consistency is key to a lasting tradition."

QUOTE "It's never going to happen. I don't have any feeling about that one way or another. You have to be dead or something." —LaVell Edwards, commenting in 1998 on the possibility of BYU's stadium being named after him, which it was in 2000

BRIGHAM YOUNG ALL-TIME SCORES

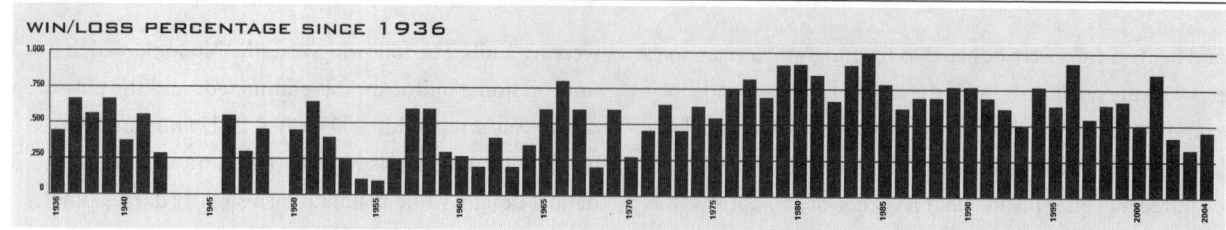

WIN/LOSS PERCENTAGE SINCE 1936

1922-1937
ROCKY MOUNTAIN

ALVIN TWITCHELL
1922-24 (.289)   5-13-1

1922   1-5-0 (1-5-0)
O7		Utah State	3	41	*
O14		at Utah	0	49	
O24		Colorado Mines	0	49	
N14	●	Wyoming	7	0	
N25		at Colorado State	0	33	
N30		at Wyoming	0	13	

1923   2-5-0 (1-5-0)
S29	●	Montana St.	16	15	
O7		at Colorado	0	41	
O13		at Colorado State	6	14	
O27		Utah	0	15	
N3	●	Western	19	0	
N12		at Utah State	0	40	
N24		at Colorado Mines	6	31	

1924   2-3-1 (0-3-1)
O4	●	at Colorado College	3	0	
O11		at Montana St.	0	13	
O25		at Utah	6	35	
N7		Utah State	9	13	
N11	●	at Western St.	26	0	
N15	=	at Colorado Mines	0	0	

C.J. HART
1925-27 (.350)   6-12-2

1925   3-3-0 (3-3-0)
O10		at Colorado State	7	21	
O17	●	Colorado College	7	6	
O24		at Utah State	0	14	
O31		Utah	0	27	
N7	●	Western St.	39	6	
N21	●	Montana St.	16	7	

1926   1-5-1 (1-4-1)
O2		Cal-Davis	0	17	
O9		at No. Colorado	6	12	
O15	=	Utah State	0	0	
O23	●	at Western St.	30	0	
N6		at Montana St.	0	27	
N13		at Utah	7	40	
N20		Colorado State	6	19	

1927   2-4-1 (2-4-0)
O8		at Colorado State	0	29	
O15	=	at Cal-Davis	0	0	
O22		No. Colorado	7	21	
O29		at Utah State	0	22	
N5	●	Western St.	60	7	
N12		Utah	0	20	
N19	●	Colorado Mines	38	19	

G. OTT ROMNEY
1928-36 (.571)   42-31-5

1928   3-3-1 (1-3-1)
S29	●	Albertson	9	6	
O6	●	Cal-Davis	7	6	
O13		at Colorado State	6	15	
O20	●	at Western St.	46	0	
O27		Utah State	0	10	
N3	●	at Montana St.	7	19	
N17	=	at Utah	0	0	

1929   5-3-0 (4-2-0)
S28	●	at Nevada	10	7	
O6		at Cal-Davis	0	19	
O12		Montana St.	12	13	
O19	●	Utah State Unk	7	6	
O26	●	Western St.	33	12	
N2		at Utah	13	45	
N11	●	No. Colorado	25	13	
N23	●	Wyoming	40	0	

1930   5-2-4 (4-1-1)
S27	●	Wyoming	19	12	
O4	=	Nevada	6	6	
O11	=	at No. Colorado	7	7	
O18		at Utah	7	34	*
O25	●	at Western St.	25	0	
N1	●	Utah State Unk	39	14	
N8	=	at Carroll	13	13	
N15	●	Montana St.	19	6	
N22	●	at Regis	18	6	
N27	=	at Albertson	13	13	
D10		at Hawaii	13	49	

1931   4-4-0 (2-3-0)
S18	●	UAY All Stars Unk	7	3	
S25		at San Francisco	0	25	
O3	●	at Nevada	18	14	
O17		at Utah	0	43	
O24	●	Western St.	31	0	
O31		at No. Colorado	0	6	
N7	●	Utah State Unk	6	0	
N13		Wyoming	7	13	

1932   8-1-0 (5-1-0)
S23	●	Montana St. Unk	6	0	
O1	●	at Western St.	28	6	
O7	●	at Occidental	46	0	
O15		at Utah	0	29	
O22	●	No. Colorado	20	2	
O29	●	at Wyoming	25	0	
N4	●	at Idaho St.	32	0	
N19	●	Utah State	18	6	
N24	●	South Dakota Unk	13	7	

1933   5-4-0 (5-3-0)
S23		at U.S. Marines	0	21	
S30	●	Montana St.	25	0	
O6		at Utah	6	21	
O14	●	at No. Colorado	6	2	
O21	●	at Western St.	13	0	
N4		at Denver	0	6	
N11	●	at Colorado College	25	0	
N18		at Utah State	0	14	
N30	●	Wyoming	3	0	*

1934   4-5-0 (3-5-0)
S22	●	Occidental	32	7	
O6	●	Montana St. Unk	20	6	
O13		at Wyoming	0	6	*
O20		at Utah	0	43	
O26		Colorado Unk	6	48	
O29	●	at Western St.	46	0	
N3		Utah State	0	15	
N10	●	at Colorado College	34	19	
N17]		at Denver	6	24	

1935   4-4-0 (3-4-0)
S28		at Montana St.	0	7	
O12	●	No. Colorado	19	3	
O19		Colorado College	12	13	
O26	●	at Wyoming	13	6	
N2		Utah	0	32	
N9	●	at Western St.	21	2	
N16		at Utah State	0	27	
N23	●	at Arizona State	13	0	

1936   4-5-0 (4-4-0)
S25		at Arizona	6	32	
O3	●	Montana St.	19	0	
O9	●	at No. Colorado	33	0	
O17		Utah State	0	13	
O31		at Utah	0	18	
N7	●	Western St.	26	12	
N14		at Denver	7	35	
N21	●	Wyoming	32	7	
N28		at Colorado College	0	6	

EDDIE KIMBALL
1937-41, '46-48 (.514) 34-32-8

1937   6-3-0 (5-2-0)
S25	●	No. Colorado	7	0	
O2		at Utah	0	14	
O9	●	Cal-Davis	34	0	
O16		at Colorado	0	14	
O23		at Portland	10	13	
O30	●	Western St.	21	0	
N6	●	at Wyoming	19	0	
N13	●	at Utah State	54	0	
N20	●	Montana St.	19	0	

1938-1947
MOUNTAIN STATES

1938   4-3-1 (3-2-1)
S24	●	No. Arizona	19	0	
S30	●	at Denver	20	0	
O8	●	Wyoming	22	13	*
O15	=	at Utah	7	7	
O22		Portland	3	6	
N5		Utah State	0	3	
N12		at Colorado	0	8	
N19	●	at Colorado State	20	12	

1939   5-2-2 (2-2-2)
S23	●	at No. Arizona	25	0	
O7	●	Colorado State	13	12	
O14		Utah	13	35	
O21	●	at Nevada	7	0	
O27	●	at Western St.	18	6	
N4	●	at Denver	21	18	
N11	=	at Utah State	0	0	
N18		Colorado	6	12	
N25	=	at Wyoming	7	7	

1940   2-4-2 (2-3-1)
S27	=	Nevada	6	6	
O5		at Utah	6	12	
O11	●	Wyoming	20	0	
O18		at Texas Tech	20	21	
N2	●	Utah State	12	7	
N9		Denver	0	9	
N16		at Colorado	2	25	
N23	=	at Colorado State	13	13	

1941   4-3-2 (3-1-2)
S26		Montana	7	20	
O3	●	Western St.	26	0	
O10	●	at Denver	13	7	
O18		at Utah	6	6	
O24		at San Francisco	13	25	
N1	●	at Utah State	28	0	
N8		at Wyoming	23	7	
N15	=	Colorado	13	13	
N22		Colorado State	7	22	

FLOYD MILLET
1942 (.286)   2-5

1942   2-5-0 (1-4-0)
S26		at Montana	12	6	
O2		Wyoming	6	13	
O10	●	at Utah	12	7	
O16		Fort Douglas	13	24	
O31		Utah State	6	9	
N7		Denver	6	26	
N14		at Colorado	0	48	

EDDIE KIMBALL
1943-1945
NO TEAM WWII

EDDIE KIMBALL

1946   5-4-1 (3-2-1)
S22	●	Western St.	13	2	
S28		at Montana St.	12	13	
O4		at Denver	13	26	
O12		Utah	6	35	
O19	●	Colorado	10	7	
O25		at San Jose State	0	14	
N2	●	Wyoming	6	3	
N9	=	at Utah State	0	0	
N16	●	at Colorado State	20	6	
N22	●	at Texas-El Paso	14	13	

1947   3-7-0 (1-5-0)
S20	●	Western St.	45	0	
S26	●	Montana St.	19	14	
O4		at Wyoming	7	12	
O11		at Utah	6	28	
O18		at Colorado	7	9	
O25	●	Utah State	20	12	*
N1		at Denver	6	20	
N8		San Jose State	19	28	
N15		Colorado State	25	27	
N22		at San Diego State	7	32	

1948-1961
SKYLINE

1948   5-6-0 (1-3-0)
S18	●	San Diego State	14	6	
S24	●	Pepperdine	13	0	
O1		Pacific Fleet	7	9	
O9		Utah	0	30	
O15		at Texas-El Paso	20	34	
O23		at Utah State	7	20	
O30	●	Montana	26	20	
N5		at San Jose State	6	21	
N15		at Colorado State	0	20	
N20	●	Wyoming	15	14	
N26	●	at Arizona State	27	25	

CHICK ATKINSON
1949-55 (.279)   18-49-3

1949   0-11-0 (0-5-0)
S17		Texas-El Paso	6	47	
S23		Pacific Fleet	13	27	
O1		San Jose State	21	40	
O8		at Utah	0	38	
O15		at Arizona State	21	49	
O22		at Denver	7	35	
O29		at Wyoming	0	45	
N5		Utah State	3	22	
N11		Colorado State	14	16	
N19		at Montana	6	25	
N26		at Pepperdine	14	28	

1950   4-5-1 (1-3-1)
S16	●	Idaho St.	14	13	
S23		Arizona State	13	41	
S29	●	Pepperdine	28	27	
O7	=	Utah	28	28	
O14		at Colorado State	14	27	
O21		at Denver	3	42	
N4	●	at Utah State	34	13	
N11		Wyoming	0	48	
N17		at Hawaii	7	39	
N25	●	Fort Hood	28	14	

1951   6-3-1 (2-2-1)
S14	●	Idaho St.	27	7	
S22	●	Western St.	67	7	
S29	●	Hawaii	20	7	
O6		at Utah	6	7	
O20	=	at Wyoming	20	20	
O27		at Denver	6	56	
N3	●	Colorado State	21	19	
N10	●	Utah State	28	27	
N17		at New Mexico	0	34	
N24	●	at Pepperdine	20	0	

1952 4-6-0 (3-4-0)

S19 ●	San Diego NAS	14	7
S27 ● |	New Mexico	14	10
O4 ● |	at Montana	28	7
O11 |	at Utah	6	34
O25 ● |	Denver	14	13
N1 |	Wyoming	13	24
N7	at San Jose State	27	44
N15 |	at Utah State	26	27
N22 |	at Colorado State	6	27
N29	at Arizona State	6	47

1953 2-7-1 (1-5-1)

S19 ● |	Montana	27	13
S25	San Jose State	25	28
O3 = |	at New Mexico	12	12
O10 ●	Idaho *Boi*	20	14
O16 |	Utah State	7	14
O23 |	at Denver	19	27
O31 |	at Wyoming	0	27
N7 |	Colorado State	12	34
N14	at Arizona State	18	26
N26 |	at Utah	32	33

1954 1-8-0 (1-6-0)

S18 |	New Mexico	12	21
S24	Arizona State	19	28
O2 |	at Colorado State	13	14
O9 |	Utah	7	12
O23 ● |	Montana	19	7
O30 |	at Utah State	13	45
N6 |	Denver	0	20
N13 |	Wyoming	13	34
N20	Idaho *Boi*	0	7

1955 1-9-0 (0-7-0)

S17	at Oregon State	0	33
S24 ●	Los Angeles St.	33	0
O1 |	at Montana	13	27
O8 |	at Utah	9	41
O21 |	at Denver	0	33
O29 |	at Wyoming	6	14
N5 |	Utah State	21	47
N11	Idaho	6	49
N19 |	Colorado State	0	35
N26 |	at New Mexico	16	21

HAL KOPP
1956-58 (.483) 13-14-3

1956 2-7-1 (1-5-1)

S15	at Wichita St.	0	13
S22	Fresno State	13	26
S29 = |	at Colorado State	0	0
O5 |	Utah	6	41
O20 |	at Montana	14	21
O27 |	at Utah State	7	33
N3 ● |	New Mexico	33	12
N10 |	at Denver	34	58
N17 |	Wyoming	6	7
N24 ●	Air Force *Unk*	34	21

1957 5-3-2 (5-1-1)

S21 =	at Arizona	14	14
S28	at Kansas State	7	36
O4 ● |	Montana	20	7
O12 |	at Utah	0	27
O19 = |	at Wyoming	0	0
O26 ● |	Denver	25	6
N2 ● |	Utah State	14	0
N9	at Fresno State	14	27
N23 ● |	Colorado State	26	9
N30 ● |	at New Mexico	14	12

1958 6-4-0 (5-2-0)

S20 ●	Fresno State	29	7
S27 ● |	at Utah	14	7
O4 |	at Colorado State	6	32
O11	at Pacific	8	28
O18	North Texas	6	12
O25 ● |	at Montana	41	12
N1 ● |	at Utah State	13	6
N8 ● |	New Mexico	36	19
N15 ● |	at Denver	22	7
N22 |	Wyoming	14	22

TALLY STEVENS
1959-60 (.286) 6-15

1959 3-7-0 (2-5-0)

S19 ●	at Arizona	18	14
S26	at Fresno State	16	27
O3 |	Montana	0	12
O9 |	at Utah	8	20
O17 |	at Wyoming	6	21
O24 |	Denver	7	14
O31 ● |	Utah State	18	0
N7 |	at New Mexico	6	21
N14	at Arizona State	8	27
N21 ● |	Colorado State	14	13

1960 3-8-0 (2-5-0)

S16 ●	Cal Poly SLO	34	14
S23	at San Jose State	8	21
O1 |	at Colorado State	7	8
O7 |	at Utah	0	17
O15	Arizona State	0	31
O22 ● |	at Montana	7	6
O29 |	at Utah State	0	34
N5 |	New Mexico	15	27
N12 ● |	at Denver	19	6
N19 |	Wyoming	6	30
N25	at Hawaii	6	13

HAL MITCHELL
1961-63 (.267) 8-22

1961 2-8-0 (2-4-0)

S16	San Jose State	13	14
S23	at West Texas St.	8	55
S30	at North Texas	30	41
O7 ● |	Montana	7	6
O14 |	at Utah	20	21
O21 |	at Wyoming	8	36
N4 |	Utah State	8	31
N11 ● |	Colorado State	30	16
N18	at Oregon State	0	35
N25 |	at New Mexico	6	34

1962-1998
WAC

1962 4-6-0 (2-2-0)

S15	at Pacific	7	26
S22 |	at Arizona	21	27
S29	George Washington	12	13
O6 ●	at Colorado State	28	7
O13 |	at Utah	20	35
O20 ●	at Montana	27	0
O27	at Utah State	21	27
N3 ● |	New Mexico	27	0
N10	at Western Michigan	20	28
N17 ● |	Wyoming	14	7

1963 2-8-0 (0-4-0)

S21	at Kansas State	7	24
S28 |	at Arizona	7	33
O5 ●	Montana	27	0
O12 |	at Utah	6	15
O19 |	at Wyoming	14	41
N2	Utah State	0	26
N9	at George Washington	6	23
N16	at Pacific	0	14
N23 ●	Colorado State	24	20
N30 |	at New Mexico	0	26

TOM HUDSPETH
1964-71 (.482) 39-42-1

1964 3-6-1 (0-4-0)

S19	at Oregon	13	20
S26 |	at Arizona	6	39
O2 |	New Mexico	14	26
O10	at Colorado State	6	7
O17 ●	Pacific	21	0
O24 =	at Texas-El Paso	18	18
O31 ●	Utah State	28	14
N7 |	at Utah	13	47
N14 ●	Western Michigan	43	8
N21 |	Wyoming	11	31

1965 6-4-0 (4-1-0)

S18 ● |	at Arizona State	24	6
S24 ●	Kansas State	21	3
O2	at Oregon	14	27
O8 ●	San Jose State	34	7
O23 |	at Wyoming	6	34
O30	at Utah State	21	34
N6 ● |	Utah	25	20
N13	Colorado State	22	36
N20 ● |	at Arizona	20	3
N27 ● |	at New Mexico	42	8

1966 8-2-0 (3-2-0)

S24 ●	at San Jose State	19	9
S30 ●	Colorado State	27	24
O8 ●	Utah State	27	7
O14 |	Arizona State	7	10
O22 ● |	at New Mexico	33	6
O29 ● |	at Arizona	16	14
N5 ●	Texas-El Paso	53	33
N12 ● |	at Utah	35	13
N19 |	Wyoming	14	47
N26 ●	Pacific	38	0

1967 6-4-0 (3-2-0)

S23 ● |	New Mexico	44	14
S29 ●	Western Michigan	44	19
O7 |	at Wyoming	10	26
O14 ●	at Oregon State	31	13
O21	at Texas-El Paso	17	47
O28 ● |	Utah	17	13
N4	at Utah State	9	30
N11 ● |	Arizona	17	14
N18 |	at Arizona State	22	31
N25 ●	San Jose State	67	8

1968 2-8-0 (1-5-0)

S21 ●	at Western Michigan	17	7
S28	Iowa State	20	28
O12 |	Wyoming	17	20
O19 |	at Arizona	3	19
O26 |	Texas-El Paso	25	31
N2 |	at Utah	21	30
N9	Utah State	8	34
N16 |	Arizona State	12	47
N23 ● |	at New Mexico	35	6
N30	at San Jose State	21	25

1969 6-4-0 (4-3-0)

S20 ● |	Colorado State	22	20
S27	at Iowa State	0	10
O4 |	at Arizona State	7	23
O11 ● |	New Mexico	41	15
O18 |	at Wyoming	7	40
O25 ● |	at Texas-El Paso	30	7
N1 ● |	Arizona	31	21
N8 ●	San Jose State	21	3
N15 ●	at Utah State	21	3
N22 |	Utah	6	16

1970 3-8-0 (1-6-0)

S12 ●	North Texas	10	7
S19	at Western Michigan	17	35
S26 |	Texas-El Paso	0	17
O3	at San Diego State	11	31
O10 |	at Arizona	17	24
O17 |	Arizona State	3	27
O24 ●	Utah State	27	20
O31 ● |	Wyoming	23	3
N7 |	at Colorado State	9	26
N14 |	at New Mexico	8	51
N21 |	at Utah	13	14

1971 5-6-0 (3-4-0)

S10 ●	North Texas *Dal*	41	13
S18 ● |	Colorado State	54	14
S25	at Kansas State	7	23
O1 |	New Mexico	0	14
O9	at Utah State	7	29
O16 ● |	at Wyoming	35	17
O23 ● |	at Tulsa	25	7
O30 ● |	at Texas-El Paso	16	0
N6 |	at Arizona State	13	38
N13 |	Arizona	14	27
N20 |	Utah	15	17

LAVELL EDWARDS
1972-2000 (.716) 257-101-3

1972 7-4-0 (5-2-0)

S16 ●	Kansas State	32	9
S23	Utah State	19	42
S30	at Oregon State	3	29
O6 ●	at Long Beach St.	38	27
O14 ● |	Texas-El Paso	21	14
O21 |	Arizona State	17	49
O28 ● |	at Colorado State	44	8
N4 ● |	Wyoming	33	14
N11 |	at Arizona	7	21
N18 ● |	at Utah	16	7
N25 ● |	at New Mexico	21	7

1973 5-6-0 (3-4-0)

S15 |	Colorado State	13	21
S29 ●	Oregon State	37	14
O6	at Utah State	7	13
O13	Iowa State	24	26
O20 |	at Arizona State	12	52
O27 |	at Wyoming	21	41
N3 ● |	New Mexico	56	21
N10 |	Arizona	10	24
N17 ●	Weber St.	45	14
N24 ● |	at Utah	46	22
D1 ● |	at Texas-El Paso	63	0

1974 7-4-1 (6-0-1)

S14	at Hawaii	13	15
S21	Utah State	6	9
S28	at Iowa State	7	34
O5 = |	at Colorado State	33	33
O12 ● |	Wyoming	38	7
O19 ● |	Texas-El Paso	45	21
O26 ● |	at Arizona	37	13
N2 ●	at Air Force	12	10
N9 ● |	Arizona State	21	18
N16 ● |	at New Mexico	36	3
N23 ● |	Utah	48	20
	FIESTA BOWL		
D28	Oklahoma State	6	16

1975 6-5-0 (4-3-0)

S13	Bowling Green	21	23
S20 |	at Colorado State	17	21
S27 |	at Arizona State	0	20
O3 ● |	New Mexico	16	15
O11 ●	Air Force	28	14
O25 ● |	at Wyoming	33	20
N1 |	Arizona	20	36
N8 ●	at Utah State	24	7
N15 ● |	Utah	51	20
N22 ● |	at Texas-El Paso	20	10
N29	Southern Miss *JaM*	14	42

1976 9-3-0 (6-1-0)

S11	at Kansas State	3	13
S18 ● |	Colorado State	42	18
S25 ● |	at Arizona	23	16
O2 ●	at San Diego State	8	0
O9 |	Wyoming	29	34
O16 ●	Southern Miss	63	19
O23 ●	Utah State	45	14
O30 ● |	Arizona State	43	21
N6 ● |	Texas-El Paso	40	27
N13 ● |	at New Mexico	21	8
N20 ● |	at Utah	34	12
	TANGERINE BOWL		
D18	Oklahoma State	21	49

1977 9-2-0 (6-1-0)

S10 ●	Kansas State	39	0
S24 ●	at Utah State	65	6
S30 ● |	New Mexico	54	19
O8	at Oregon State	19	24
O15 ● |	at Colorado State	63	17
O22 ● |	at Wyoming	10	7
O29 ● |	Arizona	34	14
N5 ● |	Utah	38	8
N12 |	at Arizona State	13	24
N19 ●	Long Beach St.	30	27
N26 ● |	at Texas-El Paso	68	19

1978 9-4-0 (5-1-0)

S9 ●	at Oregon State	10	6
S16	at Arizona State	17	24
S23 ● |	Colorado State	32	6
S30 ● |	at New Mexico	27	23
O7	Utah State	7	24
O14 ●	at Oregon	17	16
O21 ● |	Texas-El Paso	44	0
N4 ● |	Wyoming	48	14
N11 ● |	San Diego State	21	3
N18 |	at Utah	22	23
N25 ●	at Hawaii	31	13
D2 ●	Nevada-Las Vegas *Yok*	28	24
	HOLIDAY BOWL		
D22	Navy	16	23

1979 11-1-0 (7-0-0)

S8 ●	Texas A&M *Hou*	18	17
S15 ●	Weber St.	48	3
S29 ● |	Texas-El Paso	31	7
O5 ● |	Hawaii	38	15
O13 ●	at Utah State	48	24
O20 ● |	at Wyoming	54	14
O27 ● |	New Mexico	59	7
N3 ● |	at Colorado State	30	7
N9 ●	at Long Beach St.	31	17
N17 ● |	Utah	27	0
N24 ● |	at San Diego State	63	14
	HOLIDAY BOWL		
D21	Indiana	37	38

1980 12-1-0 (6-1-0)

S6	|	at New Mexico	21	25
S13	• |	San Diego State	35	11
S20	•	at Wisconsin	28	3
S27	•	Long Beach St.	41	25
O11	• |	Wyoming	52	17
O18	•	at Utah State	70	46
O25	• |	at Hawaii	34	7
N1	• |	Texas-El Paso	83	7
N8	•	North Texas	41	23
N15	• |	Colorado State	45	14
N22	• |	at Utah	56	6
N29	•	at Nevada-Las Vegas	54	14
		HOLIDAY BOWL		
D19	•	SMU	46	45

1981 11-2-0 (7-1-0)

S5	•	at Long Beach St.	31	8
S12	• |	Air Force	45	21
S19	• |	at Texas-El Paso	65	8
S26	•	at Colorado	41	20
O2	•	Utah State	32	26
O10		Nevada-Las Vegas	41	45
O17	• |	at San Diego State	27	7
O24	|	at Wyoming	20	33
O31	• |	New Mexico	31	7
N7	• |	at Colorado State	63	14
N14	• |	at Hawaii	13	3
N21	• |	Utah	56	28
		HOLIDAY BOWL		
D18	•	Washington State	38	36

1982 8-4-0 (7-1-0)

S2	•	at Nevada-Las Vegas	27	0
S11		at Georgia	14	17
S25	|	Air Force	38	39
O2	• |	at Texas-El Paso	51	3
O9	• |	at New Mexico	40	12
O16	• |	Hawaii	39	25
O23	• |	Colorado State	34	18
O30		at Utah State	17	20
N6	• |	Wyoming	23	13
N13	• |	San Diego State	58	8
N20	• |	at Utah	17	12
		HOLIDAY BOWL		
D17		Ohio State	17	47

1983 11-1-0 (7-0-0)

S10		at Baylor	36	40
S17	•	Bowling Green	63	28
S24	• |	at Air Force	46	28
O1	•	at UCLA	37	35
O8	• |	at Wyoming	41	10
O15	• |	New Mexico	66	21
O22	• |	at San Diego State	47	12
O29	•	Utah State	38	34
N5	• |	at Texas-El Paso	31	9
N12	• |	Colorado State	24	6
N19	• |	Utah	55	7
		HOLIDAY BOWL		
D23	•	Missouri	21	17

1984 13-0-0 (8-0-0)

S1	•	at Pittsburgh	20	14
S8	•	Baylor	47	13
S15	•	Tulsa	38	15
S22	• |	at Hawaii	18	13
O6	• |	at Colorado State	52	9
O13	• |	Wyoming	41	38
O20	• |	at Air Force	30	25
O25	• |	at New Mexico	48	0
N3	• |	Texas-El Paso	42	9
N10	• |	San Diego State	34	3
N17	• |	at Utah	24	14
N24	•	Utah State	38	13
		HOLIDAY BOWL		
D21	•	Michigan	24	17

1985 11-3-0 (7-1-0)

A29	•	Boston College ERUT	28	14
S7		UCLA	24	27
S14	•	Washington	31	3
S21	•	at Temple	26	24
O5	• |	at Colorado State	42	7
O12	• |	San Diego State	28	0
O19	• |	at New Mexico	45	23
O26	|	at Texas-El Paso	16	23
N2	• |	Wyoming	59	0
N9	•	at Utah State	44	0
N16	• |	Air Force	28	21
N23	• |	Utah	38	28
D7	• |	at Hawaii	26	6
		CITRUS BOWL		
D28		Ohio State	7	10

1986 8-5-0 (6-2-0)

S6	•	Utah State	52	0
S13	• |	New Mexico	31	30
S20		at Washington	21	52
S27	•	Temple	27	17
O3	|	Colorado State	20	24
O18	• |	at Wyoming	34	22
O25	• |	Texas-El Paso	37	13
N8	• |	at Hawaii	10	3
N15		Oregon State	7	10
N22	• |	at Utah	35	21
N29	|	at San Diego State	3	10
D6	• |	at Air Force	23	3
		FREEDOM BOWL		
D30		UCLA	10	31

1987 9-4-0 (7-1-0)

S2		Pittsburgh	17	27
S12	•	at Texas	22	17
S19		at TCU	12	33
S26	• |	at New Mexico	45	25
O2	•	Utah State	45	24
O10	|	Wyoming	27	29
O24	• |	at Hawaii	16	14
O31	• |	Air Force	24	13
N7	• |	San Diego State	38	21
N14	• |	at Texas-El Paso	37	24
N21	• |	Utah	21	18
D4	• |	Colorado State MEL	30	26
		ALL-AMERICAN BOWL		
D22		Virginia	16	22

1988 9-4-0 (5-3-0)

S1	|	at Wyoming	14	24
S8	•	Texas	47	6
S17	• |	Texas-El Paso	31	27
S30	•	Utah State	38	3
O8	• |	Colorado State	42	7
O15	•	TCU	31	18
O22	• |	at Hawaii	24	23
O29	• |	New Mexico	65	0
N5	|	at San Diego State	15	27
N12	• |	at Air Force	49	31
N19	|	at Utah	28	57
D3		at Miami, Fla.	17	41
		FREEDOM BOWL		
D29	•	Colorado	20	17

1989 10-3-0 (7-1-0)

S2	• |	at New Mexico	24	3
S7		Washington State	41	46
S16	•	at Navy	31	10
S30	•	at Utah State	37	10
O7	• |	Wyoming	36	20
O14	• |	at Colorado State	45	16
O21	• |	Texas-El Paso	49	24
O28	|	at Hawaii	14	56
N4	•	Oregon	45	41
N11	• |	Air Force	44	35
N18	• |	Utah	70	31
N25	• |	at San Diego State	48	27
		HOLIDAY BOWL		
D29		Penn State	39	50

1990 10-3-0 (7-1-0)

S1	• |	at Texas-El Paso	30	10
S8	•	Miami, Fla.	28	21
S15	•	Washington State	50	36
S22	• |	San Diego State	62	34
S29		at Oregon	16	32
O13	• |	Colorado State	52	9
O27	• |	New Mexico	55	31
N3	• |	at Air Force	54	7
N10	• |	at Wyoming	45	14
N17	• |	at Utah	45	22
N24	•	Utah State	45	10
D1	|	at Hawaii	28	59
		HOLIDAY BOWL		
D29		Texas A&M	14	65

1991 8-3-2 (7-0-1)

A29		Florida State	28	44
S7		at UCLA	23	27
S21		at Penn State	7	33
S28	• |	Air Force	21	7
O4	•	Utah State	38	10
O12	• |	Texas-El Paso	31	29
O19	• |	Hawaii	35	18
O26	• |	at New Mexico	41	23
O31	• |	at Colorado State	40	17
N9	• |	Wyoming	56	31
N16	= |	at San Diego State	52	52
N23	• |	Utah	48	17
		HOLIDAY BOWL		
D30	=	Iowa	13	13

1992 8-5-0 (6-2-0)

S5	• |	at Texas-El Paso	38	28
S10	|	San Diego State	38	45
S19		UCLA	10	17
S26	|	at Hawaii	32	36
O2	•	Utah State	30	9
O10	• |	Fresno State	36	24
O17	• |	at Wyoming	31	28
O24		at Notre Dame	16	42
O31	•	Penn State	30	17
N7	• |	New Mexico	35	0
N14	• |	at Air Force	28	7
N21	• |	at Utah	31	22
		ALOHA BOWL		
D25		Kansas	20	23

1993 6-6-0 (6-2-0)

S4	• |	at New Mexico	34	31
S11	• |	Hawaii	41	38
S18	• |	at Colorado State	27	22
S25	• |	Air Force	30	3
O9		at UCLA	14	68
O16		Notre Dame	20	45
O23	|	Fresno State	45	48
O30		at Utah State	56	58
N11	• |	at San Diego State	45	44
N20	|	Utah	31	34
N27	• |	Texas-El Paso	47	16
		HOLIDAY BOWL		
D30		Ohio State	21	28

1994 10-3-0 (6-2-0)

S3	• |	at Hawaii	13	12
S10	• |	at Air Force	45	21
S17	|	Colorado State	21	28
S24	• |	New Mexico	49	47
S30	•	Utah State	34	6
O8	• |	at Fresno State	32	30
O15	•	at Notre Dame	21	14
O22	• |	at Texas-El Paso	34	28
O29		Arizona State	15	36
N5	•	La. Monroe	24	10
N10	• |	San Diego State	35	28
N19	|	at Utah	31	34
		COPPER BOWL		
D29	•	Oklahoma	31	6

1995 7-4-0 (6-2-0)

S2	|	at Air Force	12	38
S9		UCLA	9	23
S16	• |	San Diego State	31	19
S30	• |	at Colorado State	28	21
O14		at Arizona State	21	29
O21	• |	Wyoming	23	20
O28	• |	Hawaii	45	7
N4	•	Tulsa	45	35
N11	• |	at New Mexico	31	14
N18	|	Utah	17	34
N25	• |	at Fresno State	45	28

1996 14-1 (9-0)

A24	•	Texas A&M	41	37
A31	•	Arkansas State	58	9
S14		at Washington	17	29
S21	• |	New Mexico	17	14
S28	• |	SMU	31	3
O4	•	at Utah State	45	17
O12	• |	Nevada-Las Vegas	63	28
O19	• |	at Tulsa	55	30
O26	• |	at TCU	45	21
N2	• |	Texas-El Paso	40	18
N9	• |	Rice	49	0
N16	• |	at Hawaii	45	14
N23	• |	at Utah	37	17
		WAC CHAMPIONSHIP		
D7	•	Wyoming LV	28	25
		COTTON BOWL		
J1	•	Kansas State	19	15

1997 6-5 (4-4)

S6		Washington	20	42
S20	•	at Arizona State	13	10
S27	• |	at SMU	19	16
O3	•	Utah State	42	35
O11	|	at Rice	14	27
O18	• |	Hawaii	17	3
O25	• |	TCU	31	10
N1	|	at Texas-El Paso	3	14
N8	• |	Tulsa	49	39
N15	|	at New Mexico	28	38
N22	|	Utah	14	20

1998 9-5 (7-1)

S5		at Alabama	31	38
S12	•	Arizona State	26	6
S19		at Washington	10	20
S26	•	Murray St.	43	9
O3	|	at Fresno State	21	31
O10	• |	Nevada-Las Vegas	38	14
O17	• |	at Hawaii	31	9
O24	• |	San Jose State	46	43
O29	• |	San Diego State	13	0
N7	• |	New Mexico	46	21
N14	• |	at Texas-El Paso	31	14
N21	• |	at Utah	26	24
		WAC CHAMPIONSHIP		
D5		Air Force LV	13	20
		LIBERTY BOWL		
D31		Tulane	27	41

1999-PRESENT MOUNTAIN WEST

1999 8-4 (5-2)

S9	•	Washington	35	28
S16	• |	Colorado State	34	13
S25		Virginia	40	45
O1	•	at Utah State	34	31
O9	•	California	38	28
O16	• |	at New Mexico	31	7
O23	• |	at Nevada-Las Vegas	29	0
O30	• |	Air Force	27	20
N6	• |	at San Diego State	30	7
N13	|	at Wyoming	17	31
N20	|	Utah	17	20
		MOTOR CITY BOWL		
D27		Marshall	3	21

2000 6-6 (4-3)

A26		Florida State JacF	3	29
S2	•	at Virginia	38	35
S9	|	at Air Force	23	31
S14		Mississippi State	28	44
S23	• |	Nevada-Las Vegas	10	7
S30		at Syracuse	14	42
O6	•	Utah State	38	14
O21	|	San Diego State	15	16
O26	• |	Wyoming	19	7
N2	|	at Colorado State	21	45
N18	• |	New Mexico	37	13
N24	• |	at Utah	34	27

GARY CROWTON
2001-04 (.531) 26-23

2001 12-2 (7-0)

A25	•	Tulane	70	35
S1	•	Nevada	52	7
S8	•	at California	44	16
S29	• |	at Nevada-Las Vegas	35	31
O5	• |	Utah State	54	34
O13	• |	at New Mexico	24	20
O20	• |	Air Force	63	33
O27	• |	at San Diego State	59	21
N1	• |	Colorado State	56	34
N10	• |	at Wyoming	41	34
N17	• |	Utah	24	21
D1	•	at Mississippi State	41	38
D8		at Hawaii	45	72
		LIBERTY BOWL		
D31		Louisville	10	28

2002 5-7 (2-5)

A29	•	Syracuse	42	21
S6	•	Hawaii	35	32
S14		at Nevada	28	31
S21		at Georgia Tech	19	28
O4	•	at Utah State	35	34
O12	|	at Air Force	9	52
O19	|	Nevada-Las Vegas	3	24
O24	|	at Colorado State	10	37
N2	• |	San Diego State	34	10
N9	• |	Wyoming	35	31
N16	|	New Mexico	16	20
N23	|	at Utah	6	13

2003 4-8 (3-4)

A28	•	Georgia Tech	24	13
S6		at Southern Cal	18	35
S13	• |	at New Mexico	10	7
S20		Stanford	14	18
S27	|	Air Force	10	24
O4	• |	at San Diego State	44	36
O9	|	Colorado State	13	58
O18	|	at Wyoming	10	13
O25	• |	at Nevada-Las Vegas	27	20
O31		Boise State	12	50
N15		at Notre Dame	14	33
N22	|	Utah	0	3

2004   5-6   (4-3)

S4	•	Notre Dame	20 17
S11		at Stanford	10 37
S18		Southern Cal	10 42
S25		at Boise State	27 28
O2	•	at Colorado State	31 21
O8		Nevada-Las Vegas	20 24
O16	•	Wyoming	24 13
O23	•	at Air Force	41 24
N6	•	San Diego State	49 16
N13		New Mexico	14 21
N20		at Utah	21 52

Neutral Site Key : *Boi* Boise, ID / *Dal* Dallas, TX / *ERut* East Rutherford, NJ / *Hou* Houston, TX / *JacF* Jacksonville, FL / *JaM* Jackson, MS / *LV* Las Vegas, NV / *Mel* Melbourne, Australia / *Unk* Unknown, Unknown / *Yok* Yokohama, Japan
ƒ Forfeit † Game Later Forfieted # Disputed Victor * Disputed Score || Designated Conference Game |2 Counted Twice in Conference Standings

BRIGHAM YOUNG ANNUAL STATISTICAL LEADERS

YR	RUSHING	YDS	ATT	AVG	PASSING	ATT	CMP	PCT	YDS	RECEIVING	REC	YDS	AVG
1952	Reed Stolworthy	436	99	4.4		NA	NA	NA	NA		NA	NA	NA
1953	Reed Stolworthy	473	86	5.5	LaVon Satterfield	92	34	.37	568		NA	NA	NA
1954	Dick Felt	379	90	4.2	Ron Bean	42	20	.48	437	Tom Verbantz	14	226	16.1
1955	Phil Oyler	366	64	5.7	Don Dixon	60	21	.35	335	Owen Skousen	10	190	19.0
1956	Steve Campora	259	34	7.6	Carroll Johnston	167	71	.43	945	Burt Bullock	22	291	13.2
1957	Weldon Jackson	605	138	4.3	Carroll Johnston	102	39	.38	447	R.K. Brown	12	183	15.3
1958	Weldon Jackson	698	101	6.9	Wayne Startin	68	28	.41	332	R.K. Brown	10	177	17.7
1959	LeGrand Young	423	83	5.1	Gary Dunn	31	10	.32	223	Howard Ringwood	10	130	13.0
1960	Bud Belnap	256	101	2.5	Bud Belnap	51	20	.39	285	Jack Gifford	6	138	23.0
1961	Eldon Fortie	422	138	3.1	Eldon Fortie	83	33	.40	469	Paul Allen	5	261	52.2
1962	Eldon Fortie	1,149	199	5.8	Eldon Fortie	100	43	.43	814	Bruce Smith	14	230	16.4
1963	Phil Brady	318	71	4.5	Ron Stewart	23	10	.43	160	Bruce Smith	13	178	13.7
1964	John Ogden	770	179	4.3	Virgil Carter	193	66	.34	1,154	Bruce Smith	24	413	17.2
1965	John Ogden	700	152	4.6	Virgil Carter	250	120	.48	1,789	Phil Odle	46	657	14.3
1966	John Ogden	906	204	4.4	Virgil Carter	293	141	.48	2,182	Phil Odle	60	920	15.3
1967	Ron Wakley	296	62	4.7	Marc Lyons	193	99	.51	1,313	Phil Odle	77	971	12.6
1968	Dave Swanson	353	94	3.8	Marc Lyons	157	66	.42	735	Ed Romero	41	495	12.1
1969	Kip Jackson	791	209	3.7	Marc Lyons	193	87	.45	1,297	Kip Jackson	25	261	10.4
1970	P. Van Valkenburg	405	103	3.9	Rick Jones	168	76	.45	851	Golden Richards	36	513	14.3
1971	P. Van Valkenburg	601	121	4.9	Bill August	87	37	.43	448	Golden Richards	14	238	17.0
1972	P. Van Valkenburg	1,386	232	6.0	Bill August	144	69	.48	891	Logan Hunter	49	555	11.3
1973	Mark Terranova	414	94	4.3	Gary Sheide	294	177	.60	2,350	Jay Miller	100	1,181	11.8
1974	Jeff Blanc	784	199	3.9	Gary Sheide	300	181	.60	2,174	John Betham	38	569	15.0
1975	Jeff Blanc	984	216	4.6	Gifford Nielsen	180	110	.61	1,471	John Van Der Wouden	29	621	21.4
1976	Jeff Blanc	625	149	4.0	Gifford Nielsen	372	207	.56	3,192	Todd Christensen	51	510	10.0
1977	Scott Phillips	325	47	6.9	Marc Wilson	277	164	.59	2,418	Todd Christensen	50	603	12.1
1978	Bill Ring	520	116	4.5	Marc Wilson	233	121	.52	1,499	Mike Chronister	52	850	16.3
1979	Eric Lane	595	94	6.3	Marc Wilson	427	250	.59	3,720	Homer Jones	46	404	8.8
1980	Eric Lane	473	96	4.9	Jim McMahon	445	284	.64	4,571	Scott Phillips	60	689	11.5
1981	Scott Pettis	499	94	5.3	Jim McMahon	423	272	.64	3,555	Gordon Hudson	67	960	14.3
1982	Casey Tiumalu	681	110	6.0	Steve Young	367	230	.63	3,100	Gordon Hudson	67	928	13.9
1983	Casey Tiumalu	851	139	6.1	Steve Young	429	306	.71	3,902	Gordon Hudson	44	596	13.5
1984	Lakei Heimuli	796	158	5.0	Robbie Bosco	458	283	.62	3,875	David Mills	60	1,023	17.1
1985	Lakei Heimuli	913	188	4.6	Robbie Bosco	511	338	.66	4,273	Mark Bellini	63	1,008	16.0
1986	Lakei Heimuli	966	230	4.2	Steve Lindsley	287	180	.63	2,247	Mark Bellini	46	839	18.2
1987	Fred Whittingham	418	129	3.2	Bob Jensen	259	144	.56	1,833	Darren Handley	52	636	12.2
1988	Fred Whittingham	513	88	5.8	Sean Covey	319	174	.55	2,607	Chuck Cutler	64	1,039	16.2
1989	Fred Whittingham	582	109	5.3	Ty Detmer	412	265	.64	4,560	Chris Smith	60	1,090	18.2
1990	Peter Tuipulotu	637	98	6.5	Ty Detmer	562	361	.64	5,188	Andy Boyce	79	1,241	15.7
1991	Peter Tuipulotu	619	125	5.0	Ty Detmer	403	249	.62	4,031	Eric Drage	46	1,018	22.1
1992	Jamal Willis	1,004	204	4.9	Ryan Hancock	288	165	.57	2,635	Eric Drage	56	1,093	19.5
1993	Kalin Hall	567	113	5.0	John Walsh	397	244	.61	3,727	Eric Drage	54	867	16.1
1994	Jamal Willis	1,042	204	5.1	John Walsh	463	284	.61	3,712	Tim Nowatzke	47	601	12.8
1995	Hema Heimuli	449	112	4.0	Steve Sarkisian	385	250	.65	3,437	Mike Johnston	40	650	16.3
1996	Brian McKenzie	950	167	5.7	Steve Sarkisian	404	278	.69	4,027	K.O. Kealaluhi	49	901	18.4
1997	Brian McKenzie	1,004	218	4.6	Kevin Feterik	208	125	.60	1,767	Ben Cahoon	57	931	16.3
1998	Ronney Jenkins	1,307	252	5.2	Kevin Feterik	336	202	.60	2,718	Margin Hooks	49	732	14.9
1999	Fahu Tahi	445	102	4.4	Kevin Feterik	452	277	.61	3,554	Margin Hooks	60	1,067	17.8
2000	Luke Staley	548	130	3.7	Charlie Peterson	260	149	.57	1,617	Margin Hooks	61	718	11.8
2001	Luke Staley	1,582	196	8.1	Brandon Doman	408	261	.64	3,542	Reno Mahe	91	1,211	13.3
2002	Marcus Whalen	918	181	5.1	Bret Engemann	215	119	.55	1,334	Reno Mahe	59	771	13.1
2003	Rey Brathwaite	812	145	5.6	Matt Berry	235	147	.63	1,445	Toby Christensen	53	547	10.3
2004	Curtis Brown	789	158	5.0	John Beck	343	192	.56	2,563	Todd Watkins	52	1,042	20.0

The NCAA began including postseason stats in 2002

THE SCHOOLS

BUFFALO

BY ED KRZEMIENSKI

AMID CAMPUS AMBIVALENCE AND disputes over athletic expenses, the State University of New York at Buffalo (now known as the University of Buffalo) dropped football as a varsity sport in January 1971. The Bulls were not dead, though, only sleeping. In 1977, students and alumni came to persuade the administration to resurrect the program. Shortly thereafter, the Bulls began what supporters termed the Run to Division I, a goal finally reached in 1999.

The transition hasn't been easy. In its first five years in the MAC, Buffalo went 7–50–0 overall and 4–36–0 in conference. With the rest of the MAC getting stronger by national standards, and the conference's ongoing efforts to take on tougher opponents in out-of-conference games, the Bulls have a tough road ahead of them.

But there are reasons for optimism. The school houses genuinely fine athletic facilities. It's located in a sports-crazy town that not only supports the NFL's Bills and NHL's Sabres, but also sets attendance records for its minor league baseball team, the Bisons. Sure, it snows some in Buffalo. But the Bulls have a lot going for them.

TRADITION Outside of Division I play, Buffalo has a long tradition. In 1894, fourteen medical students practiced in a pasture heavily trodden by grazing horses before playing the school's first football game against Hobart College on a Buffalo baseball field. More than a century later, Buffalo got its first Division I victory, beating Bowling Green 20-17 on Sept. 23, 2000. Traditions, then, are a work in progress. One of the recent additions—an a cappella rendition of the Bulls fight song at halftime of home games—still has a ways to go before it becomes a permanent fixture.

BEST PLAYER Gerry Philbin played in the North-South All-Star Shrine Game after his senior season in 1963. The two-way tackle brutalized opponents for a Bulls team that went 5–3–1, and after graduation, Philbin went on to even bigger accomplishments when he joined the New York Jets of the American Football League. There, utilized strictly as a defensive end, Philbin helped the Jets to their upset win in Super Bowl III; the following year he was inducted into the Bulls Athletic Hall of Fame. Philbin, who played in the AFL, NFL and WFL for 11 seasons, was named to the All-Time AFL Team in 1969.

BEST COACH In 1955, Buffalo Chancellor Clifford Furnas hired Dick Offenhamer to lead the Bulls back to respectability. Led by standout tackle Frank Woidzik, the Bulls posted a 4–4–1 record under the new head coach. Buffalo then reeled off four consecutive winning seasons, including back-to-back 8–1–0 seasons in 1958-59. In 11 seasons, Offenhamer's record was 58–37–5; his total victories rank second in school history, but his .605

winning percentage is the school's best for coaches with more than two seasons' service.

BEST TEAM The 1958 Bulls went 8–1–0, including a 6-3 win over powerful Harvard. Dick Offenhamer's team won the Lambert Cup for small eastern colleges and received a bid to the Tangerine Bowl. In a bold decision, the school declined the invitation to protest the bowl's discriminatory practices prohibiting black athletes from competing on its field. The team, however, received even greater publicity than the Tangerine Bowl could offer, when on Dec. 14 team captains Nick Bottini and Lou Reale appeared on *The Ed Sullivan Show* to receive the Lambert Cup. In 1993, the school honored the 1958 teams' accomplishments, both on and off the field, when it inducted the entire team, en masse, into its athletic Hall of Fame.

BIGGEST GAME Riding an 14-game losing streak as a Division I school, Buffalo hosted Bowling Green for its fourth game of the 2000 season. With 1:27 remaining and the Bulls losing by four points, it looked as if the streak might continue. But running back Marquis Dwarte managed to break off a 27-yard touchdown, and the Bulls held on for a 20-17 win.

> ## A band member recovered the original lyrics to the fight song, lost when football was eliminated in 1971.

BIGGEST UPSET On Sept. 7, 2002, the Bulls traveled to Piscataway, N.J., to take on a Rutgers team that had beaten them in their two most recent encounters by a combined score of 90-15. This particular evening, though, the Bulls dominated on both sides and scored a 34-11 victory. Though they managed the feat only for a week, Buffalo achieved .500 status (at 1–1–0) for the first, and thus far only time, in its Division I-A history.

STADIUM In 1991 the New York State Dormitory Authority financed the construction of UB Stadium for $23 million. It quickly became a center for track and field, hosting the World University Games in 1993 and the NCAA Division I Championships in 1998. Additional construction to the stadium brought it to its current capacity of 31,000.

RIVAL At the Division I level, the Bulls still lack an intense rivalry. The most likely suspect might be Rutgers. Close enough for unfriendly familiarity and on opposite sides of New York City condescension, the two schools have some necessary ingredients for a rivalry. The teams began playing regularly in 2000.

NICKNAME From 1915 to 1930, Buffalo was known as the Bisons. In 1931, though, the school changed its

RECORDS

RUSHING YARDS

	GAME
266	Alan Bell vs. Duquesne, Nov. 2, 1991 (26 att.)
	SEASON
1,189	O.D. Underwood, 1986 (229 att.)
	CAREER
3,103	Anthony Swan, 1994-97 (812 att.)

PASSING YARDS

	GAME
490	Cliff Scott vs. New Haven, Sept. 12, 1992 (29 of 51)
	SEASON
2,889	Chad Salisbury, 1997 (218 of 384)
	CAREER
7,578	Cliff Scott, 1991-94 (545 of 1,101)

RECEIVING YARDS

	GAME
218	Joe D'Amico vs. Cortland, Sept. 12, 1981 (5 rec.)
	SEASON
1,158	Drew Haddad, 1997 (67 rec.)
	CAREER
3,409	Drew Haddad, 1996-99 (240 rec.)

POINTS

	GAME
36	Lou Corriere vs. Hobart, Nov. 7, 1942 (6 TDs)
	SEASON
96	Leeland Jones, 1966 (16 TDs)
	CAREER
180	Anthony Swan, 1994-97 (30 TDs)

CONSENSUS ALL-AMERICANS

1984	Gerry Quinlivan	LB
1987	Steve Wojciechowski	LB
1995	Pete Conley	LB
1996	Michael Chichester	DB

nickname to the Bulls in order to distinguish itself from the city's professional teams.

MASCOT Big and blue, Victor E. Bull is one of the top mascots. In 2002, Vic achieved what his favorite team could not, when he was invited to compete at a New Year's Day bowl. As one of the twelve All-America mascots chosen to compete for the inaugural national Mascot of the Year, Victor joined such heady company as Otto the Orange from Syracuse, Sebastian the Ibis from Miami and Penn State's Nittany Lion.

UNIFORMS In its first game ever in 1894, Buffalo players wore blue jerseys, introducing it as the school's official color (along with white). The uniforms have always maintained this color scheme, as have the helmets, with a bit of red thrown in at various times. The helmets have been white or blue, with numbers, the letters UB or, more frequently, buffaloes in various poses: running, jumping and snorting. Currently, the helmets have images of horns on both sides.

LORE Buffalo owes a couple of debts to *Sports Illustrated*. In the March 11, 1963, issue, a drawing of an enraged bull by artist Robert Riger appeared. The school requested, and received, permission to use the image of The Fighting Bull and unveiled it as its official logo one month later. More than three decades later, another issue of *Sports Illustrated* influenced the school. In his weekly column, commentator Rick Reilly mentioned that "even Buffalo doesn't know the lyrics to Buffalo's" fight song. That spurred one of the members of the marching band to recover the original lyrics, lost when the school eliminated the football program in 1971 and marching band in 1972. Tracking down the author, a retired professor of music, the student recovered a revised version of the song and renewed a tradition in Buffalo.

QUOTE "We finally did it."—Bulls senior linebacker Chris Gray, after the team won its first game at the Division I-A level over Bowling Green in 2000

BUFFALO ALL-TIME SCORES

WIN/LOSS PERCENTAGE SINCE 1999

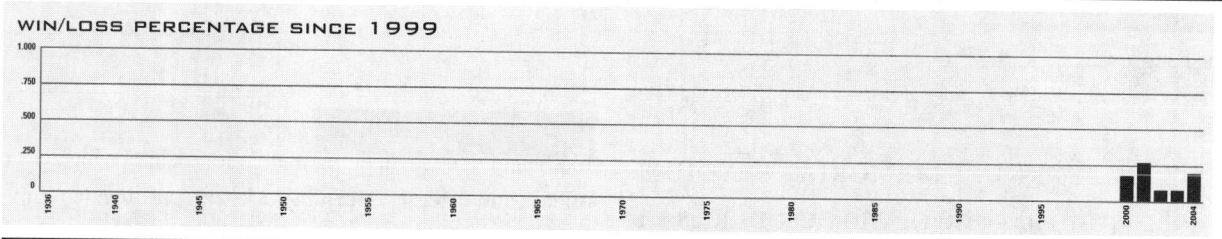

1999-PRESENT
MAC

CRAIG CIRBUS
1995-2000 (.288)   19-47

1999   0-11   (0-8)

S11	Akron	10	17
S18	at Connecticut	0	23
S25	at Ohio U.	6	45
O2	Northern Illinois	21	45
O9	Central Michigan	19	38
O16	at Western Michigan	17	45
O23	Marshall	3	59
O30	at Kent State	20	41
N6	Hofstra	13	20
N13	at Virginia	21	50
N20	at Miami, Ohio	0	43

2000   2-9   (2-6)

S2	at Syracuse	7	63
S9	at Rutgers	0	59
S16	Connecticut	21	24
S23 ●	Bowling Green	20	17
S30	at Marshall	14	47
O7	at Ohio U.	20	42
O21	Ball State	35	44
O28	at Northern Illinois	10	73
N4 ●	Kent State	20	17
N11	at Akron	14	49
N18	Miami, Ohio	16	17

JIM HOFHER
2001-PRESENT (.152)   7-39

2001   3-8   (1-7)

A30	Rutgers	15	31
S8	at Bowling Green	0	35
S22 ●	at Connecticut	37	20
S29	Central Michigan	8	16
O6	at Miami, Ohio	14	31
O13	Marshall	14	34
O20	at Kent State	13	35
O27	at Eastern Michigan	20	24
N3 ●	Ohio U.	44	0
N10 ●	at Army	26	19
N17	Akron	14	41

2002   1-11   (0-8)

A29	Lehigh	26	37
S7 ●	at Rutgers	34	11
S14	Connecticut	3	24
S21	at Minnesota	17	41
S28	at Ohio U.	32	34
O5	Western Michigan	17	31
O12	at Marshall	21	66
O19	Miami, Ohio	0	49
O26	Kent State	12	16
N9	Central Florida	21	45
N16	at Akron	10	21
N23	at Ball State	21	41

2003   1-11   (1-7)

A30	at Rutgers	10	24
S6	at Iowa	7	56
S13	Colgate	15	38
S20	Connecticut	7	38
S27	Akron	21	38
O4	at Central Florida	10	19
O11	at Miami, Ohio	3	59
O18	Marshall	16	26
O25 ●	Ohio U.	26	17
N1	at Toledo	29	56
N8	Northern Illinois	9	40
N22	at Kent State	24	34

2004   2-9   (2-6)

S2	at Eastern Michigan	34	37
S11	Syracuse	17	37
S18	at Nevada	13	38
S25	at Ohio U.	0	34
O2 ●	Central Florida	48	20
O9	at Akron	21	44
O16	Miami, Ohio	7	25
O23	at Marshall	14	48
N6	Kent State	7	33
N13 ●	Central Michigan	36	6
N20	at Connecticut	0	29

f Forfeit † Game Later Forfieted # Disputed Victor * Disputed Score || Designated Conference Game |2 Counted Twice in Conference Standings

BUFFALO ANNUAL STATISTICAL LEADERS

YR	RUSHING	YDS	ATT	AVG	PASSING	ATT	CMP	PCT	YDS	RECEIVING	REC	YDS	AVG
1999	Josh Roth	519	124	4.2	Joe Freedy	299	151	.51	1,775	Drew Haddad	85	1,158	13.6
2000	Marquis Dwarte	611	129	4.7	Joe Freedy	338	184	.54	2,060	Andre Forde	36	590	16.4
2001	Marquis Dwarte	546	141	3.9	Joe Freedy	371	187	.51	2,077	Chad Bartoszek	42	441	10.5
2002	Aaron Leeper	917	235	3.9	Randall Secky	421	204	.48	2,015	Andre Forde	54	748	13.9
2003	Dave Dawson	678	128	5.3	P.J. Piskorik	162	85	.53	824	Matt Knueven	47	622	13.2
2004	Steven King	445	94	4.7	P.J. Piskorik	133	61	.46	616	Matt Knueven	29	415	14.3

Receiving leaders by receptions
NCAA began including postseason stats in 2002

THE SCHOOLS

CALIFORNIA

BY BUD WITHERS

CALIFORNIA'S MEMORIAL STADIUM is simply one of the best places in the country to watch college football. Tucked on campus, the facility affords vistas of the Bay Area's three bridges, and the denizens of Tightwad Hill high above the stadium in Strawberry Canyon not only get those views, but get them free of charge. Until early in the 21st century, cynics might have called the spectacular surroundings window dressing. After several glorious periods in earlier times, the Golden Bears went half a century without experiencing more than two consecutive winning seasons. Then Jeff Tedford, an offensive-minded, workaholic assistant from Oregon, took over in December 2001 and got the program winning again, including a Top 10 season in 2004.

TRADITION Mounted on Tightwad Hill, Cal's victory cannon emits a deafening blast at the start of each game, after each Bears score and after each victory. Cal is also credited with the first card stunts in 1910, an ongoing student ritual.

BEST PLAYER Jackie Jensen was an All-America in both football and baseball, doing it all in football: playing offense and defense, returning kicks and punting. Jensen, Cal's first 1,000-yard rusher, gained 1,080 yards in 1948, averaging 7.3 yards per carry. All he did in a 7-6 victory over Stanford to preserve a Rose Bowl berth in 1948 was gain 170 yards on 19 carries, launch a punt 67 yards and, on fourth and 31 against a fierce punt rush late in the game, dash for 32 yards. He went on to be a star outfielder alongside Ted Williams for the Boston Red Sox, regularly driving in more than 100 runs, and won the American League Most Valuable Player award in 1958.

BEST COACH As legend has it, Andy Smith's presence at Cal in the early 1920s had its genesis in a Chicago bar. There, James Schaeffer, Cal's rugby coach, stopped for a cold one before the 1915 season, lamenting to the bartender that he was having trouble finding a man to guide the Bears through the transition from their rugby years to football. The barkeep suggested Smith, a young coach at Purdue, who came to Cal for the 1916 season. Smith was a taskmaster who annually staged Elimination Day, in which continuous scrimmaging weeded out less-committed players. In the summer of 1920, his players convinced him to do away with that tactic, and—coincidence or not—the Bears took off. Smith's Wonder Teams went 44–0–4 from 1920 to 1924, and

---

PROFILE

University of California, Berkeley
Berkeley, Calif.
Founded: 1868
Enrollment: 22,880
Colors: Blue and Gold
Nickname: Golden Bears
Stadium: Memorial Stadium
　　Opened in 1923
　　Momentum Turf; 73,981 capacity
First football game: 1882
All-time record: 592–453–53 (.563)
Bowl record: 6–8–1
Pac-10 Conference championships: 13 (9 outright)
First-round NFL draftees: 21
Website: www.calbears.com

THE BEST OF TIMES

Coach Lynn "Pappy" Waldorf's first five teams, from 1947 to 1951, went 46–6–1 and captured three conference championships.

THE WORST OF TIMES

In the four years immediately following Cal's last Rose Bowl appearance in 1959, the Bears went 6–32–2, the last three seasons under coach Marv Levy, who later would lead the Buffalo Bills to four consecutive Super Bowls in the early 1990s.

CONFERENCE

Cal became a charter member of the Pacific Coast Conference—the forerunner to the Pac-10—when it was founded in 1916.

DISTINGUISHED ALUMNI

William Randolph Hearst Jr.; Earl Warren; Joan Didion, author; John Kenneth Galbraith, economist; Maxine Hong Kingston, author; Jack London, author; Gregory Peck, actor; Dean Witter, founder, Dean Witter Financial Services

FIGHT SONG

BIG C
California!
On our rugged eastern foothills
Stands our symbol clear and bold.
Big C means to fight and strive
And win for Blue and Gold.
Golden Bear is ever watching.
Day by day he prowls.
And when he hears the tread of lowly Stanford Red,
From his lair he fiercely growls!
(Yell: gr-rr-rah, gr-rr-rah, gr-r, r-r-r, r-r-rah!)

"The most amazing ... exciting, thrilling finish in the history of college football!"

the 1920 team was a consensus national champion and is considered college football's greatest team of the first half-century.

BEST TEAM Some 15 years after Cal's Wonder Teams of the early 1920s came its Thunder Team of 1937, a 10–0–1 outfit that won some national championship acclaim while finishing No. 2 to Pittsburgh in the Associated Press poll. Coached by Leonard "Stub" Allison, it relied on power runs and a nasty, opportunistic defense that allowed only 33 points and shut out seven teams, including fourth-ranked Alabama in the Rose Bowl, 13-0. Five players made at least one All-America team that year—quarterback and captain Johnny Meek, halfback Sam Chapman, end Perry Schwartz, guard Vard Stockton and center Bob Herwig.

BIGGEST GAME Words seem inadequate to describe the finish that gave Cal its best victory ever—a 25-20 win over Stanford in 1982. Not that Bears radio play-by-play man Joe Starkey didn't try: "And the Bears ... the Bears ... have won, the Bears have won! Oh, my God! The most amazing, sensational, dramatic, heart-rending, exciting,

thrilling finish in the history of college football!"

Who would argue? Set to receive a Stanford kickoff, the Bears had apparently been victimized by a John Elway-led comeback, giving Stanford a 20-19 lead with four seconds left. But Elway called timeout with eight seconds left before Mark Harmon's 35-yard field goal, leaving Cal the slightest sliver of light. What unfolded was a priceless piece of college football lore. Kevin Moen received the Stanford kickoff at the Cal 43 and lateraled to Richard Rodgers at his 48. He gained only a yard before pitching it to Dwight Garner, whose knee may have touched before he could deal the ball back to Rodgers. But the return continued, as Rodgers carried to the Stanford 45 and tossed it back to Mariet Ford. Ford bolted another 20 yards before the most memorable of the five laterals: a blind, over-the-shoulder pitch to Moen, who took it the final 25 yards into the end zone, where he bowled over trombonist Gary Tyrrell, a member of the Stanford band assembled to celebrate a Cardinal victory. Today, Tyrrell's trombone is in the College Football Hall of Fame. He's an amateur brewer whose brand is Trombone Guy Pale Ale.

RECORDS

RUSHING YARDS

GAME
283 Jerry Drew vs. Oregon State, Nov. 13, 1954 (11 att.)
SEASON
2,018 J.J. Arrington, 2004 (289 att.)
CAREER
3,367 Russell White, 1990-92 (663 att.)

PASSING YARDS

GAME
503 Pat Barnes vs. Arizona, Nov. 2, 1996, 4 OT (35 of 46)
SEASON
3,499 Pat Barnes, 1996 (250 of 420)
CAREER
8,126 Troy Taylor, 1986-89 (683 of 1,162)

RECEIVING YARDS

GAME
289 Wesley Walker vs. San Jose State, Oct. 2, 1976 (8 rec.)
SEASON
1,504 Geoff McArthur, 2003 (85 rec.)
CAREER
3,188 Geoff McArthur, 2000-04 (202 rec.)

POINTS

GAME
36 Dick Dunn vs. Nevada, Nov. 18, 1922 (6 TDs)
SEASON
131 Duke Morrison, 1922 (18 TDs, 1 FG, 20 PATs)
CAREER
288 Doug Brien, 1991-93 (56 FGs, 120 PATs)

CONSENSUS ALL-AMERICANS

1921-22	Brick Muller, E
1921	Dan McMillan, T
1924	Edwin Horrell, C
1928	Irv Phillips, E
1930	Ted Beckett, G
1935	Larry Lutz, T
1937	Sam Chapman, B
1938	Vic Bottari, B
1948	Jackie Jensen, B
1949	Rod Franz, G
1950-51	Les Richter, G
1968	Ed White, MG
1971	Sherman White, DT
1974	Steve Bartkowski, QB
1975	Chuck Muncie, RB
1975	Steve Rivera, E
1983	Ron Rivera, LB
1991	Russell White, RB
1992	Sean Dawkins, WR
1996	Tony Gonzalez, TE
1999	Deltha O'Neal, DB
2000	Andre Carter, DL
2000	Nick Harris, P
2004	J.J. Arrington, RB

BIGGEST UPSET In 1986, the Bears (1–9) were an 18-point underdog at home against a 16th-ranked, 7-2 Stanford team. Cal sacked Cardinal quarterback John Paye seven times, allowed only 41 rushing yards and won 17-11 in fired coach Joe Kapp's final game. "I'm graduating with my seniors," said the colorful Kapp, who was 20–34–1 in his five seasons.

TRAGEDY Few figures could galvanize the eclectic mix that is California, but Joe Roth did. The Bears' passing leader in 1975 and 1976, Roth suffered a recurrence of cancer during the 1976 season, and he somehow played in the Hula Bowl only seven weeks before his death at age 21 in early 1977. A quiet and humble figure, Roth elicited this remembrance from a close friend, the Reverend Michael Hunt: "He has broken the hearts of students on one of the most cynical, far-out campuses in the country."

BEST COMEBACK Down 30-0 in the second quarter to Oregon in 1993, Cal roared back behind quarterback Dave Barr's three second-half touchdown passes to stun the Ducks 42-41, marking the biggest comeback in Pac-10 history. Cal pulled within 41-40 on Barr's 26-yard pass to Iheanyi Uwaezuoke with 1:17 left, and then took its first lead on Barr's two-point pass to tight end Mike Caldwell.

WILDEST FINISH The 1982 ending was the most chaotic of the Cal-Stanford series—or any other—but the Cardinal have shocked the Bears by winning the Big Game three times on the final play. None was more abrupt than in 1974, when Mike Langford kicked a 50-yard field goal to win for Stanford, 22-20.

STADIUM In October 1921, the university launched a fund-raising plan for a new stadium that would honor the World War I dead. Within a month, Cal supporters had pledged more than $1 million. Memorial Stadium was completed in time for the 1923 Big Game at a cost of more than $1.4 million. While the feel is thoroughly collegiate and the setting gorgeous, the facility fell into disrepair near the end of the 20th century and became the focal point of Cal's campaign to keep up with other Pac-10 facilities.

RIVAL For most of the year, those around Cal and Stanford, both highly regarded institutions, stay above the sort of diabolical hijinks that mark other rivalries. Many, however, join the silliness during Big Game week and affect at least a mock disdain for the other side. Kapp, the ultimate

Bear, once snatched a red—Stanford's color—baseball cap off somebody's head at a press conference, threw it to the ground and stomped on it. Cal students pulled off a memorable heist in 1998, stealing the Tree's costume and mailing a photograph to the *Daily Californian*, showing someone dressed as the mascot. The real Stanford Tree, a student named Chris Henderson, subsequently dared the thieves to finish the job and kidnap him, too.

DUBIOUS DISTINCTION In the 1929 Rose Bowl, "Wrong Way" Riegels scooped up a Georgia Tech fumble at the Tech 30, whirled and raced 69 yards toward the opposite goal line before teammate Benny Lom spun him in the opposite direction at the 1, after which he was swarmed by Tech tacklers. An ensuing safety provided the deciding points in an 8-7 Tech victory. Cal's ambivalence toward Riegels seems exemplified by the fact that he wasn't enshrined in the school's hall of fame until 1998.

NICKNAME In 1895, Cal had a dominant track and field team that challenged Midwest and Eastern powers in an eight-meet tour. Arthur Rodgers, a regent from the class of 1872, commissioned a blue silk banner with the state symbol, a golden grizzly bear, and the team displayed it on the tour. Since then, Cal's athletic teams have been the Golden Bears.

UNIFORMS At home, the Bears wear Yale-blue jerseys with gold numerals and gold pants. Road uniforms feature white jerseys, gold pants and blue numerals. After spending much of the 1970s with a gold helmet featuring an elongated block "C" in a blue oval as well as a lighter shade of blue for the jersey, the Bears switched back to the traditional blue in 1982. Since 1987, the blue helmets have featured a script "Cal" in gold on the side.

LORE In 1972, Vince Ferragamo, a highly recruited quarterback from Banning High in Wilmington, Calif., signed a letter of intent from Stanford. Later that day, he changed his mind. However, Vince had a problem: he had already mailed the letter to Palo Alto. Ferragamo and his brother Chris hustled to the local post office and managed to intercept the letter. He later signed with the Golden Bears. Alas, Ferragamo had a modest tenure in Berkeley before transferring to Nebraska on the way to a worthy pro career.

QUOTE "The Bear will not quit! The Bear will not die!" —Former quarterback and coach Joe Kapp, repeating a phrase he uttered often regarding California's resilience

CALIFORNIA ANNUAL STATISTICAL LEADERS

YR	RUSHING	YDS	ATT	AVG	PASSING	ATT	CMP	PCT	YDS	RECEIVING	REC	YDS	AVG
1946	Jack Jensen	189	51	3.7	Dick Erickson	23	6	.26	156	John Cunningham	8	143	17.9
1947	Johnny Graves	466	66	7.1	Bob Celeri	103	35	.34	635	Frank Van Deren	15	302	20.1
1948	Jack Jensen	1,080	148	7.3	Bob Celeri	69	27	.39	470	John Cunningham	14	222	15.9
1949	Jim Monachino	781	138	5.7	Bob Celeri	117	48	.41	1,081	Dan Begovich	14	275	19.6
1950	John Olszewski	1,008	167	6.0	Jim Marinos	49	28	.57	383	John Olszewski	9	109	12.1
1951	John Olszewski	651	89	7.3	Bill Mais	110	46	.42	758	Dave Hood	18	215	11.9
1952	John Olszewski	845	160	5.3	Bill Mais	53	30	.57	541	Don Johnson	10	142	14.2
1953	Don Marks	469	71	6.6	Paul Larson	171	85	.50	1,431	Jim Hanifan	19	247	13.0
1954	Jerry Drew	715	77	9.3	Paul Larson	195	125	.64	1,537	Jim Hanifan	44	569	12.9
1955	Ted Granger	379	83	4.6	Hugh Maguire	80	38	.48	564	Roger Ramseier	17	209	12.3
1956	Herb Jackson	462	97	4.8	Joe Kapp	112	52	.46	667	Norm Becker	22	313	14.2
1957	Jack Hart	396	101	3.9	Joe Kapp	77	38	.49	580	Jack Hart	13	276	21.2
1958	Joe Kapp	616	152	4.1	Joe Kapp	114	64	.56	775	Jack Hart	32	395	12.3
1959	Walt Arnold	351	76	4.6	Wayne Crow	67	26	.39	379	Gael Barsotti	6	111	18.5
1960	Steve Bates	384	82	4.7	Randy Gold	117	65	.56	696	George Pierovich	12	90	7.5
1961	Alan Nelson	331	59	5.6	Randy Gold	81	41	.51	403	Bob Wills	21	302	14.4
1962	Alan Nelson	334	73	4.6	Craig Morton	126	69	.55	905	Bill Turner	44	537	12.2
1963	Tom Blanchfield	387	78	5.0	Craig Morton	207	101	.49	1,475	Jack Schraub	30	467	15.6
1964	Tom Relles	519	145	3.6	Craig Morton	308	185	.60	2,121	Jack Schraub	52	663	12.8
1965	Tom Relles	485	133	3.6	Jim Hunt	63	26	.41	383	Jerry Bradley	22	360	16.4
1966	Rick Bennett	319	96	3.3	Barry Bronk	183	84	.46	965	Jerry Bradley	32	473	14.8
1967	Paul Williams	432	116	3.7	Barry Bronk	146	65	.45	708	Wayne Stewart	45	503	11.2
1968	Gary Fowler	665	162	4.1	Randy Humphries	207	98	.47	1,247	Wayne Stewart	50	679	13.6
1969	Gary Fowler	741	157	4.7	Dave Penhall	145	76	.52	874	Geoff DeLapp	25	261	10.4
1970	Stan Murphy	603	165	3.7	Dave Penhall	227	118	.52	1,785	Steve Sweeney	43	679	15.8
1971	Steve Kemnitzer	686	157	4.4	Jay Cruze	242	119	.49	1,284	Geoff DeLapp	48	464	9.7
1972	Steve Kemnitzer	434	103	4.2	Steve Bartkowski	165	70	.42	944	Steve Sweeney	52	785	15.1
1973	Chuck Muncie	801	157	5.1	Vince Ferragamo	170	82	.48	1,014	Chuck Muncie	27	283	10.5
1974	Chuck Muncie	791	164	4.8	Steve Bartkowski	325	182	.56	2,580	Steve Rivera	56	938	16.8
1975	Chuck Muncie	1,460	228	6.4	Joe Roth	226	126	.56	1,880	Steve Rivera	57	790	13.9
1976	Tom Newton	546	137	4.0	Joe Roth	295	154	.52	1,789	Jesse Thompson	37	411	11.1
1977	Paul Jones	805	189	4.3	Charlie Young	249	135	.54	1,875	Jesse Thompson	51	797	15.6
1978	Paul Jones	801	212	3.8	Rich Campbell	293	164	.56	2,281	Holden Smith	26	641	24.7
1979	Paul Jones	888	214	4.1	Rich Campbell	322	216	.67	2,618	Matt Bouza	52	717	13.8
1980	John Tuggle	580	136	4.3	Rich Campbell	273	193	.71	2,026	Matt Bouza	44	651	14.8
1981	John Tuggle	486	110	4.4	J. Torchio	363	155	.43	2,112	Mariet Ford	45	600	13.3
1982	John Tuggle	538	143	3.8	Gale Gilbert	270	147	.54	1,796	David Lewis	54	715	13.2
1983	Ron Story	435	124	3.5	Gale Gilbert	365	216	.59	2,769	Rance McDougald	46	797	17.3
1984	Ed Barbero	554	120	4.6	Gale Gilbert	308	166	.54	1,693	Dwight Garner	46	376	8.2
1985	Ed Barbero	586	126	4.7	Kevin Brown	227	122	.54	1,447	Vince Delgado	30	358	11.9
1986	Marc Hicks	357	98	3.6	Troy Taylor	160	92	.58	891	James Devers	40	582	14.6
1987	Chris Richards	668	157	4.3	Troy Taylor	278	169	.61	2,081	Brian Bedford	39	515	13.2
1988	Chris Richards	729	162	4.5	Troy Taylor	330	202	.61	2,416	Todd Powers	45	378	8.4
1989	Anthony Wallace	606	150	4.0	Troy Taylor	394	220	.56	2,738	Brian Treggs	54	746	13.8
1990	Anthony Wallace	1,002	220	4.6	Mike Pawlawski	299	179	.60	2,069	Brian Treggs	45	564	12.5
1991	Russell White	1,177	241	4.9	Mike Pawlawski	316	191	.60	2,517	Brian Treggs	43	643	15.0
1992	Russell White	1,069	206	5.2	Dave Barr	344	199	.58	2,343	Sean Dawkins	65	1,070	16.5
1993	Lindsey Chapman	1,037	207	5.0	Dave Barr	275	187	.68	2,619	Mike Caldwell	55	962	17.5
1994	Reynard Rutherford	713	163	4.4	Dave Barr	144	95	.66	1,077	Iheanyi Uwaezuoke	56	716	12.8
1995	Reynard Rutherford	868	191	4.5	Pat Barnes	362	197	.54	2,685	Na'il Benjamin	52	594	11.4
1996	Brandon Willis	701	187	3.7	Pat Barnes	420	250	.60	3,499	Bobby Shaw	58	888	15.3
1997	Tarik Smith	636	162	3.9	Justin Vedder	390	221	.57	2,718	Bobby Shaw	75	1,093	14.6
1998	Marcus Fields	734	163	4.5	Justin Vedder	386	210	.54	2,322	Dameane Douglas	100	1,150	11.5
1999	Joe Igber	694	148	4.7	Kyle Boller	259	100	.39	1,303	Phillip Pipersburg	13	85	6.5
2000	Joe Igber	901	195	4.6	Kyle Boller	349	163	.47	2,121	Derek Swafford	25	335	13.4
2001	Terrell Williams	688	160	4.3	Kyle Boller	272	134	.49	1,741	Charon Arnold	53	606	11.4
2002	Joe Igber	1,130	241	4.7	Kyle Boller	421	225	.53	2,815	Jonathan Makonner	54	682	12.6
2003	Adimchinobe Echemandu	1,195	238	5.0	Aaron Rodgers	349	215	.62	2,903	Geoff McArthur	85	1,504	17.7
2004	J.J. Arrington	2,018	289	7.0	Aaron Rodgers	316	209	.66	2,566	Geoff McArthur	57	862	15.1

Receiving leaders by receptions
The NCAA began including postseason stats in 2002

CALIFORNIA ALL-TIME SCORES

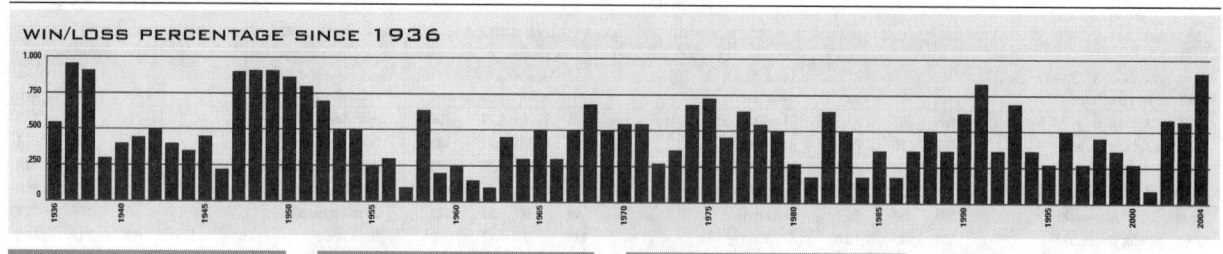

WIN/LOSS PERCENTAGE SINCE 1936

THE SCHOOLS

NO HEAD COACH

1882 0-1-0
| D2 | | Phoenix Club *SF* | 4 | 7 |

1883 2-0-1
F10	=	Allies *SF*	0	0
F24	•	Phoenix Club *SF*	7	6
P7	•	Allies *SF*	13	0

1884 2-0-0
| F9 | • | Merions *SF* | 18 | 0 |
| M1 | • | Wanderers *SF* | 9 | 0 |

1885 4-0-1
F14	•	Merions	13	0
F21	•	Merions	4	0
F28	•	Merions	4	0
M14	=	Wasps	0	0
M28	•	Wasps	2	0

OSCAR S. HOWARD
1886 (.722) 6-2-1

1886 6-2-1
J16	•	Wasps	20	2
F6		Orions	10	12
F22	•	Hastings Law	1	0 *f*
M13	•	Reliance	12	12
M27	•	Reliance	10	0
P30	•	Orions	29	2
Y5		Reliance	4	7
Y21	•	Wasps	1	0 *f*
M22	•	Hastings Law	1	0 *f*

NO HEAD COACH

1887 4-0-0
F18	•	S. F. Club	26	0
F25	•	Volunteers	14	0
M5	•	Reliance	14	6
M26	•	Reliance	12	6

1888 6-1-0
F18	•	S. F. Club	26	0
F25	•	Volunteers	6	10
M10	•	S. F. Club	20	0
M17	•	Posens	14	0
M31	•	Wasps	1	0 *f*
P21	•	Wasps	1	0 *f*
P23	•	at S. F. Club	36	0

1889
NO TEAM

1890 4-0-0
J11	•	Posens	6	4
F8	•	Posens	16	0
F15	•	Posens	11	0
M1	•	Posens	12	0

1891 4-3-0
M7		S.F. Coll.	0	36
D12	•	S. F. Boys HS	12	0
J5	•	S. F. Boys HS	14	0
J12	•	Hopkins	16	4
F3	•	Berkely Gym	30	0
F20		Olympic Club	0	6
M19		Stanford *SF*	10	14

THOMAS McCLUNG
1892 (.625) 2-1-1

1892 2-1-1
O26		Olympic Club *SF*	10	20
N5	•	Olympic Club *SF*	16	0
N12	•	Olympic Club *SF*	8	4
D17	=	Stanford *SF*	10	10

W.W. HEFFELFINGER
1893 (.786) 5-1-1

1893 5-1-1
O28	•	Reliance Club	30	0
N1	•	S.F. All Stars *SF*	14	12
N3	•	Olympic Club *SF*	22	10
N11	•	Olympic Club *SF*	12	6
N14	•	at Reliance Club	22	10
N17	•	at Reliance Club	4	16
N30	=	Stanford *SF*	6	6

CHARLES O. GILL
1894 (.333) 0-1-2

1894 0-1-2
O13	=	Reliance Club *SF*	12	12
O27	=	at Reliance Club	0	0
N29		Stanford *SF*	0	6

FRANK BUTTERWORTH
1895-96 (.700) 9-3-3

1895 3-1-1
O6		Reliance Club	0	4
O12	•	Reliance Club	12	0
O26	•	Reliance Club	8	0
N9	•	Olympic Club *SF*	20	0
N28		Stanford *SF*	6	6

1896 6-2-2
O3		Reliance Club	2	12
O6	=	Olympic Club *SF*	0	0
O10	•	Reliance Club *SF*	0	0
O17	•	Olympic Club *SF*	24	8
N3	•	Reliance Club *SF*	16	10
N26		Stanford *SF*	0	20
D25	•	at Los Angeles AC	14	0
D29	•	at Redlands HS	32	0
D31	•	at San Diego HS	52	0
J1	•	at Whittier School	10	6

CHARLES P. NOTT
1897 (.200) 0-3-2

1897 0-3-2
S25		Reliance Club	0	12
O2		Reliance Club *SF*	0	10
O9	=	Reliance Club	4	4
N6	=	Reliance Club	4	4
N25		Stanford *SF*	0	28

GARRETT COCHRAN
1898-99 (.868) 15-1-3

1898 8-0-2
O1	•	Olympic Club *SF*	17	0
O8	•	Wash. Vol.	4	0
O13	•	Wash. Vol.	44	0
O15	•	Olympic Club *SF*	18	0
O18	•	Kansas Volunteers	33	0
O31	•	Iowa Volunteers	0	0
N4	•	StateMarys	51	0
N12	•	Olympic Club *SF*	5	5
N24	•	Stanford *SF*	22	0
D26	•	at Multnomah AC	27	0

1899 7-1-1
S30	•	Olympic Club	6	0
O14	=	Olympic Club *SF*	0	0
O21	•	League Cross	11	0
N11	•	Olympic Club *SF*	15	0
N15	•	Nevada	24	0
N18	•	Oregon	12	0
N22	•	San Jose State	44	0
N30	•	Stanford *SF*	30	0
D25		Carlisle *SF*	0	2

ADDISON W. KELLY
1900 (.643) 4-2-1

1900 4-2-1
O6	=	Reliance Club	0	0
O20	•	Reliance Club	5	0
N10	•	Reliance Club	11	0
N14	•	Nevada	32	0
N17		Oregon	0	2
N22	•	San Jose State	5	0
N29		Stanford *SF*	0	5

FRANK SIMPSON
1901 (.950) 9-0-1

1901 9-0-1
S28	•	Reliance Club	0	0
O5	•	Olympic Club	5	0
O10	•	Olympic Club	6	0
O12	•	Reliance Club	6	0
O26	•	Olympic Club *SF*	6	5
O30	•	Nevada	12	0
N1	•	Mare Island Marines	16	0
N9	•	Stanford *SF*	2	0
D25	•	at So.Cal Stars	38	0
D30	•	at Perris Indians	15	10

JAMES R. WHIPPLE
1902-03 (.882) 14-1-2

1902 8-0-0
S27	•	Alumni Club	12	0
O4	•	Reliance Club	16	0
O11	•	Alumni Club	44	0
O25	•	Reliance Club	17	0
O28	•	'98-'99 Alumni	5	0
N1	•	Nevada	29	0
N8	•	Stanford *SF*	16	0
N28	•	at Perris Ind.	29	12

1903 6-1-2
S26	=	Reliance Club	0	0
O3	•	Naval Acad.	51	0
O10	•	Reliance Club	7	0
O14	•	Reliance Club	5	0
O24	•	Chemawa	40	0
O28	•	Almuni	6	0
O31	•	Multnomah AC	11	0
N7		Nevada	2	6
N14	=	Stanford *SF*	6	6

JAMES HOPPER
1904 (.813) 6-1-1

1904 6-1-1
O1	•	Sherman	6	0
O8	•	Olympic Club	10	0
O18	•	Multnomah AC	20	0
O22	•	Oregon	12	0
O29	•	Pomona	5	0
N5	•	Nevada	16	0
N12		Stanford	0	18
N24	=	at Washington	6	6

J.W. KNIBBS
1905 (.714) 4-1-2

1905 4-1-2
S30	•	StateVincent	23	0
O7	•	Willamette	0	0
O12	•	Oregon	0	0
O21	•	at Sherman	21	0
O28	•	Oregon State	10	0
N4	•	Nevada	16	0
N11		at Stanford	5	12

1906-1914
NO FOOTBALL TEAM
PLAYED RUGBY

JAMES G. SCHAEFFER
1915 (.615) 8-5

1915 8-5-0
S11	•	Olympic Club	17	0
S18	•	Commerce Club	0	10
S25	•	Olympic Club	18	2
O2	•	Olympic Club	19	9
O9	•	Originals	7	0
O16	•	Sherman Ind.	44	7
O20	•	Saint Mary's-Cal	6	7
O23	•	Southern Cal	10	28
O30	•	Saint Mary's-Cal	10	9
N6	•	Washington	0	72
N13	•	at Washington	7	13
N20	•	at Nevada	81	6
N25	•	at Southern Cal	23	21

1916-1958
Pacific Coast

ANDY SMITH
1916-25 (.799) 74-16-7

1916 6-4-1 (0-3-0)
S16	•	Olympic Club	23	0
S23	•	Originals	23	0
S30	=	Olympic Club	0	0
O7	•	Originals	13	0
O14	•	Whittier	21	17
O21		Oregon	14	39
O28	•	Occidental	13	14
N4	•	at Southern Cal	27	0
N11	•	Saint Mary's-Cal	48	6
N18		Washington	3	13
N30		at Washington	7	14

1917 5-5-1 (2-1-0)
S15		Mare Island Marines	0	27
S22		Olympic Club	2	6
S29		Mare Island Marines	0	26
O6	•	Olympic Club	40	0
O13	•	Navy Hosp. Corps	33	7
O20	•	Occidental	20	0
O27		Oregon State	14	3
N3		Washington	27	0
N10		Saint Mary's-Cal	13	14
N17		at Oregon	0	21
N29	=	at Southern Cal	0	0

1918 7-2-0 (2-0-0)
O5		Fort. MacDowell	7	21
O12	•	S.F. Presido	13	7
O19	•	Fort Scott	1	0 *f*
N9	•	Saint Mary's-Cal	40	14
N16		Mather Field	0	13
N23		Oregon	6	0
N30		Stanford	67	0
D7	•	at San Pedro Navy	20	0
D14	•	at Southern Cal	33	7

1919 6-2-1 (2-2-0)
S27	•	Olympic Club	12	0
O4	•	Olympic Club	6	6
O11	•	Saint Mary's-Cal	19	0
O18	•	Occidental	61	0
O25		Washington State	0	14
N1	•	Oregon State	21	14
N8	•	at Southern Cal	14	13
N22	•	at Stanford	14	10
N27		at Washington	0	7

1920 9-0-0 (3-0-0)

S25	●	Olympic Club	21	0
O2	●	Mare Island Marines	88	0
O9	●	Saint Mary's-Cal	127	0
O16	●	Nevada	79	7
O23	●	Utah	63	0
O30	● |	at Oregon State	17	7
N6	● |	Washington State	49	0
N20	● |	Stanford	38	0
		ROSE BOWL		
J1	●	Ohio State	28	0

1921 9-0-1 (4-0-0)

S24	●	Saint Mary's-Cal	21	0
O1	●	Olympic Club	14	0
O8	●	Nevada	51	6
O15	●	Pacific Club	21	10
O22	● |	Oregon	39	0
O29	● |	Washington State Port	14	0
N5	● |	Southern Cal	38	7
N12	● |	Washington	72	3
N19	● |	at Stanford	42	7
		ROSE BOWL		
J2	=	Wash. & Jeff.	0	0

1922 9-0-0 (4-0-0)

S30	●	Santa Clara	5	14
O7	●	Mare Island Marines	80	0
O14	●	Saint Mary's-Cal	41	0
O21	●	Olympic Club	25	0
O28	● |	Southern Cal Pas	12	0
N4	● |	Washington State	61	0
N11	● |	at Washington	45	7
N18	●	Nevada	61	13
N25	● |	at Stanford	28	0

1923 9-0-1 (5-0-0)

S22	●	Alumni All Stars	3	0
S29	●	Saint Mary's-Cal	49	0
O6	●	Santa Clara	48	0
O13	●	Olympic Club	16	0
O20	● |	Oregon State	26	0
O27	● |	Washington State Port	9	0
N3	=	Nevada	0	0
N10	● |	at Southern Cal	13	7
N17	● |	Washington	9	0
N24	● |	Stanford	9	0

1924 8-0-2 (2-0-2)

S27	●	Santa Clara	13	7
O4	●	Saint Mary's-Cal	17	7
O11	●	Pomona	28	0
O18	●	Olympic Club	9	3
O25	● |	Washington State	20	7
N1	● |	Southern Cal	7	0
N8	= |	at Washington7	7	
N15	●	Nevada	27	0
N22	= |	Stanford	20	20
J1	●	Pennsylvania	14	0

1925 6-3-0 (2-2-0)

S26	●	Santa Clara	28	0
O3	●	Nevada	54	0
O10		Olympic Club	0	15
O17	●	Saint Mary's-Cal	6	0
O24	● |	Oregon Port	28	0
O31	● |	Pomona LA	27	0
N7	● |	Washington State	35	7
N14	|	Washington	0	7
N21	|	at Stanford	14	27

CLARENCE M. PRICE
1926-30 (.606) 27-17-3

1926 3-6-0 (0-5-0)

S25	●	Santa Clara	13	6
O2	●	Olympic Club	32	0
O9		Saint Mary's-Cal	7	26
O16	|	Oregon State	7	27
O23	|	Southern Cal	0	27
O30	|	Oregon	13	21
N6	|	at Washington	7	13
N13	●	Nevada	20	6
N20	|	Stanford	6	41

1927 7-3-0 (2-3-0)

S24	●	Santa Clara	14	6
O1	●	Nevada	54	0
O8	●	Saint Mary's-Cal	13	0
O15	● |	Oregon Port	16	0
O22	●	Olympic Club	21	0
O29	|	at Southern Cal	0	13
N5	● |	Montana	33	13
N12	|	Washington	0	6
N19	|	at Stanford	6	13
D31	●	Pennsylvania	27	13

1928 6-2-2 (3-0-2)

S29	●	Santa Clara	22	0
O6	●	Saint Mary's-Cal	7	0
O13	● |	Washington State	13	3
O20	= |	Southern Cal	0	0
O27		Olympic Club	0	12
N3	● |	Oregon	13	0
N10	● |	at Washington	6	0
N17	●	Nevada	60	0
N24	= |	Stanford	13	13
		ROSE BOWL		
J1		Georgia Tech	7	8

1929 7-1-1 (4-1-0)

S28	●	Santa Clara	27	6
O5	=	Saint Mary's-Cal	0	0
O12	● |	Washington State	14	0
O19	●	at Pennsylvania	12	7
O26	●	Olympic Club	21	19
N2	● |	at Southern Cal	15	7
N9	● |	Montana	53	18
N16	● |	Washington	7	0
N23	|	at Stanford	6	21

1930 4-5-0 (1-4-0)

S27	●	Santa Clara	19	7
O4	|	Washington State	0	16
O11	●	Saint Mary's-Cal	7	6
O18		Olympic Club	7	13
O25	|	at Washington	0	13
N1	● |	Montana	46	0
N8	|	at Southern Cal	0	74
N15	●	Nevada	8	0
N22	|	Stanford	0	41

WILLIAM A. INGRAM
1931-34 (.644) 27-14-4

1931 8-2-0 (4-1-0)

S26	●	Santa Clara	6	2
O3		Saint Mary's-Cal	0	14
O10	●	Olympic Club	6	0
O17	● |	Washington State Port	13	7
O24	|	Southern Cal	0	6
O31	●	Nevada	25	6
N7	● |	Washington	13	0
N14	● |	Idaho	18	0
N21	● |	at Stanford	6	0
D26	●	at Georgia Tech	19	6 *

1932 7-3-2 (2-2-1)

S17	●	Cal State	20	6
S17	●	West Coast Army	13	0
S24		Santa Clara	0	12
O1	●	Olympic Club	22	6
O8	=	Saint Mary's-Cal	12	12
O15	|	Washington State	2	7
O22	● |	at Washington	7	6
O29	●	Nevada	38	0
N5	|	at Southern Cal	7	27
N12	● |	Idaho	21	6
N19	= |	Stanford	0	0
D17	●	Georgia Tech	27	7

1933 6-3-2 (2-2-2)

S23		Santa Clara	0	7
S30	●	Cal State	39	0
S30	●	Nevada	34	0
O7	●	Saint Mary's-Cal	14	13
O14	●	Olympic Club	23	0
O21	= |	Washington State Port	6	6
O28	|	Southern Cal	3	6
N4	= |	at UCLA	0	0
N11	● |	Washington	33	0
N18	● |	Idaho	6	0
N25	|	at Stanford	3	7

1934 6-6-0 (3-2-0)

S29	●	Cal State	54	0
S29	●	Nevada	33	0
O6		Saint Mary's-Cal	0	7
O13	●	Pacific	7	6
O20	● |	UCLA	3	0
O27	|	at Washington	7	13
N3		Santa Clara	0	20
N10	● |	at Southern Cal	7	2
N17	● |	Idaho	45	13
N24	|	Stanford	7	9
D25		at Hawaii All Stars	13	26
J1		at Hawaii	0	14

LEONARD "STUB" ALLISON
1935-44 (.578) 58-42-2

1935 9-1-0 (4-1-0)

S28	●	Cal State	47	0
S28	●	Whittier	6	0
O5	●	Saint Mary's-Cal	10	0
O12	● |	Oregon Port	6	0
O19	●	Santa Clara	6	0
O26	● |	Southern Cal	21	7
N2	● |	at UCLA	14	2
N9	● |	Washington	14	0
N16	●	Pacific	39	0
N23	|	at Stanford	0	13

1936 6-5-0 (4-3-0)

S26	●	Pacific	14	0
S26	●	Cal State	39	0
O3		Saint Mary's-Cal	0	10
O10	● |	Oregon State Port	7	0
O17	|	UCLA	6	17
O24	|	at Washington	0	13
O31	|	Washington State	13	14
N7	● |	at Southern Cal	13	7
N14	● |	Oregon	28	0
N21	● |	Stanford	20	0
D26		at Georgia Tech	7	13

1937 10-0-1 (6-0-1)

S25	●	Saint Mary's-Cal	30	7
O2	● |	Oregon State	24	6
O9	● |	Washington State	27	0
O16	●	Cal Aggies	14	0
O16	●	Pacific	20	0
O23	● |	Southern Cal	20	6
O30	● |	at UCLA	27	14
N6	= |	Washington	0	0
N13	● |	Oregon Port	26	0
N20	● |	at Stanford	13	0
		ROSE BOWL		
J1	●	Alabama	13	0

1938 10-1-0 (6-1-0)

S24	●	Saint Mary's-Cal	12	7
O1	● |	at Washington State	27	3
O8	●	Cal State	48	0
O8	●	Pacific	39	0
O15	● |	UCLA	20	7
O22	● |	at Washington	14	7
O29	● |	Oregon State	13	7
N5	|	at Southern Cal	7	13
N12	● |	Oregon	20	0
N19	● |	Stanford	6	0
D26	●	Georgia Tech	13	0

1939 3-7-0 (2-5-0)

S30	●	Cal State	32	14
S30		Pacific	0	6
O7		Saint Mary's-Cal	3	7
O14	|	Oregon	0	6
O21	● |	Washington State	13	7
O28	|	Southern Cal	0	26
N4	|	at UCLA	7	20
N11	|	Washington	6	13
N18	|	at Oregon State	0	21
N25	● |	at Stanford	32	14

1940 4-6-0 (3-4-0)

S28		Michigan	0	41
O5	●	Saint Mary's-Cal	9	6
O12	|	Washington State	6	9
O19	● |	UCLA	9	7
O26	|	at Washington	6	7
N2	|	Oregon State	13	19
N9	● |	at Southern Cal	20	7
N16	● |	Oregon	14	6
N30	|	Stanford	7	13
D28		at Georgia Tech	0	13

1941 4-5-0 (3-4-0)

S27	●	Saint Mary's-Cal	31	0
O4	|	at Washington State	6	13
O11		Santa Clara	0	13
O18	|	Oregon Port	7	19
O25	● |	Southern Cal	14	0
N1	● |	at UCLA	27	7
N8	|	Washington	6	13
N15	|	Oregon State	0	6
N29	● |	at Stanford	16	0

1942 5-5-0 (3-4-0)

S26	●	Saint Mary's-Cal	6	0
O3	|	at Oregon State	8	13
O10		Santa Clara	6	7
O17	|	UCLA	0	21
O24	● |	at Washington	19	6
O31	● |	Oregon	20	7
N7	|	at Southern Cal	7	21
N14	● |	Montana	13	0
N21	|	Stanford	7	26
D12	●	Saint Mary's Pre-Flight	12	6

1943 4-6-0 (2-2-0)

S25	●	Saint Mary's-Cal	27	12
O2	|	Southern Cal	0	7
O9		Pacific	6	12
O16	● |	at UCLA	13	0
O23		State Marys P.F.	0	39
O30	|	at Southern Cal	0	13
N6	●	San Francisco	32	0
N13	● |	UCLA	13	6
N20		Alameda CG	0	7
N27		Del Monte Pre-Flight	8	47

1944 3-6-1 (1-3-1)

S23	●	Saint Mary's-Cal	31	7
S30	● |	UCLA	6	0
O7	= |	at Southern Cal	6	6
O14	●	Pacific	14	0
O21		Fleet City	2	19
O28	|	Washington	7	33
N4		Coast Guard	6	12
N11	|	at UCLA	0	7
N18	|	Southern Cal	0	32
N25		Saint Mary's Pre-Flight	6	33

LAWRENCE T. SHAW
1945 (.450) 4-5-1

1945 4-5-1 (2-4-1)

S22		Saint Mary's-Cal	13	20
S29	|	Southern Cal	2	13
O6	● |	Washington	27	14
O13	|	at UCLA	0	13
O27	●	Nevada	19	6
N3	= |	Washington State	7	7
N10	|	at Southern Cal	0	14
N17	|	Oregon	13	20
N24	● |	UCLA	6	0
D1	●	State Marys P-f	6	0

FRANK WICKHORST
1946 (.222) 2-7

1946 2-7-0 (1-6-0)

S28		Wisconsin	7	28
O5	|	Oregon	13	14
O12	●	Saint Mary's-Cal	20	13
O19	|	UCLA	6	13
O26	|	at Washington	6	20
N2	● |	Washington State	47	14
N9	|	at Southern Cal	0	14
N16	|	Oregon State	7	28
N23	|	Stanford	6	25

LYNN "PAPPY" WALDORF
1947-56 (.670) 67-32-4

1947 9-1-0 (5-1-0)

S20	●	Santa Clara	33	7
S27	●	Navy	14	7
O4	●	Saint Mary's-Cal	45	6
O11	●	at Wisconsin	48	7
O18	● |	Washington State	21	6
O25	|	Southern Cal	14	39
N1	● |	at UCLA	6	0
N8	● |	Washington	13	7
N15	● |	Montana	60	14
N22	● |	at Stanford	21	18

1948 10-1-0 (6-0-0)

S18	●	Santa Clara	41	19
S25	●	Navy Balt	21	7
O2	●	Saint Mary's-Cal	20	0
O9	●	Wisconsin	40	14
O16	● |	Oregon State	42	0
O23	● |	at Washington	21	0
O30	● |	at Southern Cal	13	7
N6	● |	UCLA	28	13
N13	● |	Washington State	44	14
N20	● |	Stanford	7	6
		ROSE BOWL		
J1		Northwestern	14	20

1949 10-1-0 (7-0-0)

S17	●	Santa Clara	21	7
S24	●	Saint Mary's-Cal	29	7
O1	● |	Oregon State PORT	41	0
O8	●	at Wisconsin	35	20
O15	● |	Southern Cal	16	10
O22	● |	Washington	21	7
O29	● |	at UCLA	35	21
N5	● |	Washington State	33	14
N12	● |	Oregon	41	14
N19	● |	at Stanford	33	14
		ROSE BOWL		
J2		Ohio St	14	17

1950 9-1-1 (5-0-1)

S23	●	Santa Clara	27	9
S30	● |	Oregon PORT	28	7
O7	●	Pennsylvania	14	7
O14	● |	at Southern Cal	13	7
O21	● |	Oregon State PORT	27	0
O28	●	Saint Mary's-Cal	40	25
N4	● |	at Washington	14	7
N11	● |	UCLA	35	0
N18	●	San Francisco	13	7
N25	= |	Stanford	7	7
		ROSE BOWL		
J1		Michigan	6	14

1951 8-2-0 (5-2-0)

S22	●	Santa Clara	34	0
S29	●	at Pennsylvania	35	0
O6	●	Minnesota	55	14
O13	● |	at Washington State	42	35
O20	|	Southern Cal	14	21
O27	● |	Oregon State	35	14
N3	|	at UCLA	7	21
N10	● |	Washington	37	28
N17	● |	Oregon	28	26
N24	● |	at Stanford	20	7

1952 7-3-0 (3-3-0)

S20	●	Pacific	34	13
S27	●	Missouri	28	14
O4	●	at Minnesota	49	13
O11	● |	Oregon PORT	41	7
O18	●	Santa Clara	27	7
O25	|	at Southern Cal	0	10
N1	|	UCLA	7	28
N8	|	at Washington	7	22
N15	● |	Washington State	28	13
N22	● |	Stanford	26	0

1953 4-4-2 (2-2-2)

S19		Baylor	0	25
S26	● |	Oregon State PORT	26	0
O3		Ohio State	19	33
O10	●	at Pennsylvania	40	0
O17	●	San Jose State	34	14
O24	|	Southern Cal	20	32
O31	|	at UCLA	7	20
N7	● |	Washington	53	25
N14	= |	Oregon	0	0
N21	= |	at Stanford	21	21

1954 5-5-0 (4-3-0)

S18		Oklahoma	13	27
S25	●	San Jose State	45	0
O2		at Ohio State	13	21
O9	|	Oregon	27	33
O16	● |	Washington State	17	7
O23	|	at Southern Cal	27	29
O30	|	UCLA	6	27
N6	● |	at Washington	27	6
N13	● |	Oregon State	46	7
N20	● |	Stanford	28	20

1955 2-7-1 (1-5-1)

S17		at Pittsburgh	7	27
S24		Illinois	13	20
O1	●	Pennsylvania	27	7
O8	= |	Washington State	20	20
O15	|	Oregon PORT	0	21
O22	|	Southern Cal	6	33
O29	|	at UCLA	0	47
N5	● |	Washington	20	6
N12	|	Oregon	14	16
N19	|	at Stanford	0	19

1956 3-7-0 (2-5-0)

S22		Baylor	6	7
S29		at Illinois	20	32
O6	●	Pittsburgh	14	0
O13	|	at Oregon State	13	21
O20	|	UCLA	20	34
O27	● |	at Washington	16	7
N3	|	Oregon	6	28
N10	|	at Southern Cal	7	20
N17	|	Washington State	13	14
N24	● |	Stanford	20	18

PETE ELLIOTT
1957-59 (.323) 10-21

1957 1-9-0 (1-6-0)

S21		SMU	6	13
S28	|	at Washington State	7	13
O5		Michigan State	0	19
O12		Navy	6	21
O19	● |	Southern Cal	12	0
O26	|	at Oregon	6	24
N2	|	at UCLA	14	16
N9	|	Oregon State	19	21
N16	|	Washington	27	35
N23	|	at Stanford	12	14

1958 7-4-0 (6-1-0)

S20		Pacific	20	24
S27		at Michigan State	12	32
O4	● |	Washington State	34	14
O11	●	Utah	36	21
O18	● |	at Southern Cal	14	12
O25	● |	Oregon	23	6
N1	|	at Oregon State	8	14
N8	● |	UCLA	20	17
N15	● |	at Washington	12	7
N22	● |	Stanford	16	15
		ROSE BOWL		
J1		Iowa	12	38

1959-1967
AAWU

1959 2-8-0 (1-3-0)

S19	●	Washington State SPO	20	6
S26		Iowa	12	42
O3		at Texas	0	33
O10		Notre Dame	6	28
O17	|	at UCLA	12	19
O24		Oregon State	20	24
O31	|	Southern Cal	7	14
N7		Oregon PORT	18	20
N14	|	Washington	0	20
N21	● |	at Stanford	20	17

MARV LEVY
1960-63 (.238) 8-29-3

1960 2-7-1 (1-3-0)

S17		Tulane	3	7
S24		at Notre Dame	7	21
O1		Army	10	28
O8	=	Washington State	21	21
O15	|	at Southern Cal	10	27
O22		Oregon	0	20
O29	●	at Oregon State	14	6
N5	|	UCLA	0	28
N12	|	at Washington	7	27
N19	● |	Stanford	21	10

1961 1-8-1 (1-3-0)

S23		Texas	3	28
S30		at Iowa	7	28
O7	=	at Missouri	14	14
O14	● |	Washington	21	14
O21	|	Southern Cal	14	28
O28		at Penn State	16	33
N4	|	at UCLA	15	35
N11		Air Force	14	15
N18		Kansas	7	53
N25	|	at Stanford	7	20

1962 1-9-0 (0-4-0)

S22		Missouri	10	21
S29	●	San Jose State	25	8
O6		Pittsburgh	24	26
O13		at Duke	7	21
O20	|	at Southern Cal	6	32
O27		Penn State	21	23
N3	|	UCLA	16	26
N10	|	at Washington	0	27
N17		at Kansas	21	33
N24	|	Stanford	13	30

1963 4-5-1 (1-3-0)

S21	●	Iowa State	15	8
S28		at Illinois	0	10
O5		at Pittsburgh	15	35
O12	=	Duke	22	22
O19	●	San Jose State	34	13
O26	|	Southern Cal	6	36
N2	● |	at UCLA	25	0
N9	|	Washington	26	39
N16	●	at Utah	35	22
N30	|	at Stanford	17	28

RAY WILLSEY
1964-71 (.488) 40-42-1

1964 3-7-0 (0-4-0)

S19	●	Missouri	21	14
S26		Illinois	14	20
O3		Minnesota	20	26
O10	●	at Miami, Fla.	9	7
O17	●	Navy	27	13
O24	|	at Southern Cal	21	26
O31	|	UCLA	21	25
N7	|	at Washington	16	21
N14		Utah	0	14
N21	|	Stanford	3	21

1965 5-5-0 (2-3-0)

S18		Notre Dame	6	48
S25		at Michigan	7	10
O2	●	Kansas	17	0
O9	●	at Air Force	24	7
O16	● |	Washington	16	12
O23	|	at UCLA	3	56
O30	●	Penn State	21	17
N6	|	Southern Cal	0	35
N13	● |	Oregon PORT	24	0
N20	|	at Stanford	7	9

1966 3-7-0 (2-3-0)

S17	● |	Washington State SPO	21	6
S24		Michigan	7	17
O1	●	Pittsburgh	30	15
O8		San Jose State	0	24
O15	● |	at Washington	24	20
O22	|	UCLA	15	28
O29		at Penn State	15	33
N5	|	at Southern Cal	9	35
N12		Army	3	6
N19	|	Stanford	7	13

1967 5-5-0 (2-3-0)

S16	● |	Oregon	21	13
S23		at Notre Dame	8	41
S30	●	Michigan	10	9
O7	●	Air Force	14	12
O14	|	at UCLA	14	37
O21		at Syracuse	14	20
O28	|	Washington	6	23
N4	|	Southern Cal	12	31
N11	●	San Jose State	30	6
N18	● |	at Stanford	26	3

1968-PRESENT
PAC 10

1968 7-3-1 (2-2-1)

S21	●	at Michigan	21	7
S28	●	Colorado	10	0
O5	●	San Jose State	46	0
O12		at Army	7	10
O19	● |	UCLA	39	15
O26	●	Syracuse	43	0
N2	= |	at Washington	7	7
N9	|	at Southern Cal	17	35
N16	● |	Oregon	36	8
N23	|	Stanford	0	20
N30	●	at Hawaii	17	12

1969 5-5-0 (2-4-0)

S20		Texas	0	17
S27	●	at Indiana	17	14
O4	●	Rice	31	21
O11	● |	Washington	44	13
O18	|	at UCLA	0	32
O25	● |	Washington State SPO	17	0
N1	|	Southern Cal	9	14
N8	|	Oregon State	3	35
N15	●	San Jose State	31	7
N22	|	at Stanford	28	29

1970 6-5-0 (4-3-0)

S12	|	Oregon PORT	24	31
S19		at Texas	15	56
S26	●	Indiana	56	14
O3		at Rice	0	28
O10	● |	at Washington	31	28
O17	|	UCLA	21	24
O24	● |	Washington State	45	0
O31	● |	at Southern Cal	13	10
N7	|	at Oregon State	10	16
N14	●	San Jose State	35	28
N21	● |	Stanford	22	14

1971 6-5-0 (4-3-0)

S11		Arkansas LR	20	51
S18	●	West Virginia	20	10
S25	●	San Jose State	34	10
O2		at Ohio State	3	35
O9	● |	Oregon State	30	27
O16	● |	Washington State SPO	24	23
O23	● |	at UCLA	31	24
O30	|	Southern Cal	0	28
N6	|	Washington	7	30
N13	● |	at Oregon	17	10
N20	|	at Stanford	0	14

MIKE WHITE
1972-77 (.523) 34-31-1

1972 3-8-0 (3-4-0)

S9		at Colorado	10	20
S16	● |	Washington State	37	23
S23		San Jose State	10	17
S30		at Missouri	27	34
O7		Ohio State	18	35
O14	|	at Southern Cal	14	42
O21	|	UCLA	13	49
O28	|	at Washington	21	35
N4	● |	Oregon	31	12
N11	|	Oregon State PORT	23	26
N18	● |	Stanford	24	21

1973 4-7-0 (2-5-0)

S15		Alabama BIRM	0	66
S22		Illinois	7	27
S29	●	at Army	51	6
O6	● |	Washington	54	49
O13	|	at Oregon	10	41
O20	● |	Oregon State	24	14
O27	|	at UCLA	21	61
N3	|	Southern Cal	14	50
N10	●	San Jose State	19	9
N17	|	at Washington State	28	31
N24	|	at Stanford	17	26

1974 7-3-1 (4-2-1)

S14		at Florida	17	21
S21	●	San Jose State	17	16
S28	●	Army	27	14
O5	●	at Illinois	31	14
O12	● |	Oregon	40	10
O19	● |	at Oregon State	17	14
O26	|	UCLA	3	28
N2	= |	at Southern Cal	15	15
N9	● |	at Washington	52	26
N16	● |	Washington State	37	33
N23	|	Stanford	20	22

1975 8-3-0 (6-1-0)

S13		at Colorado	27	34
S20		West Virginia	10	28
S27	● |	at Washington State	33	21
O4	●	San Jose State	27	24
O11	● |	at Oregon	34	7
O18	● |	Oregon State	51	24
O25	|	at UCLA	14	28
N1	● |	Southern Cal	28	14
N8	● |	Washington	27	24
N15	●	at Air Force	31	14
N22	● |	at Stanford	48	15

1976 5-6-0 (3-4-0)

S11		at Georgia	24	36
S18		at Oklahoma	17	28
S25	●	at Arizona State	31	22
O2	●	San Jose State	43	16
O9	● |	Oregon	27	10
O16	|	at Oregon State	9	10
O23	|	UCLA	19	35
O30	|	at Southern Cal	6	20
N6	● |	at Washington	7	0
N13	● |	Washington State	23	22
N20	|	Stanford	24	27

1977 7-4-0 (3-4-0)

S10	●	at Tennessee	27	17
S17	●	Air Force	24	14
S24	●	at Missouri	28	21
O1	●	San Jose State	52	3
O8	|	at Washington State	10	17
O15	● |	Oregon State	41	17
O22	|	at UCLA	19	21 †
O29	● |	Southern Cal	17	14
N5	|	Washington	31	50
N12	● |	at Oregon	48	16
N19	|	at Stanford	3	21

ROGER THEDER
1978-81 (.378) 17-28

1978 6-5-0 (3-4-0)

S9		at Nebraska	26	36
S16	●	at Georgia Tech	34	22
S23	●	Pacific	24	6
S30	●	at West Virginia	28	21
O7	● |	Oregon	21	18
O14	● |	at Arizona	33	20
O21	|	UCLA	0	45
O28	|	at Southern Cal	17	42
N4	|	at Arizona State	21	35
N11	● |	Washington State	22	14
N18	|	Stanford	10	30

1979 6-6-0 (5-4-0)

S8	● |	at Arizona State	17	9
S15	● |	at Arizona	10	7
S22	●	San Jose State	13	10
S29		Michigan	10	14
O6	|	at Oregon	14	19
O13	● |	Oregon State	45	0
O20	|	at UCLA	27	28
O27	|	Southern Cal	14	24
N3	|	Washington	24	28
N10	● |	at Washington State	45	13
N17	● |	at Stanford	21	14
		GARDEN STATE BOWL		
D15		Temple	17	28

1980 3-8-0 (3-5-0)

S13		Florida TAM	13	41
S20		at Army	19	26
S27	|	Arizona	24	31
O4		at Michigan	13	38
O11	● |	Oregon	31	6
O18	● |	Oregon State	27	6
O25	|	UCLA	9	32
N1	|	at Southern Cal	7	60
N8	|	at Arizona State	6	34
N15	|	Washington State	17	31
N22	● |	Stanford	28	23

1981 2-9-0 (2-6-0)

S5		Texas A&M	28	29
S12		at Georgia	13	27
S19	● |	at Arizona	14	13
S26		San Jose State	24	27
O10	|	Washington	26	27
O17	|	at Arizona State	17	45
O24	|	at UCLA	6	34
O31	● |	Oregon State	45	3
N7	|	Southern Cal	3	21
N14	|	Washington State SPO	0	19
N21	|	at Stanford	21	42

JOE KAPP
1982-86 (.373) 20-34-1

1982 7-4-0 (4-4-0)

S11	●	at Colorado	31	17
S18	●	San Diego State	28	0
S25	|	Arizona State	0	15
O2	●	San Jose State	26	7
O9	|	at Washington	7	50
O16	● |	Oregon	10	7
O23	|	UCLA	31	47
O30	● |	at Oregon State	28	14
N6	|	at Southern Cal	0	42
N13	● |	Washington State	34	14
N20	● |	Stanford	25	20

1983 5-5-1 (3-4-1)

S3	●	at Texas A&M	19	17
S10		at San Diego St	14	28
S17	●	San Jose State	30	9
O1	= |	Arizona	33	33
O8	|	at Oregon	17	24
O15	● |	Oregon State	45	19
O22	|	at UCLA	16	20
O29	|	Southern Cal	9	19
N5	● |	Arizona State	26	24
N12	|	at Washington State	6	16
N27	● |	at Stanford	27	18

1984 2-9-0 (1-8-0)

S8	|	at Arizona	13	23
S15	●	Pacific	28	12
S22	|	Oregon	14	21
S29		San Jose State	18	33
O6	● |	at Arizona State	19	14
O13	|	at Oregon State	6	9
O20	|	UCLA	14	17
O27	|	at Southern Cal	7	31
N3	|	at Washington	14	44
N10	|	Washington State	7	33
N17	|	Stanford	10	27

1985 4-7-0 (2-7-0)

A31	●	San Jose State	48	21
S7	|	at Washington State	19	20
S14	|	Oregon State PORT	20	23
S21	|	Arizona	17	23
O5	●	at Missouri	39	32
O12	|	Washington	12	28
O19	● |	at Oregon	27	24
O26	|	at UCLA	7	34
N2	|	Arizona State	8	30
N9	● |	Southern Cal	14	6
N23	|	at Stanford	22	24

1986 2-9-0 (2-7-0)

S13		at Boston College	15	21
S20	● |	Washington State	31	21
S27		San Jose State	14	35
O4	|	at Washington	18	50
O11	|	Oregon State	12	14
O18	|	UCLA	10	36
O25	|	at Arizona	16	33
N1	|	Oregon	9	27
N8	|	at Arizona State	0	49
N15	|	at Southern Cal	3	28
N22	● |	Stanford	17	11

BRUCE SNYDER
1987-91 (.544) 29-24-4

1987 3-6-2 (2-3-2)

S5	●	Pacific	42	0
S12		San Jose State	25	27
S19		at Minnesota	23	32
S26	|	Southern Cal	14	31
O3		at Tennessee	12	38
O10	= |	Arizona	23	23
O24	|	at UCLA	18	42
O31	● |	at Oregon	20	6
N14	● |	Arizona State	38	20
N21	|	at Stanford	7	31
N28	= |	Washington State TOK	17	17

1988 5-5-1 (1-5-1)

S10	●	Pacific	30	7
S17	|	at Oregon State	16	17
S24	●	Kansas	52	21
O1	●	San Jose State	21	14
O8	|	at Washington State	13	44
O15	|	UCLA	21	38
O22	● |	Temple	31	14
O29	● |	at Arizona	10	7
N5	|	at Southern Cal	3	35
N12	|	at Washington	27	28
N19	= |	Stanford	19	19

1989 4-7-0 (2-6-0)

S9	|	at Oregon	19	35
S16		at Miami, Fla.	3	31
S23	●	Wisconsin	20	14
S30	|	at UCLA	6	24
O7	●	San Jose State	26	21
O14	|	Southern Cal	15	31
O21	|	Washington	16	29
O28	|	Oregon State	14	25
N4	● |	Arizona	29	28
N11	● |	Washington State	38	26
N18	|	at Stanford	14	24

1990 7-4-1 (4-3-1)

S8	●	at Wisconsin	28	12
S15		Miami, Fla.	24	52
S22	|	at Washington State	31	41
S29	● |	at Arizona	30	25
O6	●	San Jose State	35	34
O13	● |	at Arizona State	31	24
O20	● |	UCLA	38	31
O27	|	at Washington	7	46
N3	= |	at Southern Cal	31	31
N10	● |	Oregon	28	3
N17	|	Stanford	25	27
		COPPER BOWL		
D31	●	Wyoming	17	15

1991 10-2-0 (6-2-0)

S7	●	Pacific	86	24
S14	●	Purdue	42	18
S21	● |	at Arizona	23	21
O5	● |	at UCLA	27	24
O12	● |	Oregon	45	7
O19	|	Washington	17	24
O26	● |	San Jose State	41	20
N2	● |	Southern Cal	52	30
N9	● |	at Oregon State	27	14
N16	● |	Arizona State	25	6
N23	|	at Stanford	21	38
		CITRUS BOWL		
J1	●	Clemson	37	13

KEITH GILBERTSON
1992-95 (.435) 20-26

1992 4-7-0 (2-6-0)

S5	●	San Jose State	46	16
S12		at Purdue	14	41
S24	●	at Kansas	27	23
O3	● |	Oregon State	42	0
O10	|	at Washington	16	35
O17	|	at Southern Cal	24	27
O24	|	Arizona	17	24
O31	● |	UCLA	48	12
N7	|	at Oregon	17	37
N14	|	at Arizona State	12	28
N21	|	Stanford	21	41

1993 9-4-0 (4-4-0)

S4	● |	at UCLA	27	25
S11	●	San Diego State	45	25
S18	●	at Temple	58	0
S25	●	San Jose State	46	13
O2	● |	Oregon	42	41
O9	|	Washington	23	24
O16	|	at Washington State	7	34
O30	|	Southern Cal	14	42
N6	|	at Arizona State	0	41
N13	● |	Arizona	24	20
N20	● |	at Stanford	46	17
N27	●	at Hawaii	42	18
		ALAMO BOWL		
D31	●	Iowa	37	3

1994 4-7-0 (3-5-0)

S10		at San Diego State	20	22
S17		Hawaii	7	21
S24	● |	Arizona State	25	21
O1	●	San Jose State	55	0
O8	● |	UCLA	26	7
O15	|	at Oregon	7	23
O22	|	at Southern Cal	0	61
O29	|	Washington State	23	26
N5	|	at Arizona	6	13
N12	|	at Washington	19	31
N19	● |	Stanford	24	23

1995 3-8-0 (2-6-0)

S2		at San Diego State	9	33
S9		Fresno State	24	25
S23	●	San Jose State	40	7
S30	|	at Arizona	15	20
O7	|	Southern Cal	16	26
O14	|	Oregon	30	52
O21	● |	at Oregon State	13	12
O28	|	at UCLA	16	33
N4	● |	Washington State	27	11
N11	|	Arizona State	29	38
N18	|	at Stanford	24	29

STEVE MARIUCCI
1996 (.500) 6-6

1996 6-6 (3-5)

S7	●	at San Jose State	45	25
S14	●	San Diego State	42	37
S21	●	Nevada	33	15
S28	● |	Oregon State	48	42
O5	● |	at Southern Cal	22	15
O19	|	at Washington State	18	21
O26	|	UCLA	29	38
N2	● |	Arizona	56	55
N9	|	at Arizona State	7	35
N16	|	at Oregon	23	40
N23	|	Stanford	21	42
		ALOHA BOWL		
D25		Navy	38	42

TOM HOLMOE
1997-2001 (.291) 16-39

1997 3-8 (1-7)

S6	●	at Houston	35	3
S20	●	Oklahoma	40	36
S27	|	Southern Cal	17	27
O4		at Louisiana Tech	34	41
O11	|	Washington	3	30
O18	|	at Washington State	37	63
O25	|	at UCLA	17	35
N1	● |	Oregon State	33	14
N8	|	Arizona State	21	28
N15	|	at Arizona	38	41
N22	|	at Stanford	20	21

1998 5-6 (3-5)

S5	●	Houston	14	10
S12		Nebraska	3	24
S19	●	at Oklahoma	13	12
S26	● |	Washington State	24	14
O10	● |	at Southern Cal	32	31
O17	|	at Washington	13	21
O24	|	UCLA	16	28
O31	● |	at Oregon State	20	19
N7	|	at Arizona State	22	55
N14	|	Arizona	23	27
N21	|	Stanford	3	10

1999 4-7 (3-5)

S4	●	Rutgers	21	7
S11		at Nebraska	0	45
S25	●	Arizona State	24	23
O2	|	at Washington State	7	31
O9		at Brigham Young	28	38
O16	● |	at UCLA	17	0
O23	|	Washington	27	31
O30	● |	Southern Cal	17	7
N6	|	at Oregon State	7	17
N13	|	Oregon	19	24
N20	|	at Stanford	13	31

2000 3-8 (2-6)

S9	●	Utah	24	21
S16		at Illinois	15	17
S23		at Fresno State	3	17
S30	|	Washington St	17	21
O7	|	at Arizona State	10	30
O14	● |	UCLA	46	38
O21	|	at Washington	24	36
O28	● |	at Southern Cal	28	16
N4	|	Oregon State	32	38
N11	|	at Oregon	17	25
N18	|	Stanford	30	36

2001 1-10 (0-8)

S1		Illinois	17	44
S8		Brigham Young	16	44
S22	|	at Washington State	20	51
S29	|	Washington	28	31
O13	|	Oregon	7	48
O20	|	at UCLA	17	56
O27	|	at Oregon State	10	19
N3	|	Arizona	24	38
N10	|	Southern Cal	14	55
N17	|	at Stanford	28	35
N23	●	at Rutgers	20	10

JEFF TEDFORD
2002-PRESENT (.658) 25-13

2002 7-5 (4-4)

A31	●	Baylor	70	22
S7	●	New Mexico State	34	13
S14	●	at Michigan State	46	22
S21		Air Force	21	23
S28	|	Washington State	38	48
O5	● |	at Washington	34	27
O12	|	at Southern Cal	28	30
O19	● |	UCLA	17	12
O26	|	at Oregon State	13	24
N9	● |	at Arizona State	55	38
N16	|	Arizona	41	52
N23	● |	Stanford	30	7

2003 8-6 (5-3)

A23		Kansas State KC	28	42
A30	●	Southern Miss	34	2
S6		Colorado State	21	23
S11		at Utah	24	31
S20	●	at Illinois	31	24
S27	● |	Southern Cal	34	31
O4	|	Oregon State	21	35
O18	|	at UCLA	20	23
O25	● |	Arizona	42	14
N1	● |	at Arizona State	51	23
N8	|	at Oregon	17	21
N15	● |	Washington	54	7
N22	● |	at Stanford	28	16
		INSIGHT BOWL		
D26	●	Virginia Tech	52	49

2004 10-2 (7-1)

S4	●	at Air Force	56	14
S11	●	New Mexico State	41	14
O2	● |	at Oregon State	49	7
O9	|	at Southern Cal	17	23
O16	● |	UCLA	45	28
O23	● |	at Arizona	38	0
O30	● |	Arizona State	27	0
N6	● |	Oregon	28	27
N13	● |	at Washington	42	12
N20	● |	Stanford	41	6
D4	●	at Southern Miss	26	16
		HOLIDAY BOWL		
D30		Texas Tech	31	45

Neutral Site key: *TAM* Tampa, FL / *TOK* Tokyo, Japan / *LA* Los Angeles, CA / *SF* San Francisco, CA / *PORT* Portland, OR / *PAS* Pasadena, CA / *BALT* Baltimore, MD / *SPO* Spokane, WA / *LR* Little Rock, AR / *BIRM* Birmingham, AL

f Forfeit † Game Later Forfieted # Disputed Victor * Disputed Score || Designated Conference Game |2 Counted Twice in Conference Standings

CENTRAL FLORIDA
BY ED KRZEMIENSKI

CHANGE IS THE ONLY CONSTANT. Such a saying could be applied to Central Florida's football program. Starting its run in competitive football in 1979, Central Florida climbed up the NCAA division ladder quickly. In less than 20 years of play, the team went from NCAA Division III (three years) to Division II (eight years) to Division I-AA (six years) before joining Division I-A in 1996. In 2002, Central Florida joined the MAC in hopes of getting its football program into the national spotlight. Taking on any and every opponent of excellence, the Knights played memorable games against BCS powers like Nebraska, Virginia Tech and Auburn. Big upsets of college football powerhouses have been rare so far, and UCF took a step back with an 0–11 mark in 2004, but there are many reasons to believe that is a temporary condition. With a location in the heart of one of the two best recruiting states in the nation, an already impressive list of NFL players claiming UCF as their alma mater, the 2004 hiring of George O'Leary as head coach and a move to Conference USA in 2005, the future looks potentially bright in the middle of the Sunshine State.

TRADITION The Knights have not been around long enought for any of their traditions to be called historic. Still, the team follows the guidelines of their nickname with historical accuracy. The Big Stick Award is given to the UCF player who delivers the biggest hit in a game, but at one time, a player was presented a sword and dubbed a Knight by the previous week's winner after Thursday practice. Like knights during the Middle Ages, the player then ties a cloth (now a bandanna) around his left arm as a symbol of bravery. The Big Stick winner also leads the team out of the tunnel before the next game. The award extended to the national level in 1998, when Knights cornerback Jeff Fye earned the Compaq College Hit of the Year for knocking out a Northern Illinois receiver.

BEST PLAYER It will be a long time before anyone forgets Daunte Culpepper's career at Central Florida. The Knights' starting quarterback for each of his eligible seasons (1995-98) Culpepper set every major passing mark at Central Florida, most of which he still holds. In each of his first two seasons, Culpepper threw for more than 2,000 yards; in his final two, he racked up more than 3,000. He threw for 300 yards in 15 career games and for 400 yards in three. All told Culpepper passed for 11,412 yards. He not only threw often and far, but also on target. In his senior

---

PROFILE

University of Central Florida
Orlando, Fla.
Founded: 1963
Enrollment: 35,385
Colors: Black and Gold
Nickname: Golden Knights
Stadium: Florida Citrus Bowl
    Opened in 1936
    Grass; 65,432 capacity
First football game: 1979
All-time record: 142–142–1 (.500)
Website: www.ucfathletics.com

THE BEST OF TIMES

The Daunte Culpepper era (1995-98) culminated in a 9–2 senior season, but even when the Knights lost earlier in his career, it was usually close and always exciting.

THE WORST OF TIMES

In 1982, their first season in Division II, the Golden Knights went 0–10, including a 69-0 loss to VMI and a 60-10 loss to Nicholls State. Overall, it was an abysmal start to the decade, with 18 wins in six years.

CONFERENCE

After just three seasons in the Mid-American Conference, Central Florida joined Conference USA in 2005.

DISTINGUISHED ALUMNI

Michelle Akers, captain, 1996 Olympic gold medal soccer team; Bill Parsons, director, NASA; Tari Phillips, WNBA player

FIGHT SONG

BLACK AND GOLD
U-C-F charge on to the field!
With our spirit, we'll never yield!
Black and gold charge right through the line.
Victory is our cry,
V-I-C-T-O-R-Y!
Tonight our Knights will shine!
U-C-F Knights! U-C-F lets gooooooo Knights!

year, the Knights quarterback set a Division I-A record with a .736 completion percentage, breaking the mark set by Steve Young. Following his senior season, Culpepper finished sixth in the Heisman balloting and became the Minnesota Vikings' first-round pick (11th overall) in the NFL draft. At 6' 4", 255 pounds, Culpepper lived up to the lofty expectations placed on him by the likes of Nebraska coach Tom Osborne, who stated, "People may not know about Culpepper now, but the whole world will find out about him, because he'll be making big noise on Sundays."

BEST COACH Toward the end of his school-record 13 seasons at the helm, Gene McDowell coached UCF through its transition to Division I-A and recruited Culpepper. Before his resignation in 1998, McDowell set the standard for Golden Knights coaches as he compiled an 86–61 overall record. It looked as if his successor, Mike Kruczek, might surpass these marks, but after a disappointing 3–9 2003 season, the school replaced Kruczek with former Georgia Tech coach O'Leary. As it stands, McDowell has exactly 50 more total victories to his name than the second-place Kruczek.

> *Central Florida became the first collegiate team to play a Russian football team on American soil.*

BEST TEAM Led by the senior Culpepper, the 1998 Golden Knights began the season with two lopsided victories, then dropped a game to Purdue, which finished the season ranked No. 24, before ripping off five consecutive victories to bring their record to a gaudy 7–1 en route to a 9–2 finish. Only in its third season at the Division I-A level, Kruczek's squad accepted a conditional bid to the Oahu Bowl in Hawaii. When UCLA lost a late-season game at Miami, Fla., though, it forced the bowl officials to select a team from the Pac-10, leaving Central Florida out of the picture. In a season that saw Culpepper complete 296 of 402 passes for 3,690 yards with a 4:1 touchdown-to-interception ratio, with Siaha Burley catching 88 of those tosses, the nation did not get to watch the Knights and their phenomenal quarterback in a bowl game.

BIGGEST GAME Central Florida is one of the few teams in Division I football that can look to a loss as its biggest game. Yet the performance the Golden Knights put up in a losing effort against Nebraska in 1997 stands as the moment in which the program arrived on the national stage. Playing the eventual national champs on Sept. 13 in Lincoln, Culpepper threw for 318 yards and led UCF to a 17-14

RECORDS

RUSHING YARDS
GAME
242 — Willie English vs. Arkansas State, Oct. 5, 1991 (25 att.)
SEASON
1,511 — Marquette Smith, 1995 (274 att.)
CAREER
3,356 — Alex Haynes, 2001-04 (742 att.)

PASSING YARDS
GAME
497 — Ryan Schneider vs. Florida Atlantic, Sept. 13, 2003 (37 of 52)
SEASON
3,770 — Ryan Schneider, 2002 (265 of 430)
CAREER
11,412 — Daunte Culpepper, 1995-98 (889 of 1,391)

RECEIVING YARDS
GAME
266 — Siaha Burley vs. Louisiana-Lafayette, Oct. 24, 1998 (10 rec.)
SEASON
1,237 — Doug Gabriel, 2002 (75 rec.)
CAREER
3,618 — David Rhodes, 1991-94 (213 rec.)

POINTS
GAME
24 — Six tied; most recently by Doug Gabriel vs. Ohio, Sept. 30. 2002 (4 TDs).
SEASON
90 — Bret Cooper, 1992 (15 TDs)
CAREER
297 — Charlie Pierce, 1993-96 (46 FGs, 159 PATs)

CONSENSUS ALL-AMERICANS

1987	Bernard Ford	WR
1987	Ed O'Brien	PK
1993	David Rhodes	WR
1994	Charlie Pierce	PK

halftime lead, before it lost a hard-fought game, 38-24. Despite standing winless after three games, UCF received its first-ever vote in the AP weekly poll and was regarded as the "best 0–3 team in the nation." Equally impressed was Grant Wistrom, Nebraska's All-America defensive lineman, who remarked, "It was kind of a reality check. Maybe we're not as good as we thought we were on defense."

BIGGEST UPSET Traveling to face Alabama in 2000, the Knights scored their first win over a major power in a game characterized by momentum shifts. Trailing 10-0 in the first half, the Tide scored 24 unanswered points before Central Florida followed with a 27-point run of its own. Alabama responded with another 14, to take a 38-37 lead with 2:34 left. Led by redshirt freshman Ryan Schneider, playing for senior Vic Penn, who had dislocated his shoulder earlier in the season, Central Florida moved 59 yards in 12 plays to set up a game-winning field goal with three seconds left. The 37-yard kick by Javier Beorlegui made the final score 40-38.

HEARTBREAKER In 1998, Auburn invited Central Florida to be its homecoming sacrificial lamb. The Knights turned out to be wolves that day. Ahead 6-3 in the final two minutes, all Central Florida had to do was run out the clock to spoil the day for the 80,000-plus Tigers fans as well as run its own record to 8–1. But a UCF fumble was recovered by Auburn and the home team scored a late touchdown to win 10-6.

STADIUM Central Florida plays its home games in the Florida Citrus Bowl. Originally named Orlando Stadium, it was built in 1936 for about $115,000, and was renamed the Tangerine Bowl in 1947. In 1983, the facility and its annual bowl game were both renamed the Florida Citrus Bowl in conjunction with an annual sponsorship agreement with the Florida Department of Citrus. Playing in the 65,432-seat stadium can be a cavernous experience

for Central Florida. Even in it's best season, 1998, UCF averaged 27,464 and its largest home crowd, vs. Virginia Tech in 2000, still fell 20,000 short of capacity.

RIVAL As a D1-AA team, Central Florida regarded Georgia Southern as its fiercest rival. Since its shift to D1-A, no team emerged as a consistent annual foe. So what's a Florida school without a natural conference rival to do? Look for another Florida school to square off against. One candidate: South Florida. The schools have competed in other sports but have yet to meet on the football field. They meet in 2005 for the first time.

DISPUTE In 1999, after dropping its first three games—to No. 22 Purdue, No. 4 Florida and No. 12 Georgia Tech—Central Florida tried to right its ship against No. 11 Georgia. Late in the fourth quarter, Vic Penn threw a touchdown pass to Page Sessoms, but the Golden Knights missed the extra point and still trailed 24-23. Not finished yet, UCF marched down the field to the Georgia 20-yard line with 22 seconds remaining. On the verge of attempting a game-winning field goal, Central Florida was flagged on a controversial offensive pass interference call that backed it out of field goal range. The Golden Knights lost by a point.

NICKNAME The school was still known as Florida Technological University in 1970, when it instituted Operation Mascot to determine a mascot and nickname. Voters chose the name Knights of Pegasus, a name taken up by the football team in 1979 a year after the school changed its name to UCF. In 1993, Steve Sloan—who became AD at Tennessee-Chattanooga in 2002—took over as athletic director of Central Florida and started the march to Division I-A. Having previously worked for teams nicknamed the Crimson Tide, Red Raiders, Yellow Jackets and Blue Devils, Sloan helped the Knights evolve into the Golden Knights.

ALL-TIME TEAM

This 25th anniversary team was chosen by The Orlando Sentinel in conjunction with the Central Florida athletic department.

OFFENSE

1982-85	Jorge Magluta,	OG
1995-98	Marcus Jenkins,	OG
1995-98	Cornell Green,	OT
2000-01	Steve Edwards,	OT
1991-94	Mike Gruttadauria,	C
1986-87	Don Grayson,	TE
1987-90	Sean Beckton,	WR
1991-94	David Rhodes,	WR
1995-98	Daunte Culpepper,	QB
1987-90	Perry Balasis,	FB
1989-91, 1993	Willie English,	TB
1989-92	Franco Grilla,	PK
1989-92	Mike Dickinson,	PR
1983-86	Ted Wilson,	KR

DEFENSE

1991-94	Greg Jefferson,	DE
1999-02	Elton Patterson,	DE
1984-87	Sylvester Bembery,	DT
1998-01	Josh McKibben,	DT
1979-82	Bill Giovanetti,	LB
1989-92	Rich Hamilton,	LB
1993-96	Nakia Reddick,	LB
1984-87	Corris Ervin,	CB
1999-02	Asante Samuel,	CB
1986-88	Keith Evans,	S
1999-01	Ricot Joseph,	S
1993-96	Charlie Pierce,	P

MASCOT A member of the UCF cheerleading squad, Knightro is the school's mascot. He appears in full armor at all football games, usually with a jousting lance.

UNIFORMS Central Florida's colors have always been black and gold and their uniforms have always included some combination of black, gold and white. Helmets have been either gold or black base—twice solidly so—with logos on both sides. The first logo to appear on the Knights helmet was that of the winged Pegasus in 1981. Thereafter, the helmets lost their wings in favor of a UCF over an outline of the state of Florida, then just UCF. Currently, the Golden Knights sport gold helmets with a black UCF logo pierced by a knight's lance.

QUIRK No second-stringer playing for the Knights when Coach Kruczek and AD Steve Sloan ruled the roost could claim the higher-ups in the football program did not know what it was like backing up a great player. Coach Kruczek was especially familiar with staying ready as a backup, knowing they're only "one play away from being in there." In his rookie season with the Pittsburgh Steelers, Kruczek came off the bench for an injured Terry Bradshaw and led Pittsburgh to six consecutive victories. Sloan, on the other hand, stepped in at quarterback at Alabama when the Crimson Tide starter was suspended from the team for drinking on campus. That miscreant's name was Joe Willie Namath. Both starters are now enshrined in Canton.

LORE In 1992, Central Florida helped officially end the cold war when it became the first collegiate team to play a Russian football team on American soil. The Golden Knights defeated the Moscow Bears of the Russian League of American Football 42-6 in an exhibition game in Orlando. U! S! A! … er … U! C! F!

QUOTE "How come there's a pro quarterback playing in college?"—A young fan from Louisiana-Monroe wondered after watching Daunte Culpepper account for 480 yards of total offense in a game in 1997

THE SCHOOLS

CENTRAL FLORIDA ANNUAL STATISTICAL LEADERS

YR	RUSHING	YDS	ATT	AVG	PASSING	ATT	CMP	PCT	YDS	RECEIVING	REC	YDS	AVG
1996	Mike Grant	339	90	3.8	Daunte Culpepper	314	187	.60	2,565	Mark Nonsant	60	925	15.4
1997	Mike Grant	565	132	4.3	Daunte Culpepper	381	238	.63	3,086	Siaha Burley	77	1,106	14.4
1998	Mike Grant	503	110	4.6	Daunte Culpepper	402	296	.74	3,690	Siaha Burley	88	1,142	13.0
1999	Edward Mack	461	86	5.4	Vic Penn	455	262	.58	3,078	Charles Lee	87	1,133	13.0
2000	Corey Baker	417	91	4.6	Ryan Schneider	286	177	.62	2,334	Tyson Hinshaw	89	1,089	12.2
2001	Alex Haynes	690	140	4.9	Ryan Schneider	357	204	.57	2,923	Tavirus Davis	47	722	15.4
2002	Alex Haynes	1,038	204	5.1	Ryan Schneider	430	265	.62	3,770	Doug Gabriel	75	1,237	16.5
2003	Alex Haynes	774	183	4.2	Ryan Schneider	281	194	.69	1,949	Tavaris Capers	67	585	8.7
2004	Alex Haynes	854	215	4.0	Steven Moffett	229	147	.64	1,721	Luther Huggins	42	585	13.9

Receiving leaders by receptions
NCAA began including postseason stats in 2002

CENTRAL FLORIDA ALL-TIME SCORES

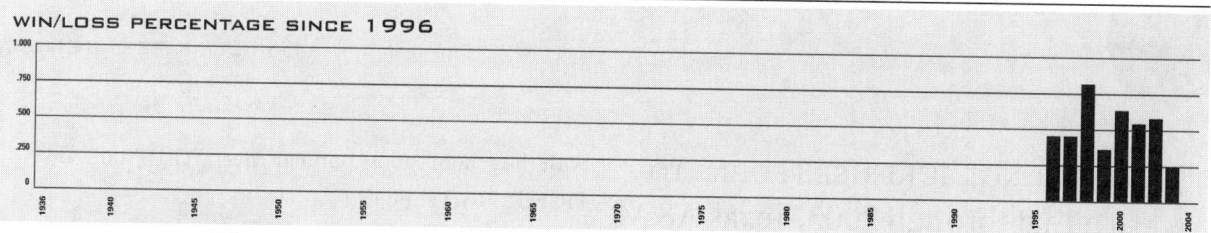

WIN/LOSS PERCENTAGE SINCE 1996

GENE McDOWELL
1985-97 (.585)   86-61

1996-2001
INDEPENDENT

1996   5-6
A29 ●	William & Mary	39	33
S7	at South Carolina	14	33
S14	at New Mexico	7	17
S21	at Ball State	10	31
S28	at East Carolina	7	28
O12 ●	Samford	38	6
O19	La. Monroe	38	39
O26	at Georgia Tech	20	27
N2 ●	Illinois St.	42	15
N9 ●	at UAB	35	13
N16 ●	Bowling Green	27	19

1997   5-6
A30	at Mississippi	23	24
S6	at South Carolina	31	33
S13	at Nebraska	24	38
S20 ●	Idaho	41	10
S27	at Auburn	14	41
O4 ●	at Kent State	59	43
O11 ●	Samford	52	7
O25	at Mississippi State	28	35
N1	at La. Monroe	41	45
N15 ●	Eastern Michigan	27	10
N22 ●	Toledo	34	17

MIKE KRUCZEK
1998-2003 (.545)   36-30

1998   9-2
S5 ●	at Louisiana Tech	64	30
S12 ●	Ea. Illinois	48	0
S19	at Purdue	7	35
S26 ●	at Bowling Green	38	31
O3 ●	at Toledo	31	24
O10 ●	Northern Illinois	38	17
O24 ●	at La. Lafayette	42	10
O31 ●	Youngstown St.	44	32
N7	at Auburn	6	10
N14 ●	Ball State	37	14
N21 ●	New Mexico	38	6

1999   4-7
S4	Purdue	13	47
S11	at Florida	27	58
S18	at Georgia Tech	10	41
S25	at Georgia	23	24
O2 ●	Ea. Illinois	31	21
O16 ●	Nicholls St.	28	0
O23	Louisiana Tech	35	46
O30 ●	Eastern Michigan	31	6
N6	at Auburn	10	28
N13 ●	at Middle Tennessee	39	14
N20	Bowling Green	30	33

2000   7-4
S2	at Georgia Tech	17	21
S9 ●	Northwestern St.	19	7
S16	at Akron	24	35
S23 ●	William & Mary	52	7
S30 ●	at Eastern Michigan	31	10
O7	at Northern Illinois	20	40
O14 ●	Ea. Kentucky	34	3
O21 ●	La. Monroe	55	0
O28 ●	at Alabama	40	38
N4 ●	at Louisiana Tech	20	16
N11	Virginia Tech	21	44

2001   6-5
S1	at Clemson	13	21
S8	at Syracuse	10	21
S22 ●	at Tulane	36	29
S29	at Virginia Tech	14	46
O6 ●	UAB	24	7
O13 ●	Liberty	63	0
O20 ●	La. Monroe	38	6
O27	at Utah State	27	30
N3 ●	Akron	57	17
N10	at Arkansas	20	27
N24 ●	La. Lafayette	31	0

2002-2004
MAC

2002   7-5   (6-2)
A31		at Penn State	24	27
S7		at Arizona State	13	46
S20	|	at Marshall	21	26
S28 ●		Liberty	48	17
O12 ●	|	at Western Michigan	31	27
O19	|	Toledo	24	27
O26 ●	|	Akron	28	17
N2		Syracuse	35	38
N9 ●	|	at Buffalo	45	21
N16 ●	|	Kent State	32	6
N23 ●	|	at Miami, Ohio	48	31
N30 ●	|	Ohio U.	42	32

ALAN GOOCH
2003 (.000)   0-2

2003   3-9   (2-6)
A31		at Virginia Tech	28	49
S13 ●		Florida Atl.	33	29
S20		at Syracuse	14	38
S27	|	at Kent State	16	36
O4 ●	|	Buffalo	19	10
O11	|	at Ohio U.	0	28
O18	|	at Akron	24	38
O25 ●	|	Central Michigan	31	13
N1		at West Virginia	18	36
N8	|	at Eastern Michigan	13	19
N19	|	Marshall	7	21
N28	|	Miami, Ohio	21	56

GEORGE O'LEARY
2004-PRESENT (.000)   0-11

2004   0-11   (0-8)
S4		at Wisconsin	6	34
S11		West Virginia	20	45
S18		at Penn State	13	37
O2	|	at Buffalo	20	48
O9		Northern Illinois	28	30
O16		Akron	21	26
O23	|	at Miami, Ohio	7	43
O30	|	at Marshall	3	20
N6	|	Ohio U.	16	17
N13	|	at Ball State	17	21
N23	|	Kent State	24	41

CENTRAL MICHIGAN

BY ED KRZEMIENSKI

IT MIGHT NOT SURPRISE PEOPLE TO learn that through 2003, Texas A&M ranked 24th in all-time Division I-A winning percentage. It would probably surprise most, though, to find out that the team directly above the Aggies is Central Michigan. With an overall .611 mark, the Chippewas ranked ahead of not just the Aggies, but also Syracuse, Michigan State and UCLA. So the Chippewas were no stranger to success on the football field. From 1965 to 1991, Central Michigan ran off 27 consecutive nonlosing seasons, including an 8–2–1 mark in its first season in Division I-A. In recent years, after four consecutive losing seasons, the team attempted to rebuild under head coach Mike DeBord. But DeBord resigned in 2003. Brian Kelly, who left nearby Grand Valley State University after compiling a 118–35–2 overall record at the D2 powerhouse, replaced him.

TRADITION The Central Michigan football team and band have a close relationship. Each fall, the band teaches the school's fight song to newcomers on the football team, and the band accompanies the squad on the walk from a nearby motel to home games. The band also came up with the school's most popular cheer: "CHIP-ooh-ah! FIGHT! FIGHT! FIGHT!"

BEST PLAYER Although quarterback Gary Hogeboom went on to the best professional career, running back Jim Podoley stands as the greatest Chippewa ever. From 1953 to 1956, Podoley ran for 2,775 yards and led the Chippewas to a combined record of 32–4–1. His 307 points, 51 touchdowns and 29-yard punt-return average still stand as CMU career records. Perhaps most impressive, though, is Podoley's career average of 7.9 yards per carry. Despite playing in the NCAA College Division, Podoley was invited to the 1956 Senior Bowl and 1957 Blue-Gray Game. After college, Podoley played four seasons for the Washington Redskins, was inducted into the CMU Athletics Hall of Fame (1984) and became the first and only Chippewa to have his number (62) retired.

BEST COACH Before retiring to become CMU's athletic director after the 1993 season, Herb Deromedi coached the Chippewas to a 110–55–10 record in 16 years. He owns the CMU record for career wins and is tied with Bill Kelly for longest tenure. Under Deromedi, the Chippewas won or shared the MAC title three times and made their first Division I postseason appearance in the 1990 California Raisin Bowl. Deromedi twice won MAC Coach of the Year

---

PROFILE

Central Michigan University
Mount Pleasant, Mich.
Founded: 1892
Enrollment: 19,934
Colors: Maroon and Gold
Nickname: Chippewas
Stadium: Kelly/Shorts Stadium
  Opened in 1972
  FieldTurf; 30,199 capacity
First football game: 1896
All-time record: 526–333–36 (.608)
Bowl record: 0–2
Mid-American Conference championships:
4 (outright)
Website: www.cmuchippewas.com

THE BEST OF TIMES

From 1979 to 1980, Central Michigan went 19–2–1 and won two MAC championships.

THE WORST OF TIMES

From 1995 to 2004, CMU had nine losing seasons in 10 years.

CONFERENCE

Central Michigan joined the MAC in 1975, when it moved up to Division I-A, and has been a member ever since.

DISTINGUISHED ALUMNI

Dick Enberg; Jeff Daniels, actor; Joseph Ralston, NATO Supreme Allied Commander General

FIGHT SONG

THE FIGHTING CHIPPEWA
(Chorus)
Come on and Fight! Central, down the field,
Fight for Victory,
Fight! Fellows never yield,
We're with you, oh Varsity,
Onward with banners bold,
To our colors we'll be true,
Fight for Maroon and Gold,
Down the field for CMU!
(Refrain)
Victory - Rah Rah!
Varsity - Rah Rah!
Chippewas we're proud of our nickname,
Hear our song - Rah Rah!
Loud and strong - Rah Rah!
Central is going to win this game!

(1980 and 1990) and retired with a .657 winning percentage as the all-time MAC leader in victories. He became a CMU Athletics Hall of Fame member in 2000.

BEST TEAM In their final year as a Division II team, the 1974 Chippewas opened the season with a loss to Kent State—a future Mid-American Conference rival—then won their next 12 straight games. In the process, Roy Kramer's CMU team defeated Boise State, Louisiana Tech and Delaware in the playoffs to win the D2 national championship. Seniors Mike Franckowiak and Matt Means led the team in passing and receiving, respectively, while junior running back Walt "Smoke" Hodges ran for 1,463 yards. Franckowiak and noseguard Rick Newsome were named Division II/Small College All-Americas. Franckowiak was also named a first-team Academic All-America.

BIGGEST GAME In 1974, the Chippewas went to the nationally televised Division II championship game, known then as the Camellia Bowl, as underdogs against powerhouse Delaware. The Blue Hens had won two of the last three College Division titles, and it looked as if the 1974 game would be a runaway. It was, but not as expected: the Chippewas

> ## *Hope the 1991 Chippewas had good-looking sisters: the team tied four games that season.*

destroyed the Hens 54-14. CMU running backs Hodges and Dick Dunham each ran for over 100 yards and combined for six of the Chippewas' seven touchdowns. Neither, however, was named Offensive Player of the Game. That honor went to quarterback Mike Franckowiak, who not only completed 11 of 13 passes for 186 yards and a touchdown, but also accounted for 12 points with his foot, kicking two field goals and six extra points.

BIGGEST UPSET After tying Ohio and squeaking past Southwestern Louisiana to start the 1991 season, it looked as if Herb Deromedi's Chippewas might not make it back alive from East Lansing after their game with No. 18 Michigan State. But on this September day, it was the Spartans who needed help off the field. Controlling all facets of the game, CMU stunned MSU 20-3. Led by running back Billy Smith's 162 yards, the Chippewas out-gained the Spartans 346–281 in a game dominated by the CMU defense. Setting the tone on the first series, CMU's defense stuffed a fourth-and-goal attempt at their own 1-yard line. Perhaps the game should not be regarded as much of an upset, though. One year later, the Chippewas, having lost their first game of the season

RECORDS

RUSHING YARDS

GAME
377	Robbie Mixon vs. Eastern Michigan, Nov. 2, 2002 (43 att.)

SEASON
1,890	Brian Pruitt, 1994 (292 att.)

CAREER
4,162	Curtis Adams, 1981-84 (761 att.)

PASSING YARDS

GAME
435	Chad Darnell vs. Bowling Green, Sept. 28, 1996 (22 of 40)

SEASON
2,921	Chad Darnell, 1996 (189 of 348)

CAREER
6,528	Jeff Bender, 1988-91 (502 of 960)

RECEIVING YARDS

GAME
284	Norm Tellar vs. Toledo, Nov. 16, 1929

SEASON
1,229	Reggie Allen, 1996 (66 rec.)

CAREER
3,242	Reggie Allen, 1995-98 (192 rec.)

POINTS

GAME
36	Jim Podoley vs. Eastern Illinois, Nov. 10, 1956 (6 TDs)

SEASON
132	Brian Pruitt, 1994 (22 TDs)

CAREER
307	Jim Podoley, 1953-56 (51 TDs, 1 PAT)

CONSENSUS ALL-AMERICANS

1942	Warren Schmakel, G
1959	Walter Beach, B
1962	Ralph Soffredine, G
1974	Rick Newsome, DL

to Kentucky, again traveled to East Lansing and again upset the Spartans, this time 24-20.

HEARTBREAKER In the 1994 Las Vegas Bowl, Central Michigan faced Nevada-Las Vegas in a rematch of the second game of the Chippewas' season, which CMU won 35-23 in Mount Pleasant. Prior to the bowl game, however, Central's All-America tailback Brian Pruitt bruised his knee in practice and was unable to play. After one quarter of play, the score stood at 14-10 in favor of UNLV. By early in the fourth quarter, the Rebels were up 52-10. The final score, a discouraging cap on an otherwise stellar season, was 52-24.

STADIUM Kelly/Shorts Stadium opened in 1972 when Central Michigan defeated Illinois State in the first collegiate game ever played on AstroTurf in Michigan. Originally named Perry Shorts Stadium, after R. Perry Shorts, a 1900 graduate who went on to a lucrative career in banking and philanthropy, the school added "Kelly" in 1983 to honor former coach Kenneth Kelly. Several renovations brought the stadium's capacity to more than 30,000. Since its opening, Kelly/Shorts has been a sweet home indeed, as the Chippewas have won some 72% of their games played there.

RIVAL As its name indicates, Central Michigan is roughly equidistant—about 140 miles—from its MAC opponents, Western and Eastern Michigan. CMU's greater rival, though, is its Western counterpart, and the Western Michigan Broncos agree. Six of the 10 biggest Kelly/Shorts Stadium crowds attended CMU-WMU games.

NICKNAME Originally known as the Normalites, Central Michigan became the Dragons in 1925, then the Bearcats two years later. In 1942, the school changed its name to Chippewas in consideration of a local Saginaw tribe. The school has maintained that nickname despite the trend throughout the sports world, including schools within the MAC, to abdicate names derived from Native American tribes and caricatures. The school states that it will "continue to use the Chippewa name with dignity and respect."

MASCOT So as not to dishonor the Saginaw Chippewa

Tribe, CMU keeps no mascot. That, however, has not kept students from independently breaking the rules. On Oct. 11, 2003, at a home game against Northern Illinois, Central Michigan freshman Jared Parko attended the game dressed in head feathers and a breastplate made of pasta, apparently of the penne rigate or mostaccioli variety. The following weekend, for a game against Toledo, school officials asked a similarly attired Parko to leave the stadium. Parko remarked that he meant no disrespect, and that "if we were the Bobcats, I would dress up as a Bobcat and try to get people going."

UNIFORMS From 1973 to 1988, CMU wore red helmets with a feathered spear on the side (like the mid-60s Washington Redskins helmets). At the end of the 1980s, though, the school edged away from Native American emblems and instituted blank red helmets. In the 1990s, the team went with red helmets adorned with the letters CMU, and then, in 1996, turned to the current design featuring a gold C on the sides.

NUMBERS Hope the 1991 Chippewas had good-looking sisters: five years before the NCAA implemented its overtime system, Central Michigan ended the season with four ties (to Ohio, Toledo, Miami and Eastern Michigan). In fact, despite losing only one game all year, the team tied more MAC games than it won, finishing its conference schedule at 3–1–4.

LORE It might not pay to play both sides against the middle in the outside world, but when the middle defeats both sides in mid-major Michigan, it'll guarantee a coach's job. Herb Deromedi beat most teams he faced as head coach of the Chippewas, but he really dominated his in-state rivals. Against Western Michigan, Deromedi posted a 13–2–1 career record, and put up a 12–2–2 mark against Eastern Michigan. That kind of mastery will keep the interested alumni at bay and future coaches looking pale by comparison.

QUOTE "I'm excited about the opportunity of waking up a sleeping giant."—Brian Kelly, upon being hired as CMU head coach in 2004

THE SCHOOLS

CENTRAL MICHIGAN ANNUAL STATISTICAL LEADERS

YR	RUSHING	YDS	ATT	AVG	PASSING	ATT	CMP	PCT	YDS	RECEIVING	REC	YDS	AVG
1951	Dave Clark	301	48	6.3	Andy MacDonald	183	114	.62	1,560	Porter Lewis	22	272	12.4
1952	Vern Hawes	540	69	7.8	Don Koleber	63	25	.40	417	Al Droth	16	302	18.9
1953	Chuck Miller	938	131	7.2	Lornie Kerr	70	27	.39	327	Jim Podoley	9	186	20.7
1954	Jim Podoley	1,079	110	9.8	Jim King	38	18	.47	399	Jerry Thomas	4	121	30.3
1955	Bernie Raterink	1,044	128	8.2	Mike Sweeney	31	15	.48	302	Ray Sine	6	140	23.3
1956	Jim Podoley	655	100	6.6	Herb Kipke	68	36	.53	490	Jim Podoley	12	211	17.6
1957	Walt Beach	1,084	140	7.7	Herb Kipke	75	34	.45	511	Walt Beach	27	313	11.6
1958	Walt Beach	929	129	7.2	Oarie Lemanski	73	33	.45	455	Walt Beach	16	264	16.5
1959	Jerry O'Neil	821	145	5.7	Oarie Lemanski	110	56	.51	962	Jerry O'Neil	12	296	24.7
1960	Bob Fisher	492	89	5.5	Wally Sadosty	112	51	.46	531	Len Jagello	10	150	15.0
1961	Chuck Koons	402	113	3.6	Gary Harrington	62	20	.32	239	Chuck Koons	21	130	6.2
1962	Bill Shuple	640	143	4.5	Dick Moffit	179	83	.46	1,109	Gary Finnin	31	361	11.6
1963	Bill Shuple	692	149	4.6	Pat Boyd	117	54	.46	817	Larry Moore	16	397	24.8
1964	Bruce Wyman	823	168	4.9	Pat Boyd	90	45	.50	607	Jamie Gent	19	422	22.2
1965	Jim Acitelli	445	99	4.5	Pat Boyd	283	146	.52	1,604	Wally Hempton	43	605	14.1
1966	Bob Rosso	662	168	3.9	Bob Miles	184	94	.51	1,368	Wally Hempton	34	574	16.9
1967	Craig Tefft	1,046	267	3.9	Gene Gilin	84	41	.49	611	Greg Hoefler	16	292	18.3
1968	Craig Tefft	1,126	239	4.7	Bob Miles	120	62	.52	918	Dave Lemere	15	325	21.7
1969	Jesse Lakes	1,263	253	5.0	Bob Miles	52	22	.42	305	Dave Lemere	18	239	13.3
1970	Jesse Lakes	1,296	250	5.2	Mick Brzezinski	123	50	.41	775	Rick Groth	31	451	14.5
1971	Jesse Lakes	1,143	211	5.4	Mick Brzezinski	162	69	.43	426	Ron Goodin	10	186	18.6
1972	Chuck Markey	1,513	290	5.2	Gary Bevington	162	69	.43	834	Matt Means	43	603	14.0
1973	Jim Sandy	1,168	209	5.6	Mike Franckowiak	88	41	.47	655	Matt Means	32	553	17.3
1974	Walt Hodges	1,463	251	5.8	Mike Franckowiak	122	63	.52	985	Matt Means	40	613	15.3
1975	Walt Hodges	1,025	186	5.5	Ron Rummel	98	37	.38	586	John Fossen	18	211	11.7
1976	Mike Gray	734	188	3.9	Ron Rummel	88	44	.50	761	Wayne Schwalbach	26	496	19.1
1977	Mose Rison	1,241	238	5.2	Ron Rummel	75	34	.45	638	Wayne Schwalbach	21	426	20.3
1978	Willie Todd	746	144	5.2	Gary Hogeboom	143	72	.50	1,095	Brian Blank	19	384	20.2
1979	Willie Todd	1,003	234	4.3	Gary Hogeboom	150	92	.61	1,404	Mike Ball	21	457	21.8
1980	Willie Todd	695	170	4.1	Kevin Northup	133	69	.52	1,011	Mike Hirn	22	388	17.6
1981	Reggie Mitchell	1,068	199	5.4	Bob DeMarco	162	85	.52	1,159	Mike Hirn	24	295	12.3
1982	Curtis Adams	1,090	204	5.3	Bob DeMarco	161	81	.50	1,113	Jaime Jackson	23	412	17.9
1983	Curtis Adams	1,431	267	5.4	Ron Fillmore	126	59	.47	915	John DeBoer	22	540	24.5
1984	Curtis Adams	1,204	222	5.4	Bob DeMarco	173	98	.57	1,427	John DeBoer	40	831	20.8
1985	Tony Brown	655	174	3.8	Ron Fillmore	185	94	.51	1,191	John DeBoer	26	494	19.0
1986	Rodney Stevenson	1,104	207	5.3	Marcelle Carruthers	138	64	.46	912	Melvin Houston	12	210	17.5
1987	John Hood	1,121	208	5.4	Marcelle Carruthers	191	108	.57	1,323	Eric Reed	43	652	15.2
1988	Donnie Riley	1,238	215	5.8	Jeff Bender	169	93	.55	1,309	Mark Hopkins	32	433	13.5
1989	Donnie Riley	1,187	269	4.4	Jeff Bender	232	108	.47	1,487	Ken Ealy	12	346	28.8
1990	Billy Smith	1,047	244	4.3	Jeff Bender	262	145	.55	1,978	Ken Ealy	44	916	20.8
1991	Billy Smith	1,440	374	3.9	Jeff Bender	297	156	.53	1,754	Ken Ealy	41	724	17.7
1992	Brian Pruitt	859	178	4.8	Joe Youngblood	278	161	.58	2,209	Terrance McMillan	43	649	15.1
1993	Brian Pruitt	944	201	4.7	Joe Youngblood	287	167	.58	2,466	D.J. Reid	47	693	14.7
1994	Brian Pruitt	1,890	292	6.5	Erik Timpf	174	90	.52	1,315	Terrance McMillan	28	398	14.2
1995	Silas Massey	1,089	225	4.8	Chad Darnell	258	130	.50	1,737	Bryan Schorman	38	604	15.9
1996	Silas Massey	1,544	312	4.9	Chad Darnell	348	189	.54	2,921	Reggie Allen	66	1,229	18.6
1997	Eric Flowers	909	216	4.2	Tim Crowley	321	148	.46	2,204	Reggie Allen	50	877	17.5
1998	Eric Flowers	1,302	292	4.5	Pete Shepherd	324	152	.47	2,005	Reggie Allen	61	832	13.6
1999	Eric Flowers	766	200	3.8	Pete Shepherd	320	171	.53	2,295	Jammarl O'Neal	59	1,085	18.4
2000	Vince Webber	458	130	3.5	Derrick Vickers	180	83	.46	1,059	David Hannah	34	411	12.1
2001	Terrence Jackson	1,194	252	4.7	Derrick Vickers	211	116	.55	1,156	Rob Turner	50	668	13.4
2002	Robbie Mixon	1,361	255	5.3	Derrick Vickers	320	175	.55	1,828	Rob Turner	43	506	11.8
2003	Jerry Seymour	1,117	205	5.4	Derrick Vickers	216	118	.55	1,345	Justin Harper	45	441	9.8
2004	Jerry Seymour	1,284	262	4.9	Kent Smith	333	188	.56	2,284	Jerry Seymour	47	413	8.8

Receiving leaders by receptions
All statistics include postseason

CENTRAL MICHIGAN ALL-TIME SCORES

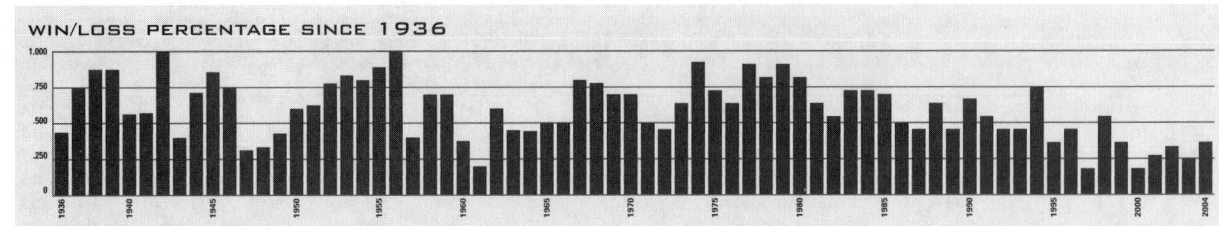

WIN/LOSS PERCENTAGE SINCE 1936

PETE McCORMICK
1896 (.750)   3-1

1896   3-1-0
U •	Alma HS*Unk*	5	14
U •	Bay City HS*Unk*	14	4
U •	Saginaw HS*Unk*	35	0
U •	Alma HS*Unk*	8	4

CARL PRAY
1897-99 (.545)   6-5

1897   2-1-0
U	Alma*Unk*	0	18
U •	Bay City HS*Unk*	10	0
U •	Ithica HS*Unk*	NA	10

1898   1-2-0
U	Alma*Unk*	0	27
U	MP Indians*Unk*	35	0
U	Mt. Pleasant HS*Unk*	2	5

1899   3-2-0
U	Alma*Unk*	0	12
U	Saginaw Stars*Unk*	0	5
U •	Cadillac HS*Unk*	12	0
U •	St. John's HS*Unk*	27	5
U •	Ferris State*Unk*	6	0

NO HEAD COACH

1900   1-0-0
U •	Cadillac HS*Unk*	20	5

1901
NO TEAM

CHARLES TAMBLING
1902-05, '18 (.900)   18-2

1902   4-0-0
U •	Marion HS*Unk*	10	0
U •	McBain HS*Unk*	51	0
N1 •	Eastern Michigan*Unk*	10	0
U •	Ferris State*Unk*	11	0

1903   6-0-0
U •	Ferris State*Unk*	12	0
U •	Alma*Unk*	23	5
U •	Elsie Giants*Unk*	15	0
U •	Hillsdale*Unk*	7	6
U •	Clare HS	NA	NA
U •	Mount Pleasant HS	NA	NA

1904   0-1-0
U	Ferris State*Unk*	6	60

1905   7-1-0
U •	Elsie Giants*Unk*	5	0
U •	Ferris State*Unk*	35	2
U •	Midland AC*Unk*	51	0
U	Alma*Unk*	6	12
N17 •	Eastern Michigan*Unk*	13	0
U •	Ferris State*Unk*	10	0
U •	W. Michigan JV*Unk*	6	0
U •	Kalamazoo	NA	NA

1906
NO TEAM

RALPH THACKER
1907 (.333)   2-4

1907   2-4-0
U	Ferris State*Unk*	0	45
U •	Flint MSD*Unk*	6	5
U •	MP Indians*Unk*	12	11 *
U	Western Michigan*Unk*	0	27
N16	Eastern Michigan*Unk*	0	39
U	Alma	NA	NA

HUGH SUTHERLAND
1908 (.571)   4-3

1908   4-3-0
U	Alma*Unk*	0	5
U •	Alma*Unk*	10	0
N7 •	Eastern Michigan*Unk*	11	0
U	Western Michigan*Unk*	5	11
U •	Elsie Giants	NA	NA
U	Hillsdale	NA	NA
U •	West Branch HS	NA	NA

HARRY HELMER
1909-12 (.652)   14-7-2

1909   4-3-0
U •	West Branch HS*Unk*	23	0
U •	Saginaw Arthur Hill HS*Unk*	8	5
U •	Alma*Unk*	15	8
U •	Michigan State JV*Unk*	6	17
U •	Ferris State*Unk*	11	0
N5	at Eastern Michigan	0	17
U	Western Michigan*Unk*	0	11

1910   6-1-1
U •	MP Indians*Unk*	18	0
U •	West Branch HS*Unk*	6	0
U =	Michigan State JV*Unk*	6	6
U •	Flint MSD*Unk*	40	0
U	Western Michigan*Unk*	6	16
N12 •	Eastern Michigan*Unk*	13	0
U •	Ferris State*Unk*	17	11
U •	Elsie Giants	NA	NA

1911   3-2-0
U •	West Branch HS*Unk*	17	6
U •	Mount Pleasant HS	NA	NA
U •	Ithica HS*Unk*	3	0
U	Flint MSD	NA	NA
U	Michigan State JV	NA	NA

1912   1-1-1
U	Michigan State JV	NA	NA
U •	Flint MSD	NA	NA
N8 •	Eastern Michigan*Unk*	0	0

1913-15
NO TEAM

BLAKE MILLER
1916 (.167)   1-5

1916   1-5-0
U •	West Branch HS*Unk*	39	0
U •	Bay City Western HS*Unk*	0	12
U •	Michigan State JV*Unk*	0	14
U •	Alma*Unk*	0	39
U	Saginaw East*Unk*	0	30
U	Alma*Unk*	0	44

FRED JOHNSON
1917 (.333)   1-2

1917   1-2-0
U •	Bay City Western HS*Unk*	7	0
O20	at Eastern Michigan	0	63
U	Mount Pleasant HS*Unk*	0	8

CHARLES TAMBLING

1918   1-0-0
U •	Traverse City HS*Unk*	41	6

GARLAND NEVITT
1919 (.500)   2-2-3

1919   2-2-3
U •	Bay City Western HS*Unk*	34	6
U =	Saginaw East*Unk*	13	13
U •	Ferris State*Unk*	7	0
U =	Grand Rapids JC*Unk*	7	7
N7 =	Eastern Michigan*Unk*	7	7
U	Michigan State JV*Unk*	0	13
U	Detroit JC*Unk*	14	42

JOE SIMMONS
1920 (.563)   4-3-1

1920   4-3-1
U •	Ferris State	80	0
O16	at Eastern Michigan	6	7
U •	at Olivet	7	0
U •	at Ferris State	34	0
U	Michigan State JV	6	14
U	at Hillsdale	10	14
U •	at Hope	17	0
U =	Detroit JC	6	6

WALLACE PARKER
1921-23, '26-28 (.729)   32-10-6

1921   5-1-1
U •	at Ferris State	7	0
U •	Olivet	35	0
O15	Eastern Michigan	6	7
U •	Ferris State	60	0
U •	at Alma	28	0
U •	at Grand Rapids JC	7	0
U =	at Detroit JC	0	0

1922   6-0-2
U •	Ferris State	40	0
U =	at St. Ignatius	6	6
U •	Grand Rapids JC	39	0
N4 •	at Eastern Michigan	0	0
U •	Northern Michigan	62	0
U •	Michigan Mlty. Acad.	7	0
U •	Alma	5	0
U •	Detroit JC	20	7

1923   5-1-2
U •	Bay City JC	37	0
U	at Albion	7	14
U =	at Grand Rapids JC	0	0
O27 •	Eastern Michigan	27	3
U •	at Northern Michigan	35	0
U •	Olivet	40	0
U =	at Alma	0	0
U •	at Detroit City	21	7

LESTER BARNARD
1924-25 (.781)   11-2-3

1924   7-1-0
U •	at Assumption	26	0
U	Albion	12	13
O25 •	at Eastern Michigan	13	0
O31 •	Bowling Green	21	0
U •	Northern Michigan	22	0
U •	at Valparaiso	13	0
U •	Alma	13	0
U •	Detroit City	38	6

1925   4-1-3
U •	Carrollton AC	29	0
U	at Alma	0	14
U •	at Northern Michigan	8	0
U =	Detroit JV	0	0
U =	at Western Michigan	0	0
U •	Valparaiso	41	0
U =	Albion	0	0
U •	Detroit City	18	6

WALLACE PARKER

1926   3-4-1
O2	at Albion	14	20
O9	at Ferris State	6	7
O16 •	Northern Michigan	24	7
O23	at Eastern Michigan	0	41
O30	at Bowling Green	0	13
N13 •	Alma	13	2
N20 =	Battle Creek	0	0
U •	Detroit City	9	0

1927   7-1-0
U •	Adrian	26	0
U •	Ferris State	20	0
O15 •	Olivet	7	0
O22 •	Western Michigan	18	12
O29 •	at Eastern Michigan	0	6
U •	at Northern Michigan	6	0
N11 •	at Alma	14	13
U •	at Detroit City	33	6

1928   6-3-0
S29 •	Detroit Tech	18	0
O6 •	at Adrian	0	9
O13 •	at Toledo	13	0
O20 •	Northern Michigan	26	0
O27 •	Eastern Michigan	0	36
N3 •	at Valparaiso	25	0
N10 •	at Ferris State	21	0
U •	at Western Michigan	0	19
N29 •	Detroit City	23	0

A.J. NOWAK
1929-30 (.600)   8-5-2

1929   2-3-2
S28 •	Detroit Tech	28	7
O5 =	Michigan JV	0	0
O12 •	at Northern Michigan	6	6
O26 •	at Eastern Michigan	0	24
N9 •	Western Michigan	6	25
N16 •	Toledo	31	12
N28 •	at Detroit City	0	6

1930   6-2-0
U •	Detroit Frosh	7	0
U •	Michigan JV	13	7
U •	at Western Michigan	0	54
U •	at Ferris State	14	0
O25 •	Eastern Michigan	0	13
N8 •	at Alma	27	7
N15 •	Northern Michigan	34	0
N27 •	at Detroit City	13	0

GEORGE VAN BIBBER
1931-33 (.565)   12-9-2

1931   4-3-0
O3	at Michigan	0	27
O10 •	Ferris State	14	6
O24 •	at Eastern Michigan	20	12
O31 •	Detroit City	42	0
N7 •	Alma	13	0
N14 •	at Bowling Green	0	6
N21 •	Western Michigan	6	7

1932   3-4-1
O1 =	at Michigan JV	0	0
O8 •	Defiance	32	9
O15 •	Purdue JV	6	13
O22 •	Eastern Michigan	0	28
O29 •	at Detroit City	13	0
N5 •	at Western Michigan	0	7
N12 •	Michigan Coll. of Mines	46	0
N19 •	at Alma	0	9

1933   5-2-1
S30 •	Saint Mary's-Cal	52	0
O7 •	at Kalamazoo	18	13
O14 =	at Hillsdale	0	0
O21 •	at Eastern Michigan	7	13 *
O28 •	Detroit City	26	13
N4 •	Western Michigan	0	13 *
N11 •	at Ferris State	33	0
N18 •	Alma	27	0

ALEX YUNEVICH
1934-36 (.438) 10-13-1

1934 — 5-3-0

S28		at Detroit	0	38
O6		Ferris State	2	6
O13	●	Hillsdale	15	6
O20	●	Eastern Michigan	13	12
O27	●	at Wayne State	13	7
N3		at Western Michigan	0	13
N10	●	Kalamazoo	12	0
N17	●	at Alma	26	0

1935 — 2-6-0

S27		at Detroit	0	43
O5		at Ferris State	7	12
O12		Wayne State	6	7
O19		at Eastern Michigan	0	7
O26	●	at Northern Michigan	7	0
N2	●	Assumption	19	0
N9		at Western Michigan	0	13
N16		Alma	0	13

1936 — 3-4-1

S26		at Baldwin-Wallace	2	65
O3	●	Ferris State	22	0
O10	=	at Wayne State	0	0
O17	●	at Northern State	7	6
O24		Eastern Michigan	7	13
O31	●	Saint Mary's-Cal	44	8
N7		at Western Michigan	0	33
N14		Detroit Tech	7	10

RON FINCH
1937-46 (.743) 53-18-1

1937 — 6-2-0

S25	●	Assumption	52	0
O2	●	at Ferris State	21	7
O9	●	Northern Michigan	32	0
O16		Wayne State	0	18
O23	●	at Eastern Michigan	27	10
O30	●	at Saint Mary's-Cal	38	0
N6		Western Michigan	0	7
N13	●	at Kalamazoo	30	0

1938 — 7-1-0

S23	●	at Lawrence Tech	44	0
O1	●	at Ferris State	68	0
O8	●	at Northern Michigan	47	0
O15	●	at Bluffton	45	0
O21	●	Eastern Michigan	7	6
O28	●	Saint Mary's-Cal	39	0
N5	●	at Wayne State	20	3
N12		at Western Michigan	0	35

1939 — 7-1-0

S22		at Detroit	7	20
S29	●	at Ferris State	20	0
S30	●	at Illinois State	14	0
O6	●	at Northern Michigan	6	0
O14	●	at Eastern Kentucky	18	14
O20	●	at Eastern Michigan	14	0
O27	●	Ball State	7	0
N11	●	at Wayne State	33	6

1940 — 4-3-1

S27	●	at Ferris State	37	0
O5	●	at Ball State	7	0
O12		at Northern Illinois	6	9
O19		at Bradley	0	19
O25	●	at Eastern Michigan	24	0
N2	=	at Wayne State	7	7
N9		Eastern Kentucky	0	25
N16	●	at DeSales	7	0

1941 — 4-3-0

O3	●	at Northern Michigan	7	6
O10		at Detroit	0	45
O18	●	at Ball State	7	6
O24	●	at Eastern Michigan	12	6
N1		at Wayne State	0	6
N8		at Grand Rapids U	6	7
N15	●	at DeSales	12	6

1942 — 6-0-0

O3	●	at Northern Michigan	21	0
O9	●	at Grand Rapids U	6	2
O15	●	at Eastern Michigan	14	0
O24	●	Ball State	19	13
O30	●	at Wayne State	13	0
N7	●	at Grand Rapids U	20	6

1943 — 2-3-0

O2		at Bowling Green	0	36
U		Western Michigan	0	19
U	●	at Alma	13	7
U		at Alma	0	8
U	●	at Alma	6	0

1944 — 5-2-0

U	●	at Alma	20	13
S1		Bowling Green	19	20
U	●	at Alma	33	13
U	●	at Michigan JV	25	12
O7		at Western Michigan	14	35
U	●	at Michigan JV	14	13
U	●	at Indiana State	25	0

1945 — 6-1-0

U	●	at Alma	13	0
S7		at Bowling Green	6	19
U	●	at Alma	26	0
S29	●	Western Michigan	6	0
O6	●	at Eastern Kentucky	14	7
U	●	at Wayne State	26	0
O20	●	at Albion	7	0

1946 — 6-2-0

S20		at Ohio Wesleyan	0	13
S28	●	at Bowling Green	7	0
O5	●	at Eastern Kentucky	20	7
O12	●	at Northern Michigan	60	0
O18	●	at Eastern Michigan	26	13
O25	●	Northern Illinois	58	7
N2		at Western Michigan	21	27
N9	●	at Great Lakes NAS	41	0

LYLE BENNETT
1947-49 (.354) 8-15-1

1947 — 2-5-1

S19		at Detroit	14	34
S27		at Bowling Green	19	20
O3	=	Northern Illinois	6	6
O11		Western Michigan	12	20
O17	●	at Northern Michigan	45	10
O24		at Youngstown	7	13
N1	●	Eastern Michigan	33	10 *
N15		at Milwaukee State	0	12

1948 — 3-6-0

S18	●	at Ferris State	27	6
O2		Bowling Green	12	13
O9		at Western Michigan	0	7
O14	●	at Northern Michigan	46	14
O16		Kent State	0	28
O23		at Youngstown	9	32
O30		Wayne State	12	27
N6		at Eastern Michigan	0	6
N13	●	at Milwaukee State	21	6

1949 — 3-4-0

S23	●	at Ferris State	33	7
O1		at Bowling Green	0	20
O8	●	at Michigan Mines	35	0
O14		at Kent State	12	26
O22		Western Michigan	8	35
O29		Hillsdale	0	8
N4	●	Eastern Michigan	18	7

WARREN SCHMAKEL
1950 (.600) 6-4

1950 — 6-4-0

S18	●	Alma	19	0
S23		at Western Illinois	7	28
S30		at Western Michigan	13	21
O7		Illinois State	13	14
O14	●	Bowling Green	12	0
O21	●	at DePauw	33	20
O28	●	at Eastern Michigan	26	7
N3	●	at Northern Illinois	27	14
N11	●	Ferris State	40	0
N18		at Hillsdale	20	21

BILL KELLY
1951-66 (.609) 91-58-2

1951 — 5-3-0

S22	●	at Southern Illinois	34	13
S28		Western Illinois	6	27
O13	●	Eastern Illinois	59	27
O20	●	at Eastern Michigan	19	13
O27	●	at Illinois State	26	0
N2		Northern Illinois	13	26
N9	●	at Ferris State	46	6
N17		at Western Michigan	25	46

1952 — 7-2-0

S13	●	at St. Ambrose	38	14
S20		at Bowling Green	7	20
S27	●	at Northern Illinois	56	7
O4		Western Michigan	0	18
O11	●	at Western Illinois	27	0
O18	●	Southern Illinois	55	7
O25	●	Eastern Michigan	26	7
N1	●	Illinois State	35	12
N8	●	at Eastern Illinois	41	0

1953 — 7-1-1

S19	●	Northern Iowa	34	20
S26	●	Western Michigan	21	0
O2	●	Eastern Illinois	33	6
O10		at Great Lakes NAS	16	39
O17	●	at Southern Illinois	19	6
O24	●	Western Illinois	13	6
O31	●	at Illinois State	29	19
N6	●	Northern Illinois	46	0
N14	=	at Eastern Michigan	33	33

1954 — 8-2-0

S11	●	at Milwaukee State	26	7
S18	●	Northern Iowa	42	21
S25	●	at Western Michigan	25	19
O2	●	at Eastern Illinois	60	0
O9		at Great Lakes NAS	28	32
O16	●	Southern Illinois	33	0
O23		at Western Illinois	7	14
O30	●	Illinois State	26	0
N6	●	at Northern Illinois	46	7
N13	●	Eastern Michigan	28	7

1955 — 8-1-0

S17	●	at Pittsburg State	33	0
S24	●	Western Michigan	27	12
O1		at Southern Illinois	13	14
O8	●	Northern Illinois	61	0
O15	●	Western Illinois	20	0
O22	●	at Illinois State	35	7
O29	●	at Milwaukee State	63	12
N5	●	at Eastern Michigan	27	20
N12	●	Eastern Illinois	48	14

1956 — 9-0-0

S15	●	at Bradley	38	33
S22	●	at Western Michigan	14	7
S29	●	Southern Illinois	32	13
O6	●	at Northern Illinois	41	0
O13	●	at Western Illinois	44	20
O20	●	Illinois State	20	0
O27	●	Milwaukee State	67	12
N3	●	Eastern Michigan	19	0
N10	●	at Eastern Illinois	38	7

1957 — 4-6-0

S14		at Bradley	7	14
S21		Western Michigan	0	33
S28		Hillsdale	14	35
O5		at Illinois State	20	24
O12		at Eastern Michigan	6	39
O19	●	Northern Illinois	52	12
O26		at Louisville	0	40
N2	●	Eastern Illinois	61	6
N9	●	at Southern Illinois	21	12
N16	●	Western Illinois	39	7

1958 — 7-3-0

S13	●	at Northern Michigan	27	14
S20	●	at Western Michigan	33	32
S27	●	at Hillsdale	19	13
O4	●	Illinois State	33	6
O11	●	Eastern Michigan	7	6
O18	●	at Northern Illinois	33	23
O25		Louisville	7	40
N1	●	at Eastern Illinois	27	8
N8		Southern Illinois	7	24
N15		at Western Illinois	23	38

1959 — 7-3-0

S12		at Bolling AFB	13	19
S19	●	Western Michigan	21	15
S25	●	at Drake	41	21
O3		Western Illinois	20	26
O10	●	at Illinois State	22	0
O17	●	at Eastern Michigan	21	8
O24	●	Northern Illinois	29	7
O31	●	Northern Michigan	20	8
N7	●	Eastern Illinois	26	0
N14		at Southern Illinois	20	51

1960 — 3-5-0

S17		at Western Michigan	0	31
S24		at Northern Michigan	3	20
O1		at Western Illinois	13	38
O8	●	Illinois State	50	0
O15	●	Eastern Michigan	28	0
O22		at Northern Illinois	15	36
N5	●	at Eastern Illinois	35	12
N12		Southern Illinois	17	28

1961 — 2-8-0

S9		at Northern Michigan	0	35
S16		Western Michigan	21	27
S21		at Youngstown	7	36
S30		at Southern Illinois	0	18
O7		Western Illinois	7	12
O14		at Illinois State	21	32
O21	●	at Eastern Michigan	13	11
O28		Northern Illinois	0	11
N4	●	Hillsdale	13	10
N11		Eastern Illinois	13	22

1962 — 6-4-0

S8		at Northern Michigan	12	20
S15		at Western Michigan	0	28
S22		Youngstown	7	14
S29		Southern Illinois	6	43
O6	●	at Western Illinois	17	8
O13	●	Illinois State	46	8
O20	●	Eastern Michigan	24	0
O27	●	at Northern Illinois	35	27
N3	●	at Hillsdale	9	0
N10	●	at Eastern Illinois	35	23

1963 — 4-5-1

S14		at Bradley	6	12
S21	=	at Youngstown	7	7
S28	●	Western Michigan	30	14
O5	●	Eastern Illinois	35	15
O12		at Northern Michigan	0	19
O19		at Western Illinois	7	28
O26	●	at Illinois State	24	22
N2	●	at Eastern Michigan	55	20
N9		Northern Illinois	22	27
N16		Hillsdale	23	31

1964 — 4-5-0

S12	●	at Whitewater State	13	7
S26	●	at Western Michigan	18	6
O3		at Eastern Illinois	14	17
O10		Northern Michigan	7	12
O17		Western Illinois	7	41
O24	●	Illinois State	12	0
O31	●	Youngstown	25	20
N7		at Northern Illinois	14	19
N14		at Hillsdale	7	26

1965 — 5-5-0

S11		at Whitewater State	13	35
S17		Youngstown	14	35
S25		Western Michigan	13	21
O2		Northern Illinois	14	19
O9	●	at Northern Michigan	13	0
O16		Hillsdale	0	13
O23	●	at Illinois State	32	8
O30	●	Western Illinois	9	6
N6	●	Eastern Illinois	48	6
N13	●	at Ferris State	37	0

1966 — 5-5-0

S10		Whitewater State	16	40
S17		Youngstown	6	7
S24		at Western Michigan	14	31
O1		at Northern Illinois	13	20
O8		Northern Michigan	14	35
O15	●	at Hillsdale	28	7
O22	●	Illinois State	20	6
O29	●	Western Illinois	28	3
N5	●	at Eastern Illinois	30	10
N19	●	Wayne State	44	0

ROY KRAMER
1967-77 (.718) 83-32-2

1967 — 8-2-0

S16	●	Bradley	23	21
S22	●	at Youngstown	24	20
S30		Northern Michigan	24	28
O7	●	Eastern Illinois	23	16
O14	●	Hillsdale	35	10
O21	●	at Central State	27	0
O28	●	at Illinois State	19	16
N4		at Western Illinois	28	30
N11	●	Morehead State	9	7
N18	●	at Wayne State	35	6

1968 — 7-2-0

S14	●	at Bradley	41	6
S21	●	Youngstown	24	20
S28		at Northern Michigan	24	28
O5	●	at Eastern Illinois	23	16
O12	●	at Hillsdale	35	10
O19	●	Central State	27	0
O26	●	at Illinois State	19	16
N2		Western Illinois	28	30
N16	●	Wayne State	35	6

1969 — 7-3-0

S13		at Western Michigan	0	24
S20	●	at Northern Iowa	28	10
S27	●	Wisconsin-Milwaukee	41	6
O4	●	at Illinois State	21	0
O11	●	Northern Michigan	40	37
O18		at Western Illinois	14	17
O25	●	Eastern Illinois	44	0
N1		Akron	6	9
N8	●	at Indiana State	25	24
N15	●	at Wayne State	35	20

1970 — 7-3-0

S12		Western Michigan	0	41
S19	●	Northern Iowa	27	9
S26	●	at Wisconsin-Milwaukee	27	0
O3	●	Illinois State	34	20
O10		at Northern Michigan	14	34
O17	●	Western Illinois	20	10
O24	●	at Eastern Illinois	58	34
O31		at Akron	19	35
N7	●	Indiana State	17	7
N14	●	at Hofstra	47	0

1971 — 5-5-0

S11		at Ball State	6	9
S18	●	Youngstown	47	19
S25		Northern Michigan	14	37
O2	●	at Indiana State	21	6
O9		at Western Illinois	0	28
O23	●	Eastern Illinois	47	14
O30	●	Akron	10	7
N6		at Illinois State	6	13
N13	●	Hofstra	24	13
N20		at Southern Illinois	8	35

1972 — 5-5-1

S9		at Ohio U.	21	26
S16		at Ball State	12	30
S23	●	at Northern Michigan	26	9
S30	●	Indiana State	34	0
O7		Western Illinois	19	20
O14	●	Eastern Kentucky	21	14
O21	●	at Eastern Illinois	63	0
O28		at Akron	10	14
N4	●	Illinois State	28	21
N11	=	at Youngstown	28	28
N18		Eastern Michigan	3	28

1973 — 7-4-0

S8		Western Michigan	13	18
S15	●	Ball State	14	7
S22		at Toledo	21	23
S29	●	at Dayton	15	6
O6	●	Illinois State	6	3
O13	●	at Indiana State	21	7
O20		at Western Illinois	18	24
N3	●	Eastern Michigan	31	21
N10	●	at Eastern Kentucky	21	7
N17	●	Northern Michigan	30	7
N24		at Kent State	7	28

1974 — 12-1-0

S7		Kent State	14	21
S14	●	at Ball State	24	17
S21	●	at Northern Michigan	21	7
S28	●	Dayton	42	8
O5	●	at Illinois State	21	14
O12	●	Indiana State	49	0
O19	●	Western Illinois	58	7
N2	●	at Eastern Michigan	28	13
N9	●	Western Michigan	42	6
N16	●	Southern Illinois	42	0
		DIVISION II PLAYOFFS		
N30	●	Boise State	20	6
D7	●	Louisiana Tech[WiFL]	35	14
D14	●	Delaware[UNK]	54	14

1975-PRESENT MAC

1975 — 8-2-1 (4-1-1)

S6	● |	Western Michigan	34	0
S13	= |	Ohio U.	6	6
S20		Northern Michigan	16	17
S27	● |	at Toledo	34	27
O4	●	at Illinois State	42	7
O11	●	Eastern Michigan	20	7
O18	|	at Ball State	13	16
O25	● |	at Kent State	17	8
N1	●	Marshall	34	0
N8	●	at Western Illinois	24	7
N15	● |	Northern Illinois	69	7

1976 — 7-4-0 (4-3-0)

S11	|	Kent State	10	20
S18	● |	Toledo	9	7
S25	●	at Marshall	22	7
O2	●	Illinois State	26	7
O9	● |	Ohio U.	17	15
O16	●	Indiana State	16	13
O23		at Northern Michigan	13	41
O30	● |	at Bowling Green	38	28
N6	|	at Eastern Michigan	27	30
N13	● |	at Northern Illinois	31	9
N20	|	at Western Michigan	14	42

1977 — 10-1-0 (7-1-0)

S3	●	Alcorn State	37	7
S10	● |	Eastern Michigan	9	3
S17	●	at Illinois State	28	7
S24	● |	at Ohio U.	31	14
O1	|	at Ball State	12	28
O8	● |	at Northern Illinois	25	21
O15	●	Akron	17	14
O29	● |	Bowling Green	35	28
N5	● |	at Kent State	49	10
N12	● |	at Toledo	44	0
N19	● |	Western Michigan	28	23

HERB DEROMEDI
1978-93 (.657) 110-55-10

1978 — 9-2-0 (8-1-0)

S9	● |	Kent State	41	0
S16	● |	at Miami, Ohio	37	18
S23		at Alcorn St.	16	24
S30	|	Ball State	0	27
O7	● |	at Ohio U.	17	3
O14	●	Illinois St.	45	7
O21	● |	Northern Illinois	34	7
O28	● |	at Bowling Green	38	7
N4	● |	Toledo	27	3
N11	● |	at Eastern Michigan	41	9
N18	● |	at Western MIchigan	35	14

1979 — 10-0-1 (8-0-1)

S8	● |	Western Michigan	10	0
S22	● |	at Bowling Green	24	0
S29	● |	Miami, Ohio	19	18
O6	● |	Ohio U.	26	0
O13	● |	Northern Illinois	31	11
O20	● |	at Ball State	31	30
O27	● |	at Kent State	44	21
N3	= |	at Toledo	7	7
N10	● |	Eastern Michigan	37	14
N17	●	at Northwestern St.	28	0
N24	●	at San Jose State	34	32

1980 — 9-2-0 (7-2-0)

S6	● |	Ball State	21	17
S13	● |	at Miami, Ohio	15	14
S20	●	Illinois St.	16	0
S27	● |	Kent State	21	6
O4	● |	Toledo	14	10
O11	|	at Ohio U.	9	24
O18	|	at Northern Illinois	0	21
O25	●	Northwestern St.	17	0
N1	● |	at Eastern Michigan	51	15
N8	● |	Bowling Green	32	10
N15	● |	at Western Michigan	22	10

1981 — 7-4-0 (7-2-0)

S5		at Pacific	3	10
S19	● |	Northern Illinois	17	10
S26		Arkansas State	23	26
O3	● |	Eastern Michigan	63	14
O10	● |	at Western Michigan	15	13
O17	|	at Toledo	3	17
O24	● |	Kent State	24	3
O31	● |	at Ohio U.	38	21
N7	|	Miami, Ohio	3	7
N14	● |	at Ball State	28	7
N21	● |	at Bowling Green	6	3

1982 — 6-4-1 (5-3-1)

S4	●	Indiana St.	35	10
S18	|	Bowling Green	30	34
S25		at East Carolina	6	24
O2	● |	at Eastern Michigan	13	8
O9	= |	Western Michigan	18	18
O16	● |	Toledo	16	12
O23	● |	at Kent State	31	20
O30	● |	Ohio U.	42	18
N6	|	at Miami, Ohio	0	23
N13	● |	Ball State	24	13
N20	|	at Northern Illinois	13	19

1983 — 8-3-0 (7-2-0)

S3		at Kentucky	14	31
S10	●	No. Michigan	37	15
S24	● |	Western Michigan	32	14
O1	● |	Kent State	13	7
O8	● |	Eastern Michigan	24	3
O15	● |	at Ohio U.	14	9
O22	|	Miami, Ohio	7	12
O29	|	at Bowling Green	14	15
N5	● |	Northern Illinois	30	14
N12	● |	at Ball State	38	10
N19	● |	at Toledo	34	8

1984 — 8-2-1 (6-2-1)

S8	●	No. Michigan	45	22
S15	●	East Carolina	17	12
S22	● |	Western Michigan	38	19
S29	● |	at Kent State	14	10
O6	= |	at Eastern Michigan	16	16
O13	● |	Ohio U.	35	3
O20	● |	at Miami, Ohio	10	9
O27	● |	Bowling Green	42	21
N3	|	at Northern Illinois	7	8
N10	● |	Ball State	51	7
N17	|	Toledo	7	14

1985 — 7-3-0 (6-3-0)

S14	●	Pacific	27	10
S28	● |	at Ohio U.	13	7
O5	● |	Kent State	21	17
O12	● |	at Western Michigan	24	17
O19	|	at Bowling Green	18	23
O26	● |	Eastern Michigan	17	10
N2	|	Miami, Ohio	14	19
N9	|	at Toledo	7	10
N16	● |	at Ball State	23	9
N23	● |	Northern Illinois	30	21

1986 — 5-5-0 (4-4-0)

S13	●	Idaho	34	21
S20	● |	Bowling Green	20	10
S27	● |	Ohio U.	56	27
O4	|	at Kent State	30	33
O11	● |	at Western Michigan	18	10
O18		at Tulsa	6	42
O25	|	at Eastern Michigan	16	34
N1	|	at Miami, Ohio	21	59
N8	|	Toledo	14	26
N15	● |	Ball State	43	22

1987 — 5-5-1 (3-4-1)

S5	|	Miami, Ohio	6	15
S12	●	at Idaho	30	18
S26		at Minnesota	10	30
O3	|	at Kent State	21	24
O10	● |	Eastern MIchigan	16	6
O17	●	Tulsa	41	18
O24	|	at Ball State	3	13
O31	● |	Western Michigan	30	27
N7	● |	at Ohio U.	31	17
N14	= |	Toledo	17	17
N21	|	at Bowling Green	17	18

1988 — 7-4-0 (5-3-0)

S3		at Kentucky	7	18
S17	●	at Akron	27	16
S24	●	Montana St.	48	10
O1	● |	Kent State	31	7
O8	● |	at Eastern Michigan	20	6
O15	● |	Bowling Green	21	3
O22	|	Ball State	20	27
O29	|	at Western Michigan	24	42
N5	● |	Ohio U.	42	10
N12	|	at Toledo	13	20
N19	● |	at Miami, Ohio	34	17

1989 — 5-5-1 (5-2-1)

S9		at La. Lafayette	20	22
S16		Akron	26	27
S23	|	at Bowling Green	20	24
S30	● |	at Miami, Ohio	20	7
O7	● |	Kent State	38	0
O14	● |	at Western Michigan	34	6
O21		Youngstown St.	3	30
O26	● |	Eastern Michigan	24	9
N4	= |	at Ball State	13	13
N11	● |	Ohio U.	24	15
N18	|	at Toledo	6	29

1990 — 8-3-1 (7-1-0)

S1		at Kentucky	17	20
S8	●	Cincinnati	34	0
S15	=	at Akron	14	14
S22	● |	Bowling Green	17	0
S29	● |	Miami, Ohio	31	7
O6	● |	at Kent State	42	0
O13	● |	Western Michigan	20	13
O20	● |	Toledo	13	12
O27	● |	at Eastern Michigan	16	12
N3	|	Ball State	3	13
N10	● |	at Ohio U.	52	7
		CALIFORNIA BOWL		
D8		San Jose State	24	48

1991 — 6-1-4 (3-1-4)

A31	= |	at Ohio U.	17	17
S7	●	La. Lafayette	27	24
S14	●	at Michigan State	20	3
S21	●	Akron	31	29
S28	= |	at Toledo	16	16
O5	|	at Bowling Green	10	17
O12	= |	Miami, Ohio	10	10
O19	● |	at Kent State	23	7
O26	● |	Ball State	10	3
N2	= |	at Eastern Michigan	14	14
N16	● |	Western Michigan	27	17

1992 — 5-6-0 (4-5-0)

S5		at Kentucky	14	21
S12	●	at Michigan State	24	20
S19	● |	Ohio U.	24	0
S26	● |	Toledo	28	9
O3	|	Bowling Green	14	17
O10	|	at Miami, Ohio	13	16
O17	● |	Kent State	35	0
O24	|	at Ball State	23	24
O31	|	at Akron	28	31
N7	● |	Eastern Michigan	30	13
N14	|	at Western Michigan	14	19

1993 — 5-6-0 (5-4-0)

S2	|	Akron	13	23
S11	● |	Ohio U.	38	0
S18		at Nevada-Las Vegas	20	33
S25		at Michigan State	34	48
O2	|	Ball State	17	20
O9	● |	at Western Michigan	23	18
O16	|	Eastern Michigan	21	28
O23	● |	at Kent State	33	28
N6	● |	at Toledo	38	7
N13	● |	Bowling Green	17	15
N20	|	at Miami, Ohio	21	24

DICK FLYNN
1994-99 (.448) 30-37

1994 — 9-3-0 (8-1-0)

S3		at Iowa	21	52
S10	●	Nevada-Las Vegas	35	23
S17	● |	at Eastern Michigan	30	29
S24	● |	Kent State	45	0
O1	|	at Ball State	28	31
O8	● |	Western Michigan	35	28
O15	● |	at Akron	47	0
O22	● |	Miami, Ohio	32	30
O29	● |	at Ohio U.	22	10
N5	● |	Toledo	45	27
N12	● |	at Bowling Green	36	33
		LAS VEGAS BOWL		
D15		Nevada-Las Vegas	24	52

1995 — 4-7-0 (2-6-0)

S9	●	Weber St.	39	31
S16		at East Carolina	17	30
S23	● |	Bowling Green	22	16
S30	|	at Akron	13	16
O7	|	at Eastern Michigan	24	34
O14	●	at Youngstown St.	46	25
O21	● |	Kent State	27	16
O28	|	Miami, Ohio	13	17
N4	|	Toledo	7	19
N11	|	at Ball State	16	24
N18	|	at Western Michigan	31	48

1996   5-6   (4-4)

A31	●	at Boise State	42	21
S7		at Virginia	21	55
S14		Louisiana Tech	37	38
S21	● |	Western Michigan	38	28
S28	|	at Bowling Green	27	31
O5	|	at Miami, Ohio	14	46
O12	● |	Akron	42	0
O19	● |	Eastern Michigan	41	36
O26	|	Ball State	17	24
N2	● |	at Kent State	52	51
N9	|	at Toledo	20	23

1997   2-9   (1-7)

A28	● |	Northern Illinois	44	10
S6		at Florida	6	82
S13	●	Boise State	44	26
S20		at Louisiana Tech	28	56
S27	|	Eastern Michigan	24	31
O4	|	at Akron	14	53
O11	|	Toledo	10	41
O18	|	at Ball State	34	37
O25	|	at Kent State	37	60
N1	|	Marshall	17	45
N8	|	at Western Michigan	24	38

1998   6-5   (5-3)

S5		at Iowa	0	38
S12	●	Western Illinois	35	14
S26	● |	Kent State	46	7
O3		at Michigan State	7	38
O10	● |	at Eastern Michigan	36	23
O17	|	at Northern Illinois	6	16
O24	● |	Western Michigan	26	24
O31	● |	Akron	28	27
N7	|	at Marshall	0	28
N14	|	at Toledo	14	17
N21	● |	Ball State	31	21

1999   4-7   (3-5)

S2	●	Eastern Illinois	33	17
S11		at Syracuse	7	47
S18		at Purdue	16	58
S25	|	Miami, Ohio	16	24
O2	|	at Western Michigan	16	38
O9	● |	at Buffalo	38	19
O16	|	Northern Illinois	27	31
O30	|	at Bowling Green	7	31
N6	|	Toledo	13	32
N13	● |	Eastern Michigan	29	26
N20	● |	at Ball State	27	21

MIKE DeBORD
2000-03 (.261)   12-34

2000   2-9   (2-6)

S2		at Purdue	0	48
S9	● |	Akron	17	7
S16		at Wyoming	10	31
S23		Boise State	10	47
S30	|	at Toledo	0	41
O7	|	Kent State	21	24
O21	|	at Ohio U.	3	52
O28	|	Ball State	34	38
N4	|	at Eastern Michigan	15	31
N11	● |	Western Michigan	21	17
N18	|	at Northern Illinois	6	40

2001   3-8   (2-6)

A30	●	Ea. Kentucky	42	28
S8		at Michigan State	21	35
S22	|	Toledo	28	52
S29	|	at Buffalo	16	8
O13	● |	Ohio U.	3	34
O20	|	at Marshall	21	42
O27	|	Northern Illinois	24	33
N3	|	at Ball State	34	38
N10	● |	Eastern Michigan	35	30
N17	|	at Western Michigan	17	20
N24	|	at Boise State	10	26

2002   4-8   (2-6)

A29	●	Sam Houston St.	34	10
S7	●	Wyoming	32	20
S14	● |	at Akron	24	17
S21		at Indiana	29	39
S28		at Boston College	0	43
O12	|	Bowling Green	35	45
O19	|	at Northern Illinois	0	49
O26	|	Marshall	18	23
N2	● |	at Eastern Michigan	47	21
N9	|	at Toledo	17	44
N16	|	Ball State	21	38
N23	|	Western Michigan	10	35

2003   3-9   (1-7)

A30		at Michigan	7	45
S6	●	New Hampshire	40	33
S13	●	Eastern Kentucky	42	41
S20	|	at Ball State	14	27
O4	|	at Bowling Green	3	23
O11	|	Northern Illinois	24	40
O18	|	Toledo	13	31
O25	|	at Central Florida	13	31
N1	● |	Eastern Michigan	38	10
N8	|	Akron	28	40
N15	|	at Western Michigan	21	44
N22		at Navy	34	63

BRIAN KELLY
2004-PRESENT (.364)   4-7

2004   4-7   (3-5)

S4		at Indiana	10	41
S11		at Michigan State	7	24
S18	●	S.E. Missouri St.	44	27
O2	|	Kent State	24	21
O9	|	Bowling Green	14	38
O16	|	at Northern Illinois	10	42
O23	|	at Toledo	22	27
O30	● |	Western Michigan	24	21
N6	|	Eastern Michigan *DET*	58	61
N13	|	at Buffalo	6	36
N20	● |	Ball State	41	40

CINCINNATI

BY KEVIN GLEASON

CINCINNATI HAS THREE CHARACteristics of a spunky college football program: a long history (since 1885), a rich coaching tradition (Sid Gillman) and a stadium with character (Nippert). But it's for one coaching character that Cincy football is best known. Arriving in 1949 after serving as an assistant under Red Blaik at Army, Gillman polished his X's and O's for six seasons before going on to the NFL, where he would become one of the most influential coaches ever. At Cincinnati, he carved out a 50–13–1 record. In doing so, he set the bar for future offensive powers such as the 1968 Bearcats, the nation's top passing team.

TRADITION Previous UC captains converge the morning of the annual spring game for the Captain's Breakfast. They're joined by seniors-to-be from the current team, marking the unofficial start of senior year.

BEST PLAYER All-America quarterback Greg Cook led the nation in total offense in 1968 with 3,210 yards. The following spring he became Cincy's first player chosen in the first round of the NFL draft when he was taken fifth overall by the Cincinnati Bengals in 1969. That year Cook was named AFL Rookie of the Year.

BEST COACH Gillman's Cincinnati teams won three Mid-American Conference titles and played in two bowl games. The secret to his success? Watching movies. His wife, Esther, revealed that Sid bought a projector at a pawnshop on their honeymoon to satisfy an insatiable thirst for watching game film. In fact, the NCAA once ruled Gillman gained an unfair advantage by having first-quarter game film sent to a studio, developed and delivered back to the stadium for halftime viewing. (The NCAA still forbids the use of film during games.) Gillman left to coach the Los Angeles Rams in 1955. In the pros, he would create the blueprint for what came to be known as the West Coast offense. He was later inducted into both the College and Pro Football halls of fame.

BEST TEAM Gillman's 1951 team set a school record with 10 wins and outscored opponents 345-112. The Bearcats missed out on a bowl game when they lost to Xavier 26-0 in their next-to-last game.

BIGGEST GAME Eventual 2002 national champion Ohio State helped Cincinnati set school and Conference USA attendance records when 63,319 fans packed Paul Brown Stadium in Cincy for their game. The Bearcats lost 23-19,

---

PROFILE

University of Cincinnati
Cincinnati, Ohio
Founded: 1819
Enrollment: 19,159
Colors: Red and Black
Nickname: Bearcats
Stadium: Nippert Stadium
　　Opened in 1916
　　FieldTurf; 35,000 capacity
First football game: 1885
All-time record: 502–523–51 (.490)
Bowl record: 3–4
First-round NFL draftees: 2
Website: www.ucbearcats.com

THE BEST OF TIMES

The Sid Gillman era produced a 50–13–1 record and three Mid-American Conference championships from 1949 to 1954.

THE WORST OF TIMES

The Bearcats endured 10 straight losing seasons from 1983 to 1992.

CONFERENCE

Cincinnati joined the Big East in 2005. Before that the Bearcats played stints in Conference USA (1996-2004), the Missouri Valley Conference ('57-69) and Mid-American Conference ('47-52).

DISTINGUISHED ALUMNI

William Howard Taft; Oscar Robertson; Sandy Koufax; John Amos, actor; Kathleen Battle, operatic diva; Charles Dawes, U.S. vice president/Nobel Peace Prize winner; Albert Sabin, developer of the polio vaccine

FIGHT SONG

CHEER CINCINNATI
Cheer Cincinnati, Cincy will win
Fight to the finish, never give in, Rah, Rah, Rah!
You do your best boys,
We'll do the rest boys —
Onward to victory!
Go Red, Go Black!
Go Bearcats, Fight, Fight, Fight!
BE-AR-CATS Go UC!

but gained the respect of the state's marquee college football team. Cincinnati won its final five league games to earn a share of the Conference USA championship, its first conference championship since 1964.

BIGGEST UPSET Cincinnati opened the 1983 season with a stunning 14-3 win over defending national champion Penn State at Beaver Stadium. The Nittany Lions were still recovering from a 44-6 Kickoff Classic thrashing at the hands of Nebraska. Despite the win, Cincinnati slumped to a 4–6–1 mark for the season.

HEARTBREAKER Cincinnati took a 21-7 lead over sixth-ranked Florida State into the fourth quarter of their 1979 game. But the Seminoles rallied for a 26-21 win.

STADIUM Nippert Stadium, on the Cincinnati campus, is the sixth-oldest continuously used stadium in college football. On Thanksgiving Day 1923, UC's Jimmy Nippert was cleated on his left leg in the season-ending game against Miami (Ohio); he died of blood poisoning on Christmas Day. His grandfather, James N. Gamble, donated the $250,000

> *Sid Gillman had an insatiable thirst for game film. His wife revealed he bought a projector at a pawnshop on their honeymoon.*

needed to complete construction of a 12,000-seat stadium a year later. Capacity was doubled in 1936, with 4,000 more seats added in 1954. The Cincinnati Bengals played their home games at Nippert before the opening of Riverfront Stadium in 1970. A $10.5 million renovation project (1991-92) boosted the capacity to 35,000, with new lighting and a new scoreboard.

RIVAL Cincinnati and Miami (Ohio) have the eighth-longest current rivalry in college football, first meeting in 1888. Through 2004, Miami led the series, 58–44–7.

DISPUTE The NCAA record book recognizes the 1902 Rose Bowl as the first college bowl game. But Cincinnati claims it played in a bowl game on Jan. 6, 1898, against the Southern Athletic Club in New Orleans. Cincy, with 14 players and coaches making the trip, beat SAC 16-0. At a victory party that night, some LSU players challenged UC to a game. Two days later, according to Cincinnati lore, the Bearcats beat LSU 28-0.

NICKNAME Cincinnati was facing the Kentucky

RECORDS

RUSHING YARDS

GAME
306	Bob Hynes vs. Case Western Reserve, Nov. 17, 1923

SEASON
1,361	DeMarco McCleskey, 2002 (315 att.)

CAREER
4,242	Reggie Taylor, 1983-86 (876 att.)

PASSING YARDS

GAME
554	Greg Cook vs. Ohio U., Nov. 16, 1968 (35 of 56)

SEASON
3,543	Gino Guidugli, 2002 (258 of 472)

CAREER
11,453	Gino Guidugli, 2001-04 (880 of 1,556)

RECEIVING YARDS

GAME
254	Tom Rossley vs. Louisville, Nov. 9, 1968 (11 rec.)

SEASON
1,114	Jon Olinger, 2002 (54 rec.)

CAREER
2,483	LaDaris Vann, 1999-2002 (204 rec.)

POINTS

GAME
51	Ike Stewart vs. Transylvania, 1912

SEASON
142	Jim O'Brien, 1968 (12 TDs, 13 FGs, 31 PATs)

CAREER
315	Jonathan Ruffin, 1999-2002 (62 FGs, 129 PATs)

CONSENSUS ALL-AMERICANS

2000	Jonathan Ruffin, PK

Wildcats on Oct. 31, 1914, when a cheerleader named Norman "Pat" Lyon took up a cheer for Cincy's star fullback, Leonard K. "Teddy" Baehr. "They may be Wildcats," Lyon shrieked, "but we have a Baehr-cat on our side." Cincy won 14-7, and a cartoon in the student newspaper, *University News*, showed a tattered Kentucky Wildcat being chased by a creature tagged the Cincinnati Bear Cat. The moniker disappeared when Baehr graduated two years later, but returned after a 1919 game at Tennessee when *Cincinnati Enquirer* writer Jack Ryder referred to UC as the Bearcats in his game story.

MASCOT The Bearcat made news late in the 2002 season when, according to Cincinnati officials, he was assaulted after the Hawaii game by its mascot, the Warrior. The brawl started after Hawaii's narrow 20-19 victory.

UNIFORMS The late 1990s and early 2000s saw Cincinnati go to the C-Paw logo on helmets, paws extending from the top of a C. The first Bearcat logo came in 1924 with an upright bear on uniforms. Six years later, a C was added.

LORE College Football Hall of Fame inductee Frank Cavanaugh began his coaching career in 1898 by leading Cincy to a 5–1–3 record. He moved on after the season and later coached at Holy Cross (1903-05) and Dartmouth (1911-16) before serving in World War I. Cavanaugh earned the nickname Iron Major for his wartime heroics; he became the subject of a 1943 movie of the same name.

QUOTE "I'd hate to have something on the football field happen that I'm not aware of."—Sid Gillman

CINCINNATI ANNUAL STATISTICAL LEADERS

YR	RUSHING	YDS	ATT	AVG	PASSING	ATT	CMP	PCT	YDS	RECEIVING	REC	YDS	AVG
1946	Roger Stephens	768	96	8.0		NA	NA	NA	NA		NA	NA	NA
1947	Roger Stephens	959	136	7.1	Tom O'Malley	81	40	.49	634	Alkie Richards	18	400	22.2
1948	Jim Dougherty	495	108	4.6	Tom O'Malley	147	71	.48	899	Joe Hauk	20	263	13.2
1949	Howie Bellamah	473	97	4.9	Tom O'Malley	225	108	.48	1,617	Jim Kelly	42	468	11.1
1950	Bob Stratton	539	93	5.8	Gene Rossi	149	68	.46	1,000	Jim Kelly	29	455	15.7
1951	Bob Daugherty	528	96	5.5	Gene Rossi	173	89	.51	1,444	Dick Jarvis	31	554	17.9
1952	Joe Concilla	488	96	5.1	Gene Rossi	170	100	.59	1,559	Dom Del Bene	28	372	13.3
1953	Dick Goist	561	64	8.8	Mike Murphy	70	44	.63	809	Glen Dillhoff	13	265	20.4
1954	Joe Miller	717	128	5.6	Mike Murphy	101	51	.50	764	Fred Maccioli	13	179	13.8
1955	Joe Miller	399	90	4.4	Mike Murphy	66	30	.45	450	Jim Niemann	9	177	19.7
1956	Bob Del Rosa	242	57	4.2	Joe Morrison	78	29	.37	438	Gene Johnson	9	200	22.2
1957	Barry Maroney	346	98	3.5	Jack Lee	52	25	.48	328	Don Reinhold	9	90	10.0
1958	Joe Morrison	467	99	4.7	Jack Lee	130	71	.55	951	Joe Morrison	27	303	11.2
1959	Ed Kovac	515	134	3.8	Jack Lee	232	132	.57	1,535	Ed Kovac	31	332	10.7
1960	Ed Banks	404	104	3.9	Larry Harp	116	39	.34	581	Fred Oblak	23	386	16.8
1961	Phil Goldner	277	70	4.0	Larry Harp	107	40	.37	426	Jim Paris	16	185	11.6
1962	Royce Starks	408	91	4.5	Bruce Vogelgesang	93	41	.44	424	Frank Shaut	12	197	16.4
1963	Brig Owens	556	121	4.6	Brig Owens	124	67	.54	974	Jim Curry	39	621	15.9
1964	Al Nelson	973	201	4.8	Brig Owens	111	54	.49	790	Al Nelson	13	133	10.2
1965	Bill Bailey	694	139	5.0	Mike Flaherty	41	20	.49	304	Mike Turner	8	76	9.5
1966	Clem Turner	840	153	5.5	Tony Jackson	127	63	.50	702	Ed Ford	25	279	11.2
1967	Lloyd Pate	658	198	3.3	Greg Cook	179	81	.45	1,221	Jim O'Brien	26	547	21.0
1968	Lloyd Pate	623	135	4.6	Greg Cook	411	219	.53	3,272	Tom Rossley	80	1,072	13.4
1969	Steve Cowan	676	165	4.1	Albert Johnson	123	50	.41	937	Jim O'Brien	34	631	18.6
1970	Steve Cowan	1,197	239	5.0	Albert Johnson	130	39	.30	516	Rod Warren	13	204	15.7
1971	Mel Riggins	663	131	5.1	Albert Johnson	101	30	.30	434	Steve Cowan	15	226	15.1
1972	Reggie Harrison	844	173	4.9	Mike Shoemaker	175	70	.40	787	Zeke Harden	29	330	11.4
1973	Reggie Harrison	883	211	4.2	Mike Campbell	83	41	.49	538	Jim Kelly	20	215	10.8
1974	Santo Atkinson	708	196	3.6	Henry Miller	140	61	.44	796	Jim Kelly	25	345	13.8
1975	Jay Bonds	567	158	3.6	Henry Miller	150	73	.49	886	Jim Kelly	31	404	13.0
1976	Curtliss Williams	399	102	3.9	Art Bailey	77	36	.47	491	Napolean Outlaw	20	309	15.5
1977	Curtliss Williams	845	162	5.2	Art Bailey	77	33	.43	524	Napolean Outlaw	14	223	15.9
1978	Allen Harvin	1,283	233	5.5	Tim Morris	139	64	.46	839	Allen Harvin	21	150	7.1
1979	James Bettis	343	75	4.6	Tony Kapetanis	224	99	.44	1,414	Aaron Hagans	27	531	19.7
1980	James Bettis	1,106	212	5.2	Danny Barrett	130	73	.56	888	Ralph Williams	34	418	12.3
1981	James Bettis	1,226	246	5.0	Danny Barrett	177	92	.52	1,186	Deno Foster	22	427	19.4
1982	Allen Harvin	1,161	191	6.1	Danny Barrett	324	179	.55	2,222	Bill Booze	36	571	15.9
1983	Reggie Taylor	784	158	5.0	Troy Bodine	209	127	.61	1,643	Don Goodman	51	343	6.7
1984	Reggie Taylor	1,021	198	5.2	Troy Bodine	350	171	.49	2,056	Deno Foster	49	754	15.4
1985	Reggie Taylor	1,112	264	4.2	Danny McCoin	201	115	.57	1,576	Joe Hice	27	358	13.3
1986	Reggie Taylor	1,325	256	5.2	Danny McCoin	369	237	.64	2,831	Joe Hice	44	584	13.3
1987	Al McKinney	950	208	4.6	Danny McCoin	268	158	.59	2,013	Bill Davis	41	626	15.3
1988	Al McKinney	829	168	4.9	Glenn Farkas	204	114	.56	1,279	Al McKinney	31	199	6.4
1989	Terry Strong	411	105	3.9	Glenn Farkas	163	84	.52	982	Bryant Hatcher	34	520	15.3
1990	Terry Strong	803	172	4.7	Paul Anderson	238	123	.52	1,453	Joe Koynock	44	496	11.3
1991	David Small	1,004	198	5.1	Lance Harp	204	107	.52	1,443	Marlon Pearce	42	758	18.0
1992	David Small	780	209	3.7	Lance Harp	292	151	.52	1,785	Marlon Pearce	56	891	15.9
1993	David Small	1,179	223	5.3	Lance Harp	292	139	.48	1,575	Albert Sweet	29	460	15.9
1994	Craedel Kimbrough	565	132	4.3	Eric Vibberts	182	114	.63	1,335	Anthony Ladd	35	446	12.7
1995	Orlando Smith	471	126	3.7	Eric Vibberts	264	136	.52	1,851	Robert Tate	46	895	19.5
1996	Daryl Royal	853	167	5.1	Chad Plummer	198	102	.52	1,335	Robert Tate	23	247	10.7
1997	Robert Cooper	611	137	4.5	Chad Plummer	190	87	.46	1,178	Cornelius Bonner	27	366	13.6
1998	DeMarco McCleskey	861	162	5.3	Deontey Kenner	270	148	.55	2,047	Chad Plummer	61	852	14.0
1999	Robert Cooper	1,245	228	5.5	Deontey Kenner	379	208	.55	2,430	Tony Smikle	45	429	9.5
2000	Ray Jackson	808	201	4.0	Deontey Kenner	265	137	.52	1,717	Antonio Chatman	46	609	13.2
2001	DeMarco McCleskey	765	179	4.3	Gino Guidugli	317	185	.58	2,573	LaDaris Vann	73	902	12.4
2002	DeMarco McCleskey	1,361	315	4.3	Gino Guidugli	472	258	.55	3,543	LaDaris Vann	71	844	11.9
2003	Richard Hall	777	185	4.2	Gino Guidugli	425	227	.53	2,704	George Murray	30	270	11.1
2004	Richard Hall	210	1,012	4.8	Gino Guidugli	342	210	.61	2,633	Hannibal Thomas	64	1,028	16.1

Receiving leaders by receptions
The NCAA began including postseason stats in 2002

THE SCHOOLS

CINCINNATI ALL-TIME SCORES

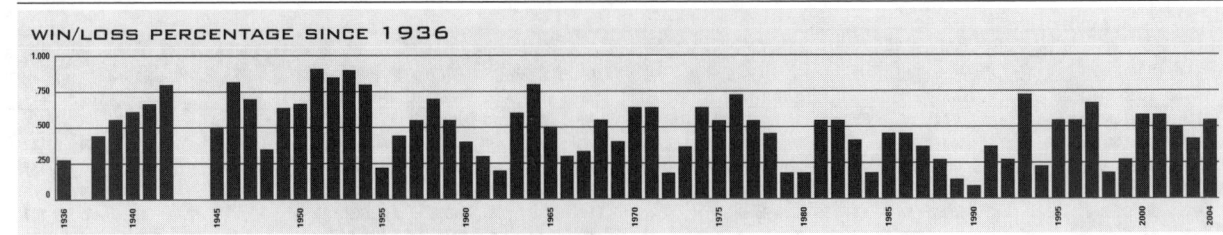

WIN/LOSS PERCENTAGE SINCE 1936

NO HEAD COACH

1885 — 1-0-1
O23	=	Mt. Auburn[UNK]	0	0
N14	●	Mt. Auburn[UNK]	26	6

1886 — 2-0-0
U	●	Mt. Auburn[UNK]	18	6
U	●	Mt. Auburn[UNK]	8	6

1887 — 1-0-0
U	●	Woodward HS[UNK]	8	4

1888 — 1-0-1
U	●	Walnut Hills Gym[UNK]	8	6
D8	●	at Miami, Ohio	0	0

1889 — 1-1-0
U	●	Avondale[UNK]	12	0
U		Miami, Ohio	0	34

1890 — 2-1-1
U	=	Franklin[UNK]	0	0
U		Woodward HS[UNK]	8	16
U	●	Wyoming, Ohio[UNK]	8	4
U	●	Wyoming, Ohio[UNK]	6	0

1891 — 4-2-1
U	●	Woodward HS[UNK]	22	0
U	●	Hughes HS[UNK]	33	0
U	●	Franklin[UNK]	38	0
U	=	Cincinnati Gym[UNK]	0	0
U		Dayton YMCA[UNK]	8	12
U		Butler[UNK]	10	34
U	●	Cincinnati Gym[UNK]	18	0

1892 — 1-2-0
U	●	Dayton YMCA[UNK]	16	6
U		Centre[UNK]	4	12
U		Centre[UNK]	0	34

1893 — 0-6-0
U		at Miami, Ohio	6	24
U		Centre[UNK]	0	16
O28		at Chicago	0	20
U		Cincinnati YMCA[UNK]	6	22
U		Miami, Ohio	0	6
N18		Ohio State	0	38

W. DURANT BERRY
1894-95 (.500) — 6-6

1894 — 3-3-0
U		Georgetown, Ky.[UNK]	4	6
U	●	Miami, Ohio	6	0
S22	●	Kentucky	32	4
U		Hanover[UNK]	14	12
N17		Ohio State[UNK]	4	6
U		Ohio Wesleyan[UNK]	4	16

1895 — 3-3-0
O12	●	Kenyon[UNK]	16	4
O19		Duquesne AC[UNK]	6	26
O26	●	Earlham[UNK]	26	0
N9		Ohio State[UNK]	0	4
N16		Miami, Ohio	0	12
N28	●	Marietta[UNK]	6	0

WILLIAM REYNOLDS
1896 (.563) — 4-3-1

1896 — 4-3-1
U		Miami, Ohio	4	6
O10	●	Ohio State	8	6
U	●	Ohio U.[UNK]	52	0
U	●	Ohio Wesleyan[UNK]	6	0
U		Indiana[UNK]	0	16
N14		at Carlisle	0	28
U	●	Wittenberg[UNK]	6	0
U	=	Centre[UNK]	12	12

TOM FENNEL
1897 (.864) — 9-1-1

1897 — 9-1-1
U	●	Ohio U.[UNK]	12	0
U	=	Nashville Guards[UNK]	6	6
U	●	at Miami, Ohio	6	0
U	●	Centre[UNK]	4	0
U	●	Ohio Nat. Guard[UNK]	20	0
U	●	Miami, Ohio[UNK]	10	6
U	●	Centre[UNK]	10	0
N13	●	Ohio State	24	0_*
N25		Carlisle	0	10
J6	●	at Southern AC	16	0
J8	●	at LSU	26	0_*

FRANK CAVANAUGH
1898 (.722) — 5-1-3

1898 — 5-1-3
U	=	Ohio U.[UNK]	12	12
U	●	at Miami, Ohio	22	0
O22	●	Vanderbilt[UNK]	10	0_*
U		Oberlin[UNK]	0	5
U	=	Indiana[UNK]	0	0
U	●	Alumni[UNK]	12	0
U	●	Ohio Wesleyan[UNK]	57	0
U	=	Indiana[UNK]	11	11
N24	●	Dartmouth	17	12

DAN REED
1899-1900 (.567) — 8-6-1

1899 — 5-2-0
U	●	Miami, Ohio[UNK]	22	0
O20	●	Vanderbilt[UNK]	6	0
U	●	Centre[UNK]	26	0
N4		at Indiana	0	35
U		Wash. & Jeff.[UNK]	0	20
U	●	Alumni[UNK]	6	0
U	●	Ohio Wesleyan[UNK]	28	5

1900 — 3-4-1
U	●	Covington YMCA[UNK]	15	10
U	=	Centre[UNK]	0	0
U		Haskell[UNK]	0	16
S29	●	Kentucky	20	6
U		Marietta[UNK]	0	25
U	●	Miami, Ohio[UNK]	16	12
O13		Ohio State	0	29
O20		at Notre Dame[UNK]	0	58_*

HENRY PRATT
1901 (.300) — 1-3-1

1901 — 1-3-1
U		Avondale[UNK]	0	13
U	●	Hanover[UNK]	10	0
O12	=	at Kentucky	0	0
U		Ohio U.[UNK]	0	16
U		Wittenberg[UNK]	0	18

ANTHONY CHEZ
1902-03 (.353) — 5-10-2

1902 — 4-2-2
U	●	Hanover[UNK]	18	0
U	●	Earlham[UNK]	12	6
U	●	Indianapolis[UNK]	6	0
U		Stumps[UNK]	0	23
U	●	Otterbein[UNK]	16	0
U	=	Wittenberg[UNK]	0	0
N15	=	at Kentucky	6	6
U		Marietta[UNK]	0	10

1903 — 1-8-0
U	●	Hanover[UNK]	28	6
U		Wittenberg[UNK]	0	6
U		Miami, Ohio	0	15
U		Earlham[UNK]	0	11
O24		at Northwestern	0	35
U		Kenyon[UNK]	0	16
U		Alumni[UNK]	0	6
N21		at Washington, Mo	11	23
U		Avondale[UNK]	0	23

AMOS FOSTER
1904-05 (.733) — 11-4

1904 — 7-1-0
U	●	Georgetown, Ky.[UNK]	33	0
U	●	Wittenberg[UNK]	29	4
U	●	Miami, Ohio	46	0
O22	●	Kentucky	11	0
U	●	Ohio Medics[UNK]	11	0
U		Stumps[UNK]	0	6
N16	●	at Tennessee	35	0
U	●	Kenyon[UNK]	17	0

1905 — 4-3-0
O10		Carlisle	5	34
U	●	DePauw[UNK]	17	0
U	●	Earlham[UNK]	12	0
N4		at Indiana	6	47
U	●	Kenyon[UNK]	23	4
U		Marietta[UNK]	0	6
U	●	Ohio Wesleyan[UNK]	24	0

WILLIAM FOLEY
1906 (.111) — 0-7-2

1906 — 0-7-2
O6	=	at Marshall	0	0
O13		Carlisle[UNK]	0	18
U	=	Miami, Ohio	0	0
U		Earlham[UNK]	0	20
U		Avondale[UNK]	0	4
U		Ohio U.[UNK]	5	16
U		Wittenberg[UNK]	0	12
N29		at Nebraska	0	41
U		Marietta[UNK]	0	51

1907
NO TEAM

RALPH INOTT
1908 (.250) — 1-4-1

1908 — 1-4-1
O17		Alabama[BIRM]	0	16
U	●	Hanover[UNK]	5	9
U	●	Lebanon[UNK]	43	0
U		Kenyon[UNK]	0	63
U		Antioch[UNK]	11	16
U	=	Wittenberg[UNK]	0	0

ROBERT BURCH
1909-11 (.654) — 16-8-2

1909 — 4-3-1
U	●	Hanover[UNK]	6	2
U	●	Wittenberg[UNK]	22	5
U	●	Otterbein[UNK]	3	15
U	=	Transylvania[UNK]	6	6
U		Centre[UNK]	0	34
N6		at Tulane	0	6
U	●	Butler[UNK]	22	0
N25	●	Miami, Ohio	10	6

1910 — 6-3-0
U	●	Transylvania[UNK]	16	0
O8		at Ohio State	0	23
U	●	Earlham[UNK]	20	0
U	●	Wittenberg[UNK]	8	0
U	●	Miami, Ohio	3	0
U		Otterbein[UNK]	6	12
U		Centre[UNK]	3	12
U	●	Antioch[UNK]	38	0
U	●	Denison[UNK]	28	12

1911 — 6-2-1
U	●	Transylvania[UNK]	12	0
U		Earlham[UNK]	0	9
U	●	Otterbein[UNK]	16	3
O28	●	at Kentucky	6	0
U	●	Butler[UNK]	23	11
U	=	Denison[UNK]	0	0
N18	●	Miami, Ohio	11	0
U	●	Wittenberg[UNK]	5	0
N30		Ohio State	6	11

LOWELL DANA
1912-13 (.529) — 8-7-2

1912 — 3-4-1
U	●	Transylvania[UNK]	124	0
U	●	Earlham[UNK]	21	0
O19		Kentucky	13	19
O26		at Ohio State	7	47_*
U	●	Otterbein[UNK]	39	7
U		Denison[UNK]	13	31
U		Kenyon[UNK]	13	22
N28	=	Miami, Ohio	21	21

1913 — 5-3-1
U	●	Georgetown, Ky.[UNK]	46	0
U	●	Wittenberg[UNK]	32	0
U	●	Ohio U.[UNK]	20	2
U	●	Ohio Wesleyan[UNK]	44	3
O25		at Kentucky	7	27
U	=	Case Western[UNK]	0	0
U		Denison[UNK]	7	14
U	●	Kenyon[UNK]	14	2
N27		Miami, Ohio	7	13

GEORGE LITTLE
1914-15 (.556) — 10-8

1914 — 6-3-0
U	●	Georgetown, Ky.[UNK]	35	0
U	●	Denison[UNK]	13	0
U		Ohio Wesleyan[UNK]	7	14
U	●	Kenyon[UNK]	47	0
O31	●	Kentucky	14	7
U	●	Western Reserve[UNK]	20	0
U		Otterbein[UNK]	0	3
U	●	Ohio U.[UNK]	15	0
N27		Miami, Ohio	13	20

1915 — 4-5-0
S26	●	Alumni	14	7
O2		Georgetown, Ky.	7	21
O9		Ohio U.	0	15
O16	●	Kenyon	27	7
O23		Denison	0	35
O30		at Kentucky	6	27
N6	●	Ohio Wesleyan	17	6
N13	●	Wittenberg	27	16
N25		Miami, Ohio	12	24

ION CORTRIGHT 1916 (.056)   0-8-1

1916   0-8-1

U	=	Wittenberg^Unk	0	0
U		Denison^Unk	0	29
U		Georgetown, Ky.^Unk	0	16
U		Ohio Northern^Unk	0	9
O28		Kentucky	0	32 *
U		Wooster^Unk	0	20
U		Ohio U.^Unk	10	33
U		Kenyon^Unk	0	27
N30		Miami, Ohio	0	33 *

FRANK MARTY 1917 (.000)   0-6

1917   0-6-0

U		Earlham^Unk	0	19
U		Wittenberg^Unk	0	7
U		Marietta^Unk	0	53
U		Ohio U.^Unk	0	22
U		Ohio Wesleyan^Unk	0	48
N29		Miami, Ohio	0	40

BOYD CHAMBERS 1918-21 (.450)   12-15-3

1918   3-0-2

N2		Fort Thomas	6	0
N9	=	at Ohio U.	6	6
N23		Georgetown, Ky.	21	7
N28	=	Miami, Ohio	0	0
D7	•	Xavier	12	0

1919   3-4-1

O4	•	Wilmington	34	0
O11		at Ohio State	0	46
O18	•	Kenyon	18	0
O25		Denison	2	9
N1		at Wittenberg	0	0
N8		Kentucky	7	0
N15		at Tennessee	12	33
N28		Miami, Ohio	0	14

1920   4-5-0

S25	•	Ky. Wesleyan	35	0
O2	•	Kenyon	45	0
O9	•	Ohio U.	6	0
O16		Denison	0	21
O23		at Carnegie Tech	17	27
O30		Wittenberg	9	13
N6		at Kentucky	6	7
N13		Marietta	0	28
N25	•	Miami, Ohio	7	0

1921   2-6-0

S24	•	Toledo	20	0
O1		at West Virginia	0	50
O15		at Pittsburgh	14	21
O22	•	Ky. Wesleyan	115	0
O29		Wittenberg	2	7
N5		at Ohio U.	6	7
N12		Denison	0	7
N24	•	Miami, Ohio	7	15

GEORGE McLAREN 1922-26 (.389)   16-26-3

1922   1-7-1

S30		Pittsburgh	0	38 *
O7		at Kentucky	0	15
O14		at Georgetown	0	37
O21		Ohio Wesleyan^Unk	7	14
O28	•	Case^Unk	16	0
N4		West Virginia	0	34
N11		Denison^Unk	0	22
N18	=	Wittenberg^Unk	6	6
N30	•	Miami, Ohio^Unk	6	9

1923   6-3-0

S29	•	Ky. Wesleyan	17	0
O6		Kentucky	0	14
O13		at Denison	7	24
O20		at Ohio U.	13	6 *
O27	•	Wooster	7	20
N3		at Oberlin	6	0
N10		Ohio Northern	15	7
N17		Case	69	0
N23	•	Miami, Ohio	23	0

1924   2-6-1

S27	=	Ky. Wesleyan	6	6
O4	•	Georgetown, Ky.	33	21
O11		at Northwestern	0	42
O18		Denison	7	13
O25		at Ohio Northern	0	9
N1		Dayton	0	21
N8		Oberlin	0	13
N15		at Wooster	0	32
N27	•	Miami, Ohio	8	7

1925   4-5-0

S26		Transylvania	15	21
O3	•	Hanover	12	0
O10	•	Georgetown, Ky.	12	6
O17	•	at Otterbein	6	0
O24		Denison	12	24
O31		Dayton	0	23
N7	•	at Wittenberg	6	2
N14		Ohio U.	2	13
N26	•	Miami, Ohio	0	33

1926   3-5-1

S25	•	Ky. Wesleyan	25	0
O2	•	Otterbein	21	6
O9		at Denison	0	14
O16	•	Marietta	22	7
O23		at Ohio U.	7	38
O30		at Western Reserve	2	14
N6		Dayton	0	52
N13		Wittenberg	13	15
N25	=	Miami, Ohio	6	6

GEORGE BABCOCK 1927-30 (.375)   12-21-3

1927   2-5-2

S24		Ky. Wesleyan	0	12
O1	•	Hanover	35	6
O8		at Wittenberg	0	45
O15		Dayton	0	9
O22	=	Marietta	6	6
O29		Denison	0	3
N5	•	Transylvania	19	0
N12	•	Ohio U	7	7
N24		Miami, Ohio	14	17

1928   1-8-0

S29	•	Hanover	20	6
O6		Ky. Wesleyan	0	6
O13		Ohio Wesleyan	0	71
O20		at Ohio U.	0	65 *
O27		Wittenberg	0	6
N3		Transylvania	6	25
N10		Dayton	6	25
N17		Denison	0	9
N29		Miami, Ohio	0	34

1929   4-4-1

S28	•	Cedarville	19	0
O2	•	at Louisville	7	0
O5	•	Ohio Northern	12	6
O12	•	at Kenyon	18	6
O19	=	Denison	6	6
O26		Ohio U.	0	35
N2		at Wittenberg	7	13
N16		Ohio Wesleyan	0	53
N28		Miami, Ohio	6	14

1930   5-4-0

S27	•	Cedarville	46	0
O3	•	Ky. Wesleyan	6	0
O11		at Michigan State	0	32
O18		Ohio Wesleyan	0	33
O25	•	Denison	13	6
N1		Ohio U.	0	48
N8	•	Marietta	20	7
N15		Wittenberg	0	12
N27	•	Miami, Ohio	6	0

DANA KING 1931-34 (.708)   25-10-1

1931   5-4-0

S26	•	Rio Grande	19	6
O3		at Ohio State	6	67
O10		DePauw	6	7
O17	•	Marietta	50	0
O24		Ohio U.	7	13
O31		Muskingum	0	15
N7		at Denison	33	0
N14	•	Heidelberg	46	7
N26	•	Miami, Ohio	20	0

1932   7-2-0

S24	•	Hanover	51	0
O1	•	Georgetown, Ky.	22	12
O8	•	Butler	13	7
O15	•	South Dakota	7	0
O22	•	Denison	6	0
O29	•	Wittenberg	25	6
N5	•	Wabash	14	0
N12		at Ohio U.	0	23
N24	•	Miami, Ohio	13	21

1933   7-2-0

S30	•	Rio Grande	20	0
O7	•	South Dakota	13	0
O14		Kentucky	0	3
O21	•	Marshall	19	0
O28	•	Butler	34	7
N4	•	at Ohio Wesleyan	7	0
N11		at Wittenberg	14	6
N18	•	Ohio U.	2	0
N30	•	Miami, Ohio	2	6

1934   6-2-1

S29	•	Otterbein	45	0
O6		Kentucky	0	27
O13		at Vanderbilt	0	32
O20	•	Ashland	32	6
O27	•	Georgetown, Ky.	45	0
N3	•	Marshall	7	0
N10		at Ohio U.	0	0
N17	•	Ohio Wesleyan	13	6
N29	•	Miami, Ohio	21	0

RUSS COHEN 1935-37 (.432)   8-11-3

1935   7-2-0

S28	•	Dayton	25	0
O5	•	South Dakota St.	38	0
O12	•	at Denison	35	0
O19	•	Indiana	7	0
O26	•	Baltimore	67	0
N2		at Ohio Wesleyan	12	13
N9	•	Marshall	39	13
N16		at Ohio U.	6	16
N28		Miami, Ohio	8	7

1936   1-5-3

S26	•	at West Virginia	6	40
O3	=	Butler	12	12
O10		Georgetown	0	7
O17	•	at Marshall	13	7
O24		Dayton	13	21
O31		at Ohio U.	7	10
N7	•	Ohio Wesleyan	0	0
N14		at Wisconsin	6	27
N26	•	Miami, Ohio	6	14

WADE WOODWORTH 1937 (.000)   0-6

1937   0-10-0

S18		Morehead	0	7
S25		Western Reserve	6	32
O2		Butler	0	13
O9		at Dayton	0	35
O16		Case	0	21
O23		at Indiana	0	27
O30		at Ohio Wesleyan	6	20
N6		Ohio U.	0	17
N13		at Marshall	0	28
N25		Miami, Ohio	6	14

JOE MEYER 1938-42 (.620)   27-16-3

1938   4-5-0

S24	•	Louisville	19	9 *
O1	•	Illinois Wesleyan	6	0
O8		Dayton	7	26
O14		at Tampa	7	6
O22		Western Reserve	0	33
O29		at Ohio U.	12	13
N5	•	Ohio Wesleyan	14	7
N12		Marshall	9	27
N24		Miami, Ohio	7	16

1939   4-3-2

S30	•	Tampa	26	7
O6		at Dayton	2	32
O14		West Virginia	0	7
O21	•	at Wayne	21	0
O27	=	at Western Reserve	0	0
N4	=	Centre	6	6
N11		Boston U.	6	13
N18	•	South Dakota	13	0
N23	•	Miami, Ohio	13	0

1940   5-3-1

S21	•	Hanover	45	0
S28	•	Louisville	7	0
O5		at Navy	0	14
O12	•	Centre	22	0
O19		at Boston U.	0	14
O26	•	Dayton	0	7
N2	•	Carnegie Tech	7	6
N9	=	at West Virginia	7	7
N21	•	Miami, Ohio	44	0

1941   6-3-0

S20	•	Transylvania	46	0
S27	•	Louisville	28	7
O4		at Boston U.	13	14
O11	•	Wayne	37	0
O18	•	Centre	18	0
O25		at Tennessee	6	21
N1		at Dayton	0	3
N8	•	Carnegie Tech	20	0
N20	•	Miami, Ohio	26	0

1942   8-2-0

S26	•	Louisville	51	0
O3	•	at Western Reserve	18	7
O10	•	Centre	21	0
O17	•	Ohio U.	26	7
O24	•	Georgia	13	35
O31	•	Boston U.	6	0
N7		at Tennessee	12	34
N14	•	Dayton	20	0
N21	•	Xavier	9	0
N26	•	Miami, Ohio	21	12

1943-44 NO TEAM

RAY NOLTING 1945-48 (.603)   23-15-1

1945   4-4-0

S22	•	Denison	30	0
S29		at Kentucky	7	13
O6	•	DePauw	7	0
O13	•	at Ohio U.	19	20
O27	•	Kentucky	16	7
N3	•	Baldwin Wallace	39	0
N10	•	at Detroit	0	20
N22	•	Miami, Ohio	14	28

1946   9-2-0

S21	•	at Indiana	15	6
S28		Kentucky	7	26
O5	•	Marshall	39	14
O12	•	at Dayton	19	0
O19	•	Ohio U.	19	0
O26	•	at Michigan St.	18	7
N2	•	at Tulsa	0	20
N9	•	Xavier	39	0
N16	•	Western Reserve	34	7
N28	•	Miami, Ohio	13	7

SUN BOWL

J1	•	Virginia Tech	18	6

1947-1952 MAC

1947   7-3-0 (3-1-0)

S27		at Kentucky	0	20
O4	•	St. Bonaventure	20	14
O11		Dayton	21	26
O18	•	Oklahoma City	20	13
O25	•	Xavier	27	25
N1	•	| at Ohio U.	34	0
N8	•	| Miami, Fla.	20	7
N15	•	| at Western Reserve	7	6
N22		| Butler	26	19
N27		| Miami, Ohio	7	38

1948   3-6-1 (3-1-0)

S25	=	Hardin Simmons	7	7
O2		Xavier	7	13
O9	•	| Ohio U.	18	13
O16		at Mississippi State	0	27
O23	•	| at Butler	16	7
O30		Kentucky	7	28
N5		at Miami, Fla.	6	36
N13	•	| Western Reserve	26	13
N20		Tulane	0	6
N25		| Miami, Ohio	19	43

214 CINCINNATI

THE SCHOOLS

SID GILLMAN
1949-54 (.789) 50-13-1

1949 7-4-0 (4-0-0)
S17 Nevada 21 41
S24 ● Hardin Simmons 27 21
O1 at Pacific 7 34
O15 ● Mississippi State 19 0
O21 ● | Western Reserve 21 13
O28 ● | at Western Michigan 27 6
O29 at Kentucky 7 14
N5 ● | at Ohio U. 34 13
N12 Xavier 14 20
N24 ● | Miami, Ohio 27 6
GLASS BOWL
D3 ● at Toledo 33 13

1950 8-4-0 (3-1-0)
S16 ● Texas-El Paso 32 0
S23 ● Hardin Simmons 9 7
S30 at William & Mary 14 20
O7 ● Louisville 28 20
O14 at Kentucky 7 41
O21 ● | Western Reserve 48 6
O28 ● | at Western Michigan 27 6
N4 ● | Ohio U. 23 0
N11 ● Pacific 14 7
N18 ● Xavier 33 20
N25 | Miami, Ohio 0 28
SUN BOWL
J1 West Texas St. 13 14

1951 10-1-0 (3-0-0)
S15 ● VMI 26 7
S22 ● at Kansas State 34 0
S29 ● Tulsa 47 35
O6 ● Hawaii 34 0
O13 ● Louisville 38 0
O20 ● | Western Reserve 41 0
O27 ● Texas-El Paso 53 18
N3 ● at Hardin Simmons 13 12
N10 ● | at Ohio U. 40 0
N17 Xavier 0 26
N24 ● | Miami, Ohio 19 14

1952 8-1-1 (3-0-0)
S20 ● Dayton 25 0
S27 ● Kansas State 13 6
O4 = at Tulsa 14 14
O11 ● Xavier 20 13
O18 ● Wabash 27 7
O25 Kentucky 6 14
N1 ● | at Western Reserve 41 2
N8 ● | Ohio U. 41 7 *
N15 ● Wash. & Lee 54 0
N27 ● | Miami, Ohio 34 9

1953-1956
INDEPENDENT

1953 9-1-0
S19 ● at Tulsa 14 7
S26 at Marquette 7 31
O3 ● William & Mary 57 7
O10 ● Toledo 41 7
O17 ● Xavier 20 6
O24 ● Western Reserve 66 0
O31 ● Dayton 27 0
N7 ● at Louisville 41 0
N14 ● VMI 67 0
N26 ● Miami, Ohio 14 0

1954 8-2-0
S18 ● at Detroit 21 13
S25 ● Dayton 42 13
O2 ● Tulsa 40 7
O9 ● at Marquette 30 13
O16 ● Hardin Simmons 27 13
O23 ● Xavier 33 0
O30 ● Pacific 13 7
N6 ● at Arizona State 34 7
N13 Wichita St. 0 13
N25 Miami, Ohio 9 21

GEORGE BLACKBURN
1955-60 (.483) 25-27-6

1955 1-6-2
S24 Dayton 14 15
O1 at Pacific 13 27
O8 Xavier 0 37
O15 ● Marquette 13 12
O22 = at Tulsa 21 21
O29 = Detroit 0 0
N5 at Wichita St. 16 20
N12 Hardin Simmons 20 53
N24 Miami, Ohio 0 14

1956 4-5-0
S22 Dayton 13 19
S29 ● Tulsa 7 6
O6 at Pacific 15 21
O13 Xavier 14 34
O20 at Navy 7 13
O27 ● at Marquette 35 13
N3 ● Detroit 33 7
N10 ● Wichita St. 21 0
N22 Miami, Ohio 13 27

1957-1969
MISSOURI VALLEY

1957 5-4-1 (1-3-0)
S21 = Dayton 13 13
S28 ● | at Wichita St. 19 13
O5 | Houston 0 7
O12 ● Xavier 23 14
O19 ● Marquette 14 0
O26 ● Pacific 7 2
N2 | Detroit 12 20
N9 ● at Indiana 21 0
N16 | at Tulsa 7 12
N28 Miami, Ohio 14 20

1958 6-2-2 (1-1-2)
S20 ● Dayton 14 0
S27 = | Wichita St. 16 16
O4 | Houston 13 34
O11 ● Xavier 14 8
O18 ● at Pacific 12 6
O25 Oklahoma State 14 19
N1 = | at North Texas 8 8
N8 ● | Tulsa 15 6
N15 ● at Marquette 15 0
N27 ● Miami, Ohio 18 7

1959 5-4-1 (0-3-1)
S19 ● at Oklahoma State 22 9
S26 ● Dayton 21 7
O3 | at Houston 12 13
O10 | North Texas 6 21
O17 = | at Wichita St. 28 28
O24 ● Pacific 21 14
O31 ● Xavier 28 0
N7 | at Tulsa 7 14
N14 Marquette 34 35
N26 ● Miami, Ohio 14 7

1960 4-6-0 (1-2-0)
S17 ● Hardin Simmons 15 14
S24 ● Dayton 27 21
O1 ● | North Texas 21 0
O7 at Detroit 0 14
O15 | at Wichita St. 8 25
O22 | Tulsa 3 34
O29 Xavier 0 5
N5 at Houston 0 14
N12 ● at Marquette 33 13
N19 Miami, Ohio 6 10

CHUCK STUDLEY
1961-66 (.450) 27-33

1961 3-7-0 (1-2-0)
S16 ● Dayton 16 12
S23 at Boston College 0 23
S30 | at Wichita St. 13 21
O7 Xavier 12 17
O14 Air Force 6 8
O21 Houston 7 13
O28 ● | North Texas 21 9
N4 | at Tulsa 0 19
N18 Miami, Ohio 3 7
N25 ● Detroit 19 13

1962 2-8-0 (1-2-0)
S22 ● Dayton 13 0
S29 Indiana 6 26
O6 ● | Wichita St. 27 15
O20 | at North Texas 8 14
O27 Richmond 20 21
N3 | Tulsa 18 24
N9 at Detroit 14 15
N17 Miami, Ohio 16 38
N24 Xavier 6 7
D1 at Houston 14 42

1963 6-4-0 (3-1-0)
S21 ● Drake 28 0
S28 at Army 0 22
O5 ● Xavier 35 22
O12 ● | at Tulsa 21 15
O19 ● Detroit 35 0
O26 at Indiana 6 20
N2 ● | Dayton 35 8
N9 ● | North Texas 39 7
N16 | at Wichita St. 20 23
N28 Miami, Ohio 19 21

1964 8-2-0 (4-0-0)
S26 ● Dayton 20 10
O2 ● at Detroit 19 0
O10 ● Xavier 35 6
O17 at Boston College 0 10
O24 ● | Tulsa 28 23
O31 George Washington 15 17
N7 ● |[2] at North Texas 27 6
N14 ● | at Wichita St. 19 7
N21 ● Miami, Ohio 28 14
N28 ● Houston 20 6

1965 5-5-0 (2-2-0)
S18 ● | Dayton 28 0
S24 at Houston 6 21
O2 ● | Wichita St. 14 6
O9 Xavier 3 14
O15 ● at George Washington 13 3
O23 | at Tulsa 6 49
O30 | North Texas 24 28
N6 ● at Kansas State 21 14
N13 ● South Dakota 41 0
N20 Miami, Ohio 7 37

1966 3-7-0 (2-2-0)
S24 Dayton 7 23
O1 ● | at Wichita St. 20 6
O8 Xavier 13 25
O15 at Tulane 21 28
O22 ● Kansas State 28 14
O29 | Tulsa 0 13
N5 | at North Texas 13 35
N12 ● | Louisville 17 3
N19 at Memphis 14 26
N26 Miami, Ohio 8 28

HOMER RICE
1967-68 (.447) 8-10-1

1967 3-6-0 (2-2-0)
S23 Dayton 13 27
S30 at Memphis 0 17
O7 ● | Wichita St. 14 6
O14 Xavier 10 15
O21 | at Tulsa 6 35
O28 | North Texas 14 34
N4 ● Boston College 27 21
N11 ● | at Louisville 13 7
N18 Miami, Ohio 14 27

1968 5-4-1 (3-2-0)
S21 = at Texas Tech 10 10
S28 ● Xavier 17 14
O4 at Houston 33 71
O12 ● Tampa 31 28
O19 ● | at Wichita St. 40 27
O26 | Tulsa 27 34
N2 | at North Texas 34 55
N9 ● | Louisville 37 7
N16 Ohio U. 48 60
N23 ● | Miami, Ohio 23 21

RAY CALLAHAN
1969-72 (.465) 20-23

1969 4-6-0 (2-3-0)
S13 at West Virginia 11 57
S20 ● William & Mary 26 18
O4 ● Xavier 17 14
O11 | Memphis 6 52
O18 ● | Wichita St. 21 14
O25 | at Tulsa 24 40
N1 | North Texas 30 31
N8 ● | at Louisville 31 21
N15 at Ohio U. 6 46
N22 Miami, Ohio 20 36

1970-1995
INDEPENDENT

1970 7-4-0
S12 at Tulsa 3 7
S19 ● Dayton 13 7
S26 ● at William & Mary 17 10
O3 Tulane 3 6
O10 ● Xavier 42 0
O17 ● at Wichita St. 35 5
O24 ● Ohio U. 29 21
N7 ● at North Texas 30 10
N14 Louisville 14 28
N21 ● Miami, Ohio 33 0
N28 at Memphis 10 14

1971 7-4-0
S11 at Dayton 3 16
S18 ● Kent State 42 20
S25 Houston 3 12
O2 ● at Texas A&M 17 0
O9 ● Xavier 30 7
O16 ● Wichita St. 20 7
O30 Memphis 21 45
N6 ● North Texas 40 7
N13 ● Ohio U. 23 15
N20 at Miami, Ohio 7 43
N27 ● at Louisville 19 16

1972 2-9-0
S9 ● at Indiana St. 10 7
S16 at Colorado 14 56
S23 Xavier 7 19
S30 ● Villanova 14 7
O7 Ohio U. 14 28
O14 at Wichita St. 17 20
O28 Louisville 13 38
N4 at North Texas 25 27
N11 at Memphis 24 49
N18 Miami, Ohio 0 23
N25 at Houston 0 49

TONY MASON
1973-76 (.568) 25-19

1973 4-7-0
S15 ● Xavier 40 7
S22 at Villanova 7 14
S29 at Tulsa 13 16
O6 at Temple 15 16
O13 ● La. Lafayette 27 0
O20 ● Wichita St. 27 6
O27 at Louisville 8 10
N3 ● North Texas 52 3
N10 at Ohio U. 8 14
N17 at Miami, Ohio 0 6
N24 Memphis 13 17

1974 7-4-0
S14 at Washington 17 21
S21 ● at Rice 28 21
S28 ● Louisville 7 6
O12 at Memphis 7 13
O19 ● at Wichita St. 43 0
O25 at Houston 6 27
N2 ● Temple 22 20
N9 ● Ohio U. 35 13
N16 Miami, Ohio 7 27
N23 ● U.T. Chattanooga 35 20
N30 ● La. Monroe 20 7

1975 6-5-0
S13 ● Richmond 19 6
S20 ● Memphis 13 3
S27 ● at Louisville 46 27
O4 at Temple 17 21
O11 at Tulsa 16 24
O18 Arkansas State 9 14
O25 ● La. Lafayette 23 17
N1 ● Houston 28 23
N8 Maryland 19 21
N15 ● at Ohio U. 6 5
N22 at Miami, Ohio 13 21

1976 8-3-0
S11 ● at Tulane 21 14
S18 La. Lafayette 3 7 †
S25 ● Miami, Ohio 17 0
O2 ● at Southern Miss 28 21
O9 ● at Arizona State 14 0
O16 ● Tulsa 16 7
O30 at Georgia 17 31
N6 at Maryland 0 21
N13 ● Ohio U. 35 0
N20 ● Vanderbilt 33 7
N27 ● Louisville 20 6

RALPH STAUB
1977-80 (.341) 14-28-2

1977 5-4-2
S10 ● N.W. La. 41 0
S17 = at Louisville 17 17
S24 ● La. Monroe 63 0
O1 ● Southern Miss 17 6
O8 at Florida State 0 14
O15 at Tulane 13 16
O22 ● Tulsa 28 0
O29 = Temple 17 17
N5 ● at Ohio U. 38 26
N19 at Vanderbilt 9 13
N24 Miami, Ohio 7 12

1978 5-6-0

S16	•	Southern Miss	26	14
S23		Louisville	14	28
S30		at Richmond	28	51
O7		at Florida State	21	26
O14		at Temple	13	16
O21		Tulsa	26	27
O28	•	at La. Lafayette	38	13
N4	•	La. Monroe	20	7
N11	•	Ohio U.	35	0
N18		at Miami, Ohio	24	28
N25	•	at Memphis	34	14

1979 2-9-0

S15		at Southern Miss	6	24
S22		at Louisville	19	22
S29	•	Villanova	27	13
O6		at North Carolina	14	35
O13		at Pittsburgh	0	35
O20		at Temple	14	35
O27	•	Richmond	17	14
N3		Florida State	21	26
N10		Ohio U.	7	27
N17		at Miami, Ohio	14	27
N24		at Memphis	17	23

1980 2-9-0

S6		at West Virginia	27	41
S13		at Tulsa	13	31
S20		at Rutgers	7	24
S27		Wichita St.	8	13
O4		at Villanova	6	23
O18		at South Carolina	7	49
O25		at Temple	7	23
N1		at Richmond	10	24
N8	•	at Memphis	14	10
N15		at Louisville	0	20
N22	•	Miami, Ohio	23	13

MIKE GOTTFRIED
1981-82 (.545) 12-10

1981 6-5-0

S5		Youngstown St.	13	19
S12		at Penn State	0	52
S19		at Pittsburgh	7	38
S26	•	Rutgers	10	0
O10	•	at Ohio U.	19	9
O17	•	Richmond	27	18
O24		Temple	13	24
O31	•	Tulane	17	13
N7	•	Memphis	38	7
N14	•	Louisville	24	0
N21		at Miami, Ohio	3	7

1982 6-5-0

S4		at Florida State	31	38
S11	•	Louisville	38	16
S25	•	Youngstown St.	52	3
O2		at South Carolina	10	37
O9	•	Long Beach St.	34	14
O16	•	at Memphis	16	7
O23		at Alabama	3	21
O30		at Temple	7	41
N13	•	Morgan St.	52	0
N18	•	Miami, Ohio	20	10
N27		at Miami, Fla.	13	19

WATSON BROWN
1983 (.409) 4-6-1

1983 4-6-1

S10	•	at Penn State	14	3
S17		Oklahoma State	17	27
S24		at Louisville	23	31
O1	•	Cornell	48	20
O8	•	Temple	31	16
O15		at Florida State	17	43
O22		Miami, Fla.	7	17
O29	=	at Kentucky	13	13
N5	•	Rutgers	18	7
N12		Memphis	10	43
N19		at Miami, Ohio	10	14

DAVE CURREY
1984-88 (.345) 19-36

1984 2-9-0

S8	•	Akron	28	27
S15		Youngstown St.	23	27
S22		at Memphis	7	47
S29		at Rutgers	15	43
O13		Miami, Fla.	25	49
O20		at Florida	17	48
O27	•	Louisville	40	21
N3		at Temple	10	42
N10		at Auburn	0	60
N17		Alabama	7	29
N22		Miami, Ohio	26	31

1985 5-6-0

A31	•	Virginia Tech	31	14
S7	•	Austin Peay	31	9
S14	•	at Youngstown St.	29	27
S21		at Alabama	10	45
S28		at Kentucky	7	27
O5		Temple	16	28
O12		at Miami, Fla.	0	38
O19	•	at Louisville	31	9
O26	•	Boston College	24	17
N9		Penn State	10	31
N23		at Miami, Ohio	10	16

1986 5-6-0

S6	•	at Virginia Tech	24	20
S13	•	Miami, Ohio	45	38
S20		at Rutgers	28	48
S27		Kentucky	20	37
O4	•	Louisville	24	17
O11		at Penn State	17	23
O18		Miami, Fla.	13	45
O25	•	at Wichita St.	24	19
N1	•	Indiana St.	46	14
N8		at Auburn	7	52
N15		at East Carolina	19	32

1987 4-7-0

S5		Rutgers	7	10
S12	•	at Louisville	25	0
S19		at Penn State	0	41
S26	•	Miami, Ohio	31	26
O10		at East Carolina	28	56
O17		at West Virginia	17	45
O24		Miami, Fla.	10	48
O31	•	Tenn. Tech	38	17
N7		Indiana St.[IND]	16	40
N14	•	Austin Peay	42	10
N21		at Virginia Tech	20	21

1988 3-8-0

S10		at Boston College	7	41
S17	•	Austin Peay	52	7
S24	•	at Miami, Ohio	34	18
O1		at Rutgers	9	38
O8		at Penn State	9	35
O15		Virginia Tech	14	41
O22		at Miami, Fla.	3	57
O29		Louisville	6	21
N5		West Virginia	13	51
N12	•	Indiana St.	40	21
N19		East Carolina	14	49

TIM MURPHY
1989-93 (.318) 17-37-1

1989 1-9-1

S2	=	Rutgers	17	17
S16		East Carolina	14	21
S23	•	at Miami, Ohio	30	14
S30		at Louisville	17	37
O7		at Miami, Fla.	0	56
O14		Memphis	17	34
O21		at West Virginia	3	69
O28		at Akron	0	31
N4		at Kentucky	0	31
N11		Morehead St.	10	13
N18		Northern Illinois	3	56

1990 1-10-0

S2		Bowling Green	20	34
S8		at Central Michigan	0	34
S15		at Iowa	10	63
S22		Miami, Ohio	12	16
S29	•	at Kent State	27	24
O13		at West Virginia	20	28
O20		at East Carolina	32	56
O27		at Tulane	7	49
N3		Louisville	16	41
N10		at Florida State	21	70
N17		Alabama[BIRM]	7	45

1991 4-7-0

S7		at Penn State	0	81
S14		at North Carolina	16	51
S21		at Bowling Green	16	20
S28		Miami, Ohio	9	22
O5	•	at Louisville	30	7
O12	•	at Kent State	38	19
O19		at Virginia Tech	9	56
O26	•	Southern Miss	17	7
N2		at Kentucky	17	20
N9	•	Middle Tennessee	30	10
N23		East Carolina	19	30

1992 3-8-0

S5		Penn State	20	24
S19		at Miami, Ohio	14	17
S26		at Tennessee	0	40
O3	•	Kent State	31	0
O10		at Memphis	14	34
O17		at East Carolina	21	42
O24		at Southern Miss	17	31
O31		Louisville	17	27
N7	•	Rutgers	26	24
N14	•	Kentucky	17	13
N21		Akron	22	24

1993 8-3-0

S4	•	Austin Peay	42	10
S11		at Bowling Green	7	21
S18	•	Miami, Ohio	30	23
S25		at Syracuse	21	24
O2	•	at Tulsa	22	15
O9		at Vanderbilt	7	17
O16	•	Ball State	44	12
O23	•	at Toledo	31	24
O30	•	Memphis	23	20
N13	•	at Houston	41	17
N20	•	East Carolina	34	14

RICK MINTER
1994-2003 (.457) 53-63-1

1994 2-8-1

S3		at Indiana	3	28
S10		Syracuse	19	34
S17	=	at Miami, Ohio	17	17
O1		Bowling Green	0	38
O8		Vanderbilt	24	34
O15		at Rutgers	9	14
O22		at Memphis	3	26
O29		at East Carolina	21	35
N5	•	Troy State	28	24
N12		at Wisconsin	7	38
N19	•	Tulsa	28	13

1995 6-5-0

S2		at Kansas	18	23
S9		Kansas State	21	23
S16	•	at Virginia Tech	16	0
S23		at Miami, Ohio	16	23
S30		Toledo	31	45
O7	•	East Carolina	13	10
O14	•	Southern Miss	16	13
O21	•	Memphis	28	3
O28	•	at Northern Illinois	55	19
N11		at Kentucky	14	33
N18	•	at Tulsa	24	5

1996-2004
C-USA

1996 6-5 (2-3)

A30	|	Tulane	14	34
S7	•	Kentucky	24	3
S14		at Kansas State	0	35
S28	•	Miami, Ohio	30	23
O5	|	at Memphis	16	18
O12		Boston College	17	24
O19	• |	Houston	31	20
O26	• |	at Louisville	10	7
N2	|	at Southern Miss	17	21
N16	•	at UAB	34	14
N23	•	La. Monroe	35	13

1997 8-4 (2-4)

A28	•	Tulsa	34	24
S6	|	at Tulane	17	31
S20	•	Kansas	34	7
S27	•	at Boston College	24	6
O4	• |	Memphis	20	17
O11	•	UAB	33	29
O18	|	at Houston	38	41
O25	•	at Miami, Ohio	34	31
N1	|	Southern Miss	17	24
N8	• |	Louisville	28	9
N13	|	at East Carolina	7	14
		HUMANITARIAN BOWL		
D29	•	Utah State	35	19

1998 2-9 (1-5)

S5	|	Tulane	34	52
S12		Miami, Fla.	12	38
S19	|	at Army	20	37
S26		Indiana	14	48
O3	|	at Louisville	19	62
O10		at Syracuse	21	63
O17	|	at Memphis	23	41
O24		Miami, Ohio	0	41
N5	|	East Carolina	21	24
N14	• |	Houston	44	43
N21	•	at Arkansas State	51	7

1999 3-8 (0-6)

S4	•	Kent State	41	3
S11		Troy State	24	31
S18	•	Wisconsin	17	12
S25		at Ohio State	20	34
O9	|	at Houston	20	23
O16	|	UAB	21	24
O23	|	at Southern Miss	20	28
O30	•	at Miami, Ohio	52	42
N6	|	Louisville	13	23
N13	|	at East Carolina	34	48
N20	|	Memphis	13	21

2000 7-5 (5-2)

S4	• |	Army	23	17
S9	•	Syracuse	12	10
S16		at Wisconsin	25	28
S23		at Indiana	6	42
S30	|	at Tulane	19	24
O7	• |	Houston	48	31
O14	|	at Louisville	24	38
O28	•	Miami, Ohio	45	15
N4	• |	UAB	33	21
N11	• |	at Memphis	13	10
N18	• |	Southern Miss	27	24
		MOTOR CITY BOWL		
D27		Marshall	14	25

2001 7-5 (5-2)

S2		Purdue	14	19
S8	• |	at Army	24	21
S22		at Miami, Ohio	14	21
O6	• |	Tulane	46	33
O13	• |	at UAB	31	17
O20	• |	at Houston	29	28
O27	|	Louisville	13	28
N3	•	Connecticut	45	28
N10	|	East Carolina	26	28
N24	• |	at Memphis	36	34
D1	•	La. Monroe	42	10
		MOTOR CITY BOWL		
D29		Toledo	16	23

2002 7-7 (6-2)

S2	• |	TCU	36	29
S14		West Virginia	32	35
S21		Ohio State	19	23
S28	•	at Temple	35	22
O5		Miami, Ohio	26	31
O12	|	at Tulane	17	35
O19	|	at Southern Miss	14	23
O26	• |	Memphis	48	10
N7	• |	at Louisville	24	14
N16	• |	Houston	47	14
N23		at Hawaii	19	20
N30	• |	UAB	31	23
D6	• |	at East Carolina	42	26
		NEW ORLEANS BOWL		
D17		North Texas	19	24

2003 5-7 (2-6)

S1	• |	East Carolina	40	3
S13	•	at West Virginia	15	13
S20	•	Temple	30	24
S27		at Miami, Ohio	37	42
O4	|	Southern Miss	20	22
O11	|	at UAB	14	31
O25	• |	Army	33	29
N1	|	at South Florida	17	24
N8	•	Rhode Island	31	24
N15	|	at TCU	10	43
N22	|	at Memphis	16	21
N28	|	Louisville	40	43

MARK DANTONIO
2004-PRESENT (.583) 7-5

2004 7-5 (5-3)

S4		at Ohio State	6	27
S11	•	Miami, Ohio	45	26
S18		at Syracuse	7	19
S25	• |	at East Carolina	24	19
O2	|	UAB	27	30
O9	|	at Army	29	48
O23	• |	Memphis	49	10
O30	• |	TCU	21	10
N6	• |	at Southern Miss	52	24
N20	• |	South Florida	45	23
N27	|	at Louisville	7	70
		FORT WORTH BOWL		
D23	•	Marshall	32	14

Neutral Site Key: *UNK* Unkown / *BIRM* Brmingham, AL / *IN* Indianapolis, IN
f Forfeit † Game Later Forfieted # Disputed Victor * Disputed Score || Designated Conference Game |2 Counted Twice in Conference Standings

CLEMSON

BY BOB HARIG

CLEMSON'S MEMORIAL STADIUM IS filled with some 80,000 fans on game day, which would make it the third-largest city in South Carolina. The crowd swells with Tiger Pride as each member of the football team touches Howard's Rock before running down a hill into the stadium to the sound of thunderous applause. The fans' rabid nature is one of the reasons Memorial Stadium long ago became known as Death Valley. There's one other reason: great teams. No school has won more ACC titles than Clemson, a charter member of the conference.

TRADITION There are two central traditions associated with Clemson football: Howard's Rock and the hill. The latter preceded the former, although now players touch the rock before running down the hill. Described as "the most exciting 25 seconds in college football from a color and pageantry standpoint," the hill entrance began out of necessity. The first 20,000 seats in Memorial Stadium were

built and ready for use for the 1942 season. The shortest entry into the stadium was through a gate at the top of the hill behind the east end zone; the team would jog down the hill for warmups, fanfare-free.

The second tradition came about in the mid-1960s. S.C. Jones, an alum from the Class of 1919, made a trip to California, where he stopped at a spot in Death Valley, and picked up a white flint rock. He presented it to coach Frank Howard, and the rock sat in the coach's office for years. One day, while cleaning up his office, Howard asked Gene Willimon, who was executive secretary of the booster organization IPTAY, to "take this rock and throw it over the fence … do something with it, but get it out of my office." Willimon, knowing the rock had been brought to Clemson by a sincere Tiger fan, had it mounted on a pedestal and placed at the top of the hill. Soon, Howard bought into the tradition.

On Sept. 24, 1966, the rock was unveiled before Clemson played Virginia. The Tigers were down 18 points with 17 minutes to play—but came back to win 40-35 on a 65-yard pass from Jimmy Addison to Jacky Jackson in the fourth quarter. Team members started rubbing the rock as a pregame ritual on Sept. 23, 1967, when Clemson defeated

PROFILE

Clemson University
Clemson, S.C.
Founded: 1889
Enrollment: 13,066
Colors: Burnt Orange and Northwestern Purple
Nickname: Tigers
Stadium: Memorial Stadium
    Opened in 1942
    Grass; 81,473 capacity
First football game: 1896
All-time record: 600–413–45 (.588)
Bowl record: 14–13
Consensus national championships, 1936-present: 1 (1981)
Atlantic Coast Conference championships: 13 (12 outright)
First-round NFL draftees: 19
Website: www.clemsontigers.com

THE BEST OF TIMES

The 1980s began with Clemson's first national championship in 1981 and ended with four straight bowl victories. The Tigers won 10 games in the 1987, 1988 and 1989 seasons and had the fifth-best winning percentage in college football in the 1980s.

THE WORST OF TIMES

From 1968 to 1976, the Tigers had just one winning season. They had their longest stretch of consecutive losing seasons, six, from 1968 to 1973.

CONFERENCE

The Tigers were charter members of the Atlantic Coast Conference in 1953. They also were charter members of the Southern Conference, joining in 1921, and of the Southern Intercollegiate Athletic Association, in 1896.

DISTINGUISHED ALUMNI

Dr. Henry Cooper, U.S. ambassador to Russia; Jane Robelot DeCarvalho, host, *CBS This Morning*; Shawn Weatherly Harris, Miss Universe; Don Logan, chairman/president/CEO, Time Warner; Strom Thurmond, U.S. senator.

FIGHT SONG

TIGER RAG
Long ago way down in the jungle
Someone got an inspiration for a tune,
And that jingle came from the jungle
Became famous mighty soon.
Thrills and chills it sends through you!
Hot so hot it burns you too!
Though it's just the growl of the Tiger
It was written in a syncopated way,
More and more they yell for the Tiger
Everywhere you go today,
They're shoutin':
Where's that Tiger?
Where's that Tiger?
Where's that Tiger?
Where's that Tiger?
Hold that Tiger!
Hold that Tiger!
Hold that Tiger!
C-L-E-M-S-O … N!

Wake Forest 23-6. "If you're going to give me 110 percent, you can rub that rock. If you're not, keep your filthy hands off it," Howard said to his players. When he told the story the next day on his television show, the story became part of Clemson legend.

Today, after Clemson's final warm-up, the team returns to its dressing room under the west end zone stands. Ten minutes before kickoff, the team boards two buses, rides around the stadium to the east end zone, and debarks at the top of the hill behind Howard's Rock. A cannon booms, the band strikes up "Tiger Rag," and the team hustles onto the field, led by a tiger's-paw flag.

BEST PLAYER Defensive back Terry Kinard (1979-1982) is Clemson's only two-time first-team Associated Press All-America. Named CBS Sports' national defensive player of the year as a senior, Kinard is also a member of *Sports Illustrated*'s Team of the Century. His 2001 induction into the College Football Hall of Fame made him just the second

> *There was once the Country Gentleman, a student dressed in purple tails and top hat, carrying a cane.*

Clemson player to be honored. "I haven't seen a player who could dominate a game from the secondary like he could," coach Danny Ford said as Kinard was inducted into the Hall of Fame.

BEST COACH In addition to being the school's best coach, Howard was considered its best ambassador, as he was associated with the Tigers for nearly 65 years. He was the Tigers' head coach for 30 seasons (1940-1969), and retired with 165 victories—the fifth-winningest coach in the nation at the time. His 66 ACC wins still rank third in league history. In 1948, his squad went 11–0, the school's first undefeated season since 1906.

Howard continued on the Clemson payroll through 1974, and kept representing Clemson long after that. The Clemson board of trustees named the playing surface of Memorial Stadium "Frank Howard Field" in honor of his long service to the school. Howard was inducted into the South Carolina Athletic Hall of Fame, the Clemson Hall of Fame and the State of Alabama Hall of Fame. His greatest

RECORDS

RUSHING YARDS
GAME	
263	Raymond Priester vs. Duke, Nov. 11, 1995 (32 att.)
SEASON	
1,345	Raymond Priester, 1996 (257 att.)
CAREER	
3,966	Raymond Priester, 1994-97 (805 att.)

PASSING YARDS
GAME	
420	Charlie Whitehurst vs. Duke, Nov. 2, 2002 (34 of 52)
SEASON	
3,561	Charlie Whitehurst, 2003 (288 of 465)
CAREER	
7,182	Charlie Whitehurst, 2002-04 (588 of 1,028)

RECEIVING YARDS
GAME	
182	Rod Gardner vs. North Carolina, Oct. 21, 2000 (7 rec.)
SEASON	
1,084	Rod Gardner, 1999 (80 rec.)
CAREER	
2,681	Terry Smith, 1990-93 (162 rec.)

POINTS
GAME	
33	Maxcey Welch vs. Newberry, Oct. 17, 1930 (5 TDs, 3 PATs)
SEASON	
108	Travis Zachery, 2000 (18 TDs)
CAREER	
329	Aaron Hunt, 2000-03 (55 FGs, 164 PATs)

CONSENSUS ALL-AMERICANS

1967	Harry Olszewski, G
1974	Bennie Cunningham, TE
1979	Jim Stuckey, DL
1981	Jeff Davis, LB
1981-82	Terry Kinard, DB
1983	William Perry, DL
1986	Terrence Flagler, RB
1987	David Treadwell, PK
1988	Donnell Woolford, DB
1990	Stacy Long, OL
1991	Jeb Flesch, OL
1991	Levon Kirkland, LB
1993	Stacy Seegars, G
1997	Anthony Simmons, LB
2000	Keith Adams, LB

honor, perhaps, was his 1989 induction into the College Football Hall of Fame, where he joined former Clemson mentors John Heisman and Jess Neely.

BEST TEAM Clemson's first national championship in any sport came in 1981, when the Tigers were the only unbeaten and untied team in the country. Led by Ford, the Tigers defeated three Top-10 teams, including fourth-ranked Georgia—the Bulldogs' only regular-season defeat in Herschel Walker's career. The Tigers also defeated eighth-ranked North Carolina in the first meeting of Top-10 teams in ACC history. As a finale, they defeated fourth-ranked Nebraska in the Orange Bowl to win the national championship. The team included 22 players who went on to play in the NFL. The Tigers were 6–5 the year before and were unranked in every major preseason poll heading into the 1981 season. Ford, who was just 33 at the time, remains the youngest coach to ever win a national championship.

BIGGEST GAME The Tigers' 1982 Orange Bowl showdown was essentially a national title game. Clemson was the last undefeated team in the country at kickoff, while Nebraska, behind sophomore quarterback Turner Gill, had rebounded from a 1–2 start to win eight straight games at the end of the regular season, and was climbing in the polls. Clemson, making its first Orange Bowl appearance in 25 years, stormed onto the field in their big-game look of orange pants and orange jerseys. Tigers QB Homer Jordan completed 11 of 22 passes for 134 yards and collected 180 yards of total offense. Nebraska played without both Gill and second-string quarterback Nate Mason (both injured), leaving third-team QB Mark Mauer to lead the sluggish attack, and Clemson's opportunistic defense allowed just one completion in the second half. The Tigers trailed 7-6 after one quarter, then went ahead at halftime when Cliff Austin scored on a two-yard run (a two-point conversion failed). The Tigers scored 10 third-quarter points to take a seemingly commanding 22-7 lead, but the Huskers pulled within seven points with 9:15 to play when Roger Craig scored on a 26-yard run and then ran for a two-point conversion. The Clemson defense, though, shut down

Nebraska for the rest of the game, securing the 22-15 win and the school's first national championship.

HEARTBREAKER Ranked third in the country and aiming to climb higher with a victory over visiting Florida State, the Tigers faltered in the rain against the Seminoles in 1988. The score was tied at 21 with less than two minutes to play in the game, and Clemson was poised to take over with good field position after an FSU punt. But the Seminoles called a risky trick play—known as the "punt-rooskie"—in which the ball was snapped to upback Dayne Williams, who sneaked the ball between the legs of LeRoy Butler. The punter faked as if the ball had sailed over his head, the entire punt team ran to the right while Butler went left. By the time Clemson defenders realized what had happened, Butler was streaking down the sideline with the ball on a 78-yard run before finally being pushed out of bounds at the 1-yard line. With 32 seconds remaining, the Seminoles kicked the winning field goal for a 24-21 victory. The Tigers would finish with a 10–2 record, their only other loss coming against NC State.

> *The Death Valley name didn't stick until Clemson coach Frank Howard began using it in the 1950s.*

DISPUTE The 1984 game against rival Georgia still rankles the Tiger faithful. The Tigers were ranked second in the country and stood at 2–0; Georgia was ranked 20th. The Bulldogs' Kevin Butler kicked a 60-yard field goal with 11 seconds remaining for a 26-23 lead. Clemson took the ensuing kickoff, and Terrance Roulhac was knocked out of bounds at the Georgia 35 with no time remaining—but Georgia was whistled for a late hit, a personal foul that meant the ball would move to the 20. From there, Clemson's kicker Donald Igwebuike, who was 16 of 17 for the year and had not missed inside the 50, would have attempted a 44-yard field goal to tie the game. However, officials ruled that since the penalty occurred after time expired, the game was over. Clemson officials maintain there were two seconds remaining when Roulhac was knocked out of bounds.

STADIUM Also known as Death Valley, Clemson's Memorial Stadium lived up to its nickname under Howard, thanks to the number of Clemson home victories. However,

the name was first used by Lonnie McMillian, head coach at Presbyterian College in Clinton, S.C., in the 1940s. McMillian and the other Presbyterian coaches who preceded him used to open each season by coming to Clemson. They seldom scored, getting shut out 24 times in 39 games, and managed to rack up only three wins and four ties. In 1948, McMillian commented to reporters that he was taking his team to play Clemson in Death Valley. Occasional references were made to Death Valley for the next few seasons, but the name didn't stick until Howard started using it in the 1950s.

Ironically, the stadium would not have been built if a former Clemson coach had had his way. When Jess Neely left for Rice after the 1939 season, he warned Clemson officials not to build a big stadium. "Put 10,000 seats behind the YMCA. That's all you'll ever need," he said. Clemson officials disregarded Neely's suggestion, building the stadium on the western part of campus. It opened in 1942 with 20,000 seats; by 1960, capacity had increased to 53,000. Later, upper decks were added to each side and by 1983 capacity had swelled to more than 80,000.

RIVAL The annual Clemson–South Carolina game is the state's Super Bowl. The game between the schools dates back to 1896 and is the fourth-longest uninterrupted series in college football, played every year since 1909. The 1977 installment ranks as one of the best: Jerry Butler made a diving, backward reception of a 20-yard pass from quarterback Steve Fuller with 49 seconds remaining to give Clemson a 31-27 victory at South Carolina. The play became known as The Catch and sent Clemson to the Gator Bowl, its first bowl bid in 18 years. The 2004 edition might rank as the worst in the series. A lengthy brawl broke out on the field between the players, prompting both schools to keep themselves out of bowl games.

NICKNAME "Tigers" goes back to the turn of the 20th century, when players wore orange-and-purple-striped jerseys and stockings. As the theory goes, the stripes resembled tigers, hence the nickname. Coach John Heisman's 1900 Clemson team was called the Tigers and used an insignia of a tiger head with bared fangs and the motto "Eat 'Em Up Clemson." Another theory centers on Clemson's first coach, Walter Riggs, who arrived at the school in 1896. Riggs came from Auburn, which was also known as the Tigers.

MASCOT Clemson is renowned for its Tiger mascot, which does pushups after every score. The school used to have two mascots, however. In addition to the Tiger, there was once the Country Gentleman, a student dressed in purple tails and top hat, carrying a cane. The concept developed from *Greenville News* sportswriter Carter "Scoop" Latimer's referring to Clemson as the "Country Gentlemen." Clemson maintained both mascots between 1954 and 1972.

UNIFORMS Although Clemson's official colors are Northwestern purple and burnt orange, many of Clemson's athletic uniforms are mostly orange and white. Clemson has worn all orange for special games, and in 1991 wore purple jerseys with white pants and orange helmets for the NC State and California games. Purple trim is now on the uniform pants and helmet, which was first graced with a distinctive tiger's paw in 1970, and evolved somewhat to the present design which premiered in 1976. According to Clemson legend, the school used to have pale purple and gold as the official colors, but Neely—who coached at the school from 1931 to 1939—changed that because he wanted colorfast uniforms. Weather and constant washing were causing the uniforms to fade, so Neely brought in deeper colors.

NUMBERS John Heisman, the man for whom the Heisman Trophy is named, was the first to bring Clemson football to prominence. He coached the Tigers to a 19–3–2 record from 1900 to 1903. His .833 winning percentage is still the best in school history … Clemson played Ohio State in the 1978 Gator Bowl, the last game for Buckeyes coach Woody Hayes. Clemson middle guard Charlie Bauman intercepted a pass and was run out-of-bounds on the OSU sideline when Hayes took a swing at him ... In 2001, Clemson quarterback Woodrow Dantzler became the only player in college football history to pass for 2,000 yards and run for 1,000 in a regular season ... Chris Gardocki is the only kicker in NCAA history to twice rank in the top 10 in the nation in punting and field goals in the same year. He did so in 1989 and 1990.

LORE Most of America knew William Perry as a household appliance: "The Refrigerator" was so nicknamed by teammate Ray Brown, who once tried to get in an elevator with Perry but said he took up as much room as a refrigerator. Brown called him GE, but Clemson assistant sports information director Tim Bourret modified the name during Perry's senior season. Perry first made his 300-plus-pound presence felt as a freshman defensive lineman during the 1981 season. He went on to become a three-time All-America and gained great fame as a rookie with the Chicago Bears in 1985, when

he helped the team to a Super Bowl victory by scoring a rushing touchdown during the game.

QUIRK The booster club is among the largest in the country (24,000 members) and goes by the name IPTAY. It originally stood for "I Pay Ten a Year." (Those who like to needle Clemson say it stands for "It's Probation Time Again Y'all.") The organization continues to provide funds for athletic and academic scholarships.

QUOTE "Even when I was little, I was big." — Former Clemson defensive tackle William "The Refrigerator" Perry

CLEMSON ANNUAL STATISTICAL LEADERS

YR	RUSHING	YDS	ATT	AVG	PASSING	ATT	CMP	PCT	YDS	RECEIVING	REC	YDS	AVG
1935	Joe Berry	457	99	4.6	Joe Berry	72	42	.58	422		NA	NA	NA
1936	Mac Fogler	522	144	3.6	Joe Berry	99	32	.32	434		NA	NA	NA
1937	Don Willis	329	99	3.3	Bob Bailey	88	35	.40	579		NA	NA	NA
1938	Don Willis	483	103	4.7	Bob Bailey	35	18	.51	272	Gus Goins	8	123	15.4
1939	Charlie Timmons	556	146	3.8	Banks McFadden	70	31	.44	581	Joe Blalock	15	322	21.5
1940	Chippy Maness	472	86	5.5	Chippy Maness	51	19	.37	388	Joe Blalock	10	211	21.1
1941	Charlie Timmons	635	149	4.3	Booty Payne	90	36	.40	582	Joe Blalock	13	240	18.5
1942	Marion Butler	616	145	4.2	Butch Butler	90	38	.42	504	Marion Craig	14	173	12.4
1943	James Whitmire	376	72	5.2	Butch Butler	34	12	.35	166	Eddis Freeman	8	175	21.9
1944	Sid Tinsley	479	126	3.8	Sid Tinsley	51	11	.22	248	Eddis Freeman	9	162	18.0
1945	Dewey Quinn	392	89	4.4	Butch Butler	45	11	.24	239	Eddis Freeman	7	156	22.3
1946	Bobby Gage	264	58	4.6	Dutch Leverman	62	26	.42	501	Eddis Freeman	15	181	12.1
1947	Bobby Gage	502	114	4.4	Bobby Gage	109	47	.43	1,002	John Poulos	6	169	28.2
1948	Ray Mathews	646	113	5.7	Bobby Gage	105	42	.40	799	Oscar Thompson	19	333	17.5
1949	Ray Mathews	728	118	6.2	Ray Mathews	72	24	.33	487	Glenn Smith	25	446	17.8
1950	Fred Cone	845	184	4.6	Billy Hair	71	29	.41	644	Glenn Smith	22	498	22.6
1951	Billy Hair	698	160	4.4	Billy Hair	164	67	.41	1,004	Glenn Smith	39	632	16.2
1952	Red Whitten	445	115	3.9	Don King	69	23	.33	317	Otis Kempson	15	220	14.7
1953	Don King	243	79	3.1	Don King	98	46	.47	706	Dreher Gaskin	21	426	20.3
1954	Joel Wells	352	74	4.8	Don King	72	32	.44	468	Scott Jackson	11	151	13.7
1955	Joel Wells	782	135	5.8	Don King	79	33	.42	586	Joe Pagliei	10	233	23.3
1956	Joel Wells	803	174	4.6	Charlie Bussey	68	26	.38	330	Dalton Rivers	5	76	15.2
1957	Bob Spooner	358	88	4.1	Harvey White	95	46	.48	841	Whitey Jordan	12	369	30.8
1958	Doug Cline	450	103	4.4	Harvey White	87	43	.49	492	George Usry	18	171	9.5
1959	Doug Cline	482	119	4.1	Harvey White	107	56	.52	770	Bill Mathis	18	319	17.7
1960	Bill McGuirt	320	99	3.2	Lowndes Shingler	145	61	.42	790	Harry Pavilack	17	272	16.0
1961	Ron Scrudato	341	99	3.4	Jim Parker	98	46	.47	735	Elmo Lam	17	237	13.9
1962	Pat Crain	348	94	3.7	Jim Parker	67	30	.45	431	Johnny Case	13	213	16.4
1963	Pat Crain	513	137	3.7	Jim Parker	117	52	.44	728	Lou Fogle	17	218	12.8
1964	Hal Davis	533	87	6.1	Thomas Ray	59	21	.36	253	Hoss Hostetler	8	103	12.9
1965	Hugh Mauldin	664	194	3.4	Thomas Ray	175	74	.42	1,019	Phil Rogers	36	466	12.9
1966	Buddy Gore	750	186	4.0	Jimmy Addison	186	103	.55	1,491	Phil Rogers	42	574	13.7
1967	Buddy Gore	1,045	230	4.5	Jimmy Addison	174	82	.47	924	Phil Rogers	28	429	15.3
1968	Buddy Gore	776	184	4.2	Billy Ammons	162	74	.46	1,006	Charlie Waters	22	411	18.7
1969	Ray Yauger	968	223	4.3	Tommy Kendrick	227	107	.47	1,457	Charlie Waters	44	738	16.8
1970	Ray Yauger	711	183	3.9	Tommy Kendrick	267	133	.50	1,407	John McMakin	40	532	13.3
1971	Rick Gilstrap	514	144	3.6	Tommy Kendrick	152	64	.42	1,040	John McMakin	29	421	14.5
1972	Wade Hughes	761	177	4.3	Ken Pengitore	131	55	.42	831	Dennis Goss	21	385	18.3
1973	Smiley Sanders	627	113	5.5	Ken Pengitore	188	82	.44	1,370	Bennie Cunningham	22	341	15.5
1974	Ken Callicutt	809	161	5.0	Mark Fellers	92	42	.46	783	Bennie Cunningham	24	391	16.3
1975	Ken Callicutt	572	145	3.9	Willie Jordan	73	40	.55	728	Joey Walters	26	394	15.2
1976	Warren Ratchford	676	119	5.7	Steve Fuller	116	58	.50	835	Jerry Butler	33	484	14.7
1977	Warren Ratchford	616	118	5.2	Steve Fuller	205	106	.52	1,655	Jerry Butler	47	824	17.5
1978	Lester Brown	1,022	202	5.1	Steve Fuller	187	101	.54	1,515	Jerry Butler	58	908	15.7
1979	Marvin Sims	743	158	4.7	Billy Lott	174	90	.52	1,184	Perry Tuttle	36	544	15.1
1980	Chuck McSwain	544	114	4.8	Homer Jordan	172	85	.49	1,311	Perry Tuttle	53	915	17.3
1981	Cliff Austin	824	163	5.1	Homer Jordan	196	107	.55	1,630	Perry Tuttle	52	883	17.0
1982	Cliff Austin	1,064	197	5.4	Homer Jordan	100	55	.55	674	Jeff Stockstill	25	247	9.9
1983	Kevin Mack	862	151	5.7	Mike Eppley	166	99	.60	1,410	Ray Williams	19	342	18.0
1984	Stacey Driver	627	139	4.5	Mike Eppley	213	116	.54	1,494	Terrance Roulhac	26	512	19.7
1985	Kenny Flower	1,200	227	5.3	Randy Anderson	123	63	.51	703	Terrance Roulhac	31	533	17.2
1986	Terrence Flagler	1,258	192	6.6	Rodney Williams	200	98	.49	1,245	Ray Williams	20	280	14.0
1987	Terry Allen	973	183	5.3	Rodney Williams	209	101	.48	1,486	Gary Cooper	34	618	18.2
1988	Terry Allen	1,192	216	5.5	Rodney Williams	186	78	.42	1,144	Keith Jennings	30	397	13.2
1989	Joe Henderson	848	178	4.8	Chris Morocco	134	79	.59	1,131	Rodney Fletcher	35	556	15.9
1990	Ronald Williams	941	178	5.3	DeChane Cameron	194	98	.51	1,185	Terry Smith	34	480	14.1
1991	Rodney Blunt	747	175	4.3	DeChane Cameron	226	126	.56	1,601	Terry Smith	52	829	15.9
1992	Rodney Blunt	812	149	5.4	Patrick Sapp	144	60	.42	750	Terry Smith	38	596	15.7
1993	Derrick Witherspoon	519	111	4.7	Patrick Sapp	133	66	.50	1,084	Terry Smith	38	776	20.4
1994	Lamont Pegues	390	92	4.2	Nealon Greene	94	51	.54	524	Antwuan Wyatt	30	282	9.4
1995	Raymond Priester	1,322	231	5.7	Nealon Greene	202	116	.57	1,537	Antwuan Wyatt	45	683	15.2
1996	Raymond Priester	1,345	257	5.2	Nealon Greene	219	111	.51	1,446	Kenya Crooks	30	444	14.8
1997	Raymond Priester	956	223	4.3	Nealon Greene	290	180	.62	2,212	Tony Horne	70	907	13.0
1998	Travis Zachery	635	158	4.0	Brandon Streeter	282	150	.53	1,948	Brian Wofford	35	535	15.3
1999	Travis Zachery	820	185	4.4	Woodrow Dantzler	201	112	.56	1,506	Rod Gardner	80	1,084	13.6
2000	Woodrow Dantzler	1,028	190	5.4	Woodrow Dantzler	244	137	.56	1,871	Rod Gardner	58	1,050	18.1
2001	Woodrow Dantzler	1,061	221	4.8	Woodrow Dantzler	334	203	.61	2,578	Derrick Hamilton	53	684	12.9
2002	Yusef Kelly	520	125	4.2	Willie Simmons	244	142	.58	1,559	Kevin Youngblood	59	591	10.0
2003	Duane Coleman	615	133	4.6	Charlie Whitehurst	465	288	.62	3,561	Kevin Youngblood	70	897	12.8
2004	Reggie Meriweather	670	136	4.9	Charlie Whitehurst	349	177	.51	2,067	Airese Currie	61	868	14.2

Receiving leaders by receptions

All statistics include postseason

CLEMSON ALL-TIME SCORES

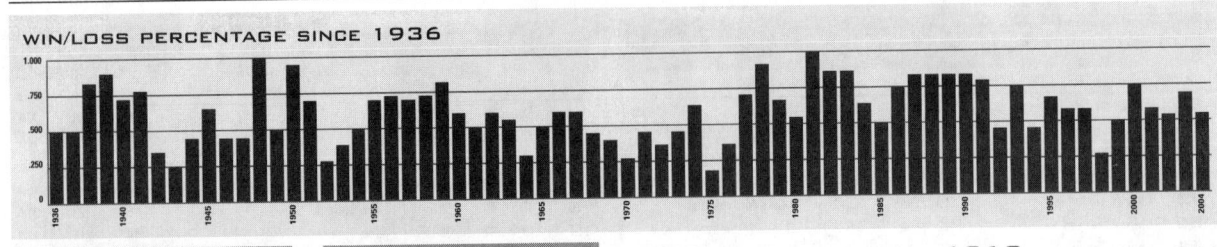

WIN/LOSS PERCENTAGE SINCE 1936

WALTER RIGGS
1896, '99 (.667)   6-3

1896   2-1-0
O31	●	at Furman	14	6
N12	●	at South Carolina	6	12
N21	●	at Wofford	16	0

W.M. WILLIAMS
1897 (.500)   2-2

1897   2-2-0
O9		at Georgia	0	24
O23	●	at Charlotte YMCA	10	0
O25	●	at North Carolina	0	28
N10	●	at South Carolina	18	6 *

JOHN PENTON
1898 (.750)   3-1

1898   3-1-0
O8		at Georgia	8	20
O20	●	Bingham	55	0
N17	●	South Carolina	24	0
N24	●	Georgia Tech *Aug*	23	0

WALTER RIGGS

1899   4-2-0
O7		at Georgia	0	11
O14	●	Davidson *RH*	10	0
O28	●	at Auburn	0	34
N9	●	at South Carolina	34	0
N18	●	North Carolina St. *RH*	24	0
N30	●	Georgia Tech *GrvSC*	41	5

JOHN HEISMAN
1900-03 (.833)   19-3-2

1900   6-0-0
O19	●	Davidson	64	0
O22	●	at Wofford	21	0
N1	●	at South Carolina	51	0
N10	●	at Georgia	39	5
N24	●	Virginia Tech *Char*	12	5
N29	●	Alabama *Birm*	35	0

1901   3-1-1
O5	●	Guilford	122	0
O19	=	at Tennessee	6	6
O26	●	at Georgia	29	5
O31		Virginia Tech *Colu*	11	17
N28	●	North Carolina *Char*	22	10

1902   6-1-0
O4	●	North Carolina St.	11	5
O18	●	at Georgia Tech	44	5
O24	●	at Furman	28	0
O30		at South Carolina	6	12
N8	●	Georgia	36	0
N15	●	at Auburn	16	0
N27	●	at Tennessee	11	0

1903   4-1-1
O10	●	at Georgia	29	0
O17	●	at Georgia Tech	73	0
O28	●	North Carolina St. *Colu*	24	0
N14		at North Carolina	6	11
N21	●	at Davidson	24	0
N26	=	Cumberland *Mont*	11	11

SHACK SHEALY
1904 (.500)   3-3-1

1904   3-3-1
O8	●	Alabama *Birm*	18	0
O15	●	Auburn	0	5
O22	●	Georgia	10	0
O27		Sewanee *Colu*	5	11
N5	=	at Georgia Tech	11	11
N12	●	at Tennessee	6	0
N24		at North Carolina St.	0	8 *

EDDIE COCHEMS
1905 (.583)   3-2-1

1905   3-2-1
O14	=	Tennessee	5	5
O21	●	at Georgia	35	0
O25	●	Alabama *Colu*	25	0
N11	●	at Auburn	6	0 *
N18	●	at Vanderbilt	0	41
N30	●	at Georgia Tech	10	17

BOB WILLIAMS
1906, '09,'13-15, (.585) 21-14-6

1906   4-0-3
O13	=	Virginia Tech	0	0
O20	●	Georgia	6	0
O25	=	North Carolina St. *Colu*	0	0
N3	●	at Davidson	0	0
N10	●	Auburn	6	4
N19	●	Tennessee	16	0
N29	●	at Georgia Tech	10	0

FRANK SHAUGHNESSY
1907 (.500)   4-4

1907   4-4-0
S28	●	Gordon	5	0
O9	●	Maryville	35	0
O21		Tennessee	0	4
O31	●	North Carolina *Colu*	15	6
N2		at Auburn	0	12
N7	●	Georgia *Aug*	0	8
N9		Davidson	6	10
N28	●	at Georgia Tech	6	5

JOHN STONE
1908 (.143)   1-6

1908   1-6-0
S26	●	Gordon	15	0
O10		Virginia Tech	0	6
O17		at Vanderbilt	0	41
O28		Davidson *Colu*	0	13
N5		Georgia *Aug*	0	8
N14		at Tennessee	5	6
N26		at Georgia Tech	6	30

BOB WILLIAMS

1909   6-3-0
S27	●	Gordon	26	0
O2		at Virginia Tech	0	6
O9	●	Davidson *Char*	17	5
O16		Alabama *Birm*	0	3
O23	●	Port Royal	19	0
N4	●	at South Carolina	6	0
N10	●	Georgia *Aug*	5	0
N13	●	at Citadel	17	0
N25		at Georgia Tech	3	29

FRANK DOBSON
1910-12 (.479)   11-12-1

1910   4-3-1
S24	●	Gordon	26	0
O1		Mercer	0	3
O8	●	at Samford	24	0
O15	●	at Citadel	32	0
O22		at Auburn	0	17
N3	●	at South Carolina	24	0
N10	=	Georgia *Aug*	0	0
N24		at Georgia Tech	0	34

1911   3-5-0
O14		Auburn	0	20 *
O21	●	Samford	15	0
O25	●	Florida	5	6
N2		at South Carolina	27	0
N4	●	at Citadel	18	0
N9		Georgia *Aug*	0	22
N18	●	Mercer *ColGa*	6	20
N30		at Georgia Tech	0	31

1912   4-4-0
O5	●	at Samford	59	0
O12	●	Riverside	26	0
O19	●	at Auburn	6	27
O26	●	Citadel	52	14
O31	●	at South Carolina	7	22
N9		Georgia *Aug*	6	27
N16	●	at Mercer	21	13
N28		at Georgia Tech	0	20 *

BOB WILLIAMS

1913   4-4-0
O4	●	Davidson	6	3
O11		at Alabama	0	20
O18		Auburn	0	20
O30	●	at South Carolina	32	0
N6		Georgia *Aug*	15	18
N8	●	at Citadel	7	3
N17	●	at Mercer	52	0
N27		at Georgia Tech	0	34

1914   5-3-1
O3	=	at Davidson	0	0
O10		at Tennessee	0	27
O17		at Auburn	0	28
O22	●	at Furman	57	0
O29	●	at South Carolina	29	6
O31	●	at Citadel	14	0
N7	●	at Georgia	35	13
N14	●	VMI *Rich*	27	23
N26		at Georgia Tech	6	26

1915   2-4-2
S25	●	at Furman	94	0
O2	=	Davidson	6	6
O9	●	at Tennessee	3	0
O16	●	Auburn *And*	0	14
O28	=	at South Carolina	0	0
N6		North Carolina *GrvSC*	7	9
N13	●	VMI *Rich*	3	6
N25		at Georgia	0	13

WAYNE HART
1916 (.333)   3-6

1916   3-6-0
S30	●	Furman	7	6
O7		Georgia *And*	0	26
O14		Tennessee	0	14
O20		at Auburn	0	28
O26	●	at South Carolina	27	0
N11		VMI *Rich*	7	37
N16	●	Citadel *Ora*	0	3
N22	●	Presbyterian	40	0
N30		Davidson *Char*	0	33

EDWARD DONAHUE
1917-20 (.625)   21-12-3

1917   6-2-0
S28	●	Presbyterian	13	0
O13	●	at Furman	38	0
O19	●	Auburn	0	7
O25	●	at South Carolina	21	13
N1	●	at Wofford	27	16
N8	●	Citadel *Ora*	20	0
N17	●	Florida *JacF*	55	7
N29	●	Davidson *Char*	9	21

1918   5-2-0
S27	●	Camp Sevier	65	0
O5		at Georgia Tech	0	28
N2	●	at South Carolina	39	0
N9		Camp Hancock	13	66
N16	●	Citadel *Colu*	7	0
N23	●	Furman	67	7
N28	●	Davidson *Char*	7	0

1919   6-2-2
S27	●	Erskine	53	0
O3	●	Davidson	7	0
O11	●	at Georgia Tech	0	28
O17	●	at Auburn	0	7
O25	●	Tennessee	14	0
O30	●	at South Carolina	19	6
N7	●	Presbyterian	19	7
N13	●	Citadel *Ora*	33	0
N21	=	at Furman	7	7
N27	=	at Georgia	0	0

1920   4-6-1
S24	●	Erskine	26	0
O1	=	Presbyterian	7	7
O2	●	Newberry	26	6
O9	●	Wofford	13	7
O15	●	Auburn	0	21
O23	●	at Tennessee	0	26
O28	●	at South Carolina	0	3
N6	●	at Georgia Tech	0	7
N11	●	Citadel *Ora*	26	0
N20	●	at Furman	0	14
N25	●	at Georgia	0	55

1921-1952 SOUTHERN CONFERENCE

E.J. STEWART
1921-22 (.389)   6-10-2

1921   1-6-2 (0-3-0)
O1		at Centre	0	14
O7	●	Presbyterian	34	0
O14		at Auburn	0	56
O21	=	at Furman	0	0
O27		at South Carolina	0	21
N5		at Georgia Tech	7	48
N10	=	Citadel *Ora*	7	7
N18		Erskine	0	13
N25		at Georgia	0	28

1922   5-4-0 (1-2-0)
S30		Centre	0	21
O7	●	Newberry	57	0
O13	●	Presbyterian	13	0
O26	●	at South Carolina	3	0
N4		at Georgia Tech	7	21
N11	●	at Citadel	18	0
N18	●	Erskine	52	0
N25		at Furman	6	20
D2		Florida *JacF*	14	47

BUD SAUNDERS
1923-26 (.318)   10-22-1

1923   5-2-1 (1-1-1)
S29	=	Auburn	0	0
O6	●	Newberry	32	0
O13		at Centre	7	28
O25	●	at South Carolina	7	6
N3		at Virginia Tech	6	25
N9	●	Davidson	12	0
N17	●	Presbyterian	20	0
N29	●	at Furman	7	6

1924   2-6-0 (0-3-0)
S27	●	Elon	60	0
O4		at Auburn	0	13
O11	●	Presbyterian	14	0
O23	●	at South Carolina	0	3
N1		Virginia Tech	6	50
N8		Davidson *Char*	0	7
N15		Citadel *And*	0	20
N27		Furman	0	3

1925 — 1-7-0 (0-4-0)

S26		Presbyterian	9	14
O3		Auburn	6	13
O10		at Kentucky	6	19
O22		at South Carolina	0	33
O29		at Wofford	0	13
N7		Florida	0	42
N14	●	at Citadel	6	0
N26		at Furman	0	26

1926 — 2-7-0 (1-3-0)

S18	●	Erskine	7	0
S25		Presbyterian	0	14
O2		at Auburn	0	47
O9	●	North Carolina St.	7	3
O21		at South Carolina	0	24
O28		at Wofford	0	3
N6		at Florida	0	33
N13		Citadel	6	15
N25		at Furman	0	30

JOSH CODY
1927-30 (.720) 29-11-1

1927 — 5-3-1 (2-2-0)

S24	=	Presbyterian	0	0
O1	●	Auburn	3	0
O8		at North Carolina St.	6	18
O14	●	Erskine	25	6
O20	●	at South Carolina	20	0
O29	●	Wofford	6	0
N5	●	at Citadel	13	0
N12		at Georgia	0	32
N24		at Furman	0	28

1928 — 8-3-0 (4-2-0)

S22	●	Newberry	30	0
S29	●	Davidson	6	0
O6	●	at Auburn	6	0
O12	●	North Carolina St. FLO	7	0
O19	●	Erskine	52	0
O25	●	at South Carolina	32	0
N3		at Mississippi	7	26
N10	●	VMI LYN	12	0
N17		Florida JACF	6	27
N29	●	at Furman	27	12
D8		at Citadel	7	12

1929 — 8-3-0 (3-3-0)

S21	●	Newberry	68	0
S28	●	Davidson CHAR	32	14
O5	●	Auburn	26	7
O11	●	North Carolina St. FLO	26	0
O18	●	Wofford	30	0
O24	●	at South Carolina	21	14
N2		at Kentucky	6	44
N9		VMI NOR	0	12
N16		at Florida	7	13
N23	●	Citadel	13	0
N28	●	Furman	7	6

1930 — 8-2-0 (3-2-0)

S20	●	Presbyterian	28	7
S27	●	Wofford	32	0
O3	●	Citadel FLO	13	7
O11	●	North Carolina St. CHAR	27	0
O17	●	Newberry	75	0
O23	●	at South Carolina	20	7
N1		at Tennessee	0	27
N8	●	VMI NOR	32	0
N15		Florida JACF	0	27
N27	●	at Furman	12	7

JESS NEELY
1931-39 (.547) 43-35-7

1931 — 1-6-2 (1-4-0)

S25	=	Presbyerian	0	0
O3		at Tennessee	0	44
O10	●	North Carolina St. CHAR	6	0
O16		Citadel FLO	0	6
O22		at South Carolina	0	21
O31		Oglethorpe	0	12
N7		VMI NOR	6	7
N14		Alabama MONT	7	74
N26	=	at Furman	0	0

1932 — 3-5-1 (0-4-0)

S23	●	Presbyterian	13	0
O1		at Georgia Tech	14	32
O8		at North Carolina St.	0	13
O14	●	Erskine	19	0
O20		at South Carolina	0	14
O29	=	at Davidson	7	7
N5	●	at Citadel	18	6
N11		Georgia	18	32
N24		at Furman	0	7

1933 — 3-6-2 (1-1-0)

S23	=	Presbyterian	6	6
S30		at Georgia Tech	2	39
O7	●	North Carolina St.	9	0
O13	=	at George Washington	0	0
O19		at South Carolina	0	7
O28		Mississippi MER	0	13
N4	●	Wake Forest CHAR	13	0
N11		at Wofford	13	14
N18		Mercer SAV	0	13
N25	●	Citadel	7	0
N30		at Furman	0	6

1934 — 5-4-0 (2-1-0)

S22	●	Presbyterian	6	0
S29		at Georgia Tech	7	12
O6		at Duke	6	20
O13		at Kentucky	0	7
O25	●	at South Carolina	19	0
N3	●	at North Carolina St.	12	6
N10		at Alabama	0	40
N17	●	Mercer SAV	32	0
N29	●	Furman	7	0

1935 — 6-3-0 (2-1-0)

S21	●	Presbyterian	25	6
S28	●	at Virginia Tech	28	7
O5	●	Wake Forest	13	7
O12		at Duke	12	38
O24	●	at South Carolina	44	0
N2	●	Mercer AUG	13	0
N9		at Alabama	0	33
N16	●	at Citadel	6	0
N28		at Furman	6	8

1936 — 5-5-0 (3-3-0)

S19	●	Presbyterian	19	0
S26	●	Virginia Tech	20	0
O3		at Alabama	0	32
O10		at Duke	0	25
O16		at Wake Forest	0	6
O22	●	at South Carolina	19	0
O31	●	at Georgia Tech	14	13
N7	●	at Citadel	20	0
N14		at Kentucky	6	7
N26		Furman	0	12

1937 — 4-4-1 (2-0-1)

S18	●	Presbyterian	46	0
S25		at Tulane	0	7
O2		at Army	6	21
O9		at Georgia	0	14
O21	●	at South Carolina	34	6
O30	●	Wake Forest	32	0
N6		at Georgia Tech	0	7
N13	●	at Florida	10	9
N25	=	at Furman	0	0

1938 — 7-1-1 (3-0-1)

S17	●	Presbyterian	26	0
S24	●	at Tulane	13	10
O1		at Tennessee	7	20
O8	=	VMI CHAR	7	7
O20	●	at South Carolina	34	12
O28	●	at Wake Forest	7	0
N5	●	George Washington GRVSC	27	0
N12	●	at Kentucky	14	0
N24	●	Furman	10	7

1939 — 9-1-0 (4-0-0)

S23	●	Presbyterian	18	0
S30		at Tulane	6	7
O7	●	North Carolina St. CHAR	25	6
O19	●	at South Carolina	27	0
O28	●	at Navy	15	7
N3	●	at George Washington	13	6
N11	●	Wake Forest	20	7
N18	●	at Southwestern	21	6
N25	●	at Furman	14	3
		COTTON BOWL		
J1	●	Boston College	6	3

FRANK HOWARD
1940-69 (.580) 165-118-12

1940 — 6-2-1 (4-0-0)

S21	●	at Presbyterian	38	0
S28	●	Wofford	26	0
O5	●	North Carolina St. CHAR	26	7
O12	●	Wake Forest	39	0
O24	●	at South Carolina	21	13
N2		at Tulane	0	13
N9		at Auburn	7	21
N16	=	at Southwestern	12	12
N23	●	at Furman	13	7

1941 — 7-2-0 (5-1-0)

S20	●	Presbyterian	41	12
S27	●	VMI LYN	36	7
O4	●	North Carolina St. CHAR	27	6
O11	●	at Boston College	26	13
O23		at South Carolina	14	18
O31	●	at George Washington	19	0
N15	●	Wake Forest	29	0
N29		at Auburn	7	28

1942 — 3-6-1 (2-3-1)

S19	●	Presbyterain	32	13
S26	=	VMI LYN	0	0
O3		North Carolina St. CHAR	6	7
O10		at Boston College	7	14
O22	●	at South Carolina	18	6
O31		at Wake Forest	6	19
N7		George Washington	0	7
N14		at Jacksonville NAS	6	24
N21	●	Furman	12	7
N28		at Auburn	13	41

1943 — 2-6-0 (2-3-0)

S25		Presbyterian	12	13
O2	●	North Carolina St. CHAR	19	7
O9		VMI ROA	7	12
O21		at South Carolina	6	33
O30		Wake Forest	12	41
N6	●	at Davidson	26	6
N13		Georgia Pre-Flight GRVSC	6	32
N20		at Georgia Tech	6	41

1944 — 4-5-0 (3-1-0)

S23	●	Presbyterian	34	0
S30		at Georgia Tech	0	51
O7	●	North Carolina St. CHAR	13	7
O19	●	at South Carolina	20	13
O28		at Tennessee	7	26
N4		at Wake Forest	7	13
N11	●	VMI	57	12
N18		at Tulane	20	36
N24		at Georgia	7	21

1945 — 6-3-1 (2-1-1)

S22	●	Presbyterain	76	0
S29		at Georgia	0	20
O6	●	at North Carolina St.	13	0
O13	●	Pensacola NAS	7	6
O25	=	at South Carolina	0	0
N2		at Miami, Fla.	6	7
N10	●	Virginia Tech	35	0
N17	●	at Tulane	47	20
N24	●	at Georgia Tech	21	7
D1		Wake Forest	6	13

1946 — 4-5-0 (2-3-0)

S21	●	Prebyterain	39	0
S27		at Georgia	12	35
O5		North Carolina St.	7	14
O12		at Wake Forest	7	19
O24		at South Carolina	14	26
N2	●	at Virginia Tech	14	7
N9		at Tulane	13	54
N16	●	Furman	20	6
N23	●	Auburn MONT	21	13

1947 — 4-5-0 (1-3-0)

S20	●	Presbyterian	42	0
S26		at Boston College	22	32
O4		Wake Forest	14	16
O11		at North Carolina St.	0	18
O23		at South Carolina	19	21
O31		at Georgia	6	21
N8	●	at Furman	35	7
N15	●	at Duquesne	34	13
N22	●	Auburn	34	18

1948 — 11-0-0 (5-0-0)

S25	●	Presbyterian	53	0
O2	●	North Carolina St.	6	0
O9	●	at Mississippi State	21	7
O21	●	at South Carolina	13	7
O29	●	at Boston College	26	19
N6	●	Furman	41	0
N13	●	Wake Forest W-S	21	14
N20	●	Citadel	20	0
N27	●	Auburn MBL	7	6
D4	●	at Duquesne	42	0
		GATOR BOWL		
J1	●	Missouri	24	23

1949 — 4-4-2 (2-2-0)

S17	●	Presbyterian	69	7
S24		at Rice	7	33
O1	●	at North Carolina St.	7	6
O8	=	Mississippi State	7	7
O20		at South Carolina	13	27
O29		Wake Forest	21	35
N5		Boston College	27	40
N12	●	Duquesne	33	20
N19	●	at Furman	28	21
N26	=	Auburn MBL	20	20

1950 — 9-0-1 (3-0-1)

S23	●	Presbyterian	55	0
S30	●	at Missouri	34	0
O7	●	North Carolina St.	27	0
O19	=	at South Carolina	14	14
O28	●	at Wake Forest	13	12
N4	●	Duquesne	53	20
N11	●	at Boston College	35	14
N18	●	Furman	57	2
N25	●	at Auburn	41	0
		ORANGE BOWL		
J1	●	Miami, Fla.	15	14

1951 — 7-3-0 (3-1-0)

S22	●	Presbyterian	53	6
S29	●	at Rice	20	14
O6	●	at North Carolina St.	6	0
O13		at Pacific	7	21
O25		at South Carolina	0	20
N3	●	Wake Forest	21	6
N10	●	Boston College	21	2
N17	●	at Furman	34	14
N24	●	Auburn	34	0
		GATOR BOWL		
J1		Miami, Fla.	0	14

1952 — 2-6-1 (0-2-0)

S20	●	Presbyterian	53	13
S27		Villanova	7	14
O4		at Maryland	0	28
O11		at Florida	13	54
O23		at South Carolina	0	6
O31	●	at Boston College	13	0
N8	=	at Fordham	12	12
N15		at Kentucky	14	27
N22		at Auburn	0	3

1953–PRESENT
ACC

1953 — 3-5-1 (1-2-0)

S19	●	Presbyterian	33	7
S26	=	at Boston College	14	14
O3		Maryland	0	20
O9		at Miami, Fla.	7	39
O22		at South Carolina	7	14
O31	●	Wake Forest	18	0
N7		at Georgia Tech	7	20
N14	●	at Citadel	34	13
N21		Auburn	19	45

1954 — 5-5-0 (1-2-0)

S18	●	Presbyterian	33	0
S25		at Georgia	7	14
O2		Virginia Tech	7	18
O9	●	Florida JACF	14	7
O21		at South Carolina	8	13
O30	●	Wake Forest CHAR	32	20
N6	●	Furman	27	6
N13		at Maryland	0	16
N20		at Auburn	6	27
N27	●	Citadel	59	0

1955 — 7-3-0 (3-1-0)

S17	●	Presbyterian	33	0
S24	●	at Virginia	20	7
O1	●	Georgia	26	7
O8		at Rice	7	21
O20	●	at South Carolina	28	14
O29	●	Wake Forest	19	13
N5	●	Virginia Tech ROA	21	16
N12		Maryland	12	25
N19		Auburn MBL	0	21
N26	●	at Furman	40	20

1956 — 7-2-2 (4-0-1)

S22		Presbyterian	27	7
S29	=	at Florida	20	20
O6	●	at North Carolina St.	13	7
O13	●	at Wake Forest	17	0
O25	●	at South Carolina	7	0
N3	●	Virginia Tech	21	6
N10	=	at Maryland	6	6
N16		at Miami, Fla.	0	21
N24	●	Virginia	7	0
		ORANGE BOWL		
D1	●	Furman	28	7

1957 — 7-3-0 (4-3-0)

S21	●		Presbyterian	66	0
S28		|	at North Carolina	0	26
O5		|	North Carolina St.	7	13
O12	●	|	at Virginia	20	6
O24	●	|	at South Carolina	13	0
N2	●		at Rice	20	7
N9	●	|	Maryland	26	7
N16		|	at Duke	6	7
N23	●	|	Wake Forest	13	6
N30	●		at Furman	45	6

1958 — 8-3-0 (5-1-0)

S20	●	|	Virginia	20	15
S27	●	|	North Carolina	26	21
O4	●	|	at Maryland	8	0
O11	●		at Vanderbilt	12	7
O23		|	at South Carolina	6	26
N1	●	|	Wake Forest	14	12
N8			at Georgia Tech	0	13
N15	●	|	at North Carolina St.	13	6
N22	●		Boston College	34	12
N29	●		Furman	36	19
			SUGAR BOWL		
J1			LSU		07

1959 — 9-2-0 (6-1-0)

S19	●	|	at North Carolina	20	18
S26	●	|	at Virginia	47	0
O3			at Georgia Tech	6	16
O10	●	|	North Carolina St.	23	0
O22	●	|	at South Carolina	27	0
O31	●		at Rice	19	0
N7	●	|	Duke	6	0
N14		|	Maryland	25	28
N21	●	|	Wake Forest	33	31
N28	●		at Furman	56	3
			BLUEBONNET BOWL		
D19	●		TCU	23	7

1960 — 6-4-0 (4-2-0)

S24	●	|	at Wake Forest	28	7
O1	●		Virginia Tech	13	7
O8	●	|	Virginia	21	7
O15		|	at Maryland	17	19
O22		|	at Duke	6	21
O29			at Vanderbilt	20	22
N5	●	|	North Carolina	24	0
N12	●	|	South Carolina	12	2
N19			at Boston College	14	25
N26	●		Furman	42	14

1961 — 5-5-0 (3-3-0)

S23			at Florida	17	21
S30		|	Maryland	21	24
O7	●	|	at North Carolina	27	0
O14		|	Wake Forest	13	17
O21	●	|	at Duke	17	7
O28			at Auburn	14	24
N4	●		Tulane	21	6
N11		|	at South Carolina	14	21
N18	●		Furman	35	6
N25	●	|	North Carolina St.	20	0

1962 — 6-4-0 (5-1-0)

S22			at Georgia Tech	9	26
S29	●	|	at North Carolina St.	7	0
O6	●	|	at Wake Forest	24	7
O13			Georgia	16	24
O20		|	Duke	0	16
O27			Auburn	14	17
N3	●	|	North Carolina	17	6
N10	●		at Furman	44	3
N17	●	|	at Maryland	17	14
N24	●	|	South Carolina	20	17

1963 — 5-4-1 (5-2-0)

S21			at Oklahoma	14	31
S28			at Georgia Tech	0	27
O5		|	North Carolina St.	3	7
O12	=		Georgia	7	7
O19		|	at Duke	30	35
O26	●	|	at Virginia	35	0
N2	●	|	Wake Forest	36	0
N9	●	|	at North Carolina	11	7
N16	●	|	Maryland	21	6
N28	●	|	at South Carolina	24	20

1964 — 3-7-0 (2-4-0)

S19	●		Furman	28	0
S26		|	at North Carolina St.	0	9
O3			at Georgia Tech	7	14
O10			at Georgia	7	19
O17	●	|	at Wake Forest	21	2
O24			at TCU	10	14
O31	●	|	Virginia	29	7
N7		|	North Carolina	0	29
N14		|	at Maryland	0	34
N28		|	South Carolina	3	7

1965 — 5-5-0 (4-3-0)

S18	●	|	North Carolina St.	21	7
S25	●	|	at Virginia	20	14
O2			at Georgia Tech	6	38
O9			at Georgia	9	23
O16	●	|	at Duke	3	2
O23	●		TCU	3	0
O30	●	|	Wake Forest	26	13
N6		|	at North Carolina	13	17
N13		|	Maryland	0	6
N20		|	at South Carolina	16	17

1966 — 6-4-0 (6-1-0)

S24	●	|	Virginia	40	35
O1			at Georgia Tech	12	13
O8			at Alabama	0	26
O15	●	|	Duke	9	6
O22			at Southern Cal	0	30
O29	●	|	at Wake Forest	23	21
N5	●	|	North Carolina	27	3
N12	●	|	at Maryland	14	10
N19		|	at North Carolina St.	14	23
N26	●	|	South Carolina	35	10

1967 — 6-4-0 (6-0-0)

S23	●	|	Wake Forest	23	6
S30			Georgia	17	24
O7			at Georgia Tech	0	10
O14			at Auburn	21	43
O21	●	|	at Duke	13	7
O28			Alabama	10	13
N4	●	|	at North Carolina	17	0
N11	●	|	Maryland	28	7
N18	●	|	North Carolina St.	14	6
N25	●	|	at South Carolina	23	12

1968 — 4-5-1 (4-1-1)

S21	=	|	at Wake Forest	20	20
S28			at Georgia	13	31
O5			at Georgia Tech	21	24
O12			Auburn	10	21
O19	●	|	Duke	39	22
O26			at Alabama	14	21
N2	●	|	at North Carolina St.	24	19
N9	●	|	at Maryland	16	0
N16	●	|	North Carolina	24	14
N23		|	South Carolina	3	7

1969 — 4-6-0 (3-3-0)

S20	●	|	at Virginia	21	14
S27			Georgia	0	30
O4	●		at Georgia Tech	21	10
O11			at Auburn	0	51
O18	●	|	Wake Forest	28	14
O25			Alabama	13	
N1	●	|	Maryland	40	0
N8		|	at Duke	27	34
N15		|	at North Carolina	15	32
N22		|	at South Carolina	13	27

HOOTIE INGRAM
1970-72 (.364) 12-21

1970 — 3-8-0 (2-4-0)

S12	●		Citadel	24	0
S19	●	|	Virginia	27	17
S26			at Georgia	0	38
O3			at Georgia Tech	7	28
O10			Auburn	0	44
O17		|	at Wake Forest	20	36
O24		|	Duke	10	21
O31	●	|	at Maryland	24	11
N7			at Florida State	13	38
N14		|	North Carolina	7	42
N21		|	South Carolina	32	38

1971 — 5-6-0 (5-2-0)

S11			Kentucky	10	13
S25			Georgia	0	28
O2			at Georgia Tech	14	24
O9	●	|	Duke *Nor*	3	0
O16	●	|	Virginia *Rich*	32	15
O23			at Auburn	13	35
O30	●	|	Wake Forest	10	9
N6		|	at North Carolina	13	26
N13	●	|	Maryland	20	14
N20		|	North Carolina St.	23	31
N27	●	|	at South Carolina	17	7

1972 — 4-7-0 (2-4-0)

S9	●		Citadel	13	0
S23			at Rice	10	29
S30			at Oklahoma	3	52
O7			at Georgia Tech	9	31
O14		|	Duke	0	7
O21	●	|	Virginia	37	21
O28	●	|	at Wake Forest	31	0
N4		|	North Carolina	10	26
N11		|	at Maryland	6	31
N18		|	at North Carolina St.	17	42
N25	●		South Carolina	7	6

RED PARKER
1973-76 (.409) 17-25-2

1973 — 5-6-0 (4-2-0)

S8	●		Citadel	14	12
S22			at Georgia	14	31
S29			at Georgia Tech	21	29
O6			Texas A&M	15	30
O13	●	|	Virginia	32	27
O20	●	|	at Duke	24	8
O27		|	North Carolina St.	6	29
N3	●	|	Wake Forest	35	8
N10	●	|	at North Carolina	37	29
N17		|	Maryland	13	28
N24			at South Carolina	20	32

1974 — 7-4-0 (4-2-0)

S14			at Texas A&M	0	24
S21		|	at North Carolina St.	10	31
S28	●		Georgia Tech	21	17
O5	●		Georgia	28	24
O12		|	at Maryland	0	41
O19	●	|	Duke	17	13
O26			at Tennessee	28	29
N2	●	|	at Wake Forest	21	9
N9	●	|	North Carolina	54	32
N16	●	|	Virginia	28	9
N23	●		South Carolina	39	21

1975 — 2-9-0 (2-3-0)

S13			Tulane	13	17
S20			at Alabama	0	56
S27			at Georgia Tech	28	33
O4			at Georgia	7	35
O11	●	|	Wake Forest	16	14
O18		|	at Duke	21	25
O25		|	North Carolina St.	7	45
N1			Florida State	7	43
N8	●	|	at North Carolina	38	35
N15		|	Maryland	20	22
N22			at South Carolina	20	56

1976 — 3-6-2 (0-4-1)

S11	●		Citadel	10	7
S18			Georgia	0	41
S25	=		at Georgia Tech	24	24
O2			at Tennessee	19	21
O9		|	at Wake Forest	14	20
O16	=	|	Duke	18	18
O23		|	at North Carolina St.	21	38
O30	●		at Florida State	15	12
N6		|	North Carolina	23	27
N13		|	at Maryland	0	20
N20	●		South Carolina	28	9

CHARLEY PELL
1977-78 (.804) 18-4-1

1977 — 8-3-1 (4-1-1)

S10		|	Maryland	14	21
S17	●		at Georgia	7	6
S24	●		Georgia Tech	31	14
O1	●		at Virginia Tech	31	13
O8	●	|	Virginia	31	0
O15	●	|	at Duke	17	11
O22	●	|	North Carolina St.	7	3
O29	●	|	Wake Forest	26	0
N5	=	|	at North Carolina	13	13
N12			Notre Dame	17	21
N19	●		at South Carolina	31	27
			GATOR BOWL		
D30			Pittsburgh	3	34

1978 — 11-1-0 (6-0-0)

S16	●		Citadel	58	3
S23			at Georgia	0	12
S30	●		Villanova	31	0
O7	●		Virginia Tech	38	7
O14	●	|	at Virginia	30	14
O21	●	|	Duke	28	8
O28	●	|	at North Carolina St.	33	10
N4	●	|	at Wake Forest	51	6
N11	●	|	North Carolina	13	9
N18	●	|	at Maryland	28	24
N25	●		South Carolina	41	23
			GATOR BOWL		
D29	●		Ohio State	17	15

DANNY FORD
1978-89 (.760) 96-29-4

1979 — 8-4-0 4-2-0

S8	●		Furman	21	0
S15		|	Maryland	0	19
S22	●		Georgia	12	7
O6	●	|	Virginia	17	7
O13	●		at Virginia Tech	21	0
O20	●	|	at Duke	28	10
O27		|	North Carolina St.	13	16
N3	●	|	Wake Forest	31	0
N10	●	|	at North Carolina	19	10
N17	●		at Notre Dame	16	10
N24			at South Carolina	9	13
			PEACH BOWL		
D31			Baylor	18	24

1980 — 6-5-0 (2-4-0)

S13	●		Rice	19	3
S20			at Georgia	16	20
S27	●		Western Carolina	17	10
O4	●		Virginia Tech	13	10
O11	●	|	at Virginia	27	24
O18		|	Duke	17	34
O25		|	at North Carolina St.	20	24
N1	●	|	at Wake Forest	35	33
N8		|	North Carolina	19	24
N15		|	at Maryland	7	34
N22	●		South Carolina	27	6

1981 — 12-0-0 (6-0-0)

S5	●		Wofford	45	10
S12	●		at Tulane	13	5
S19	●		Georgia	13	3
O3	●		at Kentucky	21	3
O10	●	|	Virginia	27	0
O17	●	|	at Duke	38	10
O24	●	|	North Carolina St.	17	7
O31	●	|	Wake Forest	82	24
N7	●	|	at North Carolina	10	8
N14	●	|	Maryland	21	7
N21	●		at South Carolina	29	13
			ORANGE BOWL		
J1	●		Nebraska	22	15

1982 — 9-1-1 (6-0-0)

S6			at Georgia	7	13
S18	=		Boston College	17	17
S25	●		Western Carolina	21	10
O2	●		Kentucky	24	6
O9	●	|	at Virginia	48	0
O16	●	|	Duke	49	14
O23	●	|	at North Carolina St.	38	29
N6	●	|	North Carolina	16	13
N13	●	|	at Maryland	24	22
N20	●		South Carolina	24	6
N27	●	|	Wake Forest *Tok*	21	17

1983 — 9-1-1 (7-0-0)

S3	●		Western Carolina	44	10
S10			at Boston College	16	31
S17	=		Georgia	16	16
S24	●	|	Georgia Tech	41	14
O8	●	|	Virginia	42	21
O15	●	|	at Duke	38	31
O22	●	|	North Carolina St.	27	17
O29	●	|	Wake Forest	24	17
N5	●	|	at North Carolina	16	3
N12	●	|	Maryland	52	27
N19	●		at South Carolina	22	13

1984 — 7-4-0 (5-2-0)

S1	●		Appalachian St.	40	7
S8	●	|	at Virginia	55	0
S22			at Georgia	23	26
S29		|	at Georgia Tech	21	28
O6	●	|	North Carolina	20	12
O20	●	|	Duke	54	21
O27	●	|	at North Carolina St.	35	34
N3	●	|	Wake Forest	37	14
N10	●		Virginia Tech	17	10
N17		|	Maryland *Balt*	23	41
N24			South Carolina	21	22

1985 — 6-6-0 (4-3-0)

Date		Opponent		
S14	●	at Virginia Tech	20	17
S21		Georgia	13	20
S28	|	Georgia Tech	3	14
O5		at Kentucky	7	26
O12	● |	Virginia	27	24
O19	●	at Duke	21	9
O26	● |	North Carolina St.	39	10
N2	● |	Wake Forest	26	10
N9		at North Carolina	20	21
N16	|	Maryland	31	34
N23		at South Carolina	24	17
		INDEPENDENCE BOWL		
D21		Minnesota	13	20

1986 — 8-2-2 (5-1-1)

Date		Opponent		
S13		Virginia Tech	14	20
S20	●	at Georgia	31	28
S27	|	at Georgia Tech	27	3
O4	●	Citadel	24	0
O11	● |	at Virginia	31	17
O18	● |	Duke	35	3
O25	|	at North Carolina St.	3	27
N1	●	Wake Forest	28	20
N8	●	North Carolina	38	10
N15	=	Maryland *BALT*	17	17
N22	=	South Carolina	21	21
		GATOR BOWL		
D27	●	Stanford	27	21

1987 — 10-2-0 (6-1-0)

Date		Opponent		
S5	●	Western Carolina	43	0
S12	●	at Virginia Tech	22	10
S19	●	Georgia	21	20
S26	|	Georgia Tech	33	12
O10	● |	Virginia	38	21
O17	|	Duke	17	10
O24	|	North Carolina St.	28	30
O31	● |	Wake Forest	31	17
N7	● |	at North Carolina	13	10
N14	● |	Maryland	45	16
N21		at South Carolina	7	20
		CITRUS BOWL		
J1	●	Penn State	35	10

1988 — 10-2-0 (6-1-0)

Date		Opponent		
S3	●	Virginia Tech	40	7
S10	●	Furman	23	3
S17		Florida State	21	24
S24	● |	at Georgia Tech	30	13
O8	● |	at Virginia	10	7
O15	● |	Duke	49	17
O22	|	at North Carolina St.	3	10
O29	● |	at Wake Forest	38	21
N5	● |	North Carolina	37	14
N12	● |	at Maryland	49	25
N19	●	South Carolina	29	10
		CITRUS BOWL		
J2	●	Oklahoma	13	6

1989 — 10-2-0 (5-2-0)

Date		Opponent		
S2	●	Furman	30	0
S9	●	at Florida State	34	23
S16	●	at Virginia Tech	27	7
S23	● |	Maryland	31	7
S30	|	at Duke	17	21
O7	|	Virginia	34	20
O14	|	Georgia Tech	14	30
O21	● |	North Carolina St.	30	10
O28	● |	Wake Forest	44	10
N4	● |	at North Carolina	35	3
N18	● |	at South Carolina	45	0
		GATOR BOWL		
D30	●	West Virginia	27	7

1990 — 10-2-0 (5-2-0)

Date		Opponent		
S1	●	Long Beach St.	59	0
S8		at Virginia	7	20
S15	● |	Maryland *BALT*	18	17
S22	● |	Appalachian St.	48	0
S29	● |	Duke	26	7
O6	● |	Georgia	34	3
O13	|	at Georgia Tech	19	21
O20	● |	at North Carolina St.	24	17
O27	● |	at Wake Forest	24	6
N3	● |	North Carolina	20	3
N17	● |	South Carolina	24	15
		HALL OF FAME BOWL		
J1	●	Illinois	30	0

1991 — 9-2-1 (6-0-1)

Date		Opponent		
S7	●	Appalachian St.	34	0
S21	●	Temple	37	7
S28	● |	Georgia Tech	9	7
O5	●	at Georgia	12	27
O12	= |	Virginia	20	20
O26	● |	North Carolina St.	29	19
N2	● |	Wake Forest	28	10
N9	● |	at North Carolina	21	6
N16	● |	Maryland	40	7
N23	● |	at South Carolina	41	24
N30	● |	Duke *TOK*	33	21
		CITRUS BOWL		
J1		California	13	37

1992 — 5-6-0 (3-5-0)

Date		Opponent		
S5	●	Ball State	24	10
S12	|	Florida State	20	24
S26	|	at Georgia Tech	16	20
O3	●	U.T. Chattanooga	54	3
O10	● |	at Virginia	29	28
O17	|	Duke	21	6
O24	|	at North Carolina St.	6	20
O31	|	at Wake Forest	15	18
N7	|	North Carolina	40	7
N14	|	at Maryland	23	53
N21	|	South Carolina	13	24

1993 — 9-3-0 (5-3-0)

Date		Opponent		
S4	●	Nevada-Las Vegas	24	14
S11		at Florida State	0	57
S25	● |	Georgia Tech	16	13
O2	● |	North Carolina St.	20	14
O9	●	at Duke	13	10
O16	|	Wake Forest	16	20
O23	●	E. Tennessee St.	27	0
O30	|	Maryland	29	0
N6	●	at North Carolina	0	24
N13	●	Virginia	23	14
N20	●	at South Carolina	16	13
		PEACH BOWL		
D31	●	Kentucky	14	13

1994 — 5-6-0 (4-4-0)

Date		Opponent		
S3	●	Furman	27	6
S10	|	North Carolina St.	12	29
S17	|	at Virginia	6	9
O1	● |	Maryland	13	0
O8		at Georgia	14	40
O15	|	at Duke	13	19
O22		at Florida State	0	17
O29	● |	Wake Forest	24	8
N5	● |	at North Carolina	28	17
N12	|	Georgia Tech	20	10
N19	|	South Carolina	7	33

1995 — 8-4-0 (6-2-0)

Date		Opponent		
S2	|	Western Carolina	55	9
S9	|	Florida State	26	45
S16	● |	at Wake Forest	29	14
S23	|	Virginia	3	22
S30	● |	at North Carolina St.	43	22
O7	|	Georgia	17	19
O21	● |	at Maryland	17	0
O28	● |	at Georgia Tech	24	3
N4	● |	North Carolina	17	10
N11	● |	Duke	34	17
N18	● |	at South Carolina	38	17
		GATOR BOWL		
J1		Syracuse	0	41

1996 — 7-5 (6-2)

Date		Opponent		
A31	|	at North Carolina	0	45
S7	●	Furman	19	3
S21		at Missouri	24	38
S28	● |	Wake Forest	21	10
O5	|	at Florida State	3	34
O12	● |	at Duke	13	6
O19	|	Georgia Tech	28	25
N2	● |	Maryland	35	3
N9	● |	at Virginia	24	16
N16	● |	North Carolina St.	40	17
N23		South Carolina	31	34
		PEACH BOWL		
D28		LSU	7	10

1997 — 7-5 (4-4)

Date		Opponent		
S6	●	Appalachian St.	23	12
S13	●	at North Carolina St.	19	17
S20	|	Florida State	28	35
S27	|	at Georgia Tech	20	23
O4		Texas El Paso	39	7
O11	|	Virginia	7	21
O25	●	at Maryland	20	9
N1	●	at Wake Forest	33	16
N8	●	Duke	29	20
N15		North Carolina	10	17
N22	●	at South Carolina	47	21
		PEACH BOWL		
J2		Auburn	17	21

1998 — 3-8 (1-7)

Date		Opponent		
S5	●	Furman	33	0
S12	|	Virginia Tech	0	37
S19	|	at Virginia	18	20
S26	|	Wake Forest	19	29
O3	|	at North Carolina	14	21
O10	● |	Maryland	23	0
O17	|	at Florida State	0	48
O24	|	at Duke	23	28
O31	|	North Carolina St.	39	46
N12	|	Georgia Tech	21	24
N21	●	South Carolina	28	19

1999 — 6-6 (5-3)

Date		Opponent		
S4	●	Marshall	10	13
S11	● |	Virginia	33	14
S23	|	at Virginia Tech	11	31
O2	● |	North Carolina	31	20
O9	|	at North Carolina St.	31	35
O16	● |	at Maryland	42	30
O23	|	Florida State	14	17
O30	● |	at Wake Forest	12	3
N6	● |	Duke	58	7
N13	|	at Georgia Tech	42	45
N20	● |	at South Carolina	31	21
		PEACH BOWL		
D30		Mississippi State	7	17

2000 — 9-3 (6-2)

Date		Opponent		
S2	●	Citadel	38	0
S9		Missouri	62	9
S16	● |	Wake Forest	55	7
S23	● |	at Virginia	31	10
S30	● |	at Duke	52	22
O7	● |	North Carolina St.	34	27
O14	● |	Maryland	35	14
O21	● |	at North Carolina	38	24
O28	|	Georgia Tech	28	31
N4	|	at Florida State	7	54
N18	● |	South Carolina	16	14
		GATOR BOWL		
J1		Virginia Tech	20	41

2001 — 7-5 (4-4)

Date		Opponent		
S1	●	Central Florida	21	13
S8	●	Wofford	38	14
S22	|	Virginia	24	26
S29	● |	at Georgia Tech	47	44
O13	● |	at North Carolina St.	45	37
O20	|	North Carolina	3	38
O27	● |	at Wake Forest	21	14
N3	|	Florida State	27	41
N10	|	at Maryland	20	37
N17	|	at South Carolina	15	20
D1	● |	Duke	59	31
		HUMANITARIAN BOWL		
D31	●	Louisiana Tech	49	24

2002 — 7-6 (4-4)

Date		Opponent		
A31		at Georgia	28	31
S7	●	Louisiana Tech	33	13
S14	● |	Georgia Tech	24	19
S21	●	Ball State	30	7
O3		at Florida State	31	48
O12		at Virginia	17	22
O19	● |	Wake Forest	31	23
O24	|	North Carolina St.	6	38
N2	● |	at Duke	34	31
N9	● |	North Carolina	42	12
N16	|	Maryland	12	30
N23	● |	South Carolina	27	20
		TANGERINE BOWL		
D23		Texas Tech	15	55

2003 — 9-4 (5-3)

Date		Opponent		
A30		Georgia	0	30
S6	●	Furman	28	17
S13	●	Middle Tennessee	37	14
S20	● |	at Georgia Tech	39	3
O4	|	at Maryland	7	21
O11	● |	Virginia	30	27
O16	|	at North Carolina St.	15	17
O25	● |	North Carolina	36	28
N1	|	at Wake Forest	17	45
N8	● |	Florida State	26	10
N15	● |	Duke	40	7
N22	● |	at South Carolina	63	17
		PEACH BOWL		
J2	●	Tennessee	27	14

2004 — 6-5 (4-4)

Date		Opponent		
S4	|	Wake Forest	37	30
S11	|	Georgia Tech	24	28
S18	●	at Texas A&M	6	27
S25	|	at Florida State	22	41
O7	|	at Virginia	10	30
O16	●	Utah State	35	6
O23	|	Maryland	10	7
O30	● |	North Carolina St.	26	20
N6	●	at Miami, Fla.	24	17
N13	●	at Duke	13	16
N20	●	South Carolina	29	7

COLORADO

BY MARK WANGRIN

THE LURE OF PRECIOUS MINERALS and a quick buck led to the founding of the city of Boulder in the Flatiron Mountains of Colorado in 1859. Hoping to make their fortunes in gold or silver, some prospectors hit it rich. Others failed miserably, dying in poverty, their dreams unfulfilled.

Such has been the story of Colorado football, which has prospered and busted in this once wide-open mining town. From an 0–4 season in the inaugural year of 1890, which included a still-record 103-0 loss to the Colorado School of Mines, to the death of quarterback Sal Aunese in 1989 and the national championship year of 1990, the Buffaloes have enjoyed ethereal highs and dreary lows—sometimes almost simultaneously.

TRADITION It's college football's version of suicide chicken. Who blinks first? The 1,300-pound live buffalo stampeding toward the Colorado opponent du jour's sideline, or the opponents themselves? Before the start of each half, the team follows Ralphie and its six handlers out on the field. Ralphie rounds the end zone and veers toward the opposing sideline, often causing teams to stop dead in their tracks.

BEST PLAYER Clayton "Sam" White was a star football player and Rhodes scholar at Colorado, but it was another of his skills—his salesmanship—that left its most profound mark on the university. White sold coach William Saunders on his younger brother, who still only received academic aid when he arrived in Boulder in the fall of 1934. Once Byron White got on the practice field and showed his varied skills, the Buffaloes took notice. Nicknamed Whizzer by a local sportswriter who had told his boss, "That guy's a real whizzer," White emerged as a star during his junior season. During his senior season he led the nation in rushing and scoring and was also an effective passer, punter and safety. But White's biggest accomplishments were yet to come. A Rhodes scholar like his brother, he played in the NFL and then graduated from Yale Law School. In 1962, he was named to the U.S. Supreme Court, where he served 31 years before retiring in 1993.

BEST COACH In 1981, Bill McCartney was in his seventh year as defensive coordinator at Michigan, waiting for the

---

PROFILE

University of Colorado
Boulder, Colo.
Founded: 1876
Enrollment: 26,182
Colors: Silver, Gold and Black
Nickname: Buffaloes
Stadium: Folsom Field
    Opened in 1924
    Grass; 53,750 capacity
First football game: 1890
All-time record: 643–397–36 (.614)
Bowl record: 12–14
Consensus national championships, 1936-present: 1 (1990)
Big 12 Conference championships: 1 (outright)
Heisman Trophy: Rashaan Salaam, 1994
First-round NFL draftees: 22
Website: www.cubuffs.com

THE BEST OF TIMES

From 1988 to 1994, Bill McCartney's Buffaloes went 66–15–4, winning a national title following the 1990 season and playing in January four out of seven seasons.

THE WORST OF TIMES

Hailed as a savior upon his arrival from the Patriots at the end of the 1978 season, Chuck Fairbanks mustered just seven wins in three seasons, leaving the program in a worse state than he'd found it.

CONFERENCE

After long stints in the Rocky Mountain (1900-1937) and Mountain States (1938-47), CU joined the Big Eight in 1948. It became a charter member of the Big 12 in 1996.

DISTINGUISHED ALUMNI

Robert Redford; Judy Collins, singer; Glenn Miller, bandleader; Trey Parker and Matt Stone, creators of *South Park*; Jack Swigert, astronaut; Bill Toomey, 1968 Olympic decathlon gold medalist; Byron "Whizzer" White, U.S. Supreme Court justice; Steve Wozniak, co-founder, Apple Computer

FIGHT SONG

CU FIGHT SONG
Fight CU down the field,
CU must win
Fight, fight for victory
CU knows no defeat
We'll roll up a mighty score
Never give in
Shoulder to shoulder
We will fight, fight
Fight, fight, fight!

In Flutie-esque fashion, Kordell Stewart heaved the ball more than 70 yards in the air to beat Michigan.

day his mentor, Bo Schembechler, would step down so he might have a shot at the UM head coaching job. Colorado called first, in 1982, and McCartney, 42, became CU's 20th head coach. His tenure was an argument for patience in what's now become an instant-gratification society. Colorado administrators stuck with McCartney after a 7–25–1 start in his first three seasons—and it paid off. In 1985, he switched offenses to the wishbone, and the program took off. During his 13-year tenure, he won three Big Eight titles and his 1989 and 1990 teams played for national championships, winning one on the second try with a 10-9 victory over Notre Dame in the 1991 Orange Bowl. But the program had its black eyes, too, and from 1986 to 1989, at least 24 football players were arrested. Concerned over the amount of time coaching was taking from his family, McCartney exercised an option in the 15-year lifetime contract he had signed in summer 1990 with his surprise announcement on Nov. 19, 1994, that he would resign after the end of the season. In 1990, McCartney helped start the evangelical Christian group Promise Keepers, which focuses on introducing men to Jesus Christ.

BEST TEAM Unbeaten Colorado cruised into the 1990 Orange Bowl against Notre Dame with a high-powered offense and a shot at the national title. Instead, the Buffaloes came out with a 21-6 loss, leaving many pundits to wonder if their run had been a fluke. The next year, facing what was considered the toughest schedule in the nation—Tennessee, Stanford, Illinois, Texas and Washington were there, along with the usual Big Eight foes—the Buffaloes would not dominate. But they ultimately earned the respect of poll voters after some had questioned the team's stature following its notorious "fifth down" victory at Missouri. Behind the option attack featuring quarterback Darian Hagan and tailback Eric Bieniemy and a smothering defense with bookend outside linebackers Kanavis McGhee and Alfred Williams, the Buffaloes went 10–1–1 and earned a rematch with the Fighting Irish. CU, which had dropped to No. 20 after its third game, won a share of its only national

RECORDS

RUSHING YARDS
GAME
342   Charlie Davis vs. Oklahoma State, Nov. 13, 1971 (34 att.)
SEASON
2,055   Rashaan Salaam, 1994 (298 att.)
CAREER
3,940   Eric Bieniemy, 1987-90 (699 att.)

PASSING YARDS
GAME
465   Mike Moschetti vs. San Jose State, Sept. 11, 1999 (25 of 32)
SEASON
3,156   Koy Detmer, 1996 (208 of 363)
CAREER
6,481   Kordell Stewart, 1991-94 (456 of 785)

RECEIVING YARDS
GAME
222   Walter Stanley vs. Texas Tech, Sept. 12, 1981 (5 rec.)
SEASON
1,149   Charles Johnson, 1992 (57 rec.)
CAREER
2,548   Michael Westbrook, 1991-94 (167 rec.)

POINTS
GAME
36   Chris Brown vs. Nebraska, Nov. 23, 2001 (6 TDs)
SEASON
144   Rashaan Salaam, 1994 (24 TDs)
CAREER
254   Eric Bieniemy, 1987-90 (42 TDs, 1 two-pt. conv.)

CONSENSUS ALL-AMERICANS

1937	Byron "Whizzer" White, B
1960-61	Joe Romig, G
1967	Dick Anderson, DB
1968	Mike Montler, OT
1969	Bob Anderson, TB
1970	Don Popplewell, C
1972	Cullen Bryant, DB
1985-86	Barry Helton, P
1988	Keith English, P
1989	Tom Rouen, P
1989-90	Joe Garten, OL
1989-90	Alfred Williams, LB
1990	Eric Bieniemy, TB
1991	Jay Leeuwenburg, OL
1992	Deon Figures, DB
1994	Michael Westbrook, WR
1994	Rashaan Salaam, RB
1994	Chris Hudson, DB
1995	Bryan Stoltenberg, C
1996	Matt Russell, LB
1996	Chris Naeole, OL
2001	Dan Graham, TE
2001	Andre Gurode, OL
2002	Mark Mariscal, P

title with a 10-9 victory. AP voted the Buffaloes No. 1, but the coaches awarded unbeaten Georgia Tech the top spot in the UPI poll, reigniting calls for a playoff.

BIGGEST GAME After failing to win the national title against Notre Dame in the 1990 Orange Bowl, the Buffaloes appeared just as doomed in 1991 in an Orange Bowl rematch. Injuries knocked out star quarterback Darian Hagan and end Kanavis McGhee right before halftime and Notre Dame rallied to take a 9-3 lead in the third quarter. Paul Rose, subbing for McGhee, recovered a fumble in Notre Dame territory and Charles Johnson, in for Hagan, led the Buffaloes' offense in for the go-ahead touchdown, a one-yard run by Bieniemy with 4:26 left in the third quarter. The game came down to the final minute, when it appeared Raghib Ismail's 91-yard punt return for a touchdown would again dash CU's hopes. But the Irish were called for clipping on the return—a call Notre Dame and some observers disputed—and Buffaloes cornerback Deon Figures intercepted a Rick Mirer pass and ran out the clock.

BIGGEST UPSET Nebraska came into its 2001 regular-season finale against Colorado with a commanding lead over No. 2 Miami in the Bowl Championship Series rankings. It left utterly embarrassed—and with the BCS embroiled in a new level of controversy. Behind a 380-yard rushing attack featuring Chris Brown and Bobby Purify, who relentlessly ran a counter play called 98-G, CU bulled to a 42-23 halftime lead. The Cornhuskers attempted a comeback, but the Buffaloes matched them on their way to a shocking 62-36 victory, their first over Nebraska in 10 seasons. "It's almost too overwhelming a win," CU coach Gary Barnett said. "If it had been a last-minute, one-point win, I think it would sink in. But 62-36? That's going to take a while."

HEARTBREAKER The Buffaloes' first national title was there for the taking in the 1990 Orange Bowl against Notre

Dame. CU came into the game 11–0 and ranked No. 1 behind an offense that averaged 6.1 yards per rush and 41.1 points per game. The Buffaloes were also riding the emotion of the off-season death of quarterback Sal Aunese, to whom they had dedicated the season. The Colorado offense started strongly, but it couldn't take advantage of three great first-half scoring opportunities. Slowly the Irish got the momentum, building a 14-0 lead on two third-quarter touchdown runs. Notre Dame put together a 17-play, 82-yard touchdown drive that ate up almost nine minutes and returned the ball to CU down 21-6 with only 1:32 remaining. "We had the opportunity of a lifetime," McCartney said.

WILDEST FINISH Before the start of the 1994 season, running back Rashaan Salaam was quoted in the Colorado media guide on what would be his favorite ESPN *SportsCenter* highlight. "It's fourth and 15 late in the game at Michigan Stadium, and we're down by five," he said. "We're on our 2-yard line, and with two seconds to go, Kordell pitches me the ball. I throw a 98-yard touchdown pass to Michael Westbrook and the Buffs win the game." Salaam almost nailed the scenario. But it was Stewart who, on Sept. 24 in the Big House, rolled out with time running out and the Buffaloes trailing the Wolverines 26-21. Stewart stopped, set and heaved the ball more than 70 yards in the air to Westbrook, who caught it in the end zone off a deflection for the game-winning touchdown. CU had trailed 26-14 with four minutes left and after scoring to cut the UM lead, got the ball back on its own 15-yard line with 14 seconds remaining and no timeouts. "Better than Doug Flutie!" CU cornerback/wide receiver T.J. Cunningham shouted, recalling the Boston College quarterback's last-second Hail Mary pass to beat Miami in 1984. "Kordell can throw the ball 85 yards on his knees—ask him," Westbrook said. Countered Stewart, "Today I could have thrown it the whole field."

CENTENNIAL TEAM

Selected by the university through public balloting in 1989.

OFFENSE

1923-26	Bill McGlone,	OL
1956-58	John Wooten,	OL
1973-75	Pete Brock,	OL
1917, 1919-21	Walt Franklin,	C/E
1956-58	Boyd Dowler,	QB
1959-61	Gale Weidner,	QB
1967-69	Bobby Anderson,	QB/TB
1970-71	Cliff Branch,	WR/KR
1972-75	Dave Logan,	WR
1935-37	Byron White,	B
1955-57	Bob Stransky,	HB
1973-76	Billy Waddy,	RB
1987-90	Eric Bieniemy,	TB

DEFENSE

1959-61	Joe Romig,	OG/LB
1969-71	Herb Orvis,	DE
1918-21	Lee Willard,	B
1923-25	Hatfield Chilson,	B
1933-35	William Lam,	B
1964-66	Hale Irwin,	DB
1965-67	Dick Anderson,	DB
1976-79	Mark Haynes,	DB
1984-87	Mickey Pruitt,	DB
1951-54	Carroll Hardy,	HB
1950-52	Zack Jordan,	HB/P
1970-72	John Stearns,	DB/P

STADIUM As interest in football grew, CU president George Norlin commissioned the construction of Colorado Stadium in 1924. Built in a natural ravine as a gesture toward saving money otherwise spent for excavation, the original facility cost $65,000 and had wooden bleachers to seat 26,000 erected on a concrete base. After the death of CU football coaching pioneer Frederick Folsom in 1944, the stadium was renamed Folsom Field. A second deck was erected around two-thirds of the stadium in 1956, increasing capacity to 45,000. A new six-story press box was added in 1968 and a series of renovations, including the change from wooden to aluminum benches and the addition of suites and club seating on the stadium's east side, has upped capacity to 53,750.

RIVAL When McCartney was named coach in 1982, the Buffaloes were pretty much without a rival, having seen theirs with Colorado State lapse in 1958. McCartney wanted to change that and selected Nebraska. He had long admired the Cornhuskers program because it had never been on probation, won with local players and was perennially in the Top 10. It wasn't much of a rivalry at first, with CU losing the first four games by a combined score of 150-47. The Buffaloes finally broke through with a 20-10 win in 1986, and they beat the Cornhuskers in 1989 and 1990 and tied them in 1991 to win back-to-back-to-back Big Eight titles. The games from 1996 to 2000 are known as the "frustrating five," with CU losing all of them by a combined margin of 15 points. The Buffaloes exacted their revenge with the record-setting 62-36 rout in 2001, ending a streak of nine straight NU victories.

DUBIOUS DISTINCTION Gary Barnett thought his biggest headache after the 2003 season would be how to rebuild after a 5–7 year, only his second losing record at CU. Instead, the sixth-year Buffaloes coach was battling to keep his job after a tumultuous off-season of scandal. At least nine women claimed they had been sexually assaulted by football players or recruits since 1997. A school panel investigated whether sex and alcohol were used as recruiting tools, leading to a series of reforms and safeguards in the program but no firings. A grand jury returned only one indictment, of former CU recruiting assistant Nathan Maxcey for misdemeanor solicitation and felony counts of theft and embezzlement. Three of the women filed civil suits against CU, all of which were eventually dropped by the spring of 2005. Barnett was suspended for three months for making insensitive comments about former female kicker Katie Hnida, one of the women who had made an accusation. In

a span from November 2004 to March 2005, athletic director Dick Tharp and president Elizabeth Hoffman resigned under pressure and chancellor Richard Byyny left to become executive director of a branch of the school's medical center. Also in early 2005, a leaked grand jury report alleged that there was a slush fund for athletic department officials. University budget officials reported the athletic department was $2.1 million in the red, in part because of "unforeseen problems with the department's image."

CONTROVERSY Trailing 31-27 at Missouri on Oct. 6, 1990, the Buffaloes found themselves with first and goal at the Tigers' 3-yard line with 30 seconds left. After a two-yard dive play by Bieniemy on second down, the officials failed to note it was third down. After Bieniemy was stopped for no gain on what should have been fourth down, quarterback Charles Johnson grounded the ball. Given an extra down, Johnson scored on a sneak. CU won the game 33-31, but lost credibility. Critics called McCartney, who was a devout Christian, a hypocrite for accepting the victory. McCartney ripped into Missouri's six-year-old artificial turf, saying it was like playing on an "ice rink." UM athletic director Dick Tamburo shot back, "If he's complaining about slipping on the turf, then I'm complaining about seven officials who can't count." The Big Eight suspended the officials for two weeks and then reinstated them, but broke up their crew. The scandal dogged the Buffaloes as they made their national title run.

NICKNAME In 1934, the school newspaper sponsored a contest to select a new official CU nickname. Boulder resident Andrew Dickson got the $5 prize as the first of the 1,000 contestants to submit Buffaloes. Previously the teams had been known as Silver and Gold, but also by a bevy of informal nicknames that included Silver Helmets, Yellow Jackets, Hornets, Arapahoes, Big Horns, Grizzlies and Frontiersmen.

MASCOT In 1934, three weeks after CU had adopted Buffaloes as its official nickname, a group of students paid $25 to rent a buffalo calf and his keeper for an afternoon football game against the University of Denver. Live buffaloes made appearances at the games on and off until 1966, when Lubbock, Texas, rancher John Lowery donated a 6-month-old buffalo calf to his son's school. Named Ralph until a subsequent physical examination revealed he was a she, the buffalo was rechristened Ralphie and has run at games ever since. In 1970, Ralphie I was kidnapped by

Air Force Academy cadets and, in a move of unadulterated anti-establishment inspiration, was voted homecoming queen in 1971. The current mascot, Ralphie IV, debuted in 1998.

UNIFORMS In 1980, CU regent Jack Kent Anderson suggested that the school's athletic uniforms reflect Colorado's "sky blue at 9,000 feet." Blue replaced black as home jersey color and remained until 1984, when McCartney broke out the black uniforms for a home game against Nebraska. By 1988, blue had disappeared from the uniforms. The pants were silver through the 1950s and early 1960s, then gold. Black pants for road games appeared in the late 1980s, and white pants for the first time in 2000. "Colorado" debuted on the front of the jerseys in 1986. In the early to mid-1960s, the Buffaloes switched from silver to gold helmets, with a horn logo giving way to numbers and then later to an interlocking CU logo in the middle of a Buffalo silhouette, the current version of which was adopted in 1980.

NUMBERS Colorado is 0–10 all time against teams ranked No. 1 in the Associated Press poll, but that doesn't mean the Buffaloes haven't played spoilers. Twice they've played No. 1 Oklahoma close enough in Norman to convince voters to drop the Sooners to No. 2, including a 14-13 loss in 1957 and a 21-20 defeat in 1975 … Salaam became the school's only Heisman Trophy winner with a school-record 2,055 yards rushing in 1994. He gained 1,040 of those yards against ranked opponents.

QUOTE "I've never wanted just part of the package, part of the prize. I want it all."—Bill McCartney

COLORADO ANNUAL STATISTICAL LEADERS

YR	RUSHING	YDS	ATT	AVG	PASSING	ATT	CMP	PCT	YDS	RECEIVING	REC	YDS	AVG
1946	Maurice Reilly	327	125	2.6	Maurice Reilly	83	35	.42	551	John Zisch	16	241	15.1
1947	Dick Schrepferman	252	78	3.2	Don Evans	35	20	.57	383	Malcolm Miller	14	188	13.4
1948	Harry Narcisian	510	126	4.0	Harry Narcisian	77	30	.39	521	Ed Pudlik	12	238	19.8
1949	Merwin Hodel	748	169	4.4	Bob Manire	48	24	.50	299	Merwin Hodel	14	174	12.4
1950	Merwin Hodel	757	169	4.5	Zack Jordan	103	55	.53	823	Chuck Mosher	18	366	20.3
1951	Merwin Hodel	597	137	4.4	Zack Jordan	123	62	.50	897	Woody Shelton	14	254	18.1
1952	Ralph Curtis	664	139	4.8	Zack Jordan	85	42	.49	567	Roger Williams	22	243	11.0
1953	Emerson Wilson	591	118	5.0	Frank Bernardi	22	11	.50	176	Gary Knafelc	22	451	20.5
1954	John Bayuk	824	145	5.7	Carroll Hardy	25	13	.52	189	Frank Bernardi	8	170	21.3
1955	John Bayuk	460	95	4.8	Dick Hyson	36	15	.42	358	Frank Clarke	13	407	31.3
1956	John Bayuk	659	127	5.2	Boyd Dowler	26	13	.50	136	Frank Clarke	7	124	17.7
1957	Bob Stransky	1,097	183	6.0	Bob Stransky	32	18	.56	290	Boyd Dowler	26	380	14.6
1958	Howard Cook	625	120	5.2	Boyd Dowler	77	35	.45	320	Boyd Dowler	10	154	15.4
1959	Dave Rife	275	96	2.9	Gale Weidner	207	100	.48	1,200	Gary Henson	11	201	18.3
1960	Chuck Weiss	391	108	3.6	Gale Weidner	111	45	.41	732	Jerry Hillebrand	11	218	19.8
1961	Ted Woods	525	107	4.9	Gale Weidner	162	73	.45	1,101	Jerry Hillebrand	17	282	16.6
1962	Bill Harris	582	157	3.7	Frank Cesarek	167	78	.47	786	John McGuire	36	376	10.4
1963	Noble Milton	487	117	4.2	Frank Cesarek	95	45	.47	612	Bill Symons	14	197	14.1
1964	Robert Lee	310	89	3.5	Bernie McCall	87	48	.55	569	Bill Symons	27	267	9.9
1965	William Harris	680	142	4.8	Bernie McCall	181	84	.46	1,175	George Lewark	18	278	15.4
1966	Wilmer Cooks	594	159	3.7	Bernie McCall	93	45	.48	588	Larry Plantz	22	354	16.1
1967	Bobby Anderson	625	166	3.8	Bob Anderson	110	63	.57	733	Monte Huber	45	486	10.8
1968	Bobby Anderson	788	183	4.3	Bob Anderson	222	112	.50	1,341	Monte Huber	38	462	12.2
1969	Bobby Anderson	954	219	4.4	Paul Arendt	75	34	.45	563	Monte Huber	28	488	17.4
1970	Ward Walsh	679	117	5.8	Jim Bratten	151	64	.42	771	Cliff Branch	23	335	14.6
1971	Charlie Davis	1,386	219	6.3	Ken Johnson	163	64	.39	1,126	Willie Nichols	16	316	19.8
1972	Charlie Davis	926	201	4.6	Ken Johnson	182	83	.46	1,044	J.V. Cain	30	407	13.6
1973	Charlie Davis	646	118	5.5	Clyde Crutchmer	89	50	.56	722	J.V. Cain	23	293	12.7
1974	Billy Waddy	765	157	4.9	David Williams	139	73	.53	899	Dave Logan	21	273	13.0
1975	Terry Kunz	882	160	5.5	David Williams	172	103	.60	1,282	Dave Logan	24	392	16.3
1976	Tony Reed	1,210	264	4.6	Jeff Knapple	136	60	.44	904	Tony Reed	19	128	6.7
1977	James Mayberry	1,299	246	5.3	Jeff Knapple	180	79	.44	1,203	Bob Niziolek	29	416	14.3
1978	James Mayberry	920	230	4.0	Bill Solomon	158	77	.49	944	Greg Howard	28	374	13.4
1979	Lance Olander	440	88	5.0	Bill Solomon	184	91	.49	1,174	Kazell Pugh	23	375	16.3
1980	Lance Olander	611	130	4.7	Scott Kingdom	113	45	.40	619	Ricky Ward	25	428	17.1
1981	Lee Rouson	656	159	4.1	Randy Essington	197	95	.48	1,199	Dave Hestera	21	202	9.6
1982	Richard Johnson	584	117	5.0	Randy Essington	219	109	.50	1,121	Dave Hestera	41	489	11.9
1983	Lee Rouson	494	120	4.1	Steve Vogel	236	110	.47	1,385	Loy Alexander	39	557	14.3
1984	Lee Rouson	725	199	3.6	Steve Vogel	224	100	.45	1,432	Jon Embree	51	680	13.3
1985	Anthony Weatherspoon	569	140	4.1	Mark Hatcher	51	16	.31	325	Jon Embree	9	140	15.6
1986	O.C. Oliver	668	136	5.0	Mark Hatcher	66	28	.42	493	Lance Carl	9	171	19.0
1987	Sal Aunese	612	122	5.0	Sal Aunese	51	23	.45	522	Lance Carl	15	270	18.0
1988	Eric Bieniemy	1,243	219	5.7	Sal Aunese	106	44	.42	1,004	Jeff Campbell	15	466	31.1
1989	J.J. Flannigan	1,187	164	7.2	Darian Hagan	85	48	.56	1,002	Mike Pritchard	12	292	24.3
1990	Eric Bieniemy	1,628	288	5.7	Darian Hagan	163	75	.46	1,538	Mike Pritchard	28	733	26.2
1991	Lamont Warren	830	157	5.3	Darian Hagan	170	88	.52	1,228	Sean Brown	24	300	12.5
1992	Lamont Warren	512	148	3.5	Kordell Stewart	252	151	.60	2,109	Michael Westbrook	76	1,060	13.9
1993	Lamont Warren	900	183	4.9	Kordell Stewart	294	157	.53	2,299	Charles Johnson	57	1,082	19.0
1994	Rashaan Salaam	2,055	298	6.9	Kordell Stewart	237	147	.62	2,071	Michael Westbrook	36	689	19.1
1995	Herchell Troutman	826	171	4.8	John Hessler	266	154	.58	2,136	Rae Carruth	53	1,008	19.0
1996	Herchell Troutman	804	193	4.2	Koy Detmer	363	208	.57	3,156	Rae Carruth	54	1,116	20.7
1997	Herchell Troutman	613	155	4.0	John Hessler	338	181	.54	2,478	Phil Savoy	43	659	15.3
1998	Marlon Barnes	572	121	4.7	Mike Moschetti	276	162	.59	2,104	Darrin Chiaverini	52	630	12.1
1999	Cortlen Johnson	835	172	4.9	Mike Moschetti	331	204	.62	2,693	Javon Green	40	663	16.6
2000	Cortlen Johnson	622	144	4.3	Craig Ochs	245	145	.59	1,778	Javon Green	48	699	14.6
2001	Chris Brown	946	190	5.0	Bobby Pesavento	139	85	.61	1,234	Daniel Graham	51	753	14.8
2002	Chris Brown	1,841	303	6.1	Robert Hodge	243	131	.54	1,542	Derek McCoy	41	643	15.7
2003	Brian Calhoun	810	195	4.2	Joel Klatt	358	233	.65	2,614	D.J. Hackett	78	1,013	13.0
2004	Bobby Purify	1,017	209	4.9	Joel Klatt	334	192	.58	2,065	Evan Judge	29	336	11.6

Receiving leaders by receptions

COLORADO ALL-TIME SCORES

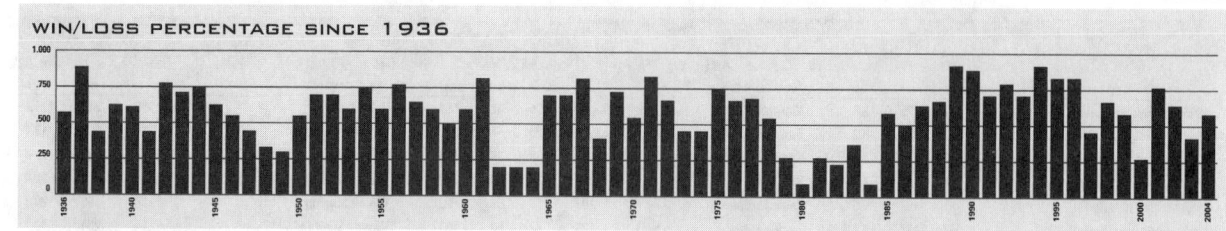

WIN/LOSS PERCENTAGE SINCE 1936

NO HEAD COACH

1890   0-4-0
N15	at Denver AC	0	20
N22	Colorado Mines	0	103
N29	at Colorado College	0	44
D13	Colorado Mines	4	50

1891   1-4-0
O24	Colorado Mines	6	10
O31	at Denver AC	0	42
N3	Denver AC	0	44
N7	at Colorado Mines	0	6
N26	at Colorado College	24	4

1892   2-2-0
O22 ●	Denver	46	0
N8 ●	Denver	46	0
N13 ●	Colorado Mines	10	16
N19 ●	at Denver AC	6	42

1893   3-3-0
F10 ●	at Colorado State	70	6
S30 ●	at Denver AC	0	14
O7 ●	Colorado State	44	6
O14 ●	at Boulder HS	4	0
N7 ●	at Colorado Mines	10	24
N18 ●	at Denver AC	4	32

HARRY HELLER
1894 (.889)   8-1

1894   8-1-0
O6 ●	at East Denver H.S.	46	0
O13 ●	at Denver AC	12	4
O20 ●	Denver	44	0
O27 ●	Colorado State	67	0
O31 ●	at West Denver H.S.	26	4
N3 ●	at Denver	49	4
N6 ●	at Colorado Mines	20	0
N13 ●	at Denver AC	6	20
N20 ●	Colorado Mines	18	0

FRED FOLSOM
1895-99, 1901-02, '08-15
77-23-2 (.765)

1895   5-1-0
O13 ●	at Denver H.S.	36	0
O26 ●	Denver Wheel Club	32	0
N5 ●	Denver	28	0
N9 ●	Denver AC	10	22
N16 ●	at Colorado College	38	10
N28 ●	Colorado Mines	14	0

1896   5-0-0
O4 ●	Denver Manual H.S.	42	0
O11 ●	East Denver H.S.	41	0
O17 ●	at Colorado Mines	30	0
O22 ●	Colorado College	50	0
N6 ●	at Denver AC	8	6

1897   7-1-0
S22 ●	East Denver H.S.	22	0
S29 ●	West Denver H.S.	52	0
O5 ●	Denver Manual H.S.	18	0
O11 ●	Littleton AC	30	0
O17 ●	at Colorado College	8	0
O25 ●	at Denver Wheel Club	22	0
N1 ●	Colorado Mines	36	2
N6 ●	at Denver AC	0	8

1898   4-4-0
S21 ●	North Denver H.S.	41	0
S28 ●	East Denver H.S.	42	0
O4 ●	at Colorado College	0	22
O11 ●	at Denver AC	5	11
O18 ●	Denver Wheel Club	29	0
O25 ●	at Colorado Mines	0	12
N17 ●	Nebraska	10	23
N24 ●	at Denver AC	23	5

1899   7-2-0
S20 ●	at Boulder HS	6	0
S27 ●	Denver Manual H.S.	46	0
O3 ●	West Denver H.S.	21	0
O10 ●	at East Denver H.S.	33	0
O15 ●	at Colorado State	63	0
O23 ●	at Denver Wheel Club	5	0
O31 ●	Colorado Mines	25	6
N7 ●	at Colorado College	5	17
N30 ●	at Denver AC	6	11

1900-1937
ROCKY MOUNTAIN

T.C. MORTIMER
1900 (.600)   1-2

1900   6-4-0 (1-2-0)
S18 ●	at Denver Manual HS	29	0
S25 ●	at West Denver H.S.	18	0
O1 ●	State Prep School	23	5
O8 ●	at No. Colorado	41	0
O15 ●	Colorado State	29	0
O22 ●	at Denver Wheel Club	0	11
O29 ●	Colorado Mines	0	11
N5 ●	Wyoming	10	6
N12 ●	at Colorado College	0	21
N19 ●	Denver AC	0	24

FRED FOLSOM

1901   5-1-1 (2-0-0)
S17 ●	Boulder HS	5	0
S24 ●	Alumni	6	0
S30 =	at Boulder HS	0	0
O8 ●	Denver Wheel Club	11	0
O15 ●	at Colorado College	11	2
O22 ●	at Colorado Mines	23	0
O29 ●	at Denver AC	0	29

1902   5-1-0 (4-0-0)
S27 ●	Boulder HS	12	0
O4 ●	Nebraska	0	10
O11 ●	Denver	24	0
O18 ●	Colorado State	11	6
O25 ●	at Colorado College	12	6
N3 ●	Colorado Mines	28	0

DAVE CROPP
1903-04 (.763)   14-4-1

1903   8-2-0 (6-0-0)
S26 ●	at Boulder HS	40	0
O3 ●	Utah	22	0
O10 ●	at Colorado State	5	0
O17 ●	Kansas	11	12
O24 ●	at Nebraska	0	31
O31 ●	at Colorado Mines	17	0
N7 ●	at Denver	10	0
N14 ●	Colorado College	31	6
N21 ●	Colorado Mines	23	5
N26 ●	Missouri Rolla	38	0

1904   6-2-1 (4-1-0)
S24 ●	Alumni	6	0
O1 ●	at Utah	32	6
O8 ●	Nebraska	6	0
O15 =	at Kansas	6	6
O29 ●	at Colorado College	23	0
N5 ●	at Colorado Mines	10	13
N12 ●	at Denver	57	0
N19 ●	Colorado State	46	0
N24 ●	at Stanford	0	33

W.S. KIENHOLZ
1905 (.889)   8-1

1905   8-1-0 (2-0-0)
S30 ●	at North Denver H.S.	28	0
O7 ●	at Regis Coll.	109	0
O14 ●	Alumni	23	0
O21 ●	Wyoming	69	0
O28 ●	Kansas *Den*	15	0
N4 ●	Utah	46	5
N11 ●	at Nebraska	0	18
N18 ●	Washburn	30	5
N30 ●	Haskell *Den*	39	0

FRANK CASTLEMAN
1906-07 (.529)   7-6-4

1906   2-3-4 (1-2-2)
S29 ●	Boulder HS	22	0
O6 =	Alumni	0	0
O13 ●	Denver	6	0
O20 =	at Washburn	0	0
O27 ●	at Kansas	0	16
N3 ●	Colorado College	0	6
N10 ●	at Colorado State	0	0
N17 ●	at Utah	0	10
N22 =	Colorado Mines	0	0

1907   5-3-0 (3-2-0)
O1 ●	Boulder HS	40	0
O5 ●	Denver	29	4
O12 ●	Alumni	5	0
O19 ●	Colorado State	17	13
O26 ●	at Nebraska	8	22
N9 ●	at Colorado College	0	10
N16 ●	Utah	24	10
N21 ●	at Colorado Mines	4	5

FRED FOLSOM

1908   5-2-0 (3-2-0)
O4 ●	at Longmont H.S.	6	0
O11 ●	at Boulder HS	29	0
O24 ●	at Colorado State	8	0
N7 ●	Colorado College	14	0
N14 ●	at Utah	14	21
N21 ●	Denver	10	14
N26 ●	Colorado Mines	15	0

1909   6-0-0 (3-0-0)
O2 ●	Boulder HS	3	0
O9 ●	Alumni	3	0
O23 ●	Colorado State	57	0
N6 ●	New Mexico	53	0
N13 ●	at Colorado College	9	0
N25 ●	at Colorado Mines	16	0

1910   6-0-0 (4-0-0)
O1 ●	Boulder HS	20	0
O8 ●	Alumni	11	0
O22 ●	Wyoming	14	3 *
O29 ●	Utah	11	0
N5 ●	at Colorado State	44	0
N24 ●	at Colorado Mines	19	0

1911   6-0-0 (5-0-0)
O14 ●	Alumni	11	0
O28 ●	Wyoming	18	3
N4 ●	Colorado College	8	2
N11 ●	Colorado State	31	0
N18 ●	at Utah	9	0
N30 ●	at Colorado Mines	11	0

1912   6-3-0 (4-2-0)
S28 ●	Alumni	20	0
O5 ●	Utah State	16	3
O12 ●	at Colorado State	0	21
O26 ●	Wyoming	75	0
N2 ●	at Colorado College	10	7
N9 ●	Utah *Den*	3	0
N16 ●	at Kansas State	6	14
N23 ●	Colorado Mines	3	24
N28 ●	Oklahoma *Den*	14	12

1913   5-1-1 (4-0-1)
O4 ●	at Wyoming	7	0
O11 ●	Alumni	6	0
O25 ●	Colorado State	16	7
N1 =	Colorado College	0	0
N8 ●	at Utah	30	12
N15 ●	at Colorado Mines	20	0
N27 ●	at Oklahoma	3	14

1914   5-1-0 (4-1-0)
O3 ●	Alumni	27	3
O10 ●	at Colorado Mines	2	6
O17 ●	at Colorado State	33	6
O31 ●	at Colorado College	10	7
N7 ●	Utah	33	0
N26 ●	at Denver	6	0

1915   1-6-0 (1-5-0)
O2 ●	Wyoming	30	0
O9 ●	Colorado State	6	23
O23 ●	Colorado College	0	44
O30 ●	at Utah	3	35
N13 ●	at Colorado Mines	6	13
N20 ●	at Denver	0	7
N26 ●	at Washington	0	46

MELBOURNE "BOB" EVANS
1916-17 (.500)   7-7-1

1916   1-5-1 (1-5-0)
S30 =	Alumni	0	0
O7 =	at Wyoming	16	10
O21 ●	Denver	0	7
O28 ●	at Utah	0	28
N11 ●	at Colorado College	0	58
N18 ●	at Colorado Mines	10	27
N30 ●	Colorado State	14	32

1917   6-2-0 (4-2-0)
S22 ●	Alumni	6	0
O6 ●	at No. Colorado	54	0
O13 ●	at Colorado State	6	0
O20 ●	at Denver	0	7
O27 ●	at Colorado Mines	12	0
N3 ●	Colorado College	18	17
N10 ●	Utah	18	9
N17 ●	at Utah State	0	23

JOE MILLS
1918-19 (.409)   4-6-1

1918   2-3-0 (0-3-0)
N16 ●	No. Colorado	0	9
N20 ●	Lieutenants	20	6
N23 ●	at Denver	0	6
N28 ●	Colorado State	16	13
D7 ●	at Colorado College	7	8

1919   2-3-1 (2-3-1)
O11 ●	at Colorado State	7	49
O18 ●	at Denver	26	7
O25 =	Colorado College	14	14
N8 ●	at Utah	0	7
N15 ●	Utah State	7	19
N29 ●	Colorado Mines	33	0

MYRON WITHAM
1920-31 (.693)   63-26-7

1920   4-1-2 (3-1-2)
O16 ●	at Denver	31	0
O23 ●	at Wyoming	7	0
O31 ●	Colorado College	7	7
N6 ●	Utah	0	7
N13 ●	at Colorado Mines	7	0
N20 =	Colorado State	7	7
N25 ●	Oklahoma State *OkC*	40	7

1921 4-1-1 (4-0-1)

O22	● |	Denver	10	7
O29		at Chicago	0	35
N5	● |	Colorado Coll.	35	14
N12	= |	at Utah	0	0
N19	● |	at Colorado State	10	0
N24	● |	Colorado Mines	10	7

1922 4-4-0 (2-3-0)

O7	●	at Regis Coll.	14	0
O14	●	New Mexico	3	0
O21	|	Utah	0	3
O29	|	at Denver	0	16
N4	● |	Colorado State	7	0
N11	|	at Colorado College	10	21
N18		at Kansas	6	39
N23	● |	at Colorado Mines	16	0

1923 9-0-0 (8-0-0)

O7	● |	Brigham Young	41	0
O14	●	Western St.	51	0
O21	● |	No. Colorado	60	0
O27	● |	at Denver	21	7
N3	● |	Colorado College	17	7
N10	● |	at Colorado Mines	47	0
N17	● |	at Utah	17	7
N24	● |	Wyoming	20	3
N28	● |	at Colorado State	6	3

1924 8-1-1 (5-0-1)

O4	●	Western St.	31	0
O11	●	Regis Coll.	39	0
O18	● |	at Colorado College	26	0
O25	● |	at Wyoming	21	0
N1	● |	Utah	3	0
N8	● |	Colorado Mines	38	0
N15	= |	at Denver	0	0
N22	● |	Colorado State	36	0
D25	●	Hawaii All Stars	43	0
J1		at Hawaii	0	13

1925 6-3-0 (5-2-0)

S26		Chadron St.	0	3
O3	● |	Montana St.	23	3
O7	● |	at Creighton	14	6
O24	|	at Utah	7	12
O31	● |	at Colorado Mines	14	3
N7	● |	Colorado College	23	6
N14	|	at Colorado State	0	12
N21	● |	Western St.	34	0
N26	● |	at Denver	41	0

1926 3-5-1 (2-5-1)

O2	●	Chadron St.	25	0
O9	|	Montana St.	3	6
O16	= |	Wyoming	13	13
O23	|	Utah	3	37
O30	|	at Colorado College	0	21
N6	● |	at Colorado Mines	12	0
N13	|	Colorado State	0	3
N20	● |	No. Colorado	12	3
N25	|	at Denver	9	20

1927 4-5-0 (4-4-0)

O1	● |	Western St.	25	6
O8	|	at Montana St.	6	12
O15	● |	No. Colorado	43	0
O22	|	at Utah	13	20
O29	● |	Colorado Mines	28	18
N5	● |	Colorado College	7	6
N12		at Southern Cal	7	46
N19	|	at Colorado State	7	39
N24	|	at Denver	0	48

1928 5-1-0 (5-1-0)

O13	● |	at No. Colorado	21	6
O20	● |	Colorado Mines	39	0
O27	|	Utah	6	25
N10	● |	Colorado State	13	7
N17	● |	at Colorado College	24	19
N29	● |	at Denver	7	0

1929 5-1-1 (4-1-1)

O5	●	Regis Coll.	27	13
O12	● |	No. Colorado	19	0
O19	|	at Utah	0	40
N2	= |	Denver	0	0
N9	● |	at Colorado Mines	13	9
N16	● |	at Colorado State	6	0
N23	● |	Colorado College	13	7

1930 6-1-1 (5-1-1)

O4	●	at Missouri	9	0
O11	= |	at Utah State	0	0
O18	● |	Colorado Mines	36	7
O25	● |	Colorado State	7	0
N1	● |	at Colorado College	14	13
N8	● |	at No. Colorado	27	7
N15	|	Utah	0	34
N27	● |	at Denver	27	7

1931 5-3-0 (3-2-0)

S26		Oregon State PORT	0	16
O10	● |	Colorado Mines	27	0
O17	●	Missouri	9	7
O24	|	at Colorado State	6	19
N7	● |	at Denver	25	6
N14	|	at Utah	0	32
N21	● |	Colorado College	17	7
N26	●	at Arizona	27	7

WILLIAM SAUNDERS
1932-34 (.667) 15-7-2

1932 2-4-0 (2-4-0)

O1	● |	at Colorado Mines	31	0
O8	● |	Utah State	26	7
O22	|	Colorado State	6	7
N5	|	Utah	0	14
N12	|	at Colorado College	0	12
N24	|	at Denver	0	6

1933 7-2-0 (5-2-0)

S30	●	Chadron St.	19	0
O6	●	at Oklahoma State	6	0
O14	● |	Colorado Mines	42	0
O21	|	at Colorado State	6	19
O28	● |	Wyoming	40	12
N4	● |	Colorado College	26	0
N11	|	at Utah	6	13
N18	● |	No. Colorado	24	0
N30	● |	at Denver	14	7

1934 6-1-2 (6-1-0)

S29	=	at Kansas	0	0
O6	=	Missouri	0	0
O12	|	at No. Colorado	7	13
O20	● |	Brigham Young UNK	48	6
O27	● |	Colorado State	27	9
N3	● |	at Colorado Mines	40	6
N10	● |	Utah	7	6
N17	● |	at Colorado College	31	0
N29	● |	at Denver	7	0

BUNNIE OAKES
1935-39 (.622) 25-15-1

1935 5-4-0 (5-1-0)

S28		at Oklahoma	0	3
O12		at Missouri	6	20
O19	● |	Colorado Mines	58	0
O26	● |	Colorado State	19	6
N2	● |	Colorado College	23	0
N9	● |	at Utah	14	0
N16		Kansas	6	12
N23	|	Wyoming	0	6
N28	● |	at Denver	14	0

1936 4-3-0 (4-2-0)

O3		Oklahoma	0	8
O17	● |	Colorado Mines	33	0
O24	● |	at Colorado State	9	7
O31	● |	at Colorado College	7	0
N7	● |	Utah	31	7
N14	|	at Utah State	13	14
N26	|	at Denver	6	7

1937 8-1-0 (7-0-0)

O2	●	Missouri	14	6
O9	● |	Utah State	33	0
O16	● |	Brigham Young	14	0
O23	● |	Colorado State	47	0
O30	● |	Colorado Mines	54	0
N6	● |	at Utah	17	7
N13	● |	Colorado College	35	6
N25	● |	at Denver	34	7
COTTON BOWL				
J1		Rice	14	28

1938-1947
MOUNTAIN STATES

1938 3-4-1 (3-2-1)

O1		at Missouri	7	14
O8	|	at Utah State	0	20
O15		George Washington	0	13
O22	● |	at Colorado State	31	6
O29	● |	Wyoming	20	6
N5	= |	Utah	0	0
N12	● |	Brigham Young	8	0
N24	|	at Denver	12	19

1939 5-3-0 (5-1-0)

S30		at Missouri	0	30
O7	|	Utah State	6	16
O14		at Kansas State	0	20
O21	● |	Colorado State	13	0
O28	● |	at Wyoming	27	7
N4	● |	at Utah	21	14
N18	● |	at Brigham Young	12	6
N30	● |	Denver	27	17

FRANK POTTS
1940, '44-45 (.660) 16-8-1

1940 5-3-1 (4-1-1)

S28		at Texas	7	39
O5	●	Kansas State	7	6
O12	● |	at Utah State	26	0
O19	● |	at Colorado State	33	14
O26	● |	Wyoming	62	0
N2	|	Utah	13	21
N9		Missouri	6	21
N16	● |	Brigham Young	25	2
N21	= |	at Denver	3	3

JIM YEAGER
1941-43, '46-47 (.581) 24-17-2

1941 3-4-1 (3-2-1)

S27		Texas	6	34
O4		at Missouri	6	21
O11	● |	Utah State	13	7
O18	● |	Colorado State	26	13
O25	● |	Wyoming	27	0
N1	|	at Utah	6	46
N15	= |	at Brigham Young	13	13
N20	|	at Denver	0	27

1942 7-2-0 (5-1-0)

S26	●	Colorado Mines	54	0
O3		at Missouri	13	26
O9	● |	Utah State	31	14
O17	●	New Mexico	12	0
O24	● |	at Colorado State	34	7
O31	● |	Wyoming	28	7
N7	|	Utah	0	13
N14	● |	Brigham Young	48	0
N26	● |	at Denver	31	6

1943 5-2-0 (2-0-0)

S25	●	Fort Warren	38	0
O2	●	Lowry AFB	19	6
O9	● |	Utah	35	0
O16	●	Salt Lake AFB	14	0
O23		Colorado College	6	16
N6	● |	at Utah	22	19
N20		at Colorado College	0	6

FRANK POTTS

1944 6-2-0 (2-0-0)

S23		Fort Warren	6	7
S30		Second Air Force	6	33
O14	● |	at Utah	26	0
O21	●	Colorado College	28	0
N4	●	New Mexico PUE	39	0
N11	●	Peru St.	40	12
N18	●	at Colorado College	40	6
N23	● |	at Denver	16	14

1945 5-3-0 (3-1-0)

S22		Fort Warren	0	6
S29	●	at Colorado College	13	0
O6	● |	Utah	18	13
O13	● |	at Colorado State	21	6
O20	●	Colorado College	31	0
N3		at New Mexico	6	12
N10	● |	Utah State	14	7
N22	|	at Denver	8	14

JIM YEAGER

1946 5-4-1 (3-2-1)

S21	●	Iowa State	13	7
S28		at Texas	0	76
O5	● |	Utah State	6	0
O12	● |	at Wyoming	20	0
O19	|	at Brigham Young	7	10
O26	●	New Mexico	14	13
N2	|	at Utah	0	7
N9		at Missouri	0	21
N16	= |	Denver	13	13
N28	● |	Colorado State	18	0

1947 4-5-0 (3-3-0)

S27	●	at Iowa State	7	0
O4		at Army	0	47
O11		Missouri	0	21
O18	● |	Brigham Young	9	7
O25	● |	at Colorado State	14	7
N1	|	Utah	7	13
N8	|	at Utah State	12	35
N15	● |	Wyoming	21	6
N27	|	at Denver	20	26

1948-1995
BIG 8

DALLAS WARD
1948-58 (.600) 63-41-6

1948 3-6-0 (2-3-0)

S25		New Mexico	6	9
O2	|	at Kansas	7	40
O9	● |	Nebraska	19	6
O16	|	at Iowa State	7	18
O23	● |	Kansas State	51	7
O30		at Utah	12	14
N6	●	Utah State	28	14
N13	|	at Missouri	13	27
N20		Colorado State	25	29

1949 3-7-0 (1-4-0)

S24	● |	Kansas	13	12
O1	|	at Kansas State	13	27
O8	|	Iowa State	6	13
O15		at Oregon	14	42
O22	●	at Utah State	20	7
O29	●	Utah	14	7
N5	|	Missouri	13	20
N12		at New Mexico	15	17
N19	|	at Nebraska	14	25
N26		Colorado State	7	14

1950 5-4-1 (2-4-0)

S23	|	at Iowa State	7	14
S30	● |	Kansas State	34	6
O7	|	at Kansas	21	27
O14	● |	Nebraska	28	19
O21	●	Arizona	28	25
O28	=	at Utah	20	20
N4	|	Oklahoma	18	27
N11	|	at Missouri	19	21
N18	●	Oregon	21	7
N25	●	at Colorado State	31	6

1951 7-3-0 (5-1-0)

S22	●	Colorado State	28	13
S29		at Northwestern	14	35
O6	● |	Kansas	35	27
O13	● |	Missouri	34	13
O20	● |	at Kansas State	20	7
O27	|	at Oklahoma	14	55
N3	● |	Iowa State	47	20
N10	●	Utah	54	0
N17	● |	at Nebraska	36	14
N24		at Michigan St.	7	45

1952 6-2-2 (2-2-2)

S20	●	San Jose State	20	14
S27	= |	Oklahoma	21	21
O4	|	at Kansas	12	21
O11	●	at Arizona	34	19
O18	● |	at Iowa State	21	12
O25	= |	Nebraska	16	16
N1	●	at Utah	20	14
N8	|	at Missouri	7	27
N15	● |	Kansas State	34	14
N29	●	Colorado State	61	0

1953 6-4-0 (2-4-0)

S19	●	at Washington	21	20
S26	●	Arizona	20	14
O3	|	Missouri	16	27
O10	|	Kansas	21	27
O17	|	at Kansas State	14	28
O24	|	at Oklahoma	20	27
O31	● |	Iowa State	41	34
N7	●	Utah	21	0
N14	● |	at Nebraska	14	10
N28	●	at Colorado State	13	7

1954 7-2-1 (3-2-1)

S18	●	Drake	61	0
S25	●	Colorado State	46	0
O2	● |	at Kansas	27	0
O9	●	at Arizona	40	18
O16	● |	at Iowa State	20	0
O23	|	Nebraska	6	20
O30	|	Oklahoma	6	13
N6	= |	at Missouri	19	19
N13	●	at Utah	20	7
N20	● |	Kansas State	38	14

1955 6-4-0 (3-3-0)

S24	●	Arizona	14	0
O1	●	Kansas	12	0
O8		at Oregon	13	6
O15	●	at Kansas State	34	13
O22		at Oklahoma	21	56
O29	●	Missouri	12	20
N5	●	Utah	37	7
N12		at Nebraska	20	37
N19	●	Iowa State	40	0
N26		at Colorado State	0	10

1956 8-2-1 (4-1-1)

S22		Oregon	0	35
S29	●	Kansas State	34	0
O6	●	at Kansas	26	25
O13	●	Colorado State	47	7
O20	●	at Iowa State	52	0
O27	●	Nebraska	16	0
N3		Oklahoma	19	27
N10	=	at Missouri	14	14
N17	●	at Utah	21	7
N24	●	at Arizona	38	7
ORANGE BOWL				
J1		Clemson	27	21

1957 6-3-1 (3-3-0)

S21	=	at Washington	6	6
S28	●	Utah	30	24
O5		Kansas	34	35
O12	●	Arizona	34	14
O19	●	at Kansas State	42	14
O26		at Oklahoma	13	14
N2		Missouri	6	9
N9	●	at Colorado State	20	0
N16	●	at Nebraska	27	0
N23	●	Iowa State	38	21

1958 6-4-0 (4-2-0)

S27		Kansas State	13	3
O4	●	at Kansas	31	0
O11	●	at Arizona	65	12
O18	●	at Iowa State	20	0
O25	●	Nebraska	27	16
N1		Oklahoma	7	23
N8		at Missouri	9	33
N15	●	at Utah	7	0
N22		Colorado State	14	15
N29		Air Force	14	20

1959 5-5-0 (3-3-0)

S19		Washington	12	21
S26		Baylor	7	15
O3		at Oklahoma	12	42
O10	●	at Kansas State	20	17
O17		Iowa State	0	27
O24	●	at Arizona	18	0
O31	●	Missouri	21	20
N7	●	Kansas	27	14
N14		at Nebraska	12	14
N28	●	Air Force	15	7

1960 6-4-0 (5-2-0)

S24		at Baylor	0	26
O1	●	Kansas State	27	7
O8	●	Arizona	35	16
O15	●	at Iowa State	21	6
O22	●	Nebraska	19	6
O29	●	Oklahoma	7	0
N5		at Missouri	6	16
N12		at Kansas	6	34 †
N19	●	at Oklahoma St.	13	6
N26		Air Force	6	16

1961 9-2-0 (7-0-0)

S30	●	Oklahoma St.	24	0
O7	●	Kansas	20	19
O13	●	at Miami, Fla.	9	7
O21	●	at Kansas State	13	0
O28	●	at Oklahoma	22	14
N4	●	Missouri	7	6
N11		Utah	12	21
N18	●	at Nebraska	7	0
N25	●	Iowa State	34	0
D2	●	at Air Force	29	12
ORANGE BOWL				
J1		LSU	7	25

1962 2-8-0 (1-6-0)

S22		at Utah	21	37
S29	●	Kansas State	6	0
O6		at Kansas	8	35
O13		at Oklahoma St.	16	36
O20		at Iowa State	19	57
O27		Nebraska	6	31
N3		Oklahoma	0	62
N10		at Missouri	0	57
N17		at Texas Tech	12	21
N24	●	Air Force	34	10

1963 2-8-0 (2-5-0)

S21		Southern Cal	0	14
S28		Oregon State _PORT_	6	41
O5	●	at Kansas State	21	7
O12	●	Oklahoma St.	25	0
O19		Iowa State	7	19
O26		at Nebraska	6	41
N2		at Oklahoma	0	35
N9		Missouri	7	28
N16		Kansas	14	43
D7		at Air Force	14	17

1964 2-8-0 (1-6-0)

S18		at Southern Cal	0	21
S26		Oregon State	7	14
O3		Kansas State	14	16
O10		at Oklahoma St.	10	14
O17	●	at Iowa State	14	7
O24		Nebraska	3	21
O31		Oklahoma	11	14
N7		at Missouri	7	16
N14		at Kansas	7	10
N21	●	Air Force	28	23

1965 6-2-2 (4-2-1)

S18		at Wisconsin	0	0
S25		Fresno State	10	7
O2	●	at Kansas State	36	0
O9	●	Oklahoma St.	34	11
O16	=	Iowa State	10	10
O23		at Nebraska	13	38
O30	●	at Oklahoma	13	0
N6		Missouri	7	20
N13	●	Kansas	21	14
N20	●	at Air Force	19	6

1966 7-3-0 (5-2-0)

S17		Miami, Fla.	3	24
S24	●	at Baylor	13	7
O1	●	Kansas State	10	0
O8	●	at Oklahoma St.	10	11
O15	●	at Iowa State	41	21
O22		Nebraska	19	21
O29	●	Oklahoma	24	21
N5	●	at Missouri	26	0
N12	●	at Kansas	35	18
N19	●	Air Force	10	9

1967 9-2-0 (5-2-0)

S16	●	Baylor	27	7
S23	●	at Oregon	17	13
O7	●	Iowa State	34	0
O14	●	Missouri	23	9
O21	●	at Nebraska	21	16
O28		Oklahoma St.	7	10
N4		at Oklahoma	0	23
N11	●	Kansas	12	8
N18	●	at Kansas State	40	6
N25	●	at Air Force	33	0
BLUEBONNET BOWL				
D23	●	Miami, Fla.	31	21

1968 4-6-0 (3-4-0)

S21		Oregon	28	7
S28		at California	0	10
O5	●	at Iowa State	28	18
O12		at Missouri	14	27
O19		Kansas State	37	14
O26	●	Oklahoma	41	27
N2		at Kansas	14	27
N9		at Oklahoma St.	17	34
N16		Nebraska	6	22
N23		Air Force	35	58

1969 8-3-0 (5-2-0)

S20	●	Tulsa	35	14
S27		at Penn State	3	27
O4	●	Indiana	30	7
O11	●	at Iowa State	14	0
O18		at Oklahoma	30	42
O25	●	Missouri	31	24
N1		at Nebraska	7	20
N8	●	at Kansas	17	14
N15	●	Oklahoma St.	17	14
N22	●	Kansas State	45	32
LIBERTY BOWL				
D13	●	Alabama	47	33

1970 6-5-0 (3-4-0)

S19	●	at Indiana	16	9
S26	●	Penn State	41	13
O3		at Kansas State	20	21
O10	●	Iowa State	61	10
O17		Oklahoma	15	23
O24		at Missouri	16	30
O31		Nebraska	13	29
N7	●	Kansas	45	29
N14	●	at Oklahoma St.	30	6
N21	●	at Air Force	49	19
LIBERTY BOWL				
D12		Tulane	3	17

1971 10-2-0 (5-2-0)

S11	●	at LSU	31	21
S18	●	Wyoming	56	13
S25	●	at Ohio State	20	14
O2	●	Kansas State	31	21
O9	●	at Iowa State	24	14
O16		at Oklahoma	17	45
O23	●	Missouri	27	7
O30		at Nebraska	7	31
N6	●	at Kansas	35	14
N13	●	Oklahoma St.	40	6
N20	●	Air Force	53	17
BLUEBONNET BOWL				
D31	●	Houston	29	17

1972 8-4-0 (4-3-0)

S9	●	California	20	10
S16	●	Cincinnati	56	14
S23	●	at Minnesota	38	6
S30		at Oklahoma St.	6	31
O7	●	at Kansas State	38	17
O14	●	Iowa State	34	22
O21	●	Oklahoma	20	14
O28		at Missouri	17	20
N4		Nebraska	10	33
N11	●	Kansas	33	8
N18	●	at Air Force	38	7
GATOR BOWL				
D30		Auburn	3	24

1973 5-6-0 (2-5-0)

S15		at LSU	6	17
S22	●	at Wisconsin	28	25
S29	●	Baylor	52	28
O6	●	at Iowa State	23	16
O13	●	Air Force	38	17
O20		at Oklahoma	7	34
O27	●	Missouri	17	13
N3		at Nebraska	16	28
N10		at Kansas	15	17
N17		Oklahoma St.	24	38
N24		Kansas State	14	17

1974 5-6-0 (3-4-0)

S14		at LSU	14	42
S21		at Michigan	0	31
S28	●	Wisconsin	24	21
O5	●	at Air Force	28	27
O12	●	Iowa State	34	7
O19		Oklahoma	14	49
O26		at Missouri	24	30
N2		Nebraska	15	31
N9	●	Kansas	17	16
N16	●	at Oklahoma St.	37	20
N23		at Kansas State	19	33

1975 9-3-0 (5-2-0)

S13	●	California	34	27
S20	●	Wyoming	27	10
S27	●	Wichita St.	52	0
O4		at Oklahoma	20	21
O10	●	at Miami, Fla.	23	10
O18	●	Missouri	31	20
O25		Nebraska	21	63
N1	●	at Iowa State	28	27
N8	●	Oklahoma State	17	7
N15	●	at Kansas	24	21
N22	●	Kansas State	33	7
BLUEBONNET BOWL				
D27		Texas	21	38

1976 8-4-0 (5-2-0)

S11		at Texas Tech	7	24
S18	●	at Washington	21	7
S25	●	Miami, Fla.	33	3
O2	●	Drake	45	24
O9		Nebraska	12	24
O16	●	at Oklahoma St.	20	10
O23	●	Iowa State	33	14
O30	●	Oklahoma	42	31
N6		at Missouri	7	16
N13	●	Kansas	40	17
N20	●	at Kansas State	35	28
ORANGE BOWL				
J1		Ohio State	10	27

1977 7-3-1 (3-3-1)

S10	●	Stanford	27	21
S17	●	Kent State	42	0
S24	●	New Mexico	42	7
O1	●	at Army	31	0
O8	●	Oklahoma St.	29	13
O15	=	at Kansas	17	17
O22		at Nebraska	15	33
O29		Missouri	14	24
N5	●	at Iowa State	12	7
N12		at Oklahoma	14	52
N19		Kansas State	23	0

1978 6-5-0 (2-5-0)

S9	●	Oregon	24	7
S16	●	Miami, Fla.	17	7
S23	●	San Jose State	22	7
S30	●	Northwestern	55	7
O7	●	Kansas	17	7
O14		at Oklahoma St.	20	24
O21		Nebraska	14	52
O28	●	at Missouri	28	27
N4		Oklahoma	7	28
N11		at Kansas State	10	20
N18		Iowa State	16	20

1979 3-8-0 (2-5-0)

S8		Oregon	19	33
S15		LSU	0	44
S22		Drake	9	13
S29	●	at Indiana	17	16
O6		at Oklahoma	24	49
O20		Missouri	7	13
O27		at Nebraska	10	38
N3		at Iowa State	10	24
N10	●	Oklahoma St.	20	21
N17	●	at Kansas	31	17
N24	●	Kansas State	21	6

1980 1-10-0 (1-6-0)

S13		at UCLA	14	56
S20		at LSU	20	23
S27		Indiana	7	49
O4		Oklahoma	42	82
O11		Drake	22	41
O18		at Missouri	7	45
O25		Nebraska	7	45
N1	●	Iowa State	17	9
N8		at Oklahoma St.	7	42
N15		Kansas	3	42
N22		at Kansas State	14	17

1981 3-8-0 (2-5-0)

S12	●	Texas Tech	45	27
S19		Washington State	10	14
S26		Brigham Young	20	41
O3		at UCLA	7	27
O10		at Nebraska	0	59
O17	●	Oklahoma St.	11	10
O24		at Iowa State	10	17
O31		at Oklahoma	0	49
N7		Missouri	14	30
N14		at Kansas	0	27
N21	●	Kansas State	24	21

BILL McCARTNEY
1982-94 (.624)   93-55-5

1982   2-8-1 (1-5-1)
S11		California	17 31
S18	●	Washington State *Spo*	12 0
S25		Wyoming	10 24
O2		UCLA	6 34
O9		Nebraska	14 40
O16	=	at Oklahoma St.	25 25
O23		Iowa State	14 31
O30		Oklahoma	10 45
N6		at Missouri	14 35
N13	●	Kansas	28 3
N20		at Kansas State	10 33

1983   4-7-0 (2-5-0)
S10		at Michigan State	17 3
S17	●	Colorado State	31 3
S24	●	Oregon State	38 14
O1		Notre Dame	3 27
O8		Missouri	20 59
O15		at Iowa State	10 22
O22		at Nebraska	19 69
O29		Oklahoma St.	14 40
N5	●	at Kansas	34 23
N12		at Oklahoma	28 41
N19	●	Kansas State	38 21

1984   1-10-0 (1-6-0)
S8		Michigan St.	21 24
S15		at Oregon	20 27
S22		at Notre Dame	14 55
S29		UCLA	16 33
O6		at Missouri	7 52
O13	●	Iowa State	23 21
O20		Nebraska	7 24
O27		at Oklahoma St.	14 20
N3		Kansas	27 28
N10		Oklahoma	17 42
N17		at Kansas State	6 38

1985   7-5-0 (4-3-0)
S7	●	Colorado State	23 10
S14	●	Oregon	21 17
S21		Ohio State	13 36
S28	●	at Arizona	14 13
O12	●	Missouri	38 7
O19	●	at Iowa State	40 6
O26		at Nebraska	7 17
N2		Oklahoma St.	11 14
N9	●	at Kansas	14 3
N16		at Oklahoma	0 31
N23	●	Kansas State	30 0
		FREEDOM BOWL	
D30		Washington	17 20

1986   6-6-0 (6-1-0)
S6		Colorado State	7 23
S13		at Oregon	30 32
S20		at Ohio State	10 13
S27		Arizona	21 24
O11	●	at Missouri	17 12
O18	●	Iowa State	31 3
O25	●	Nebraska	20 10
N1	●	at Oklahoma St.	31 14
N8	●	Kansas	17 10
N15		Oklahoma	0 28
N22	●	at Kansas State	49 3
		BLUEBONNET BOWL	
D31		Baylor	9 21

1987   7-4-0 (4-3-0)
S12		Oregon	7 10
S19	●	Stanford	31 17
S26	●	Washington State	26 17
O3		at Colorado State	29 16
O10		at Oklahoma St.	17 42
O17	●	Kansas	35 10
O24		at Oklahoma	6 24
O31	●	at Iowa State	42 10
N7	●	Missouri	27 10
N21	●	at Kansas State	41 0
N28		Nebraska	7 24

1988   8-4-0 (4-3-0)
S10	●	Fresno State	45 3
S17	●	at Iowa	24 21
S24	●	Oregon State	28 21
O1	●	at Colorado State	27 23
O8		Oklahoma St.	21 41
O15	●	at Kansas	21 9
O22		Oklahoma	14 17
O29	●	Iowa State	24 12
N5	●	at Missouri	45 8
N12		at Nebraska	0 7
N19	●	Kansas State	56 14
		FREEDOM BOWL	
D29		Brigham Young	17 20

1989   11-1-0 (7-0-0)
S4		Texas	27 6
S9		Colorado State	45 20
S16		Illinois	38 7
S30		at Washington	45 28
O7	●	Missouri	49 3
O14	●	at Iowa State	52 17
O21	●	Kansas	49 17
O28	●	at Oklahoma	20 3
N4	●	Nebraska	27 21
N11	●	at Oklahoma St.	41 17
N18	●	at Kansas State	59 11
		ORANGE BOWL	
J1		Notre Dame	6 21

1990   11-1-1 (7-0-0)
A26	=	Tennessee *Ana*	31 31
S6		Stanford	21 17
S15		at Illinois	22 23
S22	●	at Texas	29 22
S29		Washington	20 14
O6	●	at Missouri	33 31
O13	●	Iowa State	28 12
O20	●	at Kansas	41 10
O27	●	Oklahoma	32 23
N3	●	at Nebraska	27 12
N10	●	Oklahoma St.	41 22
N17		Kansas State	64 3
		ORANGE BOWL	
J1	●	Notre Dame	10 9

1991   8-3-1 (6-0-1)
S7	●	Wyoming	30 13
S14		Baylor	14 16
S21	●	Minnesota	58 0
S28		at Stanford	21 28
O12	●	Missouri	55 7
O19	●	at Oklahoma	34 17
O26	●	at Kansas State	10 0
N2	=	Nebraska	19 19
N9	●	at Oklahoma St.	16 12
N16	●	Kansas	30 24
N23	●	at Iowa State	17 14
		BLOCKBUSTER BOWL	
D28		Alabama	25 30

1992   9-2-1 (5-1-1)
S5	●	Colorado State	37 17
S12	●	at Baylor	57 38
S19	●	at Minnesota	21 20
S26	●	Iowa	28 12
O8	●	at Missouri	6 0
O17	=	Oklahoma	24 24
O24	●	Kansas State	54 7
O31		at Nebraska	7 52
N7	●	Oklahoma St.	28 0
N14	●	at Kansas	25 18
N21	●	Iowa State	31 10
		FIESTA BOWL	
J1	●	Syracuse	22 26

1993   8-3-1 (5-1-1)
S4	●	Texas	36 14
S11	●	Baylor	45 21
S18		at Stanford	37 41
S25		Miami, Fla.	29 35
O9	●	Missouri	30 18
O16	●	at Oklahoma	27 10
O23	=	at Kansas State	16 16
O30		Nebraska	17 21
N6	●	at Oklahoma St.	31 14
N13	●	Kansas	38 14
N20	●	at Iowa State	21 16
		ALOHA BOWL	
D25	●	Fresno State	41 30

1994   11-1-0 (6-1-0)
S3	●	La. Monroe	48 13
S17	●	Wisconsin	55 17
S24	●	at Michigan	27 26
O1	●	at Texas	34 31
O8	●	at Missouri	38 23
O15	●	Oklahoma	45 7
O22	●	Kansas State	35 21
O29		at Nebraska	7 24
N5	●	Oklahoma St.	17 3
N12	●	at Kansas	51 26
N19	●	Iowa State	41 20
		FIESTA BOWL	
J2	●	Notre Dame	41 24

RICK NEUHEISEL
1995-98 (.702)   33-14

1995   10-2-0 (5-2-0)
S2	●	at Wisconsin	43 7
S9	●	Colorado State	42 14
S16	●	La. Monroe	66 14
S23	●	Texas A&M	29 21
S30	●	at Oklahoma	38 17
O7		Kansas	24 40
O21	●	at Iowa State	50 28
O28		Nebraska	21 44
N4	●	at Oklahoma St.	45 32
N11	●	Missouri	21 0
N18	●	at Kansas State	27 17
		COTTON BOWL	
J1	●	Oregon	38 6

1996-Present
Big 12

1996   10-2 (7-1)
A31		Washington State	37 19
S7		at Colorado State	48 34
S14		Michigan	13 20
S28	●	at Texas A&M	24 10
O12	●	Oklahoma St.	35 13
O19	●	at Kansas	20 7
O26	●	Texas	28 24
N2	●	at Missouri	41 13
N9	●	Iowa State	49 42
N16	●	Kansas State	12 0
N29		at Nebraska	12 17
		HOLIDAY BOWL	
D30	●	Washington	33 21

1997   5-6 (3-5)
S6	●	Colorado State	31 21
S13		at Michigan	3 27
S27	●	Wyoming	20 19
O4		Texas A&M	10 16
O11		at Oklahoma St.	29 33
O18	●	Kansas	42 6
O25	●	at Texas	47 30
N1		Missouri	31 41
N8	●	at Iowa State	43 38
N15		at Kansas State	20 37
N28		Nebraska	24 27

1998   8-4 (4-4)
S5	●	Colorado State *Den*	42 14
S12	●	Fresno State	29 21
S19	●	Utah State	25 6
S26	●	Baylor	18 16
O3	●	at Oklahoma	27 25
O10	●	Kansas State	9 16
O17	●	Texas Tech	19 17
O24	●	at Kansas	17 33
N7		at Missouri	14 38
N14	●	Iowa State	37 8
N27		at Nebraska	14 16
		ALOHA BOWL	
D25	●	Oregon	51 43

GARY BARNETT
1999-Present (.560)   42-33

1999   7-5 (5-3)
S4		Colorado State *Den*	14 41
S11	●	San Jose State	63 35
S18	●	Kansas	51 17
S25		at Washington	24 31
O9	●	Missouri	46 39
O16		at Texas Tech	10 31
O23	●	at Iowa State	16 12
O30	●	Oklahoma	38 24
N6		at Kansas State	14 20
N13	●	at Baylor	37 0
N26		Nebraska	30 33
		INSIGHT.COM BOWL	
D31	●	Boston College	62 28

2000   3-8 (3-5)
S2		Colorado State *Den*	24 28
S9		at Southern Cal	14 17
S16		Washington	14 17
S30		Kansas State	21 44
O7	●	at Texas A&M	26 19
O14		Texas	14 28
O21		at Kansas	15 23
O28	●	Oklahoma St.	37 21
N4	●	at Missouri	28 18
N11		Iowa State	27 35
N24		at Nebraska	32 34

2001   10-3 (7-1)
A26		Fresno State	22 24
S1	●	Colorado State *Den*	41 14
S8	●	San Jose State	51 15
S22	●	Kansas	27 16
O6		at Kansas State	16 6
O13	●	Texas A&M	31 21
O20		at Texas	7 41
O27	●	at Oklahoma St.	22 19
N3	●	Missouri	38 24
N10	●	at Iowa State	40 27
N23		Nebraska	62 36
		BIG 12 CHAMPIONSHIP	
D1	●	Texas *Dal*	39 37
		FIESTA BOWL	
J1		Oregon	16 38

2002   9-5 (7-1)
A31	●	Colorado State *Den*	14 19
S7	●	San Diego State	34 14
S14	●	Southern Cal	3 40
S21	●	at UCLA	31 17
O5	●	Kansas State	35 31
O12	●	at Kansas	53 29
O19	●	Baylor	34 0
O26	●	Texas Tech	37 13
N2		at Oklahoma	11 27
N9	●	at Missouri	42 35
N16	●	Iowa State	41 27
N29	●	at Nebraska	28 13
		BIG 12 CHAMPIONSHIP	
D7		Oklahoma *Hou*	7 29
		ALAMO BOWL	
D28		Wisconsin	28 31

2003   5-7 (3-5)
A30	●	Colorado State *Den*	42 35
S6	●	UCLA	16 14
S13		Washington State	26 47
S20		at Florida State	7 47
O4		at Baylor	30 42
O11	●	Kansas	50 47
O18	●	at Kansas State	20 49
O25		Oklahoma	20 34
N1		at Texas Tech	21 26
N8	●	Missouri	21 16
N15	●	at Iowa State	44 10
N28		Nebraska	22 31

2004   8-5 (4-4)
S4		Colorado State	27 24
S11	●	Washington State *Sea*	20 12
S18	●	North Texas	52 21
O2		at Missouri	9 17
O9		Oklahoma State	14 42
O16	●	Iowa State	19 14
O23		at Texas A&M	26 29
O30		Texas	7 31
N6	●	at Kansas	30 21
N13	●	Kansas State	38 31
N26	●	at Nebraska	26 20
		BIG 12 CHAMPIONSHIP	
D4		Oklahoma *KC*	3 42
		HOUSTON BOWL	
D29	●	Texas-El Paso	33 28

THE SCHOOLS

COLORADO STATE

BY STU DURANDO

BACK IN THE DAY, WHEN THE SCHOOL was still known as Colorado A&M, the Aggies enjoyed decades of solid, low-profile success—and one bowl appearance, a 21-20 loss to Occidental in the penultimate Raisin Bowl in 1949. Coaches Harry Hughes (125–93–18) and Bob Davis (54–33–2) could always be counted on to field strong teams. But in 1959, four years after Davis' departure and two years after Colorado A&M became Colorado State, the Aggies became the Rams, and losing became a way of life. Seven coaches came and went over the next three decades, each with a losing record in his getaway suitcase. Then, in 1993, Sonny Lubick rode into Fort Collins …

… And, suddenly, it was morning in Colorado. After a slight stumble (5–6 his first season), Lubick turned the program around: 10 winning seasons and eight bowl games over the next 12 years.

TRADITION Rams players touch two plaques as they leave the locker room on their way to a practice or a game. One bears an inscription: "Attitude, a little thing that makes a big difference." The other is a tribute to Fum McGraw, the school's first All-America.

BEST PLAYER Thurman "Fum" McGraw was a two-time All-America at defensive tackle (1948, 1949)and he earned All-Pro honors three of his five seasons with the Detroit Lions. McGraw was student body president his senior year. He returned to his alma mater as wrestling coach in 1955 and later served as athletic director (1977-86).

BEST COACH Usually a coach has to wait until he's dead a few years before seeing his name slapped on an athletic facility. Lubick, still very much alive, had that honor bestowed on him in 2003: CSU now plays home games on Sonny Lubick Field at Hughes Stadium. A mouthful, but deemed fitting by Colorado Staters for a coach whose 1997 team—11–2, ranked in the Top 20 in both national polls—was the best in school history. So far, there've been no suggestions to remove his name after the Rams stumbled to 4–7 in 2004.

BEST TEAM Things looked gloomy in 1997 after the Rams fell to 2–2 with a 24-0 home loss to Air Force on Sept. 20. It was the team's first home shutout loss since 1973. But led by

---

PROFILE

Colorado State University
Fort Collins, Colo.
Founded: 1870
Enrollment: 21,049
Colors: Green and Gold
Nickname: Rams
Stadium: Sonny Lubick Field at Hughes Stadium
    Opened in 1968
    Grass; 35,028 capacity
First football game: 1893
All-time record: 448–481–33 (.483)
Bowl record: 4–6
Mountain West Conference championships: 3 (2 outright)
First-round NFL draftees: 5
Website: www.csurams.com

THE BEST OF TIMES

Coach Sonny Lubick, who became head coach in 1993, led the Rams to eight bowl games in his first 12 seasons. The Rams posted 10 consecutive winning seasons between 1994 and 2003 after finishing over .500 just three times in the previous 15 years. Lubick's .651 winning percentage is the best of any coach in the program's history.

THE WORST OF TIMES

The 1980s started with a winning season, but the Rams quickly hit the skids. They became the first Division I team to go 0–12 in 1981 and had only one winning campaign the remainder of the decade. Coach Leon Fuller's tenure ended with marks of 1–11 and 1–10 in 1987 and 1988.

CONFERENCE

The Rams hopped around several conferences, including lengthy stays in the Skyline Athletic Conference (1938-61) and the Western Athletic Conference (1968-98) before becoming a charter member of the Mountain West in 1999.

DISTINGUISHED ALUMNI

Wayne Allard, U.S. senator; John Amos, actor; Baxter Black, cowboy, humorist; Amy Van Dyken, Olympic swimming gold medalist; Becky Hammon, WNBA player

FIGHT SONG

COLORADO STATE FIGHT SONG
Fight on you stalwart Ram team
On to the goal!
Tear the [opponent's nickname] line asunder
As down the field we thunder.
Knights of the green and gold
Fight with all your might!
Fight on you stalwart Ram team
Fight! Fight! Fight!

> *Usually a coach has to be dead a few years before seeing his name on an athletic facility.*

quarterback Moses Moreno, the WAC Offensive Player of Year, the Rams reeled off nine straight wins, including a 35-24 Holiday Bowl victory over Missouri. CSU set a school record for points in a season with 442 and led the country in turnover ratio at plus-27. The Rams ended the season ranked No. 16 in the coaches poll and No. 17 in the Associated Press poll.

BIGGEST GAME The Rams were ranked nationally (at No. 23) for the first time since 1977 when they went on the road in 1994 to play No. 6 Arizona. CSU built a 21-6 lead in the third quarter with the help of a 77-yard fumble return for a touchdown by Sean Moran and held on for a 21-16 win. "Well, this was damn near impossible," Lubick said afterward. "It's the biggest win, I'm sure, in CSU history." The Rams went on to finish 10–2. Arizona remains the highest-ranked opponent CSU has defeated.

BIGGEST UPSET Coach Mike Lude resorted to out-and-out trickery in 1966, and it's exactly what the Rams needed to beat No. 10 Wyoming 12-10. On what became known as the Bounce Pass Play, quarterback Ron Wolfe intentionally bounced a lateral to Larry Jackson, who relaxed as if he'd been thrown an incomplete pass. The Wyoming defense also relaxed, and Jackson tossed a 36-yard TD pass to Tom Pack. Al Lavan kicked a field goal with 1:58 remaining to win the game.

HEARTBREAKER Hopes of a conference championship and bowl berth were starting to grow in 1986 after the Rams beat Colorado and snapped a 10-game losing streak against Brigham Young. The 5–2 Rams held a 26-20 lead over San Diego State with just over a minute remaining on Nov. 1. The Aztecs had no timeouts and started at their own 14-yard line, but they went the length of the field and scored with two seconds left and won 27-26. The Rams collapsed, losing two of their final three games to previously winless Utah and Texas-El Paso to finish 6–5.

LORE A rock formation on the foothills overlooking the stadium is marked by a letter A, from the days when the school was named Colorado State Agricultural College and its nickname was Aggies. The A made its debut in 1923; the following year it was expanded to its current size (450

RECORDS

RUSHING YARDS

GAME
310   Tony Alford vs. Utah, Oct. 28, 1989 (28 att.)

SEASON
1,601   Cecil Sapp, 2002 (347 att.)

CAREER
4,813   Steve Bartalo, 1983-86 (1,211 att.)

PASSING YARDS

GAME
449   Scooter Molander vs. Hawaii, Nov. 7, 1987 (31 of 43)

SEASON
3,319   Terry Nugent, 1983 (275 of 433)

CAREER
7,141   Kelly Stouffer, 1984-86 (593 of 1,027)

RECEIVING YARDS

GAME
256   Greg Primus vs. Hawaii, Sept. 28, 1991 (10 rec.)

SEASON
1,293   David Anderson, 2003 (72 rec.)

CAREER
3,163   Greg Primus, 1989-92 (191 rec.)

POINTS

GAME
24   Seven times; most recently by Todd Yert vs. UTEP, Nov. 11, 1989 (4 TDs)

SEASON
132   Calvin Branch, 1996 (22 TDs)

CAREER
294   Steve Bartalo, 1983-86 (49 TDs)

CONSENSUS ALL-AMERICANS

1978   Mike Bell, DL
1995   Greg Myers, DB

feet tall, 210 feet wide). During homecoming week every year, freshman football players join members of a campus fraternity to paint it white.

STADIUM Hughes Stadium sits at the base of the foothills of the Rocky Mountains, about two miles from campus. The stadium was named after Harry Hughes, the winningest coach in the program's history with 125 victories, and it opened in 1968 with a capacity of 30,000. It replaced a 10,000-seater, Colorado Field, that dated to 1912. Prior to that, home games were at Durkee Field, a rocky track underwritten by one Charles Durkee to the tune of $650. In 2003, the name was lengthened to Sonny Lubick Field at Hughes Stadium, which now seats 35,028.

RIVAL You might think that Colorado tops CSU's list of rivals, and certainly that matchup has taken root and started to grow in intensity since the series was revived in 1983 after a 25-year hiatus. But Colorado State's series with Wyoming has much more history: in fact, it's the oldest interstate rivalry west of the Mississippi River. The Border War has been waged since 1899, with the Rams holding a 50–39–5 lead. (No games were played for 13 years during that span.) The teams duke it out for the Bronze Boot, which was worn in Vietnam by Colorado State graduate Jeff Romero. Wyoming coach Joe Glenn underscored the importance of the rivalry when he said in 2003, "It's important to this university, it's important to this state and it's important to me. These games define you and your time at your school."

DUBIOUS DISTINCTION The 1981 Rams became the first Division I-A team to go 0–12. Obviously, CSU bit off a schedule bigger than its stomach. The average margin of defeat: 28 points. Only one game was decided by fewer than 10 points, and the Rams gave up 40 or more six times.

ALL-CENTURY TEAM

Selected by the public in 1992 in conjunction with the school's 100-Year Football Celebration. More than 10,000 ballots were submitted.

OFFENSE

1950-53	Harvey Achziger,	OL
1980-83	Kevin Call,	OL
1983-86	John Benton,	OL
1983-86	Guy Goar,	OL
1987-90	John Laurita,	OL
1932-35	Glenn Morris,	WR
1972-75	Willie Miller,	WR
1980-83	Jeff Champine,	WR
1981-84	Keli McGregor,	WR
1984-86	Kelly Stouffer,	QB
1953-55	Gary Glick,	RB
1969-72	Lawrence McCutcheon,	RB
1983-86	Steve Bartalo,	RB
1983-86	Steve DeLine,	PK

DEFENSE

1947-49	Fum McGraw,	DL
1948-51	Dale Dodrill,	DL
1974-77	Al Baker,	DL
1975-78	Mike Bell,	DL
1986-90	Eric Schaller,	DL
1975-76	Kevin McLain,	LB
1978-81	Kevin Sheesley,	LB
1983-86	Dale Carr,	LB
1985-89	Gary Thompson,	LB
1987-90	Eric Tippeconnic,	LB
1949-51	Jack Christiansen,	DB
1949-52	Jim David,	DB
1968-69	Earlie Thomas,	DB
1975-77	Keith King,	DB
1985-88	Ron Cortell,	DB
1974-77	Mike Deutsch,	P

DISPUTE On Oct. 5, 1974, after overcoming a 20-point deficit and scoring a touchdown on the game's final play, the Rams left the field thinking they had a 34-33 win over visiting Brigham Young. The touchdown tied the game, and after the ensuing extra-point attempt, one official raised his hands over his head, sparking a celebration. However, after returning to their locker room, the Rams were told that the kick had failed, and the official had merely been signaling the game's conclusion—in a tie.

NICKNAME So long as the school was named Colorado A&M, its sports teams were called Aggies. No matter that in 1945 the school had adopted as its mascot the Rambouillet ram, which was kept on campus by the animal sciences program. The reasoning was that the Rambouillet resembled the Rocky Mountain bighorn ram, the official state animal. Two years after Colorado State University, its athletic teams became the Rams.

MASCOT After the Rambouillet ram was adopted as school mascot in 1945, he obviously needed a name. The student body voted to call him Cam the Ram, an acronym for the school's name (Colorado Agricultural & Mechanical). The current Cam is the 19th to serve as Colorado State's mascot. Cam runs onto the field with the team at every home game and in-state away games; he stands on the sideline during the action.

UNIFORMS Colorado State's helmets have been adorned with ram horns since 1973. They were gold with green horns until 1982, when they were changed to green with gold horns. The combination of gold pants and green jerseys at home is also a long-standing tradition.

QUIRK After losing a 21-20 squeaker to Occidental in the Raisin Bowl on Jan. 1, 1949, the Rams had what was probably an even better team the following year. They

were 9–1 with a win over Colorado and were set to make the program's second bowl appearance. However, after losing money playing in the Raisin Bowl, the administration decided to reject an invitation. It took 41 years for the Rams to get another chance.

QUOTE "When you drive up to the stadium and see your name on the field, it makes me feel so darn inadequate. Now I'm embarrassed to lose a game."— Sonny Lubick, whose name was attached to the Colorado State stadium in 2000

COLORADO STATE ANNUAL STATISTICAL LEADERS

YR	RUSHING	YDS	ATT	AVG	PASSING	ATT	CMP	PCT	YDS	RECEIVING	REC	YDS	AVG
1951	Joe Mohorcich	450	100	4.5	Don Burroughs	160	86	.54	1,279	Jim David	46	551	12.0
1952	Jerry Zaleski	435	90	4.8	Don Burroughs	151	76	.50	866	Kirk Hinderlider	20	249	12.5
1953	Al Dorsey	428	85	5.0	Bob Rollins	71	35	.49	474	Kirk Hinderlider	11	163	14.8
1954	Gary Glick	458	150	3.1	Gary Glick	137	58	.42	811	Gary Sanders	16	285	17.8
1955	Gary Glick	579	139	4.2	Jerry Callahan	52	22	.42	302	Gary Sanders	24	351	14.6
1956	Wayne Walter	471	117	4.0	Jerry Callahan	57	14	.25	342	Ron McClary	8	188	23.5
1957	Frank Gupton	540	91	5.9	Louie Long	56	21	.38	328	Al Fortune	8	97	12.1
1958	Wayne Schneider	578	84	6.9	Fred Glick	62	28	.45	372	Wayne Schneider	11	135	12.3
1959	Wayne Schneider	457	90	5.1	Bill Wade	33	14	.42	197	Al Fortune	5	99	19.8
1960	Brady Keys	368	103	3.6	Jon Crider	64	25	.39	387	Ward Gates	16	219	13.7
1961	Dennis Wohlhueter	308	69	4.5	Leroy Guiterrez	82	37	.45	387	Kay McFarland	18	196	10.9
1962	Phil Jackson	314	66	4.8	John Christensen	133	56	.42	562	John Swanson	13	160	12.3
1963	Ken Hines	531	94	5.6	John Christensen	93	29	.31	322	Howard Knapp	8	80	10.0
1964	Jess Willis	580	145	4.0	Eddie Belt	100	33	.33	387	Bob Greathouse	17	252	14.8
1965	Oscar Reed	725	149	4.9	Bob Wolfe	109	47	.43	568	Bruce Weeter	21	276	13.1
1966	Oscar Reed	946	188	5.0	Bob Wolfe	160	65	.41	890	Tom Pack	21	276	13.1
1967	Oscar Reed	910	213	4.3	Gerry Montiel	194	76	.39	965	Larry Jackson	16	277	17.3
1968	Charles Piggee	579	137	4.2	Gerry Montiel	202	75	.37	1,031	Terry Swarn	38	563	14.8
1969	Lawrence McCutcheon	797	146	5.5	Chip Maxwell	305	190	.62	1,257	Harry Stevenson	38	493	13.0
1970	Lawrence McCutcheon	1,008	242	4.2	Wayne Smith	321	136	.42	1,861	Tim Labus	41	573	14.0
1971	Lawrence McCutcheon	1,112	261	4.3	Scott Simmons	121	55	.45	668	Greg Stemrick	24	325	13.5
1972	Reggie Leonard	481	144	3.3	Pat Juliana	166	68	.41	938	Willie Miller	42	729	17.4
1973	Kim Jones	537	125	4.3	Jan Stuebbe	310	146	.47	1,938	Willie Miller	53	793	15.0
1974	Ron Harris	956	218	4.4	Mark Driscoll	246	122	.50	2,016	Willie Miller	53	1,193	22.5
1975	Ron Harris	836	218	3.8	Mark Driscoll	227	109	.48	1,246	Dan O'Rourke	26	388	14.9
1976	Mark Davis	845	163	5.2	Dan Graham	116	55	.47	816	Mike Bachman	17	377	22.2
1977	Larry Jones	790	185	4.3	Dan Graham	228	97	.43	1,692	Mark R. Bell	40	797	19.9
1978	Larry Jones	898	189	4.8	Steve Fairchild	115	57	.50	916	Mark E. Bell	26	328	12.6
1979	Alvin Lewis	635	135	4.7	Keith Lee	166	77	.46	993	Cecil Stockdale	19	361	19.0
1980	Alvin Lewis	1,047	211	5.0	Steve Fairchild	392	200	.51	2,573	Tony Goolsby	47	838	17.8
1981	Troy Lindsay	577	172	3.4	Tom Thenell	185	80	.43	1,079	Jeff Champine	66	882	13.4
1982	Doug Jones	341	90	3.8	Terry Nugent	382	201	.53	2,595	Jeff Champine	54	904	16.7
1983	Steve Bartalo	1,113	292	3.8	Terry Nugent	433	275	.64	3,319	Keli McGregor	69	717	10.4
1984	Steve Bartalo	913	219	4.2	Kelly Stouffer	295	168	.57	2,150	Keli McGregor	47	479	10.2
1985	Steve Bartalo	1,368	338	4.0	Kelly Stouffer	346	204	.59	2,387	Steve Bartalo	40	324	8.1
1986	Steve Bartalo	1,419	362	3.9	Kelly Stouffer	374	205	.55	2,604	Steve Bartalo	40	289	7.2
1987	Scott Whitehouse	812	183	4.4	Scooter Molander	407	237	.58	3,168	J.D. Brookhart	51	683	13.4
1988	Scott Whitehouse	713	201	3.5	Scooter Molander	347	175	.50	2,232	Scott Whitehouse	41	368	9.0
1989	Tony Alford	1,035	157	6.6	Mike Gimenez	179	97	.54	1,223	Sean Willis	44	657	14.9
1990	Brian Copeland	896	169	5.3	Kevin Verdugo	154	90	.58	1,153	Greg Primus	54	971	18.0
1991	Brian Copeland	1,028	190	5.4	Kevin Verdugo	265	159	.60	2,138	Greg Primus	67	1,081	16.1
1992	Leonice Brown	1,051	156	6.7	Anthoney Hill	231	112	.48	1,669	Greg Primus	60	1,007	16.8
1993	E.J. Watson	695	115	6.0	Anthoney Hill	263	121	.46	1,636	Eric Olsen	31	546	17.6
1994	E.J. Watson	665	160	4.2	Anthoney Hill	290	154	.53	2,552	Eric Olsen	43	825	19.2
1995	E.J. Watson	885	194	4.6	Moses Moreno	175	99	.57	1,439	Paul Turner	41	678	16.5
1996	Calvin Branch	1,279	228	5.6	Moses Moreno	335	193	.58	2,921	Geoff Turner	52	921	17.7
1997	Damon Washington	1,112	180	6.2	Moses Moreno	257	157	.61	2,257	Geoff Turner	34	559	16.4
1998	Damon Washington	645	147	4.4	Ryan Eslinger	336	206	.61	2,386	Darran Hall	44	629	14.3
1999	Kevin McDougal	1,164	207	5.6	Matt Newton	324	193	.60	2,368	Dallas Davis	51	665	13.0
2000	Cecil Sapp	841	151	5.6	Matt Newton	334	198	.59	2,609	Pete Rebstock	46	768	16.7
2001	Henri Childs	841	166	5.1	Bradlee Van Pelt	194	94	.48	1,247	Pete Rebstock	28	546	19.5
2002	Cecil Sapp	1,601	347	4.6	Bradlee Van Pelt	287	150	.52	2,073	Chris Pittman	60	807	13.5
2003	Bradlee Van Pelt	909	170	5.3	Bradlee Van Pelt	297	180	.61	2,845	David Anderson	72	1,293	18.0
2004	Jimmy Green	436	132	3.3	Justin Holland	197	121	.61	1,622	David Anderson	57	940	16.5

Receiving leaders by receptions
The NCAA began inluding postseason stats in 2003

COLORADO STATE ALL-TIME SCORES

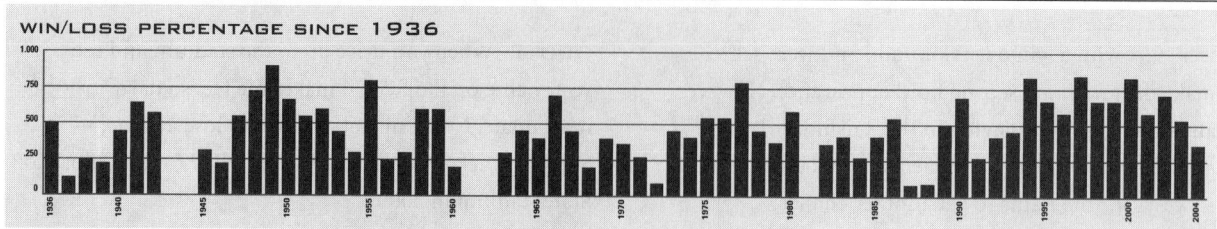

WIN/LOSS PERCENTAGE SINCE 1936

NO HEAD COACH

1893 2-4-0

U	at Longmont Acad.	8	12
U ●	Longmont Acad.	24	16
F10	Colorado	6	70
U ●	Denver	60	10
U	at Colorado Mines	6	12
O7	at Colorado	6	44

1894 0-1-0

O27	at Colorado	0	67

1895-1898

NO TEAM

W.J. FORBES
1899 (.375) 1-2-1

1899 1-2-1

O15	Colorado	0	63
U	Colorado Mines	5	49
U =	No. Colorado	5	5
N30 ●	Wyoming	12	0

1900-1937
ROCKY MOUNTAIN

GEORGE TOOMEY
1900 (.250) 1-3

1900 1-3-0 (0-3-0)

U	at Colorado College	0	53
O15	at Colorado	0	29
U	at Colorado Mines	0	27
N24 ●	Wyoming	16	0

C.J. GRIFFITH
1901-03 (.563) 8-6-2

1901 1-2-0 (0-2-0)

U ●	Denver	56	5
U	at Colorado College	0	16
U	Colorado Mines	0	11

1902 1-3-2 (1-3-2)

O11 ●	at Utah State	24	5
O18	at Colorado	6	11
O25 =	at Utah	0	0
N4	Colorado College	6	29
N15 =	at Colorado Mines	6	6
N22	Denver	5	11

1903 6-1-0 (5-1-0)

O3 ●	Denver	23	17
O10	Colorado	0	5
O24 ●	Colorado Mines	10	2
N3 ●	at Colorado College	8	5
N14 ●	Wyoming	17	0
N21 ●	at Denver	16	6
N26 ●	at Utah	16	6 *

JOHN McINTOSH
1904-05 (.292) 3-8-1

1904 0-4-1 (0-4-0)

O1	Denver	0	18
O8	at Colorado Mines	0	51
N12	Colorado College	0	4
N19	at Colorado	0	46
N24 =	at Wyoming	6	6

1905 3-4-0 (2-4-0)

O7 ●	Denver	12	0
O21 ●	at No. Colorado	6	5
O28	at Colorado Mines	10	17
N4	at Colorado College	0	33
N18	at Denver	5	11
N25 ●	Wyoming	34	5
N30	at Utah	0	24

CLAUDE ROTHGEB
1906-09 (.233) 3-11-1

1906 1-2-1 (1-2-1)

O20	at Colorado Mines	0	11
O27 ●	at Colorado College	4	0
N10 =	Colorado	0	0
N17	at Denver	0	10

1907 0-4-0 (0-4-0)

O12	Colorado College	4	20
O19	at Colorado	13	17
N2	Colorado Mines	0	35
N23	Denver	0	5

1908 1-3-0 (1-2-0)

O17	at Denver	0	17
O24	Colorado	0	8
N14 ●	Wyoming	20	0
N26	at Kansas State	10	33

1909 1-2-0 (1-2-0)

O16 ●	Wyoming	32	3
O23	at Colorado	0	57
N6	at Colorado College	6	31

GEORGE CASSIDY
1910 (.000) 0-5

1910 0-5-0 (0-5-0)

O22	at Colorado Mines	6	10
O29	Denver	0	22
N5	Colorado College	0	24
N12	Colorado	0	44
N24	at Wyoming	0	10

HARRY HUGHES
1911-41 (.568) 125-93-18

1911 0-6-0 (0-6-0)

O7	at Utah	0	51
O14	at Utah State	0	29
O28	Colorado Mines	0	29
N4	at Denver	0	49
N11	at Colorado	0	31
N30	Wyoming	0	27

1912 3-2-0 (3-2-0)

O5 ●	Denver	14	13
O12 ●	Colorado	21	0
O19	at Colorado College	0	13
N2	at Colorado Mines	0	14
N28 ●	at Wyoming	33	0

1913 3-2-0 (3-2-0)

O18 ●	at Denver	20	6
O25	at Colorado	7	16
N1	Colorado Mines	7	14
N8 ●	Utah State	20	7
N27 ●	Wyoming	61	0

1914 3-4-0 (3-3-0)

O17	Colorado	6	33
O24 ●	at Wyoming	48	10
O31 ●	at Denver	19	6
N7	Colorado College	13	24
N14 ●	at Utah State	41	7
N21	at Colorado Mines	0	19
N26	Oklahoma State OkC	0	7

1915 7-0-0 (7-0-0)

O9 ●	at Colorado	23	6
O16 ●	at Utah	21	9
O23 ●	Utah State	59	0
O30 ●	Colorado Mines	35	0
N6 ●	at Wyoming	47	0 *
N13 ●	at Colorado College	24	13
N25 ●	Denver	33	3

1916 6-0-1 (6-0-1)

S30 ●	Wyoming	40	0
O14 ●	at Utah State	53	0
O28 ●	Colorado College	14	12
N4 ●	at Denver	21	13
N11 =	at Colorado Mines	0	0
N18 ●	Utah	12	6
N30 ●	at Colorado	32	14

1917 0-7-1 (0-7-1)

O6	at Wyoming	0	6
O13	Colorado	0	6
O20 =	Montana St.	20	20
O27	Denver	6	10
N3	at Utah	12	25
N10	at Utah State	7	47
N17	at Colorado College	0	7
N29	at Colorado Mines	6	27

1918 0-2-0 (0-2-0)

N16	at Denver	0	14
N28	at Colorado	13	16

1919 7-1-0 (7-1-0)

S27 ●	at Wyoming	28	0
O4 ●	Wyoming	14	0
O11 ●	Utah	34	21
O18 ●	Colorado	49	7
N1 ●	at Denver	33	3
N8 ●	Utah State	27	7
N15 ●	at Colorado Mines	33	6
N27	at Colorado College	0	13

1920 6-1-1 (6-0-1)

O2 ●	at Wyoming	13	0
O9	at Nebraska	0	7
O16 ●	Wyoming	42	0
O23 ●	Colorado Mines	27	0
O30 ●	at Utah State	21	0
N11 ●	Colorado College	28	0
N20 =	at Colorado	7	7
N27 ●	at Denver	14	0

1921 2-3-1 (2-2-1)

O1 =	Wyoming	7	7
O15 ●	Colorado Mines	14	0
O29 ●	at Colorado College	24	0
N5	Denver	14	21
N19	Colorado	0	10
N24	at Nebraska	7	70

1922 5-2-1 (5-1-1)

O14 ●	at Wyoming	60	0
O21 =	Colorado College	0	0
O28 ●	Utah State	34	6
N4	at Colorado	0	7
N11	at Drake	6	19
N18 ●	Colorado Mines	19	0
N25 ●	Brigham Young	33	0
D2 ●	at Denver	27	6

1923 5-2-1 (5-1-1)

S29 ●	Wyoming	33	0
O6	at Chicago	0	10
O13 ●	Brigham Young	14	6
O20 =	at Colorado College	6	6
O27 ●	at Utah State	26	7
N10	Denver	25	0
N17 ●	at Colorado Mines	14	0
N28	Colorado	3	6

1924 4-2-0 (4-2-0)

O11 ●	Colorado Mines	17	0
N1 ●	Utah State	17	13
N8	Colorado College	6	7
N15 ●	at No. Colorado	22	7
N22	at Colorado	0	36
N29 ●	at Denver	19	0

1925 9-1-0 (8-0-0)

O3 ●	Regis	34	0
O10 ●	Brigham Young	21	7
O17 ●	at Denver	17	0
O24 ●	at Colorado College	7	3
O31 ●	at Utah State	13	0
N7 ●	No. Colorado	43	18
N14 ●	Colorado	12	0
N21 ●	at Colorado Mines	41	10
N26 ●	Wyoming	40	0
D12	at Hawaii	0	41

1926 6-2-1 (5-2-0)

O2 ●	Regis	39	0
O9 ●	Colorado Mines	53	0
O16 ●	at Denver	7	6
O23 ●	Colorado College	19	6
O30	at Utah	6	10
N6	Utah State	0	13
N13 ●	at Colorado	3	0
N20 ●	at Brigham Young	19	6
N27 =	at Arizona	3	3

1927 7-1-0 (7-1-0)

O1 ●	at No. Colorado	33	0
O8 ●	Brigham Young	29	0
O15	at Denver	0	6
O29 ●	Utah	12	0
N5 ●	at Utah State	6	0
N12 ●	at Colorado Mines	37	6
N19 ●	Colorado	39	7
N26 ●	at Colorado College	20	7

1928 6-2-0 (6-2-0)

O6 ●	No. Colorado	26	6
O13 ●	Brigham Young	15	6
O20	at Utah	0	6
N3 ●	Utah State	7	6
N10	at Colorado	7	13
N17 ●	at Denver	15	0
N24 ●	Colorado Mines	46	20
D1 ●	Colorado College	35	13

1929 5-4-0 (4-4-0)

S28 ●	at Regis	14	0
O4 ●	Wyoming	20	7
O12	at Colorado College	13	14
O19 ●	at Colorado Mines	12	0
O26	Utah	0	21
N2 ●	Western St.	45	14
N9 ●	at Utah State	7	6
N16	Colorado	0	6
N29	at Denver	6	20

1930 3-5-1 (3-3-1)

S27	at Regis	7	14
O11 ●	at Denver	15	7
O18 ●	at No. Colorado	26	0
O25	at Colorado	0	7
N1	Utah	0	39
N8	Wyoming	6	21
N15 ●	at Utah State	13	0
N22 =	Colorado College	0	0
N29	at Arizona	0	16

1931 5-4-0 (5-2-0)

S26	at Kansas	6	27
O10 ●	at Colorado College	32	6
O24 ●	Colorado	19	6
O31	at Utah	6	60
N7 ●	at Wyoming	26	6
N14	Utah State	0	6
N21 ●	at Denver	20	0
N28 ●	No. Colorado	21	7
D5	Nebraska Den	7	20

1932 4-3-1 (4-3-1)
- O1 ● | at No. Colorado 12 0
- O8 ● | Colorado Mines 39 0
- O15 = | at Denver 7 7
- O22 ● | at Colorado 7 6
- O29 | Colorado College 0 3
- N5 | at Utah State 12 13
- N19 | Utah 0 16
- N24 ● | Wyoming 23 0

1933 5-1-1 (5-1-1)
- S30 ● | at Wyoming 7 0
- O14 = | at Denver 0 0
- O21 ● | Colorado 19 6
- N4 ● | at Colorado Mines 19 0
- N11 ● | Utah State 3 0
- N25 ● | Colorado College DEN 30 7
- N30 | at Utah 0 13

1934 6-2-1 (6-1-1)
- S29 ● | at No. Colorado 12 0
- O6 Arizona 3 7
- O13 ● | at Denver 2 0
- O20 ● | Colorado Mines 56 0
- O27 | at Colorado 9 27
- N3 ● | Wyoming 16 0
- N10 = | at Utah State 21 21
- N17 ● | Utah 14 6
- N24 ● | Colorado College DEN 40 6

1935 3-4-1 (2-4-1)
- S28 ● | at Wyoming 12 3
- O5 | at Denver 14 20
- O12 ● | Colorado Mines 19 0
- O26 | at Colorado 6 19
- N2 | at Utah State 0 13
- N16 | Utah 0 14
- N23 = | at Colorado College 0 0
- N28 ● at New Mexico 7 6

1936 4-4-1 (3-4-1)
- S26 ● | Western St. 13 0
- O3 ● New Mexico 9 7
- O10 | at Denver 7 14
- O17 = | at Wyoming 0 0
- O24 | Colorado 7 9
- N7 | Utah State 0 13
- N14 ● | at No. Colorado 12 6
- N24 ● | Colorado College 19 12
- N26 | at Utah 0 13

1937 1-7-0 (1-6-0)
- O2 | Colorado Mines 0 7
- O9 | at Denver 0 22
- O16 | Wyoming 0 7
- O23 | at Colorado 0 47
- O30 | at Utah State 0 7
- N13 | Utah 0 45
- N20 ● | at Colorado College 6 0
- N27 at Arizona 0 47

1938-1947
MOUNTAIN STATES

1938 1-5-2 (0-4-2)
- S24 ● at Colorado Mines 12 6
- O1 = | at Wyoming 0 0
- O8 = | at Denver 0 0
- O22 | Colorado 6 31
- O29 | Utah State 0 6
- N12 | at Utah 0 13
- N19 | Brigham Young 12 20
- N24 at New Mexico 7 27

1939 2-7-0 (2-4-0)
- S30 Colorado Mines 14 19
- O7 | at Brigham Young 12 13
- O14 Kansas 0 7
- O21 | at Colorado 0 13
- O28 ● | at Utah State 9 0
- N4 ● | Wyoming 22 0
- N11 | at Denver 6 13
- N18 | Utah 7 42
- N30 at New Mexico 19 21

1940 3-5-2 (1-3-2)
- S28 ● at Colorado Mines 25 0
- O5 = | at Wyoming 0 0
- O12 | at Denver 13 14
- O19 | Colorado 14 33
- O26 ● New Mexico DEN 7 6
- N9 ● | Utah State 13 12
- N16 | at Utah 0 27
- N23 = | Brigham Young 13 13
- N28 at Kansas 0 26
- D5 at Fresno State 0 28

1941 4-2-1 (3-2-1)
- S27 ● Colorado Mines 21 6
- O4 ● | Wyoming 27 0
- O18 | at Colorado 13 26
- O25 ● | at Utah State 7 6
- N1 = | at Denver 6 6
- N15 | Utah 13 26
- N22 ● | at Brigham Young 22 7

JULIUS WAGNER
1942-46 (.354) 8-15-1

1942 4-3-0 (2-3-0)
- S26 ● | at Wyoming 10 0
- O3 ● Colorado Mines 27 0
- O10 | at Denver 0 26
- O24 | Colorado 7 34
- O31 | at Utah 14 33
- N7 ● | Utah State 25 0
- N14 ● at No. Colorado 14 6

1943-1944
NO TEAM WWII

1945 2-5-1 (0-4-0)
- S29 ● at No. Colorado 33 0
- O6 at Fort Warren 6 61
- O13 | Colorado 6 21
- O20 | at Utah State 0 13
- O27 | Utah 0 28
- N3 ● No. Colorado 25 14
- N10 | at Denver 12 35
- N17 = at Colorado College 7 7

1946 2-7-0 (1-5-0)
- S21 ● at Fort Warren 25 0
- S28 at Montana 0 27
- O5 ● | at Wyoming 7 0
- O12 | at Denver 0 33
- O19 | at Utah State 0 47 *
- O26 Colorado College 12 25
- N9 | Utah 0 13
- N16 | Brigham Young 6 20
- N28 | at Colorado 0 18

BOB DAVIS
1947-55 (.618) 54-33-2

1947 5-4-1 (2-3-1)
- S20 ● Colorado Mines 20 12
- S27 ● at Drake 23 19
- O4 | Utah State 13 26
- O11 = | at Denver 13 13
- O18 ● at Colorado College 28 7
- O25 | Colorado 7 14
- N8 | at Utah 0 19
- N15 ● | at Brigham Young 27 25
- N22 ● | Wyoming 21 6
- N29 at Montana 7 41

1948-1961
SKYLINE

1948 8-3-0 (4-1-0)
- S18 ● Colorado College 25 6
- S25 ● New Mexico State 40 6 *
- O2 ● | at Utah State 9 7
- O9 ● | at Denver 14 10
- O16 ● | at Wyoming 21 20
- O23 Drake 29 31
- O30 ● at Colorado Mines 33 0
- N6 | Utah 3 12
- N15 ● | Brigham Young 20 0
- N20 ● at Colorado 29 25

RAISIN BOWL
- J1 Occidental 20 21

1949 9-1-0 (4-1-0)
- S17 ● at Colorado College 14 7
- S24 ● | at Denver 14 13
- O1 | Wyoming 0 8
- O8 ● Montana 27 12
- O15 ● Colorado Mines 27 7
- O29 ● | Utah State 28 6
- N5 ● | at Utah 21 12
- N11 ● | at Brigham Young 16 14
- N19 ● at New Mexico State 45 0
- N26 ● at Colorado 14 7

1950 6-3-0 (4-1-0)
- S23 ● | at Denver 30 14
- S30 ● Colorado College 48 7
- O7 | at Wyoming 0 34
- O14 ● | Brigham Young 27 14
- O21 ● at Colorado Mines 26 0
- O28 ● | at Utah State 33 13
- N11 ● | Utah 32 7
- N18 at Arizona State 13 21
- N25 Colorado 6 31

1951 5-4-1 (2-3-1)
- S22 at Colorado 13 28
- S29 ● Colorado Mines 41 0
- O6 ● at Colorado College 54 13
- O13 ● | Wyoming 14 7
- O20 = | Utah State 20 20
- O27 ● at New Mexico 20 15
- N3 | at Brigham Young 19 21
- N10 ● | Montana 34 6
- N17 | at Utah 21 27
- N24 | at Denver 6 21

1952 6-4-0 (5-2-0)
- S20 ● at Colorado Mines 26 0
- S27 at Arizona State 14 40
- O4 ● | at Denver 28 6
- O11 ● | at Wyoming 14 0
- O18 ● | Montana 41 0
- O25 ● | at Utah State 21 7
- N8 | Utah 6 14
- N15 | at New Mexico 0 3
- N22 ● | Brigham Young 27 6
- N29 at Colorado 0 61

1953 4-5-0 (3-4-0)
- S26 ● Kansas State 14 13
- O3 ● | Denver 21 6
- O10 | at Wyoming 14 21
- O17 | at Montana 31 32
- O24 | Utah State 13 14
- N7 ● | at Brigham Young 34 12
- N14 | at Utah 14 35
- N21 ● | New Mexico 9 3
- N28 Colorado 7 13

1954 3-7-0 (3-4-0)
- S18 at Kansas State 0 29
- S25 at Colorado 0 46
- O2 ● | Brigham Young 14 13
- O9 | Wyoming 0 34
- O16 Pacific 7 15
- O23 | at Utah State 14 20
- O30 ● | Montana 37 34
- N6 ● | Utah 14 13
- N13 | at New Mexico 7 10
- N20 | at Denver 0 34

1955 8-2-0 (6-1-0)
- S17 at Arizona 7 20
- S24 ● | New Mexico 25 0
- O1 ● | Denver 20 19
- O8 ● | at Wyoming 14 13
- O22 ● | Utah State 26 9
- O29 ● | at Montana 12 7
- N5 ● at Oklahoma State 20 13
- N12 | at Utah 6 27
- N19 ● | at Brigham Young 35 0
- N26 ● Colorado 10 0

DON MULLISON
1956-61 (.325) 19-40-1

1956 2-7-1 (2-4-1)
- S22 at Pacific 14 39
- S29 = | Brigham Young 0 0
- O6 | Wyoming 12 20
- O13 at Colorado 7 47
- O20 | at Utah State 7 46
- O27 ● | Montana 34 20
- N3 at Xavier 14 27
- N10 | Utah 27 49
- N17 | at Denver 13 39
- D1 ● | at New Mexico 28 27

1957 3-7-0 (2-5-0)
- S28 | New Mexico 7 30
- O5 ● | Denver 27 6
- O12 | at Wyoming 13 27
- O19 at Bradley 0 19
- O26 | Utah State 14 27
- N3 | at Utah 0 55
- N9 Colorado 0 20
- N16 ● | at Montana 19 7
- N23 | at Brigham Young 9 26
- N30 ● at Air Force 20 7

1958 6-4-0 (4-3-0)
- S27 ● at Drake 21 0
- O4 ● | Brigham Young 32 6
- O11 at Air Force 6 36
- O18 | Wyoming 6 7
- O25 | at Utah State 0 15
- N1 ● | Montana 57 7
- N8 ● | Utah 20 0
- N15 | at New Mexico 12 17
- N22 ● at Colorado 15 14
- N29 ● | at Denver 9 8

1959 6-4-0 (5-2-0)
- S19 ● at Pacific 9 6
- S26 ● | New Mexico 14 9
- O3 ● | Denver 15 0
- O10 | at Wyoming 0 29
- O17 Arizona State 9 24
- O24 at Army 6 25
- O31 ● | at Montana 26 16
- N7 ● | Utah State 10 7
- N14 ● | at Utah 21 17
- N21 | at Brigham Young 13 14

1960 2-8-0 (1-6-0)
- S17 at Arizona State 0 39
- S24 at Air Force 8 32
- O1 ● | Brigham Young 8 7
- O8 ● at Drake 30 3
- O15 | Wyoming 8 40
- O22 | at Utah State 0 21
- O29 | Montana 14 26
- N5 | Utah 6 27
- N12 | at New Mexico 6 24
- N24 | at Denver 12 21

1961 0-10-0 (0-6-0)
- S16 | at Utah 0 40
- S23 at Arizona 6 28
- S30 Arizona State 6 14
- O7 at San Jose State 0 14
- O14 | at Wyoming 7 18
- O21 | Utah State 3 49
- O28 | at Montana 19 22
- N4 at Air Force 9 14
- N11 | at Brigham Young 16 30
- N18 | New Mexico 8 20

1962-1967
INDEPENDENT

MIKE LUDE
1962-69 (.364) 29-51-1

1962 0-10-0
- S22 at Air Force 0 34
- S29 at Arizona State 0 35
- O6 Brigham Young 7 28
- O12 at UCLA 7 35
- O20 at Utah State 0 21
- O27 Wyoming 7 28
- N3 Utah 8 26
- N10 at New Mexico 8 21
- N17 at Oregon State 14 25
- N24 Montana 15 16

1963 3-7-0
- S21 ● at Pacific 20 0
- S28 at Air Force 0 69
- O5 Arizona State 7 50
- O12 at Wyoming 3 21
- O19 at Utah 14 48
- O26 ● Texas-El Paso 21 14
- N2 New Mexico 0 25
- N9 Utah State 13 36
- N16 ● at Montana 20 12
- N23 at Brigham Young 20 24

1964 5-6-0
- S19 at Wyoming 7 31
- S26 ● Pacific 7 0
- O3 at Air Force 6 14
- O10 ● Brigham Young 7 6
- O17 Utah 3 13
- O24 at Utah State 13 42
- O31 at Arizona State 6 34
- N7 ● San Jose State 14 3
- N14 at New Mexico 0 42
- N26 ● at Texas-El Paso 35 8
- D4 ● at Hawaii 13 6

1965 4-6-0
- S18 ● Hawaii 54 6
- S25 Wyoming 14 33
- O2 ● New Mexico 27 22
- O9 at Texas-El Paso 10 35
- O16 at West Texas St. 12 15
- O23 Utah State 20 41
- O30 at Utah 19 22
- N6 ● South Dakota State 52 20
- N13 ● at Brigham Young 36 22
- N25 at Tulsa 20 48

1966 — 7-3-0

S24	●	at South Dakota St.	45	14
S30		at Brigham Young	24	27
O8		Tulsa	6	20
O15	●	at Utah State	10	7
O22	●	at Air Force	41	21
O29	●	Wyoming	12	10
N5	●	at New Mexico	45	6
N12	●	West Texas St.	35	26
N19		at Wichita St.	23	37
N26	●	Iowa State	34	10

1967 — 4-5-1

S23		Kansas State	7	17
S30		at Wyoming	10	13
O7		at West Texas St.	14	24
O14		at North Texas	10	21
O21	●	Utah State	17	14
O28	=	at Air Force	17	17
N4	●	at Pacific	24	15
N11		at Texas-El Paso	0	17
N18	●	Emporia St.	77	0
N25	●	Wichita St.	43	11

1968-1998
WAC

1968 — 2-8-0 (1-4-0)

S14	● |	at New Mexico	21	13
S21		at Kansas State	0	21
S28		North Texas	12	17
O5	||	at Texas Tech	13	43
O12	●	at Wichita St.	37	15
O19	||	Air Force	0	31
O26		Pacific	0	31
N2	|	Wyoming	14	46
N23		West Texas St.	17	22
N30	|	at Texas-El Paso	19	23

1969 — 4-6-0 (0-4-0)

S20	|	at Brigham Young	20	22
S27	●	Wichita St.	50	21
O4	|	at Wyoming	3	39
O11	●	at Utah State	37	33
O18	●	West Texas St.	27	7
O25		at Air Force	7	28
N1	|	Texas-El Paso	16	17
N15	●	Idaho	31	21
N22	|	at Arizona State	7	79
N27		at New Mexico State	20	21

JERRY WAMPFLER
1970-72 (.242) 8-25

1970 — 4-7-0 (1-3-0)

S12	●	at New Mexico State	28	9
S19	|	at Arizona State	9	38
S26		at Iowa State	6	37
O3		at Air Force	22	37
O10	|	Wyoming	6	16
O17	|	Texas-El Paso	37	41
O24		at West Virginia	21	24
O31	●	Utah State	20	13
N7	● |	Brigham Young	26	9
N14	●	Pacific	17	8
N21		at Toledo	14	24

1971 — 3-8-0 (1-4-0)

S18	|	at Brigham Young	14	54
S25		at Idaho	0	10
O2	|	at Wyoming	6	17
O9	|	Arizona State	0	42
O16	|	at Utah	16	42
O23		Air Force	12	17
O30		Utah State	17	18
N6		at Wichita St.	14	34
N13	●	West Texas St.	36	14
N20	● |	at Texas-El Paso	24	7
N27	●	New Mexico State	38	21

1972 — 1-10-0 (1-4-0)

S9	|	at Arizona	0	17
S16		Iowa State	0	41
S23		at West Texas St.	14	41
S30		at Utah State	0	21
O7		Air Force	13	52
O14	|	Wyoming	9	28
O21		at Florida State	0	37
O28	|	Brigham Young	8	44
N11		at Houston	13	48
N18	● |	Texas-El Paso	35	22
N25	|	at Utah	36	62

SARK ARSLANIAN
1973-81 (.490) 45-47-4

1973 — 5-6-0 (2-4-0)

S8	|	Arizona	0	31
S15	● |	at Brigham Young	21	13
S22	●	New Mexico State	31	27
S29	|	at Arizona State	14	67
O6	●	at Idaho	33	30
O13		Utah State	18	34
O20	|	at Wyoming	3	35
O27	● |	at Texas-El Paso	76	24
N3	●	Toledo	21	14
N10		Houston	20	28
N24	|	New Mexico	13	30

1974 — 4-6-1 (2-3-1)

S14	|	at New Mexico	23	32
S21	●	at Florida State	14	7
S28		Memphis	18	20
O5	= |	Brigham Young	33	33
O12		at Utah State	23	24
O19	●	Nevada	66	17
O26		Arkansas [LR]	9	43
N2	● |	Wyoming	11	6
N9	|	at Arizona	21	34
N16	● |	Texas-El Paso	56	24
N23	|	at Arizona State	21	26

1975 — 6-5-0 (4-2-0)

S13		at Texas	0	46
S20	● |	Brigham Young	21	17
S27	● |	at New Mexico	27	16
O4	● |	at Wyoming	3	0
O11	●	at Oregon State	17	8
O18	|	Arizona State	3	33
O25	●	Air Force	47	10
N1		at Tennessee	7	28
N8	● |	at Texas-El Paso	21	17
N15	|	Arizona	9	31
N22		Utah State	17	28

1976 — 6-5-0 (2-4-0)

S11		at Oregon	3	17
S18	|	at Brigham Young	18	42
S25	●	Wichita St.	24	3
O2	|	New Mexico	20	33
O9	●	at Utah State	10	7
O16	●	at Air Force	27	3
O23	● |	Texas-El Paso	28	7
O30	● |	Wyoming	19	16
N6	●	Idaho	31	14
N13	|	at Arizona	6	23
N20	|	at Arizona State	19	21

1977 — 9-2-1 (5-2-0)

S10	●	at Pacific	20	3
S17	●	at Hawaii	20	16
S24	●	No. Colorado	48	10
O1	● |	Utah	44	3
O8	● |	at Texas-El Paso	31	14
O15	|	Brigham Young	17	63
O22	● |	New Mexico	14	9
O29	|	at Wyoming	13	29
N5	● |	at Arizona	35	14
N12	=	at West Texas St.	21	21
N19	● |	Arizona State	25	14
N26	●	Utah State	13	10

1978 — 5-6-0 (2-4-0)

S16		Utah State	20	21
S23	|	at Brigham Young	6	32
S30	|	at Utah	6	30
O7	● |	Texas-El Paso	39	29
O14	●	at Air Force	31	13
O21		Nevada-Las Vegas	6	33
O28	|	Wyoming	3	13
N4	|	at San Diego State	31	34
N11	● |	at New Mexico	26	15
N18	●	West Virginia	50	14
N23	●	at Pacific	20	13

1979 — 4-7-1 (3-4-0)

S1		at Arizona	17	33
S15		Arkansas [LR]	3	36
S22		at Utah State	0	24
S29	● |	at Wyoming	20	16
O6	|	Utah	16	21
O13	● |	at Texas-El Paso	17	3
O20	● |	San Diego State	37	3
O27	●	Air Force	20	6
N3	|	Brigham Young	7	30
N10	|	New Mexico	9	24
N17	=	at Nevada-Las Vegas	21	21
N24	|	at Hawaii	10	24

1980 — 6-4-1 (5-1-1)

S6	● |	Air Force	21	9
S13		West Virginia	24	52
S20	●	at Arizona	15	13
S27		Nevada-Las Vegas	15	56
O4		at Iowa State	0	69
O11	● |	at New Mexico	31	26
O18	● |	at San Diego State	26	7
O25	= |	at Utah	21	21
N1	● |	Wyoming	28	25
N8	● |	Texas-El Paso	37	7
N15	|	at Brigham Young	14	45

CHESTER CADDAS
1981 (.000) 0-6

1981 — 0-12-0 (0-8-0)

S12	|	San Diego State	14	30
S19		at Tennessee	0	42
S26		at West Virginia	3	49
O3	|	at Air Force	14	28
O10		Mississippi State	27	37
O17	|	Utah	13	24
O24	|	at Texas-El Paso	29	35
O31	|	at Wyoming	21	55
N7	|	Brigham Young	14	63
N14	|	New Mexico	16	28
N21		at Arizona State	7	52
N28	|	at Hawaii	6	59

LEON FULLER
1982-88 (.313) 25-55

1982 — 4-7-0 (3-5-0)

S4		at Missouri	14	28
S11	● |	Wyoming	9	3
S18	|	Hawaii	13	23
S25	●	New Mexico State	28	17
O1	|	at Utah	14	35
O16	● |	at Air Force	21	11
O23	|	at Brigham Young	18	34
O30	● |	Texas-El Paso	38	13
N6		Nevada-Las Vegas	31	36
N13	|	at New Mexico	24	29
N20	|	at San Diego State	10	38

1983 — 5-7-0 (4-4-0)

S3	|	Air Force	13	34
S10	|	at Hawaii	0	34
S17		at Colorado	3	31
S24		at Iowa State	17	21
O1	● |	Utah	31	28
O8		at Arizona	21	52
O15	● |	San Diego State	17	15
O22	● |	at Texas-El Paso	31	15
O29	● |	New Mexico	25	24
N5	●	No. Colorado	41	20
N12	|	at Brigham Young	6	24
N19	|	at Wyoming	17	42

1984 — 3-8-0 (3-5-0)

S8		at Mississippi State	9	14
S15	● |	Hawaii	10	3
S22		Fullerton St.	22	34
S29	|	at Air Force	10	52
O6	|	Brigham Young	9	52
O13	● |	at New Mexico	16	10
O20	|	at San Diego State	24	41
O27	|	Wyoming	34	43
N3	|	at Utah	23	35
N10	● |	Texas-El Paso	59	31
N17		at Arizona State	14	45

1985 — 5-7-0 (4-4-0)

S7		at Colorado	10	23
S14	● |	Texas-El Paso	41	24
S21		at LSU	3	17
S28	|	at San Diego State	23	48
O5	|	Brigham Young	7	42
O12	● |	at New Mexico	45	28
O19	|	Air Force	19	35
O26	● |	at Wyoming	30	19
N2	|	at Hawaii	14	34
N9	●	Southern Miss	35	17
N16	● |	Utah	21	19
N23		at Miami, Fla.	3	24

1986 — 6-5-0 (4-4-0)

S6	●	at Colorado	23	7
S13		at Arizona	10	37
S20	●	No. Colorado	46	14
S27	|	at Air Force	7	24
O3	● |	at Brigham Young	24	20
O18	● |	Hawaii	31	7
O25	● |	Wyoming	20	15
N1	|	San Diego State	26	27
N8	|	at Utah	28	38
N15	● |	New Mexico	32	27
N22	|	at Texas-El Paso	19	21

1987 — 1-11-0 (1-7-0)

S5		at Tennessee	3	49
S12		at Texas Tech	24	33
S19	|	Texas-El Paso	6	45
S26	|	Air Force	19	27
O3		Colorado	16	29
O10	|	Utah	23	24
O17	● |	New Mexico	35	13
O31	|	at Wyoming	15	20
N7	|	at Hawaii	38	39
N14	|	at San Diego State	12	26
N21		at La. Lafayette	28	35
D4	|	Brigham Young [MEL]	26	30

1988 — 1-10-0 (1-7-0)

S3	|	Air Force	23	29
S10	|	Hawaii	23	31
S17		at Arizona State	17	28
O1		Colorado	23	27
O8	|	at Brigham Young	7	42
O15	|	at Texas-El Paso	14	34
O22	● |	San Diego State	13	7
O29	|	Wyoming	14	48
N5	|	at Utah	7	46
N12	|	at New Mexico	23	24
N26		at Tulsa	28	32

EARLE BRUCE
1989-92 (.479) 22-24-1

1989 — 5-5-1 (4-3-0)

S2		at Tennessee	14	17
S9		at Colorado	20	45
S16	●	Fullerton St.	42	14
S23	=	Eastern Michigan	35	35
S30	|	Air Force	21	46
O7	● |	at New Mexico	34	20
O14	|	Brigham Young	16	45
O21	● |	Hawaii	31	16
O28	● |	at Utah	50	10
N4	|	at Wyoming	35	56
N11	● |	at Texas-El Paso	52	0

1990 — 9-4-0 (6-1-0)

S1	● |	at Air Force	35	33
S8	●	Montana St.	41	5
S15		at Arizona State	20	31
S22	● |	Texas-El Paso	38	20
S29		Arkansas [LR]	20	31
O6	● |	Utah	22	13
O13	|	at Brigham Young	9	52
O20	● |	New Mexico	47	7
N3	● |	Wyoming	17	8
N10	●	Tulsa	31	13
N17		at Louisiana Tech	30	31
N24	● |	at Hawaii	30	27
		FREEDOM BOWL		
D29	●	Oregon	32	31

1991 — 3-8-0 (2-6-0)

A31	●	Arkansas State	38	24
S7	|	Air Force	26	31
S14		at Nebraska	14	71
S21		at Southern Miss	7	39
S28	● |	Hawaii	28	16
O5	● |	at Texas-El Paso	23	18
O19	|	at Utah	16	21
O26	|	at Wyoming	28	35
O31	|	Brigham Young	17	40
N9	|	at San Diego State	32	42
N16	|	New Mexico	36	38

1992 — 5-7-0 (3-5-0)

S5		at Colorado	17	37
S12		Idaho	34	37
S19	|	at Fresno State	21	52
S26	●	at LSU	17	14
O3	|	Utah	29	33
O10	● |	Texas-El Paso	42	24
O17	● |	at Air Force	32	28
O24	|	Wyoming	14	31
O31	|	San Diego State	13	20
N7	|	at Hawaii	13	24
N14	●	Ohio U.	35	24
N21	● |	at New Mexico	14	10

SONNY LUBICK		
1993-PRESENT # (.651)		95-51

1993

			5-6-0 (5-3-0)
S4		Oregon	9	23
S11	●	Air Force	8	5
S18	│	Brigham Young	22	27
S25		at Nebraska	13	48
O2		at Kansas	6	24
O9	●	Fresno State	34	32
O16		at San Diego State	3	30
O23	│	at Utah	21	38
O30	●	New Mexico	21	20
N13	●	at Texas-El Paso	52	0
N20	●	at Wyoming	41	21

1994

			10-2-0 (7-1-0)
S3	●	at Air Force	34	21
S10	●	Utah State	41	16
S17	●	at Brigham Young	28	21
S24	●	San Diego State	19	17
O1	●	at New Mexico	38	31
O8	●	at Arizona	21	16
O15	●	Texas-El Paso	47	9
O22		Utah	31	45
N5	│	Wyoming	35	24
N12	●	Arkansas State	48	3
N19	●	at Fresno State	44	42
		HOLIDAY BOWL	
D30		Michigan	14	24

1995

			8-4-0 (6-2-0)
S2	●	Montana St.	31	10
S9		at Colorado	14	42
S16	●	at Air Force	27	20
S30	│	Brigham Young	21	28
O7	●	at Utah State	59	17
O14	●	at Utah	19	14
O21	│	New Mexico	14	22
O28	●	at Wyoming	31	24
N4	●	Texas-El Paso	56	10
N11	●	Hawaii	22	0
N25	●	at San Diego State	24	13
		HOLIDAY BOWL	
D29		Kansas State	21	54

1996

			7-5 (6-2)
A31	●	U.T. Chattanooga	61	19
S7		Colorado	34	48
S14		at Oregon	28	35
S21	│	Nevada-Las Vegas	35	16
S28		at Nebraska	9	65
O5	●	at Hawaii	28	16
O12	│	at Tulsa	14	20
O19	●	San Jose State	36	13
O26	●	San Diego State	27	18
N2	●	at Air Force	42	41
N9	●	at Fresno State	42	20
N16	│	Wyoming	24	25

1997

			11-2 (7-1)
A30	●	Nevada	45	13
S6		at Colorado	21	31
S13	●	at Utah State	35	24
S20	│	Air Force	0	24
O4	●	Hawaii	63	0
O11	●	at San Jose State	55	20
O18	●	at Wyoming	14	7
O26	●	Tulsa	44	8
N1	●	at Nevada-Las Vegas	45	19
N8	●	Fresno State	41	3
N22	●	at San Diego State	38	17
		WAC CHAMPIONSHIP	
D6	●	New Mexico *LV*	41	13
		HOLIDAY BOWL	
D29	●	Missouri	35	24

1998

			8-4 (5-3)
A29	●	at Michigan State	23	16
S5		Colorado *DEN*	14	42
S12	●	at Nevada	26	14
S17	│	at Air Force	27	30
S26	●	Nevada-Las Vegas	38	16
O3	●	at Texas-El Paso	20	17
O10	●	Tulsa	34	7
O17	●	at New Mexico State	47	28
O24	●	TCU	42	21
O31		at Rice	23	35
N7		Wyoming	19	27
N14	●	at SMU	32	10

1999-PRESENT	
MOUNTAIN WEST	

1999

			8-4 (5-2)
S4	●	Colorado *DEN*	41	14
S11	●	Nevada	38	33
S16	│	at Brigham Young	13	34
O2	●	New Mexico State	46	7
O9		at Fresno State	13	44
O16	│	San Diego State	10	17
O23	●	at Wyoming	24	13
O28	│	Utah	31	24
N6		at New Mexico	36	22
N18	●	Air Force	41	21
N27	●	at Nevada-Las Vegas	35	17
		LIBERTY BOWL	
D31		Southern Miss	17	23

2000

			10-2 (6-1)
S2	●	Colorado *DEN*	28	24
S9	●	East Tenn. St.	41	7
S16		at Arizona State	10	13
S30	●	at Nevada	45	14
O7	●	New Mexico	17	14
O14	●	Nevada-Las Vegas	20	19
O21	●	at Utah	24	17
O28	●	at San Diego State	34	22
N2	●	Brigham Young	45	21
N11	│	at Air Force	40	44
N16	●	Wyoming	37	13
		LIBERTY BOWL	
D29	●	Louisville	22	17

2001

			7-5 (5-2)
S1	●	Colorado *DEN*	14	41
S8	●	Nevada	35	18
S22	│	San Diego State	7	14
S29	●	at Wyoming	42	14
O4		at Louisville	2	7
O13		Fresno State	22	25
O20	●	at Nevada-Las Vegas	26	24
O27	●	Utah	19	17
N1	│	at Brigham Young	34	56
N8	●	Air Force	28	21
N17	●	at New Mexico	24	17
		NEW ORLEANS BOWL	
D18	●	North Texas	45	20

2002

			10-4 (6-1)
A22	●	at Virginia	35	29
A31	●	Colorado *DEN*	19	14
S7		at UCLA	19	30
S14	●	Louisville	36	33
S28	●	at Nevada	32	28
O4		at Fresno State	30	32
O12	●	Wyoming	44	36
O19	●	at Utah	28	20
O24	│	Brigham Young	37	10
O31	●	at Air Force	31	12
N16	●	at San Diego State	49	21
N23	●	New Mexico	22	14
N30	│	Nevada-Las Vegas	33	36
		LIBERTY BOWL	
D31	●	TCU	3	17

2003

			7-6 (4-3)
A30	●	Colorado *DEN*	35	42
S6	●	at California	23	21
S13	●	Weber St.	31	7
S20		Miami, Ohio	21	41
S27	│	Utah	21	28
O4	●	Fresno State	34	10
O9	│	at Brigham Young	58	13
O16	●	Air Force	30	20
N1	│	at Wyoming	28	35
N7	│	at New Mexico	34	37
N15	●	San Diego State	21	6
N22	●	at Nevada-Las Vegas	24	23
		SAN FRANCISCO BOWL	
D31	●	Boston College	21	35

2004

			4-7 (3-4)
S4		at Colorado	24	27
S11		at Southern Cal	0	49
S18		Minnesota	16	34
S25	●	Montana St.	39	14
O2	│	Brigham Young	21	31
O16	●	at San Diego State	21	17
O22	●	Wyoming	30	7
O30	│	New Mexico	16	27
N6	│	at Utah	31	63
N13	●	Nevada-Las Vegas	45	10
N20	│	at Air Force	17	47

CONNECTICUT

BY SETH WICKERSHAM

UCONN FOOTBALL IS HAVING FUN. In 2000, the Huskies joined Division I-A as an independent. In 2003, brand-new Rentschler Field opened. In 2004, they moved up to the Big East, where a conference championship means a BCS berth. No wonder UConn advertises that the future looks bright. The past, though, is something else entirely. For 102 years, the Huskies struggled to score (the 1911 team was whipped 166-6), defend (the 1998 team gave up 413 points) and win (the program's all-time winning percentage is .484). But in recent years, the program began to grow into its own, and in 1998 UConn won 10 games for the first time in its history and qualified for the Division I-AA playoffs. After making the jump to the big time and a major conference, the Huskies are prepared for their next challenge: putting Storrs, Conn., on the college football map.

TRADITION In 2003, after 107 years of football, UConn fans finally started tailgating. Perhaps they're running a little behind, but until 2003 they didn't have a place for pregame parties at the old Memorial Stadium. In the 1930s and '40s, fans would steal rival University of Rhode Island's mascot—"ramnapping," it was called. After stealing rams grew old, fans would pack the train to the annual University of Massachusetts game. But when Rentschler Field opened, tailgating on the old Rentschler Airport landing strip was the scene. Hey, UConn: welcome to the party. Next year: goalpost removing!

BEST PLAYER Tailback Walt Trojanowski tied for the national lead in scoring as a sophomore in 1945, ringing up 132 points during the Huskies' 7–1 season. His stats that year: 761 yards on 158 carries and 22 rushing touchdowns, including games of six touchdowns (Worcester Tech) and four (Boston University). The Bridgeport product has owned UConn records for points in a game (36), rushing touchdowns in a game (six) and total points in a season (132) for almost 60 years.

BEST COACH J.O. Christian led UConn to a three-year run over the 1942, 1944 and 1945 seasons (no football was played in 1943 due to WWII) that featured a 20–4 record and 558 points scored to only 137 allowed. UConn's defense recorded a shutout in 13 of the 24 games. The Huskies had winning streaks of eight, six and five games during those seasons.

BEST TEAM Ten wins, a school record; first Atlantic 10 New England conference championship; first Division I-AA playoff berth. Not a bad way to celebrate 100 years of

PROFILE

University of Connecticut
Storrs, Conn.
Founded: 1881
Enrollment: 15,184
Colors: National Flag Blue and White
Nickname: Huskies
Stadium: Rentschler Field
　　Opened in 2003
　　Grass; 40,000 capacity
First football game: 1896
All-time record: 439–470–38 (.484)
Bowl record: 1–0
Website: www.uconnhuskies.com

THE BEST OF TIMES

Now. UConn made the transition into the Big East in 2004 with a 7–4 record, including 3–3 in conference play, capped with a 39-10 Motor City Bowl win.

THE WORST OF TIMES

The 1932 team went 0–6–2 and was shut out five times.

CONFERENCE

UConn joined the Big East in 2004 after stepping up to Division I-A in 2000. The Huskies were members of the Yankee Conference from 1949 to 1996, winning 14 titles (five outright), and the Atlantic 10 from 1997 to 1999. The program was independent from 2000 to 2003.

DISTINGUISHED ALUMNI

Ray Allen, NBA player and actor; David Lee, 1996 co-winner of Nobel Prize for Physics; Rebecca Lobo, WNBA player and TV analyst; Ron Palillo, actor; Joseph Polisi, president of Julliard School of Music

FIGHT SONG

UCONN HUSKY
UConn Husky, symbol of might to the foe.
Fight, fight Connecticut, It's vict'ry, Let's go.
Connecticut UConn Husky,
Do it again for the White and Blue
So go—go—go Connecticut, Connecticut U.
C-O-N-N-E-C-T-I-C-U-T
Connecticut, Connecticut Husky, Connecticut Husky
Connecticut C-O-N-N-U

Huskies football. In that 1998 season, UConn beat Hampton 42-34 in the Huskies' first playoff game, and finished the season ranked No. 7 among I-AA schools. Quarterback Shane Stafford finished his senior year ranked first or second in every major passing category, and needed it all; UConn's defense gave up 31.7 points per game that year.

BIGGEST GAME Division I-A can't be this easy, can it? The hard work for UConn in 2004 was finishing 7–4 in its first regular season in the Big East, including a 3–3 record in conference play. That got the Huskies a trip to Detroit to play Toledo in the Motor City Bowl—the Huskies' first bowl game. And the Huskies made it look easy again. Leading 3-0 in the first quarter, UConn went for it on fourth and six from Toledo's 32. Quarterback Dan Orlovsky rolled out and threw deep to receiver Jason Williams in the corner of the end zone for a touchdown. Two minutes later, Larry Taylor took a punt 68 yards for six, and by the end of the first quarter UConn was up 17-0. Most of the record crowd of 52,552 stormed the field after the 39-10 win. UConn coach Randy Edsall gave

> *Finally in 2003, after 107 years of football, UConn fans started tailgating. Previously, they just didn't have a place for pregame parties.*

the game ball to Connecticut governor Jodi Rell, who had been diagnosed with cancer and underwent a mastectomy the day of the game.

BIGGEST UPSET UConn was 0–16 against Yale, and on Sept. 25, 1965, it looked like it would be 0–17. The score was 6-6 with less than four minutes remaining, but Bulldogs quarterback Pete Doherty was moving Yale. The Huskies blitzed every linebacker, leaving their secondary in man coverage. Doherty passed to the left flat, right into the arms of UConn safety Eugene Campbell, who returned it 35 yards for a touchdown. Huskies fans were so excited about the 13-6 win, they ripped apart the Yale Bowl bleachers for souvenirs.

HEARTBREAKER Trailing North Carolina State 24-10 on the road in 2003 with less than nine minutes left, UConn rallied. Huskies quarterback Dan Orlovsky drove UConn on back-to-back drives of 84 and 79 yards to bring the game to 24-24; the tying score came on fourth and six with 1:34 left, when Orlovsky hit Shaun Feldeisen for an 11-yard touchdown. Orlovsky got the ball back moments later and

RECORDS

RUSHING YARDS

	GAME
277	Nick Giaquinto vs. Holy Cross, Nov. 20, 1976 (31 att.)
	SEASON
1,262	Tory Taylor, 1995 (208 att.)
	CAREER
2,624	Wilbur Gilliard, 1992-95 (484 att.)

PASSING YARDS

	GAME
413	Brian Hoffmann vs. Massachusetts, Oct. 17, 1998 (26 of 45)
	SEASON
3,485	Dan Orlovsky, 2003 (279 of 475)
	CAREER
10,706	Dan Orlovsky, 2001-04 (896 of 1,557)

RECEIVING YARDS

	GAME
236	Keith Hugger vs. Delaware, Nov. 27, 1981 (14 rec.)
	SEASON
1,354	Mark Didio, 1991 (88 rec.)
	CAREER
3,535	Mark Didio, 1988-91 (239 rec.)

POINTS

	GAME
36	Walter Trojanowski vs. Worcester Tech, Sept. 29, 1945 (6 TDs)
	SEASON
132	Walter Trojanowski, 1945 (22 TDs)
	CAREER
210	Wilbur Gilliard, 1992-95 (35 TDs)

CONSENSUS ALL-AMERICANS

1945	Walter Trojanowski, B
1973	Richard Foye, C
1980	Reggie Eccleston, WR
1983	John Dorsey, LB
1988	Glenn Antrum, WR
1989	Troy Ashley, LB
1991	Mark Didio, WR
1997	TaVarr Closs, OL

drove the Huskies to midfield before NC State linebacker Freddie Aughtry-Lindsay picked off his pass and returned it 56 yards for a touchdown with five seconds left.

STADIUM When Rentschler Field was opened in 2003, it was as if the Huskies finally had junked their black-and-white TVs for color—the program came to life. Rentschler seats 40,000, more than twice what old Memorial Stadium hosted (16,000). The $91.2 million venue has 38 club suites and more than 12,000 square feet of "function" (read: pregame party) area. The stadium is named Rentschler Field because it's built on ground formally known as Rentschler Field, an airstrip that saw visits from Charles Lindbergh and Amelia Earhart.

RIVAL Pick an era. Historically, UConn's biggest rival is Yale or Rhode Island, but the move to Division I-A has severed those ties, as the Huskies haven't played Yale since 1998 and Rhode Island since 2000. Since joining the Big East, UConn pointed to Boston College as its top competitor, but with BC off to the ACC in 2005, the Huskies will have to seek out a new antagonist.

NICKNAME From 1896 until 1934, UConn didn't have an official nickname, mostly juggling between the Aggies and the Statesmen. In 1934, UConn officially adopted the Huskies as its nickname.

MASCOT Jonathan the Husky was an all-white Siberian husky who first came to Storrs in 1934, and was named after Jonathan Trumbull, Connecticut's governor during the Revolutionary War. Jonathan I's great-grandfather traveled to the North Pole with Admiral E. Byrd in 1909, and Jonathan III was with Byrd when he carried out Operation High Jump in the Antarctic in 1946. UConn is currently showcasing Jonathan XII.

UNIFORMS The Huskies' early years were not very fashionable. In the first team photo in 1897, no two players are dressed alike. In 1901, every Husky wore horizontal blue-and-white striped shirts. Since then, the Huskies have played around with all the different combinations that National Flag Blue and White can afford, such as a large "C" on blue helmets (1960s and '70s), cursive "UConn" on a white helmet (1980s), print "UConn" on blue helmets (1990s), a large "UC" (early 2000s) and now just a "C" on blue helmets.

QUOTE "The bottom line is there is no tradition."
—Former UConn tailback Vin Clements, on Huskies football

CONNECTICUT ANNUAL STATISTICAL LEADERS

YR	RUSHING	YDS	ATT	AVG	PASSING	ATT	CMP	PCT	YDS	RECEIVING	REC	YDS	AVG
2002	Terry Caulley	1,247	220	5.7	Dan Orlovsky	366	221	.60	2,488	Tommy Collins	39	497	12.7
2003	Cornell Brockington	643	131	4.9	Dan Orlovsky	475	279	.59	3,485	Shaun Feldeisen	65	860	13.2
2004	Cornell Brockington	1,218	238	5.1	Dan Orlovsky	457	288	.63	3,354	Keron Henry	67	891	13.3

Receiving leaders by receptions
All statistics include postseason

CONNECTICUT ALL-TIME SCORES

WIN/LOSS PERCENTAGE SINCE 2000

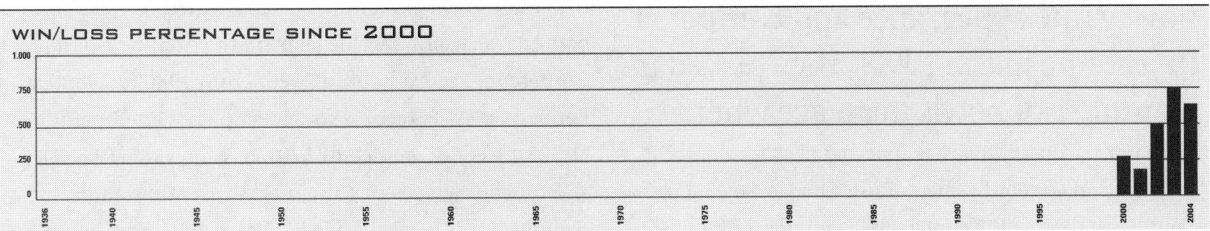

2000-2003
INDEPENDENT

RANDY EDSALL
1999-PRESENT (.464)   32-37

2000   3-8
S2		at Eastern Michigan	25	32
S9	●	Colgate	37	7
S16	●	at Buffalo	24	21
S23		Northeastern	27	35
S30		at Louisville	22	41
O7		at Boston College	3	55
O21	●	at Akron	38	35
O28		South Florida	13	21
N4		Middle Tennessee	10	66
N11		Rhode Island	21	26
N18		at Ball State	0	29

2001   2-9
S1		at Virginia Tech	10	52
S8		Ea. Washington	17	35
S22		Buffalo	20	37
S29	●	at Rutgers	20	19
O6	●	Eastern Michigan	19	0
O13		at South Florida	21	40
O27		Ball State	5	10
N3		at Cincinnati	28	45
N10		Utah State	31	38
N17		at Middle Tennessee	14	38
N24		at Temple	7	56

2002   6-6
A31		at Boston College	16	24
S7		Georgia Tech	14	31
S14	●	at Buffalo	24	3
S21	●	Ohio U.	37	19
S28		Ball State	21	24
O5		at Miami, Fla.	14	48
O19		Temple	24	38
O26		at Vanderbilt	24	48
N2	●	Fla. Atl.	61	14
N9	●	Kent State	63	21
N16	●	at Navy	38	0
N23	●	at Iowa State	37	20

2003   9-3
A30	●	Indiana	34	10
S6	●	at Army	48	21
S13	●	Boston College	14	24
S20	●	at Buffalo	38	7
S27		at Virginia Tech	13	47
O4	●	Lehigh	35	17
O11		at North Carolina St.	24	31
O18	●	at Kent State	34	31
O25	●	Akron	38	37
N1	●	Western Michigan	41	27
N8	●	Rutgers	38	31
N15	●	at Wake Forest	51	17

2004-PRESENT
BIG EAST

2004   8-4   (3-3)
S4	●	Murray St.	52	14
S11	●	Duke	22	20
S17	|	at Boston College	7	27
S25	●	Army	40	3
S30	●	Pittsburgh	29	17
O14	|	West Virginia	19	31
O23	●	Temple	45	31
O30	|	at Syracuse	30	42
N13	●	at Georgia Tech	10	30
N20	●	Buffalo	29	0
N25	●	at Rutgers	41	35

MOTOR CITY BOWL
D27		Toledo	39	10

DUKE

BY BOB HARIG

DUKE WASN'T ALWAYS KNOWN AS A basketball school, and it certainly wasn't always considered a pushover in football. Although the Blue Devils went more than 25 years without a bowl game appearance and competed in just one in the 1990s, they played in a number of bowls in an age when it was harder to do so. Duke has appeared in all four of the traditional major bowl games—Rose, Orange, Sugar and Cotton—and earned 17 conference championships in the Southern and Atlantic Coast conferences. The school boasts 11 College Football Hall of Fame inductees, a legendary coach whose name is on the stadium and an Outland Trophy winner in Mike McGee. Back when it was known as Trinity College, Duke played the first college football game below the Mason-Dixon line, taking on North Carolina in 1888. Finally, and perhaps most impressively, one Duke team (1938) did not allow a single point during the regular season.

TRADITION The best-known tradition associated with the Duke football program is playing for the Victory Bell each year against rival North Carolina. The practice began in 1948, with North Carolina earning possession in a 20-0 victory in Chapel Hill. The tradition was the brainchild of Duke head cheerleader Loring Jones and North Carolina head cheerleader Norman Spear; Jones designed the concept while Spear obtained a bell from an old railroad train. Red Lewis, then Duke's business manager for athletics, agreed to fund the bell's purchase.

BEST PLAYER Not only was Ben Bennett one of Duke's best quarterbacks, but his feats fill the Atlantic Coast Conference record book, as well. From 1980 to 1983, Bennett set ACC records for career passes attempted (1,375), passes completed (820), passing yards (9,614) and touchdown passes (55), marks that still stand as school records. Guard Mike McGee also deserves mention; in 1959 he won the Outland Trophy, given to the nation's outstanding interior lineman.

But a player from an earlier era, Ace Parker, was Duke's best. The Ace Parker Award is still given to the individual who overcomes adversity to display unparalleled prowess and commitment to the team. Parker is one of 11 former Blue Devils and coaches enshrined in the College Football Hall of Fame. A first-team All-America in 1936, Parker, a halfback, guided the Blue Devils to a 24–5 record from 1934 to 1936, finishing his career with 21 touchdowns and an average of 5.9 yards per rushing attempt. He went on to the NFL, where he was league MVP in 1940, and was inducted into the Pro Football Hall of Fame in 1972. "Ace Parker was a tremendous athlete," said Johnny Moore, a former Duke

PROFILE

Duke University
Durham, N.C.
Founded: 1838
Enrollment: 6,347
Colors: Royal Blue and White
Nickname: Blue Devils
Stadium: Wallace Wade Stadium
    Opened in 1929
    FieldTurf; 33,941 capacity
First football game: 1888
All-time record: 441–417–31 (.513)
Bowl record: 3–5
Atlantic Coast Conference championships:
7 (4 outright)
Outland Trophy: Mike McGee, 1959
First-round NFL draftees: 5
Website: www.goduke.com

THE BEST OF TIMES

From 1933 to 1941, the Blue Devils won five Southern Conference titles and never failed to win at least seven games in a season. The 1938 team did not allow a point throughout a nine-game regular season.

THE WORST OF TIMES

From 1996 to 2001, the Blue Devils had three winless seasons (1996, 2000 and 2001) and won a total of nine games. During that period, they won just five games in the ACC.

CONFERENCE

Duke was a charter member of the Atlantic Coast Conference in 1953, and has remained in the ACC since.

DISTINGUISHED ALUMNI

Elizabeth Dole, U.S. senator; Melinda Gates, co-founder of the Bill and Melinda Gates Foundation; Rik Kirkland, managing editor of *Fortune* magazine; Richard Lagos, president of Chile; Charlie Rose, talk-show host; Kenneth Starr, U.S. solicitor general, former U.S. appeals court judge

FIGHT SONG

FIGHT BLUE DEVILS
Fight, Fight Blue Devils
Fight for Duke and the Blue and White
March on through
For the touchdown's there for you
Go get 'em
Duke is out to win today
Carolina goodnight
So turn on the steam team
Fight Blue Devils Fight

sports information assistant and unofficial Duke historian. "He could shoot par at golf. He played professional football and baseball. Just a great athlete."

BEST COACH The Blue Devils' stadium is named after Wallace Wade for a reason. When he came to Duke in 1931, fresh off of eight seasons at Alabama, he helped put the Blue Devils on the college football map. It seemed a curious decision, leaving an undefeated program at Alabama—where he had won three national titles—but many years later Wade said he simply liked the idea of going to a school that valued academics and athletics. He guided Duke to two bowl games and final national rankings of No. 3 in 1938 and No. 2 in 1941. In the former season, the Blue Devils finished 9–1, but were 9–0 in the regular season and posted shutouts in every game. Wade coached Duke from 1931 to 1941, then again from 1946 to 1950 (his hiatus was due to military service during World War II), compiling a record of 110–36–7. Bill Murray's 1951-65 tenure was nearly as impressive: he went 93–51–9, led the Blue Devils to seven conference titles and eight final Top 20 rankings, and four times was voted league coach of the year. Murray,

> *There is a reason Duke still plays in a stadium named for Wallace Wade: he helped put the Blue Devils on the college football map.*

the first Duke graduate to lead the football program, also coached at Delaware; he compiled an overall record of 142–67–11, and is a member of the College Football Hall of Fame.

BEST TEAM The 1938 Blue Devils were nicknamed the Iron Dukes after going through the regular season unbeaten, untied and unscored upon. Since 1920, just three schools have accomplished the feat: Colgate in 1932, Duke in 1938 and Tennessee in 1939. Coach Wade's team won the Southern Conference title and outscored its nine regular-season opponents by a total of 114-0. Robert O'Mara was the team's top offensive player, rushing for 703 yards on 162 carries and scoring a team-high five touchdowns. The year's arguable highlight was the final game of the regular season, a 7-0 victory over No. 4 Pittsburgh before 49,138 fans at Duke Stadium. The game was played in a snowstorm, and Duke won when Bolo Perdue blocked a Pittsburgh punt and recovered it in the end zone. The game featured 16 punts by Duke's Eric Tipton, with 14 pinning the Panthers inside their 20. The season ultimately ended with a 7-3 Rose Bowl loss to Southern California.

RECORDS

RUSHING YARDS
GAME
238 — Robert Baldwin vs. Maryland, Sept. 3, 1994 (33 att.)
SEASON
1,236 — Steve Jones, 1972 (287 att.)
CAREER
3,122 — Chris Douglas, 2000-03 (695 att.)

PASSING YARDS
GAME
479 — Dave Brown vs. North Carolina, Nov. 18, 1989 (33 of 54)
SEASON
3,824 — Anthony Dilweg, 1988 (287 of 484)
CAREER
9,614 — Ben Bennett, 1980-83 (820 of 1,375)

RECEIVING YARDS
GAME
283 — Chris Castor vs. Wake Forest, Nov. 6, 1982 (10 rec.)
SEASON
1,149 — Clarkston Hines, 1989 (61 rec.)
CAREER
3,318 — Clarkston Hines, 1986-89 (189 rec.)

POINTS
GAME
36 — Tom Powers vs. Richmond, Oct. 21, 1950 (6 TDs)
SEASON
104 — Clarkston Hines, 1989 (17 TDs, 1 two-pt. conv.)
CAREER
240 — Sims Lenhardt, 1996-99 (55 FGs, 75 PATs)

CONSENSUS ALL-AMERICANS

1933	Fred Crawford	T
1936	Ace Parker	HB
1971	Ernie Jackson	DB
1989	Clarkston Hines	WR

BIGGEST GAME After going through the 1938 regular season without giving up a point, the Blue Devils traveled to Pasadena for the Rose Bowl against USC and nearly extended the streak to 10. In front of 93,000 fans, Tony Ruffa's 24-yard field goal gave the Blue Devils a 3-0 lead in the fourth quarter, but fourth-team USC quarterback Doyle Nave completed three straight passes to Al Krueger—the final one an 18-yard touchdown with 40 seconds remaining—to give No. 7 USC a 7-3 victory over No. 3 Duke. "I hated to see the boys lose it when they played such a great game," said Wade. "We did well as long as they used only two teams, but when they put in those third and fourth teams, they were too much for us."

BIGGEST UPSET Duke's 21-17 home victory over No. 7 Clemson in 1989 helped the Blue Devils claim their first ACC title since 1962. The Tigers were the highest-ranked team Duke had defeated since the 1960 season, when the Devils beat No. 4 Navy and No. 7 Arkansas (the latter in the Cotton Bowl). Going in, coach Steve Spurrier said Duke had a "million-in-one chance" of winning, but the Blue Devils came back from a 14-0 halftime deficit behind fullback Randy Cuthbert, who gained 55 yards on 10 carries, including a five-yard touchdown run in the third quarter. Quarterback Billy Ray put together an 86-yard drive and hit All-America receiver Clarkston Hines for the tying touchdown with 2:09 remaining in the third quarter. A Clemson field goal made it 17-14, but with seven minutes left, Ray engineered another drive, completing six of nine passes, including a seven-yarder to fullback Chris Brown for the winning touchdown with 3:18 remaining.

STADIUM Wallace Wade Stadium was named for the former Duke coach. Known as Duke Stadium when it opened on Oct. 5, 1929, it seats 33,941 in an intimate setting among the greenery and towering pines of the surrounding Duke Forest. The stadium was renamed in honor of Wade in 1967. The horseshoe-shaped structure still features aluminum bench seating, though modern improvements include a video scoreboard and the Yoh Football Center on the stadium's northeast corner.

RIVAL The University of North Carolina is 11 miles down the road from Durham, in Chapel Hill; predictably, the two neighbors have met every year since 1922, though they first played in 1888. The Tar Heels hold a big lead in the series, but Duke has played no opponent more often. The Blue Devils put an end to the longest streak in the series— 13 games—when they defeated the Tar Heels in 2003. Duke and North Carolina play for the Victory Bell each year, though the rivalry also includes the Carlyle Cup, a trophy at stake in an all-sports competition between the two schools.

NICKNAME The term Blue Devils was derived from the French Blue Devils, an Alpine corps that wore a striking blue uniform with a blue beret. Its adoption by Duke was slow, mostly because nothing better could be found. Dating to 1921-22, meetings of the entire student body were held to decide a name; William H. Lander, an assistant editor of *The Trinity Chronicle*, suggested Blue Devils, although he later admitted he wasn't enamored of it. No name received majority support, so by the end of the school year, Duke was still without a nickname. The following year, Lander and Mike Bradshaw were named editors of *The Chronicle*, and decided before leaving that they would use their influence to name the school and its teams the Blue Devils. Thus, from the first issue of the 1922-23 *Chronicle*, athletic teams were referred to as Blue Devils.

MASCOT The first time a Blue Devil mascot appeared was Oct. 5, 1929, when someone dressed up as a blue devil for a game against Pittsburgh on the day Duke Stadium was dedicated.

UNIFORMS Duke's team colors are royal blue and white, with blue jerseys worn at home, white on the road. Helmets

---

ALL-CENTURY TEAM

Chosen in 2000 by Blue Devil Weekly through voting by readers and visitors to GoDuke.com.

OFFENSE

1957-59	Mike McGee,	OL
1960-62	Art Gregory,	OL
1970-72	Ed Newman,	OL
1986-89	Chris Port,	OL
1936-38	Dan Hill,	C
1973-76	Billy Bryan,	C
1958-60	Tee Moorman,	WR
1968-70	Wes Chesson,	WR
1986-89	Clarkston Hines,	WR
1980-83	Ben Bennett,	QB
1934-36	Ace Parker,	RB
1937-39	George McAfee,	RB
1970-72	Steve Jones,	RB
1961-63	Jay Wilkinson,	KR
1996-99	Sims Lenhardt,	PK

DEFENSE

1931-33	Fred Crawford,	DL
1945-48	Al DeRogatis,	DL
1952-53	Ed Meadows,	DL
1958-60	Dwight Bumgarner,	LB
1962-64	Mike Curtis,	LB
1964-66	Bob Matheson,	LB
1967-70	Dick Biddle,	LB
1969-71	Ernie Jackson,	DB
1992-95	Ray Farmer,	DB
1934-36	Ace Parker,	DB
1941-44	Tom Davis,	DB
1936-38	Eric Tipton,	P

with "Duke" written in script had been a staple for years, but are now white with a blue "D."

TRAGEDY Micah Harris, a senior linebacker and defensive end, was killed in a one-car accident on June 11, 2004, at age 21. Harris played in 33 games for the Blue Devils, with 22 starts, recording 124 tackles and 6.5 quarterback sacks.

LORE Duke played in two Rose Bowl games, but only one was played at Rose Bowl Stadium in Pasadena, Calif. The other was played right at home at Duke Stadium. Following the bombing of Pearl Harbor on Dec. 7, 1941, large crowds were not allowed to assemble on the West Coast, so the Rose

Bowl had to look for another site, ultimately accepting an offer to play the game in Durham. Duke had won the Southern Conference title and was 9–0 before losing to Pacific Coast Conference champion Oregon State, 20-16. Coach Wade later blamed the loss on himself, pointing to the distractions of playing in his own stadium. The game remains the only time the Rose Bowl has not been played in California.

QUOTE "Duke wants to be successful in everything it does. Why can't we have a football program that's successful?" —Carl Franks, who went 7–45 in four-plus seasons as coach (1999-2003), including consecutive 0–11 campaigns, as the Blue Devils went 14 years with just one winning record

DUKE ANNUAL STATISTICAL LEADERS

YR	RUSHING	YDS	ATT	AVG	PASSING	ATT	CMP	PCT	YDS	RECEIVING	REC	YDS	AVG
1963	Jay Wilkinson	631	117	5.4	Scotty Glacken	201	101	.50	1,265	Stan Crisson	48	559	11.6
1964	Mike Curtis	497	121	4.1	Scotty Glacken	192	104	.54	1,178	James Scott	29	388	13.4
1965	Jay Calabrese	658	154	4.3	Todd Orvald	105	63	.60	850	Chuck Drulis	39	390	10.0
1966	Jay Calabrese	580	175	3.3	Al Woodall	71	39	.55	482	Dave Dunaway	43	614	14.3
1967	Jay Calabrese	563	136	4.1	Al Woodall	150	79	.53	1,019	Jim Dearth	20	284	14.2
1968	Phil Asack	690	168	4.1	Leo Hart	301	162	.54	2,238	Henley Carter	65	892	13.7
1969	Bob Zwirko	504	94	5.4	Leo Hart	268	145	.54	1,642	Marcel Courtillet	45	489	10.9
1970	Steve Jones	854	203	4.2	Leo Hart	308	180	.58	2,236	Wes Chesson	74	1,080	14.6
1971	Steve Jones	861	193	4.5	Dennis Satyshur	84	41	.49	631	Dan Phelan	17	273	16.1
1972	Steve Jones	1,236	287	4.3	Mark Johnson	69	30	.43	380	Mark Landon	16	206	12.9
1973	Tony Benjamin	572	114	5.0	Mark Johnson	91	38	.42	497	Ben Fordham	30	438	14.6
1974	Art Gore	627	125	5.0	Hal Spears	141	79	.56	1,132	Troy Slade	31	489	15.8
1975	Tony Benjamin	674	136	5.0	Bob Corbett	131	81	.62	1,063	Troy Slade	43	654	15.2
1976	Mike Dunn	757	176	4.3	Mike Dunn	168	90	.54	1,078	Tom Hall	44	594	13.5
1977	Stanley Broadie	579	132	4.4	Mike Dunn	191	102	.53	1,239	Tom Hall	33	418	12.7
1978	Greg Rhett	453	85	4.8	Mike Dunn	144	65	.45	688	Derrick Lewis	20	365	18.3
1979	Greg Rhett	427	121	3.5	Stanley Driskell	145	54	.37	721	Ron Frederick	28	395	14.1
1980	Greg Boone	380	94	4.0	Ben Bennett	330	174	.53	2,050	Marvin Brown	34	451	13.3
1981	Mike Grayson	744	179	4.2	Ben Bennett	202	110	.54	1,445	Cedric Jones	42	832	19.8
1982	Mike Grayson	693	136	5.1	Ben Bennett	374	236	.63	3,033	Mark Militello	52	725	13.9
1983	Mike Grayson	785	181	4.3	Ben Bennett	469	300	.64	3,086	Mike Grayson	66	582	8.8
1984	Julius Grantham	395	110	3.6	Steve Slayden	202	113	.56	1,229	Chuck Herring	37	627	16.9
1985	Tracy Smith	455	122	3.7	Steve Slayden	294	173	.59	1,937	Doug Green	51	804	15.8
1986	Julius Grantham	677	158	4.3	Steve Slayden	313	183	.58	1,914	Doug Green	46	608	13.2
1987	Roger Boone	550	137	4.0	Steve Slayden	395	230	.58	2,924	Roger Boone	62	587	9.5
1988	Roger Boone	836	185	4.5	Anthony Dilweg	484	287	.59	3,824	Roger Boone	73	630	8.6
1989	Randy Cuthbert	1,023	187	5.5	Billy Ray	274	174	.64	2,035	Clarkston Hines	61	1,149	18.8
1990	Randy Cuthbert	595	136	4.4	Dave Brown	245	129	.53	1,444	Randy Cuthbert	46	374	8.1
1991	Chris Brown	320	83	3.9	Dave Brown	437	230	.53	2,794	Chris Brown	38	302	7.9
1992	Randy Cuthbert	1,031	227	4.5	Spence Fischer	197	113	.57	1,505	Randy Cuthbert	37	345	9.3
1993	David Lowman	439	110	4.0	Spence Fischer	388	213	.55	2,563	Stanley Dorsey	44	678	15.4
1994	Robert Baldwin	1,187	276	4.3	Spence Fischer	346	204	.59	2,285	Bill Khayat	49	562	11.5
1995	Laymarr Marshall	708	188	3.8	Spence Fischer	438	256	.58	2,668	Marc Wilson	47	531	11.3
1996	Letavious Wilkins	554	116	4.8	David Green	165	88	.53	958	Corey Thomas	38	527	13.9
1997	Laymarr Marshall	359	70	5.1	Bobby Campbell	176	85	.48	925	Scottie Montgomery	51	633	12.4
1998	B.J. Hill	798	192	4.2	Bobby Campbell	206	101	.49	1,199	Scottie Montgomery	60	793	13.2
1999	Letavious Wilkins	334	95	3.5	Spencer Romine	243	123	.51	1,638	Scottie Montgomery	51	819	16.1
2000	Chris Douglas	503	110	4.6	D. Bryant	258	129	.50	1,448	Mike Hart	31	540	17.4
2001	Chris Douglas	841	218	3.9	D. Bryant	384	187	.49	2,454	Ben Erdeljac	42	684	16.3
2002	Alex Wade	979	201	4.9	Adam Smith	308	174	.56	2,031	Khary Sharpe	30	458	15.3
2003	Chris Douglas	1,138	236	4.8	Mike Schneider	208	97	.47	1,220	Reggie Love	27	290	10.7
2004	Cedric Dargan	462	125	3.7	Mike Schneider	253	150	.59	1,527	Ben Patrick	32	311	9.7

Receiving leaders by receptions
The NCAA began including postseason stats in 2002

DUKE ALL-TIME SCORES

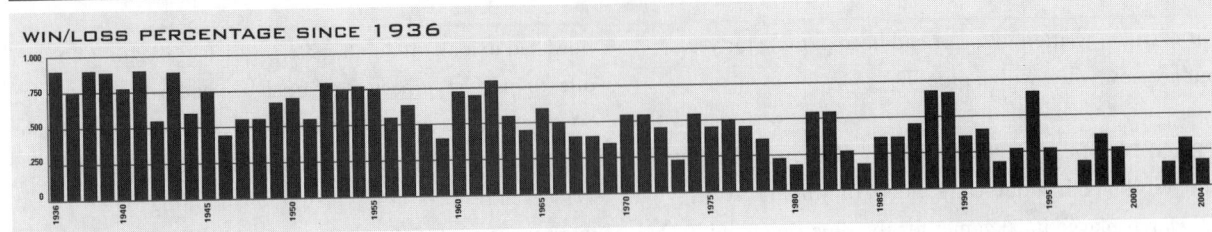

WIN/LOSS PERCENTAGE SINCE 1936

DR. JOHN CROWELL
1888-89 (.750)   3-1

1888   1-0-0
| N27 | ● | North Carolina | 16 | 0 |

1889   2-1-0
M8	●	North Carolina *RAL*	25	17
M29		Wake Forest *RAL*	0	32
N27		at Wake Forest	8	4

NO HEAD COACH

1890   0-1-0
| N29 | | Virginia *RICH* | 4 | 10 |

1891   3-0-0
N14	●	Furman *COLU*	96	0
N20	●	at North Carolina	6	4
N28	●	Virginia *RICH*	20	0

1892   1-3-0
N12		North Carolina	0	24
U		at VMI	0	32
N22	●	at Auburn	34	6
N24		Virginia *ATL*	4	46

1893   3-1-0
O18	●	at Wake Forest	12	6
O28	●	North Carolina	6	4
N4	●	Tennessee	70	0
N11		Virginia *LYN*	0	30

1894   0-1-0
| O24 | | at North Carolina | 0 | 28 |

1895-1919
NO TEAM

FLOYD J. EGAN
1920 (.900)   4-0-1

1920   4-0-1
O30	●	Guilford *UNK*	20	7
N6	●	Emory & Henry *UNK*	7	0
N13	●	Lynchburg *UNK*	13	0
N13	●	Elon	13	6
N25	=	at Wofford	0	0

JAMES BALDWIN
1921 (.778)   6-1-2

1921   6-1-2
O1	●	Lynchburg	14	13
O8		William & Mary	0	12
O15	●	Randolph Macon	6	0
O22	●	Emory & Henry	7	0
O29	=	Elon	0	0
N5	●	Guilford	28	0
N11	●	at Wake Forest	17	0
N19	=	NYU	7	7
N24	●	Wofford	68	0

HERMAN STEINER
1922 (.750)   7-2-1

1922   7-2-1
S30	●	Guilford	43	0
O7	●	Hampden-Sydney	27	0
O12		at North Carolina	0	20
O21		William & Mary	7	13
O28	●	at Davidson	12	0
N4	●	Oglethorpe	7	6
N11	●	at Wake Forest	3	0
N18	●	Randolph Macon	25	12
N25	=	at Presbyterian	6	6
D2	●	at Wofford	26	0

S.M. ALEXANDER
1923 (.556)   5-4

1923   5-4-0
S29	●	Guilford	68	0
O6	●	Randolph Macon	54	0
O12		North Carolina	6	14
O20		William & Mary	0	21
O27		at Virginia	0	33
N3	●	Elon	39	0
N10		at Wake Forest	6	16
N24	●	at Newberry	20	14
D1	●	Davidson *CHAR*	18	6

HOWARD JONES
1924 (.444)   4-5

1924   4-5-0
S27		at North Carolina St.	0	14
O4	●	Guilford	33	6
O11		at North Carolina	0	6
O18	●	at Richmond	14	0
N1		William & Mary *NOR*	3	21
N8	●	Elon	54	0
N11		Wake Forest	0	32
N22	●	Wofford	12	0
N29		Davidson	13	20

PAT HERRON
1925 (.444)   4-5

1925   4-5-0
S26	●	Guilford	33	0
O3		North Carolina St.	0	13
O10		North Carolina	0	41
O17		at William & Mary	0	41
O31	●	Richmond	10	0
N7		Wake Forest	3	21
N14	●	at Elon	6	0
N21	●	Wofford	6	0
N28		at Davidson	0	26

JAMES DeHART
1926-30 (.510)   24-23-2

1926   3-6-0
S25	●	Guilford	32	0
O2		at Richmond	7	9
O9	●	Elon	32	0
O16		at North Carolina	0	6
O23		at Columbia	0	24
O30		Wake Forest *GOL*	0	21
N13		at North Carolina St.	19	26
N20	●	Wofford	34	0
N27		Davidson	0	20

1927   4-5-0
S23		Furman	7	13
O1	●	at Boston College	25	9
O8		at Wash. & Lee	7	12
O15	●	Richmond	72	0
O22		at Navy	6	32
O29	●	at Wake Forest	32	6
N12		North Carolina St.	18	20
N19		North Carolina	0	18
N26	●	at Davidson	48	7

1928   5-5-0
S29		at Furman	0	6
O6	●	South Dakota	25	6
O12		at Boston College	0	19
O20		at Navy	0	6
O27		at Georgetown	0	35
N3	●	Mercer	38	18
N10	●	Wake Forest	38	0
N17	●	at North Carolina St.	14	12
N24	●	Davidson	33	0
D8		at North Carolina	7	14

1929   4-6-0 (2-1-0)
S28		at Mercer	19	6
O5		Pittsburgh	7	52
O19		at Navy	13	45
O26		at Villanova	12	58
N2		at Boston College	12	20
N9	●	LSU	32	6
N16	●	North Carolina St.	19	12
N23	●	Wake Forest	20	0
N30		at Davidson	12	13
D7		North Carolina	7	48

1930   8-1-2 (4-1-1)
S27		South Carolina	0	22
O4	●	Virginia	32	0
O11	●	Davidson	12	0
O18	●	at Navy	18	0
O25	●	Wofford	14	0
N1	●	Villanova *PHIL*	12	6
N8	●	Kentucky	14	7
N15	●	at North Carolina St.	18	0
N22	=	at Wake Forest	13	13
N27	●	Wash. & Lee	14	0
D6	=	at North Carolina	0	0

WALLACE WADE
1931-41, '46-50 (.742)   110-36-7

1931   5-3-2 (3-3-1)
S26		at South Carolina	0	7
O3	●	VMI	13	0
O10	●	Villanova	18	0
O17	=	at Davidson	0	0
O23	●	Wake Forest	28	0
O31		at Tennessee	2	25
N7	●	at Kentucky	7	0
N14		North Carolina St.	0	14
N21		North Carolina	0	0
N28	●	at Wash. & Lee	6	0

1932   7-3-0 (5-3-0)
S24	●	Davidson	13	0
O1	●	at VMI	44	0
O8		Auburn *BIRM*	7	18
O15	●	Maryland	34	0
O21	●	Wake Forest	9	0
O29		at Tennessee	13	16
N5	●	Kentucky	13	0
N12		at North Carolina St.	0	6
N19	●	at North Carolina	7	0
N25	●	Wash. & Lee	13	0

1933   9-1-0 (4-0-0)
S30	●	VMI *GRO*	37	6
O7	●	Wake Forest	22	0
O14	●	Tennessee	10	2
O21	●	at Davidson	19	7
O28	●	at Kentucky	14	7
N4	●	Auburn	13	7
N11	●	at Maryland	38	7
N18	●	North Carolina	21	0
N25	●	North Carolina St.	7	0
D2		at Georgia Tech	0	6

1934   7-2-0 (3-1-0)
S29	●	at VMI	46	0
O6	●	Clemson	20	6
O13	●	Georgia Tech	20	0
O20	●	at Davidson	20	0
O27		at Tennessee	6	14
N3	●	Auburn *BIRM*	13	6
N10	●	Wake Forest	28	7
N17		at North Carolina	0	7
D1	●	North Carolina St.	32	0

1935   8-2-0 (5-0-0)
S21	●	Wake Forest *GRO*	26	7
S28	●	South Carolina	47	0
O5	●	Wash. & Lee *RICH*	26	0
O12	●	at Clemson	38	12
O19		Georgia Tech	0	6
O25		Auburn	0	7
N2	●	Tennessee	19	6
N9	●	at Davidson	26	7
N16	●	North Carolina	25	0
N23	●	at North Carolina St.	7	0

1936   9-1-0 (7-0-0)
S19	●	Davidson *GRO*	13	0
S26	●	Colgate	6	0
O3	●	at South Carolina	21	0
O10	●	Clemson	25	0
O17	●	Georgia Tech	19	6
O24		at Tennessee	13	15
O31	●	Wash. & Lee *RICH*	51	0
N7	●	at Wake Forest	20	0
N14	●	at North Carolina	27	7
N26	●	North Carolina St.	13	0

1937   7-2-1 (5-1-0)
S25	●	Virginia Tech *GRO*	25	0
O2	●	at Davidson	34	6
O9	=	Tennessee	0	0
O16	●	at Georgia Tech	20	19
O23	●	at Colgate	13	0
O30	●	Wash. & Lee *RICH*	43	0
N6	●	Wake Forest	67	0
N13		North Carolina	6	14
N20	●	at North Carolina St.	20	7
N27		Pittsburgh	0	10

1938   9-1-0 (5-0-0)
S24	●	Virginia Tech *GRO*	18	0
O1	●	Davidson	27	0
O8	●	Colgate *BUF*	7	0
O15	●	Georgia Tech	6	0
O22	●	Wake Forest *W-S*	7	0
O29	●	at North Carolina	14	0
N12	●	at Syracuse	21	0
N19	●	North Carolina St.	7	0
N26	●	Pittsburgh	7	0

ROSE BOWL
| J2 | | Southern Cal | 3 | 7 |

1939   8-1-0 (5-0-0)
S30	●	at Davidson	26	6
O7	●	Colgate	37	0
O14		at Pittsburgh	13	14
O21	●	Syracuse	33	6
O28	●	Wake Forest	6	0
N4	●	at Georgia Tech	7	6
N11	●	at VMI	20	7
N18	●	North Carolina	13	3
N25	●	at North Carolina St.	28	0

1940   7-2-0 (4-1-0)
S28	●	VMI	23	0
O5		at Tennessee	0	13
O19	●	at Colgate	13	0
O26	●	at Wake Forest	23	0
N2	●	Georgia Tech	41	7
N9	●	Davidson	46	13
N16		at North Carolina	3	6
N23	●	North Carolina St.	42	6
N30	●	Pittsburgh	12	7

1941   9-1-0 (5-0-0)
S27	●	Wake Forest	43	14
O4	●	Tennessee	19	0
O11	●	Maryland *BALT*	50	0
O18	●	Colgate	27	14
O25	●	at Pittsburgh	27	7
N1	●	at Georgia Tech	14	0
N8	●	at Davidson	56	0
N15	●	North Carolina	20	0
N22	●	at North Carolina St.	55	6

ROSE BOWL
| J1 | | Oregon State *DUR* | 16 | 20 |

EDDIE CAMERON
1942-45 (.689) 25-11-1

1942 5-4-1 (3-1-1)

S26	● |	Davidson W-S	21	0
O3	|	at Wake Forest	7	20
O10		Georgia Pre-Flight	12	26
O17	●	Colgate BUF	34	0
O24	●	at Pittsburgh	28	0
O31		Georgia Tech	7	26
N7	● |	Maryland	42	0
N14	= |	at North Carolina	13	13
N21	● |	North Carolina St.	47	0
N28		at Jacksonville NAS	0	13

1943 8-1-0 (4-0-0)

S18	●	Camp Lejeune	40	0
S25	● |	Richmond	61	0
O2	●	N.C. Pre-Flight	42	0
O9		Navy BALT	13	14
O16	● |	North Carolina	14	7
O30	●	at Georgia Tech	14	7
N6	● |	at North Carolina St.	75	0
N13	●	Virginia	49	0
N20	● |	at North Carolina	27	6

1944 6-4-0 (4-0-0)

S23	● |	Richmond	61	7
S30		at Pennsylvania	7	18
O7		N.C. Pre-Flight	6	13
O14		Navy BALT	0	7
O28		Army NYC	7	27
N4	●	Georgia Tech	19	13
N11	● |	Wake Forest	34	0
N18	● |	at South Carolina	34	7
N25	● |	at North Carolina	33	0
		SUGAR BOWL		
J1	●	Alabama	29	26

1945 6-2-0 (4-0-0)

S22	● |	South Carolina	60	0
S29	●	Bogue Field	76	0
O6		Navy	0	21
O13	● |	at Wake Forest	26	19
O27		Army NYC	13	48
N3	●	at Georgia Tech	14	6
N10	● |	North Carolina St.	26	13
N24	● |	North Carolina	14	7

WALLACE WADE

1946 4-5-0 (3-2-0)

S28	|	at North Carolina St.	6	13
O5		Tennessee	7	12
O12	●	Navy BALT	21	6
O19	● |	Richmond	41	0
O26		Army NYC	0	19
N2		Georgia Tech	0	14
N9	● |	Wake Forest	13	0
N16	● |	at South Carolina	39	0
N23	|	at North Carolina	7	22

1947 4-3-2 (3-1-1)

S27	● |	North Carolina St.	7	0
O4	●	at Tennessee	19	7
O11	=	Navy BALT	14	14
O18	● |	Maryland	19	7
O25	● |	at Wake Forest	13	6
N1		at Georgia Tech	0	7
N8		Missouri	7	28
N15	= |	South Carolina	0	0
N22	|	North Carolina	0	21

1948 4-3-2 (3-2-1)

S25	= |	at North Carolina St.	0	0
O2	=	Tennessee	7	7
O9	●	Navy	28	7
O16	● |	Maryland DC	13	12
O23	● |	Virginia Tech ROA	7	0
O30		Georgia Tech	7	19
N6	|	Wake Forest	20	27
N13	● |	George Washington	62	0
N20	|	at North Carolina	0	20

1949 6-3-0 (4-2-0)

S24	● |	Richmond	67	0
O1	●	at Tennessee	21	7
O8		at Navy	14	28
O15	● |	North Carolina St.	14	13
O22	● |	Virginia Tech	55	7
O29	●	at Georgia Tech	27	14
N5	|	Wake Forest	7	27
N12	● |	at George Washington	35	0
N19	|	North Carolina	20	21

1950 7-3-0 (5-2-0)

S23	● |	at South Carolina	14	0
S30	●	Pittsburgh	28	14
O7		Tennessee	7	28
O14	● |	at North Carolina St.	7	0
O21	● |	at Richmond	41	0
O28	|	Maryland	14	26
N4	●	Georgia Tech	30	21
N11	|	Wake Forest	7	13
N18	● |	Virginia Tech W-S	47	6
N25	● |	at North Carolina	7	0

BILL MURRAY
1951-65 (.637) 93-51-9

1951 5-4-1 (4-2-0)

S22	● |	at South Carolina	34	6
S29	●	at Pittsburgh	19	14
O6		at Tennessee	0	26
O13	● |	North Carolina St.	27	21
O20	● |	Virginia Tech NOR	55	6
O27		Virginia	7	30
N3	=	at Georgia Tech	14	14
N10	|	Wake Forest	13	19
N17	|	at William & Mary	13	14
N24	● |	North Carolina	19	7

1952 8-2-0 (5-0-0)

S20	● |	Wash. & Lee	34	0
S26	●	at SMU	14	7
O4	●	Tennessee	7	0
O11	● |	at South Carolina	33	7
O18	● |	at North Carolina St.	57	0
O25	●	at Virginia	21	7
N1		Georgia Tech	7	28
N8		Navy	6	16
N15	● |	at Wake Forest	14	7
N22	● |	at North Carolina	34	0

1953-PRESENT
ACC

1953 7-2-1 (4-0-0)

S19	● |	at South Carolina	20	7
S26	● |	Wake Forest	19	0
O3	●	at Tennessee	21	7
O10	●	Purdue	20	14
O17		Army NYC	13	14
O24	● |	North Carolina St.	31	0
O31	●	Virginia NOR	48	6
N7	=	Navy BALT	0	0
N21		at Georgia Tech	10	13
N28	● |	North Carolina	35	20

1954 8-2-1 (4-0-0)

S25	●	at Pennsylvania	52	0
O2	●	Tennessee	7	6
O9	=	at Purdue	13	13
O16		Army	14	28
O23	● |	at North Carolina St.	21	7
O30	●	Georgia Tech	21	20
N6		Navy NOR	7	40
N13	● |	at Wake Forest	28	21
N20	● |	South Carolina	26	7
N27	● |	at North Carolina	47	12
		ORANGE BOWL		
J1	●	Nebraska	34	7

1955 7-2-1 (4-0-0)

S24	● |	at North Carolina St.	33	7
O1	●	at Tennessee	21	0
O8	●	William & Mary	47	7
O15	●	at Ohio State	20	14
O22		Pittsburgh	7	26
O29		at Georgia Tech	0	27
N5	=	Navy BALT	7	7
N12	● |	at South Carolina	41	7
N19	● |	Wake Forest	14	0
N26	● |	North Carolina	6	0

1956 5-4-1 (4-1-0)

S22	|	at South Carolina	0	7
S29	● |	at Virginia	40	7
O6		Tennessee	20	33
O13	●	SMU	14	6
O20		Pittsburgh NOR	14	27
O27	● |	North Carolina St.	42	0
N3		Georgia Tech	0	7
N10	=	Navy	7	7
N17	● |	at Wake Forest	26	0
N24	● |	at North Carolina	21	6

1957 6-3-2 (5-1-1)

S21	● |	at South Carolina	26	14
S28	● |	Virginia	40	0
O5	● |	Maryland	14	0
O12	●	at Rice	7	6
O19	● |	Wake Forest	34	7
O26	= |	at North Carolina St.	14	14
N2		at Georgia Tech	0	13
N9	=	Navy BALT	6	6
N16	● |	Clemson	7	6
N23	|	North Carolina	13	21
		ORANGE BOWL		
J1		Oklahoma	21	48

1958 5-5-0 (3-2-0)

S20	|	at South Carolina	0	8
S27	|	at Virginia	12	15
O4	●	Illinois	15	13
O11	●	Baylor	12	7
O18		at Notre Dame	7	9
O25	● |	North Carolina St.	20	13
N1		Georgia Tech	8	10
N8		at LSU	18	50
N15	● |	at Wake Forest	29	0
N22	● |	at North Carolina	7	6

1959 4-6-0 (2-3-0)

S19	|	at South Carolina	7	12
S26		at Ohio State	13	14
O3	●	Rice	24	7
O10		at Pittsburgh	0	12
O17		Army	6	21
O24	● |	at North Carolina St.	17	15
O31	●	at Georgia Tech	10	7
N7	|	at Clemson	0	6
N14	● |	Wake Forest	27	15
N21	|	North Carolina	0	50

1960 8-3-0 (5-1-0)

S24	● |	at South Carolina	31	0
O1	● |	at Maryland	20	7
O8		at Michigan	6	31
O15	● |	North Carolina St.	17	13
O22	● |	Clemson	21	6
O29	●	Georgia Tech	6	0
N5	●	Navy	19	10
N12	● |	at Wake Forest	34	7
N19	|	at North Carolina	6	7
D3		at UCLA	6	27
		COTTON BOWL		
J2	●	Arkansas	7	6

1961 7-3-0 (5-1-0)

S23	● |	at South Carolina	7	6
S30	● |	Virginia RICH	32	0
O7	● |	Wake Forest	23	3
O14		at Georgia Tech	0	21
O21	|	Clemson	7	17
O28	● |	at North Carolina St.	17	6
N4		at Michigan	14	28
N11	●	Navy NOR	30	9
N18	● |	North Carolina	6	3
D2	●	Notre Dame	37	13

1962 8-2-0 (6-0-0)

S22		at Southern Cal	7	14
S29	● |	South Carolina	21	8
O6	●	Florida JACF	28	21
O13	●	California	21	7
O20	● |	at Clemson	16	0
O27	● |	North Carolina St.	21	14
N3		Georgia Tech	9	20
N10	● |	Maryland	10	7
N17	● |	at Wake Forest	50	0
N24	● |	at North Carolina	16	14

1963 5-4-1 (5-2-0)

S21	● |	South Carolina	22	14
S28	● |	at Virginia	30	8
O5	● |	Maryland RICH	30	12
O12	=	at California	22	22
O19	● |	Clemson	35	30
O26	|	at North Carolina St.	7	21
N2		at Georgia Tech	6	30
N9	● |	Wake Forest	39	7
N16		Navy	25	38
N28	|	North Carolina	14	16

1964 4-5-1 (3-2-1)

S19	= |	at South Carolina	9	9
S26	● |	Virginia	30	0
O10	● |	Maryland	24	17
O17	● |	North Carolina St.	35	3
O24	●	at Army	6	0
O31		Georgia Tech	8	21
N7	|	at Wake Forest	7	20
N14		at Navy	14	27
N21	|	at North Carolina	15	21
N28		at Tulane	0	17

1965 6-4-0 (4-2-0)

S18	● |	at Virginia	21	7
S25	● |	at South Carolina	20	15
O2	●	at Rice	41	21
O9	●	Pittsburgh	21	13
O16	|	Clemson	2	3
O23		at Illinois	14	28
O30		at Georgia Tech	23	35
N6	|	at North Carolina St.	0	21
N13	● |	Wake Forest	40	7
N20	● |	North Carolina	34	7

TOM HARP
1966-70 (.441) 22-28-1

1966 5-5-0 (2-3-0)

S17	●	West Virginia	34	15
S24	●	at Pittsburgh	14	7
O1	● |	Virginia	27	8
O8	|	at Maryland	19	21
O15	|	at Clemson	6	9
O22	|	North Carolina St.	7	33
O29		Georgia Tech	7	48
N5	●	at Navy	9	7
N12		at Notre Dame	0	64
N19	● |	at North Carolina	41	25

1967 4-6-0 (2-4-0)

S16	● |	Wake Forest RAL	31	13
S23		at Michigan	7	10
S30	|	South Carolina	17	21
O7	●	at Army	10	7
O14	● |	at Virginia	13	6
O21	|	Clemson	7	13
O28	|	at North Carolina St.	7	28
N4		at Georgia Tech	7	19
N11	●	Navy NOR	35	16
N18	|	North Carolina	9	20

1968 4-6-0 (3-4-0)

S21	● |	at South Carolina	14	7
S28		Michigan	10	31
O5	● |	Maryland NOR	30	28
O12	|	Virginia	20	50
O19	|	at Clemson	22	39
O26		at Army	25	57
N2	●	Georgia Tech	46	30
N9	|	North Carolina St.	15	17
N16	● |	Wake Forest	18	3
N23	|	at North Carolina	14	25

1969 3-6-1 (3-3-1)

S20	|	at South Carolina	20	27
S27	|	at Virginia	0	10
O4		Pittsburgh	12	14
O11	● |	at Wake Forest	27	20
O18	|	at Maryland	7	20
O25	= |	at North Carolina St.	25	25
N1		at Georgia Tech	7	20
N8	● |	Clemson	34	27
N15		Virginia Tech NOR	12	48
N22	● |	North Carolina	17	13

1970 6-5-0 (5-2-0)

S12		Florida JACF	19	21
S19	● |	Maryland	13	12
S26	● |	Virginia	17	7
O3		at Ohio State	10	34
O10	●	at West Virginia	21	13
O17	● |	at North Carolina St.	22	6
O24	● |	at Clemson	21	10
O31		Georgia Tech	16	24
N7	|	Wake Forest	14	28
N14	● |	at South Carolina	42	38
N21	|	at North Carolina	34	59

MIKE McGEE
1971-78 (.443) 37-47-4

1971 6-5-0 (3-3-0)

S11	●	Florida TAM	12	6
S18	● |	South Carolina	28	12
S25	● |	at Virginia	28	0
O2	●	at Stanford	9	3
O9	|	Clemson NOR	0	3
O16	● |	North Carolina St.	41	13
O23		at Navy	14	15
O30		at Georgia Tech	0	21
N6	●	West Virginia	31	15
N13	|	at Wake Forest	7	23
N20	|	North Carolina	0	38

254 DUKE

THE SCHOOLS

1972 5-6-0 (3-3-0)

S9		Alabama Birm	12	35
S16		at Washington	6	14
S23		Stanford	6	10
S30	● |	Virginia	37	13
O7	|	at North Carolina St.	0	17
O14	● |	at Clemson	7	0
O21	● |	Maryland	20	14
O28	●	Navy Nor	17	16
N4	●	Georgia Tech	20	14
N11	|	Wake Forest	7	9
N18	|	at North Carolina	0	14

1973 2-8-1 (1-4-1)

S15		at Tennessee	17	21
S22	●	Washington	23	21
S29	|	at Virginia	3	7
O6		at Purdue	7	27
O13		Tulane	17	24
O20	|	Clemson	8	24
O27	|	Maryland Nor	10	30
N3		at Georgia Tech	10	12
N10	= |	at Wake Forest	7	7
N17	|	North Carolina St.	3	21
N24	● |	North Carolina	27	10

1974 6-5-0 (2-4-0)

S14	|	at North Carolina St.	21	35
S21	●	at South Carolina	20	14
S28	● |	Virginia	27	7
O5	●	Purdue	16	14
O12	●	Army	33	14
O19	|	at Clemson	13	17
O26		at Florida	13	30
N2	●	Georgia Tech	9	0
N9	● |	Wake Forest	23	7
N16	|	Maryland Nor	13	56
N23	|	at North Carolina	13	14

1975 4-5-2 (3-0-2)

S12		at Southern Cal	7	35
S20		South Carolina	16	24
S27	● |	Virginia	26	11
O4		at Pittsburgh	0	14
O11	●	at Army	21	10
O18	● |	Clemson	25	21
O25		at Florida	16	24
N1		at Georgia Tech	6	21
N8	● |	at Wake Forest	42	14
N15	= |	North Carolina St.	21	21
N22	= |	North Carolina	17	17

1976 5-5-1 (2-3-1)

S11	●	at Tennessee	21	18
S18		at South Carolina	6	24
S25	● |	at Virginia	21	6
O2		Pittsburgh	31	44
O9	●	at Miami, Fla.	20	7
O16	= |	at Clemson	18	18
O23	|	Maryland	3	30
O30	●	Georgia Tech	31	7
N6	|	Wake Forest	17	38
N13	● |	at North Carolina St.	28	14
N20	|	at North Carolina	38	39

1977 5-6-0 (2-4-0)

S10		East Carolina	16	17
S17		at Michigan	9	21
S24	● |	at Virginia	31	7
O1	●	Navy	28	16
O8	●	at South Carolina	25	21
O15	|	Clemson	11	17
O22	|	at Maryland	13	31
O29	●	at Georgia Tech	25	24
N5	● |	at Wake Forest	38	14
N12	|	North Carolina St.	32	37
N19	|	North Carolina	3	16

1978 4-7-0 (2-4-0)

S9	●	Georgia Tech	28	10
S23	●	South Carolina	16	12
S30		at Michigan	0	52
O7	● |	Virginia	20	13
O14		at Navy	8	31
O21	|	at Clemson	8	28
O28	|	Maryland	0	27
N4		at Tennessee	0	34
N11	● |	Wake Forest	3	0
N18	|	at North Carolina St.	10	24
N25	|	at North Carolina	15	16

SHIRLEY "RED" WILSON
1979-82 (.375) 16-27-1

1979 2-8-1 (0-6-0)

S15	●	East Carolina	28	14
S22		at South Carolina	0	35
S29	|	at Virginia	12	30
O6	=	at Army	17	17
O13	●	at Richmond	34	7
O20	|	Clemson	10	28
O27	|	Maryland	0	27
N3		at Georgia Tech	14	24
N10	|	at Wake Forest	14	17
N17	|	North Carolina St.	7	28
N24	|	North Carolina	16	37

1980 2-9-0 (1-5-0)

S6		East Carolina	10	35
S20		at Auburn	28	35
S27	|	Virginia	17	20
O4		at Indiana	21	31
O11		at South Carolina	7	20
O18	● |	at Clemson	34	17
O25	|	Maryland	14	17
N1	●	Georgia Tech	17	12
N8	|	Wake Forest	24	27
N15	|	at North Carolina St.	21	38
N22	|	at North Carolina	21	44

1981 6-5-0 (3-3-0)

S12		at Ohio State	13	34
S19		at South Carolina	3	17
S26	● |	at Virginia	29	24
O3	●	East Carolina	24	14
O10	●	Virginia Tech	14	7
O17	|	Clemson	10	38
O24	|	at Maryland	21	24
O31	●	at Georgia Tech	38	24
N7	● |	at Wake Forest	31	10
N14	● |	North Carolina St.	17	7
N21	|	North Carolina	10	31

1982 6-5-0 (3-3-0)

S4	●	at Tennessee	25	24
S18	●	at South Carolina	30	17
S25	● |	Virginia	51	17
O2		Navy	21	27
O9		Virginia Tech	21	22
O16	|	at Clemson	14	49
O23	|	at Maryland	22	49
O30	●	at Georgia Tech	38	21
N6	● |	Wake Forest	46	26
N13	|	at North Carolina St.	16	21
N20	● |	North Carolina	23	17

STEVE SLOAN
1983-86 (.295) 13-31

1983 3-8-0 (3-4-0)

S3	|	at Virginia	30	38
S10		at Indiana	10	15
S17		South Carolina	24	31
O1		Miami, Fla.	17	56
O8		at Virginia Tech	14	27
O15	|	Clemson	31	38
O22	|	at Maryland	3	38
O29	● |	Georgia Tech	32	26
N5	● |	at Wake Forest	31	21
N10	● |	North Carolina St.	27	26
N19	|	at North Carolina	27	34

1984 2-9-0 (1-6-0)

S8	●	Indiana	31	24
S22		at South Carolina	0	21
S29		at Army	9	13
O6	|	Virginia	10	38
O13		at Virginia Tech	0	27
O20	|	at Clemson	21	54
O27	|	Maryland	7	43
N3	|	at Georgia Tech	3	31
N10	|	Wake Forest	16	20
N17	● |	at North Carolina St.	16	13
N24	|	North Carolina	15	17

1985 4-7-0 (2-5-0)

S7	●	Northwestern	40	17
S14		at West Virginia	18	20
S21	●	Ohio U.	34	13
O5	|	at Virginia	14	37
O12		at South Carolina	7	28
O19	|	Clemson	9	21
O26	|	at Maryland	10	40
N2	|	Georgia Tech	0	9
N9	|	at Wake Forest	7	27
N16	● |	North Carolina St.	31	19
N23	● |	at North Carolina	23	21

1986 4-7-0 (2-5-0)

S6	●	at Northwestern	17	6
S13		at Georgia	7	31
S20	●	Ohio U.	22	7
S27	● |	Virginia	20	13
O4		at Vanderbilt	18	24
O18	|	at Clemson	3	35
O25	|	Maryland	19	27
N1	|	at Georgia Tech	6	34
N8	● |	Wake Forest	38	36
N15	|	at North Carolina St.	15	29
N22	|	North Carolina	35	42

STEVE SPURRIER
1987-89 (.603) 20-13-1

1987 5-6-0 (2-5-0)

S5	●	Colgate	41	6
S12	●	Northwestern	31	16
S19	●	Vanderbilt	35	31
S26	|	at Virginia	17	42
O3		Rutgers ERut	0	7
O17	|	at Clemson	10	17
O24	|	at Maryland	22	23
O31	● |	Georgia Tech	48	14
N7	|	at Wake Forest	27	30
N14	|	North Carolina St.	45	47
N21	● |	at North Carolina	25	10

1988 7-3-1 (3-3-1)

S3	●	Northwestern	31	21
S10	●	at Tennessee	31	26
S17	●	Citadel	41	17
S24	● |	Virginia	38	34
O1	●	at Vanderbilt	17	15
O15	|	at Clemson	17	49
O22	|	Maryland	24	34
O29	● |	at Georgia Tech	31	21
N5	|	Wake Forest	16	35
N12	= |	at North Carolina St.	43	43
N19	● |	North Carolina	35	29

1989 8-4-0 (6-1-0)

S2		at South Carolina	21	27
S9	●	Northwestern	41	31
S16		at Tennessee	6	28
S23	|	at Virginia	28	49
S30	● |	Clemson	21	17
O7	●	Army	35	29
O21	● |	at Maryland	46	25
O28	● |	Georgia Tech	30	19
N4	● |	at Wake Forest	52	35
N11	● |	North Carolina St.	35	26
N18	● |	at North Carolina	41	0
		ALL-AMERICAN BOWL		
D28		Texas Tech	21	49

BARRY WILSON
1990-93 (.307) 13-30-1

1990 4-7-0 (1-6-0)

S1		at South Carolina	10	21
S8	●	at Northwestern	27	24
S22	|	Virginia	0	59
S29	|	at Clemson	7	26
O6	●	at Army	17	16
O13	●	Western Carolina	49	18
O20	|	Maryland	20	23
O27	|	at Georgia Tech	31	48
N3	● |	Wake Forest	57	20
N10	|	at North Carolina St.	0	16
N17	|	North Carolina	22	24

1991 4-6-1 (1-6-0)

S7	=	at South Carolina	24	24
S14	●	Rutgers	42	22
S21	●	Colgate	42	14
S28	|	at Virginia	3	34
O5	●	Vanderbilt	17	13
O26	● |	at Maryland	17	13
N2	|	Georgia Tech	6	17
N9	|	at Wake Forest	14	31
N16	|	North Carolina St.	31	32
N23	|	at North Carolina	14	47
N30	|	Clemson Tok	21	33

1992 2-9-0 (0-8-0)

S5	|	at Florida State	21	48
S12		at Vanderbilt	37	42
S19	●	Rice	17	12
S26	|	Virginia	28	55
O10	●	East Carolina	45	14
O17	|	at Clemson	6	21
O24	|	Maryland	25	27
O31	|	at Georgia Tech	17	20
N7	|	Wake Forest	14	28
N14	|	at North Carolina St.	27	45
N21	|	North Carolina	28	31

1993 3-8-0 (2-6-0)

S4	|	Florida State	7	45
S11		Rutgers ERut	38	39
S18	●	Army	42	21
S25	|	at Virginia	0	35
O2		at Tennessee	19	52
O9	|	Clemson	10	13
O16	|	at Maryland	18	26
O23	● |	at Wake Forest	21	13
O30	|	Georgia Tech	14	47
N6	● |	North Carolina St.	21	20
N26	|	at North Carolina	24	38

FRED GOLDSMITH
1994-98 (.304) 17-39

1994 8-4-0 (5-3-0)

S3	● |	Maryland	49	16
S10	●	East Carolina	13	10
S15	●	Army	43	7
S24	● |	at Georgia Tech	27	12
O1	●	at Navy	47	14
O15	● |	Clemson	19	13
O22	● |	at Wake Forest	51	26
O29	|	at Florida State	20	59
N5	● |	Virginia	28	25
N12	|	at North Carolina St.	23	24
N19	|	North Carolina	40	41
		HALL OF FAME BOWL		
J2		Wisconsin	20	34

1995 3-8-0 (1-7-0)

S2	|	Florida State Orl	26	70
S9	●	Rutgers	24	14
S16	●	at Army	23	21
S23	|	at Maryland	28	41
S30		Navy	9	30
O7	|	Georgia Tech	21	37
O14	|	at Virginia	30	44
O21	|	North Carolina St.	38	41
O28	● |	Wake Forest	42	26
N11	|	at Clemson	17	34
N18	|	at North Carolina	24	28

1996 0-11 (0-8)

S7	|	at Florida State	7	44
S14		Northwestern	13	38
S21		at Army	17	35
S26	|	at Georgia Tech	22	48
O5		at Navy	27	64
O12	|	Clemson	6	13
O26	|	Maryland	19	22
N2	|	Virginia	3	27
N9	|	at North Carolina St.	22	44
N16	|	at Wake Forest	16	17
N23	|	North Carolina	10	27

1997 2-9 (0-8)

S6	|	North Carolina St.	14	45
S13		at Northwestern	20	24
S20	●	Army	20	17
S27	●	Navy	26	17
O4	|	at Maryland	10	16
O11	|	Florida State	27	51
O18	|	at Virginia	10	13
O25	|	Wake Forest	24	38
N8	|	at Clemson	20	29
N15	|	Georgia Tech	38	41
N22	|	at North Carolina	14	50

1998 4-7 (2-6)

S5	●	Western Carolina	24	10
S12	●	at Northwestern	44	10
S19	|	at Florida State	13	62
S26	|	Virginia	0	24
O3	|	at Georgia Tech	13	41
O10	● |	at Wake Forest	19	16
O17	|	at North Carolina St.	24	27
O24	● |	Clemson	28	23
O31		at Vanderbilt	33	36
N14	|	Maryland	25	42
N21	|	North Carolina	6	28

CARL FRANKS
1999-2003 (.135) 7-45

1999 3-8 (3-5)

S11		at East Carolina	9	27
S18		Northwestern	12	15
S25		Vanderbilt	14	31
O2	|	Florida State JacF	23	51
O9	● |	at Virginia	24	17
O16	|	Georgia Tech	31	38
O23	|	North Carolina St.	24	31
O30	● |	at Maryland	25	22
N6	|	at Clemson	7	58
N13	● |	Wake Forest	48	35
N20	|	at North Carolina	0	38

2000   0-11   (0-8)

S2		East Carolina	0 38
S9		at Northwestern	5 38
S16	|	Virginia	10 26
S23		at Vanderbilt	7 26
S30	|	Clemson	22 52
O14	|	at Florida State	14 63
O21	|	at Georgia Tech	10 45
O28	|	Maryland	9 20
N4	|	at Wake Forest	26 28
N11	|	at North Carolina St.	31 35
N18	|	North Carolina	21 59

2001   0-11   (0-8)

S1	|	Florida State	13 55
S8		at Rice	13 15
S22		Northwestern	7 44
S29	|	at Virginia	10 31
O6	|	Georgia Tech	10 37
O13	|	Wake Forest	35 42
O20	|	at Maryland	17 59
O27	|	Vanderbilt	28 42
N3	|	North Carolina St.	31 55
N17	|	at North Carolina	17 52
D1	|	at Clemson	31 59

2002   2-10   (0-8)

A31	●	East Carolina	23 16
S7		Louisville	3 40
S14		at Northwestern	21 26
S21	|	at Florida State	17 48
S28	●	at Navy	43 17
O5	|	Virginia	22 27
O12	|	at Wake Forest	10 36
O19	|	at North Carolina St.	22 24
O26	|	Maryland	12 45
N2	|	Clemson	31 34
N16	|	at Georgia Tech	2 17
N23	|	North Carolina	21 23

TED ROOF	
2003-Present (.250)	4-12

2003   4-8   (2-6)

A30	|	at Virginia	0 27
S6	●	Western Carolina	29 3
S13	●	Rice	27 24
S20		Northwestern	10 28
S27	|	Florida State	7 56
O11	|	at Maryland	20 33
O18	|	Wake Forest	13 42
O25	|	North Carolina St.	21 28
N1		at Tennessee	6 23
N8	● |	Georgia Tech	41 17
N15	|	at Clemson	7 40
N22	● |	at North Carolina	30 22

2004   2-9   (1-7)

S4	|	at Navy	12 27
S11		at Connecticut	20 22
S18	|	at Virginia Tech	17 41
S25	|	Maryland	21 55
O2	●	Citadel	28 10
O16	|	at Georgia Tech	7 24
O23	|	Virginia	16 37
O30	|	at Wake Forest	22 24
N6	|	at Florida State	7 29
N13	● |	Clemson	16 13
N20	|	North Carolina	17 40

Neutral Site key: *Atl* Atlanta, Ga. / *Balt* Baltimore, Md. / *Birm* Birmingham, Ala. / *Buf* Buffalo,N.Y. / *Char* Charlotte, N.C. / *Colu* Columbia, S.C. / *DC* Washington, D.C. / *Dur* Durham, N.C. / *ERut* East Rutherford, N.J. / *Gol* Goldsboro, N.C. / *Gro* Greensboro, N.C. / *JacF* Jacksonville, Fla. / *Lyn* Lynchburg, Va. / *Nor* Norfolk,Va. / *NYC* New York, N.Y. / *Orl* Orlando, Fla. / *Phil* Philadelphia, Pa. / *Ral* Raleigh, N.C. / *Rich* Richmond, Va. / *Roa* Roanoke, Va. / *Tam* Tampa, Fla. / *Tok* Tokyo, Japan / *Unk* Unknown Unknown / *W-S* Winston-Salem, N.C.
f Forfeit † Game Later Forfieted # Disputed Victor * Disputed Score || Designated Conference Game | 2 Counted Twice in Conference Standings

EAST CAROLINA

BY KEVIN GLEASON

DESPITE GARNERING LITTLE ATTEN-tion around college football nation, East Carolina has thrived in the shadow of better-known names in North Carolina. Since Clarence Stasavich led ECU to three straight nine-win seasons in the 1960s, the Pirates have been one of the more consistent outfits around.

Pat Dye (48–18–1, 1974-79) oversaw East Carolina's successful transition from the Southern Conference to independent. Bill Lewis (21–12–1, 1989-91) took the 1991 Pirates to a Top 10 ranking, an 11–1 record and a victory in the Peach Bowl before leaving for Georgia Tech. And Steve Logan (69–58, 1992-2002), East Carolina's winningest coach, led the Pirates to five bowl games. ECU seamlessly joined Conference USA in 1997, finishing at least .500 in its first six seasons in the league.

TRADITION Firing the cannon at home games goes back to at least 1967, when a Confederate cannon was shot off for pregame introductions. The cannon endured a 16-year hiatus beginning in the mid-1970s after a player scored and mistakenly ran in front of the cannon just as it was being fired. He was knocked to the ground, triggering safety questions from administrators and fans. Greenville native and longtime fan Ken Howard helped revive the

cannon in the early 1990s. Howard passed on his cannon-firing responsibilities in 1998 to a select group of Army ROTC students. The cannon is fired at the end of the national anthem, when the team runs onto the field, after the Pirates score and at the conclusion of games.

BEST PLAYER Quarterback Jeff Blake led East Carolina to its best season ever, 11–1 in 1991, and wound up seventh in Heisman Trophy voting. Among the school records set by Blake in 1991: yards passing (3,073), yards per game (279.4) and touchdown passes in a game (five vs. Southern Mississippi). Blake went on to a long NFL career with varying degrees of success, making the Pro Bowl in 1995 with the Bengals and going to the Super Bowl in 2005 with the Eagles as a backup.

BEST COACH Logan won 69 games in 11 seasons and brought East Carolina national prestige by beating top-flight programs and competing in five bowl games. But the winningest coach in school history was fired one day after a 42-26 season-ending defeat to Cincinnati in 2002 that closed a 4–8 campaign. That didn't work out so well: the Pirates went 1–11 in 2003, their first one-win season since 1957.

BEST TEAM The Pirates went 11–1 and finished ranked ninth in the country under Bill Lewis in 1991. They lost their opener at Illinois 38-31 but then reeled off 11 straight

---

wins, including a 37-34 victory over NC State in the Peach Bowl. They were led by Blake's 3,073 yards passing and 28 touchdowns.

BIGGEST GAME On its biggest stage to date—the 1992 Peach Bowl—East Carolina added a memorable ending to its most memorable season. Down 34-17 to NC State with 8:41 to play, Pirates fans began chanting, "We believe." East Carolina made them proud behind the electric leadership of Blake, who narrowed the score to 34-24 on a two-yard touchdown run with 7:26 left, then followed up by completing eight of 10 passes on an 80-yard touchdown drive, capped by a 17-yarder to Dion Johnson with 4:18 left. A two-point conversion failed but another defensive stand and more Blake magic led to the go-ahead score. "We've been called a Cinderella story all year," center Keith Arnold said after the game. "Cinderella went to a ball tonight and got married. She's queen now. Now I guess we know who's best in North Carolina."

BIGGEST UPSET The 1999 East Carolina-Miami game would have been remembered in Greenville regardless of the outcome. But the Pirates added a layer of historical significance by beating No. 9 Miami 27-23. The game

"Pirates" was expected to inspire more enthusiasm than the previous nickname, "Teachers."

was played in the aftermath of Hurricane Floyd, which devastated the Greenville area and forced the contest to be moved 85 miles west to Raleigh. East Carolina fell behind 23-3 early in the third quarter before starting a comeback capped by David Garrard's 27-yard touchdown pass to Keith Stokes with 4:51 left. Fans pulled down both goalposts and some even tried to take both sets of uprights and crossbars as souvenirs. "If I was to describe how I feel," Miami's Kenny Kelly said afterward, "the NCAA might fine me."

HEARTBREAKER The Pirates led 38-8 at halftime of the 2001 GMAC Bowl before Marshall came back to win 64-61 in two overtimes, the highest-scoring—and maybe the most exciting—bowl game in history. It's not outlandish to say that ECU took years to recover from the loss. That fall, the 2001 Pirates were set up to have one of the greatest seasons in school history. They were ranked in *Sports Illustrated*'s preseason Top 25 and took an unbeaten conference record into Game 10 against Louisville. But conference rivals Louisville and Southern Mississippi beat the Pirates on consecutive weeks in Greenville leading to the GMAC Bowl. Those three losses began a downward spiral that led to a 4–8 season in 2002 and ultimately cost Logan his job.

RECORDS

RUSHING YARDS

GAME	
351	Scott Harley vs. NC State, Nov. 30, 1996 (42 att.)
SEASON	
1,745	Scott Harley, 1996 (307 att.)
CAREER	
3,745	Junior Smith, 1991-94 (732 att.)

PASSING YARDS

GAME	
414	David Garrard vs. Memphis, Nov. 21, 1998 (33 of 44)
SEASON	
3,073	Jeff Blake, 1991 (203 of 368)
CAREER	
9,029	David Garrard, 1998-2001 (666 of 1,169)

RECEIVING YARDS

GAME	
218	Terry Gallaher vs. Appalachian State, Sept. 13, 1975 (3 rec.)
SEASON	
897	Terrance Copper, 2003 (87 rec.)
CAREER	
1,982	Troy Smith, 1995-98 (129 rec.)

POINTS

GAME	
36	Scott Harley vs. Ohio, Nov. 16, 1996 (6 TDs)
SEASON	
108	Leonard Henry, 2001 (18 TDs)
CAREER	
287	Kevin Miller, 1999-2002 (131 PATs, 52 FGs)

CONSENSUS ALL-AMERICANS

1964	Bill Cline, HB
1983	Terry Long, OL
1991	Robert Jones, LB
1999	Andrew Bayes, P

STADIUM James Skinner Ficklen Memorial Stadium was dedicated in September 1963. In 1994, when Ron and Mary Ellen Dowdy of Orlando announced a $1 million gift to the ECU Educational Foundation, it became Dowdy-Ficklen Stadium. An 8,000-seat upper deck was added in 1998, and a year later club-level seating was added to give Dowdy-Ficklen its 43,000 capacity. Along the way, average attendance has increased from 10,300 during the 1963 inaugural to a high of 42,036 in 1999.

RIVAL There are plenty of talent-rich football programs around the state, but East Carolina has faced a challenge common to successful schools in less-visible conferences. NC State, which is 85 miles west, represents the closest program geographically. North Carolina has periodically refused to schedule ECU. ECU and NC State had played every season from 1970 to 1987 before the series was halted. It was renewed in the 1992 Peach Bowl, which East Carolina won 37-34. So now East Carolina's No. 1 rival comes from out of state: Southern Miss

DISPUTE Want to get a whole bunch of high school football coaches ticked off in the Carolinas? Play a college game at home on Friday night. Schoolboy coaches across North Carolina got their headsets out of joint when East Carolina closed its 2002 season with a Friday game against Cincinnati on ESPN. Some high school coaches threatened to prohibit Pirates coaches from recruiting on their campuses. East Carolina agreed to work with the high school association before scheduling future Friday nighters.

NICKNAME East Carolina's athletic teams became the Pirates in 1934. The school's men's athletic association figured the nickname would inspire more spirit and enthusiasm than the former nickname, Teachers. The nickname derives from the school's location near the Carolina coast, where pirates often harbored their ships.

MASCOT Pee Dee the Pirate was selected in 1983 by local elementary students in a name-the-mascot contest. The name presumably came from the Pee Dee River flowing through the Carolinas. But ECU students complained they didn't have a say in naming the mascot, and by 1985 Pee Dee was changed to, simply, the Pirate.

UNIFORMS East Carolina's purple and gold colors date to 1909, when the administration asked students for suggestions on school colors. The helmets are purple, with bright gold trim, featuring the stylized letters ECU underlined by a sword. New uniforms in 2004 featured a jazzy stripe along the shoulder. The home purple uniforms have gold lettering and numbers, both of which are trimmed in white. The white visiting uniforms have purple lettering and numbers.

LORE No East Carolina player has worn jersey No. 18 since Norman Swindell, a blocking back from New Bern, N.C. The most valuable player on the 1965 team that capped a 9–1 season by beating Maine 31-0 in the Tangerine Bowl. Swindell drowned near his home over the Christmas break following that season.

QUOTE "There was a lot of tension for the long week. But we turned that tension into passion in the second half." —Steve Logan, following East Carolina's 27-23 upset of Miami in 1999 after Hurricane Floyd had caused havoc to the Greenville area the previous week

EAST CAROLINA ANNUAL STATISTICAL LEADERS

YR	RUSHING	YDS	ATT	AVG	PASSING	ATT	CMP	PCT	YDS	RECEIVING	REC	YDS	AVG
1963	Tom Michel	830	170	4.9	Bill Cline	80	44	.55	693	Dave Bumgarner	23	328	14.3
1964	Dave Alexander	869	138	6.3	Bill Cline	111	63	.57	944	Dave Bumgarner	37	408	11.0
1965	Dave Alexander	1,029	227	4.5	George Richardson	98	53	.54	680	Ruffin Odom	28	367	13.1
1966	Bill Bailey	378	91	4.2	Bill Bailey	151	62	.41	774	Nelson Gravatt	20	184	9.2
1967	Butch Colson	1,135	252	4.5	Neal Hughes	124	65	.52	805	Jimmy Adkins	19	328	17.3
1968	Butch Colson	680	180	3.8	Billy Wightman	63	29	.46	306	Jimmy Adkins	22	331	15.0
1969	Billy Wightman	835	170	4.9	Butch Colson	33	19	.58	256	Dick Corrada	19	211	11.1
1970	Billy Wallace	902	210	4.3	John Casazza	277	122	.44	1,512	Dick Corrada	46	512	11.1
1971	Billy Wallace	557	108	5.2	John Casazza	182	72	.40	1,004	Tim Dameron	25	487	19.5
1972	Carlester Crumpler	1,309	340	3.9	Carl Summerell	197	86	.44	1,275	Tim Dameron	30	648	21.6
1973	Carlester Crumpler	1,042	204	5.1	Carl Summerell	154	82	.53	1,222	Stan Eure	27	495	18.3
1974	Kenny Strayhorn	635	106	6.0	Mike Weaver	81	21	.26	443	Vic Wilfore	8	110	13.8
1975	Kenny Strayhorn	638	101	6.3	Pete Conaty	59	24	.41	463	Terry Gallaher	13	433	33.3
1976	Eddie Hicks	897	137	6.5	Mike Weaver	84	37	.44	633	Terry Gallaher	14	269	19.2
1977	Theodore Sutton	706	125	5.6	Jimmy Southerland	84	47	.56	779	Terry Gallaher	27	512	19.0
1978	Theodore Sutton	621	127	4.9	Leander Green	110	46	.42	838	Terry Gallaher	18	227	12.6
1979	Anthony Collins	1,130	154	7.3	Leander Green	141	73	.52	1,082	Vern Davenport	26	343	13.2
1980	Theodore Sutton	586	135	4.3	Greg Stewart	83	38	.46	400	Vern Davenport	14	186	13.3
1981	Carlton Nelson	489	107	4.6	Carlton Nelson	78	29	.37	484	Norwood Vann	20	288	14.4
1982	Tony Baker	827	126	6.6	Greg Stewart	114	58	.51	941	Carlton Nelson	28	526	18.8
1983	Earnest Byner	862	174	5.0	Kevin Ingram	164	90	.55	1,191	Stefon Adams	20	277	13.9
1984	Reggie Branch	521	116	4.5	Darrell Speed	132	61	.46	795	Ricky Nichols	28	513	18.3
1985	Tony Baker	951	197	4.8	Ron Jones	127	47	.37	652	Tony Smith	14	234	16.7
1986	Anthony Simpson	753	178	4.2	Charlie Libretto	148	71	.48	833	Jarrod Moody	22	252	11.5
1987	Anthony Simpson	670	153	4.4	Travis Hunter	155	76	.49	1,107	Ron Jones	23	301	13.1
1988	Tim James	787	163	4.8	Travis Hunter	118	52	.44	828	Walter Wilson	19	355	18.7
1989	Travis Hunter	398	98	4.1	Travis Hunter	223	110	.49	1,478	Walter Wilson	43	771	17.9
1990	David Daniels	553	100	5.5	Jeff Blake	219	116	.53	1,510	Luke Fisher	35	534	15.3
1991	Cedric Van Buren	351	90	3.9	Jeff Blake	368	203	.55	3,073	Hunter Gallimore	49	881	18.0
1992	Junior Smith	1,037	186	5.6	Michael Anderson	398	222	.56	2,486	Morris Letcher	47	557	11.9
1993	Junior Smith	1,352	278	4.9	Perez Mattison	183	78	.43	924	Jerris McPhail	34	410	12.1
1994	Junior Smith	1,204	226	5.3	Marcus Crandell	401	230	.57	2,687	Jason Nichols	42	450	10.7
1995	Jerris McPhail	910	185	4.9	Marcus Crandell	447	235	.53	2,751	Mitchell Galloway	46	619	13.5
1996	Scott Harley	1,745	307	5.7	Marcus Crandell	245	136	.56	1,507	Mitchell Galloway	48	554	11.5
1997	Scott Harley	457	119	3.8	Dan Gonzalez	431	253	.59	2,510	Troy Smith	54	795	14.7
1998	Jamie Wilson	647	138	4.7	David Garrard	255	157	.62	2,091	Troy Smith	44	719	16.3
1999	Jamie Wilson	865	156	5.5	David Garrard	312	181	.58	2,359	LaMont Chappell	36	558	15.5
2000	Leonard Henry	711	133	5.3	David Garrard	312	164	.53	2,332	Keith Stokes	29	442	15.2
2001	Leonard Henry	1,432	184	7.8	David Garrard	290	164	.57	2,247	Derrick Collier	31	481	15.5
2002	Art Brown	1,029	214	4.8	Paul Troth	359	177	.49	2,315	Torey Morris	38	552	14.5
2003	Marvin Townes	1,128	258	4.4	Desmore Robinson	201	133	.66	1,262	Terrance Cooper	87	897	10.3
2004	Chris Johnson	546	121	4.5	James Pinkney	335	188	.56	2,180	Bobby Good	33	427	12.9

Receiving leaders by receptions
The NCAA began including postseason stats in 2002

THE SCHOOLS

EAST CAROLINA ALL-TIME SCORES

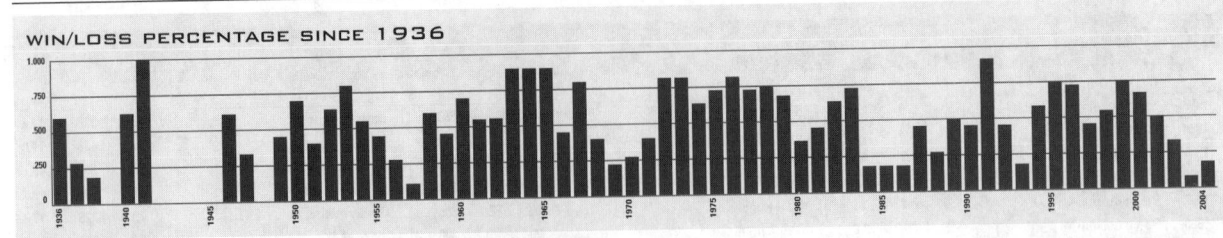

WIN/LOSS PERCENTAGE SINCE 1936

KENNETH BEATTY
1932-33 (.091)   1-10

1932   0-5-0
O29	at Presbyteria	0	39
N3	at Wake Forest JV	0	20
N12	Guilford	0	79
N19	NC State JV	0	28
N26	at Appalachian State	0	21

1933   1-5-0
O6	at NC State JV	0	18
O20	Wake Forest JV	0	27
O28	at Guilford	0	32
N3	Presbyterian	0	8
N11 •	Campbell	6	0
N25	Appalachian State	0	14

G.L. "DOC" MATHIS
1934-35 (.375)   4-7-1

1934   1-4-1
O13	Wingate	0	6
O20	at Appalachian State	6	27
N3 •	at Presbyterian	6	0
N12	Louisburg	6	7
N16 =	William & Mary	0	0
N23	at Lenoir-Rhyne	0	47

1935   3-3-0
O12	at Wingate	0	6
O26	Oak Ridge	2	6
N9 •	Chowan	46	0
N16 •	at William & Mary	10	6
N23	Appalachian State	6	14
N30 •	at Louisburg	13	0

BO FARLEY
1936 (.600)   3-2

1936   3-2-0
O24	at Western Carolina	6	7
O30 •	William & Mary	25	0
N6 •	Duke JV	14	6
N14	at Guilford	0	6
N21 •	Louisburg	19	0

J.O. ALEXANDER
1937-38 (.233)   3-11-1

1937   2-5-0
O2	Guilford	0	7
O9	at Campbell	6	7
O16 •	Belmont Abbey	7	19
O23	Western Carolina	0	7
O30	at William & Mary	6	18
N6 •	High Point	19	7
N13 •	at Louisburg	27	13

1938   1-6-1
O1	at Belmont Abbey	0	19
O8	Campbell	6	19
O15 •	at Western Carolina	7	6
O29	at High Point	7	20
N5 =	at Guilford	7	7
N11 •	William & Mary	0	6
N19	Appalachian State	6	18
N26	Norfolk Navy	7	32

D.A. HANKER
1939 (.000)   0-8

1939   0-8-0
S31	at Kutztown State	6	20
O7	at Campbell	0	13
O13	Western Carolina	6	12
O21	at William & Mary	0	7
O28	Guilford	0	20
N11	High Point	0	25
N18	at Appalachian State	0	64
N25	at Norfolk Navy	6	7

JOHN CHRISTENBURY
1940-41 (.800)   12-3

1940   5-3-0
S28 •	Kutztown State	14	6
O5 •	Presbyterian	40	0
O12 •	at William & Mary	18	0
O19 •	at Western Carolina	14	25
O26	NC State JV	0	26
N2 •	at Guilford	13	0
N16	High Point	0	6
N22 •	at Newport News	44	7

1941   7-0-0
S27 •	Tusculum	31	0
O10 •	Newport News	39	0
O18 •	Western Carolina	19	6
O24 •	Newport Navy	30	0
O31 •	at Erskine	14	7
N6 •	at Bergen	13	7
N13 •	at Belmont Abbey	13	0

1942-45
NO TEAM

JIM JOHNSON
1946-48 (.315)   8-18-1

1946   5-3-1
S30 •	at Presbyterian	20	0
O5 =	Atlantic Christian	6	6
O12	at Elon	6	13
O19 •	Erskine	21	7
O26 •	Newport News	19	7
N9 •	at Atlantic Christian	26	6
N16	Western Carolina	7	13
N23	Lenoir-Rhyne	0	6
N28 •	at Fort Bragg	53	0

1947   3-6-0
S27	Lenoir-Rhyne	9	27
O4 •	at Atlantic Christian	12	7
O11	Elon	0	7
O18	at Erskine	0	13
O25 •	at Newport News	14	6
N1 •	Fort Bragg	12	2
N8	Little Creek, Va.	7	31
N22	at NC State JV	12	20
N29	at Western Carolina	0	28

1948   0-9-0
S17	at Cherry Point Marines	6	13
S25	at Lenoir-Rhyne	6	26
O8	at Elon	0	6
O15	Western Carolina	0	39
O22	at Newport News JV	6	20
O29	Duke JV	13	19
N6	Appalachian State	0	47
N13	High Point	7	30
N20	Atlantic Christian	0	6

BILL DOLE
1949-51 (.517)   15-14-1

1949   4-5-1
S15 •	Cherry Point Marines	24	0
S24 •	Lenoir-Rhyne	20	21
O1 •	at Hampden-Sydney	7	20
O8 •	at Elon	7	33
O15 •	at Western Carolina	6	19
O21 •	at Newport News	26	21
O28 •	Edenton Flyers	67	0
N5 •	Appalachian State	18	35
N12 =	at High Point	26	26
N19 •	Atlantic Christian	6	2

1950   7-3-0
S16 •	at Newport News	21	7
S23 •	at Lenoir-Rhyne	27	19
S30 •	Hampden-Sydney	26	38
O7 •	at Elon	16	26
O14 •	Western Carolina	36	6
O20 •	at Guilford	26	7
O28 •	Cherry Point Marines	20	12
N4 •	at Appalachian State	0	20
N11 •	High Point	26	0
N18 •	Atlantic Christian	54	7

1951   4-6-0
S15 •	at Southern Miss	0	40
S22 •	at Newport News	32	6
S29 •	at Norfolk Navy	7	6
O6 •	Elon	20	34
O13 •	at Western Carolina	20	34
O20 •	Guilford	19	14
O27 •	Lenoir-Rhyne	14	41
N3 •	Appalachian State	20	24
N10 •	at Cherry Point Marines	45	0
N24 •	at The Citadel	7	21

JACK BOONE
1952-61 (.520)   49-45-5

1952   6-3-2
S13 •	Norfolk Navy	7	13
S20 •	Newport News	37	6
S27 •	at Lenoir-Rhyne	6	7
O4 =	Catawba	7	7
O11 •	at Elon	25	9
O18 •	Western Carolina	21	0
O25 •	Guilford	41	25
N1 •	at Appalachian State	22	19
N8 =	at Stetson	19	19
N15 •	West Virginia Tech	34	7

LIONS BOWL
D13	Clarion State	6	13

1953   8-2-0
S19 •	Wilson Teachers	41	0
S26 •	Lenoir-Rhyne	34	0
O3 •	at Catawba	13	6
O10 •	Elon	45	25
O17 •	at Western Carolina	26	7
O24 •	Guilford	40	0
O31 •	Appalachian State	40	7
N7 •	at Tampa	13	18
N14 •	at Stetson	40	6

ELKS BOWL
J2 •	Morris-Harvey	0	12

1954   5-4-1
S11 •	Norfolk Navy	21	0
S18 •	West Chester	4	6
S25 •	at Lenoir-Rhyne	7	6
O2 •	Catawba	26	7
O9 •	at Elon	6	20
O16 •	Western Carolina	27	13
O23 =	East Tennessee State	6	6
O30 •	at Appalachian State	7	13
N6 •	at Tampa	14	27
N13 •	Stetson	26	7

1955   4-5-0
S10 •	Norfolk Navy	6	0
S17 •	at West Chester	0	9
S24 •	Lenoir-Rhyne	6	7
O1 •	at Catawba	7	13
O8 •	Elon	13	0
O15 •	at Western Carolina	14	6
O22 •	at East Tennessee State	20	34
O29 •	Appalachian State	13	0
N5 •	Tampa	14	33

1956   2-6-1
S15 •	at Virginia Tech	2	37
S22 =	Stetson	7	7
S29 •	Catawba	13	23
O6 •	at Elon	19	7
O13 •	Western Carolina	20	19
O20 •	Morris-Harvey	0	28
O27 •	at Appalachian State	19	22
N3 •	at Lenoir-Rhyne	12	57
N17 •	Richmond	7	45

1957   1-8-0
S18 •	at Richmond	7	40
S28 •	Davidson	7	19
O5 •	at Catawba	14	36
O12 •	Elon	12	21
O19 •	at Western Carolina	7	20
O26 •	Newberry	7	20
N2 •	Appalachian State	6	7
N9 •	Lenoir-Rhyne	7	55
N16 •	at Presbyterian	6	0

1958   6-4-0
S13 •	Emory & Henry	12	0
S20 •	Presbyterian	16	24
O4 •	Catawba	6	0
O11 •	at Elon	14	6
O18 •	Western Carolina	18	7
O25 •	at Newberry	6	28
N1 •	at Appalachian State	0	14
N8 •	at Lenoir-Rhyne	14	59
N15 •	Randolph-Macon	36	6
N27 •	Guilford	20	0

1959   5-6-0
S12 •	at Presbyterian	13	18
S19 •	Albright	45	0
S26 •	at Guilford	27	0
O3 •	at Catawba	34	7
O10 •	Elon	31	8
O17 •	at Western Carolina	14	34
O24 •	at Newberry	7	34
O31 •	Appalachian State	0	28
N7 •	Lenoir-Rhyne	21	22
N14 •	Newport News	74	0
N21 •	at Wofford	13	20

1960   7-3-0
S17 •	Newport News	21	6
S24 •	Guilford	7	0
O1 •	Catawba	28	0
O8 •	at Elon	14	8
O15 •	Western Carolina	7	6
O22 •	Newberry	21	0
O29 •	at Appalachian State	17	21
N5 •	at Lenoir-Rhyne	0	17
N12 •	Presbyterian	7	27
N19 •	Richmond	22	7

1961   5-4-1
S16 •	Indiana State	19	6
S23 •	at Guilford	17	15
S30 •	at Catawba	16	0
O7 •	Elon	22	20
O14 •	Western Carolina	6	7
O21 •	at Newberry	13	7
O28 •	at Appalachian State	14	16
N4 •	Lenoir-Rhyne	19	24
N11 •	at Furman	8	29
N18 =	Wofford	20	20

CLARENCE STASAVICH
1962-69 (.647) 50-27-1

1962 5-4-0

S15		at Richmond	26	27
S29	●	Catawba	15	14
O6		at Elon	19	23
O13		at Western Carolina	16	20
O20	●	Newberry	36	8
O27	●	Appalachian State	29	16
N3		at Lenoir-Rhyne	6	7
N17	●	at Wofford	41	9
N24	●	Eastern Kentucky	29	12

1963 9-1-0

S14		at Richmond	7	10
S21	●	Wake Forest	20	10
S28	●	Wofford	34	7
O5	●	at Presbyterian	24	7
O12	●	Elon	6	0
O19	●	Western Carolina	50	0
N2	●	at The Citadel	20	6
N9	●	Lenoir-Rhyne	28	0
N23	●	at Tampa	14	8

EASTERN BOWL

D14	●	at Northeastern	27	6

1964 9-1-0

S12	●	Catawba	25	0
S19	●	at West Chester	33	7
S26	●	Howard	31	20
O10	●	at Wofford	21	0
O17	●	at Lenoir-Rhyne	33	14
O24		Richmond	20	22
O31	●	at The Citadel	19	10
N7	●	at Furman	34	14
N14	●	Presbyterian	49	8

TANGERINE BOWL

D12	●	Massachusetts	14	13

1965-76
SOUTHERN

1965 9-1-0 (3-1-0)

S25	●	West Chester	27	6
O2	|	at Furman	7	14
O9	● |	at Richmond	34	13
O16	●	at Louisville	34	20
O23	● |	The Citadel	21	0
O30	●	at La. Monroe	45	0
N6	●	Lenoir-Rhyne	44	0
N13	● |	George Washington	21	0
N20	●	at Howard	35	10

TANGERINE BOWL

D11	●	Maine	31	0

1966 4-5-1 (4-1-1)

S17	= |	at William & Mary	7	7
S24		La. Monroe	14	21
O1	● |	Furman	17	0
O8	● |	Davidson	40	7
O15	|	at George Washington	7	20
O22	● |	at The Citadel	27	17
O29		at Southern Illinois	13	31
N12	● |	Richmond	28	16
N19		Southern Miss	14	35
N25		at Louisville	7	21

1967 8-2-0 (4-1-0)

S16	● |	at William & Mary	27	7
S24	● |	at Richmond	23	7
S30	● |	at Davidson	42	17
O7	●	Southern Illinois	21	8
O14	●	Louisville	18	13
O21	●	at Parsons	27	26
O28	|	The Citadel	19	21
N4	● |	Furman	34	29
N11		West Texas State	13	37
N18	●	at Marshall	29	13

1968 4-6-0 (2-2-0)

S14	●	Parsons	37	7
S21	|	William & Mary	0	14
S28		at Louisiana Tech	7	35
O5		at Southern Miss	0	65
O26	|	Richmond	7	31
N2	● |	at Furman	24	13
N9		Tampa	21	28
N16	●	Marshall	49	20
N23	● |	at The Citadel	23	14
N30		at East Tennessee State	7	17

1969 2-7-0 (1-3-0)

S20		at East Tennessee State	0	7
S27		Louisiana Tech	6	24
O4	|	The Citadel	13	31
O18	|	at Richmond	7	24
O25	●	at Southern Illinois	17	3
N1	● |	Furman	24	21
N8	|	Davidson	27	42
N15		at Marshall	7	38
N22		Southern Miss	7	14

MIKE McGEE
1970 (.273) 3-8

1970 3-8-0 (2-2-0)

S12		at Toledo	2	35
S19		East Tennessee State	0	10
S26	|	at The Citadel	0	31
O3		at West Texas State	30	42
O10		at North Carolina St.	6	23
O17		Southern Illinois	12	14
O24	|	at Richmond	12	38
O31	● |	at Furman	7	0
N7		West Virginia	14	28
N14	●	Marshall	17	14
N28	● |	at Davidson	36	18

SONNY RANDLE
1971-73 (.622) 22-10

1971 4-6-0 (3-2-0)

S11		Toledo	0	45
S18	|	William & Mary	10	28
S25		at Bowling Green	21	47
O2	● |	The Citadel	31	25
O9	|	Richmond	7	14
O16		at West Virginia	21	44
O23	●	at North Carolina St.	31	15
O30	● |	Furman	26	13
N6	● |	Davidson	27	26
N13		at Tampa	7	43

1972 9-2-0 (6-0-0)

S9	● |	at VMI	30	3
S16	●	Southern Illinois	16	0
S23	● |	Appalachian State	35	7
O7	● |	at Richmond	21	0
O14	● |	The Citadel	27	21
O21		at North Carolina St.	16	38
O28	● |	at Furman	27	21
N4	●	Chattanooga	33	7
N11	● |	at William & Mary	21	15
N18	●	Dayton	24	22
N25		at North Carolina	19	42

1973 9-2-0 (7-0-0)

S8		at North Carolina St.	8	57
S15	●	at Southern Miss	13	0
S22	●	at Southern Illinois	42	25
S29	● |	Furman	14	3
O6	● |	at Davidson	45	0
O13	● |	VMI	42	7
O20	● |	at The Citadel	34	0
O27		at North Carolina	27	28
N3	● |	William & Mary	34	3
N10	● |	Richmond	44	14
N17	● |	Appalachian State	49	14

PAT DYE
1974-79 (.724) 48-18-1

1974 7-4-0 (3-3-0)

S14	●	Bowling Green	24	6
S21	●	East Tennessee State	24	8
S28	●	Southern Illinois	17	16
O5		at North Carolina St.	20	24
O12	● |	at Furman	15	12
O19	|	at Appalachian State	21	23
O26	●	Dayton	34	6
N2	● |	The Citadel	41	21
N9	|	at Richmond	20	28
N16	● |	at William & Mary	31	10
N23	|	at VMI	3	13

1975 8-3-0 (4-2-0)

S6		at North Carolina St.	3	26
S13	|	at Appalachian State	25	41
S20	● |	William & Mary	20	0
S27	●	at Southern Illinois	41	7
O4	|	Richmond	14	17
O11	● |	at The Citadel	3	0
O18	●	Western Carolina	42	14
O25	●	at North Carolina	38	17
N1	● |	Furman	21	10
N8	●	at Virginia	61	10
N15	● |	VMI	28	12

1976 9-2-0 (4-1-0)

S11	●	Southern Miss	48	0
S18	●	at North Carolina St.	23	14
S25	● |	at William & Mary	20	19
O2	● |	The Citadel	22	3
O9	●	Southern Illinois	49	14
O16	● |	at VMI	17	3
O23		at North Carolina	10	12
O30	●	Western Carolina	24	17
N6	●	at Richmond	20	10
N13	|	at Furman	10	17
N20	● |	Appalachian State	35	7

1977-96
INDEPENDENT

1977 8-3-0

S3	●	at North Carolina St.	28	23
S10	●	at Duke	17	16
S17	●	at Toledo	22	9
S24	●	VMI	14	13
O1		at South Carolina	16	19
O8	●	Southern Illinois	33	0
O15	●	Richmond	35	14
O22	●	at The Citadel	34	16
O29		La. Lafayette	7	9
N5	●	at Appalachian State	45	14
N12		William & MaryNor	17	21

1978 9-3-0

S2	●	Western Carolina	14	6
S9		at North Carolina St.	13	29
S16		at North Carolina	10	14
S23	●	at La. Lafayette	38	9
S30	●	Texas Arlington	23	17
O7	●	at VMI	19	6
O14		at Southern Miss	16	17
O28	●	RichmondNor	21	14
N4	●	Appalachian St.	33	8
N11	●	William & Mary	20	3
N18	●	Marshall	45	0

INDEPENDENCE BOWL

D16	●	Louisiana Tech SHRE	35	13

1979 7-3-1

S1	●	Western Carolina	31	6
S8		at North Carolina St.	20	34
S15		at Duke	14	28
S22		at Wake Forest	20	23
S29	●	VMI	45	10
O13	●	Citadel	49	7
O27	=	at North Carolina	24	24
N3	●	Appalachian St.	38	21
N10	●	Richmond	52	10
N17	●	North Texas	49	16
N24	●	at William & Mary	38	14

ED EMORY
1980-84 (.473) 26-29

1980 4-7-0

S6	●	at Duke	35	10
S13		La. Lafayette	21	27
S20		at Florida State	7	63
S27		Southern Miss	7	35
O11	●	at Richmond	24	22
O18	●	Western Carolina	24	14
O25		at North Carolina	3	31
N1	●	William & Mary	31	23
N8		at Miami, Fla.	10	23
N15		Eastern Kentucky	16	28
N22		at North Carolina St.	14	36

1981 5-6-0

S5	●	Western Carolina	42	6
S12		at North Carolina	0	56
S19		at North Carolina St.	10	31
S26	●	Toledo	28	24
O3		at Duke	14	24
O10	●	at Richmond	17	13
O17	●	La. Lafayette	35	31
O24		Miami, Fla.	6	31
O31		at West Virginia	3	20
N7	●	East Tennessee St.	66	23
N14		William & Mary	21	31

1982 7-4-0

S11		at North Carolina St.	26	33
S18	●	East Tennessee St.	30	0
S25	●	Central Michigan	24	6
O2		at Missouri	9	28
O9	●	Richmond	35	14
O16		at Florida State	17	56
O23	●	Illinois St.	21	0
O30		at West Virginia	3	30
N6	●	at Texas Arlington	40	24
N13	●	at William & Mary	31	27
N20	●	at Temple	23	10

1983 8-3-0

S3		at Florida State	46	47
S10	●	North Carolina St.	22	16
S17	●	Murray St.	50	25
O1	●	at Missouri	13	6
O8	●	La. Lafayette	21	18
O15	●	Temple	24	11
O22		at Florida	17	24
O29	●	East Tenn St.	21	9
N5		at Miami, Fla.	7	12
N12	●	William & Mary	40	6
N19	●	at Southern Miss	10	6

1984 2-9-0

S1		at Florida State	17	48
S8		Temple	0	17
S15		at Central Michigan	12	17
S22	●	Geo. Southern	34	27
S29		at North Carolina St.	22	31
O6		at Pittsburgh	10	17
O13		at Tulsa	20	31
O20	●	East Tenn. St.	24	6
O27		at South Carolina	20	42
N3		La. Lafayette	24	42
N10		Southern Miss	27	31

ART BAKER
1985-88 (.273) 12-32

1985 2-9-0

S7	●	at North Carolina St.	33	14
S14	●	Texas St.	27	16
S21		at Penn State	10	17
S28		Temple	7	21
O5		Miami, Fla.	15	27
O12		at La. Lafayette	14	16
O26		South Carolina	10	52
N2		at Southern Miss	0	27
N9		at Auburn	10	35
N16		Tulsa	20	21
D7		at LSU	15	35

1986 2-9-0

S6		at North Carolina St.	10	38
S13		West Virginia	21	24
S20		at Auburn	0	45
S27		at Penn State	17	42
O4		La. Lafayette	10	21
O11		at Temple	28	45
O18	●	Georgia Southern	35	33
O25		at South Carolina	3	38
N1		Southern Miss	21	23
N15	●	Cincinnati	32	19
N27		at Miami, Fla.	10	36

1987 5-6-0

S5	●	at North Carolina St.	32	14
S12		Florida State	3	44
S19		at Illinois	10	20
S26	●	Georgia Southern	16	13
O3		at West Virginia	0	49
O10	●	Cincinnati	56	28
O17	●	at Virginia Tech	32	23
O24		at South Carolina	12	34
O31		Miami, Fla.	3	41
N7	●	Temple	31	26
N14		at Southern Miss	34	38

1988 -3-8-0

S3	●	Tenn. Tech	52	13
S10		at Virginia Tech	16	27
S17		at South Carolina	0	17
S24		Southern Miss	42	45
O1		La. Lafayette	36	48
O8		West Virginia	10	30
O15		at Florida State	21	45
O22		Syracuse	14	38
O29		Miami, Fla.	7	31
N5	●	at Temple	34	17
N19	●	at Cincinnati	49	14

BILL LEWIS
1989-91 (.632) 21-12-1

1989 5-5-1

S9	●	Bowling Green	41	6
S16	●	at Cincinnati	21	14
S23	●	Illinois St.	56	10
S30	=	Louisiana Tech	29	29
O7		at South Carolina	14	47
O21	●	Virginia Tech	14	10
O28		at Syracuse	16	18
N4		at Miami, Fla.	10	40
N11	●	Temple	31	24
N18		at Pittsburgh	42	47
N25		at Southern Miss	27	41

1990   5-6-0

S1 ●	Louisiana Tech	27	17
S8	at Florida State	24	45
S15	Virginia Tech	23	24
S22 ●	at La. Lafayette	20	10
S29	at Georgia	15	19
O6	Southern Miss	7	16
O13	at South Carolina	7	37
O20 ●	Cincinnati	56	32
O27 ●	at Temple	27	30
N3 ●	at Memphis	24	17
N10 ●	Northern Illinois	24	20

1991   11-1-0

A31	at Illinois	31	38
S14 ●	Memphis	20	13
S21 ●	at Central Florida	47	25
S28 ●	South Carolina	31	20
O5 ●	Akron	56	20
O12 ●	at Syracuse	23	20
O26 ●	Pittsburgh	24	23
N2 ●	Tulane	38	28
N9 ●	at Southern Miss	48	20
N16 ●	at Virginia Tech	24	17
N23 ●	at Cincinnati	30	19
PEACH BOWL			
J1 ●	North Carolina St.	37	34

STEVE LOGAN
1992-2002 (.543)   69-58

1992   5-6-0

S5	Syracuse	21	42
S12 ●	Virginia Tech	30	27
S19 ●	at South Carolina	20	18
S26	at Bowling Green	34	44
O10	at Duke	14	45
O17 ●	Cincinnati	42	21
O24 ●	at Pittsburgh	37	31
O29	Southern Miss	21	38
N7	at West Virginia	28	41
N14 ●	Arkansas State	35	18
N21	at Memphis	7	42

1993   2-9-0

S9	Syracuse	22	41
S18 ●	Central Florida	41	17
S25	at Washington	0	35
O2	Memphis	7	34
O9	at South Carolina	3	27
O16 ●	Louisiana Tech	31	28
O23	at Southern Miss	16	24
O30	at Virginia Tech	12	31
N6	Tulsa	26	52
N13	at Kentucky	3	6
N20	at Cincinnati	14	34

1994   7-5-0

S10	at Duke	10	13
S17 ●	at Temple	31	14
S24	Syracuse	18	21
O1 ●	Southern Miss	31	10
O8 ●	at South Carolina	56	42
O15	Virginia Tech	20	27
O22 ●	at Tulsa	28	21
O29 ●	Cincinnati	35	21
N5	at Auburn	21	38
N12 ●	Central Florida	23	20
N19 ●	at Memphis	30	6
LIBERTY BOWL			
D31	Illinois	0	30

1995   9-3-0

S2	at Tennessee	7	27
S9 ●	at Syracuse	27	24
S16 ●	Central Michigan	30	17
S23	at Illinois	0	7
S30 ●	West Virginia	23	20
O7	at Cincinnati	10	13
O21 ●	Temple	32	22
O28 ●	at Southern Miss	36	34
N4 ●	at Army	31	25
N11 ●	Tulsa	28	7
N18 ●	Memphis	31	17
LIBERTY BOWL			
D30 ●	Stanford	19	13

1996   8-3

S7 ●	East Tenn. St.	45	21
S14 ●	at West Virginia	9	10
S21 ●	at South Carolina	23	7
S28 ●	Central Florida	28	7
O10 ●	Southern Miss	7	28
O19 ●	at Miami, Fla.	31	6
N2 ●	Arkansas State	34	16
N9 ●	at Virginia Tech	14	35
N16 ●	Ohio U.	55	45
N23 ●	at Memphis	20	10
N30 ●	North Carolina St. *CHAR*	50	29

1997-PRESENT
C-USA

1997   5-6   (4-2)

S6	at West Virginia	17	24
S13 ●	Wake Forest	25	24
S20	South Carolina	0	26
O4	at Syracuse	0	56
O11 │	Southern Miss	13	23
O18 │	at Tulane	16	33
O25 ● │	Memphis	32	10
N1 ● │	at Louisville	45	31
N8 ● │	at Houston	28	27
N13 ● │	Cincinnati	14	7
N22	at North Carolina St.	24	37

1998   6-5   (3-3)

S5	at Virginia Tech	3	38
S12 ●	U.T. Chattanooga	31	0
S19 ●	at Ohio U.	21	14
O3 ● │	Army	30	25
O10 ● │	UAB	26	7
O17	at Alabama	22	23
O24 │	at Southern Miss	7	41
O31 │	Houston	31	34
N5 ● │	at Cincinnati	24	21
N14 │	Louisville	45	63
N21 ● │	at Memphis	34	31

1999   9-3   (4-2)

S4 ●	West Virginia *CHAR*	30	23
S11 ●	Duke	27	9
S18 ●	at South Carolina	21	3
S25 ●	Miami, Fla. *RAL*	27	23
O2 ● │	at Army	33	14
O9 │	Southern Miss	22	39
O23 ● │	Tulane	52	7
O30 ● │	at Houston	19	3
N6 │	at UAB	17	36
N13 ● │	Cincinnati	48	34
N20 ● │	North Carolina St.	23	6
MOBILE BOWL			
D22	TCU	14	28

2000   8-4   (5-2)

S2 ●	at Duke	38	0
S7	Virginia Tech	28	45
S16 ● │	Tulane	37	17
S23 ●	Syracuse	34	17
O7 │	at Memphis	10	17
O14 │	Army	42	21
O19 ● │	at Louisville	28	25
O28 │	UAB	13	16
N11 │	Houston	62	20
N18 │	at West Virginia	24	42
N24 ● │	at Southern Miss	14	9
GALLERYFURNITURE.COM BOWL			
D27 ●	Texas Tech	40	27

2001   6-6   (5-2)

S1	Wake Forest	19	21
S8 ● │	at Tulane	51	24
S22 ●	William & Mary	38	23
S29	at Syracuse	30	44
O6	at North Carolina	21	24
O13 ● │	at Army	49	26
O20 ● │	Memphis	32	11
O30 ● │	at TCU	37	30
N10 ● │	at Cincinnati	28	26
N15 │	Louisville	34	39
N23 │	Southern Miss	21	28
GMAC BOWL			
D19	Marshall	61	64

2002   4-8   (4-4)

A31	at Duke	16	23
S7	at Wake Forest	22	27
S14 ● │	Tulane	24	20
S28	at West Virginia	17	37
O5 ● │	Army	59	24
O19 │	South Florida	30	46
O26 │	at Louisville	20	44
N9 ● │	at Houston	54	48
N16 │	at UAB	29	36
N23 │	TCU	31	28
N30 │	at Southern Miss	7	24
D6 │	Cincinnati	26	42

JOHN THOMPSON
2003-04 (.130)   3-20

2003   1-11   (1-7)

S1 │	at Cincinnati	3	40
S6 │	West Virginia	7	48
S13 │	at Miami, Fla.	3	38
S20 │	at Wake Forest	16	34
S30 │	Houston	13	27
O11 │	North Carolina	17	28
O18 ● │	at Army	38	32
O25 │	Louisville	20	36
N1 │	at Memphis	24	41
N8 │	South Florida	37	38
N22 │	at Tulane	18	28
N29 │	Southern Miss	21	38

2004   2-9   (2-6)

S4 │	at West Virginia	23	56
S11 │	Wake Forest	17	31
S25 │	Cincinnati	19	24
O2 │	at Louisville	7	59
O9 ● │	Tulane	27	25
O23 │	at Southern Miss	10	51
O30 ● │	Army	38	28
N6 │	at Houston	24	34
N13 │	at South Florida	17	41
N20 │	Memphis	35	38
N27 │	North Carolina St. *CHAR*	14	52

Neutral Site key: *CHAR* Charlotte, North Carolina
ƒ Forfeit † Game Later Forfieted # Disputed Victor * Disputed Score ‖ Designated Conference Game │2 Counted Twice in Conference Standings

EAST CAROLINA ANNUAL STATISTICAL LEADERS

YR	RUSHING	YDS	ATT	AVG	PASSING	ATT	CMP	PCT	YDS	RECEIVING	REC	YDS	AVG
1963	Tom Michel	830	170	4.9	Bill Cline	80	44	.55	693	Dave Bumgarner	23	328	14.3
1964	Dave Alexander	869	138	6.3	Bill Cline	111	63	.57	944	Dave Bumgarner	37	408	11.0
1965	Dave Alexander	1,029	227	4.5	George Richardson	98	53	.54	680	Ruffin Odom	28	367	13.1
1966	Bill Bailey	378	91	4.2	Bill Bailey	151	62	.41	774	Nelson Gravatt	20	184	9.2
1967	Butch Colson	1,135	252	4.5	Neal Hughes	124	65	.52	805	Jimmy Adkins	19	328	17.3
1968	Butch Colson	680	180	3.8	Billy Wightman	63	29	.46	306	Jimmy Adkins	22	331	15.0
1969	Billy Wightman	835	170	4.9	Butch Colson	33	19	.58	256	Dick Corrada	19	211	11.1
1970	Billy Wallace	902	210	4.3	John Casazza	277	122	.44	1,512	Dick Corrada	46	512	11.1
1971	Billy Wallace	557	108	5.2	John Casazza	182	72	.40	1,004	Tim Dameron	25	487	19.5
1972	Carlester Crumpler	1,309	340	3.9	Carl Summerell	197	86	.44	1,275	Tim Dameron	30	648	21.6
1973	Carlester Crumpler	1,042	204	5.1	Carl Summerell	154	82	.53	1,222	Stan Eure	27	495	18.3
1974	Kenny Strayhorn	635	106	6.0	Mike Weaver	81	21	.26	443	Vic Wilfore	8	110	13.8
1975	Kenny Strayhorn	638	101	6.3	Pete Conaty	59	24	.41	463	Terry Gallaher	13	433	33.3
1976	Eddie Hicks	897	137	6.5	Mike Weaver	84	37	.44	633	Terry Gallaher	14	269	19.2
1977	Theodore Sutton	706	125	5.6	Jimmy Southerland	84	47	.56	779	Terry Gallaher	27	512	19.0
1978	Theodore Sutton	621	127	4.9	Leander Green	110	46	.42	838	Terry Gallaher	18	227	12.6
1979	Anthony Collins	1,130	154	7.3	Leander Green	141	73	.52	1,082	Vern Davenport	26	343	13.2
1980	Theodore Sutton	586	135	4.3	Greg Stewart	83	38	.46	400	Vern Davenport	14	186	13.3
1981	Carlton Nelson	489	107	4.6	Carlton Nelson	78	29	.37	484	Norwood Vann	20	288	14.4
1982	Tony Baker	827	126	6.6	Greg Stewart	114	58	.51	941	Carlton Nelson	28	526	18.8
1983	Earnest Byner	862	174	5.0	Kevin Ingram	164	90	.55	1,191	Stefon Adams	20	277	13.9
1984	Reggie Branch	521	116	4.5	Darrell Speed	132	61	.46	795	Ricky Nichols	28	513	18.3
1985	Tony Baker	951	197	4.8	Ron Jones	127	47	.37	652	Tony Smith	14	234	16.7
1986	Anthony Simpson	753	178	4.2	Charlie Libretto	148	71	.48	833	Jarrod Moody	22	252	11.5
1987	Anthony Simpson	670	153	4.4	Travis Hunter	155	76	.49	1,107	Ron Jones	23	301	13.1
1988	Tim James	787	163	4.8	Travis Hunter	118	52	.44	828	Walter Wilson	19	355	18.7
1989	Travis Hunter	398	98	4.1	Travis Hunter	223	110	.49	1,478	Walter Wilson	43	771	17.9
1990	David Daniels	553	100	5.5	Jeff Blake	219	116	.53	1,510	Luke Fisher	35	534	15.3
1991	Cedric Van Buren	351	90	3.9	Jeff Blake	368	203	.55	3,073	Hunter Gallimore	49	881	18.0
1992	Junior Smith	1,037	186	5.6	Michael Anderson	398	222	.56	2,486	Morris Letcher	47	557	11.9
1993	Junior Smith	1,352	278	4.9	Perez Mattison	183	78	.43	924	Jerris McPhail	34	410	12.1
1994	Junior Smith	1,204	226	5.3	Marcus Crandell	401	230	.57	2,687	Jason Nichols	42	450	10.7
1995	Jerris McPhail	910	185	4.9	Marcus Crandell	447	235	.53	2,751	Mitchell Galloway	46	619	13.5
1996	Scott Harley	1,745	307	5.7	Marcus Crandell	245	136	.56	1,507	Mitchell Galloway	48	554	11.5
1997	Scott Harley	457	119	3.8	Dan Gonzalez	431	253	.59	2,510	Troy Smith	54	795	14.7
1998	Jamie Wilson	647	138	4.7	David Garrard	255	157	.62	2,091	Troy Smith	44	719	16.3
1999	Jamie Wilson	865	156	5.5	David Garrard	312	181	.58	2,359	LaMont Chappell	36	558	15.5
2000	Leonard Henry	711	133	5.3	David Garrard	312	164	.53	2,332	Keith Stokes	29	442	15.2
2001	Leonard Henry	1,432	184	7.8	David Garrard	290	164	.57	2,247	Derrick Collier	31	481	15.5
2002	Art Brown	1,029	214	4.8	Paul Troth	359	177	.49	2,315	Torey Morris	38	552	14.5
2003	Marvin Townes	1,128	258	4.4	Desmore Robinson	201	133	.66	1,262	Terrance Cooper	87	897	10.3
2004	Chris Johnson	546	121	4.5	James Pinkney	335	188	.56	2,180	Bobby Good	33	427	12.9

Receiving leaders by receptions
The NCAA began including postseason stats in 2002

THE SCHOOLS

EASTERN MICHIGAN

BY ED KRZEMIENSKI

IT'S NOT EASY FOR A COLLEGE FOOTball team to get a lot of attention when it plays just 11 miles from one of the greatest programs in the history of the sport. No one could blame Eastern Michigan if, every once in a while, it glances down the road from its home in Ypsilanti and ponders how sweet it would be to receive just half the attention that the neighboring school in Ann Arbor gets.

EMU, which in the early years of the 20th century scheduled opponents such as Ann Arbor High School and the Michigan School for the Deaf, actually became something of a force in the 1920s and 1930s. But the team has rarely done well since its lone MAC championship in 1987. Since 1990, Eastern Michigan has had one nickname change (from Hurons to Eagles)—and the same number of winning seasons. Through 2004, the Eagles had run through seven coaches in the preceding 14 seasons. Not a good sign.

TRADITION It's indicative of the Eagles' slight success on the football field that their annual awards are named not for former players but former administrators. The James M. (Bingo) Brown Award for offensive MVP, the John Borowiec Award for the defensive MVP and the Harold Sponberg Award for Scholar-Lineman honor the former dean of men, an original member of the Bust Committee and an ex-president of the school, respectively. Meanwhile, the stadium and an award for best scholar-athlete are named for former coach Elton J. Rynearson.

BEST PLAYER Gary Patton led the Hurons in rushing in each of his four varsity seasons (1984-87). Running for 1,242 yards and 13 touchdowns his senior year, he led Eastern Michigan to its only MAC championship and a victory in the California Bowl. By the end of his career, Paatton held school records for rushing (3,497 yards) and touchdowns (31).

BEST COACH Elton J. Rynearson coached Eastern Michigan for a total of 26 seasons between 1917 and 1948. He led the school to an overall record of 114–58–15, for a .650 winning percentage. From 1925 to 1938, Rynearson compiled an amazing run during which his teams went 80–19–7, including a 6–1 mark in 1930, the only loss coming in a 7-0 thriller to powerhouse neighbor Michigan. During his 46 years of service to EMU, "Rynie" coached every varsity sport at one time or another.

BEST TEAM Led by Patton and 1,500-yard passer Ron Adams, Jim Harkema's 1987 team went 10–2 overall and

PROFILE

Eastern Michigan University
Ypsilanti, Mich.
Founded: 1849
Enrollment: 19,000
Colors: Dark Green and White
Nickname: Eagles
Stadium: Rynearson Stadium
  Opened in 1969
  AstroTurf; 30,200 capacity
First football game: 1891
All-time record: 414–471–47 (.469)
Bowl record: 1–0
Mid-American Conference championships:
1 (outright)
First-round NFL draftees: 2
Website: www.emich.edu/goeagles

THE BEST OF TIMES

During the 1987 season, EMU posted a 10–2 record, taking the MAC championship and a victory in the California Bowl.

THE WORST OF TIMES

Eastern Michigan failed to achieve a single winning season from 1958 to 1963, going winless in 1960 and 1961.

CONFERENCE

EMU joined the Mid-American Conference in 1976 and has remained there since.

DISTINGUISHED ALUMNI

George "Iceman" Gervin, Basketball Hall of Famer; Shirley Spork, LPGA co-founder; Bob Welch, baseball player

FIGHT SONG

GO GREEN

Go Green, roll up the score
Go Green, let's get some more.
Raise a cheer for old Green and White
Let's show them we came here to fight.
Go Green, vict'ry we'll claim
Go Green, let's win this game.
We'll always fight for old EMU
Come on and let's go Green!

EAGLES FIGHT SONG

Eastern Eagles, Hats off to you!
Fight, Fight, Fight for ole EMU.
Look to the sky, the Eagles will fly,
The bravest we'll defy!
Rah, Rah, Rah
Hold that line for ole Green and White,
Sons and daughters show your might,
So fight, fight for ole EMU and victory!

7–1 in the MAC. Four Hurons won all-conference honors: Patton, Adams, guard Brian Clouse and defensive back Charles Gordon.

BIGGEST GAME On Dec. 12, 1987, the 9–2 Hurons traveled to Fresno to take on the 10–1 San Jose State Spartans in the California Bowl. Playing as a 17-point underdog in front of a hostile crowd, Eastern Michigan came away with a 30-27 win in a seesaw offensive thriller that saw five lead changes. The Hurons went ahead for good on a 32-yard touchdown pass from Adams to Craig Ostrander with less than four minutes left in the game. The redoubtable Patton led the team with 130 yards rushing and was named Most Valuable Player.

BIGGEST UPSET Eastern Michigan's first season in the MAC was in 1976, and the Hurons got off to a horrid 1–7 start. A 30-27 home win over archrival Central Michigan, then 6–2, salvaged a modicum of pride. It was EMU's only conference win of that first season, which saw the Hurons lose nine games by an average of more than 25 points.

In 1914, Olds had a special striped shirt made so that he would not be confused with the players. It caught on, and he is regarded as the originator of the officials' jersey.

STADIUM Eastern Michigan formally dedicated Rynearson Stadium on Oct. 25, 1969. Originally holding 15,500 spectators and a natural grass playing field, Rynearson now has a capacity of 30,200 (plus standing room in the south end zone) and AstroTurf.

RIVAL There's a huge three-way rivalry in Michigan *not* involving Wolverines and Spartans: Eastern, Central and Western Michigan fight fiercely year-round for recruits and bragging rights. As former EMU head coach Rick Rasnick once noted, "The MAC is predominantly a regional conference, so wins against rivals can really help you when it comes to signing players." In this sense, Eastern considers Central its prime rival, and Central has clearly had the upper hand: through 2004, Eastern trailed Central in their series 24-52-6.

NICKNAME EMU began its life on the football field known variously as the Normalites or Men from Ypsi. In 1929, the school held a contest for a new nickname. The winning entry of Hurons, a regional Native-American tribe,

RECORDS

RUSHING YARDS
GAME
291 Larry Ratcliff vs. Eastern Kentucky, Oct. 16, 1971 (40 att.)
SEASON
1,531 Anthony Sherrell, 2003 (338 att.)
CAREER
3,497 Gary Patton, 1984-87 (702 att)

PASSING YARDS
GAME
450 Walter Church vs. Central Michigan, Oct. 19, 1996 (30 of 62)
SEASON
3,280 Charlie Batch, 1997 (247 of 434)
CAREER
9,142 Walter Church, 1996-2000 (807 of 1,441)

RECEIVING YARDS
GAME
241 Ontario Pryor vs. Central Michigan, Oct. 19, 1996 (14 rec.)
SEASON
1,368 Kevin Walter, 2002 (93 rec.)
CAREER
2,838 Kevin Walter, 1999-2002 (211 rec.)

POINTS
GAME
26 Eric Deslauriers vs. Central Michigan, Nov. 6, 2004 (4 TDs, 1 two-pt. conv.)
SEASON
90 Ime Akpan, 2002 (15 TDs); Kerry Keating, 1957 (15 TDs)
CAREER
239 Justin Ventura, 1995-98 (42 FGs, 113 PATs)

CONSENSUS ALL-AMERICANS

1968	John Schmidt	C
1969	Robert Lints	MG
1970–71	Dave Pureifory	DT
1973	Jim Pietrzak	OT

came from two students, one of whom was additionally influenced by his place of employment, the Huron Hotel. EMU reconsidered its choice in 1988 when the Michigan Department of Civil Rights suggested schools drop the use of Native American names, logos and mascots. Three years later, the school christened another contest winner as the new and current nickname, Eagles.

UNIFORMS The school's official colors of dark green and white have remained consistent throughout the team's modern history, although the helmets have changed with the new nickname and mascot. Throughout its Huron history, the team periodically wore helmets with the profile of a Native American alongside "EMU." In 1991, as the school was trotting out its new name, helmets sported a "100" logo in honor of the team's 100th year of play. Currently, the team wears a large white E on both sides of a green helmet, with all-white outfits on the road and all-green at home.

MASCOT The school adopted an eagle named Swoop as its official mascot in 1994. A member of the EMU cheerleading squad, Swoop raised the fraternity of bird-oriented MAC mascots to five.

LORE Dr. Lloyd W. Olds served as a football coach, professor, athletic director and head of intramurals, but his principal contribution to the world of sports spread well beyond Ypsilanti. You see, he invented the Zebra. As a high school basketball referee in 1914, Olds had a special striped shirt made so that he would not be confused with the players. His striped shirt caught on in basketball. And in football, too.

QUOTE "Our economy is soaring higher than Swoop." —President Bill Clinton, in his keynote address at EMU's 2000 commencement ceremony

EASTERN MICHIGAN ANNUAL STATISTICAL LEADERS

YR	RUSHING	YDS	ATT	AVG	PASSING	ATT	CMP	PCT	YDS	RECEIVING	REC	YDS	AVG
1952	Ed Skowneski	328	80	4.1		NA	NA	NA	NA		NA	NA	NA
1953	Tom Fagan	388	93	4.2		NA	NA	NA	NA		NA	NA	NA
1954	Virgil Windom	530	122	4.3		NA	NA	NA	NA		NA	NA	NA
1955	Tom McCormick	461	86	5.4		NA	NA	NA	NA		NA	NA	NA
1956	Kerry Keating	417	67	6.2	Herman Carroll	66	31	.47	413	Kerry Keating	8	126	15.8
1957	Kerry Keating	563	96	5.9	Bill Ameel	47	19	.40	328	Kerry Keating	5	153	30.6
1958	Al Day	296	80	3.7	John Kubiak	64	29	.45	452	Jerry Wedge	10	183	18.3
1959	Al Day	226	61	3.7	Dave Longridge	122	41	.34	513	Ron Gulyas	9	191	21.2
1960	Jim Dills	231	67	3.4	George Beaudette	60	25	.42	339	Bill Yanis	21	388	18.5
1961	Don Oboza	207	75	2.8	George Beaudette	155	50	.32	696	Pat Dignan	12	195	16.3
1962	Terry Hurley	261	84	3.1	Tom Prieur	148	61	.41	854	Terry Hurley	29	534	18.4
1963	Terry Hurley	366	101	3.6	Don Oboza	150	70	.47	885	Terry Hurley	31	345	11.1
1964	Pete DiMercurio	341	78	4.4	Bill MacGillivray	104	49	.47	760	Tom Grundner	21	333	15.9
1965	Bob Edelbrock	305	71	4.3	Ed Mass	120	58	.48	716	Tom Grundner	17	282	16.6
1966	Lonny Head	350	114	3.1	Rick Krumm	81	32	.40	351	Ted LeClaire	19	295	15.5
1967	John Vaccarelli	481	106	4.5	John Vaccarelli	78	22	.28	273	Gary Matsche	16	260	16.3
1968	Dennis Hewitt	607	157	3.9	Arnold Fontes	107	49	.46	725	Chip Gooden	23	463	20.1
1969	Larry Ratcliff	649	141	4.6	Donald Stewart	148	73	.49	1,042	Gary Matsche	34	513	15.1
1970	Larry Ratcliff	1,011	171	5.9	Donald Stewart	68	31	.46	499	Chip Gooden	26	430	16.5
1971	Larry Ratcliff	1,188	166	7.2	Bob Hill	53	20	.38	278	Tim Cogswell	10	209	20.9
1972	Mike Strickland	924	182	5.1	Houston Booth	62	29	.47	513	Chip Gooden	21	259	12.3
1973	Mike Strickland	1,105	185	6.0	Frank Kolch	124	71	.57	988	Reggie Garrett	43	693	16.1
1974	Mike Strickland	1,203	282	4.3	Jerry Mucha	56	27	.48	406	Clarence Chapman	17	296	17.4
1975	Clarence Chapman	643	119	5.4	Jerry Mucha	94	37	.39	526	Clarence Chapman	13	194	14.9
1976	Bobby Windom	824	147	5.6	Steve Raklovits	199	90	.45	954	Carlos Henderson	19	328	17.3
1977	Bobby Windom	1,322	246	5.4	Steve Raklovits	228	123	.54	1,784	James Hall	40	646	16.2
1978	Doug Crisan	485	103	4.7	Burt Beaney	133	62	.47	833	Tom Parm	21	363	17.3
1979	Doug Crisan	412	128	3.2	Scott Davis	254	131	.52	1,744	Tom Parm	41	701	17.1
1980	Albert Williams	456	121	3.8	Scott Davis	227	106	.47	1,143	Jeff Dackin	27	363	13.4
1981	Ricky Calhoun	971	235	4.1	J.F. Green	226	131	.58	1,391	Jeff Dackin	35	440	12.6
1982	Ricky Calhoun	656	139	4.7	Steve Coulter	258	117	.45	1,415	Ricky Simpson	32	385	12.0
1983	Ricky Calhoun	871	217	4.0	Steve Coulter	330	147	.45	1,827	Derrin Powell	34	582	17.1
1984	Gary Patton	566	103	5.5	Robert Gordon	189	89	.47	949	Derrin Powell	16	261	16.3
1985	Gary Patton	631	142	4.4	Ron Adams	167	91	.54	977	Don Vesling	19	354	18.6
1986	Gary Patton	1,058	210	5.0	Ron Adams	251	151	.60	1,995	Don Vesling	35	653	18.7
1987	Gary Patton	1,242	247	5.0	Ron Adams	202	107	.53	1,527	Mark Ziegler	26	486	18.7
1988	Bob Foster	762	169	4.5	Tom Sullivan	205	114	.56	1,664	Craig Ostrander	33	676	20.5
1989	Perry Foster	1,087	263	4.1	Tom Sullivan	253	129	.51	1,927	Todd Bell	20	515	25.8
1990	Ed Nwagbaraocha	402	110	3.7	Shane Jackson	245	113	.46	1,454	Patrick Walsh	29	385	13.3
1991	Cameron Moss	452	119	3.8	Kwame McKinnon	149	74	.50	849	Bryan Wauldron	14	213	15.2
1992	Stephen Whitfield	377	86	4.4	Kwesi Ramsey	129	43	.33	592	Craig Thompson	19	329	17.3
1993	Melvin Green	488	129	3.8	Michael Armour	165	93	.56	1,208	Anthony Cicchelli	31	616	19.9
1994	Stephen Whitfield	1,232	284	4.3	Michael Armour	230	135	.59	1,629	Steve Clay	46	589	12.8
1995	Savon Edwards	732	148	4.9	Charlie Batch	421	244	.58	3,177	Steve Clay	63	999	15.9
1996	Mike Scott	792	145	5.5	Walter Church	355	178	.50	2,151	Ontario Pryor	62	1,031	16.6
1997	Savon Edwards	627	128	4.9	Charlie Batch	434	247	.57	3,280	Ta-if Kumasi	39	710	18.2
1998	Eric Powell	473	152	3.1	Walter Church	355	213	.60	2,650	Jermaine Sheffield	62	953	15.4
1999	Eric Powell	583	151	3.9	Walter Church	332	178	.54	2,015	Brandon Campbell	53	764	14.4
2000	John White	561	155	3.6	Walter Church	399	238	.60	2,326	Kenny Christian	78	808	10.4
2001	Chris R. Roberson	755	167	4.5	Kainoa Akina	267	140	.52	1,504	Kevin Walter	62	748	12.1
2002	Ime Akpan	1,221	267	4.6	Troy Edwards	410	232	.57	2,762	Kevin Walter	93	1,368	14.7
2003	Anthony Sherrell	1,531	338	4.5	Chinedu Okoro	251	134	.53	1,360	Anthony Sherrell	44	304	6.9
2004	Anthony Sherrell	854	194	4.4	Matt Bohnet	434	228	.53	2,807	Eric Deslauriers	84	1,257	15.0

Receiving leaders by receptions
All statistics include postseason

EASTERN MICHIGAN ALL-TIME SCORES

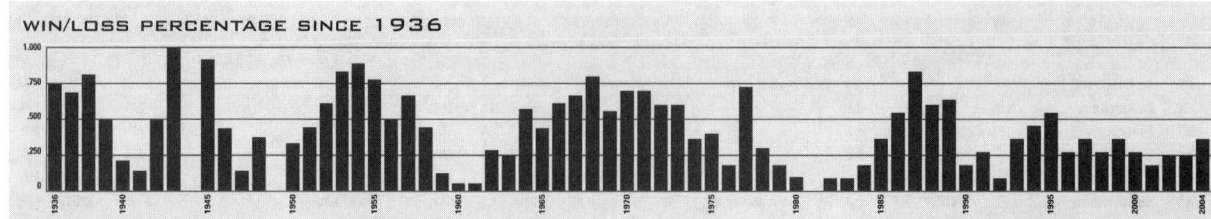

WIN/LOSS PERCENTAGE SINCE 1936

JAMES M. SWIFT
1891 (.000)   0-2

1891   0-2-0
O21		Ann Arbor HS	4	34
U		at Michigan Lit.	0	30

DEANE W. KELLEY
1892 (.667)   2-1

1892   2-1-0
O15		at Ann Arbor HS	0	16
O29	●	at Michigan Jr. Laws.	6	4
N2	●	Albion	30	10

ERNEST GOODRICH
1893 (.667)   4-2

1893   4-2-0
U	●	Lit. Students ' 96	16	8
U		at Hillsdale	0	28
U	●	at Detroit HS	14	10
U	●	at Ann Arbor HS	42	12
U		at Saint Mary's-Cal	22	30
U	●	at Fort Wayne	22	6

VERNE S. BENNETT
1894 (.714)   5-2

1894   5-2-0
S29	●	Ann Arbor HS	18	0
O6		at Olivet	0	48
O13	●	Michigan JV	18	4
O27	●	Ypsilanti HS	36	0
N3	●	Toledo AA	76	0
N17	●	at Detroit	18	6
N24	●	at Ann Arbor HS	10	12 *

MARCUS CARTER
1895 (.500)   3-3

1895   3-3-0
O4	●	at Atlantis	9	8
O5	●	at Ann Arbor HS	32	0
O12	●	at Michigan JV	0	10
O26	●	at Saint Mary's-Cal	10	24
N2	●	Michigan Lits.	56	6
N16		at Detroit AC	12	16

FRED GREEN
1896 (.800)   4-1

1896   4-1-0
U	●	Hillsdale	18	0
O3		at Michigan	0	18
U	●	at Ann Arbor HS	30	0
U	●	at Albion	52	0
U	●	at Detroit AC	10	0

A. BIRD GLASPIE
1897 (.400)   2-3

1897   2-3-0
S25	●	Michigan Alumni	24	0
O2		at Michigan	0	24
O30		at Albion	0	18
N6	●	at Toledo YMCA	12	4
N30		Kalamazoo	0	16

ENOCH C. THORNE
1898 (.250)   1-5-2

1898   1-5-2
O1		at Michigan	0	21 *
O8		at Michigan State	6	11
U		at Toledo YMCA	0	16
U	=	Toledo YMCA	0	0
U	=	Alumni	0	0
U		at Hillsdale	0	24
N15	●	at Ypsilanti HS	7	0
N19		at Michigan State	6	24

DWIGHT WATSON
1899 (.500)   1-1-1

1899   1-1-1
O30	=	at Michigan JV	5	5
N11		at Michigan State	0	18
N18	●	Toledo YMCA	24	0

CLAYTON T. TEETZEL
1900-02 (.237)   4-14-1

1900   0-4-0
O20		Orchard Lake	0	17
O27		Michigan JV	0	41
N3		D.A.C. Reserves	0	11
N10		at Kalamazoo	0	12

1901   3-5-0
O5		at Michigan JV	20	28
O19	●	at Michigan Alkali Works	6	5
O26		Michigan JV	6	12
N2	●	at Michigan Alkali Works	12	10
N9		Kalamazoo	0	39
N16		Albion	0	29
N25		Albion	6	39
N30		Michigan School-Deaf	10	5

1902   1-5-1
O18		at Detroit Univ. School	0	18
O25	●	at Detroit Bus. Univ.	32	0
N1		at Central Michigan	0	10
N8	=	Detroit Cent. HS	6	6
N15		at Hillsdale	5	29
N22		Hillsdale	0	22
N29		at Michigan School-Deaf	0	40

HUNTER FOREST
1903 (.500)   4-4

1903   4-4-0
O10		at Detroit	0	6
O17		at Mt. Clemens	0	23
O24		Olivet	0	41
O31	●	Detroit Bus. Univ.	10	6
N7		at Adrian	16	0
N12		Detroit College	5	0
N14		at Hillsdale	11	12
N21	●	Adrian	36	0

DANIEL H. LAWRENCE
1904-05 (.625)   10-6

1904   6-2-0
O8	●	Detroit Bus. Univ.	24	5
O15		at Albion	0	68
O22	●	at Michigan School-Deaf	18	11
O29	●	at Michigan JV	0	43
N5	●	at Adrian	23	11
N12	●	Michigan School-Deaf	16	0
N19	●	Adrian	28	10
N24	●	Hillsdale	12	11

1905   4-4-0
S30		Michigan JV	0	20
O7	●	Detroit Bus. Univ.	30	0
O14	●	at Michigan Military Acad.	17	12
O21	●	Alumni Game	16	0
O28		at Olivet	0	69
N4	●	at Michigan School-Deaf	6	5
N17	●	at Central Michigan	0	13
N29		at Hillsdale	12	38

HENRY F. SCHULTE
1906-08 (.594)   9-6-1

1906   5-0-1
O20	=	at Michigan School-Deaf	0	0
O25	●	Detroit	6	0
N3	●	at Adrian	6	0
N10	●	Flint	16	0
N17	●	at Western Michigan	14	5
N27	●	Hillsdale	10	6

1907   3-2-0
O12	●	Adrian	22	0
O26	●	Detroit	7	0
N9	●	at Western Michigan	0	6
N16	●	Central Michigan	39	0
N23		at Hillsdale	4	7

1908   1-4-0
O10	●	Michigan School-Deaf	5	0
O23		Alma	0	5
O31		at Adrian	0	4
N7		at Central Michigan	0	11
N21	●	Hillsdale	10	20

CLARE HUNTER
1909 (.333)   2-4

1909   2-4-0
O16		at Alma	0	5
O23		Cleary Business	0	19
O30		Adrian	2	6
N5	●	Central Michigan	17	0
N13		at Detroit	8	9
N20	●	at Hillsdale	17	6

CURRY HICKS
1910 (.083)   0-5-1

1910   0-5-1
O9	=	at Adrian	5	5
O22		Detroit Univ. School	0	6
O15		Alma	6	22
N5		at Detroit	0	16
N12		at Central Michigan	0	13
N19		Hillsdale	0	6

DWIGHT WILSON
1911 (.429)   3-4

1911   3-4-0
O14	●	at Detroit Univ. School	17	0
O21		Adrian	0	9
O28	●	Alumni	6	0
N4	●	Battle Creek Normal	17	0
N9		Detroit	0	6
U		at Culver Military Acad.	0	28
N25		at Hillsdale	6	28

LEROY BROWN
1912-13 (.538)   6-5-2

1912   4-2-1
O19	●	Michigan School-Deaf	20	7
O26	●	Alumni Game	9	0
O29	●	Cleary College	33	0
N2		at Assumption Coll.	0	12
N8	=	at Central Michigan	0	0
N15	●	Western Michigan	7	0 *
N23		Hillsdale	14	26

1913   2-3-1
O11		at Michigan JV	0	26
O18	●	Assumption Coll.	38	0
O25	=	Detroit	0	0
N1		at Western Michigan	6	12
N15		Alma	0	34
N22	●	at Hillsdale	6	0

DR. THOMAS RANSOM
1914 (.583)   3-2-1

1914   3-2-1
O10		at Michigan JV	0	7
O16	=	at Alma	0	0
O31	●	Assumption Coll.	32	10
N4	●	Saint Mary's-Cal	27	12
N14		Western Michigan	0	10
N21	●	Hillsdale	13	7

ELMER C. MITCHELL
1915-16 (.545)   5-4-2

1915   4-2-1
O9		at Assumption Coll.	33	0
O16	=	at Michigan JV	0	0
O23	●	Detroit	46	0
O30	●	Adrian	28	0
N6		at Western Michigan	0	19
N13	●	Battle Creek Tr.	47	0
N20	●	at Hillsdale	0	6

1916   1-2-1
O7		Alma	0	6
O14	=	at Michigan JV	0	0
O21	●	Kalamazoo	6	21
O28	●	at Detroit	12	6

ELTON J. RYNEARSON
1917, '19-20, '25-48 (.650) 114-58-15

1917   3-4-0
O13		at Michigan JV	0	18
O17	●	at Assumption Coll.	28	0
O20	●	Central Michigan	63	0
O27		Olivet	0	19
N3		at Alma	0	27
N10		Michigan State JV	7	13
N24	●	at Hillsdale	13	3

LYNN BELL
1918 (.333)   1-2

1918   1-2-0
O26		at Detroit JC	0	18
N2		at U-M Army Corps	6	7
N9	●	at Hillsdale	20	6

ELTON J. RYNEARSON

1919   4-2-1
O16	●	Assumption Coll.	12	0
O23		at Bowling Green	10	0
O25	●	Adrian	23	6
N1	●	Alma	14	0
N7	=	at Central Michigan	7	7
N15	●	Albion	7	30
N22		at Hillsdale	0	1

1920   6-2-0
O9	●	at Assumption Coll.	27	13
O12	●	Bowling Green	45	0 *
O16	●	Central Michigan	7	6
O23	●	at Alma	12	6
O30	●	Grand Rapids JC	20	0
N6	●	Detroit JC	21	7
N15		at Albion	0	28
N29	●	Hillsdale	0	28

JOSEPH McCULLOCH
1921-22 (.538)   6-5-2

1921   3-3-0
O8	●	Assumption Coll.	48	0
O15	●	at Central Michigan	7	6
O22	●	Alma	0	7
N12	●	at Hillsdale	13	7
N18		Albion	14	27
N29		at Wayne State	0	3

1922   3-2-2
O7	●	at Assumption Coll.	13	0
O14	●	at Grand Rapids JC	12	0
O21		at Alma	0	14
O28	=	Wayne State	0	0
N4	=	Central Michigan	0	0
N11	●	Olivet	6	0
N18		Albion	0	14

JAMES BROWN
1923-24 (.313) 4-10-2

1923 2-5-1
S29	●	Adrian	13	0
O6		at Toledo	0	13
O13	=	Hillsdale	6	6
O20		Alma	0	19
O27		at Central Michigan	3	27
N3	●	at Kalamazoo	19	3
N17		Albion	7	21
N22		at Olivet	7	15

1924 2-5-1
S27	=	at Adrian	7	7
O4		Toledo	0	7
O11		at Hillsdale	13	14
O18		at Alma	0	9
O25		Central Michigan	0	13
N1	●	Kalamazoo	14	0
N15		at Albion	0	13
N22	●	Olivet	12	6

ELTON J. RYNEARSON

1925 8-0-0
O3	●	Detroit JV	8	0
O10	●	at Bowling Green	14	0
O17	●	Albion	6	0
O24	●	Hillsdale	20	0
O31	●	Ferris State	6	0
N8	●	at Olivet	20	0
N14	●	at Alma	25	0
N21	●	at Kalamazoo	7	6

1926 6-1-0
O2	●	Detroit JV	6	0
O9		at Alma	0	12
O16	●	at Detroit City College	6	0
O23	●	Central Michigan	41	0
O30	●	at Ferris State	21	0
N6	●	Olivet	20	0
N29	●	Kalamazoo	19	0

1927 8-0-0
O1	●	Olivet	20	0
O8	●	at Northern Illinois	25	6
O15	●	at Assumption Coll.	26	7
O22	●	Valparaiso	44	0
O29	●	Central Michigan	6	0
N5	●	at Adrian	20	0
N12	●	at Western Michigan	6	0
N19	●	Wayne State	39	0

1928 7-1-0
S29		at John Carroll	9	31
O6	●	Olivet	33	0
O13	●	Michigan JV	25	3
O19	●	Adrian	38	0
O27	●	at Central Michigan	36	0
N3	●	Northern Illinois	43	0
N10	●	Western Michigan	18	9
N17	●	at Wayne State	31	0

1929 5-1-2
O5	●	Bowling Green	34	7
O12	●	at DePaul	27	0
O19	●	Notre Dame JV	13	7
O26	●	Central Michigan	24	0
N2	=	at Western Michigan	7	7
N9		Michigan JV	14	18
N16	=	John Carroll	6	6
N23	●	at Detroit City Coll.	31	0

1930 6-1-0
S27		at Michigan	0	7
O11	●	Detroit City Coll.	33	7
O18	●	Western Michigan	19	0
O25	●	at Central Michigan	13	0
N1	●	Georgetown, Ky.	45	0
N8	●	Notre Dame JV	16	0
N15	●	at No. Iowa	19	0

1931 3-2-1
O3		at Michigan	0	34
O10	●	Ohio State JV	27	0
O17	=	at Notre Dame JV	0	0
O24		Central Michigan	12	20
N7	●	Ferris State	27	0
N14	●	No. Iowa	32	0

1932 5-2-0
S30		at Detroit	7	13
O7	●	at Northern Michigan	50	0
O15	●	Alma	27	0
O22	●	at Central Michigan	28	0
O29	●	Michigan JV	15	6
N5	●	South Dakota State	12	0
N13		No. Iowa	6	12

1933 6-2-0
S23	●	at Ferris State	20	0
S29		at Detroit	0	31
O7	●	at Northern Michigan	24	0
O13	●	St. Viator	13	8
O21	●	Central Michigan	13	7 *
O28	●	Alma	19	6
N4		South Dakota State	7	13
N11	●	at No. Iowa	19	6

1934 5-2-0
O6	●	Northern Michigan	26	6
O13		at No. Iowa	0	33
O20		at Central Michigan	12	13
O27	●	Alma	15	6
N3	●	St. Viator	13	0
N10	●	Ferris State	9	7
N17	●	at Indiana State	34	14

1935 4-2-2
S28		at Northern Michigan	0	2
O5	●	at Wayne State	16	6
O12	●	No. Iowa	3	0
O19	●	Central Michigan	7	0
O26	=	at Illinois St.	0	0
N2		Valparaiso	0	19
N9	●	Indiana State	10	7
N16	=	at Hope	7	7

1936 6-2-0
S26	●	Ball State	6	0
O2	●	Northern Michigan	12	0
O10		at Bowling Green	0	6
O17		Wayne State	0	8
O24	●	at Central Michigan	13	7
O31	●	at Valparaiso	7	6
N7	●	Illinois St.	19	13
N14	●	at Indiana State	19	13

1937 5-2-1
S25	●	at Ball State	13	6
O2	●	at Northern Michigan	44	0
O9	●	Bowling Green	25	0
O15	=	at Alma	12	12
O23		Central Michigan	10	27
O30	●	at Hope	19	0
N6		at Wayne State	0	7
N13	●	Indiana State	33	7

1938 6-1-1
S24	●	at Indiana State	37	0
S30	●	at Alma	20	0
O7	●	at Illinois St.	12	6
O14	●	Wayne State	20	7
O21		at Central Michigan	6	7
O28	=	at Bowling Green	7	7
N4	●	Kalamazoo	39	7
N11	●	Northern Michigan	25	2

1939 3-3-1
O7	=	at Illinois St.	0	0
O13		Wayne State	7	9
O20		Central Michigan	0	14
O27	●	Kalamazoo	19	6
N4	●	at Wayne State	13	6
N10	●	Alma	16	6
N18		Bowling Green	13	23

1940 1-5-1
O4	=	Illinois St.	0	0
O11		at Detroit	0	47
O19		at Bowling Green	0	15
O25		at Central Michigan	0	24
N2	●	Alma	24	7
N9		Wayne State	7	19
N16		Kalamazoo	3	13

1941 0-5-2
S27	=	at Hope	0	0
O4	=	at Illinois St.	0	0
O11		at Kalamazoo	0	7
O18		Bowling Green	6	20
O24		Central Michigan	6	12
N1		Indiana State	0	14
N8		at Wayne State	0	12

1942 3-3-1
S25		at Alma	6	14
O1	●	Hope	13	9
O9	●	Illinois St.	14	7
O15		at Central Michigan	0	14
O23	=	Wayne State	12	12
O29	●	Hillsdale	19	13
N7		at Albion	0	12

1943 2-0-0
O18	●	at Wayne State	14	0
O28	●	Wayne State	14	0

1944
NO TEAM

1945 5-0-1
O6	●	Albion	6	0
O13	●	Hillsdale	13	0
O27	●	at Hillsdale	6	0
N3	●	at Albion	6	0
N9	●	at Wayne State	14	13
N16	=	Wayne State	0	0

1946 3-4-1
S28		at Illinois St.	0	10
O4		at Hope	0	13
O11	●	Alma	6	0
O18		Central Michigan	13	26
O26		at Hillsdale	7	18
N2	●	Albion	13	6
N9	=	at Ball State	7	7
N15	●	Great Lakes NAS	19	0

1947 1-6-0
S26		at Alma	0	12
O3		Illinois St.	0	6
O11		at Northern Illinois	6	21
O18		Hope	7	12
O24		Hillsdale	2	15
O31		at Central Michigan	10	33 *
N6	●	Ball State	14	7

1948 3-5-0
S24		at Hope	0	14
O2		at Illinois St.	7	40
O9	●	Northern Michigan	6	0
O16		at Ball State	14	23
O23		at Eastern Kentucky	0	20
O29		Northern Illinois	7	10
N6	●	Central Michigan	6	0
N12	●	Valparaiso	26	7

HARRY OCKERMAN
1949-51 (.269) 7-19

1949 0-8-0
S24		at Northern Michigan	0	6
O1		Akron	6	20
O8		at Northern Illinois	14	39
O15		Ball State	2	33
O21		Eastern Kentucky	6	27
O29		Hope	6	16
N4		at Central Michigan	7	18
N12		at Valparaiso	26	28

1950 3-6-0
S21	●	at Hope	19	6
S29		at Akron	7	40
O7		Northern Illinois	13	35
O14		Wayne State	6	26
O21	●	at Ball State	13	0
O28		Central Michigan	7	26
N4		at Illinois St.	0	14
N10		at Southern Illinois	13	44
N17	●	Northern Michigan	45	0

1951 4-5-0
S22	●	Hope	20	7
S29	●	Kalamazoo	20	6
O6		at Eastern Illinois	12	19
O13		at Northern Illinois	21	35
O20		Central Michigan	13	19
O27		at Western Illinois	28	63
N3	●	Illinois St.	12	0
N10	●	Southern Illinois	47	7
N17		at Wayne State	13	27

FRED TROSKO
1952-64 (.473) 50-56-4

1952 5-3-1
S19	●	at Hope	13	6
S27	●	Ball State	26	14
O4		Western Illinois	13	20
O11	●	Eastern Illinois	13	7
O18	●	Northern Illinois	19	7
O25		at Central Michigan	7	26
O31		at Wayne State	19	46
N7	=	at Illinois St.	14	14
N14	●	at Southern Illinois	30	6

1953 7-1-1
S19	●	Hope	20	7
S26	●	Hillsdale	28	13
O3	●	Wayne State	13	6
O10	●	at Eastern Illinois	34	6
O17	●	at Northern Illinois	20	14
O24	●	Southern Illinois	37	0
O31		at Western Illinois	0	20
N7	●	Illinois St.	27	6
N14	=	Central Michigan	33	33

1954 8-1-0
S17	●	at Hope	19	0
S25	●	Hillsdale	32	13
O1	●	Wayne State	7	0
O9	●	Eastern Illinois	33	0
O16	●	at Northern Illinois	34	0
O23	●	at Southern Illinois	20	0
O30	●	Western Illinois	33	19
N6	●	at Illinois St.	25	7
N13		at Central Michigan	7	28

1955 7-2-0
S17	●	Hope	27	0
S24		at Hillsdale	6	20
O1	●	at Baldwin-Wallace	20	0
O7	●	at Western Illinois	6	2
O15	●	Illinois St.	25	6
O22	●	Southern Illinois	7	2
O29	●	at Eastern Illinois	14	7
N5		Central Michigan	20	27
N12	●	at Northern Illinois	13	6

1956 4-4-0
S22		at Hillsdale	7	16
S29	●	Baldwin-Wallace	26	0
O6	●	Western Illinois	21	6
O13		at Illinois St.	7	22
O20		at Southern Illinois	7	14
O27	●	Eastern Illinois	65	0
N3		at Central Michigan	0	19
N10	●	at Northern Illinois	25	7

1957 6-3-0
S21		Hope	6	19
S28	●	at Illinois St.	33	14
O5		at Youngstown State	6	13
O12	●	Central Michigan	39	6
O19	●	at Eastern Illinois	39	0
O26	●	Southern Illinois	21	7
N2	●	at Northern Illinois	54	20
N9	●	Western Illinois	26	0
N16		at St. Joseph's	13	48

1958 4-5-0
S19		at Hope	7	19
S27	●	Illinois St.	13	0
O3	●	Youngstown State	21	12
O11		at Central Michigan	6	7
O18	●	Eastern Illinois	31	0
O25		at Southern Illinois	9	13
N1	●	at Northern Illinois	15	7
N8		Western Illinois	6	27
N15		St. Joseph's	0	3

1959 1-7-0
S30		Youngstown State	3	21
O7	●	Illinois St.	13	7
O14		at Northern Michigan	6	39
O17		Central Michigan	8	21
O24		at Eastern Illinois	6	32
O31		Southern Illinois	14	41
N7		at Northern Illinois	0	34
N14		at Western Illinois	0	22

1960 0-8-1
S17		Albion	7	21
S22		at Youngstown State	7	27
O1	=	at Illinois State	14	14
O7		Northern Michigan	0	21
O15		at Central Michigan	0	28
O22		Eastern Illinois	0	8
O29		at Southern Illinois	8	66
N5		Northern Illinois	0	19
N12		Western Illinois	2	26

1961 0-8-1
S16		at Albion	0	13
S23	=	at Ball State	0	0
S30		at Western Illinois	0	43
O6		at Illinois State	0	13
O13		Baldwin-Wallace	14	27
O21		Central Michigan	11	13
O28		at Eastern Illinois	0	7
N4		Southern Illinois	14	20
N11		at Northern Illinois	10	35

1962 2-5-0
S21		Ball State	0	14
S28		Kalamazoo	6	13
O6		at Illinois State	19	20
O13		at Baldwin-Wallace	15	27
O20		at Central Michigan	0	24
O27	●	Eastern Illinois	14	0
N10	●	Alma	30	6

1963 2-6-0

S21		at Ball State	6	22
S28	●	at Kalamazoo	13	12
O4		Ohio Northern	7	20
O11		Baldwin-Wallace	13	27
O19		at Findlay	18	48
O25	●	Adrian	13	0
N2		Central Michigan	20	55
N9		at Albion	6	17

1964 4-3-0

S26	●	Adrian	7	0
O10		at John Carroll	3	7
O17	●	Allegheny	28	7
O24		at Wayne State	0	13
O31	●	Western Reserve	17	7
N7	●	at Case Tech	48	26
N14		at Ashland	7	13

JERRY RAYMOND
1965-66 (.529) 8-7-2

1965 3-4-1

S25		Western Illinois	7	44
O1		Ohio Northern	0	7
O8		John Carroll	6	7
O16	●	at Allegheny	23	8
O23	●	Wayne State	20	0
O30	=	at Western Reserve	14	14
N6	●	Case Tech	41	20
N13		at Baldwin-Wallace	14	29

1966 5-3-1

S17		at Findlay	0	20
S24	=	Western Illinois	0	0
O1		Kentucky State	9	26
O8	●	at Western Reserve	16	3
O15	●	at John Carroll	12	2
O22	●	Ferris State	21	6
O29	●	Wayne State	16	0
N5		at Ohio Northern	9	17
N12	●	Eastern Illinois	17	13

DAN BOISTURE
1967-73 (.684) 45-20-3

1967 6-3-0

S16	●	Findlay	17	0
S23	●	Baldwin-Wallace	15	13
S30	●	at Eastern Illinois	28	12
O7	●	at Western Reserve	47	0
O14	●	John Carroll	34	0
O21	●	at Ferris State	13	6
O28		at Wayne State	3	20
N4		at La. Monroe	10	12
N11		at Northern Iowa	6	14

1968 8-2-0

S14	●	Morningside	46	16
S21	●	S. Connecticut	40	0
S28		at Arkansas State	7	26
O5	●	at Akron	16	7
O12	●	at Ball State	43	7
O19		at Tampa	0	21
O26	●	Kentucky State	7	0
N2	●	Northeastern	41	0
N9	●	Northern Iowa	34	7
N16	●	at Wittenberg	14	7

1969 5-4-0

S20		at Murray State	20	28
S27	●	Akron	10	3
O4		at Indiana State	13	14
O11	●	at Waynesburg	48	0
O18	●	Kentucky State	48	6
O25		Tampa	7	17
N1	●	at Northeastern	56	0
N8	●	Montana State	31	7
N15		at Ball State	22	31

1970 7-2-1

S12	=	at North Dakota State	14	14
S19	●	at Quantico Marines	23	0
S26	●	Waynesburg	30	0
O3	●	Indiana State	25	21
O10		at Western Kentucky	6	45
O17		at Eastern Kentucky	10	21
O24	●	Wisconsin-Milwaukee	35	0
O31	●	at Northern Michigan	14	8
N7	●	La. Monroe	20	0
N14	●	Ball State	60	0

1971 7-1-2

S11	●	Oshkosh State	50	0
S18	●	Quantico Marines	28	20
O2	●	at Idaho State	23	22
O9	●	Western Kentucky	17	14
O16	=	Eastern Kentucky	0	0
O23	●	at Wisconsin-Milwaukee	31	0
O30	●	Northern Michigan	31	3
N6	=	at La. Monroe	10	10
N13	●	South Dakota State	35	2
		PIONEER BOWL		
D11		Louisiana Tech	3	14

1972 6-4-0

S9	●	at Wisconsin-Oshkosh	26	14
S16		Toledo	0	16
S22		at Tampa	0	42
O7		Idaho State	14	21
O14	●	Quantico Marines	21	7
O21	●	at Northern Michigan	24	15
O28	●	New Mexico Highlands	30	6
N4	●	at St. Norbert	42	14
N11		at Louisiana Tech	17	24
N18	●	at Central Michigan	28	3

1973 6-4-0

S8	●	Ball State	17	14
S15	●	Louisiana Tech	21	19
S22	●	at Indiana State	25	14
S29	●	St. Norbert	47	14
O6		at Western Illinois	21	24
O20		at Kent State	20	34
O27	●	Youngstown State	42	2
N3		at Central Michigan	21	31
N10		at Bowling Green	7	31
N22	●	Weber State	44	7

GEORGE MANS
1974-75 (.405) 8-12-1

1974 4-6-1

S7		at Miami, Ohio	0	39
S14	●	Western Michigan	20	19
S21		La. Monroe	14	17
S28		Kent State	0	13
O5		at Arkansas State	7	14
O12	=	at McNeese State	6	6
O19	●	at Northern Michigan	24	0
O26	●	Ball State	17	9
N2		Central Michigan	13	28
N16		at Weber State	14	21
N23	●	at Toledo	28	12

1975 4-6-0

S6		at Ball State	14	24
S13	●	Indiana State	30	7
S20	●	at La. Monroe	27	24
S27	●	McNeese State	20	6
O11		at Central Michigan	7	20
O18		Northern Michigan	7	20
O25		Western Illinois	14	17
N1		at Youngstown State	14	15
N8	●	Illinois State	51	14
N15		at Western Michigan	14	24

1976-PRESENT
MAC

ED CHLEBEK
1976-77 (.455) 10-12

1976 2-9-0 (1-5-0)

S4	|	Ohio U.	7	23
S11	|	at Western Michigan	13	31
S18	|	at Bowling Green	12	53
S26		at McNeese State	10	23
O2		Northern Michigan	6	28
O9	●	Arkansas State	32	30
O23		at Akron	0	36
O30	|	at Kent State	13	38
N6	● |	Central Michigan	30	27
N13		at Illinois State	6	14
N20	|	Ball State	3	52

1977 8-3-0 (4-3-0)

S3	● |	at Northern Illinois	25	2
S10	|	at Central Michigan	3	9
S17	● |	Bowling Green	16	6
S24	●	McNeese State	9	7
O1	● |	Toledo	17	7
O8	● |	Ohio U.	31	14
O22	|	Kent State	13	29
O29	●	at Akron	42	28
N5	●	at North Carolina A&T	21	20
N12	●	Illinois State	41	28
N19	|	at Ball State	21	45

MIKE STOCK
1978-82 (.144) 6-38-1

1978 3-7-0 (1-5-0)

S2		at No. Michigan	3	30
S9	|	at Ohio U.	22	23
S16	|	Bowling Green	6	43
S23	●	Indiana St.	27	8
S30	● |	at Toledo	17	12
O7	●	Akron	25	14
O21	|	at Western Michigan	0	32
O28	|	Ball State	0	21
N11	|	Central Michigan	9	41
N18		at Illinois St.	13	14

1979 2-8-1 (1-6-1)

S1	●	No. Michigan	21	7
S8	|	at Bowling Green	6	32
S15	|	at Ohio U.	7	20
S22		at Illinois St.	15	24
S29	|	Toledo	7	37
O6	= |	Northern Illinois	0	0
O13		Akron	12	24
O20	● |	Kent State	14	10
N3	|	at Ball State	10	28
N10	|	at Central Michigan	14	37
N17	|	Western Michigan	7	17

1980 1-9-0 (1-7-0)

S6	|	at Western Michigan	0	37
S13	● |	at Bowling Green	18	16
S20	|	at Ohio U.	6	34
S27	|	at Toledo	7	49
O11		at Akron	10	21
O18	|	Ball State	0	26
O25	|	at Kent State	12	35
N1	|	Central Michigan	15	51
N8		Illinois St.	7	15
N22	|	at Northern Illinois	6	38

1981 0-11-0 (0-9-0)

S12		Akron	7	14
S19		at Illinois St.	7	28
S26	|	Miami, Ohio	12	18
O3	|	at Central Michigan	14	63
O10	|	Toledo	7	42
O17	|	at Ohio U.	7	29
O24	|	Northern Illinois	7	30
O31	|	at Ball State	13	35
N7	|	at Kent State	7	13
N14	|	Bowling Green	0	28
N21	|	at Western Michigan	7	38

BOB LAPOINTE
1982 (.188) 1-6-1

1982 1-9-1 (1-7-1)

S11		at Akron	7	14
S18		at Louisiana Tech	12	49
S25	|	at Miami, Ohio	0	35
O2	|	Central Michigan	8	13
O9	|	at Toledo	19	20
O16	|	Ohio U.	13	14
O23	|	at Northern Illinois	0	10
O30	|	Ball State	7	16
N6	● |	Kent State	9	7
N13	|	at Bowling Green	7	24
N20	= |	Western Michigan	3	3

JIM HARKEMA
1983-92 (.422) 41-57-5

1983 1-10-0 (0-9-0)

S3	●	Marshall	7	3
S17		Akron	0	13
S24	|	at Ohio U.	14	31
O1	|	Bowling Green	21	26
O8	|	at Central Michigan	3	24
O15	|	Northern Illinois	15	34
O22	|	Toledo	9	37
O29	|	at Ball State	20	33
N5	|	at Kent State	13	37
N12	|	Miami, Ohio	12	24
N19	|	at Western Michigan	10	14

1984 2-7-2 (2-5-2)

S8		at Youngstown St.	7	31
S15		at Marshall	17	24
S22	|	Ohio U.	13	16
S29	|	at Bowling Green	27	35
O6	= |	Central Michigan	16	16
O13	= |	at Northern Illinois	10	10
O20	|	at Toledo	7	17
O27	|	Ball State	10	17
N3	● |	Kent State	20	18
N10	|	at Miami, Ohio	0	23
N17	● |	Western Michigan	24	14

1985 4-7-0 (3-6-0)

S7	●	Youngstown St.	27	22
S21		at Akron	12	16
S28	|	at Kent State	3	28
O5	● |	Toledo	21	10
O12	|	Bowling Green	24	42
O19	● |	at Ohio U.	27	21
O26	|	at Central Michigan	10	17
N2	● |	at Ball State	27	24
N9	|	Northern Illinois	0	3
N16	|	Miami, Ohio	16	31
N23	|	at Western Michigan	21	38

1986 6-5-0 (4-4-0)

S6	● |	Western Michigan	21	14
S13	●	at Youngstown St.	18	17
S20	●	Akron	24	21
S27	|	Kent State	16	20
O4	|	at Toledo	18	23
O11	|	at Bowling Green	10	24
O18	● |	Ohio U.	33	31
O25	● |	Central Michigan	34	16
N1	● |	Ball State	14	7
N8		at Northern Illinois	14	21
N15	|	at Miami, Ohio	20	34

1987 10-2-0 (7-1-0)

S5	●	Youngstown St.	35	20
S12	● |	at Miami, Ohio	33	17
S19		at Akron	16	17
S26	● |	at Kent State	23	21
O3	●	Northern Illinois	32	21
O10	|	at Central Michigan	6	16
O17	● |	Ball State	35	28
O24	● |	at Western Michigan	23	17
O31	● |	Ohio U.	34	16
N5	● |	at Toledo	38	9
N14	● |	Bowling Green	38	18
		CALIFORNIA BOWL		
D12	●	San Jose State	30	27

1988 6-3-1 (5-2-1)

S3	● |	Miami, Ohio	24	17
S10	●	at Youngstown St.	17	12
S17	● |	Kent State	21	14
S24		at Arizona	0	55
O8	|	Central Michigan	6	20
O15	● |	at Ball State	16	12
O22	|	Western Michigan	24	31
O29	= |	at Ohio U.	17	17
N5	● |	Toledo	20	19
N12	● |	at Bowling Green	28	3

1989 7-3-1 (6-2-0)

S2	● |	Kent State	30	7
S9	●	Youngstown St.	14	3
S16	● |	at Ohio U.	30	25
S23	=	at Colorado State	35	35
S30	● |	at Western Michigan	21	20
O7	● |	Toledo	31	14
O14		Liberty	24	25
O21	● |	Bowling Green	21	13
O28	|	at Central Michigan	9	24
N4	● |	Miami, Ohio	20	7
N11	|	at Ball State	17	23

1990 2-9-0 (2-6-0)

S1		at Fresno State	10	41
S8	● |	Western Michigan	27	24
S15	● |	Ohio U.	21	18
S22		at Youngstown St.	14	24
S29		at Indiana	6	37
O6	|	at Toledo	23	37
O20	|	at Bowling Green	15	25
O27	|	Central Michigan	12	16
N3	|	at Miami, Ohio	14	34
N10	|	Ball State	13	20
N17	|	at Kent State	24	25

1991 3-7-1 (3-4-1)

A31	|	at Bowling Green	6	17
S7		at Purdue	3	49
S14	|	at Miami, Ohio	3	29
S21		Louisiana Tech	14	17
S28		at Wisconsin	6	21
O5	● |	at Kent State	21	20
O12	|	Ball State	8	10
O19	● |	Western Michigan	42	24
N2	= |	Central Michigan	14	14
N9	● |	at Ohio U.	13	10
N16	|	Toledo	14	21

JAN QUARLESS
1992 (.143)   1-6

1992
1-10-0 (1-7-0)

S5		Akron	9	27
S12		at Louisiana Tech	17	31
S19		at Penn State	7	52
S26		Kent State	14	17
O3		Miami, Ohio	7	24
O10		at Ball State	7	31
O17		at Western Michigan	19	20
O24	●	Ohio U.	7	6
O31		at Army	17	57
N7		at Central Michigan	13	30
N14		at Toledo	0	41

RON COOPER
1993-94 (.409)   9-13

1993
4-7-0 (3-5-0)

S4		at West Virginia	6	48
S9		Temple	28	31
S18	●	Western Illinois	16	14
O2	●	at Miami, Ohio	15	7
O9	●	Kent State	20	15
O16	●	at Central Michigan	28	21
O23		Western Michigan	20	21
O30		Ball State	13	18
N6		at Akron	7	19
N13		Ohio U.	10	12
N19		at Toledo	0	14

1994
5-6-0 (5-4-0)

S3		at Nevada-Las Vegas	3	17
S10		at Wisconsin	0	56
S17		Central Michigan	29	30
S24		Bowling Green	13	30
O1		Miami, Ohio	17	21
O8	●	at Kent State	24	10
O22		at Western Michigan	14	33
O29	●	at Ball State	41	20
N5	●	Akron	42	18
N12	●	at Ohio U.	24	13
N19	●	Toledo	40	37

RICK RASNICK
1995-99 (.370)   20-34

1995
6-5-0 (5-3-0)

S2	●	at Akron	49	29
S9		at Pittsburgh	30	66
S16	●	Nevada-Las Vegas	51	6
S23	●	Ohio U.	31	20
O7	●	Central Michigan	34	24
O14		at Syracuse	24	52
O21	●	at Ball State	40	35
O28		at Toledo	28	34
N4		at Miami, Ohio	23	39
N11		Western Michigan	13	23
N18	●	at Kent State	40	7

1996
3-8 (3-5)

A31		Temple	24	28
S7		at Wisconsin	3	24
S14	●	at Western Michigan	19	12
S21		Toledo	7	24
S28		at Michigan State	0	47
O5		at Ohio U.	0	7
O12		Miami, Ohio	25	35
O19		at Central Michigan	36	41
O26	●	Kent State	51	10
N2		Ball State	25	39
N9	●	Akron	20	17

1997
4-7 (4-5)

S6		at Missouri	24	44
S13		at Toledo	35	38
S20		Kent State	38	41
S27	●	at Central Michigan	31	24
O4		Ohio U.	7	47
O11	●	Ball State	38	32
O18	●	Akron	45	0
O25		at Marshall	25	48
N1		Western Michigan	38	41
N8	●	at Northern Illinois	38	10
N15		at Central Florida	10	27

1998
3-8 (3-6)

S3		No. Iowa	10	13
S12	●	at Ball State	13	7
S19		at Michigan	20	59
S26		Marshall	23	26
O3	●	at Kent State	26	17
O10		Central Michigan	23	36
O17		at Western Michigan	35	45
O24		Northern Illinois	14	26
N7		at Ohio U.	21	49
N14		at Akron	21	24
N21	●	Toledo	10	7

TONY LOMBARDI
1999 (.000)   0-1

1999
4-7 (4-4)

S11		at Michigan State	7	51
S18		at Miami, Ohio	14	35
S25	●	Akron	38	17
O2		at Louisville	10	45
O9		Western Michigan	37	40
O16	●	Ohio U.	27	26
O23	●	at Toledo	20	13
O30		at Central Florida	6	31
N6		Ball State	31	21
N13		at Central Michigan	26	29
N20		at Northern Illinois	23	30

JEFF WOODRUFF
2000-03 (.209)   9-34

2000
3-8 (2-5)

S2	●	Connecticut	32	25
S9		Miami, Ohio	17	34
S16		at South Carolina	6	41
S23		at Temple	40	49
S30		Central Florida	10	31
O7		Toledo	14	42
O14		at Ball State	14	33
O21		at Bowling Green	6	20
N4		Central Michigan	31	15
N11	●	Northern Illinois	39	32
N18		at Western Michigan	0	28

2001
2-9 (1-6)

S1	●	S.E. Missouri St.	16	12
S8		at Maryland	3	50
S22		Indiana St.	14	21
S29		Western Michigan	10	31
O6		at Connecticut	0	19
O13		Ball State	14	35
O27	●	Buffalo	24	20
N3		at Northern Illinois	17	40
N10		at Central Michigan	30	35
N17		at Toledo	7	28
N24		at Akron	62	65

2002
3-9 (1-7)

A31		at Michigan State	7	56
S7		Toledo	13	65
S14	●	S.E. Missouri St.	35	32
S21		at Maryland	3	45
S28	●	So. Illinois	48	45
O5	●	Akron	42	34
O12		at Ohio U.	27	55
O19		at Ball State	17	42
N2		Central Michigan	21	47
N9		at Western Michigan	31	33
N16		Northern Illinois	21	49
N23		at Bowling Green	21	63

AL LAVAN
2003 (.667)   2-1

2003
3-9 (2-6)

A28	●	E. Tenn. St.	28	21
S4		Western Illinois	12	34
S13		at Akron	17	24
S20		at Navy	7	39
S27		Maryland	13	37
O4		Western Michigan	3	31
O11		at Toledo	14	49
O18		Bowling Green	20	33
N1		at Central Michigan	10	38
N8	●	Central Florida	19	13
N15	●	Ball State	38	14
N22		at Northern Illinois	24	38

JEFF GENYK
2004-Present (.364)   4-7

2004
4-7 (4-4)

S2	●	Buffalo	37	34
S11		at Florida	10	49
S18		Toledo	32	42
S25		Eastern Illinois	28	31
O2		Idaho	41	45
O9	●	at Ball State	31	24
O16	●	at Western Michigan	35	31
O30		at Bowling Green	20	41
N6	●	Central Michigan DET	61	58
N13		at Kent State	17	69
N20		Northern Illinois	16	34

ƒ Forfeit † Game Later Forfieted # Disputed Victor * Disputed Score ‖ Designated Conference Game |2 Counted Twice in Conference Standings

FLORIDA

BY GEOFFREY NORMAN

THE STORY OF FOOTBALL AT FLORIDA is one of almost Sisyphean frustration. For 80-plus years, the Gators were the Great Big Team That Couldn't—couldn't win the big game, couldn't win the conference championship, couldn't put up an undefeated season, couldn't win a national title.

Until the 1990s, Florida routinely raised the hopes of its faithful fans only to dash them, often in some cruel or unusual way. In 1928, 1966, 1969 and 1985, the Gators went deep into the season with a shot at the national championship, but came up short.

Oh, sure, Florida always won a lot of games—enough to convince Gators fans that it was possible to win more. Citizens of GatorsWorld came to accept as an article of faith what Bear Bryant supposedly said about their football program, that all Florida needed was the right head man. When the Gators found him, The Bear warned, then everybody else had better watch out.

And lo, in 1990 the right head man finally arrived in Gainesville, where he had won the 1966 Heisman Trophy. Very soon, Steve Spurrier started proving Bryant right.

TRADITION Between the third and fourth quarters of every game, Gators fans stand and sway and sing "We Are the Boys of Old Florida." The "Gator Chomp"—made by extending both arms at about a 45° angle from each other and then bringing them sharply together—is another Florida trademark.

BEST PLAYER A case can be made that at Florida, the best player and the best coach are one and the same. But according to Spurrier, the best Gators player ever is Danny Wuerffel, the 1996 Heisman Trophy winner and quarterback of Florida's only national championship team that same season. Many among the Florida faithful would dispute this and go with the Gators' other Heisman-winning quarterback—Spurrier.

Spurrier was probably the better athlete, while Wuerffel put up the more impressive numbers, completing 708 of 1,170 passes for 10,875 yards in his career. His 1995 single-season rating of 178.4 was tops in major-college history. These are hard numbers to dispute, unless you want to argue that Wuerffel rang them up while playing for the most creative offensive football mind of the time. But this brings us back to Spurrier, who says the greatest is Wuerffel, no question.

A final point in Wuerffel's favor is that he bore up and prospered under Spurrier, who could be remorselessly demanding of his quarterbacks. There were some who

PROFILE

University of Florida
Gainesville, Fla.
Founded: 1853
Enrollment: 33,982
Colors: Blue and Orange
Nickname: Gators
Stadium: Ben Hill Griffin Stadium
at Florida Field
Opened in 1930
Grass; 88,548 capacity
First football game: 1906
All-time record: 597–364–40 (.616)
Bowl record: 14–18
Southeastern Conference championships:
6 (outright)
Consensus national championships, 1936-present: 1 (1996)
Heisman Trophy: Steve Spurrier, 1966; Danny Wuerffel, 1996
First-round NFL draftees: 35
Website: www.gatorzone.com/football/

THE BEST OF TIMES

The zenith of the Steve Spurrier era came in the mid-to-late 1990s. From the 1992 Gator Bowl to the middle of the 1997 season, Florida posted a 51–6–1 record and won the national championship in 1996.

THE WORST OF TIMES

From 1935 to 1951, the Gators posted only one season with a winning record.

CONFERENCE

After 11 years in the Southern Conference, Florida became a charter member of the SEC in 1933.

DISTINGUISHED ALUMNI

John Atanasoff, inventor of digital electronic computer; Faye Dunaway, actress; Buddy Ebsen, actor; Bob Graham, U.S. senator; Carl Hiaasen, author; Dara Torres, Olympic swimmer; Bob Vila, host of *This Old House*

FIGHT SONG

THE ORANGE & BLUE
On, brave old Florida, just keep on marching on your way!
On, brave old Florida, and we will cheer you on your play!
Rah! Rah! Rah!
And as you march along, we'll sing our victory song anew
With all your might go on and fight Gators
Fight for Dixie's rightly proud of you
So give a cheer for the Orange and Blue,
Waving forever, forever
Pride of old Florida, may she droop never
We'll sing a song for the flag today, cheer for the team at play!
On to the goal we'll fight our way for Florida.

"A swamp is hot and sticky and can be dangerous." Steve Spurrier should know.

could not take the \overbearing perfectionism. Wuerffel, however, was indomitable. Where others withered, he thrived.

BEST COACH When Spurrier arrived in Gainesville in 1990, the Gators were in the football doghouse, ineligible for television, bowl games and the conference championship. Florida had seen two head coaches—Charley Pell and Galen Hall—leave in disgrace. So the hiring of Spurrier was something like the return of the prodigal son, since his years as a player were among the happiest of many Gators fans' memories. By the eighth game of his 10th season as head coach, he had won 100 games at Florida (faster than any other major-college coach had accomplished the feat). In all, his teams won at least nine games in every one of his 12 seasons.

Spurrier's wide-open, creative offensive schemes, which he called the Fun 'n Gun, changed the culture not only at Florida but throughout the SEC. Florida fans loved him for the same qualities that rivals found infuriating: brashness, confidence and arrogance. He was, in a word, cocky. He was routinely accused of running up the score, a complaint he never denied with very much conviction. Other schools and coaches lusted to beat Spurrier and Florida. After the 2002

Orange Bowl, Spurrier resigned and left for an unhappy two-year stint in the NFL with the Washington Redskins. Things weren't much happier in Gainesville for Spurrier's successor, Ron Zook, who was fired during the 2004 season. But Florida was still an elite program, and proof of that came late in 2004. Urban Meyer, who'd brought BCS-crashing Utah into the top 10 in just two years, passed on an offer from Notre Dame to take the Florida job.

BEST TEAM The 1996 Gators, Florida's only national championship team, announced they were something special in the third game of the season, against Tennessee in Knoxville. The game was billed as a shootout between two top college quarterbacks—Wuerffel and Peyton Manning—and there was plenty of offense, with Florida winning 35-29. The Gators went to the top of the rankings and stayed there until the last weekend of November, when they went to Tallahassee to play No. 2 Florida State. The high stakes made the cross-state rivalry—one of football's fiercest—even more intense. Florida lost 24-21, and after the game Spurrier complained that FSU had gotten away with a number of late hits on Wuerffel. He put together a video to back up the charge and continued to make his case, adding to the already

---

RECORDS

RUSHING YARDS

	GAME
316	Emmitt Smith vs. New Mexico, Oct. 21, 1989 (31 att.)
	SEASON
1,599	Emmitt Smith, 1989 (284 att.)
	CAREER
4,163	Errict Rhett, 1989-93 (873 att.)

PASSING YARDS

	GAME
464	Rex Grossman vs. LSU, Oct. 6, 2001 (22 of 34)
	SEASON
3,896	Rex Grossman, 2001 (259 of 395)
	CAREER
10,875	Danny Wuerffel, 1993-96 (708 of 1,170)

RECEIVING YARDS

	GAME
246	Taylor Jacobs vs. UAB, Aug. 31, 2002 (8 rec.)
	SEASON
1,357	Travis McGriff, 1998 (70 rec.)
	CAREER
2,563	Carlos Alvarez, 1969-71 (172 rec.)

POINTS

	GAME
24	Seven tied; most recently by DeShawn Wynn vs. Florida A&M, Sept. 13, 2003 (4 TDs)
	SEASON
110	Reidel Anthony, 1996 (18 TDs, 1 two-pt. conv.); Tommy Durrance, 1969 (18 TDs, 1 two-pt. conv.)
	CAREER
368	Jeff Chandler, 1997-2001 (67 FGs, 167 PAT)

CONSENSUS ALL-AMERICANS

1966	Steve Spurrier, B
1969	Carlos Alvarez, E
1975	Sammy Green, LB
1980	David Little, LB
1982-83	Wilber Marshall, DL/LB
1984	Lomas Brown, OT
1988	Louis Oliver, DB
1989	Emmitt Smith, RB
1991	Brad Culpepper, DL
1994	Jack Jackson, WR
1994	Kevin Carter, DL
1995	Jason Odom, OL
1996	Danny Wuerffel, QB
1996	Ike Hilliard, WR
1996	Reidel Anthony, WR
1997	Jacquez Green, WR
1997	Fred Weary, DB
2001	Jabar Gaffney, WR
2001	Mike Pearson, OL
2001	Rex Grossman, QB
2001	Alex Brown, DL
2003	Keiwan Ratliff, DB

bitter feelings between the two schools. That made it all the sweeter when—after beating Alabama 45-30 in the SEC championship game—Florida avenged its loss by routing Florida State 52-20 in the Sugar Bowl.

BIGGEST GAME Consider what the Gators faced in the 1997 Sugar Bowl with the national title on the line. Florida needed to beat its fiercest rival, a team that was not only ranked No. 1 but that had also defeated the Gators a month earlier. Their previous bowl game had been a monumental disaster, with the national title also on the line. Nebraska's 62-24 blowout of Florida in the 1996 Fiesta Bowl was interpreted as evidence that while Florida was fast and flashy, when it came to football fundamentals, the Gators were also soft.

A year later, in New Orleans, they had a chance to correct that reputation, avenge the loss in Tallahassee and, finally, win it all. Wuerffel had a good night, and so did all the Gators. Florida whipped the No. 1 team in the nation 52-20, slaying a history of demons.

BIGGEST UPSET In 1963, Florida had opened with a loss to Georgia Tech and a tie against Mississippi State before barely beating Richmond in Gainesville, 35-28. The next week, the unranked Gators traveled to Tuscaloosa to play No. 3 Alabama. These were the early years of the age of Bryant, and Bama wasn't losing much anywhere and never at home. So what did the struggling Gators do? They went out and held Joe Namath's team to a mere six points, scored late in the fourth quarter and won 10-6. Florida, in fact, dominated the Tide. The triumph was exceedingly special to Florida fans, with some 10,000 greeting the Gators at the airport when they arrived home. The magnitude of the accomplishment grew over the years and decades. It was not until 1982 that another Bryant-coached Alabama team lost in Tuscaloosa.

HEARTBREAKER An agonizing 31-31 "loss" to FSU at Doak Campbell Stadium in Tallahassee in 1994 tops the

ALL-CENTURY TEAM		
Chosen by The Gainesville Sun *in 1999.*		
OFFENSE		
1972-74	Burton Lawless,	G
1993-96	Donnie Young,	G
1981-84	Lomas Brown,	T
1985-88	David Williams,	T
1993-96	Jeff Mitchell,	C
1966-68	Jim Yarbrough,	TE
1969-71	Carlos Alvarez,	WR
1974-77	Wes Chandler,	WR
1993-96	Danny Wuerffel,	QB
1982-85	Neal Anderson,	RB
1987-89	Emmitt Smith,	RB
1992-94	Judd Davis,	PK
1995-97	Jacquez Green,	KR
DEFENSE		
1968-70	Jack Youngblood,	DE
1991-94	Kevin Carter,	DE
1988-91	Brad Culpepper,	DT
1991-94	Ellis Johnson,	DT
1976-79	Scot Brantley,	LB
1977-80	David Little,	LB
1980-83	Wilber Marshall,	LB
1967-69	Steve Tannen,	CB
1984-87	Jarvis Williams,	CB
1963-65	Bruce Bennett,	S
1985-88	Louis Oliver,	S
1958-59	Bobby Joe Green,	P

list. Bitter doesn't even begin to describe what gleeful Florida State fans still call the Choke at the Doak. It's bad enough to finish tied with anyone when you've been up 28-3 late in the third quarter. But against Florida State? Wormwood and gall would taste sweeter. The game seemed to cast a spell over Spurrier and the Gators. They lost a Sugar Bowl rematch with the Seminoles, who went on to dominate the Gators for the rest of Spurrier's tenure. He never won in Tallahassee.

BEST COMEBACK In 1986, Auburn came to Gainesville ranked fifth in the nation and smelling blood. Kerwin Bell, the Gators' quarterback, hadn't played in a month, and when he limped onto the field in the third quarter, Florida was down 17-0. Throwing to Ricky Nattiel, who was playing with a separated shoulder, Bell brought Florida to within a point, 17-16, with 30 seconds left and the PAT still to come. Florida went for two, and when Bell dropped back to pass, Auburn covered everyone except the gimpy quarterback. Bell limped in for the win.

STADIUM The official—and rather prosaic—name of the University of Florida's facility is Ben Hill Griffin Stadium at Florida Field. But it is better and more aptly known as The Swamp. It was so named by Spurrier, who explained, "The swamp is where gators live. We feel comfortable there, but we hope our opponents feel tentative. A swamp is hot and sticky and can be dangerous." Not to mention loud. Florida home games routinely draw more than 85,000 fans, and there is something about the low-lying terrain and the bowl-like structure that captures their cheers and amplifies them in such a way that you can actually feel the sound.

RIVAL As with many programs, there is the traditional rivalry and there is the modern one. No question, Georgia is the traditional rival. The game is played in Jacksonville, on neutral turf. (Exceptions being the 1994

and 1995 seasons, when, due to stadium construction, the games were in Athens and Gainesville.) There is an epic, carnival quality to the event, which spans the week leading up to the game and is universally known as the World's Largest Outdoor Cocktail Party. Spirits flow fiercely, in drinks and in fanaticism, with some serious bragging rights at stake.

The modern rivalry is with Florida State. The upstart from Tallahassee was a girls' school until after World War II, when the veterans came home with G.I. Bill money to spend. It was years before the Gators agreed—grudgingly—to play FSU, and more years before parity was achieved on the field. In the 1990s, both schools had achieved status as national championship contenders, and the game was played for high stakes and with almost dangerously fierce emotion. There were ugly pregame incidents between players, and fan behavior had become such a concern that the respective head coaches made public service announcements urging them to "check your hate at the gate." Lots of luck.

DISPUTE The 1966 FSU game in Tallahassee will be forever remembered for the Lane Fenner catch that was ruled incomplete by an SEC official. A famous photograph makes a pretty convincing case that Fenner was inbounds. The official claimed he did not have control and waved off the apparent touchdown. The Gators held on to their 22-19 lead, and FSU fans never got over it. One Gators loyalist, who later became a U.S. senator and governor of the state, is supposed to have told one opposing fan, "You're damn right we stole it, and that just makes it sweeter."

NICKNAME According to the legend, the first Gator appeared on a little pennant in 1908, when there were probably more alligators than people in Florida. Others ascribe the name's origins to the nickname given Neal "Bo Gator" Storter, who began his career as a backup center and wound up the varsity team captain in 1911. *Florida Times-Union* columnist Laurence "Kiddo" Woltz first referred to the school as "Gators" in print in the fall of 1911.

MASCOT A 12-foot alligator named Albert served as the official mascot throughout the 1960s before dying in 1970. Not long after, the school switched to a student in a cartoonish Albert Gator costume with an orange letter sweater who roams the sidelines leading cheers. Albert was soon joined by Alberta Gator, and the couple became such a hit that in 2003, a $75,000 bronze statue of the two mascots was unveiled just across the street from Ben Hill Griffin Stadium.

UNIFORM After years with a distinctively interlocked "U" and "F" on their orange helmets, Florida switched to a script "Gators" in 1979, and that look remains today. The Gators wear blue jerseys and (usually) white pants at home, white jerseys and (usually) orange or blue pants on the road.

LORE In 1923, coached by a man named James Van Fleet, Florida traveled to Tuscaloosa to play Wallace Wade's Alabama powerhouse. A storm had turned the field into a lake. At halftime, down 6-0, Van Fleet had his starters change uniforms with the reserves and kept his players in the locker room until the last possible moment before returning for the kickoff. This little piece of psychological warfare worked and the Gators came back to score 16 unanswered points for the win. Van Fleet was then a temporary coach, moonlighting from his job as commander of the Florida ROTC unit. He was a major in the Army and later became a hero as a general in the Korean War.

In 1965, Florida kidney specialist Dr. Robert Cade invented an electrolyte beverage for the football team at the request of an assistant coach. It was called Gatorade. The university still receives 20 percent of the drink's profits, to the tune of $80 million to date.

QUOTE "Running it out to keep the shutout? No, I didn't think about that. We felt having 35 points at the half, we only needed 17 more to break 50."—Steve Spurrier, on whether he had considered running the ball instead of passing for the end zone with less than two minutes left in Florida's 52-0 rout of Mississippi State in 2001

THE SCHOOLS

FLORIDA ANNUAL STATISTICAL LEADERS

YR	RUSHING	YDS	ATT	AVG	PASSING	ATT	CMP	PCT	YDS	RECEIVING	REC	YDS	AVG
1955	Jackie Simpson	422	65	6.5	Richard Allen	56	17	.30	273	Jim Roundtree	8	110	13.8
1956	Ed Sears	370	84	4.4	Jimmy Dunn	34	15	.44	268	Jim Roundtree	9	176	19.6
1957		NA	NA	NA		NA	NA	NA	NA	Jim Roundtree	8	171	21.4
1958	Bob Milby	288	53	5.4	Mickey Ellenburg	36	15	.42	238	Don Hudson	8	118	14.8
1959	John MacBeth	257	59	4.4	Richard Allen	80	31	.39	613	Perry McGriff	14	360	25.7
1960	Don Goodman	454	95	4.8	Bobby Dodd	55	30	.55	448	Bob Hoover	10	108	10.8
1961	Don Goodman	413	111	3.7	Tom Batten	67	30	.45	460	Russ Brown	13	239	18.4
1962	Larry Dupree	604	113	5.3	Tom Shannon	100	56	.56	551	Russ Brown	15	227	15.1
1963	Larry Dupree	745	189	3.9	Tom Shannon	158	84	.53	956	Russ Brown	12	113	9.4
1964	Larry Dupree	376	101	3.7	Steve Spurrier	114	65	.57	943	Charles Casey	47	673	14.3
1965	Alan Poe	366	83	4.4	Steve Spurrier	287	148	.52	1,893	Charles Casey	58	809	13.9
1966	Larry Smith	742	162	4.6	Steve Spurrier	291	179	.62	2,012	Richard Trapp	63	872	13.8
1967	Larry Smith	754	205	3.7	Larry Rentz	140	80	.57	1,031	Richard Trapp	58	708	12.2
1968	Larry Smith	690	152	4.5	Jackie Eckdahl	125	56	.45	572	Guy McTheny	34	347	10.2
1969	Tommy Durrance	731	189	3.9	John Reaves	396	222	.56	2,896	Carlos Alvarez	88	1,329	15.1
1970	Tommy Durrance	584	167	3.5	John Reaves	376	188	.50	2,549	Carlos Alvarez	44	717	16.3
1971	Mike Rich	481	106	4.5	John Reaves	356	193	.54	2,104	Carlos Alvarez	40	517	12.9
1972	Nat Moore	845	145	5.8	David Bowden	229	198	.86	1,480	Nat Moore	25	351	14.0
1973	Vince Kendrick	516	127	4.1	David Bowden	113	62	.55	711	Lee McGriff	38	703	18.5
1974	Tony Green	856	133	6.4	Don Gaffney	87	37	.43	621	Lee McGriff	36	698	19.4
1975	Jimmy DuBose	1,307	191	6.8	Don Gaffney	90	42	.47	755	Wes Chandler	20	457	22.9
1976	Willie Wilder	654	101	6.5	Jimmy Fisher	146	83	.57	1,511	Wes Chandler	44	967	22.0
1977	Tony Green	696	119	5.8	Terry LeCount	134	62	.46	848	Wes Chandler	25	490	19.6
1978	Calvin Davis	497	126	3.9	John Brantley	170	85	.50	1,334	Cris Collinsworth	39	745	19.1
1979	Johnell Brown	306	104	2.9	Larry Ochab	185	98	.53	1,169	Cris Collinsworth	41	593	14.5
1980	James Jones	657	150	4.4	Wayne Peace	180	91	.51	1,271	Cris Collinsworth	40	599	15.0
1981	James Jones	617	166	3.7	Wayne Peace	273	159	.58	1,803	Spencer Jackson	39	449	11.5
1982	James Jones	752	150	5.0	Wayne Peace	246	174	.71	2,053	Dwayne Dixon	45	589	13.1
1983	Neal Anderson	835	162	5.2	Wayne Peace	292	186	.64	2,079	Dwayne Dixon	47	596	12.7
1984	Neal Anderson	916	157	5.8	Kerwin Bell	184	98	.53	1,614	John L. Williams	21	276	13.1
1985	Neal Anderson	1,034	238	4.3	Kerwin Bell	288	180	.63	2,687	John L. Williams	44	369	8.4
1986	Octavius Gould	562	156	3.6	Kerwin Bell	242	131	.54	1,515	Ricky Nattiel	44	679	15.4
1987	Emmitt Smith	1,341	229	5.9	Kerwin Bell	239	140	.59	1,769	Stacey Simmons	25	392	15.7
1988	Emmitt Smith	988	187	5.3	Kyle Morris	167	84	.50	1,217	Tony Lomack	22	276	12.5
1989	Emmitt Smith	1,599	284	5.6	Kyle Morris	131	65	.50	1,098	Emmitt Smith	21	207	9.9
1990	Errict Rhett	845	148	5.7	Shane Matthews	378	229	.61	2,952	Kirk Kirkpatrick	55	770	14.0
1991	Errict Rhett	1,109	224	5.0	Shane Matthews	361	218	.60	3,130	Willie Jackson	51	725	14.2
1992	Errict Rhett	903	250	3.6	Shane Matthews	463	275	.59	3,205	Willie Jackson	62	772	12.5
1993	Errict Rhett	1,289	247	5.2	Danny Wuerffel	273	159	.58	2,230	Jack Jackson	51	949	18.6
1994	Fred Taylor	873	171	5.1	Danny Wuerffel	212	132	.62	1,754	Jack Jackson	57	855	15.0
1995	Elijah Williams	858	114	7.5	Danny Wuerffel	325	210	.65	3,266	Chris Doering	70	1,045	14.9
1996	Elijah Williams	671	106	6.3	Danny Wuerffel	360	207	.58	3,625	Reidel Anthony	72	1,293	18.0
1997	Fred Taylor	1,292	214	6.0	Doug Johnson	269	148	.55	2,023	Jacquez Green	61	1,024	16.8
1998	Terry Jackson	587	105	5.6	Doug Johnson	274	154	.56	2,346	Travis McGriff	70	1,357	19.4
1999	Earnest Graham	654	117	5.6	Doug Johnson	337	190	.56	2,574	Darrell Jackson	67	1,156	17.3
2000	Robert Gillespie	678	125	5.4	Rex Grossman	223	116	.52	1,866	Jabar Gaffney	71	1,184	16.7
2001	Earnest Graham	650	125	5.2	Rex Grossman	395	259	.66	3,896	Jabar Gaffney	67	1,191	17.8
2002	Earnest Graham	1,085	240	4.5	Rex Grossman	503	287	.57	3,402	Taylor Jacobs	71	1,088	15.3
2003	Ron Carthon	595	119	5.0	Chris Leak	320	190	.59	2,435	Ben Troupe	39	638	16.4
2004	Ciatrick Fason	1,267	222	5.7	Chris Leak	399	238	.60	3,197	O.J. Small	63	719	11.4

Receiving leaders by receptions
The NCAA began including postseason stats in 2002

FLORIDA ALL-TIME SCORES

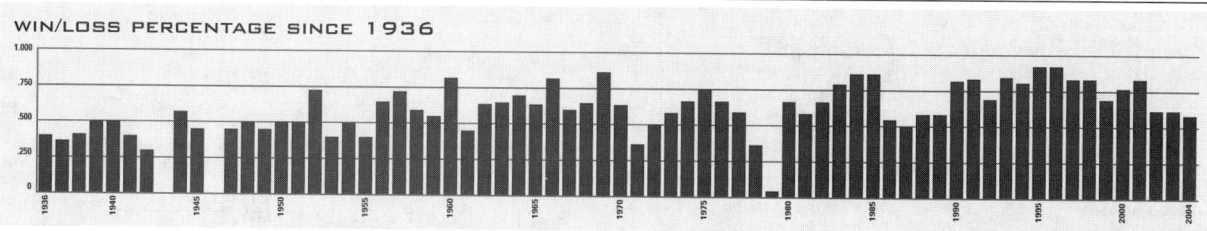

WIN/LOSS PERCENTAGE SINCE 1936

JACK FORSYTHE
1906-08 (.682)   14-6-2

1906   5-3-0

U	●	Gainesville ᵁᴺᴷ	16	6
U	●	Mercer ᵁᴺᴷ	3	27
U	●	Rollins ᵁᴺᴷ	6	0
U	●	Jacksonville AC ᵁᴺᴷ	19	0
U	●	Savannah AC ᵁᴺᴷ	2	27
U	●	Athens AC ᵁᴺᴷ	10	0
U	●	Rollins ᵁᴺᴷ	0	6
U	●	Jacksonville AC ᵁᴺᴷ	39	0

1907   4-1-1

U	●	Columbia AC ᵁᴺᴷ	6	0
U	●	Mercer ᵁᴺᴷ	0	6
U	●	Jacksonville AC ᵁᴺᴷ	21	0
U	●	Rollins ᵁᴺᴷ	9	4
U	●	Jacksonville AC ᵁᴺᴷ	17	0
U	=	Rollins ᵁᴺᴷ	0	0

1908   5-2-1

U		at Mercer	0	24
U	●	at Jacksonville AC	4	0
U	●	Gainesville	37	5
U		at Rollins	0	6
U	●	at Portland	6	0
U		Stetson	6	5
U	●	Jacksonville AC	37	0
U	=	at Stetson	0	0

G.E. PYLE
1909-13 (.764)   26-7-3

1909   6-1-1

U	●	Gainesville	5	0
U	●	Rollins	14	0
U		at Stetson	0	26
U	●	Rollins ᴼᴿᴸ	28	3
U	●	Olympics ᴶᵃᶜꟳ	11	0
U	=	Stetson	5	5
U	●	Olympics	28	0
U	●	Tallahassee	26	0

1910   6-1-0

U	●	G'ville Guards	23	0
O22		at Mercer	0	13
U	●	Georgia Coll.	52	0
N5	●	Citadel ᴶᵃᶜꟳ	6	2
U	●	at Rollins	38	0
U	●	Coll. Charleston	34	0
U	●	Portland	33	0

1911   5-0-1

O7	●	Citadel	15	3
O21	=	at South Carolina	6	6
O25	●	at Clemson	9	5
N3	●	Portland	9	0
N11	●	at Stetson	27	0
N30	●	Coll. Charleston ᴶᵃᶜꟳ	21	0

1912   5-2-1

O12		at Auburn	13	27
O19	●	South Carolina	10	6
O26		Georgia Tech ᴶᵃᶜꟳ	7	14
N4	●	Coll. of Charleston	78	0
N15	●	Stetson	23	7
N28	=	Mercer ᴶᵃᶜꟳ	0	0
D21	●	at Tampa AC	44	0
S25	●	at Vedado Club	28	0

1913   4-3-0

O6	●	Florida Southern	144	0
O11		at Auburn	0	55
O18	●	Maryville	39	0
O25		Georgia Tech ᴶᵃᶜꟳ	3	13
N8		at South Carolina	0	13
N15	●	Citadel	18	13
N27	●	Mercer	24	0

CHARLES McCOY
1914-16 (.474)   9-10

1914   5-2-0

O10		Auburn ᴶᵃᶜꟳ	0	20
O17	●	King	36	0
O24		Sewanee ᴶᵃᶜꟳ	0	26
O31	●	Florida Southern ᵀᴬᴹ	59	0
N7	●	Wofford	36	0
N14	●	at Citadel	7	0
N26	●	Mercer	14	0

1915   4-3-0

O9		at Auburn	0	7
O16	●	Sewanee ᴶᵃᶜꟳ	0	7
O30	●	Florida Southern	45	0
N6		Georgia ᴶᵃᶜꟳ	0	37
N13	●	Citadel	6	0
N18	●	Tulane	14	7
N25	●	at Mercer	34	7

1916   0-5-0

O14		at Georgia	0	21
O21		Alabama ᴶᵃᶜꟳ	0	16
O28		Tennessee ᵀᴬᴹ	0	24
N11		Auburn ᴶᵃᶜꟳ	0	20
N18		at Indiana	3	14

A.L. BUSSER
1917-19 (.467)   7-8

1917   2-4-0

O13	●	South Carolina	21	13
O20		Tulane	0	52
O27	●	Florida Southern	19	7
N3		at Auburn	0	68
N17		Clemson ᴶᵃᶜꟳ	7	55
N29		at Kentucky	0	52

1918   0-1-0

U		Camp Johnson	2	14

1919   5-3-0

O4	●	No. Georgia	33	2
O18	●	Mercer	48	0
O25	●	Georgia ᵀᴬᴹ	0	16
N1	●	Florida Southern ˢᵗᴾ	0	7
N8		at Tulane	2	14
N15	●	Stetson	64	0
N22	●	at South Carolina	13	0
N27	●	Oglethorpe	14	7

WILLIAM KLINE
1920-22 (.690)   19-8-2

1920   6-3-0

O9	●	Newberry	21	0
O16	●	Rollins	1	0 f
O23	●	Florida Southern	13	0
O29	●	Mercer ᵛᴬᴸ	30	0
N6		Tulane ᵀᴬᴹ	0	14
N11	●	Stetson ᴾᴬᴸ	26	0
N13		at Georgia	0	56
N20	●	Stetson	21	0
N25		Oglethorpe ᶜᴼᴸᴳᵃ	0	21

1921   6-3-2

O1	●	at Fort Benning	6	0
O8	●	Rollins ᴼᴿᴸ	33	0
O10		Carlestom F.	0	19
O15	●	Mercer	7	0
O22		at Tennessee	0	9
O29	●	Samford ᴹᴼⁿᵀ	34	0
N5	=	South Carolina ᵀᴬᴹ	7	7
N11	●	at Alabama	9	2
N18	=	Mississippi Coll.	7	7
N24	●	Oglethorpe	21	3
D3		North Carolina ᴶᵃᶜꟳ	10	14

1922-1932
SOUTHERN

1922   7-2-0 (2-0-0)

O7		Furman	6	7
O14	●	at Rollins	19	0
O21	●	at American Legion	14	0
O28	●	Samford	57	0
N4		at Harvard	0	24
N11	●	Mississippi Coll. ᵀᴬᴹ	58	0
N18	●	at Tulane	27	6
N25	●	at Oglethorpe	12	0
D2	●	Clemson ᴶᵃᶜꟳ	47	14

GEN. J.A. VAN FLEET
1923-24 (.737)   12-3-4

1923   6-1-2 (1-0-2)

O6		at Army	0	20
O13	=	at Georgia Tech	7	7
O20	●	Rollins	28	0
O27	●	Wake Forest ᵀᴬᴹ	16	7
N3	●	Mercer	19	7
N10	●	at Stetson	27	0
N17	●	at Florida Southern	53	0
N24	=	Mississippi State ᴶᵃᶜꟳ	13	13
N29	●	Alabama ᴮⁱʳᵐ	16	6

1924   6-2-2 (2-0-1)

O4	●	Rollins	77	0
O11	=	at Georgia Tech	7	7
O18	●	Wake Forest ᵀᴬᴹ	34	0
O25	=	at Texas	7	7
N1	●	Florida Southern	27	0
N8		at Army	7	14
N14		at Mercer	0	10
N22	●	Mississippi State ᴹᴼⁿᵀ	27	0
N27	●	Drake	10	0
D6	●	Wash. & Lee ᴶᵃᶜꟳ	16	6

H.L. SEBRING
1925-27 (.600)   17-11-2

1925   8-2-0 (3-2-0)

O3	●	Mercer	24	0
O10	●	Florida Southern	9	0
O10	●	Hampden-Sydney	22	6
O17		at Georgia Tech	7	23
O24	●	Wake Forest	24	3
O31	●	Rollins	65	0
N7	●	at Clemson	42	0
N14		Alabama ᴹᴼⁿᵀ	0	34
N21	●	Mississippi State ᵀᴬᴹ	12	0
N26	●	Wash. & Lee ᴶᵃᶜꟳ	17	14

1926   2-6-2 (1-4-1)

S25	●	Florida Southern	16	0
O2		at Chicago	6	12
O9		Mississippi	7	12
O16		at Mercer	3	7
O23		Kentucky ᴶᵃᶜꟳ	13	18
O30		at Georgia	9	32
N6	●	Clemson	33	0
N13		Alabama ᴹᴼⁿᵀ	0	49
N20	=	Hampden-Sydney ᵀᴬᴹ	0	0
N25	=	Wash. & Lee ᴶᵃᶜꟳ	7	7

1927   7-3-0 (5-2-0)

S24	●	Florida Southern	26	7
O1		Davidson	0	12
O8	●	at Auburn	33	6
O15	●	Kentucky ᴶᵃᶜꟳ	27	6
O22		North Carolina St. ᵀᴬᴹ	6	12
O29	●	Mercer	32	6
N5		Georgia ᴶᵃᶜꟳ	0	28
N12	●	Alabama ᴹᴼⁿᵀ	13	6
N24	●	Wash. & Lee ᴶᵃᶜꟳ	20	7
D3		Maryland ᴶᵃᶜꟳ	7	6

CHARLES BACHMAN
1928-32 (.594)   27-18-3

1928   8-1-0 (6-1-0)

O6	●	Florida Southern	26	0
O13	●	Auburn	27	0
O20	●	Mercer	73	0
O27	●	North Carolina St. ᴶᵃᶜꟳ	14	7
N3	●	Sewanee ᴶᵃᶜꟳ	71	6
N10	●	Georgia ˢᴬⱽ	26	6
N17	●	Clemson ᴶᵃᶜꟳ	27	6
N29	●	Wash. & Lee ᴶᵃᶜꟳ	60	6
D8		at Tennessee	12	13

1929   8-2-0 (6-1-0)

S28	●	Florida Southern	54	0
O5	●	VMI ᵀᴬᴹ	18	7
O11	●	Auburn ᴹᴼⁿᵀ	19	0
O19		at Georgia Tech	6	19
O26	●	Georgia ᴶᵃᶜꟳ	18	6
N2		at Harvard	0	14
N16	●	Clemson	13	7
N23		at South Carolina	20	7
N28	●	Wash. & Lee ᴶᵃᶜꟳ	25	7
D7	●	Oregon ᴹⁱᴬ	20	6

1930   6-3-1 (4-2-1)

S27	●	Florida Southern	45	7
O4	●	North Carolina St. ᵀᴬᴹ	27	0
O11	●	Auburn ᴶᵃᶜꟳ	7	0
O18	●	at Chicago	19	0
O25	●	Furman	13	14
N1	=	Georgia ˢᴬⱽ	0	0
N8		Alabama	0	20
N15	=	Clemson ᴶᵃᶜꟳ	27	0
N27	●	at Georgia Tech	55	7
D6		Tennessee ᴶᵃᶜꟳ	6	13

1931   2-6-2 (2-4-2)

O3	●	at North Carolina St.	34	0
O10	=	North Carolina	0	0
O17		at Syracuse	12	33
O24	●	Auburn ᴶᵃᶜꟳ	13	12
O31		Georgia	6	33
N7		Alabama ᴮⁱʳᵐ	0	41
N14	=	South Carolina	6	6
N21		at Georgia Tech	0	23
N26		at UCLA	0	13
D5		Kentucky ᴶᵃᶜꟳ	2	7

1932   3-6-0 (1-6-0)

O8	●	Sewanee ᴶᵃᶜꟳ	19	0
O15	●	Citadel	27	7
O22		North Carolina St. ᵀᴬᴹ	6	17
O29		at Georgia	12	33
N4		at North Carolina	13	18
N12		Auburn ᴹᴼⁿᵀ	6	21
N19		Georgia Tech	0	6
D3		Tennessee ᴶᵃᶜꟳ	13	32
D17	●	UCLA	12	2

1933-PRESENT
SEC

D.K. STANLEY
1933-35 (.517)   14-13-2

1933   5-3-1 (2-3-0)

S30	●	Stetson	28	0
O7	●	Sewanee ᴶᵃᶜꟳ	31	0
O14	=	at North Carolina St.	0	0
O21	●	North Carolina	9	0
O28		at Tennessee	6	13
N4		Georgia ᴶᵃᶜꟳ	0	14
N11		at Georgia Tech	7	19
N25	●	Auburn	14	7
D2	●	Maryland ᵀᴬᴹ	19	0

THE SCHOOLS

1934 — 6-3-1 (2-2-1)

S29	•	Rollins JacF	13 2
O6	•	at Virginia Tech	20 13
O13		Tulane	12 28
O20	•	North Carolina St. TAM	14 0
O27		Maryland BALT	0 21
N3		Georgia JacF	0 14
N10	=	Mississippi	13 13
N17	•	Auburn Mont	14 7
N24	•	Georgia Tech	13 12
D1	•	Stetson	14 0

1935 — 3-7-0 (1-6-0)

S28	•	Stetson	34 0
O12		at Tulane	7 19
O19		at Mississippi	6 27
O26		Maryland	6 20
N2	•	Georgia JacF	0 7
N9		at Kentucky	6 15
N16	•	Sewanee	20 0
N23		at Georgia Tech	6 39
N30	•	Auburn Mia	6 27
D7	•	South Carolina TAM	22 0

JOSH CODY
1936-39 (.419)   17-24-2

1936 — 4-6-0 (1-5-0)

O3	•	Citadel	20 14
O10		at South Carolina	0 7
O17	•	Stetson	32 0
O24		at Kentucky	0 7
O31	•	Maryland	7 6
N7		Georgia JacF	8 26
N14	•	Sewanee	18 7
N21		at Georgia Tech	14 38
N28		Auburn Mont	0 13
D5		Mississippi State	0 7

1937 — 4-7-0 (3-4-0)

S25		at LSU	0 19
O2	•	Stetson	18 0
O8		at Temple	6 7
O16	•	Sewanee	21 0
O23		at Mississippi State	13 14
O30		at Maryland	7 13
N6	•	Georgia JacF	6 0
N13		Clemson	9 10
N20		Georgia Tech	0 12
N27		Auburn JacF	0 14
D4		Kentucky	6 0

1938 — 4-6-1 (2-2-1)

S24		Stetson	14 16
O1		at Mississippi State	0 22
O8	•	Sewanee	10 6
O15		Miami, Fla.	7 19
O22	•	at Tampa	33 0
O29		at Boston College	0 33
N5		Georgia JacF	6 19
N12		Maryland	21 7
N19	=	at Georgia Tech	0 0
N26	•	Auburn JacF	9 7
D3		Temple	12 20

1939 — 5-5-1 (0-3-1)

S23	•	Stetson	21 0
S30		at Texas	0 12
O7		Mississippi State	0 14
O12	•	at Boston College	7 0
O21	•	Tampa	7 0
O28	•	at Maryland	14 0
N4		at South Carolina	0 6 *
N11	•	Georgia JacF	2 6
N18	•	at Miami, Fla.	13 0
N25		Georgia Tech	7 21
N30	=	at Auburn	7 7

TOM LIEB
1940-45 (.436)   20-26-1

1940 — 5-5-0 (2-3-0)

S28	•	Mississippi State	7 27
O5	•	at Tampa	23 0
O11		Villanova PHIL	0 28
O19	•	Maryland	19 0
O26		at Tennessee	0 14
N9	•	Georgia JacF	18 13
N16	•	at Miami, Fla.	46 6
N23	•	at Georgia Tech	16 7
N30	•	Auburn ColGA	7 20
D7		Texas	0 26

1941 — 4-6-0 (1-3-0)

S20	•	Randolph-Macon	26 0
S27		at Mississippi State	0 6
O4	•	Tampa	46 6
O11	•	Villanova	0 6
O18	•	at Maryland	12 13
O25		at LSU	7 10
N8		Georgia JacF	3 19
N15	•	at Miami, Fla.	14 0
N22	•	Georgia Tech	14 7
D20		UCLA JacF	27 30

1942 — 3-7-0 (1-3-0)

S19	•	at Jacksonville NAS	7 20
S26	•	Randolph-Macon	45 0
O3	•	at Tampa	26 6
O10	•	Auburn	6 0
O17		Villanova PHIL	3 13
O24		Mississippi State	12 26
O31		Maryland DC	0 13
N7		Georgia JacF	0 75
N14	•	at Miami, Fla.	0 12
N21		at Georgia Tech	7 20

1943
NO TEAM WWII

1944 — 4-3-0 (0-3-0)

S23	•	Mayport NAS	36 6
S30		Mississippi JacF	6 26
O7	•	Jacksonville NAS	26 20
O14	•	at Tennessee	0 40
O28	•	Maryland	14 6
N3		at Miami, Fla.	13 0
N11		Georgia JacF	12 38

1945 — 4-5-1 (1-3-1)

S22	•	Camp Blanding	31 2
S29	•	Mississippi JacF	26 13
O6	=	at Tulane	6 6
O13		Vanderbilt	0 7
O19	•	at Miami, Fla.	6 7
O27	•	La. Lafayette	45 0
N3		at Auburn	0 19
N10	•	Georgia JacF	0 34
N17	•	Presbyterian	41 0
N24	•	at U.S. Amphibians	0 12

RAYMOND WOLF
1946-49 (.359)   13-24-2

1946 — 0-9-0 (0-5-0)

S28	•	Mississippi JacF	7 13
O5		at Tulane	13 27
O12		at Vanderbilt	0 20
O19		Miami, Fla.	13 20
O26		at North Carolina	19 40
N9		Georgia JacF	14 33
N16		Villanova	20 27
N23		North Carolina St. TAM	6 37
N30		Auburn	12 47

1947 — 4-5-1 (0-3-1)

S27		Mississippi JacF	6 14
O4		North Texas	12 20
O11		Auburn Mont	14 20
O18	•	at North Carolina St.	7 6
O25		North Carolina	7 35
N1	•	Furman TAM	34 7
N8		Georgia JacF	6 34
N15	=	at Tulane	7 7
N22	•	at Miami, Fla.	7 6
N29		Kansas State	25 7

1948 — 5-5-0 (1-5-0)

S25		Mississippi	0 14
O2	•	Tulsa	28 14
O9	•	Auburn TAM	16 9
O16	•	Rollins	41 12
O23		at Georgia Tech	7 42
O30	•	at Furman	39 14
N6		Georgia JacF	12 20
N13		at Kentucky	15 34
N20	•	Miami, Fla.	27 13
N27		at Alabama	28 34

1949 — 4-5-1 (1-4-1)

S24	•	Citadel	13 0
O1	•	at Tulsa	40 7
O8	=	Auburn MBL	14 14
O15		Vanderbilt JacF	17 22
O22	•	Georgia Tech	14 43
O29		Furman	28 27
N5	•	Georgia JacF	28 7
N12		Kentucky TAM	0 35
N18	•	at Miami, Fla.	13 28
N26		Alabama	13 35

BOB WOODRUFF
1950-59 (.554)   53-42-6

1950 — 5-5-0 (2-4-0)

S23	•	Citadel	7 3
S30	•	Duquesne	27 14
O7		at Georgia Tech	13 16
O14	•	Auburn	27 7
O21	•	at Vanderbilt	31 27
O28	•	Furman	19 7
N4		at Kentucky	6 40
N11	•	Georgia JacF	0 6
N18	•	Miami, Fla.	14 20
N25		Alabama JacF	0 34

1951 — 5-5-0 (2-4-0)

S15	•	Wyoming JacF	13 0
S22	•	Citadel	27 7
S29		Georgia Tech	0 27
O6	•	at Loyola-Marymount	40 7
O13	•	at Auburn	13 14
O20	•	Vanderbilt	33 13
O27	•	Kentucky	6 14
N10	•	Georgia JacF	6 7
N17	•	at Miami, Fla.	6 21
N24	•	at Alabama	30 21

1952 — 8-3-0 (3-3-0)

S20	•	Stetson	33 6
S27	•	at Georgia Tech	14 17
O4	•	Citadel JacF	33 0
O11	•	Clemson	54 13
O18	•	at Vanderbilt	13 20
O25	•	Georgia JacF	30 0
N1	•	Auburn	31 21
N15	•	at Tennessee	12 26
N22	•	Miami, Fla.	43 6
D6		Kentucky	27 0

GATOR BOWL

J1	•	Tulsa	14 13

1953 — 3-5-2 (1-3-2)

S19	•	at Rice	16 20
S26	=	Georgia Tech	0 0
O3		at Kentucky	13 26
O10	•	Stetson	45 0
O17	•	Citadel JacF	60 0
O24	=	LSU	21 21
O31	•	at Auburn	7 16
N7	•	Georgia JacF	21 7
N14		Tennessee	7 9
N28		at Miami, Fla.	10 14

1954 — 5-5-0 (5-2-0)

S18	•	at Rice	14 34
S25	•	at Georgia Tech	13 12
O2	•	Auburn	19 13
O9		Clemson TAM	7 14
O16	•	Kentucky	21 7
O23		at LSU	7 20
O30	•	Mississippi State	7 0
N6		Georgia JacF	13 14
N13	•	at Tennessee	14 0
N27		Miami, Fla.	0 14

1955 — 4-6-0 (3-5-0)

S17	•	Mississippi State	20 14
S24	•	Georgia Tech	7 14
O1		at Auburn	0 13
O8	•	George Washington JacF	28 0
O15	•	LSU	18 14
O22		at Kentucky	7 10
N5	•	Georgia JacF	19 13
N12		Tennessee	0 20
N19	•	at Vanderbilt	6 21
N26		at Miami, Fla.	6 7

1956 — 6-3-1 (5-2-0)

S22	•	at Mississippi State	26 0
S29	•	Clemson	20 20
O6		Kentucky	8 17
O13	•	Rice	7 0
O20	•	at Vanderbilt	21 7
O27	•	at LSU	21 6
N3	•	Auburn	20 0
N10	•	Georgia JacF	28 0
N24	•	Georgia Tech JacF	0 28
D1	•	Miami, Fla.	7 20

1957 — 6-2-1 (4-2-1)

S28	•	Wake Forest	27 0
O5	•	at Kentucky	14 7
O19	•	Mississippi State	20 29
O26	•	LSU	22 14
N2	•	at Auburn	0 13
N9	•	Georgia JacF	22 0
N16	•	Vanderbilt	14 7
N23		at Georgia Tech	0 0
N30	•	at Miami, Fla.	14 0

1958 — 6-4-1 (2-3-1)

S20	•	Tulane	34 14
S27		Mississippi State	7 14
O10	•	at UCLA	21 14
O18	=	Vanderbilt	6 6
O25		at LSU	7 10
N1	•	Auburn	5 6
N8	•	Georgia JacF	7 6
N15	•	Arkansas State	51 7
N22	•	Florida State	21 7
N29	•	Miami, Fla. JacF	12 9

GATOR BOWL

D27		Mississippi	3 7

1959 — 5-4-1 (2-4-0)

S18	•	at Tulane	30 0
S26	•	Mississippi State	14 13
O3	•	Virginia	55 10
O10	=	at Rice	13 13
O17	•	at Vanderbilt	6 13
O24		LSU	0 9
O31	•	at Auburn	0 6
N7		Georgia JacF	10 21
N21	•	Florida State	18 8
N28	•	Miami, Fla. JacF	23 14

RAY GRAVES
1960-69 (.686)   70-31-4

1960 — 9-2-0 (5-1-0)

S17	•	George Washington JacF	30 7
S24	•	Florida State	3 0
O1	•	Georgia Tech	18 17
O8	•	Rice JacF	0 10
O15	•	Vanderbilt	12 0
O22	•	at LSU	13 10
O29	•	Auburn	7 10
N5	•	Georgia JacF	22 14
N12	•	Tulane	21 6
N26	•	at Miami, Fla.	18 0

GATOR BOWL

D31	•	Baylor	13 12

1961 — 4-5-1 (3-3-0)

S23	•	Clemson	21 17
S30	=	Florida State	3 3
O6	•	at Tulane	14 3
O14	•	at Rice	10 19
O21	•	at Vanderbilt	7 0
O28		LSU	0 23
N4	•	at Georgia Tech	0 20
N11	•	Georgia JacF	21 14
N25	•	at Auburn	15 32
D2		Miami, Fla.	6 15

1962 — 7-4-0 (4-2-0)

S22	•	Mississippi State JAM	19 9
S29	•	Georgia Tech	0 17
O6	•	Duke JacF	21 28
O13	•	Texas A&M	42 6
O20	•	Vanderbilt	42 7
O27	•	at LSU	0 23
N3	•	Auburn	22 3
N10	•	Georgia JacF	23 15
N17	•	Florida State	20 7
D1	•	at Miami, Fla.	15 17

GATOR BOWL

D29	•	Penn State	17 7

1963 — 6-3-1 (3-3-1)

S14		at Georgia Tech	0 9
S28	=	Mississippi State	9 9
O5	•	Richmond	35 28
O12	•	at Alabama	10 6
O19	•	at Vanderbilt	21 0
O26		LSU	0 14
N2		at Auburn	0 19
N9	•	Georgia JacF	21 14
N23	•	at Miami, Fla.	27 21
N30	•	Florida State	7 0

1964 — 7-3-0 (4-2-0)

S19	•	SMU	24 8
S26	•	Mississippi State JAM	16 13
O10	•	Mississippi	30 14
O17	•	South Carolina	37 0
O24	•	at Alabama	14 17
O31	•	Auburn	14 0
N7		Georgia JacF	7 14
N21	•	at Florida State	7 16
N28	•	Miami, Fla.	12 10
D5	•	at LSU	20 6

1965 7-4-0 (4-2-0)

S18	●	at Northwestern	24	14
S25	|	Mississippi State	13	18
O2	● |	LSU	14	7
O9	● |	at Mississippi	17	0
O16	●	North Carolina St.	28	6
O30	|	at Auburn	17	28
N6	● |	Georgia JacF	14	10
N13	● |	Tulane	51	13
N20		at Miami, Fla.	13	16
N27	●	Florida State	30	17
		SUGAR BOWL		
J1		Missouri	18	20

1966 9-2-0 (5-1-0)

S17	●	Northwestern	43	7
S24	● |	Mississippi State	28	7
O1	● |	at Vanderbilt	13	0
O8	●	at Florida State	22	19
O15	●	at North Carolina St.	17	10
O22	● |	at LSU	28	7
O29	● |	Auburn	30	27
N5	|	Georgia JacF	10	27
N12	● ||	Tulane	31	10
N26		Miami, Fla.	16	21
		ORANGE BOWL		
J2	●	Georgia Tech	27	12

1967 6-4-0 (4-2-0)

S23	●	Illinois	14	0
S30	● |	Mississippi State JaM	24	7
O7	|	LSU	6	37
O14	●	at Tulane	35	0
O28	● |	Vanderbilt	27	22
N4	|	at Auburn	21	26
N11	● |	Georgia JacF	17	16
N18	● |	Kentucky	28	12
N25		Florida State	16	21
D9		at Miami, Fla.	13	20

1968 6-3-1 (3-2-1)

S21	●	Air Force TaM	23	20
S28	●	at Florida State	9	3
O5	● |	Mississippi State	31	14
O12	● ||	Tulane	24	3
O19		at North Carolina	7	22
O26	= |	at Vanderbilt	14	14
N2	|	Auburn	13	24
N9	|	Georgia JacF	0	51
N16	● |	at Kentucky	16	14
N30	●	Miami, Fla.	14	10

1969 9-1-1 (3-1-1)

S20	●	Houston	59	34
S27	● |	Mississippi State JaM	47	35
O4	●	Florida State	21	6
O11	●	Tulane TaM	18	17
O18	●	North Carolina	52	2
O25	● |	Vanderbilt	41	20
N1	|	at Auburn	12	38
N8	= |	Georgia JacF	13	13
N15	● |	Kentucky	31	6
N29	●	at Miami, Fla.	35	16
		GATOR BOWL		
D27	●	Tennessee	14	13

DOUG DICKEY
1970-78 (.573) 58-43-2

1970 7-4-0 (3-3-0)

S12	●	Duke JacF	21	19
S19	● |	Mississippi State	34	13
S26	|	at Alabama	15	46
O3	●	North Carolina St.	14	6
O10	●	at Florida State	38	27
O17	●	Richmond	20	0
O24	|	at Tennessee	7	38
O31	|	Auburn	14	63
N7	● |	Georgia JacF	24	17
N14	● |	Kentucky TaM	24	13
N28		Miami, Fla.	13	14

1971 4-7-0 (1-6-0)

S11		Duke TaM	6	12
S18	|	Mississippi State JaM	10	13
S25	|	Alabama	0	38
O2	|	Tennessee	13	20
O9	|	at LSU	7	48
O16	●	Florida State	17	15
O23	●	Maryland	27	23
O30	|	at Auburn	7	40
N6	|	Georgia JacF	7	49
N13	● |	Kentucky	35	24
N27	●	at Miami, Fla.	45	16

1972 5-5-1 (3-3-1)

S23		SMU TaM	14	21
S30	● |	Mississippi State	28	13
O7	●	at Florida State	42	13
O14	|	at Alabama	7	4
O21	● |	at Mississippi	16	0
N4	|	Auburn	20	26
N11	|	Georgia JacF	7	10
N18	● |	Kentucky	40	0
N25	= |	LSU	3	3
D2	●	Miami, Fla.	17	6
D9		North Carolina JacF	24	28

1973 7-5-0 (3-4-0)

S15	●	Kansas State	21	10
S22	●	Southern Miss TaM	14	13
S29	|	Mississippi State JaM	12	33
O6	|	at LSU	3	24
O13	|	Alabama	14	35
O20	|	Mississippi	10	13
N3	● |	at Auburn	12	8
N10	● |	Georgia JacF	11	10
N17	● |	Kentucky	20	18
N24	●	at Miami, Fla.	14	7
D1	●	Florida State	49	0
		TANGERINE BOWL		
D22		Miami, Ohio	7	16

1974 8-4-0 (3-3-0)

S14	●	California	21	17
S21	●	Maryland TaM	17	10
S28	● |	Mississippi State	29	13
O5	● |	LSU	24	14
O12	|	at Vanderbilt	10	24
O19	●	at Florida State	24	14
O26	●	Duke	30	13
N2	● |	Auburn	25	14
N9	|	Georgia	16	17
N16	|	at Kentucky	24	41
N30	●	Miami, Fla.	31	7
		SUGAR BOWL		
D31		Nebraska	10	13

1975 9-3-0 (5-1-0)

S13	●	SMU	40	14
S20		at North Carolina St.	7	8
S27	● |	Mississippi State JaM	27	10
O4	● |	at LSU	34	6
O11	● |	Vanderbilt	35	0
O18	●	Florida State	34	8
O25	●	Duke	24	16
N1	● |	at Auburn	31	14
N8	|	Georgia JacF	7	10
N15	● |	Kentucky	48	7
N29	●	at Miami, Fla.	15	11
		GATOR BOWL		
D29		Maryland	0	13

1976 8-4-0 (4-2-0)

S11		North Carolina TaM	21	24
S18	●	Houston	49	14
S25	● |	Mississippi State	34	30
O2	● |	LSU	28	23
O16	●	at Florida State	33	26
O23	● |	at Tennessee	20	18
O30	● |	Auburn	24	19
N6	|	Georgia JacF	27	41
N13	|	at Kentucky	9	28
N20	●	Rice	50	22
N27	●	Miami, Fla. Orl	19	10
		SUN BOWL		
J2		Texas A&M	14	37

1977 6-4-1 (3-3-0)

S17	●	at Rice	48	3
S24	● |	Mississippi State JaM	24	22
O1	|	at LSU	14	36
O8	=	Pittsburgh	17	17
O22	● |	Tennessee	27	17
O29	|	at Auburn	14	29
N5	● |	Georgia JacF	22	17
N12	|	Kentucky	7	14
N19	●	Utah	38	29
N26	●	at Miami, Fla.	31	14
D3		Florida State	9	37

1978 4-7-0 (3-3-0)

S16		SMU Orl	25	35
S30	● |	Mississippi State	34	0
O7	|	LSU	21	34
O14	|	at Alabama	12	23
O21	●	Army	31	7
O28		at Georgia Tech	13	17
N4	● |	Auburn	31	7
N11	|	Georgia JacF	22	24
N18	● |	at Kentucky	18	16
N25		at Florida State	21	38
D2		Miami, Fla.	21	22

CHARLEY PELL
1979-84 (.556) 33-26-3

1979 0-10-1 (0-6-0)

S15		at Houston	10	14
S22	=	Georgia Tech	7	7
S29	|	Mississippi State JaM	10	24
O6	|	at LSU	3	20
O13	|	Alabama	0	40
O27		Tulsa	10	20
N3	|	at Auburn	13	19
N10	|	Georgia JacF	10	33
N17	|	Kentucky	3	31
N24		Florida State	16	27
D1		at Miami, Fla.	24	30

1980 8-4-0 (4-2-0)

S13	●	California TaM	41	13
S20	●	at Georgia Tech	45	12
S27	● |	Mississippi State	21	15
O4	|	LSU	7	24
O18	● |	at Mississippi	15	3
O25	●	Louisville	13	0
N1	● |	Auburn	21	10
N8	|	Georgia JacF	21	26
N15	● |	at Kentucky	17	15
N29		Miami, Fla.	7	31
D6		at Florida State	13	17
		TANGERINE BOWL		
D20	●	Maryland	35	20

1981 7-5-0 (3-3-0)

S5		at Miami, Fla.	20	21
S12	●	Furman	35	7
S19	●	Georgia Tech	27	6
S26	|	Mississippi State JaM	7	28
O3	● |	at LSU	24	10
O10	●	Maryland	15	10
O17	● |	Mississippi	49	3
O31	|	at Auburn	12	14
N7	|	Georgia JacF	21	26
N14	● |	Kentucky	33	12
N28	●	Florida State	35	3
		PEACH BOWL		
D31		West Virginia	6	26

1982 8-4-0 (3-3-0)

S4	●	Miami, Fla.	17	14
S11	●	Southern Cal	17	9
S25	● |	Mississippi State	27	17
O2	|	LSU	13	24
O9	|	at Vanderbilt	29	31
O16	●	West Texas St.	77	14
O30	● |	Auburn	19	17
N6	|	Georgia JacF	0	44
N13	● |	at Kentucky	39	13
N20	●	at Tulane	21	7
D4	●	at Florida State	13	10
		BLUEBONNET BOWL		
D31		Arkansas	24	28

1983 9-2-1 (4-2-0)

S3	●	Miami, Fla.	28	3
S10	=	at Southern Cal	19	19
S17	●	Indiana St.	17	13
S24	● |	at Mississippi State	35	12
O1	● |	at LSU	31	17
O8	● |	Vanderbilt	29	10
O22	●	East Carolina	24	17
O29	|	at Auburn	21	28
N5	|	Georgia JacF	9	10
N12	● |	Kentucky	24	7
D3	●	Florida State	53	14
		GATOR BOWL		
D30	●	Iowa	14	6

GALEN HALL
1984-89 (.686) 40-18-1

1984 9-1-1 (5-0-1)

S1		Miami, Fla. TaM	20	32
S8	= |	LSU	21	21
S15	●	Tulane	63	21
S29	● |	Mississippi State	27	12
O6	●	Syracuse	16	0
O13	● |	at Tennessee	43	30
O20	●	Cincinnati	48	17
N3	● |	Auburn	24	3
N10	● |	Georgia JacF	27	0
N17	● |	at Kentucky	25	17
D1	●	at Florida State	27	17

1985 9-1-1 (5-1-0)

S7	●	at Miami, Fla.	35	23
S14	=	Rutgers	28	28
S28	● |	at Mississippi State	36	22
O5	● |	at LSU	20	0
O12	● |	Tennessee	17	10
O19	●	La. Lafayette	45	0
O26	●	Virginia Tech	35	18
N2	● |	at Auburn	14	10
N9	|	Georgia JacF	3	24
N16	● |	Kentucky	15	13
N30	●	Florida State	38	14

1986 6-5-0 (2-4-0)

A30	●	Georgia Southern	38	14
S6		Miami, Fla.	15	23
S20	|	Alabama	7	21
S27	|	at Mississippi State	10	16
O4	|	LSU	17	28
O11	●	Kent State	52	9
O18	●	Rutgers ERut	15	3
N1	● |	Auburn	18	17
N8	● |	Georgia JacF	31	19
N15	|	at Kentucky	3	10
N29	●	at Florida State	17	13

1987 6-6-0 (3-3-0)

S5		at Miami, Fla.	4	31
S12	●	Tulsa	52	0
S19	● |	Alabama Birm	23	14
S26	● |	Mississippi State	38	3
O3	|	at LSU	10	13
O10	●	Fullerton St.	65	0
O17	●	Temple	34	3
O31	|	at Auburn	6	29
N7	|	Georgia JacF	10	23
N14	● |	Kentucky	27	14
N28		Florida State	14	28
		ALOHA BOWL		
D25		UCLA	16	20

1988 7-5-0 (4-3-0)

S3	●	Montana St.	69	0
S10	● |	Mississippi JaM	27	15
S17	●	Indiana St.	58	0
S24	● |	Mississippi State	17	0
O1	● |	LSU	19	6
O8		Memphis	11	17
O15	|	at Vanderbilt	9	24
O29	|	Auburn	0	16
N5	|	Georgia JacF	3	26
N12	● |	at Kentucky	24	19
N26		at Florida State	17	52
		ALL-AMERICAN BOWL		
D29	●	Illinois	14	10

GARY DARNELL
1989 (.429) 3-4

1989 7-5-0 (4-3-0)

S9	|	Mississippi	19	24
S16	●	Louisiana Tech	34	7
S23	●	at Memphis	38	13
S30	● |	Mississippi State TaM	21	0
O7	● |	at LSU	16	13
O14	● |	Vanderbilt	34	11
O21	●	New Mexico	27	21
N4	|	at Auburn	7	10
N11	|	Georgia JacF	10	17
N18	● |	Kentucky	38	28
D2		Florida State	17	24
		FREEDOM BOWL		
D30		Washington	7	34

STEVE SPURRIER
1990-2001 (.817) 122-27-1

1990 9-2-0 (6-1-0)

S8	●	Oklahoma State	50	7
S15	● |	at Alabama	17	13
S22	●	Furman	27	3
S29	● |	Mississippi State	34	21
O6	● |	LSU	34	8
O13	|	at Tennessee	3	45
O20	●	Akron	59	0
N3	● |	Auburn	48	7
N10	● |	Georgia JacF	38	7
N17	● |	at Kentucky	47	15
D1		at Florida State	30	45

1991 — 10-2-0 (7-0-0)

Date		Opponent		
S7	•	San Jose State	59	21
S14		Alabama	35	0
S21		at Syracuse	21	38
S28		Mississippi State _Orl_	29	7
O5	•	at LSU	16	0
O12	•	Tennessee	35	18
O19	•	Northern Illinois	41	10
N2	•	at Auburn	31	10
N9	•	Georgia _JacF_	45	13
N16	•	Kentucky	35	26
N30		Florida State	14	9
SUGAR BOWL				
J1		Notre Dame	28	39

1992 — 9-4-0 (6-2-0)

Date		Opponent		
S12	•	Kentucky	35	19
S19		at Tennessee	14	31
O1		at Mississippi State	6	30
O10		LSU	28	21
O17	•	Auburn	24	9
O24	•	Louisville	31	17
O31	•	Georgia _JacF_	26	24
N7	•	Southern Miss	24	20
N14	•	South Carolina	14	9
N21		at Vanderbilt	41	21
N28		at Florida State	24	45
SEC CHAMPIONSHIP GAME				
D5		Alabama _Birm_	21	28
GATOR BOWL				
D31	•	North Carolina St.	27	10

1993 — 11-2-0 (7-1-0)

Date		Opponent		
S4	•	Arkansas State	44	6
S11		at Kentucky	24	20
S18	•	Tennessee	41	34
O2		Mississippi State	38	24
O9		at LSU	58	3
O16		at Auburn	35	38
O30		Georgia _JacF_	33	26
N6	•	La. Lafayette	61	14
N13		at South Carolina	37	26
N20	•	Vanderbilt	52	0
N27		Florida State	21	33
SEC CHAMPIONSHIP GAME				
D4	•	Alabama _Birm_	28	13
SUGAR BOWL				
J1	•	West Virginia	41	7

1994 — 10-2-1 (7-1-0)

Date		Opponent		
S3	•	New Mexico St.	70	21
S10	•	Kentucky	73	7
S17	•	at Tennessee	31	0
O1	•	at Mississippi	38	14
O8	•	LSU	42	18
O15	•	Auburn	33	36
O29	•	Georgia	52	14
N5	•	Southern Miss	55	17
N12	•	South Carolina	48	17
N19	•	at Vanderbilt	24	7
N26	=	at Florida State	31	31
SEC CHAMPIONSHIP GAME				
D3	•	Alabama _Atl_	24	23
SUGAR BOWL				
J2		Florida State	17	23

1995 — 12-1-0 (8-0-0)

Date		Opponent		
S2	•	Houston	45	21
S9	•	at Kentucky	42	7
S16	•	Tennessee	62	37
S30	•	Mississippi	28	10
O7	•	at LSU	28	10
O14	•	at Auburn	49	38
O28	•	at Georgia	52	17
N4	•	Northern Illinois	58	20
N11	•	at South Carolina	63	7
N18	•	Vanderbilt	38	7
N25	•	Florida State	35	24
SEC CHAMPIONSHIP GAME				
D2	•	Arkansas _Atl_	34	3
FIESTA BOWL				
J2		Nebraska	24	62

1996 — 12-1 (8-0)

Date		Opponent		
A30	•	La. Lafayette	55	21
S7	•	Georgia So.	62	14
S21	•	at Tennessee	35	29
S28		Kentucky	65	0
O5	•	at Arkansas	42	7
O12	•	LSU	56	13
O19	•	Auburn	51	10
N2	•	Georgia _JacF_	47	7
N9	•	at Vanderbilt	28	21
N16	•	South Carolina	52	25
N30		at Florida State	21	24
SEC CHAMPIONSHIP GAME				
D7	•	Alabama _Atl_	45	30
SUGAR BOWL				
J2	•	Florida State	52	20

1997 — 10-2 (6-2)

Date		Opponent		
A30	•	Southern Miss	21	6
S6	•	Central Michigan	82	6
S20	•	Tennessee	33	20
S27	•	at Kentucky	55	28
O4	•	Arkansas	56	7
O11	•	at LSU	21	28
O18	•	at Auburn	24	10
N1	•	Georgia _JacF_	17	37
N8	•	Vanderbilt	20	7
N15	•	at South Carolina	48	21
N22	•	Florida State	32	29
CITRUS BOWL				
J1	•	Penn State	21	6

1998 — 10-2 (7-1)

Date		Opponent		
S5	•	Citadel	49	10
S12	•	La. Monroe	42	10
S19	•	at Tennessee	17	20
S26	•	Kentucky	51	35
O3	•	at Alabama	16	10
O10	•	LSU	22	10
O17	•	Auburn	24	3
O31	•	Georgia _JacF_	38	7
N7	•	at Vanderbilt	45	13
N14	•	South Carolina	33	14
N21	•	at Florida State	12	23
ORANGE BOWL				
J2	•	Syracuse	31	10

1999 — 9-4 (7-1)

Date		Opponent		
S4	•	Western Michigan	55	26
S11	•	Central Florida	58	27
S18	•	Tennessee	23	21
S25	•	at Kentucky	38	10
O2	•	Alabama	39	40
O9	•	at LSU	31	10
O16	•	at Auburn	32	14
O30	•	Georgia _JacF_	30	14
N6	•	Vanderbilt	13	6
N13	•	at South Carolina	20	3
N20		Florida State	23	30
SEC CHAMPIONSHIP GAME				
D4	•	Alabama _Atl_	7	34
CITRUS BOWL				
J1	•	Michigan State	34	37

2000 — 10-3 (7-1)

Date		Opponent		
S2	•	Ball State	40	19
S9	•	Middle Tennessee	55	0
S16	•	at Tennessee	27	23
S23	•	Kentucky	59	31
S30	•	at Mississippi State	35	47
O7	•	LSU	41	9
O14	•	Auburn	38	7
O28	•	Georgia _JacF_	34	23
N4	•	at Vanderbilt	43	20
N11	•	South Carolina	41	21
N18		at Florida State	7	30
SEC CHAMPIONSHIP GAME				
D2	•	Auburn _Atl_	28	6
SUGAR BOWL				
J2		Miami, Fla.	20	37

2001 — 10-2 (6-2)

Date		Opponent		
S1	•	Marshall	49	14
S8	•	La. Monroe	55	6
S22	•	at Kentucky	44	10
S29	•	Mississippi State	52	0
O6	•	at LSU	44	15
O13	•	at Auburn	20	23
O27	•	Georgia _JacF_	24	10
N3	•	Vanderbilt	71	13
N10	•	at South Carolina	54	17
N17	•	Florida State	37	13
D1		Tennessee	32	34
ORANGE BOWL				
J1	•	Maryland	56	23

RON ZOOK — 2002-04 (.622) — 23-14

2002 — 8-5 (6-2)

Date		Opponent		
A31	•	UAB	51	3
S7	•	Miami, Fla.	16	41
S14	•	Ohio U.	34	6
S21	•	at Tennessee	30	13
S28	•	Kentucky	41	34
O5	•	at Mississippi	14	17
O12	•	LSU	7	36
O19	•	Auburn	30	23
N2	•	Georgia _JacF_	20	13
N9	•	at Vanderbilt	21	17
N16	•	South Carolina	28	7
N30		at Florida State	14	31
OUTBACK BOWL				
J1	•	Michigan	30	38

2003 — 8-5 (6-2)

Date		Opponent		
A30	•	San Jose State	65	3
S6	•	at Miami, Fla.	33	38
S13	•	Florida A&M	63	3
S20		Tennessee	10	24
S27	•	at Kentucky	24	21
O4	•	Mississippi	17	20
O11	•	at LSU	19	7
O18	•	at Arkansas	33	28
N1	•	Georgia _JacF_	16	13
N8	•	Vanderbilt	35	17
N15	•	at South Carolina	24	22
N29		Florida State	34	38
OUTBACK BOWL				
J1		Iowa	17	37

CHARLIE STRONG — 2004 (.000) — 0-1

2004 — 7-5 (4-4)

Date		Opponent		
S11	•	Eastern Michigan	49	10
S18	•	at Tennessee	28	30
S25	•	Kentucky	20	3
O2	•	Arkansas	45	30
O9		LSU	21	24
O16	•	Middle Tennessee	52	16
O23	•	at Mississippi State	31	38
O30	•	Georgia _JacF_	24	31
N6	•	at Vanderbilt	34	17
N13	•	South Carolina	48	14
N20	•	at Florida State	20	13
PEACH BOWL				
D31		Miami, Fla.	10	27

FLORIDA ATLANTIC

BY DAN GALVIN

"**I**F YOU BUILD IT, THEY WILL COME." It worked for Ray Kinsella in *Field of Dreams*, and Florida Atlantic coach Howard Schnellenberger is hoping for the same for his fledgling football team, Florida Atlantic. Schnellenberger built Miami and Louisville into powerhouse programs in the 1980s and 1990s, and he couldn't refuse the ultimate challenge of building an entire football program from scratch. The man who coached alongside Bear Bryant and Don Shula took his positive attitude to Boca Raton in 1998, had his first practice in 2000 and first game in 2001. So it surprised no one when it took just 22 games for Florida Atlantic to notch its first victory over a D1-A team, the fastest journey to success in college football history. FAU will begin playing in the Sun Belt Conference in 2005, making the impossible a reality.

TRADITION They're homespun at this point. Schnellenberger combed through south Florida for his first recruiting class, trying to sell student-athletes on building a program. So on his first and each successive signing day he oversees a potluck dinner with the new signees.

BEST PLAYER Why does a kid from Edmond, Okla., travel to Boca Raton to play football? For QB Jared Allen, it's simple: he wanted to be part of history. Allen signed in 2000 as one of Schnellenberger's first recruits, with the lure of building a team from the ground up. A starter since the second game of FAU's inaugural season in 2001, Allen led the Owls to respectability. In 2003, he directed the team to 2 TDs in the final three minutes against Middle Tennessee State to give the team its first win over a Division I program. Posting a 20–6 record in 2003-04 as a starter, Allen helped make Florida Atlantic a winning program and an attractive destination to future recruits.

COACH Howard Schnellenberger played under Bear Bryant at Kentucky and was later an assistant for three of Bryant's national championship teams at Alabama. He moved to the NFL as an assistant under George Allen and was on the Miami Dolphins staff for the team's undefeated Super Bowl season. He then became a head coach in the NFL for the Baltimore Colts from 1973 to 1974. He led the University of Miami to its first national title in 1983, and later turned Louisville into a national power. Hired on May 1, 1998, Schnellenberger's unwavering confidence and enthusiasm for football quickly permeated the campus. With his distinctive white hair, pipe, boots and sport coat, Schnellenberger proved an instantly recognizable figure in the community,

PROFILE

Florida Atlantic University
Boca Raton, Fla.
Founded: 1961
Enrollment: 21,358
Colors: Blue and Red
Nickname: Owls
Stadium: Lockhart Stadium
   Opened in 1959
   Grass; 20,000 capacity
First football game: 2001
All-time record: 26–21
Website: fausports.com

THE BEST OF TIMES

Traveling 5,000 miles and upending Hawaii 35-28 in OT on Sept. 4, 2004. Easily the biggest win in the program's short history.

THE WORST OF TIMES

A 61-14 shellacking at Connecticut to begin 2002 with its eighth straight defeat in a 2–9 season. Citizens of Boca Raton were wondering why they needed another football team with three in-state behemoths.

CONFERENCE

FAU will play in the Sun Belt beginning in 2005.

DISTINGUISHED ALUMNI

Scott "Carrot Top" Thompson, comedian/actor; Donald Brewer, drummer, Grand Funk Railroad; Maynard Webb, COO of eBay; Luis Alberto Moreno, Colombian ambassador to the U.S.; Carol W. Hunstein, Georgia Supreme Court Justice

FIGHT SONG

FAU FIGHT SONG
We'll fight fight fight for FAU
There's foot-ball in pa-ra-dise
We'll fight fight fight for FAU
We know we're gonna win and it's feelin' mighty nice
Cheering our football team down the field and waving our colors too
Hoot! Hoot!
The fighting Owls are on the prowl
Go F A U hey!
Go Owls Go!
Go Owls Go!
Hit'em high, hit'em low, Go Owls Go!
(repeat)

raising the profile not just of the football program but of the university itself.

BEST TEAM With wins over Hawaii, North Texas and Middle Tennessee State, the 2004 Owls realized many of Schnellenberger's lofty goals. FAU's first recruiting class, 12 seniors who stayed with the program from its humble beginning, finished with an overall winning record of 26–21, including 20–6 over 2003 and 2004.

BIGGEST GAME With FAU trailing Middle Tennessee State 19-7 with six minutes remaining and the ball on their own 25-yard line in 2003, it looked as though the Owls were going to have to wait for their first victory over a D1-A team. Allen gave his team some hope when he connected with receiver Roosevelt Bynes on a seven-yard TD pass to close the gap to 19-14 with 2:53 remaining. The Owls' defense stuffed MTSU, forcing a punt, but the ball rolled out on FAU's 2-yard line. With the clock ticking down and the ball on FAU's 38-yard line, fourth and nine, Allen bobbled the snap, scrambled left and managed to find Bynes, who dodged a tackler and ran untouched for the winning touchdown as time expired and the FAU

> ## *The win put Florida Atlantic on the map ... Schnellenberger's program was all grown up.*

bench emptied in celebration of its first Division I-A victory.

BIGGEST UPSET Hurricane Frances was bearing down on Florida while FAU played 5,000 miles away in Hawaii, on Sept. 4, 2004. Florida Atlantic pulled off one of the biggest upsets of the year with a 35-28 overtime win against the Rainbow Warriors. Facing fourth-and-11 at the Hawaii 31 with 30 seconds remaining, QB Jared Allen hit tight end Anthony Crissinger-Hill for a touchdown to tie the score at 28. But Hawaii blocked the extra point to force overtime. Doug Parker scored on a seven-yard run to give FAU a 35-28 lead and LB Shomari Earls batted down QB Timmy Chang's fourth-down pass. It's the win that put Florida Atlantic on the college football map and let the nation know Schnellenberger's little program was all grown up.

HEARTBREAKER Looking for its sixth consecutive win to begin the 2004 season, FAU was trailing Louisiana-Monroe 17-13 in the fourth quarter. Allen was intercepted twice in the final nine minutes of the game, first at the Monroe 5-yard line and then, in the final minute, in the Monroe end zone. Allen finished with 260 yards passing, but his three

RECORDS

RUSHING YARDS

	GAME
147	Daveon Barron vs. Morris Brown, Nov. 9, 2002 (25 att.)
	SEASON
896	Doug Parker, 2004 (227 att.)
	CAREER
1,981	Doug Parker, 2001, 2003-04 (519 att.)

PASSING YARDS

	GAME
352	Jared Allen vs. Central Florida, Sept. 13, 2003 (26 of 40)
	SEASON
3,003	Jared Allen, 2003 (218 of 346)
	CAREER
8,100	Jared Allen, 2001-04 (570 of 1,003)

RECEIVING YARDS

	GAME
183	Anthony Crissinger-Hill vs. Hawaii, Sept. 4, 2004 (15 rec.)
	SEASON
1,134	Anthony Crissinger-Hill, 2003 (74 rec.)
	CAREER
2,071	Anthony Crissinger-Hill, 2001, 2003-04 (136 rec.)

POINTS

	GAME
24	Doug Parker vs. Jacksonville, Oct. 13, 2001 (4 TDs)
	SEASON
90	Mark Myers, 2004 (20 FGs, 30 PATs)
	CAREER
233	Mark Myers, 2001-04 (44 FGs, 101 PATs)

CONSENSUS ALL-AMERICANS

2003	Anthony Crissinger-Hill, TE

costly interceptions jolted the Owls back to reality after a sensational start to their season.

STADIUM Lockhart Stadium, a former high school field renovated for the now defunct Miami Fusion of Major League Soccer, is home to the Owls, though its capacity is just 20,000. When the Owls are granted full-fledged status in 2005, FAU will have the smallest stadium in Division I-A. The school had earlier proposed a 42,000-seat domed stadium on campus, but hasn't yet been able to raise the money to begin construction.

RIVAL Three meetings and three wins over Florida International, its rival just 55 miles to the south. The schools are bound together by parallel attempts to join the world of big-time college football. Since 2002, a win in the series has the added satisfaction of bringing with it the Don Shula Trophy, signifying the coaching legend's ties to coaches at both schools (Schnellenberger was a Shula assistant in the 1960s and 1970s; Florida International coach Don Strock played for Shula in the 1970s and 1980s). "Don Shula is a legend who has achieved so very much for the game of football in South Florida and the nation," said Schnellenberger before his team won the trophy for the first time. "By lending his name to this award he continues to give back to the South Florida football community. It is not very often that two start-up programs would have such wonderful support from a person of Don Shula's stature. As both universities are working to establish football traditions, Coach Shula's trophy will serve as a symbol of inspiration." Schnellenberger's Owls have the upper perch for now.

NICKNAME The National Audubon Society declared FAU's campus a sanctuary for the burrowing owl in 1971. The school adopted the nickname in 1981, when it started fielding athletic teams that competed in the NAIA.

UNIFORM The team sports a white helmet with "FAU" in block letters on either side. The uniforms feature blue jerseys and white pants, with red, white and blue trim. "The best uniforms I ever designed," said Schnellenberger.

QUIRK Keeping a D-1A football program alive is expensive. FAU students pay among the highest sport fees in the state. The average full-time student paid $11.75 a credit or $282 a year based on a 24-credit enrollment in 2004. Compare that with University of Florida students, who pay $1.90 per credit yet enjoy a tradition-rich football program. FAU expects to lose $1.7 million on sports in 2005, mainly due to the burgeoning football program.

LORE FAU's first practice on Aug. 28, 2000, took place inside the gymnasium at Palm Beach Country Club due to inclement weather. More than 160 students tried out for the team on the first day.

QUOTE "I think there have been three really, really outstanding, great coaching jobs in the history of college football. One of them is what Bill Snyder did at Kansas State to take that program from one of the worst in the nation to one of the best. The second is what George Welsh did at Navy and Virginia. The last one is Howard Schnellenberger taking a school without football and doing what he has done in a four-year period."—ESPN College GameDay analyst Lee Corso, quoted in the St. Petersburg Times, Nov. 30, 2004

FLORIDA ATLANTIC ALL-TIME SCORES

WIN/LOSS PERCENTAGE SINCE 2001

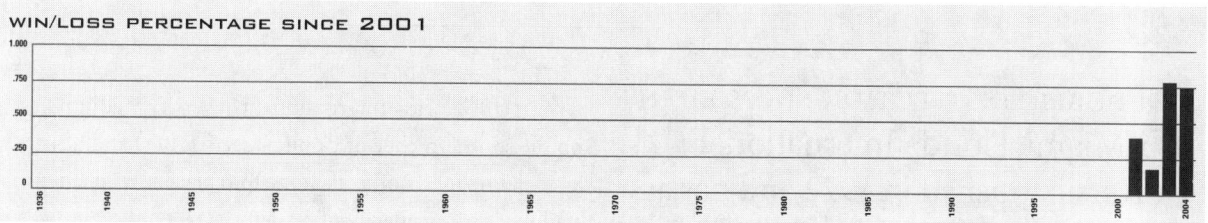

	2001-04
	DIVISION 1-AA INDEPENDENT

HOWARD SCHNELLENBERGER	
2001-04 (.553)	26-21

2001 4-6

S1		Slippery Rock	7	30
S8	●	at Bethune- Cookman	31	28
S22	●	Marist	31	9
O6		at Drake	7	31
O13	●	Jacksonville	35	12
O20		Saint Mary's-Cal	10	24
O27		Saint Peter's	0	19
N3		at Gardner-Webb	19	35
N10		Eastern Illinois	10	38
N17	●	SUNY-Albany	27	9

2002 2-9

A29		at South Florida	10	51
S7		Bethune-Cookman	17	30
S14		at James Madison	13	16
S21		at Eastern Kentucky	6	22
O5		at Nicholls St.	22	33
O12		Youngstown St.	17	24
O26		at Troy State	6	21
N2		at Connecticut	14	61
N9	●	Morris Brown	34	13
N16		at Eastern Illinois	6	47
N23	●	Florida International	31	21

2003 11-3

A28	●	at Middle Tennessee	20	19
S6		Valdosta St.	17	45
S13		at Central Florida	29	33
S20	●	at Youngstown St.	13	6
S27	●	at Illinois St.	28	10
O4	●	Texas St.	27	14
O11	●	Nicholls St.	31	23
O18	●	No. Colorado	21	19
N1	●	Gardner-Webb	31	26
N15	●	Siena	51	3
N22	●	at Florida International	32	23
DIVISION 1-AA PLAYOFFS				
N29	●	at Bethune- Cookman	32	24
D6	●	at No. Arizona	48	25
D13		Colgate	24	36

2004 9-3

S4	●	at Hawaii	35	28
S11	●	at NorthTexas	20	13
S18	●	at Middle Tennessee	27	20
O9	●	at Texas St.	20	13
O16	●	at No. Colorado	39	24
O23		La. Monroe	13	17
O30	●	at Florida A&M	38	8
N6		at Troy State	6	24
N13		New Mexico State	7	35
N20	●	Illinois St.	28	0
N27	●	Edward Waters	49	15
D4	●	Florida International	17	10

f Forfeit † Game Later Forfieted # Disputed Victor * Disputed Score || Designated Conference Game |2 Counted Twice in Conference Standings

FLORIDA INTERNATIONAL

BY CHRIS PEPUS

A PUBLIC INSTITUTION LOCATED IN Miami, Florida International University opened in 1972 and has an enrollment of 29,000. Inspired by the national prominence of the football programs at Florida, Florida State and Miami, as well as by the wealth of high school talent in its home state, FIU

started playing intercollegiate football in 2002. The Golden Panthers posted a 5–6 mark in their inaugural season, but fell to 2–10 in their second campaign. Nevertheless, the school announced in December 2003 that the program would move from Division I-AA to I-A and join the Sun Belt Conference. In 2004, Florida International played three Sun Belt opponents (Louisiana-Lafayette, Louisiana-Monroe and New Mexico State) and finished with a 3–7 mark. In 2005, FIU plays a full Sun Belt Conference schedule.

TRADITION Every year, Florida International plays cross-state rival Florida Atlantic for the Don Shula Award, named after the Dolphins' famed head coach, still a legend in South Florida.

STADIUM Florida International University Stadium lies on the southern edge of campus, seats 17,000 and has artificial turf. FIU officials hope to replace it with a new stadium with a capacity of 30,000.

BEST PLAYER Josh Padrick of Merritt Island, Fla., was a freshman in 2003 but became the starting quarterback after Jamie Burke was knocked out of the lineup by injury in the season's first game. Padrick threw for 2,493 yards and 12 touchdowns in 2003, a performance that garnered team MVP honors. While he nearly matched those numbers in 2004, the FIU MVP was running back Rashod Smith, who became the first Golden Panther to exceed the single-season 1,000-yard rushing mark, carrying for 1,133 yards and 12 touchdowns.

COACH One of the more famous backup quarterbacks in NFL history, Don Strock is best known for leading the Miami Dolphins back from a 24-0 deficit against the San Diego Chargers in a hard-fought 1982 AFC playoff game. (The Chargers won in overtime, 41–38.) Before taking the job as Florida International's first coach, Strock held head coaching positions in the Arena League. He also served as quarterbacks coach for the Baltimore Ravens

---

PROFILE

Florida International University
Miami, Fla.
Founded: 1965
Enrollment: 29,000
Colors: Blue and Gold
Nickname: Golden Panthers
Stadium: Florida International University Stadium
    Opened in 1995
    AstroPlay: 17,000 capacity
First football game: 2002
All-time record: 10–23
Website: www.fiusports.com/football

THE BEST OF TIMES

The Golden Panthers went 5–2 at home during their inaugural season in 2002.

THE WORST OF TIMES

Florida International lost its first seven games in 2003 en route to a 2–10 record. The program did not record a road victory until its third season.

CONFERENCE

FIU will play its first full SBC schedule in 2005.

DISTINGUISHED ALUMNI

Andy Garcia, actor; Tayna Lawrence, Olympic medalist; Mike Lowell, baseball player; Allen Susser, celebrity chef

FIGHT SONG

FIU FIGHT SONG
From the green fields of Tamiami,
To the north shores of Biscayne Bay,
Here's the place where we can gather
Where Golden Panthers hunt their prey.
Anyone who tries to defeat us,
Better think twice and stand aside.
Bring them here with their fear to Miami,
And when they come
we'll show our panther pride.
Golden Panthers see the paw, we will fight
you'll feel the claw.
Let's go Panthers, gold and blue, fight for FIU!

FAU is a natural measuring stick for the progress of the FIU program.

from 1996 to 1998. Unsurprisingly, Strock's Golden Panther teams have featured strong passing attacks; the 2004 unit averaged 246 pass yards per game. "I couldn't be happier. We have a tremendous opportunity to build this program from the ground up, and we're going to do it right," said Strock at the press conference announcing his appointment in 2000. "I'm eager to put my playing and coaching experience at the collegiate and professional levels to work here, developing a program that FIU's students, alumni, faculty and staff can all be proud of."

BEST TEAM The 2002 squad won its first three home games en route to a 5–6 finish. A highlight of the season was a 27-3 home victory over St. Peter's in the program's inaugural game.

BIGGEST GAME On Oct. 2, 2004, Florida International played host to a Division I-A opponent for the first time when future Sun Belt rival Louisiana-Lafayette visited. Lafayette needed nine points in the final 25 seconds to prevail, 43-34.

BIGGEST UPSET In 2003, a 1–7 Golden Panther team surprised 4–4 Jacksonville University with a 55-12 win at home. FIU rushed for 391 yards and four touchdowns in a pouring rainstorm.

NICKNAME At first, Florida International teams were known as the Sunblazers, but the school administration changed the nickname to Golden Panthers in 1987. In preparation for the opening of the football program, the university commissioned a new, more aggressive-looking panther for the athletic department's official seal.

RIVAL Though FIU's ultimate goal would be to challenge the more famous college team in its hometown, its biggest rival is Boca Raton's Florida Atlantic University. FAU is also in the process of moving up to Division I-A and the Sun Belt Conference, and is therefore a natural measuring stick for the progress of the Golden Panthers program. Though FIU has an 0–3 record against Howard Schnellenberger's fast-rising Florida Atlantic squad, the games have been close and intense. In 2003, the 2–9 Golden Panthers scared 8–2 FAU by opening up a 17-point

RECORDS

RUSHING YARDS

GAME
262 — Rashod Smith vs. Jacksonville, Oct. 31, 2002 (21 att.)

SEASON
1,133 — Rashod Smith, 2004 (230 att.)

CAREER
2,195 — Rashod Smith, 2002-04 (424 att.)

PASSING YARDS

GAME
370 — Josh Padrick vs. Georgia Southern, Oct. 4, 2003 (24 of 48)

SEASON
2,493 — Josh Padrick, 2003 (183 for 367)

CAREER
4,762 — Josh Padrick, 2003-04 (386 for 725)

RECEIVING YARDS

GAME
192 — Harold Leath vs. Georgia Southern, Oct. 4, 2003 (8 rec.)

SEASON
890 — Cory McKinney, 2002 (42 rec.)

CAREER
2,193 — Cory McKinney, 2002-04 (141 rec.)

POINTS

GAME
24 — Rashod Smith vs. New Mexico State, Oct. 30, 2004 (4 TDs)

SEASON
72 — Rashod Smith, 2004 (12 TDs)

CAREER
168 — Adam Moss, 2002-04 (30 FGs, 78 PATs)

CONSENSUS ALL-AMERICANS

None

lead before succumbing, 32-23. In 2004, Florida Atlantic won again 17-10.

UNIFORM The Golden Panthers wear blue home jerseys with white-and-gold piping on the shoulders. The pants are gold and the helmets are blue with "FIU" in white letters with gold trim on either side. The initials on the helmet form a slight arch.

QUOTE "Nothing good happens when you go half speed. That philosophy is sound, and that's the way I believe in doing things."—Coach Don Strock

FLORIDA INTERNATIONAL ALL-TIME SCORES

WIN/LOSS PERCENTAGE SINCE 2002

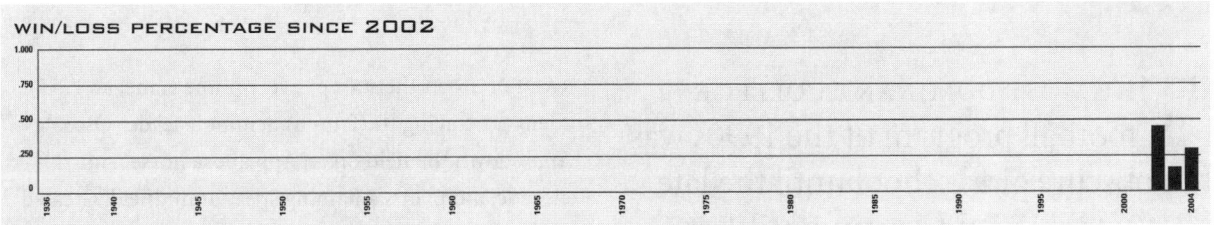

	2001-04
	DIVISION 1-AA INDEPENDENT
	DON STROCK
2002-04 (.303)	10-23

2002   5-6

A29	●	Saint Peter's	27	3
S7		at Elon	22	23
S14	●	Butler	42	0
S21		at Bethune-Cookman	0	31
S28	●	Georgetown	27	2
O12		at Western Kentucky	7	56
O19		Maine	7	33
O26		Gardner-Webb	14	17
O31	●	Jacksonville	39	6
N9	●	SUNY-Albany	35	26
N23		at Florida Atlantic	21	31

2003   2-10

S6		at Indiana St.	10	13
S13		at Maine	14	24
S20		Bethune-Cookman	14	24
S27		Carson-Newman	33	55
O4		at Georgia Southern	35	37
O9		Stephen F. Austin	13	35
O18		at Troy State	10	21
O25	●	Holy Cross	34	23
O30	●	Jacksonville	55	12
N8		at La. Lafayette	10	43
N15		at Gardner-Webb	19	22
N22		Florida Atlantic	23	32

2004   3-7

S11	●	at Youngstown St.	22	16
O2		La. Lafayette	34	43
O9	●	at Stephen F. Austin	31	24
O16		at La. Monroe	20	28
O23		McNeese State	27	30
O30		at New Mexico State	31	56
N13		Georgia Southern	32	53
N20		Western Kentucky	14	35
N27	●	Florida A&M	40	23
D4		at Florida Atlantic	10	17

ƒ Forfeit † Game Later Forfieted # Disputed Victor * Disputed Score || Designated Conference Game |2 Counted Twice in Conference Standings

FLORIDA STATE

BY BOB HARIG

THE MOST DOMINANT COLLEGE football program of the 1990s was an obscure girls' school until the late 1940s, didn't field a team until 1947 and raised doubts about its viability as recently as the mid-1970s. Florida State enjoyed fleeting success in the 1960s, when Bill Peterson led the Seminoles to four bowl games and their first win over Florida. But by the time Bobby Bowden arrived in 1976, the program was in shambles, having gone 4–29 over the previous three seasons. "I could think of only two jobs that would have been worse," Bowden wrote in *Bound for Glory,* his autobiography. "Being elected mayor of Atlanta shortly after Sherman left town or being the general who volunteers to replace George Custer during the last siege of the Little Big Horn."

The charismatic, folksy Bowden built a juggernaut by recruiting in his fertile Florida backyard, instituting a wide-open offense and playing big-name opponents on the road, where the Seminoles became giant-killers and, ultimately, giants themselves.

TRADITION At the start of every home game, an FSU student portraying the famous Seminole leader Osceola charges down the field on an Appaloosa horse named Renegade and plants a flaming spear at midfield. Created by 1965 FSU graduate Bill Durham, the routine didn't take off until Bowden embraced it during his tenure. Durham received approval from the Seminole Tribe of Florida for the portrayal of Osceola, and the tradition began at the home opener of the 1978 season against Oklahoma State. Another essential part of FSU games—to the chagrin of opponents—is the war chant, in which fans make chopping motions with their arms in unison. During the 1960s, FSU's Marching Chiefs band would chant the melody of a popular FSU cheer, but the present version of the chant is traced to a 1984 game against Auburn, where it apparently began randomly and grew into a stadium-wide happening by 1986.

The retirement, or permanent sealing, of lockers began after Deion Sanders' senior season in 1988 as a way to add more tradition to the locker room. For a locker to be retired, a player must be a two-time consensus All-American or Heisman Trophy winner. Sanders' glass-encased locker is joined by those of Ron Simmons, Marvin Jones, Derrick Brooks, Sebastian

---

Janikowski, Peter Warrick and Heisman Trophy- winners Charlie Ward and Chris Weinke. The lockers are sealed with the player's final home-game uniform and gear intact.

BEST PLAYER Ward and Weinke won Heismans, but the greatest (and most flamboyant) Seminole was Sanders, a cornerback who might have won the award were it not for an arguable bias against defensive players. "Neon" Deion, who lettered in three sports, was a game-changing presence. His smothering coverage and athleticism were reflected not only in his 14 career interceptions, but also by his effectively rendering half the field off-limits to opposing quarterbacks. As a punt returner, he led the nation in 1988, averaging a scintillating 15.2 yards per return. As a self-promoter, he was unmatched, reveling in his "Prime Time" nickname and brashly calling out opponents. "When those lights go on, it's prime time for

> *"When those lights go on, it's prime time for me. It's like Jekyll and Hyde. When I have to put on a show, I put on a show," said Deion Sanders, FSU's greatest player.*

me," he said. "It's like Jekyll and Hyde. When I have to put on a show, I put on a show." Sanders went on to be a first-round pick of the Atlanta Falcons, and he also played major league baseball. "I'm not just any defensive back," said Sanders, stumping for a big contract. "I'm three players in one. I'm a punt returner, the best cornerback you'll ever get and an entertainer."

BEST COACH In 2002, Bowden passed his coaching idol, Paul "Bear" Bryant, registering his 324th career victory—and in 2003, with 339 wins, he surpassed Joe Paterno as the all-time leader in Division I-A. He won national titles in 1993 and 1999, but his greatness is better illuminated by his remarkable consistency: he posted 14 consecutive seasons of at least 10 victories from 1987 through 2000 and won or shared the ACC title nine straight years from 1992 through 2000. He also boasted a streak of

RECORDS

RUSHING YARDS

GAME	
322	Greg Allen vs. Western Carolina, Oct. 31, 1981 (32 att.)
SEASON	
1,242	Warrick Dunn, 1995 (166 att.)
CAREER	
3,959	Warrick Dunn, 1993-96 (575 att.)

PASSING YARDS

GAME	
536	Chris Weinke vs. Duke, Oct. 14, 2000 (37 of 47)
SEASON	
4,167	Chris Weinke, 2000 (266 of 431)
CAREER	
9,839	Chris Weinke, 1997-2000 (650 of 1,107)

RECEIVING YARDS

GAME	
260	Ron Sellers vs. Wake Forest, Nov. 23, 1968 (14 rec.)
SEASON	
1,496	Ron Sellers, 1968 (86 rec.)
CAREER	
3,598	Ron Sellers, 1966-68 (212 rec.)

POINTS

GAME	
30	Ron Sellers vs. Wake Forest, Nov. 23, 1968 (5 TDs)
SEASON	
126	Greg Allen, 1982 (21 TDs)
CAREER	
393	Derek Schmidt, 1984-87 (73 FGs, 174 PATs)

CONSENSUS ALL-AMERICANS

1951	Williams Dawkins, OG
1964	Fred Biletnikoff, E
1967	Ron Sellers, FL
1979-80	Ron Simmons, NG
1983	Greg Allen, TB
1985	Jamie Dukes, OG
1987-88	Deion Sanders, CB
1989	LeRoy Butler, CB
1991-92	Marvin Jones, LB
1991	Terrell Buckley, CB
1993	Charlie Ward, QB
1993-94	Derrick Brooks, LB
1993	Corey Sawyer, CB
1994	Clifton Abraham, CB
1995	Clay Shiver, C
1996	Peter Boulware, DE
1996	Reinard Wilson, DE
1997	Sam Cowart, LB
1997	Andre Wadsworth, DE
1998-99	Sebastian Janikowski, K
1998-99	Peter Warrick, WR
1999	Jason Whitaker, OG
1999	Corey Simon, DT
2000	Marvin Minnis, FL
2000	Jamal Reynolds, DE
2000	Tay Cody, CB
2003-04	Alex Barron, OL

14 consecutive bowls without a defeat. Perhaps most impressively, from 1987 through 2000, Bowden's teams finished in the Top 5 in the national polls every year.

Born in Birmingham, Ala., in 1929, Bowden played football at small Howard College (now Samford University) and dreamed of one day coaching at Auburn or Alabama. Instead, he began coaching at his alma mater, and then took assistant positions at Florida State and West Virginia, where in 1970 he became the head coach. Bowden, who was hanged in effigy at West Virginia during his only losing season there in 1974, came to FSU in 1976. "Every job I've gotten has led to something better. But I had no idea this was a good job," Bowden said of coaching at FSU. "When I came here, I thought this was the stepping stone to something else. Then things just worked out here."

Always relishing the role of underdog, Bowden took the Seminoles on the road to build their national reputation. They won at Nebraska in 1980 and played five straight road games in 1981—against Nebraska, Ohio State, Notre Dame, Pittsburgh and LSU—going 3–2. Reverses, flea-flickers, laterals and "rooskies" all became part of the offensive arsenal. By the late 1980s, the Seminoles were rarely underdogs. From the 1982 Gator Bowl through the 1996 Orange Bowl—a span of 14 games—the Seminoles were undefeated in bowls, with 13 victories and a tie. During that time, they had an 11-game winning streak in bowl games.

BEST TEAM For all of his success, Bowden managed just one perfect season. It came in 1999, when the Seminoles went 12–0, including a 46-29 victory over Virginia Tech in the Sugar Bowl to win the national championship. The team featured quarterback Chris Weinke, who would win the Heisman the following year, and electrifying receiver Peter Warrick, the Sugar Bowl's Most Outstanding Player, who might have received consideration for the Heisman before a midseason arrest cost him two games. The

ALL-TIME TEAM	
Selected by Bob Harig of the St. Petersburg Times, after consulting with Florida State players, coaches and athletic department administrators and alumni.	
OFFENSE	
1982-85	Jamie Dukes, OG
1996-99	Jason Whitaker, OG
1994-97	Tra Thomas, OT
2002-04	Alex Barron, OT
1992-95	Clay Shiver, C
1984-87	Pat Carter, TE
1962-64	Fred Biletnikoff, WR
1966-68	Ron Sellers, WR
1996-99	Peter Warrick, SE
1989, '91-93	Charlie Ward, QB
1981-84	Greg Allen, RB
1993-96	Warrick Dunn, RB
1991-93	William Floyd, FB
1997-99	Sebastian Janikowski, PK
DEFENSE	
1992-94	Derrick Alexander, DE
1994-96	Peter Boulware, DE
1948-1949	Hugh Adams, DT
1996-99	Corey Simon, DT
1977-80	Ron Simmons, NG
1984-87	Paul McGowan, LB
1990-92	Marvin Jones, LB
1991-94	Derrick Brooks, LB
1985-88	Deion Sanders, CB
1989-91	Terrell Buckley, CB
1985-88	Stan Shiver, SS
1987-89	LeRoy Butler, FS
1978-81	Rohn Stark, P

Seminoles were the first team to be ranked first wire-to-wire in the Associated Press poll.

BIGGEST GAME Four painful losses to Miami (10-9 in 1980, 26-25 in 1987, 17-16 in 1991 and 19-16 in 1992), including two with crucial missed field goals, cost FSU potential national championship bids. The Seminoles were in danger of losing another in the 1994 Orange Bowl, when Nebraska's Byron Bennett kicked a 27-yard field goal to put the second-ranked and 17-point-underdog Huskers up 16-15 over top-ranked FSU. But Charlie Ward and the offense roared back, and when Scott Bentley's 22-yard field goal cleared the uprights with 21 seconds remaining, there was a sense of justice among the FSU faithful. An FSU kicker had converted—on Miami's home field, no less—apparently giving the Seminoles their first national title.

Not so fast. Nebraska QB Tommie Frazier completed a 29-yard pass to Trumane Bell in FSU territory as time expired, but just as FSU was celebrating its victory, officials ruled that NU had called a timeout with one second left. With the national title on the line, Nebraska's Bennett attempted a 45-yard field goal that went wide left. Finally, Florida State had won its national championship.

BIGGEST UPSET Florida State's 18-14 victory at Nebraska in 1980 put the Seminoles on the map and solidified Bowden's reputation as a coach willing to go on the road and play anyone. The Seminoles finished 10–2 that season.

HEARTBREAKER The subject is of considerable debate in Seminoles land. How about a 10-9 loss to Miami in 1980, when FSU failed on a two-point conversion late in the game for its only loss of the regular season? How about a 26-25 loss to Miami in 1987, again on a failed two-point conversion, again the only loss of the regular season? Then there are the Wide Right games of 1991, 1992 and 2000. The Seminoles missed field goals in the

waning seconds of all three Miami games to again lose to the Hurricanes. However, many agree that the 17-16 loss to Miami in Tallahassee in 1991 was most searing. The Seminoles had been ranked No. 1 all season, were 10–0 and were leading most of the game before falling behind by a point. They drove into position for the winning points, only to see walk-on kicker Gerry Thomas miss from 34 yards. The Hurricanes went on to win the national championship. It was the third one-point loss to the Hurricanes for Bowden, and his sixth defeat in seven years to UM. After the game, Bowden said, "On my tombstone, they'll put: 'But he played Miami.'"

CONTROVERSY Florida State's 22-19 loss to Florida in 1966 is a game the Seminoles still believe they won. Late in the game, FSU wide receiver Lane Fenner caught what appeared to be the go-ahead touchdown pass—but officials ruled that he was out of bounds on the sideline, short of the end zone. Printed photographs, however, showed that Fenner did, indeed, have a foot inbounds and that the catch should have stood.

STADIUM Named after a former FSU president, Doak Campbell Stadium had a capacity of 15,000 when it opened in 1950. For many years, it was derisively referred to as the Erector Set, because its steel girders were visible from the outside. It has now grown to more than 80,000 seats and a brick facade surrounds the girders, matching the architectural design of most of the buildings on the FSU campus. The north end zone seating, which consisted of wooden bleachers until the 1994 season, is topped by the coaches' offices. Bowden's teams lost just 18 home games in 26 years through 2001, the season a 52-game home unbeaten streak was snapped.

RIVAL Although the football game dates to just 1958, the Florida Gators are FSU's chief rival, the team the Seminoles have played the most in their relatively brief history. FSU perhaps initially suffered from an inferiority complex, which ultimately enhanced the rivalry. After starting a football program in 1947, FSU could not get Florida to play. The state legislature threatened to write a law mandating the teams play, but Florida yielded before it came to that. The agreement came with the stipulation that the first six games were to be played in Gainesville. FSU's 3-3 tie in 1961 was hailed as a victory, though the first win didn't come until 1964. Before Bowden arrived at FSU in 1976, the Seminoles had won just twice against the

Gators. Bowden turned the tables on the rivalry in favor of the Noles. Twice the schools met in the Sugar Bowl, one a 1995 FSU victory and the other a 1997 Florida win for the national championship.

NICKNAME After just two games in their inaugural season of 1947, calls for a nickname went out. The *Florida Flambeau* reported that a student poll preferred the nickname Seminoles over other contenders such as Statesmen, Rebels, Tarpons, Fighting Warriors and Crackers. In the 1950s, a pair of undergraduates dressed in Native American costumes joined cheerleaders on the field, which eventually evolved into the tradition of Renegade and Osceola.

UNIFORMS The school colors of garnet and gold were first used on an FSU uniform in a 14-6 loss to Stetson on Sept. 27, 1947. Over the years, the uniform has remained relatively unchanged. The helmet used to have an outline of the state of Florida with the word "State" written across it, but that was changed in the 1970s to the current design featuring feather-bedecked spears. FSU became trendsetters in the Bowden years, with many other schools with gold colors, including Notre Dame, copying the muted gold of Florida State's game pants.

LORE FSU's Sod Cemetery, where turf from other stadiums has been buried in commemoration of many FSU road victories, is next to the practice field. A tombstone above each piece of turf's resting place notes the score and date of the game. The practice began in 1962, when FSU returned from Georgia after an 18-0 victory with a piece of sod from Sanford Stadium. The turf was presented to dean Coyle E. Moore, who founded the tradition of the sod game. At first, FSU took only grass from an opponent's stadium when the Seminoles won by upset on the road. Over time, the criteria changed: it is still considered a sod game when FSU is an underdog on the road, but now all bowl games are considered sod games, as are all big road games, no matter who is favored. (If the game is played on artificial turf, an attempt is made to bring back some artifact from that stadium.)

QUOTE "At West Virginia, they sold bumper stickers that said BEAT PITT. When I came to Florida State, they sold bumper stickers that said BEAT ANYBODY."

— Bobby Bowden

FLORIDA STATE ALL-TIME SCORES

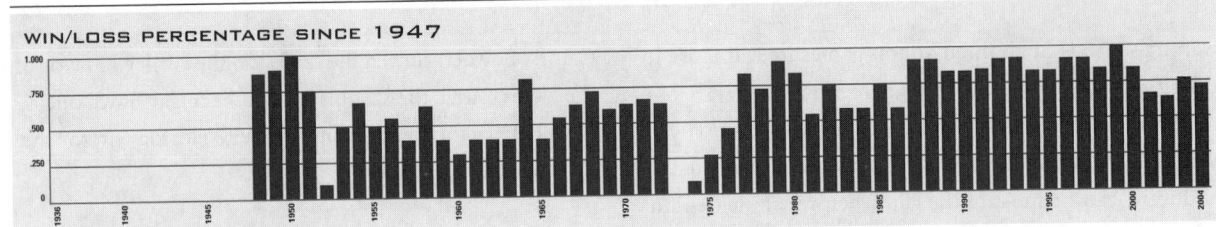

WIN/LOSS PERCENTAGE SINCE 1947

ED WILLIAMSON
1947 (.000)   0-5

1947   0-5-0
S27		Stetson	6	14
O4		at Cumberland	0	6
O11		Tennessee Tech	6	27
O18		Troy State	6	36
O25		Jacksonville St.	0	7

DON VELLER
1948-52 (.716)   31-12-1

1948   7-1-0
S24	•	Cumberland	30	0
O9	•	at Erskine	6	14
O16	•	at Millsaps	7	6
O23	•	at Stetson	18	7
O30	•	Mississippi Coll.	26	6
N6	•	Livingston St.	12	6
N13	•	at Troy State	20	13
N20	•	Tampa	33	12

1949   9-1-0
S24	•	Whiting Field	74	0
O1	•	at Mississippi Coll.	33	12
O8	•	Erskine	26	7
O15	•	at Sewanee	6	0
O22	•	Stetson	33	14
O29	•	at Livingston St.	6	13
N5	•	Millsaps	40	0
N12	•	at Tampa	34	7
N19	•	Troy State	20	0
		CIGAR BOWL		
J2	•	Wofford	19	6

1950   8-0-0
S23	•	at Troy State	26	7
S30	•	Randolph Macon	40	7
O7	•	Samford	20	6
O14	•	at Newberry	24	0
O21	•	Sewanee	14	8
O28	•	at Stetson	27	7
N4	•	Mississippi Coll.	33	0
N11	•	Tampa	35	19

1951   6-2-0
S29	•	Troy State	40	0
O6		at Miami, Fla.	13	35
O13	•	Delta St.	34	0
O20	•	Sul Ross St.	35	13
O27	•	Stetson	13	10
N3	•	at Jacksonville Navy	39	0
N10	•	Wofford	14	0
N17		Tampa	6	14

1952   1-8-1
S27	•	Louisiana Tech	13	32
O4	•	Louisville	14	41
O11	•	VMI	7	28
O25	•	at North Carolina St.	7	13
N1	=	Stetson *UNK*	6	6
N8	•	Southern Miss	21	50
N15	•	Furman	0	9
N22	•	at Georgia Tech	0	30
N29	•	at Wofford	27	13
D6		Tampa	6	39

TOM NUGENT
1953-58 (.548)   34-28-1

1953   5-5-0
S25		at Miami, Fla.	0	27
O3	•	Louisville	59	0
O17	•	Abilene Christian	7	20
O24	•	at Louisiana Tech	21	32
O31	•	VMI	12	7
N7		at Southern Miss	0	21
N14		Furman	7	14
N21	•	Stetson	13	6
N28	•	North Carolina St.	23	13
D5	•	at Tampa	41	6

1954   8-4-0
S18		Georgia	0	14
S25		Abilene Christian	0	13
O2	•	at Louisville	47	6
O9	•	Villanova	52	13
O16	•	at North Carolina St.	13	7
O23		at Auburn	0	33
O30	•	VMI *Lyn*	33	19
N13	•	Furman	33	14
N20	•	at Stetson	47	6
N27	•	Southern Miss	19	18
D4	•	at Tampa	13	0
		SUN BOWL		
J1		Texas El Paso	20	47

1955   5-5-0
S17	•	North Carolina St.	7	0
S30	•	at Miami, Fla.	0	34
O8	•	Virginia Tech	20	24
O15	•	Georgia	14	47
O22	•	at Georgia Tech	0	34
N5	•	Villanova	16	13
N11	•	at Furman	19	6
N19	•	Citadel	39	0
N25	•	at Southern Miss	6	21
D3	•	at Tampa	26	7

1956   5-4-1
S22	•	Ohio U.	47	7
S29		at Georgia	0	3
O6		Virginia Tech	7	20
O13	•	at North Carolina St.	14	0
O20	=	Wake Forest	14	14
O27	•	Villanova *Phil*	20	13
N2		at Miami, Fla.	7	20
N10	•	Furman	42	7
N17	•	Southern Miss	20	19
N24		at Auburn	7	13

1957   4-6-0
S21	•	Furman	27	7
S28		at Boston College	7	20
O5		Villanova *Phil*	7	21
O12		North Carolina St.	0	7
O19	•	Abilene Christian	34	7
O26	•	Virginia Tech	20	7
N8		Miami, Fla.	13	40
N16		at Southern Miss	0	20
N23		Auburn	7	29
N30	•	at Tampa	21	7

1958   7-4-0
S13	•	Tennessee Tech	22	7
S20	•	Furman	42	6
S26		at Georgia Tech	3	17
O4	•	Wake Forest	27	24
O11	•	Georgia *JacF*	13	28
O18	•	Virginia Tech	28	0
O25	•	at Tennessee	10	0
N1	•	Tampa	43	0
N7	•	at Miami, Fla.	17	6
N22	•	at Florida	7	21
		BLUEGRASS BOWL		
D13		Oklahoma State	6	15

PERRY MOSS
1959 (.400)   4-6

1959   4-6-0
S19		Wake Forest	20	22
S26	•	Citadel	47	6
O3		Miami, Fla.	6	7
O10	•	at Virginia Tech	7	6
O17		at Memphis	6	16
O24	•	Richmond	22	6
O31		at Georgia	0	42
N14		William & Mary	0	9
N21	•	at Florida	8	18
N28	•	Tampa	33	0

BILL PETERSON
1960-70 (.587)   62-42-11

1960   3-6-1
S17	•	Richmond	28	0
S24		at Florida	0	3
O1	•	Wake Forest	14	6
O8	=	at Citadel	0	0
O15		Southern Miss *MBl*	13	15
O22	•	William & Mary	22	0
O29		Kentucky	0	23
N4		at Miami, Fla.	7	25
N12		Houston	6	7
N19		at Auburn	21	57

1961   4-5-1
S16	•	George Washington	15	7
S30	=	at Florida	3	3
O7		at Mississippi	0	33
O14	•	Georgia	3	0
O21	•	Richmond	13	7
O28		at Virginia Tech	7	10
N4		at Kentucky	0	20
N11	•	Southern Miss	44	8
N18		Southern Miss	0	12
N25		at Houston	8	28

1962   4-3-3
S15	•	Citadel	49	0
S22	=	at Kentucky	0	0
S29	•	Furman	42	0
O5		at Miami, Fla.	6	7
O20	•	at Georgia	18	0
O27	•	Virginia Tech	20	7
N3		Houston	0	7
N10	=	at Georgia Tech	14	14
N17		at Florida	7	20
N24	=	at Auburn	14	14

1963   4-5-1
S20	•	Miami, Fla.	24	0
S28		TCU	0	13
O12	•	Wake Forest	35	0
O19	=	Southern Miss *MBl*	0	0
O26		Virginia Tech	23	31
N2	•	Furman	49	6
N9		at Georgia Tech	7	15
N16	•	North Carolina St.	14	0
N23		at Auburn	15	21
N30		at Florida	0	7

1964   9-1-1
S19	•	at Miami, Fla.	14	0
S26	•	at TCU	10	0
O3	•	New Mexico St.	36	0
O10	•	Kentucky	48	6
O17	•	at Georgia	17	14
O24	•	at Virginia Tech	11	20
O31	•	Southern Miss	34	0
N7	=	at Houston	13	13
N14	•	North Carolina St.	28	6
N21	•	Florida	16	7
		GATOR BOWL		
J2	•	Oklahoma	36	19

1965   4-5-1
S25		at TCU	3	7
O2	•	Baylor	9	7
O9		at Kentucky	24	26
O16	•	Georgia	10	3
O23		at Alabama	0	21
O30	•	Virginia Tech	7	6
N6	•	Wake Forest	35	0
N13	•	at North Carolina St.	0	3
N20	=	Houston	16	16
N27		at Florida	17	30

1966   6-5-0
S17		Houston	13	21
S24	•	at Miami, Fla.	23	20
O8		Florida	19	22
O15	•	at Texas Tech	42	33
O22	•	Mississippi State	10	0
O29	•	at Virginia Tech	21	23
N5	•	at South Carolina	32	10
N12	•	at Syracuse	21	37
N19	•	Wake Forest	28	0
N26	•	Maryland	45	21
		SUN BOWL		
D24		Wyoming	20	28

1967   7-2-2
S15		at Houston	13	33
S23	=	Alabama *Birm*	37	37
S30		North Carolina St.	10	20
O7	•	at Texas A&M	19	18
O14	•	South Carolina	17	0
O21	•	Texas Tech	28	12
O28	•	Mississippi State	24	12
N4	•	at Memphis	26	7
N11	•	Virginia Tech	38	15
N25	•	at Florida	21	16
		GATOR BOWL		
D30		Penn State	17	17

1968   8-3-0
S21	•	at Maryland	24	14
S28	•	Florida	3	9
O5	•	Texas A&M	20	14
O19	•	Memphis	20	10
O26	•	at South Carolina	35	28
N2	•	Virginia Tech	22	40
N9	•	at Mississippi State	27	14
N16	•	at North Carolina St.	48	7
N23	•	Wake Forest	42	24
N29	•	Houston *JacF*	40	20
		PEACH BOWL		
D30		LSU	27	31

1969   6-3-1
S20	•	Wichita St.	24	0
S26	•	at Miami, Fla.	16	14
O4	•	at Florida	6	21
O18	•	at Tulsa	38	20
O25	•	Mississippi State	20	17
N1	•	South Carolina	34	9
N8	=	at Virginia Tech	10	10
N15	•	Memphis	26	28
N22	•	North Carolina St.	33	22
N29		at Houston	13	41

1970   7-4-0
S12	•	Louisville	9	7
S19	•	at Georgia Tech	13	23
S26	•	Wake Forest	19	14
O10	•	Florida	27	38
O17	•	at Memphis	12	16
O24	•	at South Carolina	21	13
O30	•	at Miami, Fla.	27	3
N7	•	Clemson	38	13
N14	•	Virginia Tech	34	8
N21	•	Kansas State	33	7
N26	•	Houston *Tam*	21	53

LARRY JONES
1971-73 (.441)   15-19

1971   8-4-0

S11	●	Southern Miss [MBL]	24 9
S18	●	at Miami, Fla.	20 17
S25	●	Kansas	30 7
O2	●	at Virginia Tech	17 3
O9	●	Mississippi State	27 9
O16		at Florida	15 17
O23	●	South Carolina	49 18
O30		at Houston	7 14
N13		at Georgia Tech	6 12
N20	●	Tulsa	45 10
N27	●	Pittsburgh	31 13
FIESTA BOWL			
D27		Arizona State	38 45

1972   7-4-0

S9	●	at Pittsburgh	19 7
S16	●	at Miami, Fla.	37 14
S23	●	Virginia Tech	27 15
S30	●	at Kansas	44 22
O7		Florida	13 42
O14	●	Mississippi State [J&M]	25 21
O21	●	Colorado State	37 0
O28		at Auburn	14 27
N4		Houston	27 31
N11	●	Tulsa	23 21
N18		at South Carolina	21 24

1973   0-11-0

S15		at Wake Forest	7 9
S22		Kansas	0 28
S29		Miami, Fla.	10 14
O6		at Baylor	14 21
O13		Mississippi State	12 37
O20		Memphis	10 13
O27		at San Diego State	17 38
N3		at Houston	3 34
N10		at Virginia Tech	13 36
N17		South Carolina	12 52
D1		at Florida	0 49

DARRELL MUDRA
1974-75 (.182)   4-18

1974   1-10-0

S14		Pittsburgh	6 9
S21		Colorado State	7 14
S28		at Kansas	9 40
O5		Baylor	17 21
O12		at Alabama	7 8
O19		Florida	14 24
O26		at Auburn	6 38
N2		at Memphis	14 42
N8	●	at Miami, Fla.	21 14
N16		Virginia Tech	21 56
N23		Houston	8 23

1975   3-8-0

S13		at Texas Tech	20 31
S20	●	Utah State	17 8
S27		Iowa State	6 10
O4		at Georgia Tech	0 30
O11		at Virginia Tech	10 13
O18		at Florida	8 34
O25		Auburn	14 17
N1	●	at Clemson	43 7
N8		Memphis	14 17
N15		Miami, Fla.	22 24
N22	●	at Houston	33 22

BOBBY BOWDEN
1976-Present (.793) 277-71-4

1976   5-6-0

S11		at Memphis	12 21
S18		at Miami, Fla.	0 47
S25	●	at Oklahoma	9 24
O2	●	Kansas State	20 10
O9	●	at Boston College	28 9
O16		Florida	26 33
O23		at Auburn	19 31
O30		Clemson	12 15
N6	●	Southern Miss	30 27
N13	●	at North Texas	21 20
N20	●	Virginia Tech	28 21

1977   10-2-0

S10	●	at Southern Miss	35 6
S17	●	at Kansas State	18 10
S24		Miami, Fla.	17 23
O1	●	at Oklahoma State	25 17
O8	●	Cincinnati	14 0
O22	●	Auburn	24 3
O29	●	North Texas	35 14
N5	●	at Virginia Tech	23 21
N12	●	Memphis	30 9
N19		at San Diego State	16 41
D3	●	at Florida	37 9
TANGERINE BOWL			
D23	●	Texas Tech	40 17

1978   8-3-0

S9	●	at Syracuse	28 0
S16	●	Oklahoma State	38 20
S23	●	at Miami, Fla.	31 21
S30		Houston	21 27
O7	●	Cincinnati	26 21
O14		at Mississippi State	27 55
O21		at Pittsburgh	3 7
O28	●	at Southern Miss	38 16
N11	●	Virginia Tech	24 14
N18	●	Navy	38 6
N25	●	Florida	38 21

1979   11-1-0

S8	●	Southern Miss	17 14
S15	●	Arizona State [TAM]	31 3
S22	●	Miami, Fla.	40 23
S29	●	at Virginia Tech	17 10
O6	●	at Louisville	27 0
O13	●	Mississippi State	17 6
O27	●	at LSU	24 19
N3	●	at Cincinnati	26 21
N10	●	South Carolina	27 7
N17	●	Memphis	66 17
N24	●	at Florida	27 16
ORANGE BOWL			
J1		Oklahoma	7 24

1980   10-2-0

S6	●	at LSU	16 0
S13	●	Louisville	52 0
S20	●	East Carolina	63 7
S27	●	at Miami, Fla.	9 10
O4	●	at Nebraska	18 14
O11	●	Pittsburgh	36 22
O18	●	Boston College	41 7
O25	●	at Memphis	24 3
N1	●	Tulsa	45 2
N8	●	Virginia Tech	31 7
D6	●	Florida	17 13
ORANGE BOWL			
J1		Oklahoma	17 18

1981   6-5-0

S5	●	Louisville	17 0
S12	●	Memphis	10 5
S19		at Nebraska	14 34
O3	●	at Ohio State	36 27
O10	●	at Notre Dame	19 13
O17		at Pittsburgh	14 42
O24	●	at LSU	38 14
O31	●	Western Carolina	56 31
N7		Miami, Fla.	19 27
N14		Southern Miss	14 58
N28		at Florida	3 35

1982   9-3-0

S4	●	Cincinnati	38 31
S18		Pittsburgh	17 37
S25	●	at Southern Miss	24 17
O2	●	at Ohio State	34 17
O9	●	So. Illinois	59 8
O16	●	East Carolina	56 17
O30	●	at Miami, Fla.	24 7
N6	●	at South Carolina	56 26
N13	●	Louisville	49 14
N20		at LSU	21 55
D4		Florida	10 13
GATOR BOWL			
D30	●	West Virginia	31 12

1983   7-5-0

S3	●	East Carolina	47 46
S10	●	at LSU	40 35
S17	●	at Tulane	28 34 †
O1		at Auburn	24 27
O8		at Pittsburgh	16 17
O15	●	Cincinnati	43 17
O20	●	Louisville	51 7
O29	●	at Arizona State	29 26
N5	●	South Carolina	45 30
N12		Miami, Fla.	16 17
D3		at Florida	14 53
PEACH BOWL			
D30	●	North Carolina	28 3

1984   7-3-2

S1	●	East Carolina	48 17
S15	●	at Kansas	42 16
S22	●	at Miami, Fla.	38 3
S29	●	Temple	44 27
O6	=	at Memphis	17 17
O13	●	Auburn	41 42
O20	●	Tulane	27 6
N3	●	at Arizona State	52 44
N10		at South Carolina	26 38
N17	●	U.T. Chattanooga	37 0
D1		Florida	17 27
CITRUS BOWL			
D22	=	Georgia	17 17

1985   9-3-0

A31	●	at Tulane	38 12
S7		at Nebraska	17 13
S21	●	Memphis	19 10
S28	●	Kansas	24 20
O12	●	at Auburn	27 59
O19	●	Tulsa	76 14
O26	●	at North Carolina	20 10
N2		Miami, Fla.	27 35
N9	●	South Carolina	56 14
N16	●	Western Carolina	50 10
N30		at Florida	14 38
GATOR BOWL			
D30	●	Oklahoma State	34 23

1986   7-4-1

A30	●	Toledo	24 0
S6		at Nebraska	17 34
S20	=	North Carolina	10 10
S27		at Michigan	18 20
O11	●	Tulane	54 21
O18	●	Wichita St.	59 3
O25	●	at Louisville	54 18
N1	●	Miami, Fla.	23 41
N8	●	at South Carolina	45 28
N15	●	Southern Miss	49 13
N29		Florida	13 17
ALL-AMERICAN BOWL			
D31	●	Indiana	27 13

1987   11-1-0

S5	●	Texas Tech	40 16
S12	●	at East Carolina	44 3
S19	●	Memphis	41 24
S26	●	at Michigan State	31 3
O3		Miami, Fla.	25 26
O10	●	at Southern Miss	61 10
O17	●	Louisville	32 9
O31	●	Tulane	73 14
N7	●	at Auburn	34 6
N14	●	Furman	41 10
N28	●	at Florida	28 14
FIESTA BOWL			
J1	●	Nebraska	31 28

1988   11-1-0

S3		at Miami, Fla.	0 31
S10	●	Southern Miss	49 13
S17	●	at Clemson	24 21
S24	●	Michigan State	30 7
O1	●	at Tulane	48 28
O8	●	Georgia Southern	28 10
O15	●	East Carolina	45 21
O22	●	Louisiana Tech	66 3
N5	●	at South Carolina	59 0
N12	●	Virginia Tech	41 14
N26	●	Florida	52 17
SUGAR BOWL			
J2	●	Auburn	13 7

1989   10-2-0

S2		Southern Miss [JacF]	26 30
S9		Clemson	23 34
S16	●	at LSU	31 21
S23	●	Tulane	59 9
O7	●	at Syracuse	41 10
O14	●	at Virginia Tech	41 7
O21	●	Auburn	22 14
O28	●	Miami, Fla.	24 10
N4	●	South Carolina	35 10
N18	●	Memphis	57 20
D2	●	at Florida	24 17
FIESTA BOWL			
J1	●	Nebraska	41 17

1990   10-2-0

S8	●	East Carolina	45 24
S15	●	Georgia Southern	48 6
S22	●	at Tulane	31 13
S29	●	Virginia Tech	39 28
O6		at Miami, Fla.	22 31
O20	●	at Auburn	17 20
O27	●	LSU	42 3
N3	●	at South Carolina	41 10
N10	●	Cincinnati	70 21
N17	●	Memphis [ORL]	35 3
D1	●	Florida	45 30
BLOCKBUSTER BOWL			
D28	●	Penn State	24 17

1991   11-2-0

A29	●	Brigham Young [ANA]	44 28
S7	●	Tulane	38 11
S14	●	Western Michigan	58 0
S28	●	at Michigan	51 31
O5	●	Syracuse	46 14
O12	●	Virginia Tech [ORL]	33 20
O19	●	Middle Tennessee	39 10
O26	●	at LSU	27 16
N2	●	at Louisville	40 15
N9	●	South Carolina	38 10
N16		Miami, Fla.	16 17
N30		at Florida	9 14
COTTON BOWL			
J1	●	Texas A&M	10 2

1992-PRESENT
ACC

1992   11-1-0 (8-0-0)

S5	●	Duke	48 21
S12	●	at Clemson	24 20
S19	●	at North Carolina St.	34 13
S26	●	Wake Forest	35 7
O3		at Miami, Fla.	16 19
O10	●	North Carolina	36 13
O17	●	at Georgia Tech	29 24
O31	●	at Virginia	13 3
N7	●	Maryland	69 21
N14	●	Tulane	70 7
N28	●	Florida	45 24
ORANGE BOWL			
J1	●	Nebraska	27 14

1993   12-1-0 (8-0-0)

A28	●	Kansas [ERut]	42 0
S4	●	at Duke	45 7
S11	●	Clemson	57 0
S18	●	at North Carolina	33 7
O2	●	Georgia Tech	51 0
O9	●	Miami, Fla.	28 10
O16	●	Virginia	40 14
O30	●	Wake Forest	54 0
N6	●	at Maryland	49 20
N13		at Notre Dame	24 31
N20	●	North Carolina St.	62 3
N27	●	at Florida	33 21
ORANGE BOWL			
J1	●	Nebraska	18 16

1994   10-1-1 (8-0-0)

S3	●	Virginia	41 17
S10	●	at Maryland	52 20
S17	●	at Wake Forest	56 14
S24	●	North Carolina	31 18
O8		at Miami, Fla.	20 34
O22	●	Clemson	17 0
O29	●	Duke	59 20
N5	●	at Georgia Tech	41 10
N12	●	Notre Dame [ORL]	23 16
N19	●	at North Carolina St.	34 3
N26	=	Florida	31 31
SUGAR BOWL			
J2	●	Florida	23 17

1995   10-2-0 (7-1-0)

S2	●	Duke [ORL]	70 26
S9	●	at Clemson	45 26
S16	●	North Carolina St.	77 17
S23	●	Central Florida	46 14
O7	●	Miami, Fla.	41 17
O14	●	Wake Forest	72 13
O21	●	Georgia Tech	42 10
N2		at Virginia	28 33
N11	●	at North Carolina	28 12
N18	●	Maryland	59 17
N25		at Florida	24 35
ORANGE BOWL			
J1	●	Notre Dame	31 26

1996   11-1   (8-0)

S7	●	Duke	44	7
S19	●	at North Carolina St.	51	17
S28	●	North Carolina	13	0
O5	●	Clemson	34	3
O12	●	at Miami, Fla.	34	16
O26	●	Virginia	31	24
N2	●	at Georgia Tech	49	3
N9	●	Wake Forest *Orl*	44	7
N16	●	Southern Miss	54	14
N23	●	Maryland *Mia*	48	10
N30	●	Florida	24	21
		SUGAR BOWL		
J2		Florida	20	52

1997   11-1   (8-0)

S6	●	at Southern Cal	14	7
S13	●	Maryland	50	7
S20	●	at Clemson	35	28
O4	●	Miami, Fla.	47	0
O11	●	at Duke	51	27
O18	●	Georgia Tech	38	0
O25	●	at Virginia	47	21
N1	●	North Carolina St.	48	35
N8	●	at North Carolina	20	3
N15	●	Wake Forest	58	7
N22		at Florida	29	32
		SUGAR BOWL		
J1	●	Ohio State	31	14

1998   11-2   (7-1)

A31	●	Texas A&M *ERut*	23	14
S12		at North Carolina St.	7	24
S19	●	Duke	62	13
S26	●	Southern Cal	30	10
O3	●	at Maryland	24	10
O10	●	at Miami, Fla.	26	14
O17	●	Clemson	48	0
O24	●	at Georgia Tech	34	7
O31	●	North Carolina	39	13
N7	●	Virginia	45	14
N14	●	at Wake Forest	24	7
N21	●	Florida	23	12
		FIESTA BOWL		
J4		Tennessee	16	23

1999   12-0   (8-0)

A28	●	Louisiana Tech	41	7
S11	●	Georgia Tech	41	35
S18	●	North Carolina St.	42	11
S25	●	at North Carolina	42	10
O2	●	Duke *JacF*	51	23
O9	●	Miami, Fla.	31	21
O16	●	Wake Forest	33	10
O23	●	at Clemson	17	14
O30	●	at Virginia	35	10
N13	●	Maryland	49	10
N20	●	at Florida	30	23
		SUGAR BOWL		
J4	●	Virginia Tech	46	29

2000   11-2   (8-0)

A26	●	Brigham Young *JacF*	29	3
S9	●	at Georgia Tech	26	21
S16	●	North Carolina	63	14
S23	●	Louisville	31	0
S30	●	at Maryland	59	7
O7		at Miami, Fla.	24	27
O14	●	Duke	63	14
O21	●	Virginia	37	3
O28	●	at North Carolina St.	58	14
N4	●	Clemson	54	7
N11	●	at Wake Forest	35	6
N18	●	Florida	30	7
		ORANGE BOWL		
J3		Oklahoma	2	13

2001   8-4   (6-2)

S1	●	at Duke	55	13
S8	●	UAB	29	7
S22		at North Carolina	9	41
S29	●	Wake Forest	48	24
O13		Miami, Fla.	27	49
O20	●	at Virginia	43	7
O27	●	Maryland	52	31
N3	●	at Clemson	41	27
N10		North Carolina St.	28	34
N17		at Florida	13	37
D1	●	Georgia Tech	28	17
		GATOR BOWL		
J1	●	Virginia Tech	30	17

2002   9-5   (7-1)

A24	●	Iowa State *KC*	38	31
A31	●	Virginia	40	19
S14	●	at Maryland	37	10
S21	●	Duke	48	17
S26		at Louisville	20	26
O3	●	Clemson	48	31
O12		at Miami, Fla.	27	28
O26		Notre Dame	24	34
N2	●	at Wake Forest	34	21
N9	●	at Georgia Tech	21	13
N16	●	North Carolina	40	14
N23		at North Carolina St.	7	17
N30	●	Florida	31	14
		SUGAR BOWL		
J1		Georgia	13	26

2003   10-3   (7-1)

A30	●	at North Carolina	37	0
S6	●	Maryland	35	10
S13	●	Georgia Tech	14	13
S20	●	Colorado	47	7
S27	●	at Duke	56	7
O11		Miami, Fla.	14	22
O18	●	at Virginia	19	14
O25	●	Wake Forest	48	24
N1		at Notre Dame	37	0
N8		at Clemson	10	26
N15	●	North Carolina St.	50	44
N29	●	at Florida	38	34
		ORANGE BOWL		
J1		Miami, Fla.	14	16

2004   9-3   (6-2)

S10		at Miami, Fla.	10	16
S18	●	UAB	34	7
S25	●	Clemson	41	22
O2	●	North Carolina	38	16
O9	●	at Syracuse	17	13
O16	●	Virginia	36	3
O23		at Wake Forest	20	17
O30		at Maryland	17	20
N6	●	Duke	29	7
N11	●	at North Carolina St.	17	10
N20		Florida	13	20
		GATOR BOWL		
J1	●	West Virginia	30	18

FLORIDA STATE ANNUAL STATISTICAL LEADERS

YR	RUSHING	YDS	ATT	AVG	PASSING	ATT	CMP	PCT	YDS	RECEIVING	REC	YDS	AVG
1955	Lee Corso	431	111	3.9	Len Swantic	73	37	.51	576	Tom Feamster	18	258	14.3
1956	Bobby Renn	596	105	5.7	Lee Corso	59	32	.54	369	Joe Holt/Ron Schomburger	16	140	8.8
1957	Fred Pickard	463	86	5.4	Bobby Renn	54	23	.43	263	Bob Nellums	21	217	10.3
1958	Fred Pickard	615	122	5.0	Vic Prinzi	71	40	.56	480	Jack Espenship	18	200	11.1
1959	Fred Pickard	481	131	3.7	Joe Majors	168	90	.54	1,063	Bud Whitehead	31	320	10.3
1960	Bud Whitehead	293	81	3.6	Ed Trancygier	97	38	.39	552	Bud Whitehead	23	212	9.2
1961	Keith Kindermann	385	81	4.8	Eddie Feely	83	48	.58	471	Jim Daniel	10	113	11.3
1962	Gene Roberts	299	75	4.0	Steve Tensi	121	60	.50	796	Keith Kindermann	21	275	13.1
1963	Dave Snyder	500	107	4.7	Steve Tensi	147	71	.48	915	Fred Biletnikoff	24	358	14.9
1964	Phil Spooner	516	136	3.8	Steve Tensi	204	121	.59	1,681	Fred Biletnikoff	57	987	17.3
1965	Jim Mankins	326	85	3.8	Ed Pritchett	247	110	.45	1,225	Max Wettstein	24	365	15.2
1966	Bill Moremen	480	123	3.9	Gary Pajcic	232	125	.54	1,590	Ron Sellers	56	874	15.6
1967	Bill Moremen	439	94	4.7	Kim Hammond	241	140	.58	1,991	Ron Sellers	70	1,228	17.5
1968	Tom Bailey	570	116	4.9	Bill Cappleman	287	162	.56	2,410	Ron Sellers	86	1,496	17.4
1969	Tom Bailey	630	144	4.4	Bill Cappleman	344	183	.53	2,467	Jim Tyson	49	720	14.7
1970	Tom Bailey	514	121	4.2	Tommy Warren	190	97	.51	1,594	Rhett Dawson	54	946	17.5
1971	Paul Magalski	516	106	4.9	Gary Huff	327	184	.56	2,736	Rhett Dawson	62	817	13.2
1972	Hodges Mitchell	944	192	4.9	Gary Huff	385	206	.54	2,893	Barry Smith	69	1,243	18.0
1973	Hodges Mitchell	669	171	3.9	Billy Sexton	128	51	.40	754	Mike Shumann	21	280	13.3
1974	Larry Key	602	123	4.9	Ron Coppess	145	78	.54	817	Mike Shumann	43	515	12.0
1975	Leon Bright	675	162	4.2	Clyde Walker	203	117	.58	1,619	Mike Shumann	38	730	19.2
1976	Larry Key	712	144	4.9	Jimmy Black	179	104	.58	1,535	Ed Beckman	37	521	14.1
1977	Larry Key	1,117	239	4.7	Wally Woodham	154	94	.61	1,270	Roger Overby	38	626	16.5
1978	Homes Johnson	817	183	4.5	Jimmy Jordan	199	108	.54	1,427	Jackie Flowers	43	757	17.6
1979	Mark Lyles	1,011	225	4.5	Jimmy Jordan	180	87	.48	1,173	Jackie Flowers	37	622	16.8
1980	Sam Platt	983	224	4.4	Rick Stockstill	201	121	.60	1,377	Michael Whiting	25	203	8.1
1981	Greg Allen	888	139	6.4	Rick Stockstill	238	122	.51	1,356	Michael Whiting	29	211	7.3
1982	Ricky Williams	857	134	6.4	Kelly Lowrey	217	113	.52	1,671	Tony Johnson	30	500	16.7
1983	Greg Allen	1,134	200	5.7	Kelly Lowrey	233	131	.56	1,720	Jessie Hester	31	576	18.6
1984	Greg Allen	971	133	7.3	Eric Thomas	161	78	.48	1,218	Jessie Hester	42	832	19.8
1985	Tony Smith	678	111	6.1	Chip Ferguson	130	70	.54	990	Hassan Jones	34	738	21.7
1986	Victor Floyd	654	129	5.1	Danny McManus	112	65	.58	872	Herb Gainer	27	441	16.3
1987	Sammie Smith	1,230	172	7.2	Danny McManus	264	138	.52	1,964	Herb Gainer	30	478	15.9
1988	Sammie Smith	577	108	5.3	Chip Ferguson	194	122	.63	1,714	Terry Anthony	32	550	17.2
1989	Dexter Carter	684	131	5.2	Peter Tom Willis	346	211	.61	3,124	Lawrence Dawsey	38	683	18.0
1990	Amp Lee	825	158	5.2	Casey Weldon	182	112	.62	1,600	Lawrence Dawsey	65	999	15.4
1991	Amp Lee	977	186	5.3	Casey Weldon	313	189	.60	2,527	Shannon Baker	30	451	15.0
1992	Tiger McMillon	579	116	5.0	Charlie Ward	365	204	.56	2,647	Tamarick Vanover	42	581	13.8
1993	Sean Jackson	825	134	6.2	Charlie Ward	380	264	.69	3,032	Kez McCorvey	74	966	13.1
1994	Warrick Dunn	1,026	152	6.8	Danny Kanell	380	227	.60	2,781	Kez McCorvey	59	870	14.7
1995	Warrick Dunn	1,242	166	7.5	Danny Kanell	402	257	.64	2,957	Andre Cooper	71	1,002	14.1
1996	Warrick Dunn	1,180	189	6.2	Thad Busby	243	134	.55	1,866	E.G. Green	34	662	19.5
1997	Travis Minor	623	112	5.6	Thad Busby	390	235	.60	3,317	E.G. Green	54	1,059	19.6
1998	Travis Minor	857	191	4.5	Chris Weinke	286	145	.51	2,487	Peter Warrick	61	1,232	20.2
1999	Travis Minor	815	180	4.5	Chris Weinke	377	232	.62	3,103	Peter Warrick	71	934	13.2
2000	Travis Minor	923	181	5.1	Chris Weinke	431	266	.62	4,167	Snoop Minnis	63	1,340	21.3
2001	Greg Jones	713	134	5.3	Chris Rix	286	165	.58	2,734	Javon Walker	45	944	21.0
2002	Greg Jones	938	161	5.8	Chris Rix	225	118	.52	1,684	Anquan Boldin	65	1,011	15.6
2003	Greg Jones	618	144	4.3	Chris Rix	382	216	.57	3,107	Craphonso Thorpe	51	994	19.5
2004	Leon Washington	951	138	6.9	Wyatt Sexton	252	139	.55	1,661	Chauncey Stovall	53	780	14.7

Receiving leaders by receptions
The NCAA began including postseason stats in 2002

THE SCHOOLS

FRESNO STATE

BY DAVE REARDON

ANYBODY, ANYWHERE, ANYTIME. That's been Pat Hill's motto in his eight years at Fresno State, where the Bulldogs have established themselves as road-warrior giant-killers. In 2001, Fresno State took the college football world by storm with early nonconference victories over Colorado, Oregon State and Wisconsin. Ultimately, however, the Bulldogs faltered during the Western Athletic Conference season and fell out of BCS contention, though quarterback David Carr would go on to become the first pick of the NFL draft. Carr perpetuated the school's reputation as a quarterback factory, since it had previously produced stars and future pros Kevin Sweeney, Mark Barsotti, Trent Dilfer and Billy Volek (who each passed for at least 6,500 yards and 50 touchdowns while a Bulldog). Thanks in part to these quarterbacks, Fresno State boasts the 17th-best winning percentage in the nation since 1985, at .661 (160–81–3), despite perennially playing one of the nation's toughest nonconference schedules.

TRADITION It's only a couple of hundred yards from the visitors locker room to the field at Bulldog Stadium, but negotiating the Red Mile can seem like an endless trek for a visiting team, as fans lining the pathway toss verbal bouquets at Fresno State's opponents. Then there's the pregame soundtrack, a 1980s heavy metal blitzkrieg that helps fuel an already intimidating home atmosphere. The Bulldogs' fans are known as the Red Wave, and they are among the loudest in college football.

BEST PLAYER David Carr passed for 4,299 yards in 2001, leading the nation with what was then the sixth-highest season total in NCAA history. He also completed a nation's-best 46 TD passes that season. Of course, Carr was known for his intangibles—his maturity and affability—almost as much as for his numbers, which was part of why the Houston Texans made him the first pick in the 2002 NFL draft.

BEST COACH After a mediocre run at Washington State, Jim Sweeney became a legend at Fresno State, coaching the Bulldogs to a record of 143–75–3, including eight conference championships and a 5–2 record in bowl games. Fresno State had a winning mark every season from 1982 through 1993, with the exception of a 6–6 year in 1984.

BEST TEAM The 1985 Bulldogs went 11–0–1, including a 51-7 pasting of Bowling Green in the California Bowl.

PROFILE

California State University, Fresno
Fresno, Calif.
Founded: 1911
Enrollment: 18,560
Colors: Bulldog Red and Blue
Nickname: Bulldogs
Stadium: Bulldog Stadium
    Opened in 1980
    Grass; 41,031 capacity
First football game: 1921
All-time record: 508–342–27 (.595)
Bowl record: 9–6
Western Athletic Conference championships: 3 (shared)
First-round NFL draftees: 4
Website: www.gobulldogs.com

THE BEST OF TIMES

When Jim Sweeney led the Bulldogs to an 11–0–1 mark in 1985, it was the beginning of a seven-year stretch in which Fresno State went 65–14–2, including four seasons of 10-plus wins.

THE WORST OF TIMES

Three coaches—Ken Gleason, Alvin Pierson, Duke Jacobs—went 11–26–4 from 1947 to 1950.

CONFERENCE

After 47 years in the college division, in 1969 the Bulldogs stepped up to NCAA Division I as a charter member of the Pacific Coast Athletic Association, renamed the Big West Conference in 1988. Fresno State won or shared six PCAA/Big West titles between 1969 and 1991. The Bulldogs have competed in the Western Athletic Conference since 1992.

DISTINGUISHED ALUMNI

Marvin R. Baxter, California Supreme Court Justice; Kenny Guinn, Nevada governor; Paul H. O'Neill, U.S. Secretary of Treasury; Jerry Tarkanian, NCAA champion basketball coach

FIGHT SONG

FIGHT! VARSITY
Fight! Varsity
On your toes dig in and hit that line!
We're pulling hard for you.
So fight and give the best there is in you.
Fight! Varsity on your toes dig in and hit that line!
We'll fight on to victory
We're always true to Fresno State!

Bulldog Spellout (To be shouted between the fight song verses)
B-U-L-L-D-O-G-S
Go Dogs Go!
Fight Dogs Fight!
Go Bulldogs!

David Carr perpetuated Fresno State's reputation as a quarterback factory.

Quarterback Kevin Sweeney and wide receiver Stephen "The Touchdown Maker" Baker were among 10 Bulldogs to receive honorable mention All-America accolades from the AP, with the two connecting for a 95-yard scoring pass in an early-season 33-24 victory over Oregon State. The other honorees included noseguard Chris Pacheco and safety Michael Stewart, who led the defense. The Bulldogs also had a 1,040-yard rusher in James Williams. Safety Rod Webster picked off two passes in the California Bowl, a game that featured touchdowns by five different Fresno State players. The Bulldogs, their record tainted only by a 24-24 tie against Hawaii, finished the season ranked No. 16 in the coaches' poll.

BIGGEST GAME On Dec. 29, 1992, the Trent Dilfer-led Bulldogs went to Anaheim and chalked one up for the little guys, thrashing USC 24-7 in the Freedom Bowl with a balanced effort on offense and defense. Fresno State outgained USC 405 to 183 in total yards, and forced four turnovers from the Trojans. Despite it not being a historically great Southern California team, the Bulldogs' victory was a huge one: the Trojans might win most of the recruiting battles against State, but the Bulldogs can point to a very important W when talking about the only on-field encounter between the programs.

BIGGEST UPSET When Fresno State won 32-20 at Wisconsin in 2001, the Bulldogs became the toast of college football. In the first half, it appeared the Badgers would do what they normally did to mid-major teams at Camp Randall—win, and win big—as they took a 20-10 lead. But the Dogs fired back after halftime, as Bernard Berrian took the opening kickoff 96 yards for a TD. Carr controlled the game on offense, hitting Berrian and Rodney Wright with short passes, and defensive tackle Alan Harper took charge on defense, as Wisconsin was blanked in the second half. The victory was the upstarts' third consecutive nonconference upset and moved the Bulldogs up to No. 11 in the AP poll.

HEARTBREAKER After their fourth victory against a nonconference foe in 2001, 25-22 at Colorado State, the Bulldogs were riding high at 6–0, with a 2–0 record in the WAC. But it doesn't take much for a mid-major to be

RECORDS		
RUSHING YARDS		
	GAME	
252	Larry Willoughby vs. Nevada, Nov. 8, 1952 (9 att.)	
	SEASON	
1,586	Rodney Davis, 2002 (313 att.)	
	CAREER	
3,473	Ron Rivers, 1991-93 (525 att.)	
PASSING YARDS		
	GAME	
536	Dave Telford vs. Pacific, Oct. 24, 1987 (32 of 47)	
	SEASON	
4,839	David Carr, 2001 (343 of 532)	
	CAREER	
10,808	Kevin Sweeney, 1982-86 (740 of 1,355)	

RECEIVING YARDS		
	GAME	
299	Rodney Wright vs. Michigan State, Dec. 31, 2001 (13 rec.)	
	SEASON	
1,630	Rodney Wright, 2001 (104 rec.)	
	CAREER	
3,344	Charlie Jones, 1992-95 (187 rec.)	
POINTS		
	GAME	
30	Don Driscoll vs. Cal State Los Angeles, Oct. 2, 1954 (5 TDs)	
	SEASON	
129	Asen Asparuhov, 2001 (23 FGs, 60 PATs)	
	CAREER	
364	Derek Mahoney, 1990-93 (47 FGs, 223 PATs)	

CONSENSUS ALL-AMERICANS	
1939-40	Jack Mulkey, E
1960	Douglas Brown, G
1968	Tom McCall, LB
1968	Erv Hunt, DB

considered a fluke, and the ride came to a crashing halt on the night of Friday, Oct. 19: the Boise State Broncos came to town and stole the slipper with a 35-30 win over the Bulldogs, knocking them out of BCS consideration. To make matters worse, Fresno State lost 38-34 at Hawaii the next week, and ended up settling for second place in the WAC.

STADIUM Bulldog Stadium provides one of the more underrated homefield advantages in the nation. Fresno State has won 81% of its games on Bulldog Stadium's natural grass. Local residents raised $7 million in order to erect the 30,000-seat stadium in 1979, and in 1991 the stadium expanded to its current capacity of 41,031.

RIVAL The Bulldogs lead their series with San Jose State 34–32–3, having won the last 11 in a row. They first played each other in 1921, Fresno State's first year of football, with the Bulldogs losing to the Spartans, 14-2.

DISPUTE During a Fresno State home loss, things can happen—things like objects getting thrown onto the field in the general direction of the visiting team. In 2002, during a 31-21 victory over Fresno State, Hawaii coach June Jones said a screwdriver went whizzing by his head and stuck in the grass in front of him, quivering like a Bowie knife. Others say the screwdriver merely fell out of the tool belt of a Hawaii equipment staffer. Charges have yet to be filed.

NICKNAME In 1921, the inaugural year of Fresno State football, student body president Warren Moody encountered a white bulldog on campus and decided with his friends to make the dog the school mascot. Student representative Arids

Walker then moved to make Bulldogs the official Fresno State nickname, and the motion passed with little opposition.

MASCOT A student from the university's Spirit Team wears a Bulldog costume and appears at games and community functions as Timeout. The name was taken from the Timeout Boosters Club, which sponsored the mascot in his first year, 1981. That year, the rookie Timeout was cited by *Sports Illustrated* as one of the best mascots in college sports.

UNIFORMS The women from Fresno Normal School wanted blue and white, the men from Fresno Junior College wanted red and white; they finally agreed on blue and red as Fresno State's official colors. You could say the men won in the end, since the Bulldogs use much more red than blue in their football uniforms, especially on the helmets. Of course, you could also say the women ultimately won the argument, since technically red is no longer a team color (the color is "cardinal"). The helmets used to be white, and featured numbers during the 1960s. In the 1980s, the word "Bulldogs" was written out in script, but has since been replaced with a cartoon bulldog. Coach Pat Hill added a green V to the back of the helmet, acknowledging Fresno State's huge fan base throughout the San Joaquin Valley. The color green symbolizes the area's rich agriculture. Like most teams, the Bulldogs wear white jerseys at home.

SUPERSTITION Coach Pat Hill collects lucky pennies, and will wear the same cap game after game when he's on a winning streak.

QUOTE "I'm going to keep trying to play every major college football team at their field, with their referees, until they'll come here."—Pat Hill

FRESNO STATE ANNUAL STATISTICAL LEADERS

YR	RUSHING	YDS	ATT	AVG	PASSING	ATT	CMP	PCT	YDS	RECEIVING	REC	YDS	AVG
1959	Dale Messer	485	72	6.7	Nick Papac	102	47	.46	712	Dale Messer	17	297	17.5
1960	Dale Messer	811	131	6.2	Nick Papac	99	52	.53	936	Dale Messer	30	655	21.8
1961	Bill Kendrick	484	89	5.4	Beau Carter	114	57	.50	805	Gerald Houser	26	316	12.2
1962	Jim Long	313	58	5.4	Jon Anabo	135	70	.52	1,184	Larry Fogelstrom	24	415	17.3
1963	Herman Hamp	282	62	4.5	Beau Carter	266	115	.51	1,595	Jan Farif	35	528	15.0
1964	Jim Long	492	115	4.3	Ron Melton	142	66	.46	886	Doyle Keith	26	446	17.2
1965	Bill Wilsey	215	48	4.5	Don Robinson	211	117	.55	1,177	Jim Stewart	37	435	11.8
1966	Ken Long	297	75	4.0	Don Robinson	149	74	.50	803	Ernie Nolte	35	551	15.7
1967	Fred Figueroa	428	125	3.4	Don Robinson	319	170	.53	2,278	Lloyd Madden	53	563	10.6
1968	Mike Flores	312	NA	NA	Ron Hudson	NA	NA	NA	1,047	Mike White	33	461	13.9
1969	Walt Jensen	312	97	3.2	Ron Hudson	201	104	.52	1,462	Mike White	36	558	15.5
1970	Henry Woodson	822	200	4.1	Karl Francis	261	134	.51	1,783	John Sexton	53	753	14.2
1971	Herbie Phillips	719	169	4.3	John Behrens	159	67	.42	880	Gene Austin	35	463	13.2
1972	Isaac Glass	278	98	2.8	John Behrens	315	139	.44	1,857	Mike Harris	30	407	13.6
1973	Greg Bass	311	76	4.1	Rod Kraft	110	43	.39	695	Curt Wurst	24	295	12.3
1974	Jeff Johnson	565	135	4.2	Neftali Cortez	255	120	.47	1,916	Glenn Cotton	24	543	22.6
1975	Craig Johnson	774	185	4.2	Neftali Cortez	246	125	.51	1,674	Calvin Young	30	437	14.6
1976	Dean Jones	646	153	4.2	Dean Jones	128	65	.51	696	Kevin Spencer	27	333	12.3
1977	Steve Franklin	789	135	5.8	Dean Jones	148	56	.38	941	Tony Jackson	25	507	20.3
1978	Keith Gooch	531	108	4.9	Billy Yancy	161	66	.41	1,083	Wyatt Henderson	30	566	18.9
1979	Ken Lovely	825	182	4.5	Sergio Toscano	142	76	.54	1,084	Enis Gilbeau	40	628	15.7
1980	Ted Torosian	520	123	4.2	Sergio Toscano	247	121	.49	1,476	Henry Ellard	28	493	17.6
1981	Ted Torosian	639	155	4.1	Jeff Tedford	250	132	.53	1,879	Henry Ellard	39	808	20.7
1982	Ken Williams	436	75	5.8	Jeff Tedford	348	184	.53	2,993	Henry Ellard	62	1,510	24.4
1983	Ken Williams	391	91	4.3	Kevin Sweeney	334	166	.50	2,359	Larry Willis	63	1,009	16.0
1984	Calvin Scruggs	371	113	3.3	Kevin Sweeney	421	227	.54	3,259	Larry Willis	79	1,251	15.8
1985	James Williams	1,040	179	5.8	Kevin Sweeney	314	186	.59	2,789	Gene Taylor	30	545	18.2
1986	James Williams	896	166	5.4	Kevin Sweeney	284	160	.56	2,363	Stephen Baker	33	785	23.8
1987	Kelly Skipper	588	141	4.2	Dave Tedford	351	202	.58	2,589	Ron Jenkins	76	985	13.0
1988	Aaron Craver	1,390	247	5.6	Mark Barsotti	232	116	.50	1,795	Andre Alexander	33	703	21.3
1989	Myron Jones	760	138	5.5	Mark Barsotti	262	138	.53	1,987	Dwight Pickens	32	673	21.0
1990	Aaron Craver	1,003	224	4.5	Mark Barsotti	346	182	.53	2,534	Kelvin Means	40	492	12.3
1991	Ron Rivers	989	141	7.0	Mark Barsotti	191	123	.64	1,777	Kelvin Means	34	474	13.9
1992	Ron Rivers	1,007	154	6.5	Trent Dilfer	360	188	.52	3,000	Malcom Seabron	42	994	23.7
1993	Ron Rivers	1,477	230	6.4	Trent Dilfer	396	254	.64	3,799	Charlie Jones	47	897	19.1
1994	Jerome Oliver	1,106	258	4.3	Richie Donati	263	152	.58	2,254	Charlie Jones	54	971	18.0
1995	Reggie Brown	719	131	5.5	Jim Arellanes	172	102	.59	1,539	Charlie Jones	71	1,171	16.5
1996	Michael Pittman	1,132	214	5.3	Jim Arellanes	281	173	.62	2,487	Brian Roberson	78	1,248	16.0
1997	Michael Pittman	1,057	238	4.4	Billy Volek	318	178	.56	1,853	Jamie Kimbrough	36	368	10.2
1998	Jamie Kimbrough	1,168	213	5.5	Billy Volek	261	151	.58	1,973	Charles Smith	42	621	14.8
1999	Derrick Ward	875	147	6.0	Billy Volek	383	249	.65	2,706	Rodney Wright	74	1,062	14.4
2000	Josh Levi	397	92	4.3	David Carr	349	216	.62	2,729	Bernard Berrian	43	705	16.4
2001	Paris Gaines	1,044	220	4.7	David Carr	532	343	.64	4,839	Rodney Wright	104	1,630	15.7
2002	Rodney Davis	1,586	313	5.1	Paul Pinegar	403	230	.57	2,929	Marque Davis	64	956	14.9
2003	Dwayne Wright	1,038	190	5.5	Paul Pinegar	294	174	.59	1,773	Bernard Berman	63	668	10.6
2004	Bryson Sumlin	1,104	191	5.8	Paul Pinegar	292	173	.59	2,099	Joe Fernandez	38	546	14.4

All statistics include postseason

THE SCHOOLS

FRESNO STATE ALL-TIME SCORES

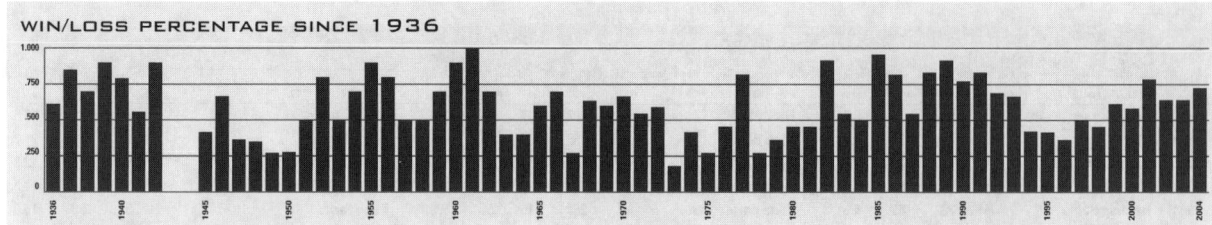

WIN/LOSS PERCENTAGE SINCE 1936

ARTHUR JONES
1921-28 (.579)   37-26-7

1921   4-4-0
U	●	La Verne	46	0
U	●	at Cal Tech	12	0
U	●	at Pacific	0	35
U	●	Cal Tech	12	0
U		Chico State	0	3
U	●	at Modesto JC	28	0
U		San Jose State	2	14
U		Fresno HS	7	62

1922   7-1-2
U	●	at Tulare HS	12	0
U	●	at Lemoore HS	25	9
U	=	Modesto JC	0	0
U	●	at Loyola-Marymount	2	0
U	●	Reedley HS	21	0
U		Stanford JV	3	7
N4	●	Cal Poly	20	0
N18	=	at UC Davis	0	0
U	●	at Bakersfield JC	31	6
U	●	Pacific	12	7

1923   7-2-0
U	●	Reedley HS	39	0
U	●	at Caruthers Legion	39	0
U	●	Sacramento JC	53	18
O27	●	at UC Davis	26	14
U	●	at Modesto JC	7	6
N10		at Nevada	3	46
U	●	Redlands	10	6
U	●	Bakersfield JC	32	6
N29		at San Diego State	2	12

1924   7-2-0
O11		at Nevada	0	16
U	●	Cal Christian	31	0
U	●	Bakersfield JC	9	0
U	●	Modesto JC	41	6
U	●	Mare Island Navy	10	0
N15	●	at Cal Poly SLO	22	6
U	●	at Pacific	12	0
N27	●	San Diego State	7	0
U		at Chico State	0	16

1925   2-6-1
U	=	at Modesto JC	6	6
O3		Occidental	10	33
O10		Santa Clara	0	6
U	●	San Jose State	23	7
U		UC Davis	0	6
N7		at Nevada	6	60
U	●	Barbarians	63	6
N26		Pacific	0	7
D5		at Saint Mary's-Cal	15	61

1926   5-3-1
S18		at Stanford	0	44
O2	●	UC Santa Barbara	26	0
O9		Nevada	6	28
O16	●	La Verne	22	7
O30	●	at San Diego State	28	7
N6	●	San Jose State	34	0
N11	●	UC Davis	23	7
N19		Saint Mary's-Cal	0	16
N25	=	at Pacific	0	0

1927   3-3-2
S17		at Stanford	7	44
O1		at UCLA	0	7
O15		Nevada	10	7
O29	=	St. Ignatius	6	6
N5	●	San Jose State	10	7
N11		UC Davis	7	13
N18		Santa Clara	6	6
N24	●	Pacific	6	0

1928   2-5-1
S29	●	Cal Poly SLO	37	0
O6	●	UC Santa Barbara	7	0
O13		St. Ignatius	0	19
O27		Stanford	0	47
N3		at Pacific	0	13
N10	=	at Nevada	12	12
N23		Santa Clara	0	33
N29		UC Davis	0	13

STANLEY BORLESKE
1929-32 (.472)   16-18-2

1929   1-7-0
S28		Loyola-Marymount	0	20
O5		at UCLA	6	56
O12		Olympic Club	0	60
O19		at Chico State	0	12
O26		at Nevada	0	48
N11		at UC Davis	0	22
N16		San Jose State	14	26
N28	●	Pacific	20	6

1930   8-0-0
S27	●	at Cal Christian	19	7
O4	●	Redlands	31	26
O10	●	at Loyola-Marymount	12	7
O18	●	Chico State	13	7
N1	●	at Pacific	19	0
N8	●	UC Davis	27	7
N15	●	at San Jose State	27	12
N27	●	Nevada	6	0

1931   4-6-0
S26		Northern Arizona	2	26
O3	●	Whittier	13	12
O10		La Verne	6	7
O17	●	San Jose State	32	0
O24		at Nevada	13	31
N7		Arizona State	0	7
N14	●	at UC Davis	20	7
N21		at Chico State	6	18
N26	●	Pacific	6	0
D5		San Diego State	0	15

1932   3-5-2
S24	●	San Diego Marines	12	0
O1		West Coast Army	6	7
O8		UC Davis	0	3
O15	●	San Francisco State	32	13
O22	=	at San Jose State	0	0
O29		at Pacific	0	35
N5	=	at Northern Arizona	0	0
N11		at Washburn	0	26
N18	●	La Verne	6	0
N24		Nevada	0	7

LEO HARRIS
1933-35 (.661)   18-9-1

1933   5-4-0
S29	●	Cal Tech	26	6
O7	●	La Verne	14	7
O14		California JV	0	7
O21	●	Cal Poly SLO-Pomona	24	0
O28	●	at UC Davis	20	0
N4		at Arizona State	7	21
N11	●	Washburn	7	0
N18		at San Jose State	7	18	*
N30		Pacific	0	12

1934   7-2-1
S22	●	San Francisco State	33	6
S29	●	Southern Cal JV	7	0
O6		California JV	6	12
O13	●	at Northern Arizona	26	14
O20	●	at Pacific	7	6
O27		Santa Clara	0	19
N3	=	San Jose State	7	7
N12	●	UC Davis	40	13
N17	●	Cal Tech	66	0
N29	●	Nevada	33	0

1935   6-3-0
S28	●	La Verne	46	0
O5		California JV	7	13
O12		Santa Clara	0	24
O19	●	at Chico State	13	0
O26	●	Cal Tech	51	7
N2	●	Pacific	20	7
N11	●	at Nevada	27	6
N16	●	at UC Davis	32	6
N30		San Francisco	3	21

JAMES BRADSHAW
1936-42, '46 (.750)   59-18-5

1936   5-3-1
S27		San Francisco	0	14
O10	●	Whittier	18	0
O17	●	Northern Arizona	31	6
O24	●	California JV	32	6
O31	●	Chico State	38	0
N7	=	Willamette	14	14
N13		at Pacific	0	17
N26	●	Nevada	13	6
D5		at Hardin-Simmons	6	28

1937   8-1-1
U	=	Southern Cal JV	13	13
O1	●	at Willamette	7	0
O9	●	California JV	20	7
O15	●	at Whittier	24	0
O22	●	at UC Davis	19	0
O30	●	Chico State	40	7
N6	●	at Nevada	46	8
N11		Hardin-Simmons	7	14
N25	●	Pacific	20	0

LITTLE ALL-AMERICAN BOWL
D25	●	at Arkansas State	27	26

1938   7-3-0
O1	●	San Diego Marines	34	14
O8	●	California JV	27	7
O15	●	Arkansas State	34	0
O22	●	at Nevada	27	0
O29	●	UC Davis	37	7
N4		at Pacific	13	18
N12		San Francisco	6	14
N18	●	Hawaii	15	13
N24	●	UC Santa Barbara	28	0
D3		Texas-El Paso	6	26

1939   9-1-0
S30	●	Texas-El Paso	10	7
O6	●	at UC Santa Barbara	13	6
O14	●	Nevada	45	0
O21	●	California JV	28	7
O28	●	San Francisco	21	2
N4	●	Pacific	7	0
N11	●	Portland	27	13
N24	●	San Jose State	7	42
D2	●	at Hawaii	38	2
U	●	at Healani AC	21	6

1940   9-2-1
S28	●	Whittier	13	7
O5	●	UC Santa Barbara	20	6
O12	●	West Texas State	15	6
O18	●	at Pacific	3	0
O25	=	at San Diego State	0	0
N2	●	Nevada	7	6
N9	●	Texas-El Paso	16	6
N16		San Jose State	7	14
N21	●	Colorado State	28	0
D7		at Arkansas State	0	13
U	●	at Healani AC	20	0

PINEAPPLE BOWL
J1	●	at Hawaii	3	0

1941   4-3-2
S27		at West Texas State	6	7
O4	=	at Camp Haan	7	7
O11	●	at UC Santa Barbara	26	0
O18	●	at Nevada	6	3
O25	●	San Diego State	26	0
N1		at San Francisco	27	47
N11	●	at Pacific	13	0
N15	=	at San Jose State	0	0
N20		at Arizona State	7	26

1942   9-1-0
S26	●	Whittier	51	0
O3	●	Occidental	53	6
O11	●	at San Diego State	66	0
O17	●	March Field	20	0
O24	●	Fort Ord	80	0
O30	●	at Pacific	13	0
N7	●	Nevada	33	0
N11		San Francisco	13	33
N26	●	San Jose State	6	0
N28	●	at Loyola-Marymount	27	6

1943   0-0-0
NO TEAM

EARL WIGHT
1944 (.000)   0-6

1944   0-6-0
U		at Minter Field	0	20
U		at Salinas JC	6	13
U		at Modesto JC	0	28
U		Minter Field	0	13
U		Tonopah AAF	6	7
U		Pacific	6	14

ALVIN PIERSON
1945, '49 (.348)   7-14-2

1945   4-6-2
S15	=	Cal Poly SLO	6	6
S21	●	at Pacific	13	0
U	=	Minter Field	0	0
U	●	at Northern Arizona	19	0
O13	●	at Cal Poly SLO	24	0
U		at S.B. Marines	0	26
O27		San Diego State	0	7
N3		at Nevada	4	7
N12		Saint Mary's-Cal	6	32
U		at Camp Beale	13	21
U	●	at Pacific	16	0

RAISIN BOWL
J1		Drake	12	13

JAMES BRADSHAW

1946   8-4-0
S28		Santa Clara	20	7
O5	●	Hawaiian All-Stars	13	6
O12		at Oklahoma City	7	46
O19	●	at UC Santa Barbara	20	13
O26		at San Diego State	0	7
N2	●	Loyola-Marymount	28	0
N11		Hawaii	2	7
N16	●	Pacific	13	12
N22		at San Jose State	2	13
N28	●	Idaho	13	12
U	●	at Molii Bears	41	0
U	●	at Leilehau Alumni	18	6

KEN GLEASON
1947-48 (.357) 6-12-3

1947 3-6-2

S20		Oklahoma City	2	27
S27	●	Molii Bears	18	7
O4		Santa Clara	19	20
O11	●	Cal Poly SLO	14	6
U		Honolulu All-Stars	7	34
N1	=	San Diego State	7	7
N8		at New Mexico	3	34
N15	=	at UC Santa Barbara	7	7
N21		at Pacific	22	47
N27	●	San Jose State	21	20
D6		at Hawaii	13	27

1948 3-6-1

S25	=	Portland	6	6
O2		Santa Clara	7	45
O9		at Cal Poly SLO	14	26
O16	●	UC Santa Barbara	28	7
O23		at Pepperdine	13	14
O30	●	New Mexico	20	14
N6	●	San Diego State	7	6
N11		Nevada	7	53
N19		at San Jose State	6	41
N25		Pacific	0	55

ALVIN PIERSON

1949 3-8-0

S24	●	Cal Poly SLO	20	7
O1		at UC Santa Barbara	7	14
O8		Santa Clara	0	53
O14		at Nevada	13	34
O22		at Loyola-Marymount	13	52
O29	●	Alameda Air Pac	55	30
N5		San Diego State	7	18
N11	●	Pepperdine	20	7
N18		at Pacific	0	45
N24		San Jose State	7	43
D2		at Hawaii	14	41

DUKE JACOBS
1950-51 (.395) 7-11-1

1950 2-6-1

O23	●	Hawaii	34	20
O6	=	at San Diego State	20	20
O13		UC Santa Barbara	7	13
O21	●	at Cal Poly SLO	31	7
O28		at San Jose State	7	33
N3		Pacific	7	52
N11		Loyola-Marymount	0	28
N18		at Pepperdine	13	27
N24		North Texas	12	31

1951 5-5-0

S22	●	at UC Davis	27	0
S29	●	Pepperdine	33	14
O6		San Jose State	6	32
O12		UC Santa Barbara	22	23
O20	●	Cal Poly SLO	42	19
O27	●	Occidental	27	6
N3		San Diego State	7	13
N10	●	at Whittier	28	0
N17		at North Texas	0	62
N24		San Francisco State	7	20

CLARK VAN GALDER
1952-58 (.671) 46-22-2

1952 8-2-0

S20	●	UC Davis	41	7
O4	●	Pepperdine	60	7
O10		at San Jose State	6	40
O18	●	Utah State	27	21
O24	●	at Occidental	20	9
N1	●	at San Diego State	49	33
N8	●	at Nevada	59	32
N15		Pacific	0	50
N22	●	San Francisco State	48	20
N29	●	Whittier	21	14

1953 4-4-2

S26		Cal Poly SLO	6	27
O3		San Jose State	21	27
O9		at Cal State LA	12	14
O17	●	Nevada	47	7
O24	●	UC Santa Barbara	20	0
O31	=	San Diego State	27	27
N7		at Utah State	6	46
N11	●	San Francisco State	41	27
N14	●	Pepperdine	54	2
N21	=	at Pacific	21	21

1954 7-3-0

S25		Hawaii	20	25
O2	●	Cal State LA	49	19
O9	●	Utah State	23	13
O16	●	at Nevada	52	6
O23	●	at UC Santa Barbara	26	20
O30	●	at San Diego State	20	0
N7	●	Cal Poly SLO	16	13
N10		San Diego Marines	0	20
N19		at San Jose State	0	28
N26	●	San Francisco State	39	20

1955 9-1-0

S23	●	at San Francisco State	20	12
O1	●	Willamette	33	7
O8	●	San Diego Navy	52	0
O15	●	Nevada	42	9
O22	●	San Diego Marines	20	0
O29		at Utah State	14	39
N5	●	San Diego State	20	6
N12	●	at Cal Poly SLO	34	6
N18	●	San Jose State	19	13
N26	●	at Hawaii	20	18

1956 8-2-0

S22	●	at Brigham Young	26	13
S29	●	at Willamette	27	12
O5	●	San Diego Marines	2	0
O13		Pacific	14	21
O20	●	San Francisco State	28	0
O27	●	Hawaii	39	20
N3		Idaho	12	24
N10	●	Cal Poly SLO	21	13
N17	●	at San Diego State	50	7
N22	●	at San Jose State	30	14

1957 5-5-0

S21		Montana State	14	27
S28		at Pacific	12	34
O5		San Diego Marines	0	53
O12	●	at San Francisco State	27	7
O19		at Cal Poly SLO	7	14
O26		at Idaho	6	20
N2	●	San Diego State	27	0
N9	●	Brigham Young	27	14
N16	●	San Jose State	13	6
N22	●	at Hawaii	31	8

1958 5-5-0

S20		at Brigham Young	7	29
S27		San Diego Marines	6	20
O4		at UC Santa Barbara	22	25
O18	●	Cal Poly SLO	14	0
O25	●	at Cal State LA	7	6
N1	●	San Diego State	22	20
N8	●	Long Beach State	22	6
N15		at San Jose State	6	48
N22	●	San Francisco State	35	0
N27		Pacific	6	52

CECIL COLEMAN
1959-63 (.740) 37-13

1959 7-3-0

S26	●	Brigham Young	27	16
O3	●	UC Santa Barbara	28	12
O10		San Diego Marines	6	13
O17		San Jose State	14	40
O24	●	at Cal Poly SLO	28	13
O31	●	San Diego State	38	13
N7		at Pacific	13	18
N14	●	at Long Beach State	29	8
N21	●	Cal State LA	21	0
N27	●	at Hawaii	22	13

1960 9-1-0

S24	●	Hawaii	17	7
S30	●	at UC Santa Barbara	33	15
O8	●	Abilene Christian	20	19
O15	●	Cal Poly SLO	33	0
O22	●	at Cal State LA	35	13
O29	●	San Diego State	60	0
N5	●	Long Beach State	21	3
N11	●	at San Jose State	27	12
N19		Montana State	20	22
N26	●	Pacific	32	7

1961 10-0-0

S23	●	at Montana State	16	13
S30	●	UC Santa Barbara	22	14
O7	●	at Pacific	20	19
O14	●	at Cal Poly SLO	42	13
O21	●	at Cal State LA	35	6
O28	●	San Diego State	27	6
N3	●	at Long Beach State	37	14
N11	●	Abilene Christian	21	7
N18	●	San Jose State	36	27
		MERCY BOWL		
N23	●	at Bowling Green	36	6

1962 7-3-0

S22	●	Whitworth	48	7
S28	●	at UC Santa Barbara	37	0
O6		at Abilene Christian	14	26
O13	●	Cal Poly SLO	51	6
O20	●	at Cal State LA	34	0
O27		at San Diego State	26	29
N3	●	Long Beach State	50	0
N10	●	at San Jose State	20	14
N17	●	Pacific	18	13
N24		Montana State	20	21

1963 4-6-0

S21		at Idaho	8	32
S28		at Montana State	7	29
O5	●	Adams State	25	7
O12	●	at Pacific	29	7
O19	●	at Cal Poly SLO	28	0
O26	●	Cal State LA	35	20
N2		at Long Beach State	14	25
N9		San Diego State	6	34
N16		San Jose State	27	56
N23		Abilene Christian	29	32

PHIL KRUEGER
1964-65 (.500) 10-10

1964 4-6-0

S19	●	South Dakota State	20	14
S26		at Montana State	13	27
O3	●	Hawaii	28	0
O10		at Idaho State	12	20
O17	●	Cal Poly SLO	23	13
O24		at Cal State LA	12	32
O31		at San Diego State	6	44
N7		Long Beach State	20	21
N14	●	Pacific	54	7
N21		at San Jose State	14	26

1965 6-4-0

S25		at Colorado	7	10
O2	●	Washburn	54	0
O9	●	Montana State	25	14
O16	●	at Cal Poly SLO	20	14
O23		Cal State LA	15	17
O30		San Diego State	7	26
N6		at Long Beach State	12	14
N13	●	at Pacific	20	0
N20	●	San Jose State	24	18
N27	●	at Hawaii	7	3

DARRYL ROGERS
1966-72 (.572) 43-32-1

1966 7-3-0

S17	●	Hawaii	28	27
S24	●	Northern Arizona	14	12
O1		at Montana State	6	55
O8	●	CS Northridge	18	17
O15	●	Cal Poly SLO	14	7
O22	●	at Cal State LA	14	7
O29		at San Diego State	13	34
N5		Long Beach State	20	28
N12	●	Pacific	16	14
N19	●	at San Jose State	15	13

1967 3-8-0

S16		Santa Clara	16	24
S23		Idaho	14	30
S30		Montana State	20	21
O7	●	at CS Northridge	31	25
O14	●	at Cal Poly SLO	41	14
O21	●	Cal State LA	14	3
O28		San Diego State	21	28
N4		at Long Beach State	14	26
N11		at Pacific	20	32
N18		San Jose State	30	35
N25		at Hawaii	19	29

1968 7-4-0

S21		Idaho State	23	38
S28		at San Jose State	21	25
O5	●	at Portland State	30	13
O12	●	CS Northridge	35	12
O19	●	Cal Poly SLO	17	0
O25	●	at Cal State LA	42	20
N2		at San Diego State	12	42
N9	●	Long Beach State	34	28
N16	●	Montana State	31	16
N23	●	Pacific	10	3
		CAMELLIA BOWL		
D14		at Humboldt State	14	29

1969-1991
BIG WEST

1969 6-4-0 (1-3-0)

S20	●	Cal Poly SLO-Pomona	27	7
S27	●	at Montana State	28	20
O4	|	at Pacific	21	40
O11	●	at CS Northridge	38	14
O18		at Cal Poly SLO	17	21
O25	● |	Cal State LA	24	0
N1	|	San Diego State	20	48
N8	|	at Long Beach State	7	37
N15	●	Northern Arizona	27	18
N22	●	Portland State	28	22

1970 8-4-0 (4-2-0)

S12	●	Hayward State	28	12
S19	● |	at UC Santa Barbara	25	10
S26		Montana State	12	26
O3	● |	Pacific	34	14
O10	●	CS Northridge	21	7
O17	●	Cal Poly SLO	23	17
O24	● |	Cal State LA	51	6
O31	|	at San Diego State	14	56
N7	|	Long Beach State	14	50
N14	●	at Northern Arizona	40	7
N21	● |	at San Jose State	27	19
N28		at Hawaii	0	49

1971 6-5-0 (3-2-0)

S11		Hayward State	14	18
S18	● |	San Jose State	14	7
S25		at Montana State	28	37
O2	●	Hawaii	19	8
O16	●	at Cal Poly SLO	13	10
O23	● |	Cal State LA	47	7
O30	● |	San Diego State	17	10
N5	|	at Long Beach State	13	30
N13	●	CS Northridge	23	7
N20	|	at Pacific	13	14
		MERCY BOWL		
U		at Fullerton St.	14	17

1972 6-4-1 (1-3-0)

S9	●	Sacramento State	24	7
S16	●	Western Michigan	41	14
S23	●	at New Mexico State	49	17
S30	● |	at San Jose State	23	21
O7	|	Pacific	0	17
O14	=	Cal Poly SLO	24	24
O21	●	Cal State LA	31	0
O28	|	at San Diego State	14	21
N4	|	Long Beach State	16	21
N11	●	at Northern Illinois	9	6
N18		Montana State	6	10

J.R. BOONE
1973-75 (.294) 10-24

1973 2-9-0 (1-3-0)

S8		Cal Poly SLO-Pomona	9	17
S15	|	San Jose State	6	24
S22		Hawaii	10	13
S29		at Montana State	6	38
O6		Northern Illinois	15	24
O13		at Wichita State	13	18
O19	● |	at Long Beach State	15	14
O27		at Cal Poly SLO	14	28
N10	|	at Pacific	0	42
N17	|	San Diego State	6	41
N24	●	CS Northridge	54	24

1974 5-7-0 (1-3-0)

S7		Cal Poly SLO-Pomona	12	13
S14	|	at San Jose State	7	28
S21		Montana State	7	14
S28		Cal Poly SLO	13	17
O5	●	at New Mexico State	9	7
O12	|	at San Diego State	21	24
O19	● |	Pacific	37	21
O26	●	at Fullerton St.	48	21
N2	●	at CS Northridge	41	0
N9	|	Long Beach State	24	28
N15	●	Wichita State	24	12
N23		at Hawaii	7	21

1975 3-8-0 (1-4-0)

S6	● |	Fullerton St.	49	7
S13		at New Mexico	0	29
S20		CS Northridge	7	13
S27	●	at Montana State	34	17
O4		at Cal Poly SLO	7	24
O11	|	San Diego State	0	29
O18	|	at Long Beach State	17	47
O25	|	at Pacific	28	45
N1	|	San Jose State	7	21
N8		at Wichita State	11	28
N15	●	Cal State LA	59	14

JIM SWEENEY
1976-77, '80-'96 (.654) 143-75-3

1976 5-6-0 (3-1-0)

S11		at La. Lafayette	14	41
S18		at San Diego State	3	7
S25	●	Montana State	24	10
O2	● |	Fullerton St.	31	12
O9		at Wichita State	24	30
O16		Cal Poly SLO	15	17
O23	|	at San Jose State	7	21
O30	● |	Pacific	35	7
N6	● |	Long Beach State	23	0
N13	●	New Mexico State	44	0
N20		at Santa Clara	17	20

1977 9-2-0 (4-0-0)

S10		at La. Lafayette	13	34
S17	●	Boise State	42	7
S24		at Montana State	14	24
O1	●	at Cal Poly SLO	52	3
O8	●	San Diego State	34	14
O15	● |	at Pacific	24	10
O22	● |	San Jose State	45	24
O29	●	Idaho State	28	7
N5	● |	at Long Beach State	23	14
N11	● |	at Fullerton St.	44	19
N19	●	Santa Clara	35	7

BOB PADILLA
1978-79 (.318) 7-15

1978 3-8-0 (1-4-0)

S9		at McNeese St.	16	21
S16	●	at Weber St.	55	14
S23	|	at Utah State	22	45
S30		Cal Poly SLO	12	24
O7		at San Diego State	14	31
O14	|	Pacific	7	27
O21	|	at San Jose State	16	26
O28	|	Fullerton St.	8	37
N4	● |	Long Beach St.	42	41
N11		Montana St.	14	35
N18	●	at Idaho	41	28

1979 4-7-0 (3-2-0)

S8	●	Idaho	30	10
S15	●	at Montana St.	22	20
S22		San Diego State	23	32
S29		at Washington	14	49
O6		at Cal Poly SLO	0	26
O13	|	San Jose State	22	35 †
O20	|	at Long Beach St.	14	24
O27	● |	at Pacific	33	10
N3		Nevada-Las Vegas	28	31
N10	● |	at Fullerton St.	28	24
N24	|	Utah State	31	41

JIM SWEENEY

1980 5-6-0 (1-4-0)

S6	|	Fullerton St.	25	39
S13		at Nevada-Las Vegas	6	35
S20	●	La. Lafayette	16	14
S27		at Utah	12	27
O4	●	Cal Poly SLO	31	25
O11	|	at San Jose State	14	26
O18	● |	Pacific	27	3
O25	|	Utah State	0	14
N1	|	Long Beach St.	9	34
N8	●	at So. Illinois	31	14
N15	●	Montana St.	21	14

1981 5-6-0 (2-3-0)

S5	●	Oregon	23	16
S12		at Oregon State	28	31
S19		at Montana St.	26	30
O3	|	San Jose State	33	65
O10	|	at Fullerton St.	10	13
O17		So. Illinois	18	24
O24	● |	at Pacific	30	27
O31	|	at Utah State	0	20
N7	●	Nevada-Las Vegas	42	26
N14	● |	at Long Beach St.	31	30
N21	●	at Arizona	23	17

1982 11-1-0 (6-0-0)

S11	●	Cal Poly SLO	26	6
S18	●	at Oregon	10	4
S25	●	Weber St.	25	9
O2	● |	Utah State	31	6
O9	● |	Pacific	49	30
O16		at Nevada	26	40
O23	● |	at San Jose State	39	27
O30	● |	Long Beach St.	40	22
N6	● |	Fullerton St.	31	14
N13	●	Montana St.	45	14
N20	● |	at Nevada-Las Vegas	30	28
		CALIFORNIA BOWL		
D18	●	Bowling Green	29	28

1983 6-5-0 (2-4-0)

S10		Bowling Green	27	35
S17	●	Nevada	24	22
S24	● |	at Pacific	34	14
O1	|	at Utah State	12	20
O8	|	San Jose State	23	41
O15	●	at Montana St.	31	12
O22	|	at Fullerton St.	17	18
O29	●	at Cal Poly SLO	30	7
N5	|	Nevada-Las Vegas	7	20
N12	● |	at Long Beach St.	7	3
N19	●	No. Arizona	30	22

1984 6-6-0 (3-4-0)

S1	●	at Arizona	27	22
S8	●	Boise State	37	21
S15	●	Cal Poly SLO	14	0
S22	● |	Long Beach St.	20	17
S29	● |	New Mexico State	53	24
O6		at Hawaii	15	27
O20	● |	Utah State	43	18
O27	|	at San Jose State	17	18
N3	|	Fullerton St.	17	20
N10	|	Pacific	6	24
N17		Montana St.	31	35
N24	|	at Nevada-Las Vegas	13	27 †

1985 11-0-1 (7-0-0)

S14	● |	Nevada-Las Vegas	26	6
S21	●	at Oregon State	33	24
S28	●	at Cal Poly SLO	59	10
O5	=	Hawaii	24	24
O12	● |	San Jose State	37	17
O19	● |	at New Mexico State	48	21
O26	● |	at Utah State	38	19
N2	● |	at Fullerton St.	42	7
N9	● |	at Pacific	43	37
N16	● |	at Long Beach St.	33	31
N23	●	Wichita St.	47	6
		CALIFORNIA BOWL		
D14	●	Bowling Green	51	7

1986 9-2-0 (6-1-0)

S6	●	Montana St.	55	2
S13	●	Oregon State	27	0
S27	●	Louisiana Tech	34	10
O4	|	at San Jose State	41	45
O11	● |	New Mexico State	17	14
O18	● |	Pacific	10	9
O25	● |	Long Beach St.	25	12
N1	● |	Fullerton St.	30	20
N8	● |	at Nevada-Las Vegas	36	7
N15		at Hawaii	13	24
N22	● |	Utah State	14	7

1987 6-5-0 (4-3-0)

S5		at Washington State	24	41
S12	●	Western Illinois	20	17
S19		at UCLA	0	17
O3	● |	Long Beach St.	30	7
O10	●	So. Illinois	35	0
O17	|	San Jose State	16	20
O24	|	at Pacific	22	23
O31	● |	Nevada-Las Vegas	45	10
N7	● |	Fullerton St.	21	17
N14	|	at Utah State	13	17
N21	● |	at New Mexico State	34	10

1988 10-2-0 (7-0-0)

S3	●	at New Mexico	68	21
S10		at Colorado	3	45
S17	● |	New Mexico State	41	0
S24	●	McNeese St.	49	0
O1		at Oregon State	10	21
O8	● |	at Fullerton St.	23	10
O15	● |	Utah State	51	10
O29	● |	at San Jose State	17	15
N5	● |	Pacific	34	0
N12	● |	at Nevada-Las Vegas	31	14
N19	● |	Long Beach St.	31	3
		CALIFORNIA BOWL		
D10	●	Western Michigan	35	30

1989 11-1-0 (7-0-0)

S2	●	Utah	52	22
S9	●	Montana	52	37
S16	● |	at Pacific	27	14
S23	● |	Long Beach St.	52	0
O7	●	Oregon State	35	18
O14	● |	at Utah State	34	7
O21	● |	Fullerton St.	33	19
O28	● |	Nevada-Las Vegas	31	17
N4	● |	San Jose State	31	30
N11	● |	at New Mexico State	45	5
N18		at New Mexico	22	45
		CALIFORNIA BOWL		
D9	●	Ball State	27	6

1990 8-2-1 (5-1-1)

S1	●	Eastern Michigan	41	10
S8	●	New Mexico	24	17
S15	●	at Utah	31	7
S22	● |	New Mexico State	42	3
S29	● |	at Fullerton St.	38	3
O6		at Northern Illinois	18	73
O13	= |	Utah State	24	24
O20	● |	Long Beach St.	28	16
N3	● |	at Nevada-Las Vegas	45	18
N10	● |	Pacific	48	17
N17	|	at San Jose State	7	42

1991 10-2-0 (6-1-0)

S7	●	Northern Illinois	55	7
S14	●	at Washington State	34	30
S21	●	at Oregon State	24	20
O5	●	New Mexico	94	17
O12	● |	Long Beach St.	42	14
O19	● |	at New Mexico State	42	28
O26	● |	Nevada-Las Vegas	48	22
N2	|	at Utah State	19	20
N9	● |	at Pacific	59	14
N16	● |	Fullerton St.	38	7
N23	● |	San Jose State	31	28
		CALIFORNIA BOWL		
D14		Bowling Green	21	28

1992-PRESENT
WAC

1992 9-4-0 (6-2-0)

S5	●	at Pacific	42	21
S12		at Oregon State	36	46
S19	● |	Colorado State	52	21
S26		Washington State	37	39
O3	●	Louisiana Tech	48	14
O10	|	at Brigham Young	24	36
O17	|	at Hawaii	45	47
O24	● |	New Mexico	31	28
O31	● |	Wyoming	42	31
N7	● |	Utah	41	15
N21	● |	at San Diego State	45	41
N28	● |	at Texas-El Paso	43	18
		FREEDOM BOWL		
D29	●	Southern Cal	24	7

1993 8-4-0 (6-2-0)

S4		at Baylor	39	42
S11	●	Oregon State	48	30
S18	● |	at New Mexico	41	24
S25	●	Utah State	30	14
O9	|	at Colorado State	32	34
O16	● |	Air Force	33	20
O23	● |	at Brigham Young	48	45
O30	|	at Wyoming	28	32
N6	● |	Texas-El Paso	30	10
N13	● |	Hawaii	45	21
N20	● |	San Diego State	63	27
		ALOHA BOWL		
D25		Colorado	30	41

1994 5-7-1 (3-4-1)

A29		Ohio State Ana	10	34
S3	●	San Jose State	45	13
S10		at Washington State	3	24
S17	●	Oregon State	24	14
S24	● |	at Hawaii	31	16
O8	|	Brigham Young	30	32
O15	● |	Wyoming	38	24
O22	|	at Air Force	7	42
O29	|	New Mexico	32	49
N5		Nevada	35	62
N12	= |	at Texas-El Paso	30	30
N19	|	Colorado State	42	44
N26	● |	at San Diego State	49	42

1995 5-7-0 (2-6-0)

S2	●	La. Monroe	31	17
S9	●	at California	25	24
S16	●	Pacific	56	24
S23	|	at Utah	21	25
S30		at UCLA	21	45
O7	● |	New Mexico	51	34
O14	|	at San Diego State	24	48
O28	|	Air Force	20	31
N4	|	at Hawaii	37	42
N11	● |	Texas-El Paso	47	14
N18	|	at Wyoming	10	38
N25	|	Brigham Young	28	45

1996 4-7 (3-5)

A31		Oregon	27	30
S7		at Auburn	0	62
S21	|	at Utah	17	45
S28	● |	Hawaii	20	0
O12	● |	San Jose State	28	18
O19	|	at Wyoming	21	42
O26	● |	at Nevada-Las Vegas	34	23
N2	●	Boise State	41	7
N9	|	Colorado State	20	42
N16	|	Air Force	38	44
N23	|	at San Diego State	21	31

PAT HILL
1997-PRESENT (.627) 64-38

1997 6-6 (5-3)

A30	●	Portland St.	35	7
S6		Baylor	35	37
S13		at Oklahoma State	0	35
S20		at Oregon	40	43
O2	● |	Utah	27	13
O11	|	at Hawaii	16	28
O18	● |	at Air Force	20	17
O25	● |	Nevada-Las Vegas	46	28
N1	● |	at San Jose State	53	12
N8	|	at Colorado State	3	41
N15	|	San Diego State	19	20
N22	● |	Wyoming	24	7

1998 5-6 (5-3)

S12		at Colorado	21	29
S19		at Texas Tech	28	34
S26		Nevada	24	27
O3	● |	Brigham Young	31	21
O10	|	at TCU	10	21
O17	|	at Utah	16	24
O24	● |	Texas-El Paso	32	6
O31	● |	at New Mexico	28	20
N7	|	at San Diego State	0	10
N14	● |	Hawaii	51	12
N21	● |	San Jose State	24	21

1999 8-5 (5-2)

S4	●	Portland St.	34	6
S11		at Oregon State	23	46
S18		at UCLA	21	35
S25	●	at Nevada	49	24
O2	● |	TCU	26	19
O9	●	Colorado State	44	13
O14	|	at SMU	14	24
O23	● |	Texas-El Paso	24	23
O30	● |	at Tulsa	28	14
N6	● |	Rice	47	18
N13	|	at Hawaii	24	31
N20	● |	San Jose State	63	12
		LAS VEGAS BOWL		
D18		Utah	16	17

2000 7-5 (6-2)

S2		at Ohio State	10	43
S9		at UCLA	21	24
S23	●	California	17	3
O5	● |	at Rice	27	24
O14	● |	Nevada	58	21
O21	|	at Texas-El Paso	13	23
O28	● |	Tulsa	34	12
N4	● |	Hawaii	45	27
N11	|	at TCU	7	24
N18	● |	SMU	14	7
N25	● |	at San Jose State	37	6
		SILICON VALLEY CLASSIC		
D31		Air Force	34	37

2001   11-3 (6-2)

A26	●	at Colorado	24	22
S2	●	Oregon State	44	24
S8	●	at Wisconsin	32	20
S22	● |	at Tulsa	37	18
S29	● |	Louisiana Tech	38	28
O13	●	at Colorado State	25	22
O19	|	Boise State	30	35
O26	|	at Hawaii	34	38
N3	● |	Rice	52	24
N10	● |	at SMU	38	13
N17	● |	at Nevada	61	14
N23	● |	San Jose State	40	21
D1	●	Utah State	70	21

SILICON VALLEY CLASSIC

D31		Michigan State	35	44

2002   9-5 (6-2)

A23		at Wisconsin	21	23
A31	●	San Diego State	16	14
S7		at Oregon	24	28
S21		at Oregon State	19	59
S28	● |	at Rice	31	28
O4	●	Colorado State	32	30
O12	● |	SMU	30	7
O19	|	at Boise State	21	67
O26	|	Hawaii	21	31
N9	● |	Tulsa	31	12
N16	● |	Nevada	38	30
N23	● |	at San Jose State	19	16
D5	● |	at Louisiana Tech	45	13

SILICON VALLEY BOWL

D31	●	Georgia Tech	30	21

2003   9-5 (6-2)

A30		at Tennessee	6	24
S5	●	Oregon State	16	14
S13		at Oklahoma	28	52
S20	● |	Louisiana Tech	16	6
S27	●	Portland St.	42	16
O4		at Colorado State	10	34
O11	|	at Hawaii	28	55
O25	● |	Rice	31	28
N1	● |	at SMU	20	11
N8	● |	at Nevada	27	10
N15	● |	San Jose State	41	7
N21	|	Boise State	17	31
N29	● |	at Texas-El Paso	23	20

SILICON VALLEY BOWL

D30	●	UCLA	17	9

2004   9-3 (5-3)

S5	●	at Washington	35	16
S11	●	at Kansas State	45	21
S18	●	Portland St.	27	17
O2	|	at Louisiana Tech	21	28
O9	|	Texas-El Paso	21	24
O23	|	at Boise State	16	33
O30	● |	SMU	42	0
N6	● |	at Rice	52	21
N13	● |	Hawaii	70	14
N20	● |	Nevada	54	17
N27	● |	at San Jose State	62	28

MPC COMPUTERS BOWL

D27	●	Virginia	37	34

ƒ Forfeit † Game Later Forfieted # Disputed Victor * Disputed Score ‖ Designated Conference Game │2 Counted Twice in Conference Standings

GEORGIA

BY GEOFFREY NORMAN

SEVERAL SCHOOLS HAVE WON national championships and fielded Heisman winners. And these accomplishments go a long way toward making a program eligible for "elite" status in the universe of college football. But a few teams have gone even further and become iconic. To get to this level, you need to have been coached, at some time, by a man whose name is mythic—like, oh, Pop Warner. You need a stadium that doesn't even have to go by its proper name, so when the team is at home, you could say it plays "between the hedges." You need a mascot that everyone in the world recognizes—an English bulldog would do nicely. And you need a war cry that has been appropriated all over the football world but resonates best in the original, "How 'bout them Dawgs!"

One team, of course, has all these things and, thus, an undeniable place in the pantheon of college football programs. It is impossible, in short, to imagine college football without the University of Georgia.

TRADITION Back in the late 1800s, when the Georgia football field was located not far from the university chapel, students began the custom of ringing the chapel bell until midnight following each Georgia win. The tradition used to dictate that only Bulldogs freshmen ring the bell, but now everyone is welcome to ring in another night of celebration following a victory.

BEST PLAYER Georgia has produced a number of All-Americas and two Heisman winners. The first to capture both honors was Frank Sinkwich, a single-wing tailback, who won the Heisman in 1942, when he set an SEC record of 2,187 yards total offense. Sinkwich was small—only 5'10" and 185 pounds—but he was shifty, and any defense that played him to run made itself vulnerable to the pass. In his career, Sinkwich ran for 30 touchdowns, passed for 30 more and accounted for more than 4,600 yards of total offense. Losing only one game in his senior year, he became the first Heisman winner from a Southern school, and the greatest back in Georgia history. That is, until the 1980s and the arrival of one Herschel Walker, who immediately lit up the college football world like a comet.

Walker was a freshman listed as the third-string tailback on the depth chart when the 1980 season started. In the first game, with Tennessee keeping the Georgia offense bottled up and leading 15-0, he got his chance and scored twice. Walker flattened future pro Bill Bates on one touchdown run to bring the Bulldogs back for a 16-15 victory. Walker never looked back—he had four 200-yard

---

PROFILE

University of Georgia
Athens, Ga.
Founded: 1785
Enrollment: 24,814
Colors: Red and Black
Nickname: Bulldogs
Stadium: Sanford Stadium
    Opened in 1929
    FleldTurf; 92,746 capacity
First football game: 1892
All-time record: 683–372–54 (.640)
Bowl record: 22–15–3
Consensus national championships, 1936-present: 2 (1942, 1980)
Southeastern Conference championships: 11 (8 outright)
Heisman Trophy: Frank Sinkwich, 1942; Herschel Walker, 1982
Outland Trophy: Bill Stanfill, 1968
First-round NFL draftees: 24
Website: www.georgiadogs.com

THE BEST OF TIMES

Vince Dooley's Dawgs won a national title and 23 straight conference games, and went 43–4–1 in the four seasons from 1980 to 1983.

THE WORST OF TIMES

From 1949 through 1956, Georgia lost to archrival Georgia Tech eight straight times.

CONFERENCE

After 12 seasons in the Southern Conference (1921-32), Georgia became a charter member of the Southeastern Conference in 1933.

DISTINGUISHED ALUMNI

Kim Basinger, actress; Pete Correll, chairman of Georgia-Pacific Corp.; Phil Gramm, U.S. senator; Pat Mitchell, president of PBS; Hala Moddelmog, president of Church's Chicken; Deborah Norville, TV journalist

FIGHT SONG

GLORY
Glory, glory to old Georgia!
Glory, glory to old Georgia!
Glory, glory to old Georgia!
G-E-O-R-G-I-A.
Glory, glory to old Georgia!
Glory, glory to old Georgia!
Glory, glory to old Georgia!
G-E-O-R-G-I-A.

rushing games that season—and the Bulldogs finished the year undefeated, untied and as consensus national champs. Walker rushed for 1,616 yards and finished third in the Heisman balloting. The next season, he finished second. As a junior, he finally won the award, then left school for the United States Football League. There has never been another three years in Bulldog history to compare with the Walker era, when the Bulldogs swept to three straight SEC titles and lost just three times in three seasons.

BEST COACH The legendary Pop Warner did coach the Bulldogs (then known as the Red and Black) briefly. And Wally Butts won a share of the national championship in 1942, and also had the face of a Georgia Bulldog. But Georgia's best coach was, without a doubt, Vince Dooley.

A former Auburn quarterback (there is a remarkable amount of cross-fertilization between these longtime rivals), Dooley was hired in 1964 at the young age of 31 to bring Georgia back to respectability. Butts had resigned in 1960 and his successor, Johnny Griffith, had his troubles, especially against the teams he needed to beat, going 1–8 against Auburn, Florida and Georgia Tech.

Twenty-five years later, Dooley left the sideline to

The origins of the Bulldogs moniker are typically linked to Georgia's ties to Yale.

become full-time athletic director. His record was 201–77–10. His teams had won one national championship and finished on top of the SEC six times. Under Dooley, the Bulldogs went to 20 bowl games.

Dooley was not an innovator. He preached the old-time religion of football fundamentals. Defense, the running game, kicking. It was never flashy but it worked, and it made believers out of Bulldog fans, who were also attracted to Dooley's homespun wisdom. After spurning an offer to coach at his alma mater in 1980, Dooley rightly said, "The overriding factor was I had too much invested here. I wouldn't leave. This has been my home for 17 years. I'm a Bulldog and proud to be one."

Dooley also earned a reputation as a player's coach. After Georgia won its first SEC title in eight years in 1976, he fulfilled a vow to his team that he'd shave his head—to mimic chrome-domed defensive coordinator Erik Russell—in honor of the accomplishment.

BEST TEAM The 1942 team won the Rose Bowl and a national championship but lost in an upset to Auburn. The 1946 team was undefeated and untied but was not consensus national champion. So the choice is the 1980

RECORDS

RUSHING YARDS
GAME
283 Herschel Walker vs. Vanderbilt, Oct. 18, 1980 (23 att.)
SEASON
1,891 Herschel Walker, 1981 (385 att.)
CAREER
5,259 Herschel Walker, 1980-82 (994 att.)

PASSING YARDS
GAME
544 Eric Zeier vs. Southern Mississippi, Oct. 9, 1993 (30 of 47)
SEASON
3,525 Eric Zeier, 1993 (269 of 425)
CAREER
11,528 David Greene, 2001-04 (849 of 1,440)

RECEIVING YARDS
GAME
201 Fred Gibson vs. Kentucky, Oct. 20, 2001 (9 rec.)
SEASON
1,004 Terrence Edwards, 2002 (59 rec.)
CAREER
3,093 Terrence Edwards, 1999-2002 (204 rec.)

POINTS
GAME
30 Robert Edwards vs. South Carolina, Sept. 2, 1995 (5 TDs)
SEASON
131 Billy Bennett, 2003 (31 FGs, 38 PATs)
CAREER
409 Billy Bennett, 2000-03 (87 FGs, 148 PATs)

CONSENSUS ALL-AMERICANS

1927	Tom Nash, E
1931	Vernon Smith, E
1941-42	Frank Sinkwich, B
1946	Charley Trippi, B
1967	Ed Chandler, T
1968	Bill Stanfill, DT
1968	Jake Scott, DB
1971	Royce Smith, G
1975	Randy Johnson, G
1976	Joel Parrish, G
1980-82	Herschel Walker, RB
1982-83	Terry Hoage, DB
1984	Kevin Butler, PK
1984	Jeff Sanchez, DB
1985	Pete Anderson, C
1988	Tim Worley, RB
1992	Garrison Hearst, RB
1998	Champ Bailey, DB
1998	Matt Stinchcomb, OL
2002, 2004	David Pollack, DE
2004	Thomas Davis, FS

team, which went undefeated and untied and was the consensus national champ. That team came from behind to beat Tennessee in the season opener. The Bulldogs beat South Carolina—in a battle of ranked teams—in the eighth game of the season to move up to No. 2. The next week, Georgia trailed rival Florida 21-20 with 63 seconds to play and the ball on the Bulldogs' 7-yard line. A 93-yard TD pass from Buck Belue to Lindsay Scott—a play that will live forever in Bulldog hearts—saved the day and the season. Georgia went to the Sugar Bowl to play Notre Dame. Herschel Walker ran for two touchdowns and the Bulldogs won 17-10 to take their throne as undisputed champions.

STORYBOOK SEASON After Herschel Walker left to join the USFL, little was expected of the Bulldogs prior to the 1983 season. The team began the campaign with gaping holes at tailback and at quarterback, where John Lastinger's main gift was for leadership. With grit and defense, the Bulldogs scrapped their way to a 9–1–1 regular season and went to the Cotton Bowl to play undefeated, untied, No. 2 Texas. The Bulldogs leaned on their defense to keep the score close and awaited their chance. That came when Texas fumbled a punt late in the game. Georgia turned opportunity into a touchdown and won 10-9 to finish No. 4 in the nation.

BIGGEST GAME A 15-0 win on Oct. 12, 1929, over Yale—reigning football power from the East—at the dedication of Sanford Stadium still resonates down the years. There were so many satisfying elements to that victory, not least that nobody expected the Bulldogs to win and that they did it in front of a crowd (30,000) that exceeded the capacity of the new stadium. The Bulldogs from New Haven were whipped so convincingly that they never came south again.

BIGGEST UPSET Defending national champion Alabama was ahead 17-10 in Athens on Sept. 18, 1965, and had Georgia pinned inside its own 30-yard line with 2:08 to play. On second and eight, quarterback Kirby Moore passed to Pat Hodgson, who then lateraled to Bob Taylor, who ran the ball in for a touchdown. The play covered 73 yards. Georgia went for two against a frustrated Tide and Moore again hit Hodgson—no lateral necessary. Georgia 18, Alabama 17. To this day, Tide fans insist that Pat Hodgson's knees were on the ground before he lateraled to Bob Taylor for the decisive touchdown. The film was pretty clearly on Alabama's side but as Bear Bryant said, "You don't win games in the movies on Monday."

TRAGEDY The University of Virginia and the University of Georgia met in Atlanta in 1897 to play football, a sport still in its infancy. Virginia owned a decisive lead when Richard Vonalbade Gammon, one of Georgia's best players, was injured badly enough to be taken from the field and delivered by horse-drawn ambulance to a nearby hospital. He died there the next morning.

Gammon's death ignited a campaign to abolish the sport of football in the state of Georgia. A bill had made it through the legislature and was on the governor's desk for his signature when he received a letter from Gammon's mother. "It would be inexpressibly sad," she pleaded, "to have the cause he held so dear injured by his sacrifice. Grant me the right to request that the boy's death should not be used to defeat the most cherished object of his life." The governor refused to sign the bill. Football in Georgia survived Gammon's death.

BEST COMEBACK Down 20-0 to Georgia Tech on Dec. 2, 1978, a true freshman named Buck Belue (could there be a better name for a Georgia quarterback?) entered the game for the Bulldogs and provided the spark they needed. But a 21-20 Georgia lead vanished when Drew Hill returned a kick 101 yards and Tech converted a two-point attempt. But Belue was undaunted, which may have been his greatest asset as a football player. He drove the Bulldogs 84 yards, including a 43-yard touchdown pass to Amp Arnold, who also took a pitch from Belue and ran it in for two and a 29-28 victory.

STADIUM A seating capacity of slightly more than 92,700 makes Sanford Stadium the fifth-largest college football stadium in the country. The stadium is now more than 75 years old and seats more than three times the number of fans (30,000) who attended the first game played there. English privet hedges surround the field and the playing surface is natural grass. Other football teams play in stadiums with shrubbery surrounding the field, but the Georgia Bulldogs' landscaping became immortal when a sportswriter of the 1930s (some insist it was Grantland Rice) observed that the Bulldogs had their opponents "between the hedges."

RIVAL A poll of the house would probably divide the Bulldog faithful into thirds on this issue. One-third would say Auburn and have a good case, since it is the South's oldest continuous football rivalry. Georgia's greatest coach, Vince Dooley, played at Auburn. And Auburn's sainted

Shug Jordan was the basketball coach at Georgia from 1947 to 1950, before becoming head football coach at Auburn (1951 to 1975). The game is played late in the season and there is generally a lot riding on it. But another game on Georgia's schedule—often the next one of the schedule—would get the votes of another third of the Bulldog faithful. Georgia Tech is, after all, an in-state rival. Lose to Tech and you'll hear about it all year long. This game means marginally less today than during the era of Bobby Dodd's powerhouse Tech teams in the two decades following World War II. Still, even as Tech's fortunes have fluctuated, the battle for in-state bragging rights has remained undeniably fierce.

And then there is Florida. The game is known as "the world's largest outdoor cocktail party." Ordinarily the game is played in Jacksonville on what is supposed to be neutral turf. The faithful come from both states for the obligatory tailgating and a game that can be decisive in the SEC and national championship picture. The intensity had always been there, but when Steve Spurrier arrived at Florida he managed to jack it up several notches. He also dominated the series and made it into an almost personal thing, which just made the Bulldogs hungrier.

NICKNAME The origins of the Bulldogs moniker are obscure and typically linked to the strong ties between the University of Georgia and Yale University. Georgia's first president, Abraham Baldwin, was a Yale man, and some of the early structures on campus were copied from Yale buildings. In 1920, a writer for the *Atlanta Journal* suggested the name, arguing that there was "a certain dignity about a bulldog, as well as ferocity." Later that year, another writer used "Bulldogs" five times in an account of a game with Virginia that ended in a scoreless tie. The name stuck.

MASCOT The English bulldog wearing the spiked collar and the red jersey is as essential to college football as the Golden Dome and the Ohio State band dotting the "i." There is simply no more recognizable mascot in all of college football. *Sports Illustrated* acknowledged this obvious fact when it put Uga V on its April 28, 1997, cover. Uga V also appeared in the Clint Eastwood film *Midnight in the Garden of Good and Evil*. His predecessor, Uga IV, joined Herschel Walker at the Downtown Athletic Club in New York for the presentation of the Heisman Trophy. Those two mascots — along with Uga I, Uga II and Uga III—are buried near the main gate in the embankment of the south stands. Before each game, flowers are placed on their graves. And if you're looking to win a bar bet, here's a nugget of trivia. The first Georgia mascot wasn't a bulldog, but a goat.

UNIFORMS Red jerseys and the famous "silver britches." Coach Wally Butts introduced these in 1939. When Vince Dooley redesigned the uniform in 1964, he went for more subdued white pants. Then, before the 1980 season, he went back to the silver britches and the Bulldogs wore them on a march to the national title.

QUOTE "Win in football. That's the bottom line. It doesn't really matter what you do in the other stuff as long as you're winning in football."—Vince Dooley, asked to give advice to his successor as athletic director before stepping down in 2004 after four decades with the Georgia program

GEORGIA ALL-TIME SCORES

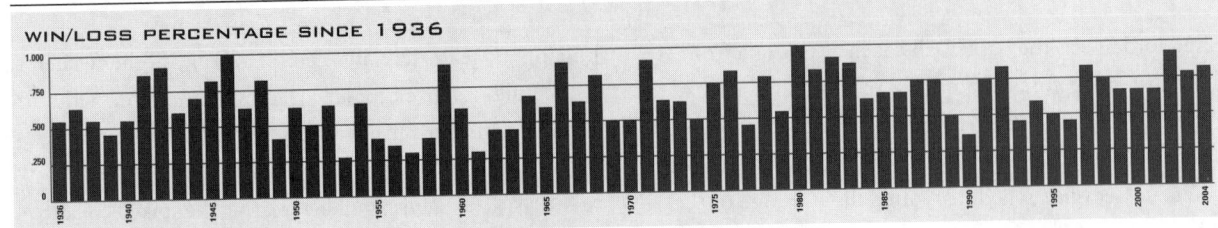

WIN/LOSS PERCENTAGE SINCE 1936

DR. CHARLES HERTY
1892 (.500)   1-1

1892   1-1-0
J30 ●	Mercer	50	0
F20 ●	Auburn *Atl*	0	10

ERNEST BROWN
1893 (.500)   2-2-1

1893   2-2-1
N4 ●	Georgia Tech	6	28
N7 ●	at Vanderbilt	10	35 *
N30 =	at Savannah AC	0	0
D1 ●	Augusta AC *Aug*	24	0
D9 ●	Furman *Aug*	22	8

ROBERT WINSTON
1894 (.833)   5-1

1894   5-1-0
O29 ●	Sewanee	8	12
N3 ●	at So. Carolina St.	40	0
N10 ●	at Wofford	10	0
N17 ●	at Augusta AC	66	0
N24 ●	Auburn *Atl*	10	8
N29 ●	at Savannah AC	22	0

GLENN "POP" WARNER
1895-96 (.636)   7-4

1895   3-4-0
O19 ●	Wofford	34	0
O26 ●	North Carolina *Atl*	0	6
O31 ●	North Carolina *Atl*	6	10
N2 ●	Alabama *ColGa*	30	6
N9 ●	Sewanee *Atl*	22	0
N23 ●	at Vanderbilt	0	6
N28 ●	Auburn *Atl*	6	16

1896   4-0-0
O24 ●	at Wofford	26	0
O31 ●	North Carolina *Atl*	24	16
N9 ●	Sewanee	26	0
N26 ●	Auburn *Atl*	12	6

CHARLES McCARTHY
1897-98 (.667)   6-3

1897   2-1-0
O9 ●	Clemson	24	0
O23 ●	Georgia Tech	28	0
N20 ●	Virginia *Atl*	4	17

1898   4-2-0
O8 ●	Clemson	20	8
O15 ●	Atlanta AC	14	0
O22 ●	Georgia Tech	15	0
O29 ●	Vanderbilt *Atl*	4	0
N12 ●	North Carolina *Mac*	0	44 *
N24 ●	Auburn	17	18

GORDON SAUSSY
1899 (.417)   2-3-1

1899   2-3-1
O7 ●	Clemson	11	0
O21 ●	Sewanee *Atl*	0	12
O28 ●	Georgia Tech	33	0 *
N11 ●	at Tennessee	0	5
N18 =	Auburn *Atl*	0	0
N30 ●	North Carolina *Atl*	0	5

E.E. JONES
1900 (.333)   2-4

1900   2-4-0
O13 ●	Georgia Tech *Atl*	12	0
O20 ●	South Carolina	5	0
O27 ●	Sewanee *Atl*	6	21
N10 ●	Clemson	5	39
N17 ●	North Carolina *Ral*	0	55
N29 ●	Auburn *Atl*	0	44

BILLY REYNOLDS
1901-02 (.433)   5-7-3

1901   1-5-2
O12 ●	South Carolina *Aug*	10	5
O19 ●	at Vanderbilt	0	47
O21 ●	at Sewanee	0	47
O26 ●	Clemson	5	29
N2 ●	North Carolina *Atl*	0	27
N9 =	Alabama *Mont*	0	0
N16 ●	Davidson	6	16
N28 ●	Auburn *Atl*	0	0

1902   4-2-1
O18 ●	Furman	11	0
O25 =	at Georgia Tech	0	0
N1 ●	Alabama *Birm*	5	0
N7 ●	Davidson	20	0
N8 ●	at Clemson	0	36
N11 ●	Sewanee *Atl*	0	11
N27 ●	Auburn *Atl*	12	5

M.M. DICKINSON
1903, '05 (.308)   4-9

1903   3-4-0
O10 ●	Clemson	0	29
O17 ●	South Carolina	0	17
O24 ●	at Georgia Tech	38	0
O31 ●	Vanderbilt	0	33
N7 ●	at Tennessee	5	0
N14 ●	at Savannah	0	6
N26 ●	Auburn *Atl*	22	13

CHARLES A. BARNARD
1904 (.167)   1-5

1904   1-5-0
O8 ●	Florida U. Club *Mac*	52	0
O22 ●	at Clemson	0	10
O26 ●	at South Carolina	0	2
N5 ●	at Alabama	5	16
N12 ●	at Georgia Tech	6	23
N24 ●	Auburn *Mac*	6	17 *

M.M. DICKINSON

1905   1-5-0
O3 ●	Cumberland	10	39
O21 ●	Clemson	0	35
N4 ●	Alabama *Birm*	0	36
N11 ●	North Georgia	16	12
N18 ●	at Georgia Tech	0	46
N30 ●	Auburn *Mac*	0	20 *

W.S. WHITNEY
1906-07 (.417)   4-6-2

1906   2-4-1
O13 ●	Davidson	0	15
O20 ●	at Clemson	0	6
N3 ●	at Mercer	55	0
N10 ●	Georgia Tech	0	17
N21 =	Tennessee	0	0
N29 ●	Auburn *Mac*	4	0
D2 ●	at Savannah AC	0	12

1907   4-3-1
O5 ●	North Georgia	57	0
O12 ●	Tennessee	0	15
O19 ●	at Mercer	26	6
O25 =	Alabama *Mont*	0	0
N2 ●	at Georgia Tech	6	10
N7 ●	Clemson *Aug*	8	0
N11 ●	Sewanee	0	16
N28 ●	Auburn *Mac*	6	0

BRANCH BOCOCK
1907-08 (.682)   7-3-1

1908   5-2-1
O3 ●	North Georgia	16	0
O17 ●	South Carolina	29	6
O24 ●	at Tennessee	0	10
O31 ●	Mercer	10	0
N5 ●	Clemson *Aug*	8	0
N14 ●	Alabama *Atl*	6	6
N21 ●	Davidson	2	0
N26 ●	Auburn *Mont*	0	23

J. COULTER/FRANK DOBSON
1909 (.286)   1-4-2

1909   1-4-2
O9 ●	at Citadel	0	0
O16 ●	Davidson	0	0
O23 ●	at Tennessee	3	0
O30 ●	Alabama *Atl*	0	14
N10 ●	Clemson *Aug*	0	5
N20 ●	at Georgia Tech	6	12
N25 ●	Auburn *Mont*	5	17 *

W.A. CUNNINGHAM
1910-19 (.679)   43-18-9

1910   6-2-1
O1 ●	Locust Grove	101	0
O8 ●	Gordon	79	0
O15 ●	Alabama *Birm*	22	0
O22 ●	Tennessee	35	5
O29 ●	Mercer	21	0
N5 ●	at Sewanee	12	15
N10 =	Clemson *Aug*	0	0
N19 ●	at Georgia Tech	11	6
N24 ●	Auburn *Sav*	0	26

1911   7-1-1
S30 ●	Alabama Presbyterian	51	0
O7 ●	South Carolina	38	0
O14 ●	Alabama *Birm*	11	3
O21 ●	Sewanee	12	3
O28 ●	Mercer	8	5
N4 ●	at Vanderbilt	0	17
N9 ●	Clemson *Aug*	22	0
N18 ●	at Georgia Tech	5	0
N29 =	Auburn *Sav*	0	0

1912   6-1-1
O5 ●	U.T. Chattanooga	33	0
O12 ●	Citadel	33	0
O19 ●	Vanderbilt *Atl*	0	46
O26 ●	Alabama *ColGa*	13	9
N2 ●	Sewanee	13	13
N9 ●	Clemson *Aug*	27	6
N16 ●	at Georgia Tech	20	0
N28 ●	Auburn	12	6

1913   6-2-0
O4 ●	Alabama Presbyterian	108	0
O11 ●	North Georgia	51	0
O18 ●	Alabama *Birm*	20	0
O25 ●	Virginia *Atl*	6	13
N1 ●	North Carolina	19	6
N6 ●	Clemson *Aug*	18	15
N15 ●	at Georgia Tech	14	0
N22 ●	Auburn *Atl*	7	21

1914   3-5-1
S26 ●	North Georgia	81	0
O3 ●	Citadel	13	0
O10 ●	at Sewanee	7	6
O17 ●	North Carolina *Atl*	6	41
O24 ●	at Virginia	0	28
O31 ●	Mississippi State	0	9
N7 ●	Clemson	13	35
N14 ●	at Georgia Tech	0	7
N21 ●	Auburn *Atl*	0	0

1915   5-2-2
S28 ●	Newberry	79	0
O1 ●	North Georgia	64	0
O9 ●	at U.T. Chattanooga	6	6
O16 ●	at Citadel	39	0
O23 ●	Virginia	7	9
O30 ●	Auburn	0	12
N6 ●	Florida *JacF*	37	0
N13 ●	at Georgia Tech	0	0
N25 ●	Clemson	13	0

1916   6-3-0
S30 ●	Citadel	6	0
O7 ●	Clemson *And*	26	0
O14 ●	Florida	21	0
O21 ●	at Virginia	13	7
O28 ●	at Navy	3	27
N4 ●	Auburn *ColGa*	0	3
N11 ●	Furman	49	0
N18 ●	Georgia Tech	0	21
N30 ●	Alabama *Birm*	3	0

1917-1918
NO TEAM WWI

1919   4-2-3
O4 ●	Citadel	28	0
O11 ●	South Carolina	14	0
O18 ●	Sewanee	13	0
O25 ●	Florida *Tam*	16	0
N1 ●	Auburn *ColGa*	0	7
N7 =	Virginia	7	7
N15 =	Tulane *Aug*	7	7
N22 ●	Alabama *Atl*	0	6
N27 =	Clemson	0	0

H.J. STEGEMAN
1920-22 (.741)   20-6-3

1920   8-0-1
O2 ●	Citadel	40	0
O9 ●	at South Carolina	37	0
O13 ●	at Furman	7	0
O23 ●	at Oglethorpe	27	3
O30 ●	Auburn *ColGa*	7	0
N6 ●	at Virginia	0	0
N13 ●	Florida	56	0
N20 ●	Alabama *Atl*	21	14
N25 ●	Clemson	55	0

1921-1932
SOUTHERN

1921   7-2-1 (4-0-0)
O1 ●	Mercer	28	0
O8 ●	Furman	27	7
O15 ●	at Harvard	7	10
O22 ●	Oglethorpe	14	0
O29		Auburn *ColGa*	7	0
N6 ●	Virginia	21	0
N13 =	at Vanderbilt	7	7
N19		Alabama *Atl*	22	0
N25		Clemson	28	0
N27 ●	Dartmouth *Atl*	0	7

GEORGIA 311

THE SCHOOLS

1922 5-4-1 (1-3-1)

S23	●	Newberry	82	13
S30	●	Mercer	41	0
O7		at Chicago	0	20
O14	●	at Furman	7	0
O21	● |	Tennessee	7	3
O28	●	Oglethorpe	26	6
N4	|	Auburn ColGa	3	7
N11	= |	at Virginia	6	6
N18	|	Vanderbilt	0	12
N25	|	Alabama Mont	6	10

GEORGE WOODRUFF
1923-27 (.649) 30-16-1

1923 5-3-1 (3-2-0)

S29	●	Mercer	7	0
O6	●	Oglethorpe	20	6
O13		at Yale	0	40
O20	● |	at Tennessee	17	0
N3	● |	Auburn ColGa	7	0
N10	● |	Virginia	13	0
N17	|	at Vanderbilt	7	35
N24	|	Alabama Mont	0	36
D1	=	Centre	3	3

1924 7-3-0 (5-1-0)

S27	●	Mercer	26	7
O4	● |	South Carolina	18	0
O11		at Yale	6	7
O18	●	Furman Aug	22	0
O25	● |	at Vanderbilt	3	0
N1	● |	Tennessee	33	0
N8	● |	at Virginia	7	0
N15	● |	Auburn ColGa	6	0
N27	|	Alabama Birm	0	33
N29		at Centre	7	14

1925 4-5-0 (2-4-0)

S26	●	at Mercer	32	0
O3	|	Virginia	6	7
O10		at Yale	7	35
O17	●	Furman Aug	21	0
O24	● |	Vanderbilt	26	7
O31	|	at Tennessee	7	12
N7	● |	Auburn ColGa	34	0
N14	|	at Georgia Tech	0	3
N26	|	Alabama Birm	0	27

1926 5-4-0 (4-2-0)

S25	●	Mercer	20	0
O2	● |	at Virginia	27	7 *
O9		at Yale	0	10
O16		Furman	7	14
O23	|	at Vanderbilt	13	14
O30	● |	Florida	32	9
N6	● |	Auburn ColGa	16	6 *
N13	● |	at Georgia Tech	14	13
N25	|	Alabama Birm	6	33

1927 9-1-0 (6-1-0)

O1	● |	Virginia	32	0
O8	●	at Yale	14	10
O15	●	Furman	32	0
O22	● |	Auburn ColGa	33	3 *
O29	● |	at Tulane	31	0
N5	● |	Florida JacF	28	0
N12	● |	Clemson	32	0
N19	●	Mercer	26	7
N27	● |	Alabama Birm	20	6
D3	|	at Georgia Tech	0	12

HARRY MEHRE
1928-37 (.626) 59-34-6

1928 4-5-0 (2-4-0)

O6	●	Mercer	52	0
O13		at Yale	6	21
O20	●	Furman	7	0
O27	● |	Tulane	20	14
N3	● |	Auburn ColGa	13	0
N10	|	Florida Sav	6	26
N17	|	LSU	12	13
N29	|	Alabama Birm	0	19
D8	|	Georgia Tech	6	20

1929 6-4-0 (4-2-0)

S28		Oglethorpe	6	13
O5	●	Furman	27	0
O12	●	Yale	15	0
O19	● |	at North Carolina	19	12
O26	|	Florida JacF	6	18
N2	|	Tulane ColGa	15	21
N9		NYU Brnx	19	27
N16	● |	Auburn	24	0
N28	● |	Alabama Birm	12	0
D7	● |	Georgia Tech	12	6

1930 7-2-1 (3-2-1)

S27	●	Oglethorpe	31	6
O4	●	Mercer	51	0
O11	●	at Yale	18	14
O18	● |	North Carolina	26	0
O25	● |	Auburn ColGa	39	7
N1	= |	Florida Sav	0	0
N8	●	NYU NYC	7	6
N15	|	at Tulane	0	25
N27	|	Alabama Birm	0	13
D6	● |	at Georgia Tech	13	0

1931 8-2-0 (6-1-0)

O3	● |	Virginia Tech	40	0
O10	●	at Yale	26	7
O17	● |	at North Carolina	32	7 *
O24	● |	Vanderbilt	9	0
O31	● |	at Florida	33	6
N7	●	NYU Brnx	7	6
N14	|	Tulane	7	20
N21	● |	Auburn ColGa	12	6
N28	● |	Georgia Tech	35	6
D12		at Southern Cal	0	60

1932 2-5-2 (2-4-2)

O1	|	Virginia Tech	6	7
O8	|	at Tulane	25	34
O15	= |	North Carolina	6	6
O22	|	at Vanderbilt	6	12
O29	● |	Florida	33	12
N5		NYU Brnx	7	13
N11	● |	at Clemson	32	18
N19	|	Auburn ColGa	7	14
N26	= |	at Georgia Tech	0	0

1933-Present
SEC

1933 8-2-0 (3-1-0)

S30	●	North Carolina St.	20	10
O7	● |	Tulane	26	13
O14	●	at North Carolina	30	0
O20	●	at Mercer	13	12
O28	●	NYU	25	0
N4	● |	Florida JacF	14	0
N11	●	at Yale	7	0
N18	|	Auburn ColGa	6	14
N25	● |	at Georgia Tech	7	6
D2		at Southern Cal	0	31

1934 7-3-0 (3-2-0)

S29	●	Stetson	42	0
O6	●	at Furman	7	2
O13		North Carolina	0	14
O20	|	at Tulane	6	7
O27	|	Alabama Birm	6	26
N3	● |	Florida JacF	14	0
N10	●	at Yale	14	7
N17	●	North Carolina St.	27	0
N24	● |	Auburn ColGa	18	0
D1	● |	Georgia Tech	7	0

1935 6-4-0 (2-4-0)

S28	●	Mercer	31	0
O5	●	at U.T. Chattanooga	40	0
O12	●	Furman	31	7
O19	●	at North Carolina St.	13	0
O26	|	Alabama	7	17
N2	● |	Florida JacF	7	0
N9	● |	at Tulane	26	13
N16	|	LSU	0	13
N23	|	Auburn ColGa	7	19
N30	|	at Georgia Tech	7	19

1936 5-4-1 (3-3-0)

S26	●	Mercer	15	6
O3	●	Furman	13	0
O10	|	at LSU	7	47
O17		Rice	6	13
O24	|	Auburn ColGa	13	20
O31	|	Tennessee	0	46
N7	● |	Florida JacF	26	8
N14	● |	at Tulane	12	6
N21	=	Fordham NYC	7	7
N28	● |	Georgia Tech	16	6

1937 6-3-2 (1-2-2)

S25	●	Oglethorpe	60	0
O2	●	at South Carolina	13	7
O9	●	Clemson	14	0
O16		at Holy Cross	6	7
O23	●	Mercer	19	0
O30	|	at Tennessee	0	32
N6	|	Florida JacF	0	6
N13	● |	Tulane	7	6
N20	= |	Auburn ColGa	0	0
N27	= |	at Georgia Tech	6	6
D10	●	at Miami, Fla.	26	8 *

JOEL HUNT
1938 (.550) 5-4-1

1938 5-4-1 (1-2-1)

S27	●	Citadel	20	0
O1	●	at South Carolina	7	6
O9	●	Furman	38	7
O17	●	Mercer	28	19
O26		at Holy Cross	6	29
N5	● |	Florida JacF	19	6
N12	|	at Tulane	6	28
N19	|	Auburn ColGa	14	23
N27	= |	Georgia Tech	0	0
D2		at Miami, Fla.	7	13

WALLACE BUTTS
1939-60 (.615) 140-86-9

1939 5-6-0 (1-3-0)

S30	●	Citadel	26	0
O7		at Furman	0	20
O14		Holy Cross	0	13
O21	|	Kentucky Lou	6	13
O28		NYU Brnx	13	14
N4	●	Mercer	16	9
N11	● |	Florida JacF	6	2
N18	●	South Carolina	33	7
N25	|	Auburn ColGa	0	7
D2	|	at Georgia Tech	0	13
D8	●	at Miami, Fla.	13	0

1940 5-4-1 (2-3-1)

S27	●	at Oglethorpe	53	0
O5	●	at South Carolina	33	2
O12	|	Mississippi	14	28
O19		at Columbia	13	19
O25	= |	Kentucky	7	7
N2	● |	Auburn ColGa	14	13
N9	|	Florida JacF	13	18
N16	|	at Tulane	13	21
N30	● |	Georgia Tech	21	19
D6	●	at Miami, Fla.	28	7

1941 9-1-1 (3-1-1)

S27	●	at Mercer	81	0
O4	●	South Carolina	34	6
O10	= |	Mississippi	14	14
O18	●	at Columbia	7	3
O25	|	Alabama Birm	14	27
N1	● |	Auburn ColGa	7	0
N8	● |	Florida JacF	19	3
N15	●	Centre	47	6
N22	●	Dartmouth	35	0
N29	● |	at Georgia Tech	21	0
		ORANGE BOWL		
J1	●	TCU	40	26

1942 11-1-0 (6-1-0)

S19	● |	Kentucky Lou	7	6
S25	●	Jacksonville NAS Mac	14	0
O3	●	Furman	40	7
O10	● |	Mississippi Mem	48	13
O17	● |	Tulane	40	0
O24	●	at Cincinnati	35	13
O31	● |	Alabama Atl	21	10
N7	● |	Florida JacF	75	0
N14	●	at U.T. Chattanooga	40	0
N21	|	Auburn ColGa	13	27
N28	● |	Georgia Tech	34	0
		ROSE BOWL		
J1	●	UCLA	9	0

1943 6-4-0 (0-3-0)

S17	●	Presbyterian	25	7
S25	|	at LSU	27	34
O1	●	Tennessee Tech	67	0
O8	●	Wake Forest	7	0
O10		at Daniel Field	7	18
O23	|	LSU ColGa	6	27
O29	●	Samford	39	0
N5	●	Presbyterian	40	12
N13	●	VMI Atl	46	7
N27	|	at Georgia Tech	0	48

1944 7-3-0 (4-2-0)

S29		Wake Forest	7	14
O6	●	Presbyterian	67	0
O13	● |	Kentucky	13	12
O20	●	Daniel Field	57	6
O28	|	LSU Atl	7	15
N4	● |	Alabama Birm	14	7
N11	● |	Florida JacF	38	12
N18	● |	Auburn ColGa	49	13
N24	●	Clemson	21	7
D2	|	Georgia Tech	0	44

1945 9-2-0 (4-2-0)

S22	●	Murray St.	49	0
S29	●	Clemson	20	0
O5	●	at Miami, Fla.	27	21
O13	● |	at Kentucky	48	6
O20	|	LSU	0	32
O27	|	Alabama Birm	14	28
N3	●	at U.T. Chattanooga	34	7
N10	● |	Florida JacF	34	0
N17	● |	Auburn ColGa	35	0
D1	● |	at Georgia Tech	33	0
		OIL BOWL		
J1	●	Tulsa	20	6

1946 11-0-0 (5-0-0)

S27	●	Clemson	35	12
O4	●	at Temple	35	7
O11	● |	Kentucky	28	13
O19	●	Oklahoma State	33	13
O26	●	at Furman	70	7
N2	● |	Alabama	14	0
N9	● |	Florida JacF	33	14
N16	● |	Auburn ColGa	41	0
N23	●	at U.T. Chattanooga	48	27
N30	● |	Georgia Tech	35	7
		SUGAR BOWL		
J1	●	North Carolina	20	10

1947 7-4-1 (3-3-0)

S19	●	Furman	13	7
S27		at North Carolina	7	14
O4	● |	LSU	35	19
O11	|	at Kentucky	0	26
O18	●	at Oklahoma State	20	7
O25	|	Alabama	7	17
O31	●	Clemson	21	6
N8	● |	Florida JacF	34	6
N15	● |	Auburn ColGa	28	6
N22	●	at U.T. Chattanooga	27	0
N29	|	at Georgia Tech	0	7
		GATOR BOWL		
J1	=	Maryland	20	20

1948 9-2-0 (6-0-0)

S25	●	U.T. Chattanooga	14	7
O2		North Carolina	14	21
O9	● |	Kentucky	35	12
O16	● |	at LSU	22	0
O22	●	at Miami, Fla.	42	21
O30	● |	Alabama Birm	35	0
N6	● |	Florida JacF	20	12
N13	● |	Auburn ColGa	42	14
N20	●	Furman	33	0
N27	● |	Georgia Tech	21	13
		ORANGE BOWL		
J1		Texas	28	41

1949 4-6-1 (1-4-1)

S16	●	Furman	25	0
S23	●	U.T. Chattanooga	42	6
O1		at North Carolina	14	21
O8	|	at Kentucky	0	25
O14	● |	LSU	7	0
O21		at Miami, Fla.	9	13
O29	|	Alabama	7	14
N5	|	Florida JacF	7	28
N12	●	Duquesne ColGa	40	0
N19	= |	Auburn	20	20
N26	|	at Georgia Tech	6	7

1950 6-3-3 (3-2-1)

S23	●	Maryland	27	7
S29	=	St. Mary's Cal. SF	7	7
O7	=	North Carolina	0	0
O14	● |	Mississippi State	27	0
O21	= |	at LSU	13	13
O27	●	at Boston College	19	7
N4	|	Alabama Birm	7	14
N11	● |	Florida JacF	6	0
N18	● |	Auburn ColGa	12	10
N25	●	Furman	40	0
D2	|	Georgia Tech	0	7
		PRESIDENTIAL CUP		
D9		Texas A&M	20	40

312 GEORGIA

THE SCHOOLS

1951 5-5-0 (2-4-0)

S22	●	George Washington	33	0
S29	●	at North Carolina	28	16
O6	|	at Mississippi State	0	6
O13		Maryland	7	43
O20	|	LSU	0	7
O27	●	Boston College	35	28
N3	|	Alabama	14	16
N10	● |	Florida JacF	7	6
N17	● |	Auburn ColGa	46	14
D1	|	at Georgia Tech	6	48

1952 7-4-0 (4-3-0)

S20	● |	at Vanderbilt	19	7
S27	● |	at Tulane	21	16
O4	●	North Carolina	49	0
O11		Maryland	0	37
O18	● |	at LSU	27	14
O25	|	Florida JacF	0	30
N1	|	Alabama BirM	19	34
N8	●	at Pennsylvania	34	27
N15	● |	Auburn ColGa	13	7
N29	|	Georgia Tech	9	23
D5	●	at Miami, Fla.	35	13

1953 3-8-0 (1-5-0)

S19	●	Villanova Phil	32	19
S26	● |	Tulane	16	14
O3		Texas A&M Dal	12	14
O10		at Maryland	13	40
O17	|	LSU	6	14
O24	●	North Carolina	27	14
O31	|	Alabama	12	33
N7	|	Florida JacF	7	21
N14	|	Auburn ColGa	18	39
N21		Southern Miss JaM	0	14
N28	|	at Georgia Tech	12	28

1954 6-3-1 (3-2-1)

S18	●	at Florida State	14	0
S25	●	Clemson	14	7
O2		Texas A&M	0	6
O9	●	at North Carolina	21	7
O16	● |	Vanderbilt	16	14
O23	● |	at Tulane	7	0
O30	= |	Alabama BirM	0	0
N6	● |	Florida JacF	14	13
N13	|	Auburn ColGa	0	35
N27	|	Georgia Tech	3	7

1955 4-6-0 (2-5-0)

S17	|	Mississippi Atl	13	26
S24	● |	Vanderbilt	14	13
O1		at Clemson	7	26
O8	●	North Carolina	28	7
O15	●	at Florida State	47	14
O22	|	Tulane	0	14
O29	● |	Alabama	35	14
N5	|	Florida JacF	13	19
N12	|	Auburn ColGa	13	16
N26	|	at Georgia Tech	3	21

1956 3-6-1 (1-6-0)

S22	|	at Vanderbilt	0	14
S29	●	Florida State	3	0
O6	|	Mississippi State	7	19
O13	●	at North Carolina	26	12
O19	=	at Miami, Fla.	7	7
O27	|	Kentucky	7	14
N3	● |	Alabama BirM	16	13
N10	|	Florida JacF	0	28
N17	|	Auburn ColGa	0	20
D1	|	Georgia Tech	0	35

1957 3-7-0 (3-4-0)

S21		Texas Atl	7	26
S28	|	Vanderbilt	6	9
O5		at Michigan	0	26
O11	● |	at Tulane	13	6
O19		Navy Nor	14	27
O26	● |	at Kentucky	33	14
N2	|	Alabama	13	14
N9	|	Florida JacF	0	22
N16	|	Auburn ColGa	0	6
N30	● |	at Georgia Tech	7	0

1958 4-6-0 (2-4-0)

S20		at Texas	8	13
S27	|	at Vanderbilt	14	21
O4		South Carolina	14	24
O11	●	Florida State JacF	28	13
O25	● |	Kentucky	28	0
N1	|	at Alabama	0	12
N8	|	Florida JacF	6	7
N15	|	Auburn ColGa	6	21
N22	●	Citadel	76	0
N29	● |	Georgia Tech	16	3

1959 10-1-0 (7-0-0)

S19	● |	Alabama	17	3
S26	● |	Vanderbilt	21	6
O3		at South Carolina	14	30
O10	●	Hardin-Simmons	35	6
O17	● |	Mississippi State Atl	15	0
O24	● |	at Kentucky	14	7
O31	●	Florida State	42	0
N7	● |	Florida JacF	21	10
N14	● |	Auburn	14	13
N28	● |	at Georgia Tech	21	14
		ORANGE BOWL		
J1	●	Missouri	14	0

1960 6-4-0 (4-3-0)

S17	|	Alabama BirM	6	21
S24	● |	at Vanderbilt	18	7
O1	●	South Carolina	38	6
O7		at Southern Cal	3	10
O15	● |	Mississippi State	20	17
O22	● |	at Kentucky	17	13
O29	●	Tulsa	45	7
N5	|	Florida JacF	14	22
N12	|	at Auburn	6	9
N26	● |	Georgia Tech	7	6

JOHNNY GRIFFITH
1961-63 (.400) 10-16-4

1961 3-7-0 (2-5-0)

S23	|	Alabama	6	32
S30	|	Vanderbilt	0	21
O7	●	South Carolina	17	14
O14		at Florida State	0	3
O21	● |	Mississippi State Atl	10	7
O28	● |	Kentucky	16	15
N3		at Miami, Fla.	7	32
N11	|	Florida JacF	14	21
N18	|	Auburn	7	10
D2	|	at Georgia Tech	7	22

1962 3-4-3 (2-3-1)

S22	|	Alabama BirM	0	35
S29	● |	at Vanderbilt	10	0
O6	=	at South Carolina	7	7
O13	●	at Clemson	24	16
O20		Florida State	0	18
O27	= |	Kentucky	7	7
N3	=	North Carolina St.	10	10
N10	|	Florida JacF	15	23
N17	● |	at Auburn	30	21
D1	|	Georgia Tech	6	37

1963 4-5-1 (2-4-0)

S21	|	Alabama	7	32
S28	● |	Vanderbilt	20	0
O5	●	South Carolina	27	7
O12	=	at Clemson	7	7
O18	●	at Miami, Fla.	31	14
O26	● |	at Kentucky	17	14
N2		at North Carolina	7	28
N9	|	Florida JacF	14	21
N16	|	Auburn	0	14
N30	|	at Georgia Tech	3	14

VINCE DOOLEY
1964-88 (.715) 201-77-10

1964 7-3-1 (3-2-0)

S19	|	at Alabama	3	31
S26	● |	at Vanderbilt	7	0
O3	=	at South Carolina	7	7
O10	●	Clemson	19	7
O17		Florida State	14	17
O24	● |	Kentucky	21	7
O31	●	North Carolina	24	8
N7	● |	Florida JacF	14	7
N14	|	at Auburn	7	14
N28	●	Georgia Tech	7	0
		SUN BOWL		
D26	●	Texas Tech	7	0

1965 6-4-0 (3-3-0)

S18	● |	Alabama	18	17
S25	● |	Vanderbilt	24	10
O2	●	at Michigan	15	7
O9	● ||	Clemson	23	9
O16		at Florida State	3	10
O23	|	at Kentucky	10	28
O30	●	at North Carolina	47	35
N6	|	Florida JacF	10	14
N13	|	Auburn	19	21
N27	●	at Georgia Tech	17	7

1966 10-1-0 (6-0-0)

S17	● |	Mississippi State JaM	20	17
S24	●	VMI Roa	43	7
O1	●	at South Carolina	7	0
O8	● |	Mississippi	9	3
O14		at Miami, Fla.	6	7
O22	● |	Kentucky	27	15
O29	● ||	North Carolina	28	3
N5	● |	Florida JacF	27	10
N12	● |	at Auburn	21	13
N26	●	Georgia Tech	23	14
		COTTON BOWL		
D31	●	SMU	24	9

1967 7-4-0 (4-2-0)

S23	● |	Mississippi State	30	0
S30	● ||	at Clemson	24	17
O7	●	South Carolina	21	0
O14	|	Mississippi JaM	20	29
O21	●	VMI	56	6
O28	● |	at Kentucky	31	7
N4		at Houston	14	15
N11	|	Florida JacF	16	17
N18	● |	Auburn	17	0
N25	●	at Georgia Tech	21	14
		LIBERTY BOWL		
D16		North Carolina St.	7	14

1968 8-1-2 (5-0-1)

S14	= |	at Tennessee	17	17
S28	●	Clemson	31	13
O5	●	at South Carolina	21	20
O12	● |	Mississippi	21	7
O19	● |	Vanderbilt	32	6
O26	● |	at Kentucky	35	14
N2	=	Houston	10	10
N9	● |	Florida JacF	51	0
N16	● |	at Auburn	17	3
N30	●	Georgia Tech	47	8
		SUGAR BOWL		
J1		Arkansas	2	16

1969 5-5-1 (2-3-1)

S20	●	Tulane	35	0
S27	●	at Clemson	30	0
O4	●	South Carolina	41	16
O11	|	Mississippi JaM	17	25
O18	● |	at Vanderbilt	40	8
O25	● |	Kentucky	30	0
N1	|	Tennessee	3	17
N8	= |	Florida JacF	13	13
N15	|	Auburn	3	16
N29		at Georgia Tech	0	6
		SUN BOWL		
D20		Nebraska	6	45

1970 5-5-0 (3-3-0)

S19		at Tulane	14	17
S26	●	Clemson	38	0
O3	|	Mississippi State JaM	6	7
O10	|	Mississippi	21	31
O17	● |	Vanderbilt	37	3
O24	● |	at Kentucky	19	3
O31	●	South Carolina	52	34
N7	|	Florida JacF	17	24
N14	● |	at Auburn	31	17
N28		Georgia Tech	7	17

1971 11-1-0 (5-1-0)

S11	●	Oregon State	56	25
S18	●	Tulane	17	7
S25	●	at Clemson	28	0
O2	● |	Mississippi State	35	7
O9	● |	Mississippi JaM	38	7
O16	● |	at Vanderbilt	24	0
O23	● |	Kentucky	34	0
O30	●	at South Carolina	24	0
N6	● |	Florida JacF	49	7
N13	|	Auburn	20	35
N25	●	at Georgia Tech	28	24
		GATOR BOWL		
D31	●	North Carolina	7	3

1972 7-4-0 (4-3-0)

S16	●	Baylor	24	14
S23		at Tulane	13	24
S30	●	North Carolina St.	28	22
O7	|	Alabama	7	25
O14	● |	Mississippi JaM	14	13
O21	● |	Vanderbilt	28	3
O28	● |	at Kentucky	13	7
N4	|	Tennessee	0	14
N11	● |	Florida JacF	10	7
N18	|	at Auburn	10	27
D2	●	Georgia Tech	27	7

1973 7-4-1 (3-4-0)

S15	=	Pittsburgh	7	7
S22	●	Clemson	31	14
S29	●	North Carolina St.	31	12
O6	|	at Alabama	14	28
O13	● |	Mississippi	20	0
O20	|	at Vanderbilt	14	18
O27	|	Kentucky	7	12
N3	● |	at Tennessee	35	31
N10	|	Florida JacF	10	11
N17	● |	Auburn	28	14
D1	●	at Georgia Tech	10	3
		PEACH BOWL		
D28	●	Maryland	17	16

1974 6-6-0 (4-2-0)

S14	●	Oregon State	48	35
S21	|	Mississippi State JaM	14	38
S28	●	South Carolina	52	14
O5		at Clemson	24	28
O12	● |	Mississippi	49	0
O19	● |	Vanderbilt	38	31
O26	● |	at Kentucky	24	20
N2		Houston	24	31
N9	● |	Florida JacF	17	16
N16	|	at Auburn	13	17
N30		Georgia Tech	14	34
		TANGERINE BOWL		
D21		Miami, Ohio	10	21

1975 9-3-0 (5-1-0)

S13		Pittsburgh	9	19
S20	● |	Mississippi State	28	6
S27	●	at South Carolina	28	20
O4	●	Clemson	35	7
O11	|	at Mississippi	13	28
O18	● |	at Vanderbilt	47	3
O25	● |	Kentucky	21	13
N1	●	Richmond	28	24
N8	● |	Florida JacF	10	7
N15	● |	Auburn	28	13
N27	●	at Georgia Tech	42	26
		COTTON BOWL		
J1		Arkansas	10	31

1976 10-2-0 (5-1-0)

S11	●	California	36	24
S18	●	at Clemson	41	0
S25	●	South Carolina	20	12
O2	● |	Alabama	21	0
O9	|	at Mississippi	17	21
O16	● |	Vanderbilt	45	0
O23	● |	at Kentucky	31	7
O30	●	Cincinnati	31	17
N6	● |	Florida JacF	41	27
N13	● |	at Auburn	28	0
N27	●	Georgia Tech	13	10
		SUGAR BOWL		
J1		Pittsburgh	3	27

1977 5-6-0 (2-4-0)

S10	●	Oregon	27	16
S17		Clemson	6	7
S24	●	at South Carolina	15	13
O1	|	at Alabama	10	18
O8	● |	Mississippi	14	13
O15	● |	at Vanderbilt	24	13
O22	|	Kentucky	0	33
O29	●	Richmond	23	7
N5	|	Florida JacF	17	22
N12	|	Auburn	14	33
N26		at Georgia Tech	7	16

1978 9-2-1 (5-0-1)

S16	●	Baylor	16	14
S23	●	Clemson	12	0
S30		at South Carolina	10	27
O7	● |	Mississippi	42	3
O14	● |	at LSU	24	17
O21	● |	Vanderbilt	31	10
O28	● |	at Kentucky	17	16
N4	●	VMI	41	3
N11	● |	Florida JacF	24	22
N18	= |	at Auburn	22	22
D2	●	Georgia Tech	29	28
		BLUEBONNET BOWL		
D31		Stanford	22	25

1979 6-5-0 (5-1-0)

S15		Wake Forest	21	22
S22		at Clemson	7	12
S29		South Carolina	20	27
O6	● |	at Mississippi	24	21
O13	● |	LSU	21	14
O20	● |	at Vanderbilt	31	10
O27	● |	Kentucky	20	6
N3		Virginia	0	31
N10	● |	Florida JacF	33	10
N17	|	Auburn	13	33
D1	●	at Georgia Tech	16	3

1980   12-0-0 (6-0-0)

S6	●	at Tennessee	16 15
S13	●	Texas A&M	42 0
S20	●	Clemson	20 16
S27	●	TCU	34 3
O11	●	Mississippi	28 21
O18	●	Vanderbilt	41 0
O25	●	at Kentucky	27 0
N1	●	South Carolina	13 10
N8	●	Florida JacF	26 21
N15	●	at Auburn	31 21
N29	●	Georgia Tech	38 20
		SUGAR BOWL	
J1	●	Notre Dame	17 10

1981   10-2-0 (6-0-0)

S5	●	Tennessee	44 0
S12	●	California	27 13
S19	●	at Clemson	3 13
S26	●	South Carolina	24 0
O10	●	at Mississippi	37 7
O17	●	at Vanderbilt	53 21
O24	●	Kentucky	21 0
O31	●	Temple	49 3
N7	●	Florida JacF	26 21
N14	●	Auburn	24 13
N28	●	at Georgia Tech	44 7
		SUGAR BOWL	
J1	●	Pittsburgh	20 24

1982   11-1-0 (6-0-0)

S6	●	Clemson	13 7
S11	●	Brigham Young	17 14
S25	●	at South Carolina	34 18
O2	●	at Mississippi State	29 22
O9	●	Mississippi	33 10
O16	●	Vanderbilt	27 13
O23	●	at Kentucky	27 14
O30	●	Memphis	34 3
N6	●	Florida JacF	44 0
N13	●	at Auburn	19 14
N27	●	Georgia Tech	38 18
		SUGAR BOWL	
J1	●	Penn State	23 27

1983   10-1-1 (5-1-0)

S3	●	UCLA	19 8
S17	=	at Clemson	16 16
S24	●	South Carolina	31 13
O1	●	Mississippi State	20 7
O8	●	at Mississippi	36 11
O15	●	at Vanderbilt	20 13
O22	●	Kentucky	47 21
O29	●	Temple	31 14
N5	●	Florida JacF	10 9
N12	●	Auburn	7 13
N26	●	at Georgia Tech	27 24
		COTTON BOWL	
J2	●	Texas	10 9

1984   7-4-1 (4-2-0)

S8	●	Southern Miss	26 19
S22	●	Clemson	26 23
S29	●	at South Carolina	10 17
O6	●	Alabama Birm	24 14
O13	●	Mississippi	18 12
O20	●	Vanderbilt	62 35
O27	●	at Kentucky	37 7
N3	●	Memphis	13 3
N10	●	Florida JacF	0 27
N17	●	at Auburn	12 21
D1	●	Georgia Tech	18 35
		CITRUS BOWL	
D22	=	Florida State	17 17

1985   7-3-2 (3-2-1)

S2		Alabama	16 20
S14		Baylor	17 14
S21	●	at Clemson	20 13
S28	●	South Carolina	35 21
O12	●	Mississippi JaM	49 21
O19	=	at Vanderbilt	13 13
O26	●	Kentucky	26 6
N2	●	Tulane	58 3
N9	●	Florida JacF	24 3
N16	●	Auburn	10 24
N30	●	at Georgia Tech	16 20
		SUN BOWL	
D28	=	Arizona	13 13

1986   8-4-0 (4-2-0)

S13	●	Duke	31 7
S20	●	Clemson	28 31
S27	●	at South Carolina	31 26
O4	●	Mississippi	14 10
O11	●	at LSU	14 23
O18	●	Vanderbilt	38 16
O25	●	at Kentucky	31 9
N1	●	Richmond	28 13
N8	●	Florida JacF	19 31
N15	●	at Auburn	20 16
N29	●	Georgia Tech	31 24
		HALL OF FAME BOWL	
D23	●	Boston College	24 27

1987   9-3-0 (4-2-0)

S5	●	Virginia	30 22
S12	●	Oregon State	41 7
S19	●	at Clemson	20 21
S26	●	South Carolina	13 6
O3	●	at Mississippi	31 14
O10	●	LSU	23 26
O17	●	at Vanderbilt	52 24
O24	●	Kentucky	17 14
N7	●	Florida JacF	23 10
N14	●	Auburn	11 27
N28	●	at Georgia Tech	30 16
		LIBERTY BOWL	
D29	●	Arkansas	20 17

1988   9-3-0 (5-2-0)

S3	●	Tennessee	28 17
S10	●	TCU	38 10
S17	●	at Mississippi State	42 35
S24	●	at South Carolina	10 23
O1	●	Mississippi	36 12
O8	●	Vanderbilt	41 22
O22	●	at Kentucky	10 16
O29	●	William & Mary	59 24
N5	●	Florida JacF	26 3
N12	●	at Auburn	10 20
N26	●	Georgia Tech	24 3
		GATOR BOWL	
J1	●	Michigan State	34 27

RAY GOFF
1989-95 (.574)   46-34-1

1989   6-6-0 (4-3-0)

S16	●	Baylor	15 3
S23	●	Mississippi State	23 6
S30	●	South Carolina	20 24
O7	●	at Tennessee	14 17
O14	●	at Mississippi	13 17
O21	●	at Vanderbilt	35 16
O28	●	Kentucky	34 23
N4	●	Temple	37 10
N11	●	Florida JacF	17 10
N18	●	Auburn	3 20
D2	●	at Georgia Tech	22 33
		PEACH BOWL	
D30	●	Syracuse	18 19

1990   4-7-0 (2-5-0)

S8	●	at LSU	13 18
S15	●	Southern Miss	18 17
S22	●	Alabama	16 17
S29	●	East Carolina	19 15
O6	●	at Clemson	3 34
O13	●	Mississippi	12 28
O20	●	Vanderbilt	39 28
O27	●	at Kentucky	24 26
N10	●	Florida JacF	7 38
N17	●	at Auburn	10 33
D1	●	Georgia Tech	23 40

1991   9-3-0 (4-3-0)

A31	●	Western Carolina	48 0
S7	●	LSU	31 10
S21	●	at Alabama	0 10
S28	●	Fullerton St.	27 14
O5	●	Clemson	27 12
O12	●	at Mississippi	37 17
O19	●	at Vanderbilt	25 27
O26	●	Kentucky	49 27
N9	●	Florida JacF	13 45
N16	●	Auburn	37 27
N30	●	at Georgia Tech	18 15
		INDEPENDENCE BOWL	
D29	●	Arkansas	24 15

1992   10-2-0 (6-2-0)

S5	●	at South Carolina	28 6
S12	●	Tennessee	31 34
S19	●	Fullerton St.	56 0
S26	●	Mississippi	37 11
O3	●	at Arkansas	27 3
O10	●	Georgia So.	34 7
O17	●	Vanderbilt	30 20
O24	●	at Kentucky	40 7
O31	●	Florida JacF	24 26
N14	●	at Auburn	14 10
N28	●	Georgia Tech	31 17
		CITRUS BOWL	
J1	●	Ohio State	21 14

1993   5-6-0 (2-6-0)

S4	●	South Carolina	21 23
S11	●	at Tennessee	6 38
S18	●	Texas Tech	52 37
S25	●	at Mississippi	14 31
O2	●	Arkansas	10 20
O9	●	Southern Miss	54 24
O16	●	at Vanderbilt	41 3
O23	●	Kentucky	33 28
O30	●	Florida JacF	26 33
N13	●	Auburn	28 42
N25	●	at Georgia Tech	43 10

1994   6-4-1 (3-4-1)

S3	●	at South Carolina	24 21
S10	●	Tennessee	23 41
S17	●	La. Monroe	70 6
S24	●	Mississippi	17 14
O1	●	Alabama Birm	28 29
O8	●	Clemson	40 14
O15	●	Vanderbilt	30 43
O22	●	at Kentucky	34 30
O29	●	at Florida	14 52
N12	=	at Auburn	23 23
N25	●	Georgia Tech	48 10

1995   6-6-0 (3-5-0)

S2	●	South Carolina	42 23
S9	●	at Tennessee	27 30
S16	●	New Mexico St.	40 13
S23	●	at Mississippi	10 18
S30	●	Alabama	0 31
O7	●	at Clemson	19 17
O14	●	at Vanderbilt	17 6
O21	●	Kentucky	12 3
O28	●	Florida	17 52
N11	●	Auburn	31 37
N23	●	at Georgia Tech	18 17
		PEACH BOWL	
D30		Virginia	27 34

JIM DONNAN
1996-2000 (.678)   40-19

1996   5-6 (3-5)

A31	●	Southern Miss	7 11
S14	●	at South Carolina	14 23
S21	●	Texas Tech	15 12
O5	●	at Mississippi State	38 19
O12	●	Tennessee	17 29
O19	●	Vanderbilt	13 2
O26	●	at Kentucky	17 24
N2	●	Florida JacF	7 47
N16	●	at Auburn	56 49
N23	●	Mississippi	27 31
N30	●	Georgia Tech	19 10

1997   10-2 (6-2)

A30	●	Arkansas State	38 7
S13	●	South Carolina	31 15
S20	●	La. Monroe	42 3
O4	●	Mississippi State	47 0
O11	●	at Tennessee	13 38
O18	●	at Vanderbilt	34 13
O25	●	Kentucky	23 13
N1	●	Florida JacF	37 17
N15	●	Auburn	34 45
N22	●	at Mississippi	21 14
N29	●	at Georgia Tech	27 24
		OUTBACK BOWL	
J1	●	Wisconsin	33 6

1998   9-3 (6-2)

S5	●	Kent	56 3
S12	●	at South Carolina	17 3
S19	●	Wyoming	16 9
O3	●	at LSU	28 27
O10	●	Tennessee	3 22
O17	●	Vanderbilt	31 6
O24	●	at Kentucky	28 26
O31	●	Florida JacF	7 38
N14	●	at Auburn	28 17
N21	●	Mississippi	24 17
N28	●	Georgia Tech	19 21
		PEACH BOWL	
D31	●	Virginia	35 33

1999   8-4 (5-3)

S4	●	Utah State	38 7
S11	●	South Carolina	24 9
S25	●	Central Florida	24 23
O2	●	LSU	23 22
O9	●	at Tennessee	20 37
O16	●	at Vanderbilt	27 17
O23	●	Kentucky	49 34
O30	●	Florida JacF	14 30
N13	●	Auburn	21 38
N20	●	at Mississippi	20 17
N27	●	at Georgia Tech	48 51
		OUTBACK BOWL	
J1	●	Purdue	28 25

2000   8-4 (5-3)

S2	●	Geo. Southern	29 7
S9	●	at South Carolina	10 21
S23	●	New Mexico St.	37 0
S30	●	at Arkansas	38 7
O7	●	Tennessee	21 10
O14	●	Vanderbilt	29 19
O21	●	at Kentucky	34 30
O28	●	Florida JacF	23 34
N11	●	at Auburn	26 29
N18	●	Mississippi	32 14
N25	●	Georgia Tech	15 27
		OAHU BOWL	
D24	●	Virginia	37 14

MARK RICHT
2001-Present (.808)   42-10

2001   8-4 (5-3)

S1	●	Arkansas State	45 17
S8	●	South Carolina	9 14
S29	●	Arkansas	34 23
O6	●	at Tennessee	26 24
O13	●	at Vanderbilt	30 14
O20	●	Kentucky	43 29
O27	●	Florida JacF	10 24
N10	●	Auburn	17 24
N17	●	at Mississippi	35 15
N24	●	at Georgia Tech	31 17
D1	●	Houston	35 7
		MUSIC CITY BOWL	
D28	●	Boston College	16 20

2002   13-1 (7-1)

A31	●	Clemson	31 28
S14	●	at South Carolina	13 7
S21	●	Northwestern St.	45 7
S28	●	New Mexico State	41 10
O5	●	at Alabama	27 25
O12	●	Tennessee	18 13
O19	●	Vanderbilt	48 17
O26	●	at Kentucky	52 24
N2	●	Florida JacF	13 20
N9	●	Mississippi	31 17
N16	●	at Auburn	24 21
N30	●	Georgia Tech	51 7
		SEC CHAMPIONSHIP GAME	
D7	●	Arkansas Atl	30 3
		SUGAR BOWL	
J1	●	Florida State	26 13

2003   11-3 (6-2)

A30	●	at Clemson	30 0
S6	●	Middle Tennessee	29 10
S13	●	South Carolina	31 7
S20	●	at LSU	10 17
O4	●	Alabama	37 23
O11	●	at Tennessee	41 14
O18	●	at Vanderbilt	27 8
O25	●	UAB	16 13
N1	●	Florida JacF	13 16
N15	●	Auburn	26 7
N22	●	Kentucky	30 10
N29	●	at Georgia Tech	34 17
		SEC CHAMPIONSHIP GAME	
D6	●	LSU Atl	13 34
		CAPITAL ONE BOWL	
J1	●	Purdue	34 27

2004   10-2   (6-2)

S4	●	Ga. Southern	48	28
S11	● |	at South Carolina	20	16
S18	●	Marshall	13	3
O2	● |	LSU	45	16
O9	|	Tennessee	14	19
O16	● |	Vanderbilt	33	3
O23	● |	at Arkansas	20	14
O30	● |	Florida *JacF*	31	24
N6	● |	at Kentucky	62	17
N13	|	at Auburn	6	24
N27	●	Georgia Tech	19	13
		OUTBACK BOWL		
J1	●	Wisconsin	24	21

Neutral Site key: *Lou* Louisville, KY / *Mem* Memphis, TN / *SF* San Francisco, CA / *Phil* Philadelphia, PA / *Dal* Dallas, TX / *JaM* Jackson, MS / *Atl* Atlanta, GA / *Nor* Norfolk, VA / *Roa* Roanoke, VA / *Sav* Savannah, GA / *And* Anderson, SC / *Aug* Augusta, GA / *Tam* Tampa, FL / *Brnx* Bronx, NY / *NYC* New York, NY / *Ral* Raleigh, NC / *ColGa* Columbus, GA / *Mac* Macon, GA / *Mont* Montgomery, AL / *Birm* Birmingham, AL / *JacF* Jacksonville, FL.
f Forfeit † Game Later Forfieted # Disputed Victor * Disputed Score ‖ Designated Conference Game |2 Counted Twice in Conference Standings

GEORGIA ANNUAL STATISTICAL LEADERS

YR	RUSHING	YDS	ATT	AVG	PASSING	ATT	CMP	PCT	YDS	RECEIVING	REC	YDS	AVG
1950	Billy Mixon	705	134	5.3	Mal Cook	68	35	.51	535	Zippy Morocco	13	206	15.8
1951	Lauren Hargrove	422	89	4.7	Zeke Bratkowski	248	116	.47	1,578	Harry Babcock	41	666	16.2
1952	Bob Clemens	460	106	4.3	Zeke Bratkowski	262	131	.50	1,824	Johnny Carson	32	467	14.6
1953	Bob Clemens	586	120	4.9	Zeke Bratkowski	224	113	.50	1,461	Johnny Carson	45	663	14.7
1954	Bobby Garrard	442	93	4.8	Jimmy Harper	71	29	.40	407	Roy Wilkins	6	70	11.7
1955	Bobby Garrard	533	107	5.0	Dick Young	97	48	.50	875	James Orr	24	443	18.5
1956	Carl Manning	348	83	4.2	William Hearn	61	26	.43	294	Roy Wilkins	9	116	12.9
1957	Theron Sapp	599	137	4.4	Charley Britt	77	31	.40	415	James Orr	16	237	14.8
1958	Theron Sapp	635	114	5.6	Charley Britt	75	31	.41	535	Norman King	8	138	17.3
1959	Bill Godfrey	319	79	4.0	Fran Tarkenton	102	62	.61	736	Bobby Towns	18	263	14.6
1960	Fred Brown	355	78	4.6	Fran Tarkenton	185	108	.58	1,189	Fred Brown	31	275	8.9
1961	Bill McKenny	328	81	4.0	Larry Rakestraw	136	88	.65	710	Bill McKenny	23	202	8.8
1962	Leon Armbrester	266	64	4.2	Larry Rakestraw	196	78	.40	1,135	Mickey Babb	20	354	17.7
1963	Larry Rakestraw	170	102	1.7	Larry Rakestraw	209	103	.50	1,297	Pat Hodgson	24	375	15.6
1964	Preston Ridlehuber	368	110	3.3	Lynn Hughes	54	17	.31	408	Leon Armbrester	7	104	14.9
1965	Preston Ridlehuber	401	142	2.8	Kirby Moore	60	32	.53	487	Pat Hodgson	26	312	12.0
1966	Ronnie Jenkins	669	171	3.9	Kirby Moore	80	36	.45	524	Billy Payne	12	144	12.0
1967	Ronnie Jenkins	646	170	3.8	Kirby Moore	116	46	.40	699	Dennis Hughes	18	356	20.0
1968	Bruce Kemp	553	140	4.0	Mike Cavan	207	116	.56	1,619	Charley Whittemore	40	608	15.2
1969	Julian Smiley	494	124	4.0	Mike Cavan	162	71	.44	946	Charley Whittemore	28	452	16.1
1970	Ricky Lake	570	135	4.2	Mike Cavan	79	42	.53	651	Charley Whittemore	46	620	13.5
1971	Andy Johnson	870	174	5.0	Andy Johnson	77	33	.43	341	Lynn Hunnicutt	14	141	10.1
1972	Jimmy Poulos	556	150	3.7	James Ray	121	55	.45	756	Bob Burns	23	389	16.9
1973	Jimmy Poulos	702	167	4.2	Andy Johnson	120	43	.36	506	Richard Appleby	12	171	14.3
1974	Glynn Harrison	959	149	6.4	Matt Robinson	121	60	.50	1,317	Richard Appleby	23	510	22.2
1975	Glynn Harrison	894	131	6.8	Matt Robinson	72	29	.40	369	Richard Appleby	13	221	17.0
1976	Kevin McLee	1,058	218	4.9	Matt Robinson	81	36	.44	609	Gene Washington	20	469	23.5
1977	Kevin McLee	717	178	4.0	Jeff Pyburn	55	25	.45	312	Jesse Murray	13	216	16.7
1978	Willie McClendon	1,312	287	4.6	Jeff Pyburn	133	72	.54	878	Lindsay Scott	36	484	13.4
1979	Matt Simon	589	152	3.9	Buck Belue	112	59	.53	719	Lindsay Scott	34	512	15.0
1980	Herschel Walker	1,616	274	5.9	Buck Belue	156	77	.49	1,314	Amp Arnold	20	357	17.9
1981	Herschel Walker	1,891	385	4.9	Buck Belue	188	114	.61	1,603	Lindsay Scott	42	728	17.3
1982	Herschel Walker	1,752	335	4.9	John Lastinger	148	62	.42	907	Clarence Kay	12	175	14.6
1983	Keith Montgomery	519	120	4.3	John Lastinger	137	68	.50	796	Herman Archie	31	355	11.5
1984	Andre Smith	665	110	6.0	Todd Williams	130	64	.49	620	Scott Williams	19	204	10.7
1985	Keith Henderson	731	108	6.8	James Jackson	112	51	.46	759	Herman Archie	10	116	11.6
1986	Lars Tate	954	188	5.1	James Jackson	181	100	.55	1,475	Lars Tate	22	214	9.7
1987	Lars Tate	1,016	208	4.9	James Jackson	132	67	.51	1,026	John Thomas	25	391	15.6
1988	Tim Worley	1,216	191	6.4	Wayne Johnson	122	66	.54	945	John Thomas	23	354	15.4
1989	Rodney Hampton	1,059	218	4.9	Greg Talley	174	92	.53	1,330	Kirk Warner	30	404	13.5
1990	Garrison Hearst	717	162	4.4	Greg Talley	123	72	.59	871	Sean Hummings	25	376	15.0
1991	Garrison Hearst	968	153	6.3	Eric Zeier	286	159	.56	1,984	Andre Hastings	48	683	14.2
1992	Garrison Hearst	1,594	228	7.0	Eric Zeier	258	151	.59	2,248	Andre Hastings	52	860	16.5
1993	Terrell Davis	824	167	4.9	Eric Zeier	425	269	.63	3,525	Brice Hunter	76	970	12.8
1994	Terrell Davis	445	97	4.6	Eric Zeier	433	259	.60	3,396	Brice Hunter	59	799	13.5
1995	Torin Kirtsey	603	134	4.5	Hines Ward	112	69	.62	872	Juan Daniels	46	726	15.8
1996	Robert Edwards	800	184	4.3	Mike Bobo	344	175	.51	2,440	Hines Ward	52	900	17.3
1997	Robert Edwards	908	165	5.5	Mike Bobo	306	199	.65	2,751	Hines Ward	55	715	13.0
1998	Olandis Gary	698	143	4.9	Quincy Carter	290	176	.61	2,484	Tony Small	48	675	14.1
1999	Jasper Sanks	896	177	5.1	Quincy Carter	380	216	.57	2,713	Terrence Edwards	53	772	14.6
2000	Brett Millican	375	67	5.6	Quincy Carter	183	91	.50	1,250	Terrence Edwards	53	704	13.3
2001	Verron Haynes	691	126	5.5	David Greene	324	192	.59	2,789	Terrence Edwards	39	613	15.7
2002	Musa Smith	1,324	260	5.1	David Greene	379	218	.58	2,924	Terrence Edwards	59	1,004	17.0
2003	Michael Cooper	673	156	4.3	David Greene	438	264	.60	3,307	Reggie Brown	49	662	13.5
2004	Thomas Brown	875	172	5.1	David Greene	299	175	.59	2,508	Reggie Brown	53	860	16.2

Receiving leaders by receptions
The NCAA began including postseason stats in 2002

THE SCHOOLS

GEORGIA TECH

BY BOB HARIG

GEORGIA TECH BOASTS SOME OF college football's strongest history. The Atlanta engineering institution was the first school to win all four traditional major bowls: Rose, Orange, Sugar and Cotton. Its first full-time coach, John Heisman, is the inspiration behind college football's most prestigious award. Its stadium, more than 90 years old, is named for another legendary coach, Bobby Dodd, who once had a 31-game unbeaten streak. Georgia Tech has had only 12 coaches since 1904—and they've guided the Yellow Jackets to 15 conference titles and four national championships.

TRADITION Before each home game, the team runs onto Grant Field behind the Rambling Wreck, a 1930 Model A. Ford Sport Coupe. After a victory, the players sing the school's fight song, "Ramblin' Wreck," to the student section. At away games, Tech band members ask the stadium's public-address announcer to page George P. Burdell, a mythical character in Tech lore. (In 1927, the fictional Burdell's name appeared on class rosters, registration forms and grade reports.)

Off the field, first-year students are instructed to decorate their "rat caps" (distinctive Tech symbols of freshman status) by writing the school's winning football scores upright on the sides of the cap—and writing the losing scores upside down. Tech's traditions aren't solely for students, either: on the way to games, Tech supporters stop by The Varsity, an Atlanta landmark, to order a chili dog, onion rings and a Frosted Orange.

BEST PLAYER Quarterback Joe Hamilton was the Heisman runner-up in 1999, matching the highest previous finish by a Tech player (quarterback Billy Lothridge finished second in the 1963 voting). An equally dangerous runner and passer, Hamilton helped the Yellow Jackets lead the nation in total offense and rank second in scoring in 1999. His 734 rushing yards were the most ever by a Division I-A quarterback who also had 3,000 yards passing. Hamilton was a consensus first-team All-America selection and ACC Player of the Year that season, as well as winner of the Davey O'Brien National Quarterback Award. He owns a number of Tech passing records and finished his career as the ACC's all-time leader in total offense and touchdown passes. For his career, Hamilton threw for 8,882 yards and 65 touchdowns.

PROFILE

Georgia Institute of Technology
Atlanta, Ga.
Founded: 1885
Enrollment: 11,251
Colors: Old Gold, White and Blue
Nickname: Yellow Jackets
Stadium: Bobby Dodd Stadium/Grant Field
    Opened in 1913
    Grass; 55,000 capacity
First football game: 1892
All-time record: 630–426–43 (.593)
Bowl record: 22–11
Consensus national championships, 1936-present: 1 (1990)
Atlantic Coast Conference championships: 2 (1 outright)
First-round NFL draftees: 7
Website: www.ramblinwreck.com

THE BEST OF TIMES

From 1951 to 1956, Tech went 59–7–3 and won six straight major bowl games.

THE WORST OF TIMES

From 1892 to 1903, Tech had just two winning seasons, compiling a record of 9–32–5.

CONFERENCE

Georgia Tech joined the Atlantic Coast Conference in 1979 (but didn't start competing in football until 1983) after three times being a charter member of other conferences: Southwest Intercollegiate Athletic Association (1894), Southern Conference (1921) and SEC (1933).

DISTINGUISHED ALUMNI

Jimmy Carter; Nomar Garciaparra; David Duval; Jeff Foxworthy, comedian; Sam Nunn, U.S. senator; Dick Truly, astronaut and head of NASA

FIGHT SONG

RAMBLIN' WRECK
I'm a Ramblin' Wreck from Georgia
  Tech and a hell of an engineer,
A helluva, helluva, helluva, helluva, hell
  of an engineer,
Like all the jolly good fellows, I drink
  my whiskey clear,
I'm a Ramblin' Wreck from Georgia
  Tech and a hell of an engineer.
Oh, if I had a daughter, sir, I'd dress her
  in White and Gold,
And put her on the campus, to cheer the
  brave and bold.
But if I had a son, sir, I'll tell you what
  he'd do.
He would yell, "To Hell with Georgia,"
  like his daddy used to do.
Oh, I wish I had a barrel of rum and
  sugar three thousand pounds,
A college bell to put it in and a clapper
  to stir it around.
I'd drink to all good fellows who come
  from far and near.
I'm a ramblin' gamblin' hell of an
  engineer

BEST COACH The chalkhead's pick is John Heisman, who coached at eight schools but carved much of his reputation at Tech, where he had a 102–29–7 record from 1904 to 1919 and brought the school its first national title in 1917. He was the first paid college coach in the country, with a salary of $2,250 plus 30 percent of the gate receipts. (He also coached baseball and basketball at the school.) He left after the 1919 season—not because of the 7–3 record, but because he was divorcing his wife and agreed to leave Atlanta.

The sentimental choice, however, is Bobby Dodd, who may be a less significant figure in football history but is peerless in Tech annals. From 1945 to 1966, Dodd went 165–64–8 (.713) and guided Tech to a 31-game unbeaten streak from 1950 to 1953. He was 9–4 in bowl games and won eight straight, including six in consecutive seasons: 1952 Orange, 1953 Sugar, 1954 Sugar, 1955 Cotton, 1956 Sugar and 1956 Gator. He also beat Georgia eight straight times. Dodd was known as an excellent sideline coach, and he emphasized finesse and well-rehearsed execution. So as not

> *Bobby Dodd was known as an excellent sideline coach, and he emphasized finesse and well-rehearsed execution.*

to wear out the players before Saturdays, practices were laid-back, with little hitting but great attention to detail. "There's no point in rough scrimmages before a bowl game," he once said. "Your top players learn nothing playing against the third team, and you risk injury."

BEST TEAM Though Georgia Tech boasts four national champion squads, the 1952 team was the only one to complete a 12–0 season. Those 12 victories, which included four shutouts, were part of an 18-game winning streak from 1951 to 1953 and a 31-game unbeaten streak from 1950 to 1953. The 1952 team had six players who were first-team on at least one All-America lineup. The Yellow Jackets completed their perfect season by defeating Mississippi 24-7 in the Sugar Bowl. "The best football team that I coached," Dodd once said. After Duke fell to Tech 28-7, Blue Devils head coach Bill Murray called Tech "the greatest team in the country." A week later, Army went down 45-6; Cadets coach Red Blaik said, "I never compare teams, but I repeat, this team could play in any league."

RECORDS

RUSHING YARDS
GAME
356   Eddie Lee Ivery vs. Air Force, Nov. 11, 1978 (26 att.)
SEASON
1,562   Eddie Lee Ivery, 1978 (267 att.)
CAREER
4,066   Robert Lavette, 1981-84 (914 att.)

PASSING YARDS
GAME
486   George Godsey vs. Virginia, Nov. 10, 2001 (39 of 55)
SEASON
3,085   George Godsey, 2001 (249 of 384)
CAREER
8,882   Joe Hamilton, 1996-99 (629 of 1,020)

RECEIVING YARDS
GAME
243   Dez White vs. Virginia, Oct. 17, 1998 (6 rec.)
SEASON
1,138   Jonathan Smith, 2003 (78 rec.)
CAREER
2,907   Kelly Campbell, 1998-2001 (195 rec.)

POINTS
GAME
24   Seven players; most recently by P.J. Daniels vs. Tulsa, Jan. 3, 2004 (4 TDs)
SEASON
114   Robert Lavette, 1982 (19 TDs)
CAREER
322   Luke Manget, 1999-2002 (54 FGs, 160 PATs)

CONSENSUS ALL-AMERICANS

1917	Everett Strupper, B
1918	Ashel Day, C
1918	Joe Guyon, T
1918, 1920	Bill Fincher, E
1928	Peter Pund, C
1942	Harvey Hardy, G
1944	Phil Tinsley, E
1946	Paul Duke, C
1947	Bob Davis, T
1952	Hal Miller, T
1953	Larry Morris, C
1959	Maxie Baughan, C
1966	Jim Breland, C
1970	Rock Perdoni, DT
1973	Randy Rhino, DB
1990	Ken Swilling, FS
1998	Craig Page, C
1999	Joe Hamilton, QB
2000	Chris Brown, OT

BIGGEST GAME This is no misprint: Georgia Tech 222, Cumberland 0. It happened on Oct. 7, 1916, an act of revenge for a 22-0 whipping Cumberland handed the Tech baseball team the previous spring. Tech scored nine touchdowns in the first quarter. Futile on offense, Cumberland began to kick the ball back to the Jackets after receiving it and never recorded a first down. Tech coach John Heisman agreed to shorten the periods from 15 to 12.5 minutes, but Tech still scored 180 points by the end of the third quarter—beating the record of 153 set by Michigan four years earlier. Tech scored 32 touchdowns, averaged 3.8 points per minute and carried the ball for 978 yards. Running up the score? The Jackets never threw a pass, nor did they make a single first down—because they scored within four downs on every possession. Cumberland provided such little opposition that Heisman put his team through a hard half-hour scrimmage afterward.

BIGGEST UPSET Tech's 7-6 victory over top-ranked Alabama on Nov. 17, 1962, ended the Crimson Tide's 26-game unbeaten streak. Bobby Dodd called it his greatest victory, as Tech thwarted Alabama comeback efforts by preventing a two-point conversion attempt and intercepting a Joe Namath pass in the end zone with just 1:05 left. It was Tech's second victory over a Bear Bryant-coached team.

STADIUM The oldest on-campus stadium in Division I-A, Grant Field (now Bobby Dodd Stadium/Grant Field) opened in 1913. A year later, the first permanent concrete stands were built on the west side of the field, thanks to a gift from Atlanta merchant and Tech trustee John W. Grant. The stadium has grown tremendously since its original 5,600-seat configuration. Nestled within Atlanta's skyline, it now has a capacity of 55,000. Following the 1985 season, the stadium's south stands were razed and replaced with the William C. Wardlaw Center, a multipurpose facility for athletic and academic departments. The name Bobby Dodd Stadium was added

ALL-TIME TEAM	
Selected in 1991 by fan balloting.	
1945-66	Bobby Dodd, coach
OFFENSE	
1958-60	Billy Shaw, G
1960-62	Rufus Guthrie, G
1976-78	Kent Hill, T
1983-86	John Davis, T
1962-64	Bill Curry, C
1961-63	Billy Martin, TE
1972-74	Jimmy Robinson, WR
1975-78	Drew Hill, WR
1961-63	Billy Lothridge, QB
1975-78	Eddie Lee Ivery, RB
1981-84	Robert Lavette, RB
1989-92	Scott Sisson, K
DEFENSE	
1960-62	Larry Stallings, DL
1969-70	Rock Perdoni, DL
1982-85	Pat Swilling, DL
1950-52	George Morris, LB
1951-54	Larry Morris, LB
1957-59	Maxie Baughan, LB
1974-77	Lucius Sanford, LB
1972-74	Randy Rhino, CB
1983-86	Reginald Rutland, CB
1975-78	Don Bessillieu, S
1988-91	Ken Swilling, S
1961-63	Billy Lothridge, P

in 1988 after the death of the legendary Tech coach and athletic director.

RIVAL Tech has played Georgia 99 times (through the 2004 season), including every year since 1925. The series began in 1893, when the Yellow Jackets traveled to Athens and won 28-6 to post the first football victory in school history. Tech is 38–56–5 overall against Georgia. Tech's 51-48 overtime win in 1999 was the highest-scoring game in the series and featured 1,104 yards of total offense. At one point under Dodd, the Yellow Jackets won eight in a row over the Bulldogs. "Old Georgia Bulldogs hated him because he made it look so easy," wrote *The Atlanta Journal-Constitution*'s Furman Bisher. "It seemed that Georgia might never beat Georgia Tech again."

STORYBOOK SEASON In 1990, the Yellow Jackets were just two seasons removed from a 3–8 campaign. While the 1989 team had posted a 7–4 record, the first winning season under coach Bobby Ross, there was little to portend what was to happen the next year. That 1990 Tech squad began the season unranked and finished as the only unbeaten team in major college football. Among the highlights of Tech's season was a dramatic 41-38 victory over No. 1 Virginia in what many consider to be the best game in ACC history. Tech rallied from 13-0 and 28-14 deficits, then scored the winning points with just seven seconds remaining on a 37-yard field goal by Scott Sisson. The Jackets defeated Nebraska 45-21 in the Florida Citrus Bowl to cap the 11–0–1 campaign and win the national title in the United Press International coaches' poll. (Colorado, which went 11–1–1 with the help of a controversial clipping penalty to beat Notre Dame in the Orange Bowl, was named champion in the Associated Press poll.)

NICKNAME The school has two official nicknames: Yellow Jackets and Rambling Wreck. Tech opened its doors in 1888, and the fight song "Ramblin' Wreck" dates back to

the school's earliest years, when a large portion of the student body traveled to Athens to watch Tech play Georgia in baseball. The legendary song was adapted from an old folk ballad, "The Sons of the Gamboliers," and was so renowned worldwide that Richard Nixon and Nikita Khrushchev sang it together during their meeting in Moscow in 1959. The Yellow Jackets nickname, which first appeared in *The Atlanta Constitution* in 1905, originally referred to Tech supporters, many of whom came to games sporting yellow coats and jackets.

MASCOT The official Rambling Wreck car made its first appearance on Grant Field before the Sept. 30, 1961, home opener against Rice, and has led the team onto the field at every home game since. The bumblebee mascot, Buzz, debuted in 1980.

UNIFORMS The Yellow Jackets are among the few teams that wear white jerseys at home. They returned to this traditional uniform in 1995, when NCAA rules permitted such a change. The uniform consists of a white jersey (with unusually thick numerals), gold pants and a gold helmet with an interlocking GT logo. During the late 1960s and early 1970s, Tech experimented with various combinations of gold jerseys, white pants and white helmets. In the mid-1970s, NCAA rules required a "dark" home jersey, so the Yellow Jackets went to a black jersey with gold or white pants and a gold helmet. When Bobby Ross became the head coach in 1987, the black was replaced with a dark blue.

QUOTE "Toe meets leather!" — Al Ciraldo, Tech's longtime radio announcer, on every kickoff

GEORGIA TECH ANNUAL STATISTICAL LEADERS

YR	RUSHING	YDS	ATT	AVG	PASSING	ATT	CMP	PCT	YDS	RECEIVING	REC	YDS	AVG
1962	Billy Lothridge	478	128	3.7	Billy Lothridge	156	83	.53	1,006	Billy Martin	21	323	15.4
1963	Ray Mendheim	427	93	4.6	Billy Lothridge	153	76	.50	1,017	Billy Martin	19	221	11.6
1964	Johnny Gresham	437	99	4.4	Jerry Priestley	77	37	.48	441	Johnny Gresham	22	290	13.2
1965	Lenny Snow	597	125	4.8	Kim King	191	112	.59	1,331	Craig Baynham	30	368	12.3
1966	Lenny Snow	761	202	3.8	Kim King	124	64	.52	690	Steve Almond	24	265	11.0
1967	Lenny Snow	385	118	3.3	Kim King	145	67	.46	742	John Sias	42	671	16.0
1968	Kenny Bounds	188	56	3.4	Larry Good	191	97	.51	1,337	John Sias	61	902	14.8
1969	Brent Cunningham	459	118	3.9	Jack Williams	59	30	.51	358	Steve Foster	19	200	10.5
1970	Brent Cunningham	740	144	5.1	Eddie McAshan	223	110	.49	1,138	Larry Studdard	29	355	12.2
1971	Greg Horne	500	123	4.1	Eddie McAshan	234	125	.53	1,186	Mike Oven	33	361	10.9
1972	Greg Horne	558	139	4.0	Eddie McAshan	241	125	.52	1,756	Jimmy Robinson	48	812	16.9
1973	Cleo Johnson	451	92	4.9	Jim Stevens	217	119	.55	1,481	Jimmy Robinson	34	597	17.6
1974	David Sims	881	144	3.8	Rudy Allen	52	28	.54	357	Jimmy Robinson	19	224	11.8
1975	David Sims	590	72	8.2	Danny Myers	27	16	.59	272	Steve Raible	13	277	21.3
1976	David Sims	803	163	4.9	Gary Lanier	33	16	.48	290	John Steele	14	233	16.6
1977	Eddie Lee Ivery	900	153	5.9	Gary Lanier	26	10	.38	182	Drew Hill	7	102	14.6
1978	Eddie Lee Ivery	1,562	267	5.9	Mike Kelley	197	96	.49	1,479	Drew Hill	36	708	19.7
1979	Ronny Cone	617	126	4.9	Mike Kelley	300	149	.50	2,051	Kris Kentera	25	526	21.0
1980	David Allen	466	134	3.5	Mike Kelley	137	68	.50	832	Marlon Heggs	29	483	16.7
1981	Robert Lavette	866	188	4.6	Mike Kelley	151	78	.52	887	Robert Lavette	45	307	6.8
1982	Robert Lavette	1,208	280	4.3	Jim Bob Taylor	232	135	.58	1,839	Robert Lavette	25	286	11.4
1983	Robert Lavette	803	186	4.3	John Dewberry	134	74	.55	790	Robert Lavette	21	123	18.5
1984	Robert Lavette	1,189	260	4.6	John Dewberry	206	126	.61	1,846	Ken Whisenhunt	27	517	19.1
1985	Cory Collier	606	139	4.4	John Dewberry	193	110	.57	1,557	Gary Lee	29	645	22.2
1986	Jerry Mays	842	148	5.7	Rick Strom	167	87	.52	1,011	Gary Lee	24	386	16.1
1987	Malcolm King	383	89	4.3	Darrell Gast	179	80	.45	1,104	Greg Lester	33	593	18.0
1988	Jerry Mays	942	194	4.9	Todd Rampley	275	154	.56	1,579	Jerry Mays	46	338	7.3
1989	Jerry Mays	1,349	249	5.4	Shawn Jones	271	142	.52	1,748	Jerry Mays	37	275	7.4
1990	William Bell	891	161	5.5	Shawn Jones	245	142	.58	2,008	Emmett Merchant	29	489	16.9
1991	Jimy Lincoln	913	199	4.6	Shawn Jones	339	178	.53	2,288	Greg Lester	35	676	19.3
1992	Michael Smith	336	74	4.5	Shawn Jones	362	190	.52	2,397	Bobby Rodriguez	51	621	12.2
1993	Dorsey Levens	823	114	7.2	Donnie Davis	237	137	.58	1,739	Omar Cassidy	26	395	15.2
1994	C.J. Williams	564	120	4.7	Tommy Luginbill	327	182	.56	2,128	Charlie Simmons	40	587	14.7
1995	C.J. Williams	1,138	245	4.6	Donnie Davis	223	124	.56	1,462	Harvey Middleton	31	444	14.3
1996	C.J. Williams	663	174	3.8	Joe Hamilton	188	108	.57	1,342	Harvey Middleton	64	804	12.6
1997	Charles Wiley	567	150	3.8	Joe Hamilton	268	173	.65	2,314	Harvey Middleton	52	839	16.1
1998	Joe Burns	474	98	4.8	Joe Hamilton	259	145	.56	2,166	Dez White	46	973	18.0
1999	Sean Gregory	837	172	4.9	Joe Hamilton	305	203	.67	3,060	Kelly Campbell	69	1,105	16.0
2000	Joe Burns	908	220	4.1	George Godsey	349	222	.64	2,906	Kelly Campbell	59	963	16.3
2001	Joe Burns	1,165	282	4.1	George Godsey	384	249	.65	3,085	Kelly Campbell	56	708	12.6
2002	Tony Hollings	633	92	6.9	A.J. Suggs	363	208	.57	2,242	Kerry Watkins	71	1,050	14.8
2003	P.J. Daniels	1,447	283	5.1	Reggie Ball	350	181	.52	1,996	Jonathan Smith	78	1,138	14.6
2004	P.J. Daniels	714	154	4.6	Reggie Ball	330	164	.50	2,147	Calvin Johnson	48	837	17.4

Receiving leaders by receptions
All statistics include postseason

THE SCHOOLS

GEORGIA TECH ALL-TIME SCORES

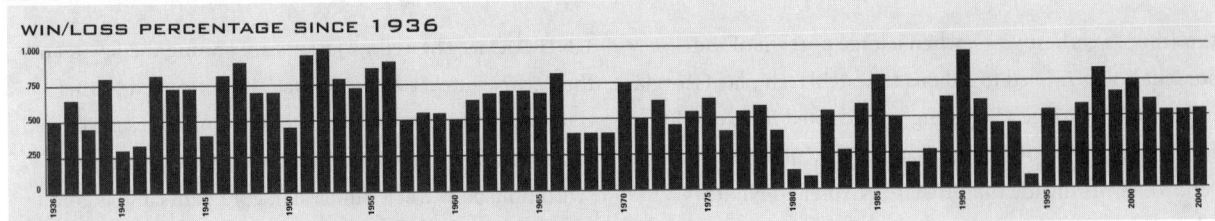

WIN/LOSS PERCENTAGE SINCE 1936

THE SCHOOLS

NO HEAD COACH

1892 0-3-0
N5		at Mercer	6	12
N19		Vanderbilt	10	20
N25		Auburn	0	26

1893 2-1-1
N4	•	at Georgia	28	6
N11	•	Mercer	10	6
N30		St. Albans	0	6
D7	•	Auburn	0	0

1894 0-3-0
O27		Savannah AA	0	8
N17		Auburn	0	94
N29		Fort McPhersons	0	34

1895
NO TEAM

1896 1-1-1
O31	•	at Mercer	6	4
N7	•	at Auburn	0	45
N21	=	Mercer	12	12

1897 0-1-0
| O23 | | at Georgia | 0 | 28 |

1898 0-3-0
O22		at Georgia	0	15
N5		at Auburn	6	29
N24		Clemson Aug	0	23

1899 0-5-0
O14		at Auburn	0	63
O23		Sewanee	0	30
O28		at Georgia	0	33 *
N11		Nashville GrvSC	0	15
N30		Clemson GrvSC	5	41

1900 0-4-0
O13		Georgia	0	12
O20		Nashville	0	23
O29		Sewanee	0	34
D7		Davidson	6	38

1901 4-0-1
O12	•	Gordon	29	0
O15	•	Furman	17	0
O18	•	Wofford Aug	33	0
O26	=	at Furman	5	5
N9	•	South Carolina	13	0

1902 0-6-2
O11		Auburn	6	18
O18		Clemson	5	44
O25		Georgia	0	0
N1	=	at Furman	0	0
N8		St. Albans	0	17
N13		Davidson	6	7
N22		Tennessee	6	10
N27		Alabama Birm	0	26

1903 2-5-0
O17		Clemson	0	73
O24		Georgia	0	38
O31	•	at Howard Coll.	37	0
N7	•	Florida Coll.	17	0
N14		Auburn	5	10
N21		at Tennessee	0	11
N26		South Carolina	0	16

JOHN HEISMAN
1904-19 (.764)   102-29-7

1904 8-1-0
O1	•	Fort Mc Phersons	11	5
O8	•	Florida State Coll.	35	0
O15	•	Mooney Sch.	51	0
O17	•	Florida U. Club	77	0
O22	•	Tennessee	2	0
O29	•	at Auburn	0	12
N5	=	Clemson	11	11
N12	•	Georgia	23	6
N16	•	Tenn. Med.	59	0
N24	•	Cumberland	18	0

1905 6-0-1
O7	•	North Georgia	54	0
O21	•	Alabama	12	5
O28	•	Cumberland	18	0
N4	•	Tennessee	45	0
N11	=	Sewanee	18	18
N18	•	Georgia	46	0
N30	•	Clemson	17	10

1906 5-3-1
S29	=	Maryville	6	6
O6	•	North Georgia	11	0
O13	•	U.T. Chattanooga	18	0
O20	•	Sewanee	0	16
O27	•	Davidson	4	0
N3	•	Auburn	11	0
N10	•	at Georgia	17	0
N17	•	Vanderbilt	6	37
N29	•	Clemson	0	10

1907 4-4-0
O5	•	Gordon	51	0
O12	•	North Georgia	70	0
O19	•	Tennessee	6	4
O26	•	Auburn	6	12
N2	•	Georgia	10	6
N9	•	Sewanee	0	18
N16	•	at Vanderbilt	0	54
N28	•	Clemson	5	6

1908 6-3-0
O3	•	Gordon	32	0
O10	•	Mooney	30	0
O17	•	Mississippi State	23	0
O24	•	Alabama	11	6
O31	•	Tennessee	5	6
N7	•	Auburn	0	44
N14	•	Sewanee	0	6
N19	•	Mercer	16	6
N26	•	Clemson	30	6

1909 7-2-0
O2	•	Gordon	18	6
O9	•	Mooney Sch.	35	6
O16	•	South Carolina	59	0
O23	•	Sewanee	0	15
O30	•	at Tennessee	29	0
N6	•	Auburn	0	9 *
N13	•	at Mercer	35	0
N20	•	Georgia	12	6
N25	•	Clemson	29	3

1910 5-3-0
O1	•	Gordon	57	0
O8	•	U.T. Chattanooga	18	0
O15	•	Mercer	46	0
O22	•	at Alabama	36	0
N5	•	Auburn	0	16
N12	•	Vanderbilt	0	23
N19	•	Georgia	6	11
N24	•	Clemson	34	0

1911 6-2-1
S30	•	11th Cavalry	22	5
O7	•	at Samford	28	0
O14	•	Tennessee	24	0
O21	•	Mercer	17	0
O29	=	Alabama	0	0
N4	•	Auburn	6	11
N11	•	Sewanee	23	0
N18	•	Georgia	0	5
N30	•	Clemson	31	0

1912 5-3-1
S28	•	11th Cavalry	0	0
O5	•	at Citadel	20	16
O12	•	Alabama	20	3
O19	•	at Mercer	16	6
O26	•	Florida JacF	14	7
N2	•	Auburn	7	27
N9	•	Sewanee	0	7
N16	•	Georgia	0	20
N28	•	Clemson	20	0 *

1913 7-2-0
S27	•	Fort McPhersons	19	0
O4	•	at Citadel	47	0
O11	•	at U.T. Chattanooga	71	6
O18	•	Mercer	33	0
O25	•	Florida JacF	13	3
N1	•	Sewanee	33	0
N8	•	Auburn	0	20
N15	•	Georgia	0	14
N27	•	Clemson	34	0 *

1914 6-2-0
O3	•	South Carolina	20	0
O10	•	Mercer	105	0
O17	•	Alabama Birm	0	13
O24	•	VMI	28	7
O31	•	Sewanee	20	0
N7	•	Auburn	0	14
N14	•	Georgia	7	0
N26	•	Clemson	26	6

1915 7-0-1
O2	•	Mercer	52	0
O9	•	Davidson	27	7
O16	•	Transylvania, Ky	67	0
O22	•	LSU NO	36	7
O30	•	North Carolina	23	3
N6	•	Alabama	21	7
N13	=	Georgia	0	0
N25	•	Auburn	7	0

1916 8-0-1
S30	•	Mercer	61	0
O7	•	Cumberland	222	0
O14	•	Davidson	9	0
O21	•	North Carolina	10	6
O28	•	Wash. & Lee	7	7
N4	•	Tulane	45	0
N11	•	Alabama	13	0
N18	•	at Georgia	21	0
N30	•	Auburn	33	7

1917 9-0-0
S29	•	Furman	25	0
S29	•	Wake Forest	33	0
O6	•	Pennsylvania	41	0
O13	•	Davidson	32	10
O20	•	Wash. & Lee	63	0
N3	•	Vanderbilt	83	0
N10	•	at Tulane	48	0
N17	•	Carlisle	98	0
N29	•	Auburn	68	7

1918 6-1-0
O5	•	Clemson	28	0
O12	•	Furman	118	0
O19	•	11th Cavalry	123	0
O26	•	Camp Gordon	28	0
N10	•	North Carolina St.	128	0
N23	•	at Pittsburgh	0	32
N28	•	Auburn	41	0

1919 7-3-0
S20	•	5th Division	48	0
S27	•	Furman	74	0
O4	•	Wake Forest	14	0
O11	•	Clemson	28	0
O18	•	Vanderbilt	20	0
O25	•	at Pittsburgh	6	16
N1	•	Davidson	33	0
N8	•	Wash. & Lee	0	3
N15	•	Georgetown	27	0
N27	•	Auburn	7	14

WILLIAM ALEXANDER
1920-44 (.580)   134-95-15

1920 8-1-0
S25	•	Wake Forest	44	0
O2	•	Oglethorpe	55	0
O9	•	Davidson	66	0
O16	•	at Vanderbilt	44	0
O23	•	at Pittsburgh	3	10
O30	•	Centre	24	0
N6	•	Clemson	7	0
N13	•	Georgetown	35	6
N25	•	Auburn	34	0

1921-1932
SOUTHERN CONFERENCE

1921 8-1-0 (2-0-0)
S24	•	Wake Forest	42	0
O1	•	Oglethorpe	41	0
O8	•	Davidson	70	0
O15	•	Furman	69	0
O22	•	Rutgers	48	14
O29	•	Penn State NYC	7	28
N5	|	Clemson	48	7
N12	|	Georgetown	21	7
N24	|	Auburn	14	0

1922 7-2-0 (4-0-0)
S30	•	Oglethorpe	31	6
O7	•	Davidson	19	0
O14	|	Alabama	33	7
O21	•	at Navy	0	13
O28	•	Notre Dame	3	13
N4	|	Clemson	21	7
N11	|	Georgetown	19	7
N18	|	North Carolina St.	17	0
N30	|	Auburn	14	6

1923 3-2-4 (0-0-4)
S29	•	Oglethorpe	28	13
O6	•	VMI	10	7
O13	|	Florida	7	7
O20	|	Georgetown	20	10
O27	•	at Notre Dame	7	35
N3	|	Alabama	0	0
N10	|	at Penn State	0	7
N17	|	Kentucky Unk	3	3
N29	|	Auburn	0	0

1924 5-3-1 (3-2-1)
S27	•	Oglethorpe	19	0
O4	|	VMI	3	0
O11	|	Florida	7	7
O18	|	Penn State	15	13
O25	|	Alabama	0	14
N1	|	at Notre Dame	3	34
N8	•	LSU	28	7
N15	|	Vanderbilt	0	3
N27	•	Auburn	7	0

1925 6-2-1 (4-1-1)
S26 ● Oglethorpe 13 7
O3 ● | VMI 33 0
O10 ● Penn State BNX 16 7
O17 ● | Florida 23 7
O24 | Alabama 0 7
O31 Notre Dame 0 13
N7 ● | at Vanderbilt 7 0
N14 ● | Georgia 3 0
N26 = | Auburn 7 7

1926 4-5-0 (4-3-0)
S25 Oglethorpe 6 7
O2 ● | VMI 13 0
O9 ● | Tulane 9 6
O16 | Alabama 0 21
O23 ● | Wash. & Lee 19 7
O30 at Notre Dame 0 12
N6 | Vanderbilt 7 13
N13 | Georgia 13 14
N25 ● | Auburn 20 7

1927 8-1-1 (7-0-1)
O1 ● | VMI 7 0
O8 ● | Tulane 13 6
O15 ● | Alabama 13 0
O22 ● | North Carolina 13 0
O29 at Notre Dame 7 26
N6 = | at Vanderbilt 0 0
N12 ● | LSU 23 0
N19 ● Oglethorpe 19 7
N24 ● | Auburn 18 0
D3 ● | Georgia 12 0

1928 10-0-0 (7-0-0)
O6 ● | VMI 13 0
O13 ● | at Tulane 12 0
O20 ● Notre Dame 13 0
O27 ● | at North Carolina 20 7
N3 ● Oglethorpe 32 7
N10 ● | Vanderbilt 19 7
N17 ● | Alabama 33 13
N29 ● | Auburn 51 0
D8 ● | Georgia 20 6
ROSE BOWL
J1 ● California 8 7

1929 3-6-0 (3-5-0)
O5 ● | Mississippi State 27 13
O12 | North Carolina 7 18
O19 ● | Florida 19 6
O26 | at Tulane 14 20
N2 Notre Dame 6 26
N9 | at Vanderbilt 7 23
N16 | Alabama 0 14
N28 ● | Auburn 19 6
D7 | at Georgia 6 12

1930 2-6-1 (2-4-1)
O4 ● | South Carolina 45 0
O11 at Carnegie Tech 0 31
O18 ● | Auburn 14 12
O25 | Tulane 0 28
N1 = | at North Carolina 6 6
N8 | Vanderbilt 0 6
N15 at Pennsylvania 7 34
N27 | Florida 7 55
D6 | Georgia 0 13

1931 2-7-1 (2-4-1)
O3 ● | South Carolina 25 13
O10 Carnegie Tech 0 13
O17 | Auburn 0 13
O24 | at Tulane 0 33
O31 | Vanderbilt 7 49
N7 = | North Carolina 19 19
N14 at Pennsylvania 12 13
N21 ● | Florida 23 0
N28 | at Georgia 6 35
D26 California 6 19 *

1932 4-5-1 (4-4-1)
O1 ● | Clemson 32 14
O8 | Kentucky 6 12
O15 | Auburn 0 6
O22 ● | at North Carolina 43 14
O29 | at Vanderbilt 0 12
N5 | Tulane 14 20
N12 ● | Alabama 6 0
N19 ● | at Florida 6 0
N26 = | Georgia 0 0
D17 at California 7 27

1933-1963
SEC

1933 5-5-0 (2-5-0)
S30 ● Clemson 39 2
O7 | at Kentucky 6 7
O14 ● | Auburn 16 6
O21 | Tulane 0 7
O28 ● at North Carolina 10 6
N4 | Vanderbilt 6 9
N11 ● | Florida 19 7
N18 | Alabama 9 12
N25 | Georgia 6 7
D2 ● Duke 6 0

1934 1-9-0 (0-6-0)
S29 ● Clemson 12 7
O6 | Vanderbilt 12 27
O13 at Duke 0 20
O20 at Michigan 2 9
O27 | at Tulane 12 20
N3 North Carolina 0 26
N10 | Auburn 6 18
N17 | Alabama 0 40
N24 | at Florida 12 13
D1 | at Georgia 0 7

1935 5-5-0 (3-4-0)
S28 ● Presbyterian 33 0
O5 ● | Sewanee 32 0
O12 | at Kentucky 6 25
O19 ● Duke 6 0
O26 at North Carolina 0 19
N2 | Vanderbilt 13 14
N9 | Auburn 7 33
N16 | Alabama BIRM 7 38
N23 ● | Florida 39 6
N30 ● | Georgia 19 7

1936 5-5-1 (3-3-1)
S26 ● Presbyterian 55 0
O3 ● | Sewanee 58 0
O10 ● | Kentucky 34 0
O17 at Duke 6 19
O24 = | at Vanderbilt 0 0
O31 Clemson 13 14
N7 | Auburn 12 13
N14 | Alabama 16 20
N21 ● | Florida 38 14
N28 | at Georgia 6 16
D26 ● California 13 7

1937 6-3-1 (3-2-1)
S24 ● Presbyterian 59 0
O2 ● Mercer 28 0
O9 ● | at Kentucky 32 0
O16 Duke 19 20
O23 | Auburn 0 21
O30 ● | Vanderbilt 14 0
N6 ● Clemson 7 0
N13 | Alabama BIRM 0 7
N20 ● | at Florida 12 0
N27 = | Georgia 6 6

1938 3-4-3 (2-1-3)
O1 ● Mercer 19 0
O8 Notre Dame 6 14
O15 at Duke 0 6
O22 ● | Auburn 7 6
O29 | at Vanderbilt 7 13
N5 ● | Kentucky 19 18
N12 = | Alabama 14 14
N19 = | Florida 0 0
N27 = | at Georgia 0 0
D26 at California 0 13

1939 8-2-0 (6-0-0)
O7 at Notre Dame 14 17
O14 ● Samford 35 0
O21 ● | Vanderbilt 14 6
O28 ● | Auburn 7 6
N4 Duke 6 7
N11 ● | Kentucky 13 6
N18 ● | Alabama BIRM 6 0
N25 ● | at Florida 21 7
D2 ● | Georgia 13 0
ORANGE BOWL
J1 ● Missouri 21 7

1940 3-7-0 (1-5-0)
O5 ● Samford 27 0
O12 at Notre Dame 20 26
O19 ● | Vanderbilt 19 0
O26 | Auburn 7 16
N2 at Duke 7 41
N9 | Kentucky LOU 7 26
N16 | Alabama 13 14
N23 | Florida 7 16
N30 | at Georgia 19 21
D28 ● California 13 0

1941 3-6-0 (2-4-0)
O4 ● U.T. Chattanooga 20 0
O11 Notre Dame 0 20
O18 | at Vanderbilt 7 14
O25 ● | Auburn 28 14
N1 Duke 0 14
N8 ● | Kentucky 20 13
N15 | Alabama BIRM 0 20
N22 | at Florida 7 14
N29 | Georgia 0 21

1942 9-2-0 (4-1-0)
S26 ● | Auburn 15 0
O3 ● at Notre Dame 13 6
O10 ● U.T. Chattanooga 30 6
O17 ● Davidson 33 0
O24 ● at Navy 21 0
O31 ● at Duke 26 7
N7 ● | Kentucky 47 7
N14 ● | Alabama 7 0
N21 ● | Florida 20 7
N28 | at Georgia 0 34
COTTON BOWL
J1 Texas 7 14

1943 8-3-0 (3-0-0)
S25 ● North Carolina 20 7
O2 at Notre Dame 13 55
O9 ● Georgia Pre-Flight 35 7
O16 ● Fort Benning 27 0
O23 Navy BALT 14 28
O30 Duke 7 14
N6 ● | LSU 42 7
N13 ● | at Tulane 33 0
N20 ● Clemson 41 6
N27 ● | Georgia 48 0
SUGAR BOWL
J1 ● Tulsa 20 18

1944 8-3-0 (4-0-0)
S30 ● Clemson 51 0
O7 ● North Carolina 28 0
O14 ● | Auburn 27 0
O21 ● Navy 17 15
O27 ● Georgia Pre-Flight 13 7
N4 at Duke 13 19
N11 ● | Tulane 34 7
N18 ● | at LSU 14 6
N25 Notre Dame 0 21
D2 ● | at Georgia 44 0
ORANGE BOWL
J1 Tulsa 12 26

BOBBY DODD
1945-66 (.713) 165-64-8

1945 4-6-0 (2-2-0)
S29 ● at North Carolina 20 14
O6 Notre Dame 7 40
O13 ● Samford 43 0
O20 Navy BALT 6 20
O27 ● | Auburn 20 7
N3 Duke 6 14
N10 ● | at Tulane 41 7
N17 | LSU 7 9
N24 Clemson 7 21
D1 | Georgia 0 33

1946 9-2-0 (4-2-0)
S28 | at Tennessee 9 13
O5 ● VMI 32 6
O12 ● | Mississippi 24 7
O19 ● | at LSU 26 7
O26 ● | Auburn 27 6
N2 ● at Duke 14 0
N9 ● Navy 28 20
N16 ● | Tulane 35 7
N23 ● Furman 41 7
N30 | at Georgia 7 35
OIL BOWL
J1 ● St. Mary's 41 19

1947 10-1-0 (4-1-0)
S27 ● | Tennessee 27 0
O4 ● | at Tulane 20 6 *
O11 ● VMI 20 0
O18 ● | Auburn 27 7
O25 ● Citadel 38 0
N1 ● Duke 7 0
N8 ● Navy BALT 16 14
N15 | Alabama BIRM 7 14
N22 ● Furman 51 0
N29 ● | Georgia 7 0
ORANGE BOWL
J1 ● Kansas 20 14

1948 7-3-0 (4-3-0)
S25 ● | at Vanderbilt 13 0
O2 ● | Tulane 13 7
O9 ● Wash. & Lee 27 0
O16 ● | Auburn 27 0
O23 ● | Florida 42 7
O30 ● at Duke 19 7
N6 | Tennessee 6 13
N13 | Alabama 12 14
N20 ● Citadel 54 0
N27 | at Georgia 13 21

1949 7-3-0 (5-2-0)
S24 ● | Vanderbilt 12 7
O1 | at Tulane 0 18
O8 ● Wash. & Lee 36 0
O15 ● | Auburn 35 21
O22 ● | at Florida 43 14
O29 Duke 14 27
N5 ● | at Tennessee 30 13
N12 | Alabama BIRM 7 20
N19 ● South Carolina 13 3
N26 ● | Georgia 7 6

1950 5-6-0 (4-2-0)
S23 at SMU 13 33
S30 South Carolina 0 7
O7 ● | Florida 16 13
O14 ● | at LSU 13 0
O21 ● | Auburn 20 0
O28 | Kentucky 14 28
N4 at Duke 21 30
N11 VMI 13 14
N18 | Alabama 19 54
N25 ● Davidson 46 14
D2 ● | at Georgia 7 0

1951 11-0-1 (7-0-0)
S22 ● SMU 21 7
S29 ● | at Florida 27 0
O6 ● | at Kentucky 13 7
O13 ● | LSU 25 7
O20 ● | Auburn 27 7
O27 ● | at Vanderbilt 8 7
N3 = Duke 14 14
N10 ● VMI 34 7
N17 ● | Alabama BIRM 27 7
N24 ● Davidson 34 7
D1 ● | Georgia 48 6
ORANGE BOWL
J1 ● Baylor 17 14

1952 12-0-0 (6-0-0)
S20 ● Citadel 54 6
S27 ● | Florida 17 14
O4 ● at SMU 20 7
O11 ● | Tulane 14 0
O18 ● | Auburn 33 0
O25 ● | Vanderbilt 30 0
N1 ● at Duke 28 7
N8 ● Army 45 6
N15 ● | Alabama 7 3
N22 ● Florida State 30 0
N29 ● | at Georgia 23 9
SUGAR BOWL
J1 ● Mississippi 24 7

1953 9-2-1 (4-1-1)
S19 ● Davidson 53 0
S26 = | at Florida 0 0
O3 ● SMU 6 4
O10 ● | at Tulane 27 13
O17 ● | Auburn 36 6
O24 at Notre Dame 14 27
O31 ● | at Vanderbilt 43 0
N7 ● Clemson 20 7
N14 | Alabama BIR 6 13
N21 ● Duke 13 10
N28 ● | Georgia 28 12
SUGAR BOWL
J1 ● West Virginia 42 19

1954 8-3-0 (6-2-0)
S18 ● | Tulane 28 0
S25 | Florida 12 13
O2 ● at SMU 10 7
O9 ● | LSU 30 20
O16 ● | Auburn 14 7
O23 | Kentucky 6 13
O30 at Duke 20 21
N6 ● | Tennessee 28 7
N13 ● | Alabama 20 0
N27 ● | at Georgia 7 3
COTTON BOWL
J1 ● Arkansas 14 6

THE SCHOOLS

THE SCHOOLS

1955 — 9-1-1 (4-1-1)

Date	Opponent		
S17	● Miami, Fla.	14	6
S24	● at Florida	14	7
O1	● SMU	20	7
O8	● at LSU	7	0
O15	Auburn	12	14
O22	● Florida State	34	0
O29	● Duke	27	0
N5	= at Tennessee	7	7
N12	● Alabama *Birm*	26	2
N26	● Georgia	21	3
SUGAR BOWL			
J2	● Pittsburgh	7	0

1956 — 10-1-0 (7-1-0)

Date	Opponent		
S22	● at Kentucky	14	6
S29	● at SMU	9	7
O13	LSU	39	7
O20	Auburn	28	7
O27	Tulane	40	0
N3	at Duke	7	0
N10	Tennessee	0	6
N17	● Alabama	27	0
N24	● Florida *JacF*	28	0
D1	at Georgia	35	0
GATOR BOWL			
D29	● Pittsburgh	21	14

1957 — 4-4-2 (3-4-1)

Date	Opponent		
S21	● Kentucky	13	0
S28	= SMU	0	0
O12	at LSU	13	20
O19	Auburn	0	3
O26	● at Tulane	20	13
N2	● Duke	13	0
N9	at Tennessee	6	21
N16	● Alabama *Birm*	10	7
N23	= Florida	0	0
N30	Georgia	0	7

1958 — 5-4-1 (2-3-1)

Date	Opponent		
S20	at Kentucky	0	13
S26	● Florida State	17	3
O4	● Tulane	14	0
O11	● Tennessee	21	7
O18	= Auburn	7	7
O25	at SMU	0	20
N1	● at Duke	10	8
N8	Clemson	13	0
N15	Alabama	8	17
N29	at Georgia	3	16

1959 — 6-5-0 (3-3-0)

Date	Opponent		
S19	● at Kentucky	14	12
S26	● SMU	16	12
O3	● Clemson	16	6
O10	● at Tennessee	14	7
O17	● Auburn	6	7
O24	● at Tulane	21	13
O31	● Duke	7	10
N7	● at Notre Dame	14	10
N14	Alabama *Birm*	7	9
N28	Georgia	14	21
GATOR BOWL			
J2	● Arkansas	7	14

1960 — 5-5-0 (4-4-0)

Date	Opponent		
S17	● Kentucky	23	13
S24	● at Rice	16	13
O1	● at Florida	17	18
O8	● LSU	6	2
O15	● Auburn *Birm*	7	9
O22	● Tulane	14	6
O29	● at Duke	0	6
N5	● Tennessee	14	7
N12	Alabama	15	16
N26	at Georgia	6	7

1961 — 7-4-0 (4-3-0)

Date	Opponent		
S22	● at Southern Cal	27	7
S30	● Rice	24	0
O7	at LSU	0	10
O14	● Duke	21	0
O21	● Auburn	7	6
O28	● at Tulane	35	0
N4	Florida	20	0
N11	at Tennessee	6	10
N18	● Alabama *Birm*	0	10
D2	● Georgia	22	7
GATOR BOWL			
D30	Penn State	15	30

1962 — 7-3-1 (5-2-0)

Date	Opponent		
S22	● Clemson	26	9
S29	● at Florida	17	0
O6	LSU	7	10
O13	Tennessee	17	0
O20	● Auburn	17	14
O27	● Tulane	42	12
N3	● at Duke	20	9
N10	= Florida State	14	14
N17	● Alabama	7	6
D1	● at Georgia	37	6
BLUEBONNET BOWL			
D22	Missouri	10	14

1963 — 7-3-0 (4-3-0)

Date	Opponent		
S14	● Florida	9	0
S28	● Clemson	27	0
O5	at LSU	6	7
O12	● at Tennessee	23	7
O19	Auburn	21	29
O26	● at Tulane	17	3
N2	Duke	30	6
N9	Florida State	15	7
N16	● Alabama *Birm*	11	27
N30	● Georgia	14	3

1964-1982 INDEPENDENT

1964 — 7-3-0 (0-0-0)

Date	Opponent		
S19	● Vanderbilt	14	2
S26	● Miami, Fla.	20	0
O3	● Clemson	14	7
O10	● Navy *JacF*	17	0
O17	● Auburn	7	3
O24	● Tulane	7	6
O31	● at Duke	21	8
N7	Tennessee	14	22
N14	Alabama	7	24
N28	at Georgia	0	7

1965 — 7-3-1 (0-0-0)

Date	Opponent		
S18	= at Vanderbilt	10	10
S25	● Texas A&M	10	14
O2	● Clemson	38	6
O9	● at Tulane	13	10
O16	● Auburn	23	14
O23	● Navy	37	16
O30	● Duke	35	23
N6	● at Tennessee	7	21
N13	● Virginia	42	19
N27	● Georgia	7	17
GATOR BOWL			
D31	● Texas Tech	31	21

1966 — 9-2-0 (0-0-0)

Date	Opponent		
S17	● Texas A&M	38	3
S24	● Vanderbilt	42	0
O1	● Clemson	13	12
O8	● Tennessee	6	3
O15	● Auburn *Birm*	17	3
O22	● Tulane	35	17
O29	● at Duke	48	7
N5	● Virginia	14	13
N12	● Penn State	21	0
N26	● at Georgia	14	23
ORANGE BOWL			
J2	● Florida	12	27

BUD CARSON — 1967-71 (.500) — 27-27

1967 — 4-6-0 (0-0-0)

Date	Opponent		
S23	● at Vanderbilt	17	10
S30	● TCU	24	7
O7	● Clemson	10	0
O14	● at Tennessee	13	24
O21	● Auburn	10	28
O28	● at Tulane	12	23
N4	● Duke	19	7
N10	● at Miami, Fla.	7	49
N18	● Notre Dame	3	36
N25	● Georgia	14	21

1968 — 4-6-0 (0-0-0)

Date	Opponent		
S21	● TCU	17	7
S28	● Miami, Fla.	7	10
O5	● Clemson	24	21
O12	● Tennessee	7	24
O19	● Auburn	21	20
O26	● Tulane	23	19
N2	● at Duke	30	46
N9	● Navy	15	35
N16	● at Notre Dame	6	34
N30	● at Georgia	8	47

1969 — 4-6-0 (0-0-0)

Date	Opponent		
S20	● SMU	24	21
S27	● Baylor	17	10
O4	● Clemson	10	21
O11	● at Tennessee	8	26
O18	● Auburn	14	17
O25	● at Southern Cal	18	29
N1	● Duke	20	7
N8	● at Tulane	7	14
N15	● Notre Dame	20	38
N29	● Georgia	6	0

1970 — 9-3-0 (0-0-0)

Date	Opponent		
S12	● South Carolina	23	20
S19	● Florida State	23	13
S26	● Miami, Fla.	31	21
O3	● Clemson	28	7
O10	● Tennessee	6	17
O17	● at Auburn	7	31
O24	● Tulane	20	6
O31	● at Duke	24	16
N7	● Navy	30	8
N14	● at Notre Dame	7	10
N28	● at Georgia	17	7
SUN BOWL			
D19	● Texas Tech	17	9

1971 — 6-6-0 (0-0-0)

Date	Opponent		
S11	● at South Carolina	7	24
S18	● Michigan State	10	0
S25	● Army	13	16
O2	● Clemson	24	14
O9	● at Tennessee	6	10
O16	● Auburn	14	31
O23	● at Tulane	24	16
O30	● Duke	21	0
N6	● Navy	34	21
N13	● Florida State	12	6
N27	● Georgia	24	28
PEACH BOWL			
D30	● Mississippi	18	41

BILL FULCHER — 1972-73 (.543) — 12-10-1

1972 — 7-4-1 (0-0-0)

Date	Opponent		
S9	● Tennessee	3	34
S16	● South Carolina	34	6
S23	● at Michigan State	21	16
S30	= Rice	36	36
O7	● Clemson	31	9
O21	● at Auburn	14	24
O28	● Tulane	21	7
N4	● at Duke	14	20
N11	● Boston College	42	10
N18	● Navy	30	7
D2	● at Georgia	7	27
LIBERTY BOWL			
D18	● Iowa State	31	30

1973 — 5-6-0 (0-0-0)

Date	Opponent		
S15	● at South Carolina	28	41
S22	● Southern Cal	6	23
S29	● Clemson	29	21
O6	● Army	14	10
O13	● at Tennessee	14	20
O20	● Auburn	10	24
O27	● at Tulane	14	23
N3	● Duke	12	10
N10	● VMI	36	7
N17	● Navy *JacF*	26	22
D1	● Georgia	3	10

FRANKLIN "PEPPER" RODGERS — 1974-79 (.522) — 34-31-2

1974 — 6-5-0 (0-0-0)

Date	Opponent		
S9	● Notre Dame	7	31
S14	● South Carolina	35	20
S21	● Pittsburgh	17	27
S28	● at Clemson	17	21
O5	● Virginia	28	24
O12	● North Carolina	29	28
O19	● at Auburn	22	31
O26	● Tulane	27	7
N2	● at Duke	0	9
N16	● Navy	22	0
N30	● at Georgia	34	14

1975 — 7-4-0 (0-0-0)

Date	Opponent		
S13	● at South Carolina	17	23
S20	● Miami, Fla.	38	23
S27	● Clemson	33	28
O4	● Florida State	30	0
O11	● VMI	38	10
O18	● Auburn	27	31
O25	● at Tulane	23	0
N1	● Duke	21	6
N8	● at Notre Dame	3	24
N15	● Navy	14	13
N27	● Georgia	26	42

1976 — 4-6-1 (0-0-0)

Date	Opponent		
S11	● South Carolina	17	27
S18	● Pittsburgh	14	42
S25	= Clemson	24	24
O2	● Virginia	35	14
O9	● Tennessee	7	42
O16	● at Auburn	28	10
O23	● Tulane	28	16
O30	● at Duke	7	31
N6	● Notre Dame	23	14
N13	● at Navy	28	34
N27	● at Georgia	10	13

1977 — 6-5-0 (0-0-0)

Date	Opponent		
S10	● at South Carolina	0	17
S17	● Miami, Fla.	10	6
S24	● at Clemson	14	31
O1	● Air Force	30	3
O8	● at Tennessee	24	8
O15	● Auburn	38	21
O22	● at Tulane	38	14
O29	● Duke	24	25
N5	● at Notre Dame	14	69
N12	● at Navy	16	20
N26	● Georgia	16	7

1978 — 7-5-0 (0-0-0)

Date	Opponent		
S9	● at Duke	10	28
S16	● California	22	34
S23	● Tulane	27	17
S30	● Citadel	28	0
O7	● South Carolina	6	3
O14	● Miami, Fla.	24	19
O21	● at Auburn	24	10
O28	● Florida	17	13
N11	● at Air Force	42	21
N18	● Notre Dame	21	38
D2	● at Georgia	28	29
PEACH BOWL			
D25	● Purdue	21	41

1979 — 4-6-1 (0-0-0)

Date	Opponent		
S8	● Alabama	6	30
S22	= at Florida	7	7
S29	● William & Mary	33	7
O6	● at Notre Dame	13	21
O13	● at Tennessee	0	31
O20	● Auburn	14	38
O27	● at Tulane	7	12
N3	● Duke	24	14
N10	● Air Force	21	0
N17	● Navy	24	14
D1	● Georgia	3	16

BILL CURRY — 1980-86 (.423) — 31-43-4

1980 — 1-9-1 (0-0-0)

Date	Opponent		
S6	● Alabama *Birm*	3	26
S20	● Florida	12	45
S27	● Memphis	17	8
O4	● at North Carolina	0	33
O11	● Tennessee	10	23
O18	● at Auburn	14	17
O25	● Tulane	14	31
N1	● at Duke	12	17
N8	= Notre Dame	3	3
N15	● Navy	8	19
N29	● at Georgia	20	38

1981 — 1-10-0 (0-0-0)

Date	Opponent		
S12	● Alabama *Birm*	24	21
S19	● at Florida	6	27
S26	● Memphis	15	28
O3	● North Carolina	7	28
O10	● at Tennessee	7	10
O17	● Auburn	7	31
O24	● at Tulane	10	27
O31	● Duke	24	38
N7	● at Notre Dame	3	35
N14	● Navy	14	20
N28	● Georgia	7	44

1982 — 6-5-0 (0-0-0)

Date		Opponent		
S11		Alabama	7	45
S18	•	Citadel	36	7
S25	•	at Memphis	24	20
O2		at North Carolina	0	41
O9	•	at Tulane	19	13
O16		at Auburn	0	24
O23	•	Tennessee	31	21
O30		Duke	21	38
N6	•	Virginia	38	32
N13	•	at Wake Forest	45	7
N27		at Georgia	18	38

1983-PRESENT ACC

1983 — 3-8-0 3-3-0

Date		Opponent		
S10		Alabama *Birm*	7	20
S17		Furman	14	17
S24		at Clemson	14	41
O1		North Carolina	21	38
O8	•	at North Carolina St.	20	10
O15		Auburn	13	31
O22		at Tennessee	3	37
O29		at Duke	26	32
N3	•	Virginia	31	27
N12	•	Wake Forest	49	33
N26		Georgia	24	27

1984 — 6-4-1 (3-2-1)

Date		Opponent		
S15	•	Alabama	16	6
S22	•	Citadel	48	3
S29	•	Clemson	28	21
O6		North Carolina St.	22	27
O13	=	at Virginia	20	20
O20		at Auburn	34	48
O27		Tennessee	21	24
N3	•	Duke	31	3
N10		at North Carolina	17	24
N17	•	at Wake Forest	24	7
D1	•	Georgia	35	18

1985 — 9-2-1 (5-1-0)

Date		Opponent		
S14	•	at North Carolina St.	28	18
S21		Virginia	13	24
S28	•	at Clemson	14	3
O5	•	North Carolina	31	0
O12	•	Western Carolina	24	17
O19		Auburn	14	17
O26	=	at Tennessee	6	6
N2	•	at Duke	9	0
N9	•	U.T. Chattanooga	35	7
N16	•	Wake Forest	41	10
N30	•	Georgia	20	16
HALL OF FAME CLASSIC				
D31	•	Michigan State	17	14

1986 — 5-5-1 (3-3-0)

Date		Opponent		
S13	=	Furman	17	17
S20	•	at Virginia	28	14
S27		Clemson	3	27
O4		at North Carolina	20	21
O11	•	North Carolina St.	59	21
O18		at Auburn	10	31
O25	•	Tennessee	14	13
N1	•	Duke	34	6
N8	•	VMI	52	6
N22		at Wake Forest	21	24
N29		at Georgia	24	31

BOBBY ROSS
1987-91 (.543)   31-26-1

1987 — 2-9-0 (0-6-0)

Date		Opponent		
S12	•	Citadel	51	12
S19		North Carolina	23	30
S26		at Clemson	12	33
O3		at North Carolina St.	0	17
O10	•	Indiana St.	38	0
O17		Auburn	10	20
O24		at Tennessee	15	29
O31		at Duke	14	48
N7		Virginia	14	23
N21		Wake Forest	6	33
N28		Georgia	16	30

1988 — 3-8-0 (0-7-0)

Date		Opponent		
S10	•	U.T. Chattanooga	24	10
S17		at Virginia	16	17
S24		Clemson	13	30
O1		North Carolina St.	6	14
O8		at Maryland	8	13
O15	•	South Carolina	34	0
O22		at North Carolina	17	20
O29		Duke	21	31
N5	•	VMI	34	7
N12		at Wake Forest	24	28
N26		at Georgia	3	24

1989 — 7-4-0 (4-3-0)

Date		Opponent		
S9		at North Carolina St.	28	38
S16		Virginia	10	17
S23		at South Carolina	10	21
O7	•	Maryland	28	24
O14	•	at Clemson	30	14
O21	•	North Carolina	17	14
O28		at Duke	19	30
N4	•	Western Carolina	34	7
N18	•	Wake Forest	43	14
N25	•	Boston College	13	12
D2	•	Georgia	33	22

1990 — 11-0-1 (6-0-1)

Date		Opponent		
S8		North Carolina St.	21	13
S22	•	U.T. Chattanooga	44	9
S29	•	South Carolina	27	6
O6	•	at Maryland	31	3
O13	•	Clemson	21	19
O20	=	at North Carolina	13	13
O27	•	Duke	48	31
N3	•	at Virginia	41	38
N10	•	Virginia Tech	6	3
N17	•	at Wake Forest	42	7
D1	•	at Georgia	40	23
CITRUS BOWL				
J1	•	Nebraska	45	21

1991 — 8-5-0 (5-2-0)

Date		Opponent		
A28		Penn State *ERut*	22	34
S14	•	at Boston College	30	14
S19	•	Virginia	24	21
S28		at Clemson	7	9
O5		at North Carolina St.	21	28
O12	•	Maryland	34	10
O19		at South Carolina	14	23
O26	•	North Carolina	35	14
N2	•	at Duke	17	6
N9	•	Furman	19	17
N16	•	Wake Forest	27	3
N30		Georgia	15	18
ALOHA BOWL				
D25	•	Stanford	18	17

BILL LEWIS
1992-94 (.367)   11-19

1992 — 5-6-0 4-4-0

Date		Opponent		
S12	•	Western Carolina	37	19
S19		at Virginia	24	55
S26	•	Clemson	20	16
O3		North Carolina St.	16	13
O10		at Maryland	28	26
O17		Florida State	24	29
O24		at North Carolina	14	26
O31	•	Duke	20	17
N7		at Baylor	27	31
N14		Wake Forest	10	23
N28		at Georgia	17	31

1993 — 5-6-0 (3-5-0)

Date		Opponent		
S11	•	Furman	37	3
S16		Virginia	14	35
S25		at Clemson	13	16
O2		at Florida State	0	51
O9	•	Maryland	38	0
O16		North Carolina	3	41
O23		at North Carolina St.	23	28
O30	•	at Duke	47	14
N6	•	Baylor	37	27
N13	•	at Wake Forest	38	28
N25		Georgia	10	43

GEORGE O'LEARY
1994-2001 (.612)   52-33

1994 — 1-10-0 (0-8-0)

Date		Opponent		
S1		Arizona	14	19
S10	•	Western Carolina	45	26
S24		Duke	12	27
O1		at North Carolina St.	13	21
O8		at North Carolina	24	31
O15		Virginia	7	24
O22		at Maryland	27	42
N5		Florida State	10	41
N12		at Clemson	10	20
N19		Wake Forest	13	20
N25		at Georgia	10	48

1995 — 6-5-0 (5-3-0)

Date		Opponent		
S2	•	Furman	51	7
S7		at Arizona	19	20
S16		at Virginia	14	41
S28	•	Maryland	31	3
O7	•	at Duke	37	21
O14	•	North Carolina	27	25
O21		at Florida State	10	42
O28		Clemson	3	24
N4	•	at Wake Forest	24	23
N11	•	North Carolina St.	27	19
N23		Georgia	17	18

1996 — 5-6 (4-4)

Date		Opponent		
S7		at North Carolina St.	28	16
S14	•	Wake Forest	30	10
S21		at North Carolina	0	16
S26	•	Duke	48	22
O5	•	Virginia	13	7
O19		at Clemson	25	28
O26	•	Central Florida	27	20
N2		Florida State	3	49
N14	•	Maryland	10	13
N23	•	Navy	26	36
N30		at Georgia	10	19

1997 — 7-5 (5-3)

Date		Opponent		
S6		at Notre Dame	13	17
S20	•	at Wake Forest	28	26
S27	•	Clemson	23	20
O4	•	at Boston College	42	14
O11	•	North Carolina St.	27	17
O18		at Florida State	0	38
O30		North Carolina	13	16
N8		at Virginia	31	35
N15	•	at Duke	41	38
N22	•	Maryland	37	18
N29		Georgia	24	27
CARQUEST BOWL				
D29	•	West Virginia	35	30

1998 — 10-2 (7-1)

Date		Opponent		
S5		Boston College	31	41
S12	•	New Mexico St.	42	7
S26	•	at North Carolina	43	21
O3	•	Duke	41	13
O10	•	at North Carolina St.	47	24
O17	•	Virginia	41	38
O24		Florida State	7	34
O31	•	Maryland *Balt*	31	14
N12	•	at Clemson	24	21
N21	•	Wake Forest	63	35
N28	•	at Georgia	21	19
GATOR BOWL				
J1	•	Notre Dame	35	28

1999 — 8-4 (5-3)

Date		Opponent		
S4	•	at Navy	49	14
S11	•	at Florida State	35	41
S18	•	Central Florida	41	10
S30	•	Maryland	49	31
O9	•	North Carolina	31	24
O16	•	at Duke	38	31
O30	•	North Carolina St.	48	21
N6		at Virginia	38	45
N13	•	Clemson	45	42
N20	•	at Wake Forest	23	26
N27	•	Georgia	51	48
GATOR BOWL				
J1	•	Miami, Fla.	13	28

2000 — 9-3 (6-2)

Date		Opponent		
S2	•	Central Florida	21	17
S9		Florida State	21	26
S16	•	Navy	40	13
S21	•	at North Carolina St.	23	30
S30	•	at North Carolina	42	28
O14	•	Wake Forest	52	20
O21	•	Duke	45	10
O28	•	at Clemson	31	28
N9	•	Virginia	35	0
N18	•	at Maryland	35	22
N25	•	at Georgia	27	15
PEACH BOWL				
D29	•	LSU	14	28

MAC McWHORTER
2001 (1.000)   1-0

2001 — 8-5 (4-4)

Date		Opponent		
A26	•	Syracuse *ERut*	13	7
S1	•	Citadel	35	7
S8		at Navy	70	7
S29	•	Clemson	44	47
O6	•	at Duke	37	10
O11		Maryland	17	20
O20	•	North Carolina St.	27	17
N1	•	North Carolina	28	21
N10	•	at Virginia	38	39
N17	•	at Wake Forest	38	33
N24		Georgia	17	31
D1		at Florida State	17	28
SEATTLE BOWL				
D27	•	Stanford	24	14

CHAN GAILEY
2002-Present (.533)   21-17

2002 — 7-6 (4-4)

Date		Opponent		
A31	•	Vanderbilt	45	3
S7		at Connecticut	31	14
S14		at Clemson	19	24
S21	•	Brigham Young	28	19
S28	•	at North Carolina	21	13
O5		Wake Forest	21	24
O17		at Maryland	10	34
O26	•	Virginia	23	15
N2	•	at North Carolina St.	24	17
N9		Florida State	13	21
N16	•	Duke	17	2
N30		at Georgia	7	51
SILICON VALLEY BOWL				
D31	•	Fresno State	21	30

2003 — 7-6 (4-4)

Date		Opponent		
A30	•	at Brigham Young	13	24
S6	•	Auburn	17	3
S13		at Florida State	13	14
S20		Clemson	3	39
S27	•	at Vanderbilt	24	17
O4	•	North Carolina St.	29	21
O11	•	at Wake Forest	24	7
O23	•	Maryland	7	3
N8		at Duke	17	41
N15	•	North Carolina	41	24
N22	•	at Virginia	17	29
N29		Georgia	17	34
HUMANITARIAN BOWL				
J3	•	Tulsa	52	10

2004 — 7-5 (4-4)

Date		Opponent		
S4	•	Samford	28	7
S11	•	at Clemson	28	24
S18		at North Carolina	13	34
O2		Miami, Fla.	3	27
O9	•	at Maryland	20	7
O16	•	Duke	24	7
O28	•	Virginia Tech	20	34
N6	•	at North Carolina St.	24	14
N13	•	Connecticut	30	10
N20	•	Virginia	10	30
N27	•	at Georgia	13	19
CHAMPS SPORTS BOWL				
D21	•	Syracuse	51	14

THE SCHOOLS

Neutral Site key: *Aug* Augusta, Ga. / *Balt* Baltimore, Md. / *Birm* Birmingham, Ala. / *Bnx* Bronx, N.Y. / *ERut* East Rutherford, N.J. / *GrvSC* Greenville, S.C. / *JacF* Jacksonville, Fla. / *Lou* Louisville, Ky. / *NO* New Orleans, La. / *NYC* New York, N.Y. / *Unk* Unknown Unknown

ƒ Forfeit   † Game Later Forfeited   # Disputed Victor   * Disputed Score || Designated Conference Game |2 Counted Twice in Conference Standings

HAWAII

BY DAVE REARDON

HAWAII HAS BECOME A PASSING-game paradise in recent years. June Jones, a former UH backup quarterback and assistant coach, returned to the islands from the NFL in 1999 and brought the run 'n shoot offense with him. A brash talker and born gambler, Jones revitalized Hawaii football by daring to predict Top 25 finishes and a Heisman Trophy award for quarterback Timmy Chang, who broke the UH career passing yardage mark in 2004. In his first six years, Jones led Hawaii to four seasons of at least nine wins—and he often says that the Warriors (né Rainbows) will play anyone, anywhere in their quest for national recognition.

TRADITION All-conference defensive back/quarterback Blane Gaison—one of the most popular players in the program's history—often gets credit for being the first to walk around Aloha Stadium after his final game in 1980 to say good-bye to the fans. In truth, though, center Ed Riewerts and walk-on defensive back Nelson Maeda did the same thing the year before. Today, the Senior Walk is an organized affair, with every senior introduced for a final time before he circles the stadium, signing autographs and receiving flower leis and other gifts.

BEST PLAYER In the fall of 1988, a kicker from Georgia arrived at Manoa with little fanfare. His name was Jason Elam, and in his first game he kicked a field goal to give the Rainbows a 27-24 upset of Iowa. He would go on to become a three-time All-WAC first-teamer, as well the conference's special-teams Player of the Year in 1992. He holds school records for points (395), longest field goal (56 yards, against BYU in 1992) and career punting average (43.5 yards). Elam, now of the Denver Broncos, has returned to Honolulu three times as a member of the AFC Pro Bowl team. In 1998, he tied the NFL record with a 63-yard field goal.

BEST COACH Dave Holmes guided Hawaii to a 46–17–1 record from 1968 to 1973. His .727 winning percentage is the best of any UH football coach since the 1920s, but team dissent at the end of the 1973 season—based on tension between both offensive/defensive and

---

PROFILE

University of Hawaii at Manoa
Honolulu, Hawaii
Founded: 1907
Enrollment: 13,755
Colors: Green, Black, White and Silver
Nickname: Warriors
Stadium: Aloha Stadium
    Opened in 1975
    FieldTurf; 50,000 capacity
First football game: 1909
All-time record: 469–358–25 (.565)
Bowl record: 4–2
Western Athletic Conference championships: 2 (shared)
First-round NFL draftees: 1
Website: uhathletics.hawaii.edu

THE BEST OF TIMES

Hawaii went unbeaten two consecutive seasons in 1924 and 1925, going 8–0 and 10–0. Most of the games were against military or town teams, but the Wonder Teams under coach Otto "Proc" Klum did notch victories against Colorado, Colorado State and Washington State.

THE WORST OF TIMES

Fred von Appen's teams went 5–31 from 1996 to 1998. The Rainbow Warriors lost 18 in a row, including all 12 games in 1998, before athletic director Hugh Yoshida fired his Linfield College teammate.

CONFERENCE

Hawaii has played in the Western Athletic Conference since the 1979 season. It's the only conference the previously independent program has ever been in.

DISTINGUISHED ALUMNI

Bette Midler; Daniel Inouye, U.S. senator; Richard Mamiya, UH quarterback and heart surgeon; Angela Perez Baraquio, Miss America

FIGHT SONG

CO-ED
Here's to our dear Hawaii
Here's to our Green and White
Here's to our Alma Mater
Here's to the team with fight
Rah! Rah! Rah!
Here's to old warriors calling
Here's to old battles won
Here's to Hawaii's victory
Here's to each valiant son.

Hawaii's relationship with Brigham Young is for the most part a one-sided hate affair.

mainlander/local factions—brought about Holmes' resignation.

BEST TEAM The 1992 Rainbows won a school-record 11 games, including a 27-17 Holiday Bowl victory over Illinois. UH opened the season with victories at Oregon and Air Force, and finished the season 7–0 at home, ranked 20th in both major polls. Four players—offensive lineman Doug Vaioleti, running back Travis Sims, Elam and defensive lineman Maa Tanuvasa—were All-WAC first-teamers.

BIGGEST GAME In 1989, after 10 consecutive losses to BYU over 11 years, Hawaii finally ended the Cougars-induced drought in a huge way, with quarterback Garrett Gabriel and linebacker Mark Odom leading UH to a 56-14 rout. The following year, UH did it again, pounding the Cougars 59-28. The second win came on the same day that BYU quarterback Ty Detmer won the Heisman Trophy; when Hawaii's Jeff Sydner scored, he struck the famous pose of the statue Detmer was awarded.

BIGGEST UPSET In 1973, coach Dave Holmes took the Rainbows to Seattle for a game against Washington. Washington was heavily favored but stumbled, plagued by five turnovers, as the Rainbows came away 10-7 winners. Hawaii cornerback Hal Stringert intercepted three passes, and UH scored on a 24-yard touchdown pass to Allen Brown from Casey Ortiz and a 27-yard field goal by Reinhold Stuprich.

HEARTBREAKER Hawaii's 1984 squad was one of the school's most talented ever, finishing 7–4 and coming agonizingly close to a win that would have altered the outcome of the national championship race. The Warriors were 0–2 when they played host to unbeaten Brigham Young on Sept. 22 of that season. With the Aloha Stadium crowd on its feet virtually throughout the game, the Warriors' defense continually stymied Robbie Bosco and the high-scoring Cougars attack. Early in the fourth quarter, Hawaii drove down to the BYU 1-yard line, but the drive stalled when

RECORDS

RUSHING YARDS

	GAME	
270	Pete Wilson vs. Brigham Young, Nov. 17, 1950	
	SEASON	
1,498	Travis Sims, 1992 (220 att.)	
	CAREER	
3,451	Gary Allen, 1978-81 (647 att.)	

PASSING YARDS

	GAME	
543	Nick Rolovich vs. Brigham Young, Dec. 8, 2001 (29 of 52)	
	SEASON	
4,474	Timmy Chang, 2002 (349 of 624)	
	CAREER	
17,072	Timmy Chang, 2000-04 (1,388 of 2,436)	

RECEIVING YARDS

	GAME	
285	Ashley Lelie vs. Air Force, Nov. 24, 2001 (9 rec.)	
	SEASON	
1,713	Ashley Lelie, 2001 (84 rec.)	
	CAREER	
3,341	Ashley Lelie, 1999-2001 (194 rec.)	

POINTS

	GAME	
30	Chad Owens vs. Northwestern, Nov. 27, 2004 (5 TDs); Heikoti Fakava vs. Yale, Oct. 3, 1987 (5 TDs)	
	SEASON	
132	Chad Owens, 2004 (22 TDs)	
	CAREER	
395	Jason Elam, 1988-92 (79 FGs, 158 PATs)	

CONSENSUS ALL-AMERICANS

1941	Nolle Smith, B
1968	Tim Buchanan, LB

BYU linebacker Kyle Morrell leaped over two offensive linemen to sack quarterback Raphel Cherry, forcing Hawaii to settle for a go-ahead field goal and a 13-12 lead. BYU responded with a touchdown to regain the lead, 18-13. Late in the fourth quarter, Hawaii's Al Noga blocked a BYU punt, giving the Warriors one last chance. But it was dashed when Walter Murray dropped a Cherry pass in the end zone in the final minute, allowing the Cougars to escape with the win, en route to a national championship. It's a loss that still haunts Warriors fans to this day.

STADIUM UH fans have fond memories of old Honolulu Stadium and its boiled peanuts. "The Termite Palace," where Hawaii played until Aloha Stadium opened in 1975, could barely hold more than 24,000, and nobody worried about parking, because there was none. Aloha Stadium, on the other hand, has been a flashpoint of controversy for several seasons, for many reasons: its distance from the university (12 miles) and difficult parking situation are blamed for small crowds and, as the stadium is state-owned, UH must pay rent.

RIVAL Hawaii's relationship with Brigham Young is for the most part a one-sided hate affair. Back when both schools were in the WAC, the Cougars would regularly beat the Rainbows (and swipe a good deal of local talent from Hawaii as well). Not only have the Cougars won 19 of the teams' 27 meetings, but it infuriates the Hawaii faithful even more that BYU thinks of UH as simply another team on the schedule, saving its wrath for in-state rival Utah.

NUMBERS Operating out of the spread option offense in 1991, quarterback Michael Carter was one of the few quarterbacks to both pass and rush for at least 1,000 yards in a season, running for 1,092 and passing for 1,172 ... Chad Owens set Hawaii single-game records for kickoff return yardage (249) and total kick return yardage (342) in Hawaii's 72-45 victory over Brigham Young on Dec. 8, 2001 ... Nick Rolovich passed for 1,548 yards and 20 touchdowns in Hawaii's last three games of the 2001 season.

TRAGEDY The Warriors' locker room is named after Shannon Shea Smith, a backup punter who drowned on March 29, 1997, after saving the life of coach Fred von Appen's 6-year-old son during a swimming outing on the island of Kauai. On Jan. 11, 1998, Smith became the seventh person to receive the NCAA's Award of Valor. Smith's locker remains decorated with football gear and draped with a lei.

NICKNAME Rainbows or Warriors? People in Hawaii tend to be agreeable sorts, but everyone seems to have an opinion on the nickname. In 1923, a rainbow appeared over Moiliili Field after Hawaii upset Oregon State 7-0, and reporters began calling them the Rainbows. In 2000, June Jones got permission to change the team's nickname to the Warriors and to drop the rainbow from the uniform; the change drew negative national attention when athletic director Hugh Yoshida publicly said that a reason for the change was that the rainbow's association with the gay community was causing UH football players to be teased. Old-time advocates of the Rainbow nickname still refuse to call the team the Warriors.

MASCOT Some might consider him politically incorrect, but the Warriors' Polynesian players say Vili Fehoko is culturally correct. They love exchanging pregame chest butts with the half-naked, face-painted "Warrior," who entertains tourists as a fire dancer and drummer in his real job. Fans enjoy his fierce appearance and intimidating style much more than they did the previous mascot, who tried to emulate the look of a Hawaiian chief by wearing a rubber suit.

UNIFORMS As part of the Rainbows-to-Warriors makeover, the rainbow piping on the uniform pants was removed. Native tapa triangle designs, often seen in Polynesian tattoos, were added to the helmet, shirt and pants. The Warriors usually wear combinations of green, black, silver and white, switching to all black for select big games.

LORE In 1935, Tommy Kaulukukui returned a kickoff 103 yards against UCLA at the Los Angeles Coliseum. The touchdown supplied Hawaii's only points in a 19-6 loss, but the five-foot, 140-pound Kaulukukui impressed legendary sportswriter Grantland Rice enough that Rice dubbed him "Grass Shack." Kaulukukui's number, 32, remains the only one retired in school history.

QUOTE "I've never known a Texan to back down from a fight before. I guess their coach isn't from Texas."—June Jones, talking about Texas coach Mack Brown after the Longhorns pulled out of a game at Hawaii in 2000

Hawaii Annual Statistical Leaders

YR	RUSHING	YDS	ATT	AVG	PASSING	ATT	CMP	PCT	YDS	RECEIVING	REC	YDS	AVG
1967	Larry Cook	362	100	3.6	Dick Hough	197	109	.55	1,419	Jim Schultz	60	956	15.9
1968	Emory Holmes	714	139	5.1	Larry Arnold	278	154	.55	1,821	McKinley Reynolds	49	711	13.9
1969	Bill Massey	840	144	5.8	Larry Arnold	211	110	.52	1,378	Dave Patterson	36	435	12.1
1970	Larry Sherrer	722	106	6.8	Howard Gay	140	68	.49	851	Henry Sovio	29	339	11.7
1971	Larry Sherrer	1,129	204	5.5	Elroy Chong	156	71	.46	1,041	Henry Sovio	36	527	14.6
1972	Albert Holmes	146	199	0.7	Mike Biscotti	110	54	.49	772	Golden Richards	23	414	18.0
1973	Albert Holmes	714	166	4.3	Casey Ortez	178	103	.58	1,385	Allen Brown	46	735	16.0
1974	Regis Grice	472	115	4.1	Alex Kaloi	240	120	.50	1,214	Mel deLaura	42	482	11.5
1975	Norris Birdsong	731	165	4.4	Alex Kaloi	132	64	.48	793	Larry Jackson	12	186	15.5
1976	Wilbert Haslip	730	139	5.3	Joe McReynolds	76	36	.47	373	Mike Fletcher	23	284	12.3
1977	Wilbert Haslip	698	134	5.2	Jeff Duva	197	105	.53	1,478	Rick Wagner	19	270	14.2
1978	Gary Allen	521	98	5.3	Jeff Duva	208	113	.54	1,463	DeWayne Jett	18	382	21.2
1979	Gary Allen	1,040	162	6.4	Mike Stennis	92	42	.46	565	DeWayne Jett	21	271	12.9
1980	Gary Allen	884	193	4.6	Mike Stennis	141	71	.50	869	Ron Pennick	23	282	12.3
1981	Gary Allen	1,006	194	5.2	Tim Lyons	142	72	.51	970	Gary Allen	21	367	17.5
1982	Anthony Edgar	900	201	4.5	Bernard Quarles	188	103	.55	1,350	Walter Murray	31	494	15.9
1983	Dino Babers	295	76	3.9	Raphel Cherry	299	170	.57	2,478	Walter Murray	44	773	17.6
1984	Raphel Cherry	424	168	2.5	Raphel Cherry	295	143	.48	2,055	Walter Murray	37	625	16.9
1985	Nuu Faaola	1,064	203	5.2	Gregg Tipton	288	156	.54	2,130	Walter Murray	66	673	10.2
1986	Danny Crowell	724	164	4.4	Gregg Tipton	377	211	.56	2,645	David Dyas	33	562	17.0
1987	Heikoti Fakava	792	163	4.9	Warren Jones	168	84	.50	1,326	Dane McArthur	24	391	16.3
1988	Heikoti Fakava	860	194	4.4	Warren Jones	259	138	.53	2,268	Chris Roscoe	44	859	19.5
1989	Jamal Farmer	986	199	5.0	Garrett Gabriel	249	143	.57	2,145	Chris Roscoe	47	1,043	22.2
1990	Jamal Farmer	664	159	4.2	Garrett Gabriel	320	165	.52	2,752	Jeff Sydner	47	820	17.4
1991	Michael Carter	1,092	221	4.9	Michael Carter	205	81	.40	1,172	Jeff Sydner	34	421	12.4
1992	Travis Sims	1,498	220	6.8	Michael Carter	115	51	.44	787	Darrick Branch	25	491	19.6
1993	Calvin Melvin	831	139	6.0	Michael Carter	179	91	.51	1,489	Brian Gordon	27	419	15.5
1994	Tupu Alualu	638	129	4.9	John Hao	152	86	.57	1,181	Brannon Kennedy	23	462	20.1
1995	Brett Washington	574	90	6.4	Johnny Macon	152	68	.45	985	Dillan Micus	31	536	17.3
1996	Carlos Shaw	394	99	4.0	Glenn Freitas	234	129	.55	1,157	Dillan Micus	27	366	13.6
1997	Charles Tharp	796	195	4.1	Josh Skinner	195	109	.56	1,416	Charles Tharp	42	435	10.4
1998	Charles Tharp	679	146	4.7	Dan Robinson	354	163	.46	2,155	Wesley Morris	51	692	13.6
1999	Avion Weaver	645	114	5.7	Dan Robinson	556	288	.52	3,853	Dwight Carter	77	1,253	16.3
2000	James Fenderson	651	113	5.8	Timmy Chang	469	245	.52	3,041	Ashley Lelie	74	1,110	15.0
2001	Mike Bass	558	108	5.2	Nick Rolovich	405	233	.58	3,361	Ashley Lelie	84	1,713	20.4
2002	John West	451	59	7.6	Timmy Chang	624	349	.53	4,474	Justin Colbert	92	1,302	14.2
2003	John West	422	64	6.6	Timmy Chang	601	353	.59	4,199	Chad Owens	85	1,134	13.3
2004	Michael Brewster	722	113	6.4	Timmy Chang	602	358	.60	4,258	Chad Owens	102	1,290	12.6

The NCAA began including postseason stats in 2002

HAWAII ALL-TIME SCORES

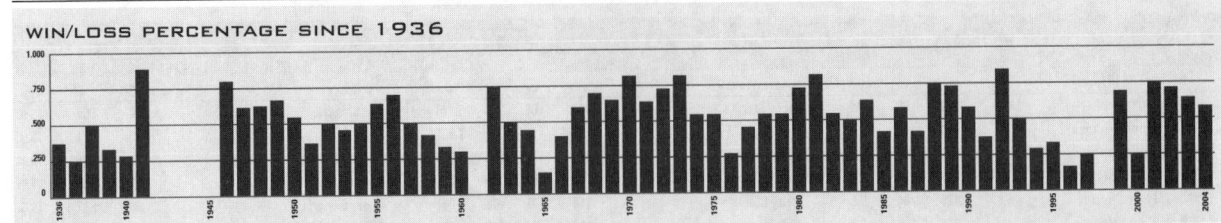

WIN/LOSS PERCENTAGE SINCE 1936

AUSTIN JONES
1909-11 (.571)   8-6

1909   2-2-0
O23 ●	McKinley HS	6	5
O30 ●	Oahu College (Punahou)	0	23
N13 ●	McKinley HS	10	0
N20 ●	Oahu College (Punahou)	0	11

1910   4-2-0
O29 ●	McKinley HS	16	0
N5 ●	McKinley HS	24	0
N12 ●	McKinley HS	36	0
N19 ●	Oahu College (Punahou)	3	2
N24 ●	Oahu College (Punahou)	0	0
D3 ●	Oahu College (Punahou)	0	5

1911   2-2-0
O28 ●	McKinley HS	21	0
N11 ●	Punahou Academy	0	17
N18 ●	McKinley HS	6	3
N30 ●	Punahou Academy	5	29

1912-14
NO TEAM

JOHN PEDEN
1915 (.786)   5-1-1

1915   5-1-1
O9 ●	Kamehameha HS	0	7
O16 ●	McKinley HS	17	0
O30 ●	Punahou Academy	15	13
N5 ●	Mills (Mid-Pacific Inst.)	50	0
N13 =	Punahou Academy	0	0
N17 ●	Kamehameha HS	20	16
N20 ●	McKinley HS	19	0

WILLIAM BRITTON
1916 (.583)   3-2-1

1916   3-2-1
O14 ●	Punahou Academy	12	12
O21 ●	McKinley HS	14	0
O27 ●	Mills (Mid-Pacific Inst.)	38	6
N4 ●	Kamehameha HS	0	10
N18 ●	Kamehameha HS	9	6
N25 ●	National Guard	6	7

DAVE CRAWFORD
1917-19 (.857)   11-1-2

1917   4-0-1
O6 ●	Punahou Academy	0	0
O13 ●	Kamehameha HS	7	6
O20 ●	McKinley HS	48	0
O27 ●	Punahou Academy	21	0
N3 ●	Kamehameha HS	12	0

1918   3-1-0
N9 ●	Aero Squadron	21	0
N16 ●	1st Infantry (Fort Shafter)	7	34
N23 ●	Aero Squadron	27	7
N28 ●	Signal Corps	7	6

1919   4-0-1
N1 =	Outrigger Canoe Club	6	6
N9 ●	Outrigger Canoe Club	27	7
N15 ●	Schofield	10	6
N29 ●	Luke Field	68	0
D6 ●	Town Team	27	2

RAYMOND ELLIOT
1920 (.750)   6-2

1920   6-2-0
N6 ●	Pearl Harbor Navy	19	0
N13 ●	Luke Field	47	0
N18 ●	Punahou Academy	21	0
N27 ●	Schofield	41	0
D4 ●	Palama	7	0
D11 ●	Outrigger Canoe Club	0	3
D15 ●	Waikiki	23	14
D18 ●	Nevada	0	14

OTTO "PROC" KLUM
1921-39 (.616)   84-51-7

1921   3-3-2
O8 ●	Honolulu AC	6	7
O14 =	Hawaii Marines	0	0
O29 ●	National Guard	29	7
N5 ●	Pearl Harbor Navy	0	35
N11 ●	Palama	13	6
N26 =	Outrigger Canoe Club	12	12
D3 ●	Town Team	7	0
D26 ●	Oregon	0	47

1922   5-1-1
O7 ●	Field Artillery	20	0
O14 =	Fort Ruger	88	0
N4 ●	National Guard	40	0
N11 ●	Palama	27	0
N25 ●	Hawaii Navy	10	13
D9 ●	Town Team	6	6
D25 ●	Cal Poly SLO-Pomona	25	6

1923   5-1-2
S29 ●	Coast Defense	83	6
O6 ●	Town Team	13	0
O20 ●	Hawaii Army	27	7
N3 ●	National Guard	10	0
N12 ●	Pearl Harbor Navy	19	19
N29 ●	at Cal Poly SLO-Pomona	7	14
D18 ●	Town Team	6	6
J1 ●	Oregon State	7	0

1924   8-0-0
O4 ●	13th Field Artillery	41	0
O11 ●	Town Team	21	6
N11 ●	Hawaii Army	37	0
N22 ●	Hawaii Navy	16	3
N29 ●	Town Team	19	0
D6 ●	Occidental	18	3
D13 ●	Healani	20	0
J1 ●	Colorado	13	0

1925   10-0-0
S26 ●	11th Field Artillery	68	0
S26 ●	27th Infantry	20	0
O3 ●	National Guard	86	0
O10 ●	Healani	74	0
O24 ●	Palama	42	0
O31 ●	Pearl Harbor Navy	43	0
N11 ●	Town Team	14	6
N26 ●	at Occidental	13	0
D12 ●	Colorado State	41	0
J1 ●	Washington State	20	11

1926   5-4-0
O2 ●	Field Artillery	101	0
O9 ●	UH Alumni	0	2
O16 ●	Healani	101	0
O30 ●	National Guard	26	7
N11 ●	Town Team	7	14
N19 ●	Hawaii Navy	33	13
D4 ●	SF Olympic Club	34	0
D18 ●	Utah	7	17
D25 ●	South Dakota State	2	9

1927   5-2-0
O8 ●	UH Alumni	2	3
O22 ●	Oahu Blues	20	13
N2 ●	Pearl Harbor Navy	24	7
N11 ●	Town Team	10	0
N24 ●	at Occidental	20	0
D17 ●	Utah State	21	20
J2 ●	Santa Clara	12	18

1928   2-5-0
O6 ●	UH Alumni	6	13
N6 ●	Mailes	13	38
N13 ●	Palama	38	0
N24 ●	Town Team	20	39
D8 ●	Occidental	32	0
D15 ●	Denver	12	13
J1 ●	Oregon	0	6

1929   4-3-0
O5 ●	UH Alumni	22	0
O15 ●	Honolulu AC	14	0
O26 ●	St. Louis Alumni	32	6
N11 ●	Town Team	13	0
N23 ●	at Oregon	0	7
D14 ●	Santa Clara	0	25
J1 ●	Washington State	7	28

1930   5-2-0
S27 ●	UH Alumni	12	6
O8 ●	Honolulu AC	28	0
O22 ●	St. Louis Alumni	19	7
O29 ●	Town Team	0	7
N15 ●	at Southern Cal	0	52
D10 ●	Brigham Young	49	13
J1 ●	Idaho	37	0

1931   3-2-1
O24 ●	St. Louis Alumni	13	20
N4 ●	McKinley Alumni	20	6
N18 ●	Town Team	6	6
D9 ●	San Francisco	18	14
D19 ●	Drake	19	13
J1 ●	Oklahoma	0	7

1932   2-1-1
O1 ●	McKinley Alumni	0	13
O19 =	Kamehameha Alumni	0	0
N2 ●	St. Louis Alumni	12	2
N19 ●	Town Team	20	13

1933   4-3-0
S27 ●	McKinley Alumni	13	7
O11 ●	St. Louis Alumni	0	14
O25 ●	Kamehameha Alumni	12	19
N11 ●	at Denver	7	6
N23 ●	Hawaii Navy	21	7
D2 ●	Town Team	13	7
J1 ●	Santa Clara	7	26

1934   6-0-0
O10 ●	McKinley Alumni	13	0
O31 ●	Town Team	26	7
O16 ●	Kamehameha Alumni	33	7
D1 ●	St. Louis Alumni	20	0
D15 ●	Denver	36	14
J1 ●	California	14	0

1935   5-3-0
S27 ●	St. Louis Alumni	18	0
O4 ●	McKinley Alumni	40	0
O16 ●	Kamehameha Alumni	19	7
O25 ●	Town Team	10	7
N9 ●	at Denver	7	14
N15 ●	at UCLA	6	19
D14 ●	Utah	21	20
PINEAPPLE BOWL			
J1 ●	Southern Cal	6	38

1936   3-5-0
O2 ●	McKinley Alumni	0	26
O9 ●	Town Team	6	13
O16 ●	Kamehameha Alumni	13	20
O23 ●	McKinley Alumni	13	0
O30 ●	Kamehameha Alumni	12	18
D2 ●	Town Team	12	7
D11 ●	San Jose State	8	13
J2 ●	Honolulu All-Stars	18	12

1937   2-6-0
O8 ●	McKinley Alumni	21	13
O15 ●	Town Team	7	19
O22 ●	Kamehameha Alumni	6	27
N12 ●	Town Team	7	21
N19 ●	Kamehameha Alumni	18	53
D4 ●	San Jose State	6	7
D18 ●	Denver	7	6
PINEAPPLE BOWL			
J1 ●	Washington	13	53

1938   4-4-0
O7 ●	Kamehameha Alumni	18	8
O14 ●	Town Team	19	12
O21 ●	Pearl Harbor Navy	33	0
N12 ●	at Denver	12	20
N18 ●	at Fresno State	13	15
D3 ●	San Jose State	13	12
D17 ●	Utah	13	14
PINEAPPLE BOWL			
J2 ●	UCLA	7	32

1939   3-6-0
O6 ●	Polar Bears	12	6
O13 ●	Healani	13	24
O20 ●	Pearl Harbor Navy	30	0
O26 ●	Polar Bears	6	7
N11 ●	at Utah	19	34
N15 ●	at San Diego State	13	0
D2 ●	Fresno State	2	38
D16 ●	Pacific	6	19
PINEAPPLE BOWL			
J1 ●	Oregon State	6	39

EUGENE "LUKE" GILL
1940 (.286)   2-5

1940   2-5-0
O18 ●	Polar Bears	28	35
O25 ●	Healani	13	28
N1 ●	Polar Bears	21	20
N15 ●	Healani	4	25
D7 ●	San Diego State	33	7
D14 ●	Denver	16	19
PINEAPPLE BOWL			
J1 ●	Fresno State	0	3

KAULUKUKUI/GILL
1941 (.889)   8-1

1941   8-1-0
S14 ●	at Pacific	14	0
S20 ●	at Portland	33	6
O10 ●	Hawaii Bears	20	6
O17 ●	Na Alii	19	6
O27 ●	Healani	6	26
N7 ●	Na Alii	33	14
N19 ●	Hawaii Bears	27	13
N26 ●	Healani	21	6
D6 ●	Willamette	20	6

1942-45
NO TEAM

TOM KAULUKUKUI
1946-50 (.645)   34-18-3

1946   8-2-0
S25	●	Hawaiian Pine	14	6
O2	●	Kaala	44	0
O9	●	Olympic	27	0
O16	●	Lanakila	73	6
N1	●	at Pacific	19	13
N11	●	at Fresno State	7	2
N27	●	Healani	58	6
D7	●	Nevada	7	26
D23	●	Stanford	7	18

PINEAPPLE BOWL
J1	●	Utah	19	16

1947   8-5-0
S17	●	Moiliili Bears	18	6
S27	●	Saint Mary's-Cal	7	27
O4	●	at Utah	0	35
O11	●	at Montana State	14	0
O22	●	Olympic	40	15
O29	●	Kaialums	65	0
N5	●	Leialums	26	0
N12	●	Mickalums	33	13
N29	●	Michigan State	19	58
D6	●	Fresno State	27	13
D13	●	Denver	0	27
D20	●	Montana	12	14

PINEAPPLE BOWL
J1	●	Redlands	33	32

1948   7-4-1
S7	●	Kauai Broncos	20	0
S17	●	Cardinals	47	0
S22	=	Islanders	20	20
O2	●	at Michigan State	21	68
O9	●	at Redlands	55	0
O21	●	Olympic	52	12
N3	●	Leilehua Vandals	53	7
N11	●	Ford Island	39	6
N24	●	Leilehua Vandals	14	7
D4	●	Texas-El Paso	6	49
D17	●	Nevada	12	73

PINEAPPLE BOWL
J1	●	Oregon State	27	47

1949   6-3-0
S23	●	Moiliili Cards	59	6
O1	●	at Texas-El Paso	7	14
O7	●	at Denver	27	14
O28	●	Islanders	98	7
N4	●	Moiliili Cards	34	0
N11	●	Leilehua	76	6
D2	●	Fresno State	41	14
D16	●	Pacific	0	75

PINEAPPLE BOWL
J2	●	Stanford	20	74

1950   5-4-2
S20	●	San Diego State	27	49
S27	=	Leilehua	6	6
O6	●	at Fresno State	20	34
O14	●	at Willamette	21	21
O20	●	College of Idaho	43	14
N8	●	Islanders	41	6
N17	●	Brigham Young	39	7
N22	●	Cardinals	24	6
D1	●	Texas-El Paso	13	46
D16	●	Utah	28	40

PINEAPPLE BOWL
J1	●	Denver	28	27

ARCHIE KODROS
1951 (.364)   4-7

1951   4-7-0
S12	●	Town Team	8	2
S22	●	at Tulsa	0	58
S29	●	at Brigham Young	7	20
O6	●	Cincinnati	0	34
O24	●	Mickalums	40	20
N7	●	Town Team	47	13
N18	●	Sub Pac (San Diego)	33	35
N30	●	College of Idaho	31	13
D16	●	Pendleton	26	31
D21	●	Arizona	21	32

PINEAPPLE BOWL
J1	●	San Diego State	13	34

HANK VASCONCELLOS
1952-60 (.484)   43-46-3

1952   5-5-2
S12	●	Town Team	42	0
S20	●	at Arizona	7	57
S26	●	at Lewis & Clark	21	7
O4	●	at Texas-El Paso	26	42
O15	●	Hawaiian AC	47	0
O22	●	Barber's Point	40	20
O30	=	Hawaii 49ers	21	21
N5	●	Town Team	40	7
N16	●	Hawaii 49ers	14	41
N28	=	Willamette	7	7
D5	●	Pacific	13	49
D13	●	Barber's Point	7	16

1953   5-6-0
S4	●	Islanders	13	6
S17	●	Kaneohe Marines	22	13
S26	●	at San Diego State	7	40
O3	●	at Utah	24	47
O10	●	at Pacific	8	26
O21	●	Pearl Harbor Navy	7	12
N1	●	Hawaii 49ers	13	27
N8	●	Pacific Army	28	6
N15	●	Barber's Point	26	0
N22	●	Pearl Harbor Marines	7	27
D4	●	Lewis & Clark	34	12

1954   4-4-0
S3	●	Prep All-Stars	14	13
S18	●	at Arizona State	14	28
S25	●	at Fresno State	25	20
O6	●	Pearl Harbor Navy	28	27
O13	●	Hawaii Rams	0	13
O24	●	Pacific Army	7	14
N14	●	Hawaii Marines	45	13
N26	●	Nebraska	0	50

1955   7-4-0
S2	●	Prep All-Stars	33	7
S17	●	at Nebraska	6	0
S23	●	at San Jose State	0	34
O7	●	Pearl Harbor Navy	19	12
O28	●	Hawaii Marines	20	19
N5	●	Pearl Harbor Navy	25	0
N16	●	Hawaii Rams	26	12
N21	●	Hawaii Marines	0	2
N26	●	Fresno State	18	20
D3	●	Arizona State	6	39
D11	●	Hawaii Rams	34	21

1956   7-3-0
A31	●	Prep All-Stars	21	7
S21	●	Pearl Harbor Navy	59	7
S28	●	Humboldt State	33	6
O7	●	Hawaii Rams	32	7
O20	●	at Iowa	0	34
O27	●	at Fresno State	20	39
N9	●	Southern Oregon	59	0
N18	●	Hawaii Marines	2	7
N24	●	Lewis & Clark	45	6
N30	●	San Jose State	20	0

1957   4-4-1
S14	●	at Utah State	12	26
S21	●	at Lewis & Clark	40	6
S28	●	at Humboldt State	26	0
O11	●	Willamette	27	0
O27	●	Pearl Harbor Navy	26	7
N3	=	Hawaii Marines	7	7
N11	●	Hawaii Rams	6	7
N22	●	Fresno State	8	31
N30	●	San Jose State	0	12

1958   5-7-0
A22	●	Honolulu All-Stars	6	0
S13	●	at Kentucky	0	51
S20	●	at Arizona State	6	47
S27	●	at San Jose State	8	6
O10	●	San Diego Marines	0	27
O19	●	Hawaii Rams	12	7
O26	●	Hawaii Marines	23	28
N2	●	Hawaii Rams	6	8
N8	●	Hawaii Marines	12	8
N14	●	Humboldt State	6	12
N29	●	Idaho State	40	19
D6	●	Utah	20	47

1959   3-6-0
A21	●	Hawaii All-Stars	0	13
S19	●	at Southern Oregon	20	13
S26	●	at Idaho State	14	8
O3	●	at San Jose State	14	44
O30	●	Pacific	0	6
N13	●	Cal State LA	27	6
N27	●	Fresno State	13	22
D4	●	Arizona State	6	14
D11	●	Utah State	6	48

1960   3-7-0
A26	●	Honolulu All-Stars	7	0
S10	●	at Cal State LA	20	7
S17	●	at Utah	6	33
S24	●	at Fresno State	7	17
O1	●	at Pacific	20	28
O23	●	Idaho	6	14
O28	●	Humboldt State	15	29
N11	●	Lewis & Clark	13	18
N25	●	Brigham Young	13	6
D2	●	San Jose State	6	48

1961
NO TEAM

JIM ASATO
1962-64 (.556)   15-12

1962   6-2-0
S12	●	Old Timers	19	14
S22	●	at Cal Western	14	8
S29	●	at Cal State LA	6	10
O17	●	Kaimuki Spartans	27	0
O31	●	Tantalus Rangers	13	0
N7	●	Waikiki Surfers	19	0
N24	●	Willamette	14	12
N30	●	San Jose State	0	19

1963   5-5-0
S19	●	AAH All-State	25	12
S28	●	at Humboldt State	13	30
O5	●	at Redlands	7	6
O17	●	AAH All-Stars	26	14
O23	●	Hawaii Colts	21	14
N2	●	Cal State LA	7	43
N13	●	Hawaii Colts	28	0
N26	●	Cal Western	13	16
N30	●	Service Stars	20	26
D6	●	Pacific	0	6

1964   4-5-0
S7	●	Hawaii 49ers	6	2
S19	●	at Cal Western	24	3
S26	●	at Cal State LA	0	43
O3	●	at Fresno State	0	28
O16	●	Humboldt State	14	19
N13	●	Redlands	26	0
N20	●	New Mexico	0	20
N27	●	Service Stars	28	3
D4	●	Colorado State	6	13

CLARK SHAUGHNESSY
1965 (.150)   1-8-1

1965   1-8-1
S4	=	Hawaii Colts	26	26
S11	●	at Utah State	12	31
S18	●	at Colorado State	6	54
S25	●	Humboldt State	6	14
O2	●	at Pacific	0	21
O30	●	Cal State LA	7	37
N13	●	UC Santa Barbara	0	3
N20	●	Cal Western	10	8
N27	●	Fresno State	3	7
D3	●	Service Stars	15	26

PHIL SARBOE
1966 (.400)   4-6

1966   4-6-0
S17	●	at Fresno State	27	28
S24	●	at UC Santa Barbara	6	24
O1	●	British Columbia	27	6
O8	●	at Air Force	0	54
O15	●	Humboldt State	7	0
O22	●	Pacific	0	41
O29	●	Cal Western	21	17
N5	●	Whitworth	12	6
N19	●	Parsons	10	21
N26	●	Utah State	0	48

DON KING
1967 (.600)   6-4

1967   6-4-0
S23	●	Linfield	13	15
S30	●	Lewis & Clark	34	3
O14	●	Central Washington	30	7
O21	●	at Humboldt State	0	13
O28	●	Cal State LA	3	9
N4	●	Idaho State	21	6
N11	●	UC Santa Barbara	15	7
N18	●	at Cal Western	40	14
N25	●	Fresno State	29	19
D2	●	Utah	20	25

DAVE HOLMES
1968-73 (.727)   46-17-1

1968   7-3-0
S21	●	Humboldt State	34	20
S28	●	Puget Sound	38	28
O5	●	British Columbia	48	0
O12	●	at UC Santa Barbara	14	49
O19	●	Santa Clara	23	12
N2	●	at Cal State LA	33	46
N9	●	Whitworth	54	14
N16	●	Linfield	35	13
N23	●	Nevada	21	0
N30	●	California	12	17

1969   6-3-1
S20	=	N.M. Highlands	16	16
S27	●	Central Washington	38	6
O4	●	at Puget Sound	30	20
O11	●	Long Beach State	14	28
O18	●	at Santa Clara	33	26
O25	●	Nevada-Las Vegas	57	19
N1	●	Cal State LA	52	28
N15	●	Linfield	41	14
N22	●	UC Santa Barbara	16	21
N29	●	Oregon	16	57

1970   9-2-0
S19	●	US International	14	13
S26	●	at Long Beach State	23	14
O3	●	Santa Clara	39	24
O10	●	Cal Poly SLO-Pomona	29	10
O24	●	at UC Santa Barbara	20	22
O31	●	Cal State LA	31	7
N7	●	at Nevada-Las Vegas	28	21
N14	●	Linfield	19	17
N21	●	Pacific	14	0
N28	●	Fresno State	49	0
D5	●	N.M. Highlands	10	21

1971   7-4-0
S25	●	Linfield	44	6
O2	●	at Fresno State	8	19
O9	●	Cal State LA	26	0
O16	●	Santa Clara	32	14
O23	●	N.M. Highlands	28	9
O30	●	UC Santa Barbara	23	14
N6	●	at Pacific	17	40
N13	●	Montana	25	11
N20	●	Long Beach State	21	46
N27	●	New Mexico	28	21
D4	●	Nebraska	3	45

1972   8-3-0
S16	●	at Portland State	38	13
S23	●	Cal Lutheran	38	10
O7	●	Puget Sound	27	10
O14	●	Fullerton St.	49	15
O21	●	Montana	30	3
O28	●	at Tennessee	2	34
N4	●	Grambling	7	46
N11	●	Northern Arizona	20	13
N18	●	Linfield	36	17
N25	●	San Jose State	28	14
D2	●	Stanford	7	39

1973   9-2-0
S15	●	at Washington	10	7
S22	●	at Fresno State	13	10
S29	●	Texas Southern	24	21
O6	●	Cal State LA	16	9
O20	●	Puget Sound	30	7
O27	●	Nevada-Las Vegas	31	29
N3	●	Cal State Northridge	28	3
N10	●	Santa Clara	40	9
N17	●	Pacific	3	28
N24	●	San Jose State	3	23
D1	●	Utah	7	6

330 HAWAII

THE SCHOOLS

LARRY PRICE
1974-76 (.455) 15-18

1974 6-5-0

S14	●	Brigham Young	15	13
S21	●	Humboldt State	35	9
O5	●	at Pacific	23	14
O19	●	Long Beach State	28	21
O26		at Nevada-Las Vegas	8	33
N2		Western Illinois	0	31
N9		San Jose State	11	32
N16		Santa Clara	3	9
N23	●	Fresno State	21	7
N30	●	Rutgers	28	16
D7		Arizona State	3	26

1975 6-5-0

S13		Texas A&I	9	43
S20		Grambling	6	20
O4		at Rutgers	3	7
O18	●	Portland State	24	7
O25	●	Santa Clara	48	40
N1	●	Fullerton St.	16	7
N8		at Long Beach State	0	10
N15	●	Texas-El Paso	21	9
N22	●	Pacific	17	10
N29	●	San Jose State	30	20
D6		Tennessee	6	28

1976 3-8-0

S11		at San Jose State	7	48
S18		Texas A&I	21	56
S25		at Pacific	12	21
O2		Grambling	23	34
O16	●	Portland State	20	17
O30	●	Fullerton St.	27	7
N6		Kent State	6	27
N13		Montana State	7	28
N20	●	Texas-El Paso	28	12
N27		Oregon State	0	59
D4		Nebraska	3	68

DICK TOMEY
1977-86 (.576) 63-46-3

1977 5-6-0

S10		New Mexico	26	35
S17		Colorado State	16	20
S24	●	Idaho	45	26
O1	●	La. Lafayette	20	6
O8		at Pacific	7	37
O15		Southern Miss	26	28
O22	●	Portland State	21	12
N5		at San Jose State	14	24
N19	●	Bowling Green	41	21
N26	●	South Carolina	24	7
D3		Arizona	10	17

1978 6-5-0

S9	●	New Mexico	22	16
S16		at Nebraska	10	56
S30	●	Fullerton St.	42	33
O7	●	San Jose State	25	11
O14		at Nevada-Las Vegas	20	30
O28		Pacific	17	27
N4	●	Texas-El Paso	35	13
N11	●	New Mexico State	35	20
N18	●	Wyoming	27	22
N25		Brigham Young	13	31
D2		Southern Cal	5	21

1979-PRESENT
WAC

1979 6-5-0 (3-3-0)

S8	|	Utah	23	27
S22	● |	New Mexico	20	3
S29		Nevada-Las Vegas	31	48
O5	|	at Brigham Young	15	38
O13	●	Santa Clara	52	3
O20	●	Prarie View A&M	65	0
O27	● |	at Texas-El Paso	27	12
N3		Temple	31	34
N17	|	Wyoming	13	21
N24	● |	Colorado State	24	10
D1	●	Arizona State	29	17

1980 8-3-0 (3-3-0)

S13	●	Abilene Christian	41	0
S20	●	Pacific	25	14
S27	|	at Wyoming	20	45
O4	|	Texas-El Paso	14	34
O11	●	West Virginia	16	13
O18	● |	at New Mexico	31	14
O25	|	Brigham Young	7	34
N1	●	Fullerton St.	31	21
N8	● |	San Diego State	31	6
N15	● ||	at Nevada-Las Vegas	24	19
N29	● |	Air Force	20	12

1981 9-2-0 (5-1-0)

S19	●	Fullerton St.	38	12
S26	●	Idaho	21	6
O10	● |	at Wyoming	14	9
O17	● |	New Mexico	23	13
O24	● |	at San Diego State	28	10
O31	● ||	Nevada-Las Vegas	57	21
N7	● |	at Texas-El Paso	35	7
N14	|	Brigham Young	3	13
N21		Pacific	17	23
N28	● |	Colorado State	59	6
D5	●	South Carolina	33	10

1982 6-5-0 (4-4-0)

S11	●	Montana	40	0
S18	● |	at Colorado State	23	13
S25	● |	Texas-El Paso	17	10
O2	|	Wyoming	10	28
O9	● |	Utah	10	7
O16	|	at Brigham Young	25	39
O30	● |	Fullerton St.	9	3
N6	|	San Diego State	28	31
N20	|	at New Mexico	17	41
N27	● |	Air Force	45	21
D4		Nebraska	16	37

1983 5-5-1 (3-3-1)

S10	● |	Colorado State	34	0
S17		Long Beach St.	21	23
S24	|	at Utah	25	28
O1	= |	San Diego State	27	27
O15	●	at Nevada-Las Vegas	23	0
O22	● |	New Mexico	25	16
O29	● |	Texas-El Paso	25	24
N5	|	at Air Force	10	45
N19	●	Pacific	31	21
N26	|	Wyoming	13	31
D3		Oklahoma	17	21

1984 7-4-0 (5-2-0)

S8		Fullerton St.	13	21
S15	|	at Colorado State	3	10
S22	|	Brigham Young	13	18
S29	●	Nevada-Las Vegas	16	12 †
O6	●	Fresno State	27	15
O13	● |	at Texas-El Paso	24	20
O20	● |	Utah	20	17
O27	● |	San Diego State	16	10
N3	● |	Wyoming	31	28
N24	● |	New Mexico	48	13
D1		Iowa	6	17

1985 4-6-2 (4-3-1)

A31		Kansas	27	33
S14	|	Utah	27	29
S21		Long Beach St.	30	33
O5	=	at Fresno State	24	24
O12	● |	at Wyoming	26	18
O19		Pacific	15	24
O26	● |	at New Mexico	27	17
N2	● |	Colorado State	34	14
N9	● |	at Texas-El Paso	23	7
N23	|	Air Force	20	27
N30	= |	San Diego State	10	10
D7	|	Brigham Young	6	26

1986 7-5-0 (4-4-0)

A30	|	at Air Force	17	24
S6	●	Wisconsin	20	17
S20	● |	Texas-El Paso	31	21
O4	● |	New Mexico	27	10
O18	|	at Colorado State	7	31
O25	●	Fullerton St.	26	15
N1	● |	at Utah	33	13
N8	|	Brigham Young	3	10
N15	●	Fresno State	24	13
N22	|	at San Diego State	5	35
N29	● |	Wyoming	35	19
D6		Michigan	10	27

BOB WAGNER
1987-95 (.541) 58-49-3

1987 5-7-0 (3-5-0)

S5	●	Fullerton St.	44	0
S12		at Wisconsin	7	28
S26	|	at Texas-El Paso	13	37
O3	●	Yale	62	10
O10	● |	at New Mexico	41	31
O17	● |	Utah	25	14
O24	|	Brigham Young	14	16
O31	|	San Diego State	21	29
N7	● |	Colorado State	39	38
N21	|	Air Force	31	34
N28	|	Wyoming	20	24
D5		Arkansas	20	38

1988 9-3-0 (5-3-0)

S3	●	Iowa	27	24
S10	● |	at Colorado State	31	23
S17	●	San Jose State	36	27
S24	● |	at Utah	48	20
O8	|	Texas-El Paso	25	42
O15	● |	at San Diego State	32	30
O22	|	Brigham Young	23	24
O29	●	Long Beach St.	34	31
N5	● |	New Mexico	45	3
N19	|	Wyoming	22	28
N26	● |	Air Force	19	14
D3	●	Oregon	41	17

1989 9-3-1 (5-2-1)

S2	●	Tulane	31	26
S9	●	Long Beach St.	63	10
S16	|	at Wyoming	15	20
S23	● |	Utah	67	20
S30	● |	New Mexico	60	14
O7	● |	San Diego State	31	24
O21	|	at Colorado State	16	31
O28	● |	Brigham Young	56	14
N4	● |	Texas-El Paso	26	7
N11	●	Pacific	34	26
N25	●	Oregon State	23	21
D9	= |	Air Force	35	35
		ALOHA BOWL		
D25		Michigan State	13	33

1990 7-5-0 (4-4-0)

S1		Texas A&M	13	28
S8	|	at Air Force	3	27
S22	● |	at Utah	19	7
O6	●	Maine	44	3
O13	|	at Texas-El Paso	10	12
O20	●	Fullerton St.	45	21
O27	●	Pacific	35	24
N3	● |	New Mexico	43	16
N10	|	at San Diego State	38	44
N17	● |	Wyoming	38	17
N24	|	Colorado State	27	30
D1	● |	Brigham Young	59	28

1991 4-7-1 (3-5-0)

A31	● |	at Wyoming	32	17
S7		at Iowa	10	53
S14	● |	New Mexico	35	13
S21	●	Pacific	30	21
S28	|	at Colorado State	16	28
O5	|	San Diego State	21	47
O19	|	at Brigham Young	18	35
N2	● |	Utah	52	26
N9	|	Texas-El Paso	24	41
N16	=	at San Jose State	35	35
N23	|	Air Force	20	24
N30		Notre Dame	42	48

1992 11-2-0 (6-2-0)

S5	●	at Oregon	24	21
S12	● |	at Air Force	6	3
S26	● |	Brigham Young	36	32
O10	|	at Utah	17	38
O17	● |	Fresno State	47	45
O24	●	Nevada-Las Vegas	55	25
O31	● |	at Texas-El Paso	41	21
N7	● |	Colorado State	24	13
N14	|	at San Diego State	28	52
N21	● |	Wyoming	42	18
N28	●	Tulsa	38	9
D5	●	Pittsburgh	36	23
		HOLIDAY BOWL		
D30	●	Illinois	27	17

1993 6-6-0 (3-5-0)

S4	●	Middle Tennessee	35	14
S11	|	at Brigham Young	38	41
S18	●	Kent State	49	17
S25	● |	Texas-El Paso	52	0
O2	|	at New Mexico	14	41
O9	|	San Diego State	14	45
O23	|	at Wyoming	10	48
N6	● |	Utah	41	30
N13	|	at Fresno State	21	45
N20	● |	Air Force	45	17
N27		California	18	42
D4	●	Tulane	56	17

1994 3-8-1 (0-8-0)

S3	|	Brigham Young	12	13
S10	●	Oregon	36	16
S17	●	at California	21	7
S24	|	Fresno State	16	31
O1	|	at Texas-El Paso	28	34
O8	|	New Mexico	21	38
O15	|	at Utah	3	14
O29	|	at San Diego State	23	38
N12	●	S.E. Missouri St.	34	0
N19	|	Wyoming	10	13
N26	=	Missouri	32	32
D3	|	Air Force	24	37

1995 4-8-0 (2-6-0)

S2		Texas	17	38
S16	|	at Wyoming	6	52
S23	● |	Texas-El Paso	42	21
S30	●	at Nevada-Las Vegas	58	30
O14	|	at New Mexico	10	24
O21	●	Central Florida	45	14
O28	|	at Brigham Young	7	45
N4	● |	Fresno State	42	37
N11	|	at Colorado State	0	22
N18	|	San Diego State	10	49
N25	|	Air Force	28	45
D2		Oklahoma State	20	24

FRED vonAPPEN
1996-98 (.139) 5-31

1996 2-10 (1-7)

A31		Boston College	21	24
S7		Ohio U.	10	21
S14	|	at Wyoming	0	66
S21	●	Boise State	20	14
S28	|	at Fresno State	0	20
O5	|	Colorado State	16	28
O11	|	at San Diego State	8	56
O19	● |	Nevada-Las Vegas	38	28
O26	|	at Air Force	7	34
N9	|	San Jose State	17	38
N16	|	Brigham Young	14	45
N30		Wisconsin	10	59

1997 3-9 (1-7)

A30	●	Minnesota	17	3
S6	●	Cal. St. Northridge	34	21
S13	|	Wyoming	6	35
S20	|	at Nevada-Las Vegas	15	25
O4	|	at Colorado State	0	63
O11	● |	Fresno State	28	16
O18	|	at Brigham Young	3	17
O25	|	San Diego State	3	10
N1	|	Air Force	27	34
N15	|	at San Jose State	14	38
N22		La. Monroe	20	23
N29		Notre Dame	22	23

1998 0-12 (0-8)

S3		Arizona	6	27
S19	|	at Utah	21	30
S26		Arkansas State	0	20
O3	|	SMU	0	28
O9	|	at San Diego State	13	35
O17	|	Brigham Young	9	31
O24	|	New Mexico	20	30
O31	|	at Texas-El Paso	13	30
N7	|	San Jose State	17	45
N14	|	at Fresno State	12	51
N21		Northwestern	21	47
N28		Michigan	17	48

JUNE JONES
1999-PRESENT (.615) 48-30

1999 9-4 (5-2)

S4		Southern Cal	7	62
S11	●	Ea. Illinois	31	27
S18	●	Boise State	34	19
S25	● |	at SMU	20	0
O2	● |	Texas-El Paso	33	3
O9	|	Rice	19	38
O23	● |	at Tulsa	35	21
O30	|	TCU	14	34
N6	● |	at San Jose State	62	41
N13	● |	Fresno State	31	24
N20	●	Navy	48	41
N27		Washington State	14	22
		OAHU BOWL		
D25	●	Oregon State	23	17

2000   3-9   (2-6)

S9		Portland St.	20 45
S23		at Texas-El Paso	7 39
S30		Tulsa	14 24
O7		at TCU	21 41
O14	●	SMU	30 15
O21		at Rice	13 38
O28		San Jose State	48 57
N4		at Fresno State	27 45
N11		Nevada	37 17
N18	●	Louisiana Tech	27 10
N25		Wisconsin	18 34
D2		Nevada-Las Vegas	32 34

2001   9-3   (5-3)

S8	●	Montana *WAI*	30 12
S22		at Nevada	20 28
S29		Rice	24 27
O6	●	at SMU	38 31
O13	●	Texas-El Paso	66 7
O20	●	at Tulsa	36 15
O26	●	Fresno State	38 34
N3	●	San Jose State	34 10
N10		Boise State	21 28
N17	●	Miami, Ohio	52 51
N24	●	Air Force	52 30
D8	●	Brigham Young	72 45

2002   10-4   (7-1)

A31	●	Ea. Illinois	61 36
S7		at Brigham Young	32 35
S21	●	at Texas-El Paso	31 6
S28	●	SMU	42 10
O5		at Boise State	31 58
O12	●	Nevada	59 34
O19	●	Tulsa	37 14
O26	●	at Fresno State	31 21
N2	●	San Jose State	40 31
N16	●	at Rice	33 28
N23	●	Cincinnati	20 19
N30		Alabama	16 21
D7	●	San Diego State	41 40
		HAWAII BOWL	
D25		Tulane	28 36

2003   9-5   (5-3)

A30	●	Appalachian St.	40 17
S13	●	at Southern Cal	32 61
S19		at Nevada-Las Vegas	22 33
S27	●	Rice	41 21
O4		at Tulsa	16 27
O11	●	Fresno State	55 28
O18	●	at Louisiana Tech	44 41
O25	●	Texas-El Paso	31 15
N1	●	at San Jose State	13 10
N15		at Nevada	14 24
N22	●	Army	59 28
N29	●	Alabama	37 29
D6		Boise State	28 45
		HAWAII BOWL	
D25	●	Houston	54 48

2004   8-5   (4-4)

S4		Florida Atlantic	28 35
S18		at Rice	29 41
O2	●	Tulsa	44 16
O9	●	Nevada	48 26
O16		at Texas-El Paso	20 51
O23	●	San Jose State	46 28
O30		at Boise State	3 69
N6	●	Louisiana Tech	34 23
N13		at Fresno State	14 70
N20	●	Idaho	52 21
N27	●	Northwestern	49 41
D4	●	Michigan State	41 38
		HAWAII BOWL	
D24	●	UAB	59 40

ƒ Forfeit   † Game Later Forfieted   # Disputed Victor   * Disputed Score || Designated Conference Game |2 Counted Twice in Conference Standings

HOUSTON

BY KEVIN GLEASON

THE GLORY DAYS OF HOUSTON FOOT-ball are synonymous with Bill Yeoman, father of the veer, who helped get Houston into the Southwest Conference in 1976. In all, Yeoman's teams went 160–108–8 from 1962 to 1986, and Yeoman broke a color barrier by signing the legendary Lone Star state running back Warren McVea, the first black football scholarship player at a major Texas school, in 1964. The program sparkled again in the late 1980s under Jack Pardee and his offensive coordinator, John Jenkins, who succeeded him as head coach. Times were tough in the ensuing years, but hopes rose again after first-year coach Art Briles took Houston to the Hawaii Bowl in 2003.

TRADITION Houston needed something extra for its first game against Texas in 1953, so the Cougars' live mascot, Shasta I, made the trip to Texas. But Shasta's front paw got caught in his cage door during the trip, and one of his toes was cut off. Texas got wind of it and naturally taunted Houston during the game—won by Texas 28-7—with four-finger hand signs. Little did the Longhorns faithful know they were inventing The Paw. Houston's official hand sign—the ring finger folded toward the palm—is a wildly popular gesture on the campus.

BEST PLAYER The Cougars have produced some big-time talent: Robert Newhouse, Elmo Wright, Mack Mitchell, Riley Odoms, Chuck Weatherspoon, Antowain Smith, David Klingler, Eugene Lockhart and Lamar Lathon. But 1989 Heisman Trophy winner Andre Ware is the greatest player in school history. Ware had a forgettable NFL career after being drafted seventh overall by Detroit, but only after he'd helped set 26 NCAA records for passing and total offense. He became the first Houston player, and fifth from the Southwest Conference, to win the Heisman. And Ware did it as a junior and without the benefit of playing before a national television audience. Ware, who bypassed his senior season to go pro, threw for a staggering 4,699 yards and 46 touchdowns in 11 games. He finished his career with 8,202 yards passing, 75 touchdowns and 28 interceptions.

BEST COACH Of course it is the legendary Yeoman, whose compassion, courage and innovation left a permanent mark on college football. Yeoman designed the veer T offense and shared the scheme with fellow coaches. Always generous,

---

PROFILE

University of Houston
Houston, Texas
Founded: 1927
Enrollment: 26,366
Colors: Scarlet and White
Nickname: Cougars
Stadium: John O'Quinn Field/Robertson Stadium
    Opened in 1942
    Grass; 32,000 capacity
First football game: 1946
All-time record: 323–302–15 (.516)
Bowl record: 7–7–1
Conference USA championships: 1 (shared)
Heisman Trophy: Andre Ware, 1989
First-round NFL draftees: 11

THE BEST OF TIMES

Most of the Bill Yeoman era. From 1962-86, his teams went 160–108–8, including 51–35–2 in the Southwestern Conference.

THE WORST OF TIMES

Kim Helton's teams went 4–28–1 from 1993-95.

CONFERENCE

Houston has played in Conference USA since its 1996 inception. Previously the Cougars were memebers of the Southwest (1976-95) and Missouri Valley (1951-59) conferences.

DISTINGUISHED ALUMNI

Fred Couples, PGA Tour golfer; Tom DeLay, U.S. representative; Elvin Hayes, Basketball Hall of Famer; Tom Landry, Hall of Fame NFL coach; Carl Lewis, nine-time Olympic gold medalist in track and field; Dennis and Randy Quaid, actors; Dan Rather, *CBS Evening News* anchor; Jack Valenti, chairman, Motion Picture Association

FIGHT SONG

COUGAR FIGHT SONG
Cougars fight for dear old U of H
For our Alma Mater cheer
Fight for Houston University
For victory is near
Where the going gets so rough and tough
We never worry cause we got the stuff
So Fight, Fight, Fight for red and white
And we will go to victory

Andre Ware had a forgettable NFL career, but the Heisman winner helped set 26 NCAA records for passing and total offense.

always humble, Yeoman said of discovering the veer, "We stumbled upon it, really. Almost by accident." He startled the Southwest Conference by tying for the 1976 league title in Houston's SWC debut. It was the first of four conference titles under Yeoman, whose teams also won the 1977 and 1980 Cotton Bowls. In 2001, Yeoman became the first Cougar inducted into the College Football Hall of Fame. Sixteen years earlier, in 1985, Yeoman was inducted into the SWC Hall of Honor.

BEST TEAM The old boys of the Southwest Conference were rather surprised in 1976 when Yeoman's first-year entry came in and won a share of the league title, with a 7–1 record. The SWC debut served as an appetizer for their 30-21 win over Maryland in the Cotton Bowl. Houston went 10–2 and finished No. 4 in both the Associated Press and United Press International polls. It had wins over Baylor, Texas A&M, SMU, TCU and Texas, which managed all of eight first downs and 24 rushing yards in Houston's 30-0 romp. The Cougars were led by

consensus All-American defensive tackle Wilson Whitley and several honorable mention All-Americas: tight end Don Bass, guard Val Belcher, quarterback Danny Davis, defensive back Anthony Francis and defensive end Vincent Greenwood. Running back Alois Blackwell averaged 6.2 yards a carry and finished with 934 yards and 8 TDs. Houston went on to win three more SWC titles.

BIGGEST GAME Houston would win 11 games in the 1979 season, tied for the most in school history. The Cougars would hold Nebraska to 227 yards, less than half its season average, in the season's grand finale. But to win that 1980 Cotton Bowl, Houston was going to have to convert on fourth-and-goal from the 6 with 19 seconds left. Quarterback Terry Elston found Eric Herring cutting across the goal line and connected to give Houston a 17-14 win over No. 7 Nebraska. The catch capped a 66-yard drive and helped Houston (11–1) finish No. 5 in the country.

BIGGEST UPSET Tying for the 1976 Southwest

RECORDS

RUSHING YARDS

GAME
300 Joffrey Reynolds vs. East Carolina, Nov. 9, 2002 (41 att.)

SEASON
1,757 Robert Newhouse, 1971 (277 att.)

CAREER
3,636 Ketric Sanford, 1996-99 (743 att.)

PASSING YARDS

GAME
716 David Klingler vs. Arizona State, Dec. 2, 1990 (41 of 70)

SEASON
5,140 David Klingler, 1990 (374 of 643)

CAREER
9,430 David Klingler, 1988-91 (726 of 1262)

RECEIVING YARDS

GAME
262 Elmo Wright vs. Wyoming, Nov. 22, 1969 (7 rec.)

SEASON
1,689 Manny Hazard, 1989 (142 rec.)

CAREER
3,347 Elmo Wright, 1968-70 (153 rec.)

POINTS

GAME
36 Antowain Smith vs. Southern Miss, Nov. 9, 1996 (6 TDs)

SEASON
134 Manny Hazard, 1989 (22 TDs, 1 two-pt. conv.)

CAREER
423 Roman Anderson, 1988-91 (70 FGs, 213 PATs)

CONSENSUS ALL-AMERICANS

1967	Rich Stotter, G
1969	Bill Bridges, G
1970	Elmo Wright, E
1976	Wilson Whitley, DT
1980	Leonard Mitchell, DL
1988	Jason Phillips, WR
1989	Andre Ware, QB

Conference title would have represented a brilliant season on its own. But the Cougars capped things off with a memorable 30-21 upset of fifth-ranked and undefeated Maryland in the Cotton Bowl. Houston led 21-0 after one quarter and continued churning yards on the ground against the nation's second-ranked rushing defense. The Cougars ran for 320 yards, with running back Alois Blackwell going for 149 yards on 22 carries to earn the offensive Most Valuable Player award. Cornerback Mark Mohr earned the defensive award with seven tackles, two pass breakups, a blocked punt and a fumble recovery.

HEARTBREAKER Long before he started breaking hearts in the NFL, Notre Dame's Joe Montana dropped a tearjerker on Houston in the 1979 Cotton Bowl. Montana capped a 23-point surge in the final 7:37 by hitting Kris Haines on an eight-yard TD pass with no time left for a 35-34 Irish victory. Montana got the final chance with 28 seconds left when Houston was stopped short on fourth-and-one at its own 29. Said Yeoman afterward, "It was my decision. I don't think anyone wanted to kick the ball away anyway."

STADIUM Houston Public School Stadium was constructed in 1941 and, as the name suggests, was used by local high schools. Lamar High beat Adamson of Dallas 26-7 before a crowd of 14,500 in the first game there on Sept. 18, 1942. Four years later the facility played host to Houston games. The Cougars played twice in newly constructed Rice Stadium, and became the first college team to play in a domed stadium upon moving into the Astrodome in 1965. Houston Public School Stadium was renamed Jeppesen Stadium in 1958 (and was the site of the historic double-overtime AFL title game between the Dallas Texans and Houston Oilers in 1962). The university bought the facility in 1970. It was rededicated as Robertson Stadium in 1980 to honor former Board of Regents member and athletics committee chairman Corbin J. Robertson, though throughout the 1970s and 1980s, the team still played some games at the Astrodome.

RIVAL Rice and Texas presumably constitute Houston's most heated rivals. But the Houston-Rice series has spanned only a shade over three decades; Houston dominates that series while Texas holds the reins over the Cougars. Houston and Texas don't meet up quite as often, though, since the SWC broke apart.

CONTROVERSY It's safe to say SMU and its fans were none too pleased when Jack Pardee's team dropped a 95-21 whipping on the Mustangs in a 1989 game at the Astrodome. Of course, Texas football historians remember that runaway scores have been part of Houston football tradition. In 1968, Yeoman's Cougars ran up a 100-6 win over Tulsa, still the last time a major-college team scored in triple digits. Throw in Elmo Wright's high-stepping, running-in-place touchdown dance, one of the game's first choreographed end zone celebrations, and the Yeoman teams of the late 1960s and early 1970s earned a reputation as a team that liked to rub it in.

NICKNAME The name is a product of outright thievery, according to the Houston media-relations department. A faculty member who once worked at Washington State —home of the Cougars—"came up with" the nickname for Houston.

MASCOT Shasta and Sasha are the cute first cougar couple of Houston football.

UNIFORMS In the 1960s, Houston was one of the first college teams to feature the school name on the front of its jerseys. The overall look—red jersey and helmet—has essentially remained the same, while stripes have come and gone on the pants like Texas rainstorms. The interlocking UH on the Cougars' helmets has grown both taller and wider over the years.

LORE Defensive tackle Wilson Whitley led the 1976 team in sacks, fumbles caused and fumbles recovered on his way to winning the Lombardi Award as the nation's outstanding college lineman. He went on to be named the Southwest Conference Player of the Decade for the 1970s. The catch? It was his only year competing in the SWC. Whitley became the eighth overall selection by Cincinnati in the 1977 NFL draft and played six seasons with the Bengals. He played a year with the Houston Oilers before serving as national director of sports marketing for Holiday Inn Inc. Whitley suffered a fatal heart attack in 1992.

NUMBERS At one time the Cougars held 78 individual and 31 team NCAA records.

QUOTE "I don't see color. I just see football players." —Former coach Bill Yeoman, who in 1964 signed the first black football scholarship player at a major Texas school

HOUSTON ALL-TIME SCORES

WIN/LOSS PERCENTAGE SINCE 1946

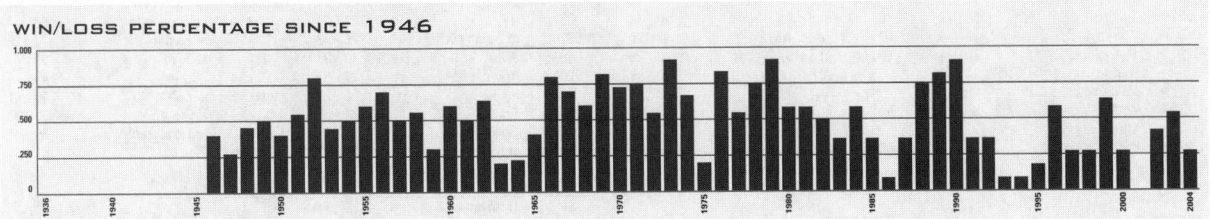

JEWELL WALLACE
1946-47 (.333)   7-14

1946 4-6-0
S21		La. Lafayette	7 13
S27	•	West Texas St.	14 12
O5	•	at Fort Hood	32 7
O12	•	Texas A&I	34 0
O19		at East Texas St.	14 20
O26		at Texas-El Paso	7 21
N9	•	Stephen F. Austin	16 7
N16		North Texas	3 7
N23		at SW. Texas	7 21
N28		Sam Houston St.	6 28

1947 3-8-0
S20	•	Centenary	19 7
S27	•	McMurry	14 13
O4	•	Daniel Baker	35 12
O11		at Texas A&I	0 13
O18		East Texas St.	7 33
O25		Trinity	0 20
N1		Hardin Simmons Cor	7 33
N8		at Stephen F. Austin	14 25
N15		at North Texas	0 33
N22		SW. Texas	0 2
N27		at Sam Houston St.	0 23

CLYDE LEE
1948-54 (.535)   37-32-2

1948 5-6-0
S18	•	Texas A&I	14 0
S25		at Texas-El Paso	7 35
O2		at La. Lafayette	7 21
O9	•	Louisiana Tech	40 33
O16	•	at East Texas St.	18 7
O23		at Trinity	7 15
O30		at West Texas St.	13 28
N6	•	Stephen F. Austin	13 21
N13	•	North Texas	8 6
N20		at SW. Texas	0 3
N25	•	Sam Houston St.	22 13

1949 5-4-1
S17		William & Mary	13 14
O1	•	Wichita St.	28 6
O8		at La. Lafayette	28 7
O15	•	West Texas St.	14 13
O22	=	Hardin Simmons	27 27
O29		at M.W. Texas St.	21 33
N5		at St. Bonaventure	14 20
N12		at North Texas	23 28
N19	•	Trinity	28 21
N24	•	at St. Louis	35 0

1950 4-6-0
S23		St. Bonaventure	14 29
S30		at Baylor	7 34
O7		at Trinity	16 20
O14	•	Louisville	27 7
O20		at Hardin Simmons	13 14
O28	•	at Wichita St.	46 6
N11		North Texas	13 16
N18	•	William & Mary	36 18
N24	•	M.W. Texas St.	40 18
D2		Tulsa	21 28

1951-1959
MISSOURI VALLEY

1951 6-5-0 (1-1-0)
S22		Baylor	0 19
S28	•	at Detroit	33 7
O6	•	Texas Tech	6 0
O13	|	at Tulsa	27 46
O20	•	Hardin Simmons	35 27
O27	•	Villanova	27 33
N3	|	at Wichita St.	14 19
N10	|	at Louisville	28 35
N24	• |	Oklahoma State	31 7
N30	• |	at North Texas	20 14
SALAD BOWL			
J1	•	Dayton	26 21

1952 8-2-0 (3-0-0)
S20		Texas A&M	13 21
S27	•	at Arkansas	17 7
O4	• |	at Oklahoma State	10 7
O11	• |	Tulsa	33 7
O25	•	at Arizona State	6 0
N1	•	at Texas Tech	20 7
N8		Mississippi	0 6
N15	•	Baylor	28 6
N29	• |	Detroit	33 19
D6	•	Wyoming	20 0

1953 4-4-1 (1-2-0)
S26	=	at Texas A&M	14 14
O3	•	at Texas	7 28
O9	• |	at Detroit	25 19
O17	|	Oklahoma State	7 14
O24	•	Arizona State	24 20
N7	|	at Tulsa	21 23
N14	•	at Baylor	37 7
N21		Texas Tech	21 41
D5	•	Tennessee	33 19

1954 5-5-0 (3-0-0)
S18		at Baylor	13 53
O9	•	Texas A&M	10 7
O16	|	at Oklahoma State	14 7
O22	•	Villanova Phil	28 7
O30	|	at Wichita St.	7 9
N6	• |	Tulsa	20 7
N13		Mississippi	0 26
N20		at Texas Tech	14 61
N27		Arkansas	0 19
D4	• |	Detroit	19 7

BILL MEEK
1955-56 (.675)   13-6-1

1955 6-4-0 (2-2-0)
S17	•	Montana	54 12
O1		at Texas A&M	3 21
O7	• |	at Detroit	7 0
O15	• |	Oklahoma State	21 13
O22	•	Texas Tech	7 0
O29	|	Wichita St.	7 21
N5	|	at Tulsa	14 17
N12		Mississippi JAM	11 27
N19	•	Villanova	26 14
D3	•	Wyoming	26 14

1956 7-2-1 (4-0-0)
S29	•	Mississippi State	18 7
O6		Mississippi JAM	0 14
O13	=	Texas A&M	14 14
O20	• |	at Oklahoma State	13 0
O27		at Auburn	0 12
N3	• |	at Wichita St.	41 16
N10	• |	Tulsa	14 0
N17	•	Villanova	26 13
N24	•	at Texas Tech	20 7
D1	• |	Detroit	39 7

HAROLD LAHAR
1957-61 (.510)   24-23-2

1957 5-4-1 (3-0-0)
S21	•	Miami, Fla.	7 0
S28		at Baylor	6 14
O5	• |	at Cincinnati	7 0
O12		at Texas A&M	6 28
O19	=	Oklahoma State	6 6
O26	•	Auburn	7 48
N2		Mississippi JAM	7 20
N9	•	Southern Miss JAM	27 12
N16	• |	at Wichita St.	27 6
N23	• |	at Tulsa	13 7

1958 5-4-0 (2-2-0)
S27	•	Texas A&M	39 14
O4	• |	at Cincinnati	34 13
O11	• |	Wichita St.	44 0
O18		Oklahoma State	0 7
N1	|	Tulsa	20 25
N8		at Mississippi	7 56
N15		at North Texas	6 10
N21	•	at Miami, Fla.	37 26
N29	•	Texas Tech	22 17

1959 3-7-0 (2-1-0)
S19		Mississippi	0 16
S26		Alabama	0 3
O3	• |	Cincinnati	13 12
O10		at Texas A&M	6 28
O17		at Oklahoma State	12 19
O24	|	North Texas	6 7
O31	• |	at Tulsa	22 13
N7	• |	at Wichita St.	28 13
N14		at Texas Tech	0 27
N26		Washington State	18 32

1960-1975
INDEPENDENT

1960 6-4-0
S17		Mississippi	0 42
S24	•	at Mississippi State	14 10
O1		Oregon State Port	20 29
O8	•	Texas A&M	17 0
O15	•	Oklahoma State	12 7
O22		at Alabama	0 14
O29	•	at North Texas	41 16
N5		Cincinnati	14 0
N12	•	at Florida State	7 6
N26		Tulsa	16 26

1961 5-4-1
S23	=	at Texas A&M	7 7
S30	•	Mississippi State	7 10
O7	•	Boston College	21 0
O14		Mississippi Mem	7 47
O21	•	at Cincinnati	13 7
O28		Alabama	0 17
N11	•	at Tulsa	14 2
N18		at Oklahoma State	24 28
N25	•	Florida State	28 8
D2	•	Oregon State	23 12

BILL YEOMAN
1962-86 (.594)   160-108-8

1962 7-4-0
S22	•	Baylor	19 0
S29	•	Texas A&M	6 3
O6		Mississippi JAM	7 40
O13		at Alabama	3 14
O20		Mississippi State	3 9
O27		at Boston College	0 14
N3	•	at Florida State	7 0
N10	•	Tulsa	35 31
N24	•	at Louisville	27 25
D1	•	Cincinnati	42 14
CITRUS BOWL			
D22	•	Miami, Ohio	49 21

1963 2-8-0
S21		Auburn	14 21
S28		at Baylor	0 27
O5		Mississippi	6 20
O12		at Texas A&M	13 23
O19		at Mississippi State	0 20
O26		at Alabama	13 21
N2	•	Detroit	55 18
N16		at Tulsa	21 22
N30		at Memphis	6 29
D14	•	Louisville	21 7

1964 2-6-1
S12	•	Trinity	34 7
S19		at Auburn	0 30
S25	•	Texas A&M	10 0
O3		at Mississippi	9 31
O10		Tulsa	23 31
O24		at Mississippi State	13 18
N7	=	Florida State	13 13
N14		Penn State	7 24
N28		Cincinnati	6 20

1965 4-5-1
S11	•	Tulsa	0 14
S18	•	Mississippi State	0 36
S24	•	Cincinnati	21 6
O9		at Texas A&M	7 10
O16		at Miami, Fla.	12 44
O23		at Tennessee	8 17
O30	•	U.T. Chattanooga	40 7
N6	•	Mississippi	17 3
N13	•	Kentucky	38 21
N20	=	at Florida State	16 16

1966 8-2-0
S17	•	at Florida State	21 13
S23	•	Washington State	21 7
O1		Oklahoma State	35 9
O15	•	Mississippi State	28 0
O22		Mississippi Mem	6 27
O29	•	Tampa	48 9
N5	•	Tulsa	73 14
N12	•	at Kentucky	56 18
N26	•	Memphis	13 14
D3	•	Utah	34 14

1967 7-3-0
S15	•	Florida State	33 13
S23	•	at Michigan State	37 7
S29	•	Wake Forest	50 6
O7		North Carolina St.	6 16
O21	•	at Mississippi State	43 6
O28		at Mississippi	13 14
N4	•	Georgia	15 14
N11	•	Memphis	35 18
N18	•	Idaho	77 6
N25		at Tulsa	13 22

1968 6-2-2
S14	•	Tulane	54 7
S21	=	at Texas	20 20
O4	•	Cincinnati	71 33
O12		Oklahoma State	17 21
O26	•	Mississippi JAM	29 7
N2	=	at Georgia	10 10
N9	•	at Memphis	27 7
N16	•	Idaho	77 3
N23	•	Tulsa	100 6
N29		Florida State JacF	20 40

1969 9-2-0
S20		at Florida	34 59
S27		at Oklahoma State	18 24
O4	•	Mississippi State	74 0
O11	•	at Arizona	34 17
O25	•	Mississippi	25 11
N1	•	Miami, Fla.	38 36
N8	•	at Tulsa	47 14
N15		at North Carolina St.	34 13
N22	•	Wyoming	41 14
N29	•	Florida State	41 14
BLUEBONNET BOWL			
D31	•	Auburn	36 7

1970 8-3-0
S19	•	Syracuse	42 15
S26	•	at Oklahoma State	17 26
O10	•	at Mississippi State	31 14
O17	•	Oregon State	19 16
O24		Alabama	21 30
O31	•	Tulsa	21 9
N7		at Mississippi	13 24
N14	•	Wyoming	28 0
N21	•	Wake Forest	26 2
N26	•	Florida State TAM	53 21
D5	•	at Miami, Fla.	36 3

THE SCHOOLS

1971 — 9-3-0

S11	● at Rice	23	21
S18	● at Arizona State	17	18
S25	● at Cincinnati	12	3
O2	● San Jose State	34	20
O15	● Villanova	42	9
O23	● at Alabama	20	34
O30	● Florida State	14	7
N6	● at Memphis	35	7
N13	● Virginia Tech	56	29
N20	● Miami, Fla.	27	6
N27	● Utah	42	16
BLUEBONNET BOWL			
D31	● Colorado	17	29)

1972 — 6-4-1

S9	● at Rice	13	14
S16	● Arizona State	28	33
S23	● at Tulsa	21	0
O7	= at Virginia Tech	27	27
O14	● San Diego State	49	14
O21	● at Miami, Fla.	13	33
O28	● at Mississippi State	13	27
N4	● at Florida State	31	27
N11	● Colorado State	48	13
N18	● New Mexico	33	14
N25	● Cincinnati	49	0

1973 — 11-1-0

S15	● Rice	24	6
S21	● South Carolina	27	19
S29	● at Memphis	35	21
O6	● at San Diego State	14	9
O12	● Virginia Tech	54	27
O19	● at Miami, Fla.	30	7
O27	● at Auburn	0	7
N3	● Florida State	34	3
N10	● at Colorado State	28	20
N24	● Wyoming	35	0
D1	● Tulsa	35	16
BLUEBONNET BOWL			
D29	● Tulane	47	7

1974 — 8-3-1

S7	● at Arizona State	9	30
S14	● at Rice	21	0
S21	● Miami, Fla.	3	20
S28	● at Virginia Tech	49	12
O5	● at South Carolina	24	14
O19	● Villanova	35	0
O25	● Cincinnati	27	6
N2	● at Georgia	31	24
N16	● Memphis	13	10
N23	● at Florida State	23	8
N30	● at Tulsa	14	30
BLUEBONNET BOWL			
D23	= North Carolina St.	31	31

1975 — 2-8-0

S6	● Lamar	20	3
S13	● Rice	7	24
S27	● SMU	16	26
O11	● North Texas Inv	0	28
O17	● at Miami, Fla.	20	24
N1	● at Cincinnati	23	28
N8	● Virginia Tech	28	34
N15	● at Memphis	7	14
N22	● Florida State	22	33
N29	● Tulsa	42	30

1976-1995 SWC

1976 — 10-2-0 (7-1-0)

S11	● at Baylor	23	5
S18	● at Florida	14	49
S25	● Texas A&M	21	10
O9	● West Texas St.	50	7
O16	● at SMU	29	6
O23	Arkansas	7	14
O30	● TCU	49	21
N6	● at Texas	30	0
N20	● at Texas Tech	27	19
N27	● at Rice	42	20
D4	● Miami, Fla.	21	16
COTTON BOWL			
J1	● Maryland	30	21

1977 — 6-5-0 (4-4-0)

S10	● UCLA	17	13
S17	● at Penn State	14	31
S24	● at Utah	34	16
O1	Baylor	28	24
O15	SMU	23	37
O22	Arkansas LR	0	34
O29	● at TCU	42	14
N5	Texas	21	35
N19	● Texas Tech	45	7
N26	● at Rice	51	21
D3	at Texas A&M	7	27

1978 — 9-3-0 (7-1-0)

S16	at Memphis	3	17
S23	● Utah	42	25
S30	● at Florida State	27	21
O7	at Baylor	20	18
O14	Texas A&M	33	0
O21	● at SMU	42	28
O28	● Arkansas	20	9
N4	TCU	63	6
N11	● at Texas	10	7
N25	at Texas Tech	21	22
D2	● Rice	49	25
COTTON BOWL			
J1	Notre Dame	34	35

1979 — 11-1-0 (7-1-0)

S8	● at UCLA	24	16
S15	● Florida	14	10
S29	● West Texas St.	49	10
O6	● Baylor	13	10
O13	● at Texas A&M	17	14
O20	● SMU	37	10
O27	● at Arkansas	13	10
N3	● at TCU	21	10
N10	● Texas	13	21
N24	● Texas Tech	14	10
D1	● at Rice	63	0
COTTON BOWL			
J1	● Nebraska	17	14

1980 — 7-5-0 (5-3-0)

S13	● at Arizona State	13	29
S20	● Miami, Fla.	7	14
S27	● North Texas	24	20
O4	at Baylor	12	24
O11	Texas A&M	17	13
O18	● at SMU	13	11
O25	● Arkansas	24	17
N1	● TCU	37	5
N8	● at Texas	13	15
N22	● at Texas Tech	34	7
N29	Rice	7	35
GARDEN STATE BOWL			
D14	● Navy	35	0

1981 — 7-4-1 (5-2-1)

S5	● New Mexico	21	10
S19	● at Miami, Fla.	7	12
S26	● Utah State	35	7
O3	Baylor	24	3
O10	at Texas A&M	6	7
O17	SMU	22	38
O24	● Arkansas	20	17
O31	● at TCU	20	16
N7	= Texas	14	14
N21	● Texas Tech	15	7
N28	● at Rice	40	3
SUN BOWL			
D26	● Oklahoma	14	40

1982 — 5-5-1 (4-3-1)

S11	● at Miami, Fla.	12	31
S18	● Arizona State	10	24
S25	● Lamar	48	3
O2	= at Baylor	21	21
O9	● Texas A&M	24	20
O16	● at SMU	14	20
O23	● Arkansas	3	38
O30	● TCU	31	27
N6	at Texas	0	50
N20	● at Texas Tech	24	7
N27	● Rice	28	21

1983 — 4-7-0 (3-5-0)

S1	at Rice	45	14
S10	Miami, Fla.	7	29
S17	● Lamar	42	35
S24	at Oregon	14	15
O1	Baylor	21	42
O8	at Texas A&M	7	30
O22	at Arkansas	3	24
O29	● at TCU	28	21
N5	Texas	3	9
N19	● Texas Tech	43	41
N26	SMU Tok	12	34

1984 — 7-5-0 (6-2-0)

S15	● Miami, Ohio	30	17
S22	● at Washington	7	35
S29	● Louisville	28	30
O6	● at Baylor	27	17
O13	● Texas A&M	9	7
O20	● at SMU	29	20
O27	● Arkansas	3	17
N3	TCU	14	21
N10	● at Texas	29	15
N24	● at Texas Tech	24	17
D1	Rice	38	26
COTTON BOWL			
J1	Boston College	28	45

1985 — 4-7-0 (3-5-0)

S7	at Tulsa	24	31
S21	Washington	12	29
S28	● at Louisville	49	27
O5	Baylor	21	24
O12	at Texas A&M	16	43
O19	SMU	13	37
O26	Arkansas LR	27	57
N2	● at TCU	26	21
N9	Texas	24	34
N23	● Texas Tech	17	16
N30	● at Rice	24	20

1986 — 1-10-0 (0-8-0)

S6	at Arizona	3	37
S20	● at Oklahoma State	28	12
S27	Tulsa	14	24
O4	at Baylor	13	27
O11	Texas A&M	7	19
O18	at SMU	3	10
O25	Arkansas	13	30
N1	TCU	14	30
N8	at Texas	10	30
N22	at Texas Tech	7	34
N29	Rice	13	14

JACK PARDEE — 1987-89 (.662) — 22-11-1

1987 — 4-6-1 (2-4-1)

S12	Oklahoma State	0	35
S26	● Sam Houston St.	38	34
O3	Baylor	18	30
O10	at Texas A&M	17	22
O17	at Wyoming	35	37
O24	at Arkansas	17	21
O31	at TCU	7	35
N7	● Texas	60	40
N14	● at Temple	37	7
N21	= at Texas Tech	10	10
N28	● at Rice	45	21

1988 — 9-3-0 (5-2-0)

S10	● Louisiana Tech Shre	60	0
S17	● at Missouri	31	7
O1	● at Baylor	27	24
O8	Texas A&M	16	30
O15	● Tulsa	82	28
O22	Arkansas	21	26
O29	● TCU	40	12
N5	at Texas	66	15
N12	● Wyoming	34	10
N19	● at Texas Tech	30	29
N26	● Rice	45	14
ALOHA BOWL			
D25	● Washington State	22	24

1989 — 9-2-0 (6-2-0)

S2	● at Nevada-Las Vegas	69	0
S23	● at Arizona State	36	7
S30	● Temple	65	7
O7	● Baylor	66	10
O14	at Texas A&M	13	17
O21	● SMU	95	21
O28	● Arkansas LR	39	45
N4	● at TCU	55	10
N11	● Texas	47	9
N25	● Texas Tech	40	24
D2	● at Rice	64	0

JOHN JENKINS — 1990-92 (.545) — 18-15

1990 — 10-1-0 (7-1-0)

S8	● Nevada-Las Vegas	37	9
S13	● at Texas Tech	51	35
S29	● Rice	24	22
O6	at Baylor	31	15
O13	● Texas A&M	36	31
O20	● at SMU	44	17
O27	Arkansas	62	28
N3	● TCU	56	35
N10	at Texas	24	45
N17	● Ea. Washington	84	21
D2	● Arizona State Tok	62	45

1991 — 4-7-0 (3-5-0)

A31	● Louisiana Tech	73	3
S12	● at Miami, Fla.	10	40
S21	● at Illinois	10	51
O5	Baylor	21	38
O12	at Arkansas	17	29
O19	● SMU	49	20
O26	● at Texas A&M	18	27
N9	Texas	23	14
N16	at Rice	41	21
N23	● at TCU	45	49
N30	Texas Tech	46	52

1992 — 4-7-0 (2-5-0)

S5	at Tulsa	25	28
S19	● Illinois	31	13
S26	● at Michigan	7	61
O3	● La. Lafayette	63	7
O17	● at Baylor	23	29
O24	● at Texas	38	45
O31	● TCU	49	46
N7	● at SMU	16	41
N12	Texas A&M	30	38
N21	● at Texas Tech	35	44
N28	● Rice	61	34

KIM HELTON — 1993-99 (.314) — 24-53-1

1993 — 1-9-1 (1-5-1)

S4	at Southern Cal	7	49
S11	Tulsa	24	38
S25	● at Michigan	21	42
O2	Baylor	24	3
O9	at Texas A&M	10	34
O16	= SMU	28	28
O30	at TCU	10	28
N4	Texas	16	34
N13	Cincinnati	17	41
N20	Texas Tech SA	7	58
N26	at Rice	7	37

1994 — 1-10-0 (1-6-0)

S1	Kansas	13	35
S10	at Louisiana Tech	7	32
S17	Missouri	0	16
S24	at Ohio State	0	52
O8	Texas A&M	7	38
O15	● at SMU	39	33
O22	TCU	10	31
O29	at Baylor	13	52
N12	at Texas	13	48
N19	Texas Tech SA	0	34
N26	Rice	13	31

1995 — 2-9-0 (2-5-0)

S2	at Florida	21	45
S9	Louisiana Tech	7	19
S16	at Southern Cal	10	45
S23	at Kansas	13	20
O7	at TCU	21	31
O14	Baylor	7	47
O21	● SMU	38	15
O28	at Texas A&M	7	31
N11	Texas	20	52
N25	Texas Tech	26	38
D2	● at Rice	18	17

1996-PRESENT C-USA

1996 — 7-5 (4-1)

A31	● Sam Houston St.	43	25
S7	at LSU	34	35
S14	● at Pittsburgh	42	35
S21	Southern Cal	9	26
O5	● at La. Lafayette	31	24
O12	Memphis	37	20
O19	at Cincinnati	20	31
O26	North Carolina	14	42
N2	● at Tulane	20	17
N9	● Southern Miss	56	49
N16	● Louisville	38	7
LIBERTY BOWL			
D27	Syracuse	17	30

1997 — 3-8 (2-4)

A30	Alabama Birm	17	42
S6	California	3	35
S13	Pittsburgh	24	35
S27	● Minnesota	45	43
O4	at UCLA	10	66
O18	at Cincinnati	41	38
O25	● Louisville	36	22
N1	at Memphis	3	24
N8	at East Carolina	27	28
N15	at Southern Miss	0	33
N22	Tulane	10	44

1998 — 3-8 (2-4)

S5	at California	10	14
S12	Minnesota	7	14
S19	UCLA	24	42
S26	at Tennessee	7	42
O3	● Memphis	35	14
O10	Army	28	38
O24	● at North Texas	31	9
O31	● at East Carolina	34	31
N7	Southern Miss	15	21
N14	at Cincinnati	43	44
N21	at Tulane	20	48

1999   7-4 (3-3-0)

S4	●	Rice	28	3
S11		Alabama *Birm*	10	37
S18	●	La. Lafayette	45	0
S25		at UAB	10	29
O9	●	Cincinnati	23	20
O16	●	at North Carolina	20	12
O23		at Louisville	33	39
O30		East Carolina	3	19
N6	●	Tulane	36	31
N13	●	at LSU	20	7
N20	●	at Army	26	14

DANA DIMEL
2000-02 (.235)   8-26

2000   3-8 (2-5)

S2		at Rice	27	30
S9		at LSU	13	28
S16	●	Army	31	30
S23		at Texas	0	48
S30	●	SMU	17	15
O7		at Cincinnati	31	48
O21	●	at Memphis	33	30
O28		Southern Miss	3	6
N4		at Tulane	23	41
N11		at East Carolina	20	62
N18		Louisville	13	32

2001   0-11 (0-7)

S1		Rice	14	21
S22		Texas	26	53
S29		TCU	17	34
O6		at Army	14	28
O13		Memphis	33	52
O20		Cincinnati	28	29
O27		at Southern Miss	14	58
N3		at South Florida	6	45
N10		at Louisville	10	34
N17		UAB	21	43
D1		at Georgia	7	35

2002   5-7 (3-5)

A31	●	at Rice	24	10
S7		Tulane	13	34
S14	●	La. Lafayette	36	17
S21		at Texas	11	41
O5		at TCU	17	34
O12		at UAB	34	51
O19	●	Army	56	42
N2	●	at Memphis	26	21
N9		East Carolina	48	54
N16		at Cincinnati	14	47
N23		South Florida	14	32
N30	●	Louisville	27	10

ART BRILES
2003- PRESENT (.417)   10-14

2003   7-6 (4-4)

A30	●	Rice	48	14
S6		at Michigan	3	50
S13	●	at La. Lafayette	21	14
S20		Mississippi State	42	35
S30	●	at East Carolina	27	13
O11	●	at Tulane	45	42
O18		Memphis	14	45
O25		TCU	55	62
N8		Southern Miss	10	31
N15	●	at Army	34	14
N22		at Louisville	45	66
N29	●	UAB	56	28

HAWAII BOWL

D25		at Hawaii	48	54

2004   3-8 (3-5)

S5	●	at Rice	7	10
S11		at Oklahoma	13	63
S18	●	Army	35	21
S23		Miami, Fla.	13	38
O2		at Memphis	14	41
O7		at Southern Miss	29	35
O23		at TCU	27	34
O30	●	Tulane	24	3
N6	●	East Carolina	34	24
N13		at UAB	7	20
N20		Louisville	27	65

Neutral Site Key: *Birm* Birmingham, AL / *Cor* Corpus Christi, TX / *Irv* Irving, TX / *JacF* Jacksonville, FL / *JaM* Jackson, MS / *LR* Little Rock, AR / *Mem* Memphis, TN / *Phil* Philadelphia, PA / *Port* Portland, OR / *SA* San Antonio, TX / *Tam* Tampa, FL / *Tok* Tokyo, Japan
f Forfeit / † Game Later Forfeited / # Disputed Victor / * Disputed Score / ‖ Designated Conference Game / 2 Counted Twice in Conference Standings

HOUSTON ANNUAL STATISTICAL LEADERS

YR	RUSHING	YDS	ATT	AVG	PASSING	ATT	CMP	PCT	YDS	RECEIVING	REC	YDS	AVG
1947	Boyd Tingle	299	54	5.5		NA	NA	NA	NA		NA	NA	NA
1948	Jack Gwin	357	78	4.6	Alan Neveux	116	46	.40	549	Ed Staggs	17	234	13.8
1949	Gene Shannon	498	88	5.7	Alan Neveux	144	63	.44	939	Maurice Elliott	13	177	13.6
1950	Max Clark	860	129	6.7	Bobby Rogers	61	28	.46	287	Max Clark	11	203	18.5
1951	Gene Shannon	1,036	143	7.2	Bobby Clatterbuck	111	57	.51	966	Vic Hampel	24	499	20.8
1952	S. M. Meeks	366	78	4.7	Bobby Clatterbuck	128	47	.37	736	Vic Hampel	19	396	20.8
1953	Donn Hargrove	407	69	5.9	Bobby Clatterbuck	61	30	.49	276	Ben Wilson	12	128	10.7
1954	Jack Patterson	361	77	4.7	Jimmy Dickey	77	32	.42	474	Ronnie Emberg	12	152	12.7
1955	Curley Johnson	469	82	5.7	Jimmy Dickey	81	32	.40	454	Ronnie Emberg	12	173	14.4
1956	Don Flynn	412	90	4.6	Don Flynn	53	22	.42	464	Bob Borah	6	73	12.2
1957	Don Brown	378	86	4.4	Sammy Blount	50	22	.44	306	Charles Mallia	9	116	12.9
1958	Claude King	439	76	5.8	Lonnie Holland	84	48	.57	542	Bob Borah	29	375	12.9
1959	Charlie Rieves	347	87	4.0	Lonnie Holland	76	45	.59	423	Randall Dorsett	12	139	11.6
1960	Ken Bolin	542	75	7.2	Don Sessions	133	65	.49	724	Erroll Linden	12	146	12.2
1961	Ken Bolin	356	60	5.9	Don Sessions	111	48	.43	549	Bill McMillan	15	244	16.3
1962	Bobby Brezina	512	102	5.0	Billy Roland	123	60	.49	753	Bill Van Osdel	14	218	15.6
1963	Joe Lopasky	353	96	3.7	Jack Skog	182	100	.55	1,145	Clem Beard	19	240	12.6
1964	Dick Post	528	116	4.6	Jack Skog	55	30	.55	436	Dick Post	12	100	8.3
1965	Dick Post	630	156	4.0	Bo Burris	175	81	.46	1,256	Ken Hebert	24	359	15.0
1966	Dick Post	1,061	185	5.7	Bo Burris	204	98	.48	1,666	Ken Hebert	38	800	21.1
1967	Paul Gipson	1,100	187	5.9	Dick Woodall	132	65	.49	1,224	Ken Hebert	28	626	22.4
1968	Paul Gipson	1,550	242	6.4	Rusty Clark	58	32	.55	650	Elmo Wright	43	1,198	27.9
1969	Jim Strong	1,293	190	6.8	Gary Mullins	166	83	.50	1,433	Elmo Wright	63	1,275	20.2
1970	Tommy Mozisek	935	153	6.1	Gary Mullins	159	68	.43	1,046	Elmo Wright	47	874	18.6
1971	Robert Newhouse	1,757	277	6.3	Gary Mullins	184	94	.51	1,616	Riley Odoms	45	730	16.2
1972	Puddin' Jones	1,216	222	5.5	D.C. Nobles	209	101	.48	1,351	Robert Ford	35	538	15.4
1973	Leonard Parker	1,123	224	5.0	D.C. Nobles	156	70	.45	1,148	Bryan Willingham	16	328	20.5
1974	John Housman	988	192	5.1	David Husmann	90	38	.42	524	Robert Lavergne	13	184	14.2
1975	John Housman	466	107	4.4	David Husmann	76	43	.57	692	Don Bass	38	646	17.0
1976	Alois Blackwell	934	151	6.2	Danny Davis	161	77	.48	1,348	Eddie Foster	26	524	20.2
1977	Alois Blackwell	1,169	213	5.5	Delrick Brown	136	69	.51	977	Don Bass	42	580	13.8
1978	Emmett King	1,095	183	6.0	Danny Davis	155	76	.49	1,053	Willis Adams	29	534	18.4
1979	Terald Clark	1,063	193	5.5	Delrick Brown	117	59	.50	737	Garrett Jurgajtis	23	275	12.0
1980	Terald Clark	859	219	3.9	Brent Chinn	109	48	.44	749	Lonell Phea	29	533	18.4
1981	Lionel Wilson	656	191	3.4	Lionel Wilson	170	85	.50	1,225	Lonell Phea	40	614	15.4
1982	Dallas Wiggins	895	169	5.3	Lionel Wilson	171	85	.50	1,386	David Roberson	48	667	13.9
1983	Donald Jordan	1,049	191	5.5	Gerald Landry	120	56	.47	957	David Roberson	32	354	11.1
1984	Raymond Tate	864	180	4.8	Gerald Landry	235	113	.48	1,503	Carl Hilton	38	517	13.6
1985	Sloan Hood	652	114	5.7	Gerald Landry	258	121	.47	1,624	Carl Hilton	34	450	13.2
1986	Sloan Hood	391	97	4.0	Mark Davis	91	45	.49	590	Jet Brown	33	556	16.8
1987	Kimble Anders	791	158	5.0	Andre Ware	83	140	1.69	996	Jason Phillips	99	875	8.8
1988	Chuck Weatherspoon	1,004	118	8.5	Andre Ware	356	212	.60	2,507	Jason Phillips	108	1,444	13.4
1989	Chuck Weatherspoon	1,146	119	9.6	Andre Ware	578	365	.63	4,699	Manny Hazard	142	1,689	11.9
1990	Chuck Weatherspoon	1,097	158	6.9	David Klingler	643	374	.58	5,140	Manny Hazard	78	946	12.1
1991	TiAndre Sanders	397	70	5.7	David Klingler	498	278	.56	3,388	Freddie Gilbert	106	957	9.0
1992	Lamar Smith	845	111	7.6	Jimmy Klingler	504	303	.60	3,818	Sherman Smith	103	923	9.0
1993	Lamar Smith	417	96	4.3	Jimmy Klingler	230	117	.51	1,291	Keith Jack	41	556	13.6
1994	Jermaine Williams	670	136	4.9	Chad O'Shea	109	59	.54	791	Ron Peters	28	342	12.2
1995	Antowain Smith	608	152	4.0	Chuck Clements	437	245	.56	2,641	Larkay James	50	706	14.1
1996	Antowain Smith	1,239	202	6.1	Chuck Clements	354	223	.63	2,417	Damion Johnson	52	708	13.6
1997	Ketric Sanford	636	151	4.2	Jason McKinley	314	166	.53	1,910	Robbie Wheeler	42	470	11.2
1998	Ketric Sanford	1,054	222	4.7	Jason McKinley	386	218	.56	2,437	Jerrian James	80	931	11.6
1999	Ketric Sanford	1,199	224	5.4	Jason McKinley	257	148	.58	1,651	Orlando Iglesias	59	750	12.7
2000	Joffrey Reynolds	534	136	3.9	Jason McKinley	431	254	.59	2,696	Brian Robinson	80	890	11.1
2001	Joffrey Reynolds	765	163	4.7	Kelly Robertson	190	105	.55	1,352	Orlando Iglesias	44	557	12.7
2002	Joffrey Reynolds	1,545	316	4.9	Nick Eddy	265	134	.51	2,054	KeyKowa Bell	35	422	12.1
2003	Anthony Evans	1,149	236	4.9	Kelly Robertson	267	134	.50	1,704	Vincent Marshall	60	812	13.5
2004	Anthony Evans	788	153	5.2	Kevin Kolb	353	198	.56	2,766	Vincent Marshall	61	1,040	17.0

Receiving leaders by receptions
The NCAA began including postseason stats in 2002

IDAHO

BY SETH WICKERSHAM

FROM 1982 TO 1999, IDAHO HAD ONE losing season. On the way to five Big Sky titles and one Big West title, a string of coaches and players who would later make names for themselves broke in at Moscow. Guys like Dennis Erickson (who went on to coach the University of Miami, the Seattle Seahawks and the San Francisco 49ers) and John Friesz (who later quarterbacked the San Diego Chargers and played 11 years in the NFL) got their starts at Idaho. Too bad for the Vandals (14–44, from 2000 to 2004) that the 20th century had to end so soon.

TRADITION Before games, students have bonfire rallies on campus near the team's practice field. Also, when Idaho plays rival Washington State, students on the losing side of the rivalry walk the eight miles home between the two campuses.

BEST PLAYER Though the Pro Football Hall of Famer Jerry Kramer of the Green Bay Packers is Idaho's best-known alum, the school's best player was Ray McDonald. A two-time All-America in 1965 and 1966, when he averaged 132.9 yards rushing per game and scored 14 touchdowns, the 6'4", 230-pound tailback was fast enough

to rush for more than 240 yards in a game twice. McDonald excelled off the field as well, as a pianist and a singer. Idaho's only NFL first-round pick, McDonald lasted only two years with the Washington Redskins.

BEST COACH Dennis Erickson remodeled Idaho from a running team to a passing team years before going on to do the same at Washington State and, to a lesser extent, Miami. He came to Moscow in 1982 and went 9–4 in his first year, leading Idaho to the Division I-AA playoffs for the first time. Erickson also showed his knack for coaching quarterbacks, as Ken Hobart became the first Idaho QB to break 3,000 yards in a season. Erickson stayed in Moscow four seasons, going 32–15, before coaching Wyoming for a year and then heading for the big time, eight miles west, to Washington State.

BEST TEAM The 1998 season looked iffy at best, with Idaho coming off a 5–6 season and facing a new year— just the school's third in Division I-A—with a freshman quarterback. But after a tough early-season loss to Washington State, followed by a 33-point trouncing at the hands of LSU, the young Vandals turned their season around, losing just once more the rest of the way as QB John Welsh emerged as a team leader. Idaho's 1998 squad was gunning for its first-ever bowl bid and a Big West Conference title when it traveled to Boise State on Nov. 21, 1998. Trailing the Broncos 14-6 in the third quarter,

Idaho started playing football— and archrival Washington State—in 1894.

the Vandals recovered a Boise fumble and the game exploded. Welsh led the charge, finishing with 326 yards passing and two touchdowns. His last completion was a two-point conversion to running back Joel Thomas that brought Idaho a 36-35 win, giving the Vandals a return trip to Boise for the 1998 Humanitarian Bowl.

BIGGEST GAME The dream season of 1998, which began with some publications rating Idaho among the worst in the nation, concluded with the Vandals, fresh off their first Big West title, playing in the second Humanitarian Bowl. Idaho was a 16½-point underdog against perennial mid-major power Southern Mississippi. But Welsh threw for four touchdowns, and the Vandals defense forced six turnovers, turning a 21-7 Southern Miss lead into a 42-35 Idaho victory. "These guys were rated 112th in the nation about 90 days ago, but it's not where you start, it's where you finish," Idaho coach Chris Tormey said. "This is the high point in Idaho football history, I think."

BIGGEST UPSET Washington State had not lost in the last 27 matchups with Idaho when the Vandals visited Pullman on Oct. 23, 1954. A 61-yard run by halfback Bill

Lawr in the second quarter set up a six-yard touchdown pass from George Eidam to Frank Teverbaugh, giving the Vandals a 7-0 lead. Then the Idaho D took over. The Cougars got into scoring position twice but couldn't get past the 15. Idaho won 10-0.

BEST COMEBACK Colorado State took a 28-0 first-quarter lead over Idaho in Fort Collins in 1992. But Idaho rallied furiously in the second half, and coach John L. Smith's key decision—to kick a field goal on fourth-and-two at the CSU 5-yard line with the Vandals trailing by 10 in the fourth quarter—proved prescient. They'd tie the game later, and then, with 42 seconds left, leave it to Mike Hollis to kick the game-winning 29-yard field goal, for an improbable 37–34 win.

HEARTBREAKER Idaho decided to take a rare trip into Alabama in 1999 to play at Auburn, and for three quarters it looked like a major mistake. The Tigers led at halftime 20-0, and after the third quarter it was 23-0. But backup Vandals quarterback Ed Dean threw three touchdown passes, and suddenly Idaho was back in it. The Vandals ended up losing 30-23, but proved that—for a day at least—they could hold their own with the big boys.

RECORDS

RUSHING YARDS

	GAME	
345	Russell Davis vs. Portland State, Oct. 3, 1981	
	SEASON	
1,393	Devon Pearce, 1990 (267 att.)	
	CAREER	
3,929	Joel Thomas, 1993-1998 (765 att.)	

PASSING YARDS

	GAME	
637	Brian Lindgren vs. Middle Tennessee, Oct. 6, 2001 (49 of 71)	
	SEASON	
4,041	John Friesz, 1989 (260 of 425)	
	CAREER	
10,824	Doug Nussmeier, 1990-93 (746 of 1,205)	

RECEIVING YARDS

	GAME	
257	Jerry Hendren vs. Idaho State, Sept. 27, 1969	
	SEASON	
1,457	Jerry Hendren, 1968 (86 rec.)	
	CAREER	
3,847	Kasey Dunn, 1988-91 (268 rec.)	

POINTS

	GAME	
33	Bob Fitzke vs. College of Idaho, 1923	
	SEASON	
150	Sherriden May, 1992 (25 TDs)	
	CAREER	
366	Sherriden May, 1990-93 (61 TDs)	

CONSENSUS ALL-AMERICANS

1983	Ken Hobart, QB
1985	Eric Yarber, WR
1988-89	John Friesz, QB
1989	Lee Allen, WR
1990-91	Kasey Dunn, WR
1992	Yo Murphy, WR
1992	Jeff Robinson, DL
1993	Doug Nussmeier, QB
1993	Mat Groshong, C
1994	Sherriden May, RB
1994	Jim Mills, OL
1995	Ryan Phillips, DL

STADIUM Neale Stadium had been Idaho's home for 75 years when it was destroyed by fire in November 1969. A new stadium, Kibbie Dome, was built on the site and has been the Vandals' home since 1971. (The dome took four more years to be completed.) It stands 14 stories tall and lists a seating capacity of 16,000, but a record 17,600 packed into the complex in 1989 for a game against Boise State. The facility is also home to the men's and women's basketball teams.

RIVAL Idaho first played Washington State in 1894. The Cougars dominated from the outset, winning the first game 10–0, and 21 straight in the rivalry from 1928 to 1949. The two teams still play every year, and the Cougars still tend to get the upper hand. "Pullman is so close that it's a clear rivalry," says Vandals radio announcer Bob Curtis, who has broadcast Idaho games for more than 55 years. "But Boise State is more of a bragging-rights game." In 1971, Idaho started playing Boise State, and the schools have produced a much more competitive rivalry, though not as storied as the one with Washington State. Through 2004, Idaho held a 17–16–1 lead in the series.

NICKNAME In 1917, Harry Lloyd McCarty, a writer at the *Argonaut* student newspaper, noted that the Idaho basketball team played so ferociously that it "vandalized" opponents. In 1921, Vandals became the official school nickname.

MASCOT Idaho has had one: Joe Vandal. He runs around on game days wearing a monstrous pirate headpiece.

UNIFORMS When Idaho first started playing football, in 1894, the squad wore a combination of dark pants and light shirts. By the 1950s, the team had black shirts with gold lettering and gold pants, and that look continued until the 1970s, when the team switched to gold jerseys and white pants. Since the 1980s, Idaho has primarily had black jerseys, gold pants and gold helmets with Vandals written in cursive.

QUOTE "No classes on Monday." —University president Dean Theophilus, after Idaho defeated Washington State in 1954

IDAHO ANNUAL STATISTICAL LEADERS

YR	RUSHING	YDS	ATT	AVG	PASSING	ATT	CMP	PCT	YDS	RECEIVING	REC	YDS	AVG
1996	Joel Thomas	1,148	222	5.2	Ryan Fien	455	267	.59	3,674	Antonio Wilson	65	1,203	18.5
1997	Anthony Tenner	573	122	4.7	Brian Brennan	387	218	.56	2,708	Antonio Wilson	77	910	11.8
1998	Joel Thomas	1,229	231	5.3	John Welsh	182	98	.54	1,387	Ryan Prestimonico	42	668	15.9
1999	Anthony Tenner	764	179	4.3	Greg Robertson	224	101	.45	1,279	Jeffrey Townsley	37	449	12.1
2000	Willie Alderson	1,245	238	5.0	John Welsh	399	251	.63	3,171	Chris Lacy	45	776	17.2
2001	Blair Lewis	509	98	5.2	John Welsh	284	183	.64	2,215	Chris Lacy	65	1,045	16.1
2002	Blair Lewis	930	176	5.3	Brian Lindgren	382	240	.63	2,763	Josh Jelmberg	64	785	12.3
2003	Zach Gerstner	1,186	256	4.6	Brian Lindgren	246	147	.60	2,077	Orlando Winston	55	807	14.7
2004	Jayson Bird	859	151	5.7	Michael Harrington	343	225	.66	2,222	Bobby Bernal-Wood	96	938	9.8

Receiving leaders by receptions
The NCAA began including postseason stats in 2002

IDAHO ALL-TIME SCORES

WIN/LOSS PERCENTAGE SINCE 1996

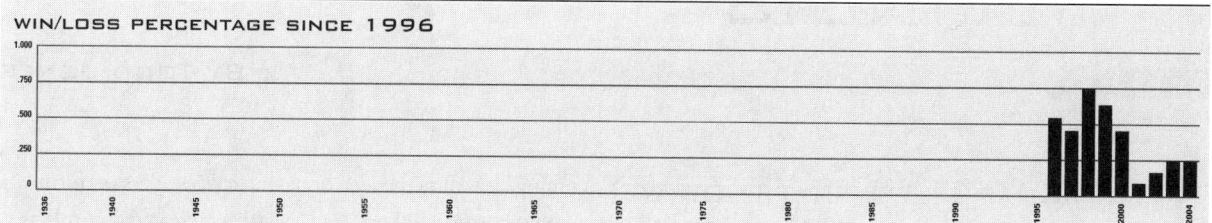

CHRIS TORMEY
1995-99 (.589)   33-23

1996-2000
BIG WEST

1996   6-5   (3-2)
A31		at Wyoming	38 40
S7		at San Diego State	21 40
S14	●	Saint Mary's-Cal	52 17
S28		at Texas St.	21 27
O5	●	Cal Poly SLO	38 33
O19	●	Nevada	24 15
O26		at Utah State	28 35
N2	●	Ea. Washington	37 27
N9	●	New Mexico State	34 19
N16		at North Texas	17 24
N23	●	at Boise State	64 19

1997   5-6   (2-3)
A30		at Air Force	10 14
S6	●	Portland St.	46 0
S13	●	at Idaho St.	43 0
S20		at Central Florida	10 41
O4		North Texas	30 17
O11	●	Cal Davis	44 14
O18		at Nevada	23 42
O25		Utah State	17 63
N1		Ea. Washington *Spo*	21 24
N14	●	at New Mexico State	35 18
N22		Boise State	23 30

1998   9-3   (4-1)
S5	●	Ea. Washington	31 14
S12	●	at San Jose State	17 12
S19		at Washington State	16 24
S26		at LSU	20 53
O3	●	Idaho St.	52 3
O10	●	at Arkansas State	52 14
O17	●	at Utah State	26 14
O24		Nevada	23 58
O31	●	at North Texas	41 23
N14	●	New Mexico State	36 32
N21	●	at Boise State	36 35
HUMANITARIAN BOWL			
D30	●	Southern Miss	42 35

1999   7-4   (4-2)
S2	●	Ea. Washington *Spo*	48 21
S11		at Auburn	23 30
S18	●	Washington State *Pull*	28 17
O2		at Wyoming	13 28
O9	●	North Texas *Pull*	28 10
O16	●	at Arkansas State	30 24
O23	●	Utah State *Pull*	31 3
O30		at New Mexico State	14 42
N6	●	at Nevada	42 33
N13	●	at Montana	33 30
N20		Boise State *Pull*	14 45

TOM CABLE
2000-03 (.239)   11-35

2000   5-6   (3-2)
S2		at Washington	20 44
S9		Montana	38 45
S16		at Oregon	13 42
S23	●	at Washington State	38 34
S30	●	Montana St.	56 7
O7		at West Virginia	16 28
O14	●	Arkansas State	42 25
O21		at Utah State	14 31
N4	●	at North Texas	16 14
N11	●	New Mexico State	44 41
N18		at Boise State	24 66

2001-2004
SUN BELT

2001   1-10   (1-5)
A30		at Washington State	7 36
S8		at Arizona	29 36
S22		at Washington	3 53
S29		Boise State *Pull*	13 45
O6		at Middle Tennessee	58 70
O13		at New Mexico State	39 46
O20		La. Lafayette *Pull*	37 54
O27		at Arkansas State	31 34
N3	●	La. Monroe	42 38
N17		North Texas	19 43
N24		at Montana	27 33

2002   2-10   (1-5)
A31		at Boise State	21 38
S7		at Washington State	14 49
S14		at Oregon	21 58
S21	●	San Diego State	48 38
S28		at Washington	27 41
O5		Montana	31 38
O12		at La. Monroe	14 34
O26	●	Middle Tennessee	21 18
N2		at La. Lafayette	28 31
N9		at North Texas	0 10
N16		Arkansas State	29 38
N23		New Mexico State	31 35

2003   3-9   (3-4)
A30		at Washington State	0 25
S6		Ea. Washington	5 8
S13		Boise State	10 24
S20		at Washington	14 45
S27		at Montana	28 41
O4	●	at New Mexico State	35 31
O11		North Texas	14 24
O18		Middle Tennessee	21 28
O25		at La. Lafayette	20 31
N8		at Arkansas State	23 24
N15	●	at La. Monroe	58 20
N22	●	Utah State	20 13

NICK HOLT
2004-PRESENT (.250)   3-9

2004   3-9   (2-5)
S4		at Boise State	7 65
S11		at Utah State	7 14
S18		Washington State	8 49
S25		at Oregon	10 48
O2	●	at Eastern Michigan	45 41
O9		La. Monroe	14 16
O16	●	La. Lafayette	38 25
O23		at Middle Tennessee	14 34
O30		at Troy State	7 47
N2	●	Arkansas State *Pull*	45 31
N13		at North Texas	29 51
N20		at Hawaii	21 52

ILLINOIS

BY TODD JONES

ILLINOIS HAS HELPED SHAPE HOW WE look at football. The Fighting Illini gave us the game's first true superstar, the prototypical linebacker and another player who later became the ideal autocratic coach in the professional ranks. The trio—Red Grange, Dick Butkus and George Halas, respectively —molded our perception of offense, defense and coaching. The innovative Robert Zuppke coached Illinois to four national championships from 1914 to 1927 and forever created a standard of success in Champaign-Urbana. History reassures the future hopes of the Fighting Illini. As Ray Eliot, one of the school's great coaches, once told his players: "Anything you think you can do, you can do." It has all been done before at Illinois.

TRADITION Homecoming weekend originated at Illinois in 1910, created by undergraduates W. Elmer Ekblaw and C.F. "Dab" Williams. The first celebration was held Oct. 14-16, and the Fighting Illini beat Chicago 3-0 in a game that served as the weekend's main event. Other schools adopted home-

coming, as well as the idea of having cheerleaders perform acrobatic stunts. Robert "Red" Matthews created that role as an Illinois cheerleader from 1899 to 1900. Illinois has celebrated "Dad's Day" since 1920, when it crowns a "King Dad" (nominated by a student) on the field at halftime of one game each season. The Fighting Illini have three trophy games, the oldest dating to 1925, when they began competing against Ohio State for a wooden replica of a turtle known as the Illibuck Trophy. The Purdue Cannon has been up for grabs since 1943 whenever the Illini play the Boilermakers. In 1945, the winner of the Illinois-Northwestern game earned a bulky wooden Indian trophy called Sweet Sioux, but since 1947 the schools have played for the Tomahawk instead.

BEST PLAYER The man who would become one of sports' great legends arrived at Illinois in the fall of 1922. Harold "Red" Grange quit before his first practice ended, convinced he was too small to play at 5'10" and 170 pounds. He returned a day later and accepted No. 77 because all other jerseys had been given out. Three years later, the school retired that number after his final game. By then, people were writing poetry about the man Grantland Rice dubbed the Galloping Ghost. Grange was as big a sports star in the Roaring '20s as Babe Ruth

PROFILE

University of Illinois at Urbana-Champaign
Champaign-Urbana, Ill.
Founded: 1867
Enrollment: 27,770
Colors: Orange and Blue
Nickname: Fighting Illini
Stadium: Memorial Stadium
   Opened in 1923
   AstroPlay; 69,249 capacity
First football game: 1890
All-time record: 542–485–50 (.526)
Bowl record: 6–8
Big Ten Conference championships:
15 (8 outright)
First-round NFL draftees: 16
Website: www.fightingillini.com

THE BEST OF TIMES

A record of 20–2–2 from 1927 to 1929 can't match the excitement of 1923, when sophomore sensation Red Grange ran wild in new Memorial Stadium. The Illini went 8–0 and won the Big Ten championship that season, and Grange's teams had a 19–4–1 record from 1923 to 1925.

THE WORST OF TIMES

Eight consecutive losing seasons from 1966 to 1973 with a 25–58 record. Six consecutive losing seasons from 1975 to 1980 with a 19–43–4 record. But the worst winning percentage (.152) occurred from 1996 to 1998, when a 5–28 record included a school-worst 0–11 in 1997. The Illini also were winless (0–9) in 1961 and 1969 (0–10).

CONFERENCE

Charter member of the Western Conference in 1896 and has remained in the league since then. Popularly known as the Big Ten since 1917, but didn't officially change its name to the Big Ten Conference until 1987.

DISTINGUISHED ALUMNI

Marc Andreessen, co-founder, Netscape Communications; Jerry Colangelo, owner, Phoenix Suns and Arizona Diamondbacks; Roger Ebert, film critic; Hugh Hefner, founder, *Playboy* magazine; Robert Johnson, CEO, Black Entertainment TV; Ang Lee, film director

FIGHT SONG

ILLINOIS LOYALTY
We're loyal to you Illinois,
We're "Orange and Blue," Illinois,
We'll back you so stand
'Gainst the best in the land,
For we know you have sand, Illinois,
Rah! Rah!
So crack out that ball Illinois,
We're backing you all Illinois;
Our team is our fame protector,
On! boys, for we expect a vict'ry from you Illinois!
For honest Labor and for Learning we stand,
And unto thee we pledge our heart and hand,
Dear Alma Mater Illinois.

> ## Red Grange gave credibility to pro football as a Chicago Bear, but his fame began at Illinois.

and Jack Dempsey. The small, shy man from Wheaton, Ill., ran with the football like no one had before and few have since. He single-handedly gave credibility to pro football as a barnstorming member of the Chicago Bears, but his fame began at Illinois. There he gained 2,071 rushing yards, passed for 575 yards and scored 31 touchdowns in 20 games over three seasons. With muscles toned from working on a hometown ice truck, the Wheaton Iceman ran with extraordinary speed, balance and power. Grange burst into stardom on Oct. 18, 1924, by scoring the first four times he touched the ball in the first 12 minutes against Michigan. He later scored a fifth touchdown and passed for a sixth. His legend became solidified a year later when the eastern press saw him gain 363 total yards and score 3 TDs in a 24-2 win at powerful Penn. "This man Red Grange of Illinois is three or four men and a horse rolled into one," Damon Runyon wrote of the performance. In 1999, an Associated Press panel voted Grange the fourth-best football player of the 20th century. He was a charter member of both the college and pro football halls of fame and a unanimous selection on the all-time All-America team.

BEST COACH He was born in Berlin, Germany, and never played varsity football. He looked out of place—a stubby 5'7" with a cowlick hanging on his youthful face—in such a bruising game. His mind, however, made up for what he lacked in physique. Robert Zuppke, who loved to paint, is remembered as one of football's most creative thinkers. He invented the huddle, the screen pass, the flea-flicker, spring practice and the spiral snap from center. Zuppke named his offensive plays Razzle Dazzle and the Flying Trapeze and once said his defense was "on loan from Barnum and Bailey." And he created all expectations for Illinois football. Grange and others who played for the Little Dutchman raved about his ability to inspire a team with motivational speeches. "Shoot at the moon," he often urged his team. Once, Zuppke even told his players that "the only man who comes out of the game today is a dead man." The Illini had won only one Big Ten title when he was hired in 1913, but they won seven in Zuppke's 29 seasons. He led Illinois to its only four national championships: 1914, 1919, 1923 and 1927.

RECORDS

RUSHING YARDS

GAME
- 315 Robert Holcombe vs. Minnesota, Nov. 16, 1996 (43 att.)

SEASON
- 1,330 Antoineo Harris, 2002 (278 att.)

CAREER
- 4,105 Robert Holcombe, 1994-97 (943 att.)

PASSING YARDS

GAME
- 621 Dave Wilson vs. Ohio State, Nov. 8, 1980 (43 of 69)

SEASON
- 3,671 Tony Eason, 1982 (313 of 505)

CAREER
- 8,725 Jack Trudeau, 1981-85 (797 of 1,245)

RECEIVING YARDS

GAME
- 208 David Williams vs. Northwestern, Sept. 1, 1984 (11 rec.)

SEASON
- 1,278 David Williams, 1984 (101 rec.)

CAREER
- 3,392 David Williams, 1983-85 (262 rec.)

POINTS

GAME
- 48 Howard Griffith vs. Southern Illinois, Sept. 22, 1990 (8 TDs)

SEASON
- 110 Neil Rackers, 1999 (20 FGs, 44 PATs, 1 TD)

CAREER
- 262 Chris White, 1983-85 (53 FGs, 103 PATs)

CONSENSUS ALL-AMERICANS

1914	Perry Graves	E
1914	Ralph Chapman	G
1915	Bart Macomber	B
1918	John Depler	C
1920	Charles Carney	E
1923	James McMillen	G
1923-25	Red Grange	HB
1926	Bernie Shively	G
1946	Alex Agase	G
1951	Johnny Karras	B
1953	J.C. Caroline	B
1959	Bill Burrell	G
1963-64	Dick Butkus	C
1965	Jim Grabowski	FB
1984-85	David Williams	WR
1989-90	Moe Gardner	NT
1994	Dana Howard	LB
1995	Kevin Hardy	LB

BEST TEAM The 1914 Fighting Illini are revered for sharing the national championship with Army and Texas after going 7–0 and outscoring opponents 224-22. Zuppke once said he never had a quarterback as good as that team's George "Potsy" Clark, and the team also had All-Americas in Perry Graves and Ralph Chapman. However, those who favor the modern era consider the 1951 squad the school's best. That team, led by fullback Bill Tate and linebacker Chuck Boerio, went 9–0–1—the school's last undefeated season—and outscored opponents 220-83. Only a 0-0 tie against Ohio State spoiled a perfect season. Illinois beat Stanford 40-7 in the Rose Bowl by scoring 34 unanswered points in the second half. Still, Illinois finished No. 4 in the final 1951 AP poll.

BIGGEST GAME Fans and the media greeted Illinois with little respect when it arrived for the 1947 Rose Bowl in Pasadena to fulfill the first contract calling to match the champions of the Big Ten and Pac-8. Many people wanted Pac-8 champ UCLA to play Army. Illinois coach Ray Eliot made his players read every negative article and convinced them they were playing for the Big Ten's pride as well as their school. UCLA, ranked No. 4 and favored by 11, led 7-6 after one quarter, but the Fighting Illini erupted for a 45-14 victory. Six different Illinois players scored TDs and the team set a Rose Bowl record with 326 rushing yards. Julius Rykovich and Buddy Young each gained 103 yards behind the blocking of All-America tackle Alex Agase. "You wanted an army. Well you got an army today," the Illinois players chanted at UCLA throughout the game.

BIGGEST UPSET The headline on the *Chicago Herald*'s game story screamed: "Hold On Tight When You Read This!" Such was the shock of Illinois' 14-9 victory over 40-point favorite Minnesota on Nov. 4, 1916. The Gophers had five All-America candidates and outscored opponents 236-14 while going 4–0. Illinois traveled to Minnesota with a 2–2 record, but Zuppke delivered a

ALL-TIME TEAM	
In the fall of 1990, Illinois fans cast nearly 5,000 ballots to select the school's 25-man All-Century football team. The team was chosen as part of the university's celebration of 100 years of football.	
FIRST TEAM	
1923-25	Red Grange, HB
1962-64	Dick Butkus, LB/C
1963-65	Jim Grabowski, FB
1944, 1946	Buddy Young, HB
1955-57	Ray Nitschke, FB/LB
1981-82	Tony Eason, QB
1953-54	J.C. Caroline, HB
1973, 1975-76	Scott Studwell, LB
1917	George Halas, E
1987-90	Moe Gardner, NT
SECOND TEAM	
1917-19	Burt Ingwersen, T
1932-34	Chuck Bennis, G
1941-42, 1946	Alex Agase, G
1946-48	Dike Eddleman, P
1949-51	John Karras, HB
1950-52	Al Brosky, DB
1959-60	Ed O'Bradovich, E/P
1968-70	Doug Dieken, TE
1973-76	Dan Beaver, PK
1980	Dave Wilson, QB
1980-82	Mike Bass, PK
1980-83	Don Thorp, DT
1982-85	Jim Juriga, G
1983-85	David Williams, WR
1988-89	Jeff George, QB

passionate pregame speech. "I am Louis XIV, and you are my court," he told his players. "After us, the deluge. Let them eat their cake today. We'll live on bread." The Illini went up 14-0 and held on despite using only 11 players. When the game ended, injured Illinois player George Halas threw his crutches into the air in celebration. Up in the press box, Walter Camp said: "Will somebody please tell me how something like this could happen?"

HEARTBREAKER Illinois won the 1983 Big Ten championship by going 9–0 in league play, including victories over No. 4 Iowa, No. 6 Ohio State and No. 8 Michigan. The Illini earned their first Rose Bowl berth in 20 years. Six players were named first-team All-Big Ten, including defensive tackle Don Thorp, the league's MVP. Mike White won the Big Ten's Coach of the Year honor. The storybook season, however, ended with a horrible final chapter. UCLA, led by quarterback Rick Neuheisel, crushed the Illini 45-9 in the Rose Bowl. The Bruins gained 511 yards of total offense. Illinois finished 10–2.

WILDEST FINISH Another year, another loss in Ann Arbor. Or so it seemed on Oct. 23, 1993, when the Fighting Illini trailed Michigan 21-10 early in the fourth quarter and 21-17 with less than two minutes to play. Illinois linebacker Kevin Hardy, however, forced Michigan's Ricky Powers to fumble, and linebacker Simeon Rice recovered at the Wolverines' 44 with 1:13 remaining. Three completions later, the Illini faced fourth down and six. Johnny Johnson rolled left and split two defenders with a TD pass to tight end Jim Klein for a 24-21 lead. Michigan answered by driving to the Illini 25, but time ran out before the Wolverines could try a field goal. Maybe the pregame switch from orange pants to blue ones, done to change the team's luck, had worked for Illinois.

BEST GOAL-LINE STAND Two different stands earned an 18-16 win at Ohio State on Oct. 10, 1992. Linebacker

Dana Howard and safety Jeff Arneson forced OSU's Eddie George, who won the Heisman three years later, to fumble on the Illini 1 on the game's opening series. Arneson recovered the ball and ran 96 yards for a touchdown. Ohio State bounced back and led 16-15 early in the fourth quarter when it again had the ball on the Illini 1. Howard and safety Tyrone Washington caused another George fumble. Illinois recovered, drove 86 yards, and ended the scoring with a Chris Richardson field goal.

BEST COMEBACK The Fighting Illini, a 24-point underdog, trailed 27-7 midway through the third period at No. 9 Michigan in 1999. Quarterback Kurt Kittner then rallied the Illini to four consecutive TDs. The last two scores came in the game's final 2:42 when Kittner hit Rocky Harvey with a 59-yard TD pass and Harvey followed with a 54-yard TD run. Illinois safety Muhammad Abdulah intercepted a last-second pass by Michigan's Tom Brady in the end zone. The Wolverines scored a safety on the play, but fell 35-29.

STADIUM The 200 granite columns on the east and west sides of Memorial Stadium link fans to the past, which includes Red Grange running wild in the stadium's 1924 dedication game. Illinois athletic director George Huff pushed for a new stadium after the 1920 season. School president David Kinley agreed with the idea, saying he wanted one that could "bring a touch of Greek glory to the prairie." The wish came true when the 60,632-seat Memorial Stadium opened Nov. 3, 1923, thanks to public donations that accounted for some $1.7 million of the stadium's $2.5 million cost. Zuppke suggested the new field honor the 184 Illinois students who died in World War I, so the names of those 183 men and one woman were etched on separate columns. Little changed about the stadium until 1966, when the playing field was named Zuppke Field. Memorial Stadium received $7 million worth of improvements in 1985 and another $7 million of upgrades seven years later. It now seats 69,249. Grange Rock, a memorial to Red Grange, sits at the north end zone of Zuppke Field. Ray Eliot, the coach known as Mr. Illini, is buried in Mt. Hope Cemetery, located across Fourth Street from Memorial Stadium.

RIVAL In basketball, it's simple: Illinois hates Indiana and vice versa. All Fighting Illini football fans, however, don't aim their ill will at the same opponent. Some detest in-state rival Northwestern. The Illini have played the Wildcats 96 times, more than any other school, and hold a 51-42-5 lead in the series. Other Illinois fans can't stand Purdue, their closest geographical Big Ten opponent. And still other Illini fans consider Michigan the school's biggest rival, although the Wolverines don't share that feeling.

CONTROVERSY Ohio State trailed visiting Illinois 24-20 early in the fourth quarter in 1990 when Buckeyes kicker Tim Williams attempted a 51-yard field goal. Mel Agee blocked the kick. Illinois defensive tackle Mike Poloskey picked up the ball, began running and was tripped by Ohio State holder Kirk Herbstreit. Poloskey then pitched the ball to teammate Quintin Parker, who ran 43 yards for a TD. The Buckeyes protested that Poloskey had made an illegal forward lateral. Game officials huddled at midfield, discussed the matter, and signaled touchdown for Illinois. They're still grumbling about it in Columbus.

NICKNAME The Illini Indian tribe were the first inhabitants of what later became the state of Illinois. University officials adopted the name Illini because the word means "brave men." It's believed that *Chicago Tribune* writer Harvey Woodruff first used the moniker Fighting Illini in an account of Illinois' 7-0 upset win at Ohio State in 1921.

MASCOT Chief Illiniwek was created when Ray Dvorak, assistant director of the Illinois marching band, proposed that an Illini Indian do a dance at halftime during a 1926 game against Penn. A student has since played the role of chief every year.

UNIFORMS The University of Illinois convocation and faculty officially adopted orange and navy blue as the school's colors on Nov. 1, 1894. Those colors replaced Dartmouth green, which had been used to honor E.K. Hall, a Dartmouth graduate who served as Illinois football coach from 1892 to 1893. Illinois doesn't have a traditional logo and uniform design. Both have changed many times throughout the school's history.

NUMBERS Illinois running back Howard Griffith scored 8 TDs against Southern Illinois on Sept. 22, 1990 ... Al Brosky set an NCAA record with an interception in 15 consecutive games (1950-52) ... QB Dave Wilson set 44 different school, Big Ten and NCAA records in a 49-42 loss at Ohio State on Nov. 8, 1980. The senior completed 43 of 69 passes to 10 different receivers for 621 yards and 6 TDs against an OSU

defense ranked No. 1 in the conference against the pass ... Zero fans saw Illinois beat Municipal Pier 7-0 on Oct. 26, 1918. Spectators were not permitted at the game because of an influenza epidemic in Champaign-Urbana.

LORE The greatest 12 minutes of individual performance in the history of college football occurred on Oct. 18, 1924. Illinois was dedicating its new Memorial Stadium against mighty Michigan. Grange returned the game's opening kickoff 95 yards for a touchdown. On Illinois' next possession, the junior ran around left end, cut back off tackle and raced 67 yards for a score. Grange scored again when he ran 56 yards, cutting across the field after starting around the right end. Two minutes later, he ran 44 yards for yet another TD. In 12 minutes, he had scored all four times he touched the ball and totaled 265 yards. The crowd of 67,000 was roaring when Grange asked for a rest. He didn't return to play until the third quarter, then scored on a 13-yard run. He capped his day by throwing a TD pass. Grange totaled 402 yards, including 126 in kickoff returns. Illinois won 39-14 to end Michigan's 22-game winning streak, and the legend of the Galloping Ghost was born.

QUOTE "We'll have the will to win, and if we go down, we'll go down fighting hard and clean. That's the Illinois way."
—Ray Eliot

ILLINOIS ANNUAL STATISTICAL LEADERS

YR	RUSHING	YDS	ATT	AVG	PASSING	ATT	CMP	PCT	YDS	RECEIVING	REC	YDS	AVG
1946	Buddy Young	456			Perry Moss		23		298	Bill Heiss	5	132	26.4
1947	Ruck Steger	447	125	3.6	Perry Moss	127	71	.56	719	Sam Zatkoff	13	147	11.3
1948	Ruck Steger	265	68	3.9	Bernie Krueger	106	52	.49	703	Walt Kersulis	22	329	15.0
1949	John Karras	826	127	6.5	Bernie Krueger	90	42	.47	477	Ronnie Clark	11	105	9.5
1950	Dick Raklovits	709	133	5.3	Fred Major	65	32	.49	464	Tony Klimek	13	200	15.4
1951	John Karras	716	159	4.5	Tom O'Connell	120	62	.52	692	Rex Smith	22	343	15.6
1952	Pete Bachouros	484	95	5.1	Tom O'Connell	224	133	.59	1,761	Rocky Ryan	45	714	15.9
1953	J.C. Caroline	1,256	194	6.5	Elry Falkenstein	72	36	.50	577	Rocky Ryan	16	308	19.3
1954	J.C. Caroline	440	93	4.7	Em Lindbeck	66	38	.58	476	Dean Renn	17	246	14.5
1955	Harry Jefferson	514	97	5.3	Em Lindbeck	86	39	.45	588	Bob DesEnfants	12	206	17.2
1956	Abe Woodson	599	110	5.4	Hiles Stout	39	20	.51	278	Abe Woodson	12	257	21.4
1957	Ray Nitschke	514	79	6.5	Tom Haller	100	51	.51	675	Rich Kreitling	12	203	16.9
1958	Marshall Starks	303	65	4.7	John Eastbrook	66	34	.52	656	Rich Kreitling	23	688	29.9
1959	Bill Brown	504	89	5.7	Mel Meyers	63	32	.51	495	John Counts	19	314	16.5
1960	Bill Brown	531	128	4.1	John Eastbrook	87	40	.46	538	Ed O'Bradovich	21	233	11.1
1961	Al Wheatland	230	73	3.2	Dave McGann	49	27	.55	269	Dick Newell	16	184	11.5
1962	Ken Zimmerman	225	55	4.1	Mike Taliaferro	212	80	.38	1,139	Jim Warren	18	230	12.8
1963	Jim Grabowski	616	141	4.4	Mike Taliaferro	87	35	.40	450	Jim Warren	10	121	12.1
1964	Jim Grabowski	1,004	186	5.4	Fred Custardo	159	86	.54	1,012	Bob Trumpy	28	428	15.3
1965	Jim Grabowski	1,258	252	5.0	Fred Custardo	170	90	.53	1,124	John Wright Sr.	47	755	16.1
1966	Bill Huston	420	89	4.7	Bob Naponic	162	70	.43	998	John Wright Sr.	60	831	13.9
1967	Rich Johnson	768	195	3.9	Dean Volkman	183	77	.42	1,005	John Wright Sr.	52	698	13.4
1968	Rich Johnson	973	186	5.2	Bob Naponic	213	83	.39	813	Doug Dieken	21	223	10.6
1969	Dave Jackson	465	118	3.9	Steve Livas	131	42	.32	705	Doug Dieken	29	486	16.8
1970	Darrell Robinson	749	193	3.9	Mike Wells	170	71	.42	906	Doug Dieken	39	537	13.8
1971	John Wilson	543	115	4.7	Mike Wells	179	84	.47	1,007	Garvin Roberson	28	372	13.3
1972	George Uremovich	611	152	4.0	Mike Wells	158	76	.48	837	Garvin Roberson	31	569	18.4
1973	George Uremovich	519	141	3.7	Jeff Hollenbach	178	78	.44	916	Garvin Roberson	25	416	16.6
1974	Chubby Phillips	772	175	4.4	Jeff Hollenbach	131	64	.49	1,037	Joe Smalzer	29	525	18.1
1975	Lonnie Perrin	907	171	5.3	Kurt Steger	166	80	.48	1,136	Jeff Chrystal	22	261	11.9
1976	James Coleman	687	170	4.0	Kurt Steger	187	87	.47	1,243	Frank Johnson	24	306	12.8
1977	James Coleman	715	143	5.0	Mike McCray	60	36	.60	418	Tom Schooley	15	231	15.4
1978	Wayne Strader	389	74	5.3	Rich Weiss	109	58	.53	665	Jeff Barnes	22	270	12.3
1979	Mike Holmes	792	147	5.4	Lawrence McCullough	228	130	.57	1,254	Mike Holmes	25	127	5.1
1980	Mike Holmes	305	69	4.4	Dave Wilson	463	245	.53	3,154	Greg Dentino	40	512	12.8
1981	Calvin Thomas	390	110	3.5	Tony Eason	406	248	.61	3,360	Darrell Smith	43	495	11.5
1982	Dwight Beverly	396	74	5.4	Tony Eason	505	313	.62	3,671	Mike Martin	77	1,068	13.9
1983	Thomas Rooks	863	156	5.5	Jack Trudeau	324	226	.70	2,624	David Williams	69	958	13.9
1984	Thomas Rooks	1,056	219	4.8	Jack Trudeau	378	247	.65	2,724	David Williams	101	1,278	12.7
1985	Thomas Rooks	753	133	5.7	Jack Trudeau	446	322	.72	3,339	David Williams	92	1,156	12.6
1986	Keith Jones	534	133	4.0	Shane Lamb	227	115	.51	1,414	Stephen Pierce	43	602	14.0
1987	Keith Jones	322	110	2.9	Scott Mohr	212	106	.50	1,436	Darryl Usher	43	723	16.8
1988	Keith Jones	1,196	206	5.8	Jeff George	366	232	.63	2,451	Keith Jones	48	388	8.1
1989	Howard Griffith	747	164	4.6	Jeff George	386	242	.63	2,738	Mike Bellamy	59	927	15.7
1990	Howard Griffith	1,115	201	5.5	Jason Verduzco	355	226	.64	2,567	Shawn Wax	60	863	14.4
1991	Kameno Bell	664	140	4.7	Jason Verduzco	420	252	.60	3,014	Kameno Bell	64	503	7.9
1992	Darren Boyer	593	157	3.8	Jason Verduzco	282	184	.65	1,779	John Wright Jr.	47	508	10.8
1993	Ty Douthard	599	153	3.9	Johnny Johnson	287	135	.47	1,688	Ty Douthard	43	406	9.4
1994	Ty Douthard	765	179	4.3	Johnny Johnson	333	198	.59	2,495	Jason Dulick	52	550	10.6
1995	Robert Holcombe	1,051	264	4.0	Johnny Johnson	199	99	.50	1,110	Jason Dulick	36	453	12.6
1996	Robert Holcombe	1,281	260	4.9	Scott Weaver	314	176	.56	1,701	Jason Dulick	53	614	11.6
1997	Robert Holcombe	1,253	294	4.3	Mark Hoekstra	219	115	.53	1,029	Robert Holcombe	35	277	7.9
1998	Rocky Harvey	634	134	4.7	Kurt Kittner	162	72	.44	782	Lenny Willis	26	301	11.6
1999	Steve Havard	790	179	4.4	Kurt Kittner	396	216	.55	2,702	Michael Dean	45	608	13.5
2000	Antoineo Harris	772	192	4.0	Kurt Kittner	297	173	.58	1,982	Greg Lewis	40	544	13.6
2001	Antoineo Harris	629	169	3.7	Kurt Kittner	409	221	.54	3,256	Brandon Lloyd	65	1,062	16.3
2002	Antoineo Harris	1,330	278	4.8	Jon Beutjer	327	193	.59	2,511	Brandon Lloyd	65	1,010	15.5
2003	E.B. Halsey	525	140	3.8	Jon Beutjer	257	162	.63	1,597	Kelvin Hayden	52	592	11.4
2004	Pierre Thomas	893	152	5.9	Jon Beutjer	188	107	.57	1,082	Kendrick Jones	47	687	14.6

Receiving leaders by receptions
All statistics include postseason

ILLINOIS ALL-TIME SCORES

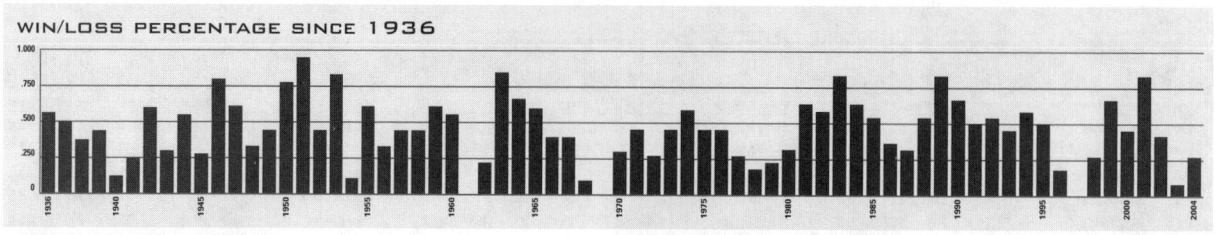

WIN/LOSS PERCENTAGE SINCE 1936

SCOTT WILLIAMS
1890 (.333)   1-2

1890   1-2-0
O2		at Ill. Wesleyan	0	16
N22		at Purdue	0	62
N27	•	Ill. Wesleyan	12	6

ROBERT LACKEY
1891 (.833)   5-1

1891   5-1-0
O1	•	at Lake Forest	0	8
O17	•	Bloomington	26	0
N7	•	Eureka Coll.	40	0
N13	•	Illinois Wesley	44	4
N21	•	Knox Coll.	12	0
N26	•	at Bloomington	20	12

E.K. HALL
1892-93 (.600)   10-6-4

1892   7-4-1
O8		Purdue	6	12
O12	=	Northwestern	16	16
O21	•	at Washington, Mo.	22	0
O22	•	Doane Coll. *Oma*	20	0
O24		at Nebraska	0	6
O26	•	at Baker U.	26	10
O27		at Kansas	4	26
O29	•	at Kansas City AC	42	0
N5	•	Englewood HS	38	0
N16		at Chicago	4	10
N18	•	DePauw	34	0
N24	•	Chicago	28	12

1893   3-2-3
S30	•	Wabash	60	6
O7	•	at DePauw	14	4
O21	=	at Northwestern	0	0
O28		Chicago AA	4	10
N6		Oberlin	24	34
N11	•	Pastime AC	18	16
N25	=	at Purdue	26	26
N30		Lake Forest	10	10

LOUIS D. VAIL
1894 (.571)   5-3

1894   5-3-0
O6	•	at Wabash	36	6
O13		at Chicago AC	0	14
O20	•	Lake Forest	54	6
N3	•	Northwestern	66	0
N17		Purdue	2	22
N21	•	Chicago	1	0
N24		Indianapolis Artillery.	14	18
N29	•	Pastime AC *StL*	10	0

GEORGE A. HUFF
1895-99 (.563)   21-16-3

1895   4-2-1
O5	•	Wabash	48	0
O12		at Chicago AC	0	8
O19	•	Illinois College	79	0
O26	=	at Wisconsin	10	10
N2	•	Lake Forest	38	0
N23	•	Northwestern	38	4
N28		at Purdue	2	6

1896-PRESENT
BIG 10

1896   4-2-1 (0-2-1)
O3	•	Lake Forest	38	0
O10	•	Knox	70	4
O17	•	Missouri *StL*	10	0
O21	•	Oberlin	22	6
O31		at Chicago	0	12
N7		Northwestern	4	10
N25	=	at Purdue	4	4

1897   6-2-0 (1-1-0)
O2	•	Eureka	26	0
O9	•	Phys. & Surg.	6	0
O16	•	Lake Forest	36	0
O23	•	Purdue	34	4
O30		Chicago	12	18
N12	•	Knox	64	0
N20	•	Carlisle *Peo*	6	23
N25	•	Eureka	6	0

1898   4-5-0 (1-1-0)
S28	•	Illinois Wesleyan	18	0
O1	•	Phys. & Surg.	6	11
O8	•	Notre Dame	0	5
O15	•	DePauw	16	0
O22	•	Alumni	10	6
N4	•	Alumni	17	23
N12		Michigan *Det*	5	12
N19		Carlisle *Chi*	0	11
N24	•	Minnesota	11	10

1899   3-5-1 (0-3-0)
S30	•	Ill. Wesleyan	6	0
O7	•	at Knox	5	0
O14		Indiana	0	5	*
O28		Michigan	0	5
N6	=	Alumni	0	0
N11		Wisconsin *Mil*	0	23
N22		Purdue	0	5
N25	•	at St. Louis	29	0
N30		Iowa *RI*	0	58

FRED L. SMITH
1900 (.667)   7-3-2

1900   7-3-2 (1-3-2)
S29	•	Rose Poly	26	0
O3	•	DePauw	63	0
O6	•	Illinois Wesleyan	21	0
O10	•	Phys. & Surg.	6	0
O13	•	Knox	16	0
O16	•	Lombard	35	0
O20	=	at Northwestern	0	0
O27		Michigan *Chi*	0	12
N3		Purdue	17	5
N10		at Minnesota	0	23
N17	=	Indiana *Ind*	0	0
N24		at Wisconsin	0	27

EDGAR G. HOLT
1901-02 (.804)   18-4-1

1901   8-2-0 (4-2-0)
S28	•	Englewood HS	39	0
O5	•	Marion Sims	52	0
O11	•	Phys. & Surg.	23	0
O12	•	Washington, Mo.	21	0
O19	•	at Chicago	24	0
O26		Northwestern	11	17
N2	•	Indiana *Ind*	18	0
N9	•	at Iowa	27	0
N16	•	at Purdue	28	6
N28		Minnesota	0	16

1902   10-2-1 (4-2-0)
S20	•	North Div. HS	34	6
S27	•	Englewood HS	45	0
O1	•	Osteopaths	22	0
O4	•	Monmouth	33	0
O8	•	Haskell	24	10
O11	•	Washington, Mo.	44	0
O18	•	Purdue	29	5
O25		at Chicago	0	6
N1	•	Indiana	47	0
N8		at Minnesota	5	17
N15	=	at Ohio State	0	0
N22	•	at Northwestern	17	0
N27	•	Iowa	80	0

GEORGE WOODRUFF
1903 (.571)   8-6

1903   8-6-0 (1-5-0)
S19	•	Englewood HS	45	5
S26	•	Lombard	43	0
S30	•	Osteopaths	36	0
O3	•	Knox	29	5
O7	•	Phys. & Surg.	40	0
O10	•	Rush	64	0
O14	•	Chicago Dental	54	0
O17		at Purdue	24	0
O24		at Chicago	6	18
O31		Northwestern	11	12
N6		at Indiana	0	17
N14		Minnesota	0	32
N21		at Iowa	0	12
N26		at Nebraska	0	16

NO HEAD COACH

1904   9-2-1 (3-1-1)
S24	•	North Central	10	0
S28	•	Wabash	23	2
O1	•	Knox	11	0
O5	•	Phys. & Surg.	26	0
O8	•	at Washington, Mo.	31	0
O15	•	Indiana	10	0
O22	•	at Purdue	24	6
O29	=	at Chicago	6	6
N5	•	at Ohio State	46	0
N12		at Northwestern	6	12
N19	•	Iowa	29	0
N24		at Nebraska	10	16

FRED LOWENTHAL
1905 (.556)   5-4

1905   5-4-0 (0-3-0)
S30	•	Knox	6	0
O4	•	Wabash	6	0
O7	•	North Central	24	0
O14	•	St. Louis	12	6
O21	•	Purdue	0	29
O28	•	Phys. & Surg.	30	0
N4		Michigan	0	33
N18	•	at Chicago	0	44
N30	•	at Nebraska	6	24

JUSTA LINDGREN
1906 (.300)   1-3-1

1906   1-3-1 (1-3-0)
O13	=	Wabash	0	0
O27		at Michigan	9	28
N10		Wisconsin	6	16
N17		at Chicago	0	63
N25	•	at Purdue	5	0

ARTHUR R. HALL
1907-12 (.713)   27-10-3

1907   3-2-0 (3-2-0)
O19		Chicago	6	42
O26		at Wisconsin	15	4
N2	•	Purdue	21	4
N9		at Iowa	12	25
N22	•	at Indiana	10	6

1908   5-1-1 (4-1-0)
O3	•	Monmouth	17	6
O10	=	Marquette	6	6
O17	•	at Chicago	6	11
O31	•	Indiana	10	0
N7	•	Iowa	22	0
N14	•	at Purdue	15	6
N21	•	Northwestern	64	8

1909   5-2-0 (3-1-0)
O2	•	James Millikin	23	0
O9	•	Kentucky	2	6
O16	•	at Chicago	8	14
O30	•	Purdue	24	6
N6	•	Indiana	6	5
N13	•	at Northwestern	35	0
N20	•	at Syracuse	17	8

1910   7-0-0 (4-0-0)
O1	•	James Millikin	13	0
O8	•	Drake	29	0
O15	•	Chicago	3	0
O29	•	at Purdue	11	0
N5	•	at Indiana	3	0
N12	•	at Northwestern	27	0
N19	•	Syracuse	3	0

1911   4-2-1 (2-2-1)
O7	•	James Millikin	33	0
O14	•	St. Louis	9	0
O21		at Chicago	0	24
N4	•	Purdue	12	3
N11	=	at Indiana	0	0
N18		Northwestern	27	13
N25		Minnesota	0	11

1912   3-3-1 (1-3-1)
O5	•	Illinois Wesleyan	87	3
O12	•	Washington, Mo.	13	0
O19	•	Indiana	13	7
N2		at Minnesota	0	13
N9	=	at Purdue	9	9
N16		Chicago	0	10
N23		at Northwestern	0	6

ROBERT C. ZUPPKE
1913-41 (.611)   131-81-13

1913   4-2-1 (2-2-1)
O4	•	Kentucky	21	0
O11	•	Missouri	24	7
O18	•	Northwestern	37	0
O25	•	at Indiana	10	0
N1		at Chicago	7	28
N15	=	Purdue	0	0
N22		Minnesota	9	19

1914   7-0-0 (6-0-0)
O3	•	Christian Brothers	37	0
O10		Indiana	51	0	*
O17		Ohio State	37	0
O24		at Northwestern	33	0
O31		at Minnesota	21	6
N14	•	Chicago	21	7
N21	•	at Wisconsin	24	9

1915   5-0-2 (3-0-2)
O2	•	Haskell	36	0
O9	•	Rolla Mines	75	7
O16	=	at Ohio State	3	3
O23	•	Northwestern	36	6
N6		Minnesota	6	6
N13	•	Wisconsin	17	3
N20	•	at Chicago	10	0

1916   3-3-1 (2-2-1)
O7	•	Kansas	30	0
O14		Colgate	3	15
O21	•	Ohio State	6	7
O28	•	at Purdue	14	7
N4	•	at Minnesota	14	9
N18	•	Chicago	7	20
N25	•	at Wisconsin	0	0

1917   5-2-1 (2-2-1)
O6	•	Kansas	22	0
O13	•	Oklahoma	44	0
O20		Wisconsin	7	0
O27		Purdue	27	0
N3	=	at Chicago	0	0
N17		at Ohio State	0	13
N24		Minnesota	6	27
N29	•	at Camp Funston	28	0

THE SCHOOLS

1918 — 5-2-0 (4-0-0)
O4	●	at Chanute Field	3	0
O12		Great Lakes NAS	0	7
O26		Municipal Pier	0	7
N2	●	at Iowa	19	0
N9	●	at Wisconsin	22	0
N16	●	Ohio State	13	0
N23	●	at Chicago	29	0

1919 — 6-1-0 (6-1-0)
O11	●	at Purdue	14	7
O18	●	Iowa	9	7
O25	●	Wisconsin	10	14
N1	●	Chicago	10	0
N8	●	at Minnesota	10	6
N15	●	Michigan	29	7
N22	●	at Ohio State	9	7

1920 — 5-2-0 (4-2-0)
O9	●	Drake	41	0
O16	●	Iowa	20	3
O23	●	at Michigan	7	6
O30	●	Minnesota	17	7
N6	●	at Chicago	3	0
N13	●	at Wisconsin	9	14
N20	●	Ohio State	0	7

1921 — 3-4-0 (1-4-0)
O8	●	South Dakota	52	0
O15		at Iowa	2	14
O22		Wisconsin	0	20
O29		Michigan	0	3
N5	●	DePauw	21	0
N12		Chicago	6	14
N19		at Ohio State	7	0

1922 — 2-5-0 (2-4-0)
O14		Butler	7	10
O21		Iowa	7	8
O28		at Michigan	0	24
N4	●	Northwestern	6	3
N11	●	at Wisconsin	3	0
N18		at Chicago	0	9
N25		Ohio State	3	6

1923 — 8-0-0 (5-0-0)
O6	●	Nebraska	24	7
O13	●	Butler	21	7
O20	●	at Iowa	9	6
O27	●	Northwestern CHI	29	0
N3	●	Chicago	7	0
N10	●	Wisconsin	10	0
N17	●	Mississippi State	27	0
N24	●	at Ohio State	9	0

1924 — 6-1-1 (3-1-1)
O4	●	at Nebraska	9	6
O11	●	Butler	40	10
O18	●	Michigan	39	14
O25	●	DePauw	45	0
N1	●	Iowa	36	0
N8	=	at Chicago	21	21
N15	●	at Minnesota	7	20
N22	●	Ohio State	7	0

1925 — 5-3-0 (2-2-0)
O3	●	Nebraska	0	14
O10	●	Butler	16	13
O17		at Iowa	10	12
O24		Michigan	0	3
O31	●	at Pennsylvania	24	2
N7	●	Chicago	13	6
N14	●	Wabash	21	0
N21	●	at Ohio State	14	9

1926 — 6-2-0 (2-2-0)
O2	●	Coe	27	0
O9	●	Butler	38	7
O16	●	Iowa	13	6
O23		at Michigan	0	13
O30	●	Pennsylvania	3	0
N6	●	at Chicago	7	0
N13	●	Wabash	27	13
N20		Ohio State	6	7

1927 — 7-0-1 (5-0-0)
O1	●	Bradley	19	0
O8	●	Butler	58	0
O15	=	Iowa State	12	12
O22	●	at Northwestern	7	6
O29	●	Michigan	14	0
N5	●	at Iowa	14	0
N12	●	Chicago	15	6
N19	●	at Ohio State	13	0

1928 — 7-1-0 (4-1-0)
O6	●	Bradley	33	6
O13	●	Coe	31	0
O20	●	Indiana	13	7
O27	●	Northwestern	6	0
N3		at Michigan	0	3
N10	●	at Butler	14	0
N17	●	at Chicago	40	0
N24		Ohio State	8	0

1929 — 6-1-1 (3-1-1)
O5	●	Kansas	25	0
O12	●	Bradley	45	0
O20	=	at Iowa	7	7
O26	●	Michigan	14	0
N2		at Northwestern	0	7
N9	●	Army	17	7
N16	●	Chicago	20	6
N23	●	at Ohio State	27	0

1930 — 3-5-0 (1-4-0)
O4	●	Iowa State	7	0
O11	●	Butler	27	0
O18		Northwestern	0	32
O25		at Michigan	7	15
N1		Purdue	0	25
N8		Army BRNX	0	13
N15	●	at Chicago	28	0
N22		Ohio State	9	12

1931 — 2-6-1 (0-6-1)
O3	●	St. Louis	20	6
O10		at Purdue	0	7
O17	●	Bradley	20	0
O24		Michigan	0	35
O31		at Northwestern	6	32
N7		Wisconsin	6	7
N14		Chicago	6	13
N21		at Ohio State	0	40
N26	=	Indiana CHI	0	0

1932 — 5-4-0 (2-4-0)
O1	●	Miami, Ohio	20	7
O1	●	Coe	13	0
O8	●	Bradley	20	0
O15		Northwestern	0	26
O22		at Michigan	0	32
O29	●	at Chicago	13	7
N5		at Wisconsin	12	20
N12	●	Indiana	18	6
N19		Ohio State	0	3

1933 — 5-3-0 (3-2-0)
S30	●	Drake	13	6
O7	●	at Washington, Mo.	21	6
O14	●	Wisconsin	21	0
O21		Army CLEV	0	6
N4	●	Michigan	6	7
N11	●	at Northwestern	3	0
N18	●	Chicago	7	0
N25		at Ohio State	6	7

1934 — 7-1-0 (4-1-0)
S29	●	Bradley	40	7
O6	●	at Washington, Mo.	12	7
O13	●	Ohio State	14	13
O27		at Michigan	7	6
N3	●	Army	7	0
N10	●	at Northwestern	14	3
N17		at Wisconsin	3	7
N24	●	at Chicago	6	0

1935 — 3-5-0 (1-4-0)
S28	●	Ohio U.	0	6
O5	●	Washington, Mo.	28	6
O12	●	at Southern Cal	19	0
O26		Iowa	0	19
N2		at Northwestern	3	10
N9	●	Michigan	3	0
N16		at Ohio State	0	6
N23		Chicago	6	7

1936 — 4-3-1 (2-2-1)
S26	●	DePaul	9	6
O3	●	Washington, Mo.	13	7
O10		Southern Cal	6	24
O17	=	at Iowa	0	0
O24		Northwestern	2	13
O31	●	at Michigan	9	6
N14		Ohio State	0	13
N21	●	at Chicago	18	7

1937 — 3-3-2 (2-3-0)
S25	●	Ohio U.	20	6
O2	=	DePaul	0	0
O9	=	Notre Dame	0	0
O16		at Indiana	6	13
O30		Michigan	6	7
N6	●	at Northwestern	6	0
N13		at Ohio State	0	19
N20		Chicago	21	0

1938 — 3-5-0 (2-3-0)
S24		Ohio U.	0	6
O1	●	DePaul	44	7
O8		Indiana	12	2
O15	●	at Notre Dame	6	14
O22		Northwestern	0	13
O29		at Michigan	0	14
N12		Ohio State	14	32
N19	●	at Chicago	34	0

1939 — 3-4-1 (3-3-0)
S30	=	Bradley	0	0
O14		at Southern Cal	0	26
O21		Indiana	6	7
O28		at Northwestern	0	13
N4	●	Michigan	16	7
N11	●	Wisconsin	7	0
N18		at Ohio State	0	21
N25		at Chicago	46	0

1940 — 1-7-0 (0-5-0)
O5	●	Bradley	31	0
O12		Southern Cal	7	13
O19		at Michigan	0	28
O26		Notre Dame	0	26
N2		at Wisconsin	6	13
N9		at Northwestern	14	32
N16		Ohio State	6	14
N23		at Iowa	7	18

1941 — 2-6-0 (0-5-0)
O4	●	Miami, Ohio	45	0
O11		at Minnesota	6	34
O18	●	Drake	40	0
O25		at Notre Dame	14	49
N1		Michigan	0	20
N8		Iowa	0	21
N15		at Ohio State	7	12
N22		at Northwestern	0	27

RAY ELIOT
1942-59 (.530)   83-73-11

1942 — 6-4-0 (3-2-0)
S26	●	South Dakota	46	0
O3	●	Butler	67	0
O10		Minnesota	20	13
O17	●	at Iowa	12	7
O24		Notre Dame	14	21
O31		at Michigan	14	28
N7	●	at Northwestern	14	7
N14		Ohio State CLEV	20	44
N21		Great Lakes NAS	0	6
N28	=	at Camp Grant	20	0

1943 — 3-7-0 (2-4-0)
S11		Camp Grant	0	23
S18		Iowa Pre-Flight	18	32
O2	●	at Purdue	21	40
O9	●	at Wisconsin	25	7
O16	●	Pittsburgh	33	25
O23		at Notre Dame	0	47
O30		Michigan	6	42
N6	●	at Iowa	19	10
N13		at Ohio State	26	29
N20		at Northwestern	6	53

1944 — 5-4-1 (3-3-0)
S16	●	Illinois St.	79	6
S23	●	Indiana	26	18
S30	=	at Great Lakes NAS	26	26
O7		Purdue	19	35
O14	●	Iowa	40	6
O21	●	at Pittsburgh	39	5
O28		Notre Dame	7	13
N11		at Michigan	0	14
N18		Ohio State CLEV	12	26
N25	●	at Northwestern	25	6

1945 — 2-6-1 (1-4-1)
S22	●	Pittsburgh	23	6
S29		at Notre Dame	0	7
O6		Indiana	0	6
O20	=	at Wisconsin	7	7
O27		Michigan	0	19
N3		Great Lakes NAS	6	12
N10	●	Iowa	48	7
N17		at Ohio State	2	27
N24		at Northwestern	7	13

1946 — 8-2-0 (6-1-0)
S21	●	at Pittsburgh	33	7
S28		Notre Dame	6	26
O5	●	Purdue	43	7
O12		at Indiana	7	14
O19	●	Wisconsin	27	21
O26		at Michigan	13	9
N2	●	at Iowa	7	0
N16		Ohio State	16	7
N23	●	at Northwestern	20	0

ROSE BOWL
| J1 | ● | UCLA | 45 | 14 |

1947 — 5-3-1 (3-3-0)
S27	●	Pittsburgh	14	0
O4		at Iowa	35	12
O11	=	Army BRNX	0	0
O18	●	Minnesota	40	13
O25		at Purdue	7	14
N1		Michigan	7	14
N8	●	Western Michigan	60	14
N15	●	at Ohio State	28	7
N22		Northwestern	13	28

1948 — 3-6-0 (2-5-0)
S25	●	Kansas State	40	0
O2		at Wisconsin	16	20
O9		Army	21	26
O16	●	at Minnesota	0	6
O23	●	Purdue	10	6
O30		at Michigan	20	28
N6	●	Iowa	14	0
N13		Ohio State	7	34
N20		at Northwestern	7	20

1949 — 3-4-2 (3-3-1)
S24		Iowa State	20	20
O1	=	Wisconsin	13	13
O8	●	at Iowa	20	14
O15		Missouri	20	27
O22	●	at Purdue	19	0
O29		Michigan	0	13
N5	●	Indiana	33	14
N12		at Ohio State	17	30
N19		Northwestern	7	9

1950 — 7-2-0 (4-2-0)
S30	●	Ohio U.	28	2
O7		Wisconsin	6	7
O13	●	at UCLA	14	6
O21	●	Washington	20	13
O28	●	Indiana	20	0
N4	●	at Michigan	7	0
N11	●	at Iowa	21	7
N18	●	Ohio State	14	7
N25	●	at Northwestern	7	14

1951 — 9-0-1 (5-0-1)
S29	●	UCLA	27	13
O6	●	Wisconsin	14	10
O13	●	at Syracuse	41	20
O20	●	at Washington	27	20
O27	●	at Indiana	21	0
N3		Michigan	7	0
N10	●	Iowa	40	13
N17	=	at Ohio State	0	0
N24	●	at Northwestern	3	0

ROSE BOWL
| J1 | ● | Stanford | 40 | 7 |

1952 — 4-5-0 (2-5-0)
S27	●	Iowa State	33	7
O4		at Wisconsin	6	20
O11	●	Washington	48	14
O18		at Minnesota	7	13
O25		Purdue	12	40
N1		at Michigan	22	13
N8	●	at Iowa	33	13
N15		Ohio State	7	27
N22		Northwestern	26	28

1953 — 7-1-1 (5-1-0)
S26	=	Nebraska	21	21
O3		Stanford	33	21
O10	●	at Ohio State	41	20
O17	●	Minnesota	27	7
O24	●	Syracuse	20	13
O31	●	Purdue	21	0
N7	●	Michigan	19	3
N14		at Wisconsin	7	34
N21	●	at Northwestern	39	14

350 ILLINOIS

THE SCHOOLS

1954 1-8-0 (0-6-0)

S25		Penn State	12	14
O2		at Stanford	2	12
O9		Ohio State	7	40
O16		at Minnesota	6	19
O23	●	Syracuse	34	6
O30		at Purdue	14	28
N6		at Michigan	7	14
N13		Wisconsin	14	27
N20		Northwestern	7	20

1955 5-3-1 (3-3-1)

S24	●	at California	20	13
O1	●	Iowa State	40	0
O8		at Ohio State	12	27
O15	●	Minnesota	21	13
O22		at Michigan State	7	21
O29		Purdue	0	13
N5	●	Michigan	25	6
N12	●	at Wisconsin	17	14
N19	=	at Northwestern	7	7

1956 2-5-2 (1-4-2)

S29	●	California	32	20
O6		at Washington	13	28
O13		Ohio State	6	26
O20		at Minnesota	13	16
O27	●	Michigan State	20	13
N3	=	at Purdue	7	7
N10		at Michigan	7	17
N17	=	Wisconsin	13	13
N24		at Northwestern	13	14

1957 4-5-0 (3-4-0)

S27		at UCLA	6	16
O5	●	Colgate	40	0
O12		at Ohio State	7	21
O19	●	Minnesota	34	13
O26		at Michigan State	14	19
N2		Purdue	6	21
N9	●	Michigan	20	19
N16		at Wisconsin	13	24
N23	●	Northwestern	27	0

1958 4-5-0 (4-3-0)

S27		UCLA	14	18
O4		at Duke	13	15
O11		Ohio State	13	19
O18	●	at Minnesota	20	8
O25	●	Michigan State	16	0
N1		at Purdue	8	31
N8	●	at Michigan	21	8
N15		Wisconsin	12	31
N22	●	Northwestern	27	20

1959 5-3-1 (4-2-1)

S26		at Indiana	0	20
O3	●	Army	20	14
O10	●	at Ohio State	9	0
O17	●	Minnesota	14	6
O24		Penn State CLEV	9	20
O31	=	Purdue	7	7
N7		Michigan	15	20
N14	●	at Wisconsin	9	6
N21	●	Northwestern	28	0

PETE ELLIOTT
1960-66 (.477) 31-34-1

1960 5-4-0 (3-4-0)

S24	●	Indiana	17	6
O1	●	West Virginia	33	0
O8		Ohio State	7	34
O15		at Minnesota	10	21
O22	●	Penn State	10	8
O29	●	at Purdue	14	12
N5		at Michigan	7	8
N12	●	Wisconsin	35	14
N19		at Northwestern	7	14

1961 0-9-0 (0-7-0)

S30		Washington	7	20
O7		Northwestern	7	28
O14		at Ohio State	0	44
O21		Minnesota	0	33
O28		at Southern Cal	10	14
N4		Purdue	9	23
N11		Michigan	6	38
N18		at Wisconsin	7	55
N25		at Michigan State	7	34

1962 2-7-0 (2-5-0)

S29		at Washington	7	28
O6		at Northwestern	0	45
O13		Ohio State	15	51
O20		at Minnesota	0	17
O27		Southern Cal	16	28
N3	●	at Purdue	14	10
N10		at Michigan	10	14
N17		Wisconsin	6	35
N24	●	Michigan State	7	6

1963 8-1-1 (5-1-1)

S28	●	California	10	0
O5	●	Northwestern	10	9
O12	=	at Ohio State	20	20
O19	●	Minnesota	16	6
O25	●	at UCLA	18	12
N2	●	Purdue	41	21
N9		Michigan	8	14
N16	●	at Wisconsin	17	7
N28	●	at Michigan State	13	0
		ROSE BOWL		
J1	●	Washington	17	7

1964 6-3-0 (4-3-0)

S26	●	at California	20	14
O3	●	at Northwestern	17	6
O10		Ohio State	0	26
O17	●	at Minnesota	14	0
O24	●	UCLA	26	7
O31		at Purdue	14	26
N7		at Michigan	6	21
N14	●	Wisconsin	29	0
N21	●	Michigan State	16	0

1965 6-4-0 (4-3-0)

S18		Oregon State	10	12
S25	●	SMU	42	0
O2		at Michigan State	12	22
O9		at Ohio State	14	28
O16	●	Indiana	34	13
O23	●	Duke	28	14
O30	●	Purdue	21	0
N6		Michigan	3	23
N13	●	at Wisconsin	51	0
N20	●	at Northwestern	20	6

1966 4-6-0 (4-3-0)

S17		at SMU	7	26
S24		Missouri	14	21
O1		Michigan State	10	26
O8	●	Ohio State	10	9
O15	●	at Indiana	24	10
O22		Stanford	3	6
O29		at Purdue	21	25
N5	●	at Michigan	28	21
N12	●	Wisconsin	49	14
N19		at Northwestern	7	35

JIM VALEK
1967-70 (.200) 8-32

1967 4-6-0 (3-4-0)

S23		at Florida	0	14
S30	●	Pittsburgh	34	6
O7		Indiana	7	20
O14		Minnesota	7	10
O21		Notre Dame	7	47
O28	●	at Ohio State	17	13
N4		Purdue	9	42
N11		Michigan	14	21
N18	●	at Northwestern	27	21
N25	●	at Iowa	21	19

1968 1-9-0 (1-6-0)

S21		Kansas	7	47
S28		Missouri	0	44
O5		at Indiana	14	28
O12		at Minnesota	10	17
O19		at Notre Dame	8	58
O26		Ohio State	24	31
N2		at Purdue	17	35
N9		at Michigan	0	36
N16	●	Northwestern	14	0
N23		Iowa	13	37

1969 0-10-0 (0-7-0)

S20		Washington State	18	19
S27		Missouri STL	6	37
O4		at Iowa State	20	48
O11		Northwestern	6	10
O18		at Indiana	20	41
O25		at Ohio State	0	41
N1		Purdue	22	49
N8		Michigan	0	57
N15		at Wisconsin	14	55
N22		Iowa	0	40

1970 3-7-0 (1-6-0)

S19	●	Oregon	20	16
S26		Tulane	9	23
O3	●	Syracuse	27	0
O10		at Northwestern	0	48
O17		Indiana	24	30
O24		Ohio State	29	48
O31	●	at Purdue	23	21
N7		at Michigan	0	42
N14		Wisconsin	17	29
N21		at Iowa	16	22

BOB BLACKMAN
1971-76 (.447) 29-36-1

1971 5-6-0 (5-3-0)

S11		at Michigan State	0	10
S18		North Carolina	0	27
S25		at Southern Cal	0	28
O2		Washington	14	52
O9		Ohio State	10	24
O16		at Michigan	6	35
O23	●	Purdue	21	7
O30	●	Northwestern	24	7
N6	●	at Indiana	22	21
N13	●	at Wisconsin	35	27
N20	●	Iowa	31	0

1972 3-8-0 (3-5-0)

S16		Michigan State	0	24
S23		Southern Cal	20	55
S30		at Washington	11	31
O7		Penn State	17	35
O14		at Ohio State	7	26
O21		Michigan	7	31
O28		at Purdue	14	20
N4	●	at Northwestern	43	13
N11	●	Indiana	37	20
N18	●	Wisconsin	27	7
N25		at Iowa	14	15

1973 5-6-0 (4-4-0)

S15	●	at Indiana	28	14
S22	●	at California	27	7
S29		West Virginia	10	17
O6		Stanford	0	24
O13	●	Purdue	15	13
O20	●	at Michigan State	6	3
O27	●	Iowa	50	0
N3		Ohio State	0	30
N10		at Michigan	6	21
N17		Minnesota	16	19
N24		at Northwestern	6	9

1974 6-4-1 (4-3-1)

S14	●	Indiana	16	0
S21	●	at Stanford	41	7
S28	●	Washington State	21	19
O5		California	14	31
O12	●	at Purdue	27	23
O19	=	Michigan State	21	21
O26		at Iowa	12	14
N2		at Ohio State	7	49
N9		Michigan	6	14
N16	●	at Minnesota	17	14
N23	●	Northwestern	28	14

1975 5-6-0 (4-4-0)

S13	●	at Iowa	27	12
S20		Missouri	20	30
S27		at Texas A&M	13	43
O4	●	Washington State	27	21
O11	●	Minnesota	42	23
O18		Purdue	24	26
O25	●	at Michigan State	21	19
N1		at Wisconsin	9	18
N8		Ohio State	3	40
N15		Michigan	15	21
N22	●	at Northwestern	28	7

1976 5-6-0 (4-4-0)

S11	●	Iowa	24	6
S18	●	at Missouri	31	6
S25		Baylor	19	34
O2		Texas A&M	7	14
O9		at Minnesota	14	29
O16	●	at Purdue	21	17
O23		Michigan State	23	31
O30	●	Wisconsin	31	25
N6		at Ohio State	10	42
N13		at Michigan	7	38
N20	●	Northwestern	48	6

GARY MOELLER
1977-79 (.277) 6-24-3

1977 3-8-0 (2-6-0)

S10		Michigan	9	37
S17	●	Missouri	11	7
S24		at Stanford	24	37
O1		Syracuse	20	30
O8		at Wisconsin	0	26
O15	●	at Purdue	29	22
O22	●	Indiana	21	7
O29		at Michigan State	20	49
N5		Ohio State	0	35
N12		Minnesota	0	21
N19		at Northwestern	7	21

1978 1-8-2 (0-6-2)

S9	=	Northwestern	0	0
S16		at Michigan	0	31
S23		Stanford	10	35
S30	●	at Syracuse	28	14
O7		at Missouri	3	45
O14	=	Wisconsin	20	20
O21		Purdue	0	13
O28		at Indiana	10	31
N4		Michigan State	19	59
N11		at Ohio State	7	45
N18		at Minnesota	6	24

1979 2-8-1 (1-6-1)

S8		at Michigan State	16	33
S15		Missouri	6	14
S22	●	at Air Force	27	19
S29		Navy	12	13
O6		Iowa	7	13
O13		at Purdue	14	28
O20		Michigan	7	27
O27	=	at Minnesota	17	17
N3		Ohio State	7	44
N10		Indiana	14	45
N17	●	at Northwestern	29	13

MIKE WHITE
1980-87 (.533) 47-41-3

1980 3-7-1 (3-5-0)

S6	●	Northwestern	35	9
S13	●	Michigan State	20	17
S20		at Missouri	7	52
S27	=	Air Force	20	20
O4		Mississippi State	21	28
O11	●	at Iowa	20	14
O18		Purdue	20	45
O25		at Michigan	14	45
N1		Minnesota	18	21
N8		at Ohio State	42	49
N15		at Indiana	24	26

1981 7-4-0 (6-3-0)

S5		at Pittsburgh	6	26
S12	●	at Michigan State	27	17
S19	●	Syracuse	17	14
O3	●	Minnesota	38	29
O10		at Purdue	20	44
O17		at Ohio State	27	34
O24	●	Wisconsin	23	21
O31	●	Iowa	24	7
N7		at Michigan	21	70
N14	●	Indiana	35	14
N21	●	at Northwestern	49	12

1982 7-5-0 (6-3-0)

S4	●	Northwestern	49	13
S11	●	Michigan State	23	16
S18	●	at Syracuse	47	10
S25		Pittsburgh	3	20
O2	●	at Minnesota	42	24
O9	●	Purdue	38	34
O16		Ohio State	21	26
O23	●	at Wisconsin	29	28
O30		at Iowa	13	14
N6		Michigan	10	16
N13	●	at Indiana	48	7
		LIBERTY BOWL		
D29		Alabama	15	21

1983 10-2-0 (9-0-0)

S10		at Missouri	18	28
S17	●	Stanford	17	7
S24	●	at Michigan State	20	10
O1	●	Iowa	33	0
O8	●	at Wisconsin	27	15
O15	●	Ohio State	17	13
O22	●	at Purdue	35	21
O29	●	Michigan	16	6
N5	●	at Minnesota	50	23
N12	●	Indiana	49	21
N19	●	at Northwestern	56	24
		ROSE BOWL		
J2		UCLA	9	45

1984 7-4-0 (6-3-0)

S1	●	Northwestern	24	16
S8	●	Missouri	30	24
S15		at Stanford	19	34
S22	●	Michigan State	40	7
S29		at Iowa	16	21
O6	●	Wisconsin	22	6
O13		at Ohio State	38	45
O20	●	Purdue	34	20
O27		at Michigan	18	26
N3	●	Minnesota	48	3
N10	●	Indiana IND	34	7

1985   6-5-1 (5-2-1)

S7		Southern Cal	10	20
S14	●	So. Illinois	28	25
S21		at Nebraska	25	52
O5	●	Ohio State	31	28
O12		at Purdue	24	30
O19	●	at Michigan State	30	17
O26	●	Wisconsin	38	25
N2	=	Michigan	3	3
N9		at Iowa	0	59
N16	●	Indiana	41	24
N23	●	at Northwestern	45	20
PEACH BOWL				
D31		Army	29	31

1986   4-7-0 (3-5-0)

S6	●	Louisville	23	0
S13		at Southern Cal	16	31
S20		Nebraska	14	59
O4		at Ohio State	0	14
O11	●	Purdue	34	27
O18		Michigan State	21	29
O25		at Wisconsin	9	15
N1		at Michigan	13	69
N8	●	Iowa	20	16
N15	●	at Indiana	21	16
N22		Northwestern	18	23

1987   3-7-1 (2-5-1)

S5		at North Carolina	14	34
S12		Arizona State	7	21
S19	●	East Carolina	20	10
O3		Ohio State	6	10
O10		at Purdue	3	9
O17	●	Wisconsin	16	14
O24	=	at Michigan State	14	14
O31		Minnesota	27	17
N7		at Indiana	22	34
N14		Michigan	14	17
N21		at Northwestern	10	28

1988   6-5-1 (5-2-1)

S3		Washington State	7	44
S10		at Arizona State	16	21
S17	●	Utah	35	24
O1		at Ohio State	31	12
O8	●	Purdue	20	0
O15	●	at Wisconsin	34	6
O22		Michigan State	21	28
O29	=	at Minnesota	27	27
N5	●	Indiana	21	20
N12		at Michigan	9	38
N19	●	Northwestern	14	9
ALL-AMERICAN BOWL				
D29		Florida	10	14

1989   10-2-0 (7-1-0)

S4	●	at Southern Cal	14	13
S16		at Colorado	7	38
S23	●	Utah State	41	2
O7		Ohio State	34	14
O14		at Purdue	14	2
O21		at Michigan State	14	10
O28	●	Wisconsin	32	9
N4	●	at Iowa	31	7
N11		Michigan	10	24
N18	●	Indiana	41	28
N25	●	at Northwestern	63	14
CITRUS BOWL				
J1	●	Virginia	31	21

1990   8-4-0 (6-2-0)

S8		at Arizona	16	28
S15	●	Colorado	23	22
S22	●	So. Illinois	56	21
O6	●	at Ohio State	31	20
O13	●	Purdue	34	0
O20	●	Michigan State	15	13
O27	●	at Wisconsin	21	3
N3		Iowa	28	54
N10		at Michigan	17	22
N17	●	at Indiana	24	10
N24	●	Northwestern	28	23
HALL OF FAME BOWL				
J1		Clemson	0	30

1991   6-6-0 (4-4-0)

A31	●	East Carolina	38	31
S14		at Missouri	19	23
S21	●	Houston	51	10
O5		Minnesota	24	3
O12	●	Ohio State	10	7
O19		at Iowa	21	24
O26		at Northwestern	11	17
N2	●	Wisconsin	22	6
N9	●	at Purdue	41	14
N16		Michigan	0	20
N23		at Michigan State	24	27
SUN BOWL				
D31		UCLA	3	6

1992   6-5-1 (4-3-1)

S5	●	Northern Illinois	30	14
S12	●	Missouri	24	17
S19		at Houston	13	31
O3		at Minnesota	17	18
O10	●	at Ohio State	18	16
O17		Iowa	14	24
O24		Northwestern	26	27
O31	●	at Wisconsin	13	12
N7		Purdue	20	17
N14	=	at Michigan	22	22
N21	●	Michigan State	14	10
HOLIDAY BOWL				
D30		Hawaii	17	27

1993   5-6-0 (5-3-0)

S11		at Missouri	3	31
S18		Arizona	14	16
S25		Oregon	7	13
O2	●	at Purdue	28	10
O9		Ohio State	12	20
O16	●	at Iowa	49	3
O23	●	at Michigan	24	21
O30	●	Northwestern	20	13
N6	●	Minnesota	23	20
N13		at Penn State	14	28
N20		Wisconsin	10	35

1994   7-5-0 (4-4-0)

S1		Washington State *CHI*	9	10
S10	●	Missouri	42	0
S17	●	Northern Illinois	34	10
O1		Purdue	16	22
O8	●	at Ohio State	24	10
O15	●	Iowa	47	7
O22		Michigan	14	19
O29	●	at Northwestern	28	7
N5	●	at Minnesota	21	17
N12		Penn State	31	35
N19		at Wisconsin	13	19
LIBERTY BOWL				
D31	●	East Carolina	30	0

1995   5-5-1 (3-4-1)

S2		Michigan	14	38
S9		at Oregon	31	34
S16	●	Arizona	9	7
S23	●	East Carolina	7	0
O7	●	at Indiana	17	10
O14		Michigan State	21	27
O28		Northwestern	14	17
N4	●	at Iowa	26	7
N11		at Ohio State	3	41
N18	●	Minnesota	48	14
N25	=	at Wisconsin	3	3

1996   2-9 (1-7)

A31		at Michigan	8	20
S7		Southern Cal	3	55
S14		at Arizona	0	41
S21	●	Akron	38	7
O5		Indiana	46	43
O12		at Michigan State	14	42
O26		at Northwestern	24	27
N2		Iowa	21	31
N9		Ohio State	0	48
N16		at Minnesota	21	23
N23		Wisconsin	15	35

1997   0-11 (0-8)

S6		Southern Miss	7	24
S13		at Louisville	14	26
S20		Washington State	22	35
S27		at Iowa	10	38
O4		Penn State	6	41
O11		at Wisconsin	7	31
O25		Purdue	3	48
N1		at Indiana	6	23
N8		Northwestern	21	34
N15		at Ohio State	6	41
N22		Michigan State	17	27

1998   3-8 (2-6)

S5		at Washington State	13	20
S12	●	Middle Tennessee	48	20
S19		Louisville	9	35
S26		Iowa	14	37
O3	●	at Northwestern	13	10
O10		Ohio State	0	41
O17		Wisconsin	3	37
O24		at Purdue	9	42
O31		at Penn State	0	27
N7	●	Indiana	31	16
N21		at Michigan State	9	41

1999   8-4 (4-4)

S4		Arkansas State	41	3
S11	●	San Diego State	38	10
S18	●	at Louisville	41	36
S25		Michigan State	10	27
O2	●	at Indiana	31	34
O16		Minnesota	7	37
O23	●	at Michigan	35	29
O30		Penn State	7	27
N6	●	at Iowa	40	24
N13	●	at Ohio State	46	20
N20	●	Northwestern	29	7
MICRON PC BOWL				
D30	●	Virginia	63	21

2000   5-6 (2-6)

S2	●	Middle Tennessee	35	6
S9		at San Diego State	49	13
S16	●	California	17	15
S23		Michigan	31	35
S30		at Minnesota	10	44
O14	●	Iowa	31	0
O21		at Penn State	25	39
O28		at Michigan State	10	14
N4	●	Indiana	42	35
N11		Ohio State	21	24
N18		at Northwestern	23	61

2001   10-2 (7-1)

S1	●	at California	44	17
S8	●	Northern Illinois	17	12
S22	●	Louisville	34	10
S29		at Michigan	20	45
O6	●	Minnesota	25	14
O13	●	at Indiana	35	14
O20	●	Wisconsin	42	35
N3	●	at Purdue	38	13
N10		Penn State	33	28
N17	●	at Ohio State	34	22
N24	●	Northwestern	34	28
SUGAR BOWL				
J1		LSU	34	47

2002   5-7 (4-4)

A31		Missouri *StL*	20	33
S7		at Southern Miss	20	23
S14	●	Arkansas State	59	7
S21		San Jose State	35	38
S28		Michigan	28	45
O3		at Minnesota	10	31
O12	●	Purdue	38	31
O26	●	Indiana	45	14
N2		at Penn State	7	18
N9	●	at Wisconsin	37	20
N16		Ohio State	16	23
N23	●	at Northwestern	31	24

2003   1-11 (0-8)

A30		StLMissouri	15	22
S6	●	Illinois St.	49	22
S13		at UCLA	3	6
S20		California	24	31
S27		Wisconsin	20	38
O4		at Purdue	10	43
O11		Michigan State	14	49
O18		at Michigan	14	56
O25		Minnesota	10	36
N1		at Iowa	10	41
N8		at Indiana	14	17
N22		Northwestern	20	37

2004   3-8 (1-7)

S4	●	Florida A&M	52	13
S11		UCLA	17	35
S18	●	Western Michigan	30	27
S25		Purdue	30	38
O2		at Wisconsin	7	24
O9		at Michigan State	25	38
O16		Michigan	19	30
O23		at Minnesota	0	45
O30		Iowa	13	23
N6	●	Indiana	26	22
N20		at Northwestern	21	28

INDIANA

BY TODD JONES

FOOTBALL STRUGGLED FOR ACCEPTance at Indiana University from the very start, long before the sport became overshadowed by the school's basketball success. IU first played football in 1887, but the Hoosiers had only three games in three years. Interest improved but never reached the passionate levels seen at other Big Ten schools. From 1931 to 1933, the Hoosiers were coached by E.C. "Billy" Hayes, a famous track and field coach, at the request of IU president William L. Bryan. Bo McMillin is the only one of 15 Indiana coaches since 1922 to finish his career in Bloomington with a winning record. Still, there have been some magical moments at IU— produced by exciting players such as Bill Hillenbrand, Pete Pihos, George Taliaferro, John Isenbarger, Anthony Thompson, Vaughn Dunbar and Antwaan Randle El.

TRADITION Indiana and Purdue decided 34 years after they first played that they should "discuss the possibility of undertaking a worthy joint enterprise on behalf of the two schools." Alumni clubs from both schools formed a joint committee, and IU's Dr. Clarence Jones suggested a trophy for the winner of the annual football game. The schools agreed on an old oaken bucket. IU's Wiley J. Huddle and Fritz Ernst of Purdue found a suitable bucket on Bruner Farm in southern Indiana. Besides the Old Oaken Bucket, the Hoosiers also play for a trophy against Michigan State. Since 1950, the winner has been awarded the Old Brass Spittoon, which came from one of Michigan's earliest trading posts and supposedly was around when both schools were formed. Indiana and Kentucky used to play for the Bourbon Barrel, but they ended that tradition in 1999. The 1991 season was the first time in 23 years IU had possession of the Bourbon Barrel, the Old Brass Spittoon and the Old Oaken Bucket all at once.

BEST PLAYER Indiana fans attending a basketball game against Kentucky broke into a chorus of boos when it was announced on the Hoosier Dome scoreboard that Houston QB Andre Ware had won the 1989 Heisman Trophy. Such was the love for native son Anthony Thompson, runner-up in that Heisman balloting and the Hoosiers' all-time leading rusher (5,299 yards from 1986 to 1989). The running back from Terre Haute had led the NCAA in rushing (1,793 yards) and scoring (154 points) as a senior in 1989. He was named the Walter Camp Foundation's Player of the Year and the AFCA "Coaches' Choice" Player of the Year, and he won the Maxwell Award as the nation's finest college player. Thompson was Big Ten rushing champion and first-team All-America in his junior and senior seasons, when he totaled 3,579 rushing yards and 50 touchdowns. He set a then-NCAA record in 1989 with 377 rushing yards against Wisconsin. He held the NCAA record

PROFILE

Indiana University, Bloomington
Bloomington, Ind.
Founded: 1820
Enrollment: 29,549
Colors: Cream and Crimson
Nickname: Hoosiers
Stadium: Memorial Stadium
　　Opened in 1960
　　AstroPlay; 52,180 capacity
First football game: 1887
All-time record: 419–574–45 (.425)
Bowl record: 3–5
Big Ten Conference championships: 2
(1 outright)
First-round NFL draftees: 11
Website: www.iuhoosiers.com

THE BEST OF TIMES

The 1945 Hoosiers went 9–0–1 to win the Big Ten title, and finished No. 4 in the AP poll as Bo McMillin was named national coach of the year. But '67 ranks as the most magical season because the Hoosiers, 1–8–1 the previous year, rebounded under coach John Pont to go 9–2, win the Big Ten and earn the school's first bowl trip, losing the Rose Bowl to USC, 14-3.

THE WORST OF TIMES

Clyde Smith and former Notre Dame star Bernie Crimmins struggled as IU coaches. Under them the Hoosiers went 21–59–1 with nine straight losing seasons from 1948 to 1956.

CONFERENCE

Joined Western Conference in 1900. The Western Conference had been known as the Big Ten since 1917, but didn't officially change its name until 1987.

DISTINGUISHED ALUMNI

Isiah Thomas; Dick Enberg; John Mellencamp; Joshua Bell, world-renowned violinist; Mark Cuban, owner Dallas Mavericks; Kevin Kline, actor; Jane Pauley, broadcast journalist

FIGHT SONG

INDIANA, OUR INDIANA
Indiana, our Indiana
Indiana, we're all for you!
We will fight for the cream and crimson
For the glory of old IU
Never daunted, we cannot falter
In the battle, we're tried and true
Indiana, our Indiana,
Indiana we're all for you! I-U!

for career touchdowns (65) until 1998, and held the Big Ten record for career points (412) until 1999. Thompson is the only player to lead Indiana in rushing four seasons and he took the Hoosiers to three consecutive bowl games.

History books easily explain why Indiana fans detest in-state foe Purdue.

BEST COACH Reaction to defeat is a defining moment in Bill Mallory's coaching career at Indiana. His Hoosiers went into Michigan on Oct. 19, 1991, and lost valiantly to the No. 4-ranked Wolverines 24-16. Immediately after the defeat, Mallory ripped the game officials with so much venom that the Big Ten suspended him for one game. The tirade showed Mallory wasn't going to allow his Hoosiers to simply accept their role as cannon fodder for the league's big guns. He would fight for his players and do so in a fiery manner that belied IU's low-key football history. In his 13 seasons at Bloomington, Mallory won more games (68) than any other Indiana coach. He took the Hoosiers to six bowl games in an eight-year span. In the end, Mallory became a victim of the IU expectations he had raised himself. On Oct. 31, 1996, athletic director Clarence Doninger announced Mallory would be replaced at the end of the 1996 season. Three weeks later, the IU players carried Mallory off the field after his final game as their coach, a 33-16 win at Purdue. He went 68–78–3 from 1984 to 1996. Indiana hasn't had a winning season since 1994.

BEST TEAM The end of World War II had a direct effect on Indiana winning its first Big Ten championship in 1945, which is still the school's only outright conference title. Hoosiers coach Bo McMillin picked up two extra players after opening the season with a 13-7 win at Michigan. The military allowed Howard Brown, who was stationed in Europe, to return to Bloomington to play on 60 days' leave. The guard earned second-team All-America honors that season. Pete Pihos, an All-America end in 1943, returned to IU on permanent leave from the military. He earned All-America honors again, this time as a fullback, and finished sixth in the Heisman voting. Other top players were running back George Taliaferro, end Bob Ravensberg, guard Howard Brown, quarterback Ben Raimondi, tackle Russ Deal and end Ted Kluszewski, later a major league baseball slugger. Northwestern tied IU 7-7 in Week 2, but the Hoosiers then won their final eight games. The final three wins were shutouts by a combined score of 94-0 over No. 20 Minnesota, Pittsburgh and No. 18 Purdue. Indiana outscored its opponents 279-56 while going 9–0–1 as the only undefeated team in school history.

BIGGEST GAME Indiana's first bowl game is still the school's only Rose Bowl appearance, and it came a season after a 1–8–1 finish. Hoosiers coach John Pont took his

RECORDS

RUSHING YARDS
GAME
377 Anthony Thompson vs. Wisconsin, Nov. 11, 1989 (52 att.)
SEASON
1,805 Vaughn Dunbar, 1991 (364 att.)
CAREER
5,299 Anthony Thompson, 1986-89 (1,161 att.)

PASSING YARDS
GAME
408 Jay Rodgers vs. Ball State, Sept. 13, 1997 (27 of 39)
SEASON
2,627 Trent Green, 1991 (200 of 339)
CAREER
7,469 Antwaan Randle El, 1998-2001 (528 of 1,060)

RECEIVING YARDS
GAME
285 Thomas Lewis vs. Penn State, Nov. 6, 1993 (12 rec.)
SEASON
1,265 Ernie Jones, 1987 (66 rec.)
CAREER
2,361 Ernie Jones, 1984-87 (133 rec.)

POINTS
GAME
36 Levron Williams vs. Wisconsin, Oct. 6, 2001 (6 TDs)
SEASON
156 Anthony Thompson, 1988 (26 TDs)
CAREER
412 Anthony Thompson, 1986-89 (68 TDs, 2 two-pt. conv.)

CONSENSUS ALL-AMERICANS
1942 Billy Hillenbrand, B
1944 John Tavener, C
1945 Bob Ravensberg, E
1988-89 Anthony Thompson, RB
1991 Vaughn Dunbar, RB

surprising 9–1 team, along with 20,000 Indiana fans, to Pasadena to meet No. 1-ranked Southern California on New Year's Day 1968. For the first time, the Rose Bowl parade and game were shown via satellite to other parts of the world. USC junior tailback O.J. Simpson thrilled the crowd of 102,946 by rushing for 128 yards and 2 TDs in an otherwise defensive game won by Southern Cal 14-3.

BIGGEST UPSET The Hoosiers had won just 14 games from 1960 through 1966 when the unthinkable happened: they entered a game with a chance to earn a Rose Bowl berth. One year after going 1–8–1, Indiana entered the 1967 regular-season finale—the annual grudge game against Purdue—with an 8–1 record. The Hoosiers had earned the name the Cardiac Kids for winning six games by seven points or less, but their magic carpet ride was expected to end against Purdue. One week earlier, IU had lost 33-7 at Minnesota to fall from No. 5 to No. 14. The Boilermakers were the nation's No. 3-ranked team and came to Bloomington as 14-point favorites. They didn't, however, have an answer for Indiana running back Terry Cole. He rushed for 155 yards on 15 carries. Indiana won another thriller, 19-14, to earn its first bowl game berth as Big Ten trichampion.

HEARTBREAKER The Purdue game of 1980 still rankles the IU faithful. Indiana trailed 24-17 when it put together a 65-yard drive on its final possession of the game. The visiting Hoosiers converted three fourth-down situations. The third time was the charm as quarterback Tim Clifford threw a 10-yard touchdown pass to Steve Corso with 17 seconds remaining. Indiana coach Lee Corso decided his team had come too far to settle for a tie. He ordered a two-point conversion attempt, but the pass was deflected incomplete. Purdue escaped with a 24-23 win.

WILDEST FINISH Indiana played gallantly as homecoming opponent for Michigan in 1979. Trailing 21-14, IU quarterback Tim Clifford threw a two-yard TD pass to Dave Harangody with 55 seconds remaining in the game. Indiana radio announcer Don Fischer became so excited he set himself on fire when cigarette ash burned the sleeve of his sports coat. He kept on announcing the game. An extra-point kick tied the score. Michigan took the kickoff and drove to IU's 45-yard line. Six seconds remained. Wolverine QB John Wangler then completed a pass to Anthony Carter near the 20. Indiana defenders Bart Ramsey and Stoner Gray hit the skinny freshman, but he

bounced off and headed into the end zone. IU safety Tim Wilbur grabbed Carter but couldn't stop him. "Oh my god, Carter scored!" screamed Michigan radio announcer Bob Ufer as the Wolverines won 27-21.

BEST COMEBACK Iowa bolted to a 26-3 halftime lead over Indiana on Sept. 8, 1979. The Hawkeyes should have recalled their game against IU from two years earlier, when freshman QB Tim Clifford came off the bench and rallied the Hoosiers from a 14-point deficit to a 24-21 win. Now a junior, Clifford once again brought IU back against Iowa. He threw for two touchdowns, the second a 66-yarder to Lonnie Johnson with 58 seconds remaining. The Hoosiers pulled out a 30-26 victory. No other Indiana team has ever overcome such a large deficit to win.

STADIUM Jordan Field was home to the Hoosiers for 38 years before the original Memorial Stadium opened in 1925. Three years of fund-raising produced $250,000 to finance the building of that 22,000-seat horseshoe, named in honor of IU students and alumni who served in World War I. The Hoosiers played at Memorial Stadium for 35 years. Indiana began building new athletic facilities in the late 1950s on a 160-acre site on the northern edge of campus. A $1.5 million football stadium opened in 1960 and was originally named Indiana University Stadium, although it was often referred to as the 17th Street Stadium. Indiana changed the official name to Memorial Stadium in 1971 to honor the school's veterans of World War I, World War II and subsequent wars. The stadium capacity is 52,180.

RIVAL History books easily explain why Indiana fans detest in-state foe Purdue. The Boilermakers beat the Hoosiers 60-0 in their first game in 1891 and followed that up with a 68-0 win the next year and a 64-0 win the year after that. Indiana forfeited the 1894 game and lost two more to the Boilermakers before breaking through with a 17-5 win in 1899. The Hoosiers have won just 15 of 56 games in the series since 1948. No wonder the basketball rivalry is more intriguing.

NICKNAME There are over 30 theories about the origin of the word Hoosier but none of them is conclusive. Historians agree that the nickname for Indiana residents was popularized in the 1800s by novels, poetry and newspaper articles. Former governor Robert D. Orr may have best summed up all the conjecture. In a 1987 letter to *The Wall Street Journal*, Orr wrote, "Those unfortunate

souls who, for some reason, live elsewhere may continue to speculate as to the origin of our name; and we Hoosiers will continue to enjoy their doing so."

UNIFORMS Indiana officially made cream and crimson its school colors in 1888, but red and white have also been part of the uniforms. During the early 1960s, IU was one of the first schools to use something other than stripes or numerals on its helmets. From 1967 through 1996, the Hoosiers' headgear was varying shades of red and (except for 1983) sported a white block "I" on the side. They wore black helmets from 1997 to 2001, though when the team's fortunes didn't change, they switched back to crimson helmets in 2002 with a white interlocking "IU" on the side.

LORE Lee Corso left them laughing during his 10 seasons as Indiana coach. Once, with his team mired in a losing streak, he emerged from a coffin on his coach's TV show and said, "We aren't dead yet." Corso also paused during a game against Ohio State to have his photograph taken with the scoreboard behind him showing the Hoosiers leading the Buckeyes. After a win over Purdue, he took the Old Oaken Bucket home and slept with it in his bed. Few were smiling, however, when his tenure as Hoosiers coach got off to an infamous start on Sept. 15, 1973. Corso had his players warm up in the fieldhouse before the game and then board a double-decker bus to be driven onto the field. The team's bus was nearly late for the game's opening kickoff because of traffic. Illinois won 28-14.

QUOTE "This has got to be the darkest day for Ohio State football since I've been associated with it." —Ohio State coach Earle Bruce after Indiana beat the Buckeyes 31-10 in 1987, the Hoosiers' first victory over Ohio State in 36 years

INDIANA ANNUAL STATISTICAL LEADERS

YR	RUSHING	YDS	ATT	AVG	PASSING	ATT	CMP	PCT	YDS	RECEIVING	REC	YDS	AVG
1963	Tom Nowatzke	756	160	4.7	Richie Badar	94	55	.59	679	Bill Malinchak	25	353	14.1
1964	Tom Nowatzke	545	150	3.6	Richie Badar	245	121	.49	1,571	Bill Malinchak	46	634	13.8
1965	Terry Cole	286	91	3.1	Frank Stavroff	159	74	.47	1,045	Bill Malinchak	44	699	15.9
1966	Mike Krivoshia	675	179	3.8	Frank Stavroff	224	119	.53	1,406	Bill Couch	45	546	12.1
1967	John Isenbarger	579	120	4.8	Harry Gonso	143	67	.47	931	Jade Butcher	38	654	17.2
1968	John Isenbarger	669	130	5.1	Harry Gonso	163	76	.47	1,109	Jade Butcher	44	713	16.2
1969	John Isenbarger	1,217	233	5.2	Harry Gonso	207	107	.52	1,336	Jade Butcher	37	552	14.9
1970	John Motil	358	101	3.5	Ted McNulty	126	55	.44	488	John Andrews	29	268	9.2
1971	Ken St. Pierre	760	181	4.2	Ted McNulty	201	95	.47	1,140	Alan Dick	25	312	12.5
1972	Ken Starling	781	196	4.0	Ted McNulty	132	74	.56	906	Glenn Scolnick	53	727	13.7
1973	Ken Starling	676	180	3.8	Willie Jones	135	76	.56	881	Trent Smock	36	505	14.0
1974	Courtney Snyder	1,254	291	4.3	Terry Jones	220	129	.59	1,347	Trent Smock	31	549	17.7
1975	Courtney Snyder	1,103	248	4.4	Terry Jones	135	65	.48	787	Trent Smock	25	427	17.1
1976	Mike Harkrader	1,003	192	5.2	Scott Arnett	93	42	.45	398	Keith Calvin	26	319	12.3
1977	Ric Enis	978	199	4.9	Scott Arnett	151	73	.48	796	Keith Calvin	41	604	14.7
1978	Mike Harkrader	880	198	4.4	Tim Clifford	130	60	.46	726	Mike Friede	17	412	24.2
1979	Mike Harkrader	807	210	3.8	Tim Clifford	288	160	.56	2,078	Bob Stephenson	49	564	11.5
1980	Lonnie Johnson	1,075	200	5.4	Tim Clifford	198	105	.53	1,391	Bob Stephenson	26	337	13.0
1981	Tim Hines	271	67	4.0	Babe Laufenberg	252	144	.57	1,788	Bob Stephenson	32	230	7.2
1982	Orlando Brown	580	136	4.3	Babe Laufenberg	364	217	.60	2,468	Duane Gunn	35	764	21.8
1983	Orlando Brown	312	72	4.3	Steve Bradley	355	182	.51	2,298	Duane Gunn	50	815	16.3
1984	Bobby Howard	268	78	3.4	Steve Bradley	402	208	.52	2,544	Len Kenebrew	41	750	18.3
1985	Bobby Howard	967	194	5.0	Steve Bradley	266	142	.53	1,737	Kenny Allen	55	929	16.9
1986	Anthony Thompson	806	191	4.2	Dave Kramme	180	98	.54	1,334	Tony Buford	26	416	16.0
1987	Anthony Thompson	1,014	257	3.9	Dave Schnell	207	121	.58	1,707	Ernie Jones	66	1,265	19.2
1988	Anthony Thompson	1,686	355	4.7	Dave Schnell	225	119	.53	1,877	Rob Turner	36	814	22.6
1989	Anthony Thompson	1,793	358	5.0	Dave Schnell	258	146	.57	1,608	Eddie Thomas	38	559	14.7
1990	Vaughn Dunbar	1,224	250	4.9	Trent Green	128	60	.47	934	Rob Turner	33	717	21.7
1991	Vaughn Dunbar	1,805	364	5.0	Trent Green	339	200	.59	2,627	Eddie Thomas	54	687	12.7
1992	Brett Law	541	130	4.2	Trent Green	278	154	.55	1,780	Thomas Lewis	54	685	12.7
1993	Jermaine Chaney	716	186	3.8	John Paci	258	133	.52	1,796	Thomas Lewis	55	1,058	19.2
1994	Alex Smith	1,475	265	5.6	John Paci	176	96	.55	996	Eddie Baety	45	559	12.4
1995	Alex Smith	769	166	4.6	Chris Dittoe	196	102	.52	1,214	Sean Glover	33	239	7.2
1996	Alex Smith	1,248	292	4.3	Chris Dittoe	159	83	.52	1,035	Dorian Wilkerson	40	490	12.3
1997	De'Wayne Hogan	506	149	3.4	Jay Rodgers	330	192	.58	2,156	Chris Gall	54	422	7.8
1998	Antwaan Randle El	873	227	3.8	Antwaan Randle El	273	127	.47	1,745	Tyrone Browning	47	764	16.3
1999	Levron Williams	817	118	6.9	Antwaan Randle El	279	150	.54	2,277	Versie Gaddis	35	633	18.1
2000	Antwaan Randle El	1,270	218	5.8	Antwaan Randle El	277	133	.48	1,783	Versie Gaddis	29	554	19.1
2001	Levron Williams	1,401	212	6.6	Antwaan Randle El	231	118	.51	1,664	Levron Williams	26	289	11.1
2002	Yamar Washington	688	174	4.0	Gibran Hamdan	293	152	.52	2,115	Courtney Roby	59	1,039	17.6
2003	BenJarvus Green-Ellis	938	225	4.2	Matt LoVecchio	291	155	.53	1,778	Courtney Roby	45	504	11.2
2004	BenJarvus Green-Ellis	794	231	3.4	Matt LoVecchio	271	153	.57	1,951	Courtney Roby	55	810	14.7

All statistics include postseason

INDIANA ALL-TIME SCORES

WIN/LOSS PERCENTAGE SINCE 1936

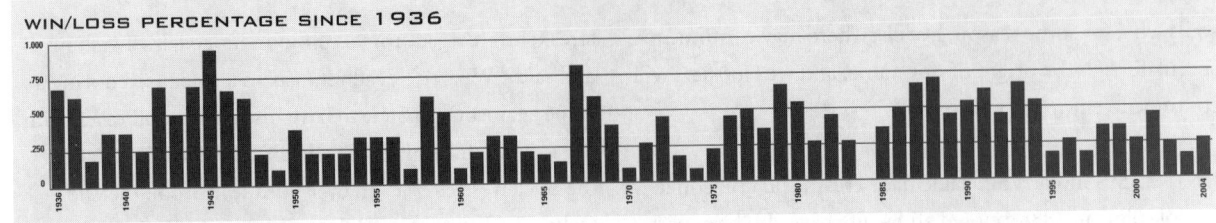

A.B. WOODFORD
1887-88 (.250)   0-1-1

1887   0-1-0
U		Franklin *Unk*	8	10

1888   0-0-1
U	=	DePauw *Unk*	6	6

EVANS WOLLEN
1889 (.000)   0-1

1889   0-1-0
U		Wabash *Unk*	2	40

1890
NO TEAM

BILLY HEROD
1891 (.167)   1-5

1891   1-5-0
U	●	Louisville AC *Unk*	30	0
U		Butler *Unk*	6	52
U		DePauw *Unk*	4	62
N14		at Purdue	0	60
U		Butler *Unk*	6	26
U		Wabash *Unk*	0	25

NO HEAD COACH

1892   2-2-0
U	●	Butler *Unk*	11	10
N5		at Purdue	0	68
U	●	Wabash *Unk*	36	24
U		DePauw *Unk*	0	1 f

1893   1-4-1
O14		at Purdue	0	64
U		Butler *Unk*	0	38
U	●	Danville AC *Unk*	18	0
U		DePauw *Unk*	0	34
N30	=	at Kentucky	24	24
U		Wabash *Unk*	12	24

FERBERT & HUDDLESTON
1894 (.000)   0-4

1894   0-4-0
U		Butler *Unk*	0	58
U		DePauw *Unk*	10	20
U		Wabash *Unk*	0	46
N24		at Purdue	0	1 f

OSGOOD & WREN
1895 (.563)   4-3-1

1895   4-3-1
U	●	Louisville AC *Unk*	36	0
U		Indianapolis *Unk*	8	16
U	●	Noblesville AC *Unk*	30	0
U		DePauw *Unk*	0	14
U	=	DePauw *Unk*	14	14
U		Butler *Unk*	2	34
U	●	Rose Poly *Unk*	8	4
U	●	Wabash *Unk*	12	10

M.G. GONTERMAN
1896-97 (.781)   12-3-1

1896   6-2-0
U		DePauw *Unk*	4	22
U		Noblesville *Unk*	6	8
U	●	Knightstown *Unk*	50	0
U		Butler *Unk*	22	6
U	●	Cincinnati *Unk*	16	0
U	●	Wabash *Unk*	38	0
U	●	Louisville AC *Unk*	38	24
U	●	DePauw *Unk*	12	0

1897   6-1-1
U	=	Rose Poly	6	6
U	●	at Rose Poly	12	0
U	●	Bedford	40	0
U	●	Louisville Manual HS	30	0
O30		at Purdue	6	20
U	●	DePauw	18	0
U	●	Miami ,Ohio	22	6
U	●	DePauw	14	0

JAMES H. HORNE
1898-1904 (.602)   33-21-5

1898   4-1-2
U	●	Rose Poly	16	0
U	●	Indiana Training Sch.	20	0
U	=	Cincinnati	0	0
N5	●	at Notre Dame	11	5
U	●	at DePauw	32	0
N12		at Purdue	0	14
U	=	at Cincinnati	11	11

1899   6-2-0
O7	●	Rose Poly	16	0
O14	●	at Illinois	5	0 *
O23		at Notre Dame	0	17
O28	●	at Vanderbilt	20	0
N4	●	Cincinnati	35	0
N11	●	DePauw	34	0
N18		at Northwestern	6	11
N30		at Purdue	17	5

1900-PRESENT
BIG 10

1900   4-2-2 (1-2-1)
S29	=	Alumni	0	0
O6	●	Earlham	18	0
O13		at Northwestern	0	12
O20	●	Vinncennes	62	0
O25	●	Notre Dame	6	0
N3		at Michigan	0	12
N17		Illinois *Ind*	0	0
N29	●	at Purdue	24	5

1901   6-3-0 (1-2-0)
S28	●	Wabash	24	6
O5	●	Rose Poly	56	0
O12		at Michigan	0	33
O19	●	Franklin	76	0
O26	●	Purdue	11	6
N2		Illinois *Ind*	0	18
N16		at Notre Dame	5	18
N23		at Ohio State	18	6
N28	●	DePauw	24	0

1902   3-5-1 (0-4-0)
O4	●	Wabash	34	0
O11		at Michigan	0	60
O18	●	DePauw	16	5
O25		Notre Dame	5	11
N1		at Illinois	0	47
N8		at Chicago	0	39
N15		at Purdue	0	39
N22	●	Vinncennes	33	0
N27	=	at Ohio State	6	6

1903   4-4-0 (1-2-0)
S26		Wabash	0	5
O3		at Chicago	0	34
O10	●	Earlham	39	0
O17		at Michigan	0	51
N6	●	Illinois	17	0
N14	●	DePauw	70	0
N21		at Transylvania, Ky	5	18
N28	=	at Ohio State	17	16

1904   6-4-0 (0-3-0)
S24	●	Alumni	11	5
S28	●	Indiana Medical	12	0
O1		at Chicago	0	56
O8		Kentucky	0	12
O15		at Illinois	0	10
O22	●	at Washington, Mo.	22	6
O29	●	Ohio State	8	0
N5	●	at Wabash	4	0
N12		Purdue *Ind*	0	27
N19	●	Kent	27	0

JAMES M. SHELDON
1905-13 (.570)   35-26-3

1905   8-1-1 (0-1-1)
S23	●	Alumni	5	0
S30	●	Butler	31	0
O7	●	Kentucky	29	0
O14		at Chicago	5	16
O21	●	Washington, Mo.	39	0
O28	=	Purdue *Ind*	11	11
N4	●	Cincinnati	47	6
N11	●	Notre Dame	22	5
N18	●	Wabash	40	0
N30	●	at Ohio State	11	0

1906   4-2-0 (0-2-0)
O13	●	Alumni	16	0
O20	●	at Wabash	12	5
O27		at Chicago	8	33
N3	●	DePauw	55	0
N10	●	Notre Dame *Unk*	12	0
N24		at Minnesota	6	8

1907   2-3-1 (0-3-0)
O5	●	DePauw	25	9
O12		at Chicago	6	27
O19	●	Alumni	40	0
N2	=	at Notre Dame	0	0
N9		at Wisconsin	8	11
N22		Illinois	6	10

1908   3-4-0 (1-3-0)
S26	●	Alumni	11	0
O3	●	DePauw	16	0
O10		at Chicago	6	29
O17		Wisconsin	0	16
O31		at Illinois	0	10
N7		Notre Dame *Unk*	0	11
N21	●	at Purdue	10	4

1909   4-3-0 (1-3-0)
O2	●	DePauw	28	5
O9		at Chicago	0	28
O16	●	Lake Forest	27	5
O23		at Wisconsin	3	6
O30	●	at St. Louis	30	0
N6		at Illinois	5	6
N20	●	at Purdue	36	3

1910   6-1-0 (3-1-0)
O1	●	DePauw	12	0
O8		at Chicago	6	0
O15	●	James Millikin	33	0
O22	●	Wisconsin *Ind*	12	3
O29	●	Butler	33	0
N5		Illinois	0	3
N19	●	at Purdue	15	0

1911   3-3-1 (0-3-1)
S30	●	DePauw	9	6
O7		at Chicago	6	23
O14	●	at Franklin	42	0
O21		at Northwestern	0	5
O28	●	Washington, Mo.	12	0
N11	=	Illinois	0	0
N25		Purdue	5	12

1912   2-5-0 (0-5-0)
S28	●	DePauw	20	0
O5		at Chicago	0	13
O19		at Illinois	7	13
O26	●	Earlham	33	7
N2		Iowa	6	13
N9		Northwestern	6	21
N24		at Purdue	7	34

1913   3-4-0 (2-4-0)
S27	●	DePauw	48	3
O4		at Chicago	7	21
O25		Illinois	0	10
N1		at Ohio State	7	6
N8		at Iowa	0	60
N15		at Northwestern	21	20
N23		Purdue	7	42

CLARENCE C. CHILDS
1914-15 (.464)   6-7-1

1914   3-4-0 (1-4-0)
S26	●	DePauw	13	6
O3		at Chicago	0	34
O10		at Illinois	0	51 *
O17	●	Northwestern	27	0
O31	●	Miami, Ohio	48	3
N7		Ohio State	3	13
N21		at Purdue	13	23

1915   3-3-1 (1-3-0)
O2	●	DePauw	7	0
O9	●	Miami, Ohio	41	0
O16		at Chicago	7	13
O30	=	Wash. & Lee *Ind*	7	7
N6		at Ohio State	9	10
N13	●	at Northwestern	14	6
N20		Purdue	0	7

EWALD O. STIEHM
1916-21 (.526)   20-18-1

1916   2-4-1 (0-3-1)
S30	●	DePauw	20	0
O14		at Chicago	0	22
O21		at Tufts	10	12
N4		Northwestern	0	7
N11		at Ohio State	7	46
N18	●	Florida	14	3
N25	=	at Purdue	0	0

1917   5-2-0 (1-2-0)
S29	●	Franklin	50	0
O6	●	Wabash	51	0
O13	●	St. Louis	40	0
O27		at Minnesota	9	33
N3		Ohio State	3	26
N10	●	DePauw	35	0
N24		at Purdue	37	0

1918   2-2-0 (0-0-0)
O5		Kentucky	7	24
N2		at Camp Taylor	3	7
N9	●	Fort Harrison	41	0
N16	●	DePauw	13	0

1919   3-4-0 (0-2-0)
S27	●	Wabash	20	7
O4		Centre	3	12
O11	●	at Kentucky	24	0
O18		Minnesota	6	20
N1		Notre Dame *Ind*	3	16
N15		at Northwestern	2	3
N22	●	Syracuse	12	6

1920   5-2-0 (3-1-0)
S25	●	Franklin	47	0
O2		Iowa	7	14
O9	●	Mississippi State	24	0
O23		at Minnesota	21	7
O30	●	Northwestern *Ind*	10	7
N13		Notre Dame *Ind*	10	13
N20	●	at Purdue	10	7

1921   3-4-0 (1-2-0)

S24	●	Franklin	47	0
O1	●	Kalamazoo	29	0
O8		at Harvard	0	19
O22		at Minnesota	0	6
O29		Notre Dame IND	7	28
N12		at Iowa	0	41
N19		Purdue	3	0

JAMES P. HERRON
1922 (.286) 1-4-2

1922   1-4-2 (0-2-1)

O7	=	DePauw	0	0
O14		Minnesota	0	20
O21		at Wisconsin	0	20
O28	●	Michigan State	14	6
N4		at Notre Dame	0	27
N11		West Virginia	0	33
N25	=	at Purdue	7	7

WILLIAM A. INGRAM
1923-25 (.457) 10-12-1

1923   3-4-0 (2-2-0)

O6		DePauw	0	3
O13	●	Northwestern IND	7	6
O20		Wisconsin	0	52
O27	●	Hanover	32	0
N10		at Chicago	0	27
N17		Wabash	6	29
N24		Purdue	3	0

1924   4-4-0 (1-3-0)

S27	●	Rose Poly	65	0
O4	●	DePauw	21	0
O11		LSU IND	14	20
O18		at Chicago	0	23
N1		at Northwestern	7	17
N8	●	at Ohio State	12	7
N15	●	Wabash	21	7
N22		at Purdue	7	26

1925   3-4-1 (0-3-1)

O3	●	Indiana Normal	31	0
O10		at Michigan	0	63
O17		Syracuse	0	14
O24	●	Miami, Ohio	25	7
O31		at Northwestern	14	17
N7		at Ohio State	0	7
N14	●	Rose Poly	32	7
N21	=	Purdue	0	0

H.O. (PAT) PAGE
1926-30 (.378) 14-24-3

1926   3-5-0 (0-4-0)

O2	●	DePauw	31	7
O9		Kentucky	14	6
O16		at Northwestern	0	20
O23		at Wisconsin	2	27
O30		Northwestern	0	21
N6		at Notre Dame	0	26
N13	●	Mississippi State	19	6
N20		at Purdue	14	24

1927   3-4-1 (1-2-1)

O1	●	at Kentucky	21	0
O8		at Chicago	0	13
O15	=	Minnesota	14	14
O22		Notre Dame	6	19
O29		at Harvard	6	26
N5	●	Michigan State	33	7
N12	●	at Northwestern	18	7
N19		Purdue	6	21

1928   4-4-0 (2-4-0)

S29	●	Wabash	14	0
O6	●	Oklahoma	10	7
O13	●	at Michigan	6	0
O20		at Illinois	7	13
O27		Ohio State	0	13
N10		at Minnesota	12	21
N17	●	Northwestern	6	0
N24		at Purdue	0	14

1929   2-6-1 (1-3-1)

S21	●	Wabash	19	2
S28		Ohio U.	0	18
O5		Notre Dame	0	14
O12		at Chicago	7	13
O19		Colgate	6	21
O26	=	at Ohio State	0	0
N2		at Minnesota	7	19
N16	●	at Northwestern	19	14
N23		Purdue	0	32

1930   2-5-1 (1-3-0)

S27	●	Miami, Ohio	14	0
O4		at Ohio State	0	23
O11	=	Oklahoma State	7	7
O18		at Minnesota	0	6
O25		at SMU	0	27
N1		at Notre Dame	0	27
N8		Northwestern	0	25
N22	●	at Purdue	7	6

BILLY HAYES
1931-33 (.340) 6-14-5

1931   2-5-2 (1-4-2)

S26	●	Ohio U.	7	6
O3		Notre Dame	0	25
O17	=	at Iowa	0	0
O24	●	at Chicago	32	6
O31		Ohio State	6	13	*
N7		at Michigan	0	22
N14		at Northwestern	6	7
N21		Purdue	0	19
N26	=	Illinois CHI	0	0

1932   3-4-1 (1-4-1)

O1	●	Ohio U.	7	6
O8	=	at Ohio State	7	7
O15	●	Iowa	12	0
O22		at Chicago	7	13
O27	●	Mississippi State	19	0
N5		Michigan	0	7
N12		at Illinois	6	18
N19		at Purdue	7	25

1933   1-5-2 (0-3-2)

S30	●	Miami, Ohio	7	0
O7	=	at Minnesota	6	6
O14		Notre Dame	2	12
O21		Northwestern CHI	0	25
N4		at Ohio State	0	21
N11	=	at Chicago	7	7
N18		at Xavier	0	6
N25		Purdue	3	19

A.N. (BO) McMILLIN
1934-47 (.561) 63-48-11

1934   3-3-2 (1-3-1)

S29	●	Ohio U.	27	0
O6		at Ohio State	0	33
O13	=	at Temple	6	6
O20		at Chicago	0	21
N3	=	Iowa	0	0
N10		at Minnesota	0	30
N17	●	Maryland	17	14
N24	●	at Purdue	17	6

1935   4-3-1 (2-2-1)

O5	●	Centre	14	0
O12		at Michigan	0	7
O19		at Cincinnati	0	7
O26		Ohio State	6	28
N2	=	at Iowa	6	6
N9	●	Maryland BALT	13	7	*
N16	●	at Chicago	24	0
N23	●	Purdue	7	0

1936   5-2-1 (3-1-1)

O3	●	Centre	38	0
O10	●	at Michigan	14	3
O17		at Nebraska	9	13
O24		at Ohio State	0	7
O31	●	Iowa	13	6
N7		Syracuse	9	7
N14	●	at Chicago	20	7
N21	=	at Purdue	20	20

1937   5-3-0 (3-2-0)

O2	●	Centre	12	0
O9		at Minnesota	0	6
O16	●	Illinois	13	6
O23	●	Cincinnati	27	0
O30		at Nebraska	0	7
N6	●	at Ohio State	10	0
N13	●	at Iowa	3	0
N20		Purdue	7	13

1938   1-6-1 (1-4-1)

O1		at Ohio State	0	6
O8		at Illinois	2	12
O15	=	at Nebraska	0	0
O22		Kansas State	6	13
O29		at Wisconsin	0	6
N5		Boston College BOS	0	14
N12	●	Iowa	7	3
N19		at Purdue	6	13

1939   2-4-2 (2-3-0)

S30	=	Nebraska	7	7
O7		at Iowa	29	32
O14	●	at Wisconsin	14	0
O21	●	at Illinois	7	6
N4		at Ohio State	0	24
N11		Fordham NYC	0	13
N18	=	at Michigan State	7	7
N25		Purdue	6	7

1940   3-5-0 (2-3-0)

O5		Texas	6	13
O12		at Nebraska	7	13
O19	●	Iowa	10	6
O26		at Northwestern	7	20
N2		at Ohio State	6	21
N9	●	Michigan State	20	0
N16		at Wisconsin	10	27
N23	●	at Purdue	3	0

1941   2-6-0 (1-3-0)

S27		Detroit	7	14
O4		at Notre Dame	6	19
O11		TCU	14	20
O18	●	at Nebraska	21	13
O25		at Wisconsin	25	27
N1		at Iowa	7	13
N8		at Northwestern	14	20
N22	●	Purdue	7	0

1942   7-3-0 (2-2-0)

S26	●	Butler	53	0
O3		at Ohio State	21	32
O10	●	at Nebraska	12	0
O17	●	at Pittsburgh	19	7
O24	●	Iowa	13	14
O31		Iowa Pre-Flight	6	26
N7	●	at Minnesota	7	0
N14	●	Kansas State	54	0
N21	●	at Purdue	20	0
N28	●	at Fort Knox	51	0

1943   4-4-2 (2-3-1)

S18	●	Miami, Ohio	7	7
S25		at Northwestern	6	14
O2	●	Wabash	52	0
O9	●	at Nebraska	54	13
O16	=	at Iowa	7	7
O23	●	Wisconsin	34	0
O30	●	at Ohio State	20	14
N6		at Michigan	6	23
N13		Great Lakes NAS	7	21
N20		Purdue	0	7

1944   7-3-0 (4-3-0)

S16	●	Fort Knox	72	0
S23		at Illinois	18	26
S30	●	at Michigan	20	0
O14	●	Nebraska	54	0
O21	●	at Northwestern	14	7
O28		Iowa	32	0
N4		at Ohio State	7	21
N11		at Minnesota	14	19
N18	●	Pittsburgh	47	0
N25	●	at Purdue	14	6

1945   9-0-1 (5-0-1)

S22	●	at Michigan	13	7
S29	=	at Northwestern	7	7
O6	●	at Illinois	6	0
O13	●	Nebraska	54	14
O20	●	at Iowa	52	20
O27	●	Tulsa	7	2
N3	●	Cornell Coll.	46	6
N10	●	at Minnesota	49	0
N17	●	at Pittsburgh	19	0
N24	●	Purdue	26	0

1946   6-3-0 (4-2-0)

S21		Cincinnati	6	15
S28		at Michigan	0	21
O5	●	at Minnesota	21	0
O12	●	Illinois	14	7
O19		Iowa	0	13
O26	●	at Nebraska	27	7
N2	●	Pittsburgh	20	6
N9	●	at Northwestern	7	6
N23	●	at Purdue	34	20

1947   5-3-1 (2-3-1)

S27	●	at Nebraska	17	0
O4	=	Wisconsin	7	7
O11		at Iowa	14	27
O18	●	Pittsburgh	41	6
O25	●	at Northwestern	6	7
N1	●	at Ohio State	7	0
N8		at Michigan	0	35
N15	●	Marquette	48	6
N22	●	Purdue	16	14

CLYDE SMITH
1948-51 (.236) 8-27-1

1948   2-7-0 (2-4-0)

S25		at Wisconsin	35	7
O2	●	Iowa	7	0
O9		TCU	6	7
O16		Ohio State	0	17
O23		at Pittsburgh	14	21
O30		at Minnesota	7	30
N6		Notre Dame	6	42
N13		at Michigan	0	54
N20		at Purdue	0	39

1949   1-8-0 (0-6-0)

S24		at Notre Dame	6	49
O1		at Ohio State	7	46
O8		TCU	6	13
O15		at Iowa	9	35
O22	●	Pittsburgh	48	14
O29		Wisconsin	14	30
N5		at Illinois	14	33
N12		at Michigan	7	20
N19		Purdue	6	14

1950   3-5-1 (1-4-0)

S30	=	at Nebraska	20	20
O7	●	Iowa	20	7
O14		Ohio State	14	26
O21		Notre Dame	20	7
O28		at Illinois	0	20
N4		at Michigan State	0	35
N11		at Michigan	7	20
N18	●	Marquette	18	7
N25		at Purdue	0	13

1951   2-7-0 (1-5-0)

S29		at Notre Dame	6	48
O6	●	Pittsburgh	13	6
O13		at Michigan	14	33
O20	●	at Ohio State	32	10
O27		Illinois	0	21
N3		at Wisconsin	0	6
N10		at Minnesota	14	16
N17		Michigan State	26	30
N24		Purdue	13	21

BERNIE CRIMMINS
1952-56 (.289) 13-32

1952   2-7-0 (1-5-0)

S27		at Ohio State	13	33
O4	●	Iowa	20	13
O11		at Michigan	13	28
O18	●	Temple	33	0
O25		at Northwestern	13	23
N1		at Pittsburgh	7	28
N8		Michigan State	14	41
N15		Wisconsin	14	37
N22		at Purdue	16	21

1953   2-7-0 (1-5-0)

S26		at Ohio State	12	36
O2		at Southern Cal	14	27
O10	●	Marquette	21	20
O17		at Michigan State	18	47
O24		at Iowa	13	19
O31		Missouri	7	14
N7		at Minnesota	20	28
N14	●	Northwestern	14	6
N21		Purdue	0	30

1954   3-6-0 (2-4-0)

S25		at Ohio State	0	28
O2	●	Pacific	34	6
O9		Michigan State	14	21
O16		at Missouri	14	20
O23		Iowa	14	27
O30	●	at Michigan	13	9
N6		Miami, Ohio	0	6
N13	●	at Northwestern	14	13
N20		at Purdue	7	13

1955   3-6-0 (1-5-0)

S24		Michigan State	13	20
O1		at Notre Dame	0	19
O8		at Iowa	6	20
O15	●	Villanova	14	7
O22	●	at Northwestern	20	14
O29	●	Ohio U.	21	14
N5		at Ohio State	13	20
N12		at Michigan	0	30
N19		Purdue	4	6

1956 3-6-0 (1-5-0)

S29	|	Iowa	0	27
O6		at Notre Dame	6	20
O13	|	at Michigan State	6	53
O20	•	at Nebraska	19	14
O27	• |	Northwestern	19	13
N3	•	Marquette	14	35
N17	|	at Michigan	26	49
N24	|	at Purdue	20	39

BOB HICKS
1957 (.111) 1-8

1957 1-8-0 (0-6-0)

S28	|	at Michigan State	0	54
O5		at Notre Dame	0	26
O12	|	Iowa	7	47
O19	|	at Ohio State	0	56
O26	•	Villanova	14	7
N2	|	at Minnesota	0	34
N9		Cincinnati	0	21
N16	|	at Michigan	13	27
N23	|	Purdue	13	35

PHIL DICKENS
1958-64 (.333) 20-41-2

1958 5-3-1 (3-2-1)

S27		at Notre Dame	0	18
O4	•	West Virginia	13	12
O11	|	at Iowa	13	34
O18	|	at Ohio State	8	49
O25	•	Miami, Ohio	12	7
N1	• |	Minnesota	6	0
N8	• |	Michigan State	6	0
N15	• |	at Michigan	8	6
N22	= |	at Purdue	15	15

1959 4-4-1 (2-4-1)

S26	• |	Illinois	20	0
O3	|	at Minnesota	14	24
O10	•	Marquette	33	13
O17	•	at Nebraska	23	7
O24	|	at Michigan State	6	14
O31	|	at Northwestern	13	30
N7	= |	at Ohio State	0	0
N14	• |	Michigan	26	7
N21	|	Purdue	7	10

1960 1-8-0 (0-7-0)

S24	|	at Illinois	6	17
O1	|	at Minnesota	0	42
O8		Oregon State	6	20
O15	•	Marquette	34	8
O22	|	Michigan State	0	35
O29	|	Northwestern	3	21
N5	|	at Ohio State	7	36
N12	|	at Michigan	7	29
N19	|	at Purdue	6	35

1961 2-7-0 (0-6-0)

S23		at Kansas State	8	14
O7	|	Wisconsin	3	6
O14	|	at Iowa	8	27
O21	•	Washington State	33	7
O28	|	at Michigan State	0	35
N4	|	at Northwestern	8	14
N11	|	Ohio State	7	16
N18	•	at West Virginia	17	9
N25	|	Purdue	12	34

1962 3-6-0 (1-5-0)

S22	•	Kansas State	21	0
S29	•	at Cincinnati	26	6
O6	|	at Wisconsin	6	30
O13	|	Iowa	10	14
O20		Washington State SPO	15	21
O27	|	Michigan State	8	26
N3	|	Northwestern	21	26
N10	|	at Ohio State	7	10
N24	• |	at Purdue	12	7

1963 3-6-0 (1-5-0)

S28	|	at Northwestern	21	34
O5	|	Ohio State	0	21
O12	|	at Iowa	26	37
O19	|	at Michigan State	3	20
O26	•	Cincinnati	20	6
N2	• |	at Minnesota	24	6
N9	•	Oregon State	20	15
N16		Oregon PORT	22	28
N30	|	Purdue	15	21

1964 2-7-0 (1-5-0)

S26	|	Northwestern	13	14
O3	|	at Ohio State	9	17
O10	|	Iowa	20	21
O17	• |	Michigan State	27	20
O23	•	at Miami, Fla.	28	14
O31	|	Minnesota	0	21
N7		at Oregon State	14	24
N14		Oregon	21	29
N21	|	at Purdue	22	28

JOHN PONT
1965-72 (.380) 31-51-1

1965 2-8-0 (1-6-0)

S18	•	Kansas State	19	7
S25	|	Northwestern	0	20
O2		at Texas	12	27
O9	|	at Minnesota	18	42
O16	|	at Illinois	13	34
O23		Washington State	7	8
O30	• |	Iowa	21	17
N6	|	at Ohio State	10	17
N13	|	at Michigan State	13	27
N20	|	Purdue	21	26

1966 1-8-1 (1-5-1)

S17		Miami, Ohio	10	20
S24	• |	at Northwestern	26	14
O1		at Texas	0	35
O8	= |	Minnesota	7	7
O15	|	Illinois	10	24
O22		at Miami, Fla.	7	14
O29	|	at Iowa	19	20
N5	|	at Ohio State	0	7
N12	|	Michigan State	19	37
N19	|	at Purdue	6	51

1967 9-2-0 (6-1-0)

S23	•	Kentucky	12	10
S30	•	Kansas	18	15
O7	• |	at Illinois	20	7
O14	• |	Iowa	21	17
O21	• |	at Michigan	27	20
O28	•	at Arizona	42	7
N4	• |	Wisconsin	14	9
N11	• |	at Michigan State	14	13
N18	|	at Minnesota	7	33
N25	• |	Purdue	19	14
		ROSE BOWL		
J1		Southern Cal	3	14

1968 6-4-0 (4-3-0)

S21	•	Baylor	40	36
S28		at Kansas	20	38
O5	• |	Illinois	28	14
O12	• |	at Iowa	38	34
O19	|	Michigan	22	27
O26	•	Arizona	16	13
N2	• |	at Wisconsin	21	20
N9	• |	at Michigan State	24	22
N16	|	Minnesota	6	20
N23	|	at Purdue	35	38

1969 4-6-0 (3-4-0)

S20	•	at Kentucky	58	30
S27		California	14	17
O4		at Colorado	7	30
O11	• |	Minnesota	17	7
O18	• |	Illinois	41	20
O25	|	at Wisconsin	34	36
N1	• |	at Michigan State	16	0
N8	|	Iowa	17	28
N15	|	at Northwestern	27	30
N22	|	Purdue	21	44

1970 1-9-0 (1-6-0)

S19		Colorado	9	16
S26		at California	14	56
O3		West Virginia	10	16
O10	|	at Minnesota	0	23
O17	• |	at Illinois	30	24
O24	|	Wisconsin	12	30
O31	|	Michigan State	7	32
N7	|	at Iowa	13	42
N14	|	Northwestern	7	21
N21	|	at Purdue	0	40

1971 3-8-0 (2-6-0)

S11	|	at Minnesota	0	28
S18	•	Kentucky	26	8
S25		at Baylor	0	10
O2		Syracuse	0	7
O9	|	at Wisconsin	29	35
O16	|	Ohio State	7	27
O23	|	Northwestern	10	24
O30	|	at Michigan	7	61
N6	|	Illinois	21	22
N13	• |	at Iowa	14	7
N20	• |	Purdue	38	31

1972 5-6-0 (3-5-0)

S16	• |	Minnesota	27	23
S23		TCU	28	31
S30	•	at Kentucky	35	34
O7	•	at Syracuse	10	2
O14	• |	Wisconsin	33	7
O21	|	at Ohio State	7	44
O28	|	at Northwestern	14	23
N4	|	Michigan	7	21
N11	|	at Illinois	20	37
N18	• |	Iowa	16	8
N25	|	at Purdue	7	42

LEE CORSO
1973-82 (.378) 41-68-2

1973 2-9-0 (0-8-0)

S15	|	Illinois	14	28
S22		at Arizona	10	26
S29	•	Kentucky	17	3
O6	•	at West Virginia	28	14
O13	|	at Minnesota	3	24
O20	|	Ohio State	7	37
O27	|	at Wisconsin	7	31
N3	|	at Michigan	13	49
N10	|	Northwestern	20	21
N17	|	at Michigan State	9	10
N24	|	Purdue	23	28

1974 1-10-0 (1-7-0)

S14	|	at Illinois	0	16
S21		Arizona	20	35
S28		at Kentucky	22	28
O5		West Virginia	0	24
O12	• |	Minnesota	34	3
O19	|	at Ohio State	9	49
O26	|	Wisconsin	25	35
N2	|	Michigan	7	21
N9	|	at Northwestern	22	24
N16	|	Michigan State	10	19
N23	|	at Purdue	17	38

1975 2-8-1 (1-6-1)

S13	• |	Minnesota	20	14
S20		at Nebraska	0	45
S27	•	Utah	31	7
O4		at North Carolina St.	0	27
O11	|	at Northwestern	0	30
O18	|	Iowa	10	20
O25	|	at Michigan	7	55
N1	|	at Ohio State	14	24
N8	|	Michigan State	6	14
N15	= |	at Wisconsin	9	9
N22	|	Purdue	7	9

1976 5-6-0 (4-4-0)

S11	|	at Minnesota	13	32
S18		Nebraska	13	45
S25	•	at Washington	20	13
O2		North Carolina St.	21	24
O9	• |	Northwestern	7	0
O16	• |	at Iowa	14	7
O23	|	Michigan	0	35
O30	|	Ohio State	7	47
N6	|	at Michigan State	0	23
N13	• |	Wisconsin	15	14
N20	• |	at Purdue	20	14

1977 5-5-1 (4-3-1)

S10	|	Wisconsin	14	30
S17	•	LSU	24	21
S24		Miami, Ohio	20	21
O1		at Nebraska	13	31
O8	• |	at Northwestern	28	3
O15	= |	Michigan State	13	13
O22	|	at Illinois	7	21
O29	• |	Minnesota	34	22
N5	• |	at Iowa	24	21
N12	|	at Ohio State	7	35
N19	• |	Purdue	21	10

1978 4-7-0 (3-5-0)

S16		at LSU	17	24
S23	•	Washington	14	7
S30		Nebraska	17	69
O7	|	at Wisconsin	7	34
O14	• |	Northwestern	38	10
O21	|	at Michigan State	14	49
O28	• |	Illinois	31	10
N4	|	at Minnesota	31	32
N11	• |	Iowa	34	14
N18	|	Ohio State	18	21
N25	|	at Purdue	7	20

1979 8-4-0 (5-3-0)

S8	• |	at Iowa	30	26
S15	•	Vanderbilt	44	13
S22	•	Kentucky	18	10
S29		Colorado	16	17
O6	• |	at Wisconsin	3	0
O13	|	at Ohio State	6	47
O20	• |	Northwestern	30	0
O27	|	at Michigan	21	27
N3	• |	Minnesota	42	24
N10	• |	at Illinois	45	14
N17	|	Purdue	21	37
		HOLIDAY BOWL		
D21	•	Brigham Young	38	37

1980 6-5-0 (3-5-0)

S13	|	Iowa	7	16
S20	•	at Kentucky	36	30
S27	•	at Colorado	49	7
O4	•	Duke	31	21
O11	• |	Wisconsin	24	0
O18	|	at Ohio State	17	27
O25	• |	at Northwestern	35	20
N1	|	Michigan	0	35
N8	|	at Minnesota	7	31
N15	• |	Illinois	26	24
N22	|	at Purdue	23	24

1981 3-8-0 (3-6-0)

S12	• |	at Northwestern	21	20
S19		Southern Cal	0	21
S26		at Syracuse	7	21
O3	|	Michigan	17	38
O10	|	at Iowa	28	42
O17	• |	Minnesota	17	16
O24	|	at Ohio State	10	29
O31	|	at Michigan State	3	26
N7	|	Wisconsin	7	28
N14	|	at Illinois	14	35
N21	• |	Purdue	20	17

1982 5-6-0 (4-5-0)

S11	• |	Northwestern	30	0
S18		at Southern Cal	7	28
S25	•	Syracuse	17	10
O2	|	at Michigan	10	24
O9	|	Iowa	20	24
O16	• |	at Minnesota	40	21
O23	|	Ohio State	25	49
O30	|	Michigan State	14	22
N6	• |	at Wisconsin	20	17
N13	|	Illinois	7	48
N20	• |	at Purdue	13	7

SAM WYCHE
1983 (.273) 3-8

1983 3-8-0 (2-7-0)

S10	•	Duke	15	10
S17		at Kentucky	13	24
S24	|	Northwestern	8	10
O1	|	at Michigan	18	43
O8	• |	Minnesota	38	31
O15	• |	Michigan State	24	12
O22	|	at Wisconsin	14	45
O29	|	at Iowa	3	49
N5	|	Ohio State	17	56
N12	|	at Illinois	21	49
N19	|	Purdue	30	31

BILL MALLORY
1984-96 (.466) 68-78-3

1984 0-11-0 (0-9-0)

S8		at Duke	24	31
S15		Kentucky	14	48
S22	|	at Northwestern	37	40
S29	|	Michigan	6	14
O6	|	at Minnesota	24	33
O13	|	at Michigan State	6	13
O20	|	Wisconsin	16	20
O27	|	Iowa	20	24
N3	|	at Ohio State	7	50
N10	|	Illinois IND	7	34
N17	|	at Purdue	24	31

1985 4-7-0 (1-7-0)

S14	•	Louisville	41	28
S21	•	Navy	38	35
S28	•	at Missouri	36	17
O5	• |	Northwestern	26	7
O12	|	at Ohio State	7	48
O19	|	Minnesota	7	22
O26	|	at Michigan	15	42
N2	|	at Wisconsin	20	31
N9	|	Michigan State	16	35
N16	|	at Illinois	24	41
N23	|	Purdue	21	34

1986   6-6-0 (3-5-0)

Date		Opponent		
S13	●	Louisville	21	0
S20	●	Navy	52	29
S27	●	at Missouri	41	24
O4	●	at Northwestern	24	7
O11		Ohio State	22	24
O18		at Minnesota	17	19
O25		Michigan	14	38
N1	●	Wisconsin	21	7
N8	●	at Michigan State	17	14
N15		Illinois	16	21
N22		at Purdue	15	17
ALL-AMERICAN BOWL				
D31		Florida State	13	27

1987   8-4-0 (6-2-0)

Date		Opponent		
S12	●	Rice	35	13
S19		at Kentucky	15	34
S26		Missouri	20	17
O3		Northwestern	35	18
O10	●	at Ohio State	31	10
O16	●	at Minnesota	18	17
O24		Michigan	14	10
O31		at Iowa	21	29
N7	●	Illinois	34	22
N14		at Michigan State	3	27
N21	●	Purdue	35	14
PEACH BOWL				
J2		Tennessee	22	27

1988   8-3-1 (5-3-0)

Date		Opponent		
S10	●	at Rice	41	14
S17	●	Kentucky	36	15
S24	=	at Missouri	28	28
O1	●	at Northwestern	48	17
O8	●	Ohio State	41	7
O15	●	Minnesota	33	13
O22		at Michigan	6	31
O29	●	Iowa	45	34
N5		at Illinois	20	21
N12		Michigan State	12	38
N19	●	at Purdue	52	7
LIBERTY BOWL				
D28		South Carolina	34	10

1989   5-6-0 (3-5-0)

Date		Opponent		
S9		at Kentucky	14	17
S16	●	Missouri	24	7
S30	●	Toledo	32	12
O7	●	Northwestern	43	11
O14		at Ohio State	31	35
O21	●	Minnesota	28	18
O28		at Michigan	10	38
N4		Michigan State	20	51
N11	●	at Wisconsin	45	17
N18		at Illinois	28	41
N25		Purdue	14	15

1990   6-5-1 (3-4-1)

Date		Opponent		
S15	●	at Kentucky	45	24
S22	●	Missouri	58	7
S29	●	Eastern Michigan	37	6
O6	●	at Northwestern	42	0
O13	=	Ohio State	27	27
O20		at Minnesota	0	12
O27		Michigan	19	45
N3		at Michigan State	20	45
N10	●	Wisconsin	20	7
N17		Illinois	10	24
N24	●	at Purdue	28	14
PEACH BOWL				
D29		Auburn	23	27

1991   7-4-1 (5-3-0)

Date		Opponent		
S7		at Notre Dame	27	49
S21	●	Kentucky	13	10
S28	=	at Missouri	27	27
O5	●	Michigan State	31	0
O12	●	Northwestern	44	6
O19		at Michigan	16	24
O26	●	at Wisconsin	28	20
N2	●	Minnesota	34	8
N9		at Iowa	21	38
N16		at Ohio State	16	20
N23	●	Purdue	24	22
COPPER BOWL				
D31	●	Baylor	24	0

1992   5-6-0 (3-5-0)

Date		Opponent		
S12	●	Miami, Ohio	16	0
S19		at Kentucky	25	37
S26	●	Missouri	20	10
O3		at Michigan State	31	42
O10	●	at Northwestern	28	3
O17		Michigan	3	31
O24	●	Wisconsin	10	3
O31	●	at Minnesota	24	17
N7		Iowa	0	14
N14		Ohio State	10	27
N21	●	at Purdue	10	13

1993   8-4-0 (5-3-0)

Date		Opponent		
S4	●	Toledo	27	0
S11	●	Northern Illinois	28	10
S18	●	Kentucky	24	8
S25		Wisconsin	15	27
O2	●	at Minnesota	23	19
O9	●	Iowa	16	10
O23	●	at Northwestern	24	0
O30	●	Michigan State	10	0
N6		at Penn State	31	38
N13		at Ohio State	17	23
N20	●	Purdue	24	17
INDEPENDENCE BOWL				
D31		Virginia Tech	20	45

1994   6-5-0 (3-5-0)

Date		Opponent			
S3	●	Cincinnati	28	3	
S10	●	Miami, Ohio	35	14	
S17	●	at Kentucky	59	29	
S24		at Wisconsin	13	62	
O1	●	Minnesota	25	14	
O8	●	at Iowa	27	20	
O22		Northwestern	7	20	
O29		at Michigan State	21	27	†
N5		Penn State	29	35	
N12		Ohio State	17	32	
N19	●	at Purdue	33	29	

1995   2-9-0 (0-8-0)

Date		Opponent		
S9	●	Western Michigan	24	10
S16		Kentucky	10	17
S23	●	Southern Miss	27	26
S30		at Northwestern	7	31
O7		Illinois	10	17
O14		at Iowa	13	22
O21		Michigan	17	34
O28		at Penn State	21	45
N11		Michigan State	13	31
N18		at Ohio State	3	42
N24		Purdue	14	51

1996   3-8 (1-7)

Date		Opponent		
S7	●	at Toledo	40	6
S14	●	Miami, Ohio	21	14
S21		at Kentucky	0	3
S28		Northwestern	17	35
O5		at Illinois	43	46
O12		Iowa	10	31
O19		at Michigan	20	27
O26		Penn State	26	48
N9		at Michigan State	15	38
N16		Ohio State	17	27
N23	●	at Purdue	33	16

CAM CAMERON
1997-2001 (.327)   18-37

1997   2-9 (1-7)

Date		Opponent		
S6		at North Carolina	6	23
S13	●	Ball State	33	6
S20		Kentucky	7	49
S27		at Wisconsin	26	27
O4		Michigan	0	37
O11		Michigan State	6	38
O18		at Ohio State	0	31
O25		at Iowa	0	62
N1	●	Illinois	23	6
N15		at Minnesota	12	24
N22		Purdue	7	56

1998   4-7 (2-6)

Date		Opponent		
S12	●	Western Michigan	45	30
S19		at Kentucky	27	31
S26	●	at Cincinnati	48	14
O3		Wisconsin	20	24
O10		at Michigan State	31	38
O17	●	Iowa	14	7
O24		at Michigan	10	21
O31		Ohio State	7	38
N7		at Illinois	16	31
N14	●	Minnesota	20	19
N21		at Purdue	7	52

1999   4-7 (3-5)

Date		Opponent		
S4	●	Ball State	21	9
S11		North Carolina	30	42
S18		Kentucky	35	44
S25		at Penn State	24	45
O2	●	Illinois	34	31
O9	●	Northwestern	34	17
O16		at Wisconsin	0	59
O23	●	at Iowa	38	31
O30		Michigan	31	34
N13		at Minnesota	20	44
N20		Purdue	24	30

2000   3-8 (2-6)

Date		Opponent		
S9		North Carolina St.	38	41
S16		at Kentucky	34	41
S23	●	Cincinnati	42	6
S30	●	Iowa	45	33
O7		at Northwestern	33	52
O14		at Michigan	0	58
O21	●	Minnesota	51	43
O28		Penn State *IND*	24	27
N4		at Illinois	35	42
N11	●	Wisconsin	22	43
N18		at Purdue	13	41

2001   5-6 (4-4)

Date		Opponent		
S6		at North Carolina St.	14	35
S22		Utah	26	28
S29		Ohio State	14	27
O6	●	at Wisconsin	63	32
O13		Illinois	14	35
O20		at Iowa	28	42
N3	●	Northwestern	56	21
N10	●	at Michigan State	37	28
N17		at Penn State	14	28
N24	●	Purdue	13	7
D1		Kentucky	26	15

GERRY DiNARDO
2002-04 (.229)   8-27

2002   3-9 (1-7)

Date		Opponent		
A31	●	William & Mary	25	17
S7		at Utah	13	40
S14		at Kentucky	17	27
S21	●	Central Michigan	39	29
S28		at Ohio State	17	45
O12	●	Wisconsin	32	29
O19		Iowa	8	24
O26		at Illinois	14	45
N2		at Northwestern	37	41
N9		Michigan State	21	56
N16		Penn State	25	58
N23		at Purdue	10	34

2003   2-10 (1-7)

Date		Opponent		
A30		at Connecticut	10	34
S6		at Washington	13	38
S13	●	Indiana St.	33	3
S20		Kentucky	17	34
S27		at Michigan	17	31
O4		at Michigan State	3	31
O11		Northwestern	31	37
O25		Ohio State	6	35
N1		at Minnesota	7	55
N8	●	Illinois	17	14
N15		at Penn State	7	52
N22		Purdue	16	24

2004   3-8 (1-7)

Date		Opponent		
S4		Central Michigan	41	10
S11	●	at Oregon	30	24
S18		at Kentucky	32	51
S25		Michigan State	20	30
O2		Michigan	14	35
O9		at Northwestern	24	31
O23		at Ohio State	7	30
O30	●	Minnesota	30	21
N6		at Illinois	22	26
N13		Penn State	18	22
N20		at Purdue	24	63

IOWA

BY TODD JONES

THE HISTORY OF IOWA FOOTBALL has reflected the agricultural nature of America's heartland. Some years there's been only drought with minimal production, while others have been filled with a bounty of excitement, awards and championships. Memories of Aubrey Devine and Duke Slater starring for Howard Jones in the 1920s and Alex Karras and Randy Duncan starring for Forest Evashevski in the 1950s alleviate the pain of tough times. Hayden Fry showed in the 1980s that Iowa can reap as much success as any program. When his teams stumbled in his final years in the 1990s, his successor, Kirk Ferentz, proved there's always a chance for new life. Through it all, good times and bad, there has never been any doubt about the passion of the Hawkeyes' fans and the sustenance of their teams. Iowa always pushes on, like the enduring memory of its 1939 Heisman winner, Nile Kinnick.

TRADITION In 1935, Iowa governor Clyde Herring and Minnesota governor Floyd B. Olson wagered on the game between the state universities as a way to cool bad feelings and promote sportsmanship. Iowa lost, so Herring walked into Olson's office and presented him with Floyd of Rosedale—a full-blooded award-winning pig named for Olson, raised by Iowa farmer Allen Loomis and the brother of Blueboy from Will Rogers' movie *State Fair*. Olson, in turn, offered up Floyd as the grand prize in a statewide essay-writing contest. The winner, Robert Jones, then sold the hog to the University of Minnesota. Olson commissioned St. Paul artist Charles Brioschi to sculpt Floyd's image. The bronze pig, 21 inches long and 15 inches high, became the annual prize for the winner of the Iowa-Minnesota game. The Hawkeyes also play for the Cy-Hawk Trophy, awarded to the Iowa-Iowa State winner. Donated in 1977 by the Des Moines Athletic Club, the trophy features a running back and the school mascots, Herky the Hawkeye and Cy the Cardinal. Iowa didn't play Iowa State for 43 years until the rivalry resumed in 1977.

BEST PLAYER The coins tossed by officials at the start of some Big Ten games bear Nile Kinnick's face. He won the Heisman, Walter Camp and Maxwell trophies in 1939 as a runner, passer, kicker and defender on Iowa's legendary Ironmen team. The humble Iowa native was also Phi Beta Kappa with a 3.4 GPA. His play as a junior was hampered by an ankle injury that Kinnick, a Christian Scientist, would

PROFILE

University of Iowa
Iowa City, Iowa
Founded: 1847
Enrollment: 20,135
Colors: Old Gold and Black
Nickname: Hawkeyes
Stadium: Kinnick Stadium
   Opened in 1929
   Grass; 70,397 capacity
First football game: 1889
All-time record: 538–489–39 (.523)
Bowl record: 11–8–1
Big Ten Conference championships:
11 (4 outright)
Heisman Trophy: Nile Kinnick, 1939
Outland Trophy: Calvin Jones, 1955; Alex Karras, 1957; Robert Gallery, 2003
First-round NFL draftees: 15
Website: www.hawkeyesports.com

THE BEST OF TIMES

Coach Forest Evashevski led the Hawkeyes to a 24–3–2 record, including two Rose Bowl wins, from 1956 to 1958. The 1958 team finished No. 2 in the final AP and UPI polls. The Hawkeyes went 8–1 in 1960 and won their third Big Ten title in five years as Evashevski's tenure came to an end.

THE WORST OF TIMES

Four different coaches were part of 11 consecutive losing seasons from 1970 to 1980. An 0–11 finish in 1973 was the worst mark in a span that produced a 33–85–2 record.

CONFERENCE

Started playing in the Western Conference in 1900, and has remained in the league since then (also belonged to Missouri Valley Intercollegiate Athletic Association from 1907 to 1910.) The Western Conference was popularly known as the Big Ten since 1917, but didn't officially change its name to the Big Ten Conference until 1987.

DISTINGUISHED ALUMNI

Tennessee Williams; Tom Brokaw; George Gallup; Charles Guggenheim, filmmaker; John Irving, novelist; E.F. Lindquist, co-founder of the ACT test; Gene Wilder, actor

FIGHT SONG

THE IOWA FIGHT SONG
The word is "Fight! Fight! Fight! for Iowa,"
Let every loyal Iowan sing
The word is "Fight! Fight! Fight! for Iowa";
Until the walls and rafters ring. (Rah! Rah!)

Come on and cheer, cheer, cheer for Iowa
We're gonna cheer until we hear the final gun.
The word is "Fight! Fight! Fight! for Iowa,"
Until the game is won.

Fry redesigned the uniforms for 1979 to change the mind-set of a losing program.

not allow to be examined, much less treated. He returned healthy as a senior and led the Hawkeyes to a 6–1–1 record by rushing for 5 TDs and throwing for 11, drop-kicking 11 extra points and scoring 107 of the team's 130 points. Kinnick played all 60 minutes in six games and led the country in kickoff-return yardage (377) and tied for the lead in interceptions (8). The Associated Press named the Cornbelt Comet the nation's top male athlete for 1939. His Heisman acceptance speech is renowned for its eloquence. After a year of law school, Kinnick enlisted in the Naval Air Corps reserve. On June 2, 1943, above the Gulf of Paria in the Caribbean Sea, he crashed his oil-leaking fighter plane into the sea. Kinnick, 24, chose not to attempt to land on the USS *Lexington* because it would have endangered planes spotted for takeoff. His body was never found.

BEST COACH Evashevski took Iowa to grand heights in the 1950s, but Fry is the man most identified today with the program. Previously of North Texas State, Fry didn't know the state of Iowa's location when he inherited a struggling football program in December 1978. Everyone knew Iowa football when he retired as Hawkeyes coach

in 1998. Fry led Iowa to three Big Ten titles, three Rose Bowl trips and six other top-three league finishes. The ex-Marine from Eastland, Texas, altered Iowa's losing culture by immediately changing the team's logo and uniform design and creating The Swarm, where players hold hands and walk slowly onto the field. His innovations included painting the visitors' locker room pink to pacify Iowa opponents, and his homespun humor and endearing Texas drawl made him popular. So did his wide-open passing attack. In 1981, his third season, Iowa ended a streak of 19 nonwinning seasons, won its first Big Ten title in 21 years and went to the Rose Bowl for the first time since 1959. Rose Bowl berths in the 1985 and 1990 seasons sealed Fry's reputation. His Iowa tenure ended with a school-record 143 wins and 14 bowl trips in 20 seasons. The athletic department named all the football offices and facilities, except the stadium, the Hayden Fry Complex.

BEST TEAM Evashevski constructed a wing-T offensive machine in 1958. Randy Duncan, All-America quarterback and Big Ten MVP, teamed with a strong line, a deep stable of backs and a group of ends known as the Gluefingers

RECORDS

RUSHING YARDS
GAME
314 — Tavian Banks vs. Tulsa, Sept. 13, 1997 (29 att.)
SEASON
1,691 — Tavian Banks, 1997 (260 att.)
CAREER
4,156 — Sedrick Shaw, 1993-96 (837 att.)

PASSING YARDS
GAME
558 — Chuck Hartlieb vs. Indiana, Oct. 29, 1988 (44 of 60)
SEASON
3,738 — Chuck Hartlieb, 1988 (288 of 460)
CAREER
10,461 — Chuck Long, 1981-85 (782 of 1,203)

RECEIVING YARDS
GAME
256 — Quinn Early vs. Northwestern, Nov. 7, 1987 (10 rec.)
SEASON
1,037 — Keith Chappelle, 1980 (64 rec.)
CAREER
2,271 — Tim Dwight, 1994-97 (139 rec.)

POINTS
GAME
24 — Six tied; most recently by Tavian Banks vs. Iowa State, Sept. 20, 1997 (4 TDs)
SEASON
120 — Nate Kaeding, 2002 (21 FGs, 57 PATs)
CAREER
373 — Nate Kaeding, 2000-03 (1 TD, 67 FGs, 166 PATs)

CONSENSUS ALL-AMERICANS

1919	Lester Belding	E
1921	Aubrey Devine	B
1922	Gordon Locke	B
1939	Nile Kinnick	B
1954-55	Calvin Jones	G
1957	Alex Karras	T
1958	Randy Duncan	B
1981	Andre Tippett	DL
1981	Reggie Roby	P
1984-85	Larry Station	LB
1985	Chuck Long	QB
1988	Marv Cook	TE
1991	Leroy Smith	DL
1997	Tim Dwight	KR
1998	Jared DeVries	DL
2002	Dallas Clark	TE
2002	Eric Steinbach	OL
2003	Robert Gallery	OL
2003	Nate Kaeding	PK

Gang to lead the conference in scoring, total yards, first downs, rushing, passing and pass-completion percentage. Iowa went 8–1–1 while averaging 416.7 yards per game, second-best in the nation. The Hawkeyes won the Big Ten title despite a 38-28 home loss to Ohio State in a November game in which the teams combined to gain 889 yards. Iowa rolled to a 38-12 win over California in the Rose Bowl as Bob Jeter ran for 194 yards on nine carries. The Hawkeyes finished No. 2 to LSU for the school's highest-ever season-ending ranking. Evashevski's seniors finished a three-year run of 24–3–2.

BIGGEST GAME Portable lights cast an eerie, reflective glare on Kinnick Stadium's artificial turf on Oct. 19, 1985, as No. 1 Iowa hosted No. 2 Michigan in a nationally televised Poll Bowl that would live up to its hype. Iowa fans swarmed the field at game's end to celebrate a 12-10 victory after Hawkeyes kicker Rob Houghtlin made a 29-yard field goal as time expired. The kick capped a 16-play drive, engineered by QB Chuck Long, that began on Iowa's 22 with 5:27 remaining. Michigan coach Bo Schembechler called time out to rattle Houghtlin, but as Fry said of his kicker, a former walk-on, "That rascal, he wanted to kick it."

BIGGEST UPSET Evashevski's coaching tenure began with Iowa being outscored 129-54 in four losses. Ohio State, ranked No. 16, then rolled into Iowa City on Oct. 25, 1952, as a homecoming opponent. The Buckeyes had defeated Iowa the previous two seasons by a combined score of 130-42. The Hawkeyes, however, scored first on a second-quarter safety, and they stymied OSU's offense. The Buckeyes gained just 216 total yards, including 42 rushing, and never crossed Iowa's 28-yard line. A one-yard TD run by Binkey Broeder with 2:17 left in the fourth quarter sealed the 8-0 win. "It was like my 8-year-old granddaughter out-boxing Sugar Ray Robinson," wrote *Des Moines Register* sports editor Sec Taylor.

STADIUM Iowa Stadium opened in 1929 near the Iowa River at a cost of nearly $500,000, all financed by athletic

ALL-TIME TEAM		

The Gannett News Service selected this team at the start of 2000.

OFFENSE

1918-21	Duke Slater,	OL
1956-57	Alex Karras,	OL
1963-65	John Niland,	OL
1980-83	John Alt,	OL
1951-53	Jerry Hilgenberg,	C
1985-88	Marv Cook,	TE
1994-97	Tim Dwight,	WR
1981-85	Chuck Long,	QB
1937-39	Nile Kinnick,	RB
1982-85	Ronnie Harmon,	RB
1949-51	Bill Reichardt,	FB

DEFENSE

1918-21	Lester Belding,	DL
1938-40	Mike Enich,	DL
1953-55	Calvin Jones,	DL
1983-85	Dave Haight,	DL
1995-98	Jared DeVries,	DL
1979-81	Andre Tippett,	LB
1982-85	Larry Station,	LB
1989-91	Leroy Smith,	LB
1920-22	Gordon Locke,	DB
1927-29	Willis Glassgow,	DB
1961-63	Paul Krause,	DB

event income. The Great Depression began nine days after the Hawkeyes tied Illinois 7-7 in the stadium's dedication game, and 10 years passed before the school could pay its debt on the facility. The stadium's brick facade and bleacher seats remain, but the original capacity of 53,000 has grown to 70,397 because of expansions, one of which enclosed the north end zone in 1983. The school changed the name to Kinnick Stadium in 1972.

HEARTBREAKER The 1985 regular season played out like a Grimm's fairy tale, written by Fry and his consensus All-Americas, Long and linebacker Larry Station. Long finished runner-up in the Heisman race to Bo Jackson while leading the Hawkeyes to a school-record 10 wins. Iowa was ranked No. 1 for five weeks until losing 22-13 at No. 8 Ohio State on Nov. 2. The Hawkeyes rallied with three straight wins to earn the Big Ten championship. They were 10–1 heading into their second Rose Bowl in four years. The giddiness ended in Pasadena. Senior running back Ronnie Harmon lost four fumbles and dropped a certain TD pass as Iowa fell behind UCLA 24-10 at halftime. The Bruins cruised to a 45-28 win as freshman tailback Eric Ball came off the bench to run for 227 yards and 4 TDs. A season of Heisman dreams and national title hopes ended with Iowa settling for a No. 10 ranking in the final AP poll.

WILDEST FINISH Less than five seconds remained in the Capital One Bowl on Jan. 1, 2005, when Iowa center Mike Elgin snapped the ball. The game seemed lost. LSU had taken a 25-24 led with 46 seconds remaining on a three-yard touchdown pass from JaMarcus Russell to Skyler Green. And now here were the Hawkeyes, forgetting to call one of their final two timeouts, scrambling on their final play—but magic happened. Hawkeyes quarterback Drew Tate took the snap on his own 44 and dropped back to pass. He had called "All Up," a play sending four receivers toward the end zone. LSU slot defender Ronnie Prude was supposed to hit receiver Warren Holloway, but instead Prude gave chase for a few

yards and turned to cover the flat. Holloway raced down the middle of the field untouched, wide open. He caught Tate's pass near the 17-yard line. "All I saw was the end zone," said Holloway, a fifth-year senior who had never scored a TD in his career. Tate said, "I was scared that I overthrew him." Holloway kept his balance after the reception and sprinted into the end zone as time expired for a 30-25 Iowa victory. Teammates mobbed Holloway after his game-ending score. "The hardest part was being underneath the pile," he said. "Scoring was the easiest part, believe it or not." Iowa's victory ended the five-year tenure of LSU coach Nick Saban, who had been named head coach of the Miami Dolphins one week earlier.

BEST GOAL-LINE STAND Fry's first Big Ten victory at Iowa came in dramatic fashion in 1979. The Hawkeyes led 13-7 with 30 seconds left, but Illinois had first-and-goal at the Iowa 5. Illini QB Lawrence McCullough threw an incomplete pass on first down and ran for two yards on the next play. McCullough tried a keeper on third down but was thrown for a three-yard loss as time expired. "The ol' Hawks are coming on," Fry said afterward.

BEST COMEBACK Iowa trailed 20-0 in the fourth quarter of the 1951 Minnesota game. Fullback Bill Reichardt, known as The Bull, then went wild. He rushed for two touchdowns, sandwiched around a "tackle eligible" scoring pass from Burt Britzmann to Hubert Johnson. Reichardt's final TD came on a 36-yard run with 1:47 remaining. He kicked the extra point and the game ended in a 20-20 tie. Reichardt had rushed a school-record 31 times and gained a career-high 166 yards—a performance that helped him earn Big Ten MVP honors that season.

RIVAL The Hawkeyes' most frequent opponent has been Minnesota. Iowa first played the Gophers in 1891, and the border-state schools have met almost every season since 1901. Minnesota became unpopular in Iowa by outscoring the Hawkeyes 463-30 while winning the first 12 games of the series. The Gophers had other long stretches of dominance until losing 21-16 in 1982. Iowa coach Fry celebrated that victory, his first over Minnesota, by meeting with reporters after the game dressed up like a farmer and yelling, "Soo-eee." The Hawkeyes then won the Floyd of Rosedale 15 times in 22 meetings.

CONTROVERSY Iowa had a fit after being tied 14-14 by No. 1 Notre Dame in 1953. The visiting Hawkeyes led 7-0

when an official called timeout with one second left in the first half because a Fighting Irish player was apparently injured. Notre Dame QB Ralph Guglielmi then threw a 12-yard TD pass to Dan Shannon. Iowa led 14-7 with less than a minute remaining in the game when two more official timeouts were called as Irish players fell down with suspicious injuries. Guglielmi hit Shannon for a nine-yard TD pass with six seconds remaining. Notre Dame was described as the "Fainting Irish" and dropped to No. 2 in the polls. At a campus pep rally the day after the tie, Evashevski said his team had been "gypped at Notre Dame."

NICKNAME James Fenimore Cooper named a character Hawkeye in his 1826 novel, *The Last of the Mohicans*. People living in the Iowa territory then began referring to themselves as Hawkeyes even though no such bird exists. Territorial officials formally approved usage of the name, and the school later adopted it for its teams.

MASCOT Iowa journalism instructor Richard Spencer III created a cartoon character of the Hawkeye in 1948. The athletic department later conducted a statewide contest to name the mascot and settled on Herky the Hawk, suggested by alumnus John Franklin. Herky became a mascot at Iowa games in the mid-1950s. His depiction was the insignia of the 124th Fighter Squadron during the Korean War.

UNIFORMS When Fry became Iowa coach in 1978 he immediately redesigned the team's uniforms as a psychological ploy to change the mind-set of a program that hadn't had a winning season in 17 years. He was a fan of the Pittsburgh Steelers, who had just won their third of four Super Bowls in the decade, and received permission from the NFL team for Iowa to mimic its black-and-gold designed uniforms. Fry changed the school logo to a meaner-looking hawk and placed it on black helmets.

NUMBERS Calvin Jones was the first college football player and the first African-American to grace the cover of *Sports Illustrated* in the fall of 1954. His No. 62 jersey was retired by Iowa. Jones was a three-time All-Big Ten selection and a two-time All-America offensive lineman, and won the Outland Trophy as a senior in 1955. He died on Dec. 9, 1956, in an airline crash in the Canadian mountains … There were 32 fumbles in the 1925 Iowa-Wisconsin game, played during a snowstorm. The Hawkeyes lost 10 of their 20 fumbles in a 6-0 defeat … Zero fans attended Iowa's 27-0 victory over Coe in 1918 because the influenza epidemic caused the

War Department to bar spectators … Thirteen Hawkeyes known as The Ironmen played all 60 minutes of at least one game in 1939 … Chuck Long set a then-NCAA record by completing 22 consecutive passes in a 24-20 win over Indiana on Oct. 27, 1984 … Eight Hawkeyes have been selected Big Ten Lineman of the Year since 1984 and four QBs have been named All-Big Ten a total of eight times in the past 20 seasons.

LORE Near the end of his sophomore season in 1955, an out-of-shape Alex Karras showed up late for practice. Evashevski told him to leave and never come back. After Karras apologized to his teammates a day later they voted unanimously for his reinstatement. Karras played little in the season's final three games, then withdrew from school and returned home to Gary, Ind. His mother, Emiline Schofield, talked him into returning to Iowa. Karras was named All-America as an offensive and defensive tackle as a junior and led the Hawkeyes to the 1956 Big Ten title and a Rose Bowl win. He won the Outland Trophy, finished second in the Heisman Trophy voting and became a two-time All-America his senior year.

QUOTE "Scratch where it itches." —Hayden Fry, describing how Iowa's style of play was to do whatever it took to win

IOWA ANNUAL STATISTICAL LEADERS

YR	RUSHING	YDS	ATT	AVG	PASSING	ATT	CMP	PCT	YDS	RECEIVING	REC	YDS	AVG
1933	Dick Crayne	655	161	4.1		NA	NA	NA	NA		NA	NA	NA
1934	Dick Crayne	432	128	3.4		NA	NA	NA	NA		NA	NA	NA
1935	Ozzie Simmons	580	113	5.1		NA	NA	NA	NA		NA	NA	NA
1936	Ozzie Simmons	592	98	6.0		NA	NA	NA	NA		NA	NA	NA
1937	Nile Kinnick	214	95	2.3		NA	NA	NA	NA		NA	NA	NA
1938	Jerry Niles	176	51	3.5		NA	NA	NA	NA		NA	NA	NA
1939	Nile Kinnick	374	106	3.5		NA	NA	NA	NA		NA	NA	NA
1940	Bill Green	483	115	4.2		NA	NA	NA	NA		NA	NA	NA
1941	Bill Green	420	114	3.7		NA	NA	NA	NA		NA	NA	NA
1942	Charles Uknes	445	84	5.3		NA	NA	NA	NA		NA	NA	NA
1943	Bill Gallagher	314	72	4.4	Roger Stephens		12		231	Bill Barbour	10	179	17.9
1944	Bill Kersten	301	106	2.8	Dick Woodard		11		128	John Stewart	7	46	6.6
1945	Arthur Johnson	290	65	4.5	Jerry Niles		63		889	Harold Loehlein	11	165	15.0
1946	Bob Smith	503	109	4.6	Emlen Tunnell	58	28	.48	228	Dick Hoerner	6	72	12.0
1947	Bob Smith	395	110	3.6	Al DiMarco	100	49	.49	644	Emlen Tunnell	12	262	21.8
1948	Jerry Faske	491	73	6.7	Al DiMarco	161	64	.40	1,105	Bob McKenzie	22	382	17.4
1949	Ralph Doran	342	53	6.5	Glenn Drahn	145	51	.35	735	Bob McKenzie	22	313	14.2
1950	Bill Reichardt	585	138	4.2	Glenn Drahn	168	55	.33	835	Bill Reichardt	11	95	8.6
1951	Bill Reichardt	737	178	4.1	Burt Britzmann	150	68	.45	942	Fred Ruck	25	274	11.0
1952	George Broeder	311	86	3.6	Burt Britzmann	94	37	.39	515	Dan McBride	29	448	15.4
1953	George Broeder	410	96	4.3	Lou Matykiewicz	44	18	.41	234	Frank Gilliam	12	71	5.9
1954	Eddie Vincent	618	95	6.5	Jerry Reichow	73	34	.47	386	Frank Gilliam	15	223	14.9
1955	Eddie Vincent	381	73	5.2	Jerry Reichow	88	48	.55	722	Jim Gibbons	16	257	16.1
1956	Ken Ploen	487	86	5.7	Ken Ploen	64	33	.52	386	Jim Gibbons	17	255	15.0
1957	Collins Hagler	456	67	6.8	Randy Duncan	119	70	.59	1,124	Jim Gibbons	36	587	16.3
1958	Ray Jauch	524	76	6.9	Randy Duncan	179	106	.59	1,397	Don Norton	25	374	15.0
1959	Bob Jeter	609	108	5.6	Olen Treadway	147	86	.59	1,014	Don Norton	30	428	14.3
1960	Larry Ferguson	665	90	7.4	Wilburn Hollis	62	22	.35	289	Felton Rogers	8	96	12.0
1961	Bill Perkins	380	62	6.1	Matt Szykowny	120	79	.66	1,078	Cloyd Webb	25	425	17.0
1962	Larry Ferguson	547	113	4.8	Matt Szykowny	115	59	.51	737	Paul Krause	16	214	13.4
1963	Bobby Grier	406	98	4.1	Gary Snook	90	34	.38	667	Cloyd Webb	24	424	18.0
1964	Dalton Kimble	284	68	4.2	Gary Snook	311	151	.49	2,062	Karl Noonan	59	933	15.8
1965	Silas McKinnie	286	89	3.2	Gary Snook	230	95	.41	1,009	Karl Noonan	43	545	12.7
1966	Silas McKinnie	516	124	4.2	Ed Podolak	191	77	.40	1,041	Al Bream	30	418	13.9
1967	Silas McKinnie	588	166	3.5	Ed Podolak	162	79	.49	1,014	Al Bream	55	703	12.8
1968	Ed Podolak	937	154	6.1	Larry Lawrence	156	88	.56	1,307	Ray Manning	35	426	12.2
1969	Steve Penney	484	102	4.7	Larry Lawrence	239	113	.47	1,680	Kerry Reardon	43	738	17.2
1970	Levi Mitchell	900	205	4.4	Roy Bash	70	32	.46	473	Kerry Reardon	27	438	16.2
1971	Levi Mitchell	623	149	4.2	Frank Sunderman	235	109	.46	1,297	Dave Triplett	28	426	15.2
1972	Dave Harris	621	136	4.6	Kyle Skogman	57	24	.42	356	Brian Rollins	29	378	13.0
1973	Jim Jensen	509	111	4.6	Butch Caldwell	99	36	.36	549	Brian Rollins	33	408	12.4
1974	Jim Jensen	659	163	4.0	Rob Fick	165	79	.48	1,059	Bill Schultz	25	432	17.3
1975	Dave Schick	482	90	5.4	Tom McLaughlin	87	23	.26	358	Bill Schultz	8	238	30.0
1976	Jon Lazar	392	95	4.1	Butch Caldwell	101	37	.37	616	Tom Grine	12	195	16.3
1977	Jon Lazar	411	100	4.1	Tom McLaughlin	152	78	.51	1,081	Mike Brady	26	357	13.7
1978	Jon Lazar	423	108	3.9	Jeff Green	103	41	.40	556	Jon Lazar	18	72	4.0
1979	Dennis Mosley	1,267	270	4.7	Phil Suess	159	88	.55	1,165	Brad Reid	25	290	11.6
1980	Jeff Brown	673	132	5.1	Phil Suess	166	87	.52	1,031	Keith Chappelle	64	1,037	16.2
1981	Phil Blatcher	708	145	4.9	Gordy Bohannon	142	72	.51	999	Jeff Brown	20	301	15.1
1982	Eddie Phillips	806	166	4.9	Chuck Long	227	148	.65	1,678	Dave Moritz	41	605	14.8
1983	Owen Gill	798	129	6.2	Chuck Long	265	157	.59	2,601	Dave Moritz	50	912	18.2
1984	Owen Gill	920	199	4.6	Chuck Long	322	216	.67	2,871	Bill Happel	47	632	13.4
1985	Ronnie Harmon	1,166	223	5.2	Chuck Long	388	260	.67	3,297	Ronnie Harmon	60	699	11.7
1986	Rick Bayless	1,150	216	5.3	Mark Vlasic	180	108	.60	1,456	Jim Mauro	30	600	20.0
1987	Kevin Harmon	715	151	4.7	Chuck Hartlieb	334	217	.65	3,092	Quinn Early	63	1,004	15.9
1988	Tony Stewart	1,036	215	4.8	Chuck Hartlieb	460	288	.63	3,738	Marv Cook	63	767	12.2
1989	Nick Bell	603	117	5.1	Matt Rodgers	312	178	.57	2,222	Travis Watkins	36	583	16.2
1990	Nick Bell	1,009	166	6.1	Matt Rodgers	310	187	.60	2,228	Danan Hughes	29	410	14.1
1991	Mike Saunders	1,022	216	4.7	Matt Rodgers	283	185	.65	2,275	Danan Hughes	43	757	17.6
1992	Marvin Lampkin	653	171	3.8	Jim Hartlieb	226	144	.64	1,579	Alan Cross	55	640	11.6
1993	Ryan Terry	664	157	4.2	Paul Burmeister	309	184	.60	2,152	Harold Jasper	38	641	16.9
1994	Sedrick Shaw	1,002	170	5.9	Ryan Driscoll	154	78	.51	1,018	Harold Jasper	33	621	18.8
1995	Sedrick Shaw	1,477	316	4.7	Matt Sherman	295	170	.58	2,546	Tim Dwight	46	816	17.7
1996	Sedrick Shaw	1,116	224	5.0	Matt Sherman	264	154	.58	1,918	Tim Dwight	51	751	14.7
1997	Tavian Banks	1,691	260	6.5	Matt Sherman	158	82	.52	1,199	Tim Dwight	42	704	16.8
1998	Ladell Betts	679	188	3.6	Kyle McCann	159	86	.54	1,179	Kahlil Hill	35	432	12.3
1999	Ladell Betts	857	189	4.5	Scott Mullen	226	126	.56	1,415	Kevin Kasper	60	664	11.1
2000	Ladell Betts	1,090	232	4.7	Scott Mullen	141	74	.52	877	Kevin Kasper	82	1,010	12.3
2001	Ladell Betts	1,060	222	4.7	Kyle McCann	252	167	.66	2,028	Kahlil Hill	59	841	14.3
2002	Fred Russell	1,264	220	5.7	Brad Banks	294	170	.58	2,573	Maurice Brown	48	966	20.1
2003	Fred Russell	1,355	282	4.8	Nathan Chandler	308	165	.54	2,040	Maurice Brown	33	507	15.4
2004	Sam Brownlee	227	94	2.4	Drew Tate	375	233	.62	2,786	Ed Hinkel	63	744	11.8

All statistics include postseason

THE SCHOOLS

IOWA ALL-TIME SCORES

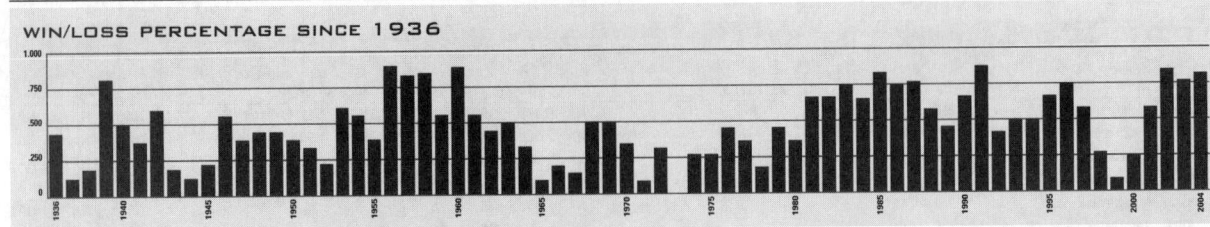

WIN/LOSS PERCENTAGE SINCE 1936

NO HEAD COACH

1889   0-1-0
| N16 | | at Grinnell | 0 | 24 |

1890   1-1-0
| U | | Grinnell | 6 | 11 |
| U | ● | at Iowa Wesleyan | 91 | 0 |

1891   2-3-0
O24	●	Cornell Coll.	64	6
N2		Minnesota	4	42
N9		at Grinnell	4	6
N26	●	Nebraska [Oma]	22	0
D5		Kansas [KC]	12	14 #

E.A. DALTON
1892 (.583)   3-2-1

1892   3-2-1
O21	●	Knox	44	0
O29	●	at Coe	48	0
N5		Kansas [KC]	4	24
N12		at Missouri	0	22 *
N16	●	Grinnell	18	12
N24	=	Nebraska [Oma]	10	10

BEN DONNELLY
1893 (.429)   3-4

1893   3-4-0
O7	●	at Coe	56	0
O14		at Denver AC	0	58
O21	●	Luther	32	0
N4		Kansas [KC]	24	35
N11		at Grinnell	14	36
N18	●	Missouri	34	12*
N30		Nebraska [Oma]	18	20

ROGER SHERMAN
1894 (.500)   4-4-1

1894   4-4-1
S29		Iowa State	8	16
O13	●	at Cornell Coll	60	0
O20	●	at Augustana	34	0
O27	=	at Chicago	18	18
O29		at Wisconsin	0	44
N3	●	Kansas	14	12
N10	●	Grinnell	6	0
N17		at Missouri	16	32 *
N29		Nebraska [Oma]	0	36

NO HEAD COACH

1895   2-5-0
O12	●	Doane	0	10
O19	●	at Parsons	28	0
O28		Iowa State	0	24
N2		at Kansas	0	52 *
N18		at Missouri	0	34
N19		at Penn Coll.	14	12
N28		Nebraska [Oma]	0	6

ALFRED BULL
1896 (.833)   7-1-1

1896   7-1-1
O3	●	Drake	32	0
O10		at Chicago	0	6
O25	●	Kansas	6	0
N4	●	Wilton	27	0
N9		at Missouri	12	0
N14	●	at Grinnell	15	6
N21	●	at Des Moines YMCA	34	0
N26	=	Nebraska [Oma]	0	0
N28	●	Nebraska [Oma]	6	0

OTTO WAGONHURST
1897 (.500)   4-4

1897   4-4-0
O2	●	Wilton	22	4
O16	●	at Northwestern	12	6
O23		Phys. & Surg.	0	14
O30		at Kansas	0	56
N5		Iowa State	0	6 *
N13	●	at Drake	16	0
N20	●	Grinnell	16	12
N25		Nebraska [Cou]	0	6

ALDEN KNIPE
1898-1902 (.705)   29-11-4

1898   3-4-2
O1	=	at Knox	0	0
O8		at Chicago	0	38
O15	●	Drake	5	18
O22	●	Upper Iowa	23	5
O29		at Rush	11	15
N5		at No. Iowa	5	11
N12		at Grinnell	5	5
N17	●	Simpson	12	0
N24	●	Nebraska [Cou]	6	5

1899   8-0-1
S23	●	No. Iowa	22	0
O7	=	at Chicago	5	5
O14	●	William Penn	35	0
O21	●	Rush	17	0
O28	●	Iowa State	5	0
N4	●	Nebraska [Oma]	30	0
N11	●	Grinnell	16	0
N18	●	at Knox	33	0
N30	●	Illinois [RI]	58	0

1900-Present
BIG 10

1900   7-0-1 (2-0-1)
S28	●	Upper Iowa	57	0
O6	●	No. Iowa	68	0
O12	●	Simpson	47	0
O26	●	Drake	26	0
N3	●	at Chicago	17	0
N10	●	Michigan [DET]	28	5
N16	●	Grinnell	63	2
N29	=	at Northwestern	5	5

1901   6-3-0 (0-3-0)
O5	●	No. Iowa	16	0
O11	●	at Drake	6	5
O18	●	Iowa State	6	0 *
O26		at Minnesota	0	16
O30	●	Coe	11	0
N2	●	Knox	23	6
N9		Illinois	0	27
N16	●	Grinnell	17	11
N28		Michigan [CHI]	0	50

1902   5-4-0 (0-3-0)
O4	●	No. Iowa	26	5
O11	●	at Drake	12	0
O18	●	at Simpson	10	0
O25		Minnesota	0	34
N1	●	Iowa State	12	6
N8		at Michigan	0	107
N15	●	at Washington, Mo.	61	0
N20		Missouri	0	6
N27		at Illinois	0	80

JOHN CHALMERS
1903-05 (.750)   24-8

1903   9-2-0 (1-1-0)
S27	●	Cornell Coll.	6	0
S29	●	Coe	16	0
O3	●	No. Iowa	29	0
O10	●	Drake	22	6
O17		at Minnesota	0	75
O24	●	at Grinnell	17	0
O31		Nebraska	6	17
N6	●	Simpson	35	2
N14	●	at Missouri	16	0
N21	●	Illinois	12	0
N26	●	at Washington, Mo.	12	2

1904   7-4-0 (0-3-0)
S24	●	Coe	17	0
S27	●	Augustana	33	2
O1	●	Cornell Coll.	88	0
O6	●	at Drake	17	0
O15		at Chicago	0	39
O22	●	No. Iowa	11	5
O29	●	Iowa State	10	6
N5		at Nebraska	6	17
N12	●	Grinnell	69	0
N19		at Illinois	0	29
N24		Minnesota	0	11

1905   8-2-0 (0-2-0)
S26	●	Coe	27	0
S30	●	Monmouth	40	0
O7		at Chicago	0	42
O21		at Minnesota	0	39
O28	●	No. Iowa	41	5
N4	●	Grinnell	46	0
N11	●	Des Moines	72	0
N18	●	Drake	44	0
N24	●	at Iowa State	8	0
N30	●	at St. Louis	31	0

MARK CATLIN
1906-08 (.412)   7-10

1906   2-3-0 (0-1-0)
O27	●	Missouri	24	4
N3		at Wisconsin	4	18
N10	●	Coe	15	12
N24		Iowa State	0	2
N29		at St. Louis	0	39

1907   3-2-0 (1-1-0)
O19	●	Missouri	21	6
O26	●	at Drake	25	4
N2		Wisconsin	5	6
N9	●	Illinois	25	12
N23		at Iowa State	14	20 *

1908   2-5-0 (0-1-0)
O10	●	Coe	92	0
O17		at Missouri	5	10
O24	●	at Morningside	16	0
O31		Nebraska	8	11
N7		at Illinois	0	22
N14	●	Drake	6	12
N21		Kansas	5	52

JOHN GRIFFITH
1909 (.357)   2-4-1

1909   2-4-1 (0-1-0)
O2		at Minnesota	0	41
O9	●	Cornell Coll.	3	0
O23	=	at Nebraska	6	6
O30		Missouri	12	13
N6		at Drake	14	17
N13	●	Iowa State	13	0 *
N20		at Kansas	7	20

JESSE HAWLEY
1910-15 (.571)   24-18

1910   5-2-0 (1-1-0)
O2	●	Morningside	12	0
O8		at Northwestern	5	10
O15		at Missouri	0	5
O22	●	Purdue	16	0
N5		at Iowa State	2	0
N12	●	Drake	21	0
N19		at Washington, Mo.	38	0

1911   3-4-0 (2-2-0)
O14	●	at Morningside	11	5
O21		at Cornell Coll.	0	3
O28		Minnesota	6	24
N4		at Wisconsin	0	12
N11	●	at Purdue	11	0
N18	●	Iowa State	0	9
N25		Northwestern	6	0

1912   4-3-0 (1-3-0)
O7	●	No. Iowa	35	7
O12	●	Cornell Coll.	31	0
O19		at Chicago	14	34
O26		at Minnesota	7	56
N9	●	at Indiana	13	6
N16	●	at Iowa State	20	7
N23		Wisconsin	10	28

1913   5-2-0 (2-1-0)
O8	●	No. Iowa	45	3
O15	●	Cornell Coll.	76	0
O18		at Chicago	6	23
O25	●	at Northwestern	78	6
N8		Indiana	60	0
N15	●	Iowa State	45	7
N22		at Nebraska	0	12

1914   4-3-0 (1-2-0)
O3	●	No. Iowa	95	0
O10	●	Cornell Coll.	49	0
O17		at Chicago	0	7
O24		Minnesota	0	7
N7		at Northwestern	27	0
N14	●	at Iowa State	26	6
N21		Nebraska	7	16

1915   3-4-0 (1-2-0)
O2	●	at Cornell Coll.	33	0
O9	●	at Morningside	17	6
O16		Northwestern	9	6
O23		at Minnesota	13	51
N6		at Purdue	13	19
N13		Iowa State	0	16
N20		at Nebraska	7	52

HOWARD JONES
1916-23 (.708)   42-17-1

1916   4-3-0 (1-2-0)
O7	●	Cornell Coll.	31	6
O14	●	Grinnell	17	7
O21		Purdue	24	6
O28		at Minnesota	0	67
N10	●	at Northwestern	13	20
N18	●	at Iowa State	19	16
N25		Nebraska	17	34

1917   3-5-0 (0-2-0)
O6	●	Cornell Coll.	22	13
O13		at Nebraska	0	47
O20		Grinnell	0	10
O27		at Wisconsin	0	20
N3		at Great Lakes NAS	14	23
N10	●	South Dakota	35	0
N17		at Northwestern	14	25
N24	●	Iowa State	6	3

IOWA 367

1918 6-2-1 (2-1-0)

S28		Great Lakes NAS	0	10
O5	●	at Nebraska	12	0
O12	●	Coe	27	0
O19	●	Cornell Coll.	34	0
N2	|	Illinois	0	19
N9	● |	Minnesota	6	0
N16	●	Iowa State	21	0
N23	● |	Northwestern	23	7
N30	=	at Camp Dodge	0	0

1919 5-2-0 (2-2-0)

O4	●	Nebraska	18	0
O18	|	at Illinois	7	9
O25	● |	at Minnesota	9	6
N1	●	South Dakota	26	13
N8	● |	at Northwestern	14	7
N15	|	at Chicago	6	9
N22	●	Iowa State	10	0

1920 5-2-0 (3-2-0)

O2	● |	at Indiana	14	7
O9	●	Cornell Coll.	63	0
O16	|	at Illinois	3	20
O23	|	at Chicago	0	10
N6	● |	Northwestern	20	0
N13	● |	Minnesota	28	7
N20	●	at Iowa State	14	10

1921 7-0-0 (5-0-0)

O1	●	Knox	52	14
O8	●	Notre Dame	10	7
O15	● |	Illinois	14	2
O29	● |	at Purdue	13	6
N5	● |	at Minnesota	41	7
N12	● |	Indiana	41	0
N19	● |	at Northwestern	14	0

1922 7-0-0 (5-0-0)

O7	●	Knox	61	0
O14	●	at Yale	6	0
O21	● |	at Illinois	8	7
O28	● |	Purdue	56	0
N11	● |	Minnesota	28	14
N18	● |	at Ohio State	12	9
N25	● |	Northwestern	37	3

1923 5-3-0 (3-3-0)

S29	●	Oklahoma State	20	0
O6	●	Knox	44	3
O13	● |	Purdue	7	0
O20	|	at Illinois	6	9
O27	● |	Ohio State	20	0
N3	|	at Michigan	3	9
N17	|	at Minnesota	7	20
N24	● |	Northwestern	17	14

BURT INGWERSEN 1924-31 (.547) 33-27-4

1924 6-1-1 (3-1-1)

O4	●	S.E. Oklahoma	43	0
O11	= |	Ohio State	0	0
O18	●	Lawrence	13	5
O25	● |	Minnesota	13	0
N1	|	at Illinois	0	36
N8	●	Butler	7	0
N15	● |	at Wisconsin	21	7
N22	● |	at Michigan	9	2

1925 5-3-0 (2-2-0)

O3	●	Arkansas	25	0 *
O10	●	St. Louis	41	0
O17	● |	Illinois	12	10
O24	● |	at Ohio State	15	0
O31	●	Wabash	28	7
N7	|	Wisconsin	0	6
N14	|	at Minnesota	0	33
N21		at Southern Cal	0	18

1926 3-5-0 (0-5-0)

O2	●	Colorado Teachers	24	0
O9	●	North Dakota	40	7
O16	|	at Illinois	6	13
O23	|	at Ohio State	6	23
O30	●	Carroll	21	0
N6	|	Minnesota	0	41
N13	|	at Wisconsin	10	20
N20	|	Northwestern	6	13

1927 4-4-0 (1-4-0)

O1	●	Monmouth	32	6
O8	|	Ohio State	6	13
O15	●	Wabash	38	0
O22	|	at Minnesota	0	38
O29	●	Denver	15	0
N5	|	Illinois	0	14
N12	● |	at Wisconsin	16	0
N19	|	at Northwestern	0	12

1928 6-2-0 (3-2-0)

O7	●	Monmouth	26	0
O13	● |	at Chicago	13	0
O20	●	Ripon	61	6
O27	● |	Minnesota	7	6
N3	●	South Dakota	19	0
N10	● |	at Ohio State	14	7
N17	|	Wisconsin	0	13
N24	|	at Michigan	7	10

1929 4-2-2 (2-2-2)

S29	●	Carroll	46	0
O6	●	Monmouth	46	0
O12	|	at Ohio State	6	7
O20	= |	Illinois	7	7
O26	● |	at Wisconsin	14	0
N9	● |	Minnesota	9	7
N16	|	at Purdue	0	7
N23	= |	at Michigan	0	0

1930 4-4-0 (0-1-0)

S27	●	Bradley Tech	38	12
O4		Oklahoma State	0	6
O11		Centenary	12	19
O18	|	Purdue	0	20
N1	●	at Detroit	7	3
N8		at Marquette	0	7
N15	●	Penn State	19	0
N22	●	Nebraska	12	7

1931 1-6-1 (0-3-1)

O3		Pittsburgh	0	20
O10		Texas A&M DAL	0	29
O17	= |	Indiana	0	0
O24	|	at Minnesota	0	34
O31	●	George Washington	7	0
N7		at Nebraska	0	7
N12	|	at Purdue	0	22
N21	|	Northwestern	0	19

OSSIE SOLEM 1932-36 (.425) 15-21-4

1932 1-7-0 (0-5-0)

O1	●	Bradley Tech	31	7
O8	|	at Wisconsin	0	34
O15	|	at Indiana	0	12
O22	|	Minnesota	6	21
O28		at George Washington	6	21
N5		Nebraska	13	14
N12	|	Purdue	0	18
N19	|	at Northwestern	6	44

1933 5-3-0 (3-2-0)

O7	● |	Northwestern CHI	7	0
O14	●	Bradley Tech	38	0
O21	● |	Wisconsin	26	7
O28	|	at Minnesota	7	19
N4	●	Iowa State	27	7
N11	|	at Michigan	6	10
N18	● |	at Purdue	14	6
N25		at Nebraska	6	7

1934 2-5-1 (1-3-1)

S29	●	South Dakota	34	0
O6	● |	at Northwestern	20	7
O13		at Nebraska	13	14
O20		at Iowa State	6	31
O28	|	Minnesota	12	48
N3	= |	at Indiana	0	0
N10	|	Purdue	6	13
N24	|	at Ohio State	7	40

1935 4-2-2 (1-2-2)

S28	●	Bradley	26	0
O5	●	South Dakota	47	2
O12	●	Colgate	12	6
O26	● |	at Illinois	19	0
N2	= |	Indiana	6	6
N9	|	Minnesota	6	13
N16	|	at Purdue	6	12
N23	= |	at Northwestern	0	0

1936 3-4-1 (0-4-1)

S26	●	Carleton	14	0
O3	|	at Northwestern	7	18
O10	●	South Dakota	33	7
O17	= |	Illinois	0	0
O31	|	at Indiana	6	13
N7	|	at Minnesota	0	52
N14	|	Purdue	0	13
N21	●	at Temple	25	0

IRL TUBBS 1937-38 (.156) 2-13-1

1937 1-7-0 (0-5-0)

S25		at Washington	0	14
O9	●	Bradley Tech	14	7
O16	|	at Wisconsin	6	13
O23	|	Michigan	6	7
O30	|	at Purdue	0	13
N6	|	Minnesota	10	35
N13	|	Indiana	0	3
N20		at Nebraska	0	28

1938 1-6-1 (1-3-1)

S23		at UCLA	3	27
O8	|	Wisconsin	13	31
O15	● |	at Chicago	27	14
O22		Colgate	0	14
O29	= |	Purdue	0	0
N5	|	at Minnesota	0	28
N12	|	at Indiana	3	7
N19		Nebraska	0	14

EDDIE ANDERSON 1939-42 '46-49 (.514) 35-33-2

1939 6-1-1 (4-1-1)

S30	●	South Dakota	41	0
O7	● |	Indiana	32	29
O14	|	at Michigan	7	27
O28	● |	at Wisconsin	19	13
N4	● |	at Purdue	4	0
N11	●	Notre Dame	7	6
N18	● |	Minnesota	13	9
N25	= |	at Northwestern	7	7

1940 4-4-0 (2-3-0)

O5	●	South Dakota	46	0
O12	● |	Wisconsin	30	12
O19	|	at Indiana	6	10
O26	|	at Minnesota	6	34
N2	|	Purdue	6	21
N9		at Nebraska	6	14
N16	●	at Notre Dame	7	0
N23	● |	Illinois	18	7

1941 3-5-0 (2-4-0)

S27	●	Drake	25	8
O4	|	at Michigan	0	6
O18	|	at Wisconsin	0	23
O25	|	at Purdue	6	7
N1	● |	Indiana	13	7
N8	● |	at Illinois	21	0
N15	|	Minnesota	13	34
N22		at Nebraska	13	14

1942 6-4-0 (3-3-0)

S19	●	Washington, Mo.	26	7
S26	●	Nebraska	27	0
O3		Great Lakes NAS	0	25
O10	●	Camp Grant	33	16
O17	|	Illinois	7	12
O24	● |	at Indiana	14	13
O31	● |	Purdue	13	7
N7	● |	Wisconsin	6	0
N14	|	at Minnesota	7	27
N28	|	at Michigan	14	28

SLIP MADIGAN 1943-44 (.156) 2-13-1

1943 1-6-1 (0-4-1)

S25		at Great Lakes NAS	7	21
O2	|	Wisconsin	5	7
O9		Iowa Pre-Flight	0	25
O16	= |	Indiana	7	7
O23	|	at Purdue	7	28
N6	|	Illinois	10	19
N13	|	at Minnesota	14	33
N20	●	at Nebraska	33	13

1944 1-7-0 (0-6-0)

O7	|	at Ohio State	0	34
O14	|	at Illinois	6	40
O21	|	Purdue	7	26
O28	|	at Indiana	0	32
N4	●	at Nebraska	27	6
N11	|	at Wisconsin	7	26
N18	|	Minnesota	0	46
N25		Iowa Pre-Flight	6	30

CLEM CROWE 1945 (.222) 2-7

1945 2-7-0 (1-5-0)

S29	●	Berg AAf	14	13
O6	|	at Ohio State	0	42
O13	|	at Purdue	0	40
O20	|	Indiana	20	52
O27		at Notre Dame	0	56
N3	|	Wisconsin	7	27
N10	|	at Illinois	7	48
N17	● |	Minnesota	20	19
N24		at Nebraska	6	13

EDDIE ANDERSON

1946 5-4-0 (3-3-0)

S21	●	North Dakota St.	39	0
S28	● |	Purdue	16	0
O5	|	at Michigan	7	14
O12	●	Nebraska	21	7
O19	● |	at Indiana	13	0
O26		Notre Dame	6	41
N2	|	Illinois	0	7
N9	● |	at Wisconsin	21	7
N16	|	at Minnesota	6	16

1947 3-5-1 (2-3-1)

S20	●	North Dakota St.	59	0
S26		at UCLA	7	22
O4	|	Illinois	12	35
O11	● |	Indiana	27	14
O18	= |	at Ohio State	13	13
O25		at Notre Dame	0	21
N1	|	at Purdue	0	21
N8	|	at Wisconsin	14	46
N15	● |	Minnesota	13	7

1948 4-5-0 (2-4-0)

S25	●	Marquette	14	12
O2	|	at Indiana	0	7
O9	● |	at Ohio State	14	7
O16	|	Purdue	13	20
O23		Notre Dame	12	27
O30	● |	Wisconsin	19	13
N6	|	at Illinois	0	14
N13	|	Minnesota	21	28
N20	●	at Boston U.	34	14

1949 4-5-0 (3-3-0)

S24		UCLA	25	41
O1	● |	at Purdue	21	7
O8	|	Illinois	14	20
O15	● |	Indiana	35	9
O22	● |	Northwestern	28	21
O29	●	Oregon	34	31
N5	|	at Minnesota	7	55
N12	|	at Wisconsin	13	35
N19		at Notre Dame	7	28

LEONARD RAFFENSPERGER 1950-51 (.361) 5-10-3

1950 3-5-1 (2-4-0)

S29	●	at Southern Cal	20	14
O7	|	at Indiana	7	20
O14	|	Wisconsin	0	14
O21	● |	Purdue	33	21
O28	|	at Ohio State	21	83
N4	● |	at Minnesota	13	0
N11	|	Illinois	7	21
N18	=	Notre Dame	14	14
N24		at Miami, Fla.	6	14

1951 2-5-2 (0-5-1)

S29	●	Kansas State	16	0
O6	|	at Purdue	30	34
O13	●	Pittsburgh	34	17
O20	|	Michigan	0	21
O27	|	at Ohio State	21	47
N3	= |	Minnesota	20	20
N10	|	at Illinois	13	40
N17	|	at Wisconsin	7	34
N24	=	at Notre Dame	20	20

FOREST EVASHEVSKI 1952-60 (.651) 52-27-4

1952 2-7-0 (2-5-0)

S27		at Pittsburgh	14	26
O4	|	at Indiana	13	20
O11	|	at Purdue	14	41
O18	|	Wisconsin	13	42
O25	● |	Ohio State	8	0
N1	|	at Minnesota	7	17
N8	|	Illinois	13	33
N15	● |	at Northwestern	39	14
N22		Notre Dame	0	27

THE SCHOOLS

368 IOWA

THE SCHOOLS

1953 5-3-1 (3-3-0)

S26		|	Michigan State	7	21
O3	●		Washington State	54	12
O10		|	at Michigan	13	14
O17	●		Wyoming	21	7
O24	●	|	Indiana	19	13
O31		|	at Wisconsin	6	10
N7	●	|	at Purdue	26	0
N14	●	|	Minnesota	27	0
N21	=		at Notre Dame	14	14

1954 5-4-0 (4-3-0)

S25	●	|	Michigan State	14	10
O2	●		Montana	48	6
O9		|	at Michigan	13	14
O16		|	at Ohio State	14	20
O23	●	|	at Indiana	27	14
O30	●	|	Wisconsin	13	7
N6	●	|	Purdue	25	14
N13		|	at Minnesota	20	22
N20			Notre Dame	18	34

1955 3-5-1 (2-3-1)

S24	●		Kansas State	28	7
O1		|	at Wisconsin	14	37
O8	●	|	Indiana	20	6
O15	=	|	Purdue	20	20
O21			at UCLA	13	33
O29		|	at Michigan	21	33
N5	●	|	Minnesota	26	0
N12		|	at Ohio State	10	20
N19			at Notre Dame	14	17

1956 9-1-0 (5-1-0)

S29	●	|	at Indiana	27	0
O6	●		Oregon State	14	13
O13	●	|	Wisconsin	13	7
O20	●		Hawaii	34	0
O27	●	|	at Purdue	21	20
N3		|	Michigan	14	17
N10	●	|	at Minnesota	7	0
N17	●	|	Ohio State	6	0
N24	●		Notre Dame	48	8
			ROSE BOWL		
J1	●		Oregon State	35	19

1957 7-1-1 (4-1-1)

S28	●		Utah State	70	14
O5	●		Washington State	20	13
O12	●	|	at Indiana	47	7
O19	●	|	Wisconsin	21	7
O26	●	|	at Northwestern	6	0
N2	=	|	at Michigan	21	21
N9	●	|	Minnesota	44	20
N16		|	at Ohio State	13	17
N23	●		at Notre Dame	21	13

1958 8-1-1 (5-1-0)

S27	●		TCU	17	0
O4	=		Air Force	13	13
O11	●	|	Indiana	34	13
O18	●	|	at Wisconsin	20	9
O25	●	|	Northwestern	26	20
N1	●	|	at Michigan	37	14
N8	●	|	at Minnesota	28	6
N15		|	Ohio State	28	38
N22	●		Notre Dame	31	21
			ROSE BOWL		
J1	●		California	38	12

1959 5-4-0 (3-3-0)

S26	●		at California	42	12
O3		|	Northwestern	10	14
O10	●	|	Michigan State	37	8
O17		|	at Wisconsin	16	25
O24		|	at Purdue	7	14
O31	●		Kansas State	53	0
N7	●	|	Minnesota	33	0
N14	●	|	at Ohio State	16	7
N21			Notre Dame	19	20

1960 8-1-0 (5-1-0)

S24	●		Oregon State	22	12
O1	●	|	at Northwestern	42	0
O8	●	|	at Michigan State	27	15
O15	●	|	Wisconsin	28	21
O22	●	|	Purdue	21	14
O29	●		Kansas	21	7
N5		|	at Minnesota	10	27
N12	●	|	Ohio State	35	12
N19	●		at Notre Dame	28	0

JERRY BURNS
1961-65 (.378) 16-27-2

1961 5-4-0 (2-4-0)

S30	●		California	28	7
O7	●		at Southern Cal	35	34
O14	●	|	Indiana	27	8
O21	●	|	Wisconsin	47	15
O28		|	at Purdue	0	9
N4		|	at Ohio State	13	29
N11		|	Minnesota	9	16
N18		|	at Michigan	14	23
N25	●		Notre Dame	42	21

1962 4-5-0 (3-3-0)

S29	●		Oregon State	28	8
O6			Southern Cal	0	7
O13	●	|	at Indiana	14	10
O20		|	at Wisconsin	14	42
O27		|	Purdue	3	26
N3	●	|	Ohio State	28	14
N10		|	at Minnesota	0	10
N17	●	|	Michigan	28	14
N24			at Notre Dame	12	35

1963 3-3-2 (2-3-1)

S28	=		Washington State	14	14
O5	●		at Washington	17	7
O12	●	|	Indiana	37	26
O19		|	Wisconsin	7	10
O26		|	at Purdue	0	14
N2		|	at Ohio State	3	7
N9	●	|	Minnesota	27	13
N16	=	|	at Michigan	21	21

1964 3-6-0 (1-5-0)

S26	●		Idaho	34	24
O3	●		Washington	28	18
O10	●	|	at Indiana	21	20
O17		|	at Wisconsin	21	31
O24		|	Purdue	14	19
O31		|	Ohio State	19	21
N7		|	at Minnesota	13	14
N14		|	Michigan	20	34
N21			at Notre Dame	0	28

1965 1-9-0 (0-7-0)

S18			Washington State	0	7
S25	●		Oregon State^PORT	27	7
O2		|	at Wisconsin	13	16
O9		|	Purdue	14	17
O16		|	Minnesota	3	14
O23		|	at Northwestern	0	9
O30		|	at Indiana	17	21
N6		|	Michigan State	0	35
N13		|	at Ohio State	0	38
N20			North Carolina St.	20	28

RAY NAGEL
1966-70 (.340) 16-32-2

1966 2-8-0 (1-6-0)

S17	●		Arizona	31	20
S24			Oregon State	3	17
O1		|	Wisconsin	0	7
O8		|	at Purdue	0	35
O15		|	at Minnesota	0	17
O22		|	Northwestern	15	24
O29	●	|	Indiana	20	19
N5		|	at Michigan State	7	56
N12		|	Ohio State	10	14
N18			at Miami, Fla.	0	44

1967 1-8-1 (0-6-1)

S23	●		TCU	24	9
S30			Oregon State	18	38
O7			at Notre Dame	6	56
O14		|	at Indiana	17	21
O21	=	|	at Wisconsin	21	21
O28		|	Purdue	22	41
N4		|	Minnesota	0	10
N11		|	at Northwestern	24	39
N18		|	at Ohio State	10	21
N25		|	Illinois	19	21

1968 5-5-0 (4-3-0)

S21	●		Oregon State	21	20
S28			at TCU	17	28
O5			Notre Dame	28	51
O12		|	Indiana	34	38
O19	●	|	Wisconsin	41	0
O26		|	at Purdue	14	44
N2	●	|	at Minnesota	35	28
N9	●	|	Northwestern	68	34
N16		|	Ohio State	27	33
N23	●	|	at Illinois	37	13

1969 5-5-0 (3-4-0)

S20			Oregon State	14	42
S27	●		Washington State	61	35
O4	●		Arizona	31	19
O11		|	at Wisconsin	17	23
O18		|	at Purdue	31	35
O25	●	|	Michigan State	19	18
N1		|	Minnesota	8	35
N8	●	|	at Indiana	28	17
N15		|	Michigan	6	51
N22	●	|	at Illinois	40	0

1970 3-6-1 (3-3-1)

S19			Oregon State^PORT	14	21
S26			Southern Cal	0	48
O3			at Arizona	10	17
O10	●	|	Wisconsin	24	14
O17		|	Purdue	3	24
O24		|	at Michigan State	0	37
O31	=	|	at Minnesota	14	14
N7	●	|	Indiana	42	13
N14		|	at Michigan	0	55
N21	●	|	Illinois	22	16

FRANK LAUTERBUR
1971-73 (.136) 4-28-1

1971 1-10-0 (1-8-0)

S11		|	at Ohio State	21	52
S18			at Oregon State	19	33
S25			Penn State	14	44
O2		|	at Purdue	13	45
O9		|	Northwestern	3	28
O16		|	Minnesota	14	19
O23		|	at Michigan State	3	34
O30	●	|	Wisconsin	20	16
N6		|	at Michigan	7	63
N13		|	Indiana	7	14
N20		|	at Illinois	0	31

1972 3-7-1 (2-6-1)

S16		|	at Ohio State	0	21
S23	●		Oregon State	19	11
S30			at Penn State	10	14
O7		|	Purdue	0	24
O14	●	|	at Northwestern	23	12
O21		|	at Minnesota	14	43
O28	=	|	Michigan State	6	6
N4		|	at Wisconsin	14	16
N11		|	Michigan	0	31
N18		|	at Indiana	8	16
N25	●	|	Illinois	15	14

1973 0-11-0 (0-8-0)

S15		|	Michigan	7	31
S22			at UCLA	18	55
S29			at Penn State	8	27
O6			Arizona	20	23
O13		|	at Northwestern	15	31
O20		|	Minnesota	23	31
O27		|	at Illinois	0	50
N3		|	Purdue	23	48
N10		|	at Wisconsin	7	35
N17		|	at Ohio State	13	55
N24		|	Michigan State	6	15

BOB COMMINGS
1974-78 (.309) 17-38

1974 3-8-0 (2-6-0)

S14		|	at Michigan	7	24
S21	●		UCLA	21	10
S28			Penn State	0	27
O5			at Southern Cal	3	41
O12	●	|	Northwestern	35	10
O19		|	at Minnesota	17	23
O26	●	|	Illinois	14	12
N2		|	at Purdue	14	38
N9		|	Wisconsin	15	28
N16		|	Ohio State	10	35
N23		|	at Michigan State	21	60

1975 3-8-0 (3-5-0)

S13		|	Illinois	12	27
S20			at Syracuse	7	10
S27			Penn State	10	30
O4			Southern Cal	16	27
O11		|	at Ohio State	0	49
O18	●	|	at Indiana	20	10
O25		|	Minnesota	7	31
N1	●	|	at Northwestern	24	21
N8	●	|	Wisconsin	45	28
N15		|	at Purdue	18	19
N22		|	Michigan State	23	27

1976 5-6-0 (3-5-0)

S11		|	at Illinois	6	24
S18	●		Syracuse	41	3
S25	●		at Penn State	7	6
O2			at Southern Cal	0	55
O9		|	Ohio State	14	34
O16		|	Indiana	7	14
O23	●	|	at Minnesota	22	12
O30	●	|	Northwestern	13	10
N6		|	at Wisconsin	21	38
N13		|	Purdue	0	21
N20	●	|	at Michigan State	30	17

1977 4-7-0 (3-5-0)

S10	●	|	Northwestern	24	0
S17	●		Iowa State	12	10
S24			Arizona	7	41
O1			at UCLA	16	34 †
O8	●	|	Minnesota	18	6
O15		|	Ohio State	6	27
O22		|	at Purdue	21	34
O29		|	at Michigan	6	23
N5		|	Indiana	21	24
N12	●	|	at Wisconsin	24	8
N19		|	Michigan State	16	22

1978 2-9-0 (2-6-0)

S16	●	|	Northwestern	20	3
S23			Iowa State	0	31
S30			at Arizona	3	23
O7			Utah	9	13
O14		|	at Minnesota	20	22
O21		|	at Ohio State	7	31
O28		|	Purdue	7	34
N4		|	Michigan	0	34
N11		|	at Indiana	14	34
N18	●	|	Wisconsin	38	24
N25		|	at Michigan State	7	42

HAYDEN FRY
1979-98 (.613) 143-89-6

1979 5-6-0 (4-4-0)

S8		|	Indiana	26	30
S15			at Oklahoma	6	21
S22			Nebraska	21	24
S29	●		Iowa State	30	14
O6	●	|	at Illinois	13	7
O13	●	|	at Northwestern	58	6
O20		|	Minnesota	7	24
O27	●	|	at Wisconsin	24	13
N3		|	Purdue	14	20
N10		|	at Ohio State	7	34
N17	●	|	Michigan State	33	23

1980 4-7-0 (4-4-0)

S13	●	|	at Indiana	16	7
S20			at Nebraska	0	57
S27			Iowa State	7	10
O4			Arizona	3	5
O11		|	Illinois	14	20
O18	●	|	Northwestern	25	3
O25		|	at Minnesota	6	24
N1	●	|	Wisconsin	22	13
N8		|	at Purdue	13	58
N15		|	Ohio State	7	41
N22	●	|	at Michigan State	41	0

1981 8-4-0 (6-2-0)

S12	●		Nebraska	10	7
S19			at Iowa State	12	23
S26	●		UCLA	20	7
O3	●	|	at Northwestern	64	0
O10	●	|	Indiana	42	28
O17	●	|	at Michigan	9	7
O24		|	Minnesota	10	12
O31		|	at Illinois	7	24
N7	●	|	Purdue	33	7
N14	●	|	at Wisconsin	17	7
N21	●	|	Michigan State	36	7
			ROSE BOWL		
J1			Washington	0	28

1982 8-4-0 (6-2-0)

S11			at Nebraska	7	42
S18			Iowa State	7	19
S25	●		at Arizona	17	14
O2	●	|	Northwestern	45	7
O9	●	|	at Indiana	24	20
O16		|	Michigan	7	29
O23	●	|	at Minnesota	21	16
O30	●	|	Illinois	14	13
N6		|	at Purdue	7	16
N13	●	|	Wisconsin	28	14
N20	●	|	at Michigan State	24	18
			PEACH BOWL		
D31	●		Tennessee	28	22

1983   9-3-0 (7-2-0)

S10	●	at Iowa State	51 10
S17	●	at Penn State	42 34
S24	●	Ohio State	20 14
O1		at Illinois	0 33
O8	●	Northwestern	61 21
O15	●	Purdue	31 14
O22		at Michigan	13 16
O29	●	Indiana	49 3
N5	●	at Wisconsin	34 14
N12		at Michigan State	12 6
N19	●	Minnesota	61 10
GATOR BOWL			
D30	●	Florida	6 14

1984   8-4-1 (5-3-1)

S8	●	Iowa State	59 21
S15		Penn State	17 20
S22		at Ohio State	26 45
S29	●	Illinois	21 16
O6	●	at Northwestern	31 3
O13	●	at Purdue	40 3
O20	●	Michigan	26 0
O27		at Indiana	24 20
N3	=	Wisconsin	10 10
N10		Michigan State	16 17
N17		at Minnesota	17 23
D1	●	at Hawaii	17 6
FREEDOM BOWL			
D26	●	Texas	55 17

1985   10-2-0 (7-1-0)

S14	●	Drake	58 0
S21	●	Northern Illinois	48 20
S28	●	at Iowa State	57 3
O5	●	Michigan State	35 31
O12	●	at Wisconsin	23 13
O19	●	Michigan	12 10
O26	●	at Northwestern	49 10
N2		at Ohio State	13 22
N9	●	Illinois	59 0
N16	●	at Purdue	27 24
N23		Minnesota	31 9
ROSE BOWL			
J1		UCLA	28 45

1986   9-3-0 (5-3-0)

S13	●	Iowa State	43 7
S20	●	Northern Illinois	57 3
S27	●	Texas El Paso	69 7
O4		at Michigan State	24 21
O11	●	Wisconsin	17 6
O18		at Michigan	17 20
O25	●	Northwestern	27 20
N1		Ohio State	10 31
N8		at Illinois	16 20
N15	●	Purdue	42 14
N22	●	at Minnesota	30 27
HOLIDAY BOWL			
D30	●	San Diego State	39 38

1987   10-3-0 (6-2-0)

A30		Tennessee ERut	22 23
S12	●	at Arizona	15 14
S19	●	at Iowa State	48 9
S26	●	Kansas State	38 13
O3		Michigan State	14 19
O10	●	at Wisconsin	31 10
O17		at Michigan	10 37
O24	●	Purdue	38 14
O31	●	Indiana	29 21
N7	●	at Northwestern	52 24
N14		at Ohio State	29 27
N21	●	Minnesota	34 20
HOLIDAY BOWL			
D30	●	Wyoming	20 19

1988   6-4-3 (4-1-3)

S3		at Hawaii	24 27
S10	●	at Kansas State	45 10
S17		Colorado	21 24
S24	●	Iowa State	10 3
O1	=	at Michigan State	10 10
O8	●	Wisconsin	31 6
O15	=	Michigan	17 17
O22	●	at Purdue	31 7
O29		at Indiana	34 45
N5	●	Northwestern	35 10
N12	=	Ohio State	24 24
N19	●	at Minnesota	31 22
PEACH BOWL			
D31		North Carolina St.	23 28

1989   5-6-0 (3-5-0)

S16		Oregon	6 44
S23	●	at Iowa State	31 21
S30	●	Tulsa	30 22
O7		Michigan State	14 17
O14	●	at Wisconsin	31 24
O21		Michigan	12 26
O28	●	at Northwestern	35 22
N4		Illinois	7 31
N11		at Ohio State	0 28
N18	●	at Purdue	24 0
N25		Minnesota	7 43

1990   8-4-0 (6-2-0)

S15	●	Cincinnati	63 10
S22	●	Iowa State	45 35
S29		at Miami, Fla.	21 48
O6	●	at Michigan State	12 7
O13	●	Wisconsin	30 10
O20	●	at Michigan	24 23
O27	●	Northwestern	56 14
N3	●	at Illinois	54 28
N10		Ohio State	26 27
N17	●	Purdue	38 9
N24		at Minnesota	24 31
ROSE BOWL			
J1		Washington	34 46

1991   10-1-1 (7-1-0)

S7	●	Hawaii	53 10
S14	●	at Iowa State	29 10
S28	●	Northern Illinois	58 7
O5		Michigan	24 43
O12	●	at Wisconsin	10 6
O19	●	Illinois	24 21
O26	●	at Purdue	31 21
N2	●	at Ohio State	16 9
N9	●	Indiana	38 21
N16	●	at Northwestern	24 10
N23	●	Minnesota	23 8
HOLIDAY BOWL			
D30	=	Brigham Young	13 13

1992   5-7-0 (4-4-0)

A29		North Carolina St. ERut	14 24
S5		Miami, Fla.	7 24
S12	●	Iowa State	21 7
S26		at Colorado	12 28
O3		at Michigan	28 52
O10	●	Wisconsin	23 22
O17	●	at Illinois	24 14
O24		Purdue	16 27
O31		Ohio State	15 38
N7	●	at Indiana	14 0
N14	●	Northwestern	56 14
N21		at Minnesota	13 28

1993   6-6-0 (3-5-0)

S4	●	Tulsa	26 25
S11	●	at Iowa State	31 28
S18		Penn State	0 31
O2		at Michigan	7 24
O9		at Indiana	10 16
O16		Illinois	3 49
O23		at Michigan State	10 24
O30	●	Purdue	26 17
N6	●	Northern Illinois	54 20
N13	●	at Northwestern	23 19
N20	●	Minnesota	21 3
ALAMO BOWL			
D31		California	3 37

1994   5-5-1 (3-4-1)

S3	●	Central Michigan	52 21
S10	●	Iowa State	37 9
S17		at Penn State	21 61
S24		at Oregon	18 40
O1		Michigan	14 29
O8		Indiana	20 27
O15		at Illinois	7 47
O22	●	Michigan State	19 14
O29	=	at Purdue	21 21
N12	●	Northwestern	49 13
N19	●	at Minnesota	49 42

1995   8-4-0 (4-4-0)

S9	●	No. Iowa	34 13
S16	●	at Iowa State	27 10
S30	●	New Mexico St.	59 21
O7	●	at Michigan State	21 7
O14	●	Indiana	22 13
O21		Penn State	27 41
O28		at Ohio State	35 56
N4		Illinois	7 26
N11		at Northwestern	20 31
N18	●	at Wisconsin	33 20
N25	●	Minnesota	45 3
SUN BOWL			
D29	●	Washington	38 18

1996   9-3 (6-2)

S7	●	Arizona	21 20
S14	●	Iowa State	38 13
S21		at Tulsa	20 27
O5		Michigan State	37 30
O12	●	at Indiana	31 10
O19	●	at Penn State	21 20
O26		Ohio State	26 38
N2	●	at Illinois	31 21
N9		Northwestern	13 40
N16	●	Wisconsin	31 0
N23	●	at Minnesota	43 24
ALAMO BOWL			
D29	●	Texas Tech	27 0

1997   7-5 (4-4)

S6	●	No. Iowa	66 0
S13	●	Tulsa	54 16
S20	●	at Iowa State	63 20
S27	●	Illinois	38 10
O4		at Ohio State	7 23
O18		at Michigan	24 28
O25	●	Indiana	62 0
N1	●	Purdue	35 17
N8		at Wisconsin	10 13
N15		at Northwestern	14 15
N22	●	Minnesota	31 0
SUN BOWL			
D31		Arizona State	7 17

1998   3-8 (2-6)

S5	●	Central Michigan	38 0
S12		Iowa State	9 27
S19		at Arizona	11 35
S26	●	at Illinois	37 14
O3		Michigan	9 12
O10	●	Northwestern	26 24
O17		at Indiana	7 14
O24		Wisconsin	0 31
O31		at Purdue	14 36
N14		Ohio State	14 45
N21		at Minnesota	7 49

1999   1-10 (0-8)

S4		Nebraska	7 42
S11		at Iowa State	10 17
S18	●	Northern Illinois	24 0
O2		at Michigan State	3 49
O9		Penn State	7 31
O16		at Northwestern	21 23
O23		Indiana	31 38
O30		at Ohio State	11 41
N6		Illinois	24 40
N13		at Wisconsin	3 41
N20		Minnesota	21 25

2000   3-9 (3-5)

A26		Kansas State KC	7 27
S9		Western Michigan	21 27
S16		Iowa State	14 24
S23		at Nebraska	13 42
S30		at Indiana	33 45
O7	●	Michigan State	21 16
O14		at Illinois	0 31
O21		Ohio State	10 38
O28		Wisconsin	7 13
N4	●	at Penn State	26 23
N11	●	Northwestern	27 17
N18		at Minnesota	24 27

2001   7-5 (4-4)

S1	●	Kent	51 0
S8	●	Miami, Ohio	44 19
S29		Penn State	24 18
O6		at Purdue	14 23
O13		at Michigan State	28 31
O20	●	Indiana	42 28
O27		Michigan	26 32
N3		at Wisconsin	28 34
N10	●	at Northwestern	59 16
N17	●	Minnesota	42 24
N24		at Iowa State	14 17
ALAMO BOWL			
D29	●	Texas Tech	19 16

2002   11-2 (8-0)

A31	●	Akron	57 21
S7	●	at Miami, Ohio	29 24
S14		Iowa State	31 36
S21	●	Utah State	48 7
S28	●	at Penn State	42 35
O5	●	Purdue	31 28
O12	●	Michigan State	44 16
O19	●	at Indiana	24 8
O26	●	at Michigan	34 9
N2	●	Wisconsin	20 3
N9	●	Northwestern	62 10
N16	●	at Minnesota	45 21
ORANGE BOWL			
J2		Southern Cal	17 38

2003   10-3 (5-3)

A30	●	Miami, Ohio	21 3
S6	●	Buffalo	56 7
S13	●	at Iowa State	40 21
S20	●	Arizona State	21 2
S27		at Michigan State	10 20
O4	●	Michigan	30 27
O18		at Ohio State	10 19
O25	●	Penn State	26 14
N1	●	Illinois	41 10
N8		at Purdue	14 27
N15	●	Minnesota	40 22
N22	●	at Wisconsin	27 21
OUTBACK BOWL			
J1	●	Florida	37 17

2004   10-2 (7-1)

S4	●	Kent State	39 7
S11	●	Iowa State	17 10
S18		at Arizona State	7 44
S25		at Michigan	17 30
O2	●	Michigan State	38 16
O16	●	Ohio State	33 7
O23	●	at Penn State	6 4
O30	●	Illinois	23 13
N6	●	Purdue	23 21
N13	●	at Minnesota	29 27
N20	●	Wisconsin	30 7
CAPITAL ONE BOWL			
J1	●	LSU	30 25

IOWA STATE

BY MARK WANGRIN

IOWA AGRICULTURAL COLLEGE WAS looking to go big time in 1895, so its administrators sent letters back East to the hotbeds of college football hoping to find a coach. One found its way to a former Cornell player by the name of Glenn "Pop" Warner, who had become a lawyer in Buffalo, N.Y. Intrigued by the lure of coaching, he accepted the promise of $25 a week, plus expenses, to begin that August.

Figuring he needed to test the market, the enterprising young man sent out inquiry letters of his own. Georgia also needed a coach and offered him $35 a week to start in September. Warner took that job, too.

He ultimately worked out a deal to coach for one month in Iowa before leaving for Georgia, with this scenario repeated the following summer. Warner would also go on to coach Cornell, Carlisle Indian School, Pittsburgh, Stanford and Temple. He became the winningest coach in major college football and currently ranks sixth overall. Unfortunately, the Iowa State program has been marked by mediocrity, due at least partly to the unofficial tradition that began with Warner of Cyclones coaches moving through the school on their way to bigger and better things. These include Johnny Majors, Earle Bruce, Mack Brown, Pete Carroll, Jimmy Johnson, Glen Mason and Jackie Sherrill.

TRADITION A good year at ISU means a full trophy case. Since the series was resumed in 1977, the winner of the annual Iowa-Iowa State game receives the Cy-Hawk Trophy. Presented by the Des Moines Athletic Club, the ungainly award features a bronze replica of a stiff-armed running back and a large football. One of the most unusual stakes in college football is the Telephone Trophy, which goes to the winner of the ISU-Missouri game. Topped with a replica of an old-fashioned dial phone, the award was inspired by a 1959 game, when a test of phone lines before the contest revealed each team could hear the other's plays. Although the lines were fixed before the game, neither coaching staff trusted them. Coach Dan McCarney created the Senior Bowl Trophy before the 1998 season. The trophy is engraved with the names of the senior class and displayed at the Gary Thompson Hall of Honor for the next season if ISU wins its last home game of the year.

PROFILE

Iowa State University
Ames, Iowa
Founded: 1858
Enrollment: 21,354
Colors: Cardinal and Gold
Nickname: Cyclones
Stadium: Jack Trice Stadium
    Opened in 1975
    Grass; 45,814 capacity
First football game: 1892
All-time record: 465–543–46 (.463)
Bowl record: 2–6
First-round NFL draftees: 1
Website: www.cyclones.com

THE BEST OF TIMES

From 1902 to 1917, the Cyclones had only two nonwinning seasons. The span also included ISU's only two conference championships, Missouri Valley Intercollegiate Athletic Association titles in 1911 and 1912.

THE WORST OF TIMES

During the stretch from 1990 to 1999, the Cyclones went 27–80–3, including an 0–10–1 record in 1994, one of only two winless seasons since 1918.

CONFERENCE

Along with fellow Big Eight members Oklahoma, Nebraska, Oklahoma State, Missouri, Kansas, Kansas State and Colorado, the Cyclones merged with former Southwest Conference schools Texas, Texas A&M, Texas Tech and Baylor to form the Big 12 in 1996. Iowa State joined the Missouri Valley Intercollegiate Athletic Association in 1908. The MVIAA evolved into the Big Six in 1928 when Oklahoma A&M, Washington, Drake and Grinnell dropped out. The league became the Big Seven in 1948 with the addition of Colorado and the Big Eight in 1960 when Oklahoma State—formerly Oklahoma A&M—joined.

DISTINGUISHED ALUMNI

George Washington Carver; Carrie Chapman Catt, suffragette; Tom Harkin, U.S. senator; Cael Sanderson, NCAA champion and Olympic gold medal-winning wrestler; Henry A. Wallace, U.S. vice president

FIGHT SONG

IOWA STATE FIGHT SONG
O we will fight, fight, fight for Iowa State,
And may her colors ever fly.
Yes, we will fight with might for Iowa State,
With a will to do or die,
Rah! Rah! Rah!
Loyal sons forever true,
And we will fight the battle through.
And when we hit that line we'll hit it hard ev'ry yard for ISU.

THE SCHOOLS

Feuding caused Iowa to rebuff most attempts to continue the ISU series, with only two games played from 1921 to 1976.

BEST PLAYER Troy Davis was homesick after his freshman year in 1994 and was mulling over a transfer after an unspectacular debut season that got him only 187 yards rushing on a 0–10–1 team. New coach Dan McCarney talked him out of it, making the 5'8", 185-pounder the focus of his offense. It turned out better than either one expected. Davis became the first Division I-A player to rush twice for at least 2,000 yards, following his 2,010-yard effort in 1995 with a 2,185-yard season in 1996. He was a two-time Heisman Trophy finalist and inaugural Big 12 player of the year. Davis entered the NFL draft after his junior year, leaving the halfback spot in the capable hands of younger brother, Darren.

BEST COACH After Johnny Majors left for Pittsburgh, the Cyclones turned to Earle Bruce, a former Ohio State assistant. Bruce inherited a team that returned 10 starters from Majors' 1972 Liberty Bowl squad. Still, he struggled early in his ISU tenure with three straight 4–7 seasons before leading his 1976 team to an 8–3 record and No. 18 ranking. The Cyclones won eight games each during the next two years, which did more than whet the appetites of ISU faithful. Ohio State hired Bruce to replace the legendary Woody Hayes in early 1979. Bruce coached the Buckeyes from 1979 to 1987, compiling an 81–26–1 record. With a 36–32 overall mark in six seasons in Ames, he remains the only one of 19 ISU coaches since 1919 to post an overall winning record with the Cyclones.

BEST TEAM A veteran nucleus of seniors plus a smattering of talented sophomores helped Earle Bruce finally put it together in 1976. Behind a prolific I-formation attack that featured sophomore halfback Dexter Green, the Cyclones led the Big Eight and were second in the nation in total offense. The Cyclones went 8–3 and set school records for points, touchdowns, rushing yardage and total offense. Safety Tony Hawkins and lineman Maynard Stensrud led the defense. A 42-21 loss to Oklahoma State in the regular-

RECORDS

RUSHING YARDS

GAME
378 Troy Davis vs. Missouri, Sept. 28, 1996 (41 att.)

SEASON
2,185 Troy Davis, 1996 (402 att.)

CAREER
4,382 Troy Davis, 1994-96 (782 att.)

PASSING YARDS

GAME
437 Todd Bandhauer vs. Texas, Oct. 3, 1998 (30 of 62)

SEASON
3,245 Seneca Wallace, 2002 (244 of 443)

CAREER
5,307 Alex Espinoza, 1984-86 (455 of 891)

RECEIVING YARDS

GAME
217 Tracy Henderson vs. Texas A&M, Sept. 22, 1984 (11 rec.)

SEASON
1,073 Lane Danielsen, 2002 (63 rec.)

CAREER
2,690 Lane Danielsen, 2000-03 (163 rec.)

POINTS

GAME
30 Troy Davis vs. Northern Iowa, Sept. 21, 1996 (5 TDs); Troy Davis vs. UNLV, Sept. 23, 1995 (5 TDs); Joe Henderson vs. Kansas, Oct. 22, 1988 (5 TDs)

SEASON
126 Troy Davis, 1996 (21 TDs)

CAREER
266 Jeff Shudak, 1987-90 (58 FGs, 92 PATs)

CONSENSUS ALL-AMERICANS

1938	Ed Bock,	G
1989	Mike Busch,	TE
1995-96	Troy Davis,	RB

season finale cost the Cyclones a share of the Big Eight championship. Though they finished the season ranked No. 19, the Cyclones were passed over by the bowls.

BIGGEST GAME Heading into the 2000 Insight.com Bowl, it had been 24 years since the Cyclones finished the season ranked. Standing in their way was a 7–4 Pittsburgh Panthers team that featured Biletnikoff Award-winning receiver Antonio Bryant, who gave the Panthers a quick 7-0 lead with a 72-yard touchdown catch. The Cyclones took a 27-7 halftime lead behind quarterback Sage Rosenfels, who led them to score on four straight drives. Pitt had cut the lead to 27-20 late in the third quarter when JaMaine Billups took his first collegiate punt return 72 yards for a touchdown. ISU hung on for a 37-29 victory, which allowed the team to finish No. 25 in the AP Poll.

BIGGEST UPSET No. 7 Nebraska came steamrolling into its annual game against ISU on Nov. 14, 1992, having just beaten No. 8 Colorado 52-7 and No. 13 Kansas 49-7. ISU, meanwhile, was 3–6 and couldn't even settle on a starting quarterback. Coach Jim Walden finally tabbed Marv Seiler, and it would be one of the most rewarding decisions of his career. Seiler led the Cyclones into position for four first-half field goals to take an unlikely 12-10 halftime lead. Seiler's 78-yard run on an option keeper to the NU 2 set up the Cyclones only touchdown. ISU's defense stonewalled NU on two possessions and Seiler led the Cyclones on a drive that chewed up the last 5:14 of a 19-10 victory. "You always dream about something like this," Seiler said, "but this was almost an unbelievable story. I am just glad it happened to me."

ALL-TIME TEAM	
The players—either All-Americas or multiple first-team all-conference selections—were selected by the ISU sports information department in 2004.	
OFFENSE	
1916-17, 1919	Dick Barker, OG
1933-35	Ike Hayes, OG
1943-46	Jack Fathauer, OG
1970-72	Geary Murdock, OG
1987-90	Gene Williams, OG
1962-64	John Van Sicklen, OT
1979-82	Karl Nelson, OT
1990-93	Doug Skartvedt, OT
1917, 1920-21	Leigh "Polly" Wallace, C
1997-2000	Ben Bruns, C
1971-73	Keith Krepfle, TE
1986-89	Mike Busch, TE
1949-50	Jim Doran, WR
1964-66	Eppie Barney, WR
1982-84	Tracy Henderson, WR
1936-38	Everett "Rabbit" Kischer, QB
1957-59	Dwight Nichols, QB
1960-62	Dave Hoppmann, QB
1970-72	George Amundson, QB
1962-64	Tom Vaughn, RB
1972-74	Mike Strachan, RB
1975-78	Dexter Green, RB
1980-81	Dwayne Crutchfield, RB
1989-90	Blaise Bryant, RB
1994-96	Troy Davis, RB
1998-2001	Ennis Haywood, RB
1958-60	Tom Watkins, FB
1987-90	Jeff Shudak, PK
1991-94	Ty Stewart, PK
1974-76	Luther Blue, KR
1989, 1991-93	James McMillion, PR
DEFENSE	
1970-72	Merv Krakau, DE
1936-38	Ed Bock, DT
1937-38	Clyde Shugart, DT
1974, 1976-78	Mike Stensrud, DT
1973-75, 1977	Ron McFarland, NG
1971-73	Matt Blair, LB
1968-70	Tony Washington, DB
1972-74	Barry Hill, DB
1976-79	Mike Schwartz, DB
1987-90	Marcus Robertson, DB
1989-92	Mark DouBrava, DB
1934-36	Fred Poole, P

HEARTBREAKER Trailing 12-7 late against Oklahoma in 1944, the Cyclones' hopes for an unbeaten season hinged on a crucial fourth-and-goal play. Joe Noble found Dick Howard with a short pass and Howard headed for the goal line, where he collided with an OU defender. Referee Jack North, who was standing at the 15, ruled Howard out-of-bounds just short of the goal line. According to ISU, the game films later showed he crossed the line. The Cyclones would have to settle for a 6–1–1 record instead of what would have been the only unbeaten multiwin season in school history.

BEST COMEBACK The Cyclones came into their 1990 game against 5–1 and No. 16 Oklahoma as a 24-point underdog. Twice in the first half they fell behind by 14 points but rallied to draw within 31-20 to start the fourth quarter. Sherman Williams scored on a seven-yard run, but the Cyclones missed the two-point conversion. After OU missed a field goal, ISU took over on its own 20-yard line with only 2:50 remaining. Sparked by a 20-yard run from quarterback Chris Pedersen on fourth-and-8 at their own 22, the Cyclones drove 80 yards for the winning touchdown. Pedersen scored on a sneak with just over 30 seconds left and ISU won 33-31, its first win over the Sooners since 1961.

STADIUM Jack Trice Stadium, the newest football facility in the Big 12, opened on Sept. 20, 1975, with a Cyclones victory over Air Force. Built for $7.4 million, the stadium originally had grandstands on both sides of the field that held 42,500. End zone bleachers were added in 1976 and subsequent renovations have pushed the capacity to 45,814. A three-level, $6.2 million press box was added in 1997, including 23 skybox suites. From 1914 to 1974, the Cyclones played

at Clyde Williams Field, constructed on the Horticulture Department's prize orchard. Built for $35,000, the stadium underwent a series of renovations that enlarged capacity from 5,600 to 36,000.

RIVAL It's not the most played series in Cyclones history but it's clearly the most hotly contested. ISU's annual meeting with cross-state rival Iowa first heated up in 1906, when the Cyclones beat the Hawkeyes 2-0, the first time Iowa had lost to an in-state team in 40 games. Merchants back in Ames greeted the team with a bonfire that included the town's entire supply of gunpowder. The next year, ISU's Phil Reppert knocked over Carroll Kirk on a punt return after the Hawkeyes claimed he had signaled for a fair catch. Incensed, Iowa refused to play the Cyclones for the next season. Bad blood and feuding caused Iowa to rebuff most attempts to continue the series—the Iowa Board in Control of Athletics adopted a resolution that stated any activity that pitted the schools against each other should be "discouraged"—and the schools played only twice from 1921 to 1976. In 1968, Iowa athletic director Forrest Evashevski and his counterpart, Clay Stapleton, agreed on a six-year series to begin in 1977. But after Evashevski resigned in 1970, Iowa refused to honor the last four years of the contract and only did so when forced to by an arbitrator's ruling. The Hawkeyes have dominated the series 35–17 through 2004, but the Cyclones have risen to the challenge in recent years.

WILDEST FINISH Nebraska came to Ames on Veterans Day 1972 ranked No. 3 in the nation and winners of its last seven games by a combined margin of 348-24. ISU was ranked 17th, but few gave the Cyclones much of a chance against a Cornhuskers team that featured eventual Heisman Trophy winner Johnny Rodgers. NU kicked a field goal to go up 23-17 with 63 seconds left to go, forcing ISU to try for a touchdown. ISU returned the kickoff to its 26, and quarterback George Amundson hit 4 of 6 passes, including the game-tying touchdown throw to Willie Jones with 23 seconds left. Fans swarmed the field and when order was finally restored sophomore Tom Goedjen lined up to kick the extra point. He missed. Goedjen wouldn't miss for the remainder of his career, but that was no solace for the Cyclones, who settled for a 23-23 tie instead of what would have been a shocking upset.

CONTROVERSY The Cyclones played Nebraska on Nov. 2, 1907, in Lincoln in a game *The Des Moines Register* called "the fiercest, most thrilling football game ever waged on the Nebraska field." It may still be the most controversial. Trailing 10-9, the Cyclones tried a four-point dropkick in the closing seconds that bounced once before clearing the crossbar. The referee disallowed the play. The Cyclones protested, appealing to rules and coaching expert Walter Camp, whose nonbinding opinion was that the kick should have been allowed. To this day Nebraska lists the game as a 10-9 victory; ISU as a 13-10 win.

TRAGEDY When East Tech High School coach Sam Willaman was hired by Iowa State in 1922, he brought seven of his players with him from Cleveland. One of them was a young black halfback whose goal was to study animal husbandry and then help other blacks farm the south. On Oct. 6, 1923, at Minnesota, Jack Trice tried to break up a play with a roll block when he was trampled. He didn't return to the game but was deemed well enough to accompany the team on its train ride back to Ames. However, Trice developed respiratory problems on Sunday and died Monday of bleeding in his lungs and abdomen. A memorial scholarship fund was created and Cyclone Stadium was renamed Jack Trice Stadium in 1997.

NICKNAME In the summer and early fall of 1895, Iowa was hit by an unusually high number of whirling windstorms then called "cyclones." That fact was not lost on an editor for the *Chicago Tribune*, who after Iowa State rolled to a 36-0 rout at Northwestern, laid out the headline, "Struck by a Cyclone. It Comes From Iowa and Devastates Evanston Town." Taken by the image the headline made, the school decided to go with Cyclones over Cardinals, as the teams had originally been known.

MASCOT Building school spirit was the goal in 1954 when a student group led by pep council president Chuck Duncan decided the Cyclones needed a costumed mascot. Unsure how to "stuff a cyclone," they approached Collegiate Manufacturing of Ames for ideas. Ultimately, they decided to hearken back to the team's original nickname and created a bird in the school's cardinal and gold colors. Named Cy in a school-wide contest, the bird made its debut at the 1954 homecoming pep rally.

UNIFORMS ISU has used a variety of cardinal-and-gold uniform combinations throughout the program's history. Pants have switched between gold, white and cardinal with the home jersey being cardinal and the road jersey white.

The school name was added to the front of the uniforms in the late 1980s. The Cyclones have used 14 different helmet designs since 1962, using cardinal, yellow and metallic gold shells with a cardinal logo, script nickname, school letters or a cyclone on the side. The current model, with a cardinal shell and a cardinal-and-black cyclone logo on the sides, was introduced in 1995. The face mask changed from blue to white in 2003.

NUMBERS Troy Davis is one of only ten Division I-A players to rush for at least 2,000 yards in a season and the only player to do it twice. His 2,185 in 1996 ranks third, behind Barry Sanders and Marcus Allen. His 2,010-yard season in 1995 ranks 11th.

QUIRK ISU was leading Oklahoma State 14-0 in 1973 and looked to increase its lead when Buddy Hardeman broke a long run along the Cowboys sideline. S.L. Stephens came off the OSU bench to tackle Hardeman. Officials conferred and awarded ISU a 74-yard touchdown run. ISU won, 28-12 ... In 1966, Larry Spealler, a pickup soccer player who had just walked on that week, kicked a field goal against Kansas in full football uniform—except he was wearing gym shorts instead of pants. It was the only game Spealler played for the Cyclones.

LORE Injuries hit the Cyclones hard in 1959, whittling the roster to only 30 players when the season opened against Drake in a withering rainstorm on September 19. As the players came into the locker room after a 41-0 win, trainer Warren Ariail yelled, "Here comes the dirty 30!" The name stuck. Led by All-America halfback Dwight Nichols the undermanned Cyclones went 7–3 and the Dirty 30 earned a warm spot in the hearts of Cyclones fans. "I'd rather be coach of the Dirty 30 than president of the United States," coach Clay Stapleton said.

QUOTE "I boil it down to the fact that even the officials are so used to seeing Iowa State lose that they don't hesitate at all to call them against us."—ISU Coach Mike Michalske, bemoaning a disallowed touchdown that would have given the Cyclones a huge upset win over Oklahoma in 1944

IOWA STATE ANNUAL STATISTICAL LEADERS

YR	RUSHING	YDS	ATT	AVG	PASSING	ATT	CMP	PCT	YDS	RECEIVING	REC	YDS	AVG
1943	Meredith Warner	401	74	5.4	Howard Tippee	122	56	.46	637	Hal Crisler	8	139	17.4
1944	Meredith Warner	260	42	6.2	Joe Noble	30	13	.43	162	Dick Howard	7	108	15.4
1945		NA	NA	NA		NA	NA	NA	NA		NA	NA	NA
1946	Dick Howard	335	69	4.9	Ron Norman	82	33	.40	356	Dean Laun	23	322	14.0
1947	Webb Halbert	464	109	4.3	Ron Norman	110	35	.32	504	Dean Laun	11	246	22.4
1948	Bill Chauncey	428	90	4.8	Don Ferguson	71	32	.45	367	Dean Laun	17	225	13.2
1949	Bill Chauncey	544	134	4.1	Bill Weeks	176	79	.45	1,247	Jim Doran	34	689	20.3
1950	Maury Schnell	490	131	3.7	Bill Weeks	220	116	.53	1,552	Jim Doran	42	652	15.5
1951	Frank Congiardo	315	99	3.2	Rich Mann	212	104	.49	1,296	Mal Schmidt	33	548	11.6
1952	Dick Cherpinsky	278	62	4.5	Rich Mann	72	36	.50	389	Bob Rohwedder	11	167	16.6
1953	Max Burkett	342	109	3.1	Bill Plantan	100	57	.57	723	Gary Lutz	15	249	15.2
1954	Max Burkett	528	97	5.4	John Breckenridge	76	35	.46	236	Mell Westoupal	12	151	16.6
1955	Donn Lorenzen	179	32	5.6	John Breckenridge	89	36	.40	354	Harold Potts	14	173	12.6
1956	Bob Harden	244	70	3.5	Phil Hill	38	14	.37	205	John Scheldrup	6	140	12.4
1957	Dwight Nichols	668	211	3.2	Dwight Nichols	99	50	.51	751	Brian Dennis	15	256	17.1
1958	Dwight Nichols	815	220	3.7	Dwight Nichols	55	26	.47	357	Gale Gibson	9	148	16.4
1959	Tom Watkins	843	161	5.3	Dwight Nichols	80	43	.54	609	Don Webb	24	309	12.9
1960	Dave Hoppmann	844	161	5.2	Dave Hoppmann	40	17	.43	214	Don Webb	13	203	15.6
1961	Dave Hoppmann	920	229	4.0	Dave Hoppmann	91	41	.45	718	Dick Limerick	21	555	26.4
1962	Dave Hoppmann	798	198	4.0	Dave Hoppmann	89	40	.45	679	Dick Limerick	17	296	17.4
1963	Tom Vaughn	795	190	4.2	Ken Bunte	70	26	.37	347	Dick Limerick	24	339	14.1
1964	Tom Vaughn	497	129	3.9	Tim Van Galder	105	35	.33	354	Tony Baker	6	76	12.6
1965	Les Webster	498	137	3.6	Tim Van Galder	228	100	.44	1,418	Eppie Barney	35	495	14.1
1966	Les Webster	572	149	3.8	Tim Van Galder	245	124	.51	1,645	Eppie Barney	56	783	14.0
1967	Ben King	388	110	3.5	John Warder	196	80	.41	949	Tom Busch	33	429	13.0
1968	Ben King	437	124	3.5	John Warder	201	89	.44	1,184	Otto Stowe	34	421	12.4
1969	Jock Johnson	427	98	4.4	Obert Tisdale	189	79	.42	896	Otto Stowe	39	508	13.0
1970	George Amundson	440	111	4.0	Dean Carlson	220	105	.48	1,391	Otto Stowe	59	822	13.9
1971	George Amundson	1,260	272	4.6	Dean Carlson	285	141	.49	1,867	Keith Krepfle	40	570	14.3
1972	Mike Strachan	1,260	268	4.7	George Amundson	332	155	.47	2,110	Willie Jones	36	671	18.6
1973	Mike Strachan	1,103	272	4.1	Wayne Stanley	116	49	.42	723	Keith Krepfle	30	436	14.5
1974	Mike Strachan	647	189	3.4	Wayne Stanley	121	58	.48	842	Luther Blue	26	450	17.3
1975	Jim Wingender	1,070	195	5.5	Tom Mason	128	42	.33	725	Forry Smith	31	493	15.9
1976	Dexter Green	1,074	208	5.2	Wayne Stanley	146	70	.48	1,084	Luther Blue	33	644	19.5
1977	Dexter Green	1,240	271	4.6	Terry Rubley	142	83	.58	1,037	Dexter Green	25	203	8.1
1978	Dexter Green	991	230	4.3	Walter Grant	154	66	.43	992	Stan Hixon	26	474	18.2
1979	Jack Seabrooke	441	105	4.2	Terry Rubley	132	70	.53	716	Mickey Leafblad	18	168	9.3
1980	Dwayne Crutchfield	1,312	284	4.6	John Quinn	153	69	.45	835	Jerry Lorenzen	15	203	13.5
1981	Dwayne Crutchfield	1,189	307	3.9	John Quinn	251	140	.56	1,576	Michael Wade	27	343	12.7
1982	Tommy Davis	832	193	4.3	David Archer	244	125	.51	1,465	Frankie Leaks	25	427	17.1
1983	Jason Jacobs	490	99	4.9	David Archer	403	234	.58	2,639	Tracy Henderson	81	1,051	13.0
1984	Richard Hanson	507	155	3.3	Alex Espinoza	262	143	.55	1,580	Tracy Henderson	64	941	14.7
1985	Andrew Jackson	415	113	3.7	Alex Espinoza	330	159	.48	1,704	Jeff Wodka	35	390	11.1
1986	Andrew Jackson	455	143	3.2	Alex Espinoza	299	153	.51	2,023	Robbie Minor	35	592	16.9
1987	Joe Henderson	1,232	262	4.7	Brett Sadek	229	117	.51	1,443	Dennis Ross	53	673	12.7
1988	Joe Henderson	1,040	242	4.3	Bret Oberg	179	99	.55	1,360	Dennis Ross	39	506	13.0
1989	Blaise Bryant	1,516	299	5.1	Bret Oberg	245	152	.62	2,242	Steve Lester	46	612	13.3
1990	Blaise Bryant	753	187	4.0	Chris Pedersen	206	114	.55	1,601	Chris Spencer	31	485	15.6
1991	Sundiata Patterson	471	100	4.7	Chris Pedersen	90	46	.51	598	Chris Spencer	25	356	14.2
1992	Chris Ulrich	474	103	4.6	Bob Utter	86	50	.58	712	Chris Spencer	26	437	16.8
1993	Calvin Branch	478	84	5.7	Bob Utter	105	60	.57	893	Calvin Branch	16	350	21.9
1994	Todd Doxzon	375	148	2.5	Todd Doxzon	90	51	.57	745	Calvin Branch	19	370	19.5
1995	Troy Davis	2,010	345	5.8	Todd Doxzon	100	58	.58	730	Ed Williams	46	639	13.9
1996	Troy Davis	2,185	402	5.4	Todd Doxzon	231	124	.54	1,498	Ed Williams	34	491	14.4
1997	Darren Davis	1,005	212	4.7	Todd Brandhauer	374	180	.48	2,514	Ty Watley	50	827	16.5
1998	Darren Davis	1,166	294	4.0	Todd Brandhauer	355	179	.50	2,206	Damien Groce	47	640	13.6
1999	Darren Davis	1,388	287	4.8	Sage Rosenfels	235	127	.54	1,781	Chris Anthony	37	432	11.7
2000	Ennis Haywood	1,237	229	5.4	Sage Rosenfels	333	172	.52	2,298	J.J. Moses	53	775	14.6
2001	Ennis Haywood	1,169	258	4.5	Seneca Wallace	269	167	.62	2,044	Lane Danielsen	49	694	14.2
2002	Hiawatha Rutland	614	160	3.8	Seneca Wallace	443	244	.55	3,245	Lane Danielsen	63	1,073	17.0
2003	Stevie Hicks, Jr.	471	123	3.8	Austin Flynn	212	99	.47	1,238	Lane Danielsen	46	772	16.8
2004	Stevie Hicks, Jr.	1,062	270	3.9	Bret Meyer	290	149	.51	1,926	Todd Blythe	39	833	21.4

The NCAA began including postseason stats in 2002

THE SCHOOLS

IOWA STATE ALL-TIME SCORES

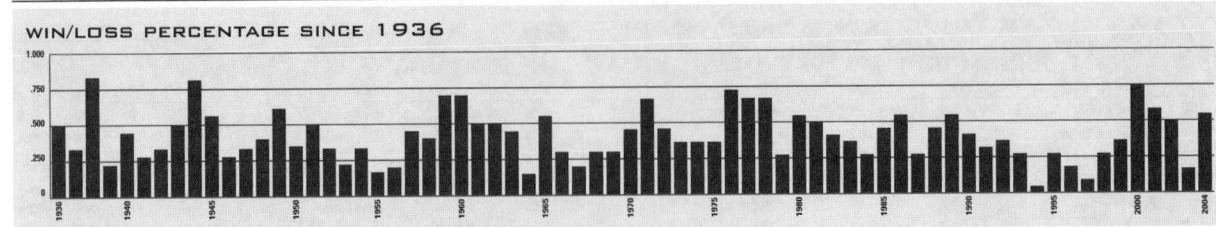

WIN/LOSS PERCENTAGE SINCE 1936

IRA C. BROWNLIE
1892 (.750)   1-0-1

1892   1-0-1
U	=	State Center	6	6
U	●	Des Moines YMCA	30	0

W.F. FINNEY
1893 (.000)   0-3

1893   0-3-0
U		Grinnell	6	36
U		Cornell Coll.	6	14
U		Grinnell	2	6

BERT GERMAN
1894 (.833)   5-1

1894   5-1-0
S2	●	Fort Dodge	46	0
S3	●	at Des Moines YMCA	18	4
S29	●	at Iowa	16	8
O1		at Grinnell	6	12
O13	●	at Simpson	28	0
N9	●	Panora	66	0

GLENN "POP" WARNER
1895-99 (.692)   18-8

1895   3-3-0
S15	●	at Butte AC	10	12
S28	●	at Northwestern	36	0
S30	●	at Wisconsin	6	28 *
O12	●	at Sioux City AC	6	0
O19		at Minnesota	0	24
O28	●	at Iowa	24	0

1896   8-2-0
S4	●	Iowa Falls	46	0
S5	●	Cornell Coll.	50	0
O2	●	at Missouri	12	0
O17	●	at Des Moines YMCA	24	16
O24		at Minnesota	6	18
O30	●	Simpson	44	0
N7	●	Grinnell	42	0
N19		Nebraska	4	12
N21	●	Des Moines YMCA	15	0
N28	●	at Eldora	62	0

1897   3-1-0
O8	●	Nebraska	10	0
O23	●	at Minnesota	12	10
O30		at Grinnell	6	12
N5	●	at Iowa	6	0 *

1898   3-2-0
O1	●	Rush Medical	10	0
O8	●	at Nebraska	20	23 *
O15		at Kansas	6	11
O22	●	at Minnesota	6	0
O29	●	Drake	17	16

JOE MEYERS
1899 (.500)   4-4-1

1899   5-4-1
S16	●	at Panora	23	0
S30	●	at Cornell Coll.	32	0
O6	●	Nebraska	33	0 *
O11	●	at Simpson	18	0
O14	●	South Dakota *Sio*	11	5
O21		at Minnesota	0	6
O28		at Iowa	0	5
N4	=	Grinnell *Des*	0	15
N11	●	at No. Iowa	0	5
N18		Grinnell	0	6

C.E. WOODRUFF
1900 (.313)   2-5-1

1900   2-5-1
S29	●	at William Penn	16	0
O6		at Minnesota	0	27
O13		at Nebraska	0	30
O27	=	at Simpson	0	0
N3		Grinnell	5	22
N10		at Drake	0	16
N17		at No. Iowa	0	5
N24	●	at Cornell Coll.	17	0

EDGAR CLINTON
1901 (.300)   2-6-2

1901   2-6-2
S28	=	Grinnell *Mar*	0	0
O5	●	Still Coll.	23	0
O12	=	at No. Iowa	0	0
O18		at Iowa	0	6 *
O26		at Nebraska	0	17
N2		Missouri	0	23
N9		at Wisconsin	0	45
N16		Drake	5	12
N21	●	Cornell Coll.	28	12
N28		at Simpson	0	12

A.W. RISTINE
1902-06 (.777)   36-10-1

1902   6-3-1
S28	●	Still College	35	0
O4		at Minnesota	0	16
O11	●	at No. Iowa	52	0
O18	●	Grinnell	23	0
O25		at Cornell Coll.	15	17
N1		at Iowa	6	12
N8	●	Coe	53	0
N15	=	at Drake	0	0
N22	●	at William Penn	44	0
N28	●	at Simpson	18	11

1903   8-1-0
S25	●	Highland Park	16	0
O6	●	at Omaha Lt.G.	18	0
O10		at Minnesota	0	46
O17	●	Coe	36	5
O31	●	South Dakota	23	0
N7	●	at Grinnell	41	6
N14	●	at Simpson	11	2
N20	●	at Cornell Coll.	41	0
N26	●	at Drake	16	0

1904   7-2-0
O1	●	Coe	22	0
O8	●	Northern Iowa	17	0
O15		at Minnesota	0	32
O22	●	Simpson	87	0
O29	●	at Iowa	6	10
N5	●	Grinnell	40	0
N12	●	Des Moines	16	0
N18	●	Cornell Coll.	41	6
N24	●	at Drake	19	0

1905   6-3-0
S30	●	Coe	29	0
O7	●	Northern Iowa	28	0
O14		at Minnesota	0	42
O21	●	Simpson	63	0
N4		at Nebraska	0	21
N11	●	at Grinnell	38	4
N18	●	Coe	28	6
N24		Iowa	0	8
N30	●	at Drake	17	12

1906   9-1-0
S29	●	Cornell Coll.	81	0
O5	●	Coe	36	0
O6	●	Des Moines	45	0
O13	●	Morningside	32	0
O20	●	at Nebraska	14	2
O27		at Minnesota	4	22
N3	●	South Dakota	22	0
N17	●	Grinnell	25	6
N24	●	at Iowa	2	0
N29	●	at Drake	7	0

CLYDE WILLIAMS
1907-12 (.694)   33-14-2

1907   7-1-0
O4	●	Coe	18	0
O12		at Minnesota	0	8
O19	●	at Morningside	12	0
O26	●	Cornell Coll.	17	0
N2	●	at Nebraska	13	10 #
N9	●	at Grinnell	49	0
N23	●	Iowa	20	14 *
N30	●	at Drake	13	8

1908-1927
MISSOURI VALLEY

1908   6-3-0 (2-1-0)
S26	●	Morningside	18	0
O3	●	Coe	34	0
O10		at Minnesota	10	15
O17		at Cornell Coll.	0	6
O24	●	South Dakota	26	0
O31	●		at Missouri	16	0
N7		Nebraska *Oma*	17	23
N14	●		Grinnell	53	0
N26	●		at Drake	12	6

1909   4-3-1 (0-2-1)
O2	●	Coe	11	5
O9		at Minnesota	0	18
O16	●	at Grinnell	24	0
O23	=		Missouri	6	6
O30	●	Des Moines Coll.	23	0
N6	●	Cornell Coll.	18	6
N13			at Iowa	0	13 *
N25			at Drake	0	11

1910   4-4-0 (2-2-0)
O1	●	Coe	12	0
O8		at Minnesota	0	49
O15	●	Des Moines	17	0
O22	●		at Missouri	6	5
O29		Morningside	0	5
N5			Iowa	0	2
N12			at Nebraska	0	24
N24	●		at Drake	2	0

1911   6-1-1 (2-0-1)
S30		at Minnesota	0	5
O7	●	Coe	25	0
O21	●		Missouri	6	3
O28	●	at Grinnell	21	6
N4	=		Nebraska	6	6
N11	●		Cornell Coll.	15	0
N18	●		at Iowa	9	0
N25	●		at Drake	6	0

1912   6-2-0 (2-0-0)
O5		at Minnesota	0	5
O12	●	Simpson	24	7
O19	●		at Missouri	29	0
O26	●		Grinnell	31	7
N2		Morningside	16	3
N9	●		at Cornell Coll.	21	0
N16			Iowa	7	20
N23	●		at Drake	27	3

HOMER C. HUBBARD
1913-14 (.533)   8-7

1913   4-4-0 (2-2-0)
S27	●	at Grinnell	6	0
O4		at Minnesota	0	25
O18	●		at Washington, Mo.	37	7
O25			Missouri	13	21
N1		Nebraska	9	18
N8	●		Cornell Coll.	14	0
N15			at Iowa	7	45
N22	●		at Drake	26	3

1914   4-3-0 (2-1-0)
O3	●	Coe	27	6
O10		at Minnesota	0	26
O24	●		at Missouri	6	0
O31			at Nebraska	7	20
N7	●	Cornell Coll.	69	0
N14		Iowa	6	26
N21	●		at Drake	52	0

CHARLES MAYSER
1915-19 (.647)   21-11-2

1915   6-2-0 (2-1-0)
S25	●	Ellsworth	31	0
O2	●	Simpson	27	0
O9		at Minnesota	6	34
O23			Missouri	14	6
O30			Nebraska	0	21
N6	●	Morningside	7	0
N13	●		at Iowa	16	0
N25	●		at Drake	28	14

1916   5-2-1 (2-1-1)
S30	●	Northern Iowa	19	0
O7	●	Highland Park	19	0
O14	●		Kansas	13	0
O21	=		at Missouri	0	0
N4			at Nebraska	0	3
N11	●		at Morningside	7	0
N18	●		Iowa	16	19
N30	●		Drake	32	14

1917   5-2-0 (3-1-0)
S29	●	Simpson	47	0
O6	●	Coe	7	0
O20	●		Missouri	15	0
O27		at Kansas	0	7
N10	●		Kansas State	10	7
N24			at Iowa	3	6
N29	●		at Drake	47	0

1918   0-3-0 (0-1-0)
N9		Camp Dodge	0	6
N16		at Iowa	0	21
N23			at Kansas State	0	11

1919   5-2-1 (3-1-1)
O4	●	Coe	3	0
O11	●		Grinnell	7	0
O18			at Missouri	0	10
O25	=		Kansas	0	0
N1	●		at Nebraska	3	0
N15	●		Kansas State	46	0
N22			at Iowa	0	10
N27			at Drake	14	0

NORMAN C. PAINE
1920 (.500)   4-4

1920   4-4-0 (3-2-0)
O2		Coe	0	6
O9	●		at Grinnell	28	0
O16			Missouri	2	14
O23			at Kansas	0	7
O30	●		Washington, Mo.	24	7
N6	●		at Creighton	17	0
N13	●		at Kansas State	17	0
N20			Iowa	10	14

MAURY KENT
1921 (.500) 4-4

1921 4-4-0 (3-4-0)
O1 ● Coe 28 3
O8 ● | Grinnell 21 3
O15 | at Missouri 14 17
O22 | Kansas 7 14
O29 | at Washington, Mo. 0 2
N5 ● | at Drake 7 0
N11 ● | Kansas State 7 0
N19 | Nebraska 3 35

SAM F. WILLAMAN
1922-25 (.484) 14-15-3

1922 2-6-0 (2-4-0)
O7 Coe 0 24
O14 | Missouri 3 6
O21 ● | at Grinnell 7 0
O28 ● | Washington, Mo. 13 0
N4 | at Drake 7 14
N11 | at Kansas State 2 12
N18 Central Oklahoma 13 14
N25 | at Nebraska 6 54

1923 4-3-1 (3-2-1)
S29 ● Simpson 14 6
O6 at Minnesota 17 20
O13 ● | at Missouri 2 0
O20 = | Kansas State 7 7
O27 ● | at Washington, Mo. 54 7
N3 | at Drake 0 21
N17 | Nebraska 14 26
N24 ● | Grinnell 13 6

1924 4-3-1 (3-2-0)
S27 ● Nebraska Wesleyan 23 13
O4 at Wisconsin 0 17
O11 ● | at Kansas 13 10
O18 | Missouri 0 7
N1 ● | at Kansas State 21 0
N8 = at Minnesota 7 7
N15 | at Grinnell 13 14
N22 ● | Drake 10 0

1925 4-3-1 (3-2-1)
S26 ● Simpson 28 0
O3 at Wisconsin 0 30
O10 ● | Kansas 20 0
O24 ● | Washington, Mo. 28 13
O31 | at Missouri 8 23
N7 = | Grinnell 9 9
N21 ● | at Drake 7 6
N26 | Kansas State 7 12 *

NOEL WORKMAN
1926-30 (.305) 11-27-3

1926 4-3-1 (3-3-1)
O4 ● | at Washington, Mo. 6 0
O9 | Oklahoma State 0 13
O16 = | at Grinnell 0 0
O23 | Missouri 3 7
O30 | at Nebraska 6 31
N13 ● | Drake 13 7
N20 ● | at Kansas State 3 2
N27 ● at UCLA 20 0

1927 4-3-1 (3-2-0)
O1 | at Nebraska 0 6
O8 ● Simpson 26 6
O15 = at Illinois 12 12
O29 ● | Kansas State 12 7
N5 ● | at Drake 7 0
N11 | Missouri 6 13
N19 ● | Grinnell 14 0
N24 at Marquette 0 34

1928-1995
BIG 8

1928 2-5-1 (2-2-1)
O6 | Nebraska 0 12
O13 at Grinnell 0 3
O20 | at Missouri 19 28
O27 = | at Kansas 0 0
N3 ● | Oklahoma 13 0
N17 ● | Kansas State 7 0
N24 at Drake 0 18
N29 at Marquette 0 6

1929 1-7-0 (0-5-0)
O5 ● Grinnell 27 7
O12 | Missouri 0 19
O18 at Marquette 6 14
O26 | Kansas 0 33
N2 | at Oklahoma 7 21
N9 | at Kansas State 2 3
N16 Drake 0 7
N28 | at Nebraska 12 31

1930 0-9-0 (0-5-0)
O4 at Illinois 0 7
O18 | Nebraska 12 14
O25 | at Kansas 6 20
N1 | Oklahoma 13 19
N8 | at Missouri 0 14
N15 | Kansas State 0 13
N22 at Drake 19 20
N29 at Loyola, New Orleans 7 13
D6 at Rice 7 14

GEORGE VEENKER
1931-36 (.490) 21-22-8

1931 5-3-0 (3-1-0)
S26 ● Simpson 6 0
O3 ● at Morningside 20 6
O9 at Detroit 0 20
O24 ● | Missouri 20 0
O31 ● | at Oklahoma 13 12
N7 ● | Kansas State 7 6
N14 Drake 6 7
N21 | at Nebraska 0 23

1932 3-4-1 (0-4-1)
S24 ● Simpson 21 0
O1 ● Morningside 32 0
O8 | at Nebraska 6 12
O15 | Kansas 0 26
O22 = | at Missouri 0 0
N5 | at Kansas State 0 31
N12 | Oklahoma 12 19
N19 ● Drake 34 13

1933 3-5-1 (1-4-0)
S23 ● Central St. 14 0
S29 ● at Denver 18 13
O14 | Nebraska 0 20
O21 | at Oklahoma 7 19
O28 ● | Missouri 14 7
N4 at Iowa 7 27
N11 | Kansas State 0 7
N18 | at Kansas 6 20
N25 = at Drake 7 7

1934 5-3-1 (1-3-1)
S29 ● Luther 23 3
O6 ● Grinnell 26 6
O13 ● | at Missouri 13 0
O20 ● Iowa 31 6
O27 | at Nebraska 6 7
N3 = | Kansas 0 0
N10 | at Oklahoma 0 12
N17 ● Drake 33 12
N24 | at Kansas State 0 20

1935 2-4-3 (1-3-1)
S28 = Cornell Coll. 6 6
O5 | Nebraska 7 20
O12 ● Upper Iowa 23 0
O19 | at Oklahoma 0 16
O26 = | Missouri 6 6
N2 at Marquette 12 28
N9 | Kansas State 0 6
N16 = at Drake 7 7
N23 ● | at Kansas 21 12

1936 3-3-2 (1-3-1)
S26 = Northern Iowa 0 0
O3 | at Nebraska 0 34
O10 ● | Kansas 21 7
O17 ● Cornell Coll. 38 0
O24 | at Missouri 0 10
O31 = | Oklahoma 7 7
N14 | at Kansas State 7 47
N21 ● Drake 21 7

JIM YEAGER
1937-40 (.458) 16-19-1

1937 3-6-0 (1-4-0)
S25 ● Northern Iowa 14 12
O2 at Northwestern 0 33
O9 | Nebraska 7 20
O16 | at Kansas 6 14
O23 at Drake 0 30
O30 | Missouri 0 12
N6 | at Oklahoma 7 33
N13 ● at Marquette 3 0
N20 ● | Kansas State 13 7

1938 7-1-1 (3-1-1)
S23 ● at Denver 14 7
O1 ● Luther 32 7
O8 ● | at Nebraska 8 7
O15 ● | at Missouri 16 13
O22 ● | Kansas 21 7
O29 ● at Marquette 7 0
N5 ● Drake 14 0
N12 = | at Kansas State 13 13
N19 | Oklahoma 0 10

1939 2-7-0 (1-4-0)
S23 ● Coe 19 0
S29 at Denver 0 6
O7 | at Kansas 0 14
O14 | Nebraska 7 10
O21 at Drake 0 7
O28 | Missouri 6 21
N4 | at Oklahoma 6 38
N11 at Marquette 2 21
N18 ● | Kansas State 10 0

1940 4-5-0 (2-3-0)
S21 ● Luther 27 0
S27 at Denver 7 14
O5 ● | Kansas 7 0
O11 at Marquette 25 41
O19 | at Missouri 14 30
O26 | Oklahoma 7 20
N9 ● Drake 7 6
N16 ● | at Kansas State 12 0
N23 | at Nebraska 12 21

RAY DONELS
1941-42 (.292) 3-8-1

1941 2-6-1 (0-4-1)
S26 ● at Denver 7 6
O4 | Nebraska 0 14
O18 | Missouri 13 39
O25 | at Kansas 0 13
N1 ● South Dakota 27 0
N8 | at Oklahoma 0 55
N15 at Drake 13 14
N22 = | Kansas State 12 12
N29 at Marquette 13 20

MIKE MICHALSKE
1942-46 (.500) 18-18-3

1942 3-6-0 (1-4-0)
S25 ● at Denver 7 0
O3 | at Nebraska 0 26
O10 Marquette 12 34
O17 ● Drake 29 6
O24 | at Missouri 6 45
O31 | Oklahoma 7 14
N6 Villanova PHIL 7 32
N14 ● | Kansas 20 13
N21 | at Kansas State 6 7

1943 4-4-0 (3-2-0)
O2 Iowa Pre-Flight 13 33
O9 ● | at Kansas 13 6
O16 ● | Nebraska 27 6
O23 at Ottumwa Pre Flight 12 13
O30 | at Oklahoma 7 21
N6 | Missouri 7 25
N13 ● Drake 20 0
N20 ● | Kansas State 48 0

1944 6-1-1 (3-1-1)
S29 ● Gustavas Adolphus 49 0
O7 ● Doane 59 0
O14 ● | Kansas 25 0
O21 = | at Missouri 21 21
O28 ● | at Kansas State 14 0
N4 | Oklahoma 7 12
N11 ● | at Nebraska 19 6
N18 ● Drake 9 0

1945 4-3-1 (2-2-1)
S22 at Northwestern 6 18
S29 ● Northern Iowa 48 13
O6 = | at Kansas 13 13
O13 | Missouri 7 13
O20 ● | Nebraska 27 7
N3 ● | Kansas State 40 13
N10 | at Oklahoma 7 14
N17 ● at Drake 8 6

1946 2-6-1 (1-4-0)
S21 at Colorado 7 13
S28 at Northwestern 9 41
O5 ● Northern Iowa 20 18
O12 | Kansas 8 24
O19 | at Missouri 13 33
O26 | Oklahoma 0 63
N2 ● | at Kansas State 13 7
N9 = Drake 7 7
N16 | at Nebraska 0 33

ABE STUBER
1947-53 (.392) 24-38-3

1947 3-6-0 (1-4-0)
S20 ● Northern Iowa 31 14
S27 Colorado 0 7
O4 | at Kansas 7 27
O11 | Nebraska 7 14
O18 at Michigan State 0 20
O25 | Missouri 7 26
N1 | at Oklahoma 9 27
N8 ● at Drake 36 6
N15 ● | Kansas State 14 0

1948 4-6-0 (2-4-0)
S18 ● Northern Iowa 27 7
S25 | at Nebraska 15 19
O2 ● | at Kansas State 20 0
O9 | Kansas 7 20
O16 ● | Colorado 18 7
O23 | at Missouri 7 49
O30 | Oklahoma 6 33
N6 ● Drake 2 0
N13 Michigan State 7 48
N20 at Arizona 7 14

1949 5-3-1 (3-3-0)
S17 ● Dubuque 64 0
S24 = at Illinois 20 20
O1 ● | at Kansas 19 6
O8 ● | at Colorado 13 6
O15 ● | Kansas State 25 21
O22 | Missouri 0 32
O29 | at Oklahoma 7 34
N5 ● | at Drake 21 8
N12 | Nebraska 0 7

1950 3-6-1 (2-3-1)
S23 ● | Colorado 14 7
S30 at Northwestern 13 23
O7 ● Northern Iowa 26 8
O14 | Kansas 21 33
O21 = | at Missouri 20 20
O28 | Oklahoma 7 20
N4 ● | at Kansas State 13 7
N11 Drake 21 35
N18 | at Nebraska 13 20
N25 at Arizona 26 27

1951 4-4-1 (2-4-0)
S22 ● Wayne St. 53 21
S29 | at Kansas 33 53
O6 = at Marquette 6 6
O13 ● | Kansas State 32 6
O20 ● | Missouri 21 14
O27 ● at Drake 13 0
N3 | at Colorado 20 47
N10 | Nebraska 27 34
N17 | at Oklahoma 6 35

1952 3-6-0 (1-5-0)
S20 ● South Dakota St. 57 19
S27 at Illinois 7 33
O4 | at Nebraska 0 16
O11 | Kansas 0 43
O18 | Colorado 12 21
O25 | at Missouri 0 19
N1 | Oklahoma 0 41
N8 ● Drake 55 7
N22 ● | at Kansas State 27 0

1953 2-7-0 (1-5-0)
S19 ● South Dakota 35 0
S26 at Northwestern 0 35
O3 | at Kansas 0 23
O10 | Kansas State 12 20
O17 ● | Missouri 13 6
O24 at Drake 7 12
O31 | at Colorado 34 41
N7 | Nebraska 19 27
N14 | at Oklahoma 0 47

VINCE DiFRANCESCA
1954-56 (.232) 6-21-1

1954 3-6-0 (1-5-0)

S18	●		South Dakota St.	34	6
S25			at Northwestern	14	27
O2		|	at Nebraska	14	39
O9	●	|	Kansas	33	6
O16		|	Colorado	0	20
O23		|	at Missouri	14	32
O30	●		Drake	35	0
N6		|	Oklahoma	0	40
N13		|	at Kansas State	7	12

1955 1-7-1 (1-4-1)

S17			Denver	7	19
O1			at Illinois	0	40
O8	=	|	at Kansas	7	7
O15	●	|	Missouri	20	14
O22		|	Kansas State	7	9
O29			at Drake	21	27
N5		|	Nebraska	7	10
N12		|	at Oklahoma	0	52
N19		|	at Colorado	0	40

1956 2-8-0 (0-6-0)

S15	●		at Denver	13	10
S29			at Northwestern	13	14
O6		|	at Nebraska	7	9
O13		|	Kansas	14	25
O20		|	Colorado	0	52
O27		|	at Missouri	0	34
N3	●		Drake	39	14
N10		|	Oklahoma	0	44
N17		|	at Kansas State	6	32
N24			at Villanova	0	26

JIM MYERS
1957 (.450) 4-5-1

1957 4-5-1 (2-4-0)

S21	●		Denver	10	0
S28	=		at Syracuse	7	7
O5		|	at Oklahoma	14	40
O12	●	|	at Kansas	21	6
O19		|	Missouri	13	35
O26		|	Kansas State	10	14
N2			at Drake	0	20
N9	●	|	Nebraska	13	0
N16	●		South Dakota	33	0
N23		|	at Colorado	21	38

CLAY STAPLETON
1958-67 (.444) 42-53-4

1958 4-6-0 (0-6-0)

S20	●		Drake	33	0
S27	●		at Arizona	14	0
O4		|	at Nebraska	6	7
O11		|	Kansas	0	7
O18		|	Colorado	0	20
O25		|	at Missouri	6	14
N1	●		South Dakota	53	0
N8		|	Oklahoma	0	20
N15		|	at Kansas State	6	14
N21	●		at San Jose State	9	6

1959 7-3-0 (3-3-0)

S19	●		Drake	41	0
S25	●		at Denver	28	12
O3		|	Missouri	0	14
O10	●		South Dakota	41	6
O17	●	|	at Colorado	27	0
O24	●	|	Kansas State	26	0
O31		|	at Kansas	0	7
N7	●	|	Nebraska	18	6
N14	●		San Jose State	55	0
N21		|	at Oklahoma	12	35

1960 7-3-0 (4-3-0)

S17	●		Drake	46	0
S23	●		at Detroit	44	21
O1	●	|	at Nebraska	10	7
O8		|	Kansas	14	28
O15		|	Colorado	6	21
O22		|	at Missouri	8	34
O29	●	|	at Oklahoma State	13	6
N5	●	|	Oklahoma	10	6
N12	●	|	at Kansas State	20	7
N19	●		at Pacific	14	6

1961 5-5-0 (3-4-0)

S16	●		at Drake	21	0
S23	●	|	Oklahoma State	14	7
O7	●	|	at Oklahoma	21	15
O14		|	at Kansas	7	21
O21		|	Missouri	7	13
O28	●	|	Kansas State	31	7
N4			at Boston College	10	14
N11		|	Nebraska	13	16
N18	●		at Tulsa	27	6
N25		|	at Colorado	0	34

1962 5-5-0 (3-4-0)

S15	●		Drake	14	7
S22			Oregon State PORT	35	39
O6		|	at Nebraska	22	36
O13		|	Kansas	8	29
O20	●	|	Colorado	57	19
O27		|	at Missouri	6	21
N3	●	|	at Oklahoma State	34	7
N10		|	Oklahoma	0	41
N17	●	|	at Kansas State	28	14
N24	●		Ohio U.	31	22

1963 4-5-0 (3-4-0)

S21			at California	8	15
S28	●		VMI	21	6
O5		|	at Nebraska	7	21
O12	●	|	at Kansas	17	14
O19	●	|	at Colorado	19	7
O26		|	Missouri	0	7
N2	●	|	Oklahoma State	33	28
N9		|	at Oklahoma	14	24
N16		|	Kansas State	10	21

1964 1-8-1 (0-7-0)

S19	●		Drake	25	0
S26		|	at Oklahoma State	14	29
O3		|	Nebraska	7	14
O10		|	Kansas	6	42
O17		|	Colorado	7	14
O24		|	at Missouri	0	10
O31			at Army	7	9
N7		|	at Oklahoma	0	30
N14		|	at Kansas State	6	7
N21	=		at Arizona	0	0

1965 5-4-1 (3-3-1)

S18	●		Drake	21	0
S25	●		Pacific	38	13
O2		|	at Nebraska	0	44
O9	●	|	at Kansas	21	7
O16	=	|	at Colorado	10	10
O23		|	Missouri	7	23
O30	●	|	Oklahoma State	14	10
N6		|	at Oklahoma	20	24
N13	●	|	Kansas State	38	6
N20			at New Mexico	9	10

1966 2-6-2 (2-3-2)

S17			at Wisconsin	10	20
S24		|	Oklahoma	11	33
O1		|	Nebraska	6	12
O8	●	|	Kansas	24	7
O15		|	Colorado	21	41
O22	=	|	at Missouri	10	10
O29	=	|	at Oklahoma State	14	14
N12	●	|	at Kansas State	30	13
N19			at Arizona	24	27
N26			at Colorado State	10	34

1967 2-8-0 (1-6-0)

S16			at South Carolina	3	34
S23			at Texas Tech	0	52
S30	●		New Mexico	17	12
O7		|	at Colorado	0	34
O14	●	|	Kansas State	17	0
O21		|	Missouri	7	23
O28		|	at Kansas	14	28
N4		|	at Nebraska	0	12
N11		|	Oklahoma	14	52
N18		|	Oklahoma State	14	28

JOHN MAJORS
1968-72 (.445) 24-30-1

1968 3-7-0 (1-6-0)

S14	●		Buffalo	28	10
S21			Arizona	12	21
S28	●		at Brigham Young	28	20
O5		|	Colorado	18	28
O12	●	|	at Kansas State	23	14
O19		|	at Oklahoma	7	42
O26		|	Kansas	25	46
N2		|	Nebraska	13	24
N9		|	at Missouri	7	42
N16		|	at Oklahoma State	17	26

1969 3-7-0 (1-6-0)

S20			at Syracuse	13	14
S27	●		Brigham Young	10	0
O4	●		Illinois	48	20
O11		|	Colorado	0	14
O18		|	at Kansas State	7	34
O25	●	|	Kansas	44	20
N1		|	at Oklahoma	14	37
N8		|	at Nebraska	3	17
N15		|	Missouri	13	40
N22		|	Oklahoma State	0	35

1970 5-6-0 (1-6-0)

S19	●		at New Mexico	32	3
S26	●		Colorado State	37	6
O3	●		at Utah	16	13
O10		|	at Colorado	10	61
O17		|	Kansas State	0	17
O24		|	at Kansas	10	24
O31		|	Oklahoma	28	29
N7		|	Nebraska	29	54
N14	●	|	at Missouri	31	19
N21		|	at Oklahoma State	27	36
N28	●		at San Diego State	28	22

1971 8-4-0 (4-3-0)

S18	●		Idaho	24	7
S25	●		at New Mexico	44	20
O2	●		at Kent State	17	14
O9		|	Colorado	14	24
O16	●	|	at Kansas State	24	0
O23	●	|	Kansas	40	24
O30		|	at Oklahoma	12	43
N6		|	at Nebraska	0	37
N13	●	|	Missouri	45	17
N20	●	|	Oklahoma State	54	0
N27	●		at San Diego State	48	31
			SUN BOWL		
D18			LSU	15	33

1972 5-6-1 (2-4-1)

S16	●		at Colorado State	41	0
S23	●		Utah	44	22
S30	●		New Mexico	31	0
O14		|	at Colorado	22	34
O21	●	|	Kansas State	55	22
O28	●	|	at Kansas	34	8
N4		|	Oklahoma	6	20
N11	=	|	Nebraska	23	23
N18		|	at Missouri	5	6
N25		|	at Oklahoma State	14	45
D2			at San Diego State	14	27
			LIBERTY BOWL		
D18			Georgia Tech	30	31

EARLE BRUCE
1973-78 (.529) 36-32

1973 4-7-0 (2-5-0)

S22	●		Idaho	48	0
S29			at Arkansas	19	21
O6		|	Colorado	16	23
O13	●		at Brigham Young	26	24
O20		|	at Kansas State	19	21
O27		|	Kansas	20	22
N3		|	at Oklahoma	17	34
N10		|	at Nebraska	7	31
N17	●	|	Missouri	17	7
N24	●	|	Oklahoma State	28	12
D1			at San Diego State	28	41

1974 4-7-0 (2-5-0)

S14			at Texas Tech	3	24
S21			at Washington	28	31
S28	●		Brigham Young	34	7
O5	●		New Mexico	27	3
O12		|	at Colorado	7	34
O19	●	|	Kansas State	23	18
O26	●	|	at Kansas	22	6
N2		|	Oklahoma	10	28
N9		|	Nebraska	13	23
N16		|	at Missouri	7	10
N23		|	at Oklahoma State	12	14

1975 4-7-0 (1-6-0)

S13			at UCLA	21	37
S20	●		Air Force	17	12
S27	●		at Florida State	10	6
O4	●		at Utah	31	3
O11	●	|	at Kansas State	17	7
O18		|	Kansas	10	21
O25		|	at Oklahoma	7	39
N1		|	Colorado	27	28
N8		|	Missouri	14	44
N15		|	at Nebraska	0	52
N22		|	Oklahoma State	7	14

1976 8-3-0 (4-3-0)

S11	●		Drake	58	14
S18	●		at Air Force	41	6
S25	●		Kent State	47	7
O2		|	Oklahoma	10	24
O9	●		Utah	44	14
O16	●	|	at Missouri	21	17
O23		|	at Colorado	14	33
O30	●	|	Kansas State	45	14
N6	●	|	at Kansas	31	17
N13	●	|	Nebraska	37	28
N20		|	at Oklahoma State	21	42

1977 8-4-0 (5-2-0)

S10	●		Wichita St.	35	9
S17			at Iowa	10	12
S24	●		at Bowling Green	35	21
O1	●		Dayton	17	13
O8	●	|	Missouri	7	0
O15	●	|	at Nebraska	24	21
O22		|	at Oklahoma	16	35
O29	●	|	Kansas	41	3
N5		|	Colorado	7	12
N12	●	|	at Kansas State	22	15
N19	●	|	Oklahoma State	21	13
			PEACH BOWL		
D31			North Carolina St.	14	24

1978 8-4-0 (4-3-0)

S9	●		at Rice	23	19
S16	●		San Diego State	14	13
S23	●		at Iowa	31	0
S30	●		Drake	35	7
O7		|	Nebraska	0	23
O14		|	at Missouri	13	26
O21		|	Oklahoma	6	34
O28	●	|	at Kansas	13	7
N4	●	|	Kansas State	24	0
N11	●	|	at Oklahoma State	28	15
N18	●	|	at Colorado	20	16
			HALL OF FAME CLASSIC		
D20			Texas A&M	12	28

DONNIE DUNCAN
1979-82 (.432) 18-24-2

1979 3-8-0 (2-5-0)

S15	●		Bowling Green	38	10
S22			at Texas	9	17
S29			at Iowa	14	30
O6			Pacific	7	24
O13	●	|	at Kansas State	7	3
O20		|	Kansas	7	24
O27		|	at Oklahoma	9	38
N3	●	|	Colorado	24	10
N10		|	Missouri	9	18
N17		|	at Nebraska	3	34
N24		|	Oklahoma State	10	13

1980 6-5-0 (2-5-0)

S13	●		La. Monroe	42	7
S20	●		San Jose State	27	6
S27	●		at Iowa	10	7
O4	●		Colorado State	69	0
O11	●	|	Kansas State	31	7
O18		|	at Kansas	17	28
O25		|	Oklahoma	7	42
N1		|	at Colorado	9	17
N8		|	at Missouri	10	14
N15		|	Nebraska	0	35
N22	●	|	at Oklahoma State	23	21

1981 5-5-1 (2-4-1)

S12	●		West Texas St.	17	13
S19	●		Iowa	23	12
S26	●		Kent State	28	19
O3	=	|	at Oklahoma	7	7
O10			at San Diego State	31	52
O17	●	|	Missouri	34	13
O24	●	|	Colorado	17	10
O31		|	at Kansas State	7	10
N7		|	Kansas	11	24
N14		|	at Nebraska	7	31
N21		|	Oklahoma State	7	27

1982 4-6-1 (1-5-1)

S11			at Tennessee	21	23
S18	●		at Iowa	19	7
S25	●		Drake	35	10
O2		|	Oklahoma	3	13
O9	●		Kent State	44	7
O16	=	|	at Missouri	17	17
O23	●	|	at Colorado	31	14
O30		|	Kansas State	3	9
N6		|	at Kansas	17	24
N13		|	Nebraska	10	48
N20		|	at Oklahoma State	13	49

JIM CRINER
1983-86 (.405)   16-24-2

1983   4-7-0 (3-4-0)
S10		Iowa	10 51
S17		at Vanderbilt	26 29
S24	●	Colorado State	21 17
O1		New Mexico St.	17 24
O8	●	Kansas	38 35
O15	●	Colorado	22 10
O22		at Oklahoma	11 49
O29		Missouri	18 41
N5		at Nebraska	29 72
N12	●	at Kansas State	49 27
N19		Oklahoma State	7 30

1984   2-7-2 (0-5-2)
S8		at Iowa	21 59
S15	●	Drake	21 17
S22		at Texas A&M	17 38
S29		West Texas St.	14 0
O6		at Kansas	14 33
O13		at Colorado	21 23
O20		Oklahoma	10 12
O27	=	at Missouri	14 14
N3		Nebraska	0 44
N10	=	Kansas State	7 7
N17		at Oklahoma State	10 16

1985   5-6-0 (3-4-0)
S14		Utah State	10 3
S21	●	Vanderbilt	20 17
S28	●	Iowa	3 57
O5		Drake	17 20
O12	●	Kansas	22 21
O19		Colorado	6 40
O26		at Oklahoma	14 59
N2		Missouri	27 28
N9		at Nebraska	0 49
N16		at Kansas State	21 14
N23		Oklahoma State	15 10

CHUCK BANKER
1986 (.500)   1-1

1986   6-5-0 (3-4-0)
S13		at Iowa	7 43
S20	●	Indiana St.	64 9
S27	●	Wichita St.	36 14
O4	●	Wyoming	21 10
O11	●	at Kansas	13 10
O18		at Colorado	3 31
O25		Oklahoma	0 38
N1	●	at Missouri	37 14
N8		Nebraska	14 35
N15		Kansas State	48 19
N22		at Oklahoma State	14 21

JIM WALDEN
1987-94 (.335)   28-57-3

1987   3-8-0 (2-5-0)
S12		at Tulane	12 25
S19		Iowa	9 48
S26		at Wyoming	17 34
O3		Oklahoma	3 56
O10	●	Northern Iowa	39 38
O17		Missouri	17 42
O24	●	at Kansas	42 28
O31		Colorado	10 42
N7		at Nebraska	3 42
N14	●	Kansas State	16 14
N21		at Oklahoma State	27 48

1988   5-6-0 (3-4-0)
S10	●	Tulane	30 13
S17		Baylor	0 35
S24		at Iowa	3 10
O1		at Oklahoma	7 35
O8	●	Northern Iowa	20 17
O15	●	at Missouri	21 3
O22	●	Kansas	42 14
O29		at Colorado	12 24
N5		Nebraska	16 51
N12	●	at Kansas State	16 7
N19		Oklahoma State	28 49

1989   6-5-0 (4-3-0)
S9	●	Ohio U.	28 3
S16		Minnesota	20 30
S23		Iowa	21 31
S30	●	at Tulane	25 24
O7	●	at Kansas	24 20
O14		Colorado	17 52
O21		Oklahoma	40 43
O28		at Nebraska	17 49
N4	●	Kansas State	36 11
N11	●	at Missouri	35 21
N18	●	at Oklahoma State	31 21

1990   4-6-1 (2-4-1)
S8	●	Northern Iowa	35 6
S15		at Minnesota	16 20
S22		at Iowa	35 45
S29	●	Western Michigan	34 20
O6	=	Kansas	34 34
O13		at Colorado	12 28
O20	●	at Oklahoma	33 31
O27		Nebraska	13 45
N3		at Kansas State	14 28
N10	●	Missouri	27 25
N17		Oklahoma State	17 25

1991   3-7-1 (1-5-1)
S7	●	Eastern Illinois	42 13
S14		Iowa	10 29
S21		at Wisconsin	6 7
S28	●	at Rice	28 27
O5		Oklahoma	8 29
O19		at Kansas	0 41
O26	=	Oklahoma State	6 6
N2	●	at Missouri	23 22
N9		Kansas State	7 37
N16		at Nebraska	13 38
N23		Colorado	14 17

1992   4-7-0 (2-5-0)
S5	●	Ohio U.	35 9
S12		at Iowa	7 21
S19	●	Tulane	38 14
S26		Northern Iowa	10 27
O3		at Oklahoma	3 17
O17		Kansas	47 50
O24		at Oklahoma State	21 27
O31	●	Missouri	28 14
N5		at Kansas State	13 22
N14	●	Nebraska	19 10
N21		at Colorado	10 31

1993   3-8-0 (2-5-0)
S2	●	Northern Illinois	54 10
S11		Iowa	28 31
S18		at Wisconsin	7 28
S25		at Rice	21 49
O2		Oklahoma	7 24
O16		at Kansas	20 35
O23	●	Oklahoma State	20 17
O30		at Missouri	34 37
N6	●	Kansas State	27 23
N13		at Nebraska	17 49
N20		Colorado	16 21

1994   0-10-1 (0-6-1)
S3		Northern Iowa	14 28
S10		at Iowa	9 37
S17		Western Michigan	19 23
S24		Rice	18 28
O1		at Oklahoma	6 34
O15		Kansas	23 41
O22	=	at Oklahoma State	31 31
O29		Missouri	20 34
N5		at Kansas State	20 38
N12		Nebraska	12 28
N19		at Colorado	20 41

DAN McCARNEY
1995-PRESENT (.385)   45-72

1995   3-8-0 (1-6-0)
A31	●	Ohio U.	36 21
S9		at TCU	10 27
S16		Iowa	10 27
S23	●	Nevada-Las Vegas	57 30
O7		Oklahoma	26 39
O14		at Kansas	7 34
O21		Colorado	28 50
O28	●	Oklahoma State	38 14
N4		at Nebraska	14 73
N11		Kansas State	7 49
N18		at Missouri	31 45

1996-PRESENT BIG 12

1996   2-9 (1-7)
S7		Wyoming	38 41
S14		at Iowa	13 38
S21	●	Northern Iowa	42 23
S28		Missouri	45 31
O12		Texas A&M	21 24
O19		at Oklahoma State	27 28
O26		at Baylor	21 49
N2		Kansas	31 34
N9		at Colorado	42 49
N16		Nebraska	14 49
N23		at Kansas State	20 35

1997   1-10   (1-7)
A30		Oklahoma State	14 21
S6		at Wyoming	10 56
S13		at Minnesota	29 53
S20		Iowa	20 63
O4		at Missouri	21 45
O11		at Texas A&M	17 56
O25	●	Baylor	24 17
N1		at Kansas	24 34
N8		Colorado	38 43
N15		at Nebraska	14 77
N22		Kansas State	3 28

1998   3-8   (1-7)
S5		TCU	21 31
S12	●	at Iowa	27 9
S19	●	Ball State	38 0
S26		Texas Tech	24 31
O3		at Texas	33 54
O10		Missouri	19 35
O24		at Kansas State	7 52
O31		at Oklahoma	14 17
N7		Nebraska	7 42
N14		at Colorado	8 37
N21	●	Kansas	23 20

1999   4-7   (1-7)
S2	●	Indiana St.	33 7
S11	●	Iowa	17 10
S18	●	at Nevada-Las Vegas	24 0
S25		Kansas State	28 35
O9		at Nebraska	14 49
O16	●	at Missouri	24 21
O23		Colorado	12 16
O30		Texas	41 44
N6		at Texas Tech	16 28
N13		Oklahoma	10 31
N20		at Kansas	28 31

2000   9-3   (5-3)
S2	●	Ohio U.	25 15
S9	●	Nevada-Las Vegas	37 22
S16	●	at Iowa	24 14
S30	●	at Baylor	31 17
O7		Nebraska	27 49
O14	●	at Oklahoma State	33 26
O21		Texas A&M	7 30
O28	●	Missouri	39 20
N4		at Kansas State	10 56
N11	●	at Colorado	35 27
N18	●	Kansas	38 17

INSIGHT.COM BOWL
D28	●	Pittsburgh	37 29

2001   7-5   (4-4)
S8	●	Northern Iowa	45 0
S22	●	at Ohio U.	31 28
S29		Baylor	41 0
O6		at Nebraska	14 48
O13		at Missouri	20 14
O20	●	Oklahoma State	28 14
O27		at Texas A&M	21 24
N3		Kansas State	3 42
N10	●	Colorado	27 40
N17	●	at Kansas	49 7
N24	●	Iowa	17 14

INDEPENDENCE BOWL
D27		Alabama	13 14

2002   7-7   (4-4)
A24		Florida State KC	31 38
A31	●	Kansas	45 3
S7		Tennessee Tech	58 6
S14		at Iowa	36 31
S21		Troy State	42 12
S28		Nebraska	36 14
O12	●	Texas Tech	31 17
O19		at Oklahoma	3 49
O26		at Texas	10 21
N2	●	Missouri	42 35
N9		at Kansas State	7 58
N16		at Colorado	27 41
N23		Connecticut	20 37

HUMANITARIAN BOWL
D31		Boise State	16 34

2003   2-10   (0-8)
A30		No. Iowa	17 10
S6	●	Ohio U.	48 20
S13		Iowa	21 40
S27		at Northern Illinois	16 24
O4		Oklahoma	7 53
O11		at Texas Tech	21 52
O18		Texas	19 40
O25		at Nebraska	0 28
N8		Kansas State	0 45
N15		Colorado	10 44
N22		at Kansas	7 36
N29		at Missouri	7 45

2004   7-5   (4-4)
S4	●	No. Iowa	23 0
S11		at Iowa	10 17
S18	●	Northern Illinois	48 41
O2		at Oklahoma State	7 36
O9		Texas A&M	3 34
O16		at Colorado	14 19
O23	●	at Baylor	26 25
O30	●	Kansas	13 7
N6	●	Nebraska	34 27
N20	●	at Kansas State	37 23
N27		Missouri	14 17

INDEPENDENCE BOWL
D28	●	Miami, Ohio	17 13

THE SCHOOLS

KANSAS

BY MARK WANGRIN

S ANDLOT FOOTBALL WAS PLAYED IN Lawrence, Kan., more than a full decade before 1898, when James Naismith first brought basketball to the region. Yet when basketball got its grip on the Sunflower State's oldest state university, it wouldn't let go, and it never let football out of its formidable shadow.

Despite great players such as Gale Sayers, John Hadl and Nolan Cromwell, the Jayhawks have been down more than they've been up. While the university's basketball team was making appearances in the Final Four, the football team won only five conference titles, including just one since 1947. Rival Kansas State's remarkable renaissance in the 1990s further marginalized Kansas football, though the Jayhawks showed signs of reemerging under Glen Mason in the mid-1990s, only to fall back down.

TRADITION E.H.S. Bailey was a KU chemistry professor trying to come up with a cheer for his Science Club when he patterned a chant after the cadence of the train he and several associates were riding on in 1886. The original cheer was "Rah, Rah, Jayhawk, KU," but "Rah, Rah" was later substituted with "Rock Chalk" because it alluded to the limestone formations found on nearby Mount Oread—and because it rhymed. After touchdowns, KU fans wave their arms in the air, a gesture called Waving the Wheat.

BEST PLAYER Nicknamed the Kansas Comet for his blazing speed, Gale Sayers also possessed an uncanny ability—like a butterfly's—to change direction in an instant. The two-time All-America player led the Jayhawks in rushing, touchdowns and kickoff returns in his three seasons as a starter. His 99-yard touchdown run against Nebraska in 1963 ties him with four others, including Jayhawk Eric Vann, for the NCAA record for longest run from scrimmage. "Gale was a very unselfish player," said former teammate Bobby Skahan. "I was always intrigued by that, because he was so talented. He could do it all. He was the best player in the nation, and it's sad he didn't win the Heisman Trophy." Sayers was a first-round draft pick of the NFL Chicago Bears and AFL Kansas City Chiefs. Though he played only four full seasons for the Bears, Sayers, at age 34, became the youngest player ever inducted into the Pro Football Hall of Fame.

PROFILE
University of Kansas
Lawrence, Kan.
Founded: 1866
Enrollment: 20,213
Colors: Crimson and Blue
Nickname: Jayhawks
Stadium: Memorial Stadium
    Opened in 1921
    AstroPlay; 50,071 capacity
First football game: 1890
All-time record: 529–527–58 (.501)
Bowl record: 3–6
First-round NFL draftees: 8
Website: www.kuathletics.com

THE BEST OF TIMES
Under coach A.R. Kennedy, the Jayhawks were 53–9–4 from 1904 to 1910, including a 10–1 record in 1905.

THE WORST OF TIMES
1982 to 1990. Four coaches, nine straight non-winning seasons and only two finishes higher than sixth place in the Big Eight.

CONFERENCE
Along with fellow Big Eight members Oklahoma, Nebraska, Oklahoma State, Missouri, Kansas State, Colorado and Iowa State, the Jayhawks merged with former Southwest Conference schools Texas, Texas A&M, Texas Tech and Baylor to form the Big 12 in 1996. Kansas was a charter member of the Missouri Valley Intercollegiate Athletic Assocation when it was formed in 1907. The MVIAA evolved into the Big Six in 1928 when six teams left the MVIAA. The league became the Big Seven in 1948 with the addition of Colorado and the Big Eight in 1960 when Oklahoma State—formerly Oklahoma A&M—joined.

DISTINGUISHED ALUMNI
Bob Dole; Nancy Kassebaum Baker, U.S. senator; Don Johnson, actor; Bill Kurtis, broadcaster; Sara Paretsky, mystery writer; Paul Pierce, NBA player; Jim Ryun, track star and U.S. representative; Clyde Tombaugh, the discoverer of planet Pluto

FIGHT SONG
I'M A JAYHAWK
Talk about the Sooners, the Cowboys and the Buffs,
Talk about the Tiger and his tail,
Talk about the Wildcats, and those Cornhuskin' boys,
But I'm the bird to make 'em weep and wail.
Chorus: 'Cause I'm a Jay, Jay, Jay, Jay Jayhawk
Up at Lawrence on the Kaw
'Cause I'm a Jay, Jay, Jay, Jay Jayhawk
With a sis-boom, hip hoorah.
Got a bill that's big enough to twist the Tiger's tail,
Husk some corn and listen to the Cornhusker's wail,
'Cause I'm a Jay, Jay, Jay, Jay Jayhawk,
Riding on a Kansas gale.

Gale Sayers possessed a butterfly's uncanny ability to change direction in an instant.

BEST COACH Jack Mitchell knew he could win if he got the best in-state talent. "Jack was probably the greatest recruiter in the history of recruiting—period," said John Hadl, who played quarterback for him. "He had a lot of enthusiasm and made you believe that everything was going to happen, that the team was going to be good in a short period of time ... As it turned out, pretty much everything he said would happen did happen." In his nine seasons he went 44–42–5, including KU's first bowl win in the 1961 Bluebonnet Bowl. His 1960 team won the Big Eight, KU's first conference title in 30 years, but the title was vacated when the Jayhawks were forced to forfeit two wins because of an ineligible player. "All my life my ambition was to go to KU," Mitchell said. "I thought that that's where you died and went to heaven, in Lawrence, Kan."

BEST TEAM In 1968, a quarterback named Bobby Douglass was the perfect man to guide KU's single-wing, T-formation attack. Behind Douglass' passing and running and the emergence of a sophomore fullback named John

Riggins, the Jayhawks won their first seven games and climbed to No. 3 in the nation before a 27-23 home loss to unranked Oklahoma. KU finished the regular season 9–1 and with a share of the Big Eight title. Led by coach Pepper Rodgers, the Jayhawks earned a bid to the Orange Bowl, where they nearly upset No. 3 Penn State before falling 15-14. Joining Douglass on the All-America teams was defensive end John Zook.

BIGGEST GAME Kansas had two cracks at the No. 1 team in the nation in 1960. The Jayhawks lost 21-7 to Iowa, but on Nov. 19 they got another chance when they traveled to Columbia to take on rival Missouri, where school secretaries were answering the phones by saying, "We're No. 1." Defensively, KU crowded the line and strung out Missouri's option attack. Offensively, the Jayhawks rode a backfield of John Hadl, Curtis McClinton and Bert Coan to a 23-7 victory. The Faurot Field public-address announcer comforted the home fans, telling them not to worry due to a pending investigation of KU recruiting violations. Weeks later,

RECORDS

RUSHING YARDS

	GAME
396	Tony Sands vs. Missouri, Nov. 23, 1991 (58 att.)
	SEASON
1,442	Tony Sands, 1991 (273 att.)
	CAREER
3,841	June Henley, 1993-96 (823 att.)

PASSING YARDS

	GAME
480	Mike Norseth vs. Vanderbilt, Sept. 14, 1985 (24 of 38)
	SEASON
2,995	Mike Norseth, 1985 (227 of 408)
	CAREER
6,410	Frank Seurer, 1980-83 (467 of 934)

RECEIVING YARDS

	GAME
221	Quintin Smith vs. Louisville, Sept. 9, 1989 (11 rec.)
	SEASON
1,144	Bob Johnson, 1983 (58 rec.)
	CAREER
2,266	Willie Vaughn, 1985-88 (133 rec.)

POINTS

	GAME
24	June Henley vs. TCU, Sept. 14, 1996; tied with four others (4 TDs)
	SEASON
108	June Henley, 1996 (18 TDs)
	CAREER
302	Dan Eichloff, 1990-93 (62 FGs, 116 PATs)

CONSENSUS ALL-AMERICANS

1963-64	Gale Sayers, B
1968	John Zook, DE
1973	David Jaynes, QB

the Jayhawks were stripped of the victory when it was ruled that Coan had improperly accepted a plane ticket to the College All-Star Game from a KU alumnus.

BIGGEST UPSET Oklahoma had gone unbeaten for 37 games—including 28 straight wins—when it hosted a 5–3 Kansas team on Nov. 8, 1975. Suddenly, everything that had gone right for the Sooners for the better part of three seasons went desperately wrong, leading to the Jayhawks' 23-3 victory. They turned the ball over on eight possessions, including seven in the second half, and had a punt and field goal attempt blocked. The Sooners also couldn't stop a KU wishbone attack keyed by quarterback Nolan Cromwell—who didn't need to throw a single pass.

STADIUM In 1919, a movement began on the KU campus to build a bigger football venue and to honor the KU students who had fought and died in World War I. In 1920, KU hoops coaching legend Phog Allen took a shot at directing the football team. Led by quarterback Dutch Lonborg and halfback John Bunn—two men who would later be inducted into the Basketball Hall of Fame—the Jayhawks rallied from a 20-0 halftime deficit to tie Nebraska. Two days later, wildly inspired by the tie, students and faculty gathered to celebrate while, over a three-day period, more than $200,000 was pledged to begin building a new concrete stadium. Although it opened the prior season, Memorial Stadium was formally dedicated on Nov. 11, 1922—Armistice Day. The north end of the structure was closed to form a horseshoe shape in 1927, raising capacity to 35,000. Renovations that extended the grandstands in 1963 and 1965 increased seating to 51,500, though subsequent renovations reduced it to 50,071. In the late 1990s and early 2000s, a $30 million dollar renovation added new lights, locker rooms, press box and MegaVision video board.

LANDMARK Located near the southeast corner of Memorial Stadium, Potter Lake is traditionally the final resting place for the remnants of the crossbars and uprights

downed after big home victories. Fans also congregate on nearby Campanile Hill during games, where they barbecue and recline on blankets to watch the game.

ALL-TIME TEAM	

Selected by the Lawrence Journal-World *in June 2004.*

OFFENSE

1948-50	Mike McCormack, OL
1950-52	George Mrkonic, OL
1950-52	Oliver Spencer, OL
1959-60	Fred Hageman, OL
1968-70	Larry Brown, OL
1942, 1946-47	Otto Schnellbacher, TE
1985-88	Willie Vaughn, WR
1959-61	John Hadl, QB
1941-42, 1946-47	Ray Evans, HB
1962-64	Gale Sayers, HB
1968-70	John Riggins, FB
1980, 1982-83	Bruce Kallmeyer, PK

DEFENSE

1966-68	John Zook, DL
1973-76	Mike Butler, DL
1989-92	Gilbert Brown, DL
1990-92	Dana Stubblefield, DL
1950-52	Galen Fiss, LB
1967-69	Emery Hicks, LB
1982-85	Willie Pless, LB
1952	Gil Reich, DB
1972-75	Kurt Knoff, DB
1973-76	Nolan Cromwell, DB
1976-79	LeRoy Irvin, DB
1980-82	Bucky Scribner, P

HEARTBREAKER Kansas was up 14-7 on Penn State as the clock ran down in the 1969 Orange Bowl. The Nittany Lions had the ball on the 50 and no timeouts. Before Penn State completed a long pass to the 3, KU assistant Dave McClain sent tackle Karl Salb into the game. Salb forgot to tell linebacker Rick Abernathy he was coming in. Undetected, KU played with 12 men for five downs, with Penn State finally scoring on third down. The Nittany Lions went for the two-point conversion and failed, and it was then that the officials noticed the extra Jayhawks player. Given another chance because of the penalty, Penn State got the two-point conversion and the 15-14 victory. "He'd been on the field for five plays. The officials didn't catch it. If they'd been doing their job, if they would have called the penalty when it originally happened, we would have won the game," said KU coach Pepper Rodgers, employing some twisted logic. Kansas finished the season ranked seventh.

WILDEST FINISH A premature celebration nearly cost the Jayhawks their first win over rival Missouri in four seasons in 1981. An interception return by Roger Foote and a touchdown run by Garfield Taylor gave KU a 19-3 lead with just over a minute left. With 27 seconds remaining, fans swarmed the field and tore down the north goalposts. The officials penalized the Jayhawks twice for unsportsmanlike conduct, setting the Tigers up for a short touchdown and two-point conversion that brought them within eight points. Missouri recovered the onside kick, but the drive stalled. KU fans pelted the field with tangerines to taunt the Tigers, who had received a bid to the Tangerine Bowl the week before.

RIVAL The only argument more vehement than those between Kansas fans and Missouri fans or Kansas fans and Kansas State fans is the one between Kansas fans themselves

over which rival is more hated. Before the Jayhawks played Missouri in 1988, former coach Don Fambrough gave his annual pre-Missouri speech to the team. "You have your damn rivalry. Your rivalry is with Kansas State. This is a war! Playing Missouri is a war that goes back to the 1860s." One of the Jayhawks' most delicious moments came in 1991, when halfback "Tuxedo" Tony Sands—so nicknamed because he wore a tuxedo to every game—ran for a then-NCAA-record 396 yards on 58 carries in a 53-29 victory over the Tigers. The KSU-KU rivalry was often marked with mediocrity, culminating in the 1987 game, when 1–7 KU met 0–8 KSU. The game, billed by the *Topeka Capital-Journal* as the Toilet Bowl and described as a meeting between "the resistible force and the moveable object," ended in—what else?—a 17-17 tie.

TRAGEDY Tommy Johnson was already a basketball star at Kansas when he decided to give football a try in 1908, becoming a key player at quarterback. In the 1909 season finale against Missouri, Johnson took a blow to the head. Disoriented, he played poorly and the Tigers won 12-6 to ruin KU's perfect season and end their 18-game winning streak. The next year Johnson, who had been bothered by a kidney ailment as a kid, took a few shots to the lower back against the Tigers, aggravating the condition. He never recovered and exactly a year to the day after he played his last football game for the Jayhawks, he died in a Kansas City hospital. His memorial in the 1931 *Jayhawker Yearbook* read, "There is glory, there is tragedy, in the story of Tommy Johnson, whose name has rightly gone down in university annals as KU's greatest athlete. Many a victorious Jayhawker received the inspiration necessary to come from behind against overwhelming odds from the 'Man Who Died for Kansas.'"

NICKNAME A Civil War regiment commissioned by Kansas governor Charles Robinson called themselves the Independent Mounted Jayhawks. By the end of the war, the name had become synonymous with the "spirit of camaraderie and the courageous fighting qualities that characterized efforts to keep Kansas a free state." By 1886, KU had adopted the nickname as part of a school yell, and when KU fielded its first football team in 1890 they were tabbed Jayhawks.

MASCOT The Jayhawk is a mythical bird that combines the

traits of two birds indigenous to Kansas, the blue jay and the sparrow hawk. The blue jay is a noisy, contentious nest raider; the sparrow hawk a stealthy hunter. The intended message is, "Don't turn your back on this bird." In 1912, Henry Maloy, a cartoonist for the school paper, drew up a Jayhawk, complete with shoes for kicking opponents. Over the next three decades, the Jayhawk was revised several times with Harold D. Sandy's 1946 version of a smiling Jayhawk finally sticking as the basic design. The KU Alumni Association created a costumed mascot in the 1960s. During halftime of the homecoming game in 1971, a large egg was hauled out to midfield and the crowd watched mascot sidekick Baby Jay hatch. In September 1978, the Baby Jay costume was kidnapped before the homecoming game but returned in time for kickoff.

UNIFORMS KU's original school colors, maize and blue, were the same as Michigan's at the time. But when football started up in 1890, a push was made to adopt crimson, in honor of the Harvard pedigree of Colonel John. J. McCook, who had donated money for the first stadium. Faculty members who had graduated from Yale balked, and insisted that Yale blue also be adopted. In 1896, the school colors became crimson and blue. When Jack Mitchell became head coach in 1958, his first impulse was to ditch the red jerseys because so many other Big Seven teams—Iowa State, Nebraska, Oklahoma—wore red. He learned the other school color was blue, and he remembered how much he liked North Carolina's blue uniforms when he played against them for OU in the Sugar Bowl. So he switched the Jayhawks to sky-blue jerseys, pants and helmets. By the time Pepper Rodgers replaced Mitchell in 1967, the Jayhawks had gone to darker blue jerseys, though in various shades from royal to navy. The helmets have also had a variety of incarnations, from white to blue, with Kansas, the Jayhawk logo and the interlocking KU appearing on the sides at different times. A plan to go to red helmets in 1965 was scrapped after fan protest.

QUOTE "I flashed him the peace sign and he gave half of it back to me."—Pepper Rodgers, on his greeting of Missouri coach Dan Devine following the Tigers' 69-21 romp in 1969. Rodgers later admitted he had made up the story

THE SCHOOLS

KANSAS ANNUAL STATISTICAL LEADERS

YR	RUSHING	YDS	ATT	AVG	PASSING	ATT	CMP	PCT	YDS	RECEIVING	REC	YDS	AVG
1937	Clarence Douglass	376	72	5.2	Lyman Diven	60	21	.35	207	Max Replogle	18	180	10.0
1938	Dick Amerine	277	58	4.8	Ralph Miller	53	25	.47	407	Max Replogle	12	259	21.6
1939	Ed Hall	189	44	4.3	Ralph Miller	37	23	.62	261	Jake Fry	11	137	12.5
1940	Ed Hall	294	109	2.7	Ed Hall	52	22	.42	251	Don Pollom	14	158	11.3
1941	Ray Niblo	241	87	2.8	Ralph Miller	100	54	.54	657	Ray Evans	18	235	13.1
1942	Ray Evans	293	111	2.6	Ray Evans	200	101	.51	1,117	Otto Schnellbacher	25	366	14.6
1943	Bob George	180	42	4.3	Bob George	37	18	.49	288	Charlie Moffatt	15	230	15.3
1944	Charlie Moffatt	300	80	3.8	Charlie Moffatt	58	24	.41	222	Dwight Sutherland	8	148	18.5
1945	Dick Bertuzzi	360	76	4.7	George Gear	58	21	.36	223	Norm Pumphrey	12	212	17.7
1946	Ray Evans	459	112	4.1	Ray Evans	39	17	.44	379	Otto Schnellbacher	16	342	21.4
1947	Forrest Griffith	483	86	5.6	Ray Evans	60	30	.50	598	Otto Schnellbacher	17	361	21.2
1948	Forrest Griffith	368	96	3.8	Dick Gilman	129	44	.34	945	Bryan Sperry	21	343	16.3
1949	Bud French	510	86	5.9	Dick Gilman	118	49	.42	885	Lyn Smith	20	358	17.9
1950	Wade Stinson	1,129	167	6.8	Chet Strehlow	88	32	.36	651	Lyn Smith	14	309	22.1
1951	Bob Brandeberry	649	136	4.8	Jerry Robertson	113	54	.48	925	Orban Tice	19	363	19.1
1952	Charlie Hoag	469	93	5.0	Jerry Robertson	101	55	.54	868	Charlie Hoag	16	380	23.8
1953	Don Hess	369	83	4.4	John McFarland	79	28	.35	343	Harold Patterson	10	179	17.9
1954	Bud Laughlin	339	94	3.6	Bev Buller	51	18	.35	303	Joe Held	5	116	23.2
1955	John Francisco	459	107	4.3	Wally Strauch	76	28	.37	498	Jim Letcavits	9	169	18.8
1956	Homer Floyd	638	134	4.8	Wally Strauch	80	32	.40	596	Jim Letcavits	14	246	17.6
1957	Homer Floyd	505	127	4.0	Wally Strauch	43	26	.60	320	Homer Floyd	9	189	21.0
1958	Homer Floyd	391	103	3.8	Larry McKnown	23	10	.43	219	Homer Floyd	15	307	20.5
1959	Curtis McClinton	472	91	5.2	Lee Flachsbarth	27	14	.52	345	John Hadl	7	126	18.0
1960	Bert Coan	488	73	6.7	John Hadl	87	43	.49	566	Curtis McClinton	11	184	16.7
1961	Ken Coleman	656	130	5.0	John Hadl	93	44	.47	665	Curtis McClinton	10	166	16.6
1962	Gale Sayers	1,125	158	7.1	R. McFarland	86	28	.33	366	Lloyd Buzzi	6	118	19.7
1963	Gale Sayers	917	132	6.9	Steve Renko	86	31	.36	505	Gale Sayers	11	155	14.1
1964	Gale Sayers	633	122	5.2	Bobby Skahan	78	41	.53	550	Gale Sayers	17	182	10.7
1965	Dan Miller	356	66	5.4	Bill Fenton	104	35	.34	500	Sim Stokes	25	271	10.8
1966	Donnie Shanklin	732	182	4.0	Bobby Skahan	47	23	.49	299	Halley Kampschroeder	18	278	15.4
1967	Bobby Douglass	415	175	2.4	Bobby Douglass	173	82	.47	1,326	John Mosier	37	495	13.4
1968	John Riggins	866	139	6.2	Bobby Douglass	168	84	.50	1,316	George McGowan	32	592	18.5
1969	John Riggins	662	170	3.9	Phil Basler	110	40	.36	746	John Mosier	25	339	13.6
1970	John Riggins	1,131	209	5.4	Dan Heck	188	81	.43	1,169	Ron Jessie	18	308	17.1
1971	Delvin Williams	509	102	5.0	David Jaynes	137	64	.47	748	John Schroll	40	491	12.3
1972	Jerome Nelloms	684	179	3.8	David Jaynes	287	153	.53	2,253	Bruce Adams	39	704	18.1
1973	Delvin Williams	762	198	3.8	David Jaynes	330	172	.52	2,131	Emmett Edwards	49	802	16.4
1974	Laverne Smith	1,181	176	6.7	Scott McMichael	156	74	.47	1,044	Emmett Edwards	30	542	18.1
1975	Nolan Cromwell	1,124	218	5.2	Nolan Cromwell	49	20	.41	333	Waddell Smith	9	197	21.9
1976	Laverne Smith	978	148	6.6	Nolan Cromwell	43	13	.30	273	Waddell Smith	10	221	22.1
1977	Norris Banks	655	162	4.0	Brian Bethke	53	23	.43	384	David Verser	11	220	20.0
1978	Mike Higgins	270	68	4.0	Harry Sydney	107	44	.41	605	Kevin Murphy	20	346	17.3
1979	Harry Snydey	541	123	4.4	Brian Bethke	108	59	.55	874	David Verser	21	463	22.0
1980	Kerwin Bell	1,114	228	4.9	Frank Seurer	146	64	.44	797	David Verser	30	576	19.2
1981	Garfield Taylor	728	167	4.4	Frank Seurer	176	89	.51	1,199	Wayne Capers	36	629	17.5
1982	Dino Bell	370	110	3.4	Frank Seurer	259	127	.49	1,625	Bob Johnson	18	428	23.8
1983	Kerwin Bell	498	115	4.3	Frank Seurer	353	187	.53	2,789	Bob Johnson	58	1,144	19.7
1984	Lynn Williams	776	172	4.5	Mike Norseth	239	136	.57	1,682	Richard Estell	25	500	20.0
1985	Lynn Williams	373	172	2.2	Mike Norseth	408	227	.56	2,995	Richard Estell	70	1,109	15.8
1986	Arnold Snell	672	163	4.1	Mike Orth	290	144	.50	1,548	Ronnie Caldwell	39	423	10.8
1987	Arnold Snell	691	184	3.8	Kelly Donohoe	144	72	.50	981	John Baker	27	300	11.1
1988	Tony Sands	480	103	4.7	Kelly Donohoe	258	131	.51	1,844	Willie Vaughn	39	812	20.8
1989	Tony Sands	1,109	216	5.1	Kelly Donohoe	256	141	.55	2,125	Quintin Smith	50	898	18.0
1990	Tony Sands	757	186	4.1	Chip Hilleary	224	129	.58	1,730	Kenny Drayton	34	506	14.9
1991	Tony Sands	1,442	273	5.3	Chip Hilleary	188	98	.52	1,267	Kenny Drayton	34	439	12.9
1992	Maurice Douglas	899	198	4.5	Chip Hilleary	215	106	.49	1,583	Matt Gay	30	425	14.2
1993	June Henley	1,127	233	4.8	Asheiki Preston	159	97	.61	1,233	Ashaundai Smith	27	256	9.5
1994	L.T. Levine	803	128	6.3	Asheiki Preston	156	88	.56	1,168	Ashaundai Smith	22	426	19.4
1995	L.T. Levine	841	156	5.4	Mark Williams	282	174	.62	1,957	Isaac Byrd	48	604	12.6
1996	June Henley	1,349	302	4.5	Matt Johner	185	96	.52	1,232	Isaac Byrd	53	840	15.8
1997	Eric Vann	796	196	4.1	Zac Wegner	144	66	.46	970	Michael Chandler	21	311	14.8
1998	David Winbush	974	209	4.7	Zac Wegner	186	91	.49	1,367	Harrison Hill	28	391	14.0
1999	David Winbush	595	123	4.8	Dylen Smith	263	135	.51	1,599	Michael Chandler	36	473	13.1
2000	David Winbush	701	163	4.3	Dylen Smith	306	140	.46	1,963	Harrison Hill	47	591	12.6
2001	Reggie Duncan	739	181	4.1	Mario Kinsey	202	88	.44	1,215	Roger Ross	39	493	12.6
2002	Clark Green	883	197	4.5	Bill Whittemore	305	151	.50	1,666	Byron Gasaway	39	490	12.6
2003	Clark Green	1,015	147	3.7	Bill Whittemore	263	159	.60	2,385	Charles Gordon	57	769	13.5
2004	John Randle	572	204	4.7	Adam Barmann	262	141	.54	1,427	Brandon Rideau	51	597	11.7

Receiving leaders by receptions
The NCAA began including postseason stats in 2002

KANSAS ALL-TIME SCORES

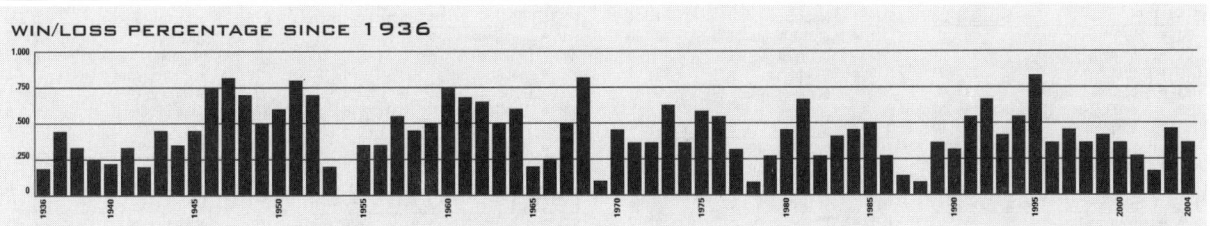

WIN/LOSS PERCENTAGE SINCE 1936

NO HEAD COACH

1890   1-2-0
N22	at Baker	9	22
N27	at K.C. YMCA	10	18
D8 ●	Baker	14	12

E.M. HOPKINS
1891 (.938)   7-0-1

1891   7-0-1
O31 ●	Missouri *KC*	22	10	*
N17 ●	at Washburn	32	10	
N21 ●	Washburn	38	10	
N26 ●	Kansas City YMCA *KC*	22	4	
N28 ●	at Baker	18	4	
D5 ●	Iowa *KC*	14	12	#
D17 ●	Baker	8	0	
D22 =	Washington, Mo. *KC*	6	6	

A.W. SHEPARD
1892-93 (.600)   9-6

1892   7-1-0
O15 ●	at Denver AC	20	6
O20 ●	Baker	14	0
O27 ●	Illinois	26	4
O28 ●	Washburn	36	0
N5 ●	Iowa *KC*	24	4
N12 ●	at Nebraska	12	0
N19 ●	at Baker	0	18
N26 ●	Missouri *KC*	12	4

1893   2-5-0
O14 ●	at Minnesota	6	12
O25 ●	Baker	12	14
O28 ●	at Denver AC	10	24
N4 ●	Iowa *KC*	35	24
N18 ●	at Nebraska	18	0
N25 ●	Michigan *KC*	0	22
N30 ●	Missouri *KC*	4	12

HECTOR COWAN
1894-96 (.674)   15-7-1

1894   2-3-1
O14 ●	Doane	22	12
O28 =	Ottawa	6	6
N3 ●	at Iowa	12	14
N10 ●	Michigan *KC*	12	22
N17 ●	at Nebraska	6	12
N30 ●	Missouri *KC*	18	12

1895   6-1-0
S21 ●	at Midland Lutheran	28	0	
O5 ●	Midland Lutheran	56	0	
O11 ●	at Emporia St.	10	0	
N2 ●	Iowa	52	0	*
N9 ●	Doane *KC*	32	0	
N16 ●	at Nebraska	8	4	
N28 ●	Missouri *KC*	6	10	

1896   7-3-0
S27 ●	Haskell	32	0
O4 ●	Abilene	6	0
O11 ●	Emporia St.	26	0
O18 ●	at Denver AC	8	6
O25 ●	at Iowa	0	6
N1 ●	K.C. Med. Coll. *KC*	0	8
N7 ●	Nebraska	18	4
N14 ●	Doane	16	4
N26 ●	Missouri *KC*	30	0
N28 ●	Minnesota *KC*	0	12

WYLIE G. WOODRUFF
1897-98 (.833)   15-3

1897   8-2-0
O6 ●	at K.C. Med. Coll.	22	8	
O8 ●	Midland Lutheran	40	0	
O9 ●	Haskell	40	0	
O16 ●	Warrennsburg	23	0	
O23 ●	at Glasco	23	0	
O30 ●	Iowa	56	0	
N6 ●	at St. Mary's, Kan.	28	0	
N13 ●	at Nebraska	5	6	*
N20 ●	K.C. Med. Coll. *KC*	0	2	
N25 ●	Missouri *KC*	16	0	

1898   7-1-0
S24 ●	Haskell	15	0
O5 ●	at K.C. Med. Coll.	6	0
O15 ●	Iowa State	11	6
O22 ●	at Central Mo. St.	33	0
O29 ●	at Ensworth Med.	40	0
N5 ●	Nebraska	6	18
N12 ●	K.C. Med. Coll.	6	0
N24 ●	Missouri *KC*	12	0

FIELDING H. YOST
1899 (1.000)   10-0

1899   10-0-0
S30 ●	Haskell	12	0
O7 ●	Washburn U.	35	0
O14 ●	Ottawa	29	6
O21 ●	Drake	29	5
O28 ●	Haskell	18	0
N4 ●	at Ottawa	29	0
N11 ●	at Emporia St.	35	0
N18 ●	at Nebraska	36	20
N25 ●	Washburn	23	0
N30 ●	Missouri *KC*	34	6

CHARLES BOYNTON
1900 (.333)   2-5-2

1900   2-5-2
O1 ●	at Ottawa	6	0
O6 ●	Washburn	0	24
O20 =	Emporia St.	6	6
O27 ●	at South Dakota	42	0
N3 ●	at K.C. Med. Coll.	15	23
N10 ●	Washburn	0	29
N17 ●	Nebraska	0	12
N21 ●	at Emporia Coll.	0	18
N29 =	Missouri *KC*	6	6

JOHN OUTLAND
1901 (.400)   3-5-2

1901   3-5-2
S29 ●	Ottawa	5	16
O5 ●	Emporia St.	36	10
O14 ●	at American Osteopath	17	6
O19 =	at Washburn	0	0
O26 ●	at Wisconsin	0	50
O29 ●	at Beloit	0	0
N9 ●	Haskell	5	18
N16 ●	at Nebraska	5	29
N23 ●	Texas	12	0
N28 ●	Missouri *KC*	12	18

ARTHUR CURTIS
1902 (.600)   6-4

1902   6-4-0
S29 ●	Wichita St.	6	0
O4 ●	Kansas State	16	0
O11 ●	Washburn	34	0
O18 ●	K.C. Med. Coll.	13	0
O25 ●	at Wisconsin	0	38
O29 ●	at Knox Coll.	0	5
N8 ●	at Nebraska	0	16
N15 ●	Haskell	5	24
N20 ●	at Emporia St.	17	5
N27 ●	Missouri *KC*	17	5

HARRISON WEEKS
1903 (.667)   6-3

1903   6-3-0
S28 ●	Emporia Coll.	32	0
O3 ●	Kansas State	34	0
O10 ●	Emporia St.	12	0
O17 ●	at Colorado	12	11
O24 ●	Haskell	6	12
O31 ●	at Washburn	0	5
N7 ●	Oklahoma	17	5
N14 ●	Nebraska	0	6
N26 ●	Missouri *KC*	5	0

A.R. KENNEDY
1904-10 (.833)   53-9-4

1904   8-1-1
S24 ●	Emporia Coll.	6	0
O1 ●	Emporia St.	34	0
O6 ●	Haskell	6	23
O15 ●	Colorado	6	6
O21 ●	at Oklahoma	16	0
O29 ●	at Washburn	5	0
N5 ●	Notre Dame	24	5
N12 ●	at Washington, Mo.	12	0
N19 ●	at Kansas State	41	4
N24 ●	Missouri *KC*	29	0

1905   10-1-0
S23 ●	William-Jewell	31	0
O4 ●	Emporia Coll.	45	0
O7 ●	at Arkansas	6	0
O9 ●	at Drury Coll.	11	0
O14 ●	at Emporia St.	32	0
O21 ●	Oklahoma	34	0
O28 ●	Colorado *DEN*	0	15
N4 ●	Washington, Mo.	21	0
N11 ●	at Washburn	18	11
N25 ●	Kansas State	28	0
N30 ●	Missouri *KC*	24	0

1906   7-2-2
S22 ●	William-Jewell	18	0
O3 ●	Emporia Coll.	25	0
O6 ●	St. Mary's, Kan.	18	0
O13 ●	Arkansas	37	5
O20 ●	Oklahoma	20	4
O27 ●	Colorado	16	0
N3 ●	at St. Louis	2	34
N10 =	at Washington, Mo.	0	0
N17 ●	at Nebraska	8	6
N24 ●	at Kansas State	4	6
N29 =	Missouri *KC*	0	0

1907-1927
MISSOURI VALLEY

1907   5-3-0 (1-1-0)
O5 ●	William-Jewell	38	0
O12 ●	St. Mary's, Kan.	14	2
O19 ●	at Oklahoma	15	0
O26 ●	Kansas State	29	10
N2 ●	at Washburn	5	12
N9 |	Nebraska	6	16
N16 ●	at St. Louis	0	17
N28 ● |	Missouri *StJ*	4	0

1908   9-0-0 (4-0-0)
S26 ●	Emporia St.	11	0
O3 ●	St. Mary's, Kan.	24	0
O10 ●	Kansas State	12	6
O17 ●	Oklahoma	11	0
O24 ● |	Washington, Mo.	10	0
N7 ●	Washburn	23	0
N14 ●	at Nebraska	20	5
N21 ●	at Iowa	10	5
N26 ● |	Missouri *KC*	10	4

1909   8-1-0 (3-1-0)
S25 ●	Emporia St.	55	0
O2 ●	St. Mary's, Kan.	29	0
O9 ●	Oklahoma	11	0
O16 ●	at Kansas State	5	3
O23 ● |	Washington, Mo.	23	0
O30 ● |	at Washburn	17	0
N6 ●	at Nebraska	6	0
N20 ●	Iowa	20	7
N25 ● |	Missouri *KC*	6	12

1910   6-1-1 (1-1-1)
O1 ●	Ottawa	11	0
O8 ●	St. Mary's, Kan.	9	5
O15 ●	Baker	21	0
O22 ● |	at Drake	6	0
O29 ●	Washburn	21	6
N5 ●	Nebraska	0	6
N12 ●	at Oklahoma	2	0
N24 = |	Missouri *KC*	5	5

RALPH W. SHERWIN
1911 (.625)   4-2-2

1911   4-2-2 (1-1-1)
O7 =	Baker	0	0
O14 ●	St. Mary's, Kan.	47	0
O21 ●	at Kansas State	6	0
O28 ●	Drake	11	3
N4 ●	at Washburn	14	6
N11 ●	Oklahoma	0	3
N18 ●	Nebraska	0	29
N25 ● |	at Missouri	3	3

ARTHUR MOSSE
1912-13 (.563)   9-7

1912   4-4-0 (1-2-0)
O5 ●	St. Mary's, Kan.	62	0
O12 ●	C. Missouri St.	27	0
O19 ● |	at Drake	2	0
O26 ●	Kansas State	19	6
N2 ●	Oklahoma	5	6
N9 ●	at Washburn	0	10
N16 ●	at Nebraska	3	14
N23 ● |	Missouri	12	3

1913   5-3-0 (3-2-0)
O4 ●	William Jewell	7	0
O11 ● |	Washington, Mo.	55	7
O18 ●	Drake	11	0
O25 ● |	at Kansas State	26	0
N1 ●	at Oklahoma	7	21
N8 ●	Washburn	14	0
N15 ● |	Nebraska	0	9
N22 ● |	at Missouri	0	3

H.M. WHEATON
1914 (.688)   5-2-1

1914   5-2-1 (2-2-0)
O3 ●	William-Jewell	48	2	
O10 ●	Emporia Coll.	7	0	
O17 ● |	at Drake	32	7	
O26 ● |	Kansas State	27	0	*
O31 = |	Oklahoma	16	16	
N7 ●	at Washburn	20	14	
N14 ●	at Nebraska	0	35	
N21 ● |	Missouri	7	10	

386 KANSAS

HERMAN OLCOTT
1915-17 (.688) 16-7-1

1915 6-2-0 (3-1-0)
O2 ● William-Jewell 20 0
O9 ● Emporia St. 21 3
O16 ● | Drake 30 7
O23 ● | at Kansas State 19 7
O30 at Oklahoma 14 23
N6 ● Washburn 41 0
N13 | Nebraska 0 33
N25 ● | at Missouri 8 6

1916 4-3-1 (1-2-1)
S30 ● Emporia St. 13 0
O7 at Illinois 0 30
O14 | at Iowa State 0 13
O28 = | Kansas State 0 0
N4 ● Oklahoma 21 13
N11 ● at Washburn 27 0
N18 ● | at Nebraska 7 3
N30 | Missouri 0 13

1917 6-2-0 (3-1-0)
O6 at Illinois 0 22
O13 ● Emporia St. 33 0
O20 ● Washburn 34 2
O27 ● | Iowa State 7 0
N3 ● | at Kansas State 9 0
N10 ● at Oklahoma 13 6
N17 | Nebraska 3 13
N29 ● | at Missouri 27 3

JAY BOND
1918 (.500) 2-2

1918 2-2-0 (1-1-0)
N9 Oklahoma 0 33
N16 | at Nebraska 0 20
N23 ● Baker 20 6
N28 ● | Kansas State 13 7

LEON McCARTY
1919 (.563) 3-2-3

1919 3-2-3 (1-1-1)
O4 ● Pittsburg St. 42 0
O11 ● Emporia St. 14 0
O18 = at Washburn 0 0
O25 = | at Iowa State 0 0
N1 ● | Kansas State 16 3
N8 = Oklahoma 0 0
N15 at Nebraska 7 19
N27 | Missouri 6 13

FORREST C. ALLEN
1920 (.688) 5-2-1

1920 5-2-1 (3-2-0)
O2 ● Emporia St. 47 0
O9 ● Washburn 6 0
O16 ● | Drake 7 3
O23 ● | Iowa State 7 0
O30 ● at Kansas State 14 0
N6 | at Oklahoma 9 21
N13 = Nebraska 20 20
N25 | at Missouri 7 16

POTSY CLARK
1921-25 (.487) 16-17-6

1921 4-3-0 (3-3-0)
O1 ● at Washburn 28 7
O15 | Drake 7 15
O22 ● | at Iowa State 14 7
O29 ● | Kansas State 21 7
N5 | at Oklahoma 7 24
N12 | at Nebraska 0 28
N24 ● | Missouri 15 9

1922 3-4-1 (1-3-1)
O7 at Army 0 13
O14 | at Drake 0 6
O21 ● Washburn 32 3
O28 = | at Kansas State 7 7
N4 ● | Oklahoma 19 3
N11 | Nebraska 0 28
N18 ● Colorado 39 6
N30 | at Missouri 7 9

1923 5-0-3 (3-0-3)
O6 ● Creighton 6 0
O13 ● Oklahoma State 9 0
O20 = | at Nebraska 0 0
O27 = | Kansas State 0 0
N3 ● | at Oklahoma 7 3
N10 ● | Washington, Mo. 83 0
N17 ● | Drake 17 0
N29 = | Missouri 3 3

1924 2-5-1 (2-4-1)
O4 Oklahoma State 0 3
O11 | Iowa State 10 13
O18 | at Kansas State 0 6
O25 | Nebraska 7 14
N1 ● | at Washington, Mo. 48 0
N8 = | at Drake 6 6
N15 ● | Oklahoma 20 0
N27 | at Missouri 0 14

1925 2-5-1 (2-5-1)
O3 ● | Oklahoma State 13 3
O10 | at Iowa State 0 20
O17 | Kansas State 7 14
O24 | at Nebraska 0 14
O31 | Drake 0 7
N7 = | at Oklahoma 0 0
N14 | at Grinnell 0 3
N21 ● | Missouri 10 7

FRANKLIN CAPPON
1926-27 (.344) 5-10-1

1926 2-6-0 (1-5-0)
O2 ● Washburn 14 6
O9 at Wisconsin 0 13
O16 | at Kansas State 0 27
O23 | Nebraska 3 20
O30 | at Drake 0 13
N6 | Grinnell 7 32
N11 ● | Oklahoma 10 9
N20 | at Missouri 0 15

1927 3-4-1 (3-3-1)
O1 ● | at Grinnell 19 0
O8 Wisconsin 6 26
O15 | Kansas State 2 13
O22 = | Washington, Mo. 21 21
O29 ● | Drake 7 6
N5 | at Nebraska 13 47
N12 | at Oklahoma 7 26
N19 ● | Missouri 14 7

1928-1995
Big 8

BILL HARGISS
1928-32 (.528) 18-16-2

1928 2-4-2 (1-3-1)
O6 ● Grinnell 14 0
O13 = at Washington, Mo. 7 7
O20 ● | at Kansas State 7 0
O27 = | Iowa State 0 0
N3 | Nebraska 0 20
N10 at Marquette 0 7
N17 | Oklahoma 0 7
N24 | at Missouri 6 25

1929 4-4-0 (2-3-0)
O5 at Illinois 0 25
O12 ● Emporia St. 38 0
O19 | Kansas State 0 6
O26 ● | at Iowa State 33 0
N2 | at Nebraska 6 12
N9 ● | at Oklahoma 7 0
N16 ● Washington, Mo. 13 0
N23 | Missouri 0 7

1930 6-2-0 (4-1-0)
O4 ● at Creighton 26 0
O10 ● at Haskell 33 7
O18 ● | at Kansas State 14 0
O25 ● | Iowa State 20 6
N1 at Pennsylvania 6 21
N8 | Nebraska 0 16
N15 ● | Oklahoma 13 0
N22 ● | at Missouri 32 0

1931 5-5-0 (1-3-0)
S26 ● Colorado State 27 6
O2 Haskell 0 6
O10 ● James Milikin 30 0
O17 | Kansas State 0 13
O24 | at Nebraska 0 6
O31 Oklahoma State 7 13
N7 | at Oklahoma 0 10
N14 ● at Washington, Mo. 28 0
N21 ● | Missouri 14 0
D5 ● at Washburn 6 0

ADRIAN LINDSEY
1932-38 (.443) 23-30-8

1932 5-3-0 (3-2-0)
S30 ● at Denver 13 12
O8 | Oklahoma 6 21
O15 ● | at Iowa State 26 0
O22 | Nebraska 6 20
O28 ● at St. Louis 6 0
N5 Notre Dame 6 24
N12 ● | at Missouri 7 0
N19 ● | at Kansas State 19 0

1933 5-4-1 (2-3-0)
S23 ● Central Mo. St. 34 0
S30 ● at Creighton 14 0
O7 = at Notre Dame 0 0
O21 at Tulsa 0 7
O28 | Kansas State 0 6
N4 | at Oklahoma 0 20
N11 | at Nebraska 0 12
N18 ● | Iowa State 20 6
N30 ● | Missouri 27 0
D2 ● at George Washington 7 0

1934 3-4-3 (1-2-2)
S29 = Colorado 0 0
O6 at Tulsa 0 7
O13 ● St. Benedict 34 12
O20 | at Kansas State 0 13
O27 = | Oklahoma 7 7
N3 = | at Iowa State 0 0
N10 ● at Washington, Mo. 13 0
N17 | Nebraska 0 3
N24 Michigan State 0 6
N29 ● | at Missouri 20 0

1935 4-4-1 (2-2-1)
S28 at Notre Dame 7 28
O5 ● St. Benedict 42 0
O12 at Michigan State 0 42
O26 ● | Kansas State 9 2
N2 ● | at Oklahoma 7 0
N9 | at Nebraska 13 19
N16 ● at Colorado 12 6
N23 | Iowa State 12 21
N28 = | Missouri 0 0

1936 1-6-1 (0-5-0)
O3 ● Washburn 19 6
O10 | at Iowa State 7 21
O17 | Oklahoma 0 14
O24 | at Kansas State 6 26
O31 = Arizona 0 0
N7 | Nebraska 0 26
N14 Michigan State 0 41
N26 | at Missouri 3 19

1937 3-4-2 (2-1-2)
O1 ● at Washburn 25 2
O9 at Wichita St. 7 18
O16 ● | Iowa State 14 6
O23 ● | at Oklahoma 6 3
O30 at Michigan State 0 16
N6 = | at Nebraska 13 13
N13 | Kansas State 0 7
N20 at Arizona 7 9
N25 = | Missouri 0 0

1938 3-6-0 (1-4-0)
S24 ● Texas 19 18
O1 at Notre Dame 0 52
O8 ● Washburn 58 14
O15 | Oklahoma 0 19
O22 | at Iowa State 7 21
O29 ● | at Kansas State 27 7
N5 | Nebraska 7 16
N12 at George Washington 7 9
N24 | at Missouri 7 13

GWINN HENRY
1939-42 (.250) 9-27

1939 2-6-0 (1-4-0)
S29 at Drake 6 12
O7 ● | Iowa State 14 0
O14 ● at Colorado State 7 0
O21 | at Oklahoma 7 27
N4 | Kansas State 6 27
N11 | at Nebraska 0 7
N18 George Washington 7 14
N25 | Missouri 0 20

1940 2-7-0 (0-5-0)
O5 | at Iowa State 0 7
O12 ● Drake 20 6
O19 | Nebraska 2 53
O26 | at Kansas State 0 20
N1 Villanova PHIL 7 33
N9 | Oklahoma 0 13
N16 at George Washington 0 6
N21 | at Missouri 20 45
N28 ● Colorado State 26 0

1941 3-6-0 (2-3-0)
S26 at Temple 9 31
O4 ● Washington, Mo. 19 6
O11 | at Nebraska 0 32
O18 at Marquette 7 33
O25 ● | Iowa State 13 0
N1 | at Oklahoma 0 38
N8 at West Virginia 0 21
N15 ● | Kansas State 20 16
N22 | Missouri 6 45

1942 2-8-0 (1-4-0)
S19 Iowa Pre-Flight 0 61
S26 Marquette 0 14
O2 at Denver 0 17
O10 at TCU 6 41
O17 | Oklahoma 0 25
O24 ● | at Kansas State 19 7
O31 | Nebraska 7 14
N7 ● Washington, Mo. 19 7
N14 | at Iowa State 13 20
N26 | at Missouri 13 42

HENRY SHENK
1943-45 (.417) 11-16-3

1943 4-5-1 (2-3-0)
S24 = at Washburn 0 0
O1 at Denver 6 19
O9 | Iowa State 6 13
O16 ● Washburn 13 0
O23 | at Nebraska 6 7
O30 ● | Kansas State 25 2
N6 | at Oklahoma 13 26
N13 ● Central Mo. St. 13 12
N20 ● | Missouri 7 6
N25 at Fort Riley 7 22

1944 3-6-1 (1-4-0)
S15 ● Washburn 47 0
S23 TCU KC 0 7
S29 = at Denver 14 14
O7 at Tulsa 0 27
O14 | at Iowa State 0 25
O21 ● | Nebraska 20 0
N4 ● Olathe NAS 33 14
N11 | at Kansas State 14 18
N18 | Oklahoma 0 20
N23 | Missouri KC 0 28

1945 4-5-1 (1-3-1)
S22 TCU KC 0 18
S29 ● at Denver 20 19
O6 = | Iowa State 13 13
O12 ● Washburn 34 0
O20 | at Oklahoma 7 39
O27 ● at Wichita St. 13 0
N3 | at Nebraska 13 27
N10 at Marquette 0 26
N17 ● | Kansas State 27 0
N24 | Missouri KC 12 33

GEORGE SAUER
1946-47 (.786) 15-3-3

1946 7-2-1 (4-1-0)
S21 = TCU KC 0 0
S27 ● at Denver 21 13
O5 ● Wichita St. 14 7
O12 ● | at Iowa State 24 8
O19 | Nebraska 14 16
O26 at Tulsa 0 56
N2 ● Oklahoma State 14 13
N9 ● | Oklahoma 16 13
N16 ● | at Kansas State 34 0
N28 ● | at Missouri 20 19

THE SCHOOLS

1947 8-1-2 (4-0-1)

S20	=		TCU KC	0	0
S26	●		at Denver	9	0
O4	●	│	Iowa State	27	7
O11	●		South Dakota St.	86	6
O18	=	│	at Oklahoma	13	13
N1	●	│	Kansas State	55	0
N8	●	│	at Nebraska	13	7
N15	●		at Oklahoma State	13	7
N22	●	│	Missouri	20	14
N29	●		at Arizona	54	28
			ORANGE BOWL		
J1			Georgia Tech	14	20

J.V. SIKES
1948-53 (.583) 35-25

1948 7-3-0 (4-2-0)

S18			TCU	13	14
S24	●		at Denver	40	0
O2	●	│	Colorado	40	7
O9	●	│	at Iowa State	20	7
O15	●		at George Washington	12	0
O23	●	│	Nebraska	27	7
O30	●		Oklahoma State	13	7
N13	●	│	at Kansas State	20	14
N20		│	Oklahoma	7	60
N25		│	at Missouri	7	21

1949 5-5-0 (2-4-0)

S17			TCU	0	28
S24		│	at Colorado	12	13
O1		│	Iowa State	6	19
O8	●		George Washington	21	14
O15		│	at Oklahoma	26	48
O22	●		at Oklahoma State	55	14
O29	●	│	Kansas State	38	0
N5	●	│	at Nebraska	27	13
N19		│	Missouri	28	34
N26	●		at Arizona	46	0

1950 6-4-0 (3-3-0)

S23			TCU	7	14
S29	●		at Denver	46	6
O7	●	│	Colorado	27	21
O14	●	│	at Iowa State	33	21
O21	●		Oklahoma State	40	7
O28		│	Nebraska	26	33
N4	●		at Utah	39	26
N11		│	Oklahoma	13	33
N18	●	│	at Kansas State	47	7
N23		│	at Missouri	6	20

1951 8-2-0 (4-2-0)

S22	●		at TCU	27	13
S29	●	│	Iowa State	53	33
O6		│	at Colorado	27	35
O13	●		Utah	26	7
O20		│	at Oklahoma	21	33
O27	●	│	Kansas State	33	14
N3	●	│	at Nebraska	27	7
N10	●		Loyola Marymount	34	26
N17	●		at Oklahoma State	27	12
D1	●	│	Missouri	41	28

1952 7-3-0 (3-3-0(

S20	●		TCU	13	0
S27	●		Santa Clara	21	9
O4	●	│	Colorado	21	12
O11	●	│	at Iowa State	43	0
O18		│	Oklahoma	20	42
O25	●		at SMU	26	0
N1	●	│	at Kansas State	26	6
N8		│	Nebraska	13	14
N15	●		Oklahoma State	12	7
N22		│	at Missouri	19	20

1953 2-8-0 (2-4-0)

S19			at TCU	0	13
S25			at UCLA	7	19
O3	●	│	Iowa State	23	0
O10	●	│	at Colorado	27	21
O17		│	at Oklahoma	0	45
O24			SMU	6	14
O31		│	at Nebraska	0	9
N7		│	Kansas State	0	7
N14			Oklahoma State	14	41
N21		│	Missouri	6	10

CHUCK MATHER
1954-57 (.313) 11-26-3

1954 0-10-0 (0-6-0)

S18			TCU	6	27
S25			UCLA	7	32
O2		│	Colorado	0	27
O9		│	at Iowa State	6	33
O16		│	Oklahoma	0	65
O23			at SMU	18	36
O30		│	at Kansas State	6	28
N6		│	Nebraska	20	41
N13			at Oklahoma State	12	47
N20		│	at Missouri	18	41

1955 3-6-1 (1-4-1)

S17			at TCU	14	47
S24	●		Washington State	13	0
O1		│	at Colorado	0	12
O8	=	│	Iowa State	7	7
O15		│	at Oklahoma	6	44
O22			SMU	14	33
O29		│	at Nebraska	14	19
N5		│	Kansas State	0	46
N12	●		Oklahoma State	12	7
N19	●	│	Missouri	13	7

1956 3-6-1 (2-4-0)

S22			TCU	0	32
S29	=		Pacific	27	27
O6		│	Colorado	25	26
O13	●	│	at Iowa State	25	14
O20		│	Oklahoma	12	34
O26	●		at Oklahoma State	21	13
N3	●	│	at Kansas State	20	15
N10		│	Nebraska	20	26
N17			at UCLA	0	13
D1		│	at Missouri	13	15

1957 5-4-1 (4-2-0)

S21	=		at TCU	13	13
S28			Oregon State	6	34
O5	●	│	at Colorado	35	34
O12		│	Iowa State	6	21
O19		│	at Oklahoma	0	47
O25			at Miami, Fla.	6	48
N2	●	│	at Nebraska	14	12
N9	●	│	Kansas State	13	7
N16	●		Oklahoma State	13	7
N23	●	│	Missouri	9	7

JACK MITCHELL
1958-66 (.511) 44-42-5

1958 4-5-1 (3-2-1)

S20			TCU	0	42
S27			Oregon State PORT	0	12
O4		│	Colorado	0	31
O11	●	│	at Iowa State	7	0
O18		│	Oklahoma	0	43
O25	●		Tulane	14	9
N1	●	│	at Kansas State	21	12
N8	●	│	Nebraska	29	7
N15			at Oklahoma State	3	6
N22	=	│	at Missouri	13	13

1959 5-5-0 (3-3-0)

S19			at TCU	7	14
S26			at Syracuse	21	35
O3	●		Boston U.	28	7
O10	●	│	at Nebraska	10	3
O17	●	│	Kansas State	33	14
O24		│	at Oklahoma	6	7
O31	●	│	Iowa State	7	0
N7		│	at Colorado	14	27
N14	●		Oklahoma State	28	14
N21		│	Missouri	9	13

1960 7-2-1 (6-0-1)

S17	●		TCU	21	7
S24	●	│	at Kansas State	41	0
O1			Syracuse	7	14
O8	●	│	at Iowa State	28	14
O15	=	│	Oklahoma	13	13
O22	●	│	at Oklahoma State	14	7
O29			at Iowa	7	21
N5	●	│	Nebraska	31	0
N12	●	│	Colorado	34	6 †
N19	●	│	at Missouri	23	7 †

1961 7-3-1 (5-2-0)

S23			at TCU	16	17
S30	=		Wyoming	6	6
O7		│	at Colorado	19	20
O14	●	│	Iowa State	21	7
O21	●	│	at Oklahoma	10	0
O28	●	│	Oklahoma State	42	8
N4	●	│	at Nebraska	28	6
N11	●	│	Kansas St.	34	0
N18	●		at California	53	7
N25		│	Missouri	7	10
			BLUEBONNET BOWL		
D16	●		Rice	33	7

1962 6-3-1 (4-2-1)

S22			TCU	3	6
S29	●		at Boston U.	14	0
O6	●	│	Colorado	35	8
O13	●	│	at Iowa State	29	8
O20		│	Oklahoma	7	13
O27	●	│	at Oklahoma State	36	17
N3	●	│	at Kansas State	38	0
N10		│	Nebraska	16	40
N17	●		California	33	21
N24	=	│	at Missouri	3	3

1963 5-5-0 3-4-0

S21			at TCU	6	10
S28	●		Syracuse	10	0
O5	●		at Wyoming	25	21
O12		│	Iowa State	14	17
O19		│	at Oklahoma	18	21
O26	●	│	Oklahoma State	41	7
N2	●	│	Kansas State	34	0
N9		│	at Nebraska	9	23
N16	●	│	at Colorado	43	14
N23		│	Missouri	7	9

1964 6-4-0 (5-2-0)

S19	●		TCU	7	3
S26			at Syracuse	6	38
O3			Wyoming	14	17
O10	●	│	at Iowa State	42	6
O17	●	│	Oklahoma	15	14
O24	●	│	at Oklahoma State	14	13
O31	●	│	at Kansas State	7	0
N7		│	Nebraska	7	14
N14	●	│	Colorado	10	7
N21		│	at Missouri	14	34

1965 2-8-0 (2-5-0)

S18			at Texas Tech	7	26
S25			Arizona	15	23
O2			at California	0	17
O9		│	Iowa State	7	21
O16		│	at Oklahoma	7	21
O23	●	│	Oklahoma State	9	0
O30	●	│	Kansas State	34	0
N6		│	at Nebraska	6	42
N13		│	at Colorado	14	21
N20		│	Missouri	20	44

1966 2-7-1 (0-6-1)

S17			Texas Tech	7	23
S24	●		at Arizona	35	13
O1	●		at Minnesota	16	14
O8		│	at Iowa State	7	24
O15		│	Oklahoma	0	35
O22		│	at Oklahoma State	7	10
O29	=	│	at Kansas State	3	3
N5		│	Nebraska	13	24
N12		│	Colorado	18	35
N19		│	at Missouri	0	7

PEPPER RODGERS
1967-70 (.476) 20-22

1967 5-5-0 (5-2-0)

S23			at Stanford	20	21
S30			at Indiana	15	18
O7			Ohio U.	15	30
O14	●	│	Nebraska	10	0
O21	●	│	at Oklahoma State	26	15
O28	●	│	Iowa State	28	14
N4	●	│	Kansas State	17	16
N11		│	at Colorado	8	12
N18		│	at Oklahoma	10	14
N25	●	│	Missouri	17	6

1968 9-2-0 (6-1-0)

S21	●		at Illinois	47	7
S28	●		Indiana	38	20
O5	●		New Mexico	68	7
O12	●	│	at Nebraska	23	13
O19	●	│	Oklahoma State	49	14
O26	●	│	at Iowa State	46	25
N2	●	│	Colorado	27	14
N9		│	Oklahoma	23	27
N16	●	│	at Kansas State	38	29
N23	●	│	at Missouri	21	19
			ORANGE BOWL		
J1			Penn State	14	15

1969 1-9-0 (0-7-0)

S20			at Texas Tech	22	38
S27	●		Syracuse	13	0
O4			at New Mexico	7	16
O11		│	Kansas State	22	26
O18		│	at Nebraska	17	21
O25		│	at Iowa State	20	44
N1		│	Oklahoma State	25	28
N8		│	Colorado	14	17
N15		│	at Oklahoma	15	31
N22		│	Missouri	21	69

1970 5-6-0 (2-5-0)

S12	●		Washington State	48	31
S19			Texas Tech	0	23
S26	●		at Syracuse	31	14
O3	●		New Mexico	49	23
O10	●	│	at Kansas State	21	15
O17		│	Nebraska	20	41
O24	●	│	Iowa State	24	10
O31		│	at Oklahoma State	7	19
N7		│	at Colorado	29	45
N14		│	Oklahoma	24	28
N21		│	at Missouri	17	28

DON FAMBROUGH
1971-74, '79-82 (.428) 36-49-5

1971 4-7-0 (2-5-0)

S11	●		Washington State	34	0
S18	●		Baylor	22	0
S25			at Florida State	7	30
O2			at Minnesota	20	38
O9	●	│	Kansas State	39	13
O16		│	at Nebraska	0	55
O23		│	at Iowa State	24	40
O30		│	Oklahoma State	10	17
N6		│	Colorado	14	35
N13		│	at Oklahoma	10	56
N20	●	│	Missouri	7	2

1972 4-7-0 (2-5-0)

S9			Washington State	17	18
S23	●		Wyoming	52	14
S30			Florida State	22	44
O7	●		at Minnesota	34	28
O14		│	at Kansas State	19	20
O21		│	Nebraska	0	56
O28		│	Iowa State	8	34
N4	●	│	at Oklahoma State	13	10
N11		│	at Colorado	8	33
N18		│	Oklahoma	7	31 †
N25	●	│	at Missouri	28	17

1973 7-4-1 (4-2-1)

S15	●		Washington State	29	8
S22	●		at Florida State	28	0
S29	●		Minnesota	34	19
O6			Tennessee MEM	27	28
O13	●	│	Kansas State	25	18
O20		│	at Nebraska	9	10
O27	●	│	at Iowa State	22	20
N3	=	│	Oklahoma State	10	10
N10	●	│	Colorado	17	15
N17		│	at Oklahoma	20	48
N24	●	│	Missouri	14	13
			LIBERTY BOWL		
D17			North Carolina St.	18	31

1974 4-7-0 (1-6-0)

S14	●		Washington State SPO	14	7
S21			at Tennessee	3	17
S28	●		Florida State	40	9
O5	●		Texas A&M	28	10
O12	●	│	at Kansas State	20	13
O19		│	Nebraska	0	56
O26		│	Iowa State	6	22
N2		│	at Oklahoma State	13	24
N9		│	at Colorado	16	17
N16		│	Oklahoma	14	45
N23		│	at Missouri	3	27

388 KANSAS

THE SCHOOLS

BUD MOORE
1975-78 (.389) 17-27-1

1975 — 7-5-0 (4-3-0)

S13			Washington State	14	18	
S20	●		at Kentucky	14	10	
S27	●		Oregon State	20	0	
O4	●		at Wisconsin	41	7	
O11		|	at Nebraska	0	16	
O18	●	|	at Iowa State	21	10	
O25		|	Oklahoma State	19	35	
N1	●	|	Kansas State	28	0	
N8	●	|	at Oklahoma	23	3	
N15		|	Colorado	21	24	
N22	●	|	Missouri	42	24	
			SUN BOWL			
D26			Pittsburgh	19	33	

1976 — 6-5-0 (2-5-0)

S4	●		at Oregon State	28	16	
S11	●		Washington State	35	16	
S18	●		Kentucky	37	16	
O2	●		Wisconsin	34	24	
O9		|	at Oklahoma State	14	21	
O16		|	Oklahoma	10	28	
O23	●	|	at Kansas State	24	14	
O30		|	Nebraska	3	31	
N6		|	Iowa State	17	31	
N13		|	at Colorado	17	40	
N20	●	|	at Missouri	41	14	

1977 — 3-7-1 (2-4-1)

S10			at Texas A&M	14	28	
S17			at UCLA	7	17	†
S24	●		Washington State	14	12	
O1		|	at Oklahoma	9	24	
O8			at Miami, Fla.	7	14	
O15	=	|	Colorado	17	17	
O22		|	Oklahoma State	0	21	
O29		|	at Iowa State	3	41	
N5	●	|	Kansas State	29	21	
N12		|	at Nebraska	7	52	
N19	●	|	Missouri	24	22	

1978 — 1-10-0 (0-7-0)

S9			Texas A&M	10	37	
S16			at Washington	2	31	
S23	●		UCLA	28	24	
S30			Miami, Fla.	6	38	
O7		|	at Colorado	7	17	
O14		|	Oklahoma	16	17	
O21		|	at Oklahoma State	7	21	
O28		|	Iowa State	7	13	
N4		|	Nebraska	21	63	
N11		|	at Missouri	0	48	
N18		|	at Kansas State	20	36	

DON FAMBROUGH

1979 — 3-8-0 (2-5-0)

S15			at Pittsburgh	0	24	
S22			at Michigan	7	28	
S29	●		North Texas	37	18	
O6			Syracuse	27	45	
O13		|	at Nebraska	0	42	
O20	●	|	at Iowa State	24	7	
O27		|	Oklahoma State	17	30	
N3	●	|	Kansas State	36	28	
N10		|	at Oklahoma	0	38	
N17		|	Colorado	17	31	
N24		|	Missouri	7	55	

1980 — 4-5-2 (3-3-1)

S13	=		at Oregon	7	7	
S20			Pittsburgh	3	18	
S27			Louisville	9	17	
O4	●		at Syracuse	23	8	
O11		|	Nebraska	0	54	
O18	●	|	Iowa State	28	17	
O25	=	|	at Oklahoma State	14	14	†
N1	●	|	at Kansas State	20	18	†
N8		|	Oklahoma	19	21	
N15	●	|	at Colorado	42	3	
N22		|	at Missouri	6	31	

1981 — 8-4-0 (4-3-0)

S5	●		at Tulsa	15	11	†
S12	●		Oregon	19	10	
S26	●		Kentucky	21	16	
O3	●		Arkansas State	17	16	
O10		|	Oklahoma State	7	20	
O17		|	at Oklahoma	7	45	
O24	●	|	Kansas State	17	14	
O31		|	at Nebraska	15	31	
N7	●	|	at Iowa State	24	11	
N14	●	|	Colorado	27	0	
N21	●	|	Missouri	19	11	
			HALL OF FAME CLASSIC			
D31			Mississippi St	0	10	

1982 — 2-7-2 (1-5-1)

S11			Wichita St.	10	13	
S18	●		TCU	30	19	
S25	=		at Kentucky	13	13	
O2			Tulsa	15	20	
O9	=	|	at Oklahoma State	24	24	
O16		|	Oklahoma	14	38	
O23		|	at Kansas State	7	36	
O30		|	Nebraska	0	52	
N6	●	|	Iowa State	24	17	
N13		|	at Colorado	3	28	
N20		|	at Missouri	10	16	

MIKE GOTTFRIED
1983-85 (.456) 15-18-1

1983 — 4-6-1 (2-5-0)

S3			Northern Illinois	34	37	
S10	=		at TCU	16	16	
S17	●		Wichita St.	57	6	
S24	●		at Southern Cal	26	20	
O8		|	at Iowa State	35	38	
O15	●	|	Kansas State	31	3	
O22		|	Oklahoma State	10	27	
O29		|	at Oklahoma	14	45	
N5		|	Colorado	23	34	
N12		|	at Nebraska	13	67	
N19	●	|	Missouri	37	27	

1984 — 5-6-0 (4-3-0)

S8	●		Wichita St.	31	7	
S15			Florida State	16	42	
S22			at Vanderbilt	6	41	
S29			at North Carolina	17	23	
O6	●	|	Iowa State	33	14	
O13		|	at Kansas State	7	24	
O20		|	at Oklahoma State	10	47	
O27	●	|	Oklahoma	28	11	
N3	●	|	at Colorado	28	27	
N10		|	Nebraska	7	41	
N17	●	|	at Missouri	35	21	

1985 — 6-6-0 (2-5-0)

A31	●		at Hawaii	33	27	
S14	●		Vanderbilt	42	16	
S21	●		Indiana St.	37	10	
S28			at Florida State	20	24	
O5	●		Eastern Illinois	44	20	
O12		|	at Iowa State	21	22	
O19	●	|	Kansas State	38	7	
O26		|	Oklahoma State	10	17	
N2		|	at Oklahoma	6	48	
N9		|	Colorado	3	14	
N16		|	at Nebraska	6	56	
N23	●	|	Missouri	34	20	

BOB VALESENTE
1986-87 (.205) 4-17-1

1986 — 3-8-0 (0-7-0)

S13			North Carolina	0	20	
S20	●		Utah State	16	13	
S27	●		Indiana St.	20	6	
O4	●		So. Illinois	35	23	
O11		|	Iowa State	10	13	
O18		|	at Kansas State	12	29	
O25		|	at Oklahoma State	6	24	
N1		|	Oklahoma	3	64	
N8		|	at Colorado	10	17	
N15		|	Nebraska	0	70	
N22		|	at Missouri	0	48	

1987 — 1-9-1 (0-6-1)

S12			at Auburn	0	49	
S19			Kent State	17	31	
S26			Louisiana Tech	11	16	
O3	●		So. Illinois	16	15	
O10		|	at Nebraska	2	54	
O17		|	at Colorado	10	35	
O24		|	Iowa State	28	42	
O31		|	Oklahoma	10	71	
N7	=	|	at Kansas State	17	17	
N14		|	Oklahoma State	17	49	
N21		|	at Missouri	7	19	

GLEN MASON
1988-96 (.466) 47-54-1

1988 — 1-10-0 (1-6-0)

S10			Baylor	14	27	
S17			at Auburn	7	56	
S24			at California	21	52	
O1			New Mexico St.	29	42	
O8		|	Nebraska	10	63	
O15		|	Colorado	9	21	
O22		|	at Iowa State	14	42	
O29		|	at Oklahoma	14	63	
N5	●	|	Kansas State	30	12	
N12		|	at Oklahoma State	24	63	
N19		|	Missouri	17	55	

1989 — 4-7-0 (2-5-0)

S2	●		Montana St.	41	17	
S9			Louisville	28	33	
S16	●		Kent State	28	21	
S23			at Baylor	3	46	
S30		|	Oklahoma	6	45	
O7		|	Iowa State	20	24	
O21		|	at Colorado	17	49	
O28	●	|	at Kansas State	21	16	
N4		|	Oklahoma State	24	37	
N11		|	at Nebraska	14	51	
N18	●	|	at Missouri	46	44	

1990 — 3-7-1 (2-4-1)

S1			Virginia	10	59	
S8	●		Oregon State	38	12	
S15			at Louisville	16	28	
S29		|	at Oklahoma	17	31	
O6	=	|	at Iowa State	34	34	
O13			at Miami, Fla.	0	34	
O20		|	Colorado	10	41	
O27	●	|	Kansas State	27	24	
N3	●	|	at Oklahoma State	31	30	
N10		|	Nebraska	9	41	
N17		|	Missouri	21	31	

1991 — 6-5-0 (3-4-0)

S7	●		at Toledo	30	7	
S14	●		Tulsa	23	17	
S21	●		New Mexico St.	54	14	
O5			at Virginia	19	31	
O12		|	at Kansas State	12	16	
O19	●	|	Iowa State	41	0	
O26		|	at Oklahoma	3	41	
N2	●	|	at Oklahoma State	31	0	
N9		|	Nebraska	23	59	
N16		|	at Colorado	24	30	
N23	●	|	Missouri	53	29	

1992 — 8-4-0 (4-3-0)

S5	●		at Oregon State	49	20	
S12	●		Ball State	62	10	
S19	●		at Tulsa	40	7	
S26			California	23	27	
O10	●	|	Kansas State	31	7	
O17	●	|	at Iowa State	50	47	
O24	●	|	Oklahoma	27	10	
O31	●	|	Oklahoma State	26	18	
N7		|	at Nebraska	7	49	
N14		|	Colorado	18	25	
N21		|	at Missouri	17	22	
			ALOHA BOWL			
D25	●		Brigham Young	23	20	

1993 — 5-7-0 (3-4-0)

A28			Florida State *ERut*	0	42	
S4	●		Western Carolina	46	3	
S11			at Michigan State	14	31	
S18			Utah	16	41	
O2	●		Colorado State	24	6	
O9		|	at Kansas State	9	10	
O16	●	|	Iowa State	35	20	
O23		|	at Oklahoma	23	38	
O30	●	|	at Oklahoma State		136	
N6		|	Nebraska	20	21	
N13		|	at Colorado	14	38	
N20	●	|	Missouri	28	0	

1994 — 6-5-0 (3-4-0)

S1	●		at Houston	35	13	
S10	●		Michigan State	17	10	
S17			at TCU	21	31	
S24	●		UAB	72	0	
O6		|	Kansas State	13	21	
O15	●	|	at Iowa State	41	23	
O22		|	Oklahoma	17	20	
O29	●	|	Oklahoma State	24	14	
N5		|	at Nebraska	17	45	
N12		|	Colorado	26	51	
N19	●	|	at Missouri	31	14	

1995 — 10-2-0 (5-2-0)

S2	●		Cincinnati	23	18	
S9	●		North Texas *Irv*	27	10	
S14	●		TCU	38	20	
S23	●		Houston	20	13	
O7	●	|	at Colorado	40	24	
O14	●	|	Iowa State	34	7	
O21	●	|	at Oklahoma	38	17	
O28		|	at Kansas State	7	41	
N4	●	|	Missouri	42	23	
N11		|	Nebraska	3	41	
N18	●	|	at Oklahoma State	22	17	
			ALOHA BOWL			
D25	●		UCLA	51	30	

1996-PRESENT BIG 12

1996 — 4-7 (2-6)

A29	●		Ball State	35	10	
S14	●		at TCU	52	17	
S28			at Utah	42	45	
O5	●	|	at Oklahoma	52	24	
O12		|	Texas Tech	17	30	
O19		|	Colorado	7	20	
O26		|	at Nebraska	7	63	
N2	●	|	at Iowa State	34	31	
N9		|	Kansas State	12	38	
N16		|	Texas	17	38	
N23		|	at Missouri	25	42	

TERRY ALLEN
1997-2001 (.377) 20-33

1997 — 5-6 (3-5)

A28	●		UAB	24	0	
S6	●		TCU	17	10	
S13	●	|	Missouri	15	7	
S20			at Cincinnati	7	34	
O4	●	|	Oklahoma	20	17	
O11		|	at Texas Tech	7	17	
O18		|	at Colorado	6	42	
O25		|	Nebraska	0	35	
N1	●	|	Iowa State	34	24	
N8		|	at Kansas State	16	48	
N15		|	at Texas	31	45	

1998 — 4-7 (1-7)

S5		|	Oklahoma State	28	38	
S12		|	at Missouri	23	41	
S19	●		Illinois St.	63	21	
S26	●		at UAB	39	37	
O3		|	Texas A&M	21	24	
O10		|	at Baylor	24	31	
O17		|	at Nebraska	0	41	
O24	●	|	Colorado	33	17	
O31		|	Kansas State	6	54	
N7	●		North Texas	23	14	
N21		|	at Iowa State	20	23	

1999 — 5-7 (3-5)

A28			at Notre Dame	13	48	
S11	●		Cal St. Northridge	71	14	
S18		|	at Colorado	17	51	
S25			San Diego State	13	41	
O2	●		SMU	27	9	
O9		|	at Kansas State	9	50	
O16		|	at Texas A&M	17	34	
O23	●	|	Missouri	21	0	
O30		|	Nebraska	17	24	
N6	●	|	Baylor	45	10	
N13		|	at Oklahoma State	13	45	
N20	●	|	Iowa State	31	28	

2000 — 4-7 (2-6)

S2			at SMU	17	31	
S16	●		UAB	23	20	
S23	●		So. Illinois	42	0	
S30		|	at Oklahoma	16	34	
O7		|	Kansas State	13	52	
O14	●	|	at Missouri	38	17	
O21	●	|	Colorado	23	15	
O28		|	Texas Tech	39	45	
N4		|	at Nebraska	17	56	
N11		|	Texas	16	51	
N18		|	at Iowa State	17	38	

TOM HAYES
2001 (.333) 1-2

2001 — 3-8 (1-7)

S1	●		S.W. Missouri St.	24	10	
S8			UCLA	17	41	
S22		|	at Colorado	16	27	
O6	●	|	at Texas Tech	34	31	
O13		|	Oklahoma	10	38	
O20		|	Missouri	34	38	
O27		|	at Kansas State	6	40	
N3		|	Nebraska	7	51	
N10		|	at Texas	0	59	
N17		|	Iowa State	7	49	
N24	●		Wyoming	27	14	

MARK MANGINO
2002-Present (.333)   12-24

2002   2-10   (0-8)

A31		at Iowa State	3	45
S7		at Nevada-Las Vegas	20	31
S14	●	S.W. Missouri St.	44	24
S21		Bowling Green	16	39
S28	●	at Tulsa	43	33
O5		at Baylor	32	35
O12		Colorado	29	53
O19		Texas A&M	22	47
O26		at Missouri	12	36
N2		Kansas State	0	64
N9		at Nebraska	7	45
N16		Oklahoma State	20	55

2003   6-7   (3-5)

A30		Northwestern	20	28
S6	●	Nevada-Las Vegas	46	24
S13	●	at Wyoming	42	35
S20	●	Jacksonville St.	41	6
S27	●	Missouri	35	14
O11		at Colorado	47	50
O18	●	Baylor	28	21
O25		at Kansas State	6	42
N1		at Texas A&M	33	45
N8		Nebraska	3	24
N15		at Oklahoma State	21	44
N22	●	Iowa State	36	7
		TANGERINE BOWL		
D22		North Carolina St.	26	56

2004   4-7   (2-6)

S4	●	Tulsa	21	3
S11	●	Toledo	63	14
S18		at Northwestern	17	20
S25		Texas Tech	30	31
O2		at Nebraska	8	14
O9	●	Kansas State	31	28
O23		at Oklahoma	10	41
O30		at Iowa State	7	13
N6		Colorado	21	30
N13		Texas	23	27
N20	●	at Missouri	31	14

KANSAS STATE

BY MARK WANGRIN

WHEN BILL SNYDER TOOK OVER A moribund Kansas State program in 1989, he found a place where few people even cared enough to be apathetic. The Wildcats had been trying for their 300th all-time win—fewest among major-college programs at the time—for 27 consecutive games. *Sports Illustrated* called them the Tamecats and anointed Manhattan, Kan., "home of the worst major-college program."

"Kansas State is flat on its back," athletic director Steve Miller told Snyder when he hired him away from Iowa. "You may have heard it's one of the toughest jobs in the country. It's not. It's the toughest."

The bespectacled Snyder was more than up for the job, rebuilding with attention to detail, junior-college athletes and a soft schedule. By convincing those around him that the smallest victories would eventually lead to big ones, Snyder slowly transformed the program into a national power that won 11 games and finished in the Associated Press Top 10 in five of seven seasons from 1997 to 2003 before a 4–7 hiccup in 2004.

TRADITION Mascot Willie Wildcat leads the "K-S-U Wildcats" cheer, in which Willie forms the letters K-S-U with his body and then pumps his fist twice for "Wildcats." During pregame festivities and after every kickoff following a KSU score, the Pride of Wildcat Land band plays "Wabash Cannonball." The tuba players bob back and forth during the song, a motion the students imitate. The song became a staple when the music department building burned down in 1969 just before a football game. The only item salvaged from the smoldering ruins was the band director's briefcase, inside of which was sheet music for "Wabash Cannonball." Unable to locate other sheet music before the game, the band played the tune early and often. In 1993, public-address announcer Ivan Wilkinson began saying "Good for a Wildcat first down" every time the KSU offense moved the chains. Gradually, the crowd began to join in, shouting the phrase and mimicking the first-down arm motion. And Wilkinson's distinctive call made it all the way to the NFL: at Arrowhead Stadium in Kansas City, when the PA announcer says, "That's a Chiefs ... " the crowd chimes in, "first down!" In Manhattan, the call is also punctuated by the playing of a cat growl on the PA system.

BEST PLAYER Nicknamed Joe because friends considered him as tough as boxer Joe Louis, Veryl Switzer stands out as much for his impact on changing the face of the Big Seven Conference as for his prodigious accomplishments. One of the first African-American

---

players in the league, Switzer was already one of the nation's top cornerbacks in 1953, when he became an offensive force, leading KSU in rushing, receiving, scoring and punt returns, leading the nation in the latter category with a remarkable 31.0-yard average. He almost single-handedly lifted KSU from a last-place finish in 1952 to a 6–3–1 record and second place in the conference in 1953. Cornerback Terence Newman, linebacker Gary Spani and quarterbacks Lynn Dickey and Michael Bishop also deserve consideration.

> *Bill Snyder transformed KSU into a national power that finished in the AP Top 10 in five of seven seasons.*

like Bill Snyder. I would have to say that the Lord sent him here."

BEST TEAM The 1998 Wildcats team went into the season with tremendous talent and high hopes. Quarterback Michael Bishop, who would finish second in the Heisman Trophy voting, was surrounded by versatile halfback Eric Hickson and game-breaking receiver Darnell McDonald. Defensively, the Wildcats were talented, with perhaps the best linebacking corps in the nation in Jeff Kelly, Travis Ochs and Mark Simoneau. Punt returner David Allen, who would tie the NCAA career record for punt returns for a touchdown with seven (a record broken in 2003 by Texas Tech's Wes Walker), and kicker Martin Gramatica, who booted a 65-yarder that season, led the great special teams. Some pundits felt only a soft nonconference schedule—Indiana State, Northern Illinois and Louisiana-Monroe—could deprive the Wildcats of a spot in the BCS title game. But the Wildcats' best team was also its most star-crossed. After celebrating its ascension to No. 1 in the *ESPN/USA Today* coaches poll with its first victory over Nebraska in 30 games, the Wildcats fell apart with an upset loss to Texas A&M in the Big 12 Championship game and a flat performance against Purdue in the Alamo Bowl.

BEST COACH Critics call him media unfriendly and say he's a control freak. But even his harshest detractors marvel at the job Bill Snyder's done. The Wildcats went 1–10 in 1989, Snyder's first season, but he coaxed the beaten-down program to take baby steps. In 1993, the Wildcats earned a Copper Bowl berth, only the second postseason appearance in school history. By the late 1990s and early 2000s, they were fixtures in the national Top 10, winning the Big 12 title in 2003. "How many football coaches can accomplish what he's accomplished? Oh, one out of 10,000," said Kansas State president Jon Wefald. "Believe me, even with all the support from the administration, you have to have a rare individual

RECORDS

RUSHING YARDS

	GAME	
273	Darren Sproles vs. Missouri, Nov. 22, 2003 (43 att.)	
	SEASON	
1,986	Darren Sproles, 2003 (306 att.)	
	CAREER	
4,979	Darren Sproles, 2001-04 (815 att.)	

PASSING YARDS

	GAME	
489	Chad May vs. Nebraska, Oct. 16, 1993 (30 of 51)	
	SEASON	
2,844	Michael Bishop, 1998 (164 of 295)	
	CAREER	
6,208	Lynn Dickey, 1968-70 (501 of 994)	

RECEIVING YARDS

	GAME	
206	Darnell McDonald vs. Syracuse, Dec. 31, 1997 (7 rec.)	
	SEASON	
1,232	James Terry, 2003 (64 rec.)	
	CAREER	
3,032	Kevin Lockett, 1993-96 (217 rec.)	

POINTS

	GAME	
30	Jonathan Beasley vs. North Texas, Sept. 23, 2000 (5 TDs)	
	SEASON	
135	Martin Gramatica, 1998 (69 PATs, 22 FGs)	
	CAREER	
349	Martin Gramatica, 1994-95, 1997-98 (187 PATs, 54 FGs)	

CONSENSUS ALL-AMERICANS

1977	Gary Spani, LB	
1992	Sean Snyder, P	
1995-96	Chris Canty, DB	
1997	Martin Gramatica, K	
1998	David Allen, KR	
1998	Michael Bishop, QB	
1998	Jeff Kelly, LB	
1999	Mark Simoneau, LB	
2002	Terence Newman, CB	

BIGGEST GAME Dozens of former Wildcats players scored sideline credentials at Wagner Field on Nov. 14, 1998, hoping for a close-up view of something they had never experienced—a victory over Nebraska. K-State, unbeaten and recently elevated to the top spot in the ESPN/*USA Today* coaches poll, had the oddsmakers on their side against the No. 11 and twice-beaten Cornhuskers—but not history. The Wildcats had lost 29 games straight to NU by an aggregate score of 1,234-337, but the presence of do-everything quarterback Michael Bishop and a stout defense gave the sellout crowd hope. Bishop did a little bit of everything—he threw an interception and lost three fumbles, ran for two touchdowns and passed for two more, rolled up 442 yards total offense and got a face-masking penalty. But midway through the fourth quarter NU led 30-27, and Bishop needed more heroics. Stepping into the huddle on the first play of what would be the game-winning drive, Bishop told his teammates he would lead them to a score, and "then I'm going to help the fans tear down the goalposts." Bishop's 11-yard touchdown pass to Darnell McDonald with 5:25 left put K-State ahead to stay. After the final gun sounded with K-State up 40-30, the crowd rushed the field and—without Bishop's help—tore down the north goalpost.

BIGGEST UPSET Much of the debate heading into the 2003 Big 12 Championship game in Kansas City was about whether the North Division-winning Oklahoma squad was the best Sooners team of all time, which by extension would make it one of the best college football teams of all time. No. 13 KSU, meanwhile, lost quarterback Ell Roberson early in the year, and its cornerbacks were routinely getting burned. The Wildcats started out Big 12 play 0–2 for the first time ever and looked to be out of the league race by mid-October. But after OU scored to go up 7-0, KSU took control. The Wildcats defense began blitzing OU quarterback and eventual Heisman Trophy winner Jason White into making mistakes; Wildcats halfback Darren

Sproles busted the highly regarded Sooner defense for 235 yards rushing; and a healthy Roberson threw four touchdown passes in a 35-7 KSU rout. "We shocked the world," Wildcats defense tackle Jermaine Berry said.

ALL-TIME TEAM

Selected in fall 2004 by the editors of Powercat Illustrated *and* GoPowercat.com.

OFFENSE

1932-34	George Maddox, OL
1994-97	Kendyl Jacox, OL
1995-97	Todd Weiner, OL
1995-98	Ryan Young, OL
2000-03	Nick Leckey, C
1975-77	Paul Coffman, TE
1993-96	Kevin Lockett, WR
1999-00	Quincy Morgan, WR
1997-98	Michael Bishop, QB
1951-53	Veryl Switzer, RB
2001-04	Darren Sproles, RB
1994-98	Martin Gramatica, PK
1997-00	David Allen, KR

DEFENSE

1929-31	Henry Cronkite, DE
1996-99	Darren Howard, DE
1981-83	Reggie Singletary, DT
1992-95	Tim Colston, DT
1974-77	Gary Spani, LB
1996-99	Mark Simoneau, LB
1997-98	Jeff Kelly, LB
1968-70	Clarence Scott, DB
1990-93	Jaime Mendez, DB
1994-96	Chris Canty, DB
1999-02	Terence Newman, DB
1991-92	Sean Snyder, P

STADIUM In 1918, the Kansas State Agricultural College faculty, moved by the sacrifice of 45 of their former students who died in World War I, looked for a way to honor them. Work began in 1922 on Memorial Stadium. Original plans included a horseshoe-shaped grandstand that would seat 22,500, but the price tag to finish the horseshoe rose from $350,000 to $500,000 and it was never finished. In 1968, the school used student fees, gate receipts and donations to finance KSU Stadium, a $1.6 million replacement across campus. Snyder's arrival and the Wildcats' subsequent successes spawned several notable renovations, including the addition of a football complex in the north end zone (1989-92), a new press box (1993) and an expansion project after the 1998 season that added two decks and sky suites. In 1991, a new artificial surface was installed and named Wagner Field in honor of Dave and Carol Wagner, two former KSU students who donated $800,000 of their $35 million state lottery pot.

HEARTBREAKER Call the 2003 Big 12 Championship a little karmic revenge for what unfolded in 1998, when unbeaten and top-ranked K-State went into St. Louis needing only a win over a banged-up Texas A&M team to punch its ticket for the national title game. With 12 minutes left and K-State up 27-12, it appeared the crowd at the Trans World Dome in St. Louis was going to see exactly what was expected. But a long A&M drive and then a fumble by KSU quarterback Michael Bishop quickly changed the complexion of the game. A late touchdown pass and two-point conversion pass, both from Branndon Stewart to Sirr Parker, tied the score. KSU had a shot to win in regulation, but time expired before KSU could capitalize on a Hail Mary pass from Bishop to Everett Burnett that took the ball to the Aggie 2. Then Stewart and Parker

connected on a touchdown pass in the second overtime for a shocking 36-33 A&M victory.

BEST GOAL-LINE STAND The No. 13 Wildcats found themselves in a tight spot in Lubbock on Nov. 1, 1997, leading only 6-2 in the fourth quarter, so they opted for what was supposed to be a simple low-risk screen pass designed to move the ball and protect the lead. But Michael Bishop threw it directly to Texas Tech end Montae Reagor at the KSU 13-yard line, and his touchdown-saving tackle at the 3 seemed only to delay the inevitable Red Raiders score. On first down, Tech quarterback Zebbie Lethridge kept around left end for a 2-yard gain. On second-and-goal at the 1, he tried to dive over the middle, but KSU linebacker Jeff Kelly swatted the ball out before it crossed the goal line and safety Lamar Chapman recovered. KSU hung on to win 13-2 and keep alive a win streak that would eventually reach 19 games.

BEST COMEBACK Iowa State, looking for a big win to validate its rebuilding effort, was ready for an ambush in Ames, Iowa, on Sept. 25, 1999. The Cyclones dominated the first half, building a 28-7 lead over the No. 15 Wildcats. At halftime, Snyder benched starting quarterback Jonathan Beasley in favor of Adam Helm and emphasized a short passing game to take advantage of the Cyclones' soft coverage. KSU scored on its first drive of the second half, and after a stop by the defense, David Allen returned a punt 94 yards for a touchdown to steal the momentum. KSU scored twice in the fourth quarter for a 35-28 victory.

WILDEST FINISH On Nov. 11, 1944, KSU was poised to end a three-game losing streak to rival Kansas, leading by four points with only seconds remaining. KU halfback Chuck Moffett broke loose on a long run, with the gun sounding before he reached the end zone. Kansas fans, certain he was headed for the winning touchdown, stormed the field even as Moffett reached the end zone. As the fans celebrated, the officials—minus one member of the crew who had already made it to the locker room and started his shower—met with both coaches. A clipping penalty had been called on KU, negating the run but giving the Jayhawks one final play. KSU stopped it, hanging on for an 18-14 victory that turned out to be the only Jayhawks loss in the series from 1941 to 1952.

RIVAL Though games with Nebraska have been more competitive and meaningful since the mid-1990s, nothing

gets the juices flowing in Manhattan or Lawrence like the Kansas-Kansas State game. Going into the 2005 season, KU leads 62–35–5. In 1941, the schools' student councils, hoping to dilute the bad blood between the fans, bought a trophy with a miniature set of bronze goalposts, with the idea that it would influence the winning team's fans to refrain from tearing down the real thing. In 1969, the trophy was replaced by the Governor's Cup. The rivalry was darkest in 1984, when fans stormed the field to tear down the goalposts after a KSU victory and later gathered 8,000-strong in Aggieville, Manhattan's entertainment district, where a riot ensued that injured seven police officers and led to the arrest of 23 students.

NICKNAME Like many universities with an agricultural mandate, Kansas State Agricultural College used the nickname Aggies in its infancy. New coach John Bender, inspired that his team played "like a bunch of wildcats," gave his 1915 squad the Wildcats nickname, but it lasted only as long as he did—one year. KSAC reverted back to another agrarian moniker, Farmers, before coach Charles Bachman arrived from Northwestern (also nicknamed the Wildcats) in 1920. He revived the Wildcats and dumped the Farmers nickname.

MASCOT In 1922, two years after restoring the Wildcats nickname, Coach Bachman asked alumni to find a living wildcat to serve as a school mascot. Alums and veterinarians Herbert R. Groome and John E. McCoy donated a convalescing bobcat, named Touchdown, who died from wounds suffered in a scuffle with a porcupine before he could serve. Subsequent bobcats, like many KSU fans during the bleak years, stopped attending games and have been replaced by Willie Wildcat, a student in a No. 0 football jersey, shoulder pads and oversize plush cat head.

UNIFORMS In 1896, a committee of senior students chose Royal Purple as the school color, and although a variety of complementary colors have been used, from white to silver to gray and even gold, it remains the only official school color. The uniforms have remained fairly constant since the 1940s—purple home and white road jerseys over white or silver pants—but the helmet design changed with the frequency of springtime tornadoes on the Kansas plains. From 1967 to 1988, the Wildcats changed helmet designs 10 times, as if trying to avoid association with the team that had stunk it up the year or two before. During that span, the color went from light gray to purple to white and back to purple. It went from a

traditional wildcats' face to the school's initials in stepladder form to a script "Cats," all with stripes in a variety of numbers and widths down the middle. Shortly after becoming head coach in 1989, Snyder commissioned a KSU graphic design instructor named Tom Bookwalter to create a more modern wildcat's-head logo.

NUMBERS Number 11 is the only number in KSU history to have been retired. Quarterbacks Lynn Dickey (1968-70) and Steve Grogan (1972-74), both of whom wore it, went on to productive NFL careers ... Entering the 2005 season the Wildcats are second in the Big 12 in regular-season winning percentage (.708, 51-21) ... KSU shows up four times on the list of major-college football's 33 longest losing streaks, including separate skids of 28—third longest all time—18, 17 and 16.

QUOTE "This thing didn't rise out of the sand like Las Vegas. We have a solid foundation. We've done it by getting a little bit better each day in everything we do." —Bill Snyder, on the staying power of Kansas State's rebuilt program

KANSAS STATE ANNUAL STATISTICAL LEADERS

YR	RUSHING	YDS	ATT	AVG	PASSING	ATT	CMP	PCT	YDS	RECEIVING	REC	YDS	AVG
1948	Gerald Hackney	598	114	5.2	Dana Atkins	73	28	.38	363	Dick Johnson	8	NA	NA
1949	Hi Faubion	605	120	5.0	Dana Atkins	99	44	.44	626	Hi Faubion	21	247	11.8
1950	Ted Maupin	321	96	3.3	Frank Hooper	129	46	.36	709	Dick Johnson	22	382	17.4
1951	Ted Maupin	300	56	5.4	Lane Brown	96	36	.38	500	Ted Maupin	14	149	10.6
1952	Veryl Switzer	201	54	3.7	Carl Albacker	119	55	.46	559	Jack McShulskis	14	104	7.4
1953	Veryl Switzer	558	95	5.9	Bob Dahnke	28	14	.50	415	Veryl Switzer	8	211	26.4
1954	Corky Taylor	529	72	7.3	Jim Logsdon	39	18	.46	260	Corky Taylor	14	334	23.9
1955	Doug Roether	272	74	3.7	Dick Corbin	42	14	.33	156	Don Zadnik	9	110	12.2
1956	Keith Wilson	341	103	3.3	Dick Corbin	49	16	.33	378	Gene Keady	14	247	17.6
1957	Ralph Pfeifer	468	115	4.1	Dick Corbin	61	24	.39	287	Ralph Pfeifer	11	109	9.9
1958	Max Falk	295	74	4.0	Les Krull	106	57	.54	661	Joe Vader	21	219	10.4
1959	Dale Evans	245	70	3.5	John Solmes	114	49	.43	585	Dale Evans	23	224	9.7
1960	Jack Richardson	219	38	5.8	John Solmes	83	32	.39	378	Willis Crenshaw	18	190	10.6
1961	Joel Searles	252	73	3.5	Larry Corrigan	30	13	.43	234	Spencer Puls	7	123	17.6
1962	Willis Crenshaw	331	88	3.8	Larry Corrigan	84	28	.33	441	Jack King	13	137	10.5
1963	Ron Barlow	293	58	5.1	Larry Corrigan	127	58	.46	634	Ralph McFillen	29	328	11.3
1964	Jerry Condit	450	122	3.7	Ed Danieley	79	36	.46	358	Jerry Condit	10	170	17.0
1965	Henry Howard	279	84	3.3	Vic Castillo	159	60	.38	734	Richard Balducci	13	172	13.2
1966	Cornelius Davis	1,028	210	4.9	Vic Castillo	113	44	.39	617	Dave Jones	13	721	55.5
1967	Cornelius Davis	628	210	3.0	Bill Nossek	216	111	.51	1,220	Dave Jones	35	561	16.0
1968	Larry Brown	402	111	3.6	Lynn Dickey	258	125	.48	1,569	Dave Jones	46	622	13.5
1969	Mack Herron	506	127	4.0	Lynn Dickey	372	196	.53	2,476	Mack Herron	46	652	14.2
1970	Bill Butler	497	127	3.9	Lynn Dickey	364	180	.49	2,163	Mike Montgomery	51	386	7.6
1971	Bill Butler	838	204	4.1	Dennis Morrison	333	157	.47	1,780	Henry Childs	36	396	11.0
1972	Don Calhoun	608	131	4.6	Dennis Morrison	300	136	.45	1,596	John Goerger	30	612	20.4
1973	Isaac Jackson	1,137	225	5.1	Steve Grogan	164	72	.44	1,050	Henry Childs	57	502	8.8
1974	Roscoe Scobey	401	80	5.0	Steve Grogan	144	67	.47	834	John Tuttle	32	346	10.8
1975	Verdell Jones	373	78	4.8	Joe Hatcher	93	34	.37	432	Stan Ross	24	192	8.0
1976	Tony Brown	368	123	3.0	Wendell Henrikson	149	73	.49	1,066	Manzy King	13	273	21.0
1977	Mack Green	707	192	3.7	Wendell Henrikson	163	72	.44	882	Charlie Green	21	634	30.2
1978	Mack Green	561	113	5.0	Dan Manucci	237	122	.51	1,808	Charlie Green	33	616	18.7
1979	L. J. Brown	668	148	4.5	Darrell Dickey	140	71	.51	895	John Liebe	39	423	10.8
1980	L. J. Brown	575	165	3.5	Darrell Dickey	168	80	.48	1,004	John Liebe	22	400	18.2
1981	Masi Toluao	531	114	4.7	Darrell Dickey	158	75	.47	974	Ernie Coleman	25	229	9.2
1982	Iosefatu Faraimo	404	99	4.1	Darrell Dickey	174	93	.53	1,225	Mike Wallace	13	693	53.3
1983	Greg Dageforde	677	153	4.4	Doug Bogue	119	61	.51	851	Mike Wallace	37	466	12.6
1984	Stan Weber	406	98	4.1	Stan Weber	114	58	.51	602	Eric Bailey	15	171	11.4
1985	Ray Wilson	367	112	3.3	John Welch	116	55	.47	659	Gerald Alphin	14	524	37.4
1986	Tony Jordan	738	202	3.7	Randy Williams	197	68	.35	1,069	Dan Hughes	34	413	12.1
1987	Tony Jordan	692	169	4.1	Gary Swim	235	115	.49	1,304	Kent Dean	28	481	17.2
1988	Lee Pickett	736	144	5.1	Carl Straw	358	191	.53	1,947	Greg Washington	38	928	24.4
1989	Pat Jackson	328	93	3.5	Carl Straw	192	101	.53	1,095	Michael Smith	69	816	11.8
1990	Pat Jackson	721	177	4.1	Carl Straw	277	153	.55	2,156	Michael Smith	70	796	11.4
1991	Eric Gallon	1,161	224	5.2	Paul Watson	304	172	.57	2,312	Michael Smith	46	768	16.7
1992	Eric Gallon	705	178	4.0	Jason Smargiasso	149	72	.48	990	Gerald Benton	55	603	11.0
1993	J. J. Smith	758	190	4.0	Chad May	350	185	.53	2,682	Kevin Lockett	50	770	15.4
1994	J. J. Smith	1,073	232	4.6	Chad May	337	200	.59	2,571	Tyson Schwieger	44	564	12.8
1995	Eric Hickson	816	158	5.2	Matt Miller	240	154	.64	2,059	Kevin Lockett	56	797	14.2
1996	Mike Lawrence	982	209	4.7	Brian Kavanagh	284	167	.59	1,893	Kevin Lockett	72	882	12.3
1997	Eric Hickson	750	169	4.4	Michael Bishop	185	80	.43	1,557	Darnell McDonald	21	441	21.0
1998	Eric Hickson	902	169	5.3	Michael Bishop	295	164	.56	2,844	Darnell McDonald	75	1,092	14.6
1999	Joe Hall	613	121	5.1	Jonathan Beasley	203	80	.39	1,805	Quincy Morgan	42	1,007	24.0
2000	Josh Scobey	718	169	4.2	Jonathan Beasley	313	156	.50	2,636	Quincy Morgan	64	1,166	18.2
2001	Josh Scobey	1,263	240	5.3	Ell Roberson	136	54	.40	855	Aaron Lockett	24	357	14.9
2002	Darren Sproles	1,465	237	6.2	Ell Roberson	175	91	.52	1,365	Taco Wallace	39	704	18.1
2003	Darren Sproles	1,986	306	6.5	Ell Roberson	294	152	.52	2,545	James Terry	64	1,232	19.2
2004	Darren Sproles	1,318	244	5.4	Dylan Meier	220	127	.58	1,436	Jermaine Moreira	39	406	10.4

Receiving leaders by receptions
The NCAA began including postseason stats in 2002

KANSAS STATE ALL-TIME SCORES

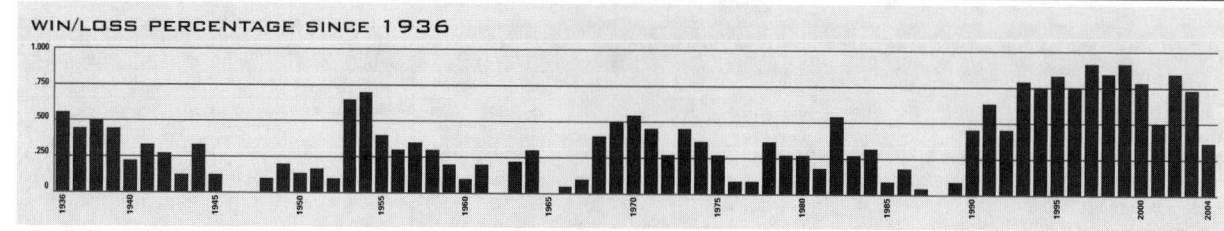

WIN/LOSS PERCENTAGE SINCE 1936

IRA PRATT
1896 (.250) 0-1-1

1896 — 0-1-1
N28	at Fort Riley	0	14
D5 =	Fort Riley	6	6

A.W. EHRSAM
1897 (.375) 1-2-1

1897 — 1-2-1
N1 ●	Dickinson HS	4	0
N8	Washburn U.	0	4
U =	Chapman HS	0	0
N20	at Washburn	0	36

W.P. WILLIAMSON
1898 (.500) 1-1-2

1898 — 1-1-2
O28 =	at Chapman HS	0	0
N5 ●	Junction City HS	26	0
N12 =	Chapman HS	0	0
N28	Ottawa	6	16

ALBERT HANSON
1899 (.400) 2-3

1899 — 2-3-0
O14	at Washburn U.	0	24
O16	at St. Mary's Kan.	0	23
O30 ●	Kansas Weslayan	17	5
N11 ●	at Emporia Coll.	6	0
N30	at Emporia St.	0	20

F.G. MOULTON
1900 (.333) 2-4

1900 — 2-4-0
O22 ●	at Wichita U.	11	5
O26	at Emporia St.	0	28
O29	Ottawa	0	28
N10	Emporia St.	0	11
N17 ●	Kansas Weslayan	30	0
N30	at St. Mary's Kan.	6	28

WADE MOORE
1901 (.438) 3-4-1

1901 — 3-4-1
O7 ●	at Bethany	12	5
O14 ●	Emporia Coll.	11	0
O21	Bethany	0	17
N6 ●	KC Medical Coll.	6	24
N9	at Emporia St.	0	24
N11	at Emporia Coll.	0	11
N20 ●	Manhattan HS	30	0
D1 =	at Washington HS	6	6

C.E. DIETZ
1902 (.250) 2-6

1902 — 2-6-0
S27	at Emporia St.	0	16
O4	at Kansas	0	16
O11	Haskell	0	23
O23	Fort Riley	0	6
N1	Ottawa	0	15
N10	at Bethany	0	40
N22 ●	Haskell	24	0
N27 ●	Chapman	22	5

G.O. DIETZ
1903 (.438) 3-4-1

1903 — 3-4-1
S26 =	Emporia St.	0	0
O3	at Kansas	0	34
O24	Bethany	0	18
O30 ●	Clyde HS	11	0
N7	Washburn U.	0	34
N14 ●	Fort Riley	11	0
N21	Emporia Coll.	0	11
N26 ●	Haskell	34	6

A.A. BOOTH
1904 (.143) 1-6

1904 — 1-6-0
O8 ●	Fort Riley	28	0
O22	at St. Mary's Kan.	5	10
O28	Bethany	5	28
O31	at Washburn	0	56
N12	Fort Hayes St.	0	17
N19	Kansas	4	41
N24	at Emporia St.	6	34

MIKE AHEARN
1905-10 (.765) 39-12

1905 — 6-2-0
O7 ●	Ottawa	20	0
O14 ●	Washburn U.	5	12
O21 ●	at Kansas Wesleyan	24	0
O23 ●	St. Mary's Kan.	10	5
O31 ●	Wichita St.	11	6
N17 ●	Haskell	60	0
N25	at Kansas	0	28
N30 ●	Emporia St.	10	0

1906 — 5-2-0
O22 ●	Emporia Coll.	35	0
O13 ●	Haskell	10	5
O27 ●	at Washburn	4	5
N5 ●	Wichita St.	6	12
N12 ●	Ottawa	32	11
N24 ●	at Kansas	6	4
N29 ●	Emporia St.	10	0

1907 — 5-3-0
O7 ●	Emporia Coll.	46	0
O12 ●	Haskell	0	10
O19 ●	KC Vet Coll.	32	0
O26 ●	Kansas	10	29
N4 ●	Ottawa	16	6
N9 ●	Washburn	0	5
N18 ●	Wichita St.	10	6
N28 ●	Emporia St.	21	0

1908 — 6-2-0
O3 ●	Kansas Wesleyan	28	5
O10 ●	at Kansas	6	12
O23 ●	Oklahoma	4	33
O28 ●	Southwestern	17	0
N7 ●	at Creighton	31	0
N14 ●	Oklahoma State	40	10
N21 ●	at Washburn	23	4
N26 ●	Colorado State	33	10

1909 — 7-2-0
O2 ●	Kansas Wesleyan	35	0
O9 ●	at Missouri	0	3
O16 ●	Kansas	3	5
O23 ●	Oklahoma State	9	0
O30 ●	Southwestern	60	0
N6 ●	at Emporia St.	44	0
N13 ●	Creighton	58	3
N20 ●	Wichita St.	71	0
N25 ●	at Washburn	40	0

1910 — 10-1-0
S28 ●	William Jewel	57	0
O1 ●	Haskell	39	0
O8 ●	at Emporia St.	22	0
O15 ●	at Arkansas	5	0
O17 ●	at Drury Coll.	75	0
O22 ●	Missouri Mines	23	0
O29 ●	at Creighton	6	2
N5 ●	at Colorado College	8	15
N12 ●	Wichita St.	33	6
N18 ●	Baker	35	0
N24 ●	Washburn	33	0

GUY LOWMAN
1911-14 (.529) 17-15-3

1911 — 5-4-1
S30 =	Southwestern	6	6
O7 ●	Emporia St.	0	3
O14 ●	at Nebraska	0	59
O21 ●	Kansas	0	6
O28 ●	Wichita St.	9	5
N4 ●	at Baker	0	3
N11 ●	Creighton	12	0
N18 ●	Arkansas KC	3	0
N24 ●	Oklahoma State	11	0
N30 ●	at Washburn	6	5

1912 — 8-2-0
S28 ●	Southwestern	19	7
O5 ●	Haskell	21	14
O12 ●	at Nebraska	6	30
O19 ●	Emporia St.	22	7
O26 ●	at Kansas	6	19
N2 ●	at Wichita St.	54	0
N8 ●	Emporia Coll.	28	7
N16 ●	Colorado	14	6
N20 ●	at Texas A&M	13	10
N28 ●	Washburn	21	3

1913-1927 MISSOURI VALLEY

1913 — 3-4-1 (0-2-0)
O3	Southwestern	10	13
O11	at Nebraska	6	24
O18	Emporia St.	33	0
O25	Kansas	0	26
N1 ●	Wichita St.	30	7
N8 ●	Texas A&M	12	0
N18	at Texas	0	46
N27 =	at Washburn	6	6

1914 — 1-5-1 (0-3-0)
O3 ●	Southwestern	15	0
O10 =	Emporia St.	0	0
O17	Nebraska	0	31
O26	at Kansas	0	27 *
O31	at Missouri	3	13
N13	Oklahoma	10	52
N25	Washburn	16	26

JOHN BENDER
1915 (.438) 3-4-1

1915 — 3-4-1 (0-2-1)
O1 ●	Southwestern	9	0
O9	at Nebraska	0	31
O15	at Emporia St.	0	13
O23	Kansas	7	19
O29 =	at Missouri	0	0
N6 ●	Friends	14	0
N12	at Washburn	6	0
N19	Oklahoma	7	21

Z.G. CLEVENGER
1916-19 (.667) 19-9-2

1916 — 6-1-1 (1-1-1)
S30 ●	Baker	20	0
O6 ●	Southwestern	53	0
O14	at Nebraska	0	14
O21 ●	Emporia St.	13	3
O28 =	at Kansas	0	0
N11	Missouri	7	6
N17	at Oklahoma	14	13
N23 ●	Washburn	47	0

1917 — 6-2-0 (2-2-0)
S29 ●	Baker	28	0
O6 ●	Oklahoma State	23	0
O13 ●	at Missouri	7	6
O20 ●	Washington, Mo.	61	0
N3	Kansas	0	9
N10	at Iowa State	7	10
N22 ●	Emporia St.	51	0
N29 ●	Washburn	38	0

1918 — 4-1-0 (1-1-0)
S27 ●	Baker	22	0
O5 ●	Fort Riley	27	7
N9 ●	Washburn	28	9
N23 ●	Iowa State	11	0
N28	at Kansas	7	13

1919 — 3-5-1 (0-3-1)
S27 ●	Baker	16	0
O4 ●	Camp Funston	20	6
O11 =	Missouri	6	6
O18	Washington, Mo.	9	14
O24 ●	Fort Hayes St.	12	0
N1	at Kansas	3	16
N8	Haskell	3	7
N15	at Iowa State	0	46
N22	Oklahoma	3	14

CHARLES BACHMAN
1920-27 (.577) 33-23-9

1920 — 3-3-3 (0-3-1)
O1 ●	Fort Hayes St.	14	0
O8 ●	Camp Funston	55	0
O15 =	Emporia St.	7	7
O22 ●	at Creighton	3	0
O30	Kansas	0	14
N6	at Missouri	7	10
N13	Iowa State	0	17
N19 =	Oklahoma	7	7
N26	Washburn	0	0

1921 — 5-3-0 (4-2-0)
O1 ●	Emporia Coll.	7	3
O8 ●	Washington, Mo.	21	0
O15	at Creighton	7	14
O22 ●	Missouri	7	5
O29	at Kansas	7	21
N5 ●	Grinnell	21	7
N11	at Iowa State	0	7
N19	Oklahoma	14	7

1922 — 5-1-2 (3-1-2)
O6 ●	Washburn	47	0
O14 ●	at Washington, Mo.	22	14
O21 =	at Oklahoma	7	7
O28 =	Kansas	7	7
N4 ●	at Missouri	13	10 *
N11 ●	Iowa State	12	2
N18	at Nebraska	0	21
N30 ●	TCU	45	0

1923 — 4-2-2 (2-2-2)

O5	•	Washburn	25	0
O13	•	Creighton	6	0
O20	=	at Iowa State	7	7
O27	•	at Kansas	0	0
N3		Missouri	2	4
N10	•	at Grinnell	34	7
N23	•	Oklahoma	21	20
N29		at Nebraska	12	34

1924 — 3-4-1 (1-4-1)

O3	•	at Washburn	23	0
O10	•	Emporia St.	19	6
O18	•	Kansas	6	0
O25	•	at Missouri	7	14
N1		Iowa State	0	21
N15	•	Drake	6	7
N22		Nebraska	0	24
N26	=	at Oklahoma	7	7

1925 — 5-2-1 (3-2-1)

S26	•	Emporia St.	26	7
O3	•	Oklahoma	16	0
O10	•	at Drake	0	19
O17	•	at Kansas	14	7
O24		Missouri	0	3
N7	•	at Marquette	2	0
N14	=	Nebraska	0	0
N26	=	at Iowa State	12	7 *

1926 — 5-3-0 (2-2-0)

O2	•	Texas	13	3
O9	•	at Creighton	12	0
O16	•	Kansas	27	0
O23	•	at Oklahoma	15	12
O30	•	Arkansas	16	7
N6		at Marquette	0	14
N13	•	at Nebraska	0	3
N20		Iowa State	2	3

1927 — 3-5-0 (2-4-0)

S24	•	Fort Hayes St.	30	6
O1		at Missouri	6	13
O15	•	at Kansas	13	2
O22	•	Oklahoma	20	14
O29	•	at Iowa State	7	12
N12		at Texas	7	41
N19		Nebraska	0	33
N24		Oklahoma State	18	25

1928-1995 BIG 8

BO McMILLIN
1928-33 (.578)   29-21-1

1928 — 3-5-0 (0-5-0)

S29	•	Bethany	32	7
O6	•	at Oklahoma State	13	6
O13	•	Fort Hayes St.	22	7
O20		Kansas	0	7
O27	•	at Oklahoma	21	33
N10		Missouri	6	19
N17	•	at Iowa State	0	7
N29		at Nebraska	0	8

1929 — 3-5-0 (3-2-0)

O5		at Purdue	14	26
O12		Texas A&M *Dal*	0	19
O19	•	at Kansas	6	0
O26	•	Oklahoma	13	14
N2	•	at Missouri	7	6
N9	•	Iowa State	3	2
N23	•	Nebraska	6	10
N25	•	at Marquette	6	25

1930 — 5-3-0 (3-2-0)

O4	•	Washburn	14	0
O18	•	Kansas	0	14
O25	•	at Oklahoma	0	7
N1	•	Missouri	20	13
N8	•	at West Virginia	7	23
N15	•	at Iowa State	13	0
N22	•	Centre	27	0
N27	•	at Nebraska	10	9

1931 — 8-2-0 (3-2-0)

O3	•	Pittsburg St.	28	7
O10	•	at Missouri	20	7
O17	•	at Kansas	13	0
O24	•	Oklahoma	14	0
O31	•	at West Virginia	19	0
N7		at Iowa State	6	7
N14	•	Nebraska	3	6
N21	•	North Dakota St.	19	6
N26	•	at Washburn	22	0
D5	•	at Wichita	20	6

1932 — 4-4-0 (2-3-0)

S24	•	Wichita St.	26	0
O1		at Purdue	13	29
O7	•	at Kansas Wesleyan	52	6
O15	•	Missouri	25	0
O22		at Oklahoma	13	20
O29		at Nebraska	0	6
N5	•	Iowa State	31	0
N19		Kansas	0	19

1933 — 6-2-1 (4-1-0)

S30	•	Emporia St.	25	0
O6	•	at Washington, Mo.	20	14
O14	•	at Missouri	33	0
O21		Nebraska	0	9
O28	•	at Kansas	6	0
N4	•	at Michigan State	0	0
N11	•	at Iowa State	7	0
N18	•	Oklahoma	14	0
N30		at Texas Tech	0	6

LYNN WALDORF
1934 (.750)   7-2-1

1934 — 7-2-1 (5-0-0)

S29	•	Fort Hayes St.	13	0
O6	=	at Manhattan Coll.	13	13
O12	•	at Marquette	20	27
O20	•	Kansas	13	0
O27		at Tulsa	0	21
N3	•	at Washburn	14	6
N10	•	Missouri	29	0
N17	•	at Oklahoma	8	7
N24	•	Iowa State	20	0
N29	•	at Nebraska	19	7

WES FRY
1935-39 (.467)   18-21-6

1935 — 2-4-3 (1-2-2)

S27	•	at Duquesne	12	0
O5		Fort Hayes St.	0	3
O11	•	at Washburn	0	14
O19	=	Nebraska	0	0
O26		at Kansas	2	9
N2	=	at Tulsa	13	13
N9	•	at Iowa State	6	0
N16	•	Oklahoma	0	3
N23	=	at Missouri	7	7

1936 — 4-3-2 (2-1-2)

S26	•	Fort Hayes St.	13	0
O3	•	at Oklahoma State	31	0
O10	=	Missouri	7	7
O17	•	at Marquette	0	13
O24	•	Kansas	26	6
O31		at Tulsa	7	10
N7	•	at Oklahoma	6	6
N14	•	Iowa State	47	7
N21		at Nebraska	0	40

1937 — 4-5-0 (1-4-0)

O2		at Boston College	7	21
O9	•	at Missouri	7	14
O16	•	Marquette	13	0
O23	•	at Creighton	15	7
O30		Oklahoma	0	19
N6	•	Washburn	20	7
N13	•	at Kansas	7	0
N20	•	at Iowa State	7	13
N27		Nebraska	0	3

1938 — 4-4-1 (1-3-1)

O1		at Northwestern	0	21
O8	•	Missouri	21	13
O14	•	Marquette	6	0
O22	•	at Indiana	13	6
O29		Kansas	7	27
N5		at Oklahoma	0	26
N12	•	Iowa State	13	13
N19	•	Washburn	41	14
N24		at Nebraska	7	14

1939 — 4-5-0 (1-4-0)

S30	•	Fort Hayes St.	34	7
O6	•	at Marquette	3	0
O14	•	Colorado	20	0
O21		at Missouri	7	9
O28		Nebraska	9	25
N4	•	at Kansas	27	6
N11		Oklahoma	10	13
N18	•	at Iowa State	0	10
N25		at Boston College	7	38

HOBBS ADAMS
1940-41, '46 (.185)   4-21-2

1940 — 2-7-0 (1-4-0)

S28	•	Emporia St.	21	16
O5		at Colorado	6	7
O12		Missouri	13	24
O19		at Oklahoma	0	14
O26	•	Kansas	20	0
N2		at Michigan State	0	32
N9		at South Carolina	13	20
N16		Iowa State	0	12
N30		at Nebraska	0	20

1941 — 2-5-2 (1-3-1)

S27	=	Fort Hayes St.	0	0
O4		at Northwestern	3	51
O11		at Missouri	0	35
O18		Oklahoma	0	16
N1	•	Nebraska	12	6
N8	•	South Carolina	3	0
N15	•	at Kansas	16	20
N22	•	at Iowa State	12	12
N29		at Arizona	21	28

WARD HAYLETT
1942-44 (.250)   6-20-2

1942 — 3-8-0 (2-3-0)

S19	•	at Kansas Wesleyan	37	6
S26		at Texas	0	64
O3		Fort Riley	7	21
O10	•	Duquesne *Phil*	0	33
O17		Missouri	2	46
O24		Kansas	7	19
O31	•	at Wichita St.	0	9
N7		at Oklahoma	0	76
N14		at Indiana	0	54
N21	•	Iowa State	7	6
N28	•	at Nebraska	19	0

1943 — 1-7-0 (0-5-0)

O2	•	Washburn	13	7
O9		at Missouri	14	47
O16		William-Jewell	6	19
O23		Oklahoma	0	37
O30		at Kansas	2	25
N6		Nebraska	7	13
N12	•	Washburn	6	13
N20		at Iowa State	0	48

1944 — 2-5-2 (1-4-0)

S30	•	Wichita St.	6	6
O7		Missouri	0	33
O14		at Michigan State	6	45
O21		at Oklahoma	0	68
O28		Iowa State	0	14
N4	•	at Wichita St.	15	0
N11	•	Kansas	18	14
N18	•	Olathe NAS	0	0
N25		at Nebraska	0	35

LUD FISER
1945 (.125)   1-7

1945 — 1-7-0 (0-5-0)

S29	•	Wichita St.	13	6
O6	•	Olathe NAS	12	34
O13	•	at Marquette	13	55
O20	•	at Missouri	7	41
O27	•	Oklahoma	13	41
N3	•	at Iowa State	13	40
N10	•	Nebraska	0	24
N17	•	at Kansas	0	27

HOBBS ADAMS

1946 — 0-9-0 (0-5-0)

S28	•	at Hardin Simmons	7	21
O5	•	at Nebraska	0	31
O12		Missouri	0	26
O19	•	at Oklahoma	7	28
N2	•	Iowa State	7	13
N9	•	at San Francisco	6	38
N16	•	Kansas	0	34
N23	•	at New Mexico	7	14
N30	•	at Arizona	7	28

SAM FRANCIS
1947 (.000)   0-10

1947 — 0-10-0 (0-5-0)

S20	•	Oklahoma State	0	12
S26	•	at Texas El Paso	6	20
O4	•	New Mexico	18	20
O10	•	at Boston College	13	49
O18	•	at Missouri	7	47
O25	•	Nebraska	7	14
N1	•	at Kansas	0	55
N8	•	Oklahoma	13	27
N15	•	at Iowa State	0	14
N29	•	at Florida	7	25

RALPH GRAHAM
1948-50 (.145)   4-26-1

1948 — 1-9-0 (0-6-0)

S25	•	at Illinois	0	40
O2		Iowa State	0	20
O9	•	Arkansas State	37	6
O16		at Oklahoma	0	42
O23		at Colorado	7	51
O30		Missouri	7	49
N6		at Nebraska	0	32
N13		Kansas	14	20
N20		at Oklahoma State	6	42
N25		at Washington, Mo.	7	21

1949 — 2-8-0 (1-5-0)

S24	•	Fort Hayes St.	55	0
O1	•	Colorado	27	13
O8	•	Nebraska	6	13
O15	•	at Iowa State	21	25
O22	•	at Memphis	14	21
O29	•	at Kansas	0	38
N5	•	Oklahoma	0	39
N12	•	Oklahoma State	14	26
N19	•	at Tulsa	27	48
N24	•	at Missouri	27	34

1950 — 1-9-1 (0-6-0)

S16	•	Baker	55	0
S23	•	at Washington	7	33
S30	•	at Colorado	6	34
O7	•	at Marquette	6	46
O14	•	Missouri	7	28
O21	•	at Oklahoma	0	58
N4	•	Iowa State	7	13
N11	•	at Nebraska	21	49
N18	•	Kansas	7	47
N25	•	at Oklahoma State	0	41
D2	•	at Wichita St.	6	6

BILL MEEK
1951-54 (.410)   15-22-2

1951 — 1-7-1 (1-4-1)

S22	•	Cincinnati	0	34
S29	•	at Iowa	0	16
O6	=	Nebraska	6	6 †
O13	•	at Iowa State	6	32
O20	•	Colorado	7	20
O27	•	at Kansas	14	33
N3	•	Oklahoma	0	33
N10	•	at Tulsa	26	42
N17	•	at Missouri	14	12 †

1952 — 1-9-0 (0-6-0)

S20	•	Bradley	21	7
S27	•	at Cincinnati	6	13
O4		Missouri	0	26
O11	•	at Nebraska	14	27
O18	•	at Tulsa	7	26
O25	•	at Oklahoma	6	49
N1	•	Kansas	6	26
N8	•	Wyoming	7	20
N15	•	at Colorado	14	34
N22	•	Iowa State	0	27

1953 — 6-3-1 (4-2-0)

S19	•	Drake	50	0
S26	•	at Colorado State	13	14
O3	•	Nebraska	27	0
O10	•	at Iowa State	20	12
O17	•	Colorado	28	14
O24	•	Wichita St.	21	0
O31		Oklahoma	0	34
N7	•	at Kansas	7	0
N14		at Missouri	6	16
N21	=	at Arizona	26	26

THE SCHOOLS

1954 7-3-0 (3-3-0)

S18	●	Colorado State	29	0
S25	●	at Wyoming	21	13
O2	|	Missouri	7	35
O9	● |	at Nebraska	7	3
O16	●	at Tulsa	20	13
O23	|	at Oklahoma	0	21
O30	● |	Kansas	28	6
N6	●	at Drake	53	18
N13	● |	Iowa State	12	7
N20	|	at Colorado	14	38

BUS MERTES
1955-59 (.310) 15-34-1

1955 4-6-0 (3-3-0)

S17		Wyoming	20	38
S24		at Iowa	7	28
O1	|	Nebraska	0	16
O8	●	at Marquette	41	0
O15	|	Colorado	13	34
O22	● |	at Iowa State	9	7
O29	|	Oklahoma	7	40
N5	● |	at Kansas	46	0
N12	● |	at Missouri	21	0
N19		at Oklahoma State	0	28

1956 3-7-0 (2-4-0)

S22		Oklahoma State	7	27
S29	|	at Colorado	0	34
O6	|	at Oklahoma	0	66
O13	● |	at Nebraska	10	7
O20	|	Missouri	6	20
O27		at Wyoming	15	27
N3	|	Kansas	15	20
N10	●	at Marquette	41	14
N17	● |	Iowa State	32	6
N24		at Michigan State	17	38

1957 3-6-1 (2-4-0)

S21		at Wyoming	7	12
S28	●	Brigham Young	36	7
O5	|	Nebraska	7	14
O12	=	at Pacific	7	7
O19	|	Colorado	14	42
O26	● |	at Iowa State	14	10
N2	|	Oklahoma	0	13
N9	|	at Kansas	7	13
N16	● |	at Missouri	23	21
N23		at Michigan State	9	27

1958 3-7-0 2-4-0

S20	●	Wyoming	17	14
S27	|	at Colorado	3	13
O4		Utah State	13	20
O11	● |	at Nebraska	23	6
O18	|	Missouri	8	32
O25	|	at Oklahoma	6	40
N1	|	Kansas	12	21
N8		at Oklahoma State	7	14
N15	● |	Iowa State	14	6
N22		at Michigan State	7	26

1959 2-8-0 (1-5-0)

S19		Wichita St.	0	19
S26	●	at South Dakota St.	28	12
O3		Oklahoma State	21	27
O10	|	Colorado	17	20
O17	|	at Kansas	14	33
O24	|	at Iowa State	0	26
O31		at Iowa	0	53
N7	|	Oklahoma	0	36
N14	|	at Missouri	0	26
N21	● |	Nebraska	29	14

DOUG WEAVER
1960-66 (.123) 8-60-1

1960 1-9-0 (0-7-0)

S17	●	South Dakota St.	20	6
S24	|	Kansas	0	41
O1	|	at Colorado	7	27
O8	|	at Nebraska	7	17
O15	|	Missouri	0	45
O22	|	at Oklahoma	7	49
O29		at Minnesota	7	48
N5	|	Oklahoma State	7	28
N12	|	Iowa State	7	20
N19		at Arizona	16	35

1961 2-8-0 (0-7-0)

S23	●	Indiana	14	8
S30	●	at Air Force	14	12
O7	|	Nebraska	0	24
O14		at Kentucky	8	21
O21	|	Colorado	0	13
O28	|	at Iowa State	7	31
N4	|	Oklahoma	6	17
N11	|	at Kansas	0	34
N18	|	at Missouri	9	27
N25	|	at Oklahoma State	0	45

1962 0-10-0 (0-7-0)

S22		at Indiana	0	21
S29	|	at Colorado	0	6
O6		at Washington	0	41
O13	|	Missouri	0	32
O20	|	at Nebraska	6	26
O27	|	at Oklahoma	0	47
N3	|	Kansas	0	38
N10		at Arizona	13	14
N17	|	Iowa State	14	28
N24	|	Oklahoma State	6	30

1963 2-7-0 (1-5-0)

S21	●	Brigham Young	24	7
S28		at San Jose State	0	16
O5	|	Colorado	7	21
O12	|	at Missouri	11	21
O19	|	Nebraska	6	28
O26	|	Oklahoma	9	34
N2	|	at Kansas	0	34
N9		at Texas Tech	13	51
N16	● |	at Iowa State	21	10

1964 3-7-0 (3-4-0)

S19		at Wisconsin	7	17
O3	● |	at Colorado	16	14
O10	|	Missouri	0	7
O17	|	at Nebraska	0	47
O24	|	at Oklahoma	0	44
O31	|	Kansas	0	7
N7		at Arizona State	10	21
N14	● |	Iowa State	7	6
N21	● |	Oklahoma State	17	14
N28		at New Mexico	7	9

1965 0-10-0 (0-7-0)

S18		at Indiana	7	19
S24		at Brigham Young	3	21
O2	|	Colorado	0	36
O9	|	at Missouri	6	28
O16	|	Nebraska	0	41
O23	|	Oklahoma	0	27
O30	|	at Kansas	0	34
N6		Cincinnati	14	21
N13	|	at Iowa State	6	38
N20	|	at Oklahoma State	7	31

1966 0-9-1 (0-6-1)

S17		at Army	6	21
S24		New Mexico	8	28
O1	|	at Colorado	0	10
O8	|	Missouri	0	27
O15	|	at Nebraska	10	21
O22		at Cincinnati	14	28
O29	= |	Kansas	3	3
N5	|	at Oklahoma	6	37
N12	|	Iowa State	13	30
N19	|	Oklahoma State	6	21

VINCE GIBSON
1967-74 (.388) 33-52

1967 1-9-0 (0-7-0)

S23	●	at Colorado State	17	7
S30		Virginia Tech	3	15
O7	|	Nebraska	14	16
O14	|	at Iowa State	0	17
O21	|	Oklahoma	7	46
O28		Arkansas [LR]	7	28
N4	|	at Kansas	16	17
N11	|	at Missouri	6	28
N18	|	Colorado	6	40
N25	|	at Oklahoma State	14	49

1968 4-6-0 (2-5-0)

S21	●	Colorado State	21	0
S28		at Penn State	9	25
O5	●	at Virginia Tech	34	19
O12	|	Iowa State	14	23
O19	|	at Colorado	14	37
O26	|	Missouri	20	56
N2	|	at Oklahoma	20	35
N9	● |	at Nebraska	12	0
N16	|	Kansas	29	38
N23	● |	Oklahoma State	21	14

1969 5-5-0 (3-4-0)

S20	●	at Baylor	45	15
S27	●	at Arizona	42	27
O4		Penn State	14	17
O11	● |	at Kansas	26	22
O18	● |	Iowa State	34	7
O25	● |	Oklahoma	59	21
N1	|	at Missouri	38	41
N8	|	at Oklahoma State	19	28
N15	|	Nebraska	7	10
N22	|	at Colorado	32	45

1970 6-5-0 (5-2-0)

S12	●	at Utah State	37	0
S19		at Kentucky	3	16
S26		at Arizona State	13	35
O3	● |	Colorado	21	20
O10	|	Kansas	15	21
O17	● |	at Iowa State	17	0
O24	● |	at Oklahoma	19	14
O31	● |	Missouri	17	13
N7	● |	Oklahoma State	28	15
N14	|	at Nebraska	13	51
N21		at Florida State	7	33

1971 5-6-0 (2-5-0)

S11		Utah State	7	10
S18	●	at Tulsa	19	10
S25	●	Brigham Young	23	7
O2	|	at Colorado	21	31
O9	|	at Kansas	13	39
O16	|	Iowa State	0	24
O23	|	Oklahoma	28	75
O30	● |	at Missouri	28	12
N6	● |	at Oklahoma State	35	23
N13	|	Nebraska	17	44
N20	●	at Memphis	28	21

1972 3-8-0 (1-6-0)

S9	●	Tulsa	21	13
S16		at Brigham Young	9	32
S23		at Arizona State	14	56
S30	●	Tampa	31	7
O7	|	Colorado	17	38
O14	● |	Kansas	20	19
O21	|	at Iowa State	22	55
O28	|	at Oklahoma	0	52
N4	|	Missouri	14	31
N11	|	Oklahoma State	14	45
N18	|	at Nebraska	7	59

1973 5-6-0 (2-5-0)

S15		at Florida	10	21
S22	●	Tulsa	21	0
S29	●	at Tampa	17	0
O6	●	Memphis	21	16
O13	|	at Kansas	18	25
O20	● |	Iowa State	21	19
O27	|	Oklahoma	14	56
N3	|	at Missouri	7	31
N10	|	at Oklahoma State	9	28
N17	|	Nebraska	21	50
N24	● |	at Colorado	17	14

1974 4-7-0 (1-6-0)

S14	●	Tulsa	31	14
S21	●	Wichita St.	17	0
S28	●	Pacific	38	7
O5		at Mississippi State	16	21
O12	|	Kansas	13	20
O19	|	at Iowa State	18	23
O26	|	at Oklahoma	0	63
N2	|	Missouri	15	52
N9	|	Oklahoma State	5	29
N16	|	at Nebraska	7	35
N23	● |	Colorado	33	19

ELLIS RAINSBERGER
1975-77 (.152) 5-28

1975 3-8-0 (0-7-0)

S13	●	at Tulsa	17	16
S20	●	Wichita St.	32	0
S27	●	at Wake Forest	17	16
O4		Texas A&M	0	10
O11	|	Iowa State	7	17
O18	|	Oklahoma	3	25
O25	|	at Missouri	3	35
N1	|	at Kansas	0	28
N8	|	Nebraska	0	12
N15	|	at Oklahoma State	3	56
N22	|	at Colorado	7	33

1976 1-10-0 (0-7-0)

S11	●	Brigham Young	13	3
S18		at Texas A&M	14	34
S25		Wake Forest	0	13
O2		at Florida State	10	20
O9	|	Missouri	21	28
O16	|	at Nebraska	0	51
O23	|	Kansas	14	24
O30	|	at Iowa State	14	45
N6	|	at Oklahoma	20	49
N13	|	Oklahoma State	21	45
N20	|	Colorado	28	35

1977 1-10-0 (0-7-0)

S10		at Brigham Young	0	39
S17		Florida State	10	18
S24	●	at Wichita St.	21	14
O1		Mississippi State	21	24 †
O8	|	Nebraska	9	26
O15	|	at Oklahoma State	14	21
O22	|	at Missouri	13	28
O29	|	Oklahoma	7	42
N5	|	at Kansas	21	29
N12	|	Iowa State	15	22
N19	|	at Colorado	0	23

JIM DICKEY
1978-85 (.305) 24-56-2

1978 4-7-0 (3-4-0)

S9		at Arizona	0	31
S16		Auburn	32	45
S23		at Tulsa	14	24
S30	●	Air Force	34	21
O7	● |	Oklahoma State	18	7
O14	|	at Nebraska	14	48
O21	|	Missouri	14	56
O28	|	at Oklahoma	19	56
N4	|	at Iowa State	0	24
N11	● |	Colorado	20	10
N18	● |	Kansas	36	20

1979 3-8-0 (1-6-0)

S15		at Auburn	18	26
S22	●	Oregon State	22	16
S29	●	at Air Force	19	6
O6		Tulsa	6	9
O13	|	Iowa State	3	7
O20	|	Oklahoma	6	38
O27	● |	at Missouri	19	3
N3	|	at Kansas	28	36
N10	|	Nebraska	12	21
N17	|	at Oklahoma State	15	42
N24	|	at Colorado	6	21

1980 3-8-0 (1-6-0)

S13		at LSU	0	21
S20	●	South Dakota	24	3
S27	●	Arkansas State	31	7
O4		at Tulsa	0	3
O11	|	at Iowa State	7	31
O18	|	at Oklahoma	21	35
O25	|	Missouri	3	13
N1	|	Kansas	18	20 †
N8	|	at Nebraska	8	55
N15	|	Oklahoma State	0	10
N22	● |	Colorado	17	14

1981 2-9-0 (1-6-0)

S12	●	South Dakota	31	10
S19		at Washington	3	20
S26		Drake	17	18
O3		at Tulsa	21	35
O10	|	at Missouri	13	58
O17	|	Nebraska	3	49
O24	|	at Kansas	14	17
O31	● |	Iowa State	10	7
N7	|	Oklahoma	21	28
N14	|	at Oklahoma State	10	31
N21	|	at Colorado	21	24

1982 6-5-1 (3-3-1)

S11	●	Kentucky	23	9
S18	●	South Dakota	42	3
S25	●	Wichita St.	31	7
O2		at Arizona State	7	30
O9	= |	Missouri	7	7
O16	|	at Nebraska	13	42
O23	● |	Kansas	36	7
O30	● |	at Iowa State	9	3
N6	|	at Oklahoma	10	24
N13	|	Oklahoma State	16	24
N20	● |	Colorado	33	10
		INDEPENDENCE BOWL		
D11		Wisconsin	3	14

1983 — 3-8-0 (1-6-0)

Date		Opponent		
S3		Long Beach St.	20	28
S10		at Kentucky	12	31
S17	•	TCU	20	3
S24	•	Wyoming	27	25
O1	|	Oklahoma	10	29
O15	|	at Kansas	3	31
O22	|	at Missouri	0	38
O29	|	Nebraska	25	51
N5	• |	at Oklahoma State	21	20
N12	|	Iowa State	27	49
N19	|	at Colorado	21	38

1984 — 3-7-1 (2-4-1)

Date		Opponent		
S8		at Vanderbilt	14	26
S15	•	Tennessee Tech	28	12
S22		at TCU	10	42
S29	|	at Oklahoma	6	24
O6		at South Carolina	17	49
O13	• |	Kansas	24	7
O20	|	Missouri	21	61
O27	|	at Nebraska	14	62
N3	|	Oklahoma State	6	34
N10	= |	at Iowa State	7	7
N17	• |	Colorado	38	6

LEE MOON
1985 (.111) 1-8

1985 — 1-10-0 (1-6-0)

Date		Opponent		
S7		Wichita St.	10	16
S14		Northern Iowa	6	10
S21		TCU	22	24
S28		North Texas	10	22
O5	|	Oklahoma	6	41
O19	|	at Kansas	7	38
O26	• |	at Missouri	20	17
N2	|	Nebraska	3	41
N9	|	at Oklahoma State	3	35
N16	|	Iowa State	14	21
N23	|	at Colorado	0	30

STAN PARRISH
1986-88 (.076) 2-30-1

1986 — 2-9-0 (1-6-0)

Date		Opponent		
A30	•	Western Illinois	35	7
S6		at Texas Tech	7	41
S13		Northern Iowa	0	17
S20		at TCU	22	35
O4	|	at Oklahoma	10	56
O18	• |	Kansas	29	12
O25	|	Missouri	6	17
N1	|	at Nebraska	0	38
N8	|	Oklahoma State	3	23
N15	|	at Iowa State	19	48
N22	|	Colorado	3	49

1987 — 0-10-1 (0-6-1)

Date		Opponent		
S5		Austin Peay	22	26
S19		Army	14	41
S26		at Iowa	13	38
O3		Tulsa	25	37
O10	|	at Missouri	10	34
O17	|	Oklahoma	10	59
O24	|	at Nebraska	3	56
O31	|	at Oklahoma State	7	56
N7	= |	Kansas	17	17
N14	|	at Iowa State	14	16
N21	|	Colorado	0	41

1988 — 0-11-0 (0-7-0)

Date		Opponent		
S3		at Tulsa	9	35
S10		Iowa	10	45
S17		at Tulane	16	20
O1		Louisiana Tech	28	31
O8	|	Missouri	21	52
O15	|	at Oklahoma	24	70
O22	|	Nebraska	3	48
O29	|	Oklahoma State	27	45
N5	|	at Kansas	12	30
N12	|	Iowa State	7	16
N19	|	at Colorado	14	56

BILL SNYDER
1989-Present (.678) 131-62-1

1989 — 1-10-0 (0-7-0)

Date		Opponent		
S9		at Arizona State	0	31
S16		Northern Iowa	8	10
S23		Northern Illinois	20	37
S30	•	North Texas	20	17
O7	|	at Nebraska	7	58
O14	|	at Oklahoma State	13	17
O21	|	Missouri	9	21
O28	|	Kansas	16	21
N4	|	at Iowa State	11	36
N11	|	at Oklahoma	19	42
N18	|	Colorado	11	59

1990 — 5-6-0 (2-5-0)

Date		Opponent		
S8	•	Western Illinois	27	6
S15	•	New Mexico St.	52	7
S22		at Northern Illinois	35	42
S29	•	New Mexico	38	6
O6		Nebraska	8	45
O13	•	Oklahoma State	23	17
O20		at Missouri	10	31
O27		at Kansas	24	27
N3	•	Iowa State	28	14
N10		at Oklahoma	7	34
N17		at Colorado	3	64

1991 — 7-4-0 (4-3-0)

Date		Opponent		
S7	•	Indiana St.	26	25
S14	•	Idaho St.	41	7
S21	•	Northern Illinois	34	17
S28		at Washington	3	56
O12	•	Kansas	16	12
O19		at Nebraska	31	38
O26		Colorado	0	10
N2		at Oklahoma	7	28
N9	•	at Iowa State	37	7
N16	•	Missouri	32	0
N23		at Oklahoma State	36	26

1992 — 5-6-0 (2-5-0)

Date		Opponent		
S19	•	Montana	27	12
S26	•	Temple	35	14
O3	•	New Mexico St.	19	0
O10		at Kansas	7	31
O17		at Utah State	16	28
O24		at Colorado	7	54
O31		at Oklahoma	14	16
N5	•	Iowa State	22	13
N14		at Missouri	14	27
N21	•	Oklahoma State	10	0
D6		Nebraska Tok	24	38

1993 — 9-2-1 (4-2-1)

Date		Opponent		
S4	•	New Mexico St.	34	10
S11	•	Western Kentucky	38	13
S18	•	at Minnesota	30	25
S25	•	Nevada-Las Vegas	36	20
O9	•	Kansas	10	9
O16		at Nebraska	28	45
O23	=	Colorado	16	16
O30	•	Oklahoma	21	7
N6	•	at Iowa State	23	27
N13	•	Missouri	31	21
N20	•	at Oklahoma State	21	17
COPPER BOWL				
D29	•	Wyoming	52	17

1994 — 9-3-0 (5-2-0)

Date		Opponent		
S3	•	La. Lafayette	34	6
S17	•	Rice	27	18
S24	•	Minnesota	35	0
O6		at Kansas	21	13
O15	|	Nebraska	6	17
O22	|	at Colorado	21	35
O29	• |	at Oklahoma	37	20
N5	• |	Iowa State	38	20
N12	• |	at Missouri	21	18
N19	• |	Oklahoma State	23	6
N26	• |	at Nevada-Las Vegas	42	3
ALOHA BOWL				
D25	•	Boston College	7	12

1995 — 10-2-0 (5-2-0)

Date		Opponent		
S2	•	Temple	34	7
S9	•	at Cincinnati	23	21
S23	•	Akron	67	0
S30	•	Northern Illinois	44	0
O7	• |	Missouri	30	0
O14	• |	at Oklahoma State	23	17
O21	|	at Nebraska	25	49
O28	• |	Kansas	41	7
N4	• |	Oklahoma	49	10
N11	• |	at Iowa State	49	7
N18	|	Colorado	17	27
HOLIDAY BOWL				
D29	•	Colorado State	54	21

1996-PRESENT
BIG 12

1996 — 9-3 (6-2)

Date		Opponent		
A31	• |	Texas Tech	21	14
S7	• |	Indiana St.	59	3
S14	• |	Cincinnati	35	0
S21	• |	at Rice	34	7
O5	|	Nebraska	3	39
O12	• |	at Missouri	35	10
O19	• |	at Texas A&M	23	20
O26	• |	Oklahoma	42	35
N9	• |	at Kansas	38	12
N16	|	at Colorado	0	12
N23	• |	Iowa State	35	20
COTTON BOWL				
J1	|	Brigham Young	15	19

1997 — 11-1 (7-1)

Date		Opponent		
S6	• |	at Northern Illinois	47	7
S13	• |	Ohio U.	23	20
S27	• |	Bowling Green	58	0
O4	|	Nebraska	26	56
O11	• |	at Missouri	41	11
O18	• |	Texas A&M	36	17
O25	• |	at Oklahoma	26	7
N1	• |	at Texas Tech	13	2
N8	• |	Kansas	48	16
N15	• |	Colorado	37	20
N22	• |	at Iowa State	28	3
FIESTA BOWL				
D31	• |	Syracuse	35	18

1998 — 11-2 (8-0)

Date		Opponent		
S5	• |	Indiana St.	66	0
S12	• |	Northern Illinois	73	7
S19	• |	Texas	48	7
S26	• |	La. Monroe	62	7
O10	• |	at Colorado	16	9
O17	• |	Oklahoma State	52	20
O24	• |	Iowa State	52	7
O31	• |	at Kansas	54	6
N7	• |	at Baylor	49	6
N14	• |	Nebraska	40	30
N21	• |	at Missouri	31	25
BIG 12 CHAMPIONSHIP				
D5	|	Texas A&M StL	33	36
ALAMO BOWL				
D29	• |	Purdue	34	37

1999 — 11-1 (7-1)

Date		Opponent		
S11	• |	Temple	40	0
S18	• |	Texas El Paso	40	7
S25	• |	at Iowa State	35	28
O2	• |	at Texas	35	17
O9	• |	Kansas	50	9
O16	• |	Utah State	40	0
O23	• |	at Oklahoma State	44	21
O30	• |	Baylor	48	7
N6	• |	Colorado	20	14
N13	• |	at Nebraska	15	41
N20	|	Missouri	66	0
HOLIDAY BOWL				
D29	• |	Washington	24	20

2000 — 11-3 (6-2)

Date		Opponent		
A26	• |	Iowa KC	27	7
S2	• |	Louisiana Tech	54	10
S16	• |	Ball State	76	0
S23	• |	North Texas	55	10
S30	• |	at Colorado	44	21
O7	• |	at Kansas	52	13
O14	• |	Oklahoma	31	41
O21	• |	Texas Tech	28	23
O28	• |	at Texas A&M	10	26
N4	• |	Iowa State	56	10
N11	• |	Nebraska	29	28
N18	• |	at Missouri	28	24
BIG 12 CHAMPIONSHIP				
D2	|	Oklahoma KC	24	27
COTTON BOWL				
J1	• |	Tennessee	35	21

2001 — 6-6 (3-5)

Date		Opponent		
S8	• |	at Southern Cal	10	6
S22	• |	New Mexico St.	64	0
S29	• |	at Oklahoma	37	38
O6	|	Colorado	6	16
O13	|	at Texas Tech	19	38
O20	|	Texas A&M	24	31
O27	• |	Kansas	40	6
N3	• |	at Iowa State	42	3
N10	|	at Nebraska	21	31
N17	• |	Louisiana Tech	40	7
N24	• |	Missouri	24	3
INSIGHT. COM				
D29	|	Syracuse	3	26

2002 — 11-2 (6-2)

Date		Opponent		
A31	• |	Western Kentucky	48	3
S7	• |	La. Monroe	68	0
S14	• |	Eastern Illinois	63	13
S21	• |	Southern Cal	27	20
O5	|	at Colorado	31	35
O12	• |	Oklahoma State	44	9
O19	|	Texas	14	17
O26	• |	at Baylor	44	10
N2	• |	at Kansas	64	0
N9	• |	Iowa State	58	7
N16	• |	Nebraska	49	13
N23	• |	at Missouri	38	0
HOLIDAY BOWL				
D27	• |	Arizona State	34	27

2003 — 11-4 (6-2)

Date		Opponent		
A23	• |	California KC	42	28
A30	• |	Troy State	41	5
S6	• |	McNeese State	55	14
S13	• |	Massachusetts	38	7
S20	• |	Marshall	20	27
O4	|	at Texas	20	24
O11	• |	at Oklahoma State	34	38
O18	• |	Colorado	49	20
O25	• |	Kansas	42	6
N1	• |	Baylor	38	10
N8	• |	at Iowa State	45	0
N15	• |	at Nebraska	38	9
N22	• |	Missouri	24	14
BIG 12 CHAMPIONSHIP				
D6	|	Oklahoma KC	35	7
FIESTA BOWL				
J2	|	Ohio State	28	35

2004 — 4-7 (2-6)

Date		Opponent		
S4	• |	W. Kentucky	27	13
S11	• |	Fresno State	21	45
S18	• |	La. Lafayette	40	20
O2	|	at Texas A&M	30	42
O9	|	at Kansas	28	31
O16	|	Oklahoma	21	31
O23	• |	Nebraska	45	21
O30	|	Texas Tech	25	35
N6	• |	at Missouri	35	24
N13	|	at Colorado	31	38
N20	|	Iowa State	23	37

KENT STATE

BY ED KRZEMIENSKI

KENT STATE UNIVERSITY SITS IN northeastern Ohio, one of the nation's premier regions for football recruiting. It maintains state-of-the-art athletic facilities, and has a football-mad student body the size of most Big Ten schools—all of the ingredients necessary for a successful program. Yet the Golden Flashes have been to just two bowl games, have won just one conference title in 54 years and own Division I-A football's lowest overall winning percentage. However, the school has a proud coaching tradition, which includes Trevor Rees and Don James. The latest to try to push Kent State to the top of the Mid-American Conference is Doug Martin, who had served as Kent State's offensive coordinator and took over as head coach prior to the 2004 season, inheriting a team that had won only 17 games over the previous six years.

TRADITION Kent State plays two trophy games, one against Akron for the Wagon Wheel and the other against Bowling Green for the Anniversary Award. Periodically, Kent and Youngstown State play in the Schwebel Challenge Series, named after the Schwebel Baking Company. The Flashes now play in front of a sea of gold, thanks in large part to a campaign to popularize the team's new logo, Flash the Golden Eagle. Since 2001, KSU has sold more than 30,000 gold T-shirts, worn by fans at KSU home games.

BEST PLAYER Recruited out of Crestwood (Ohio) High School as a quarterback, Jack Lambert played linebacker for the rest of his career. At Kent he led the Flashes in tackles in each of his three varsity years, from 1971 to 1973, was a unanimous All-MAC selection his last two years and won the Vern Smith Award as MAC Player of the Year in 1972. Defensive coach Dennis Fitzgerald remarked that Lambert "had complete disdain for pain … He played in one game with hip-pointers on both hips, a bruised chest and a swollen elbow." And head coach James summed up Lambert's intensity as well as anyone when he quipped, "Every time they gain an inch, he feels responsible."

BEST COACH Before heading west to become head coach of the University of Washington in 1975, Don James stopped off at Kent State to jump-start its floundering football program. Inheriting a team that had gone 34–60–3 over the previous 10 years, James immediately led the Flashes to a 3–8 season in 1971. But he got better—in 1972, he coached the Flashes to a 6–5–1 season that included the school's first MAC championship, a Tangerine Bowl appearance and MAC Coach of the Year

---

PROFILE

Kent State University
Kent, Ohio
Founded: 1910
Enrollment: 19,173
Colors: Navy Blue and Gold
Nickname: Golden Flashes
Stadium: Dix Stadium
    Opened in 1969
    AstroTurf; 29,287 capacity
First football game: 1920
All-time record: 286–452–28 (.392)
Mid-American Conference championships:
1 (outright)
Website: www.kentstatesports.com

THE BEST OF TIMES

From 1946 to 1956, the team had no losing and 10 winning seasons and an appearance in the 1954 Refrigerator Bowl (honest). In 1972, during the Jack Lambert and Larry Poole years, the school won its only MAC championship and a Tangerine Bowl berth.

THE WORST OF TIMES

Most others, but especially 1978-85, when the team went 20–68, and 1989-93, an even worse stretch with a cumulative record of 5–50. The former era ended tragically in 1986, when head coach Dick Scesniak died of a heart attack while running around the stadium.

CONFERENCE

KSU joined the Mid-American Conference in 1951, five years after the league's charter. Prior to joining the MAC, Kent State played independently from 1920 to 1930 as Kent State Normal College and in the Ohio Conference from 1931 to 1950 (as Kent State College until 1935 and as Kent State University afterward). The school is currently in the East Division of the MAC.

DISTINGUISHED ALUMNI

Lou Holtz; Drew Carey, comedian; Arsenio Hall, comedian; Chrissie Hynde, musician; Michael Keaton, actor; Joe Walsh, musician

FIGHT SONG

KENT STATE FIGHT SONG
Fight on for KSU;
Fight for the Blue and Gold.
We're out to beat the foe;
Fight on brave and bold.
Fight on to victory;
Don't stop 'til we're through.
We're all together;
Let's go forward KSU!

honors for James. The next year the Flashes went 9–2; in 1974, they were 7–4. James left for Seattle with a 25–19–1 career record at Kent State—22 of those wins in his last three years. James was inducted into the College Football Hall of Fame in 1998.

BEST TEAM The 1972 Flashes won the MAC and appeared in the Tangerine Bowl, but the 1973 team was even better. Like the year before, Kent State went 4–1 in MAC play, but unlike the 1972 team, it had a winning record in out-of-conference games, including a 10-3 win over Louisville to begin the season, and finished with a 9–2 record. On defense, Lambert served as a senior captain, led the team in tackles and received unanimous first-team All-MAC honors. Joining him from a defense that gave up an average of 11.9 points per game on the first team All-MAC team defense were defensive linemen Walt Vrabel and Larry Faulk (the future Abdul Salaam of New York Jets Sack Exchange fame). The 1973 team had an offense to go with its stingy defense: Larry Poole ran for over 1,000 yards and scored 18 touchdowns, and Greg Kokal threw

> *The 1954 team earned a trip to the Refrigerator Bowl—the players actually ran through a backless refrigerator placed on the field before the game.*

for 1,776 yards. All told, the 1973 Flashes placed 18 players on the three All-MAC lists. KSU's only conference loss was 20-10 against undefeated Miami (Ohio), which finished 15th in the final AP poll. Had there been more bowl games in 1973, this Flashes team would certainly have received a bid.

BIGGEST GAME The Flashes finished the 1972 season needing a victory over Toledo to claim the MAC championship. In front of a frenzied home crowd, Kent State held a 6-3 lead at the break, but blew the game open in the second half. Eddie Woodard started the second half with a 95-yard kickoff return for a touchdown, Poole ran for a game-high 144 yards and two touchdowns and Lambert had 15 tackles and 14 assists on defense. The final score was 27-9, and Kent State got its first and as yet only conference title.

BIGGEST UPSET In 1972, the Flashes traveled to Bowling Green with a 1–3–1 record and little hope of salvaging a successful season. Bowling Green, on the other

RECORDS

RUSHING YARDS

	GAME
373	Astron Whatley vs. Eastern Michigan, Sept. 20, 1997 (42 att.)
	SEASON
1,325	Eric Wilkerson, 1988 (247 att.)
	CAREER
3,989	Astron Whatley, 1994-97 (878 att.)

PASSING YARDS

	GAME
551	Jose Davis vs. Central Florida, Oct. 4, 1997 (32 of 51)
	SEASON
2,707	Jose Davis, 1997 (194 of 365)
	CAREER
7,169	Joshua Cribbs, 2001-04 (616 of 1,123)

RECEIVING YARDS

	GAME
243	Eugene Baker at Western Michigan, Nov. 16, 1996 (14 rec.)
	SEASON
1,549	Eugene Baker, 1997 (103 rec.)
	CAREER
3,513	Eugene Baker, 1995-98 (229 rec.)

POINTS

	GAME
30	Jack Mancos vs. Western Michigan, Sept. 22, 1951 (5 TDs); Carmen Falcone vs. Buffalo, Oct. 22, 1938 (5 TDs)
	SEASON
110	Eugene Baker, 1997 (18 TDs, 1 two-pt. conv.)
	CAREER
246	Joshua Cribbs, 2001-04 (41 TDs)

CONSENSUS ALL-AMERICANS

None

hand, was 3–0–1, including an opening-game victory over Purdue. The Flashes won the game 14-10 and turned their season around, winning five of their last six games to claim the conference title.

HEARTBREAKER In 1972, following its MAC championship, Kent State traveled to Orlando to play the University of Tampa in the Tangerine Bowl—its first Division I postseason appearance. In what would have been a fitting conclusion to a great turnaround season (the Flashes went 0–5 in the MAC the previous year), Kent State fell short of victory by three points, losing 21-18.

STADIUM Kent State plays its games at Dix Stadium, a 29,287-capacity facility named for Robert C. Dix, a former member of the Kent State Board of Trustees. Although used the previous year, Dix Stadium was officially dedicated on Sept. 19, 1970, in a game against Ohio University, and sported natural grass until 1997, when the school changed the surface to artificial turf.

RIVAL Located just 14 miles apart, the students of Kent State and the University of Akron share a lot of stomping grounds. Naturally, this interaction extends to the football field, where many players and fans rekindle rivalries at the collegiate level. Every year the teams play for the Wagon Wheel trophy, a game based on a legendary story in which the founder of the forerunner to the University of Akron lost a wheel in the mud at the present-day site of Kent State. Found in 1902, the wheel became the reward for the winner in 1946 when it was painted blue and gold. That neither team has played well in recent years makes the rivalry all the more significant. Akron leads the series 26-19-2 (through 2004).

NICKNAME Although it started out as Kent State Normal School, no one can accuse Kent State of normality when it comes to its nickname, the Golden Flashes. There is some debate as to who should be credited with its origin. Originally dubbed the Silver Foxes by university president John McGilvrey, the school offered a $25 prize in a 1926 contest for a new name following McGilvrey's dismissal. Golden Flashes won and was first used by the basketball team in 1927. Another story reports that Oliver Wolcott, sports editor of the *Kent Courier Tribune*, thought the name Silver Foxes a bit delicate for the gridiron and began referring to the football team as the Golden Flashes beginning, conveniently for school historians, in 1927.

Regardless of its absolute origin, 1927 saw the birth of one of collegiate football's most colorful and unique nicknames.

MASCOT Now the more important question: what exactly is a Golden Flash and how does a team create a mascot from such an intangible name? Moreover, how does one invest a Golden Flash with a sense of force? Whether prompted by a contest winner or newspaper editor, the 1927 name-change did not raise the bar much in terms of ferocity. Ultimately, though, the school came up with a choice both accurate and daunting. Flash the Golden Eagle is represented by a costumed student and was briefly symbolized by an actual eagle after 9/11.

UNIFORMS Thank god for hot water. In 1910, the school's official colors were, by state charter, purple and orange. When washing the basketball uniforms, though, a local laundry faded the obnoxious combination to a more palatable blue and gold. Needless to say, the athletes and student body found the harsh wash an undeniable improvement. With the arrival of the moniker Golden Flashes 17 years later, the uniforms happily, if accidentally, matched the team's nickname. As helmet technology improved, Kent State used, variously, Kent, KSU and K on the side of the headgear. Most famously, Kent State used a golden lightning bolt that in various seasons mimicked precisely the helmet design of the NFL's San Diego Chargers. Currently, the team combines its three most prominent logos on a blue helmet: an uppercase K atop an image of Flash the Golden Eagle, which has a lightning bolt tail. On the shoulders and along the pant-leg run lightning bolts—gold on blue at home and blue on white for road games.

QUIRK After not fielding a team in the final two years of World War II, Kent State experienced a bit of a renaissance, racking up 13 winning seasons from 1946 to 1960. The 1954 team earned a trip to Evansville, Ind., to play the University of Delaware in the Refrigerator Bowl—the players actually ran through a backless refrigerator placed on the field before the game. The Blue Hens defeated the Golden Flashes, 19-7.

NUMBERS In 2001, Joshua Cribbs became the first freshman in Division I-A history to run and pass for 1,000 yards each in a single season. He repeated the feat in his sophomore season, and then attempted to become the

first player to achieve a three-peat. Cribbs, however, fell short with 701 yards rushing in 2003.

TRAGEDY It is impossible and improper to discuss any aspect of Kent State University without mentioning the events of May 4, 1970. No American college is identified more with a single event in its history than Kent State. That day, in the wake of a student protest over the American invasion of Cambodia, Ohio National Guardsmen shot into a crowd of students, killing four and wounding nine. Understandably and correctly, nothing will ever surpass this event as the defining and illustrative moment in Kent State's history. In 1986, the football team endured its own misfortune when head coach Dick Scesniak died of a heart attack while jogging around the stadium.

QUOTE "You'd better hope he goes outside the Mid-American Conference, because someday he's gonna come back and beat you."—Gerry Myers, high school coach of Jack Lambert, to Miami (Ohio) head coach Bill Mallory, who rejected Lambert for being too slow. Three years later, Lambert made four straight tackles inside the 2-yard line against the Redskins

KENT STATE ALL-TIME SCORES

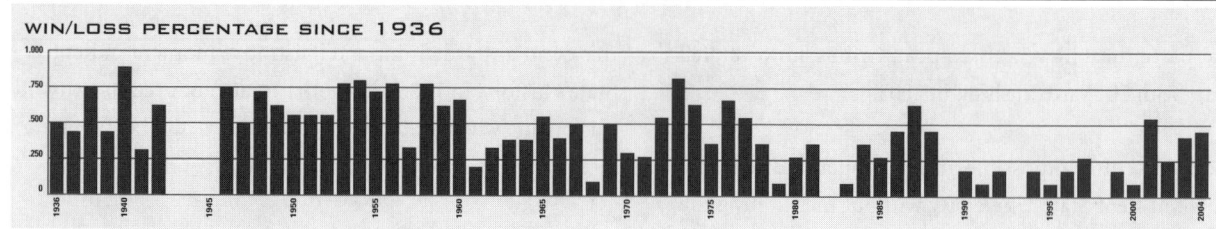

WIN/LOSS PERCENTAGE SINCE 1936

PAUL G. CHANDLER
1920-22 (.115)   **1-11-1**

1920   1-2-0
O30	at Ashland	0	6
N6	Bowling Green	0	7
U ●	St. Ignatius	1	0 *f*

1921   0-2-1
O1 =	Bowling Green	0	0
U	John Carroll	0	13
U	Ashland	0	7

1922   0-7-0
U	at Hiram	0	14
U	at Mt. Union	0	32
U	St. Ignatius	0	34
U	Ashland	0	14
U	at Baldwin-Wallace	0	32
U	at California, Pa.	0	14
N11	Bowling Green	0	6

FRANK HARSH
1923-24 (.000)   **0-9**

1923   0-5-0
U	at Akron	0	32
U	at Baldwin-Wallace	0	118
U	West Liberty	6	7
U	Slippery Rock	0	82
U	Indiana STC	0	21

1924   0-4-0
U	Indiana STC	0	29
U	at Ashland	0	20
U	Hiram	0	14
U	at West Liberty	0	26

MERLE WAGONER
1925-32 (.342)   **15-33-9**

1925   1-1-3
U =	Hiram	0	0
U =	at Edinboro	0	0
U =	at Indiana STC	6	6
N14 ●	West Liberty	7	6
U	Findlay	0	12

1926   2-6-0
S25	at Wittenberg	0	27
O9	West Liberty	2	25
O16	at Heidelberg	0	25
O23	at Ashland	0	55
O30 ●	Edinboro	12	0
N6	at Findlay	6	7
N13	Indiana STC	0	23
N20 ●	Wilmington	15	14

1927   1-5-1
S24 =	at Kenyon	6	6
O8	Slippery Rock	0	6
O15	Bowling Green	0	13
O22 ●	Cedarville	19	18
N5	Edinboro *Unk*	0	6
N12	at Indiana STC	0	7
N19	at Wilmington	0	24

1928   4-2-2
S29 ●	at Kenyon	25	6
O6	at John Carroll	0	12
O13 =	at Defiance	0	0
O20	at Akron	6	8
O27 ●	Cedarville	26	0
N3 ●	Rio Grande	13	0
N10 ●	Indiana STC	13	0
N26 =	at Bowling Green	6	6

1929   1-7-0
S28	at Oberlin	0	19
O5	at Akron	0	25
O12	at Heidelberg	2	25
O19	at Kenyon	15	21
O25	at John Carroll	0	32
N11 ●	Rio Grande	3	0
N16	Baldwin-Wallace	0	18
N23	at Indiana STC	0	21

1930   3-3-1
O3	at Mt. Union	6	18
O11	at Akron	6	12
O18	at Case Tech	0	6
O25 =	Ashland	0	0
N1 ●	Hiram	6	0
N8 ●	at Capital	33	0
N15 ●	Defiance	13	6

1931   3-4-0
O3	at Oberlin	6	12
O10	at Akron	6	12
O16	at Mt. Union	0	25
O31	at Baldwin-Wallace	0	31
N7 ●	Capital	33	0
N14 ●	Otterbein	6	0
N21 ●	Hiram	7	0

1932   0-5-2
S22	Hiram	0	6
O8	Otterbein	0	19
O15	Baldwin-Wallace	0	21
O22 =	at Akron	0	0
O29	at John Carroll	0	28
N5 =	at Capital	0	0
N12	Ashland	0	6

JOE BEGALA
1933-34 (.467)   **4-5-6**

1933   2-2-3
S29	at Muskingum	0	12
O7	Akron	6	19
O14 ●	Capital	13	0
O20 =	at Ashland	0	0
O28 =	at Hiram	0	0
N4 ●	Marietta	12	0
N18 =	Mt. Union	0	0

1934   2-3-3
S28 =	at Muskingum	6	6
O6	at Akron	0	26
O13 =	at Bowling Green	0	0
O20 ●	Otterbein	7	6
O27 =	Ashland	0	0
N3 ●	Hiram	26	6
N10	Baldwin-Wallace	0	39
N18	at Mt. Union	6	7

G. DONALD STARN
1935-42 (.546)   **34-28-3**

1935   3-5-0
S27	at Mt. Union	0	19
O5	Heidlberg	6	21
O11	at Akron	0	3
O19 ●	Otterbein	6	0
O26 ●	Bowling Green	45	0
N2 ●	at Hiram	45	6
N9	at Baldwin-Wallace	18	40
N16	at Ashland	7	19

1936   4-4-0
S25 ●	at John Carroll	34	7
O3	Heidelberg	0	19
O9	at Akron	0	6
O17	at Ohio U.	0	6
O24 ●	at Bowling Green	6	0
O30 ●	at Findlay	19	0
N7	Marietta	12	14
N14 ●	Ashland	14	7

1937   3-4-1
S25	at Baldwin-Wallace	0	13
O2	Heidelberg	7	13
O9 ●	Otterbein	13	6
O16	at Wooster	6	15
O25	at John Carroll	0	13
O30 =	Bowling Green	13	13
N6 ●	Findlay	26	0
N11 ●	at Ashland	14	0

1938   6-2-0
S24 ●	Albion	17	0
O1 ●	at Heidelberg	22	6
O7 ●	at Findlay	13	7
O15 ●	Holbrook	49	0
O22 ●	Buffalo	54	0
O28	at John Carroll	6	27
N5 ●	at Bowling Green	7	3
N11	Baldwin-Wallace	6	26

1939   3-4-1
S30 ●	Lawrence Tech	20	6
O7 ●	Heidelberg	19	0
O14 =	at Mt. Union	6	6
O21	Findlay	7	10
O28 ●	at Hobart	8	6
N4	Bowling Green	0	34
N11	at Western Reserve	0	38
N18	at Baldwin-Wallace	6	40

1940   8-1-0
S21 ●	Bluffton	37	0
S28 ●	Assumption	26	0
O5 ●	Hiram	26	0
O12 ●	Mt. Union	26	0
O18 ●	at Findlay	13	0
O26 ●	at Wash & Jeff	31	0
N2 ●	at Bowling Green	13	0
N9	at Akron	7	23
N16 ●	at Baldwin-Wallace	14	7

1941   2-5-1
S27 ●	Bluffton	58	0
O3 ●	at Findlay	26	0
O10	at Case Tech	6	7
O17 =	West Liberty	0	0
O24	at Western Reserve	0	28
N1	Bowling Green	6	12
N8	John Carroll	0	12
N15	at Akron	13	41

1942   5-3-0
S26	at Toledo	14	26
O3 ●	Findlay	6	0
O10	at Miami, Ohio	7	53
O17 ●	Patterson Field	24	0
O24	Western Reserve	13	28
O31 ●	at Bowling Green	7	0
N7 ●	at Hiram	20	0
N14 ●	at Akron	23	6

1943-45
NO TEAM—WWII

TREVOR J. REES
1946-63 (.591)   **92-63-5**

1946   6-2-0
S28 ●	at Hiram	40	0
O5 ●	at John Carroll	20	7
O12 ●	Bluffton	39	0
O19	Bowling Green	0	13
O26	at Baldwin-Wallace	12	21
N2 ●	at Kalamazoo	12	0
N9 ●	at Ohio Wesleyan	7	0
N16	at Akron	13	6

1947   4-4-0
S27 ●	at Mt. Union	13	6
O4	Miami, Ohio	7	35
O11	at Wooster	6	13
O18 ●	Kalamazoo	13	0
O25	at Bowling Green	18	21
N1 ●	John Carroll	26	7
N14 ●	Akron	6	0
N21	at Youngstown	0	13

1948   6-2-1
S24 ●	at Mt. Union	18	0
O2 ●	Wooster	39	0
O8 ●	Waynesburg	34	7
O16 ●	at Central Michigan	28	0
O23 =	at Western Reserve	14	14
O29 ●	Youngstown	7	19
N6	Bowling Green	14	23
N12 ●	at Akron	31	0
N20 ●	at Connecticut	42	26

1949   5-3-0
S23 ●	Western Reserve	20	23
S30 ●	Mt. Union	13	11
O7	at Ohio U.	6	34
O14 ●	Central Michigan	26	12
O29 ●	Connecticut	27	0
N5	at Bowling Green	6	27
N12 ●	Akron	47	0
N18 ●	at Northern Illinois	21	19

1950   5-4-0
S22	at Morris-Harvey	0	7
S29 ●	at Mt. Union	14	19
O7	at John Carroll	7	48
O14 ●	Marietta	57	0
O21 ●	Ohio U.	35	13
O27 ●	Northern Illinois	56	7
N4 ●	Bowling Green	19	6
N11 ●	at Akron	19	7
N18	at New Hampshire	7	13

1951-PRESENT
MAC

1951   4-3-2 (2-1-0)
S22 ●	at Western Michigan	48	19
S28 ●	Mt. Union	28	27
O6 ●	at Western Reserve	42	20
O13 ●	Bucknell	7	13
O20 ●	Morris-Harvey	14	14
O27 ●	at Ohio U.	27	28
N3 =	at Bowling Green	27	27
N10 ●	Akron	48	7
N17	New Hampshire	0	7

1952   5-4-0 (2-2-0)
S20 ●	Western Michigan	20	13
S26 ●	at Mt. Union	26	7
O3 ●	Western Reserve	25	19
O11 ●	at Baldwin-Wallace	13	19
O18 ●	Ohio U.	18	27
O25 ●	at Marshall	26	14
N1 ●	Bowling Green	21	44
N7 ●	at Akron	34	14
N15 ●	at New Hampshire	21	23

1953   7-2-0 (3-1-0)
S19 ●	at Waynesburg	20	10
S25 ●	Fort Belvoir	6	7
O3 ●	at Western Reserve	27	0
O9 ●	Baldwin-Wallace	14	13
O17 ●	at Ohio U.	21	40
O24 ●	Marshall	27	7
O31 ●	at Bowling Green	41	7
N7 ●	Akron	54	19
N14 ●	at Western Michigan	40	0

1954 8-2-0 (4-1-0)

S18	●	Waynesburg	26	0
O1	● |	Western Reserve	65	0
O8	●	at Baldwin-Wallace	52	7
O16	|	Ohio U.	7	14
O23	● |	at Marshall	41	20
O30	● |	Bowling Green	28	25
N6	●	at Akron	58	18
N13	●	John Carroll	27	14
N20	● |	Western Michigan	20	13
REFRIGERATOR BOWL				
D5		Delaware	7	19

1955 6-2-1 (4-1-1)

S23	= |	Bowling Green	6	6
O1		at Dayton	13	26
O7	●	Baldwin-Wallace	33	2
O15	● |	at Ohio U.	20	14
O22	● |	Marshall	39	6
O29	|	Miami, Ohio	7	19
N5	● |	at Toledo	27	0
N12	●	Waynesburg	14	0
N19	● |	at Western Michigan	25	14

1956 7-2-0 (4-2-0)

S22	|	at Bowling Green	0	17
S29	●	at Louisville	7	0
O6	●	Waynesburg	19	6
O13	● |	Ohio U.	32	13
O20	● |	at Marshall	25	7
O27	|	at Miami, Ohio	0	14
N3	● |	Toledo	52	6
N10	●	at Baldwin-Wallace	46	0
N17	● |	Western Michigan	27	13

1957 3-6-0 (1-5-0)

S21		at Xavier	7	13
S27	●	Baldwin-Wallace	26	13
O5	● |	at Ohio U.	14	9
O12	|	Miami, Ohio	14	27
O19	|	at Marshall	6	7
O26	|	Bowling Green	7	13
N2	|	at Toledo	7	21
N9	●	Louisville	13	7
N16	|	at Western Michigan	20	28

1958 7-2-0 (5-1-0)

S20	●	at Xavier	6	0
S27	●	at Baldwin-Wallace	21	14
O4	● |	Ohio U.	14	6
O11	|	at Miami, Ohio	0	35
O18	● |	Marshall	24	0
O25	● |	at Bowling Green	8	7
N1	● |	Toledo	32	6 *
N8		at Louisville	0	21
N15	● |	Western Michigan	32	6

1959 5-3-0 (3-3-0)

S25	●	Baldwin-Wallace	46	12
O3	|	at Ohio U.	0	46
O10	● |	Miami, Ohio	14	6
O17	● |	at Marshall	46	7
O24	|	Bowling Green	8	25
O31	● |	at Toledo	14	7
N7	|	at Western Michigan	0	7
N21	●	Louisville	16	14

1960 6-3-0 (4-2-0)

S24	●	at Baldwin-Wallace	16	6
O1	|	Ohio U.	8	25
O8	● |	at Miami, Ohio	22	19
O15	● |	Marshall	22	6
O22	|	at Bowling Green	0	28
O29	● |	Toledo	18	13
N5	● |	Western Michigan	10	3
N11		at Louisville	8	22
N19	●	at Dayton	14	7

1961 2-8-0 (1-5-0)

S16	●	Dayton	38	14
S23		at Xavier	8	16
S30	● |	at Ohio U.	23	17
O7	|	Miami, Ohio	0	21
O14	|	at Marshall	8	14
O21	|	Bowling Green	6	21
O28	|	at Toledo	22	31
N4	|	at Western Michigan	0	14
N11		Louisville	15	19
N18		Baldwin-Wallace	6	14

1962 3-6-0 (2-4-0)

S15	●	at Dayton	22	7
S22		Xavier	8	9
S29	|	Ohio U.	0	21
O6	|	at Miami, Ohio	14	23
O13	● |	Marshall	23	14
O20	|	at Bowling Green	6	45
O27	● |	Toledo	20	18
N3	|	Western Michigan	6	19
N10		at Louisville	8	29

1963 3-5-1 (1-5-0)

S28	=	at Xavier	7	7
O5	|	at Ohio U.	0	20
O12	|	Miami, Ohio	8	30
O19	|	at Western Michigan	12	26
O26	|	Bowling Green	3	18
N2	● |	at Toledo	20	0
N9	●	Louisville	26	7
N16	|	Marshall	8	14
N23	●	Dayton	23	0

LEO STRANG
1964-67 (.462) 17-20-2

1964 3-5-1 (1-4-1)

S26	●	Xavier	15	2
O3	= |	Ohio U.	3	3
O10	|	Miami, Ohio	14	17
O17	|	Western Michigan	9	12
O24	|	at Bowling Green	0	41
O31	● |	Toledo	14	11
N7	●	at Louisville	14	7
N14	|	at Marshall	7	12
N21		at Dayton	11	16

1965 5-4-1 (3-2-1)

S18		at Xavier	14	21
S25	●	Dayton	14	6
O2	● |	at Ohio U.	27	10
O9	● |	Miami, Ohio	24	13
O16	= |	at Western Michigan	10	10
O23	|	Bowling Green	6	7
O30	|	at Toledo	3	7
N6		at Penn State	6	21
N13	● |	Marshall	33	13
N20	●	Louisville	7	6

1966 4-6-0 (2-4-0)

S17		Buffalo	23	27
S25	●	at Northern Illinois	26	7
O1	|	Ohio U.	10	12
O8	|	at Miami, Ohio	0	7
O15	|	Western Michigan	20	23
O22	● |	at Bowling Green	35	12
O29	● |	Toledo	28	20
N5		at Louisville	20	23
N12	|	at Marshall	7	16
N19	●	Xavier	42	14

1967 5-5-0 (2-4-0)

S16		at Buffalo	6	30
S23	●	Northern Illinois	35	0
S30	● |	at Ohio U.	21	14 †
O7	|	Miami, Ohio	7	21
O14	|	at Western Michigan	7	16
O21	|	Bowling Green	6	7
O28	|	at Toledo	13	14
N4	●	Louisville	28	21
N11	● |	Marshall	41	2
N18	●	at Xavier	31	19

DAVE PUDDINGTON
1968-70 (.300) 9-21

1968 1-9-0 (1-5-0)

S14		at Dayton	10	24
S21		Buffalo	13	21
S28	|	Ohio U.	7	31
O5	|	at Miami, Ohio	0	24
O12	|	Western Michigan	0	14
O19	|	at Bowling Green	7	30
O26	|	Toledo	12	28
N2		at Louisville	9	23
N9	● |	at Marshall	36	12
N16		Xavier	7	23

1969 5-5-0 (1-4-0)

S13	●	Dayton	24	14
S20	|	at Ohio U.	0	35
S27	●	at Xavier	23	7
O4	●	at Buffalo	17	8
O11	|	at Western Michigan	13	33
O18	|	Bowling Green	0	7
O25	|	at Toledo	17	43
N1	●	Louisville	35	6
N8		Marshall	20	31
N15	● |	Miami, Ohio	17	14

1970 3-7-0 (1-4-0)

S19	|	Ohio U.	14	24
S26	●	Buffalo	27	21
O3		at Pittsburgh	6	27
O10	● |	Western Michigan	25	22
O17	|	at Bowling Green	0	44
O24	|	Toledo	17	34
O31		at Louisville	13	14
N7		at Marshall	17	20
N14	|	at Miami, Ohio	8	10
N21	●	Xavier	34	6

DON JAMES
1971-74 (.566) 25-19-1

1971 3-8-0 (0-5-0)

S11	●	at North Carolina St.	23	21
S18		at Cincinnati	20	42
S25	|	at Ohio U.	21	37
O2		Iowa State	14	17
O9	|	at Western Michigan	0	31
O16	|	Bowling Green	33	46
O23	●	at Xavier	24	13
O30		Northern Illinois	7	26
N6	●	Marshall	21	0
N13	|	Miami, Ohio	0	30
N20	|	at Toledo	6	41

1972 6-5-1 (4-1-0)

S9	=	at Akron	13	13
S16		at Louisville	0	34
S23	● |	Ohio U.	37	14
S30		San Diego State	0	14
O7	|	Western Michigan	12	13
O14	● |	at Bowling Green	14	10
O21	●	Xavier	26	16
O28		at Northern Illinois	7	28
N4	●	at Marshall	16	14
N11	● |	at Miami, Ohio	21	10
N18	● |	Toledo	27	9
TANGERINE BOWL				
D29		Tampa	18	21

1973 9-2-0 (4-1-0)

S15	●	Louisville	10	3
S22	● |	at Ohio U.	35	7
S30		at San Diego State	9	17
O6	● |	at Western Michigan	39	15
O13	● |	Bowling Green	21	7
O20	●	Eastern Michigan	34	20
O27	●	at Utah State	27	16
N3	●	Marshall	35	3
N10	|	Miami, Ohio	10	20
N17	● |	at Toledo	52	16
N24	●	Central Michigan	28	7

1974 7-4-0 (2-3-0)

S7	●	at Central Michigan	21	14
S14	●	at Syracuse	20	14
S21	|	Ohio U.	0	20
S28	●	at Eastern Michigan	13	0
O5	● |	Western Michigan	28	6
O12	|	at Bowling Green	10	26
O19		Utah State	24	27
O26	●	Akron	51	14
N2	●	at Marshall	35	7
N9	|	at Miami, Ohio	17	19
N16	● |	Toledo	35	14

DENNIS FITZGERALD
1975-77 (.529) 18-16

1975 4-7-0 (1-6-0)

S13	●	at La. Monroe	31	29
S20	●	Virginia Tech	17	11
S27	|	at Ohio U.	21	23
O4	|	at Northern Illinois	15	38
O11	● |	at Western Michigan	22	17
O18	|	Bowling Green CLEV	9	35
O25	|	Central Michigan	8	17
N1		at West Virginia	13	38
N8	●	Marshall	30	21
N15	|	Miami, Ohio	8	27
N22	|	at Toledo	28	33

1976 8-4-0 (6-2-0)

S11	● |	at Central Michigan	20	10
S18	|	Ohio U.	12	14
S25		at Iowa State	7	47
O2	●	Air Force	24	19
O9	● |	Western Michigan	24	12
O16	|	at Bowling Green	13	17
O23		at Virginia Tech	14	42
O30	● |	Eastern Michigan	38	13
N6	●	at Hawaii	27	6
N13	● |	at Miami, Ohio	24	17
N20	● |	Toledo	35	9
N25	● |	Northern Illinois	42	0

1977 6-5-0 (5-4-0)

S12	●	Illinois St.	33	14
S17		at Colorado	0	42
S24	● |	Ball State	13	12
O1	● |	at Ohio U.	44	23
O8	● |	at Western Michigan	20	16
O15	|	Bowling Green	10	14
O22	● |	at Eastern Michigan	29	13
O29	|	Northern Illinois	18	21
N5	|	Central Michigan	10	49
N12	|	Miami, Ohio	0	25
N19	● |	at Toledo	23	12

RON BLACKLEDGE
1978-80 (.242) 8-25

1978 4-7-0 (2-6-0)

S9	|	at Central Michigan	0	41
S16	|	at Ball State	3	27
S23	●	Illinois St.	34	3
S30	● |	Ohio U.	20	14
O7	|	Western Michigan	0	14
O14	|	at Bowling Green	20	28
O21	●	Marshall	20	17
O28		at Air Force	10	26
N4	|	at Northern Illinois	21	27
N11	|	at Miami, Ohio	13	38
N18	● |	Toledo	17	13

1979 1-10-0 (1-7-0)

S8		Eastern Kentucky	14	17
S15		at Akron	13	15
S22		Ball State	10	35
S29	|	at Ohio U.	13	43
O6	● |	at Western Michigan	18	13
O13	|	Bowling Green	17	28
O20	|	at Eastern Michigan	10	14
O27	|	Central Michigan	21	44
N3	|	at Northern Illinois	0	25
N10	|	Miami, Ohio	8	35
N17	|	at Toledo	3	29

1980 3-8-0 (3-6-0)

S13		at Marshall	7	17
S20		at Navy	3	31
S27	|	at Central Michigan	6	21
O4	● |	Ohio U.	15	14
O11	|	Western Michigan	21	28
O18	|	at Bowling Green	3	24
O25	● |	Eastern Michigan	35	12
N1	|	Northern Illinois	14	35
N8	|	at Ball State	7	34
N15	|	at Miami, Ohio	14	49
N22	● |	Toledo	34	14

ED CHLEBEK
1981-82 (.182) 4-18

1981 4-7-0 (3-6-0)

S12	|	Western Michigan	17	20
S19	●	Akron	17	6
S26		at Iowa State	19	28
O3	|	at Miami, Ohio	13	20
O10	● |	Northern Illinois	31	10
O17	● |	at Ball State	17	7
O24	|	at Central Michigan	3	24
O31	|	at Bowling Green	7	13
N7	● |	Eastern Michigan	13	7
N14	|	at Toledo	0	17
N21	|	Ohio U.	7	20

1982 0-11-0 (0-9-0)

S4		at Marshall	21	30
S18	|	at Northern Illinois	15	23
S25	|	at Western Michigan	14	24
O2	|	Miami, Ohio	0	20
O9		at Iowa State	7	44
O16	|	Ball State	3	21
O23	|	Central Michigan	20	31
O30	|	Bowling Green	7	41
N6	|	at Eastern Michigan	7	9
N13	|	Toledo	0	3
N20	|	at Ohio U.	20	24

DICK SCESNIAK
1983-85 (.242) 8-25

1983 1-10-0 (1-8-0)

S3		at Akron	6	13
S10		at Syracuse	10	22
S24	|	Northern Illinois	7	38
O1	|	at Central Michigan	7	13
O8	|	at Miami, Ohio	7	27
O15	|	Ball State	13	17
O22	|	Ohio U.	20	21
O29	|	at Toledo	34	37
N5	● |	Eastern Michigan	37	13
N12	|	Western MIchigan	13	21
N19	|	at Bowling Green	3	38

1984 4-7-0 (3-6-0)

S1	●	Akron	24	17
S8		at Kentucky	0	42
S22	|	at Northern Illinois	10	24
S29	|	Central Michigan	10	14
O6	|	Miami, Ohio	3	19
O13	● |	at Ball State	15	10
O20	● |	at Ohio U.	19	7
O27	● |	Toledo	17	6
N3	|	at Eastern Michigan	18	20
N10	|	at Western Michigan	9	13
N17	|	Bowling Green	10	27

THE SCHOOLS

1985 — 3-8-0 (2-6-0)

S14	at Akron	0	24
S21	at Syracuse	0	34
S28 •	Eastern Michigan	28	3
O5	at Central Michigan	17	21
O12	Texas-El Paso	51	24
O19	Ball State	45	16
O26	at Bowling Green	14	26
N2	Ohio U.	23	33
N9	at Miami, Ohio	24	52
N16	Western Michigan	3	34
N23	at Toledo	7	10

GLEN MASON — 1986-87 (.545) — 12-10

1986 — 5-6-0 (5-3-0)

S6 •	Toledo	18	16
S13	Akron	7	17
S20	at Kentucky	12	37
S27 •	at Eastern Michigan	20	16
O4 •	Central Michigan	33	30
O11	at Florida	9	52
O18	at Ball State	17	26
O25	Bowling Green	15	31
N1 •	at Ohio U.	17	13
N8 •	Miami, Ohio	24	23
N15	at Western Michigan	7	27

1987 — 7-4-0 (5-3-0)

S12 •	at Akron	27	23
S19 •	at Kansas	31	17
S26	Eastern Michigan	21	23
O3 •	Central Michigan	24	21
O10	at Ball State	23	24
O17 •	Western Michigan	27	13
O24 •	at Ohio U.	24	10
O31	Toledo	17	13
N7	at Bowling Green	20	30
N14 •	Miami, Ohio	14	10
N21	at Pittsburgh	5	28

DICK CRUM — 1988-90 (.212) — 7-26

1988 — 5-6-0 (3-5-0)

S3 •	Youngstown St.	34	3
S10 •	Akron	32	12
S17	at Eastern Michigan	14	21
S24	at Kentucky	14	38
O1	at Central Michigan	7	31
O8	Ball State	20	31
O15 •	at Western Michigan	45	28
O22	Ohio U.	14	21
O29	at Toledo	28	35
N5 •	Bowling Green	31	19
N12 •	at Miami, Ohio	17	11

1989 — 0-11-0 (0-8-0)

S2	at Eastern Michigan	7	30
S9	at Akron	7	40
S16	at Kansas	21	28
S23	Western Michigan	4	26
S30	at North Carolina St.	22	42
O7	at Central Michigan	0	38
O14	Ball State	21	23
O21	at Ohio U.	14	37
O28	Toledo	42	47
N4	at Bowling Green	28	51
N11	Miami, Ohio	13	15

1990 — 2-9-0 (2-6-0)

S1	at West Virginia	24	35
S8	Akron	10	38
S22	at Western Michigan	10	37
S29	Cincinnati	24	27
O6	Central Michigan	0	42
O13	at Ball State	0	31
O20 •	Ohio U.	44	15
O27	at Toledo	14	28
N3	Bowling Green	16	20
N10	at Miami, Ohio	10	31
N17 •	Eastern Michigan	25	24

PETE CORDELLI — 1991-93 (.091) — 3-30

1991 — 1-10-0 (1-7-0)

A31	at Western Michigan	10	13
S14	at North Carolina St.	0	47
S21	at Ball State	27	28
S28	at Kentucky	6	24
O5	Eastern Michigan	20	21
O12	Cincinnati	19	38
O19	Central Michigan	7	23
O26	at Ohio U.	40	45
N2 •	Toledo	14	13
N9	at Bowling Green	7	35
N16	Miami, Ohio	9	20

1992 — 2-9-0 (2-7-0)

S5	at Pittsburgh	10	51
S12	Ohio U.	14	27
S19	Ball State	6	10
S26 •	at Eastern Michigan	17	14
O3	at Cincinnati	0	31
O10 •	Akron	20	16
O17	at Central Michigan	0	35
O24	Western Michigan	13	26
O31	at Toledo	17	32
N7	Bowling Green	22	28
N14	at Miami, Ohio	14	31

1993 — 0-11-0 (0-9-0)

S4	at Kentucky	0	35
S11	at Akron	7	42
S18	at Hawaii	17	49
O2	Western Michigan	21	27
O9	at Eastern Michigan	15	20
O16	at Ohio U.	10	15
O23	Central Michigan	28	33
O30	Toledo	27	45
N6	at Bowling Green	7	40
N13	Miami, Ohio	14	23
N20	at Ball State	3	28

JIM CORRIGALL — 1994-97 (.193) — 8-35-1

1994 — 2-9-0 (2-7-0)

S3	at Rutgers	6	28
S17 •	Akron	32	16
S24	at Central Michigan	0	45
O1	at Western Michigan	10	24
O8	Eastern Michigan	10	24
O15	at Youngstown St.	14	28
O22 •	Ohio U.	24	0
O29	at Toledo	14	48
N5	Bowling Green	16	22
N12	at Miami, Ohio	14	24
N19	Ball State	0	34

1995 — 1-9-1 (0-7-1)

S2 •	Youngstown St.	17	14
S9	Miami, Ohio	0	39
S16 =	at Ohio U.	28	28
S23	at West Virginia	6	45
S30	Western Michigan	6	52
O7	at South Carolina	14	77
O21	at Central Michigan	16	27
O28	at Akron	6	14
N4	Ball State	13	28
N11	Bowling Green	15	26
N18	Eastern Michigan	7	40

1996 — 2-9 (1-7)

A31	at Miami, Ohio	6	64
S7	at Pittsburgh	14	52
S14 •	Youngstown St.	28	12
S28	at Nevada	42	63
O5 •	Akron	32	17
O12	at Bowling Green	24	31
O19	Ohio U.	15	24
O26	at Eastern Michigan	10	51
N2	Central Michigan	51	52
N9	at Ball State	6	50
N16	at Western Michigan	27	76

1997 — 3-8 (3-5)

A28	at Ohio U.	7	31
S6	at Youngstown St.	23	44
S13	Marshall	17	42
S20 •	at Eastern Michigan	41	38
O4	Central Florida	43	59
O11	Miami, Ohio	26	62
O18	at Western Michigan	27	50
O25 •	Central Michigan	60	37
N1 •	Bowling Green	29	20
N8	at Akron	35	45
N22	at Navy	29	62

DEAN PEES — 1998-2003 (.250) — 17-51

1998 — 0-11 (0-8)

S5	at Georgia	3	56
S12	Youngstown St.	10	24
S19	at Navy	24	38
S26	at Central Michigan	7	46
O3	Eastern Michigan	17	26
O10	Akron	16	45
O17	at Marshall	7	42
O24	at Bowling Green	21	42
O31	Western Michigan	23	48
N14	at Miami, Ohio	0	56
N21	Ohio U.	21	31

1999 — 2-9 (2-6)

S4	at Cincinnati	3	41
S11	Navy	28	48
S18	at Pittsburgh	23	30
S25 •	Bowling Green	41	27
O2	at Ohio U.	3	31
O9	at Toledo	7	47
O16	Miami, Ohio	10	17
O23	at Northern Illinois	7	50
O30 •	Buffalo	41	20
N6	Marshall	16	28
N13	at Akron	34	37

2000 — 1-10 (1-7)

S2	at Pittsburgh	7	30
S9	at Purdue	10	45
S16	Youngstown St.	20	26
S23	at Miami, Ohio	14	45
S30	Bowling Green	11	18
O7 •	at Central Michigan	24	21
O14	Ohio U.	7	44
O21	at Marshall	12	34
O28	Western Michigan	0	42
N4	at Buffalo	17	20
N18	Akron	6	34

2001 — 6-5 (5-3)

S1	at Iowa	0	51
S8 •	Bucknell	38	17
S22	at West Virginia	14	34
S29	at Akron	10	14
O6	at Bowling Green	17	24
O13 •	Northern Illinois	44	34
O20 •	Buffalo	35	13
O27 •	at Ohio U.	24	14
N3	Marshall	21	42
N10 •	at Ball State	31	18
N24 •	Miami, Ohio	24	20

2002 — 3-9 (1-7)

A29 •	New Hampshire	34	7
S7	at Ohio State	17	51
S14	Cal Poly SLO	37	34
S21	at Miami, Ohio	20	27
S28	at Northern Illinois	6	13
O5	Marshall	21	42
O19	Ohio U.	0	50
O26 •	at Buffalo	16	12
N2	Bowling Green	14	45
N9	at Connecticut	21	63
N16	at Central Florida	6	32
N23	Akron	10	48

2003 — 5-7 (4-4)

A28 •	at Akron	41	38
S6	at Pittsburgh	3	43
S13 •	Youngstown St.	16	13
S20	at Penn State	10	32
S27 •	Central Florida	36	16
O4	Ball State	17	34
O11	at Marshall	33	49
O18	Connecticut	31	34
O25	Miami, Ohio	30	38
N8 •	at Ohio U.	37	33
N15	at Bowling Green	33	42
N22 •	Buffalo	34	24

DOUG MARTIN — 2004-Present (.455) — 5-6

2004 — 5-6 (4-4)

S4	at Iowa	7	39
S11 •	Liberty	38	10
S18	at Rutgers	21	29
S23	Akron	19	24
O2	at Central Michigan	21	24
O9	at Miami, Ohio	27	47
O16	Marshall	17	27
O30 •	Ohio U.	42	16
N6 •	at Buffalo	33	7
N13 •	Eastern Michigan	69	17
N23 •	at Central Florida	41	24

KENT STATE ANNUAL STATISTICAL LEADERS

YR	RUSHING	YDS	ATT	AVG	PASSING	ATT	CMP	PCT	YDS	RECEIVING	REC	YDS	AVG
1946		NA	NA	NA	John Moore	74	45	.46	644		NA	NA	NA
1947	Wilbur Little	559	73	7.7	Neil Nelson	71	34	.48	360	Bob Evans	7	122	17.4
1948	Wilbur Little	758	108	7.0	Jerry Tuttle	91	40	.44	749		NA	NA	NA
1949	Jack Mancos	725	100	7.3	NA	NA	NA	NA	NA	Jack Mancos	12	229	19.1
1950	Dick Pitts	757	128	5.9	Nick Dellerba	84	42	.50	574	Jim Betteker	17	227	13.4
1951	Jack Mancos	778	108	7.2		NA	NA	NA	NA	Bob Scott	10	154	15.4
1952	Jim Cullom	822	159	5.2		NA	NA	NA	NA	Jim Cullom	9	74	8.2
1953	Lou Mariano	816	98	8.3	Don Burke	78	26	.33	577	Gino Gioia	6	84	14.0
1954	Lou Mariano	1,037	95	10.9	Bob Stimac	36	17	.47	434	Bill Whitley	9	239	26.6
1955	Mike Norcia	600	82	7.3	Bob Stimac	66	26	.39	428	Ken Redin	6	102	17.0
1956	Ron Fowler	522	91	5.7	Ken Horton	61	35	.57	703	Dick Mihalus	9	238	26.4
1957	Ron Fowler	508	112	4.5	Ken Horton	71	23	.32	304	Dick Mihalus	7	100	14.3
1958	John Martin	386	85	4.5	Dick Mostardo	60	30	.50	542	Dick Mihalus	7	231	33.0
1959	John Martin	391	84	4.7	Dick Mostardo	43	12	.28	164	Lou Perry	5	141	28.2
1960	Marty Grosjean	482	90	5.4	Jim Flynn	79	38	.48	423	Bob Gusbar	25	301	12.0
1961	Cullen Bowen	275	80	3.4	George Jenkins	74	34	.46	387	Dick Wolf	18	288	16.0
1962	Dick Merschman	555	140	4.0	Jim Flynn	116	50	.43	605	Dick Wolf	12	119	9.9
1963	Bill Asbury	849	94	9.0	Ron Mollric	63	24	.38	293	Tom Zuppke	6	122	20.3
1964	Tom Clements	444	112	4.0	Ron Mollric	58	30	.52	384	Fred Gissendaner	17	258	15.2
1965	Bill Asbury	998	238	4.2	Ron Mollric	80	35	.44	407	Billy Blunt	30	337	11.2
1966	Don Fitzgerald	1,245	296	4.2	Ron Swartz	125	63	.50	879	Billy Blunt	26	287	11.0
1967	Don Fitzgerald	891	230	3.9	Ron Swartz	177	79	.45	1,029	Will Perry	45	601	13.4
1968	Don Nottingham	727	163	4.5	Steve Trustdorf	138	64	.46	773	Doug Smith	21	247	11.8
1969	Don Nottingham	990	231	4.3	Steve Trustdorf	81	35	.43	442	Doug Smith	15	166	11.1
1970	Don Nottingham	798	208	3.8	Steve Broderick	120	61	.51	757	Jeff Murrey	18	165	9.2
1971	Renard Harmon	566	115	4.9	Larry Hayes	155	67	.43	848	Jeff Murrey	23	259	11.3
1972	Larry Poole	588	126	4.7	Greg Kokal	107	54	.50	792	Gary Pinkel	34	477	14.0
1973	Larry Poole	1,010	261	3.9	Greg Kokal	234	133	.57	1,776	Gary Pinkel	36	409	11.4
1974	Larry Poole	1,070	212	5.0	Greg Kokal	169	85	.50	1,265	Ken Dooner	35	451	12.9
1975	Dan Watkins	916	189	4.8	Greg Kokal	276	133	.48	1,754	Kim Featsent	42	563	13.4
1976	Art Best	1,030	194	5.3	Mike Whalen	102	55	.54	822	Kim Featsent	26	415	16.0
1977	Tom Roper	630	122	5.2	Mike Whalen	91	46	.51	534	Kim Featsent	39	549	14.1
1978	Tom Delaney	440	144	3.1	Tom Delaney	79	25	.32	400	Mike Moore	13	250	19.2
1979	J.C. Stafford	497	130	3.8	Jeff Morrow	236	111	.47	1,284	Mike Moore	27	334	12.4
1980	Ron Pittman	485	115	4.2	Pat Gladfelter	162	72	.44	745	Darren Brown	27	419	15.5
1981	Ron Pittman	648	147	4.4	Bill Willows	146	65	.45	913	Darren Brown	19	333	17.5
1982	Dana Wright	363	123	3.0	Walter Kroan	259	113	.44	1,304	Todd Feldman	28	519	18.5
1983	O.D. Underwood	531	106	5.0	Stu Rayburn	217	117	.54	1,461	Joe Rucky	34	287	8.4
1984	Derrick Nix	720	212	3.4	Stu Rayburn	266	125	.47	1,381	Ken Hughes	40	621	15.5
1985	Eric Wilkerson	594	131	4.5	Steve Poth	184	98	.53	1,221	Jim Kilbane	53	806	15.2
1986	Patrick Young	779	190	4.1	Patrick Young	131	58	.44	756	Eric Dye	28	425	15.2
1987	Eric Wilkerson	1,221	244	5.0	Tim Phillips	248	141	.57	1,625	Eric Dye	40	606	15.2
1988	Eric Wilkerson	1,325	247	5.4	Patrick Young	103	41	.40	650	Fermin Olivera	10	180	18.0
1989	Terry Daniel	304	82	3.7	Joe Dalpra	191	86	.45	1,089	Andre Palmer	26	417	16.0
1990	Marcus Haywood	672	178	3.8	Joe Dalpra	252	125	.50	1,533	Tony Gucciardo	29	339	11.7
1991	Brad Smith	645	142	4.5	Kevin Shuman	164	82	.50	943	Shawn Barnes	33	558	16.9
1992	Troy Robinson	422	107	3.9	Kevin Shuman	281	124	.44	1,518	Jimmie Woody	54	714	13.2
1993	Raeshaun Jernigan	856	169	5.1	Kevin Shuman	166	89	.54	1,022	Brian Dusho	72	890	12.4
1994	Astron Whatley	1,003	241	4.2	Mike Challenger	162	81	.50	842	Chris Amill	9	247	27.4
1995	Astron Whatley	978	231	4.2	Todd Goebbel	164	75	.46	792	Kantroy Walker	28	328	11.7
1996	Astron Whatley	1,132	254	4.5	Todd Goebbel	354	188	.53	2,419	Eugene Baker	69	1,215	17.6
1997	Astron Whatley	876	152	5.8	Jose Davis	365	194	.53	2,707	Eugene Baker	103	1,549	15.0
1998	DeMarlo Rozier	621	185	3.4	Jose Davis	320	178	.56	2,046	Eugene Baker	49	685	14.0
1999	Chante Murphy	676	162	4.2	Jose Davis	315	180	.57	1,969	Jason Gavadza	47	654	13.9
2000	Chante Murphy	800	199	4.0	Zach Williams	213	114	.54	1,120	Jurron Kelly	37	393	10.6
2001	Joshua Cribbs	1,019	164	6.2	Joshua Cribbs	238	131	.55	1,516	Jurron Kelly	37	479	12.9
2002	Joshua Cribbs	1,057	137	7.7	Joshua Cribbs	186	91	.49	1,014	Darrell Dowery	34	348	10.2
2003	Joshua Cribbs	701	161	4.4	Joshua Cribbs	364	178	.49	2,424	Darrell Dowery	41	783	19.1
2004	Joshua Cribbs	893	170	5.3	Joshua Cribbs	335	216	.64	2,215	Darrell Dowery	68	712	10.5

Receiving leaders by receptions

The NCAA began including postseason stats in 2002

THE SCHOOLS

KENTUCKY

BY GEOFFREY NORMAN

CASUAL SPORTS FANS KNOW Kentucky as a school that has had a bit of success in basketball. The large shadow cast by Wildcats hoops has obscured the school's football accomplishments and even chased away a coach who decided there simply was not enough oxygen in Lexington for both him and Adolph Rupp to breathe. In 1953, Bear Bryant left Kentucky for Texas A&M, then moved on to Alabama and immortality.

Kentucky may have lost an opportunity to become a permanent first-class football power, but it has made tantalizing moves in the half-century since Bryant's departure. There have been some very good years— including a 10–1 season and a No. 6 ranking in 1977— and a reputation as the school you should never overlook. With parity increasingly the name of the college football game, there's no doubt good things are ahead.

TRADITION Kentucky plays its October home games at night, under the lights, so fans can enjoy an unusual "daily double." This consists of the racing card at the Keeneland Race Course in the afternoon and the football game later at Commonwealth Stadium. And when those fans make it to the game they can check out the cheerleading squad, which Kentucky claims, with some justice, is the best in America. In 2004, the Wildcat cheerleaders won an unprecedented 13th national championship in the annual competition held by the University Cheerleaders Association.

BEST PLAYER Kentucky fans would doubtless vote for Tim Couch, the Wildcats' All-America quarterback who finished fourth in the 1998 Heisman balloting. Couch is, hands down, the most popular player in UK history. As a sophomore he led the nation in pass attempts, completions, yardage and completion percentage. Wildcat fans can only wonder what he might have accomplished had he not given up his senior year of eligibility to enter the NFL draft, where he was the No. 1 pick of the Cleveland Browns. In his slightly abbreviated career, Couch set seven NCAA records, 14 SEC records and 26 school records. The runners-up would be quarterback Babe Parilli, lineman Bob Gain—winner of the 1950 Outland Trophy— and Art Still, the outstanding defensive player on the great Kentucky teams of the mid-1970s. Still was the first pick of the Kansas City Chiefs in 1978 and went on to a distinguished 12-year NFL career.

BEST COACH Bryant coached the Wildcats from 1946 to 1953. His teams had winning seasons in all of those years and his 60 wins are the best of any Kentucky coach. His

---

PROFILE

University of Kentucky
Lexington, Ky.
Founded: 1865
Enrollment: 18,492
Colors: Blue and White
Nickname: Wildcats
Stadium: Commonwealth Stadium
    Opened in 1973
    Grass; 67,606 capacity
First football game: 1881
All-time record: 533–529–44 (.502)
Bowl record: 5–5
Southeastern Conference championships:
2 (1 outright)
Outland Trophy: Bob Gain, 1950
First-round NFL draftees: 13
Official website: www.ukathletics.com

THE BEST OF TIMES

Eight straight winning seasons and three major bowl bids during the eight-year tenure of Paul "Bear" Bryant, from 1946 to 1953.

THE WORST OF TIMES

The past two decades have been grim. Kentucky has won more than six games in a season only twice since 1984.

CONFERENCE

After 12 years in the Southern Conference, Kentucky became a charter member of the SEC in 1933.

DISTINGUISHED ALUMNI

Pat Riley; Ashley Judd; George Blanda, Pro Football Hall of Famer; Mitch McConnell, U.S. senator; Story Musgrave, astronaut

FIGHT SONG

ON, ON U OF K
On, on, U of K, we are right for the fight today,
Hold that ball and hit that line;
Ev'ry Wildcat star will shine;
We'll fight, fight, fight
For the blue and white
As we roll to that goal, varsity,
And we'll kick, pass and run
'til the battle is won,
And we'll bring home the victory.

Kentucky was the first team to go from a winless record to a bowl in successive seasons.

1950 squad finished on top in the SEC, the first of two conference championships won by the Wildcats. Bryant's Kentucky teams went to four bowl games, including successive Orange, Sugar and Cotton bowls during the 1949-51 seasons.

BEST TEAM The 1950 team went 10–1 during the regular season and was rewarded with an invitation to the Sugar Bowl, where it faced Bud Wilkinson's Oklahoma team, the colossus of college football and winner of 31 straight. The Wildcats won 13-7 and might have been named national champions except that the final rankings were determined before the bowl games during those days. (Jeff Sagarin's retrospective computer ratings rank the Wildcats No. 1 for that season.) As it was, Kentucky finished No. 7 in the AP poll. The 1950-51 school year was especially sweet at Kentucky, since Rupp's basketball team took the national title, beating Kansas State 68-58 and finishing 32–2. The only other Kentucky team with a legitimate claim as best Wildcat squad would be coach Fran Curci's 1977 bunch that defeated Penn State, LSU, Georgia, Florida and Tennessee. All on the road. The Wildcats' final record was 10–1 and they were ranked No. 6 in the nation. However, since the team was on probation, it did not play in a bowl game.

BIGGEST GAME On Oct. 4, 1997, Kentucky trailed Alabama late in the fourth quarter. The Wildcats returned a blocked field goal for a touchdown to take the lead—only to see Alabama send it into overtime with a field goal. On Kentucky's first possession in overtime, Couch hit Craig Yeast for the game-winning touchdown to give the Wildcats a 40-34 victory. It was the first time Kentucky had beaten Alabama in 75 years, inspiring the fans to storm the field and tear down the goalposts for the first, and only, time in school history.

BIGGEST UPSET In 1964, on the road against top-ranked Mississippi, the Wildcats had to come from behind twice in the second half to pull out a 27-21 victory. Rick Kestner caught nine balls, three of them for touchdowns—two from QB Rick Norton, the other a halfback pass from Rodger Bird—and a team under the whip of coach Charlie Bradshaw tasted glory.

HEARTBREAKER In 1965, after turning down a Gator Bowl bid in hopes of an invitation to the more prestigious Cotton Bowl, Kentucky lost to 3–5 Houston in the next-to-last game of the season and then lost to Tennessee in the finale. The Wildcats stayed home for the holidays.

RECORDS

RUSHING YARDS

	GAME
299	Moe Williams vs. South Carolina, Sept. 23, 1995 (40 att.)
	SEASON
1,600	Moe Williams, 1995 (294 att.)
	CAREER
3,835	Sonny Collins, 1972-75 (777 att.)

PASSING YARDS

	GAME
528	Jared Lorenzen vs. Georgia, Oct. 21, 2000 (39 of 58)
	SEASON
4,275	Tim Couch, 1998 (400 of 553)
	CAREER
10,354	Jared Lorenzen, 2000-03 (862 of 1,514)

RECEIVING YARDS

	GAME
269	Craig Yeast vs. Vanderbilt, Nov. 14, 1998 (16 rec.)
	SEASON
1,311	Craig Yeast, 1998 (85 rec.)
	CAREER
2,899	Craig Yeast, 1995-98 (208 rec.)

POINTS

	GAME
25	Calvin Bird vs. Hawaii, Sept. 13, 1958 (4 TD, 1 PAT)
	SEASON
102	Moe Williams, 1995 (17 TD)
	CAREER
246	Joey Worley, 1984-87 (57 FGs, 75 PATs)

CONSENSUS ALL-AMERICANS

1950	Bob Gain, T
1950-51	Babe Parilli, B
1956-57	Lou Michaels, T
1965	Sam Ball, T
1977	Art Still, DL
1998	Tim Couch, QB
1999	James Whalen, TE
2002	Derek Abney, AP/KR

BEST COMEBACK In Kentucky's case, the most memorable reversal of fortune was from one season to the next. Coach Jerry Claiborne, a Wildcat during the Bryant years, had taken over a demoralized program. In his first year, 1982, the team went 0–10–1. The following year, the Wildcats were 6–5–1 and played in the Hall of Fame Bowl, making them the first team in NCAA history to go from a winless record to a bowl game in one year.

STADIUM Commonwealth Stadium was built in 1973 with a seating capacity of 57,800, some 20,000 more than that of Stoll Field, which had been the Wildcats' home for 56 years. Commonwealth was expanded in 1999 and now accommodates 67,606 fans. On sellout days, it is the third-largest "city" in the entire state. The Bermuda grass surface of C.M. Newton Field (named after the longtime Kentucky AD) was laid down in 2001.

RIVAL Tennessee would garner the most votes among the SEC candidates, but the game against Louisville—resurrected in 1994 after 70 dormant years—generates more passion. Unlike most fierce in-state rivalries, this game is not the last of the season but the first, which means your season can be tarnished right out of the box. The winner gets the Governor's Cup, and its fans have the right to gloat insufferably all season long.

NICKNAME The "Wildcat" nickname came into coinage after a 6-2 win over Illinois in 1909. In a chapel service that followed the game, Commandant Carbusier, head of the school's military department, said the team had "fought like wildcats."

MASCOT The first costumed mascot, Wildcat, appeared

in 1976. The second, Scratch, made his debut in 1996. There is a live mascot who resides with the Kentucky Department of Fish and Wildlife. His name is Blue. His predecessors have included TNT, Whiskers, Hot Tamale, Colonel and the first of the line, a cat named Tom.

UNIFORMS Kentucky's uniforms have changed several times over the years, but the colors date to 1892. They were originally blue and yellow. When a student asked what shade of blue, a player pulled off his necktie and held it up for approval. So the blue in his necktie it was. The yellow was dropped in favor of white one year later. An odd addendum to the uniform came under Bryant, who gave the Jones twins, Harry and Larry, the numbers 1A and 1B. Harry, 1A, led the Wildcats in all-purpose yards in 1951 and Larry was tops in kickoff returns the following season.

QUIRK The game itself wasn't a nail-biter, but there was definitely something wild about it. Kentucky held Kansas State to an SEC-record minus-93 yards rushing in September of 1970. The Wildcats sacked quarterbacks Lynn Dickey and Max Arreguin seven times and came up with three interceptions. KSU still gained 307 through the air but Kentucky won the game 16-3.

LORE Known as The Immortals, the 1898 squad remains the only undefeated, untied team in school history, outscoring its opponents 180-0 while running up a 7–0–0 record.

QUOTE "If I weren't so old, I'd have torn them down myself." —Athletic director C.M. Newton, after celebrating fans tore down the goalposts in the wake of Kentucky's 1997 win over Alabama, its first victory over the Tide in 75 years

---

CENTENNIAL TEAM

Chosen by the Lexington Herald-Leader *in 1990 for the 100th season of Kentucky football.*

OFFENSE

1949-51	Doug Moseley,	OL
1951-53	Ray Correll,	OL
1959-61	Irv Goode,	OL
1963-65	Sam Ball,	OL
1973-76	Warren Bryant,	OL
1951-53	Steve Meilinger,	E
1960-62	Tom Hutchinson,	E
1949-51	Babe Parilli,	QB
1929-31	Shipwreck Kelly,	B
1963-65	Rodger Bird,	B
1972-75	Sonny Collins,	B
1984-87	Joey Worley,	PK

DEFENSE

1947-50	Bob Gain,	DL
1955-57	Lou Michaels,	DL
1966-68	Jeff Van Note,	DL
1968-70	Dave Roller,	DL
1974-77	Art Still,	DL
1942, 1946-47	Jay Rhodemyre,	LB
1969-71	Joe Federspiel,	LB
1946, 1948-49	Jerry Claiborne,	DB
1971-73	Darryl Bishop,	DB
1974-77	Mike Siganos,	DB
1982-84	Paul Calhoun,	DB
1966-68	Dicky Lyons,	RET

KENTUCKY ALL-TIME SCORES

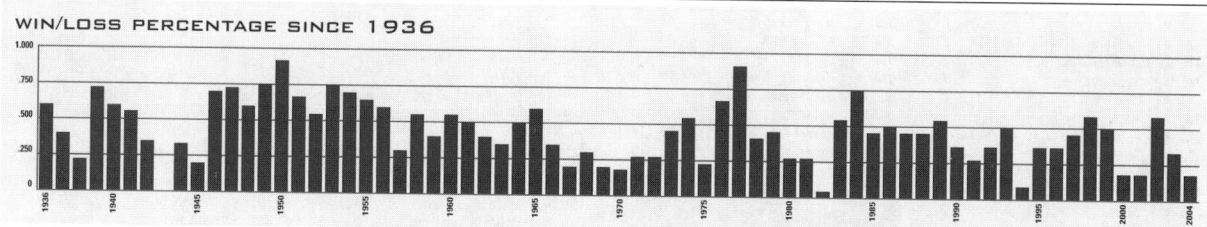

WIN/LOSS PERCENTAGE SINCE 1936

NO HEAD COACH

1881 — 1-2-0

N12	●	Transylvania, Ky	7	1
N19	●	Transylvania, Ky	1	2
D3	●	Transylvania, Ky	2	3

1882-1890

NO TEAM

S.M. POTTINGER/J.P. SELBY 1891 (.500) — 1-1

1891 — 1-1-0

P10	●	Georgetown	8	2
D19		Centre	0	10

A.M. MILLER/JOHN A. THOMPSON 1892 (.357) — 2-4-1

1892 — 2-4-1

O29	=	Transylvania, Ky	0	0
N5		Central U.	6	8
N12		at Central U.	4	8
N19	●	at Louisville	14	10
N26		at VMI	0	34
D3		Central U.	6	10
D10	●	Transylvania, Ky	10	4

JOHN A. THOMPSON 1893 (.688) — 5-2-1

1893 — 5-2-1

O14	●	Georgetown	80	0
O21	●	at Tennessee	56	0
O28		at Centre Coll.	4	6
N4		Transylvania, Ky	28	0
N11		Central U.	36	48
N18	●	Cincinnati YMCA	14	4
N25	●	Transylvania, Ky	38	28
N30	=	Indiana	24	24

W.P. FINNEY 1894 (.714) — 5-2

1894 — 5-2-0

S22		at Cincinnati	4	32
O6	●	Georgetown	40	6
O13	●	Miami, Ohio	28	6
O20	●	Jefferson AC	64	0
N10	●	Kentucky U.	44	0
N17		Centre Coll.	0	67
N29	●	Central University	38	10

CHARLES MASON 1895 (.444) — 4-5

1895 — 4-5-0

O5	●	at Frankfort AC	10	0
O12		at Purdue	0	32
O14		at DePauw	0	18
O19	●	at Centre Coll.	6	0
O26		at Georgetown	0	10
N3	●	Kentucky U.	26	0
N15		Ohio State	6	8
N23	●	Louisville AC	16	10
N28		Centre Coll.	0	16

DUDLEY SHORT 1896 (.333) — 3-6

1896 — 3-6-0

O3		Lexington AC	0	10
O10		at Vanderbilt	0	6
O17		at Cateletts AC	4	6
O24	●	Transylvania, Ky	36	6
O31		at Centre Coll.	0	32
N7	●	Central Univ.	62	0
N14		Centre Coll.	0	44
N21	●	at Georgetown	16	0
N27		at Louisville	4	30

LYMAN B. EATON 1897 (.333) — 2-4

1897 — 2-4-0

O2	●	Transylvania, Ky	8	6
O11		at Ky. Wesleyan	0	4
O23	●	Georgetown	20	4
O30		at Vanderbilt	0	50
N6		Central U.	0	18
N25		Centre Coll.	0	36

W.R. BASS 1898-99 (.813) — 12-2-2

1898 — 7-0-0

O1	●	Transylvania, Ky	18	0
O8	●	at Georgetown	28	0
O15	●	Co.H of 8th	59	0
O29	●	at Louisville AC	16	0
N5	●	Centre Coll.	6	0
N12	●	160th Indiana	17	0
N19	●	New Castle AC	36	0

1899 — 5-2-2

O7	●	Transylvania, Ky	23	6
O18	●	Miami, Ohio	18	5
O21	=	at Centre Coll.	11	11
N4		at Tennessee	0	12
N11		Central U.	0	5
N18	●	Georgetown	34	0
N21	=	Wash. & Lee	0	0
N22	●	Wash. & Lee	6	0
N30		Alumni	6	5

W.H. KILER 1900-01 (.342) — 6-12-1

1900 — 4-6-0

S29		at Cincinnati	6	20
O6	●	Louisville YMCA	12	6
O13		at Centre Coll.	0	5
O20		All-Kentucky	0	5
O27		Central U.	0	6
N3	●	at Louisville YMCA	12	0
N10		Avondale	5	11
N17	●	Georgetown	12	0
N24	●	at Central U.	0	11
N29	●	Transylvania, Ky	12	0

1901 — 2-6-1

O5		at Vanderbilt	0	22
O12	=	Cincinnati	0	0
O19	●	at Georgetown	17	0
O26		Transylvania, Ky	0	27
N2		at Avondale AC	6	17
N9		at Louisville YMCA	0	11
N16		Central U.	0	5
N23		at Tennessee	0	5
N28	●	Cincinnati AC	16	0

E.W. McLEOD 1902 (.389) — 3-5-1

1902 — 3-5-1

S27	●	Q&C RR	22	0
O4	●	Miami, Ohio	11	5
O18	●	Georgetown	28	0
O25		at Nashville	0	11
O27		at Mooney School	0	23
N1		at Central U.	0	15
N8		at Louisville YMCA	0	17
N15		Cincinnati	6	6
N27		Transylvania, Ky	5	6

C.A. WRIGHT 1903 (.875) — 7-1

1903 — 7-1-0

S25	●	Cynthiana	39	0
O3	●	Xavier	21	0
O10	●	Berea Coll.	17	0
O17	●	KMI	18	0
O24	●	Miami, Ohio	47	0
N2	●	Georgetown	51	0
N7	●	Marietta	11	5
N26		Transylvania, Ky	0	17

F.E. SCHACT 1904-05 (.775) — 15-4-1

1904 — 9-1-0

S30	●	Paris AC	28	0
O8	●	at Indiana	12	0
O12	●	at Central U.	40	0
O15	●	Berea Coll.	42	0
O18	●	Bethany W. Va.	6	0
O22		at Cincinnati	0	11
N5	●	KMI	11	0
N12	●	at Georgetown	35	0
N19	●	Central U.	81	0
N24	●	Transylvania, Ky	21	4

1905 — 6-3-1

S27	●	Cynthiana	52	0
S30	●	Cattleburg A	23	0
O7		at Indiana	0	29
O14	●	KMI	12	4
O28	●	Berea Coll.	46	0
N2	●	at Marshall	53	0
N4		at West Virginia	0	45
N11	●	Cumberland	12	0
N18		at St. Louis	0	82
N25	=	Central U.	11	11

J. WHITE GUYN 1906-08 (.700) — 17-7-1

1906 — 4-3-0

O6		at Vanderbilt	0	28
O13	●	Eminence AC	48	0
O27	●	KMI	16	11
N2		Marietta	0	16
N10	●	Tennessee	21	0
N24	●	at Georgetown	19	0
N29	●	Centre Coll.	6	12

1907 — 9-1-1

S21	●	at Ky. Wesleyan	17	0
S28	●	Winchester AC	6	0
S28	●	Louisville Manual	30	0
O5		at Vanderbilt	0	40
O12	●	Morris-Harvey	29	0
O21	●	Hanover	40	0
N9	=	at Tennessee	0	0
N11	●	at Maryville	5	2
N16	●	Georgetown	38	0
N28	●	Centre	11	0
D5	●	Transylvania, Ky	5	0

1908 — 4-3-0

O10	●	Berea Coll.	17	0
O17		at Tennessee	0	7
O19	●	at Maryville	18	0
O31		Sewanee	0	12
N7		at Michigan	0	62
N14	●	Rose Poly	12	0
N26	●	Centre Coll.	40	0

E.R. SWEETLAND 1909-10, '12 (.821) — 23-5

1909 — 9-1-0

S25	●	Ky Wesleyan	18	0
O2	●	Berea Coll.	28	0
O9	●	at Illinois	6	2
O16	●	Tennessee	17	0
O22	●	at North Carolina St.	6	15
O28	●	Rose Poly	43	0
N3	●	at Georgetown	22	6
N6	●	St. Mary's Coll.	29	0
N13	●	Transylvania, Ky	77	0
N25	●	Centre Coll.	15	6

1910 — 7-2-0

S24	●	Ohio U.	12	0
O1	●	Maryville	12	5
O8	●	North Carolina	11	0
O15	●	at Ky. Wesleyan	42	0
O22	●	Georgetown	37	0
O29	●	Tulane	10	3
N5	●	at Tennessee	10	0
N12		at St. Louis	0	9
N24	●	Centre Coll.	6	12

P.P. DOUGLASS 1911 (.700) — 7-3

1911 — 7-3-0

S30	●	Maryville	13	0
O7	●	Morris-Harvey	12	0
O14	●	at Miami, Ohio	12	0
O21	●	Lexington HS	17	0
O28		Cincinnati	0	6
N4	●	at Georgetown	18	0
N11		at Vanderbilt	0	18
N18		Transylvania, Ky	5	12
N23	●	Centre Coll.	8	5
N30	●	Tennessee	12	0

E.R. SWEETLAND

1912 — 7-2-0

S28	●	Maryville	34	0
O5	●	Marshall	13	6
O12		Miami, Ohio	8	13
O19	●	at Cincinnati	19	13
O26	●	Louisville	41	0
N2		VMI	2	3
N9	●	Hanover	64	0
N16	●	at Tennessee	13	6
N28	●	at YMI of Cincy	56	0

ALPHA BRUMAGE 1913-14 (.688) — 11-5

1913 — 6-2-0

S27	●	Butler	21	7
O4		at Illinois	0	21
O18	●	Ohio Northern	21	0
O25	●	Cincinnati	27	7
N1	●	Earlham	28	10
N8	●	Willington	33	0
N22	●	at Louisville	20	0
N27		Tennessee	7	13

1914 — 5-3-0

S26	●	Wilmington	87	0
O3	●	Maryville	80	0
O17	●	Mississippi State	19	13
O24	●	Earlham	81	3
O31		at Cincinnati	7	14
N7		at Purdue	6	40
N14	●	Louisville	42	0
N26		at Tennessee	6	23

J.J. TIGERT
1915-16 (.767) — 10-2-3

1915 — 6-1-1
O2	●	Butler	33 0
O9	●	Earlham	54 13
O16		at Mississippi State	0 12
O23	=	Sewanee	7 7
O30	●	Cincinnati	27 6
N6		at Louisville	15 0
N13	●	Purdue	7 0
N25	●	Tennessee	6 0

1916 — 4-1-2
S30	●	Butler	39 3
O7	●	Centre	68 0
O14		Vanderbilt	0 45
O21	●	Sewanee	0 0
O28	●	at Cincinnati	32 0 *
N18	●	Mississippi State	13 3
N30		at Tennessee	0 0

S.A. BOLES
1917 (.389) — 3-5-1

1917 — 3-5-1
S29	●	Butler	33 0
O6	●	Maryville	19 0
O13	=	Miami, Ohio	0 0
O20	●	Vanderbilt	0 5
O27	●	Sewanee *Chat*	0 7
N3	●	at Centre	0 3
N10	●	at Mississippi State	0 14
N17	●	Alabama	0 27
N29	●	Florida	52 0

ANDY GILL
1918-19 (.500) — 5-5-1

1918 — 2-1-0
O5	●	at Indiana	24 7
N2		at Vanderbilt	0 33
N9		at Georgetown	21 3

1919 — 3-4-1
O4	●	Georgetown	12 0
O11		Indiana	0 24
O18		at Ohio State	0 49
O25	●	at Sewanee	6 0
N1	=	Vanderbilt	0 0
N8		at Cincinnati	0 7
N15		at Centre	0 56
N27	●	Tennessee	13 0

W.J. JUNEAU
1920-22 (.560) — 13-10-2

1920 — 3-4-1
O2	●	Southwestern	62 0
O9	●	Maryville	31 0
O16		at Miami, Ohio	0 14
O23	=	Sewanee	6 6
O30		at Vanderbilt	0 20
N6	●	Cincinnati	7 6
N13		Centre	0 49
N25		at Tennessee	7 14

1921-1932 — SOUTHERN

1921 — 4-3-1 (0-0-1)
O1	●	Ky. Wesleyan	68 0
O8	●	Marshall	28 0
O15	●	Vanderbilt	14 21
O22	●	Georgetown	33 0
O29	●	Sewanee *Lou*	0 6
N5		at Centre	0 55
N12	●	VMI *Lou*	14 7
N24	=	Tennessee	0 0

1922 — 6-3-0 (2-2-0)
S30	●	Marshall	16 0
O7	●	Cincinnati	15 0
O14	●	Louisville	73 0 *
O21	●	at Georgetown	40 6
O28	●	Sewanee	7 0
N4		Centre	3 27
N11	●	at Vanderbilt	0 9
N18	●	Alabama	6 0
N30		at Tennessee	7 14

J. WINN
1923 (.556) — 4-3-2

1923 — 4-3-2 (0-2-2)
S29	●	Marshall	41 0
O6	●	at Cincinnati	14 0
O13	=	Wash. & Lee	6 6
O20	●	Maryville	28 0
O27	●	Georgetown	35 0
N3	●	at Centre	0 10
N10	●	at Alabama	8 16
N17	=	Georgia Tech *Unk*	3 3
N29		Tennessee	0 18

FRED J. MURPHY
1924-26 (.463) — 12-14-1

1924 — 4-5-0 (2-3-0)
O4	●	Louisville	29 0
O11	●	Georgetown	42 0
O18	●	Wash. & Lee	7 10
O25	●	Sewanee	7 0
N1		Centre	0 7
N8	●	at Alabama	7 42
N15		VMI	3 10
N27	●	at Tennessee	27 6
D6		W. V. Wesleyan *ChWV*	7 24

1925 — 6-3-0 (4-2-0)
S26	●	Maryville	13 6
O3		at Chicago	0 9
O10	●	Clemson	19 6
O17		Wash. & Lee	0 25
O24	●	Sewanee	14 0
O31	●	at Centre	16 0
N7		Alabama *Birm*	0 31
N14	●	VMI *ChWV*	7 0
N26	●	Tennessee	23 20

1926 — 2-6-1 (1-4-1)
O2	●	Maryville	25 0
O9	●	at Indiana	6 14
O16		Wash. & Lee	13 14
O23	●	Florida *JacF*	18 13
O30	=	Virginia Tech	13 13
N6		Alabama *Birm*	0 14
N13	●	VMI *ChWV*	9 10
N20		Centre	0 7
N25		at Tennessee	0 6

HARRY GAMAGE
1927-33 (.556) — 32-25-5

1927 — 3-6-1 (1-5-0)
S24		Maryville	6 6
O1	●	Indiana	0 21
O8	●	Ky. Wesleyan	13 7
O15		Florida *JacF*	6 27
O22	●	Wash. & Lee	0 25
O29		at Vanderbilt	6 34
N5	●	Alabama *Birm*	6 21
N12	●	VMI *ChWV*	25 0
N19	●	at Centre	53 0
N24		Tennessee	0 20

1928 — 4-3-1 (2-2-1)
O6	●	Carson-Newman	61 0
O13	●	Wash. & Lee	6 0
O20	●	at Northwestern	0 7
O27	●	Centre	8 0
N3		at Vanderbilt	7 14
N10		Alabama *Mont*	0 14
N17	●	VMI	18 6
N29	=	at Tennessee	0 0

1929 — 6-1-1 (3-1-1)
O5	●	Maryville	40 0
O12	●	Wash. & Lee	20 6
O19	●	Carson-Newman	58 0
O26	●	at Centre	33 0
N2	●	Clemson	44 6
N9		Alabama *Mont*	13 24
N16	●	at VMI	23 12
N28	=	Tennessee	6 6

1930 — 5-3-0 (4-3-0)
O4	●	Sewanee	37 0
O11	●	Maryville	57 0
O18	●	Wash. & Lee	33 14
O25	●	Virginia	47 0
N1		Alabama	0 19
N8		at Duke	7 14
N15	●	VMI	26 0
N27		at Tennessee	0 8

1931 — 5-2-2 (4-2-2)
O3	●	Maryville	19 0
O10	●	Wash. & Lee	45 0
O17	=	at Maryland	6 6
O24	●	Virginia Tech	20 6
O31	●	at Alabama	7 9
N7		Duke	0 7
N14	●	at VMI	20 12
N26	●	Tennessee	6 6
D5	●	Florida *JacF*	7 2

1932 — 4-5-0 (4-5-0)
S24	●	VMI	23 0
O1	●	Sewanee	18 0
O8	●	at Georgia Tech	12 6
O15	●	Wash. & Lee	53 7
O22	●	at Virginia Tech	0 7
O29	●	Alabama	7 12
N5		at Duke	0 13
N12		Tulane	3 6
N24		at Tennessee	0 26

1933-PRESENT — SEC

1933 — 5-5-0 (2-3-0)
S23	●	Maryville	46 2
S30	●	Sewanee	7 0
O7	●	Georgia Tech	7 6
O14	●	at Cincinnati	3 0
O21	●	Wash. & Lee *Roa*	0 7
O28	●	Duke	7 14
N4	●	Alabama *Birm*	0 20
N11	●	VMI	21 6
N18	●	at Tulane	0 34
N30		Tennessee	0 27

C.A. WYNNE
1934-37 (.513) — 20-19

1934 — 5-5-0 (1-3-0)
S22	●	Maryville	26 0
S29	●	Wash. & Lee	0 7
O6	●	at Cincinnati	27 0
O13	●	Clemson	7 0
O20		at North Carolina	0 6
O27	●	Auburn	9 0
N3		Alabama	14 34
N10	●	at Southwestern	33 0
N17		Tulane	7 20
N29		at Tennessee	0 19

1935 — 5-4-0 (3-3-0)
S21	●	Maryville	60 0
S27	●	at Xavier	21 7
O5		at Ohio State	6 19
O12	●	Georgia Tech	25 6
O19	●	Auburn *Mont*	0 23
N2		Alabama *Birm*	0 13
N9	●	Florida	15 6
N16		at Tulane	13 20
N28	●	Tennessee	27 0

1936 — 6-4-0 (1-3-0)
S19	●	Maryville	54 3
S25	●	at Xavier	21 0
O3	●	VMI	38 0
O10		at Georgia Tech	0 34
O17	●	at Wash. & Lee	39 7
O24	●	Florida	7 0
O31		Alabama	0 14
N7		Manhattan *Bkln*	7 13
N14	●	Clemson	7 6
N26		at Tennessee	6 7

1937 — 4-6-0 (0-5-0)
S25		at Vanderbilt	0 12
O2	●	at Xavier	6 0
O9		Georgia Tech	0 32
O16	●	Wash. & Lee	41 6
O23	●	Manhattan	19 0
O30		Alabama	0 41
N6		South Carolina	27 7
N13		at Boston College	0 13
N25		Tennessee	0 13
D4		at Florida	0 6

A.D. KIRWAN
1938-44 (.464) — 24-28-4

1938 — 2-7-0 (0-4-0)
S24	●	Maryville	46 7
O1	●	Oglethorpe	66 0
O8		Vanderbilt	7 14
O15		Wash. & Lee	0 8
O22		at Xavier	7 26
O29		Alabama	6 26
N5		at Georgia Tech	18 19
N12		Clemson	0 14
N24		at Tennessee	0 46

1939 — 6-2-1 (2-2-1)
S30	●	VMI	21 0
O7		at Vanderbilt	21 13
O14	●	Oglethorpe	59 0
O21	●	Georgia *Lou*	13 6
O28	●	at Xavier	21 0
N4	●	Alabama *Birm*	7 7
N11		at Georgia Tech	6 13
N18	●	West Virginia	13 6
N30		Tennessee	0 19

1940 — 5-3-2 (1-2-2)
S21	●	Baldwin Wallace	59 7
S27	●	at Xavier	13 0
O5	●	Wash. & Lee	47 12
O12	=	at Vanderbilt	7 7
O19	●	George Washington	24 0
O25	=	at Georgia	7 7
N2		Alabama	0 25
N9	●	Georgia Tech *Lou*	26 7
N16		at West Virginia	7 9
N23		at Tennessee	0 33

1941 — 5-4-0 (0-4-0)
S27	●	Virginia Tech *Lou*	37 14
O4	=	at Wash. & Lee	7 0
O11	●	Vanderbilt	15 39
O18	●	at Xavier	21 6
O25	●	West Virginia	18 6
N1		at Alabama	0 30
N8		at Georgia Tech	13 20
N15	●	Southwestern	33 19
N22		Tennessee	7 20

1942 — 3-6-1 (0-5-0)
S19		Georgia *Lou*	6 7
S25		at Xavier	35 19
O3	●	Wash. & Lee	53 0
O10	●	Vanderbilt	6 7
O17	=	Virginia Tech *Roa*	21 21
O24		Alabama	0 14
O30	●	at George Washington	27 6
N7		at Georgia Tech	7 47
N14		West Virginia	0 7
N21		at Tennessee	0 26

1943
NO TEAM WWII

1944 — 3-6-0 (1-5-0)
S23	●	Mississippi	27 7
S30		at Tennessee	13 26
O7		Michigan State	0 2
O13		at Georgia	12 13
O20	●	VMI	262
O27		Alabama *Mont*	0 41
N4		Mississippi State *Mem*	0 26
N18	●	West Virginia	40 9
N25		Tennessee	7 21

BERNIE SHIVELY
1945 (.200) — 2-8

1945 — 2-8-0 (0-5-0)
S21	●	Mississippi *Mem*	7 21
S29	●	Cincinnati	13 7
O6		at Michigan State	6 7
O13		Georgia	6 48
O20		at Vanderbilt	6 19
O27		at Cincinnati	7 16
N3		Alabama *Lou*	19 60
N10	●	at West Virginia	19 6
N17		Marquette	13 19
N24		Tennessee	0 14

PAUL "BEAR" BRYANT
1946-53 (.710) — 60-23-5

1946 — 7-3-0 (2-3-0)
S21	●	Mississippi	20 7 *
S28	●	at Cincinnati	26 7
O5	●	Xavier	70 0
O11		at Georgia	13 28
O19	●	Vanderbilt	10 7
O26		Alabama *Mont*	7 21
N2	●	Michigan State	39 14
N9	●	at Marquette	35 0
N16	●	West Virginia	13 0
N23		at Tennessee	0 7

KENTUCKY 413

1947 — 8-3-0 (2-3-0)

S20	|	at Mississippi	7	14
S27	●	Cincinnati	20	0
O4	●	at Xavier	20	7
O11	● |	Georgia	26	0
O18	● |	at Vanderbilt	14	0
O25	●	at Michigan State	7	6
N1	|	Alabama	0	13
N8	●	at West Virginia	15	6
N15	●	Evansville	36	0
N22	|	Tennessee	6	13
		GREAT LAKES BOWL		
D6	●	Villanova	24	14

1948 — 5-3-2 (1-3-1)

S25	●	Xavier	48	7
O2	|	Mississippi	7	20
O9	|	at Georgia	12	35
O16	|	Vanderbilt	7	26
O23	●	at Marquette	25	0
O30	●	at Cincinnati	28	7
N6	=	Villanova	13	13
N13	● |	Florida	34	15
N20	= |	at Tennessee	0	0
N26	●	at Miami, Fla.	25	5

1949 — 9-3-0 (4-1-0)

S17	●	Southern Miss	71	7
S24	● |	at LSU	19	0
O1	● |	at Mississippi	47	0
O8	● |	Georgia	25	0
O15	●	Citadel	44	0
O22		at SMU	7	20
O29	●	Cincinnati	14	7
N5	●	at Xavier	21	7
N12	● |	Florida *TAM*	35	0
N19	|	Tennessee	0	6
N25	●	at Miami, Fla.	21	6
		ORANGE BOWL		
J2		Santa Clara	13	21

1950 — 11-1-0 (5-1-0)

S16	●	North Texas	25	0
S23	● |	LSU	14	0
S30	● |	Mississippi	27	0
O7	●	Dayton	40	0
O14	●	Cincinnati	41	7
O21	●	Villanova *PHIL*	34	7
O28	● |	at Georgia Tech	28	14
N4	● |	Florida	40	6
N11	● |	at Mississippi State	48	21
N18	●	North Dakota	83	0
N25	|	at Tennessee	0	7
		SUGAR BOWL		
J1	●	Oklahoma	13	7

1951 — 8-4-0 (3-3-0)

S15	●	Tennessee Tech	72	13
S22		at Texas	6	7
S29	|	at Mississippi	17	21
O6	|	Georgia Tech	7	13
O13	● |	Mississippi State	27	0
O20	●	Villanova	35	13
O27	● |	at Florida	14	6
N3	●	Miami, Fla.	32	0
N10	● |	at Tulane	37	0
N17	●	George Washington	47	13
N24	|	Tennessee	0	28
		COTTON BOWL		
J1	●	TCU	20	7

1952 — 5-4-2 (1-3-2)

S20		Villanova	6	25
S27	= |	Mississippi	13	13
O4	●	at Texas A&M	10	7
O11	|	LSU	7	34
O18	|	at Mississippi State	14	27
O25	●	at Cincinnati	14	6
O31	●	at Miami, Fla.	29	0
N8	● |	Tulane	27	6
N15	●	Clemson	27	14
N22	= |	at Tennessee	14	14
D6	|	at Florida	0	27

1953 — 7-2-1 (4-1-1)

S19		Texas A&M	6	7
S26	|	at Mississippi	6	22
O3	● |	Florida	26	13
O10	= |	at LSU	6	6
O17	● |	Mississippi State	32	13
O24	●	Villanova	19	0
O31	●	at Rice	19	13
N7	● |	at Vanderbilt	40	14
N14	●	Memphis	20	7
N21	● |	Tennessee	27	21

BLANTON COLLIER
1954-61 (.531) 41-36-3

1954 — 7-3-0 (5-2-0)

S18		Maryland	0	20
S25	|	Mississippi *MEM*	9	28
O2	● |	LSU	7	6
O9	● |	Auburn	21	14
O16	|	at Florida	7	21
O23	● |	at Georgia Tech	13	6
O30	●	Villanova	28	3
N6	● |	Vanderbilt	19	7
N13	●	Memphis	33	7
N20	● |	at Tennessee	14	13

1955 — 6-3-1 (3-3-1)

S17	|	at LSU	7	19
S24	● |	Mississippi	21	14
O1	●	Villanova	28	0
O8	= |	Auburn *BIRM*	14	14
O15	|	Mississippi State	14	20
O22	● |	Florida	10	7
O29	●	Rice	20	16
N5	|	at Vanderbilt	0	34
N12	●	Memphis	41	7
N19	● |	Tennessee	23	0

1956 — 6-4-0 (4-4-0)

S22	|	Georgia Tech	6	14
S29	|	Mississippi *MEM*	7	37
O6	● |	at Florida	17	8
O13	|	Auburn	0	13
O20	● |	LSU	14	0
O27	● |	at Georgia	14	7
N3	●	at Maryland	14	0
N10	● |	Vanderbilt	7	6
N17	●	Xavier	33	0
N24	|	at Tennessee	7	20

1957 — 3-7-0 (1-7-0)

S21	|	at Georgia Tech	0	13
S28	|	Mississippi	0	15
O5	|	Florida	7	14
O12	|	at Auburn	0	6
O19	|	at LSU	0	21
O26	|	Georgia	14	33
N2	●	Memphis	53	7
N9	|	at Vanderbilt	7	12
N16	●	Xavier	27	0
N23	● |	Tennessee	20	6

1958 — 5-4-1 (3-4-1)

S13	●	Hawaii *LOU*	51	0
S20	● |	Georgia Tech	13	0
S27	|	Mississippi *MEM*	6	27
O11	|	Auburn	0	8
O18	|	at LSU	7	32
O25	|	at Georgia	0	28
N1	● |	Mississippi State	33	12
N8	= |	Vanderbilt	0	0
N15	●	Xavier	20	6
N22	● |	at Tennessee	6	2

1959 — 4-6-0 (1-6-0)

S19	|	Georgia Tech	12	14
S26	|	Mississippi	0	16
A2	●	Detroit	32	7
A10	|	Auburn	0	33
O17	|	LSU	0	9
O24	|	Georgia	7	14
O30	●	at Miami, Fla.	22	3
N7	|	at Vanderbilt	6	11
N14	●	Xavier	41	0
N21	● |	Tennessee	20	0

1960 — 5-4-1 (2-4-1)

S17	|	at Georgia Tech	13	23
S24	|	Mississippi *MEM*	6	21
O1	|	Auburn	7	10
O8	●	Marshall	55	0
O15	● |	LSU	3	0
O22	|	Georgia	13	17
O29	●	at Florida State	23	0
N5	● |	Vanderbilt	27	0
N12	●	Xavier	49	0
19	= |	at Tennessee	10	10

1961 — 5-5-0 (2-4-0)

S23		Miami, Fla.	7	14
S30	|	Mississippi	6	20
O7	● |	at Auburn	14	12
O14	●	Kansas State	21	8
O21	|	at LSU	14	24
O28	|	at Georgia	15	16
N4	●	Florida State	20	0
N11	● |	at Vanderbilt	16	3
N18	●	Xavier	9	0
N25	|	Tennessee	16	26

CHARLIE BRADSHAW
1962-68 (.386) 25-41-4

1962 — 3-5-2 (2-3-1)

S22	=	Florida State	0	0
S29	|	Mississippi *JAM*	0	14
O6	|	Auburn	6	16
O12	●	at Detroit	27	8
O20	|	LSU	0	7
O27	= |	at Georgia	7	7
N2		at Miami, Fla.	17	25
N10	● |	Vanderbilt	7	0
N17		Xavier	9	14
N24	● |	at Tennessee	12	10

1963 — 3-6-1 (0-5-1)

S21	●	Virginia Tech	33	14
S28	|	Mississippi	7	31
O5	|	at Auburn	13	14
O12	●	Detroit	35	18
O19	|	at LSU	7	28
O26	|	Georgia	14	17
N2		Miami, Fla.	14	20
N9	= |	at Vanderbilt	0	0
N16	●	at Baylor	19	7
N23	|	Tennessee	0	19

1964 — 5-5-0 (4-2-0)

S19	●	Detroit	13	6
S26	● |	Mississippi *JAM*	27	21
O3	● |	Auburn *BIRM*	20	0
O10		at Florida State	6	48
O17	|	LSU	7	27
O24	|	at Georgia	7	21
O31		at West Virginia	21	26
N7	● |	Vanderbilt	22	21
N14		Baylor	15	17
N21	● |	at Tennessee	12	7

1965 — 6-4-0 (3-3-0)

S18	●	at Missouri	7	0
S25	● |	Mississippi	16	7
O2	|	at Auburn	18	23
O9	●	Florida State	26	24
O16	|	at LSU	21	31
O23	● |	Georgia	28	10
O30	●	West Virginia	28	8
N6	● |	at Vanderbilt	34	0
N13		at Houston	21	38
N20	|	Tennessee	3	19

1966 — 3-6-1 (2-4-0)

S17	●	North Carolina	10	0
S24	|	Mississippi *JAM*	0	17
O1	● |	Auburn	17	7
O8		Virginia Tech	0	7
O15	|	LSU	0	30
O22	|	at Georgia	15	27
O29	=	at West Virginia	14	14
N5	● |	Vanderbilt	14	10
N12		Houston	18	56
N19	|	at Tennessee	19	28

1967 — 2-8-0 (1-6-0)

S23		at Indiana	10	12
S30	|	Mississippi	13	26
O7	|	at Auburn	7	48
O14		Virginia Tech	14	24
O21	|	at LSU	7	30
O28	|	Georgia	7	31
N4	●	West Virginia	22	7
N11	● |	at Vanderbilt	12	7
N18	|	at Florida	12	28
N25	|	Tennessee	7	17

1968 — 3-7-0 (0-7-0)

S21	●	Missouri	12	6
S28	|	Mississippi *JAM*	14	30
O5	|	Auburn	7	26
O12	●	Oregon State	35	34
O19	|	at LSU	3	13
O26	|	Georgia	14	35
N2	●	at West Virginia	35	16
N9	|	Vanderbilt	0	6
N16	|	Florida	14	16
N23	|	at Tennessee	7	24

JOHN RAY
1969-72 (.233) 10-33

1969 — 2-8-0 (1-6-0)

S20		Indiana	30	58
S27	● |	Mississippi	10	9
O4	|	at Auburn	3	44
O11	●	at Virginia Tech	7	6
O18	|	LSU	10	37
O25	|	at Georgia	0	30
N1		West Virginia	6	7
N8	|	at Vanderbilt	6	42
N15	|	at Florida	6	31
N22	|	Tennessee	26	31

1970 — 2-9-0 (0-7-0)

S12		at North Carolina	10	20
S19	●	Kansas State	16	3
S26	|	Mississippi *JAM*	17	20
O3	|	Auburn	15	33
O10		Utah State	6	35
O17	|	at LSU	7	14
O24	|	Georgia	3	19
O31	●	North Carolina St.	27	2
N7	|	Vanderbilt	17	18
N14	|	Florida *TAM*	13	24
N21	|	at Tennessee	0	45

1971 — 3-8-0 (1-6-0)

S11	●	at Clemson	13	10
S18		at Indiana	8	26
S25	|	Mississippi	20	34
O2	|	at Auburn	6	38
O9		Ohio U.	6	35
O16	|	LSU	13	17
O23	|	at Georgia	0	34
O30	●	Virginia Tech	33	27
N6	● |	at Vanderbilt	14	7
N13	|	at Florida	24	35
N20	|	Tennessee	7	21

1972 — 3-8-0 (2-5-0)

S16	●	Villanova	25	7
S23	|	Alabama *BIRM*	0	35
S30		Indiana	34	35
O7	● |	Mississippi State	17	13
O14		at North Carolina	20	31
O21	|	at LSU	0	10
O28	|	Georgia	7	13
N4		at Tulane	7	18
N11	● |	Vanderbilt	14	13
N18	|	at Florida	0	40
N25	|	at Tennessee	7	17

FRAN CURCI
1973-81 (.470) 46-52-2

1973 — 5-6-0 (3-4-0)

S15	●	Virginia Tech	31	26
S22	|	Alabama	14	28
S29		at Indiana	3	17
O6	● |	Mississippi State *JAM*	42	14
O13		North Carolina	10	16
O20	|	at LSU	21	28
O27	● |	at Georgia	12	7
N3	●	Tulane	34	7
N10	● |	at Vanderbilt	27	17
N17	|	at Florida	18	20
N24	|	Tennessee	14	16

1974 — 6-5-0 (3-3-0)

S14	●	at Virginia Tech	38	7
S21		at West Virginia	3	16
S28	●	Indiana	28	22
O5		Miami, Ohio	10	14
O12	|	at Auburn	13	31
O19	● |	LSU	20	13
O26	|	Georgia	20	24
N2	●	at Tulane	30	7
N9	● |	Vanderbilt	38	12
N16	● |	Florida	41	24
N23	|	at Tennessee	7	24

1975 — 2-8-1 (0-6-0)

S13	●	Virginia Tech	27	8
S20		Kansas	10	14
S27	=	Maryland	10	10
O4		at Penn State	3	10
O11	|	Auburn	9	15
O18	|	at LSU	14	17
O25	|	at Georgia	13	21
N1	●	Tulane	23	10
N8	|	at Vanderbilt	3	13
N15	|	at Florida	7	48
N22	|	Tennessee	13	17

1976 — 8-4-0 (4-2-0)

S11	●	Oregon State	38	13
S18		at Kansas	16	37
S25	●	West Virginia	14	10
O2	●	Penn State	22	6
O9	|	Mississippi State *JAM*	7	14 †
O16	● |	LSU	21	7
O23	|	Georgia	7	31
O30		at Maryland	14	24
N6	● |	Vanderbilt	14	0
N13	● |	Florida	28	9
N20	● |	at Tennessee	7	0
		PEACH BOWL		
D31	●	North Carolina	21	0

THE SCHOOLS

1977   10-1-0 (6-0-0)

S10 ●	North Carolina	10	7
S17 ●	at Baylor	6	21
S24 ●	West Virginia	28	13
O1 ●	at Penn State	24	20
O8 ●	Mississippi State	23	7
O15 ●	at LSU	33	13
O22 ●	at Georgia	33	0
O29 ●	Virginia Tech	32	0
N5 ●	at Vanderbilt	28	6
N12 ●	at Florida	14	7
N19 ●	Tennessee	21	17

1978   4-6-1 (2-4-0)

S16 =	at South Carolina	14	14
S23 ●	Baylor	25	21
S30 ●	at Maryland	3	20
O7	Penn State	0	30
O14 ●	at Mississippi	24	17
O21	LSU	0	21
O28	Georgia	16	17
N4 ●	at Virginia Tech	28	0
N11 ●	Vanderbilt	53	2
N18	Florida	16	18
N25	at Tennessee	14	29

1979   5-6-0 (3-3-0)

S15 ●	Miami, Ohio	14	15
S22	at Indiana	10	18
S29 ●	Maryland	14	7
O6	at West Virginia	6	10
O13 ●	Mississippi	14	3
O20	at LSU	19	23
O27	at Georgia	6	20
N3 ●	Bowling Green	20	14
N10 ●	at Vanderbilt	29	10
N17 ●	at Florida	31	3
N24	Tennessee	17	20

1980   3-8-0 (1-5-0)

S6 ●	Utah State	17	10
S13	at Oklahoma	7	29
S20	Indiana	30	36
S27 ●	Bowling Green	21	20
O3	Alabama *Birm*	0	45
O18	LSU	10	17
O25	Georgia	0	27
N1	at Tulane	22	24
N8 ●	Vanderbilt	31	10
N15	Florida	15	17
N22	at Tennessee	14	45

1981   3-8-0 (2-4-0)

S5 ●	North Texas	28	6
S19	Alabama	10	19
S26	at Kansas	16	21
O3	Clemson	3	21
O10	South Carolina	14	28
O17	at LSU	10	24
O24	at Georgia	0	21
O31	Virginia Tech	3	29
N7 ●	at Vanderbilt	17	10
N14	at Florida	12	33
N21 ●	Tennessee	21	10

1982   0-10-1 (0-6-0)

S11	at Kansas State	9	23
S18	Oklahoma	8	29
S25 =	Kansas	13	13
O2	at Clemson	6	24
O9	at Auburn	3	18
O16	LSU	10	34
O23	Georgia	14	27
O30	at Virginia Tech	3	29
N6	Vanderbilt	10	23
N13	Florida	13	39
N20	at Tennessee	7	28

1983   6-5-1 (2-4-0)

S3 ●	Central Michigan	31	14
S10 ●	Kansas State	31	12
S17 ●	Indiana	24	13
S24 ●	Tulane	26	14
O8	Auburn	21	49
O15 ●	at LSU	21	13
O22	at Georgia	21	47
O29 =	Cincinnati	13	13
N5 ●	at Vanderbilt	17	8
N12	at Florida	7	24
N19	Tennessee	0	10

D22	West Virginia	16	20

1984   9-3-0 (3-3-0)

S8 ●	Kent State	42	0
S15 ●	at Indiana	48	14
S22 ●	at Tulane	30	26
O6 ●	Rutgers	27	14
O13 ●	at Mississippi State	17	13
O20	LSU	10	36
O27	Georgia	7	37
N3 ●	North Texas	31	7
N10 ●	Vanderbilt	27	18
N17	Florida	17	25
N24 ●	at Tennessee	17	12

D29 ●	Wisconsin	20	19

1985   5-6-0 (1-5-0)

S14 ●	Bowling Green	26	30
S21 ●	Tulane	16	11
S28 ●	Cincinnati	27	7
O5 ●	Clemson	26	7
O12 ●	Mississippi State	33	19
O19	at LSU	0	10
O26	at Georgia	6	26
N2 ●	East Tenn. St.	23	13
N9	at Vanderbilt	24	31
N16	at Florida	13	15
N23	Tennessee	0	42

1986   5-5-1 (2-4-0)

S13 =	Rutgers	16	16
S20 ●	Kent State	37	12
S27 ●	at Cincinnati	37	20
O4 ●	Southern Miss	32	0
O11	Mississippi *JaM*	13	33
O18	LSU	16	25
O25	Georgia	9	31
N1	at Virginia Tech	15	17
N8 ●	Vanderbilt	34	22
N15	Florida	10	3
N22	at Tennessee	9	28

1987   5-6-0 (1-5-0)

S12 ●	Utah State	41	0
S19 ●	Indiana	34	15
S26 ●	Rutgers *ERut*	18	19
O3 ●	Ohio U.	28	0
O10 ●	Mississippi	35	6
O17	at LSU	9	34
O24	at Georgia	14	17
O31 ●	Virginia Tech	14	7
N7	at Vanderbilt	29	38
N14	at Florida	14	27
N21	Tennessee	22	24

1988   5-6-0 (2-5-0)

S3 ●	Central Michigan	18	7
S10	at Auburn	10	20
S17	at Indiana	15	36
S24 ●	Kent State	38	14
O1	Alabama	27	31
O15	at LSU	12	15
O22 ●	Georgia	16	10
O29 ●	So. Illinois	24	10
N5 ●	Vanderbilt	14	13
N12	Florida	19	24
N19	at Tennessee	24	28

1989   6-5-0 (2-5-0)

S9 ●	Indiana	17	14
S16 ●	North Carolina	13	6
S23	at Alabama	3	15
O7	Auburn	12	24
O14 ●	Rutgers	33	26
O21 ●	LSU	27	21
O28	at Georgia	23	34
N4 ●	Cincinnati	31	0
N11 ●	at Vanderbilt	15	11
N18	at Florida	28	38
N25	Tennessee	10	31

1990   4-7-0 (3-4-0)

S1 ●	Central Michigan	20	17
S8 ●	Rutgers *ERut*	8	24
S15	Indiana	24	45
S22	at North Carolina	13	16
O6	at Mississippi	29	35
O13 ●	Mississippi State	17	15
O20	at LSU	20	30
O27 ●	Georgia	26	24
N10 ●	Vanderbilt	28	21
N17	Florida	15	47
N24	at Tennessee	28	42

1991   3-8-0 (0-7-0)

S7 ●	Miami, Ohio	23	20
S21	at Indiana	10	13
S28 ●	Kent State	24	6
O5	Mississippi	14	35
O12	at Mississippi State	6	31
O19	LSU	26	29
O26	at Georgia	27	49
N2 ●	Cincinnati	20	17
N9 ●	at Vanderbilt	7	17
N16	at Florida	26	35
N23	Tennessee	7	16

1992   4-7-0 (2-6-0)

S5 ●	Central Michigan	21	14
S12	at Florida	19	35
S19 ●	Indiana	37	25
S26 ●	South Carolina	13	9
O3	at Mississippi	14	24
O17 ●	at LSU	27	25
O24	Georgia	7	40
O31	Mississippi State	36	37
N7	Vanderbilt	7	20
N14	at Cincinnati	13	17
N21	at Tennessee	13	34

1993   6-6-0 (4-4-0)

S4 ●	Kent State	35	0
S11	Florida	20	24
S18	at Indiana	8	24
S23 ●	at South Carolina	21	17
O2 ●	Mississippi	21	0
O16 ●	LSU	35	17
O23	at Georgia	28	33
O30 ●	at Mississippi State	26	17
N6	at Vanderbilt	7	12
N13 ●	East Carolina	6	3
N20	Tennessee	0	48

D31	Clemson	13	14

1994   1-10-0 (0-8-0)

S3 ●	Louisville	20	14
S10	at Florida	7	73
S17	Indiana	29	59
S24	South Carolina	9	23
S29	at Auburn	14	41
O15	at LSU	13	17
O22	Georgia	30	34
O29	Mississippi State	7	47
N5	Vanderbilt	6	24
N12	La. Monroe	14	21
N19	at Tennessee	0	52

1995   4-7-0 (2-6-0)

S2 ●	Louisville	10	13
S9	Florida	7	42
S16 ●	at Indiana	17	10
S23 ●	at South Carolina	35	30
S30	Auburn	21	42
O14 ●	LSU	24	16
O21	at Georgia	3	12
O28	at Mississippi State	32	42
N4	at Vanderbilt	10	14
N11 ●	Cincinnati	33	14
N18	Tennessee	31	34

1996   4-7 (3-5)

A31	Louisville	14	38
S7	at Cincinnati	3	24
S21 ●	Indiana	3	0
S28	at Florida	0	65
O5	at Alabama	7	35
O12	South Carolina	14	25
O19	at LSU	14	41
O26 ●	Georgia	24	17
N9 ●	Mississippi State	24	21
N16 ●	Vanderbilt	25	0
N23	at Tennessee	10	56

1997   5-6 (2-6)

A30	Louisville	38	24
S6	at Mississippi State	27	35
S20 ●	at Indiana	49	7
S27	Florida	28	55
O4 ●	Alabama	40	34
O11	at South Carolina	24	38
O18 ●	La. Monroe	49	14
O25	at Georgia	13	23
N1	LSU	28	63
N15 ●	at Vanderbilt	21	10
N22	Tennessee	31	59

1998   7-5 (4-4)

S5 ●	at Louisville	68	34
S12 ●	Ea. Kentucky	52	7
S19 ●	Indiana	31	27
S26	at Florida	35	51
O3 ●	Arkansas *LR*	20	27
O10 ●	South Carolina	33	28
O17 ●	at LSU	39	36
O24	Georgia	26	28
N7 ●	Mississippi State	37	35
N14 ●	Vanderbilt	55	17
N21	at Tennessee	21	59

J1	Penn State	14	26

1999   6-6 (4-4)

S4 ●	Louisville	28	56
S11 ●	Connecticut	45	14
S18 ●	at Indiana	44	35
S25 ●	Florida	10	38
O2 ●	Arkansas	31	20
O9 ●	at South Carolina	30	10
O16 ●	LSU	31	5
O23 ●	at Georgia	34	49
N4	at Mississippi State	22	23
N13 ●	at Vanderbilt	19	17
N20	Tennessee	21	56

D29	Syracuse	13	20

2000   2-9 (0-8)

S2	at Louisville	34	40
S9 ●	South Florida	27	9
S16 ●	Indiana	41	34
S23	at Florida	31	59
S30	at Mississippi	17	35
O7	South Carolina	17	20
O14	at LSU	0	34
O21	Georgia	30	34
N4	Mississippi State	17	35
N11	Vanderbilt	20	24
N18	at Tennessee	20	59

2001   2-9 (1-7)

S1	Louisville	10	36
S8 ●	Ball State	28	20
S22	Florida	10	44
S29	Mississippi	31	42
O6	at South Carolina	6	42
O13	LSU	25	29
O20	at Georgia	29	43
N3	at Mississippi State	14	17
N10 ●	at Vanderbilt	56	30
N17	Tennessee	35	38
D1	at Indiana	15	26

2002   7-5 (3-5)

S1 ●	at Louisville	22	17
S7 ●	Texas-El Paso	77	17
S14 ●	Indiana	27	17
S21 ●	Middle Tennessee	44	22
S28	at Florida	34	41
O12	South Carolina	12	16
O19 ●	at Arkansas	29	17
O26	Georgia	24	52
N2 ●	at Mississippi State	45	24
N9	LSU	30	33
N16 ●	Vanderbilt	41	21
N30	at Tennessee	0	24

2003   4-8 (1-7)

A31 ●	Louisville	24	40
S6 ●	Murray St.	37	6
S13	at Alabama	17	27
S20 ●	at Indiana	34	17
S27	Florida	21	24
O9	at South Carolina	21	27
O18 ●	Ohio U.	35	14
O25 ●	Mississippi State	42	17
N1	Arkansas	63	71
N15 ●	at Vanderbilt	17	28
N22	at Georgia	10	30
N29	Tennessee	7	20

2004   2-9   (1-7)

S5	at Louisville	0	28
S18 ●	Indiana	51	32
S25	at Florida	3	20
O2	Ohio U.	16	28
O9	Alabama	17	45
O16	South Carolina	7	12
O23	at Auburn	10	42
O30	at Mississippi State	7	22
N6	Georgia	17	62
N13 ●	Vanderbilt	14	13
N27	at Tennessee	31	37

Neutral Site key: *Unk* Unknown Unknown / *Phil* Philadelphia, PA / *Birm* Birmingham, AL / *JaM* Jackson, MS / *ERut* East Rutherford, NJ / *LR* Little Rock, AR / *Chat* Chattanooga, TN / *ChWV* Charleston, WV / *Lou* Louisville, KY / *JacF* Jacksonville, FL / *Bkln* Brooklyn, NY / *Roa* Roanoke, VA / *Mont* Montgomery, AL / *Mem* Memphis, TN / *Tam* Tampa, FL

ƒ Forfeit † Game Later Forfieted # Disputed Victor * Disputed Score || Designated Conference Game |2 Counted Twice in Conference Standings

KENTUCKY ANNUAL STATISTICAL LEADERS

YR	RUSHING	YDS	ATT	AVG	PASSING	ATT	CMP	PCT	YDS	RECEIVING	REC	YDS	AVG
1946	Don Phelps	271	57	4.8	Phil Cutchin	56	26	.46	399		NA	NA	NA
1947	Don Phelps	416	80	5.2	George Blanda	114	53	.46	484	Wallace Jones	9	93	10.3
1948	Ralph Genito	327	54	6.1	George Blanda	128	67	.52	967	Wallace Jones	19	243	12.8
1949	Bill Leskovar	722	152	4.8	Babe Parilli	150	81	.54	1,081	Al Bruno	12	224	18.7
1950	Bill Leskovar	673	118	5.7	Babe Parilli	203	114	.56	1,627	Al Bruno	38	589	15.5
1951	Tom Fillion	671	117	5.7	Babe Parilli	239	136	.57	1,643	Steve Meilinger	41	576	14.0
1952	Allen Felch	623	130	4.8	Dick Shatto	54	19	.35	221	Steve Meilinger	16	326	20.4
1953	Ralph Paolone	620	108	5.7	Bob Hardy	47	24	.51	418	Steve Meilinger	18	308	17.1
1954	Dick Rushing	369	75	4.9	Bob Hardy	108	57	.53	887	H. Schnellenberger	19	254	13.4
1955	Bob Dougherty	401	94	4.3	Bob Hardy	106	58	.55	777	H. Schnellenberger	20	287	14.4
1956	Bobby Cravens	338	78	4.3	Delmar Hughes	42	14	.33	206	Doug Shively	7	107	15.3
1957	Bobby Cravens	669	141	4.7	Lowell Hughes	83	40	.48	447	Jim Urbaniak	13	194	14.9
1958	Bobby Cravens	441	104	4.2	Lowell Hughes	72	36	.50	437	Calvin Bird	21	373	17.8
1959	Charles Sturgeon	417	101	4.1	Lowell Hughes	67	30	.45	375	Calvin Bird	16	151	9.4
1960	Charles Sturgeon	291	58	5.0	Jerry Woolum	125	63	.50	767	Tom Hutchinson	30	455	15.2
1961	Gary Steward	285	79	3.6	Jerry Woolum	125	70	.56	892	Tom Hutchinson	32	543	17.0
1962	Darrell Cox	363	81	4.5	Jerry Woolum	157	83	.53	1,100	Tom Hutchinson	32	485	15.2
1963	Rodger Bird	382	85	4.5	Rick Norton	182	79	.43	1,177	Darrell Cox	20	333	16.7
1964	Rodger Bird	671	133	5.0	Rick Norton	202	106	.52	1,514	Rick Kestner	42	639	15.2
1965	Rodger Bird	646	179	3.6	Rick Norton	214	113	.53	1,823	Bob Windsor	30	426	14.2
1966	Bob Windsor	356	101	3.5	Terry Beadles	113	47	.42	725	Larry Seiple	28	499	17.8
1967	Dicky Lyons	473	138	3.4	Dave Bair	164	66	.40	634	Phil Thompson	36	377	10.5
1968	Dicky Lyons	392	134	2.9	Stan Forston	129	48	.37	643	Phil Thompson	29	397	13.7
1969	Roger Gann	646	180	3.6	Bernie Scruggs	183	80	.44	969	Jim Grant	33	344	10.4
1970	Lee Clymer	441	118	3.7	Bernie Scruggs	209	115	.55	1,181	Jim Grant	24	251	10.5
1971	Lee Clymer	455	96	4.7	Bernie Scruggs	102	44	.43	554	Jim Grant	10	205	20.5
1972	Sonny Collins	502	128	3.9	Dinky McKay	185	80	.43	879	Jack Alvarez	41	487	11.9
1973	Sonny Collins	1,213	224	5.4	Mike Fanuzzi	84	33	.39	572	Elmore Stephens	16	282	17.6
1974	Sonny Collins	970	177	5.5	Mike Fanuzzi	83	32	.39	438	Randy Burke	12	127	10.6
1975	Sonny Collins	1,150	248	4.6	Cliff Hite	101	35	.35	430	Vin Hoover	18	198	11.0
1976	Derrick Ramsey	771	187	4.1	Derrick Ramsey	103	51	.50	659	Randy Burke	15	152	10.1
1977	Derrick Ramsey	618	159	3.9	Derrick Ramsey	156	74	.47	892	Dave Trosper	25	340	13.6
1978	Freddie Williams	313	89	3.5	Larry McCrimmon	106	35	.33	752	Felix Wilson	43	727	16.9
1979	Shawn Donigan	847	187	4.5	Terry Henry	76	30	.39	408	Felix Wilson	33	534	16.2
1980	Randy Brooks	578	166	3.5	Larry McCrimmon	137	69	.50	1,060	Jim Campbell	33	394	11.9
1981	Lawrence Lee	275	78	3.5	Randy Jenkins	170	84	.49	1,079	Rick Massie	29	448	15.4
1982	George Adams	720	185	3.9	Randy Jenkins	187	92	.49	933	Robert Mangas	22	293	13.3
1983	George Adams	763	166	4.6	Randy Jenkins	203	118	.58	1,272	Oliver White	26	252	9.7
1984	George Adams	1,085	253	4.3	Bill Ransdell	266	148	.56	1,748	George Adams	33	330	10.0
1985	Marc Logan	715	175	4.1	Bill Ransdell	231	133	.58	1,744	Marc Logan	32	314	9.8
1986	Ivy Joe Hunter	621	103	6.0	Bill Ransdell	256	151	.59	1,610	Cornell Burbage	24	331	13.8
1987	Mark Higgs	1,278	193	6.6	Glenn Fohr	163	74	.45	973	Charlie Darrington	26	365	14.0
1988	Alfred Rawls	477	101	4.7	Glenn Fohr	201	91	.45	1,260	Ivy Joe Hunter	17	160	9.4
1989	Alfred Rawls	893	185	4.8	Freddie Maggard	231	130	.56	1,515	Phil Logan	28	337	12.0
1990	Al Baker	780	170	4.6	Freddie Maggard	188	109	.58	1,051	Phil Logan	37	565	15.3
1991	Terry Samuels	307	77	4.0	Pookie Jones	138	81	.59	954	Neal Clark	47	647	13.8
1992	Terry Samuels	380	98	3.9	Pookie Jones	203	97	.48	1,434	Kurt Johnson	20	318	15.9
1993	Moe Williams	928	164	5.7	Pookie Jones	163	85	.52	1,071	Alfonzo Browning	20	335	16.8
1994	Moe Williams	805	160	5.0	Antonio O'Ferral	107	48	.45	642	Leon Smith	27	375	13.9
1995	Moe Williams	1,600	294	5.4	Billy Jack Haskins	154	93	.60	1,176	Craig Yeast	24	337	14.0
1996	Derick Logan	700	190	3.7	Billy Jack Haskins	175	93	.53	967	Craig Yeast	26	378	14.5
1997	Anthony White	723	129	5.6	Tim Couch	547	363	.66	3,884	Craig Yeast	73	873	12.0
1998	Derek Homer	716	137	5.2	Tim Couch	553	400	.72	4,275	Craig Yeast	85	1,311	15.4
1999	Anthony White	562	121	4.6	Dusty Bonner	465	303	.65	3,266	James Whalen	90	1,019	11.3
2000	Chad Scott	611	130	4.7	Jared Lorenzen	559	321	.57	3,687	Derek Smith	50	716	14.3
2001	Artose Pinner	441	100	4.4	Jared Lorenzen	292	167	.57	2,179	Derek Abney	66	741	11.2
2002	Artose Pinner	1,414	283	5.0	Jared Lorenzen	327	183	.56	2,267	Aaron Boone	41	706	17.2
2003	Arliss Beach	366	103	3.6	Jared Lorenzen	336	191	.57	2,221	Derek Abney	51	616	12.1
2004	Shane Boyd	297	102	2.9	Shane Boyd	263	138	.52	1,328	Glenn Holt	49	415	8.5

Receiving leaders by receptions

The NCAA began including postseason stats in 2002

THE SCHOOLS

LSU

By Geoffrey Norman

THERE IS SOMETHING ABOUT LSU football that is special and, well, different—just like the spelling on the "Geaux Tigers" bumper stickers you see all over the state. Tigers football is as much a part of Louisiana's unique culture and history as jambalaya and Bourbon Street. The state's mythic political figure, governor Huey P. Long, was a devout fan and often used his considerable political muscle to help the team. The Kingfish once informed the Ringling Brothers circus that if it brought its show to town on the same night that LSU was playing, he would have no choice but to enforce an obscure "animal-dipping" law. The circus canceled. On another occasion, Long leaned on the railroads to discount tickets for students traveling to an LSU game. His argument about reassessing the value of railroad bridges was especially persuasive, and the kids rode cheap.

The fervor for LSU football has not diminished since those days. You can sense a little something different in the air—an undeniable electricity that makes your skin tingle—when you are in Baton Rouge on game day. People come from all over the state to see the game. And since the Tigers famously play at night, these fans have all day to, well, prepare. Tailgaters eat and drink like they are in the French Quarter, and the fragrances of crawfish étouffé and cochon du lait fill the air around Tiger Stadium. By the time the Tigers come onto the field, emotions are on a roaring boil.

TRADITION Under the lights. Louisiana is a passionate place—part French and part antebellum South—and football is an emotional sport. Nowhere is the evidence greater than at a Death Valley night game in Baton Rouge. The Tigers began playing most of their home games at night in 1931, which seems appropriate, Louisiana being a nocturnal sort of place. With the entire day to get pumped, at kickoff the fans are so loud that the stadium— indeed, the whole city—fairly throbs with noise. After one crucial LSU score against Auburn in 1988, the celebration was loud enough to move the seismograph at the university's geology department.

BEST PLAYER Billy Cannon was an unusual blend of size and speed during the days of two-way football. Cannon had no problem playing defense, but it was as a running back that he made his reputation. And his

---

PROFILE

Louisiana State University
Baton Rouge, La.
Founded: 1860
Enrollment: 26,387
Colors: Purple and Gold
Nickname: Tigers
Stadium: Tiger Stadium
    Opened in 1924
    Grass; 91,600 capacity
First football game: 1893
All-time record: 656–374–47 (.631)
Bowl record: 17–18–1
Consensus national championships, 1936-present: 2 (1958, 2003)
Southeastern Conference championships: 9 (7 outright)
Heisman Trophy: Billy Cannon, 1959
First-round NFL draftees: 25
Website: www.lsusports.net

THE BEST OF TIMES

Billy Cannon's last two years at LSU were the high point, featuring a national title (1958), Cannon's Heisman Trophy (1959) and a 20–2 record.

THE WORST OF TIMES

From 1989 to1994 the Tigers had six straight losing seasons and never won more than three conference games in any single season.

CONFERENCE

After 11 years in the Southern Conference, LSU became a charter member of the SEC in 1933.

DISTINGUISHED ALUMNI

Shaquille O'Neal; James Carville; Elizabeth Ashley, actress; John Breaux, U.S. senator; Bill Conti, composer; Carlos Roberto Flores, president of Honduras; Rex Reed, drama critic

FIGHT SONG

FIGHT FOR LSU
Like knights of old, let's fight to hold
The glory of the Purple and Gold
Let's carry through, let's die or do
To win this game for LSU
Keep trying for the high score
Come on and fight
We want some more, some more
Come on you Tigers, fight, fight, fight
For dear old LSU.
Rah!

HEY FIGHTING TIGER
Hey! Fightin' Tigers, fight all the way!
Hey! Fightin' Tigers, win the game today!
You've got the know how, you're doing fine,
Hang on to the ball, as you hit the wall,
And smash right through the line!
You've got to go for the touchdown, run up the score,
Make Mike the Tiger stand right up and roar!
ROAR!
Give it all of your might as you fight tonight
And keep the goal in view!
Victory for LSU!

The mascot's cage is left near the visitors' locker room, where opponents are sure to walk by.

versatility didn't stop there. In the 1959 Sugar Bowl he helped LSU cap an undefeated, untied, national championship season by throwing a touchdown pass and kicking the extra point in a 7-0 victory over Clemson. He also punted and returned kicks, as everyone in Louisiana and Mississippi can still tell you. Cannon won the 1959 Heisman Trophy and was drafted by both the NFL and the AFL. He went with the AFL's Houston franchise and had a long, distinguished career with the Oilers, Raiders and Chiefs. Cannon ran into difficulties after football, serving a term in prison for his role in a counterfeiting scheme. Still, the Tigers faithful never abandoned him. No LSU fan would ever turn his back on Billy Cannon, and he remains, easily, the most beloved player in LSU history.

BEST COACH Great way to start a fight in Baton Rouge. Some still argue for Paul Dietzel and the national title of 1958. Others swear by the lengthy reign of Charlie McClendon, the beloved Cholly Mac, who presided over Tiger football from 1962 to 1979. But for pure unadorned

accomplishment, you have to go with Nick Saban. When he arrived in Baton Rouge from Michigan State in 2000, it had been more than a decade since LSU's last SEC championship. The team had gone 3–8 the previous season and the 1958 team was a fading, sepia-toned memory. With stout defense and a recruiting effort that kept the best players in-state, Saban promptly got the Tigers winning again. They were 8–4 in his first year, and in 2001, LSU won the SEC and then beat Illinois in the Sugar Bowl. It was the first Top 10 finish for the Tigers since 1987. In 2003, Saban's team topped that, losing just one game early in the season before toppling Oklahoma 21-14 in the Sugar Bowl, the BCS championship game. In four years, he'd taken the Tigers all the way to the summit. They were national champions. At the end of the 2004 season, Saban accepted an NFL job, leaving with a record of 48–16. Tiger fans loved him—and their second consensus national championship—too much to be angry.

BEST TEAM The 1958 champs were young—mostly juniors and sophomores—with mild expectations. Add the

RECORDS

RUSHING YARDS
GAME
250 Alley Broussard vs. Mississippi, Nov. 20, 2004 (26 att.)
SEASON
1,686 Charles Alexander, 1977 (311 att.)
CAREER
4,557 Kevin Faulk, 1995-98 (856 att.)

PASSING YARDS
GAME
528 Rohan Davey vs. Alabama, Nov. 3, 2001 (35 of 44)
SEASON
3,347 Rohan Davey, 2001 (217 of 367)
CAREER
9,115 Tommy Hodson, 1986-89 (674 of 1,163)

RECEIVING YARDS
GAME
293 Josh Reed vs. Alabama, Nov. 3, 2001 (19 rec.)
SEASON
1,740 Josh Reed, 2001 (94 rec.)
CAREER
2,708 Wendell Davis, 1984-87 (183 rec.)

POINTS
GAME
30 Kevin Faulk vs. Kentucky, Nov. 1, 1997 (5 TDs); Carlos Carson vs. Rice, Sept. 24, 1977 (5 TDs)
SEASON
114 LaBrandon Toefield, 2001 (19 TDs)
CAREER
318 Kevin Faulk, 1995-98 (53 TDs)

CONSENSUS ALL-AMERICANS

1935-36	Gaynell Tinsley	E
1939	Ken Kavanaugh	E
1954	Sid Fournet	T
1958-59	Billy Cannon	B
1961	Roy Winston	G
1962	Jerry Stovall	B
1970	Mike Anderson	LB
1970-71	Tommy Casanova	DB
1972	Bert Jones	QB
1977-78	Charles Alexander	RB
1987	Wendell Davis	SE
1987	Nacho Albergamo	C
1997	Alan Faneca	OG
1997	Chad Kessler	P
2001	Josh Reed	WR
2003	Chad Lavalais	DL
2004	Ben Wilkerson	OL
2004	Marcus Spears	DL

fact that coach Paul Dietzel hadn't exactly set fire to the world in his three previous seasons (5–5, 3–7, 3–5–2) and what they accomplished becomes all the more remarkable. Dietzel had a kind of gimmick in those days before unlimited substitution. He played three units: the White Team went both ways, the Go Team specialized in offense and the defense was a unit called the Chinese Bandits.

The three-platoon system worked, and it didn't hurt that Billy Cannon was in the White Team's backfield. The Tigers won every game and were named national champions in both major polls at the end of the regular season, which was customary in those days. The Tigers crowned the perfect season by shutting out Clemson 7-0 in the Sugar Bowl.

STORYBOOK SEASON Before the 2001 season, Saban's second, the Tigers were considered strong contenders for the SEC West and a first-time appearance in the conference title game. After two warmup wins against non-conference opponents, the Tigers were ready to begin their run. But the Auburn game was postponed until December in the wake of the Sept. 11 terrorist attacks. So LSU played its first conference game in Knoxville, losing to the Vols 26-18 and then losing its home opener to Florida 44-15. Another conference loss, this one to Mississippi, looked like the last nail in the coffin. Somehow the Tigers hung on, beating Alabama and Arkansas. The rescheduled game against Auburn was now for the Western division title.

LSU won easily and went on to a rematch with Tennessee in the SEC championship game. With a win the Vols would go to the Rose Bowl, where they would play Miami for the national championship. During the game,

LSU starting quarterback Rohan Davey went down with an injury, as did running back LaBrandon Toefield. No matter. Backup QB Matt Mauck stood strong and the defense made crucial stops. With a remarkable 31-20 upset, the Tigers won the conference title, just as so many LSU fans originally thought they would. The Tigers just took the long way to get there.

BIGGEST GAME The 1959 Tigers were defending national champions and riding an 18-game winning streak on Halloween night against a very tough Mississippi team. Both the Rebels and Tigers played field position and defense, sometimes punting the ball on first down. LSU trailed 3-0 in the fourth quarter and the Tiger Stadium crowd could feel the glory slipping away. Facing third and 17 on their own 42, the Rebels' Jake Gibbs punted. Billy Cannon took the ball on the 11 and started down the sideline against what looked like solid coverage. Fans still listen to J.C. Politz's frantic radio call of Cannon's immortal run 45 years later. According to legend, seven Mississippi players had a shot at Cannon, but none were able to bring him down. Cannon's legendary return lifted LSU to a 7-3 win, and though the Tigers didn't repeat as national champions, the game and the run have attained something close to immortality.

BIGGEST UPSET The 1965 Arkansas Razorbacks were the nation's No. 2-ranked team, winners of 22 straight prior to the 1966 Cotton Bowl. LSU, with a record of 7–3, seemed overmatched, especially when Arkansas went 87 yards for a touchdown on its second possession. But with little Joe Labruzzo scooting through holes, LSU mounted two touchdown drives in the second quarter and held on for a 14-7 win, denying Arkansas the national title.

ALL-CENTENNIAL TEAMS

Fans statewide selected the players from the 1893-1993 teams.

OFFENSE

1971-73	Tyler LaFauci	OG
1984-87	Eric Andolsek	OG
1958-60	Charles "Bo" Strange	OT
1981-84	Lance Smith	OT
1984-87	Nacho Albergamo	C
1981-84	Eric Martin	WR
1984-87	Wendell Davis	WR
1970-72	Bert Jones	QB
1956-57	Jimmy Taylor	RB
1957-59	Billy Cannon	RB
1975-78	Charles Alexander	RB
1982-85	Dalton Hilliard	RB
1986-89	David Browndyke	PK

DEFENSE

1960-62	Fred Miller	DT
1969-71	Ronnie Estay	DT
1973-76	A.J. Duhe	DT
1983-86	Henry Thomas	DT
1959-61	Roy "Moonie" Winston	LB
1968-70	Mike Anderson	LB
1971-73	Warren Capone	LB
1980-84	Liffort Hobley	LB
1983-86	Michael Brooks	LB
1957-59	Johnny Robinson	DB
1960-62	Jerry Stovall	DB
1969-71	Tommy Casanova	DB
1953-58	Tommy Davis	P

The early-day team of the century (1893 to 1936), as selected by a panel of journalists and others close to the program.

1933-35	W. Jeff Barrett	E
1934-36	Gaynell Tinsley	E
1912-13	Thomas Dutton	L
1926-28	Jess Tinsley	L
1931-33	Jack Torrance	L
1933-35	Justin Rukas	L
1934-36	Martin "Moose" Stewart	L
1907-09	G.E. "Doc" Fenton	QB
1933-35	Jesse Fatherree	B
1933-35	Abe Mickal	B
1935-37	Charles "Pinky" Rohm	B

WILDEST FINISH With time running out—or perhaps, having run out—against Mississippi on Nov. 4, 1972, Bert Jones completed a game-winning touchdown pass to Brad Davis in the south end zone of Tiger Stadium. Rebel fans swear that time did not merely stand still that night but actually moved backward. According to game accounts, four seconds remained when Jones dropped back 10 yards, pump-faked and then threw incomplete. Incredibly, the clock still showed one second. Jones then threw the fabled score for a 17-16 LSU victory. The finish prompted Ole Miss fans to erect a sign at the Mississippi-Louisiana state line: "You are now entering Louisiana. Set your clocks back four seconds."

BEST GOAL-LINE STAND For sheer Homeric drama, it would be hard to beat Billy Cannon and Warren Rabb stopping a Mississippi runner on the 1 in the 1959 Halloween epic. For sheer nocturnal madness, it would be the time in 1988 when LSU stopped Texas A&M on the 2. A bank of stadium lights went out after that series, giving birth to the Lights Out Defense.

BEST COMEBACK The Bluegrass Miracle. Down 30-27 at Kentucky on Nov. 9, 2002, LSU had 11 seconds to go 87 yards. The Tigers got 12 yards on one play. Then, with fireworks going off, Kentucky players dumping Gatorade on their coach's head and students streaming onto the field to tear down the goalposts, quarterback Marcus Randall completed a 75-yard touchdown pass to Devery Henderson for the improbable win.

STADIUM Tiger Stadium is among the legendary venues of college football. The structure is one of those places that leaves an imprint on visiting players, fans, coaches and broadcasters. Famously known as "Death Valley," it is routinely cited as one of the toughest places for visitors to play. *Sports Illustrated*'s Rick Reilly put it about as plainly as possible: "College football is LSU's Tiger Stadium at night." The official capacity is 91,600, but more than 92,000 fans regularly pile in for games of special importance. As the sixth-largest on-campus stadium, Tiger Stadium annually ranks in the top 10 for average attendance.

The original 12,000-seat stadium opened Thanksgiving 1924 with a game against then-rival Tulane. By 1936, it held 46,000 and one end had been closed to give the stadium a horseshoe shape. The other end was closed in 1953 to form a bowl of 68,000 seats. Additional expansions and renovations raised capacity further, made seating more comfortable and added skyboxes. A new press facility and club seats were completed for the 2005 season.

RIVAL There was a time, certainly, when in-state rival Tulane was the team that LSU fans wanted most to beat. LSU's first football game was against Tulane, a 34-0 loss in 1893. The game was played for state bragging rights and something called The Rag. The Rag was a flag splitting the teams' colors: purple, gold, green and white. The original flag was lost but a new one was awarded to the Tigers after their 48-17 win over Tulane in 2001.

With time, Tulane's football fortunes ebbed and LSU has now won three times more often than not in the series. Meanwhile, the rivalry with Mississippi has gained intensity. They are neighboring states and SEC West rivals. And then there is the Halloween tradition. Five years after the 1959 game, on another Halloween, LSU won an 11-10 thriller on a late touchdown and two-point conversion. An overtime game at Oxford on Halloween 1998 ended in a Mississippi win. The Halloween series stands at 3–3–1 and surely qualifies as a rivalry.

NICKNAME After a 6–0 season in 1896, the LSU football team adopted the nickname Tigers, a typical choice at a time when football teams commonly used ferocious animals as monikers. The LSU Tigers, however, had a slightly different pedigree that went back to the Civil War and a battalion of troops from New Orleans who had dressed gaudily (as Zouaves) and fought fiercely in Virginia. These soldiers were the ancestors of the football Fighting Tigers.

MASCOT There have been five Mike the Tigers. The first served for 20 years and died during a six-game losing streak in 1956. His death was kept a secret until the streak was broken. Mike V's quarters, just north of the stadium, are equipped with a pool, scratching post and climbing platform. Before home games, Mike rides in a cage to a spot near the visiting locker room where opposing players are sure to walk past him. Just in case they forgot where they were.

UNIFORMS Old Gold and Royal Purple made their first official appearance in 1893 on the uniforms of LSU's baseball team. Later that year, the football coach and some players wanted some ribbon to adorn their jerseys for decorations on the occasion of the program's first game.

The stores were stocking ribbons in Mardi Gras colors—purple, gold and green. The green, however, was in short supply so the players and their coach bought up all the purple and gold. The rest, as they say, is history.

LORE The championship seasons of 1958 and 2003 are fresher and more vivid in the memory of LSU fans, but there was another one of those mythic teams way back in 1908. The Tigers went 10–0 that season and were known as the "point a minute team" for scoring 442 points in 450 minutes of play. Their star, G. Ellwood "Doc" Fenton, scored a remarkable 125 of those points himself.

QUOTE There is an LSU cheer that is brilliantly alliterative and culturally perfect, somehow working both Cajun cuisine and football into the chant:

> *Hot boudin*
> *Cold coosh-coosh*
> *Come on, Tigers*
> *Poosh, poosh, poosh*

LSU ANNUAL STATISTICAL LEADERS

YR	RUSHING	YDS	ATT	AVG	PASSING	ATT	CMP	PCT	YDS	RECEIVING	REC	YDS	AVG
1937	Young Bussey	371	97	3.8	Young Bussey	78	35	.45	712	Ken Kavanaugh	11	310	28.2
1938	Jabbo Stell	277	78	3.6	Young Bussey	52	18	.35	285	Ken Kavanaugh	17	294	17.3
1939	Charley Anastasio	287	79	3.6	Leo Bird	77	35	.45	574	Ken Kavanaugh	30	470	15.7
1940	Adrian Dodson	556	142	3.9	Leo Bird	55	20	.36	246	Odell Weaver	7	139	19.9
1941	Walter Gorinski	280	88	3.2	Leo Bird	76	27	.36	358	Dudley Pillow	16	214	13.4
1942	Alvin Dark	433	60	7.2	Alvin Dark	106	40	.38	556	Jim McLeod	15	278	18.5
1943	Steve Van Buren	847	150	5.6	Gene Knight	51	19	.37	190	Carroll Griffith	6	67	11.2
1944	Elwyn Rowan	288	69	4.2	Y.A. Tittle	62	36	.58	552	Don Sandifer	10	241	24.1
1945	Gene Knight	667	85	7.8	Y.A. Tittle	77	35	.45	404	Clyde Lindsey	11	147	13.4
1946	Gene Knight	473	95	5.0	Y.A. Tittle	92	45	.49	780	Sam Lyle	7	162	23.1
1947	Rip Collins	315	73	4.3	Y.A. Tittle	96	49	.51	489	Ray Bullock	12	188	15.7
1948	Rip Collins	277	58	4.8	Charlie Pevey	99	37	.37	607	Abner Wimberly	10	197	19.7
1949	Billy Baggett	481	87	5.5	Charlie Pevey	86	36	.42	521	Sam Lyle	20	268	13.4
1950	Billy Baggett	778	119	6.5	Norm Stevens	108	42	.39	551	Warren Virgets	25	455	18.2
1951	Leroy Labat	574	152	3.8	Jim Barton	75	29	.39	417	Warren Virgets	17	263	15.5
1952	Al Doggett	382	71	5.4	Norm Stevens	97	52	.54	583	Jim Mitchell	17	209	12.3
1953	Jerry Marchand	696	137	5.1	Al Doggett	142	68	.48	822	Jerry Marchand	13	192	14.8
1954	Chuck Jons	408	88	4.6	Al Doggett	104	34	.33	459	Joe Tuminello	13	181	13.9
1955	O.K. Ferugson	465	117	4.0	M.C. Reynolds	115	51	.44	660	Chuck Johns	14	217	15.5
1956	Jimmy Taylor	552	117	4.7	M.C. Reynolds	70	30	.43	385	J.W. Brodnax	13	123	9.5
1957	Jimmy Taylor	762	162	4.7	Win Turner	41	16	.39	231	Billy Cannon	11	199	18.1
1958	Billy Cannon	686	115	6.0	Warren Rabb	90	45	.50	591	Johnny Robinson	16	235	14.7
1959	Billy Cannon	598	139	4.3	Warren Rabb	65	33	.51	422	Johnny Robinson	16	181	11.3
1960	Jerry Stovall	298	65	4.6	Lynn Amedee	67	31	.46	438	Jerry Stovall	12	114	9.5
1961	Earl Gros	406	90	4.5	Lynn Amedee	94	40	.43	485	Wendell Harris	10	177	17.7
1962	Jerry Stovall	368	89	4.1	Lynn Amedee	63	24	.38	457	Jerry Stovall	9	213	23.7
1963	Don Schwab	553	108	5.1	Pat Screen	38	22	.58	194	Billy Truax	10	112	11.2
1964	Don Schwab	583	160	3.6	Pat Screen	99	55	.56	561	Doug Moreau	33	391	11.8
1965	Joe Labruzzo	509	103	4.9	Nelson Stokley	50	32	.64	468	Doug Moreau	29	468	16.1
1966	Jimmy Dousay	441	104	4.2	Fred Haynes	91	39	.43	424	Billy Masters	24	241	10.0
1967	Tommy Allen	535	106	5.0	Nelson Stokley	130	71	.55	939	Tommy Morel	28	404	14.4
1968	Kenny Newfield	441	85	5.2	Mike Hillman	118	64	.54	787	Tommy Morel	42	564	13.4
1969	Eddie Ray	591	115	5.1	Mike Hillman	167	93	.56	1,180	Lonny Myles	43	559	13.0
1970	Art Cantrelle	892	247	3.6	Buddy Lee	138	73	.53	1,162	Andy Hamilton	39	870	22.3
1971	Art Cantrelle	649	133	4.9	Bert Jones	119	66	.55	945	Andy Hamilton	45	854	19.0
1972	Chris Dantin	707	165	4.3	Bert Jones	199	103	.52	1,446	Gerald Keigley	27	433	16.0
1973	Brad Davis	904	173	5.2	Mike Miley	107	60	.56	978	Brad Boyd	16	259	16.2
1974	Brad Davis	701	169	4.1	Billy Broussard	103	41	.40	700	Brad Boyd	18	275	15.3
1975	Terry Robiskie	765	214	3.6	Pat Lyons	168	72	.43	457	Carl Otis Trimble	16	177	11.1
1976	Terry Robiskie	1,117	224	5.0	Pat Lyons	133	54	.41	685	Carl Otis Trimble	14	211	15.1
1977	Charles Alexander	1,686	311	5.4	Steve Ensminger	159	71	.45	952	Carlos Carson	23	552	24.0
1978	Charles Alexander	1,172	281	4.2	David Woodley	153	79	.52	995	Mike Quintela	30	352	11.7
1979	Hokie Gajan	568	134	4.2	Steve Ensminger	174	80	.46	1,168	Carlos Carson	39	608	15.6
1980	Jesse Myles	403	76	5.3	Alan Risher	143	82	.57	971	Greg LaFleur	18	243	13.5
1981	Jesse Myles	202	72	2.8	Alan Risher	238	150	.63	1,780	Orlando McDaniel	41	719	17.5
1982	Dalton Hilliard	901	193	4.7	Alan Risher	234	149	.64	1,834	Eric Martin	45	817	18.2
1983	Dalton Hilliard	747	177	4.2	Jeff Wickersham	337	193	.57	2,542	Eric Martin	52	1,064	20.5
1984	Dalton Hilliard	1,268	254	5.0	Jeff Wickersham	312	178	.57	2,165	Eric Martin	47	668	14.2
1985	Dalton Hilliard	1,134	258	4.4	Jeff Wickersham	346	209	.60	2,145	Garry James	50	414	8.3
1986	Harvey Williams	700	178	3.9	Tommy Hodson	288	175	.61	2,261	Wendell Davis	80	1,244	15.6
1987	Harvey Williams	1,001	154	6.5	Tommy Hodson	265	162	.61	2,125	Wendell Davis	72	993	13.8
1988	Eddie Fuller	647	153	4.2	Tommy Hodson	293	154	.53	2,074	Tony Moss	55	957	17.4
1989	Eddie Fuller	649	140	4.6	Tommy Hodson	317	183	.58	2,655	TonyMoss	59	934	15.8
1990	Harvey Williams	953	205	4.6	Chad Loup	141	75	.53	975	Todd Kinchen	34	660	19.4
1991	Odell Beckham	397	81	4.9	Chad Loup	174	102	.59	1,181	Todd Kinchen	53	855	16.1
1992	Robert Davis	527	123	4.3	Jamie Howard	200	101	.51	1,349	Scott Ray	38	534	14.1
1993	Jay Johnson	558	106	5.3	Jamie Howard	248	106	.43	1,319	Brett Bech	30	429	14.3
1994	Jermaine Sharp	750	135	5.6	Jamie Howard	274	140	.51	1,997	Brett Bech	45	772	17.2
1995	Kevin Faulk	852	174	4.9	Jamie Howard	212	112	.53	1,493	Sheddrick Wilson	60	845	14.1
1996	Kevin Faulk	1,282	248	5.2	Herb Tyler	187	109	.58	1,688	David LaFleur	30	439	14.6
1997	Kevin Faulk	1,144	205	5.6	Herb Tyler	209	127	.61	1,581	Larry Foster	43	579	13.5
1998	Kevin Faulk	1,279	229	5.6	Herb Tyler	250	153	.61	2,018	Larry Foster	56	722	12.9
1999	Rondell Mealey	637	170	3.7	Josh Booty	333	162	.49	1,830	Jerel Myers	64	854	13.3
2000	LaBrandon Toefield	682	165	4.1	Josh Booty	290	145	.50	2,121	Josh Reed	65	1,127	17.3
2001	LaBrandon Toefield	992	230	4.3	Rohan Davey	367	217	.59	3,347	Josh Reed	94	1,740	18.5
2002	Domanick Davis	931	193	4.8	Marcus Randall	181	87	.48	1,173	Michael Clayton	57	749	13.1
2003	Justin Vincent	1,001	154	6.5	Matt Mauck	358	229	.64	2,825	Michael Clayton	78	1,079	13.8
2004	Alley Broussard	867	142	6.1	Marcus Randall	162	102	.63	1,269	Craig Davis	43	659	15.3

The NCAA began including postseason stats in 2002

LSU All-Time Scores

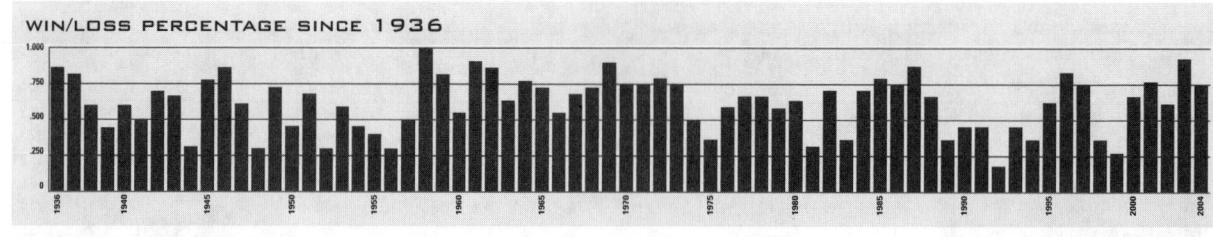

WIN/LOSS PERCENTAGE SINCE 1936

DR. CHARLES E. COATES
1893 (.000)   0-1

1893 — 0-1-0
N25		at Tulane	0	34

ALBERT P. SIMMONS
1894-95 (.833)   5-1

1894 — 2-1-0
N30	●	at Natchez AC	26	0
D3		Mississippi	6	26
D21		Centenary	30	0

1895 — 3-0-0
O26	●	Tulane	8	4
N2		Centenary Jal	16	6
N18	●	Alabama	12	6

ALLEN W. JEARDEAU
1896-97 (.875)   7-1

1896 — 6-0-0
O10	●	Centenary	46	0
O24	●	at Tulane	1	0 f
N13	●	Mississippi Vic	12	4
N16	●	Texas	14	0
N20	●	Mississippi State	52	0
N28	●	at Southern AC	6	0

1897 — 1-1-0
D20	●	Montgomery AC	28	6
J8		Cincinnati	0	26 *

EDMOND A. CHAVANNE
1898, 1900 (.600)   3-2

1898 — 1-0-0
D14	●	Tulane	37	0

JOHN P. GREGG
1899 (.200)   1-4

1899 — 1-4-0
N1		Mississippi Mer	0	11
N12		Sewanee	0	34
N30		at Texas	0	29
D2		at Texas A&M	0	52
D8	●	Tulane	38	0

EDMOND A. CHAVANNE

1900 — 2-2-0
N11	●	Millsaps	70	0
N17	●	at Tulane	0	29
N30		Millsaps Jal	5	6
D5	●	LSU Alumni	10	0

W.S. BORELAND
1901-03 (.681)   15-7

1901 — 5-1-0
O28	●	at Louisiana Tech	57	0
N7	●	Mississippi	46	0
N16	●	at Tulane	11	0 #
N20	●	Auburn	0	28
N22	●	Arkansas	15	0
N28	●	New Orleans YMCA	38	0

1902 — 6-1-0
O16	●	at La. Lafayette	42	0
O18	●	Texas SA	5	0
O27	●	Auburn	5	0
N8	●	Mississippi NO	6	0
N17	●	Vanderbilt	5	27
N27	●	at Mississippi State	6	0
N29	●	at Alabama	11	0

1903 — 4-5-0
O14	●	LSU Alumni	16	0
O24	●	Eagles - New Orleans	33	0
O30	●	at Louisiana Tech	16	0
O31	●	at Shreveport AC	5	0
N7		at Mississippi State	0	11
N9		at Alabama	0	18
N11		at Auburn	0	12
N16		Cumberland	0	41
N21		Mississippi NO	0	11

D.A. KILLIAN
1904-06 (.563)   8-6-2

1904 — 3-4-0
O16	●	Louisiana Tech	17	0
O22		at Shreveport AC	0	16
O29		at Louisiana Tech	0	6
N5		Mississippi	5	0
N10		Nashville Med.	16	0
N19		at Tulane	0	5
D2		Alabama	0	11

1905 — 3-0-0
N18	●	Louisiana Tech	16	0
N25	●	at Tulane	5	0
D2	●	Mississippi State	15	0

1906 — 2-2-2
O10	●	Monroe AC	5	0
O20		Mississippi	0	9
O27	=	Mississippi State ColMs	0	0
N9	●	Louisiana Tech	17	0
N19	●	Texas A&M	12	21
N29	●	Arkansas	6	6

EDGAR R. WINGARD
1907-08 (.850)   17-3

1907 — 7-3-0
O11	●	Louisiana Tech	28	0
O19		at Texas	5	12
O21		at Texas A&M	5	11
O28	●	Samford	57	0
N6		Arkansas	17	12
N9	●	Mississippi State	23	11
N16	●	Mississippi JaM	23	0
N23	●	Alabama MbL	4	6
N30	●	Baylor	48	0
D25	●	at Havana U.	56	0

1908 — 10-0-0
O3	●	N.O. Gym Club	41	0
O11	●	Jackson Br.- N.O.	81	5
O17	●	Texas A&M NO	26	0
O26	●	Southwestern	55	0
O31	●	at Auburn	10	2
N7	●	Mississippi State	50	0
N10	●	Baylor	89	0
N16	●	Haskell NO	32	0
N23	●	at Louisiana Tech	22	0
N26	●	Arkansas LR	36	4

JOE G. PRITCHARD
1909 (.800)   4-1

JOHN W. MAYHEW
1909-10 (.333)   3-6

1909 — 6-2-0
O2	●	Jackson Br.-N.O.	70	0
O9	●	Mississippi	10	0
O16	●	Mississippi State	15	0
O30	●	Sewanee NO	6	15
N4	●	Louisiana Tech AlexL	23	0
N13		Arkansas Mem	0	16
N18	●	Transylvania, Ky	52	0
N25	●	Alabama Birm	12	6

1910 — 1-5-0
O15	●	Mississippi Coll.	40	0
O21	●	Mississippi State ColMs	0	3
O29	●	Sewanee NO	5	31
N5		at Vanderbilt	0	22
N19		at Texas	0	12
N24		Arkansas LR	0	51

JAMES K. (PAT) DWYER
1911-13 (.680)   16-7-2

1911 — 6-3-0
O7	●	La. Lafayette	42	0
O14	●	Northwestern St.	46	0
O20	●	Mississippi Coll.	40	0
O28	●	Meteor AC	40	0
N4		at Baylor	6	0
N12		Mississippi State Gul	0	6
N18	●	Southwestern Texas Hou	6	17
N30	●	Arkansas LR	0	11
D9	●	Tulane	6	0

1912 — 4-3-0
O5	●	La-Lafayette	85	3
O11	●	Mississippi Coll.	45	0
O19	●	Mississippi	7	10
N2	●	Mississippi State	0	7
N9	●	Auburn MbL	0	7
N16	●	Arkansas LR	7	6
N28	●	at Tulane	21	3

1913 — 6-1-2
O4	●	at Louisiana Tech	20	2
O11	●	at La. Lafayette	26	0
O18	●	Jefferson Coll.	45	6
O23	●	Baylor	50	0
N1	●	Auburn MbL	0	7
N8	●	Arkansas Shre	12	7
N15	=	at Mississippi State	0	0
N22	=	Tulane	40	0
N27	=	Texas A&M Hou	7	7

E.T. McDONALD
1914-16 (.659)   14-7-1

1914 — 4-4-1
S27	●	La. Lafayette	54	0
O3	●	Louisiana Tech	60	0
O10	●	Mississippi Coll.	14	0
O17		Mississippi	0	21
O24	●	Jefferson Coll.	14	13
O31	●	Texas A&M Dal	9	63
N7	●	Arkansas Shre	12	20
N14		Haskell NO	0	31
N26	=	at Tulane	0	0

1915 — 6-2-0
O1	●	Jefferson Coll.	42	0
O8	●	Mississippi Coll.	14	0
O15	●	at Mississippi	28	0
O22	●	Georgia Tech NO	7	36
O30	●	Mississippi State	10	0
N5	●	Arkansas Shre	13	7
N17		at Rice	0	6
N25	●	Tulane	12	0

IRVING R. PRAY
1916, '19, '22 (.550)   11-9

D.X. BIBLE
1916 (.667)   1-0-0

1916 — 7-1-2
S30	●	at La. Lafayette	24	0
O7	●	Jefferson Coll.	59	0
O14	●	Texas A&M Gal	13	0
O21	●	Mississippi Coll.	50	7
O28	●	Sewanee NO	0	7
N5	●	Arkansas Shre	17	7
N11	●	at Mississippi State	13	3
N18	●	Mississippi	41	0
N24	=	Rice	7	7
N30	=	at Tulane	14	14

WAYNE SUTTON
1917 (.375)   3-5

1917 — 3-5-0
O6	●	La. Lafayette	20	6
O13	●	at Mississippi	52	7
O20	●	Sewanee NO	0	3
O27		Texas A&M SA	0	27
N3		Arkansas Shre	0	14
N10	●	Mississippi Coll.	34	0
N17		Mississippi State	0	9
N29		Tulane	6	28

1918
NO TEAM WWI

IRVING R. PRAY

1919 — 6-2-0
O4	●	La. Lafayette	39	0
O11	●	Jefferson Coll.	38	0
O18	●	Mississippi	12	0 *
O25	●	Arkansas Shre	20	0
N1		at Mississippi State	0	6
N8	●	Mississippi Coll.	24	0
N15		Alabama	0	23
N22		at Tulane	27	6

BRANCH BOCOCK
1920-21 (.706)   11-4-2

1920 — 5-3-1
O2	●	Jefferson Coll.	81	0
O2	●	Northwestern St.	34	0
O9	●	Spring Hill	40	0
O16	=	at Texas A&M	0	0
O23	●	Mississippi State	7	12
O30	●	Mississippi Coll.	41	9
N6	●	Arkansas Shre	3	0
N13		at Alabama	0	21
N25		Tulane	0	21

1921 — 6-1-1
O8	●	Northwestern St.	78	0
O15	●	Texas A&M	6	0
O22	●	Spring Hill	41	7
O29	=	Alabama NO	7	7
N5	●	Arkansas Shre	10	7
N12	●	Mississippi	21	0
N19		at Tulane	0	21
D3	●	at Mississippi State	17	14

1922-1932
SOUTHERN

IRVING R. PRAY

1922 — 3-7-0 (1-2-0)
S30		Northwestern St.	13	0
O7		Loyola-New Orleans	0	7
O14		at SMU	0	51
O20		at Texas A&M	0	47
O28		Arkansas Shre	6	40
N2	●	Spring Hill	25	7
N7		Rutgers NYC	0	25
N10		at Alabama	3	47
N18		Mississippi State	0	7
N30	●	Tulane	25	14

MIKE DONAHUE
1923-27 (.544)   23-19-3

1923 — 3-5-1 (0-3-0)
S29		Northwestern St.	40	0
O6	●	La. Lafayette	7	3
O13	●	Spring Hill	33	0
O20		Texas A&M	0	28
O27		Arkansas Shre	13	26
N2	=	Mississippi Coll. Vic	3	0
N16		Alabama Mont	3	30
N24		at Tulane	0	20
D1		at Mississippi State	7	14

1924 5-4-0 (0-3-0)
S27	•	Spring Hill	7	6
O4	•	La. Lafayette	31	7
O11	•	Indiana IND	20	14
O18	•	at Rice	12	0
O25		Auburn BIRM	0	3
N1		Arkansas SHRE	7	10
N8		at Georgia Tech	7	28
N15	•	Northwestern St.	40	0
N27		Tulane	0	13

1925 5-3-1 (0-2-1)
S26	•	Northwestern St.	27	0
O3	•	La. Lafayette	38	0
O10		Alabama	0	42
O17	•	LSU JV	6	0
O24	=	at Tennessee	0	0
O31		Arkansas SHRE	0	12
N7	•	Rice	6	0
N14	•	at Loyola-New Orleans	13	0
N21		Tulane	0	16

1926 6-3-0 (3-3-0)
S25	•	Northwestern St.	47	0
O2	•	La. Lafayette	34	0
O9		Tennessee	7	14
O16	•	Auburn MONT	10	0
O23		Mississippi State JAL	6	7
O30		at Alabama	0	24
N6	•	Arkansas SHRE	14	0
N13	•	Mississippi	3	0
N25	•	at Tulane	7	0

1927 4-4-1 (2-3-1)
S24	•	Louisiana Tech	45	0
O1	•	La. Lafayette	52	0
O8	=	Alabama BIRM	0	0
O15	•	Auburn MONT	9	0
O22	•	Mississippi State JAL	9	7
O29		Arkansas SHRE	0	28
N5		at Mississippi	7	12
N12		at Georgia Tech	0	23
N24		Tulane	6	13

RUSS COHEN
1928-31 (.635)   23-13-1

1928 6-2-1 (3-1-1)
O6	•	La. Lafayette	46	0
O13	•	Louisiana Coll.	41	0
O20		Mississippi State JAL	31	0
O27	•	Spring Hill	30	7
N3		Arkansas SHRE	0	7
N10	•	Mississippi	19	6
N17		at Georgia	13	12
N29	=	at Tulane	0	0
D8		Alabama BIRM	0	13

1929 6-3-0 (3-2-0)
S28	•	Louisiana Coll.	58	0
O5	•	La. Lafayette	58	0
O12	•	Sewanee	27	14
O19		Mississippi State JAL	31	6
O26	•	Louisiana Tech	53	7
N2		Arkansas SHRE	0	32
N9		at Duke	6	32
N16	•	Mississippi	13	6
N28		Tulane	0	21

1930 6-4-0 (2-4-0)
S20	•	S.D. Wesleyan	76	0
S27	•	Louisiana Tech	71	0
O4	•	La. Lafayette	85	0
O11		at South Carolina	6	7
O18		Mississippi State JAL	6	8
O25	•	Sewanee	12	0
N1	•	Arkansas SHRE	27	12
N8	•	Mississippi	6	0
N15		Alabama MONT	0	33
N27		at Tulane	7	12

1931 5-4-0 (3-2-0)
S26		at TCU	0	3
O3	•	Spring Hill	35	0
O10	•	South Carolina	19	12
O17	•	Mississippi State	31	0
O24	•	Arkansas SHRE	13	6
O31		Sewanee	6	12
N7		at Army	0	20
N14	•	Mississippi JAL	26	3
N28		at Tulane	7	34

BIFF JONES
1932-34 (.742)   20-5-6

1932 6-3-1 (4-0-0)
S24	=	TCU	3	3
O1		at Rice	8	10
O8	•	Spring Hill	80	0
O15	•	Mississippi State MOR	24	0
O22	•	Arkansas SHRE	14	0
O29	•	Sewanee	38	0
N5	•	at South Carolina	6	0
N12		at Centenary	0	6
N26	•	Tulane	14	0
D17	•	Oregon	0	12

1933-Present
SEC

1933 7-0-3 (3-0-2)
S30	•	Rice	13	0
O7	•	Millsaps	40	0
O14	=	Centenary	0	0
O21	•	Arkansas SHRE	20	0
O28	=	Vanderbilt	7	7
N4	•	South Carolina	30	7
N18	•	Mississippi	31	0
N25	•	Mississippi State MOR	21	6
D2	•	at Tulane	7	7
D9	•	Tennessee	7	0

1934 7-2-2 (4-2-0)
S29	=	at Rice	9	9
O6	=	SMU	14	14
O13	•	Auburn	20	6
O20	•	Arkansas SHRE	16	0
O27	•	at Vanderbilt	29	0
N3	•	Mississippi State	25	3
N10	•	at George Washington	6	0
N17	•	Mississippi JAL	14	0
D1		Tulane	12	13
D8		at Tennessee	13	19
D15	•	Oregon	14	13

BERNIE MOORE
1935-47 (.672)   83-39-6

1935 9-2-0 (5-0-0)
S28	•	Rice	7	10
O5	•	Texas	18	6
O12	•	Manhattan BKLN	32	0
O19	•	Arkansas SHRE	13	7
O26	•	at Vanderbilt	7	2
N2	•	Auburn	6	0
N9	•	Mississippi State	28	13
N16	•	at Georgia	13	0
N23	•	La. Lafayette	56	0
N30	•	at Tulane	41	0
SUGAR BOWL				
J1		TCU	2	3

1936 9-1-1 (6-0-0)
S26	•	Rice	20	7
O3	=	at Texas	6	6
O10	•	Georgia	47	7
O17	•	Mississippi	13	0
O24	•	Arkansas SHRE	19	7
O31	•	at Vanderbilt	19	0
N7	•	Mississippi State	12	0
N14	•	Auburn BIRM	19	6
N21	•	La. Lafayette	93	0
N28	•	Tulane	33	0
SUGAR BOWL				
J1		Santa Clara	14	21

1937 9-2-0 (5-1-0)
S25	•	Florida	19	0
O2	•	Texas	9	0
O9	•	at Rice	13	0
O16	•	Mississippi	13	0
O23	•	at Vanderbilt	6	7
O30	•	Loyola-New Orleans	52	6
N6	•	Mississippi State	41	0
N13	•	Auburn	9	7
N20	•	Northwestern St.	52	0
N27	•	at Tulane	20	7
SUGAR BOWL				
J1		Santa Clara	0	6

1938 6-4-0 (2-4-0)
S24		Mississippi	7	20
O1		at Texas	20	0
O8		Rice	3	0
O15	•	Loyola-New Orleans	47	0
O22		Vanderbilt	7	0
O29		at Tennessee	6	14
N5		Mississippi State	32	7
N12		Auburn BIRM	6	28
N19		La. Lafayette	32	0
N26		Tulane	0	14

1939 4-5-0 (1-5-0)
S30		Mississippi	7	14
O7		at Holy Cross	26	7
O14		Rice	7	0
O21	•	Loyola-New Orleans	20	0
O28		at Vanderbilt	12	6
N4		Tennessee	0	20
N11		Mississippi State	12	15
N18		Auburn	7	21
D2		at Tulane	20	33

1940 6-4-0 (3-3-0)
S21	•	Louisiana Tech	39	7
S28	•	Mississippi	6	19
O5	•	Holy Cross	25	0
O12		at Rice	0	23
O19	•	Mercer	20	0
O26		Vanderbilt	7	0
N2		at Tennessee	0	28
N9		Mississippi State	7	22
N16	•	Auburn BIRM	21	13
N30		Tulane	14	0

1941 4-4-2 (2-2-2)
S20	•	Louisiana Tech	25	0
S27		Holy Cross	13	19
O4		at Texas	0	34
O11	=	Mississippi State	0	0
O18	•	Rice	27	0
O25	•	Florida	10	7
N1		Tennessee	6	13
N8		Mississippi	12	13
N15	•	Auburn	7	7
N29		at Tulane	19	0

1942 7-3-0 (3-2-0)
S19	•	Northwestern St.	40	0
S26	•	Texas A&M	16	7
O3		at Rice	14	27
O10	•	Mississippi State	16	6
O17	•	Mississippi	21	7
O24	•	Georgia Pre-Flight	34	0
O31		at Tennessee	0	26
N7	•	Fordham NYC	26	13
N14	•	Auburn BIRM	7	25
N26		Tulane	18	6

1943 6-3-0 (2-2-0)
S25	•	Georgia	34	27
O2	•	Rice	20	7
O9		Texas A&M	13	28
O16	•	Louisiana Army	28	7
O23	•	Georgia COLGA	27	6
O30		TCU	14	0
N6		at Georgia Tech	7	42
N20		at Tulane	0	27
ORANGE BOWL				
J1	•	Texas A&M	19	14

1944 2-5-1 (2-3-1)
S30	=	Alabama	27	27
O7		at Rice	13	14
O14		Texas A&M	0	7
O21		Mississippi State	6	13
O28	•	Georgia ATL	15	7
N4		Tennessee	0	13
N18		Georgia Tech	6	14
N25	•	Tulane	25	6

1945 7-2-0 (5-2-0)
S29	•	Rice	42	0
O6		Alabama	7	26
O13	•	Texas A&M	31	12
O20	•	at Georgia	32	0
O27	•	Vanderbilt	39	7
N3	•	Mississippi	32	13
N10	•	Mississippi State	20	27
N17	•	at Georgia Tech	9	7
D1	•	at Tulane	33	0

1946 9-1-1 (5-1-0)
S28	•	at Rice	7	6
O5	•	Mississippi State	13	6
O12	•	Texas A&M	33	9
O19		Georgia Tech	7	26
O26	•	at Vanderbilt	14	0
N2	•	Mississippi	34	21
N9	•	Alabama	31	21
N15	•	at Miami, Fla.	20	7
N22	•	Fordham	40	0
N30	•	Tulane	41	27
COTTON BOWL				
J1	=	Arkansas	0	0

1947 5-3-1 (2-3-1)
S27	•	Rice	21	14
O4		at Georgia	19	35
O11	•	Texas A&M	19	13
O17	•	at Boston College	14	13
O25	•	Vanderbilt	19	13
N1		Mississippi	18	20
N15	•	Mississippi State	21	6
N22		at Alabama	12	41
D6	•	at Tulane	6	6

GAYNELL (GUS) TINSLEY
1948-54 (.507)   35-34-6

1948 3-7-0 (1-5-0)
S18	•	at Texas	0	33
O2	•	at Rice	26	13
O9	•	Texas A&M	14	13
O16		Georgia	0	22
O23		at North Carolina	7	34
O30		Mississippi	19	49
N6	•	at Vanderbilt	7	48
N13		Mississippi State	0	7
N20	•	Alabama	26	6
N27		Tulane	0	46

1949 8-3-0 (4-2-0)
S24		Kentucky	0	19
O1	•	Rice	14	7
O8	•	Texas A&M	34	0
O14		at Georgia	0	7
O22	•	North Carolina	13	7
O29	•	Mississippi	34	7
N5	•	Vanderbilt	33	13
N12	•	Mississippi State	34	7
N19	•	S.E. Louisiana	48	7
N26	•	at Tulane	21	0
SUGAR BOWL				
J2		Oklahoma	0	35

1950 4-5-2 (2-3-2)
S23		at Kentucky	0	14
S30	•	Pacific	19	0
O7		at Rice	20	35
O14		Georgia Tech	0	13
O21	=	Georgia	13	13
N4	•	Mississippi	40	14
N11	•	at Vanderbilt	33	7
N18		Mississippi State	7	13
N24	•	Villanova	13	7
D2		at Tulane	14	14
D9		at Texas	6	21

1951 7-3-1 (4-2-1)
S22		Southern Miss	13	0
S29		Alabama MBL	13	7
O6	•	Rice	7	6 *
O13		at Georgia Tech	7	25
O20	•	at Georgia	7	0
O27		Maryland	0	27
N3	•	Mississippi	6	6
N10	•	Vanderbilt	13	20
N17	•	Mississippi State	3	0
N24	•	Villanova SHRE	45	7
D1	•	Tulane	14	13

1952 3-7-0 (2-5-0)
S20		Texas	14	35
S27		Alabama	20	21
O4	•	at Rice	27	7
O11	•	at Kentucky	34	7
O18		Georgia	14	27
O25	•	at Maryland	6	34
N1	•	at Mississippi	0	28
N8		Tennessee	3	22
N15	•	Mississippi State	14	33
N29	•	at Tulane	16	0

1953 — 5-3-3 (2-3-3)

S19	●	Texas	20	7
S26	= |	Alabama [MBL]	7	7
O3	●	Boston College	42	6
O10	= |	Kentucky	6	6
O17	● |	at Georgia	14	6
O24	= |	at Florida	21	21
O31	|	Mississippi	16	27
N7	|	at Tennessee	14	32
N14	|	Mississippi State	13	26
N21	●	Arkansas [LR]	9	8
N28	● |	Tulane	32	13

1954 — 5-6-0 (2-5-0)

S18		at Texas	6	20
S25	|	Alabama	0	12
O2	|	at Kentucky	6	7
O9	|	at Georgia Tech	20	30
O16	●	Texas Tech	20	13
O23	● |	Florida	20	7
O30	|	Mississippi	6	21
N6	●	U.T. Chattanooga	26	19
N13	|	Mississippi State	0	25
N20	●	Arkansas [SHRE]	7	6
N27	● |	at Tulane	14	13

PAUL DIETZEL
1955-61 (.651) 46-24-3

1955 — 3-5-2 (2-3-1)

S17	● |	Kentucky	19	7
S24		Texas A&M [DAL]	0	28
O1	=	at Rice	20	20
O8	|	Georgia Tech	0	7
O15	|	at Florida	14	18
O29	|	Mississippi	26	29
N5		at Maryland	0	13
N12	● |	Mississippi State	34	7
N19	●	Arkansas [LR]	13	7
N26	= |	Tulane	13	13

1956 — 3-7-0 (1-5-0)

S29		Texas A&M	6	9
O6		at Rice	14	23
O13	|	at Georgia Tech	7	39
O20	|	at Kentucky	0	14
O27	|	Florida	6	21
N3	|	Mississippi	17	46
N10	●	Oklahoma State	13	0
N17	|	Mississippi State	13	32
N24	●	Arkansas [SHRE]	21	7
D1	● |	at Tulane	7	6

1957 — 5-5-0 (4-4-0)

S21		Rice	14	20
S28	● |	Alabama	28	0
O5	●	at Texas Tech	19	14
O12	● |	Georgia Tech	20	13
O19	● |	Kentucky	21	0
O26	|	at Florida	14	22
N2	|	at Vanderbilt	0	7
N9	|	at Mississippi	12	14
N16	|	Mississippi State	6	14
N30	● |	Tulane	25	6

1958 — 11-0-0 (6-0-0)

S20	●	at Rice	26	6
S27	● |	Alabama [MBL]	13	3
O4	●	Hardin-Simmons	20	6
O10	●	at Miami, Fla.	41	0
O18	● |	Kentucky	32	7
O25	● |	Florida	10	7
N1	● |	Mississippi	14	0
N8	●	Duke	50	18
N15	● |	Mississippi State [JAM]	7	6
N22	● |	at Tulane	62	0
		SUGAR BOWL		
J1	●	Clemson	7	0

1959 — 9-2-0 (5-1-0)

S19	●	Rice	26	3
S26	●	TCU	10	0
O3	●	Baylor [SHRE]	22	0
O10	●	Miami, Fla.	27	3
O17	● |	at Kentucky	9	0
O24	● |	at Florida	9	0
O31	● |	Mississippi	7	3
N7	|	at Tennessee	13	14
N14	● |	Mississippi State	27	0
N21	● |	Tulane	14	6
		SUGAR BOWL		
J1		Mississippi	0	21

1960 — 5-4-1 (2-3-1)

S17	●	Texas A&M	9	0
O1		Baylor	3	7
O8	|	at Georgia Tech	2	6
O15	|	at Kentucky	0	3
O22	|	Florida	10	13
O29	= |	at Mississippi	6	6
N5	●	South Carolina	35	6
N12	● |	Mississippi State	7	3
N19	●	Wake Forest	16	0
N26	● |	at Tulane	17	6

1961 — 10-1-0 (6-0-0)

S23		at Rice	3	16
S30	●	Texas A&M	16	7
O7	● |	Georgia Tech	10	0
O14	●	at South Carolina	42	0
O21	● |	Kentucky	24	14
O28	● |	at Florida	23	0
N4	● |	Mississippi	10	7
N11	●	at North Carolina	30	0
N18	● |	Mississippi State	14	6
N25	● |	Tulane	62	0
		ORANGE BOWL		
J1	●	Colorado	25	7

CHARLES McCLENDON
1962-79 (.682) 135-61-7

1962 — 9-1-1 (5-1-0)

S22	●	Texas A&M	21	0
S29	=	Rice	6	6
O6	● |	at Georgia Tech	10	7
O13	●	Miami, Fla.	17	3
O20	● |	at Kentucky	7	0
O27	● |	Florida	23	0
N3	|	Mississippi	7	15
N10	●	TCU	5	0
N17	● |	Mississippi State [JAM]	28	0
N24	● |	at Tulane	38	3
		COTTON BOWL		
J1	●	Texas	13	0

1963 — 7-4-0 (4-2-0)

S21	●	Texas A&M	14	6
S28		at Rice	12	21
O5	● |	Georgia Tech	7	6
O11	●	at Miami, Fla.	3	0
O19	● |	Kentucky	28	7
O26	● |	at Florida	14	0
N2	|	Mississippi	3	37
N9	●	TCU	28	14
N16	|	Mississippi State [JAM]	6	7
N23	● |	Tulane	20	0
		BLUEBONNET BOWL		
D21		Baylor	7	14

1964 — 8-2-1 (4-2-1)

S19	●	Texas A&M	9	6
S26	●	at Rice	3	0
O10	●	North Carolina	20	3
O17	● |	at Kentucky	27	7
O24	= |	Tennessee	3	3
O31	● |	Mississippi	11	10
N7	|	Alabama [BIRM]	9	17
N14	● |	Mississippi State	14	10
N21	● |	at Tulane	13	3
D5	|	Florida	6	20
		SUGAR BOWL		
J1	●	Syracuse	13	10

1965 — 8-3-0 (3-3-0)

S18	●	Texas A&M	10	0
S25	●	Rice	42	14
O2	|	at Florida	7	14
O9	●	at Miami, Fla.	34	27
O16	● |	Kentucky	31	21
O23	●	South Carolina	21	7
O30	|	Mississippi [JAM]	0	23
N6	|	Alabama	7	31
N13	● |	Mississippi State	37	20
N20	● |	Tulane	62	0
		COTTON BOWL		
J1	●	Arkansas	14	7

1966 — 5-4-1 (3-3-0)

S17	●	South Carolina	28	12
S24		at Rice	15	17
O1	●	Miami, Fla.	10	8
O8	=	Texas A&M	7	7
O15	● |	at Kentucky	30	0
O22	|	Florida	7	28
O29	|	Mississippi	0	17
N5	|	Alabama [BIRM]	0	21
N12	● |	Mississippi State	17	7
N19	● ||	at Tulane	21	7

1967 — 7-3-1 (3-2-1)

S23	●	Rice	20	14
S30	●	Texas A&M	17	6
O7	● |	at Florida	37	6
O14		Miami, Fla.	15	17
O21	● |	Kentucky	30	7
O28	|	at Tennessee	14	17
N4	= |	Mississippi [JAM]	13	13
N11	|	Alabama	6	7
N18	● |	Mississippi State	55	0
N25	●	Tulane	41	27
		SUGAR BOWL		
J1	●	Wyoming	20	13

1968 — 8-3-0 (4-2-0)

S21	●	Texas A&M	13	12
S28	●	at Rice	21	7
O5	●	Baylor	48	16
O11		at Miami, Fla.	0	30
O19	● |	Kentucky	13	3
O26	● ||	TCU	10	7
N2	|	Mississippi	24	27
N9	|	Alabama [BIRM]	7	16
N16	● |	Mississippi State	20	16
N23	● ||	Tulane	34	10
		PEACH BOWL		
D30	●	Florida State	31	27

1969 — 9-1-0 (4-1-0)

S20	●	Texas A&M	35	6
S27	●	at Rice	42	0
O4	●	Baylor	63	8
O10	●	at Miami, Fla.	20	0
O18	● |	at Kentucky	37	10
O25	● |	Auburn	21	20
N1	|	Mississippi [JAM]	23	26
N8	● |	Alabama	20	15
N15	● |	Mississippi State	61	6
N22	●	Tulane	27	0

1970 — 9-3-0 (5-0-0)

S19		Texas A&M	18	20
S26	●	Rice	24	0
O3	●	Baylor	31	10
O10	●	Pacific	34	0
O17	● |	Kentucky	14	7
O24	● |	at Auburn	17	9
N7	● |	Alabama [BIRM]	14	9
N14	● |	Mississippi State	38	7
N21		at Notre Dame	0	3
N28	●	at Tulane	26	14
D5	● |	Mississippi	61	17
		ORANGE BOWL		
J1		Nebraska	12	17

1971 — 9-3-0 (3-2-0)

S11		Colorado	21	31
S18	●	Texas A&M	37	0
S25	●	at Wisconsin	38	28
O2	●	Rice	38	3
O9	● |	Florida	48	7
O16	● |	at Kentucky	17	13
O30	|	Mississippi [JAM]	22	24
N6	|	Alabama	7	14
N13	● |	Mississippi State [JAM]	28	3
N20	●	Notre Dame	28	8
N27	●	Tulane	36	7
		SUN BOWL		
D18	●	Iowa State	33	15

1972 — 9-2-1 (4-1-1)

S16	●	Pacific	31	13
S23	●	Texas A&M	42	17
S30	●	Wisconsin	27	7
O7	●	at Rice	12	6
O14	● |	Auburn	35	7
O21	● |	Kentucky	10	0
N4	● |	Mississippi	17	16
N11	|	Alabama [BIRM]	21	35
N18	● |	Mississippi State	28	14
N25	= |	at Florida	3	3
D2	●	at Tulane	9	3
		BLUEBONNET BOWL		
D30		Tennessee	17	24

1973 — 9-3-0 (5-1-0)

S15	●	Colorado	17	6
S22	●	Texas A&M	28	23
S29	●	Rice	24	9
O6	● |	Florida	24	3
O13	● |	at Auburn	20	6
O20	● |	Kentucky	28	21
O27	●	at South Carolina	33	29
N3	● |	Mississippi [JAM]	51	14
N17	● |	Mississippi State	26	7
N22	|	Alabama	7	21
D1		at Tulane	0	14
		ORANGE BOWL		
J1		Penn State	9	16

1974 — 5-5-1 (2-4-0)

S14	●	Colorado	42	14
S21		Texas A&M	14	21
S28	=	at Rice	10	10
O5	|	at Florida	14	24
O12	● |	Tennessee	20	10
O19	|	at Kentucky	13	20
N2	● |	Mississippi	24	0
N9	|	Alabama [BIRM]	0	30
N16	|	Mississippi State [JAM]	6	7
N23	●	Tulane	24	22
N30	●	Utah	35	10

1975 — 4-7-0 (1-5-0)

S13		at Nebraska	7	10
S20		Texas A&M	8	39
S27	●	Rice [SHRE]	16	13
O4	|	Florida	6	34
O11	|	at Tennessee	10	24
O18	● |	Kentucky	17	14
O25	●	South Carolina	24	6
N1	|	Mississippi [JAM]	13	17
N8	|	Alabama	10	23
N15	|	Mississippi State	6	16 †
N22	●	at Tulane	42	6

1976 — 6-4-1 (2-4-0)

S11	=	Nebraska	6	6
S18	●	Oregon State	28	11
S25	●	Rice	31	0
O2	|	at Florida	23	28
O9	● |	Vanderbilt	33	20
O16	|	at Kentucky	7	21
O30	● |	Mississippi	45	0
N6	|	Alabama [BIRM]	17	28
N13	|	Mississippi State [JAM]	13	21 †
N20	●	Tulane	17	7
N27	●	Utah	35	7

1977 — 8-4-0 (4-2-0)

S17		at Indiana	21	24
S24	●	Rice	77	0
O1	● |	Florida	36	14
O8	● |	at Vanderbilt	28	15
O15	|	Kentucky	13	33
O22	●	Oregon	56	17
O29	● |	Mississippi [JAM]	28	21
N5	|	Alabama	3	24
N12	● |	Mississippi State	27	24
N19	●	at Tulane	20	17
N26	●	Wyoming	66	7
		SUN BOWL		
D31		Stanford	14	24

1978 — 8-4-0 (3-3-0)

S16	●	Indiana	24	17
S23	●	Wake Forest	13	11
S30	●	at Rice	37	7
O7	● |	at Florida	34	21
O14	|	Georgia	17	24
O21	● |	at Kentucky	21	0
N4	● |	Mississippi	30	8
N11	|	Alabama [BIRM]	10	31
N18	|	Mississippi State [JAM]	14	16
N25	●	Tulane	40	21
D2	●	Wyoming	24	17
		LIBERTY BOWL		
D23		Missouri	15	20

1979 — 7-5-0 (4-2-0)

S15	●	at Colorado	44	0
S22	●	Rice	47	3
S29		Southern Cal	12	17
O6	● |	Florida	20	3
O13	|	at Georgia	14	21
O20	● |	Kentucky	23	19
O27		Florida State	19	24
N3	● |	Mississippi [JAM]	28	24
N10	|	Alabama	0	3
N17	● |	Mississippi State	21	3
N24		at Tulane	13	24
		TANGERINE BOWL		
D22	●	Wake Forest	34	10

JERRY STOVALL
1980-83 (.511) 22-21-2

1980 — 7-4-0 (4-2-0)

S6		Florida State	0	16
S13	●	Kansas State	21	0
S20	●	Colorado	23	20
S27		at Rice	7	17
O4	● |	at Florida	24	7
O11	● |	Auburn	21	17
O18	● |	at Kentucky	17	10
N1	● |	Mississippi	38	16
N8	|	at Alabama	7	28
N15	|	Mississippi State [JAM]	31	55
N22	●	Tulane	24	7

LSU 425

THE SCHOOLS

1981 3-7-1 (1-4-1)

S5	|	Alabama	7	24
S12		at Notre Dame	9	27
S19	●	Oregon State	27	24
S26	●	Rice	28	14
O3	|	Florida	10	24
O10	|	at Auburn	7	19
O17	● |	Kentucky	24	10
O24		Florida State	14	38
O31	= |	Mississippi *JaM*	27	27
N14	|	Mississippi State	9	17
N28		at Tulane	7	48

1982 8-3-1 (4-1-1)

S18	●	Oregon State	45	7
S25	●	Rice	52	13
O2	● |	at Florida	24	13
O9	= |	Tennessee	24	24
O16	● |	at Kentucky	34	10
O23	●	South Carolina	14	6
O30	● |	Mississippi	45	8
N6	● |	Alabama *Birm*	20	10
N13	|	at Mississippi State	24	27
N20	●	Florida State	55	21
N27		Tulane	28	31
		ORANGE BOWL		
J1		Nebraska	20	21

1983 4-7-0 (0-6-0)

S10		Florida State	35	40
S17	●	at Rice	24	10
S24	●	Washington	40	14
O1	|	Florida	17	31
O8	|	at Tennessee	6	20
O15	|	Kentucky	13	21
O22	●	South Carolina	20	6
O29	|	Mississippi *JaM*	24	27
N5	|	Alabama	26	32
N12	|	Mississippi State	26	45
N19	●	at Tulane	20	7

BILL ARNSPARGER
1984-86 (.750) 26-8-2

1984 8-3-1 (4-1-1)

S8	= |	at Florida	21	21
S15	●	Wichita St.	47	7
S22	●	Arizona	27	26
S29	●	at Southern Cal	23	3
O13	● |	Vanderbilt	34	27
O20	● |	at Kentucky	36	10
O27		Notre Dame	22	30
N3	● |	Mississippi	32	29
N10	● |	Alabama *Birm*	16	14
N17	|	at Mississippi State	14	16
N24	●	Tulane	33	15
		SUGAR BOWL		
J1		Nebraska	10	28

1985 9-2-1 (4-1-1)

S14	●	at North Carolina	23	13
S21	●	Colorado State	17	3
O5	|	Florida	0	20
O12	● |	at Vanderbilt	49	7
O19	● |	Kentucky	10	0
N2	● |	Mississippi *JaM*	14	0
N9	= |	Alabama	14	14
N16	● |	Mississippi State	17	15
N23	●	at Notre Dame	10	7
N30	●	at Tulane	31	19
D7	●	East Carolina	35	15
		LIBERTY BOWL		
D27		Baylor	7	21

1986 9-3-0 (5-1-0)

S13	●	Texas A&M	35	17
S20		Miami, Ohio	12	21
O4	● |	at Florida	28	17
O11	● |	Georgia	23	14
O18	● |	at Kentucky	25	16
O25	●	North Carolina	30	3
N1	|	Mississippi	19	21
N8	● |	Alabama *Birm*	14	10
N15	● |	Mississippi State *JaM*	47	0
N22	●	Notre Dame	21	19
N29	●	Tulane	37	17
		SUGAR BOWL		
J1		Nebraska	15	30

MIKE ARCHER
1987-90 (.598) 27-18-1

1987 10-1-1 (5-1-0)

S5	●	at Texas A&M	17	3
S12	●	Fullerton St.	56	12
S19	●	Rice	49	16
S26	=	Ohio State	13	13
O3	● |	Florida	13	10
O10	● |	at Georgia	26	23
O17	● |	Kentucky	34	9
O31	● |	Mississippi *JaM*	42	13
N7	|	Alabama	10	22
N14	● |	Mississippi State	34	14
N21	●	at Tulane	41	36
		GATOR BOWL		
D31	●	South Carolina	30	13

1988 8-4-0 (6-1-0)

S3	●	Texas A&M	27	0
S17	● |	at Tennessee	34	9
S24		at Ohio State	33	36
O1	|	at Florida	6	19
O8	● |	Auburn	7	6
O15	● |	Kentucky	15	12
O29	● |	Mississippi	31	20
N5	● |	at Alabama	19	18
N12	● |	at Mississippi State	20	3
N19		Miami, Fla.	3	44
N26	●	Tulane	44	14
		HALL OF FAME BOWL		
J2		Syracuse	10	23

1989 4-7-0 (2-5-0)

S2		at Texas A&M	16	28
S16		Florida State	21	31
S30	●	Ohio U.	57	6
O7	|	Florida	13	16
O14	|	at Auburn	6	10
O21	|	at Kentucky	21	27
O28	|	Tennessee	39	45
N4	● |	at Mississippi	35	30
N11	|	Alabama	16	32
N18	● |	Mississippi State	44	20
N25	●	at Tulane	27	7

1990 5-6-0 (2-5-0)

S8	● |	Georgia	18	13
S15	●	Miami, Ohio	35	7
S22	|	at Vanderbilt	21	24
S29	●	Texas A&M	17	8
O6	|	at Florida	8	34
O20	● |	Kentucky	30	20
O27		at Florida State	3	42
N3	|	Mississippi	10	19
N10	|	at Alabama	3	24
N17	|	Mississippi State *JaM*	22	34
N24	●	Tulane	16	13

CURLEY HALLMAN
1991-94 (.364) 16-28

1991 5-6-0 (3-4-0)

S7	|	at Georgia	10	31
S14		at Texas A&M	7	45
S21	● |	Vanderbilt	16	14
O5	|	Florida	0	16
O12	●	Arkansas State	70	14
O19	● |	at Kentucky	29	26
O26		Florida State	16	27
N2	● |	Mississippi *JaM*	25	22
N9	|	Alabama	17	20
N16	|	Mississippi State	19	28
N23	●	at Tulane	39	20

1992 2-9-0 (1-7-0)

S5		Texas A&M	22	31
S12	● |	Mississippi State	24	3
S19	|	at Auburn	28	30
S26		Colorado State	14	17
O3	|	Tennessee	0	20
O10	|	at Florida	21	28
O17	|	Kentucky	25	27
O31	|	Mississippi *JaM*	0	32
N7	|	Alabama	11	31
N21	●	Tulane	24	12
N27	|	at Arkansas	6	30

1993 5-6-0 (3-5-0)

S4		at Texas A&M	0	24
S11	● |	at Mississippi State	18	16
S18	|	Auburn	10	34
S25	|	at Tennessee	20	42
O2	●	Utah State	38	17
O9	|	Florida	3	58
O16	|	at Kentucky	17	35
O30	● |	Mississippi	19	17
N6	● |	at Alabama	17	13
N20	●	Tulane	24	10
N27	|	Arkansas	24	42

1994 4-7-0 (3-5-0)

S3		Texas A&M	13	18
S10	● |	Mississippi State	44	24
S17	|	at Auburn	26	30
O1	|	South Carolina	17	18
O8	|	at Florida	18	42
O15	● |	Kentucky	17	13
O29	|	at Mississippi	21	34
N5	|	Alabama	17	35
N12		Southern Miss	18	20
N19	●	at Tulane	49	25
N26	● |	Arkansas *LR*	30	12

GERRY DiNARDO
1995-99 (.570) 32-24-1

1995 7-4-1 (4-3-1)

S2		at Texas A&M	17	33
S9	● |	at Mississippi State	34	16
S16	● |	Auburn	12	6
S23	●	Rice	52	7
S30	= |	at South Carolina	20	20
O7	|	Florida	10	28
O14	|	at Kentucky	16	24
O21	●	North Texas	49	7
N4	|	at Alabama	3	10
N11	● |	Mississippi	38	9
N18	● |	Arkansas	28	0
		INDEPENDENCE BOWL		
D29	●	Michigan State	45	26

1996 10-2 (6-2)

S7	●	Houston	35	34
S21	● |	at Auburn	19	15
S28	●	New Mexico St.	63	7
O5	● |	Vanderbilt	35	0
O12	|	at Florida	13	56
O19	● |	Kentucky	41	14
O26	● |	Mississippi State	28	20
N9	|	Alabama	0	26
N16	● |	at Mississippi	39	7
N23	●	Tulane	35	17
N29	● |	Arkansas *LR*	17	7
		PEACH BOWL		
D28	●	Clemson	10	7

1997 9-3 (6-2)

S6	●	Texas El Paso	55	3
S13	● |	at Mississippi State	24	9
S20	|	Auburn	28	31
S27	●	Akron	56	0
O4	● |	at Vanderbilt	7	6
O11	● |	Florida	28	21
O18	|	Mississippi	21	36
N1	● |	at Kentucky	63	28
N8	● |	at Alabama	27	0
N15		Notre Dame	6	24
N28	● |	Arkansas	31	21
		INDEPENDENCE BOWL		
D28	●	Notre Dame	27	9

1998 4-7 (2-6)

S12	●	Arkansas State	42	6
S19	● |	at Auburn	31	19
S26	●	Idaho	53	20
O3	|	Georgia	27	28
O10	|	at Florida	10	22
O17	|	Kentucky	36	39
O24	● |	Mississippi State	41	6
O31	|	at Mississippi	31	37
N7	|	Alabama	16	22
N21		at Notre Dame	36	39
N27	|	Arkansas *LR*	14	41

HAL HUNTER
1999 (1.000) 1-0

1999 3-8 (1-7)

S4	●	San Jose State	29	21
S11	●	North Texas	52	0
S18	|	Auburn	7	41
O2	|	at Georgia	22	23
O9	|	Florida	10	31
O16	|	at Kentucky	5	31
O23	|	at Mississippi State	16	17
O30	|	Mississippi	23	42
N6	|	at Alabama	17	23
N13		Houston	7	20
N26	● |	Arkansas	35	10

NICK SABAN
2000-04 (.750) 48-16

2000 8-4 (5-3)

S2	●	Western Carolina	58	0
S9	●	Houston	28	13
S16	|	at Auburn	17	34
S23		UAB	10	13
S30	● |	Tennessee	38	31
O7	|	at Florida	9	41
O14	● |	Kentucky	34	0
O21	● |	Mississippi State	45	38
N4	● |	Alabama	30	28
N11	● |	at Mississippi	20	9
N25	|	Arkansas *LR*	3	14
		PEACH BOWL		
D29	●	Georgia Tech	28	14

2001 10-3 (5-3)

S1	●	Tulane	48	17
S8	●	Utah State	31	14
S29	|	at Tennessee	18	26
O6	|	Florida	15	44
O13	● |	at Kentucky	29	25
O20	● |	at Mississippi State	42	0
O27	|	Mississippi	24	35
N3	● |	at Alabama	35	21
N10	●	Middle Tennessee	30	14
N23	● |	Arkansas	41	38
D1	● |	Auburn	27	14
		SEC CHAMPIONSHIP GAME		
D8	●	Tennessee *Atl*	31	20
		SUGAR BOWL		
J1	●	Illinois	47	34

2002 8-5 (5-3)

S1		at Virginia Tech	8	26
S7	●	Citadel	35	10
S14	●	Miami, Ohio	33	7
S28	● |	Mississippi State	31	13
O5	●	La. Lafayette	48	0
O12	● |	at Florida	36	7
O19	● |	South Carolina	38	14
O26	|	at Auburn	7	31
N9	● |	at Kentucky	33	30
N16	|	Alabama	0	31
N23	● |	Mississippi	14	13
N29	|	at Arkansas	20	21
		COTTON BOWL		
J1		Texas	20	35

2003 13-1 (7-1)

A30	●	La. Monroe	49	7
S6	●	at Arizona	59	13
S13	●	Western Illinois	35	7
S20	● |	Georgia	17	10
S27	● |	at Mississippi State	41	6
O11	|	Florida	7	19
O18	● |	at South Carolina	33	7
O25	● |	Auburn	31	7
N1	●	Louisiana Tech	49	10
N15	● |	at Alabama	27	3
N22	● |	at Mississippi	17	14
N29	● |	Arkansas	55	24
		SEC CHAMPIONSHIP GAME		
D6	●	Georgia *Atl*	34	13
		SUGAR BOWL		
J4	●	Oklahoma	21	14

2004 9-3 (6-2)

S4	●	Oregon State	22	21
S11	●	Arkansas State	53	3
S18	|	at Auburn	9	10
S25	● |	Mississippi State	51	0
O2	|	at Georgia	16	45
O9	● |	at Florida	24	21
O23	●	Troy State	24	20
O30	● |	Vanderbilt	24	7
N13	● |	Alabama	26	10
N20	● |	Mississippi	27	24
N26	● |	Arkansas *LR*	43	14
		CAPITAL ONE BOWL		
J1		Iowa	25	30

Neutral Site key: *Mbl* Mobile, AL / *JaM* Jackson, MS / *LR* Little Rock, AR / *Birm* Birmingham, AL / *Mem* Memphis, TN / *AlexL* Alexandria, LA / *NYC* New York, NY / *ColGa* Columbus, GA / *Atl* Atlanta, GA / *Nat* Natchez, MS / *Dal* Dallas, TX / *Shre* Shreveport, LA / *Hou* Houston, TX / *Gul* Gulfport, MS / *Gal* Galveston, TX / *Mont* Montgomery, AL / *JaL* Jackson, LA / *Ind* Indianapolis, IN / *Mor* Monroe, LA / *Bkln* Brooklyn, NY / *Vic* Vicksburg, MS / *Mer* Meridian, MS / *NO* New Orleans, LA / *SA* San Antonio, TX / *ColMs* Columbus, MS / *Hav* Havana, Cuba
f Forfeit † Game Later Forfieted # Disputed Victor * Disputed Score || Designated Conference Game |2 Counted Twice in Conference Standings

LOUISIANA TECH

WITH A PROPENSITY FOR high-octane offense and the willingness to take on all comers, the Bulldogs embody the frontier bravado of the Western Athletic Conference. The same, however, can't be said of their location—and with the exodus of Rice, Tulsa, SMU and UTEP from the WAC after the 2004 season, the Bulldogs' conference membership makes even less sense. Still, Louisiana Tech went through a lot to get to their hallowed spot in Division I-A, so the Bulldogs are all-too happy to endure some long road trips. This is a school that has historically operated in the shadow of neighboring Louisiana State University, going without any of the tradition, facilities or funding that LSU boasts. They've responded by trying harder and, more often than not, filling the air with footballs.

TRADITION In 1989, the statue of a bulldog titled *The Spirit of 1988* was unveiled, celebrating the fighting spirit of the 1988 team that ushered Louisiana Tech into D1-A. The treacherous 1988 schedule included road games at Florida State and Texas A&M. Tech won its first 18 home games over the first five seasons with the bulldog statue. Each player now touches the statue as he comes down a ramp toward the field.

BEST PLAYER Other Bulldogs quarterbacks have put up much bigger numbers, but none is as famous as Shreveport native Terry Bradshaw. Bradshaw (1966-69) is better known for what he did in his pro career with the Pittsburgh Steelers, but his exploits at Louisiana Tech are the reason he was the first overall pick in the 1970 NFL draft—an event that earned the Tech program its first intense national media attention. Bradshaw led the Bulldogs to a 17–4 mark during his junior and senior years, including a Gulf States Conference championship in 1969. He also led Tech to victory in its first bowl game, the 1968 Grantland Rice Bowl. Tech beat Akron 33-13, with Bradshaw passing for two scores and rushing for two more.

BEST COACH Joe Aillet led Tech to a 151–86–8 record from 1940 to 1966, including 12 seasons in which Tech won or shared the conference championship. Aillet, who died in 1971, later served as the school's athletic director and is a charter member of the Louisiana Tech Hall of

PROFILE

Louisiana Tech University
Ruston, La.
Founded: 1894
Enrollment: 9,331
Colors: Red and Blue
Nickname: Bulldogs
Stadium: Joe Aillet Stadium
    Opened in 1968
    Grass; 30,600 capacity
First football game: 1901
All-time record: 523–378–37 (.577)
Bowl record: 1–2–1
Western Athletic Conference championships:
1 (outright)
First-round NFL draftees: 4
Website: www.latechsports.com

THE BEST OF TIMES

Louisiana Tech was a Division II powerhouse in the early 1970s. The Bulldogs were 44–4 from 1971 to 1974, winning the Southland Conference championship all four years. Tech was also named co-national champion by the National Football Foundation after a 12–0 record in 1972, and swept through the Division II playoffs in 1973 for the national championship. UPI named the Bulldogs the 1974 college division national champions despite a 35-14 loss to Central Michigan in the playoffs.

THE WORST OF TIMES

The Bulldogs suffered four consecutive losing seasons from 1992 to 1995 (the only other time was in the program's infancy, 1901 to 1905). Louisiana Tech went 15–29 (4–23 on the road) during this stretch. The 2–9 campaign of 1993 opened with a 50-0 loss at Tennessee.

CONFERENCE

Louisiana Tech has played in the Western Athletic Conference since 2001. The Bulldogs have had three stints as an independent (1901-24, 1982-92 and 1996-2000). Louisiana Tech was a member of the Southern Intercollegiate Athletic Association (1925-38), Louisiana Intercollegiate Conference (1939-47), Gulf States Conference (1948-70), Southland Conference (1971-86) and Big West Conference (1993-95).

DISTINGUISHED ALUMNI

Karl Malone; Trace Adkins, country music star; Joseph Waggoner, nine-term U.S. congressman; Teresa Weatherspoon, WNBA All-Star and Olympian

FIGHT SONG

TECH FIGHT SONG
Fight! Fight! Fight! for old Red and Blue;
Show your might and we'll root for you.
Get on your toes when you meet your foes
And don't let them go through.
Tech! Tech! Tech!
Hit those lines like good old Canines.

Fame. Aillet's successor, Maxie Lambright, was 95–36–2 in 12 seasons (1967-78). His 1973 team routed Tennessee Tech 34-0 to win the first NCAA College Division championship, while his 1977 and 1978 teams made back-to-back trips to the Independence Bowl. Lambright's teams won or shared seven league titles.

BEST TEAM The 1972 team went 12–0, won the Southland Conference title and was named National Football Foundation small college co-champion along with Delaware. The Bulldogs allowed more than 20 points in only one game—and happened to score their season-high output in that game, whipping host Northern Arizona 41-21.

BIGGEST GAME Louisiana Tech completed its perfect 1972 season with a nearly perfect game, a 35-0 blanking of Tennessee Tech in the nationally televised Grantland

Tech has healthy giant-killing aspirations as well, but the long-awaited 2003 showdown with LSU resulted in a 49-10 rout at the hands of the eventual national champs.

Rice Bowl in Baton Rouge. Any semblance of a close game disappeared after the Bulldogs scored three touchdowns in the second quarter to take a 28-0 halftime lead. Future pro star Roger Carr (who would go on to connect with LSU alum Bert Jones as Colts teammates) caught six passes for 141 yards, including a 29-yard touchdown, and linebacker Joe McNeely had 12 solo tackles, recovered a fumble and scored on a 31-yard interception return.

BIGGEST UPSET In 1999, first-year Tech coach Jack Bicknell was no stranger to miracles; after all, it was he who had snapped the ball to Doug Flutie when the Boston College quarterback threw the famous Hail Mary pass to beat Miami 15 years earlier. This time, Bicknell was on the sideline of Legion Field in Birmingham, Ala, when backup quarterback Brian Stallworth threw a 28-yard touchdown

RECORDS

RUSHING YARDS
GAME
302 Jason Davis vs. Louisiana-Lafayette, Sept. 29, 1990 (47 att.)
SEASON
1,774 Ryan Moats, 2004 (288 att.)
CAREER
3,342 Jason Cooper, 1991-94 (739 att.)

PASSING YARDS
GAME
590 Tim Rattay vs. Nebraska, Aug. 29, 1998 (46 of 68)
SEASON
4,943 Tim Rattay, 1998 (380 of 559)
CAREER
12,746 Tim Rattay, 1997-99 (1,015 of 1552)

RECEIVING YARDS
GAME
405 Troy Edwards vs. Nebraska, Aug. 29, 1998 (21 rec.)
SEASON
1,996 Troy Edwards, 1998 (140 rec.)
CAREER
4,352 Troy Edwards, 1996-98 (280 rec.)

POINTS
GAME
30 Three tied; most recently by Troy Edwards vs. Boise State, Oct. 3, 1998 (5 TDs)
SEASON
188 Troy Edwards, 1998 (31 TDs, 1 two-pt. conv.)
CAREER
343 Josh Scobee, 2000-03 (66 FGs, 145 PATs)

CONSENSUS ALL-AMERICANS
1941	Garland Gregory, G
1946	Mike Reed, G
1968-69	Terry Bradshaw, QB
1972-73	Roger Carr, WR/FL
1974	Mike Barber, TE
1974	Fred Dean, DT
1982	Matt Dunigan, QB
1984-85	Doug Landry, LB
1984, 1986	Walter Johnson, DE/LB
1987-88	Glenell Sanders, LB
1992	Willie Roaf, OL
1998	Troy Edwards, WR

pass to a leaping Sean Cangelosi on fourth and 26 with two seconds left, tying Alabama at 28. Kicker Kevin Pond, who had missed one earlier extra point and had another blocked, converted for a shocking upset of the Shaun Alexander-led Tide, who at the time were ranked 18th in the country.

HEARTBREAKER The 1990 team was a potent one, going 8–3–1 and earning a trip to the Independence Bowl. But that season included the One That Got Away: a regular-season contest at No. 5 Auburn in which the Bulldogs held their own for almost 60 minutes before Jim Von Wyl's 30-yard field goal with three seconds left allowed the Tigers to escape with a 16-14 win.

STADIUM Joe Aillet Stadium was named after the legendary Louisiana Tech coach in 1972—four years after it opened with a capacity of 23,000, and four years after Bradshaw christened the stadium with its first touchdown pass. A skybox was added to the press box in 1985, and in 1989 seats were added to bring the facility to its current capacity of 30,600. The Bulldogs have enjoyed two 18-game home winning streaks over the years.

RIVAL Louisiana-Monroe is just 30 miles down the road, but lately the Bulldogs' rival might as well be in a different solar system. They haven't played each other since 2000, when Tech won 42-19. The Bulldogs lead the series 30-13, but the school administration would rather use its nonconference dates to play big names for big bucks. Tech has healthy giant-killing aspirations as well, but it's long-awaited 2003 showdown with LSU resulted in a 49-10 rout at the hands of the eventual national champs.

NICKNAME In 1899, the legend goes, five Louisiana Tech students befriended a stray bulldog that followed them home. Their house caught fire that night, and the bulldog awoke and roused all the students except one. The bulldog reentered the house for the last student, but the young man had already found his way to safety. The dog, sadly, could not, and died in the fire. The students buried the dog in two jackets—one red and one blue. Two years later, when Tech started a football team, it was easy to choose the nickname and colors.

UNIFORMS Louisiana Tech's distinctive red helmet has changed little since the late 1960s. The traditional state outline T logo is one of the longest-standing designs in college football. There have been minor adjustments to the shape and hue of the state outline, and perhaps also to the T, during this period, but the basic design has not changed. In recent years, the Bulldogs have worn all-blue uniforms for home games and blue pants and white jerseys on the road. Tech is one of the few programs that stuck with the old-school look of stripe-ringed shoulders, although that retro look has grown more popular in the 21st century.

NUMBERS Two Tech quarterbacks of recent vintage are fourth and fifth on the all-time passing yardage list: Tim Rattay (12,746) and Luke McCown (12,666). In 2004, the year after McCown's final season, junior tailback Ryan Moats rushed for 1,774 rushing yards.

QUOTE "We run for fun and throw to go."—Billy Ryckman, Tech wide receiver (1973-76)

ALL-CENTURY TEAM

Selected in 2001 by a 20-member committee comprised of current and former Tech coaches, players, administrators and fans.

OFFENSE

1934-37	Johnny Wyss	OL/DL
1940-41	Garland Gregory	OL/DL
1951-54	Jessie Storts	OL/DL
1953-56	Pat Hinton	OL/DL
1954-57	Tommy Hinton	OL/DL
1958-61	Herschel Vinyard	OL/DL
1971-74	Randy Crouch	OL
1971-74	Roy Waters	OL
1989-92	Willie Roaf	OL
1962-65	Wayne Davis	TE/DL
1972-75	Mike Barber	TE
1966-69	Tommy Spinks	WR
1970-73	Roger Carr	WR
1972-75	Pat Tilley	WR
1973-76	Billy Ryckman	WR
1993-96	Chad Mackey	WR
1996-98	Troy Edwards	WR/KR
1959-62	Mickey Slaughter	QB/DB
1966-69	Terry Bradshaw	QB
1979-82	Matt Dunigan	QB
1997-99	Tim Rattay	QB
1953-56	A.L. Williams	RB/DB/KR
1957-59	J.W. Slack	RB/DB
1957-60	Paul Hynes	RB/DB/KR
1964-67	Bob Brunet	RB
1971-74	Charles "Quick Six" McDaniel	RB
1971-74	Roland Harper	RB
1974-77	John Henry White	RB
1973-76	Jerry Pope	K/P
1986-89	Matt Stover	PK
1990-93	Chris Boniol	PK

DEFENSE

1941-42, 1946-47	Charles "Hoss" Newman	DL/OL
1947-50	Leo Sanford	DL/OL
1971-74	Fred Dean	DL
1977-80	Johnny Robinson	DL
1983-86	Walter Johnson	DL
1942, 1945-47	Mike Reed	LB/OL
1957-60	Joe Hinton	LB/OL
1960-63	John Williamson	LB
1967-70	Ron Alexander	LB
1970-73	Joe McNeely	LB
1982-85	Doug "Tank" Landry	LB
1982-85	Doyle Adams	DB
1986-89	Glenell Sanders	LB
1989-92	Myron Baker	LB
1971-73	John Causey	DB
1971-74	Wenford Wilborn	DB/KR
1974-77	Larry Anderson	DB
1989-92	Doug Evans	DB
1961-64	David Lee	P/WR/DL

LOUISIANA TECH ANNUAL STATISTICAL LEADERS

YR	RUSHING	YDS	ATT	AVG	PASSING	ATT	CMP	PCT	YDS	RECEIVING	REC	YDS	AVG
1948	Jimmy Harrison	643	117	5.5		NA	NA	NA	NA	Lenny Vogt	8	87	10.9
1949	Jimmy Harrison	606	131	4.6		NA	NA	NA	NA	Joe Strother	15	197	13.1
1950	Joe Rabb	738	163	4.5		NA	NA	NA	NA	Anthony Cefalu	14	215	15.4
1951	Gene Knecht	374	109	3.4		NA	NA	NA	NA	Ken Bates	18	416	23.1
1952	Jackie Martin	416	86	4.8		NA	NA	NA	NA	Larry Grissom	15	296	19.7
1953	James Oliver	515	74	7.0		NA	NA	NA	NA	Pat Patterson	8	147	18.4
1954	Russell Rainbolt	383	69	5.6		NA	NA	NA	NA	Ken Bates	13	185	14.2
1955	Russell Rainbolt	615	111	5.5		NA	NA	NA	NA	A.L. Williams	14	294	21.0
1956	Jerry Frasier	428	98	4.4		NA	NA	NA	NA	A.L. Williams	8	137	17.1
1957	Paul Hynes	359	79	4.5		NA	NA	NA	NA	Charlie Garris	4	115	28.8
1958	Paul Hynes	633	96	6.6		NA	NA	NA	NA	Tom Causey	10	163	16.3
1959	J.W. Slack	588	134	4.4		NA	NA	NA	NA	Tom Causey	17	516	30.4
1960	Paul Hynes	359	83	4.3	Mickey Slaughter	114	64	.56	834	Tom Causey	39	516	13.2
1961	Jack Lestage, Andy Farless	213	57	3.7	Mickey Slaughter	127	82	.65	856	Jerry Griffin	45	435	9.7
1962	Wayne Noland	285	70	4.1	Mickey Slaughter	138	79	.57	932	Jerry Griffin	25	283	11.3
1963	Gerald McDowell	358	94	3.8	Billy Laird	157	90	.57	1,103	Wayne Davis	23	309	13.4
1964	Gerald McDowell	427	118	3.6	Billy Laird	205	106	.52	1,361	Wayne Davis	26	372	14.3
1965	Robert Brunet	477	100	4.8	Billy Laird	179	109	.61	1,285	Wayne Davis	50	611	12.2
1966	Eddie Taylor	434	107	4.1	Phil Robertson	205	90	.44	1,011	Tommy Spinks	20	272	12.1
1967	Robert Brunet	631	106	6.0	Terry Bradshaw	139	78	.56	981	Tommy Spinks	62	811	13.1
1968	Buster Herren	591	133	4.4	Terry Bradshaw	339	176	.52	2,890	Tommy Spinks	54	885	16.4
1969	Buster Herren	556	128	4.3	Terry Bradshaw	248	136	.55	2,314	Tommy Spinks	46	995	21.6
1970	Mike Lord	458	136	3.4	Ken Lantrip	326	170	.52	2,156	Eric Johnson	40	606	15.2
1971	Charles McDaniel	913	166	5.5	Ken Lantrip	221	119	.54	2,105	Roger Carr	29	738	26.4
1972	Glen Berteau	569	142	4.0	Denny Duron	217	104	.48	1,891	Roger Carr	40	1,018	25.5
1973	Charles McDaniel	690	123	5.6	Denny Duron	199	93	.47	1,607	Roger Carr	30	587	19.6
1974	Charles McDaniel	700	143	4.9	Randy Robertson	91	50	.55	830	Pat Tilley	29	497	17.1
1975	John Henry White	835	152	5.5	Randy Robertson	114	72	.66	1,079	Pat Tilley	53	926	17.5
1976	John Henry White	767	145	5.3	Steve Haynes	216	120	.56	1,981	Billy Ryckman	77	1,382	17.9
1977	John Henry White	1,094	261	4.2	Keith Thibodeaux	260	137	.53	2,384	Rod Foppe	59	1,274	21.6
1978	George Yates	637	155	4.1	Keith Thibodeaux	198	81	.41	1,128	Scooter Spruiell	37	642	17.4
1979	Jessie Clark	443	92	4.8	Matt Buchanan	128	60	.47	840	Freddie Brown	21	300	14.3
1980	Earl James Greer	517	127	4.1	Matt Dunigan	313	149	.48	1,939	Leland Padgett	34	547	16.1
1981	Carlton Jacobs	688	134	5.1	Matt Dunigan	313	153	.49	1,898	Freddie Brown	26	464	17.7
1982	Carlton Jacobs	360	88	4.1	Matt Dunigan	413	222	.54	2,843	Freddie Brown	30	647	21.6
1983	Nate Williams	357	115	3.1	David Brewer	329	161	.49	1,848	Karl Terrebone	43	523	12.2
1984	Garlon Powell	608	160	3.8	Kyle Gamby	115	53	.46	804	Todd Breske	20	493	24.7
1985	Garlon Powell	591	139	4.3	Jordan Stanley	238	123	.52	1,544	Lifford Jackson	19	425	22.4
1986	Garlon Powell	970	233	4.2	Jordan Stanley	150	74	.49	863	Paddy Doyle	47	705	15.0
1987	Garlon Powell	458	109	4.2	David McKinney	198	78	.39	908	Roderick Wright	26	351	13.5
1988	Derrick Douglas	602	133	4.5	Conroy Hines	262	116	.44	1,286	Bobby Slaughter	49	623	12.7
1989	Derrick Douglas	1,232	281	4.4	Gene Johnson	296	147	.50	1,779	Bobby Slaughter	60	832	13.9
1990	Michael Richardson	1,114	222	5.0	Gene Johnson	297	165	.56	2,129	Bobby Slaughter	78	994	12.7
1991	Jason Davis	1,351	244	5.5	Gene Johnson	207	118	.57	1,281	Paul Bland	29	366	12.6
1992	Jason Cooper	733	174	4.2	Aaron Ferguson	184	99	.54	1,025	Corey Parham	65	741	11.4
1993	Jason Cooper	590	177	3.3	Jason Martin	193	92	.48	1,218	Chad Mackey	50	564	11.3
1994	Jason Cooper	1,189	243	4.9	Jason Martin	342	160	.47	1,882	Dean Jackson	62	790	12.7
1995	Lee Ragsdale	768	108	7.1	Jason Martin	370	206	.56	2,606	Chad Mackey	90	1,253	13.9
1996	Lee Ragsdale	808	176	4.6	Jason Martin	415	247	.60	3,360	Chad Mackey	85	1,466	17.2
1997	Bobby Ray Tell	800	118	6.8	Tim Rattay	477	293	.61	3,881	Troy Edwards	102	1,707	16.7
1998	Bobby Ray Tell	584	101	5.8	Tim Rattay	559	380	.68	4,943	Troy Edwards	140	1,996	14.3
1999	Bobby Ray Tell	552	94	5.9	Tim Rattay	516	342	.66	3,922	James Jordan	81	824	10.2
2000	John Simon	598	109	5.5	Luke McCown	369	244	.66	2,544	James Jordan	109	1,003	9.2
2001	Joe Smith	931	186	5.0	Luke McCown	521	302	.58	3,665	John Simon	78	839	10.8
2002	Joe Smith	1,216	208	5.8	Luke McCown	505	296	.59	3,337	Chris Norwood	61	748	12.3
2003	Ryan Moats	1,300	199	6.5	Luke McCown	432	246	.57	3,246	D.J. Curry	53	668	12.6
2004	Ryan Moats	1,774	288	6.2	Matt Kubik	242	123	.51	1,818	Tramissi Davis	25	527	21.1

The NCAA began including postseason stats in 2002

LOUISIANA TECH ALL-TIME SCORES

WIN/LOSS PERCENTAGE SINCE 1936

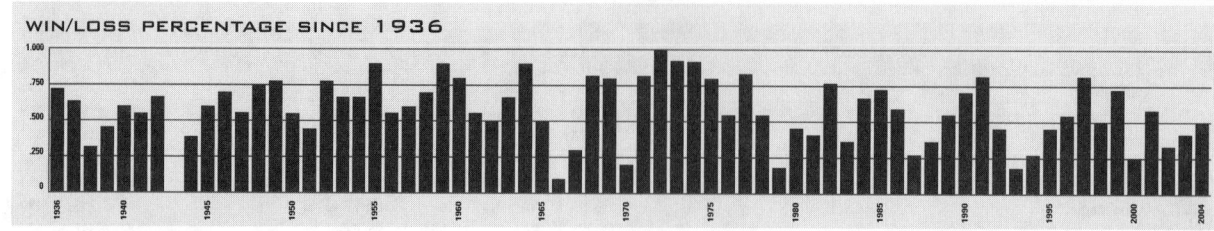

EDWIN BARBER
1901 (.000)   0-2

1901   0-2-0
| O28 | | LSU | 0 | 57 |
| N23 | | Arkansas | 0 | 16 |

1902
NO TEAM

NO HEAD COACH

1903   0-1-0
| O30 | | LSU | 0 | 16 |

E.G. PIERCE
1904 (.250)   1-3

1904   1-3-0
O16		at LSU	0	17
O23		at Tulane	0	11
O29	●	LSU	6	0
N25		at Mississippi State	5	32

J.Y. BRAGG
1905 (.000)   0-1

1905   0-1-0
| N18 | | at LSU | 0 | 16 |

Z.T. YOUNG
1906 (.583)   2-1-3

1906   2-1-3
U	=	Monroe AC	0	0
U	●	Ouachita Baptist	5	0
N9		at LSU	0	17
U		Ruston AC	26	0
U	=	Henderson St.	5	5
U	=	YMCA	0	0

GEORGE L. WATKINS
1907 (.900)   9-1

1907   9-1-0
U	●	Monroe AC	11	0
U	●	Monroe AC	11	0
O11		at LSU	0	28
U	●	Ouachita Baptist	37	0
U	●	Northwestern St	43	4
U	●	Henderson St.	21	0
U	●	Ruston AC	49	0
U	●	Jackson Milty. Coll.	35	5
U	●	Arkansas Coll.	23	0
U	●	Mississippi Coll.	18	0

A.L. CORNELL
1908 (.563)   4-3-1

1908   4-3-1
U	●	16th US Infantry	28	0
O10		at Mississippi State	0	47
U	=	Shreveport AC	0	0
U	●	Hendrix	72	0
U		Henderson St.	10	11
U	●	16th US Infantry	18	6
U	●	Ouachita Baptist	77	5
N23		LSU	0	22

PERCY S. PRINCE
1909-15, '19 (.589)   24-16-5

1909   4-1-0
U	●	Monroe AC	28	0
U	●	Centenary	60	0
N4		LSU *AlexL*	0	23
U	●	Henderson St.	3	0
U	●	Northwestern St.	45	0

1910   7-0-0
U	●	Winnfield HS	75	0
U	●	Mississippi Coll.	6	0
U	●	Ouachita Baptist	6	0
U	●	Louisiana Coll.	60	0
U	●	La. Lafayette	75	0
U	●	Henderson St.	11	6
U	●	Northwestern St.	32	0

1911   4-2-1
O13		at Mississippi	0	15
O21		at Tulane	0	45
U	●	at Ouachita Baptist	6	0
U	=	at Hendrix	5	5
U	●	Northwestern St.	39	0
N4	●	Mississippi Coll.	24	0
U	●	Henderson St.	24	3

1912   1-2-1
U	=	Ouachita	0	0
U	●	Centenary	20	0
N9		Mississippi Coll.	13	14
U		Henderson St.	0	28

1913   3-4-1
O4		LSU	2	20
N1		at Mississippi	0	26
U	●	Centenary	7	0
U	=	Ouachita	0	0
U		Ouachita	0	19
U		Mississippi Coll.	3	7
U	●	Louisiana Coll.	53	0
U	●	Louisiana Normal	40	0

1914   2-4-0
O3		at LSU	0	60
U		Henderson St.	0	28
U		Hendrix	0	20
U	●	Centenary	33	7
U		Mississippi Coll.	8	14
U	●	Centenary	14	0

1915   3-1-2
U	●	Northwestern St.	20	7
N3	=	La. Lafayette	7	7
U		Ouachita	0	19
N20	●	Mississippi Coll.	0	0
U	●	Louisiana Coll.	40	0
U	●	Henderson St	43	0

A. FLACK
1916 (.333)   2-4

1916   2-4-0
N18		La. Lafayette	0	26
U		Henderson St.	0	14
U	●	Ouachita	10	6
U		Mississippi Coll.	0	13
U	●	Northwestern St.	24	0
U		Hendrix	6	7

V.S. PUGH
1917 (.400)   2-3

1917   2-3-0
U		La. Lafayette	0	57
U		Ouachita	10	53
U		Northwestern St.	0	6
U	●	St. Charles Coll.	43	7
U	●	Henderson St.	19	13

1918
NO TEAM

PERCY S. PRINCE

1919   0-2-0
| U | | Henderson St. | 7 | 14 |
| U | | Northwestern St. | 0 | 27 |

R.F. CLARK
1920-21 (.917)   11-1

1920   5-1-0
U		Northwestern St.	0	12
O30	●	La. Lafayette	1	0 *f*
U	●	So. Arkansas	3	0
U	●	St. Charles Coll.	13	7
U	●	at Louisiana Coll.	14	0
U	●	Louisiana Coll.	7	0

1921   6-0-0
U	●	Arkansas A&M	13	0
O29	●	at So. Arkansas	22	13
N4	●	Ouachita Baptist	20	0
N11	●	La. Lafayette	20	0
N19	●	Northwestern St.	17	0
N24	●	at Centenary	14	7

WILLIAM H. DIETZ
1922-23 (.767)   11-3-1

1922   5-1-1
U	●	Hendrix	34	0
U	●	Clark Coll.	100	0
O19		at Northwestern St.	0	0
U	●	Henderson St.	34	0
U	●	at Louisiana Coll.	33	6
U	●	So. Arkansas	89	0
U		at Centenary	0	22

1923   6-2-0
O6	●	Little Rock Coll.	26	0
O12	●	at Henderson St.	7	3
O20		at Tulane	7	13
O27	●	Millsaps	20	0
N3	●	at Louisiana Coll.	40	7
N10	●	at Northwestern St.	66	7
N17	●	Loyola-New Orleans	28	6
N29		at Centenary	0	27

PHILLIP H. ARBUCKLE
1924 (.188)   1-6-1

1924   1-6-1
O4	=	Louisiana Coll.	0	0
O11		at Tulane	12	42
O18		Dallas U.	0	9
O25	●	Little Rock Coll.	12	0
N1		at St. Edwards Coll.	12	28
N8		Ouachita Coll.	0	13
N15		at La. Lafayette	6	20
N27		at Loyola-New Orleans	0	27

R.C. KENNEY
1925 (.222)   1-6-2

1925   1-6-2
S26	=	Henderson-Brown	0	0
O3	●	at Mississippi Coll.	6	0
O10		Little Rock Coll.	0	10
O17		Millsaps	2	13
O24	=	at Louisiana Coll.	0	0
O30		Ouachita Baptist	0	28
N7		at Tulane	9	37 *
N20		La. Lafayette	13	22
D5		at Fort Benning	7	66

HUGH E. WILSON
1926-27 (.529)   8-7-2

1926   5-2-2
S25		at Tulane	0	40
O2	●	Northwestern St.	28	0
O9	●	Clark Coll.	36	0
O16	=	Tenn. Doctors	0	0
O30	●	Millsaps	13	7
N5	●	at La. Lafayette	23	0
N11	●	at Centenary	0	7
N19	=	Sam Houston St.	6	6
N25	●	Louisiana coll.	28	0

1927   3-5-0
S24		at LSU	0	45
O1	●	Clark Coll.	30	0
O8		at Mississippi State	0	14
O15	●	at Northwestern St.	33	0
O29		Mississippi Coll. Mor	0	7
N5	●	La. Lafayette	13	0
N11		at Stetson	7	19
N19		at Centenary	0	33

F.A. ROCKWELL
1928-29 (.368)   6-11-2

1928   2-7-0
S29		Coll. Of Ozarks	0	18
O6	●	Clark Mem. Memphis	19	6
O13		at Northwestern St.	0	6
O20		Samford Mor	0	52
O27		Union U.	0	26
N4		La. Lafayette	6	45 *
N10	●	Millsaps	15	7
N17		at Centenary	2	63
N29		Mississippi Coll. *Mor*	0	12

1929   4-4-2
O5	●	Clark Coll.	21	12
O12	=	at So. Arkansas	6	6
O19	●	Ouachita Baptist *EdoA*	13	0
O26		at LSU	7	53
N2		Northwestern St.	0	0
N9		at Millsaps Coll.	6	0
N16		at Mississippi Coll.	6	21
N23		at Centenary	0	19
N30		at Louisiana Coll.	13	19
D7	●	La. Lafayette	24	7

GEORGE M. BOHLER
1930-33 (.469)   15-17

1930   3-6-0
S27		at LSU	0	71
O4		at Loyola-New Orleans	0	26
O11	●	Arkansas A&M	12	0
O17		Mississippi Coll. *JacM*	0	39
O25	●	La. Lafayette		70
N1		at Northwestern St.	14	19
N8		at Millsaps	0	19
N22		Centenary	0	13
N27	●	Louisiana Coll.	6	0

1931   7-0-0
O3	●	Copiah-Lincoln JC	13	7
O10	●	at Union U.	39	0
O17	●	La. Lafayette	38	0
O23	●	Millsaps	13	7
O30	●	Northwestern St.	18	2
N14	●	Mississippi Coll.	19	13
N21	●	at Louisiana Coll.	27	7

1932   4-4-0
O1		Copiah-Lincoln JC	0	2
O8	●	Union U.	46	7
O15	●	Delta St.	20	0
O21	●	at La. Lafayette	15	0
O28		at Northwestern St.	0	33
N5	●	Millsaps	19	14
N12		at Mississippi Coll.	7	14
N19		Louisiana Coll.	6	13

1933 1-7-0

S23		Copiah-Lincoln JC	9	10
O7		Henderson St.	0	7
O14		La. Lafayette	7	13
O20		at Texas Tech	10	40
O28	●	Northwestern St.	6	0
N4		Millsaps	0	3
N11		Coll. Of Ozarks	0	40
N18		Louisiana Coll.	0	30

L.P. "EDDIE" McLANE
1934-38 (.580) 27-19-4

1934 4-6-0

S22	●	Holmes JC	7	0
S29	●	So. Arkansas	7	0
O5		at Henderson St.	0	27
O12		at La. Lafayette	0	25
O20	●	Lambuth Coll.	41	0
O26		at Northwestern St.	0	6
N3	●	Millsaps	7	13
N10		at Mississippi Coll.	0	32
N17	●	Delta St.	26	0
N23		Louisiana Coll.	0	13

1935 8-1-0

O5	●	Tenn. Tech	44	0
O11	●	La. Lafayette	25	0
O19	●	Union U.	27	0
O26	●	Northwestern St.	32	0
N2		Millsaps	20	21
N9	●	Mississippi Coll.	21	7
N23	●	at Louisiana Coll.	25	7
N28	●	Southern Miss	27	0
D7	●	at Tampa	32	7

1936 6-2-1

O2	●	W. Tenn. Teachers	44	0
O8	●	at La. Lafayette	20	7
O16		Southern Miss	7	12
O24	●	at Northwestern St.	32	0
O31		at Tulane	13	22
N6	●	Tampa	6	0
N14	●	Millsaps	13	0
N21	=	Louisiana Coll.	6	6
N26	●	Illinois Wesleyan	12	0

1937 6-3-2

S17	●	Oklahoma City	27	6
S25		at Mississippi	0	13
O2		Illinois Wesleyan	0	2
O8	●	Millsaps	7	0
O15	●	Southern Miss	7	0
O23	●	Northwestern St. SHRE	14	0
N6	●	at Tampa	26	13
N12	=	La. Lafayette	0	0
N20		at Louisiana Coll.	12	13
N25	●	South Dakota	20	6
D4	=	Centenary	7	7

1938 3-7-1

S17	●	Millsaps	19	7
S23		Mississippi Coll.	13	26
O1		at Mississippi	7	27
O8		at Mississippi State	0	48
S22		Northwestern St. SHRE	6	7
S28		at Oklahoma City	6	7
N4		La. Lafayette	7	27
N11	●	Louisiana Coll.	7	0
N19	●	Cornell Coll.	26	0
N22		at Centenary	7	14
D3	=	at S.E. Louisiana	0	0

RAY E. DAVIS
1939 (.455) 5-6

1939 5-6-0

S16	●	Arkansas A&M	32	0
S23	●	Illinois Wesleyan	12	7
S29	●	Alabama St. Teachers	39	0
O7		at W. Kentucky Teachers	7	20
O13		at Birmingham South	6	7
O21		Northwestern St. SHRE	0	26
O28	●	Tampa	13	0
N4		La. Lafayette	6	12
N11	●	at Louisiana Coll.	10	9
N18		at Texas-El Paso	0	27
D9		Centenary	0	19

JOE AILLET
1940-66 (.633) 151-86-8

1940 6-4-0

S21		at LSU	7	39
S28		Ouachita Coll. EDOA	0	17
O5	●	Texas-El Paso	19	7
O11	●	W. Kentucky Teachers	7	6
O19		Northwestern St. SHRE	0	13
O26	●	Illinois Wesleyan	20	14
N1		at La. Lafayette	6	7
N8	●	Louisiana Coll.	15	6
N15	●	S.E. Louisiana	26	6
N30	●	at Centenary	6	0

1941 5-4-1

S20		at LSU	0	25
S27	=	at Texas-El Paso	0	0
O3		Southern Miss	7	19
O11		at Auburn	0	34
O18	●	Northwestern St. SHRE	10	0
O25	●	at S.E. Louisiana	21	14
O31	●	La. Lafayette	12	0
N8	●	at Louisiana Coll.	45	0
N15		Hardin-Simmons	0	13
N29	●	Centenary	39	7

1942 6-3-0

S25	●	Texas-El Paso	20	0
O2	●	Waco Army	45	0
O9	●	Marshall	26	0
O16	●	Sam Houston St.	46	0
O24		Northwestern St. SHRE	6	10
O30		at La. Lafayette	7	12
N7	●	S.E. Luoisiana	56	14
N14		at Hardin-Simmons	13	47
N21	●	at Memphis	33	7

1943

NO TEAM

1944 3-5-1

S16		Texas St.	0	26
S23		Selman Army	6	13
S30	●	Marine OCS	72	0
O7		Fort Benning	0	33
O14		La. Lafayette	0	15
O28	●	at Northwestern St.	21	7
N4		Arkansas A&M	14	20
N11	=	Northwestern St.	0	0
N18	●	at La. Lafayette	7	0

1945 6-4-0

S22	●	LC Army	7	2
S29	●	Howard Coll.	32	6
O5	●	La. Lafayette	14	12
O13		at Mississippi	21	26
O20	●	Texas St.	20	14
O27	●	Northwestern St.	18	7
N3		Barksdale	7	12
N10	●	at Northwestern St.	7	2
N17		La. Lafayette	7	13
N24		Auburn MONT	0	29

1946 7-3-0

S21		at Southern Miss	0	7 *
S26	●	Howard Payne	13	7
O5	●	Louisiana Coll.	33	6
O12	●	Arkansas State	38	0
O19	●	at Mississippi	7	6
O26	●	Northwestern St. SHRE	14	7
N2	●	at La. Lafayette	34	6
N8		S.E. Louisiana	14	22
N15		Oklahoma City	2	6
N30	●	Texas St.	34	20

1947 5-4-0

S27		Howard Payne	0	14
O4		at Auburn	0	14
O11		Southern Miss	6	7
O18	●	at Louisiana Coll.	30	12
O25	●	Northwestern St. SHRE	24	0
N1	●	La. Lafayette	9	0
N8	●	at S.E. Louisiana	20	18
N15		at Oklahoma City	13	28
N27	●	Centenary	52	14

1948 7-2-1

S18	●	Howard Payne	20	0
S25	●	Bradley	17	14
O2	=	at Auburn	13	13
O9		at Houston	33	40
O16	●	Louisiana Coll.	21	7
O23	●	Northwestern St. SHRE	10	7
O30	●	at La. Lafayette	24	14
N6	●	S.E. Louisiana	19	13
N13		at Southern Miss	6	20
N25	●	Memphis	20	14

1949 7-2-0

S17		at Howard Payne	18	22
S24		at Bradley	18	20
O1	●	Texas St.	20	0
O15	●	at Louisiana Coll.	26	7
O22	●	Northwestern St. SHRE	28	21
O29	●	La. Lafayette	21	0
N5	●	at S.E. Louisiana	20	14
N12	●	Southern Miss	34	13
N19	●	Oklahoma City	45	0

1950 5-4-1

S23	●	Howard Payne	27	20
S30	=	at East Texas St.	0	0
O7	●	at S.F. Austin	21	6
O14		at Xavier	21	35
O21	●	Northwestern St. SHRE	15	7
O28	●	Louisiania Coll.	21	9
N4		at La. Lafayette	13	41
N11	●	S.E. Louisiana	14	0
N18		at Southern Miss	20	41
D1		Memphis	0	6

1951 4-5-0

S22	●	at Howard Payne	34	27
S29		East Texas St.	7	27
O6		at Memphis	14	26
O13	●	at S.E. Okla. St.	40	6
O20	●	Northwestern St. SHRE	21	6
O27	●	Louisiana Coll.	20	14
N3		La. Lafayette	7	34
N10		at S.E. Loiisiana	7	19
N17		Southern Miss	7	33 *

1952 6-1-2

S20	●	McNeese State	6	0
S27	●	at Florida State	32	13
O4	●	Memphis	26	7
O11	●	Central Okla. St.	34	6
O18	●	Northwestern St. SHRE	22	0
O25	●	Louisiana Coll.	35	13
N1	=	at La. Lafayette	19	19
N8	=	S.E. Louisiana	7	7
N15		at Southern Miss	0	52

1953 6-3-0

S19	●	La. Monroe	61	6
S26	●	at Louisiana Coll.	20	6
O3		at Memphis	7	13
O17		Northwestern St. SHRE	7	15
O24	●	Florida State	32	21
O31	●	La. Lafayette	27	7
N7	●	S.E. Louisiana	12	0
N14		Southern Miss	0	30
N28	●	at McNeese State	56	21

1954 6-3-0

S18	●	Louisiana Coll.	27	0
S25		at Southern Miss	0	28
O9	●	McNeese State	21	10
O16	●	Howard Payne	13	7
O23	●	Northwestern St. SHRE	13	6
O30		at La. Lafayette	0	25
N6		S.E. Louisiana	24	35
N13	●	Austin Coll.	40	14
N20	●	at La. Monroe	51	6

1955 9-1-0

S17	●	at Louisiana Coll.	39	7
S24		Southern Miss	6	7
O1	●	Abilene Christian	21	7
O8	●	at McNeese State	14	0
O15	●	at Howard Payne	26	7
O22	●	Northwestern St. SHRE	21	20
O29	●	La. Lafayette	28	14
N5	●	at S.E. Louisiana	21	0
N12	●	Austin Coll.	40	21
N19	●	La. Monroe	34	14

1956 4-3-2

S15	=	Louisiana Coll.	0	0
S22		at Southern Miss	0	14
S29	●	S.F. Austin	37	14
O6	●	McNeese State	6	0
O13		at Arkansas State	13	21
O20	=	Northwestern St. SHRE	0	0
O27	●	at La. Lafayette	33	6
N3	●	S.E. Louisiana	12	6
N17		at La. Monroe	0	7

1957 6-4-0

S21		Southern Miss	0	7
S28	●	at S.F. Austin	19	13
O5		at McNeese State	6	13
O12	●	La. Lafayette	28	13
O19	●	Northwestern St. SHRE	20	13
O26	●	Arkansas State	25	19
N2		at Mc Murray	24	26
N9	●	at S.E. Louisiana	21	14
N16		Memphis	7	17
N23	●	La. Monroe	15	6

1958 7-3-0

S20		at Southern Miss	0	14
S27	●	at Arkansas State	14	7
O4	●	McNeese State	17	0
O11	●	at La. Lafayette	33	0
O18		Northwestern St. SHRE	14	18
O25	●	Arkansas A&M	40	0
N1		at Memphis	12	26
N8	●	S.E. Louisiana	10	6
N15	●	Mc Murray	20	12
N22	●	at La. Monroe	46	21

1959 9-1-0

S19		at Lamar	6	13
S26	●	Arkansas State	35	0
O3	●	at McNeese State	28	0
O10	●	La. Lafayette	21	13
O24	●	Northwestern St. SHRE	27	14
O31	●	at Pensacola Navy	7	0
N7	●	at S.E. Louisiana	14	0
N14	●	Memphis	10	8
N21	●	La. Monroe	27	0
N28	●	Southern Miss	16	0

1960 8-2-0

S17	●	Lamar	20	0
S24		at Arkansas State	3	7
O1	●	McNeese State	15	14
O8		at La. Lafayette	2	6
O15	●	Pensacola Navy	28	19
O22	●	Northwestern St. SHRE	13	7
O29	●	Mc Murray	23	7
N5	●	S.E. Louisiana	17	14
N12	●	at Southern Miss	10	7
N19	●	at La. Monroe	20	15

1961 5-4-0

S23	●	Arkansas State	47	8
S30	●	at McNeese State	21	16
O7	●	La. Lafayette	12	0
O14		at Texas Arlington	7	8
O21		Northwestern St. SHRE	7	19
O28	●	at Tenn. Tech	21	10
N4		at S.E. Louisiana	14	34
N11		Southern Miss	0	7
N18	●	La. Monroe	27	7

1962 4-4-0

S29	●	McNeese State	14	6
O6		at La. Lafayette	6	13
O13	●	Texas Arlington	19	9
O20		Northwestern St. SHRE	2	19
O27	●	Tenn. Tech	33	20
N3	●	S.E. Louisiana	27	15
N10		at La. Monroe	6	13
N17		at Southern Miss	14	22 *

1963 6-3-0

S28		at McNeese State	6	27
O5	●	Louisiana Coll.	12	6
O12	●	La. Lafayette	45	0
O19	●	Northwestern St. SHRE	27	13
O26	●	at Texas Arlington	34	13
N2		at Tenn. Tech	19	21
N9		at S.E. Louisiana	7	15
N16	●	Southern Miss	10	0
N23	●	La. Monroe	28	7

1964 9-1-0

S19	●	at Louisiana Coll.	8	7
S26	●	McNeese State	10	6
O3	●	East Texas St.	15	7
O10	●	at La. Lafayette	6	3
O17	●	Texas Arlington	19	7
O24	●	Northwestern St. SHRE	16	7
O31	●	Tenn. Tech	25	6
N7	●	S.E. Louisiana	28	7
N14		at Southern Miss	7	14
N21	●	at La. Monroe	23	0

1965 4-4-0

S18		at Rice	0	14
O2		at McNeese State	14	20
O9		La. Lafayette	8	16
O23	●	Northwestern St. Shre	42	14
O30	●	at Tenn. Tech	20	6
N6	●	at S.E. Louisiana	16	14
N13		Southern Miss	7	31
N20	●	La. Monroe	52	7

1966 1-9-0

S17		at Southern Miss	0	14
S24		Alabama Birm	0	34
O1		McNeese State	7	10
O8		at Arkansas State	13	26
O15		at La. Lafayette	12	21
O22		Northwestern St. Shre	7	28
O29		at Tenn. Tech	9	21
N5	●	S.E. Louisiana	13	6
N12		at Lamar	16	31
N19		at La. Monroe	6	14

MAXIE LAMBRIGHT
1967-78 (.722) 95-36-2

1967 3-7-0

S23	●	at Delta St.	34	7
S30		at McNeese State	12	20
O7		La. Lafayette	14	20
O14	●	Arkansas State	6	3
O21		Northwestern St. Shre	0	7
O28		at New Mexico State	7	48
N4		at S.E. Louisiana	21	27
N11	●	Lamar	41	31
N18		La. Monroe	14	21
N23		Southern Miss	7	58

1968 9-2-0

S21	●	at Mississippi State	20	13
S28	●	East Carolina	35	7
O5		McNeese State	20	27
O12		at La. Lafayette	24	28
O19	●	Northwestern St. Shre	42	39
N2	●	at Southern Miss	27	20
N9	●	S.E. Louisiana	35	7
N16	●	at Lamar	34	7
N23	●	at La. Monroe	25	10
N28	●	New Mexico State	42	24
		GRANTLAND RICE BOWL		
D14	●	Akron	33	13

1969 8-2-0

S27	●	at East Carolina	24	6
O4	●	at McNeese State	35	18
O11	●	La. Lafayette	34	21
O18	●	Northwestern St. Shre	42	21
O25	●	at U.T. Chattanooga	23	7
N1		Southern Miss	23	24
N8	●	at S.E. Louisiana	25	24
N15	●	Lamar	77	40
N22	●	La. Monroe	34	6
		GRANTLAND RICE BOWL		
D13		E. Tennessee St.	14	34

1970 2-8-0

S19	●	U.T. Chattanooga	28	3
S26		at Lamar	0	6
O3		McNeese State	14	16
O10		at La. Lafayette	10	20
O17		at Arkansas State	17	38
O24		Northwestern St. Shre	17	20
O31		Tampa	10	14
N7		S.E. Louisiana	21	24
N14	●	at Southern Miss	27	6
N21		at La. Monroe	21	28

1971 9-2-0

S18	●	at Tampa	28	20
S25	●	Lamar	26	7
O2		at McNeese State	22	29
O9	●	La. Lafayette	35	15
O16	●	Arkansas State	28	27
O23	●	Northwestern St. Shre	33	21
O30	●	at S.E. Louisiana	24	9
N6	●	at U.T. Chattanooga	35	20
N13		Southern Miss	20	24
N20	●	La. Monroe	23	0
		PIONEER BOWL		
D11	●	Eastern Michigan	14	3

1972 12-0-0

S9	●	at La. Lafayette	7	0
S16	●	at Southern Miss	33	14
S23	●	McNeese State	34	17
S30	●	Abilene Christian	35	12
O7	●	at Texas Arlington	35	14
O14	●	Arkansas State. LR	38	17
O21	●	Northwestern St. Shre	20	16
O28	●	S.E. Louisiana	21	0
N4	●	at No. Arizon	41	21
N11	●	Eastern Michigan	24	17
N18	●	at La. Monroe	10	6
		GRANTLAND RICE BOWL		
D10	●	Tenn. Tech	35	0

1973 12-1-0

S15		at Eastern Michigan	19	21
S22	●	La. Lafayette	23	0
S29	●	at McNeese State	10	7
O6	●	No. Arizona	37	7
O13	●	Arkansas State	23	7
O20	●	Northwestern St. Shre	26	7
O27	●	at S.E. Louisiana	26	7
N3	●	Texas Arlington	44	0
N10	●	at Lamar	17	3
N17	●	La. Monroe	40	0
		DIVISION II PLAYOFFS		
D1	●	Western Illinois	18	13
D8	●	Boise State WiFl	38	34
D15	●	Western Kentucky Sac	34	0

1974 11-1-0

S7	●	Illinois St.	16	7
S21	●	at Texas Arlington	42	15
S28	●	at Arkansas State	20	7
O12	●	at La. Lafayette	35	20
O19	●	Northwestern St. Shre	34	0
O26	●	McNeese State	24	17
N2	●	S.E. Louisiana	34	13
N9	●	Lamar	28	0
N16	●	at U.T. Chattanooga	35	14
N23	●	at La. Monroe	26	10
		DIVISION II PLAYOFFS		
N30	●	Western Carolina	10	7
D7		Central Michigan WiFl	14	35

1975 8-2-0

S13	●	at McNeese State	21	14
S20	●	Texas Arlington	37	8
S27	●	at Lamar	24	10
O11	●	La. Lafayette	24	14
O18	●	Northwestern St. Shre	41	14
O25		Southern Miss	14	24
N1	●	at S.E. Louisiana	33	28
N8	●	La. Monroe	41	23
N15	●	U.T. Chattanooga	49	20
N29		Arkansas State	13	30

1976 6-5-0

S11		at Ball State	28	41
S18		McNeese State	13	15
S25	●	at Arkansas State	27	13
O2		at La. Lafayette	26	31
O9		at Texas Arlington	35	56
O16	●	Lamar	37	7
O23	●	Northwestern St. Shre	35	6
O30		North Texas Shre	8	14
N6	●	at U.T. Chattanooga	49	7
N13	●	Southern Miss	23	22
N20	●	at La. Monroe	55	35

1977 9-1-2

S17	●	Cal St. Sacremento Shre	56	0
S24	=	at Illinois St.	21	21
O1	●	at McNeese State	14	7
O8	=	La. Lafayette	21	21
O15	●	at Arkansas State	20	7
O22	●	Northwestern St.	30	8
O29	●	Texas Arlington	34	12
N5	●	at Lamar	23	6
N12	●	at Southern Miss	28	10
N19		North Texas Shre	14	41
N26	●	La. Monroe	20	0
		INDEPENDENCE BOWL		
D17	●	Louisville	24	14

1978 6-5-0

S16		U.T. Chattanooga	7	12
S23	●	at Texas Arlington	28	21
S30	●	McNeese State	34	20
O7		at La. Lafayette	6	24
O14	●	Ball State	17	7
O21	●	Northwestern St. Shre	45	20
O28		North Texas Shre	14	16
N4	●	Lamar	40	3
N11	●	Arkansas State	24	10
N18		La. Monroe	0	18
D16		East Carolina	13	35

LARRY BEIGHTOL
1979 (.100) 1-9

PAT PATTERSON
1979 (1.000) 1-0

1979 2-9-0

S1		at New Mexico	0	34 †
S15		at U.T. Chattanooga	7	24
S22		at Lamar	7	19
S29		at Miami, Fla.	0	6
O6	●	La. Lafayette	17	0
O13		Arkansas State	7	14
O20		Northwestern St. Shre	21	25
O27		Texas Arlington	16	30
N3		North Texas Shre	17	19
N10		at McNeese State	7	41
N17	●	La. Monroe	13	10

BILLY BREWER
1980-82 (.557) 19-15-1

1980 5-6-0

S13		at Mississippi State	11	31
S20		at Southern Miss	11	38
S27	●	Western Illinois	42	6
O4	●	at E. Tennessee St.	7	3
O11	●	Lamar	16	7
O18	●	Northwestern St. Shre	27	23
O25		Texas Arlington	20	21
N1	●	at Arkansas State	28	0
N8		McNeese State	8	45
N15		at La. Lafayette	9	27
N22		at La. Monroe	14	19

1981 4-6-1

S5		at West Texas St.	10	17
S12	●	E. Tennessee St.	31	3
S19		Baylor Shre	21	28
S26		at Texas A&M	7	43
O3		La. Monroe	0	35
O10		at Texas Arlington	14	31
O17	●	at Lamar	16	7
O24	●	Northwestern St.	37	33
O31	=	La. Lafayette	17	17
N7		at McNeese State	20	27
N14	●	Arkansas State	32	0

1982 10-3-0

S11	●	West Texas St.	28	7
S18	●	Eastern Michigan	49	12
S25		at Texas A&M	27	38
O2	●	at Texas Arlington	17	14
O9	●	at La. Monroe	17	10
O16	●	Lamar	40	13
O23	●	Northwestern St. Shre	33	0
O30	●	at Arkansas State	24	14
N6	●	McNeese State	35	14
N13		at La. Lafayette	19	29
N20	●	at Southern Miss	13	6
		DIVISION I-AA PLAYOFFS		
D4	●	So. Carolina St.	38	3
D11		Delaware	0	17

A.L. WILLIAMS
1983-86 (.594) 28-19-1

1983 4-7-0

S10		at New Mexico State	7	15
S17		at Southern Miss	10	28
S24		Lamar	12	18
O1	●	U.T. Chattanooga	17	14
O8		McNeese State	20	24
O15		at Arkansas State	7	21
O22	●	at North Texas	25	18
O29	●	Northwestern St. Shre	21	10
N5		La. Monroe	0	17
N12	●	at Texas Arlington	24	17
N19		at La. Lafayette	9	13

1984 10-5-0

S1	●	at S.E. Louisiana	17	9
S8		La. Lafayette	16	17
S15		at Southern Miss	0	34
S22		at Mississippi	8	14
S29	●	North Texas	17	12
O6	●	at McNeese State	24	17
O13	●	Arkansas State	20	10
O20	●	Northwestern St. Shre	5	0
O27	●	at Lamar	22	7
N3		at La. Monroe	10	12
N10	●	Texas Arlington	34	0
		DIVISION I-AA PLAYOFFS		
N24	●	Mississippi Valley	66	19
D1	●	Alcorn St.	44	21
D8	●	Middle Tennessee	21	13
D15		Montana St. ChSC	6	19

1985 8-3-0

S7		at Southern Miss	0	28
S14	●	La. Lafayette	24	23
S21	●	at West Texas St.	20	10
S28	●	S.E. Louisiana	40	7
O5	●	at North Texas	33	8
O12	●	McNeese State	35	3
O19		at Arkansas State	13	31
O26	●	Northwestern St. Shre	33	17
N2	●	Lamar	23	22
N9		La. Monroe	9	13
N16	●	at Texas Arlington	29	14

1986 6-4-1

A30	●	at Tulsa	22	17
S13		at Baylor	7	38
S20	●	West Texas St.	24	21
S27		at Fresno State	10	34
O4	●	North Texas	17	10
O11	●	at McNeese State	28	16
O18		Arkansas State	17	20
O25	=	Northwestern St. Shre	13	13
N1	●	at Lamar	39	20
N8		at La. Monroe	6	20
N22	●	at La. Lafayette	23	14

CARL TORBUSH
1987 (.273) 3-8

1987 3-8-0

S5		at Baylor	3	13
S12		La. Monroe	7	44
S19		at Mississippi State	13	14
S26	●	at Kansas	16	11
O3		at U.T. Chattanooga	18	20
O10	●	McNeese State	7	3
O17		at Arkansas State	3	37
O24	●	Northwestern St.	23	0
O31		at Texas A&M	3	32
N14		S.W. Missouri	10	13
N21		at North Texas	5	10

1988-1992
INDEPENDENT

JOE RAYMOND PEACE
1988-95 (.477) 40-44-4

1988 4-7-0

S3		at Mississippi State	14	21
S10		Houston Shre	0	60
S17		at Wyoming	6	38
S24	●	Nicholls St.	31	10
O1	●	at Kansas State	31	28
O8	●	La. Lafayette	19	16
O22		at Florida State	3	66
O29		Arkansas State Shre	22	31
N5		at Texas A&M	17	56
N12		Southern Miss	19	26
N19	●	at La. Monroe	23	0

1989   5-4-1

S2	●	at La. Lafayette	40 14
S9		at Western Michigan	20 24
S16		at Florida	7 34
S30	=	at East Carolina	29 29
O7		at Akron	24 31
O14	●	Northern Illinois	42 21
O21		at Arkansas State	40 37
O28		Tulsa	34 31
N4		La. Monroe	24 6
N11		at Auburn	23 38

1990   8-3-1

S1		at East Carolina	17 27
S8		at McNeese State	51 3
S15		at Western Michigan	21 27
S22		Arkansas State	40 7
S29		La. Lafayette	24 10
O6		at Auburn	14 16
O13		at Tulsa	35 21
O27		S.F. Austin	31 22
N3		at La. Monroe	31 7
N10		Akron	36 15
N17		Colorado State	31 30

INDEPENDENCE BOWL

D15	=	Maryland	34 34

1991   8-1-2

A31		at Houston	3 73
S14	●	Montana	21 11
S21	●	at Eastern Michigan	17 14
S28	●	at Arkansas State	42 10
O5		at Northern Illinois	37 3
O12	=	at South Carolina	12 12
O26	=	at La. Lafayette	14 14
N2	●	La. Monroe	35 10
N9	●	So. Illinois	48 16
N16	●	Southern Miss	30 14
N23		at Texas-El Paso	21 17

1992   5-6-0

S5	●	at Baylor	10 9
S12	●	Eastern Michigan	31 17
S19		at Southern Miss	13 16
S26		Alabama *Birm*	0 13
O3		at Fresno State	14 48
O10	●	La. Lafayette	21 7
O17	●	East Tennessee St.	65 7
O31	●	Arkansas State	23 0
N7		at South Carolina	13 14
N14		at Mississippi	6 13
N21		at West Virginia	3 23

1993-1995
BIG WEST

1993   2-9-0 (2-4-0)

S4		at Tennessee	0 50
S18		at South Carolina	3 34
S25		Alabama *Birm*	3 56 †
O2	●	Arkansas State	17 3
O16		at East Carolina	28 31
O23	|	at San Jose State	6 31
O30	●	Northern Illinois	17 16
N6	|	Nevada-Las Vegas	23 28
N13	|	at Utah State	13 24
N20	|	Central Florida	16 38
N27	|	at La. Lafayette	17 21

1994   3-8-0 (1-5-0)

S3		at Baylor	3 44
S10	●	Houston	32 7
S17		at South Carolina	6 31
O1	|	La. Lafayette	3 13
O8	|	at Nevada-Las Vegas	20 24
O15	|	Utah State	3 7
O22	|	at Northern Illinois	17 27
O29		at West Virginia	16 52
N5	●	Northwestern St.	38 28
N12	|	San Jose State	6 27
N19	● |	at Arkansas State	20 14

1995   5-6-0 (2-4-0)

A31	●	at Bowling Green	28 21
S9	●	at Houston	19 7
S16		at South Carolina	21 68
S23	● |	Arkansas State	28 25
S30	●	Tulsa	27 23
O7	|	at New Mexico State	13 48
O14	|	at Pacific	41 47
O21	|	Nevada	45 49
N4	|	at La. Lafayette	33 40
N11		at Vanderbilt	6 29
N18	● |	Northern Illinois	59 14

1996-2000
INDEPENDENT

GARY CROWTON	
1996-98 (.618)	21-13

1996   6-5

A31	●	Middle Tennessee	20 0
S7		Baylor *Shre*	16 24
S14	●	at Central Michigan	38 37
S21		at Mississippi State	38 23
S28		La. Lafayette	31 37
O5		at Texas A&M	13 63
O12		Arkansas *LR*	21 38
O19		Toledo	61 20
O26	●	UAB	35 31
N2	●	at Northern Illinois	40 14
N9		Arkansas State *LR*	38 55

1997   9-2

A30	●	Bowling Green	30 23
S13	●	La. Monroe	17 16
S20	●	Central Michigan	56 28
S27		Arkansas *LR*	13 17
O4	●	California	41 34
O11		at Auburn	13 49
O18		Arkansas State	42 14
O25		at Boise State	31 27
N1		at Alabama	26 20
N8	●	at UAB	32 29
N15	●	at La. Lafayette	63 24

1998   6-6

A29		at Nebraska	27 56
S5		Central Florida	30 64
S12		at Texas A&M	7 28
S19	●	at La. Lafayette	77 14
S26		at Wyoming	19 31
O3	●	Boise State	63 28
O10	●	at La. Monroe	44 14
O17	●	UAB	54 23
O24		at Auburn	17 32
O31	●	Nicholls St.	56 28
N7	●	at Arkansas State	69 21
N26		at Tulane	30 63

JACK BICKNELL III	
1999-Present (.465)	33-38

1999   8-3

A28		at Florida State	7 41
S4		Texas A&M	17 37
S11	●	Sam Houston St.	55 17
S18	●	Alabama *Birm*	29 28
O2	●	at La. Lafayette	41 31
O16	●	Middle Tennessee	42 18
O23	●	at Central Florida	46 35
O30	●	at Toledo	34 17
N6	●	La. Monroe	58 17
N13	●	at UAB	41 20
N26		at Southern Cal	19 45

2000   3-9

A26	●	Miss. Valley St.	63 10
S2		at Kansas State	10 54
S9		at Penn State	7 67
S16		S.F. Austin	31 34
S23		at Tulsa	10 22
O7		at Middle Tennessee	21 49
O14	●	La. Lafayette	48 14
O21		at Auburn	28 38
O28		at Miami, Fla.	31 42
N4		Central Florida	16 20
N11	●	at La. Monroe	42 19
N18		at Hawaii	10 27

2001-Present
WAC

2001   7-5 (7-1)

S1	● |	SMU *Shre*	36 6
S8		at Oklahoma State	23 30
S29	|	at Fresno State	28 38
O6	● |	San Jose State	41 20
O13	● |	at Nevada	45 42
O20	|	at Auburn	41 48
O27	● |	Rice	41 38
N3	● |	Boise State	48 42
N10	● |	at Texas-El Paso	53 30
N17		at Kansas State	7 40
N24	● |	at Tulsa	19 7

HUMANITARIAN BOWL

D31		Clemson	24 49

2002   4-8 (3-5)

A31	●	Oklahoma State *Shre*	39 36
S7		at Clemson	13 33
S14	● |	Tulsa	53 9
S21		at Penn State	17 49
S28		at Texas A&M	3 31
O5		at Rice	20 37
O19		at SMU	34 37
O26	●	Nevada	50 47
N9		at San Jose State	30 42
N16		at Boise State	10 36
N23	|	Texas-El Paso *Shre*	38 24
D5	|	Fresno State	13 45

2003   5-7 (3-5)

A28	|	Miami, Fla. *Shre*	9 48
S6	●	at La. Lafayette	34 3
S13	●	at Michigan State	20 19
S20	|	at Fresno State	6 16
O4	|	Boise State	37 43
O11	●	at Texas-El Paso	38 35
O18	|	Hawaii	41 44
O25	●	at Nevada	42 34
N1	|	at LSU	10 49
N8	● |	SMU	41 6
N15	|	at Tulsa	18 48
N29	|	Rice	14 49

2004   6-6 (5-3)

S6	● |	Nevada	38 21
S11	● |	La. Lafayette	24 20
S18	|	at Miami, Fla.	0 48
S25	|	at Tennessee	17 42
O2	● |	Fresno State	28 21
O9	|	at Auburn	7 52
O16	● |	at SMU	41 10
O23	|	Texas-El Paso	27 44
N6	|	at Hawaii	23 34
N13	● |	Tulsa *Shre*	38 21
N20	|	at Boise State	14 55
N29	|	at Rice	51 14

LOUISIANA-LAFAYETTE

BY RYAN HOCKENSMITH

GIVE LOUISIANA-LAFAYETTE CREDIT. The Ragin' Cajuns' list of All-Americas isn't long, but the school sure knows how to develop quarterbacks. First came Christian Keener Cagle, a three-year starter from 1922 to 1925, back when the school was known as Southwestern Louisiana. Long before the NCAA eligibility restraints were conceived, Cagle then joined the Army and became a three-time All-America there, too, winning the Helms Hall Award, a precursor to the Heisman Trophy. Next came Alvin "The Swamp Fox" Dark, who led the school to its last undefeated mark, 5–0–1 in 1943, after he had transferred from LSU. Later came all-everything quarterback Brian Mitchell, who went on to fame as one of the NFL's finest return specialists ever.

Yet despite the success of the quarterbacks that came before him, no player in Louisiana-Lafayette history rallied the Cajuns faithful like Lafayette-born Jake Delhomme, who still holds school records for passing yards, touchdowns, attempts and completions. From his first game, the Golden Boy captivated fans with his Southern charm and guts, the same traits that endeared him to Carolina Panthers fans forever after the team's Super Bowl run in the 2003 season. It's the fans' loyalty to Delhomme that best typifies their commitment to Lafayette football. When Delhomme was projected as a backup in Carolina, local Lafayette ESPN Radio affiliate, KPEL 1420, aired Panthers' games. "He's still this area's favorite player," says school sports information director Daryl Cetnar. "Just on the off-chance he'd be the starter, people went crazy to be able to follow the Golden Boy. They're just drawn to him." And they're drawn to this gritty, striving football program, of which Delhomme is perhaps the best reflection.

TRADITION Even with a $75 tailgating fee and evening home games, hundreds of fans start firing up their barbecue grills at 8 a.m. in the Cajun Field parking lot. The tailgating atmosphere, ranked the Sun Belt's best, has led to some fans never making it to the game, which has kept Louisiana-Lafayette's attendance around the 14,000 mark in recent years. Coach Rickey Bustle's Ragin' Cajun Walk, in which the players walk through a heavily populated section of the parking lot, has helped show the fans the way into the stadium.

BEST PLAYER It's tough to pick against a bonafide Cajun demigod like Delhomme. But on raw performance

PROFILE

University of Louisiana at Lafayette
Lafayette, La.
Founded: 1900
Enrollment: 15,043
Colors: Vermilion and White
Nickname: Ragin' Cajuns
Stadium: Cajun Field
    Opened in 1971
    Grass; 31,000 capacity
First football game: 1901
All-time record: 451–472–34 (.489)
Website: www.ragincajuns.com

THE BEST OF TIMES

Fans nicknamed quarterback Jake Delhomme the Golden Boy, and his unprecedented four-year run can fittingly be called UL Lafayette's golden era. Coming off back-to-back two-win seasons before his arrival, Delhomme helped his team win two Big West titles from 1993 to 1996. The team hasn't had a winning season since.

THE WORST OF TIMES

The program has never been as low as after Delhomme left in 1996. UL Lafayette has endured two 1–10 marks, two 2–9 records, one 3–8 and one 3–9 season. An 0–7 start in 2003 looked like rock-bottom until third-year coach Rickey Bustle rallied his team to a 4–1 finish to end the season.

CONFERENCE

The Ragin' Cajuns joined the Sun Belt in 2001 after affiliations with the Big West (1993-95), Southland (1971-81) and Gulf States (1948-70) conferences. The program was independent from 1982 to 1992 and from 1996 to 2000.

DISTINGUISHED ALUMNI

James Lee Burke, author; Kathleen Babineaux Blanco, governor of Louisiana; Ron Guidry, baseball player; Ali Landry, actress/Miss USA; John Kennedy Toole, author

FIGHT SONG

RAGIN' CAJUN FIGHT SONG
Fight on, Cajuns, fight on to victory,
For the Red and White,
We will sing of triumph and glory
For our team tonight,
You will hear the rage of the Cajuns,
So let's give a yell,
Justle up and bustle up and
Fight on to victory U of L.

It doesn't take a BCS computer to figure out why they call Cajun Field "The Swamp."

alone, Mitchell gets the nod. He has gained more yards than any player in NFL history with the exception of Jerry Rice, most coming on punt and kickoff returns. But get this: in four years in Lafayette, Mitchell never returned a kick. Nah, all he did was throw for 5,447 yards, run for 3,335 and account for a combined 70 rushing and passing touchdowns. He became the first player in NCAA history to throw for 5,000 yards and run for 3,000, and Mitchell still holds school records in rushing and scoring. Delhomme took the Cajuns from 2–9 in 1992 to 8–3 in 1993, rousing fans with three single-digit wins, capped by a comeback 21-17 win against rival Louisiana Tech in the season finale. Two outstanding years later, Delhomme locked up his place in Louisiana-Lafayette lore by rallying the Cajuns from a 23-10 halftime deficit against Louisiana Tech. He left Lafayette with a 25–19 career mark and two Big West championships.

BEST COACH Of Louisiana-Lafayette's four Gulf State Conference championships, three came under Russ Faulkinberry. His 13-year run (1961-73) ended with an 0–10 final season and a 66–62–2 record. However, Faulkinberry guided the Ragin' Cajuns to their longest streak of non-losing seasons—eight—and one of the school's two bowl appearances, a gut-busting 26-25 loss to Tennessee State in the 1970 Grantland Rice Bowl. He even instigated the school's name change, from Bulldogs to Raging Cajuns in the mid-1960s, and a move to Cajun Field in 1971, ushering in a new era of football in Lafayette.

BEST TEAM Alvin Dark spent only one year, 1943, as Lafayette's quarterback, but what a year it was (he lettered in four other sports as well). Dark did a little bit of everything: running, passing and even kicking, to help Louisiana-Lafayette go 5–0–1 and qualify for the school's only January football game. In that Oil Bowl, Dark helped avenge the team's only blemish, a 20-20 tie in November against Arkansas A&M, with two touchdowns, one rushing and one passing, a field goal and three extra points in a 24-7 win. He capped an outstanding athletics career by becoming Major League Baseball's 1948 Rookie of the Year with the Boston Braves and later a World Series-winning manager with the Oakland Athletics.

RECORDS

RUSHING YARDS
GAME
271 Brian Mitchell vs. Colorado State, Nov. 21, 1987 (26 att.)
SEASON
1,311 Brian Mitchell, 1989 (237 att.)
CAREER
3,335 Brian Mitchell, 1986-89 (678 att.)

PASSING YARDS
GAME
473 Eric Rekieta vs. Louisiana-Monroe, Oct. 11, 2003 (33 of 54)
SEASON
2,901 Jake Delhomme, 1996 (201 of 377)
CAREER
9,216 Jake Delhomme, 1993-96 (655 of 1,246)

RECEIVING YARDS
GAME
220 Willie Culpepper vs. McNeese State, Nov. 15, 1986 (8 rec.)
SEASON
1,173 Brandon Stokley, 1998 (65 rec.)
CAREER
3,702 Brandon Stokley, 1995-98 (241 rec.)

POINTS
GAME
30 Brian Mitchell vs. Lamar, Nov. 11, 1989 (5 TDs); Jim Barton vs. Delta State, Oct. 19, 1968 (5 TDs)
SEASON
114 Brian Mitchell, 1989 (19 TDs)
CAREER
286 Brian Mitchell, 1986-89 (47 TDs, 2 two-pt. conv.)

CONSENSUS ALL-AMERICANS
1969 Glenn LaFleur, LB

BIGGEST GAME At each open end of bowl-shaped Cajun Field, grassy space allows for overflow fans to stand and watch games. The Ragin' Cajuns rarely have needed it, but they certainly did on Oct. 6, 1990, when they welcomed a vulnerable 1–3 Alabama team in what was hyped as the biggest game in school history. About 2,500 fans packed in behind both end zones to watch Louisiana-Lafayette—then still named Southwestern Louisiana—give the Crimson Tide everything they could handle before falling 25-6. Bama went on to win five of its last six and qualify for the Fiesta Bowl.

BIGGEST UPSET An overflow crowd of 38,783 was on hand six years later, in 1996, when No. 25 Texas A&M, a heavy favorite, visited Cajun Field. The Aggies would soon be unranked, as a carnivorous Louisiana-Lafayette defense forced eight turnovers and scored three defensive touchdowns. After a 30-yard interception return for a touchdown by defensive back Britt Jackson and a two-point conversion gave the Cajuns a 29-22 lead with 6:30 left in the game, the crowd watched as the Aggies drove to the Cajuns' 26-yard line with 31 seconds left. But defensive back Damon Mason stepped in front of a pass down the middle of the field and snagged perhaps the most important interception in school history, sealing the first win over a ranked foe. By the time the surge of Cajuns fans got done romping across the field, one of the goalposts was gone, found in pieces a few days later and a mile away from the stadium.

HEARTBREAKER Late in the 1970 Grantland Rice Bowl, the Ragin' Cajuns overcame a barrage of eight interceptions and eight penalties to take a 25-14 lead over Tennessee State in the fourth quarter. But a blocked extra point, the second botched one of the game, kept the lead at 11. That allowed Tennessee State to squeeze past the Ragin' Cajuns 26-25 with two late touchdowns.

STADIUM It doesn't take a BCS computer to figure out why they call Cajun Field "The Swamp," and it has nothing to do with Gainesville's Gators. Surrounded by wetlands and bayous and dug in a perfect bowl shape two feet below sea level, Cajun Field requires four 60-horsepower pumps and a high-tech drainage system to keep the field playable, especially during hurricane season. The only things missing are college football's Hurricanes and Gators. Neither Miami nor Florida has ever visited.

RIVAL With a matchup that dates back to 1910, Louisiana-Lafayette has no love lost for cross-state foe Louisiana Tech, which holds a 46-33-6 advantage in the series. The Ragin' Cajuns always will savor the 1993 game, though, when Louisiana Tech, which hadn't lost to Lafayette since 1984, came to Cajun Field with the Big West title on the line. Tech led 17-14 at halftime, but the Ragin' Cajuns took a 21-17 lead on tailback Steve Mocek's one-yard touchdown plunge at the end of the third quarter. The advantage held up and Louisiana-Lafayette secured its first Big West championship.

NICKNAME In the early 1960s, coach Russ Faulkinberry and sports information director Bob Henderson put their heads together to come up with a name change. Almost 90% of Faulkinberry's teams were made up of Louisiana players of French-speaking Acadian backgrounds, so the two came up with Raging Cajuns to replace Bulldogs. The name stuck, though decades later the school ditched the second "g." Eventually every athletics team at Louisiana-Lafayette adopted the nickname.

MASCOT Well after the nickname switch, the school kept a live bulldog as the team mascot. In the late 1970s, though, when the bulldog died, the mascot job went up for grabs for the first of many times. First, the school had the Cajun Chicken, dressed in a tuxedo with an oversize chicken head. After three years, his name changed to Cajun Man, but he kept his outfit. The school reverted back to a live bulldog again from 1995 to 1997, but switched in 1998 to Cayenne, the Cajun Pepper. Cayenne, dressed in an enormous pepper suit, has been on the sideline ever since.

UNIFORMS In the mid-1960s, the school used the Acadian flag as part of its helmet design, before switching to a dark red shell with the letters USL in the mid-1970s. The full nickname, Ragin' Cajuns, debuted on the helmet in 1999. The teams' uniforms used to feature plain block lettering with the player's number on the front. In the last five years, though, the school's jerseys have been livened up considerably and now feature a flaming chili pepper above the numbers.

QUOTE "There's never been anything this sweet."
—Coach Nelson Stokley, after Louisiana-Lafayette's 1996 upset of Texas A&M

LOUISIANA-LAFAYETTE ANNUAL STATISTICAL LEADERS

YR	RUSHING	YDS	ATT	AVG	PASSING	ATT	CMP	PCT	YDS	RECEIVING	REC	YDS	AVG
1978	Allen Strambler	336	92	3.7	David Guidry	108	45	.42	745	Rodney Smith	19	424	22.3
1979	Rodney Smith	782	185	4.2	Dwight Prudhomme	121	46	.38	594	Curtis Calhoun	18	202	11.2
1980	Ed Blanco	478	102	4.7	Phil Reynolds	277	128	.46	1,680	Curtis Calhoun	32	443	13.8
1981	Greg Davis	401	85	4.7	Curt Calderera	199	98	.49	1,426	Brent Anderson	31	358	11.5
1982	Trinion Smith	247	61	4.0	Dwight Prudhomme	191	94	.49	1,320	Doug Waddell	21	276	13.1
1983	Thomas Jackson	739	130	5.7	Donnie Schexnider	164	89	.54	1,016	Clarence Verdin	30	276	9.2
1984	Dwayne Williams	460	121	3.8	Don Wallace	167	88	.53	1,127	Pierre Perkins	26	508	19.5
1985	Thomas Jackson	700	130	5.4	Thomas King	250	59	.24	658	Pierre Perkins	13	153	11.8
1986	Brian Mitchell	514	111	4.6	Richard Pannell	167	81	.49	989	Willie Culpepper	30	651	21.7
1987	Brian Mitchell	767	150	5.1	Brian Mitchell	156	72	.46	1,100	Willie Culpepper	31	586	18.9
1988	Brian Mitchell	743	180	4.1	Brian Mitchell	273	129	.47	1,807	Willie Culpepper	34	603	17.7
1989	Brian Mitchell	1,311	237	5.5	Brian Mitchell	312	143	.46	1,966	Quent McCollum	43	670	15.6
1990	Damon Denaburg	440	97	4.5	James Freeman	209	99	.47	1,332	Wayde Butler	43	398	9.3
1991	Tyjuan Hayes	445	119	3.7	Tyjuan Hayes	84	36	.43	502	Wayde Butler	38	491	12.9
1992	Damon Denaburg	269	53	5.1	Tyjuan Hayes	147	79	.54	1,033	Wayde Butler	50	671	13.4
1993	Steve Mocek	490	126	3.9	Jake Delhomme	259	145	.56	1,842	Marcus Carter	53	801	15.1
1994	Steve Mocek	686	172	4.0	Jake Delhomme	259	119	.46	1,712	Donald Richard	41	723	17.6
1995	Marcus Prier	979	222	4.4	Jake Delhomme	351	190	.54	2,761	Brandon Stokley	75	1,121	14.9
1996	Kenyon Cotton	858	194	4.4	Jake Delhomme	377	201	.53	2,901	Brandon Stokley	81	1,160	14.3
1997	Elvis Joseph	532	139	3.8	Lance Domec	143	72	.50	925	Franco Smith	28	404	14.4
1998	Darren Brister	646	153	4.2	Barton Folse	132	68	.52	848	Brandon Stokley	65	1,173	18.0
1999	Darren Brister	729	195	3.7	Derek Dyer	203	90	.44	1,066	Marcus Wilridge	37	504	13.6
2000	Darren Brister	512	116	4.4	Lance Domec	139	74	.53	806	Marcus Wilridge	38	524	13.8
2001	Jerome Coleman	625	162	3.9	Jon Van Cleave	407	224	.55	2,499	Nick Dugas	60	616	10.3
2002	Jerome Coleman	483	171	2.8	Jon Van Cleave	316	169	.53	2,081	Fred Stamps	54	1,002	18.6
2003	Chester Johnson	421	108	3.9	Jerry Babb	259	146	.56	1,502	Fred Stamps	62	973	15.7
2004	Jerry Babb	498	101	4.9	Jerry Babb	385	223	.58	2,365	Bill Sampy	57	776	13.6

The NCAA began including postseason stats in 2002

Louisiana-Lafayette All-Time Scores

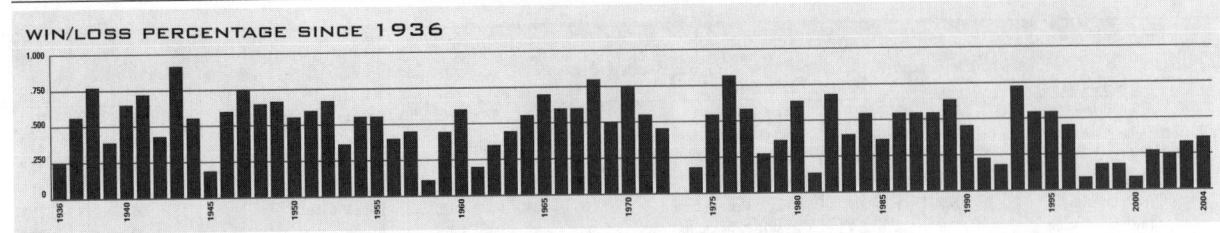

WIN/LOSS PERCENTAGE SINCE 1936

THE SCHOOLS

ASHBY WOODSON
1901-02 (.600)   3-2

1901   2-0
D21		at Opelousas	6	5
J12	●	Opelousas	21	0

1902   1-2
O16	LSU	0	42
N1	Lake Charles	5	0
D13	New Orleans AC	0	32

J. OVEY HERPIN
1903 (.500)   1-1

1903   1-1
N4	●	Delcambre Acad.	105	0
N25		at Lake Charles	0	5

EDWIN F. GAYLE
1904 (.833)   2-0-1

1904   2-0-1
N5	at Franklin	11	5
N12	Lake Charles	17	0
N24	at Company K	0	0

1905
NO TEAM

HERBERT McNASPY
1906 (.750)   1-0-1

1906   1-0-1
O27	St. Martinville	28	0
N9	Lake Charles	0	0

JEFFERSON CAFFERY
1907 (1.000)   1-0

1907   1-0
N2	at Crowley	11	5

CLEMENT J. McNASPY
1908-11, '13, '17-18 (.683)   34-15-4

1908   6-0-0
O24	●	St. Martinville *Unk*	11	10
O31	●	Crowley *Unk*	17	6
N7	●	New Iberia *Unk*	21	0
N21	●	St. Martinville *Unk*	16	0
N26	●	Lake Charles *Unk*	12	0
N27	●	Vinton *Unk*	16	0

1909   5-2-2
U	=	at St. Martinville	0	0
U	●	St. Martinville	17	0
U	●	Crowley *Unk*	36	2
U	●	Lake Arthur *Unk*	36	0
N6	●	Abbeville	62	0
N13	●	at Abbeville	49	0
U	●	Lake Charles	5	5
N25		at Northwestern St.	0	47
D11		at Northwestern St.	0	11

1910   6-2-1
U	●	LSU JV *Unk*	6	0
U	●	Jennings *Unk*	48	0
U	●	Tulane JV *Unk*	3	0
U	=	Tulane JV *Unk*	0	0
U		at Louisiana Tech	0	75
U	●	Louisiana Coll. *Unk*	18	5
U		LSU JV *Unk*	5	43
U	●	Jefferson Coll. *Unk*	11	0
U	●	Louisiana Coll. *Unk*	19	0

1911   1-4-1
O7		at LSU	0	42
O18	●	Tulane *Unk*	0	27
U		Louisiana Coll.	0	9
U	=	at Louisiana Coll.	0	0
U	●	Northwestern St. *Unk*	30	6
U		Jefferson Coll. *Unk*	5	11

H. LEE PRATHER
1912 (.429)   3-4

1912   3-4-0
S28	●	Morgan City	33	0
O5		at LSU	3	85
O12		at Tulane	0	95 *
U		at Jefferson Coll.	0	46
U	●	at Loyola-New Orleans	29	0
U	●	Louisiana Coll.	19	0
N20		Northwestern St.	6	13

CLEMENT J. McNASPY

1913   4-4-0
U	●	Lake Charles *Unk*	23	0
O11		LSU	0	26
U	●	Loyola-New Orleans *Unk*	42	0
U	●	Louisiana Coll. *Unk*	13	6
U	●	New Iberia *Unk*	55	7
U		Jefferson Coll. *Unk*	3	32
U		Jefferson Coll. *Unk*	0	59
U		Northwestern St. *Unk*	12	26

R.B. DUNBAR
1914-15 (.656)   10-5-1

1914   5-3-0
S27		at LSU	0	54
U		LSU JV *Unk*	7	13
O17		at Tulane	0	33
U	●	Louisiana Coll. *Unk*	45	0
U	●	St. Charles Coll. *Unk*	26	0
U	●	Louisiana Coll. *Unk*	89	0
U	●	St. Charles Coll. *Unk*	26	6
U	●	Northwestern St. *Unk*	12	0

1915   5-2-1
O2	●	at St. Charles College	12	0
O9		at Tulane	0	13
O16	●	LSU JV	7	0
O23	●	Chamberlain-Hunt *Unk*	25	0
O30	●	St. Charles Coll. *Unk*	28	7
N3	=	at Louisiana Tech	7	7
N6	●	at Louisiana Coll.	48	0
N25		Northwestern St. *Unk*	0	14

T. RAY MOBLEY
1916, '19, '21-30 (.540)   57-48-7

1916   7-1-0
S30		LSU	0	24
O7	●	LSU JV *Unk*	6	0
O14	●	Louisiana Coll. *Unk*	65	0
O21	●	St. Charles Coll. *Unk*	95	0
N4	●	Tulane JV *Unk*	14	0
N18	●	at Louisiana Tech	26	0
N25	●	Jefferson Coll. *Unk*	12	6
N30	●	Northwestern St. *Unk*	20	0

CLEMENT J. McNASPY

1917   8-2-0
U	●	St. Charles Coll. *Unk*	26	0
O6		at LSU	6	20
U	●	Louisiana Coll. *Unk*	36	0
U	●	Crowley *Unk*	54	0
U		Spring Hill *Unk*	0	26
U	●	St. Martinville *Unk*	69	0
U	●	Jefferson Coll. *Unk*	32	0
U	●	at Louisiana Tech	57	0
U	●	Northwestern St. *Unk*	34	0
U	●	LSU JV *Unk*	22	0

1918   4-1-0
U	●	Louisiana Coll. *Unk*	20	13
N28		at Tulane	0	74
U	●	Louisiana Coll. *Unk*	13	7
U	●	Patterson *Unk*	107	6
U	●	Lake Charles *Unk*	26	0

T. RAY MOBLEY

1919   2-4-2
S27	=	Alumni	7	7
O4		at LSU	0	39
O11		at Tulane	0	73
O18	=	Louisiana Coll. *Unk*	0	0
N1		LSU JV *Unk*	0	18
N8		Centenary *Unk*	0	6
N15	●	St. Charles *Unk*	44	3
N27		Northwestern St. *Unk*	13	0

H.O. TUDOR
1920 (.200)   2-8

1920   2-8-0
S25	●	Abbeville *Unk*	34	0
O2		at Tulane	0	79 *
O9		Patterson *Unk*	13	14
O16		LSU JV *Unk*	0	13
O23	●	Louisiana Coll. *Unk*	22	14
O30		at Louisiana Tech	0	1 *f*
N6		Louisiana Coll. *Unk*	0	14
N11		Spring Hill *Unk*	7	42
N18		St. Charles	7	35
N25		at Northwestern St.	0	13

T. RAY MOBLEY

1921   9-2-0
S24	●	Patterson *Unk*	26	0
O1		at Rice	0	54
O3	●	St. Charles	40	21
O8	●	Jefferson	35	0
O10	●	Centenary	1	0 *f*
O15	●	LSU JV	3	0
O22	●	at Tulane JV	13	7
O29	●	Louisiana Coll.	46	0
N4	●	at Loyola-New Orleans	20	0
N11		at Louisiana Tech	0	20
N24	●	Northwestern St.	33	2

1922   3-4-2
S30	●	Patterson	12	0
O7	=	at Jefferson	0	0
O14	●	Tulane JV	31	6
O21	●	Loyola-New Orleans	9	9
O28		at Louisiana Coll.	0	7
N4	●	at St. Stanislaus	14	0
N11		at LSU JV	0	6
N18		Spring Hill	12	13
N30		at Northwestern St.	6	13

1923   7-3-0
S22		at Centenary	0	35
S29		at Tulane	2	20
O6		at LSU	3	7
O13	●	Jefferson	81	0
O20	●	Louisiana Coll.	31	10
O27	●	at Lamar	19	16
N3	●	at Spring Hill	40	7
N10	●	St. Stanislaus	14	0
N17	●	Southern Miss	66	0
N29		Northwestern St.	14	12

1924   6-2-1
S27		at Tulane	0	14
O4		at LSU	7	31
O11	●	Jefferson	66	0
O18	●	Sam Houston State	28	7
O25	●	at Louisiana Coll.	32	7
N1	=	at Pensacola Navy	21	21
N8	●	Lamar	20	8
N15	●	Louisiana Tech	20	6
N27	●	at Northwestern St.	20	0

1925   7-2-0
S26	●	at Loyola-New Orleans	17	0
O3		at LSU	0	38
O10	●	Lamar	14	0
O17		at Sam Houston State	2	7
O24	●	Southern Miss	40	0 *
O31	●	Louisiana Coll.	31	0
N14	●	Stephen F. Austin	26	7
N20	●	at Louisiana Tech	22	13
N26	●	Northwestern St.	24	7

1926   6-3-1
S25	●	Southern Miss	33	6
O2		at LSU	0	34
O9		at Millsaps	0	12
O16	●	Sam Houston State	15	0
O23	●	Lamar	19	0
O30	●	at Louisiana Coll.	33	7
N5		at Louisiana Tech	0	23
N12	●	Stephen F. Austin	33	0
N20	=	at Northwestern St.	0	0
N25	●	at Mississippi Coll.	20	16

1927   2-7-1
S24	●	Southern Miss	6	0
O1		at LSU	0	52
O8		Spring Hill *Unk*	0	19
O14		at Sam Houston State	0	25
O22		at Loyola-New Orleans	0	28
O29		Louisiana Coll.	6	19
N5		at Louisiana Tech	0	13
N12	●	Millsaps	12	6
N18		at Mississippi Coll.	0	27
N24	=	at Northwestern St.	6	6

1928   4-5-0
S29		at Centenary	0	45
O6		at LSU	0	46
O13		Mississippi Coll.	0	19
O20	●	at Spring Hill	6	0
O27	●	Southern Miss	37	7
N4	●	at Louisiana Tech	45	6 *
N10		at Louisiana Coll.	7	14
N17		at Millsaps	7	31
N24	●	Northwestern St.	13	6

1929   2-7-0
S28	●	Southern Miss	7	0
O5		at LSU	0	58
O12	●	Spring Hill	6	28
O19		at Tulane	0	60
N2	●	Miami, Fla.	14	0
N9		Louisiana Coll. *Unk*	12	20
N23		Millsaps *Unk*	6	7
N30		at Northwestern St.	0	6
D7		at Louisiana Tech	7	24

1930   2-8-0
S27		at Tulane	0	84
O4		at LSU	0	85
O11		Marshall JC *Unk*	0	19
O18	●	Southern Miss	14	0
O25		at Louisiana Tech	0	7
N7		at Louisiana Coll.	13	18
N8		at Spring Hill	6	20
N11	●	at S.E. Louisiana	13	0
N14		at Miami, Fla.	0	6
N27		Northwestern St.	6	18

T.F. WILBANKS
1931-36 (.377)   19-32-2

1931   1-6-1
O3	=	S.E. Louisiana	6	6
O10		Marshall JC	0	25
O17		at Louisiana Tech	0	38
O24		Spring Hill	0	25
O31	●	Louisiana Coll.	7	6
N7		at Southern Miss	0	54
N14		Lon Morris	7	20
N26		at Northwestern St.	2	38

1932   3-4-0
S30	●	S.E. Louisiana	6	0
O7		Southern Miss	7	12
O14	●	Stephen F. Austin	19	6
O21		Louisiana Tech	0	15
N5		at Lamar	0	6
N11	●	at Louisiana Coll.	14	6
N24		at Northwestern St.	0	8

1933 6-3

S22	●	S.E. Louisiana	34	0
S29		at Loyola-New Orleans	0	12
O6		Lamar	7	8
O14	●	at Louisiana Tech	13	7
O21		at Southern Miss	0	6
O27	●	Spring Hill	21	0
N11	●	Louisiana Coll.	26	0
N17	●	at Stephen F. Austin	17	0
N30	●	at Northwestern St.	10	2

1934 5-4-0

S28		at Millsaps	2	9
O5		Spring Hill	6	7
O12	●	at Louisiana Tech	25	0
O20		at Southern Miss	6	12
O26	●	S.E. Louisiana	10	0
N3		at Louisiana Coll.	7	12
N9	●	Stephen F. Austin	39	13
N16	●	Sam Houston State	30	7
N29	●	Northwestern St.	6	0

1935 2-8-0

S27	●	at Stephen F. Austin	6	0
O4		S.E. Louisiana	7	13
O11		at Louisiana Tech	0	25
O18		Spring Hill	7	20
O25		Millsaps	3	19
N1	●	Louisiana Coll.	18	7
N8		at Southern Miss	7	19
N15		at Sam Houston State	0	7
N23		at LSU	0	56
N28		at Northwestern St.	0	6

1936 2-7-1

S25	=	Mississippi Coll.	13	13
O3	●	Lamar	13	6
O8		Louisiana Tech	7	20
O16		at Spring Hill	0	6
O23	●	Sam Houston State	7	6
O31		at Louisiana Coll.	0	12
N6		S.E. Louisiana	0	19
N13		at Southern Miss	14	44
N21		at LSU	0	93
N26		Northwestern St.	0	6

JOHNNY L. CAIN
1937-41, '46 (.623) 33-19-5

1937 4-3-1

S25		at Mississippi Coll.	0	13
O1	●	Stephen F. Austin	7	6
O8		Southern Miss	0	13
O15	●	Spring Hill	19	6
O22	●	at Millsaps	7	0
O29	●	Louisiana Coll.	26	6
N12	=	at Louisiana Tech	0	0
N25		at Northwestern St.	0	7

1938 8-2-1

S16	●	at S.E. Louisiana	8	0
S23	●	Delta State	19	0
S30	●	at Stephen F. Austin	7	0
O7	●	Sam Houston State	14	0
O14	●	at Spring Hill	33	7
O21	●	Millsaps	13	0
O29	=	at Louisiana Coll.	7	7
N4	●	at Louisiana Tech	27	7
N11		at Southern Miss	6	15
N19		at LSU	0	32
N24	●	Northwestern St.	7	0

1939 3-5-1

S22	●	at Delta State	19	6
S29	=	Stephen F. Austin	0	0
O4		at East Texas State	0	6
O13	●	Spring Hill	20	0
O27		Louisiana Coll.	6	7
N4	●	at Louisiana Tech	12	6
N10		Loyola-New Orleans	18	0
N18		Southern Miss	7	9
N30		at Northwestern St.	0	6

1940 6-3-1

S20	●	S.E. Louisiana	7	0
S27	●	at Stephen F. Austin	6	0
O5		at Mississippi State	0	20
O11	=	Millsaps	0	0
O18		at Spring Hill	7	13
O26	●	at Louisiana Coll.	6	0
N1	●	Louisiana Tech	7	6
N8	●	Delta State	18	7
N15		at Southern Miss	14	21
N28	●	Northwestern St.	12	7

1941 6-2-1

S19	●	at S.E. Louisiana	19	7
S27		at Alabama	6	47
O10	●	Millsaps	6	0
O18	●	Spring Hill	39	0
O24	●	Louisiana Coll.	23	7
O31		at Louisiana Tech	0	12
N7	●	Stephen F. Austin	25	0
N14	=	Southern Miss	0	0
N27	●	at Northwestern St.	6	0

LOUIS WHITMAN
1942-45 (.500) 14-14-2

1942 3-4-0

S25		at Alabama	0	54
O9	●	S.E. Louisiana	35	13
O16		Ouachita College	0	6
O23	●	Camp Beauregard	62	0
O30	●	Louisiana Tech	12	7
N6		Northwestern St.	6	11
N21		at Sam Houston State	0	7

1943 5-0-1

O15	●	Fort Benning, Ga.	20	7
O23	●	at Southwestern, Tx.	27	6
N6	=	Arkansas A&M *MEM*	20	20
N13	●	Lake Charles AAF	75	0
N27	●	at Randolph Field	6	0
		OIL BOWL		
D1	●	Arkansas A&M	24	7

1944 5-4-0

S22	●	LaGarde Hospital	53	0
S30		Keesler Army AFB	0	13
O7		Arkansas A&M	6	18
O14	●	at Louisiana Tech	15	0
O21	●	Northwestern State	19	7
N4		Millsaps	0	19
N11	●	at Lake Charles AAF	24	0
N18		Louisiana Tech	0	7
N25	●	at Northwestern State	7	6

1945 1-6-1

S22		Lake Charles AAF	7	21
S29		at Mississippi State	0	31
O5		Louisiana Tech	12	14
O20	=	at Northwestern	0	0
O27		at Florida	0	45
N10		at Auburn	0	52
N17	●	at Louisiana Tech	13	7
N22		Northwestern State	0	13

JOHNNY L. CAIN

1946 6-4-0

S21	●	at Houston	13	7
S28	●	Stephen F. Austin	13	2
O4		at S.E. Louisiana	13	27
O12		at Alabama	0	54
O18		at Southern Miss	0	6
O26	●	at Louisiana Coll.	40	0
N2		Louisiana Tech	6	34
N8	●	Troy State	64	0
N23	●	at Northwestern State	14	0
N29	●	Union, Tn.	26	0

GEORGE MITCHELL
1947-49 (.685) 18-8-1

1947 6-2-0

S27	●	at Stephen F. Austin	24	6
O4	●	S.E. Louisiana	40	7
O11	●	Troy State	26	0
O18		Southern Miss	7	15
O25	●	Louisiana Coll.	38	7
N1		at Louisiana Tech	0	9
N8	●	at Centenary	21	7
N27	●	Northwestern State	9	7

1948 6-3-1

S18		at Austin Coll.	0	14
S25	●	Troy State	26	19
O2	●	Houston	21	7
O8	●	at S.E. Louisiana	19	12
O15		at Southern Miss	6	26
O23	●	at Louisiana Coll.	26	7
O30		Louisiana Tech	14	24
N6	=	Sam Houston State	12	12
N13	●	Pensacola Navy	27	6
N20	●	at Northwestern State	28	7

1949 6-3-0

S17	●	Austin Coll.	30	0
S24	●	Troy State	48	25
O1	●	at S.E. Louisiana	27	20
O8		Houston	7	28
O15		Southern Miss	0	25
O22	●	Louisiana Coll.	7	0
O29		at Louisiana Tech	0	21
N12	●	at Pensacola Navy	28	12
N19	●	Northwestern State	27	14

A.L. "RED" SWANSON
1950 (.556) 5-4

1950 5-4-0

S23	●	East Texas Baptist	25	0
S30	●	S.E. Louisiana	6	0
O7	●	Troy State	40	14
O14		at Southern Miss	0	6
O21		at Memphis	0	20
O28	●	Stephen F. Austin	20	13
N4	●	Louisiana Tech	41	13
N11		at Louisiana Coll.	20	22
N18		at Northwestern State	7	12

RAYMOND DIDIER
1951-56 (.517) 29-27-2

1951 6-4-0

S15		La. Monroe	7	13
S22	●	at McNeese State	35	14
S29		at S.E. Louisiana	0	14
O6	●	at Troy State	44	7
O13		Southern Miss	0	41
O20		Memphis State	7	41
O27	●	at Stephen F. Austin	32	14
N3	●	at Louisiana Tech	34	7
N10	●	Louisiana Coll.	27	21
N17	●	Northwestern State	41	26

1952 5-2-2

S20	●	Lamar	14	13
S27	=	S.E. Louisiana	13	13
O4	●	Troy State	54	14
O11		at Southern Miss	12	32
O25		Stephen F. Austin	19	20
N1	=	Louisiana Tech	19	19
N8	●	at Louisiana Coll.	18	7
N15	●	at Northwestern State	34	0
N22	●	at McNeese State	20	13

1953 4-7-0

S19	●	at Lamar	22	13
S26		at S.E. Louisiana	13	39
O3		East Texas State	7	41
O10		Southern Miss	14	41
O14	●	at Stephen F. Austin	14	7
O17		at Arkansas State	12	13
O31		at Louisiana Tech	7	27
N7	●	Louisiana Coll.	19	6
N14		Northwestern State	7	12
N21	●	McNeese State	47	13
N28		at La. Monroe	6	35

1954 5-4-0

S18		Lamar	20	26
S25		S.E. Louisiana	0	32
O2		at East Texas State	13	33
O9	●	La. Monroe	41	7
O16	●	Arkansas State	36	2
O30	●	Louisiana Tech	25	0
N6	●	at Louisiana Coll.	25	13
N13		at Northwestern State	7	34
N20	●	at McNeese State	55	12

1955 5-4-0

S17		at Lamar	6	19
S24		at S.E. Louisiana	0	20
O1	●	East Texas State	20	15
O8	●	at La. Monroe	26	6
O15	●	Corpus Christi	49	12
O29		at Louisiana Tech	14	28
N5	●	Louisiana Coll.	21	14
N12	●	Northwestern State	27	13
N19		McNeese State	7	12

1956 4-6-0

S15		Lamar	14	21
S22		S.E. Louisiana	0	42
S29	●	at East Texas State	33	27
O6		La. Monroe	19	45
O13	●	Corpus Christi	67	14
O20	●	at Southern Arkansas	32	12
O27		Louisiana Tech	6	33
N3		at Louisiana Coll.	14	34
N10		at Northwestern State	19	38
N17	●	at McNeese State	35	33

JOHN R. BELL
1957 (.450) 4-5-1

1957 4-5-1

S14	●	Sam Houston State	14	7
S21	=	at S.E. Louisiana	7	7
S28		at Lamar	20	36
O5	●	at La. Monroe	6	0
O12		at Louisiana Tech	13	28
O19	●	Southern Arkansas	25	6
O26		Trinity *UNK*	7	27
N2	●	Louisiana Coll.	7	0
N9		Northwestern State	0	19
N23		McNeese State	0	13

JIM "RED" HOGGATT
1958-60 (.393) 11-17

1958 1-8-0

S20		S.E. Louisiana	6	14
S27		at Sam Houston State	0	6
O4		La. Monroe	8	29
O11		Louisiana Tech	0	33
O18		at Abilene Christian	8	27
O25	●	Trinity	22	18
N1		at Southern Arkansas	7	13
N8		at Northwestern State	8	27
N22		at McNeese State	8	9

1959 4-5-0

S18		at S.E. Louisiana	13	18
S25	●	Sam Houston State	19	7
O3	●	Stephen F. Austin	22	14
O10		at Louisiana Tech	13	21
O24		at Louisiana Coll.	6	21
O31		at La. Monroe	20	34
N7		Abilene Christian	12	14
N14	●	Northwestern State	34	14
N21	●	McNeese State	19	14

1960 6-4-0

S17		S.E. Louisiana	10	20
S24	●	at Sam Houston State	8	3
O1	●	at Stephen F. Austin	36	0
O8	●	Louisiana Tech	6	2
O15		Texas-Arlington	7	13
O22		Louisiana Coll.	7	13
O29	●	La. Monroe	8	7
N5	●	Pensacola Navy	20	14
N12	●	at Northwestern State	17	7
N19		at McNeese State	10	29

RUSS FAULKINBERRY
1961-73 (.515) 66-62-2

1961 2-8-0

S16		at S.E. Louisiana	0	27
S23		at Texas-Arlington	0	26
S30		Southern Miss	6	22
O7		at Louisiana Tech	0	12
O21		Louisiana Coll.	9	14
O28		at La. Monroe	20	27
N4	●	at Pensacola Navy	9	7
N11		Northwestern State	14	27
N18		McNeese State	0	25
N25	●	Henderson State	41	7

1962 4-5-1

S15	●	Mexico Poly Institute	21	0
S21		S.E. Louisiana	6	21
S29		at Southern Miss	0	29
O6	●	Louisiana Tech	13	6
O13	=	Tampa	14	14
O20		at Louisiana Coll.	6	12
O27	●	La. Monroe	18	10
N2	●	Austin Coll.	38	12
N10		at Northwestern State	0	20
N17		at McNeese State	0	19

1963 4-5-0

S10		at S.E. Louisiana	0	14
S28	●	Hardin-Simmons	16	6
O5	●	at Tampa	19	17
O12		at Louisiana Tech	0	45
O26	●	Louisiana Coll.	7	6
N2		Southern Miss	0	28
N9		at La. Monroe	6	7
N16	●	Northwestern State	19	13
N23		McNeese State	7	14

1964 5-4-0

S26		at Southern Miss	0	30
O10		Louisiana Tech	3	6
O17	●	Tampa	37	6
O24	●	at Louisiana Coll.	14	7
O30	●	Lenoir-Rhyne	20	6
N7	●	La. Monroe	23	7
N14	●	at Northwestern State	27	17
N21		at McNeese State	9	24
D12		S.E. Louisiana	7	12

1965 7-3-0

S18	●	Louisiana Coll.	30	0
O2		at S.E. Louisiana	0	13
O9	●	at Louisiana Tech	16	8
O16		at Tampa	6	7
O23	●	at Samford	7	0
O30	●	at Lamar	20	6
N6	●	at La. Monroe	14	10
N13	●	Northwestern State	41	7
N20	●	McNeese State	14	7
N25		U.T. Chattanooga	25	27

1966 6-4-0

S17	•	at Louisiana Coll.	24	0
S24		at Delta State	3	28
O1	•	S.E. Louisiana	35	6
O8	•	Lamar	14	6
O15	•	Louisiana Tech	21	12
O22	•	Samford	6	3
O29		at La. Monroe	7	10
N5		Arkansas State	14	17
N12		at Northwestern State	8	21
N19	•	at McNeese State	7	0

1967 6-4-0

S16	•	at Louisiana Coll.	28	14
S23		at Lamar	13	14
S30	•	Pensacola Navy	13	3
O7	•	at Louisiana Tech	20	14
O14	•	at S.E. Louisiana	9	0
O21		at Memphis	6	28
O28		La. Monroe	6	17
N4	•	at Arkansas State	7	6
N11		Northwestern State	9	24
N18	•	McNeese State	31	6

1968 8-2-0

S21	•	at Louisiana Coll.	28	0
S28		at Pensacola Navy	35	39
O5	•	S.E. Louisiana	31	6
O12	•	Louisiana Tech	28	24
O19	•	Delta State	32	27
O26	•	Lamar	20	14
N2		at La. Monroe	7	20
N9	•	Arkansas State	20	9
N16	•	at Northwestern State	14	7
N23	•	at McNeese State	12	7

1969 5-5-0

S20		at North Texas	6	40
S27		East Texas State	13	24
O4	•	at S.E. Louisiana	9	3
O11		at Louisiana Tech	21	34
O18		Arkansas State *UNK*	0	26
O25	•	at Lamar	24	16
N1	•	at La. Monroe	9	7
N8	•	St. Norbert	48	37
N15		Northwestern State	28	33
N22	•	McNeese State	21	17

1970 9-3-0

S12		Southern Miss	14	16
S19	•	S.E. Louisiana	17	6
S26	•	at U.T. Chattanooga	24	20
O3	•	Doane	49	0
O10	•	Louisiana Tech	20	10
O17	•	at Texas-Arlington	28	7
O24	•	Lamar	15	6
O31	•	at La. Monroe	9	7
N7		Tampa	38	50
N14	•	at Northwestern State	24	21
N21	•	at McNeese State	13	7
		GRANTLAND RICE BOWL		
D12		Tennessee State	25	26

1971 5-4-1

S18	•	at S.E. Louisiana	7	6
S25	•	Santa Clara	21	0
O2		Trinity	21	27
O9		at Louisiana Tech	15	35
O16	•	Texas-Arlington	16	0
O23	•	at Lamar	21	20
O30	•	La. Monroe	31	7
N6	=	at Arkansas State	10	10
N13		Northwestern State	19	27
N19		McNeese State	10	20

1972 5-6-0

S9		Louisiana Tech	0	7
S16	•	S.E. Louisiana	30	7
S23		at Trinity	10	13
S30		Arkansas State	18	21
O7	•	Abilene Christian	35	14
O14	•	at U.T. Chattanooga	22	21
O21		Lamar	0	3
O28		at Texas-Arlington	0	7
N4	•	Santa Clara	27	7
N11		at Northwestern State	8	24
N25	•	at McNeese State	10	0

DAN "SONNY" ROY
1973 (.000) 0-1

1973 0-10-0

S15		at Arkansas State	13	27
S22		at Louisiana Tech	0	23
S29		U.T. Chattanooga	10	21
O6		Xavier	14	17
O13		at Cincinnati	0	27
O20		at Lamar	0	31
O27		Texas-Arlington	22	31
N10		Northwestern State	10	20
N17		Memphis State	6	41
N24		McNeese State	0	37

AUGIE TAMMARIELLO
1974-79 (.463) 30-35-2

1974 2-9-0

S14		at Tulane	16	17
S21		at McNeese State	0	38
O5		Lamar	13	38
O12		Louisiana Tech	20	35
O19		at Tampa	13	14
O26	•	U.T. Chattanooga	21	20
N2		Southern Miss	7	41
N9		at Texas-Arlington	17	21
N16	•	at Northwestern State	14	10
N22		San Jose State	22	25
N29		Arkansas State	6	28

1975 6-5-0

S6	•	at Long Beach State	22	17
S13	•	Southern Illinois	27	10
S27	•	New Mexico State	31	7
O4		at Arkansas State	17	39
O11		at Louisiana Tech	14	24
O18	•	Lamar	21	12
O25		at Cincinnati	17	23
N1	•	Texas-Arlington	35	32
N8		Pacific	14	19
N15	•	Northwestern State	40	17
N22		McNeese State	21	33

1976 9-2-0

S11	•	Fresno State	41	14
S18	•	Cincinnati	7	3 †
O2	•	Louisiana Tech	31	26
O9	•	at Lamar	34	9
O16	•	Furman	27	16
O23	•	Pacific	38	10
O30	•	at Texas-Arlington	31	24
N6	•	Arkansas State	23	14
N13		at Northwestern State	3	7
N20		at McNeese State	19	20
D4	•	La. Monroe	7	5

1977 6-4-2

S3	•	Tulsa	48	21
S10	•	Fresno State	34	13
S17	•	at Lamar	10	6
S24	•	Texas-Arlington	30	20
O1		at Hawaii	6	20
O8	=	at Louisiana Tech	21	21
O15	•	Southern Illinois	24	0
O22		at Temple	20	27
O29	•	at East Carolina	9	7
N5		at Arkansas State	15	17
N12		Northwestern State	13	20
N25	=	McNeese State	9	9

1978 3-8-0 (0-0-0)

S9		Long Beach St.	0	10
S16		at Tulsa	3	10
S23		East Carolina	9	38
S30	•	Lamar	23	16
O7	•	Louisiana Tech	24	6
O14		at Texas Arlington	3	24
O28		Cincinnati	13	38
N4		Arkansas State	6	16
N11	•	at Northwestern St.	19	17
N18		So. Illinois	9	10
N25		at McNeese State	18	44

1979 4-7-0 (0-0-0)

S1	•	La. Monroe	17	13
S8		at So. Illinois	7	17
S15		at Tulsa	20	28
S22	•	West Texas St.	19	10
S29	•	at Arkansas State	13	9
O6		at Louisiana Tech	0	17
O13		Pacific	7	10
O20		at Lamar	17	21
O27	•	Cal Poly Pomona	31	19
N10		Texas Arlington	10	24
N17		McNeese State	6	10

SAM ROBERTSON
1980-85 (.462) 29-34-2

1980 7-4-0 (0-0-0)

S6	•	New Mexico State	14	12
S13	•	at East Carolina	27	21
S20		at Fresno State	14	16
S27		La. Monroe	0	24
O4		at North Texas	20	22
O11	•	Arkansas State	3	0
O25	•	Lamar	38	10
N1	•	So. Illinois	21	3
N8	•	at Texas Arlington	30	13
N15	•	Louisiana Tech	27	9
N22		at McNeese State	0	14

1981 1-9-1 (0-0-0)

S5		at Southern Miss	7	33
S12		S.E. Louisiana	0	7
S19		at La. Monroe	17	20
S26	•	North Texas	34	11
O10		at Arkansas State	3	14
O17		at East Carolina	31	35
O24		at So. Illinois	0	41
O31	=	Louisiana Tech	17	17
N7		Texas Arlington	7	23
N14		at Lamar	12	14
N21		McNeese State	7	14

1982-1992
INDEPENDENT

1982 7-3-1

S11	•	at Rice	21	14
S18	•	West Texas St.	31	18
S25	•	at North Texas	31	14
O2	•	So. Illinois	20	10
O9		Arkansas State	13	20
O16		at Texas Arlington	29	30
O23	•	Lamar	24	0
O30		at Southern Miss	0	36
N6	•	La. Monroe	40	26
N13	•	Louisiana Tech	29	19
N20	=	at McNeese State	10	10

1983 4-6-0

S10		at La. Monroe	6	31
S17		U.T. Chattanooga	14	38
S24		at Rice	21	22
O8		East Carolina	18	21
O15		at Tulane	15	17
O22	•	at Lamar	31	6
O29		at Southern Miss	3	31
N12	•	McNeese State	48	16
N19	•	at Louisiana Tech	13	9
N26	•	at San Jose State	25	21

1984 6-5-0

S1		at U.T. Chattanooga	7	9
S8	•	Louisiana Tech	17	16
S15		La. Monroe	6	7
S22		at Alabama	14	37
O6	•	Wichita St.	31	3
O13		at Memphis	7	20
O20	•	at San Jose State	35	28
O27	•	Southern Miss	13	7
N3	•	at East Carolina	42	24
N10		McNeese State	17	30
N17	•	at Tulsa	18	17

1985 4-7-0

A31		Memphis	6	37
S7		at Auburn	7	49
S14		at Louisiana Tech	23	24
S21	•	Idaho St.	31	30
S28	•	at Wichita St.	23	15
O5		at Southern Miss	16	38
O12	•	East Carolina	16	14
O19		at Florida	0	45
O26	•	Nevada-Las Vegas	20	13
N9		at Tulane	17	27
N16		at McNeese State	3	14

NELSON STOKLEY
1986-98 (.437) 62-80-1

1986 6-5-0

S6		Oklahoma State	20	21
S13	•	La. Monroe	24	20
S20	•	at Memphis	26	10
O4	•	at East Carolina	21	10
O11	•	Tulsa	17	13
O18		at Mississippi	20	21
O25	•	Stephen F. Austin	28	14
N1		at Tulane	39	42
N8		at Southern Miss	0	17
N15	•	at McNeese State	33	13
N22		Louisiana Tech	14	23

1987 6-5-0

S5		at Mississippi State	3	31
S12	•	Nevada-Las Vegas	21	10
S26		at Oklahoma State	0	36
O3		Alabama *BIRM*	10	38
O10	•	Northwestern St.	13	3
O17		at Mississippi	14	24
O24	•	at La. Monroe	17	7
N7	•	Memphis	31	7
N14		at Tulane	10	38
N21	•	Colorado State	35	28
N28	•	Southern Miss	37	30

1988 6-5-0

S3	•	Fullerton St.	24	9
S17	•	Sam Houston St.	33	8
S24	•	Rice	41	16
O1	•	at East Carolina	48	36
O8		at Louisiana Tech	16	19
O15	•	No Illinois	45	0
O22		Southern Miss	14	27
O29	•	at Tulane	51	34
N5		at Memphis	3	20
N12		Alabama *BIRM*	0	17
N19		Arkansas State	21	38

1989 7-4-0

S2		Louisiana Tech	14	40
S9	•	Central Michigan	22	20
S16		at Tulane	10	17
S23	•	at Rice	18	3
S30	•	at La. Monroe	24	10
O7	•	Tulsa	21	13
O14		at Alabama	17	24
O21	•	at Southern Miss	24	21
N4		at Northern Illinois	20	23
N11	•	Lamar	42	33
N18	•	Arkansas State	29	28

1990 5-6-0

S1	•	at Tulane	48	6
S8	•	Nicholls St.	24	21
S15		at Texas A&M	14	63
S22		East Carolina	10	20
S29		at Louisiana Tech	10	24
O6		Alabama	6	25
O20	•	at Tulsa	25	13
O27		at Memphis	6	20
N3		Southern Miss	13	14
N10	•	at Arkansas State	17	16
N17	•	Northern Illinois	24	20

1991 2-8-1

A31		La. Monroe	10	21
S7		at Central Michigan	24	27
S14		at Wyoming	15	28
S21		at Arkansas	7	9
S28		at Texas A&M	7	34
O5		Miami, Ohio	14	27
O12		Tulsa	20	34
O26	=	Louisiana Tech	14	14
N2	•	at Northern Illinois	13	12
N9		at Auburn	7	50
N16	•	at Arkansas State	17	13

1992 2-9-0

S5		at Tennessee	3	38
S12	•	La. Monroe	31	23
S19		at San Jose State	13	38
S26	•	Western Kentucky	17	14
O3		at Houston	7	63
O10		at Louisiana Tech	7	21
O17		Fullerton St.	10	14
O24		at Auburn	24	25
O31		at Tulsa	9	27
N7		Northern Illinois	15	23
N21		Arkansas State	7	20

1993-1995
BIG WEST

1993 8-3-0 (5-1-0)

S4	|	Utah State	13	34
S11		at Miami, Ohio	28	29
S18	•	Memphis	17	15
O2	•	Southern Miss	13	7
O9	•	at Tulane	36	15
O16	• |	at Arkansas State	19	3
O23	• |	at Northern Illinois	33	19
O30	• |	San Jose State	24	13
N6		at Florida	14	61
N20	• |	at Nevada-Las Vegas	31	14
N27	• |	Louisiana Tech	21	17

1994 6-5-0 (5-1-0)

S3		at Kansas State	6	34
S10	• |	Northern Illinois	29	9
S17		Troy State	20	39
S24	|	at San Jose State	28	31
O1	• |	at Louisiana Tech	13	3
O8	• |	Arkansas State	26	0
O15		at Southern Miss	20	43
O22	• |	at Utah State	27	25
N5	• |	Nevada-Las Vegas	28	27
N12		at Texas Tech	7	39
N19	•	Western Michigan	17	14

1995   6-5-0 (4-2-0)

S2	at Nevada	14	38
S9 ●	UAB	56	21
S16	at Memphis	19	33
S23	at Northern Illinois	24	25
O7 ●	at Arkansas State	33	9
O14 ●	New Mexico State	43	26
O21 ●	Pacific	45	3
O28 ●	at Tulane	32	28
N4 ●	Louisiana Tech	40	33
N11	at Arkansas	13	24
N18	Southern Miss	32	35

1996-2000
INDEPENDENT

1996   5-6

A30	at Florida	21	55
S14 ●	Texas A&M	29	22
S21	at Southern Miss	27	52
S28 ●	at Louisiana Tech	37	31
O5	Houston	24	31
O12 ●	Arkansas State	42	31
O19	at UAB	29	39
O26 ●	Memphis	13	9
N2	at Virginia Tech	16	47
N9 ●	Northern Illinois	45	31
N16	at Texas Tech	21	56

1997   1-10

A30	at Pittsburgh	13	45
S6	Oklahoma State	7	31
S13	at Texas Tech	14	59
S20	at Texas A&M	0	66
S27	UAB	7	42
O4 ●	at Arkansas State	41	38
O11	No. Alabama	42	48
O25	La. Monroe	21	28
N1	Tulane	0	56
N8	at Washington State	7	77
N15	Louisiana Tech	24	63

1998   2-9

S5	at Arkansas	17	38
S12	Northwestern St.	22	24
S19	at Louisiana Tech	14	77
S26	at Southern Miss	0	55
O3	at UAB	13	24
O17 ●	Arkansas State	21	19
O24	Central Florida	10	42
O31	at Tulane	20	72
N7	at La. Monroe	24	34
N14	at Oklahoma State	20	44
N21 ●	Western Kentucky	38	24

JERRY BALDWIN
1999-2001 (.182)   6-27

1999   2-9

S4	at Oklahoma State	7	24
S11	Texas Tech	17	38
S18	at Houston	0	45
S25 ●	Middle Tennessee	45	31
O2	Louisiana Tech	31	41
O9	at Washington State	0	44
O16	at Tulane	32	48
O23	La. Monroe	7	31
O30	at Arkansas State	27	31
N13	at Southern Miss	0	48
N20 ●	Wofford	37	34

2000   1-10

S2	Sam Houston St.	14	21
S9	at Texas	10	52
S16	at Texas Tech	0	26
S23	Northwestern St.	21	23
S30	at UAB	2	47
O7	Tulane	37	38
O14	at Louisiana Tech	14	48
O28	North Texas	0	13
N4 ●	at La. Monroe	21	18
N11	Jacksonville St.	14	28
N18	at Middle Tennessee	38	41

2001-PRESENT
SUN BELT

2001   3-8 (2-4)

S1 ●	Nicholls St.	20	0
S8	at Minnesota	14	44
S22	Southern Miss	10	35
S29	Middle Tennessee	9	26
O6	at Arizona State	27	63
O13	at Arkansas State	20	26
O20 ●	Idaho *PULL*	54	37
O27 ●	La. Monroe	17	12
N10	at North Texas	17	42
N17	New Mexico State	46	49
N24	at Central Florida	0	31

RICKEY BUSTLE
2002-PRESENT (.314)   11-24

2002   3-9 (2-4)

A31	at Texas A&M	7	31
S7	Minnesota	11	35
S14	at Houston	17	36
S21 ●	UAB	34	0
O5	at LSU	0	48
O12	at New Mexico State	28	31
O19	at Middle Tennessee	35	48
O26	North Texas	0	27
N2 ●	Idaho	31	28
N9 ●	Arkansas State	13	10
N16	at Arkansas	17	24
N23	at La. Monroe	10	34

2003   4-8 (3-2)

A30	at South Carolina	7	14
S6	Louisiana Tech	3	34
S13	Houston	14	21
S20	at Minnesota	14	48
S27	at North Texas	23	44
O4	at Oklahoma State	3	56
O11	La. Monroe	42	45
O16 ●	New Mexico State	26	24
O25 ●	Idaho	31	20
N1	at Southern Miss	3	48
N8 ●	Florida Intl.	43	10
N15	at Middle Tennessee	57	51

2004   4-7 (2-5)

S4 ●	Northwestern St.	14	7
S11	at Louisiana Tech	20	24
S18	at Kansas State	20	40
S25 ●	Middle Tennessee	24	17
O2 ●	at Florida Intn'l	43	34
O9	at New Mexico State	32	35
O16	at Idaho	25	38
O23 ●	Arkansas State	27	24
N6	North Texas	17	27
N13	Troy State	10	13
N20	at La. Monroe	10	13

THE SCHOOLS

f Forfeit   † Game Later Forfieted   # Disputed Victor   * Disputed Score || Designated Conference Game |2 Counted Twice in Conference Standings

LOUISIANA-MONROE

BY RYAN HOCKENSMITH

STARING DOWN THE GREAT DEPRESsion, Louisiana-Monroe's football team began play in 1931. At the time, the school had 416 students and 12 faculty members, and players rode a trolley across town to practice at Monroe High School because there was no field on campus. The prep field had been burned to get rid of high grass, and players' shoes kicked up so much ash and soot that many players left the field looking like they'd been swimming in chocolate syrup. But then-Northeast Louisiana shrugged off the program's miniscule resources and finished 4–1–1 that year, exhibiting the scrappy qualities they've been known for during the past seven decades. Within two years, Monroe had a dominant junior college program, spurring a move in 1951 into the senior college ranks, despite having the smallest student body (674) among the state's nine senior colleges and no recruiting hope against eight bigger, more established next-door neighbors. From 1951 to 1981, the Indians posted 10 winning seasons before a drop to Division I-AA in 1982. There, Louisiana-Monroe went 90–48–2, with a national title and four playoff appearances, before a return to Division I-A in 1994. In the last decade, the Indians have yet to post a winning season. But if history is any indication, don't expect that to last much longer.

TRADITION Many schools have adopted a pregame crowd walk-through for their teams, where players and coaches maneuver past hordes of screaming fans before taking the field. At Louisiana-Monroe, that 10-year-old tradition includes an interesting twist: The Grove. At the south end of Malone Stadium, a small wooded section of the tailgating area becomes a boisterous place for the team to come through before every home game. Hundreds of fans congregate there for everything from pregame pep rallies to shrimp cookouts.

BEST PLAYER Running back Joe Profit is the Gulf States Conference's career leading rusher with 2,818 yards from 1967 to 1970, second-best in Louisiana-Monroe history. He's one of two players in school history to have his jersey, No. 40, retired. (Stan Humphries is the other.) But Profit's greatest accomplishment can't be measured with any

PROFILE

University of Louisiana at Monroe
Monroe, La.
Founded: 1931
Enrollment: 7,231
Colors: Maroon and Old Gold
Nickname: Indians
Stadium: Malone Stadium
    Opened in 1978
    Grass; 30,427 capacity
First football game: 1931
All-time record: 244–318–8 (.435)
First-round NFL draftees: 1
Website: www.ulmathletics.com

THE BEST OF TIMES

The greatest era of Louisiana-Monroe football isn't John David Crow's head coaching tenure from 1976 to 1980. Crow went 20–34–1 and managed only two winning seasons, but what he provided for the downtrodden program—taking over after five straight losing seasons—goes beyond wins and losses. Crow, the 1957 Heisman Trophy winner, brought instant credibility and, when his assistant coach, Pat Collins, took over in 1981, the foundation was set for a decade of unparalleled success. After dropping into Division I-AA in 1982, Louisiana-Monroe reeled off five winning seasons through the rest of the decade, including the national title season in 1987.

THE WORST OF TIMES

Coach Dixie B. White would go on to post back-to-back 7–3 seasons in 1966 and 1967, and lead winning teams in 1968 and 1970. But his first two years, 1964 and 1965, were disastrous, with the Indians never scoring three touchdowns in a game and reaching double-digits just five times in 17 games. Even with a stout defense, White's Indians wobbled to 0–8 and 1–8 marks during this period.

CONFERENCE

The Indians joined the Sun Belt in 2001 after being an independent the prior seven seasons. As a member of the I-AA Southland Conference (1982-1993), Louisiana-Monroe won four titles (three outright). From 1978 to 1981, the program was a I-A independent. Dating back to 1931, Louisiana-Monroe was a junior college before becoming a senior college independent in 1951.

DISTINGUISHED ALUMNI

Tim McGraw, country musician; Calvin Natt, NBA player; Bill Pryor, Alabama attorney general; Ben Sheets, baseball player

FIGHT SONG

ULM FIGHT SONG
Cheer for the ULM Indians,
With their fighting spirit bold,
We will keep our banners waving,
The old maroon and gold.
Our battle cry rings to the sky,
Our goal is victory.
But win or lose, we'll stand by you,
And ever loyal we will be.

Chief Brave Spirit gained a spot in the imaginary Mascot Hall of Fame after a second-quarter brawl with Vic the Demon.

statistic—in 1967, he became the first African-American player in school history, paving the way for future greats such as Roosevelt Potts and Irving Spikes to come along and surpass his records. "Joe was a great player and a significant player," says longtime sports information director and Louisiana-Monroe historian Bob Anderson. "What he accomplished at ULM goes beyond what he did on the football field."

BEST COACH Jim Malone coached at Louisiana-Monroe for 20 years and won 94 games, both school records. These are the reasons the stadium is named in his honor. He had 14 winning seasons and coached one of the school's best-ever teams, the undefeated 1935 squad that won the junior college national championship. That team posted seven shutouts and outscored opponents for the season 180-6. Though hardly the most successful era in the school's history, John David Crow's tenure as head coach from 1976 to 1980 still deserves quite a bit of praise. The former

Heisman Trophy winner took over after five straight losing seasons. He went 20–34–1 and managed only two winning seasons, but what he provided for the downtrodden program went beyond wins and losses. Crow brought instant credibility, and when his assistant coach, Pat Collins, took over in 1981, the foundation was set for a decade of success unparalleled in school history.

BEST TEAM Despite the exploits of the undefeated teams of 1935 and 1937, the school's best team ever, by a nose, is the 1987 bunch that won the Division I-AA national title. Led by quarterback Humphries, the Southland Conference's top passer with 2,622 yards, and Collins, who was named by *Football News* as national Coach of the Year, the team went 13–2 and beat Division I-A opponent Southern Miss 34-24. Doug Pederson, the Indians' backup quarterback, barely played that season, but was one of eight Louisiana-Monroe players to eventually sign NFL contracts. Five members of the 1987 team—Collins, Humphries, Pederson,

RECORDS

RUSHING YARDS

	GAME
254	Irving Spikes vs. North Texas, Nov. 20, 1993 (32 att.)
	SEASON
1,563	Irving Spikes, 1993 (246 att.)
	CAREER
3,061	Roosevelt Potts, 1990-92 (658 att.)

PASSING YARDS

	GAME
619	Doug Pederson vs. Stephen F. Austin, Nov. 11, 1989 (46 of 71)
	SEASON
3,008	Robert Cobb, 1993 (197 of 345)
	CAREER
7,827	John Holman, 1979-82 (593 of 1,201)

RECEIVING YARDS

	GAME
264	Stepfret Williams vs. Nevada, Oct. 14, 1995 (10 rec.)
	SEASON
1,198	Mack Vincent, 2002 (79 rec.)
	CAREER
3,177	Stepfret Williams, 1992-95 (168 rec.)

POINTS

	GAME
24	Marquis Williams vs. Louisiana-Lafayette, Oct. 25, 1997 (4 TDs); Stepfret Williams vs. Nevada, Oct. 14, 1995 (4 TDs)
	SEASON
94	Teddy Garcia, 1987 (20 FGs, 34 PATs)
	CAREER
246	Teddy Garcia, 1984-87 (56 FGs, 78 PATs)

CONSENSUS ALL-AMERICANS

1967	Vic Bender, C
1970	Joe Profit, RB
1972	Jimmy Edwards, RB
1973-74	Glenn Fleming, MG
1982	Arthur Christophe C
1982	Bruce Daigle, DB
1983-84	Mike Grantham, OG
1985	Mike Turner, DB
1987	John Clement, OT
1987	Claude Brumfield, DT
1988	Cyril Crutchfield, DB
1989	Jackie Harris, E
1992	Jeff Blackshear, OL
1992	Vic Zordan, OL
1992	Roosevelt Potts, RB
1993	Raymond Batiste, OL
1993	James Folston, OL

tight end Jackie Harris and kicker Teddy Garcia—were later elected to the Louisiana-Monroe Hall of Fame.

BIGGEST GAME Even with a 3–0 record in 1987, the Indians had to beat rival Northwestern State on the road to accomplish anything that season. Down 31-27 and at his own 13-yard line, Humphries took the ball with 30 seconds left. A 39-yard pass from Humphries to running back Jeff Steele moved the ball to midfield, and a spike stopped the clock with one second left. On the game's final play, Humphries heaved a Hail Mary pass into the end zone, where Harris, nestled between two defenders, got his hands on the ball but couldn't pull it in. The ball bounced between the two Demons and into Harris' hands in the end zone. The Indians would later win the Division I-AA national title.

BIGGEST UPSET After consecutive losing seasons in 1971 and 1972, the Indians brought back a strong core of players and expected 1973 to be different. It wasn't. The inconsistent bunch opened with two ties, beat Northwestern State, then suffered through three brutal losses—two by shutout—that destroyed the team's high hopes. At the same time, Richmond was unbeaten, the winner of 10 straight games dating back to 1972, and had just upended ranked West Virginia to move into the AP's No. 20 spot. But when the two teams tangled in Week 7, everything came together for the Indians. Tailback Joe Mitchell rushed for 184 yards and quarterback Boyd Cole ran for 147 more (attempting only five passes for two yards), to strangle the Spiders 14-8. One week later, the Indians went to Jacksonville State and got crushed 66-24, symbolic of that topsy-turvy 3–5–2 season.

STADIUM In 1978, sparkling new Malone Stadium opened. It was just a field, surrounded by an oval seating area with a skyscraper sitting at the west end. By 1982, the school had experienced its third boost in seating availability, accommodating 18,000 fans per game. In 1983, the east-side stands were expanded from 20,000 capacity to 23,277. Ten

years later, the east-side bleachers again grew, bringing the total seating size of the stadium to 30,427. At 27, Malone Stadium is aging gracefully, with the recent additions of 20 open-air corporate boxes, a student-athlete computer lab, a weight room and coaching offices.

ALL-TIME TEAM		
Chosen by the sports information department in 2004.		
OFFENSE		
1966-67	Vic Bender,	OL
1981-84	Mike Grantham,	OL
1984-87	John Clement,	OL
1991-92	Jeff Blackshear,	OL
1995-96	Orlando Bobo,	OL
1986-89	Jackie Harris,	TE
1992-95	Stepfret Williams,	WR
1995-98	Marty Booker,	WR
1986-87	Stan Humphries,	QB
1967-70	Joe Profit,	RB
1990-92	Roosevelt Potts,	RB
1984-87	Teddy Garcia,	PK
1987-90	Cisco Richard,	KR
DEFENSE		
1955-58	Joe Driskill,	DE
1995-97	Steve Foley,	DE
1973-75	Glenn Fleming,	DT
1993-94	Shawn King,	DT
1950	George Tarasovic,	LB
1958-59	Smokey Stover,	LB
1982-84	Ronnie Washington,	LB
1975, 1977-79	David Dumars,	DB
1976-79	Vic Minor,	DB
1980-83	Bruce Daigle,	DB
1997-99	Pat Dennis,	DB
1993-94	Brian Lambert,	P

RIVAL The town of Ruston rests about 30 miles from Monroe, setting up a perfect geographical rivalry between the Indians and their neighbor, Louisiana Tech. The Indians and Techsters have battled 43 times on the field, with Louisiana Tech winning 29 of those games, along with countless other contests on the recruiting trail. The Techsters won eight of the series' first nine games, and seven in a row from 1971 to 1977. That began to change, though, when Louisiana Tech passed over Collins, a Tech graduate and then-assistant coach, for its head coaching job in 1979. Collins left to join Crow's coaching staff, taking over the program after the 1980 season when Crow retired. For eight seasons, Collins and Louisiana-Monroe enjoyed an intrastate heyday, winning six times against Louisiana Tech. The series stalled in 1992 and was revived from 1997 to 2000, with Tech winning all four meetings.

NICKNAME Little is certain about the origin of Indians as the team's nickname. But in Anderson's 2003 book, *Indian Territory: The Story of ULM Athletics*, he details the accepted account of how the team got its name. It supposedly originated in the 1930s, when the school was called Ouachita Parish Junior College. It's believed the nickname derives from the legendary stories of the Ouachita Indians, a subtribe of the Caddo Indians, as they roamed the area along the Ouachita river basin.

MASCOT Louisiana-Monroe's mascot, Chief Brave Spirit, gained a spot in the imaginary Mascot Hall of Fame in 1992 after a second-quarter brawl with rival Vic the Demon, Northwestern State's mascot. In that scuffle, later voted by viewers as CNN's No. 4 sports play of the year, Chief Brave

Spirit knocked The Demon's headpiece off, but then, by most accounts, lost the scrap, which momentarily stopped the game. The Indians went on to win that homecoming game 28-18, and Chief Brave Spirit gained infamy. Now, despite the spreading furor over mascots that some feel are offensive to Native Americans, Chief Brave Spirit remains headdressed on the Louisiana-Monroe sideline.

LORE Tag Rome is Louisiana-Monroe's version of Rudy. Rome, who grew up 30 miles away in Jonesboro, La., walked on in 1980 when nearby school Louisiana Tech—and everybody else—passed on offering him a scholarship. At Louisiana-Monroe he lettered four times, went on to set a school record with 117 career receptions and earned first-team All-Southland Conference honors. He secured his legend status when he returned to Monroe as an assistant coach and helped the Indians go 38–19–2 with two conference titles and three Division I-AA playoff berths. Rome now serves as a sideline reporter on radio broadcasts of Louisiana-Monroe football games.

QUOTE "Man, the Indians have arrived."—Assistant coach Pat Collins, as he walked into sparkling-new Malone Stadium. Collins left Louisiana Tech at the end of the 1978 season and later became one of Louisiana-Monroe's best coaches

THE SCHOOLS

THE SCHOOLS

LOUISIANA-MONROE ANNUAL STATISTICAL LEADERS

YR	RUSHING	YDS	ATT	AVG	PASSING	ATT	CMP	PCT	YDS	RECEIVING	REC	YDS	AVG
1978	Nathan Johnson	731	123	5.9	Kirby Arceneaux	171	79	.46	1,229	John Floyd	29	649	22.4
1979	George Johns	602	140	4.3	John Holman	94	42	.45	511	Tony Morrison	19	276	14.5
1980	Nathan Johnson	763	151	5.1	John Holman	350	187	.53	2,444	Tag Rome	41	562	13.7
1981	Dewayne Robinson	463	80	5.8	John Holman	296	146	.49	1,908	Alfred Kinney	44	782	17.8
1982	Feotis Moore	447	101	4.4	John Holman	461	218	.47	2,964	Tag Rome	46	604	13.1
1983	Bobby Craighead	982	209	4.7	Rodney Horn	144	64	.44	1,067	Joey Evans	23	381	16.6
1984	Jimmy Harris	400	98	4.1	Rodney Horn	248	115	.46	1,436	Joey Evans	47	672	14.3
1985	Jimmy Harris	541	108	5.0	Bubby Brister	342	191	.56	2,880	Chris Jones	33	774	23.5
1986	Tommy Minvielle	548	128	4.3	Stan Humphries	249	117	.47	1,773	Benny Mitchell	30	518	17.3
1987	Tommy Minvielle	656	143	4.6	Stan Humphries	338	176	.52	2,622	Jackie Harris	37	709	19.2
1988	Tommy Minvielle	408	106	3.9	Doug Pederson	226	121	.54	1,549	Jackie Harris	43	512	11.9
1989	Cisco Richard	585	148	4.0	Doug Pederson	436	243	.56	2,603	Cisco Richard	61	481	7.9
1990	Roosevelt Potts	954	218	4.4	Doug Pederson	341	190	.56	2,152	Cisco Richard	65	617	9.5
1991	Roosevelt Potts	1,103	239	4.6	Wendal Lowrey	136	80	.59	1,309	Erich Cox	49	535	10.9
1992	Greg Robinson	1,011	159	6.4	Wendal Lowrey	227	147	.65	2,190	Vincent Brisby	56	1,050	18.8
1993	Irving Spikes	1,563	246	6.4	Robert Cobb	345	197	.57	3,008	Stepfret Williams	40	929	23.2
1994	Eric Foster	447	107	4.2	Raymond Philyaw	243	131	.54	1,893	Stepfret Williams	57	1,106	19.4
1995	Carson Fields	632	144	4.4	Raymond Philyaw	320	167	.52	2,627	Stepfret Williams	66	1,056	16.0
1996	Marquis Williams	613	165	3.7	Raymond Philyaw	351	173	.49	2,445	Marty Booker	51	857	16.8
1997	Marquis Williams	977	231	4.2	Daniel Jeremiah	229	120	.52	1,450	Marty Booker	44	621	14.1
1998	Alan Ricard	383	100	3.8	Andre Vige	284	136	.48	1,967	Marty Booker	75	1,168	15.6
1999	Michael Mitchell	683	158	4.3	Andy Chance	246	141	.57	1,327	Sean Brown	37	304	8.2
2000	Mark Henderson	436	88	5.0	Andy Chance	210	111	.53	1,149	Kevin Stevenson	40	432	10.8
2001	Bryant Jacobs	305	103	3.0	Andy Chance	196	103	.53	1,054	Mack Vincent	47	619	13.2
2002	Bryant Jacobs	1,043	205	5.1	Steven Jyles	368	181	.49	2,318	Mack Vincent	79	1,198	15.2
2003	Kevin Payne	976	248	3.9	Steven Jyles	360	201	.56	2,112	Mack Vincent	62	700	11.3
2004	Steven Jyles	587	150	3.9	Steven Jyles	366	204	.56	2,322	Drouzon Quillen	44	758	17.2

Receiving leaders by receptions
The NCAA began including postseason stats in 2002

LOUISIANA-MONROE ALL-TIME SCORES

WIN/LOSS PERCENTAGE SINCE 1994

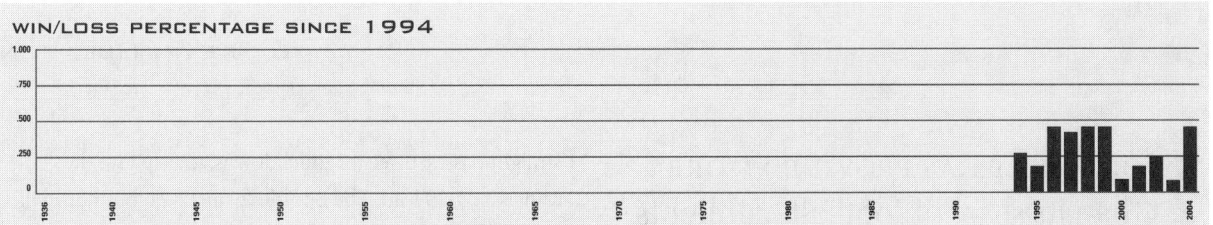

ED ZAUNBRECHER			
1994-98 (.357)			**20-36**

1994-2000
INDEPENDENT

1994 — 3-8-0
S3	at Colorado	13	48
S10	at Auburn	12	44
S17	at Georgia	6	70
S24	at Nevada	22	34
O1 ●	Weber St.	62	37
O8	at Wyoming	14	28
O15	Central Florida	16	33
O22	Jacksonville St.	28	32
N5	at Brigham Young	10	24
N12 ●	at Kentucky	21	14
N19 ●	North Texas	38	20

1995 — 2-9-0
S2	at Fresno State	17	31
S9 ●	Nicholls St.	34	21
S16	at Colorado	14	66
S23	at Missouri	22	31
S30 ●	at Mississippi State	34	32
O7	Troy State	10	20
O14	at Nevada	35	59
O21	Northwestern St.	39	42
O28	Central Florida	14	34
N4	at Auburn	14	38
N11	at Louisville	0	39

1996 — 5-6
A29 ●	Nicholls St.	14	12
S7	Minnesota	3	30
S14	at UCLA	0	44
S21 ●	Sam Houston St.	34	31
S28	Arkansas LR	21	38
O5 ●	Northwestern St.	13	10
O19	at Central Florida	39	38
N2	at Mississippi State	0	59
N9	at Auburn	24	28
N16 ●	Jacksonville St.	31	28
N23	at Cincinnati	13	35

1997 — 5-7
A30 ●	Nicholls St.	28	0
S6	at Arkansas	16	28
S13	at Louisiana Tech	16	17
S20	at Georgia	3	42
S27	at Oklahoma State	7	38
O4 ●	NW. La. St.	17	7
O11	at Mississippi State	10	24
O18	at Kentucky	14	49
O25 ●	at La. Lafayette	28	21
N1 ●	Central Florida	45	41
N15	Western Michigan	19	32
N22	at Hawaii	23	20

1998 — 5-6
S5 ●	Nicholls St.	44	10
S12	at Florida	10	42
S19 ●	Stephen F. Austin	21	10
S26	at Kansas State	7	62
O3	at Western Michigan	14	27
O10	Louisiana Tech	14	44
O24	at Arizona	7	45
O31 ●	UAB	20	14
N7 ●	La. Lafayette	34	24
N14	at Arkansas State	13	17
N21 ●	Portland St.	43	27

BOBBY KEASLER			
1999-2002 (.242)			**8-28**

1999 — 5-6
S4 ●	Nicholls St.	27	10
S11	at Minnesota	0	35
S18	Arkansas LR	6	44
S25 ●	Northwestern St.	38	7
O2	at UAB	0	47
O9	at Utah	0	42
O16	Wyoming	20	38
O23 ●	at La. Lafayette	31	7
O30 ●	Middle Tennessee	10	0
N6	at Louisiana Tech	17	58
N13 ●	at Tulsa	37	34

2000 — 1-10
S2	at Minnesota	10	47
S9	at Memphis	0	28
S16 ●	Nicholls St.	27	21
S23	at Tennessee	3	70
S30	Texas St.	7	27
O7	at Arkansas	6	52
O14	at Middle Tennessee	0	28
O21	at Central Florida	0	55
N4	La. Lafayette	18	21
N11	Louisiana Tech	19	42
N18	Wofford	6	24

2001-PRESENT
SUN BELT

2001 — 2-9 (2-4)
S1	Sam Houston St.	9	20
S8	at Florida	6	55
S22 │	Middle Tennessee	20	38
S29 │	New Mexico State	0	31
O6 ● │	North Texas	19	17
O20 │	at Central Florida	6	38
O27 │	at La. Lafayette	12	17
N3 │	at Idaho	38	42
N10 │	Troy State	12	44
N17 ● │	Arkansas State	16	7
D1 │	at Cincinnati	10	42

MIKE COLLINS			
2002 (.333)			**3-6**

2002 — 3-9 (2-4)
A31	at Mississippi	3	31
S7	at Kansas State	0	68
S14	McNeese State	19	24
S21 │	Arkansas State	21	33
O5	Tulane	9	52
O12 ● │	Idaho	34	14
O19 │	at New Mexico State	21	34
O26 ●	Utah State	51	48
N2 │	at North Texas	2	41
N9	at Auburn	14	52
N16 │	at Middle Tennessee	28	44
N23 ● │	La. Lafayette	34	10

CHARLIE WEATHERBIE			
2003-PRESENT (.261)			**6-17**

2003 — 1-11 (1-5)
A30	at LSU	7	49
S6	S. F. Austin	21	23
S13	at Mississippi	14	59
S20	Northwestern St.	10	14
S27 │	at Utah State	10	28
O4 │	Arkansas State LR	41	44
O11 ● │	at La. Lafayette	45	42
O25 │	New Mexico State	14	21
N1	at Auburn	7	73
N8 │	North Texas	26	28
N15 │	Idaho	20	58
N22	at Troy State	24	28

2004 — 5-6 (3-3)
S4	at Auburn	0	31
S18	Arkansas LR	20	49
S25 │	Arkansas State	21	28
O2	at Wyoming	10	31
O9 ● │	at Idaho	16	14
O16 ●	Florida Intn'l	28	20
O23 │	at Florida Atlantic	17	13
O30 │	at North Texas	30	45
N6 ●	Utah State	32	25
N13	at Middle Tennessee	24	37
N20 ● │	La. Lafayette	13	10

LOUISVILLE

BY KEVIN GLEASON

L OUISVILLE HAS PROVIDED MORE than its share of football highlights despite being overshadowed for decades by Denny Crum's powerhouse basketball program. Johnny Unitas played his college football here, for starters, though he did it largely in obscurity. John L. Smith changed some of the hoops-school perception after being named coach prior to the 1998 season. Still, there were five bowl games before Smith arrived, and the Frank Camp era produced a 118–95–2 record (1946-68). ESPN's own Lee Corso coached Louisville to a 28–11–3 record from 1969 to 1972.

TRADITION Louisville and Kentucky meet annually for the Governor's Cup, and Louisville faces former Conference USA rival Cincinnati for the Keg of Nails. If that doesn't suggest a hard-fought game, nothing does.

BEST PLAYER Hints: strong arm, quick release, one of the best quarterbacks in NFL history, No. 19—though he wore 16 at Louisville. Yes, Johnny Unitas, who began growing his legend five games into his freshman season. St. Bonaventure was leading Louisville 19-0 when Unitas came on and completed

11 straight passes, three for touchdowns, to help give the Cardinals a 21-19 lead. The Bonnies won 22-21, but Louisville won its next four games, including a 35-28 triumph over Houston as a 19-point underdog. Unitas went on to pass for 2,612 yards and 27 TDs before being taken by the Pittsburgh Steelers in the ninth round of the 1955 draft. After more than 40,000 passing yards, 290 TDs and a 47-game TD passing streak in his 18-year NFL career, Unitas was inducted into the Hall of Fame in 1979.

BEST COACH Louisville was coming off a 1–10 season in 1997 when Smith took over. He proceeded to lead the Cardinals to the first of five straight winning seasons and five consecutive bowl games, as well as to their first 11-win season and a 41–21 record, during his tenure.

BEST TEAM With all due respect to the 2001 team that went 11–2 and beat Brigham Young in the Liberty Bowl, the 2004 Cardinals turned in the finest season in school history. Louisville finished 11–1 (8–0 in Conference USA), and came within a few plays of perfection. The only blemish was a 41-38 loss to then-No. 3 Miami. The Cardinals capped the year by snapping Boise State's 22-game win streak with a 44-40 victory in the Liberty Bowl as safety Kerry Rhodes intercepted a pass in the end zone as time expired. Under second-year coach Bobby Petrino (20–5 in his first two

---

PROFILE

University of Louisville
Louisville, Ky.
Founded: 1798
Enrollment: 14,983
Colors: Red and Black
Nickname: Cardinals
Stadium: Papa John's Cardinal Stadium
　　Opened in 1998
　　FieldTurf; 42,000 capacity
First football game: 1912
All-time record: 405–401–17 (.502)
Bowl record: 5–6–1
First-round NFL draftees: 6
Website: www.uoflsports.com

THE BEST OF TIMES

John L. Smith's teams from 1998 to 2002 went 41–21, won two conference titles and played in five bowl games.

THE WORST OF TIMES

Louisville went 20–35 under Bob Weber (1980-84), who was fired for failing to deliver on president Donald Swain's demand that the athletic department be self-sufficient.

CONFERENCE

Louisville was in the Missouri Valley Conference from 1963 to 1974 and an independent from 1975 to 1995. The Cardinals became a charter member of Conference USA in 1996. They moved on to the Big East in 2005.

DISTINGUISHED ALUMNI

Mitch McConnell and Christopher Dodd, U.S. senators; Howard Fineman, *Newsweek* chief political correspondent; Marsha Norman, Pulitzer Prize-winning playwright

FIGHT SONG

FIGHT! U OF L
Fight! Now for vict'ry and show them
how we sure will win this game
Fight! On you Card'nals and prove to them
that we deserve our fame.
Roll up the score now and beat the foe
so we can give a yell
With a fight! Give them all you've got
for we are with you U of L!

> *Johnny Unitas began his legend five games into his freshman season, completing 11 straight passes, three for touchdowns.*

seasons), the Cardinals topped the nation in scoring with 49.8 points per game and finished first in total offense (539 yards per game) and pass efficiency. Senior quarterback Stefan LeFors completed 73.5 % of his passes for 2,596 yards with 20 touchdowns and just three interceptions. Louisville's rankings of No. 6 in the final Associated Press poll and No. 7 in the ESPN/*USA Today* poll were its highest to date.

BIGGEST GAME Browning Nagle had one of the best games in bowl history, passing for 451 yards as Louisville beat Alabama 34-7 in the 1991 Fiesta Bowl. His 451 yards are a Fiesta Bowl record; 225 came in a 25-point first quarter. The Cardinals finished the season 10–1–1.

BIGGEST UPSET Southern Miss was ranked No. 9 after upsetting Florida State on national television. Louisville was on its way to a mediocre 5–6 record. Conditions were so raw the game became known locally as the Ice Bowl. Louisville put an exclamation mark on a frustrating 1981 season with a 13-10 win.

STADIUM They love their Papa John's Cardinal Stadium, perhaps because they spent a decade raising funds toward the $63 million tab. The facility opened in 1998 and lays claim as the only university-owned-and-operated stadium in the nation in which every seat—42,000 of them—is of the chair-back variety.

HEARTBREAKER Southern Mississippi was on its own 21 with six seconds left in a 10-10 game in October 1989 when a strong-armed quarterback named Brett Favre let loose with a Hail Mary. The ball was deflected, then bounced off the helmet of Louisville's Michael Jackson before sliding into the hands of Southern Miss' Darryl Tillman on a dead run. Tillman's game-ending 79-yard touchdown gave the Golden Eagles a 16-10 win. The play was later voted among the top five most memorable in college football history in an online vote at espn.com.

RIVAL Howard Schnellenberger, who left Miami to coach at Louisville, didn't bring any national titles. But Schnellenberger's legacy must include resurrecting the program enough to force the revival of the Louisville-Kentucky game. The 1994

RECORDS

RUSHING YARDS

	GAME
269	Nathan Poole vs. Wichita State, Nov. 4, 1978 (40 att.)
	SEASON
1,429	Howard Stevens, 1971 (250 att.)
	CAREER
3,204	Walter Peacock, 1972-75 (811 att.)

PASSING YARDS

	GAME
592	Chris Redman vs. East Carolina, Nov. 14, 1998 (44 of 56)
	SEASON
4,042	Chris Redman, 1998 (309 of 473)
	CAREER
12,541	Chris Redman, 1996-99 (1,031 of 1,679)

RECEIVING YARDS

	GAME
214	Ibn Green vs. East Carolina, Nov. 14, 1998 (15 rec.)
	SEASON
1,209	Arnold Jackson, 1999 (101 rec.)
	CAREER
3,670	Arnold Jackson, 1997-2000 (200 rec.)

POINTS

	GAME
40	Roger Black vs. Washington (Tenn.), Oct. 18, 1913
	SEASON
132	Lenny Lyles, 1957 (21 TDs, 6 PATs)
	CAREER
300	Lenny Lyles, 1954-57 (49 TDs, 6 PATs)

CONSENSUS ALL-AMERICANS

1957	Leonard Lyles, B

game, won by Kentucky 20-14, ended a 70-year hiatus in the rivalry. They have played each year since.

DISPUTE Louisville was tied at 27 with less than two minutes left against Southern Mississippi with the 1999 Conference USA title on the line. Facing fourth and five at the Louisville 37, Southern Miss went into punt formation. Southern Miss receiver Shawn Mills was leaving the field when he appeared to be getting into a heated discussion with coach Jeff Bower. The ball was snapped and punter Jamie Purser threw a 26-yard pass to Mills, which led to Brant Hanna's 27-yard field goal with 1:07 left, giving Southern Miss a 30-27 victory. C-USA officials admitted later they had missed penalties for Southern Miss not having enough players on the line of scrimmage and Mills' shoulders not being parallel to the line.

NICKNAME A few years before World War I, Louisville was looking for a nickname to give the university statewide identification. What better identifier than the state bird of Kentucky, the cardinal?

UNIFORMS Petrino took over as coach prior to the 2003 season and immediately changed Louisville's look. A large Louisville inscription went across the chest, and colored stripes on the shoulders were added. The pants also have a stripe down each leg.

LORE Former Louisville player Larry Ball is one of two players in NFL history to play for both an undefeated team, the 1972 Miami Dolphins, and a winless team, the 1976 Tampa Bay Buccaneers.

QUOTE "This is huge for the program. It's unbelievable ... but we knew we could do it."—John L. Smith, after the Cardinals' 26-20 OT win over No. 4 Florida State in 2002

LOUISVILLE ANNUAL STATISTICAL LEADERS

YR	RUSHING	YDS	ATT	AVG	PASSING	ATT	CMP	PCT	YDS	RECEIVING	REC	YDS	AVG
1947	Tom Lucia	407	43	9.5	Frank Gitschier	47	31	.66	422		NA	NA	NA
1948	Tom Lucia	659	87	7.6		NA	NA	NA	NA		NA	NA	NA
1949	Tom Lucia	800	115	7.0		NA	NA	NA	NA		NA	NA	NA
1950	Jim Williams	693	126	5.5	Bill Karns	50	27	.54	517		NA	NA	NA
1951	Jim Williams	642	138	4.7	Johnny Unitas	99	46	.47	602		NA	NA	NA
1952		NA	NA	NA	Johnny Unitas	198	106	.54	1,540	Dave Riverbank	40	521	13.0
1953	Mike McDonald	336	67	5.0	Johnny Unitas	95	49	.52	470	Mike McDonald	9	101	11.2
1954	John Sowa	259	47	5.5	Jim Houser	86	39	.45	560	Gene Sartini	17	235	13.8
1955	Lenny Lyles	780	101	7.7	Bob Williams	25	13	.52	361	Lenny Lyles	6	163	27.2
1956	Lenny Lyles	610	119	5.1	Bob Williams	67	28	.42	699	Ed Young	13	358	27.5
1957	Lenny Lyles	1,207	177	6.8	Dale Orem	56	26	.46	483	Ed Young	10	263	26.3
1958	Ken Porco	561	107	5.2		NA	NA	NA	NA		NA	NA	NA
1959	Ernie Green	510	114	4.5		NA	NA	NA	NA		NA	NA	NA
1960		NA	NA	NA		NA	NA	NA	NA		NA	NA	NA
1961	Lee Calland	600	108	5.6	John Giles	172	78	.45	1,209	Don Hockensmith	20	392	19.6
1962	Lee Calland	650	125	5.2	John Giles	181	90	.50	1,222	Don Hockensmith	32	408	12.8
1963	Larry Compton	199	69	2.9	Tom LaFramboise	204	104	.51	1,205	Charlie Mudd	25	367	14.7
1964	Ron Hall	301	86	3.5	Tom LaFramboise	242	122	.50	1,380	Roger Whitehead	33	370	11.2
1965	Wayne Patrick	428	99	4.3	Benny Russell	246	115	.47	1,791	Al MacFarlane	35	524	15.0
1966	Benny Russell	273	117	2.3	Benny Russell	310	142	.46	2,016	Jim Zamberlan	59	747	12.7
1967	Wayne Patrick	582	155	3.8	Wally Oyler	192	83	.43	1,039	Jim Zamberlan	45	559	12.4
1968	Herbie Phelps	468	96	4.9	Wally Oyler	240	112	.47	1,410	Larry Hart	25	375	15.0
1969	Lee Bouggess	1,064	267	4.0	Gary Inman	182	78	.43	843	Cookie Brinkman	25	357	14.3
1970	Bill Gatti	981	207	4.7	John Madeya	244	121	.50	1,750	Cookie Brinkman	48	647	13.5
1971	Howard Stevens	1,429	250	5.7	John Madeya	201	97	.48	1,045	Tony Burdock	33	361	10.9
1972	Howard Stevens	1,294	259	5.0	John Madeya	301	146	.49	1,709	Gary Barnes	52	655	12.6
1973	Walter Peacock	1,294	290	4.5	Len DePaola	168	73	.43	808	Dale Kaminski	18	262	14.6
1974	Walter Peacock	827	237	3.5	Len DePaola	97	32	.33	428	Kevin Miller	25	361	14.4
1975	Walter Peacock	1,013	262	3.9	John Darling	137	66	.48	946	Tony Smith	26	382	14.7
1976	Calvin Prince	1,028	213	4.8	Stu Stram	93	36	.39	394	Marc Mitchell	15	147	9.8
1977	Calvin Prince	1,050	218	4.8	Stu Stram	78	36	.46	455	Marc Mitchell	24	358	14.9
1978	Nathan Poole	1,394	212	6.6	Stu Stram	149	70	.47	929	Ken Robinson	29	534	18.4
1979	Greg Hickman	648	150	4.3	Stu Stram	118	52	.44	806	Randy Butler	20	347	17.4
1980	Don Craft	687	140	4.9	Pat Patterson	167	69	.41	933	Ken Robinson	26	401	15.4
1981	Don Craft	475	136	3.5	Dean May	105	41	.39	589	Mark Clayton	27	596	22.1
1982	Ron Davenport	526	120	4.4	Dean May	311	141	.45	2,034	Mark Clayton	53	1,112	21.0
1983	Willie Shelby	447	107	4.2	Dean May	263	139	.53	1,609	David Hatfield	49	543	11.1
1984	Ron Davenport	501	130	3.9	Ed Rubbert	363	184	.51	2,465	Ernest Givins	33	689	20.9
1985	John Adams	514	140	3.7	Ed Rubbert	256	120	.47	1,475	Ernest Givins	34	577	17.0
1986	Deon Booker	537	112	4.8	Ed Rubbert	210	103	.49	1,304	Eric Vaughn	34	697	20.5
1987	Deon Booker	671	135	5.0	Jay Gruden	397	209	.53	2,481	Rodney Knighton	43	409	9.5
1988	Deon Booker	1,011	217	4.7	Jay Gruden	382	224	.59	2,605	Deon Booker	41	391	9.5
1989	Carwell Gardner	595	139	4.3	Browning Nagle	334	187	.56	2,503	Carwell Gardner	46	614	13.3
1990	Ralph Dawkins	542	121	4.5	Browning Nagle	263	146	.56	2,150	Anthony Cummings	28	473	16.9
1991	Ralph Dawkins	622	154	4.0	Erik Watts	260	115	.44	1,294	Ralph Dawkins	44	297	6.8
1992	Anthony Shelman	418	85	4.9	Jeff Brohm	297	155	.52	2,008	Ralph Dawkins	43	506	11.8
1993	Ralph Dawkins	579	129	4.5	Jeff Brohm	304	185	.61	2,626	Jamie Asher	52	658	12.7
1994	Anthony Shelman	1,084	241	4.5	Marty Lowe	319	186	.58	2,091	Jamie Asher	70	794	11.3
1995	Calvin Arrington	1,016	255	4.0	Marty Lowe	350	195	.56	2,268	Miguel Montano	50	694	13.9
1996	Donnell Gordon	482	115	4.2	Chris Redman	272	144	.53	1,773	Miguel Montano	48	602	12.5
1997	Frank Moreau	573	120	4.8	Chris Redman	445	261	.59	3,079	Miguel Montano	67	875	13.1
1998	Leroy Collins	1,134	218	5.2	Chris Redman	473	309	.65	4,042	Arnold Jackson	90	1,165	12.9
1999	Frank Moreau	1,289	233	5.5	Chris Redman	489	317	.65	3,647	Arnold Jackson	101	1,209	12.0
2000	Tony Stallings	810	181	4.5	Dave Ragone	354	216	.61	2,621	Deion Branch	71	1,016	14.3
2001	T.J. Patterson	576	118	4.9	Dave Ragone	383	231	.60	3,056	Deion Branch	72	1,188	16.5
2002	Henry Miller	594	139	4.3	Dave Ragone	441	237	.54	2,880	Damien Dorsey	52	753	14.5
2003	Lionel Gates	817	144	5.8	Stefan LeFors	357	219	.61	3,145	J.R. Russell	75	1,213	16.2
2004	Eric Shelton	146	938	6.4	Stefan LeFors	257	189	.74	2,596	J.R. Russell	73	968	13.3

Receiving leaders by receptions
The NCAA began including postseason stats in 2002

LOUISVILLE ALL-TIME SCORES

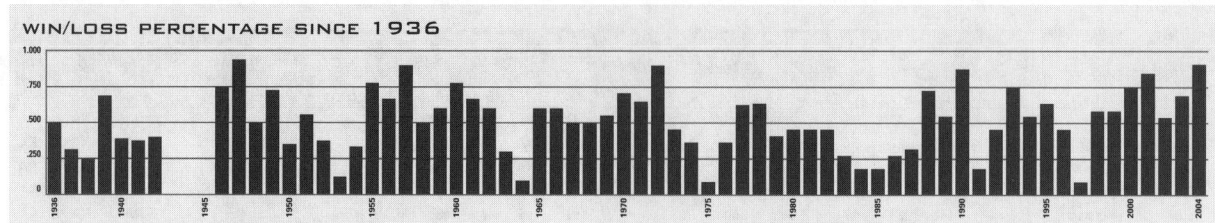

WIN/LOSS PERCENTAGE SINCE 1936

LESTER LARSON
1912-13 (.800)   8-2

1912   3-1-0
O11	●	at Transylvania	32	0
O17	●	Centre	23	6
O26		at Kentucky	0	41
N15	●	Hanover	73	0

1913   5-1-0
O4	●	Bethel	48	0
O11	●	at Moore's Hill	77	0
O18	●	Washington, Tn.	100	0
O25	●	Cumberland	6	0
N1	●	Butler	20	0
N22		Kentucky	0	20

DR. BRUCE BAKER
1914 (.200)   1-4

1914   1-4-0
O17		Tennessee	0	66
O31		Wabash	3	7
N7		at Cumberland	0	20
N14		at Kentucky	0	42
N21	●	at Rose Poly	23	0

WILL DUFFY
1915-16 (.308)   3-8-2

1915   1-5-1
O2	=	Centre	0	0
O9		at Wabash	0	38
O16		U.T. Chattanooga	6	21
O30	●	Rose Poly	22	6
N6		Kentucky	0	15
N13		Franklin	7	13
N25		Transylvania	0	26

1916   2-3-1
O14	=	Centre	0	0
O21	●	U.T. Chattanooga	6	0
O28	●	Butler	19	7
N4		Georgetown, Ky.	0	41
N18		Franklin	12	16
N30		Transylvania	0	13

1917-20
NO TEAM

BILL DUNCAN
1921-22 (.321)   4-9-1

1921   2-2-1
O22	●	Hanover	19	8
O29	=	at Bethel	0	0
N5		at Transylvania	0	7
N18	●	Kentucky Wesleyan	30	0
N26		at Marshall	0	14

1922   2-7-0
S30		Western Kentucky	0	6
O7		Bethel	12	14
O14		at Kentucky	0	73 *
O21		Franklin	6	27
O28		at Centre	7	32
N4	●	Cincinnati AC	28	0
N11	●	at Rose Poly	6	0
N18		Centenary	13	39
N30		at Marshall	7	21

FRED ENKE
1923-24 (.500)   8-8-1

1923   5-3-0
S29		at Western Kentucky	7	19
O6		at Union, Ky.	6	13
O13	●	Morris Harvey	27	0
O20		Franklin	0	35
O27	●	Rose Poly	13	0
N3	●	Transylvania	12	0
N10	●	Kentucky Wesleyan	7	0
N17	●	at Georgetown, Ky.	12	6

1924   3-5-1
O4		at Kentucky	0	29
O11	●	Western Kentucky	12	7
O18	●	at Georgetown, Ky.	9	6
O25		Transylvania	0	3
N1		at Rose Poly	6	18
N8	=	at Kentucky Wesleyan	0	0
N15		King	0	16
N22	●	U.T. Chattanooga	10	0
N27		at Marshall	6	16

TOM KING
1925-30 (.563)   27-21

1925   8-0-0
O3	●	Evansville	20	0
O10	●	at Western Kentucky	6	0
O17	●	at Hanover	24	0
O24	●	Kentucky Wesleyan	6	0
O30	●	at Transylvania	7	0
N7	●	Rose Poly	30	0
N21	●	Toledo	33	0 *
N26	●	at Marshall	7	2

1926   6-2-0
O2	●	at Ogden	79	0
O9	●	at Rose Poly	49	0
O16		at Xavier	7	20
O30		Centre	0	6
N6	●	Western Kentucky	26	10
N13	●	at Kentucky Wesleyan	25	12
N20	●	Marshall	27	3
N25	●	at Florida Southern	13	0

1927   4-4-0
O8	●	Transylvania	25	6
O15	●	Murray St.	14	0
O22		at Marshall	6	37
O29	●	Centre	40	7
N5		at Western Kentucky	6	7
N12	●	at Eastern Kentucky	21	13
N19		Davis & Elkins	0	32
N24		at Centenary	2	59

1928   1-7-0
O6	●	Eastern Kentucky	72	0
O13		at Detroit	0	46
O20		at U.T. Chattanooga	0	70
O27		Transylvania	0	18
N3		at Western Kentucky	0	20
N10		Centre	0	7
N17		at St. Loius	0	12
N24		Marshall	0	13

1929   3-5-0
O2		Cincinnati	0	7
O11		at Transylvania	0	9
O19		Western Kentucky	0	13
O26		at Marshall	6	25
N2	●	at Eastern Kentucky	19	6
N9		Centre	0	41
N16	●	Earlham	6	0
N23	●	Georgetown, Ky.	6	0

1930   5-3-0
O4	●	Hanover	32	12
O11	●	Transylvania	18	0
O17	●	Eastern Kentucky	52	0
O25	●	at Western Kentucky	6	7
N1		Centre	0	28
N8		at DePaul	0	14
N15	●	at Marshall	13	12
N22	●	Earlham	13	0

JACK McGRATH
1931 (.250)   2-6

1931   2-6-0
O2		Hanover	0	3
O9	●	Transylvania	13	12 †
O16		at Butler	6	61
O24	●	Eastern Kentucky	19	14 †
O31		at Western Kentucky	6	20
N7		DePaul	0	46
N14		at Georgetown, Ky.	6	20
N21		Centre	0	75

C.V. MONEY
1932 (.000)   0-9

1932   0-9-0
S24		at Marshall	0	60
O1		Union, Ky.	6	32
O8		at Murray St.	0	105
O15		at Eastern Kentucky	0	38
O22		Transylvania	12	34
O28		Morehead St.	0	20
N4		at Oakland City	0	19
N12		Georgetown, Ky.	0	20
N19		at Western Kentucky	0	58

BEN CREGOR
1933-35 (.196)   4-18-1

1933   1-7-0
S30		Centre	0	30
O6		at Georgetown, Ky.	0	13
O13		at Union, Ky.	0	19
O21		Western Kentucky	0	45
O28		at Morehead St.	0	13
N4		Murray St.	6	54
N10		at Miami, Fla.	7	33
N18	●	Eastern Kentucky	13	7

1934   2-5-0
O6	●	Georgetown, Ky.	14	6
O13		at Toledo	7	19
O27		at Hanover	6	7
N3		Centre	0	46
N10		at Transylvania	0	13
N17	●	at Eastern Kentucky	13	6
N24		Union, Ky.	0	7

1935   1-6-1
S28		at Butler	0	29
O5		Transylvania	7	14
O11		at Union, Ky.	7	13
O19	=	at Hanover	6	6
O26		Eastern Kentucky	0	9
N2		at Georgetown, Ky.	0	21
N9		Toledo	7	41
N16	●	Morehead St.	20	0

LAURIE APITZ
1936-42 (.435)   22-29-3

1936   4-4-0
O3	●	Union, Ky.	13	0
O10	●	at Hanover	12	2
O17	●	at Eastern Kentucky	6	9
O24		at Union U.	7	27
O30	●	Georgetown, Ky.	12	8
N7	●	Alfred Holbrook	31	7
N14		at Morehead St.	7	14
N21		Baldwin Wallace	0	67

1937   2-5-1
S25		Hanover	7	13
O2		at Transylvania	6	19
O9		at Wayne St.	0	32
O15	●	Union U.	14	6
O23	●	St. Joseph's	13	6
O30		at Georgetown, Ky.	7	12
N11	●	Centre	7	20
N20	=	Eastern Kentucky	6	6

1938   2-6-0
S24		at Cincinnati	9	19 *
O7	●	Wayne St.	14	12
O15		at St. Joseph's	0	2
O22		Georgetown, Ky.	0	6
O29		Transylvania	7	13
N4	●	at Evansville	6	0
N11		Hanover	13	14
N19		at Centre	0	14

1939   5-2-1
S22	●	at Transylvania	25	0
S30		at Indiana St.	0	7
O6	●	Evansville	7	6
O13	●	Alfred Holbrook	20	3
O19	●	St. Joseph's	13	0
O28	=	at Centre	0	0
N4		at Georgetown, Ky.	7	14
N18	●	Hanover	20	0

1940   3-5-1
S21	=	Indiana St.	0	0
S28		at Cincinnati	0	7
O5	●	at Evansville	13	7
O12	●	at St. Joseph's	6	24
O18		Centre	0	28
O25	●	Alfred Holbrook	38	7
N2		Georgetown, Ky.	14	19
N9	●	at Hanover	14	13
N16		at Long Island	6	29

1941   4-4-0
S22	●	Rio Grande	58	0
S27		at Cincinnati	7	28
O4	●	Evansville	31	6
O17	●	Transylvania	13	0
O23		at Georgetown, Ky.	6	13
N1		at DePauw	6	13
N8	●	at Hanover	21	6
N15		Vanderbilt	0	68

1942   2-3-0
S17	●	Rio Grande	25	0
S26		at Cincinnati	0	51
O10	●	at Evansville	20	0
O17		DePauw	6	19
O24		Indiana St.	7	25

1943-45
NO TEAM

FRANK CAMP
1946-68 (.553)   118-95-2

1946   6-2-0
S26		at Evansville	13	7
O4	●	Wittenberg	19	0
O11	●	at Georgetown, Ky.	20	0
O19		at Western Kentucky	19	20
O25	●	Georgetown, Ky.	20	0
N2	●	St. Joseph's	13	7
N9		at Eastern Kentucky	7	28
N16	●	Union U.	25	0

1947   7-0-1
S26	●	Wittenberg	40	3
O4	●	at DePauw	37	0
O10	●	Evansville	20	7
O24	●	Western Kentucky	19	13
N1	●	at St. Joseph's	7	7
N7	●	Eastern Kentucky	14	13
N14	●	at S.E. Louisiana	23	0
N22	●	Washington, Mo.	33	20

1948   5-5-0

S25	at Memphis	7	13
O2 ●	St. Joseph's	20	0
O8	at Xavier	26	47
O16 ●	at Akron	13	0
O23 ●	Western Kentucky	19	6
O30	Buffalo	19	48
N6 ●	Catawba	33	21
N13	at Evansville	6	18
N20 ●	Bradley	31	14
N27	at Washington, Mo.	12	27

1949   8-3-0

S17 ●	St. Joseph's	33	7
S24 ●	at Western Kentucky	47	7
S30 ●	Murray St.	34	14
O8 ●	Miami, Fla.	0	26
O15 ●	Akron	62	6
O21 ●	Xavier	7	19
O29 ●	at Bradley	35	12
N3 ●	at Catawba	41	7
N12 ●	Washington, Mo.	35	12
N19 ●	Evansville	28	7
N25 ●	at Southern Miss	21	26

1950   3-6-1

S23 ●	St. Francis, Pa.	34	14
S30 ●	Buffalo	48	19
O7	at Cincinnati	20	28
O14 ●	at Houston	7	27
O21 ●	at Xavier	13	36
O28 ●	Duquesne	20	27
N4 ●	at Washington, Mo.	28	7
N10 =	at Miami, Fla.	13	13
N18 ●	Wash. & Lee	28	33
N25 ●	at Southern Miss	28	34

1951   5-4-0

S29 ●	at Wayne St.	28	12
O5	Boston U.	7	39
O13 ●	at Cincinnati	0	38
O19 ●	Xavier	6	47
O27 ●	at St. Bonaventure	21	22
N2 ●	North Carolina St.	26	2
N10 ●	Houston	35	28
N17 ●	Wash. & Lee	14	7
N23 ●	Southern Miss	14	13

1952   3-5-0

S27 ●	Wayne St.	19	12
O4 ●	at Florida State	41	14
O11 ●	Dayton	0	20
O18 ●	at Xavier	13	27
O31 ●	at U.T. Chattanooga	14	47
N8 ●	at Memphis	25	29
N15 ●	Eastern Kentucky	34	20
N22 ●	at Southern Miss	26	55

1953   1-7-0

S19 ●	at Murray St.	19	14
O3	at Florida State	0	59
O10 ●	Xavier	13	19
O17 ●	at Dayton	13	20
O24 ●	at Tennessee	6	59
O30 ●	at U.T. Chattanooga	6	44
N7 ●	Cincinnati	0	41
N14 ●	Eastern Kentucky	13	20

1954   3-6-0

S18 ●	Murray St.	13	33
S24 ●	at Wayne St.	0	13
O2 ●	Florida State	6	47
O9 ●	at Dayton	7	27
O16 ●	Evansville	26	6
O23 ●	Centre	27	6
O30 ●	at Western Kentucky	7	25
N6 ●	Morehead St.	24	0
N13 ●	at Eastern Kentucky	6	20

1955   7-2-0

S17 ●	at Murray St.	14	33
S24 ●	at Xavier	20	49
O1 ●	Wayne St.	72	0
O8 ●	Dayton	19	7
O15 ●	at Evansville	29	7
O29 ●	Western Kentucky	20	0
N5 ●	Morehead St.	37	12
N12 ●	at Eastern Kentucky	45	13
N19 ●	Toledo	33	13

1956   6-3-0

S22 ●	at Toledo	27	12
S29 ●	Kent State	0	7
O6 ●	Evansville	41	13
O13 ●	Murray St.	7	6
O20 ●	at Morehead St.	19	7
O27 ●	at Ohio U.	25	19
N3 ●	Dayton	6	7
N10 ●	Xavier	14	34
N17 ●	Eastern Kentucky	14	6

1957   9-1-0

S21 ●	at Evansville	33	7
S27 ●	at Eastern Kentucky	40	14
O5 ●	Toledo	48	20
O12 ●	at Murray St.	35	0
O19 ●	Dayton	33	19
O26 ●	Central Michigan	40	0
N9 ●	at Kent State	7	13
N16 ●	Ohio U.	40	7
N22 ●	Morehead St.	40	6
SUN BOWL			
J1 ●	Drake	34	20

1958   4-4-0

S27 ●	Eastern Kentucky	20	7
O4 ●	at Toledo	7	13
O11 ●	Murray St.	27	0
O18 ●	at Dayton	13	26
O25 ●	at Central Michigan	40	7
N8 ●	Kent State	21	0
N15 ●	at Ohio U.	6	23
N22 ●	North Texas	10	21

1959   6-4-0

S15 ●	Western Kentucky	19	0
S19 ●	at Xavier	13	28
S25 ●	at Eastern Kentucky	14	7
O3 ●	at Bradley	28	8
O10 ●	at Murray St.	28	0
O17 ●	Dayton	32	6
O31 ●	Marshall	48	6
N7 ●	at North Texas	7	39
N14 ●	Ohio U.	15	22
N21 ●	at Kent State	14	16

1960   7-2-0

S17 ●	at Tennessee Tech	7	21
S23 ●	Eastern Kentucky	28	7
S30 ●	Bradley	40	6
O7 ●	Murray St.	12	6
O15 ●	at Dayton	36	0
O21 ●	Western Kentucky	44	0
O29 ●	at Marshall	7	0
N5 ●	Xavier	0	29
N11 ●	Kent State	22	8

1961   6-3-0

S16 ●	Tennessee Tech	29	13
S22 ●	at Eastern Kentucky	33	6
S30 ●	Marshall	32	7
O7 ●	Memphis	13	28
O14 ●	Dayton	6	7
O21 ●	Western Kentucky	20	0
N4 ●	at Xavier	8	16
N11 ●	at Kent State	19	15
N18 ●	at North Texas	20	0

1962   6-4-0

S15 ●	at Wichita St.	21	20
S22 ●	Western Michigan	27	21
S29 ●	at Marshall	18	0
O6 ●	at Memphis	0	49
O13 ●	at Dayton	21	0
O20 ●	at Tulsa	7	25
N3 ●	Xavier	12	13
N10 ●	Kent State	29	8
N17 ●	North Texas	14	10
N24 ●	Houston	25	27

1963-1974   MISSOURI VALLEY

1963   3-7-0 (1-3-0)

S28	at North Texas	6	26
O5	So. Illinois	7	13
O12	Dayton	13	12
O19	Wichita St.	14	47
O26	Marshall	27	14
N2	Memphis	0	25
N9	at Kent State	7	26
N16	at Western Michigan	21	7
D7	at Tulsa	16	22
D14	at Houston	7	21

1964   1-9-0 (0-4-0)

S19	Western Michigan	7	10
S26	So. Illinois	6	7
O3	North Texas	0	22
O10	at Dayton	21	7
O17	Tulsa	0	58
O24	at Marshall	6	28
O31	at Wichita St.	15	23
N7	Kent State	7	14
N14	at Memphis	0	34
N21	Drake	8	14

1965   6-4-0 (3-1-0)

S18 ●	at Western Michigan	13	17
S25 ●	So. Illinois	13	0
O2 ●	at North Texas	29	21
O9	Dayton	34	0
O16 ●	East Carolina	20	34
O23 ●	Marshall	23	7
O30 ●	Wichita St.	30	10
N6 ●	at Tulsa	18	51
N13 ●	at Drake	32	17
N20 ●	at Kent State	6	7

1966   6-4-0 (1-3-0)

S24 ●	at So. Illinois	16	7
O1	North Texas	19	20
O8	at Dayton	17	20
O15 ●	Drake	66	26
O22 ●	at Marshall	35	15
O29	at Wichita St.	2	9
N5 ●	Kent State	23	20
N12	at Cincinnati	3	17
N19 ●	Tulsa	29	18
N26 ●	East Carolina	21	7

1967   5-5-0 (1-3-0)

S16 ●	at Drake	46	7
S23 ●	So. Illinois	26	0
S30 ●	at North Texas	28	30
O7 ●	Dayton	29	7
O14 ●	at East Carolina	13	18
O21 ●	Marshall	43	7
O28	Wichita St.	24	17
N4	at Kent State	21	28
N11	Cincinnati	7	13
D2	at Tulsa	23	35

1968   5-5-0 (2-3-0)

S21 ●	at So. Illinois	33	10
O5	at Dayton	14	28
O12	Tulsa	16	7
O19	at Marshall	13	10
O26	at Wichita St.	21	14
N2	Kent State	23	9
N9	at Cincinnati	7	37
N16	North Texas	14	36
N23	Drake	37	38
N30	Memphis	14	44

LEE CORSO   1969-72 (.702)   28-11-3

1969   5-4-1 (2-3-0)

S13 =	at Drake	24	24
S20 ●	So. Illinois	17	13
O4	Dayton	24	17
O18 ●	Marshall	34	17
O25	at North Texas	13	31
N1	at Kent State	6	35
N8	Cincinnati	21	31
N15 ●	Wichita St.	13	7
N22	at Memphis	19	69
N27 ●	at Tulsa	35	29

1970   8-3-1 (4-0-0)

S12	at Florida State	7	9
S19	at So. Illinois	28	31
S26	North Texas	13	2
O3	at Dayton	11	28
O10	Tulsa	14	8
O17	at Marshall	16	14
O31	Kent State	14	13
N7	Memphis	40	27
N14	at Cincinnati	28	14
N21	Drake	23	14
N28 ●	at Wichita St.	34	24
PASADENA BOWL			
D19 =	Long Beach St.	24	24

1971   6-3-1 (3-2-0)

S18 =	at Vanderbilt	0	0
S25	at Drake	7	10
O2 ●	Dayton	41	13
O9 ●	at Memphis	6	20
O16 ●	at North Texas	17	20
O23 ●	Wichita St.	21	5
O30 ●	Tampa	21	10
N6 ●	at Tulsa	17	0
N13 ●	So. Illinois	24	14
N27 ●	Cincinnati	16	19

1972   9-1-0 (4-1-0)

S16 ●	Kent State	34	0
S30 ●	at Dayton	28	11
O7 ●	at Tampa	17	14
O14	North Texas	56	6
O21 ●	at Wichita St.	46	3
O28 ●	at Cincinnati	38	13
N4	Tulsa	26	28
N11 ●	at So. Illinois	20	16
N18 ●	Memphis	17	0
N25 ●	Drake	27	0

T.W. ALLEY   1973-74 (.409)   9-13

1973   5-6-0 (3-2-0)

S8 ●	at Memphis	21	28
S15 ●	at Kent State	3	10
S22 ●	at Drake	27	17
O6 ●	Wichita St.	24	10
O13 ●	at North Texas	6	7
O20 ●	Mississippi State	7	18
O27 ●	Cincinnati	10	8
N3	at Tulsa	9	17
N10	Dayton	9	10
N17 ●	Furman	35	14
N24 ●	at West Texas St.	21	9

1974   4-7-0 (3-2-0)

S7 ●	Memphis	10	16
S14 ●	Auburn BIRM	3	16
S28 ●	at Cincinnati	6	7
O5 ●	at Wichita St.	14	7
O12 ●	at North Texas	24	10
O19	Drake	35	38
O26	at Mississippi State	7	56
N2	Tulsa	7	37
N9 ●	Dayton	20	15
N23 ●	Vanderbilt	0	44
N30	West Texas St.	10	8

1975-1995   INDEPENDENT

VINCE GIBSON   1975-79 (.429)   23-31-2

1975   1-10-0

S13	Western Kentucky	17	21
S20	at Drake	7	31
S27	Cincinnati	27	46
O4	at Wichita St.	10	13
O11 ●	U.T. Chattanooga	6	3
O18	at Memphis	7	41
O25	Mississippi State	14	28 †
N1	at Tulsa	14	38
N8	Dayton	13	32
N15	at La. Monroe	10	14
N22	at West Texas St.	23	49

1976   4-7-0

S18 ●	at Mississippi State	21	30 †
S25 ●	Drake	37	24
O2 ●	Wichita St.	28	14
O9	at Pittsburgh	6	27
O16 ●	La. Monroe	36	8
O23	at Alabama	3	24
O30	Tulsa	10	20
N6	at Rutgers	0	34
N13	Memphis	14	26
N20 ●	Boston U.	16	7
N27	at Cincinnati	6	20

1977   7-4-1

S10	No. Illinois	38	0
S17 =	Cincinnati	17	17
S24 ●	William & Mary	7	21
O1 ●	at Memphis	14	13
O8 ●	Tulsa	33	0
O15 ●	at Dayton	10	14
O22 ●	at Alabama	6	55
O29 ●	at Marshall	56	0
N5 ●	Wichita St.	51	21
N12 ●	Drake	18	13
N20 ●	Indiana St.	27	16
INDEPENDENCE BOWL			
D17 ●	Louisiana Tech	14	24

1978   7-4-0

S9 ●	South Dakota St.	54	7
S16 ●	Maryland	17	24
S23 ●	at Cincinnati	28	14
S30 ●	Indiana St.	31	12
O7 ●	at Tulsa	7	24
O14 ●	Northwestern St.	51	7
O21 ●	Boston U.	35	7
O28 ●	William & Mary	33	21
N4 ●	at Wichita St.	38	20
N11 ●	Memphis	22	29
N18 ●	at Southern Miss	3	37

THE SCHOOLS

1979 4-6-1

S8		Virginia Tech	14	15
S15		at Miami, Fla.	12	24
S22	●	Cincinnati	22	19
S29	●	at Drake	31	21
O6		Florida State	0	27
O13	●	Tulsa	24	7
O20	●	at Indiana St.	34	10
N3	=	Southern Miss	10	10
N10		at Memphis	6	10
N17		at Maryland	7	28
N25		Rutgers	7	31

BOB WEBER
1980-84 (.364) 20-35

1980 5-6-0

S6		Miami, Fla.	10	24
S13		at Florida State	0	52
S20		Murray St.	9	13
S27	●	at Kansas	17	9
O11	●	Memphis	38	14
O18	●	Indiana St.	27	17
O25		at Florida	0	13
N1		Temple	12	17
N8		at Pittsburgh	23	41
N15	●	Cincinnati	20	0
N22	●	at Southern Miss	6	3

1981 5-6-0

S5		at Florida State	0	17
S12	●	Toledo	31	6
S19	●	Long Beach St.	35	13
S26		at Missouri	3	34
O3	●	Marshall	36	0
O10	●	at Memphis	14	7
O17		Tennessee St.	30	42
O24		at Oklahoma State	11	19
N7		La. Monroe	7	40
N14		at Cincinnati	0	24
N21	●	Southern Miss	13	10

1982 5-6-0

S4	●	Western Kentucky	20	10
S11		at Cincinnati	16	38
S25	●	Oklahoma State	28	22
O2		Miami, Fla.	6	28
O9		Temple	14	55
O16	●	Richmond	35	0
O23		at Southern Miss	0	48
O30		at Pittsburgh	14	63
N6	●	Indiana St.	35	23
N13		at Florida State	14	49
N20	●	at Memphis	38	19

1983 3-8-0

S3		at SMU	6	24
S10	●	Western Kentucky	41	22
S17	●	Army	31	7
S24	●	Cincinnati	31	23
O1		at Virginia Tech	0	31
O8		at Miami, Fla.	14	42
O15		Pittsburgh	10	55
O20		at Florida State	7	51
N5		Southern Miss	3	27
N12		at Temple	7	24
N24		Memphis	7	45

1984 2-9-0

S1		Murray St.	23	26
S8		at West Virginia	6	30
S15		SMU	7	41
S29	●	at Houston	30	28
O6	●	Western Kentucky	45	17
O13		Indiana St.	21	44
O20		at Rutgers	21	38
O27		at Cincinnati	21	40
N3		Miami, Fla.	23	38
N10		Tennessee St.	15	24
N17		at Southern Miss	25	34

H. SCHNELLENBERGER
1985-94 (.491) 54-56-2

1985 2-9-0

S7		at West Virginia	13	52
S14		at Indiana	28	41
S21	●	Western Kentucky	23	14
S28		Houston	27	49
O5		at Syracuse	0	48
O12		Southern Miss	12	42
O19		Cincinnati	9	31
O26		at Miami, Fla.	7	45
N2	●	Central Florida	42	21
N9		at Virginia Tech	17	41
N16		Eastern Kentucky	21	45

1986 3-8-0

S6		at Illinois	0	23
S13		at Indiana	0	21
S20	●	Western Kentucky	45	6
S27	●	Memphis	34	8
O4		at Cincinnati	17	24
O18		at Boston College	7	41
O25		Florida State	18	54
N1		Rutgers	0	41
N8	●	at Tulane	23	12
N15		West Virginia	19	42
N22		at Southern Miss	16	31

1987 3-7-1

S5	●	Tulane	42	40
S12		Cincinnati	0	25
S19	=	at Purdue	22	22
S26	●	Murray St.	34	10
O3		Southern Miss	6	65
O10		Marshall	31	34
O17		at Florida State	9	32
O24	●	Akron	31	10
O31		at Tulsa	22	26
N7		at Tennessee	10	41
N14		at Memphis	8	43

1988 8-3-0

S3		at Maryland	16	27
S8		Wyoming	9	44
S17	●	Memphis	29	18
S24	●	at North Carolina	38	34
O1		at Southern Miss	23	30
O8	●	Tulsa	9	3
O15	●	Virginia	30	28
O22	●	at Tulane	38	35
O29	●	at Cincinnati	21	6
N5	●	Virginia Tech	13	3
N12	●	Western Kentucky	35	17

1989 6-5-0

S2	●	at Wyoming	28	21
S9	●	at Kansas	33	28
S23		West Virginia	21	30
S30	●	Cincinnati	37	17
O14		Southern Miss	10	16
O21		at Tulsa	24	31
O28		at Virginia	15	16
N4	●	Western Kentucky	55	7
N11	●	at Memphis	40	10
N18	●	at Boston College	36	22
D4		Syracuse TOK	13	24

1990 10-1-1

S1	=	at San Jose State	10	10
S8	●	Murray St.	68	0
S15	●	Kansas	28	16
S22	●	at West Virginia	9	7
S29		at Southern Miss	13	25
O6	●	Tulsa	38	14
O13	●	Memphis	19	17
O20	●	at Pittsburgh	27	20
O27	●	Western Kentucky	41	7
N3	●	at Cincinnati	41	16
N10	●	Boston College	17	10
		FIESTA BOWL		
J1	●	Alabama	34	7

1991 2-9-0

A31	●	Eastern Kentucky	24	14
S5		Tennessee	11	28
S14		at Ohio State	15	23
S28	●	Southern Miss	28	14
O5		Cincinnati	7	30
O12		at Boston College	3	33
O19		Army	12	37
O26		at Virginia Tech	13	41
N2		Florida State	15	40
N9		at Memphis	7	35
N16		at Tulsa	0	40

1992 5-6-0

S5		at Ohio State	19	20
S12	●	Memphis	16	15
S19		at Arizona State	0	19
S26		Wyoming	24	26
O3		Syracuse	9	15
O10	●	Virginia Tech	21	17
O17	●	Tulsa	32	27
O24		at Florida	17	31
O31	●	at Cincinnati	27	17
N7		at Texas A&M	18	40
N14	●	at Pittsburgh	31	16

1993 9-3-0

S4	●	San Jose State	31	24
S11	●	at Memphis	54	28
S18	●	Arizona State	35	17
S25	●	Texas	41	10
O2	●	at Pittsburgh	29	7
O9		at West Virginia	34	36
O16	●	Southern Miss	35	27
O23	●	Navy	28	0
N6		at Tennessee	10	45
N13		at Texas A&M	7	42
N25	●	at Tulsa	28	0
		LIBERTY BOWL		
D28	●	Michigan State	18	7

1994 6-5-0

S3		at Kentucky	14	20
S10		at Texas	16	30
S17	●	at Arizona State	25	22
O1	●	Pittsburgh	33	29
O8	●	North Carolina St.	35	14
O15		at Army	29	30
O22	●	at Navy	35	14
O29	●	Memphis	10	6
N3		Boston College	14	35
N12		Texas A&M	10	26
N26	●	Tulsa	34	27

RON COOPER
1995-97 (.394) 13-20

1995 7-4-0

S2	●	at Kentucky	13	10
S9	●	at No. Illinois	34	21
S16		Michigan State	7	30
S21		North Carolina	10	17
S30	●	at Memphis	17	7
O7		at Southern Miss	21	25
O14		at Wyoming	20	27
O28	●	Maryland	31	0
N4	●	Tulane	34	14
N11	●	La. Monroe	39	0
N18	●	North Texas	57	14

1996-2004
C-USA

1996 5-6 (2-3)

A31	●	at Kentucky	38	14
S7		at Penn State	7	24
S14		Baylor	13	14
S21	●	at Michigan State	30	20
S28	|	Southern Miss	7	24
O12	● |	at Tulane	23	20
O19	●	No. Illinois	27	3
O26	|	Cincinnati	7	10
N2	● |	Memphis	13	10
N9		at North Carolina	10	28
N16	|	at Houston	7	38

1997 1-10 (0-6)

A30		at Kentucky	24	38
S6		Utah	21	27
S13	●	Illinois	26	14
S20		Penn State	21	57
S27		at Oklahoma	14	35
O4	|	at Southern Miss	24	42
O11	|	Tulane	33	64
O25	|	Houston	22	36
N1	|	East Carolina	31	45
N8	|	at Cincinnati	9	28
N15	|	at Memphis	20	21

JOHN L. SMITH
1998-2002 (.661) 41-21

1998 7-5 (4-2)

S5		Kentucky	34	68
S12		at Utah	22	45
S19	●	at Illinois	35	9
S26	●	Boston College	52	28
O3	● |	Cincinnati	62	19
O10	|	at Southern Miss	21	56
O17	|	at Tulane	22	28
O24	● |	Memphis	35	32
O31	●	W. Kentucky	63	34
N14	● |	at East Carolina	63	45
N21	● |	Army	35	23
		MOTOR CITY BOWL		
D23		Marshall	29	48

1999 7-5 (4-2)

S4	●	at Kentucky	56	28
S11	●	U.T. Chattanooga	58	30
S18		Illinois	36	41
S25		Oklahoma	21	42
O2	●	Eastern Michigan	45	10
O7	|	at Army	52	59
O16	● |	at Memphis	32	31
O23	● |	Houston	39	33
O30	● |	UAB	23	14
N6	● |	at Cincinnati	23	13
N20	|	Southern Miss	27	30
		HUMANITARIAN BOWL		
D30		Boise State	31	34

2000 9-3 (6-1)

S2	●	Kentucky	40	34
S9	●	Grambling	52	0
S23		at Florida State	0	31
S30	●	Connecticut	41	22
O7	● |	at UAB	38	17
O14	● |	Cincinnati	38	24
O19	|	East Carolina	25	28
O28	● |	Tulane	35	32
N4	● |	at Southern Miss	49	28
N11	● |	Army	38	17
N18	● |	at Houston	32	13
		LIBERTY BOWL		
D29		Colorado State	17	22

2001 11-2 (6-1)

A23	●	New Mexico State	45	24
S1	●	at Kentucky	36	10
S8	●	Western Carolina	31	7
S22		at Illinois	10	34
S29	● |	Memphis	38	21
O4	●	Colorado State	7	2
O16	● |	Southern Miss	24	14
O27	● |	at Cincinnati	28	13
N3	● |	at Tulane	52	7
N10	● |	Houston	34	10
N15	● |	at East Carolina	39	34
N23	|	at TCU	22	37
		LIBERTY BOWL		
D31	●	Brigham Young	28	10

2002 7-6 (5-3)

S1		Kentucky	17	22
S7	●	at Duke	40	3
S14		at Colorado State	33	36
S21	● |	at Army	45	14
S26	●	Florida State	26	20
O8	● |	at Memphis	38	32
O19	|	TCU	31	45
O26	● |	East Carolina	44	20
N7	|	Cincinnati	14	24
N14	● |	at Southern Miss	20	17
N23	● |	UAB	41	21
N30	|	at Houston	10	27
		GMAC BOWL		
D18		Marshall	15	38

BOBBY PETRINO
2003-PRESENT (.800) 20-5

2003 9-4 (5-3)

A31	●	at Kentucky	40	24
S13	●	at Syracuse	30	20
S20	●	Texas-El Paso	42	14
S27	●	Temple	21	12
O4	|	at South Florida	28	31
O11	● |	Army	34	10
O17	● |	Tulane	47	28
O25	● |	at East Carolina	36	20
N5	|	at TCU	28	31
N15	|	Memphis	7	37
N22	● |	Houston	66	45
N28	● |	at Cincinnati	43	40
		GMAC BOWL		
D18		Miami, Ohio	28	49

2004 11-1 (8-0)

S5	●	Kentucky	28	0
S11	● |	at Army	52	21
S25	●	at North Carolina	34	0
O2	● |	East Carolina	59	7
O14		at Miami, Fla.	38	41
O22	● |	South Florida	41	9
N2	● |	at Memphis	56	49
N9	● |	TCU	55	28
N20	● |	at Houston	65	27
N27	● |	Cincinnati	70	7
D4	● |	at Tulane	55	7
		LIBERTY BOWL		
D31	●	Boise State	44	40

f Forfeit † Game Later Forfeited # Disputed Victor * Disputed Score || Designated Conference Game |2 Counted Twice in Conference Standings

MARSHALL

BY ED KRZEMIENSKI

IN 1997, MARSHALL UNIVERSITY jumped from Division I-AA to Division I-A when it joined the Mid-American Conference. Immediately, the Thundering Herd became a successful mid-major program, using the skills that had brought them attention in the lower division. Yet the fact that Marshall began its first five years of Division I-A membership with 54 wins and five bowl bids is not nearly as impressive as the fact that the school even had a team.

On Nov. 14, 1970, the probation-strapped Thundering Herd suffered a 17-14 loss at East Carolina in a game that eight Marshall players missed with injuries, a ninth missed for a funeral and a 10th, Rich Taglang, missed by oversleeping and failing to catch the team bus to the airport. They were lucky. Flying back after the defeat, the team's charter encountered rain and fog as it approached Tri-State Airport in Huntington, W.Va. The weather and instrument failure caused the plane to crash into a hillside. All 75 people aboard were killed, including the coaches and 36 members of the team. The community was devastated, and the painful rebuilding of the football program became a symbol of its own efforts to heal.

TRADITION Although it's named for the fourth chief justice of the United States, John Marshall, the school is more closely affiliated with the railroad industry than with the law. Rolling Thunder, a 40-ton CSX train painted green and white, pulls onto side tracks near Marshall Stadium for home games and travels to as many road games as tracks will allow. On the way onto their home field, Marshall players touch a real stuffed buffalo head and then a sign with former coach Bob Pruett's personal mantra, "We play for championships!"

BEST PLAYER Although Randy Moss tied a Division I-AA record in 1996 with 28 touchdown receptions and went on to an All-Pro NFL career, it was the man who threw 24 of those TDs to Moss—another record—who stands as the greatest player in Marshall history. Quarterback Chad Pennington, who set the career passing mark at a pass-happy school, was a finalist for the Heisman Trophy in 1999 and was chosen 18th in the 2000 NFL draft by the New York Jets.

BEST COACH "At Marshall, we play for championships!" So said Bob Pruett not long after his arrival in 1996. And he delivered: in his first six years, Pruett amassed a 69–11 record, including two undefeated seasons and a string of four consecutive MAC championships. A close second would be Jim Donnan, who, in the six seasons before Pruett, had coached Marshall to a 64–21 record. Still, for leading

---

PROFILE

Marshall University
Huntington, W. Va.
Founded: 1837
Enrollment: 9,958
Colors: Green and White
Nickname: Thundering Herd
Stadium: Joan C. Edwards Stadium
  Opened in 1991
  FieldTurf; 38,019 capacity
First football game: 1895
All-time record: 498–461–47 (.518)
Bowl record: 5–2–0
First-round NFL draftees: 3
Website: www.herdzone.com

THE BEST OF TIMES

In the 1990s, known to Marshall fans as "the decade, the dynasty," the team set a college football record with 114 victories.

THE WORST OF TIMES

In 1970, the team plane crashed, killing all 75 people aboard, including 36 members of the football team. The team's record between 1966 and 1983 was 38–150–2.

CONFERENCE

The Thundering Herd is well-traveled, with stops in several conferences. The longest stays were in the Mid-American Conference (1953-68) and later the Southern Conference (1977-96). After rejoining the the Mid-American Conference upon its return to Division I-A (1997-2004), Marshall joins Conference USA in 2005.

DISTINGUISHED ALUMNI

Billy Crystal; Robert Byrd, U.S. senator; Hal Greer, Basketball Hall of Famer; Soupy Sales, actor

FIGHT SONG

SONS OF MARSHALL
We are the sons of Marshall
Sons of the great John Marshall
Year after year we go to Marshall U.,
Cheering for our team
and gaining knowledge, too
Proudly we wear our colors,
Love and loyalty we share
Sure from far and near,
You always hear
The wearing of the green,
But it is the green and white of Marshall U.!

Marshall into Division I-A success, it's Pruett by a neck.

BEST TEAM Although the school had a great deal of lower-division success, the 1999 Thundering Herd stands alone. Led by Pennington, the team began the season with a 13-10 win over Clemson at Death Valley, rolled through the MAC and beat Brigham Young 21-3 in the Motor City Bowl to complete an undefeated 13–0 season. They finished the year 10th in the polls. Pennington's individual statistics were just as remarkable, as he completed nearly 68% of his passes, threw for 37 touchdowns and averaged 316 yards passing per game.

BIGGEST GAME Forget bowl games, forget conference championships—there will never be a bigger win in the history of Marshall than its 15-13 defeat of Xavier on Sept. 25, 1971, at Fairfield Stadium in Huntington. It was the Thundering Herd's first home game following the tragedy that ended the 1970 season. At Morehead State the week before, Marshall had lost 29-6, and most felt that its single score was a

> *In 1971, Reggie Oliver dropped back to pass as the gun sounded. He threw across the field for a touchdown to beat Xavier. Marshall football had returned.*

moral victory. Now, in front of an emotional crowd of 13,000, the Herd trailed 13-9 with 1:18 left to play and the ball on their own 48-yard line. Three incompletions later, Marshall faced fourth and 10, but quarterback Reggie Oliver completed an 11-yard pass to keep the drive alive. Out of timeouts and with the clock running, Marshall made it inside the 20. Assistant coach Red Dawson signaled from the sideline for a "213 bootleg screen." As Oliver dropped back to pass from the 13, the gun sounded. Rolling right, he turned back and threw across the field to freshman fullback Terry Gardner for a touchdown and the win. It was a great finish, but an even greater beginning. Marshall football had returned.

BIGGEST UPSET In 1941, heavily favored Wake Forest visited Marshall a year after soundly defeating the Thundering Herd in Winston-Salem. Trailing 6-0 at halftime, Marshall coach Cam Henderson motivated his team by sucker-punching one of his players, Jackie Hunt, in the gut on the way out of the locker room. "Damn it, Hunt,"

RECORDS

RUSHING YARDS

GAME
262 Ron Darby vs. Western Carolina, Nov. 12, 1988 (47 att.)

SEASON
1,833 Chris Parker, 1995 (349 att.)

CAREER
5,924 Chris Parker, 1991-95 (1,110 att.)

PASSING YARDS

GAME
496 Michael Payton vs. VMI, Nov. 16, 1991 (22 of 28)

SEASON
4,902 Tony Petersen, 1987 (340 of 622)

CAREER
13,143 Chad Pennington, 1995-99 (1,026 of 1,619)

RECEIVING YARDS

GAME
288 Randy Moss vs. Delaware, Nov. 30, 1996 (8 rec.)

SEASON
1,757 Mike Barber, 1987 (106 rec.)

CAREER
4,262 Mike Barber, 1985-88 (242 rec.)

POINTS

GAME
38 Doug Freutal vs. Greenbriar Military Academy, Oct. 18, 1919

SEASON
174 Randy Moss, 1996 (29 TDs)

CAREER
428 Chris Parker, 1991-95 (71 TDs, 1 two-pt. conv.)

CONSENSUS ALL-AMERICANS

1937	William Smith	E
1940-41	Jackie Hunt	HB
1987-88	Mike Barber	WR
1987-88	Sean Doctor	TE
1990	Eric Ihnat	TE
1991-92	Phil Ratliff	OL
1992	Michael Payton	QB
1992	Troy Brown	WR
1993-94	Roger Johnson	DB
1993	Chris Deaton	OL
1993	William King	LB
1994-95	William Pannell	OL
1994	Travis Colquitt	P
1995	Chris Parker	RB
1995-96	Melvin Cunningham	DB
1995-96	Billy Lyon	DL
1996-97	Randy Moss	WR
1996	Aaron Ferguson	OL
1996	B.J. Cohen	DL
1996	Jermaine Swafford	LB
1996	Eugene McAleer	LB

Henderson shouted, "wake up!" It worked. Louis dePolo scored twice and future Pro Football Hall of Famer Frank "Gunner" Gatski added a safety, as the Herd defeated the heavily favored Demon Deacons 16-6—a game witnessed by approximately 15,000 in the 10,000 seat stadium. Hunt later said that Henderson's halftime punch was the hardest hit he took all day.

HEARTBREAKER The Herd played host to the University of Montana for the D1-AA championship on Dec. 16, 1995. With four minutes left, running back Chris Parker ran one in from 26 yards, putting Marshall ahead 20-19. But Montana answered by kicking a 25-yard field goal with 39 seconds remaining for a 22-20 victory.

BEST COMEBACK In the 2001 GMAC Bowl in Mobile, Ala., Marshall trailed East Carolina 38-8 at halftime. Coming off a demoralizing 41-36 defeat to Toledo in the MAC championship game, which Marshall had led 23-0, the Herd seemed spent. In the third quarter, though, Marshall transformed itself. The team scored four touchdowns, including two on interception returns, and outscored ECU 28-3 to cut the lead to 41-36. With 50 seconds left, Marshall still trailed 51-45 and had the ball on its own 20. In an amazing display of field leadership, junior quarterback Byron Leftwich led the Herd on a six-play scoring drive with seven seconds to spare. But Curtis Head missed the extra point, and the game went to overtime tied at 51. After trading touchdowns in the first OT, Marshall held ECU to a field goal in the second and won the game on another Leftwich touchdown pass. The final score was 64-61, the highest-scoring game in bowl history and one of the most exciting games in recent memory. Leftwich completed 41 of 70 passes for 576 yards and four touchdowns and ran for another.

WILDEST FINISH Late in the 1915 game against West Virginia, Marshall coach Boyd Chambers sent in a trick play as a last chance to avoid a humiliating shutout. The Tower Pass involved serious teamwork: Dayton "Runt" Carter ran into the end zone, climbed on the shoulders of tackle Okey

Taylor and caught a touchdown pass from Brad Workman—cutting the deficit to 92-6. Chambers used it again that year to avoid a shutout to Ohio University. Both the Mountaineers and the Bobcats protested the play. The American Football Rules Committee, headed by Walter Camp, ruled in favor of Marshall but made the Tower Pass illegal beginning in 1916.

NICKNAME In 1925, Zane Grey wrote one of his many novels of the American West, this one titled *The Thundering Herd*. A local sports editor thought the name fit the University well, since the campus was located in a former grazing area for herds of bison. In the 1930s, the name gained support when Randolph Scott starred in a movie version of the book. Other ideas for the team's nickname included Judges, in honor of the school's namesake, and Boogercats. For years people referred to Marshall as Big Green, until a vote in the mid-1960s finally ended the confusion and Thundering Herd was adopted as the school's official nickname.

MASCOT The getup for Marco the Buffalo used to be made of papier-mâché and was draped over two people, but in 1985 it became a standing, furry, friendly buffalo with a jersey covering a single person. For a short time in the 1970s Marco had a date on game day—a female mascot named Marsha. There used to be a live buffalo as well, but during a game in 1971 he got out of his travel cage at halftime and tried to eat the new turf.

UNIFORMS Marshall adopted its current green and white colors in 1903. Home jerseys are green with white lettering and the word Herd across the front. On the road the team wears similarly fashioned white jerseys and either white or green pants. Helmets are white with a very large green M on the sides. In 1990, Donnan arranged a deal with Nike for a supply of closeout shoes at $10 a pair. Few of the 200 pairs of shoes, however, had green swooshes to match the team uniform, so Marshall equipment managers had to paint and repaint the shoes throughout

ALL-CENTURY TEAM	
Chosen in 1999 by the Charleston Daily Mail.	
OFFENSE	
1936-38	Frank Huffman, OL
1938-41	Ed Ulinski, OL
1940-42	Frank "Gunner" Gatski, OL
1989-92	Phil Ratliff, OL
1994-97	John Wade, OL
1985-88	Mike Barber, WR
1996-97	Randy Moss, WR
1987-88	Sean Doctor, TE
1995-99	Chad Pennington, QB
1931-34	John Zontini, RB
1938-41	Jackie Hunt, RB
1992-95	Chris Parker, HB
1988-91	Dewey Klein, PK
1991-92	Troy Brown, KR
DEFENSE	
1941	Jim Pearcy, DL
1947-49	Norm Willey, DL
1990-92	Keenan Rhodes, DL
1993-96	Billy Lyon, DL
1994-97	B.J. Cohen, DL
1963-65	Tom Good, LB
1990-93	William King, LB
1994-97	Larry McCloud, LB
1962-64	Larry Coyer, DB
1969-70	Larry Sanders, DB
1979-82	Carl Lee, CB
1986-88	Reggie Giles, CB
1982-83	Pat Velarde, P

the season. The team now has a more lucrative deal with Nike and receives green swooshes prepainted.

STADIUM Marshall University Stadium opened in 1991. It has a capacity of 38,019, but the school intends to expand the seating to 55,000 in the near future. To arrive at the stadium, one travels along Marshall Memorial Boulevard, the site of Spring Hill Cemetery, where six unidentified bodies from the crash are buried, then along Third Avenue, where 75 flags fly representing each of the deceased. There are also bronze statues of three 1970-attired players rising out of the ground from the waist up, next to buffaloes—representing the rebirth of Marshall football.

RIVAL Ohio University, 80 miles northeast of Huntington across the Ohio River, seems a world away. OU and Marshall began their annual Battle for the Bell—a traveling trophy kept on a river towboat—in 1905, and even when the MAC expelled Marshall in 1969 for recruiting violations, the two teams maintained their rivalry.

LORE The Nov. 2, 2002, game may not have looked particularly interesting when Marshall released its schedule: another MAC matchup and more than likely another Marshall blowout against the undermanned Akron Zips. What happened on the field that day, though, placed Byron Leftwich in the annals of college football heroics. In the first quarter, Leftwich left the game with an injured left shin. After X-rays revealed no fracture, Leftwich hobbled back into the game with 7:06 left in the third quarter and led the Herd to a touchdown and a field goal. He finished the game 26 of 38 for 307 yards, but it was not enough to defeat the Zips. The Akron victory, however, stood only as a backdrop to Leftwich's grit. In what quickly became one of college football's most indelible images, Leftwich completed a long pass and then, unable to run to the new line of scrimmage, was carried by two of his offensive linemen to his position in shotgun formation. The injury may have caused professional scouts to think twice about investing in the Marshall quarterback, but no one could question his desire.

QUOTE "All the great things that have happened to us, the inspiration and the momentum, all started after the plane crash."—Bob Pruett

MARSHALL ANNUAL STATISTICAL LEADERS

YR	RUSHING	YDS	ATT	AVG	PASSING	ATT	CMP	PCT	YDS	RECEIVING	REC	YDS	AVG
1970	Art Harris	413	113	3.6	Ted Shoebridge	212	78	.37	1,000	Art Harris	29	242	8.3
1971	John Johnstonbaugh	285	58	4.9	Reggie Oliver	177	77	.44	835	Lanny Steed	35	483	13.8
1972	Ned Burks	346	96	3.6	Reggie Oliver	200	78	.39	993	Lanny Steed	37	509	13.8
1973	Jon Lockett	593	173	3.4	Reggie Oliver	185	91	.49	1,058	John Filliez	40	383	9.6
1974	Bob Tracey	408	108	3.8	Bob Wilt	63	27	.43	345	John Filliez	34	426	12.5
1975	Bud Nelson	382	193	2.0	Bud Nelson	146	70	.48	972	John Filliez	54	657	12.2
1976	Mike Bailey	605	128	4.7	Bud Nelson	171	78	.46	991	John Filliez	40	488	12.2
1977	C.W. Geiger	1,039	247	4.2	Bud Nelson	158	76	.48	1,187	Ray Crisp	33	594	18.0
1978	Danny Wright	652	195	3.3	Danny Wright	89	32	.36	469	Todd Ellwood	17	303	17.8
1979	Ron Lear	1,162	241	4.8	Danny Wright	71	36	.51	329	Mike Natale	21	247	11.8
1980	Ron Lear	617	134	4.6	Tony Konopka	131	55	.42	605	Darnel Richardson	31	376	12.1
1981	Larry Fourqurean	843	197	4.3	Ted Carpenter	114	55	.48	758	Darnel Richardson	50	690	13.8
1982	Gilbert Orr	549	104	5.3	Ted Carpenter	105	50	.47	549	Tony Stott	36	549	15.3
1983	Larry Fourqurean	899	204	4.4	Carl Fodor	127	60	.47	802	Brian Swisher	32	560	17.5
1984	Randy Clarkson	467	131	3.6	Carl Fodor	411	218	.53	2,888	Robert Surratt	55	642	11.7
1985	Mike McCoy	335	94	3.6	Carl Fodor	400	196	.49	2,438	Randy Clarkson	49	460	9.4
1986	Darryl DeBoes	489	122	4.0	John Gregory	124	63	.51	958	Mike Barber	64	1,180	18.4
1987	Ron Darby	1,587	313	5.1	Tony Petersen	622	340	.55	4,902	Mike Barber	106	1,757	16.6
1988	Ron Darby	1,282	289	4.4	John Gregory	386	217	.56	3,127	Mike Barber	79	1,325	16.8
1989	Ron Darby	788	172	4.6	John Gregory	351	198	.56	2,778	Andre Motley	59	908	15.4
1990	Orlando Hatchett	626	132	4.7	Michael Payton	347	199	.57	2,409	Eric Ihnat	55	592	10.8
1991	Orlando Hatchett	855	146	5.9	Michael Payton	346	222	.64	3,392	Brian Dowler	62	1,197	19.3
1992	Glenn Pedro	974	187	5.2	Michael Payton	415	268	.65	3,610	Troy Brown	101	1,654	16.4
1993	Chris Parker	1,750	339	5.2	Todd Donnan	372	211	.57	2,591	Ricky Carter	69	766	11.1
1994	Chris Parker	1,728	321	5.4	Todd Donnan	375	239	.64	3,019	Tim Martin	67	889	13.3
1995	Chris Parker	1,833	349	5.3	Chad Pennington	354	219	.62	2,445	Jermaine Wiggins	58	681	11.7
1996	Erik Thomas	1,296	187	6.9	Eric Kresser	375	226	.60	3,407	Randy Moss	78	1,709	21.9
1997	Doug Chapman	908	157	5.8	Chad Pennington	428	253	.59	3,480	Randy Moss	90	1,647	18.3
1998	Doug Chapman	1,184	252	4.7	Chad Pennington	432	279	.65	3,419	Nate Poole	48	616	12.8
1999	Doug Chapman	686	164	4.2	Chad Pennington	405	275	.68	3,799	Nate Poole	71	1,122	15.8
2000	Franklin Wallace	555	100	5.6	Byron Leftwich	457	279	.61	3,358	Nate Poole	70	818	11.7
2001	Franklin Wallace	796	152	5.2	Byron Leftwich	470	315	.67	4,132	Darius Watts	91	1,417	15.6
2002	Brandon Carey	657	150	4.4	Byron Leftwich	491	331	.67	4,268	Denero Marriott	86	993	11.5
2003	Earl Charles	1,039	205	5.1	Stan Hill	191	133	.70	1,767	Darius Watts	74	968	13.1
2004	Earl Charles	824	177	4.7	Stan Hill	397	233	.59	2,387	Josh Davis	86	914	10.6

Receiving leaders by receptions
The NCAA began including postseason stats in 2002

MARSHALL ALL-TIME SCORES

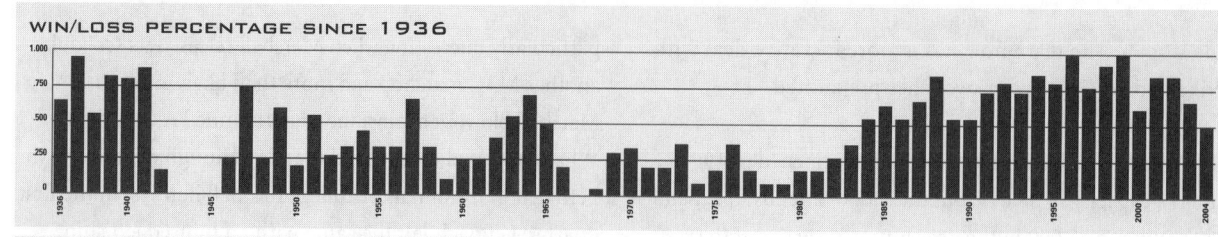

WIN/LOSS PERCENTAGE SINCE 1936

NO HEAD COACH

1895 — 0-1-1
N14		Ashland HS	0 36
N28	=	Kingbury HS	0 0

1896
NO TEAM

1897 — 0-3-0
O23		Huntington Tigers	10 14
O30		Kingsbury HS	0 4
N13		Ironton HS	6 14

1898 — 4-1-0
O22	•	Kingbury HS	12 0
N5	•	Kingbury HS	1 0 *
N9		at Catlettsburg	5 11
N18	•	Catlettsburg	17 0
N25	•	Ashland HS	6 0

1899 — 0-0-1
N30	=	at Catlettsburg	0 0

1900 — 1-0-2
O19	=	Catlettsburg JV	0 0
N19	•	Charleston	20 0
N29	=	Catlettsburg	0 0

1901 — 2-0-1
O26	•	Charleston	6 0
N22	•	Second HS	19 0
N28	=	Charleston	0 0

1902 — 5-0-2
O10	•	Huntington HS	5 2
O17	=	Ashland HS	0 0
O24	•	Gallipolis HS	34 0
N1	•	Ashland HS *CAT*	16 0
N8	•	at Charleston HS	5 0
N14	=	Charleston HS	0 0
N27	•	at Middleport HS	5 0

GEORGE FORD
1903-04 (.500) — 4-4-4

1903 — 3-1-1
O10	=	at Middleport HS	0 0
O24	•	Ashland HS	11 5
N14	•	Huntington Semi-Pro	11 5
N21		at Ashland HS	0 15
N24	•	Shelton Coll.	15 0

1904 — 1-3-3
O8		Portsmouth HS	0 6
O15	=	at Ashland HS	0 0
O19	•	Bethany Coll.	5 10
O22	=	at Portsmouth HS	0 0
O29		Charleston HS	0 5
N12	=	at Charleston HS	0 0
N24	•	Georgetown Coll.	11 5

ALFRED McCARY
1905 (.750) — 6-2

1905 — 6-2-0
S30	•	Ashland HS	1 0 *
O5	•	at Kenova	15 5
O7	•	Portsmouth HS	5 0
O18	•	Ironton HS	12 0
O21	•	Charleston HS	1 0 *
N2		Kentucky	0 53
N11	•	Ohio U.	6 5
N30	•	Miami, Ohio	5 35

PEARL RARDIN
1906 (.900) — 4-0-1

1906 — 4-0-1
O6	=	Cincinnati	0 0
O20	•	Portsmouth AC	24 0
O27	•	Georgetown Coll.	10 0
N10	•	Ashland HS	10 0
N29	•	Morris-Harvey	12 5

NO HEAD COACH

1907 — 3-2-1
O12	=	Ashland YMCA	0 0
O19	•	at Georgetown Coll.	11 5
N2	•	Mountain St. Bus. Coll.	22 0
N9	•	W.V. Wesleyan *RAV*	0 18
N16	•	Charleston AC	0 12
N28	•	Morris-Harvey	5 0

W.G. VINAL
1908 (.000) — 0-6

1908 — 0-6-0
O3		at Ohio U.	0 59
O10		Charleston YMCA	4 6
O17		at Charleston YMCA	0 12
O24		Ashland YMCA	5 6
N7		at Morris-Harvey	0 10
N28		Morris-Harvey	5 11

BOYD CHAMBERS
1909-16 (.550) — 31-25-4

1909 — 3-2-1
O16	•	Charleston AC	12 0
O23	•	Portsmouth	66 0
O25		at W.V. Wesleyan	6 25
N6		at Marietta	0 70
N14	=	Glenville	0 0
N25	•	Morris-Harvey	23 0

1910 — 5-1-1
O8	•	Charleston HS	28 0
O15		W.V. Wesleyan *GRA*	0 5
O22	=	at Morris-Harvey	0 0
O29	•	Davis & Elkins	6 3
N2	=	at Glenville	9 0
N12	•	Kentucky Wesleyan	40 0
N24	•	Georgetown	8 6

1911 — 4-1-1
O14	•	Marietta	6 0
O21	=	at Ohio U.	5 5
O28	•	at West Virginia	15 17
N4	•	Glenville	32 0
N18	•	W.V. Wesleyan	14 0
N30	•	Georgetown	50 0

1912 — 3-4-0
S28	•	Ironton	46 0
O5	•	at Kentucky	6 13
O19	•	Transylvania	87 0
O26	•	Marietta	0 14
N9	•	Wheeling Staats	6 8
N16	•	at W.V. Wesleyan	0 59
N28	•	Muskingum	52 0

1913 — 3-4-0
O10	•	Transylvania	14 2
O18	•	at Georgetown	7 0
O25	•	Marietta	12 7
N1	•	at Wheeling Staats	6 26
N8	•	at Virginia Tech	0 47
N22	•	Morris-Harvey	0 6
N27	•	W.V. Wesleyan	0 13

1914 — 5-4-0
O3	•	West Virginia	0 20
O10	•	at W.V. Wesleyan	0 34
O17	•	Davis & Elkins	6 0
O24	•	Ohio Northern	7 0
O31	•	Wilmington	94 0
N7	•	at Virginia Tech	6 53
N14	•	at Marietta	7 20
N21	•	Sandy Valley Seminary	79 0
N26	•	Morris-Harvey	32 6

1915 — 1-7-0
O2		at Denison	0 52
O9		at Washington & Lee	0 27
O16		Marietta	0 20
O22		Central U. *LexK*	6 10
O30		Otterbein	0 18
N6		West Virginia	6 92
N20		at Ohio U.	7 18
N24		Kentucky Wesleyan	61 7

1916 — 7-2-1
S29	•	at Rio Grande	26 12
O7	•	2nd Regiment	15 0
O14	•	at Muskingum	19 0
O21	•	Kentucky Wesleyan	101 0
O28	•	at Transylvania	19 19
N4	•	Otterbein	12 6 *
N11	•	Marietta *PARK*	13 40
N18	•	at Davis & Elkins	0 24
N24	•	Morris-Harvey	55 0
N30	•	Ohio Northern	7 0

CARL SHIPLEY
1917 (.167) — 1-7-1

1917 — 1-7-1
S30	•	Rio Grande	1 0
O6	•	at Denison	0 94
O13	•	at Marietta	0 68
O20	•	Otterbein	0 37
O27	•	at Georgetown	0 61
N10	•	at Greenbriar MA	0 38
N17	•	at Muskingum	0 28
N24	•	Morris-Harvey	7 7
N29	•	Huntington HS	0 12

1918
NO TEAM

ARCHER REILLY
1919 (1.000) — 8-0

1919 — 8-0
O4	•	Morris-Harvey	76 0
O11	•	at Broaddus Coll.	27 0
O18	•	Greenbriar MA	65 0
O25	•	at Davis & Elkins	33 0 *
N7	•	at Transylvania	20 0
N15	•	at Greenbriar MA	29 7
N22	•	Muskingum	19 6
N27	•	Kentucky Wesleyan	33 0

HERBERT CRAMER
1920 (.000) — 0-8

1920 — 0-8-0
O2	•	at Army	0 38 *
O9	•	Kentucky Wesleyan	0 13
O16	•	Ohio U.	0 55
O23	•	Davis & Elkins	0 16
N6	•	Ironton YMCA	0 13
N13	•	Rio Grande	0 28
N20	•	Muskingum	0 37
N25	•	Morris-Harvey	0 47

KEMPER SHELTON
1921-22 (.618) — 10-6-1

1921 — 5-2-1
S24	•	at Marietta	0 0
S30	•	Salem Coll.	6 0
O8	•	at Kentucky	0 28
O15	•	Rio Grande	33 3
O29	•	Transylvania	13 0
N4	•	Broaddus Coll.	13 3
N20	•	New River St.	0 7
N26	•	Louisville	13 0

1922 — 5-4-0
S23	•	Alderson-Broaddus	71 6
S30	•	at Kentucky	0 16
O7	•	Transylvania	56 0
O14	•	Marietta	0 14
O27	•	W.V. Wesleyan	21 48
N4	•	Georgetown	30 0
N11	•	at Rio Grande	27 3
N18	•	at Muskingum	0 6
N30	•	Louisville	21 7

HARRISON BRIGGS
1923 (.125) — 1-7

1923 — 1-7-0
S29	•	at Kentucky	0 41
O6	•	Rio Grande	6 20
O13	•	Marietta	0 33
O20	•	at West Virginia	0 81
O27	•	at Concord Coll.	6 9
N3	•	Muskingum	9 34
N10	•	Wilmington	0 53
N22	•	Morris-Harvey	7 0

RUSSELL MEREDITH
1924 (.500) — 4-4

1924 — 4-4-0
O4	•	New River St.	13 3
O11	•	Marietta	0 3
O17	•	Salem	9 7
O25	•	at Muskingum	3 0
N1	•	Concord	0 23
N15	•	at Davis & Elkins	0 43
N22	•	at Transylvania	7 28
N27	•	Louisville	16 6

CHARLES TALLMAN
1925-28 (.671) — 22-9-7

1925 — 4-1-4
S26	•	Glenville	26 0
O3	•	Concord	13 0
O10	=	at Marietta	0 0
O18	=	New River St.	6 6
O24	=	Transylvania	0 0
O31	•	at Salem	14 14
N7	•	Wilmington	19 0
N14	•	Morris-Harvey	58 2
N26	•	Louisville	2 7

1926 — 5-4-1
S25	•	Alderson-Broaddus	14 0
O1	•	Eastern Kentucky	34 0
O9	•	at Transylvania	32 6
O16	•	Grove City	0 27
O23	•	Concord	0 6
O30	•	at Xavier	6 20
N6	•	New River St.	6 0
N12	•	Fairmont St.	55 13
N20	•	at Louisville	3 27
N25	•	Hampden-Sydney	0 0

1927 — 5-3-1
S24	•	Alderson-Broaddus	33 6
O1	=	at John Carroll	6 6
O8	•	Concord	18 6
O14	•	at Ohio Wesleyan	0 7
O22	•	at Louisville	37 6
O29	•	at Canisius	0 19
N3	•	at New River St.	65 0
N12	•	Fairmont St.	35 6
N24	•	W.V. Wesleyan	0 19

1928 8-1-1
S30	=	at William & Mary	0	0
O6	●	Fairmont St.	27	0
O13	●	Morehead St. *AshK*	26	0
O20		at Wittenberg	6	0
O26	●	Morris-Harvey	45	0
N3		at Centre	6	20
N9		at New River St.	13	0
N17		Bethany	26	6
N24		at Louisville	13	0
N29		W.V. Wesleyan	13	7

JOHN MAULBETSCH
1929-30 (.500) 8-8-2

1929 5-3-1
S28	●	Glenville	40	6
O5	●	Morris-Harvey	59	6
O12		at Penn State	7	26
O19		at Bethany	8	0
O26	●	Louisville	25	6
N2	=	Emory-Henry *BLU*	0	0
N9	●	Fairmont St.	39	0
N16		Grove City	6	7
N28		W.V. Wesleyan	0	28

1930 3-5-1
S27		at Ohio Wesleyan	6	26
O4	●	Morris-Harvey	7	0
O11		at Penn State	0	65
O18	●	Bethany	37	0
O25		Emory-Henry *BLU*	0	13
N1		Wittenberg	0	7
N7	●	at Fairmont St.	43	0
N15		Louisville	12	13
N27	=	W.V. Wesleyan	6	6

TOM DANDELET
1931-34 (.528) 18-16-2

1931 6-3-0
S25	●	Morris-Harvey	20	6
O3	●	at Bethany	31	6
O10		Washington & Jefferson	0	19
O15	●	Salem *CLX*	6	0
O24	●	Marietta	40	0
O31	●	Emory-Henry *BLU*	44	13
N7	●	Fairmont St.	60	0
N14		at Wittenberg	13	27
N26		W. V. Wesleyan	0	13

1932 6-2-1
S23	●	Louisville	60	0
S30	●	Morris-Harvey	13	0
O8	=	Western Maryland	13	13
O14	●	at Georgetown	7	0
O21		at Dayton	7	13
O28		Geneva	0	12
N5	●	Emory-Henry *BLU*	14	6
N11	●	Salem	19	14
N24	●	W.V. Wesleyan	22	0

1933 3-5-1
S30	●	Transylvania	38	0
O7	●	Wittenberg	19	0
O14		at Miami, Ohio	14	42
O21		at Cincinnati	0	19
O28	●	Georgetown	32	6
N4	●	Emory-Henry *BLU*	0	12
N11	=	Ohio U.	0	0
N18		at Ohio Wesleyan	0	12
N30		W.V. Wesleyan	6	12

1934 3-6-0
S29	●	Transylvania	12	0
O6	●	Bethany	39	0
O13		Ohio Wesleyan	7	43
O19	●	Morris-Harvey	29	0
O27		at Ohio U.	0	8
N3		at Cincinnati	0	7
N10		Emory-Henry *BLU*	6	7
N17		Miami, Ohio	0	7
N29		W.V. Wesleyan	0	39

CAM HENDERSON
1935-49 (.592) 68-46-5

1935 4-6-0
S28	●	Concord	31	0
O4	●	Morris-Harvey	18	0
O11		at Dayton	6	20
O19		at Ohio U.	13	20
O26		at Miami, Ohio	13	20
N2	●	Emory-Henry *BLU*	14	0
N9		Cincinnati	13	39
N16		at Ohio Wesleyan	0	6
N22	●	Rio Grande	25	0
N28		W.V. Wesleyan	6	12

1936 6-3-1
S18	●	at Morris-Harvey	58	0
S26	●	Dayton	14	0
O2	●	Valparaiso	81	0
O10	=	at Ohio U.	13	13
O17		at Cincinnati	7	13
O24	●	Ohio Wesleyan	41	14
O31	●	Emory-Henry	52	12
N6	●	Cumberland	41	6
N14	●	Miami, Ohio	7	14
N26	●	W.V. Wesleyan	0	6

1937 9-0-1
S25	●	Salem	47	0
O1	●	Western Maryland	21	0
O9	●	at Miami, Ohio	7	0
O16	●	at Ohio Wesleyan	21	6
O22	●	Georgetown	90	0
O30	=	Ohio U.	13	13
N6	●	Centre	36	0
N13	●	Cincinnati	28	0
N20	●	at Dayton	7	0
N25	●	W.V. Wesleyan	27	0

1938 5-4-0
S24	●	Carson-Newman	44	0
O1	●	Ohio Wesleyan	62	0
O8	●	Miami, Ohio	41	0
O15	●	Oklahoma City	66	0
O22		at Toledo	7	13
O30		at Dayton	7	13
N5	●	Furman	13	18
N12	●	at Cincinnati	27	9
N19		at Ohio U.	7	14

1939 9-2-0
S23	●	Geneva	41	13
S30	●	Virginia Tech	20	0
O7	●	Salem	64	0
O14	●	at Miami, Ohio	21	0
O21		at Dayton	19	13
O28		at Scranton	0	20
N4	●	Wake Forest	13	14
N11	●	Toledo	14	12
N18	●	at Xavier	20	0
N23	●	W.V. Wesleyan	47	13
N25	●	at Morris-Harvey	27	0

1940 8-2-0
S21	●	Morehead St.	13	6
S28	●	Virginia Tech	13	7
O5	●	Dayton	25	12
O12		at Toledo	6	7
O19		at Wake Forest	19	31
O26	●	Scranton	50	6
N1	●	Morris-Harvey	33	6
N8	●	Detroit Tech	67	0
N16	●	Xavier	41	0
N21	●	W.V. Wesleyan	67	0

1941 7-1-0
S20	●	Omaha	62	6
S27	●	Illinois Wesleyan	51	7
O4		at Dayton	0	7
O11	●	Toledo	13	7
O18	●	Western Kentucky	34	7
O25	●	at Scranton	13	0
N1	●	Wake Forest	16	6
N8	●	Morehead St.	28	7

1942 1-7-1
S27	=	Morehead St.	13	19
O3		at Kentucky Wesleyan	13	19
O9		at Louisiana Tech	0	26
O17		Fort Knox	6	20
O24		at Toledo	0	7
O31		at Dayton	13	20
N7		at Xavier	7	13
N13		Morris-Harvey	0	6
N26	●	Bradley	13	7

1943-45
NO TEAM

1946 2-7-1
S28	●	W. V. Wesleyan	29	12
O5		at Cincinnati	14	39
O12	=	Toledo	14	14
O19		Evansville	0	7
O26		at Scranton	6	14
N2	●	at Morris-Harvey	34	0
N9		at Murray	0	19
N16		Morehead St.	20	29
N23		at Dayton	7	29
N28		Xavier	21	27

1947 9-3-0
S20	●	Steubenville	60	6
S27	●	Morehead St.	38	12
O4	●	at Eastern Kentucky	7	6
O11		Canisius	20	25
O18	●	at Evansville	24	0
O25		Indiana St.	33	0
N1	●	St. Vincent	39	6
N8	●	Murray	41	20
N15		at Xavier	7	18
N22	●	Bradley	33	19
N27	●	Morris-Harvey	40	6

TANGERINE BOWL
J1		Catawba	0	7

1948 2-7-1
S18		at Miami, Ohio	6	38
S25	●	Morehead St.	19	7
O2		Eastern Kentucky	7	20
O9		at Dayton	0	33
O15		at Murray	0	27
O30		at Bradley	6	15
N6		John Carroll	0	20
N13		at Vanderbilt	0	56
N20	●	at Xavier	26	20
N25	=	Canisius	7	7

1949 6-4-0
S24	●	Morehead St.	20	15
O1	●	at Eastern Kentucky	24	7
O8	●	Dayton	23	40
O15	●	Murray	13	6
O21	●	at John Carroll	7	26
O29	●	Ohio U.	14	6
N5	●	at Tenn. Tech	20	7
N11	●	Milligan	34	0
N19		at Vanderbilt	6	27
N24		Xavier	7	13

PETE PEDERSON
1950-52 (.339) 9-19-3

1950 2-8-0
S23	●	Morehead St.	6	51
S30		Eastern Kentucky	0	34
O7	●	at Western Kentucky	47	13
O14		at Murray	0	14
O21		Youngstown St.	13	28
O28		John Carroll	2	39
N4	●	Tenn. Tech	13	0
N11		at Evansville	14	21
N18		at Dayton	6	35
N23		at Ohio U.	6	14

1951 5-4-1
S22	●	Morehead St.	21	6
S29		at Eastern Kentucky	6	13
O6	●	Western Kentucky	35	21
O13		Murray	13	28
O20		at Toledo	14	32
O27	●	at Morris-Harvey	19	0
N3	●	at Tenn. Tech	20	13
N10	●	Evansville	52	13
N17		Dayton	13	37
N22	=	Ohio U.	13	13

1952 2-7-2
S13		at Virginia Tech	14	19
S20	●	Morehead St.	48	14
S27	●	Eastern Kentucky	19	26
O4	●	John Carroll	16	7
O11		Morris-Harvey	13	14
O18	=	at Youngstown St.	6	6
O25		Kent State	14	26
N1		Tenn. Tech	7	28
N8		at Dayton	14	31
N15		at Wofford	21	41
N22	●	at Ohio U.	21	21

HERB ROYER
1953-58 (.407) 21-31-2

1953 2-5-2
S19		at Virginia Tech	0	7
S26	●	Morehead St.	40	0
O3		at John Carroll	0	31
O10	=	at Morris-Harvey	14	14
O17		Miami, Ohio	6	48
O24		at Kent State	7	27
N7		Dayton	7	21
N14	=	Wofford	26	26
N21	●	Ohio U.	9	6

1954-1968
MAC

1954 4-5-0 (2-5-0)
S25	●	Morehead St.	19	7
O2		Western Michigan	47	13
O9		Morris-Harvey	25	14
O16		at Miami, Ohio	0	46
O23		Kent State	20	41
O30		at Western Reserve	20	21
N6	●	at Bowling Green	26	19
N12		Toledo	21	27
N20		at Ohio U.	25	26

1955 3-6-0 (1-5-0)
S24		at Ohio U.	6	13
O1	●	at Morris-Harvey	46	7
O8		at Western Michigan	28	0
O15		Miami, Ohio	7	46
O22		at Kent State	6	39
O29		Bowling Green	26	27
N5	●	Youngstown St.	20	12
N12		at Toledo	20	27
N19		Xavier	0	21

1956 3-6-0 (2-4-0)
S22		at Xavier	6	30
S29	●	Morris-Harvey	25	13
O6	●	Western Michigan	13	0
O13		at Miami, Ohio	14	21
O20		Kent State	7	25
O27		at Bowling Green	12	34
N3		at Youngstown St.	13	33
N9	●	Toledo	32	13
N17		at Ohio U.	0	16

1957 6-3-0 (4-2-0)
S21	●	West Virginia St.	12	7
S28	●	Morehead St.	21	0
O5	●	at Western Michigan	12	7
O12	●	at Toledo	14	7
O19		Kent State	7	6
O26		Ohio U.	34	28
N2		at Xavier	0	18
N9		at Miami, Ohio	13	25
N16		Bowling Green	7	14

1958 3-6-0 (1-5-0)
S20	●	at West Virginia St.	9	0
S27	●	at Morehead St.	30	16
O4		Western Michigan	24	30
O11	●	Toledo	35	12
O18		at Kent State	0	24
O25		at Ohio U.	0	22
N1		Xavier	6	14
N8		Miami, Ohio	0	26
N15		at Bowling Green	7	21

CHARLIE SNYDER
1959-67 (.331) 28-58-3

1959 1-8-0 (1-4-0)
S19		VMI	0	46
S26		Bowling Green	7	51
O3		Western Michigan	0	51
O10	●	at Toledo	20	13
O17		at Kent State	7	46
O24		at Delaware	6	30
O31		at Louisville	6	48
N7		Ohio U.	14	21
N21		at Buffalo	12	37

1960 2-7-1 (1-4-0)
S17		Wittenberg	0	3
S24		at Bowling Green	7	14
O1	●	Toledo	14	0
O8		at Kentucky	0	55
O15		at Kent State	6	22
O22	=	Delaware	6	6
O29		Louisville	0	7
N5		at Ohio U.	0	19
N12		at Western Michigan	12	34
N19	●	Eastern Kentucky *AshK*	13	0

1961 2-7-1 (1-4-0)
S16		VMI	6	33
S23		Bowling Green	0	40
S30		at Louisville	7	32
O7		at Toledo	6	33
O14	●	Kent State	14	8
O21	=	Morehead St.	0	0
O28		at Western Michigan	0	20
N4		Ohio U.	7	14
N11		at Xavier	2	3
N18	●	Eastern Kentucky *AshK*	20	0

THE SCHOOLS

1962 4-6-0 (0-5-0)

S15	•	Findlay	40	22
S22	|	at Bowling Green	6	48
S29		Louisville	0	18
O6	|	Toledo	12	42
O13	|	at Kent State	14	23
O20	•	Morehead St.	26	18
O27	|	Western Michigan	0	12
N3	|	at Ohio U.	0	35
N10	•	Xavier	13	6
N17	•	Butler	26	13

1963 5-4-1 (3-2-1)

S21		Morehead St.	6	19
S28	= |	at Miami, Ohio	14	14
O5	• |	Toledo	19	18
O12	•	Buffalo	10	8
O19	•	Kentucky St.	28	0
O26		at Louisville	14	27
N2	• |	at Western Michigan	20	7
N9	|	Bowling Green	14	21
N16	• |	at Kent State	14	8
N23	|	Ohio U.	0	17

1964 7-3-0 (4-2-0)

S19		at Morehead St.	0	6
S26	|	Miami, Ohio	0	21
O3	• |	at Toledo	13	0
O10	•	Buffalo	14	12
O17	•	Kentucky St.	27	6
O24	•	Louisville	28	6
O31	• |	Western Michigan	16	7
N6	|	at Bowling Green	0	28
N14	• |	Kent State	12	7
N21	• |	at Ohio U.	10	0

1965 5-5-0 (2-4-0)

S18	•	Morehead St.	22	12
S25	•	at Eastern Kentucky	28	12
O2	• |	Toledo	14	0
O9	•	Quantico	10	9
O16	|	at Miami, Ohio	7	28 *f*
O23		at Louisville	7	23
O30	|	at Western Michigan	14	17
N6	|	Bowling Green	7	20
N13	|	at Kent State	13	33
N20	• |	Ohio U.	29	14

1966 2-8-0 (1-5-0)

S17	•	Morehead St.	27	20
S24		Eastern Kentucky	6	26
O1	|	at Toledo	7	23
O8		at Quantico	7	10
O15	|	Miami, Ohio	0	12
O22		Louisville	15	35 *f*
O29	|	Western Michigan	29	35
N5	|	at Bowling Green	6	14
N12	• |	Kent State	16	7
N19	|	at Ohio U.	6	28

1967 0-10-0 (0-6-0)

S16		at Morehead St.	6	30
S23	|	Ohio U.	14	48
S30	|	Toledo	7	14
O7		Xavier	0	7
O14	|	at Miami, Ohio	6	48
O21		at Louisville	7	43
O28	|	at Western Michigan	10	42
N4	|	Bowling Green	7	9
N11	|	at Kent State	2	41
N18		East Carolina	13	29

PERRY MOSS
1968 (.050) 0-9-1

1968 0-9-1 (0-6-0)

S14	=	Morehead St.	7	7
S21	|	at Ohio U.	8	48
S28	|	at Toledo	12	35
O5		at Xavier	20	30
O12	|	Miami, Ohio	0	46
O19		Louisville	10	13
O26	|	Western Michigan	12	40
N2	|	at Bowling Green	28	54
N9	|	Kent State	12	36
N16		at East Carolina	20	49

1969-1976 INDEPENDENT

RICK TOLLEY
1969-70 (.316) 6-13

1969 3-7-0

S20		at Morehead St.	14	27
S27		Toledo	13	38
O4		Northern Illinois	17	18
O11		at Miami, Ohio	7	35
O18		at Louisville	17	34
O25		at Western Michigan	14	48
N1	•	Bowling Green	21	16
N8	•	at Kent State	31	20
N15	•	East Carolina	38	7
N22		Ohio U.	35	38

1970 3-6-0

S19	•	Morehead St.	17	7
S26		at Toledo	3	52
O3	•	at Xavier	31	14
O10		Miami, Ohio	12	19
O17		Louisville	14	16
O24		Western Michigan	3	34
O31		at Bowling Green	24	26
N7	•	Kent State	20	17
N14		at East Carolina	14	17

JACK LENGYEL
1971-74 (.214) 9-33

1971 2-8-0

S18		at Morehead St.	6	29
S25	•	Xavier	15	13
O2		at Miami, Ohio	6	66
O9		at Northern Illinois	18	33 *
O16		Dayton	0	13
O23		at Western Michigan	0	37
O30	•	Bowling Green	12	10
N6		at Kent State	0	21
N13		Toledo	0	43
N20		Ohio U.	0	30

1972 2-8-0

S16	•	Morehead St.	27	24
S23		at Dayton	0	39
S30		Northern Illinois	7	24
O7		Miami, Ohio	7	22
O14		at Xavier	0	14
O21		Western Michigan	0	34
O28		at Bowling Green	7	46
N4		Kent State	14	16
N11		at Toledo	0	21
N18	•	at Ohio U.	31	14

1973 4-7-0

S15	•	Morehead St.	24	17
S21		at Nevada-Las Vegas	9	31
S29		Xavier	28	30
O6		at Miami, Ohio	6	31
O13	•	at Northern Illinois	39	36
O20		at Western Michigan	7	21
O27		Bowling Green	21	24
N3		at Kent State	3	35
N10	•	Toledo	17	14
N17	•	Dayton	37	14
N22		Ohio U.	21	35

1974 1-10-0

S14		at Morehead St.	12	14
S21	•	Akron	17	7
S28		Miami, Ohio	0	42
O5		at Temple	10	31
O12		Northern Illinois	17	20
O19		Western Michigan	17	20
O26		at Bowling Green	3	28
N2		Kent State	7	35
N9		at Toledo	14	45
N16		at Dayton	13	14
N23		at Ohio U.	0	35

FRANK ELLWOOD
1975-78 (.205) 9-35

1975 2-9-0

S6		at Akron	8	20
S13		at Miami, Ohio	0	50
S20		Morehead St.	16	19
S27	•	Illinois St.	36	3
O4		McNeese St.	3	33
O18		at Villanova	14	21
O25	•	Western Michigan	21	19
N1		at Central Michigan	0	34
N8		at Kent State	21	30
N15		at Dayton	8	29
N22		Ohio U.	21	38

1976 4-7-0

S4		at Morehead St.	14	31 †
S11	•	Miami, Ohio	21	16
S18	•	at Illinois St.	23	13
S25		Central Michigan	7	22
O2		at McNeese St.	9	34
O16	•	Dayton	9	0
O23		at Western Michigan	21	31
O30	•	Akron	13	0
N6		Villanova	10	23
N13		at Toledo	8	39
N20		So. Illinois	16	44

1977-1996 SOUTHERN

1977 2-9-0 (0-4-0)

S10		Ohio U.	27	49
S17	•	Morehead St.	38	26
S24	•	Toledo	24	0
O1	|	at Appalachian St.	20	28
O8		at Miami, Ohio	19	29
O15	|	at Furman	24	42
O22		at Western Michigan	29	53
O29		Louisville	0	56
N5		at Akron	7	28
N12	|	Western Carolina	26	41
N19	|	at U.T. Chattanooga	20	37

1978 1-10-0 (0-5-0)

S9	•	at Toledo	17	0
S16	|	Appalachian St.	7	28
S23	|	U.T. Chattanooga	23	27
S30	|	at Western Carolina	14	21
O7	|	at Citadel	0	41
O14		Miami, Ohio	3	29
O21		at Kent State	17	20
O28	|	Furman	12	42
N4		Western Michigan	6	24
N11		at So. Illinois	14	15
N18		at East Carolina	0	45

SONNY RANDLE
1979-83 (.227) 12-42-1

1979 1-10-0 (0-6-0)

S8	•	Toledo	31	14
S15	|	Western Carolina	0	24
S22		at Ohio U.	0	35
S29	|	at U.T. Chattanooga	0	27
O6		Miami, Ohio	0	28
O13	|	at Furman	24	34
O20		at Mississippi State	0	48
O27		Villanova	14	24
N3	|	Citadel	16	17
N10	|	VMI	3	13
N17	|	at Appalachian St.	7	45

1980 2-8-1 (0-5-1)

S6	•	at Morehead St.	35	8
S13	•	Kent State	17	7
S20	|	at VMI	3	17
O4	|	Appalachian St.	6	23
O11		at Miami, Ohio	6	34
O18	|	U.T. Chattanooga	11	21
O25	= |	at Western Carolina	13	13
N1	|	Furman CHWV	0	35
N8		at Ohio U.	20	28
N15		Toledo	10	38
N22	|	at East Tenn. St.	16	21

1981 2-9-0 (1-5-0)

S12	•	Morehead St.	20	17
S19		at Western Michigan	3	14
S26	|	East Tenn. St.	0	14
O3		at Louisville	0	36
O10	|	at U.T. Chattanooga	0	20
O17		at William & Mary	7	38
O24	|	VMI	16	20
O31	|	at Furman	3	35
N7	• |	at Appalachian St.	17	10
N14	|	Western Carolina	28	38
N21		Indiana St.	0	42

1982 3-8-0 (1-6-0)

S4	•	Kent State	30	21
S11		Western Michigan	0	34
S18		at Toledo	9	17
O2	|	U.T. Chattanooga	7	17
O8	|	Appalachian St.	13	21
O16	|	at Western Carolina	13	21
O23	•	Akron	12	10
O30	|	at Citadel	7	24
N6	• |	at VMI	22	20
N13	|	Furman	7	45
N20	|	at East Tenn. St.	0	28

1983 4-7-0 (3-4-0)

S3		at Eastern Michigan	3	7
S10		Illinois St.	3	27
S17	•	at Morehead St.	35	0
S24	|	at Furman	7	33
O1	|	Western Carolina	7	21
O8	• |	East Tenn. St.	13	10
O22	|	at U.T. Chattanooga	16	23
O29	• |	Citadel	26	10
N5		William & Mary	24	48
N12	|	at Appalachian St.	19	28
N19	• |	VMI	56	7

STAN PARRISH
1984-85 (.614) 13-8-1

1984 6-5-0 (2-4-0)

S1	•	West Virginia Tech	33	10
S8	•	Morehead St.	40	6
S15	•	Eastern Michigan	24	17
S22	|	Furman	28	38
S29		at Western Michigan	7	42
O13	• |	Appalachian St.	35	7
O20	|	at Citadel	17	28
O27	|	U.T. Chattanooga	13	17
N3	|	Western Carolina	0	30
N10	•	at Illinois St.	10	3
N17	• |	at East Tenn. St.	31	28

1985 7-3-1 (3-3-1)

A31	•	West Virginia Tech	30	0
S7	•	at Morehead St.	27	10
S14	•	Ohio U.	31	7
S21	•	at Eastern Kentucky	13	7
S28	• |	Citadel	17	14
O5	= |	Western Carolina	10	10
O12	|	at Furman	3	34
O19	• |	VMI	21	16
N2	|	at U.T. Chattanooga	7	38
N9	• |	East Tenn. St.	34	21
N16	|	at Appalachian St.	0	40

GEORGE CHAUMP
1986-89 (.670) 33-16-1

1986 6-4-1 (4-3-0)

A30	•	West Virginia Tech	42	0
S6		Morehead St.	10	19
S13	•	at Ohio U.	21	7
S20	=	Eastern Kentucky	13	13
S27	|	Furman	10	38
O4	• |	at VMI	16	9
O18	• |	at East Tenn. St.	34	19
O25	• |	Davidson	63	14
N1	• |	U.T. Chattanooga	41	20
N8	|	Appalachian St.	17	27
N15	|	at Western Carolina	20	33

1987 10-5-0 (4-2-0)

S5	•	Morehead St.	29	0
S12		at Ohio U.	15	23
S19		at Eastern Kentucky	34	37
S26	•	Youngstown St.	38	13
O3	|	at Furman	36	42
O10	•	at Louisville	34	31
O17	• |	East Tenn. St.	27	7
O24	• |	VMI	42	7
O31	• |	at U.T. Chattanooga	28	26
N7	|	at Appalachian St.	10	17
N14	• |	Western Carolina	47	16
		DIVISION I-AA PLAYOFFS		
N28	•	James Madison	41	12
D5	•	Weber St.	51	23
D12	•	at Appalachian St.	24	10
D19		La. Monroe Poc	42	43

1988 11-2-0 (6-1-0)

S3	•	at Morehead St.	30	17
S10	•	Ohio U.	31	14
S17	•	Eastern Kentucky	34	32
S24	• |	at VMI	24	20
O8	• |	Furman	24	10
O15	• |	at East Tenn. St.	50	14
O22	• |	U.T. Chattanooga	38	7
O29	• |	Appalachian St.	30	27
N5	|	at Citadel	3	20
N12	• |	at Western Carolina	52	45
N19	•	at Youngstown St.	38	15
		DIVISION I-AA PLAYOFFS		
N26	•	North Texas	7	0
D3		Furman	9	13

1989   6-5-0 (4-3-0)

S2	●	Catawba	48	0
S9	●	Morehead St.	30	7
S16	●	East Tenn. St.	31	21
S23		at U.T. Chattanooga	0	14
O7	●	at Furman	13	34
O14	●	Citadel	40	17
O21		at Eastern Kentucky	23	38
O28	●	VMI	40	10
N4	●	at Appalachian St.	7	28
N11	●	Western Carolina	35	22
N18		at Georgia Southern	31	63

JIM DONNAN
1990-95 (.753)   64-21

1990   6-5-0 (4-3-0)

S1	●	Morehead St.	28	14
S8	●	West Virginia Tech	52	0
S22		at Citadel	10	21
S29	●	Furman	10	7
O6		Georgia Southern	14	17
O13		at East Tenn. St.	17	38
O20		U.T. Chattanooga	23	29
O27	●	at VMI	52	7
N3	●	Appalachian St.	50	0
N10		Eastern Kentucky	12	15
N17	●	at Western Carolina	42	14

1991   11-4-0 (5-2-0)

A31		at Appalachian St.	3	9
S7	●	New Hampshire	24	23
S14	●	Morehead St.	70	11
S28	●	Brown	46	0
O12		at Furman	38	35
O19		at North Carolina St.	14	15
O26		at U.T. Chattanooga	31	38
N2	●	Western Carolina	27	24
N9	●	Citadel	37	31
N16	●	VMI	61	0
N23		East Tenn. St.	63	9
	DIVISION I-AA PLAYOFFS		
N30	●	Western Illinois	20	17
D7	●	No. Iowa	41	13
D14	●	Eastern Kentucky	14	7
D21	●	Youngstown St. ⁵ᵗˢᴳ	17	25

1992   12-3-0 (5-2-0)

S5	●	Morehead St.	49	7
S12	●	Eastern Illinois	63	28
S19	●	at VMI	34	16
O3		at Missouri	21	44
O10		Furman	48	6
O17	●	at Citadel	34	13
O24		U.T. Chattanooga	52	23
O31		at Western Carolina	30	38
N7		Appalachian St.	34	37
N14		Tenn. Tech	52	14
N21	●	at East Tenn. St.	49	10
	DIVISION I-AA PLAYOFFS		
N28	●	Eastern Kentucky	44	0
D5	●	Middle Tennessee	35	21
D12	●	Delaware	28	7
D19	●	Youngstown St.	31	28

1993   11-4-0 (6-2-0)

S4	●	Morehead St.	56	0
S11	●	Murray St.	29	3
S18	●	Georgia Southern	13	3
O2		at U.T. Chattanooga	31	33
O9	●	VMI	51	0
O16		at North Carolina St.	17	24
O23	●	Appalachian St.	35	3
O30		at Citadel	35	15
N6		East Tenn. St.	33	9
N13		at Furman	3	17
N20	●	Western Carolina	20	16
	DIVISION I-AA PLAYOFFS		
N27	●	Howard	28	14
D4	●	Delaware	34	31
D11	●	Troy State	24	21
D18	●	Youngstown St.	5	17

1994   12-2-0 (7-1-0)

S3	●	Morehead St.	71	7
S10	●	Tenn. Tech	24	10
S17	●	at Georgia Southern	34	10
S24	●	West Virginia St.	48	0
O1	●	U.T. Chattanooga	62	21
O8	●	at VMI	49	7
O15	●	Western Carolina	38	14
O22		at Appalachian St.	14	24
O29	●	Citadel	42	30
N5	●	at East Tenn. St.	42	12
N12		Furman	35	14
	DIVISION I-AA PLAYOFFS		
N26	●	Middle Tennessee	49	14
D3	●	James Madison	28	21
D10		at Boise State	24	28

1995   12-3-0 (7-1-0)

A31		at North Carolina St.	16	33
S9	●	Tenn. Tech	45	14
S16	●	Georgia Southern	37	7
S30	●	at U.T. Chattanooga	35	32
O7	●	VMI	56	21
O14	●	at Western Carolina	42	3
O21		Appalachian St.	3	10
O28	●	at Citadel	21	19
N4	●	East Tenn. St.	52	0
N11		at Furman	31	6
N18		Hofstra	30	28
	DIVISION I-AA PLAYOFFS		
N25	●	Jackson St.	38	8
D2	●	No. Iowa	41	14
D9	●	McNeese St.	25	13
D16		Montana	20	22

BOB PRUETT
1996-2004 (.803)   94-23

1996   15-0 (8-0)

S7	●	Howard	55	27
S14	●	West Virginia St.	42	7
S21	●	at Georgia Southern	29	13
S28	●	Western Kentucky	37	3
O5	●	U.T. Chattanooga	45	0
O12	●	at VMI	45	20
O19	●	Western Carolina	56	21
O26	●	at Appalachian St.	24	10
N2	●	Citadel	56	25
N9	●	at East Tenn. St.	34	10
N16	●	Furman	42	17
	DIVISION I-AA PLAYOFFS		
N30	●	Delaware	59	14
D7	●	Furman	54	0
D14	●	No. Iowa	31	14
D21	●	Montana	49	29

1997-2004
MAC

1997   10-3 (7-1)

A30		at West Virginia	31	42
S6	●	at Army	35	25
S13	●	at Kent State	42	17
S20	●	Western Illinois	48	7
S27	●	at Ball State	42	16
O11	●	Akron	52	17
O18	●	at Miami, Ohio	21	45
O25	●	Eastern Michigan	48	25
N1	●	at Central Michigan	45	17
N8	●	Bowling Green	28	0
N15	●	Ohio U.	27	0
	MAC CHAMPIONSHIP GAME		
D5	●	Toledo	34	14
	MOTOR CITY BOWL		
D26	●	Mississippi	31	34

1998   12-1 (7-1)

S5	●	at Akron	27	16
S12	●	Troy State	42	12
S19	●	at South Carolina	24	21
S26	●	at Eastern Michigan	26	23
O3	●	Miami, Ohio	31	17
O10	●	at Ohio U.	30	23
O17	●	Kent State	42	7
O24	●	Ball State	42	10
O31	●	at Bowling Green	13	34
N7	●	Central Michigan	28	0
N21	●	Wofford	29	27
	MAC CHAMPIONSHIP GAME		
D4	●	Toledo	23	17
	MOTOR CITY BOWL		
D23	●	Louisville	48	29

1999   13-0 (8-0)

S4	●	at Clemson	13	10
S11	●	Liberty	63	3
S18	●	Bowling Green	35	16
S25	●	Temple	34	0
O2	●	at Miami, Ohio	32	14
O14	●	Toledo	38	13
O23	●	at Buffalo	59	3
O30	●	Northern Illinois	41	9
N6	●	at Kent State	28	16
N13	●	at Western Michigan	31	17
N26	●	Ohio U.	34	3
	MAC CHAMPIONSHIP GAME		
D3	●	Western Michigan	34	30
	MOTOR CITY BOWL		
D27	●	Brigham Young	21	3

2000   8-5 (5-3)

A31	●	S. E. Missouri St.	63	7
S9	●	at Michigan State	24	34
S23		at North Carolina	15	20
S30	●	Buffalo	47	14
O5		Western Michigan	10	30
O14		at Toledo	0	42
O21	●	Kent State	34	12
O28	●	at Akron	31	28
N4	●	at Bowling Green	20	13
N11	●	Miami, Ohio	51	31
N18		at Ohio U.	28	38
	MAC CHAMPIONSHIP GAME		
D2	●	Western Michigan	19	14
	MOTOR CITY BOWL		
D27	●	Cincinnati	25	14

2001   11-2 (8-0)

S1		at Florida	14	49
S8	●	Massachusetts	49	20
S29	●	Bowling Green	37	31
O6	●	at Northern Illinois	37	15
O13	●	at Buffalo	34	14
O20	●	Central Michigan	42	21
O27	●	Akron	50	33
N3	●	at Kent State	42	21
N10	●	at Miami, Ohio	27	21
N17	●	Ohio U.	42	18
N24	●	Youngstown St.	38	24
	MAC CHAMPIONSHIP GAME		
N30	●	at Toledo	36	41
	GMAC BOWL		
D19	●	East Carolina	64	61

2002   11-2 (7-1)

A31	●	Appalachian St.	50	17
S12		at Virginia Tech	21	47
S20		Central Florida	26	21
O5	●	at Kent State	42	21
O12	●	Buffalo	66	21
O19	●	Troy State	24	7
O26	●	at Central Michigan	23	18
N2		at Akron	20	34
N12	●	Miami, Ohio	36	34
N23	●	at Ohio U.	24	21
N30	●	Ball State	38	14
	MAC CHAMPIONSHIP GAME		
D7	●	Toledo	49	45
	GMAC BOWL		
D18	●	Louisville	38	15

2003   8-4 (6-2)

A30	●	Hofstra	45	21
S6		at Tennessee	24	34
S12		Toledo	17	24
S20	●	at Kansas State	27	20
S27	●	at Troy State	24	33
O11	●	Kent State	49	33
O18	●	at Buffalo	26	16
O25	●	at Western Michigan	41	21
N1	●	Akron	42	24
N12		at Miami, Ohio	6	45
N19	●	at Central Florida	21	7
N28	●	Ohio U.	28	0

2004   6-6 (6-2)

S4	●	Troy State	15	17
S11	●	at Ohio State	21	24
S18		at Georgia	3	13
S29	●	Miami, Ohio	33	25
O9	●	at Ohio U.	16	13
O16	●	at Kent State	27	17
O23	●	Buffalo	48	14
O30	●	Central Florida	20	3
N5		at Akron	28	31
N13		at Bowling Green	35	56
N20	●	Western Michigan	31	21
	FORT WORTH BOWL		
D23		Cincinnati	14	32

ƒ Forfeit   † Game Later Forfieted   # Disputed Victor   * Disputed Score || Designated Conference Game |2 Counted Twice in Conference Standings

MARYLAND

BY BOB HARIG

SINCE ITS INCEPTION IN 1892, Maryland's football program has had a star-crossed history. Its best team, the 1953 squad, won the national championship only to lose a heart-breaking bowl game to Oklahoma (in a time when final voting ended before the postseason). Its best coach, Jim Tatum, left the school for his alma mater, Maryland rival North Carolina, when the Terrapins were seemingly at the height of their powers. The team went on to post just three winning seasons in the next 17 years. Paul "Bear" Bryant made a one-year stop in College Park (1945), as did vagabond coach Lou Saban (1966). Jerry Claiborne and Bobby Ross returned glory to the school for a time in the 1970s and 1980s, leading the Terps to six ACC titles. In 2001, new coach and alum Ralph Friedgen took the helm and garnered the first back-to-back 10-victory seasons in school history. In his first year, the Terps became the first team other than Florida State to win an outright ACC title since the Seminoles joined the ACC.

TRADITION Before each home game, Maryland players and coaches walk 200 yards to the locker room through an area known as Terp Alley, in which players touch a bronze turtle known as Testudo.

BEST PLAYER Randy White was regarded as one of the game's quickest defensive linemen, both with the Terrapins and again in a Hall of Fame NFL career with the Dallas Cowboys. In 1974, White won the Lombardi and Outland trophies, was named the ACC Player of the Year and was a unanimous first-team All-America. The Cowboys made White a first-round draft choice, and he shared Super Bowl MVP honors with teammate Harvey Martin when Dallas defeated Denver in Super Bowl XII. White's No. 94 was retired at Maryland, and he was inducted into both the College and the Pro Football halls of fame in 1994.

BEST COACH Jim Tatum's Maryland teams were 51–8–2 from 1950 to 1955, with a 10–0 record and a Sugar Bowl victory in 1951. The Terrapins also posted 10–0 regular seasons in 1953 and 1955. The 1953 team was national champion, and Tatum was named national coach of the year. During his Maryland tenure, Tatum guided the Terps to 19 consecutive victories and an unbeaten streak of 22 games (21–0–1) from 1950 to 1952. Tatum's overall record at Maryland was 73–15–4. "I think he was revered by Maryland fans as much as Bear Bryant was by the Alabama fans," said former Maryland sports information

PROFILE

University of Maryland
College Park, Md.
Founded: 1807
Enrollment: 25,446
Colors: Red, White, Black and Gold
Nickname: Terrapins
Stadium: Byrd Stadium
  Opened in 1950
  FieldTurf; 48,055 capacity
First football game: 1892
All-time record: 573–498–43 (.534)
Bowl record: 8–10–2
Consensus national championships, 1936-present: 1 (1953)
Atlantic Coast Conference championships: 9 (7 outright)
Outland Trophy: Dick Modzelewski, 1952; Randy White, 1974
First-round NFL draftees: 13
Website: www.umterps.com

THE BEST OF TIMES

From 1947 to 1955, the Terrapins were 73–15–4 under coach Jim Tatum, including a 10–0 regular season and national title in 1953.

THE WORST OF TIMES

From 1963 to 1971, the Terrapins had no winning seasons and posted a .500 record just once.

CONFERENCE

Maryland was a charter member of the Atlantic Coast Conference in 1953, and has remained in the ACC since. The Terrapins were previously members of the Southern Conference and the Southern Atlantic Intercollegiate Athletic Association.

DISTINGUISHED ALUMNI

Carl Bernstein, reporter, author; Connie Chung, TV journalist; Larry David, comedian, *Seinfeld* co-creator; Jim Henson, creator of the Muppets

FIGHT SONGS

MARYLAND VICTORY SONG
Maryland, we're all behind you.
Wave high the BLACK and GOLD,
For there is nothing half so glorious
As to see our team victorious.
We've got the team, Terps,
We've got the steam, Terps,
So keep on fighting, don't give in!
M-A-R-Y-L-A-N-D
Maryland will win!

MARYLAND FIGHT SONG
Fight, fight, fight for Maryland!
Honor now her name again,
Push up the score, keep on fighting for more,
For Maryland. GO TERPS!
Go on and fight, fight, fight for Terrapin,
Keep on fighting 'til we win,
So sing out our song as we go marching along
To Victory!

director Jack Zane. "People around here looked upon him as the Redskins fans do Joe Gibbs." Tatum was considered a solid coach on both offense and defense. He could be tough on his players, but employed enough diplomatic assistants that both sides avoided lingering hard feelings. Tatum was inducted into the College Football Hall of Fame in 1984. Both Jerry Claiborne (1972-81, 77–37–3) and Bobby Ross (1982-86, 39–19–1) matched Tatum with three conference titles.

While playing for Maryland as a senior in 1984, Frank Reich came off the bench to lead what then ranked as the biggest comeback in NCAA history.

The Terps began the season ranked ninth in the Associated Press poll and moved to No. 1 after winning their final regular-season game against No. 11 Alabama, 21-0. The Terps were awarded the national title before a 7-0 loss to Oklahoma in the Orange Bowl.

BIGGEST GAME Third-ranked Maryland never trailed in its 28-13 victory over national champion Tennessee in the Sugar Bowl on Jan. 1, 1952. Ed Modzelewski had 28 carries for 153 yards, and Ed Fullerton scored on a two-yard run and 46-yard interception return. Jack Scarbath scored on a one-yard run, and Bob Shemonski caught a six-yard pass from halfback Fullerton for Maryland's other touchdown. Maryland led 21-0 and 28-6 in the fourth quarter.

BEST TEAM Not only did the 1953 group go 10–0 in the regular season, but Maryland scored 298 points while allowing only 31. Using the split T, Maryland ranked sixth in total offense with 359.5 yards per game. The defense allowed just 193.2 yards and led the country in rushing (83.9) and scoring defense (3.1). The 1953 Terps also avenged two losses from the prior year, defeating Mississippi and Alabama. A 30-0 victory over Miami prompted Hurricanes coach Andy Gustafson to say, "Maryland has one of the greatest teams I've ever seen."

BIGGEST UPSET The unranked Terrapins trailed sixth-ranked Miami 31-0 at halftime of a 1984 game at the Orange Bowl but rallied for a 42-40 victory. Quarterback Frank Reich entered the game in the second half and completed 12 of 16 passes for 260 yards and three

RECORDS

RUSHING YARDS

	GAME
306	LaMont Jordan vs. Virginia, Nov. 20, 1999 (37 att.)
	SEASON
1,632	LaMont Jordan, 1999 (266 att.)
	CAREER
4,147	LaMont Jordan, 1997-2000 (807 att.)

PASSING YARDS

	GAME
498	Scott Milanovich vs. Virginia Tech, Sept. 25, 1993 (29 of 57)
	SEASON
3,499	Scott Milanovich, 1993 (279 of 431)
	CAREER
7,301	Scott Milanovich, 1992-95 (650 of 982)

RECEIVING YARDS

	GAME
251	Marcus Badgett vs. Pittsburgh, Oct. 3, 1992 (11 rec.)
	SEASON
1,240	Marcus Badgett, 1992 (75 rec.)
	CAREER
2,932	Jermaine Lewis, 1992-95 (193 rec.)

POINTS

	GAME
30	Bob Shemonski vs. Virginia Tech, Dec. 2, 1950 (5 TDs)
	SEASON
125	Nick Novak, 2002 (24 FGs, 53 PATs)
	CAREER
393	Nick Novak, 2001-04 (80 FGs, 153 PATs)

CONSENSUS ALL-AMERICANS

1951	Bob Ward, G
1952	Dick Modzelewski, T
1952	Jack Scarbath, B
1953	Stan Jones, T
1955	Bob Pellegrini, C
1961	Gary Collins, E
1974	Randy White, DL
1976	Joe Campbell, DT
1979	Dale Castro, PK
1985	J.D. Maarleveld, OT
2001-02	E.J. Henderson, LB

touchdowns. The game's key moment occurred during the third quarter, after the Terps had cut the lead to 31-14. The Hurricanes were driving for a touchdown but Maryland kept them out of the end zone, forcing Miami to settle for a 19-yard field goal that made the score 34-14. Miami didn't score again until Maryland had completed its comeback.

HEARTBREAKER In 1953, Maryland was declared national champion after a 10–0 regular season. At the time, poll voting was conducted before bowl games, and the Terps lost 7-0 to Oklahoma in the Orange Bowl. It was the first year of a contract pitting the ACC against the Big Eight. Maryland had two drives end scoreless, despite picking up first downs inside the Sooners' 10.

DISPUTE A 7-3 Liberty Bowl loss to Tennessee in 1974 ended with an apparent touchdown reception by Maryland's Frank Russell on the Terps' second-to-last play of the game, but the play was ruled out of the end zone. One official seemingly started to give the touchdown signal while the other called it out-of-bounds. The Terrapins had fallen behind late in the game after a bad punt snap led to a Tennessee touchdown with just 2:38 left.

STADIUM Situated at the foot of the campus' North Hill, Byrd Stadium is named for Dr. H.C. Byrd, a multisport athlete at Maryland who later became the school's longest-tenured head football coach, from 1911 to 1934. (He would also go on to become the school's president.) The stadium opened on Sept. 30, 1950, when Maryland defeated Navy 35-21 in the dedication game before a record crowd of 43,386 fans. The stadium has undergone a number of major renovations, three of which occurred in the 1990s. Seating capacity increased to more than 48,000 when a massive upper deck was added on the stadium's north side. If needed, bleachers can increase capacity to 62,000.

RIVAL For years, the Terrapins considered Penn State their biggest rival, though the feeling couldn't have been mutual: Maryland's overall record against the Nittany Lions was 1–35–1, with the only victory coming in 1961. Although the series featured several excruciatingly close calls, it ended in 1993 with a 70-7 defeat that symbolized the lopsidedness. Currently, the Terps consider Virginia their biggest rival. The two teams first played in 1919 and have met every year since 1957, with Maryland holding a 39–28–2 edge through 2004.

NICKNAME Maryland started out referring to itself as Old Liners, perhaps a reference to a distinguished Revolutionary War troop of Maryland soldiers. Another theory said the name referred to a squabble with Pennsylvanians over the states' borders. The school newspaper was already called *The Diamondback*, but when the Class of 1933 donated a bronze version of what became the school mascot, a diamondback terrapin, the name Terrapins gained popularity. In 1935, the student yearbook changed its name from *The Reveille* to *The Terrapin*, and newspapers began referring to Maryland athletic teams as Terps instead of Old Liners.

MASCOT Testudo is a diamondback turtle, although the name's origin is cloudy. Some believe it comes from the scientific classification for turtle, testudines. Coach Byrd recommended the diamondback as mascot in 1932 in response to the student newspaper's search for an "official" leader. The mascot was unveiled in 1933, after more than 50 years of intercollegiate competition, and in 1994, the diamondback terrapin was made the state reptile and official mascot of the University of Maryland-College Park.

UNIFORMS Maryland's four colors come from the state flag: red, white, black and gold. After years of black-and-gold uniforms, the team changed to red and white in 1942. The school's athletic council had adopted red and white as the varsity uniform for all sports, with black and gold the freshman team colors. Coach Jim Tatum retained red as the main color, but coach Tom Nugent instituted occasional twists. Over the years, the rule was further bent or ignored by various coaches. For example, coach Ron Vanderlinden went to black game uniforms for one season. Helmets also changed with coaches. Tatum had plain white helmets, then switched to single-striped white helmets in 1949 and the next year changed to three stripes down the middle. Jerry Claiborne had single-striped white helmets but added a block M on each side. After Claiborne's addition, the helmets switched in 1982 to a script "Terps" on the sides. That was followed by a block M in 1992 and an M with a flag in 1997. The script "Terps" reappeared in 2001.

LORE Quarterback Frank Reich led the biggest comebacks in college and NFL history. While playing for Maryland as a senior in 1984, Reich came off the bench to lead the Terrapins to what then ranked as the biggest comeback in NCAA history (see Biggest Upset). Then, in 1993, Reich led the Buffalo Bills to the greatest comeback in pro football.

He again came off the bench, against the Houston Oilers, who were ahead 35-3 early in the third quarter of an AFC playoff game. Reich, filling in for injured quarterback Jim Kelly, threw for a career-high 289 yards and four touchdowns as the Bills went on to win a thriller, 41-38 in overtime.

QUOTE "Dictator, president, athletic director, football coach, comptroller, chief lobbyist and glamour boy supreme ... Curley is the most-hated and most-beloved man in Maryland." — Journalist Bob Considine, in his 1941 book *Curley Byrd Catches the Worm*

MARYLAND ANNUAL STATISTICAL LEADERS

YR	RUSHING	YDS	ATT	AVG	PASSING	ATT	CMP	PCT	YDS	RECEIVING	REC	YDS	AVG
1947	Lu Gambino	904	125	7.2	Vic Turyn	59	32	.54	504	Elmer Wingate	12	145	12.1
1948	Hubert Werner	554	101	5.5	Vic Turyn	111	45	.41	595	Elmer Wingate	9	32	3.6
1949	Dick Modzelewski	589	120	4.9	Stan Lavine	65	35	.54	554	Stan Karnash	16	245	15.3
1950	Bob Shemonski	560	101	5.5	Jack Scarbath	80	32	.40	463	Pete Augsberger	25	422	16.9
1951	Ralph Felton	485	83	5.8	Jack Scarbath	67	34	.51	675	Lou Weidensaul	18	249	13.8
1952	Jack Scarbath	237	103	2.3	Jack Scarbath	113	59	.52	1,149	Lloyd Colteryahn	32	593	18.5
1953	Ralph Felton	558	100	5.6	Bernie Faloney	68	31	.46	599	Chet Hanulak	10	152	15.2
1954	Ron Waller	592	66	9.0	Charlie Boxold	59	23	.39	525	Bill Walker	13	209	16.1
1955	Ed Vereb	642	113	5.7	Frank Tamburello	58	28	.48	497	Jack Healy	10	182	18.2
1956	Tom Selep	315	62	5.1	John Fritsch	52	23	.44	219	Bill Turner	7	74	10.6
1957	Ted Kershner	227	41	5.5	Bob Rusevlyan	58	26	.45	297	Ed Cooke	14	137	9.8
1958	Jim Joyce	406	97	4.2	Bob Rusevlyan	109	59	.54	657	Ben Scotti	18	282	15.7
1959	Jim Joyce	567	137	4.1	Dale Betty	76	39	.51	552	Gary Collins	14	350	25.0
1960	Pat Drass	297	76	3.9	Dale Betty	132	82	.62	796	Gary Collins	30	404	13.5
1961	Ernie Arizzi	375	79	4.7	Dick Shiner	111	58	.52	921	Gary Collins	30	428	14.3
1962	Len Chiaverini	602	156	3.9	Dick Shiner	203	121	.60	1,324	Tom Brown	47	557	11.9
1963	Jerry Fishman	480	116	4.1	Dick Shiner	222	108	.49	1,165	Darryl Hill	43	516	12.0
1964	Bo Hickey	894	182	4.9	Phil Petry	162	73	.45	809	Dick Absher	22	268	12.2
1965	Ernie Torain	370	93	4.0	Phil Petry	135	65	.48	763	Dick Absher	33	382	11.6
1966	Billy Lovett	451	98	4.6	Alan Pastrana	195	102	.52	1,499	Billy Van Heusen	25	536	21.4
1967	Billy Lovett	499	137	3.6	Chuck Drimal	123	54	.44	669	Rick Carlson	24	309	12.9
1968	Billy Lovett	963	217	4.4	Alan Pastrana	172	81	.47	1,053	Bernard Demczuk	23	215	9.3
1969	Tom Miller	629	169	3.7	Jeff Shugars	114	47	.41	716	Roland Merritt	19	499	26.3
1970	Art Seymore	981	221	4.4	Jeff Shugars	175	75	.43	836	Don Ratliff	26	242	9.3
1971	Monte Hinkle	472	117	4.0	Al Neville	204	107	.52	1,275	Dan Bungori	32	490	15.3
1972	Louis Carter	474	119	4.0	Bob Avellini	170	98	.58	1,251	Don Ratliff	36	515	14.3
1973	Louis Carter	801	218	3.7	Al Neville	92	51	.55	554	Frank Russell	39	468	12.0
1974	Louis Carter	991	224	4.4	Bob Avellini	189	112	.59	1,648	Frank Russell	31	404	13.0
1975	Steve Atkins	491	87	5.6	Larry Dick	158	90	.57	1,190	Kim Hoover	38	532	14.0
1976	Alvin Maddox	678	141	4.8	Mark Manges	139	81	.58	1,145	Charlie White	23	402	17.5
1977	George Scott	894	188	4.8	Larry Dick	135	83	.61	1,351	Eugene Kinney	32	505	15.8
1978	Steve Atkins	1,261	283	4.5	Tim O'Hare	192	105	.55	1,388	Dean Richards	35	575	16.4
1979	Charlie Wysocki	1,140	247	4.6	Mike Tice	154	75	.49	897	Jan Carinci	30	275	9.2
1980	Charlie Wysocki	1,359	334	4.1	Mike Tice	140	71	.51	928	Chris Havener	29	436	15.0
1981	Charlie Wysocki	715	159	4.5	Boomer Esiason	242	122	.50	1,635	John Tice	31	353	11.4
1982	Willie Joyner	1,039	177	5.9	Boomer Esiason	314	176	.56	2,302	John Tice	34	396	11.6
1983	Willie Joyner	908	198	4.6	Boomer Esiason	294	163	.55	2,322	Russell Davis	29	465	18.5
1984	Rick Badanjek	832	173	4.8	Frank Reich	169	108	.64	1,446	Greg Hill	51	820	16.1
1985	Alvin Blount	828	171	4.8	Stan Gelbaugh	311	166	.53	2,475	Azizuddin Abdur-Ra'oof	35	671	19.2
1986	Alvin Blount	517	119	4.3	Dan Henning	353	196	.56	2,725	James Milling	33	650	19.7
1987	Bren Lowery	556	168	3.3	Dan Henning	287	157	.55	1,835	Bren Lowery	44	252	5.7
1988	Ricky Johnson	635	136	4.7	Neil O'Donnell	267	160	.60	1,973	Vernon Joines	29	433	14.9
1989	Bren Lowery	482	100	4.8	Neil O'Donnell	280	156	.56	2,103	Barry Johnson	43	689	16.0
1990	Troy Jackson	662	176	3.8	Scott Zolak	418	225	.54	2,589	Frank Wycheck	58	509	8.8
1991	Mark Mason	452	82	5.5	Jim Sandwisch	291	142	.49	1,499	Frank Wycheck	45	438	9.7
1992	Mark Mason	523	96	5.4	John Kaleo	482	286	.59	3,392	Marcus Badgett	75	1,240	16.5
1993	Mark Mason	616	158	3.9	Scott Milanovich	431	279	.65	3,499	Jermaine Lewis	52	957	18.4
1994	Allen Williams	649	129	5.0	Scott Milanovich	333	229	.69	2,394	Geroy Simon	77	891	11.6
1995	Buddy Rodgers	718	158	4.5	Brian Cummings	166	98	.59	1,193	Jermaine Lewis	66	937	14.2
1996	Brian Underwood	449	97	4.6	Brian Cummings	173	92	.53	1,127	Geroy Simon	35	534	15.3
1997	LaMont Jordan	689	159	4.3	Brian Cummings	255	154	.60	1,760	Moises Cruz	29	337	11.6
1998	LaMont Jordan	906	169	5.4	Ken Mastrole	131	59	.45	632	Jermaine Arrington	23	366	15.9
1999	LaMont Jordan	1,632	266	6.1	Calvin McCall	179	93	.52	1,264	Guilian Gary	24	257	10.7
2000	LaMont Jordan	920	213	4.3	Calvin McCall	199	105	.53	1,533	Guilian Gary	40	568	14.2
2001	Bruce Perry	1,242	219	5.7	Shaun Hill	329	197	.60	2,380	Guilian Gary	49	727	14.8
2002	Chris Downs	1,154	208	5.5	Scott McBrien	284	162	.57	2,497	Scooter Monroe	37	614	16.6
2003	Josh Allen	922	186	5.0	Scott McBrien	314	173	.55	2,672	Latrez Harrison	39	558	14.3
2004	Sammy Maldonado	560	138	4.1	Joel Statham	234	126	.54	1,590	Derrick Fenner	35	430	12.3

Receiving leaders by receptions
The NCAA began including postseason stats in 2002

MARYLAND ALL-TIME SCORES

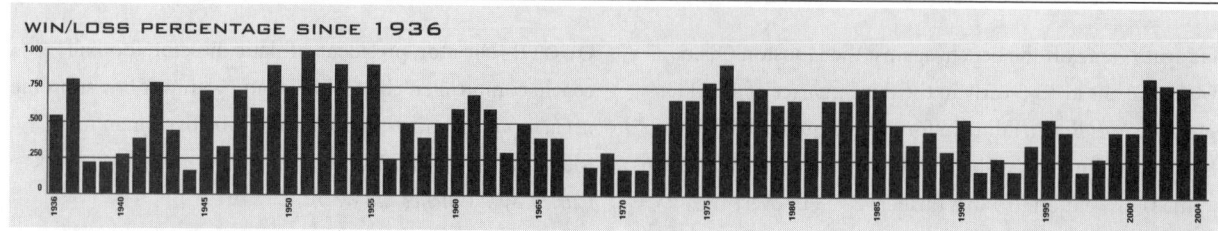

WIN/LOSS PERCENTAGE SINCE 1936

WILL SKINNER
1892 (.000)   0-3

1892   0-3-0
O15		at St. John's	0	50
N5		Johns Hopkins *Balt*	0	62
N19		Episcopal HS	0	16

SAMUEL HARDING
1893 (1.000)   6-0

1893   6-0-0
O12	●	Eastern HS	36	0
O21	●	Central HS	10	0
O26	●	Baltimore City Coll.	18	0
N1	●	St. John's	6	0
N11	●	Western Maryland	18	10
N17	●	Orient AC	16	6

J.G. BANNON
1894 (.571)   4-3

1894   4-3-0
O10	●	Orient AC	30	0
O12	●	W. Md. Coll.	52	0
O20		at Washington College	12	0
O27		at St. John's	6	22
N7	●	Georgetown	6	4
N21		College AC	0	26
N29		at Mount St. Mary's	0	24

1895
NO TEAM

GRENVILLE LEWIS
1896-97 (.563)   8-6-2

1896   6-2-2
O10		Eastern HS *Unk*		06
O17	=	Gallaudet *Unk*	0	0
O21	●	Business High *Unk*	32	0
O29	●	Central High *Unk*	10	6
N4	●	Alexandra High *Unk*	18	0
N7		Episcopal High *Unk*	0	6
N10	●	Bethel Mill AA *Unk*	20	10
N14	●	Western Maryland *Unk*	16	6
N17	●	Central High *Unk*	14	0
N21	=	Maryland U. *Unk*	0	0

1897   2-4-0
O16	●	Central High *Unk*	24	6
O20	●	Eastern High *Unk*	4	0
O30		Johns Hopkins *Unk*	0	30
N13		St. John's *Unk*	4	6
N17	●	Gallaudet *Unk*	6	16
N20		Baltimore Med. Coll. *Unk*	0	10

FRANK KENLY
1898 (.313)   2-5-1

1898   2-5-1
O13		Columbian Univ.	5	17
O15		Western Maryland	0	32
O18	●	Eastern HS	4	0
O22		Gallaudet	0	33
O26	=	Rock Hill	12	12
O29		Johns Hopkins	0	16
N2		Episcopal HS	0	37
N5	●	Rock Hill College	27	0

S.M. COOKE
1899 (.200)   1-4

1899   1-4-0
O14		Western Maryland	0	21
O25	●	Eastern Hills	26	0
O28		Johns Hopkins	0	40
N8		Delaware Coll. *Wil*	0	34
N11		St. John's	0	62

F.H. PETERS
1900 (.438)   3-4-1

1900   3-4-1
O13	=	Western High *Unk*	0	0
O21		Gib AC *Unk*	0	17
N10		Georgetown Prep *Unk*	0	5
N17	●	Georgetown Prep *Unk*	15	0
O30		Episcopal High *Unk*	6	34
N13		Gonzaga *Unk*	5	11
N24	●	Gonzaga *Unk*	21	0
N29	●	Charl. Hall AC *Unk*	21	0

EMMONS DUNBAR
1901 (.125)   1-7

1901   1-7-0
O5		Delware Coll. *Unk*	6	24
O16		Gallaudet *Unk*	10	11
O19		Johns Hopkins *Unk*	0	6
O26		Rock Hill *Unk*	6	11
N2		Central HS *Unk*	0	11
N12	●	U.S. Marines *Unk*	27	0
N16		Walbrook AC *Unk*	0	36
N23		Western Maryland *Unk*	0	30

D. JOHN MARKEY
1902-04 (.483)   12-13-4

1902   3-5-2
O15		Georgetown	0	27
O18	●	Mt. St. Joseph's *Unk*	5	0
O22	●	Columbia U. *Unk*	11	10
O25	●	Olympia AA *Unk*	6	0
N1	=	at Washington Coll. *Unk*	0	0
N8	=	at Mt. St. Mary's *Unk*	0	5
N15		at Western Maryland *Unk*	6	26
N19		Maryland U. *Unk*	0	5
N22		Johns Hopkins *Unk*	0	17
N29	=	Delaware *Unk*	0	0

1903   7-4-0
O11	●	Maryland U.	11	0
O14	●	Tech Hi	27	0
O22	●	at Columbian U.	6	0
O27		Georgetown	0	28
U	●	Clifton AC	5	0
U	●	Gunton Tem.	21	0
U		at St. John's	0	18
N2	●	Wash. Coll.	28	0
N15	●	Western Maryland.	6	0
N18		at Mt. St. Mary's	0	2
N27	●	Delaware Coll. *Wil*	0	16

1904   2-4-2
S26		at Georgetown	0	22
O3	=	Randolph Macon	0	0
U		Fortress Mon.		
O7	●	at Mt. St.Marys	11	6
O14		Western Maryland	0	5
U	●	Gallaudet	22	5
N3		Maryland U.	0	6
N26		Delaware	0	18

FRED NEILSEN
1905-06 (.611)   11-7

1905   6-4-0
O7	●	Baltimore Poly *Balt*	20	0
O14	●	Gallaudet	16	0
O21	●	Western Maryland.	0	10
O25		at Navy	0	17
O28	●	Mt St. Joseph's	28	0
N4		at William & Mary	17	0
N11	●	St. John's	27	5
N18		at Wash. Coll.	0	17
N25	●	U.of Maryland	23	5
N30		at Delaware Coll.	0	12

1906   5-3-0
S29		Tech Hi	5	0
O6	●	Baltimore City Coll. *Balt*	22	0
O10		at Navy	0	12
O13		Georgetown *DC*	0	28
O20		at Mt. Wash. Coll.	0	29
N10	●	at St. John's	20	4
N17	●	at Rock Hill	16	0
N24	●	Washington Coll.	35	0

CHARLES MELICK
1907 (.333)   3-6

1907   3-6-0
S28	●	Tech High	13	0
O3		Georgetown *DC*	0	10
O5		at Richmond Coll.	5	11
O9		at Navy	0	12
O12		at Mt. St. Mary's	6	12
O26	●	George Washington	10	0
N96	●	at Wash. Coll.	10	5
N16		St. John's	0	16
N23		at Gallaudet	0	5

BILL LANG
1908 (.364)   4-7

1908   4-7-0
S26		Tech HS	5	6
S30	●	Central HS	5	0
O3		at Richmond	0	22
O10		at Johns Hopkins	0	10
O14		Navy	0	57
O17	●	Gallaudet	5	0
O24		George Washington	0	57
O31	●	at Fredricksburg Coll.	10	0
N7	●	Baltimore Poly *Balt*	12	0
N14		St. John's	0	31
N21		Washington Coll.	0	11

BILL LANG / E. LARKIN
1909 (.286)   2-5

1909   2-5-0
S25		Tech High	0	11
O2		at Richmond Coll.	0	12
O9		at Johns Hopkins	0	9
O16	●	Rock Hill	5	0
O23		George Washington *DC*	0	26
O30		North Carolina St.	0	31
N6	●	at Gallaudet	14	12

ROYAL ALSTON
1910 (.563)   4-3-1

1910   4-3-1
S24	●	Central HS	12	0
O1	●	at Richmond	22	0
O85	=	at Johns Hopkins	11	11
O15	●	Catholic U.	20	0
O19	●	at George Washington	6	0
N12		at VMI	0	8
N19		at St. John's	0	6
N24		at Western Maryland	3	17

CHARLEY DONNELLY/ H.C. "CURLEY" BYRD
1911 (.500)   4-4-2

1911   4-4-2
S16		Central High	0	14
S23	●	Tech High	6	0
S30	=	Richmond	0	0
O14		Fredricksburgh Coll.	5	0
O21		Johns Hopkins	3	6
O28	=	Catholic U.	6	6
N4		St. John's	0	27
N11	●	at Washington Coll.	5	17
N18	●	Western Maryland	6	0
N25	●	Gallaudet	6	2

H.C. "CURLEY" BYRD
1912-34 (.582)   117-82-15

1912   6-1-1
S28	●	Tech HS *Unk*	6	0
O5	●	Richmond *Unk*	13	0
O13	●	Johns Hopkins *Unk*	58	0
O19		Maryland U. *Unk*	0	27
O26	●	St. John's *Unk*	13	6
N9	●	Gallaudet *Unk*	17	7
N23	=	Western Maryland *Unk*	13	13
N30	●	Penn. Milt. Coll. *Unk*	42	0

1913   6-3-0
S27	●	Baltimore City Coll. *Balt.*	27	0
O4	●	Richmond	45	0
O11	●	at Johns Hopkins	26	0
O18	●	Western Maryland	46	0
O25		at Navy	0	76
N8	●	St. John's	13	0
N14	●	Washington Coll.	20	0
N22		Gallaudet	0	13
N27	●	Penn. Milt. Coll.	7	27

1914   5-3-0
S26		Baltimore Poly	0	6
O3	●	Catholic U.	6	0
O10		at Western Maryland	13	20
O24	●	at Johns Hopkins	14	0
O27	●	at St. John's	27	14
N6		at Washington Coll.	3	0
N14		at Gallaudet	0	23
N26	●	Penn Mil Coll.	26	0

1915   6-3-0
S25	●	Baltimore Poly *Balt.*	31	0
O2		at Haverford	0	7
O9		Catholic U.	0	16
O16	●	Gallaudet	10	3
O23	●	Penn. Milt. Coll.	14	13
O30	●	St. John's	27	14
N6	●	Wash. Coll.	28	13
N13	●	Western Maryland	51	0
N25		at Johns Hopkins	0	3

1916   6-2-0
O6	●	Dickinson	6	0
O11	●	Navy	15	9
O18	●	VMI	6	7
O25		Haverford	7	14
N9	●	St. John's	31	6
N16	●	Catholic U.	10	7
N23		at NYU	13	9
N30	●	at Johns Hopkins	54	0

1917   4-3-1
O6	●	Delaware	20	0
O13		at Navy	0	62
O20	●	at VMI	14	14
O27	●	Wake Forest	29	13
N3		North Carolina St. *DC*	6	10
N10	●	St. John's	13	3
N17		at Penn State	0	57
N30	●	at Johns Hopkins	7	0

1918   4-1-1
O26		American	6	13
N2	●	at VMI	7	6
N9	●	Western Maryland *Balt*	10	0
N16	●	NYU	6	2
N23	●	St. John's *Balt*	19	14
N28	=	at Johns Hopkins	0	0

1919   5-4-0
O4		Swarthmore	6	10
O11	●	at Virginia	13	0
O18		West Virginia	0	27
O25		Virginia Tech	0	6
N1		at Yale	0	31
N8	●	at St. John's	27	0
N15	●	Catholic U.	13	0
N22	●	Western Maryland	20	0
N27	●	at Johns Hopkins	13	0

MARYLAND 469

THE SCHOOLS

1920 7-2-0

S25	●	Randolph Macon	54	0	
O2		at Rutgers	0	6	
O9		at Princeton	0	35	
O16	●	Wash. Coll.	27	0	
O23	●	at Virginia Tech	7	0	
O30	●	at North Carolina	13	0	
N6	●	at Catholic U.	14	0	
N13	●	at Syracuse	10	7	*
N25	●	Johns Hopkins	24	7	

1921-1952 Southern Conference

1921 3-5-1 (1-1-1)

O1	●	at Rutgers	3	0	
O8		at Syracuse	0	42	
O15		St. John's	3	7	
O22	● |	Virginia Tech DC	10	7	
O29	|	North Carolina BALT	7	16	
N5		at Yale	0	28	
N12	●	at Catholic U.	16	0	
N19		at Carnegie Tech	0	21	
N24	= |	North Carolina St. BALT	6	6	

1922 4-5-1 (1-2-0)

S30	●	3rd Army Corps	7	0	
O7	=	at Richmond	0	0	
O14		at Pennsylvania	0	12	
O21		at Princeton	0	26	
O28	|	at North Carolina	3	27	
N4	|	at Virginia Tech	0	21	
N11		at Yale	3	45	
N18	●	at Johns Hopkins	3	0	
N25	●	at Catholic U.	54	0	
N30	● |	at North Carolina St.	7	6	

1923 7-2-1 (2-1-0)

S29	●	Randolph Macon	53	0	
O6	●	at Pennsylvania	3	0	
O13	●	Richmond DC	23	0	
O20	|	Virginia Tech DC	9	16	*
O27	● |	North Carolina	14	0	
N3	●	St. John's	28	0	
N10		at Yale	14	16	
N17	● |	at North Carolina St.	26	12	
N24	●	Catholic U.	40	6	
N29	=	Johns Hopkins BALT	6	6	

1924 3-3-3 (1-2-1)

S27	●	Washington Coll.	23	0	
O4	|	Wash. & Lee DC	7	19	
O11	●	Richmond	38	0	
O18	|	Virginia Tech DC	0	12	
O25	● |	at North Carolina	6	0	
N1	=	at Catholic U.	0	0	
N8		at Yale	0	47	
N15	= |	North Carolina St.	0	0	
N27	=	Johns Hopkins BALT	0	0	

1925 2-5-1 (0-4-0)

S26	●	Wash. Coll.	13	0	
O10	●	Rutgers PHIL	16	0	
O17	|	Virginia Tech DC	0	3	
O24	|	at Virginia	0	6	
O31	|	North Carolina BALT	0	16	
N7		at Yale	14	43	
N14	|	Wash. & Lee	3	7	
N26	=	Johns Hopkins BALT	7	7	

1926 5-4-1 (1-3-1)

S25	●	Washington Coll.	63	0	
O2	|	at South Carolina	0	12	
O9		at Chicago	0	21	
O16	|	Virginia Tech NOR	8	24	
O23	● |	North Carolina	14	6	
O30	●	Gallaudet	38	7	
N6	●	at Yale	15	0	
N13	= |	Virginia	6	6	
N20	|	at Wash. & Lee	0	3	
N25	●	Johns Hopkins BALT	17	14	

1927 4-7-0 (3-5-0)

S24	●	Washington Coll.	80	0	
O1	● |	South Carolina	26	0	
O8	|	at North Carolina	6	7	
O15	● |	Virginia Tech NOR	13	7	
O22	● |	VMI RICH	10	6	
O29	|	Wash. & Lee	6	13	
N5		at Yale	6	30	
N12	|	at Virginia	0	21	
N19	|	at Vanderbilt	20	39	
N24		Johns Hopkins BALT	13	14	
D3	|	Florida JACF	6	7	

1928 6-3-1 (2-3-1)

S29	●	Washington Coll.	31	0	
O6	|	North Carolina	19	26	
O13	|	at South Carolina	7	21	
O20	●	Western Maryland	13	6	
O27	= |	VMI RICH	0	0	
N3	|	Virginia Tech NOR	6	9	
N10	●	at Yale	6	0	
N17	● |	Virginia	18	2	
N24	● |	at Wash. & Lee	6	0	
N29	●	Johns Hopkins BALT	26	6	

1929 4-4-2 (1-3-1)

S27	●	Washington Coll.	34	7	
O5	|	North Carolina	0	43	
O12	|	South Carolina	6	26	
O19	●	Gallaudet	13	6	
O26	|	VMI	6	7	
N2	= |	Virginia RICH	13	13	
N9	=	at Yale	13	13	
N16	● |	Virginia Tech NOR	24	0	
N28	●	Johns Hopkins	39	6	
D7		Western Maryland BALT	0	12	

1930 7-5-0 (4-2-0)

S27	●	Washington Coll.	60	6	
O4		at Yale	13	40	
O11	|	at North Carolina	21	28	
O18	●	St. John's	21	13	
O25	● |	VMI RICH	20	0	
N1	● |	at Virginia	14	6	
N8	● |	Wash. & Lee	41	7	
N15	● |	Virginia Tech NOR	13	7	
N22		at Navy	0	6	
N27	●	Johns Hopkins	21	0	
D1	|	at Vanderbilt	7	22	
D6		Western Maryland BALT	0	7	

1931 8-1-1 (4-1-1)

S26	●	Washington Coll.	13	0	
O3	● |	Virginia	7	6	
O10	●	Navy DC	6	0	
O17	= |	Kentucky	6	6	
O24	● |	VMI RICH	24	20	
O31	● |	at Virginia Tech	20	0	
N7	|	at Vanderbilt	12	39	
N21	● |	Wash. & Lee	13	7	
N26	●	Johns Hopkins BALT	35	14	
D5	●	Western Maryland BALT	41	6	

1932 5-6-0 (2-4-0)

S25	●	Washington Coll.	63	0	
O1	|	at Virginia	6	7	
O8	|	Virginia Tech	0	23	
O15	|	at Duke	0	34	
O22	●	St. John's	24	7	
O29	● |	VMI RICH	12	7	
N5	|	Vanderbilt DC	0	13	
N12		Navy BALT	7	28	
N19	● |	Wash. & Lee BALT	6	0	
N24	●	Johns Hopkins BALT	23	0	
D3		Western Maryland	7	39	

1933 3-7-0 (1-4-0)

S30	●	St. John's	20	0	
O7	|	Virginia Tech RICH	0	14	*
O14		at Tulane	0	20	
O21	|	at VMI	13	19	
O28		Western Maryland BALT	7	13	
N4	|	at Virginia	0	6	
N11	|	Duke	7	38	
N18	●	at Johns Hopkins	27	7	
N23	● |	Wash. & Lee	33	13	
D2		Florida TAM	0	19	

1934 7-3-0 (3-1-0)

S29	●	St. John's	13	0	
O6	|	at Wash. & Lee	0	7	
O13		at Navy	13	16	
O20	● |	Virginia Tech NOR	14	9	
O27	●	Florida BALT	21	0	
N3	● |	Virginia	20	0	
N10	● |	VMI BALT	23	0	
N17		Indiana	14	17	
N24	●	Georgetown	6	0	
N29	●	Johns Hopkins BALT	19	0	

JACK FABER
1935, '40-41 (.483) 12-13-4

1935 7-2-2 (3-1-0)

S28	●	St. John's	39	6	
O5	● |	Virginia Tech BALT	7	0	
O12	|	North Carolina	0	33	
O19	● |	at VMI	6	0	
O26	●	at Florida	20	6	
N2	● |	at Virginia	14	7	
N9		Indiana BALT	7	13	*
N16	= |	Wash. & Lee	0	0	
N23	●	Georgetown DC	12	6	
N28	=	Syracuse BALT	0	0	
D4	●	Western Maryland	22	7	

FRANK DOBSON
1936-39 (.462) 18-21

1936 6-5-0 (3-2-0)

S28	●	St. John's	28	0	
O3	● |	Virginia Tech ROA	6	0	
O10	|	at North Carolina	0	14	
O17	●	at Virginia	21	0	
O24	●	Syracuse NYC	20	0	
O31		at Florida	6	7	
N7	● |	at Richmond	12	0	*
N14	|	VMI	7	13	
N21		Georgetown	6	7	
N26	● |	Wash. & Lee BALT	19	6	
D5		Western Maryland	0	12	

1937 8-2-0 (2-0-0)

S25	●	St. John's	25	0	
O2		at Pennsylvania	21	28	
O9	●	Western Maryland	6	0	
O16	●	at Virginia	3	0	
O23	●	Syracuse BALT	13	0	
O30	●	Florida	13	7	
N6	● |	at VMI	9	7	
N13		at Penn State	14	21	
N20	●	Georgetown DC	12	2	
N25	● |	Wash. & Lee BALT	8	0	

1938 2-7-0 (1-2-0)

S24	|	Richmond	6	19	
O1		at Penn State	0	33	
O8		at Syracuse	0	53	
O15	●	Western Maryland BALT	14	8	
O22		Virginia	19	27	
O29	|	VMI	14	47	
N12		at Florida	7	21	
N19		Georgetown	7	14	
N24	● |	Wash. & Lee BALT	19	13	

1939 2-7-0 (0-1-0)

S30	●	Hampden-Sydney	26	0	
O7	●	Western Maryland BALT	12	0	
O14		at Virginia	7	12	
O21		at Rutgers	12	25	
O28		Florida	0	14	
N4		at Penn State	0	12	
N11		Georgetown DC	0	20	
N18	|	VMI NOR	14	47	
N30		Syracuse	7	10	

JACK FABER

1940 2-6-1 (0-1-1)

S28		Hampden-Sydney	6	7	
O5		at Pennsylvania	0	51	
O12		Virginia	6	19	
O19		at Florida	0	19	
O25	●	Western Maryland BALT	6	0	
N9		Georgetown	0	41	
N16	|	VMI LYN	0	20	
N21	●	Rutgers BALT	14	7	
N30	= |	Wash. & Lee	7	7	

1941 3-5-1 (1-2-0)

S27	●	Hampden-Sydney	18	0	
O4	=	Western Maryland	6	6	
O11	|	Duke BALT	0	50	
O18	●	Florida	13	12	
O25		at Pennsylvania	6	55	*
N1		at Rutgers	0	20	
N8		Georgetown DC	0	26	
N15	|	VMI	0	27	
N20	● |	Wash. & Lee BALT	6	0	

CLARK SHAUGHNESSY
1942, '46 (.556) 10-8

1942 7-2-0 (1-2-0)

S26	●	Connecticut	34	0	
O3	●	Lakehurst NAS	14	0	
O10	●	Rutgers	27	13	
O17	|	at VMI	0	29	
O24	●	Western Maryland	51	0	
O31	●	Florida DC	13	0	
N7	|	at Duke	0	42	
N14	●	at Virginia	27	12	*
N21	● |	Wash. & Lee	32	28	

CLARENCE SPEARS
1943-44 (.306) 5-12-1

1943 4-5-0 (2-0-0)

S25		Curtis Bay CG	7	13	
O2	● |	Wake Forest	13	7	
O9	●	Richmond Army Base	19	6	
O16		at West Virginia	2	6	
O23		Penn State	0	45	
O30	●	at Greenville Air Base	43	18	
N6		at Virginia	0	39	
N13		Bainbridge NTS	0	46	
N25	● |	VMI ROA	24	21	

1944 1-7-1 (1-1-0)

S29		Hampden-Sydney	0	12	
O7	|	at Wake Forest	0	39	
O14	=	West Virginia	6	6	
O21		Michigan State	0	8	
O28		at Florida	6	14	
N4		Virginia DC	7	18	
N11		at Michigan State	0	33	
N18		at Penn State	19	34	
N30	● |	VMI ROA	8	6	

PAUL "BEAR" BRYANT
1945 (.722) 6-2-1

1945 6-2-1 (3-2-0)

S28	●	Guilford	60	6	
O6	● |	at Richmond	21	0	
O13	●	Merchant Marines	22	6	
O20	|	at Virginia Tech	13	21	
O27	=	at West Virginia	13	13	
N3	|	William & Mary	14	33	
N10	● |	VMI	38	0	
N24	●	Virginia	19	13	
D1	● |	at South Carolina	19	13	

CLARK SHAUGHNESSY

1946 3-6-0 (2-5-0)

S28	●	Brianbridge NAS	54	0	
O4	|	Richmond	7	37	
O12	|	at North Carolina	0	33	
O18	● |	Virginia Tech	6	0	
N2	|	at William & Mary	7	41	
N9	|	South Carolina	17	21	
N16	● |	Wash. & Lee BALT	24	7	
N23		at Michigan State	14	26	
N30	|	at North Carolina St.	7	28	

JIM TATUM
1947-55 (.815) 73-15-4

1947 7-2-2 (3-2-1)

S27	● |	at South Carolina	19	13	
O3	●	Delaware DC	43	19	
O10	● |	Richmond DC	18	6	
O18	|	at Duke	7	19	
O25	● |	at Virginia Tech	21	19	
N1	●	West Virginia DC	27	0	
N8	●	at Duquesne	32	0	
N15	|	North Carolina DC	0	19	
N22	●	at Vanderbilt	20	6	
N29	= |	North Carolina St. DC	0	0	
		GATOR BOWL			
J1	=	Georgia	20	20	

1948 6-4-0 (4-2-0)

S25	● |	at Richmond	19	0	
O2	●	at Delaware	21	0	
O9	● |	Virginia Tech DC	28	0	
O16	|	Duke DC	12	13	
O23	● |	George Washington DC	47	0	
O29	●	at Miami, Fla.	27	13	
N6	● |	at South Carolina	19	7	
N13	|	North Carolina	20	49	
N20		Vanderbilt DC	0	34	
N27		at West Virginia	14	16	

1949 9-1-0 (4-0-0)

S24	● |	at Virginia Tech	34	7	
S30	●	Georgetown	33	7	
O8		at Michigan State	7	14	
O22	● |	at North Carolina St.	14	6	
O29	● |	South Carolina	44	7	
N5	● |	George Washington	40	14	
N12	●	at Boston U.	14	13	
N24	●	West Virginia	47	7	
D2	●	at Miami, Fla.	13	0	
		GATOR BOWL			
J2	●	Missouri	20	7	

1950 7-2-1 (4-1-1)

S23		at Georgia	7	27	
S30	●	Navy	35	21	
O7	●	at Michigan State	34	7	
O14	●	Georgetown DC	25	14	
O21	|	North Carolina St.	13	16	
O28	● |	at Duke	26	14	
N4	● |	George Washington	23	7	
N11	= |	at North Carolina	7	7	
N18	● |	at West Virginia	41	0	
D2	● |	Virginia Tech	63	7	

1951 10-0-0 (5-0-0)

S29	•	at Wash. & Lee	54	14
O6	•	George Washington	33	6
O13	•	at Georgia	43	7
O20	•	North Carolina	14	7
O27	•	at LSU	27	0
N3	•	Missouri	35	0
N10	•	Navy BALT	40	21
N17	•	North Carolina St.	53	0
N24	•	West Virginia	54	7
SUGAR BOWL				
J1		Tennessee	28	13

1952 7-2-0 (1-0-0)

S20	•	at Missouri	13	10
S27	•	Auburn BIRM	13	7
O4	•	Clemson	28	0
O11	•	at Georgia	37	0
O18	•	Navy	38	7
O25	•	LSU	34	6
N1	•	at Boston U.	34	7
N15	•	at Mississippi	14	21
N22	•	Alabama MBL	7	27

1953-PRESENT ACC

1953 10-1-0 (3-0-0)

S19	•	at Missouri	20	6
S26	•	Wash. & Lee	52	0
O3	•	at Clemson	20	0
O10	•	Georgia	40	13
O17	•	at North Carolina	26	0
O23	•	at Miami, Fla.	30	0
O31	•	South Carolina	24	6
N7	•	George Washington	27	6
N14	•	Mississippi	38	0
N21	•	Alabama	21	0
ORANGE BOWL				
J1		Oklahoma	0	7

1954 7-2-1 (4-0-1)

S18	•	at Kentucky	20	0
O1	•	UCLA	7	12
O9	=	Wake Forest W-S	13	13
O16	•	North Carolina	33	0
O22	•	at Miami, Fla.	7	9
O30	•	at South Carolina	20	0
N6	•	North Carolina St.	42	14
N13	•	Clemson	16	0
N20	•	George Washington	48	6
N25	•	Missouri	74	14

1955 10-1-0 (4-0-0)

S17	•	at Missouri	13	12
S24	•	UCLA	7	0
O1	•	at Baylor	20	6
O8	•	Wake Forest	28	7
O15	•	at North Carolina	25	7
O22	•	at Syracuse	34	13
O29	•	South Carolina	27	0
N5	•	LSU	13	0
N12	•	at Clemson	25	12
N19	•	George Washington	19	0
ORANGE BOWL				
J2		Oklahoma	6	20

TOMMY MONT 1956-58 (.383) 11-18-1

1956 2-7-1 (2-2-1)

S22		Syracuse	12	26
S29	•	at Wake Forest	6	0
O6		Baylor	0	14
O12		at Miami, Fla.	6	13
O20		at North Carolina	6	34
O27		at Tennessee	7	34
N3		Kentucky	0	14
N10	=	Clemson	6	6
N17		at South Carolina	0	13
N22	•	at North Carolina St.	25	14

1957 5-5-0 (4-3-0)

S21		Texas A&M DAL	13	21
S28		North Carolina St.	13	48
O5		at Duke	0	14
O12		Wake Forest	27	0
O19		North Carolina	21	7
O26		Tennessee	0	16
N2		at South Carolina	10	6
N9		at Clemson	7	26
N15		at Miami, Fla.	16	6
N23		Virginia	12	0

1958 4-6-0 (3-3-0)

S20		at Wake Forest	0	34
S27	•	at North Carolina St.	21	6
O4		Clemson	0	8
O11		Texas A&M	10	14
O18		at North Carolina	0	27
O25		at Auburn	7	20
N1	•	South Carolina	10	6
N8		Navy BALT	14	40
N14	•	at Miami, Fla.	26	14
N22	•	at Virginia	44	6

TOM NUGENT 1959-65 (.514) 36-34

1959 5-5-0 (4-2-0)

S19	•	West Virginia	27	7
S26		at Texas	0	26
O3		at Syracuse	0	29
O10		Wake Forest	7	10
O17	•	North Carolina	14	7
O31		at South Carolina	6	22
N7		Navy BALT	14	22
N14	•	at Clemson	28	25
N21	•	Virginia	55	12
D5	•	North Carolina St.	33	28

1960 6-4-0 (5-2-0)

S17	•	at West Virginia	31	8
S24		Texas	0	34
O1	•	Duke	7	20
O8		at North Carolina St.	10	13
O15	•	Clemson	19	17
O22	•	at Wake Forest	14	13
O29	•	South Carolina	15	0
N5		at Penn State	9	28
N12	•	at North Carolina	22	19
N19	•	at Virginia	44	12

1961 7-3-0 (3-3-0)

S23	•	at SMU	14	6
S30	•	at Clemson	24	21
O7	•	Syracuse	22	21
O14		North Carolina	8	14
O21	•	at Air Force	21	0
O28	•	at South Carolina	10	20
N4	•	Penn State	21	17
N11	•	North Carolina St.	10	7
N18	•	Wake Forest	10	7
N25		at Virginia	16	28

1962 6-4-0 (5-2-0)

S22	•	SMU	7	0
S29	•	Wake Forest	13	2
O6	•	North Carolina St.	14	6
O13	•	at North Carolina	31	13
O19	•	at Miami, Fla.	24	28
O27	•	South Carolina	13	11
N3		at Penn State	7	23
N10		at Duke	7	10
N17		Clemson	14	17
N24	•	Virginia	40	18

1963 3-7-0 (2-5-0)

S21	•	North Carolina St.	14	36
S28	•	at South Carolina	13	21
O5		Duke RICH	12	30
O12		North Carolina	7	14
O19		Air Force	21	14
O26	•	at Wake Forest	32	0
N2		Penn State	15	17
N9		at Navy	7	42
N16		at Clemson	6	21
N23	•	Virginia	21	6

1964 5-5-0 (4-3-0)

S19		Oklahoma	3	13
S26	•	South Carolina	24	6
O3		at North Carolina St.	13	14
O10		at Duke	17	24
O17	•	North Carolina NOR	10	9
O24		Wake Forest	17	21
O31		at Penn State	9	17
N7		Navy	27	22
N14	•	Clemson	34	0
N21	•	at Virginia	10	0

1965 4-6-0 (3-3-0)

S25	•	Ohio U.	24	7
O2		Syracuse	7	24
O9	•	at Wake Forest	10	7
O16		at North Carolina	10	12
O23	•	North Carolina St.	7	29
O30	•	at South Carolina	27	14
N6		at Navy	7	19
N13	•	at Clemson	6	0
N20		Virginia	27	33
D4		Penn State	7	19

LOU SABAN 1966 (.400) 4-6

1966 4-6-0 (3-3-0)

S17		at Penn State	7	15
S24	•	Wake Forest	34	7
O1		at Syracuse	7	28
O8	•	Duke	21	19
O15		West Virginia	28	9
O29	•	South Carolina	14	2
N5		at North Carolina St.	21	24
N12		Clemson	10	14
N19		at Virginia	17	41
N26		at Florida State	21	45

BOB WARD 1967-68 (.105) 2-17

1967 0-9-0 (0-6-0)

S30		at Oklahoma	0	35
O7		Syracuse	3	7
O14		North Carolina St.	9	31
O21		at North Carolina	0	14
O28		at South Carolina	0	31
N4		Penn State	3	38
N11		at Clemson	7	28
N17		at Wake Forest	17	35
N25		Virginia	7	12

1968 2-8-0 (2-5-0)

S21		Florida State	14	24
S28		at Syracuse	14	32
O5		Duke NOR	28	30
O12	•	North Carolina	33	24
O19	•	South Carolina	21	19
O26		at North Carolina St.	11	31
N2		at Wake Forest	14	38
N9		Clemson	0	16
N16		Penn State	13	57
N23		at Virginia	23	28

ROY LESTER 1969-71 (.219) 7-25

1969 3-7-0 (3-3-0)

S20		at West Virginia	7	31
S27		North Carolina St.	7	24
O4	•	at Wake Forest	19	14
O11		Syracuse	9	20
O18	•	Duke	20	7
O25		at South Carolina	0	17
N1		at Clemson	0	40
N8		Miami, Ohio	21	34
N15		at Penn State	0	48
N22	•	Virginia	17	14

1970 2-9-0 (2-4-0)

S12		Villanova	3	21
S19		at Duke	12	13
S26		North Carolina	20	53
O2		at Miami, Fla.	11	18
O10		at Syracuse	7	23
O17	•	South Carolina	21	15
O24		North Carolina St. NOR	0	6
O31		Clemson	11	24
N7		Penn State	0	34
N21	•	at Virginia	17	14
N28		West Virginia	10	20

1971 2-9-0 (1-5-0)

S11		Villanova	13	28
S18	•	North Carolina St.	35	7
S25		at North Carolina	14	35
O2		Wake Forest	14	18
O9		Syracuse	13	21
O16		at South Carolina	6	35
O23		at Florida	23	27
O30	•	VMI	38	0
N6		at Penn State	27	63
N13		at Clemson	14	20
N20		Virginia	27	29

JERRY CLAIBORNE 1972-81 (.671) 77-37-3

1972 5-5-1 (3-2-1)

S9	=	at North Carolina St.	24	24
S16		North Carolina	26	31
S23	•	VMI	28	16
S30		at Syracuse	12	16
O7	•	Wake Forest	23	0
O14		Villanova	37	7
O21		at Duke	14	20
O28	•	at Virginia	24	23
N4		at Penn State	16	46
N11	•	Clemson	31	6
N25		at Miami, Fla.	8	28

1973 8-4-0 (5-1-0)

S15		West Virginia	13	20
S22	•	at North Carolina	23	3
S29	•	Villanova	31	3
O6		Syracuse	38	0
O13	•	at North Carolina	22	24
O20	•	at Wake Forest	37	0
O27	•	Duke NOR	30	10
N3		Penn State	22	42
N10	•	Virginia	33	0
N17	•	at Clemson	28	13
N24	•	Tulane	42	9
PEACH BOWL				
D28		Georgia	16	17

1974 8-4-0 (6-0-0)

S14		Alabama	16	21
S21		Florida TAM	10	17
S28		North Carolina	24	12
O5		at Syracuse	31	0
O12		Clemson	41	0
O19		Wake Forest	47	0
O26		North Carolina St.	20	10
N2		at Penn State	17	24
N9		Villanova	41	0
N16		Duke NOR	56	13
N23		at Virginia	10	0
LIBERTY BOWL				
D16		Tennessee	3	7

1975 9-2-1 (5-0-0)

S6	•	Villanova	41	0
S13		at Tennessee	8	26
S20	•	at North Carolina	34	7
S27	=	at Kentucky	10	10
O4		Syracuse	24	7
O11		North Carolina St.	37	22
O18	•	at Wake Forest	27	0
N1		Penn State	13	15
N8		Cincinnati CIN	21	19
N15		at Clemson	22	20
N22	•	Virginia	62	24
GATOR BOWL				
D29		Florida	13	0

1976 11-1-0 (5-0-0)

S11	•	Richmond	31	7
S18		at West Virginia	24	3
S25		at Syracuse	42	28
O2	•	Villanova	20	9
O9		at North Carolina St.	16	6
O16		Wake Forest	17	15
O23		at Duke	30	3
O30		Kentucky	24	14
N6	•	Cincinnati	21	0
N13		Clemson	20	0
N20	•	at Virginia	28	0
COTTON BOWL				
J1		Houston	21	30

1977 8-4-0 (4-2-0)

S10	•	at Clemson	21	14
S17		West Virginia	16	24
S24		at Penn State	9	27
O1		at North Carolina St.	20	24
O8	•	Syracuse	24	10
O15		at Wake Forest	35	7
O22	•	Duke	31	13
O29		North Carolina	7	16
N5	•	Villanova	19	13
N12		at Richmond	27	24
N19	•	Virginia	28	0
HALL OF FAME CLASSIC				
D22	•	Minnesota	17	7

1978 9-3-0 (5-1-0)

S9	•	Tulane	31	7
S16		at Louisville	24	17
S23	•	at North Carolina	21	20
S30	•	Kentucky	20	3
O7	•	North Carolina St.	31	7
O14		at Syracuse	24	9
O21	•	Wake Forest	39	0
O28	•	at Duke	27	0
N4		at Penn State	3	27
N11	•	at Virginia	17	7
N18	•	Clemson	24	28
SUN BOWL				
D23		Texas	0	42

1979 — 7-4-0 (4-2-0)

S8	●		Villanova	24	20
S15	●	‖	at Clemson	19	0
S22	●		Mississippi State	35	14
S29			at Kentucky	7	14
O6			Penn State	7	27
O13		‖	at North Carolina St.	0	7
O20		‖	at Wake Forest	17	25
O27	●	‖	at Duke	27	0
N3	●	‖	North Carolina	17	14
N17	●		Louisville	28	7
N24	●	‖	Virginia	17	7

1980 — 8-4-0 (5-1-0)

S6	●		Villanova	7	3
S13	●		Vanderbilt	31	6
S20	●		at West Virginia	14	11
S27		‖	at North Carolina	3	17
O4			at Pittsburgh	9	38
O11			Penn State	10	24
O18	●	‖	Wake Forest	11	10
O25	●	‖	at Duke	17	14
N1	●	‖	North Carolina St.	24	0
N15	●	‖	Clemson	34	7
N22	●	‖	at Virginia	31	0
			TANGERINE BOWL		
D20			Florida	20	35

1981 — 4-6-1 (4-2-0)

S12			at Vanderbilt	17	23
S19			West Virginia	13	17
S26	●	‖	at North Carolina St.	34	9
O3	=		Syracuse	17	17
O10			at Florida	10	15
O17	●	‖	at Wake Forest	45	33
O24	●	‖	Duke	24	21
O31		‖	North Carolina	10	17
N7			at Tulane	7	14
N14		‖	at Clemson	7	21
N21	●	‖	Virginia	48	7

BOBBY ROSS
1982-86 (.669) 39-19-1

1982 — 8-4-0 (5-1-0)

S11			at Penn State	31	39
S18			at West Virginia	18	19
S25	●	‖	North Carolina St.	23	6
O2	●		at Syracuse	26	3
O9	●		Indiana St.	38	0
O16	●	‖	Wake Forest	52	31
O23	●	‖	Duke	49	22
O30	●	‖	at North Carolina	31	24
N6	●		Miami, Fla.	18	17
N13		‖	Clemson	22	24
N20	●	‖	at Virginia	45	14
			ALOHA BOWL		
D25			Washington	20	21

1983 — 8-4-0 (5-1-0)

S10	●		at Vanderbilt	21	14
S17			West Virginia	21	31
S24	●		Pittsburgh	13	7
O1	●	‖	Virginia	23	3
O8	●		Syracuse	34	13
O15	●	‖	at Wake Forest	36	33
O22	●	‖	Duke	38	3
O29	●	‖	North Carolina	28	26
N5			at Auburn	23	35
N12		‖	at Clemson	27	52
N19	●	‖	at North Carolina St.	29	6
			CITRUS BOWL		
D27			Tennessee	23	30

1984 — 9-3-0 (6-0-0)

S8			Syracuse	7	23
S15			Vanderbilt	14	23
S22	●		at West Virginia	20	17
S29	●	‖	Wake Forest	38	17
O6			at Penn State	24	25
O13	●	‖	North Carolina St.	44	21
O27	●	‖	at Duke	43	7
N3	●	‖	at North Carolina	34	23
N10	●		at Miami, Fla.	42	40
N17	●	‖	Clemson *Balt*	41	23
N24	●	‖	at Virginia	45	34
			SUN BOWL		
D22	●		Tennessee	28	27

1985 — 9-3-0 (6-0-0)

S7			Penn State	18	20
S14	●		Boston College *Fox*	31	13
S21	●		West Virginia	28	0
S28			at Michigan	0	20
O5	●	‖	at North Carolina St.	31	17
O19	●	‖	at Wake Forest	26	3
O26	●	‖	Duke	40	10
N2	●	‖	North Carolina	28	10
N9			Miami, Fla. *Balt*	22	29
N16	●	‖	at Clemson	34	31
N29	●	‖	Virginia	33	21
			CHERRY BOWL		
D21	●		Syracuse	35	18

1986 — 5-5-1 (2-3-1)

S1	●		at Pittsburgh	10	7
S13	●		Vanderbilt	35	21
S20	●		at West Virginia	24	3
S27		‖	North Carolina St.	16	28
O11			Boston College	25	30
O18		‖	Wake Forest	21	27
O25	●	‖	at Duke	27	19
N1		‖	at North Carolina	30	32
N8			at Penn State	15	17
N15	=	‖	Clemson *Balt*	17	17
N28	●	‖	at Virginia	42	10

JOE KRIVAK
1987-91 (.375) 20-34-2

1987 — 4-7-0 (3-3-0)

S5			at Syracuse	11	25
S12	●	‖	Virginia	21	19
S19	●		West Virginia	25	20
S26		‖	at North Carolina St.	14	42
O10			at Miami, Fla.	16	46
O17	●	‖	at Wake Forest	14	0
O24	●	‖	Duke	23	22
O31		‖	North Carolina	14	27
N7			Penn State *Balt*	16	21
N14		‖	at Clemson	16	45
N21			at Vanderbilt	24	34

1988 — 5-6-0 (4-3-0)

S3	●		Louisville	27	16
S17			at West Virginia	24	55
S24	●	‖	North Carolina St.	30	26
O1			at Syracuse	9	20
O8	●	‖	Georgia Tech	13	8
O15		‖	Wake Forest	24	27
O22	●	‖	at Duke	34	24
O29	●	‖	at North Carolina	41	38
N5			at Penn State	10	17
N12		‖	Clemson	25	49
N19		‖	at Virginia	23	24

1989 — 3-7-1 (2-5-0)

S2		‖	at North Carolina St.	6	10
S9			West Virginia	10	14
S16	●		Western Michigan	23	0
S23		‖	at Clemson	7	31
S30			at Michigan	21	41
O7		‖	at Georgia Tech	24	28
O14	●	‖	at Wake Forest	27	7
O21		‖	Duke	25	46
O28	●	‖	North Carolina	38	0
N11	=		Penn State *Balt*	13	13
N18		‖	Virginia	21	48

1990 — 6-5-1 (4-3-0)

S1	●		Virginia Tech	20	13
S8	●		at West Virginia	14	10
S15		‖	Clemson *Balt*	17	18
S22	●	‖	North Carolina St.	13	12
S29			at Michigan	17	45
O6		‖	Georgia Tech	3	31
O13	●	‖	Wake Forest	41	13
O20	●	‖	at Duke	23	20
O27		‖	at North Carolina	10	34
N10			at Penn State	10	24
N17	●	‖	at Virginia	35	30
			INDEPENDENCE BOWL		
D15	=		Louisiana Tech	34	34

1991 — 2-9-0 (2-5-0)

S7	●	‖	Virginia	17	6
S14			Syracuse	17	31
S21			West Virginia	7	37
O5			at Pittsburgh	20	24
O12		‖	at Georgia Tech	10	34
O19	●	‖	at Wake Forest	23	22
O26		‖	Duke	13	17
N2		‖	at North Carolina	0	24
N9			Penn State *Balt*	7	47
N16		‖	at Clemson	7	40
N23		‖	at North Carolina St.	17	20

MARK DUFFNER
1992-96 (.364) 20-35

1992 — 3-8-0 (2-6-0)

S5		‖	at Virginia	15	28
S12		‖	North Carolina St.	10	14
S19			at West Virginia	33	34
S26			at Penn State	13	49
O3	●		Pittsburgh	47	34
O10		‖	Georgia Tech	26	28
O17		‖	Wake Forest	23	30
O24	●	‖	at Duke	27	25
O31		‖	North Carolina	24	31
N7		‖	at Florida State	21	69
N14	●	‖	Clemson	53	23

1993 — 2-9-0 (2-6-0)

S4		‖	Virginia	29	43
S11		‖	at North Carolina	42	59
S18			West Virginia	37	42
S25			at Virginia Tech	28	55
O2			Penn State	7	70
O9		‖	at Georgia Tech	0	38
O16	●	‖	Duke	26	18
O30		‖	at Clemson	0	29
N6		‖	Florida State	20	49
N13		‖	at North Carolina St.	21	44
N20	●	‖	at Wake Forest	33	32

1994 — 4-7-0 (2-6-0)

S3		‖	at Duke	16	49
S10		‖	Florida State	20	52
S17	●		at West Virginia	24	13
S23	●	‖	Wake Forest	31	7
O1		‖	at Clemson	0	13
O15		‖	at North Carolina	17	41
O22	●	‖	Georgia Tech	42	27
O29	●		Tulane	38	10
N5		‖	North Carolina St.	45	47
N12		‖	at Virginia	21	46
N19			at Syracuse	16	21

1995 — 6-5-0 (4-4-0)

S2	●		at Tulane	29	10
S9	●	‖	North Carolina	32	18
S16	●		West Virginia	31	17
S23	●	‖	Duke	41	28
S28		‖	at Georgia Tech	3	31
O7	●	‖	at Wake Forest	9	6
O21		‖	Clemson	0	17
O28			at Louisville	0	31
N4	●	‖	at North Carolina St.	30	13
N11		‖	Virginia	18	21
N18		‖	at Florida State	17	59

1996 — 5-6 (3-5)

A31	●		Northern Illinois	30	6
S7	●		UAB	39	15
S14		‖	at Virginia	3	21
S28			at West Virginia	0	13
O5		‖	North Carolina St.	8	34
O12		‖	at North Carolina	7	38
O19	●	‖	Wake Forest	52	0
O26	●	‖	at Duke	22	19
N2		‖	at Clemson	3	35
N14	●	‖	Georgia Tech	13	10
N23		‖	Florida State *Mia*	10	48

RON VANDERLINDEN
1997-2000 (.341) 15-29

1997 — 2-9 (1-7)

S6			Ohio U.	14	21
S13		‖	at Florida State	7	50
S20		‖	North Carolina	14	40
S27	●		Temple *Phil*	24	21
O4	●	‖	Duke	16	10
O11			West Virginia	14	31
O18		‖	at Wake Forest	17	35
O25		‖	Clemson	9	20
N1		‖	Virginia	0	45
N8		‖	at North Carolina St.	28	45
N22		‖	at Georgia Tech	18	37

1998 — 3-8 (1-7)

S5	●		James Madison	23	15
S12		‖	at Virginia	19	31
S19			at West Virginia	20	42
S26	●		Temple	30	20
O3		‖	Florida State	10	24
O10		‖	at Clemson	0	23
O17		‖	Wake Forest	10	20
O31		‖	Georgia Tech *Balt*	14	31
N7		‖	at North Carolina	13	24
N14	●	‖	at Duke	42	25
N21		‖	North Carolina St.	21	35

1999 — 5-6 (2-6)

S2	●		at Temple	6	0
S11	●		Western Carolina	51	10
S18	●		West Virginia	33	0
S30		‖	at Georgia Tech	31	49
O9	●	‖	at Wake Forest	17	14
O16		‖	Clemson	30	42
O23	●	‖	North Carolina	45	7
O30		‖	Duke	22	25
N6		‖	at North Carolina St.	17	30
N13		‖	at Florida State	10	49
N20		‖	Virginia	30	34

2000 — 5-6 (3-5)

S9	●		Temple	17	10
S16			at West Virginia	17	30
S23	●		Middle Tennessee	45	27
S28		‖	Florida State	7	59
O7		‖	at Virginia	23	31
O14		‖	at Clemson	14	35
O21	●	‖	Wake Forest	37	7
O28	●	‖	at Duke	20	9
N4	●	‖	North Carolina St.	35	28
N11		‖	at North Carolina	10	13
N18		‖	Georgia Tech	22	35

RALPH FRIEDGEN
2001-PRESENT (.720) 36-14

2001 — 10-2 (7-1)

S1	●	‖	North Carolina	23	7
S8	●		Eastern Michigan	50	3
S22	●	‖	at Wake Forest	27	20
S29	●		West Virginia	32	20
O6	●	‖	Virginia	41	21
O11	●	‖	at Georgia Tech	20	17
O20	●	‖	Duke	59	17
O27		‖	at Florida State	31	52
N3	●		Troy State	47	14
N10	●	‖	Clemson	37	20
N17	●	‖	at North Carolina St.	23	19
			ORANGE BOWL		
J2			Florida	23	56

2002 — 11-3 (6-2)

A31			Notre Dame *ERut*	0	22
S7	●		Akron	44	14
S14		‖	Florida State	10	37
S21	●		Eastern Michigan	45	3
S28	●		Wofford	37	8
O5	●		at West Virginia	48	17
O17	●	‖	Georgia Tech	34	10
O26	●	‖	at Duke	45	12
N2	●	‖	at North Carolina	59	7
N9	●	‖	North Carolina St.	24	21
N16	●	‖	at Clemson	30	12
N23		‖	at Virginia	13	48
N30	●	‖	Wake Forest	32	14
			PEACH BOWL		
D31	●		Tennessee	30	3

2003 — 10-3 (6-2)

A28			at Northern Illinois	13	20
S6		‖	at Florida State	10	35
S13	●		Citadel	61	0
S20	●		West Virginia	34	7
S27	●		at Eastern Michigan	37	13
O4	●	‖	Clemson	21	7
O11	●	‖	Duke	33	20
O23		‖	at Georgia Tech	3	7
N1	●	‖	North Carolina	59	21
N13	●	‖	Virginia	27	17
N22	●	‖	at North Carolina St.	26	24
N29	●	‖	at Wake Forest	41	28
			GATOR BOWL		
J1	●		West Virginia	41	7

2004 — 5-6 (3-5)

S4	●		Northern Illinois	23	20
S11	●		Temple	45	22
S18			at West Virginia	16	19
S25	●	‖	at Duke	55	21
O9		‖	Georgia Tech	7	20
O16		‖	North Carolina St.	3	13
O23		‖	at Clemson	7	10
O30	●	‖	Florida State	20	17
N6		‖	at Virginia	0	16
N18		‖	at Virginia Tech	6	55
N27	●	‖	Wake Forest	13	7

f Forfeit † Game Later Forfieted # Disputed Victor * Disputed Score ‖ Designated Conference Game ‖2 Counted Twice in Conference Standings

MEMPHIS

BY KEVIN GLEASON

MEMPHIS HAS HAD FIVE DIFFER-ent names: West Tennessee State Normal School (1912), West Tennessee State Teachers College (1925), Memphis State College (1941), Memphis State University (1957) and, finally, the University of Memphis (1994). So it stands to reason that the football program has spent years searching for an identity.

The Tigers play in the shadow of in-state giant Tennessee. But Memphis has had its share of high points since the football program began in 1912. The 1929 Tigers went 8–0–2. In the 1940s, after the program was disbanded during World War II, Memphis had a strong return, going 9–1 in 1949. After a period in the 1980s and 1990s in which there was some doubt whether Memphis could remain competitive in major college football, the school rebounded in the new century under former Clemson coach Tommy West, who led the school to bowls in back-to-back seasons (2003 and 2004) for the first time in school history.

TRADITION During the 1950s, Memphis and Arkansas State came up with the Ole Paint Bucket trophy for the winner, in an attempt to keep students from painting their rival school's buildings the week before the game. Memphis won the first two Ole Paint Bucket games in 1956-57 by identical 34-0 scores before the series was ended. They next played 18 years later.

BEST COACH Billy J. Murphy had only two sub-.500 seasons as coach from 1958 to 1971 and remains Memphis' winningest coach at 91–44–1. Murphy recruited nationally while landing local stars such as early-1960s quarterback Russ Vollmer. Murphy was the 15th-winningest active coach in the country when he retired in 1972 to dedicate himself full-time to duties as the school's athletic director. Murphy promised to build a winner in five years. It took him one. Following a 4–5 record in Murphy's debut, Memphis rattled off five straight seasons with at least six wins. Murphy's other losing season was a 5–6 record in 1971. Memphis hasn't forgotten Murphy's effect on Tigers football. The school's 140-acre athletics complex—home of football, baseball, soccer and track—is known as the Billy J. Murphy Complex.

BEST PLAYER Running back Dave Casinelli, a star in the early 1960s, had eye-popping career numbers: 2,636 yards rushing, 36 rushing touchdowns. But tackle Harry Schuh

---

PROFILE

University of Memphis
Memphis, Tenn.
Founded: 1912
Enrollment: 15,928
Colors: Blue and Gray
Nickname: Tigers
Stadium: Liberty Bowl Memorial Stadium
  Opened in 1965
  Grass; 62,380 capacity
First football game: 1912
All-time record: 409–420–32 (.494)
Bowl record: 2–1
First-round NFL draftees: 4
Website: www.gotigersgo.com

THE BEST OF TIMES

Memphis survived the 1960s without a single losing record, going a combined 70–25–1 under legendary coach Billy J. Murphy. Only one team finished without a winning record, the 5–5 squad of 1965.

THE WORST OF TIMES

The Tigers lost 17 straight games in consecutive 1–10 seasons in 1981-82 under coach Rex Dockery. He led Memphis to a 6–4–1 record the following year. Dockery, offensive coordinator Chris Faros and DB Charles Greenhill were killed in a plane crash in Lawrenceburg, Tenn., on their way to an all-star banquet.

CONFERENCE

Memphis joined the Missouri Valley Conference in 1968 and won the league title that year. Memphis became a charter member of Conference USA in 1996. Though Memphis has never won a C-USA title, it finished in a second-place tie (4–2) in 1999 and was tied for third (5–3) in 2003.

DISTINGUISHED ALUMNI

Dixie Carter, actress; Kelly Cash, Miss America 1987; Anfernee "Penny" Hardaway, NBA player; Bill and Nancy Walton Laurie, owners, NHL St. Louis Blues; Fred Thompson, actor and U.S. senator

FIGHT SONG

THE U of M FIGHT SONG
Go Tigers Go, Go On To Victory,
Be A Winner Thru and Thru;
Fight Tigers, Fight Cause We're
Going All The Way
Fight, Fight
For The Blue And Gray And Say
Let's Go Tigers Go,
Go On To Victory.
See Our Colors Bright And True;
It's Fight Now Without A Fear,
Fight Now Let's Shout A Cheer,
Shout For Dear Memphis U.
(Yell)
Go Tigers Go
Go Tigers Go
Yea—Tiger Go!

Memphis may play in the shadow of Tennessee, but it's had some high points.

(1962-64) was the first Memphis player to receive first-team All-America recognition since the program became a major college in 1960. Selected seventh overall in the 1965 AFL draft, he gets the nod as the best player in Memphis history.

BEST TEAM The 1963 team was the first Memphis team since 1938 to go unbeaten. The Tigers beat such daunting opponents as Mississippi State, Southern Mississippi, Tulsa, Louisville and Houston. The one blemish to the 9–0–1 season came against second-ranked Ole Miss at Crump Stadium in Memphis. The Rebels hadn't been shut out in 47 games, the Tigers in 24 games, but they played to a 0-0 tie. Memphis wound up with five shutouts and allowed just 56 points. Running back Dave Casinelli became the only Memphis player to lead Division I-A in rushing (1,016 yards) and scoring (84 points). Billy J. Murphy was named national coach of the year by *The Detroit News* and Memphis received its first major bowl bid when the Sun Bowl called. But Memphis players and coaches voted to chase the more lucrative Gator. The bid never came, and Memphis stayed home.

BIGGEST GAME Memphis' 27-17 win over Mississippi in 1967 broke a 0–19–1 streak against Ole Miss; the only previous cause for cheering in Memphis was a 0-0 tie in 1963. Outside the tie, Memphis never got within 10 points of Ole Miss during the streak, losing by such scores of 92-0 (1935) and 82-0 (1921).

BIGGEST UPSET Tennessee, led by Peyton Manning, was ranked No. 6 in the country when it traveled to Memphis on a sunny November afternoon in 1996. Tennessee had beaten Memphis in all 15 games in the series. Tennessee led 7-0 late in the first half when Memphis' Keith Spann intercepted Manning's pass and went 76 yards to the 1. Quarterback Qadry Anderson took it in to tie the score at halftime. Tennessee again took a seven-point lead in the third quarter, and again Memphis answered emphatically, this time on kick returner Kevin Cobb's 95-yard return for a touchdown. Down 17-14, Memphis put together a 12-play, 70-yard drive capped by Chris Powers' touchdown catch with 34 seconds left to give the Tigers a 21-17 win. Cobb's return would win an ESPY as Play of the Year in college football.

RECORDS

RUSHING YARDS

	GAME
263	DeAngelo Williams vs. South Florida, Nov. 27, 2004 (28 att.)

	SEASON
1,948	DeAngelo Williams, 2004 (313)

	CAREER
4,062	DeAngelo Williams, 2002-04 (659 att.)

PASSING YARDS

	GAME
398	Danny Wimprine vs. Mississippi State, Oct. 11, 2003 (32 of 60)

	SEASON
3,174	Danny Wimprine, 2003 (246 of 440)

	CAREER
10,215	Danny Wimprine, 2001-04 (808 of 1,469)

RECEIVING YARDS

	GAME
186	Bob Sherlog vs. Mississippi State, Oct. 16, 1965 (10 rec.)

	SEASON
1,054	Isaac Bruce, 1993 (74 rec.)

	CAREER
2,126	Ernest Gray, 1975-78 (97 rec.)

POINTS

	GAME
24	Dante Brown vs. Houston, Oct. 13, 2001 (4 TDs)

	SEASON
138	DeAngelo Williams, 2004 (23 TDs)

	CAREER
263	Joe Allison, 1990-93 (51 FGs, 110 PATs)

CONSENSUS ALL-AMERICANS

1954	Robert Patterson, G
1992	Joe Allison, K

DISPUTE In 1963, Memphis quarterback Russ Vollmer was forced out of bounds on the Mississippi State sideline during a punt return. As he went to return to the playing field, a Mississippi State player tackled Vollmer, knocking him over the bench and down a concrete stairwell leading to the dressing rooms under Memphis' Crump Stadium. Vollmer hurt his back but, after a trip to the hospital, returned to the game to lead Memphis to a 17-10 win.

HEARTBREAKER In 1999, Memphis was up 16-10 in the closing minutes in Knoxville, headed for its second straight win over Tennessee. The Vols, ranked No. 7 and favored by 25 points, had one final drive. On fourth-and-long in Vols territory, quarterback Tee Martin was about to be sacked when he launched a 53-yard completion to Bobby Graham. Two plays later, Tennessee scored to win 17-16.

STADIUM In football circles, the Liberty Bowl is best known as the site of the bowl game of the same name, dedicated to the veterans of both World Wars and the Korean War. Memphis opened the stadium in 1965 with a 34-14 loss to 17th-ranked Mississippi. Major renovations in 1987 included a new lighting system, a fresh playing surface and the addition of 12,000 seats, bringing capacity to 62,380. The largest crowd for a Memphis game at the Liberty Bowl came in 1996, when 65,885 were on hand to see the Tigers' 21-17 upset of sixth-ranked Tennessee.

RIVAL For much of the Tigers' history, Mississippi was Memphis' greatest rival despite manhandling the Tigers in winning 19 of their first 20 meetings. The one blemish was a 0-0 tie in 1963. Memphis coach Billy J. Murphy and Ole Miss' John Vaught became close friends, and Ole Miss helped give the Tigers' program credibility by playing them almost annually. The same couldn't be said for Tennessee, which balked at playing the Tigers. Memphis had to take its argument to local government before Tennessee agreed to start the series in 1968. Memphis was about to attempt to have a bill passed forcing Tennessee to play when the two schools' presidents met with governor Buford Ellington and forged an agreement. They now meet on a semiregular basis.

NICKNAME The name dates to 1915, when Memphis, then known as West Tennessee State Normal School, finished with four wins. A student parade followed the last win and several students shouted, "We fight like tigers!" But the nickname went on a 14-year hiatus when the school's name was changed to West Tennessee State Teachers College, leading to the team being called Teachers and Tutors. Tigers wouldn't return until 1939.

MASCOT The Bengal tiger has been the Memphis mascot for three decades. The first tiger, TOM (the acronym for Tigers of Memphis) took over in 1972 and lived for 20 years. At 550 pounds, TOM was once the largest Bengal tiger in captivity. When TOM arrived in Memphis, a press conference was held for him in athletic director Billy J. Murphy's office. Memphis held a contest to rename the tiger, originally named Shane. TOM prevailed. TOM II came to Memphis in 1992 and is housed at Nixon Farms in Collierville, Tenn., a 3,500-square-foot setting that includes two pools, a waterfall and a den box complete with heat and air-conditioning.

UNIFORMS Students in Memphis' first class, 1912, chose blue and gray as school colors. The colors commemorate members of the opposing armies during the Civil War to symbolize the reuniting of the country following the historical conflict. In 1972, the Tigers went to a Dallas Cowboys look: blue jerseys and silver helmets featuring white letters outlined in navy that formed an interlocking MSU. The helmet changed often, featuring "Tigers" on both sides during the Rex Dockery era in the early 1990s. Later that decade, the helmet featured a tiger's head on both sides meeting in the back, reminiscent of the hawk design on the helmets of the NFL Seattle Seahawks. In the early 1990s, Memphis went to royal blue (jersey) and gray (pants). The helmet was silver with MSU on the side again. The main changes since then have been a blue helmet and a new logo: an M with a leaping tiger coming up over the center. As previously noted, Memphis has always struggled to find an identity. And hang onto it.

QUOTE "No one else would have been tough enough to build a program there. Billy Murphy built Memphis State football into what it is today. If he had been on my staff, we would have won the world."

—Mississippi coach John Vaught

MEMPHIS ANNUAL STATISTICAL LEADERS

YR	RUSHING	YDS	ATT	AVG	PASSING	ATT	CMP	PCT	YDS	RECEIVING	REC	YDS	AVG
1953	Sonny Rodgers	448	NA	NA		NA	NA	NA	NA		NA	NA	NA
1954	Jim Shelton	366	81	4.5		NA	NA	NA	NA		NA	NA	NA
1955	Bobby Brooks	293	63	4.7		NA	NA	NA	NA		NA	NA	NA
1956	Bobby Brooks	378	67	5.6	James Armstrong	49	18	.37	338	Carlos Brooks	67	378	5.6
1957	Frank Massa	261	60	4.4	Jim Leonard	27	11	.41	149	John Ruth	5	93	18.6
1958		NA	NA	NA		NA	NA	NA	NA		NA	NA	NA
1959	James Wright	310	66	4.7	Fred Hearn	30	13	.43	184	Don Coffey	8	192	24.0
1960	Lennie Kaplan	324	69	4.7	Nick Bouni	62	26	.42	475	Don Coffey	10	188	18.8
1961	Dave Casinelli	646	117	5.5	James Earl Wright	67	35	.52	604	Don Coffey	18	312	17.3
1962	Dave Casinelli	826	173	4.8	Russell Vollmer	87	39	.45	555	John Griffin	14	220	15.7
1963	Dave Casinelli	1,016	219	4.6	Russell Vollmer	58	29	.50	466	Bob Sherlag	8	183	22.9
1964	Billy Fletcher	367	92	4.0	Billy Fletcher	160	69	.43	921	Billy Ray Farmer	19	222	11.7
1965	Billy Fletcher	556	109	5.1	Billy Fletcher	256	92	.36	1,239	Bob Sherlag	46	673	14.6
1966	Terry Padgett	539	142	3.8	Terry Padgett	73	26	.36	348	Dale Brady	11	176	16.0
1967	Ricky Thurow	394	88	4.5	Terry Padgett	70	31	.44	436	Rich Coady	18	260	14.4
1968	Ray Jamieson	573	123	4.7	Danny Pierce	137	56	.41	925	Preston Riley	21	484	23.0
1969	Paul Skeeter Gowen	715	117	6.1	Danny Pierce	139	61	.44	1,049	Frank Blackwell	31	591	19.1
1970	Paul Skeeter Gowen	868	145	6.0	Rick Strawbridge	80	39	.49	557	Bill Wright	17	206	12.1
1971	Paul Skeeter Gowen	644	149	4.3	John Robinson	80	31	.39	496	Stan Davis	34	509	15.0
1972	Dornell Harris	698	132	5.3	Al Harvey	179	90	.50	961	Stan Davis	39	476	12.2
1973	Dornell Harris	564	109	5.2	Joe Bruner	118	61	.52	785	Bobby Ward	43	744	17.3
1974	Reuben Gibson	493	116	4.3	David Fowler	193	103	.53	1,266	James Thompson	40	395	9.9
1975	Terdell Middleton	586	138	4.2	Lloyd Patterson	72	30	.42	371	Ricky Rivas	18	224	12.4
1976	Terdell Middleton	919	160	5.7	Lloyd Patterson	178	87	.49	1,563	Earnest Gray *	29	529	18.2
1977	James King	626	168	3.7	Lloyd Patterson	169	73	.43	1,336	Earnest Gray	28	826	29.5
1978	Eddie Hill	739	126	5.9	Lloyd Patterson	141	56	.40	931	Earnest Gray	35	690	19.7
1979	Leo Cage	599	128	4.7	Kevin Betts	154	64	.42	884	Tony Hunt	15	234	15.6
1980	Richard Williams	438	80	5.5	Darrell Martin	185	73	.39	888	Jerry Knowlton	27	470	17.4
1981	Tony Wiley	497	123	4.0	Tom Smith	96	43	.45	466	Jerry Knowlton	18	244	13.6
1982	Richard Williams	480	89	5.4	Trell Hooper	201	112	.56	1,194	Derrick Crawford	32	523	16.3
1983	Punkin Williams	546	123	4.4	Danny Sparkman	216	105	.49	1,390	Derrick Crawford	31	594	19.2
1984	Punkin Williams	832	137	6.1	Danny Sparkman	174	81	.47	1,315	Edwin Lovelady	19	345	18.2
1985	Jeff Womack	306	89	3.4	Danny Sparkman	272	142	.52	1,606	Jerry Harris	30	519	17.3
1986	Wayne Pryor	501	129	3.9	Tom Branner	84	41	.49	412	Jerry Harris	29	338	11.7
1987	Wayne Pryor	647	145	4.5	Tim Jones	95	54	.57	709	Charles Wilson	20	393	19.7
1988	Wayne Pryor	412	111	3.7	Rusty Trail	152	79	.52	1,231	Charles Wilson	33	554	16.8
1989	Marvin Cox	844	193	4.4	Tim Jones	144	73	.51	1,017	Russell Copeland	22	333	15.1
1990	Keith Benton	612	148	4.1	Keith Benton	176	76	.43	1,265	Russell Jones	33	684	20.7
1991	Larry Porter	454	116	3.9	Keith Benton	199	90	.45	1,203	John Bush	25	420	16.8
1992	Larry Porter	732	140	5.2	Steve Matthews	286	175	.61	2,084	Russell Copeland	61	736	12.1
1993	Larry Porter	540	126	4.3	Steve Matthews	273	166	.61	1,896	Isaac Bruce	74	1,054	14.2
1994	Marcus Holliday	618	145	4.3	Tony Scarpino	148	70	.47	738	Ryan Roskelly	44	602	13.7
1995	Quitman Spaulding	383	100	3.8	Joe Borich	161	81	.50	896	Ryan Roskelly	34	361	10.6
1996	Teofilo Riley	572	145	3.9	Qadry Anderson	287	141	.49	1,557	Richie Floyd	43	600	14.0
1997	Gerald Arnold	613	145	4.2	Bernard Oden	316	170	.54	2,249	Richie Floyd	38	617	16.2
1998	Gerald Arnold	1,059	208	5.1	Neil Suber	124	61	.49	930	Damien Dodson	42	753	17.9
1999	Gerald Arnold	706	146	4.8	Travis Anglin	125	68	.54	856	Damien Dodson	39	507	13.0
2000	Sugar Sanders	646	167	3.9	Scott Scherer	154	85	.55	857	Bunkie Perkins	33	314	9.5
2001	Dante Brown	902	184	4.9	Danny Wimprine	196	102	.52	1,329	Antoine Harden	31	589	19.0
2002	DeAngelo Williams	684	103	6.6	Danny Wimprine	435	235	.54	2,820	Travis Anglin	55	740	13.5
2003	DeAngelo Williams	1,430	243	5.9	Danny Wimprine	440	246	.56	3,174	Maurice Avery	49	742	15.1
2004	DeAngelo Williams	1,948	313	6.2	Danny Wimprine	398	225	.57	2,892	Tavares Gideon	54	665	12.3

* Tied with Ricky Rivas in yardage (26-529-20.3)

The NCAA began including postseason stats in 2002

MEMPHIS ALL-TIME SCORES

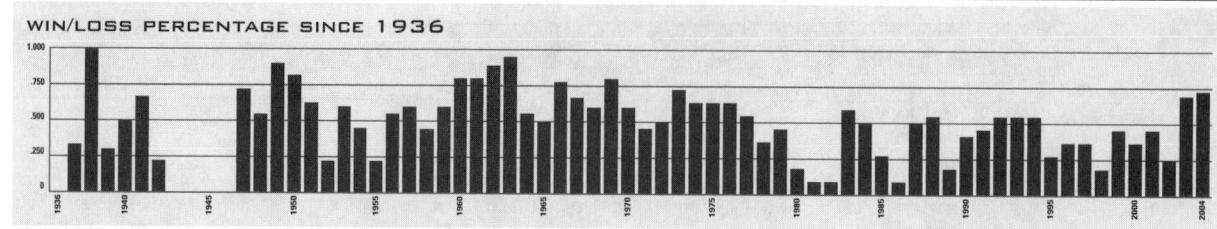

WIN/LOSS PERCENTAGE SINCE 1936

CLYDE WILSON
1912-15 (.409)   9-12-1

1912   1-2-1
O5	=	Memphis U.	0	2
O26	●	Bolten Coll.	13	0
N8		Christian Bro.	0	13
N16		Memphis U. Sch	0	2

1913   1-2-0
O17		Memphis Central HS	0	67
N8	=	M. U. Sch.	6	19
N15	●	Somerville HS	13	0

1914   3-5-0
O9	●	at Oscelo AC	14	0
O16		Memphis Central HS	0	19
O24		CBC	0	9
O27		at Arkansas State	6	18
O31	●	at Bolton HS	13	9
N7		Somerville HS	26	0
N21		at Ole Miss JV	0	31
N25		at Jackson HS	6	16

1915   4-3-0
O8		at Arkansas State	0	41
O16	●	Somerville HS	75	0
O22		Memphis Central HS	0	59
N5		Memphis U.	0	14
N8	●	CBC	53	18
N13		1st Bat. Tn. Guard	45	0
N25		at Brownsville HS	13	7

TOM SHEA
1916 (.417)   2-3-1

1916   2-3-1
O14	●	Somerville HS	115	0
O21	●	Jackson HS	24	0
O27	=	at Haywood HS	7	7
N11		at Union	6	7
N19		Memphis Central HS	0	49
N30		at Arkansas State	0	27

V.M. "BIC" CAMPBELL
1917, '19 (.500)   6-6

1917   3-2-0
O19		at Arkansas State	0	19
O27	●	Jackson HS	14	3
N5	●	at Union	14	6
N17		Memphis U. Sch.	20	6
N24		Memphis Central HS	0	33

JOHN CHILDERSON
1918 (.333)   2-4

1918   2-4-0
N2		Castle Heights	6	36
N9		Memphis U. Sch.	0	11
N16		Memphis Central HS	0	30
N23	●	at Union	18	0
N28	=	at Arkansas JV	37	6
D7		Central All Stars	7	13

V.M. "BIC" CAMPBELL

1919   3-4-0
O10		at Union	0	7
O17		at Arkansas State	0	6
N1	●	CBC	27	0
N8		Memphis U. Sch.	6	12
N15	●	Memphis Central HS	26	0
N21	●	Vocational HS	25	6
N27		at McKenzie-McTyeire	7	35

ELMORE GEORGE
1920 (.000)   0-5

1920   0-5-0
O11		at Arkansas State	0	13
O23		Union	0	19
O30		at Little Rock Coll.	0	41
N1		at Central Arkansas	0	35
N11		at Paragould HS	7	35

ROLLIN WILSON
1921 (.450)   4-5-1

1921   4-5-1
O1		at Mississippi	0	82
O15	●	Ford Kelvington	20	0
O18		Memphis U. Sch.	0	32
O28		at Union	7	28
N4	●	Memphis Central HS	13	6
N11		at Arkansas State	0	19
N18		CBC	13	25
N22	●	at Wilson HS	14	0
N24	●	at Haywood HS	12	7
N26	=	Tennessee JV	7	7

LESTER BARNHARD
1922-23 (.657)   11-5-3

1922   5-2-3
S29	●	Tupelo Military	6	0
O6		Memphis U. Sch.	6	7
O13	=	at Blytheville HS	6	6
O15	=	at Wilson HS	0	0
O21		at Arkansas Coll.	0	13
O27	●	CBC	36	0
N3	=	at Central Arkansas	0	0
N10	●	Southwestern	26	0
N24	●	Arkansas State	68	0
N30	●	at Bethel	26	0

1923   6-3-0
S29		at Springfield	0	20
O6		Tenn. Doctors	7	19
O12	●	at Hendrix	9	6
O19	●	Bethel	12	0
O22	●	Southwestern	15	0
O25	●	Mississippi Heights	14	0
O27	●	at Arkansas State	6	0
N3		at Little Rock Coll.	0	3
N10	●	at Central Arkansas	14	7

ZACH CURLIN
1924-36 (.427)   43-60-14

1924   1-7-1
O3		at Hendrix	0	51
O10		at Arkansas Coll.	0	49
O17	●	Arkansas State	33	6
O25		at Union	0	25
O31		Mississippi Heights	7	18
N15		at Bethel	0	6
N22		Hall Moody	0	26
N23		Tenn. Doctors	0	58
N27	=	at Murray Normal	0	0

1925   0-7-1
S25	=	at Arkansas State	6	6
O3		at Union	13	50
O9		at Arkansas State	0	19
O23		Hall Moody	6	15
O29		at Hendrix	6	54
N6		at Bethel	0	7
N13		at Middle Tennessee	7	57
N26		Southwestern	6	31

1926   1-8-0
S25		at Jonesboro Coll.	19	0
O2		Tenn. Doctors	0	21
O9		Arkansas State	0	7
O16		at Lambuth	0	7
O22		Middle Tennessee	0	27
O29		Bethel	0	13
N6		at Union	0	21
N13		Southwestern	6	27
N19		at Little Rock Coll.	14	48

1927   5-3-1
S24	●	Arkansas State	48	0
O1		Will Mayfield	7	0
O8	●	Delta St.	21	0
O14		at Middle Tennessee	7	47
O22	●	Bethel	27	13
O29	●	Lambuth	20	7
N5		at Araknsas A&M	6	9
N12		Southwestern	6	26
N24	=	at Murray St.	14	14

1928   5-3-2
S28	●	Sunflower JC	19	0
O6		Tennessee JC	60	0
O13	●	at Delta St.	12	0
O19	●	at Will Mayfield	34	0
O26		Middle Tennessee	13	13
N3		Arkansas State	19	14
N10		Southwestern	0	47
N16	=	Bethel	0	0
N24		Murray St.	0	40
N29		at Cumberland	0	6

1929   8-0-2
S27	●	Sunflower JC	20	0
O4	=	SE. Missouri St.	0	0
O11	●	Caruthersville JC	26	0
O19	●	at Tennessee JC	13	2
O25	●	Cumberland	12	6
N1	●	at Arkansas State	6	0
N8	●	at Bethel	10	0
N15	=	Delta St.	0	0
N23	●	at Murray St.	27	13
N28	●	Little Rock Coll.	32	6

1930   6-3-1
S27		at Milsaps	0	40
O4	●	Arkansas State	73	0
O11	●	Caruthersville JC	25	13
O17	●	at Lambuth	14	6
O24	=	at SE. Missouri St.	0	0
N1		Arkansas State	6	13
N8		at Delta St.	0	7
N14	●	Bethel	20	0
N22	●	Murray St.	10	0
N28	●	Tennessee JC	14	13

1931   2-5-2
O3	●	Lambuth	13	0
O9	=	at Bethel	0	0
O17	=	at Caruthersville JC	0	0
O24		Tennessee Tech	0	13
O30		at Arkansas State	6	14
N7		at Middle Tennessee	0	15
N14		Delta St.	6	32
N20	●	at Bethel	6	0
N27		at Murray St.	2	28

1932   4-5-0
O1	●	at Arkansas Coll.	20	0
O8		Bethel	0	6
O15		at Tennessee Tech	7	24
O21		at SE. Missouri St.	7	0
N2		Arkansas State	6	12
N5		Middle Tennessee	0	6
N11	●	at Delta St.	13	0
N19	●	Tennessee JC	6	0
N24		Murray St.	2	6

1933   7-1-1
S30	●	SE. Missouri St.	18	0
O6	●	at Bethel	20	13
O12	●	at Arkansas Coll.	18	6
O21	●	Freed Hardeman	51	0
O28	●	Western Kentucky	0	19
N3	●	at Middle Tennessee	20	6
N18	●	Tennessee Tech	13	0
N24	=	at Arkansas State	0	0
N30	●	at Union	7	0

1934   3-3-2
S29		at Mississippi	0	44
O6	=	at Western Kentucky	0	0
O13	●	Arkansas State	18	0
O19		at SE. Missouri St.	0	6
O26		at Union	6	13
N3	●	Middle Tennessee	18	0
N16	=	at Tennessee Tech	0	0
N24	●	Sunflower JC	33	0

1935   1-6-1
S28		at Mississippi	0	92
O4		at Arkansas State	0	18
O12		Arkansas Teachers	0	19
O18		at Middle Tennessee	0	35
O26		Southern Miss	0	12
N8		Union	0	33
N16	=	Tennessee Tech	0	0
N23	●	Delta St.	30	0

1936   0-9-0
S25		at Delta St.	7	33
O2		at Louisiana Tech	0	44
O9		at Tennessee Tech	0	25
O17		Louisiana Coll.	0	12
O23		Southern Miss	0	25
O31		Middle Tennessee	0	19
N7		Murray St.	6	20
N14		at Arkansas Teachers	0	54
N21		Union	0	50

ALLYN McKEEN
1937-38 (.684)   13-6

1937   3-6-0
S24		at Middle Tennessee	6	20
O2	●	Austin Peay	26	0
O8	●	at Union	13	2
O16		Delta St.	14	19
O23		at Louisiana Coll.	0	7
O29	●	Jacksonville	46	0
N5		at Murray St.	0	19
N12		Tennessee Tech	13	14
N19		Troy State	6	12

1938   10-0-0
S16	●	at Milsaps	19	0
S24	●	Louisiana Coll.	14	6
O1	●	at Arkansas State	38	2
O7	●	Cumberland	68	0
O15	●	Middle Tennessee	25	7
O21	●	at Tennessee Tech	26	13
O29	●	Arkansas State	50	0
N5	●	Troy State	20	6
N11	●	Union	13	7
N18	●	at Delta St.	8	0

C.C. HUMPHREYS
1939-41 (.483)   14-15

1939   3-7-0
S23		at Louisiana Coll.	15	19
S29	●	Arkansas State	6	7
O6		at Union	12	13
O13	●	at Middle Tennessee	25	6
O21		Western Kentucky	0	12
O28		Tennessee Tech	0	15
N3	●	at Troy State	13	7
N11	●	Delta St.	7	0
N18		at Mississippi	7	46
N25		Milsaps	0	2

1940 5-5-0
S21	•	Austin Peay	40	0
S28		Southwestern	0	34
O4		at Tennessee Tech	13	16
O12	•	Middle Tennessee	14	7
O19	•	Louisiana Coll.	26	13
O26	•	at Delta St.	7	0
N2	•	at Troy State	31	7
N9		at Murray St.	6	35
N16		Mississippi	7	38
N23		Union	6	22

1941 6-3-0
S23		Southwestern	7	13
O3	•	Milsaps	21	6
O11	•	Livingston St.	38	0
O17	•	at Union	7	6
O24	•	Delta St.	23	7
O31		at Middle Tennessee	12	13
N8		at Murray St.	6	31
N15	•	Troy State	32	0
N21	•	at Austin Peay	26	0

CHARLIE JAMERSON
1942 (.222) 2-7

1942 2-7-0
S24		Middle Tennessee	13	21
O2		Ouachita	7	32
O9	•	at Springfield	6	0
O17		Union	0	39
O24		at U.T. Chattanooga	19	44
O31		at Mississippi	0	48
N5	•	Murray St.	21	0
N13		at SE. Louisiana	14	38
N21		Louisiana Tech	7	33

1943-1945
NO TEAM WWII

1946
NO TEAM

RALPH HATLEY
1947-57 (.575) 59-43-5

1947 6-2-1
S25		at Middle Tennessee	0	20
O4	•	Missouri Mines	13	0
O11	•	Centenary	26	7
O17		at Murray St.	7	14
O23	•	at Union	21	0
N1	•	Pensacola NAS	54	0
N7	•	at NATTC	58	0
N17	=	Arkansas State	19	19
N22	•	Austin Peay	40	0

1948 6-5-0
S18		at Missouri Mines	0	6
S25	•	Louisville	13	7
O1		Murray St.	14	26
O9	•	Tampa	43	16
O16		at Pensacola NAS	21	27
O23	•	at Athens Coll.	45	0
O30	•	Union	21	0
N6	•	Middle Tennessee	13	0
N11		at NATTC	0	14
N19	•	Arkansas State	34	13
N25		at Louisiana Tech	14	20

1949 9-1-0
S16		Mississippi	7	40
S23	•	at Tampa	70	6
O1	•	at Washington, Mo.	34	0
O8	•	Delta St.	47	0
O15	•	Pensacola NAS	49	0
O22	•	Kansas State	21	14
O29	•	at Murray St.	34	6
N5	•	Louisiana Coll.	27	0
N12	•	at Arkansas State	61	7
N19	•	at Union	35	0

1950 9-2-0
S16	•	Union	64	0
S22		Mississippi	7	39
S30	•	Memphis Navy	76	7
O6	•	at U.T. Chattanooga	26	8
O14	•	Washington, Mo.	54	0
O21	•	La. Lafayette	20	0
O28	•	at Murray St.	23	6
N4	•	at Louisiana Coll.	25	12
N11	•	Arkansas State	60	7
N18		Vanderbilt	13	29
D1	•	at Louisiana Tech	6	0

1951 5-3-0
S21		Mississippi	0	32
O6	•	Louisiana Tech	26	14
O20	•	at La. Lafayette	41	7
O27	•	Western Kentucky	38	0
N3	•	Ea. Cent. Okla.	61	0
N10		Mississippi State	20	27
N17	•	U.T. Chattanooga	13	0
N24		at Vanderbilt	7	13

1952 2-7-0
S19		Mississippi	6	54
S27		at Southern Miss	20	27
O4		at Louisiana Tech	7	26
O11	•	Murray St.	34	7
O17		at U.T. Chattanooga	6	23
O25		North Texas	14	38
N8	•	Louisville	29	25
N15		at Tennessee Tech	0	35
N22		SE. Louisiana	25	28

1953 6-4-0
S19		Mississippi State	6	34
S25	•	at U.T. Chattanooga	7	6
O3	•	Louisiana Tech	13	7
O10	•	at Murray St.	20	0
O17	•	Tennessee Tech	14	7
O24		at Middle Tennessee	20	26
O31	•	Southern Miss	27	13
N7		Arkansas State	0	20
N14		Kentucky	7	20
N21	•	at SE. Louisiana	21	7

1954 3-4-3
S18		at Mississippi State	7	27
S25	=	at Tulane	13	13
O2	=	Abilene Christian	6	6
O9	•	Murray St.	34	6
O16	=	at Tennessee Tech	25	25
O23	•	Middle Tennessee	27	7
O30	•	Arkansas State	26	7
N6		Mississippi	0	51
N13		at Kentucky	7	33
N20		at Southern Miss	21	34

1955 2-7-0
S24		Trinity	0	6
O1		at Mississippi State	0	33
O8	•	at Murray St.	20	7
O15	•	Tennessee Tech	20	12
O21		Southern Miss	14	34
O29		Arkansas State	20	21
N5		Mississippi	6	39
N12		at Kentucky	7	41
N24		at U.T. Chattanooga	7	25

1956 5-4-1
S15	•	Arkansas State	32	21
S22	=	at Tennessee Tech	14	14
S29		at Trinity	0	19
O6		U.T. Chattanooga	13	14
O13	•	Austin Peay	42	19
O20		at Southern Miss	0	27
O27	•	Western Kentucky	42	0
N3	•	at Arkansas State	34	0
N10		Mississippi	0	26
N22	•	at Ea. Tenn. St.	32	12

1957 6-4-0
S21	•	Arkansas State	20	6
S28		at Mississippi State	6	10
O5	•	Austin Peay	41	0
O12	•	Tennessee Tech	40	7
O19		Southern Miss	6	14
N2		at Kentucky	7	53
N9	•	Arkansas State	34	0
N16	•	at Louisiana Tech	17	7
N23	•	Ea. Tenn. St.	24	7
N28		at U.T. Chattanooga	0	7

BILLY J. MURPHY
1958-71 (.673) 91-44-1

1958 4-5-0
S20		Mississippi	0	17
S27	•	at Tennessee Tech	13	0
O4		at Southern Miss	22	24
O11		at Mississippi State	6	28
O18		Citadel	26	28
O25	•	U.T. Chattanooga	22	7
N1	•	Louisiana Tech	26	12
N8	•	Louisiana Coll.	27	14
N22		at Alabama	0	14

1959 6-4-0
S19	•	Stephen F. Austin	25	6
S26	•	Tennessee Tech	14	3
O3		at Mississippi	0	43
O10	•	Abilene Christian	13	7
O17	•	Florida State	16	6
O24		at Mississippi State	23	28
O31	•	Southern Miss	21	6
N14		at Louisiana Tech	8	10
N21		at Alabama	7	14
N26	•	at U.T. Chattanooga	15	9

1960 8-2-0
S17	•	Texas Arlington	35	0
S24	•	Tennessee Tech	37	6
O1		Mississippi	20	31
O8	•	at North Texas	44	0
O15	•	Hardin Simmons	42	7
O22		at Mississippi State	0	21
O29	•	VMI	21	8
N5	•	Abilene Christian	55	6
N12	•	U.T. Chattanooga	42	0
N18	•	at Southern Miss	7	6

1961 8-2-0
S16	•	Citadel	40	0
S23	•	at Tulsa	48	12
S30	•	Hardin Simmons	56	0
O7	•	at Louisville	28	13
O14	•	Southern Miss	21	7
O21	•	Abilene Christian	35	0
O28		Mississippi State	16	23
N4		Furman	6	7
N11	•	North Texas	41	0
N23	•	at U.T. Chattanooga	41	13

1962 8-1-0
S15	•	Tennessee Tech	12	6
S22		Mississippi	7	21
S29	•	at North Texas	14	6
O6	•	Louisville	49	0
O13	•	Southern Miss	8	6
O27	•	at Mississippi State	28	7
N10	•	at Citadel	60	13
N17	•	Texas Arlington	50	0
N24	•	Detroit	33	8

1963 9-0-1
S14	•	Southern Miss *JaM*	28	7
S21	=	Mississippi	0	0
O5	•	Tulsa	28	15
O12	•	North Texas	21	0
O19	•	at West Texas St.	29	14
O26	•	Mississippi State	17	10
N2	•	at Louisville	25	0
N9	•	South Carolina	9	0
N16	•	U.T. Chattanooga	13	0
N30	•	Houston	29	6

1964 5-4-0
S19		at Mississippi	0	30
O3	•	Tampa	13	0
O10		Southern Miss	14	20
O17	•	at West Texas St.	41	0
O24	•	Mc Neese St.	23	0
O31	•	Wake Forest	23	14
N7		at Tulsa	7	19
N14	•	Louisville	34	0
N21		Southern Miss *JaM*	18	20

1965 5-5-0
S18		Mississippi	14	34
S25		Southern Miss *JaM*	16	21
O9		at Tulsa	28	32
O16	•	Mississippi State	33	13
O23	•	Mc Neese St.	28	0
O30	•	West Texas St.	27	12
N6	•	Utah State	7	0
N13	•	at North Texas	28	0
N20		Wake Forest	20	21
N27		at Quantico Marines	14	20

1966 7-2-0
S17		Mississippi	0	13
S24	•	at South Carolina	16	7
O1	•	Southern Miss	6	0
O15	•	Quantico Marines	20	14
O22	•	Tulsa	6	0
O29	•	at West Texas St.	26	14
N12		at Wake Forest	7	21
N19	•	Cincinnati	26	14
N26	•	at Houston	14	13

1967 6-3-0
S23	•	Mississippi	27	17
S30	•	Cincinnati	17	0
O7		Utah State *SLC*	14	28
O14	•	Wake Forest	42	10
O21	•	La. Lafayette	28	6
O28	•	Southern Miss *JaM*	24	8
N4		Florida State	7	26
N11		at Houston	18	35
N25	•	North Texas	29	20

1968-1972
MISSOURI VALLEY

1968 6-4-0 (5-0-0)
S21		Mississippi	7	21
S28		at Tennessee	17	24
O5	• |	at North Texas	30	12
O12	•	West Texas St.	42	21
O19		at Florida State	10	20
O26	• |	Southern Miss	29	7
N2	• |	at Tulsa	32	6
N9		Houston	7	27
N16	• |	Wichita St.	40	18
N30	• |	at Louisville	44	14

1969 8-2-0 (4-0-0)
S20		at Mississippi	3	28
S27	• |	North Texas	15	13
O4		Tennessee	16	55
O11	• |	at Cincinnati	52	6
O18	•	Miami, Fla.	26	13
O25	•	at Utah State	40	0
N1	• |	Tulsa	42	24
N8	•	Southern Miss	37	7
N15	•	at Florida State	28	26
N22	• |	Louisville	69	19

1970 6-4-0 (2-2-0)
S19		Mississippi	13	47
S26	•	at Virginia Tech	21	20
O3	|	at Tulsa	12	27
O17	•	Florida State	16	12
O24	• |	at North Texas	28	7
O31	•	Southern Miss	33	0
N7	|	at Louisville	27	40
N14	• |	Wichita St.	51	6
N21		Utah State	12	15
N28	•	Cincinnati	14	10

1971 5-6-0 (2-1-0)
S11	• |	West Texas St.	30	0
S18		Mississippi	21	49
O2		South Carolina	3	7
O9	|	Louisville	20	26
O16		at Utah State	6	7
O23	•	Southern Miss	27	12
O30	•	at Cincinnati	45	21
N6		Houston	7	35
N13	• |	North Texas	47	8
N20		Kansas State	21	28
		PASADENA BOWL		
D18	•	San Jose State	28	9

FRED PANCOAST
1972-74 (.621) 20-12-1

1972 5-5-1 (3-2-0)
S16		Mississippi	29	34
S23	|	Drake	7	23
S30		at South Carolina	7	34
O7		Tennessee	7	38
O14	•	Utah State	38	29
O21	• |	North Texas *IRV*	7	6
O28	• |	Tulsa	49	21
N4	• |	Wichita St.	58	14
N11	•	Cincinnati	49	24
N18	|	at Louisville	0	17
D2	=	Southern Miss *JaM*	14	14

1973-1995
INDEPENDENT

1973 8-3-0
S8	•	Louisville	28	21
S15	•	North Texas	24	3
S22	•	Mississippi *JaM*	17	13
S29		Houston	21	35
O6		at Kansas State	16	21
O13	•	Tulsa	28	16
O20	•	at Florida State	13	10
N3	•	Virginia Tech	49	16
N10		Southern Miss	10	13
N17	•	La. Lafayette	41	6
N24	•	at Cincinnati	17	13

1974 — 7-4-0

S7	●	at Louisville	16	10
S14		Southern Miss	0	6
S21	●	Mississippi	15	7
S28		at Colorado State	20	18
O12		Cincinnati	13	7
O19	●	Mississippi State	28	29
O26	●	at North Texas	41	0
N2	●	Florida State	42	14
N9		at Tennessee	6	34
N16	●	at Houston	10	13
N23	●	Wichita St.	34	10

RICHARD WILLIAMSON
1975-80 (.470)   31-35

1975 — 7-4-0

S6		Mississippi State	7	17
S13	●	at Auburn	31	20
S20		at Cincinnati	3	13
S27		Arkansas State	10	29
O4	●	North Texas	21	19
O11	●	Southern Miss	7	21
O18	●	Louisville	41	7
O25		at Tulsa	16	14
N1	●	at Wichita St.	13	7
N8	●	at Florida State	17	14
N15		Houston	14	7

1976 — 7-4-0

S4	●	Mississippi	21	16
S11	●	Florida State	21	12
S18	●	at Tulsa	14	16
O2	●	SMU	27	13
O9	●	Auburn	28	27
O16		Mississippi State	33	42 †
O23	●	Wichita St.	31	0
O30	●	at Tulane	14	7
N6		Tennessee	14	21
N13	●	at Louisville	26	14
N20		at Southern Miss	12	14

1977 — 6-5-0

S3		Mississippi JaM	3	7
S10	●	Tulane	27	9
S17	●	Utah State	31	26
S24	●	Virginia Tech	21	20
O1		Louisville	13	14
O15	●	Mississippi State	21	13
O22	●	North Texas	19	20
O29	●	Southern Miss	42	14
N5		at Tennessee	14	27
N12	●	at Florida State	9	30
N19	●	at Wichita St.	28	14

1978 — 4-7-0

S9	●	Mississippi JaM	7	14
S16	●	Houston	17	3
S23	●	Mississippi State	14	44
S30		at Texas A&M	0	58
O14	●	Wichita St.	26	13
O21	●	Southern Miss	10	13
O28		at Tulane	24	41
N4	●	Vanderbilt	35	14
N11	●	at Louisville	29	22
N18	●	North Texas	24	41
N25		Cincinnati	14	34

1979 — 5-6-0

S8	●	Mississippi State JaM	14	13
S15	●	Mississippi	34	38
S22	●	at Wichita St.	16	10
S29		Texas A&M	7	17
O13		La. Monroe	20	21
O20		at Southern Miss	0	22
O27	●	North Texas	22	0
N3		at Vanderbilt	3	13
N10	●	Louisville	10	6
N17		at Florida State	17	66
N24	●	Cincinnati	23	17

1980 — 2-9-0

S6		Mississippi State	7	34
S13		at Mississippi	7	61
S27		at Georgia Tech	8	17
O4	●	Arkansas State	24	3
O11		at Louisville	14	38
O18	●	North Texas	10	29
O25		Florida State	3	24
N1		Vanderbilt	10	14
N8		at Cincinnati	10	14
N15		at Tulane	16	21
N22	●	Wichita St.	6	0

REX DOCKERY
1981-83 (.258)   8-24-1

1981 — 1-10-0

S5		Mississippi State JaM	3	20
S12		at Florida State	5	10
S19		Mississippi	3	7
S26	●	at Georgia Tech	28	15
O3		at Virginia Tech	13	17
O10		Louisville	7	14
O17		Southern Miss	0	10
O24		Tennessee	9	28
O31		at Vanderbilt	0	26
N7		at Cincinnati	7	38
N14		Tulane	7	24

1982 — 1-10-0

S4		at Mississippi	10	27
S11		Vanderbilt	14	24
S18		Mississippi State	17	41
S25		Georgia Tech	20	24
O2		at Southern Miss	14	34
O16		Cincinnati	7	16
O23		at Tulane	10	17
O30		at Georgia	3	34
N6		at Tennessee	3	29
N20		Louisville	19	38
N27		Arkansas State	12	0

1983 — 6-4-1

S3	●	Mississippi	37	17
S10		at North Carolina	10	24
S17		Virginia Tech	10	17
O1		at Alabama	13	44
O8	●	Tulane	28	25
O15		Southern Miss	20	27
O29	●	at Vanderbilt	24	7
N5	●	at Mississippi State	30	13
N12	●	at Cincinnati	43	10
N19	=	Arkansas State	14	14
N26	●	at Louisville	45	7

REY DEMPSEY
1984-85 (.386)   7-12-3

1984 — 5-5-1

S1	●	Arkansas State	17	2
S8	●	at Mississippi	6	22
S22	●	Cincinnati	47	7
S29	=	Southern Miss	23	13
O6	—	Florida State	17	17
O13	●	La. Lafayette	20	7
O20	●	Mississippi State	23	12
O27		North Carolina	27	30
N3		at Georgia	3	13
N10		at Tennessee	9	41
N17		at Tulane	9	14

1985 — 2-7-2

A31	●	at La. Lafayette	37	6
S7	=	Mississippi	17	17
S14	=	Murray St.	10	10
S21		at Florida State	10	19
O5		at Mississippi State	28	31
O12	●	Tulane	38	21
O19		Southern Miss	7	14
O26		Alabama	9	28
N2		at Virginia Tech	10	31
N9		Tennessee	7	17
N16		at Army	7	49

CHARLIE BAILEY
1986-88 (.379)   12-20-1

1986 — 1-10-0

S6		Mississippi JaM	6	28
S13		Arkansas State	10	30
S20		La. Lafayette	10	26
S27		at Louisville	8	34
O4		Mississippi State	17	34
O11		at Alabama	0	37
O18		at Southern Miss	9	14
N1	●	at Vanderbilt	22	21
N8		at Tennessee	3	33
N15		at Tulane	6	15
N22		New Mexico	13	20

1987 — 5-5-1

S5	●	Mississippi	16	10
S12		at Vanderbilt	17	27
S19		at Florida State	24	41
O3		at Mississippi State	6	9
O10	●	Alabama	13	10
O17	●	Tulane	45	36
O24		Southern Miss	14	17
O31	=	Arkansas State	21	21
N7		at La. Lafayette	7	31
N14	●	Louisville	43	8
N21	●	at Tulsa	14	0

1988 — 6-5-0

S3	●	Mississippi JaM	6	24
S10	●	Arkansas State	9	7
S17	●	at Louisville	18	29
S24	●	at Tulane	19	20
O1	●	Mississippi State	31	10
O8	●	at Florida	17	11
O22		Tennessee	25	38
O29	●	at Southern Miss	27	34
N5	●	La. Lafayette	20	3
N12	●	Tulsa	26	20
N19	●	Vanderbilt	28	9

CHUCK STOBART
1989-94 (.447)   29-36-1

1989 — 2-9-0

S2		Mississippi	13	20
S9		Arkansas State	13	17
S16		Alabama Birm	7	35
S23		Florida	13	38
O7		Vanderbilt	13	10
O14	●	at Cincinnati	34	17
O21		at Mississippi State	10	35
O28		Southern Miss	7	31
N4		at Tulane	34	38
N11		Louisville	10	40
N18		at Florida State	20	57

1990 — 4-6-1

S1	=	Arkansas State	24	24
S8	●	at Mississippi	21	23
S22	●	Central Florida	37	28
S29	●	at Tulsa	22	10
O6		Tulane	21	14
O13		at Louisville	17	19
O20		at Southern Miss	7	23
O27	●	La. Lafayette	20	6
N3		East Carolina	17	24
N10		Mississippi State	23	27
N17		Florida State Orl	3	35

1991 — 5-6-0

S2	●	at Southern Cal	24	10
S7		Mississippi	0	10
S14		at East Carolina	13	20
S21	●	Arkansas State	31	21
O5		at Missouri	21	31
O12	●	Southern Miss	17	12
O19	●	at Mississippi State	28	23
O26		Tulsa	28	33
N2		at Tennessee	24	52
N9	●	Louisville	35	7
N16		Alabama	7	10

1992 — 6-5-0

S4		at Southern Miss	21	23
S12		at Louisville	15	16
S19		Mississippi State	16	20
S26	●	Arkansas	22	6
O10	●	Cincinnati	34	14
O17	●	Arkansas State	37	7
O24	●	at Tulsa	30	25
O31	●	at Tulane	62	20
N7		at Mississippi	12	17
N14		Tennessee	21	26
N21	●	East Carolina	42	7

1993 — 6-5-0

S4	●	at Mississippi State	45	35
S11		Louisville	28	54
S18	●	at La. Lafayette	15	17
S25	●	Arkansas LR	6	0
O2	●	at East Carolina	34	7
O9	●	Arkansas State	45	3
O16	●	Tulsa	19	23
O30		at Cincinnati	20	23
N6		Mississippi	19	3
N13	●	Southern Miss	20	9
N27		at Miami, Fla.	17	41

1994 — 6-5-0

S3		Mississippi State	6	17
S10	●	at Tulsa	42	18
S17	●	at Southern Miss	3	20
S24	●	Arkansas	16	15
O8	●	Tulane	13	0
O15	●	Arkansas State	15	6
O22	●	Cincinnati	26	3
O29	●	at Louisville	6	10
N5	●	at Mississippi	17	16
N12	●	at Tennessee	13	24
N19	●	East Carolina	6	30

RIP SCHERER
1995-2000 (.333)   22-44

1995 — 3-8-0

S2		at Mississippi State	18	28
S9	●	at Michigan	7	24
S16	●	La. Lafayette	33	19
S23	●	Arkansas LR	20	27
S30	●	Louisville	7	17
O14	●	at Tulane	23	8
O21	●	at Cincinnati	3	28
O28	●	Tulsa	10	7
N4		Mississippi	3	34
N11	●	Southern Miss	9	17
N18		at East Carolina	17	31

1996-PRESENT
C-USA

1996 — 4-7 (2-3)

A31		Miami, Fla.	7	30
S7		Mississippi State	10	31
S14	●	at Missouri	19	16
S21	|	Tulane	17	10
O5	|	Cincinnati	18	16
O12	|	at Houston	20	37
O19	|	at Southern Miss	0	16
O26	|	at La. Lafayette	9	13
N2	|	at Louisville	10	13
N9	|	Tennessee	21	17
N23	|	East Carolina	10	20

1997 — 4-7 (2-4)

A30	|	at Mississippi State	10	13
S6	●	UAB	28	7
S13	|	at Michigan State	21	51
S20	|	Minnesota	17	20
O4	|	at Cincinnati	17	20
O11	|	Arkansas State	38	9
O25	|	at East Carolina	10	32
N1	●	Houston	24	3
N8	|	at Tulane	14	26
N15	●	Louisville	21	20
N22	|	Southern Miss	18	42

1998 — 2-9 (1-5)

S5	|	at Mississippi	10	30
S12	|	Mississippi State	6	14
S19	|	at Minnesota	14	41
O3	|	at Houston	14	35
O10	|	Arkansas	9	23
O17	|	Cincinnati	41	23
O24	|	at Louisville	32	35
O31	|	Arkansas State	35	19
N7	|	Tulane	31	41
N14	|	at Southern Miss	3	45
N21	|	East Carolina	31	34

1999 — 5-6 (4-2)

S4	|	Mississippi	0	3
S11	|	at Mississippi State	10	13
S18	●	Arkansas State	31	26
S25	|	at Tennessee	16	17
O2	|	Missouri	17	27
O9	● |	at UAB	38	14
O16	|	Louisville	31	32
O30	● |	at Tulane	49	7
N6	|	Southern Miss	5	20
N13	● |	Army	14	10
N20	● |	at Cincinnati	21	13

2000 — 4-7 (2-5)

S2	|	Mississippi State	3	17
S9	|	La. Monroe	28	0
S16	● |	at Arkansas State	19	17
S23	● |	at Army	26	16
S30	|	at Southern Miss	3	24
O7	|	East Carolina	17	10
O14	|	at UAB	9	13
O21	|	Houston	30	33
N4	|	Tennessee	17	19
N11	|	Cincinnati	10	13
N18	|	at Tulane	14	37

2000 4-7 (2-5)

S2		Mississippi State	3	17
S9	●	La. Monroe	28	0
S16	●	at Arkansas State	19	17
S23	|	at Army	21	38
S30	● |	at Southern Miss	22	17
O7	● |	East Carolina	17	10
O14	|	at UAB	9	13
O21	|	Houston	30	33
N4	|	Tennessee	17	19
N11	|	Cincinnati	10	13
N18	|	at Tulane	14	37

TOMMY WEST
2001-Present (.521)   25-23

2001 5-6 (3-4)

S3		at Mississippi State	10	30
S8	●	U.T. Chattanooga	43	10
S22	●	South Florida	17	9
S29	|	at Louisville	21	38
O6	● |	Southern Miss	22	17
O13	● |	at Houston	52	33
O20	|	at East Carolina	11	32
O27	|	UAB	14	17
N10	|	at Tennessee	28	49
N17	● |	Army	42	10
N24	|	Cincinnati	34	36

2002 3-9 (2-6)

A31	●	Murray St.	52	6
S7		at Mississippi	16	38
S14	|	at Southern Miss	14	33
S21	● |	Tulane	38	10
S28	|	at UAB	17	31
O8	|	Louisville	32	38
O19	|	Mississippi State	17	29
O26	|	at Cincinnati	10	48
N2	|	Houston	21	26
N9	|	at South Florida	28	31
N23	● |	Army	38	10
N30	|	at TCU	20	27

2003 9-4 (5-3)

A30	●	Tenn. Tech	40	10
S6	●	Mississippi	44	34
S13	|	at Southern Miss	6	23
S27	●	Arkansas State	38	16
O4	|	UAB	10	24
O11	|	at Mississippi State	27	35
O18	● |	at Houston	45	14
O25	● |	at Tulane	41	9
N1	● |	East Carolina	41	24
N15	● |	at Louisville	37	7
N22	● |	Cincinnati	21	16
N29	|	South Florida	16	21

NEW ORLEANS BOWL

D16	●	North Texas	27	17

2004 8-4 (5-3)

S4	●	at Mississippi	20	13
S11	●	U.T. Chattanooga	52	21
S18	●	at Arkansas State	47	35
S25	|	at UAB	28	35
O2	● |	Houston	41	14
O16	● |	Tulane	49	24
O23	|	at Cincinnati	10	49
N2	|	Louisville	49	56
N13	● |	Southern Miss	30	26
N20	● |	at East Carolina	38	35
N27	● |	at South Florida	31	15

GMAC BOWL

D22		Bowling Green	35	52

Neutral Site Key: *Birm* Birmingham, AL / *Irv* Irving, TX / *JaM* Jackson, MS / *LR* Little Rock, AR / *Orl* Orlando, FL / *SLC* Salt Lake City, UT
ƒ Forfeit † Game Later Forfieted # Disputed Victor * Disputed Score ‖ Designated Conference Game |2 Counted Twice in Conference Standings

MIAMI (FLA.)

THEY WERE A PART OF COLLEGE football's yesterdays, a yellowing pile of newspaper clippings. The Miami Hurricanes won four national championships from 1983 to 1991, under three different head coaches, but it was easy to believe their time had come and gone.

By 1997, Miami football seemed in disarray. The program had always relished its outlaw image; now it seemed passé. The Hurricanes had landed on probation, and their players too often landed on the police blotter. *Sports Illustrated* famously called for Miami to abolish its program. And on the field, things were just as bad: a 5–6 record, the first losing season since 1979 and a humiliating 47-0 loss to archrival Florida State. Miami, so many believed, was now just another humbled power.

But even as the program was suffering the consequences of the devastating probation, rejuvenation had begun with the hiring of Butch Davis as head coach in 1995. Davis worked to rehabilitate Miami's foundation and image and soon had the Hurricanes back among the elite. The first flicker of new life came in 1998, when Miami knocked UCLA out of the national title picture with a late-season upset. Two years later, Miami served notice of its return with 10 straight wins, capped by a 37-20 thrashing of Florida in the Sugar Bowl.

That streak would grow under Davis' successor, Larry Coker, to 34 straight, including the 2001 national championship—Miami's fifth—and wouldn't be stopped until Ohio State's spine-tingling 31-24 triumph in the 2003 Fiesta Bowl. Losing out on a sixth championship by such a whisker stung, no question. But few could argue this: the Hurricanes were back—an NFL-record six first-round draft picks in 2004 confirmed it—and they had officially assumed their proper place among the greatest college football powers of all time.

TRADITION There was a time when the state of Miami football was best summed up by the fatigue-wearing group of players who showed up at a dinner prior to the 1987 Fiesta Bowl against Penn State. The Hurricanes loved the perception of themselves as college football's version of the Oakland Raiders: outrageous and eager to stomp you on game day. This was Miami's answer to the staid, age-old traditions of the more established Southern teams. Now, with the black hats and eye patches apparently gone for good, the one lasting tradition from that period is the way the Hurricanes enter the Orange Bowl during pregame introductions, through plumes

---

PROFILE

University of Miami
Coral Gables, Fla.
Founded: 1925
Enrollment: 9,794
Colors: Orange, Green and White
Nickname: Hurricanes
Stadium: Orange Bowl
　Opened in 1937
　Prescription Athletic Turf; 72,319 capacity
First football game: 1926
All-time record: 516–288–19 (.639)
Bowl record: 17–12
Consensus national championships, 1936-present: 5 (1983, 1987, 1989, 1991, 2001)
Heisman Trophy: Vinny Testaverde, 1986; Gino Torretta, 1992
Outland Trophy: Russell Maryland, 1990; Bryant McKinnie, 2001
First-round NFL draftees: 54
Website: www.hurricanesports.com

THE BEST OF TIMES

The Hurricanes welcomed back the good old days by playing in four straight BCS bowls from 2001 to 2004, but they will still have to accomplish a little more to match the run, from 1987 through 1991, when the Canes won three national championships in five years—likely missing a fourth by one point in a still-controversial 31-30 loss to Notre Dame in 1988—and compiled a 56–4–0 record.

THE WORST OF TIMES

In the 10 years from 1968 to 1977, the Hurricanes mustered only one winning season and went through six coaches. The nadir was from 1975 to 1977, when the Canes won only eight of 32 games and were outscored 697-489.

CONFERENCE

Miami joined the ACC in 2004 after dominating the Big East from 1991 to 2003. The football program had flown solo since it began playing varsity in 1927.

DISTINGUISHED ALUMNI

Sylvester Stallone; Gloria Estefan; The Rock (Dwayne Johnson); Sandy Freedman, first female mayor of Tampa; Charles Grodin, actor; Enrique Iglesias, singer; Patricia Ireland, president, NOW; Al Rosen, baseball player/executive; Jon Secada, singer

FIGHT SONG

HAIL TO THE SPIRIT OF MIAMI U
Hail to the spirit of Miami U
Hail to her pride and glory free
Hail to the orange, green and white so true
Hail to the fighting Varsity
Long may her banners wave
Over vanquished foes
In our hearts may she always be
Hail to the spirit of Miami U
We pledge our faith and loyalty

> *The Hurricanes loved their perception as college football's version of the Raiders.*

of smoke. It may seem kitschy, an MTV throwback, but Miami fans still love it, paired with the whirling rush of a hurricane sound effect piped through the stadium's public address system.

BEST PLAYER He is not one of the five quarterbacks (Bernie Kosar, Steve Walsh, Craig Erickson, Gino Torretta and Ken Dorsey) to have led the Hurricanes to a national championship. He is not the school's career passing leader (Dorsey is). He hasn't had the program's most storied pro quarterback career (Jim Kelly had that). But Vinny Testaverde, the 1986 Heisman Trophy winner, in many ways was the quintessential representative of Quarterback U. When he arrived in 1982, Testaverde had to wait his turn behind Kelly and Kosar. But he went 20–1 in two regular seasons as a starter, and over his career he threw for 6,058 yards and 48 touchdowns. Testaverde is also the only Hurricane of recent vintage to have his uniform number retired, primarily because it was under his stewardship that the program proved it had staying power.

BEST COACH It's a deep list, especially when you consider the records of Jimmy Johnson (52–9) and Dennis

Erickson (63–9). But Howard Schnellenberger, the pipe-smoking Captain Kangaroo double, is the man who started it all and stands alone at the top. When he arrived at Miami in January 1979 after a long stint as Don Shula's offensive coordinator with the Miami Dolphins, the Hurricanes were finishing off the most turbulent decade in their history—Schnellenberger was the team's seventh coach since 1970. He immediately installed a pro-style attack and slowly brought the team from credibility to respectability. After a 10–1 regular season in 1983, the Hurricanes won the national championship by shocking Nebraska 31-30 in the 1984 Orange Bowl. On the eve of the game, Schnellenberger deadpanned, "I don't gamble with my money, just my life," and then proceeded to engineer one of the greatest upsets in college football history. Schnellenberger left for the USFL four months later, leaving behind a 41–16 record and the keys to college football's newest dynasty.

BEST TEAM It's a wonderful dilemma for Miami fans, picking among three undefeated national champions (1987, 1991, 2001). But the 1987 team stands out for several

RECORDS

RUSHING YARDS
GAME
299 Edgerrin James vs. UCLA, Dec. 5, 1998 (39 att.)
SEASON
1,753 Willis McGahee, 2002 (282 att.)
CAREER
3,331 Ottis Anderson, 1975-78 (691 att.)

PASSING YARDS
GAME
485 Gino Torretta vs. San Diego State, Nov. 30, 1991 (23 of 44)
SEASON
3,642 Bernie Kosar, 1984 (262 of 416)
CAREER
9,565 Ken Dorsey, 1999-2002 (668 of 1,153)

RECEIVING YARDS
GAME
220 Eddie Brown vs. Boston College, Nov. 23, 1984 (10 rec.)
SEASON
1,114 Eddie Brown, 1984 (59 rec.)
CAREER
2,546 Santana Moss, 1997-2000 (143 rec.)

POINTS
GAME
36 Willis McGahee vs. Virginia Tech, Dec. 7, 2002 (6 TDs)
SEASON
168 Willis McGahee, 2002 (28 TDs)
CAREER
397 Carlos Huerta, 1988-91 (73 FGs, 178 PATs)

CONSENSUS ALL-AMERICANS

1945	Ed Cameron	G
1945	William Levitt	C
1961	Bill Miller	E
1966	Tom Beier	DB
1967-68	Ted Hendricks	DE
1973	Tony Cristiani	DL
1974	Rubin Carter	MG
1981	Fred Marion	DB
1984	Eddie Brown	WR
1985	Willie Smith	TE
1986	Vinny Testaverde	QB
1986	Jerome Brown	DL
1986-87	Bennie Blades	DB
1987	Daniel Stubbs	DL
1988	Steve Walsh	QB
1988	Bill Hawkins	DL
1989	Greg Mark	DL
1990	Maurice Crum	LB
1990	Russell Maryland	DL
1991	Carlos Huerta	PK
1991	Darryl Williams	DB

(Continued on next page)

reasons. It was the school's first unbeaten varsity team, for one thing. For another, the Hurricanes beat six ranked teams, opening the season with back-to-back thrashings of No. 20 Florida (31-4) and No. 10 Arkansas (51-7) and ending it with a 20-14 Orange Bowl win over No. 1 Oklahoma. Not only did the team include such future NFL stars as Michael Irvin, Russell Maryland and Brian and Bennie Blades, the coaching staff included four future NFL head coaches: Jimmy Johnson, Dave Wannstedt, Butch Davis and Dave Campo.

BIGGEST GAME It has become a staple of ESPN Classic, because it contained everything a great game is supposed to have: drama, a last-second ending, unexpected heroes, lasting stars, a classic venue and, not incidentally, an upset winner. Before Jan. 2, 1984, Miami was considered an up-and-coming program. But after the Hurricanes' 31-30 upset of undefeated Nebraska in the 50th Orange Bowl, no one would ever look at Miami the same way again. Redshirt freshman quarterback Bernie Kosar threw two first-quarter touchdown passes to Glenn Dennison as Miami stormed to a 17-0 lead. But season-long No. 1 Nebraska, whose record-setting "Scoring Explosion" offense was led by quarterback Turner Gill, running back Mike Rozier and receiver Irving Fryar, showed why it had been unstoppable all year. NU roared back twice, first tying the game 17-17. After again falling behind, 31-17, Nebraska rallied for two touchdowns, the second coming on Jeff Smith's 24-yard touchdown run on fourth and eight with less than a minute left to play. In a move that came to define the standing of the two programs for years to come, Nebraska coach Tom Osborne chose to go for the victory rather than a tie that would have secured the Huskers the national championship. Gill tried to pass to Smith for the two-point conversion, but Miami rover Ken Calhoun tipped the pass away and the upstart Hurricanes had their first national title. "There are some times you know the moment you walk off the field that you've been involved in something people are gonna talk about for a long, long time," said Schnellenberger. "Well, I think people are gonna talk about this game 20, 50, 100 years from now. And they should. That was the best game I've ever been involved in."

BIGGEST UPSET With all due respect to that thrilling

CONSENSUS ALL-AMERICANS (CONT.)		
1992	Gino Torretta,	QB
1992	Micheal Barrow,	LB
1992	Ryan McNeil,	DB
1994	Warren Sapp,	DL
2000	Santana Moss,	WR/PR
2000	Dan Morgan,	LB
2000	Edward Reed,	DB
2001	Bryant McKinnie,	OL
2001	Edward Reed,	DB
2002	Willis McGahee,	RB
2002	Brett Romberg,	C
2003	Kellen Winslow,	TE
2003	Sean Taylor,	DB
2004	Antrel Rolle,	DB

Nebraska game, the 26-10 stunner the Hurricanes pulled off against Penn State on Nov. 3, 1979, may well have been the point at which everything turned around in Miami's football history. This was a Nittany Lions team that just 10 months earlier had played for the national championship. And Schnellenberger's team was at that point struggling in his first season. But Schnellenberger gave Pennsylvania native Jim Kelly—whom Penn State had recruited as a linebacker—his first career start, and the result was better than anyone could have imagined. "We were 3–4 and had not beaten a team of any stature," Schnellenberger said in 1999. "We beat Penn State, and suddenly the nonbelievers were believers."

HEARTBREAKER Maybe the only college football scene that has been rebroadcast more than the 1984 Orange Bowl took place in the Orange Bowl 11 months later, on Nov. 23, 1984. With six seconds left in the game, Boston College's Doug Flutie heaved a prayer from midfield toward the end zone. As time ran out, the ball landed in Gerard Phelan's arms, and BC had a 47-45 win that football fans will talk about forever. It was the second straight gut-wrencher for the No. 12-ranked Hurricanes—following a 42-40 loss to Maryland in which Miami had blown a 31-0 halftime lead.

STADIUM Few football stadiums hold more history than the Orange Bowl—where Joe Namath made good on his fabled Super Bowl guarantee, where a spectacular halftime show climaxed a half-century of New Year's Nights and where the Hurricanes won 58 consecutive games from 1985 to 1994. Efforts to build an on-campus home for the Hurricanes go back to 1926. But on Sept. 17, 1926, one day after work began on a temporary 8,000-seat facility, a hurricane hammered South Florida, killing 130 people, damaging 10,000 homes and, perhaps forever, consigning the Hurricanes to this off-campus home. Though the namesake stadium didn't open until 1937, Miami played in the first Orange Bowl game on Jan. 1, 1935.

RIVAL Miami used to have a sizzling rivalry with Florida, but tensions (if not genuine hatred) forced the suspension of their matchups after the 1987 season. Although the series was temporarily renewed in 2002, Florida State

came to dominate the Hurricanes' thoughts in the meantime, and Miami-Florida State has become one of the signature rivalries in all of college football. Miami has ended many FSU championship runs, most recently in 2003. From 1990 to 1992, Miami three times knocked off the Seminoles when they were ranked in the top three. In shorthand, Miami's three greatest moments against Florida State are known as Wide Right I (Nov. 16, 1991, in Tallahassee, when FSU kicker Gerry Thomas' 34-yard field goal missed with 25 seconds to go as No. 2 Miami beat No. 1 FSU 17-16); Wide Right II (Oct. 3, 1992, in Miami, when FSU's Dan Mowrey missed from 39 yards on the game's final play, ensuring a 19-16 Miami win); and Wide Right III (Oct. 7, 2000, when it was Matt Munyon's turn to miss wide right, this time from 49 yards, clinching a 27-24 Miami win). Then, to add a twist to this fascinating pattern, Florida State kicker Xavier Beitia pulled a 43-yard field goal at the Orange Bowl on Oct. 12, 2002, sealing a 28-27 win for Miami after it had trailed by 13 points with 11:44 left in the game. Immediately, and inevitably, the game was dubbed Wide Left I. "I simply can't believe we lost the game like that again," FSU coach Bobby Bowden lamented. "I thought we had it. I went out to shake [Beitia's] hand. I thought he hit it. I've had that picture so many times before in my career. I can't stand it."

NICKNAME Local lore recalls that the 1927 Miami football team came to its nickname by choosing to emulate the terrible 1926 storm that flattened so much of South Florida. An alternate version of the story has *Miami News* columnist Jack Bell asking Porter Norris, a 1926 team member, what the team should be called, and Norris replying, "Hurricanes," because the season opener had been postponed by the famous storm. From time to time, school officials have blanched at the association between the university and the storms that have periodically tormented the area. But as one UM official said in the 1960s: "Does anyone think Chicago is overrun by bears just because the town has a football team by that name?"

MASCOT Sebastian the Ibis may be at once the oddest and most recognizable mascot in college football. According to legend, the ibis, a bird found in the Everglades and a symbol of knowledge, is the last wildlife to take shelter before a hurricane and the first to reappear after. The ibis debuted as a symbol at Miami when it was chosen for the title of the 1926 school yearbook. Students living in San Sebastian Hall 31 years later sponsored an ibis entry in the homecoming parade, and the name stuck.

UNIFORMS In 1926, Miami's school colors of orange, green and white were selected because they are the colors of the Florida orange tree. Orange symbolizes the fruit of the tree, green represents the leaves and white the blossoms. Those colors have been virtually unchanged, although the dominant home color has alternated between green and orange. The team helmet features a wide "U," which resulted from boosters in the early 1970s wanting to give Miami a recognizable logo apart from other schools that have UM for initials (Michigan, Missouri, Montana, etc.). "U" attained that icon status, though it has also inspired some unfortunate slogans through the years ("U gotta believe" and "U is great" among them). Miami also was one of the first schools to enter into an annual deal with Nike (for $8 million in 1995), which brought a jolt of MTV-flavored styling to the uniform.

LORE In Schnellenberger's first year at Miami, the team became known as the Jet Lag Kids, both because of Miami's embrace of a passing offense and because the Hurricanes traveled more than 28,000 miles that season. That included trips to Penn State, Syracuse and San Diego State, and to Japan for a date with Notre Dame.

QUOTE "When I came out of that tunnel, wearing those colors, in front of that crowd … let me tell you something. There's no drug you can ever take that matches the feeling of being a Miami Hurricane, kicking tail and taking names." — All-America linebacker Micheal Barrow

MIAMI (FLA.) ANNUAL STATISTICAL LEADERS

YR	RUSHING	YDS	ATT	AVG	PASSING	ATT	CMP	PCT	YDS	RECEIVING	REC	YDS	AVG
1947	Harry Ghaul	310	53	5.8	Hal Johnston	38	19	.50	239	Andy Novak	8	146	18.3
1948	Frank Smith	250	71	3.5	Jack DelBello	101	45	.45	455	Al Hudson	5	190	38.0
1949	Bob Campbell	482	98	4.9	Jack Hackett	76	28	.37	302	Ralph Fieler	14	151	10.8
1950	Jim Dooley	532	98	5.4	Jack Hackett	107	52	.49	612	Tom Jelley	24	399	16.6
1951	Harry Mallios	494	138	3.6	Jack Hackett	71	34	.48	544	Ed Lutes	16	409	25.6
1952	Pud Constantino	400	81	4.9	Don James	144	82	.57	913	Frank McDonald	32	418	13.1
1953	Gordon Malloy	342	90	3.8	Don James	75	39	.52	450	Frank McDonald	20	235	11.8
1954	Gordon Malloy	492	87	5.7	Carl Garrigus	47	27	.57	305	Frank McDonald	15	181	12.1
1955	Don Bosseler	435	104	4.2	Sam Scarnecchia	49	31	.63	485	Jack Losch	7	206	29.4
1956	Don Bosseler	723	161	4.5	Sam Scarnecchia	59	27	.46	357	John Varone	10	107	10.7
1957	John Varone	460	79	5.8	Fran Curci	85	41	.48	476	John Varone	11	108	9.8
1958	Frank Bouffard	289	77	3.8	Bonnie Yarbrough	80	32	.40	509	Bill Hildebrandt	12	177	14.8
1959	Frank Bouffard	387	105	3.7	Fran Curci	195	100	.51	1,068	Bill Miller	33	395	12.0
1960	Eddie Johns	521	123	4.2	Eddie Johns	91	54	.59	657	Bill Miller	26	413	15.9
1961	James Vollenweider	538	112	4.8	George Mira	172	81	.47	1,000	Bill Miller	44	648	14.7
1962	Nick Ryder	702	155	4.5	George Mira	306	146	.48	1,893	Nick Spinelli	33	506	15.3
1963	Pete Banaszak	461	97	4.8	George Mira	334	172	.51	2,155	Nick Spinelli	41	501	12.2
1964	Russell Smith	370	84	4.4	Bob Biletnikoff	159	85	.53	920	Tom Coughlin	22	294	13.4
1965	Pete Banaszak	473	111	4.3	Bill Miller	141	72	.51	856	Jerry Daanen	29	367	12.7
1966	Doug McGee	377	100	3.8	Bill Miller	155	84	.54	1,114	James Cox	41	627	15.3
1967	John Acuff	572	112	5.1	David Olivo	140	62	.44	729	James Cox	39	552	14.2
1968	Vincent Opalsky	446	152	2.9	David Olivo	248	137	.55	1,727	David Kalina	43	628	14.6
1969	Vincent Opalsky	453	109	4.2	Kelly Cochrane	243	121	.50	1,673	David Kalina	45	532	11.8
1970	Tom Sullivan	461	156	3.0	Kelly Cochrane	287	127	.44	1,328	Joe Schmidt	37	549	14.8
1971	Chuck Foreman	951	191	5.0	John Hornibrook	179	73	.41	1,006	Witt Beckman	21	288	13.7
1972	Chuck Foreman	484	107	4.5	Ed Carney	209	94	.45	1,399	Chuck Foreman	37	557	15.1
1973	Woody Thompson	802	189	4.2	Ed Carney	94	41	.44	658	Steve Marcantonio	35	568	16.2
1974	Woody Thompson	343	78	4.4	Kary Baker	146	61	.42	805	Steve Marcantonio	22	337	15.3
1975	Ottis Anderson	365	67	5.4	E.J. Baker	130	66	.51	999	Phil August	25	419	16.8
1976	Ottis Anderson	918	213	4.3	E.J. Baker	131	64	.49	907	Larry Cain	18	444	24.7
1977	Ottis Anderson	782	187	4.2	E.J. Baker	84	35	.42	515	Steve Alvers	14	249	17.8
1978	Ottis Anderson	1,266	224	5.7	Kenny McMillian	108	53	.49	611	James Joiner	15	235	15.7
1979	Chris Hobbs	406	105	3.9	Mike Rodrigue	201	94	.47	1,197	Larry Brodsky	30	495	16.5
1980	Lorenzo Roan	669	152	4.4	Jim Kelly	206	109	.53	1,519	Larry Brodsky	33	570	17.3
1981	Lorenzo Roan	388	111	3.5	Jim Kelly	285	168	.59	2,403	Larry Brodsky	37	631	17.1
1982	Keith Griffin	473	131	3.6	Mark Richt	149	71	.48	838	Rocky Belk	35	646	18.5
1983	Albert Bentley	722	144	5.0	Bernie Kosar	327	201	.61	2,329	Glenn Dennison	54	594	11.0
1984	Alonzo Highsmith	906	146	6.2	Bernie Kosar	416	262	.63	3,642	Eddie Brown	59	1,114	18.9
1985	Warren Williams	522	89	5.9	Vinny Testaverde	352	216	.61	3,238	Michael Irvin	46	840	18.3
1986	Alonzo Highsmith	442	105	4.2	Vinny Testaverde	276	175	.63	2,557	Michael Irvin	53	868	16.4
1987	Warren Williams	673	135	5.0	Steve Walsh	298	176	.59	2,249	Michael Irvin	44	715	16.3
1988	Cleveland Gary	480	117	4.1	Steve Walsh	390	233	.60	3,115	Andre Brown	47	746	15.9
1989	Leonard Conley	529	134	3.9	Craig Erickson	273	147	.54	2,007	Dale Dawkins	54	833	15.4
1990	Stephen McGuire	621	150	4.1	Craig Erickson	393	225	.57	3,363	Wesley Carroll	61	952	15.6
1991	Stephen McGuire	608	123	4.9	Gino Torretta	371	205	.55	3,095	Lamar Thomas	39	623	16.0
1992	Donnell Bennett	421	97	4.3	Gino Torretta	402	228	.57	3,060	Horace Copeland	47	769	16.4
1993	James Stewart	639	112	5.7	Ryan Collins	203	117	.58	1,605	Chris T. Jones	51	798	15.6
1994	James Stewart	724	147	4.9	Frank Costa	313	168	.54	2,443	Chris T. Jones	39	664	17.0
1995	Danyell Ferguson	1,069	212	5.0	Ryan Clement	201	119	.59	1,638	Jammi German	41	730	17.8
1996	Dyral McMillan	565	111	5.1	Ryan Clement	272	164	.60	2,257	Yatil Green	44	746	17.0
1997	Edgerrin James	1,098	184	6.0	Ryan Clement	267	157	.59	2,089	Reggie Wayne	48	640	13.3
1998	Edgerrin James	1,416	242	5.9	Scott Covington	270	159	.59	2,301	Reggie Wayne	42	629	15.0
1999	Clinton Portis	839	143	5.9	Kenny Kelly	259	141	.54	1,913	Santana Moss	54	899	16.6
2000	James Jackson	1,006	201	5.0	Ken Dorsey	322	188	.58	2,737	Santana Moss	45	748	16.6
2001	Clinton Portis	1,200	220	5.5	Ken Dorsey	318	184	.58	2,652	Jeremy Shockey	40	519	13.0
2002	Willis McGahee	1,753	282	6.2	Ken Dorsey	393	222	.56	3,369	Kellen Winslow	57	726	12.7
2003	Jarrett Payton	985	182	5.4	Brock Berlin	352	211	.60	2,419	Kellen Winslow	60	605	10.1
2004	Frank Gore	945	197	4.8	Brock Berlin	348	195	.56	2,680	Roscoe Parrish	43	693	16.1

Receiving leaders by receptions
All statistics include postseason

MIAMI (FLA.) ALL-TIME SCORES

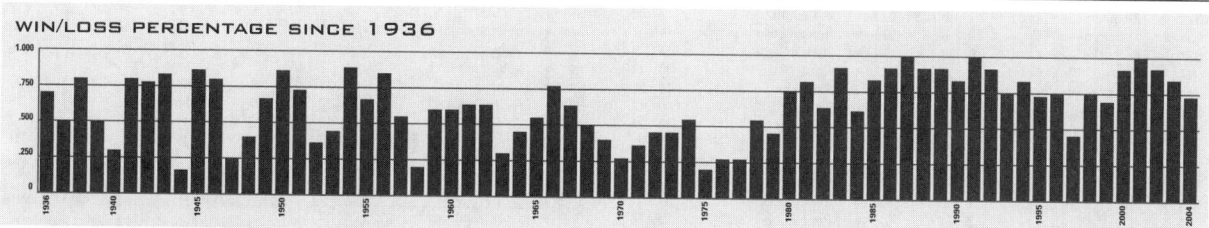

WIN/LOSS PERCENTAGE SINCE 1936

HOWARD BUCK 1927-28 (.421)   7-10-2

1927   3-6-1
O29	●	Rollins	39	3
N5	●	Piedmont	46	0
N11		Spring Hill	0	6
N19		Stetson	0	36
N24		Samford	0	52
D3		Oglethorpe	0	13
D10	=	Georgetown	7	7
D17		Millsaps	0	31
D26	●	Louisiana Coll.	7	0
J2		Furman	7	39

1928   4-4-1
O27	●	Havana	62	0
N3	●	Rollins	31	0
N10		Elon	18	21
N27		Stetson	6	15
N29		Samford	0	7
D8	●	Louisiana Coll.	20	0
D15	●	Union	7	6
D22		Wake Forest	6	13
J1	=	Florida Southern *Unk*	13	13

J. BURTON RIX 1929 (.600)   3-2

1929   3-2-0
O19	●	Florida Southern	6	0
O26	●	Rollins	32	0
N2		at La. Lafayette	0	14
N16		at Stetson	0	12
N28	●	Howard	7	0

ERNEST BRETT 1930 (.438)   3-4-1

1930   3-4-1
O24	●	Florida Southern	13	6
O31	●	Bowden	7	0
N8		at Temple	0	34
N11		at Howard	0	24
N14	●	at La. Lafayette	6	0
N21	=	Rollins	0	0
N28		Stetson	0	19
D5		Western Kentucky	0	19

TOM McCANN 1931-34 (.541)   18-15-4

1931   4-8-0
O9		Bowden	7	12
O16		Southern Georgia	12	13
O23	●	Rollins	7	0
O30		Florida Southrern	20	31
N7		at West Kentucky	0	20
N11		at Murray St.	0	15
N14		at Middle Tennessee	6	25
N20		Alabama JV	0	16
N27	●	Erskine	9	0
D4	●	Parris Island	12	6
D11	●	Jacksonville St.	14	13
D18		Norman Park	9	19

1932   4-3-1
O14	●	William & Mary	6	2
O28	●	Piedmont	30	6
N4		Southern Georgia	6	19
N10		at Rollins	0	6
N18	=	Murray St.	0	0
N24	●	La. Lafayette	7	0
D3		Middle Tennessee	0	7
J1	●	Manhattan	7	0

1933   5-1-2
O14	●	Southern Georgia	20	0
O28	●	Piedmont	71	6
N4	●	Bowden	48	0
N10	●	Louisville	33	7
N18	●	Rollins	18	0
N24	=	Tampa	0	0
D3	=	Stetson	0	0
J1		Duquesne	7	33

1934   5-3-1
O12	●	SE. Louisiana	26	7
O18	●	Florida Southern	26	6
O26	●	Wofford	42	14
N2	●	Stetson	6	6
N10	●	at Rollins	0	14
N16	●	Oglethorpe	19	6
N23	●	at Tampa	6	7
N30	●	Baltimore	25	6
ORANGE BOWL				
J1		Bucknell	0	26

IRL TUBBS 1935-36 (.667)   11-5-2

1935   5-3-0
O11	●	SE. Louisiana	2	0
O19	●	at Georgetown	0	13
O25	●	Tampa	7	13
N1	●	Stetson	12	13
N15	●	Wake Forest	3	0
N22	●	Rollins	29	0
N29	●	Boston U.	17	0
D6	●	Oglethorpe	21	13

1936   6-2-2
S25	●	Georgia Southern	44	0
O2	=	Tampa	0	0
O9	●	at Bucknell	6	0
O17	●	at Rollins	26	0
O31	=	at Boston U.	7	7
N6	●	Stetson	20	6
N20	●	Mercer	13	0
N27	●	Mississippi	0	14
D4	●	Georgetown	10	6
D11	●	South Carolina	3	6

JACK HARDING 1937-42, '45-47 (.624) 54-32-

1937   4-4-1
O1	●	Georgia Southern	40	0
O8	●	Spring Hill	26	0
O15	=	at Bucknell	6	6
O29	●	Tampa	0	12
N5	●	Stetson	25	13
N12	●	Catholic U.	21	0
N26	●	Drake	0	7
D3	●	South Carolina	0	3 *
D10	●	Georgia	8	26

1938   8-2-0
S30	●	Spring Hill	46	0
O7	●	Tampa	32	6
O15	●	at Florida	19	7
O22	●	at Drake	6	18
O28	●	Rollins	19	0
N4	●	Oglethorpe	44	0
N11	●	at Catholic U.	0	7
N18	●	Duquesne	21	7
N24	●	Bucknell	19	0
D2	●	Georgia	13	7

1939   5-5-0
O6		Wake Forest	0	33
O14		at Tampa	32	7
O20		Rollins	14	6
O27		Catholic U.	0	14
N3		Texas Tech	19	0
N10		Drake	33	6
N18		Florida	0	13
N25		at South Carolina	6	7
D1		North Carolina St.	27	7
D8		Georgia	0	13

1940   3-7-0
O4		Stetson	19	0
O11		Tampa	27	0
O18		Catholic U.	18	20
O25		Elon	31	7
N1		at Texas Tech	14	61
N8		Rollins	0	7
N16		Florida	6	46
N22		at South Carolina	2	7
N29		Mississippi	7	21
D6		Georgia	7	28

1941   8-2-0
O3	●	Elon	38	0
O10	●	at Tampa	20	6
O17	●	Rollins	21	0
O24	●	Samford	19	0
O31	●	Texas Tech	6	0
N7	●	W. V. Wesleyan	34	0
N15	●	Florida	0	14
N21	●	South Carolina	7	6
N28	●	Alabama	7	21
D5	●	VMI	10	7

1942   7-2-0
O3		Jacksonville NAS	0	14
O10	●	Tampa	65	6
O16	●	at St. Louis	31	6
O24	●	Rollins	21	0
O31	●	Furman	32	13
N7	●	North Carolina St.	0	2
N14	●	Florida	12	0
N21	●	South Carolina	13	6
N28	●	West Virginia	21	13

EDDIE DUNN 1943-44 (.433)   6-8-1

1943   5-1-0
O2	●	at Jacksonville NATTC	6	0
O16		Camp Gordon *Unk*	52	6
O23		Charleston CG *Unk*	13	6
N6		Jacksonville NATTC *Unk*	0	20
N13		Presbyterian *Unk*	32	13
N20		Fort Benning *Unk*	21	7

1944   1-7-1
O7	=	South Carolina	0	0
O20	●	Fort Pierce	0	38
O27	●	Wake Forest	0	27
N3		Florida	0	13
N10		North Carolina St.	7	28
N17		Presbyterian	31	12
N24		Auburn	19	38
D1		Tulsa	2	48
D8		Texas A&M	14	70

JACK HARDING

1945   9-1-1
S29	●	at U.T. Chattanooga	27	7
O5	●	Georgia	21	27
O12	●	St. Louis	21	0
O19	●	Florida	7	6
O26	●	Miami, Ohio	27	13
N2	●	Clemson	7	6
N9	=	South Carolina	13	13
N16	●	North Carolina St.	21	7
N23	●	Michigan State	21	7
N30	●	Auburn	33	7
ORANGE BOWL				
J1	●	Holy Cross	13	6

1946   8-2-0
S27	●	William & Mary	13	3
O4		North Carolina	0	21
O11	●	TCU	20	12
O19	●	at Florida	20	13
O25	●	U.T. Chattanooga	33	13
N1	●	Villanova *Phil*	26	21
N8	●	Miami, Ohio	20	17
N15		LSU	7	20
N22	●	Wash. & Lee	40	20
N29	●	Detroit	21	7

1947   2-7-1
S26	●	Baylor	7	18
O3	=	Villanova *Phil*	7	7
O10	●	TCU	6	19
O17	●	Rollins	6	0
O24	●	George Washington	28	7
O31	●	South Carolina	0	8
N8		at Cincinnati	7	20
N14		Vanderbilt	7	33
N22		Florida	6	7
N29		Alabama	6	21

ANDY GUSTAFSON 1948-63 (.587)   93-65-3

1948   4-6-0
O1	●	Rollins	25	0
O8	●	Villanova	10	19
O15	●	at Detroit	6	0
O22	●	Georgia	21	42
O29	●	Maryland	13	27
N5	●	Cincinnati	36	6
N12	●	U.T. Chattanooga	19	0
N20	●	at Florida	13	27
N26	●	Kentucky	5	25
D3	●	Vanderbilt	6	33

1949   6-3-0
S30	●	Rollins	52	13
O8	●	at Louisville	26	0
O14	●	Purdue	0	14
O21	●	Georgia	13	9
N4	●	Detroit	27	6
N11	●	South Carolina	13	7
N18	●	Florida	28	13
N25	●	Kentucky	6	21
D2	●	Maryland	0	13

1950   9-1-1
S29	●	Citadel	21	0
O60	●	Villanova	18	12
O14	●	at Purdue	20	14
O20	●	Boston U.	34	7
O28	●	at Pittsburgh	28	0
N3	●	Georgetown	42	7
N10	=	Louisville	13	13
N18	●	at Florida	20	14
N24	●	Iowa	14	6
D1	●	Missouri	27	9
ORANGE BOWL				
J1		Clemson	14	15

1951   8-3-0
S29		at Tulane	7	21
O5	●	Florida State	35	13
O12	●	Purdue	7	0
O19	●	Wash. & Lee.	32	12
O26	●	Mississippi	20	7
N3		at Kentucky	0	32
N90	●	U.T. Chattanooga	34	7
N17	●	Florida	21	6
N30	●	Nebraska	19	7
D7		Pittsburgh	7	21
GATOR BOWL				
J1	●	Clemson	14	0

486 MIAMI (FLA.)

THE SCHOOLS

1952 4-7-0

S26	●	VMI	45	0
O3		Alabama	7	21
O10		at Boston U.	7	9
O17	●	Richmond	41	6
O24	●	Marquette	20	6
O31		Kentucky	0	29
N7		Vanderbilt	0	9
N14	●	Stetson	35	0
N22		at Florida	6	43
N28		North Carolina	7	34
D5		Georgia	13	35

1953 4-5-0

S25	●	Florida State	27	0
O2		Baylor	13	21
O9	●	Clemson	39	7
O17		at Nebraska	16	20
O23		Maryland	0	30
O31		Fordham NYC	0	20
N6		Auburn	20	29
N13	●	Virginia Tech	26	0
N28	●	Florida	14	10

1954 8-1-0

S24	●	Furman	51	13
O1	●	Baylor	19	13
O8	●	Holy Cross	26	20
O15	●	Mississippi State	27	13
O22	●	Maryland	9	7
O29	●	Fordham	75	7
N6		Auburn BIRM	13	14
N19	●	Alabama	23	7
N27	●	at Florida	14	0

1955 6-3-0

S17		at Georgia Tech	6	14
S30	●	Florida State	34	0
O7		Notre Dame	0	14
O21		TCU	19	21
O29	●	at Pittsburgh	21	7
N4	●	Boston College	14	7
N11	●	Bucknell	46	0
N18	●	Alabama	34	12
N26	●	Florida	7	6

1956 8-1-1

S28	●	South Carolina	14	6
O5	●	Boston College	27	6
O12	●	Maryland	13	6
O19	=	Georgia	7	7
O27	●	at TCU	14	0
N2	●	Florida State	20	7
N16	●	Clemson	21	0
N23	●	West Virginia	18	0
D1	●	at Florida	20	7
D8		Pittsburgh	7	14

1957 5-4-1

S21		at Houston	0	7
O5	●	Baylor	13	7
O11		North Carolina	13	20
O18	=	North Carolina St.	0	0
O25	●	Kansas	48	6
N1	●	Villanova	13	7
N8	●	at Florida State	40	13
N15		Maryland	6	16
N30		Florida	0	14
D7	●	Pittsburgh	28	13

1958 2-8-0

S26		Wisconsin	0	20
O4	●	at Baylor	14	8
O10		LSU	0	41
O25		at Boston College	2	6
O31		Vanderbilt	15	28
N7		Florida State	6	17
N14		Maryland	14	26
N21		Houston	26	37
N29		Florida JacF	9	12
D5	●	Oregon	2	0

1959 6-4-0

S25	●	Tulane	26	7
O3	●	at Florida State	7	6
O10		at LSU	3	27
O16	●	Navy	23	8
O23		Auburn	6	21
O30		Kentucky	3	22
N6	●	North Carolina	14	7
N13	●	South Carolina	26	6
N20	●	Michigan State	18	13
N28		Florida JacF	14	23

1960 6-4-0

S30	●	North Carolina	29	12
O8		at Pittsburgh	6	17
O14	●	South Carolina	21	6
O22		at Auburn	7	20
O28	●	Boston College	10	7
N4	●	Florida State	25	7
N12	●	Notre Dame	28	21
N18		Syracuse	14	21
N26		Florida	0	18
D2	●	Air Force	23	14

1961 7-4-0

S16		Pittsburgh	7	10
S23	●	at Kentucky	14	7
S29	●	Penn State	25	8
O6		Navy	6	17
O13		Colorado	7	9
O27	●	North Carolina	10	0
N3	●	Georgia	32	7
N11	●	at Tulane	6	0
N24	●	Northwestern	10	6
D2	●	at Florida	15	6
		LIBERTY BOWL		
D16		Syracuse	14	15

1962 7-4-0

S15	●	at Pittsburgh	23	14
S29	●	TCU	21	20
O5	●	Florida State	7	6
O13		at LSU	3	17
O19	●	Maryland	28	24
O27	●	at Air Force	21	3
N2	●	Kentucky	25	17
N10		at Alabama	3	36
N23		Northwestern	7	29
D1	●	Florida	17	15
		GOTHAM BOWL		
D15		Nebraska	34	36

1963 3-7-0

S20		at Florida State	0	24
S28	●	Purdue	3	0
O4	●	at Tulane	10	0
O11		LSU	0	3
O18		Georgia	14	31
N2	●	at Kentucky	20	14
N16		at North Carolina	16	27
N23		Florida	21	27
N30		Pittsburgh	20	31
D7		Alabama	12	17

CHARLIE TATE
1964-70 (.555) 34-27-3

1964 4-5-1

S19		Florida State	0	14
S26		at Georgia Tech	0	20
O10		California	7	9
O17	=	Pittsburgh	20	20
O23		Indiana	14	28
O30	●	at Detroit	10	7
N6	●	Tulane	21	0
N13	●	Boston College	30	6
N20	●	Vanderbilt	35	17
N28		at Florida	10	12

1965 5-4-1

S18		SMU	3	7
S25	●	at Syracuse	24	0
O2		at Tulane	16	24
O9		LSU	27	34
O16	●	Houston	44	12
O23		at Pittsburgh	14	28
N5	●	Boston College	27	6
N13	●	at Vanderbilt	28	14
N20	●	Florida	16	13
N27	=	Notre Dame	0	0

1966 8-2-1

S17	●	at Colorado	24	3
S24		Florida State	20	23
O1		at LSU	8	10
O14	●	Georgia	7	6
O21	●	Indiana	14	7
O28	●	Southern Cal	10	7
N5	=	at Tulane	10	10
N11	●	Pittsburgh	38	14
N18	●	Iowa	44	0
N26	●	at Florida	21	16
		LIBERTY BOWL		
D10	●	Virginia Tech	14	7

1967 7-4-0

S23		at Northwestern	7	12
S29		Penn State	8	17
O6	●	Tulane	34	14
O14	●	at LSU	17	15
O21	●	at Pittsburgh	58	0
O27	●	Auburn	7	0
N4	●	at Virginia Tech	14	7
N10	●	Georgia Tech	49	7
N24		Notre Dame	22	24
D9	●	Florida	20	13
		BLUEBONNET BOWL		
D23		Colorado	21	31

1968 5-5-0

S20	●	Northwestern	28	7
S28	●	at Georgia Tech	10	7
O5		at Southern Cal	3	28
O11	●	LSU	30	0
O18	●	Virginia Tech	13	8
O26		at Auburn	6	31
N1	●	Pittsburgh	48	0
N9		at Penn State	7	22
N16		Alabama	6	14
N30		at Florida	10	14

1969 4-6-0

S26		Florida State	14	16
O3	●	North Carolina St.	23	13
O10		LSU	0	20
O18		at Memphis	13	26
O24	●	TCU	14	9
N1		at Houston	36	38
N7	●	Navy	30	10
N15		at Alabama	6	42
N21	●	Wake Forest	49	7
N29		Florida	16	35

WALT KICHEFSKI
1970 (.222) 2-7

1970 3-8-0

S18	●	William & Mary	36	14
S26		at Georgia Tech	21	31
O2	●	Maryland	18	11
O16		Tampa	14	31
O24		at Pittsburgh	17	28
O30		Florida State	3	27
N7		at Tulane	16	31
N14		Alabama	8	32
N21		at Syracuse	16	56
N28	●	at Florida	14	13
D5		Houston	3	36

FRAN CURCI
1971-72 (.409) 9-13

1971 4-7-0

S18		Florida State	17	20
S25	●	at Wake Forest	29	10
O1	●	Baylor	41	15
O9		Notre Dame	0	17
O15	●	Navy	31	16
O29	●	Army	24	13
N5		North Carolina St.	7	13
N13		at Alabama	3	31
N20		at Houston	6	27
N27		Florida	16	45
D4		Syracuse	0	14

1972 5-6-0

S16		Florida State	14	37
S23		at Texas	10	23
O7		at Baylor	3	10
O14	●	Tulane	24	21
O21	●	Houston	33	13
O28	●	at Army	28	7
N4	●	Nevada-Las Vegas	51	7
N11		at Tampa	0	7
N18		at Notre Dame	17	20
N25	●	Maryland	28	8
D2		at Florida	6	17

PETE ELLIOTT
1973-74 (.500) 11-11

1973 5-6-0

S21	●	Texas	20	15
S29	●	at Florida State	14	10
O6		at Oklahoma	20	24
O12	●	Boston College	15	10
O19		Houston	7	30
O27	●	at Syracuse	34	23
N2		West Virginia	14	20
N10	●	at Army	19	7
N17		at Alabama	13	43
N24		Florida	7	14
D1		Notre Dame	0	44

1974 6-5-0

S21	●	at Houston	20	3
S28	●	at Tampa	28	26
O4		Auburn	0	3
O11	●	Pacific	35	6
O19	●	at West Virginia	21	20
O26		at Notre Dame	7	38
N1	●	Virginia Tech	14	7
N8		Florida State	14	21
N16		Alabama	7	28
N22	●	Syracuse	14	7
N30		at Florida	7	31

CARL SELMER
1975-76 (.238) 5-16

1975 2-8-0

S20		at Georgia Tech	23	38
S26		Oklahoma	17	20
O4		at Nebraska	16	31
O10		Colorado	10	23
O17	●	Houston	24	20
N1		at Boston College	7	21
N7		Navy	16	17
N15	●	at Florida State	24	22
N22		Notre Dame	9	32
N29		Florida	11	15

1976 3-8-0

S18	●	Florida State	47	0
S25		at Colorado	3	33
O2		at Nebraska	9	17
O9		Duke	7	20
O16		at Pittsburgh	19	36
O23	●	TCU	49	0
N6	●	Boston College	13	6
N13		Penn State	7	21
N20		at Notre Dame	27	40
N27		Florida ORL	10	19
D4		at Houston	16	21

LOU SABAN
1977-78 (.409) 9-13

1977 3-8-0

S10		at Ohio State	0	10
S17		at Georgia Tech	6	10
S24	●	at Florida State	23	17
O1	●	Pacific	24	3
O8	●	Kansas	14	7
O22		at TCU	17	21
O29		at Penn State	7	49
N5		Tulane	10	13
N12		at Alabama	0	36
N26		Florida	14	31
D3		Notre Dame	10	48

1978 6-5-0

S16		at Colorado	7	17
S23		Florida State	21	31
S30	●	at Kansas	38	6
O7	●	at Auburn	17	15
O14		at Georgia Tech	19	24
O21	●	Utah St.	17	16
O28		at Notre Dame	0	20
N4		at Tulane	16	20
N18	●	San Diego State	16	14
N25	●	Syracuse	21	9
D2	●	at Florida	22	21

HOWARD SCHNELLENBERGER
1979-83 (.719) 41-16

1979 5-6-0

S15	●	Louisville	24	12
S22		at Florida State	23	40
S29	●	Louisiana Tech	6	0
O6		at Florida A&M	13	16
O13		at San Diego State	20	31
O20	●	Boston College	19	8
O27		Syracuse BUF	15	25
N3	●	at Penn State	26	10
N17		at Alabama	0	30
N24		Notre Dame TOK	15	40
D1	●	Florida	30	24

1980 9-3-0

S6	●	at Louisville	24	10
S13	●	Florida A&M	49	0
S20	●	at Houston	14	7
S27	●	Florida State	10	9
O11		at Notre Dame	14	32
O18		Mississippi State	31	34
N1		at Penn State	12	27
N8	●	East Carolina	23	10
N15	●	at Vanderbilt	24	17
N22	●	North Texas	26	8
N29	●	at Florida	31	7
		PEACH BOWL		
J2	●	Virginia Tech	20	10

1981 — 9-2-0

S5	●	Florida	21	20
S19	●	Houston	12	7
S26		at Texas	7	14
O3	●	Vanderbilt	48	16
O17		at Mississippi State	10	14
O24	●	at East Carolina	31	6
O31	●	Penn State	17	14
N7	●	at Florida State	27	19
N14	●	Virginia Tech	21	14
N21	●	at North Carolina St.	14	6
N27	●	Notre Dame	37	15

1982 — 7-4-0

S4		at Florida	14	17
S11	●	Houston	31	12
S18	●	at Virginia Tech	14	8
S25	●	Michigan State	25	22
O2	●	at Louisville	28	6
O9		at Notre Dame	14	16
O16	●	Mississippi State	31	14
O30		Florida State	7	24
N6		at Maryland	17	18
N20	●	North Carolina St.	41	3
N27	●	Cincinnati	19	13

1983 — 11-1-0

S3		at Florida	3	28
S10	●	at Houston	29	7
S17	●	Purdue	35	0
S24	●	Notre Dame	20	0
O1	●	at Duke	56	17
O8	●	Louisville	42	14
O15	●	at Mississippi	31	7
O22	●	at Cincinnati	17	7
O29	●	West Virginia	20	3
N5	●	East Carolina	12	7
N12	●	at Florida State	17	16
		ORANGE BOWL		
J2	●	Nebraska	31	30

JIMMY JOHNSON
1984-88 (.852) 52-9

1984 — 8-5-0

A27	●	Auburn [ERut]	20	18
S1	●	Florida [Tam]	32	20
S8		at Michigan	14	22
S15	●	at Purdue	28	17
S22		Florida State	3	38
S29	●	Rice	38	3
O6	●	at Notre Dame	31	13
O13	●	at Cincinnati	49	25
O20	●	Pittsburgh	27	7
N3	●	at Louisville	38	23
N10		Maryland	40	42
N23		Boston College	45	47
		FIESTA BOWL		
J1		UCLA	37	39

1985 — 10-2-0

S7		Florida	23	35
S14	●	at Rice	48	20
S28	●	Boston College [Fox]	45	10
O5	●	at East Carolina	27	15
O12	●	Cincinnati	38	0
O19	●	at Oklahoma	27	14
O26	●	Louisville	45	7
N2	●	at Florida State	35	27
N9	●	Maryland [Balt]	29	22
N23	●	Colorado State	24	3
N30	●	Notre Dame	58	7
		SUGAR BOWL		
J1		Tennessee	7	35

1986 — 11-1-0

A30	●	at South Carolina	34	14
S6	●	at Florida	23	15
S13	●	Texas Tech	61	11
S27	●	Oklahoma	28	16
O4	●	Northern Illinois	34	0
O11	●	at West Virginia	58	14
O18	●	at Cincinnati	45	13
N1	●	Florida State	41	23
N8	●	at Pittsburgh	37	10
N15	●	Tulsa	23	10
N27	●	East Carolina	36	10
		FIESTA BOWL		
J2		Penn State	10	14

1987 — 12-0-0

S5	●	Florida	31	4
S26	●	Arkansas [OB]	51	7
O3	●	at Florida State	26	25
O10	●	Maryland	46	16
O24	●	at Cincinnati	48	10
O31	●	at East Carolina	41	3
N7	●	Miami, Ohio	54	3
N14	●	Virginia Tech	27	13
N21	●	Toledo	24	14
N28	●	Notre Dame	24	0
D5	●	South Carolina	20	16
		ORANGE BOWL		
J1	●	Oklahoma	20	14

1988 — 11-1-0

S3	●	Florida State	31	0
S17	●	at Michigan	31	30
S24	●	Wisconsin	23	3
O1	●	Missouri	55	0
O15		at Notre Dame	30	31
O22	●	Cincinnati	57	3
O29	●	at East Carolina	31	7
N5	●	Tulsa	34	3
N19	●	at LSU	44	3
N26	●	Arkansas	18	16
D3	●	Brigham Young	41	17
		ORANGE BOWL		
J2	●	Nebraska	23	3

DENNIS ERICKSON
1989-94 (.875) 63-9

1989 — 11-1-0

S9	●	at Wisconsin	51	3
S16	●	California	31	3
S23	●	at Missouri	38	7
S30	●	at Michigan State	26	20
O7	●	Cincinnati	56	0
O14	●	San Jose State	48	16
O28		at Florida State	10	24
N4	●	East Carolina	40	10
N11	●	at Pittsburgh	24	3
N18	●	San Diego State	42	6
N25	●	Notre Dame	27	10
		SUGAR BOWL		
J1	●	Alabama	33	25

1990 — 10-2-0

S8		at Brigham Young	21	28
S15	●	at California	52	24
S29	●	Iowa	48	21
O6	●	Florida State	31	22
O13	●	Kansas	34	0
O20		at Notre Dame	20	29
O27	●	at Texas Tech	45	10
N3	●	Pittsburgh	45	0
N17	●	Boston College	42	12
N24	●	Syracuse	33	7
D1	●	at San Diego State	30	28
		COTTON BOWL		
J1	●	Texas	46	3

1991-2003
Big East

1991 — 12-0-0 (2-0-0)

A31	●	Arkansas [OB]	31	3
S12	●	Houston	40	10
S28	●	at Tulsa	34	10
O5	●	Oklahoma State	40	3
O12	●	Penn State	26	20
O19	●	Long Beach St.	55	0
O26	●	at Arizona	36	9
N9	● ‖	West Virginia	24	3
N16	●	at Florida State	17	16
N23	● ‖	at Boston College	19	14
N30	●	San Diego State	39	12
		ORANGE BOWL		
J1	●	Nebraska	22	0

1992 — 11-1-0 (4-0-0)

S5	●	at Iowa	24	7
S19	●	Florida A&M	38	0
S26	●	Arizona	8	7
O3	●	Florida State	19	16
O10	●	at Penn State	17	14
O17	●	TCU	45	10
O24	● ‖	at Virginia Tech	43	23
O31	● ‖	West Virginia	35	23
N14	● ‖	Temple	48	0
N21	● ‖	at Syracuse	16	10
N28	●	at San Diego State	63	17
		SUGAR BOWL		
J1		Alabama	13	34

1993 — 9-3-0 (6-1-0)

S4	● ‖	at Boston College	23	7
S18	● ‖	Virginia Tech	21	2
S25	●	at Colorado	35	29
O2	●	Georgia Southern	30	7
O9		at Florida State	10	28
O23	● ‖	Syracuse	49	0
O30	● ‖	Temple	42	7
N6	● ‖	at Pittsburgh	35	7
N13	● ‖	Rutgers	31	17
N20	‖	at West Virginia	14	17
N27	●	Memphis	41	17
		FIESTA BOWL		
J1		Arizona	0	29

1994 — 10-2-0 (7-0-0)

S3	●	Georgia Southern	56	0
S10	●	at Arizona State	47	10
S24		Washington	20	38
O1	● ‖	at Rutgers	24	3
O8	●	Florida State	34	20
O22	● ‖	at West Virginia	38	6
O29	● ‖	Virginia Tech	24	3
N5	● ‖	at Syracuse	27	6
N12	● ‖	Pittsburgh	17	12
N19	● ‖	at Temple	38	14
N26	● ‖	Boston College	23	7
		ORANGE BOWL		
J1		Nebraska	17	24

BUTCH DAVIS
1995-2000 (.718) 51-20

1995 — 8-3-0 (6-1-0)

S2		at UCLA	8	31
S9	●	Florida A&M	49	3
S23	‖	at Virginia Tech	7	13
O7		at Florida State	17	41
O14	● ‖	Rutgers	56	21
O21	● ‖	at Pittsburgh	17	16
O28	● ‖	Temple	36	12
N4	●	Baylor	35	14
N11	● ‖	at Boston College	17	14
N18	● ‖	West Virginia	17	12
N25	● ‖	Syracuse	35	24

1996 — 9-3 (6-1)

A31	●	at Memphis	30	7
S7	●	Citadel	52	6
S12	● ‖	at Rutgers	33	0
S28	● ‖	Pittsburgh	45	0
O12		Florida St	16	34
O19		East Carolina	6	31
O26	● ‖	at West Virginia	10	7
N2	● ‖	at Temple	57	26
N16	‖	Virginia Tech	7	21
N23	● ‖	Boston College	43	26
N30	● ‖	at Syracuse	38	31
		CARQUEST BOWL		
D27	●	Virginia	31	21

1997 — 5-6 (3-4)

A30	●	at Baylor	45	14
S13		Arizona State	12	23
S18	‖	at Pittsburgh	17	21
S27	‖	West Virginia	17	28
O4		at Florida State	0	47
O18	● ‖	at Boston College	45	44
O25	● ‖	Temple	47	15
N1	●	ArKansas State	42	10
N8	‖	at Virginia Tech	25	27
N15	● ‖	Rutgers	51	23
N29	‖	Syracuse	13	33

1998 — 9-3 (5-2)

S5	●	East Tenn. St.	66	17
S12	●	at Cincinnati	38	12
S19	‖	Virginia Tech	20	27
O3	● ‖	at Rutgers	53	17
O10		Florida State	14	26
O24	● ‖	at West Virginia	34	31
O31	● ‖	Boston College	35	17
N14	● ‖	at Temple	42	7
N19	● ‖	Pittsburgh	38	10
N28	‖	at Syracuse	13	66
D5	●	UCLA	49	45
		MICRON PC BOWL		
D29	●	North Carolina St.	46	23

1999 — 9-4 (6-1)

A29	●	Ohio State [ERut]	23	12
S4	●	Florida A&M	57	3
S18		Penn State	23	27
S25		East Carolina [Ral]	23	27
O9		at Florida State	21	31
O23	● ‖	at Boston College	31	28
O30	● ‖	West Virginia	28	20
N6	● ‖	at Pittsburgh	33	3
N13	‖	at Virginia Tech	10	43
N20	● ‖	Rutgers	55	0
N27	● ‖	Syracuse	45	13
D4	● ‖	Temple	55	0
		GATOR BOWL		
J1	●	Georgia Tech	28	13

2000 — 11-1 (7-0)

A31	●	McNeese St.	61	14
S9		at Washington	29	34
S23	● ‖	at West Virginia	47	10
S30	● ‖	at Rutgers	64	6
O7	●	Florida State	27	24
O21	● ‖	at Temple	45	17
O28	●	Louisiana Tech	42	31
N4	● ‖	Virginia Tech	41	21
N11	● ‖	Pittsburgh	35	7
N18	● ‖	at Syracuse	26	0
N25	● ‖	Boston College	52	6
		SUGAR BOWL		
J2	●	Florida	37	20

LARRY COKER
2001-Present (.880) 44-6

2001 — 12-0 (7-0)

S1	●	at Penn State	33	7
S8	● ‖	Rutgers	61	0
S27	● ‖	at Pittsburgh	43	21
O6	●	Troy St.	38	7
O13	●	at Florida State	49	27
O25	● ‖	West Virginia	45	3
N3	● ‖	Temple	38	0
N10	● ‖	at Boston College	18	7
N17	● ‖	Syracuse	59	0
N24	●	Washington	65	7
D1	● ‖	at Virginia Tech	26	24
		ROSE BOWL		
J3	●	Nebraska	37	14

2002 — 12-1 (7-0)

A31	●	Florida A&M	63	17
S7	●	at Florida	41	16
S14	● ‖	at Temple	44	21
S21	● ‖	Boston College	38	6
O5	●	Connecticut	48	14
O12	●	Florida State	28	27
O26	● ‖	at West Virginia	40	23
N2	● ‖	at Rutgers	42	17
N9	●	at Tennessee	26	3
N21	● ‖	Pittsburgh	28	21
N30	● ‖	at Syracuse	49	7
D7	● ‖	Virginia Tech	56	45
		FIESTA BOWL		
J3		Ohio State	24	31

2003 — 11-2 (6-1)

A28	●	Louisiana Tech [Shre]	48	9
S6	●	Florida	38	33
S13	●	East Carolina	38	3
S20	● ‖	at Boston College	33	14
O2	● ‖	West Virginia	22	20
O11	●	at Florida State	22	14
O18	● ‖	Temple	52	14
N1	‖	at Virginia Tech	7	31
N8		Tennessee	6	10
N15	● ‖	Syracuse	17	10
N22	● ‖	Rutgers	34	10
N29	● ‖	at Pittsburgh	28	14
		ORANGE BOWL		
J1	●	Florida State	16	14

2004-Present
ACC

2004 — 9-3 (5-3)

S10	● ‖	Florida State	16	10
S18	●	Louisiana Tech	48	0
S23	●	at Houston	38	13
O2	● ‖	at Georgia Tech	27	3
O14	●	Louisville	41	38
O23	● ‖	at North Carolina St.	45	31
O30	‖	at North Carolina	28	31
N6	‖	Clemson	17	24
N13	● ‖	at Virginia	31	21
N20	● ‖	Wake Forest	52	7
D4	‖	Virginia Tech	10	16
		PEACH BOWL		
D31	●	Florida	27	10

THE SCHOOLS

Neutral Site key: *Balt* Baltimore, MD / *Birm* Birmingham, AL / *Buf* Buffalo, NY / *ERut* East Rutherford, NJ / *Fox* Foxboro, MA / *JacF* Jacksonville, FL / *OB* Miami (Orange Bowl), FL / *NYC* New York, NY / *Orl* Orlando, FL / *Phil* Philadelphia, PA / *Ral* Raleigh, NC / *Tam* Tampa, FL / *Tok* Tokyo, Japan / *Unk* Unknown

ƒ Forfeit † Game Later Forfeited # Disputed Victor * Disputed Score ‖ Designated Conference Game |2 Counted Twice in Conference Standings

MIAMI (OHIO)

BY ED KRZEMIENSKI

WHEN ROBERT FROST REFERS TO a school as "the most beautiful college there is," it must have something going for it. Along with Frost's praise, Miami University in Oxford, Ohio, consistently receives accolades as one of the nation's "public Ivies" for its strong academics. But where Miami sheds any resemblance to the Ivy League is on the football field, where the RedHawks stand tall in Division I-A. In total, Miami (Ohio) has more victories and the same winning percentage as its more celebrated namesake to the south, the University of Miami. The school also has perhaps the greatest coaching bloodlines in the sport. Known as the Cradle of Coaches, Miami played a part in the development of more than two dozen successful head coaches, including such legends as Paul Brown, Sid Gillman, Weeb Ewbank, Bo Schembechler, Ara Parseghian, Woody Hayes and the group's most recent national champion, Jim Tressel. In 2003, Miami head coach Terry Hoeppner looked ready to join the cradle. In his fifth year at the helm, Hoeppner led the RedHawks to a No. 10 national ranking, the Mid-American Conference Championship, a GMAC Bowl win and the nation's longest winning streak, with 13 straight

victories. He left for Indiana following the 2004 season, in which the RedHawks went 8–5. Offensive coordinator Shane Montgomery took over as head coach.

TRADITION Miami and Cincinnati play each year for the Victory Bell, a traveling trophy that originally hung in Miami's Harrison Hall (Old Main). The two teams met for the first time in 1888 and began the Victory Bell tradition sometime in the 1890s when some Cincinnati fans "borrowed" the bell from the Miami campus. The game is fifth on the list of most-played rivalries and is the oldest rivalry west of the Allegheny Mountains.

STADIUM Fred C. Yager Stadium came into being in 1983. Named in honor of a 1914 graduate who supported the stadium project, it holds 30,012 people. The facilities include a Cradle of Coaches room on the second level honoring all coaches once affiliated with Miami, including more than 40 from football programs around the nation.

BEST PLAYER In three magical seasons from 2001 to 2003, quarterback Ben Roethlisberger rewrote all of Miami's passing records. After one season at the helm, Roethlisberger passed his way into sixth place on the school's career list with 3,105 yards. Following his 3,238-yard sophomore season, Roethlisberger was less than 200 yards behind Mike Bath's

PROFILE

Miami University
Oxford, Ohio
Founded: 1809
Enrollment: 15,059
Colors: Red and White
Nickname: RedHawks
Stadium: Yager Stadium
   Opened in 1983
   FieldTurf; 30,012 capacity
First football game: 1888
All-time record: 632–348–44 (.639)
Bowl record: 6–3
Mid-American Athletic Conference championships: 14 (12 outright)
First-round NFL draftees: 2
Website: www.muredhawks.com

THE BEST OF TIMES

From 1973 to 1975, the then-Redskins had a great run: a 32–1–1 record, three consecutive MAC championships, three consecutive Tangerine Bowl victories and final AP rankings of 15, 10 and 12. The only loss was a 14-13 heartbreaker to Michigan State.

THE WORST OF TIMES

Sandwiched between two one-loss MAC championship seasons, in 1976 the Redskins went 3–8, marking the school's first losing season in 34 years.

CONFERENCE

Miami was a charter member of the Mid-American Conference in 1946 (the conference began play in 1947), but did not compete in football until 1948.

DISTINGUISHED ALUMNI

R. Michael DeWine, U.S. senator; Rita Dove, U.S. poet laureate; Benjamin Harrison, U.S. president; P.J. O'Rourke, political satirist; Paul Smucker, jelly company founder

FIGHT SONG

MIAMI FIGHT SONG
Love and honor to Miami,
Our college old and grand.
Proudly we shall ever hail thee,
Over all the land.
Alma mater now we praise thee,
Sing joyfully this lay.
Love and honor to Miami,
Forever and a day.

career lead. As a junior, the 6'5" QB shattered the school record, passing for 4,486 yards with a 165.8 passer rating. (His junior season's total alone would have placed him third on the all-time list.) MAC opponents let out a collective sigh of relief when Roethlisberger announced his plan to forego his senior season and enter the NFL draft in 2004. Bowling Green coach Gregg Brandon articulated the feeling after Roethlisberger threw for 440 yards against his Falcons, saying, "I can't wait to play them when he's gone." Roethlisberger passed for 10,829 yards and 84 touchdowns in his career, led Miami to a 27–11 overall record and took the RedHawks to their first bowl game in 17 years—the 2003 GMAC Bowl, in which Miami beat Louisville 49-28.

BEST COACH Although he was not in Oxford as long as many of his celebrated brethren, Dick Crum did as much at Miami as any head coach. From 1974 to 1977, Crum won 34 games and built a .767 winning percentage. Neither of those marks constitutes a record for the school, but sometimes wins need to be weighed as well as counted. In his three winning seasons at Miami, Crum led the then-Redskins to three MAC titles, two Tangerine Bowl victories, two appearances in the final national rankings—No. 10 in 1974 and No. 12 in 1975—and compiled a gaudy 31–2–1 record.

There is no Miami, Ohio. The school is in Oxford, Ohio.

Crum ended his Miami career with a 34–10–1 record before leaving in 1978 to become the head coach at North Carolina.

BEST TEAM Bill Mallory's last season in Oxford was the school's best—not only did the team go undefeated in 1973, but they did so against some serious competition. Out of conference, Miami won at Purdue, at South Carolina and at Florida in the Tangerine Bowl. Senior Bob Hitchens led in rushing with 591 yards, but the strength of this team was its defense. Miami gave up an average of 178.5 yards per game and a total of just 76 points in 11 games. The defensive standout was middle guard Brad Cousino, who had 195 tackles, including a team-leading 32 for loss. For his efforts, Cousino was named the MAC Player of the Year. Miami was No. 15 in the final AP poll, but arguably deserved a higher place. Mallory left after the season to take over Colorado's program.

BIGGEST GAME On Nov. 10, 1973, Miami traveled to Kent State to play the Golden Flashes in a game that would determine the MAC championship. Both teams were undefeated in league play, and for the first time in the history of the MAC, two of its members were meeting as nationally ranked teams. At 7–1, defending conference champion Kent State

RECORDS

RUSHING YARDS

GAME

376 Travis Prentice vs. Akron, Nov. 6, 1999 (41 att.)

SEASON

1,787 Travis Prentice, 1998 (365 att.)

CAREER

5,596 Travis Prentice, 1996-99 (1,138 att.)

PASSING YARDS

GAME

525 Ben Roethlisberger vs. No. Illinois, Oct. 12, 2002 (41 of 61)

SEASON

4,486 Ben Roethlisberger, 2003 (342 of 495)

CAREER

10,829 Ben Roethlisberger, 2001–03 (854 of 1,398)

RECEIVING YARDS

GAME

198 Jeremy Patterson vs. Louisiana-Lafayette, Sept. 11, 1993 (10 rec.)

SEASON

1,498 Martin Nance, 2003 (90 rec.)

CAREER

2,772 Michael Larkin, 2001-04 (200 rec.)

POINTS

GAME

31 Wilbur Cartwright vs. Ashland, Nov. 1, 1930 (5 TDs, 1 PAT)

SEASON

150 Travis Prentice, 1997 (25 TDs)

CAREER

468 Travis Prentice, 1996-99 (78 TDs)

CONSENSUS ALL-AMERICANS

1982 Brian Pillman, MG

was ranked No. 19 while the undefeated Redskins were No. 17. Miami got all of the scoring it needed from fullback Chuck Varner, who scored on a two-yard run and a nine-yard pass. Leading 17-10 after three quarters, Miami finished off the Flashes when sophomore David Draudt kicked a school-record 52-yard field goal in the final quarter. It would be 30 years before two MAC opponents were simultaneously ranked again.

BIGGEST UPSET Defeating Northwestern is usually not something even a MAC team regards as an upset. But in 1995, Northwestern had beaten Notre Dame in its opening game and was ranked No. 25 in the nation, so 1–1 Miami entered as an underdog. Randy Walker's Redskins won a close one, 30-28, but the enormity of the upset became clear only after Northwestern completed the rest of its regular season without a loss. Commenting on his team's improbable run, Northwestern head coach Gary Barnett said that the only game he felt for certain the Wildcats would win going into the regular season was the one against Miami. After losing in the Rose Bowl, Northwestern ended the season 10–2 and ranked No. 8. Miami ended its year 8–2–1 and unranked.

HEARTBREAKER On Sept. 20, 1975, Miami traveled to East Lansing to play Michigan State riding not only a three-game undefeated streak against Big Ten opponents, but also a 24-game unbeaten streak. Leading 13-7 with 1:08 left in the game, it looked as if the Redskins would continue their roll. But Michigan State ended that dream with a late rally capped by a 56-yard touchdown pass for a 14-13 win. Miami won the rest of its games, though, and ended up No. 12 in the final AP poll.

RIVAL Miami's first game was against Cincinnati in 1888, a 0-0 tie that constituted Miami's entire season. Since then, the teams have met 108 times. Perhaps most memorable was the 1973 meeting in Oxford. After Miami's Larry Harper returned the opening kickoff 95 yards for a touchdown, the offense took the day off. Fortunately, Miami's top-ranked

defense shut down the Bearcats and the Redskins won 6-0, preserving their undefeated season. Through the 2004 season, Miami leads the series with a record of 58–44–7.

QUIRK The school is very particular as to how others refer to it. When referring to Miami, the school advises, one is to use Miami University, Miami University (Ohio) or Miami (Ohio). (How one speaks in parentheses, the school omits.) More specifically, Miami of Ohio is not proper. Also, there is no Miami, Ohio; the school is in Oxford, Ohio. Sportscasters will likely take heed of these distinctions when America goes metric. Incidentally, Miami (Ohio) has played Miami (Fla.) on three occasions: Miami leads the series 3–0 … the Florida one, that is.

DISPUTE Following a last-second loss to Marshall in 2002, Miami defensive coordinator Jon Wauford was arrested by West Virginia state troopers for shoving a fan who had rushed the field. Nor was Wauford the only out-of-control Miami coach that night. In the box, Miami's linebackers coach, Taver Johnson, destroyed a desk and sent several chairs through the walls after the game. Making matters significantly worse, it was the RedHawks' first game on national television.

NICKNAME At the urging of the Oklahoma-based Miami Tribe, for whom the school is named, Miami abandoned its traditional nickname of Redskins and became the RedHawks in 1997. Official use of the name Redskins began in the 1930-31 school year, because Big Red, a common appellation for Miami, caused some confusion with Denison University. Previously, the team was also known as the Miami Boys, the Big Reds, the Reds and Whites and the Big Red-Skinned Warriors.

MASCOT When Miami switched its nickname to RedHawks, it needed a new mascot as well. Enter a giant red bird named Swoop that, according to school lore, was born in the spring of 1972 and followed the team from afar (and above) until

ALL-CENTURY TEAM	
The greatest RedHawks as chosen by The Cincinnati Enquirer in 1999.	
1951-55	Ara Parseghian, coach
OFFENSE	
1946-47	Paul Dietzel, OL
1952-54	Tom Jones, OL
1972-74	Mike Biehle, OL
1995-97	Mike Bird, G
1983-86	Dan Dalrymple, T
1947-50	Doc Urich, TE
1967-69	Gary Arthur, TE
1995-98	Jay Hall, WR
1949-51	John Pont, RB
1996-99	Travis Prentice, TB
1972-75	Sherman Smith, QB
1984-87	Gary Gussman, K
DEFENSE	
1974-77	Jack Glowik, DL
1988-91	Jon Wauford, DE
1966-68	Bob Babich, LB
1972-74	Brad Cousino, LB
1980-83	Brian Pillman, LB
1989-92	Curt McMillan, LB
1993-96	Dee Osborne, LB
1968-70	Dick Adams, DB
1977-79	Kirk Springs, S
1984-87	Sheldon White, CB
1990-92	Ron Carpenter, S
1991-94	Gary Layton, P

the fortuitous 1997 nickname shift. The costumed-student Swoop brought the total number of bird-oriented MAC mascots to five and, defying all mathematical probability, the number of MAC mascots named Swoop to two.

UNIFORMS As Redskins and RedHawks, Miami has always maintained its red-and-white color scheme. Just about as consistent have been the team's helmets; since 1960, the helmets have been white with a red insignia. Except for a brief period in the latter half of the 1960s, when each player had his number on the side of his helmet, Miami helmets sported a red upper-case M of varying thickness on both sides. From 1966 to 1971 and then again in the early 1980s, a silhouette of an Indian appeared near the front of the headgear.

NUMBERS Miami represents one of two mid-major programs (the other is Army) in the top 25 for all-time NCAA Division I-A victories. Most successful was the school's three-year run from 1973 to 1975, which ended with a 32–1–1 record, a mark surpassed only by Oklahoma during that span.

QUOTE "People keep calling us the giant killers. But today we proved we're the giants."—Kicker John Scott in 1998, after unranked Miami beat No. 12 North Carolina 13-10 on a 37-yard Scott field goal with one second left to play

MIAMI (OHIO) ANNUAL STATISTICAL LEADERS

YR	RUSHING	YDS	ATT	AVG	PASSING	ATT	CMP	PCT	YDS	RECEIVING	REC	YDS	AVG
1957	Dave Thelen	755	115	6.6	Ernie Jarvis	35	13	.37	197	Harold Williams	9	118	13.1
1958	Harold Williams	566	87	6.5	Nick Mourouzis	32	14	.44	191	David Girbert	6	65	10.8
1959	David Girbert	332	55	6.0	Thomas Kilmurray	79	42	.53	454	Howie Millisor	11	132	12.0
1960	John Moore	616	94	6.5	Jack Gayheart	87	34	.39	441	Howie Millisor	17	261	15.4
1961	Bill Triplett	648	145	4.5	Jack Gayheart	77	34	.44	551	Robert Jencks	20	359	18.0
1962	Scott Tyler	538	77	7.0	Ernie Kellerman	133	61	.46	856	Robert Jencks	26	426	16.4
1963	Tom Longsworth	642	173	3.7	Ernie Kellerman	134	68	.51	895	Jack Himebauch	15	226	15.1
1964	Don Peddie	691	162	4.3	Ernie Kellerman	149	88	.59	1,260	Jack Himebauch	27	379	14.0
1965	Al Moore	677	155	4.4	Bruce Matte	146	70	.48	1,016	John Erisman	32	433	13.5
1966	Joe Kozar	633	178	3.6	Bruce Matte	111	60	.54	845	John Erisman	41	600	14.6
1967	Al Moore	717	135	5.3	Kent Thompson	106	38	.36	460	Gary Arthur	14	145	10.4
1968	Cleve Dickerson	736	161	4.6	Kent Thompson	159	76	.48	970	Mike Palija	22	334	15.2
1969	Cleve Dickerson	622	169	3.7	Jim Bengala	187	101	.54	1,276	Mike Palija	43	567	13.2
1970	Tim Fortney	1,063	265	4.0	Jim Bengala	236	107	.45	1,265	Mike Palija	41	639	15.6
1971	Bob Hitchens	1,192	271	4.4	Stu Showalter	109	43	.39	464	John Viher	24	251	10.5
1972	Bob Hitchens	1,370	326	4.3	Steve Williams	93	49	.53	676	John Viher	29	414	14.3
1973	Bob Hitchens	591	176	3.4	Steve Sanna	149	76	.51	927	John Wiggins	27	414	15.3
1974	Randy Walker	873	214	4.1	Steve Sanna	106	60	.57	724	Larry Harper	25	352	14.1
1975	Rob Carpenter	1,082	235	4.3	Sherman Smith	123	54	.44	592	Steve Joecken	17	225	13.2
1976	Rob Carpenter	1,064	240	4.4	Larry Fortner	202	88	.44	1,219	Steve Joecken	23	404	17.6
1977	Mark Hunter	809	170	4.8	Larry Fortner	186	109	.59	1,473	Paul Warth	26	450	17.3
1978	Mark Hunter	1,046	210	5.0	Larry Fortner	166	80	.48	975	Mark Angelo	21	299	14.2
1979	Paul Drennan	503	128	3.9	Chuck Hauck	207	97	.47	1,258	Keith Dummitt	17	395	23.2
1980	Greg Jones	952	201	4.7	Mark Kelly	86	41	.48	517	Don Treadwell	30	661	22.0
1981	Greg Jones	1,134	253	4.5	John Appold	171	80	.47	929	Don Treadwell	21	391	18.6
1982	Jay Peterson	1,250	271	4.3	John Appold	191	104	.54	1,051	Keith Dummitt	25	333	13.3
1983	Jay Peterson	842	224	3.8	Todd Rollins	212	110	.52	1,262	Tom Murphy	39	610	15.6
1984	George Swarn	1,281	269	4.8	Todd Rollins	140	77	.55	951	Tom Murphy	32	492	15.4
1985	George Swarn	1,511	309	4.9	Terry Morris	202	121	.60	1,471	George Swarn	29	430	14.8
1986	George Swarn	1,112	251	4.4	Terry Morris	308	193	.63	2,365	George Swarn	46	955	20.8
1987	Jon Gist	429	117	3.7	Mike Bates	359	218	.61	2,218	Chris Thomas	39	574	14.7
1988	Chris Alexander	816	164	5.0	Chris Ondrula	219	128	.58	1,304	John Stofa	32	450	14.1
1989	Chris Alexander	551	126	4.4	Joe Napoli	342	191	.56	1,988	Steve Fumi	25	426	17.0
1990	Terry Carter	858	197	4.4	Jim Clement	196	84	.43	1,184	Milt Stegall	32	590	18.4
1991	Kevin Ellerbe	708	184	3.8	Jim Clement	178	81	.46	938	Milt Stegall	45	489	10.9
1992	Deland McCullough	1,026	227	4.5	Neil Dougherty	291	148	.51	1,486	Jeremy Patterson	31	370	11.9
1993	Deland McCullough	612	174	3.5	Danny Smith	195	92	.47	982	Jim Clement	42	426	10.1
1994	Deland McCullough	1,103	227	4.9	Neil Dougherty	201	120	.60	1,431	Eric Henderson	43	560	13.0
1995	Deland McCullough	1,627	321	5.1	Sam Ricketts	211	108	.51	1,337	Tremayne Banks	44	733	16.7
1996	Ty King	1,065	247	4.3	Sam Ricketts	234	125	.53	1,333	Tremayne Banks	52	617	11.9
1997	Travis Prentice	1,549	296	5.2	Sam Ricketts	324	188	.58	2,466	Jay Hall	54	861	15.9
1998	Travis Prentice	1,787	365	4.9	Mike Bath	209	108	.52	1,500	Trevor Gaylor	38	653	17.2
1999	Travis Prentice	1,659	354	4.7	Mike Bath	295	138	.47	2,525	Trevor Gaylor	53	1,028	19.4
2000	Steve Little	986	189	5.2	Mike Bath	384	189	.49	2,415	Sly Johnson	37	620	16.8
2001	Steve Little	587	135	4.3	Ben Roethlisberger	381	241	.63	3,105	Mike Larkin	37	672	18.2
2002	Luke Clemens	1,009	223	4.5	Ben Roethlisberger	428	271	.63	3,238	Jason Branch	40	505	12.6
2003	Cal Murray	1,056	186	5.5	Ben Roethlisberger	495	342	.69	4,486	Martin Nance	90	1,498	16.6
2004	Luke Clemens	899	213	4.2	Josh Betts	444	268	.60	3,518	Ryne Robinson	64	932	14.6

Receiving leaders by receptions
The NCAA began including postseason stats in 2002

MIAMI (OHIO) ALL-TIME SCORES

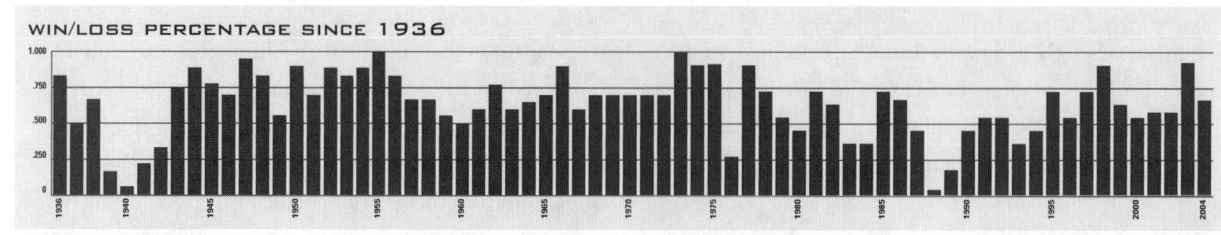

WIN/LOSS PERCENTAGE SINCE 1936

NO HEAD COACH

1888   0-0-1
D8	=	Cincinnati	0	0

1889   4-0-0
U	●	at Cincinnati	34	0
U	●	at Dayton HS	44	0
U	●	at Earlham	8	0
U	●	Dayton AC	14	4

1890
NO TEAM

1891   1-1-0
U	●	at Ohio Wesleyan	0	104
U	●	Hamilton AC	38	0

1892   2-2-0
U	●	at Earlham	0	12
U	●	at Centre	6	12
U	●	Cincinnati YMCA UNK	8	0
U	●	Hamilton AC	28	0

1893   3-0-0
U	●	Cincinnati	24	6
U	●	Earlham	28	6
U	●	at Cincinnati	6	0

1894   1-2-0
U	●	at Hamilton AC	18	0
U	●	at Cincinnati	0	6
O13		at Kentucky	6	28

C.K. FAUVER
1895 (1.000)   3-0

1895   3-0-0
N16	●	at Cincinnati	12	0
U	●	at Wittenberg	12	4
U	●	Butler	6	0

ERNEST MERRILL
1896 (.750)   3-1

1896   3-1-0
U	●	at Cincinnati	6	4
U	●	at Dayton	10	0
U	●	Earlham	26	0
U		Butler	4	16

HERBERT McINTYRE
1897 (.357)   2-4-1

1897   2-4-1
U		Cincinnati	0	6
U		Cincinnati UNK	6	10
U	=	Dayton AC UNK	0	0
U	●	at Earlham	10	0
U	●	Nashville Guards	10	0
U		at Indiana	6	22
U		at Centre	0	18

NO HEAD COACH

1898   0-2-0
U		Cincinnati	0	22
U		Dayton HS	6	11

1899   1-5-0
U		Cincinnati UNK	0	22
U		at Centre	12	15
U	●	Wittenberg	6	0
U		Earlham	0	6
O13		at Vanderbilt	0	12
O18		at Kentucky	5	18

ALONZO BRANCH
1900 (.000)   0-2

1900   0-2-0
U		at Wittenberg	0	33
U		at Cincinnati	12	16

THOMAS HAZZARD
1901 (.300)   1-3-1

1901   1-3-1
U		Denison UNK	0	6
U		Wittenberg	0	12
U	=	at Earlham	0	0
U		Dayton AC UNK	0	5
U	●	Antioch	23	6

PETER McPHERSON
1902-03 (.500)   6-6-1

1902   5-2-1
U	●	Denison UNK	24	5
O4		at Kentucky	5	11
U	●	Earlham	12	0
U	=	at Xavier	0	0
U		at Centre	6	12
U	●	at Wittenberg	11	0
U	●	Otterbein UNK	6	5
U	●	at Earlham	22	0

1903   1-4-0
U		at Ohio Wesleyan	6	19
U		at DePauw	6	11
U	●	at Cincinnati	15	0
O24		at Kentucky	0	47
U		at Xavier	0	33

ARTHUR SMITH
1904 (.167)   1-5

1904   1-5-0
O1		at Ohio State	0	80
U	●	Hamilton AC	12	6
U		at Cincinnati	0	46
U		Butler	0	32
U		at Indiana Medics	0	51
U		at Wittenberg	0	68

NO HEAD COACH

1905   4-3-0
U	●	Hamilton AC	52	0
U	●	Georgetown, Ky.	42	0
U		at Butler	0	17
U		at Wittenberg	0	35
U		at Centre	0	24
U	●	Antioch	9	0
N30	●	at Marshall	35	5	*

ARTHUR PARMALEE
1906 (.214)   1-5-1

1906   1-5-1
U	●	Georgetown, Ky.	16	0
U	=	at Cincinnati	0	0
U		Wittenberg	0	11
U		at Centre	0	8
U		Marietta	0	6
U		at Earlham	0	11
U		at DePauw	0	19

AMOS FOSTER
1907-08 (.929)   13-1

1907   6-1-0
U	●	Antioch	38	0
U	●	at Earlham	11	10
U		at DePauw	6	17
U	●	Centre UNK	10	0
U	●	Otterbein	32	0
U	●	at Marietta	12	10
U	●	at Cincinnati Gym	6	0

1908   7-0-0
O3	●	Wilmington	34	0
O10	●	at Centre	6	0
O17	●	at Ohio U.	5	0
O31	●	at Oberlin	11	10
N7	●	Wabash	6	0
N21	●	Ohio Wesleyan	24	0
N26	●	at Transylvania	27	0

HAROLD IDDINGS
1909-10 (.393)   5-8-1

1909   3-4-0
O2	●	Wilmington	35	2
O9	●	at Western Reserve	0	3
O16	●	Ohio U.	45	0
O23	●	Marietta	10	0
N6		at St. Louis	0	22
N16		at Notre Dame	0	46
N25		at Cincinnati	6	10

1910   2-4-1
U	●	Wilmington	5	0
U		at Centre	2	12
U		DePauw	0	10
U		at Cincinnati	0	3
U		at Marietta	0	17
U	=	at Butler	0	0
U	●	Wittenberg	19	0

EDWIN SWEETLAND
1911 (.375)   2-4-2

1911   2-4-2
S30	●	Wilmington	46	0
O7		at Ohio State	0	3
O14		Kentucky	0	12
O21	●	at Wittenberg	6	3
N4		at Ohio Wesleyan	0	11
N11	=	at DePauw	0	0
N18		at Cincinnati	0	11
N25	=	Western Reserve	5	5

JAMES DONNELLY
1912-14 (.625)   14-8-2

1912   3-3-2
S28	●	Wilmington	30	0
O5	=	at Wittenberg	0	0
O12	●	at Kentucky	13	8
O26		at St. Louis	0	35
N2		at DePauw	7	23
N9	●	Ohio U.	18	6
N16		Denison	0	13
N28	=	at Cincinnati	21	21

1913   6-2-0
S27	●	Wilmington	33	0
O4	●	Georgetown, Ky.	26	0
O11		at Oberlin	7	48
O25	●	at Denison	19	0
N1	●	Ohio Wesleyan	12	0
N8	●	Ohio U.	44	6
N15		at Western Reserve	0	7
N27	●	at Cincinnati	13	7

1914   5-3-0
S26	●	Otterbein	40	0
O3	●	at Oberlin	9	0
O10	●	at Ohio U.	0	6
O24	●	at Mount Union	16	14
O31		at Indiana	3	48
N7	●	at Ohio Wesleyan	10	3
N14		Denison	33	40
N27	●	at Cincinnati	20	13

C.J. ROBERTS
1915 (.750)   6-2

1915   6-2-0
S25	●	Ohio Northern	41	0
O2	●	at Akron	23	6
O9		at Indiana	0	41
O23	●	at Mount Union	17	0
O30	●	Ohio Wesleyan	19	7
N6		Denison UNK	0	14
N13	●	Ohio U.	13	7	*
N25	●	at Cincinnati	24	12

GEORGE LITTLE
1916, '19-21 (.875)   27-3-2

1916   7-0-1
S30	●	Ohio Northern	27	0
O7	●	Earlham	58	0
O14	●	at Wooster	10	6
O21	●	Kenyon	66	0
N4	=	Denison UNK	0	0
N11	●	at Ohio Wesleyan	9	0
N18	●	Western Reserve	35	6
N30	●	at Cincinnati	33	0	*

GEORGE RIDER
1917-18 (.893)   11-0-3

1917   6-0-2
O6	●	Ohio Northern	32	0
O13	=	at Kentucky	0	0
O20	●	Earlham	91	0
O27	●	Ohio Wesleyan	20	0
N3	●	Denison UNK	13	0
N10	●	at Mount Union	6	0
N17	=	Wooster	0	0
N29	●	at Cincinnati	40	0

1918   5-0-1
S28	●	Ohio Northern	47	0
N2	●	Kenyon	62	0
N9	●	at Ohio Wesleyan	14	7
N16	●	Denison	20	6
N23	●	Butler	52	0
N28	=	at Cincinnati	0	0

GEORGE LITTLE

1919   7-1-0
O4	●	Kenyon	26	0
O11	●	at Case	7	2
O18	●	Ohio Wesleyan	13	7
O25		Oberlin	0	13
N1	●	Denison UNK	14	0
N8	●	Ohio Northern	60	0
N15	●	at Mount Union	13	10
N28	●	at Cincinnati	14	0

1920   5-2-1
O2	●	Xavier	31	0
O9	●	Kenyon	41	7
O16	●	Kentucky	14	0
O23		at Wittenberg	0	17
O30	=	at Denison UNK	7	7
N6	●	at Ohio Wesleyan	7	0
N17	●	Mount Union	14	0
N25		at Cincinnati	0	7

1921   8-0-0
O1	●	Dayton	55	0
O8	●	Wittenberg	14	0
O15	●	at Ohio Northern	27	0
O22	●	Ohio Wesleyan	56	0
O29	●	Denison UNK	21	6
N5	●	Otterbein	21	0
N12	●	at Mount Union	29	0
N24	●	Cincinnati	15	7

HARRY EWING
1922-23 (.500)   7-7-2

1922   4-3-1
U	●	Alumni	0	0
U	●	Akron	20	12
U	●	Ohio Northern	6	0
U		Denison UNK	6	12
U		at Ohio Wesleyan	0	6
U	●	Mount Union	20	6
U		at Oberlin	0	3
N30	●	Cincinnati UNK	9	6

1923 — 3-4-1

S29	●	Georgetown, Ky.	22	0
O6	●	Alumni & JV	25	6
O13		at Wooster	0	13
O20		Oberlin	7	13
O27		Denison *Unk*	9	6
N10		at Mount Union	6	7
N17	=	Akron	13	13
N23		at Cincinnati	0	23

CHESTER PITTSER
1924-31 (.618)   41-25-2

1924 — 2-6-0

S27	●	Georgetown, Ky.	7	0
O4		at Michigan	0	55
O11		Mount Union	6	15
O18		Wooster	6	20
N1		Denison *Unk*	13	12
N8		Western Reserve	21	24
N15		at Oberlin	2	13
N27		at Cincinnati	7	8

1925 — 5-3-0

O3	●	Georgetown, Ky.	19	0
O10	●	Wittenberg	30	0
O17	●	Transylvania	19	0
O24		at Indiana	7	25
O31		Denison *Unk*	0	6
N7		at Mount Union	8	6
N14		Oberlin	7	18
N26		at Cincinnati	33	0

1926 — 5-2-1

S25	●	Wilmington	9	0
O2		Ohio Wesleyan	7	14
O9		Ohio Northern	34	12
O16		at Wittenberg	0	7
O30	●	Denison *Unk*	16	0
N6		Mount Union	27	19
N13		at Oberlin	13	0
N25	=	at Cincinnati	6	6

1927 — 8-1-0

S24	●	Hanover	80	0
O1	●	Otterbein	33	0
O8		at Ohio Wesleyan	35	7
O15		Denison	26	0
O22	●	Oberlin	23	0
O29		Wittenberg	0	23
N5		at Ohio Northern	34	6
N12		at Dayton	7	6
N24		at Cincinnati	17	14

1928 — 6-2-0

S29	●	Defiance	42	0
O6	●	Transylvania	8	0
O13		at Denison	0	21
O20		Ohio Wesleyan	0	12
N3	●	Ohio U.	20	13
N10		at Oberlin	18	0
N17		at Wittenberg	18	0
N29		at Cincinnati	34	0

1929 — 7-2-0

S28	●	Earlham	57	0
O5	●	at Western Reserve	18	0
O12		Kentucky Wesleyan	24	0
O19		at Ohio Wesleyan	12	20
O26	●	Wittenberg	3	0
N2		at Ohio U.	0	14
N9		Oberlin	20	0
N16	●	Denison	31	0
N28		at Cincinnati	14	6

1930 — 4-4-1

S27		at Indiana	0	14
O4	=	Illinois JV	6	6
O11	●	Kentucky Wesleyan	20	0
O18		at Denison	19	6
O25		Ohio U.	6	27
N1		Ashland	48	0
N8		Ohio Wesleyan	20	23
N15		at Oberlin	12	0
N27		at Cincinnati	0	6

1931 — 4-5-0

S26		at Pittsburgh	0	61
O3	●	Ball State	47	6	*
O10	●	Wabash	37	0
O17	●	Georgetown, Ky.	45	0
O24		at Ohio Wesleyan	7	12
O31	●	Denison	19	0
N7		Wittenberg	6	10
N14		at Ohio U.	0	13
N26		at Cincinnati	0	20

FRANK WILTON
1932-41 (.528)   44-39-5

1932 — 7-1-0

O1		at Illinois	7	20
O8	●	DePauw	33	13
O15	●	at Denison	27	7
O22	●	Ohio U.	16	0
O29	●	at Wabash	33	0
N5	●	Ohio Wesleyan	26	3
N12	●	at Wittenberg	19	0
N24	●	at Cincinnati	21	13

1933 — 7-2-0

S30		at Indiana	0	7
O7	●	Hanover	14	0
O14	●	Marshall	42	14
O21		at Ohio U.	0	6
O28	●	Wittenberg	44	7
N4	●	Georgetown, Ky.	51	0
N11	●	at Ohio Wesleyan	24	0
N18	●	Heidelberg	42	0
N30	●	at Cincinnati	6	2

1934 — 5-4-0

S29	●	Eastern Kentucky	19	0
O6		at Carnegie Tech	7	13
O13	●	Hanover	39	6
O20	●	Ohio U.	7	0
O26		at John Carroll	0	20
N3		Ohio Wesleyan	6	10
N10	●	at Wittenberg	33	0
N17	●	at Marshall	7	0
N29		at Cincinnati	0	21

1935 — 5-3-1

S28	●	Eastern Kentucky	33	7
O5	●	at Case	21	6
O12		Ohio Wesleyan	0	8
O19	●	John Carroll	28	12
O26	●	Marshall	20	13
N2		at Ohio U.	0	20
N9	●	Adrian	59	0
N16	=	at Dayton	6	6
N28		at Cincinnati	7	8

1936 — 7-1-1

S26	●	DePauw	14	6
O3	●	at Case	20	7
O10	●	Western Michigan	6	0	*
O17	●	Dayton	14	7
O24	●	Ohio U.	3	0
O31		at Ohio Wesleyan	0	13
N7	●	Toledo	13	0
N14	●	at Marshall	14	7
N26	=	at Cincinnati	0	0

1937 — 4-4-1

S25	●	Alma	27	0
O2	●	Marietta	75	6
O9		Marshall	0	7
O16		at Ohio U.	0	19
O23		at Toledo	7	13
O30	=	Case	13	13
N6	●	Ohio Wesleyan	32	0
N13		at Dayton	7	21
N25	●	at Cincinnati	14	6

1938 — 6-3-0

S24	●	Alma	51	0
O1	●	at Mount Union	40	0
O8		at Marshall	0	41
O15	●	Findlay	53	0
O22	●	Dayton	14	0
O29		at Ohio Wesleyan	16	20
N5		Ohio U.	12	20
N12	●	at Case	27	12
N24	●	at Cincinnati	16	7

1939 — 1-7-1

S30	●	Mount Union	7	0
O7		at Western Michigan	0	6
O14		Marshall	0	21
O21		Akron	0	14
O28	=	Ohio Wesleyan	0	0
N4		Detroit Tech	7	19
N11		at Ohio U.	7	20
N18		at Dayton	0	20
N23		at Cincinnati	0	13

1940 — 0-7-1

S21	=	Ball State	0	0
S28		Case	0	10
O5		at Ohio Wesleyan	7	24
O19		Dayton	6	28
O26		at Western Reserve	6	47
N2		Ohio U.	0	27
N9		Western Michigan	13	20
N21		at Cincinnati	0	44

1941 — 2-7-0

S20	●	Hanover	53	0
S27	●	Wabash	26	0
O4		at Illinois	0	45
O11		Bowling Green	0	9
O18		at Dayton	0	16
O25		Ohio Wesleyan	6	26
N1		at Ohio U.	0	26
N8		Western Reserve	13	28
N20		at Cincinnati	0	26

STU HOLCOMB
1942-43 (.553)   10-8-1

1942 — 3-6-0

S26	●	Centre	28	6
O3		at Dartmouth	7	58
O10	●	Kent State	53	7
O17		Dayton	0	20
O24		at Bowling Green	6	7
O31		Ohio U.	13	39
N7	●	at Ohio Wesleyan	28	25
N14		at Western Reserve	7	12
N26		at Cincinnati	12	21

1943 — 7-2-1

S18	=	at Indiana	7	7
U	●	Bethany	34	12
U	●	at Xavier	60	6
U	●	Wooster *Unk*	20	6
U		at Western Michigan	0	6
U	●	Ohio Wesleyan	35	0
U		Arkansas Monticello *Unk*	0	35
N6	●	Bowling Green	45	6
U		at Baldwin Wallace	40	6
U	●	Xavier *Unk*	52	7

SID GILLMAN
1944-47 (.829)   31-6-1

1944 — 8-1-0

S9	●	at Bowling Green	28	7
U	●	Oberlin	13	7
U	●	Western Michigan	32	6
U	●	at Rochester	19	7
U	●	DePauw	12	0
U	●	at Murray St.	26	14
U		Denison *Unk*	16	0
U	●	at Ohio Wesleyan	32	20
U		at DePauw	7	13

1945 — 7-2-0

S22	●	Bowling Green	26	0
U	●	Notre Dame JV	13	0
U	●	Wright Field *Unk*	14	0
U		at Western Michigan	21	13
U	●	Ohio U.	34	0
U		at Miami, Fla.	13	27
U	●	Indiana Normal	51	0
U		at Purdue	7	21
N22	●	at Cincinnati	28	14

1946 — 7-3-0

U		at Purdue	7	13
U	●	Memphis NATC	42	0
U	●	at Dayton	35	0
O12	●	at Bowling Green	6	0
U	●	Xavier	28	6
U	●	at Ohio U.	23	14
U	●	Bradley	35	6
U		at Miami, Fla.	17	20
U	●	Western Michigan	20	0
N28	●	at Cincinnati	7	13

1947 — 9-0-1

U	●	Murray St.	28	12
O4	●	at Kent State	35	7
O11	●	Bowling Green	33	19
U	=	at Xavier	6	6
U	●	Ohio U.	21	0
U	●	at Bradley	32	27
U	●	Dayton	12	0
U	●	at Wichita	22	7
N27	●	at Cincinnati	38	7
		SUN BOWL		
U	●	Texas Tech	13	12

1948-Present
MAC

GEORGE BLACKBURN
1948 (.833)   7-1-1

1948 — 7-1-1 (4-0-0)

S18	●	Marshall	38	6
S25	=	at Virginia	14	14
O2	●	at Western Reserve	49	0
O16	●	Xavier	9	0
O23	●	at Ohio U.	21	0
O30	●	Western Michigan	34	28
N6		at Dayton	0	7
N13	●	Wichita	41	16
N25	●	at Cincinnati	43	19

WOODY HAYES
1949-50 (.737)   14-5

1949 — 5-4-0 (3-1-0)

S24	●	at Wichita	23	6
O1		at Virginia	18	21
O8		Xavier	19	27
O15		at Pittsburgh	26	35
O22	●	Ohio U.	26	0
O29	●	at Western Michigan	34	20
N5	●	Western Reserve	46	7
N12	●	Dayton	52	20
N24		at Cincinnati	6	27

1950 — 9-1-0 (4-0-0)

S30	●	at Bowling Green	54	6
O7		Xavier	0	7
O14	●	Western Michigan	35	0
O21	●	at Butler	42	7
O28	●	at Ohio U.	28	20
N4	●	Wichita	39	13
N11	●	Dayton	27	12
N18	●	at Western Reserve	69	14
N25	●	at Cincinnati	28	0
		SALAD BOWL		
J1	●	Arizona State	34	21

ARA PARSEGHIAN
1951-55 (.859)   39-6-1

1951 — 7-3-0 (3-1-0)

S22	●	at Wichita	21	13
S29	●	Bowling Green	46	7
O6		Xavier	14	32
O13	●	at Western Michigan	34	27
O20	●	Ohio U.	7	0
O27	●	at Marquette	7	27
N3	●	Buffalo	27	7
N10	●	at Dayton	21	20
N17	●	Western Reserve	34	7
N24	●	at Cincinnati	14	19

1952 — 8-1-0 (4-1-0)

S27	●	at Bowling Green	42	7
O4	●	Xavier	26	7
O11	●	Western Michigan	55	6
O18	●	at Wichita	56	7
O25	●	at Ohio U.	20	0
N1	●	Toledo	27	13
N7	●	at Marquette	22	21
N15	●	Dayton	27	13
N27	●	at Cincinnati	9	34

1953 — 7-1-1 (3-0-1)

S26	●	Bowling Green	47	0
O3	●	Xavier	28	6
O10	●	at Western Michigan	52	6
O17	●	at Marshall	48	6
O24	=	Ohio U.	7	7
O31	●	at Toledo	81	0
N7	●	Tennessee Tech	44	6
N14	●	at Dayton	20	7
N26		at Cincinnati	0	14

1954 — 8-1-0 (4-0-0)

S25	●	at Bowling Green	46	7
O2	●	at Marquette	27	26
O9	●	Xavier	42	7
O16	●	Marshall	46	0
O23	●	at Ohio U.	46	13
O31	●	Western Michigan	48	0
N6	●	at Indiana	6	0
N13	●	Dayton	12	20
N25	●	at Cincinnati	21	9

1955 — 9-0-0 (5-0-0)

S24	●	at Northwestern	25	14
O1	●	Xavier	13	12
O8	●	Toledo	47	0
O15	●	at Marshall	46	7
O22	●	Ohio U.	34	7
O29	●	at Kent State	19	7
N5	●	Bowling Green	7	0
N12	●	at Dayton	21	0
N24	●	at Cincinnati	14	0

JOHN PONT
1956-62 (.657) 43-22-2

1956 7-1-1 (4-0-1)
S22 George Washington 6 7
S29 ● Xavier 14 7
O6 ● | Toledo 33 14
O13 ● | Marshall 21 14
O20 ● | at Ohio U. 16 7
O27 ● | Kent State 14 0
N3 = | at Bowling Green 7 7
N10 ● Dayton 21 14
N22 ● at Cincinnati 27 13

1957 6-3-0 (5-0-0)
S28 ● | at Western Michigan 20 0
O5 Xavier 19 39
O12 ● | at Kent State 27 14
O19 ● | Ohio U. 26 0
O26 at Purdue 6 37
N2 ● | at Bowling Green 13 7
N9 ● | Marshall 25 13
N16 at Dayton 7 13
N28 ● at Cincinnati 20 14

1958 6-3-0 (5-0-0)
S27 ● | Western Michigan 34 20
O4 Xavier 8 22
O11 ● | Kent State 35 0
O18 ● | at Ohio U. 14 10
O25 at Indiana 7 12
N1 ● | Bowling Green 28 14
N8 ● | at Marshall 26 0
N15 ● Dayton 34 0
N27 at Cincinnati 7 18

1959 5-4-0 (3-2-0)
S26 ● | at Western Michigan 21 0
O3 ● Xavier 33 7
O10 | at Kent State 6 14
O17 ● Villanova 26 6
O24 ● | Ohio U. 24 0
O31 | at Bowling Green 16 33
N7 ● | Toledo 25 7
N14 at Dayton 0 13
N26 at Cincinnati 7 14

1960 5-5-0 (2-3-0)
S17 at Xavier 6 17
S24 ● | Western Michigan 15 14
O1 | Bowling Green 12 21
O8 | Kent State 19 22
O15 ● at Villanova 17 7
O22 | at Ohio U. 0 21
O29 at Army 7 30
N5 ● | at Toledo 30 13
N12 ● Dayton 23 8
N19 ● at Cincinnati 10 6

1961 6-4-0 (3-2-0)
S16 Villanova 0 33
S23 ● Xavier 3 0
S30 | at Western Michigan 3 6
O7 ● | at Kent State 21 0
O14 at Purdue 6 19
O21 | Ohio U. 18 28
O28 ● | at Bowling Green 7 6
N4 ● | Toledo 40 14
N11 ● at Dayton 48 6
N18 ● at Cincinnati 7 3

1962 8-2-1 (3-1-1)
S15 ● at Xavier 23 14
S22 ● Quantico Marines 16 0
S29 ● | Western Michigan 17 7
O6 ● | Kent State 23 14
O13 ● at Purdue 10 7
O20 | at Ohio U. 6 12
O27 = | Bowling Green 24 24
N3 ● | at Toledo 21 12
N10 ● Dayton 42 10
N17 ● at Cincinnati 38 16
TANGERINE BOWL
D22 Houston 21 49

BO SCHEMBECHLER
1963-68 (.692) 40-17-3

1963 5-3-2 (4-1-1)
S21 Xavier 12 21
S28 = | Marshall 14 14
O5 ● | at Western Michigan 27 19
O12 ● | at Kent State 30 8
O19 at Northwestern 6 37
O26 | Ohio U. 10 13
N2 ● | at Bowling Green 21 12
N9 ● | Toledo 40 8
N16 = at Dayton 27 27
N28 ● at Cincinnati 21 19

1964 6-3-1 (4-2-0)
S19 = at Xavier 7 7
S26 ● | at Marshall 21 0
O3 ● | Western Michigan 35 0
O10 ● | Kent State 17 14
O17 ● at Northwestern 28 27
O24 | at Ohio U. 7 10
O31 | Bowling Green 18 21
N7 ● | at Toledo 35 14
N14 ● Dayton 27 21
N21 at Cincinnati 14 28

1965 7-3-0 (5-1-0)
S18 at Purdue 0 38
S25 Xavier 28 29
O2 ● | at Western Michigan 36 9
O9 | at Kent State 13 24
O16 ● | Marshall 28 7
O23 ● | Ohio U. 34 0
O30 ● | at Bowling Green 23 7
N6 ● | Toledo 20 16
N13 ● at Dayton 28 0
N20 ● at Cincinnati 37 7

1966 9-1-0 (5-1-0)
S17 ● at Indiana 20 10
S24 ● at Xavier 27 3
O1 ● | Western Michigan 26 7
O8 ● | Kent State 7 0
O15 ● | at Marshall 12 0
O22 ● | at Ohio U. 33 13
O29 | Bowling Green 14 17
N5 ● | at Toledo 24 12
N12 ● Dayton 38 6
N26 ● at Cincinnati 28 8

1967 6-4-0 (4-2-0)
S16 | at Western Michigan 14 24
S23 ● at Tulane 14 3
S30 Xavier 6 7
O7 ● | at Kent State 21 7
O14 ● | Marshall 48 6
O21 ● | Ohio U. 22 15
O28 ● | at Bowling Green 9 7
N4 | Toledo 14 24
N11 at Dayton 6 7
N18 ● at Cincinnati 27 14

1968 7-3-0 (5-1-0)
S14 ● at Xavier 28 7
S21 at Pacific 20 21
S28 ● | Western Michigan 28 0
O5 ● | Kent State 24 0
O12 ● | at Marshall 46 0
O19 | at Ohio U. 7 24
O26 ● | Bowling Green 31 7
N2 ● | at Toledo 21 17
N9 ● Dayton 14 0
N23 at Cincinnati 21 23

BILL MALLORY
1969-73 (.765) 39-12

1969 7-3-0 (2-3-0)
S13 ● Xavier 35 7
S20 ● at Dayton 19 9
S27 ● | at Western Michigan 24 20
O11 ● Marshall 35 7
O18 ● | Ohio U. 24 21
O25 | at Bowling Green 0 3
N1 | Toledo 10 14
N8 ● at Maryland 34 21
N15 | at Kent State 14 17
N22 ● at Cincinnati 36 20

1970 7-3-0 (3-2-0)
S19 ● at Xavier 28 7
S26 ● | Western Michigan 23 12
O3 ● Northern Illinois 48 0
O10 ● at Marshall 19 12
O17 | at Ohio U. 22 23
O24 ● | Bowling Green 7 3
O31 | at Toledo 13 14
N7 ● Dayton 17 0
N14 ● | Kent State 10 8
N21 at Cincinnati 0 33

1971 7-3-0 (2-3-0)
S11 ● at Pacific 17 10
S18 ● at Xavier 17 7
S25 ● at Dayton 14 0
O2 ● Marshall 66 6
O16 | Ohio U. 0 3
O23 | at Bowling Green 7 33
O30 | Toledo 6 45
N6 ● | at Western Michigan 7 6
N13 ● | at Kent State 30 0
N20 ● Cincinnati 43 7

1972 7-3-0 (2-3-0)
S16 ● Dayton 34 7
S23 | Bowling Green 7 16
S30 ● Xavier 25 7
O7 ● at Marshall 22 7
O14 ● | at Ohio U. 31 7
O21 ● at South Carolina 21 8
O28 | at Toledo 21 35
N4 ● | Western Michigan 38 8
N11 | Kent State 10 21
N18 ● at Cincinnati 23 0

1973 11-0-0 (5-0-0)
S15 ● Dayton 32 0
S22 ● at Purdue 24 19
S29 ● at South Carolina 13 11
O6 ● Marshall 31 6
O13 ● | Ohio U. 10 6
O20 ● | at Bowling Green 31 8
O27 ● | Toledo 16 0
N3 ● | at Western Michigan 24 9
N10 ● | at Kent State 20 10
N17 ● Cincinnati 6 0
TANGERINE BOWL
D22 ● Florida 16 7

DICK CRUM
1974-77 (.767) 34-10-1

1974 10-0-1 (5-0-0)
S7 ● Eastern Michigan 39 0
S21 = at Purdue 7 7
S28 ● at Marshall 42 0
O5 ● at Kentucky 14 10
O12 ● | at Ohio U. 31 3
O19 ● | Bowling Green 34 10
O26 ● | at Toledo 38 22
N2 ● | Western Michigan 31 0
N9 ● | Kent State 19 17
N16 ● at Cincinnati 27 7
TANGERINE BOWL
D21 ● Georgia 21 10

1975 11-1-0 (6-0-0)
S13 ● Marshall 50 0
S20 at Michigan State 13 14
S27 ● | Ball State 35 28
O4 ● at Purdue 14 3
O11 ● at Dayton 10 0
O18 ● | Ohio U. 17 9
O25 ● | at Bowling Green 20 17
N1 ● | Toledo 35 21
N8 ● | at Western Michigan 44 21
N15 ● | at Kent State 27 8
N22 ● Cincinnati 21 13
TANGERINE BOWL
D20 ● South Carolina 20 7

1976 3-8-0 (2-4-0)
S4 at North Carolina 10 14
S11 at Marshall 16 21
S18 | Ball State 6 23
S25 at Cincinnati 0 17
O2 at Purdue 20 42
O16 | at Ohio U. 14 28
O23 ● | Bowling Green 9 7
O30 | at Toledo 9 24
N6 ● | Western Michigan 31 0
N13 | Kent State 17 24
N20 ● Dayton 28 8

1977 10-1-0 (5-0-0)
S3 ● Dayton 26 23
S17 at South Carolina 19 42
S24 ● at Indiana 21 20
O1 ● at Yale 28 14
O8 ● Marshall 29 19
O15 ● | Ohio U. 28 24
O22 ● | at Bowling Green 33 13
O29 ● | Toledo 27 3
N5 ● | at Western Michigan 14 8
N12 ● | at Kent State 25 0
N24 ● at Cincinnati 12 7

TOM REED
1978-82 (.636) 34-19-2

1978 8-2-1 (5-2-0)
S9 | at Ball State 14 38
S16 | Central Michigan 18 37
S23 ● | Western Michigan 7 3
S30 = Dayton 10 10
O7 ● at North Carolina 7 3
O14 ● at Marshall 29 3
O21 ● | Bowling Green 18 7
O28 ● | at Toledo 28 7
N4 ● | at Ohio U. 31 16
N11 ● | Kent State 38 13
N18 ● Cincinnati 28 24

1979 6-5-0 (3-4-0)
S8 ● | Ball State 27 3
S15 ● at Kentucky 15 14
S22 at Michigan State 21 24
S29 | at Central Michigan 18 19
O6 ● at Marshall 28 0
O13 | Ohio U. 7 9
O20 ● | at Bowling Green 21 3
O27 | Toledo 21 24
N3 | at Western Michigan 3 24
N10 ● | at Kent State 35 8
N17 ● Cincinnati 27 14

1980 5-6-0 (4-3-0)
S13 | Central Michigan 14 15
S20 at Syracuse 24 36
S27 ● | at Ball State 42 9
O4 at Purdue 3 28
O11 ● Marshall 34 6
O18 | at Ohio U. 7 17
O25 ● | Bowling Green 7 3
N1 | at Toledo 14 17
N8 ● | Western Michigan 34 24
N15 ● | Kent State 49 14
N22 at Cincinnati 13 23

1981 8-2-1 (6-1-1)
S12 ● at William & Mary 33 14
S19 at North Carolina 7 49
S26 ● | at Eastern Michigan 18 12
O3 ● | Kent State 20 13
O10 = | at Bowling Green 7 7
O17 ● | Western Michigan 20 19
O24 ● | Ohio U. 40 14
O31 | at Toledo 10 17
N7 ● | at Central Michigan 7 3
N14 ● | Northern Illinois 30 3
N21 ● Cincinnati 7 3

1982 7-4-0 (5-3-0)
S11 ● William & Mary 35 17
S18 ● at Northwestern 27 13
S25 ● | Eastern Michigan 35 0
O2 ● | at Kent State 20 0
O9 ● | Bowling Green 17 12
O16 | at Western Michigan 0 10
O23 | at Ohio U. 0 20
O30 ● | Toledo 21 17
N6 ● | Central Michigan 23 0
N13 | at Northern Illinois 7 12
N18 at Cincinnati 10 20

TIM ROSE
1983-89 (.417) 31-44-3

1983 4-7-0 (3-5-0)
S10 at South Carolina 3 24
S17 at North Carolina 17 48
S24 | at Bowling Green 14 17
O1 | Western Michigan 18 20
O8 ● | Kent State 27 7
O15 | at Toledo 9 10
O22 ● | at Central Michigan 12 7
O29 | Northern Illinois 0 17
N5 | Ohio U. 14 17
N12 ● | at Eastern Michigan 24 12
N19 ● Cincinnati 14 10

1984 4-7-0 (3-5-0)
S8 | at Western Michigan 13 17
S15 at Houston 17 30
S22 | Bowling Green 10 41
S29 at Washington 7 53
O6 ● | at Kent State 19 3
O13 | Toledo 7 10
O20 | Central Michigan 9 10
O27 ● | at Northern Illinois 20 7
N3 | at Ohio U. 19 24
N10 ● | Eastern Michigan 23 0
N22 ● at Cincinnati 31 26

1985 8-2-1 (7-1-1)
S14 ● | at Ball State 17 13
S21 | at Bowling Green 24 28
S28 at Oklahoma State 10 45
O5 ● | Ohio U. 29 22
O12 ● | at Toledo 26 14
O19 = | Western Michigan 10 10
O26 ● | Northern Illinois 32 15
N2 ● | at Central Michigan 19 14
N9 ● | Kent State 52 24
N16 ● | at Eastern Michigan 31 16
N23 ● Cincinnati 16 10

1986   8-4-0 (6-2-0)

S6 ●	Ball State	45	7
S13	at Cincinnati	38	45
S20	at LSU	21	12
S27 ●	Bowling Green	24	7
O4	at Ohio U.	34	14
O11 ●	Toledo	24	8
O18	at Western Michigan	17	27
O25 ●	at Northern Illinois	20	6
N1 ●	Central Michigan	59	21
N8	at Kent State	23	24
N15 ●	Eastern Michigan	34	20

CALIFORNIA BOWL

D13	San Jose State	7	37

1987   5-6-0 (5-3-0)

S5 ●	at Central Michigan	15	6
S12	Eastern Michigan	17	33
S19	at Syracuse	10	24
S26	at Cincinnati	26	31
O3 ●	Ball State	30	20
O10 ●	at Western Michigan	17	0
O17 ●	Ohio U.	10	9
O24	at Toledo	25	37
O31 ●	Bowling Green	17	7
N7	at Miami, Fla.	3	54
N14	at Kent State	10	14

1988   0-10-1 (0- 7-1(

S3	at Eastern Michigan	17	24
S10	at Oklahoma State	20	52
S17	at Minnesota	3	35
S24	Cincinnati	18	34
O1	at Ball State	14	45
O8	Western Michigan	18	41
O15	at Ohio U.	21	38
O22	Toledo	7	20
O29 =	at Bowling Green	21	21
N12	Kent State	11	17
N19	Central Michigan	17	34

1989   2-8-1 (2-5-1)

S9	at Purdue	10	27
S16	at Michigan State	0	49
S23	Cincinnati	14	30
S30	Central Michigan	7	20
O7	at Ball State	9	37
O14 =	Ohio U.	22	22
O21	at Toledo	14	17
O28 ●	Bowling Green	17	13
N4	at Eastern Michigan	7	20
N11 ●	at Kent State	15	13
N18	Western Michigan	7	14

**RANDY WALKER
1990-98 (.611)   58-36-5**

1990   5-5-1 (4-3-1)

S1	at North Carolina	0	34
S8	Toledo	14	20
S15	at LSU	7	35
S22 ●	at Cincinnati	16	12
S29	at Central Michigan	7	31
O6 ●	Ball State	24	10
O13 ●	at Ohio U.	40	18
O27 =	at Bowling Green	10	10
N3 ●	Eastern Michigan	34	14
N10 ●	Kent State	31	10
N17	at Western Michigan	17	31

1991   6-4-1 (4-3-1)

A31 ●	Ball State	15	7
S7	at Kentucky	20	23
S14 ●	Eastern Michigan	29	3
S28 ●	at Cincinnati	22	9
O5 ●	at La. Lafayette	27	14
O12 =	at Central Michigan	10	10
O19 ●	Ohio U.	34	0
O26	at Toledo	7	24
N2	Bowling Green	7	17
N9	at Western Michigan	23	24
N16 ●	at Kent State	20	9

1992   6-4-1 (5-3-0)

S5 =	at West Virginia	29	29
S12	at Indiana	0	16
S19 ●	Cincinnati	17	14
S26	at Ball State	9	19
O3 ●	at Eastern Michigan	24	7
O10 ●	Central Michigan	16	13
O17 ●	at Ohio U.	23	21
O24	Toledo	17	20
O31 ●	at Bowling Green	24	44
N7 ●	Western Michigan	20	7
N14 ●	Kent State	31	14

1993   4-7-0 (3-6-0)

S11 ●	La. Lafayette	29	28
S18	at Cincinnati	23	30
S25	at Western Michigan	0	17
O2	Eastern Michigan	7	15
O9	at Akron	13	31
O16 ●	at Toledo	22	19
O23	Ohio U.	20	22
O30	Bowling Green	25	30
N6	at Ball State	0	21
N13 ●	at Kent State	23	14
N20 ●	Central Michigan	24	21

1994   5-5-1 (5-3-0)

S3	Western Michigan	25	28
S10	at Indiana	14	35
S17 =	Cincinnati	17	17
S24	at Michigan State	10	45 †
O1 ●	at Eastern Michigan	21	17
O8 ●	Akron	50	14
O15 ●	at Ohio U.	31	10
O22 ●	at Central Michigan	30	32
O29 ●	at Bowling Green	16	27
N5 ●	Ball State	24	21
N12 ●	Kent State	24	14

1995   8-2-1 (6-1-1)

A31 ●	Ball State	15	17
S9 ●	at Kent State	39	0
S16 ●	at Northwestern	30	28
S23 ●	Cincinnati	23	16
S30 ●	at Michigan	19	38
O7 ●	at Bowling Green	21	0
O14 =	Toledo	28	28
O28 ●	at Central Michigan	17	13
N4 ●	Eastern Michigan	39	23
N11 ●	at Ohio U.	30	2
N18 ●	Akron	65	0

1996   6-5 (6-2)

A31 ●	Kent State	64	6
S7 ●	at Ball State	16	6
S14 ●	at Indiana	14	21
S21 ●	Bowling Green	10	14
S28 ●	at Cincinnati	23	30
O5 ●	Central Michigan	46	14
O12 ●	at Eastern Michigan	35	25
O19 ●	at Akron	7	10
O26 ●	Army	7	27
N2 ●	at Toledo	27	7
N9 ●	Ohio U.	24	8

1997   8-3 (6-2)

A30 ●	Ball State	27	10
S6 ●	at Bowling Green	21	28
S13 ●	Akron	49	20
S27 ●	at Army	38	14
O4 ●	at Virginia Tech	24	17
O11 ●	at Kent State	62	26
O18 ●	Marshall	45	21
O25 ●	Cincinnati	31	34
N1 ●	at Toledo	28	35
N8 ●	at Ohio U.	45	21
N15 ●	Northern Illinois	42	0

1998   10-1 (7-1)

S5 ●	at North Carolina	13	10
S12 ●	at Army	14	13
S26 ●	Toledo	28	14
O3	at Marshall	17	31
O10 ●	Bowling Green	24	12
O17 ●	at Ball State	28	17
O24 ●	at Cincinnati	41	0
O31 ●	Ohio U.	35	21
N7 ●	at Northern Illinois	41	10
N14 ●	Kent State	56	0
N21 ●	at Akron	20	14

**TERRY HOEPPNER
1999-2004 (.658)   48-25**

1999   7-4 (6-2)

S4 ●	at Northwestern	28	3
S11	at West Virginia	27	43
S18 ●	Eastern Michigan	35	14
S25 ●	at Central Michigan	24	16
O2	Marshall	14	32
O9 ●	at Bowling Green	45	31
O16 ●	at Kent State	17	10
O30	Cincinnati	42	52
N6 ●	Akron	32	23
N13	at Ohio U.	28	40
N20 ●	Buffalo	43	0

2000   6-5 (5-3)

S2	at Vanderbilt	33	30
S9 ●	at Eastern Michigan	34	17
S16	at Ohio State	16	27
S23 ●	Kent State	45	14
S30	at Akron	20	37
O7	Ball State	10	15
O14 ●	Bowling Green	24	10
O28	at Cincinnati	15	45
N4 ●	Ohio U.	27	24
N11	at Marshall	31	51
N18	at Buffalo	17	16

2001   7-5 (6-2)

S1	at Michigan	13	31
S8	at Iowa	19	44
S22 ●	Cincinnati	21	14
S29 ●	at Ball State	28	20
O6	Buffalo	31	14
O13	Akron	30	27
O20 ●	at Ohio U.	36	24
O27 ●	Western Michigan	25	11
N3 ●	at Bowling Green	24	21
N10	Marshall	21	27
N17	at Hawaii	51	52
N24	at Kent State	20	24

2002   7-5 (5-3)

A31	at North Carolina	27	21
S7	Iowa	24	29
S14	at LSU	7	33
S21 ●	Kent State	27	20
S28 ●	at Akron	48	31
O5 ●	at Cincinnati	31	26
O12	Northern Illinois	41	48
O19 ●	at Buffalo	49	0
O26 ●	at Toledo	27	13
N2 ●	Ohio U.	38	20
N12	at Marshall	34	36
N23	Central Florida	31	48

2003   13-1 (8-0)

A30	at Iowa	3	21
S13 ●	at Northwestern	44	14
S20 ●	at Colorado State	41	21
S27 ●	Cincinnati	42	37
O4 ●	Akron	45	20
O11 ●	Buffalo	59	3
O18 ●	at Ball State	49	3
O25 ●	at Kent State	38	30
N4 ●	Bowling Green	33	10
N12 ●	Marshall	45	6
N22 ●	at Ohio U.	49	31
N28 ●	at Central Florida	56	21

MAC CHAMPIONSHIP GAME

D4 ●	at Bowling Green	49	27

GMAC BOWL

D18 ●	Louisville	49	28

2004   8-5 (7-1)

A28 ●	Indiana St.	49	0
S4	at Michigan	10	43
S11	at Cincinnati	26	45
S18 ●	Ohio U.	40	20
S29	at Marshall	25	33
O9 ●	Kent State	47	24
O16 ●	at Buffalo	25	7
O23	Central Florida	43	7
N3 ●	Toledo	23	16
N13 ●	at Western Michigan	42	21
N20 ●	at Akron	37	27

MAC CHAMPIONSHIP GAME

D2	Toledo *DET*	27	35

INDEPENDENCE BOWL

D28	Iowa State	13	17

f Forfeit † Game Later Forfieted # Disputed Victor * Disputed Score || Designated Conference Game |2 Counted Twice in Conference Standings

MICHIGAN

BY TODD JONES

EVERYTHING ABOUT MICHIGAN football looms as large as the Great Lakes. The Wolverines have the most Division I-A victories (842 through 2004), the most Big Ten championships (42) and the nation's largest stadium (107,501). The Wolverines have won nine national titles, have a .746 all-time winning percentage (highest in Division I-A) and have played in more televised games (332) than any other school. But numbers speak only to the cold efficiency of the powerful football machine. Its heart has been warmed by the play of such stars as Bennie Oosterbaan, Benny Friedman, Tom Harmon, Rick Leach, Anthony Carter, Desmond Howard and Charles Woodson, as well as by the coaching fire of Fielding Yost, Fritz Crisler, Bo Schembechler and Lloyd Carr, men who have built a lasting legacy and a tradition matched by few other schools.

TRADITION Nothing sounds quite like "The Victors." Louis Elbel created one of college football's most recognizable fight songs in 1899 after he watched Michigan upset Amos Alonzo Stagg's powerhouse Chicago team. Today, the University of Michigan Marching Band, a 225-member outfit, blasts the song when the Wolverines run out of the Michigan Stadium tunnel and touch the "Go Blue" banner as they take the field. It blares after every Michigan score, accompanied by cheerleaders doing back flips off the rail of the brick wall surrounding the home field. Since 1953, the Wolverines and Michigan State annually have played for the Paul Bunyan Trophy—a four-foot wooden statue donated by then-governor G. Mennen Williams. The Little Brown Jug, however, is the oldest of college football's 57 trophy-game traditions. Yost, who feared his Wolverines might be served contaminated water at Minnesota in 1903, ordered team manager Tommy Roberts to buy a five-gallon jug from a Minneapolis store. Michigan drank from it during a 6-6 tie, and then left the jug behind. When Yost asked for it back, Minnesota athletic director L.J. Cooke replied, "If you want it, you'll have to come up and win it." Michigan did so in 1909, and the two teams have played for the jug every year since 1929.

BEST PLAYER He was "Ol' 98," the needle-nosed, square-jawed, gregarious fellow who learned how to play rough as

---

PROFILE

University of Michigan
Ann Arbor, Mich.
Founded: 1817
Enrollment: 23,312
Colors: Maize and Blue
Nickname: Wolverines
Stadium: Michigan Stadium
    Opened in 1927
    FieldTurf; 107,501 capacity
First football game: 1879
All-time record: 842–275–36 (.746)
Bowl record: 18–18
Consensus national championships, 1936-present: 3 (1947, 1948, 1997)
Big Ten Conference championships: 42 (16 outright)
Heisman Trophy: Tom Harmon, 1940; Desmond Howard, 1991; Charles Woodson, 1997
First-round NFL draftees: 39
Website: www.mgoblue.com

THE BEST OF TIMES

Bo Schembechler's 50–4–1 record and four Big Ten championships from 1970 to 1974 is impressive, but it pales compared to the "Point a Minute" Wolverines, who went 55–1–1 from 1901 to 1905. They outscored opponents 2,821-42 while winning four consecutive national championships.

THE WORST OF TIMES

Four years without a winning record as coach Harry G. Kipke went 10–22 (5–17 in the Big Ten) from 1934 to 1937. His 1934 and 1936 clubs each went 1–7.

CONFERENCE

The Wolverines were charter members of the Big 10 (then called the Western Conference) in 1896, but left to become an independent from 1907-1916. In 1917, they rejoined the conference, where they've remained since.

DISTINGUISHED ALUMNI

Clarence Darrow; Gerald Ford; Arthur Miller; Branch Rickey; Madonna; Mike Wallace; James Earl Jones; Nancy Kassebaum, U.S. senator; Lucy Liu, actress

FIGHT SONG

THE VICTORS
Now for a cheer they are here, triumphant!
Here they come with banners flying,
In stalwart step they're nighing,
With shouts of vict'ry crying,
We hurrah, hurrah, we greet you now, Hail!
Far we their praises sing
For the glory and fame they've brought us
Loud let the bells them ring
For here they come with banners flying
Here they come, Hurrah!
Hail! to the victors valiant
Hail! to the conqu'ring heroes
Hail! Hail! to Michigan
The leaders and best!
Hail! to the victors valiant
Hail! to the conqu'ring heroes
Hail! Hail! to Michigan
The champions of the West!

a child on the sandlots of Gary, Ind., and eventually ended up on a *Life* magazine cover under the headline, "Michigan's Great Harmon." That was November 1940, shortly before senior Tom Harmon won the Heisman Trophy. He was 6'1", 195 pounds, and played tailback, defensive back, kicker and punter. Twice he led the nation in scoring, something no one had ever done before. His versatility was unstoppable at California on Sept. 28, 1940. There, he ran the opening kickoff back 94 yards for a touchdown, returned a punt 72 yards for a TD, ran 86 and eight yards for two other scores and threw a TD pass in a 41-0 win over the Bears. Nothing could stop him, not even a drunken Cal fan named Bud Brennan, who ran out of the stands and tried to tackle Harmon during his 86-yard score. In World War II, Harmon was shot down and listed as missing twice in the Pacific jungles while serving as an Army Air Force pilot. He won the Silver Star and Purple Heart, and then played briefly in the pro ranks with the Los Angeles Rams before becoming a nationally known sportscaster.

> **The men in maize and blue have built a tradition matched by few other schools.**

BEST COACH "Meeshegan," as he pronounced it, might have been just another football school without the influence of Fielding H. Yost. It became a beast, however, when the man from West Virginia arrived in Michigan at the turn of the 20th century and told everyone to "hurry up." Yost was a lawyer, a nondrinker and a cigar-chompin' son of a Confederate soldier. He was also one of football's first giants—the creator of the linebacker position and the first to use offensive motion as a decoy. Some called his style of play, which sometimes called for quick-kicking to achieve field position, boring and referred to his offense as "punt, pass and pray." Yost coached the incredible "Point a Minute" Michigan teams that went 55–1–1 (with 50 shutouts) and outscored opponents 2,821-42 from 1901 to 1905. In all, he went 165–29–10, had eight undefeated teams and won four national championships from 1901 to 1926 (he didn't coach in 1924). His seven Big Ten titles would have been more if the Wolverines had not dropped out of the league for 10 years because the school was upset with rules

RECORDS

RUSHING YARDS
GAME
347 Ron Johnson vs. Wisconsin, Nov. 16, 1968 (31 att.)
SEASON
1,818 Tim Biakabutuka, 1995 (303 att.)
CAREER
4,472 Anthony Thomas, 1997-2000 (924 att.)

PASSING YARDS
GAME
375 Tom Brady vs. Ohio State, Nov. 21, 1998 (31 of 56)
SEASON
3,331 John Navarre, 2003 (270 of 456)
CAREER
8,983 John Navarre, 2000-03 (738 of 1,320)

RECEIVING YARDS
GAME
197 Jack Clancy vs. Oregon State, Sept. 17, 1966 (10 rec.)
SEASON
1,330 Braylon Edwards, 2004 (97 rec.)
CAREER
3,541 Braylon Edwards, 2001-04 (252 rec.)

POINTS
GAME
30 Ron Johnson vs. Wisconsin, Nov. 16, 1968 (5 TDs)
SEASON
138 Desmond Howard, 1991 (23 TDs)
CAREER
336 Anthony Thomas, 1997-2000 (56 TDs)

CONSENSUS ALL-AMERICANS

1898	William Cunningham, C
1901	Neil Snow, E
1903-04	Willie Heston, B
1907	Adolph Schulz, C
1909-10	Albert Benbrook, G
1910	Stanfield Wells, E
1913	Miller Pontius, T
1913	Jim Craig, B
1914	John Maulbetsch, B
1922	Harry Kipke, B
1923	Jack Blott, C
1925-27	Bennie Oosterbaan, E
1925-26	Benny Friedman, B
1928	Otto Pommerening, T
1932	Harry Newman, B
1933	Francis Wistert, T
1933	Chuck Bernard, C
1938	Ralph Heikkinen, G
1939-40	Tom Harmon, B
1941	Bob Westfall, B
1942	Albert Wistert, T
1942	Julie Franks, G
1943	Bill Daley, B
1947	Bob Chappuis, B

(Continued on next page)

limiting a season to five games and proposals to allow players only three seasons of varsity status.

BEST TEAM It's difficult to argue against Yost's "Point a Minute" machines, but "Michigan's Mad Magicians" in 1947 are still revered for their 10–0 record and a national title. Crisler, known as Gimlet Eye for his ability to stare through his players, devised an intricate single-wing offense that led the nation in total yards (412.7 average) and passing yards (173.9). Michigan outscored its regular-season opponents 345-53. Crisler wore teams down with depth by using a two-platoon system he had introduced two years earlier against Army. All-America halfback Bob Chappuis, who appeared on the cover of *Time* magazine during the season, was the Heisman runner-up after leading the league in total offense for the second consecutive year. Bump Elliot, a two-way player who later coached the Wolverines, earned Big Ten MVP honors.

BIGGEST GAME Notre Dame had been voted No. 1 after the 1947 regular season, so undefeated Michigan had something to prove in the 1948 Rose Bowl. The Wolverines, 15-point favorites, smashed USC 49-0. It was the Trojans' worst defeat in 60 years of football and remained so until 1966. Michigan set nine Rose Bowl records, including 491 total yards. Despite an injured hamstring, Chappuis set Rose Bowl marks for total offense (188 yards passing and 91 rushing) and pass completions (14). Wolverines fullback Jack Weisenburger scored 3 TDs. Michigan was so impressive, the Associated Press conducted a special poll after the game. The Wolverines were crowned national champs, receiving 226 votes to 119 for Notre Dame, which had beaten USC 38-7 earlier that season.

BIGGEST UPSET First-year coach Bo Schembechler was not intimidated by his former boss, Ohio State coach Woody

CONSENSUS ALL-AMERICANS (CONT.)	
1948	Dick Rifenburg, E
1948-49	Alvin Wistert, T
1955-56	Ron Kramer, E
1965	Bill Yearby, DT
1966	Jack Clancy, E
1969	Jim Mandich, E
1969	Tom Curtis, DB
1970	Dan Dierdorf, T
1971	Reggie McKenzie, G
1971	Mike Taylor, LB
1972	Paul Seymour, T
1972	Randy Logan, DB
1973	Dave Gallagher, DL
1973-74	Dave Brown, DB
1976	Rob Lytle, RB
1976-77	Mark Donahue, G
1979	Ron Simpkins, LB
1981-82	Anthony Carter, WR
1981	Ed Muransky, OL
1981	Kurt Becker, OL
1985	Mike Hammerstein, DL
1985	Brad Cochran, DB
1986	Garland Rivers, DB
1987	John "Jumbo" Elliott, OL
1988	John Vitale, C
1988	Mark Messner, DL
1989-90	Tripp Welborne, DB
1991	Greg Skrepenak, OL
1991	Desmond Howard, WR
1996	Jarrett Irons, LB
1997	Charles Woodson, DB
2000	Steve Hutchinson, OL
2003	Chris Perry, RB
2004	Braylon Edwards, WR
2004	David Baas, OL
2004	Marlin Jackson, DB
2004	Ernest Shazor, DB

Hayes, when "the old man" brought his most powerful OSU team to Michigan Stadium on Nov. 22, 1969. The Buckeyes had won 50-14 the previous year, providing a rallying cry for Schembechler. He made every member of Michigan's scout team wear No. 50 during practices for the 1969 rematch. A national TV audience and a record crowd of 103,588 saw the 17-point-underdog Wolverines stun Ohio State 24-12, ending a 22-game winning streak for the Buckeyes that included 17 straight Big Ten wins. Michigan's defense recovered a fumble and intercepted six passes—three by Barry Pierson. Crisler watched the game on TV and wrote the new Michigan coach a letter telling how he shed tears of pride and joy over "the greatest upset I have ever witnessed."

HEARTBREAKER Michigan went 30–2–1 from 1972 to 1974 and didn't play in a bowl game. The tie was a 10-10 home game against Ohio State in the 1973 regular-season finale. The Wolverines entered the game 10–0 and ranked No. 4; the Buckeyes were 9–0 and No. 1. Michigan's Mike Lantry missed field goal attempts of 58 and 48 yards in the final 1:06. The next day, Big Ten commissioner Wayne Duke took a poll of the league's athletic directors to decide whether the Wolverines or Buckeyes should go to the Rose Bowl. The ADs chose Ohio State, 6-4. Michigan State's first-year AD, Burt Smith, voted against his in-state rival. Michigan QB Dennis Franklin had broken his collarbone in the Ohio State game, so some voted for the Buckeyes, reasoning they had a better chance to win the Rose Bowl. "This is the lowest day of my career as a player and a coach," Schembechler said.

WILDEST FINISH The words "Rocket Left" still cut Michigan fans like a stiletto. That was the name of Colorado's final play in Michigan's 27-26 home loss on Sept. 24, 1994. The Wolverines led by five points with six seconds left and had the Buffaloes 64 yards from the end

zone. Colorado coach Bill McCartney, a former Michigan assistant, called for three Buffaloes receivers—Michael Westbrook, Blake Anderson and Rae Carruth—to split wide left. James Kidd lined up wide right. Quarterback Kordell Stewart then threw the ball 73 yards into the wind. It came down at the goal line, where Anderson tipped it straight up over the Wolverines. Westbrook caught the ball in the end zone. More than 100,000 fans in Michigan Stadium fell silent as Colorado players jumped on each other in joy.

BEST COMEBACK What occurred in the final quarter at Minnesota on Oct. 10, 2003, confused even the No. 20 Wolverines. "We still don't know what happened," Michigan defensive end Larry Stevens said after the game. "How many points did we score in the fourth quarter? I don't even know." Michigan scored 31 fourth-quarter points to defeat the Gophers 38-35. Minnesota, ranked No. 17, was on the verge of going 7–0 when it led 28-7 at the start of the fourth quarter. The Wolverines got within 28-14 when QB John Navarre hit Chris Perry with a 10-yard TD pass, and they sliced off another seven points from the deficit when safety Jacob Stewart intercepted Minnesota QB Asad Abdul-Khaliq and returned it 34 yards for a TD. Abdul-Khaliq answered with a 52-yard scoring run to push the Gophers' lead to 35-21. Navarre tossed a 52-yard TD to Braylon Edwards, and Perry added a 10-yard TD run to tie the game. Freshman Garrett Rivas completed the comeback by kicking a 33-yard field goal with 47 seconds left to give the Wolverines their first lead of the game.

STADIUM ABC-TV announcer Keith Jackson dubbed it The Big House, but the nation's largest football facility is actually a deep crater. Nearly three-fourths of Michigan Stadium sits below ground that once had a strawberry patch and barn sitting atop an underground spring. Yost fashioned the stadium after the Yale Bowl and opened it in 1927 at a cost of $950,000. More than 37 million people have filed through

the iron gates of the brick stadium to cheer from the wooden bleachers. Every home game since Oct. 25, 1975 (a 55-7 homecoming rout of Indiana) has drawn in excess of 100,000. Fans have come to a place at the corner of Main Street and Stadium Boulevard that is neither glamorous nor luxurious. Originally designed for 84,401, the stadium now holds 107,501. The capacity is always listed with a final digit of 1, signifying an extra seat for Crisler. The location of that seat remains a secret.

RIVAL Michigan coach Gary Moeller, a former Ohio State player, caused a stir in the early 1990s when he suggested that Michigan State—not OSU—was the Wolverines' biggest game because it was against an in-state opponent. But the Wolverines and Buckeyes have shared hatred since first meeting in 1897. From 1928 through 1990, the annual series was tied 30–30–3, with OSU scoring 909 points and Michigan 903. The game's winner determined the Rose Bowl participant every year from 1972 to 1981. During that span, Michigan fans had rolls of toilet paper with Hayes' picture on them and a caption that read, "Put Woody where he belongs." The Wolverines dominated the series early, going 14–0–1 and outscoring OSU 369-21 through 1918. Michigan also dominated the 1990s, costing the Buckeyes possible national championships three times between 1993 and 1996. The Wolverines' 10–2–1 record against John Cooper got the OSU coach fired in 2000. Michigan, though, has had less luck against Buckeyes coach Jim Tressel, who won his first two games against the Wolverines, with the second one catapulting the Buckeyes to the 2002 national title.

DUBIOUS DISTINCTION Schembechler had more wins (194) than any other coach in Michigan history and won 13 Big Ten titles in 21 seasons from 1969 to 1989. But Bo knew woes in postseason games, with a 5–12 bowl record, including 2–8 in the Rose Bowl. He had a heart attack on the morning of his first Rose Bowl, at the end of the 1970

ALL-CENTENNIAL TEAM

Fans cast votes on the school's athletic website to determine Michigan's all-20th-century team.

1969-89	Bo Schembechler, coach

OFFENSE

1968-70	Dan Dierdorf, OL
1969-71	Reggie McKenzie, OL
1984-87	John "Jumbo" Elliott, OL
1988-91	Greg Skrepenak, OL
1995-98	Jon Jansen, OL
1925-27	Bennie Oosterbaan, WR
1979-82	Anthony Carter, WR
1989-91	Desmond Howard, WR
1975-78	Rick Leach, QB
1938-40	Tom Harmon, RB
1991-94	Tyrone Wheatley, RB
1994-96	Remy Hamilton, PK

DEFENSE

1985-88	Mark Messner, DL
1994-97	Glen Steele, DL
1989-92	Chris Hutchinson, DL
1988-91	Erick Anderson, LB
1993-96	Jarrett Irons, LB
1976-79	Ron Simpkins, LB
1995-98	Sam Sword, LB
1995-97	Charles Woodson, DB
1992-94	Ty Law, DB
1987-90	Tripp Welborne, DB
1967-69	Tom Curtis, DB
1984-87	Monte Robbins, P

season, and was hospitalized during the 10-3 loss to USC. Schembechler lost his first five Rose Bowls before beating Washington in the 1981 game. That was the first time one of his Michigan teams finished a season with a victory, even though his 96–10–3 regular-season record was the nation's best during the 1970s. Bo's Wolverines went 5–15–1 in the final games of a season, including nonbowl years.

NICKNAME Michigan students and alumni have referred to themselves as "Wolverines" since the school's earliest history. Yost credited use of the name to the fur trading that took place at Sault St. Marie. The *Michigan Quarterly Review* said in 1952 that the moniker stemmed from the eating habits of the French who settled Michigan in the late 1700s. A third theory dates to the state's border dispute with Ohio in 1803.

MASCOT Wolverines don't live in Michigan, and the school doesn't use a furry mascot. In 1927, however, Alaska donated three wolverines to the Detroit zoo. Two were taken to a game that year at Michigan Stadium, but they were so ferocious the school decided not to bring them back.

UNIFORMS A committee of students from the school's literary department selected maize and blue as Michigan's colors in 1867. The Wolverines wore plain black helmets until Fritz Crisler decided in 1938 that a new look would help end a streak of four consecutive losing seasons. He painted them blue and put gold on the wings and stripes on the Spalding FH5 leather helmets, which were the only helmets being used that had three straps running from front to back. The Michigan football uniform was voted the best in all sports in an ESPN.com poll in 2003.

NUMBERS QB Rick Leach made 48 consecutive starts from 1975 to 1978 while being named All-Big Ten three times and earning All-America and Big Ten MVP honors as a

> *Michigan radio announcer Bob Ufer's call—"Oh, my god! Carter scored!"—still reverberates.*

senior ... Gerald Ford, the 38th president of the United States, wore No. 48 while playing center on the Wolverines' national championship teams in 1932 and 1933. He was the team's MVP as a senior and graduated from Michigan in 1935 ... The Wolverines have played in 19 Rose Bowls, more than any other Big Ten school ... Desmond Howard carried only 176 pounds on a 5'9" frame, but he became the first receiver in Big Ten history to lead the league in scoring (90 points) as he won the 1991 Heisman. His 640 first-place votes (85%) were the most ever for a Heisman winner.

QUIRK Michigan tried to generate more revenue by scheduling a doubleheader to open the 1929 season. The Wolverines beat Albion 39-0 in the first game and Mount Union 16-6 in the second. However, only 16,412 fans attended. Undeterred, Michigan opened its next two seasons with doubleheaders: Denison (33-0) and Eastern Michigan (7-0) were defeated on the same day in 1930 and Central Michigan (27-0) and Eastern Michigan (34-0) lost to the Wolverines in 1931.

LORE Michigan radio announcer Bob Ufer's screaming call of the final play of the 1979 homecoming game—"Oh, my god! Carter scored!"—still reverberates. Anthony Carter went on to become a three-time All-America, but he was just a 5'11", 160-pound freshman on the day he sent Ufer and Michigan Stadium into frenzy. The Wolverines were at the Indiana 45-yard line with six seconds remaining in a 21-21 game. Carter ran a post pattern through IU's wide-split defense, and QB John Wangler hit him with a pass at the 20. The skinny-legged flanker bounced off two defenders and then squirted free of Hoosiers safety Tim Wilbur to dance into the end zone for a game-winning TD.

QUOTE "Who are they that they should beat a Michigan team?"—Fielding H. Yost

MICHIGAN ALL-TIME SCORES

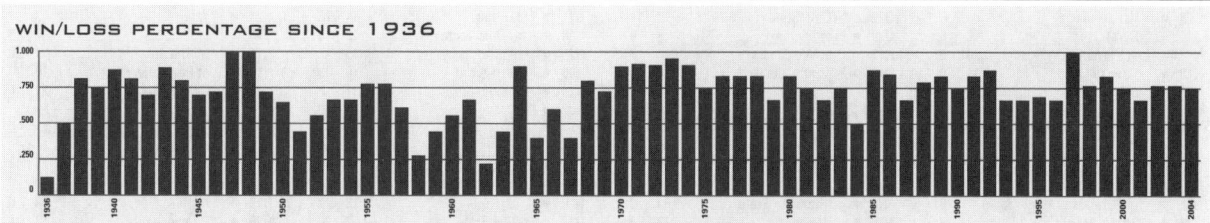

WIN/LOSS PERCENTAGE SINCE 1936

NO HEAD COACH

1879   1-0-1
M30	●	Racine *CHI*	1	0
N1	=	Toronto *DET*	0	0

1880   1-0-0
N5		at Toronto	13	6

1881   0-3-0
O31		Harvard *BOS*	0	1
N2		at Yale	0	2
N4		at Princeton	0	1

1882
NO TEAM

1883   1-4-0
M12	●	Detroit AC	40	5
N19		at Wesleyan	6	14
N21		at Yale	0	46
N22		at Harvard	0	3
N27		at Stevens	1	5

1884   2-0-0
N15	●	Albion	18	0
N22	●	U. Club Chicago	18	10

1885   3-0-0
N7	●	at Windsor Club	10	0
N14	●	Windsor Club	30	0
N26	●	at Peninsular Club *DET*	42	0

1886   2-0-0
O16	●	at Albion	50	0
O30	●	Albion	24	0

1887   3-0-0
N12	●	Albion	32	0
N23	●	at Notre Dame	8	0
N24	●	at Harvard Club	26	0

1888   4-1-0
P20	●	at Notre Dame	26	6
P21	●	at Notre Dame	10	4
N17	●	at Detroit AC	14	6
N24	●	Albion	76	4
N29		at U. Club Chicago	4	26

1889   1-2-0
N9	●	Albion	33	4
N23		Cornell *BUF*	0	56
N28		Chicago AA	0	20

1890   4-1-0
O11	●	Albion	56	10
O18	●	at Detroit A. C.	18	0
O25	●	Albion	16	0
N1	●	Purdue	34	6
N15		Cornell *DET*	5	20

M. MURPHY & F. CRAWFORD
1891 (.444)   4-5

1891   4-5-0
O10	●	Ann Arbor HS	62	0
O17	●	Albion	4	10
O19	●	at Olivet	18	6
O24	●	Oberlin	26	6
O31	●	Butler	42	6
N14		at Chicago AC	0	10
N21		Cornell *CHI*	12	58
N26		at Cleveland AA	4	8
N28		Cornell *DET*	0	10

FRANK E. BARBOUR
1892-93 (.636)   14-8

1892   7-5-0
O8	●	Michigan AA	74	0
O12	●	Michigan AA *DET*	68	0
O15	●	at Wisconsin	10	6
O17		at Minnesota	6	14
O22	●	DePauw *IND*	18	0
O24		at Purdue	0	24
O29		Northwestern *CHI*	8	10
N5	●	Albion	60	8
N8		at Cornell	0	44
N12	●	Chicago *TOL*	18	10
N19	●	Oberlin	26	24
N22		Cornell	10	30

1893   7-3-0
O7	●	Detroit AC	6	0
O14	●	at Detroit AC	26	0
O21		at Chicago	6	10
O28	●	Minnesota	20	34
N4	●	Wisconsin	18	34
N11	●	at Purdue	46	8
N13	●	at DePauw	34	0
N18	●	Northwestern	72	6
N25	●	Kansas *KC*	22	0
N30	●	at Chicago	28	0

WILLIAM L. McCAULEY
1894-95 (.875)   17-2-1

1894   9-1-1
O6	=	Michigan M.A.	12	12
O13	●	Albion	26	10
O17	●	Olivet	48	0
O21	●	Michigan M.A.	40	6
O24	●	Adrian	46	0
O28		at Case	18	8
N3		at Cornell	0	22
N10	●	Kansas *KC*	22	12
N17	●	Oberlin	14	6
N24	●	Cornell	12	4
N29	●	at Chicago	6	4

1895   8-1-0
O5	●	Michigan M.A.	34	0
O12	●	Detroit AC	42	0
O19	●	Adelbert	64	0
O26	●	Rush Lake Forest	40	0
N2	●	Oberlin	42	0
N9		at Harvard	0	4
N16	●	Purdue	12	10
N23	●	Minnesota *DET*	20	0
N28	●	at Chicago	12	0

1896-1906
BIG 10

WILLIAM D. WARD
1896 (.900)   9-1

1896   9-1-0 (2-1-0)
O3	●	Eastern Michigan	18	0
O10	●	Grand Rapids	44	0
O15	●	Phys & Surg.	28	0
O17	●	Lake Forest	66	0
O24		at Purdue	16	0
O31	●	Lehigh *DET*	40	0
N7	●	at Minnesota	6	4
N14	●	Oberlin	10	0
N21	●	Wittenberg	28	0
N26		Chicago *CHI*	6	7

GUSTAVE H. FERBERT
1897-99 (.875)   24-3-1

1897   6-1-1 (2-1-0)
O2	●	Eastern Michigan	24	0
O9	=	Ohio Wesleyan	0	0
O16	●	Ohio State	34	0 *
O23	●	Oberlin	16	6
N6	●	Purdue	34	4
N13	●	Minnesota *DET*	14	0
N20	●	Wittenberg	32	0
N25		Chicago *CHI*	12	21

1898   10-0-0 (3-0-0)
O1	●	Eastern Michigan	21	0 *
O8	●	Kenyon	29	0
O12	●	Michigan State	39	0
O17	●	Western Reserve	18	0
O19	●	Case	23	5
O23	●	Notre Dame	23	0
N5	●	Northwestern *CHI*	6	5
N12	●	Minnesota *DET*	12	5
N19	●	Beloit	22	0
N24	●	at Chicago	12	11

1899   8-2-0 (1-1-0)
S30	●	Hillsdale	11	0
O7	●	Albion	26	0
O11	●	Western Reserve	17	0
O18	●	Notre Dame	12	0
O28	●	at Illinois	5	0
N4	●	Virginia *DET*	38	0
N11		at Pennsylvania	10	11
N18	●	Case	28	6
N25	●	Kalamazoo	24	9
N30		Wisconsin *CHI*	5	17

LANGDON "BIFF" LEA
1900 (.750)   7-2-1

1900   7-2-1 (3-2-0)
S29	●	Hillsdale	29	0
O6	●	Kalamazoo	11	0
O13	●	Case	24	6
O20	●	Purdue	11	6
O27	●	Illinois *CHI*	12	0
N3	●	Indiana	12	0
N10		Iowa *DET*	5	28
N17	●	Notre Dame	7	0
N24	=	Ohio State	0	0
N29		at Chicago	6	15

FIELDING H. YOST
1901-23 '25-26 (.833)   165-29-10

1901   11-0-0 (4-0-0)
S28	●	Albion	50	0
O5	●	Case	57	0
O12	●	Indiana	33	0
O19	●	Northwestern	29	0
O26	●	Buffalo	128	0
N2	●	Carlisle *DET*	22	0
N9	●	at Ohio State	21	0
N16	●	Chicago	22	0
N23	●	Beloit	89	0
N28	●	Iowa *CHI*	50	0
ROSE BOWL				
J1	●	Stanford	49	0

1902   11-0-0 (5-0-0)
S27	●	Albion	88	0
O4	●	Case	48	6
O8	●	Michigan State	119	0
O11	●	Indiana	60	0
O18	●	Notre Dame *TOL*	23	0
O25	●	Ohio State	86	0
N1	●	Wisconsin *CHI*	6	0
N8	●	Iowa	107	0
N15	●	at Chicago	21	0
N22	●	Oberlin	63	0
N27	●	Minnesota	23	6

1903   11-0-1 (3-0-1)
O3	●	Case	31	0
O8	●	Albion	76	0
O10	●	Beloit	79	0
O14	●	Ohio Northern	65	0
O17	●	Indiana	51	0
O21	●	Ferris St.	88	0
O24	●	Drake	47	0
O31	=	at Minnesota	6	6
N7	●	Ohio State	36	0
N14	●	Wisconsin	16	0
N21	●	Oberlin	42	0
N26	●	at Chicago	28	0

1904   10-0-0 (2-0-0)
O1	●	Case	33	0
O5	●	Ohio Northern	48	0
O8	●	Kalamazoo	95	0
O12	●	P&S Chicago	72	0
O15	●	at Ohio State	31	6
O19	●	Am. Med. Chicago	72	0
O22	●	West Virginia	130	0
O29	●	at Wisconsin	28	0
N5	●	Drake	36	4
N12	●	Chicago	22	12

1905   12-1-0 (2-1-0)
S30	●	Ohio Wesleyan	65	0
O4	●	Kalamazoo	44	0
O7	●	Case	36	0
O11	●	Ohio Northern	23	0
O14	●	Vanderbilt	18	0
O21	●	Nebraska	31	0
O25	●	Albion	70	0
O28	●	Drake	48	0
N4	●	at Illinois	33	0
N11	●	Ohio State	40	0
N18	●	Wisconsin	12	0
N25	●	Oberlin	75	0
N30		at Chicago	0	2

1906   4-1-0 (1-0-0)
O6	●	Case	28	0
O20	●	at Ohio State	6	0
O27	●	Illinois	28	9
N3	●	Vanderbilt	10	4
N17		at Pennsylvania	0	17

1907-1916
INDEPENDENT

1907   5-1-0
O5	●	Case	9	0
O12	●	Michigan State	46	0
O19	●	Wabash *IND*	22	0
O26	●	Ohio State	22	0
N2	●	at Vanderbilt	8	0
N16		Pennsylvania	0	6

1908   5-2-1
O3	●	Case	16	6
O10	=	at Michigan State	0	0
O17	●	Notre Dame	12	6
O24	●	at Ohio State	10	6
O31	●	Vanderbilt	24	6
N7	●	Kentucky	62	0
N14		Pennsylvania	0	29
N21		at Syracuse	4	28

1909   6-1-0
O9	●	Case	3	0
O16	●	Ohio State	33	6
O23	●	at Marquette	6	5
O30	●	Syracuse	43	0
N6		Notre Dame	3	11
N13	●	at Pennsylvania	12	6
N20	●	at Minnesota	15	6

1910   3-0-3
O8	=	Case	3	3
O15	●	Michigan State	6	3
O22	=	at Ohio State	3	3
O29	●	at Syracuse	11	0
N12	=	at Pennsylvania	0	0
N19	●	Minnesota	6	0

502 MICHIGAN

THE SCHOOLS

1911 — 5-1-2

O7	●		Case	24	0
O14	●		at Michigan State	15	3
O21	●		Ohio State	19	0
O28	●		Vanderbilt	9	8
N4	=		Syracuse	6	6
N11			at Cornell	0	6
N18	●		Pennsylvania	11	9
N25	=		at Nebraska	6	6

1912 — 5-2-0

O5	●		Case	34	0
O12	●		Michigan State	55	7
O19	●		at Ohio State	14	0
O26			at Syracuse	7	18
N2	●		South Dakota	7	6
N9			at Pennsylvania	21	27
N16	●		Cornell	20	7

1913 — 6-1-0

O4	●		Case	48	0
O11	●		Mt. Union	14	0
O18			Michigan State	7	12
O25	●		at Vanderbilt	33	2
N1	●		Syracuse	43	7
N8	●		at Cornell	17	0
N15	●		Pennsylvania	13	0

1914 — 6-3-0

S30	●		DePauw	58	0
O3	●		Case	69	0
O7	●		Mt. Union	27	7
O10	●		Vanderbilt	23	3
O17	●		at Michigan State	3	0
O24			at Syracuse	6	20
O31			at Harvard	0	7
N7	●		Pennsylvania	34	3
N14			Cornell	13	28

1915 — 4-3-1

O6	●		Lawrence	39	0
O9	●		Mt. Union	35	0
O13	●		Marietta	28	6
O16	●		Case	14	3
O23			Michigan State	0	24
O30			Syracuse	7	14
N6			Cornell	7	34
N13	=		at Pennsylvania	0	0

1916 — 7-2-0

O4	●		Marietta	30	0
O7	●		Case	19	3
O11	●		Carroll	54	0
O14	●		Mt. Union	26	0
O21	●		Michigan State	9	0
O28	●		Syracuse	14	13
N4	●		Washington, Mo.	66	7
N11			at Cornell	20	23
N18			Pennsylvania	7	10

1917-Present
Big 10

1917 — 8-2-0 (0-1-0)

O6	●		Case	41	0
O10	●		Western Michigan	17	13
O13	●		Mt. Union	69	0
O17	●		Detroit	14	3
O20	●		at Michigan State	27	0
O27	●		Nebraska	20	0
N3	●		Kalamazoo	62	0
N10	●		Cornell	42	0
N17			at Pennsylvania	0	16
N24		│	at Northwestern	12	21

1918 — 5-0-0 (2-0-0)

O5	●		Case	33	0
N9	●	│	at Chicago	13	0
N16	●		Syracuse	15	0
N23	●		Michigan State	21	6
N30	●	│	Ohio State	14	0

1919 — 3-4-0 (1-4-0)

O4	●		Case	34	0
O18	●		Michigan State	26	0
O25		│	Ohio State	3	13
N1	●	│	Northwestern	16	13
N8		│	at Chicago	0	13
N15		│	at Illinois	7	29
N22		│	Minnesota	7	34

1920 — 5-2-0 (2-2-0)

O9	●		Case	35	0
O16	●		Michigan State	35	0
O23		│	Illinois	6	7
O30	●		Tulane	21	0
N6		│	at Ohio State	7	14
N13	●	│	Chicago	14	0
N20	●	│	at Minnesota	3	0

1921 — 5-1-1 (2-1-1)

O1	●		Mt. Union	44	0
O8	●		Case	65	0
O15	●		Michigan State	30	0
O22		│	Ohio State	0	14
O29	●	│	at Illinois	3	0
N12	=	│	at Wisconsin	7	7
N19	●	│	Minnesota	38	0

1922 — 6-0-1 (4-0-0)

O7	●		Case	48	0
O14	=		at Vanderbilt	0	0
O21	●	│	at Ohio State	19	0
O28	●	│	Illinois	24	0
N4	●		Michigan State	63	0
N18	●	│	Wisconsin	13	6
N25	●	│	at Minnesota	16	7

1923 — 8-0-0 (4-0-0)

O6	●		Case	36	0
O13	●		Vanderbilt	3	0
O20	●	│	Ohio State	23	0
O27	●		Michigan State	37	0
N3	●	│	at Iowa	9	3
N10	●		Quantico Marines	26	6
N17	●	│	at Wisconsin	6	3
N24	●	│	Minnesota	10	0

GEORGE LITTLE
1924 (.750) 6-2

1924 — 6-2-0 (4-2-0)

O4	●		Miami, Ohio	55	0
O11	●		at Michigan State	7	0
O18		│	at Illinois	14	39
O25	●	│	Wisconsin	21	0
N1	●	│	at Minnesota	13	0
N8	●	│	Northwestern	27	0
N15	●	│	at Ohio State	16	6
N22		│	Iowa	2	9

FIELDING H. YOST

1925 — 7-1-0 (5-1-0)

O3	●		Michigan State	39	0
O10	●	│	Indiana	63	0
O17	●	│	at Wisconsin	21	0
O24	●	│	at Illinois	3	0
O31	●		Navy	54	0
N7		│	Northwestern *Chi*	2	3
N14	●	│	Ohio State	10	0
N21	●	│	Minnesota	35	0

1926 — 7-1-0 (5-0-0)

O2	●		Oklahoma State	42	3
O9	●		Michigan State	55	3
O16	●	│	Minnesota	20	0
O23	●	│	Illinois	13	0
O30			Navy *Balt*	0	10
N6	●	│	Wisconsin	37	0
N13	●	│	at Ohio State	17	16
N20	●	│	at Minnesota	7	6

ELTON E. "TAD" WIEMAN
1927-28 (.594) 9-6-1

1927 — 6-2-0 (3-2-0)

O1	●		Ohio Wesleyan	33	0
O8	●		Michigan State	21	0
O15	●	│	at Wisconsin	14	0
O22	●	│	Ohio State	21	0
O29		│	at Illinois	0	14
N5	●	│	at Chicago	14	0
N12	●		Navy	27	12
N19		│	Minnesota	7	13

1928 — 3-4-1 (2-3-0)

O6			Ohio Wesleyan	7	17
O13		│	Indiana	0	6
O20		│	at Ohio State	7	19
O27		│	Wisconsin	0	7
N3	●	│	Illinois	3	0
N10	=		Navy *Balt*	6	6
N17	●		Michigan State	3	0
N24	●	│	Iowa	10	7

HARRY G. KIPKE
1929-37 (.632) 46-26-4

1929 — 5-3-1 (1-3-1)

S28	●		Albion	39	0
S28	●		Mt. Union	16	6
O5	●		Michigan State	17	0
O12		│	at Purdue	16	30
O19		│	Ohio State	0	7
O26		│	at Illinois	0	14
N9	●		Harvard	14	12
N16	●	│	at Minnesota	7	6
N23	=	│	Iowa	0	0

1930 — 8-0-1 (5-0-0)

S27	●		Denison	33	0
S27	●		Eastern Michigan	7	0
O4	=		Michigan State	0	0
O11	●	│	Purdue	14	13
O18	●	│	at Ohio State	13	0
O25	●	│	Illinois	15	7
N8	●		at Harvard	6	3
N15	●	│	Minnesota	7	0
N22	●	│	Chicago	16	0

1931 — 8-1-1 (5-1-0)

O3	●		Central St. Teachers	27	0
O3	●		Eastern Michigan	34	0
O10	●	│	Chicago	13	7
O17		│	Ohio State	7	20
O24	●	│	at Illinois	35	0
O31	●		at Princeton	21	0
N7	●	│	Indiana	22	0
N14	=		Michigan State	0	0
N21	●	│	Minnesota	6	0
N28	●	│	Wisconsin	16	0

1932 — 8-0-0 (6-0-0)

O1	●		Michigan State	26	0
O8	●	│	Northwestern	15	6
O15	●	│	at Ohio State	14	0
O22	●	│	Illinois	32	0
O29	●		Princeton	14	7
N5	●	│	at Indiana	7	0
N12	●	│	Chicago	12	0
N19	●	│	at Minnesota	3	0

1933 — 7-0-1 (5-0-1)

O7	●		Michigan State	20	6
O14	●		Cornell	40	0
O21	●	│	Ohio State	13	0
O28	●	│	at Chicago	28	0
N4	●	│	at Illinois	7	6
N11	●	│	Iowa	10	6
N18	=	│	Minnesota	0	0
N25	●	│	at Northwestern	13	0

1934 — 1-7-0 (0-6-0)

O6			Michigan State	0	16
O13		│	at Chicago	0	27
O20	●		Georgia Tech	9	2
O27		│	Illinois	6	7
N3		│	at Minnesota	0	34
N10		│	Wisconsin	0	10
N17		│	at Ohio State	0	34
N24		│	Northwestern	6	13

1935 — 4-4-0 (2-3-0)

O5			Michigan State	6	25
O12	●	│	Indiana	7	0
O19	●	│	at Wisconsin	20	12
O26	●		at Columbia	19	7
N2	●		Pennsylvania	16	6
N9		│	at Illinois	0	3
N16		│	Minnesota	0	40
N23		│	Ohio State	0	38

1936 — 1-7-0 (0-5-0)

O3			Michigan State	7	21
O10		│	Indiana	3	14
O17		│	at Minnesota	0	26
O24	●		Columbia	13	0
O31		│	Illinois	6	9
N7			at Pennsylvania	7	27
N14		│	Northwestern	0	9
N21		│	at Ohio State	0	21

1937 — 4-4-0 (3-3-0)

O2			Michigan State	14	19
O9		│	at Northwestern	0	7
O16		│	Minnesota	6	39
O23	●	│	at Iowa	7	6
O30	●	│	at Illinois	7	6
N6	●	│	Chicago	13	12
N13	●		at Pennsylvania	7	0
N20		│	Ohio State	0	21

HERBERT O. "FRITZ" CRISLER
1938-47 (.806) 71-16-3

1938 — 6-1-1 (3-1-1)

O1	●		Michigan State	14	0
O8	●	│	Chicago	45	7
O15		│	at Minnesota	6	7
O22	●		at Yale	15	13
O29	●	│	Illinois	14	0
N5	●		Pennsylvania	19	13
N12	=	│	Northwestern	0	0
N19	●	│	at Ohio State	18	0

1939 — 6-2-0 (3-2-0)

O7	●		Michigan State	26	13
O14	●	│	Iowa	27	7
O21	●	│	at Chicago	85	0
O28	●		Yale	27	7
N4		│	at Illinois	7	16
N11		│	Minnesota	7	20
N18	●		at Pennsylvania	19	17
N25	●	│	Ohio State	21	14

1940 — 7-1-0 (3-1-0)

S28	●		at California	41	0
O5	●		Michigan State	21	14
O12	●		at Harvard	26	0
O19	●	│	Illinois	28	0
O26	●		Pennsylvania	14	0
N9		│	at Minnesota	6	7
N16	●	│	Northwestern	20	13
N23	●	│	at Ohio State	40	0

1941 — 6-1-1 (3-1-1)

S27	●		Michigan State	19	7
O4	●	│	Iowa	6	0
O11	●		Pittsburgh	40	0
O18	●	│	at Northwestern	14	7
O25		│	Minnesota	0	7
N1	●	│	at Illinois	20	0
N15	●		at Columbia	28	0
N22	=	│	Ohio State	20	20

1942 — 7-3-0 (3-2-0)

S26	●		Great Lakes NAS	9	0
O3	●		Michigan State	20	0
O10			Iowa Pre-Flight	14	26
O17	●	│	Northwestern	34	16
O24		│	at Minnesota	14	16
O31	●	│	Illinois	28	14
N7	●		Harvard	35	7
N14	●		at Notre Dame	32	20
N21		│	at Ohio State	7	21
N28	●	│	Iowa	28	14

1943 — 8-1-0 (6-0-0)

S18	●		at Camp Grant	26	0
S25	●		Western Michigan	57	6
O2	●	│	at Northwestern	21	7
O9			Notre Dame	12	35
O23	●	│	Minnesota	49	6
O30	●	│	at Illinois	42	6
N6	●	│	Indiana	23	6
N13	●	│	Wisconsin	27	0
N20	●	│	Ohio State	45	7

1944 — 8-2-0 (5-2-0)

S16	●		Iowa Pre-Flight	12	7
S23	●		at Marquette	14	0
S30		│	Indiana	0	20
O7	●	│	at Minnesota	28	13
O14	●	│	Northwestern	27	0
O28	●	│	Purdue	40	14
N4	●		at Pennsylvania	41	19
N11	●	│	Illinois	14	0
N18	●	│	Wisconsin	14	0
N25		│	at Ohio State	14	18

1945 — 7-3-0 (5-1-0)

S15	●		Great Lakes NAS	27	2
S22		│	Indiana	7	13
S29	●		Michigan State	40	0
O6	●	│	at Northwestern	20	7
O13			Army *Brnx*	7	28
O27	●	│	at Illinois	19	0
N3	●	│	Minnesota	26	0
N10			Navy *Balt*	7	33
N17	●	│	Purdue	27	13
N24	●	│	Ohio State	7	3

1946 — 6-2-1 (5-1-1)

S28	●	│	Indiana	21	0
O5	●	│	Iowa	14	7
O12			Army	13	20
O19	=	│	Northwestern	14	14
O26		│	Illinois	9	13
N2	●	│	at Minnesota	21	0
N9	●		Michigan State	55	7
N16	●	│	Wisconsin	28	6
N23	●	│	at Ohio State	58	6

1947 — 10-0-0 (6-0-0)

S27	●		Michigan State	55	0
O4	●		Stanford	49	13
O11	●		Pittsburgh	69	0
O18	●	│	at Northwestern	49	21
O25	●	│	Minnesota	13	6
N1	●	│	at Illinois	14	7
N8	●	│	Indiana	35	0
N15	●	│	at Wisconsin	40	6
N22	●	│	Ohio State	21	0
			ROSE BOWL		
J1	●		Southern Cal	49	0

BENNIE G. OOSTERBAAN
1948-58 (.650)   63-33-4

1948   9-0-0 (6-0-0)
S25	●	at Michigan State	13 7
O2	●	Oregon	14 0
O9	●	at Purdue	40 0
O16	●	Northwestern	28 0
O23	●	at Minnesota	27 14
O30	●	Illinois	28 20
N6	●	Navy	35 0
N13	●	Indiana	54 0
N20	●	at Ohio State	13 3

1949   6-2-1 (4-1-1)
S24	●	Michigan State	7 3
O1	●	at Stanford	27 7
O8	●	Army	7 21
O15	●	at Northwestern	20 21
O22	●	Minnesota	14 7
O29	●	at Illinois	13 0
N5	●	Purdue	20 12
N12	●	Indiana	20 7
N19	=	Ohio State	7 7

1950   6-3-1 (4-1-1)
S30	●	Michigan State	7 14
O7	●	Dartmouth	27 7
O14	●	Army *Brnx*	6 27
O21	●	Wisconsin	26 13
O28	=	at Minnesota	7 7
N4	●	Illinois	0 7
N11	●	Indiana	20 7
N18	●	Northwestern	34 23
N25	●	at Ohio State	9 3
ROSE BOWL			
J1	●	California	14 6

1951   4-5-0 (4-2-0)
S29	●	Michigan State	0 25
O6	●	Stanford	13 23
O13	●	Indiana	33 14
O20	●	at Iowa	21 0
O27	●	Minnesota	54 27
N3	●	at Illinois	0 7
N10	●	at Cornell	7 20
N17	●	Northwestern	0 6
N24	●	Ohio State	7 0

1952   5-4-0 (4-2-0)
S27	●	Michigan State	13 27
O4	●	at Stanford	7 14
O11	●	Indiana	28 13
O18	●	at Northwestern	48 14
O25	●	Minnesota	21 0
N1	●	Illinois	13 22
N8	●	Cornell	49 7
N15	●	Purdue	21 10
N22	●	at Ohio State	7 27

1953   6-3-0 (3-3-0)
S26	●	Washington	50 0
O3	●	Tulane	26 7
O10	●	Iowa	14 13
O17	●	Northwestern	20 12
O24	●	at Minnesota	0 22
O31	●	Pennsylvania	24 14
N7	●	at Illinois	3 19
N14	●	at Michigan State	6 14
N21	●	Ohio State	20 0

1954   6-3-0 (5-2-0)
S25	●	at Washington	14 0
O2	●	Army	7 26
O9	●	Iowa	14 13
O16	●	at Northwestern	7 0
O23	●	Minnesota	34 0
O30	●	Indiana	9 13
N6	●	Illinois	14 7
N13	●	Michigan State	33 7
N20	●	at Ohio State	7 21

1955   7-2-0 (5-2-0)
S24	●	Missouri	42 7
O1	●	Michigan State	14 7
O8	●	Army	26 2
O15	●	Northwestern	14 2
O22	●	at Minnesota	14 13
O29	●	Iowa	33 21
N5	●	at Illinois	6 25
N12	●	Indiana	30 0
N19	●	Ohio State	0 17

1956   7-2-0 (5-2-0)
S29	●	UCLA	42 13
O6	●	Michigan State	0 9
O13	●	Army	48 14
O20	●	Northwestern	34 20
O27	●	Minnesota	7 20
N3	●	at Iowa	17 14
N10	●	Illinois	17 7
N17	●	Indiana	49 26
N24	●	at Ohio State	19 0

1957   5-3-1 (3-3-1)
S28	●	at Southern Cal	16 6
O5	●	Georgia	26 0
O12	●	Michigan State	6 35
O19	●	Northwestern	34 14
O26	●	at Minnesota	24 7
N2	=	Iowa	21 21
N9	●	at Illinois	19 20
N16	●	Indiana	27 13
N23	●	Ohio State	14 31

1958   2-6-1 (1-5-1)
S27	●	Southern Cal	20 19
O4	=	at Michigan State	12 12
O11	●	Navy	14 20
O18	●	at Northwestern	24 55
O25	●	Minnesota	20 19
N1	●	Iowa	14 37
N8	●	Illinois	8 21
N15	●	Indiana	6 8
N22	●	at Ohio State	14 20

BUMP ELLIOTT
1959-68 (.547)   51-42-2

1959   4-5-0 (3-4-0)
S26	●	Missouri	15 20
O3	●	Michigan State	8 34
O10	●	Oregon State	18 7
O17	●	Northwestern	7 20
O24	●	at Minnesota	14 6
O31	●	Wisconsin	10 19
N7	●	at Illinois	20 15
N14	●	at Indiana	7 26
N21	●	Ohio State	23 14

1960   5-4-0 (3-4-0)
S24	●	Oregon	21 0
O1	●	at Michigan State	17 24
O8	●	Duke	31 6
O15	●	Northwestern	14 7
O22	●	Minnesota	0 10
O29	●	at Wisconsin	13 16
N5	●	Illinois	8 7
N12	●	Indiana	29 7
N19	●	at Ohio State	0 7

1961   6-3-0 (3-3-0)
S30	●	UCLA	29 6
O7	●	Army	38 8
O14	●	Michigan State	0 28
O21	●	Purdue	16 14
O28	●	at Minnesota	20 23
N4	●	Duke	28 14
N11	●	at Illinois	38 6
N18	●	Iowa	23 14
N25	●	Ohio State	20 50

1962   2-7-0 (1-6-0)
S29	●	Nebraska	13 25
O6	●	Army	17 7
O13	●	at Michigan State	0 28
O20	●	at Purdue	0 37
O27	●	Minnesota	0 17
N3	●	Wisconsin	12 34
N10	●	Illinois	14 10
N17	●	at Iowa	14 28
N24	●	at Ohio State	0 28

1963   3-4-2 (2-3-2)
S28	●	SMU	27 16
O5	●	Navy	13 26
O12	=	Michigan State	7 7
O19	●	Purdue	12 23
O26	●	at Minnesota	0 6
N2	●	Northwestern	27 6
N9	●	at Illinois	14 8
N16	=	Iowa	21 21
N23	●	Ohio State	10 14

1964   9-1-0 (6-1-0)
S26	●	Air Force	24 7
O3	●	Navy	21 0
O10	●	at Michigan State	17 10
O17	●	Purdue	20 21
O24	●	Minnesota	19 12
O31	●	Northwestern	35 0
N7	●	Illinois	21 6
N14	●	at Iowa	34 20
N21	●	at Ohio State	10 0
ROSE BOWL			
J1	●	Oregon State	34 7

1965   4-6-0 (2-5-0)
S18	●	at North Carolina	31 24
S25	●	California	10 7
O2	●	Georgia	7 15
O9	●	Michigan State	7 24
O16	●	Purdue	15 17
O23	●	at Minnesota	13 14
O30	●	Wisconsin	50 14
N6	●	at Illinois	23 3
N13	●	at Northwestern	22 34
N20	●	Ohio State	7 9

1966   6-4-0 (4-3-0)
S17	●	Oregon State	41 0
S24	●	at California	17 7
O1	●	North Carolina	7 21
O8	●	at Michigan State	7 20
O15	●	Purdue	21 22
O22	●	Minnesota	49 0
O29	●	at Wisconsin	28 17
N5	●	Illinois	21 28
N12	●	Northwestern	28 20
N19	●	at Ohio State	17 3

1967   4-6-0 (3-4-0)
S23	●	Duke	10 7
S30	●	at California	9 10
O7	●	Navy	21 26
O14	●	Michigan State	0 34
O21	●	Indiana	20 27
O28	●	at Minnesota	15 20
N4	●	Northwestern	7 3
N11	●	at Illinois	21 14
N18	●	at Wisconsin	27 14
N25	●	Ohio State	14 24

1968   8-2-0 (6-1-0)
S21	●	California	7 21
S28	●	at Duke	31 10
O5	●	Navy	32 9
O12	●	Michigan State	28 14
O19	●	at Indiana	27 22
O26	●	Minnesota	33 20
N2	●	at Northwestern	35 0
N9	●	Illinois	36 0
N16	●	Wisconsin	34 9
N23	●	at Ohio State	14 50

BO SCHEMBECHLER
1969-89 (.796)   194-48-5

1969   8-3-0 (6-1-0)
S20	●	Vanderbilt	42 14
S27	●	Washington	45 7
O4	●	Missouri	17 40
O11	●	Purdue	31 20
O18	●	at Michigan State	12 23
O25	●	at Minnesota	35 9
N1	●	Wisconsin	35 7
N8	●	at Illinois	57 0
N15	●	at Iowa	51 6
N22	●	Ohio State	24 12
ROSE BOWL			
J1	●	Southern Cal	3 10

1970   9-1-0 (6-1-0)
S19	●	Arizona	20 9
S26	●	at Washington	17 3
O3	●	Texas A&M	14 10
O10	●	at Purdue	29 0
O17	●	Michigan State	34 20
O24	●	Minnesota	39 13
O31	●	at Wisconsin	29 15
N7	●	Illinois	42 0
N14	●	Iowa	55 0
N21	●	at Ohio State	9 20

1971   11-1-0 (8-0-0)
S11	●	at Northwestern	21 6
S18	●	Virginia	56 0
S25	●	UCLA	38 0
O2	●	Navy	46 0
O9	●	at Michigan State	24 13
O16	●	Illinois	35 6
O23	●	at Minnesota	35 7
O30	●	Indiana	61 7
N6	●	Iowa	63 7
N13	●	at Purdue	20 17
N20	●	Ohio State	10 7
ROSE BOWL			
J1	●	Stanford	12 13

1972   10-1-0 (7-1-0)
S16	●	Northwestern	7 0
S23	●	at UCLA	26 9
S30	●	Tulane	41 7
O7	●	Navy	35 7
O14	●	Michigan State	10 0
O21	●	at Illinois	31 7
O28	●	Minnesota	42 0
N4	●	at Indiana	21 7
N11	●	at Iowa	31 0
N18	●	Purdue	9 6
N25	●	at Ohio State	11 14

1973   10-0-1 (7-0-1)
S15	●	at Iowa	31 7
S22	●	Stanford	47 10
S29	●	Navy	14 0
O6	●	Oregon	24 0
O13	●	at Michigan State	31 0
O20	●	Wisconsin	35 6
O27	●	at Minnesota	34 7
N3	●	Indiana	49 13
N10	●	Illinois	21 6
N17	●	at Purdue	34 9
N24	=	Ohio State	10 10

1974   10-1-0 (7-1-0)
S14	●	Iowa	24 7
S21	●	Colorado	31 0
S28	●	Navy	52 0
O5	●	at Stanford	27 16
O12	●	Michigan State	21 7
O19	●	at Wisconsin	24 20
O26	●	Minnesota	49 0
N2	●	at Indiana	21 7
N9	●	at Illinois	14 6
N16	●	Purdue	51 0
N23	●	at Ohio State	10 12

1975   8-2-2 (7-1-0)
S13	●	at Wisconsin	23 6
S20	=	Stanford	19 19
S27	=	Baylor	14 14
O4	●	Missouri	31 7
O11	●	at Michigan State	16 6
O18	●	Northwestern	69 0
O25	●	Indiana	55 7
N1	●	at Minnesota	28 21
N8	●	Purdue	28 0
N15	●	at Illinois	21 15
N22	●	Ohio State	14 21
ORANGE BOWL			
J1	●	Oklahoma	6 14

1976   10-2-0 (7-1-0)
S11	●	Wisconsin	40 27
S18	●	Stanford	51 0
S25	●	Navy	70 14
O2	●	Wake Forest	31 0
O9	●	Michigan State	42 10
O16	●	at Northwestern	38 7
O23	●	at Indiana	35 0
O30	●	Minnesota	45 0
N6	●	at Purdue	14 16
N13	●	Illinois	38 7
N20	●	at Ohio State	22 0
ROSE BOWL			
J1	●	Southern Cal	6 14

1977   10-2-0 (7-1-0)
S10	●	at Illinois	37 9
S17	●	Duke	21 9
S24	●	Navy	14 7
O1	●	Texas A&M	41 3
O8	●	at Michigan State	24 14
O15	●	Wisconsin	56 0
O22	●	at Minnesota	0 16
O29	●	Iowa	23 6
N5	●	Northwestern	63 20
N12	●	at Purdue	40 7
N19	●	Ohio State	14 6
ROSE BOWL			
J2	●	Washington	20 27

THE SCHOOLS

1978 — 10-2-0 (7-1-0)

S16	•	Illinois	31 0
S23	•	at Notre Dame	28 14
S30	•	Duke	52 0
O7	•	Arizona	21 17
O14		Michigan State	15 24
O21	•	at Wisconsin	42 0
O28	•	Minnesota	42 10
N4	•	at Iowa	34 0
N11	•	at Northwestern	59 14
N18	•	Purdue	24 6
N25	•	at Ohio State	14 3
ROSE BOWL			
J1		Southern Cal	10 17

1979 — 8-4-0 (6-2-0)

S8	•	Northwestern	49 7
S15	•	Notre Dame	10 12
S22	•	Kansas	28 7
S29	•	at California	14 10
O6	•	at Michigan State	21 7
O13	•	Minnesota	31 21
O20	•	at Illinois	27 7
O27	•	Indiana	27 21
N3	•	Wisconsin	54 0
N10	•	at Purdue	21 24
N17	•	Ohio State	15 18
GATOR BOWL			
D28		North Carolina	15 17

1980 — 10-2-0 (8-0-0)

S13	•	Northwestern	17 10
S20	•	at Notre Dame	27 29
S27	•	South Carolina	14 17
O4	•	California	38 13
O11	•	Michigan State	27 23
O18	•	at Minnesota	37 14
O25	•	Illinois	45 14
N1	•	at Indiana	35 0
N8	•	at Wisconsin	24 0
N15	•	Purdue	26 0
N22	•	at Ohio State	9 3
ROSE BOWL			
J1		Washington	23 6

1981 — 9-3-0 (6-3-0)

S12		at Wisconsin	14 21
S19	•	Notre Dame	25 7
S26	•	Navy	21 16
O3	•	at Indiana	38 17
O10	•	at Michigan State	38 20
O17	•	Iowa	7 9
O24	•	Northwestern	38 0
O31	•	at Minnesota	34 13
N7	•	Illinois	70 21
N14	•	at Purdue	28 10
N21	•	Ohio State	9 14
BLUEBONNET BOWL			
D31		UCLA	33 14

1982 — 8-4-0 (8-1-0)

S11	•	Wisconsin	20 9
S18	•	at Notre Dame	17 23
S25	•	UCLA	27 31
O2	•	Indiana	24 10
O9	•	Michigan State	31 17
O16	•	at Iowa	29 7
O23	•	at Northwestern	49 14
O30	•	Minnesota	52 14
N6	•	at Illinois	16 10
N13	•	Purdue	52 21
N20	•	Ohio State	14 24
ROSE BOWL			
J1		UCLA	14 24

1983 — 9-3-0 (8-1-0)

S10	•	Washington State	20 17
S17	•	at Washington	24 25
S24	•	at Wisconsin	38 21
O1	•	Indiana	43 18
O8	•	at Michigan State	42 0
O15	•	Northwestern	35 0
O22	•	Iowa	16 13
O29	•	at Illinois	6 16
N5	•	Purdue	42 10
N12	•	at Minnesota	58 10
N19	•	Ohio State	24 21
SUGAR BOWL			
J2		Auburn	7 9

1984 — 6-6-0 (5-4-0)

S8	•	Miami, Fla.	22 14
S15	•	Washington	11 20
S22	•	Wisconsin	20 14
S29	•	at Indiana	14 6
O6	•	Michigan State	7 19
O13	•	Northwestern	31 0
O20	•	at Iowa	0 26
O27	•	Illinois	26 18
N3	•	at Purdue	29 31
N10	•	Minnesota	31 7
N17	•	at Ohio State	6 21
HOLIDAY BOWL			
D21		Brigham Young	17 24

1985 — 10-1-1 (6-1-1)

S14	•	Notre Dame	20 12
S21	•	at South Carolina	34 3
S28	•	Maryland	20 0
O5	•	Wisconsin	33 6
O12	•	at Michigan State	31 0
O19	•	at Iowa	10 12
O26	•	Indiana	42 15
N2	=	at Illinois	3 3
N9	•	Purdue	47 0
N16	•	at Minnesota	48 7
N23	•	Ohio State	27 17
FIESTA BOWL			
J1		Nebraska	27 23

1986 — 11-2-0 (7-1-0)

S13	•	at Notre Dame	24 23
S20	•	Oregon State	31 12
S27	•	Florida State	20 18
O4	•	at Wisconsin	34 17
O11	•	Michigan State	27 6
O18	•	Iowa	20 17
O25	•	at Indiana	38 14
N1	•	Illinois	69 13
N8	•	at Purdue	31 7
N15	•	Minnesota	17 20
N22	•	at Ohio State	26 24
D6	•	at Hawaii	27 10
ROSE BOWL			
J1		Arizona State	15 22

1987 — 8-4-0 (5-3-0)

S12	•	Notre Dame	7 26
S19	•	Washington State	44 18
S26	•	Long Beach St.	49 0
O3	•	Wisconsin	49 0
O10	•	at Michigan State	11 17
O17	•	Iowa	37 10
O24	•	at Indiana	10 14
O31	•	Northwestern	29 6
N7	•	at Minnesota	30 20
N14	•	at Illinois	17 14
N21	•	Ohio State	20 23
HALL OF FAME BOWL			
J2		Alabama	28 24

1988 — 9-2-1 (7-0-1)

S10	•	at Notre Dame	17 19
S17	•	Miami, Fla.	30 31
S24	•	Wake Forest	19 9
O1	•	at Wisconsin	62 14
O8	•	Michigan State	17 3
O15	=	at Iowa	17 17
O22	•	Indiana	31 6
O29	•	at Northwestern	52 7
N5	•	Minnesota	22 7
N12	•	Illinois	38 9
N19	•	at Ohio State	34 31
ROSE BOWL			
J2		Southern Cal	22 14

1989 — 10-2-0 (8-0-0)

S16	•	Notre Dame	19 24
S23	•	at UCLA	24 23
S30	•	Maryland	41 21
O7	•	Wisconsin	24 0
O14	•	at Michigan State	10 7
O21	•	at Iowa	26 12
O28	•	Indiana	38 10
N4	•	Purdue	42 27
N11	•	at Illinois	24 10
N18	•	at Minnesota	49 15
N25	•	Ohio State	28 18
ROSE BOWL			
J1		Southern Cal	10 17

GARY O. MOELLER — 1990-94 (.758) — 44-13-3

1990 — 9-3-0 (6-2-0)

S15	•	at Notre Dame	24 28
S22	•	UCLA	38 15
S29	•	Maryland	45 17
O6	•	at Wisconsin	41 3
O13	•	Michigan State	27 28
O20	•	Iowa	23 24
O27	•	at Indiana	45 19
N3	•	at Purdue	38 13
N10	•	Illinois	22 17
N17	•	Minnesota	35 18
N24	•	at Ohio State	16 13
GATOR BOWL			
J1		Mississippi	35 3

1991 — 10-2-0 (8-0-0)

S7	•	at Boston College	35 13
S14	•	Notre Dame	24 14
S28	•	Florida State	31 51
O5	•	at Iowa	43 24
O12	•	at Michigan State	45 28
O19	•	Indiana	24 16
O25	•	at Minnesota	52 6
N2	•	Purdue	42 0
N9	•	Northwestern	59 14
N16	•	at Illinois	20 0
N23	•	Ohio State	31 3
ROSE BOWL			
J1		Washington	14 34

1992 — 9-0-3 (6-0-2)

S12	=	at Notre Dame	17 17
S19	•	Oklahoma State	35 3
S26	•	Houston	61 7
O3	•	Iowa	52 28
O10	•	Michigan State	35 10
O17	•	at Indiana	31 3
O24	•	Minnesota	63 13
O31	•	at Purdue	24 17
N7	•	at Northwestern	40 7
N14	=	Illinois	22 22
N21	•	at Ohio State	13 13
ROSE BOWL			
J1		Washington	38 31

1993 — 8-4-0 (5-3-0)

S4	•	Washington State	41 14
S11	•	Notre Dame	23 27
S25	•	Houston	42 21
O2	•	Iowa	24 7
O9	•	at Michigan State	7 17
O16	•	at Penn State	21 13
O23	•	Illinois	21 24
O30	•	at Wisconsin	10 13
N6	•	Purdue	25 10
N13	•	at Minnesota	58 7
N20	•	Ohio State	28 0
HALL OF FAME BOWL			
J1	•	North Carolina St.	42 7

1994 — 8-4-0 (5-3-0)

S3	•	Boston College	34 26
S10	•	at Notre Dame	26 24
S24	•	Colorado	26 27
O1	•	at Iowa	29 14
O8	•	Michigan State	40 20
O15	•	Penn State	24 31
O22	•	at Illinois	19 14
O29	•	Wisconsin	19 31
N5	•	at Purdue	45 23
N12	•	Minnesota	38 22
N19	•	at Ohio State	6 22
HOLIDAY BOWL			
D30	•	Colorado State	24 14

LLOYD H. CARR — 1995-Present (.766) — 95-29

1995 — 9-4-0 (5-3-0)

A26	•	Virginia	18 17
S2	•	at Illinois	38 14
S9	•	Memphis	24 7
S16	•	at Boston College	23 13
S30	•	Miami, Ohio	38 19
O7		Northwestern	13 19
O21		at Indiana	34 17
O28		Minnesota	52 17
N4		at Michigan State	25 28
N11		Purdue	5 0
N18		at Penn State	17 27
N25		Ohio State	31 23
ALAMO BOWL			
D28		Texas A&M	20 22

1996 — 8-4 (5-3)

A31	•	Illinois	20 8
S14	•	at Colorado	20 13
S21	•	Boston College	20 14
S28	•	UCLA	38 9
O5		at Northwestern	16 17
O19	•	Indiana	27 20
O26	•	at Minnesota	44 10
N2	•	Michigan State	45 29
N9	•	at Purdue	3 9
N16	•	Penn State	17 29
N23	•	at Ohio State	13 9
OUTBACK BOWL			
J1	•	Alabama	14 17

1997 — 12-0 (9-0)

S13	•	Colorado	27 3
S20	•	Baylor	38 3
S27	•	Notre Dame	21 14
O4	•	at Indiana	37 0
O11	•	Northwestern	23 6
O18	•	Iowa	28 24
O25	•	at Michigan State	23 7
N1	•	Minnesota	24 3
N8	•	at Penn State	34 8
N15	•	at Wisconsin	26 16
N22	•	Ohio State	20 14
ROSE BOWL			
J1	•	Washington State	21 16

1998 — 10-3 (7-1)

S5	•	at Notre Dame	20 36
S12	•	Syracuse	28 38
S19	•	Eastern Michigan	59 20
S26	•	Michigan State	29 17
O3	•	at Iowa	12 9
O17	•	at Northwestern	12 6
O24	•	Indiana	21 10
O31	•	at Minnesota	15 10
N7	•	Penn State	27 0
N14	•	Wisconsin	27 10
N21	•	at Ohio State	16 31
N28	•	at Hawaii	48 17
CITRUS BOWL			
J1	•	Arkansas	45 31

1999 — 10-2 (6-2)

S4	•	Notre Dame	26 22
S11	•	Rice	37 3
S18	•	at Syracuse	18 13
S25	•	at Wisconsin	21 16
O2	•	Purdue	38 12
O9	•	at Michigan State	31 34
O23	•	Illinois	29 35
O30	•	at Indiana	34 31
N6	•	Northwestern	37 3
N13	•	at Penn State	31 27
N20	•	Ohio State	24 17
ORANGE BOWL			
J1	•	Alabama	35 34

2000 — 9-3 (6-2)

S2	•	Bowling Green	42 7
S9	•	Rice	38 7
S16	•	at UCLA	20 23
S23	•	at Illinois	35 31
S30	•	Wisconsin	13 10
O7	•	at Purdue	31 32
O14	•	Indiana	58 0
O21	•	Michigan State	14 0
N4	•	at Northwestern	51 54
N11	•	Penn State	33 11
N18	•	at Ohio State	38 26
CITRUS BOWL			
J1	•	Auburn	31 28

2001 — 8-4 (6-2)

S1	•	Miami, Ohio	31 13
S8		at Washington	18 23
S22		Western Michigan	38 21
S29		Illinois	45 20
O6		at Penn State	20 0
O13		Purdue	24 10
O27		at Iowa	32 26
N3		at Michigan State	24 26
N10		Minnesota	31 10
N17		at Wisconsin	20 17
N24		Ohio State	20 26
CITRUS BOWL			
J1		Tennessee	17 45

2002 10-3 (6-2)
A31	●	Washington	31	29
S7	●	Western Michigan	35	12
S14		at Notre Dame	23	25
S21	●	Utah	10	7
S28	●|	at Illinois	45	28
O12	● |	Penn State	27	24
O19	● |	at Purdue	23	21
O26	|	Iowa	9	34
N2	|	Michigan State	49	3
N9	|	at Minnesota	41	24
N16	|	Wisconsin	21	14
N23	|	at Ohio State	9	14
		OUTBACK BOWL		
J1	●	Florida	38	30

2003 10-3 (7-1)
A30	●	Central Michigan	45	7
S6	●	Houston	50	3
S13	●	Notre Dame	38	0
S20		at Oregon	27	31
S27	●|	Indiana	31	17
O4	|	at Iowa	27	30
O10	● |	at Minnesota	38	35
O18	● |	Illinois	56	14
O25	● |	Purdue	31	3
N1	● |	at Michigan State	27	20
N15	● |	at Northwestern	41	10
N22	● |	Ohio State	35	21
		ROSE BOWL		
J1		Southern Cal	14	28

2004 9-3 (7-1)
S4	●	Miami, Ohio	43	10
S11		at Notre Dame	20	28
S18	●	San Diego State	24	21
S25	● |	Iowa	30	17
O2	● |	at Indiana	35	14
O9	● |	Minnesota	27	24
O16	● |	at Illinois	30	19
O23	● |	at Purdue	16	14
O30	● |	Michigan State	45	37
N13	● |	Northwestern	42	20
N20	|	at Ohio State	21	37
		ROSE BOWL		
J1		Texas	37	38

Neutral Site key: *Unk* Unknown, Unknown / *Brnx* Bronx, N.Y. / *Det* Detroit, Mich. / *Ind* Indianapolis, Ind. / *Chi* Chicago, Ill. / *Tol* Toledo, Ohio / *KC* Kansas City, Mo. / *Buf* Buffalo, N.Y. / *Balt* Baltimore, Md.
ƒ Forfeit † Game Later Forfeited # Disputed Victor * Disputed Score ‖ Designated Conference Game 2 Counted Twice in Conference Standings

MICHIGAN ANNUAL STATISTICAL LEADERS

YR	RUSHING	YDS	ATT	AVG	PASSING	ATT	CMP	PCT	YDS	RECEIVING	REC	YDS	AVG
1938	Tom Harmon	398	77	5.2	Tom Harmon	45	21	.47	310	Paul Kromer	9	72	8.0
1939	Tom Harmon	884	130	6.8	Tom Harmon	94	37	.39	488	Forest Evashevski	14	134	9.6
1940	Tom Harmon	852	191	4.5	Tom Harmon	94	43	.46	506	Ed Frutig	12	181	15.1
1941	Bob Westfall	688	156	4.4	Tom Kuzma	59	26	.44	317	George Ceithaml	10	77	7.7
1942	Bob Wiese	466	133	3.5	Bob Chappuis	64	28	.44	358	George Ceithaml	18	232	12.9
1943	Bill Daley	817	120	6.8	Elroy Hirsch	22	9	.41	213	Farnham Johnson	4	109	27.3
1944	Bob Nussbaumer	502	78	6.4	Bill Culligan	39	12	.31	245	Dick Rifenburg	8	232	29.0
1945	Wally Teninga	317	66	4.8	Pete Elliott	52	19	.37	393	Hank Fonde	11	148	13.5
1946	Bob Chappuis	502	116	4.3	Bob Chappuis	92	52	.57	734	Bobby Mann	14	285	20.4
1947	J. Weisenburger	773	121	6.4	Bob Chappuis	110	62	.56	1,164	Bump Elliott	18	318	19.9
1948	Tom Peterson	330	109	3.0	Chuck Ortmann	87	41	.47	856	Dick Rifenburg	22	508	23.1
1949	Don Dufek	392	122	3.2	Chuck Ortmann	126	45	.36	627	Harry Allis	23	338	14.7
1950	Don Dufek	702	174	4.0	Chuck Ortmann	120	56	.47	736	Lowell Perry	24	374	15.6
1951	Don Peterson	549	152	3.6	Bill Putich	77	32	.42	380	Lowell Perry	16	395	24.7
1952	Ted Kress	623	135	4.6	Ted Kress	85	45	.53	559	Lowell Perry	31	492	15.9
1953	Tony Branoff	501	101	5.0	Lou Baldacci	51	21	.41	302	Bob Topp	23	331	14.4
1954	Fred Baer	439	107	4.1	Jim Maddock	35	16	.46	293	Ron Kramer	23	303	13.2
1955	Tony Branoff	387	86	4.5	Jim Maddock	52	20	.39	343	Ron Kramer	12	253	21.1
1956	Jim Pace	498	103	4.8	Bob Ptacek	23	15	.65	245	Ron Kramer	18	353	19.6
1957	Jim Pace	664	123	5.4	Jim Van Pelt	80	42	.53	629	Gary Prahst	15	233	15.5
1958	Darrell Harper	309	55	5.6	Bob Ptacek	115	65	.57	763	Gary Prahst	22	313	14.2
1959	Fred Julian	289	72	4.0	Stan Noskin	115	61	.53	747	Bob Johnson	20	264	13.2
1960	Bennie McRae	352	80	4.4	Dave Glinka	124	54	.44	755	Bob Johnson	15	230	15.3
1961	Dave Raimey	496	99	5.0	Dave Glinka	96	46	.48	588	George Mans	15	149	9.9
1962	Dave Raimey	385	124	3.1	Bob Chandler	63	29	.46	401	Harvey Chapman	11	223	20.3
1963	Mel Anthony	394	103	3.8	Bob Timberlake	98	47	.48	593	John Henderson	27	330	12.2
1964	Mel Anthony	702	145	4.8	Bob Timberlake	137	70	.51	884	John Henderson	31	427	13.8
1965	Carl Ward	639	112	5.7	Wally Gabler	125	58	.46	825	Jack Clancy	52	762	14.7
1966	Dave Fisher	637	131	4.9	Dick Vidmer	226	117	.52	1,611	Jack Clancy	76	1,079	14.2
1967	Ron Johnson	1,005	220	4.6	Dennis Brown	156	82	.53	913	Jim Berline	54	624	11.6
1968	Ron Johnson	1,391	255	5.5	Dennis Brown	229	109	.48	1,562	Jim Mandich	43	576	13.4
1969	Bill Taylor	864	141	6.1	Don Moorhead	210	103	.49	1,261	Jim Mandich	50	662	13.2
1970	Bill Taylor	911	197	4.6	Don Moorhead	190	87	.46	1,167	Paul Staroba	35	519	14.8
1971	Bill Taylor	1,297	249	5.2	Tom Slade	63	27	.43	364	Glenn Doughty	16	203	12.7
1972	Ed Shuttlesworth	723	157	4.6	Dennis Franklin	123	59	.48	818	Paul Seal	18	243	13.5
1973	Ed Shuttlesworth	745	193	3.9	Dennis Franklin	67	36	.54	534	Paul Seal	14	254	18.1
1974	Gordon Bell	1,048	174	6.0	Dennis Franklin	104	58	.56	933	Gil Chapman	23	378	16.4
1975	Gordon Bell	1,388	273	5.1	Rick Leach	100	32	.32	680	Jim Smith	24	553	23.0
1976	Rob Lytle	1,469	221	6.6	Rick Leach	105	50	.48	973	Jim Smith	26	714	27.5
1977	Russell Davis	1,092	225	4.9	Rick Leach	174	90	.52	1,348	Ralph Clayton	24	477	19.9
1978	Harlan Huckleby	741	154	4.8	Rick Leach	158	78	.49	1,283	Ralph Clayton	25	546	21.8
1979	Butch Woolfolk	990	191	5.2	John Wangler	130	78	.60	1,431	Doug Marsh	33	612	18.5
1980	Butch Woolfolk	1,042	196	5.3	John Wangler	212	117	.55	1,522	Anthony Carter	51	818	16.0
1981	Butch Woolfolk	1,459	253	5.8	Steve Smith	210	97	.46	1,661	Anthony Carter	50	952	19.0
1982	Lawrence Ricks	1,388	266	5.2	Steve Smith	227	118	.52	1,735	Anthony Carter	43	844	19.6
1983	Rick Rogers	1,002	209	4.8	Steve Smith	205	106	.52	1,420	Sim Nelson	41	494	12.0
1984	Jamie Morris	574	118	4.9	Jim Harbaugh	111	60	.54	718	Sim Nelson	40	459	11.5
1985	Jamie Morris	1,030	197	5.2	Jim Harbaugh	227	145	.64	1,976	Eric Kattus	38	582	15.3
1986	Jamie Morris	1,086	212	5.1	Jim Harbaugh	277	180	.65	2,729	Gerald White	38	408	10.7
1987	Jamie Morris	1,703	282	6.0	Demetrius Brown	168	80	.48	1,251	Greg McMurtry	21	474	22.6
1988	Tony Boles	1,408	262	5.4	Michael Taylor	122	76	.62	957	Greg McMurtry	27	470	17.4
1989	Tony Boles	839	131	6.4	Michael Taylor	121	74	.61	1,081	Greg McMurtry	41	711	17.3
1990	Jon Vaughn	1,416	216	6.6	Elvis Grbac	266	155	.58	1,911	Desmond Howard	63	1,025	16.3
1991	Ricky Powers	1,364	240	5.7	Elvis Grbac	254	165	.65	2,085	Desmond Howard	62	985	15.9
1992	Tyrone Wheatley	1,357	185	7.3	Elvis Grbac	199	129	.65	1,640	Derrick Alexander	50	740	14.8
1993	Tyrone Wheatley	1,129	207	5.5	Todd Collins	296	189	.64	2,509	Derrick Alexander	35	621	17.7
1994	Tyrone Wheatley	1,144	210	5.4	Todd Collins	288	186	.65	2,518	Amani Toomer	54	1,096	20.3
1995	Tim Biakabutuka	1,818	303	6.0	Brian Griese	238	127	.53	1,577	Mercury Hayes	48	923	19.2
1996	Clarence Williams	837	202	4.1	Scott Dreisbach	269	149	.55	2,025	Tai Streets	44	730	16.6
1997	Chris Howard	938	199	4.7	Brian Griese	307	193	.63	2,293	Chris Howard	37	276	7.5
1998	Anthony Thomas	893	167	5.3	Tom Brady	350	214	.61	2,636	Tai Streets	67	1,035	15.4
1999	Anthony Thomas	1,297	301	4.3	Tom Brady	341	214	.63	2,586	David Terrell	71	1,038	14.6
2000	Anthony Thomas	1,733	319	5.4	Drew Henson	237	146	.62	2,146	David Terrell	67	1,130	16.9
2001	B.J. Askew	902	199	4.5	John Navarre	385	207	.54	2,435	Marquise Walker	86	1,143	13.3
2002	Chris Perry	1,110	267	4.2	John Navarre	448	248	.55	2,905	Braylon Edwards	67	1,035	15.4
2003	Chris Perry	1,674	338	5.0	John Navarre	456	270	.59	3,331	Braylon Edwards	85	1,138	13.4
2004	Michael Hart	1,455	282	5.2	Chad Henne	399	240	.60	2,743	Braylon Edwards	97	1,330	13.7

Receiving leaders by receptions
All statistics include postseason

MICHIGAN STATE

T HE STANDARD FOR MICHIGAN STATE was set in 1896, when the school was known as Michigan Agricultural College and its president, Jonathan L. Snyder, declared, "If we must have football, I want the kind that wins." Many great victories have since been part of Spartans lore, especially during the 1950s under coach Clarence "Biggie" Munn and his successor Hugh "Duffy" Daugherty. Michigan State has often been at or near the forefront of college football, whether by playing in a classic game such as the one against Notre Dame in 1966 or by producing a litany of top players. Some of those Spartans—such as Lynn Chandnois, Earl Morrall, Charles "Bubba" Smith, George Webster, Lorenzo White, Tony Mandarich and Charles Rogers—set a standard of achievement not only for their school, but for college football in general.

TRADITION Fans gather on campus at The Spartan, a 10'6" ceramic figure that weighs three tons and stands on a 5'4" brick-and-concrete base. The statue, also known as

Sparty, was dedicated in 1945. Four years later, the Detroit alumni clubs of Michigan State and Notre Dame presented the first Megaphone Trophy, since awarded to the winner of that rivalry. Since 1950, the Spartans and Indiana Hoosiers have played for the Old Brass Spittoon. The Michigan-Michigan State game winner has earned the Paul Bunyan Trophy since 1953, when the governor, G. Mennen Williams, donated the four-foot wooden statue—which rests on a five-foot stand—to honor the Spartans' entry into the Big Ten. Michigan State and Penn State have played for the Land-Grant Trophy, first awarded when their series renewed in 1993.

BEST PLAYER He came from Anderson, S.C., and by the time he left East Lansing after the 1966 season he had changed the position of roverback. George Webster was fast and athletic at 6'4", 218 pounds, and his hard-hitting style epitomized two legendary Michigan State defenses. "George Webster is not only the finest football player I've ever seen, but he symbolizes our great 1965 and '66 teams," said his coach, Duffy Daugherty. Webster's play as a junior helped the Spartans set school records, which still stand, for total defense (169.9 yards allowed per game) and rushing defense (45.6 yards). He had 93

PROFILE

Michigan State University
East Lansing, Mich.
Founded: 1855
Enrollment: 35,408
Colors: Green and White
Nickname: Spartans
Stadium: Spartan Stadium
   Opened in 1923
   Grass; 75,000 capacity
First football game: 1896
All-time record: 590–389–44 (.598)
Bowl record: 7–10
Consensus national championships, 1936-present: 2 (1952, 1965)
Big Ten Conference championships: 6 (3 outright)
Outland Trophy: Ed Bagdon, 1949
First-round NFL draftees: 33
Website: www.msuspartans.com

THE BEST OF TIMES

The Spartans' consecutive national championships in 1965 and 1966 brought back memories of the previous decade, when they won four national titles and went 62–12 from 1950 to 1957.

THE WORST OF TIMES

All Spartan fans want to forget the 2–9 debacle of 1982, part of a span of five straight losing seasons from 1979 to 1983 that yielded a cumulative record of 19–35–1.

CONFERENCE

Michigan State joined the Western Conference in 1953. The Western Conference was popularly known as the Big Ten since 1917, but didn't officially change its name to the Big Ten Conference until 1987.

DISTINGUISHED ALUMNI

Magic Johnson; James Caan, actor; John Engler, Michigan governor; Jim Harrison, writer; James P. Hoffa, president of the Teamsters; R. Drayton McClane Jr., Houston Astros owner; Sam Raimi, director and producer

FIGHT SONG

MSU FIGHT SONG
On the banks of the Red Cedar,
There's a school that's known to all;
Its specialty is winning,
And those Spartans play good ball;
Spartan teams are never beaten,
All through the game they'll fight;
Fight for the only colors,
Green and White.
Go right through for MSU,
Watch the points keep growing.
Spartan teams are bound to win,
They're fighting with a vim.
Rah! Rah! Rah!
See their team is weakening,
We're going to win this game.
Fight! Fight! Rah! Team, Fight!
Victory for MSU.

Michigan State has often been at or near the forefront of college football.

tackles, including 10 for losses, as a senior on a unit that allowed 9.9 points and 51.4 yards rushing per game. The school retired Webster's No. 90 in 1967, and two years later Michigan State fans voted the two-time All-America as the Spartans' greatest player ever. In 1996, he was chosen for the school's Centennial Super Squad.

BEST COACH Laughter always followed in the wake of Hugh "Duffy" Daughtery, the man Biggie Munn entrusted to maintain his national powerhouse. Hardship gave perspective to Duffy's humor. As a teenager, he worked in a Pennsylvania coal mine, just like his father. Daughtery later enlisted in the Army and spent three years fighting in the South Pacific, earning the Bronze Star during his rise from private to major. So he always found time as Michigan State coach from 1954 to 1972 to see the lighter side of a serious game. Daughtery not only enjoyed talking to sportswriters, he even wrote a column for the Associated Press for three years. All of the one-liners and great quotes, known as Duffyisms, masked a demanding perfectionism in Daughtery. There was nothing funny about his teams,

which finished in the national Top 10 seven times, and included African-American players—Jimmy Raye was the starting quarter-back in 1966—before it was popular to recruit them. The Spartans went 19–1–1 and won Big Ten titles in 1965 and '66. The 1965 team finished No. 1 in the UPI poll.

BEST TEAM The high-water mark of Biggie Munn's successful tenure came in 1952, when the Spartans went 9–0 for the second consecutive year and finished No. 1 in both wire-service polls to earn the school's first national championship. The 1952 Spartans, one season from beginning Big Ten play, had All-Americas in guard Frank Kush, center Richard Tamburo and halfback Donald McAuliffe. Waves of other talent caused opponents to lose by an average score of 34.6 to 9.3. "It isn't so much what their first and second teams do to you, but the third, fourth and fifth teams simply murder you," said Ray George after his Texas A&M team lost 48-6 to Michigan State. The Spartans' depth helped in the season's second game, at Oregon State, when reserve fullback Eugene Lekenta came off the bench to kick a

RECORDS

RUSHING YARDS

	GAME	
350	Eric Allen vs. Purdue, Oct. 30, 1971 (29 att.)	
	SEASON	
2,066	Lorenzo White, 1985 (419 att.)	
	CAREER	
4,887	Lorenzo White, 1984-87 (1,082 att.)	

PASSING YARDS

	GAME	
400	Bill Burke vs. Michigan, Oct. 9, 1999 (21 of 36)	
	SEASON	
3,395	Jeff Smoker, 2003 (302 of 488)	
	CAREER	
8,932	Jeff Smoker, 2000-03 (685 of 1,150)	

RECEIVING YARDS

	GAME	
270	Charles Rogers vs. Fresno State, Dec. 31, 2001 (10 rec.)	
	SEASON	
1,470	Charles Rogers, 2001 (67 rec.)	
	CAREER	
2,992	Andre Rison, 1985-88 (146 rec.)	

POINTS

	GAME	
42	George E. "Carp" Julian vs. Akron, Oct. 31, 1914 (7 TDs)	
	SEASON	
114	Blake Ezor, 1989 (19 TDs)	
	CAREER	
334	Dave Rayner, 2001-04 (62 FGs, 148 PATs)	

CONSENSUS ALL-AMERICANS

1915	Neno Jerry DaPrato, B
1935	Sidney Wagner, G
1949	Ed Bagdon, G
1951	Bob Carey, E
1951	Don Coleman, T
1953	Don Dohoney, E
1955	Norman Masters, T
1955	Earl Morrall, B
1957	Dan Currie, C
1957	Walt Kowalczyk, B
1958	Sam Williams, E
1962	George Saimes, B
1963	Sherman Lewis, B
1965-66	Bubba Smith, DE
1965-66	George Webster, DB
1966	Clint Jones, B
1972	Brad Van Pelt, DB
1985, 1987	Lorenzo White, RB
1988	Tony Mandarich, OL
1989	Bob Kula, OL
1989	Percy Snow, LB
2002	Charles Rogers, WR
2004	Brandon Fields, P

24-yard field goal with eight seconds remaining to give the Spartans a 17-14 victory. Munn was named 1952 national coach of the year.

BIGGEST GAME The frenzy over Michigan State's showdown against Notre Dame on Nov. 19, 1966, crackled with unprecedented intensity. The Poll Bowl between the No. 1 Fighting Irish and No. 2 Spartans was scheduled for regional broadcast by ABC-TV, until the network received one legal suit and 50,000 letters asking it to be shown nationally. The NCAA finally told ABC it could show the game nationally if the telecast was delayed in some areas. A crowd of 80,011—more than 4,000 over capacity—crammed into Spartan Stadium on a cold, overcast afternoon. Michigan State had issued 745 media credentials, the most ever for a college football game. The ferocity of play on the field matched the pregame buildup off it. Michigan State defenders Bubba Smith and Charley Thornhill knocked Notre Dame quarterback Terry Hanratty out of the game with a separated shoulder midway through the first quarter. The Spartans went up 10-0 but the Fighting Irish eventually tied the game at 10 on the first play of the fourth quarter. Both defenses ruled from there. Notre Dame coach Ara Parseghian ordered his offense to run out the clock in the final minutes instead of risking a turnover. Fans booed as Michigan State's final game of the season ended in a 10-10 tie. Notre Dame beat USC 51-0 a week later to finish No. 1 in both polls.

BIGGEST UPSET The Michigan Wolverines were ranked No. 1 when the Spartans went into Ann Arbor in 1990. Both teams combined for four touchdowns in the game's final

ALL-CENTENNIAL TEAM	
Selected from an 850-ballot reader poll conducted by the Lansing State Journal *in 1996.*	
1954-72	Duffy Daugherty, coach
OFFENSE	
1953-55	Buck Nystrom, OL
1955-57	Dan Currie, OL
1960-62	Dave Behrman, OL
1970-72	Joe DeLamielleure, OL
1985-88	Tony Mandarich, OL
1964-66	Gene Washington, WR
1975-78	Kirk Gibson, WR
1953-55	Earl Morrall, QB
1964-66	Clinton Jones, RB
1969-71	Eric Allen, RB
1984-87	Lorenzo White, RB
1978-81	Morten Andersen, PK
1993-96	Derrick Mason, KR
DEFENSE	
1956-58	Sam Williams, DE
1964-66	Bubba Smith, DE
1974-77	Larry Bethea, DL
1964-66	George Webster, LB
1976-79	Dan Bass, LB
1980-83	Carl Banks, LB
1986-89	Percy Snow, LB
1958-60	Herb Adderley, DB
1966-68	Allen Brenner, DB
1970-72	Brad Van Pelt, DB
1971-73	Bill Simpson, DB
1985-87	Greg Montgomery, P

PRE-BIG TEN ERA	
1933-35	Sid Wagner, L
1946-49	Ed Bagdon, L
1950-52	Frank Kush, L
1949-51	Don Coleman, L
1950-52	Dick Tamburo, L
1949-51	Bob Carey, E
1951-53	Don Dohoney, E
1936-38	John Pingel, B
1946-49	Lynn Chandnois, B
1948-50	Sonny Grandelius, B
1950-52	Don McAuliffe, B

6:03. Hyland Hickson gave Michigan State a 21-14 lead with a 26-yard TD run, but Desmond Howard tied the score by taking the ensuing kickoff back 95 yards. A nine-yard TD run by Tico Duckett gave the Spartans a 28-21 lead with 1:59 remaining. Michigan quarterback Elvis Grbac hit Derrick Alexander with a seven-yard TD pass with six seconds left, but a pass to Howard on the two-point conversion attempt fell incomplete, giving Michigan State a 28-27 victory.

HEARTBREAKER Danny Pobojewski wasn't good enough to earn a letter at Michigan State so the Grand Rapids native transferred to Purdue. His playing time didn't increase with the Boilermakers, but the reserve fullback did manage to get on the field long enough to haunt the Spartans in the fifth game of 1953. He scored the only touchdown in a 6-0 upset that ended Michigan State's 28-game winning streak. The Spartans answered Pobojewski's score with a 95-yard kickoff return by All-America LeRoy Bolden, but the apparent TD was nullified by a clipping penalty. Michigan State didn't suffer another loss in its first season of Big Ten play and its final season under coach Biggie Munn. The Spartans tied Illinois for the league title and defeated UCLA in the Rose Bowl to finish 9–1.

WILDEST FINISH On Nov. 9, 1974, Michigan State scored two touchdowns, including an 88-yard scoring run by Levi Jackson, in the game's final 10 minutes to wipe out a 13-3 deficit against No. 1-ranked Ohio State. With the visiting Buckeyes inches from the goal line as the final seconds ticked down, a snap went through the legs of quarterback Cornelius Greene. Ohio State wingback Brian Baschnagel picked up the ball and ran it into the end zone. The head linesman signaled touchdown, but the back judge

and field judge ruled time had expired before the play began. No one was certain which team had won until 46 minutes later, when the officials declared Michigan State a 16-13 victor.

BEST COMEBACK Ohio State, 8–0 and ranked No. 1 in the polls since the preseason, had a 17-3 lead on visiting Michigan State after one quarter on Nov. 7, 1998. The Spartans' deficit was 24-9 at the 9:51 mark of the third quarter after Buckeyes safety Damon Moore returned an interception 73 yards for a touchdown. "I told them it was going to be a 15-round fight and we needed to be Rocky in that 15th round," said Michigan State coach Nick Saban. The Spartans, despite their 4–4 record, kept slugging and scored the game's final 19 points. They led 28-24 when Ohio State drove down to the Michigan State 15-yard line with 1:29 remaining to play. With all 93,595 in Ohio Stadium standing, the Spartans forced three incomplete passes and an interception to hold onto an improbable win.

STADIUM Spartan Stadium, a state-funded replacement for Old College Field, had no name when it opened on Oct. 6, 1923, with a win against Lake Forest. Fans called it College Field and College Stadium and Spartan Stadium until 1935, when the concrete stadium on the Grand River's south shore officially became Macklin Field in honor of former Spartans coach John Macklin. Four expansions in 22 years increased the original capacity of 14,000 to 76,000 by 1957, and that year the name changed to Spartan Stadium. Capacity dropped to 72,027 in 1994 because of the first of two renovations that decade. In October 2001, Spartan Stadium was site of a world-record crowd for an outdoor hockey game when 74,544 turned out to watch the Spartans play Michigan on ice. A $61 million expansion will add 3,000 seats and 24 suites for the 2005 season.

RIVAL Michigan State has had a long, legendary rivalry with Notre Dame, but even that heated series doesn't generate the animosity the Spartans feel toward their neighbors in Ann Arbor. The Michigan Wolverines have been detested since the series began in 1898 because of their dominance and their depiction of land-grant Michigan State as Moo U. The Spartans went 2–23–3 and were outscored 726-64 in their first 28 games against Michigan. Biggie Munn's first game as Michigan State coach was a 55-0 road loss to the Wolverines in 1947. At game's end, the Michigan band played "Old MacDonald Had a Farm" and the Spartans found their locker room inches deep with overflowed toilet water. Munn

was so mad he cried, vowed he'd recruit the state better and get revenge. From 1950 through 1969, Munn and Daugherty combined to go 14–4–2 against the Wolverines. Bo Schembechler answered by ushering in another age of Michigan dominance that continues today. The Spartans, however, will always have 1973, when Michigan tied Ohio State for the Big Ten title. League athletic directors were asked to name the conference's Rose Bowl representative. Michigan State cast the deciding vote, sending the Buckeyes to Pasadena and Schembechler into a fit of anger.

NICKNAME Michigan State players proudly called themselves Farmers or Fighting Farmers in the school's early years, although Aggies was the official nickname. The school sponsored a contest in 1925 to replace Aggies. Voters selected the Michigan Staters as the name, but *Lansing State Journal* sports editor George S. Alderton decided it was too cumbersome. He picked out Spartans from the list of entries, and newspapers popularized the use in 1926.

MASCOT A Michigan State student wears a 40-pound Sparty costume that resembles a Spartan warrior. Several versions of the costume have been used since Theta Xi fraternity created Sparty in 1955. Sigma Phi Epsilon originated his current look in 1984. For one season in 1909, the school used a live brown bear named Brewer's Bruin as its mascot.

UNIFORMS On April 11, 1899, the Athletic Association of the Michigan Agricultural College adopted the green monogram "to be worn only by athletes who subsequently take part in intercollegiate events." Chester L. Brewer popularized the use of green and white as school colors when he became the school's first full-time athletics director in 1903. In 1939, the Spartans wore four different colored jerseys (green, white, black and red) and the freshman team wore blue.

NUMBERS Jersey No. 46 was retired in 1969 to honor former Michigan State president John Hannah, who was instrumental in getting the Spartans into the Big Ten during his 46 years of school service ... Michigan State won the 1987 Big Ten title under George Perles, played in its first Rose Bowl in 22 years, and won it (20-17 over USC) for the first time in 32 years ... Sherman Lewis had TD receptions of 88 and 87 yards, a TD run of 87 yards, an 85-yard run and an 84-yard punt return in 1963 ... Dan Bass was credited with a school-record 32 tackles against Ohio State in 1979 and also had 24 tackles against Notre Dame ... Lorenzo White rushed for over 200 yards in

four games in 1985 while setting the all-time NCAA rushing record for sophomores with 2,066 yards. That total led the NCAA and set the single-season Big Ten record … Andre Rison had 252 receiving yards and 3 TDs on nine receptions against Georgia in the 1989 Gator Bowl … Derrick Mason returned a kickoff 100 yards against Penn State in 1994 and also did it against LSU in the 1995 Independence Bowl.

QUIRK He was named the nation's Outstanding Offensive End after his senior season in 1978. He finished his career as the Spartans' leader in receptions (112), reception yardage (2,347), average yards per reception (21.0) and touchdown catches (24). He was named All-America in 1978. But Kirk Gibson will always be best remembered by sports fans for his walk-off—actually, limp-off—home run against Dennis Eckersley in Game 1 of the 1988 World Series.

LORE He was called The Flea because he was 5'9" and 161 pounds, but Eric Allen's ability belied his stature. He rushed for a then-NCAA-record 350 yards on Oct. 30, 1971, at Purdue. His 29 carries included 4 TD runs in Michigan State's 43-10 victory. Allen had totaled 325 yards when Daugherty removed him from the game early in the fourth quarter. The coach had a message for his little tailback: "They tell me in the press box that you need just 23 yards to break the collegiate rushing record. You're going back and you're going to carry the ball on every play until you get it." Two carries later, Allen ran for a 25-yard score to break the NCAA mark of 347 yards set by Michigan's Ron Johnson.

QUOTE "The alumni are always with you, win or tie."
—Duffy Daugherty

MICHIGAN STATE ANNUAL STATISTICAL LEADERS

YR	RUSHING	YDS	ATT	AVG	PASSING	ATT	CMP	PCT	YDS	RECEIVING	REC	YDS	AVG
1945	Jack Breslin	361	112	3.2	Russ Reader	90	53	.59	613	Steve Cantos	31	265	8.5
1946	George Guerre	337	46	7.3	George Guerre	60	25	.42	396	Warren Huey	11	214	19.5
1947	George Guerre	354	47	7.5	Gene Glick	26	8	.31	139	Warren Huey	7	60	8.6
1948	George Guerre	734	118	6.2	Gene Glick	56	26	.46	692	Ed Sobczak	20	465	23.3
1949	Lynn Chandnois	885	129	6.9	Gene Glick	71	38	.54	776	Robert Carey	26	523	20.1
1950	Sonny Grandelius	1,023	163	6.3	Al Dorow	105	45	.43	654	Robert Carey	19	268	14.1
1951	Don McAuliffe	566	124	4.6	Al Dorow	114	64	.56	842	Robert Carey	20	263	13.2
1952	Billy Wells	585	118	5.0	Tom Yewcic	95	41	.43	941	Ellis Duckett	10	323	32.3
1953	LeRoy Bolden	691	127	5.4	Tom Yewcic	80	34	.43	489	Ellis Duckett	10	169	16.9
1954	Clarence Peaks	321	45	7.1	Earl Morrall	99	39	.39	795	John Lewis	10	338	33.8
1955	Walt Kowalczyk	584	82	7.1	Earl Morrall	68	42	.62	941	David Kaiser	12	343	28.6
1956	Dennis Mendyk	495	85	5.8	Pat Wilson	39	20	.51	414	Tony Kolodziej	7	221	31.6
1957	Walt Kowalczyk	545	101	5.4	Jim Ninowski	79	45	.57	718	David Kaiser	19	267	14.1
1958	Dean Look	238	90	2.6	Mike Panitch	37	16	.43	250	Sam Williams	15	242	16.1
1959	Herb Adderly	419	93	4.5	Dean Look	100	49	.49	785	Herb Adderly	13	265	20.4
1960	Ron Hatcher	361	59	6.1	Tom Wilson	109	46	.42	761	Herb Adderly	9	154	17.1
1961	George Saimes	451	82	5.5	Pete Smith	94	42	.45	630	Lonnie Sanders	15	247	16.5
1962	George Saimes	642	122	5.3	Pete Smith	52	18	.35	241	Lonnie Sanders	7	109	15.6
1963	Roger Lopes	601	138	4.4	Steve Juday	68	30	.44	509	Sherman Lewis	11	303	27.5
1964	Dick Gordon	741	123	6.0	Steve Juday	148	79	.53	894	Gene Washington	35	542	15.5
1965	Clinton Jones	787	165	4.8	Steve Juday	168	89	.53	1,173	Gene Washington	40	638	16.0
1966	Clinton Jones	784	159	4.9	Jimmy Raye	123	62	.50	1,110	Gene Washington	27	677	25.1
1967	Dwight Lee	497	116	4.3	Jimmy Raye	107	42	.39	580	Allen Brenner	26	462	17.8
1968	Tommy Love	729	177	4.1	William Triplett	90	47	.52	714	Frank Foreman	29	456	15.7
1969	Don Highsmith	937	209	4.5	William Triplett	117	37	.32	715	Frank Foreman	22	537	24.4
1970	Eric Allen	811	186	4.4	Mike Rasmussen	199	91	.46	1,344	Gordon Bowdell	34	495	14.6
1971	Eric Allen	1,494	259	5.8	Mike Rasmussen	88	32	.36	642	Billy Joe DuPree	25	414	16.6
1972	David E. Brown	575	123	4.7	George Mihaiu	55	25	.45	367	Billy Joe DuPree	23	406	17.7
1973	Clarence Bullock	496	113	4.4	Charles Baggett	94	38	.40	516	Michael Hurd	11	163	14.8
1974	Levi Jackson	942	153	6.2	Charles Baggett	105	48	.46	965	Michael Hurd	18	373	20.7
1975	Levi Jackson	1,063	230	4.6	Charles Baggett	88	42	.48	854	Eugene Byrd	10	266	26.6
1976	Richard Baes	931	187	5.0	Ed Smith	257	132	.51	1,749	Kirk Gibson	39	748	19.2
1977	Leroy McGee	720	162	4.4	Ed Smith	240	117	.49	1,731	Kirk Gibson	22	531	24.1
1978	Steve Smith	772	115	6.7	Ed Smith	292	169	.58	2,226	Kirk Gibson	42	806	19.2
1979	Steve Smith	972	204	4.8	Bryan Clark	131	64	.49	800	Eugene Byrd	30	559	18.6
1980	Steve Smith	667	154	4.3	John Leister	247	103	.42	1,569	Ted Jones	40	568	14.2
1981	Aaron Roberts	461	94	4.9	Bryan Clark	294	109	.37	1,521	Ted Jones	44	624	14.2
1982	Tony Ellis	671	179	3.7	John Leister	251	119	.47	1,321	Otis Grant	36	547	15.2
1983	Carl Butler	549	126	4.4	Clark Brown	141	82	.58	837	Daryl Turner	26	549	21.1
1984	Lorenzo White	616	142	4.3	Dave Yarema	222	119	.54	1,477	Mark Ingram	22	499	22.7
1985	Lorenzo White	2,066	419	4.9	Dave Yarema	116	66	.57	840	Mark Ingram	34	745	21.9
1986	Lorenzo White	633	164	3.9	Dave Yarema	297	202	.68	2,581	Andre Rison	54	966	17.9
1987	Lorenzo White	1,572	357	4.4	Bobby McAllister	139	71	.51	1,171	Andre Rison	34	785	23.1
1988	Blake Ezor	1,496	322	4.6	Bobby McAllister	154	80	.52	1,406	Andre Rison	39	961	24.6
1989	Blake Ezor	1,299	267	4.9	Dan Enos	240	153	.64	2,066	Courtney Hawkins	60	1,080	18.0
1990	Tico Duckett	1,394	257	5.4	Dan Enos	220	137	.62	1,677	James Bradley	32	517	16.2
1991	Tico Duckett	1,204	272	4.4	Jim Miller	210	130	.62	1,368	Courtney Hawkins	47	656	14.0
1992	Tico Duckett	1,021	204	5.0	Jim Miller	191	122	.64	1,400	Mill Coleman	37	586	15.8
1993	Duane Goulbourne	973	196	5.0	Jim Miller	336	215	.64	2,269	Mill Coleman	48	671	14.0
1994	Duane Goulbourne	930	214	4.3	Tony Banks	238	145	.61	2,040	Scott Greene	42	452	10.8
1995	Marc Renaud	1,057	216	4.9	Tony Banks	258	156	.60	2,089	Derrick Mason	53	787	14.8
1996	Sedrick Irvin	1,067	237	4.5	Todd Schultz	209	130	.62	1,693	Derrick Mason	53	865	16.3
1997	Sedrick Irvin	1,270	246	5.2	Todd Schultz	299	177	.59	2,003	Gari Scott	41	680	16.6
1998	Sedrick Irvin	1,167	272	4.3	Bill Burke	358	195	.54	2,595	Plaxico Burress	65	1,013	15.6
1999	Lloyd Clemons	959	191	5.0	Bill Burke	312	173	.55	2,214	Plaxico Burress	66	1,142	17.3
2000	T.J. Duckett	1,353	240	5.6	Jeff Smoker	197	103	.52	1,365	Lavaile Richardson	40	459	11.5
2001	T.J. Duckett	1,420	263	5.4	Jeff Smoker	262	166	.63	2,579	Charles Rogers	67	1,470	21.9
2002	David Richard	654	133	4.9	Jeff Smoker	203	114	.56	1,593	Charles Rogers	68	1,351	20.4
2003	Jaren Hayes	609	145	4.2	Jeff Smoker	488	302	.62	3,395	Agim Shabaj	57	692	12.1
2004	DeAndra Cobb	728	96	7.6	Drew Stanton	220	141	.64	1,601	Jerramy Scott	39	444	11.4

Receiving leaders by receptions
All statistics include postseason

MICHIGAN STATE ALL-TIME SCORES

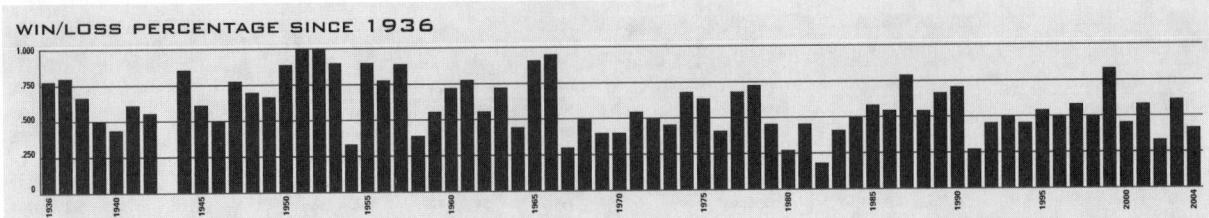

NO HEAD COACH

1896   1-2-1
S26	●	Lansing High	10 0
O17		at Kalamazoo	0 24
O25	=	Alma	0 0
N11		Kalamazoo	16 18

HENRY KEEP
1897-1898 (.607)   8-5-1

1897   4-2-1
S25	●	Lansing High	28 0
O2	●	Olivet	26 6
O9	●	Kalamazoo	0 28
O16	=	at Olivet	18 18
O30	●	at Alma	30 16
N6	●	Alma	38 4
N25		at Notre Dame	6 34

1898   4-3-0
O8	●	Eastern Michigan	11 6
O12		at Michigan	0 39
O15		at Notre Dame	0 53
O20	●	Albion	62 6
O29	●	at Olivet	45 0
N19	●	Eastern Michigan	24 6
N24		at Kalamazoo	0 17

CHARLES O. BEMIES
1899-1900 (.318)   3-7-1

1899   2-4-1
S30		at Notre Dame	0 40
O7		at Detroit AC	6 16
O14	●	Kalamazoo	6 10
O21	=	at Alma	11 11
N11		at Ypsilanti	18 0
N25		at Olivet	17 18
N30	●	DePauw	23 6

1900   1-3-0
S29	●	Albion	0 23
O10	●	Adrian	45 0
O20		at Detroit AC	6 21
O27		Alma	0 23

GEORGE E. DENMAN
1901-02 (.441)   7-9-1

1901   3-4-1
S28		at Alma	5 6
O5	●	Hillsdale	22 0
O12	●	at Albion	11 0
O19		at Detroit AC	0 33
O26	●	Kalamazoo	42 0
N2	=	Albion	17 17
N16		at Kalamazoo	5 15
N28		Olivet	18 23

1902   4-5-0
S27		at Notre Dame	0 32
O4	●	Detroit	11 0
O8		at Michigan	0 119
O11	●	Hillsdale	35 0
O18	●	Michigan Freshmen	2 0
O25		DePauw	12 17
N1		at Olivet	6 11
N15		at Albion	22 11
N22		Alma	5 16

CHESTER L. BREWER
1903-10, '17, '19 (.699) 58-23-7

1903   6-1-1
O3		at Notre Dame	0 12
O10	●	at Alma	11 0
O14	●	Michigan JV	11 0
O17	●	Kalamazoo	11 0
O31	●	Detroit YMCA	51 6
N7	●	at Hillsdale	43 0
N14	●	Albion	6 6
N21	=	Olivet	45 0

1904   8-1-0
O1	●	Michigan Deaf School	47 0
O8	●	Ohio Northern	28 6
O15	●	Port Huron YMCA	29 0
O22		at Albion	0 4
O29	●	Hillsdale	104 0
N5	●	Michigan Freshmen	39 0
N12	●	at Olivet	35 6
N19	●	at Alma	40 0
N26	●	Kalamazoo	58 0

1905   9-2-0
S30	●	Michigan Deaf School	42 0
O3	●	Port Huron YMCA	43 0
O7		at Notre Dame	0 28
O14	●	Michigan Freshmen	24 0
O21	●	Olivet	30 0
O23	●	Hillsdale	18 0
O28	●	Armour Inst.	18 0
N4	●	at Kalamazoo	30 0
N11	●	Albion	46 10
N18		at Northwestern	11 37
N25	●	at Alma	18 0

1906   7-2-2
S29	●	Olivet	23 0
O6	●	Albion	37 0
O13	=	at Alma	0 0
O20	●	Kalamazoo	38 0
O27	●	DePauw	33 0
N3		at Notre Dame	0 5
N10	●	at Albion	5 0
N12	●	Alma	12 0
N17	●	at Hillsdale	35 9
N24	●	at Olivet	6 8
N29	=	at Detroit AC	6 6

1907   4-2-1
O3	●	Detroit	17 0
O5	●	Michigan Deaf School	40 0
O12		at Michigan	0 46
O26	●	Wabash	15 6
N16	●	Olivet	55 4
N23	=	at Alma	0 0
N28		at Detroit AC	0 4

1908   6-0-2
O10	=	Michigan	0 0
O10	●	Western Michigan	35 0
O17	●	Michigan Deaf School	51 0
O24	=	at DePaul	0 0
O31	●	Wabash	6 0
N7	●	at Olivet	46 2
N21	●	Saginaw Navy	30 6
N26	●	at Detroit AC	37 14

1909   8-1-0
O7	●	Detroit	27 0
O9	●	Alma	34 0
O16	●	Wabash	28 0
O23		at Notre Dame	0 17
O30	●	at Culver	29 0
N6	●	DePaul	51 0
N10	●	Marquette	10 0
N13	●	Olivet	20 0
N25	●	at Detroit AC	34 0

1910   6-1-0
O6	●	Detroit AC	35 0
O8	●	Alma	11 0
O15		at Michigan	3 6
O22	●	Lake Forest	37 0
O29	●	Notre Dame	17 0
N5		at Marquette	3 2
N19	●	Olivet	62 0

JOHN F. MACKLIN
1911-15 (.853)   29-5

1911   5-1-0
O7	●	Alma	12 0
O14		Michigan	3 15
O28	●	Olivet	29 3
N4	●	at DePauw	6 0
N11	●	Mt. Union	26 6
N30	●	Wabash	17 5

1912   7-1-0
O5	●	Alma	14 3
O12		at Michigan	7 55
O19	●	Olivet	52 0
O26	●	DePauw	58 0
N2	●	Ohio Wesleyan	46 0
N9	●	Mt. Union	61 20
N16	●	Wabash	24 0
N28		at Ohio State	35 20

1913   7-0-0
O4	●	Olivet	26 0
O11	●	Alma	57 0
O18	●	Michigan	12 7
O25		at Wisconsin	12 7
N1	●	Akron	41 0
N8	●	Mt. Union	13 7
N15	●	South Dakota	19 7

1914   5-2-0
O3	●	Olivet	26 7
O10	●	Alma	60 0
O17		Michigan	0 3
O24		at Nebraska	0 24
O31	●	Akron	75 6
N7	●	Mt. Union	21 14
N13		at Penn State	6 3

1915   5-1-0
O2	●	Olivet	34 0
O9	●	Alma	77 12
O16	●	Carroll	56 0
O23	●	at Michigan	24 0
O30		Oregon State	0 20
N6	●	Marquette	68 6

FRANK SOMMERS
1916 (.643)   4-2-1

1916   4-2-1
S30	●	Olivet	40 0
O7	●	Carroll	20 0
O14	●	at Alma	33 0
O21		at Michigan	0 9
O28	●	North Dakota St.	30 0
N4	=	at South Dakota	3 3
N18		Notre Dame	0 14

CHESTER L. BREWER

1917   0-9-0
O6		Alma	7 14
O13		Kalamazoo	3 7
O20		at Michigan	0 27
O27		Detroit	0 14
N3		Western Michigan	0 14
N10		at Northwestern	6 39
N17		at Notre Dame	0 23
N24		Syracuse	7 21
N29		Camp MacArthur	0 20

GEORGE E. GAUTHIER
1918 (.571)   4-3

1918   4-3-0
O5	●	Albion	21 6
O12	●	Hillsdale	66 6
N2	●	Western Michigan	16 7
N9		Purdue	6 14
N16	●	Notre Dame	13 7
N23		at Michigan	6 21
N28		at Wisconsin	6 7

CHESTER L. BREWER

1919   4-4-1
O4	●	Albion	14 13
O8	●	Alma	46 6
O11	●	Western Michigan	18 21
O18		at Michigan	0 26
O25	●	DePauw	27 0
N1		at Purdue	7 13
N8	●	South Dakota	13 0
N15		at Notre Dame	0 13
N27	=	Wabash	7 7

GEORGE "POTSY" CLARK
1920 (.400)   4-6

1920   4-6-0
S25	●	Kalamazoo	2 21
O2	●	Albion	16 0
O6	●	Alma	48 0
O9		at Wisconsin	0 27
O16		at Michigan	0 35
O23	●	Marietta	7 23
O30	●	Olivet	109 0
N13	●	Chicago YMCA	81 0
N20		at Nebraska	7 35
N25	●	Notre Dame	0 25

ALBERT M. BARRON
1921-22 (.389)   6-10-2

1921   3-5-0
O1	●	Alma	28 0
O8	●	Albion	7 24
O15		at Michigan	0 30
O22	●	Western Michigan	17 14
O27		at Marquette	0 7
N5	●	South Dakota	14 0
N12		at Butler	2 3
N24		at Notre Dame	0 48

1922   3-5-2
S30	●	Alma	33 0
O7	=	Albion	7 7
O14		at Wabash	0 26
O21	●	South Dakota	7 0
O28		at Indiana	6 14
N4		at Michigan	0 63
N11	●	Ohio Wesleyan	6 9
N18		at Creighton	0 9
N25	●	Massachusetts St.	45 0
N30		at St. Louis	7 7

RALPH H. YOUNG
1923-27 (.451)   18-22-1

1923   3-5-0
S29		at Chicago	0 34
O6	●	Lake Forest	21 6
O13		at Wisconsin	0 21
O20	●	Albion	13 0
O27		at Michigan	0 37
N3		Ohio Wesleyan	14 19
N10	●	Creighton	7 27
N17	●	at Detroit	2 0

1924   5-3-0
S26	●	North Central	59 0
O4	●	Olivet	54 3
O11	●	Michigan	0 7
O17	●	Chicago YMCA	34 3
O25	●	at Northwestern	9 13
N1	●	Lake Forest	42 13
N8	●	at St. Louis	3 9
N15	●	South Dakota St.	9 0

1925 — 3-5-0
S26	•	Adrian	16 0
O3		at Michigan	0 39
O10		Lake Forest	0 6
O17	•	Centre	15 13
O24		at Penn State	6 13
N1		Colgate	0 14
N7	•	Toledo	58 0
N14		at Wisconsin	10 21

1926 — 3-4-1
S26	•	Adrian	16 0
O2	•	Kalamazoo	9 0
O9		at Michigan	3 55
O16		at Cornell	14 24
O23	=	Lake Forest	0 0
O30		at Colgate	6 38
N6	•	Centre	42 14
N20	•	Haskell	7 40

1927 — 4-5-0
S24	•	Kalamazoo	12 6
O1	•	Ohio U.	27 0
O8		at Michigan	0 21
O15		at Cornell Coll.	13 19
O29		Detroit	7 24
N5		at Indiana	7 33
N11	•	Albion	20 6
N19	•	Butler	25 0
D3		at North Carolina St.	0 19

HARRY G. KIPKE
1928 (.438)   3-4-1

1928 — 3-4-1
S29	•	Kalamazoo	103 0
O6	•	Albion	0 2
O13	•	Chicago YMCA	37 0
O20	•	Colgate	0 16
N3	=	Mississippi State	6 6
N10	•	at Detroit	0 39
N17	•	at Michigan	0 3
N24	•	North Carolina St.	7 0

JAMES H. CROWLEY
1929-32 (.712)   22-8-3

1929 — 5-3-0
S28	•	Alma	59 6
O5		at Michigan	0 17
O12		at Colgate	0 31
O19	•	Adrian	74 0
O26	•	North Carolina St.	40 6
N2	•	Case	38 0
N9	•	Mississippi State _JAM_	33 19
N16	•	Detroit	0 25

1930 — 5-1-2
S27	•	Alma	28 0
O4	=	at Michigan	0 0
O11	•	Cincinnati	32 0
O18	•	Colgate	14 7
O25	•	Case	45 0
O31		at Georgetown	13 14
N8	•	North Dakota St.	19 11
N22	=	Detroit	0 0

1931 — 5-3-1
S26	•	Alma	74 0
O3	•	Cornell Coll.	47 0
O10		at Army	7 20
O17	•	Illinois Wesleyan	34 6
O24	•	Georgetown	6 0
O31	•	Syracuse	10 15
N7	•	Ripon	100 0
N14		at Michigan	0 0
N21		at Detroit	13 20

1932 — 7-1-0
S24	•	Alma	93 0
O1		at Michigan	0 26
O8	•	Grinnell	27 6
O15	•	Illinois Wesleyan	27 0
O22	•	Fordham _NYC_	19 13
O29		at Syracuse	27 13
N5	•	South Dakota	20 6
N19	•	Detroit	7 0

CHARLES W. BACHMAN
1933-46 (.658)   70-34-10

1933 — 4-2-2
S30	•	Grinnell	14 0
O7		at Michigan	6 20
O14	•	Illinois Wesleyan	20 12
O21		at Marquette	6 0
O28	•	Syracuse	27 3
N4	=	Kansas State	0 0
N11	=	Carnegie Tech	0 0
N25		at Detroit	0 14

1934 — 8-1-0
S29	•	Grinnell	33 20
O6	=	at Michigan	16 0
O13	•	Carnegie Tech	13 0
O20		at Manhattan	39 0
N3	•	Marquette	13 7
N10		at Syracuse	0 10
N17	•	Detroit	7 6
N24		at Kansas	6 0
D8	•	Texas A&M _SA_	26 13

1935 — 6-2-0
S28	•	Grinnell	41 0
O5	•	at Michigan	25 6
O12	•	Kansas	42 0
O19		at Boston College	6 18
O26	•	Washington, Mo.	47 13
N2		at Temple	12 7
N9	•	Marquette	7 13
N16	•	at Loyola Marymount	27 0

1936 — 6-1-2
S26	•	Wayne St.	27 0
O3	•	at Michigan	21 7
O10	•	at Carnegie Tech	7 0
O17	•	Missouri	13 0
O24	•	Marquette	7 13
O31	=	at Boston College	13 13
N7	=	at Temple	7 7
N14		at Kansas	41 0
N21	•	Arizona	7 0

1937 — 8-2-0
S25	•	Wayne St.	19 0
O2	•	at Michigan	19 14
O9	•	Manhattan _NYC_	0 3
O16		at Missouri	2 0
O23	•	Marquette	21 7
O30	•	Kansas	16 0
N6	•	at Temple	13 6
N13	•	Carnegie Tech	13 6
N27		at San Francisco	14 0
		ORANGE BOWL	
J1	•	Auburn	0 6

1938 — 6-3-0
S24	•	Wayne St.	34 6
O1		at Michigan	0 14
O8	•	Illinois Wesleyan	18 0
O15	•	at West Virginia	26 0
O22	•	Syracuse	19 12
O29	•	Santa Clara	6 7
N5		at Missouri	0 6
N12	•	at Marquette	20 14
N19	•	Temple	10 0

1939 — 4-4-1
S30	•	Wayne St.	16 0
O7		at Michigan	13 26
O14	•	Marquette	14 17
O21		at Purdue	7 20
O28	•	Illinois Wesleyan	13 6
N4	•	at Syracuse	14 3
N11		at Santa Clara	0 6
N18	=	Indiana	7 7
N25	•	Temple	18 7

1940 — 3-4-1
O5		at Michigan	14 21
O12	•	Purdue	20 7
O18	•	at Temple	19 21
O25	=	Santa Clara	0 0
N2	•	Kansas State	32 0
N9		at Indiana	0 20
N16	•	at Marquette	6 7
N23	•	West Virginia	17 0

1941 — 5-3-1
S27		at Michigan	7 19
O11	•	Marquette	13 7
O18	•	at Santa Clara	0 7
O25	•	Wayne St.	39 6
N1	•	Missouri	0 19
N8	=	at Purdue	0 0
N15	•	Temple	46 0
N22	•	Ohio Wesleyan	31 7
N29	•	at West Virginia	14 12

1942 — 4-3-2
O3		at Michigan	0 20
O10	•	Waynes St.	46 6
O17		Marquette	7 28
O24	•	Great Lakes NAS	14 0
O31	=	at Temple	7 7
N7		Washington State _SPO_	13 25
N14	•	Purdue	19 6
N21	•	West Virginia	7 0
N28	=	Oregon State	7 7

1943
NO TEAM WWII

1944 — 6-1-0
S30	•	Scranton	40 12
O7	•	at Kentucky	2 0
O14	•	Kansas State	45 6
O21	•	at Maryland	8 0
O27	•	at Wayne St.	32 0
N4	•	at Missouri	7 13
N11	•	Maryland	33 0

1945 — 5-3-1
S29	•	at Michigan	0 40
O6	•	Kentucky	7 6
O13	•	at Pittsburgh	12 7
O20	•	Waynes St.	27 7
O27	=	Marquette	13 13
N3	•	Missouri	14 7
N10		Great Lakes NAS	7 27
N17	•	Penn State	33 0
N23	•	at Miami, Fla.	7 21

1946 — 5-5-0
S28	•	Wayne St.	42 0
O5		Boston College	20 34
O12		Mississippi State	0 6
O19	•	at Penn State	19 16
O26		Cincinnati	7 18
N2		at Kentucky	14 39
N9		at Michigan	7 55
N16	•	Marquette	20 0
N23	•	Maryland	26 14
N30	•	Washington State	26 20

CLARENCE "BIGGIE" MUNN
1947-53 (.846)   54-9-2

1947 — 7-2-0
S27		at Michigan	0 55
O4	•	Mississippi State	7 0
O11	•	at Washington State	21 7
O18	•	Iowa State	20 0
O25	•	Kentucky	6 7
N1	•	Marquette	13 7
N8	•	Santa Clara	28 0
N15	•	at Temple	14 6
N29	•	at Hawaii	58 19

1948 — 6-2-2
S25	•	Michigan	7 13
O2	•	Hawaii	68 21
O9	•	at Notre Dame	7 26
O16	•	Arizona	61 7
O23	=	at Penn State	14 14
O30	•	at Oregon State	46 21
N6	•	Marquette	47 0
N13	•	at Iowa State	48 7
N20	•	Washington State	40 0
N27	=	at Santa Clara	21 21

1949 — 6-3-0
S24	•	at Michigan	3 7
O1	•	Marquette	48 7
O8	•	Maryland	14 7
O15	•	William & Mary	42 13
O22	•	Penn State	24 0
O29	•	Temple	62 14
N5		Notre Dame	21 34
N12	•	Oregon State _PORT_	20 25
N19	•	at Arizona	75 0

1950 — 8-1-0
S23	•	Oregon State	38 13
S30	•	at Michigan	14 7
O7		Maryland	7 34
O14	•	William & Mary	33 14
O21	•	Marquette	34 6
O28	•	at Notre Dame	36 33
N4	•	Indiana	35 0
N11	•	Minnesota	27 0
N18	•	at Pittsburgh	19 0

1951 — 9-0-0
S22	•	Oregon State	6 0
S29	•	at Michigan	25 0
O6	•	at Ohio State	24 20
O13	•	Marquette	20 14
O20	•	at Penn State	32 21
O27	•	Pittsburgh	53 26
N10	•	Notre Dame	35 0
N17	•	at Indiana	30 26
N24	•	Colorado	45 7

1952 — 9-0-0
S27	•	at Michigan	27 13
O4	•	Oregon State _PORT_	17 14
O11	•	Texas A&M	48 6
O18	•	Syracuse	48 7
O25	•	Penn State	34 7
N1	•	at Purdue	14 7
N8	•	at Indiana	41 14
N15	•	Notre Dame	21 3
N22	•	Marquette	62 13

1953-PRESENT
BIG 10

1953 — 9-1-0 (5-1-0)
S26	•	at Iowa	21 7
O3	•	at Minnesota	21 0
O10	•	TCU	26 19
O17	•	Indiana	47 18
O24		at Purdue	0 6
O31	•	Oregon State	34 6
N7	•	at Ohio State	28 13
N14	•	Michigan	14 6
N21	•	Marquette	21 15
		ROSE BOWL	
J1	•	UCLA	28 20

HUGH DUFFY DAUGHERTY
1954-72 (.609)   109-69-5

1954 — 3-6-0 (1-5-0)
S25		at Iowa	10 14
O2		Wisconsin	0 6
O9	•	at Indiana	21 14
O16		at Notre Dame	19 20
O23		Purdue	13 27
O30		at Minnesota	13 19
N6	•	Washington State	54 6
N13		at Michigan	7 33
N20	•	Marquette	40 10

1955 — 9-1-0 (5-1-0)
S24	•	at Indiana	20 13
O1		at Michigan	7 14
O8		Stanford	38 14
O15	•	Notre Dame	21 7
O22		Illinois	21 7
O29		at Wisconsin	27 0
N5		at Purdue	27 0
N12		Minnesota	42 14
N19	•	Marquette	33 0
		ROSE BOWL	
J2	•	UCLA	17 14

1956 — 7-2-0 (4-2-0)
S29	•	at Stanford	21 7
O6	•	at Michigan	9 0
O13	•	Indiana	53 6
O20	•	at Notre Dame	47 14
O27		at Illinois	13 20
N3		Wisconsin	33 0
N10	•	Purdue	12 9
N17		at Minnesota	13 14
N24	•	Kansas State	38 17

1957 — 8-1-0 (5-1-0)
S28	•	Indiana	54 0
O5	•	at California	19 0
O12	•	at Michigan	35 6
O19		Purdue	13 20
O26	•	Illinois	19 14
N2	•	at Wisconsin	21 7
N9	•	Notre Dame	34 6
N16	•	Minnesota	42 13
N23	•	Kansas State	27 9

1958 — 3-5-1 (0-5-1)
S27	•	California	32 12
O4	=	Michigan	12 12
O11	•	Pittsburgh	22 8
O18	•	at Purdue	6 14
O25	•	at Illinois	0 16
N1		Wisconsin	7 9
N8	•	at Indiana	0 6
N15	•	at Minnesota	12 39
N22	•	Kansas State	26 7

1959 — 5-4-0 (4-2-0)
S26	•	Texas A&M	7 9
O3	•	at Michigan	34 8
O10	•	at Iowa	8 37
O17	•	Notre Dame	19 0
O24	•	Indiana	14 6
O31	•	at Ohio State	24 30
N7	•	Purdue	15 0
N14	•	Northwestern	15 10
N20	•	at Miami, Fla.	13 18

1960 6-2-1 (4-2-0)

S24	=	at Pittsburgh	7	7
O1	● |	Michigan	24	17
O8	|	Iowa	15	27
O15	●	at Notre Dame	21	0
O22	● |	at Indiana	35	0
O29	|	Ohio State	10	21
N5	● |	at Purdue	17	13
N12	● |	at Northwestern	21	18
N19	●	Detroit	43	15

1961 7-2-0 (5-2-0)

S30	● |	at Wisconsin	20	0
O7	●	Stanford	31	3
O14	● |	at Michigan	28	0
O21	●	Notre Dame	17	7
O28	● |	Indiana	35	0
N4	|	at Minnesota	0	13
N11	|	at Purdue	6	7
N18	● |	Northwestern	21	13
N25	● |	Illinois	34	7

1962 5-4-0 (3-3-0)

S29		at Stanford	13	16
O6	●	North Carolina	38	6
O13	● |	Michigan	28	0
O20	●	at Notre Dame	31	7
O27	● |	at Indiana	26	8
N3	|	Minnesota	7	28
N10	|	Purdue	9	17
N17	● |	at Northwestern	31	7
N24	|	at Illinois	6	7

1963 6-2-1 (4-1-1)

S28	●	North Carolina	31	0
O4		at Southern Cal	10	13
O12	= |	at Michigan	7	7
O19	● |	Indiana	20	3
O26	● |	at Northwestern	15	7
N2	● |	Wisconsin	30	13
N9	● |	at Purdue	23	0
N16	●	Notre Dame	12	7
N28	|	Illinois	0	13

1964 4-5-0 (3-3-0)

S26		at North Carolina	15	21
O3	●	Southern Cal	17	7
O10	|	Michigan	10	17
O17	|	at Indiana	20	27
O24	● |	Northwestern	24	6
O31	● |	at Wisconsin	22	6
N7	● |	Purdue	21	7
N14		at Notre Dame	7	34
N21	|	at Illinois	0	16

1965 10-1-0 (7-0-0)

S18	●	UCLA	13	3
S25	●	at Penn State	23	0
O2	● |	Illinois	22	12
O9	● |	at Michigan	24	7
O16	● |	Ohio State	32	7
O23	● |	at Purdue	14	10
O30	● |	Northwestern	49	7
N6	● |	at Iowa	35	0
N13	● |	Indiana	27	13
N20	●	at Notre Dame	12	3
		ROSE BOWL		
J1		UCLA	12	14

1966 9-0-1 (7-0-0)

S17	●	North Carolina St.	28	10
S24	●	Penn State	42	8
O1	● |	at Illinois	26	10
O8	● |	Michigan	20	7
O15	● |	at Ohio State	11	8
O22	● |	Purdue	41	20
O29	● |	at Northwestern	22	0
N5	● |	Iowa	56	7
N12	● |	at Indiana	37	19
N19	=	Notre Dame	10	10

1967 3-7-0 (3-4-0)

S23		Houston	7	37
S30		Southern Cal	17	21
O7	● |	Wisconsin	35	7
O14	● |	at Michigan	34	0
O21	|	at Minnesota	0	21
O28		at Notre Dame	12	24
N4	|	Ohio State	7	21
N11	|	Indiana	13	14
N18	|	at Purdue	7	21
N25	● |	Northwestern	41	27

1968 5-5-0 (2-5-0)

S21	●	Syracuse	14	10
S28	●	Baylor	28	10
O5	● |	at Wisconsin	39	0
O12	|	at Michigan	14	28
O19	|	Minnesota	13	14
O26	●	Notre Dame	21	17
N2	|	at Ohio State	20	25
N9	|	Indiana	22	24
N16	|	Purdue	0	9
N23	● |	at Northwestern	31	14

1969 4-6-0 (2-5-0)

S20	●	Washington	27	11
S27	●	SMU	23	15
O4		at Notre Dame	28	42
O11	|	at Ohio State	21	54
O18	● |	Michigan	23	12
O25	|	at Iowa	18	19
N1	|	Indiana	0	16
N8	|	at Purdue	13	41
N15	|	Minnesota	10	14
N22	● |	at Northwestern	39	7

1970 4-6-0 (3-4-0)

S19		at Washington	16	42
S26	●	Washington State	28	14
O3		Notre Dame	0	29
O10	|	Ohio State	0	29
O17	|	at Michigan	20	34
O24	● |	Iowa	37	0
O31	● |	at Indiana	32	7
N7	● |	Purdue	24	14
N14	|	at Minnesota	13	23
N21	|	Northwestern	20	23

1971 6-5-0 (5-3-0)

S11	● |	Illinois	10	0
S18		at Georgia Tech	0	10
S25	●	Oregon State	31	14
O2		at Notre Dame	2	14
O9	|	Michigan	13	24
O16	|	at Wisconsin	28	31
O23	● |	Iowa	34	3
O30	● |	at Purdue	43	10
N6	● |	at Ohio State	17	10
N13	● |	Minnesota	40	25
N20	|	at Northwestern	7	28

1972 5-5-1 (5-2-1)

S16	● |	at Illinois	24	0
S23		Georgia Tech	16	21
S30		at Southern Cal	6	51
O7		Notre Dame	0	16
O14	|	at Michigan	0	10
O21	● |	Wisconsin	31	0
O28	= |	at Iowa	6	6
N4	● |	Purdue	22	12
N11	● |	Ohio State	19	12
N18	|	at Minnesota	10	14
N25	● |	Northwestern	24	14

DENNIS E. STOLZ
1973-75 (.591) 19-13-1

1973 5-6-0 (4-4-0)

S15	|	at Northwestern	10	14
S22	●	at Syracuse	14	8
S29		UCLA	21	34
O6		at Notre Dame	10	14
O13	|	Michigan	0	31
O20	|	Illinois	3	6
O27	● |	at Purdue	10	7
N3	● |	Wisconsin	21	0
N10	|	at Ohio State	0	35
N17	● |	Indiana	10	9
N24	● |	at Iowa	15	6

1974 7-3-1 (6-1-1)

S14	● |	Northwestern	41	7
S21	●	Syracuse	19	0
S28		at UCLA	14	56
O5		Notre Dame	14	19
O12	|	at Michigan	7	21
O19	= |	at Illinois	21	21
O26	● |	Purdue	31	7
N2	● |	at Wisconsin	28	21
N9	● |	Ohio State	16	13
N16	● |	at Indiana	19	10
N23	● |	Iowa	60	21

1975 7-4-0 (4-4-0)

S13	|	Ohio State	0	21
S20	●	Miami, Ohio	14	13
S27	●	North Carolina St.	37	15
O4	●	at Notre Dame	10	3
O11	|	Michigan	6	16
O18	● |	at Minnesota	38	15
O25	|	Illinois	19	21
N1	|	at Purdue	10	20
N8	● |	at Indiana	14	6
N15	● |	Northwestern	47	14
N22	● |	at Iowa	27	23

DARRYL D. ROGERS
1976-79 (.568) 24-18-2

1976 4-6-1 (3-5-0)

S11	|	at Ohio State	21	49
S18	●	Wyoming	21	10
S25	=	at North Carolina St.	31	31
O2		Notre Dame	6	24
O9	|	at Michigan	10	42
O16	|	Minnesota	10	14
O23	● |	at Illinois	31	23
O30	● |	Purdue	45	13
N6	● |	Indiana	23	0
N13	|	at Northwestern	21	42
N20	|	Iowa	17	30

1977 7-3-1 (6-1-1)

S10	● |	Purdue	19	14
S17		Washington State	21	23
S24	●	Wyoming	34	16
O1		at Notre Dame	6	16
O8	|	Michigan	14	24
O15	= |	at Indiana	13	13
O22	● |	at Wisconsin	9	7
O29	● |	Illinois	49	20
N5	● |	at Minnesota	29	10
N11	● |	Northwestern	44	3
N19	● |	at Iowa	22	16

1978 8-3-0 (7-1-0)

S16	|	at Purdue	14	21
S23	●	Syracuse	49	21
S29		at Southern Cal	9	30
O7		Notre Dame	25	29
O14	● |	at Michigan	24	15
O21	● |	Indiana	49	14
O28	● |	Wisconsin	55	2
N4	● |	at Illinois	59	19
N11	● |	Minnesota	33	9
N18	● |	at Northwestern	52	3
N25	● |	Iowa	42	7

1979 5-6-0 (3-5-0)

S8	● |	Illinois	33	16
S15	●	Oregon	41	17
S22	●	Miami, Ohio	24	21
S29		at Notre Dame	3	27
O6	|	Michigan	7	21
O13	|	at Wisconsin	29	38
O20	|	Purdue	7	14
O27	|	at Ohio State	0	42
N3	● |	at Northwestern	42	7
N10	● |	Minnesota	31	17
N17	|	at Iowa	23	33

FRANK "MUDDY" WATERS
1980-82 (.303) 10-23

1980 3-8-0 (2-6-0)

S13	|	at Illinois	17	20
S20		at Oregon	7	35
S27	●	Western Michigan	33	7
O4		Notre Dame	21	26
O11	|	at Michigan	23	27
O18	|	Wisconsin	7	17
O25	|	at Purdue	25	36
N1	|	Ohio State	16	48
N8	● |	Northwestern	42	10
N15	● |	at Minnesota	30	12
N22	|	Iowa	0	41

1981 5-6-0 (4-5-0)

S12	|	Illinois	17	27
S19	|	at Ohio State	13	27
S26	●	Bowling Green	10	7
O3		at Notre Dame	7	20
O10	|	Michigan	20	38
O17	● |	Wisconsin	33	14
O24	|	at Purdue	26	27
O31	● |	Indiana	26	3
N7	● |	at Northwestern	61	14
N14	● |	Minnesota	43	36
N21	|	at Iowa	7	36

1982 2-9-0 (2-7-0)

S11	|	at Illinois	16	23
S18	|	Ohio State	10	31
S25		at Miami, Fla.	22	25
O2		Notre Dame	3	11
O9	|	at Michigan	17	31
O16	|	at Wisconsin	23	24
O23	|	Purdue	21	24
O30	● |	at Indiana	22	14
N6	|	Northwestern	24	28
N13	● |	at Minnesota	26	7
N20	|	Iowa	18	24

GEORGE J. PERLES
1983-94 (.540) 73-62-4

1983 4-6-1 (2-6-1)

S10	●	Colorado	23	17
S17	●	at Notre Dame	28	23
S24	|	Illinois	10	20
O1	= |	at Purdue	29	29
O8	|	Michigan	0	42
O15	|	at Indiana	12	24
O22	|	at Ohio State	11	21
O29	● |	Minnesota	34	10
N5	● |	at Northwestern	9	3
N12	|	Iowa	6	12
N19	|	at Wisconsin	0	32

1984 6-6-0 (5-4-0)

S8	●	at Colorado	24	21
S15		Notre Dame	20	24
S22	|	at Illinois	7	40
S29	|	Purdue	10	13
O6	● |	at Michigan	19	7
O13	● |	Indiana	13	6
O20	|	Ohio State	20	23
O27	● |	at Minnesota	20	13
N3	● |	Northwestern	27	10
N10	● |	at Iowa	17	16
N17	|	Wisconsin	10	20
		CHERRY BOWL		
D22		Army	6	10

1985 7-5-0 (5-3-0)

S14	●	Arizona State	12	3
S21		at Notre Dame	10	27
S28	●	Western Michigan	7	3
O5	|	at Iowa	31	35
O12	|	Michigan	0	31
O19	|	Illinois	17	30
O26	● |	at Purdue	28	24
N2	● |	Minnesota	31	26
N9	● |	at Indiana	35	16
N16	● |	Northwestern	32	0
N23	● |	at Wisconsin	41	7
		HALL OF FAME CLASSIC		
D31		Georgia Tech	14	17

1986 6-5-0 (4-4-0)

S13		at Arizona State	17	20
S20	●	Notre Dame	20	15
S27	●	Western Michigan	45	10
O4	|	Iowa	21	24
O11	|	at Michigan	6	27
O18	● |	at Illinois	29	21
O25	● |	Purdue	37	3
N1	● |	at Minnesota	52	23
N8	|	Indiana	14	17
N15	|	at Northwestern	21	24
N22	● |	Wisconsin	23	13

1987 9-2-1 (7-0-1)

S7	●	Southern Cal	27	13
S19		at Notre Dame	8	31
S26		Florida State	3	31
O3	● |	at Iowa	19	14
O10	● |	Michigan	17	11
O17	● |	at Northwestern	38	0
O24	= |	Illinois	14	14
O31	● |	at Ohio State	13	7
N7	● |	Purdue	45	3
N14	● |	Indiana	27	3
N21	● |	at Wisconsin	30	9
		ROSE BOWL		
J1	●	Southern Cal	20	17

1988 6-5-1 (6-1-1)

S10		Rutgers	13	17
S17		Notre Dame	3	20
S24		at Florida State	7	30
O1	= |	Iowa	10	10
O8	|	at Michigan	3	17
O15	● |	Northwestern	36	3
O22	● |	at Illinois	28	21
O29	● |	Ohio State	20	10
N5	● |	at Purdue	48	3
N12	● |	at Indiana	38	12
N19	● |	Wisconsin	36	0
		GATOR BOWL		
J1		Georgia	27	34

1989 — 8-4-0 (6-2-0)

S16	●	Miami, Ohio	49	0
S23		at Notre Dame	13	21
S30		Miami, Fla.	20	26
O7	●	at Iowa	17	14
O14		Michigan	7	10
O21		Illinois	10	14
O28	●	at Purdue	28	21
N4	●	at Indiana	51	20
N11		Minnesota	21	7
N18	●	Northwestern	76	14
N25	●	at Wisconsin	31	3
		ALOHA BOWL		
D25	●	Hawaii	33	13

1990 — 8-3-1 (6-2-0)

S15	=	at Syracuse	23	23
S22		Notre Dame	19	20
S29	●	Rutgers *ERut*	34	10
O6		Iowa	7	12
O13	●	at Michigan	28	27
O20		at Illinois	13	15
O27	●	Purdue	55	33
N3	●	Indiana	45	20
N10	●	at Minnesota	28	16
N17	●	at Northwestern	29	22
N24	●	Wisconsin	14	9
		SUN BOWL		
D31	●	Southern Cal	17	16

1991 — 3-8-0 (3-5-0)

S14		Central Michigan	3	20
S21		at Notre Dame	10	49
S28		Rutgers	7	14
O5		at Indiana	0	31
O12		Michigan	28	45
O19	●	Minnesota	20	12
O26		at Ohio State	17	27
N2		Northwestern	13	16
N9	●	at Wisconsin	20	7
N16	●	at Purdue	17	27
N23	●	Illinois	27	24

1992 — 5-6-0 (5-3-0)

S12		Central Michigan	20	24
S19		Notre Dame	31	52
S26		at Boston College	0	14
O3	●	Indiana	42	31
O10		at Michigan	10	35
O17	●	at Minnesota	20	15
O24		Ohio State	17	27
O31	●	at Northwestern	27	26
N7		Wisconsin	26	10
N14	●	Purdue	35	13
N21		at Illinois	10	14

1993 — 6-6-0 (4-4-0)

S11	●	Kansas	31	14
S18		at Notre Dame	14	36
S25	●	Central Michigan	48	34
O9	●	Michigan	17	7
O16		at Ohio State	21	28
O23	●	Iowa	24	10
O30		at Indiana	0	10
N6	●	Northwestern	31	29
N13	●	at Purdue	27	24
N27		Penn State *Tok*	37	38
D5		Wisconsin *Tok*	20	41
		LIBERTY BOWL		
D28		Louisville	7	18

1994 — 5-6-0 (4-4-0)

S10		at Kansas	10	17	
S17		Notre Dame	20	21	
S24	●	Miami, Ohio	45	10	†
O1	●	Wisconsin	29	10	†
O8		at Michigan	20	40	
O15		Ohio State	7	23	
O22		at Iowa	14	19	
O29	●	Indiana	27	21	†
N5	●	at Northwestern	35	17	†
N12	●	Purdue	42	30	†
N26		at Penn State	31	59	

1995 — 6-5-1 (4-3-1)

S9		Nebraska	10	50
S16	●	at Louisville	30	7
S23	=	at Purdue	35	35
S30	●	Boston College	25	21
O7		Iowa	7	21
O14	●	at Illinois	27	21
O21	●	Minnesota	34	31
O28		at Wisconsin	14	45
N4	●	Michigan	28	25
N11	●	at Indiana	31	13
N25		Penn State	20	24
		INDEPENDENCE BOWL		
D29		LSU	26	45

1996 — 6-6 (5-3)

A31	●	Purdue	52	14
S7		at Nebraska	14	55
S21		Louisville	20	30
S28	●	Eastern Michigan	47	0
O5		at Iowa	30	37
O12	●	Illinois	42	14
O19	●	at Minnesota	27	9
O26	●	Wisconsin	30	13
N2		at Michigan	29	45
N9	●	Indiana	38	15
N23		at Penn State	29	32
		SUN BOWL		
D31		Stanford	0	38

1997 — 7-5 (4-4)

S6	●	Western Michigan	42	10
S13	●	Memphis	51	21
S20	●	at Notre Dame	23	7
O4	●	Minnesota	31	10
O11	●	at Indiana	38	6
O18		at Northwestern	17	19
O25		Michigan	7	23
N1		Ohio State	13	37
N8		at Purdue	21	22
N22	●	at Illinois	27	17
N29	●	Penn State	49	14
		ALOHA BOWL		
D25	●	Washington	23	51

1998 — 6-6 (4-4)

A29	●	Colorado State	16	23
S5		at Oregon	14	48
S12	●	Notre Dame	45	23
S26		at Michigan	17	29
O3	●	Central Michigan	38	7
O10	●	Indiana	38	31
O24		at Minnesota	18	19
O31	●	Northwestern	29	5
N7		at Ohio State	28	24
N14		Purdue	24	25
N21	●	Illinois	41	9
N28		at Penn State	28	51

1999 — 10-2 (6-2)

S2	●	Oregon	27	20
S11	●	Eastern Michigan	51	7
S18	●	at Notre Dame	23	13
S25	●	at Illinois	27	10
O2	●	Iowa	49	3
O9	●	Michigan	34	31
O16		at Purdue	28	52
O23		at Wisconsin	10	40
N6	●	Ohio State	23	7
N13	●	at Northwestern	34	0
N20	●	Penn State	35	28
		CITRUS BOWL		
J1	●	Florida	37	34

2000 — 5-6 (2-6)

S9	●	Marshall	34	24
S16	●	at Missouri	13	10
S23		Notre Dame	27	21
S30		Northwestern	17	37
O7		at Iowa	16	21
O14		Wisconsin	10	17
O21		at Michigan	0	14
O28	●	Illinois	14	10
N4		at Ohio State	13	27
N11	●	Purdue	30	10
N18		at Penn State	23	42

2001 — 7-5 (3-5)

S8	●	Central Michigan	35	21
S22	●	at Notre Dame	17	10
S29		at Northwestern	26	27
O13	●	Iowa	31	28
O20		at Minnesota	19	28
O27	●	at Wisconsin	42	28
N3	●	Michigan	26	24
N10		Indiana	28	37
N17	●	at Purdue	14	24
N24	●	Penn State	37	42
D1	●	Missouri	55	7
		SILICON VALLEY CLASSIC		
D31	●	Fresno State	44	35

2002 — 4-8 (2-6)

A31	●	Eastern Michigan	56	7
S7	●	Rice	27	10
S14		California	22	46
S21		Notre Dame	17	21
S28	●	Northwestern	39	24
O12		at Iowa	16	44
O19		Minnesota	7	28
O26		Wisconsin	24	42
N2		at Michigan	3	49
N9	●	at Indiana	56	21
N16		Purdue	42	45
N23		at Penn State	7	61

2003 — 8-5 (5-3)

A30	●	Western Michigan	26	21
S6	●	Rutgers	44	28
S13		Louisiana Tech	19	20
S20	●	at Notre Dame	22	16
S27	●	Iowa	20	10
O4	●	Indiana	31	3
O11	●	at Illinois	49	14
O18	●	at Minnesota	44	38
N1		Michigan	20	27
N8		at Ohio State	23	33
N15		at Wisconsin	21	56
N22	●	Penn State	41	10
		ALAMO BOWL		
D29		Nebraska	3	17

2004 — 5-7 (4-4)

S4		at Rutgers	14	19
S11	●	Central Michigan	24	7
S18		Notre Dame	24	31
S25	●	at Indiana	30	20
O2		at Iowa	16	38
O9	●	Illinois	38	25
O16	●	Minnesota	51	17
O30		at Michigan	37	45
N6		Ohio State	19	32
N13	●	Wisconsin	49	14
N20		at Penn State	13	37
D4		at Hawaii	38	41

THE SCHOOLS

MIDDLE TENNESSEE

BY RYAN HOCKENSMITH

I N 1912, THE MIDDLE TENNESSEE Normal School decided to field a football team. The Normals, or Pedagogues, as they were alternately called, were coached by L.E. "Mutt" Weber, a student/player at Middle Tennessee. No records exist about how the team fared, or if it ever played an opponent. But football had landed in Murfreesboro, and it's remained ever since. In 1952, the program joined the Ohio Valley Conference and immediately emerged as a power, with four conference titles and an overall record of 59–20–4 from 1952 to 1959. The NCAA's reclassification in 1978 gave Middle Tennessee State Division I-AA status. But again, it didn't take the Blue Raiders long to make an impact. In 1984, coach Boots Donnelly led Middle Tennessee State to the NCAA semifinals in the first of the school's seven playoff berths in 11 years. In 1999, Middle Tennessee State joined the big boys of D1-A. The Blue Raiders played two seasons as an independent before accepting an invitation to become a member of the Sun Belt Conference.

TRADITION Ninety minutes before each home game, Blue Raiders coaches and players walk through the stadium parking lot. They're surrounded by two rows of cheerleaders, fans and the school band as they get set to enter Floyd Stadium and begin pregame preparations. When the Blue Raiders run onto the field before the game, they pay homage to those well-wishers by slapping a sign that reads, "Represent."

BEST COACH It's hard to top the legacy of former coach Boots Donnelly. After lettering on the 1962-64 teams that went a combined 22–8–1, Donnelly became Middle Tennessee State's head coach in 1979. He went 140–87–1 and presided over arguably the school's best-ever decade before accepting an administrative role in 1999. Two years later, he took over as athletic director.

BEST PLAYER Even with his smallish, 5'9", 170-pound frame, two-time all-state high school running back Joe Campbell was quite the recruiting catch for then-D1-AA Middle Tennessee State. Campbell pinballed through defenses from 1988 to 1991, becoming the Blue Raiders' first two-time All-America. When Campbell left Murfreesboro, he held school records for rushing yards (3,823) and touchdowns (45). The Los Angeles Rams used a sixth-round pick on Campbell, but injuries curtailed his pro career.

PROFILE

Middle Tennessee State University
Murfreesboro, Tenn.
Founded: 1911
Enrollment: 20,288
Colors: Royal Blue and White
Nickname: Blue Raiders
Stadium: Floyd Stadium
    Opened in 1933
    AstroTurf; 30,788 capacity
First football game: 1912
All-time record: 488–344–28 (.584)
Sun Belt Conference championships:
1 (shared)
Website: www.goblueraiders.com

THE BEST OF TIMES

The raw data make an overwhelming case: six Ohio Valley Conference Players of the Year; two conference titles; three D1-AA playoff appearances; four All-Americas; the most important coach in school history, Boots Donnelly; arguably the best player in school history, running back Joe Campbell. Yep, it's hard to argue against the 1980s as the best era in Middle Tennessee State football history.

THE WORST OF TIMES

The end of the Boots Donnelly era began almost five years before he stepped aside as Middle Tennessee State's coach—on Oct. 9, 1993. The No. 4 Blue Raiders traveled to face traditional intrastate roadkill Tennessee-Martin and suffered a devastating 24-14 loss. Middle Tennessee State tumbled from the rankings and slumped to a 5–6 mark, Donnelly's first losing record in more than a decade. After going 39–13 from 1989 to 1992, Donnelly struggled to a 35–29–1 mark before he stepped down in 1998.

CONFERENCE

The Blue Raiders joined the Sun Belt in 2001. The program upgraded to D1-A in 1999 and was independent that year and in 2000. The program was affiliated with the Ohio Valley Conference from 1952 to 1998.

DISTINGUISHED ALUMNI

George Clinton, musician; Albert Gore Sr., U.S. senator; James Buchanan, Nobel Prize winner, economics; Pete Fisher, general manager, Grand Ole Opry

FIGHT SONG

MTSU FIGHT SONG
Blue Raiders ride on to vic-t'ry
Never failing in the fight
Upholding honor and tradition
Of the name that's held most high
M-T-S-U marching onward
This will be our battle cry
For the one, true bride of the Blue
M-T-S-U Raiders Ride!

BEST TEAM When the 1984 season ended after three playoff games, the table was set for a monster year in 1985, and what a ride it would be. Led by cornerback Don Griffin, the Ohio Valley Conference's defensive player of the year, the Blue Raiders won two overtime games and routed always-dangerous Georgia Southern on the road 35-10 in a huge September clash. They entered the D1-AA playoffs 11–0, ranked No. 1 and hosting Georgia Southern. But after an Eagles touchdown drive to start the game, Middle Tennessee State lost a fumble at its own 7-yard line. Georgia Southern punched in a score, then another, to lead 21-0 at halftime. A valiant Middle Tennessee State comeback fell one touchdown short 28-21. Still, eight players were named all-conference, and fullback Tony Burse, center Bill Cherry, wide receiver Dwight Stone and Griffin all went on to play in the NFL.

BIGGEST GAME In 2001, with only two years of D1-A football under their belts, the Blue Raiders were Sun Belt Conference and big-time football rookies. That changed on Aug. 30, 2001, after Middle Tennessee State notched a 37-28

> *When the Blue Raiders run onto the field, they pay homage to well-wishers by slapping a sign that reads, "Represent."*

win at Vanderbilt. The Commodores scored 28 second-quarter points to go up 28-24 at the half, but Middle Tennessee State shut them out the rest of the way and relied on Dwone Hicks' 203 rushing yards and four touchdowns to clinch the school's first win in 15 tries against SEC teams. The Blue Raiders went on to post an 8–3 mark.

BIGGEST UPSET In October 1981, undefeated Murray State came to Murfreesboro. Coached by Frank Beamer, with the help of an assistant head coach named Ralph Friedgen, the Racers were 5–0 and ranked No. 1 in the country. Though Middle Tennessee State mustered only 31 yards of total offense, the Red Raiders suffocated the Racers offense and squeaked out a 14-9 stunner.

HEARTBREAKER The Blue Raiders were flying high in October 1998, after a 35-14 rout of No. 13 Murray State. The win evened Middle Tennessee State's record at 3–3 and gave coach Boots Donnelly two weeks to prep for No. 21 Eastern Illinois. Donnelly's team took a 32-21 lead on two fourth-quarter field goals, but squandered the advantage in

RECORDS

RUSHING YARDS

GAME
311   Dwone Hicks vs. Louisiana Tech, Oct. 7, 2000 (32 att.)

SEASON
1,439   Vince Hall, 1984 (260 att.)

CAREER
3,823   Joe Campbell, 1988-91 (638 att.)

PASSING YARDS

GAME
459   Wes Counts vs. Idaho, Oct. 6, 2001 (23 of 28)

SEASON
2,749   Clint Marks, 2004 (259 of 368)

CAREER
8,007   Wes Counts, 1998-2001 (706 of 1079)

RECEIVING YARDS

GAME
244   Demetric Mostiller vs. Tennessee-Martin, Nov. 4, 1995 (8 rec.)

SEASON
1,280   Kerry Wright, 2003 (73 rec.)

CAREER
3,074   Kendall Newson, 1998-2001 (238 rec.)

POINTS

GAME
36   Dwone Hicks vs. Louisiana Tech, Oct. 7, 2000 (6 TDs)

SEASON
148   Dwone Hicks, 2001 (24 TDs; 2 two-pt. conv.)

CAREER
358   Dwone Hicks, 1999-2002 (59 TDs, 2 two-pt. conv.)

CONSENSUS ALL-AMERICANS

1964	Jimbo Pearson	S
1965	Keith Atchley	LB
1983	Roger Carroll	OL
1984	Kelly Potter	PK
1985	Don Griffin	DB
1988	Don Thomas	LB
1990-91	Joe Campbell	RB
1991-92	Steve McAdoo	OL
1993	Pat Hicks	OL
1995	Nathanial Claybrooks	DL

the final 1:25. After the Panthers scored to make it 32-27, a botched two-point conversion made an Eastern Illinois victory seem impossible. It wasn't. After an onside kick, running back Justin Lynch scored his second touchdown of the game with 38 seconds to go, giving Eastern Illinois a stunning 35-32 win. The Blue Raiders won two of their last three games but finished 5–5. The Eastern Illinois loss cost Middle Tennessee State an Ohio Valley Conference title and a playoff trip. Donnelly retired after the season.

STADIUM In 1933, Middle Tennessee State built Horace Jones Field. During the 1960s, a series of renovations increased capacity to 15,000, and in 1979 the building was named Floyd Stadium, in honor of longtime athletic director and head coach Johnny "Red" Floyd. When the school announced that it would be moving up to D1-A in 1995, Floyd Stadium received a $25 million facelift. Now the stadium seats 30,788, and has been a daunting arena for Middle Tennessee State's foes.

RIVAL How ugly did the Middle Tennessee State-Tennessee Tech rivalry become? The mutual dislike between the two schools spilled over onto the basketball court on two fight-marred occasions in the mid-1980s, resulting in multiple player suspensions. On the football field, the two schools disagreed for decades over the name of the game's trophy. Middle Tennessee State called it the Totem Pole. Tennessee Tech insisted on the Shinny Ninny. Whatever it was called, the Blue Raiders claimed it more often than their rival, leading the series 35–32–2 through 2004. The football series was discontinued after 1998, when Middle Tennessee State moved to D1-A.

NICKNAME Before 1934, Middle Tennessee State athletics teams were referred to by a wide range of names. But during the 1934 season, the *Murfreesboro Daily News* held a contest to find an official name for the sports teams. A player on the team, Charles Sarver, took home the $5 contest prize with his entry, Blue Raiders. The name has stuck ever since.

MASCOT Though the team nickname has lasted from 1934 until now, the mascot has undergone almost constant changes. In the mid-1940s, the school had a student portray Confederate general Nathan Bedford Forrest on horseback. Around 1970, though, the school cited sensitivity concerns in discontinuing the symbol of Forrest as the team mascot. For the next 25 years or so, the Blue Raiders unofficially adopted a costumed, cartoonish dog mascot, Ole Blue, which most resembled a bluetick hound. But on Jan.17, 1998, the school unveiled Lightning, a winged blue horse.

UNIFORMS The school uniforms remained the same through 1979, when coach Boots Donnelly decided to spruce things up. He added silver helmets to top off the royal blue-and-white uniforms. When the school switched its logo in 1998, the simple MT logo that had been plastered on helmets since the program's first game had a snazzy winged horse and lightning bolt added above it.

QUOTE "If we don't pick up the enthusiasm and intensity against Florida State, we'll have the Humane Society breathing down our necks. If FSU wants to run that horse [Renegade] after every touchdown, we're liable to get him killed."—Boots Donnelly, before Middle Tennessee State's 39-10 loss to the Seminoles in 1991

MIDDLE TENNESSEE ANNUAL STATISTICAL LEADERS

YR	RUSHING	YDS	ATT	AVG	PASSING	ATT	CMP	PCT	YDS	RECEIVING	REC	YDS	AVG
1999	Jamison Palmer	548	117	4.7	Wes Counts	390	249	.64	2,603	Kendall Newson	69	918	13.3
2000	Dwone Hicks	1,277	186	6.9	Wes Counts	218	127	.58	1,536	Kendall Newson	74	945	12.8
2001	Dwone Hicks	1,143	191	6.0	Wes Counts	259	188	.73	2,327	Kendall Newson	65	796	12.2
2002	Dwone Hicks	1,011	184	5.5	Andrico Hines	243	142	.58	1,753	Tyrone Calico	45	606	13.5
2003	Eugene Gross	735	189	3.9	Andrico Hines	253	153	.61	1,742	Kerry Wright	73	1,280	17.5
2004	Eugene Gross	412	103	4.0	Clint Marks	368	259	.70	2,749	Kerry Wright	76	1,048	13.8

Receiving leaders by receptions
The NCAA began including postseason stats in 2002

MIDDLE TENNESSEE ALL-TIME SCORES

WIN/LOSS PERCENTAGE SINCE 1999

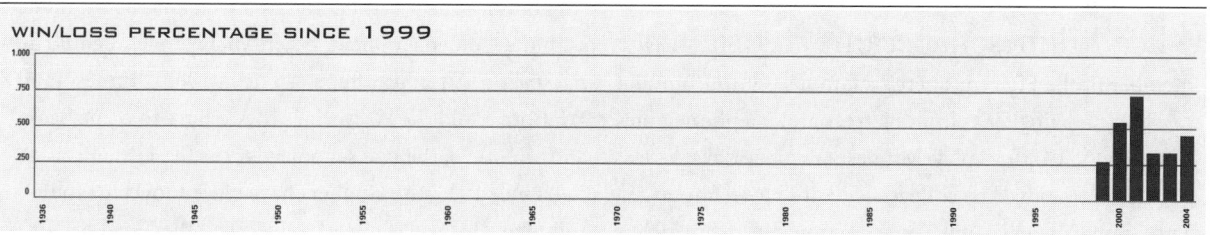

ANDY McCOLLUM	
1999-PRESENT (.441)	30-38

1999-2000
INDEPENDENT

1999   3-8
S4		at Mississippi State	7	40
S11		at Arizona	19	34
S18	●	Wofford	52	42
S25		at La. Lafayette	31	45
O2		Troy State	31	48
O9		at Arkansas	6	58
O16		at Louisiana Tech	18	42
O30		at La. Monroe	0	10
N6	●	Tenn. Martin	70	14
N13		Central Florida	14	39
N20	●	East Tenn. St.	24	7

2000   6-5
S2		at Illinois	6	35
S9		at Florida	0	55
S16	●	Murray St.	44	28
S23		at Maryland	27	45
O7	●	Louisiana Tech	49	21
O14	●	La. Monroe	28	0
O21		at UAB	9	14
O28		at Mississippi State	35	61
N4	●	at Connecticut	66	10
N11	●	South Florida	45	9
N18	●	La. Lafayette	41	38

2001-PRESENT
SUN BELT

2001   8-3   (5-1)
A30	●	at Vanderbilt	37	28
S8	●	Troy State	54	17
S22	●	at La. Monroe	38	20
S29	●	at La. Lafayette	26	9
O6	●	Idaho	70	58
O13		at North Texas	21	24
O20		at Mississippi	17	45
O27	●	New Mexico State	39	35
N3	●	Arkansas State	54	6
N10		at LSU	14	30
N17	●	Connecticut	38	14

2002   4-8   (2-4)
A31		Alabama *Birm*	34	39
S7		at Tennessee	3	26
S21		at Kentucky	22	44
S28		S.E. Missouri St.	14	24
O5		at Arkansas State	7	13
O12	●	at Vanderbilt	21	20
O19	●	La. Lafayette	48	35
O26		at Idaho	18	21
N2		at New Mexico State	21	24
N16	●	La. Monroe	44	28
N23		North Texas	20	30
N30	●	Utah State	45	28

2003   4-8   (3-3)
A28		Florida Atlantic	19	20
S6		at Georgia	10	29
S13		at Clemson	14	37
S20		at Missouri	40	41
O4		Temple	36	44
O11	●	New Mexico State	35	18
O18	●	at Idaho	28	21
O25		North Texas	28	33
N1		at Utah State	20	41
N8	●	Troy State	27	20
N15		La. Lafayette	51	57
N20	●	at Arkansas State	24	14

2004   5-6   (4-4)
S11	●	at Akron	31	24
S18		Florida Atlantic	20	27
S25		at La. Lafayette	17	24
O2		at North Texas	21	30
O9	●	Arkansas State	45	17
O16		at Florida	16	52
O23	●	Idaho	34	14
O30	●	Utah State	21	0
N6		at New Mexico State	10	44
N13	●	La. Monroe	37	24
N20		at Troy State	17	37

MINNESOTA

BY TODD JONES

RESEARCHERS AT THE UNIVERSITY of Minnesota invented the pacemaker. Good thing, since fans of the Golden Gophers have had their hearts broken many times since the school last won a Big Ten title in 1967.

Passion for football dates to 1896, when Minnesota became an original member of the Big Ten. There's a famous photo from that early era showing fans climbing trees and telephone poles to watch the Gophers play. Minnesota's glory days were as good as any enjoyed by college football's powerhouses. The Gophers won six Big Ten championships from 1934 to 1941, and won three national titles under Bernie Bierman in the final eight seasons of that magical span. The Gophers have tried and failed to live up to that tradition ever since. At times the past can be both wonderful and a burden. Minnesota never stops striving to make the present count, too.

TRADITION Cheerleading in college football originated at Minnesota in 1898. Some credit a student named Johnny Campbell for organizing cheers with fellow "yell leaders" at a home game against Northwestern. Others credit a professor for asking students to support the team before its game at Wisconsin with a rallying cry of, "Go to Madison! Go to Madison! Apply the summation of stimuli!"

Besides cheerleading, the trophy game also originated with the Golden Gophers. When Michigan left behind a five-gallon water jug after a 6-6 tie in 1903, Minnesota AD L.J. Cooke told the Wolverines they'd have to come back and win it. So, the two schools play for the Little Brown Jug. Since 1935, the Gophers have played Iowa for the rights to a bronze statue of a pig called the Floyd of Rosedale. Minnesota and Wisconsin have played for the Paul Bunyan Axe since 1948. The original axe, with a six-foot handle, was donated to the College Football Hall of Fame in 2003 and replaced by a new axe. Minnesota and Wisconsin first competed for the Slab of Bacon trophy in 1930. The slab was lost during the 1940s but found in a

PROFILE

University of Minnesota, Twin Cities
Minneapolis, Minn.
Founded: 1851
Enrollment: 28,740
Colors: Maroon and Gold
Nickname: Golden Gophers
Stadium: Hubert H. Humphrey Metrodome
   Opened in 1982
   FieldTurf; 64,172 capacity
First football game: 1882
All-time record: 613–427–44 (.586)
Bowl record: 5–5
Consensus national championships,
1936-present: 4 (1936, 1940, 1941, 1960)
Big Ten Conference championships:
18 (7 outright)
Heisman Trophy: Bruce Smith, 1941
Outland Trophy: Tom Brown, 1960;
Bobby Bell, 1962
First-round NFL draftees: 16
Website: www.gophersports.com

THE BEST OF TIMES

One of college football's great dynasties reigned in Minnesota from 1934 to 1941, when the Gophers won five national championships and went 8–0 in four of those seasons. Also don't forget 1900-05, when they went 65–4–5 and outscored opponents 2,702-121.

THE WORST OF TIMES

Minnesota's opponents enjoyed payback in the 1950s. The Gophers stumbled to six losing seasons and a 34–49–9 record. The 1990s, however, proved worst, with eight consecutive losing seasons and a 26–63 record from 1991 to 1998.

CONFERENCE

Minnesota was a charter member of the Western Conference in 1896, and has remained in the league since then. Popularly known as the Big Ten since 1917, the league didn't officially change its name to the Big Ten Conference until 1987.

DISTINGUISHED ALUMNI

Hubert H. Humphrey; Walter Mondale; Loni Anderson, actress; Dr. Christiaan Barnard, performed world's first human heart transplant; Herb Brooks, coach of 1980 gold medal-winning U.S. hockey team; Tom Lehman, pro golfer; Alford Pillsbury, founder of Pillsbury Corporation; Carl Rowan, syndicated newspaper columnist; Roy Wilkins, executive director, NAACP; Yanni (Chisomallis), New Age pianist

FIGHT SONG

MINNESOTA ROUSER
Minnesota, hats off to thee,
To thy colors true we shall ever be,
Firm and strong, united are we.
Rah! Rah! Rah! For Ski-U-Mah,
RAH! RAH! RAH! RAH!
Rah for the U. of M.
Minnesota, hats off to thee,
To thy colors true we shall ever be,
Firm and strong, united are we.
Rah! Rah! Rah! For Ski-U-Mah,
RAH! RAH! RAH! RAH!
Rah for the U. of M.
M-I-N-N-E-S-O-T-A!
Minnesota! Minnesota!
Yeaaaaaaaaaaaaaaaaah GOPHERS!

Minnesota was the first major-college team to have a black All-America quarterback.

Wisconsin storage room in 1994. Finally, the winner of the Gophers' game against Penn State receives the Governor's Victory Bell.

BEST PLAYER Bruce Smith won the school's only Heisman Trophy in 1941, but Bronko Nagurski is more of a legend. His career began without a scholarship and ended with unprecedented acclaim. As a senior in 1929, Nagurski became the only player to be named All-America at two different positions (fullback and defensive tackle) in the same season. At 6'2" and 228 pounds, Nagurski had a kind nature and high-pitched voice, but a brutish style of play. He was first called Bronko while growing up in International Falls, Minn., when a teacher misunderstood his Ukrainian mother's pronunciation of Bronislaw. His name was spoken with awe after he cracked a transverse vertebra in his back during a 1928 game against Iowa but played the rest of that game. He played lineman in parts of the next three games while wearing a corset for protection. Still suffering

from the injury, Nagurski demanded to play fullback in the season finale against Wisconsin. Wearing a special brace for his ribs and back, Nagurski caused a fumble that led to the only TD in a 6-0 Minnesota win that cost the Badgers the Big Ten title. Nagurski also knocked down a pass at the goal line and had three interceptions, the last of which ended the game. Such tales are recounted in an International Falls museum dedicated to him.

BEST COACH The truest testament of Bernie Bierman's character doesn't involve football. The Minnesota native served as a Marine in World War I and World War II. The second stint in the service was a three-year interruption to a glorious coaching career at Minnesota that ran from 1932 to 1941 and 1945 to 1950. Bierman created one of college football's great dynasties before going off to war a second time. Bierman never yelled at players but would inspect the practice grass to make certain their footsteps

RECORDS		
RUSHING YARDS		
	GAME	
294	Chris Darkins vs. Purdue, Oct. 7, 1995 (38 att.)	
	SEASON	
1,443	Chris Darkins, 1994 (277 att.)	
	CAREER	
4,654	Darrell Thompson, 1986-89 (936 att.)	
PASSING YARDS		
	GAME	
478	Tim Schade vs. Penn State, Sept. 4, 1993 (28 of 42)	
	SEASON	
2,600	Cory Sauter, 1995 (204 of 338)	
	CAREER	
6,834	Cory Sauter, 1994-97 (539 of 945)	

RECEIVING YARDS	
GAME	
228	Ryan Thelwell vs. Ball State, Sept. 14, 1996 (8 rec.)
SEASON	
1,125	Ron Johnson, 2000 (61 rec.)
CAREER	
2,989	Ron Johnson, 1998-2001 (198 rec.)
POINTS	
GAME	
30	Omar Douglas vs. Purdue, Oct. 9, 1993 (5 TDs)
SEASON	
109	Dan Nystrom, 2000 (25 FGs, 34 PATs)
CAREER	
367	Dan Nystrom, 1999-2002 (71 FGs, 154 PATs)

CONSENSUS ALL-AMERICANS	
1903	Fred Schacht, T
1909	John McGovern, B
1910	James Walker, T
1916	Bert Baston, E
1917	George Hauser, T
1923	Ray Ecklund, E
1926-27	Herb Joesting, B
1929	Bronko Nagurski, T
1931	Biggie Munn, G
1934	Frank Larson, E
1934	Bill Bevan, G
1934	Pug Lund, B
1935-36	Ed Widseth, T
1940	Urban Odson, T
1940	George Franck, B
1941	Bruce Smith, B
1941-42	Dick Wildung, T
1948-49	Leo Nomellini, T
1949	Clayton Tonnemaker, C
1953	Paul Giel, B
1960	Tom Brown, G
1961	Sandy Stephens, QB
1962	Bobby Bell, T
1963	Carl Eller, T
1965	Aaron Brown, DE
1999	Tyrone Carter, DB
1999-2000	Ben Hamilton, C/OL

were where they should be on a play. The Golden Gophers flattened defenses with a single-wing backfield running behind an unbalanced line. Their defense allowed only two opponents in 10 seasons to score 20 points or more in a game. Minnesota won three national championships and six Big Ten titles from 1934 to 1941 under the man known as the Grey Eagle or the Silver Fox. Minnesota went undefeated in five of those seasons, shut out 23 opponents and had a 21-game winning streak.

BEST TEAM "Bierman's Monsters" went 8–0 in 1934, were named national champions and were called one of the greatest teams ever at the time. All of the team's 514 yards of offense in a 48-12 win at Iowa came on the ground. Bierman used his roster's superior depth to grind opponents into sawdust. Eight different Gophers rushed for a TD during the season. Team captain Francis "Pug" Lund, Butch Larson and Bill Bevan—the last Big Ten player not to wear a helmet—were named All-Americas. Guard Bud Wilkinson later went on to fame as a coach at Oklahoma. While quarterback Glenn Seidel led an offense that averaged 33.7 points, the Minnesota defense gave up just 4.8 points and 103 yards a game. Four opponents were shut out and two others scored just seven points. Indiana gained zero yards in a 30-0 loss. Minnesota's only scare of the season came in its third game, when it trailed at Pittsburgh 7-0 after three quarters before pulling out a 13-7 win. Each of the Gophers' other seven wins was by at least 20 points.

BIGGEST GAME Minnesota was 7–0 and had outscored opponents 236-38 when it went to Wisconsin on Nov. 24, 1934. The Badgers were 4–3, but had won two in a row. They also had split the previous four games of the Border Battle. Minnesota thwarted upset plans with a potent running attack. The Gophers scored 34 points against Wisconsin, which had yielded just 50 in the season's first seven games while holding five opponents to a touchdown

ALL-TIME TEAM		
Selected by sports information director Shane Sandersfeld in 2005.		
OFFENSE		
1934-36	Ed Widseth, OL	
1940-42	Richard Wildung, OL	
1946-49	Clayton Tonnemaker, OL	
1958-60	Tom Brown, OL	
1997-2000	Ben Hamilton, OL	
1998-2001	Ron Johnson, WR	
1994-97	Chatarius Atwell, WR	
1970-72	Doug Kingsriter, TE	
1959-61	Sandy Stephens, QB	
1939-41	Bruce Smith, RB	
1951-53	Paul Giel, RB	
1986-89	Darrell Thompson, RB	
1999-2002	Dan Nystrom, K	
DEFENSE		
1927-29	Bronko Nagurski, DL	
1946-49	Leo Nomellini, DL	
1960-62	Bobby Bell, DL	
1961-63	Carl Eller, DL	
1966-68	Robert Stein, LB	
1969-71	William Light, LB	
1978-81	Jim Fahnhorst, LB	
1968-70	Jeff Wright, DB	
1988-91	Sean Lumpkin, DB	
1996-99	Tyrone Carter, DB	
1998-2000	Willie Middlebrooks, DB	
1984-85	Adam Kelly, P	

or less. Minnesota held the Badgers scoreless. The victory made the Gophers national champions for the first time.

BIGGEST UPSET The 5–3 Golden Gophers trailed No. 2 Penn State 23-21 on Nov. 6, 1999. They faced fourth and 16 at the Nittany Lions' 40-yard line late in the fourth quarter and seemed destined for a third consecutive defeat and fourth in five games. Minnesota QB Billy Cockerham, under a heavy blitz, tossed up a desperation pass into the wind. The ball bounced off the hands of receiver Ron Johnson, ricocheted behind him and was caught by Arland Bruce. The 27-yard gain silenced the Penn State crowd of 96,753. Dan Nystrom capped the last-minute drive by kicking a 32-yard field goal. The 24-23 victory clinched the Gophers' first winning season since 1990. Penn State fell to 9–1, and its 11-game winning streak and Joe Paterno's hopes for another national championship ended.

HEARTBREAKER No game in the Little Brown Jug series ended with as much disappointment for Minnesota as a 38-35 loss to Michigan in 2003. The Golden Gophers were 6–0, ranked No. 17, and primed for a breakout moment in Glen Mason's seventh season as coach. Minnesota led 14-0 at halftime and 28-7 after three quarters. Michigan responded with its biggest comeback in school history. Minnesota's defense gave up 24 points in the fourth quarter and the Wolverines added another seven when safety Jacob Stewart returned an interception 34 yards for a TD. Michigan won after taking its only lead with 47 seconds remaining on freshman kicker Garrett Rivas' 33-yard field goal. The Gophers suffered their 15th consecutive loss in the series despite rushing for 423 yards, including 197 by Marion Barber III and 106 by QB Asad Abdul-Khaliq.

WILDEST FINISH The pigskin seemed greased late in Minnesota's 1952 game at Wisconsin as the teams combined for seven turnovers in the fourth quarter. The

Golden Gophers came up with two interceptions by Gino Cappelletti and recovered a fumble by Badgers halfback Gerald Witt. Wisconsin had two interceptions by Paul Shwaiko and one by Burt Hable, and recovered a fumble by Minnesota quarterback Paul Giel. Hable intercepted Giel three times during the game, the final one coming in the Wisconsin end zone on the game's last play. The 21-21 tie sent the No. 13 Badgers to the Rose Bowl and ended Minnesota's season at 4–3–2.

BEST COMEBACK The entire 1960 season was a comeback. Minnesota was 2–7 the previous year, last in the Big Ten, and fans hung coach Murray Warmath in effigy after his third consecutive losing season. The Golden Gophers began 1960 unranked, but opened the season with a 26-14 win at No. 12 Nebraska. They went on to win their next six games and rose to No. 1 after winning 27-10 at No. 1 Iowa on Nov. 5. Minnesota lost to unranked Purdue 23-14 one week later but regained the No. 1 ranking by beating unranked Wisconsin 26-7 in the regular-season finale. The Gophers won the national championship, then lost 17-7 to Washington in the Rose Bowl to finish 8–2.

STADIUM Attendance and revenue have been problematic for the Golden Gophers since 1982 when they moved their home games downtown to the 64,172-seat Hubert H. Humphrey Metrodome. Minnesota is the only Big Ten school to play its home games off campus. Fans long for the days when the Gophers played outdoors in afternoons at Memorial Stadium, their campus home for 58 seasons before they moved to the dome. Memorial Stadium, built with over one million bricks, was named in honor of the school's 3,527 veterans of World War I. The Old Brickhouse opened in 1924 and in successful seasons would draw crowds of 66,000 despite having 52,736 permanent seats. By 1975, attendance had slipped to 31,000 and the old stadium was in need of $10 million in renovations. The Board of Regents instead decided to help Minneapolis build a downtown dome. The school's alumni band played "Taps" in 1992 as Memorial Stadium was torn down.

RIVAL Emotions of Minnesota fans reach fever pitch for two border-state rivalries. The Golden Gophers play Iowa and Wisconsin late each season for bragging rights and tradition-laden trophies. There was so much rancor in the Iowa series that Iowa governor Clyde Herring and Minnesota governor Floyd Olson agreed in 1935 to play for a pig—which turned out to be the legendary Floyd of Rosedale—to cool heads.

The real Floyd was replaced by a bronze likeness the next year. Minnesota has played Wisconsin 114 times, the most meetings between two major colleges. Such history makes it the premier rivalry for Gopher fans. Minnesota first met the Badgers in 1890 and bad blood quickly bubbled over. President Theodore Roosevelt canceled the 1906 game because there had been too many injuries and deaths on the field. The Wisconsin series resumed the next season and has been played annually ever since. Wisconsin was Minnesota's first homecoming opponent, in 1914, and the Gophers were the first homecoming opponents of the Badgers, in 1919.

CONTROVERSY About four minutes remained in the 1962 Border Battle at Wisconsin. Minnesota led 9-7 when Badgers quarterback Ron Vander Kelen had a pass intercepted by Jack Perkovich. The Golden Gophers celebrated, but an official nullified the turnover by calling All-America tackle Bobby Bell for roughing Vander Kelen. Minnesota coach Murray Warmath protested and drew an unsportsmanlike conduct penalty. Those 30 penalty yards gave Wisconsin a first down at the Gophers' 13-yard line. Three plays later, Ralph Kurek ran five yards for a TD. Wisconsin's 14-9 victory sent the Badgers to the Rose Bowl.

NICKNAME The university adopted the name Gophers after Minnesota was called the Gopher State in an 1857 newspaper cartoon. The drawing was in response to legislative action for a $5 million railroad proposal and depicted nine Gophers with the heads of local politicians pulling a locomotive. During the 1930s, the football team wore gold jerseys and pants and KSTP-AM radio announcer Halsey Hall began referring to the players as Golden Gophers. The moniker stuck.

MASCOT Goldy the Gopher became the school's mascot during the 1940s. He resembles a chipmunk more than a gopher because his original designer had never seen a gopher and instead used a chipmunk as a model.

UNIFORMS In the spring of 1880, Minnesota president William Watts Folwell asked English instructor Augusta Norwood Smith—"a woman of excellent taste," Folwell said—to choose permanent school colors for graduation ribbons. She chose maroon and gold. The school's board of regents gave official approval to the use of those colors in March 1940. Minnesota has historically worn maroon jerseys at home game. The Gophers have had an "M" on their helmets since 1968, the year they switched the helmet color

from white to gold. The Gophers wore gold helmets from 1968 to 1975 and again from 1992 to 1996. The helmets have been maroon since 1997, as they were from 1977 to 1991. The size, shape and outline of the "M" on the helmets have changed over the last three-plus decades.

NUMBERS Minnesota went 65–4–5 from 1900 to 1905 and outscored opponents 2,702-121, including 618-12 in 1903. The Golden Gophers beat Grinnell 146-0 in 1904 by scoring 73 points in each half ... All-America quarterback John McGovern played every minute of every game except one in 1909 ... Alfred Pillsbury played at Minnesota for eight seasons from 1885 to 1892 because there were no governing bodies regulating collegiate eligibility ... Minnesota has retired four numbers: Bronko Nagurski (72), Bruce Smith (54), Paul Giel (10) and Sandy Stephens (15) ... The Gophers' 16-0 upset of No. 1 Michigan on Oct. 22, 1977, vaulted them into the national rankings at No. 19. They lost 34-22 at Indiana the next week, fell out of the polls and were unranked for 15 years ... Minnesota trailed Indiana 24-0 in the second quarter on Nov. 4, 1978, before rallying to win its homecoming game 32-31 when Paul Rogind kicked a 31-yard field goal in the final seconds ... Tony Dungy was a two-time Academic All-Big Ten selection while playing quarterback at Minnesota from 1974 to 1976.

LORE Minnesota became the first major college team to have a black All-America quarterback when Sandy Stephens earned the honor in 1961, one year after he led the Golden Gophers to the national title. Minnesota coach Murray Warmath, a Tennessee native and former Mississippi State coach, began recruiting black players to Minneapolis in the late 1950s, before it was nationally popular. Besides Stephens, he gave scholarships over the next decade to Judge Dickson, Bob NcNeil, Bobby Bell, Bill Munsey, Carl Eller, Aaron Brown, John Williams, Ezell Jones, Ed Duren, Charlie Sanders and McKinley Boston. "The only people I discriminate against are people who can't play football," said Warmath, who coached the Gophers to the 1960 Big Ten and national titles, Rose Bowl trips in 1961 and 1962, and the school's last league title in 1967.

QUOTE "I was going to be more than a Big Ten quarterback who was black. I was going to be a Big Ten quarterback who took his team to the Rose Bowl." —Sandy Stephens, QB of Minnesota's 1961 and 1962 Rose Bowl teams

THE SCHOOLS

MINNESOTA ANNUAL STATISTICAL LEADERS

YR	RUSHING	YDS	ATT	AVG	PASSING	ATT	CMP	PCT	YDS	RECEIVING	REC	YDS	AVG
1925	Shorty Almquist	505	97	5.2		NA	NA	NA	NA		NA	NA	NA
1926	Herb Joesting	962	188	5.1		NA	NA	NA	NA		NA	NA	NA
1927	Shorty Almquist	687	138	5.0		NA	NA	NA	NA		NA	NA	NA
1928	Win Brockmeyer	549	91	6.0		NA	NA	NA	NA		NA	NA	NA
1929	Art Pharmer	570	109	5.2		NA	NA	NA	NA		NA	NA	NA
1930	Jack Manders	413	102	4.0		NA	NA	NA	NA		NA	NA	NA
1931	Jack Manders	459	128	3.6		NA	NA	NA	NA		NA	NA	NA
1932	Francis Lund	867	163	5.3		NA	NA	NA	NA		NA	NA	NA
1933	Francis Lund	730	153	4.8		NA	NA	NA	NA		NA	NA	NA
1934	Francis Lund	667	100	6.7		NA	NA	NA	NA		NA	NA	NA
1935	George Roscoe	648	123	5.3		NA	NA	NA	NA		NA	NA	NA
1936	Andy Uram	456	64	7.1		NA	NA	NA	NA		NA	NA	NA
1937	Harold Van Every	526	91	5.8		NA	NA	NA	NA		NA	NA	NA
1938	Wilbur Moore	555	98	5.7		NA	NA	NA	NA		NA	NA	NA
1939	Harold Van Every	733	133	5.5		NA	NA	NA	NA		NA	NA	NA
1940	Bruce Smith	542	76	7.1		NA	NA	NA	NA		NA	NA	NA
1941	Bill Daley	726	157	4.6		NA	NA	NA	NA		NA	NA	NA
1942	Bill Daley	552	88	6.3		NA	NA	NA	NA		NA	NA	NA
1943	Red Williams	561	99	5.7		NA	NA	NA	NA		NA	NA	NA
1945	Vic Kulbitski	485	112	4.3		NA	NA	NA	NA		NA	NA	NA
1946	Billy Bye	467	70	6.7	Ev Faunce	36	31	.86	335		NA	NA	NA
1947	Billy Bye	433	87	5.0	Ev Faunce	44	15	.34	234		NA	NA	NA
1948	Ev Faunce	558	116	4.8	Ev Faunce	85	44	.52	567		NA	NA	NA
1949	Billy Bye	561	138	4.1	Billy Bye	77	41	.53	571		NA	NA	NA
1950	Dick Gregory	315	66	4.8	George Hudak	45	17	.38	131		NA	NA	NA
1951	Paul Giel	789	152	5.2	Paul Giel	124	57	.46	689		NA	NA	NA
1952	Paul Giel	650	201	3.2	Paul Giel	101	42	.42	643	Donald Swanson	16	169	10.6
1953	Paul Giel	749	198	3.8	Paul Giel	93	50	.54	590	Bob McNamara	15	204	13.6
1954	Bob McNamara	708	112	6.3	Geno Cappelletti	65	28	.43	434	Richard McNamara	12	107	8.9
1955	Dick Borstad	440	96	4.6	Dick Larson	27	12	.44	253	Thomas Juhl	11	172	15.6
1956	Bobby Cox	553	130	4.3	Bob Cox	53	18	.34	240	David Lindblom	12	156	13.0
1957	Bobby Blakely	324	65	5.0	Bob Cox	53	19	.36	268	Robert Schultz	7	94	13.4
1958	Bill Kauth	361	92	3.9	Larry Johnson	51	17	.33	406	Robert Soltis	11	172	15.6
1959	Tom Robbins	339	93	3.6	Larry Johnson	92	39	.42	497	Thomas Hall	22	322	14.6
1960	Roger Hagberg	443	101	4.4	Sandy Stephens	62	22	.35	326	Thomas Hall	11	150	13.6
1961	Sandy Stephens	534	122	4.4	Sandy Stephens	153	54	.35	869	Thomas Hall	10	207	20.7
1962	Jerry Jones	453	98	4.6	Duane Blaska	154	71	.46	862	Jim Cairns	14	221	15.8
1963	Mike Reid	392	102	3.8	Bob Sadek	128	58	.45	647	Gerald Pelletier	9	105	11.7
1964	Fred Farthing	433	113	3.8	John Hankinson	178	86	.48	1,084	Aaron Brown	27	207	7.7
1965	Joe Holmberg	352	106	3.3	John Hankinson	214	111	.52	1,477	Ken Last	31	463	14.9
1966	Curtis Wilson	546	138	4.0	Larry Carlson	108	56	.52	599	Ken Last	30	356	11.9
1967	Jim Carter	519	142	3.7	Curtis Wilson	76	33	.43	543	Charley Sanders	21	276	13.1
1968	Barry Mayer	662	130	5.1	Phil Hagen	157	75	.48	771	Ray Parson	30	333	11.1
1969	Barry Mayer	745	162	4.6	Phil Hagen	208	109	.52	1,266	Ray Parson	27	391	14.5
1970	Ernie Cook	495	107	4.6	Craig Curry	228	103	.45	1,315	Doug Kingsriter	26	362	13.9
1971	Ernie Cook	881	177	5.0	Craig Curry	266	118	.44	1,691	Doug Kingsriter	28	379	13.5
1972	John King	1,164	237	4.9	Bob Morgan	89	32	.36	475	Doug Kingsriter	16	178	11.1
1973	Rick Upchurch	841	141	6.0	John Lawing	48	23	.48	276	Keith Fahnhorst	10	102	10.2
1974	Rick Upchurch	942	153	6.2	Tony Dungy	94	39	.41	612	Rick Upchurch	14	209	14.9
1975	Bubby Holmes	573	132	4.3	Tony Dungy	225	123	.55	1,515	Ron Kullas	42	545	13.0
1976	Kent Kitzmann	696	168	4.1	Tony Dungy	234	104	.44	1,291	Ron Kullas	33	372	11.3
1977	Kent Kitzmann	723	175	4.1	Wendell Avery	99	45	.45	591	Jeff Anhorn	21	266	12.7
1978	Marion Barber	1,210	247	4.9	Mark Carlson	113	64	.57	736	Elmer Bailey	27	464	17.2
1979	Garry White	861	135	6.4	Mark Carlson	300	177	.59	2,188	Elmer Bailey	37	552	14.9
1980	Garry White	959	177	5.4	Tim Salem	170	81	.48	887	Chester Cooper	14	210	15.0
1981	Frank Jacobs	636	147	4.3	Mike Hohensee	362	182	.50	2,112	Chester Cooper	58	1,012	17.4
1982	Tony Hunter	395	69	5.7	Mike Hohensee	360	210	.58	2,380	Dwayne McMullen	41	640	15.6
1983	David Puk	287	73	3.9	Greg Murphy	242	115	.48	1,410	Jay Carroll	37	459	12.4
1984	Rickey Foggie	647	145	4.5	Rickey Foggie	121	57	.47	1,036	Dwayne McMullen	26	594	22.8
1985	Valdez Baylor	680	112	6.1	Rickey Foggie	162	74	.46	1,493	Melvin Anderson	26	554	21.3
1986	Darrell Thompson	1,376	242	5.7	Rickey Foggie	216	97	.45	1,401	Melvin Anderson	27	384	14.2
1987	Darrell Thompson	1,229	224	5.5	Rickey Foggie	175	83	.47	1,232	Craig Otto	22	309	14.0
1988	Darrell Thompson	910	210	4.3	Scott Schaffner	191	106	.55	1,234	Chris Gaithers	42	564	13.4
1989	Darrell Thompson	1,139	260	4.4	Scott Schaffner	190	101	.53	1,373	Chris Gaithers	31	366	11.8
1990	Mark Smith	700	196	3.6	Marquel Fleetwood	171	95	.56	1,199	Kevin Grant	28	413	14.8
1991	Antonio Carter	660	165	4.0	Marquel Fleetwood	264	155	.59	1,643	Patt Evans	35	454	13.0
1992	Antonio Carter	572	133	4.3	Marquel Fleetwood	385	192	.50	2,168	Omar Douglas	61	669	11.0
1993	Chris Darkins	610	124	4.9	Tim Schade	286	135	.47	1,648	Omar Douglas	60	880	14.7
1994	Chris Darkins	1,443	277	5.2	Tim Schade	341	187	.55	2,338	Chuck Rios	52	436	8.4
1995	Chris Darkins	825	164	5.0	Cory Sauter	338	204	.60	2,600	Ryan Thelwell	58	775	13.4
1996	Thomas Hamner	883	195	4.5	Cory Sauter	352	200	.57	2,578	Tutu Atwell	62	822	13.3
1997	Thomas Hamner	663	170	3.9	Cory Sauter	234	126	.54	1,576	Tutu Atwell	58	924	15.9
1998	Thomas Hamner	838	209	4.0	Billy Cockerham	180	92	.51	1,150	Luke Leverson	60	854	14.2
1999	Thomas Hamner	1,426	308	4.6	Billy Cockerham	276	147	.53	2,091	Ron Johnson	43	574	13.3
2000	Tellis Redmon	1,368	293	4.7	Travis Cole	252	147	.58	1,982	Ron Johnson	61	1,125	18.4
2001	Tellis Redmon	1,091	185	6.4	Asad Abdul-Khaliq	187	107	.57	1,393	Ron Johnson	56	895	16.0
2002	Terry Jackson II	1,317	239	5.5	Asad Abdul-Khaliq	314	164	.52	2,184	Antoine Burns	44	526	12.0
2003	Marion Barber	1,196	207	5.8	Asad Abdul-Khaliq	250	158	.64	2,401	Jared Ellerson	44	909	20.7
2004	Laurence Maroney	1,348	217	6.2	Bryan Cupito	261	123	.47	2,097	Jared Ellerson	37	521	14.1

Receiving leaders by receptions
All statistics include postseason

MINNESOTA ALL-TIME SCORES

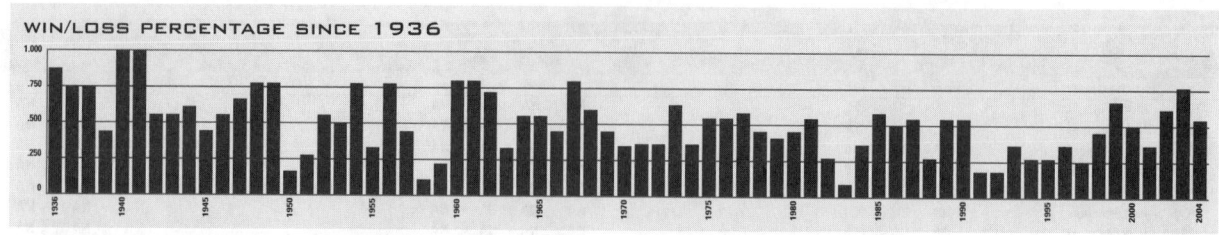

WIN/LOSS PERCENTAGE SINCE 1936

THE SCHOOLS

NO HEAD COACH

1882   1-1-0
| S30 | ● | at Hamline | 4 | 0 |
| O16 | ● | at Hamline | 0 | 2 |

THOMAS PEEBLES
1883 (.333)   1-2

1883   1-2-0
U		at Carleton	2	4
N4	●	at Hamline	5	0
U		Alumni	2	4

1884-1885
NO TEAM

FREDERICK JONES
1886-88 (.500)   3-3

1886   0-2-0
| U | | at Shattuck | 5 | 9 |
| U | | Shattuck | 8 | 18 |

1887   2-0-0
| U | ● | Minneapolis HS | 8 | 0 |
| U | ● | Alumni | 14 | 0 |

1888   1-1-0
| O28 | ● | at Shattuck | 8 | 16 |
| O31 | ● | Shattuck | 14 | 0 |

NO HEAD COACH

1889   3-1-0
O5	●	Alumni	2	0
O26	●	Alumni	10	0
N11	●	at Shattuck	8	28
N20	●	Shattuck	26	0

TOM ECK
1890 (.786)   5-1-1

1890   5-1-1
O27	●	at Hamline	44	0
N3	●	at Shattuck	58	0
N5	=	Alumni	0	0
N8	●	Grinnell	18	13
N15	●	Wisconsin	63	0
N19	●	Alumni	11	14
N29	●	Alumni	14	6

ED "DAD" MOULTON
1891 (.700)   3-1-1

1891   3-1-1
O17	●	Alumni	0	4
O24	●	Wisconsin	26	12
O31	=	at Grinnell	12	12
N2	●	at Iowa	42	4
N14	●	Grinnell	22	14

NO HEAD COACH

1892   5-0-0
O8	●	Alumni	18	10
O17	●	Michigan	14	6
O22	●	Grinnell	40	24
O29	●	at Wisconsin	32	4
N8	●	Northwestern	18	12

WALLIE WINTER
1893 (1.000)   6-0

1893   6-0-0
O14	●	Kansas	12	6
O21	●	Grinnell	36	6
O25	●	at Hamline	10	6
O28	●	at Michigan	34	20
O30	●	at Northwestern	16	0
N11	●	Wisconsin	40	0

TOM COCHRANE, JR.
1894 (.750)   3-1

1894   3-1-0
O20	●	Grinnell	10	2
O27	●	Purdue	24	0
N10	●	Beloit	40	0
N17	●	at Wisconsin	0	6

WALT "PUDGE" HEFFELFINGER
1895 (.700)   7-3

1895   7-3-0
S28	●	at Minneapolis Central HS	20	0
O5	●	Grinnell	4	6
O12	●	at Boat Club	6	0
O19	●	Iowa State	24	0
O26	●	at Chicago	10	6
O29	●	at Purdue	4	16	*
N2	●	at Macalester	40	0
N16	●	Wisconsin	14	10
N23		Michigan *DET*	0	20
N28	●	Alumni	14	0

1896-PRESENT
BIG 10

ALEXANDER JERREMS
1896-97 (.667)   12-6

1896   8-2-0 (1-2-0)
S19	●	at Minneapolis South HS	34	0
S26	●	at Miineapolis Central HS	50	0
O3	●	Carleton	16	6
O10	●	Grinnell	12	0
O17		Purdue	14	0
O24	●	Iowa State	18	6
O31	●	Alumni	8	0
N7		Michigan	4	6
N21		at Wisconsin	0	6
N28	●	Kansas *KC*	12	0

1897   4-4-0 (0-3-0)
S25	●	Minneapolis South HS	22	0
O2	●	Macalester	26	0
O9	●	Carleton	48	6
O16	●	Grinnell	6	0
O23	●	Iowa State	10	12
O30	●	Wisconsin	0	39
N13		Michigan *DET*	0	14
N20		at Purdue	0	6

JACK MINDS
1898 (.444)   4-5

1898   4-5-0 (1-2-0)
S24	●	Carleton	32	0
O1	●	Alumni	0	5
O8	●	Rush Medical	12	0
O15	●	Grinnell	6	16
O22	●	Iowa State	0	6
O29		at Wisconsin	0	28	*
N5	●	North Dakota St.	15	0
N12	●	Northwestern	17	6
N24		at Illinois	10	11

JOHN HARRISON, BILL LEARY
1899 (.636)   6-3-2

1899   6-3-0 (0-3-0)
S23	●	Minneapolis Central HS	20	0
S30	●	Macalester	29	0
O7	●	Shattuck	40	0
O14	●	Carleton	35	5
O21	●	Iowa State	6	0
O28	=	Grinnell	5	5
N4		Northwestern	5	11
N8	●	Alumni	6	5
N11	●	Beloit	5	5
N18		Wisconsin	0	19
N25		at Chicago	0	29

HENRY L. WILLIAMS
1900-21 (.786)   136-33-11

1900   10-0-2 (3-0-1)
S22	=	Minneapolis Central HS	0	0
S26	=	St. Paul Central HS	26	0
S29	●	Macalester	66	0
O3	●	Carleton	44	0
O6	●	Iowa State	27	0
O13	=	Chicago	6	6
O20	●	Grinnell	26	0
O27	●	North Dakota	34	0
N3		Wisconsin	6	5
N10	●	Illinois	23	0
N17		Northwestern	21	0
N29	●	at Nebraska	20	12

1901   9-1-1 (3-1-0)
S21	=	Minneapolis Central HS	0	0
S25	●	St. Paul Central HS	16	0
S28	●	Carleton	35	0
O5	●	Chicago Coll.	27	0
O12	●	Nebraska	19	0
O26	●	Iowa	16	0
N2	●	Haskell	28	0
N9	●	North Dakota St.	10	0
N16		Wisconsin	0	18
N23	●	Northwestern *CHI*	16	0
N28		at Illinois	16	0

1902   9-2-1 (3-1-0)
S20	=	St. Paul Central HS	0	0
S24	●	Minneapolis Central HS	28	0
S27	●	Carleton	33	0
O4	●	Iowa State	16	0
O8	●	Hamline	59	0
O11	●	Beloit	29	0
O18	●	Nebraska	0	6
O25	●	at Iowa	34	0
N1	●	Grinnell	102	0
N8	●	Illinois	17	5
N15	●	Wisconsin	11	0
N27		at Michigan	6	23

1903   14-0-1 (3-0-1)
S16	●	Minneapolis Central HS	21	6
S19	●	St. Paul Central HS	36	0
S23	●	Minneapolis Eastern HS	37	0
S26	●	Carleton	29	0
S30	●	Macalester	112	0
O3	●	Grinnell	39	0
O7	●	Hamline	65	0
O10	●	Iowa State	46	0
O17	●	Iowa	75	0
O24	●	Beloit	46	0
O31	=	Michigan	6	6
N7	●	at Lawrence	46	0
N14	●	at Illinois	32	0
N21	●	at North Dakota St.	11	0
N26		Wisconsin	17	0

1904   13-0-0 (3-0-0)
S17	●	Twin Cities HS	107	0
S24	●	South Dakota	77	0
O1	●	Carleton	65	0
O8	●	North Dakota	35	0
O15	●	Iowa State	32	0
O22	●	Grinnell	146	0
O29	●	Nebraska	16	12
N5	●	Lawrence	69	0
N12	●	Wisconsin	28	0
N19	●	Northwestern *CHI*	17	0
N24	●	at Iowa	11	0
N26	●	at Shattuck	75	0
D3	●	at St. Thomas	47	0

1905   10-1-0 (2-1-0)
S23	●	Twin Cities HS	74	0
S26	●	Shattuck	54	0
S30	●	St. Thomas	42	0
O7	●	North Dakota	45	0
O14	●	Iowa State	42	0
O21	●	Iowa	39	0
O28	●	Lawrence	46	0
N4		Wisconsin	12	16
N11	●	South Dakota	81	0
N18	●	Nebraska	35	0
N25	●	Northwestern	72	6

1906   4-1-0 (2-0-0)
O27	●	Iowa State	22	4
N3	●	Nebraska	13	0
N10	●	at Chicago	4	2
N17	●	Carlisle	0	17
N24	●	Indiana	8	6

1907   2-2-1 (0-1-1)
O12	●	Iowa State	8	0
O19	●	Nebraska	8	5
N2		Chicago	12	18
N16	●	Carlisle	10	12
N23	=	at Wisconsin	17	17

1908   3-2-1 (0-2-0)
O3	●	Lawrence	6	0
O10	●	Iowa State	15	10
O17	=	Nebraska	0	0
O31	●	at Chicago	0	29
N7		Wisconsin	0	5
N21	●	Carlisle	11	6

1909   6-1-0 (3-0-0)
S25	●	Lawrence	25	0
O2		Iowa	41	0
O9		Iowa State	18	0
O16	●	Nebraska *OMA*	14	0
O30		Chicago	20	6
N13	●	at Wisconsin	34	6
N20		Michigan	6	15

1910   6-1-0 (2-0-0)
S24	●	Lawrence	34	0
O1	●	South Dakota	17	0
O8	●	Iowa State	49	0
O15	●	Nebraska	27	0
O29	●	at Chicago	24	0
N12	●	Wisconsin	28	0
N19	●	at Michigan	0	6

1911   6-0-1 (3-0-1)
S30	●	Iowa State	5	0
O7	●	South Dakota	5	0
O21	●	Nebraska	21	3
O28	●	at Iowa	24	6
N4	●	Chicago	30	0
N18	=	at Wisconsin	6	6
N25	●	at Illinois	11	0

1912   4-3-0 (2-2-0)
S28	●	South Dakota	0	10
O5	●	Iowa State	5	0
O19	●	Nebraska	13	0
O26		Iowa	56	7
N2		Illinois	13	0
N16		Wisconsin	0	14
N23		at Chicago	0	7

1913   5-2-0 (2-1-0)
S27	●	South Dakota	14	0
O4	●	Iowa State	25	0
O18	●	at Nebraska	0	7
O25	●	North Dakota	30	0
N1		at Wisconsin	21	3
N15		Chicago	7	13
N22	●	at Illinois	19	9

1914 — 6-1-0 (3-1-0)

O3	• North Dakota	28	6
O10	• Iowa State	26	0
O17	• South Dakota	29	7
O24	• at Iowa	7	0
O31	| Illinois	6	21
N14	• Wisconsin	14	3
N21	• at Chicago	13	7

1915 — 6-0-1 (3-0-1)

O2	• North Dakota	41	0
O9	• Iowa State	34	6
O16	• South Dakota	19	0
O23	• Iowa	51	13
N6	= at Illinois	6	6
N13	• Chicago	20	7
N20	• at Wisconsin	20	3

1916 — 6-1-0 (3-1-0)

O7	• South Dakota St.	41	7
O14	• North Dakota	47	7
O21	• South Dakota	81	0
O28	• Iowa	67	0
N4	| Illinois	9	14
N18	• Wisconsin	54	0
N25	• at Chicago	49	0

1917 — 4-1-0 (3-1-0)

O20	• South Dakota St.	64	0
O27	| Indiana	33	9
N3	| at Wisconsin	7	10
N17	• Chicago	33	0
N24	• at Illinois	27	6

1918 — 5-2-1 (2-1-0)

O5	= All Stars	0	0
O12	• Overland Station	30	0
O19	• at St. Thomas	25	7
O26	• Carleton St. Olaf	59	6
N9	| at Iowa	0	6
N16	• Wisconsin	6	0
N23	| Municipal Pier	6	20
N30	| at Chicago	7	0

1919 — 4-2-1 (3-2-0)

O4	• North Dakota	39	0
O11	= Nebraska	6	6
O18	• at Indiana	20	6
O25	• Iowa	6	9
N1	• at Wisconsin	19	7
N8	| Illinois	6	10
N22	• at Michigan	34	7

1920 — 1-6-0 (0-6-0)

O2	• North Dakota	41	3
O9	• at Northwestern	0	17
O23	| Indiana	7	21
O30	| at Illinois	7	17
N6	| Wisconsin	0	3
N13	| at Iowa	7	28
N20	| Michigan	0	3

1921 — 3-4-0 (2-4-0)

O1	• North Dakota	19	0
O8	• Northwestern	28	0
O15	| at Ohio State	0	27
O22	• Indiana	6	0
O29	| at Wisconsin	0	35
N5	| Iowa	7	41
N19	| at Michigan	0	38

WILLIAM SPAULDING — 1922-24 (.591) — 11-7-4

1922 — 3-3-1 (2-3-1)

O7	• North Dakota	22	0
O14	• at Indiana	20	0
O21	= at Northwestern	7	7
O28	• Ohio State	9	0
N4	| Wisconsin	0	14
N11	| at Iowa	14	28
N25	| Michigan	7	16

1923 — 5-1-1 (2-1-1)

O6	• Iowa State	20	17
O13	• Haskell	13	12
O20	• North Dakota	27	0
O27	= at Wisconsin	0	0
N3	| Northwestern	34	14
N17	• Iowa	20	7
N24	| at Michigan	0	10

1924 — 3-3-2 (1-2-1)

O4	• North Dakota	14	0
O11	• Haskell	20	0
O18	= at Wisconsin	7	7
O25	• at Iowa	0	13
N1	| Michigan	0	13
N8	= Iowa State	7	7
N15	• Illinois	20	7
N22	| Vanderbilt	0	16

CLARENCE SPEARS — 1925-29 (.738) — 28-9-3

1925 — 5-2-1 (1-1-1)

O3	• North Dakota	25	0
O10	• Grinnell	34	6
O17	• Wabash	32	6
O24	• Notre Dame	7	19
O31	= | Wisconsin	12	12
N7	| Butler	33	7
N14	• Iowa	33	0
N21	• at Michigan	0	35

1926 — 5-3-0 (2-2-0)

O2	• North Dakota	51	0
O9	• Notre Dame	7	20
O16	| at Michigan	0	20
O23	• Wabash	67	7
O30	• at Wisconsin	16	10
N6	• at Iowa	41	0
N13	• Butler	81	0
N20	| Michigan	6	7

1927 — 6-0-2 (3-0-1)

O1	• North Dakota	57	10
O8	• Oklahoma State	40	0
O15	= | at Indiana	14	14
O22	• Iowa	38	0
O29	• Wisconsin	13	7
N5	| at Notre Dame	7	7
N12	• Drake	27	6
N19	• at Michigan	13	7

1928 — 6-2-0 (4-2-0)

O6	• Creighton	49	0
O13	• Purdue	15	0
O20	• Chicago	33	7
O27	• at Iowa	6	7
N3	| at Northwestern	9	10
N10	• Indiana	21	12
N17	• Haskell	52	0
N24	• at Wisconsin	6	0

1929 — 6-2-0 (3-2-0)

O5	• Coe	39	0
O12	• Vanderbilt	15	6
O19	• at Northwestern	26	14
O26	• Ripon	54	0
N2	• Indiana	19	7
N9	| at Iowa	7	9
N16	• Michigan	6	7
N23	• Wisconsin	13	12

HERBERT "FRITZ" CRISLER — 1930-31 (.583) — 10-7-1

1930 — 3-4-1 (1-3-0)

S27	• South Dakota St.	48	0
O4	• Vanderbilt	7	33
O11	= Stanford	0	0
O18	• Indiana	6	0
N1	| Northwestern	6	27
N8	• South Dakota	59	0
N15	| at Michigan	0	7
N22	| at Wisconsin	0	14

1931 — 7-3-0 (3-2-0)

S19	• Ripon	30	0
S26	• North Dakota St.	13	7
O3	• Oklahoma State	20	0
O10	| at Stanford	0	13
O24	• Iowa	34	0
O31	• Wisconsin	14	0
N7	| at Northwestern	14	32
N14	• Cornell Coll.	47	7
N21	| at Michigan	0	6
N28	| Ohio State	19	7

BERNIE BIERMAN — 1932-41, '45-50 (.716) — 93-35-6

1932 — 5-3-0 (2-3-0)

O1	• South Dakota St.	12	0
O8	| Purdue	0	7
O15	• Nebraska	7	6
O22	• | at Iowa	21	6
O29	| Northwestern	7	0
N5	| Mississippi	26	0
N12	• at Wisconsin	13	20
N19	| Michigan	0	3

1933 — 4-0-4 (2-0-4)

S30	• South Dakota St.	19	6
O7	= | Indiana	6	6
O14	= | Purdue	7	7
O21	• Pittsburgh	7	3
O28	• | Iowa	19	7
N4	= | at Northwestern	0	0
N18	= | at Michigan	0	0
N25	• | Wisconsin	26	3

1934 — 8-0-0 (5-0-0)

S29	• North Dakota St.	56	12
O3	• Nebraska	20	0
O20	• at Pittsburgh	13	7
O28	• | at Iowa	48	12
N3	| Michigan	34	0
N10	• | Indiana	30	0
N17	• | Chicago	35	7
N24	• | at Wisconsin	34	0

1935 — 8-0-0 (5-0-0)

O5	• North Dakota St.	26	6
O12	• at Nebraska	12	7
O19	• Tulane	20	0
O26	• Northwestern	21	13
N2	• | Purdue	29	7
N9	• | at Iowa	13	6
N16	• | at Michigan	40	0
N23	• | Wisconsin	33	7

1936 — 7-1-0 (4-1-0)

S26	• at Washington	14	7
O10	• Nebraska	7	0
O17	• | Michigan	26	0
O24	• | Purdue	33	0
O31	• | at Northwestern	0	6
N7	• | Iowa	52	0
N14	• | Texas	47	19
N21	• | at Wisconsin	24	0

1937 — 6-2-0 (5-0-0)

S25	• North Dakota St.	69	7
O2	• at Nebraska	9	14
O9	• | Indiana	6	0
O16	• | at Michigan	39	6
O30	• | Notre Dame	6	7
N6	• | at Iowa	35	10
N13	• | Northwestern	7	0
N20	• | Wisconsin	13	6

1938 — 6-2-0 (4-1-0)

S24	• Washington	15	0
O1	• Nebraska	16	7
O8	• | Purdue	7	0
O15	• | Michigan	7	6
O29	• | at Northwestern	3	6
N5	• | Iowa	28	0
N12	• at Notre Dame	0	19
N19	• | at Wisconsin	21	0

1939 — 3-4-1 (2-3-1)

S30	• Arizona	62	0
O7	| at Nebraska	0	6
O14	= | Purdue	13	13
O21	• | Ohio State	20	23
N4	• | Northwestern	7	14
N11	• | at Michigan	20	7
N18	• | at Iowa	9	13
N25	• | Wisconsin	23	6

1940 — 8-0-0 (6-0-0)

S28	• Washington	19	14
O5	• Nebraska	13	7
O19	• | at Ohio State	13	7
O26	• | Iowa	34	6
N2	• | at Northwestern	13	12
N9	• | Michigan	7	6
N16	• | Purdue	33	6
N23	• | at Wisconsin	22	13

1941 — 8-0-0 (5-0-0)

S27	• at Washington	14	6
O11	• | Illinois	34	6
O18	• | Pittsburgh	39	0
O25	• | at Michigan	7	0
N1	• | Northwestern	8	7
N8	• | Nebraska	9	0
N15	• | at Iowa	34	13
N22	• | Wisconsin	41	6

GEORGE HAUSER — 1942-44 (.574) — 15-11-1

1942 — 5-4-0 (3-3-0)

S26	• Pittsburgh	50	7
O3	| Iowa Pre-Flight	6	7
O10	| at Illinois	13	20
O17	• | at Nebraska	15	2
O24	• | Michigan	16	14
O31	• | Northwestern	19	7
N7	| Indiana	0	7
N14	• | Iowa	27	7
N21	• | at Wisconsin	6	20

1943 — 5-4-0 (2-3-0)

S25	• Missouri	26	13
O2	• Nebraska	54	0
O16	• Camp Grant	13	7
O23	| at Michigan	6	49
O30	| at Northwestern	6	42
N6	| Purdue	7	14
N13	• Iowa	33	14
N20	• Wisconsin	25	13
N27	| Iowa Pre-Flight	0	32

1944 — 5-3-1 (3-2-1)

S23	• Iowa Pre-Flight	13	19
S30	• Nebraska	39	0
O7	| Michigan	13	28
O14	• Missouri	39	27
O28	| at Ohio State	14	34
N4	= | Northwestern	14	14
N11	• Indiana	19	14
N18	• | at Iowa	46	0
N25	• | at Wisconsin	28	26

BERNIE BIERMAN

1945 — 4-5-0 (1-5-0)

S22	• Missouri	34	0
O6	• at Nebraska	61	7
O13	• Fort Warren	14	0
O20	• Northwestern	30	7
O27	| Ohio State	7	20
N3	| at Michigan	0	26
N10	• Indiana	0	49
N17	• at Iowa	19	20
N24	• Wisconsin	12	6

1946 — 5-4-0 (3-4-0)

S28	• Nebraska	33	6
O5	| Indiana	0	21
O12	• at Northwestern	7	14
O19	• Wyoming	46	0
O26	• at Ohio State	9	39
N2	| Michigan	0	21
N9	• Purdue	13	7
N16	• Iowa	16	6
N23	• at Wisconsin	6	0

1947 — 6-3-0 (3-3-0)

S27	• Washington	7	6
O4	• at Nebraska	28	13
O11	| Northwestern	37	21
O18	• at Illinois	13	40
O25	• at Michigan	6	13
N1	• Pittsburgh	29	0
N8	• | Purdue	26	21
N15	• at Iowa	7	13
N22	• Wisconsin	21	0

1948 — 7-2-0 (5-2-0)

S25	• at Washington	20	0
O2	• Nebraska	39	13
O9	• at Northwestern	16	19
O16	• Illinois	6	0
O23	• Michigan	14	27
O30	• Indiana	30	7
N6	• Purdue	34	7
N13	• at Iowa	28	21
N20	• Wisconsin	16	0

1949 — 7-2-0 (4-2-0)

S24	• Washington	48	20
O1	• at Nebraska	28	6
O8	| Northwestern	21	7
O15	• at Ohio State	27	0
O22	• at Michigan	7	14
O29	• Purdue	7	13
N5	• Iowa	55	7
N12	• at Pittsburgh	24	7
N19	• | Wisconsin	14	6

1950 — 1-7-1 (1-4-1)

S30	• at Washington	13	28
O7	• Nebraska	26	32
O14	| at Northwestern	6	13
O21	| Ohio State	0	48
O28	= | Michigan	7	7
N4	| Iowa	0	13
N11	• at Michigan State	0	27
N18	• | Purdue	27	14
N25	• | at Wisconsin	0	14

WES FESLER
1951-53 (.444)   10-13-4

1951   2-6-1 (1-4-1)
S29	Washington	20	25
O6	at California	14	55
O13	Northwestern	7	21
O20 ●	Nebraska	39	20
O27 ●	at Michigan	27	54
N3 ●	at Iowa	20	20
N10 ●	Indiana	16	14
N17 ●	at Purdue	13	19
N24	Wisconsin	6	30

1952   4-3-2 (3-1-2)
S27	at Washington	13	19
O4	California	13	49
O11 ●	Northwestern	27	26
O18 ●	Illinois	13	7
O25 ●	at Michigan	0	21
N1 ●	Iowa	17	7
N8 ●	Purdue	14	14
N15 ●	at Nebraska	13	7
N22 =	at Wisconsin	21	21

1953   4-4-1 (3-3-1)
S26	at Southern Cal	7	17
O3	Michigan State	0	21
O10 ●	at Northwestern	30	13
O17	at Illinois	7	27
O24 ●	Michigan	22	0
O31 ●	Pittsburgh	35	14
N7 ●	Indiana	28	20
N14 ●	at Iowa	0	27
N21 =	Wisconsin	21	21

MURRAY WARMATH
1954-71 (.526)   87-78-7

1954   7-2-0 (4-2-0)
S25 ●	Nebraska	19	7
O2 ●	at Pittsburgh	46	7
O9 ●	Northwestern	26	7
O16 ●	Illinois	19	6
O23 ●	at Michigan	0	34
O30 ●	Michigan State	19	13
N6 ●	Oregon State	44	6
N13 ●	Iowa	22	20
N20 ●	at Wisconsin	0	27

1955   3-6-0 (2-5-0)
S24 ●	Washington	0	30
O1	Purdue	6	7
O8 ●	at Northwestern	18	7
O15 ●	at Illinois	13	21
O22	Michigan	13	14
O29 ●	Southern Cal	25	19
N5 ●	at Iowa	0	26
N12 ●	at Michigan State	14	42
N19 ●	Wisconsin	21	6

1956   6-1-2 (4-1-2)
S29 ●	at Washington	34	14
O6 ●	Purdue	21	14
O13 =	Northwestern	0	0
O20 ●	Illinois	16	13
O27 ●	at Michigan	20	7
N3 ●	Pittsburgh	9	6
N10 ●	Iowa	0	7
N17 ●	Michigan State	14	13
N24 =	at Wisconsin	13	13

1957   4-5-0 (3-5-0)
S28 ●	Washington	46	7
O5 ●	Purdue	21	17
O12 ●	at Northwestern	41	6
O19	at Illinois	13	34
O26	Michigan	7	24
N2 ●	Indiana	34	0
N9 ●	at Iowa	20	44
N16 ●	at Michigan State	13	42
N23	Wisconsin	6	14

1958   1-8-0 (1-6-0)
S27 ●	at Washington	21	24
O4	Pittsburgh	7	13
O11 ●	Northwestern	3	7
O18 ●	Illinois	8	20
O25 ●	at Michigan	19	20
N1	at Indiana	0	6
N8	Iowa	6	28
N15 ●	Michigan State	39	12
N22	at Wisconsin	12	27

1959   2-7-0 (1-6-0)
S26	Nebraska	12	32
O3 ●	Indiana	24	14
O10 ●	at Northwestern	0	6
O17 ●	at Illinois	6	14
O24	Michigan	6	14
O31 ●	Vanderbilt	20	6
N7 ●	at Iowa	0	33
N14 ●	at Purdue	23	29
N21 ●	Wisconsin	7	11

1960   8-2-0 (6-1-0)
S24 ●	at Nebraska	26	14
O1 ●	Indiana	42	0
O8 ●	Northwestern	7	0
O15 ●	Illinois	21	10
O22 ●	at Michigan	10	0
O29 ●	Kansas State	48	7
N5 ●	Iowa	27	10
N12 ●	Purdue	14	23
N19 ●	at Wisconsin	26	7

ROSE BOWL
J2	Washington	7	17

1961   8-2-0 (6-1-0)
S30	Missouri	0	6
O7 ●	Oregon	14	7
O14 ●	at Northwestern	10	3
O21 ●	at Illinois	33	0
O28 ●	Michigan	23	20
N4 ●	Michigan State	13	0
N11 ●	at Iowa	16	9
N18 ●	Purdue	10	7
N25 ●	Wisconsin	21	23

ROSE BOWL
J1 ●	UCLA	21	3

1962   6-2-1 (5-2-0)
S29 =	Missouri	0	0
O6 ●	Navy	21	0
O13 ●	Northwestern	22	34
O20 ●	Illinois	17	0
O27 ●	at Michigan	17	0
N3 ●	at Michigan State	28	7
N10 ●	Iowa	10	0
N17 ●	Purdue	7	6
N24	at Wisconsin	9	14

1963   3-6-0 (2-5-0)
S28	Nebraska	7	14
O5 ●	Army	24	8
O12 ●	at Northwestern	8	15
O19 ●	at Illinois	6	16
O26 ●	Michigan	6	0
N2	Indiana	6	24
N9 ●	at Iowa	13	27
N16 ●	at Purdue	11	13
N28 ●	Wisconsin	14	0

1964   5-4-0 (4-3-0)
S26	Nebraska	21	26
O3 ●	at California	26	20
O10 ●	Northwestern	21	18
O17 ●	Illinois	0	14
O24 ●	at Michigan	12	19
O31 ●	at Indiana	21	0
N7 ●	Iowa	14	13
N14 ●	Purdue	14	7
N21	at Wisconsin	7	14

1965   5-4-1 (5-2-0)
S17 =	at Southern Cal	20	20
S25 ●	Washington State	13	14
O2	Missouri	6	17
O9 ●	Indiana	42	18
O16 ●	at Iowa	14	3
O23 ●	Michigan	14	13
O30 ●	at Ohio State	10	11
N6 ●	Northwestern	27	22
N13 ●	at Purdue	0	35
N20 ●	Wisconsin	42	7

1966   4-5-1 (3-3-1)
S17	at Missouri	0	24
S24 ●	Stanford	35	21
O1	Kansas	14	16
O8 =	at Indiana	7	7
O15 ●	Iowa	17	0
O22 ●	at Michigan	0	49
O29 ●	Ohio State	17	7
N5 ●	at Northwestern	28	13
N12 ●	Purdue	0	16
N19 ●	at Wisconsin	6	7

1967   8-2-0 (6-1-0)
S23 ●	Utah	13	12
S30	at Nebraska	0	7
O7 ●	SMU	23	3
O14 ●	at Illinois	10	7
O21 ●	Michigan State	21	0
O28 ●	Michigan	20	15
N4 ●	Iowa	10	0
N11 ●	at Purdue	12	41
N18 ●	Indiana	33	7
N25 ●	Wisconsin	21	14

1968   6-4-0 (5-2-0)
S21 ●	Southern Cal	20	29
S28	Nebraska	14	17
O5 ●	Wake Forest	24	19
O12 ●	Illinois	17	10
O19 ●	at Michigan State	14	13
O26 ●	at Michigan	20	33
N2 ●	Iowa	28	35
N9 ●	Purdue	27	13
N16 ●	at Indiana	20	6
N23 ●	at Wisconsin	23	15

1969   4-5-1 (4-3-0)
S20 ●	at Arizona State	26	48
S27 =	Ohio U.	35	35
O4 ●	Nebraska	14	42
O11 ●	at Indiana	7	17
O18 ●	Ohio State	7	34
O25 ●	Michigan	9	35
N1 ●	at Iowa	35	8
N8 ●	Northwestern	28	21
N15 ●	at Michigan State	14	10
N22 ●	Wisconsin	35	10

1970   3-6-1 (2-4-1)
S19 ●	at Missouri	12	34
S26 ●	Ohio U.	49	7
O3 ●	Nebraska	10	35
O10 ●	Indiana	23	0
O17 ●	at Ohio State	8	28
O24 ●	at Michigan	13	39
O31 =	Iowa	14	14
N7 ●	at Northwestern	14	28
N14 ●	Michigan State	23	13
N21 ●	at Wisconsin	14	39

1971   4-7-0 (3-5-0)
S11 ●	Indiana	28	0
S18 ●	at Nebraska	7	35
S25 ●	Washington State	20	31
O2 ●	Kansas	38	20
O9 ●	at Purdue	13	27
O16 ●	at Iowa	19	14
O23 ●	Michigan	7	35
O30 ●	Ohio State	12	14
N6 ●	at Northwestern	20	41
N13 ●	at Michigan State	25	40
N20 ●	Wisconsin	23	21

CAL STOLL
1972-78 (.500)   39-39

1972   4-7-0 (4-4-0)
S16 ●	at Indiana	23	27
S23	Colorado	6	38
S30	at Nebraska	0	49
O7	Kansas	28	34
O14	Purdue	3	28
O21 ●	Iowa	43	14
O28 ●	at Michigan	0	42
N4	at Ohio State	19	27
N11 ●	Northwestern	35	29
N18 ●	Michigan State	14	10
N25 ●	at Wisconsin	14	6

1973   7-4-0 (6-2-0)
S15	at Ohio State	7	56
S22 ●	North Dakota	41	14
S29	at Kansas	19	34
O6	Nebraska	7	48
O13 ●	Indiana	24	3
O20 ●	at Iowa	31	23
O27	Michigan	7	34
N3 ●	at Northwestern	52	43
N10 ●	Purdue	34	7
N17 ●	at Illinois	19	16
N24 ●	Wisconsin	19	17

1974   4-7-0 (2-6-0)
S14 ●	Ohio State	19	34
S21 ●	North Dakota	42	30
S28 ●	TCU	9	7
O5	at Nebraska	0	54
O12	at Indiana	3	34
O19 ●	Iowa	23	17
O26 ●	at Michigan	0	49
N2	Northwestern	13	21
N9 ●	at Purdue	24	20
N16 ●	Illinois	14	17
N23	at Wisconsin	14	49

1975   6-5-0 (3-5-0)
S13	at Indiana	14	20
S20 ●	Western Michigan	38	0
S27 ●	Oregon	10	7
O4 ●	Ohio U.	21	0
O11 ●	at Illinois	23	42
O18	Michigan State	15	38
O25 ●	at Iowa	31	7
N1	Michigan	21	28
N8 ●	Northwestern	33	9
N15 ●	at Ohio State	6	38
N22 ●	Wisconsin	24	3

1976   6-5-0 (4-4-0)
S11 ●	Indiana	32	13
S18 ●	Washington State	28	14
S25 ●	Western Michigan	21	10
O2	at Washington	7	38
O9 ●	Illinois	29	14
O16 ●	at Michigan State	14	10
O23 ●	Iowa	12	22
O30 ●	at Michigan	0	45
N6 ●	at Northwestern	38	10
N13 ●	Ohio State	3	9
N20 ●	at Wisconsin	17	26

1977   7-5-0 (4-4-0)
S10 ●	Western Michigan	10	7
S17 ●	at Ohio State	7	38
S24 ●	UCLA	27	13
O1 ●	Washington	19	17
O8 ●	at Iowa	6	18
O15 ●	Northwestern	13	7
O22 ●	Michigan	16	0
O29 ●	at Indiana	22	34
N5 ●	Michigan State	10	29
N12 ●	at Illinois	21	0
N19 ●	Wisconsin	13	7

HALL OF FAME CLASSIC
D22	Maryland	7	17

1978   5-6-0 (4-4-0)
S16 ●	Toledo	38	12
S23 ●	Ohio State	10	27
S30 ●	at UCLA	3	17
O7	Oregon State	14	17
O14 ●	Iowa	22	20
O21 ●	at Northwestern	38	14
O28 ●	at Michigan	10	42
N4 ●	Indiana	32	31
N11 ●	at Michigan State	9	33
N18 ●	Illinois	24	6
N25 ●	at Wisconsin	10	48

JOE SALEM
1979-83 (.355)   19-35-1

1979   4-6-1 (3-5-1)
S8 ●	Ohio U.	24	10
S15	Ohio State	17	21
S22	at Southern Cal	14	48
S29 ●	Northwestern	38	8
O6 ●	Purdue	31	14
O13 ●	at Michigan	21	31
O20 ●	at Iowa	24	7
O27 =	Illinois	17	17
N3 ●	at Indiana	24	42
N10 ●	at Michigan State	17	31
N17 ●	Wisconsin	37	42

1980   5-6-0 (4-5-0)
S13 ●	Ohio U.	38	14
S20 ●	at Ohio State	0	47
S27 ●	Southern Cal	7	24
O4 ●	at Northwestern	49	21
O11 ●	at Purdue	7	21
O18 ●	Michigan	14	37
O25 ●	Iowa	24	6
N1 ●	at Illinois	21	18
N8 ●	Indiana	31	7
N15 ●	Michigan State	12	30
N22 ●	at Wisconsin	7	25

MINNESOTA 529

THE SCHOOLS

1981 6-5-0 (4-5-0)

S12	●	Ohio U.	19	17
S19	● |	Purdue	16	13
S26	●	Oregon State	42	12
O3	|	at Illinois	29	38
O10	● |	Northwestern	35	23
O17	|	at Indiana	16	17
O24	● |	at Iowa	12	10
O31	|	Michigan	13	34
N7	● |	Ohio State	35	31
N14	|	at Michigan State	36	43
N21	|	Wisconsin	21	26

1982 3-8-0 (1-8-0)

S11	●	Ohio U.	57	3
S18	● |	at Purdue	36	10
S25	●	Washington State	41	11
O2	|	Illinois	24	42
O9	|	at Northwestern	21	31
O16	|	Indiana	21	40
O23	|	Iowa	16	21
O30	|	at Michigan	14	52
N6	|	at Ohio State	10	35
N13	|	Michigan State	7	26
N20	|	at Wisconsin	0	24

1983 1-10-0 (0-9-0)

S10	●	at Rice	21	17
S17		Nebraska	13	84
S24	|	Purdue	20	32
O1	|	at Ohio State	18	69
O8	|	at Indiana	31	38
O15	|	Wisconsin	17	56
O22	|	at Northwestern	8	19
O29	|	at Michigan State	10	34
N5	|	Illinois	23	50
N12	|	Michigan	10	58
N19	|	at Iowa	10	61

LOU HOLTZ
1984-85 (.455) 10-12

1984 4-7-0 (3-6-0)

S8	●	Rice	31	24
S15		at Nebraska	7	38
S22	|	at Purdue	10	34
S29	|	Ohio State	22	35
O6	● |	Indiana	33	24
O13	● |	at Wisconsin	17	14
O20	|	Northwestern	28	31
O27	|	Michigan State	13	20
N3	|	at Illinois	3	48
N10	|	at Michigan	7	31
N17	● |	Iowa	23	17

1985 7-5-0 (4-4-0)

S14	●	Wichita St.	28	14
S21	●	Montana	62	17
S28		Oklahoma	7	13
O5	● |	Purdue	45	15
O12	● |	at Northwestern	21	10
O19	● |	at Indiana	22	7
O26	|	Ohio State	19	23
N2	|	at Michigan State	26	31
N9	● |	Wisconsin	27	18
N16	|	Michigan	7	48
N23	|	at Iowa	9	31
		INDEPENDENCE BOWL		
D21	●	Clemson	20	13

JOHN GUTEKUNST
1985-91 (.441) 29-37-2

1986 6-6-0 (5-3-0)

S13	●	Bowling Green	31	7
S20		at Oklahoma	0	63
S27		Pacific	20	24
O4	● |	at Purdue	36	9
O11	● |	Northwestern	44	23
O18	● |	Indiana	19	17
O25	|	at Ohio State	0	33
N1	|	Michigan State	23	52
N8	● |	at Wisconsin	27	20
N15	● |	at Michigan	20	17
N22	|	Iowa	27	30
		LIBERTY BOWL		
D29		Tennessee	14	21

1987 6-5-0 (3-5-0)

S12	●	No. Iowa	24	7
S19	●	California	32	23
S26	●	Central Michigan	30	10
O3	● |	Purdue	21	19
O10	● |	at Northwestern	45	33
O16	|	Indiana	17	18
O24	|	at Ohio State	9	42
O31	|	at Illinois	17	27
N7	|	Michigan	20	30
N14	● |	Wisconsin	22	19
N21	|	at Iowa	20	34

1988 2-7-2 (0-6-2)

S10		Washington State	9	41
S17	●	Miami, Ohio	35	3
S24	●	Northern Illinois	31	20
O1	|	at Purdue	10	14
O8	= |	Northwestern	28	28
O15	|	at Indiana	13	33
O22	|	Ohio State	6	13
O29	= |	Illinois	27	27
N5	|	at Michigan	7	22
N12	|	at Wisconsin	7	14
N19	|	Iowa	22	31

1989 6-5-0 (4-4-0)

S16	●	at Iowa State	30	20
S23		Nebraska	0	48
S30	●	Indiana St.	34	14
O7	● |	Purdue	35	15
O14	● |	at Northwestern	20	18
O21	|	at Indiana	18	28
O28	|	Ohio State	37	41
N4	● |	Wisconsin	24	22
N11	|	at Michigan State	7	21
N18	|	Michigan	15	49
N25	● |	at Iowa	43	7

1990 6-5-0 (5-3-0)

S8		Utah	29	35
S15	●	Iowa State	20	16
S22		at Nebraska	0	56
O6	● |	at Purdue	19	7
O13	● |	Northwestern	35	25
O20	● |	Indiana	12	0
O27	|	at Ohio State	23	52
N3	● |	at Wisconsin	21	3
N10	|	Michigan State	16	28
N17	|	at Michigan	18	35
N24	● |	Iowa	31	24

1991 2-9-0 (1-7-0)

S14	●	San Jose State	26	20
S21		at Colorado	0	58
S28		Pittsburgh	13	14
O5	|	at Illinois	3	24
O12	● |	Purdue	6	3
O19	|	at Michigan State	12	20
O25	|	Michigan	6	52
N2	|	at Indiana	8	34
N9	|	Ohio State	6	35
N16	|	Wisconsin	16	19
N23	|	at Iowa	8	23

JIM WACKER
1992-96 (.291) 16-39

1992 2-9-0 (2-6-0)

S12		San Jose State	30	39
S19		Colorado	20	21
S26		at Pittsburgh	33	41
O3	● |	Illinois	18	17
O10	|	at Purdue	20	24
O17	|	Michigan State	15	20
O24	|	at Michigan	13	63
O31	|	Indiana	17	24
N7	|	at Ohio State	0	17
N14	|	at Wisconsin	6	34
N21	● |	Iowa	28	13

1993 4-7-0 (3-5-0)

S4	|	at Penn State	20	38
S11	●	Indiana St.	27	10
S18		Kansas State	25	30
S25		at San Diego State	17	48
O2	|	Indiana	19	23
O9	● |	Purdue	59	56
O16	● |	at Northwestern	28	26
O23	● |	Wisconsin	28	21
N6	|	at Illinois	20	23
N13	|	Michigan	7	58
N20	|	at Iowa	3	21

1994 3-8-0 (1-7-0)

S3	|	Penn State	3	56
S10	●	Pacific	33	7
S17	●	San Diego State	40	17
S24		at Kansas State	0	35
O1	|	at Indiana	14	25
O8	|	at Purdue	37	49
O15	|	Northwestern	31	37
O22	● |	at Wisconsin	17	14
N5	|	Illinois	17	21
N12	|	at Michigan	22	38
N19	|	Iowa	42	49

1995 3-8-0 (1-7-0)

S16	●	Ball State	31	7
S23		at Syracuse	17	27
S30	●	Arkansas State	55	7
O7	● |	Purdue	39	38
O14	|	Northwestern	17	27
O21	|	at Michigan State	31	34
O28	|	at Michigan	17	52
N4	|	Ohio State	21	49
N11	|	Wisconsin	27	34
N18	|	at Illinois	14	48
N25	|	at Iowa	3	45

1996 4-7 (1-7)

S7	●	at La. Monroe	30	3
S14	●	Ball State	26	23
S21	●	Syracuse	35	33
O5	|	at Purdue	27	30
O12	|	at Northwestern	24	26
O19	|	Michigan State	9	27
O26	|	Michigan	10	44
N2	|	at Ohio State	0	45
N9	|	at Wisconsin	28	45
N16	● |	Illinois	23	21
N23	|	Iowa	24	43

GLEN MASON
1997-Present (.531) 51-45

1997 3-9 (1-7)

A30		at Hawaii	3	17
S13	●	Iowa State	53	29
S20	●	at Memphis	20	17
S27		Houston	43	45
O4	|	at Michigan State	10	31
O11	|	Purdue	43	59
O18	|	at Penn State	15	16
O25	|	Wisconsin	21	22
N1	|	at Michigan	3	24
N8	|	Ohio State	3	31
N15	● |	Indiana	24	12
N22	|	at Iowa	0	31

1998 5-6 (2-6)

S5	●	Arkansas State	17	14
S12	●	at Houston	14	7
S19	●	Memphis	41	14
O3	|	at Purdue	21	56
O10	|	Penn State	17	27
O17	|	at Ohio State	15	45
O24	● |	Michigan State	19	18
O31	|	Michigan	10	15
N7	|	at Wisconsin	7	26
N14	|	at Indiana	19	20
N21	● |	Iowa	49	7

1999 8-4 (5-3)

S4	●	Ohio U.	33	7
S11	●	La. Monroe	35	0
S18	●	Illinois St.	55	7
O2	● |	at Northwestern	33	14
O9	|	Wisconsin	17	20
O16	● |	at Illinois	37	7
O23	|	Ohio State	17	20
O30	|	Purdue	28	33
N6	● |	at Penn State	24	23
N13	● |	Indiana	44	20
N20	● |	at Iowa	25	21
		SUN BOWL		
D31		Oregon	20	24

2000 6-6 (4-4)

S2	●	La. Monroe	47	10
S9		Ohio U.	17	23
S16	●	at Baylor	34	9
S23	|	at Purdue	24	38
S30	● |	Illinois	44	10
O7	● |	Penn State	25	16
O14	● |	at Ohio State	29	17
O21	|	at Indiana	43	51
O28	|	Northwestern	35	41
N4	|	at Wisconsin	20	41
N18	● |	Iowa	27	24
		MICRON PC.COM BOWL		
D28		North Carolina St.	30	38

2001 4-7 (2-6)

A30		at Toledo	7	38
S8	●	La. Lafayette	44	14
S29	|	Purdue	28	35
O6	|	at Illinois	14	25
O13	|	at Northwestern	17	23
O20	● |	Michigan State	28	19
O27	●	Murray St.	66	10
N3	|	Ohio State	28	31
N10	|	at Michigan	10	31
N17	|	at Iowa	24	42
N24	● |	Wisconsin	42	31

2002 8-5 (3-5)

A31	●	Texas St.	42	0
S7	●	at La. Lafayette	35	11
S14	●	Toledo	31	21
S21	●	Buffalo	41	17
S28	|	at Purdue	15	28
O3	● |	Illinois	31	10
O10	● |	Northwestern	45	42
O19	● |	at Michigan State	28	7
N2	|	at Ohio State	3	34
N9	|	Michigan	24	41
N16	|	Iowa	21	45
N23	|	at Wisconsin	31	49
		MUSIC CITY BOWL		
D30	●	Arkansas	29	14

2003 10-3 (5-3)

A30	●	Tulsa	49	10
S6	●	Troy State	48	7
S13	●	at Ohio U.	42	20
S20	●	La. Lafayette	48	14
S27	● |	at Penn State	20	14
O4	● |	at Northwestern	42	17
O10	|	Michigan	35	38
O18	|	Michigan State	38	44
O25	● |	at Illinois	36	10
N1	● |	Indiana	55	7
N8	● |	Wisconsin	37	34
N15	|	at Iowa	22	40
		SUN BOWL		
D31	●	Oregon	31	30

2004 7-5 (3-5)

S4	●	Toledo	63	21
S11	●	Illinois St.	37	21
S18	●	at Colorado State	34	16
S25	● |	Northwestern	43	17
O2	● |	Penn State	16	7
O9	|	at Michigan	24	27
O16	|	at Michigan State	17	51
O23	● |	Illinois	45	0
O30	|	at Indiana	21	30
N6	|	at Wisconsin	14	38
N13	|	Iowa	27	29
		MUSIC CITY BOWL		
D31	●	Alabama	20	16

Neutral Site key: *Unk* Unknown, Unknown / *Brnx* Bronx, N.Y. / *Det* Detroit, Mich. / *Ind* Indianapolis, Ind. / *Chi* Chicago, Ill. / *Tol* Toledo, Ohio / *KC* Kansas City, Mo. / *Buf* Buffalo, N.Y. / *Balt* Baltimore, Md.
f **Forfeit** † **Game Later Forfeited** # **Disputed Victor** * **Disputed Score** || **Designated Conference Game** |2 **Counted Twice in Conference Standings**

MISSISSIPPI

BY GEOFFREY NORMAN

NO PLACE IS MORE QUINTESSENTIALLY Southern than Oxford, where William Faulkner wrote his novels and the Ole Miss Rebels play their home games. As Faulkner famously said, "The past isn't really dead. It is not even past." Mississippi football, which is drenched in nostalgia, might be one of the best arguments for this proposition. The team's nickname, of course, speaks volumes. As does the fact that on game day, the stadium was, until recently, filled with Confederate flags. (Since the school couldn't legally ban flags without getting into First Amendment difficulties, it did the next best thing and banned sticks.) Mississippi was, needless to say, one of the last of the all-white football teams. Mercifully, those days are largely forgotten and unmourned. Leaving the troubling questions of race aside, there is something about Mississippi football that seems to long for the past and its glories, both real and imagined. As the 21st century approached, it appeared the Rebels' best seasons were behind them. The 1950s—when Ole Miss ruled the SEC—was the golden epoch. Now, it seemed, time had passed Ole Miss by. SEC powers like Florida, Tennessee and Georgia

were too big, too powerful, too "New South." Mississippi was still a small, rural, largely agrarian state and couldn't hope to compete. And then a quarterback arrived and, of course, he had a storied name out of the Ole Miss past— Manning. Glory became possible again.

TRADITION Near the center of the Ole Miss campus, there's a 10-acre plot shaded by oak trees and carpeted in lush grass. This is The Grove and it is where fans gather on game day to tailgate in a fashion that is redolent of the South. The women are drop-dead gorgeous, wearing dresses and sometimes even hats, just like it's still 1959. The men wear ties. There are cocktails—plenty of them. And, of course, there is mouthwatering food, some served on china with linen napkins to dab that spot of mayonnaise from your cheek. It is, easily, the most gracious, civilized tailgating scene in all of football and it is so seductive that at kickoff many seats still remain empty. Some people just can't quit the party. In 1983 coach Billy Brewer was looking for a way to let his players in on The Grove experience. So two hours before kickoff, he walked the team from the athletic dormitory, across the campus, to the stadium. The walk took them through The Grove, down a gauntlet of adoring fans. In 1998, the 1962 team, whose 10–0 record remains the Rebels' only perfect season, made a gift to Ole

---

PROFILE

University of Mississippi
Oxford, Miss.
Founded: 1844
Enrollment: 11,224
Colors: Cardinal Red and Navy Blue
Nickname: Rebels
Stadium: Vaught-Hemingway Stadium/Hollingsworth Field
    Opened in 1915
    AstroPlay; 60,580 capacity
First football game: 1893
All-time record: 583–439–35 (.568)
Bowl record: 19–12
Consensus national championships, 1936-present: 1 (1960)
Southeastern Conference championships: 6 (outright)
First-round NFL draftees: 15
Website:
www.olemisssports.collegesports.com

THE BEST OF TIMES

At the height of John Vaught's reign, from 1954 to 1963, the Rebels went 90–13–4, and played in eight major bowl games.

THE WORST OF TIMES

From 1972 to 1985, the Rebels were ineffectual, never able to win more than six games in any single season.

CONFERENCE

In 1933, after 11 years in the Southern Conference, Ole Miss became a charter member of the SEC.

DISTINGUISHED ALUMNI

Haley Barbour, Mississippi governor; Kate Jackson, actress; Robert Khayat, university chancellor; Trent Lott, U.S. senator; Gerald McRaney, actor; Jeanne Shaheen, New Hampshire governor; Roosevelt Skerrit, prime minister of Dominica

FIGHT SONG

FORWARD REBELS
Forward, Rebels, march to fame,
Hit that line and win this game
We know that you'll fight it through,
For your colors red and blue.
Rah, rah, rah!
Rebels you are the Southland's pride,
Take that ball and hit your stride,
Don't stop till the victory's won
for your Ole Miss.
Fight, fight for your Ole Miss!

Archie Manning never won a national or an SEC title, but he is a legend in the state.

Miss of an arch, erected at the east end of The Grove. Now the players enter The Grove under the Walk of Champions Arch.

STADIUM Naturally, a program so in love with the past plays in a stadium born way back when. In 1915, students helped lay the foundation and erect the first grandstand of what is now Vaught-Hemingway Stadium at Hollingsworth Field. In 1950, an 80-yard press box was added, and by 1980 capacity was 41,000. Recent renovations have brought capacity to 60,580, making it the state's largest facility. Judge William Hemingway, professor of law and longtime chairman of the Committee on Athletics, is the namesake. John Howard Vaught, legendary Ole Miss coach, was added in 1982. In 1998, the field was named for Dr. Jerry Hollingsworth for "his continuing generous support to the entire Ole Miss athletic department."

BEST PLAYER Archie Manning never won a national championship or an SEC title. His most memorable performance was in a nationally televised, prime-time loss. He is, nevertheless, a legend in Mississippi, where his gutsiness is considered the ideal to which all Rebel players should aspire. Manning lost games, but somehow he was never defeated. In his career, Manning threw for 4,753 yards and ran—mostly in wonderfully improvised and daring scrambles— for another 823. The second player selected in the 1971 NFL draft, Manning played brilliantly for the hapless New Orleans Saints. He is the only Ole Miss player whose jersey (No. 18) has been retired. There was recently talk of retiring the jersey worn by another Manning—Eli— but that died down. In tribute to the legendary Ole Miss family, the road leading to the new $18 million indoor practice facility was named Manning Way.

BEST COACH In 1946, Harold "Red" Drew was head coach at Mississippi and the fans were expecting big things. Then, after just one season, Drew left for Alabama to replace Frank Thomas and Vaught, his line coach, took over. Vaught's team won the SEC in his first year as head coach, going 9–2. Quarterback Charlie Conerly finished fourth in the Heisman voting and life was good at Ole Miss. Vaught won another five SEC titles before he stepped down for health reasons in 1970. He returned to the sideline three games into the 1973 season and then retired for good. Three of Vaught's teams were named national champions by various ratings services.

RECORDS

RUSHING YARDS
GAME
242 Dou Innocent vs. Mississippi State, Nov. 25, 1995 (39 att.)
SEASON
1,312 John Dottley, 1949 (208 att.)
CAREER
3,060 Deuce McAllister, 1997-2000 (616 att.)

PASSING YARDS
GAME
436 Archie Manning vs. Alabama, Oct. 4, 1969 (33 of 52)
SEASON
3,600 Eli Manning, 2003 (275 of 441)
CAREER
10,119 Eli Manning, 2000-03 (829 of 1,363)

RECEIVING YARDS
GAME
210 Eddie Small vs. Vanderbilt, Sept. 18, 1993 (6 rec.)
SEASON
949 Chris Collins, 2003 (77 rec.)
CAREER
2,621 Chris Collins, 2000-03 (198 rec.)

POINTS
GAME
42 Showboat Boykin vs. Mississippi State, Dec. 1, 1951 (7 TDs)
SEASON
124 Jonathan Nichols, 2003 (25 FGs, 49 PATs)
CAREER
344 Jonathan Nichols, 2001-04 (63 FGs, 155 PATs)

CONSENSUS ALL-AMERICANS

1947	Charlie Conerly, B
1953	Crawford Mims, G
1959	Charlie Flowers, B
1960	Jake Gibbs, B
1962	Jim Dunaway, T
1979	Jim Miller, P
1992	Everett Lindsay, OL
1998	Rufus French, TE
2001	Terrence Metcalf, OL

From 1950 to 1959, Ole Miss was 80–21–5. Only Oklahoma had a better record in that decade. Vaught's teams put up just one losing record in his near quarter century at Ole Miss, leaving a final mark of 190–61–12. Still, Vaught was more than numbers. On the one hand, the man was an innovator who brought the split-T to southern football and won games on the arms of passing quarterbacks like Conerly, Jake Gibbs and Manning. But defense is what fans remember Vaught's teams for (and this being Mississippi, they do remember). In 1959, Ole Miss gave up exactly three touchdowns on the way to a 10–1 record. This team routinely punted the ball on first or second down, because the best offense truly was a good—make that phenomenal—defense.

BEST TEAM The 1959 group was named SEC Team of the Decade in an AP poll. Rightfully so. Those Rebels led the nation in scoring defense, allowing 2.1 points per game, and shut out eight opponents. The Rebels were named national champions by four different ratings services. Had it not been for their one loss, they would doubtless have been consensus national champs. They did, however, avenge that loss in a bowl game rematch with LSU. Fittingly, the Rebels allowed the Tigers just six first downs and 74 yards total offense in a 21-0 shutout. Case closed.

STORYBOOK SEASON Things got off on the wrong foot in 2003. The Rebels were 2–2, staring mediocrity in the face afer high preseason hopes. Then quarterback Eli Manning, son of the sainted Archie, took control. Mississippi finished with a 10–3 record and tied for the lead in the SEC West (with eventual co-national champion LSU). The Rebels beat Oklahoma State in the Cotton Bowl, and Eli outdid his father, getting picked one spot higher—first overall—in the 2004 NFL draft.

BIGGEST GAME Ole Miss was unranked on Oct. 5, 2002, when mighty Florida came to town ranked sixth in

ALL-CENTENNIAL TEAM	
Chosen from the teams of 1893 through 1992 by fan voting.	
1947-70, 1973	John Vaught, coach
OFFENSE	
1942, 1947-48	Barney Poole, E
1968-70	Floyd Franks, E
1955-57	Gene Hickerson, OL
1957-59	Marvin Terrell, OL
1960-62	Jim Dunaway, OL
1963-65	Stan Hindman, OL
1989-92	Everett Lindsay, OL
1987-90	Dawson Pruett, C
1968-70	Archie Manning, QB
1942, 1946-47	Charlie Conerly, RB
1947-50	John "Kayo" Dottley, RB
1957-59	Charlie Flowers, RB
1957-59	Robert Khayat, PK
DEFENSE	
1935-37	Frank "Bruiser" Kinard, DL
1972-75	Ben Williams, DL
1988-90	Kelvin Pritchett, DL
1957-59	Larry Grantham, LB
1961-63	Kenny Dill, LB
1981-84	Freddie Joe Nunn, LB
1984-87	Jeff Herrod, LB
1986-89	Tony Bennett, LB
1952-54	Jimmy Patton, DB
1957-59	Billy Brewer, DB
1967-69	Glenn Cannon, DB
1987-90	Chris Mitchell, DB
1987-90	Todd Sandroni, DB
1976-79	Jim Miller, P

the country. The Gators had a national championship on their minds, and quarterback Rex Grossman was a leading Heisman contender. Ole Miss and Eli Manning stood as 13-point underdogs. The crowd of 61,000—the second-highest to ever attend a game on the Mississippi campus—saw Manning complete 18 of 33 attempts for 254 yards and Mississippi come back from a 14-2 halftime deficit to surprise the Gators 17-14. The next season, Manning and the confident Rebels did it to the Gators again, this time in The Swamp by a similar score, 20-17. The Gators were No. 24 and Ole Miss, again, was unranked.

BIGGEST UPSET One of many powerful Notre Dame squads came to Jackson on Sept. 17, 1977. An Irish backup quarterback named Montana watched helplessly from the bench as Rebels fullback James Storey caught two touchdown passes in the 20-13 Ole Miss victory. The Irish went on to run the table, finishing with a win over Texas in the Cotton Bowl that earned them a national championship.

HEARTBREAKER On Oct. 4, 1969, Mississippi played Alabama at Legion Field in Birmingham in the first regular-season college football game televised in prime time. The halftime score, 14-7 Tide, was ordinary enough. But in the second half, a shoot-out erupted between Archie Manning and Alabama's Scott Hunter, each matching the other touchdown for touchdown. Two coaches raised on the old SEC religion of defense and running had, it appeared, lost their minds. In the final minutes, Alabama trailed by five facing fourth and 18. Bear Bryant told his quarterback, "Run the best thing you've got." It went for a touchdown and Ole Miss lost 33-32, in what ABC's Chris Schenkel said was "the greatest duel two quarterbacks ever had. You had to be there to believe it." Manning was 33 of 52 for 436 yards. He ran for 104 and was responsible for five touchdowns all told. When Bryant greeted Vaught, an old friend, in the middle

of the field after the game, he said, "Wasn't that the worst college football game you've ever seen?" Vaught, also a disciple of defense, agreed.

WILDEST FINISH Another loss, this time to Arkansas, after seven overtimes and by a mountain-high 58-56 score. Ole Miss was going for the two-point conversion that would have sent the marathon into an eighth overtime when Jermaine Petty stopped tight end Doug Zeigler just shy of the goal line. The media had been invited to come down to the sideline from the press box with five minutes to go in regulation. An hour and 10 minutes later the game finally ended, lasting a total of 4:14; the Nov. 3, 2001, contest was the longest game in Division I-A that season.

BEST GOAL-LINE STAND On Nov. 28, 1992, Ole Miss defeated rival Mississippi State 17-10. Not overly impressive until you consider that the Bulldogs ran 11 plays inside the Rebels' 10-yard line in the final 2½ minutes, failing to even the score.

BEST COMEBACK Trailing Southern Methodist on Sept. 26, 1998, at one point by a 41-19 margin, Ole Miss scored 22 unanswered points in the final 10 minutes of regulation. Ole Miss finished the job in overtime, taking an improbable 48-41 victory.

RIVAL LSU gets the nod with Mississippi State finishing a close second. The Tigers and Rebels battled for SEC and national championships in the late 1950s, adding heat to the rivalry. In 1959, Mississippi might have gone undefeated had it not been for one sensational punt return by LSU's Billy Cannon that led to a 7-3 loss. The in-state rivalry with the Bulldogs is known as the Battle for the Golden Egg. The "egg" is actually a trophy in the shape of an old-time football, which Ole Miss has won consistently over the years.

NICKNAME The team became the Rebels in 1936. A student newspaper-sponsored contest yielded 200 entries and this one, from a Vicksburg judge, was the clear winner among newsmen asked to choose from five finalists. While the flying of the Confederate battle flag rubbed emotions in the state exceedingly raw during the 1980s and hurt Ole Miss' recruiting of black players, the nickname has not seemed to inspire the same kind of ill feelings.

UNIFORMS In 1893, when Ole Miss was about to field its first football team and play a five-game season, a discussion about school colors took place. The team manager suggested that a union of the crimson of Harvard and navy blue of Yale would be "very harmonious and that it was well to have the spirit of both of these good colleges." There has long been gray in the color scheme, a tribute to the large contingent of Rebels players who have played for the New York Giants. The players once wore the Colonel Rebel logo on their helmets. Colonel Rebel, however, isn't an officially sanctioned sideline mascot—though he has made appearances in The Grove. The logo is licensed by Ole Miss and appears on stationery, coffee cups and other booster paraphernalia.

TRAGEDY Defensive back Chucky Mullins, paralyzed in the 1989 homecoming game, became a national hero for his demonstration of courage and good cheer. During rehab, President George H. W. Bush, among other notables, visited Mullins. Shortly after returning to the university to resume work on his degree, he stopped breathing, lost consciousness and died on May 1, 1991. An award in his name is given to the Rebels' outstanding defensive player and an annual banquet in his honor raises funds to assist Ole Miss students who are victims of serious accidents.

QUOTE "I may give out but I'll never give up."

—Chucky Mullins

MISSISSIPPI ANNUAL STATISTICAL LEADERS

YR	RUSHING	YDS	ATT	AVG	PASSING	ATT	CMP	PCT	YDS	RECEIVING	REC	YDS	AVG
1946	Clayton Blount	280	49	5.7	Charlie Conerly	124	65	.52	609	Ray Poole	29	282	9.7
1947	Charlie Conerly	435	114	3.8	Charlie Conerly	232	133	.57	1,366	Barney Poole	52	511	9.8
1948	Jerry Tiblier	379	70	5.4	Farley Salmon	79	36	.46	415	Barney Poole	18	253	14.1
1949	Kayo Dottley	1,312	208	6.3	Rocky Byrd	85	42	.49	918	Jack Stribling	22	598	27.2
1950	Kayo Dottley	1,007	191	5.3	Rocky Byrd	83	42	.51	771	Jack Stribling	22	457	20.8
1951	Allen Murihead	501	105	4.8	Jimmy Lear	91	34	.37	727	James Slay	7	179	25.6
1952	Harol Lofton	698	137	5.1	Jimmy Lear	118	55	.47	975	James Slay	14	274	19.6
1953	Slick McCool	564	127	4.4	Lea Pasley	66	32	.48	713	Earl Blair	10	213	21.3
1954	Allen Murihead	443	63	7.0	Eagle Day	85	40	.47	879	Earl Blair	18	472	26.2
1955	Paige Cothren	520	93	5.6	Eagle Day	95	47	.49	724	Billy Kinard	23	371	16.1
1956	Paige Cothren	560	115	4.9	Raymond Brown	85	40	.47	653	Leroy Reed	14	278	19.9
1957	Allen Brown	530	99	5.4	Raymond Brown	53	24	.45	308	Billy Lott	5	71	14.2
1958	Charlie Flowers	559	107	5.2	Bobby Ray Franklin	121	56	.46	710	Kent Lovelace	14	178	12.7
1959	Charlie Flowers	733	141	5.2	Jake Gibbs	94	46	.49	755	Dewey Partridge	13	142	10.9
1960	Jim Anderson	505	104	4.9	Jake Gibbs	109	66	.61	970	Bobby Crespino	30	408	13.6
1961	Billy Ray Adams	575	91	6.3	Doug Elmore	84	50	.60	741	Ralph Smith	14	254	18.1
1962	Glynn Griffing	278	74	3.8	Glynn Griffing	122	72	.59	882	Louis Guy	24	295	12.3
1963	Fred Roberts	273	70	3.9	Perry Lee Dunn	89	51	.57	820	Allen Brown	16	221	13.8
1964	Mike Dennis	571	134	4.3	Jimmy Weatherly	170	91	.54	1,034	Mike Dennis	29	276	9.5
1965	Mike Dennis	525	152	3.5	Jimmy Heidel	95	52	.55	586	Mike Dennis	23	246	10.7
1966	Doug Cunningham	653	139	4.7	Bruce Newell	101	54	.53	702	Mac Hiak	20	267	13.4
1967	Stephen Hindman	829	215	3.9	Bruce Newell	121	53	.44	663	Mac Hiak	33	475	14.4
1968	Stephen Hindman	475	129	3.7	Archie Manning	263	127	.48	1,510	Hank Shows	27	276	10.2
1969	Archie Manning	502	124	4.0	Archie Manning	265	154	.58	1,762	Floyd Franks	54	720	13.3
1970	Randy Reed	668	157	4.3	Archie Manning	233	121	.52	1,481	Floyd Franks	46	668	14.5
1971	Stephen Ainsworth	629	134	4.7	Norris Weese	102	56	.55	650	Riley Myers	27	390	14.4
1972	Stephen Ainsworth	634	161	3.9	Norris Weese	163	77	.47	917	Burney Veazey	29	374	12.9
1973	Paul Hofer	642	123	5.2	Norris Weese	55	32	.58	401	Rick Kimbrough	29	459	15.8
1974	James Reed	461	110	4.2	Kenny Lyons	132	51	.39	583	Rick Kimbrough	23	271	11.8
1975	Michael Sweet	653	146	4.5	Tim Ellis	92	49	.53	621	Rick Kimbrough	31	407	13.1
1976	Michael Sweet	513	118	4.3	Tim Ellis	132	59	.45	740	Robert Frabis	20	220	11.0
1977	James Storey	564	143	3.9	Tim Ellis	78	35	.45	551	Curtis Weathers	23	395	17.2
1978	Leon Perry	673	148	4.5	John Fourcade	86	36	.42	461	Freddie Williams	30	232	7.7
1979	Leon Perry	678	160	4.2	John Fourcade	196	115	.59	1,521	Ken Toler	23	441	19.2
1980	William Hooper	619	155	4.0	John Fourcade	286	157	.55	1,897	Breck Tyler	33	535	16.2
1981	Andre Thomas	548	128	4.3	John Fourcade	251	137	.55	1,533	Michael Harmon	46	750	16.3
1982	Andre Thomas	686	173	4.0	Kent Austin	307	186	.61	2,026	Buford McGee	42	365	8.7
1983	Buford McGee	580	141	4.1	Kent Austin	211	107	.51	1,077	Buford McGee	39	272	7.0
1984	Nathan Wonsley	479	116	4.1	Kent Austin	302	177	.59	1,889	Nathan Wonsley	36	248	6.9
1985	Nathan Wonsley	462	116	4.0	Kent Austin	147	89	.61	1,116	J.R. Ambrose	38	708	18.6
1986	Willie Goodloe	526	119	4.4	Mark Young	178	87	.49	1,154	J.R. Ambrose	32	578	18.1
1987	Shawn Sykes	379	88	4.3	Mark Young	261	140	.54	1,490	J.R. Ambrose	42	515	12.3
1988	Joe Mickles	528	115	4.6	Mark Young	312	156	.50	1,969	Willie Green	38	648	17.1
1989	Randy Baldwin	642	107	6.0	John Darnell	301	167	.55	2,326	Willie Green	41	816	19.9
1990	Randy Baldwin	970	163	6.0	Russ Shows	126	57	.45	953	Darrick Owens	18	305	16.9
1991	Tyrone Ashley	503	82	6.1	Russ Shows	198	99	.50	1,369	Darrick Owens	23	329	14.3
1992	Cory Philpot	994	190	5.2	Russ Shows	224	118	.53	1,400	Eddie Small	39	558	14.3
1993	Marvin Courtney	343	71	4.8	Lawrence Adams	195	110	.56	1,415	Roell Preston	35	455	13.0
1994	Dou Innocent	910	182	5.0	Josh Nelson	308	168	.55	2,028	Ta'Boris Fisher	41	483	11.8
1995	Dou Innocent	868	192	4.5	Josh Nelson	250	143	.57	1,675	LeMay Thomas	56	801	14.3
1996	John Avery	788	181	4.4	Paul Head	172	104	.60	1,014	Ta'Boris Fisher	40	417	10.4
1997	John Avery	862	166	5.2	Stewart Patridge	352	228	.65	2,667	Rufus French	43	345	8.0
1998	Deuce McAllister	1,082	212	5.1	Romaro Miller	326	184	.56	2,273	Cory Peterson	41	601	14.7
1999	Joe Gunn	951	182	5.2	Romaro Miller	270	147	.54	1,999	Cory Peterson	46	610	13.3
2000	Deuce McAllister	767	159	4.8	Romaro Miller	295	161	.55	2,012	Grant Heard	44	655	14.9
2001	Joe Gunn	870	200	4.4	Eli Manning	408	259	.63	2,948	Chris Collins	54	692	12.8
2002	Ronald McClendon	378	96	3.9	Eli Manning	481	279	.58	3,401	Chris Collins	55	812	14.8
2003	Tremaine Turner	809	173	4.7	Eli Manning	441	275	.62	3,600	Chris Collins	77	949	12.3
2004	Vashon Pearson	807	158	5.1	Ethan Flatt	220	123	.56	1,530	Mario Hill	36	426	11.8

Receiving leaders by receptions
The NCAA began including postseason stats in 2002

MISSISSIPPI ALL-TIME SCORES

WIN/LOSS PERCENTAGE SINCE 1936

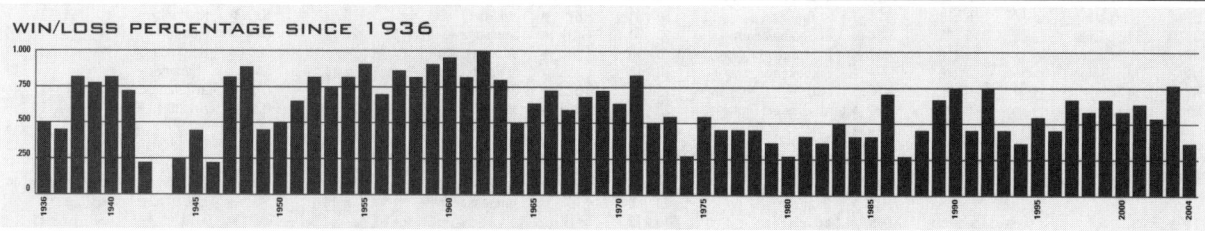

DR. A.L. BONDURANT
1893 (.800) — 4-1

1893 — 4-1-0

		Opponent		
N11	•	SWBU	56	0
N18	•	Memphis *Mem*	16	0
N25	•	SWBU *JaTn*	36	0
N30		at So. AC	0	24
D2	•	at Tulane	12	4

C.D. CLARK
1894 (.857) — 6-1

1894 — 6-1-0

		Opponent		
O20	•	St. Thomas HS	62	0
O27	•	Alabama *JaM*	6	0
N10		at Vanderbilt	0	40
N17		at Memphis AC	12	0
N29		at Tulane	8	2
D1	•	at So. AC	6	0
D3		at LSU	26	6

H.L. FAIRBANKS
1895 (.667) — 2-1

1895 — 2-1-0

		Opponent		
O12		St. Thomas Hall	18	0
N23		at Memphis AC	2	0
N28		Tulane	4	28

J.W. HOLLISTER
1896 (.333) — 1-2

1896 — 1-2-0

		Opponent		
N6		St.Thomas HS	20	0
N13		LSU *Vic*	4	12
N26		at Tulane	0	10

1897
NO TEAM

T.G. SCARBROUGH
1898 (.500) — 1-1

1898 — 1-1-0

		Opponent		
D12		at Tulane	9	14
D17	•	St.Thomas HS	9	2

W.H. LYON
1899 (.429) — 3-4

1899 — 3-4-0

		Opponent		
O27		at Central U.	13	6
O28		U. Of Nashville	0	11
N1	•	LSU *Mer*	11	0
N4		Vanderbilt *Mem*	0	11
N12		Sewanee *Mem*	0	12
N24		Alabama *JaM*	5	7
N30	•	at Tulane	15	0

Z.N. ESTES, JR.
1900 (.000) — 0-3

1900 — 0-3-0

		Opponent		
O6		at Vanderbilt	0	6
O26		at Alabama	5	12
N29		at Tulane	0	12

WILLIAM SHIBLEY / DANIEL S. MARTIN
1901 (.333) — 2-4

1901 — 2-4-0

		Opponent		
O19	•	Memphis U. Sch.	6	0
O26		at Alabama	0	41
O28		at Mississippi State	0	17
N2	•	SWBU	17	0
N7		at LSU	0	46
N28		at Tulane	11	25

DANIEL S. MARTIN
1902 (.571) — 4-3

1902 — 4-3-0

		Opponent		
O11		at Vanderbilt	0	29
O18	•	Cumberland	38	0
O25		at Mississippi State	21	0
N1	•	Memphis U. Sch.	42	0
N8		LSU *No*	0	6
N15		Tennessee *Mem*	10	11
N27		at Tulane	10	0

MIKE HARVEY
1903-04 (.591) — 6-4-1

1903 — 2-1-1

		Opponent		
O24		at Vanderbilt	0	33
N7	•	at Memphis Med. Coll.	17	0
N14	=	Mississippi State	6	6
N21	•	LSU *No*	11	0

1904 — 4-3-0

		Opponent		
O15		at Vanderbilt	0	69
O22	•	Mississippi State *CoLMs*	17	5
O29	•	SWBU	114	0
N5		at LSU	0	5
N12	•	Memphis Med. Coll. *JaM*	42	0
N19	•	Nashville *Mem*	12	5
N24		at Tulane	0	22

NO HEAD COACH

1905 — 0-2-0

		Opponent		
N20		Cumberland	0	18
N30		Mississippi State *JaM*	0	11

T.S. HAMMOND
1906 (.667) — 4-2

1906 — 4-2-0

		Opponent		
O4	•	Maryville	16	6
O13		at Vanderbilt	0	29
O20	•	at LSU	9	0
N3	•	at Tulane	17	0
N12		Sewanee *Mem*	0	24
N29	•	Mississippi State *JaM*	29	5

FRANK MASON
1907 (.000) — 0-6

1907 — 0-6-0

		Opponent		
O12		Alabama *CoLMs*	0	20
O19		S.E. Missouri. St.	6	12
O26		Sewanee *Mem*	0	65
N9		Vanderbilt *Mem*	0	60
N16		LSU *No*	0	23
N28		Mississippi State *JaM*	0	15

FRANK KYLE
1908 (.375) — 3-5

1908 — 3-5-0

		Opponent		
O3	•	Memphis U. Sch.	30	0
O10		at Arkansas	0	33
O17	•	S.E. Missouri. St. *Mem*	17	0
O24		at Vanderbilt	0	29
O29	•	Mississippi Coll. *JaM*	41	0
O31		at Tulane	0	10
N10		Southwestern	5	9
N26		Mississippi State *JaM*	6	44

DR. N.P. STAUFFER
1909-11 (.692) — 17-7-2

1909 — 4-3-2

		Opponent		
O2	•	Memphis U. Sch.	18	0
O5	•	Memphis Med. Coll..	15	0
O9		at LSU	0	10
O16		at Tulane	0	5
O23	•	Alabama *JaM*	0	16
O30		at Vanderbilt	0	17
N13	=	at Henderson-Brown	12	12
N18	•	Union	45	0
N25	•	Mississippi State *JaM*	9	5

1910 — 7-1-0

		Opponent		
O1	•	Memphis HS	10	0
O5	•	Memphis Med. Coll..	2	0
O13	•	at Tulane	16	0
O21	•	at Mississippi Coll.	24	0
O29		at Vanderbilt	2	9
N5	•	Alabama *GrvMS*	16	0
N12	•	at Memphis Med. Coll.	44	0
N24	•	Mississippi State *JaM*	30	0

1911 — 6-3-0

		Opponent		
S30	•	Memphis HS	42	0
O5	•	Southwestern	41	0
O13	•	Louisiana Tech	15	0
O24		at Henderson St.	24	11
O27		at Texas A&M	0	17
O30	•	Mississippi Coll. *JaM*	28	0
N4	•	Mercer	34	0
N18		at Vanderbilt	0	21
N30	•	Mississippi State *JaM*	0	6

LEO DeTRAY
1912 (.625) — 5-3

1912 — 5-3-0

		Opponent		
O5	•	Memphis HS	34	0
O12	•	Castle Heights	1	0 f
O19	•	at LSU	10	7
O26		at Vanderbilt	0	24
N1	•	Mississippi Coll.	12	0
N9		at Alabama	9	10
N13		Texas *Hou*	14	53
N16		at Memphis Med. Coll..	47	6

WILLIAM DRIVER
1913-14 (.600) — 11-7-2

1913 — 6-3-1

		Opponent		
O8		at VMI	0	14
O11		at Virginia Tech	14	35 *
O15	•	at Virginia Med.	7	6
O23	•	Union	46	0
N1	•	Louisiana Tech	26	0
N7	•	at Hendrix	6	8
N15	•	Arkansas *LR*	21	10
N22	•	Cumberland *Mem*	7	0
N27	•	at Southern Miss	13	7
N29	=	at Ouachita	0	0

1914 — 5-4-1

		Opponent		
O3	•	Arkansas State	20	0
O10	•	Southwestern	14	0
O17	•	at LSU	21	0
O28	=	Mississippi Coll. *JaM*	7	7
O31	•	Ouachita *Mem*	0	7
N7	•	at Tulane	21	6
N14	•	Arkansas *LR*	13	7
N17		at Texas	7	66
N20	•	Southwestern *Geo*	0	18
N26		Texas A&M *Beau*	7	14

FRED ROBBINS
1915-16 (.294) — 5-12

1915 — 2-6-0

		Opponent		
O1		Arkansas State	0	10
O8	•	Southwestern	13	6
O15		LSU	0	28
O23		Vanderbilt *Mem*	0	91
O30	•	Hendrix	32	7
N6		Mississippi State *Tup*	0	65
N13		Mississippi Coll. *JaM*	6	74
N25		Alabama *Birm*	0	53

1916 — 3-6-0

		Opponent		
S30	•	Union	30	0
O7	•	Arkansas State	20	0
O14	•	Hendrix	61	0
O21	•	at Vanderbilt	0	35
O28	•	at Alabama	0	27
N3		Mississippi State *Tup*	0	36
N11		at Transylvania, Ky	3	13
N18		at LSU	0	41
N30	•	Mississippi Coll. *JaM*	14	36

C.R. "DUDY" NOBLE
1917-18 (.250) — 2-7-1

1917 — 1-4-1

		Opponent		
O6	=	Arkansas State	0	0
O13	•	LSU	7	52
O27		at Alabama	0	64
N3	•	Mississippi State *Tup*	14	41
N10		at Sewanee	7	69
N29	•	Mississippi Coll. *JaM*	21	0

1918 — 1-3-0

		Opponent		
N9		Payne Field *WPt*	0	6
N16	•	Union	39	0
N28	•	at Mississippi State	0	34
D7	•	Mississippi State	0	13

R.L. SULLIVAN
1919-21 (.458) — 11-13

1919 — 4-4-0

		Opponent		
O4	•	Arkansas State	32	0
O11		at Alabama	0	49
O18	•	at LSU	0	12 *
O25		at Tulane	12	27
O31	•	Union	25	6
N8	•	Mississippi State *CLAR*	0	33
N15	•	Southwestern	30	0
N27	•	Mississippi Coll. *JaM*	6	0

1920 — 4-3-0

		Opponent		
O2	•	Arkansas State	33	0
O9	•	at Southern Miss	54	0
O16	•	at B'ham Southern	6	27
O23		at Tulane	0	32
O29	•	Union	86	0
N6	•	Mississippi State *Grn*	0	20
N12	•	Southwestern	38	6

1921 — 3-6-0

		Opponent		
O1	•	Memphis	82	0
O8	•	at Tulane	0	26
O15	•	Millsaps	49	0
O22	•	Southwestern	35	0
O29	•	Mississippi State *Grn*	0	21
N5	•	Mississippi Coll. *Vic*	7	27
N12	•	at LSU	0	21
N19	•	at Tenn. Doctors	6	24
D31	•	at Havanna U.	0	14

1922-1932 SOUTHERN

R.A. COWELL
1922-23 (.425) — 8-11-1

1922 — 4-5-1 (0-2-0)

		Opponent		
S30	=	Union	0	0
O7	•	at Centre	0	55
O14	•	Southwestern	23	0
O21	|	Mississippi State *JaM*	13	19
O28	|	at Tennessee	0	49
N4	•	B'ham Southern	6	0
N11	•	Hendrix	13	7
N18	•	at Tenn. Doctors	0	32
N25	•	Fort Benning *ColGa*	13	14
N30	•	at Millsaps	19	7

1923 4-6-0 (0-4-0)

S29	●	Bethel Coll.	14	6
O6	|	at Alabama	0	56
O13	●	Southwestern	33	0
O20	|	Mississippi State [JaM]	6	13
O27		at St. Louis	3	28
N3	●	B'ham Southern	6	0
N10		Mississippi Coll. [Mer]	0	6
N17	|	at Tulane	0	19
N24	|	at Tennessee	0	10
D1	●	Fort Benning [ColGa]	19	7

CHESTER BARNARD
1924 (.444) 4-5

1924 4-5-0 (0-3-0)

O4	●	Arkansas State	10	7
O11	●	Southwestern	7	0
O18	|	Mississippi State [JaM]	0	20
O25		Arkansas [LR]	0	20
N1	|	Alabama [Mont]	0	61
N8	|	Sewanee [Mem]	0	21
N15		at Furman	2	7
N22	●	Mississippi Coll.	10	6
N27	●	at Millsaps	7	0

HOMER HAZEL
1925-29 (.489) 21-22-3

1925 5-5-0 (0-4-0)

S26	●	Arkansas State	53	0
O3		at Texas	0	25
O10	|	at Tulane	7	26
O17	●	Union	7	6
O24	|	Mississippi State [JaM]	0	6
O31	|	at Vanderbilt	0	7
N7	|	Sewanee [Chat]	9	10
N14	●	at Mississippi Coll.	19	7
N21	●	Southwestern	31	0
N26	●	at Millsaps	21	0

1926 5-4-0 (2-2-0)

S25	●	Arkansas State	28	0
O2		at Arkansas	6	21
O9	● |	at Florida	12	7
O16	●	Loyola-Chicago	13	7
O23		at Drake	15	33
O30	|	at Tulane	0	6
N6	●	at Southwestern	32	27
N13	|	at LSU	0	3
N25	● |	at Mississippi State	7	6

1927 5-3-1 (3-2-0)

S24	●	Coll. Of Ozarks	58	0
O1	|	at Tulane	7	19
O7	=	Hendrix	0	0
O15	|	at Tennessee	7	21
O22	●	at Southwestern	39	0
O29	● |	at Sewanee	28	14
N5	● |	LSU	12	7
N11		Loyola-Chicago [JaM]	6	7
N24	● |	Mississippi State	20	12

1928 5-4-0 (3-3-0)

S29	●	Arkansas	25	0
O6	|	at Alabama	0	27
O13	|	at Tennessee	12	13
O20	● |	Auburn [Birm]	19	0
O27		at Loyola-New Orleans	14	34
N3	● |	Clemson	26	7
N10	|	at LSU	6	19
N17	●	at Southwestern	34	2
N29	● |	at Mississippi State	20	19

1929 1-6-2 (0-4-2)

S28	|	at Vanderbilt	7	19
O5	|	at Alabama	7	22
O12	|	at Tennessee	7	52
O18	●	at Loyola-New Orleans	26	24
O26		at SMU	0	52
N2	= |	Sewanee	6	6
N9		at Purdue	7	27
N16	|	at LSU	6	13
N28	= |	Mississippi State	7	7

ED WALKER
1930-37 (.500) 38-38-8

1930 3-5-1 (1-5-0)

S26	●	Union	64	0
O4	|	at Alabama	0	64
O11	|	at Tennessee	0	27
O18	|	Sewanee	7	13
O25	=	at Chicago	0	0
N1	|	at Vanderbilt	0	24
N8	|	at LSU	0	6
N14	●	Southwestern	37	6
N27	● |	at Mississippi State	20	0

1931 2-6-1 (1-5-0)

S19	●	Western Kentucky	13	6
S26	|	at Tulane	0	31
O3	|	at Alabama	6	55
O10	|	at Tennessee	0	38
O24	=	at Southwestern	20	20
O30		at Marquette	6	13
N7	|	Sewanee	0	7
N14	|	LSU [JaM]	3	26
N26	● |	Mississippi State	25	14

1932 5-6-0 (2-3-0)

S24	●	Southern Miss	49	0
O1	|	at Tennessee	0	33
O8	●	Samford	26	6
O15		at Centenary	6	13
O22	|	at Alabama	13	24
O29	|	Auburn [Mont]	7	14
N5		at Minnesota	0	26
N12	● |	Sewanee	27	6
N19	●	at Southwsetern	7	0
N24	● |	at Mississippi State	13	0
D3		at Tulsa	0	26

1933-Present
SEC

1933 6-3-2 (2-2-1)

S23	=	at Southwestern	6	6
S30	●	Southern Miss	45	0
O7	= |	Alabama [Birm]	0	0
O14	●	at Marquette	7	0
O21	● |	Sewanee	41	0
O28	●	Clemson [Mer]	13	0
N4	●	B'Ham Southern	12	0
N11	|	at Tennessee	6	35
N18	|	at LSU	0	31
N25		Centenary [JaM]	6	7
D2	● |	Mississippi State	31	0

1934 4-5-1 (2-3-1)

S29	●	Memphis	44	0
O5	●	Southwestern [Clar]	19	0
O13	|	at Tennessee	0	27
O20		Samford	6	7
O27	● |	Sewanee	19	6
N3	|	at Tulane	0	15
N10	= |	at Florida	13	13
N17	|	LSU [JaM]	0	14
N24		at Centenary	6	13
D1	● |	Mississippi State [JaM]	7	3

1935 9-3-0 (3-1-0)

S20	●	at Millsaps	20	0
S28	●	Memphis	92	0
O5	●	Southwestern	33	0
O11	● |	Sewanee [Clar]	33	0
O19	● |	Florida	27	6
O26		at Marquette	7	33
N1	●	at St. Louis	21	7
N9	|	Tennessee [Mem]	13	14
N16	●	at Centre	26	0
N23	●	Centenary [JaM]	6	0
N30	● |	Mississippi State	14	6
		ORANGE BOWL		
J1		Catholic U.	19	20

1936 5-5-2 (0-3-1)

S19	●	Union	45	0
S26	|	at Tulane	6	7
O2		at Temple	7	12
O9	=	at George Washington	0	0
O17	|	at LSU	0	13
O24	●	Catholic U.	14	0
O31	●	at Centenary	24	7
N7	●	Loyola-New Orleans	34	0
N14		at Marquette	0	33
N21	|	at Mississippi State	6	26
N27	●	at Miami, Fla.	14	0
D5	= |	Tennessee [Mem]	0	0

1937 4-5-1 (0-4-0)

S25	●	Louisiana Tech	13	0
O1	=	at Temple	0	0
O9	●	St. Louis	21	0
O16	|	at LSU	0	13
O23	●	Ouachita	46	0
O30	|	at Tulane	7	14
N5	●	at George Washington	27	6
N13		Arkansas [Mem]	6	32
N25	|	Mississippi State	7	9
D4	|	Tennessee [Mem]	0	32

HARRY J. MEHRE
1938-45 (.598) 39-26-1

1938 9-2-0 (3-2-0)

S24	● |	at LSU	20	7
O1	●	Louisiana Tech	27	7
O8	●	Southern Miss	14	0
O15	|	at Vanderbilt	7	13
O22	●	Centenary	47	14
O29	●	at George Washington	25	0
N5	●	at St. Louis	14	12
N12	● |	Sewanee	39	0
N16	●	Arkansas [Mem]	20	14
N26	● |	at Mississippi State	19	6
D3	|	Tennessee [Mem]	0	47

1939 7-2-0 (2-2-0)

S30	● |	at LSU	14	7
O7	●	at Southwestern	41	0
O14	●	at Centenary	34	0
O21	●	St. Louis	42	0
O28	|	at Tulane	6	18
N4	● |	Vanderbilt [Mem]	14	7
N11	●	at Southern Miss	27	7
N18	●	Memphis	46	7
N25	|	Mississippi State	6	18

1940 9-2-0 (3-1-0)

S21	●	Union	37	0
S28	● |	at LSU	19	6
O5	●	at Southwestern	27	6
O12	● |	at Georgia	28	14
O19	●	Duquesne	14	6
O26		Arkansas [Mem]	20	21
N2	● |	at Vanderbilt	13	7
N9	●	at Holy Cross	34	7
N16	●	Memphis	38	7
N23	|	at Mississippi State	0	19
N29	●	at Miami, Fla.	21	7

1941 6-2-1 (2-1-1)

S26		at Georgetown	6	16
O4	●	Southwestern	27	0
O10	= |	at Georgia	14	14
O18	●	at Holy Cross	21	0
O25	● |	at Tulane	20	13
N1	●	at Marquette	12	6
N8	● |	at LSU	13	12
N22	●	Arkansas [Mem]	18	0
N29	|	Mississippi State	0	6

1942 2-7-0 (0-5-0)

S26	●	Kentucky Teachers	39	6
O2		at Georgetown	6	14
O10	|	Georgia [Mem]	13	48
O17	|	at LSU	7	21
O24		Arkansas [Mem]	6	7
O31	●	Memphis	48	0
N7	|	Vanderbilt [Mem]	0	19
N14	|	Tennessee [Mem]	0	14
N28	|	at Mississippi State	13	34

1943
NO TEAM WWII

1944 2-6-0 (2-3-0)

S23	|	at Kentucky	7	27
S30	● |	Florida [JacF]	26	6
O7	|	Tennessee [Mem]	7	20
O21		Tulsa [Mem]	0	47
O28		Arkansas [Mem]	18	26
N4		Jackson AAB	0	10
N11	|	Alabama [Mbl]	6	34
N25	● |	Mississippi State	13	8

1945 4-5-0 (3-3-0)

S21	● |	Kentucky [Mem]	21	7
S29	|	Florida [JacF]	13	26
O6	● |	at Vanderbilt	14	7
O13	●	Louisiana Tech	26	21
O27		Arkansas [Mem]	0	19
N3	|	at LSU	13	32
N10	|	Tennessee [Mem]	0	34
N24	● |	at Mississippi State	7	6
N29		at U.T. Chattanooga	6	31

HAROLD "RED" DREW
1946 (.222) 2-7

1946 2-7-0 (1-6-0)

S21	|	at Kentucky	7	20 *
S28	● |	Florida [JacF]	13	7
O5	|	Vanderbilt [Mem]	0	7
O12	|	at Georgia Tech	7	24
O19		Louisiana Tech	6	7
O26	●	Arkansas [Mem]	9	7
N2	|	at LSU	21	34
N9	|	Tennessee [Mem]	14	18
N23	|	Mississippi State	0	20

JOHN H. VAUGHT
1947-70, '73 (.745) 190-61-12

1947 9-2-0 (6-1-0)

S20	● |	Kentucky	14	7
S27	● |	Florida [JacF]	14	6
O4	●	South Carolina [Mem]	33	0
O11	|	at Vanderbilt	6	10
O18	● |	at Tulane	27	14
O25		Arkansas [Mem]	14	19
N1	● |	at LSU	20	18
N8	● |	Tennessee [Mem]	43	13
N15	●	U.T. Chattanooga	52	0
N29	● |	at Mississippi State	33	14
		DELTA BOWL		
J1	●	TCU	13	9

1948 8-1-0 (6-1-0)

S25	● |	at Florida	14	0
O2	● |	at Kentucky	20	7
O9	● |	Vanderbilt	20	7
O16	|	at Tulane	7	20
O23	●	Boston College [Mem]	32	13
O30	● |	at LSU	49	19
N6	●	at U.T. Chattanooga	34	7
N13	● |	Tennessee [Mem]	16	13
N27	● |	Mississippi State	34	7

1949 4-5-1 (2-4-0)

S16	●	at Memphis	40	7
S23	● |	Auburn [Mont]	40	7
O1	|	Kentucky	0	47
O8	|	at Vanderbilt	27	28
O14	=	at Boston College	25	25
O22		at TCU	27	33
O29	|	at LSU	7	34
N5	●	U.T. Chattanooga	47	27
N12	|	Tennessee [Mem]	7	35
N26	● |	at Mississippi State	26	0

1950 5-5-0 (1-5-0)

S22	●	at Memphis	39	7
S30	|	at Kentucky	0	27
O7	●	Boston College	54	0
O14	|	at Vanderbilt	14	20
O21	|	at Tulane	20	27
O28	●	TCU [Mem]	19	7
N4	|	at LSU	14	40
N11	●	U.T. Chattanooga	20	0
N18	|	at Tennessee	0	35
D2	● |	Mississippi State	27	20

1951 6-3-1 (4-2-1)

S21	●	at Memphis	32	0
S29	● |	Kentucky	21	17
O5	●	Boston College [Mem]	34	7
O13	|	Vanderbilt [Mem]	20	34
O20	● |	Tulane	25	6
O26		at Miami, Fla.	7	20
N3	= |	at LSU	6	6
N10	● |	Auburn [Mbl]	39	14
N17	|	Tennessee	21	46
D1	● |	at Mississippi State	49	7

1952 8-1-2 (4-0-2)

S19	●	at Memphis	54	6
S27	= |	at Kentucky	13	13
O4	● |	Auburn [Mem]	20	7
O11	= |	at Vanderbilt	21	21
O18	● |	at Tulane	20	14
O25	●	Arkansas [LR]	34	7
N1	● |	LSU	28	0
N8	●	at Houston	6	0
N15	●	Maryland	21	14
N29	● |	Mississippi State	20	14
		SUGAR BOWL		
J1		Georgia Tech	7	24

1953 7-2-1 (4-1-1)

S19	●	U.T. Chattanooga [JaM]	39	6
S26	● |	Kentucky	22	6
O3	|	at Auburn	0	13
O10	● |	Vanderbilt	28	6
O17	● |	at Tulane	45	14
O24	●	Arkansas [Mem]	28	0
O31	● |	at LSU	27	16
N7	●	North Texas	40	7
N14		at Maryland	0	38
N28	= |	at Mississippi State	7	7

1954 9-2-0 (5-1-0)
S17 ● North Texas MEM 35 12
S25 ● | Kentucky MEM 28 9
O2 ● Villanova PHIL 52 0
O9 ● | at Vanderbilt 22 7
O16 ● | Tulane 34 7
O23 || Arkansas LR 0 6
O30 ● | at LSU 21 6
N6 ● at Memphis 51 0
N13 ● at Houston 26 0
N27 ● | Mississippi State 14 0
SUGAR BOWL
J1 Navy 0 21

1955 10-1-0 (5-1-0)
S17 ● | Georgia ATL 26 13
S24 | at Kentucky 14 21
O1 ● North Texas 33 0
O8 ● | Vanderbilt MEM 13 0
O15 ● | at Tulane 27 13
O22 ● Arkansas 17 7
O29 ● | at LSU 29 26
N5 ● at Memphis 39 6
N12 ● Houston JAM 27 11
N26 ● | at Mississippi State 26 0
COTTON BOWL
J2 ● TCU 14 13

1956 7-3-0 (4-2-0)
S22 ● North Texas 45 0
S29 ● | Kentucky MEM 37 7
O6 ● Houston JAM 14 0
O13 ● | Vanderbilt 16 0
O20 | Tulane JAM 3 10
O27 Arkansas LR 0 14
N3 ● | at LSU 46 17
N10 ● at Memphis 26 0
N17 | at Tennessee 7 27
D1 ● | Mississippi State 13 7

1957 9-1-1 (5-0-1)
S21 ● at Trinity 44 0
S28 ● | at Kentucky 15 0
O5 ● Hardin-Simmons 34 7
O12 ● | at Vanderbilt 28 0
O18 ● | at Tulane 50 0
O26 Arkansas MEM 6 12
N2 ● Houston JAM 20 7
N9 ● | LSU 14 12
N16 ● | Tennessee MEM 14 7
N30 = | at Mississippi State 7 7
SUGAR BOWL
J1 ● Texas 39 7

1958 9-2-0 (4-2-0)
S20 ● at Memphis 17 0
S27 ● | Kentucky MEM 27 6
O4 ● at Trinity 21 0
O11 ● | at Tulane 19 8
O18 ● Hardin-Simmons 24 0
O25 ● Arkansas LR 14 12
N1 | at LSU 0 14
N8 ● || Houston 56 7
N15 | at Tennessee 16 18
N29 ● | Mississippi State 21 0
GATOR BOWL
D27 ● Florida 7 3

1959 10-1-0 (5-1-0)
S19 ● at Houston 16 0
S26 ● | at Kentucky 16 0
O3 ● Memphis 43 0
O10 ● | at Vanderbilt 33 0
O17 ● | Tulane 53 7
O24 ● Arkansas MEM 28 0
O31 | at LSU 3 7
N7 ● U.T. Chattanooga 58 0
N14 ● | Tennessee MEM 37 7
N28 ● | at Mississippi State 42 0
SUGAR BOWL
J1 ● LSU 21 0

1960 10-0-1 (5-0-1)
S17 ● at Houston 42 0
S24 ● | Kentucky MEM 21 6
O1 ● at Memphis 31 20
O8 ● | at Vanderbilt 26 0
O15 ● | at Tulane 26 13
O22 ● Arkansas LR 10 7
O29 = | LSU 6 6
N5 ● U.T. Chattanooga 45 0
N12 ● | at Tennessee 24 3
N26 ● | Mississippi State 35 9
SUGAR BOWL
J2 ● Rice 14 6

1961 9-2-0 (5-1-0)
S23 ● Arkansas JAM 16 0
S30 ● | at Kentucky 20 6
O7 ● Florida State 33 0
O14 ● Houston MEM 47 7
O21 ● | Tulane JAM 41 0
O28 ● | Vanderbilt 47 0
N4 | at LSU 7 10
N11 ● U.T. Chattanooga 54 0
N18 ● | Tennessee MEM 24 10
D2 ● | at Mississippi State 37 7
COTTON BOWL
J1 Texas 7 12

1962 10-0-0 (6-0-0)
S22 ● at Memphis 21 7
S29 ● | Kentucky JAM 14 0
O6 ● Houston JAM 40 7
O20 ● | Tulane JAM 21 0
O27 ● | Vanderbilt MEM 35 0
N3 ● | at LSU 15 7
N10 ● U.T. Chattanooga 52 7
N17 ● | at Tennessee 19 6
D1 ● | Mississippi State 13 6
SUGAR BOWL
J1 ● Arkansas 17 13

1963 7-1-2 (5-0-1)
S21 = at Memphis 0 0
S28 ● | at Kentucky 31 7
O5 ● at Houston 20 6
O19 ● | at Tulane 21 0
O26 ● | Vanderbilt 27 0
N2 ● | at LSU 37 3
N9 ● Tampa 41 0
N16 ● | Tennessee MEM 20 0
N30 = | at Mississippi State 10 10
SUGAR BOWL
J1 Alabama 7 12

1964 5-5-1 (2-4-1)
S19 ● Memphis 30 0
S26 | Kentucky JAM 21 27
O3 ● Houston 31 9
O10 | at Florida 14 30
O17 ● | at Tulane 14 9
O24 = | at Vanderbilt 7 7
O31 | at LSU 10 11
N7 ● Tampa 36 0
N14 ● | at Tennessee 30 0
D5 | Mississippi State 17 20
BLUEBONNET BOWL
D19 Tulsa 7 14

1965 7-4-0 (5-3-0)
S18 ● at Memphis 34 14
S25 | at Kentucky 7 16
O2 | Alabama BIRM 16 17
O9 | Florida 0 17
O16 ● | Tulane JAM 24 7
O23 ● | Vanderbilt 24 7
O30 ● | LSU JAM 23 0
N6 at Houston 3 17
N13 ● | Tennessee MEM 14 13
N27 ● | at Mississippi State 21 0
LIBERTY BOWL
D18 ● Auburn 13 7

1966 8-3-0 (5-2-0)
S17 ● at Memphis 13 0
S24 ● | Kentucky JAM 17 0
O1 | Alabama JAM 7 17
O8 | at Georgia 3 9
O15 ● Southern Miss 14 7
O22 ● Houston MEM 27 6
O29 ● | at LSU 17 0
N12 ● | at Tennessee 14 7
N19 ● | Vanderbilt JAM 34 0
N26 ● | Mississippi State 24 0
BLUEBONNET BOWL
D17 Texas 0 19

1967 6-4-1 (4-2-1)
S23 at Memphis 17 27
S30 ● | at Kentucky 26 13
O7 | Alabama BIRM 7 21
O14 ● | Georgia JAM 29 20
O21 ● Southern Miss MEM 23 14
O28 ● Houston 14 13
N4 = | LSU JAM 13 13
N18 | Tennessee MEM 7 20
N25 ● | at Vanderbilt 28 7
D2 ● | at Mississippi State 10 3
SUN BOWL
D30 Texas El Paso 7 14

1968 7-3-1 (3-2-1)
S21 ● at Memphis 21 7
S28 ● | Kentucky JAM 30 14
O5 ● | Alabama JAM 10 8
O12 | at Georgia 7 21
O19 ● Southern Miss 21 13
O26 Houston JAM 7 29
N2 ● | at LSU 27 24
N9 ● U.T. Chattanooga 38 16
N16 | at Tennessee 0 31
N30 = | Mississippi State 17 17
LIBERTY BOWL
D14 ● Virginia Tech 34 17

1969 8-3-0 (4-2-0)
S20 ● Memphis 28 3
S27 | at Kentucky 9 10
O4 | Alabama BIRM 32 33
O11 ● | Georgia JAM 25 17
O18 ● Southern Miss 69 7
O25 at Houston 11 25
N1 ● | LSU JAM 26 23
N8 ● U.T. Chattanooga 21 0
N15 ● | Tennessee JAM 38 0
N27 ● | at Mississippi State 48 22
SUGAR BOWL
J1 ● Arkansas 27 22

1970 7-4-0 (4-2-0)
S19 ● at Memphis 47 13
S26 ● | Kentucky JAM 20 17
O3 ● | Alabama JAM 48 23
O10 ● | at Georgia 31 21
O17 Southern Miss 14 30
O24 ● | at Vanderbilt 26 16
N7 ● Houston 24 13
N14 ● U.T. Chattanooga 44 7
N26 | Mississippi State 14 19
D5 | at LSU 17 61
GATOR BOWL
J2 Auburn 28 35

BILLY R. KINARD
1971-73 (.640) 16-9

1971 10-2-0 (4-2-0)
S11 ● Long Beach St. JAM 29 13
S18 ● at Memphis 49 21
S25 ● | at Kentucky 34 20
O2 | Alabama BIRM 6 40
O9 | Georgia JAM 7 38
O16 ● Southern Miss 20 6
O23 ● | Vanderbilt 28 7
O30 ● | LSU JAM 24 22
N6 ● at Tampa 28 27
N13 ● U.T. Chattanooga 49 10
N25 ● | at Mississippi State 48 0
PEACH BOWL
D30 ● Georgia Tech 41 18

1972 5-5-0 (2-5-0)
S16 ● at Memphis 34 29
S23 ● at South Carolina 21 0
S30 ● Southern Miss 13 9
O7 | Auburn JAM 13 19
O14 | Georgia JAM 13 14
O21 | Florida 0 16
O28 ● | at Vanderbilt 31 7
N4 | at LSU 16 17
N18 | at Tennessee 0 17
N25 ● | Mississippi State 51 14

JOHN H. VAUGHT

1973 6-5-0 (4-3-0)
S8 ● Villanova JAM 24 6
S15 at Missouri 0 17
S22 Memphis JAM 13 17
S29 ● Southern Miss 41 0
O6 | at Auburn 7 14
O13 | at Georgia 0 20
O20 ● | at Florida 13 10
O27 ● | Vanderbilt 24 14
N3 | LSU JAM 14 51
N17 ● | Tennessee JAM 28 18
N24 ● | Mississippi State JAM 38 10

KEN COOPER
1974-77 (.432) 19-25

1974 3-8-0 (0-6-0)
S14 ● Missouri JAM 10 0
S21 at Memphis 7 15
S28 ● Southern Miss 20 14
O5 | Alabama JAM 21 35
O12 | at Georgia 0 49
O19 South Carolina 7 10
O26 | at Vanderbilt 14 24
N2 | at LSU 0 24
N16 | Tennessee MEM 17 29
N23 | Mississippi State JAM 13 31
N30 ● at Tulane 26 10

1975 6-5-0 (5-1-0)
S6 at Baylor 10 20
S13 at Texas A&M 0 7
S20 at Tulane 3 14
S27 ● Southern Miss 24 8
O4 | Alabama BIRM 6 32
O11 ● | Georgia 28 13
O18 South Carolina JAM 29 35
O25 ● | Vanderbilt 17 7
N1 ● | LSU JAM 17 13
N15 ● | Tennessee MEM 23 6
N22 ● | Mississippi State JAM 13 7

1976 5-6-0 (3-4-0)
S4 at Memphis 16 21
S11 ● | Alabama JAM 10 7
S18 ● Tulane 34 7
S25 ● at Southern Miss 28 0
O2 | Auburn JAM 0 10
O9 ● | Georgia 21 17
O16 at South Carolina 7 10
O23 ● | at Vanderbilt 20 3
O30 | at LSU 0 45
N13 | at Tennessee 6 32
N20 | Mississippi State JAM 11 28 †

1977 5-6-0 (2-5-0)
S3 ● Memphis JAM 7 3
S10 | Alabama BIRM 13 34
S17 ● Notre Dame JAM 20 13
S24 Southern Miss 19 27
O1 | at Auburn 15 21
O8 | at Georgia 13 14
O15 ● South Carolina 17 10
O22 ● | Vanderbilt 26 14
O29 | LSU JAM 21 28
N12 ● | Tennessee MEM 43 14
N19 | Mississippi State JAM 14 18 †

STEVE SLOAN
1978-82 (.373) 20-34-1

1978 5-6-0 (2-4-0)
S9 ● Memphis JAM 14 7
S23 at Missouri 14 45
S30 ● Southern Miss JAM 16 13
O7 | at Georgia 3 42
O14 | Kentucky 17 24
O21 at South Carolina 17 18
O28 ● | at Vanderbilt 35 10
N4 | at LSU 8 30
N11 ● Tulane 13 3
N18 | at Tennessee 17 41
N25 ● | Mississippi State JAM 27 7

1979 4-7-0 (3-3-0)
S15 ● at Memphis 38 34
S22 Missouri JAM 7 33
S29 Southern Miss JAM 8 38
O6 | Georgia 21 24
O13 | at Kentucky 3 14
O20 at South Carolina 14 21
O27 ● | Vanderbilt 63 28
N3 | LSU JAM 24 28
N10 at Tulane 15 49
N17 ● | Tennessee JAM 44 20
N24 ● | Mississippi State JAM 14 9

1980 3-8-0 (2-4-0)
S6 Texas A&M JAM 20 23
S13 ● Memphis 61 7
S20 Alabama JAM 35 59
S27 Tulane 24 26
O4 Southern Miss JAM 22 28
O11 | at Georgia 21 28
O18 | Florida 3 15
O25 ● | at Vanderbilt 27 14
N1 | at LSU 16 38
N15 ● | Tennessee MEM 20 9
N22 | Mississippi State JAM 14 19

1981 4-6-1 (1-4-1)

S5	●		at Tulane	19	18
S12	●		at South Carolina	20	13
S19	●		at Memphis	7	3
S26			Arkansas JaM	13	27
O3			at Alabama	7	38
O10		|	Georgia	7	37
O17		|	at Florida	3	49
O24		|	Vanderbilt	23	27
O31	=	|	LSU JaM	27	27
N14		|	at Tennessee	20	28
N21	●	|	Mississippi State JaM	21	17

1982 4-7-0 (0-6-0)

S4	●		Memphis	27	10
S11	●		Southern Miss	28	19
S18		|	Alabama JaM	14	42
S25			Arkansas LR	12	14
O9		|	at Georgia	10	33
O16	●		TCU	27	9
O23		|	at Vanderbilt	10	19
O30		|	at LSU	8	45
N6	●		Tulane JaM	45	14
N13		|	Tennessee JaM	17	30
N20		|	Mississippi State JaM	10	27

BILLY BREWER
1983-93 (.536) 66-57-3

1983 6-6-0 (4-2-0)

S3			at Memphis	17	37	
S10			at Tulane	23	27	†
S17		|	at Alabama	0	40	
S24	●		Arkansas JaM	13	10	
O1			Southern Miss	7	27	
O8		|	Georgia	11	36	
O15	●		at TCU	20	7	
O22	●	|	Vanderbilt	21	14	
O29	●	|	LSU JaM	27	24	
N12	●	|	at Tennessee	13	10	
N19	●	|	Mississippi State JaM	24	23	
			INDEPENDENCE BOWL			
D10			Air Force	3	9	

1984 4-6-1 (1-5-0)

S8	●		Memphis	22	6
S15	=		Arkansas LR	14	14
S22	●		Louisiana Tech	14	8
S29	●		Tulane	19	14
O6		|	Auburn	13	17
O13		|	at Georgia	12	18
O20			Southern Miss JaM	10	13
O27		|	at Vanderbilt	20	37
N3		|	at LSU	29	32
N17		|	Tennessee JaM	17	41
N24	●	|	Mississippi State JaM	24	3

1985 4-6-1 (2-4-0)

S7	=		at Memphis	17	17
S14			Arkansas JaM	19	24
S21	●		Arkansas State	18	16
S28	●		at Tulane	27	10
O5		|	at Auburn	0	41
O12		|	Georgia JaM	21	49
O26	●	|	Vanderbilt	35	7
N2		|	LSU JaM	0	14
N9			at Notre Dame	14	37
N16		|	at Tennessee	14	34
N23	●	|	Mississippi State JaM	45	27

1986 8-3-1 (4-2-0)

S6	●		Memphis JaM	28	6
S13			Arkansas LR	0	21
S20	=		Arkansas State	10	10
S27	●		Tulane	35	10
O4		|	at Georgia	10	14
O11	●	|	Kentucky JaM	33	13
O18	●		La. Lafayette	21	20
O25	●	|	at Vanderbilt	28	12
N1	●	|	at LSU	21	19
N15		|	Tennessee JaM	10	22
N22	●	|	Mississippi State JaM	24	3
			INDEPENDENCE BOWL		
D20	●		Texas Tech	20	17

1987 3-8-0 (1-5-0)

S5			at Memphis	10	16
S12			Arkansas JaM	10	31
S19	●		Arkansas State	47	10
S26			at Tulane	24	31
O3		|	Georgia	14	31
O10		|	at Kentucky	6	35
O17	●		La. Lafayette	24	14
O24	●	|	Vanderbilt	42	14
O31		|	LSU JaM	13	42
N14		|	at Tennessee	13	55
N21		|	Mississippi State JaM	20	30

1988 5-6-0 (3-4-0)

S3	●		Memphis JaM	24	6
S10		|	Florida JaM	15	27
S17			Arkansas LR	13	21
O1		|	at Georgia	12	36
O8	●	|	at Alabama	22	12
O15	●		Arkansas State	25	22
O22	●	|	at Vanderbilt	36	28
O29		|	at LSU	20	31
N5			Tulane	9	14
N12		|	Tennessee	12	20
N26	●	|	Mississippi State JaM	33	6

1989 8-4-0 (4-3-0)

S2	●		at Memphis	20	13
S9	●	|	at Florida	24	19
S16	●		Arkansas State	34	31
S23			Arkansas JaM	17	24
O7		|	Alabama JaM	27	62
O14	●	|	Georgia	17	13
O21	●		at Tulane	32	28
O28	●	|	Vanderbilt	24	16
N4		|	LSU	30	35
N18		|	at Tennessee	21	33
N25	●	|	Mississippi State JaM	21	11
			LIBERTY BOWL		
D28	●		Air Force	42	29

1990 9-3-0 (5-2-0)

S8	●		Memphis	23	21
S15		|	Auburn JaM	10	24
S22	●		Arkansas LR	21	17
S29	●		Tulane	31	21
O6	●	|	Kentucky	35	29
O13	●	|	at Georgia	28	12
O20	●		Arkansas State	42	13
O27	●	|	at Vanderbilt	14	13
N3	●	|	at LSU	19	10
N17		|	Tennessee Mem	13	22
N24	●	|	Mississippi State JaM	21	9
			GATOR BOWL		
J1			Michigan	3	35

1991 5-6-0 (1-6-0)

A31	●		at Tulane	22	3
S7	●		at Memphis	10	0
S14		|	at Auburn	13	23
S21	●		Ohio U.	38	14
S28	●		Arkansas JaM	24	17
O5	●	|	at Kentucky	35	14
O12		|	Georgia	17	37
O26		|	Vanderbilt	27	30
N2		|	LSU JaM	22	25
N16		|	at Tennessee	25	36
N23		|	at Mississippi State	9	24

1992 9-3-0 (5-3-0)

S5	●	|	Auburn	45	21
S12	●		Tulane	35	9
S19		|	at Vanderbilt	9	31
S26		|	at Georgia	11	37
O3	●	|	Kentucky	24	14
O17	●	|	Arkansas LR	17	3
O24		|	at Alabama	10	31
O31	●	|	LSU JaM	32	0
N7	●		Memphis	17	12
N14	●		Louisiana Tech	13	6
N28	●	|	Mississippi State	17	10
			LIBERTY BOWL		
D31	●		Air Force	13	0

1993 5-6-0 (3-5-0)

S2		|	at Auburn	12	16	
S11	●		U.T. Chattanooga	40	7	
S18	●	|	Vanderbilt	49	7	
S25	●	|	Georgia	31	14	
O2		|	at Kentucky	0	21	
O16	●	|	Arkansas JaM	19	0	
O23		|	Alabama	14	19	†
O30		|	at LSU	17	19	
N6			at Memphis	3	19	
N13	●		Northern Illinois	44	0	
N27		|	at Mississippi State	13	20	

JOE LEE DUNN
1994 (.364) 4-7

1994 4-7-0 (2-6-0)

S3		|	Auburn	17	22
S10	●		So. Illinois	59	3
S17	●	|	at Vanderbilt	20	14
S24		|	at Georgia	14	17
O1		|	Florida	14	38
O15		|	at Arkansas	7	31
O22		|	at Alabama	10	21
O29	●	|	LSU	34	21
N5			Memphis	16	17
N12	●		at Tulane	38	0
N26		|	Mississippi State	17	21

TOMMY TUBERVILLE
1995-98 (.556) 25-20

1995 6-5-0 (3-5-0)

S2		|	at Auburn	13	46
S9	●		Indiana St.	56	10
S23	●	|	Georgia	18	10
S30		|	at Florida	10	28
O7	●		Tulane	20	17
O14		|	Arkansas Mem	6	13
O21		|	Alabama	9	23
O28	●	|	Vanderbilt	21	10
N4	●		at Memphis	34	3
N11		|	at LSU	9	38
N25	●	|	at Mississippi State	13	10

1996 5-6 (2-6)

A31	●		Idaho St.	38	14
S7	●		VMI JaM	31	7
S14		|	Auburn	28	45
S21	●	|	at Vanderbilt	20	9
O3		|	Tennessee Mem	3	41
O19		|	at Alabama	0	37
O26	●		Arkansas State	38	21
N9		|	at Arkansas	7	13
N16		|	LSU	7	39
N23	●	|	at Georgia	31	27
N30		|	Mississippi State	0	17

1997 8-4 (4-4)

A30	●		Central Florida	24	23
S6	●		SMU	23	15
S13		|	at Auburn	9	19
S27	●	|	Vanderbilt	15	3
O4		|	at Tennessee	17	31
O18	●	|	at LSU	36	21
O25		|	Alabama	20	29
N6	●	|	Arkansas	19	9
N15	●		at Tulane	41	24
N22		|	Georgia	14	21
N29	●	|	at Mississippi State	15	14
			MOTOR CITY BOWL		
D26	●		Marshall	34	31

1998 7-5 (3-5)

S5	●		Memphis	30	10
S12		|	Auburn	0	17
S19	●	|	at Vanderbilt	30	6
S26	●		at SMU	48	41
O3	●	|	South Carolina	30	28
O10		|	at Alabama	17	20
O24	●		Arkansas State	30	17
O31	●	|	LSU	37	31
N7		|	at Arkansas	0	34
N21		|	at Georgia	17	24
N26		|	Mississippi State	6	28
			INDEPENDENCE BOWL		
D31	●		Texas Tech	35	18

DAVID CUTCLIFFE
1998-2004 (.603) 44-29

1999 8-4 (4-4)

S4	●		at Memphis	3	0
S11	●		Arkansas State	38	14
S18		|	Vanderbilt	34	37
S25	●	|	at Auburn	24	17
O2	●	|	at South Carolina	36	10
O9	●		Tulane	20	13
O16		|	Alabama	24	30
O30	●	|	at LSU	42	23
N6	●	|	Arkansas	38	16
N20		|	Georgia	17	20
N25		|	at Mississippi State	20	23
			INDEPENDENCE BOWL		
D31	●		Oklahoma	27	25

2000 7-5 (4-4)

S2	●		Tulane	49	20
S9		|	Auburn	27	35
S16	●	|	at Vanderbilt	12	7
S30	●	|	Kentucky	35	17
O7	●		Arkansas State	35	10
O14		|	at Alabama	7	45
O28	●		Nevada-Las Vegas	43	40
N4	●	|	at Arkansas	38	24
N11		|	LSU	9	20
N18		|	at Georgia	14	32
N23	●	|	Mississippi State	45	30
			MUSIC CITY BOWL		
D28			West Virginia	38	49

2001 7-4 (4-4)

S1	●		Murray St.	49	14
S8		|	at Auburn	21	27
S29	●	|	at Kentucky	42	31
O6	●		at Arkansas State	35	17
O13	●	|	Alabama	27	24
O20	●		Middle Tennessee	45	17
O27	●	|	at LSU	35	24
N3		|	Arkansas	56	58
N17		|	Georgia	15	35
N22		|	at Mississippi State	28	36
D1	●	|	Vanderbilt	38	27

2002 7-6 (3-5)

A31	●		La. Monroe	31	3
S7	●		Memphis	38	16
S14			at Texas Tech	28	42
S21	●	|	Vanderbilt	45	38
O5	●	|	Florida	17	14
O12	●		Arkansas State	52	17
O19		|	at Alabama	7	42
O26		|	at Arkansas	28	48
N2		|	Auburn	24	31
N9		|	at Georgia	17	31
N23		|	at LSU	13	14
N28	●	|	Mississippi State	24	12
			INDEPENDENCE BOWL		
D27	●		Nebraska	27	23

2003 10-3 (7-1)

A30	●	|	at Vanderbilt	24	21
S6			at Memphis	34	44
S13	●		La. Monroe	59	14
S27			Texas Tech	45	49
O4	●	|	at Florida	20	17
O11	●		Arkansas State	55	0
O18	●	|	Alabama	43	28
O25	●	|	Arkansas	19	7
N1	●	|	South Carolina	43	40
N8	●	|	at Auburn	24	20
N22		|	LSU	14	17
N27	●	|	at Mississippi State	31	0
			COTTON BOWL		
J2	●		Oklahoma State	31	28

2004 4-7 (3-5)

S4			Memphis	13	20
S11		|	at Alabama	7	28
S18	●	|	Vanderbilt	26	23
S25			at Wyoming	32	37
O2	●		Arkansas State	28	21
O9	●	|	at South Carolina	31	28
O16		|	Tennessee	17	21
O30		|	Auburn	14	35
N13		|	at Arkansas	3	35
N20		|	at LSU	24	27
N27	●	|	Mississippi State	20	3

Neutral Site key: *MBL* Mobile, AL / *MONT* Montgomery, AL / *PHIL* Philadelphia, PA / *LR* Little Rock, AR / *ATL* Atlanta, GA / *HOU* Houston, TX / *BIRM* Birmingham, AL / *MEM* Memphis, TN / *GRVMS* Greenville, MS / *GEO* Georgetown, TX / *BEAU* Beaumont, TX / *TUP* Tupelo, MS / *WPT* West Point, MS / *CLAR* Clarksdale, MS / *HAV* Havana, Cuba / *GRN* Greenwood, MS / *JAM* Jackson, MS / *COLGA* Columbus, GA / *CHAT* Chattanooga, TN / *JATN* Jackson, TN / *VIC* Vicksburg, MS / *MER* Meridian, MS / *NO* New Orleans, LA / *COLMS* Columbus, MS / *JACF* Jacksonville, F

ƒ **Forfeit** † **Game Later Forfeited** # **Disputed Victor** * **Disputed Score** || **Designated Conference Game** |2 **Counted Twice in Conference Standings**

THE SCHOOLS

MISSISSIPPI STATE

By Geoffrey Norman

THE HISTORY OF MISSISSIPPI STATE football might best be characterized by the word "struggle." No program in the SEC has had to reinvent and rebuild itself more often than the Bulldogs. This, perhaps, accounts for an abiding toughness and a reputation as the school that other, more successful SEC programs, overlook at their peril. MSU keeps picking itself up, coming back and searching for new ways to break through. This includes hiring, in 2003, Sylvester Croom—the SEC's first African-American head coach.

The first football game played at what was then Mississippi A&M College took place on Thanksgiving Day 1892. A team made up of faculty members defeated one composed of students 4-0. On Nov. 16, 1895, the school played, and lost, its first intercollegiate game, 21-0, to Southwestern Baptist (now Union University), in Jackson, Tenn. The Aggies, as they were then called, lost their first home game the next season. There was no football the following year, in 1897, when an epidemic of yellow fever swept the state. And the next year the cadets of A&M were involved in the Spanish-American War. Football would have to wait. In 1901, though, A&M fielded a team that, in its first game, fought to a scoreless tie against Christian Brothers College in Memphis. The first victory in school history, 17-0, came at home two days later, on Oct. 28, 1901, against the best of all possible opponents—the University of Mississippi.

This was the first of many highs that have sustained the program, and kept the cowbells ringing right up to the present with the promise that Croom has brought to Starkville.

TRADITION Nobody quite knows where MSU's famed cowbells originated. The consensus is that the ringing of cowbells to support Mississippi State's fortunes began in the late 1930s and early 1940s, a period still considered the golden age of Bulldog football. According to legend, during a home game against Mississippi, a Jersey cow wandered onto the playing field. MSU won the game convincingly and some fans viewed this as an omen, bringing the cow to every game from then on. After awhile, they dropped the cow and settled on the cowbell as a kind of good luck talisman. Because the folks from Oxford disparaged State as the "aggie school," there was something defiant in the choice of the cowbell symbol, which MSU fans adopted with relish. The cowbell flourished during the 1950s and 1960s—throughout long droughts in Bulldogs fortune. The addition of a handle permitted fans to really ring that thing and make some

---

PROFILE

Mississippi State University
Mississippi State, Miss.
Founded: 1878
Enrollment: 12,495
Colors: Maroon and White
Nickname: Bulldogs
Stadium: Davis Wade Stadium at Scott Field
    Opened in 1914
    Prescription Athletic Turf; 55,082 capacity
First football game: 1895
All-time record: 484–479–40 (.502)
Bowl record: 6–6
Southeastern Conference championships:
1 (outright)
First-round NFL draftees: 8
Website: www.mstateathletics.com

THE BEST OF TIMES

In the first three years of the Allyn McKeen era (1939-1941), MSU went 26–3–2, won its only SEC title and at one point fashioned a 21-game unbeaten streak.

THE WORST OF TIMES

From 1982 to 1990, the Bulldogs posted just one winning record (6–5 in 1986) and made no bowl trips.

CONFERENCE

After 12 years in the Southern Conference, Mississippi State became a charter member of the SEC in December 1932.

DISTINGUISHED ALUMNI

Rafael Palmeiro; John Grisham; Jerry Clower, comedian; Bailey Howell, Hall of Fame basketball player; G.V. "Sonny" Montgomery, U.S. Congressman; John Stennis, U.S. senator

FIGHT SONG

HAIL STATE!
Hail dear 'ole State!
Fight for that victory today.
Hit that line and tote that ball,
Cross the goal before you fall!
And then we'll yell, yell, yell, yell!
For dear 'ole State we'll yell like H-E-L-L!
Fight for Mis-sis-sip-pi State,
Win that game today.

> ## Life *magazine and 2,500 mourners attended Bully I's funeral in 1939 after he was hit by a bus.*

noise. But the practice proved too distracting for the SEC, which imposed a ban on artificial noisemakers at conference football and basketball games in 1974. The rule, however, does not apply to nonconference games. Ring away.

BEST PLAYER linebacker Johnie Cooks led MSU to its first-ever back-to-back bowl appearances and was SEC Defensive Player of the Year in 1981. He also earned the defensive MVP in that year's Hall of Fame Bowl. In his 45 games at MSU, Cooks made 392 tackles and went on to a 10-year NFL career with the Colts, Giants and Browns. Cooks was inducted into the Mississippi Sports Hall of Fame in 2004.

BEST COACH On the advice of Tennessee's Robert Neyland, MSU hired a young assistant coach named Allyn McKeen in 1939. In 1940 McKeen's squad went 10–0–1, which remains MSU's only undefeated season. McKeen's 1941 Bulldogs won the SEC title with an 8–1–1 overall record and a 4–0–1 conference mark. That 1941 team played the kind of tough defense one would expect from a Neyland protégé, shutting out Florida, Alabama, LSU and Mississippi—the last three on the road. McKeen coached

the Bulldogs until 1948, when he was fired after losing to Mississippi in consecutive seasons. Still, his winning percentage of .764 (65–19–3) is the best of any MSU coach, a group that includes, among others, Murray Warmath, Darrell Royal and Jackie Sherrill.

BEST TEAM McKeen picked the 1940 squad, which featured a defense anchored by All-America end Buddy Elrod. The only blemish—if it could be called that—was an early-season tie in Birmingham with Auburn, after which the Bulldogs ran the table in such dominant fashion that the AP crowned MSU "undisputed king of football in the Deep South." The team finished the season ranked No. 9 by the AP and beat Georgetown 14-7 in the Orange Bowl on New Year's Day, 1941, for the first bowl victory in school history.

STORYBOOK SEASON The 1998 Bulldogs, recovering from the effects of NCAA penalties for recruiting violations, went on a late-season run that included wins over Alabama, Arkansas and Mississippi to win the SEC Western Division— their first SEC championship of any kind since 1941. In the conference title game, the Bulldogs led Tennessee 14-10 in the

RECORDS

RUSHING YARDS

	GAME
237	James Johnson vs. Alabama, Nov. 14, 1998 (36 att.)

	SEASON
1,383	James Johnson, 1998 (236 att.)

	CAREER
2,820	Walter Packer, 1973-76 (483 att.)

PASSING YARDS

	GAME
466	Derrick Taite vs. Tulane, Oct. 22, 1994 (21 of 30)

	SEASON
2,422	Dave Marler, 1978 (163 of 287)

	CAREER
6,336	Wayne Madkin, 1998-2001 (462 of 887)

RECEIVING YARDS

	GAME
215	David Smith vs. Texas Tech, Oct. 17, 1970 (12 rec.)

	SEASON
1,035	Mardye McDole, 1978 (48 rec.)

	CAREER
2,214	Mardye McDole, 1977-80 (116 rec.)

POINTS

	GAME
42	Harry McArthur vs. Cumberland, Oct. 10, 1914 (7 TDs)

	SEASON
120	Jackie Parker, 1952 (16 TDs, 24 PATs)

	CAREER
218	Brian Hazelwood, 1995-98 (43 FGs, 89 PATs)

CONSENSUS ALL-AMERICANS

1974	Jimmy Webb, DL
2000	Fred Smoot, DB

fourth quarter before the eventual national champion Vols pulled it out 24-14. Mississippi State then played Texas in the Cotton Bowl, the first time in nearly 60 years that the Bulldogs went to a New Year's Day bowl.

BIGGEST GAME Rebuilding and recovering from a scandal that resulted in forfeits of all but two Bulldog victories from 1975 to 1977, MSU hired Emory Bellard in 1979 to turn things around. Bellard brought the wishbone formation, which he was credited with inventing, from Texas A&M, and after a rough first season things began to look up. The Bulldogs stood at 6–2 on Nov. 1, 1980, when defending national champion Alabama came to Jackson riding a 28-game winning streak. Defenders Johnie Cooks and Glen Collins shut down the Bama offense, and QB John Bond did enough with the modified formation Bellard called the wingbone to give MSU a 6-3 lead well into the fourth quarter. And a Bulldog goal-line stand in the final minute preserved the score. Billy Jackson, a freshman defensive end, recovered a fumble by Alabama's Don Jacobs with six seconds left and the Tide at the Bulldogs' 3-yard line. The victory was MSU's first over Alabama since 1957.

BIGGEST UPSET MSU was not considered a first-class football power in the South, much less the nation, on the last day of October in 1935, when the Maroons (as they were then known) faced powerful Army at West Point, where MSU coach Major Ralph Sasse had previously served. These were the days when eastern schools like Army dominated college football. But the Maroons hung on and hung around, and in the final minute of the game trailed Army just 7-6. Then quarterback Pee Wee Armstrong threw a 65-yard touchdown pass to Fred Waters to shock the sporting world and put MSU on the football map with the 13-7 win over the mighty Cadets.

HEARTBREAKER The 1997 game against Ole Miss would determine which of the schools would make it to a bowl game. MSU held a 14-7 lead with time winding down. The Rebels drove the field to score a touchdown, and then converted a two-point attempt for a one-point win. For many Bulldogs fans, the bitter taste from that loss still lingers.

STADIUM Davis Wade Stadium at Scott Field is the second oldest on-campus stadium in Division I-A, dating back to 1914 when it was called, merely, New Athletic Field. In 1920, the name was changed to Scott Field, in honor of Don

Magruder Scott, an Olympic sprinter and one of Mississippi State's first football stars. Improvements in 1928, 1936 and 1948 raised capacity to 35,000. The most recent expansion, begun in 2000, increased seating to 55,082, including some 50 skyboxes and 1,700 club-level seats. The bill for this project came in at more than $30 million and was made possible, in large part, through the generosity of the late Floyd Davis Wade Sr. of Meridian, an alumnus and booster for whom the stadium is named.

RIVAL Ole Miss, of course. Passions ran so high in the early days of the rivalry that, after a brawl in 1927, the student bodies got together and came up with a trophy for the winner. This was done, of course, in the name of sportsmanship. The trophy is in the shape of an old-time football and looks, remarkably, like an egg. Hence the Golden Egg was hatched.

NICKNAME MSU's teams were known as the Aggies until 1932, when the school's name changed from Mississippi A&M to Mississippi State College. Then the nickname became the Maroons, a reference to the school's maroon and white uniforms. The official nickname changed to Bulldogs in 1961 when the school attained university status.

MASCOT Bully XIX represents Mississippi State at football games. Unlike his predecessors, who roamed the Starkville campus at will or bedded down in frat houses, XIX is housed at the School of Veterinary Medicine. The original Bully debuted shortly after MSU's 1935 upset of Army. His tenure came to a sad end on Nov. 19, 1939, when he was killed by a campus school bus. Three days later, 2,500 mourners paid their final respects to Bully I, who was buried under the bench at the 50-yard line of Scott Field. *Life* magazine covered the funeral.

UNIFORMS Before Mississippi A&M's 1895 game at Southwestern Baptist, W.M. Mathews, the Aggie coach/captain/QB, chose maroon and white as the team's colors. Since then, nobody has seen reason for change, though from time to time some gray has been added to the scheme. In 1938 coach Spike Nelson decked the team in gold uniforms, but neither the gold, nor Nelson, returned in 1939, the first year, ironically, of the golden age of MSU football.

QUOTE "There ain't but one color that matters here, and that color is maroon." —Sylvester Croom, first African-American head coach in the SEC

MISSISSIPPI STATE ANNUAL STATISTICAL LEADERS

YR	RUSHING	YDS	ATT	AVG	PASSING	ATT	CMP	PCT	YDS	RECEIVING	REC	YDS	AVG
1946	Tom McWilliams	347	77	4.5	Billy Murphy	60	21	.35	279	Kermit Davis	11	158	14.4
1947	Tom McWilliams	625	137	4.6	Tom McWilliams	61	30	.49	360	Harper Davis	15	229	15.3
1948	Tom McWilliams	436	121	3.6	Tom McWilliams	74	41	.55	412	Harper Davis	12	94	7.8
1949	Wally Beech	403	90	4.5	Don Robinson	105	29	.28	303	Murray Alexander	14	131	9.4
1950	Wally Beech	529	111	4.8	Frank Branch	40	24	.60	313	Steve Clark	14	150	10.7
1951	Wally Beech	421	98	4.3	Frank Branch	44	20	.45	198	John Katusa	10	73	7.3
1952	Joe Fortunato	779	128	6.1	Jackie Parker	97	45	.46	811	Norm Duplain	14	265	18.9
1953	Charles Evans	549	109	5.0	Jackie Parker	69	41	.59	603	Art Davis	11	150	13.6
1954	Art Davis	670	132	5.1	Bobby Collins	45	20	.44	337	Levaine Hollingshead	11	180	16.4
1955	Jim Harness	497	90	5.5	Bill Stanton	57	27	.47	554	Ron Bennett	12	248	20.7
1956	Billy Stacy	613	138	4.4	Bill Stacy	71	32	.45	464	Ron Bennett	15	227	15.1
1957	Molly Halbert	386	76	5.1	Bill Stacy	41	13	.32	248	Gil Peterson	7	95	13.6
1958	Jack Batte	292	62	4.7	Bill Stacy	70	32	.46	388	P.L. Blake	6	85	14.2
1959	Billy Hill	257	63	4.1	John Correro	44	21	.48	251	Lee Welch	14	127	9.1
1960	Mackie Weaver	354	88	4.0	Charlie Furlow	114	63	.55	599	Lee Welch	12	98	8.2
1961	Billy Hill	337	85	4.0	Charlie Furlow	65	36	.55	389	Johnny Baker	22	323	14.7
1962	Ode Burrell	310	71	4.4	Charlie Furlow	111	62	.56	744	Ode Burrell	24	204	8.5
1963	Hoyle Granger	481	113	4.3	Sonny Fisher	74	36	.49	353	Tommy Inman	12	179	14.9
1964	Hoyle Granger	604	129	4.7	Ashby Cook	61	35	.57	426	Tommy Inman	21	338	16.1
1965	Hoyle Granger	449	108	4.2	Ashby Cook	162	78	.48	1,032	Don Saget	24	373	15.5
1966	Andy Rhoades	295	75	3.9	Don Saget	166	69	.42	753	Marcus Rhoden	31	365	11.8
1967	Tommy Pharr	326	136	2.4	Tommy Pharr	71	26	.37	279	Johnny Woitt	8	82	10.3
1968	Tommy Pharr	239	141	1.7	Tommy Pharr	319	173	.54	1,838	Sammy Milner	64	909	14.2
1969	Steve Whaley	275	89	3.1	Tommy Pharr	258	140	.54	1,603	Sammy Milner	64	745	11.6
1970	Lewis Grubbs	644	155	4.2	Joe Reed	294	138	.47	1,616	David Smith	74	987	13.3
1971	Lewis Grubbs	419	134	3.1	Hal Chealander	155	66	.43	937	Eric Hoggatt	28	365	13.0
1972	Melvin Barkum	522	132	4.0	Rockey Felker	161	74	.46	992	Bill Buckley	47	776	16.5
1973	Wayne Jones	1,193	212	5.6	Rockey Felker	106	60	.57	782	Bill Buckley	41	661	16.1
1974	Walter Packer	994	157	6.3	Rockey Felker	155	73	.47	1,147	Howard Lewis	21	330	15.7
1975	Walter Packer	1,012	180	5.6	Bruce Threadgill	123	43	.35	575	Gavin Rees	18	292	16.2
1976	Dennis Johnson	859	152	5.7	Bruce Threadgill	89	45	.51	807	Robert Chatman	15	277	18.5
1977	Dennis Johnson	529	114	4.6	Bruce Threadgill	219	91	.42	1,317	Mardye McDole	29	510	17.6
1978	James Jones	687	130	5.3	Dave Marler	287	163	.57	2,422	Mardye McDole	48	1,035	21.6
1979	Fred Collins	591	128	4.6	Tony Black	62	23	.37	363	Mardye McDole	20	380	19.0
1980	Michael Haddix	724	133	5.4	John Bond	133	59	.44	849	Mardye McDole	19	289	15.2
1981	Michael Haddix	622	110	5.7	John Bond	144	65	.45	875	Glen Young	19	263	13.8
1982	Michael Haddix	813	122	6.7	John Bond	183	91	.50	1,591	Danny Knight	37	924	25.0
1983	John Bond	612	164	3.7	John Bond	205	92	.45	1,306	Danny Knight	34	671	19.7
1984	Don Smith	545	128	4.3	Don Smith	176	75	.43	1,236	Mikel Williams	23	177	7.7
1985	Don Smith	554	190	2.9	Don Smith	312	143	.46	2,332	Jeff Patton	34	416	12.2
1986	Don Smith	740	159	4.7	Don Smith	244	120	.49	1,609	Fred Hadley	28	529	18.9
1987	Hank Phillips	848	184	4.6	Mike Davis	129	60	.47	779	Fred Hadley	28	499	17.8
1988	Jesse Anderson	468	102	4.6	Tony Shell	335	153	.46	1,884	Fred Hadley	29	477	16.4
1989	Kenny Roberts	511	108	4.7	Tony Shell	87	45	.52	499	Jesse Anderson	21	230	11.0
1990	Kenny Roberts	523	93	5.6	Tony Shell	293	151	.52	1,909	Jerry Bouldin	32	447	14.0
1991	Sleepy Robinson	543	154	3.5	Sleepy Robinson	141	77	.55	1,167	Willie Harris	24	529	22.0
1992	Kenny Roberts	597	106	5.6	Greg Plump	129	54	.42	863	Willie Harris	35	574	16.4
1993	Michael Davis	883	205	4.3	Todd Jordan	294	131	.45	1,935	Chris Jones	24	541	22.5
1994	Michael Davis	929	196	4.7	Derrick Taite	220	110	.50	1,806	Eric Moulds	39	845	21.7
1995	Keffer McGee	1,072	235	4.6	Derrick Taite	309	165	.53	2,241	Eric Moulds	62	779	12.6
1996	Robert Isaac	527	117	4.5	Derrick Taite	171	75	.44	1,009	Lamont Woodberry	27	305	11.3
1997	James Johnson	1,069	217	4.9	Matt Wyatt	201	92	.46	1,369	Lamont Woodberry	24	342	14.3
1998	James Johnson	1,383	236	5.9	Wayne Madkin	199	96	.48	1,532	Kevin Prentiss	38	681	17.9
1999	Dontae Walker	384	76	5.1	Wayne Madkin	257	135	.53	1,884	Kelvin Lowe	43	834	19.4
2000	Dicenzo Miller	1,005	160	6.3	Wayne Madkin	246	138	.56	1,908	Terrell Grindle	31	436	14.1
2001	Dicenzo Miller	676	132	5.1	Kevin Fant	170	94	.55	1,352	Justin Jenkins	42	661	15.7
2002	Justin Griffith	471	91	5.2	Kevin Fant	311	163	.52	1,918	Ray Ray Bivines	40	511	12.8
2003	Nick Turner	696	123	5.7	Kevin Fant	351	186	.53	2,151	Justin Jenkins	62	880	14.2
2004	Jerious Norwood	1,050	195	5.4	Omarr Conner	206	107	.52	1,224	Will Prosser	24	328	13.7

Receiving leaders by receptions
The NCAA began including postseason stats in 2002

THE SCHOOLS

MISSISSIPPI STATE ALL-TIME SCORES

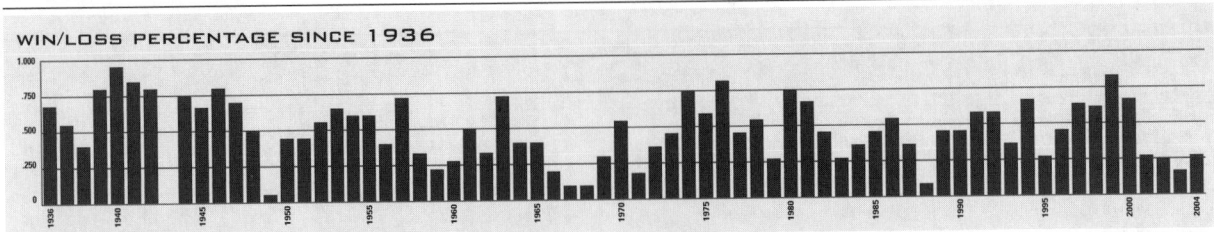

WIN/LOSS PERCENTAGE SINCE 1936

W.M. MATTHEWS
1895 (.000)   0-2

1895   0-2-0
N16	at Union	0	21
D7	at Memphis AC	0	16

J.B. HILDEBRAND
1896 (.000)   0-4

1896   0-4-0
O10	Union	0	8
N14	at Alabama	a	20
N20	at LSU	0	52
N21	at New Orleans AC	0	55

1897-1900
NO TEAM

L.B. HARVEY
1901 (.500)   2-2-1

1901   2-2-1
O26	=	at Christian Brothers	0	0
O28	●	Mississippi	17	0
N2		at Meridian AC	11	5
N9		at Tulane	6	24
N26		at Alabama	0	45

L. GWINN
1902 (.250)   1-4-1

1902   1-4-1
O17	Cumberland	6	15
O25	Mississippi	0	21
N1	at Tulane	11	11
N8	at Alabama	0	27
N15 ●	at Samford	26	0
N27	LSU	0	6

DAN MARTIN
1903-06 (.479)   10-11-3

1903   3-0-2
O16	●	Alabama ColMs	11	0
O24	=	at Meridian AC	43	0
N7		LSU	11	0
N14	=	at Mississippi	6	6
D5		at Tulane	0	0

1904   2-5-0
O1	Vanderbilt ColMs	0	61
O15	Alabama ColMs	0	6
O22	Mississippi ColMs	5	17
O29	at Tulane	0	10
N11 ●	Tenn. Med. Coll.	59	0
N18	Cumberland	5	27
N25 ●	Louisiana Tech	32	5

1905   3-4-0
O14	at Alabama	0	34
O20 ●	at Marion Inst.	38	0
O27	Auburn JaM	0	18
N11 ●	Samford	44	0
N18	Cumberland	5	27
N30 ●	Mississippi JaM	11	0
D2	at LSU	0	15

1906   2-2-1
S29 ●	Samford	30	0
O13 ●	Marion Inst.	62	0
O27	LSU ColMs	0	0
N3	Alabama	4	16
N29 ●	Mississippi JaM	5	29

FRED FURMAN
1907-08 (.563)   9-7

1907   6-3-0
O2	●	Southwestern	7	0
O10		at Sewanee	0	38
O12	●	at Samford	12	5
O19	●	Union	80	0
O24	●	Mercer ColMs	75	0
O30	●	Drury Coll.	6	0
N9		at LSU	11	23
N16		Tennessee Mem	4	11
N28	●	Mississippi JaM	15	0

1908   3-4-0
O10	●	Louisiana Tech	47	0
O17		at Georgia Tech	0	23
O23	●	La. Lafayette ColMs	5	6
O31	●	Transylvania, Ky	12	5
N7		at LSU	0	50
N14		at Tulane	0	23
N26	●	Mississippi JaM	44	6

W.D. CHADWICK
1909-13 (.698)   29-12-2

1909   5-4-0
O2	●	B'ham Southern	21	0
O9	●	Cumberland	34	6
O16		at LSU	0	15
O22	●	Southwestern ColMs	31	0
O30		at Tulane	0	2
N2	●	Union ColMs	25	0
N8		at Samford	0	6
N13	●	U.T. Chattanooga	37	0
N25	●	Mississippi JaM	5	9

1910   7-2-0
O1	●	Mississippi Coll.	24	0
O8		at Auburn	0	6
O15	●	Memphis U. Sch.	6	0
O21	●	LSU ColMs	3	0
O31	●	Tennessee	48	0
N5		at Tulane	10	0
N12	●	B'ham Southern	46	0
N18	●	Samford	82	0
N24	●	Mississippi JaM	0	30

1911   7-2-1
S29	●	Mississippi Coll.	27	6
O7	●	Southwestern	30	0
O14	●	Samford	48	0
O21	=	Alabama ColMs	6	6
O28	●	Auburn Birm	5	11
N3	●	B'ham Southern	62	0
N12	●	LSU Gul	6	0
N20	●	Tulane	4	5
N30	●	Mississippi JaM	6	0
J1	●	Havana AC Hav	12	0

1912   4-3-0
O4	●	Mississippi Coll.	19	0
O12	●	Tenn. Med. Coll.	32	0
O18	●	Alabama Abe	7	0
O26	●	Auburn Birm	0	7
N2	●	at LSU	7	0
N9		at Tulane	24	27
N16		Texas A&M Hou	7	41

1913   6-1-1
O4	●	Samford	66	0
O10	●	Mississippi Coll.	1	0 f
O17	●	Transylvania, Ky ColMs	31	0
O25	●	Auburn Birm	0	34
N1	●	at Texas A&M	6	0
N8	●	Tulane	32	0
N15	=	LSU	0	0
N27	●	Alabama Birm	7	0

E.C. HAYES
1914-16 (.640)   15-8-2

1914   6-2-0
O3	●	Marion Inst.	54	0
O10	●	Cumberland	77	0
O17		at Kentucky	13	19
O24		Auburn Birm	0	19
O31	●	at Georgia	9	0
N7	●	Mercer	66	0
N14	●	Tulane JaM	61	0
N26	●	Alabama Birm	9	0

1915   5-2-1
O2	●	Mississippi Coll. JaM	12	0
O9	=	Transylvania, Ky	0	0
O16	●	Kentucky	12	0
O23	●	Auburn Birm	0	26
O30		at LSU	0	10
N6	●	Mississippi Tup	65	0
N13	●	Tennessee	14	0
N25	●	Texas A&M Dal	7	0

1916   4-4-1
O6	●	Mississippi Coll. Abe	6	13
O14		at U.T. Chattanooga	33	0
O21	●	Transylvania, Ky	13	0
O28	●	Auburn Birm	3	7
N3	●	Mississippi Tup	36	0
N11	●	LSU	3	13
N18		at Kentucky	3	13
N20	=	at Maryville	7	7
N30	●	Arkansas Mem	20	7

SID ROBINSON
1917-19 (.750)   15-5

1917   6-1-0
O5	●	Marion Inst.	18	6
O13	●	Mississippi Coll.	68	0
O27	●	Auburn Birm	6	13
N3	●	Mississippi Tup	41	14
N10	●	Kentucky	14	0
N17		at LSU	9	0
N29	●	Haskell Mem	7	6

1918   3-2-0
N2	●	Payne Field	6	7
N9	●	Camp Shelby	12	0
N16		Park Field	0	6
N28	●	Mississippi	34	0
D7	●	at Mississippi	13	0

1919   6-2-0
O4	●	Spring Hill	12	6
O11	●	Mississippi Coll.	56	7
O18	●	at Tennessee	6	0
O25	●	Samford	39	0
N1	●	LSU	6	0
N8	●	Mississippi Clar	33	0
N15	●	Auburn Birm	0	7
N27	●	Alabama Birm	6	14

FRED HOLTKAMP
1920-21 (.559)   9-7-1

1920   5-3-0
O2	●	Mississippi Coll.	27	0
O9		at Indiana	0	24
O16	●	So. Military Acad.	33	0
O23		at LSU	12	7
O30	●	Tennessee	13	7
N6	●	Mississippi Grn	20	0
N13		at Tulane	0	6
N25	●	Alabama Birm	7	24

1921-1932
SOUTHERN

1921   4-4-1 (0-1-1)
O1	●	B'ham Southern	20	7
O8	●	Ouachita	21	6
O15	●	Mississippi Coll. JaM	14	13
O22		at Tulane	0	7
O29	●	Mississippi Grn	21	0
N5		Tennessee Mem	7	14
N11		at Texas	7	54
N24	=	Alabama Birm	7	7
D3		LSU	14	17

C.R. "DUDY" NOBLE
1922 (.444)   3-4-2

1922   3-4-2 (2-3-0)
O7	●	B'ham Southern	14	0
O14	=	Samford	0	0
O21	●	Mississippi JaM	19	13
O28		at Tulane	0	26
N4	=	Ouachita	7	7
N11	●	Tennessee Mem	3	31
N18	●	at LSU	7	0
N25	●	Drake	6	48
N30	●	Alabama Birm	0	59

EARL ABLE
1923-24 (.611)   10-6-2

1923   5-2-2 (2-1-2)
O6	●	Millsaps	28	6
O13	●	Ouachita	6	0
O20	●	Mississippi JaM	13	6
O27	●	Tennessee Mem	3	7
N3	=	at Vanderbilt	0	0
N10	●	Union	6	0
N17		at Illinois	0	27
N24	=	Florida JacF	13	13
D1	●	LSU	14	7

1924   5-4-0 (3-2-0)
O4	●	Millsaps	28	6
O11	●	Ouachita	0	12
O18	●	Mississippi JaM	20	0
O25	●	Tennessee Mem	7	2
N1	●	at Tulane	14	6
N8	●	at Vanderbilt	0	18
N15	●	Mississippi Coll.	7	6
N22	●	Florida Mont	0	27
N27		at Washington, Mo.	6	12

BERNIE BIERMAN
1925-26 (.500)   8-8-1

1925   3-4-1 (1-4-0)
O3	●	Millsaps	34	0
O10	=	Ouachita	3	3
O17		at Tulane	3	25
O24	●	Mississippi JaM	6	0
O31		at Alabama	0	6
N7	●	Mississippi Coll.	46	0
N14		at Tennessee	9	14
N21		Florida Tam	0	12

1926   5-4-0 (2-3-0)
S25	●	at B'ham Southern	19	7
O2	●	Mississippi Coll.	41	0
O9		Alabama Mer	7	26
O16	●	Millsaps	34	0
O23	●	LSU JaM	7	6
O30		Tennessee	0	33
N6	●	at Tulane	14	0
N13		at Indiana	6	19
N25		Mississippi	6	7

J.W. HANCOCK — 1927-29 (.417) · 8-12-4

1927 — 5-3-0 (2-3-0)

Date	Opponent		
O1 •	B'ham Southern	27	0
O8 •	Louisiana Tech	14	0
O15 •	at Tulane	13	6
O22	LSU JAM	7	9
O29	at Alabama	7	13
N12 •	Auburn BIRM	7	0
N18 •	Millsaps	6	0
N24	at Mississippi	12	20

1928 — 2-4-2 (1-4-0)

Date	Opponent		
S29 •	Ouachita	20	6
O6	Tulane JAM	6	51
O13	Alabama	0	46
O20	LSU JAM	0	31
N3 =	at Michigan State	6	6
N10	Centenary	6	6
N17	Auburn BIRM	13	0
N29	Mississippi	19	20

1929 — 1-5-2 (0-3-1)

Date	Opponent		
S27	Henderson-Brown	0	7
O5	at Georgia Tech	13	27
O12	at Tulane	0	34
O19	LSU JAM	6	31
N2 •	Mississippi Coll.	6	0
N9	Michigan State JAM	19	33
N16 =	Millsaps	0	0
N28	at Mississippi	7	7

CHRIS CAGLE — 1930 (.222) · 2-7

1930 — 2-7-0 (2-3-0)

Date	Opponent		
S27	Southwestern	0	14
O4	Mississippi Coll. JAM	12	13
O11	Millsaps	13	19
O18 •	LSU JAM	8	6
O25	at North Carolina St.	0	14
N1	at Tulane	0	53
N8	Henderson St.	7	25
N15 •	Auburn BIRM	7	6
N27	Mississippi	0	20

RAY DAUBER — 1931-32 (.313) · 5-11

1931 — 2-6-0 (0-5-0)

Date	Opponent		
S26	at Millsaps	10	7
O3	Mississippi Coll.	2	6
O10	Alabama MER	0	53
O17	at LSU	0	31
O31	at Tulane	7	59
N7	North Carolina St.		
N14 •	Southwestern	14	0
N26	at Mississippi	14	25

1932 — 3-5-0 (0-4-0)

Date	Opponent		
O1	Alabama MONT	0	53
O8	Mississippi Coll. JAM	18	7
O15	LSU MOR	0	24
O22 •	Millsaps	9	8
O27	at Indiana	0	19
N5	at Tennessee	0	31
N12 •	Southwestern	6	0
N24	Mississippi	0	13

1933-Present · SEC

ROSS McKECHNIE — 1933-34 (.375) · 7-12-1

1933 — 3-6-1 (1-5-1)

Date	Opponent		
S30	Millsaps	12	0
O7	at Tennessee	0	20
O14	at Alabama	0	18
O21 =	at Vanderbilt	7	7
O27	at Southwestern	0	6
N4 •	Mississippi Coll.	18	0
N11	at Tulane	0	33
N18 •	Sewanee	26	13
N25	LSU MOR	6	21
D2	at Mississippi	0	31

1934 — 4-6-0 (0-5-0)

Date	Opponent		
S21 •	at Samford	13	7
S29	at Vanderbilt	0	7
O5	Millsaps	6	7
O13 •	at Alabama	0	41
O20 •	at Southwestern	21	6
O26 •	Mississippi Coll.	13	6
N3	at LSU	3	25
N10	at Tennessee	0	14
N17 •	at Loyola-New Orleans	20	6
D1	Mississippi	3	7

RALPH SASSE — 1935-37 (.656) · 20-10-2

1935 — 8-3-0 (2-3-0)

Date	Opponent		
S20 •	Samford	19	6
S28	at Vanderbilt	9	14
O4 •	Millsaps	45	0
O12 •	at Alabama	20	7
O18 •	at Loyola-New Orleans	6	0
O26 •	at Xavier	7	0
N2 •	at Army	13	7
N9	at LSU	13	28
N15 •	at Southern Miss	27	0
N23 •	Sewanee	25	0
N30 •	at Mississippi	6	14

1936 — 7-3-1 (3-2-0)

Date	Opponent		
S26 •	Millsaps	20	0
O3 •	Samford	35	0
O10	at Alabama	0	7
O17 •	Loyola-New Orleans MER	32	0
O24 =	TCU DAL	0	0
O31 •	Sewanee JAM	68	0
N7	at LSU	0	12
N21 •	Mississippi	26	6
N28 •	Mercer	32	0
D5 •	at Florida	7	0

ORANGE BOWL

Date	Opponent		
J1	Duquesne	12	13

1937 — 5-4-1 (3-2-0)

Date	Opponent		
S25 •	Delta St.	39	0
O2 •	Samford	38	0
O9	Texas A&M TYL	0	14
O16 •	Auburn BIRM	7	33
O23 •	Florida	14	13
O30 =	at Centenary	0	0
N6	at LSU	0	41
N12 •	Sewanee	12	0
N25 •	at Mississippi	9	7
D4	Duquesne	0	9

SPIKE NELSON — 1938 (.400) · 4-6

1938 — 4-6-0 (1-4-0)

Date	Opponent		
S25 •	Samford	19	0
O1	Florida	22	0
O8 •	Louisiana Tech	48	0
O14 •	Auburn MONT	6	20
O21 •	at Duquesne	12	7
O29	at Tulane	0	27
N5	at LSU	7	32
N12	Centenary MER	0	19
N19	at Southwestern	3	7
N26	Mississippi	6	19

ALLYN McKEEN — 1939-48 (.764) · 65-19-3

1939 — 8-2-0 (3-2-0)

Date	Opponent		
S23 •	Samford	45	0
S30 •	Arkansas MEM	19	0
O7 •	at Florida	14	0
O14 •	Auburn BIRM	0	7
O21 •	Southwestern	37	0
O28	at Alabama	0	7
N4 •	B'ham Southern	28	0
N11 •	at LSU	15	12
N18 •	Millsaps	40	0
N25 •	at Mississippi	18	6

1940 — 10-0-1 (4-0-1)

Date	Opponent		
S28 •	at Florida	27	7
O5 •	La. Lafayette	20	0
O12 =	Auburn BIRM	7	7
O19 •	Samford	40	7
O26 •	at North Carolina St.	26	10
N2 •	at Southwestern	13	0
N9 •	at LSU	22	7
N16 •	Millsaps	46	13
N23 •	Mississippi	19	0
N30 •	at Alabama	13	0

ORANGE BOWL

Date	Opponent		
J1 •	Georgetown	14	7

1941 — 8-1-1 (4-0-1)

Date	Opponent		
S27	Florida	6	0
O4 •	at Alabama	14	0
O11 =	at LSU	0	0
O25 •	Union	56	7
N1 •	at Southwestern	20	6
N8 •	Auburn BIRM	14	7
N15 •	at Duquesne	0	16
N22 •	Millsaps	49	6
N29 •	at Mississippi	6	0
D6 •	at San Francisco	26	13

1942 — 8-2-0 (5-2-0)

Date	Opponent		
S26 •	Union	35	2
O3	at Alabama	6	21
O10	at LSU	6	16
O17 •	at Vanderbilt	33	0
O24 •	at Florida	26	12
O31 •	Auburn BIRM	6	0
N7	at Tulane	7	0
N14	Duquesne	28	6
N28	Mississippi	34	13
D5 •	San Francisco MEM	19	7

1943

NO TEAM WWII

1944 — 6-2-0 (3-2-0)

Date	Opponent		
S30 •	Jackson AAB	41	0
O7 •	Millsaps	56	0
O14 •	Arkansas State	49	20
O21	at LSU	13	6
N4 •	Kentucky MEM	26	0
N11 •	Auburn BIRM	26	21
N18	at Alabama	0	19
N25	at Mississippi	8	13

1945 — 6-3-0 (2-3-0)

Date	Opponent		
S29 •	La. Lafayette	31	0
O6 •	Auburn BIRM	20	0
O13 •	Detroit MEM	41	6
O20 •	Maxwell	16	6
N3	at Tulane	13	14
N10	at LSU	27	20
N17 •	Northwestern St.	54	0
N24	Mississippi	6	7
D1	at Alabama	13	55

1946 — 8-2-0 (3-2-0)

Date	Opponent		
S28 •	U.T. Chattanooga	41	7
O5	at LSU	6	13
O12 •	at Michigan State	6	0
O19 •	San Francisco MEM	48	20
O26 •	at Tulane	14	7
N2 •	Murray St.	69	0
N9 •	Auburn BIRM	33	0
N16 •	Northwestern St.	27	0
N23 •	at Mississippi	20	0
N30	at Alabama	7	24

1947 — 7-3-0 (2-2-0)

Date	Opponent		
S26 •	U.T. Chattanooga	19	0
O4	at Michigan State	0	7
O11 •	at San Francisco	21	14
O18 •	Duquesne	34	0
O25 •	Hardin-Simmons	27	7
N1 •	at Tulane	20	0
N8 •	Auburn BIRM	14	0
N15	at LSU	6	21
N22 •	Southern Miss	14	7
N29	Mississippi	14	33

1948 — 4-4-1 (3-3-0)

Date	Opponent		
S25	at Tennessee	21	6
O2 =	Baylor MEM	7	7
O9	Clemson	7	21
O16 •	Cincinnati	27	0
O23	Alabama	7	10
O30	at Tulane	0	9
N6 •	Auburn BIRM	20	0
N13 •	at LSU	7	0
N27	at Mississippi	7	34

SLICK MORTON — 1949-51 (.315) · 8-18-1

1949 — 0-8-1 (0-6-0)

Date	Opponent		
S24	at Tennessee	0	10
O1	Baylor	6	14
O8 =	at Clemson	7	7
O15	at Cincinnati	0	19
O22	at Alabama	6	35
O29	at Tulane	6	54
N5	at Auburn	6	25
N12	at LSU	7	34
N26	Mississippi	0	26

1950 — 4-5-0 (3-4-0)

Date	Opponent		
S23 •	Arkansas State	67	0
S30	Tennessee	7	0
O7	Baylor SHRE	7	14
O14	at Georgia	0	27
O28	at Alabama	7	14
N4 •	Auburn	27	0
N11	Kentucky	21	48
N18 •	at LSU	13	7
D2	at Mississippi	20	27

1951 — 4-5-0 (2-5-0)

Date	Opponent		
S22 •	Arkansas State	32	0
S29	at Tennessee	0	14
O6 •	Georgia	6	0
O13	at Kentucky	0	27
O27	Alabama	0	7
N3	at Tulane	10	7
N10 •	at Memphis	27	20
N17	at LSU	0	3
D1	Mississippi	7	49

MURRAY WARMATH — 1952-53 (.605) · 10-6-3

1952 — 5-4-0 (3-4-0)

Date	Opponent		
S27	Tennessee MEM	7	14
O4 •	Arkansas State	41	14
O11 •	North Texas	14	0
O18	Kentucky	27	14
O25	at Alabama	19	42
N1	at Tulane	21	34
N8	at Auburn	49	4
N15 •	at LSU	33	14
N29	at Mississippi	14	20

1953 — 5-2-3 (3-1-3)

Date	Opponent		
S19 •	at Memphis	34	6
S26	at Tennessee	26	0
O3 •	North Texas	21	6
O10 =	Auburn	21	21
O17	at Kentucky	13	32
O24 =	at Alabama	7	7
O31	Texas Tech JAM	20	27
N7	at Tulane	21	0
N14 •	at LSU	26	13
N28	Mississippi	7	7

DARRELL ROYAL — 1954-55 (.600) · 12-8

1954 — 6-4-0 (3-3-0)

Date	Opponent		
S18 •	Memphis	27	7
S25	Tennessee MEM	7	19
O2 •	Arkansas State	46	13
O9 •	at Tulane	14	0
O15 •	at Miami, Fla.	13	27
O23 •	at Alabama	12	7
O30	at Florida	0	7
N6 •	North Texas	48	26
N13 •	at LSU	25	0
N27	at Mississippi	0	14

1955 — 6-4-0 (4-4-0)

Date	Opponent		
S17 •	at Florida	14	20
S24 •	at Tennessee	13	7
O1 •	Memphis	33	0
O8 •	Tulane	14	0
O15 •	at Kentucky	20	14
O22 •	at Alabama	26	7
O29 •	North Texas	20	7
N5	at Auburn	26	27
N12	at LSU	7	34
N26	Mississippi	0	26

WADE WALKER — 1956-61 (.411) · 22-32-2

1956 — 4-6-0 (2-5-0)

Date	Opponent		
S22	Florida	0	26
S29 •	at Houston	7	18
O6 •	at Georgia	19	7
O13 •	Trinity	18	6
O20 •	Arkansas State	19	9
O27	at Alabama	12	13
N3	at Tulane	14	20
N10 •	at Auburn	20	7
N17 •	at LSU	32	13
D1	at Mississippi	7	13

1957 — 6-2-1 (4-2-1)

Date	Opponent		
S28 •	Memphis	10	6
O5	at Tennessee	9	14
O12 •	Arkansas State	47	13
O19 •	at Florida	29	20
O26 •	at Alabama	25	13
N2 •	Tulane JAM	27	6
N9	Auburn BIRM	7	15
N16 •	at LSU	14	6
N30 =	Mississippi	7	7

1958 — 3-6-0 (1-6-0)

Date	Opponent		
S27 •	at Florida	14	7
O4	Tennessee MEM	8	13
O11 •	Memphis	28	6
O18 •	Arkansas State	38	0
O25	Alabama	7	9
N1	at Kentucky	12	33
N8	at Auburn	14	33
N15	LSU JAM	6	7
N29	at Mississippi	0	21

THE SCHOOLS

1959　2-7-0 (0-7-0)
S26	at Florida	13	14
O3	at Tennessee	6	22
O10 ●	Arkansas State	49	14
O17	Georgia ATL	0	15
O24 ●	Memphis	28	23
O31	at Alabama	0	10
N7	Auburn BIRM	0	31
N14	at LSU	0	27
N28	Mississippi	0	42

1960　2-6-1 (0-5-1)
S24	Houston	10	14
O1 =	Tennessee MEM	0	0
O8 ●	Arkansas State	29	9
O15	at Georgia	17	20
O22 ●	Memphis	21	0
O29	Alabama	0	7
N5	at Auburn	12	27
N12	at LSU	3	7
N26	at Mississippi	9	35

1961　5-5-0 (1-5-0)
S23 ●	Texas Tech JAM	6	0
S30	at Houston	10	7
O7	at Tennessee	3	17
O14 ●	Arkansas State	38	0
O21	Georgia ATL	7	10
O28 ●	at Memphis	23	16
N4	at Alabama	0	24
N11 ●	Auburn BIRM	11	10
N18	at LSU	6	14
D2	Mississippi	7	37

PAUL DAVIS
1962-66 (.420)　20-28-2

1962　3-6-0 (2-5-0)
S22	Florida JAM	9	19
O6 ●	Tennessee MEM	7	6
O12 ●	at Tulane	35	6
O20 ●	at Houston	9	3
O27	Memphis	7	28
N3	Alabama	0	20
N10	at Auburn	3	9
N17	LSU JAM	0	28
D1	at Mississippi	6	13

1963　7-2-2 (4-1-2)
S21 ●	Samford	43	0
S28 =	at Florida	9	9
O5 =	at Tennessee	7	0
O12 ●	Tulane JAM	31	10
O19 ●	Houston	20	0
O26	at Memphis	10	17
N2	at Alabama	19	20
N9 ●	Auburn JAM	13	10
N16 ●	LSU JAM	7	6
N30	Mississippi	10	10

LIBERTY BOWL
| D21 ● | North Carolina St. | 16 | 12 |

1964　4-6-0 (2-5-0)
S19	at Texas Tech	7	21
S26	Florida JAM	13	16
O3	Tennessee MEM	13	14
O10 ●	Tulane	17	6
O17 ●	Southern Miss	48	7
O24 ●	Houston	18	13
O31	Alabama JAM	6	23
N7	at Auburn	3	12
N14	at LSU	10	14
D5	at Mississippi	20	17

1965　4-6-0 (1-5-0)
S18 ●	at Houston	36	0
S25 =	at Florida	18	13
O2 ●	Tampa	48	7
O9 ●	Southern Miss	27	9
O16	at Memphis	13	33
O22	at Tulane	15	17
O30	Alabama JAM	7	10
N6	Auburn BIRM	18	25
N13	at LSU	20	37
N27	Mississippi	0	21

1966　2-8-0 (0-6-0)
S17	Georgia JAM	17	20
S24	at Florida	7	28
O1 ●	Richmond	20	0
O8 ●	Southern Miss	10	9
O15	at Houston	0	28
O22	at Florida State	0	10
O29	at Alabama	14	27
N5	Auburn JAM	0	13
N12	at LSU	7	17
N26	at Mississippi	0	24

CHARLEY SHIRA
1967-72 (.270)　16-45-2

1967　1-9-0 (0-6-0)
S23	at Georgia	0	30
S30	Florida JAM	7	24
O7	at Texas Tech	7	3
O14	Southern Miss	14	21
O21	Houston	6	43
O28	at Florida State	12	24
N4	at Alabama	0	13
N11	at Auburn	0	36
N18	at LSU	0	55
D2	Mississippi	3	10

1968　0-8-2 (0-4-2)
S21	Louisiana Tech	13	20
S28 ●	Auburn JAM	0	26
O5	at Florida	14	31
O12	Southern Miss	14	47
O19 = ‖	Texas Tech JAM	28	28
O26	at Tampa	17	24
N2	at Alabama	13	20
N9	Florida State	14	27
N16	at LSU	16	20
N30 =	at Mississippi	17	17

1969　3-7-0 (0-5-0)
S20 ●	Richmond	17	14
S27	Florida JAM	35	47
O4	at Houston	0	74
O11 ●	Southern Miss	34	20
O18 ●	at Texas Tech	30	26
O25	at Florida State	17	20
N1	Alabama JAM	19	23
N8	at Auburn	13	52
N15	at LSU	6	61
N27	Mississippi	22	48

1970　6-5-0 (3-4-0)
S12 ●	Oklahoma State JAM	14	13
S19	at Florida	13	34
S26 ●	Vanderbilt MEM	20	6
O3 ●	Georgia JAM	7	6
O10	Houston	14	31
O17 ●	Texas Tech JAM	20	16
O24 ●	Southern Miss	51	15
O31	at Alabama	6	35
N7	Auburn BIRM	0	56
N14	at LSU	7	38
N26	at Mississippi	19	14

1971　2-9-0 (1-7-0)
S11	at Oklahoma State	7	26
S18	Florida JAM	13	10
S25	Vanderbilt	19	49
O2 ●	at Georgia	7	35
O9	at Florida State	9	27
O16 ●	Lamar	24	7
O23	Tennessee MEM	10	41
O30	Alabama JAM	10	41
N6	at Auburn	21	30
N13	LSU JAM	3	28
N25	Mississippi	0	48

1972　4-7-0 (1-6-0)
S9	Auburn JAM	3	14
S16 ●	La. Monroe	42	7
S23 ●	at Vanderbilt	10	6
S30	at Florida	13	28
O7	at Kentucky	13	17
O14 ●	Florida State JAM	21	25
O21 ●	Southern Miss	26	7
O28	Houston	27	13
N4	at Alabama	14	58
N18	at LSU	14	28
N25	at Mississippi	14	51

BOB TYLER
1973-78 (.604)　39-25-3

1973　4-5-2 (2-5-0)
S15 =	La. Monroe	21	21
S22 ●	Vanderbilt	52	21
S29 ●	Florida JAM	33	12
O6	Kentucky JAM	14	42
O13 ●	at Florida State	37	12
O20 ●	at Louisville	18	7
O27	Southern Miss	10	10
N3	Alabama	0	35
N10	at Auburn	17	31
N17	at LSU	7	26
N24	Mississippi	10	38

1974　9-3-0 (3-3-0)
S7 ●	William & Mary JAM	49	7
S21 ●	Georgia JAM	38	14
S28	at Florida	13	29
O5 ●	Kansas State	21	16
O12 ●	at Lamar	37	21
O19 ●	at Memphis	29	28
O26 ●	Louisville	56	7
N2	at Alabama	0	35
N9 ●	Auburn JAM	20	24
N16 ●	LSU JAM	7	6
N23 ●	Mississippi JAM	31	13

SUN BOWL
| D28 ● | North Carolina | 26 | 24 |

1975　6-4-1 (1-4-1)
S6 ●	at Memphis	17	7
S20	at Georgia	6	28
S27	Florida JAM	10	27
O4 ●	Southern Miss	7	3 †
O11 ●	at Rice	28	14 †
O18 ●	North Texas	15	12
O25 ●	at Louisville	28	14 †
N1	Alabama JAM	10	21
N8 = ●	at Auburn	21	21 †
N15 ●	at LSU	16	6 †
N22	Mississippi	7	13

1976　9-2-0 (4-2-0)
S4 ●	North Texas	7	0 †
S18 ●	Louisville	30	21 †
S25 ●	at Florida	30	34
O2 ●	Cal Poly Pomona	38	0 †
O9 ●	Kentucky JAM	14	7 †
O16 ●	at Memphis	42	33 †
O23 ●	at Southern Miss	14	6 †
O30	at Alabama	17	34
N6 ●	Auburn JAM	28	19 †
N13 ●	LSU JAM	21	13 †
N20 ●	Mississippi JAM	28	11 †

1977　5-6-0 (2-4-0)
S3 ●	North Texas	17	15 †
S10 ●	at Washington	27	18 †
S24 ●	Florida JAM	22	24
O1 ●	at Kansas State	24	21 †
O8	at Kentucky	7	23
O15	at Memphis	13	21
O22	Southern Miss	7	14
O29	Alabama JAM	7	37
N5 ●	at Auburn	27	13 †
N12	at LSU	24	27
N19 ●	Mississippi JAM	18	14 †

1978　6-5-0 (2-4-0)
S2 ●	West Texas St.	28	0
S9 ●	North Texas IRV	17	5
S23 ●	at Memphis	44	14
S30	at Florida	0	34
O7	at Southern Miss	17	22
O14 ●	Florida State	55	27
O28 ●	Tennessee MEM	34	21
N4	Alabama BIRM	14	35
N11	Auburn	0	6
N18 ●	LSU JAM	16	14
N25	Mississippi JAM	7	27

EMORY BELLARD
1979-85 (.468)　37-42

1979　3-8-0 (2-4-0)
S8	Memphis JAM	13	14
S22	at Maryland	14	35
S29 ●	Florida JAM	24	10
O6 ●	Tennessee MEM	28	9
O13	at Florida State	6	17
O20 ●	Marshall	48	0
O27	Southern Miss	7	21
N3	at Alabama	7	24
N10	at Auburn	3	14
N17	at LSU	3	21
N24	Mississippi JAM	9	14

1980　9-3-0 (5-1-0)
S6 ●	at Memphis	34	7
S13 ●	Louisiana Tech	31	11
S20 ●	at Vanderbilt	24	14
S27	at Florida	15	21
O4 ●	at Illinois	28	21
O11	Southern Miss	14	42
O18 ●	at Miami, Fla.	34	31
O25 ●	Auburn JAM	24	21
N1 ●	Alabama JAM	6	3
N15 ●	LSU JAM	55	31
N22 ●	Mississippi JAM	19	14

SUN BOWL
| D27 | Nebraska | 17 | 31 |

1981　8-4-0 (4-2-0)
S5 ●	Memphis JAM	20	3
S19 ●	Vanderbilt	29	9
S26 ●	Florida JAM	28	7
O3	Missouri JAM	3	14
O10 ●	at Colorado State	37	27
O17 ●	Miami, Fla.	14	10
O24 ●	at Auburn	21	17
O31	at Alabama	10	13
N7	Southern Miss JAM	6	7
N14	at LSU	17	9
N21 ●	Mississippi JAM	17	21

HALL OF FAME BOWL
| D31 ● | Kansas | 10 | 0 |

1982　5-6-0 (2-4-0)
S4 ●	at Tulane	30	21
S11 ●	Arkansas State	31	10
S18 ●	at Memphis	41	17
S25	at Florida	17	27
O2	Georgia	22	29
O9 ●	Southern Miss JAM	14	20
O16 ●	at Miami, Fla.	14	31
O23	Auburn	17	35
O30	Alabama JAM	12	20
N13 ●	LSU	27	24
N20 ●	Mississippi JAM	27	10

1983　3-8-0 (1-5-0)
S3 ●	Tulane	14	9
S17 ●	Navy JAM	38	10
S24	Florida	12	35
O1	at Georgia	7	20
O8 ●	Southern Miss JAM	6	31
O15	Miami, Fla.	7	31
O22	at Auburn	13	28
O29	at Alabama	18	35
N5	Memphis	13	30
N12 ●	at LSU	45	26
N19	Mississippi JAM	23	24

1984　4-7-0 (1-5-0)
S1 ●	at Tulane	30	3
S8 ●	Colorado State	14	9
S22	at Missouri	30	47
S29	at Florida	12	27
O6 ●	Southern Miss JAM	27	18
O13	Kentucky	13	17
O20	at Memphis	12	23
O27	Auburn	21	24
N3	Alabama JAM	20	24
N17 ●	LSU	16	14
N24	Mississippi JAM	3	24

1985　5-6-0 (0-6-0)
S7 ●	Arkansas State	22	14
S14 ●	Syracuse	30	3
S21 ●	Southern Miss JAM	23	20
S28 ●	Florida	22	36
O5 ●	Memphis	31	28
O12	at Kentucky	19	33
O19 ●	Tulane	31	27
O26	at Auburn	9	21
N2	at Alabama	28	44
N16	at LSU	15	17
N23	Mississippi JAM	27	45

ROCKEY FELKER
1986-90 (.382)　21-34

1986　6-5-0 (2-4-0)
S6 ●	at Syracuse	24	17
S13 ●	at Tennessee	27	23
S20 ●	Southern Miss JAM	24	28
S27 ●	Florida	16	10
O4 ●	at Memphis	34	17
O11 ●	Arkansas State	24	9
O18 ●	at Tulane	34	27
O25	Auburn	6	35
N1	Alabama	3	38
N15 ●	LSU JAM	0	47
N22	Mississippi JAM	3	24

1987　4-7-0 (1-5-0)
S5 ●	La. Lafayette	31	3
S12	Tennessee	10	38
S19 ●	Louisiana Tech	14	13
S26	at Florida	3	38
O3 ●	Memphis	9	6
O17 ●	Southern Miss JAM	14	18
O24	at Auburn	7	38
O31	Alabama BIRM	18	21
N7	Tulane	19	30
N14	at LSU	14	34
N21 ●	Mississippi JAM	30	20

1988   1-10-0 (0-7-0)

S3	•	Louisiana Tech	21 14
S10		at Vanderbilt	20 24
S17		Georgia	35 42
S24		at Florida	0 17
O1		at Memphis	10 31
O15		Southern Miss *JAM*	21 38
O22		at Auburn	0 33
O29		Alabama	34 53
N12		LSU	3 20
N19		at Tulane	22 27
N26		Mississippi *JAM*	6 33

1989   5-6-0 (1-6-0)

S2	•	Vanderbilt	42 7
S9	•	at Southern Miss	26 23
S23		at Georgia	6 23
S30		Florida *TAM*	0 21
O7		La. Monroe	28 14
O21	•	Memphis	35 10
O28		at Auburn	0 14
N4		Alabama *BIRM*	10 23
N11	•	Tulane	27 7
N18		at LSU	20 44
N25		Mississippi *JAM*	11 21

1990   5-6-0 (1-6-0)

S8		Tennessee	7 40
S15	•	Fullerton St.	27 13
S22	•	Southern Miss	13 10
S29		at Florida	21 34
O13		at Kentucky	15 17
O20	•	at Tulane	38 17
O27		Auburn	16 17
N3		Alabama	0 22
N10	•	at Memphis	27 23
N17	•	LSU *JAM*	34 22
N24		Mississippi *JAM*	9 21

JACKIE SHERRILL
1991-2003 (.493)   74-76-2

1991   7-5-0 (4-3-0)

A31	•	Fullerton St.	47 3
S7	•	Texas	13 6
S14	•	Tulane	48 0
S21		at Tennessee	24 26
S28		Florida *ORL*	7 29
O12	•	Kentucky	31 6
O19		Memphis	23 28
O26	•	at Auburn	24 17
N2		at Alabama	7 13
N16	•	at LSU	28 19
N23	•	Mississippi	24 9
		LIBERTY BOWL	
D29		Air Force	15 38

1992   7-5-0 (4-4-0)

S5	•	at Texas	28 10
S12		at LSU	3 24
S19	•	at Memphis	20 16
O1	•	Florida	30 6
O10	•	Auburn	14 7
O17		at South Carolina	6 21
O24	•	Arkansas State	56 6
O31	•	at Kentucky	37 36
N7	•	Arkansas	10 3
N14		Alabama	21 30
N28		at Mississippi	10 17
		PEACH BOWL	
J2		North Carolina	17 21

1993   3-6-2 (2-5-1)

S4	•	Memphis	35 45
S11		LSU	16 18
S25	•	at Tulane	36 10
O2		at Florida	24 38
O9		at Auburn	17 31
O16	•	South Carolina	23 0
O23	=	Arkansas State	15 15
O30		Kentucky	17 26
N6	=	Arkansas *LR*	13 13
N13		at Alabama	25 36 †
N27	•	Mississippi	20 13

1994   8-4-0 (5-3-0)

S3	•	at Memphis	17 6
S10		at LSU	24 44
S24	•	Tennessee	24 21
O1	•	Arkansas State	49 3
O8		Auburn	18 42
O15	•	at South Carolina	41 36
O22	•	Tulane	66 22
O29	•	at Kentucky	47 7
N5	•	Arkansas	17 7
N12	•	Alabama	25 29
N26	•	at Mississippi	21 17
		PEACH BOWL	
J1		North Carolina St.	24 28

1995   3-8-0 (1-7-0)

S2	•	Memphis	28 18
S9		LSU	16 34
S16	•	at Baylor	30 21
S23		at Tennessee	14 52
S30		La. Monroe	32 34
O7		at Auburn	20 48
O14		South Carolina	39 65
O28	•	Kentucky	42 32
N4		Arkansas *LR*	21 26
N11		at Alabama	9 14
N25		Mississippi	10 13

1996   5-6 (3-5)

S7	•	at Memphis	31 10
S21		Louisiana Tech	23 38
S28	•	at South Carolina	14 10
O5		Georgia	19 38
O12		Auburn	15 49
O26		at LSU	20 28
N2		La. Monroe	59 0
N9		at Kentucky	21 24
N16	•	Alabama	17 16
N23		Arkansas	13 16
N30	•	at Mississippi	17 0

1997   7-4 (4-4)

A30	•	Memphis	13 10
S6	•	Kentucky	35 27
S13		LSU	9 24
S27		South Carolina	37 17
O4		at Georgia	0 47
O11	•	La. Monroe	24 10
O25	•	Central Florida	35 28
N1		at Auburn	20 0
N15	•	at Alabama	32 20
N22		at Arkansas	7 17
N29		Mississippi	14 15

1998   8-5 (6-2)

S5	•	Vanderbilt	42 0
S12	•	at Memphis	14 6
S19		at Oklahoma State	23 42
S26	•	at South Carolina	38 0
O10	•	Auburn	38 21
O17	•	East Tenn. St.	53 6
O24		at LSU	6 41
N7		at Kentucky	35 37
N14	•	Alabama	26 14
N21	•	Arkansas	22 21
N26	•	at Mississippi	28 6
		SEC CHAMPIONSHIP GAME	
D5		Tennessee *ATL*	14 24
		COTTON BOWL	
J1		Texas	11 38

1999   10-2 (6-2)

S4	•	Middle Tennessee	40 7
S11	•	Memphis	13 10
S18	•	Oklahoma State	29 11
S25	•	South Carolina	17 0
O2	•	at Vanderbilt	42 14
O9	•	at Auburn	18 16
O23	•	LSU	17 16
N4	•	Kentucky	23 22
N13		at Alabama	7 19
N20		Arkansas *LR*	9 14
N25	•	Mississippi	23 20
		PEACH BOWL	
D30	•	Clemson	17 7

2000   8-4 (4-4)

S2	•	at Memphis	17 3
S14	•	at Brigham Young	44 28
S23	•	at South Carolina	19 23
S30	•	Florida	47 35
O7	•	Auburn	17 10
O21	•	at LSU	38 45
O28	•	Middle Tennessee	61 35
N4	•	at Kentucky	35 17
N11	•	Alabama	29 7
N18	•	Arkansas	10 17
N23	•	at Mississippi	30 45
		INDEPENDENCE BOWL	
D31	•	Texas A&M	43 41

2001   3-8 (2-6)

S3	•	Memphis	30 10
S20	•	South Carolina	14 16
S29		at Florida	0 52
O6		at Auburn	14 16
O13	•	Troy State	9 21
O20		LSU	0 42
N3	•	Kentucky	17 14
N10		at Alabama	17 24
N17		at Arkansas	21 24
N22	•	Mississippi	36 28
D1		Brigham Young	38 41

2002   3-9 (0-8)

A31		at Oregon	13 36
S14	•	Jacksonville St.	51 13
S19		Auburn	14 42
S28		at LSU	13 31
O5		at South Carolina	10 34
O12	•	Troy State	11 8
O19	•	at Memphis	29 17
N2		Kentucky	24 45
N9		at Alabama	14 28
N16		Tennessee	17 35
N23		Arkansas	19 26
N28		at Mississippi	12 24

2003   2-10 (1-7)

A30		Oregon	34 42
S13		at Tulane	28 31
S20		at Houston	35 42
S27		LSU	6 41
O4	•	Vanderbilt	30 21
O11	•	Memphis	35 27
O18		at Auburn	13 45
O25		at Kentucky	17 42
N8		Alabama	0 38
N15		at Tennessee	21 59
N22		at Arkansas	6 52
N27		Mississippi	0 31

SYLVESTER CROOM
2004-PRESENT (.278)   3-8

2004   3-8 (2-6)

S4	•	Tulane	28 7
S11		Auburn	14 43
S18		Maine	7 9
S25		at LSU	0 51
O2		at Vanderbilt	13 31
O9		UAB	13 27
O23	•	Florida	38 31
O30	•	Kentucky	22 7
N6		at Alabama	14 30
N20		Arkansas	21 24
N27		at Mississippi	3 20

Neutral Site key: *INV* Irving, TX / *TAM* Tampa, FL / *ORL* Orlando, FL / *LR* Little Rock, AR / *DAL* Dallas, TX / *HAV* Havana, Cuba / *GUL* Gulfport, MS / *ABE* Aberdeen, MS / *HOU* Houston, TX / *COLMS* Columbus, MS / *TUP* Tupelo, MS / *CLAR* Clarksdale, MS / *GRN* Greenwood, MS / *JACF* Jacksonville ,FL *MONT* Montgomery, AL / *MER* Meridian, MS / *MOR* Monroe, LA / *TYL* Tyler, TX / *JAM* Jackson, MS / *MEM* Memphis, TN / *BIRM* Birmingham, AL / *SHRE* Shreveport, LA / *ATL* Atlanta, GA
ƒ Forfeit / † Game Later Forfieted / # Disputed Victor / * Disputed Score / ‖ Designated Conference Game / |2 Counted Twice in Conference Standings

MISSOURI

BY MARK WANGRIN

THERE IS A CERTAIN IMPLIED CYNIcism in a population that would call its home the Show Me State. Given the history of Missouri Tigers football, where heartache has been a persistent theme, that shouldn't come as much of a surprise. Such was the atmosphere when the first group of Missouri students banded together in 1890 to field the school's first football team.

"Many of the student body preferred to stand on the sideline and hurl derisive comments at our efforts," recalled the team's fullback, Burton Thompson, "which they considered huge comedy."

And they would also take a spin at tragedy. For all of the highs—the powerful team of 1960, the Big Six title team of "Pitchin'" Paul Christman in 1939—there were dreadful and prolonged lows. Missouri last finished in the AP Top 10 in 1969, a long absence for a school with considerable football tradition. From the 1960 loss to Kansas, which cost the Tigers a dream season, to the infamous Fifth Down loss to Colorado in 1990 to the Flea-Kicker overtime defeat by Nebraska in 1997, the Tigers' experience at pain and despair has run the gamut,

proving that, as the albatross flies, it's not far from Missouri to misery.

TRADITION Legend has it that the homecoming tradition began at Missouri in 1911, when director of athletics Chester L. Brewer called on Tigers alums and former players to "come home" and support the team in its season-ending game against Kansas.

Looking to jazz up the Marching Mizzou band, director Charles Emmons created a twirling line of six to eight majorettes and two feature twirlers, known as the Golden Girls. The group began dancing in 1966, when they dropped their batons and broke into a rendition of the Charleston. In 2002, Mizzou introduced the Tiger Walk, where the players cross the Tiger Walk Bridge over Providence Road on the way to their locker room and are greeted outside Faurot Field by band and spirit groups. The Tigers play for four trophies each season against Big 12 foes, including the Bass Drum (Kansas), Bell (Nebraska), Peace Pipe (Oklahoma) and Telephone (Iowa State).

BEST PLAYER Johnny Roland originally signed with Oklahoma out of Corpus Christi, Texas, but switched to Missouri when he decided a young black man would have an easier time getting a job in St. Louis or Kansas City than in Oklahoma. As a Tiger, he would become the

---

PROFILE

University of Missouri-Columbia
Columbia, Mo.
Founded in 1839
Enrollment: 20,883
Colors: Old Gold and Black
Nickname: Tigers
Stadium: Faurot Field/Memorial Stadium
   Opened in 1926
   FieldTurf; 68,349 capacity
First football game: 1890
All-time record: 562–496–52 (.530)
Bowl record: 9–13
First-round NFL draftees: 12
Website: www.mutigers.com

THE BEST OF TIMES

1957-69. For one year under Frank Broyles and the rest under Dan Devine, Mizzou put together 13 consecutive winning seasons, including two Big Eight titles.

THE WORST OF TIMES

1930-1934. The Tigers won only 6 of 46 games during this span under coaches Gwinn Henry and Frank Carideo. They were shut out in 24 games and held to 7 or fewer points 15 other times.

CONFERENCE

Along with fellow Big Eight members Oklahoma, Nebraska, Oklahoma State, Kansas, Kansas State, Colorado and Iowa State, the Tigers merged with former Southwest Conference schools Texas, Texas A&M, Texas Tech and Baylor to form the Big 12 in 1996. Missouri was a charter member of the Missouri Valley Intercollegiate Athletic Association when it was formed in 1907. The MVIAA evolved into the Big Six in 1928 when Oklahoma A&M, Washington, Drake and Grinnell dropped out. The league became the Big Seven in 1948, with the addition of Colorado and the Big Eight in 1960, when Oklahoma State—formerly Oklahoma A&M—joined.

DISTINGUISHED ALUMNI

Jim Lehrer; George C. Scott; Sam Walton; Tom Berenger, actor; Kate Capshaw, actress; Chris Cooper, actor; Sheryl Crow, singer; Mort Walker, cartoonist, creator of "Beetle Bailey"

FIGHT SONG

FIGHT TIGERS
Fight, Tigers, fight for Old Mizzou,
Right behind you, everyone is with you,
Break the line and follow down the field,
And, you'll be, on the top, upon the top;
Fight, Tigers, you will always win,
Proudly keep the colors flying skyward,
In the end, we'll win the victory,
So Tigers, fight for Old Mizzou!

versatile, selfless player who was Missouri's leading rusher and scorer as a sophomore halfback but switched to primarily defensive back his final two seasons because that's where coach Dan Devine needed him. Roland earned All-America honors in the secondary in 1965 and was named to the *College Football News*' All-Time Big Eight team. Roland returned to offense in the NFL, earning Rookie of the Year honors in 1966 and playing for eight seasons, seven with the St. Louis Cardinals.

BEST COACH Missouri had 23 head coaches in the program's first 45 seasons, so when a 33-year-old former three-sport Tigers letterman was hired in 1935, it was with the hope of long-sought stability. Don Faurot didn't disappoint. Except for a three-year stint in the Navy during World War II—he joined up after his brother Bob was killed in the South Pacific—Faurot never left, coaching the Tigers to a 100–80–10 record through 1956 and continuing on as athletic director until 1967. In 1941, Faurot, a tremendous innovator, created the split-T-formation, an option attack that eventually spun off into

> ## To Mizzou fans, Colorado got five tries from the goal line in the final seconds in 1990—and still didn't score.

the wishbone, veer and I-option. The Thin Man led the Tigers to three Big Six titles and two Top 10 finishes. Faurot attended practices and maintained an office at Mizzou until he died on Oct. 19, 1995, of congestive heart failure.

BEST TEAM Dan Devine had lost a group of talented seniors following the 1968 season, but he returned a solid nucleus led by eventual all-conference selections Mel Gray (WR), Larron Jackson (OT), Mark Kuhlmann (DT) and Dennis Poppe (S). The Tigers went 9–1 in the regular season with impressive wins over Michigan, Nebraska and Kansas. The biggest victory may have been a 44-10 rout of Oklahoma. The Tigers finished the season ranked No. 6 and earned a spot in the Orange Bowl against Penn State, which was riding a 29-game winning streak. Despite nine turnovers, including seven interceptions, Missouri lost only 10-3, with a final drive collapsing at the Nittany Lions' 14-yard line.

BIGGEST GAME Hopes were high when the 4–1 Tigers hosted the No. 10 Nebraska Cornhuskers and their top-ranked defense on Oct. 11, 2003, but there was also the

RECORDS

RUSHING YARDS

GAME
319 — Devin West vs. Kansas, Sept. 12, 1998 (33 att.)

SEASON
1,578 — Devin West, 1998 (283 att.)

CAREER
3,198 — Zach Abron, 2000-03 (692 att.)

PASSING YARDS

GAME
480 — Jeff Handy vs. Oklahoma State, Oct. 17, 1992 (43 of 73)

SEASON
2,463 — Jeff Handy, 1992 (196 of 329)

CAREER
6,959 — Jeff Handy, 1991-94 (618 of 1,058)

RECEIVING YARDS

GAME
236 — Justin Gage vs. Bowling Green, Sept. 14, 2002 (16 rec.); Gage vs. Baylor, Nov. 10, 2001 (13 rec.)

SEASON
1,210 — Victor Bailey, 1992 (75 rec.)

CAREER
2,704 — Justin Gage, 1999-2002 (200 rec.)

POINTS

GAME
30 — Brad Smith vs. Texas Tech, Oct. 25, 2003 (5 TDs)

SEASON
121 — Bob Steuber, 1942 (18 TDs, 13 PATs)

CAREER
252 — Zack Abron, 2000-03 (42 TDs)

CONSENSUS ALL-AMERICANS

1941	Darold Jenkins	C
1960	Danny LaRose	E
1965	Johnny Roland	DB
1968	Roger Wehrli	DB
1978	Kellen Winslow	TE
1986	John Clay	OL
1999	Rob Riti	C

stark realism that it had been 25 years since they'd beaten the Cornhuskers. Calling on a little historical mojo, Missouri scheduled a ceremony to honor former coach Warren Powers—the last Tigers coach to beat NU. The Cornhuskers were not impressed, scoring two third-quarter touchdowns to wipe out a 14-10 halftime deficit. Brad Smith's 39-yard run on the first play of the fourth quarter cut the NU lead to 24-21, and after a Mizzou drive stalled at the NU 14, the Tigers lined up for a tying field goal. Holder Sonny Riccio took the snap, ran right and tossed to tight end Victor Sesay for a touchdown to put Missouri up 28-24. Inspired, the Tigers defense stymied the Cornhuskers and Smith added two more touchdowns to key a 41-24 rout. "This was a win for all the fans who have been waiting for this for 20-something years," said linebacker James Kinney.

BIGGEST UPSET The record crowd of 30,892 crammed into Memorial Stadium on Oct. 9, 1948, to glimpse one of the nation's most electrifying running backs. SMU's Doak Walker was everything he was billed to be, scoring twice and making several huge defensive plays, but it was the Tigers who provided the biggest gasps. A 13-point underdog to a Mustang team ranked No. 4 and riding a 15-game winning streak, Missouri scored three touchdowns in the second half and used a late interception by Lloyd Brinkman to escape with a 20-14 upset victory. "This is one of my biggest football thrills," coach Don Faurot said.

LANDMARK Blessed with a surplus of stone from the construction of Memorial Stadium, Mizzou students were inspired to build a 90'x95' whitewashed rock M behind the north end zone. Before the Tigers played Kansas State on Oct. 1, 1927, a group of freshmen were conscripted to create the giant consonant. Traditionally, a group of freshmen slap a new coat of whitewash on the rocks the week before the season opener. In 1957, Nebraska

pranksters changed the M to an N the night before the Cornhuskers played the Tigers. The Mizzou groundskeeper offered some young fans free admission in return for their manual labor and restored the M before kickoff.

HEARTBREAKER This is akin to picking your favorite kick in the groin. There is no shortage of candidates, but the one that may stick out above the others came in 1960 against the Tigers' bitterest rival, Kansas. Fresh off a victory over Oklahoma, the Tigers were unbeaten and ranked No. 1 for the first time in school history when they hosted the 6–2–1 Jayhawks on Nov. 19. KU jumped to a 17-0 lead and crushed the Tigers 23-7. Two weeks later, the Big Eight ruled that KU had to forfeit two games—including the Missouri win—for using an ineligible player, halfback Bert Coan. But the Tigers, who finished the season ranked No. 5, were unbeaten in name only. "They may have chalked up one in the win column but that is not a win to me," said the Tigers' Norm Beal. "We lost the game on the field and, with it, the national championship."

BEST GOAL-LINE STAND Ask a Tigers backer what was the best goal-line stand in school history and he'll point to the infamous Fifth Down game. Missouri led 31-27 in 1990 when Colorado got a first and goal at the Tigers' 3 with 30 seconds left. On first down, quarterback Charles Johnson spiked the ball to stop the clock. On second down, halfback Eric Bieniemy gained two yards. CU called time out. Inexplicably, the officials again signaled second down. Bieniemy was stopped for no gain. When the ball was set, Johnson spiked it again. On fourth down—actually fifth—Johnson ran off right tackle for the touchdown, though Missouri will forever claim his buttocks hit the ground before the ball reached the end zone. Colorado won 33-31. "If we screwed this up, nobody's going away from here feeling any worse than we are," said umpire Frank Gaines. The officials were

CENTENNIAL TEAM	
Selected by the school through 4,031 fan ballots in 1990. Voters were asked to select at least two players from five eras of Tigers football, regardless of position.	
1958-70	Dan Devine, coach
1919-20	Ed Travis, OT
1964-65	Francis Peay, OT
1940-41	Darold Jenkins, C
1978-81	Brad Edelman, C
1965-67	Russ Washington, OL
1976-78	Kellen Winslow, TE
1968-70	Mel Gray, WR
1972, 1974-75	Henry Marshall, WR
1975-78	Leo Lewis, WR
1915-16, 1919	Anton Stankowski, QB
1938-40	Paul Christman, QB
1968-69	Terry McMillan, QB
1977-80	Phil Bradley, QB
1940-41	Harry Ice, RB
1940-42	Bob Steuber, RB
1968-70	Joe Moore, RB
1974-75	Tony Galbreath, RB
1978-80	James Wilder, RB
1960-62	Andy Russell, LB
1962-64	Gus Otto, LB
1979-81	Van Darkow, LB
1962, 1964-65	Johnny Roland, DB
1966-68	Roger Wehrli, DB
1978-80	Eric Wright, DB
1984-87	Erik McMillan, DB

THE SCHOOLS

wrong again. "I got hacked off," said Mizzou coach Bob Stull. "It makes you ill. I kept saying to myself, 'How in the world could this happen?'"

BEST COMEBACK If everything had gone according to expectation in 1976, quarterback Pete Woods would have redshirted. However, if everything had gone as expected, the Tigers wouldn't have been in position to stun No. 2 Ohio State in Columbus, where the Buckeyes hadn't lost in five years. With injured quarterback Steve Pisarkiewicz in street clothes, the Tigers played along with the expectations early. Three Pete Johnson touchdowns gave the Buckeyes a 21-7 halftime lead. Curtis Brown's four-yard TD run cut into the OSU lead. With 4:42 remaining in the game the Tigers took over at their own 20-yard line. On third-and-goal at the 2, Woods hit Leo Lewis in the corner of the end zone with 12 seconds left for a touchdown. Coach Al Onofrio decided to go for two. The crowd of 87,936, then the third-largest in Ohio Stadium history, created such a din that Woods turned to the officials for relief. Buckeyes coach Woody Hayes stepped on the field and called for the crowd to quiet. Woods overthrew Brown, but the Buckeyes were called for holding. Woods rolled out again, but this time he kept knifing into the end zone to put Missouri up 22-21. Asked repeatedly about the penalty in the postgame press conference, Hayes said, "Nuts, nuts, nuts, nuts," and stormed out. Back in Columbia, police were called to Memorial Stadium to prevent the students from tearing down the goalposts.

STADIUM Carved out of a valley between two bluffs, Memorial Stadium was built in the wake of Missouri's championship seasons of 1924-25 for a cost of $350,000. Named for the 112 Mizzou students and alumni killed in World War I, it was opened in 1926 and sat 25,000. Several expansion projects increased capacity to 68,349. The field was renamed for Don Faurot in 1972 and a large statue of the legendary coach was erected outside the North entrance gates in 1999. That same year a six-level, $13.1 million press box was built atop the west stands, including a 418-seat Tiger Lounge and 35 luxury suites.

RIVAL It may have been the best opening line in Tigers history. "I understand you want to beat Kansas," new coach William Roper said to a group of 400 fans who greeted him at the Columbia train depot in 1909. The crowd roared. From the first game at Kansas City's Exposition Park in 1891 to recent history, the rivalry has been short on national

import—in only three games have both teams been ranked, with KU winning all of them—but not local vitriol. In 1930, Missouri led a conference investigation into the Jayhawks' program, based on charges they used a professional player. Four of the five other schools in the Big Six voted not to schedule KU if the Jayhawks didn't declare Jim Bausch ineligible, which KU reluctantly did. In 1960, the Jayhawks got a measure of revenge, though only temporarily. A couple of weeks after upsetting the No. 1 Tigers, the Jayhawks were forced to forfeit the game for using an ineligible player. "We play two seasons. We play our regular schedule, and then we play Missouri," former Kansas coach Don Fambrough once said. "If we win that game the winter won't be that cold." In October 2004, in deference to the war in Iraq and the post-9/11 climate, the schools changed the official name of the series from the Border War to the Border Showdown.

NICKNAME In the pre-Civil War era, Columbia, like many small Missouri towns, was often raided by bands of outlaws. Facing a rumored attack by notorious raider Bill Anderson's band in 1854, townspeople formed a home guard to fight off the marauders. The group was nicknamed the Missouri Tigers. The expected raid never occurred, but the Tigers' willingness to defend their homes convinced the University of Missouri's athletic committee to adopt the name when the first football team was organized in 1890.

MASCOT Missouri had two mascots, one female and one male, but neither had a name. That changed in 1984, when an on-campus contest selected Truman the Tiger, after Harry S. Truman, the tenacious, Missouri-bred 33rd president. A plush tiger-costumed mascot was introduced in 1986 at the Utah State game. Truman is a three-time winner of Best Mascot by the National Cheerleading Association.

UNIFORMS Early jerseys were black with gold horizontal stripes on the sleeves. The Tigers wore gold jerseys at home in the 1940s and 1950s before returning to black in the late '50s. Gary Pinkel replaced the gold pants with black when he arrived in 2001. Missouri's helmets have remained fairly consistent, with a black shell split by white and gold stripes. A block M replaced the jersey number in the early 1970s, evolving into the current gold M trimmed in black and white.

QUOTE "I don't know one thing, not a single thing, more overconfident than for a Missouri football coach to buy a house."—Don Faurot, 1935

MISSOURI ANNUAL STATISTICAL LEADERS

YR	RUSHING	YDS	ATT	AVG	PASSING	ATT	CMP	PCT	YDS	RECEIVING	REC	YDS	AVG
1947	Harold Entsminger	446	88	5.1	Bus Entsminger	50	22	.44	372	Mel Sheehan	14	218	15.6
1948	Dick Braznell	484	89	5.4	Bus Entsminger	90	43	.48	633	Mel Sheehan	23	346	15.0
1949	Dick Braznell	766	145	5.3	Phil Klein	122	55	.45	808	Gene Ackermann	42	621	14.8
1950	John Glorioso	503	106	4.7	Phil Klein	84	50	.60	625	Gene Ackermann	31	400	12.9
1951	Junior Wren	451	103	4.4	Tony Scardino	96	42	.44	653	Harold Carter	24	456	19.0
1952	Jim Hook	741	141	5.3	Tony Scardino	129	62	.48	781	Jim Jennings	14	219	15.6
1953	Robert Bauman	405	90	4.5	Vic Eaton	53	24	.45	364	Elmer Corpeny	12	179	14.9
1954	Robert Bauman	293	60	4.9	Vic Eaton	74	36	.49	774	Harold Burnine	22	405	18.4
1955	Loyd Roll	432	99	4.4	Dave Doane	113	52	.46	774	Harold Burnine	44	594	13.5
1956	Hank Khulmann	440	87	5.1	Jim Hunter	91	42	.46	567	Charley James	30	362	12.1
1957	Hank Khulmann	554	136	4.1	Phil Snowden	57	24	.42	299	Charley James	12	132	11.0
1958	Mel West	642	131	4.9	Phil Snowden	86	46	.53	548	Danny LaRose	14	215	15.4
1959	Mel West	556	122	4.6	Phil Snowden	83	33	.40	415	Russ Sloan	13	128	9.8
1960	Mel West	650	138	4.7	Ron Taylor	44	23	.52	302	Danny LaRose	10	151	15.1
1961	Andy Russell	412	100	4.1	Ron Taylor	62	31	.50	428	Conrad Hitchler	8	124	15.5
1962	Johnny Roland	830	159	5.2	Jim Johnson	33	12	.36	198	Bill Tobin	3	75	25.0
1963	Carl Reese	300	67	4.5	Gary Lane	113	51	.45	710	Ted Saussele	8	115	14.4
1964	Gary Lane	432	100	4.3	Gary Lane	119	50	.42	770	Earl Denny	10	222	22.2
1965	Charlie Brown	937	174	5.4	Gary Lane	106	45	.42	544	Monroe Phelps	17	207	12.2
1966	Charlie Brown	576	139	4.1	Gary Kombrink	77	32	.42	433	Chuck Weber	14	157	11.2
1967	Barry Lischner	647	174	3.7	Gary Kombrink	97	34	.35	452	Chuck Weber	15	212	14.1
1968	Greg Cook	693	161	4.3	Terry McMillan	113	56	.50	745	Jon Staggers	19	171	9.0
1969	Joe Moore	1,312	260	5.0	Terry McMillan	223	105	.47	1,963	Mel Gray	26	705	27.1
1970	James Harrison	702	127	5.5	Chuck Roper	235	101	.43	1,097	John Henley	39	481	12.3
1971	Don Johnson	360	98	3.7	Chuck Roper	131	62	.47	613	John Henley	25	247	9.9
1972	Tommy Reamon	454	115	3.9	John Cherry	131	52	.40	861	Jack Bastable	29	362	12.5
1973	Tommy Reamon	610	149	4.1	John Cherry	120	59	.49	743	Mark Miller	17	256	15.1
1974	Tony Galbreath	870	197	4.4	Steve Pisarkiewicz	156	70	.45	828	Mark Miller	38	522	13.7
1975	Tony Galbreath	777	183	4.2	Steve Pisarkiewicz	232	113	.49	1,792	Henry Marshall	44	945	21.5
1976	Curtis Brown	844	169	5.0	Pete Woods	131	59	.45	996	Joe Stewart	45	834	18.5
1977	Earl Gant	769	144	5.3	Pete Woods	127	65	.51	785	Joe Stewart	27	384	14.2
1978	James Wilder	873	160	5.5	Phil Bradley	226	136	.60	1,780	Kellen Winslow	29	479	16.5
1979	James Wilder	645	155	4.2	Phil Bradley	236	127	.54	1,448	Andy Gibler	23	316	13.7
1980	James Wilder	839	172	4.9	Phil Bradley	242	132	.55	1,632	Ron Fellows	33	586	17.8
1981	Bob Meyer	791	180	4.4	Mike Hyde	249	123	.49	1,471	James Caver	33	509	15.4
1982	Tracey Mack	484	120	4.0	Marlon Adler	140	79	.56	1,242	James Caver	41	634	15.5
1983	Eric Drain	684	167	4.1	Marlon Adler	175	102	.58	1,603	George Shorthose	32	483	15.1
1984	Jon Redd	668	119	5.6	Marlon Adler	144	77	.53	1,128	George Shorthose	33	601	18.2
1985	Darrell Wallace	1,120	226	5.0	Marlon Adler	183	89	.49	1,258	Herbert Johnson	49	806	16.4
1986	Darrell Wallace	872	211	4.1	Ronnie Cameron	111	49	.44	654	Herbert Johnson	17	167	9.8
1987	Robert Delpino	750	115	6.5	John Stollenwerck	137	60	.44	831	Craig Lammers	16	253	15.8
1988	Tommie Stowers	667	143	4.7	Corey Welch	53	23	.43	524	Tim Bruton	26	447	17.2
1989	Tommie Stowers	547	142	3.9	Kent Kiefer	314	183	.58	2,314	Linzy Collins	46	803	17.5
1990	Michael Jones	485	100	4.9	Kent Kiefer	275	165	.60	2,183	Linzy Collins	56	957	17.1
1991	Mike Washington	420	101	4.2	Phil Johnson	311	167	.54	2,029	Byron Chamberlain	39	464	11.9
1992	Joe Freeman	360	98	3.7	Jeff Handy	329	196	.60	2,463	Victor Bailey	75	1,210	16.1
1993	Joe Freeman	675	136	5.0	Jeff Handy	291	174	.60	1,901	Kenny Holly	58	623	10.7
1994	Brock Olivo	614	142	4.3	Jeff Handy	349	200	.57	2,030	Brian Sallee	58	616	10.6
1995	Brock Olivo	985	232	4.2	Brandon Corso	136	59	.43	623	Brock Olivo	17	101	5.9
1996	Brock Olivo	749	157	4.8	Kent Skornia	118	61	.52	701	Rahsetnu Jenkins	29	419	14.4
1997	Corby Jones	887	183	4.8	Corby Jones	191	102	.53	1,658	Eddie Brooks	24	311	13.0
1998	Devin West	1,578	283	5.6	Corby Jones	178	87	.49	1,281	Kent Layman	26	495	19.0
1999	Zain Gilmore	764	188	4.1	Jim Dougherty	219	109	.50	1,304	Travis Garvin	36	608	16.9
2000	Zain Gilmore	632	139	4.5	Darius Outlaw	225	105	.47	1,391	Justin Gage	44	709	16.1
2001	Zack Abron	783	157	5.0	Kirk Farmer	285	135	.47	1,567	Justin Gage	74	920	12.4
2002	Brad Smith	1,029	193	5.3	Brad Smith	366	196	.54	2,333	Justin Gage	82	1,075	13.1
2003	Brad Smith	1,406	212	6.6	Brad Smith	350	211	.60	1,977	Thomson Omboga	52	466	9.0
2004	Damien Nash	792	164	4.8	Brad Smith	369	191	.52	2,185	Sean Coffey	39	648	16.6

Receiving leaders by receptions
The NCAA began including postseason stats in 2002

MISSOURI ALL-TIME SCORES

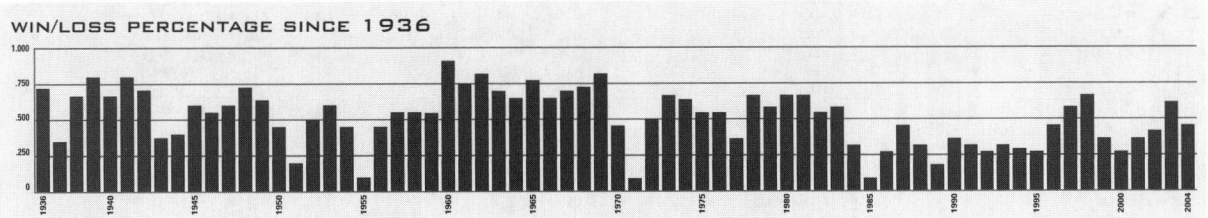

WIN/LOSS PERCENTAGE SINCE 1936

A.L. McRAE — 1890 (.667) — 2-1

1890 — 2-1-0
O20	●	Picked Team	22	6	
N27		at Washington, Mo.	0	28	
D1	●	Engineers	90	0	

HAL REID — 1891 (.750) — 3-1

1891 — 3-1-0
O31		Kansas *KC*	10	22	*
N5		Kansas City YMCA	8	0	
N24		Washburn	36	6	
D1		Drury Coll.	54	0	

E.H. JONES — 1892 (.333) — 1-2

1892 — 1-2-0
N5		Nebraska *OMA*	0	1	f
N12	●	Iowa	22	0	*
N26		Kansas *KC*	4	12	

H.O. ROBINSON — 1893-94 (.571) — 8-6

1893 — 4-3-0
O14	●	Baker *KC*	0	28	
O22		at Denver AC	0	40	
N6	●	Missouri Valley	76	0	
N11	●	Nebraska *KC*	30	18	*
N18		at Iowa	12	34	*
N25		at Pastime AC	24	12	
N30		Kansas *KC*	12	4	

1894 — 4-3-0
O16	●	Sedalia AC	44	6	
O27		at Denver AC	0	26	
N3	●	Nebraska *KC*	18	14	
N10		at Ottawa	0	28	
N17	●	Iowa	32	16	*
N30		Kansas *KC*	12	18	
D14		at Texas	28	0	

C.D. "POP" BLISS — 1895 (.875) — 7-1

1895 — 7-1-0
O7	●	Sedalia AC	10	0	
O12	●	Vanderbilt	16	0	
O19	●	Purdue *StL*	16	6	
O26	●	DePauw *StL*	38	0	
N2		Nebraska *OMA*	10	12	
N9		Northwestern *StL*	22	18	
N18	●	Iowa	34	0	
N28		Kansas *KC*	10	6	

FRANK PATTERSON — 1896 (.583) — 7-5

1896 — 7-5-0
O2		Iowa State	0	12	
O12	●	Tarkio	72	0	
O17		Illinois *KC*	0	10	
O26		Nebraska	4	8	
N7	●	Vanderbilt *StL*	26	6	
N9		Iowa	0	12	
N14		at Wentworth	42	0	
N26		Kansas *KC*	0	30	
D12		at Dallas AC	26	0	
D14		at Texas	10	0	
D16		at Austin Mutes	39	0	
D21		at San Antonio YMCA	29	0	

CHARLES YOUNG — 1897 (.455) — 5-6

1897 — 5-6-0
O4	●	Central Mo. St.	10	0	
O9		Kansas City Medical *KC*	0	4	
O11		at Central Mo. St.	0	10	
O18	●	Iowa Wesleyan	6	4	
O30		at Nebraska	0	41	
N1		at Tarkio	0	34	
N2		at Amity	8	4	
N5	●	Westminster	60	0	
N13		at Purdue	12	30	
N15		Christian Bro. *StL*	16	0	
N25		Kansas *KC*	0	16	

DAVID L. FULTZ — 1898-99 (.618) — 10-6-1

1898 — 1-4-1
O3	=	Wentworth M.A.	0	0	
O8		K.C. Med. Coll. *KC*	0	16	
O17		K.C. Med. Coll. *KC*	15	5	
O24		Nebraska	6	47	
O29		Washington, Mo. *StL*	12	18	
N24		Kansas *KC*	0	12	

1899 — 9-2-0
O1	●	Central Mo. St.	21	0	
O9	●	Wentworth M.A.	45	0	
O14	●	Haskell	17	0	
O21	●	at Nebraska	11	0	
O23	●	at Tarkio	23	0	
O24	●	at Amity	18	0	
O28	●	Christian Bro. *StL*	29	0	
N4	●	at Drake	0	11	
N11	●	Missouri Valley	39	0	
N18	●	Washington, Mo. *StL*	33	11	
N30	●	Kansas *KC*	6	34	

FRED MURPHY — 1900-01 (.389) — 6-10-2

1900 — 4-4-1
O1	●	American Osteopath	13	0	
O8	●	Haskell	0	11	
O15	●	Central Mo. St.	11	6	
O20	●	K.C. Med. Coll.	12	18	
O27	●	Missouri Rolla *StL*	12	5	
N5		at Nebraska	0	12	
N12	●	Washington, Mo.	6	5	
N17		at Texas	11	17	*
N29	=	Kansas *KC*	6	6	

1901 — 2-6-1
O5		American Osteopath	5	22	
O11		Simpson	0	10	
O19		Central Mo. St.	1	0	f
O26		at Drake	0	24	
N2		Ottawa	6	6	
N9		Nebraska *OMA*	0	51	
N16		Texas	0	10	
N18		Haskell	0	19	
N28		Kansas *KC*	18	12	

PAT O'DEA — 1902 (.625) — 5-3

1902 — 5-3-0
O11	●	Simpson	11	6	
O18	●	Haskell *KC*	0	40	
O25	●	Nebraska *StJ*	0	12	
N1	●	Washburn	28	0	
N8	●	at Washington, Mo.	27	0	
N12	●	Oklahoma	22	5	
N20	●	at Iowa	6	0	
N27		Kansas *KC*	5	17	

JOHN F. McCLAIN — 1903-05 (.352) — 9-17-1

1903 — 1-7-1
O3	●	Missouri Rolla	40	0	
O12	●	Grinnell	6	15	
O17	●	Drake	0	17	
O23	●	Simpson	0	12	
O31	●	Haskell *KC*	0	12	
N7	=	at Washington, Mo.	0	0	
N14	●	Iowa	0	16	
N18	●	Washburn	0	6	
N26	●	Kansas *KC*	0	5	

1904 — 3-6-0
O1	●	Truman St.	6	0	
O7	●	Simpson	7	0	
O15	●	Haskell *KC*	0	39	
O22	●	Transylvania, Ky	37	6	
O28	●	Purdue *StL*	0	11	
N5	●	at Washington, Mo.	0	10	
N12	●	St. Louis	0	17	
N16	●	Washburn	0	18	
N24	●	Kansas *KC*	0	29	

1905 — 5-4-0
S30	●	Truman St.	6	0	
O6	●	Simpson	26	0	
O14	●	Missouri Rolla	28	0	
O21	●	Haskell	6	0	
O28	●	Tarkio	18	0	
N4	●	at Purdue	0	24	
N11	●	St. Louis	0	17	
N18	●	at Washington, Mo.	10	14	
N30	●	Kansas *KC*	0	24	

W.J. MONILAW — 1906-08 (.740) — 18-6-1

1906 — 5-2-1
O2	●	Truman St.	23	4	
O6	●	Central Mo. St.	41	2	
O13	●	Missouri Rolla	26	0	
O20	●	Drury Coll.	11	0	
O27	●	at Iowa	4	26	
N10	●	Arkansas	11	0	
N19	●	at Washington, Mo.	0	12	
N29	=	Kansas *KC*	0	0	

1907-1927 MISSOURI VALLEY

1907 — 7-2-0 (1-2-0)
O5	●	Central Methodist	39	0	
O9	●	at Central Methodist	46	0	
O12	●	Central Mo. St.	38	6	
O19	|	at Iowa	6	21	
O26	●	William-Jewell	47	0	
N2	●	Texas	5	4	
N9	●	Tarkio	70	6	
N16	|	Washington, Mo.	27	0	
N28	|	Kansas *StJ*	0	4	

1908 — 6-2-0 (3-2-0)
O3	●	Central Mo. St.	57	6	
O10	●	Missouri Rolla	16	0	
O17	●	Iowa	10	5	
O24	●	Westminster	58	0	
O31	●	Iowa State	0	16	
N11	●	at Drake	11	8	
N14	●	Washington, Mo.	40	0	
N26	|	Kansas *KC*	4	10	

WILLIAM ROPER — 1909 (.938) — 7-0-1

1909 — 7-0-1 (4-0-1)
O1	●	Monmouth	12	6	
O9	●	Kansas State	3	0	
O16	●	Missouri Rolla	13	0	
O23	=	at Iowa State	6	6	
O30	●	at Iowa	13	12	
N6	●	at Washington, Mo.	5	0	
N13	●	Drake	22	6	
N25	|	Kansas *KC*	12	6	

W. HOLLENBECK — 1910 (.625) — 4-2-2

1910 — 4-2-2 (2-1-1)
S30	●	Monmouth	9	0	
O8	=	Missouri Rolla	0	0	
O15	●	Iowa	5	0	
O22	●	Iowa State	5	6	
O28	●	Oklahoma *JOP*	26	0	
N5		at St. Louis	0	3	
N12	●	Washington, Mo.	27	3	
N24	=	Kansas *KC*	5	5	

CHESTER L. BREWER — 1911-13 (.625) — 14-8-2

1911 — 2-4-2 (0-2-2)
S30	●	William-Jewell	15	0	
O7	●	Missouri Rolla	29	0	
O21	|	at Iowa State	3	6	
O28	|	at Nebraska	0	34	
N4	|	Oklahoma	6	14	
N11	=	at Washington, Mo.	5	5	
N18	|	at St. Louis	0	5	
N25	|	Kansas	3	3	

1912 — 5-3-0 (2-3-0)
S28	●	Central Methodist	55	7	
O12	●	Missouri Rolla	13	0	
O19	●	Iowa State	0	29	
O25	●	at Oklahoma	14	0	
N2	|	Nebraska	0	7	
N9	●	at Drake	17	14	
N16	●	Washington, Mo.	33	0	
N23	|	at Kansas	3	12	

1913 — 7-1-0 (4-0-0)
O4	●	Drury Coll.	69	0	
O11	●	at Illinois	7	24	
O18	●	Oklahoma	20	17	
O25	●	at Iowa State	21	13	
N1	●	Missouri Rolla	44	13	
N8	|	Drake	10	0	
N15	●	at Washington, Mo.	19	0	
N22	●	Kansas	3	0	

HENRY F. SCHULTE — 1914-17 (.531) — 16-14-2

1914 — 5-3-0 (4-1-0)
O3		Missouri Rolla	0	9	
O10	●	William-Jewell	46	0	
O17		at Oklahoma	0	13	
O24		Iowa State	0	6	
O31	●	Kansas State	13	3	
N7	●	at Drake	33	7	
N14	●	Washington, Mo.	26	3	
N21	●	at Kansas	10	7	

1915 — 2-5-1 (1-3-1)
O2	●	Oklahoma State	13	6	
O9	|	at Washington, Mo.	0	13	
O16	|	Oklahoma	0	24	
O23	|	at Iowa State	6	14	
O29	= |	Kansas State	0	0	
N6	|	at Northwestern	6	24	
N13	● |	Drake	41	13	
N25	|	Kansas	6	8	

1916   6-1-1 (3-1-1)

O7 ●	Central Methodist	40	0
O14 ●	Washington, Mo.	13	0
O21 =	Iowa State	0	0
O28 ●	at Oklahoma	23	14
N4 ●	Texas	3	0
N11 ●	at Kansas State	6	7
N18 ●	Drake	14	0
N30 ●	at Kansas	13	0

1917   3-5-0 (2-4-0)

O6 ●	William-Jewell	14	6
O13	Kansas State	6	7
O20	at Iowa State	0	15
O27 ●	Drake	49	0
N3	Oklahoma	7	14
N10	at Nebraska	0	52
N17 ●	at Washington, Mo.	19	3
N29	Kansas	3	27

1918   0-0-0 (0-0-0)
NO TEAM WWI

JOHN F. MILLER
1919 (.750)   5-1-2

1919   5-1-2 (4-0-1)

O4 ●	Drury Coll.	41	12
O11 =	at Kansas State	6	6
O18 ●	Iowa State	10	0
O25 ●	Drake	3	0
N1 ●	at Oklahoma	6	6
N8 ●	Nebraska	5	12
N15 ●	at Washington, Mo.	7	0
N27 ●	at Kansas	13	6

JOHN F. MILLER/JAMES PHELAN
1920 (.875)   7-1

1920   7-1-0 (5-1-0)

O2 ●	Missouri Wesleyan	41	0
O9 ●	at St. Louis	44	0
O16 ●	at Iowa State	14	2
O23 ●	at Drake	10	7
O30 ●	Oklahoma	7	28
N6 ●	Kansas State	10	7
N13 ●	Washington, Mo.	14	10
N25 ●	Kansas	16	7

JAMES PHELAN
1921 (.750)   6-2

1921   6-2-0 (4-2-0)

O1 ●	Oklahoma State	36	0
O8 ●	at St. Louis	32	0
O15 ●	Iowa State	17	14
O22 ●	at Kansas State	5	7
O29 ●	Drake	6	0
N5 ●	at Washington, Mo.	7	0
N12 ●	Oklahoma	24	14
N24 ●	at Kansas	9	15

THOMAS KELLY
1922 (.625)   5-3

1922   5-3-0 (4-3-0)

O7 ●	Grinnell	23	0	
O14 ●	at Iowa State	6	3	
O21 ●	at Nebraska	0	48	
O28 ●	at St. Louis	9	0	
N4	Kansas State	10	13	*
N11 ●	at Oklahoma	14	18	
N18 ●	Washington, Mo.	27	0	
N30 ●	Kansas	9	7	

GWINN HENRY
1923-31 (.578)   40-28-9

1923   2-3-3 (1-3-2)

O6 ●	S.W. Mo. St.	10	0
O13	Iowa State	0	2
O20 =	at St. Louis	0	0
O27 =	Nebraska	7	7
N3 ●	at Kansas State	4	2
N10 ●	Oklahoma	0	13
N17 ●	at Washington, Mo.	7	13
N29	at Kansas	3	3

1924   7-2-0 (5-1-0)

O4 ●	at Chicago	3	0
O11 ●	Missouri Wesleyan	14	0
O18 ●	at Iowa State	7	0
O25 ●	Kansas State	14	7
N1	at Nebraska	6	14
N8 ●	at Oklahoma	10	0
N15 ●	Washington, Mo.	35	0
N27 ●	Kansas	14	0

CHRISTMAS FESTIVAL
D25	Southern Cal	7	20

1925   6-1-1 (5-1-0)

O3 =	at Tulane	6	6
O10 ●	Nebraska	9	6
O17 ●	Missouri Rolla	32	0
O24 ●	at Kansas State	3	0
O31 ●	Iowa State	23	8
N7 ●	at Washington, Mo.	14	0
N14 ●	Oklahoma	16	14
N21	at Kansas	7	10

1926   5-1-2 (4-1-0)

O2 =	Tulane	14	7
O9 ●	at Nebraska	14	7
O16 ●	SMU	7	7
O23 ●	at Iowa State	7	3
O30 ●	at West Virginia	27	0
N6	at Oklahoma	7	10
N13 ●	Washington, Mo.	45	6
N20 ●	Kansas	15	0

1927   7-2-0 (5-1-0)

O1 ●	Kansas State	13	6
O8 ●	Nebraska	7	6
O15 ●	at Washington, Mo.	13	0
O22 ●	at SMU	9	32
O29 ●	at Northwestern	34	19
N5 ●	West Virginia	13	0
N11 ●	at Iowa State	13	6
N19 ●	at Kansas	7	14
N24 ●	Oklahoma	20	7

1928-1995
BIG 8

1928   4-4-0 (3-2-0)

O13 ●	Centre	60	0
O20 ●	Iowa State	8	19
O27 ●	at Nebraska	0	24
N3	Drake	0	6
N10 ●	at Kansas State	19	6
N17	NYU Brnx	6	27
N24 ●	Kansas	25	6
N29	at Oklahoma	0	14

1929   5-2-1 (3-1-1)

O12 ●	at Iowa State	19	0
O19 ●	Drake	20	0
O26 =	Nebraska	7	7
N2	Kansas State	6	7
N9 ●	at Washington, Mo.	6	0
N16	at NYU	0	14
N23 ●	at Kansas	7	0
N28 ●	Oklahoma	13	0

1930   2-5-2 (1-2-2)

O4	Colorado	0	9
O11	at St. Louis	0	20
O18	NYU Brnx	0	38
O25 ●	Drake	14	13
N1	at Kansas State	13	20
N8 ●	Iowa State	14	0
N15 =	at Nebraska	0	0
N22	Kansas	0	32
N27 =	at Oklahoma	0	0

1931   2-8-0 (1-4-0)

O3	at Texas	0	31
O10	Kansas State	7	20
O17	at Colorado	7	9
O24	at Iowa State	0	20
O31	Nebraska	7	10
N6	at Drake	32	20
N14 ●	Oklahoma	7	0
N21	at Kansas	0	14
N28	Temple KC	6	38
D5	at St. Louis	6	21

FRANK CARIDEO
1932-34 (.111)   2-23-2

1932   1-7-1 (1-3-1)

O1	at Northwestern	0	27
O8	Texas	0	65
O15	at Kansas State	0	25
O22 =	Iowa State	0	0
O29	Washington , Mo.	6	14
N5 ●	at Oklahoma	14	6
N12	Kansas	0	7
N24	at Nebraska	6	21
D3	at St. Louis	6	19

1933   1-8-0 (0-5-0)

O6 ●	Central Methodist	31	0
O7	Kirksville Teachers	6	26
O14	Kansas State	0	33
O21	at St. Louis	7	13
O28	at Iowa State	7	14
N4	Nebraska	0	26
N11	Oklahoma	0	21
N18	at Washington, Mo.	7	33
N30	at Kansas	0	27

1934   0-8-1 (0-5-0)

O6 =	at Colorado	0	0
O13	Iowa State	0	13
O20	St. Louis	0	7
O27	at Chicago	6	19
N3	at Oklahoma	0	31
N10	at Kansas State	0	29
N17	Washington, Mo.	13	40
N24	at Nebraska	6	13
N29	Kansas	0	20

DON FAUROT
1935-42, '46-56 (.553)   100-80-10

1935   3-3-3 (0-2-3)

S28 ●	William-Jewell	39	0
O5 ●	Central Mo. St.	7	0
O12 ●	Colorado	20	6
O26 =	at Iowa State	6	6
N2	Nebraska	6	19
N9	Oklahoma	6	20
N16	at Washington, Mo.	6	19
N23 =	Kansas State	7	7
N28 =	at Kansas	0	0

1936   6-2-1 (3-1-1)

O3 ●	S.E. Missouri St.	20	0
O10 =	at Kansas State	7	7
O17	at Michigan State	0	13
O24 ●	Iowa State	10	0
O31	at Nebraska	0	20
N7 ●	at St. Louis	13	7
N14 ●	at Oklahoma	21	14
N21 ●	Washington, Mo.	17	10
N26 ●	Kansas	19	3

1937   3-6-1 (2-2-1)

O2	at Colorado	6	14
O9 ●	Kansas State	14	7
O16	Michigan State	0	2
O23	Nebraska	0	7
O30 ●	at Iowa State	12	0
N6	at St. Louis	7	14
N13	Oklahoma	0	7
N20 ●	at Washington, Mo.	3	0
N25 =	at Kansas	0	0
N27	at UCLA	0	13

1938   6-3-0 (2-3-0)

O1 ●	Colorado	14	7
O8 ●	at Kansas State	13	21
O15 ●	Iowa State	13	16
O22 ●	at Washington, Mo.	13	0
O29 ●	at Nebraska	13	10
N5 ●	Michigan State	6	0
N12 ●	at Oklahoma	0	21
N19 ●	at St. Louis	26	0
N24 ●	Kansas	13	7

1939   8-2-0 (5-0-0)

S30 ●	Colorado	30	0
O7	at Ohio State	0	19
O14 ●	at Washington, Mo.	14	0
O21 ●	Kansas State	9	7
O28 ●	at Iowa State	21	6
N4 ●	at Nebraska	27	13
N11 ●	NYU Brnx	20	7
N18 ●	Oklahoma	7	6
N25 ●	at Kansas	20	0

ORANGE BOWL
J1	Georgia Tech	7	21

1940   6-3-0 (3-2-0)

S28 ●	St. Louis	40	26
O5	at Pittsburgh	13	19
O12 ●	at Kansas State	24	13
O19 ●	Iowa State	30	14
O26 ●	at Nebraska	7	20
N2 ●	NYU	33	0
N9 ●	at Colorado	21	6
N16	at Oklahoma	0	7
N21 ●	Kansas	45	20

1941   8-2-0 (5-0-0)

S27	at Ohio State	7	12
O4 ●	Colorado	21	6
O11 ●	Kansas State	35	0
O18 ●	at Iowa State	39	13
O25 ●	Nebraska	6	0
N1 ●	at Michigan State	19	0
N8 ●	NYU Brnx	26	0
N15 ●	Oklahoma	28	0
N22 ●	at Kansas	45	6

SUGAR BOWL
J1	Fordham	0	2

1942   8-3-1 (4-0-1)

S19 ●	Fort Riley StJ	31	0
S26 =	St. Louis	38	7
O3 ●	Colorado	26	13
O10	at Wisconsin	9	17
O17 ●	at Kansas State	46	2
O24 ●	Iowa State	45	6
O31	Great Lakes NAS StL	0	17
N7 ●	at Nebraska	26	6
N14 =	at Oklahoma	6	6
N21	Fordham Brnx	12	20
N26 ●	Kansas	42	13
D5	Iowa Pre-Flight KC	7	0

CHAUNCEY SIMPSON
1943-45 (.464)   12-14-2

1943   3-5-0 (3-2-0)

S25	at Minnesota	13	26
O2	at Ohio State	6	27
O9 ●	Kansas State	17	14
O16	Iowa Pre-Flight KC	6	21
O30	Nebraska	54	20
N6	at Iowa State	25	7
N13	Oklahoma	13	20
N20	at Kansas	6	7

1944   3-5-2 (2-1-2)

S23	Arkansas StL	6	7
S30	at Ohio State	0	54
O7	at Kansas State	33	0
O14	at Minnesota	27	39
O21 =	Iowa State	21	21
O28	at Nebraska	20	24
N4 ●	Michigan State	13	7
N11 =	at Oklahoma	21	21
N18	Iowa Pre-Flight	7	51
N23 =	Kansas KC	28	0

1945   6-4-0 (5-0-0)

S22	at Minnesota	0	34
S29	Ohio State	6	47
O6 ●	at SMU	10	7
O13 ●	at Iowa State	13	7
O20 ●	Kansas State	41	7
O27 ●	Nebraska	19	0
N3	at Michigan State	7	14
N17 ●	Oklahoma	14	6
N24 ●	Kansas KC	33	12

COTTON BOWL
J1	Texas	27	40

DON FAUROT

1946   5-4-1 (3-2-0)

S21	at Texas	0	42
S28 =	at Ohio State	13	13
O4 ●	at St. Louis	19	14
O12 ●	at Kansas State	26	0
O19 ●	Iowa State	33	13
O26	SMU	0	17
N2 ●	at Nebraska	21	20
N9 ●	Colorado	21	0
N16 ●	at Oklahoma	6	27
N28 ●	Kansas	19	20

1947   6-4-0 (3-2-0)

S20 ●	St. Louis	19	0
S27 ●	at Ohio State	7	13
O4	at SMU	19	35
O11 ●	at Colorado	21	0
O18 ●	Kansas State	47	7
O25 ●	at Iowa State	26	7
N1 ●	Nebraska	47	6
N8 ●	at Duke	28	7
N15 ●	Oklahoma	12	21
N22	at Kansas	14	20

1948 8-3-0 (5-1-0)

S25		at Ohio State	7	21
O1	●	at St. Louis	60	7
O9	●	SMU	20	14
O16	●	Navy BALT	35	14
O23	● |	Iowa State	49	7
O30	● |	at Kansas State	49	7
N6	|	at Oklahoma	7	41
N13	● |	Colorado	27	13
N20	● |	at Nebraska	33	6
N25	● |	Kansas	21	7
		GATOR BOWL		
J1		Clemson	23	24

1949 7-4-0 (5-1-0)

S24		at Ohio State	34	35
O1		at SMU	27	28
O8	●	Oklahoma State	21	7
O15	●	at Illinois	27	20
O22	● |	at Iowa State	32	0
O29	● |	Nebraska	21	20
N5	● |	at Colorado	20	13
N12	|	Oklahoma	7	27
N19	● |	at Kansas	34	28
N24	● |	Kansas State	34	27
		GATOR BOWL		
J2		Maryland	7	20

1950 4-5-1 (3-2-1)

S30		Clemson	0	34
O7		SMU	0	21
O14	● |	at Kansas State	28	7
O21	= |	Iowa State	20	20
O28	●	at Oklahoma State	27	0
N4	|	at Nebraska	34	40
N11	● |	Colorado	21	19
N18	|	at Oklahoma	7	41
N23	● |	Kansas	20	6
D1		at Miami, Fla.	9	27

1951 2-8-0 (1-5-0)

S22		Fordham	20	34
S29	●	Oklahoma State	27	26
O6		at SMU	0	34
O13	|	at Colorado	13	34
O20	|	at Iowa State	14	21
O27	● |	Nebraska	35	19
N3		at Maryland	0	35
N10	|	Oklahoma	20	34
N17	|	Kansas State	12	14 †
D1	|	at Kansas	28	41

1952 5-5-0 (5-1-0)

S20		Maryland	10	13
S27		at California	14	28
O4	● |	at Kansas State	26	0
O11		SMU	7	25
O18		at Oklahoma State	7	14
O25	● |	Iowa State	19	0
N1	● |	at Nebraska	10	6
N8	● |	Colorado	27	7
N15	|	at Oklahoma	7	47
N22	● |	Kansas	20	19

1953 6-4-0 (4-2-0)

S19		Maryland	6	20
S26	●	Purdue	14	7
O3	● |	at Colorado	27	16
O10		at SMU	7	20
O17	|	at Iowa State	6	13
O24	● |	Nebraska	23	7
O31	●	at Indiana	14	7
N7	|	Oklahoma	7	14 *
N14	● |	Kansas State	16	6
N21	● |	at Kansas	10	6

1954 4-5-1 (3-2-1)

S25		at Purdue	0	31
O2	● |	at Kansas State	35	7
O9		SMU	6	25
O16	●	Indiana	20	14
O23	● |	Iowa State	32	14
O30	|	at Nebraska	19	25
N6	= |	Colorado	19	19
N13	|	at Oklahoma	13	34
N20	● |	Kansas	41	18
N25		at Maryland	13	74

1955 1-9-0 (1-5-0)

S17		Maryland	12	13
S24		at Michigan	7	42
O1		Utah	14	20
O7		at SMU	6	13
O15	|	at Iowa State	14	20
O22	|	Nebraska	12	18
O29	● |	at Colorado	20	12
N5	|	Oklahoma	0	20
N12	|	Kansas State	0	21
N19	|	at Kansas	7	13

1956 4-5-1 (3-2-1)

S22		Oregon State	13	19
S29		at Purdue	7	16
O6		SMU	27	33
O13	●	North Dakota St.	42	0
O20	● |	at Kansas State	20	6
O27	● |	Iowa State	34	0
N3	|	at Nebraska	14	15
N10	= |	Colorado	14	14
N17	|	at Oklahoma	14	67
D1	● |	Kansas	15	13

FRANK BROYLES
1957 (.550) 5-4-1

1957 5-4-1 (3-3-0)

S21	=	at Vanderbilt	7	7
S28	●	Arizona	35	13
O5		Texas A&M	0	28
O11	●	at SMU	7	6
O19	● |	at Iowa State	35	13
O26	● |	Nebraska	14	13
N2	● |	at Colorado	9	6
N9	|	Oklahoma	14	39
N16	|	Kansas State	21	23
N23	|	at Kansas	7	9

DAN DEVINE
1958-70 (.697) 92-38-7

1958 5-4-1 (4-1-1)

S20		Vanderbilt	8	12
S27	●	Idaho	14	10
O4		at Texas A&M	0	12
O11		SMU	19	32
O18	● |	at Kansas State	32	8
O25	● |	Iowa State	14	6
N1	● |	at Nebraska	31	0
N8	● |	Colorado	33	9
N15	|	at Oklahoma	0	39
N22	= |	Kansas	13	13

1959 6-5-0 (4-2-0)

S19		Penn State	8	19
S26	●	at Michigan	20	15
O3	● |	at Iowa State	14	0
O9		at SMU	2	23
O17	|	Oklahoma	0	23
O24	● |	Nebraska	9	0
O31	|	at Colorado	20	21
N7	●	Air Force	13	0
N14	● |	Kansas State	26	0
N21	● |	at Kansas	13	9
		ORANGE BOWL		
J1		Georgia	0	14

1960 10-1-0 (6-1-0)

S17	●	SMU	20	0
S24	● |	Oklahoma State	28	7
O1	●	at Penn State	21	8
O8	●	Air Force DEN	34	8
O15	● |	at Kansas State	45	0
O22	● |	Iowa State	34	8
O29	● |	at Nebraska	28	0
N5	● |	Colorado	16	6
N12	● |	at Oklahoma	41	19
N19	|	Kansas	7	23 †
		ORANGE BOWL		
J2	●	Navy	21	14

1961 7-2-1 (5-2-0)

S23	●	Washington State	28	6
S30	●	at Minnesota	6	0
O7	=	California	14	14
O14	● |	at Oklahoma State	10	0
O21	● |	at Iowa State	13	7
O28	● |	Nebraska	10	0
N4	|	at Colorado	6	7
N11	|	Oklahoma	0	7
N18	● |	Kansas State	27	9
N25	● |	at Kansas	10	7

1962 8-1-2 (5-1-1)

S22	●	at California	21	10
S29	=	at Minnesota	0	0
O6	●	Arizona	17	7
O13	● |	at Kansas State	32	0
O20	● |	Oklahoma State	23	6
O27	● |	Iowa State	21	6
N3	● |	at Nebraska	16	7
N10	● |	Colorado	57	0
N17	|	at Oklahoma	0	13
N24	= |	Kansas	3	3
		BLUEBONNET BOWL		
D22	●	Georgia Tech	14	10

1963 7-3-0 (5-2-0)

S21		Northwestern	12	23
S28	●	Arkansas LR	7	6
O5	●	Idaho	24	0
O12	● |	Kansas State	21	11
O19	● |	at Oklahoma State	28	6
O26	● |	at Iowa State	7	0
N2	|	Nebraska	12	13
N9	● |	at Colorado	28	7
N16	|	Oklahoma	3	13
N23	● |	at Kansas	9	7

1964 6-3-1 (4-2-1)

S19		at California	14	21
S26	●	Utah	23	6
O3	|	Oklahoma State	7	10
O10	● |	at Kansas State	7	0
O17	●	at Air Force	17	7
O24	● |	Iowa State	10	0
O31	|	at Nebraska	0	9
N7	● |	Colorado	16	7
N14	= |	at Oklahoma	14	14
N21	● |	Kansas	34	14

1965 8-2-1 (6-1-0)

S18		Kentucky	0	7
S25	● |	at Oklahoma State	13	0
O2	●	at Minnesota	17	6
O9	● |	Kansas State	28	6
O16	=	UCLA	14	14
O23	● |	at Iowa State	23	7
O30	|	Nebraska	14	16
N6	● |	at Colorado	20	7
N13	● |	Oklahoma	30	0
N20	● |	at Kansas	44	20
		SUGAR BOWL		
J1	●	Florida	20	18

1966 6-3-1 (4-2-1)

S17	●	Minnesota	24	0
S24	●	at Illinois	21	14
O1		at UCLA	15	24
O8	● |	at Kansas State	27	0
O15	● |	Oklahoma State	7	0
O22	= |	Iowa State	10	10
O29	|	at Nebraska	0	35
N5	|	Colorado	0	26
N12	● |	at Oklahoma	10	7
N19	● |	Kansas	7	0

1967 7-3-0 (4-3-0)

S23	●	SMU	21	0
S30	●	at Northwestern	13	6
O7	●	Arizona	17	3
O14	|	at Colorado	9	23
O21	● |	at Iowa State	23	7
O28	|	Oklahoma	0	7
N4	● |	at Oklahoma State	7	0
N11	● |	Kansas State	28	6
N18	● |	Nebraska	10	7
N25	|	at Kansas	6	17

1968 8-3-0 (5-2-0)

S21		at Kentucky	6	12
S28	●	at Illinois	44	0
O5	●	Army	7	3
O12	● |	Colorado	27	14
O19	● |	at Nebraska	16	14
O26	● |	at Kansas State	56	20
N2	● |	Oklahoma State	42	7
N9	● |	Iowa State	42	7
N16	|	at Oklahoma	14	28
N23	|	Kansas	19	21
		GATOR BOWL		
D28	●	Alabama	35	10

1969 9-2-0 (6-1-0)

S20	●	Air Force	19	17
S27	●	Illinois StL	37	6
O4	●	at Michigan	40	17
O11	● |	Nebraska	17	7
O18	● |	Oklahoma State	31	21
O25	|	at Colorado	24	31
N1	● |	Kansas State	41	38
N8	● |	Oklahoma	44	10
N15	● |	at Iowa State	40	13
N22	● |	at Kansas	69	21
		ORANGE BOWL		
J1		Penn State	3	10

1970 5-6-0 (3-4-0)

S11	●	Baylor StL	38	0
S19	●	Minnesota	34	12
S26		Air Force StL	14	37
O3	● |	at Oklahoma State	40	20
O10	|	at Nebraska	7	21
O17		Notre Dame	7	24
O24	● |	Colorado	30	16
O31	|	at Kansas State	13	17
N7	|	at Oklahoma	13	28
N14	|	Iowa State	19	31
N21	● |	Kansas	28	17

AL ONOFRIO
1971-77 (.481) 38-41

1971 1-10-0 (0-7-0)

S11		Stanford	0	19
S18		at Air Force	6	7
S25	●	SMU	24	12
O2		at Army	6	22
O9	|	Nebraska	0	36
O16	|	Oklahoma State	16	37
O23	|	at Colorado	7	27
O30	|	Kansas State	12	28
N6	|	Oklahoma	3	20
N13	|	at Iowa State	17	45
N20	|	at Kansas	2	7

1972 6-6-0 (3-4-0)

S9	●	Oregon	24	22
S23		Baylor	0	27
S30	●	California	34	27
O7	|	at Oklahoma State	16	17
O14	|	at Nebraska	0	62
O21	●	at Notre Dame	30	26
O28	● |	Colorado	20	17
N4	● |	at Kansas State	31	14
N11	|	at Oklahoma	6	17 †
N18	● |	Iowa State	6	5
N25	|	Kansas	17	28
		FIESTA BOWL		
D23		Arizona State	35	49

1973 8-4-0 (3-4-0)

S15	●	Mississippi	17	0
S22	●	Virginia	31	7
S29	●	at North Carolina	27	14
O6	●	at SMU	17	7
O13	● |	Nebraska	13	12
O20	● |	Oklahoma State	13	9
O27	|	at Colorado	13	17
N3	● |	Kansas State	31	7
N10	|	Oklahoma	3	31
N17	|	at Iowa State	7	17
N24	|	at Kansas	13	14
		SUN BOWL		
D29	●	Auburn	34	17

1974 7-4-0 (5-2-0)

S14		Mississippi JAM	0	10
S21	●	Baylor	28	21
S28	●	Arizona State	9	0
O5		at Wisconsin	20	59
O12	● |	at Nebraska	21	10
O19	|	at Oklahoma State	7	31
O26	● |	Colorado	30	24
N2	● |	at Kansas State	52	15
N9	|	at Oklahoma	0	37
N16	● |	Iowa State	10	7
N23	● |	Kansas	27	3

1975 6-5-0 (3-4-0)

S8	●	Alabama BIRM	20	7
S20	●	at Illinois	30	20
S27	●	Wisconsin	27	21
O4		at Michigan	7	31
O11	● |	Oklahoma State	41	14
O18	|	at Colorado	20	31
O25	● |	Kansas State	35	3
N1	|	Nebraska	7	30
N8	● |	at Iowa State	44	14
N15	|	Oklahoma	27	28
N22	|	at Kansas	24	42

556 MISSOURI
THE SCHOOLS

1976 6-5-0 (3-4-0)

S11 ● at Southern Cal 46 25
S18 Illinois 6 31
S25 ● at Ohio State 22 21
O2 ● North Carolina 24 3
O9 ● | at Kansas State 28 21
O16 | Iowa State 17 21
O23 ● | at Nebraska 34 24
O30 | at Oklahoma State 19 20
N6 ● | Colorado 16 7
N13 | at Oklahoma 20 27
N20 | Kansas 14 41

1977 4-7-0 (3-4-0)

S10 Southern Cal 10 27
S17 at Illinois 7 11
S24 California 21 28
O1 ● at Arizona State 15 0
O8 | at Iowa State 0 7
O15 | Oklahoma 17 21
O22 ● | Kansas State 28 13
O29 ● | at Colorado 24 14
N5 | Nebraska 10 21
N12 ● | Oklahoma State 41 14
N19 | at Kansas 22 24

WARREN POWERS
1978-84 (.579) 46-33-3

1978 8-4-0 (4-3-0)

S9 ● at Notre Dame 3 0
S16 Alabama 20 38
S23 ● Mississippi 45 14
S30 | at Oklahoma 23 45
O7 ● Illinois 45 3
O14 ● | Iowa State 26 13
O21 ● | at Kansas State 56 14
O28 | Colorado 27 28
N4 | at Oklahoma State 20 35
N11 ● | Kansas 48 0
N18 ● | at Nebraska 35 31
LIBERTY BOWL
D23 ● LSU 20 15

1979 7-5-0 (3-4-0)

S8 ● San Diego State 45 15
S15 ● at Illinois 14 6
S22 ● Mississippi JaM 33 7
S29 Texas 0 21
O13 | Oklahoma State 13 14
O20 ● | at Colorado 13 7
O27 | Kansas State 3 19
N3 | Nebraska 20 23
N10 ● | at Iowa State 18 9
N17 | Oklahoma 22 24
N24 ● | at Kansas 55 7
HALL OF FAME CLASSIC
D29 ● South Carolina 24 14

1980 8-4-0 (5-2-0)

S13 ● New Mexico 47 16
S20 ● Illinois 52 7
S27 ● at San Diego State 31 7
O4 Penn State 21 29
O11 ● | at Oklahoma State 30 7
O18 ● | Colorado 45 7
O25 ● | at Kansas State 13 3
N1 | at Nebraska 16 38
N8 ● | Iowa State 14 10
N15 | at Oklahoma 7 17
N22 ● | Kansas 31 6
LIBERTY BOWL
D27 Purdue 25 28

1981 8-4-0 (3-4-0)

S12 ● Army 24 10
S19 ● Rice 42 10
S26 ● Louisville 34 3
O3 ● Mississippi State JaM 14 3
O10 ● | Kansas State 58 13
O17 | at Iowa State 13 34
O24 | Nebraska 0 6
O31 | Oklahoma State 12 16
N7 ● | at Colorado 30 14
N14 ● | Oklahoma 19 14
N21 | at Kansas 11 19
TANGERINE BOWL
D19 ● Southern Miss 19 17

1982 5-4-2 (2-3-2)

S4 ● Colorado State 28 14
S11 ● Army 23 10
S25 at Texas 0 21
O2 ● East Carolina 28 9
O9 = | at Kansas State 7 7
O16 = | Iowa State 17 17
O23 | at Nebraska 19 23
O30 | at Oklahoma State 20 30
N6 ● | Colorado 35 14
N13 | at Oklahoma 14 41
N20 ● | Kansas 16 10

1983 7-5-0 (5-2-0)

S10 ● Illinois 28 18
S17 at Wisconsin 20 21
S24 ● Utah State 17 10
O1 East Carolina 6 13
O8 ● | at Colorado 59 20
O15 | Nebraska 3 34
O22 ● | Kansas State 38 0
O29 ● | at Iowa State 41 18
N5 ● | Oklahoma 10 0
N12 ● | Oklahoma State 16 10
N19 | at Kansas 27 37
HOLIDAY BOWL
D23 Brigham Young 17 21

1984 3-7-1 (2-4-1)

S8 at Illinois 24 30
S15 Wisconsin 34 35
S22 ● Mississippi State 47 30
S29 Notre Dame 14 16
O6 ● | Colorado 52 7
O13 | at Nebraska 23 33
O20 ● | at Kansas State 61 21
O27 = | Iowa State 14 14
N3 | at Oklahoma 7 49
N10 | at Oklahoma State 13 31
N17 | Kansas 21 35

WOODY WIDENHOFER
1985-88 (.284) 12-31-1

1985 1-10-0 (1-6-0)

S14 Northwestern 23 27
S21 at Texas 17 21
S28 Indiana 17 36
O5 California 32 39
O12 | at Colorado 7 38
O19 | Nebraska 20 28
O26 | Kansas State 17 20
N2 ● | at Iowa State 28 27
N9 | Oklahoma 6 51
N16 | Oklahoma State 19 21
N23 | at Kansas 20 34

1986 3-8-0 (2-5-0)

S13 ● Utah State 24 10
S20 Texas 25 27
S27 Indiana 24 41
O4 at Syracuse 9 41
O11 | Colorado 12 17
O18 | at Nebraska 17 48
O25 ● | at Kansas State 17 6
N1 | Iowa State 14 37
N8 | at Oklahoma 0 77
N22 ● | Kansas 48 0
D4 | at Oklahoma State 6 10

1987 5-6-0 (3-4-0)

S12 ● Baylor 23 18
S19 ● Northwestern 28 3
S26 at Indiana 17 20
O3 Syracuse 13 24
O10 ● | Kansas State 34 10
O17 ● | at Iowa State 42 17
O24 | Oklahoma State 20 24
O31 | Nebraska 7 42
N7 | at Colorado 10 27
N14 | at Oklahoma 13 17
N21 ● | Kansas 19 7

1988 3-7-1 (2-5-0)

S10 ● Utah State 35 21
S17 Houston 7 31
S24 = Indiana 28 28
O1 at Miami, Fla. 0 55
O8 ● | at Kansas State 52 21
O15 | Iowa State 3 21
O22 | at Oklahoma State 21 49
O29 | at Nebraska 18 26
N5 | Colorado 8 45
N12 | Oklahoma 7 16
N19 ● | at Kansas 55 17

BOB STULL
1989-93 (.291) 15-38-2

1989 2-9-0 (1-6-0)

S9 ● TCU 14 10
S16 at Indiana 7 24
S23 Miami, Fla. 7 38
S30 at Arizona State 3 19
O7 | at Colorado 3 49
O14 | Nebraska 7 50
O21 ● | at Kansas State 21 9
O28 | Oklahoma State 30 31
N4 | at Oklahoma 14 52
N11 | Iowa State 21 35
N18 | Kansas 44 46

1990 4-7-0 (2-5-0)

S8 TCU 19 20
S15 ● Utah State 45 10
S22 at Indiana 7 58
S29 ● Arizona State 30 9
O6 | Colorado 31 33
O13 | at Nebraska 21 69
O20 ● | Kansas State 31 10
O27 | at Oklahoma State 28 48
N3 | Oklahoma 10 55
N10 | at Iowa State 25 27
N17 ● | at Kansas 31 21

1991 3-7-1 (1-6-0)

S14 ● Illinois 23 19
S21 at Baylor 21 47
S28 = Indiana 27 27
O5 ● Memphis 31 21
O12 | at Colorado 7 55
O19 ● | Oklahoma State 41 7
O26 | at Nebraska 6 63
N2 | Iowa State 22 23
N9 | Oklahoma 16 56
N16 | at Kansas State 0 32
N23 | at Kansas 29 53

1992 3-8-0 (2-5-0)

S12 at Illinois 17 24
S19 Texas A&M 13 26
S26 at Indiana 10 20
O3 ● Marshall 44 21
O8 | Colorado 0 6
O17 | at Oklahoma State 26 28
O24 | Nebraska 24 34
O31 | at Iowa State 14 28
N7 | at Oklahoma 17 51
N14 ● | Kansas State 27 14
N21 ● | Kansas 22 17

1993 3-7-1 (2-5-0)

S11 ● Illinois 31 3
S18 at Texas A&M 0 73
S25 at West Virginia 3 35
O2 = SMU 10 10
O9 | at Colorado 18 30
O16 ● | Oklahoma State 42 9
O23 | at Nebraska 7 49
O30 ● | Iowa State 37 34
N6 | Oklahoma 23 42
N13 | at Kansas State 21 31
N20 | at Kansas 0 28

LARRY SMITH
1994-2000 (.419) 33-46-1

1994 3-8-1 (2-5-0)

S3 Tulsa 17 20
S10 at Illinois 0 42
S17 ● at Houston 16 0
O1 West Virginia 10 34
O8 | Colorado 23 38
O15 ● | at Oklahoma State 24 15
O22 | Nebraska 7 42
O29 ● | at Iowa State 34 20
N5 | at Oklahoma 13 30
N12 | Kansas State 18 21
N19 | Kansas 14 31
N26 = at Hawaii 32 32

1995 3-8-0 (1-6-0)

S2 ● North Texas 28 7
S9 Bowling Green 10 17
S16 at Texas Tech 14 41
S23 ● La. Monroe 31 22
O7 | at Kansas State 0 30
O14 | at Nebraska 0 57
O21 | Oklahoma State 26 30
O28 | Oklahoma 9 13
N4 | at Kansas 23 42
N11 | at Colorado 0 21
N18 ● | Iowa State 45 3

1996-PRESENT
BIG 12

1996 5-6 (3-5)

A31 | at Texas 10 40
S14 Memphis 16 19
S21 ● Clemson 38 24
S28 | at Iowa State 31 45
O5 ● at SMU 27 26
O12 | Kansas State 10 35
O26 ● | Oklahoma State 35 28
N2 | Colorado 13 41
N9 | at Nebraska 7 51
N16 ● | at Baylor 49 42
N23 ● | Kansas 42 25

1997 7-5 (5-3)

S6 ● Eastern Michigan 44 24
S13 | at Kansas 7 15
S20 ● at Tulsa 42 21
S27 Ohio State 10 31
O4 ● | Iowa State 45 21
O11 | at Kansas State 11 41
O18 ● | Texas 37 29
O25 ● | at Oklahoma State 51 50
N1 ● | at Colorado 41 31
N8 | Nebraska 38 45
N15 ● | Baylor 42 24
HOLIDAY BOWL
D29 Colorado State 24 35

1998 8-4 (5-3)

S5 ● Bowling Green 37 0
S12 ● | Kansas 41 23
S19 at Ohio State 14 35
O3 ● Northwestern St. 35 14
O10 ● | at Iowa State 35 19
O17 ● | Oklahoma 20 6
O24 | at Nebraska 13 20
O31 ● | at Texas Tech 28 26
N7 ● | Colorado 38 14
N14 | at Texas A&M 14 17
N21 | Kansas State 25 31
INSIGHT.COM
D26 ● West Virginia 34 31

1999 4-7 (1-7)

S4 ● UAB 31 28
S18 ● Western Michigan 48 34
S25 | Nebraska 10 40
O2 ● at Memphis 27 17
O9 | at Colorado 39 46
O16 | Iowa State 21 24
O23 | at Kansas 0 21
O30 ● | Texas Tech 34 7
N6 | at Oklahoma 0 37
N13 | Texas A&M 14 51
N20 | at Kansas State 0 66

2000 3-8 (2-6)

S2 ● Western Ill. 50 20
S9 at Clemson 9 62
S16 Michigan State 10 13
S30 | at Nebraska 24 42
O7 ● | Oklahoma State 24 10
O14 | Kansas 17 38
O21 | at Texas 12 46
O28 | at Iowa State 20 39
N4 | Colorado 18 28
N11 ● | at Baylor 47 22
N18 | Kansas State 24 28

GARY PINKEL
2001-PRESENT (.468) 22-25

2001 4-7 (3-5)

S1 Bowling Green 13 20
S8 ● Texas St. 40 6
S29 | Nebraska 3 36
O6 ● | at Oklahoma State 41 38
O13 | Iowa State 14 20
O20 ● | at Kansas 38 34
O27 | Texas 16 35
N3 | at Colorado 24 38
N10 ● | Baylor 41 24
N24 | at Kansas State 3 24
D1 at Michigan State 7 55

2002
5-7   (2-6)

A31	●	Illinois *StL*	33	20
S7	●	Ball State	41	6
S14		at Bowling Green	28	51
S28	●	Troy State	44	7
O5	|	Oklahoma	24	31
O12	|	at Nebraska	13	24
O19	|	at Texas Tech	38	52
O26	● |	Kansas	36	12
N2	|	at Iowa State	35	42
N9	|	Colorado	35	42
N16	● |	at Texas A&M	33	27
N23	|	Kansas State	0	38

2003
8-5   (4-4)

A30	●	Illinois *StL*	22	15
S6	●	at Ball State	35	7
S13	●	Eastern Illinois	37	0
S20	●	Middle Tennessee	41	40
S27	|	at Kansas	14	35
O11	● |	Nebraska	41	24
O18	|	at Oklahoma	13	34
O25	● |	Texas Tech	62	31
N8	|	at Colorado	16	21
N15	● |	Texas A&M	45	22
N22	|	at Kansas State	14	24
N29	● |	Iowa State	45	7
		INDEPENDENCE BOWL		
D31		Arkansas	14	27

2004
5-6   (3-5)

S4	●	Arkansas State	52	20
S9	●	at Troy State	14	24
S18	●	Ball State	48	0
O2	● |	Colorado	17	9
O9	● |	at Baylor	30	10
O16	|	at Texas	20	28
O23	|	Oklahoma State	17	20
O30	|	at Nebraska	3	24
N6	|	Kansas State	24	35
N20	|	Kansas	14	31
N27	● |	at Iowa State	17	14

THE SCHOOLS

NAVY

BY SETH WICKERSHAM

N AVY FOOTBALL USED TO MATTER, back when the program was featured on the cover of *Time* magazine, when the Army-Navy game was frequently between Top 10 teams, when the Midshipmen were anything but in the middle. From the 1920s until the 1960s, when they had Heisman Trophy winners Joe Bellino (1960) and Roger Staubach (1963), the Midshipmen were one of the glamour teams in college football. Newspapers would send scores of reporters to cover the Army-Navy game, which featured the one-time national champion Mids against the three-time champ Cadets. Today, the Midshipmen may no longer be at the center of the sport—though the Army-Navy game remains a national television staple—but the program still has its virtues.

Navy's program seems virginal when set against the rest of Division I-A college football. The Midshipmen still make their beds, shine their shoes and prepare to defend their country. Despite three bowl games in the 1970s and early 1980s, Navy football slid at the turn of the century, going 3–30 from 2000 to 2002. Talk went from 10-win seasons to a 10-win decade. But coach Paul Johnson has revived the school's fortunes with a refined triple-option attack and a ball-hawking defense. In 2003 and 2004, Navy won a combined 18 games and, for only the second time in school history, competed in consecutive bowl contests. And, as anyone close to Annapolis can tell you, they've now taken five of the past six from Army.

TRADITION Before home games, the 4,000 members of the Brigade of Midshipmen march on the field. During home games, the freshmen do push-ups—one for every point Navy scores. After each score, a cannon is fired and students in the stands throw their caps into the air. Navy's mascot, Bill the Goat (not to be confused with the Billy Goat from Wrigley Field), always faces the direction the offense is going.

BEST PLAYER No team Roger Staubach quarterbacked was ever out of a game. Not in the pros with Dallas, and especially not in college with Navy. Staubach was so good that in 1963, he was on the cover of *Time* in his football uniform and *Sports Illustrated* in his military uniform. In that year, his junior season, he led No. 2 Navy to the Cotton Bowl and was awarded the Heisman, Maxwell and Walter Camp trophies and was named first team All-America. "He came along in the age of television and performed best when the lights were on," says Jack Clary, author of two books on Navy football. Following four years in the U.S. Navy, Staubach joined the Dallas Cowboys and became one of the finest players of his era. In 11 seasons, he led the Cowboys to a 90–31 record and

---

PROFILE

United States Naval Academy
Annapolis, Md.
Founded: 1845
Enrollment: 4,000
Colors: Navy Blue and Gold
Nickname: Midshipmen
Stadium: Jack Stephens Field at Navy-Marine Corps Memorial Stadium
   Opened in 1959
   Grass; 34,000 capacity
First football game: 1879
All-time record: 599–498–57 (.544)
Bowl record: 5–5–1
Heisman Trophy: Joe Bellino, 1960; Roger Staubach, 1963
Website: www.navysports.com

THE BEST OF TIMES

Navy went 55–30–9 in the 1950s, with only two losing seasons, highlighted by a Cotton Bowl win against Rice in 1958.

THE WORST OF TIMES

From 2000 to 2002, Navy went 3–30. The low point was a winless 2001 season in which coach Charlie Weatherbie was fired after seven games.

CONFERENCE

Since its first game in 1879, Navy has remained independent.

DISTINGUISHED ALUMNI

Jimmy Carter; John McCain; H. Ross Perot; David Robinson, NBA player; Alan Shepard, astronaut

FIGHT SONG

ANCHORS AWEIGH
Stand, Navy, out to sea, fight our battle cry;
We'll never change our course, So vicious foe steer shy-y-y-y.
Roll out the TNT, Anchors Aweigh.
Sail on to victory
And sink their bones to Davy Jones, hooray!
Anchors Aweigh, my boys, Anchors Aweigh.
Farewell to college joys, we sail at break of day-ay-ay-ay.
Through our last night on shore, drink to the foam,
Until we meet once more.
Here's wishing you a happy voyage home.

guided them to Super Bowl wins over Miami and Denver. Staubach retired with a then-NFL-record 23 fourth-quarter comeback wins and was inducted into both the college and Pro Football halls of fame.

BEST COACH George Welsh was a crafty, cunning, practical quarterback when he led Navy to an 8–2 record in 1954, capped by a Sugar Bowl win over Mississippi. He had the same attributes as a coach. He became Navy's head coach in 1973, and guided the Midshipmen to three bowls in nine years. Welsh was known as a tough coach, but as a graduate of Navy he knew what and how much he could demand from his players. "He had their respect," Clary says. "He didn't con them, and they didn't con him." Welsh left for the University of Virginia in 1982 with a 55–46–1 record, still good enough to be Navy's all-time winningest coach. At Virginia, he was named ACC Coach of the Year five times and National Coach of the Year three times.

BEST TEAM In 1926, Bill Ingram became head coach of a Navy football program that had won only seven games combined in its previous two seasons. To say he turned it around immediately is an understatement. Behind the coaching of Ingram and the play of three offensive stars— tackle Frank Wickhorst, quarterback Tom Hamilton and

> *Roger Staubach was on the covers of* Time *in his football uniform and SI in his military uniform in 1963.*

running back Henry Caldwell—the Midshipmen raced to a 5–0 record. The man the team followed was Hamilton, a natural leader who went on to become an admiral. Against Michigan on Oct. 30, before 80,000 fans in Baltimore, Hamilton led Navy up and down the field, and Caldwell's one-yard touchdown run beat the Wolverines 10-0. A 21-21 tie against Army four weeks later ruined Navy's unblemished record, but the Midshipmen were still good enough to finish 9–0–1 and claim a share of the national championship.

BIGGEST GAME The Midshipmen had been 7–34–2 since the 1946 season and were 2–6 on the year when they met Army on Dec. 2, 1950. Army was ranked No. 2 in the country and was a three-touchdown favorite. But before 101,000 spectators, including President Harry S. Truman, an 813-foot good-luck telegram signed by 824 Midshipmen was delivered to Philadelphia's Municipal Stadium. Navy ran with the luck. Quarterback Bob "Zug" Zastrow contributed two second-half touchdowns, one a seven-yard run and another a 30-yard pass to receiver Jim Baldinger, and Navy led 14-0. The Midshipmen's defense allowed the Cadets inside the Navy 20-yard line seven times in the third and fourth quarters, but didn't permit a score, helping Navy to a 14-2 win.

RECORDS

RUSHING YARDS

	GAME	
298	Eddie Meyers vs. Syracuse, Nov. 7, 1981 (42 att.)	

	SEASON	
1,587	Napoleon McCallum, 1983 (331 att.)	

	CAREER	
4,179	Napoleon McCallum, 1981-85 (908 att.)	

PASSING YARDS

	GAME	
406	Jim Kubiak vs. Wake Forest, Nov. 23, 1991 (36 of 54)	

	SEASON	
2,628	Jim Kubiak, 1993 (248 of 401)	

	CAREER	
6,008	Jim Kubiak, 1991-94 (558 of 969)	

RECEIVING YARDS

	GAME	
179	Dave King vs. Notre Dame, Oct. 30, 1976; Rob Taylor vs. Vanderbilt, Nov. 18, 1967 (10 rec.)	

	SEASON	
818	Rob Taylor, 1967 (61 rec.)	

	CAREER	
1,736	Rob Taylor, 1965-67 (129 rec.)	

POINTS

	GAME	
38	Bill Ingram vs. Villanova, Nov. 17, 1917	

	SEASON	
174	Bill Ingram, 1917 (21 TDs, 48 PATs)	

	CAREER	
268	Chris McCoy, 1995-97 (44 TDs, 2 two-pt. conv.)	

CONSENSUS ALL-AMERICANS

1907	Bill Dague, E
1908	Ed Lange, QB
1908	Percy Northcroft, T
1911	Jack Dalton, B
1913	John Brown, G
1918	Lyman Perry, G
1918	Wolcott Roberts, B
1922	Wendell Taylor, E
1926	Frank Wickhorst, T
1928	Ed Burke, G
1934	Fred Borries, B
1943-44	Don Whitmire, T
1944	Ben Chase, G
1944	Bobby Jenkins, HB
1945	Dick Duden, E
1954-55	Ron Beagle, E
1960	Joe Bellino, HB
1963	Roger Staubach, QB
1975	Chet Moeller, DB
1983, 1985	Napoleon McCallum, HB

BIGGEST UPSET How can a tie be an upset? It was on Nov. 27, 1948, when Navy was 0–8 and Army was 8–0 and a 20-point favorite. The Cadets went ahead 14-7 early on short touchdown runs by Rudolph Cosentino and Harold Shultz. But Navy's Bill Hawkins plunged over from one yard out late in the third quarter to tie the game. Army quarterback Arnold Galiffa countered by scoring on a 10-yard bootleg, but Hawkins was the difference late, scoring to tie it 21-21 and knocking down Galiffa's fourth-down pass to end the game.

HEARTBREAKER Navy hadn't beaten Notre Dame for 36 years, but on Oct. 30, 1999, the Mids were ahead 24-21 with 1:20 remaining and Notre Dame facing fourth and 10 from the Navy 37. With the home crowd behind him, Irish quarterback Jarious Jackson hit receiver Bobby Brown, who fell near the first-down marker. Irish eyes saw that he twisted his body and cleared the first-down line by inches. Navy eyes saw that he was short. The officials said Brown got the first down, and Notre Dame scored two plays later to win 28-24.

STADIUM Jack Stephens Field at Navy-Marine Corps Memorial Stadium, with bleachers sprouting out of the inset field and end zone grass seating areas, is in its 47th season as Navy's home. It was finished in 1959, at a cost of $3 million, all raised through private donations. Since then, more than four million fans have watched the Midshipmen play. The stadium has been through a few face-lifts recently. In 1992, $800,000 was spent for new locker rooms and a stadium-side Walk of Fame, highlighted by Navy's Heisman and Maxwell trophy winners, Hall of Fame selectees and All-America picks.

RIVAL Army-Navy no longer determines national champions, but it's still nationally broadcast, still attended by the entire student bodies of both teams, still features a unique pageantry and is still the most important game every year for both schools. Everything at the Naval Academy, from weights to stationery, says, "Beat Army!" For the week leading up to the game, many rules at the two academies are called off. Statues are painted, curfews are broken, and school officials really don't care. According to John Feinstein's 1996 book *A Civil War*, plebes answer all questions from upperclassmen the week of the Army game with, "Beat Army!" The schools first played in 1890, and the series stood at 49–49–7 through 2004.

> *Army-Navy no longer determines national champions, but it's still attended by the entire student bodies of both schools.*

NICKNAME Navy has virtually always been known as the Midshipmen, a name that first came into the English language in the 17th century for men who were stationed "amidships"—in the middle portion of a vessel. In the American Navy's early days, one could become a midshipman only by training aboard the boat and being commissioned, but in 1845 it became possible to reach that designation straight from civilian life. In 1902, Navy football players became officially known as the Midshipmen.

MASCOT Going through Navy's mascots is like going through a zoo. Navy's first mascot was a goat named El Cid (The Chief), and it cheered on Navy as the Midshipmen beat Army 6-4 in 1893. In the next 10 years, the mascot moved from being a dog to a cat to a carrier pigeon. Finally, in 1904, a goat was handed the role, and since then there have been 33 Bill the Goats. Bill is a well-attended goat: 15 handlers care for him, and all have to be trained for the position.

UNIFORMS In the Midshipmen's first year, 1879, they wore white canvas jackets laced tightly. These were supposedly the first real uniforms ever used. By 1890, blue-and-white stocking caps were added. In the early 1900s, the uniforms were all blue. By 1926, the Midshipmen wore jerseys with vertical blue-and-gold stripes. During Navy's one-loss 1943 season, the uniforms were changed to gold pants and blue or white jerseys with stripes on the sleeves. By the 1990s, "Navy" was put on the front, above the numbers. In 1962, there was a skull-and-bones logo added to the front of the helmet, an idea of then-SID Budd Thalman, who used the pirate symbol of Jolly Roger—Staubach's nickname. For the 1963 Army game, a "Beat Army" sticker was added to the side of the helmet. For the past 30 years, the helmet has been plain gold.

QUOTE "Now that's a tough schedule."—Lou Holtz, then-coach of William & Mary, when looking at the battles the U.S. Navy has fought, as documented along the facade of Memorial Stadium

NAVY ALL-TIME SCORES

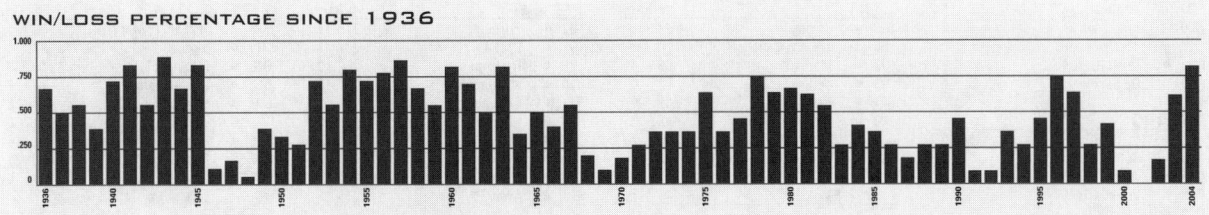

WIN/LOSS PERCENTAGE SINCE 1936

NO HEAD COACH

1879   0-0-1
D11	=	Baltimore AC *Unk*	0	0

1880-1881
NO TEAM

VAUX CARTER
1882 (1.000)   1-0

1882   1-0-0
U		Johns Hopkins *Unk*	8	0

NO HEAD COACH

1883   0-1-0
U		Johns Hopkins *Unk*	0	2

1884   1-0-0
U	●	Johns Hopkins *Unk*	9	6

1885   1-2-0
U		St. John's *Unk*	46	10
U		Johns Hopkins *Unk*	8	12
U		Princeton JV *Unk*	0	10

1886   3-3-0
U	●	St. John's *Unk*	12	0
U	●	Johns Hopkins *Unk*	6	0
U	●	St. John's *Unk*	0	4
U	●	Johns Hopkins *Unk*	15	14
U		Princeton JV *Unk*	0	30
U		Gallaudet *Unk*	0	16

1887   3-1-0
U	●	St. John's *Unk*	4	0
U	●	St. John's *Unk*	24	0
U	●	Johns Hopkins *Unk*	8	0
U		Princeton JV *Unk*	5	22

1888   1-3-0
U		St. John's *Unk*	4	6
U	●	Gallaudet *Unk*	4	0
U		Johns Hopkins *Unk*	12	25
D1		Pennsylvania	9	20
D9		St. John's *Unk*	6	22

1889   4-1-1
U	●	St. John's *Unk*	20	10
U	●	Johns Hopkins *Unk*	36	0
N9	=	Dickinson *Unk*	0	0
N28		Lehigh	6	26
D7	●	Virginia	22	12 *
U		Washington Stars *Unk*	24	0

1890   5-1-1
U	●	St. John's *Unk*	45	0
U	●	Georgetown *Unk*	70	4
N8	●	Dickinson *Unk*	32	6
U	=	Columbia AC *Unk*	6	6
U	●	Kendall *Unk*	24	0
N27		Lehigh	4	24
N29	●	at Army	24	0

EDGAR A. POE
1891 (.714)   5-2

1891   5-2-0
O24	●	St. John's	28	6
O31	●	Rutgers	20	12 *
N7	●	Gallaudet	6	0
N11	●	Georgetown	16	4
N14	●	Dickinson	34	4
N21		Lafayette	0	4
N28		Army	16	32

BEN CROSBY
1892 (.714)   5-2

1892   5-2-0
O12	●	Pennsylvania	0	16
O15	●	Princeton	0	28
O22	●	Lafayette	22	4
O29	●	Franklin & Marshall	24	0
N5	●	Rutgers	48	12
N19	●	Georgetown	40	0
N26	●	at Army	12	4

JOSH HARTWELL
1893 (.625)   5-3

1893   5-3-0
O11	●	Pennsylvania	0	34
O14	●	Dickinson *Unk*	26	0
O21	●	Virginia	28	0
O28	●	Lehigh	6	12
U	●	Georgetown *Unk*	22	10
U	●	Franklin & Marshall *Unk*	34	6
N22	●	Virginia	0	12
D2	●	Army	6	4

BILL WURTENBURG
1894 (.714)   4-1-2

1894   4-1-2
U	=	Elizabeth AC *Unk*	6	6
U	●	Georgetown *Unk*	12	0
O27	●	Pennsylvania	0	12
U	●	Carlisle	8	0
N11	=	Lehigh *Unk*	10	0
N10	=	Penn State	6	6
U	●	Baltimore City Coll. *Unk*	30	6

MATT McCLUNG
1895 (.714)   5-2

1895   5-2-0
U	●	Elizabeth AC *Unk*	6	0
U	●	New Jersey AC *Unk*	34	0
U	●	Franklin & Marshall *Unk*	68	0
U	●	Carlisle	34	0
U	●	Virginia Coll. *Unk*	1	0 *f*
U	●	Orange AC *Unk*	6	10
N16	●	Lehigh	4	6

JOHNNY POE
1896 (.625)   5-3

1896   5-3-0
O7	●	Pennsylvania	0	8
O10	●	Franklin & Marshall	49	0
O17	●	St. John's	50	0
O24	●	Penn Reserves	0	6
O31	●	Rutgers	40	6
N7	●	Lehigh	24	10
N23	●	White Squadron	11	5
N26	●	Lafayette	6	18

BILL ARMSTRONG
1897-99 (.800)   20-5

1897   8-1-0
U	●	Rutgers	1	0 *f*
O9	●	Princeton	0	28
O13	●	Penn Reserves	22	0
O16	●	Princeton AC	6	0
O23	●	Penn State	4	0
N6	●	Virginia	4	0
N13	●	Maryland Coll.	38	0
N20	●	Lehigh	28	6
N25	●	White Squadron	8	0

1898   7-1-0
O8	●	Bucknell	11	0
O15	●	Princeton	0	30
O22	●	Penn State	16	11
O29	●	Lafayette	18	0
N5	●	Columbia AC	52	5
N12	●	Lehigh	6	5
N19	●	at Virginia	6	0
N24	●	VMI	21	5

1899   5-3-0
O7	●	Princeton	0	5
O14	●	Georgetown	12	0
O21	●	Penn State	6	0
O28	●	Lafayette	0	5
N4	●	North Carolina	12	0
N11	●	Trinity	35	0
N18	●	Lehigh	24	0
D2	●	Army *Phil*	5	17

GARRETT COCHRAN
1900 (.667)   6-3

1900   6-3-0
O6	●	Baltimore Med. Coll.	6	0
O13	●	Princeton	0	5
O20	●	Georgetown	6	0
O24	●	Lehigh	15	0
N3	●	Wash. & Jeff.	18	0
N10	●	Penn State	44	0
N17	●	Columbia	0	11
N21	●	Pennsylvania	6	28
D1	●	Army *Phil*	11	7

DOC HILLEBRAND
1901-02 (.429)   8-11-2

1901   6-4-1
O5	=	Georgetown	0	0
O9	●	St. John's	28	2
O12	●	Yale	0	24
O19	●	Lehigh	18	0
O21	●	Pennsylvania	6	5
O26	●	Penn State	6	11
N2	●	Dickinson	12	6
N9	●	Carlisle	16	5
N16	●	Wash. & Jeff.	17	11
N22	●	Columbia	5	6
N30	●	Army *Phil*	5	11

1902   2-7-1
S27	●	Georgetown	0	4
O4	●	Princeton	0	11
O15	=	Lehigh	5	5
O22	●	Pennsylvania	10	6
O25	●	Dickinson	0	6
N1	●	Penn State	0	6
N8	●	Lafayette	12	11
N15	●	Bucknell	0	23
N19	●	Columbia	0	5
N29	●	Army *Phil*	8	22

BURR CHAMBERLAIN
1903 (.375)   4-7-1

1903   4-7-1
O10	●	Virginia	6	5
O14	●	Gallaudet	18	0
O17	●	Dickinson	5	0
O21	=	Baltimore Med. Coll.	0	0
O24	●	Lafayette	5	6
O28	●	Georgetown	5	12
O31	●	Penn State	0	17
N4	●	N.Y. Navy	28	0
N7	●	Wash. & Jeff.	0	16
N14	●	Bucknell	5	23
N21	●	Virginia Tech	0	11
N28	●	Army *Phil*	5	40

PAUL DASHIELL
1904-06 (.794)   25-5-4

1904   7-2-1
O8	●	VMI	12	0
O12	●	Marine Officers	68	0
O15	●	Princeton	10	9
O19	●	St. John's	23	0
O22	=	Dickinson	0	0
O29	●	Swarthmore	0	9
N5	●	Penn State	20	9
N12	●	at Virginia	5	0
N19	●	Virginia Tech	11	0
N26	●	Army *Phil*	0	11

1905   10-1-1
O7	●	VMI	34	0
O11	●	St. John's	29	0
O14	●	Dickinson	6	0
O18	●	Western Maryland	29	0
O21	●	North Carolina	38	0
O25	●	Maryland	17	0
O28	●	Swarthmore	5	6
N4	●	Penn State	11	5
N11	●	Bucknell	34	0
N18	●	Virginia	22	0
N25	●	Virginia Tech	12	6
D2	=	Army *Pri*	6	6

1906   8-2-2
O6	=	Dickinson	0	0
O10	●	Maryland	12	0
O13	●	Princeton	0	5
O17	●	St. John's	34	5
O20	●	Lehigh	12	0
O24	●	Western Maryland	31	0
O27	=	Bucknell	0	0
N3	●	Penn State	0	5
N10	●	Swarthmore	5	4
N17	●	North Carolina	40	0
N24	●	Virginia Tech	5	0
D1	●	Army *Phil*	10	0

JOE REEVES
1907 (.792)   9-2-1

1907   9-2-1
O2	●	St. John's	26	0
O5	●	Dickinson	15	0
O9	●	Maryland	12	0
O12	=	Vanderbilt	6	6
O16	●	St. John's	12	0
O19	●	Harvard	0	6
O26	●	Lafayette	17	0
N2	●	West Virginia	6	0
N9	●	Swarthmore	0	18
N16	●	Penn State	6	4
N23	●	Virginia Tech	12	0
N30	●	Army *Phil*	6	0

FRANK BERRIEN
1908-10 (.776)   21-5-3

1908   9-2-1
O3	●	Rutgers	18	0
O4	●	St. John's	22	0
O10	●	Dickinson	22	0
O14	●	at Maryland	57	0
O17	●	Lehigh	16	0
O24	=	Harvard	6	6
O28	●	George Washington	17	0
O31	●	Carlisle	6	16
N7	●	Villanova	30	0
N14	●	Penn State	5	0
N21	●	Virginia Tech	15	4
N28	●	Army *Phil*	4	6

1909 4-3-1

O6	●	St. John's	16	6
O9	●	Rutgers	12	3
O16	●	Villanova	6	11
O23	●	Virginia	0	5
O30	●	Princeton	3	5
N6	=	Wash. & Jeff.	0	0
N13	●	West Reserve	17	6
N20	●	Davidson	45	6

1910 8-0-1

O1	●	St. John's	16	0
O8	●	Rutgers	0	0
O15	●	Wash. & Jeff.	15	0
O22	●	Virginia Tech	3	0
O29	●	West Reserve	17	0
N5	●	Lehigh	30	0
N12	●	Carlisle	6	0
N19	●	NYU	9	0
N26	●	Army *Phil*	3	0

DOUG HOWARD
1911-14 (.750) 25-7-4

1911 6-0-3

O7	●	Johns Hopkins	27	5
O11	●	St. John's	21	0
O14	●	Wash. & Jeff.	16	0
O21	=	Princeton	0	0
O28	●	West Reserve	0	0
N4	●	North Carolina St.	17	6
N11	●	West Virginia	32	0
N18	●	Penn State	0	0
N24	●	Army *Phil*	3	0

1912 6-3-0

O5	●	Johns Hopkins	7	3
O12	●	Lehigh	0	14
O19	●	Swarthmore	6	21
O26	●	Pittsburgh	13	6
N1	●	West Reserve	7	0
N9	●	Bucknell	7	17
N16	●	North Carolina St.	40	0
N23	●	NYU	39	0
N30	●	Army *Phil*	6	0

1913 7-1-1

O4	=	Pittsburgh	0	0
O11	●	Georgetown	23	0
O18	●	Dickinson	29	0
O25	●	Maryland	76	0
N1	●	Lehigh	39	0
N8	●	Bucknell	70	7
N15	●	Penn State	10	0
N22	●	NYU	48	0
N29	●	Army *NYC*	9	22

1914 6-3-0

O3	●	Georgetown	13	0
O10	●	Pittsburgh	6	13
O17	●	at Pennsylvania	6	13
O24	●	West Reserve	48	0
O31	●	North Carolina St.	14	12 *
N7	●	Fordham	21	0
N14	●	Colby	31	21
N21	●	Ursinus	33	2
N28	●	Army *Phil*	0	20

JONAS INGRAM
1915-16 (.526) 9-8-2

1915 3-5-1

O2	●	Georgetown	0	9
O9	●	Pittsburgh	12	47
O16	●	Pennsylvania	7	7
O23	●	Virginia Tech	20	0
O30	●	North Carolina St.	12	14
N6	●	Bucknell	13	3
N13	●	Colby	28	14
N20	●	Ursinus	7	10
N27	●	Army *NYC*	0	14

1916 6-3-1

S30	=	Dickinson	0	0
O7	●	Georgetown	13	7
O11	●	at Maryland	14	7
O14	●	Pittsburgh	19	20
O21	●	West Virginia	12	7
O28	●	Georgia	27	3
N4	●	Wash. & Lee	0	10
N11	●	North Carolina St.	50	0
N18	●	Villanova	57	7
N25	●	Army *NYC*	7	15

GIL DOBIE
1917-19 (.850) 17-3

1917 7-1-0

S29	●	Davidson	27	6
O6	●	West Virginia	0	7
O13	●	Maryland	62	0
O20	●	Carlisle	62	0
O27	●	Haverford	89	0
N3	●	West Reserve	95	0
N10	●	Georgetown	28	7
N17	●	Villanova	80	3

1918 4-1-0

O26	●	New Port NTS	47	7
N2	●	St. Helena NTS	66	0
N9	●	Norfolk Navy	37	6
N16	●	Ursinus	127	0
N23	●	Great Lakes NAS	6	7

1919 6-1-0

O4	●	North Carolina St.	49	0
O11	●	Johns Hopkins	66	0
O25	●	Bucknell	21	6
N1	●	W.V. Wesleyan	20	6
N8	●	Georgetown	0	6
N15	●	Colby	121	0
N29	●	Army *NYC*	6	0

BOB FOLWELL
1920-24 (.654) 24-12-3

1920 6-2-0

O2		North Carolina St.	7	14
O9	●	Lafayette	12	7
O16	●	Bucknell	7	2
O23	●	at Princeton	0	14
O30	●	West Reserve	47	0
N6	●	Georgetown	21	6
N13	●	South Carolina	63	0
N27	●	Army *NYC*	7	0

1921 6-1-0

O1	●	North Carolina St.	40	0
O8	●	Western Reserve	53	0
O15	●	Princeton	13	0
O29	●	Bethany	21	0
N5	●	Bucknell	6	0
N12	●	Penn State *Phil*	7	13
N26	●	Army *NYC*	7	0

1922 5-2-0

O7	●	Western Reserve	71	0
O14	●	Bucknell	14	7
O21	●	Georgia Tech	13	0
O28	●	at Pennsylvania	7	13
N3	●	Penn State *DC*	14	0
N11	●	Xavier	52	0
N25	●	Army *Phil*	14	17

1923 5-1-3

S29	●	William & Mary	39	10
O6	●	Dickinson	13	7
O13	●	W.V. Wesleyan	26	7
O20	●	at Penn State	3	21
O27	=	Princeton *Balt*	3	3
N3	●	Colgate	9	0
N10	●	Xavier	61	0
N24	=	Army *NYC*	0	0

ROSE BOWL
J1	=	Washington	14	14

1924 2-6-0

O4	●	William & Mary	14	7
O11	●	Marquette	3	21
O18	●	at Princeton	14	17
O25	●	W.V. Wesleyan	7	10
N1	●	Penn State	0	6
N8	●	Vermont	53	0
N15	●	Bucknell	0	6
N29	●	Army *Balt*	0	12

JACK OWSLEY
1925 (.688) 5-2-1

1925 5-2-1

O3	●	William & Mary	25	0
O10	●	Marquette	19	0
O17	●	Princeton *Balt*	10	10
O24	●	Washington Coll.	37	0
O31	●	at Michigan	0	54
N7	●	Western Maryland	27	0
N14	●	Bucknell	13	7
N28	●	Army *NYC*	3	10

BILL INGRAM
1926-30 (.694) 32-13-4

1926 9-0-1

O2	●	Purdue	17	13
O9	●	Drake	24	7
O9	●	Richmond	26	0
O16	●	at Princeton	27	13
O23	●	Colgate	13	7
O30	●	Michigan *Balt*	10	0
N6	●	W.V. Wesleyan	53	7
N13	●	Georgetown	10	7
N20	●	Loyola-Baltimore	35	13
N27	=	Army *Chi*	21	21

1927 6-3-0

O1	●	Davis & Elkins	27	0
O8	●	Drake	35	6
O15	●	Notre Dame *Balt*	6	19
O22	●	Duke	32	6
O29	●	at Pennsylvania	12	6
N5	●	W.V. Wesleyan	26	0
N12	●	at Michigan	12	27
N19	●	Loyola-Baltimore	33	6
N26	●	Army *NYC*	9	14

1928 5-3-1

S29	●	Davis & Elkins	0	2
O6	●	Boston College	0	6
O13	●	Notre Dame *CHI*	0	7
O20	●	Duke	6	0
O27	●	at Pennsylvania	6	0
N3	●	W.V. Wesleyan	37	0
N10	=	Michigan *Balt*	6	6
N17	●	Loyola-Baltimore	57	0
N24	●	Princeton *Phil*	9	0

1929 6-2-2

S28	●	Denison	47	0
O5	●	William & Mary	15	0
O12	●	Notre Dame *Balt*	7	14
O19	●	Duke	45	13
O26	=	at Princeton	13	13
N2	●	at Pennsylvania	2	7
N9	=	Georgetown	0	0
N16	●	Wake Forest	61	0
N23	●	W.V. Wesleyan	30	6
N30	●	Dartmouth *Phil*	13	6

1930 6-5-0

O4	●	William & Mary	19	6
O11	●	at Notre Dame	2	26
O18	●	Duke	0	18
O25	●	at Princeton	31	0
N1	●	W.V. Wesleyan	37	14
N8	●	Ohio State *Balt*	0	27
N15	●	SMU *Balt*	7	20
N22	●	Maryland	6	0
N29	●	George Washington	20	0
D6	●	at Pennsylvania	26	0
D13	●	Army *Bnx*	0	6

RIP MILLER
1931-33 (.448) 12-15-2

1931 5-5-1

O3	●	William & Mary	13	6
O10	●	Maryland *DC*	0	6
O17	●	Delaware	12	7
O24	●	at Princeton	15	0
O31	●	W.V. Wesleyan	0	0
N7	●	at Ohio State	0	20
N14	●	Notre Dame *Balt*	0	20
N21	●	at SMU	7	13 *
N28	●	Wooster	19	6
D5	●	at Pennsylvania	6	0
D12	●	Army *Bnx*	7	17

1932 2-6-1

O1	●	William & Mary	0	6
O8	●	Wash. & Lee	33	0
O15	●	Ohio U.	0	14
O22	=	at Princeton	0	0
O29	●	at Pennsylvania	0	14
N5	●	Columbia	6	7
N12	●	Maryland *Balt*	28	7
N19	●	Notre Dame *CLEV*	0	12
D3	●	Army *Phil*	0	20

1933 5-4-0

S30	●	William & Mary	12	0
O7	●	Mercer	25	6
O14	●	at Pittsburgh	6	34
O21	●	Virginia	13	7
O28	●	at Pennsylvania	13	0
N4	●	Notre Dame *Balt*	7	0
N11	●	at Columbia	7	14
N18	●	at Princeton	0	13
N25	●	Army *Phil*	7	12

TOM HAMILTON
1934-36, '46-47 (.478) 21-23-1

1934 8-1-0

S29	●	William & Mary	20	7
O6	●	Virginia *DC*	21	6
O13	●	Maryland	16	13
O20	●	at Columbia	18	7
O27	●	at Pennsylvania	17	0
N3	●	Wash. & Lee	26	0
N10	●	Notre Dame *CLEV*	10	6
N17	●	Pittsburgh	7	31
D1	●	Army *Phil*	3	0

1935 5-4-0

S28	●	William & Mary	30	0
O5	●	Mercer	27	0
O10	●	Virginia	26	7
O19	●	at Yale	6	7
O26	●	Notre Dame *Balt*	0	14
N2	●	at Princeton	0	26
N9	●	at Pennsylvania	13	0
N16	●	Columbia	28	7
N30	●	Army *Phil*	6	28

1936 6-3-0

S26	●	William & Mary	18	6
O3	●	Davidson	19	6
O10	●	Virginia	35	14
O17	●	Yale *Balt*	7	12
O24	●	at Princeton	0	7
O31	●	at Pennsylvania	6	16
N7	●	Notre Dame *Balt*	3	0
N14	●	at Harvard	20	13
N28	●	Army *Phil*	7	0

HANK HARDWICK
1937-38 (.528) 8-7-3

1937 4-4-1

S25	●	William & Mary	45	0
O2	●	Citadel	32	0
O9	●	Virginia	40	13
O16	=	Harvard *Balt*	0	0
O23	●	at Notre Dame	7	9
O30	●	at Pennsylvania	7	14
N6	●	Columbia	13	6
N20	●	at Princeton	6	26
N27	●	Army *Phil*	0	6

1938 4-3-2

S24	●	William & Mary	26	0
O1	●	VMI	26	0
O8	●	Virginia	33	0
O15	●	at Yale	7	9
O22	=	Princeton *Balt*	13	13
O29	=	at Pennsylvania	0	0
N5	●	Notre Dame *Balt*	0	15
N12	●	at Columbia	14	9
N26	●	Army *Phil*	7	14

SWEDE LARSON
1939-41 (.648) 16-8-3

1939 3-5-1

S30	●	William & Mary	31	6
O7	●	Virginia	14	12
O14	=	Dartmouth *Balt*	0	0
O21	●	Notre Dame *CLEV*	7	14
O28	●	Clemson	7	15
N4	●	at Pennsylvania	6	13
N11	●	Columbia	13	19
N25	●	at Princeton	0	28
D2	●	Army *Phil*	10	0

1940 6-2-1

S28	●	William & Mary	19	7
O5	●	Cincinnati	14	0
O12	●	at Princeton	12	6
O19	●	Drake	19	0
O26	●	at Yale	21	0
N2	●	at Pennsylvania	0	20
N9	●	Notre Dame *Balt*	7	13
N16	●	at Columbia	0	0
N30	●	Army *Phil*	14	0

1941 7-1-1

S27	●	William & Mary	34	0
O4	●	West Virginia	40	0
O11	●	Lafayette	41	2
O18	●	Cornell *Balt*	14	0
O25	=	at Harvard	0	0
N1	●	at Pennsylvania	13	6
N8	●	Notre Dame *Balt*	13	20
N22	●	at Princeton	23	0
N29	●	Army *Phil*	14	6

THE SCHOOLS

BILLICK WHELCHEL
1942-43 (.722) — 13-5

1942 — 5-4-0
S26	William & Mary	0	3
O3 •	Virginia	35	0
O10	Princeton *NYC*	0	10
O17	Yale *BALT*	13	6
O24	Georgia Tech	0	21
O31	Notre Dame *Clev*	0	9
N7	at Pennsylvania	7	0
N14	Columbia *BALT*	13	9
N28	Army	14	0

1943 — 8-1-0
S25 •	N.C. Pre-Flight	31	0
O2 •	Cornell *BALT*	46	7
O9 •	Duke *BALT*	14	13
O16 •	Penn State	14	6
O23 •	Georgia Tech *BALT*	28	14
O30 •	Notre Dame *Clev*	6	33
N6 •	at Pennsylvania	24	7
N13 •	at Columbia	61	0
N27 •	at Army	13	0

OSCAR HAGBERG
1944-45 (.750) — 13-4-1

1944 — 6-3-0
S30	N.C. Pre-Flight	14	21
O7 •	Penn State	55	14
O14 •	Duke *BALT*	7	0
O21	at Georgia Tech	15	17
O28 •	at Pennsylvania	26	0
N4 •	Notre Dame *BALT*	32	13
N11 •	Cornell *BALT*	48	0
N18 •	Purdue *BALT*	32	0
D2 •	Army *BALT*	7	23

1945 — 7-1-1
S29 •	Villanova	49	0
O6 •	at Duke	21	0
O13 •	Penn State	28	0
O20 •	Georgia Tech *BALT*	20	6
O27 •	at Pennsylvania	14	7
N3 = •	Notre Dame *Clev*	6	6
N10 •	Michigan *BALT*	33	7
N17 •	Wisconsin *BALT*	36	7
D1 •	Army *PHIL*	13	32

TOM HAMILTON

1946 — 1-8-0
S28 •	Villanova	7	0
O5 •	at Columbia	14	23
O12 •	Duke *BALT*	6	21
O19 •	North Carolina *BALT*	14	21
O26 •	at Pennsylvania	19	32
N2 •	Notre Dame *BALT*	0	28
N9 •	at Georgia Tech	20	28
N16 •	Penn State	7	12
N30 •	Army *PHIL*	18	21

1947 — 1-7-1
S27 •	at California	7	14
O4 •	Columbia	6	13
O11 = •	Duke *BALT*	14	14
O18 •	at Cornell	38	19
O25 •	at Pennsylvania	0	21
N1 •	Notre Dame *Clev*	0	27
N8 •	Georgia Tech *BALT*	14	16
N15 •	Penn State *BALT*	7	20
N29 •	Army *PHIL*	0	21

GEORGE SAUER
1948-49 (.222) — 3-13-2

1948 — 0-8-1
S25 •	California *BALT*	7	21
O2 •	Cornell *BALT*	7	13
O9 •	at Duke	7	28
O16 •	Missouri *BALT*	14	35
O23 •	at Pennsylvania	14	20
O30 •	Notre Dame *BALT*	7	41
N6 •	at Michigan	0	35
N13 •	at Columbia	0	13
N27 = •	Army *PHIL*	21	21

1949 — 3-5-1
S24 •	at Southern Cal	20	42
O1 •	Princeton *BALT*	28	7
O8 •	Duke *BALT*	28	14
O15 •	at Wisconsin	13	48
O22 •	at Pennsylvania	7	28
O29 •	Notre Dame *BALT*	0	40
N5 = •	at Tulane	21	21
N12 •	Columbia	34	0
N26 •	Army *PHIL*	0	38

EDDIE ERDELATZ
1950-58 (.643) — 50-26-8

1950 — 3-6-0
S30	at Maryland	21	35
O7	Northwestern *BALT*	0	22
O14	at Princeton	14	20
O21 •	Southern Cal *BALT*	27	14
O28 •	at Pennsylvania	7	30
N4	Notre Dame *Clev*	10	19
N11	Tulane *BALT*	0	27
N18 •	at Columbia	29	7
D2	Army *PHIL*	14	2

1951 — 2-6-1
S29 =	at Yale	7	7
O6	Princeton	20	24
O13	at Rice	14	21
O20	at Northwestern	7	16
O27 •	at Pennsylvania	0	14
N3	Notre Dame *BALT*	0	19
N10	Maryland *BALT*	21	40
N17	at Columbia	21	7
D1	Army *PHIL*	42	7

1952 — 6-2-1
S27	Yale *BALT*	31	7
O4	at Cornell	31	7
O11	William & Mary	14	0
O18	at Maryland	7	38
O25 =	at Pennsylvania	7	7
N1	Notre Dame *Clev*	6	17
N8	at Duke	16	6
N15	Columbia	28	0
N29	Army *PHIL*	7	0

1953 — 4-3-2
S26 =	William & Mary	6	6
O3	Dartmouth	55	7
O10	Cornell *BALT*	26	6
O17	at Princeton	65	7
O24	at Pennsylvania	6	9
O31	at Notre Dame	7	38
N7 =	Duke *BALT*	0	0
N14	at Columbia	14	6
N28	Army *PHIL*	7	20

1954 — 8-2-0
S25 •	William & Mary	27	0
O2 •	at Dartmouth	42	7
O9 •	at Stanford	25	0
O16 •	at Pittsburgh	19	21
O23 •	at Pennsylvania	52	6
O30 •	Notre Dame *BALT*	0	6
N6 •	Duke *Nor*	40	7
N13 •	Columbia	51	6
N27 •	Army *PHIL*	27	20
SUGAR BOWL			
J1 •	Mississippi	21	0

1955 — 6-2-1
S24 •	William & Mary	7	0
O1 •	at South Carolina	26	0
O8 •	Pittsburgh *BALT*	21	0
O15 •	at Penn State	34	14
O22 •	at Pennsylvania	33	0
O29 •	at Notre Dame	7	21
N5 •	Duke *BALT*	7	7
N12 •	at Columbia	47	0
N26 •	Army *PHIL*	6	14

1956 — 6-1-2
S29 •	William & Mary	39	14
O6 •	at Cornell	14	0
O13 •	at Tulane	6	21
O20 •	Cincinnati	13	7
O27 •	at Pennsylvania	54	6
N3 •	Notre Dame *BALT*	33	7
N10 •	at Duke	7	7
N17 •	Virginia *BALT*	34	7
D1 •	Army *PHIL*	7	7

1957 — 9-1-1
S21 •	at Boston College	46	6
S28 •	William & Mary	33	6
O5 •	at North Carolina	7	13
O12 •	at California	21	6
O19 •	Georgia *Nor*	27	14
O26 •	at Pennsylvania	35	7
N2 •	at Notre Dame	20	6
N9 •	Duke *BALT*	6	6
N16 •	George Washington *BALT*	52	0
N30 •	Army *PHIL*	14	0
COTTON BOWL			
J1 •	Rice	20	7

1958 — 6-3-0
S27 •	William & Mary	14	0
O4 •	at Boston U.	28	14
O11 •	at Michigan	20	14
O18 •	Tulane *Nor*	6	14
O25 •	at Pennsylvania	50	8
N1 •	Notre Dame *BALT*	20	40
N8 •	Maryland *BALT*	40	14
N15 •	at George Washington	28	8
N29 •	Army *PHIL*	6	22

WAYNE HARDIN
1959-64 (.629) — 38-22-2

1959 — 5-4-1
S19 •	at Boston College	24	8
S26 •	William & Mary	29	2
O3 •	at SMU	7	20
O10 •	Syracuse *Nor*	6	32
O16 •	at Miami, Fla.	8	23
O24 = •	at Pennsylvania	22	22
O31 •	at Notre Dame	22	25
N7 •	Maryland *BALT*	22	14
N14 •	George Washington	16	8
N28 •	Army *PHIL*	43	12

1960 — 9-2-0
S17 •	at Boston College	22	7
S24 •	Villanova	41	7
O1 •	at Washington	15	14
O8 •	SMU *Nor*	26	7
O15 •	Air Force *BALT*	35	3
O22 •	at Pennsylvania	27	0
O29 •	Notre Dame *PHIL*	14	7
N5 •	at Duke	10	19
N12 •	Virginia	41	6
N26 •	Army *PHIL*	17	12
ORANGE BOWL			
J2	Missouri	14	21

1961 — 7-3-0
S23 •	at Penn State	10	20
S30 •	William & Mary	44	6
O6 •	at Miami, Fla.	17	6
O14 •	at Cornell	31	7
O20 •	at Detroit	37	19
O28 •	at Pittsburgh	14	28
N4 •	at Notre Dame	13	10
N11 •	Duke *Nor*	9	30
N18 •	Virginia	13	3
D1 •	Army *PHIL*	13	7

1962 — 5-5-0
S22 •	at Penn State	7	41
S29 •	William & Mary	20	16
O6 •	at Minnesota	0	21
O13 •	Cornell	41	0
O20 •	at Boston College	26	6
O27 •	Pittsburgh *Nor*	32	9
N3 •	Notre Dame *PHIL*	12	20
N10 •	at Syracuse	6	34
N17 •	at Southern Cal	6	13
D1 •	Army *PHIL*	34	14

1963 — 9-2-0
S21 •	at West Virginia	51	7
S28 •	William & Mary	28	0
O5 •	at Michigan	26	13
O11 •	at SMU	28	32
O19 •	VMI *Nor*	21	12
O26 •	Pittsburgh	24	12
N2 •	at Notre Dame	35	14
N9 •	Maryland	42	7
N16 •	at Duke	38	25
D7 •	Army *PHIL*	21	15
COTTON BOWL			
J1 •	Texas	6	28

1964 — 3-6-1
S19 •	at Penn State	21	8
S26 •	William & Mary	35	6
O3 •	at Michigan	0	21
O10 •	Georgia Tech *JacF*	0	17
O17 •	at California	13	27
O24 = •	at Pittsburgh	14	14
O31 •	Notre Dame *PHIL*	0	40
N7 •	at Maryland	22	27
N14 •	Duke	27	14
N28 •	Army *PHIL*	8	11

BILL ELIAS
1965-68 (.413) — 15-22-3

1965 — 4-4-2
S18 •	Syracuse	6	14
S25 =	at Stanford	7	7
O2 •	at Oklahoma	10	0
O9 •	William & Mary	42	14
O16 •	Pittsburgh *DC*	12	0
O23 •	at Georgia Tech	16	37
O30 •	at Notre Dame	3	29
N6 •	Maryland	19	7
N13 •	at Penn State	6	14
N27 = •	Army *PHIL*	7	7

1966 — 4-6-0
S17 •	Boston College	27	7
S24 •	at SMU	3	21
O1 •	at Air Force	7	15
O8 •	at Syracuse	14	28
O15 •	at Pittsburgh	24	7
O22 •	William & Mary	21	0
O29 •	Notre Dame *PHIL*	7	31
N5 •	Duke	7	9
N12 •	at Vanderbilt	30	14
N26 •	Army *PHIL*	7	20

1967 — 5-4-1
S23 •	Penn State	23	22
S30 •	at Rice	7	21
O7 •	at Michigan	26	21
O14 •	Syracuse	27	14
O21 •	William & Mary	16	27
O28 •	at Pittsburgh	22	21
N4 •	at Notre Dame	14	43
N11 •	Duke *Nor*	16	35
N18 = •	Vanderbilt	35	35
D2 •	Army *PHIL*	19	14

1968 — 2-8-0
S21 •	at Penn State	6	31
S28 •	Boston College	15	49
O5 •	at Michigan	9	32
O12 •	Air Force *CHI*	20	26
O19 •	Pittsburgh	17	16
O26 •	Virginia	0	24
N2 •	Notre Dame *PHIL*	14	45
N9 •	at Georgia Tech	35	15
N16 •	at Syracuse	6	44
N30 •	Army *PHIL*	14	21

RICK FORZANO
1969-72 (.233) — 10-33

1969 — 1-9-0
S20 •	Penn State	22	45
S27 •	at Boston College	14	21
O4 •	at Texas	17	56
O11 •	at Pittsburgh	19	46
O18 •	at Rutgers	6	20
O25 •	Virginia	10	0
N1 •	at Notre Dame	0	47
N7 •	at Miami, Fla.	10	30
N15 •	Syracuse	0	15
N29 •	Army *PHIL*	0	27

1970 — 2-9-0
S12 •	Colgate	48	22
S19 •	at Penn State	7	55
S26 •	Boston College	14	28
O3 •	at Washington	7	56
O10 •	Pittsburgh	8	10
O17 •	Air Force *DC*	3	26
O24 •	at Syracuse	8	23
O31 •	Notre Dame *PHIL*	7	56
N7 •	at Georgia Tech	8	30
N14 •	Villanova	10	14
N28 •	Army *PHIL*	11	7

1971 — 3-8-0
S11 •	at Virginia	10	6
S18 •	Penn State	3	56
S25 •	at Boston College	6	49
O2 •	at Michigan	0	46
O9 •	at Pittsburgh	35	36
O15 •	at Miami, Fla.	16	31
O23 •	Duke	15	14
O30 •	at Notre Dame	0	21
N6 •	at Georgia Tech	21	34
N13 •	Syracuse	17	14
N27 •	Army *PHIL*	23	24

564 NAVY

THE SCHOOLS

1972 4-7-0

S16	●	William & Mary	13	9
S23		at Penn State	10	21
S30	●	Boston College	27	20
O7		at Michigan	7	35
O14		at Syracuse	14	30
O21	●	at Air Force	21	17
O28		Duke NOR	16	17
N4		Notre Dame PHIL	23	42
N11	●	Pittsburgh	28	13
N18		at Georgia Tech	7	30
D2		Army PHIL	15	23

GEORGE WELSH
1973-81 (.544) 55-46-1

1973 4-7-0

S15	●	at VMI	37	6
S22		Penn State	0	39
S29		at Michigan	0	14
O6		at Boston College	7	44
O13	●	Syracuse	23	14
O20	●	Air Force	42	6
O27		at Pittsburgh	17	22
N3		at Notre Dame	7	44
N10		at Tulane	15	17
N17		Georgia Tech JACF	22	26
D1	●	Army PHIL	51	0

1974 4-7-0

S14	●	Virginia	35	28
S21	●	at Penn State	7	6
S28		at Michigan	0	52
O5		Boston College	0	37
O12		at Syracuse	9	17
O19		at Air Force	16	19
O26		Pittsburgh	11	13
N2		Notre Dame PHIL	6	14
N9	●	Citadel	28	21
N16		at Georgia Tech	0	22
N30	●	Army PHIL	19	0

1975 7-4-0

S13	●	at Virginia	42	14
S20	●	Connecticut	55	7
S27		at Washington	13	14
O4	●	Air Force DC	17	0
O11	●	Syracuse	10	6
O18		at Boston College	3	17
O25	●	at Pittsburgh	17	0
N1		at Notre Dame	10	31
N7	●	at Miami, Fla.	17	16
N15		at Georgia Tech	13	14
N29	●	Army PHIL	30	6

1976 4-7-0

S11		Rutgers	3	13
S18	●	at Connecticut	21	3
S25		at Michigan	14	70
O2		Boston College	13	17
O9		at Air Force	3	13
O16		William & Mary	13	21
O23		Pittsburgh	0	45
O30		Notre Dame CLEV	21	27
N6	●	at Syracuse	27	10
N13	●	Georgia Tech	34	28
N27	●	Army PHIL	38	10

1977 5-6-0

S10	●	Citadel	21	2
S17	●	Connecticut	38	7
S24		at Michigan	7	14
O1		at Duke	16	28
O8	●	Air Force	10	7
O15		at Pittsburgh	17	34
O22	●	William & Mary	42	17
O29		at Notre Dame	10	43
N5		Syracuse	34	45
N12	●	Georgia Tech	20	16
N26		Army PHIL	14	17

1978 9-3-0

S16	●	at Virginia	32	0
S23	●	at Connecticut	30	0
S30	●	at Boston College	19	8
O7	●	at Air Force	37	8
O14	●	Duke	31	8
O21	●	William & Mary	9	0
O28	●	Pittsburgh	21	11
N4		Notre Dame CLEV	7	27
N11		at Syracuse	17	20
N18		at Florida State	6	38
D2	●	Army PHIL	28	0
		HOLIDAY BOWL		
D22	●	Brigham Young	23	16

1979 7-4-0

S15	●	Citadel	26	7
S22	●	Connecticut	21	10
S29	●	at Illinois	13	12
O6	●	Air Force	13	9
O13	●	William & Mary NOR	24	7
O20	●	Virginia	17	10
O27		at Pittsburgh	7	24
N3		at Notre Dame	0	14
N10		Syracuse	14	30
N17		at Georgia Tech	14	24
D1	●	Army PHIL	31	7

1980 8-4-0

S13		at Virginia	3	6
S20	●	Kent State	31	3
S27	●	William & Mary	45	6
O4	●	Boston College	21	0
O11		at Air Force	20	21
O18	●	Villanova	24	15
O25	●	at Washington	24	10
N1		Notre Dame ERUT	0	33
N8	●	at Syracuse	6	3
N15	●	at Georgia Tech	19	8
N29	●	Army PHIL	33	6
		GARDEN STATE BOWL		
D14		Houston	0	35

1981 7-4-1

S12	●	Citadel	17	7
S19	●	Ea. Kentucky	24	0
S26		at Michigan	16	21
O3		at Yale	19	23
O10	●	Air Force	30	13
O17	●	at Boston College	25	10
O24	●	William & Mary	27	0
O31		at Notre Dame	0	38
N7	●	Syracuse	35	23
N14	●	at Georgia Tech	20	14
N28	=	Army PHIL	3	3
		LIBERTY BOWL		
D30		Ohio State	28	31

GARY TRANQUILL
1982-86 (.373) 20-34-1

1982 6-5-0

S11	●	Virginia	20	16
S18		Arkansas LR	17	29
S25		Boston College	0	31
O2	●	at Duke	27	21
O9		at Air Force	21	24
O16	●	William & Mary	39	3
O23	●	Citadel	28	3
O30		Notre Dame ERUT	10	27
N6	●	at Syracuse	20	18
N13		at South Carolina	14	17
D4	●	Army PHIL	24	7

1983 3-8-0

S10		at Virginia	16	27
S17		Mississippi State JAM	10	38
S24	●	Lehigh	30	0
O1		at Washington	10	27
O8		Air Force	17	44
O15	●	at Princeton	37	29
O22		Pittsburgh	14	21
O29		at Notre Dame	12	28
N5		Syracuse	7	14
N12		at South Carolina	7	31
N25	●	Army PAS	42	13

1984 4-6-1

S15	●	at North Carolina	33	30
S22		Virginia	9	21
S29		Arkansas LR	10	33
O6		at Air Force	22	29
O13	●	Lehigh	31	14
O20	●	Princeton	41	3
O27	=	at Pittsburgh	28	28
N3		Notre Dame ERUT	17	18
N10		at Syracuse	0	29
N17	●	South Carolina	38	21
D1		Army PHIL	11	28

1985 4-7-0

S7		North Carolina	19	21
S14		at Delaware	13	16
S21		at Indiana	35	38
S28	●	at Virginia	17	13
O12		Air Force	7	24
O19	●	Lafayette	56	14
O26	●	Pittsburgh	21	7
N2		at Notre Dame	17	41
N9		Syracuse	20	24
N16		at South Carolina	31	34
D7	●	Army PHIL	17	7

1986 3-8-0

S13	●	Virginia	20	10
S20		at Indiana	29	52
S27	●	Lehigh	41	0
O4	●	Dartmouth	45	0
O11		at Air Force	6	40
O18		Pennsylvania	26	30
O25		at Pittsburgh	14	56
N1		Notre Dame BALT	14	33
N8		at Syracuse	22	31
N15		Delaware	14	27
D6		Army PHIL	7	27

ELLIOT UZELAC
1987-89 (.242) 8-25

1987 2-9-0

S12		William & Mary	12	27
S19		Lehigh	9	24
S26		North Carolina	14	45
O3		at Virginia Tech	11	31
O10		Air Force	13	23
O17	●	at Pennsylvania	38	28
O24		Pittsburgh	6	10
O31		at Notre Dame	13	56
N7		Syracuse	10	34
N14	●	at Delaware	31	22
D5		Army PHIL	3	17

1988 3-8-0

S3	●	James Madison	27	14
S10	●	Delaware	30	3
S17		Temple	7	12
S24		at Citadel	35	42
O1	●	Yale	41	7
O8		at Air Force	24	34
O22		at Pittsburgh	6	52
O29		Notre Dame BALT	7	22
N5		at Syracuse	21	49
N12		at South Carolina	8	19
D3		Army PHIL	15	20

1989 3-8-0

S16		Brigham Young	10	31
S23		Citadel	10	14
S30	●	at North Carolina	12	7
O7		Air Force	7	35
O14		at Pittsburgh	14	31
O21	●	at Boston College	27	24
O28		James Madison	20	24
N4		at Notre Dame	0	41
N11		Syracuse	17	38
N18		at Delaware	9	10
D9	●	Army ERUT	19	17

GEORGE CHAUMP
1990-94 (.255) 14-41

1990 5-6-0

S8	●	Richmond	28	17
S15		at Virginia	14	56
S22	●	Villanova	23	21
S29		Boston College	17	28
O6		at Air Force	7	24
O13	●	Akron	17	13
O27		James Madison	7	16
N3		Notre Dame ERUT	31	52
N10	●	at Toledo	14	10
N17	●	Delaware	31	27
D8		Army PHIL	20	30

1991 1-10-0

S7		Ball State	10	33
S14		at Virginia	10	17
S21		William & Mary	21	26
S28		Bowling Green	19	22
O12		Air Force	6	46
O19		at Temple	14	21
O26		Delaware	25	29
N2		at Notre Dame	0	38
N9		at Tulane	7	34
N23		Wake Forest	24	52
D7	●	Army PHIL	24	3

1992 1-10-0

S12		Virginia	0	53
S19		at Boston College	0	28
S26		Rutgers	0	40
O3		at North Carolina	14	28
O10		at Air Force	16	18
O24		at Delaware	21	37
O31		Notre Dame ERUT	7	38
N7	●	Tulane	20	17
N14		Vanderbilt	7	27
N21		at Rice	22	27
D5		Army PHIL	24	25

1993 4-7-0

S11		at Virginia	0	38
S18	●	Ea. Illinois	31	10
S25	●	Bowling Green	27	20
O2		at Tulane	25	27
O9	●	Air Force	28	24
O16	●	Colgate	31	3
O23		at Louisville	0	28
O30		Notre Dame PHIL	27	58
N13		at Vanderbilt	7	41
N20		SMU	13	42
D4		Army ERUT	14	16

1994 3-8-0

S3		at San Diego State	14	56
S10		Virginia	10	47
S17		at Bowling Green	21	59
O1		Duke	14	47
O8		at Air Force	21	43
O15	●	Lafayette	7	0
O22		Louisville	14	35
O29		at Notre Dame	21	58
N5	●	at Tulane	17	15
N19	●	Rice	29	17
D3		Army PHIL	20	22

CHARLIE WEATHERBIE
1995-2001 (.400) 30-45

1995 5-6-0

S9	●	at SMU	33	2
S16		at Rutgers	17	27
S23		Wake Forest	7	30
S30	●	at Duke	30	9
O7		Virginia Tech	0	14
O14		Air Force	20	30
O21	●	Villanova	20	14
N4		at Notre Dame	17	35
N11	●	Delaware	31	7
N18	●	Tulane	35	7
D2		Army PHIL	13	14

1996 9-3-0

S7	●	at Rutgers	10	6
S21	●	SMU	19	17
S28		at Boston College	38	43
O5	●	Duke	64	27
O12	●	Air Force DUB	20	17
O26	●	at Wake Forest	47	18
N2		Notre Dame DUB	27	54
N9	●	Delaware	30	14
N16	●	Tulane	35	21
N23	●	at Georgia Tech	36	26
D7		Army PHIL	24	28
		ALOHA BOWL		
D25	●	California	42	38

1997 7-4-0

S5		at San Diego State	31	45
S13	●	Rutgers	36	7
S20	●	at SMU	46	16
S27		at Duke	17	26
O11		Air Force	7	10
O18	●	VMI	42	7
N1		at Notre Dame	17	21
N8	●	Temple	49	17
N15	●	Colgate	52	24
N22	●	Kent State	62	29
D6	●	Army ERUT	39	7

1998 3-8-0

S10		at Wake Forest	14	26
S19	●	Kent State	38	24
S26		at Tulane	24	42
O3		West Virginia	24	45
O10		at Air Force	7	49
O17	●	Colgate	42	35
O24	●	at Boston College	32	31
N7		Rutgers	33	36
N14		Notre Dame RAJ	0	30
N21		SMU	11	24
D5		Army PHIL	30	34

1999 5-7-0

S4		Georgia Tech	14	49
S11	●	at Kent State	48	28
S18		Boston College	10	14
S25		at Rice	17	20
O2	●	at West Virginia	31	28
O9		Air Force LAN	14	19
O23		Akron	29	35
O30		at Notre Dame	24	28
N6	●	at Rutgers	34	7
N13	●	Tulane	45	21
N20		at Hawaii	41	48
D4	●	Army PHIL	19	9

2000   1-10-0

S2	Temple	6	17
S16	at Georgia Tech	13	40
S23	at Boston College	7	48
S30	TCU	0	24
O7	at Air Force	13	27
O14	Notre Dame *ORL*	14	45
O21	Rutgers	21	28
O28	Toledo	14	35
N11	at Tulane	38	50
N18	Wake Forest	26	49
D2 ●	Army *BALT*	30	28

RICK LANTZ
2001 (.000)   0-3

2001   0-1 0-0

A30	at Temple	26	45
S8	Georgia Tech	7	70
S22	Boston College	21	38
O6	Air Force *LAN*	18	24
O13	Rice	13	21
O20	at Rutgers	17	23
O27	at Toledo	20	21
N10	Tulane	28	42
N17	at Notre Dame	16	34
D1	Army *PHIL*	17	26

PAUL JOHNSON
2002-Present (.541)   20-17

2002   2-10 (0-0)

A31 ●	at SMU	38	7
S7	North Carolina St.	19	65
S21	Northwestern	40	49
S28	Duke	17	43
O5	at Air Force	7	48
O12	Rice	10	17
O19	at Boston College	21	46
O26	at Tulane	30	51
N9	Notre Dame *BALT*	23	30
N16	Connecticut	0	38
N23	at Wake Forest	27	30
D7 ●	Army *ERUT*	58	12

2003   8-5 (0-0)

A30 ●	VMI	37	10
S6	at TCU	3	17
S20 ●	Eastern Michigan	39	7
S27	at Rutgers	27	48
O4 ●	Air Force *LAN*	28	25
O11	at Vanderbilt	37	27
O18 ●	at Rice	38	6
O25	Delaware	17	21
N1 ●	Tulane	35	17
N8	at Notre Dame	24	27
N22 ●	Central Michigan	63	34
D6 ●	Army *PHIL*	34	6
HOUSTON BOWL			
D30 ●	Texas Tech	14	38

2004   10-2 (0-0)

S4 ●	Duke	27	12
S11 ●	Northeastern	28	24
S18	at Tulsa	29	0
S25 ●	Vanderbilt	29	26
S30 ●	at Air Force	24	21
O16	Notre Dame *NYC*	9	27
O23 ●	Rice	14	13
O30 ●	Delaware	34	20
N6	at Tulane	10	42
N20 ●	Rutgers	54	21
D4 ●	Army *PHIL*	42	13
EMERALD BOWL			
D30 ●	New Mexico	34	19

Neutral Site Key: *BALT* Baltimore, MD / *BNX* Bronx, NY / *CHI* Chicago, IL / *CLEV* Cleveland, OH / *DC* Washington, DC / *DUB* Dublin, Ireland / *ERUT* East Rutherford, NJ / *JACF* Jacksonville, FL / *JAM* Jackson, MS / *LR* Little Rock, AR / *NOR* Norfolk, VA / *NYC* New York, NY / *ORL* Orlando, FL / *PAS* Pasadena, CA / *PHIL* Philadelphia, PA / *PRI* Princeton, NJ / *RAL* Raljon, MD / *UNK* Unknown, Unknown
f Forfeit   † Game Later Forfieted   # Disputed Victor   * Disputed Score || Designated Conference Game |2 Counted Twice in Conference Standings

NAVY ANNUAL STATISTICAL LEADERS

YR	RUSHING	YDS	ATT	AVG	PASSING	ATT	CMP	PCT	YDS	RECEIVING	REC	YDS	AVG
1955	Ned Oldham	404	86	4.7	George Welsh	150	94	.63	1,319	Ron Beagle	30	451	15.0
1956	Ned Oldham	393	90	4.4	Tom Forrestal	106	57	.54	808	Earle Smith	14	151	10.8
1957	Harry Hurst	634	112	5.7	Tom Forrestal	183	93	.51	1,270	Pete Jokanovich	32	386	12.1
1958	Joe Matalavage	271	40	6.8	Joe Tranchini	118	67	.57	837	Joe Bellino	19	240	12.6
1959	Joe Bellino	564	99	5.7	Jim Maxfield	123	55	.45	711	Dick Pariseau	20	228	11.4
1960	Joe Bellino	834	168	5.0	Hal Spooner	111	65	.59	805	Jim Luper	22	307	14.0
1961	John Sai	472	95	5.0	Ron Klemick	183	84	.46	1,035	Jim Stewart	23	498	21.7
1962	Pat Donnelly	338	102	3.3	Roger Staubach	98	67	.68	966	Jim Stewart	24	399	16.6
1963	Pat Donnelly	603	99	6.1	Roger Staubach	161	107	.66	1,474	Ed Orr	25	321	12.8
1964	Kip Paskewich	363	65	5.6	Roger Staubach	204	119	.58	1,131	Ed Orr	31	299	9.6
1965	Terry Murray	391	117	3.3	John Cartwright	172	82	.48	943	Phil Norton	35	429	12.3
1966	Terry Murray	663	171	3.9	John Cartwright	188	96	.51	1,146	Rob Taylor	55	727	13.2
1967	Jeri Balsly	559	159	3.5	John Cartwright	241	129	.54	1,537	Rob Taylor	61	818	13.4
1968	Dan Pike	500	123	4.1	Mike McNallen	280	124	.44	1,342	Bill Newton	29	358	12.3
1969	Dan Pike	329	117	2.8	Mike McNallen	304	120	.39	1,312	Mick Barr	19	189	9.9
1970	Andy Pease	399	92	4.3	Mike McNallen	234	105	.45	1,342	Mick Barr	34	403	11.9
1971	Dan Howard	411	118	3.5	Fred Stuvek	186	92	.49	1,125	Larry Van Loan	41	589	14.4
1972	Cleveland Cooper	1,046	192	5.4	Fred Stuvek	109	54	.50	583	Bert Calland	61	650	10.7
1973	Cleveland Cooper	898	221	4.1	Al Glenny	207	101	.49	1,295	Larry Van Loan	33	542	16.4
1974	Cleveland Cooper	638	166	3.8	Phil Poirier	143	58	.41	656	Robin Ameen	26	403	15.5
1975	Bob Jackson	849	184	4.6	Phil Poirier	104	49	.47	729	Kevin Sullivan	19	336	17.7
1976	Joe Gattuso Jr.	591	142	4.2	Bob Leszczynski	158	84	.53	1,154	Dave King	27	443	16.4
1977	Joe Gattuso Jr.	1,292	266	4.9	Bob Leszczynski	223	110	.49	1,509	Phil McConkey	34	596	17.5
1978	Steve Callahan	766	175	4.4	Bob Leszczynski	161	77	.48	1,282	Phil McConkey	22	532	24.2
1979	Eddie Meyers	651	106	6.1	Bob Powers	154	65	.42	983	Dave Dent	17	269	15.8
1980	Eddie Meyers	957	204	4.7	Fred Reitzel	163	76	.47	908	Curt Gainer	24	340	14.2
1981	Eddie Meyers	1,318	277	4.8	Marco Pagnanelli	140	80	.57	1,010	Greg Papajohn	35	517	14.8
1982	Napoleon McCallum	739	165	4.5	Marco Pagnanelli	169	98	.58	1,133	Bill Cebak	26	415	16.0
1983	Napoleon McCallum	1,587	331	4.8	Rick Williamson	249	123	.49	1,394	Mark Stevens	41	483	11.8
1984	Rich Clouse	557	134	4.2	Bill Byrne	213	109	.51	1,425	Chris Weiler	44	711	16.2
1985	Napoleon McCallum	1,327	287	4.6	Bill Byrne	269	151	.56	1,694	Napoleon McCallum	44	358	8.1
1986	Chuck Smith	933	190	4.9	Bill Byrne	229	121	.53	1,463	Mike Ray	30	403	13.4
1987	Alton Grizzard	519	152	3.4	Alton Grizzard	73	30	.41	490	Don Hughes	13	261	20.1
1988	Alton Grizzard	633	190	3.3	Gary McIntosh	81	35	.43	504	Carl Jordan	29	511	17.6
1989	Alton Grizzard	626	190	3.3	Alton Grizzard	147	67	.46	1,109	Shane Smith	23	356	15.5
1990	Jason Pace	565	136	4.2	Alton Grizzard	240	121	.50	1,438	Jerry Dawson	46	649	14.1
1991	Jason Van Matre	544	141	3.9	Jim Kubiak	154	93	.60	957	Tom Pritchard	35	569	16.3
1992	Jason Van Matre	632	188	3.4	Jason Van Matre	151	72	.48	955	Tom Pritchard	30	404	13.5
1993	Jason Van Matre	428	88	4.9	Jim Kubiak	401	248	.62	2,628	Jason Van Matre	59	393	6.7
1994	Monty Williams	215	74	2.9	Jim Kubiak	399	211	.53	2,388	Damon Dixon	51	556	10.9
1995	Chris McCoy	803	168	4.8	Ben Fay	144	73	.51	869	Cory Schemm	25	327	13.1
1996	Chris McCoy	1,228	268	4.6	Chris McCoy	109	49	.45	759	Astor Heaven	19	396	20.8
1997	Chris McCoy	1,370	246	5.6	Chris McCoy	135	69	.51	1,203	Pat McGrew	18	407	22.6
1998	Brian Broadwater	679	162	4.2	Brian Broadwater	98	47	.48	838	Ryan Read	17	433	25.5
1999	Brian Madden	897	180	5.0	Brian Broadwater	107	50	.47	806	Matt O'Donnell	22	347	15.8
2000	Brian Broadwater	597	151	4.0	Brian Broadwater	137	73	.53	858	Brandon Rampani	22	324	14.7
2001	Brian Madden	905	217	4.2	Brian Madden	145	62	.43	902	Jeff Gaddy	24	365	15.2
2002	Craig Candeto	775	177	4.4	Craig Candeto	103	51	.50	843	Eric Roberts	17	429	25.2
2003	Kyle Eckel	1,249	236	5.3	Craig Candeto	131	64	.49	1,140	Eric Roberts	20	493	24.7
2004	Kyle Eckel	1,151	235	4.9	Aaron Polanco	114	61	.54	1,131	Jason Tomlinson	16	273	17.1

Receiving leaders by receptions
The NCAA began including postseason stats in 2002

NEBRASKA

BY MARK WANGRIN

THE CORNHUSKERS YEARBOOK ONCE included a job description for the team's quarterback. To fill that position a player was required to "run fast, to dodge and twist [his] way through a broken field." That was written in 1907. Nearly a century later, it was still gospel in the Cornhusker State.

When coach Tom Osborne developed his I-formation option attack, he looked for quarterbacks with speed. From Jeff Quinn (1978-80) to Turner Gill (1981-83) to Jammal Lord (2003), the Cornhuskers turned to quarterbacks more apt to beat opponents with their feet than with their arms.

That began to change on Nov. 23, 2001, when then-No. 1 Nebraska was taken apart by Colorado 62-36 in Boulder. The Cornhuskers still made the Rose Bowl national championship game—amidst renewed howls that the BCS needed to be overhauled—only to get thrashed by Miami. Their mystique tarnished, the Cornhuskers lost six games by 17 or more points over the next two seasons, and even many proponents of the I-option could see it was time for a change.

Enter new coach Bill Callahan, a disciple of the West Coast offense, who came to Lincoln in January 2004 with promises to again fill the air with footballs—forward passes, not pitchouts. The last time the Cornhuskers altered their option attack was in 1968, after back-to-back 6–4 seasons. Two years later, coach Bob Devaney won the first of his consecutive national championships.

TRADITION The idea was a simple one—to differentiate the starting defensive players from their backups. But since Devaney first began assigning black practice jerseys in the 1960s, the routine has evolved to one of total reverence, with the pullovers presented to first-teamers in a ceremony at the start of the season. The unit is known widely as the Blackshirts. "The thing could be a rag and you'd still look at it as a shrine," says former defensive end Chad Kelsay. Before each game the team touches a horseshoe hanging above the locker room door and then walks under Memorial Stadium and out of the tunnel to the sound of "Sirius," a 1982 progressive rock song by the Alan Parsons Project.

PROFILE

University of Nebraska
Lincoln, Neb.
Founded: 1869
Enrollment: 15,742
Colors: Scarlet and Cream
Nickname: Cornhuskers
Stadium: Memorial Stadium/
Tom Osborne Field
    Opened in 1923
    FieldTurf; 73,918 capacity
First football game: 1890
All-time record: 784–318–41 (.704)
Bowl record: 21–21
Consensus national championships, 1936-present: 5 (1970, 1971, 1994, 1995, 1997)
Big 12 Conference championships: 2
Heisman Trophy: Johnny Rodgers, 1972; Mike Rozier, 1983; Eric Crouch, 2001
Outland Trophy: Larry Jacobson, 1971; Rich Glover, 1972; Dave Rimington, 1981-82; Dean Steinkuhler, 1983; Will Shields, 1992; Zach Wiegert, 1994; Aaron Taylor, 1997
First-round NFL draftees: 30
Website: www.huskers.com

THE BEST OF TIMES

From 1994 to 1997, the Cornhuskers won three national titles and had a 49–2 record plus two Outland, one Lombardi and a Johnny Unitas Trophy. They also had nine All-Americas.

THE WORST OF TIMES

In the 1940s, the Cornhuskers had six coaches, a .374 winning percentage and only one winning season.

CONFERENCE

A charter member of the Missouri Valley Conference, Nebraska joined the Big Six in 1928, which eventually grew to the Big Eight, before absorbing four SWC schools to become the Big 12 in 1996.

DISTINGUISHED ALUMNI

Johnny Carson; Warren Buffett; Gen. John J. "Black Jack" Pershing; George W. Beadle, Nobel Prize-winning geneticist; Willa Cather, Pulitzer Prize-winning author; Bob Kerrey, U.S. senator; Merlene Ottey, Olympic track star

FIGHT SONG

HAIL VARSITY
Hail to the team
The stadium rings as everyone sings,
The Scarlet and Cream.
Cheers for a victory, echo our loyalty;
So, on mighty men,
The eyes of the land, upon every hand,
Are looking at you.
Fight on for victory
Hail to the men of Nebraska U.

DEAR OLD NEBRASKA U
(NO PLACE LIKE NEBRASKA)
There is no place like Nebraska
Dear old Nebraska U.
Where the girls are the fairest,
The boys are the squarest,
Of any old school that I knew.
There is no place like Nebraska,
Where they're all true blue.
We'll all stick together,
In all kinds of weather,
For Dear old Nebraska U!

Nebraska's 1995 team was selected by a computer analyst as the best major-college team since 1956, with the 1971 Cornhuskers second.

BEST PLAYER Walking home from Horace Mann Junior High School in Omaha, Johnny "The Jet" Rodgers was often targeted by bullies jealous of his athletic success. "I was tougher than they thought, but it wasn't just one or two guys; several were jumping on me," Rodgers said. "So I had to get up and run." And run he did. Too small to follow his dream and win a Heisman at Southern California—the Trojans backed off on their scholarship offer—the 5'9", 173-pound Rodgers displayed uncanny elusiveness for the Cornhuskers, particularly on punt returns, where he often followed his own instincts rather than the designed return. His 5,586 career all-purpose yards set an NCAA record and he won NU's first Heisman Trophy in 1972.

BEST COACH Conventional wisdom says it's not wise to follow a legend, but Tom Osborne had little choice when Bob

Devaney handpicked his former graduate assistant to be his successor in 1973, after Devaney had won two national titles in 11 seasons as NU coach. A straight-laced doctor of education, Osborne was haunted early on by not being able to beat Oklahoma, a legacy he was finally able to escape. While he finished with a sterling 255–49–3 career record, he'll always be remembered for putting together one of the most dominant runs in modern college football history. Osborne's last five Nebraska teams went 60–3, and won three national titles in four seasons (1994, 1995 and 1997). Osborne retired after the last title and in 2000 won a seat in the U.S. House of Representatives.

BEST TEAM In 1996, the Cornhuskers' 1995 national championship team was selected by computer analyst Jeff Sagarin as the best major college team since 1956, with

RECORDS

RUSHING YARDS

GAME
294   Calvin Jones vs. Kansas, Nov. 9, 1991 (27 att.)

SEASON
2,148   Mike Rozier, 1983 (275 att.)

CAREER
4,780   Mike Rozier, 1981-83 (668 att.)

PASSING YARDS

GAME
342   Joe Dailey vs. Baylor, Oct. 16, 2004 (13 of 20)

SEASON
2,074   Dave Humm, 1972 (140 of 266)

CAREER
5,035   Dave Humm, 1972-74 (353 of 637)

RECEIVING YARDS

GAME
167   Matt Davison vs. Texas A&M, Oct. 10, 1998 (10 rec.)

SEASON
942   Johnny Rodgers, 1972 (55 rec.)

CAREER
2,479   Johnny Rodgers, 1970-72 (143 rec.)

POINTS

GAME
36   Calvin Jones vs. Kansas, Nov. 9, 1991 (6 TDs)

SEASON
174   Mike Rozier, 1983 (29 TDs)

CAREER
388   Kris Brown, 1995-98 (57 FGs, 217 PATs)

CONSENSUS ALL-AMERICANS

1915	Guy Chamberlin, E
1924-25	Ed Weir, T
1933	George Sauer, B
1936	Sam Francis, B
1963	Bob Brown, G
1964	Larry Kramer, T
1965	Freeman White, E
1965	Walt Barnes, DT
1966	LaVerne Allers, G
1966-67	Wayne Meylan, MG
1970	Bob Newton, T
1971	Larry Jacobson, DT
1971-72	Johnny Rodgers, FL
1971-72	Willie Harper, DE
1972	Rich Glover, MG
1973	John Dutton, DL
1974	Marvin Crenshaw, OT
1975	Rik Bonness, C
1976	Dave Butterfield, DB
1978	Kelvin Clark, OT
1979	Junior Miller, TE
1980	Randy Schleusener, OL
1980	Jarvis Redwine, RB
1981-82	Dave Rimington, C
1982-83	Mike Rozier, RB
1983	Irving Fryar, WR

(Continued on next page)

the 1971 NU team second. Which is better? Take your pick. Behind quarterback Tommie Frazier, the 1995 team won its regular-season games by an average of 38.7 points, led the nation in scoring with a school-record 52.4 points and was second in total offense. It routed No. 2 Florida 62-24 in the Fiesta Bowl. Six players on the 1971 team earned All-America honors, including game-breaking wingback Johnny Rodgers. Those Cornhuskers went 13–0 despite perhaps the toughest conference schedule ever— OU finished the season ranked No. 2 by the AP and Colorado was No. 3.

BIGGEST GAME Like many a college football showdown since, the 1971 Nebraska-Oklahoma game was hyped as the Game of the Century. Unlike the other versions, the 1971 game is still known as such. On Nov. 25, more than 61,000 fans filled Owen Field to see the nation's top two teams square off. OU was No. 1 on offense, NU No. 1 on defense. Between the two teams they accounted for 17 of the 22 first-team All-Big Eight players. Rodgers returned a punt 72 yards for a touchdown to open the scoring, but just as vital was his diving catch to keep the Cornhuskers' game-winning drive alive. Jeff Kinney capped a 74-yard drive with a two-yard touchdown run with 1:38 left and noseguard Rich Glover deflected a fourth-down pass by Jack Mildren to seal the game, a 35-31 NU victory. The Cornhuskers beat Alabama 38-6 in the Orange Bowl to win their second consecutive national title.

BIGGEST UPSET There was no love lost between NU Coach Bill Jennings and his former boss, OU head coach Bud Wilkinson. As a Sooners assistant Jennings was embroiled in a controversy over an NCAA investigation that put the Sooners on probation.

He also clashed with Wilkinson over recruiting ethics. Jennings' first two NU teams won only one game each and lost to OU by a combined 72-14, but in 1959 he got his revenge. His Cornhuskers were 2–4 heading into an Oct. 31, 1959, date with a Sooners team that had beaten NU 16 straight and had gone unbeaten in 74 straight Big Eight games. NU broke up and intercepted late passes in the end zone and won 25-21 at Memorial Stadium. A patient Wilkinson followed the mob of Cornhuskers supporters carrying Jennings off the field so he could shake his former protégé's hand.

STADIUM The goal in the fall of 1922 was to raise $430,000 from faculty, students, alumni and friends of Nebraska to build a football stadium, a total that was quickly reached. The building was named Memorial Stadium, to honor the Nebraskans who had served in the Civil and Spanish-American Wars and the 751 Nebraskans who had died in World War I. Built in just over 90 working days, the stadium was dedicated on Oct. 20, 1923, with a homecoming game against Kansas that ended in a scoreless tie. Since then it has undergone several major renovations, the most recent (1997-99) a $36 million upgrade that included the addition of 42 skyboxes, club seating and a new press box. On April 24, 1998, the stadium was rededicated and the field named for Hall of Fame coach Tom Osborne. NU holds the NCAA record with 268 straight home sellouts through 2004, a streak that began in 1962, Devaney's first season. On game days, Memorial Stadium is the third largest population center in the state, behind Omaha and Lincoln.

CONSENSUS ALL-AMERICANS (cont.)

1983	Dean Steinkuhler, OL
1984	Mark Traynowicz, C
1986	Danny Noonan, DL
1988-89	Jake Young, C
1988	Broderick Thomas, LB
1992	Will Shields, OL
1993	Trev Alberts, LB
1994	Zach Wiegert, OL
1994	Brenden Stai, OL
1994	Ed Stewart, LB
1995	Tommie Frazier, QB
1996-97	Aaron Taylor, OL
1996-97	Grant Wistrom, DL
1997	Jason Peter, DL
1999	Ralph Brown, DB
2000	Dominic Raiola, C
2001	Toniu Fonoti, OL

ALL-CENTURY TEAM

Nearly 10,000 Huskers fans selected the team on the Internet during 1999 and 2000.

OFFENSE

1969-70	Bob Newton, OT
1991-94	Zach Wiegert, OT
1981-83	Dean Steinkuhler, OG
1989-92	Will Shields, OG
1994-97	Aaron Taylor, OG/C
1979-82	Dave Rimington, C
1977-79	Junior Miller, TE
1970-72	Johnny Rodgers, WR
1981-83	Irving Fryar, WR
1992-95	Tommie Frazier, QB
1979-82	Roger Craig, IB
1981-83	Mike Rozier, IB
1983-85	Tom Rathman, FB
1995-98	Joel Makovicka, FB
1995-98	Kris Brown, PK
1989-92	Tyrone Hughes, KR

DEFENSE

1985-87	Neil Smith, DT
1994-97	Jason Peter, DT
1970-72	Rich Glover, NT
1985-88	Broderick Thomas, DE/OLB
1990-93	Trev Alberts, DE/OLB
1994-97	Grant Wistrom, DE
1946-49	Tom Novak, LB
1984-86	Marc Munford, LB
1991-94	Ed Stewart, LB
1994-96	Michael Booker, CB
1996-99	Ralph Brown, CB
1993-96	Mike Minter, S
1996-99	Mike Brown, S
1994-97	Jesse Kosch, P
1970-72	Johnny Rodgers, PR

HEARTBREAKER In a press conference the day before the 1984 Orange Bowl against Miami, Osborne was asked if he'd go for the tie if faced with the situation late in the game. Did he figure that the Cornhuskers' regular-season body of work would be enough to earn them the national title, or would he go for the win to erase any doubt? "If it came down to a two-pointer or if I were inside their 10-yard line," he said, "I'd have to go for it." Faced with that exact situation the following evening after rallying from a 13-point deficit to draw within 31-30 with 48 seconds left, Osborne didn't hesitate. Turner Gill's two-point conversion pass to Jeff Smith was tipped away. Miami escaped with sole possession of the national title, though the Cornhuskers, who finished second, still received 4½ first-place votes in the AP poll and six in the UPI coaches poll.

WILDEST FINISH Down seven points with 1:02 left at Missouri in 1997, Nebraska found its 35-game conference winning streak and No. 1 ranking in peril. But Scott Frost drove the Cornhuskers 43 yards to the Tigers' 12, where his pass in the end zone appeared to glance harmlessly off the hands of wingback Shevin Wiggins as he was being hit. The ball glanced high off Wiggins' foot, where freshman receiver Matt Davison snagged it as time expired—and as unsuspecting Missouri fans swarmed the field to celebrate the upset. NU went on to win 45-38 in overtime.

BEST COMEBACK If you buy the axiom that option attacks are not built for comebacks, then the No. 1 Cornhuskers appeared finished after Miami jumped to a 10-0 first-quarter lead in the 1995 Orange Bowl. The third-ranked Hurricanes extended the lead to 17-7 early in the second half, but the Cornhuskers' defense, ranked in the top 10 in all four major categories during the regular season, turned the tide when Dwayne Harris sacked Miami quarterback Frank Costa for a safety. Behind Tommie Frazier, who replaced Brook Berringer in the fourth quarter, the Cornhuskers marched for two fourth-quarter touchdown runs by fullback Cory Schlesinger. Kareem Moss' interception on fourth down with 1:01 left ended Miami's comeback hopes and NU had its first national title for Osborne, who had lost with the title on the line in the 1982, 1984 and 1994 Orange Bowls.

RIVAL Nine times since 1971, both Nebraska and Oklahoma were ranked in the AP Top 5 when they met, with OU winning six. From 1970 to 1988 the two schools finished first or second in the Big Eight in 17 of 19 seasons. From 1976 to 1986 Oklahoma scored in the final minute three times to take a come-from-behind victory. NU played spoiler of its own in 2001, using a fourth-quarter throwback TD pass to quarterback Eric Crouch to solidify a 20-10 win over the defending national champions. When the Big 12 was formed in 1996, the Cornhuskers were put in the North Division, the Sooners in the South. The unbalanced schedule meant the teams played only two out of every four years, which has partly diminished what had been one of the fiercest rivalries in college football and opened the door for a fellow Big 12 counterpart, Kansas State, to perhaps someday take OU's place.

CONTROVERSY On Jan. 3, 2002, a Nebraska team that in its last game had allowed more points than in any other game in school history, and didn't even win the Big 12 North Division, found itself playing for the national title to a cacophony of protest and disbelief. NU had sailed through the season, knocking off No. 3 Oklahoma in Lincoln before heading into its regular-season finale at Colorado. The Buffaloes ripped apart the Blackshirt defense and ran away with a 62-36 victory and the North title. But after a series of upsets knocked Oklahoma, Texas, Florida and Tennessee out of a shot at Miami in the Rose Bowl, the Cornhuskers emerged as the No. 2 team in the BCS rankings. Critics of the BCS thought once-beaten Oregon and coach Mike Bellotti—who had referred to the BCS as "a cancer"—deserved the shot because they ranked No. 2 in the coaches' and writers' polls. BCS backers got a break when the Hurricanes jumped to a 34-0 halftime lead on their way to a 37-14 dismantling of the Cornhuskers. BCS handlers responded with another in a series of off-season formula tweakings, dropping margin of victory from the computer polls that helped determine the title game participants.

NICKNAME In the early years, Nebraska was known by a host of nicknames, including Treeplanters, Rattlesnake Boys, Antelopes, Old Gold Knights and the infamous sobriquet Bugeaters. Legend has it that the latter nickname was applied after an East Coast newspaper writer lauded the toughness of Nebraskans facing drought and a grasshopper plague, which left them with not much left to eat but bugs. Less noble is the explanation from those who say the nickname simply came from the favored meal of the bullbats that hovered over the plains during that time. In 1900, Charles "Cy" Sherman, a staff writer at the *Lincoln Journal* and later the sports editor at the *Lincoln Star*, picked up the nickname Cornhuskers.

Strangely, the Nebraska student newspaper had tagged the University of Iowa football team with that derisive moniker in 1894, but when Sherman suggested it be applied to the NU teams it was quickly and widely embraced.

MASCOT Though not the official mascot, Herbie Husker has been the face of NU football off and on since 1975. Former Huskers SID Don Bryant was captivated by a cartoon penned by Dirk West of Lubbock, Texas, for the Cotton Bowl press headquarters, and the school adopted Herbie, who appeared on the sideline resembling a giant plush cowboy. Li'l Red, a wide-eyed and oversized inflated rubber character in red overalls, came on as Herbie was banished in 1994. But in 2003, the university announced that after "a rigorous exercise routine, resulting in a loss of 70 pounds of fat and an increase of 50 pounds in muscle mass," Herbie would make a comeback. Buffed and revitalized—and with a fiberglass head—he returned to the sideline for the Cornhuskers 2003 season opener.

UNIFORMS From the first football team in 1890, which wore canvas uniforms and black stockings, NU has undergone few changes, though some of them have been drastic. From the turn of the century, NU wore horizontal stripes, then vertical stripes, then a big "N" on the front of the jersey. Originally, the Cornhuskers had red helmets, before switching to white ones under Devaney. For much of the 1960s their uniforms were distinctive for their skinny, fluid numbers. In 1970, the "NU" on the helmet was changed to an "N." The Cornhuskers have traditionally worn scarlet jerseys at home and cream-colored jerseys on the road. Trifling with that style—a large, modern stripe and white pants on the road—was greeted with derision by fans in 2002 and the Cornhuskers returned to the classic look in 2003.

NUMBERS In 2002, the Cornhuskers went 7–7, which caused more teeth-gnashing in Nebraska than a biblical infestation of rootworm beetles. As if the losing wasn't bad enough, the

> ## The 7–7 record in 2002 caused more teeth-gnashing in Nebraska than a biblical infestion of rootworm beetles.

season saw a slew of streaks end, including winning seasons (40), nine-win seasons (33), consecutive home wins (26) and consecutive appearances in the Associated Press rankings (348). Even though Coach Frank Solich's team improved to 9–3 in 2003, it still cost the former NU fullback his job ... NU has led major colleges in rushing in 15 seasons since 1963 ... The school has had 47 different players earn a total of 59 first-team Academic All-America honors as selected by the College Sports Information Directors of America.

QUIRK Osborne's I-formation option attack may have been simple in scheme, but that didn't mean he didn't put some spice in the playbook. Twice Osborne called for the "fumbleroosky." The play was designed for the center to snap the ball to the quarterback—who would touch it but not take it—and then leave the ball on the ground while a pulling guard snatched it up and ran. The first time, in 1979, Randy Schleusener scooted 15 yards for a touchdown against OU in a 17-14 defeat. In the 1984 Orange Bowl, trailing Miami by 17 points, Osborne called for it again and Dean Steinkuhler ran 19 yards for a touchdown. The play—inspired by the "Bummeroosky," a similar gimmick scripted by Bum Phillips when he was an assistant coach at Texas A&M—became a relic in 1992 when it was outlawed by the NCAA.

LORE. Walk-ons give Nebraska a sort of Ellis Island flavor. Not good enough for a scholarship? Come to Lincoln and we'll make you a football player. That was the theme for the Cornhuskers under Osborne, who encouraged a walk-on program so successful that NU wound up starting five former walk-ons in the 1996 Fiesta Bowl victory over Florida that gave them the national title. Ends Jared Tomich (1995-96) and Jimmy Williams (1981) came to NU as walk-ons but left as All-Americas.

QUOTE "We're the only undefeated team. I can't see how the pope himself would vote for Notre Dame."

—Bob Devaney, 1971

NEBRASKA ALL-TIME SCORES

WIN/LOSS PERCENTAGE SINCE 1936

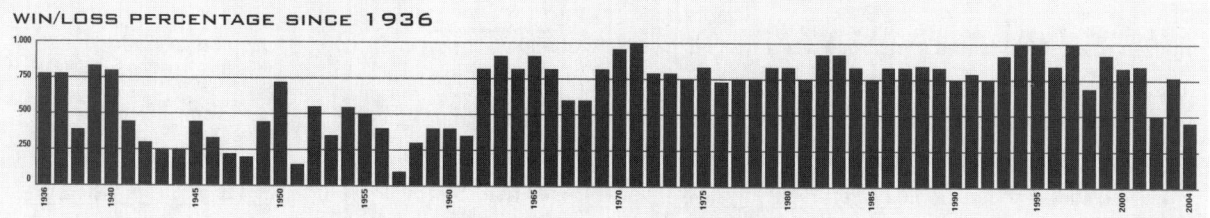

DR. LANGDON FROTHINGHAM
1890 (1.000)   2-0

1890   2-0-0
| N27 | • | at Omaha | 10 | 0 |
| F14 | • | at Doane | 18 | 0 |

NO HEAD COACH

1891   2-2-0
O31	•	Doane	28	4
N14	•	at Doane	12	14
N26	•	Iowa Oma	0	22
D5	•	at Doane	32	0

1892   2-2-1
O24	•	Illinois	6	0
O29	•	at Denver AC	4	18
N5	•	Missouri Oma	1	0 f
N12	•	Kansas	0	12
N24	=	Iowa Oma	10	10

FRANK CRAWFORD
1893-94 (.679)   9-4-1

1893   3-2-1
O21	•	Doane	28	0
O28	=	Baker	10	10
N4	•	at Denver AC	1	0 f
N11	•	at Missouri	18	30 *
N18	•	Kansas	0	18
N30	•	Iowa Oma	20	18

1894   6-2-0
O20	•	Grinnell	22	0
O27	•	Doane	0	12
N3	•	Missouri KC	14	18
N10	•	at Omaha YMCA	36	6
N17	•	at Kansas	12	6
N19	•	at Ottawa	6	0
N29	•	Iowa Oma	36	0
D25	•	at Omaha YMCA	10	6

CHARLES THOMAS
1895 (.667)   6-3

1895   6-3-0
O12	•	at Sioux City AC	38	0
O16	•	at Butte	6	16
O19	•	at Denver AC	12	4
O26	•	at Omaha U. Club	36	0
N2	•	Missouri Oma	12	10
N16	•	Kansas	4	8
N19	•	at Doane	24	0
N22	•	at Grinnell	0	24
N28	•	Iowa Oma	6	0

E.N. ROBINSON
1896-97 (.719)   11-4-1

1896   6-3-1
O17	•	Doane	20	0
O26	•	at Missouri	8	4
O31	•	Nebraska Wesleyan	18	8
N7	•	at Kansas	4	18
N9	•	at K.C. Med. Coll.	6	4
N12	•	Butte	6	20
N19	•	Iowa State	12	4
N23	•	Nebraska Wesleyan	28	0
N26	=	Iowa Oma	0	0
N28	•	Iowa Oma	0	6

1897   5-1-0
O8	•	at Iowa State	0	10
O18	•	Tarkio	16	0
O23	•	Nebraska Wesleyan	11	0
O30	•	Missouri	41	0
N13	•	Kansas	6	5 *
N25	•	Iowa Cou	6	0

FIELDING H. YOST
1898 (.727)   8-3

1898   8-3-0
O1	•	Hastings	76	0
O8	•	Iowa State	23	20 *
O15	•	Tarkio	24	0
O22	•	at William-Jewell	38	0
O24	•	at Missouri	47	6
N5	•	at Kansas	18	6
N7	•	at K.C. Medics	0	24
N12	•	Drake	5	6
N17	•	at Colorado	23	10
N19	•	at Denver AC	11	10
N24	•	Iowa Cou	5	6

A. EDWIN BRANCH
1899 (.167)   1-7-1

1899   1-7-1
O6	•	at Iowa State	0	33 *
O14	=	K.C. Medics	6	6
O21	•	Missouri	0	11
O28	•	at K.C. Medics	0	24
N4	•	Iowa Oma	0	30
N11	•	at Drake	12	6
N18	•	Kansas	20	36
N24	•	at South Dakota	5	6
N30	•	Grinnell Oma	0	12

WALTER C. BOOTH
1900-05 (.845)   46-8-1

1900   6-1-1
O13	•	Iowa State	30	0
O20	•	Drake	8	0
O27	=	at K.C. Med. Coll.	0	0
O29	•	at Tarkio	5	0
N5	•	at Missouri	12	0
N10	•	Grinnell	33	0
N17	•	at Kansas	12	0
N29	•	Minnesota	12	20

1901   6-2-0
S28	•	at American Osteopath	5	0
O59	•	Doane	29	0
O12	•	at Minnesota	0	19
O26	•	Iowa State	17	0
N2	•	Wisconsin Mil	0	18
N9	•	Missouri Oma	51	0
N16	•	Kansas	29	5
N28	•	Haskell	18	10

1902   9-0-0
S27	•	Doane	51	0
O4	•	at Colorado	10	0
O11	•	Grinnell	17	0
O18	•	at Minnesota	6	0
O25	•	Missouri StJ	12	0
N1	•	Haskell	28	0
N8	•	Kansas	16	0
N15	•	Knox	7	0
N27	•	Northwestern	12	0

1903   10-0-0
S26	•	Grand Island	64	0
O3	•	South Dakota	23	0
O10	•	at Denver	10	0
O17	•	Haskell	16	0
O24	•	Colorado	31	0
O31	•	at Iowa	17	6
N7	•	Knox	33	5
N14	•	at Kansas	6	0
N21	•	Bellvue	52	0
N26	•	Illinois	16	0

1904   7-3-0
S24	•	Grand Island	72	0
O1	•	Grinnell	46	0
O8	•	at Colorado	0	6
O15	•	at Creighton	39	0
O22	•	Knox	34	0
O29	•	at Minnesota	12	16
N5	•	Iowa	17	6
N12	•	Haskell KC	6	14
N19	•	Bellvue	51	0
N24	•	Illinois	16	10

1905   8-2-0
S23	•	Grande Island	30	0
O7	•	S. Dakota	42	6
O14	•	Knox	16	0
O21	•	at Michigan	0	31
O28	•	at Creighton	102	0
N4	•	Iowa State	21	0
N11	•	Colorado	18	0
N18	•	at Minnesota	0	35
N25	•	Doane	43	5
N30	•	Illinois	24	6

AMOS FOSTER
1906 (.600)   6-4

1906   6-4-0
S29	•	Hastings	56	0
O6	•	S. Dakota	4	0
O13	•	Drake	5	0
O20	•	Iowa State	2	14
O27	•	Doane	28	0
N3	•	at Minnesota	0	13
N10	•	at Creighton	17	0
N17	•	Kansas	6	8
N24	•	at Chicago	5	38
N29	•	Cincinnati	41	0

1907-1918
MISSOURI VALLEY

W.C. COLE
1907-10 (.708)   24-9-3

1907   7-3-0 (1-0-0)
S28	•	Peru St.	53	0
O5	•	South Dakota	39	0
O12	•	Grinnell	30	4
O19	•	at Minnesota	5	8
O26	•	Colorado	22	8
N2	•	Iowa State	10	13 #
N9	•	| at Kansas	16	6
N16	•	at Denver	63	0
N23	•	Doane	85	0
N28	•	at St. Louis	0	34

1908   7-2-1 (2-1-0)
S26	•	Peru St.	20	0
O3	•	Doane	43	0
O10	•	Grinnell	20	5
O17	=	at Minnesota	0	0
O24	•	Haskell	10	0
O31	•	| at Iowa	11	8
N7	•	| Iowa State Oma	23	17
N14	•	Kansas	5	20
N26	•	Wabash	27	6
D2	•	Carlisle	6	37

1909   3-3-2 (0-1-1)
O2	=	South Dakota	6	6
O9	•	Knox	34	0
O16	•	Minnesota Oma	0	14
O23	=	| Iowa	6	6
O30	•	Doane	12	0
N6	•	Kansas	0	6
N20	•	at Denver	6	5
N25	•	Haskell	5	16

1910   7-1-0 (2-0-0)
O1	•	Peru St.	66	0
O8	•	South Dakota	12	9
O15	•	at Minnesota	0	27
O22	•	Denver	27	0
O29	•	Doane	6	0
N5	•	| at Kansas	6	0
N12	•	| Iowa State	24	0
N24	•	Haskell	119	0

E.O. STIEHM
1911-15 (.913)   35-2-3

1911   5-1-2 (2-0-1)
O7	•	Kearney St.	117	0
O14	•	Kansas State	59	0
O21	•	at Minnesota	3	21
O28	•	| Missouri	4	0
N4	=	| at Iowa State	6	6
N11	•	Doane	27	0
N18	•	| at Kansas	29	0
N25	•	Michigan	6	6

1912   7-1-0 (2-0-0)
O5	•	Bellvue	81	0
O12	•	Kansas State	30	6
O19	•	at Minnesota	0	13
O26	•	Adrian	41	0
N2	•	| at Missouri	7	0
N9	•	Doane	54	6
N16	•	Kansas	14	3
N23	•	Oklahoma	13	9

1913   8-0-0 (3-0-0)
O4	•	Washburn	19	0
O11	•	| Kansas State	24	6
O18	•	Minnesota	7	0
O25	•	Haskell	7	6
N1	•	| at Iowa State	18	9
N8	•	Nebraska Wesleyan	42	7
N15	•	| at Kansas	9	0
N22	•	Iowa	12	0

1914   7-0-1 (3-0-0)
O3	•	Washburn	14	7
O10	=	South Dakota	0	0
O17	•	at Kansas State	31	0
O24	•	Michigan State	24	0
O31	•	| Iowa State	20	7
N7	•	Morningside	34	7
N14	•	| Kansas	35	0
N21	•	at Iowa	16	7

1915   8-0-0 (4-0-0)
O2	•	| Drake	48	13
O9	•	| Kansas State	31	0
O16	•	Wasburn	47	0
O23	•	| Notre Dame	20	19
O30	•	at Iowa State	21	0
N6	•	Nebraska Wesleyan	30	0
N13	•	| at Kansas	33	0
N20	•	| Iowa	52	7

E.J. STEWART
1916-17 (.733)   11-4

1916   6-2-0 (3-1-0)
O7	•	| Drake	53	0
O14	•	| Kansas State	14	0
O21	•	| Oregon State Port	17	7
O28	•	| Nebraska Wesleyan	21	0
N4	•	| Iowa State	3	0
N18	•	| Kansas	3	7
N25	•	at Iowa	34	17
N30	•	Notre Dame	0	20

THE SCHOOLS

1917 — 5-2-0 (2-0-0)

	Opponent		
O6	• Nebraska Wesleyan	100	0
O13	• Iowa	47	0
O20	• Notre Dame	7	0
O27	at Michigan	0	20
N10	• Missouri	52	0
N17	at Kansas	13	3
N29	Syracuse	9	10

WILLIAM G. KLINE
1918 (.417) — 2-3-1

1918 — 2-3-1 (2-0-0)

	Opponent		
O5	Iowa	0	12
N9	• Omaha Balloon	19	0
N16	• Kansas	20	0
N23	Camp Dodge	7	23
N28	= Notre Dame	0	0
D7	at Washington, Mo.	7	20

1919-1920
INDEPENDENT

HENRY F. SCHULTE
1919-20 (.559) — 8-6-3

1919 — 3-3-2

	Opponent		
O4	at Iowa	0	18
O11	= at Minnesota	6	6
O18	Notre Dame	9	14
O25	• Oklahoma *OMA*	7	7
N1	Iowa State	0	3
N8	at Missouri	12	5
N15	Kansas	19	7
N27	• Syracuse	3	0

1920 — 5-3-1

	Opponent		
O2	• Washburn	14	0
O9	• Colorado State	7	0
O16	Notre Dame	7	16
O23	• South Dakota	20	0
N2	Rutgers *NYC*	28	0
N6	at Penn State	0	20
N13	= at Kansas	20	20
N20	• Michigan State	35	7
N25	Washington State	20	21

1921-1927
MISSOURI VALLEY

FRED DAWSON
1921-24 (.750) — 23-7-2

1921 — 7-1-0 (3-0-0)

	Opponent		
O1	• Nebraska Wesleyan	55	0
O15	• Haskell	41	0
O22	at Notre Dame	0	7
O29	• | Oklahoma	44	0
N5	• at Pittsburgh	10	0
N12	• | Kansas	28	0
N19	• | at Iowa State	35	3
N24	• Colorado State	70	7

1922 — 7-1-0 (5-0-0)

	Opponent		
O7	• South Dakota	66	0
O21	• | Missouri	48	0
O28	• at Oklahoma	39	7
N4	at Syracuse	6	9
N11	• | at Kansas	28	0
N18	• | Kansas State	21	0
N25	• | Iowa State	54	6
N30	• Notre Dame	14	6

1923 — 4-2-2 (3-0-2)

	Opponent		
O6	• at Illinois	7	24
O13	• | Oklahoma	24	0
O20	= | Kansas	0	0
O27	= | at Missouri	7	7
N10	• Notre Dame	14	7
N17	• | at Iowa State	26	14
N24	Syracuse	0	7
N29	• | Kansas State	34	12

1924 — 5-3-0 (3-1-0)

	Opponent		
O4	Illinois	6	9
O11	| at Oklahoma	7	14
O18	| Colgate	35	7
O25	• | at Kansas	14	7
N1	• | Missouri	14	6
N15	at Notre Dame	6	34
N22	• | at Kansas State	24	0
N27	• Oregon State	14	0

ERNEST E. BEARG
1925-28 (.742) — 23-7-3

1925 — 4-2-2 (2-2-1)

	Opponent		
O3	• | at Illinois	14	0
O10	| at Missouri	6	9
O17	= | Washington	6	6
O24	• | Kansas	14	0
O31	• | Oklahoma	12	0
N7	| at Drake	0	12
N14	= | at Kansas State	0	0
N26	• Notre Dame	17	0

1926 — 6-2-0 (5-1-0)

	Opponent		
O2	• | Drake	21	0
O9	| Missouri	7	14
O16	• | at Washington, Mo.	20	3
O23	• | at Kansas	20	3
O30	| Iowa State	31	6
N13	• | Kansas State	3	0
N20	• | NYU	15	7
N25	| at Washington	6	10

1927 — 6-2-0 (4-1-0)

	Opponent		
O1	• | Iowa State	6	0
O8	| at Missouri	6	7
O15	• | Grinnell	58	0
O29	• | Syracuse	21	0
N5	• | Kansas	47	13
N12	• | at Pittsburgh	13	21
N19	• | at Kansas State	33	0
N24	• | NYU	27	18

1928-1995
BIG 8

1928 — 7-1-1 (5-0-0)

	Opponent		
O6	• | at Iowa State	12	0
O13	• | Montana St.	26	6
O20	• | Syracuse	7	6
O27	• | Missouri	24	0
N3	| at Kansas	20	0
N10	• | at Oklahoma	44	6
N17	| Pittsburgh	0	0
N24	| at Army	3	13
N29	• | Kansas State	8	0

D.X. BIBLE
1929-36 (.743) — 50-15-7

1929 — 4-1-3 (3-0-2)

	Opponent		
O5	= | SMU	0	0
O12	• | at Syracuse	13	6
O19	| Pittsburgh	7	12
O26	= | at Missouri	7	7
N2	• | Kansas	12	6
N16	• | Oklahoma	13	13
N23	• | at Kansas State	10	6
N28	• | Iowa State	31	12

1930 — 4-3-2 (2-2-1)

	Opponent		
O4	• | Texas A&M	13	0
O11	| at Oklahoma	7	20
O18	• | at Iowa State	14	12
O25	• | Montana St.	53	7
N1	• | Pittsburgh	0	0
N8	• | at Kansas	16	0
N15	= | Missouri	0	0
N22	• | at Iowa	7	12
N27	| Kansas State	9	10

1931 — 8-2-0 (5-0-0)

	Opponent		
S26	• | South Dakota	44	6
O3	| at Northwestern	7	19
O10	• | Oklahoma	13	0
O24	• | Kansas	6	0
O31	• | at Missouri	10	7
N7	• | Iowa	7	0
N14	• | at Kansas State	6	3
N21	• | Iowa State	23	0
N26	| at Pittsburgh	0	40
D5	• | Colorado State *N25*	20	7

1932 — 7-1-1 (5-0-0)

	Opponent		
O8	• | Iowa State	12	6
O15	| at Minnesota	6	7
O22	• | at Kansas	20	6
O29	• | Kansas State	6	0
N5	• | at Iowa	14	13
N12	= | Pittsburgh	0	0
N19	• | at Oklahoma	5	0
N24	• | Missouri	21	6
D3	| at SMU	21	14

1933 — 8-1-0 (5-0-0)

	Opponent		
O7	• | Texas	26	0
O14	• | at Iowa State	20	0
O21	• | at Kansas State	9	0
O28	• | Oklahoma	16	7
N4	• | at Missouri	26	0
N11	• | Kansas	12	0
N18	• | at Pittsburgh	0	6
N25	• | Iowa	7	6
N30	| Oregon State	22	0

1934 — 6-3-0 (4-1-0)

	Opponent		
S29	• | Wyoming	50	0
O3	| at Minnesota	0	20
O13	• | Iowa	14	13
O20	• | at Oklahoma	6	0
O27	• | Iowa State	7	6
N10	• | Pittsburgh	6	25
N17	• | at Kansas	3	0
N24	• | Missouri	13	6
N29	| Kansas State	7	19

1935 — 6-2-1 (4-0-1)

	Opponent		
S28	• | Chicago	28	7
O5	• | at Iowa State	20	7
O12	| Minnesota	7	12
O19	= | at Kansas State	19	0
O26	• | Oklahoma	19	0
N2	• | at Missouri	19	6
N9	• | Kansas	19	13
N16	• | at Pittsburgh	0	6
N28	• | Oregon State	26	20

1936 — 7-2-0 (5-0-0)

	Opponent		
O3	• | Iowa State	34	0
O10	• | at Minnesota	0	7
O17	• | Indiana	13	9
O24	• | at Oklahoma	14	0
O31	• | Missouri	20	0
N7	• | at Kansas	26	0
N14	• | Pittsburgh	6	19
N21	• | Kansas State	40	0
N28	• | Oregon State *Port*	32	14

L. M. JONES
1937-41 (.652) — 28-14-4

1937 — 6-1-2 (3-0-2)

	Opponent		
O2	• | Minnesota	14	9
O9	• | at Iowa State	20	7
O16	= | Oklahoma	0	0
O23	• | at Missouri	7	0
O30	• | Indiana	7	0
N6	= | Kansas	13	13
N13	• | at Pittsburgh	7	13
N20	• | Iowa	28	0
N27	• | at Kansas State	3	0

1938 — 3-5-1 (2-3-0)

	Opponent		
O1	• | at Minnesota	7	16
O8	| Iowa State	7	8
O15	= | Indiana	0	0
O22	• | at Oklahoma	0	14
O29	• | Missouri	10	13
N5	• | at Kansas	16	7
N12	• | Pittsburgh	0	19
N19	• | at Iowa	14	0
N24	• | Kansas State	14	7

1939 — 7-1-1 (4-1-0)

	Opponent		
S30	= | at Indiana	7	7
O7	• | Minnesota	6	0
O14	• | at Iowa State	10	7
O21	• | Baylor	20	0
O28	• | at Kansas State	25	9
N4	• | at Missouri	13	27
N11	• | Kansas	7	0
N18	• | at Pittsburgh	14	13
N25	• | Oklahoma	13	7

1940 — 8-2-0 (5-0-0)

	Opponent		
O5	• | at Minnesota	7	13
O12	• | Indiana	13	7
O19	• | at Kansas	53	2
O26	• | Missouri	20	7
N2	• | at Oklahoma	13	0
N9	• | Iowa	14	6
N16	• | at Pittsburgh	9	7
N23	• | Iowa State	21	12
N30	• | Kansas State	20	0
ROSE BOWL			
J1	| Stanford	13	21

1941 — 4-5-0 (3-2-0)

	Opponent		
O4	• | at Iowa State	14	0
O11	• | Kansas	32	0
O18	• | Indiana	13	21
O25	| at Missouri	0	6
N1	| at Kansas State	6	12
N8	| at Minnesota	0	9
N15	| Pittsburgh	7	14
N22	• | Iowa	14	13
N29	• | Oklahoma	7	6

GLENN PRESNELL
1942 (.300) — 3-7

1942 — 3-7-0 (3-2-0)

	Opponent		
S26	| at Iowa	0	27
O3	• | Iowa State	26	0
O10	| Indiana	0	12
O17	| Minnesota	2	15
O24	• | at Oklahoma	7	0
O31	• | at Kansas	14	7
N7	| Missouri	6	26
N14	| at Pittsburgh	0	6
N21	| at Iowa Pre-Flight	0	46
N28	| Kansas State	0	19

ADOLPH LEWANDOWSKI
1943-44 (.250) — 4-12

1943 — 2-6-0 (2-3-0)

	Opponent		
O2	| at Minnesota	0	54
O9	| Indiana	13	54
O16	| at Iowa State	6	27
O23	• | Kansas	7	6
O30	| at Missouri	20	54
N6	• | at Kansas State	13	7
N20	| Iowa	13	33
N27	| Oklahoma	7	26

1944 — 2-6-0 (2-3-0)

	Opponent		
S30	| at Minnesota	0	39
O14	| at Indiana	0	54
O21	| at Kansas	0	20
O28	| Missouri	24	20
N4	| at Iowa	6	27
N11	| Iowa State	6	19
N25	• | Kansas State	35	0
D2	| Oklahoma *OkC*	12	31

GEORGE CLARK
1945, '48 (.316) — 6-13

1945 — 4-5-0 (2-3-0)

	Opponent		
S29	| Oklahoma	0	20
O6	| Minnesota	7	61
O13	| at Indiana	14	54
O20	| at Iowa State	7	27
O27	| at Missouri	0	19
N3	• | Kansas	27	13
N10	• | at Kansas State	24	0
N17	• | South Dakota	53	0
N24	• | Iowa	13	6

BERNIE MASTERSON
1946-47 (.278) — 5-13

1946 — 3-6-0 (3-2-0)

	Opponent		
S28	| at Minnesota	6	33
O5	• | Kansas State	31	0
O12	| at Iowa	7	21
O19	• | at Kansas	16	14
O26	| Indiana	7	27
N2	| Missouri	20	21
N16	• | Iowa State	33	0
N23	| at Oklahoma	6	27
N30	| at UCLA	0	18

1947 — 2-7-0 (2-3-0)

	Opponent		
S27	| Indiana	0	17
O4	| Minnesota	13	28
O11	• | at Iowa State	14	7
O18	| at Notre Dame	0	31
O25	• | at Kansas State	14	7
N1	| at Missouri	6	47
N8	| Kansas	7	13
N22	| Oklahoma	13	14
N29	| Oregon State	6	27

NEBRASKA 573

GEORGE CLARK

1948 2-8-0 (2-4-0)
S25 ● | Iowa State 19 15
O2 at Minnesota 13 39
O9 | at Colorado 6 19
O16 Notre Dame 13 44
O23 | at Kansas 7 27
O30 UCLA 15 27
N6 ● | Kansas State 32 0
N13 | at Oklahoma 14 41
N20 | Missouri 6 33
N27 Oregon State PORT 12 28

BILL GLASSFORD
1949-55 (.464) 30-35-4

1949 4-5-0 (3-3-0)
S24 ● South Dakota 33 6
O1 Minnesota 6 28
O8 ● | at Kansas State 13 6
O15 at Penn State 7 22
O22 | Oklahoma 0 48
O29 | at Missouri 20 21
N5 | Kansas 13 27
N12 ● | at Iowa State 7 0
N19 ● | Colorado 25 14

1950 6-2-1 (4-2-0)
S30 = Indiana 20 20
O7 ● at Minnesota 32 26
O14 | at Colorado 19 28
O21 ● Penn State 19 0
O28 ● | at Kansas 33 26
N4 ● | Missouri 40 34
N11 ● | Kansas State 49 21
N18 ● | Iowa State 20 13
N25 | at Oklahoma 35 49

1951 1-8-1 (1-4-1)
S29 TCU 7 28
O6 = | at Kansas State 6 6 †
O13 Penn State 7 15
O20 at Minnesota 20 39
O27 | at Missouri 19 35
N3 | Kansas 7 27
N10 ● | at Iowa State 34 27
N17 | Colorado 14 36
N24 | Oklahoma 0 27
N30 at Miami, Fla. 7 19

1952 5-4-1 (3-2-1)
S20 ● South Dakota 46 0
S27 ● Oregon PORT 28 13
O4 ● | Iowa State 16 0
O11 ● | Kansas State 27 14
O18 at Penn State 0 10
O25 = | at Colorado 16 16
N1 | Missouri 6 10
N8 ● | at Kansas 14 13
N15 Minnesota 7 13
N22 | at Oklahoma 13 34

1953 3-6-1 (2-4-0)
S19 Oregon 12 20
S26 = at Illinois 21 21
O3 | at Kansas State 0 27
O10 at Pittsburgh 6 14
O17 ● Miami, Fla. 20 16
O24 | at Missouri 7 23
O31 ● | Kansas 9 0
N7 ● | at Iowa State 27 19
N14 | Colorado 10 14
N21 | Oklahoma 7 30

1954 6-5-0 (4-2-0)
S25 at Minnesota 7 19
O2 ● | Iowa State 39 14
O9 | Kansas State 3 7
O16 ● Oregon State 27 7
O23 ● | at Colorado 20 6
O30 ● | Missouri 25 19
N6 ● | at Kansas 41 20
N13 Pittsburgh 7 21
N20 | at Oklahoma 7 55
N26 ● at Hawaii 50 0
ORANGE BOWL
J1 Duke 7 34

1955 5-5-0 (5-1-0)
S17 Hawaii 0 6
S24 at Ohio State 20 28
O1 ● | at Kansas State 16 0
O8 Texas A&M 0 27
O15 at Pittsburgh 7 21
O22 ● | at Missouri 18 12
O29 ● | Kansas 19 14
N5 ● | at Iowa State 10 7
N12 ● | Colorado 37 20
N19 | Oklahoma 0 41

PETE ELLIOTT
1956 (.400) 4-6

1956 4-6-0 (3-3-0)
S22 ● South Dakota 34 6
S29 at Ohio State 7 34
O6 ● | Iowa State 9 7
O13 | Kansas State 7 10
O20 Indiana 14 19
O27 | at Colorado 0 16
N3 ● | Missouri 15 14
N10 ● | at Kansas 26 20
N17 Baylor 7 26
N24 | at Oklahoma 6 54

BILL JENNINGS
1957-61 (.310) 15-34-1

1957 1-9-0 (1-5-0)
S21 Washington State 12 34
S28 at Army 0 42
O5 ● | at Kansas State 14 7
O12 at Pittsburgh 0 34
O19 Syracuse 9 26
O26 | at Missouri 13 14
N2 | Kansas 12 14
N9 | at Iowa State 0 13
N16 | Colorado 0 27
N23 | Oklahoma 7 32

1958 3-7-0 (1-5-0)
S20 ● Penn State 14 7
S27 at Purdue 0 28
O4 ● | Iowa State 7 6
O11 | Kansas State 6 23
O18 at Syracuse 0 38
O25 | at Colorado 16 27
N1 | Missouri 0 31
N8 | at Kansas 7 29
N15 ● Pittsburgh 14 6
N22 | at Oklahoma 7 40

1959 4-6-0 (2-4-0)
S19 Texas 0 20
S26 ● at Minnesota 32 12
O3 ● Oregon State 7 6
O10 | Kansas 3 10
O17 Indiana 7 23
O24 | at Missouri 0 9
O31 ● | Oklahoma 25 21
N7 | at Iowa State 6 18
N14 ● | Colorado 14 12
N21 | at Kansas State 14 29

1960 4-6-0 (2-5-0)
S17 ● at Texas 14 13
S24 Minnesota 14 26
O1 | Iowa State 7 10
O8 ● | Kansas State 17 7
O15 ● Army 14 9
O22 | at Colorado 6 19
O29 | Missouri 0 28
N5 | at Kansas 0 31
N12 | Oklahoma State 6 7
N19 ● | at Oklahoma 17 14

1961 3-6-1 (2-5-0)
S23 ● North Dakota 33 0
S30 = Arizona 14 14
O7 ● | at Kansas State 24 0
O14 Syracuse 6 28
O21 | at Oklahoma State 6 14
O28 | at Missouri 0 10
N4 | Kansas 6 28
N11 ● | at Iowa State 16 13
N18 | Colorado 0 7
N25 | Oklahoma 14 21

BOB DEVANEY
1962-72 (.829) 101-20-2

1962 9-2-0 (5-2-0)
S22 ● South Dakota 53 0
S29 ● at Michigan 25 13
O6 ● | Iowa State 36 22
O13 ● North Carolina St. 19 14
O20 ● | Kansas State 26 6
O27 ● | at Colorado 31 6
N3 | Missouri 7 16
N10 ● | at Kansas 40 16
N17 ● | Oklahoma State 14 0
N24 | at Oklahoma 6 34
GOTHAM BOWL
D15 ● Miami, Fla. 36 34

1963 10-1-0 (7-0-0)
S21 ● South Dakota 58 7
S28 ● at Minnesota 14 7
O5 ● | Iowa State 21 7
O12 Air Force 13 17
O19 ● | at Kansas State 28 6
O26 ● | Colorado 41 6
N2 ● | at Missouri 13 12
N9 ● | Kansas 23 9
N16 ● | at Oklahoma State 20 16
N23 ● | Oklahoma 29 20
ORANGE BOWL
J1 ● Auburn 13 7

1964 9-2-0 (6-1-0)
S19 ● South Dakota 56 0
S26 ● at Minnesota 26 21
O3 ● | at Iowa State 14 7
O10 ● South Carolina 28 6
O17 ● | Kansas State 47 0
O24 ● | at Colorado 21 3
O31 ● | Missouri 9 0
N7 ● | at Kansas 14 7
N14 ● | Oklahoma State 27 14
N21 | at Oklahoma 7 17
COTTON BOWL
J1 Arkansas 7 10

1965 10-1-0 (7-0-0)
S18 ● TCU 34 14
S25 ● at Air Force 27 17
O2 ● | Iowa State 44 0
O9 ● Wisconsin 37 0
O16 ● | at Kansas State 41 0
O23 ● | Colorado 38 13
O30 ● | at Missouri 16 14
N6 ● | Kansas 42 6
N13 ● | at Oklahoma State 21 17
N25 ● | Oklahoma 21 9
ORANGE BOWL
J1 Alabama 28 39

1966 9-2-0 (6-1-0)
S17 ● TCU 14 10
S24 ● Utah State 28 7
O1 ● | at Iowa State 12 6
O8 ● at Wisconsin 31 3
O15 ● | Kansas State 21 10
O22 ● | at Colorado 21 19
O29 ● | Missouri 35 0
N5 ● | at Kansas 24 13
N12 ● | Oklahoma State 21 6
N24 | at Oklahoma 9 10
SUGAR BOWL
J2 Alabama 7 34

1967 6-4-0 (3-4-0)
S16 ● at Washington 17 7
S30 ● Minnesota 7 0
O7 ● | at Kansas State 16 14
O14 | at Kansas 0 10
O21 | Colorado 16 21
O28 ● at TCU 29 0
N4 ● | Iowa State 12 0
N11 ● | Oklahoma State 9 0
N18 | at Missouri 7 10
N25 | Oklahoma 14 21

1968 6-4-0 (3-4-0)
S14 ● Wyoming 13 10
S21 ● Utah 31 0
S28 ● at Minnesota 17 14
O12 | Kansas 13 23
O19 | Missouri 14 16
O26 ● | at Oklahoma State 21 20
N2 ● | at Iowa State 24 13
N9 | Kansas State 0 12
N16 ● | at Colorado 22 6
N23 | at Oklahoma 0 47

1969 9-2-0 (6-1-0)
S20 Southern Cal 21 31
S27 ● Texas A&M 14 0
O4 ● at Minnesota 42 14
O11 | at Missouri 7 17
O18 ● | Kansas 21 17
O25 ● | Oklahoma State 13 3
N1 ● | Colorado 20 7
N8 ● | Iowa State 17 3
N15 ● | at Kansas State 10 7
N22 ● | at Oklahoma 44 14
SUN BOWL
D20 ● Georgia 45 6

1970 11-0-1 (7-0-0)
S12 ● Wake Forest 36 12
S19 = at Southern Cal 21 21
S26 ● Army 28 0
O3 ● at Minnesota 35 10
O10 ● | Missouri 21 7
O17 ● | at Kansas 41 20
O24 ● | Oklahoma State 65 31
O31 ● | at Colorado 29 13
N7 ● | at Iowa State 54 29
N14 ● | Kansas State 51 13
N21 ● | Oklahoma 28 21
ORANGE BOWL
J1 ● LSU 17 12

1971 13-0-0 (7-0-0)
S11 ● Oregon 34 7
S18 ● Minnesota 35 7
S25 ● Texas A&M 34 7
O2 ● Utah State 42 6
O9 ● | at Missouri 36 0
O16 ● | Kansas 55 0
O23 ● | at Oklahoma State 41 13
O30 ● | Colorado 31 7
N6 ● | Iowa State 37 0
N13 ● | at Kansas State 44 17
N25 ● | at Oklahoma 35 31
D4 ● at Hawaii 45 3
ORANGE BOWL
J1 ● Alabama 38 6

1972 9-2-1 (5-1-1)
S9 at UCLA 17 20
S16 ● Texas A&M 37 7
S23 ● at Army 77 7
S30 ● Minnesota 49 0
O14 ● | Missouri 62 0
O21 ● | at Kansas 56 0
O28 ● | Oklahoma State 34 0
N4 ● | at Colorado 33 10
N11 = | at Iowa State 23 23
N18 ● | Kansas State 59 7
N23 | Oklahoma 14 17
ORANGE BOWL
J1 ● Notre Dame 40 6

TOM OSBORNE
1973-97 (.836) 255-49-3

1973 9-2-1 (4-2-1)
S8 ● UCLA 40 13
S22 ● North Carolina St. 31 14
S29 ● Wisconsin 20 16
O6 ● at Minnesota 48 7
O13 | at Missouri 12 13
O20 ● | Kansas 10 9
O27 = | at Oklahoma State 17 17
N3 ● | Colorado 28 16
N10 ● | Iowa State 31 7
N17 ● | at Kansas State 50 21
N23 | at Oklahoma 0 27
COTTON BOWL
J1 ● Texas 19 3

1974 9-3-0 (5-2-0)
S14 ● Oregon 61 7
S21 at Wisconsin 20 21
S28 ● Northwestern 49 7
O5 ● Minnesota 54 0
O12 | Missouri 10 21
O19 ● | at Kansas 56 0
O26 ● | Oklahoma State 7 3
N2 ● | at Colorado 31 15
N9 ● | at Iowa State 23 13
N16 ● | Kansas State 35 7
N23 | Oklahoma 14 28
SUGAR BOWL
D31 ● Florida 3 10

THE SCHOOLS

574 NEBRASKA

THE SCHOOLS

1975 10-2-0 (6-1-0)

S13	●	LSU	10	7
S20	●	Indiana	45	0
S27	●	TCU	56	14
O4	●	Miami, Fla.	31	16
O11	● |	Kansas	16	0
O18	● |	at Oklahoma State	28	20
O25	● |	Colorado	63	21
N1	● |	at Missouri	30	7
N8	● |	at Kansas State	12	0
N15	● |	Iowa State	52	0
N22	|	at Oklahoma	10	35
		FIESTA BOWL		
D26		Arizona State	14	17

1976 9-3-1 (4-3-0)

S11	=	at LSU	6	6
S18	●	at Indiana	45	13
S25	●	TCU	64	10
O2	●	Miami, Fla.	17	9
O9	● |	at Colorado	24	12
O16	● |	Kansas State	51	0
O23	|	Missouri	24	34
O30	● |	at Kansas	31	3
N6	● |	Oklahoma State	14	10
N13	|	at Iowa State	28	37
N26	|	Oklahoma	17	20
D4	●	at Hawaii	68	3
		BLUEBONNET BOWL		
D31	●	Texas Tech	27	24

1977 9-3-0 (5-2-0)

S10		Washington State	10	19
S17	●	Alabama	31	24
S24	●	Baylor	31	10
O1	●	Indiana	31	13
O8	● |	at Kansas State	26	9
O15	|	Iowa State	21	24
O22	● |	Colorado	33	15
O29	● |	at Oklahoma State	31	14
N5	● |	at Missouri	21	10
N12	● |	Kansas	52	7
N25	|	at Oklahoma	7	38
		LIBERTY BOWL		
D19	●	North Carolina	21	17

1978 9-3-0 (6-1-0)

S2		Alabama [Birm]	3	20
S9	●	California	36	26
S16	●	Hawaii	56	10
S30	●	at Indiana	69	17
O7	● |	at Iowa State	23	0
O14	● |	Kansas State	48	14
O21	● |	at Colorado	52	14
O28	● |	Oklahoma State	22	14
N4	● |	at Kansas	63	21
N11	● |	Oklahoma	17	14
N18	|	Missouri	31	35
		ORANGE BOWL		
J1		Oklahoma	24	31

1979 10-2-0 (6-1-0)

S15	●	Utah State	35	14
S22	●	at Iowa	24	21
S29	●	Penn State	42	17
O6	●	New Mexico St.	57	0
O13	● |	Kansas	42	0
O20	● |	at Oklahoma State	36	0
O27	● |	Colorado	38	10
N3	● |	at Missouri	23	20
N10	● |	at Kansas State	21	12
N17	● |	Iowa State	34	3
N24	|	at Oklahoma	14	17
		COTTON BOWL		
J1		Houston	14	17

1980 10-2-0 (6-1-0)

S13	●	Utah	55	9
S20	●	Iowa	57	0
S27	●	at Penn State	21	7
O4		Florida State	14	18
O11	● |	at Kansas	54	0
O18	● |	Oklahoma State	48	7
O25	● |	at Colorado	45	7
N1	● |	Missouri	38	16
N8	● |	Kansas State	55	8
N15	● |	at Iowa State	35	0
N22	|	Oklahoma	17	21
		SUN BOWL		
D27	●	Mississippi State	31	17

1981 9-3-0 (7-0-0)

S12		at Iowa	7	10
S19	●	Florida State	34	14
S26		Penn State	24	30
O3	●	Auburn	17	3
O10	● |	Colorado	59	0
O17	● |	at Kansas State	49	3
O24	● |	at Missouri	6	0
O31	● |	Kansas	31	15
N7	● |	at Oklahoma State	54	7
N14	● |	Iowa State	31	7
N21	● |	at Oklahoma	37	14
		ORANGE BOWL		
J1		Clemson	15	22

1982 12-1-0 (7-0-0)

S11	●	Iowa	42	7
S18	●	New Mexico St.	68	0
S25		at Penn State	24	27
O2	●	at Auburn	41	7
O9	● |	at Colorado	40	14
O16	● |	Kansas State	42	13
O23	● |	Missouri	23	19
O30	● |	at Kansas	52	0
N6	● |	Oklahoma State	48	10
N13	● |	at Iowa State	48	10
N26	● |	Oklahoma	28	24
D4	●	at Hawaii	37	16
		ORANGE BOWL		
J1	●	LSU	21	20

1983 12-1-0 (7-0-0)

A29	●	Penn State [ERut]	44	6
S10	●	Wyoming	56	20
S17	●	at Minnesota	84	13
S24	●	UCLA	42	10
O1	●	Syracuse	63	7
O8	● |	at Oklahoma State	14	10
O15	● |	at Missouri	34	13
O22	● |	Colorado	69	19
O29	● |	at Kansas State	51	25
N5	● |	Iowa State	72	29
N12	● |	Kansas	67	13
N26	● |	at Oklahoma	28	21
		ORANGE BOWL		
J2		Miami, Fla.	30	31

1984 10-2-0 (6-1-0)

S8	●	Wyoming	42	7
S15	●	Minnesota	38	7
S22	●	at UCLA	42	3
S29		at Syracuse	9	17
O6	● |	Oklahoma State	17	3
O13	● |	Missouri	33	23
O20	● |	at Colorado	24	7
O27	● |	Kansas State	62	14
N3	● |	at Iowa State	44	0
N10	● |	at Kansas	41	7
N17	|	Oklahoma	7	17
		SUGAR BOWL		
J1	●	LSU	28	10

1985 9-3-0 (6-1-0)

S7		Florida State	13	17
S21	●	Illinois	52	25
S28	●	Oregon	63	0
O5	●	New Mexico	38	7
O12	● |	at Oklahoma State	34	24
O19	● |	at Missouri	28	20
O26	● |	Colorado	17	7
N2	● |	at Kansas State	41	3
N9	● |	Iowa State	49	0
N16	● |	Kansas	56	6
N23	|	at Oklahoma	7	27
		FIESTA BOWL		
J1		Michigan	23	27

1986 10-2-0 (5-2-0)

S6	●	Florida State	34	17
S20	●	at Illinois	59	14
S27	●	Oregon	48	14
O4	●	at South Carolina	27	24
O11	● |	Oklahoma State	30	10
O18	● |	Missouri	48	17
O25	|	at Colorado	10	20
N1	● |	Kansas State	38	0
N8	● |	at Iowa State	35	14
N15	● |	at Kansas	70	0
N22	|	Oklahoma	17	20
		SUGAR BOWL		
J1	●	LSU	30	15

1987 10-2-0 (6-1-0)

S5	●	Utah State	56	12
S12	●	UCLA	42	33
S26	●	at Arizona State	35	28
O3	●	South Carolina	30	21
O10	● |	Kansas	54	2
O17	● |	at Oklahoma State	35	0
O24	● |	Kansas State	56	3
O31	● |	at Missouri	42	7
N7	● |	Iowa State	42	3
N21	|	Oklahoma	7	17
N28	● |	at Colorado	24	7
		FIESTA BOWL		
J1		Florida State	28	31

1988 11-2-0 (7-0-0)

A27	●	Texas A&M [ERut]	23	14
S3	●	Utah State	63	13
S10		at UCLA	28	41
S24	●	Arizona State	47	16
O1	●	Nevada-Las Vegas	48	6
O8	● |	at Kansas	63	10
O15	● |	Oklahoma State	63	42
O22	● |	at Kansas State	48	3
O29	● |	Missouri	26	18
N5	● |	at Iowa State	51	16
N12	● |	Colorado	7	0
N19	● |	at Oklahoma	7	3
		ORANGE BOWL		
J2		Miami, Fla.	3	23

1989 10-2-0 (6-1-0)

S9	●	Northern Illinois	48	17
S16	●	Utah	42	30
S23	●	at Minnesota	48	0
S30	●	Oregon State	35	7
O7	● |	Kansas State	58	7
O14	● |	at Missouri	50	7
O21	● |	at Oklahoma State	48	23
O28	● |	Iowa State	49	17
N4	|	at Colorado	21	27
N11	● |	Kansas	51	14
N18	● |	Oklahoma	42	25
		FIESTA BOWL		
J1		Florida State	17	41

1990 9-3-0 (5-2-0)

S1	●	Baylor	13	0
S8	●	Northern Illinois	60	14
S22	●	Minnesota	56	0
S29	●	Oregon State	31	7
O6	● |	at Kansas State	45	8
O13	● |	Missouri	69	21
O20	● |	Oklahoma State	31	3
O27	● |	at Iowa State	45	13
N3	|	Colorado	12	27
N10	● |	at Kansas	41	9
N23	|	at Oklahoma	10	45
		CITRUS BOWL		
J1		Georgia Tech	21	45

1991 9-2-1 (6-0-1)

S7	●	Utah State	59	28
S14	●	Colorado State	71	14
S21		Washington	21	36
S28	●	at Arizona State	18	9
O12	● |	at Oklahoma State	49	15
O19	● |	Kansas State	38	31
O26	● |	Missouri	63	6
N2	= |	at Colorado	19	19
N9	● |	at Kansas	59	23
N16	● |	Iowa State	38	13
N29	● |	Oklahoma	19	14
		ORANGE BOWL		
J1		Miami, Fla.	0	22

1992 9-3-0 (6-1-0)

S5	●	Utah	49	22
S12	●	Middle Tennessee	48	7
S19		at Washington	14	29
S26	●	Arizona State	45	24
O10	● |	Oklahoma State	55	0
O24	● |	at Missouri	34	24
O31	● |	Colorado	52	7
N7	● |	Kansas	49	7
N14	|	at Iowa State	10	19
N27	● |	at Oklahoma	33	9
D6	● |	Kansas State [Tok]	38	24
		ORANGE BOWL		
J1		Florida State	14	27

1993 11-1-0 (7-0-0)

S4	●	North Texas	76	14
S11	●	Texas Tech	50	27
S18	●	at UCLA	14	13
S25	●	Colorado State	48	13
O7	● |	at Oklahoma State	27	13
O16	● |	Kansas State	45	28
O23	● |	Missouri	49	7
O30	● |	at Colorado	21	17
N6	● |	at Kansas	21	20
N13	● |	Iowa State	49	17
N26	● |	Oklahoma	21	7
		ORANGE BOWL		
J1		Florida State	16	18

1994 13-0-0 (7-0-0)

A28	●	West Virginia [ERut]	31	0
S8	●	at Texas Tech	42	16
S17	●	UCLA	49	21
S24	●	Pacific	70	21
O1	●	Wyoming	42	32
O8	● |	Oklahoma State	32	3
O15	● |	at Kansas State	17	6
O22	● |	at Missouri	42	7
O29	● |	Colorado	24	7
N5	● |	Kansas	45	17
N12	● |	at Iowa State	28	12
N25	● |	at Oklahoma	13	3
		ORANGE BOWL		
J1	●	Miami, Fla.	24	17

1995 12-0-0 (7-0-0)

A31	● |	at Oklahoma State	64	21
S9	●	at Michigan State	50	10
S16	●	Arizona State	77	28
S23	●	Pacific	49	7
S30	●	Washington State	35	21
O14	● |	Missouri	57	0
O21	● |	Kansas State	49	25
O28	● |	at Colorado	44	21
N4	● |	Iowa State	73	14
N11	● |	at Kansas	41	3
N24	● |	Oklahoma	37	0
		FIESTA BOWL		
J2	●	Florida	62	24

1996-PRESENT
BIG 12

1996 11-2 (8-0)

S7	●	Michigan State	55	14
S21		at Arizona State	0	19
S28	●	Colorado State	65	9
O5	● |	at Kansas State	39	3
O12	● |	Baylor	49	0
O19	● |	at Texas Tech	24	10
O26	● |	Kansas	63	7
N2	● |	at Oklahoma	73	21
N9	● |	Missouri	51	7
N16	● |	at Iowa State	49	14
N29	● |	Colorado	17	12
		BIG 12 CHAMPIONSHIP		
D7		Texas [StL]	27	37
		ORANGE BOWL		
D31	●	Virginia Tech	41	21

1997 13-0 (8-0)

A30	●	Akron	59	14
S13	●	Central Florida	38	24
S20	●	at Washington	27	14
O4	● |	Kansas State	56	26
O11	● |	at Baylor	49	21
O18	● |	Texas Tech	29	0
O25	● |	at Kansas	35	0
N1	● |	Oklahoma	69	7
N8	● |	at Missouri	45	38
N15	● |	Iowa State	77	14
N28	● |	at Colorado	27	24
		BIG 12 CHAMPIONSHIP		
D6	●	Texas A&M [SA]	54	15
		ORANGE BOWL		
J2	●	Tennessee	42	17

FRANK SOLICH
1998-2003 (.753)   58-19

1998   9-4   (5-3)

A29 •	Louisiana Tech	56	27
S5 •	UAB	38	7
S12 •	at California	24	3
S26 •	Washington	55	7
O3 •	Oklahoma State *KC*	24	17
O10	at Texas A&M	21	28
O17 •	Kansas	41	0
O24 •	Missouri	20	13
O31	Texas	16	20
N7 •	at Iowa State	42	7
N14 •	at Kansas State	30	40
N27 •	Colorado	16	14
	HOLIDAY		
D30 •	Arizona	20	23

1999   12-1   (7-1)

S4 •	at Iowa	42	7
S11 •	California	45	0
S18 •	Southern Miss	20	13
S25 •	at Missouri	40	10
O2 •	Oklahoma State	38	14
O9 •	Iowa State	49	14
O23 •	at Texas	20	24
O30 •	at Kansas	24	17
N6 •	Texas A&M	37	0
N13 •	Kansas State	41	15
N26 •	at Colorado	33	30
	BIG 12 CHAMPIONSHIP		
D4 •	Texas *SA*	22	6
	FIESTA BOWL		
J2 •	Tennessee	31	21

2000   10-2   (6-2)

S2 •	San Jose State	49	13
S9 •	at Notre Dame	27	24
S23 •	Iowa	42	13
S30 •	Missouri	42	24
O7 •	at Iowa State	49	27
O14 •	at Texas Tech	56	3
O21 •	Baylor	59	0
O28	at Oklahoma	14	31
N4 •	Kansas	56	17
N11 •	at Kansas State	28	29
N24 •	Colorado	34	32
	ALAMO BOWL		
D30 •	Northwestern	66	17

2001   11-2   (7-1)

A25 •	TCU	21	7
S1 •	Troy State	42	14
S8 •	Notre Dame	27	10
S20 •	Rice	48	3
S29 •	at Missouri	36	3
O6 •	Iowa State	48	14
O13 •	at Baylor	48	7
O20 •	Texas Tech	41	31
O27 •	Oklahoma	20	10
N3 •	at Kansas	51	7
N10 •	Kansas State	31	21
N23 •	at Colorado	36	62
	ROSE BOWL		
J3 •	Miami, Fla.	14	37

2002   7-7   (3-5)

A24 •	Arizona State	48	10
A31 •	Troy State	31	16
S7 •	Utah State	44	13
S14 •	at Penn State	7	40
S28 •	at Iowa State	14	36
O5 •	McNeese State	38	14
O12 •	Missouri	24	13
O19 •	at Oklahoma State	21	24
O26 •	at Texas A&M	38	31
N2 •	Texas	24	27
N9 •	Kansas	45	7
N16 •	at Kansas State	13	49
N29 •	Colorado	13	28
	INDEPENDENCE BOWL		
D27 •	Mississippi	23	27

BO PELINI
2003 (1.000)   1-0

2003   10-3   (5-3)

A30 •	Oklahoma State	17	7
S6 •	Utah State	31	7
S13 •	Penn State	18	10
S25 •	at Southern Miss	38	14
O4 •	Troy State	30	0
O11 •	at Missouri	24	41
O18 •	Texas A&M	48	12
O25 •	Iowa State	28	0
N1 •	at Texas	7	31
N8 •	at Kansas	24	3
N15 •	Kansas State	9	38
N28 •	at Colorado	31	22
	ALAMO BOWL		
D29 •	Michigan State	17	3

BILL CALLAHAN
2004-Present (.455)   5-6

2004   5-6   (3-5)

S4 •	W. Illinois	56	17
S11 •	Southern Miss	17	21
S18 •	at Pittsburgh	24	17
O2 •	Kansas	14	8
O9 •	at Texas Tech	10	70
O16 •	Baylor	59	27
O23 •	at Kansas State	21	45
O30 •	Missouri	24	3
N6 •	at Iowa State	27	34
N13 •	at Oklahoma	3	30
N26 •	Colorado	20	26

Neutral Site key: *Port* Portland, OR / *Birm* Birmingham, AL / *ERut* East Rutherford, NJ / *Oma* Omaha, NE / *StL* St. Louis, MO / *KC* Kansas City, MO / *SA* San Antonio, TX / *NYC* New York, NY / *Tok* Tokyo, Japan / *StJ* St. Joseph, MO / *Mil* Milwaukee, WI / *Cou* Council Bluffs, IA / *OkC* Oklahoma City, OK
ƒ Forfeit / † Game Later Forfeited / # Disputed Victor / * Disputed Score / || Designated Conference Game / |2 Counted Twice in Conference Standings

NEBRASKA ANNUAL STATISTICAL LEADERS

YR	RUSHING	YDS	ATT	AVG	PASSING	ATT	CMP	PCT	YDS	RECEIVING	REC	YDS	AVG
1962	Willie Ross	431	89	4.8	Dennis Claridge	128	56	.44	829	Jim Huge	11	208	18.9
1963	Rudy Johnson	573	91	6.3	Dennis Claridge	66	31	.47	440	Tony Jeter	9	151	16.8
1964	Frank Solich	444	87	5.1	Bob Churchich	102	54	.53	893	Tony Jeter	18	219	12.2
1965	Harry Wilson	672	120	5.6	Fred Duda	110	46	.42	632	Freeman White	28	458	16.4
1966	Harry Wilson	635	138	4.6	Bob Churchich	174	96	.55	1,136	Tom Penney	24	286	11.9
1967	Dick Davis	717	162	4.4	Frank Patrick	233	116	.50	1,449	Dennis Richnafsky	36	422	11.7
1968	Joe Orduna	677	186	3.6	Ernie Sigler	144	73	.51	907	Tom Penney	25	424	17.0
1969	Jeff Kinney	546	177	3.1	Jerry Tagge	177	101	.57	1,302	Jeff Kinney	41	433	10.6
1970	Joe Orduna	834	187	4.5	Jerry Tagge	165	104	.63	1,383	Johnny Rodgers	35	665	19.0
1971	Jeff Kinney	1,037	222	4.7	Jerry Tagge	239	143	.60	2,019	Johnny Rodgers	53	872	16.5
1972	Gary Dixon	506	130	3.9	Dave Humm	266	140	.53	2,074	Johnny Rodgers	55	942	17.1
1973	Tony Davis	1,008	254	4.0	Dave Humm	196	109	.56	1,526	Ritch Bahe	30	406	13.5
1974	Monte Anthony	587	109	5.4	Dave Humm	175	104	.59	1,435	Don Westbrook	33	508	15.4
1975	Monte Anthony	723	161	4.5	Vince Ferragamo	134	79	.59	1,153	Bobby Thomas	24	501	20.9
1976	Rick Berns	854	155	5.5	Vince Ferragamo	254	145	.57	2,071	Chuck Malito	30	615	20.5
1977	I.M. Hipp	1,301	197	6.6	Randy Garcia	94	38	.40	568	Tim Smith	23	371	16.1
1978	I.M. Hipp	936	173	5.4	Tom Sorley	174	102	.59	1,571	Junior Miller	30	560	18.7
1979	Jarvis Redwine	1,042	148	7.0	Tim Hager	90	46	.51	680	Tim Smith	30	477	15.9
1980	Jarvis Redwine	1,119	156	7.2	Jeff Quinn	157	96	.61	1,337	Todd Brown	28	416	14.9
1981	Roger Craig	1,060	173	6.1	Turner Gill	91	47	.52	619	Jamie Williams	22	282	12.8
1982	Mike Rozier	1,689	242	7.0	Turner Gill	166	90	.54	1,182	Irving Fryar	24	346	14.4
1983	Mike Rozier	2,148	275	7.8	Turner Gill	170	94	.55	1,516	Irving Fryar	40	780	19.5
1984	Doug DuBose	1,040	156	6.7	Craig Sundberg	84	53	.63	740	Shane Swanson	16	203	12.7
1985	Doug DuBose	1,161	203	5.7	McCathorn Clayton	78	28	.36	602	Robb Schnitzler	16	382	23.9
1986	Keith Jones	830	161	5.2	Steve Taylor	124	52	.42	808	Dana Brinson	14	208	14.9
1987	Keith Jones	1,232	170	7.2	Steve Taylor	123	57	.46	902	Rod Smith	21	329	15.7
1988	Ken Clark	1,497	232	6.5	Steve Taylor	151	72	.48	1,067	Morgan Gregory	20	239	12.0
1989	Ken Clark	1,196	198	6.0	Gerry Gdowski	136	71	.52	1,326	Morgan Gregory	19	282	14.8
1990	Leodis Flowers	940	149	6.3	Mickey Joseph	78	34	.44	624	Jon Bostick	19	375	19.7
1991	Derek Brown	1,313	230	5.7	Keithen McCant	168	97	.58	1,454	Johnny Mitchell	31	534	17.2
1992	Calvin Jones	1,210	168	7.2	Tommie Frazier	100	44	.44	727	Calvin Jones	14	162	11.6
1993	Calvin Jones	1,043	185	5.6	Tommie Frazier	162	77	.48	1,159	Abdul Muhammad	25	383	15.3
1994	Lawrence Phillips	1,722	286	6.0	Brook Berringer	151	94	.62	1,295	Abdul Muhammad	23	360	15.7
1995	Ahman Green	1,086	141	7.7	Tommie Frazier	163	92	.56	1,362	Clester Johnson	22	367	16.7
1996	Ahman Green	917	155	5.9	Scott Frost	200	104	.52	1,440	Brendan Hobein	23	335	14.6
1997	Ahman Green	1,877	278	6.8	Scott Frost	159	88	.55	1,237	Kenny Cheatham	14	191	13.6
1998	Correll Buckhalter	799	142	5.6	Bobby Newcombe	79	50	.63	712	Matt Davison	32	394	12.3
1999	Eric Crouch	889	180	4.9	Eric Crouch	160	83	.52	1,269	Matt Davison	29	441	15.2
2000	Dan Alexander	1,154	182	6.3	Eric Crouch	156	75	.48	1,101	Matt Davison	21	389	18.5
2001	Dahrran Diedrick	1,299	233	5.6	Eric Crouch	189	105	.56	1,510	Wilson Thomas	37	616	16.6
2002	Jammal Lord	1,412	251	5.6	Jammal Lord	204	95	.47	1,362	Wilson Thomas	30	353	11.8
2003	Jammal Lord	948	215	4.4	Jammal Lord	176	85	.48	1,305	Matt Herian	22	484	22.0
2004	Cory Ross	1,102	207	5.3	Joe Dailey	310	153	.49	2,025	Ross Pilkington	27	337	12.5

Receiving leaders by receptions
All statistics include postseason

NEVADA

BY DAVE REARDON

RENO, THE SELF-PROCLAIMED Biggest Little City in the World, was for many years home to one of the best little college football teams in the country. During Chris Ault's first two hitches as coach, Nevada was a regular in the Division I-AA playoffs. In 2004, Ault again picked up the whistle after some of coach Chris Tormey's recruits were arrested and Tormey was fired. But times have changed, and the Wolf Pack's found the going a lot rougher since joining the Western Athletic Conference in 2000.

TRADITION Each year, Nevada and UNLV play for the Fremont Cannon, a replica of a gun that captain John C. Fremont took with him on an expedition through Oregon, Nevada and Canada in 1843 and 1844. The Nevada Mines Division of Kennecott Copper Corp., using technical drawings from the U.S. Army archives, built the cannon in 1970 and donated it to the two schools. The Wolf Pack won the first game between the universities in 1969, but the Rebels were the first team to capture the cannon in 1970. Today, the team in possession of the cannon fires it every time it scores at home.

BEST PLAYER The great Marion Motley, who played fullback and linebacker at Nevada from 1940 to 1942 after transferring from South Carolina State, scored 129 points in three seasons, and also ran track and boxed. Motley was one of the few black players in college football at the time. When Mississippi State said it would not play against the Wolf Pack because of Motley, the rest of the Nevada team voted to not make the trip, and the game was canceled. Motley helped pave the way for African-Americans in pro football, going on to star for the Cleveland Browns. He usually played fullback in the pros, but was also used in key situations at linebacker, even after the platoon system was fully established. Motley was enshrined in the Pro Football Hall of Fame in 1968.

BEST COACH Ault has led Nevada to a 168–70–1 record over 20 seasons and three tenures as head coach, winning seven conference championships. One of those titles came in 1992, when the Wolf Pack captured the Big West crown during their first year in Division I-A. Ault was inducted into the College Football Hall of Fame in 2002. He became athletic director in 1986 and held both positions concurrently until 1992, when he relinquished the

---

PROFILE

University of Nevada
Reno, Nev.
Founded: 1874
Enrollment: 12,118
Colors: Navy Blue and Silver
Nickname: Wolf Pack
Stadium: Mackay Stadium
Opened in 1965
FieldTurf; 31,900 capacity
First football game: 1896
All-time record: 452–407–33 (.525)
Bowl record: 2–3
First-round NFL draftees: 1
Website: www.nevadawolfpack.com

THE BEST OF TIMES

In 1986, Chris Ault led Nevada to a 13–1 record and the Division I-AA championship game. The Pack lost the title game to Georgia Southern 48-38.

THE WORST OF TIMES

After the 1905 season, in which Nevada scored no points and had an 0–3–1 record, there was no football team from 1906 to 1914. In 1915, the program was re-established and the team went 0–5. Nevada went 11 seasons between wins.

CONFERENCE

Nevada has been a member of the Western Athletic Conference since 2000, after entering Division I-A in 1992 as part of the Big West Conference. The Wolf Pack competed in the Big Sky Conference from 1979 to 1991.

DISTINGUISHED ALUMNI

Richard Bryan, U.S. senator and Nevada governor; Evelyn de la Rose, opera singer; Susan Desmond-Hellmann, cancer and AIDS researcher; Mills Lane, boxing referee; Robert Laxalt, author

FIGHT SONG

HAIL TO OUR STURDY MEN
Hail to our sturdy men, loyal and true,
March, march on down that field, O' Silver and Blue.
We'll give a long cheer for Nevada's men,
See them break through again.
Fighting for our own U of N—to victory!
Hurrah, hurray, hurrah, hurray—
NEVAAAA-DA!
We'll give a long cheer for Nevada's men,
See them break through again,
Fighting for our own U of N—to victory!

coaching job. He returned to the sideline the following year, then resigned again after the 1995 season. This is Ault's third go-around as coach.

BEST TEAM The 1986 Wolf Pack won their first 13 games before losing to Georgia Southern 48-38 in the Division I-AA title game. Nevada's hallmark was its diverse offense, led by running backs Lucius Floyd (1,066 yards, with 305 of them and four touchdowns against Montana State) and Charvez Foger (827 yards and 14 TDs). But the Pack were also dangerous through the air, with quarterback Eric Beavers throwing for 25 of his school-record 78 career touchdowns. Kicker Marty Zendejas made 14 of 18 field goals and 53 of 54 PATs on his way to 95 points, and Joe Peterson led the defense, snagging seven interceptions. Zendejas and linebacker Henry Rolling received All-America recognition.

BIGGEST GAME On Dec. 6, 1986, Nevada soundly beat Tennessee State 33-6 to advance to the D1-AA national

The Nevada-UNLV rivalry is one of the more intense in the West, and it can get ugly. In 2003, Rebels coach John Robinson was hit in the head with a bottle.

championship game. Tennessee State scored in the second quarter, narrowing the score to 14-6, but Zendejas hit four consecutive field goals to put the game out of reach.

BIGGEST UPSET Nevada arrived at Husky Stadium on Oct. 11, 2003, as a 17-point underdog against Washington, where Wolf Pack head coach Chris Tormey had been an assistant for 10 years. Nevada dominated from the outset on both defense and special teams. Defensive end Jorge Cordova had five of the Pack's eight sacks and one of their three blocked field goals; Chris Barry blocked the other two. Nevada's offense, which had scored just 12 points in each of the previous two games, performed ably and the Wolf Pack won 28–17.

HEARTBREAKER In its first Division I-A bowl game, Nevada lost to Bowling Green 35–34 in the 1992 Las Vegas Bowl. Bowling Green jumped out to a 28-3 halftime lead, but after the break, Nevada scored five consecutive times behind quarterback Chris Vargas and took a 34-28 lead in

RECORDS

RUSHING YARDS

	GAME
327	Chance Kretschmer vs. UTEP, Nov. 24, 2001 (45 att.)
	SEASON
1,732	Chance Kretschmer, 2001 (302 att.)
	CAREER
5,333	Frank Hawkins, 1977, 80 (947 att.)

PASSING YARDS

	GAME
611	David Neill vs. New Mexico State, Oct. 10, 1998 (30 of 57)
	SEASON
4,265	Chris Vargas, 1993 (331 of 490)
	CAREER
10,903	David Neill, 1998-2001 (763 of 1,374)

RECEIVING YARDS

	GAME
326	Nate Burleson vs. San Jose State, Nov. 10, 2001 (12 rec.)
	SEASON
2,060	Trevor Insley, 1999 (134 rec.)
	CAREER
5,005	Trevor Insley, 1996-99 (298 rec.)

POINTS

	GAME
36	Chance Kretschmer vs. UTEP, Nov. 24, 2001 (6 TDs)
	SEASON
115	Damon Shea, 1996 (20 FGs, 55 PATs)
	CAREER
367	Marty Zendejas, 1984-87 (66 FGs, 169 PATs)

CONSENSUS ALL-AMERICANS

1952	Neil Garrett, DB
1974	Greg Grouwinkel, DB
1978	James Curry, MG
1978-80	Frank Hawkins, RB
1979	Lee Fobbs, DB
1980	Bubba Puha, DL
1981	John Ramatici, LB
1981-83	Tony Zendejas, K
1982	Charles Mann, DT
1983	Jim Werbeckes, OG
1983	Tony Shaw, DB
1985	Greg Rea, OL
1985	Marty Zendejas, PK
1985	Pat Hunter, DB
1986	Henry Rolling, DE/LB
1988, 1990	Bernard Ellison, DB
1990	Treamelle Taylor, KR
1991	Matt Clafton, LB

the fourth quarter. A bad punt snap gave Bowling Green the ball at Nevada's 15 with less than two minutes to play. The Falcons got a first down at the Wolf Pack 3, and on fourth down, with less than 30 seconds left, Bowling Green quarterback Eric White hit David Hankins in the end zone for the game-tying points. The PAT was good.

STADIUM Mackay Stadium, named for university benefactor Clarence Mackay, opened in 1966 with a capacity of 4,500. It was expanded several times and now officially seats 31,900. But the facility has accommodated up to 33,391, such as when the Wolf Pack beat UNLV 55-32 on Oct. 28, 1995. In 2000, FieldTurf was installed, and field lights were added prior to the 2003 season. The Wolf Pack opened that season with the first night home game in school history, a 24-23 win over Southern Utah.

RIVAL The Nevada-UNLV rivalry is one of the more intense in the West, and it can get ugly. At the end of UNLV's 16-12 victory over Nevada in 2003 at Mackay Stadium, Rebels coach John Robinson was hit in the head with a bottle. On a less sinister note, after the Wolf Pack lost 21-17 in 2002, Reno mayor Bob Cashell was forced to wear a red UNLV jersey in keeping with his bet with Las Vegas mayor Oscar Goodman.

DISPUTE It's more an off-field argument than anything else, but many UNLV backers have a problem with Nevada calling itself Nevada, and not UNR or Nevada-Reno. Nevada is the name on Wolf Pack uniforms, and so the team and school are consistently referred to as "Nevada" by the media. "I think everything from the jerseys to the stationery to the name on the school should be University of Nevada, Reno," University of Nevada Regent Steve Sisolak said in a *Reno Gazette-Journal* article. "They are equal." Wolf Pack athletic director Cary Groth sees no reason to change: "The market dictates what you are called. The University of Nevada, Las Vegas, everyone calls UNLV. Everyone calls us Nevada."

NICKNAME In 1923, students voted for the name Wolf Pack a couple of years after a writer reported that Nevada played like a pack of wolves. One thing's certain—they'll never go back to the names Nevada teams were called in the 1890s and early 1900s: Sagebrushers and Sage Hens.

MASCOT Alphie, a student dressed in a cartoonish wolf costume, performs at games and appears at parades and other functions.

UNIFORMS For much of the 1970s, the Wolf Pack wore silver, (later blue) helmets with an elongated N on the side. That was replaced in 1986 by the word Pack written in script, which remained in place through the 1990s. Today, the blue helmets sport a silver-hued wolf on the side, and the blue home jerseys have numbers—and the name Nevada—in white with a silver shadow.

QUOTE "If I don't get you now, I'll get you later."
—Marion Motley

ALL-CENTENNIAL TEAM

In conjunction with the school's celebration of 100 years of athletics in 1998, five committees representing different eras of Wolf Pack football turned over their findings to a committee for selection of the team.

1976-92, 1994-95, 2004-present	Chris Ault, coach

OFFENSE

1921-24	Leslie "Spud" Harrison, OL
1932-33	Vic Carroll, OL
1976-79	Robert Selden, OL
1978-81	Todd Wilcks, OL
1981-83	Derek Kennard, OL
1982-85	Greg Rea, OL
1946-48	Scott Beasley, TE
1994-95	Alex Van Dyke, WR
1947-48	Stan Heath, QB
1990-93	Chris Vargas, QB
1920-21	James "Rabbit" Bradshaw, RB
1940-42	Marion Motley, RB
1946-48	Tommy Kalmanir, RB
1977-80	Frank Hawkins, RB
1981-83	Tony Zendejas, PK

DEFENSE

1943-46	Buster McClure, DL
1980-82	Charles Mann, DL
1987-90	Neil Hulbert, DL
1994-97	James Cannida, DL
1944, 1946-48	Ken Sinofsky, LB
1983-86	Henry Rolling, LB
1988-91	Matt Clafton, LB
1994-97	Deshone Myles, LB
1972-74	Greg Grouwinkle, DB
1980-83	Tony Shaw, DB
1982-85	Patrick Hunter, DB
1986-88, 1990	Bernard Ellison, DB
1949-50	Pat Brady, P
1926-28	Jim Bailey, ALL-PURPOSE
1946-48	Richard Trachok, ALL-PURPOSE

NEVADA ANNUAL STATISTICAL LEADERS

YR	RUSHING	YDS	ATT	AVG	PASSING	ATT	CMP	PCT	YDS	RECEIVING	REC	YDS	AVG
1992	Dedric Holmes	521	130	4.0	Chris Vargas	316	171	.54	2,094	Bryan Reeves	81	1,114	13.8
1993	Marcellus Chrison	809	136	5.9	Chris Vargas	490	331	.68	4,265	Bryan Reeves	91	1,362	15.0
1994	Marcellus Chrison	1,076	189	5.7	Mike Maxwell	447	221	.49	3,537	Alex Van Dyke	98	1,246	12.7
1995	Kin Minor	1,052	218	4.8	Mike Maxwell	409	227	.56	3,611	Alex Van Dyke	129	1,854	14.4
1996	Chris Lemon	867	163	5.3	John Dutton	334	222	.66	2,750	Damond Wilkins	114	1,121	9.8
1997	Chris Lemon	1,112	250	4.4	John Dutton	367	225	.61	3,526	Geoff Noisy	86	1,184	13.8
1998	Chris Lemon	1,154	253	4.6	David Neill	344	199	.58	3,249	Geoff Noisy	94	1,405	14.9
1999	Chris Lemon	1,170	238	4.9	David Neill	423	247	.58	3,402	Trevor Insley	134	2,060	15.4
2000	Marquis Starks	457	158	2.9	David Neill	353	179	.51	2,334	Nate Burleson	57	921	16.2
2001	Chance Kretschmer	1,732	302	5.7	David Neill	256	138	.54	1,918	Nate Burleson	53	737	13.9
2002	Matt Milton	1,108	225	4.9	Zack Threadgill	451	275	.61	3,418	Nate Burleson	138	1,629	11.8
2003	Chance Kretschmer	1,162	245	4.7	Andy Heiser	326	164	.50	2,294	Maurice Mann	35	594	17.0
2004	Chance Kretschmer	813	176	4.6	Jeff Rowe	394	230	.58	2,633	Nichiren Flowers	91	1,126	12.4

Receiving leaders by receptions
The NCAA began including postseason stats in 2002

NEVADA ALL-TIME SCORES

WIN/LOSS PERCENTAGE SINCE 1992

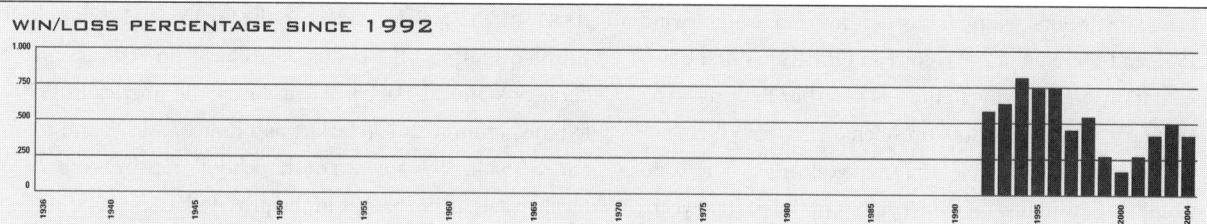

CHRIS AULT
1976-92, '94-95 '04-Present
168-70-1 (.705)

1992-1999 BIG WEST

1992 7-5-0 (5-1-0)
S5	•	at Wyoming	6	25
S12	•	Pacific	20	14
S19	•	McNeese State	31	21
S26	•	at Tulane	17	34
O3	•	at Fullerton St.	19	0
O17	•	at Nevada-Las Vegas	14	10
O24	•	New Mexico State	35	21
O31	•	Weber St.	21	23
N7	•	at San Jose State	35	39
N14	•	Utah State	48	47
N21	•	Texas Southern	38	14

LAS VEGAS BOWL
| D18 | | Bowling Green | 34 | 35 |

JEFF HORTON 1993 (.636) 7-4

1993 7-4-0 (5-2-0)
S4	•	at Wisconsin	17	35
S11	•	Boise State	38	10
S18	•	Texas Southern	63	14
S25		Northern Illinois	42	46
O2	•	Nevada-Las Vegas	49	14
O16	•	at Utah State	48	44
O23		Weber St.	30	47
O30	•	at Pacific	31	23
N6	•	San Jose State	46	45
N13	•	at New Mexico State	34	14
N20		at Arkansas State	21	23

CHRIS AULT

1994 9-2-0 (6-1-0)
S3	•	No. Arizona	30	27
S10	•	Arkansas State	18	0
S17		at Boise State	27	37
S24	•	La. Monroe	34	22
O1	•	at Northern Illinois	35	31
O8	•	Pacific	38	26
O15	•	New Mexico State	45	24
O22	•	at San Jose State	42	10
N5	•	at Fresno State	62	35
N12	•	Utah State	56	28
N19	•	at Nevada-Las Vegas	27	32

1995 9-3-0 (7-0-0)
S2	•	La. Lafayette	38	14
S9	•	at New Mexico State	45	24
S23		Toledo	35	49
S28		at San Diego State	27	30
O7	•	North Texas	56	24
O14	•	La. Monroe	59	35
O21	•	at Louisiana Tech	49	45
O28	•	Nevada-Las Vegas	55	32
N4	•	at Utah State	30	25
N11	•	at Pacific	45	29
N18		San Jose State	45	28

LAS VEGAS BOWL
| D14 | | Toledo | 37 | 40 |

JEFF TISDEL 1996-99 (.511) 23-22

1996 9-3 (4-1)
S7	•	at Oregon	30	44
S14	•	Montana St.	31	7
S21	•	at California	15	33
S28	•	Kent State	63	42
O5	•	at Nevada-Las Vegas	54	17
O12	•	Boise State	66	28
O19	•	at Idaho	15	24
O26	•	at North Texas	40	13
N2	•	New Mexico State	63	14
N9	•	at Utah State	54	27
N16	•	Arkansas State	66	14

LAS VEGAS BOWL
| D19 | • | Ball State | 18 | 15 |

1997 5-6 (4-1)
A30	•	at Colorado State	13	45
S6	•	Nevada-Las Vegas	31	14
S13		Oregon	20	24
S20		at Southern Miss	19	35
S27	•	at Toledo	13	31
O11	•	Wyoming	30	34
O18	•	Idaho	42	23
O25	•	North Texas	65	10
N1	•	at New Mexico State	45	24
N8	•	at Boise State	56	42
N15		Utah State	19	38

1998 6-5 (3-2)
S5	•	at Oregon State	6	48
S12	•	Colorado State	14	26
S26	•	at Fresno State	27	24
O3	•	at Nevada-Las Vegas	31	20
O10		New Mexico State	45	48
O17		at North Texas	21	27
O24	•	at Idaho	58	23
O31	•	Boise State	52	24
N7	•	at Utah State	26	21
N14	•	Cal Poly SLO SLO	63	0
N21	•	Southern Miss	28	55

1999 3-8 (2-4)
S4		Oregon State	13	28
S11		at Colorado State	33	38
S18		at Oregon	10	72
S25		Fresno State	24	49
O2	•	Nevada-Las Vegas	26	12
O9	•	at New Mexico State	23	16
O23	•	at Boise State	17	52
O30	•	North Texas	41	28
N6		Idaho	33	42
N13	•	at Arkansas State	28	44
N20		Utah State	35	37

2000-PRESENT WAC

CHRIS TORMEY 2000-03 (.340) 16-31

2000 2-10 (1-7)
S2	•	at Oregon	7	36
S9		TCU	10	41
S23	•	at Wyoming	35	28
S30		Colorado State	14	45
O7	•	at Nevada-Las Vegas	7	38
O14		at Fresno State	21	58
O21		San Jose State	30	49
O28		at SMU	7	21
N4		Texas-El Paso	22	45
N11	•	at Hawaii	17	37
N18	•	Rice	34	28
N25		at Tulsa	3	38

2001 3-8 (3-5)
S1	•	at Brigham Young	7	52
S8	•	at Colorado State	18	35
S22	•	Hawaii	28	20
O6		Nevada-Las Vegas	12	27
O13		Louisiana Tech	42	45
O20		at Rice	30	33
O27		at Boise State	7	49
N3	•	SMU	35	14
N10	•	at San Jose State	45	65
N17	•	Fresno State	14	61
N24	•	at Texas-El Paso	48	31

2002 5-7 (4-4)
A31	•	at Washington State *SEA*	7	31
S14	•	Brigham Young	31	28
S21	•	Rice	31	21
S28	•	Colorado State	28	32
O5		at Nevada-Las Vegas	17	21
O12		at Hawaii	34	59
O19	•	San Jose State	52	24
O26	•	at Louisiana Tech	47	50
N2	•	at SMU	24	6
N9	•	Texas-El Paso	23	17
N16	•	at Fresno State	30	38
N23		Boise State	7	44

2003 6-6 (4-4)
A30	•	So. Utah	24	23
S6		at Oregon	23	31
S18	•	at San Jose State	42	30
S27		SMU	12	9
O4		Nevada-Las Vegas	12	16
O11	•	at Washington	28	17
O18	•	at Tulsa	28	21
O25		Louisiana Tech	34	42
N1	•	at Rice	42	52
N8		Fresno State	10	27
N15	•	Hawaii	24	14
N29		at Boise State	3	56

CHRIS AULT

2004 5-7 (3-5)
S6	•	at Louisiana Tech	21	38
S11	•	at Sacramento St.	59	7
S18	•	Buffalo	38	13
S25		at San Diego State	10	27
O2		at Nevada-Las Vegas	13	48
O9		at Hawaii	26	48
O16	•	Rice	35	10
O23	•	Tulsa	54	48
N6	•	San Jose State	42	24
N13	•	at SMU	20	38
N20	•	at Fresno State	17	54
N27	•	Boise State	21	58

THE SCHOOLS

NEW MEXICO

BY DERRICK GOOLD

BELIEVED TO BE THE FIRST COLLEGE football team to hop a plane and fly to an away game, the New Mexico Lobos have had a turbulent history. Each time the program has attempted to ascend, it has been stripped of importance, either by its own administration or by being the No. 2 sport behind the Lobos-mania of men's basketball. After six seasons without a winning record, the Lobos caught wind in 1952 and soared to a 7–2 record and the team's first bowl invitation since playing in the 1947 Harbor Bowl against Montana State. The school president, who was a former football star, would not let the team go in 1952. The Lobos would appear in just two bowl games in the next 50 years. One longtime Lobos booster grumbled, "So close, yet always so far." In 1998, optimism swooped in when, for the first time, the Lobos hired a Lobo to lead them. Former New Mexico quarterback Rocky Long, the 1971 Western Athletic Conference offensive player of the year, had dreamed of becoming the team's head coach. He bragged about the Lobos even when he was on another coaching staff and once made a pact with a former teammate that he would one day become the Lobos' coach. And he did. From 1999 to 2003, the Lobos increased their wins total each year—the only Division I-A program to make such a climb. "I can sell this product better than anybody," Long said when he was introduced as coach, "because I believe in it."

TRADITION Nothing on the football side of New Mexico's campus rivals the reputation of The Pit, the raucous home of the men's basketball team—renowned for its steep steps and loco Lobo crowd. But in the past decade, football season ticket sales have more than tripled (to 15,022 for 2004) and the Lobos have drawn seven of the eight largest football crowds in school history since 2001.

BEST PLAYER Brian Urlacher, the highest NFL draft pick (ninth overall) for the Lobos, edges out Don Perkins and Terance Mathis. Urlacher, a consensus All-America in 1999, led the nation with 178 tackles as a junior in 1998 and added 154 in 1999 for two of the school's top-five season tackle totals. A linebacker in the pros, Urlacher was considered a defensive back in college—though he played what Long nicknamed the Lobo position. A linebacker-safety hybrid, the Lobo continued after Urlacher's departure, though not with the same success.

BEST COACH Bill Weeks made his debut the same day University Stadium opened and Don Perkins' No. 43 jersey was retired. Weeks replaced famed Buffalo Bills coach Marv Levy, who turned two 7–3 seasons at UNM into a head coach position at the University of California. The Lobos became a charter member of the Western Athletic Conference in 1962,

PROFILE

University of New Mexico
Albuquerque, N.M.
Founded: 1889
Enrollment: 16,968
Colors: Cherry and Silver
Nickname: Lobos
Stadium: University Stadium
  Opened in 1960
  Grass; 38,634 capacity
First football game: 1892
All-time record: 425–488–31 (.467)
Bowl record: 2–6–1
First-round NFL draftees: 2
Website: www.golobos.com

THE BEST OF TIMES

In the WAC's first three seasons, New Mexico won the conference title in 1962 and 1963 and shared it in 1964, with an average of more than seven victories a season.

THE WORST OF TIMES

Anchored by an 0–11 season in 1987 and a 94-17 loss to Fresno State in 1991, the Lobos had nine consecutive losing seasons from 1984 to 1992 (an average of 2.6 wins per season).

CONFERENCE

Prior to the formation of the WAC, New Mexico had been a member of two conferences: the Border (1931-51) and the Skyline (1952-61). In the WAC from 1962 to 1998, the Lobos became a charter member of the Mountain West in 1999.

DISTINGUISHED ALUMNI

Pete Domenici, U.S. senator; Tony Hillerman, author; Brian Levant, screenwriter/film director; John Lewis, jazz musician/composer; Dana Miller-Mackie, Women's International Bowling Congress Hall of Famer

FIGHT SONG

THE UNM FIGHT SONG
Hail to thee, New Mexico,
Thy loyal sons are we.
Marching down the field we go,
Fighting for thee.
RAH! RAH! RAH!
Now we pledge our faith to thee,
Never shall we fail.
Fighting ever, yielding never.
HAIL! HAIL! HAIL!

Nothing Lobos football has done compares with the legacy forged by New Mexico's men's basketball team.

on the heels of Weeks' first two seasons and a 1961 bowl victory. Weeks led the team to the first of three consecutive WAC titles, twice outright. Weeks was 40–41–1 in eight seasons from 1960 to 1967, his record dropping as the university de-emphasized football and reduced the roster. The Lobos were 1–9 (0–5 in conference) in his final season.

BEST TEAM Though some recent teams have quality claims on the title—the 1982 squad was 10–1, but didn't go to a bowl; the 1952 team allowed just 46 points in nine games—the 1927 Lobos get the nod. Quarterbacked by Malcolm Long, powered by halfback John Dolzadelli and fueled by fullback/defensive lineman Jack McFarland, the 1927 Lobos finished 8–0–1, the last unbeaten team in school history. The Lobos shut out five teams and allowed only 28 points during the season. The coach, Roy Johnson, served as athletic director, head coach of all the university's sports, groundskeeper, equipment manager and custodian throughout the 1920s.

BIGGEST GAME On Nov. 21, 1959, the Lobos concluded their season with a come-from-behind victory against the Air Force Academy in Denver. Down 21-7, Perkins caught two touchdown passes and ignited a three-touchdown rally for a 28-27 win. When the Lobos arrived home, 5,000 to 7,500 fans awaited the team, flooding an airport that could accommodate only 2,000. The Lobos finished the season 7–3, but the win kindled interest that carried over into (and no doubt contributed players to) Bill Weeks' three-year run of WAC titles.

BIGGEST UPSET On Sept. 6, 1980, defensive alchemist Joe Lee Dunn's frenzied blitz package resulted in nine sacks against Brigham Young quarterback Jim McMahon as the Lobos won coach Joe Morrison's debut, 25-21. New Mexico had not defeated BYU in eight previous games, and the Lobos would go another 17 seasons before doing it again.

HEARTBREAKER The high-powered 1982 Lobos concluded their regular-season schedule with an emphatic 41-17 rout of Hawaii, giving them a 10–1 record and the most wins in school history. But no bowl invite was forthcoming. The Lobos' lone loss to BYU gave the Cougars the WAC title and automatic berth in the Holiday Bowl. A Justice Bowl was calculated with the help of a computer pitting the 10–1 Lobos against 10–1 Tulsa, which didn't receive a bowl invite either. A radio station in Albuquerque, N.M., carried the play-by-play of the game—a script built from comparing the team's statistics. Sound effects simulated fan noise, fight

RECORDS

RUSHING YARDS

	GAME
265	Quincy Wright vs. Weber State, Aug. 31, 2002 (27 att.)
	SEASON
1,450	DonTrell Moore, 2003 (276 att.)
	CAREER
3,862	Mike Williams, 1975-78 (857 att.)

PASSING YARDS

	GAME
622	Jeremy Leach vs. Utah, Nov. 11, 1989 (41 of 68)
	SEASON
3,573	Jeremy Leach, 1989 (282 of 511)
	CAREER
9,460	Stoney Case, 1991-94 (677 of 1,237)

RECEIVING YARDS

	GAME
257	Emilio Vallez vs. Texas-El Paso, Oct. 27, 1967 (17 rec.)
	SEASON
1,315	Terance Mathis, 1989 (88 rec.)
	CAREER
4,254	Terance Mathis, 1985-87, 1989 (263 rec.)

POINTS

	GAME
32	Reginal Johnson vs. Tulsa, Nov. 2, 1996 (5 TDs; 1 two-pt. conv.)
	SEASON
126	DonTrell Moore, 2003 (21 TDs)
	CAREER
252	DonTrell Moore, 2001-03 (42 TDs)

CONSENSUS ALL-AMERICANS

1989	Terance Mathis, WR
1999	Brian Urlacher, DB

songs and even vendors. The Lobos won—virtually—30-27. In Tulsa, over KGTO-AM, the Golden Hurricanes prevailed 27-24. Justice aside, coach Joe Morrison left at season's end for South Carolina, and it would be 10 seasons before New Mexico's next winning season and 15 until its next shot at a conference title.

CONTROVERSY The 1952 Lobos shut out five opponents and finished 7–2 with a spot in the Sun Bowl assured. But school president Tom Popejoy, who kicked a 12-yard field goal in 1924 to give New Mexico a 3-0 victory against rival Arizona, continued his deemphasis of athletics and rejected the bowl invitation. Head coach Dudley DeGroot publicly criticized Popejoy's decision and was fired before the next season. The program spiraled but didn't learn. After the three WAC titles in the early 1960s, another deemphasis rocked the program. The team was not allowed to expand to two platoons until late in the decade. Each Lobo played two ways while most opponents did not. New Mexico won six games between 1965 and 1968, punctuating the policy-propelled plummet with an 0–10 record in 1968.

STADIUM University Stadium opened Sept. 17, 1960, with the Lobos hosting the National University of Mexico. New Mexico's 77-6 win remains its most lopsided on the field. By the start of the 2001 season, $3.5 million in renovations had expanded the stadium by 5,700 seats to 37,370. Prior to the 2004 season, capacity was increased to 38,634. Before 1960, the Lobos played at Zimmerman Field (1938-59) and University Field (1892-1937).

RIVAL New Mexico State and the University of New Mexico had already played six games by the time New Mexico became a state in 1912. The Lobos hold a 62–28–5 edge in the 95 meetings between the schools before the 2005 game. Since 1969, New Mexico has won 29 of the 36 games.

NICKNAME In 1917, the student body sought both a nickname and a new name for the student newspaper,

ALL-TIME TEAM	
Selected in 1998 by fans and media for 100th anniversary of the football program.	
OFFENSE	
1985-87, 1989	Terance Mathis, WR
1974-77	Preston Dennard, WR
1976-79	Walt Arnold, TE
1962-64	Jack Abendschan, OL
1964-65	Dave Hettema, OL
1951-54	Larry White, C
1955-57	Jerry Nesbitt, OL
1970-71	Tom Walker, OL
1991-94	Stoney Case, QB
1975-78	Mike Williams, FB
1992-95	Winslow Oliver, RB
1957-59	Don Perkins, RB
1989-92	David Margolis, K
DEFENSE	
1987-90	John Bell, DL
1973-76	Robin Cole, DL
1974-76	Andy Frederick, DL
1965, '67	Paul Smith, DL
1994-97	Blake Irwin, LB
1981-84	Johnny Jackson, LB
1969-71	Houston Ross, LB
1981-84	Ray Hornfeck, DB
1994-97	Scott McGarrahan, DB
1963-65	Stan Quintana, DB
1972-75	Randy Rich, DB
1995-98	Jason Bloom, P

U.N.M. Weekly. Several names—including *The Rattler*, the *Sand Devil*, *The Ki-yo-te*—were recommended, but three years later the paper remained *U.N.M. Weekly*. In 1920, the paper's editor, George S. Bryan, who was also the student manager of the football team, proposed Lobos, after the Spanish word for wolves. "The Lobo is respected for his cunning, feared for his prowess and is the leader of the pack. It is the ideal name for the varsity boys who go forth to battle for the glory of the school," the paper's announcement of the nickname read. "All together now; 15 rahs for the LOBOS." The student paper also adopted the nickname and is still known as *The Daily Lobo*.

MASCOT Soon after the team's christening, a real wolf became the mascot. Jim Young, a government trapper, captured a wolf near Mount Taylor. The wolf would come on a leash to football games. In the late 1920s, a child teased the harnessed wolf at a game and was bitten. The school had to dispose of the mascot "for fear other ill-bred brats might become tempted to play with the wolf and bring a damage suit," wrote a historian. A human mascot, Lobo Louie, arrived in the 1960s and a female mascot, Lobo Lucy, debuted in the 1980s.

UNIFORMS Other than a brief flirtation with turquoise as the color of home jerseys from 1973 to 1979, cherry and silver have been the school's colors for more than 100 years. As suggested by a professor, cherry was for the evening glow of the Sandia Mountains and silver was for the ribbon of the Rio Grande running at their base. The sun from the state flag originally appeared on the silver helmets, but a wolf's head has been the more recent logo.

LORE For its first night game in school history, New Mexico flew to Los Angeles to play Occidental College in 1929—believed to be the first time a team took a plane to a game. Well, half of the team, that is. Johnson put the second string and team manager on the two Ford Tri-Motor planes. Cautious, he and the first team took the train. After losing

26-0 to Occidental—which used a white-dyed football so it could be seen at night—Johnson and the first string flew back to Albuquerque. The second string took the train. On Christmas Day 2002, junior kicker Katie Hnida became the first woman to play in an NCAA Division I-A football game. Hnida attempted a point-after kick in the first quarter of the Las Vegas Bowl against UCLA. It was blocked. In her senior season, Hnida attempted and made two point-after kicks.

QUOTE "There have been years around here where we won a damn football game and we acted like we had changed the state of the union."—Coach Dennis Franchione, 1997

NEW MEXICO ANNUAL STATISTICAL LEADERS

YR	RUSHING	YDS	ATT	AVG	PASSING	ATT	CMP	PCT	YDS	RECEIVING	REC	YDS	AVG
1946	Lou Cullen	287	56	5.1	Bryan Brock	27	11	.41	326	Lou Cullen	7	230	32.9
1947	Rudy Krall	513	124	4.1	Bryan Brock	86	26	.30	488	Rudy Camunez	9	162	18.0
1948	Rudy Krall	756	164	4.6	Jerry McKown	51	20	.39	342	Bill Speer	10	134	13.4
1949	Bob Cooke	272	78	3.5	Herbie Hughes	33	14	.42	176	Bill Speer	10	82	8.2
1950	Chuck Hill	346	65	5.3	Milton Price	114	49	.43	520	Chuck Hill	19	321	16.9
1951	Chuck Hill	394	105	3.8	Chuck Hill	60	31	.52	359	Dick Brett	26	276	10.6
1952	Bobby Arnett	360	109	3.3	Bobby Arnett	37	13	.35	195	Dick Brett	15	205	13.7
1953	Bobby Lee	624	110	5.7	Bob Burns	24	10	.42	127	Ray Guerrette	11	147	13.4
1954	A.L. Terpening	227	79	2.9	Jerry Lott	45	19	.42	271	Ray Guerrette	8	136	17.0
1955	Jerry Apodaca	224	64	3.5	Jerry Lott	74	34	.46	422	Dick Drake	14	174	12.4
1956	Phil Spear	625	123	5.1	Jerry Lott	41	19	.46	281	John Barefoot	6	156	26.0
1957	Don Perkins	744	112	6.6	Chuck Roberts	47	22	.47	305	Don Perkins	10	162	16.2
1958	Don Perkins	621	112	5.5	Chuck Roberts	53	19	.36	337	Don Black	14	303	21.6
1959	Billy Brown	740	95	7.8	George Friberg	68	26	.38	361	Don Perkins	8	226	28.3
1960	Bobby Santiago	596	98	6.1	Jim Cromartie	57	30	.53	343	Bobby Santiago	11	187	17.0
1961	Bobby Santiago	535	98	5.5	Jim Cromartie	60	28	.47	533	Larry Jasper	5	161	32.2
1962	Bobby Santiago	806	151	5.3	Jim Cromartie	33	12	.36	245	George Heard	6	255	42.5
1963	Bucky Stallings	553	126	4.4	Stan Quintana	32	15	.47	221	Claude Ward	7	181	25.9
1964	Joe Harris	582	152	3.8	Stan Quintana	86	45	.52	794	Gary Plumlee	19	316	16.6
1965	Carl Jackson	665	166	4.0	Stan Quintana	96	29	.30	444	Woody Dame	11	198	18.0
1966	Carl Jackson	348	105	3.3	Rick Beitler	162	67	.41	763	Sherman Seiders	27	351	13.0
1967	David Bookert	671	148	4.5	Terry Stone	336	160	.48	1,946	Ace Hendricks	67	1,094	16.3
1968	David Bookert	872	209	4.2	Terry Stone	147	58	.39	769	Bob Fowler	26	265	10.2
1969	Sam Scarber	534	162	3.3	Rocky Long	125	61	.49	865	John Stewart	19	391	20.6
1970	Sam Scarber	961	184	5.2	Rocky Long	115	48	.42	649	Fred Henry	10	73	7.3
1971	Fred Henry	1,129	176	6.4	Rocky Long	105	54	.51	876	Ken Smith	17	281	16.5
1972	Fred Henry	977	164	6.0	Bruce Boone	103	35	.34	540	Ken Smith	24	382	15.9
1973	Don Woods	971	220	4.4	Don Woods	124	52	.42	869	Paul Labarrere	16	374	23.4
1974	Floyd Perry	294	103	2.9	Steve Myer	196	105	.54	1,103	Pete Robison	20	236	11.8
1975	Mike Williams	511	121	4.2	Steve Myer	353	190	.54	2,501	Preston Dennard	59	962	16.3
1976	Mike Williams	1,240	258	4.8	Noel Mazzone	188	89	.47	1,427	Preston Dennard	42	783	18.6
1977	Mike Williams	1,096	265	4.1	Noel Mazzone	159	77	.48	1,085	Preston Dennard	26	341	13.1
1978	Mike Williams	1,015	213	4.8	Brad Wright	251	126	.50	1,925	Ricky Martin	21	594	28.3
1979	Jimmy Sayers	696	145	4.8	Casey Miller	82	42	.51	555	Jimmy Sayers	19	145	7.6
1980	Jimmy Sayers	691	166	4.2	Robin Gabriel	170	75	.44	1,083	Ricky Martin	43	850	19.8
1981	Mike Carter	595	158	3.8	Robin Gabriel	277	123	.44	1,783	Keith Magee	44	706	16.0
1982	Mike Carter	722	107	6.7	David Osborn	216	105	.49	1,609	Keith Magee	39	641	16.4
1983	Michael Johnson	739	143	5.2	Buddy Funck	204	110	.54	1,521	Derwin Williams	37	677	18.3
1984	Willie Turral	1,064	190	5.6	Buddy Funck	106	52	.49	922	Kenneth Whitehead	34	713	21.0
1985	Willie Turral	800	181	4.4	Billy Rucker	268	134	.50	2,475	Terance Mathis	49	852	17.4
1986	Kevin Burgess	1,023	181	5.7	Ned James	215	125	.58	1,777	Terance Mathis	53	955	18.0
1987	Shane Hall	315	83	3.8	Barry Garrison	489	277	.57	3,163	Terance Mathis	73	1,132	15.5
1988	Andre Wooten	801	160	5.0	Jeremy Leach	323	165	.51	1,986	Al Owens	49	774	15.8
1989	Dion Morrow	664	148	4.5	Jeremy Leach	511	282	.55	3,573	Terance Mathis	88	1,315	14.9
1990	Aaron Givens	546	128	4.3	Jeremy Leach	380	180	.47	2,428	Eric Morgan	80	1,043	13.0
1991	Marc Wilson	245	73	3.4	Stoney Case	216	103	.48	1,564	Carl Winston	76	1,177	15.5
1992	Winslow Oliver	1,063	245	4.3	Stoney Case	308	164	.53	2,289	Carl Winston	34	389	11.4
1993	Winslow Oliver	648	146	4.4	Stoney Case	304	177	.58	2,490	Carl Winston	50	766	15.3
1994	Eric Young	732	128	5.7	Stoney Case	409	233	.57	3,117	Gavin Pearlman	52	866	16.7
1995	Winslow Oliver	915	162	5.6	Donald Sellers	195	121	.62	1,693	Steve Pagador	33	492	14.9
1996	Lennox Gordon	1,008	196	5.1	Donald Sellers	256	157	.61	2,048	Larry Brown	38	518	13.6
1997	Graham Leigh	528	135	3.9	Graham Leigh	276	166	.60	2,318	Pascal Volz	69	1,229	17.8
1998	Lennox Gordon	571	130	4.4	Graham Leigh	276	198	.72	2,608	Martinez Williams	49	760	15.5
1999	Holmon Wiggins	601	138	4.4	Sean Stein	272	141	.52	1,584	Martinez Williams	60	609	10.2
2000	Holmon Wiggins	727	180	4.0	Rudy Caamano	192	107	.56	1,270	Ted Iacenda	28	257	9.2
2001	Jarrod Baxter	907	203	4.5	Casey Kelly	228	107	.47	1,559	Dwight Counter	43	774	18.0
2002	DonTrell Moore	1,134	245	4.6	Casey Kelly	314	181	.58	1,904	Joe Manning	36	413	11.5
2003	DonTrell Moore	1,450	276	5.3	Casey Kelly	274	146	.53	2,223	Adrian Boyd	41	581	14.2
2004	DonTrell Moore	1,091	232	4.7	Kole McKamey	210	103	.49	1,272	Hank Baskett	54	908	16.8

Receiving leaders by receptions
The NCAA began including postseason stats in 2002

NEW MEXICO ALL-TIME SCORES

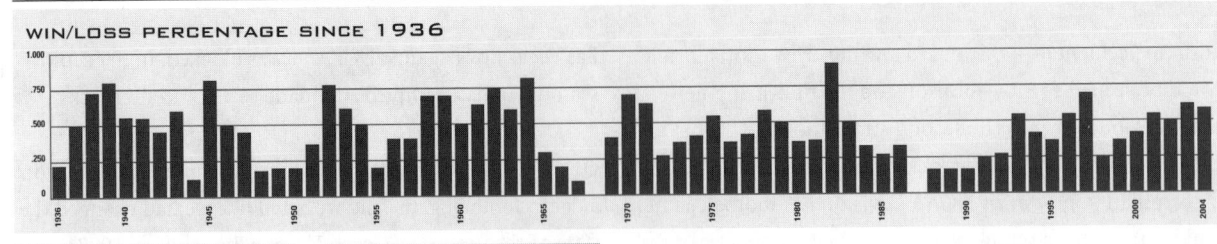

WIN/LOSS PERCENTAGE SINCE 1936

NO HEAD COACH

1892   0-2-0
O7		Albuq. HS	0	5
O28		Albuq. HS	0	8

1893   3-1-0
N18	●	Albuq. HS	4	0
N30		Albuq. Indian Sch.	4	10
D25	●	Albuq. Town Team	6	0
J1	●	New Mexico State	18	6 *

W.A. ZIMMER
1894 (.500)   1-1-1

1894   1-1-1
O27		Albuq. Indian Sch.	0	4
N10	=	Albuq. Indian Sch.	0	0
N29	●	Albuq. HS	5	0

1895-1898
NO TEAM

NO HEAD COACH

1899   1-1-0
N11	●	Albuq. HS	5	0
N30		Albuq. HS	0	5

1900
NO TEAM

JOE NAPIER
1901 (.125)   0-3-1

1901   0-3-1
N9	●	Albuq. HS	0	11
N16		at N.M. Highlands	0	32
N28		Albuq. HS	0	11
D7		Albuq. Indian Sch.	7	11

1902
NO TEAM

WALTER McEWAN
1903-04 (.900)   4-0-1

1903   3-0-1
O3		Albuq. Minors	8	0
O12	●	Albuq. Indian Sch.	11	0
N7	=	Albuq. Minors	0	0
N21	●	Santa Fe Indian Sch.	11	0

1904   1-0-0
O19	●	Menual HS	11	0

MARTIN F. ANGEL
1905-07 (.792)   9-2-1

1905   5-1-1
O7	●	Menual HS	5	5
O14	●	Albuq. HS	16	0
O21	●	Albuq. HS	15	0
O28	●	Menual HS	15	0
N11	●	Albuq. Indian Sch.	27	0
N18	●	Santa Fe Indian Sch.	12	0
N30		at New Mexico State	0	40

1906   3-1-0
O13	●	Albuq. Indian Sch.	27	5
O27	●	N.M. Mines	5	0
N17	●	Santa Fe Indian Sch.	22	0
N29	●	New Mexico State	5	25

1907   1-0-0
O21	●	Albuq. Indian Sch.	44	0

H.H. CONWELL
1908 (.833)   5-1

1908   5-1-0
O24	●	Albuq. Indian Sch.	33	0
O30	●	Albuq. Indian Sch.	12	6
N7	●	N.M. Mines	30	6
N13		at N.M. Military	16	12
N21	●	at New Mexico State	10	6
N26		Arizona	6	10 *

C.L. McBIRNIE
1909 (.667)   4-2

1909   4-2-0
O1		at El Paso Military	0	11
O15	●	El Paso Military	15	0
O30	●	N.M. Military	28	2
N6	●	at Colorado	0	53
N13	●	at Arizona	23	11
N25	●	New Mexico State	51	0

CARL HAMILTON
1910 (.000)   0-3

1910   0-3-0
O21	●	N.M. Mines	0	9
N4		at N.M. Military	0	80
N24		at Arizona	0	1 *f*

R.F. HUTCHINSON
1911-16 (.500)   13-13-2

1911   1-3-1
O29		at El Paso Military	0	6
N5	=	N.M. Military	0	0
N12		at New Mexico State	6	10
N19	●	at N.M. Highlands	56	0
N30		Arizona	0	6

1912   0-4-0
N2		at N.M. Military	0	20
N9		Albuq. Indian Sch.	6	7
N16		New Mexico State	0	27
N30		at Arizona	9	22 *

1913   3-2-0
O18	●	Menual HS	28	0
O25	●	Albuq. Indian Sch.	44	0
N1	●	N.M. Military	9	7
N8	●	at New Mexico State	0	13
N21		Arizona	3	7

1914   3-1-1
O23		at N.M. Military	3	12
O31	●	Albuq. Indian Sch.	46	0
N13	●	N.M. Military	9	7
N21	●	Albuq. Indian Sch.	18	7
D5	=	New Mexico State	7	7

1915   3-1-0
O30	●	N.M. Military	3	6
N13	●	Albuq. Indian Sch.	55	0
N20	●	New Mexico State	13	0
D4	●	Albuq. Indian Sch.	26	0

1916   3-2-0
O7		Colorado College	2	47
O14		at Colorado Mines	0	23
N11	●	No. Arizona	108	0
N18	●	Albuq. Indian Sch.	55	0
N30	●	New Mexico State	51	0

FRANK E. WORTH
1917 (.333)   1-2

1917   1-2-0
O20	●	Menual HS	38	0
N3		Albuq. HS	6	19
N24		at New Mexico State	3	110

1918
NO TEAM WWI

JOHN F. McGOUGH
1919 (.800)   3-0-2

1919   3-0-2
O18	●	N.M. Mines	55	0
O25	=	Colorado Mines	0	0
N1	=	at N.M. Military	0	0
N15	●	at Texas-El Paso	57	13
N27	●	New Mexico State	24	2

ROY JOHNSON
1920-30 (.557)   41-32-6

1920   3-3-0
O16		at Colorado College	3	42
O30	●	Fort Bliss	12	0
N6	●	Texas-El Paso	67	0
N11	●	N.M. Military	9	7
N20		at Arizona	7	28
D4		at New Mexico State	7	14

1921   2-2-0
O15		at Colorado College	0	7
N12	●	Fort Bliss	35	0
N19		Arizona	0	24
N24	●	New Mexico State	6	0

1922   3-4-0
S30	●	Albuq. Indian Sch.	33	0
O7		Denver	0	41
O14		at Colorado	0	3
O28	●	Texas-El Paso	13	0
N4	●	West Texas St.	12	0
N18		at Arizona	0	10
N30		at New Mexico State	0	7

1923   3-5-0
S29	●	N.M. Highlands	82	7
O6		at Denver	7	10
O15	●	Montezuma Coll.	75	6
O20		at West Texas St.	8	21
O27		at Texas-El Paso	3	0
N3		Arizona	7	14
N17		New Mexico State	0	6
N29		Montana St.	7	34

1924   5-1-0
O11	●	Montezuma Coll.	56	0
O18	●	West Texas St.	12	6
O25	●	Texas-El Paso	18	0
N11	●	at Arizona	3	0
N15		at New Mexico State	0	6
N27	●	Western St.	14	0

1925   2-4-1
O3	=	at Colorado College	0	0
O10	●	Montezuma Coll.	10	0
O17		at West Texas St.	7	9
O24		at Texas-El Paso	2	19
N7		Arizona	0	24
N21	●	New Mexico State	20	9
N26		Western St.	13	16

1926   4-2-1
O2	●	N.M. Mines	20	0
O9	●	Montezuma Coll.	41	7
O16		at Texas A&M	0	63
O23		at Texas-El Paso	19	7
N6		Arizona	0	21
N13	●	New Mexico State	6	6
N20	●	Western St.	35	6

1927   8-0-1
O1	●	N.M. Mines	35	0
O8	●	Montezuma Coll.	47	0
O15	●	N.M. Military	26	0
O22	●	at Texas-El Paso	6	6
N5	●	Arizona	7	6
N11	●	No. Arizona	24	7
N18	●	New Mexico State	26	9
N24	●	at Western St.	32	0
D3	●	at N.M. Highlands	12	0

1928   5-2-1
S29	●	N.M. Mines	45	0
O6	●	Montezuma Coll.	36	0
O13	●	N.M. Military	6	7
O20	●	No. Arizona	0	12
O27	●	at New Mexico State	14	13
N3	=	at Arizona	6	6
N17	●	Texas-El Paso	33	0
N29	●	Colorado Mines	32	13

1929   2-4-2
O5	●	N.M. Mines	46	0
O11		at Occidental	0	26
O19		at N.M. Military	20	28
N2		No. Arizona	6	26
N9	●	Montezuma Coll.	47	0
N16	=	at New Mexico State	7	7
N23		Arizona	0	6
N28		Lombard	7	7

1930   4-5-0
O4		at Oklahoma	0	47
O11	●	N.M. Highlands	45	0
O18	●	N.M. Mines	51	0
O25	●	at No. Arizona	25	0
N1		Texas-El Paso	13	20
N8		New Mexico State	6	14
N15		at Arizona	0	33
N22	●	N.M. Military	2	0
N29		Wyoming	6	19

1931-1951
BORDER

CHARLES RILEY
1931-33 (.370)   7-13-3

1931   3-3-1 (1-1-1)
O17	●	at N.M. Military	25	0
O24	●	Occidental	14	0
O31	●	No. Arizona	20	6
N7	|	at New Mexico State	6	13
N14	= |	Arizona	7	7
N20	|	at Texas Tech	6	32
N26	|	Wyoming	2	12

1932   1-6-1 (1-3-1)
O8	● |	No. Arizona	6	0
O15	|	at No. Colorado	6	30
O22	= |	New Mexico State	7	7 *
O29	|	N.M. Military	0	7
N4	|	at Loyola-Marymount	0	52
N11	|	Arizona	6	13
N19	|	Texas Tech	6	39
D3	|	at Arizona State	0	40 *

1933   3-4-1 (2-2-0)
O6	|	No. Arizona	0	14
O14	= |	at N.M. Military	6	6
O21	|	Arizona State	13	26
O28	|	Loyola-Marymount	7	43
N4	|	N.M. Highlands	45	6
N11	● |	Arizona	7	0
N18	● |	at New Mexico State	14	7
N26	|	No. Colorado	0	6

NEW MEXICO 585

THE SCHOOLS

GWINN HENRY
1934-36 (.571) 16-12

1934 8-1-0 (3-1-0)

S29	●	N.M. Highlands	76	7
O5	● |	No. Arizona	33	6
O13	●	at Texas-El Paso	21	15
O20	● |	at Arizona State	18	12
O27	●	N.M. Military	26	7
N3	|	at Arizona	6	14 *
N12	●	Western New Mexico	26	0
N17	● |	New Mexico State	12	6
N29	●	Colorado College	33	6

1935 6-4-0 (3-2-0)

S21	●	Western New Mexico	46	0
S28	● |	Texas-El Paso	20	0
O5		at Oklahoma	0	25
O12	●	at Colorado College	13	0
O19	● |	No. Arizona	20	0
O26	●	at N.M. Military	21	0
N2	● |	Arizona State	13	0
N11	|	at New Mexico State	0	32
N23	|	Arizona	6	38
N28		Colorado State	6	7

1936 2-7-0 (1-4-0)

S26		Western New Mexico	0	6
O3		at Colorado State	7	9
O10		West Texas St.	7	13
O17	|	at Texas-El Paso	7	12
O24	●	N.M. Military	13	7
O31	|	at Arizona State	6	7
N7	|	at Arizona	0	28
N14	|	New Mexico State	6	7
N26	● |	No. Arizona	15	6

TED SHIPKEY
1937-41 (.633) 30-17-2

1937 4-4-1 (2-3-1)

S25	●	Western New Mexico	14	0
O1		at Denver	0	12
O8	|	at New Mexico State	0	5
O16	= |	Texas-El Paso	7	7
O23	|	at Texas Tech	0	27
O30	● |	Arizona State	15	7
N6	●	at Colorado State Coll.	26	6
N13	|	Arizona	0	23
N25	● |	No. Arizona	7	6

1938 8-3-0 (4-2-0)

S23	●	Western Mew Mexico	40	0
S30	● |	Arizona State	21	0
O7	●	Colorado College	45	0
O15	|	at Texas-El Paso	6	7
O22	● |	at No. Arizona	20	0
O29	● |	at Arizona	20	7
N5	●	Denver	7	6
N12	● |	New Mexico State	6	2
N19	|	Texas Tech	7	17
N24	●	Colorado State	27	7
		SUN BOWL		
J2		Utah	0	26

1939 8-2-0 (4-2-0)

S22	●	Western New Mexico	29	7
S29	●	Wyoming	34	7
O6	●	at Denver	7	6
O12	● |	Texas-El Paso	14	0
O21	|	at Texas Tech	7	19
O27	● |	No. Arizona	33	0
N10	● |	at New Mexico State	9	6
N18	|	at Arizona State	6	28
N25	● |	Arizona	7	6
N30	●	Colorado State	21	19

1940 5-4-0 (4-2-0)

S28		at Wyoming	3	7
O4	●	Western New Mexico	28	0
O11	|	Arizona State	6	13
O19	|	at Texas-El Paso	7	9
O26		Colorado State DEN	6	7
N9	● |	New Mexico State	39	6
N16	● |	No. Arizona	45	26
N23	● |	at Arizona	13	12
N30	● |	Texas Tech	19	14

1941 5-4-1 (3-2-1)

S26	● |	No. Arizona	12	6
O4	● |	Texas-El Paso	16	14
O11	= |	at Arizona State	0	0
O18	|	Arizona	6	31
O24	|	at Texas Tech	0	36
N1	●	Nevada	23	7
N8	● |	at New Mexico State	28	0
N15		at Marquette	0	34
N22		Loyola-Marymount	3	7
N29	●	Wyoming	28	0

WILLIS BARNES
1942-46 (.489) 19-20-5

1942 4-5-2 (3-4-0)

S19	●	Kirtland AFB	7	6
S26	● |	No. Arizona	26	6
O2	|	Texas-El Paso	0	7
O10	● |	New Mexico State	32	0
O17		Colorado	0	12
O24	|	Texas Tech	0	20 *
O31	=	Nevada	0	0
N7	|	Arizona	13	14
N14	|	West Texas St.	7	13
N21	=	at Loyola-Marymount	14	14
N28	● |	Arizona State	35	7

1943 3-2-0 (1-0-0)

S25		at Colorado College	7	20
O2	●	Kirtland AFB	19	13
O16	● |	No. Arizona	26	6
N13	●	at Denver	33	13
		SUN BOWL		
J1		Southwestern	0	7

1944 1-7-0 (1-2-0)

S16		Amarillo AFB	2	21
S23	● |	No. Arizona	47	14
S30		Colorado College	7	25
O7	|	West Texas St.	0	6
O14		Second Air Force ELP	6	89
N4		Colorado PUE	0	39
N11		Denver	6	41
N18	|	at Texas Tech	7	13

1945 6-1-1 (1-0-1)

S22	●	Ea. New Mexico	78	0
S29	●	Lubbock AFB	39	0
O6	● |	at West Texas St.	13	0
O13	●	at Colorado College	6	4
N3	●	Colorado	12	6
N10		Utah	20	21
N24	= |	Texas Tech	6	6
		SUN BOWL		
J1	●	Denver	34	24

1946 5-5-2 (4-2-1)

S21	● |	No. Arizona	12	7
S28		at Utah	14	56
O4	● |	West Texas St.	6	0
O12	● |	at New Mexico State	7	6
O18	|	Hardin-Simmons	0	49
O26		at Colorado	13	14
N2	● |	Texas-El Paso	21	13
N9	|	Texas Tech	0	27
N16	= |	Arizona	13	13
N23	●	Kansas State	14	7
D22		at Hawaii All Stars	14	19
		HARBOR BOWL		
J1	=	Montana St.	13	13

BERL HUFFMAN
1947-49 (.274) 8-22-1

1947 4-5-1 (1-5-1)

S27	|	Arizona State	12	25
O4	●	at Kansas State	20	18
O11	● |	New Mexico State	20	0
O18	|	at Hardin-Simmons	7	33
O25	|	at Arizona	12	22
N1	= |	at Texas-El Paso	20	20
N8	●	Fresno State	34	3
N15	●	Drake	8	7
N22	|	Texas Tech	20	26
N29	|	West Texas St.	18	28

1948 2-9-0 (1-6-0)

S25	●	at Colorado	9	6
O2		at Texas	0	47
O9	● |	New Mexico State	61	0
O16	|	Hardin-Simmons	19	28
O23	|	Texas-El Paso	13	27
O30		at Fresno State	14	20
N6	|	Arizona	6	14
N13		at Drake	0	14
N20	|	at Texas Tech	7	14
N27	|	at West Texas St.	0	19
D14	|	at Arizona State	17	28

1949 2-8-0 (1-6-0)

S24		Wyoming	14	41
S30	● |	at New Mexico State	14	13
O8		at Rice	0	55
O15	|	Hardin-Simmons ODE	7	34
O22	|	at Texas-El Paso	0	7
O29	|	Arizona State	19	28
N5	|	at Arizona	14	46
N12	●	Colorado	17	15
N19	|	Texas Tech	0	27
N26	|	West Texas St.	13	41

DUDLEY DEGROOT
1950-52 (.433) 13-17

1950 2-8-0 (2-5-0)

S23	● |	No. Arizona	78	0
S30	|	at Arizona State	6	41 *
O7	● |	New Mexico State	26	13
O14	|	West Texas St. AMAR	6	45
O21	|	Texas-El Paso	13	41
O28		at Wyoming	0	44
N4	|	Arizona	0	38
N11		at Army	0	51
N18		Bradley	19	20
N25	|	at Texas Tech	12	37

1951 4-7-0 (2-3-0)

S22	● |	No. Arizona	55	6
S29		at Montana	7	25
O6	● |	at New Mexico State	20	0
O13		at Denver	17	33
O20	|	at Texas-El Paso	7	32
O27		Colorado State	15	20
N3	|	at Arizona	20	32
N10		Wyoming	7	41
N17	●	Brigham Young	34	0
N24	|	Texas Tech	14	60
D1	●	Utah State	17	13

1952-1961
SKYLINE

1952 7-2-0 (5-1-0)

S27	|	at Brigham Young	10	14
O4	●	New Mexico State	23	0
O18	● |	at Wyoming	7	0
O25	●	at Texas-El Paso	14	13
N1		Arizona	7	13
N8	● |	at Denver	15	0
N15	● |	Colorado State	3	0
N22	● |	Montana	12	6
D6	● |	Utah State	28	0

BOB TITCHENAL
1953-55 (.431) 12-16-1

1953 5-3-1 (3-2-1)

S26	|	at Utah State	0	6
O3	= |	Brigham Young	12	12
O10		at Arizona	0	20
O17	●	San Diego State	41	12
O24	● |	at Montana	41	13
O31	● |	Denver	20	18
N7	●	at New Mexico State	28	6
N14	● |	Wyoming	9	7
N21	|	at Colorado State	3	9

1954 5-5-0 (3-3-0)

S18	● |	at Brigham Young	21	12
S25	●	at San Diego State	28	7
O2	|	Utah State	0	6
O16	|	at Wyoming	7	9
O23		Arizona	7	41
O29	|	at Denver	6	19
N6	● |	Montana	20	14
N13	● |	Colorado State	10	7
N20	●	New Mexico State	39	27
N27		at San Jose State	14	16

1955 2-8-0 (1-5-0)

S17	●	New Mexico State	14	7
S24	|	at Colorado State	0	25
O1		Texas-El Paso	0	34
O8	|	at Utah State	0	18
O15		San Jose State	0	14
O22	|	at Montana	14	19
O29	|	Denver	6	33
N12	|	Wyoming	0	20
N19		at Arizona	6	27
N26	● |	Brigham Young	21	16

DICK CLAUSEN
1956-57 (.400) 8-12

1956 4-6-0 (2-4-0)

S22	●	at New Mexico State	14	6
S29	● |	Utah State	27	19
O6		at Texas-El Paso	0	34
O13	|	at Wyoming	13	20
O20		Arizona	12	26
O26	|	at Denver	14	20
N3	|	at Brigham Young	12	33
N17	● |	Montana	14	13
N24	●	San Diego State	34	6
D1	|	Colorado State	27	28

1957 4-6-0 (2-4-0)

S21	●	New Mexico State	25	7
S28	● |	at Colorado State	30	7
O5		Texas-El Paso	13	15
O12	● |	at Utah State	14	10
O19	●	at Arizona	27	0
O26	|	at Montana	6	21
N1	|	Denver	0	19
N16	|	Wyoming	13	20
N23		at Air Force	0	31
N30	|	Brigham Young	12	14

MARV LEVY
1958-59 (.700) 14-6

1958 7-3-0 (5-1-0)

S20	●	at New Mexico State	16	7
S27		at Texas-El Paso	7	15
O4	● |	Montana	44	16
O11	● |	Utah State	34	14
O18	●	Arizona	33	13
O25	● |	at Wyoming	13	12
O31	● |	at Denver	21	15
N8	|	at Brigham Young	19	36
N15	● |	Colorado State	17	12
N22		Air Force	7	45

1959 7-3-0 (4-2-0)

S19		New Mexico State	12	29
S26	|	at Colorado State	9	14
O3	●	Texas-El Paso	17	7
O10	● |	at Utah State	28	6
O17	●	at Arizona	28	7
O24	● |	at Montana	55	14
O31	● |	Denver	42	0
N7	● |	Brigham Young	21	6
N14	|	Wyoming	20	25
N21	●	Air Force DEN	28	27

BILL WEEKS
1960-67 (.494) 40-41-1

1960 5-5-0 (4-2-0)

S17	●	U. of Mexico	77	6
S24	|	at Wyoming	3	13
O1		at Texas-El Paso	17	23
O8		New Mexico State	0	34
O15	|	Utah State	7	46
O22		Arizona	14	26
O28	● |	at Denver	41	6
N5	● |	at Brigham Young	27	15
N12	● |	Colorado State	24	6
N19	● |	Montana	24	7

1961 7-4-0 (3-3-0)

S23	●	New Mexico State	41	7
S30	|	at Montana	8	40
O7	●	Texas-El Paso	7	6
O14	|	at Utah State	7	41
O21		at Arizona	21	22
O28	●	Air Force	21	6
N4	● |	Utah	21	16
N11	|	Wyoming	7	33
N18	● |	at Colorado State	20	8
N25	● |	Brigham Young	34	6
		AVIATION BOWL		
D9	●	Western Michigan	28	12

1962-1998
WAC

1962 7-2-1 (2-1-1)

S15	●	New Mexico State	28	17
S22	● |	at Wyoming	25	21
S29	● |	Arizona	35	25
O6		at Texas-El Paso	14	16
O13	●	Utah State	14	13
O20	= |	at Utah	7	7
O27	●	at San Jose State	25	13
N3	|	at Brigham Young	0	27
N10	●	Colorado State	21	8
N17	●	Montana	41	12

1963 6-4-0 (3-1-0)

S28	●	Texas-El Paso	23	7
O5	|	Utah	6	19
O12		at Utah State	14	47
O19		at New Mexico State	12	13
O26	●	Montana	24	6
N2	●	at Colorado State	25	0
N9	● |	Wyoming	17	6
N16		Air Force	8	30
N30	● |	Brigham Young	26	0
D7	● |	at Arizona	22	15

586 NEW MEXICO

THE SCHOOLS

1964 9-2-0 (3-1-0)

S19		at Utah	0	16
S26	•	Montana	20	0
O2	•	at Brigham Young	26	14
O10	•	Arizona	10	7
O17		Utah State	3	14
O24	•	New Mexico State	18	14
O31	•	at Wyoming	17	6
N7	•	at Texas-El Paso	20	12
N14	•	Colorado State	42	0
N20	•	at Hawaii	20	0
N28	•	Kansas State	9	7

1965 3-7-0 (2-3-0)

S25		Texas-El Paso	14	35
O2		at Colorado State	22	27
O9	•	at Arizona	24	2
O16	•	Utah	13	10
O23		at Arizona State	14	27
O30		San Jose State	7	27
N6		Wyoming	9	27
N13		at New Mexico State	6	20
N20	•	Iowa State	10	9
N27		Brigham Young	8	42

1966 2-8-0 (0-5-0)

S17	•	Utah State	17	8
S24	•	at Kansas State	28	8
O1		at Texas-El Paso	3	51
O8		Arizona	15	36
O15		at Wyoming	7	37
O22		Brigham Young	6	33
O29		at Utah	0	27
N5		Colorado State	6	45
N12		New Mexico State	12	47
N19		at Arizona State	7	28

1967 1-9-0 (0-5-0)

S16	•	Idaho St.	24	3
S23		at Brigham Young	14	44
S30		at Iowa State	12	17
O7		Utah	27	42
O14		Arizona State	23	56
O21		at San Jose State	14	52
O27		Texas-El Paso	12	75
N4		at Arizona	13	48
N11		Wyoming	6	42
N18		New Mexico State	7	54

RUDY FELDMAN
1968-73 (.397) 24-37-2

1968 0-10-0 (0-7-0)

S14		Colorado State	13	21
S21		at Texas-El Paso	15	44
S28		Arizona	8	19
O5		at Kansas	7	68
O12		at Utah	7	30
O19		San Jose State	24	55
O26		at Wyoming	6	35
N2		at Arizona State	28	63
N16		New Mexico State	6	33
N23		Brigham Young	6	35

1969 4-6-0 (1-5-0)

S20		at Army	14	31
S27		Texas-El Paso	6	21
O4	•	Kansas	16	7
O11		at Brigham Young	15	41
O18		Utah	0	24
O25		at Arizona	28	52
N1	•	at San Jose State	27	24
N8		Arizona State	17	48
N15	•	Wyoming	24	12
N22	•	at New Mexico State	24	21

1970 7-3-0 (5-1-0)

S19		Iowa State	3	32
S26	•	at Utah	34	28
O3		at Kansas	23	49
O10	•	San Jose State	48	25
O17	•	New Mexico State	24	17
O24	•	at Wyoming	17	7
O31	•	at Texas-El Paso	35	16
N7	•	Arizona	35	7
N14	•	Brigham Young	51	8
N21		at Arizona State	21	33

1971 6-3-2 (5-1-0)

S18	•	at Texas Tech	13	10
S25		Iowa State	20	44
O1	•	at Brigham Young	14	0
O9	=	New Mexico State	35	35
O16	=	at San Jose State	21	21
O23		Arizona State	28	60
O30	•	at Arizona	34	28
N6	•	Utah	57	39
N13	•	Texas-El Paso	49	13
N20	•	Wyoming	49	14
N27		at Hawaii	21	28

1972 3-8-0 (2-4-0)

S16	•	New Mexico State	55	20
S23		Texas Tech	16	41
S30		at Iowa State	0	31
O7	•	at Wyoming	17	14
O14		Arizona	15	27
O21	•	at Texas-El Paso	56	7
O28		at Utah	14	59
N4		San Jose State	7	14
N11		at Arizona State	7	60
N18		at Houston	14	33
N25		Brigham Young	7	21

1973 4-7-0 (3-4-0)

S15	•	New Mexico State	48	6
S22		at Texas Tech	7	41
S29		at Air Force	6	10
O6		Arizona State	24	67
O13		at Arizona	14	22
O20	•	Texas-El Paso	49	0
O27		at San Jose State	0	15
N3		at Brigham Young	21	56
N10		Utah	35	36
N17	•	Wyoming	23	21
N24	•	at Colorado State	30	13

BILL MONDT
1974-79 (.471) 32-36-1

1974 4-6-1 (3-4-0)

S14	•	Colorado State	32	23
S21	=	Texas Tech	21	21
S28		Arizona	10	15
O5		at Iowa State	3	27
O12		San Jose State	11	13
O19	•	at Wyoming	32	21
O26		at Arizona State	7	41
N2	•	New Mexico State	26	24
N9		at Utah	10	21
N16		Brigham Young	3	36
N23	•	at Texas-El Paso	37	21

1975 6-5-0 (4-3-0)

S13	•	Fresno State	29	0
S20		at Texas Tech	17	24
S27		Colorado State	16	27
O4		at Brigham Young	15	16
O11		Arizona State	10	16
O18	•	Utah	27	23
O25	•	at Arizona	44	34
N1	•	Texas-El Paso	23	3
N8		at San Jose State	20	29
N15	•	Wyoming	38	32
N22	•	at New Mexico State	52	28

1976 4-7-0 (3-4-0)

S18	•	at Texas-El Paso	25	7
S25		Texas Tech	16	20
O2	•	at Colorado State	33	20
O9	•	San Jose State	36	30
O16		at Wyoming	23	24
O23		at Arizona State	15	31
O30		New Mexico State	7	16
N6		at Utah	31	34
N13		Brigham Young	8	21
N20	•	Arizona	21	15
N27		at San Diego State	14	17

1977 5-7-0 (2-5-0)

S10	•	at Hawaii	35	26
S17		at Texas Tech	14	49
S24		at Colorado	7	42
S30		at Brigham Young	19	54
O8		Arizona State	24	45
O15	•	Wichita St.	22	17
O22		at Colorado State	9	14
O29	•	at New Mexico State	35	13
N5	•	Texas-El Paso	33	17
N12		at Arizona	13	15
N19		Wyoming	21	23
N26	•	Utah	41	24

1978 7-5-0 (3-3-0)

S9		at Hawaii	16	22
S16	•	at Wichita St.	16	14
S23	•	Nevada-Las Vegas	24	0
S30		Brigham Young	23	27
O7	•	at Wyoming	19	15
O14		Texas Tech	23	36
O21	•	New Mexico State	35	20
O28	•	at Texas-El Paso	21	0
N4	•	at Utah	24	12
N11		Colorado State	15	26
N18	•	Pacific	44	6
N25		at San Diego State	24	27

1979 6-6-0 (3-4-0)

S1	•	Louisiana Tech	34	0 †
S8	•	Oregon State	35	16
S15		at Texas Tech	7	17
S22		at Hawaii	3	20
S29	•	at New Mexico State	30	16
O6		San Diego State	7	35
O13		at Nevada-Las Vegas	20	28
O20	•	Texas-El Paso	20	0
O27		at Brigham Young	7	59
N3		Utah	7	26
N10	•	at Colorado State	24	9
N24	•	Wyoming	17	3

JOE MORRISON
1980-82 (.544) 18-15-1

1980 4-7-0 (3-4-0)

S6	•	Brigham Young	25	21
S13		at Missouri	16	47
S20		at Texas Tech	17	28
S27	•	New Mexico State	52	19
O4	•	at Wyoming	24	21
O11		Colorado State	26	31
O18		Hawaii	14	31
O25	•	at Texas-El Paso	22	21
N1		Nevada-Las Vegas	7	72
N8		at Utah	21	49
N22		at San Diego State	22	24

1981 4-7-1 (3-4-1)

S5		at Houston	10	21
S12		at Nevada-Las Vegas	42	49
S19		at Texas Tech	21	28
S26	•	Air Force	27	10
O3		San Diego State	15	17
O10	•	Texas-El Paso	26	3
O17		at Hawaii	13	23
O24	•	at New Mexico State	17	13
O31		at Brigham Young	7	31
N7	=	Utah	7	7
N14	•	at Colorado State	28	16
N21		Wyoming	12	13

1982 10-1-0 (6-1-0)

S4	•	at Wyoming	41	20
S11	•	Texas Tech	14	0
S18	•	Nevada-Las Vegas	49	21
O2	•	at Air Force	49	37
O9		Brigham Young	12	40
O16	•	at San Diego State	22	17
O23	•	New Mexico State	66	14
O30	•	at North Texas	20	17
N6	•	at Texas-El Paso	31	18
N13	•	Colorado State	29	24
N20	•	Hawaii	41	17

JOE LEE DUNN
1983-86 (.362) 17-30

1983 6-6-0 (4-3-0)

S3	•	Utah	17	7
S10		at Tennessee	6	31
S17		Arkansas LR	0	17
S24	•	at New Mexico State	31	10
O1		North Texas	8	18
O8	•	at Texas Tech	30	10
O15		at Brigham Young	21	66
O22		at Hawaii	16	25
O29		at Colorado State	24	25
N5	•	Wyoming	17	10
N12	•	Texas-El Paso	35	0
N19	•	San Diego State	34	14

1984 4-8-0 (1-7-0)

S8	•	New Mexico State	61	21
S15	•	West Texas St.	27	0
S22	•	Texas Tech	29	24
S29	•	at Texas-El Paso	34	7
O5		at Utah	14	38
O13		Colorado State	10	16
O20		at Wyoming	21	59
O25		Brigham Young	0	48
N3		at Baylor	2	38
N10		Air Force	9	23
N17		at San Diego State	31	37
N24		at Hawaii	13	48

1985 3-8-0 (2-6-0)

S7		at Texas Tech	31	32
S14	•	at New Mexico State	34	27
S28		Air Force	12	49
O5		at Nebraska	7	38
O12		Colorado State	28	45
O19		Brigham Young	23	45
O26		Hawaii	17	27
N2	•	at Texas-El Paso	27	23
N9		at Utah	49	58
N16	•	Wyoming	41	16
N23		San Diego State	20	55

1986 4-8-0 (2-5-0)

S6		at Tennessee	21	35
S13		at Brigham Young	30	31
S20		at Texas Tech	7	14
S27		San Diego State	34	38
O4		at Hawaii	10	24
O11	•	Texas-El Paso	24	22
O18	•	Utah	47	43
O25	•	New Mexico State	45	14
N1		at Wyoming	25	35
N8		Tulsa	27	34
N15		at Colorado State	27	32
N22	•	at Memphis	20	13

MIKE SHEPPARD
1987-91 (.153) 9-50

1987 0-11-0 (0-8-0)

S5		at Utah	20	24
S12		at New Mexico State	14	17
S19		at Arizona	9	20
S26		Brigham Young	25	45
O10		Hawaii	31	41
O17		at Colorado State	13	35
O31		at Texas-El Paso	0	34
N7		Wyoming	16	59
N14		Air Force	26	73
N21		at San Diego State	30	53
N28		Arkansas LR	25	43

1988 2-10-0 (1-7-0)

S3		Fresno State	21	68
S10	•	at New Mexico State	36	34
S17		at Texas	0	47
S24		Akron	28	30
O1		at Air Force	14	63
O8		Utah	27	33
O15		at Wyoming	7	55
O22		Texas-El Paso	0	37
O29		at Brigham Young	0	65
N5		at Hawaii	3	45
N12	•	Colorado State	24	23
N19		San Diego State	10	18

1989 2-10-0 (0-7-0)

S2		Brigham Young	3	24
S9	•	New Mexico State	45	13
S16		at Texas Tech	20	27
S23		at Tulsa	33	35
S30		at Hawaii	14	60
O7		Colorado State	20	34
O14		at Texas-El Paso	7	26
O21		at Florida	21	27
O28		Wyoming	23	24
N4		at San Diego State	28	45
N11		at Utah	39	41
N18	•	Fresno State	45	22

1990 2-10-0 (1-6-0)

S1	•	at New Mexico State	29	12
S8		at Fresno State	17	24
S15		Arizona	10	25
S22		Texas Tech	32	34
S29		at Kansas State	6	38
O6	•	Texas-El Paso	48	28
O13		at Wyoming	22	25
O20		at Colorado State	7	47
O27		at Brigham Young	31	55
N3		at Hawaii	16	43
N10		Utah	27	29
N17		San Diego State	34	40

1991   3-9-0 (2-6-0)

Date	Opponent			
A31		at Texas-El Paso	19	35
S7		at TCU	7	60
S14		at Hawaii	13	35
S21		Nevada-Las Vegas	22	23
S28	●	New Mexico State	17	10
O5		at Fresno State	17	94
O12		at San Diego State	24	38
O19		Wyoming	19	39
O26		Brigham Young	23	41
N2	●	Air Force	34	32
N9		at Utah	7	30
N16	●	at Colorado State	38	36

DENNIS FRANCHIONE
1992-97 (.478)   33-36

1992   3-8-0 (2-6-0)

Date		Opponent		
S5	●	TCU	24	7
S12		at New Mexico State	39	42
S19		SMU	13	20
S26		at Air Force	32	33
O3		San Diego State	21	49
O10		at Wyoming	21	35
O17	●	Utah	24	7
O24		at Fresno State	28	31
N7		at Brigham Young	0	35
N14	●	Texas-El Paso	35	14
N21		Colorado State	10	14

1993   6-5-0 (4-4-0)

Date		Opponent		
S4		Brigham Young	31	34
S11		at TCU	34	35
S18		Fresno State	24	41
S25	●	New Mexico State	42	7
O2	●	Hawaii	41	14
O9		at Utah	42	35
O23		at San Diego State	17	20
O30		at Colorado State	20	21
N6		Idaho St.	39	13
N13	●	Wyoming	10	7
N20	●	at Texas-El Paso	35	29

1994   5-7-0 (4-4-0)

Date		Opponent		
S3		at Texas Tech	31	37
S10		TCU	29	44
S17		at SMU	31	34
S24		at Brigham Young	47	49
O1		Colorado State	31	38
O8	●	at Hawaii	38	21
O15		San Diego State	13	20
O22	●	at New Mexico State	56	31
O29	●	at Fresno State	49	32
N5		Utah	23	21
N12		at Wyoming	28	38
N19	●	Texas-El Paso	25	21

1995   4-7-0 (2-6-0)

Date		Opponent		
S2		No. Arizona	45	21
S16		Utah	9	36
S23		New Mexico State	36	24
S30		Air Force	24	27
O7		at Fresno State	34	51
O14	●	Hawaii	24	10
O21	●	at Colorado State	22	14
O28		Texas Tech	7	34
N4		at San Diego State	29	38
N11		Brigham Young	14	31
N18		at Texas-El Paso	12	17

1996   6-5 (3-5)

Date		Opponent		
A29	●	at New Mexico State	28	7
S7		No. Arizona	49	33
S14	●	Central Florida	17	7
S21		at Brigham Young	14	17
S28	●	TCU	27	7
O5		at Rice	21	38
O19		San Diego State	42	48
O26		at SMU	31	52
N2	●	at Tulsa	34	23
N9		Utah	24	31
N23	●	Texas-El Paso	44	17

1997   9-4 (6-2)

Date		Opponent		
A30		No. Arizona	33	10
S6	●	New Mexico State	61	24
S13	●	at Texas-El Paso	38	20
S20	●	at Utah State	25	22
O4	●	SMU	22	15
O11	●	at San Diego State	36	21
O18		Rice	23	35
O25		at Utah	10	15
N1	●	at TCU	40	10
N15	●	Brigham Young	38	28
N22	●	Tulsa	51	13
WAC CHAMPIONSHIP				
D6		Colorado State *LV*	13	41
INSIGHT.COM BOWL				
D27		Arizona	14	20

ROCKY LONG
1998-Present (.471)   40-45

1998   3-9 (1-7)

Date		Opponent		
S5	●	Idaho St.	38	9
S12	●	Utah State	39	36
S19		at New Mexico State	27	28
S26		at San Jose State	20	37
O3		at Air Force	14	56
O10		Texas-El Paso	19	22
O17		San Diego State	33	36
O24	●	at Hawaii	30	20
O31		Fresno State	20	28
N7		at Brigham Young	21	46
N14		Utah	7	41
N21		at Central Florida	6	38

1999-Present
MOUNTAIN WEST

1999   4-7 (3-4)

Date		Opponent		
S4		at Texas-El Paso	10	13
S11		New Mexico State	28	35
S18	●	No. Arizona	45	14
S25		at Boise State	9	20
O9	●	at San Diego State	24	21
O16		Brigham Young	7	31
O30	●	Nevada-Las Vegas	27	6
N6		Colorado State	22	36
N13		at Utah	7	52
N20		at Wyoming	28	42
N27	●	Air Force	33	28

2000   5-7 (3-4)

Date		Opponent		
A26		at Texas Tech	3	24
S2		Boise State	14	31
S9		Oregon State	20	28
S16	●	at New Mexico State	16	13
S23	●	No. Arizona	35	28
S30	●	Wyoming	45	10
O7		at Colorado State	14	17
O21	●	at Air Force	29	23
O28	●	Utah	10	3
N4		San Diego State	16	17
N11	●	at Nevada-Las Vegas	14	18
N18	●	at Brigham Young	13	37

2001   6-5 (4-3)

Date		Opponent		
S1	●	Texas-El Paso	26	6
S8		at Texas Tech	30	42
S22		at Baylor	13	16
S29		at Utah	16	37
O6		at Wyoming	30	29
O13		Brigham Young	20	24
O27	●	Air Force	52	33
N3		at San Diego State	20	15
N10	●	Nevada-Las Vegas	27	17
N17		Colorado State	17	24
N24	●	New Mexico State	53	0

2002   7-7 (5-2)

Date		Opponent		
A24		at North Carolina St.	14	34
A31	●	Weber St.	38	24
S7		at Air Force	31	38
S14		Baylor	23	0
S21		at New Mexico State	13	24
S27		Texas Tech	0	49
O12	●	at Nevada-Las Vegas	25	16
O19		at Utah State	44	45
O26	●	Utah	42	35
N9		San Diego State	15	8
N16	●	at Brigham Young	20	16
N23	●	at Colorado State	14	22
N30	●	Wyoming	49	20
LAS VEGAS BOWL				
D25		UCLA	13	27

2003   8-5 (5-2)

Date		Opponent		
A30	●	Texas St.	72	8
S6		at Texas Tech	28	42
S13		Brigham Young	7	10
S20		at Washington State	13	23
S27	●	New Mexico State	24	17
O4		Utah State	34	7
O18	●	at San Diego State	30	7
O25	●	at Utah	47	35
N1		Nevada-Las Vegas	35	37
N7	●	Colorado State	37	34
N15	●	Air Force	24	12
N22	●	at Wyoming	26	3
LAS VEGAS BOWL				
D24		Oregon State	14	55

2004   7-5 (5-2)

Date		Opponent		
S3		Washington State	17	21
S11	●	Texas Tech	27	24
S18		at Oregon State	7	17
S25	●	at New Mexico State	38	3
O2		Utah	7	28
O9		at Air Force	23	28
O16	●	at Nevada-Las Vegas	24	20
O23	●	San Diego State	19	9
O30	●	at Colorado State	26	17
N13	●	at Brigham Young	21	14
N20	●	Wyoming	16	9
EMERALD BOWL				
D30		Navy	19	34

THE SCHOOLS

Neutral Site Key: *Ama* Amarillo, TX / *Den* Denver, CO / *ElP* El Paso, TX / *LR* Little Rock, AR / *LV* Las Vegas, NV / *Ode* Odessa, TX / *Pue* Pueblo, CO
f Forfeit † Game Later Forfeited # Disputed Victor * Disputed Score || Designated Conference Game 2 Counted Twice in Conference Standings

NEW MEXICO STATE

BY SETH WICKERSHAM

HOW STARVED ARE NEW MEXICO State football fans? After the Aggies' road upset of No. 22 Arizona State in 1999, liquored-up honky-tonkers back in Las Cruces stormed Memorial Stadium, and in the pitch black they sawed off the goalposts as a keepsake. It has been so long since the modest glory days—back-to-back Sun Bowl wins in 1959 and 1960—one can hardly blame Aggies fans for snaring whatever tokens of victory are available. Since 1967, New Mexico State has enjoyed just four winning seasons. The coach who was responsible for two of those, Tony Samuel, was fired after the 2004 campaign. But there's hope: Samuel's replacement, Hal Mumme, has a 97–64–1 record in 14 seasons as a college head coach.

TRADITION Fans hike up Tortuga Mountain to paint and polish an A (for Aggie) composed of rocks. The A is supposed to be a blessing, but in the 1980s, folks considered it a curse. With a 27-game losing streak hanging over New Mexico State in November 1990, a few football players knocked the rocks out of line. The entire team hiked up to reassemble the landmark. Feeding off its clean,

crisp A, New Mexico State beat Cal State-Fullerton, 43-9. But, after the Aggies broke their 20-game road losing streak the following year, players couldn't remember the words to the school fight song.

BEST PLAYER In 1958, sophomore quarterback Charley Johnson joined a program that hadn't gone bowling in 22 years. Two years later, he left Las Cruces as the only two-time Sun Bowl MVP. In his final two years, Johnson threw 31 touchdown passes and only 15 interceptions, and his 128.09 career-efficiency rating stood for 32 years as the school's best. After 15 professional seasons spent with the Cardinals, Oilers and Broncos, he ultimately returned to Las Cruces in 2000 as the head of the chemical engineering department.

BEST COACH Picture Woody Hayes with a cowboy hat. That would be hard-bitten Warren Woodson—spitting, sneering, grabbing jerseys—who took over New Mexico State in 1958 and posted a 63–36–3 record over the next 10 seasons. His mouth was as loud as his .632 winning percentage; after being denied a favor by the university president, he once yelled, "If I ran my football team the way you run this university, we wouldn't win a game." Woodson, who was inducted into the College Football Hall of Fame in 1989, won seven games or more in five of his

---

PROFILE

New Mexico State University
Las Cruces, N.M.
Founded: 1888
Enrollment: 12,145
Colors: Crimson and White
Nickname: Aggies
Stadium: Aggie Memorial Stadium
   Opened in 1978
   Grass; 30,343 capacity
First football game: 1893
All-time record: 392–508–30 (.438)
Bowl record: 2–0–1
Conference: Joined Western Athletic Conference in 2005
Website: www.nmstatesports.com

THE BEST OF TIMES

Back-to-back Sun Bowl wins, 1959 and 1960.

THE WORST OF TIMES

A 27-game losing streak from October 1988 to November 1990.

CONFERENCE

New Mexico State joined the Sun Belt Conference in 2001 and remained there until joining the WAC in 2005. From 1894 to 1931, it was an independent, then joined the Border Conference in 1931. Thirty years later, it was an independent again. From 1972 until 1982 it was a member of the Missouri Valley, and from 1984 to 2000 it was in the Big West.

DISTINGUISHED ALUMNI

Rich Beem, golfer; Danny Villanueva, founder of Telemundo and Univision networks

FIGHT SONG

AGGIES, OH AGGIES
Aggies, Oh Aggies
The hills send back the cry
We're here to do or die
Aggies, Oh Aggies
We'll win this game or know the reason why
And when we win this game
We'll buy a keg of booze
And we'll drink to the Aggies
'Til we wobble in our shoes
A-G-G-I-E-S
Aggies, Aggies, go Aggies
Aggies, Oh Aggies
The hills send back the cry
We're here to do or die
Aggies, Oh Aggies
We'll win this game or know the reason why.

A look east to the 9,000-foot peaks of the Organ Mountains is often a prettier sight than the scoreboard.

10 seasons, but he was let go despite going 7–2–1 in his final season, reportedly because of conflicts with his superiors.

BEST TEAM Led by the nation's top-rated offense and a backfield that sent all three starters—Charley Johnson and running backs Pervis Atkins and Bob Gaiters—to the pros, New Mexico State finished the 1960 season with an 11–0 record. One of only three Aggie teams to go undefeated during a full regular season, they capped the campaign with a second straight Sun Bowl win, over Utah State. New Mexico State finished the season ranked No. 17 in the AP poll and No. 18 in the UPI rankings.

BIGGEST GAME With its undefeated season on the line in the 1960 Sun Bowl, New Mexico State trailed Utah State 13-7 at halftime. Led by future Hall of Famer Merlin Olsen, Utah State held the Aggies to just 234 total yards, but in the second half New Mexico State broke through. Gaiters ran 32 yards for the go-ahead score, and Johnson sealed the win with a 7-yard touchdown pass in the fourth quarter, as the Aggies prevailed, 20-13.

BIGGEST UPSET Going into Tempe, Arizona, for a September 1999 game against the No. 22-ranked Sun Devils, New Mexico State was 0–14 against ranked teams. But, led by backup quarterback K.C. Enzminger, the Aggies scored three touchdowns in an eight-minute span in the third quarter to rout Arizona State 35-7. The backfield of Walter Taylor, Keeon Johnson and Chris Barnes combined to run for 295 yards. J.R. Redmond, the Sun Devils' preseason Heisman Trophy candidate, rushed for only 62 yards on 24 carries.

HEARTBREAKER In 1998, New Mexico State seemed on the verge of snapping its 13-game road losing streak, with a 31-10 lead over Arkansas State early in the fourth quarter. But Indians quarterback Cleo Lemon threw three touchdown passes in nine minutes to tie. Trailing 34-31 in overtime, Aggies tailback Denvis Manns took the carry on second and goal at the 2, and lunged for the end zone. Hit high and low by a pair of Arkansas State defenders, he fumbled the ball at the goal line, and the Aggies lost. Encouraged by their performance, though, they snapped the streak a week later, with a 48-45 win at Nevada.

RECORDS

RUSHING YARDS

	GAME
319	James Pilot, vs. Hardin-Simmons, Nov. 25, 1961 (45 att.)
	SEASON
1,469	Denvis Manns, 1998 (269 att.)
	CAREER
4,692	Denvis Manns, 1995-98 (889 att.)

PASSING YARDS

	GAME
546	Cody Ledbetter vs. UNLV, Nov. 18, 1995 (34 of 56)
	SEASON
3,501	Cody Ledbetter, 1995 (259 of 453)
	CAREER
7,480	Cody Ledbetter, 1991-95 (556 of 1039)

RECEIVING YARDS

	GAME
316	Jeff Evans vs. Southern Illinois, Sept. 30, 1978 (15 rec.)
	SEASON
1,111	Hank Cook, 1973 (65 rec.)
	CAREER
2,769	Lucious Davis, 1992-95 (147 rec.)

POINTS

	GAME
42	Robert Foster vs. New Mexico, Nov. 24, 1917 (7 TDs)
	SEASON
145	Bob Gaiters, 1960 (23 TDs, 7 PATs)
	CAREER
262	Dario Aguiniga, 2000-03 (47 FGs, 121 PATs]

CONSENSUS ALL-AMERICANS

None

STADIUM *The Sporting News* once rated Aggie Memorial Stadium, New Mexico State's home since 1978, as the Sun Belt Conference's best. Even so, all the losing over the years has taken its toll, and fans come and go during games; former tight end Todd Cutler remembers the crowd doubling after halftime in a 1991 game after word got out of a tie score. More often than not, a look east to the 9,000-foot peaks of the Organ Mountains is a prettier sight than the scoreboard.

RIVAL Thanks to proximity, UTEP, only 45 miles away from Las Cruces, developed into the Aggies' rival instead of the University of New Mexico (225 miles away). But for two years, money meant more than the brass spittoon and the silver spade given to the winner: in 2000, after the 80th game in the series, UTEP turned up its nose at playing the Aggies on the road so it could schedule Texas Southern at home, which brought in a bigger payday to the athletic department. In 2002, the battle of I-10 returned. The year off was sandwiched by two classics: in 2000, after perceived cheap shots, UTEP coach Gary Nord told his team not to shake hands with any Aggie players. Two years later, New Mexico State got payback, whipping UTEP 49-14.

NICKNAME As if all the talk on campus about playing the "city kids" at the University of New Mexico doesn't give it away, New Mexico State is primarily known as an agriculture school. It started in 1888 as the New Mexico College of Agriculture and Mechanic Arts. Until 2000, the men's nickname was the Aggies and the women's was the Roadrunners. Now, all are called Aggies.

MASCOT Pistol Pete derives from an Old West gunman named Frank Eaton. Driven mad by his father's murder in 1868, Eaton became one of the fastest draws around and earned the nickname Pistol Pete from fellow marksmen at Fort Gibson. During a gunfight in Albuquerque in 1881, Eaton got revenge, killing the last of the six men involved in his father's death.

UNIFORMS New Mexico State swore by its vertically striped jerseys until the uniforms were changed in 1973. The helmets have changed 12 times, the most drastic being from a white helmet to a crimson one in 1973, back to white in 1986 and back to crimson in 1990. In the last 10 years, black has been added to the usual colors of crimson and white. For the 2005 season, a new helmet design was unveiled: a white helmet with crimson stripes down the middle and a crimson "Aggies" written on the sides.

QUOTE "Coach, you haven't been an Aggie long enough." —Wide receiver Larry Harriston in 1990, when irate first-year coach Jim Hess questioned how he could have fallen out-of-bounds untouched while running toward the end zone

NEW MEXICO STATE ANNUAL STATISTICAL LEADERS

YR	RUSHING	YDS	ATT	AVG	PASSING	ATT	CMP	PCT	YDS	RECEIVING	REC	YDS	AVG
1954	Gary Walton	320	63	5.1	Charles Sanford	NA	NA	NA	314	Dick Holmes	12	260	21.7
1955	Joe Kelly	775	149	5.2	Vernon Duenas	71	27	.38	388	Dick Holmes	13	261	20.1
1956	Joe Kelly	587	126	4.7	Foy Lowery	56	27	.48	388	Bill Floyd	16	242	15.1
1957	Wally Ferguson	741	139	5.3	Ricky Alba	114	41	.36	223	Louis Kelly	11	197	17.9
1958	Dick Cohee	566	118	4.8	Charley Johnson	179	97	.54	1,184	Bob Kelly	28	343	12.3
1959	Pervis Atkins	971	130	7.5	Charley Johnson	199	105	.53	1,449	Pervis Atkins	22	301	13.7
1960	Bob Gaiters	1,338	197	6.8	Charley Johnson	199	109	.55	1,511	E.A. Sims	30	415	13.8
1961	James Pilot	1,278	191	6.7	Ron Logback	105	51	.49	796	Royce Cassell	29	519	17.9
1962	James Pilot	1,247	208	6.0	Armando Alba	101	37	.37	605	Lee Sampson	21	283	13.5
1963	James Pilot	478	91	5.3	Armando Alba	132	55	.42	860	Fred Smith	28	510	18.2
1964	Jim Bohl	519	90	5.8	Rick Norman	133	69	.52	1,049	Hartwell Menefee	24	373	15.5
1965	Jim Bohl	1,191	184	6.5	Sal Olivas	141	52	.37	594	Hartwell Menefee	40	577	14.4
1966	Jim Bohl	1,148	218	5.3	Sal Olivas	173	83	.48	1,154	Mike Carroll	15	431	28.7
1967	Doug Dalton	1,123	177	6.3	Sal Olivas	321	155	.48	2,225	Howard Taylor	49	639	13.0
1968	Ron James	1,291	225	5.7	Loy Hayes	156	67	.43	1,068	Howard Taylor	40	545	13.6
1969	Ron James	1,182	257	4.6	Rhett Putman	109	56	.51	942	Al Barnes	21	458	21.8
1970	Ron James	641	135	4.7	Rhett Putman	203	91	.45	1,435	Al Barnes	28	463	16.5
1971	Ron James	771	200	3.9	Joe Pisarcik	333	152	.46	1,973	Skip Stephenson	39	513	13.2
1972	Otis Register	525	116	4.5	Joe Pisarcik	384	183	.48	2,179	Jack Warren	43	555	12.9
1973	Jim Germany	513	117	4.4	Joe Pisarcik	221	111	.50	1,618	Hank Cook	65	1,111	17.1
1974	Jim Germany	1,096	202	5.4	Bill Bowerman	134	59	.44	1,007	Duriel Harris	29	701	24.2
1975	Jim Ringer	437	86	5.1	Cliff Olander	99	41	.41	642	Duriel Harris	34	607	17.9
1976	Jim Ringer	320	88	3.6	Cliff Olander	117	56	.48	665	Stanley Sam	31	392	12.6
1977	Rick Horacek	423	128	3.3	Rick Horacek	182	84	.46	1,111	Stanley Sam	36	514	14.3
1978	Ray Locklin	863	179	4.8	David Spriggs	318	170	.53	2,574	Jeff Evans	48	926	19.3
1979	Ray Locklin	814	176	4.6	Butch Kelly	205	99	.48	1,350	Chris Holloway	40	572	14.3
1980	Rudy Rudison	749	183	4.1	Jamie McAlister	212	106	.50	1,219	Al Tanner	32	423	13.2
1981	Rudy Rudison	559	157	3.6	Jamie McAlister	180	91	.51	1,046	Al Tanner	20	346	17.3
1982	James Hebert	781	139	5.6	Jamie McAlister	338	165	.49	1,950	Al Tanner	38	534	14.1
1983	Kim Locklin	727	139	5.2	Mark Huago	100	44	.44	460	Kim Locklin	31	279	9.0
1984	Kim Locklin	747	166	4.5	Pierre Cooper	143	64	.45	862	Kim Locklin	23	168	7.3
1985	Joe Rowley	459	80	5.7	Jim Miller	338	179	.53	2,024	Joe Rowley	57	530	9.3
1986	Pat Brown	351	73	4.8	Jim Miller	241	114	.47	1,207	Bennie Thomas	37	416	11.2
1987	Anthony Singleton	415	83	5.0	Phil Vinson	275	114	.41	1,256	Larry Harriston	35	491	14.0
1988	Anthony Singleton	652	135	4.8	Mike Reneau	214	94	.44	1,179	Alvin Warren	38	462	12.2
1989	Anthony Singleton	608	166	3.7	Phil Vinson	289	144	.50	1,723	Jim Williams	45	445	9.9
1990	Jimmie Mitchell	832	171	4.9	David Chisum	374	187	.50	2,277	Alvin Warren	49	707	14.4
1991	Jimmie Mitchell	385	99	3.9	David Chisum	205	112	.55	1,524	Todd Cutler	44	718	16.3
1992	Lawerence Truehill	593	146	4.1	Charles Puleri	349	189	.54	2,788	Atlas Reagor	35	635	18.1
1993	Troy Dublin	856	208	4.1	Cody Ledbetter	300	158	.53	2,177	Lucious Davis	36	766	21.3
1994	Brian Pizula	564	126	4.5	Cody Ledbetter	247	120	.49	1,578	Lucious Davis	54	985	18.2
1995	Denvis Manns	1,120	157	7.1	Cody Ledbetter	453	259	.57	3,501	Lucious Davis	57	1,018	17.9
1996	Denvis Manns	1,086	269	4.0	Chad Salisbury	341	172	.50	2,291	Duane Gregory	68	890	13.1
1997	Denvis Manns	1,017	194	5.2	Ty Houghtaling	301	152	.50	1,985	Duane Gregory	46	628	13.7
1998	Denvis Manns	1,469	269	5.5	Ty Houghtaling	267	130	.49	1,829	Ryan Shaw	43	672	15.6
1999	Chris Barnes	519	104	5.0	K.C. Enzminger	236	112	.47	1,878	Ryan Shaw	44	844	19.2
2000	Chris Barnes	1,131	171	6.6	K.C. Enzminger	236	111	.47	1,454	P.J. Winston	34	553	16.3
2001	Kenton Keith	839	183	4.6	K.C. Enzminger	235	121	.51	1,160	P.J. Winston	46	570	12.4
2002	Paul Dombrowski	868	189	4.6	Paul Dombrowski	158	95	.60	1,327	H.B. Briscoe	50	880	17.6
2003	Eric Higgins	753	146	5.2	Buck Pierce	170	118	.69	1,510	Ronshay Jenkins	57	928	16.3
2004	Muammar Ali	572	137	4.2	Buck Pierce	285	191	.67	2,253	Tim Tolbert	28	420	15.0

Receiving leaders based on receptions
The NCAA began including postseason stats in 2002

THE SCHOOLS

NEW MEXICO STATE ALL-TIME SCORES

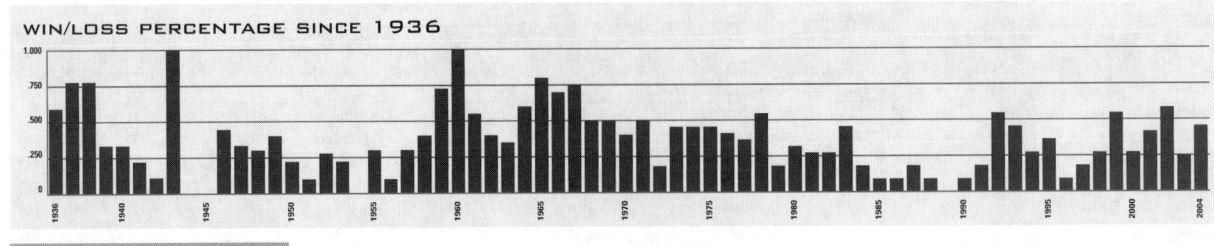

WIN/LOSS PERCENTAGE SINCE 1936

W.M. CLUTE
1893 (.000)   0-1

1893   0-1-0
J1		at New Mexico	6	18 *

1894
NO TEAM

ALFRED HOLT
1895 (1.000)   2-0

1895   2-0-0
U	●	El Paso AC	1	0 *f*
U	●	El Paso HS	10	4

NO HEAD COACH

1896   0-2-0
U		Fort Bliss	0	10
U		Las Cruces	0	6

CHARLES M. BARBER
1897-98 (.700)   3-1-1

1897   1-0-1
U	=	at Fort Bliss	0	0
U	●	Fort Bliss	10	0

1898   2-1-0
U	●	El Paso	46	0
U	●	at Albuquerque AC	11	0
U		at Albuq. Indian Sch.	0	6

JOHN O. MILLER
1899, 1901-07 (.750)   16-4-4

1899   1-0-0
U	●	U.S. Indian Sch.	38	0

WILLIAM A. SUTHERLAND
1900 (.500)   3-3-1

1900   3-3-1
U		at N.M. Highlands	5	6
U		Albuq. Indian Sch.	0	11
U		Las Cruces	16	0
U	●	Las Cruces	6	0
U	●	Organ	22	5
U		at El Paso	0	5
U	=	at El Paso	0	0

JOHN O. MILLER

1901   2-1-0
U		at N.M. Highlands	0	6
U	●	at Albuq. Indian Sch.	5	0
U	●	at Albuq. Guard	33	0

1902   0-1-2
U	=	at Albuq. Indian Sch.	0	0
U	=	Santa Fe Indian Sch.	0	0
U		Albuq. Indian Sch.	0	6

1903   2-0-1
U	●	Las Cruces	23	0
U	=	Santa Fe Indian Sch.	0	0
U	●	El Paso AA	11	0

1904   1-2-1
U	●	Mesilla	36	0
U	=	at El Paso AA	0	0
U		Albuquerque AC	0	22
U		Fort Bliss	6	11

1905   3-0-0
U	●	Fort Bliss	17	0
N30	●	New Mexico	40	0
U	●	New Mexico Tech	39	0

1906   4-0-0
U	●	El Paso AA	5	0
U	●	New Mexico Tech	19	5
U	●	at New Mexico Tech	22	2
N29	●	at New Mexico	25	5

1907   3-0-0
U	●	El Paso AA	31	6
U	●	at El Paso AA	29	0
U	●	N.M. Military	28	0

W.G. HUMMELL
1908 (.667)   4-2

1908   4-2-0
U		El Paso AA	0	5
U	●	at New Mexico Tech	62	5
U	●	Fort Bliss	35	0
U	●	at New Mexico Tech	39	10
N21		New Mexico	6	10
U	●	at N.M. Military	37	12

J.H. SQUIRES
1909 (.300)   1-3-1

1909   1-3-1
U	=	El Paso Military	0	0
U		Arizona	0	6
U	●	New Mexico Tech	19	0
U		at N.M. Military	0	34
N25		at New Mexico	0	51

ARTHUR H. BADENOCH
1910-13 (.865)   22-3-1

1910   3-2-0
U	●	at El Paso Military	12	0
U	●	El Paso Military	35	0
U	●	at New Mexico Tech	12	0
U		at Arizona	2	18
U		N.M. Military	0	5

1911   7-0-0
U	●	El Paso Military	3	0
U	●	El Paso YMCA	37	0
U	●	Arizona	3	0
U	●	El Paso HS	75	0
N12	●	New Mexico	10	6
U	●	at El Paso YMCA	28	0
U	●	at N.M. Military	36	0

1912   5-1-0
U	●	El Paso HS	43	0
U	●	El Paso Military	49	0
U	●	2nd Cavalry	116	0
U	●	Arizona	21	7 *
N16	●	at New Mexico	27	0
U		N.M. Military	0	10

1913   7-0-1
U	●	El Paso HS	7	2
U	●	13th Cavalry	51	6
U	=	El Paso HS	0	0
U	●	at Arizona	12	6
U	●	El Paso HS	13	3
U	●	Catholic AA	13	0
N8	●	New Mexico	13	0
U	●	at N.M. Military	15	7

CLARENCE W. RUSSELL
1914-16 (.500)   7-7-1

1914   4-2-1
U		at El Paso HS	0	6
U	●	El Paso HS	17	0
U	●	at El Paso YMCA	5	0
O31	●	Texas-El Paso	19	0
U	●	N.M. Military	32	6
U		at Arizona	0	10
D5	=	at New Mexico	7	7

1915   3-1-0
O30	●	Texas-El Paso	33	0 *
U	●	Arizona	3	0
U	●	at N.M. Military	17	7
N20		at New Mexico	0	13

1916   0-4-0
U		N.M. Military	7	16
U		at Arizona	0	74
N25		Texas-El Paso	3	6
N30		at New Mexico	0	51

JOHN G. GRIFFITH
1917 (.667)   4-2

1917   4-2-0
U	●	7th Cavalry	3	0
U	●	El Paso HS	21	0
U	●	7th Cavalry	84	0
U		at Arizona	7	26
U		at N.M. Military	6	46
N24	●	New Mexico	110	3

1918
NO TEAM WWI

ANTHONY SAVAGE
1919 (.417)   2-3-1

1919   2-3-1
U		Quartermaster Corps	0	6
U	●	82nd Aty.	27	6
U		Arizona	0	33
U	●	New Mexico Tech	54	0
U	=	N.M. Military	0	0
N27		at New Mexico	2	24

ARTHUR J. BERGMAN
1920-22 (.694)   12-5-1

1920   5-1-1
U		at Arizona	0	41
N11	●	at Texas-El Paso	12	7
U	●	8th Cavalry	19	0
U	●	Quartermaster Corps	27	0
U	●	New Mexico Tech	80	0
U	=	at N.M. Military	7	7
D4	●	New Mexico	14	7

1921   2-2-0
O21	●	New Mexico Tech	32	0
N5		Arizona	0	31
N11	●	at Texas-El Paso	13	0
N24		at New Mexico	0	6

1922   5-2-0
S30	●	at Hardin-Simmons	6	0
O14	●	Menual Indian Sch.	56	0
O28		at Saint Mary's-Cal	6	19
N4		at Arizona	7	21
N11	●	Texas-El Paso	64	0
N18	●	at N.M. Military	25	7
N30	●	New Mexico	7	0

ROBERT R. BROWN
1923-25 (.759)   20-6-1

1923   8-0-0
O6	●	El Paso HS	10	0
O13	●	E.P. Garden Grocers	33	0
O20	●	Hardin-Simmons	13	6
O27	●	Beaumont Army Hosp.	32	6
N3	●	at Montezuma Coll.	73	3
N10	●	at Texas-El Paso	23	2
N17	●	at New Mexico	6	0
U	●	N.M. Military	7	0

1924   7-3-0
U		Las Cruces HS	6	7
S26	●	Beaumont Army Hosp.	45	7
O4	●	El Paso HS	33	2
O11	●	El Paso JC	36	0
O18	●	El Paso Grocers	7	0
O25		at Arizona	0	7
N1	●	Montezuma Coll.	89	0
N8		at Texas-El Paso	19	0
N15	●	New Mexico	6	0
N27		at N.M. Military	0	7

1925   5-3-1
S26	●	Las Cruces HS	44	0
O3		at El Paso HS	7	3
O10	●	Beaumont Army Hosp.	40	0
O17	●	Western New Mexico	14	0
O24		Sul Ross	12	13
O31		at Arizona	0	33
N7	=	at Texas-El Paso	6	6
N21		at New Mexico	9	20
N27	●	N.M. Military	19	0

ARTHUR L. BURKHOLDER
1926 (.611)   5-3-1

1926   5-3-1
O2	●	El Paso HS	7	0
O9	●	El Paso JC	20	0
O16		at Sul Ross	7	37
U	●	El Paso Grocers	7	0
O23		Arizona	0	7
O30	●	Western New Mexico	27	0
N6		at Texas-El Paso	10	8
N13	=	New Mexico	6	6
N30		at N.M. Military	6	7

TED R. COFFMAN
1927-28 (.412)   7-10

1927   3-5-0
U	●	Beaumont Army Hosp.	80	0
O8	●	New Mexico Tech	40	0
O15		Sul Ross	6	19
O21	●	Western New Mexico	31	0
O29		at Arizona	6	33
N11		at Texas-El Paso	7	19
N18		New Mexico	9	26
N24		N.M. Military	6	10

1928   4-5-0
S26	●	Army Artillery	57	0
O4	●	Western New Mexico	92	0
O13		at Sul Ross	0	33
O20	●	Montezuma Coll.	25	0
O27		at New Mexico	13	14
N2	●	New Mexico Tech	39	7
N9		at Texas-El Paso	0	6
N17		at Arizona	0	40
N29		at N.M. Military	0	40

GERALD H. HINES
1929-39 (.590)   54-36-10

1929   3-2-3
S28	●	Gila JC	60	0
O12	●	Sul Ross	6	0
O18	=	Montezuma Coll.	0	0
O26		at Arizona	0	28
N1	●	New Mexico Tech	52	7
N9		at Texas-El Paso	0	8
N16	=	New Mexico	7	7
N21	=	N.M. Military	7	7

1930 — 5-3-0

Date		Opponent		
S28	●	N.M. Highlands	25	0
O3		at Texas Tech	0	14
O18	●	No. Arizona	6	9
O25	●	Arizona State	7	0
N1	●	Gila JC	38	0
N8	●	at New Mexico	14	6
N15		Texas-El Paso	0	25
N27	●	at N.M. Military	25	19

1931-1961
BORDER

1931 — 6-4-0 (1-2-0)

S19	●	El Paso Nat. Guard	19	0
S26	●	at N.M. Highlands	33	6
O3	●	Texas Tech	0	7
O10		at No. Arizona	6	13
O17		at Arizona State	7	25
O30	●	Gila JC	45	0
N7		New Mexico	13	6
N14	●	Wayland	20	6
N21		at Texas-El Paso	0	20
N28	●	N.M. Military	12	7

1932 — 4-5-1 (1-2-1)

S24	●	El Paso Nat. Guard	24	0
O1		at San Diego Marines	0	12
O8		at Arizona	7	12
O15	●	at New Mexico Tech	108	0
O22	=	at New Mexico	7	7 *
O29		Texas-El Paso	6	31
N5		Arizona State	6	7
N11	●	No. Arizona	7	0
N18	●	N.M. Highlands	39	0
N26		at N.M. Military	6	19

1933 — 2-6-0 (0-4-0)

S29	●	Wayland	63	0
O6	●	at N.M. Highlands	14	4
O14		at No. Arizona	7	13
O27		Arizona	0	6
N4		Texas-El Paso	0	9
N11		at Arizona State	7	19
N18		New Mexico	7	14
N30		N.M. Military	2	7

1934 — 4-1-3 (0-1-3)

S28	●	Wayland	52	0
O6	●	N.M. Highlands	59	0
O13	●	Sul Ross	13	0
O19	=	No. Arizona	6	6
O26	=	at Arizona	0	0
N10	=	Arizona State	7	7
N17	●	at New Mexico	6	12
N26	●	N.M. Military	26	0

1935 — 7-1-2 (4-1-0)

S28	●	Ea. New Mexico	34	0
O5	●	at No. Arizona	7	0
O12	●	at N.M. Highlands	56	6
O19		Arizona State	7	6
O26		at Arizona	6	9
N2	●	N.M. Military	47	7
N11	●	New Mexico	32	0
N22	=	Western New Mexico	0	0
N28	●	Texas-El Paso	7	0
SUN BOWL				
J1	=	Hardin-Simmons	14	14

1936 — 6-4-1 (3-2-0)

S25	●	Panhandle St.	58	6
O2	●	Adams St.	58	0
O9		No. Arizona	41	0
O17		at N.M. Military	6	13
O24		at Arizona	7	28
O31	=	San Diego State	7	7
N7	●	at Arizona State	20	6
N14	●	at New Mexico	7	6
N20	●	Western New Mexico	27	0
N26		at Texas-El Paso	7	27
D25		at Santa Barbara	14	25

1937 — 7-2-0 (4-1-0)

S24		Texas-El Paso	14	0
O1	●	Western New Mexico	34	0
O8	●	New Mexico	5	0
O16	●	at No. Arizona	7	0
O23		at San Diego State	0	20
O30		at Arizona	12	27
N13	●	Western St.	33	6
N25	●	Arizona State	14	0
D4	●	Santa Barbara	9	7

1938 — 7-2-0 (4-1-0)

S23		Montana St.	27	7
S30		Central Arkansas	6	12
O8	●	at Arizona	7	6
O22		at Arizona State	14	12
O28	●	No. Arizona	34	0
N4	●	Western New Mexico	43	7
N12		at New Mexico	2	6
N24	●	at Texas-El Paso	13	9
D2	●	Drake	20	16

1939 — 3-6-0 (1-4-0)

S22	●	Fort Hayes	33	7
S28		at Central Arkansas	12	3
O7	●	at No. Arizona	26	13
O14		at Arizona	3	20
O20		Arizona State	0	7
N4		at Oklahoma State	0	20
N10		New Mexico	6	9
N17		Hardin-Simmons	13	28
N25		Texas-El Paso	0	34

1940 — 3-6-0 (1-4-0)

S20	●	Western New Mexico	12	0
S27	●	Howard Payne	0	10
O5		at Arizona	0	41
O19		at Arizona State	6	42
O25	●	No. Arizona	13	0
N1		Bradley	7	14
N9		at New Mexico	6	39
N23	●	Redlands	25	14
N28		at Texas-El Paso	26	40

1941 — 2-7-0 (0-6-0)

S19	●	N.M. Highlands	52	0
S26	●	Western New Mexico	7	6
O4		at Arizona	0	47
O11		at West Texas St.	0	51
O18		Arizona State	14	19
O25		at Bradley	0	26
N1		at No. Arizona	7	27
N8		New Mexico	0	28
N22		at Texas-El Paso	13	24 *

1942 — 1-8-0 (0-6-0)

S19	●	Western New Mexico	27	6
S26		at Arizona	0	53
O3		McMurry	0	12
O10		at New Mexico	0	32
O24		at Arizona State	0	20
O31		West Texas St.	0	23
N11		Kirtland AFB	0	13
N21		No. Arizona	0	3
N26		at Texas-El Paso	6	61

1943 — 4-0-0 (0-0-0)

S25	●	El Paso All Stars	32	6
O2	●	Station Hospital	21	14
O9	●	51st General Hosp.	27	0
O16	●	51st General Hosp.	21	0

1944-1945
NO TEAM WWII

1946 — 4-5-0 (1-4-0)

S21	●	Western New Mexico	37	0
S28		at Tulsa	0	52
O12		New Mexico	6	7
O19		at No. Arizona	6	14
O26		at West Texas St.	14	21
N2		Arizona State	7	14
N9		Sul Ross	26	25
N16	●	No. Colorado	20	7
N28	●	at Texas-El Paso	14	7

1947 — 3-6-0 (1-4-0)

S19	●	McMurry	7	22
S26	●	at No. Colorado	13	14
O3	●	Western New Mexico	48	0
O11		at New Mexico	0	20
O17	●	Sul Ross	27	14
O24		West Texas St.	7	34
N1		at Arizona State	12	33
N8	●	No. Arizona	26	6
N22		at Texas-El Paso	0	26

1948 — 3-7-0 (0-4-0)

S18		at No. Arizona	7	13
S25	●	at Colorado State	6	40 *
O2	●	Fort Bliss	33	12
O9		at New Mexico	0	61
O16		at Sul Ross	12	47
O29	●	N.M. Highlands	26	0
N5		Arizona State	7	52
N12	●	Fort Hayes St.	27	12
N19		W. Colo. St.	13	61
N25		at Texas-El Paso	7	92

1949 — 4-6-0 (1-4-0)

S17	●	White Sands	68	0
S24		at Arizona	7	40
S30	●	New Mexico	13	14
O6	●	N.M. Military	45	28
O15		at San Diego State	18	39
O29	●	N.M. Highlands	40	12
N5		at Arizona State	32	68
N12	●	No. Arizona	35	0
N19		Colorado State	0	45
N26		at Texas-El Paso	7	69

1950 — 2-7-0 (1-4-0)

S16		Hardin-Simmons	0	48
S23		at Texas-El Paso	0	40
S29		Howard Payne	6	33
O7		at New Mexico	13	26
O14	=	at No. Arizona	20	14
O21	●	N.M. Military	27	7
O28		at Arizona State	0	49
N11		SW. Oklahoma	16	18
N18		Colorado Mines	13	14

1951 — 1-9-0 (1-5-0)

S15		at Arizona	13	67
S22		Stephen F. Austin	7	27
S29		at Texas-El Paso	7	41
O6		New Mexico	0	20
O12		at Colorado Mines	0	7
O20		at Bradley	6	34
O27		at Arizona State	0	46
N3	●	No. Arizona	48	12
N10		West Texas St.	20	50
N17		McMurry	14	33

1952 — 2-6-1 (1-2-1)

S20		Howard Payne	20	7
S27		Arizona	12	62
O4		New Mexico	0	23
O11		West Texas St.	7	45
O18	=	Texas-El Paso	20	20
N1	●	No. Arizona	33	9
N8		McMurry	14	27
N15		Midwestern Texas	6	28
N27		Wichita St.	6	34

1953 — 2-7-0 (1-4-0)

S19		at Wyoming	0	47
S26	●	Colorado College	12	7
O3		at Arizona	7	46
O10		McMurry	12	26
O17		at Texas-El Paso	0	39
O24		at Texas Tech	0	71
N7		New Mexico	6	28
N14		at Hardin-Simmons	0	39
N21	●	West Texas St.	19	13

1954 — 0-9-0 (0-4-0)

S18		at Arizona	0	58
S25		Hardin-Simmons	0	27
O2		Sul Ross Pec	18	42
O9		Howard Payne	7	34
O16		at West Texas St.	7	41
O23		San Diego Marines	7	33
O30		Texas-El Paso	7	12
N13		SW. Oklahoma	14	20
N20		at New Mexico	27	39

1955 — 3-7-0 (0-4-0)

S17		at New Mexico	7	14
S24		N.M. Highlands	12	19
O1		at Hardin-Simmons	0	39
O8		at Howard Payne	12	34
O15		West Texas St.	6	32
O22	●	Corpus Christi NAS	19	7
O29		at Texas-El Paso	6	41
N5	●	Adams St.	47	8
N12	●	San Diego State	26	6
N19		at Arizona State	6	26

1956 — 1-9-0 (0-4-0)

S15		at Tulsa	6	27
S22		New Mexico	6	14
S29		at Cal Poly SLO	7	32
O6		Arizona State	7	28
O13		McMurry	13	14
O20		at West Texas St.	0	45
O27		Texas-El Paso	7	51
N10		at Nebraska Omaha	20	21
N16	●	Nebraska Wesleyan	46	6
N24		Hardin-Simmons	19	38

1957 — 3-7-0 (0-4-0)

S21		at New Mexico	7	25
S28		Cal Tech	8	10
O5	●	Corpus Christi NAS	32	0
O19		West Texas St.	7	25
O26		at Texas-El Paso	12	42
N2		at Arizona State	0	21
N9		McMurry	6	26
N16		Nebraska Omaha	39	6
N23	●	Western St.	26	21
N28		at Hardin-Simmons	20	29

1958 — 4-6-0 (1-3-0)

S13		Trinity	0	20
S20		New Mexico	7	16
S26	●	U. of Mexico	28	14
O4		at North Texas	12	43
O11	●	at Western St.	27	24
O25		Texas-El Paso	17	16
N1		at Arizona State	19	33
N8	●	McMurry	10	7
N22	●	at West Texas St.	32	39
N28		at Hardin-Simmons	20	26

1959 — 8-3-0 (2-2-0)

S12	●	No. Arizona	35	0
S19	●	at New Mexico	29	12
S26		at Tulsa	27	28
O3	●	McMurry	43	11
O10	●	at Trinity	20	18
O24		at Texas-El Paso	15	20
O31		at Arizona State	31	35
N14	●	Hardin-Simmons	42	13
N21	●	West Texas St.	35	13
N28	●	at U. of Mexico	55	0
SUN BOWL				
D31	●	North Texas	28	8

1960 — 11-0-0 (4-0-0)

S10	●	U. of Mexico	41	0
S17	●	Tulsa	38	18
S24	●	Trinity	45	0
O8	●	New Mexico	34	0
O15	●	McMurry	47	17
O22	●	Wichita St.	40	8
O29	●	Arizona State	27	24
N12	●	West Texas St.	35	15
N19	●	Hardin-Simmons	40	3
N26	●	Texas-El Paso	27	15
SUN BOWL				
D31	●	Utah State	20	13

1961 — 5-4-1 (2-1-0)

S16	●	No. Arizona	56	6
S23	●	at New Mexico	7	41
S30	●	McMurry	35	7
O7	=	at North Texas	14	14
O14	●	Pacific	70	19
O21		at Wichita St.	27	42
O28	●	at Texas-El Paso	42	6
N4		at Trinity	14	17
N18		West Texas St.	22	35
N25	●	Hardin-Simmons	54	8

1962-1971 INDEPENDENT

1962 4-6-0 (0-0-0)

S15		at New Mexico	17	28
S22	●	Pacific	28	6
S29		at Wisconsin	13	69
O5	●	at Detroit	21	14
O13		at Wichita St.	6	24
O20		at West Texas St.	12	20
O27	●	North Texas	48	12
N3	●	Trinity	26	20
N10		Texas-El Paso	0	21
N17		at Arizona State	20	45

1963 3-6-1

S14	●	Ea. New Mexico	21	0
S28		at Arizona State	13	14
O5		at Texas-El Paso	13	14
O12	●	at Trinity	40	8
O19	●	New Mexico	13	12
O26		Hardin-Simmons	6	41
N2		Wichita St.	7	47
N9	=	at West Texas St.	24	24
N16		Utah State	6	7
N28		Sul Ross	15	42

1964 6-4-0

S19	●	Texas Arlington	3	0
S26		at Utah State	0	76
O3		at Florida State	0	36
O10	●	Trinity	14	6
O17	●	at North Texas	13	7
O24		at New Mexico	14	18
O31	●	at Ea. New Mexico	20	0
N7		at Lamar	14	21
N14	●	West Texas St.	40	0
N21	●	Texas-El Paso	13	7

1965 8-2-0

S18	●	Texas Arlington	27	10
S25	●	Louisiana Tech	21	20
O2		at Texas-El Paso	6	21
O9	●	at Pacific	14	6
O16	●	at Wichita St.	45	20
O23	●	at West Texas St.	10	2
O30	●	Ea. New Mex. St.	41	7
N6		at Texas Tech	9	48
N13	●	New Mexico	20	6
N20	●	North Texas	43	13

1966 7-3-0

S10	●	Howard Payne	35	7
S17		at North Texas	21	25
S24	●	Texas Arlington	23	10
O1	●	at Utah State	23	7
O8	●	Pacific	49	23
O15	●	Wichita St.	45	7
O22		at West Texas St.	14	17
O29	●	at Ea. New Mexico	50	13
N12	●	at New Mexico	47	12
N19		at Texas-El Paso	14	28

1967 7-2-1

S16	●	Lamar	17	6
S23		at Texas Arlington	14	15
S30	●	Utah State	10	9
O7	=	North Texas	31	31
O14	●	at Wichita St.	27	14
O21	●	West Texas St.	31	10
O28	●	Louisiana Tech	48	7
N4		at Texas-El Paso	24	46
N11	●	No. Arizona	90	0
N18	●	at New Mexico	54	7

JIM WOOD
1968-72 (.413) 21-30-1

1968 5-5-0

S14		at Utah State	12	28
S21		at North Texas	20	47
S28	●	Texas Arlington	21	20
O5	●	at Lamar	16	14
O19		Texas-El Paso	14	30
O26	●	at Northern Illinois	27	13
N2		West Texas St.	14	23
N9	●	Wichita St.	47	21
N16	●	at New Mexico	33	6
N28		at Louisiana Tech	24	42

1969 5-5-0

S20	●	Howard Payne	21	14
S27	●	at Texas Arlington	16	7
O4		at Lamar	7	9
O11	●	at Wichita St.	23	6
O18		North Texas	12	30
O25		at West Texas St.	16	17
N8	●	at Texas-El Paso	41	38
N15		at San Diego State	21	70
N22		New Mexico	21	24
N27	●	Colorado State	21	20

1970 4-6-0

S12		Colorado State	9	28
S19	●	Texas Arlington	35	7
S26		at SMU	21	34
O3		at Texas-El Paso	14	21
O10	●	No. Arizona	57	13
O17		at New Mexico	17	24
O24		at West Texas St.	7	37
O31	●	at North Texas	32	31
N14	●	Lamar	69	37
N28		Utah State	21	45

1971 5-5-1

S11	●	Drake	7	3
S18		at Utah State	0	34
S25	●	North Texas	10	0
O2		at SMU	25	28
O9	=	at New Mexico	35	35
O16		Texas-El Paso	7	14
O23	●	at Texas Arlington	20	6
O30		Idaho	14	19
N6	●	West Texas St.	50	24
N13	●	at Wichita St.	31	7
N27		at Colorado State	21	38

1972-1982 MISSOURI VALLEY

1972 2-9-0 (1-3-0)

S9		Utah State	14	48
S16		at New Mexico	20	55
S23		Fresno State	17	49
S30		at Texas-El Paso	20	21
O7		at SMU	6	55
O14	|	at West Texas St.	14	63
O21	●	at Texas Arlington	17	12
O28	|	Drake	10	28
N4		Lamar	19	24
N11	● |	at North Texas	36	22
N18	|	Wichita St.	20	23

JIM BRADLEY
1973-77 (.427) 23-31-1

1973 5-6-0 (3-2-0)

S1	● |	at Drake	27	12
S8	●	Lamar	24	7
S15		at New Mexico	6	48
S22		at Colorado State	27	31
S29	● |	Wichita St.	44	18
O6	●	at Texas-El Paso	27	23
O13		at San Diego State	0	27
O20	|	at Tulsa	14	52
O27	|	North Texas	7	27
N3	● |	West Texas St.	56	14
N10		Utah State	12	40

1974 5-6-0 (2-3-0)

S7	● |	at Wichita St.	13	12
S14	●	So. Illinois	28	9
S21	● |	at West Texas St.	41	0
S28	●	Texas Arlington	42	14
O5		Fresno State	7	9
O12	●	Texas-El Paso	14	13
O19	|	at North Texas	19	24
O26	|	Drake	28	29
N2		at New Mexico	24	26
N9	|	at Tulsa	7	28
N16		at San Diego State	14	35

1975 5-6-0 (2-2-0)

S6	● |	Drake	14	10
S13	●	at Texas-El Paso	31	24
S20	●	at Lamar	17	14
S27		at La. Lafayette	7	31
O4	|	Tulsa	7	35
O11	● |	at Wichita St.	26	24
O18		at San Diego State	3	48
O25	●	Texas Arlington	16	0
N8	|	at West Texas St.	10	38
N15		North Texas	20	24
N22		New Mexico	28	52

1976 4-6-1 (2-1-1)

S4	● |	at Drake	30	29
S11	●	Texas-El Paso	13	10
S18		at Texas Arlington	10	21
S25		Lamar	17	21
O2	|	at Tulsa	7	32
O9		at Idaho	6	33
O23		North Texas	14	25
O30	●	at New Mexico	16	7
N6	● |	Wichita St.	26	6
N13		at Fresno State	0	44
N20	= |	West Texas St.	13	13

1977 4-7-0 (3-2-0)

S3	● |	So. Illinois	29	7
S10	†	Arkansas LR	10	53
S17	● |	Wichita St.	24	12
S24	● |	Drake	35	9
O1		at Texas-El Paso	21	23
O8	|	West Texas St.	14	17
O22	●	at Texas Arlington	7	6
O29		New Mexico	13	35
N5		at North Texas	17	45
N12	|	at Tulsa	24	27
N19		Idaho	44	47

GIL KRUEGER
1978-82 (.318) 17-37-1

1978 6-5-0 (5-1-0)

S9	● |	at Indiana St.	14	9
S16	●	Texas-El Paso	35	32
S23		North Texas	21	22
S30	|	at So. Illinois	39	43
O7		Texas Arlington	17	28
O14	● |	Tulsa	23	20
O21		at New Mexico	20	35
O28	● |	at Wichita St.	31	21
N4	● |	Drake	21	20
N11		at Hawaii	20	35
N25	● |	at West Texas St.	33	31

1979 2-9-0 (1-4-0)

S1	● |	Wichita St.	23	13
S8	|	at Drake	13	14
S15	●	at Texas-El Paso	14	13
S22		Indiana St.	23	40
S29		New Mexico	16	30
O6		at Nebraska	0	57
O13		at North Texas	7	21
O20		Texas Arlington	14	42
N3	|	West Texas St.	21	54
N10	|	at Tulsa	16	38
N17	|	at So. Illinois	28	45

1980 3-7-1 (1-4-1)

S6		at La. Lafayette	12	14
S13	●	Texas-El Paso	6	3
S20	● |	So. Illinois	18	17
S27		at New Mexico	19	52
O4	|	at West Texas St.	15	17
O18	●	at Texas Arlington	30	10
O25	|	Drake	22	28
N1		North Texas	28	38
N8	= |	at Wichita St.	14	14
N15	|	at Indiana St.	28	33
N22	|	Tulsa	20	21

1981 3-8-0 (1-5-0)

S5	●	at Texas-El Paso	14	7
S12		at Texas Arlington	13	26
S19	|	Indiana St.	6	41
O3	|	Wichita St.	20	24
O10		at North Texas	16	38
O17	● |	at Illinois St.	20	10
O24		New Mexico	13	17
O31	●	Western Illinois	31	24
N7	|	at Tulsa	0	31
N14	|	So. Illinois	16	23
N21	|	West Texas St.	9	45

1982 3-8-0 (1-4-0)

S4		Texas-El Paso	17	20
S11	|	at Indiana St.	10	14
S18		at Nebraska	0	68
S25		at Colorado State	17	28
O2	● |	Illinois St.	26	17
O9	|	Tulsa	14	31
O16	|	at Wichita St.	26	28
O23		at New Mexico	14	66
O30	●	No. Arizona	34	32
N6	●	North Texas	30	19
N13	|	at West Texas St.	28	30

1983 INDEPENDENT

FRED ZECHMAN
1983-85 (.242) 8-25

1983 5-6-0

S3		at Texas-El Paso	9	20
S10	●	Louisiana Tech	15	7
S17		at North Texas	3	49
S24		New Mexico	10	31
O1	●	at Iowa State	24	17
O8		at Tulsa	10	24
O15	●	Drake	42	23
O22		at Texas Arlington	7	28
O29		at So. Illinois	3	41
N5	●	Wichita St.	62	28
N19	●	West Texas St.	26	24

1984-2000 BIG WEST

1984 2-9-0 (1-6-0)

S1	|	at San Jose State	0	14
S8		at New Mexico	21	61
S15	|	Nevada-Las Vegas	21	28 †
S22		at Drake	28	35
S29	|	at Fresno State	24	53
O6	● ||	Texas-El Paso	27	16
O13	|	at Pacific	7	21
O20	|	Long Beach St.	13	43
O26		West Texas St.	13	21
N3	●	at Wichita St.	31	24
N17	|	Fullerton St.	0	20

1985 1-10-0 (0-7-0)

S7	|	at San Jose State	3	32
S14		New Mexico	27	34
S21	●	at Texas-El Paso	22	20
S28		Arkansas LR	13	45
O5	|	Pacific	10	19
O19	|	Fresno State	21	48
O26	|	at Long Beach St.	17	38
O31	|	at Nevada-Las Vegas	12	17
N9	|	at Fullerton St.	17	21
N16		West Texas St.	25	55
N23	|	Utah State	23	40

MIKE KNOLL
1986-89 (.091) 4-40

1986 1-10-0 (1-6-0)

A30		Angelo St.	14	20
S6	● |	Fullerton St.	24	21
S13		Texas-El Paso	33	47
S20	|	at Pacific	14	41
S27		Arkansas LR	11	42
O4	|	at Utah State	9	42
O11	|	at Fresno State	14	17
O18	|	Long Beach St.	7	38
O25		at New Mexico	14	45
N1	|	San Jose State	7	45
N15	|	Nevada-Las Vegas	42	58

1987 2-9-0 (0-7-0)

S5		at Texas-El Paso	0	31
S12	●	New Mexico	17	14
S26		Angelo St.	17	21
O3	|	at Pacific	7	23
O10	|	at San Jose State	6	57
O17	|	at Long Beach St.	6	33
O24	●	McNeese State	32	13
O31	|	at Fullerton St.	14	48
N7	|	Utah State	6	25
N14	|	Nevada-Las Vegas	6	29
N21	|	Fresno State	10	34

1988 1-10-0 (0-7-0)

S3	|	San Jose State	0	51
S10		New Mexico	34	36
S17	|	at Fresno State	0	41
S24	|	at Utah State	20	32
O1	●	at Kansas	42	29
O15	|	at Nevada-Las Vegas	20	28
O22	|	Fullerton St.	3	24
O29		Texas-El Paso	9	42
N5		at Akron	7	52
N12	|	Long Beach St.	16	21
N19	|	at Pacific	20	21

1989 0-11-0 (0-7-0)

S2		at Oklahoma	3	73
S9		at New Mexico	13	45
S16		Texas-El Paso	27	29
S23	|	at Nevada-Las Vegas	14	26
O7	|	at Long Beach St.	48	55
O14		at Tulsa	13	34
O21	|	Utah State	13	28
O28	|	at San Jose State	6	34
N4	|	at Fullerton St.	10	45
N11	|	Fresno State	5	45
N18	|	Pacific	10	14

JIM HESS
1990-96 (.286)   22-55

1990   1-10-0 (1-6-0)
S1		New Mexico	12 29
S8		at Texas-El Paso	24 27
S15		at Kansas State	7 52
S22		at Fresno State	3 42
O6		at Long Beach St.	27 31
O13		Nevada-Las Vegas	20 24
O20		at Pacific	24 62
O27		Tulsa	10 35
N3		at Utah State	10 55
N10		San Jose State	20 56
N17	●	Fullerton St.	43 9

1991   2-9-0 (2-5-0)
S14		Texas-El Paso	21 22
S21		at Kansas	14 54
S28		at New Mexico	10 17
O5		at Oregon	6 29
O12		San Jose State	13 39
O19		Fresno State	28 42
O26		at Pacific	20 27
N2	●	at Fullerton St.	35 12
N9	●	Long Beach St.	28 24
N16		at Nevada-Las Vegas	28 38
N23		Utah State	21 46

1992   6-5-0 (3-3-0)
S5	●	Weber St.	37 21
S12	●	New Mexico	42 39
S19	●	at Texas-El Paso	30 24
S26		at Utah State	21 48
O3		at Kansas State	0 19
O10	●	Nevada-Las Vegas	40 10
O17		Pacific	17 49
O24		at Nevada	21 35
O31		at Arizona	0 30
N14	●	Fullerton St.	44 31
N21	●	at San Jose State	34 24

1993   5-6-0 (4-3-0)
S4		at Kansas State	10 34
S11	●	at Arkansas State	22 19
S18	●	Texas-El Paso	31 14
S25		at New Mexico	7 42
O9	●	Northern Illinois	24 17
O16		San Jose State	13 52
O23	●	at Pacific	27 23
O30	●	at Nevada-Las Vegas	52 40
N6		at Auburn	14 55
N13		Nevada	14 34
N20		Utah State	17 20

1994   3-8-0 (2-5-0)
S3		at Florida	21 70
S10		at Arizona	0 44
S17	●	at Texas-El Paso	23 22
S24		Arkansas State	24 17
O1		Nevada-Las Vegas	27 31
O8		at Northern Illinois	27 48
O15		at Nevada	24 45
O22		New Mexico	31 56
N5	●	at San Jose State	24 21
N12		Pacific	14 21
N19		at Utah State	20 47

1995   4-7-0   3-4-0
S2	●	Texas-El Paso	45 17
S9		Nevada	24 45
S16		at Georgia	13 40
S23		at New Mexico	24 36
S30		at Iowa	21 59
O7	●	Louisiana Tech	48 13
O14		at La. Lafayette	26 43
O21		Utah State	14 27
N4	●	at Pacific	39 37
N11		San Jose State	37 38
N18	●	at Nevada-Las Vegas	58 34

1996   1-10   (0-5)
A29		New Mexico	7 28
S7		at Texas	7 41
S14		at Texas-El Paso	7 14
S21		Cal St. Northridge	0 33
S28		at LSU	7 63
O12		Utah State	21 53
O19		at North Texas	0 13
O26	●	So. Utah	52 21
N2		at Nevada	14 63
N9		at Idaho	19 34
N16		Boise State	32 33

TONY SAMUEL
1997-2004 (.374)   34-57

1997   2-9   (0-5)
A30		at Arizona State	10 41
S6		at New Mexico	24 61
S13		Cal St. Northridge	28 18
S27		at Texas-El Paso	16 24
O4		Cal Poly SLO	35 38
O11		at Boise State	10 52
O18		at Utah State	7 38
O25	●	Arkansas State	34 20
N1		Nevada	24 45
N8		North Texas	15 26
N14		Idaho	18 35

1998   3-8   (1-4)
S5		at Texas	36 66
S12		at Georgia Tech	7 42
S19	●	New Mexico	28 27
S26	●	Texas-El Paso	33 24
O3		at Arkansas State	31 34
O10	●	at Nevada	48 45
O17		Colorado State	28 47
O31		Utah State	26 29
N7		Boise State	51 55
N14		at Idaho	32 36
N21		at North Texas	11 19

1999   6-5   (3-2)
S2	●	N.M. Highlands	73 7
S11	●	at New Mexico	35 28
S18	●	at Arizona State	35 7
S25		at Texas-El Paso	23 54
O2		at Colorado State	7 46
O9		Nevada	16 23
O23		at Army	18 35
O30	●	Idaho	42 14
N6	●	at Utah State	14 6
N13		at Boise State	26 45
N20	●	North Texas	22 9

2000   3-8   (1-4)
S2		at South Carolina	0 31
S16		New Mexico	13 16
S23		at Georgia	0 37
S30		at Texas-El Paso	31 41
O7	●	Army	42 23
O14	●	Tulsa	42 28
O21	●	at Arkansas State	35 29
O28		Boise State	31 34
N4		Utah State	37 44
N11		at Idaho	41 44
N18		at North Texas	23 30

2001-2004
SUN BELT

2001   5-7   (4-2)
A23		at Louisville	24 45
S1		at Texas	7 41
S8		Oregon State	22 27
S22		at Kansas State	0 64
S29	●	at La. Monroe	31 0
O6	●	at Tulsa	24 7
O13	●	Idaho	46 39
O27		at Middle Tennessee	35 39
N3		North Texas	20 22
N10	●	Arkansas State	28 17
N17	●	at La. Lafayette	49 46
N24		at New Mexico	0 53

2002   7-5   5-1
A31		at South Carolina	24 34
S7		at California	13 34
S21	●	New Mexico	24 13
S28		at Georgia	10 41
O5	●	Texas-El Paso	49 14
O12	●	La. Lafayette	31 28
O19	●	La. Monroe	34 21
O26	●	at Arkansas State	26 21
N2	●	Middle Tennessee	24 21
N9		at Utah State	30 32
N16	●	at North Texas	27 38
N23	●	at Idaho	35 31

2003   3-9   (2-5)
A31		at Texas	7 66
S6	●	W. New Mexico	48 3
S13		at Oregon State	16 28
S27		at New Mexico	17 24
O4		Idaho	31 35
O11		at Middle Tennessee	18 35
O16		at La. Lafayette	24 26
O25	●	at La. Monroe	21 14
N1		Arkansas State	24 28
N6		Utah State	26 21
N15		at Arkansas	20 48
N25		North Texas	10 13

2004   5-6   (3-2)
S4		at Arkansas	13 63
S11		at California	14 41
S18	●	Troy State	22 18
S25		New Mexico	3 38
O2		at Texas-El Paso	0 45
O9	●	La. Lafayette	35 32
O23		at North Texas	26 36
O30		Florida Int'l	56 31
N6	●	Middle Tennessee	44 10
N13		at Florida Atlantic	35 7
N20		at Utah State	25 34

NORTH CAROLINA

BY BOB HARIG

A MONG THE BIGGEST NAMES TO wear Carolina blue and play in Kenan Stadium's idyllic setting were Charlie "Choo-Choo" Justice and Lawrence Taylor, two stars who came to symbolize the Tar Heels program despite playing markedly different games. Justice was a triple-threat quarterback; Taylor was a defensive specialist, revolutionizing the way linebackers play football. And yet, the program might be even better known for its slew of 1,000-yard rushers—the school holds the NCAA record for such feats. One coach, Carl Snavely, went on to the College Football Hall of Fame, while others such as Dick Crum, Mack Brown and Bill Dooley reside at the top of the UNC record book for victories.

TRADITION The Old Well Walk is a relatively new tradition begun by coach John Bunting; players walk to Kenan Stadium from the Old Well, the most recognizable landmark on campus. The route passes through Tar Heel Town, where fans congregate for pregame festivities.

BEST PLAYER More than five decades after he played at Carolina, Justice is still spoken of with reverence. From 1946 to 1949, Justice helped guide the Tar Heels to three major bowls. Carolina was ranked No. 1 for a week during the 1948 season, and finished third, the best in school history, thanks largely to Justice's contributions in numerous phases of the game. He ran, he passed, he punted—and played special teams as well, returning kicks and punts. During his four years, the Tar Heels won 32 games, with just seven defeats and two ties. It was in the Navy where Justice got his nickname. Playing on the Bainbridge Navy squad he was described as "[running] along just like a choo-choo train." After spurning pro offers, Justice enrolled at Carolina, where he thrived as a tailback but was also an excellent passer and master of the quick kick. In his career, Justice scored 234 points and passed or ran for 53 touchdowns, tacking on 2,634 yards as a ballcarrier. Justice was runner-up for the 1948 Heisman Trophy to Doak Walker of SMU and second to Notre Dame's Leon Hart in 1949. What was perhaps his finest moment came in the College All-Star Game in 1950 at Soldier Field in Chicago; Justice was voted the game's MVP after gaining 133 yards in a 17-7 victory over the Philadelphia Eagles, the NFL champs.

BEST COACH Carl Snavely coached the UNC teams of the Justice era and is in the College Football Hall of Fame, also by virtue of having coached at Bucknell, Cornell and Washington University in St. Louis. However, the best-coach nod ultimately goes to Bill Dooley, who revitalized

---

PROFILE

University of North Carolina at Chapel Hill
Chapel Hill, N.C.
Founded: 1789
Enrollment: 16,144
Colors: Carolina Blue and White
Nickname: Tar Heels
Stadium: Kenan Memorial Stadium
     Opened in 1927
     Grass; 60,000 capacity
First football game: 1888
All-time record: 618–455–54 (.572)
Bowl record: 12–13
Atlantic Coast Conference championships:
5 (4 outright)
First-round NFL draftees: 16
Website: www.tarheelblue.com

THE BEST OF TIMES

From 1971 to '77 under coach Bill Dooley, the Tar Heels won three ACC titles, including back-to-back championships in 1971-72 when North Carolina went 20–4. The Tar Heels also finished second twice during that time.

THE WORST OF TIMES

In 1988-89, the Tar Heels suffered back-to-back 1–10 seasons under Mack Brown, the worst records at the school since Carolina started football in 1888 and had 0–2 records in two of its first three seasons.

CONFERENCE

North Carolina was a charter member of the Atlantic Coast Conference in 1953, and has remained in the ACC since. Previously, the Tar Heels were in the Southern Conference, which they joined in 1921.

DISTINGUISHED ALUMNI

Michael Jordan; Mia Hamm; Marion Jones; Lawrence Taylor; James K. Polk, U.S. president; Erskine Bowles, White House chief of staff; Andy Griffith, actor; Charles Kuralt, journalist; Davis Love III, pro golfer

FIGHT SONG

HERE COMES CAROLINA
Here comes Carolina-lina
Here comes Carolina-lina
We hail from NCU.
We've got the spirit in it
We've got the team to win it
We wear the colors White and Blue—
So it's fight! Fight! for Carolina
As Davie did in days of old.
As we gather 'round the Well
Cheer that Tar Heel team like hell—
For the glory of NCU

UNC players have rushed for 1,000 yards or more 24 times, an NCAA record.

the program in the early 1970s, winning ACC titles in 1971 and 1972. Dooley—whose 11-year tenure was the longest of any Carolina football coach—is tied with Mack Brown for second-most wins at the school, 69. Brown never won an ACC title, but in 10 years as Carolina's coach, he led the Tar Heels to eight consecutive winning seasons. His last two teams were 10–2 in 1996 and 11–1 in 1997. Both he and Dooley rebuilt programs that were in pitiable condition.

BEST TEAM The 1997 Tar Heels went 11–1, including a Gator Bowl victory over Virginia Tech, losing only to national power Florida State, and finished fourth in the *ESPN/USA Today* coaches poll. A close second was the 1948 team, featuring Justice: the team finished third in the Associated Press poll after being ranked No. 1 for one week during the regular season and losing to Oklahoma in the Sugar Bowl. The 1980 team also deserves mention for finishing 11–1; although the squad suffered a 41-7 loss at Oklahoma, it boasted future Pro Football Hall of Famer Lawrence Taylor and two 1,000-yard rushers, Amos Lawrence and Kelvin Bryant.

BIGGEST GAME Longtime UNC fans regard the 34-7 victory over Texas in 1948 as the biggest in school history.

Having lost to the Longhorns 34-0 a year earlier in Austin, the stage was set for a Chapel Hill rematch. The game was billed as the greatest intersectional battle of the season, but after just 12 minutes Carolina had run up a 21-0 lead, keyed by two Charlie Justice touchdown passes and another scoring run. Justice added another touchdown run in the fourth quarter.

BIGGEST UPSET The Tar Heels had never defeated a Top 5 opponent until their 2004 victory over Miami at Kenan Stadium. The Hurricanes, in their first season as part of the ACC, entered 6–0 and ranked fourth in the country with designs on playing for another national championship. UNC had other ideas. Despite entering the game 3–4 and with a defense ranked 116th in the country, the Tar Heels managed to stay with the Hurricanes. In fact, they led 28-21 late in the game before UM drove 89 yards to tie the score. With the game apparently headed to overtime, UNC quarterback Darian Durant led the Tar Heels on a 65-yard drive for the winning points. He completed all four passes and scrambled five yards to set up a field goal attempt. Connor Barth converted from 42 yards on the final play of the game for the 31-28 victory. "It's the best feeling in the world," Barth said. "I've never made a game-winner like that. That was the first one, and what a game to do it in."

RECORDS

RUSHING YARDS

	GAME	
328	Derrick Fenner vs. Virginia, Nov. 15, 1986 (39 att.)	
	SEASON	
1,720	Don McCauley, 1970 (324 att.)	
	CAREER	
4,391	Amos Lawrence, 1977-80 (881 att.)	

PASSING YARDS

	GAME	
417	Darian Durant vs. Arizona State, Oct. 5, 2002 (25 of 40)	
	SEASON	
2,551	Darian Durant, 2003 (234 of 389)	
	CAREER	
8,755	Darian Durant, 2001-04 (701 of 1,159)	

RECEIVING YARDS

	GAME	
247	Randy Marriott vs. Georgia Tech, Sept. 19, 1987 (9 rec.)	
	SEASON	
990	Sam Aiken, 2002 (68 rec.)	
	CAREER	
2,447	Corey Holliday, 1989-93 (155 rec.)	

POINTS

	GAME	
36	Kelvin Bryant vs. East Carolina, Sept. 12, 1981 (6 TDs)	
	SEASON	
126	Don McCauley, 1970 (21 TDs)	
	CAREER	
306	Leon Johnson, 1993-96 (50 TDs, 3 two-pt. conv.)	

CONSENSUS ALL-AMERICANS

1937	Andy Bershak	E
1948	Charlie Justice	B
1970	Don McCauley	B
1972	Ron Rusnak	G
1974	Ken Huff	G
1977	Dee Hardison	DL
1980	Lawrence Taylor	LB
1983	William Fuller	DL
1995	Marcus Jones	DL
1996-97	Dre' Bly	DB
1997	Greg Ellis	DL
1997	Brian Simmons	LB
2001	Julius Peppers	DL

HEARTBREAKER UNC was 8-1 heading into its 1996 game against Virginia, the only defeat being a 13-0 loss at Florida State. With a win over the Cavaliers and against rival Duke, the Tar Heels would be headed to the Fiesta Bowl—and they were seemingly on their way, ahead 17-3 with 10 minutes remaining and holding the ball first and goal at the Virginia 9. But a third-down pass by quarterback Chris Keldorf was picked off by Antwan Harris and returned 95 yards for a touchdown. The Cavs converted a pair of fourth-down plays to score the tying touchdown, with quarterback Tim Sherman scrambling in from the 7 on fourth and six. Then, with 2:11 remaining, Sherman completed a 41-yard pass, setting up Rafael Garcia's winning 32-yard field goal with 39 seconds left.

DISPUTE In Choo-Choo Justice's last game against Duke in 1949, he threw for one touchdown and caught another, but the Tar Heels were still in trouble; it was late in the game, and the Blue Devils had driven deep into UNC territory. The clock ran out, fans stormed the field and Carolina celebrated a 21-20 victory—Duke athletic officials, though, argued that the scoreboard clock, which was difficult to read, still had four seconds on it. Game officials agreed, and after a long wait to clear the field, play resumed. After Mike Souchak (who later gained fame as a professional golfer) came in to kick what could have been the winning field goal for Duke, UNC's Art Weiner rushed in untouched and smothered the ball before it ever left the ground, preserving the win.

STADIUM Considered to be one of college football's best settings, Kenan Stadium sits among the pine trees in the heart of the UNC campus and has been home to Carolina football since it was completed in 1927. William Rand Kenan Jr., an 1894 Carolina graduate, is credited with its genesis: the stadium was built as a memorial to his parents, William R. Kenan and Mary Hargrave Kenan. A $1 million gift from Kenan in the 1950s led to the construction of a second deck. Originally, the stadium seated 24,000, but portable stands and a second deck increased capacity to 48,000 in 1963. Four more expansions, the last in 1998, brought capacity to 60,000.

RIVAL For years, Carolina's biggest rival was Virginia, with the two playing the last game of the season. Since the 1950s, however, the team's biggest rival has been Duke. The Tar Heels and Blue Devils, located just 11 miles apart, now play the final game of the regular season against each other. NC State is another big rival, as the Wolfpack are also within a short drive. The rivalry heated up during the days of Bill Dooley and State coach Lou Holtz.

NICKNAME North Carolina athletic teams are known as the Tar Heels—a nickname also given to the school's home state. Legend has it that the name dates to the Revolutionary War, when troops of British general Charles Cornwallis were fording what is now known as the Tar River, between Rocky Mount and Battleboro. The soldiers discovered that tar had been dumped into the stream to stall their crossing; when they got to the other side, their feet were completely covered with black tar, leading to the observation that anyone who waded through Carolina rivers would acquire tar heels. Another story attributes the nickname to the Civil War and General Robert E. Lee, who was quoted in a letter as saying that men from North Carolina involved in a fight stood "as if they have tar on their heels." His remarks came after a battle on the outskirts of Petersburg, Va., in 1864.

MASCOT The players might be Tar Heels, but the team mascot is a ram. The ram dates to 1924, when head cheerleader Vic Huggins looked at other teams—Georgia had a bulldog, NC State a wolf—and realized UNC needed a symbol. Huggins thought back two years earlier, to when the Tar Heels compiled a 9–1 record, led by a fullback named Jack Merritt. Merritt was nicknamed the Battering Ram for his running style; Huggins thought the name a natural fit. The athletic business manager came up with $25 to purchase a mascot, and Rameses the First arrived from Texas, just in time to be introduced before a game against VMI. Today, another Rameses walks the sideline during games at Kenan Stadium.

UNIFORMS Among the most distinctive color schemes in college sports, UNC's powder blue, white and navy dates back to the 19th century, when the school reopened following the Civil War. The helmets have had an interlocking NC for years, although in the past the initials UNC had been stepladdered.

NUMBERS UNC players have rushed for 1,000 yards or more 24 times—an NCAA record. From 1973 to 1984, Carolina had at least one player break the 1,000-yard mark each season. There are 19 former UNC players who have been honored by having their names and jersey numbers placed on the facade at Kenan Stadium.

TRAGEDY After winning the national championship at Maryland, coach Jim Tatum returned to his alma mater in

1956 to rebuild the Tar Heels program. His recruiting was starting to pay off when he died of Rocky Mountain spotted fever just prior to the 1959 season.

QUOTE "I'll get up from my desk, walk by that beautiful stadium of ours, and the hair raises on the back of my neck and my blood gets hot—I'm just tickled to death to be there. I still sometimes just can't realize that I've made my dream come true."—John Bunting, on returning to his alma mater as coach in 2001

NORTH CAROLINA ANNUAL STATISTICAL LEADERS

YR	RUSHING	YDS	ATT	AVG	PASSING	ATT	CMP	PCT	YDS	RECEIVING	REC	YDS	AVG
1946	Charlie Justice	943	131	7.2	Charlie Justice	50	19	.38	274	Jack Fitch	6	129	21.5
1947	Charlie Justice	548	125	4.4	Charlie Justice	50	27	.54	390	Bob Cox	22	297	13.5
1948	Charlie Justice	766	147	5.2	Charlie Justice	122	62	.51	854	Art Weiner	31	481	15.5
1949	Billy Hayes	447	148	3.0	Charlie Justice	99	51	.52	731	Art Weiner	52	762	14.7
1950	Dick Bunting	401	106	3.8	Billy Hayes	104	49	.47	528	Benny Walser	16	260	16.3
1951	Dick Wiess	339	82	4.1	Frank Wissman	65	35	.54	396	Skeet Hesmer	14	109	7.8
1952	Larry Parker	215	83	2.6	Marshall Newman	92	34	.37	564	Benny Walser	12	186	15.5
1953	Ken Keller	432	83	5.2	Marshall Newman	81	26	.32	297	Tom Adler	13	145	11.2
1954	Don Klochak	361	55	6.6	Len Bullock	55	31	.56	283	Will Frye	12	100	8.3
1955	Ken Keller	353	105	3.4	Dave Reed	73	25	.34	418	Will Frye	13	181	13.9
1956	Ed Sutton	748	120	6.2	Dave Reed	54	22	.41	313	Ed Sutton	14	159	11.4
1957	Ed Lipski	305	50	6.1	Jack Cummings	76	39	.51	640	Buddy Payne	12	204	17.0
1958	Wade Smith	449	102	4.4	Jack Cummings	134	68	.51	1,139	Al Goldstein	24	490	20.4
1959	Wade Smith	414	87	4.8	Jack Cummings	144	63	.44	889	Al Goldstein	20	328	16.4
1960	Bob Elliott	356	88	4.0	Ray Farris	143	63	.44	865	John Schroeder	15	202	13.5
1961	Gib Carson	406	116	3.5	Ray Farris	159	71	.45	875	Jimmy Addison	16	110	6.9
1962	Ken Willard	466	119	3.9	Junior Edge	185	103	.56	1,234	Bob Lacey	44	668	15.2
1963	Ken Willard	648	167	3.9	Junior Edge	170	89	.52	1,163	Bob Lacey	48	533	11.1
1964	Ken Willard	835	228	3.7	Gary Black	174	82	.47	1,038	Ronnie Jackson	34	512	15.1
1965	Tom Lampman	444	108	4.1	Danny Talbott	207	103	.50	1,080	Bob Hume	30	263	8.8
1966	David Riggs	399	110	3.6	Danny Talbott	122	69	.57	691	Charlie Carr	52	490	9.4
1967	Gayle Bomar	529	193	2.7	Gayle Bomar	158	79	.50	873	Peter Davis	30	338	11.3
1968	Gayle Bomar	495	165	3.0	Gayle Bomar	189	87	.46	1,229	Don McCauley	23	313	13.6
1969	Don McCauley	1,092	204	5.4	John Swofford	74	33	.45	487	Tony Blanchard	23	320	13.9
1970	Don McCauley	1,720	324	5.3	Paul Miller	80	48	.60	728	Lewis Jolley	20	358	17.9
1971	Lewis Jolley	712	117	6.1	Paul Miller	146	75	.51	1,041	Lewis Jolley	23	367	16.0
1972	Ike Oglesby	707	148	4.8	Nick Vidnovic	143	69	.48	1,096	Jimmy Jerome	22	326	14.8
1973	Sammy Johnson	1,006	183	5.5	Bill Paschall	116	65	.56	837	Jimmy Jerome	24	309	12.9
1974	James Betterson	1,082	209	5.2	Chris Kupec	150	104	.69	1,474	Jimmy Jerome	47	837	17.8
1975	Mike Voight	1,250	259	4.8	Bill Paschall	180	93	.52	1,195	Charlie Williams	24	290	12.1
1976	Mike Voight	1,407	315	4.5	Matt Kupec	99	52	.53	751	Mel Collins	14	185	13.2
1977	Amos Lawrence	1,211	193	6.3	Matt Kupec	105	59	.56	715	Brooks Williams	19	218	11.5
1978	Amos Lawrence	1,043	234	4.5	Matt Kupec	121	71	.59	787	Bob Loomis	31	432	13.9
1979	Amos Lawrence	1,019	225	4.5	Matt Kupec	227	123	.54	1,587	Mike Chatham	29	448	15.4
1980	Amos Lawrence	1,118	229	4.9	Rod Elkins	160	81	.51	1,002	Mike Chatham	20	239	12.0
1981	Kelvin Bryant	1,015	152	6.7	Rod Elkins	136	69	.51	994	Jon Richardson	28	373	13.3
1982	Kelvin Bryant	1,064	228	4.7	Scott Stankavage	158	78	.49	1,124	Victor Harrison	30	489	16.3
1983	Ethan Horton	1,107	200	5.5	Scott Stankavage	249	147	.59	1,721	Mark Smith	40	580	14.5
1984	Ethan Horton	1,247	238	5.2	Kevin Anthony	265	146	.55	1,786	Earl Winfield	34	527	15.5
1985	William Humes	515	115	4.5	Kevin Anthony	249	142	.57	1,546	Earl Winfield	47	696	14.8
1986	Derrick Fenner	1,250	200	6.3	Mark Maye	176	110	.63	1,401	Eric Streater	37	601	16.2
1987	Eric Starr	550	142	3.9	Mark Maye	270	143	.53	1,965	Randy Marriott	36	634	17.6
1988	Kennard Martin	1,146	193	5.9	Todd Burnett	97	52	.54	497	Randy Marriott	34	498	14.6
1989	Aaron Staples	463	114	4.1	Jonathan Hall	113	50	.44	581	Randall Felton	37	495	13.4
1990	Natrone Means	849	168	5.1	Todd Burnett	219	112	.51	1,339	Corey Holliday	28	488	17.4
1991	Natrone Means	1,030	201	5.1	Chuckie Burnette	130	81	.62	939	Corey Holliday	40	504	12.6
1992	Natrone Means	1,195	236	5.1	Jason Stanicek	144	84	.58	1,082	Corey Holliday	37	588	15.9
1993	Curtis Johnson	1,034	173	6.0	Jason Stanicek	217	139	.64	1,878	Corey Holliday	50	867	17.3
1994	Leon Johnson	805	151	5.3	Jason Stanicek	166	96	.58	1,222	Octavus Barnes	32	609	19.0
1995	Leon Johnson	963	225	4.3	Mike Thomas	332	185	.56	2,436	Leon Johnson	54	408	7.6
1996	Leon Johnson	913	242	3.8	Chris Keldorf	338	201	.59	2,347	Na Brown	52	534	10.3
1997	Jonathan Linton	1,004	248	4.0	Oscar Davenport	183	115	.63	1,380	Na Brown	55	610	11.1
1998	Rufus Brown	534	133	4.0	Oscar Davenport	182	100	.55	1,208	Na Brown	55	897	16.3
1999	Daniel Davis	303	69	4.4	Ronald Curry	110	54	.49	682	Kory Bailey	25	418	16.7
2000	Brandon Russell	508	145	3.5	Ronald Curry	304	163	.54	2,325	Bosley Allen	40	634	15.9
2001	Andre' Williams	520	170	3.1	Darian Durant	223	142	.64	1,843	Sam Aiken	46	789	17.2
2002	Jacque Lewis	574	130	4.4	Darian Durant	248	147	.59	2,123	Sam Aiken	68	990	14.6
2003	Ronnie McGill	654	128	5.1	Darian Durant	389	234	.60	2,551	Jarwarski Pollock	71	745	10.5
2004	Chad Scott	796	143	5.6	Darian Durant	299	178	.60	2,238	Jarwarski Pollock	45	408	9.1

Receiving leaders by receptions
The NCAA began including postseason stats in 2002

NORTH CAROLINA ALL-TIME SCORES

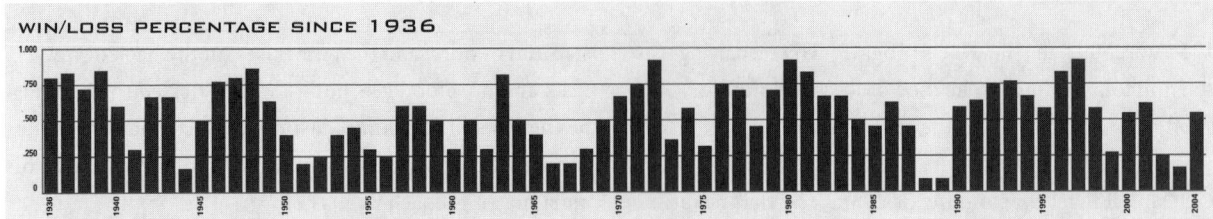

WIN/LOSS PERCENTAGE SINCE 1936

NO HEAD COACH

1888   0-2-0
O18	Wake Forest *Ral*	4	6
N27	Duke *Ral*	0	16

HECTOR COWAN
1889 (.333)   1-2

1889   1-2-0
M1 •	Wake Forest *Ral*	33	0
M8 •	Duke *Ral*	17	25
N22 •	Wake Forest *Ral*	8	18

1890
NO TEAM

NO HEAD COACH

1891   0-2-0
N10 •	Wake Forest *Ral*	0	1	f
N20 •	Duke	4	6	

1892   5-1-0
O21 •	at Richmond	40	0
O22 •	at Virginia	18	30
N12 •	at Duke	24	0
N23 •	Auburn *Atl*	64	0
N24 •	at Vanderbilt	24	0
N26 •	Virginia *Atl*	26	0

1893   3-4-0
O20 •	at Wash. & Lee	44	0
O21 •	at VMI	4	10
O28 •	at Duke	4	6
N7 •	Tennessee	60	0
N18 •	Wake Forest *Ral*	40	0
N25 •	Lehigh *NYC*	0	34
N30 •	Virginia *Rich*	0	16

V.K. IRVINE
1894 (.667)   6-3

1894   6-3-0
O12 •	North Carolina St.	44	0
O20 •	at North Carolina St.	16	0
O24 •	Duke	28	0
O27 •	Sewanee *Ashe*	36	4
O31 •	at Lehigh	6	24
N1 •	at Rutgers	0	5
N3 •	at Georgetown	20	4
N10 •	Richmond *Gro*	28	0
N22 •	Virginia *Rich*	0	34

T.C. TRENCHARD
1895, 1913-15 (.730)   26-9-2

1895   7-1-1
O12 •	North Carolina St.	36	0
O19 •	Richmond	34	0
O26 •	Georgia *Atl*	6	0
O28 •	at Vanderbilt	12	0
O29 =	at Sewanee	0	0
O31 •	Georgia *Atl*	10	6
N2 •	Wash. & Lee *Lyn*	16	0
N16 •	Virginia Tech *Char*	32	5
N28 •	Virginia *Rich*	0	6

GORDON JOHNSTON
1896 (.438)   3-4-1

1896   3-4-1
O10 •	Guilford	26	4
O17 •	at Guilford	34	0
O24 =	Virginia Tech *Dan*	0	0
O31 •	Georgia *Atl*	16	24
N3 •	at Charlotte AC	0	8
N7 •	at Hampton	0	18
N11 •	Greensboro AC	30	0
N26 •	Virginia *Rich*	0	46

W.A. REYNOLDS
1897-1900 (.763)   27-7-4

1897   7-3-0
O2 •	North Carolina St.	40	0
O9 •	Guilford	16	0
O22 •	Greensboro AA	24	0
O25 •	Clemson	28	0
O30 •	Virginia Tech *Dan*	0	4
N5 •	Sewanee *Cow*	12	6
N6 •	at Vanderbilt	0	31
N8 •	at Tennessee	16	0
N9 •	at Bingham	14	0
N22 •	Virginia *Rich*	0	12

1898   9-0-0
O1 •	Guilford	18	0	
O15 •	North Carolina St.	34	0	
O20 •	Greensboro AA	11	0	
O29 •	Oak Ridge	11	0	
N4 •	Virginia Tech *W-S*	28	6	
N5 •	Davidson *Rich*	11	0	
N12 •	Georgia *Mac*	44	0	*
N15 •	at Auburn	24	0	*
N24 •	Virginia *Rich*	6	2	

1899   7-3-1
O7 •	North Carolina St.	34	0
O12 •	Oak Ridge	16	0
O14 •	Guilford	45	0
O21 •	Davidson *Char*	10	0
O23 •	Horners Sch.	46	0
O28 =	at North Carolina St.	11	11
O31 •	Maryland Coll.	6	0
N4 •	at Navy	0	12
N8 •	at Princeton	0	30
N30 •	Georgia *Atl*	5	0
D2 •	Sewanee *Atl*	0	5

1900   4-1-3
O6 •	Deaf & Dumb Inst.	38	0
O27 =	Virginia Tech	0	0
N1 •	at Tennessee	22	5
N3 •	at Vanderbilt	48	0
N5 =	Sewanee *Atl*	0	0
N17 •	Georgia *Ral*	55	0
N24 •	Virginia *Nor*	0	17
N29 =	at Georgetown	0	0

CHARLES JENKINS
1901 (.778)   7-2

1901   7-2-0
O12 •	Oak Ridge	28	0
O16 •	North Carolina St.	39	0
O19 •	Guilford	42	0
O26 •	Davidson *Char*	6	0
N2 •	Georgia *Atl*	27	0
N4 •	at Auburn	10	0
N19 •	at North Carolina St.	30	0
N23 •	Virginia	6	23
N28 •	Clemson *Char*	10	22

H.B. OLCOTT
1902-03 (.694)   11-4-3

1902   5-1-3
S24 •	Guilford	16	0
O4 •	Oak Ridge	35	0
O11 •	Furman	10	0
O18 •	Davidson *Char*	27	0
O25 =	Virginia Tech *Roa*	0	0
N1 •	VMI *Lyn*	17	10
N8 =	at North Carolina St.	0	0
N15 •	Georgetown *Nor*	5	12
N27 =	Virginia *Rich*	12	12

1903   6-3-0
S26 •	Guilford	15	0
O3 •	Oak Ridge	45	0
O10 •	at South Carolina	17	0
O14 •	VMI *Roa*	28	6
O17 •	Georgetown *Nor*	0	33
O31 •	Transylvania, Ky *Gro*	5	6
N7 •	Virginia Tech *Roa*	0	21
N14 •	Clemson	11	6
N25 •	Virginia *Rich*	16	0

R.R. BROWN
1904 (.667)   5-2-2

1904   5-2-2
O1 •	Guilford	29	0
O8 =	Davidson *Char*	0	0
O12 •	Bingham	50	0
O15 •	South Carolina	27	0
O22 •	Norfolk AC *Gro*	41	0
O29 •	at Virginia Tech	6	0
N5 •	Georgetown *Nor*	0	16
N16 =	North Carolina St.	6	6
N24 •	Virginia *Rich*	11	12

WILLIAM WARNER
1905 (.563)   4-3-1

1905   4-3-1
O7 •	Davidson *Char*	6	0
O14 •	at Pennsylvania	0	17
O21 •	at Navy	0	38
O28 •	Virginia Tech *Rich*	6	35
N4 •	Georgetown *Rich*	36	0
N12 =	at North Carolina St.	0	0
N18 •	VMI *W-S*	17	0
N30 •	Virginia *Nor*	17	0

W.S. KIENHOLZ
1906 (.286)   1-4-2

1906   1-4-2
S29 =	Davidson *Char*	0	0
O6 •	at Pennsylvania	0	11
O12 •	Richmond	12	0
O20 •	Lafayette *Rich*	6	28
O27 =	Virginia Tech *Rich*	0	0
N3 •	Georgetown *Nor*	0	4
N17 •	at Navy	0	40

OTIS LAMSON
1907 (.500)   4-4-1

1907   4-4-1
S28 •	at Pennsylvania	0	37
O5 =	Wash. & Lee *NN*	0	0
O12 •	Oak Ridge	38	0
O19 •	William & Mary	14	0
O26 •	Virginia *Rich*	4	9
O31 •	Clemson *Colu*	6	15
N9 •	at Georgetown	12	5
N16 •	Richmond	13	11
N28 •	Virginia Tech *Rich*	6	20

EDWARD GREEN
1908 (.500)   3-3-3

1908   3-3-3
S26 •	Wake Forest	17	0
O3 •	at Tennessee	0	12
O10 =	Wash. & Lee *NN*	0	0
O17 =	Davidson *Wil*	0	0
O26 =	at Georgetown	6	6
O31 •	Richmond	17	12
N7 •	Virginia Tech *Rich*	0	10
N14 •	South Carolina	22	0
N26 •	Virginia *Rich*	0	31

A.E. BRIDES
1909-10 (.500)   8-8

1909   5-2-0
O2 •	Wake Forest	18	0
O9 •	at Tennessee	3	0
O16 •	VMI *Lyn*	0	3
O23 •	at Georgetown	5	0
O31 •	Richmond	22	0
N6 •	Virginia Tech *Rich*	0	15
N13 •	Wash. & Lee *NN*	6	0

1910   3-6-0
O1 •	VMI	6	0	
O8 •	at Kentucky	0	11	
O15 •	Davidson *Char*	0	6	
O22 •	Wake Forest	37	0	
O29 •	at Georgetown	0	12	
N5 •	Virginia Tech *Rich*	0	20	
N12 •	Wash. & Lee *Nor*	0	5	
N19 •	South Carolina *Dur*	23	6	*
N24 •	Virginia *Rich*	0	7	

BRANCH BOCOCK
1911 (.813)   6-1-1

1911   6-1-1
O7 •	Wake Forest	12	3
O14 •	Bingham	12	0
O21 •	Davidson *Char*	5	0
O28 •	USS Franklin	12	0
N4 =	Virginia Tech *Rich*	0	0
N11 •	South Carolina	21	0
N18 •	Wash. & Lee *Unk*	4	0
N30 •	Virginia *Rich*	0	28

W.C. MARTIN
1912 (.438)   3-4-1

1912   3-4-1
O5 •	Davidson *Char*	13	0
O12 •	Wake Forest	9	2
O19 •	Bingham	47	0
O26 •	Virginia Tech *Ral*	0	26
N2 •	Georgetown *Unk*	10	37
N9 =	South Carolina	6	6
N16 •	Wash. & Lee *Gro*	0	31
N26 •	Virginia *Rich*	0	66

T.C. TRENCHARD

1913   5-4-0
S27 •	Wake Forest	7	0
O4 •	Virginia Med.	15	0
O11 •	Davidson *Gro*	7	0
O18 •	at South Carolina	13	3
O25 •	Virginia Tech *W-S*	7	14
N1 •	at Georgia	6	19
N8 •	Wash. & Lee *Lyn*	0	14
N15 •	Wake Forest *Dur*	29	0
N27 •	Virginia *Rich*	7	26

1914   10-1-0
S29 •	Richmond	41	0
O3 •	VA. Medical	65	0
O8 •	Wake Forest *Dur*	53	0
O12 •	South Carolina	48	0
O17 •	Georgia *Atl*	41	6
O20 •	Riverside Acad. *Unk*	40	0
O24 •	at Vanderbilt	10	9
O31 •	Davidson *W-S*	16	3
N7 •	VMI *Char*	30	7
N14 •	Wake Forest *Ral*	12	7
N26 •	Virginia *Rich*	3	20

1915   4-3-1
O2 •	Citadel	14	7
O9 •	Wake Forest	35	0
O16 •	Georgetown	0	38
O23 =	VMI *Gro*	3	3
O30 •	at Georgia Tech	3	23
N6 •	Clemson *GrvSC*	9	7
N13 •	Davidson *W-S*	41	6
N25 •	Virginia *Rich*	0	14

THOMAS CAMPBELL
1916-19 (.559) 9-7-1

1916 5-4-0

S30	●	Wake Forest	20	0
O7		at Princeton	0	29
O14		at Harvard	0	21
O21		at Georgia Tech	6	10
O28	●	VMI	38	13
N4		Virginia Tech ROA	7	14
N11	●	Davidson W-S	10	6
N18	●	Furman	46	0
N30	●	Virginia RICH	7	0

1917-1918
NO TEAM WWI

1919 4-3-1

O4		at Rutgers	0	19
O11		at Yale	7	34
O18	●	Wake Forest	6	0
O23	●	at North Carolina St.	13	12
N1	=	at Tennessee	0	0
N8		VMI	7	29
N15	●	Davidson W-S	10	0
N27	●	Virginia	6	0

M.E. FULLER
1920 (.250) 2-6

1920 2-6-0

O2	●	Wake Forest	6	0
O9		at Yale	0	21
O16	●	South Carolina	7	0
O21		at North Carolina St.	3	13
O30		Maryland	0	13
N6		VMI	0	23
N13		Davidson W-S	0	7
N25		at Virginia	0	14

1921-1952
SOUTHERN CONFERENCE

BOB & BILL FETZER
1921-25 (.696) 30-12-4

1921 5-2-2 (2-1-0)

O1	●	Wake Forest	21	0
O8		at Yale	0	34
O15	=	at South Carolina	7	7
O20	|	at North Carolina St.	0	7
O29	● |	Maryland BALT	16	7
N5	●	VMI RICH	20	7
N12	=	Davidson W-S	0	0
N24	● |	Virginia	7	3
D3	●	Florida JACF	14	10

1922 9-1-0 (5-0-0)

S30	●	Wake Forest UNK	62	3
O7		at Yale	0	18
O12	●	Duke	20	0
O14	● |	South Carolina	10	7
O19	● |	at North Carolina St.	14	9
O28	● |	Maryland	27	3
N4	● |	at Tulane RICH	19	12
N11	●	VMI	9	7
N18	●	Davidson CHAR	29	6
N30	● |	at Virginia	10	7

1923 5-3-1 (2-1-1)

S29	●	Wake Forest	22	0
O6		at Yale	0	53
O12	●	at Duke	14	6
O18	● |	at North Carolina St.	14	0
O27	|	at Maryland	0	14
N3	● |	at South Carolina	13	0
N10		VMI RICH	0	9
N17	●	Davidson	14	3
N29	= |	Virginia	0	0

1924 4-5-0 (2-3-0)

S27		at Wake Forest	6	7
O4		at Yale	0	27
O11	●	Duke	6	0
O16	● |	at North Carolina St.	10	0
O25	|	Maryland	0	6
N1	|	South Carolina	7	10
N8	● |	VMI	3	0
N15	●	at Davidson	6	0
N27	|	at Virginia	0	7

1925 7-1-1 (4-0-1)

S26		Wake Forest	0	6
O3	● |	at South Carolina	7	0
O10	●	at Duke	41	0
O15	● |	at North Carolina St.	17	6 *
O24	●	at Mercer	3	0
O31	● |	Maryland BALT	16	0
N7	● |	VMI RICH	23	11
N14	●	Davidson	13	0
N26	= |	Virginia	3	3

CHUCK COLLINS
1926-33 (.545) 38-31-9

1926 4-5-0 (3-3-0)

S25		at Wake Forest	0	13 *
O2	|	at Tennessee	0	34
O9	● |	South Carolina	7	0
O16	●	Duke	6	0
O23	|	at Maryland	6	14
O30	● |	North Carolina St.	12	0
N6	● |	VMI	28	0
N13		at Davidson	0	10
N23	|	at Virginia	0	3

1927 4-6-0 (2-5-0)

S24		Wake Forest	8	9
O1	|	Tennessee	0	26
O8	● |	Maryland	7	6
O15	|	at South Carolina	6	14
O22	|	at Georgia Tech	0	13
O29	|	at North Carolina St.	6	19
N5	|	at VMI	0	7
N12	●	Davidson	27	0
N19	●	at Duke	18	0
N24	● |	Virginia	14	13

1928 5-3-2 (2-2-2)

S29	●	Wake Forest	65	0
O6	● |	at Maryland	26	19
O13		at Harvard	0	20
O20	|	Virginia Tech	14	16
O27	|	Georgia Tech	7	20
N3	= |	at North Carolina St.	6	6
N10	= |	South Carolina	0	0
N17	●	at Davidson	30	7
N29	● |	at Virginia	24	20
D8	●	Duke	14	7

1929 9-1-0 (7-1-0)

S28	●	Wake Forest	48	0
O5	● |	at Maryland	43	0
O12	● |	at Georgia Tech	18	7
O19	|	Georgia	12	19
O26	● |	Virginia Tech	38	13
N2	● |	North Carolina St.	32	0
N9	● |	at South Carolina	40	0
N16	●	Davidson CHAR	26	7
N28	● |	Virginia	41	7
D7	● |	at Duke	48	7

1930 5-3-2 (4-2-2)

S27	●	Wake Forest	13	7
O4	● |	at Virginia Tech	39	21
O11	● |	Maryland	28	21
O18	|	at Georgia	0	26
O25	|	at Tennessee	7	9
N1	= |	Georgia Tech	6	6
N7	● |	North Carolina St.	13	6
N15		at Davidson	6	7
N27	● |	at Virginia	41	0
D6	= |	Duke	0	0

1931 4-3-3 (2-3-3)

S26	●	Wake Forest	37	0
O3	|	at Vanderbilt	0	13
O10	= |	at Florida	0	0
O17	|	Georgia	7	32 *
O24	|	Tennessee	0	7
O31	● |	at North Carolina St.	18	15
N7	= |	at Georgia Tech	19	19
N14	●	Davidson	20	0
N21	= |	at Duke	0	0
N26	● |	Virginia	13	6

1932 3-5-2 (2-5-1)

S24	=	Wake Forest	0	0
O1	|	Vanderbilt	7	39
O8	|	at Tennessee	7	20 *
O15	= |	at Georgia	6	6
O22	|	Georgia Tech	14	43
O29	● |	North Carolina St.	13	0
N4	● |	Florida	18	13
N12	●	at Davidson	12	0
N19	|	Duke	0	7
N24	|	at Virginia	7	14

1933 4-5-0 (2-1-0)

S30	●	Davidson	6	0
O7		at Vanderbilt	13	20
O14		Georgia	0	30
O21		at Florida	0	9
O28		Georgia Tech	6	10
N4	● |	at North Carolina St.	6	0
N11	●	Wake Forest	26	0
N18	|	at Duke	0	21
N30	● |	Virginia	14	0

CARL SNAVELY
1934-35, '45-52 (.621) 59-35-5

1934 7-1-1 (2-0-1)

S29	●	Wake Forest	21	0
O6		Tennessee	7	19
O13	●	at Georgia	14	0
O20	●	Kentucky	6	0
O27	= |	North Carolina St.	7	7
N3	●	at Georgia Tech	26	0
N10	●	at Davidson	12	2
N17	● |	Duke	7	0
N24	● |	at Virginia	25	6

1935 8-1-0 (4-1-0)

S28	●	Wake Forest	14	0
O5	●	at Tennessee	38	13
O12	● |	at Maryland	33	0
O19	●	at Davidson	14	0
O26	●	Georgia Tech	19	0
N2	● |	at North Carolina St.	35	6
N9	● |	VMI	56	0
N16	|	at Duke	0	25
N28	● |	Virginia	61	0

RAY WOLF
1936-41 (.681) 38-17-3

1936 8-2-0 (5-1-0)

S26	● |	Wake Forest CHAR	14	7
O3	●	Tennessee	14	6
O10	● |	Maryland	14	0
O17	●	NYU BNX	14	13
O24		at Tulane	7	21
O31	● |	North Carolina St.	21	6
N7	● |	at Davidson	26	6
N14		Duke	7	27
N21	● |	at South Carolina	14	0
N26	●	at Virginia	59	14

1937 7-1-1 (4-0-1)

S25	= |	South Carolina	13	13
O2	● |	at North Carolina St.	20	0
O9	●	NYU BNX	19	6
O16	● |	at Wake Forest	28	0
O23	●	Tulane	13	0
O30		Fordham	0	14
N6	● |	at Davidson	26	0
N13	● |	at Duke	14	6
N27	●	Virginia	40	0

1938 6-2-1 (4-1-0)

S24	● |	Wake Forest	14	6
O1	● |	at North Carolina St.	21	0
O8		Tulane	14	17
O15	●	NYU BNX	7	0
O22	● |	at Davidson	34	0
O29	|	Duke	0	14
N5	● |	Virginia Tech	7	0
N12	=	Fordham NYC	0	0
N24	●	at Virginia	20	0

1939 8-1-1 (5-1-0)

S23	● |	Citadel	50	0
S30	● |	Wake Forest	36	6
O7	● |	Virginia Tech NOR	13	6
O14	●	NYU	14	7
O21	=	at Tulane	14	14
O28	●	at Pennsylvania	30	6
N4	● |	North Carolina St.	17	0
N11	● |	Davidson W-S	32	0
N18	|	at Duke	3	13
N30	●	Virginia	19	0

1940 6-4-0 (3-2-0)

S21	●	Appalachian St.	56	6
S28	|	Wake Forest	0	12
O5	● |	Davidson W-S	27	7
O12	●	TCU	21	14
O19	● |	at North Carolina St.	13	7
O26		Tulane	13	14
N2		Fordham NYC	0	14
N9	|	at Richmond	13	14
N16	● |	Duke	6	3
N23	●	at Virginia	10	7

1941 3-7-0 (2-4-0)

S20	●	Lenoir-Rhyne	42	6
S27	|	South Carolina	7	13
O4	● |	at Davidson	20	0
O11		Fordham	14	27
O18		at Tulane	6	52
O25	|	at Wake Forest	0	13
N1	|	North Carolina St.	7	13
N8	● |	at Richmond	27	0
N15	|	at Duke	0	20
N20		Virginia	7	28

JIM TATUM
1942, '56-58 (.526) 19-17-3

1942 5-2-2 (3-1-1)

S26	● |	Wake Forest	6	0
O3	● |	South Carolina	18	6
O10	=	Fordham NYC	0	0
O17	●	Duquesne	13	6
O24		at Tulane	14	29
O31	|	at North Carolina St.	14	21
N7	● |	Davidson CHAR	43	14
N14	= |	Duke	13	13
N21	●	at Virginia	28	13

TOM YOUNG
1943 (.667) 6-3

1943 6-3-0 (2-2-0)

S25		at Georgia Tech	7	20
O2	●	Penn State	19	0
O9	●	Jacksonville NAS	23	0
O16	|	at Duke	7	14
O30	● |	North Carolina St.	27	13
N6	● |	at South Carolina	21	6
N13	●	at Pennsylvania	9	6
N20	|	Duke	6	27
N27	●	Virginia	54	7

GENE McEVER
1944 (.167) 1-7-1

1944 1-7-1 (0-3-1)

S23	|	Wake Forest	0	7
S30		at Army	0	46
O7		at Georgia Tech	0	28
O14	●	Cherry Point Marines	20	14
N4	|	South Carolina	0	6
N11	= |	William & Mary	0	0
N18		at Yale	6	13
N25	|	Duke	0	33
D2		Virginia NOR	7	26

CARL SNAVELY

1945 5-5-0 (2-2-0)

S22	●	at Camp Lee	6	0
S29		Georgia Tech	14	20
O6	● |	Virginia Tech ROA	14	0
O13		at Pennsylvania	0	49
O20	●	Cherry Point Marines	20	14
N3		at Tennessee	6	20
N10	● |	William & Mary NOR	6	0
N17	|	Wake Forest	13	14
N24	|	at Duke	7	14
D1	●	Virginia	27	18

1946 8-2-1 (4-0-1)

S28	= |	Virginia Tech	14	14
O4	●	at Miami, Fla.	21	0
O12	● |	Maryland	33	0
O19	●	Navy BALT	21	14
O26	●	Florida	40	19
N2		at Tennessee	14	20
N9	● |	William & Mary RICH	21	7
N16	● |	Wake Forest	26	14
N23	● |	Duke	22	7
N30	●	at Virginia	49	14
		SUGAR BOWL		
J1		Georgia	10	20

1947 8-2-0 (4-1-0)

S27	●	Georgia	14	7
O4		at Texas	0	34
O11	|	Wake Forest	7	19
O18	● |	at William & Mary	13	7
O25	●	at Florida	35	7
N1	●	Tennessee	20	6
N8	● |	North Carolina St.	41	6
N15	● |	Maryland DC	19	0
N22	● |	at Duke	21	0
N29	●	Virginia	40	7

1948 9-1-1 (4-0-1)

S25	●	Texas	34	7
O2	●	at Georgia	21	14
O9	● |	at Wake Forest	28	6
O16	● |	North Carolina St.	14	0
O23	●	LSU	34	7
O30	●	at Tennessee	14	7
N6	= |	William & Mary	7	7
N13	● |	at Maryland	49	20
N20	● |	Duke	20	0
N27	●	at Virginia	34	12
		SUGAR BOWL		
J1		Oklahoma	6	14

1949 7-4-0 (5-0-0)

S24	● |	North Carolina St.	26	6
O1	●	Georgia	21	14
O8	● |	at South Carolina	28	13
O15	● |	Wake Forest	28	14
O22		at LSU	7	13
O29		Tennessee	6	35
N5	● |	at William & Mary	20	14
N12		Notre Dame BNX	6	42
N19	● |	at Duke	21	20
N26	●	Virginia	14	7
		COTTON BOWL		
J2		Rice	13	27

1950 3-5-2 (3-2-1)

S23	● |	North Carolina St.	13	7
S30		at Notre Dame	7	14
O7	=	at Georgia	0	0
O14	|	Wake Forest	7	13
O28	● |	William & Mary	40	7
N4		at Tennessee	0	16
N11	= |	Maryland	7	7
N18	● |	at South Carolina	14	7
N25	|	Duke	0	7
D2		at Virginia	13	44

1951 2-8-0 (2-3-0)

S22	● |	North Carolina St.	21	0
S29		Georgia	16	28
O6		at Texas	20	45
O13	● |	South Carolina	21	6
O20	|	at Maryland	7	14
O27	|	at Wake Forest	7	39
N3		Tennessee	0	27
N10		at Virginia	14	34
N17		Notre Dame	7	12
N24	|	at Duke	7	19

1952 2-6-0 (1-2-0)

S27		Texas	7	28
O18	|	Wake Forest	7	9
O25		at Notre Dame	14	34
N1		at Tennessee	14	41
N8		Virginia	7	34
N15	● |	at South Carolina	27	19
N22	|	Duke	0	34
N28	●	at Miami, Fla.	34	7

1953- PRESENT
ACC

GEORGE BARCLAY
1953-55 (.383) 11-18-1

1953 4-6-0 (2-3-0)

S26	● |	North Carolina St.	29	7
O3	●	Wash. & Lee	39	0
O10	● |	at Wake Forest	18	13
O17	|	Maryland	0	26
O24		at Georgia	14	27
O31		Tennessee	6	20
N7	|	at South Carolina	0	18
N14		Notre Dame	14	34
N21	●	at Virginia	33	7
N28	|	at Duke	20	35

1954 4-5-1 (4-2-0)

S25	● |	North Carolina St.	20	6
O2	=	at Tulane	7	7
O9		Georgia	7	21
O16	|	at Maryland	0	33
O23	● |	Wake Forest	14	7
O30		at Tennessee	20	26
N6	● |	South Carolina	21	19
N13		at Notre Dame	13	42
N20	● |	at Virginia	26	14
N27	|	Duke	12	47

1955 3-7-0 (3-3-0)

S24		Oklahoma	6	13
O1	● |	at North Carolina St.	25	18
O8		at Georgia	7	28
O15	|	Maryland	7	25
O22	|	at Wake Forest	0	25
O29		Tennessee	7	48
N5	● |	South Carolina NOR	32	14
N12		Notre Dame	7	27
N19	● |	Virginia	26	14
N26	|	at Duke	0	6

JIM TATUM

1956 2-7-1 (2-3-1)

S22	|	North Carolina St.	6	26
S29		at Oklahoma	0	36
O6	|	at South Carolina	0	14
O13		Georgia	12	26
O20	● |	Maryland	34	6
O27	= |	Wake Forest	6	6
N3		at Tennessee	0	20
N10	● |	at Virginia	21	7 †
N17		at Notre Dame	14	21
N24	|	Duke	6	21

1957 6-4-0 (4-3-0)

S21	|	North Carolina St.	0	7
S28	● |	Clemson	26	0
O5	●	Navy	13	7
O11	●	at Miami, Fla.	20	13
O19	|	at Maryland	7	21
O26	● |	at Wake Forest	14	7
N2		Tennessee	0	35
N9	● |	South Carolina	28	6
N23	● |	at Duke	21	13
N30	|	Virginia	13	20

1958 6-4-0 (4-3-0)

S20	|	North Carolina St.	14	21
S27	|	at Clemson	21	26
O3	●	at Southern Cal	8	7
O11	● |	South Carolina	6	0
O18	● |	Maryland	27	0
O25	● |	Wake Forest	26	7
N1	●	at Tennessee	21	7
N8	● |	at Virginia	42	0
N15		at Notre Dame	24	34
N22	|	Duke	6	7

JIM HICKEY
1959-66 (.444) 36-45

1959 5-5-0 (5-2-0)

S19	|	Clemson	18	20
S26		at Notre Dame	8	28
O3	● |	North Carolina St.	20	12
O10	● |	South Carolina	19	6
O17	|	at Maryland	7	14
O24	● |	at Wake Forest	21	19
O31		Tennessee	7	29
N6		at Miami, Fla.	7	14
N14	● |	Virginia	41	0
N21	● |	at Duke	50	0

1960 3-7-0 (2-5-0)

S24	|	North Carolina St.	0	3
S30		at Miami, Fla.	12	29
O8	●	Notre Dame	12	7
O15	|	Wake Forest	12	13
O22	|	at South Carolina	6	22
O29		at Tennessee	14	27
N5	|	at Clemson	0	24
N12	|	Maryland	19	22
N19	● |	Duke	7	6
N26	● |	at Virginia	35	8

1961 5-5-0 (4-3-0)

S30	● |	North Carolina St.	27	22
O7	|	Clemson	0	27
O14	● |	at Maryland	14	8
O21	● |	at South Carolina	17	0
O27		at Miami, Fla.	0	10
N4	●	Tennessee	22	21
N11		LSU	0	30
N18	|	at Duke	3	6
N25	|	at Wake Forest	14	17
D2	● |	Virginia	24	0

1962 3-7-0 (3-4-0)

S22	|	North Carolina St.	6	7
S29		at Ohio State	7	41
O6		at Michigan State	6	38
O13	|	Maryland	13	31
O20	● |	South Carolina	19	14
O27	● |	Wake Forest	23	14
N3	|	at Clemson	6	17
N10	● |	at Virginia	11	7
N17		at Notre Dame	7	21
N24	|	Duke	14	16

1963 9-2-0 (6-1-0)

S21	● |	Virginia	11	7
S28		at Michigan State	0	31
O5	● |	at Wake Forest	21	0
O12	● |	at Maryland	14	7
O19	● |	North Carolina St.	31	10
O26	● |	at South Carolina	7	0
N2	●	Georgia	28	7
N9	|	Clemson	7	11
N16	●	Air Force	27	16
N28	● |	at Duke	16	14
		GATOR BOWL		
D28	●	Air Force	35	0

1964 5-5-0 (4-3-0)

S19	|	North Carolina St.	13	14
S26	●	Michigan State	21	15
O3	● |	Wake Forest	23	0
O10		at LSU	3	20
O17	|	Maryland NOR	9	10
O24	● |	South Carolina	24	6
O31		at Georgia	8	24
N7	● |	at Clemson	29	0
N14	|	at Virginia	27	31
N21	● |	Duke	21	15

1965 4-6-0 (3-3-0)

S18		Michigan	24	31
S25	●	at Ohio State	14	3
O2	|	Virginia	17	21
O9	● |	at North Carolina St.	10	7
O16	● |	Maryland	12	10
O23	|	at Wake Forest	10	12
O30		Georgia	35	47
N6	● |	Clemson	17	13
N13		at Notre Dame	0	17
N20	|	at Duke	7	34

1966 2-8-0 (1-4-0)

S17		at Kentucky	0	10
S24	● |	North Carolina St.	10	7
O1	●	at Michigan	21	7
O15		at Notre Dame	0	32
O22	|	Wake Forest	0	3
O29		at Georgia	3	28
N5	|	at Clemson	3	27
N12		Air Force	14	20
N19	|	Duke	25	41
N26	|	Virginia	14	21

BILL DOOLEY
1967-77 (.565) 69-53-2

1967 2-8-0 (2-5-0)

S16	|	at North Carolina St.	7	13
S23	|	at South Carolina	10	16
S30		Tulane	11	36
O7		Vanderbilt	7	21
O14		at Air Force	8	10
O21	● |	Maryland	14	0
O28	|	Wake Forest	10	20
N4	|	Clemson	0	17
N11	|	at Virginia	17	40
N18	● |	at Duke	20	9

1968 3-7-0 (1-6-0)

S21	|	North Carolina St.	6	38
S28	|	South Carolina	27	32
O5	●	at Vanderbilt	8	7
O12	|	at Maryland	24	33
O19	●	Florida	22	7
O26	|	at Wake Forest	31	48
N2		at Air Force	15	28
N9	|	Virginia	6	41
N16	|	at Clemson	14	24
N23	● |	Duke	25	14

1969 5-5-0 (3-3-0)

S20	|	at North Carolina St.	3	10
S27	|	at South Carolina	6	14
O4	●	Vanderbilt	38	22
O11		Air Force	10	20
O18		at Florida	2	52
O25	● |	Wake Forest	23	3
N1	● |	at Virginia	12	0
N8	●	VMI	61	11
N15	● |	Clemson	32	15
N22	|	at Duke	13	17

1970 8-4-0 (5-2-0)

S12	●	Kentucky	20	10
S19	● |	North Carolina St.	19	0
S26	● |	at Maryland	53	20
O3	●	at Vanderbilt	10	7
O10	|	South Carolina	21	35
O17		at Tulane	17	24
O24	|	at Wake Forest	13	14
O31	● |	Virginia	30	15
N7	●	VMI	62	13
N14	● |	at Clemson	42	7
N21	● |	Duke	59	34
		PEACH BOWL		
D30		Arizona State	26	48

1971 9-3-0 (6-0-0)

S11	●	at Richmond	28	0
S18	●	at Illinois	27	0
S25	● |	Maryland	35	14
O2	● |	at North Carolina St.	27	7
O9		Tulane	29	37
O16		at Notre Dame	0	16
O23	● |	Wake Forest	7	3
O30	●	William & Mary	36	35
N6	● |	Clemson	26	13
N13	● |	at Virginia	32	20
N20	● |	at Duke	38	0
		GATOR BOWL		
D31		Georgia	3	7

1972 11-1-0 (6-0-0)

S9	●	Richmond	28	18
S16	● |	at Maryland	31	26
S23	● |	North Carolina St.	34	33
S30		at Ohio State	14	29
O14	●	Kentucky	31	20
O21	● |	at Wake Forest	21	0
N4	● |	at Clemson	26	10
N11	● |	Virginia	23	3
N18	● |	Duke	14	0
N25	●	East Carolina	42	19
D9	●	Florida	28	24
		SUN BOWL		
D30	●	Texas Tech	32	28

1973 4-7-0 (1-5-0)

S15	●	William & Mary	34	27
S22	|	Maryland	3	23
S29		Missouri	14	27
O6	|	at North Carolina St.	26	28
O13	●	at Kentucky	16	10
O20		at Tulane	0	16
O27	●	East Carolina	28	27
N3	|	at Virginia	40	44
N10	|	Clemson	29	37
N17	● |	Wake Forest	42	0
N24	|	at Duke	10	27

1974 7-5-0 (4-2-0)

S14	●	Ohio U.	42	7
S21	● |	at Wake Forest	31	0
S28	|	at Maryland	12	24
O5	●	Pittsburgh	45	29
O12		at Georgia Tech	28	29
O19	● |	North Carolina St.	33	14
O26		at South Carolina	23	31
N2	● |	Virginia	24	10
N9	|	at Clemson	32	54
N16	●	Army	56	42
N23	● |	Duke	14	13
		SUN BOWL		
D28		Mississippi State	24	26

1975 3-7-1 (1-4-1)

S6	●	William & Mary	33	7
S20	|	Maryland	7	34
S27		at Ohio State	7	32
O4	● |	at Virginia	31	28
O11		Notre Dame	14	21
O18	|	at North Carolina St.	20	21
O25		East Carolina	17	38
N1	|	Wake Forest	9	21
N8	|	Clemson	35	38
N15	●	at Tulane	17	15
N22	= |	at Duke	17	17

1976 9-3-0 (4-1-0)

S4	●	Miami, Ohio	14	10
S11	●	Florida TAM	24	21
S18	●	Northwestern	12	0
S25	●	at Army	34	32
O2		at Missouri	3	24
O16	|	North Carolina St.	13	21
O23	●	East Carolina	12	10
O30	● |	at Wake Forest	34	14
N6	● |	at Clemson	27	23
N13	● |	Virginia	31	6
N20	● |	Duke	39	38
		PEACH BOWL		
D31		Kentucky	0	21

1977 8-3-1 (5-0-1)

S10		at Kentucky	7	10
S17	●	Richmond	31	0
S24	●	at Northwestern	41	7
O1		Texas Tech	7	10
O8	● |	Wake Forest	24	3
O15	● |	at North Carolina St.	27	14
O22	●	South Carolina	17	0
O29	● |	at Maryland	16	7
N5	= |	Clemson	13	13
N12	● |	at Virginia	35	14
N19	● |	at Duke	16	3
		LIBERTY BOWL		
D19		Nebraska	17	21

DICK CRUM
1978-87 (.634) 72-41-3

1978 5-6-0 (3-3-0)

S16	●	East Carolina	14	10
S23	|	Maryland	20	21
S30		at Pittsburgh	16	20
O7		Miami, Ohio	3	7
O14	● |	at Wake Forest	34	29
O21	|	North Carolina St.	7	34
O28	●	at South Carolina	24	22
N4		at Richmond	18	27
N11	|	at Clemson	9	13
N18	● |	Virginia	38	20
N25	● |	Duke	16	15

1979 — 8-3-1 (3-3-0)

S8	•	South Carolina	28	0
S22	•	Pittsburgh	17	7
S29	•	at Army	41	3
O6	•	Cincinnati	35	14
O13	|	Wake Forest	19	24
O20	• |	at North Carolina St.	35	21
O27	=	East Carolina	24	24
N3	|	at Maryland	14	17
N10	|	Clemson	10	19
N17	• |	at Virginia	13	7
N24	• |	at Duke	37	16
		GATOR BOWL		
D28	•	Michigan	17	15

1980 — 11-1-0 (6-0-0)

S6	•	Furman	35	13
S13	•	at Texas Tech	9	3
S27	• |	Maryland	17	3
O4	• |	Georgia Tech	33	0
O11	• |	at Wake Forest	27	9
O18	• |	North Carolina St.	28	8
O25	•	East Carolina	31	3
N1		at Oklahoma	7	41
N8	• |	at Clemson	24	19
N15	• |	Virginia	26	3
N22	• |	Duke	44	21
		BLUEBONNET BOWL		
D31	•	Texas	16	7

1981 — 10-2-0 (5-1-0)

S12	•	East Carolina	56	0
S19	•	Miami, Ohio	49	7
S26	•	Boston College	56	14
O3	•	at Georgia Tech	28	7
O10	• |	Wake Forest	48	10
O17	• |	at North Carolina St.	21	10
O24		South Carolina	13	31
O31	• |	at Maryland	17	10
N7	|	Clemson	8	10
N14	• |	at Virginia	17	14
N21	• |	at Duke	31	10
		GATOR BOWL		
D28	•	Arkansas	31	27

1982 — 8-4-0 (3-3-0)

S9		at Pittsburgh	6	7
S18	•	Vanderbilt	34	10
S25	•	Army	62	8
O2	•	Georgia Tech	41	0
O9	• |	at Wake Forest	24	7
O16	• |	North Carolina St.	41	9
O30	|	Maryland	24	31
N6	|	at Clemson	13	16
N13	• |	Virginia	27	14
N20	|	at Duke	17	23
N25	• |	Bowling Green	33	14
		SUN BOWL		
D25	•	Texas	26	10

1983 — 8-4-0 (4-3-0)

S3	•	at South Carolina	24	8
S10	•	Memphis	24	10
S17	•	Miami, Ohio	48	17
S24	•	William & Mary	51	20
O1	• |	at Georgia Tech	38	21
O8	• |	Wake Forest	30	10
O15	• |	at North Carolina St.	42	14
O29	|	at Maryland	26	28
N5	|	Clemson	3	16
N12	|	at Virginia	14	17
N19	• |	Duke	34	27
		PEACH BOWL		
D30		Florida State	3	28

1984 — 5-5-1 (3-3-1)

S15		Navy	30	33
S22		at Boston College	20	52
S29	•	Kansas	23	17
O6	|	at Clemson	12	20
O13	|	at Wake Forest	3	14
O20	• |	North Carolina St.	28	21
O27	•	at Memphis	30	27
N3	|	Maryland	23	34
N10	• |	Georgia Tech	24	17
N17	= |	Virginia	24	24
N24	• |	at Duke	17	15

1985 — 5-6-0 (3-4-0)

S7	•	at Navy	21	19
S14		LSU	13	23
S28	•	VMI	51	7
O5	|	at Georgia Tech	0	31
O12	• |	Wake Forest	34	14
O19	• |	at North Carolina St.	21	14
O26		Florida State	10	20
N2	|	at Maryland	10	28
N9	• |	Clemson	21	20
N16	|	at Virginia	22	24
N23	|	Duke	21	23

1986 — 7-4-1 (5-2-0)

S6	•	Citadel	45	14
S13	•	at Kansas	20	0
S20	=	at Florida State	10	10
O4	• |	Georgia Tech	21	20
O11	• |	at Wake Forest	40	30
O18	|	North Carolina St.	34	35
O25		at LSU	3	30
N1	• |	Maryland	32	30
N8	|	at Clemson	10	38
N15	• |	Virginia	27	7
N22	• |	at Duke	42	35
		ALOHA BOWL		
D27		Arizona	21	30

1987 — 5-6-0 (3-4-0)

S5	•	Illinois	34	14
S12		at Oklahoma	0	28
S19	• |	at Georgia Tech	30	23
S26	•	at Navy	45	14
O3		Auburn	10	20
O10	|	Wake Forest	14	22
O17	• |	at North Carolina St.	17	14
O31	• |	at Maryland	27	14
N7	|	Clemson	10	13
N14	|	at Virginia	17	20
N21	|	Duke	10	25

MACK BROWN
1988-97 (.599) 69-46-1

1988 — 1-10-0 (1-6-0)

S3		at South Carolina	10	31
S10		Oklahoma	0	28
S24		Louisville	34	38
O1		at Auburn	21	47
O8	|	at Wake Forest	24	42
O15	|	North Carolina St.	3	48
O22	• |	Georgia Tech	20	17
O29	|	Maryland	38	41
N5	|	at Clemson	14	37
N12	|	Virginia	24	27
N19	|	at Duke	29	35

1989 — 1-10-0 (0-7-0)

S9	•	VMI	49	7
S16		at Kentucky	6	13
S23	|	at North Carolina St.	6	40
S30		Navy	7	12
O7	|	Wake Forest	16	17
O14	|	at Virginia	17	50
O21	|	at Georgia Tech	14	17
O28	|	at Maryland	0	38
N4	|	Clemson	3	35
N11		South Carolina	20	27
N18	|	Duke	0	41

1990 — 6-4-1 (3-3-1)

S1	•	Miami, Ohio	34	0
S8		at South Carolina	5	27
S15	•	Connecticut	48	21
S22	•	Kentucky	16	13
S29	|	North Carolina St.	9	12
O6	• |	at Wake Forest	31	24
O20	= |	Georgia Tech	13	13
O27	• |	Maryland	34	10
N3	|	at Clemson	3	20
N10	|	Virginia	10	24
N17	• |	at Duke	24	22

1991 — 7-4-0 (3-4-0)

S14	•	Cincinnati	51	16
S21	•	at Army	20	12
S28	|	at North Carolina St.	7	24
O5	•	William & Mary	59	36
O12	• |	Wake Forest	24	10
O19	|	at Virginia	9	14
O26	|	at Georgia Tech	14	35
N2	• |	Maryland	24	0
N9	|	Clemson	6	21
N16	•	South Carolina	21	17
N23	• |	Duke	47	14

1992 — 9-3-0 (5-3-0)

S5	• |	at Wake Forest	35	17
S12	•	Furman	28	0
S19	•	Army	22	9
S26	|	North Carolina St.	20	27
O3	•	Navy	28	14
O10	|	at Florida State	13	36
O17	• |	Virginia	27	7
O24	• |	Georgia Tech	26	14
O31	• |	at Maryland	31	24
N7	|	at Clemson	7	40
N21	• |	at Duke	31	28
		PEACH BOWL		
J2	•	Mississippi State	21	17

1993 — 10-3-0 (6-2-0)

A29	•	Southern Cal ANA	31	9
S4	•	Ohio U.	44	3
S11	• |	Maryland	59	42
S18	|	Florida State	7	33
S25	• |	at North Carolina St.	35	14
O2	•	Texas El Paso	45	39
O9	• |	Wake Forest	45	35
O16	• |	at Georgia Tech	41	3
O23	|	at Virginia	10	17
N6	• |	Clemson	24	0
N13	•	at Tulane	42	10
N26	• |	Duke	38	24
		GATOR BOWL		
D31		Alabama	10	24

1994 — 8-4-0 (5-3-0)

S3	•	TCU	27	17
S17	•	Tulane	49	0
S24	|	at Florida State	18	31
O1	•	at SMU	28	24
O8	• |	Georgia Tech	31	24
O15	• |	Maryland	41	17
O22	|	at Virginia	10	34
O29	• |	North Carolina St.	31	17
N5	|	Clemson	17	28
N12	• |	at Wake Forest	50	0
N19	• |	at Duke	41	40
		SUN BOWL		
D30		Texas	31	35

1995 — 7-5-0 (4-4-0)

S2		Syracuse	9	20
S9	|	at Maryland	18	32
S21	•	at Louisville	17	10
S30	•	Ohio U.	62	0
O7	• |	Virginia	22	17
O14	|	at Georgia Tech	25	27
O21	• |	Wake Forest	31	7
N4	|	at Clemson	10	17
N11	|	Florida State	12	28
N18	• |	Duke	28	24
N24	• |	at North Carolina St.	30	28
		CARQUEST BOWL		
D30	•	Arkansas	20	10

1996 — 10-2 (6-2)

A31	• |	Clemson	45	0
S7	•	at Syracuse	27	10
S21	• |	Georgia Tech	16	0
S28	|	at Florida State	0	13
O5	• |	at Wake Forest	45	6
O12	• |	Maryland	38	7
O26	•	at Houston	42	14
N2	• |	North Carolina St.	52	20
N9	•	Louisville	28	10
N16	|	at Virginia	17	20
N23	• |	at Duke	27	10
		GATOR BOWL		
J1	•	West Virginia	20	13

1997 — 11-1 (7-1)

S6	•	Indiana	23	6
S13	•	Stanford	28	17
S20	• |	at Maryland	40	14
S27	• |	Virginia	48	20
O4	•	at TCU	31	10
O11	• |	Wake Forest	30	12
O18	• |	at North Carolina St.	20	7
O30	• |	at Georgia Tech	16	13
N8	|	Florida State	3	20
N15	• |	at Clemson	17	10
N22	• |	Duke	50	14
		GATOR BOWL		
J1	•	Virginia Tech	42	3

CARL TORBUSH
1997-2000 (.486) 17-18

1998 — 7-5 (5-3)

S5		Miami, Ohio	10	13
S19		at Stanford	34	37
S26	|	Georgia Tech	21	43
O3	• |	Clemson	21	14
O10	•	Pittsburgh	29	10
O24	• |	at Wake Forest	38	31
O31	|	at Florida State	13	39
N7	• |	Maryland	24	13
N14	|	at Virginia	13	30
N21	• |	at Duke	28	6
N28	• |	North Carolina St. CHAR	37	34
		LAS VEGAS BOWL		
D19	•	San Diego State	20	13

1999 — 3-8 (2-6)

S4	|	Virginia	17	20
S11	•	at Indiana	42	30
S25	|	Florida State	10	42
O2	|	at Clemson	20	31
O9	|	at Georgia Tech	24	31
O16		Houston	12	20
O23	|	at Maryland	7	45
O30		Furman	3	28
N6	|	Wake Forest	3	19
N13	• |	North Carolina St. CHAR	10	6
N20	• |	Duke	38	0

2000 — 6-5 (3-5)

S2	•	Tulsa	30	9
S9	• |	at Wake Forest	35	14
S16	|	at Florida State	14	63
S23	•	Marshall	20	15
S30	|	Georgia Tech	28	42
O14	|	North Carolina St.	20	38
O21	|	Clemson	24	38
O28	|	at Virginia	6	17
N4	•	at Pittsburgh	20	17
N11	• |	Maryland	13	10
N18	• |	at Duke	59	21

JOHN BUNTING
2001-Present (.388) 19-30

2001 — 8-5 (5-3)

A25		at Oklahoma	27	41
S1	|	at Maryland	7	23
S8		at Texas	14	44
S22	• |	Florida State	41	9
S29	• |	at North Carolina St.	17	9
O6	•	East Carolina	24	21
O13	• |	Virginia	30	24
O20	• |	at Clemson	38	3
N1	|	at Georgia Tech	21	28
N10	|	Wake Forest	31	32
N17	• |	Duke	52	17
D1	•	SMU	19	10
		PEACH BOWL		
D31	•	Auburn	16	10

2002 — 3-9 1-7

A31		Miami, Ohio	21	27
S7	•	at Syracuse	30	22
S14		Texas	21	52
S28	|	Georgia Tech	13	21
O5	•	at Arizona State	38	35
O12	|	North Carolina St.	17	34
O19	|	at Virginia	27	37
O26	|	at Wake Forest	0	31
N2	|	Maryland	7	59
N9	|	Clemson	12	42
N16	|	at Florida State	14	40
N23	• |	at Duke	23	21

2003 — 2-10 (1-7)

A30	|	Florida State	0	37
S6		Syracuse	47	49
S20		at Wisconsin	27	38
S27	|	at North Carolina St.	34	47
O4	|	Virginia	13	38
O11	•	at East Carolina	28	17
O18		Arizona State	31	33
O25	|	at Clemson	28	36
N1	|	at Maryland	21	59
N8	• |	Wake Forest	42	34
N15	|	at Georgia Tech	24	41
N22	|	Duke	22	30

2004 — 6-6 (5-3)

S4	•	William & Mary	49	38
S11	|	at Virginia	24	56
S18	• |	Georgia Tech	34	13
S25		Louisville	0	34
O2	|	at Florida State	16	38
O9	• |	North Carolina St.	30	24
O16		at Utah	16	46
O30	• |	Miami, Fla.	31	28
N6	|	Virginia Tech	24	27
N13	• |	at Wake Forest	31	24
N20	• |	at Duke	40	17
		CONTINENTAL TIRE BOWL		
D30		Boston College	24	37

f Forfeit † Game Later Forfeited # Disputed Victor * Disputed Score || Designated Conference Game |2 Counted Twice in Conference Standings

NORTH CAROLINA STATE

BY BOB HARIG

NORTH CAROLINA STATE BEGAN playing football in the late 1800s wearing pink uniforms, and one of its most formidable defenses wore white shoes. For the most part, though, opponents have seen red—if not in the uniform, then simply in the frustration of playing the Wolfpack program, which has featured both notable coaches and some excellent players. Three of them—halfback Jack McDowell, quarterback Roman Gabriel and center Jim Ritcher—were inducted into the College Football Hall of Fame. Halfback Ted Brown is the only ACC player named all-conference for four years. Halfback Dick Christy led the Wolfpack to their first ACC title almost single-handedly, and two-time all-ACC honoree Torry Holt set the conference reception yardage record, only to see it eclipsed by Florida State's Peter Warrick a year later. Earle Edwards coached State to its first ACC title, despite having to play most games on the road (thanks to a small home stadium). A young Lou Holtz began to forge his reputation at the school. And a former Wolfpack player, Chuck Amato, guided the Wolfpack to the most wins for a season in school history in 2002.

TRADITION Players sing the NC State fight song in the locker room following games, a tradition that's been continued by Amato. Tailgating is also a major part of NC State football, as attested to by the numerous parking spaces surrounding Carter-Finley Stadium. The practice was featured in a 1969 *Southern Living* magazine story.

BEST PLAYER Most NC State fans have trouble settling on one of the team's three College Football Hall of Fame members: halfback Jack McDowell (1925-27), quarterback Roman Gabriel (1959-61) and center Jim Ritcher (1976-79), who won the Outland Trophy in 1979. But longtime observers of the program consider the best to be McDowell, who in 1927 led NC State to its only Southern Conference title. Given the competition, it's quite a distinction. Gabriel was a two-time ACC Player of the Year in 1960 and '61, and went on to be the 1969 NFL Most Valuable Player with the Los Angeles Rams. Ritcher was twice a consensus All-America and was honored as a center on the Walter Camp All-Century Team. He played in four Super Bowls and was All-Pro five times for the Buffalo Bills.

BEST COACH Earle Edwards' 17-year tenure (1954-70) was monumental for Wolfpack football, though his overall record of 77–88–8 might not suggest it. He revitalized the program's grim financial situation and brought a measure of

---

PROFILE

North Carolina State University
Raleigh, N.C.
Founded: 1887
Enrollment: 21,134
Colors: Red and White
Nickname: Wolfpack
Stadium: Carter-Finley Stadium
   Opened in 1966
   Grass; 51,500 capacity
First football game: 1892
All-time record: 508–492–55 (.508)
Bowl record: 11–10–1
Atlantic Coast Conference championships:
7 (5 outright)
Outland Trophy: Jim Ritcher, 1979
First-round NFL draftees: 12
Website: www.gopack.com

THE BEST OF TIMES

The Wolfpack were 33–12–3 from 1972 to 1975, including 20–1–1 at home, under Lou Holtz.

THE WORST OF TIMES

From 1951 to 1956, the Wolfpack never won more than four games in a season and went their first three seasons in the ACC (1953-55) without winning a conference game.

CONFERENCE

NC State was a charter member of the Atlantic Coast Conference in 1953, and has remained in the ACC since. The Wolfpack were previously members of the Southern Conference from 1921 to 1952.

DISTINGUISHED ALUMNI

John Edwards, U.S. senator; Dr. James Goodnight, co-founder and CEO of SAS Institute, world's largest privately held software company; Dr. Jerry Punch, trauma specialist and sportscaster; Cyma Rubin, producer, director, writer; General Hugh Shelton, chairman of the joint chiefs of staff; John Tesh, musician

FIGHT SONG

THE RED AND WHITE
We're the Red and White from State
And we know we are the best.
A hand behind our back,
We can take on all the rest.
Come o'er the hill, Caroline.
Devils and Deacs stand in line.
The Red and White from NC State.
Go State!!

Earle Edwards' tenure was the most significant, revitalizing a bad financial situation and bringing respectability.

respectability to the school's level of play as well. Edwards won NC State's first ACC title in 1957, and then collected a number of first-place (1963, '64, '65 and '68) and second-place (1960, '66, '67 and '69) finishes in the ACC standings.

Making his run more impressive is the fact that his teams played in Riddick Stadium until 1965; during his 17 seasons the Wolfpack played more home games than road games only once. Six times, his teams played three home games and seven away in order to collect a paycheck. During one stretch—the end of the 1960 season and the start of the 1961 season—his team played 10 consecutive road games. His most significant legacy, then, might well be his lead role in the construction of Carter-Finley Stadium.

BEST TEAM The Wolfpack in 1967 collected back-to-back major upsets, over No. 18 Florida State (20-10) and No. 2 Houston (16-6), and ascended to their highest ranking, No. 3. With 17 senior starters on Edwards' team, the Wolfpack finished 9–2. The season saw NC State sweep its four biggest rivals—North Carolina, Maryland, Wake Forest and Duke— for the first time. The Wolfpack suffered defeats to Penn State and Clemson, which cost them the ACC title, but this team is considered the best, especially after a 14-7 Liberty Bowl victory over Georgia. Eight other Wolfpack teams won at least nine times, and the 2002 team under coach Chuck Amato finished 11–3, the most victories ever for the school in one season. That team won its first nine games, the longest winning streak in school history.

BIGGEST GAME Dick Christy scored every one of NC State's points, kicking a late field goal, scoring four touchdowns and booting two extra points in a 29-26 victory over South Carolina that clinched the Wolfpack's first ACC title in 1957. NC State fell behind the Gamecocks 19-6 in the second quarter, but a one-yard run by Christy with just 57 seconds remaining in the half cut the deficit. The Pack took the second-half kickoff and drove to tie the game 19-19, then took the lead with a touchdown early in the fourth quarter. But the Gamecocks came back again, evening the score at 26-26 with just 1:09 remaining. Then things got interesting.

With less than 10 seconds remaining, the Pack threw a desperation pass that was intercepted by South Carolina's

RECORDS

RUSHING YARDS

	GAME
251	Ted Brown vs. Penn State, Nov. 5, 1977 (37 att.)

	SEASON
1,350	Ted Brown, 1978 (302 att.)

	CAREER
4,602	Ted Brown, 1975-78 (860 att.)

PASSING YARDS

	GAME
535	Shane Montgomery vs. Duke, Nov. 11, 1989 (37 of 73)

	SEASON
4,491	Philip Rivers, 2003 (348 of 483)

	CAREER
13,484	Philip Rivers, 2000-03 (1,087 of 1,710)

RECEIVING YARDS

	GAME
255	Torry Holt vs. Baylor, Sept. 19, 1998 (11 rec.)

	SEASON
1,604	Torry Holt, 1998 (88 rec.)

	CAREER
3,379	Torry Holt, 1995-98 (191 rec.)

POINTS

	GAME
30	Three players; most recently by T.A. McLendon vs. Texas Tech, Sept. 21, 2002 (5 TDs)

	SEASON
108	T.A. McLendon, 2002 (18 TDs)

	CAREER
312	Ted Brown, 1975-78 (52 TDs)

CONSENSUS ALL-AMERICANS

1967	Dennis Byrd	DT
1973	Bill Yoest	G
1978	Ted Brown	RB
1978-79	Jim Ritcher	C
1996	Marc Primanti	PK
1998	Torry Holt	WR

Alex Hawkins. But interference was called, and State was given one final play at the South Carolina 30-yard line. While fans were being cleared from the playing field, Christy approached Edwards and asked to attempt a 46-yard field goal. He had never attempted a field goal in a game—but it was State's only remaining chance to win the ACC title. "I held my head down for a moment," Christy said afterward. "Then I looked up and saw the official raise his arms. Man, I was stunned. But, oohh, it felt good."

BIGGEST UPSET The 1967 squad was ranked 20th when it traveled to Houston to play the second-ranked Cougars in what was back then a futuristic Astrodome. Houston had scored 120 points in its first three games and was listed as a 21-point favorite over the Wolfpack. The crowd of 52,483 was the largest ever to see an indoor football game at that time, but State's White Shoes defense smothered Houston and the Wolfpack rallied from a 6-0 halftime deficit to win, 16-6. Back in Raleigh, students celebrated on Hillsborough Street, and some 7,000 fans went to the airport to greet the team the next day. The win boosted the Wolfpack to ninth in the AP poll, with four first-place votes.

HEARTBREAKER A victory over Penn State in 1967 would have assured the Wolfpack a trip to either the Orange Bowl or the Sugar Bowl. Instead, NC State fell behind 13-0 and trailed 13-6 as the clock wound down. The Wolfpack drove to the Penn State 13 in the final minutes, only to have a pass intercepted in the end zone. But the defense held, giving the offense another shot, and the Wolfpack moved to the 1-yard line, where fullback Tony Barchuk was stopped on fourth and goal. Penn State took a safety and won 13-8. Running a close second is a 2003 visit to Ohio State, home of the defending national champions. The Wolfpack, trailing 24-7 in the fourth quarter, forced a tie but fell in triple overtime 44-38.

TRAGEDY Bo Rein had completed four seasons as coach at NC State, compiling a record of 27–18–1, when he left for LSU following the 1979 season. Six weeks later, on Jan. 11, 1980, Rein was killed when the private plane that he was riding from Shreveport, La., to Baton Rouge veered off course and crashed into the Atlantic Ocean.

STADIUM Carter-Finley Stadium is named for Harry and Nick Carter, textile executives and NC State alumni, and the late Raleigh philanthropist A.E. Finley. Built at a cost of $3.7 million, it holds 51,500. Before the stadium opened in

1966, the Wolfpack played at Riddick Stadium, which never seated more than 20,000 fans and often forced NC State to play road games for paychecks.

RIVAL NC State has played Wake Forest more than any other opponent, with the schools meeting every year since 1910; the Wolfpack lead the series 60-32-6. The two schools used to be neighbors when the Deacons were in the town of Wake Forest, just 14 miles north of Raleigh. However, the more bitter rivalry over the years has been with North Carolina. The schools have played each year since 1953, when the ACC was formed. But the series started in 1894, and proximity—the schools are only 24 miles apart—has stoked a natural rivalry in all sports. From 1943 to 1964, all but one of the 18 games were played in Chapel Hill. Once the Wolfpack moved to Carter-Finley Stadium in 1966, it became a home-and-home series.

NICKNAME A disgruntled fan lodged a complaint with the school in 1922, saying the student body behaved "like a wolfpack." The name stuck. Prior to that comment, NC State's teams were known as the Farmers, the Aggies, the Techs and the Red Terrors. In 1945, during World War II, the German U-boat fleet was commonly referred to as the Wolfpack. Due to the negative connotation, NC State chancellor J.W. Harrelson attempted to get the student body to agree to a name change. The suggestion went unheeded.

MASCOT NC State has the rare distinction of having married mascots. Going back to the 1920s, cheerleaders experimented with mascots to represent the Wolfpack. The school took on a female wolf when women's athletics got started in the 1970s; later, after varying adventures with a live wolf (actually a coyote), a metal wolf and a costumed, single, strutting male wolf, the pair was married in the late 1980s.

UNIFORMS When NC State fielded its first football team in 1892, the players took the field in pink-and-blue uniforms. In 1895, after three years of the not-so-imposing color scheme, the team voted to wear brown and white. That lasted only a year before the student body decided on red and white for the school colors. The logo has been modified over the years, but the basic one has been a large block S with smaller N and C letters inside the S. At times, just an S was used on the helmets, but a major change took place between 1986 and 1999, when coaches Dick Sheridan and Mike O'Cain used a diamond logo. Later, Chuck Amato went back to what most consider the traditional logo: the N and C inside a large S.

LORE In a Nov. 5, 1994, game at Maryland, NC State scored on nine of its 10 possessions. And yet the Wolfpack needed a 35-yard field goal from Steve Videtich with six seconds left to win the game 47-45. The game featured 62 first downs, and the teams gained 1,030 yards in total offense … Two former Wolfpack standouts, Alex Webster and Bill Cowher, became head coaches in the NFL. Webster played both offense and defense at NC State, went on to the CFL and then played for the NFL's New York Giants from 1955 to 1964. He coached the Giants from 1969 to 1973. Cowher, a linebacker at NC State from 1975 to 1978, played for the Cleveland Browns and Philadelphia Eagles. He became head coach of the Pittsburgh Steelers in 1992 … Coach Gus Tebell pulled off an interesting double play at NC State when he won the Southern Conference football title with a 9–1 record in 1927 and then won the Wolfpack's first Southern Conference basketball title in 1929. No other head coach in either the Southern or ACC has duplicated the feat.

QUOTE "I don't know about that. The players we had were only 'all-ours'—and they were good enough to win today." —NC State coach Earle Edwards in 1956, following a 26-6 victory over rival and favorite North Carolina, with its slew of preseason All-Americas

NORTH CAROLINA STATE ANNUAL STATISTICAL LEADERS

YR	RUSHING	YDS	ATT	AVG	PASSING	ATT	CMP	PCT	YDS	RECEIVING	REC	YDS	AVG
1957	Dick Christy	626	144	4.3	Tom Katich	29	11	.38	182	Dick Christy	10	211	21.1
1958	Ken Trowbridge	495	113	4.4	Frank Cackovic	108	42	.39	487	Bob Pepe	15	203	13.5
1959	Ron Podwika	379	96	3.9	Roman Gabriel	134	81	.60	832	Ron Podwika	23	181	7.9
1960	Al Taylor	303	93	3.3	Roman Gabriel	186	105	.56	1,182	John Morris	18	218	12.1
1961	Jim D'Antonio	232	47	4.9	Roman Gabriel	186	99	.53	937	John Morris	24	325	13.5
1962	Tony Koszarsky	244	64	3.8	Jim Rossi	130	66	.51	792	Joe Scarpati	18	214	11.9
1963	Jim Rossi	423	139	3.0	Jim Rossi	141	70	.50	873	Joe Scarpati	24	273	11.4
1964	Pete Falzarano	324	78	4.2	Ron Skosnik	93	45	.48	566	Gary Rowe	16	210	13.1
1965	Shelby Mansfield	618	175	3.5	Charlie Noggle	109	55	.50	533	Gary Rowe	20	270	13.5
1966	Don DeArment	727	175	4.2	Jim Donnan	158	74	.47	859	Gary Rowe	47	571	12.1
1967	Tony Barchuk	600	186	3.2	Jim Donnan	156	79	.51	980	Harry Martell	27	390	14.4
1968	Charlie Bowers	706	197	3.6	Jack Klebe	120	57	.48	746	Bobby Hall	17	231	13.6
1969	Charlie Bowers	693	180	3.9	Darrell Moody	101	44	.44	434	Wayne Lewis	15	148	9.9
1970	Pat Kenney	310	66	4.7	Pat Korsnick	91	46	.51	427	Pat Kenney	19	249	13.1
1971	Willie Burden	910	227	4.0	Bruce Shaw	127	53	.42	681	Mike Schultz	24	481	20.0
1972	Stan Fritts	689	145	4.8	Bruce Shaw	175	91	.52	1,708	Pat Kenney	36	832	23.1
1973	Willie Burden	1,014	150	6.8	Dave Buckey	101	53	.52	762	Don Buckey	24	439	18.3
1974	Stan Fritts	1,169	245	4.8	Dave Buckey	162	105	.65	1,481	Don Buckey	26	452	17.4
1975	Ted Brown	913	142	6.4	Dave Buckey	201	113	.56	1,511	Don Buckey	34	551	16.2
1976	Ted Brown	1,088	198	5.5	Johnny Evans	163	77	.47	942	Ted Brown	25	239	9.6
1977	Ted Brown	1,251	218	5.7	Johnny Evans	203	93	.46	1,357	Ted Brown	24	164	6.8
1978	Ted Brown	1,350	302	4.5	Scott Smith	101	50	.50	741	Ted Brown	17	197	11.6
1979	Dwight Sullivan	665	150	4.4	Scott Smith	138	75	.54	1,093	Mike Quick	30	524	17.5
1980	Wayne McLean	706	147	4.8	Tol Avery	184	98	.53	1,114	Mike Quick	43	632	14.7
1981	Joe McIntosh	1,190	222	5.4	Tol Avery	139	70	.50	825	Mike Quick	32	508	15.9
1982	Joe McIntosh	780	183	4.3	Tol Avery	224	126	.56	1,396	Ricky Wall	23	412	17.9
1983	Joe McIntosh	1,081	217	5.0	Tim Esposito	323	190	.59	2,234	Jeff Brown	41	354	8.6
1984	Vince Evans	883	198	4.5	Tim Esposito	262	143	.55	1,751	Jeff Brown	33	243	7.4
1985	Vince Evans	712	172	4.1	Erik Kramer	339	189	.56	2,510	Haywood Jeffires	36	542	15.1
1986	Bobby Crumpler	581	152	3.8	Erik Kramer	277	145	.52	2,092	Nasrallah Worthen	41	686	16.7
1987	Bobby Crumpler	571	143	4.0	Shane Montgomery	153	81	.53	1,144	Mack Jones	23	403	17.5
1988	Tyrone Jackson	464	120	3.9	Shane Montgomery	198	123	.62	1,522	Nasrallah Worthen	55	856	15.6
1989	Anthony Barbour	412	108	3.8	Shane Montgomery	395	217	.55	2,632	Mike Kavulic	46	745	16.2
1990	Greg Manior	406	97	4.2	Terry Jordan	179	101	.56	1,221	Aubrey Shaw	34	288	8.5
1991	Anthony Barbour	769	124	6.2	Geoff Bender	167	76	.46	949	Charles Davenport	33	558	16.9
1992	Anthony Barbour	1,204	199	6.1	Terry Jordan	256	164	.64	1,963	Eddie Goines	46	580	12.6
1993	Gary Downs	835	173	4.8	Terry Harvey	235	131	.56	1,837	Eddie Goines	48	928	19.3
1994	Tremayne Stephens	791	125	6.3	Terry Harvey	199	116	.58	1,466	Eddie Goines	39	624	16.0
1995	Tremayne Stephens	849	186	4.6	Terry Harvey	279	155	.56	2,099	Mike Guffie	49	810	16.5
1996	Tremayne Stephens	771	165	4.7	Jamie Barnette	226	102	.45	1,594	Jimmy Grissett	50	751	15.0
1997	Tremayne Stephens	1,142	204	5.6	Jamie Barnette	302	171	.57	2,378	Torry Holt	62	1,099	17.7
1998	Ray Robinson	822	154	5.3	Jamie Barnette	377	193	.51	3,169	Torry Holt	88	1,604	18.2
1999	Rahshon Spikes	636	140	4.5	Jamie Barnette	338	171	.51	2,320	Koren Robinson	48	853	17.8
2000	Ray Robinson	788	193	4.1	Philip Rivers	441	237	.54	3,054	Koren Robinson	62	1,061	17.1
2001	Ray Robinson	733	190	3.9	Philip Rivers	368	240	.65	2,586	Ray Robinson	52	376	7.2
2002	T.A. McLendon	1,101	245	4.5	Philip Rivers	418	262	.63	3,353	Jerricho Cotchery	67	1,192	17.8
2003	T.A. McLendon	608	130	4.7	Philip Rivers	483	348	.72	4,491	Jerricho Cotchery	86	1,369	15.9
2004	T.A. McLendon	770	167	4.6	Jay Davis	313	175	.56	2,104	T.J. Williams	31	382	12.3

Receiving leaders by receptions
The NCAA began including postseason stats in 2002

NORTH CAROLINA STATE ALL-TIME SCORES

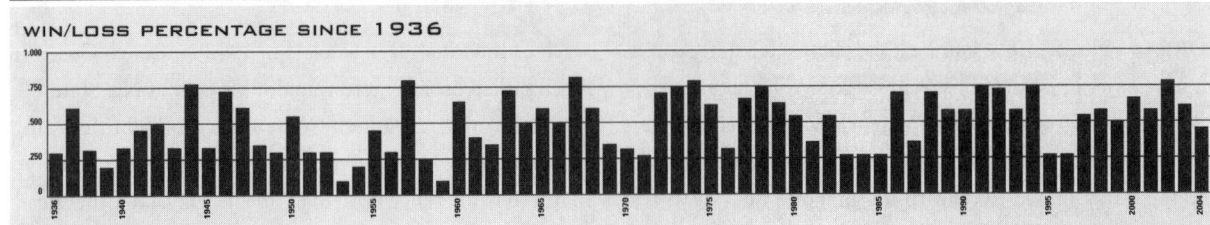

WIN/LOSS PERCENTAGE SINCE 1936

PERRIN BUSBEE
1892, '96-97 (.600)   3-2

1892   1-0-0
| U • | Raleigh Academy | 14 | 6 |

BART GATLING
1893-95 (.437)   3-4-1

1893   2-0-0
| U • | Tennessee Coll. | 12 | 6 |
| U • | Raleigh Academy | 13 | 0 |

1894   0-2-0
| O12 | at North Carolina | 0 | 44 |
| O20 | North Carolina | 0 | 16 |

1895   1-2-1
O12	at North Carolina	0	36
O19 =	Wake Forest	4	4
O25	VMI *Atl*	6	42
N18 •	Richmond	40	0

PERRIN BUSBEE

1896   1-0-0
| U • | Guilford | 6 | 0 |

1897   1-2-0
U •	Guilford	0	18
O2	at North Carolina	0	40
U •	Davidson	19	0

W.C. RIDDICK
1898-99 (.333)   1-3-2

1898   0-1-0
| O15 | at North Carolina | 0 | 34 |

1899   1-2-2
O7	at North Carolina	0	34
U •	Bingham *Ashe*	18	0
O28 =	North Carolina	11	11
U •	Davidson	0	0
N18 •	Clemson *RH*	0	24

DR. JOHN McGEE
1900-01 (.143)   1-6

1900   0-4-0
O25	Virginia Tech	2	18
N10	at South Carolina	0	12
U	Davidson	0	17
N29	South Carolina	5	17

1901   1-2-0
O16	at North Carolina	0	39
N19	North Carolina	0	30
U •	Davidson	27	6

ARTHUR DEVLIN
1902-03 (.471)   7-8-2

1902   3-4-2
O4	at Clemson	5	11
O6 =	at Furman	0	0
O13	Furman	2	5
O18	at Virginia Tech	6	10 *
O25 •	St. Albans *Roa*	10	0
N1 •	Guilford	28	5
N8 •	North Carolina	0	0
N22 •	Davidson	0	5
N27 •	Richmond	30	5

1903   4-4-0
U •	Guilford	50	0
U •	at VMI	0	6
O17 •	at Virginia Tech	0	21
U •	DMI *Dan*	33	0
O28 •	Clemson *Colu*	0	24
U •	Transylvania, Ky	0	18
N12 •	at Richmond	53	0
N14 •	South Carolina	6	5

W.S. KIENHOLZ
1904 (.667)   3-1-2

1904   3-1-2
S24 •	Guilford	59	0
O1 •	at VMI	6	0
O22 •	at Virginia	0	5
N5 =	South Carolina	0	0
N16 =	at North Carolina	6	6
N24 •	Clemson	8	0 *

GEORGE WHITNEY
1905 (.750)   4-1-1

1905   4-1-1
U •	VMI	5	0
O7 •	at Virginia	0	10
O26 •	at South Carolina	29	0
N12 =	North Carolina	0	0
U •	Wash. & Lee	21	0
U •	Davidson *W-S*	10	0

WILLIE HESTON
1906 (.625)   3-1-4

1906   3-1-4
U •	Randolph Macon	39	0
U =	at Virginia	0	0
O11 =	Richmond	0	0
U •	VMI	17	0
U =	Wash. & Lee	4	4
U •	William & Mary	40	0
O25 •	Clemson *Colu*	0	0
N29 •	Virginia Tech *Rich*	0	6

MICKEY WHITEHURST
1907-08 (.893)   12-1-1

1907   6-0-1
U •	Randolph Macon	20	0
O12 •	at Richmond	7	4
U •	Roanoke Coll.	22	0
O26 •	Richmond	11	0
N16 •	Davidson *Char*	6	0
U •	N.C. All Stars	5	5
N23 •	Virginia *Nor*	10	4

1908   6-1-0
S30 •	Wake Forest	76	0
O10 •	William & Mary	24	0
O17 •	Georgetown	5	0
N7 •	Davidson *Char*	21	0
N14 •	Virginia	0	6
N21 •	at Wake Forest	25	0
N26 •	Virginia Tech *Nor*	6	5

EDDIE GREEN
1909-13 (.743)   25-8-2

1909   6-1-0
O9 •	Maryville	39	0
O16 •	Maryland AC *Nor*	12	0
O22 •	Kentucky	15	6
O30 •	Maryland	31	0
N6 •	at Wash. & Lee	3	0
N20 •	USS Franklin	5	0
N25 •	Virginia Tech *Nor*	5	18

1910   4-0-2
O8 =	Georgetown	0	0
O15 =	Villanova	6	6
O22 •	Eastern	33	0
N12 •	Richmond	53	0
N19 •	Wake Forest	28	3
N24 •	Virginia Tech *Nor*	5	3

1911   5-3-0
O7 •	USS Franklin	23	0
O14 •	at VMI	5	6
O21 •	Bucknell	6	0
O28 •	Tennessee	16	0
N4 •	at Navy	6	17
N11 •	Wash. & Lee	15	3
N18 •	at Wake Forest	13	6 *
N30 •	Virginia Tech *Nor*	0	3

1912   4-3-0
O5 •	USS Franklin	21	0
O12 •	VA. Medical Coll.	7	0
O19 •	Georgetown	0	48
O26 •	at Davidson	7	0
N2 •	at Wake Forest	12	0
N16 •	at Navy	0	40
N28 •	Wash. & Lee *Nor*	6	16

1913   6-1-0
O11 •	USS Franklin	54	0
O18 •	at Davidson	26	6
O25 •	at Georgetown	12	0
N1 •	at Wake Forest	37	0
N8 •	VMI *Rich*	7	14
N15 •	Virginia Med.	13	7
N27 •	Wash. & Lee *Nor*	6	0

JACK HEGARTY
1914-15 (.461)   5-6-2

1914   2-3-1
O3 •	Wake Forest	51	0
O22 •	West Virginia	26	13
O31 •	at Navy	12	14 *
N7 •	Virginia Tech	0	3
N14 •	Wash. & Lee *Roa*	0	7
N26 =	Georgetown	7	7

1915   3-3-1
O9 =	Roanoke Coll.	0	0
O16 •	at Wake Forest	7	0
O21 •	South Carolina	10	19
O30 •	at Navy	14	12
N6 •	Gallaudet	27	7
N9 •	Georgetown	0	28
N25 •	Wash. & Lee *Nor*	13	48

BRIT PATTERSON
1916 (.286)   2-5

1916   2-5-0
S30 •	Roanoke Coll.	13	3
O7 •	at Davidson	0	16
O19 •	at Wake Forest	6	0
O28 •	Virginia Tech *Nor*	0	40
N11 •	at Navy	0	50
N18 •	Georgetown	5	61
N30 •	Wash. & Lee	0	28

HARRY HARTSELL
1917, '21-23 (.474)   16-18-4

1917   6-2-1
S29 •	at Guilford	19	0
O6 •	Davidson	7	3
O13 •	Roanoke Coll.	28	0
O18 •	Wake Forest	17	6
O27 •	at Wash. & Lee	7	27
N3 •	Maryland *DC*	10	6
N10 •	VMI *Rich*	17	0
N17 =	Virginia Tech *Nor*	7	7
N29 •	at West Virginia	0	21

TAL STAFFORD
1918 (.250)   1-3

1918   1-3-0
N2 •	Guilford	54	0
N10 •	at Georgia Tech	0	128
N16 •	Virginia Tech *Nor*	0	25
N23 •	Wake Forest	0	21

BILL FETZER
1919-20 (.737)   14-5

1919   7-2-0
S27 •	Guilford	80	0
O4 •	at Navy	0	49
O11 •	Hampton Roads	100	0
O18 •	Roanoke Coll.	78	0
O23 •	North Carolina	12	13
N1 •	VMI *Roa*	21	0
N8 •	Davidson	36	6
N15 •	Virginia Tech *Nor*	3	0
N27 •	Wake Forest	21	7

1920   7-3-0
S25 •	Davidson	23	0
O2 •	at Navy	14	7
O9 •	at Georgetown	0	27
O16 •	at Penn State	0	41
O21 •	North Carolina	13	3
O30 •	VMI *Pet*	0	14
N6 •	William & Mary	81	0
N11 •	Virginia Tech *Nor*	14	6
N20 •	Wofford	90	7
N25 •	at Wake Forest	49	7

1921-1952
SOUTHERN CONFERENCE

HARRY HARTSELL

1921   3-3-3 (1-1-1)
S24 •	Randolph Macon	21	0
O1 •	at Navy	0	40
O8 •	at Penn State	0	35
O20 •	North Carolina	7	0
O29 =	VMI	7	7
N5 =	Davidson *Char*	3	3
N11	Virginia Tech *Nor*	3	7
N19	at Wake Forest	14	0
N24	Maryland *Balt*	6	6

1922   4-6-0 (0-5-0)
S30 •	Randolph Macon	20	2
O7	at Wash. & Lee	6	14
O14	Roanoke Coll.	13	0
O19	North Carolina	9	14
O28	VMI *Nor*	0	14
N4	Davidson	15	0
N11	Virginia Tech *Nor*	0	24
N18	at Georgia Tech	0	17
N25	at Wake Forest	32	0
N30	Maryland	6	7

1923   3-7-0 (1-4-0)
S29 •	Roanoke Coll.	6	0
O6	at Penn State	0	16
O13	South Carolina	7	0
O18	North Carolina	0	14
O27	at VMI	7	22
N3	Davidson *Char*	12	6
N10	Virginia Tech *Nor*	0	16
N17	Maryland	12	26
N24	at Wake Forest	0	14
N29	Wash. & Lee *Nor*	12	20

BUCK SHAW
1924 (.300) 2-6-2

1924 — 2-6-2 (1-4-1)

S27	●	Duke	14	0
O4		at Penn State	6	51
O11		at South Carolina	0	10
O16		North Carolina	0	10
O25		VMI *Rich*	7	17
N1	=	Davidson *Pin*	10	10
N8	●	Virginia Tech	6	3
N15	=	at Maryland	0	0
N22		Wake Forest	0	12
N27		Wash. & Lee	0	34

GUS TEBELL
1925-29 (.479) 21-25-2

1925 — 3-5-1 (0-4-1)

S25	●	Richmond	20	0
O3	●	at Duke	13	0
O11		South Carolina	6	7
O15		North Carolina	6	17 *
O24		at Davidson	0	9
O31		VMI *Rich*	6	27
N7	=	at Virginia Tech	0	0
N14	●	Wake Forest	6	0
N21		at Wash. & Lee	0	14

1926 — 4-6-0 (0-4-0)

S25	●	Elon	10	0
O2		Furman	0	31
O9		at Clemson	3	7
O16		Davidson	0	3
O23		VMI *Rich*	0	7
O30		at North Carolina	0	12
N6	●	Lenoir Rhyne	6	0
N13	●	Duke	26	19
N20		at South Carolina	14	20
N27	●	Wake Forest	7	3

1927 — 9-1-0 (4-0-0)

S24	●	Elon	39	0
S30		at Furman	0	20
O8	●	Clemson	18	6
O13	●	Wake Forest	30	7
O22	●	Florida *Tam*	12	6
O29	●	North Carolina	19	6
N5	●	Davidson *Gro*	25	6
N12	●	at Duke	20	18
N24	●	at South Carolina	34	0
D3	●	Michigan State	19	0

1928 — 4-5-1 (1-3-1)

S29	●	Elon	57	0
O6		at Wash. & Lee	6	38
O12		Clemson *Flo*	0	7
O18	●	Wake Forest	37	0
O27		Florida *JacF*	7	14
N3	=	North Carolina	6	6
N10	●	Davidson *Gro*	14	7
N17		Duke	12	14
N24		at Michigan State	0	7
N29	●	South Carolina	18	7

1929 — 1-8-0 (0-5-0)

O4		Wash. & Lee	6	27
O11		Clemson *Flo*	0	26
O17	●	Wake Forest	8	6
O26		at Michigan State	6	40
N2		at North Carolina	0	32
N9		Davidson	0	13
N16		at Duke	12	19
N23		Villanova *Phil*	6	24
N30		South Carolina	6	20

JOHN VAN LIEW
1930 (.200) 2-8

1930 — 2-8-0 (1-5-0)

S20	●	High Point	34	0
S27		Davidson	0	12
O4		Florida *Tam*	0	27
O11		Clemson *Char*	0	27
O16		Wake Forest	0	7
O25	●	Mississippi State	14	0
N1		Presbyterian	0	2
N7		at North Carolina	6	13
N15		Duke	0	18
N22		at South Carolina	0	19

CLIPPER SMITH
1931-33 (.463) 10-12-5

1931 — 3-6-0 (2-4-0)

S26	●	Davidson *Nor*	18	7
O3		Florida	0	34
O10		Clemson *Gro*	0	6
O16		Wake Forest	0	6
O24		Catholic U.	7	12
O31		North Carolina	15	18
N7	●	at Mississippi State	6	0
N14	●	at Duke	14	0
N21		at South Carolina	0	21

1932 — 6-1-2 (3-1-1)

S24	●	Appalachian St.	31	0
O1	●	at Richmond	9	0
O8	●	Clemson	13	0
O15	=	Wake Forest	0	0
O22	●	Florida *Tam*	17	6
O29		at North Carolina	0	13
N5	●	Davidson *Char*	7	3
N12	●	Duke	6	0
N24	=	South Carolina	7	7

1933 — 1-5-3 (0-4-0)

S23	●	Catawba	7	0
S30		at Georgia	10	20
O7		at Clemson	0	9
O14	=	Florida	0	0
O21	=	Wake Forest	0	0
O28	=	Davidson	6	6
N4		North Carolina	0	6
N11		at South Carolina	0	14
N25		at Duke	0	7

HEARTLEY "HUNK" ANDERSON
1934-36 (.396) 11-17-1

1934 — 2-6-1 (1-3-1)

S29	●	Davidson *Gro*	7	0
O6		Wake Forest	12	13
O13	●	South Carolina	6	0
O20		Florida *Tam*	0	14
O27	=	at North Carolina	7	7
N3		Clemson	6	12
N10		Virginia Tech *Pts*	6	7
N17		at Georgia	0	27
D1		at Duke	0	32

1935 — 6-4-0 (2-2-0)

S28	●	Davidson	14	7
O5	●	at South Carolina	14	0
O12	●	Wake Forest	21	6
O19		Georgia	0	13
O26	●	Manhattan *Bkln*	20	0
N2		North Carolina	6	35
N9	●	Virginia Tech *Pts*	6	0
N16	●	at Richmond	6	0
N23		Duke	0	7
N30		at Catholic U.	0	8

1936 — 3-7-0 (2-4-0)

S19	●	Elon	12	0
S26		Davidson	2	6
O3		Wake Forest	0	9
O9		Manhattan *Bkln*	6	13
O17	●	Furman	27	0
O24	●	Virginia Tech	13	0
O31		at North Carolina	6	21
N7		at Boston College	3	7
N14		at Catholic U.	6	7
N26		at Duke	0	13

DOC NEWTON
1937-43 (.391) 24-39-6

1937 — 5-3-1 (4-2-1)

S18	●	Davidson *Gro*	6	2
O2		North Carolina	0	20
O9	=	at Furman	7	7
O16	●	Virginia Tech	13	7
O23	●	at Wake Forest	20	0
O30	●	at Boston College	12	7
N6	●	Citadel	26	14
N13		Manhattan *Bkln*	0	15
N20		Duke	7	20

1938 — 3-7-1 (3-3-1)

S24	●	Davidson *Char*	19	7
O1		North Carolina	0	21
O8		at Alabama	0	14
O15	●	Wake Forest	19	7
O22	=	Furman	7	7
O29		at Virginia Tech	0	7
N5		Manhattan *Bnx*	0	3
N12		Detroit	0	7
N19		at Duke	0	7
N26		Carnegie Tech	0	14
D3	●	Citadel *Wil*	14	6

1939 — 2-8-0 (2-4-0)

S23	●	Davidson *Gro*	18	14
S29		Tennessee	0	13
O7		Clemson *Char*	6	25
O14		Wake Forest	0	32
O21		at Detroit	6	21
N4		at North Carolina	0	17
N11		Duquesne	0	7
N18	●	at Furman	12	7
N25		Duke	0	28
D1		at Miami, Fla.	7	27

1940 — 3-6-0 (3-5-0)

S21	●	William & Mary	16	0
S28	●	at Davidson	34	0
O5		Clemson *Char*	7	26
O19		North Carolina	7	13
O26		Mississippi State	10	26
N2		Furman	6	20
N9		Wake Forest	14	20
N16	●	Citadel	20	14
N23		at Duke	6	42

1941 — 4-5-2 (3-4-2)

S20	●	Richmond	14	7
S27	=	Davidson *Gro*	6	6
O4		Clemson *Char*	6	27
O11	=	at Furman	0	0
O18		Wake Forest	0	7
O25	●	Newberry	44	0
N1	●	at North Carolina	13	7
N8		Virginia Tech *W-S*	13	14
N15		at Georgetown	7	20
N22		Duke	6	55
N29	●	at William & Mary	13	0

1942 — 4-4-2 (3-1-2)

S19	=	Davidson *Wil*	0	0
S26	●	Richmond	13	0
O3	●	Clemson *Char*	7	6
O10		N.C. Pre-Flight	7	19
O17	=	Wake Forest	0	0
O24		at Holy Cross	0	28
O31	●	North Carolina	21	14
N7	●	at Miami, Fla.	2	0
N14		Georgetown	20	28
N21		at Duke	0	47

1943 — 3-6--0 (1-4-0)

S25	●	Newport News	18	0
O2		Clemson *Char*	7	19
O9		at Camp Davis	0	27
O16		Wake Forest	6	54
O23	●	at Greenville Air Base	7	6
O30		at North Carolina	13	27
N6		Duke	0	75
N13	●	at Davidson	10	0
N25		N.C. Pre-Flight	7	19

BEATTIE FEATHERS
1944-51 (.494) 37-38-3

1944 — 7-2-0 (3-2-0)

S23	●	Milligan	27	7
S30	●	Virginia *Nor*	13	0
O7		Clemson *Char*	7	13
O14	●	Catawba	12	7
O21		Wake Forest	7	21
O28	●	William & Mary	19	2
N4	●	at VMI	21	6
N10	●	at Miami, Fla.	28	7
N18	●	Richmond *Nor*	39	0

1945 — 3-6-0 (2-4-0)

S22	●	Milligan	47	12
S29		Virginia *Nor*	6	26
O6		Clemson	0	13
O13		VMI	14	21
O20		Wake Forest	18	19
O27	●	William & Mary	20	6
N3	●	Virginia Tech	6	0
N10		at Duke	13	26
N16		at Miami, Fla.	7	21

1946 — 8-3-0 (6-1-0)

S28	●	Duke	13	6
O5	●	at Clemson	14	7
O12	●	Davidson	25	0
O19	●	at Wake Forest	14	6
O26		at Virginia Tech	6	14
N2	●	VMI *Nor*	49	7
N9		at Vanderbilt	0	7
N16	●	Virginia	27	7
N23	●	Florida *Tam*	37	6
N30	●	Maryland	28	7
		GATOR BOWL		
J1		Oklahoma	13	34

1947 — 5-3-1 (3-2-1)

S27		at Duke	0	7
O4	●	Davidson *Char*	14	0
O11	●	Clemson	18	0
O18		Florida	6	7
N1	●	U.T. Chattanooga	21	0
N8		at North Carolina	6	41
N15	●	Wake Forest	20	0
N22	●	at Virginia	7	2
N29	=	Maryland *DC*	0	0

1948 — 3-6-1 (1-4-1)

S25	=	Duke	0	0
O2		at Clemson	0	6
O9	●	at Davidson	40	0
O16		at North Carolina	0	14
O23	●	at U.T. Chattanooga	7	0
O30		at Wake Forest	13	34
N6		Virginia	14	21
N16	●	at Duquesne	20	6
N20		at William & Mary	6	26
N27		Villanova	7	21

1949 — 3-7-0 (3-6-0)

S24		at North Carolina	6	26
O1		Clemson	6	7
O8		Davidson *Char*	14	20
O15		at Duke	13	14
O22		Maryland	6	14
O29	●	Virginia Tech *Nor*	14	13
N5	●	Richmond	20	6
N12	●	Wake Forest	27	14
N19		Villanova *Phil*	21	45
N26		at William & Mary	7	33

1950 — 5-4-1 (4-4-1)

S23		at North Carolina	7	13
S30	●	Catawba	7	6
O7		at Clemson	0	27
O14		Duke	0	7
O21	●	at Maryland	16	13
O28	●	Virginia Tech	34	6
N4	●	at Richmond	7	0
N11	●	Davidson	15	7
N18	=	at Wake Forest	6	6
N25		William & Mary *Nor*	0	34

1951 — 3-7-0 (2-6-0)

S15	●	Catawba	34	0
S22		at North Carolina	0	21
S29		Wake Forest	6	21
O6		Clemson	0	6
O13		at Duke	21	27
O20		William & Mary	28	35
O27	●	at Virginia Tech	19	14
N2		at Louisville	2	26
N10	●	Davidson *Char*	31	0
N17		at Maryland	0	53

HORACE HENDRICKSON
1952-53 (.200) 4-16

1952 — 3-7-0 (2-4-0)

S27		George Washington	0	39
O4		at Georgia	0	49
O11	●	Davidson	28	6
O18		Duke	0	57
O25	●	Florida State	13	7
N1		at Wake Forest	6	21
N8	●	at Wash. & Lee	25	14
N15		at Pittsburgh	6	48
N22		at William & Mary	6	41
N29		at Texas Tech	7	54

1953-PRESENT
ACC

1953 — 1-9-0 (0-3-0)

S26		at North Carolina	7	29
O3		at George Washington	7	20
O10	●	Davidson	27	7
O17		Wake Forest	7	20
O24		at Duke	0	31
O31		William & Mary	6	7
N7		at Army	7	27
N14		at Pittsburgh	6	40
N21		West Virginia	0	61
N28		at Florida State	13	23

EARLE EDWARDS
1954-70 (.468) 77-88-8

1954 2-8-0 (0-4-0)

S18			at Virginia Tech	21	30
S25		|	at North Carolina	6	20
O2		|	at Wake Forest	0	26
O9	●		at William & Mary	26	0
O16			Florida State	7	13
O23		|	Duke	7	21
O30			Furman	6	7
N6		|	at Maryland	14	42
N13	●		Richmond	14	6
N20			at West Virginia	3	28

1955 4-5-1 (0-2-1)

S17			at Florida State	0	7
S24		|	Duke	7	33
O1		|	North Carolina	18	25
O15	=	|	Wake Forest	13	13
O22	●		at Villanova	34	13
O29	●		at Furman	33	7
N5	●		at Boston U.	40	13
N12			Virginia Tech *Blu*	26	34
N19	●		William & Mary	28	21
N25			West Virginia	7	27

1956 3-7-0 (2-4-0)

S22	●	|	at North Carolina	26	6
S29			Virginia Tech *Nor*	6	35
O6		|	Clemson	7	13
O13			Florida State	0	14
O20	●		at Dayton	20	0
O27		|	at Duke	0	42
N3		|	at Wake Forest	0	13
N10	●	|	South Carolina	14	7
N17			at Penn State	7	14
N22		|	Maryland	14	25

1957 7-1-2 (5-0-1)

S21	●	|	at North Carolina	7	0
S28	●	|	at Maryland	48	13
O5	●	|	at Clemson	13	7
O12	●		at Florida State	7	0
O18	=		at Miami, Fla.	0	0
O26	=	|	Duke	14	14
N2	●	|	Wake Forest	19	0
N9			William & Mary	6	7
N16	●		Virginia Tech *Roa*	12	0
N23	●	|	at South Carolina	29	26

1958 2-7-1 (2-5-0)

S20	●	|	at North Carolina	21	14
S27		|	Maryland	6	21
O4	●	|	at Virginia	26	14
O11		|	at Wake Forest	7	13
O18			at William & Mary	6	13
O25		|	at Duke	13	20
N1	=		Virginia Tech	14	14
N8			Southern Miss *Mbl*	14	26
N15		|	Clemson	6	13
N22		|	at South Carolina	7	12

1959 1-9-0 (0-6-0)

S19	●		Virginia Tech *Nor*	15	13
O3		|	at North Carolina	12	20
O10		|	at Clemson	0	23
O17		|	Wake Forest	14	17
O24		|	Duke	15	17
O31			Wyoming	0	26
N7			Southern Miss *Mbl*	14	19
N13			at UCLA	12	21
N21		|	at South Carolina	7	12
D5		|	at Maryland	28	33

1960 6-3-1 (4-1-1)

S17	●		Virginia Tech	29	14
S24	●	|	at North Carolina	3	0
O1	●	|	Virginia	26	7
O8	●	|	Maryland	13	10
O15		|	at Duke	13	17
O22	●		at Southern Miss	20	13
O29			at UCLA	0	7
N5	●	|	at Wake Forest	14	12
N12			at Arizona State	22	25
N19	=	|	at South Carolina	8	8

1961 4-6-0 (3-4-0)

S23			at Wyoming	14	15
S30		|	at North Carolina	22	27
O7	●	|	at Virginia	21	14
O14			at Alabama	7	26
O21	●	|	Wake Forest	7	0
O28		|	Duke	6	17
N4	●		Southern Miss *Mbl*	7	6
N11		|	at Maryland	7	10
N18	●	|	South Carolina	38	14
N25		|	at Clemson	0	20

1962 3-6-1 (3-4-0)

S22	●	|	at North Carolina	7	6
S29		|	Clemson	0	7
O6		|	at Maryland	6	14
O13			at Nebraska	14	19
O20			Southern Miss *Mbl*	0	30
O27		|	at Duke	14	21
N3	=		at Georgia	10	10
N10		|	at South Carolina	6	17
N17	●	|	Virginia	24	12
N22	●	|	at Wake Forest	27	3

1963 8-3-0 (6-1-0)

S21	●	|	at Maryland	36	14
S28	●		at Southern Miss	14	0
O5	●	|	at Clemson	7	3
O12	●	|	at South Carolina	18	6
O19		|	at North Carolina	10	31
O26	●	|	Duke	21	7
N2	●	|	Virginia *Nor*	15	9
N9	●		Virginia Tech	13	7
N16			at Florida State	0	14
N22	●	|	Wake Forest	42	0
			LIBERTY BOWL		
D21			Mississippi State	12	16

1964 5-5-0 (5-2-0)

S19	●	|	at North Carolina	14	13
S26	●	|	Clemson	9	0
O3	●	|	Maryland	14	13
O10			at Alabama	0	21
O17		|	at Duke	3	35
O24	●	|	at Virginia	24	15
O31	●	|	South Carolina	17	14
N7			at Virginia Tech	19	28
N14			at Florida State	6	28
N20		|	at Wake Forest	13	27

1965 6-4-0 (4-3-0)

S18		|	at Clemson	7	21
S25	●	|	Wake Forest	13	11
O2		|	at South Carolina	7	13
O9		|	North Carolina	7	10
O16			at Florida	6	28
O23	●	|	at Maryland	29	7
O30	●	|	at Virginia	13	0
N6	●	|	Duke	21	0
N13	●		Florida State	3	0
N20	●		at Iowa	28	20

1966 5-5-0 (5-2-0)

S17			at Michigan State	10	28
S24		|	at North Carolina	7	10
O1	●	|	at Wake Forest	15	12
O8		|	South Carolina	21	31
O15			Florida	10	17
O22	●	|	at Duke	33	7
O29	●	|	Virginia	42	21
N5	●	|	Maryland	24	21
N12			Southern Miss *Nor*	6	7
N19	●	|	Clemson	23	14

1967 9-2-0 (5-1-0)

S16	●	|	North Carolina	13	7
S23	●		Buffalo	24	6
S30	●		at Florida State	20	10
O7	●		at Houston	16	6
O14	●	|	at Maryland	31	9
O21	●	|	Wake Forest	24	7
O28	●	|	Duke	28	7
N4	●	|	at Virginia	30	8
N11			at Penn State	8	13
N18		|	at Clemson	6	14
			LIBERTY BOWL		
D16	●		Georgia	14	7

1968 6-4-0 (6-1-0)

S14	●	|	at Wake Forest	10	6
S21	●	|	at North Carolina	38	6
S28			at Oklahoma	14	28
O5			at SMU	14	35
O12	●	|	South Carolina	36	12
O19	●	|	Virginia	19	0
O26	●	|	Maryland	31	11
N2		|	Clemson	19	24
N9	●	|	at Duke	17	15
N16			Florida State	7	48

1969 3-6-1 (3-2-1)

S13		|	Wake Forest	21	22
S20	●	|	North Carolina	10	3
S27	●	|	at Maryland	24	7
O3			at Miami, Fla.	13	23
O11		|	at South Carolina	16	21
O18	●	|	at Virginia	31	0
O25	=	|	Duke	25	25
N15			Houston	13	34
N22			at Florida State	22	33
N29			Penn State	8	33

1970 3-7-1 (2-3-1)

S12			at Richmond	6	21
S19		|	at North Carolina	0	19
S26	=	|	South Carolina	7	7
O3			at Florida	6	14
O10	●		East Carolina	23	6
O17		|	Duke	6	22
O24	●	|	Maryland *Nor*	6	0
O31			at Kentucky	2	27
N7	●	|	Virginia	21	16
N14		|	at Wake Forest	13	16
N21			at Tulane	0	31

AL MICHAELS
1971 (.273) 3-8

1971 3-8-0 (2-5-0)

S11			Kent State	21	23
S18		|	at Maryland	7	35
S25		|	at South Carolina	6	24
O2		|	North Carolina	7	27
O9	●	|	Wake Forest	21	14
O16		|	at Duke	13	41
O23			East Carolina	15	31
O30		|	Virginia	10	14
N6	●		at Miami, Fla.	13	7
N13			at Penn State	3	35
N20	●	|	at Clemson	31	23

LOU HOLTZ
1972-75 (.719) 33-12-3

1972 8-3-1 (4-1-1)

S9	=	|	Maryland	24	24
S16	●		Syracuse	43	20
S23		|	at North Carolina	33	34
S30			at Georgia	22	28
O7	●	|	Duke	17	0
O14	●	|	at Wake Forest	42	13
O21	●		East Carolina	38	16
O28	●		South Carolina	42	24
N4	●	|	at Virginia	35	14
N11			at Penn State	22	37
N18	●	|	Clemson	42	17
			PEACH BOWL		
D29	●		West Virginia	49	13

1973 9-3-0 (6-0-0)

S8	●		East Carolina	57	8
S15	●	|	Virginia	43	23
S22			at Nebraska	14	31
S29			at Georgia	12	31
O6	●	|	North Carolina	28	26
O13	●	|	Maryland	24	22
O27	●	|	at Clemson	29	6
N3	●		at South Carolina	56	35
N10			at Penn State	29	35
N17	●	|	at Duke	21	3
N24	●	|	Wake Forest	52	13
			LIBERTY BOWL		
D17	●		Kansas	31	18

1974 9-2-1 (4-2-0)

S7	●	|	at Wake Forest	33	15
S14	●	|	Duke	35	21
S21	●	|	Clemson	31	10
S28	●		at Syracuse	28	22
O5	●		East Carolina	24	20
O12	●	|	at Virginia	22	21
O19		|	at North Carolina	14	33
O26		|	at Maryland	10	20
N2	●		South Carolina	42	27
N9	●		Penn State	12	7
N16	●		at Arizona State	35	14
			BLUEBONNET BOWL		
D23	=		Houston	31	31

1975 7-4-1 (2-2-1)

S6	●		East Carolina	26	3
S13		|	Wake Forest	22	30
S20	●		Florida	8	7
S27			at Michigan State	15	37
O4	●		Indiana	27	0
O11		|	at Maryland	22	37
O18	●	|	North Carolina	21	20
O25	●	|	at Clemson	45	7
N1	●		South Carolina	28	21
N8	●		at Penn State	15	14
N15	=	|	at Duke	21	21
			PEACH BOWL		
D31			West Virginia	10	13

BO REIN
1976-79 (.619) 27-18-1

1976 3-7-1 (2-3-0)

S4			Furman	12	17
S11		|	at Wake Forest	18	20
S18			East Carolina	14	23
S25	=		Michigan State	31	31
O2	●		at Indiana	24	21
O9		|	Maryland	6	16
O16	●	|	at North Carolina	21	13
O23	●	|	Clemson	38	21
O30			at South Carolina	7	27
N6			at Penn State	20	41
N13		|	Duke	14	28

1977 8-4-0 (4-2-0)

S3			East Carolina	23	28
S10	●	|	Virginia	14	0
S17	●		at Syracuse	38	0
S24	●	|	Wake Forest	41	14
O1	●	|	Maryland	24	20
O8	●		at Auburn	17	15
O15		|	North Carolina	14	27
O22		|	at Clemson	3	7
O29	●		South Carolina	7	3
N5			Penn State	17	21
N12	●	|	at Duke	37	32
			PEACH BOWL		
D31	●		Iowa State	24	14

1978 9-3-0 (4-2-0)

S9	●		East Carolina	29	13
S16	●		Syracuse	27	19
S23	●		West Virginia	29	15
S30	●	|	at Wake Forest	34	10
O7		|	at Maryland	7	31
O21	●	|	at North Carolina	34	7
O28		|	Clemson	10	33
N4	●		South Carolina	22	13
N11			at Penn State	10	19
N18	●	|	Duke	24	10
N25	●	|	at Virginia	24	21
			TANGERINE BOWL		
D23	●		Pittsburgh	30	17

1979 7-4-0 (5-1-0)

S8	●		East Carolina	34	20
S15	●	|	Virginia	31	27
S22	●		at West Virginia	38	14
S29	●	|	Wake Forest	17	14
O6			at Auburn	31	44
O13	●	|	Maryland	7	0
O20		|	North Carolina	21	35
O27	●	|	at Clemson	16	13
N3			at South Carolina	28	30
N10			Penn State	7	9
N17	●	|	at Duke	28	7

MONTE KIFFIN
1980-82 (.485) 16-17

1980 6-5-0 (3-3-0)

S6	●		William & Mary	42	0
S20	●	|	at Virginia	27	13
S27		|	Wake Forest	7	27
O4			at South Carolina	10	30
O11	●		Appalaichain St.	17	14
O18		|	at North Carolina	8	28
O25	●	|	Clemson	24	20
N1		|	at Maryland	0	24
N8			at Penn State	13	21
N15	●	|	Duke	38	21
N22	●		East Carolina	36	14

1981 4-7-0 (2-4-0)

S5	●		Richmond	27	21
S12	●	|	at Wake Forest	28	23
S19	●		East Carolina	31	10
S26		|	Maryland	9	34
O3	●	|	Virginia	30	24
O17		|	North Carolina	10	21
O24		|	at Clemson	7	17
O31			at South Carolina	12	20
N7			Penn State	15	22
N14		|	at Duke	7	17
N21			Miami, Fla.	6	14

1982 6-5-0 (3-3-0)

S4	●		Furman	26	0
S11	●		East Carolina	33	26
S18	●	|	Wake Forest	30	0
S25		|	at Maryland	6	23
O2	●	|	at Virginia	16	13
O16		|	at North Carolina	9	41
O23		|	Clemson	29	38
O30	●		South Carolina	33	3
N6			at Penn State	0	54
N13	●	|	Duke	21	16
N20			at Miami, Fla.	3	41

THE SCHOOLS

TOM REED
1983-85 (.273)   9-24

1983   3-8-0 (1-6-0)
S10		at East Carolina	16	22
S17	•	Citadel	45	0
S24		Virginia	14	26
O1	•	at Wake Forest	38	15
O8		Georgia Tech	10	20
O15		North Carolina	14	42
O22		at Clemson	17	27
O29		at South Carolina	17	31
N5		Appalachian St.	33	7
N10		at Duke	26	27
N19		Maryland	6	29

1984   3-8-0 (1-6-0)
S8	•	Ohio U.	43	6
S15		Furman	30	34
S22		Wake Forest	15	24
S29	•	East Carolina	31	22
O6	•	at Georgia Tech	27	22
O13	•	at Maryland	21	44
O20	•	at North Carolina	21	28
O27		Clemson	34	35
N3		South Carolina	28	35
N10		at Virginia	0	45
N17		Duke	13	16

1985   3-8-0 (2-5-0)
S7		East Carolina	14	33
S14		Georgia Tech	18	28
S21	•	at Wake Forest	20	17
S28		Furman	20	42
O5		Maryland	17	31
O12		at Pittsburgh	10	24
O19		North Carolina	14	21
O26		at Clemson	10	39
N2	•	at South Carolina	21	17
N9		Virginia	23	22
N16		at Duke	19	31

DICK SHERIDAN
1986-92 (.637)   52-29-3

1986   8-3-1 (5-2-0)
S6	•	East Carolina	38	10
S13	=	Pittsburgh	14	14
S20	•	Wake Forest	42	38
S27	•	at Maryland	28	16
O11	•	at Georgia Tech	21	59
O18	•	at North Carolina	35	34
O25	•	Clemson	27	3
N1	•	South Carolina	23	22
N8		at Virginia	16	20
N15	•	Duke	29	15
N22	•	Western Carolina	31	18
PEACH BOWL				
D31		Virginia Tech	24	25

1987   4-7-0 (4-3-0)
S5		East Carolina	14	32
S12		at Pittsburgh	0	34
S19		at Wake Forest	3	21
S26	•	Maryland	42	14
O3	•	Georgia Tech	17	0
O17	•	North Carolina	14	17
O24	•	at Clemson	30	28
O31	•	at South Carolina	0	48
N7		East Tenn. St.	14	29
N14	•	at Duke	47	45
N21		Virginia	31	34

1988   8-3-1 (4-2-1)
S3	•	Western Carolina	45	6
S17	•	Wake Forest	14	6
S24		at Maryland	26	30
O1	•	at Georgia Tech	14	6
O8	•	East Tenn. St.	49	0
O15	•	at North Carolina	48	3
O22	•	Clemson	10	3
O29		South Carolina	7	23
N5		at Virginia	14	19
N12	=	Duke	43	43
N19	•	Pittsburgh	14	3
PEACH BOWL				
D31	•	Iowa	28	23

1989   7-5-0 (4-3-0)
S2	•	Maryland	10	6
S9	•	Georgia Tech	38	28
S16	•	at Wake Forest	27	17
S23	•	North Carolina	40	6
S30	•	Kent State	42	22
O7	•	Middle Tennessee	35	14
O21		at Clemson	10	30
O28	•	at South Carolina	20	10
N4		Virginia	9	20
N11		at Duke	26	35
N18		Virginia Tech	23	25
COPPER BOWL				
D31	•	Arizona	10	17

1990   7-5-0 (3-4-0)
S1	•	Western Carolina	67	0
S8		at Georgia Tech	13	21
S15	•	Wake Forest	20	15
S22		at Maryland	12	13
S29	•	at North Carolina	12	9
O6	•	Appalachian St.	56	0
O13		at Virginia	0	31
O20		Clemson	17	24
O27	•	South Carolina	38	29
N3		at Virginia Tech	16	20
N10	•	Duke	16	0
ALL-AMERICAN BOWL				
D28	•	Southern Miss	31	27

1991   9-3-0 (5-2-0)
S7	•	Virginia Tech	7	0
S14	•	Kent State	47	0
S21	•	at Wake Forest	30	3
S28	•	North Carolina	24	7
O5	•	Georgia Tech	28	21
O19	•	Marshall	15	14
O26		at Clemson	19	29
N2	•	at South Carolina	38	21
N9		Virginia	10	42
N16	•	at Duke	32	31
N23	•	Maryland	20	17
PEACH BOWL				
J1		East Carolina	34	37

1992   9-3-1 (6-2-0)
A29	•	Iowa *ERut*	24	14
S5	•	Appalachian St.	35	10
S12	•	at Maryland	14	10
S19		Florida State	13	34
S26	•	at North Carolina	27	20
O3		at Georgia Tech	13	16
O10	•	Texas Tech	48	13
O17	=	at Virginia Tech	13	13
O24	•	Clemson	20	6
N7		at Virginia	31	7
N14	•	Duke	45	27
N21	•	Wake Forest	42	14
GATOR BOWL				
D31	•	Florida	10	27

MIKE O'CAIN
1993-99 (.506)   41-40

1993   7-5-0 (4-4-0)
S4	•	Purdue	20	7
S11	•	at Wake Forest	34	16
S25		North Carolina	14	35
O2	•	at Clemson	14	20
O9	•	at Texas Tech	36	34
O16	•	Marshall	24	17
O23	•	Georgia Tech	28	23
O30	•	Virginia	34	29
N6		at Duke	20	21
N13	•	Maryland	44	21
N20	•	at Florida State	3	62
HALL OF FAME BOWL				
J1	•	Michigan	7	42

1994   9-3-0 (6-2-0)
S1	•	Bowling Green	20	15
S10	•	at Clemson	29	12
S24	•	Western Carolina	38	13
O1	•	Georgia Tech	21	13
O8		at Louisville	14	35
O15	•	Wake Forest	34	3
O29		at North Carolina	17	31
N5	•	at Maryland	47	45
N12	•	Duke	24	23
N19		Florida State	3	34
N25	•	at Virginia	30	27
PEACH BOWL				
J1	•	Mississippi State	28	24

1995   3-8-0 (2-6-0)
A31	•	Marshall	33	16
S9		Virginia	24	29
S16		at Florida State	17	77
S23		Baylor	0	14
S30		Clemson	22	43
O7		at Alabama	11	27
O21	•	at Duke	41	38
N4		Maryland	13	30
N11		at Georgia Tech	19	27
N18	•	at Wake Forest	52	23
N24		North Carolina	28	30

1996   3-8 (3-5)
S7		Georgia Tech	16	28
S19		Florida State	17	51
S28		at Purdue	21	42
O5	•	at Maryland	34	8
O12		Alabama	19	24
O19		at Virginia	14	62
N2		at North Carolina	20	52
N9		Duke	44	22
N16		at Clemson	17	40
N23	•	Wake Forest	37	22
N30		East Carolina *Char*	29	50

1997   6-5 (3-5)
A30	•	at Syracuse	32	31
S6	•	at Duke	45	14
S13		Clemson	17	19
S20	•	Northern Illinois	41	14
S25		at Wake Forest	18	19
O11	•	at Georgia Tech	17	27
O18		North Carolina	7	20
N1		at Florida State	35	48
N8	•	Maryland	45	28
N15	•	Virginia	31	24
N22	•	East Carolina	37	24

1998   7-5 (5-3)
S3	•	Ohio U.	34	31
S12	•	Florida State	24	7
S19		at Baylor	30	33
O1	•	Syracuse	38	17
O10		Georgia Tech	24	47
O17	•	Duke	27	24
O24		at Virginia	13	23
O31	•	at Clemson	46	39
N7	•	Wake Forest	38	27
N21	•	at Maryland	45	28
N28	•	North Carolina *Char*	34	37
MICRON PC.COM BOWL				
D29	•	Miami, Fla.	23	46

1999   6-6 (3-5)
A28	•	at Texas	23	20
S4	•	South Carolina	10	0
S11	•	William & Mary	38	9
S18		at Florida State	11	42
S25	•	at Wake Forest	7	31
O9		Clemson	35	31
O16		Virginia	26	47
O23	•	at Duke	31	24
O30		at Georgia Tech	21	48
N6	•	Maryland	30	17
N11	•	North Carolina *Char*	6	10
N20		at East Carolina	6	23

CHUCK AMATO
2000-Present (.629)   39-23

2000   8-4 (4-4)
S2	•	Arkansas State	38	31
S9	•	at Indiana	41	38
S16	•	SMU	41	0
S21	•	Georgia Tech	30	23
O7		at Clemson	27	34
O14	•	at North Carolina	38	20
O28		Florida State	14	58
N4		at Maryland	28	35
N11	•	Duke	35	31
N18	•	at Virginia	17	24
N25	•	Wake Forest	32	14
MICRON PC.COM BOWL				
D28	•	Minnesota	38	30

2001   7-5 (4-4)
S6	•	Indiana	35	14
S22	•	at SMU	26	17
S29		North Carolina	9	17
O6	•	at Wake Forest	17	14
O13		Clemson	37	45
O20		at Georgia Tech	17	27
O27	•	Virginia	24	0
N3	•	at Duke	55	31
N10	•	at Florida State	34	28
N17		Maryland	19	23
N24	•	Ohio U.	27	20
FLORIDA TANGERINE BOWL				
D20	•	Pittsburgh	19	34

2002   11-3 (5-3)
A24	•	New Mexico	34	14
A31	•	E. Tennessee St.	34	0
S7		at Navy	65	19
S14	•	Wake Forest	32	13
S21	•	at Texas Tech	51	48
S28	•	Massachusetts	56	24
O12	•	at North Carolina	34	17
O19	•	Duke	24	22
O24	•	at Clemson	38	6
N2		Georgia Tech	17	24
N9		at Maryland	21	24
N16		at Virginia	9	14
N23	•	Florida State	17	7
GATOR BOWL				
J1	•	Notre Dame	28	6

2003   8-5 (4-4)
A30	•	Western Carolina	59	26
S6	•	at Wake Forest	24	38
S13	•	at Ohio State	38	44
S20	•	Texas Tech	49	21
S27	•	North Carolina	47	34
O4		at Georgia Tech	21	29
O11	•	Connecticut	31	24
O16	•	Clemson	17	15
O25	•	at Duke	28	21
N1	•	Virginia	51	37
N15	•	at Florida State	44	50
N22	•	Maryland	24	26
TANGERINE BOWL				
D22	•	Kansas	56	26

2004   5-6 (3-5)
S4	•	Richmond	42	0
S18		Ohio State	14	22
S25	•	at Virginia Tech	17	16
O2	•	Wake Forest	27	21
O9		at North Carolina	24	30
O16	•	at Maryland	13	3
O23	•	Miami, Fla.	31	45
O30		at Clemson	20	26
N6		Georgia Tech	14	24
N11		Florida State	10	17
N27	•	East Carolina *Char*	52	14

NORTH TEXAS

BY RYAN HOCKENSMITH

HE'D WRITTEN LETTERS TO EVERY football college he'd ever heard of, asking if they'd give a kid from an all-black high school a shot. North Texas coach Odus Mitchell opened one of those pleadings and called a dentist he knew from the kid's hometown. It just so happened that the kid's mom worked for the dentist, who thought highly of the young man. The dentist put the kid on a bus to Denton, Texas, and when the kid arrived, he rushed into the bathroom, ripped off his shirt's sleeves and cranked out 20 push-ups, so that when he sat down with the coaching staff five minutes later his arms would look a little bigger. That's how badly an 18-year-old named Charles Edward Greene wanted to play college football in 1965. Luckily, the coaches wanted him, too. "Mean" Joe Greene grabbed a scholarship and proceeded to captivate the university by leading the team to a 23–5–1 record from 1966 to 1968. Almost four decades later, the men's athletic teams are named after the school's greatest athlete. After drifting into mediocrity in the 1970s and

dropping to Division I-AA from 1982 to 1994, the Mean Green returned to big-time college football in 1995. The bumpy return (North Texas went 24–54 in its first seven seasons back) was justified in 2002, with the second of two straight Sun Belt Conference titles and the Mean Green's first bowl win in 56 years, a 24-19 New Orleans Bowl triumph against Conference USA co-champion Cincinnati.

TRADITION Each Mean Green score is celebrated with a blast from a Civil War replica cannon. The original cannon, Boomer I, was introduced in 1970 by The Talons, North Texas' spirit group, and was retired in the late 1980s after a crack developed in its barrel. Boomer II has been used ever since.

STADIUM The Mean Green's modest home, Fouts Field, expanded from 20,000 to 30,000 seats in a 1994 renovation; it now accommodates 30,500. The stadium was used for scenes in the 1991 film *Necessary Roughness* and doubled as Berlin Olympic Stadium in *The Jesse Owens Story*, a made-for-TV movie.

BEST PLAYER Who else? For three years, Mean Joe Greene was a wrecking ball on the line of scrimmage. He's

---

PROFILE

University of North Texas
Denton, Texas
Founded: 1890
Enrollment: 22,323
Colors: Green and White
Nickname: Mean Green
Stadium: Fouts Field
  Opened in 1952
  All-Pro Turf; 30,500 capacity
First football game: 1913
All-time record: 456–395–32 (.535)
Bowl record: 2–5
Sun Belt Conference championships: 4
(3 outright)
First-round NFL draftees: 3
Website: www.meangreensports.com

THE BEST OF TIMES

In 1973, North Texas looked to former SMU coach Hayden Fry to bring its flagging program credibility. In six seasons (1973 to 1978), Fry guided the Mean Green to a 40–23–3 record, winning the Missouri Valley Conference title in his first year and going 9–2 in 1977 as an independent.

THE WORST OF TIMES

The program reached its low point in 1981, when first-year coach and athletic director Bob Tyler's team went 2–9. After going 6–5 in 1980 under coach Jerry Moore, the Mean Green dropped its first five games of the 1981 season under Tyler. The disastrous campaign (UNT averaged just 10 points per game and was shut out three times) cost Tyler both the coach and AD jobs.

CONFERENCE

North Texas moved to the major-college ranks in 1957 when it joined the Missouri Valley Conference. In 18 years (1957-75), the Mean Green won five MVC titles. UNT competed an independent from 1975 until 1982, when it dropped to NCAA Division I-AA. North Texas, which returned to Division I-A in 1995, joined the Sun Belt Conference in 2001.

DISTINGUISHED ALUMNI

Pat Boone; Joan Blondell, actress; Phyllis George, Miss America and TV personality; Larry McMurtry, novelist; Roy Orbison, singer/songwriter; Ann Sheridan, actress

FIGHT SONG

FIGHT, NORTH TEXAS
Let's give a cheer for U of NT!
Cheer for the Green and White.
Victory's in store, whate'er the score,
Our team will ever fight. Fight, fight, fight!
Shoulder to shoulder we march along,
Striving for victory,
Playing the game for the honor
And fame and glory of UNT!
U-N-T Eagles! U-N-T Eagles,
Fight! Fight! Fight!

As Joe Greene became an NFL legend, the school eventually renamed the men's athletic programs after its former star.

responsible for the team's name and most of the football program's reputation and was inducted into the Pro Football Hall of Fame. "Joe Greene could not be blocked," former sports information director Fred Graham says. "If he didn't make the tackle, he created enough havoc that somebody else could." He generated enough mayhem in the middle that new Pittsburgh Steelers coach Chuck Noll decided to build a defense around Greene, who had been his first draft pick. (He was No. 4 overall in 1969.) That worked out well.

BEST COACH While Hayden "Flat Top" Fry was better known for his 38–25–3 record in six seasons at North Texas, Odus Mitchell had laid the groundwork. In 1946, Mitchell inherited a program that hadn't put a team on the field in three years because of World War II, but he quickly reconstructed football into the fabric of North Texas. He won 122 games from 1946 to 1966, took the school to all three of its 20th-century bowl games and ushered in the integration of college football in the Southwest. In 1956, two years after North Texas lost a lawsuit preventing black undergraduates from attending the school, Mitchell let black players Abner Haynes and Leon King walk on for his team that season. It would be almost a decade before most of his North Texas neighbors would allow the same to happen at their schools. Mitchell instructed his players and coaching staff to welcome Haynes and King as they would any other teammate and they followed his instructions. When restaurants refused service to Haynes and King, the team went somewhere else. When Houston hotels wouldn't allow them to stay with their white teammates on a road trip, Mitchell leased railroad sleeping cars for the entire team. And when Mississippi declared it wouldn't play against a team with black players, Mitchell declared he wouldn't play Mississippi. Mitchell's groundbreaking stance opened the door for black student-athletes across the Southwest.

RECORDS

RUSHING YARDS

GAME
247 Malcolm Jones vs. Louisiana-Monroe, Nov. 15, 1980 (29 att.)

SEASON
1,801 Jamario Thomas, 2004 (285 att.)

CAREER
3,120 Ja'Quay Wilburn, 1997-2000 (647 att.)

PASSING YARDS

GAME
495 Steve Ramsey vs. Louisiana-Lafayette, Sept. 20, 1969 (35 of 52)

SEASON
3,103 Mitch Maher, 1994 (231 of 370)

CAREER
8,256 Mitch Maher, 1991-94 (640 of 1,149)

RECEIVING YARDS

GAME
231 Scott Ford vs. Abilene Christian, Sept. 5, 1992 (9 rec.)

SEASON
1,130 Barry Moore, 1969 (71 rec.); John Love, 1966 (68 rec.)

CAREER
2,567 Troy Redwine, 1992-96 (138)

POINTS

GAME
45 Fred Cobb vs. University of Dallas, Oct. 11, 1919 (6 TDs, 6 PATs, 1 FG)

SEASON
126 Patrick Cobbs, 2003 (21 TDs)

CAREER
236 Keith Chapman, 1985-89 (49 FGs, 89 PATs)

CONSENSUS ALL-AMERICANS

1947	Frank Whitlow, T
1951	Ray Renfro, DB
1968	Joe Greene, DT
1983	Ronnie Hickman, DE
1983	Rayford Cooks. DL
1988	Rex Johnson, DL
1990	Mike Davis, DL

BEST TEAM Fry guided his 1977 team to a 9–2 record as a major independent, losing only to Mississippi State and Florida State. Mississippi State, however, later forfeited its win over the Mean Green because of NCAA sanctions. Quarterback Ken Washington led a balanced attack with 1,413 yards of total offense. Washington racked up two touchdowns and 241 total yards to help the Mean Green defeat Southern Methodist University for the first time in 44 years, 24-13. But in the days of fewer than 30 bowl games, with no conference affiliation and a poor strength of schedule, North Texas wasn't invited to participate in the postseason.

BIGGEST GAME In its third game since returning to Division I-A, North Texas rallied to nip Oregon State 30-27 on Sept. 16, 1995. Trailing 27-16, the Mean Green scored a touchdown with 10:22 left, then made a huge fourth-down stop at its own 29-yard line. Quarterback Jason Mills proceeded to lead an 11-play, 72-yard scoring drive, capped by Troy Redwine's four-yard TD catch with 13 seconds left.

BIGGEST UPSET Sears Woods stunned 72,670 Volunteer diehards with a 98-yard kickoff return in the final five minutes of the Mean Green's 21-14 shocker at Tennessee in 1975. Woods, who played just one season, had a career day, running for 121 yards and two touchdowns.

HEARTBREAKER In 1988, intrastate big boy Texas welcomed its northern neighbor into Austin for a late-September clash. The Longhorns were in the midst of their worst season since 1956 (they'd win just four games), and North Texas was Division I-AA's top-ranked team. A win at Texas would have been enormous for the Mean Green, and they came incredibly close. Trailing the entire game, Texas drove down the field in the fourth quarter and took a 27-24 lead—its first of the day—with 45 seconds left on a 10-yard touchdown pass to Keith Cash. Replays show Cash almost certainly landed out-of-bounds, but officials ruled it a touchdown and Texas held on for a win North Texas fans still grumble about.

RIVAL No game sums up the North Texas rivalry with New Mexico State like the 2001 contest. Down 20-16 with 1:54 left,

North Texas took over on its own 30-yard line needing a touchdown. On the Mean Green's second play, Aggies safety Shiddeeq Shabazz grabbed what appeared to be a game-clinching interception, only to see a roughing-the-passer penalty nullify the play. North Texas then marched down the field and scored on a fourth-down, 15-yard touchdown pass with 18 seconds left. Receiver George Marshall split through two Aggies defensive backs down the middle of the field and galloped into the end zone. The win catapulted North Texas to the Sun Belt Conference title and kept the Aggies home for December. The Mean Green are 8–2 against New Mexico State in games decided by one score or less, and 22–9–2 overall.

NICKNAME In a 1922 vote to establish a school nickname, the students selected Eagles. That name stuck until the wife of North Texas' sports information director stood up at a 1966 game and yelled, "Way to go, mean Greene" as the standout defensive tackle bulldozed an opposing punt returner. As North Texas' defense gained a national reputation and Greene later became an NFL star, the school eventually renamed all of its men's athletic programs after him.

MASCOT The Mean Green mascot has undergone numerous face-lifts. The old eagle mascot used to go by Scrappy before Mean Green took hold in the form of an eagle named Eppy. In 1995, the university unveiled a modified eagle and changed its name back to Scrappy.

UNIFORMS In 2001, Mean Green players started wearing dark green uniforms with North Texas written across the front of the jersey. This marked the fifth uniform change in five decades. In the 1960s, players wore white jerseys with a green NT on the front, followed by a change in the 1970s to lime green jerseys. In the 1980s, North Texas switched to dark green jerseys with NT lettering. In 1973, the school scrapped the lettering for an Eagle logo, which remained in some form until 2000, when it was replaced by North Texas written in white script.

QUOTE "Do you believe in the Mean Green?"—Radio play-by-play announcer George Dunham

NORTH TEXAS ANNUAL STATISTICAL LEADERS

YR	RUSHING	YDS	ATT	AVG	PASSING	ATT	CMP	PCT	YDS	RECEIVING	REC	YDS	AVG
1950	Ken Bahnsen	568	94	6.0	Zeke Martin	109	48	.44	822	Wendell Swann	26	434	16.7
1951	Ray Renfro	959	127	7.6	Richard Harvey	131	61	.47	1,194	Wendell Swann	23	472	20.5
1952	Tom Gray	829	140	5.9	Bobby Hughes	70	28	.40	385	Winton Criswell	12	157	13.1
1953	Dean Renfro	700	101	6.9	Bobby Hughes	115	59	.51	757	Ken Hall	18	288	16.0
1954	Dean Renfro	499	97	5.1	Don Baker	98	46	.47	630	Char. McGinty	25	376	15.0
1955	Tommy Runnels	570	83	6.9	Don Baker	85	40	.47	700	Dennis Shaw	13	225	17.3
1956	Ben Boehnke	483	107	4.5	Ray Toole	66	29	.44	485	Dennis Shaw	15	279	18.6
1957	Abner Haynes	639	112	5.7	Ray Toole	72	26	.36	367	Abner Haynes	11	50	4.5
1958	Abner Haynes	495	117	4.2	Vernon Cole	98	48	.49	589	Abner Haynes	19	298	15.7
1959	Abner Haynes	730	116	6.3	Vernon Cole	58	29	.50	304	Abner Haynes	16	231	14.4
1960	Arthur Perkins	441	101	4.4	Robert Duty	109	49	.45	614	Billy Christle	12	161	13.4
1961	Bobby Smith	541	120	4.5	Billy Ryan	50	20	.40	179	Winston Freeman	6	63	10.5
1962	Dwain Bean	657	140	4.7	Billy Ryan	49	17	.35	189	A.D. Whitfield	7	116	16.6
1963	Dwain Bean	770	152	5.1	Billy Ryan	59	21	.36	277	Herb Carr	7	88	12.6
1964	A.D. Whitfield	592	148	4.0	Corkey Boland	116	49	.42	608	Carl Lockhart	29	341	11.8
1965	Willie Cherry	397	75	5.3	Vidal Carlin	341	159	.47	1,723	John Love	76	994	13.1
1966	Willie Cherry	218	75	2.9	Vidal Carlin	292	117	.40	1,510	John Love	68	1,130	16.6
1967	Vic Williams	606	157	3.9	Steve Ramsey	269	119	.44	1,732	James Russell	44	624	14.2
1968	Leo Taylor	1,017	246	4.1	Steve Ramsey	332	177	.53	2,516	Barry Moore	69	1,053	15.3
1969	Leo Taylor	545	150	3.6	Steve Ramsey	414	195	.47	2,828	Barry Moore	71	1,130	15.9
1970	Nap Landry	191	64	3.0	Joe Milton	296	138	.47	1,852	Ret Little	43	733	17.0
1971	Fred Woods	417	121	3.4	Rick Shaw	124	41	.33	666	David Yaege	35	631	18.0
1972	Charles Johnson	685	164	4.2	Rick Shaw	177	47	.27	734	David Yaege	42	738	17.6
1973	Reggie Turner	366	105	3.5	Phil Shotland	176	72	.41	959	David Kervin	34	641	18.9
1974	John Brown	674	152	4.4	Ken Washington	201	78	.39	1,042	J.T. Hollins	27	374	13.9
1975	Sears Woods	446	131	3.4	Glen Ray	65	26	.40	472	Jeff Webb	23	375	16.3
1976	Michael Jones	411	86	4.8	Ken Smith	111	47	.42	630	J.T. Hollins	22	331	15.0
1977	Michael Jones	940	187	5.0	Ken Washington	129	81	.63	1,155	Tim Loftin	33	523	15.8
1978	Bernard Jackson	1,453	269	5.4	Jordan Case	179	105	.59	1,360	Charlie Murray	32	546	17.1
1979	Bernard Jackson	749	152	4.9	Jordan Case	167	103	.62	1,152	Pete Harvey	37	424	11.5
1980	Malcolm Jones	1,144	254	4.5	Joe Stevenson	236	129	.55	1,582	Pete Harvey	47	496	10.6
1981	Carlen Charleston	420	106	4.0	Greg Carter	138	73	.53	782	Pete Harvey	57	743	13.0
1982	Bobby Daniels	455	127	3.6	Rusty Hill	292	177	.61	1,704	Marvin Walker	91	934	10.3
1983	Nathan Williams	691	164	4.2	Greg Carter	185	93	.50	1,275	Tim Wasson	37	553	14.9
1984	Monty Moon	464	106	4.4	Scott Toman	112	35	.31	494	Tim Wasson	28	453	16.2
1985	Monty Moon	507	119	4.3	Mike Rhone	94	30	.32	487	Marcus Camper	17	332	19.5
1986	Darrin Collins	603	125	4.8	Bron Beal	95	43	.45	664	Marcus Camper	16	247	15.4
1987	Darrin Collins	851	208	4.1	Scott Davis	127	64	.50	1,023	Marcus Camper	24	422	17.6
1988	Scott Davis	439	160	2.7	Scott Davis	270	158	.59	2,409	Marcus Camper	54	938	17.4
1989	Erric Pegram	513	119	4.3	Scott Davis	263	155	.59	1,941	Tony Cook	45	523	11.6
1990	Erric Pegram	957	212	4.5	Scott Davis	262	142	.54	1,550	Erric Pegram	55	444	8.1
1991	Travis Gibson	370	85	4.4	Wendell Mosley	169	75	.44	861	David Brown	45	531	11.8
1992	Terrance Brown	976	233	4.2	Mitch Maher	292	151	.52	2,090	Clayton George	36	563	15.6
1993	Terrance Brown	1,101	235	4.7	Mitch Maher	324	176	.54	2,595	David Brown	45	497	11.0
1994	Eteka Huckaby	435	97	4.5	Mitch Maher	370	231	.62	3,103	David Brown	66	1,013	15.3
1995	Bo Harrison	455	161	2.8	Jason Mills	216	105	.49	1,183	Troy Redwine	50	800	16.0
1996	Hut Allred	907	210	4.3	Jason Mills	211	91	.43	1,016	Brian Waters	28	272	9.7
1997	Ja'Quay Wilburn	594	112	5.3	Jason Mills	245	127	.52	1,667	Jay Young	36	552	15.3
1998	Ja'Quay Wilburn	754	128	5.9	Jason Attaway	109	51	.47	680	Jay Young	32	428	13.4
1999	Ja'Quay Wilburn	1,016	234	4.3	Richard Bridges	150	54	.36	621	Broderick McGrew	32	601	18.8
2000	Ja'Quay Wilburn	756	173	4.4	Scott Hall	154	75	.49	937	Byron Curtis	21	336	16.0
2001	Kevin Galbreath	1,119	264	4.2	Scott Hall	194	102	.53	1,453	George Marshall	32	546	17.1
2002	Kevin Galbreath	1,298	272	4.8	Andrew Smith	196	91	.46	1,206	George Marshall	30	398	13.3
2003	Patrick Cobbs	1,680	307	5.5	Scott Hall	186	107	.58	1,732	Johnny Quinn	34	709	20.9
2004	Jamario Thomas	1,801	285	6.3	Scott Hall	237	134	.58	1,818	Johnny Quinn	49	785	16.0

Receiving leaders by receptions
NCAA began including postseason stats in 2002

NORTH TEXAS ALL-TIME SCORES

WIN/LOSS PERCENTAGE SINCE 1936

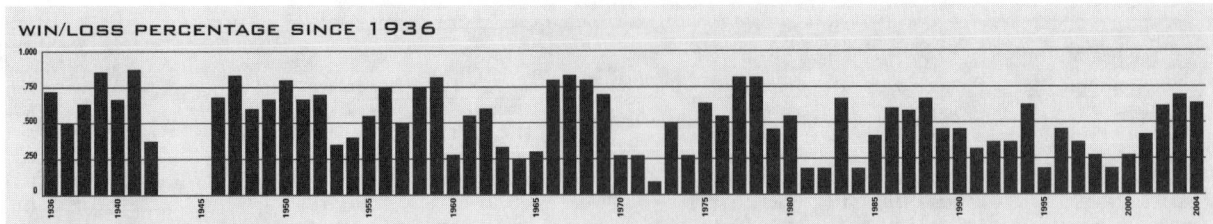

J.W. PENDER
1913-14 (.429)   3-4

1913   0-1-0
U		TCU	0	40

1914   3-3-0
S26		at TCU	0	40
U		SE. Oklahoma _Unk_	0	39
U	●	Burleson Coll. _Unk_	25	0
U	●	Dallas U. _Unk_	13	2
U		Terrell Acad. _Unk_	0	6
U	●	Sam Houston St. _Unk_	18	0

J.W. ST. CLAIR
1915-19 (.656)   20-10-2

1915   4-1-0
U	●	Sam Houston St. _Unk_	6	0
U	●	Decatur Baptist _Unk_	75	0
U	●	Texas St. _Unk_	14	0
U	●	Decatur Baptist _Unk_	53	0
U		Dallas U. _Unk_	0	6

1916   4-3-1
U	●	SE. Oklahoma _Unk_	6	0
U	●	Decatur Baptist _Unk_	12	0
U		Dallas U. _Unk_	0	42
U		Trinity _Unk_	7	12
U	=	Texas St. _Unk_	0	0
U	●	Thorp Springs _Unk_	48	0
U		Meridian _Unk_	12	13
U	●	East Texas St. _Unk_	40	7

1917   6-1-0
O1		at Burleson Coll.	0	14
O8	●	at Hardin-Simmons	14	8
O15		SE. Oklahoma	27	0
O29		at Austin Coll.	19	13
N5	●	at Decatur Baptist	48	0
N19	●	Dallas U.	13	0
N23	●	Meridian	25	7

1918   1-2-1
U		Austin Coll.	7	9
N2		at TCU	0	39
U	=	at SE. Oklahoma	7	7
U	●	Decatur Baptist	25	3

1919   5-3-0
O4		at TCU	6	14
O11	●	Dallas U.	87	6
O18	●	at Tarleton St.	44	0
O25	●	SE. Oklahoma	53	6
N1		at Hardin-Simmons	0	23
N8		at Burleson Coll.	0	16
N15		at Austin Coll.	0	1 _f_
N22	●	at Edmond Normal	35	6

THERON FOUTS
1920-24 (.615)   23-14-2

1920   7-1-0
U	●	at Burleson Coll.	48	12
U	●	at Hardin-Simmons	7	6
U	●	Oklahoma Baptist	29	0
U	●	Meridian	41	0
U	●	SE. Oklahoma	47	0
U		at Tarleton St.	7	20
U	●	Baylor JV	28	0
U	●	Texas St.	20	6

1921   3-3-0
U	●	at Grubbs Voc.	41	6
U		Hardin-Simmons	0	6
U		Tarleton St.	0	13
U	●	at Wesley Coll.	33	6
U	●	Burleson Coll.	61	12
U		at Texas St.	0	14

1922   5-2-1
S30		at Baylor	0	55
O7		at SMU	0	66
U	●	Burleson Coll. _Unk_	13	9
U	=	Grubbs Voc. _Unk_	7	7
U	●	East Texas St. _Unk_	30	0
U	●	Trinity _Unk_	13	6
U	●	Grubbs Voc. _Unk_	6	0
U	●	Texas St. _Unk_	16	13

1923   3-5-0
S29		at SMU	0	41
O6		at Baylor	7	33
U		Grubbs Voc. _Unk_	12	30
U		Trinity _Unk_	0	6
U	●	Sam Houston St. _Unk_	18	6
U	●	West Texas St. _Unk_	14	6
U		Austin Coll. _Unk_	0	7
U	●	Texas St. _Unk_	12	7

1924   5-3-1
S27		at SMU	0	7
O4		at Baylor	0	30
U	●	Decatur Baptist _Unk_	15	3
U	●	Daniel Baker _Unk_	10	0
U		Texas St. _Unk_	6	10
U	●	Sam Houston St. _Unk_	7	0
U	●	Hardin-Simmons _Unk_	12	7
U	●	West Texas St. _Unk_	14	7
U	=	Trinity _Unk_	0	0

JOHN REID
1925-28 (.473)   16-18-3

1925   6-4-0
S26		at SMU	0	48
O3		at Baylor	6	20
O10	●	Decatur Baptist _Unk_	27	0
O17	●	Stephen F. Austin _Unk_	10	0
O23	●	East Texas St. _Unk_	33	13
O30	●	West Texas St. _Unk_	6	0
N6		Hardin-Simmons _Unk_	0	10
N11	●	Daniel Baker _Unk_	13	8
N19	●	Texas St. _Unk_	10	6
N26		Trinity _Unk_	6	16

1926   5-3-1
S24		at SMU	0	42
U	●	Decatur Baptist	16	0
U	●	at Stephen F. Austin	9	6
O23		Abilene Christian	10	13
O30	●	West Texas St.	16	3
U	=	Hardin-Simmons	7	7
U	●	at East Texas St.	21	7
N18	●	Texas St.	13	12
U		at Trinity	7	14

1927   1-6-2
S24		at SMU	0	68
U		at Hardin-Simmons	0	14
U	●	Decatur Baptist	12	0
U	=	Stephen F. Austin	12	12
U		Abilene Christian	0	33
O29		at Texas St.	0	38
U		at McMurry	0	15
U	=	East Texas St.	7	7
U		at Trinity	0	37

1928   4-5-0
S22		at SMU	6	60
S29		at Baylor	0	45 *
U	●	Decatur Baptist _Unk_	33	0
U	●	Stephen F. Austin _Unk_	14	7
O27		Texas St.	17	0
N3		at Texas A&M	0	44
U		East Texas St. _Unk_	12	13
U		McMurry _Unk_	0	2
U	●	Austin Coll. _Unk_	6	0

JACK SISCO
1929-41 (.653)   74-37-10

1929   4-3-2
S21		at SMU	3	13
S28		at Baylor	0	32
U	●	Decatur Baptist _Unk_	97	0
U	●	Stephen F. Austin _Unk_	31	0
U	●	Trinity _Unk_	7	0
U	●	East Texas St. _Unk_	34	0
N2		at TCU	0	25
U	=	Sam Houston St. _Unk_	6	6
N29	=	Texas St. _Unk_	0	0

1930   5-4-1
S20		TCU	0	47
S27		at Baylor	0	33
O3		Austin Coll.	0	6
O10	=	at Southwestern	13	13
O17		Trinity _H_	9	6
O24		at Abilene Christian	20	12
N1	●	Stephen F. Austin _Unk_	13	6
N11	●	East Texas St. _Unk_	19	0
N18	●	Sam Houston St. _Unk_	0	13
N28	●	Texas St. _Unk_	13	0

1931   8-3-0
S19		at TCU	6	33
S26		at SMU	0	13
O2	●	at Austin Coll.	21	6
O9	●	Southwestern	25	0
O17		at Trinity	0	7
O23		Abilene Christian	6	0
O31	●	at Stephen F. Austin	33	0
N11	●	East Texas St.	13	0
N16	●	Sam Houston St.	19	0
N25	●	at Texas St.	20	0
U	●	Daniel Baker _Unk_	32	13

1932   8-1-1
S17		at TCU	2	14
S24	=	at SMU	0	0
U	●	Austin Coll. _Unk_	54	0
U	●	Southwestern _Unk_	20	0
O14		Abilene Christian	13	0
U	●	Stephen F. Austin _Unk_	31	0
U	●	East Texas St. _Unk_	27	6
U	●	Sam Houston St. _Unk_	7	6
U	●	Trinity _Unk_	20	0
N23	●	Texas St.	6	0

1933   3-4-2
S23	●	at SMU	7	0
S30		TCU	0	13
O6	=	Southwestern _Unk_	0	0
O13		Abilene Christian _Unk_	0	6
U	●	Stephen F. Austin _Unk_	22	6
U		Sam Houston St. _Unk_	7	19
U		East Texas St. _Unk_	0	6
N17	●	at Trinity	13	0
N24	=	Texas St.	0	0

1934   5-4-0
S22		at SMU	0	33
S29		at TCU	0	27
O5	●	at Southwestern	6	0
O15	●	Abilene Christian	6	0
O26	●	Stephen F. Austin	14	0
N1		at Sam Houston St.	0	7
N9		at East Texas St.	0	3
N16	●	Trinity	21	9
N23	●	at Texas St.	3	0

1935   5-3-1
S21		at SMU	0	29 *
S28		at TCU	11	28
O4	●	Southwestern	34	0
O11	=	at Abilene Christian	13	13
O25	●	at Sam Houston St.	20	0
N1		Stephen F. Austin	7	9
N8	●	East Texas St.	30	6
N15	●	at Trinity	13	8
N22	●	at Texas St.	6	0

1936   6-2-1
S26		at SMU	0	6
O3		at Southwestern	7	12
O9		Abilene Christian	18	0
O16	●	Stephen F. Austin	27	7
O22	=	at Austin Coll.	0	0
O30	●	at Sam Houston St.	27	0
N6		at East Texas St.	6	0
N13	●	Trinity	26	6
N20	●	Texas St.	14	0

1937   4-4-2
S18		Austin Coll.	0	6
S25		at SMU	3	14 *
O1		Southwestern	6	7
O8	●	Abilene Christian	22	14
O16		at McMurry	0	0
O23	=	at Stephen F. Austin	6	6
O29	●	Sam Houston St.	13	6
N5	●	at Texas St.	10	3
N12	●	at Trinity	14	7
N20	●	East Texas St.	0	20

1938   7-4-0
S18	●	at Howard Payne	13	0
S24		at SMU	7	34
O1	●	at Southwestern	27	6
O8		at Abilene Christian	0	6
O14	●	McMurry	46	7
O21	●	Stephen F. Austin	27	6
O28	●	at Sam Houston St.	0	18
N4	●	at Texas St.	7	6
N12	●	at Austin Coll.	32	2
N19	●	at East Texas St.	3	7
D2	●	Pittsburg St.	28	0

1939   6-1-0
S23	●	at Abilene Christian	9	0
O7		at SMU	0	16
O20	●	at Stephen F. Austin	14	0
O29	●	Sam Houston St.	24	13
N3	●	at Texas St.	26	0
N11	●	Austin Coll.	27	0
N18	●	East Texas St.	16	13

1940   6-3-0
S21	●	at Abilene Christian	13	19
S28		at Baylor	20	27
O5		at SMU	7	20
O11	●	Arkansas Coll.	79	0
O18	●	Stephen F. Austin	27	0
O25	●	at Sam Houston St.	7	6
N1	●	Texas St.	22	0
N8	●	Austin Coll.	14	0
N16	●	at East Texas St.	10	7

1941   7-1-0
S27		at SMU	0	54
O4	●	at Hardin-Simmons	7	3
O10	●	Arkansas State	60	0
O17	●	at Stephen F. Austin	28	0
O24	●	Sam Houston St.	19	0
O31	●	at Texas St.	10	6
N7	●	Austin Coll.	26	6
N15	●	East Texas St.	15	8

NORTH TEXAS 617

LLOYD RUSSELL
1942 (.375) 3-5

1942 3-5-0
S18 at Howard Payne 0 14
S26 at SMU 7 26
O3 at Hardin-Simmons 0 34
O10 ● Fort Hood 47 0
O24 at Sam Houston St. 20 21
O30 ● Texas St. 10 6
N6 ● Austin Coll. 32 12
N13 at East Texas St. 7 16

1943-1945
NO TEAM WWII

ODUS MITCHELL
1946-66 (.586) 122-85-9

1946 7-3-1
S21 at Texas A&M 0 47
S28 ● Austin Coll. 14 0
O5 at Abilene Christian 0 6
O12 ● at Fort Sam Houston 23 7
O19 Sam Houston St. 0 12
O26 ● at Stephen F. Austin 9 0
N2 ● at Texas St. 6 0
N9 = at McMurry 7 7
N16 ● at Houston 7 3
N23 ● East Texas St. 47 7
OPTIMIST BOWL
D21 ● Pacific 14 13

1947 10-2-0
S13 ● at Midwestern Texas 27 6
S20 ● Brooke Gen. Hosp. 44 0
S27 Arkansas [LR] 0 12
O4 ● at Florida 20 12
O18 ● Stephen F. Austin 13 7
O25 ● at Sam Houston St. 27 0
N1 ● Texas St. 27 7
N7 ● at Trinity 33 7
N15 ● Houston 33 0
N22 ● at East Texas St. 12 6
N27 ● at U.T. Chattanooga 14 7
SALAD BOWL
J1 Nevada 6 13

1948 6-4-0
S17 at Oklahoma City 6 14
S25 ● Randolph AFB 86 0
O2 ● at West Texas St. 20 7
O9 at Nevada 7 48
O16 ● at Stephen F. Austin 19 6
O23 ● Sam Houston St. 37 7
O30 at Texas St. 14 24
N6 ● Trinity 27 12
N13 at Houston 6 8
N20 ● East Texas St. 27 7

1949 8-4-0
S10 ● at Howard Payne 34 14
S17 at Hardin-Simmons 7 13
S24 Arkansas [LR] 19 33
S30 ● at Oklahoma City 26 7
O8 Midwestern Texas 17 20
O15 ● Stephen F. Austin 25 6
O22 ● at Sam Houston St. 41 14
O29 ● Texas St. 41 7
N5 ● at Trinity 32 21
N12 ● Houston 28 23
N19 ● at East Texas St. 59 6
N24 at Nevada 7 28

1950 7-2-1
S16 at Kentucky 0 25
S23 ● at East Texas St. 42 20
S30 at Arkansas 6 50
O6 ● at SW. Oklahoma 76 6
O13 = at Midwestern Texas 7 7
O20 ● at U.T. Chattanooga 19 14
N3 ● Trinity 35 6
N10 ● at Houston 16 13
N18 ● Nevada 34 21
N25 ● at Fresno State 31 12

1951 8-4-0
S15 ● at Lamar 54 6
S22 ● at Texas-El Paso 33 0
S29 ● at Sul Ross 62 6
O5 ● East Texas St. 48 7
O12 ● at West Texas St. 42 14
O19 Carswell AFB 6 13
O27 at Pacific 0 34
N3 ● at Trinity 32 0
N10 ● Midwestern Texas 61 0
N17 ● Fresno State 62 0
N22 at U.T. Chattanooga 20 32
N30 Houston 14 20

1952 7-3-0
S20 ● Texas-El Paso [ODE] 27 14
S27 ● North Dakota 55 0
O4 at Dayton 14 20
O11 at Mississippi State 0 14
O18 Hardin-Simmons 13 38
O25 ● at Memphis 38 14
N1 ● Trinity 34 7
N8 ● Texas Tech 34 19
N15 ● Carswell AFB 28 14
N27 ● at Midwestern Texas 33 7

1953 3-6-1
S26 Arizona State 0 14
O3 at Mississippi State 6 21
O9 ● San Diego NAS 27 12
O17 ● Midwestern Texas 39 7
O24 at Texas-El Paso 21 26
O31 = at San Jose State 13 13
N7 at Mississippi 7 40
N14 ● West Texas St. 38 6
N21 at Hardin-Simmons 10 14
N28 at Trinity 6 14

1954 4-6-0
S17 Mississippi [MEM] 12 35
O2 ● Southern Miss 15 7
O9 ● Hardin-Simmons 20 7
O15 at U.T. Chattanooga 19 20
O23 Texas-El Paso 0 6
O30 San Jose State 20 27
N6 at Mississippi State 26 48
N13 ● at Arizona State 20 13
N20 Trinity 0 13
N24 ● at Midwestern Texas 19 0

1955 5-4-1
S24 = at Texas-El Paso 7 7
O1 at Mississippi 0 33
O8 at Southern Miss 0 26
O15 ● Hardin-Simmons 30 19
O22 ● Midwestern Texas 40 13
O29 at Mississippi State 7 20
N5 U.T. Chattanooga 6 14
N12 ● McMurry 38 21
N19 ● Emporia St. 62 0
N26 ● Trinity 7 6

1956 7-2-1
S22 at Mississippi 0 45
S29 at Arizona State 7 27
O6 ● San Diego NAS 65 6
O13 ● at Midwestern Texas 14 7
O20 ● Texas-El Paso 13 6
O26 ● at Youngstown St. 19 12
N3 = Trinity 7 7
N10 ● McMurry 23 7
N17 ● Abilene Christian 20 7
N22 ● at U.T. Chattanooga 20 7

1957-1974
MISSOURI VALLEY

1957 5-5-0 (1-0-0)
S21 at Texas-El Paso 13 14
S28 Oklahoma State 19 25
O5 Drake 6 19
O12 at Abilene Christian 20 28
O19 ● | at Tulsa 14 12
O26 ● at San Jose State 12 6
N2 at Trinity 13 26
N9 ● U.T. Chattanooga 12 0
N16 ● Youngstown St. 68 13
N23 ● McMurry 14 7

1958 7-2-1 (2-0-1)
S20 ● Texas-El Paso 26 8
S27 at Oklahoma State 14 21
O4 ● New Mexico State 43 12
O11 ● at Drake 42 0
O18 ● at Brigham Young 12 6
O25 ● | Tulsa 8 7
N1 = | Cincinnati 8 8
N8 | at Wichita St. 13 15
N15 ● | Houston 10 6
N22 ● at Louisville 21 10

1959 9-2-0 (3-1-0)
S19 ● at Hardin-Simmons 46 24
S26 ● at Texas-El Paso 31 7
O3 ● West Texas St. 28 6
O10 ● | at Cincinnati 21 6
O17 ● Pensacola NAS 43 0
O24 ● | at Houston 7 6
O31 ● | Wichita St. 12 0
N7 ● Louisville 39 7
N14 | at Tulsa 6 17
N21 ● Drake 62 2
SUN BOWL
D31 New Mexico State 8 28

1960 2-6-1 (0-3-0)
S24 = Texas-El Paso 16 16
O1 | Cincinnati 0 21
O8 Memphis 0 44
O15 at West Texas St. 6 14
O22 ● Drake 29 7
O29 Houston 16 41
N5 ● Hardin-Simmons 26 19
N12 | at Tulsa 8 12
N19 | at Wichita St. 6 34

1961 5-4-1 (1-2-0)
S23 ● at Hardin-Simmons 9 7
S30 ● Brigham Young 41 30
O7 = New Mexico State 14 14
O14 | Wichita St. 14 26
O21 ● | Tulsa 23 12
O28 | at Cincinnati 9 21
N4 ● Drake 28 21
N11 at Memphis 0 41
N18 Louisville 0 20
N25 ● at Texas-El Paso 24 14

1962 6-4-0 (2-1-0)
S22 ● Texas-El Paso 19 6
S29 Memphis 6 14
O6 ● Hardin-Simmons 29 8
O13 | at Tulsa 0 34
O20 ● | Cincinnati 14 8
O27 at New Mexico State 12 48
N3 ● | at Wichita St. 9 7
N10 ● West Texas St. 20 13
N17 at Louisville 10 14
N24 ● at So. Illinois 55 30

1963 3-6-0 (2-2-0)
S21 at Texas-El Paso 7 34
S28 ● | Louisville 26 6
O5 at West Texas St. 16 38
O12 at Memphis 0 21
O19 | Tulsa 21 22
O26 ● | Wichita St. 7 3
N2 at Abilene Christian 6 20
N9 | at Cincinnati 7 39
N16 ● Hardin-Simmons 18 12

1964 2-7-1 (1-3-0)
S19 = Texas-El Paso 0 0
S26 Bowling Green 7 21
O3 ● | at Louisville 22 0
O10 West Texas St. 13 21
O17 New Mexico State 7 13
O24 at San Diego Marines 3 16
O31 ● at So. Illinois 14 13
N7 | Cincinnati 6 27
N14 | at Tulsa 0 47
N21 | at Wichita St. 6 14

1965 3-7-0 (2-2-0)
S18 at Texas-El Paso 15 61
S25 ● Parsons 26 7
O2 | Louisville 21 29
O9 at Tampa 14 17
O16 | Tulsa 20 27
O23 Arkansas [LR] 20 55
O30 ● | at Cincinnati 28 24
N6 ● | Wichita St. 24 21
N13 Memphis 0 28
N20 at New Mexico State 13 43

1966 8-2-0 (3-1-0)
S17 ● New Mexico State 25 21
S24 ● Texas-El Paso 12 9
O1 ● | at Louisville 20 19
O8 ● Tampa 41 6
O15 | at Tulsa 27 30
O22 ● So. Illinois 53 6
O29 at Drake 13 17
N5 ● | Cincinnati 35 13
N12 ● | at Wichita St. 30 13
N19 ● U.T. Chattanooga 42 7

ROD RUST
1967-72 (.476) 29-32-1

1967 7-1-1 (4-0-0)
S23 ● Drake 31 0
S30 ● | Louisville 30 28
O7 = at New Mexico State 31 31
O14 ● Colorado State 21 10
O21 ● at So. Illinois 37 0
O28 ● | at Cincinnati 34 14
N11 ● | Wichita St. 20 14
N18 ● | Tulsa 54 12
N25 at Memphis 20 29

1968 8-2-0 (4-1-0)
S21 ● New Mexico State 47 20
S28 ● at Colorado State 17 12
O5 | Memphis 12 30
O12 ● No. Michigan 17 3
O19 ● | at Tulsa 20 17
O26 Arkansas [LR] 15 17
N2 ● | Cincinnati 55 34
N9 ● at Texas-El Paso 34 31
N16 ● | at Louisville 36 14
N23 ● | at Wichita St. 44 6

1969 7-3-0 (4-1-0)
S20 ● La. Lafayette 40 6
S27 | at Memphis 13 15
O4 at Drake 23 27
O11 ● Weber St. 35 13
O18 ● at New Mexico State 30 12
O25 ● | Louisville 31 13
N1 ● | at Cincinnati 31 30
N8 ● | Wichita St. 47 0
N15 ● | Tulsa 42 16
N22 at San Diego State 24 42

1970 3-8-0 (1-3-0)
S12 at Brigham Young 7 10
S19 San Diego State 0 23
S26 | at Louisville 2 13
O3 ● Drake 37 13
O10 at Tampa 7 18
O17 ● at West Texas St. 11 10
O24 | Memphis 7 28
O31 New Mexico State 31 32
N7 Cincinnati 10 30
N21 ● | at Wichita St. 41 24
D5 | at Tulsa 20 26

1971 3-8-0 (3-1-0)
S10 Brigham Young [DAL] 13 41
S18 at Weber St. 0 20
S25 at New Mexico State 0 10
O9 Akron 6 20
O16 ● | Louisville [IRV] 20 17
O23 at Arkansas 21 60
O30 ● | Drake 21 12
N6 at Cincinnati 7 40
N13 | at Memphis 8 47
N20 ● | Wichita St. [IRV] 31 10
D4 at San Diego State 28 44

1972 1-10-0 (0-7-0)
S16 at Long Beach St. 21 24
S23 San Diego State [IRV] 0 25
S30 | at Drake 8 54
O7 | at Wichita St. 6 23
O14 | at Louisville 6 56
O21 | Memphis [IRV] 6 7
O28 Arkansas [LR] 16 42
N4 ● Cincinnati [IRV] 27 25
N11 | New Mexico State 22 36
N18 | West Texas St. [IRV] 14 17
N25 | at Tulsa 22 45

HAYDEN FRY
1973-78 (.598) 38-25-3

1973 5-5-1 (5-1-0)
S8 Texas Arlington [IRV] 7 31
S15 at Memphis 3 24
S22 ● | West Texas St. 32 15
S29 = Long Beach St. 0 0
O13 ● | Louisville 7 6
O20 ● | Drake 19 7
O27 ● | at New Mexico State 27 7
N3 at Cincinnati 3 52
N10 ● | Wichita St. 31 21
N17 | Tulsa 15 24
N24 at San Diego State 9 56

1974 2-7-2 (1-3-2)
S14 at SMU 6 7
S21 | at Tulsa 6 31
S28 Lamar 7 27
O5 = | at Drake 24 24
O12 | Louisville 10 24
O19 ● | New Mexico State 24 19
O26 Memphis 0 41
N2 ● San Diego State 14 9
N9 = | at Wichita St. 10 10
N16 | at West Texas St. 14 21
N23 Long Beach St. 19 35

THE SCHOOLS

1975-1982 Independent

1975 7-4-0

S4	●	Texas Arlington [IRV]	27	14
S13	●	at Drake	7	3
S20		at San Diego State	12	30
S27		at Oklahoma State	7	61
O4		at Memphis	19	21
O11	●	Houston [IRV]	28	0
O18		at Mississippi State	12	15
O25	●	at Tennessee	21	14
N8	●	Cal Poly Pomona	27	17
N15	●	at New Mexico State	24	20
N29	●	West Texas St.	16	15

1976 6-5-0

S4		at Mississippi State	0	7 †
S11	●	Texas Arlington	24	7
S18		at Texas	14	17
S25		at SMU	31	38
O2		at Oklahoma State	10	16
O9	●	at Cal Poly Pomona	21	10
O16	●	at West Texas St.	10	7
O23	●	at New Mexico State	25	14
O30	●	Louisiana Tech [SHRE]	14	8
N13		Florida State	20	21
N20	●	Drake	63	0

1977 9-2-0

S3		at Mississippi State	15	17 †
S10	●	at Texas-El Paso	41	10
S17	●	SMU	24	13
S24	●	West Texas St.	31	20
O1	●	at Richmond	47	14
O8	●	at Southern Miss	27	14
O15	●	Texas Arlington [IRV]	15	6
O22	●	at Memphis	20	19
O29		at Florida State	14	35
N5	●	New Mexico State	45	17
N19	●	at Louisiana Tech	41	14

1978 9-2-0

S2	●	Texas-El Paso	49	0
S9		Mississippi State [IRV]	5	17
S16	●	Texas Arlington [IRV]	28	23
S23	●	at New Mexico State	22	21
S30	●	Oklahoma State [IRV]	12	7
O7	●	at West Texas St.	35	0
O14		at Texas	16	26
O28	●	at Louisiana Tech	16	14
N4	●	Southern Miss	25	12
N11	●	La. Monroe	28	6
N18	●	at Memphis	41	24

JERRY MOORE
1979-80 (.500) 11-11

1979 5-6-0

S1	●	Texas-El Paso	35	0
S8		at Oklahoma State	7	25
S15	●	Texas Arlington [IRV]	19	14
S22		at SMU	9	20
S29		at Kansas	18	37
O6		at Southern Miss	10	30
O13	●	New Mexico State	21	7
O20	●	West Texas St.	28	14
O27		at Memphis	0	22
N3	●	at Louisiana Tech	19	17
N17		at East Carolina	16	49

1980 6-5-0

S6	●	at Texas Arlington	31	14
S13		at SMU	9	28
S20	●	at Texas-El Paso	35	15
S27		at Houston	17	24
O4	●	La. Lafayette	22	20
O11		at Tulsa	27	28
O18	●	at Memphis	29	10
N1	●	at New Mexico State	38	28
N8		at Brigham Young	23	41
N15	●	La. Monroe	26	18
N22		at Miami, Fla.	8	26

BOB TYLER
1981 (.182) 2-9

1981 2-9-0

S5		at Kentucky	6	28
S12		at SMU	7	34
S19		at Texas	10	23
S26		at La. Lafayette	11	34
O3		Oklahoma State [IRV]	0	9
O10	●	New Mexico State	38	16
O24		Texas Arlington [IRV]	6	7
O31		Southern Miss	0	22
N7		at Auburn	0	20
N14	●	at La. Monroe	17	14
N28		at San Jose State	16	28

CORKY NELSON
1982-90 (.480) 48-52-1

1982 2-9-0

S4		at Baylor	17	21
S11		at Oklahoma State	6	27
S18		La. Monroe	15	38
S25		La. Lafayette	14	31
O2		at SMU	10	38
O9	●	at Texas Arlington	17	3
O23		at West Texas St.	22	24
O30		New Mexico	17	20
N6		at New Mexico State	19	30
N13	●	at Richmond	22	13
N20		Tulsa	20	38

1983-1994 Division 1-AA

1983 8-4-0

S3	●	West Texas St.	32	3
S10		at Oklahoma State	13	20
S17	●	New Mexico State	49	3
S24		at Texas	2	26
O1	●	at New Mexico	18	2
O8	●	at Arkansas State	17	0
O15	●	at McNeese State	17	10
O22		Louisiana Tech	18	25
O29	●	Lamar	10	0
N5	●	at N.E. Louisiana	27	7
N12	●	UT-Arlington	52	15
		DIVISION I-AA PLAYOFF		
N19		at Nevada-Reno	17	20

1984 2-9-0

S1	●	Angelo St.	7	3
S15		at Lamar	6	10
S22		at SMU	6	24
S29		at Louisiana Tech	12	17
O6		at Arkansas State	9	14
O13		McNeese State	7	26
O20		at TCU	3	34
O27		Texas St.	19	27
N3		at Kentucky	7	31
N10	●	N.E. Louisiana	10	3
N17		at UT-Arlington	0	22

1985 4-6-1

S7	●	Northwestern St.	34	14
S14		at Oklahoma State	9	10
S21		at Texas Tech	7	28
S28	●	at Kansas State	22	10
O5		Louisiana Tech	8	33
O12		at Arkansas State	0	56
O19		at TCU	10	14
O26	=	at McNeese State	0	0
N9	●	Lamar	20	0
N16		at N.E. Louisiana	17	18
N23	●	UT-Arlington	23	20

1986 6-4-0

S6	●	at Texas St.	7	0
S20		at Texas A&M	28	48
S27	●	McNeese State	21	13
O4		at Louisiana Tech	10	17
O11	●	Northwestern St.	24	3
O18	●	at TCU	24	20
O25	●	at Lamar	33	13
N1		at Nevada-Las Vegas	26	27
N8		Arkansas State	21	43
N15	●	N.E. Louisiana	28	20

1987 7-5-0

S5		at Oklahoma	14	69
S12	●	Texas St.	20	3
S19	●	at Northwestern St.	15	13
S26	●	at McNeese State	38	16
O3	●	Abilene Christian	26	3
O10	●	at Sam Houston St.	41	24
O17		at TCU	10	19
O31	●	at Stephen F. Austin	16	14
N7		at Arkansas State	20	27
N14		at N.E. Louisiana	23	24
N21	●	Louisiana Tech	10	5
		DIVISION I-AA PLAYOFF		
N28		N.E. Louisiana	9	30

1988 8-4-0

S3	●	at Texas Tech	29	24
S17	●	Arkansas State	49	21
S24		at Texas	24	27
O1	●	EA. Washington	51	0
O8	●	N.E. Louisiana	26	23
O15	●	McNeese State	37	0
O22	●	at Sam Houston St.	24	3
O29		at Stephen F. Austin	10	17
N5		Northwestern St.	17	25
N12	●	at Texas St.	30	10
N19	●	at Rice	33	17
		DIVSION I-AA PLAYOFF		
N25		at Marshall	0	7

1989 5-6-0

S9	●	Abilene Christian	35	19
S16	●	Murray St.	28	14
S23	●	at Arkansas State	20	17
S30		at Kansas State	17	20
O7		at Northwestern St.	7	30
O14		Stephen F. Austin	16	35
O21		Sam Houston St.	6	14
O28		at SMU	9	35
N4	●	at McNeese State	31	19
N11		Texas St.	20	25
N18	●	at N.E. Louisiana	28	25

1990 6-5-0

S8	●	Alcorn St.	20	7
S15	●	Abilene Christian	38	6
S22		at Texas A&M	8	40
S29		Northwestern St.	18	28
O6	●	SMU	14	7
O13	●	at Stephen F. Austin	31	24
O20		McNeese State	14	16
O27		at Sam Houston St.	14	26
N2	●	Arkansas State	35	26
N10	●	at Texas St.	16	15
N24		N.E. Louisiana	15	16

DENNIS PARKER
1991-93 (.348) 11-21-1

1991 3-7-1

S7	●	Abilene Christian	24	0
S14		at Oklahoma	2	40
S21		at Nevada	0	72
S28	=	SW. Missouri St.	21	21
O12		at Northwestern St.	10	24
O19	●	Stephen F. Austin	18	14
O26		Sam Houston St.	6	14
N2		at McNeese State	3	41
N9	●	at Nicholls St.	24	19
N16		Texas St.	6	38
N23		at N.E. Louisiana	21	44

1992 4-7-0

S5	●	Abilene Christain	41	0
S12		at SMU	14	28
S19		at SW. Missouri St.	10	35
S26		at Texas	15	33
O10	●	Northwestern St.	37	34
O17	●	at Stephen F. Austin	21	11
O24		at Sam Houston St.	14	34
O31		McNeese State	25	26
N7	●	Nicholls St.	31	3
N14	●	at Texas St.	13	10
N21		N.E. Louisiana	25	47

1993 4-7-0

S4		at Nebraska	14	76
S11		at No. Arizona	23	24
S18	●	SW. Missouri St.	34	33
S25	●	Abilene Christian	33	13
O9	●	Texas St.	35	28
O16		at McNeese State	17	18
O23		Northwestern St.	37	38
O30		at Sam Houston St.	14	24
N6		Stephen F. Austin	27	29
N13	●	Nicholls St.	63	21
N20		at N.E. Louisiana	31	61

MATT SIMON
1994-97 (.411) 18-26-1

1994 7-4-1

S1	●	Abilene Christain	48	0
S10	●	at SW. Missouri	26	20
S24		Montana	17	21
O1		at Oklahoma State	34	36
O8	●	at Texas St.	27	14
O15	●	McNeese State	38	17
O22	●	at Northwestern St.	28	25
O29	●	Sam Houston St.	21	16
N4	=	at Stephen F. Austin	33	33
N12	●	at Nicholls St.	31	17
N19		at N.E. Louisiana	20	38
		DIVISION I-AA PLAYOFF		
N26		at Boise State	20	24

1995 Independent

1995 2-9-0

S2		at Missouri	7	28
S9		Kansas [IRV]	10	27
S16	●	Oregon State	30	27
S23		at Oklahoma	10	51
O7		at Nevada	24	56
O14		UAB	14	19
O21		at LSU	7	49
O28		at Alabama	19	38
N4		at Nevada-Las Vegas	24	34
N11	●	Idaho St.	41	38
N18		at Louisville	14	57

1996-2000 Big West

1996 5-6 (3-2)

S7	●	Illinois St.	20	14
S14		at Arizona State	7	52
S21		at Texas A&M	0	55
S28		Army [IRV]	10	27
O5	●	at Northern Illinois	24	21
O12		Vanderbilt	7	19
O19	● |	New Mexico State	13	0
O26	|	Nevada	13	40
N2	|	at Utah State	13	21
N9	● |	at Boise State	30	27
N16	● |	Idaho	24	17

1997 4-7 (2-3)

A30		at Vanderbilt	12	29
S6		at Oregon State	7	33
S13	●	Indiana St.	41	6
S20	●	at Texas Tech	30	27
S27		Texas A&M [IRV]	10	36
O4	|	at Idaho	17	30
O18	|	Boise State	14	17
O25	|	at Nevada	10	65
N8	● |	at New Mexico State	26	15
N15		at Army	14	25
N22	● |	Utah State	51	48

DARRELL DICKEY
1998-PRESENT (.446) 37-46

1998 3-8 (3-2)

S5		at Oklahoma	9	37
S12		Texas Tech [IRV]	0	30
S19		at Arizona State	15	34
S26		at Texas A&M	9	28
O10	● |	at Boise State	21	13
O17	● |	Nevada	27	21
O24		Houston	9	31
O31	|	Idaho	23	41
N7		at Kansas	14	23
N14	|	at Utah State	27	28
N21	● |	New Mexico State	19	11

1999 2-9 (1-5)

S2		Nevada-Las Vegas	3	26
S11		at LSU	0	52
S18	●	at Texas Tech	21	14
O2		at Baylor	10	23
O9	|	Idaho [PULL]	10	28
O16	● |	Boise State	17	10
O23	|	Arkansas State	10	14
O30	|	at Nevada	28	41
N13		at TCU	3	27
N20	|	at New Mexico State	9	22
N27	|	Utah State	7	34

2000 3-8 (1-4)

A31		Baylor	7	20
S9		at Texas Tech	7	13
S16		at Nevada-Las Vegas	0	38
S23		at Kansas State	10	55
O5	●	Samford	41	6
O14	|	Utah State	12	17
O21	|	at Boise State	0	59
O28	●	at La. Lafayette	13	0
N4	|	Idaho	14	16
N11	|	at Arkansas State	28	53
N18	● |	New Mexico State	30	23

2001-Present Sun Belt

2001 5-7 (5-1)

S1		TCU	5	19
S8		at Oklahoma	10	37
S22		Texas Tech [IRV]	14	42
S29		at South Florida	10	28
O6	|	at La. Monroe	17	19
O13	● |	Middle Tennessee	24	21
O20	● |	Arkansas State	45	0
N3	● |	at New Mexico State	22	20
N10	● |	La. Lafayette	42	17
N17	● |	at Idaho	50	27
D1		at Troy State	16	18
		NEW ORLEANS BOWL		
D18		Colorado State	20	45

2002   8-5   (6-0)

A31		at Texas	0	27
S7	●	Nicholls St.	23	0
S14		at Alabama	7	33
S21		at TCU	10	16
S28		at Arizona	9	14
O5		South Florida	17	24
O19	● |	at Arkansas State	13	10
O26	● |	at La. Lafayette	27	0
N2	● |	La. Monroe	41	2
N9	● |	Idaho	10	0
N16	● |	New Mexico State	38	27
N23	● |	at Middle Tennessee	30	20
		NEW ORLEANS BOWL		
D17	●	Cincinnati	24	19

2003   9-4   (7-0)

A30		at Oklahoma	3	37
S6	●	Baylor	52	14
S13		at Air Force	21	34
S20		Arkansas *LR*	7	31
S27	● |	La. Lafayette	44	23
O11	● |	at Idaho	24	14
O18	● |	Utah State	37	27
O25	● |	at Middle Tennessee	33	28
N1	● |	Troy State	21	0
N8	● |	at La. Monroe	28	26
N15	● |	Arkansas State	58	14
N25	● |	at New Mexico State	13	10
		NEW ORLEANS BOWL		
D16		Memphis	17	27

2004   7-5   (7-0)

S4		at Texas	0	65
S11		Florida Atlantic	13	20
S18		at Colorado	21	52
S25		at Baylor	14	37
O2	● |	Middle Tennessee	30	21
O9	● |	at Utah State	31	23
O23	● |	New Mexico State	36	26
O30	● |	La. Monroe	45	30
N6	● |	at La. Lafayette	27	17
N13	● |	Idaho	51	29
N18	● |	at Arkansas State	31	7
		NEW ORLEANS BOWL		
D14		Southern Miss	10	31

NORTHERN ILLINOIS

BY ED KRZEMIENSKI

NORTHERN ILLINOIS KNOWS THE pitfall of being a successful conference-affiliated mid-major. In 2003, after upsetting two perennial power-houses, the Huskies found themselves in the byzantine confines of the Bowl Championship Series as they tried to make a push into the national spotlight. Losses to MAC opponents left 10–2 NIU out of the Motor City Bowl, but its initial success highlighted one of many reasons the BCS continues to evolve. All of that, of course, is a backward way of saying that NIU, under head coach Joe Novak, has quickly become one of the top teams in a conference growing in power and recognition.

TRADITION In addition to the team's gridiron success, the Huskies faithful have had much to celebrate. NIU's cheerleading squad usually ends up among the top groups in the national championships. Band Day brings 20 or so groups to DeKalb, where they play a high-decibel version of the "Huskie Fight Song." Longtime Huskies fans shake their car keys during kickoffs, perhaps letting their dogs know it's time to go for a ride.

BEST PLAYER LeShon Johnson was dubbed the biggest thing to hit DeKalb since Cindy Crawford. Known as The Cowboy because he came from Haskell, Okla., Johnson ran the football an awful lot like a couple of guys who played in his home state, Billy Sims and Barry Sanders. In his 1993 senior season, Johnson ran for a national-best 1,976 yards on 327 carries, for an average of 179.6-yards per game. He ended the season sixth in the Heisman race and as only the seventh football player from an Illinois college to make unanimous first-team All-America. (The other six, including Red Grange and Dick Butkus, all played for the University of Illinois.) Johnson played just two years at NIU, but his total yards mark of 3,314 still places him fifth on the school's all-time list. A third-round pick of the Green Bay Packers in 1994, Johnson battled lymphoma but played professionally until 2001.

BEST COACH Howard Fletcher coached NIU for 13 years from 1956 to 1968 and won 74 games. More significant than his seven winning seasons, though, was the excitement Fletcher brought to the DeKalb campus. Three of his squads played in the Mineral Water Bowl for the NCAA College Division Championship. In 1963, Fletcher's Huskies won that title. Innovative in his approach to the game, "Fletch" taught his 1963 squad the blitz-T formation, which resulted in their leading the nation in passing. Fletcher corresponded regularly on the intricacies of this

PROFILE

Northern Illinois University
DeKalb, Ill.
Founded: 1895
Enrollment: 18,275
Colors: Cardinal and Black
Nickname: Huskies
Stadium: Brigham Field at Huskie Stadium
　　Opened in 1965
　　FieldTurf; 28,000 capacity
First football game: 1899
All-time record: 472–423–51 (.526)
Bowl record: 2–0
Mid-American Conference championships:
1 (outright)
Website: www.niu.edu/athletics

THE BEST OF TIMES

The threes have it: in 1963, undefeated NIU won the college division national title; in 1973, Mark Kellar led the nation in rushing; in 1983, NIU won a MAC title and the California Bowl; in 1993, LeShon Johnson led the nation in rushing; in 2003, the Huskies dropped Maryland, Alabama and Iowa State in a 10–2 campaign.

THE WORST OF TIMES

1996 to 1998: the team went 3–30, bookending a 23-game losing streak.

CONFERENCE HISTORY

Northern Illinois entered the MAC in 1975 but left after a decade. The Huskies returned in 1997 to stay. NIU played as an independent (1899-21, 1926-27, 1966-74, 1986-92 and 1996), in the Little 19 Conference (1922-25, 1928-46), the Illinois Intercollegiate Athletic Conference (1947-49), the Interstate Intercollegiate Athletic Conference (1950-65) and the Big West (1993-95).

DISTINGUISHED ALUMNI

Joan Allen, actress; Dan Castellaneta, actor and voice of Homer Simpson; J. Dennis Hastert, Speaker of the House; Paul Sereno, paleontologist

FIGHT SONG

HUSKIE FIGHT SONG
Huskies, come on you Huskies
And make a score or two
Huskies, you're Northern Huskies
The team to pull us through
Forward, together forward
There's victory in view
Come on you Huskies, Fight on you
Huskies and win for N.I.U.

LeShon Johnson was dubbed the biggest thing to hit DeKalb since Cindy Crawford.

shotgun-style offense with a coaching friend of his named Tom Landry.

BEST TEAM The 1963 Huskies went undefeated and won the NCAA College Division Championship by defeating Southwest Missouri State 21-14 in the Mineral Water Bowl at Excelsior Springs, Mo. In an era of the rushing play, the 1963 Huskies became synonymous with the forward pass. Running a shotgun offense led by George Bork, who became the first collegiate passer to reach 3,000 yards in a single season, the Huskies put up some amazing numbers: final scores of 55-7 and 61-0, a 445-yard passing game, a seven-touchdown passing game and a 17-reception game for Gary Stearns. Fletcher summed up his philosophy succinctly: "We believe in putting the ball in the air and spreading out our opponents." In 1986, the school inducted the entire 1963 squad into its Huskies Hall of Fame.

BIGGEST GAME Bill Mallory's 1983 Huskies brought NIU its only MAC championship and California Bowl bid. Against Cal State-Fullerton on Dec. 17, the Huskies won a thriller 20-13. Led by Lou Wicks, the NIU fullback who gained a career-best 119 yards on 14 carries and won the game's MVP, the Huskies sealed a victory when its defense stopped CSF on a fourth-and-one with 35 seconds left in the

game. NIU ended its season at 10–2 and just outside the Top 20. Moreover, the California Bowl team sent 19 players to myriad professional leagues and was inducted en masse into the Huskie Hall of Fame in 1995.

BIGGEST UPSET On Aug. 28, 2003, the Huskies hosted No. 15 Maryland. Falling behind twice, the Huskies battled back to tie the game with an 18-play, 84-yard drive late in the fourth quarter. In overtime, NIU beat the Terps 20-13, when Randee Drew intercepted a pass that ricocheted off a Maryland receiver's foot. The upset set the tone for NIU; it later won at Alabama and ended the season at 10–2.

HEARTBREAKER In 1992, Northern Illinois led Wisconsin 17-3 in the fourth quarter and looked to be on its way to a second straight win over the Badgers. But Wisconsin cut the lead to 17-16, and then, in the final seconds of the game, attempted a two-point conversion for the win. On a play the NIU faithful felt the officials blew, Badgers quarterback Darrell Bevell sneaked into the end zone to give Wisconsin an 18-17 win.

STADIUM In 1965, Huskie Stadium, a.k.a. The Doghouse, a.k.a. The House That George Bork Built (the latter in honor of

RECORDS

RUSHING YARDS
GAME	
325	Garrett Wolfe vs. Eastern Michigan, Nov. 20, 2004 (43 att.)
SEASON	
1,976	LeShon Johnson, 1993 (327 att.)
CAREER	
4,941	Michael Turner, 2000-03 (940 att.)

PASSING YARDS
GAME	
445	George Bork vs. Illinois State, Oct. 19, 1963 (38 of 53)
SEASON	
3,077	George Bork, 1963 (244 of 374)
CAREER	
6,782	George Bork, 1960-63 (577 of 902)

RECEIVING YARDS
GAME	
234	P.J. Fleck vs. Ohio, Oct. 4, 2003 (14 rec.)
SEASON	
1,215	Dave Petzke, 1978 (91 rec.)
CAREER	
2,991	Justin McCareins, 1997-2000 (204 rec.)

POINTS
GAME	
42	Bill Anderson vs. Wheaton, Oct. 19, 1912 (7 TDs)
SEASON	
126	Garrett Wolfe, 2004 (21 TDs)
CAREER	
370	Steve Azar, 2000-03 (73 FGs, 151 PATs)

CONSENSUS ALL-AMERICANS
1962-63	George Bork, QB
1993	LeShon Johnson, TB

the school's former Little All-America quarterback), replaced cozy but outdated Glidden Field as the home for NIU football. Originally seating 20,257, the structure remained half-built. Beginning with head coach Howard Fletcher in the mid-1960s and continuing with his seven immediate successors, the promise of a completed stadium served as a recruiting tool. "Son," the mantra went, "by the time you graduate, we will build the other side of the stadium." That dream became reality in 1995, when the east grandstand joined the existing west superstructure and gave Huskie Stadium its current capacity of 28,000.

RIVAL Because it reentered competition in the MAC only in 1997 and remains the only conference school from Illinois, NIU has yet to establish much in the way of a rivalry in the conference. Traditional in-state rivals, moreover, fell off NIU's schedule as it rose to Division I-A play. Historically, Illinois State served as the Huskies' greatest foe. The schools began meeting in 1906 and have played 55 times since then. Alas, maintaining the rivalry has been difficult, as NIU plays in Division I-A and Illinois State resides in I-AA, and the teams have not met since 2000. NIU holds a 25–22–9 advantage in the series. Perhaps an annual game with the University of Illinois could create a new tradition. Certainly, the Huskies have nothing to fear from the Illini on the gridiron.

DISPUTE Following the 2003 season, Northern Illinois was overlooked for a bowl game. Miami and Bowling Green represented the MAC in postseason play, but the 10–2 Huskies stayed home. Novak was hot: "I don't think a .500 team should get in over a team that won 10 games. Are you telling me they had a better season than us? Baloney." The .500 team was a slightly veiled reference to a 6–6 Northwestern team that received a bid to the Motor City Bowl.

NICKNAME Northern Illinois ran through a series of nicknames before finally solidifying its current moniker. Early on, the teachers college teams became known as The Profs. Later the school was the

Cardinals, Evansmen (for head coach Chick Evans), Northerners and Teachers, before a committee was appointed to find "a term with a trifle more dash" in 1940. The result was a pretty and powerful dog, and the nickname Huskies, a name regarded as apt to the school's varsity teams, became official. A notable stipulation of the original name is that the team forever became known, in its singular collective, as Husk-IE instead of the traditional Husk-Y form.

MASCOT NIU's mascot is Victor E. Huskie, a student-in-costume chosen as part of the cheerleading squad. Laura Schlembach, 2002's Victor E. Huskie, noted that the job was not all milk bones and fire hydrants, though, especially in the dog days of summer. Commenting on the first day she was issued the outfit, Schlembach remarked, "They just handed me this large bag … and it was the worst smell ever. The next game I came prepared. I brought Febreze. I brought dryer sheets. I made that thing smell so nice." In previous years, the school kept a series of real dogs for its mascot.

UNIFORMS The Huskies wear a mix of red (cardinal), white and black. Throughout most of its history, NIU emblazoned its helmets with a block N overlaid with an I. Currently, the team wears black helmets with a cardinal NIU and white mascot profile on the side. The team jerseys are cardinal at home and white on the road; pants are solid black both at home and on the road.

TRAGEDY On the second day of conditioning drills in February 2002, Jawan Jackson collapsed and died. The 19-year-old freshman was attempting to make the Huskies squad as a walk-on.

DUBIOUS DISTINCTION In 1982, Northern Illinois lost to Northwestern 31-6, ending the Wildcats' 34-game losing streak.

LORE In 1983, the city of Chicago experienced its own Heidi Bowl. With temperatures below zero, the local television station carrying the California Bowl game between NIU and

---

ALL-CENTURY TEAM

The team was selected in 1999 by an NIU committee chaired by sports information director Michael Korcek.

OFFENSE

1977-79	Randy Clark,	OL
1983-86	Todd Peat,	OG
1984-87	Ted Karamanos,	OG
1980-83	Scott Bolzan,	OT
1988-90	Eric Wenckowski,	C
1977-80	Jim Hannula,	TE
1960-63	Hugh Rohrschneider,	WR
1966-68	John Spilis,	WR
1960-63	George Bork,	QB
1992-93	LeShon Johnson,	TB
1985-88	Rodney Taylor,	HB
1971-73	Mark Kellar,	FB
1980-83	Vince Scott,	PK
1948-51	Fran Cahill,	KR

DEFENSE

1945-47	Larry Brink,	DL
1982-85	Scott Kellar,	DT
1983-86	Doug Bartlett,	DT
1993-95	Hollis Thomas,	NG
1970-72	Larry Clark,	LB
1973-75	Bob Gregolunas,	LB
1976-79	Frank Lewandoski,	ILB
1959-61	Tom Beck,	HB
1971-73	Rich Marks,	SS
1977-80	Dave Petway,	FS
1985, 87-89	Brett Tucker,	CB
1969-71	Tom Wittum,	P

Cal State-Fullerton lost its signal when the transmitter on top of the John Hancock Center froze in the third quarter. A station spokesman said they received thousands of complaints.

QUOTE "I thought I was in Norman, Okla."—Fresno State coach Jim Sweeney in 1990, after NIU's wishbone offense shredded his team by a score of 73-18

NORTHERN ILLINOIS ANNUAL STATISTICAL LEADERS

YR	RUSHING	YDS	ATT	AVG	PASSING	ATT	CMP	PCT	YDS	RECEIVING	REC	YDS	AVG
1948	Bob Brigham	786	138	5.7	Don Fortunato	164	66	.40	1,214	Floyd Hunsberger	22	401	18.2
1949	Ernie Wickstrom	452	63	7.2	Bob Heimerdinger	115	45	.54	779	Bill Russell	19	334	17.6
1950	Hugh Helms	506	94	5.4	Bob Heimerdinger	210	102	.49	1,597	Ernie Wickstrom	29	504	17.4
1951	Bill Graham	395	64	6.2	Bob Heimerdinger	225	103	.46	1,710	Fran Cahill	40	876	21.9
1952	Jack Pheanis	339	69	4.9	Jim Harmes	106	46	.43	694	Jim McKinzie	44	703	16.0
1953	Wes Luedeking	330	97	3.4	Paul Smith	62	23	.37	275	Wes Luedeking	24	247	10.3
1954	Bill Graham	236	91	2.6	Ron Hicks	108	45	.42	617	Tom Skubich	14	147	10.5
1955	Bob Snider	242	66	3.7	Don Coulom	90	37	.41	402	Bob Snider	16	202	12.6
1956	Tom Skubich	404	89	4.5	Joe Plaskas	44	12	.27	154	Bob Soltis	6	117	19.5
1957	Ron Hansen	211	41	5.1	Lew Flinn	103	40	.39	897	Jim Caldwell	16	497	31.1
1958	Joe Plaskas	511	136	3.8	Lew Flinn	137	64	.47	916	Al Eck	32	486	15.2
1959	Joe Plaskas	698	140	5.0	Lew Flinn	174	93	.53	1,420	Al Eck	34	586	17.2
1960	Bob Soltis	559	77	7.3	Tom Beck	156	77	.49	1,176	Al Eck	45	740	16.4
1961	Mickey Stevens	225	50	4.5	George Bork	121	72	.60	841	Rich Bader	33	430	13.0
1962	Jack Dean	504	100	5.0	George Bork	356	232	.65	2,506	Hugh Rohrschneider	76	795	10.5
1963	Jack Dean	516	78	6.6	George Bork	374	244	.65	3,077	Hugh Rohrschneider	75	1,036	13.8
1964	Jack Dean	733	160	4.6	Jack Dean	110	59	.54	716	Bill Pelkey	26	436	16.8
1965	Leigh Gilbert	473	97	4.9	Ron Christian	323	173	.54	2,101	Bob Stark	58	525	9.1
1966	Jim Wendler	358	78	4.6	Mike Griesman	283	141	.50	1,899	Jack Frost	48	796	16.6
1967	Bruce Bray	344	76	4.5	Bob Carpenter	203	88	.43	1,169	John Spilis	46	620	13.5
1968	John Lalonde	866	177	4.9	Bob Carpenter	259	128	.49	1,421	John Spilis	46	629	13.7
1969	John Lalonde	813	187	4.3	Steve Parker	181	85	.47	827	Tom Bastable	26	357	13.7
1970	John Lalonde	548	145	3.8	Terry Drugan	117	58	.50	561	Willie Hatter	35	418	11.9
1971	Mark Kellar	710	168	4.2	Terry Drugan	174	77	.44	957	Willie Hatter	50	615	12.3
1972	Mark Kellar	1,316	285	4.6	Terry Drugan	77	34	.44	390	Willie Hatter	17	268	15.8
1973	Mark Kellar	1,719	291	5.9	Bob Gregolunas	58	27	.47	362	Dan Gentile	15	319	21.3
1974	Vince Smith	720	131	5.5	Jerry Golsteyn	138	62	.45	712	Gary Hosier	27	375	13.9
1975	Ed Johnson	814	179	4.5	Jerry Golsteyn	221	117	.53	1,539	Ken Moore	30	425	14.2
1976	Vince Smith	448	105	4.3	Pete Kraker	152	47	.31	525	Scott Paplham	15	208	13.9
1977	Allen Ross	1,043	273	3.8	Pete Kraker	183	103	.56	1,034	Dave Petzke	57	743	13.0
1978	Allen Ross	1,033	259	4.0	Pete Kraker	283	134	.47	1,731	Dave Petzke	91	1,215	13.4
1979	Allen Ross	751	194	3.9	John Gibbons	124	44	.35	747	Mike Pinckney	34	601	17.7
1980	Allen Ross	673	141	4.8	John Gibbons	179	102	.57	1,119	Jim Latanski	30	421	14.0
1981	Joe Law	596	143	4.2	Rick Bridges	104	49	.47	636	Joe Law	20	156	7.8
1982	Pete Roth	1,008	220	4.6	Tim Tyrrell	93	38	.41	458	Greg Spicher	14	208	14.9
1983	Darryl Richardson	1,204	235	5.1	Tim Tyrrell	189	91	.48	1,260	Reggie Sims	27	279	10.3
1984	Pete Roth	557	137	4.1	Darryl Taylor	132	62	.47	938	Reggie Sims	39	475	12.2
1985	Darryl Richardson	585	121	4.8	Marshall Taylor	186	94	.51	1,162	Curt Pardridge	26	409	15.7
1986	Antonio Davis	648	141	4.6	Marshall Taylor	130	67	.52	993	Virgil Gerin	18	210	11.7
1987	Marshall Taylor	826	157	5.3	Marshall Taylor	139	76	.55	1,039	Virgil Gerin	28	366	13.1
1988	Adam Dach	906	192	4.7	Marshall Taylor	127	63	.50	973	Mark Clancy	13	315	24.2
1989	Stacey Robinson	1,443	223	6.5	Stacey Robinson	128	65	.51	863	Kurt Cassidy	12	137	11.4
1990	Stacey Robinson	1,238	193	6.4	Stacey Robinson	118	58	.49	861	Kurt Cassidy	13	198	15.2
1991	Adam Dach	847	165	5.1	Rob Rugai	86	47	.55	624	Larry Wynn	21	415	19.8
1992	LeShon Johnson	1,338	265	5.0	Rob Rugai	132	76	.58	987	Larry Wynn	37	538	14.5
1993	LeShon Johnson	1,976	327	6.0	Scott Crabtree	141	80	.57	1,163	Raymond Roberts	31	401	12.9
1994	Brian Grimes	876	169	5.2	Aaron Gilbert	185	93	.50	1,437	Vaurice Patterson	34	578	17.0
1995	Charles Talley	1,540	285	5.4	Aaron Gilbert	184	79	.43	1,057	Ralph Strickland	38	664	17.5
1996	Charles Talley	1,008	241	4.2	Brandon Barker	203	105	.52	1,223	Deon Mitchell	36	524	14.6
1997	Ivory Bryant	828	224	3.7	Chris Finlen	149	87	.58	1,107	Deon Mitchell	45	588	13.1
1998	Ivory Bryant	655	187	3.5	Craig Harmon	172	81	.47	795	Justin McCareins	54	486	9.0
1999	William Andrews	1,127	240	4.7	Chris Finlen	199	118	.59	1,551	Justin McCareins	57	906	15.9
2000	Thomas Hammock	1,083	215	5.0	Chris Finlen	231	131	.57	1,857	Justin McCareins	66	1,168	17.7
2001	Thomas Hammock	1,096	268	4.1	Chris Finlen	331	166	.50	2,036	P.J. Fleck	59	732	12.4
2002	Michael Turner	1,915	338	5.7	Josh Haldi	254	130	.51	2,027	Dan Sheldon	40	783	19.6
2003	Michael Turner	1,648	310	5.3	Josh Haldi	336	199	.59	2,544	P.J. Fleck	77	1,028	13.4
2004	Garrett Wolfe	1,656	256	6.5	Josh Haldi	179	94	.53	1,384	Dan Sheldon	40	936	23.4

Receiving leaders by receptions
All statistics include postseason

NORTHERN ILLINOIS ALL-TIME SCORES

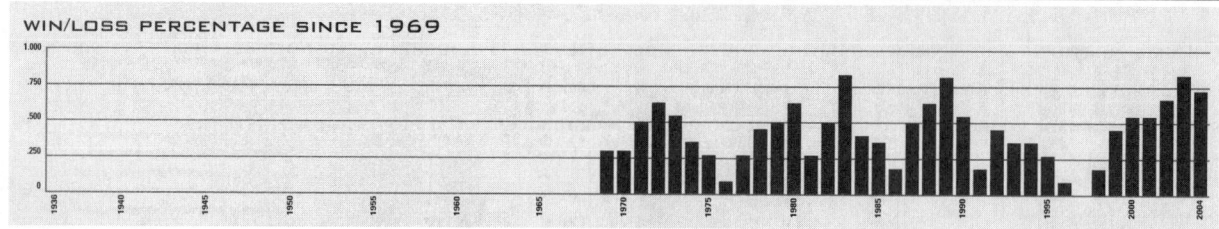

WIN/LOSS PERCENTAGE SINCE 1969

RICHARD URICH
1969-70 (.300) 6-14

1969 3-7-0
S13		at N. Dakota St.	0	28
S20	●	Idaho	47	30
S27		at West Texas St.	7	22
O4		at Marshall	18	17
O11		Western Kentucky	12	14
O18		at Dayton	24	56
O25		Ball State	17	13
N8		Toledo	21	35
N15		Western Michigan	22	31
N22		at Bowling Green	23	38

1970 3-7-0
S12		San Diego State	3	35
S19		Montana	6	30
S26	●	at Xavier	18	0
O3		Miami, Ohio	0	48
O10		West Texas St.	22	24
O24	●	at Ball State	31	14
O31		Dayton	20	21
N7		at Toledo	7	45
N14		at Western Michigan	18	38
N21	●	Buffalo	43	26

JERRY IPPOLITI
1971-75 (.464) 25-29-1

1971 5-5-1
S11		at Wisconsin	0	31
S18	●	Long Beach St.	48	38
S25		at Western Michigan	17	27
O2		at San Diego State	10	30
O9	●	Marshall	33	18 *
O16	●	at West Texas St.	22	19
O23	=	Ball State	10	10
O30		at Kent State	26	7
N6		Toledo	8	23
N13		at Boston College	10	20
N20	●	Xavier	14	9

1972 7-4-0
S9		Illinois St.	21	7
S16		at Wisconsin	7	31
S23		Western Michigan	10	14
S30	●	at Marshall	24	7
O7	●	Xavier	20	7
O14		at Idaho	13	31
O21	●	West Texas State	17	8
O28	●	Kent State	28	7
N4	●	at Toledo	30	7
N11		Fresno State	6	9
N17	●	at Long Beach St.	22	13

1973 6-5-0
S8	●	Indiana St.	42	24
S15	●	So. Illinois	34	28
S22		at Western Michigan	14	28
S29	●	at West Texas St.	21	14
O6		at Fresno State	24	15
O13		Marshall	36	39
O20	●	Ball State	45	17
O27		at Illinois St.	28	14
N3		Western Illinois	27	30
N10		at Xavier	36	40
N17		at Bowling Green	20	21

1974 4-7-0
S7		at McNeese State	16	19
S14	●	Long Beach St.	16	14
S21		Western Michigan	13	30
S28		Indiana St.	14	23
O5		at Ohio U.	14	31
O12		at Marshall	20	17
O19	●	at So. Illinois	17	7
O26		Illinois St.	14	24
N2		at Toledo	14	44
N9		at Ball State	21	31
N16	●	Idaho	27	21

1975-1985 MAC

1975 3-8-0 (2-3-0)
S13		Long Beach St.	7	24
S20		at Northwestern	3	10
S27	●	at Western Michigan	20	0
O4		Kent State	38	15
O11		at Indiana St.	10	21
O18	●	So. Illinois	52	12
O25		Ball State	0	3
N1		at Illinois St.	10	27
N8		Toledo	22	24
N15		at Central Michigan	7	69
N22		at Idaho	24	25

PAT CULPEPPER
1976-79 (.330) 14-29-1

1976 1-10-0 (0-6-0)
S11		at Wichita St.	0	21
S18		Western Michigan	6	37
S25		at Long Beach St.	0	37
O9		at Indiana St.	10	28
O16	●	Illinois St.	7	3
O23		at So. Illinois	0	54
O30		Ball State	7	33
N6		at Toledo	2	17
N13		Central Michigan	9	31
N20		at Ohio U.	15	63
N25		at Kent State	0	42

1977 3-8-0 (2-5-0)
S3		Eastern Michigan	2	25
S10		at Louisville	0	38
S17		at Wisconsin	3	14
S24		at Western Michigan	21	49
O1		at Illinois St.	7	16
O8		Central Michigan	21	25
O15		at Ball State	6	31
O22	●	So. Illinois	28	0
O29	●	at Kent State	21	18
N5		Toledo	9	27
N19	●	Ohio U.	20	6

1978 5-6-0 (2-4-0)
S16		Western Michigan	30	44
S23		at La. Monroe	10	27
S30	●	Illinois St.	49	21
O7		at Long Beach St.	19	24
O14	●	Western Illinois	24	20
O21		at Central Michigan	7	34
O28	●	at So. Illinois	14	13
N4	●	Kent State	27	11
N11		at Toledo	16	35
N18		Ball State	13	31
N25		at Ohio U.	23	14

1979 5-5-1 (3-3-1)
S15	●	E. Tennessee St.	21	14
S22		at Western Michigan	17	45
S29		Long Beach St.	3	9
O6	=	at Eastern Michigan	0	0
O13		at Central Michigan	11	31
O20	●	at Illinois St.	33	7
O27		So. Illinois	11	21
N3	●	Kent State	25	0
N10	●	Toledo	28	10
N17		at Ball State	0	42
N24	●	Ohio U.	28	27

BILL MALLORY
1980-83 (.568) 25-19

1980 7-4-0 (4-3-0)
S5	●	at Long Beach St.	16	9
S13	●	Ball State	17	18
S20		Western Michigan	6	35
S27	●	at Ohio U.	22	21
O4		at So. Illinois	20	17
O11		Illinois St.	18	28
O18	●	Central Michigan	21	0
O25		at Wichita St.	17	14
N1		at Kent State	35	14
N8		at Toledo	6	13
N22		Eastern Michigan	38	6

1981 3-8-0 (2-7-0)
S12		Long Beach St.	7	17
S19		at Central Michigan	10	17
S26	●	Illinois St.	40	7
O3		at Ball State	0	23
O10		at Kent State	10	31
O17		Bowling Green	10	17
O24	●	at Eastern Michigan	30	7
O31		Western Michigan	12	23
N7	●	Ohio U.	38	14
N14		at Miami, Ohio	3	30
N21		Toledo	0	31

1982 5-5-0 (5-4-0)
S4		at Toledo	3	9
S18	●	Kent State	23	15
S25		at Northwestern	6	31
O2		Ball State	7	14
O16		at Bowling Green	18	20
O23	●	Eastern Michigan	10	0
O30		at Western Michigan	3	27
N6	●	at Ohio U.	36	0
N13	●	Miami, Ohio	12	7
N20	●	Central Michigan	19	13

1983 10-2-0 (8-1-0)
S3	●	at Kansas	37	34
S10		at Wisconsin	9	37
S24	●	at Kent State	38	7
O1	●	at Ball State	27	14
O8	●	Western Michigan	27	3
O15	●	at Eastern Michigan	34	15
O22	●	Bowling Green	24	23
O29	●	at Miami, Ohio	17	0
N5		at Central Michigan	14	30
N12	●	Toledo	26	10
N19	●	Ohio U.	41	17
CALIFORNIA BOWL				
D17	●	Fullerton St.	20	13

LEE CORSO
1984 (.409) 4-6-1

1984 4-6-1 (3-5-1)
S1	●	West Texas St.	40	33
S8		at Wisconsin	14	27
S22	●	Kent State	24	10
S29		Ball State	14	15
O6	●	at Western Michigan	20	15
O13	=	Eastern Michigan	10	10
O20		at Bowling Green	6	28
O27		Miami, Ohio	7	20
N3	●	Central Michigan	8	7
N10		at Toledo	7	13
N17		at Ohio U.	3	10

JERRY PETTIBONE
1985-90 (.508) 33-32-1

1985 4-7-0 (4-4-0)
S7	●	Western Michigan	17	0
S14		at Wisconsin	17	38
S21		at Iowa	20	48
S28		at Northwestern	16	38
O5		at Ball State	0	29
O19	●	Toledo	16	3
O26		at Miami, Ohio	15	32
N2		Bowling Green	14	34
N9	●	at Eastern Michigan	3	0
N16	●	Ohio U.	35	7
N23		at Central Michigan	21	30

1986-1992 INDEPENDENT

1986 2-9-0
A30		Ball State	10	20
S6		at West Virginia	14	47
S13		at Wisconsin	20	35
S20		at Iowa	3	57
S27		Western Illinois	0	10
O4		at Miami, Fla.	0	34
O18		at Toledo	28	29
O25		at Miami, Ohio	6	20
N1	●	at Bowling Green	16	8
N8	●	Eastern Michigan	21	14
N15		at Ohio U.	26	34

1987 5-5-1
S12		Lamar	35	39
S19	●	at Western Michigan	34	14
S26	=	at Northwestern	16	16
O3		at Eastern Michigan	31	32
O10	●	Toledo	41	5
O17	●	S.W. Missouri St.	27	21
O24		Fullerton St.	20	21
O31		at Ball State	17	42
N7	●	Western Illinois	29	14
N14		Akron	21	27
N28	●	at Nevada-Las Vegas	34	31

1988 7-4-0
S3	●	Akron	7	6
S10	●	Middle Tennessee	14	10
S17	●	at Wisconsin	19	17
S24		at Minnesota	20	31
O1	●	S.W. Missouri St.	17	3
O8		at Toledo	20	33
O15		at La. Lafayette	0	45
O22	●	at So. Illinois	10	9
O29		Ball State	17	18
N5	●	Western Illinois	16	6
N12	●	Western Michigan	15	7

1989 9-2-0
S2	●	Fullerton St.	26	17
S9		at Nebraska	17	48
S23	●	at Kansas State	37	20
S30	●	Western Illinois	34	27
O7	●	So. Illinois	29	24
O14		at Louisiana Tech	21	42
O21	●	Nevada-Las Vegas	42	24
O28	●	at Temple	20	17
N4	●	La. Lafayette	23	20
N11	●	Toledo	39	27
N18	●	at Cincinnati	56	3

1990 6-5-0
S1	●	Ea. Illinois	28	17
S8		at Nebraska	14	60
S15		at Toledo	14	23
S22	●	Kansas State	42	35
S29		at Northwestern	7	24
O6	●	Fresno State	73	18
O13	●	Arkansas State	35	0
O20	●	Murray St.	49	7
N3	●	at Akron	31	28
N10		at East Carolina	20	24
N17		at La. Lafayette	20	24

CHARLIE SADLER
1991-95 (.327) 18-37

1991 2-9-0
S7		at Fresno State	7	55
S14	●	Arkansas State	22	21
S21		at Kansas State	17	34
S28		at Iowa	7	58
O5		Louisiana Tech	3	37
O12		Western Michigan	10	22
O19		at Florida	10	41
O26		at Akron	7	17
N2	●	La. Lafayette	12	13
N16	●	Illinois St.	27	24
N23		at Toledo	21	42

1992   5-6-0

S5	at Illinois	14	30
S12 •	Illinois St.	26	19
S19 •	at Arkansas State	31	0
S26	at Wisconsin	17	18
O3	Middle Tennessee	13	21
O10 •	Southern Miss	23	10
O24 •	Liberty	27	21
O31	at Western Michigan	7	13
N7 •	at La. Lafayette	23	15
N14	at Army	14	21
N21	Toledo	8	25

1993-1995
BIG WEST

1993   4-7-0 (3-3-0)

S2	at Iowa State	10	54
S11	at Indiana	10	28
S18 •	Arkansas State	23	7
S25 •	at Nevada	46	42
O2 •	So. Illinois	45	15
O9	at New Mexico State	17	24
O16 •	Pacific	21	16
O23	La. Lafayette	19	33
O30	at Louisiana Tech	16	17
N6	at Iowa	20	54
N13	at Mississippi	0	44

1994   4-7-0 (3-3-0)

S1	Oklahoma State	14	31
S10	at La. Lafayette	9	29
S17	at Illinois	10	34
S24 •	Ea. Illinois	49	17
O1	Nevada	31	35
O8 •	New Mexico State	48	27
O15	at Pacific	32	41
O22 •	Louisiana Tech	27	17
O29	at Vanderbilt	16	17
N5 •	at Arkansas State	38	16
N12	at Arkansas	27	30

1995   3-8-0 (3-3-0)

A31	at Southern Miss	13	45
S9	Louisville	21	34
S16 •	at San Jose State	18	17
S23 •	La. Lafayette	25	24
S30	at Kansas State	0	44
O7 •	Nevada-Las Vegas	62	14
O14	at Utah State	7	42
O28	Cincinnati	19	55
N4	at Florida	20	58
N11	Arkansas State	21	28
N18	at Louisiana Tech	14	59

1996
INDEPENDENT

JOE NOVAK		
1996-PRESENT (.461)	47-55	

1996   1-10

A31	at Maryland	6	30
S7	Western Ill.	0	17
S14	at Penn State	0	49
S21 •	at Arkansas State	31	30
S28	Texas-El Paso	6	37
O5	North Texas	21	24
O19	at Louisville	3	27
O26	Akron	17	34
N2	Louisiana Tech	14	40
N9	at La. Lafayette	31	45
N16	at Oregon State	28	67

1997-PRESENT
MAC

1997   0-11 (0-8)

A28	at Central Michigan	10	44
S6	Kansas State	7	47
S13	Western Michigan	13	21
S20	at North Carolina St.	14	41
O4	at Bowling Green	10	35
O11	Vanderbilt	7	17
O18	at Toledo	14	41
O25	Ball State	14	21
N1	Ohio U.	30	35
N8	Eastern Michigan	10	38
N15	at Miami, Ohio	0	42

1998   2-9 (2-6)

S3	at Western Michigan	23	37
S12	at Kansas State	7	73
S19	Eastern Illinois	10	24
O3	at Ball State	13	18
O10	at Central Florida	17	38
O17 •	Central Michigan	16	6
O24 •	at Eastern Michigan	26	14
O31	Toledo	3	16
N7	Miami, Ohio	10	41
N14	at Ohio U.	12	28
N21	Bowling Green	23	34

1999   5-6 (5-3)

S2	Western Illinois	21	27
S11	at Vanderbilt	31	34
S18	at Iowa	0	24
S25	Western Michigan	21	24
O2 •	at Buffalo	45	21
O9 •	Ball State	37	17
O16 •	at Central Michigan	31	27
O23 •	Kent State	50	7
O30	at Marshall	9	41
N13	at Toledo	14	44
N20 •	Eastern Michigan	30	23

2000   6-5 (4-3)

A31	at Northwestern	17	35
S9 •	Illinois St.	52	0
S23	at Auburn	14	31
S30 •	at Ball State	43	14
O7 •	Central Florida	40	20
O14 •	at Akron	52	35
O21	at Western Michigan	22	52
O28 •	Buffalo	73	10
N4	Toledo	24	38
N11	at Eastern Michigan	32	39
N18 •	Central Michigan	40	6

2001   6-5 (4-3)

A30 •	South Florida	20	17
S8 •	at Illinois	12	17
S22 •	Sam Houston St.	41	16
S29 •	at Toledo	20	41
O6	Marshall	15	37
O13	at Kent State	34	44
O20 •	Western Michigan	20	12
O27 •	at Central Michigan	33	24
N3 •	Eastern Michigan	40	17
N17 •	Ball State	33	29
N24 •	at Wake Forest	35	38

2002   8-4 (7-1)

A29 •	Wake Forest	42	41
S7	at South Florida	6	37
S14	at Wisconsin	21	24
S21	Western Illinois	26	29
S28 •	Kent State	13	6
O5 •	at Ball State	41	29
O12 •	at Miami, Ohio	48	41
O19 •	Central Michigan	49	0
O26 •	at Western Michigan	24	20
N9 •	Bowling Green	26	17
N16 •	at Eastern Michigan	49	21
N23 •	Toledo	30	33

2003   10-2 (6-2)

A28 •	Maryland	20	13
S6 •	Tenn. Tech	42	17
S20 •	at Alabama	19	16
S27 •	Iowa State	24	16
O4 •	Ohio U.	30	23
O11 •	at Central Michigan	40	24
O18 •	Western Michigan	37	10
O25 •	at Bowling Green	18	34
N1 •	Ball State	48	23
N8 •	at Buffalo	40	9
N15 •	at Toledo	30	49
N22 •	Eastern Michigan	38	24

2004   9-3 (7-1)

S4	at Maryland	20	23
S11 •	So. Illinois	23	22
S18	at Iowa State	41	48
S24 •	Bowling Green	34	17
O2 •	Akron	49	19
O9 •	at Central Florida	30	28
O16 •	Central Michigan	42	10
O23 •	at Western Michigan	59	38
O30 •	at Ball State	38	31
N10 •	Toledo	17	31
N20 •	at Eastern Michigan	34	16
	SILICON VALLEY BOWL		
D30 •	Troy State	34	21

NORTHWESTERN

BY TODD JONES

NORTHWESTERN HAS ALWAYS BEEN miscast as the only private institution in the Big Ten. Such a disadvantage has tested any optimism on the campus along Lake Michigan, just north of Chicago. The Wildcats, however, have persevered even though their football history includes six seasons without a victory, and 13 others with only one win. They trudged on through 23 consecutive losing seasons from 1972 to 1994, reaching their nadir with a record 34-game losing streak. Then, like Northwestern alum Charlton Heston playing Moses, coach Gary Barnett led the Wildcats out of the wilderness in 1995. That stunning year of success—featuring NU's first conference title and Rose Bowl berth in more than four decades—hearkened back to such joyous times as 1930 and 1931, when the Wildcats won consecutive Big Ten titles; the 1948 season, when they went to the Rose Bowl; and 1962, when they were briefly ranked No. 1. It's not likely that Northwestern will ever consistently challenge perennial powers such as Michigan and Ohio State, but three Big Ten titles from 1995 to 2000 showed the Wildcats can do more than just hope to overcome.

TRADITION Northwestern's team crosses the Wisconsin border every August and gathers at the University of Wisconsin-Parkside, about 55 miles north of Evanston. There, the Wildcats hold two weeks of preseason workouts. Gary Barnett began the tradition of going to Camp Kenosha when he became Northwestern coach in 1992. Randy Walker, his successor, placed a 2x4 piece of wood in the team's locker room in Evanston. The word "trust" is painted on it, and each player slaps the board before taking the field or after leaving it. Touchdowns and significant plays are celebrated with the playing of a Wildcat "growl" on the Ryan Field PA system.

BEST PLAYER Northwestern coach Pappy Waldorf saw a freshman playing intramural football on campus in 1940. The kid from Waukegan, Ill., was Otto Graham, attending Northwestern on a basketball scholarship. Waldorf convinced him to play varsity football in 1941. Good idea. Graham went on to break every Big Ten passing record, was named league MVP as a senior and twice earned All-America honors. The QB known as Automatic Otto threw for 2,072 yards and 15 TDs and rushed for 823 yards and 17 scores in his career. His 1,326 total yards in 1942 was a Northwestern record for 20 years, and his 61 points the next season stood as the school record for 43 years. Graham's 27

PROFILE

Northwestern University
Evanston, Ill.
Founded: 1851
Enrollment: 7,840
Colors: Purple and White
Nickname: Wildcats
Stadium: Ryan Field
    Opened in 1926
    Grass; 47,130 capacity
First football game: 1876
All-time record: 440–592–44 (.429)
Bowl record: 1–4
Big Ten Conference championships: 8
(2 outright)
First-round NFL draftees: 8
Website: www.nusports.com

THE BEST OF TIMES

A miracle seemed to happen in 1995 when the longtime Big Ten doormats went to the Rose Bowl. The Wildcats finished that magical season 10–2 overall, 8–0 in the league. The next season they went 9–3, earning a share of a Big Ten title with a 7–1 league mark.

THE WORST OF TIMES

Where to start? Okay, try 23 consecutive losing seasons from 1972-94. Everything bottomed out from 1976-81, when the Wildcats went 3–62–1.

CONFERENCE

Northwestern was a charter member of the Western Conference in 1896, and has remained in the league since then. Popularly known as the Big Ten since 1917, the league didn't officially change its name to the Big Ten Conference until 1987.

DISTINGUISHED ALUMNI

Kenesaw Mountain Landis; Charlton Heston; Julia Louis-Dreyfus, actress; Richard Gephardt, U.S. congressman; Garry Marshall, TV and movie producer; John Paul Stevens, U.S. Supreme Court justice; Adlai Stevenson II, statesman; David Schwimmer, actor

FIGHT SONG

GO U NORTHWESTERN
Go U Northwestern,
Break right through that line,
With our colors flying, we will cheer you all the time,
U Rah, Rah,
Go U Northwestern, fight for victory
Spread far the fame of our fair name,
Go Northwestern, win that Game! (whistle)
Go Northwestern, go!
Go Northwestern, go!
Hit 'em hard,
Hit 'em low,
Go Northwestern, go!

> *In 1995, NU embarked on one of the great storybook seasons in college football history.*

points in a 41-0 win over Wisconsin in 1943 is still a Northwestern record. He scored three TDs and kicked three extra points in that game's first 12 minutes, and later he returned a punt 55 yards for a TD and threw a TD pass. Graham was also All-America in basketball and earned two letters in baseball. The music major served in World War II for two years as a commissioned officer in the U.S. Navy Air Corps. After returning from the war, he signed with the Cleveland Browns of the new All-American Football Conference. Graham was the player around whom coach Paul Brown built his new team, which won four straight AAFC titles, then went to six consecutive NFL title games, winning three.

BEST COACH Ara Parseghian is best known as a Notre Dame coach, but he earned his spurs with a stint at Northwestern. The Wildcats went 11–40–3 from 1952 to 1957, including 0–9 in Parseghian's second season as coach in '57. Five years later, he had Northwestern ranked No. 1 in the nation. Parseghian had excellent tutors, playing for Sid Gillman at Miami (Ohio) and for Paul Brown in the NFL, before returning to Miami for his first coaching job as a

member of Woody Hayes' staff. Parseghian's acquired knowledge led Northwestern to winning records in five of his final six seasons. The Wildcats had success throwing the ball, especially in 1962. The Wildcats started 6–0 and were ranked No. 1 for two weeks because of the passing combination of QB Tom Myers to flanker Paul Flatley. NU's 35-6 win over Notre Dame in 1962 was the fourth straight over the Fighting Irish under Parseghian. The Irish made Parseghian their coach before the 1964 season. After a three-year hiatus, the series resumed in 1965 and Parseghian then won nine consecutive games against Northwestern as Notre Dame coach. Parseghian went 95–17–4 in 11 seasons with the Fighting Irish. Northwestern went 17–41–1 in six seasons after he left for South Bend.

BEST TEAM The Wildcats were coming off a 3–7–1 year, their 23rd consecutive losing season, when they embarked on one of the great storybook seasons in college football history. In 1995, Gary Barnett's fourth NU squad produced the school's best regular-season record (10–1) and a Big Ten title as the Wildcats went to the Rose Bowl for the first time since 1948. Linebacker Pat Fitzgerald was the team's corner-

RECORDS

RUSHING YARDS
GAME
316 Mike Adamle vs. Wisconsin, Oct. 18, 1969 (40 att.)
SEASON
2,063 Damien Anderson, 2000 (311 att.)
CAREER
4,485 Damien Anderson, 1998-2001 (953 att.)

PASSING YARDS
GAME
446 Mike Greenfield vs. No. Illinois, Sept. 28, 1985 (26 of 43)
SEASON
2,735 Sandy Schwab, 1982 (234 of 416)
CAREER
7,487 Len Williams, 1990-93 (644 of 1,076)

RECEIVING YARDS
GAME
226 Todd Sheets vs. Purdue, Nov. 1, 1980 (11 rec.), Jim Lash vs. Michigan State, Nov. 25, 1972 (9 rec.)
SEASON
1,245 D'Wayne Bates, 1998 (83 rec.)
CAREER
3,370 D'Wayne Bates, 1995-98 (210 rec.)

POINTS
GAME
27 Otto Graham vs. Wisconsin, Nov. 6, 1943 (4 TDs, 3 PATs)
SEASON
138 Damien Anderson, 2000 (23 TDs)
CAREER
262 Brian Gowins, 1995-98 (58 FGs, 88 PATs)

CONSENSUS ALL-AMERICANS

1926	Ralph Baker	B
1930	Frank Baker	E
1931	Jack Riley	T
1931	Dallas Marvil	T
1931	Pug Rentner	B
1936	Steve Reid	G
1940	Alf Bauman	T
1945	Max Morris	E
1959	Ron Burton	B
1962	Jack Cvercko	G
1995-96	Pat Fitzgerald	LB
2000	Damien Anderson	RB

stone, earning the first of his two National Defensive Player of the Year awards. Quarterback Steve Schnur threw for 1,792 yards and Darnell Autry ran for 1,785. The team began to jell in the off-season. Defensive back Marcel Price was killed in a shooting over the summer, and teammates put his nickname, Big Six, in patches on their jerseys. They also ended every preseason practice by singing the Frank Sinatra song "High Hopes." The Wildcats opened the season by winning 17-15 at 27½-point favorite Notre Dame, then lost 30-28 to Miami (Ohio). Nine consecutive victories followed. Autry was pictured on the cover of *Sports Illustrated* after a 21-10 win over Penn State on Nov. 4, and when Ohio State was upset by Michigan two weeks later, NU was alone atop the Big Ten standings. "We're not any dumber now than when we stunk," said NU defensive tackle Matt Rice. A 41-32 loss to Southern California in the Rose Bowl couldn't dull the shine of 1995.

BIGGEST GAME With the 1995 season opener approaching, Notre Dame coach Lou Holtz was asked about his team's opponent, Northwestern. "I have a great deal of respect for Leon Burtnett," he said. Of course, he meant Gary Barnett, coach of the Wildcats. Northwestern hadn't had a winning season since 1971, and hadn't defeated Notre Dame in 33 years. Barnett, however, sensed an upset brewing. "I do not want you to carry me off the field after this game. I want you to act like you've been here before," he told his team before the game in South Bend. Northwestern took a 7-0 lead on a seven-yard TD pass from Steve Schnur to David Beazley, and led 10-9 at halftime. Schnur threw a TD pass to D'Wayne Bates early in the third quarter. Notre Dame scored with 6:16 left but failed on a two-point conversion. The Wildcats held on for a 17-15 victory. The *Chicago Tribune* ranked this game No. 13 on its list of the greatest moments in Chicago-area sports.

BIGGEST UPSET Bernie Bierman brought his Minnesota Golden Gophers and their 21-game winning streak to Evanston on Oct. 31, 1936. Minnesota was defending national champion, ranked No. 1 at 4–0, and hadn't lost in 28 games, since the final game of the 1932 season. Lynn "Pappy" Waldorf had his second Northwestern team ranked No. 3. Rain and wind made playing conditions treacherous, and the teams were scoreless after three quarters. In the fourth, Minnesota halfback Julius Alfonse mishandled a pitchout and fumbled. DeWitt Gibson recovered for Northwestern at the Gophers' 13-yard line. Wildcats reserve fullback Don Geyer fumbled on the ensuing play, but Minnesota All-America

tackle Ed Widseth was penalized for punching Geyer in the scramble for the loose ball. The penalty put the ball on the 1-yard line, and halfback Steve Toth scored from there on third down. Minnesota drove inside Northwestern's 20 on its next three possessions but couldn't score. The crowd of 48,347 rejoiced over a 6-0 victory that propelled the Wildcats to the Big Ten championship.

STADIUM William Dyche was Northwestern's vice president and business manager in the early 1920s when he saw a need for the Wildcats to play in a larger place than their 10,000-seat wooden facility. His desire became reality in 1926 when 45,000-seat Dyche Stadium opened at a cost of $1.4 million. The south end was enclosed after the 1948 Wildcats went to the Rose Bowl. Occasionally, capacity reached 55,000 when temporary bleachers were put in the north end. A $30 million fund-raising campaign produced major stadium renovations in 1996-97, adding a new sound system, locker rooms and press box, and dropping capacity to 47,130. Board of Trustees chairman Patrick Ryan donated $10 million, and Northwestern president Henry Bienen renamed the stadium Ryan Field in his honor.

WILDEST FINISH Northwestern's game against Michigan on Nov. 4, 2000, played out like an amusement park ride at Ryan Field. The two ranked teams combined for 105 points, 171 plays and 1,189 total yards of offense. Michigan led 51-46 with less than two minutes remaining in the fourth quarter when Wildcats running back Damien Anderson dropped a fourth-down pass while alone in the end zone. Northwestern found new life 46 seconds later when it recovered a fumble by Wolverines running back Anthony Thomas. Zak Kustok promptly completed three consecutive passes, the final one a 12-yard touchdown to Sam Simmons on a crossing pattern with 20 seconds left. Kustok made a two-point conversion pass to Teddy Johnson to give No. 21-ranked Northwestern a 54-51 lead. The No. 12 Wolverines answered with one final drive and set up for a 57-yard field goal attempt by Hayden Epstein, who earlier in the game had made a 52-yarder. This time he never kicked because the snap was mishandled. Fans stormed the field. NU went on to earn a share of the Big Ten title with an 8–4 season under second-year coach Randy Walker.

RIVAL The University of Chicago, when it was a member of the Big Ten, served as Northwestern's main foil. The teams played 37 times between 1892 and 1926. Today, the Wildcats call Illinois their top rival, in part because the schools battle

for in-state recruits. Northwestern and Illinois first met in 1892 and have played for the Sweet Sioux Tomahawk since 1945. Originally designed as a wooden Indian, the trophy proved too difficult to take on road trips. A tomahawk replaced the Indian as the game's memento. The series has traditionally been close. Even in its worst era, the Wildcats beat the Illini 9-6 in 1973, won 21-7 in 1977 and tied 0-0 in 1978.

NICKNAME Northwestern was known as the Purple until 1924, when the football team lost a hard-fought 3-0 game to the University of Chicago. The effort displayed by Northwestern prompted *Chicago Tribune* sportswriter Wallace Abbey to write that "football players had not come down from Evanston; Wildcats would be a name better suited." The school then adopted Wildcats as its nickname.

MASCOT In 1923, one year before adopting the Wildcats moniker, students at Northwestern brought a caged bear cub named Furpaw from the Lincoln Park Zoo to its home games. Northwestern went 2–6 that season. Furpaw was deemed to be bad luck and was never brought to another game. The current mascot, Willie the Wildcat, began as an advertising firm's caricature in 1933. Fourteen years later, four members of the Alpha Delta fraternity dressed up as Willie the Wildcat for their homecoming float.

UNIFORMS A Northwestern special committee selected purple as the school's official color in 1894. The traditional purple used was a deep indigo blue, but was changed to royal purple in the mid-1970s. Silver was added to the purple-and-white uniforms in 1980. Black replaced silver in 1988 and has remained part of the uniform look.

QUOTE "We're going to take the Purple to Pasadena." —Gary Barnett, when introduced to the student body as Northwestern's new coach on Jan. 11, 1992

NORTHWESTERN ANNUAL STATISTICAL LEADERS

YR	RUSHING	YDS	ATT	AVG	PASSING	ATT	CMP	PCT	YDS	RECEIVING	REC	YDS	AVG
1966	Bob McKelvey	459	128	3.6	Bill Melzer	176	94	.53	1,171	Roger Murphy	51	777	15.2
1967	Bob Olson	507	143	3.5	Bill Melzer	215	101	.47	1,146	Don Anderson	33	376	11.4
1968	Bob Olson	342	90	3.8	Dave Shelbourne	251	105	.42	1,358	Bruce Hubbard	33	551	16.7
1969	Mike Adamle	666	140	4.8	Maurie Daigneau	191	85	.45	1,276	Bruce Hubbard	25	384	15.4
1970	Mike Adamle	1,255	304	4.1	Maurie Daigneau	204	88	.43	1,228	Barry Pearson	33	552	16.7
1971	Al Robinson	881	277	3.2	Maurie Daigneau	264	125	.47	1,733	Barry Pearson	48	674	14.0
1972	Greg Boykin	625	159	3.9	Mitch Anderson	187	95	.51	1,333	Jim Lash	36	667	18.5
1973	Stan Key	894	197	4.5	Mitch Anderson	197	91	.46	1,224	Steve Craig	30	479	16.0
1974	Jim Pooler	949	216	4.4	Mitch Anderson	225	101	.45	1,282	Scott Yelvington	37	417	11.3
1975	Greg Boykin	1,105	239	4.6	Randy Dean	200	101	.51	1,315	Scott Yelvington	50	686	13.7
1976	Pat Geegan	537	154	3.5	Randy Dean	177	87	.49	1,384	Scott Yelvington	34	649	19.1
1977	Dave Mishler	520	115	4.5	Scott Stranski	95	37	.39	541	Mark Bailey	22	347	15.8
1978	Mike Cammon	322	73	4.4	Kevin Strasser	307	151	.49	1,526	Tim Hill	24	122	5.1
1979	Jeff Cohn	426	117	3.6	Mike Kerrigan	195	82	.42	961	Todd Sheets	43	614	14.3
1980	Jeff Cohn	503	137	3.7	Mike Kerrigan	337	173	.51	1,816	Todd Sheets	33	570	17.3
1981	Jim Browne	162	52	3.1	Mike Kerrigan	265	124	.47	1,317	Jim Browne	24	140	5.8
1982	Ricky Edwards	688	157	4.4	Sandy Schwab	416	234	.56	2,735	Jon Harvey	52	807	15.5
1983	Ricky Edwards	561	183	3.1	Sandy Schwab	334	188	.56	1,838	Ricky Edwards	83	570	6.9
1984	Casey Cummings	386	79	4.9	Sandy Schwab	198	93	.47	845	Casey Cummings	28	131	4.7
1985	Stanley Davenport	598	149	4.0	Mike Greenfield	335	199	.59	2,152	Brian Nuffer	40	328	8.2
1986	Stanley Davenport	703	181	3.9	Mike Greenfield	250	126	.50	1,653	Curtis Duncan	29	437	15.1
1987	Byron Sanders	778	187	4.2	Mike Greenfield	199	92	.46	1,265	George Jones	40	668	16.7
1988	Byron Sanders	1,062	264	4.0	Greg Bradshaw	257	129	.50	1,550	Richard Buchanan	41	514	12.5
1989	Bob Christian	1,291	277	4.7	Tim O'Brien	334	207	.62	2,218	Richard Buchanan	94	1,115	11.9
1990	Bob Christian	939	237	4.0	Len Williams	262	150	.57	1,700	Richard Buchanan	60	834	13.9
1991	Eric Dixon	227	64	3.5	Len Williams	212	131	.62	1,630	Mark Benson	45	831	18.5
1992	Len Williams	148	119	0.8	Len Williams	286	181	.63	2,110	Lee Gissendaner	68	846	12.4
1993	Robbie Glanton	159	36	4.4	Len Williams	316	182	.58	2,047	Lee Gissendaner	58	669	11.5
1994	Darnell Autry	556	120	4.6	Steve Schnur	117	61	.52	899	Michael Senters	28	385	13.8
1995	Darnell Autry	1,785	387	4.6	Steve Schnur	257	141	.55	1,792	D'Wayne Bates	49	889	18.1
1996	Darnell Autry	1,452	280	5.2	Steve Schnur	368	221	.60	2,632	D'Wayne Bates	75	1,196	15.9
1997	Adrian Autry	1,049	244	4.3	Tim Hughes	270	142	.53	1,862	Brian Musso	58	865	14.9
1998	Damien Anderson	537	164	3.3	Gavin Hoffman	323	176	.54	2,199	D'Wayne Bates	83	1,245	15.0
1999	Damien Anderson	1,128	306	3.7	Nick Kreinkbrink	158	60	.38	774	Teddy Johnson	23	354	15.4
2000	Damien Anderson	2,063	311	6.6	Zak Kustok	363	206	.57	2,389	Teddy Johnson	33	595	18.0
2001	Damien Anderson	757	172	4.4	Zak Kustok	404	231	.57	2,692	Sam Simmons	50	807	16.1
2002	Jason Wright	1,234	219	5.6	Brett Basanez	325	190	.58	2,204	Jon Schweighardt	58	719	12.4
2003	Jason Wright	1,388	267	5.2	Brett Basanez	302	162	.54	1,916	Roger Jordan	31	442	14.3
2004	Noah Herron	1,381	247	5.6	Brett Basanez	460	247	.54	2,838	Mark Philmore	54	633	11.7

All statistics include postseason

NORTHWESTERN ALL-TIME SCORES

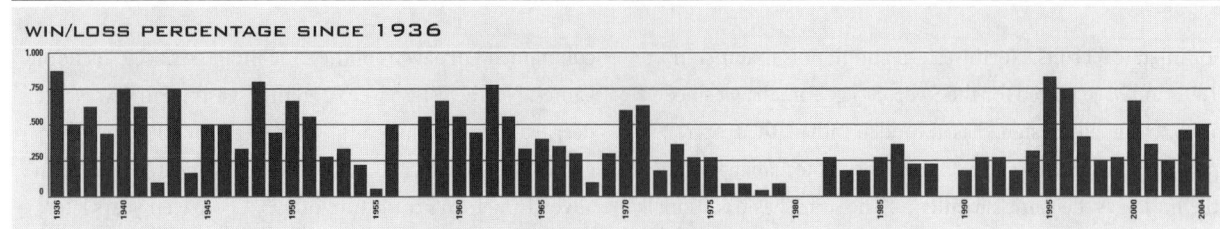

WIN/LOSS PERCENTAGE SINCE 1936

NO HEAD COACH

1876
			0-1-0
F22	at Chicago Club	0	3

1877-1881
NO TEAM

1882
			1-1-0
N11	at Lake Forest	0	1
N18 •	Lake Forest	1	0

1883-1885
NO TEAM

1886
			0-1-0
O30	Harvard Prep	4	32

1887
NO TEAM

1888
			2-1-0
N20 •	W. Division HS	16	6
N29	at Lake Forest	4	18
D1 •	Lake Forest	12	6

1889
			2-2-0
N9	Evanston H.S	18	4
N14	Notre Dame	9	0
N23	Alumni	0	25
D7	at Chicago Wanderers	22	0

1890
			4-1-1
O10 •	Evanston HS	16	4
O22 •	Evanston HS	18	0
O30 •	S. Division HS	0	0
N1	Alumni	0	24
N15 •	Beloit	22	6
N26 •	at Wisconsin	22	10

KNOWLTON AMES
1891-92 (.559)   7-5-5

1891
			2-2-3
S30 •	Evanston HS	8	0
O17 •	Lake Forest	0	0
O31 •	at Wisconsin	0	0
N5 •	Chicago YMCA	22	0
N14 =	at Beloit	12	12
N21	Lake Forest *UNK*	0	20
N29 •	at Wisconsin	0	40

1892
			5-3-2
O1 •	Chicago YMCA	16	0
O12 =	at Illinois	16	16
O15 •	Beloit	36	0
O22 =	at Chicago	0	0
O29 •	Michigan *CHI*	10	8
N2 •	Chicago	6	4
N8	at Minnesota	12	18
N12 •	at Lake Forest	18	0
N19	Wisconsin	6	26
N24	Wisconsin *MIL*	6	20

PAUL NOYES
1893 (.350)   2-5-3

1893
			2-5-3
O4	Denver AC *CHI*	0	8
O18	at Chicago	6	12
O21 =	Illinois	0	0
O27 =	Lake Forest	12	12
O30	Minnesota	0	16
N4 =	Beloit	10	6
N8 =	Chicago	6	6
N11 •	Lake Forest	38	22
N18	at Michigan	6	72
D16	at Chicago	14	22

AA EWING
1894 (.444)   4-5

1894
			4-5-0
O6	at Chicago	0	46
O11 •	Evanston HS	14	0
O13	at Lake Forest	6	24
O17 •	Evanston HS	12	0
O20	Beloit	6	42
O24 •	Evanston HS	22	6
O26 •	Lake Forest	12	8
N3	at Illinois	0	66
N24	Chicago	0	36

ALVIN H. CULVER
1895-96 (.650)   12-6-2

1895
			6-5-0
S21 •	Wisconsin *MIL*	6	12
S28 •	Iowa State	0	36
O3 •	Evanston HS	16	0
O5 •	Beloit	34	6
O12 •	Armour	44	0
O19 •	at Chicago	22	6
O31 •	Lake Forest	24	0
N2 •	at Purdue	24	6
N9 •	Missouri *STL*	18	22
N16 •	Chicago	0	6
N23 •	at Illinois	4	38

1896-Present
Big 10

1896
			6-1-2 (2-1-1)
O1 •	Englewood HS	25	0
O3 •	Chicago AC	4	0
O7 •	Armour	42	0
O10 •	Beloit	6	6
O17 •	Phys. & Surg.	16	6
O24 •	Chicago *CHI*	46	6
N7 •	at Illinois	10	4
N14	Chicago	6	18
N26 =	Wisconsin	6	6

JESSE VAN DOOZER
1897 (.625)   5-3

1897
			5-3-0 (0-2-0)
S29 •	Evanston HS	6	0
O9 •	Beloit *ROC*	6	0
O16 •	Iowa	6	12
O23	at Chicago	6	21
O30 •	Phys & Surg	16	0
N6 •	Rush	16	0
N13 •	Alumni	25	0
N25	Wisconsin	0	22

W.H. BANNARD
1898 (.679)   9-4-1

1898
			9-4-1 (0-4-0)
S21 •	N.W. Division HS	34	0
S24 •	Englewood HS	22	0
S28 •	Hyde Park HS	18	0
O1 •	Dixon	57	0
O8 •	Beloit	17	11
O12 •	Hahnemann Medical	22	6
O15 •	Phys & Surg	11	2
O18 •	Chicago AC	5	0
O22	at Chicago	5	34
O29 •	Lake Forest	27	0
N5	Michigan *CHI*	5	6
N12	at Minnesota	6	17
N19 =	Armour	0	0
N24	Wisconsin	0	47

C.M. HOLLISTER
1899-1902 (.625)   28-16-4

1899
			7-6-0 (2-2-0)
S21 •	N.U. Dental	24	0
S23 •	Englewood HS	29	0
S30 •	Alumni	0	18
O4 •	Lake Forest AC.	24	5
O7 •	Rush Medical	0	6
O14 •	at Wisconsin	0	38
O21 •	at Beloit	0	11
O25 •	Lake Forest	16	0
O28 •	at Notre Dame	0	12
N4 •	at Minnesota	11	5
N11	at Chicago	0	76
N18 •	Indiana	11	6
N25	Purdue	29	0

1900
			7-2-3 (2-1-2)
S22 •	North Central	26	0
S26 •	North Division HS	18	6
S29 •	Phys. & Surg.	0	6
O6 •	Rush Medical	6	0
O13 •	Indiana	12	0
O17 •	Lake Forest Academy	23	0
O20 =	Illinois	0	0
O27 =	Beloit	6	6
N3 •	Knox	11	5
N10 •	at Chicago	5	0
N17 •	at Minnesota	0	21
N29 •	Iowa	5	5

1901
			8-2-1 (3-2-0)
S18 •	Fort Sheridan	27	0
S21 •	North Central	30	0
S28 •	Lombard	47	0
O5 •	Lake Forest	11	0
O12 •	Notre Dame	2	0
O19 •	at Michigan	0	29
O26 •	at Illinois	17	11
N9 •	at Chicago	6	5
N16 •	Beloit	11	11
N23 •	Minnesota *CHI*	0	16
N28 •	at Purdue	10	5

1902
			6-6-0 (0-4-0)
S20 •	Fort Sheridan	15	0
S27 •	North Central	10	5
O1 •	Chicago Dental	11	0
O4 •	Lake Forest	26	0
O11 •	Rush Medical	11	0
O18 •	Chicago *CHI*	0	12
O25 •	Knox	0	15
N1 •	Purdue	0	5
N8 •	Wisconsin	0	51
N15 •	Beloit	10	0
N22 •	Illinois	0	17
N27 •	at Nebraska	0	12

WALTER McCORNACK
1903-05 (.800)   26-5-4

1903
			10-1-3 (1-0-2)
S19 •	N.Division HS	22	5
S22 •	Fort Sheridan	28	0
S23 •	Englewood HS	35	0
S26 •	North Central	22	6
S30 •	Alumni	5	0
O3 •	Lombard	23	0
O7 •	Chicago Dental	18	11
O10 •	at Washington, Mo.	23	0
O17 =	at Chicago	0	0
O24 •	at Cincinnati	35	0
O31 •	at Illinois	12	11
N14 •	Notre Dame *CHI*	0	0
N21 =	Wisconsin *CHI*	6	6
N26 •	Carlisle *CHI*	0	28

1904
			8-2-0 (1-2-0)
S24 •	Fort Sheridan	17	0
O1 •	North Central	34	0
O5 •	N. Division HS	18	0
O8 •	Lombard	55	0
O15 •	Beloit	34	0
O22 •	at Chicago	0	32
O29 •	DePauw	45	0
N5 •	Oshkosh Normal	97	0
N12 •	Illinois	12	6
N19	Minnesota *CHI*	0	17

1905
			8-2-1 (0-2-0)
S20 •	Evanston HS	32	0
S23 •	at N. Division HS	11	0
S30 •	St. Viator	41	0
O7 •	Wabash	5	0
O14 •	at Beloit	18	2
O21 =	Transylvania, Ky	0	0
O28	Chicago	0	32
N4 •	Marquette	30	5
N11 •	Ohio Northern	34	0
N18 •	Michigan State	37	11
N25	at Minnesota	6	72

1906-1907
NO TEAM

ALTON JOHNSON
1908 (.500)   2-2

1908
			2-2-0 (0-2-0)
O10 •	Alumni	10	6
O24 •	Beloit	44	4
N7 •	Purdue	10	16
N21	at Illinois	8	64

BILL HORR
1909 (.300)   1-3-1

1909
			1-3-1 (1-3-0)
O2 =	Illinois Wesleyan	0	0
O9 •	at Purdue	14	5
O30	Wisconsin	11	21
N6	at Chicago	0	34
N13	Illinois	0	35

C.E. HAMMETT
1910-12 (.389)   6-10-2

1910
			1-3-1 (1-2-1)
O1	Illinois Wesleyan	0	3
O8 •	Iowa	10	5
O22	at Chicago	0	10
O29 =	at Wisconsin	0	0
N12	Illinois	0	27

1911
			3-4-0 (1-4-0)
O7 •	Monmouth	26	0
O14 •	Illinois Wesleyan	10	0
O21 •	Indiana	5	0
O28 •	Wisconsin	3	28
N11 •	Chicago	3	9
N18 •	at Illinois	13	27
N25 •	at Iowa	0	6

1912
			2-3-1 (2-3-0)
O5 =	Lake Forest	0	0
O12 •	at Wisconsin	0	56
O26 •	at Indiana	20	7
N2 •	Purdue	6	21
N9 •	at Chicago	0	3
N23 •	Illinois	6	0

DENNIS GRADY
1913 (.143) · 1-6

1913 — 1-6-0 (0-6-0)
O4	•	Lake Forest	10	0
O11		at Purdue	0	34
O18		at Illinois	0	37
O25		Iowa	6	78
N8		Chicago	0	14
N15		Indiana	20	21
N22		at Ohio State	0	58

FRED MURPHY
1914-18 (.500) · 16-16-1

1914 — 1-6-0 (0-6-0)
O3	•	Lake Forest	7	0
O10		at Chicago	0	28
O17		at Indiana	0	27
O24		Illinois	0	33
N7		Iowa	0	27
N14		Purdue	6	34
N21		at Ohio State	0	27

1915 — 2-5-0 (0-5-0)
O2	•	Lake Forest	27	6
O9		Chicago	0	7
O16		at Iowa	6	9
O23		at Illinois	6	36
N6	•	Missouri	24	6
N13		Indiana	6	14
N20		Ohio State	0	34

1916 — 6-1-0 (4-1-0)
O7	•	Lake Forest	26	7
O21	•	at Chicago	10	0
O28	•	Drake	40	6
N4	•	at Indiana	7	0
N10	•	Iowa	20	13
N18	•	Purdue	38	6
N25	•	at Ohio State	3	23

1917 — 5-2-0 (3-2-0)
O6	•	Lake Forest	48	0
O13		at Ohio State	0	40
O27		at Chicago	0	7
N3	•	at Purdue	12	6
N10	•	Michigan State	39	6
N17	•	Iowa	25	14
N24	•	Michigan	21	12

1918 — 2-2-1 (1-1-0)
O26	=	at Great Lakes NAS	0	0
N2		Chicago Navy	0	25
N9	•	Knox	47	7
N16	•	Chicago	21	6
N23		at Iowa	7	23

CHARLES BACHMAN
1919 (.286) · 2-5

1919 — 2-5-0 (1-4-0)
O11	•	DePauw	20	0
O18		Wisconsin	6	10
O25		at Chicago	0	41
N1		at Michigan	13	16
N8		Iowa	7	14
N15	•	Indiana	3	2
N27		Rutgers Nwk	0	28

ELMER MCDEVITT
1920-21 (.286) · 4-10

1920 — 3-4-0 (2-3-0)
O2	•	Knox	14	0
O9		Minnesota	17	0
O16		at Wisconsin	7	27
O30		Indiana IND	7	10
N6		at Iowa	0	20
N13	•	Purdue	14	0
N20		Notre Dame	7	33

1921 — 1-6-0 (0-5-0)
S24		Beloit	0	7
O1		at Chicago	0	41
O8		at Minnesota	0	28
O15		Wisconsin	0	27
O29	•	DePaul	34	0
N5		at Purdue	0	3
N19		Iowa	0	14

G. THISTLETHWAITE
1922-26 (.551) · 21-17-1

1922 — 3-3-1 (1-3-1)
O7	•	Beloit	17	0
O14		at Chicago	7	15
O21	=	Minnesota	7	7
N4		at Illinois	3	6
N11	•	Purdue	24	13
N18	•	Monmouth	58	14
N25		at Iowa	3	37

1923 — 2-6-0 (0-6-0)
O6	•	Beloit	21	6
O13		Indiana IND	6	7
O20		at Chicago	0	13
O27		Illinois CHI	0	29
N3		at Minnesota	14	34
N10	•	Lake Forest	32	0
N17		at Purdue	3	6
N24		Iowa	14	17

1924 — 4-4-0 (1-3-0)
O4	•	South Dakota	28	0
O11	•	Cincinnati	42	0
O18		Purdue	3	7
O25	•	Michigan State	13	9
N1	•	Indiana	17	7
N8		at Michigan	0	27
N15		at Chicago	0	3
N22		Notre Dame CHI	6	13

1925 — 5-3-0 (3-1-0)
O3	•	South Dakota	14	7
O10	•	Carleton	17	0
O17		at Chicago	0	6
O24		Tulane CHI	7	18
O31	•	Indiana	17	14
N7	•	Michigan CHI	3	2
N14	•	at Purdue	13	9
N21		at Notre Dame	10	13

1926 — 7-1-0 (5-0-0)
O2	•	South Dakota	34	0
O9	•	Carleton	31	3
O16	•	Indiana	20	0
O23		Notre Dame	0	6
O30	•	at Indiana	21	0
N6	•	Purdue	22	0
N13	•	Chicago	38	7
N20	•	at Iowa	13	6

DICK HANLEY
1927-34 (.576) · 36-26-4

1927 — 4-4-0 (2-3-0)
O1	•	South Dakota	47	2
O8	•	Utah	13	6
O15	•	at Ohio State	19	13
O22		Illinois	6	7
O29		Missouri	19	34
N5		at Purdue	6	18
N12		Indiana	7	18
N19	•	Iowa	12	0

1928 — 5-3-0 (2-3-0)
O6	•	Butler	14	0
O13		Ohio State	0	10
O20	•	Kentucky	7	0
O27		at Illinois	0	6
N3	•	Minnesota	10	9
N10	•	Purdue	7	6
N17		at Indiana	0	6
N24	•	Dartmouth	27	6

1929 — 6-3-0 (3-2-0)
O5	•	Cornell Coll.	27	18
O5	•	Butler	13	0
O12	•	at Wisconsin	7	0
O19		Minnesota	14	26
O26	•	Wabash	66	0
N2	•	Illinois	7	0
N9	•	at Ohio State	18	6
N16	•	Indiana	14	19
N23		Notre Dame	6	26

1930 — 7-1-0 (5-0-0)
O4	•	Tulane	14	0
O11	•	Ohio State	19	2
O18	•	at Illinois	32	0
O25	•	Centre	45	7
N1	•	at Minnesota	27	6
N8	•	at Indiana	25	0
N15	•	Wisconsin	20	7
N22		Notre Dame	0	14

1931 — 7-1-1 (5-1-0)
O3	•	Nebraska	19	7
O10	=	Notre Dame CHI	0	0
O17	•	UCLA	19	0
O24	•	at Ohio State	10	0
O31	•	Illinois	32	6
N7	•	Minnesota	32	14
N14	•	Indiana	7	6
N21	•	at Iowa	19	0
N28		Purdue CHI	0	7

1932 — 3-4-1 (2-3-1)
O1	•	Missouri	27	0
O8		at Michigan	6	15
O15	•	at Illinois	26	0
O22	=	Purdue	7	7
O29		at Minnesota	0	7
N5	•	Ohio State	6	20
N12		Notre Dame CHI	0	21
N19	•	Iowa	44	6

1933 — 1-5-2 (1-4-1)
O7		Iowa CHI	0	7
O14	=	Stanford	0	0
O21	•	Indiana CHI	25	0
O28		at Ohio State	0	12
N4	=	Minnesota	0	0
N11	•	Illinois	0	3
N18		Notre Dame	0	7
N25		Michigan	0	13

1934 — 3-5-0 (2-3-0)
S29	•	Marquette	21	12
O6		Iowa	7	20
O13		at Stanford	0	20
O27		Ohio State	6	28
N3	•	Wisconsin	7	0
N10	•	Illinois	3	14
N17		Notre Dame	7	20
N24		at Michigan	13	6

LYNN WALDORF
1935-46 (.520) · 49-45-7

1935 — 4-3-1 (2-3-1)
S28	•	DePaul	14	0
O5		Purdue	0	7
O19		at Ohio State	7	28
O26		at Minnesota	13	21
N2	•	Illinois	10	3
N9		at Notre Dame	14	7
N16	•	Wisconsin	32	13
N23	=	Iowa	0	0

1936 — 7-1-0 (6-0-0)
O3		Iowa	18	7
O10	•	North Dakota St.	40	7
O17	•	Ohio State	14	13
O24		at Illinois	13	2
O31	•	Minnesota	6	0
N7	•	Wisconsin	26	18
N14		at Michigan	9	0
N21		at Notre Dame	6	26

1937 — 4-4-0 (3-3-0)
O2	•	Iowa State	33	0
O9	•	Michigan	7	0
O16	•	Purdue	14	7
O23		at Ohio State	0	7
O30	•	at Wisconsin	14	6
N6		Illinois	0	6
N13		at Minnesota	0	7
N20		Notre Dame	0	7

1938 — 4-2-2 (2-1-2)
O1	•	Kansas State	21	0
O8		Drake	33	0
O15	=	Ohio State	0	0
O22	•	at Illinois	13	0
O29		Minnesota	6	3
N5		Wisconsin	13	20
N12	=	at Michigan	0	0
N19		Notre Dame	7	9

1939 — 3-4-1 (3-2-1)
O7		Oklahoma	0	23
O14		at Ohio State	0	13
O21	•	Wisconsin	13	7
O28	•	Illinois	13	0
N4	=	at Minnesota	14	7
N11		Purdue	0	3
N18		at Notre Dame	0	7
N25	=	Iowa	7	7

1940 — 6-2-0 (4-2-0)
O5	•	at Syracuse	40	0
O12	•	Ohio State	6	3
O19	•	at Wisconsin	27	7
O26	•	Indiana	20	7
N2		Minnesota	12	13
N9	•	Illinois	32	14
N16		at Michigan	13	20
N23	•	Notre Dame	20	0

1941 — 5-3-0 (4-2-0)
O4	•	Kansas State	51	3
O11	•	Wisconsin	41	14
O18		Michigan	7	14
O25	•	at Ohio State	14	7
N1		at Minnesota	7	8
N8	•	Indiana	20	14
N15		Notre Dame	6	7
N22	•	Illinois	27	0

1942 — 1-9-0 (0-6-0)
S26		Iowa Pre-Flight	12	20
O3	•	Texas	3	0
O10		Purdue	6	7
O17		at Michigan	16	34
O24		Ohio State	6	20
O31		at Minnesota	7	19
N7		Illinois	7	14
N14		Wisconsin	19	20
N21		at Notre Dame	20	27
N26		Great Lakes NAS	0	48

1943 — 6-2-0 (5-1-0)
S25	•	Indiana	14	6
O2		Michigan	7	21
O16	•	Great Lakes NAS	13	0
O23	•	at Ohio State	13	0
O30	•	Minnesota	42	6
N6	•	at Wisconsin	41	0
N13	•	Notre Dame	6	25
N20	•	Illinois	53	6

1944 — 1-7-1 (0-5-1)
S23	•	DePauw	62	0
S30		Wisconsin	6	7
O7		Great Lakes NAS	0	25
O14		at Michigan	0	27
O21		Indiana	7	14
N4	=	at Minnesota	14	14
N11		Purdue	7	27
N18		at Notre Dame	0	21
N25		Illinois	6	25

1945 — 4-4-1 (3-3-1)
S22	•	Iowa State	18	6
S29	=	Indiana	7	7
O6		Michigan	7	20
O20		at Minnesota	7	30
O27	•	Purdue	26	14
N3		at Ohio State	14	16
N10	•	at Wisconsin	28	14
N17		Notre Dame	7	34
N24	•	Illinois	13	7

1946 — 4-4-1 (2-3-1)
S28	•	Iowa State	41	9
O5	•	Wisconsin	28	0
O12	•	Minnesota	14	7
O19	=	at Michigan	14	14
O26	•	Pacific	26	13
N2		Ohio State	27	39
N9		Indiana	6	7
N16		at Notre Dame	0	27
N23		Illinois	0	20

BOB VOIGTS
1947-54 (.459) · 33-39-1

1947 — 3-6-0 (2-4-0)
S27		Vanderbilt	0	3
O4	•	UCLA	27	26
O11		at Minnesota	21	37
O18		Michigan	21	49
O25	•	Indiana	7	6
N1		Wisconsin	0	29
N8		at Ohio State	6	7
N15		Notre Dame	19	26
N22	•	at Illinois	28	13

1948 — 8-2-0 (5-1-0)
S25	•	at UCLA	19	0
O2	•	Purdue	21	0
O9	•	Minnesota	19	16
O16		at Michigan	0	28
O23	•	Syracuse	48	0
O30	•	Ohio State	21	7
N6	•	at Wisconsin	16	7
N13		at Notre Dame	7	12
N20	•	Illinois	20	7
ROSE BOWL				
J1	•	California	20	14

1949 4-5-0 (3-4-0)

S24	●	Purdue	20	6
O1		Pittsburgh	7	16
O8		at Minnesota	7	21
O15	●	Michigan	21	20
O22		at Iowa	21	28
O29		at Ohio State	7	24
N5		Wisconsin	6	14
N12	●	Colgate	39	20
N19	●	at Illinois	9	7

1950 6-3-0 (3-3-0)

S30	●	Iowa State	23	13
O7	●	Navy BALT	22	0
O14	●	Minnesota	13	6
O21	●	Pittsburgh	28	23
O28		at Wisconsin	13	14
N4		Ohio State	0	32
N11	●	at Purdue	19	14
N18		at Michigan	23	34
N25	●	Illinois	14	7

1951 5-4-0 (2-4-0)

S29	●	Colorado	35	14
O6	●	Army	20	14
O13	●	at Minnesota	21	7
O20	●	Navy	16	7
O27		Wisconsin	0	41
N3		at Ohio State	0	3
N10		Purdue	14	35
N17	●	at Michigan	6	0
N24		Illinois	0	3

1952 2-6-1 (2-5-0)

S26		at Southern Cal	0	31
O4	=	Vanderbilt	20	20
O11		at Minnesota	26	27
O18		Michigan	14	48
O25	●	Indiana	23	13
N1		Ohio State	21	24
N8		at Wisconsin	20	24
N15		Iowa	14	39
N22	●	at Illinois	28	26

1953 3-6-0 (0-6-0)

S26	●	Iowa State	35	0
O3	●	Army	33	20
O10		Minnesota	13	30
O17		at Michigan	12	20
O24	●	Pittsburgh	27	21
O31		at Ohio State	13	27
N7		Wisconsin	13	34
N14		at Indiana	6	14
N21		Illinois	14	39

1954 2-7-0 (1-5-0)

S25	●	Iowa State	27	14
O2		Southern Cal	7	12
O9		at Minnesota	7	26
O16		Michigan	0	7
O23		at Pittsburgh	7	14
O30		Ohio State	7	14
N6		at Wisconsin	13	34
N13		Indiana	13	14
N20	●	at Illinois	20	7

LOU SABAN
1955 (.056) 0-8-1

1955 0-8-1 (0-6-1)

S24		Miami, Ohio	14	25
O1		at Tulane	0	21
O8		Minnesota	7	18
O15		at Michigan	2	14
O22		Indiana	14	20
O29		at Ohio State	0	49
N5		Wisconsin	14	41
N12		at Purdue	8	46
N19	=	Illinois	7	7

ARA PARSEGHIAN
1956-63 (.507) 36-35-1

1956 4-4-1 (3-3-1)

S29	●	Iowa State	14	13
O6		Tulane	13	20
O13	=	at Minnesota	0	0
O20		at Michigan	20	34
O27		at Indiana	13	19
N3		Ohio State	2	6
N10	●	at Wisconsin	17	7
N17	●	Purdue	14	0
N24	●	Illinois	14	13

1957 0-9-0 (0-7-0)

S28		at Stanford	6	26
O5		Oregon State	13	22
O12		Minnesota	6	41
O19		at Michigan	14	34
O26		Iowa	0	6
N2		at Ohio State	6	47
N9		Wisconsin	12	41
N16		at Purdue	0	27
N23		at Illinois	0	27

1958 5-4-0 (3-4-0)

S27	●	Washington State	29	28
O4	●	Stanford	28	0
O11	●	at Minnesota	7	3
O18	●	Michigan	55	24
O25		at Iowa	20	26
N1	●	Ohio State	21	0
N8		at Wisconsin	13	17
N15		Purdue	6	23
N22		at Illinois	20	27

1959 6-3-0 (4-3-0)

S26	●	Oklahoma	45	13
O3	●	at Iowa	14	10
O10	●	Minnesota	6	0
O17	●	at Michigan	20	7
O24	●	at Notre Dame	30	24
O31	●	Indiana	30	13
N7		Wisconsin	19	24
N14		at Michigan State	10	15
N21		at Illinois	0	28

1960 5-4-0 (3-4-0)

S24	●	at Oklahoma	19	3
O1		Iowa	0	42
O8		at Minnesota	0	7
O15		at Michigan	7	14
O22	●	Notre Dame	7	6
O29	●	at Indiana	21	3
N5	●	at Wisconsin	21	0
N12		Michigan State	18	21
N19	●	Illinois	14	7

1961 4-5-0 (2-4-0)

S30	●	Boston College	45	0
O7	●	at Illinois	28	7
O14		Minnesota	3	10
O21		Ohio State	0	10
O28	●	at Notre Dame	12	10
N4	●	Indiana	14	8
N11		Wisconsin	10	29
N18		at Michigan State	13	21
N24		at Miami, Fla.	6	10

1962 7-2-0 (4-2-0)

S22	●	South Carolina	37	20
O6	●	Illinois	45	0
O13	●	at Minnesota	34	22
O20	●	at Ohio State	18	14
O27	●	Notre Dame	35	6
N3	●	at Indiana	26	21
N10		at Wisconsin	6	37
N17		Michigan State	7	31
N23	●	at Miami, Fla.	29	7

1963 5-4-0 (3-4-0)

S21	●	at Missouri	23	12
S28	●	Indiana	34	21
O5		at Illinois	9	10
O12	●	Minnesota	15	8
O19	●	Miami, Ohio	37	6
O26		Michigan State	7	15
N2		at Michigan	6	27
N9		at Wisconsin	14	17
N16	●	at Ohio State	17	8

ALEX AGASE
1964-72 (.357) 32-58-1

1964 3-6-0 (2-5-0)

S19	●	Oregon State	7	3
S26	●	at Indiana	14	13
O3		Illinois	6	17
O10		at Minnesota	18	21
O17		Miami, Ohio	27	28
O24		at Michigan State	6	24
O31		at Michigan	0	35
N7	●	Wisconsin	17	13
N14		at Ohio State	0	10

1965 4-6-0 (3-4-0)

S18		Florida	14	24
S25	●	at Indiana	20	0
O2		at Notre Dame	7	38
O9	●	Oregon State	15	7
O16		Wisconsin	7	21
O23	●	Iowa	9	0
O30		at Michigan State	7	49
N6		at Minnesota	22	27
N13	●	Michigan	34	22
N20		Illinois	6	20

1966 3-6-1 (2-4-1)

S17		at Florida	7	43
S24		Indiana	14	26
O1		Notre Dame	7	35
O8	●	at Oregon State	14	6
O15	=	at Wisconsin	3	3
O22	●	at Iowa	24	15
O29		Michigan State	0	22
N5		Minnesota	13	28
N12		at Michigan	20	28
N19	●	Illinois	35	7

1967 3-7-0 (2-5-0)

S23	●	Miami, Fla.	12	7
S30		Missouri	6	13
O7		at Purdue	16	25
O14		at Rice	6	50
O21		Ohio State	2	6
O28	●	at Wisconsin	17	13
N4		at Michigan	3	7
N11	●	Iowa	39	24
N18		Illinois	21	27
N25		at Michigan State	27	41

1968 1-9-0 (1-6-0)

S20		at Miami, Fla.	7	28
S28		Southern Cal	7	24
O5		Purdue	6	43
O12		at Notre Dame	7	27
O19		at Ohio State	21	45
O26	●	Wisconsin	13	10
N2		Michigan	0	35
N9		at Iowa	34	68
N16		at Illinois	0	14
N23		Michigan State	14	31

1969 3-7-0 (3-4-0)

S20		at Notre Dame	10	35
S27		at Southern Cal	6	48
O4		UCLA	0	36
O11	●	at Illinois	10	6
O18	●	Wisconsin	27	7
O25		at Purdue	20	45
N1		Ohio State	6	35
N8		at Minnesota	21	28
N15	●	Indiana	30	27
N22		Michigan State	7	39

1970 6-4-0 (6-1-0)

S19		Notre Dame	14	35
S26		at UCLA	7	12
O3		SMU	20	21
O10	●	Illinois	48	0
O17	●	at Wisconsin	24	14
O24	●	Purdue	38	14
O31		at Ohio State	10	24
N7	●	Minnesota	28	14
N14	●	at Indiana	21	7
N21	●	at Michigan State	23	20

1971 7-4-0 (6-3-0)

S11		Michigan	6	21
S18		at Notre Dame	7	50
S25	●	Syracuse	12	6
O2	●	Wisconsin	24	11
O9	●	at Iowa	28	3
O16		Purdue	20	21
O23	●	at Indiana	24	10
O30		at Illinois	7	24
N6	●	Minnesota	41	20
N13	●	at Ohio State	14	10
N20	●	Michigan State	28	7

1972 2-9-0 (1-8-0)

S16		at Michigan	0	7
S23		Notre Dame	0	37
S30	●	at Pittsburgh	27	22
O7		at Wisconsin	14	21
O14		Iowa	12	23
O21		at Purdue	0	37
O28	●	Indiana	23	14
N4		Illinois	13	43
N11		at Minnesota	29	35
N18		Ohio State	14	27
N25		at Michigan State	14	24

JOHN PONT
1973-77 (.218) 12-43

1973 4-7-0 (4-4-0)

S15	●	Michigan State	14	10
S22		at Notre Dame	0	44
S29		Pittsburgh	14	21
O6		Ohio U.	12	14
O13	●	Iowa	31	15
O20		at Purdue	10	21
O27		at Ohio State	0	60
N3		Minnesota	43	52
N10	●	at Indiana	21	20
N17		at Wisconsin	34	36
N24	●	Illinois	9	6

1974 3-8-0 (2-6-0)

S14		at Michigan State	7	41
S21		Notre Dame	3	49
S28		at Nebraska	7	49
O5	●	Oregon	14	10
O12		at Iowa	10	35
O19		Purdue	26	31
O26		Ohio State	7	55
N2	●	at Minnesota	21	13
N9	●	Indiana	24	22
N16		Wisconsin	7	52
N23		at Illinois	14	28

1975 3-8-0 (2-6-0)

S13	●	Purdue	31	25
S20	●	Northern Illinois	10	3
S27		at Notre Dame	7	31
O4		at Arizona	6	41
O11	●	Indiana	30	0
O18		at Michigan	0	69
O25		at Wisconsin	14	17
N1		Iowa	21	24
N8		at Minnesota	9	33
N15		at Michigan State	14	47
N22		Illinois	7	28

1976 1-10-0 (1-7-0)

S11		at Purdue	19	31
S18		at North Carolina	0	12
S25		Notre Dame	0	48
O2		Arizona	15	27
O9		at Indiana	0	7
O16		Michigan	7	38
O23		Wisconsin	25	28
O30		at Iowa	10	13
N6		Minnesota	10	38
N13	●	Michigan State	42	21
N20		at Illinois	6	48

1977 1-10-0 (1-8-0)

S10		at Iowa	0	24
S17		at Arizona State	3	35
S24		North Carolina	7	41
O1		at Wisconsin	7	19
O8		Indiana	3	28
O15		at Minnesota	7	13
O22		Ohio State	15	35
O29		Purdue	16	28
N5		at Michigan	20	63
N11		at Michigan State	3	44
N19	●	Illinois	21	7

RICK VENTURI
1978-80 (.045) 1-31-1

1978 0-10-1 (0-8-1)

S9	=	at Illinois	0	0
S16		at Iowa	3	20
S23		Wisconsin	7	28
S30		at Colorado	7	55
O7		Arizona State	14	56
O14		at Indiana	10	38
O21		Minnesota	14	38
O28		at Ohio State	20	63
N4		at Purdue	0	31
N11		Michigan	14	59
N18		Michigan State	3	52

1979 1-10-0 (0-9-0)

S8		at Michigan	7	49
S15	●	Wyoming	27	22
S22		Syracuse	21	54
S29		at Minnesota	8	38
O6		at Ohio State	7	16
O13		Iowa	6	58
O20		at Indiana	0	30
O27		at Purdue	16	20
N3		Michigan State	7	42
N10		at Wisconsin	3	28
N17		Illinois	13	29

1980   0-11-0 (0-9-0)

Date	Opponent		
S6	at Illinois	9	35
S13	at Michigan	10	17
S20	at Washington	7	45
S27	at Syracuse	21	42
O4	Minnesota	21	49
O11	Ohio State	0	63
O18	at Iowa	3	25
O25	Indiana	20	35
N1	Purdue	31	52
N8	at Michigan State	10	42
N15	Wisconsin	19	39

DENNIS GREEN
1981-85 (.182)   10-45

1981   0-11-0 (0-9-0)

Date	Opponent		
S12	Indiana	20	21
S19	Arkansas *LR*	7	38
S26	Utah	0	42
O3	Iowa	0	64
O10	at Minnesota	23	35
O17	Purdue	0	35
O24	at Michigan	0	38
O31	at Wisconsin	0	52
N7	Michigan State	14	61
N14	at Ohio State	6	70
N21	Illinois	12	49

1982   3-8-0 (2-7-0)

Date	Opponent		
S4	at Illinois	13	49
S11	at Indiana	0	30
S18	Miami, Ohio	13	27
S25 ●	Northern Illinois	31	6
O2 ●	at Iowa	7	45
O9 ●	Minnesota	31	21
O16	at Purdue	21	34
O23	Michigan	14	49
O30	at Wisconsin	20	54
N6 ●	at Michigan State	28	24
N13	Ohio State	28	40

1983   2-9-0 (2-7-0)

Date	Opponent		
S10	Washington	0	34
S17	at Syracuse	0	35
S24 ●	at Indiana	10	8
O1	Wisconsin	0	49
O8	at Iowa	21	61
O15	at Michigan	0	35
O22 ●	Minnesota	19	8
O29	at Purdue	17	48
N5	Michigan State	3	9
N12	at Ohio State	7	55
N19	Illinois	24	56

1984   2-9-0 (2-7-0)

Date	Opponent		
S1	at Illinois	16	24
S8	at Washington	0	26
S15	Syracuse	12	13
S22 ●	Indiana	40	39
S29	at Wisconsin	16	31
O6	Iowa	3	31
O13	at Michigan	0	31
O20 ●	at Minnesota	31	28
O27	Purdue	7	49
N3	at Michigan State	10	27
N10	Ohio State	3	52

1985   3-8-0 (1-7-0)

Date	Opponent		
S7	at Duke	17	40
S14 ●	at Missouri	27	23
S28 ●	Northern Illinois	38	16
O5	at Indiana	7	26
O12	Minnesota	10	21
O19 ●	at Wisconsin	17	14
O26	Iowa	10	49
N2	at Purdue	7	31
N9	Ohio State	17	35
N16	at Michigan State	0	32
N23	Illinois	20	45

FRANCIS PEAY
1986-91 (.212)   13-51-2

1986   4-7-0 (2-6-0)

Date	Opponent		
S6	Duke	6	17
S20 ●	Army	25	18
S27 ●	at Princeton	37	0
O4	Indiana	7	24
O11	at Minnesota	23	44
O18	Wisconsin	27	35
O25	at Iowa	20	27
N1	Purdue	16	17
N8	at Ohio State	9	30
N15 ●	Michigan State	24	21
N22 ●	at Illinois	23	18

1987   2-8-1 (2-6-0)

Date	Opponent		
S12	at Duke	16	31
S19	at Missouri	3	28
S26 =	Northern Illinois	16	16
O3	at Indiana	18	35
O10	Minnesota	33	45
O17	Michigan State	0	38
O24 ●	at Wisconsin	27	24
O31	at Michigan	6	29
N7	Iowa	24	52
N14	at Purdue	15	20
N21 ●	Illinois	28	10

1988   2-8-1 (2-5-1)

Date	Opponent		
S3	Duke	21	31
S17	at Air Force	27	62
S24	at Army	7	23
O1	Indiana	17	48
O8 =	at Minnesota	28	28
O15	at Michigan State	3	36
O22 ●	Wisconsin	35	14
O29	Michigan	7	52
N5	at Iowa	10	35
N12 ●	Purdue	28	7
N19	at Illinois	9	14

1989   0-11-0 (0-8-0)

Date	Opponent		
S9	at Duke	31	41
S16	Air Force	31	48
S23	Rutgers	27	38
O7	at Indiana	11	43
O14	Minnesota	18	20
O21	at Wisconsin	31	35
O28	Iowa	22	35
N4	Ohio State	27	52
N11	at Purdue	15	46
N18	at Michigan State	14	76
N25	Illinois	14	63

1990   2-9-0 (1-7-0)

Date	Opponent		
S8	Duke	24	27
S22	at Rice	14	31
S29 ●	Northern Illinois	24	7
O6	Indiana	0	42
O13	at Minnesota	25	35
O20 ●	Wisconsin	44	34
O27	at Iowa	14	56
N3	at Ohio State	7	48
N10	Purdue	13	33
N17	Michigan State	22	29
N24	at Illinois	23	28

1991   3-8-0 (2-6-0)

Date	Opponent		
S14	Rice	7	36
S21	at Rutgers	18	22
S28 ●	Wake Forest	41	14
O5	Purdue	14	17
O12	at Indiana	6	44
O19	Ohio State *CLEV*	3	34
O26 ●	Illinois	17	11
N2 ●	at Michigan State	16	13
N9	at Michigan	14	59
N16	Iowa	10	24
N23	at Wisconsin	14	32

GARY BARNETT
1992-98 (.438)   35-45-1

1992   3-8-0 (3-5-0)

Date	Opponent		
S5	Notre Dame *CHI*	7	42
S12	at Boston College	0	49
S19	at Stanford	24	35
O3 ●	at Purdue	28	14
O10	Indiana	3	28
O17	at Ohio State	7	31
O24 ●	at Illinois	27	26
O31	Michigan State	26	27
N7	Michigan	7	40 *f*
N14	at Iowa	14	56
N21 ●	Wisconsin	27	25

1993   2-9-0 (0-8-0)

Date	Opponent		
S4	at Notre Dame	12	27
S18 ●	Boston College	22	21
S25 ●	Wake Forest	26	14
O2	at Ohio State	3	51
O9	at Wisconsin	14	53
O16	Minnesota	26	28
O23	Indiana	0	24
O30	at Illinois	13	20
N6	at Michigan State	29	31
N13	Iowa	19	23
N20	Penn State	21	43

1994   3-7-1 (2-6-0)

Date	Opponent		
S3	Notre Dame *CHI*	15	42
S10 =	Stanford	41	41
S17 ●	at Air Force	14	10
O1	Ohio State	15	17
O8	Wisconsin	14	46
O15 ●	at Minnesota	37	31
O22 ●	at Indiana	20	7
O29	Illinois	7	28
N5	Michigan State	17	35 †
N12	at Iowa	13	49
N19	at Penn State	17	45

1995   10-2-0 (8-0-0)

Date	Opponent		
S2	at Notre Dame	17	15
S16	Miami, Ohio	28	30
S23 ●	Air Force	30	6
S30 ●	Indiana	31	7
O7	at Michigan	19	13
O14 ●	at Minnesota	27	17
O21 ●	Wisconsin	35	0
O28 ●	at Illinois	17	14
N4 ●	Penn State	21	10
N11 ●	Iowa	31	20
N18 ●	at Purdue	23	8

ROSE BOWL

Date	Opponent		
J1	Southern Cal	32	41

1996   9-3 (7-1)

Date	Opponent		
S7	at Wake Forest	27	28
S14 ●	at Duke	38	13
S21 ●	Ohio U.	28	7
S28 ●	at Indiana	35	17
O5 ●	Michigan	17	16
O12 ●	Minnesota	26	24
O19 ●	at Wisconsin	34	30
O26 ●	Illinois	27	24
N2	at Penn State	9	34
N9 ●	at Iowa	40	13
N16 ●	Purdue	27	24

CITRUS BOWL

Date	Opponent		
J1	Tennessee	28	48

1997   5-7 (3-5)

Date	Opponent		
A23 ●	Oklahoma *CHI*	24	0
S6	at Wake Forest	20	27
S13 ●	Duke	24	20
S20	Rice	34	40
S27	at Purdue	9	21
O4	Wisconsin	25	26
O11	at Michigan	6	23
O18 ●	Michigan State	19	17
O25	at Ohio State	6	49
N1	Penn State	27	30
N8 ●	at Illinois	34	21
N15 ●	Iowa	15	14

1998   3-9 (0-8)

Date	Opponent		
S5	Nevada-Las Vegas	41	7
S12	Duke	10	44
S19	at Rice	23	14
S26	at Wisconsin	7	38
O3	Illinois	10	13
O10	at Iowa	24	26
O17	Michigan	6	12
O24	Ohio State	10	36
O31	at Michigan State	5	29
N7	Purdue	21	56
N14	at Penn State	10	41
N21 ●	at Hawaii	47	21

RANDY WALKER
1999-Present (.423)   30-41

1999   3-8 (1-7)

Date	Opponent		
S4	Miami, Ohio	3	28
S11	TCU	17	7
S18 ●	at Duke	15	12
S25	at Purdue	23	31
O2	Minnesota	14	33
O9	at Indiana	17	34
O16 ●	Iowa	23	21
O30	Wisconsin	19	35
N6	at Michigan	3	37
N13	Michigan State	0	34
N20	at Illinois	7	29

2000   8-4 (6-2)

Date	Opponent		
A31 ●	Northern Illinois	35	17
S9 ●	Duke	38	5
S16	at TCU	14	41
S23 ●	at Wisconsin	47	44
S30 ●	at Michigan State	37	17
O7 ●	Indiana	52	33
O14	Purdue	28	41
O28 ●	at Minnesota	41	35
N4 ●	Michigan	54	51
N11	at Iowa	17	27
N18 ●	Illinois	61	23

ALAMO BOWL

Date	Opponent		
D30	Nebraska	17	66

2001   4-7 (2-6)

Date	Opponent		
S7 ●	at Nevada-Las Vegas	37	28
S22 ●	at Duke	44	7
S29 ●	Michigan State	27	26
O6	at Ohio State	20	38
O13 ●	Minnesota	23	17
O20	Penn State	35	38
O27	at Purdue	27	32
N3	at Indiana	21	56
N10	Iowa	16	59
N17	Bowling Green	42	43
N22 ●	at Illinois	28	34

2002   3-9 (1-7)

Date	Opponent		
A31	at Air Force	3	52
S7	TCU	24	48
S14 ●	Duke	26	21
S21 ●	at Navy	49	40
S28	at Michigan State	24	39
O5	Ohio State	16	27
O10	at Minnesota	42	45
O19	at Penn State	0	49
O26	Purdue	13	42
N2 ●	Indiana	41	37
N9	at Iowa	10	62
N23	Illinois	24	31

2003   6-7 (4-4)

Date	Opponent		
A30 ●	at Kansas	28	20
S6	Air Force	21	22
S13	Miami, Ohio	14	44
S20 ●	at Duke	28	10
S27	at Ohio State	0	20
O4	Minnesota	17	42
O11 ●	at Indiana	37	31
O25 ●	Wisconsin	16	7
N1	at Purdue	14	34
N8 ●	Penn State	17	7
N15	Michigan	10	41
N22 ●	at Illinois	37	20

MOTOR CITY BOWL

Date	Opponent		
D26	Bowling Green	24	28

2004   6-6 (5-3)

Date	Opponent		
S2	at TCU	45	48
S11	Arizona State	21	30
S18 ●	Kansas	20	17
S25 ●	at Minnesota	17	43
O2	Ohio State	33	27
O9 ●	Indiana	31	24
O23	at Wisconsin	12	24
O30	Purdue	13	10
N6 ●	at Penn State	14	7
N13	at Michigan	20	42
N20 ●	Illinois	28	21
N27	at Hawaii	41	49

Neutral Site key: *UNK* Unknown, Unknown / *BRNX* Bronx, N.Y. / *DET* Detroit, Mich. / *IND* Indianapolis, Ind. / *CHI* Chicago, Ill. / *TOL* Toledo, Ohio / *KC* Kansas City, Mo. / *BUF* Buffalo, N.Y. / *BALT* Baltimore, Md.
f Forfeit † Game Later Forfeited ● Disputed Victor * Disputed Score ‖ Designated Conference Game |2 Counted Twice in Conference Standings

NOTRE DAME

BY MIKE VACCARO

EVERY SPORT NEEDS ITS KINGS. Kings define excellence and provide a standard for everyone else in the sport to measure themselves against. They are loved and hated, respected and feared, revered and reviled. They are royalty, regardless of the year, regardless of the era. Baseball has the Yankees, pro basketball the Celtics, pro hockey the Canadiens. And college football has Notre Dame.

The sheer breadth of the history that's taken place on this Indiana campus is enough to take your breath away. Coaches? Put it this way: Dan Devine went 53–16–1 and won one national title in six years at Notre Dame, yet his .764 winning percentage puts him only sixth on the all-time Irish list (among men who coached more than five seasons). Ahead of him: Lou Holtz (.765), Elmer Layden (.770), Ara Parseghian (.836), Frank Leahy (.855) and Knute Rockne (.881).

Players? Where do you start? With George Gipp, subject of the most famous pep talk in history? With Paul Hornung, or Leon Hart, or any of the seven Irish players who have won the Heisman Trophy? Oh, you want college football icons? Well take your pick: there's Touchdown Jesus. The Golden Dome. The Four Horsemen. For kicks, we'll throw in Rudy, too.

And maybe we should mention the 11 national championships the Irish have won outright, or the 10 other times they finished a season with a partial stake in the title. "The first time you walk onto the field here," former Irish nose tackle Chris Zorich said, "you wonder if the goose bumps will ever leave your arm. Then you realize: you have a lot of history to live up to."

Sometimes that history can be overwhelming. Ty Willingham learned that after three seasons, when his 21–15 record wasn't enough to satisfy the echoes and the ghosts. Beginning in 2005, Charlie Weis will see it for himself. It really is a lot of history.

The most history, in fact.

TRADITION Where to begin? Notre Dame is the very definition of college football tradition. Before each game, as players descend the locker room tunnel to the field at Notre Dame Stadium, each player touches an overhanging sign that reads, "Play like a champion today." Once they reach

Notre Dame is the very definition of college football tradition.

the field, their senses are assaulted by the leprechaun mascot and Touchdown Jesus, the mural that covers the south side of Hesburgh Library and is visible from inside Notre Dame Stadium. If it's an especially big game, there may be an extra surprise awaiting the players: the green jerseys that are broken out only for extra-special occasions. And, of course, there is the Notre Dame Victory March endlessly emanating from the band section, which is only the most famous song in college football history, and one of the most recognizable in all of American song. Is that enough?

BEST PLAYER He has become famous mostly because of a tear-jerking (and perhaps apocryphal) deathbed speech and because Ronald Reagan portrayed him in the movies. But Gipp may well have been one of the finest all-around college football players ever. Rockne often called Gipp "the most versatile player I've ever seen," and that was evident on both sides of the ball. As a defensive back, he was one of the original "lockdown" cover men, and opposing quarterbacks rarely ventured into his territory. As a running back on offense, Gipp led the Irish in rushing

and passing his final three years. His career total of 2,341 rushing yards stood as a record for some 58 years, until Jerome Heavens broke it in 1978. Eighty-four years after he last carried a ball for Notre Dame, Gipp still ranks No. 6 all time on the rushing list. In 1920, he was named the college football player of the year by Walter Camp. But it was during a game with Northwestern that year—a game in which he stepped in at quarterback and completed five of six passes for 157 yards and two touchdowns—that he contracted the strep throat that would contribute to his death three weeks later. On Dec. 13, 1920, the day before he died, Gipp made a simple plea to Rockne: "Sometime, Rock, when the team is up against it, when things are wrong and the breaks are beating the boys, tell them to go in there with all they've got and win just one for The Gipper. I don't know where I'll be then, Rock, but I'll know about it, and I'll be happy." While scholars have questioned whether Gipp actually made the speech—or even called himself The Gipper—his words nevertheless have become an iconic part of American sporting lore. Gipp's legend was solidified by Reagan's performance in the film *Knute Rockne, All American*.

RECORDS

RUSHING YARDS
GAME
262 Julius Jones vs. Pittsburgh, Oct. 11, 2003 (24 att.)
SEASON
1,437 Vagas Ferguson, 1979 (301 att.)
CAREER
4,318 Autry Denson, 1995-98 (854 att.)

PASSING YARDS
GAME
526 Joe Theisman vs. USC, Nov. 28, 1970 (33 of 58)
SEASON
2,753 Jarious Jackson, 1999 (184 of 316)
CAREER
7,602 Ron Powlus, 1994-97 (558 of 969)

RECEIVING YARDS
GAME
276 Jim Seymour vs. Purdue, Sept. 24, 1966 (13 rec.)
SEASON
1,123 Tom Gatewood, 1970 (77 rec.)
CAREER
2,512 Derrick Mayes, 1992-95 (129 rec.)

POINTS
GAME
37 Art Smith vs. Loyola (Ill.), Oct. 28, 1911 (7 TDs, 2 PATs)
SEASON
120 Jerome Bettis, 1991 (20 TDs)
CAREER
320 Allen Pinkett, 1982-85 (53 TDs; 1 two-pt. conv.)

CONSENSUS ALL-AMERICANS

1913	Gus Dorais, B
1917	Frank Rydzewski, C
1920	George Gipp, B
1921	Eddie Anderson, E
1924	Harry Stuhldreher, B
1924	Jim Crowley, B
1924	Elmer Layden, B
1926	Bud Boeringer, C
1927	John Smith, G
1929	Jack Cannon, G
1929-30	Frank Carideo, B
1930-31	Marchy Schwartz, HB
1931	Tommy Yarr, C
1932	Joe Kurth, T
1934	Jack Robinson, C
1935	Wayne Millner, E
1937	Chuck Sweeney, E
1938	Ed Beinor, T
1941-42	Bob Dove, E
1943	Angelo Bertelli, B
1943	Pat Filley, G
1943	Creighton Miller, B
1943	Jim White, T
1943	John Yonakor, E

(Continued on next page)

BEST COACH Rockne may have first achieved a measure of notoriety as a player, teaming with quarterback Gus Dorais to stun Army 35-13 in 1913 in the game that popularized the forward pass. But it was as the coach at his alma mater that Rockne grew into a fable. He succeeded Jesse Harper as coach in 1918; over the next 13 years he would guide Notre Dame to five unbeaten, untied seasons and 105 wins (against 12 losses and five ties). His .881 winning percentage is still unequaled by anyone who has ever coached at the major-college or professional level. But Rockne was an innovator as well as a winner. He all but invented the notion of intersectional games by instituting yearly matchups with Southern California. He designed his own uniforms and streamlined football equipment. He made far more use of substitutes than most coaches of the day (foreshadowing two-platoon football, which was still a quarter century away from becoming standard). And, of course, he was eager to use the forward pass at a time when most coaches were devoted to keeping the ball safely wrapped in their running backs' arms. There's no telling how vast the numbers Rockne would have compiled had he been afforded a complete career. But on March 31, 1931, he boarded Transcontinental-Western Flight 599 in Kansas City, bound for Los Angeles, where he was to complete a football instructional movie. Shortly after takeoff, the plane hit bad weather and went down in a wheat field near Bazaar, Kan. Rockne was 43 years old.

BEST TEAM When you've won 11 national championships, it's a happy dilemma trying to figure out which is the best of the best. Perhaps it's best to listen to Rockne, who always considered the 1924 team his finest—and his

CONSENSUS ALL-AMERICANS (CONT.)	
1946-47	John Lujack, B
1946-47	George Connor, T
1947-48	Bill Fischer, G
1948-49	Leon Hart, E
1948-49	Emil Sitko, B
1949	Bob Williams, B
1950	Jerry Groom, C
1952-53	Johnny Lattner, B
1953	Art Hunter, T
1954	Ralph Guglielmi, B
1955	Paul Hornung, B
1957	Al Ecuyer, G
1959	Monty Stickles, E
1964	Jack Snow, E
1964	John Huarte, B
1965	Dick Arrington, G
1965	Nick Rassas, B
1966	Nick Eddy, B
1966	Jim Lynch, LB
1966	Alan Page, DE
1966	Tom Regner, G
1967	Tom Schoen, DB
1968	Terry Hanratty, QB
1968	George Kunz, T
1969	Mike McCoy, DT
1970	Larry DiNardo, G
1970	Tom Gatewood, E
1971	Clarence Ellis, DB
1971	Walt Patulski, DE
1972	Greg Marx, DT
1973	Dave Casper, TE
1973	Mike Townsend, DB
1974	Pete Demmerle, WR
1974	Gerry DiNardo, G
1975	Steve Niehaus, DT
1976-77	Ross Browner, DE
1976-77	Ken MacAfee, TE
1977	Luther Bradley, DB
1978	Bob Golic, LB
1978	Dave Huffman, C
1979	Vagas Ferguson, RB
1980	John Scully, C
1980-81	Bob Crable, LB
1987	Tim Brown, WR
1988	Frank Stams, DE
1988, 1990	Michael Stonebreaker, LB
1990	Raghib Ismail, WR
1989-90	Chris Zorich, DT/DL
1989-90	Todd Lyght, DB
1991	Mirko Jurkovic, OL
1992-93	Aaron Taylor, OL
1993	Jeff Burris, DB
1994	Bobby Taylor, DB
2002	Shane Walton, DB

favorite. It was also the first Notre Dame squad to capture the consensus national title. In the Oct. 19, 1924, *New York Herald-Tribune*, Grantland Rice immortalized Notre Dame's wondrous backfield of Harry Stuhldreher, Don Miller, Jim Crowley and Elmer Layden, dubbing them the Four Horsemen. The 1924 squad outscored its nine regular-season opponents 258-44, then pounded Stanford 27-10 in the Rose Bowl. It was the last bowl game Notre Dame would play for 45 years. "I think I sensed that the backfield was a product of destiny," Rockne would say later. "At times, they caused me a certain amount of pain and exasperation, but mainly they brought me great joy."

BIGGEST GAME The Army-Notre Dame game of Nov. 9, 1946, at Yankee Stadium was one of the most hotly anticipated college football games ever. Army was No. 1, Notre Dame No. 2, and 74,121 fans shoehorned their way into the stadium. What followed was the most famous scoreless tie in football history, maybe in all sports history. Notre Dame drove to the Army 4 in the second quarter, but the Cadets held. Just before the fourth-down play, Notre Dame coach Frank Leahy turned to kicker Fred Earley. "Can you make it?" he asked of the possible 21-yard field goal. "Sir, it's like an extra point to me," Earley replied, grabbing for his helmet before Leahy replied, "No. We need six, not three. Three points will never win this game." Later, Army's "Mr. Inside," Doc Blanchard, broke into the clear and seemed headed for a sure score, but Johnny Lujack's sensational open-field tackle saved the day for the Irish. Army emerged from the game with its No. 1 ranking intact, but Notre Dame, on the strength of beating Northwestern, Tulane and USC by a combined

94-6 to close out the season, wound up passing Army in the polls by season's end. Still, the 0-0 score burned both teams. "I suppose I should be elated over the tie," Leahy said after the game. "After all, we didn't lose. But I'm not." Added Army's Red Blaik: "There is no jubilation in this dressing room."

BIGGEST UPSET Notre Dame had been the last team to defeat Oklahoma, a 28-21 victory in Norman on Sept. 26, 1953. Four years had passed. Oklahoma had played 47 games in the meantime and had not lost any, the longest unbeaten streak in college football history. And there seemed no end in sight to the Sooners' dominance. In fact, if you picked up a copy of *Sports Illustrated* on the morning of Nov. 16, 1957, you would have seen this headline: "Why Oklahoma Is Unbeatable." Notre Dame, coming off its first losing season in 23 years in 1956, was a pedestrian 4–2 coming into the game, riding a two-game losing streak in which it had been outscored 54-12 by Navy and Michigan State. There seemed little chance Notre Dame would pose an impediment to the Sooners at Norman's Memorial Stadium. And Oklahoma drove the ball breezily on its first possession, driving to the Irish 13. But the drive stalled there and, stunningly, the Sooners would never get that close to the end zone the rest of the day. "I was willing to settle for a scoreless tie," Oklahoma coach Bud Wilkinson would admit later. But Notre Dame had other ideas. With 3:50 left in the game, the Irish had fourth and goal at the Oklahoma 3. Quarterback Bob Williams faked a dive to fullback Nick Pietrosante, then pitched to halfback Dick Lynch, who scampered into the end zone for the staggering, game-winning score. The game ended 7-0. The Sooners' streak was over at 47. And Terry Brennan, the embattled Irish coach who'd been under fire for two years, called the game "the greatest thrill of my athletic career."

STADIUM It's enough to get the football poets kicked into overdrive. Is it a shrine? A cathedral? A football mecca? What it is, is the most recognizable college football stadium in the world, a formerly cozy 59,075-seat bandbox that is now a fortress for 80,795 strong. Notre Dame first played its home games at Cartier Field, a 30,000-seat facility located just north of the present stadium, but as the program grew to national prominence in the 1920s, it was clear a bigger home was necessary. The Osborn Engineering Company of Cleveland, which had built Yankee Stadium, designed the new stadium and it was completed in only four months. The sod from Cartier Field was transplanted into the new stadium, and Rockne carefully oversaw every minute detail, from how much sideline space was available (to limit game-day intruders) to parking and traffic systems. Ironically, Rockne would get to coach only one year in the new palace before his tragic plane crash, although he did earn the stadium's first win, a 20-14 decision over SMU on Oct. 4, 1930. Notre Dame won its first eight games there, in fact, before falling to USC 16-14 on Nov. 21, 1931, a loss that also snapped a 26-game unbeaten streak. Since 1966, every home game has been a sellout, except for a Thanksgiving Day game with Air Force in 1973, which was about 1,800 shy of capacity due to the absence of students.

HEARTBREAKER Parseghian had been the answer to the prayers offered up by a nation filled with subway alumni. Notre Dame hadn't had a winning season in six years and was coming off a desultory 2–7 mark in 1963, but Parseghian turned that all around in one short year. By early November, the Irish had ascended to No. 1 in both polls, and by Nov. 28, as they traveled to Los Angeles for their annual date with USC, they knew they needed but one more victory to wrap up the program's most improbable national championship. And thanks to Heisman Trophy winner John Huarte and his favorite receiver, Jack Snow, the Irish raced to a 17-0 first-half lead. But in the second half, unheralded Trojans

---

ALL-CENTURY TEAM

In 2000, Blue & Gold Illustrated *magazine assembled its 25-player "All 20th Century" Notre Dame team. Criteria used in each player's selection included his standing in lore, impact on the team's success and lifetime achievement, including achievement away from the field.*

OFFENSE

1918-21	Heartley "Hunk" Anderson	LG
1945-48	Bill Fischer	G
1946-47	George Connor	T
1946-49	Jim Martin	T
1922-24	Adam Walsh	C
1971-73	Dave Casper	TE
1984-87	Tim Brown	WR
1988-90	Raghib Ismail	FL
1975, 1977-78	Joe Montana	QB
1917-20	George Gipp	TB
1990-92	Jerome Bettis	FB
1983-86	John Carney	PK

DEFENSE

1946-49	Leon Hart	DE
1973, 1975-77	Ross Browner	DE
1964-66	Alan Page	DT
1988-90	Chris Zorich	DT
1964-66	Jim Lynch	LB
1975-78	Bob Golic	LB
1978-81	Bob Crable	LB
1973, 1975-77	Luther Bradley	DB
1951-53	John Lattner	DB
1987-90	Todd Lyght	DB
1943, 1946-47	John Lujack	DB
1989-92	Craig Hentrich	P
1954-56	Paul Hornung	UTILITY

quarterback Craig Fertig began heating up, and so did an emerging USC tailback named Mike Garrett. Suddenly, USC found itself within 17-13 as it began its final drive of the day. And with just 1:33 left in the game, Fertig found Sherman for a 15-yard touchdown pass that crushed Notre Dame's title hopes. Parseghian would have to wait two more years to win a championship. "After the game," Fertig would recall years later, "someone sent me papers from Paris, London, Frankfurt and a bunch of other countries. The game was on the front page of all of them."

CONTROVERSY It was billed as the Game of the Century, and by the time it was over it would leave a nation grumbling. Notre Dame took its No. 1 ranking into East Lansing on Nov. 19, 1966, where second-ranked Michigan State was lying in wait. The Spartans, behind quarterback Jimmy Raye, seized a quick 10-0 lead before the Irish slowly began clawing their way back into the game. Notre Dame was without its best running back Nick Eddy, who'd slipped getting off the train in East Lansing and aggravated his shoulder. Quarterback Terry Hanratty had to leave the game in the first quarter after State's Bubba Smith banged up his shoulder. Coley O'Brien, a diabetic who required two insulin shots a day, stepped in to call the signals. O'Brien hooked up with Bob Gladieux, a seldom-used sophomore, on a 34-yard touchdown to make the score 10-7 at the half, and Joe Azzaro kicked a 28-yard field goal on the first play of the fourth quarter to knot the score. Azzaro would miss a 41-yarder with 4:39 to play that could have won the game. Notre Dame's defense held the Spartans, and the Irish got the ball back on their own 30 with 1:24 to play, still plenty of time to take a crack at reaching field goal range. But Parseghian, in a decision that is still ripped to this day in East Lansing and much talked-about elsewhere, ordered his players to dive into the line and take the tie, which all but wrapped up Parseghian's first national title. "We'd fought hard to come back and tie it up," the coach would explain later. "After all that, I didn't want to risk giving it to them cheap. They get reckless and it could cost them the game. I wasn't going to do a jackass thing like that at this point."

RIVALRY Through the years, many different programs have emerged as heated rivals for Notre Dame. The annual game with Army, in fact, became such a heated affair that both schools opted to discontinue the rivalry following the 1947 season, and they've met only 14 times since. In the 1980s, when Miami emerged as a significant power, the Hurricanes and Irish engaged in some memorable showdowns. Through

it all, the Notre Dame-USC rivalry remains the most colorful in all of football. The schools have met every year since 1926 (with the exception of a three-year hiatus during World War II). Notre Dame holds a commanding 42–29–5 lead in the series, which has produced a slew of unforgettable moments. None has had the lasting impact of the 1974 game, a 55-24 USC rout. Notre Dame had a 24-0 lead late in the second quarter when Pat Haden found Anthony Davis—who two years earlier, as a sophomore, had scored 6 TDs in South Bend—for a seven-yard scoring pass. Then Davis promptly returned the second-half kickoff 102 yards for another touchdown, and one of the most remarkable routs in football history was under way. USC would score 55 unanswered points—49 of them in a span of 16:44. "We turned into madmen" is the only way Davis could describe it.

NICKNAME There are several theories to explain the origin of Fighting Irish as one of the most famous monikers in American sports. One story suggests it was born during an 1899 game with Northwestern, when Wildcats fans started chanting "Kill the Fighting Irish!" Others credit an angry Notre Dame player who, at halftime of a 1909 game with Michigan, looked around at a room filled with Gaelic surnames and sneered, "What's the matter with you guys? You're all Irish and you're not fighting worth a lick." Notre Dame had played under the nickname Catholics in the 1880s and 1890s, and the Four Horsemen-era teams would also be referred to as the Ramblers. But the explanation most believed to be official comes from the *Notre Dame Scholastic*, in a 1929 edition: "The term 'Fighting Irish' has been applied to Notre Dame for years. It first attached itself ... when the school, comparatively unknown, sent its athletic teams away to play in another city ... At that time the title 'Fighting Irish' held no glory or prestige." The years passed and, according to the *Scholastic*, "the unkind appellation became symbolic of the struggle for supremacy of the field ... The term, while given in irony, has become our heritage." The university officially adopted the nickname for good in 1927.

MASCOT Befitting the Fighting Irish nickname, Notre Dame officially adopted the leprechaun as its mascot in 1965. Hard as it may be to imagine it, before that the Irish's official mascot had been a series of Irish terrier dogs, beginning with one named Brick Top Shaun-Rhu in 1930. Most of the succeeding terriers went by the name Clashmore Mike.

UNIFORMS Notre Dame's iconic solid-gold helmet has

been the only one the program has used, with two notable exceptions: from 1959 to 1962 a green shamrock was featured on each side, and in 1963 a white number was stenciled over the gold. It should probably be noted that Notre Dame was 19–30 during this interlude, which may explain why solid gold returned for good when Parseghian arrived in 1964 and has remained ever since.

LORE Green is the school's unofficial third color. The tradition of the occasional green jersey began under Rockne in the 1920s, but at first there was nothing mystical about it; Rockne merely opted for green whenever he would play another team whose colors too closely matched his own. By 1927, however, Rockne could sense other teams would occasionally get psyched out by the ploy, and so he used it to his advantage. Leahy also used green periodically during his tenure. But the most famous instance of green as a motivational tool came on Oct. 22, 1977, when Devine surprised everyone inside Notre Dame Stadium—including most of his own players—by ordering special green jerseys for the USC game. Twenty minutes before kickoff, Devine handed out the jerseys, and when the crowd first glimpsed the "Green Machine" tops, it exploded and propelled the Irish to a 49-19 win that helped carry them to the national championship. Later, Gerry Faust twice used green jerseys in wins over USC (once ordering the switch at halftime), although the ploy hasn't always worked: Notre Dame was 8–0 and ranked fourth in 2002 when Willingham broke out the green jerseys against Boston College on Nov. 2. BC won 14-7.

NUMBERS No program in college football history has more national titles (11), Heisman Trophy winners (seven) or consensus All-American selections (94) than Notre Dame. It is also the only school to ever have one national network (NBC) televise all its home games.

QUOTE "Outlined against a blue, gray October sky, the Four Horsemen rode again. In dramatic lore, they are known as famine, pestilence, destruction and death. These are only aliases. Their real names are Stuhldreher, Miller, Crowley and Layden." —Grantland Rice, *New York Herald-Tribune*, Oct. 19, 1924

NOTRE DAME ANNUAL STATISTICAL LEADERS

YR	RUSHING	YDS	ATT	AVG	PASSING	ATT	CMP	PCT	YDS	RECEIVING	REC	YDS	AVG
1918	George Gipp	541	98	5.5	George Gipp	45	19	.42	293	Bernie Kirk	7	102	14.6
1919	George Gipp	729	106	6.9	George Gipp	72	41	.57	727	Bernie Kirk	21	372	17.7
1920	George Gipp	827	102	8.1	George Gipp	62	30	.48	709	Eddie Anderson	17	293	17.2
1921	John Mohardt	781	136	5.7	John Mohardt	98	53	.54	995	Eddie Anderson	26	394	15.2
1922	Jim Crowley	566	75	7.5	Jim Crowley	21	10	.48	154	Don Miller	6	144	24.0
1923	Don Miller	698	89	7.8	Jim Crowley	36	13	.36	154	Don Miller	9	149	16.6
1924	Don Miller	763	107	7.1	Harry Stuhldreher	33	25	.76	471	Don Miller	16	297	18.6
1925	Christie Flanagan	556	99	5.6	Harry O'Boyle	21	7	.33	107	Gene Edwards	4	28	7.0
1926	Christie Flanagan	535	68	7.9	Christie Flanagan	29	12	.41	207	Ike Voedisch	6	95	15.8
1927	Christie Flanagan	731	118	6.2	John Niemiec	33	14	.42	187	John Colrick	11	126	11.5
1928	Jack Chevigny	539	120	4.5	John Niemiec	108	37	.34	456	John Colrick	18	199	11.1
1929	Joe Savoldi	597	112	5.3	Jack Elder	25	8	.32	187	John Colrick	4	90	22.5
1930	Marchy Schwartz	927	124	7.5	Marchy Schwartz	56	17	.30	319	Ed Kosky	4	76	19.0
1931	Marchy Schwartz	692	146	4.7	Marchy Schwartz	51	9	.18	174	Paul Host	6	48	8.0
1932	George Melinkovich	503	88	5.7	Nick Lukats	28	13	.46	252	George Melinkovich	7	106	15.1
1933	Nick Lukats	339	107	3.2	Nick Lukats	67	21	.31	329	Steve Banas	6	59	9.8
1934	George Melinkovich	324	73	4.4	Bill Shakespeare	29	9	.31	230	Dom Vairo	4	135	33.8
1935	Bill Shakespeare	374	104	3.6	Bill Shakespeare	66	19	.29	267	Wally Fromhart	11	174	15.8
1936	Bob Wilke	434	132	3.3	Bob Wilke	52	19	.37	365	Joe O'Neil	8	140	17.5
1937	Bunny McCormick	347	91	3.8	Jack McCarthy	53	16	.30	225	Andy Puplis	5	86	17.2
1938	Bob Saggau	353	60	5.9	Bob Saggau	28	8	.29	179	Earl Brown	6	192	32.0
1939	Milt Piepul	414	82	5.0	Harry Stevenson	50	14	.28	236	Bud Kerr	6	129	21.5
1940	Steve Juzwik	407	71	5.7	Bob Saggau	60	21	.35	483	Bob Hargrave	9	98	10.9
1941	Fred Evans	490	141	3.5	Angelo Bertelli	123	70	.57	1,027	Steve Juzwik	18	307	17.1
1942	Corwin Clatt	698	138	5.1	Angelo Bertelli	159	72	.45	1,039	Bob Livingstone	17	272	16.0
1943	Creighton Miller	911	151	6.0	Johnny Lujack	71	34	.48	525	John Yonakor	15	323	21.5
1944	Bob Kelly	681	136	5.0	Frank Dancewicz	163	68	.42	989	Bob Kelly	18	283	15.7
1945	Elmer Angsman	616	87	7.1	Frank Dancewicz	90	30	.33	489	Bob Skoglund	9	100	11.1
1946	Emil Sitko	346	53	6.5	Johnny Lujack	100	49	.49	778	Terry Brennan	10	154	15.4
1947	Emil Sitko	426	60	7.1	Johnny Lujack	109	61	.56	777	Terry Brennan	16	181	11.3
1948	Emil Sitko	742	129	5.8	Frank Tripuka	91	53	.58	660	Leon Hart	16	231	14.4
1949	Emil Sitko	712	120	5.9	Bob Williams	147	83	.56	1,374	Leon Hart	19	257	13.5
1950	Jack Landry	491	109	4.5	Bob Williams	210	99	.47	1,035	Jim Mutscheller	35	426	12.2
1951	Neil Worden	676	181	3.7	John Mazur	110	48	.44	645	Jim Mutscheller	20	305	15.3
1952	John Lattner	732	148	4.9	Ralph Guglielmi	143	62	.43	725	Joe Heap	29	437	15.1
1953	Neil Worden	859	145	5.9	Ralph Guglielmi	113	52	.46	792	Joe Heap	22	335	15.2
1954	Don Schaefer	766	141	5.4	Ralph Guglielmi	127	68	.54	1,162	Joe Heap	18	369	20.5
1955	Don Schaefer	638	145	4.4	Paul Hornung	103	46	.45	743	Jim Morse	17	424	24.9
1956	Paul Hornung	420	94	4.5	Paul Hornung	111	59	.53	917	Jim Morse	20	442	22.1
1957	Nick Pietrosante	449	90	5.0	Bob Williams	106	53	.50	565	Dick Lynch	13	128	9.8
1958	Nick Pietrosante	549	117	4.7	George Izo	118	68	.58	1,067	Monty Stickles	20	328	16.4
1959	Gerry Gray	256	50	5.1	George Izo	95	44	.46	661	Bob Scarpitto	15	297	19.8
1960	Angelo Dabiero	325	80	4.1	George Haffner	108	30	.28	548	Les Traver	14	225	16.1
1961	Angelo Dabiero	637	92	6.9	Frank Budka	95	40	.42	636	Les Traver	17	349	20.5
1962	Don Hogan	454	90	5.0	Daryle Lamonica	128	64	.50	821	Jim Kelly	41	523	12.8
1963	Joe Kantor	330	88	3.8	Frank Budka	40	21	.53	239	Jim Kelly	18	264	14.7
1964	Bill Wolski	657	136	4.8	John Huarte	205	114	.56	2,062	Jack Snow	60	1,114	18.6
1965	Nick Eddy	582	115	5.1	Bill Zloch	88	36	.41	558	Nick Eddy	13	233	17.9
1966	Nick Eddy	553	78	7.1	Terry Hanratty	147	78	.53	1,247	Jim Seymour	48	862	18.0
1967	Jeff Zimmerman	591	133	4.4	Terry Hanratty	206	110	.53	1,439	Jim Seymour	37	515	13.9
1968	Bob Gladieux	713	152	4.7	Terry Hanratty	197	116	.59	1,466	Jim Seymour	53	736	13.9
1969	Denny Allan	612	148	4.1	Joe Theismann	192	108	.56	1,531	Tom Gatewood	47	743	15.8
1970	Ed Gulyas	534	118	4.5	Joe Theismann	268	155	.58	2,429	Tom Gatewood	77	1,123	14.6
1971	Bob Minnix	337	78	4.3	Cliff Brown	111	56	.50	669	Tom Gatewood	33	417	12.6
1972	Eric Penick	726	124	5.9	Tom Clements	162	83	.51	1,163	Willie Townsend	25	369	14.8
1973	Wayne Bullock	752	162	4.6	Tom Clements	113	60	.53	882	Pete Demmerle	26	404	15.5
1974	Wayne Bullock	855	203	4.2	Tom Clements	215	122	.57	1,549	Pete Demmerle	43	667	15.5
1975	Jerome Heavens	756	129	5.9	Rick Slager	139	66	.47	686	Ken MacAfee	26	333	12.8
1976	Al Hunter	1,058	233	4.5	Rick Slager	172	86	.50	1,281	Ken MacAfee	34	483	14.2
1977	Jerome Heavens	994	229	4.3	Joe Montana	189	99	.52	1,604	Ken MacAfee	54	797	14.8
1978	Vagas Ferguson	1,192	211	5.6	Joe Montana	260	141	.54	2,010	Kris Haines	32	699	21.8
1979	Vagas Ferguson	1,437	301	4.8	Rusty Lisch	208	108	.52	1,781	Dean Masztak	28	428	15.3
1980	Jim Stone	908	192	4.7	Blair Kiel	124	48	.39	531	Tony Hunter	23	303	13.2
1981	Phil Carter	727	165	4.4	Blair Kiel	151	67	.44	936	Tony Hunter	28	387	13.8
1982	Phil Carter	715	179	4.0	Blair Kiel	219	118	.54	1,273	Tony Hunter	42	507	12.1
1983	Allen Pinkett	1,394	252	5.5	Steve Beuerlein	145	75	.52	1,061	Allen Pinkett	28	288	10.3
1984	Allen Pinkett	1,105	275	4.0	Steve Beuerlein	232	140	.60	1,920	Mark Bavaro	32	395	12.3
1985	Allen Pinkett	1,100	255	4.3	Steve Beuerlein	214	107	.50	1,335	Tim Brown	25	397	15.9
1986	Mark Green	406	96	4.2	Steve Beuerlein	259	151	.58	2,211	Tim Brown	45	910	20.2
1987	Mark Green	861	146	5.9	Tony Rice	82	35	.43	663	Tim Brown	39	846	21.7
1988	Tony Rice	700	121	5.8	Tony Rice	138	70	.51	1,176	Rickey Watters	15	286	19.1
1989	Tony Rice	884	174	5.1	Tony Rice	137	68	.50	1,122	Raghib Ismail	27	535	19.8
1990	Rodney Culver	710	150	4.7	Rick Mirer	200	110	.55	1,824	Raghib Ismail	32	699	21.8

YR	RUSHING	YDS	ATT	AVG	PASSING	ATT	CMP	PCT	YDS	RECEIVING	REC	YDS	AVG
1991	Jerome Bettis	972	168	5.8	Rick Mirer	234	132	.56	2,117	Tony Smith	42	789	18.8
1992	Reggie Brooks	1,343	167	8.0	Rick Mirer	234	120	.51	1,876	Lake Dawson	25	462	18.5
1993	Lee Becton	1,044	164	6.4	Kevin McDougal	159	98	.62	1,541	Lake Dawson	25	395	15.8
1994	Randy Kinder	702	119	5.9	Ron Powlus	222	119	.54	1,729	Derrick Mayes	47	847	18.0
1995	Randy Kinder	809	143	5.7	Ron Powlus	217	124	.57	1,853	Derrick Mayes	48	881	18.4
1996	Autry Denson	1,179	202	5.8	Ron Powlus	232	133	.57	1,942	Pete Chryplewicz	27	331	12.3
1997	Autry Denson	1,268	264	4.8	Ron Powlus	298	182	.61	2,078	Bobby Brown	45	543	12.1
1998	Autry Denson	1,176	251	4.7	Jarious Jackson	188	104	.55	1,740	Malcolm Johnson	43	642	14.9
1999	Tony Fisher	783	156	5.0	Jarious Jackson	316	184	.58	2,753	Bobby Brown	36	608	16.9
2000	Julius Jones	657	162	4.1	Matt LoVecchio	125	73	.58	980	David Givens	25	310	12.4
2001	Julius Jones	718	168	4.3	Carlyle Holiday	144	73	.51	784	Javin Hunter	37	387	10.5
2002	Ryan Grant	1,085	261	4.2	Carlyle Holiday	257	129	.50	1,788	Arnaz Battle	58	786	13.6
2003	Julius Jones	1,341	229	5.9	Brady Quinn	411	195	.47	2,149	Rhema McKnight	47	600	12.8
2004	Darius Walker	786	185	4.2	Brady Quinn	353	191	.54	2,586	Rhema McKnight	42	610	14.6

Receiving leaders by receptions
The NCAA began including postseason stats in 2002

THE SCHOOLS

NOTRE DAME ALL-TIME SCORES

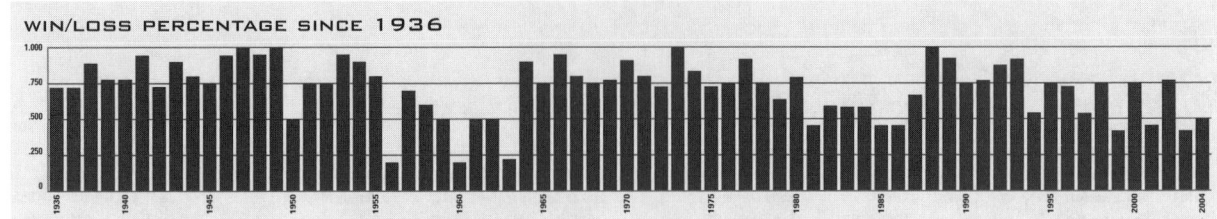

WIN/LOSS PERCENTAGE SINCE 1936

NO HEAD COACH

1887   0-1-0
N23	Michigan	0	8

1888   1-2-0
P20	Michigan	6	26
P21	Michigan	4	10
D6 ●	Harvard Prep	20	0

1889   1-0-0
N14 ●	at Northwestern	9	0

1890-1891
NO TEAM

1892   1-0-1
O19 ●	South Bend HS	56	0
N24 =	Hillsdale	10	10

1893   4-1-0
O25 ●	Kalamazoo	34	0
N11 ●	Albion	8	6
N23 ●	De LaSalle	28	0
N30 ●	Hillsdale	22	10
J1	at Chicago	0	8

J.L. MORRISON
1894 (.700)   3-1-1

1894   3-1-1
O13 ●	Hillsdale	14	0
O20 =	Albion	6	6
N15 ●	Wabash	30	0
N22 ●	Rush Medical	18	6
N29 ●	Albion	12	19

H.G. HADDEN
1895 (.750)   3-1

1895   3-1-0
O19 ●	Northwestern Law	20	0
N7 ●	Ill. Cycle Club	18	2
N22	Indianapolis Artillery	0	18
N28 ●	Chicago P&S	32	0

FRANK E. HERING
1896-98 (.658)   12-6-1

1896   4-3-0
O8	Chicago Phys. & Surg.	0	4
O14 ●	Chicago	0	18
O27 ●	South Bend AC	46	0
O31 ●	Albion	24	0
N14 ●	Purdue	22	28
N20 ●	Highland Views	82	0
N26 ●	Beloit	8	0

1897   4-1-1
O13 =	Rush Medical	0	0
O23 ●	DePauw	4	0
O28 ●	Chicago Dental	62	0
N6	at Chicago	5	34
N13 ●	St. Viator	60	0
N25 ●	Michigan State	34	6

1898   4-2-0
O8 ●	Illinois	5	0
O15 ●	Michigan State	53	0
O23 ●	at Michigan	0	23
O29 ●	DePauw	32	0
N5 ●	Indiana	5	11
N19 ●	at Albion	60	0

JAMES McWEENEY
1899 (.650)   6-3-1

1899   6-3-1
O27 ●	Englewood HS	29	5
S30 ●	Michigan State	40	0
O4 ●	at Chicago	6	23
O14 ●	Lake Forest	38	0
O18 ●	at Michigan	0	12
O23 ●	Indiana	17	0
O28 ●	Northwestern	12	0
N4 ●	Rush Medical	17	0
N18 =	at Purdue	10	10
N30 ●	Chicago P&S	0	5

PATRICK O'DEA
1900-01 (.750)   14-4-2

1900   6-3-1
S29 ●	Goshen	55	0
O6 ●	Englewood HS	68	0
O13 ●	S.B. Howard Park	64	0
O20 ●	Cincinnati	58	0 *
O25 ●	at Indiana	0	6
N3 =	Beloit	6	6
N10 ●	at Wisconsin	0	54
N17 ●	at Michigan	0	7
N24 ●	Rush Medical	5	0
N29 ●	Chicago P&S	5	0

1901   8-1-1
S28 =	South Bend AC	0	0
O5 ●	at Ohio Medical	6	0
O12 ●	at Northwestern	0	2
O19 ●	Chicago Medical	32	0
O26 ●	at Beloit	5	0
N2 ●	Lake Forest	16	0
N9 ●	Purdue	12	6
N16 ●	Indiana	18	5
N23 ●	Chicago P&S	34	0
N28 ●	South Bend AC	22	6

JAMES FARAGHER
1902-03 (.833)   14-2-2

1902   6-2-1
S27 ●	Michigan State	32	0
O11 ●	Lake Forest	28	0
O18 ●	Michigan *Tol*	0	23
O25 ●	at Indiana	11	5
N1 ●	at Ohio Medical	6	5
N8 ●	Knox *RI*	5	12
N15 ●	American Medical	92	0
N22 ●	DePauw	22	0
N27 =	at Purdue	6	6

1903   8-0-1
O3 ●	Michigan State	12	0
O10 ●	Lake Forest	28	10
O17 ●	DePauw	56	0
O24 ●	American Medical	52	0
O29 ●	Chicago P&S	46	0
N7 ●	Missouri Osteopaths	28	0
N14 =	at Northwestern	0	0
N21 ●	at Ohio Medical	35	0
N26 ●	at Wabash	35	0

LOUIS SALMON
1904 (.625)   5-3

1904   5-3-0
O1 ●	Wabash	12	4
O8 ●	American Medical	44	0
O15 ●	Wisconsin *Mil*	0	58
O22 ●	at Ohio Medical	17	5
O27 ●	Toledo AA	6	0
N5 ●	at Kansas	5	24
N19 ●	DePauw	10	0
N24 ●	at Purdue	0	36

HENRY J. McGLEW
1905 (.556)   5-4

1905   5-4-0
S30 ●	N.Division HS	44	0
O7 ●	Michigan State	28	0
O14 ●	Wisconsin *Mil*	0	21
O21 ●	Wabash	0	5
O28 ●	American Medical	142	0
N4 ●	DePauw	71	0
N11 ●	at Indiana	5	22
N18 ●	Bennette Medical	22	0
N24 ●	at Purdue	0	32

THOMAS BARRY
1906-07 (.893)   12-1-1

1906   6-1-0
O6 ●	Franklin	26	0
O13 ●	Hillsdale	17	0
O20 ●	Chicago P&S	28	0
O27 ●	Michigan State	5	0
N3 ●	at Purdue	2	0
N10 ●	Indiana *Ind*	0	12
N24 ●	Beloit	29	0

1907   6-0-1
O12 ●	Chicago P&S	32	0
O19 ●	Franklin	23	0
O26 ●	Olivet	22	4
N2 ●	Indiana	0	0
N9 ●	Knox	22	4
N23 ●	Purdue	17	0
N28 ●	at St. Vincents	21	12

VICTOR M. PLACE
1908 (.889)   8-1

1908   8-1-0
O3 ●	Hillsdale	39	0
O10 ●	Franklin	64	0
O17 ●	at Michigan	6	12
O24 ●	Chicago P&S	88	0
O29 ●	Ohio Northern	58	4
N7 ●	Indiana *Ind*	11	0
N13 ●	at Wabash	8	4
N18 ●	St. Viator	46	0
N26 ●	at Marquette	6	0 *

FRANK C. LONGMAN
1909-10 (.857)   11-1-2

1909   7-0-1
O9 ●	Olivet	58	0
O16 ●	Rose Poly	60	11
O23 ●	Michigan State	17	0
O30 ●	at Pittsburgh	6	0
N6 ●	at Michigan	11	3
N16 ●	Miami, Ohio	46	0
N20 ●	Wabash	38	0
N25 =	at Marquette	0	0

1910   4-1-1
O8 ●	Olivet	48	0
O22 ●	Butchel	51	0
N5 ●	at Michigan State	0	17
N12 ●	at Rose Poly	41	3
N19 ●	Ohio Northern	47	0
N24 =	at Marquette	5	5

JOHN L. MARKS
1911-12 (.933)   13-0-2

1911   6-0-2
O7 ●	Ohio Northern	32	6
O14 ●	St. Viator	43	0
O21 ●	Butler	27	0
O28 ●	Loyola-Chicago	80	0
N4 ●	at Pittsburgh	0	0
N11 ●	St. Bonaventure	34	0
N20 ●	at Wabash	6	3
N30 =	at Marquette	0	0

1912   7-0-0
O5 ●	St. Viator	116	7
O12 ●	Adrian	74	7
O19 ●	Morris Harvey	39	0
O26 ●	Wabash	41	6
N2 ●	at Pittsburgh	3	0
N9 ●	at St. Louis	47	7
N28 ●	Marquette *Chi*	69	0

JESSE C. HARPER
1913-17 (.863)   34-5-1

1913   7-0-0
O4 ●	Ohio Northern	87	0
O18 ●	South Dakota	20	7
O25 ●	Alma	62	0
N1 ●	at Army	35	13
N8 ●	at Penn State	14	7
N22 ●	at Christian Brothers	20	7
N27 ●	at Texas	30	7

1914   6-2-0
O3 ●	Alma	56	0
O10 ●	Rose Poly	103	0
O17 ●	at Yale	0	28
O24 ●	South Dakota *Unk*	33	0
O31 ●	Haskell	20	7
N7 ●	at Army	7	20
N14 ●	Carlisle *Chi*	48	6
N26 ●	at Syracuse	20	0

1915   7-1-0
O2 ●	Alma	32	0
O9 ●	Haskell	34	0
O23 ●	at Nebraska	19	20
O30 ●	South Dakota	6	0
N6 ●	at Army	7	0
N13 ●	at Creighton	41	0
N25 ●	at Texas	36	7
N27 ●	at Rice	55	2

1916   8-1-0
S30 ●	Case Tech	48	0
O7 ●	at Western Reserve	48	0
O14 ●	Haskell	26	0
O28 ●	Wabash	60	0
N4 ●	at Army	10	30
N11 ●	South Dakota *Unk*	21	0
N18 ●	at Michigan State	14	0
N25 ●	Alma	46	0
N30 ●	at Nebraska	20	0

1917   6-1-1
O6 ●	Kalamazoo	55	0
O13 =	at Wisconsin	0	0
O20 ●	at Nebraska	0	7
O27 ●	South Dakota	40	0
N3 ●	at Army	7	2
N10 ●	at Morningside	13	0
N17 ●	Michigan State	23	0
N24 ●	at Wash. & Jeff.	3	0

KNUTE ROCKNE
1918-30 (.881)   105-12-5

1918   3-1-2
S28 ●	at Case Tech	26	6
N2 ●	at Wabash	67	7
N9 =	Great Lakes NAS	7	7
N16 ●	at Michigan State	7	13
N23 ●	at Purdue	26	6
N28 =	at Nebraska	0	0

1919   9-0-0
O4 ●	Kalamazoo	14	0
O11 ●	Mt. Union	60	7
O18 ●	at Nebraska	14	9
O25 ●	Western Michigan	53	0
N1 ●	Indiana *Ind*	16	3
N8 ●	at Army	12	9
N15 ●	Michigan State	13	0
N22 ●	at Purdue	33	13
N27 ●	at Morningside	14	6

THE SCHOOLS

1920 — 9-0-0
O2	● Kalamazoo	39	0
O9	● Western Michigan	42	0 *
O16	● at Nebraska	16	7
O23	● Valparaiso	28	3
O30	● at Army	27	17
N6	● Purdue	28	0
N13	● Indiana IND	13	10
N20	● at Northwestern	33	7
N25	● at Michigan State	25	0

1921 — 10-1-0
S24	● Kalamazoo	56	0
O1	● DePauw	57	10
O8	● at Iowa	7	10
O15	● at Purdue	33	0
O22	● Nebraska	7	0
O29	● Indiana IND	28	7
N5	● at Army	28	0
N8	● Rutgers NYC	48	0
N12	● Haskell	42	7
N19	● at Marquette	21	7
N24	● Michigan State	48	0

1922 — 8-1-1
S30	● Kalamazoo	46	0
O7	● St. Louis	26	0
O14	● at Purdue	20	0
O21	● DePauw	34	7
O28	● at Georgia Tech	13	3
N4	● Indiana	27	0
N11	= at Army	0	0
N18	● at Butler	31	3
N25	● at Carnegie Tech	19	0
N30	● at Nebraska	6	14

1923 — 9-1-0
S29	● Kalamazoo	74	0
O6	● Lombard	14	0
O13	● Army BKLN	13	0
O20	● at Princeton	25	2
O27	● Georgia Tech	35	7
N3	● Purdue	34	7
N10	● at Nebraska	7	14
N17	● Butler	34	7
N24	● at Carnegie Tech	26	0
N29	● at St. Louis	13	0

1924 — 10-0-0
O4	● Lombard	40	0
O11	● Wabash	34	0
O18	● Army NYC	13	7
O25	● at Princeton	12	0
N1	● Georgia Tech	34	3
N8	● at Wisconsin	38	3
N15	● Nebraska	34	6
N22	● Northwestern CHI	13	6
N29	● at Carnegie Tech	40	19
ROSE BOWL			
J1	● Stanford	27	10

1925 — 7-2-1
S26	● Baylor	41	0
O3	● Lombard	69	0
O10	● Beloit	19	3
O17	● Army BRNX	0	27
O24	● at Minnesota	19	7
O31	● at Georgia Tech	13	0
N7	● at Penn State	0	0
N14	● Carnegie Tech	26	0
N21	● Northwestern	13	10
N26	● at Nebraska	0	17

1926 — 9-1-0
O2	● Beloit	77	0
O9	● at Minnesota	20	7
O16	● Penn State	28	0
O23	● at Northwestern	6	0
O30	● Georgia Tech	12	0
N6	● Indiana	26	0
N13	● Army BRNX	7	0
N20	● Drake	21	0
N27	● at Carnegie Tech	0	19
D4	● at Southern Cal	13	12

1927 — 7-1-1
O1	● Coe	28	7
O8	● at Detroit	20	0
O15	● Navy BALT	19	6
O22	● at Indiana	19	6
O29	● Georgia Tech	26	7
N5	= Minnesota	7	7
N12	● Army BRNX	0	18
N19	● at Drake	32	0
N26	● Southern Cal CHI	7	6

1928 — 5-4-0
S29	● Loyola, La.	12	6
O6	● at Wisconsin	6	22
O13	● Navy CHI	7	0
O20	● at Georgia Tech	0	13
O27	● Drake	32	6
N3	● Penn State PHIL	9	0
N10	● Army BRNX	12	6
N17	● Carnegie Tech	7	27
D1	● at Southern Cal	14	27

1929 — 9-0-0
O5	● at Indiana	14	0
O12	● Navy BALT	14	7
O19	● Wisconsin CHI	19	0
O26	● at Carnegie Tech	7	0
N2	● at Georgia Tech	26	6
N9	● Drake CHI	19	7
N16	● Southern Cal CHI	13	12
N23	● at Northwestern	26	6
N30	● Army BRNX	7	0

1930 — 10-0-0
O4	● SMU	20	14
O11	● Navy	26	2
O18	● Carnegie Tech	21	6
O25	● at Pittsburgh	35	19
N1	● Indiana	27	0
N8	● at Pennsylvania	60	20
N15	● Drake	28	7
N22	● at Northwestern	14	0
N29	● Army CHI	7	6
D6	● at Southern Cal	27	0

HEARTLEY "HUNK" ANDERSON
1931-33 (.630)   16-9-2

1931 — 6-2-1
O3	● at Indiana	25	0
O10	= Northwestern CHI	0	0
O17	● Drake	63	0
O24	● Pittsburgh	25	12
O31	● at Carnegie Tech	19	0
N7	● Pennsylvania	49	0
N14	● Navy BALT	20	0
N21	● Southern Cal	14	16
N28	● Army BRNX	0	12

1932 — 7-2-0
O8	● Haskell	73	0
O15	● Drake	62	0
O22	● Carnegie Tech	42	0
O29	● at Pittsburgh	0	12
N5	● at Kansas	24	6
N12	● Northwestern CHI	21	0
N19	● Navy CLEV	12	0
N26	● Army BRNX	21	0
D10	● at Southern Cal	0	13

1933 — 3-5-1
O7	= Kansas	0	0
O14	● at Indiana	12	2
O21	● at Carnegie Tech	0	7
O28	● Pittsburgh	0	14
N4	● Navy BRNX	0	7
N11	● Purdue	0	19
N18	● at Northwestern	7	0
N25	● Southern Cal	0	19
D2	● Army BRNX	13	12

ELMER LAYDEN
1934-40 (.770)   47-13-3

1934 — 6-3-0
O6	● Texas	6	7
O13	● Purdue	18	7
O20	● Carnegie Tech	13	0
O27	● Wisconsin	19	0
N3	● at Pittsburgh	0	19
N10	● Navy BALT	6	10
N17	● at Northwestern	20	7
N24	● Army BRNX	12	6
D8	● at Southern Cal	14	0

1935 — 7-1-1
S28	● Kansas	28	7
O5	● at Carnegie Tech	14	3
O12	● at Wisconsin	27	0
O19	● Pittsburgh	9	6
O26	● Navy BALT	14	0
N2	● at Ohio State	18	13
N9	● Northwestern	7	14
N16	= Army BRNX	6	6
N23	● Southern Cal	20	13

1936 — 6-2-1
O3	● Carnegie Tech	21	7
O10	● Washington, Mo.	14	6
O17	● Wisconsin	27	0
O24	● at Pittsburgh	0	26
O31	● Ohio State	7	2
N7	● Navy BALT	0	3
N14	● Army BRNX	20	6
N21	● Northwestern	26	6
D5	= at Southern Cal	13	13

1937 — 6-2-1
O2	● Drake	21	0
O9	● at Illinois	0	0
O16	● at Carnegie Tech	7	9
O23	● Navy	9	7
O30	● at Minnesota	7	6
N6	● Pittsburgh	6	21
N13	● Army BRNX	7	0
N20	● at Northwestern	7	0
N27	● Southern Cal	13	6

1938 — 8-1-0
O1	● Kansas	52	0
O8	● at Georgia Tech	14	6
O15	● Illinois	14	6
O22	● Carnegie Tech	7	0
O29	● Army BRNX	19	7
N5	● Navy BALT	15	0
N12	● Minnesota	19	0
N19	● at Northwestern	9	7
D3	● at Southern Cal	0	13

1939 — 7-2-0
S30	● Purdue	3	0
O7	● Georgia Tech	17	14
O14	● SMU	20	19
O21	● Navy BALT	14	7
O28	● at Carnegie Tech	7	6
N4	● Army BRNX	14	0
N11	● at Iowa	6	7
N18	● Northwestern	7	0
N25	● Southern Cal	12	20

1940 — 7-2-0
O5	● Pacific	25	7
O12	● Georgia Tech	26	20
O19	● Carnegie Tech	61	0
O26	● at Illinois	26	0
N2	● Army BRNX	7	0
N9	● Navy BALT	13	7
N16	● Iowa	0	7
N23	● at Northwestern	0	20
D7	● at Southern Cal	10	6

FRANK LEAHY
1941-43, '46-53 (.855)   87-11-9

1941 — 8-0-1
S27	● Arizona	38	7
O4	● Indiana	19	6
O11	● at Georgia Tech	20	0
O18	● at Carnegie Tech	16	0
O25	● Illinois	49	14
N1	● Army BRNX	0	0
N8	● Navy BALT	20	13
N15	● at Northwestern	7	6
N22	● Southern Cal	20	18

1942 — 7-2-2
S26	● at Wisconsin	7	7
O3	● Georgia Tech	6	13
O10	● Stanford	27	0
O17	● Iowa Pre-Flight	28	0
O24	● at Illinois	21	14
O31	● Navy CLEV	9	0
N7	● Army BRNX	13	0
N14	● Michigan	20	32
N21	● Northwestern	27	20
N28	● at Southern Cal	13	0
D5	= Great Lakes NAS CHI	13	13

1943 — 9-1-0
S25	● at Pittsburgh	41	0
O2	● Georgia Tech	55	13
O9	● at Michigan	35	12
O16	● at Wisconsin	50	0
O23	● Illinois	47	0
O30	● Navy CLEV	33	6
N6	● Army BRNX	26	0
N13	● at Northwestern	25	6
N20	● Iowa Pre-Flight	14	13
N27	● Great Lakes NAS CHI	14	19

ED McKEEVER
1944 (.800)   8-2

1944 — 8-2-0
S30	● at Pittsburgh	58	0
O7	● Tulane	26	0
O14	● Dartmouth BOS	64	0
O21	● Wisconsin	28	13
O28	● at Illinois	13	7
N4	● Navy BALT	13	32
N11	● Army BRNX	0	59
N18	● Northwestern	21	0
N25	● at Georgia Tech	21	0
D2	● Great Lakes NAS	28	7

HUGH DEVORE
1945, '63 (.500)   9-9-1

1945 — 7-2-1
S29	● Illinois	7	0
O6	● at Georgia Tech	40	7
O13	● Dartmouth	34	0
O20	● at Pittsburgh	39	9
O27	● Iowa BRNX	56	0
N3	= Navy CLEV	6	6
N10	● Army	0	48
N17	● at Northwestern	34	7
N24	● at Tulane	32	6
D1	● at Great Lakes NAS	7	39

FRANK LEAHY

1946 — 8-0-1
S28	● at Illinois	26	6
O5	● Pittsburgh	33	0
O12	● Purdue	49	6
O26	● at Iowa	41	6
N2	● Navy BALT	28	0
N9	= Army BRNX	0	0
N16	● Northwestern	27	0
N23	● at Tulane	41	0
N30	● Southern Cal	26	6

1947 — 9-0-0
O4	● at Pittsburgh	40	6
O11	● at Purdue	22	7
O18	● Nebraska	31	0
O25	● Iowa	21	0
N1	● Navy CLEV	27	0
N8	● Army	27	7
N15	● at Northwestern	26	19
N22	● Tulane	59	6
D6	● at Southern Cal	38	7

1948 — 9-0-1
S25	● Purdue	28	27
O2	● at Pittsburgh	40	0
O9	● Michigan State	26	7
O16	● at Nebraska	44	13
O23	● at Iowa	27	12
O30	● Navy BALT	41	7
N6	● at Indiana	42	6
N13	● Northwestern	12	7
N27	● Washington	46	0
D4	● at Southern Cal	14	14

1949 — 10-0-0
S24	● Indiana	49	6
O1	● at Washington	27	7
O8	● at Purdue	35	12
O15	● Tulane	46	7
O29	● Navy BALT	40	0
N5	● at Michigan State	34	21
N12	● North Carolina BRNX	42	6
N19	● Iowa	28	7
N26	● Southern Cal	32	0
D3	● at SMU	27	20

1950 — 4-4-1
S30	● North Carolina	14	7
O7	● Purdue	14	28
O14	● at Tulane	13	9
O21	● at Indiana	7	20
O28	● Michigan State	33	36
N4	● Navy CLEV	19	10
N11	● Pittsburgh	18	7
N18	● at Iowa	14	14
D2	● at Southern Cal	7	9

1951 — 7-2-1
S29	● Indiana	48	6
O5	● Detroit DET	40	6
O13	SMU	20	27
O20	● at Pittsburgh	33	0
O27	● Purdue	30	9
N3	● Navy BALT	19	0
N10	● at Michigan State	0	35
N17	● at North Carolina	12	7
N24	= Iowa	20	20
D1	● at Southern Cal	19	12

THE SCHOOLS

1952 — 7-2-1
Date	Opponent		
S27 =	at Pennsylvania	7	7
O4 •	at Texas	14	3
O11	Pittsburgh	19	22
O18 •	at Purdue	26	14
O25	North Carolina	34	14
N1	Navy BALT	17	6
N8	Oklahoma	27	21
N15	at Michigan State	3	21
N22	at Iowa	27	0
N29	Southern Cal	9	0

1953 — 9-0-1
Date	Opponent		
S26 •	at Oklahoma	28	21
O3 •	at Purdue	37	7
O17	Pittsburgh	23	14
O24	Georgia Tech	27	14
O31	Navy	38	7
N7	at Pennsylvania	28	20
N14	at North Carolina	34	14
N21 =	Iowa	14	14
N28	at Southern Cal	48	14
D5	SMU	40	14

TERRY BRENNAN
1954-58 (.640)   32-18

1954 — 9-1-0
Date	Opponent		
S25 •	Texas	21	0
O2	Purdue	14	27
O9 •	at Pittsburgh	33	0
O16	Michigan State	20	19
O30	Navy BALT	6	0
N6	at Pennsylvania	42	7
N13	North Carolina	42	13
N20	at Iowa	34	18
N27 •	Southern Cal	23	17
D4	at SMU	26	14

1955 — 8-2-0
Date	Opponent		
S24 •	SMU	17	0
O1 •	Indiana	19	0
O7	at Miami, Fla.	14	0
O15	at Michigan State	7	21
O22	at Purdue	22	7
O29	Navy	21	7
N5	at Pennsylvania	46	14
N12	at North Carolina	27	7
N19	Iowa	17	14
N26	at Southern Cal	20	42

1956 — 2-8-0
Date	Opponent		
S22	at SMU	13	19
O6 •	Indiana	20	6
O13	Purdue	14	28
O20	Michigan State	14	47
O27	Oklahoma	0	40
N3	Navy BALT	7	33
N10	at Pittsburgh	13	26
N17	North Carolina	21	14
N24	at Iowa	8	48
D1	at Southern Cal	20	28

1957 — 7-3-0
Date	Opponent		
S28 •	at Purdue	12	0
O5 •	Indiana	26	0
O12 •	Army PHIL	23	21
O26 •	Pittsburgh	13	7
N2	Navy	6	20
N9	at Michigan State	6	34
N16 •	at Oklahoma	7	0
N23	Iowa	13	21
N30 •	Southern Cal	40	12
D7 •	at SMU	54	21

1958 — 6-4-0
Date	Opponent		
S27 •	Indiana	18	0
O4 •	at SMU	14	6
O11	Army	2	14
O18 •	Duke	9	7
O25	Purdue	22	29
N1	Navy BALT	40	20
N8	at Pittsburgh	26	29
N15	North Carolina	34	24
N22	at Iowa	21	31
N29	at Southern Cal	20	13

JOE KUHARICH
1959-62 (.425)   17-23

1959 — 5-5-0
Date	Opponent		
S26 •	North Carolina	28	8
O3	at Purdue	7	28
O10 •	at California	28	6
O17	at Michigan State	0	19
O24	Northwestern	24	30
O31 •	Navy	25	22
N7	Georgia Tech	10	14
N14	at Pittsburgh	13	28
N21 •	at Iowa	20	19
N28 •	Southern Cal	16	6

1960 — 2-8-0
Date	Opponent		
S24 •	California	21	7
O1	Purdue	19	51
O8	at North Carolina	7	12
O15	Michigan State	0	21
O22	at Northwestern	6	7
O29	Navy PHIL	7	14
N5	Pittsburgh	13	20
N12	at Miami, Fla.	21	28
N19	Iowa	0	28
N26	at Southern Cal	17	0

1961 — 5-5-0
Date	Opponent		
S30 •	Oklahoma	19	6
O7 •	at Purdue	22	20
O14 •	Southern Cal	30	0
O21	at Michigan State	7	17
O28	Northwestern	10	12
N4	Navy	10	13
N11 •	at Pittsburgh	26	20
N18 •	Syracuse	17	15
N25	at Iowa	21	42
D2	at Duke	13	37

1962 — 5-5-0
Date	Opponent		
S29 •	at Oklahoma	13	7
O6	Purdue	6	24
O13	at Wisconsin	8	17
O20	Michigan State	7	31
O27	at Northwestern	6	35
N3	Navy PHIL	20	12
N10	Pittsburgh	43	22
N17	North Carolina	21	7
N24	Iowa	35	12
D1	at Southern Cal	0	25

HUGH DEVORE

1963 — 2-7-0
Date	Opponent		
S28	Wisconsin	9	14
O5	at Purdue	6	7
O12 •	Southern Cal	17	14
O19 •	UCLA	27	12
O26	at Stanford	14	24
N2	Navy	14	35
N9	Pittsburgh	7	27
N16	at Michigan State	7	12
N28	Syracuse BRNX	7	14

ARA PARSEGHIAN
1964-74 (.836)   95-17-4

1964 — 9-1-0
Date	Opponent		
S26 •	at Wisconsin	31	7
O3 •	Purdue	34	15
O10 •	at Air Force	34	7
O17 •	UCLA	24	0
O24 •	Stanford	28	6
O31 •	Navy	40	0
N7 •	at Pittsburgh	17	15
N14 •	Michigan State	34	7
N21 •	Iowa	28	0
N28	at Southern Cal	17	20

1965 — 7-2-1
Date	Opponent		
S18 •	at California	48	6
S25 •	at Purdue	21	25
O2 •	Northwestern	38	7
O9 •	Army FLU	17	0
O23 •	Southern Cal	28	7
O30 •	Navy	29	3
N6 •	at Pittsburgh	69	13
N13 •	North Carolina	17	0
N20 •	Michigan State	3	12
N27 =	at Miami, Fla.	0	0

1966 — 9-0-1
Date	Opponent		
S24 •	Purdue	26	14
O1 •	at Northwestern	35	7
O8 •	Army	35	0
O15 •	North Carolina	32	0
O22 •	at Oklahoma	38	0
O29 •	Navy PHIL	31	7
N5 •	Pittsburgh	40	0
N12 •	Duke	64	0
N19 =	at Michigan State	10	10
N26 •	at Southern Cal	51	0

1967 — 8-2-0
Date	Opponent		
S23 •	California	41	8
S30 •	at Purdue	21	28
O7 •	Iowa	56	6
O14 •	Southern Cal	7	24
O21 •	at Illinois	47	7
O28 •	Michigan State	24	12
N4 •	Navy	43	14
N11 •	at Pittsburgh	38	0
N18 •	at Georgia Tech	36	3
N24 •	at Miami, Fla.	24	22

1968 — 7-2-1
Date	Opponent		
S21 •	Oklahoma	45	21
S28 •	Purdue	22	37
O5 •	at Iowa	51	28
O12 •	Northwestern	27	7
O19 •	Illinois	58	8
O26 •	at Michigan State	17	21
N2 •	Navy PHIL	45	14
N9 •	Pittsburgh	56	7
N16 •	Georgia Tech	34	6
N30 =	at Southern Cal	21	21

1969 — 8-2-1
Date	Opponent		
S20 •	Northwestern	35	10
S27 •	at Purdue	14	28
O4 •	Michigan State	42	28
O11 •	Army BRNX	45	0
O18 •	Southern Cal	14	14
O25 •	at Tulane	37	0
N1 •	Navy	47	0
N8 •	at Pittsburgh	49	7
N15 •	at Georgia Tech	38	20
N22 •	Air Force	13	6
COTTON BOWL			
J1	Texas	17	21

1970 — 10-1-0
Date	Opponent		
S19 •	at Northwestern	35	14
S26 •	Purdue	48	0
O3 •	at Michigan State	29	0
O10 •	Army	51	10
O17 •	at Missouri	24	7
O31 •	Navy PHIL	56	7
N7 •	Pittsburgh	46	14
N14 •	Georgia Tech	10	7
N21 •	LSU	3	0
N28 •	at Southern Cal	28	38
COTTON BOWL			
J1	Texas	24	11

1971 — 8-2-0
Date	Opponent		
S18 •	Northwestern	50	7
S25 •	at Purdue	8	7
O2 •	Michigan State	14	2
O9 •	at Miami, Fla.	17	0
O16 •	North Carolina	16	0
O23 •	Southern Cal	14	28
O30 •	Navy	21	0
N6 •	at Pittsburgh	56	7
N13 •	Tulane	21	7
N20 •	at LSU	8	28

1972 — 8-3-0
Date	Opponent		
S23 •	at Northwestern	37	0
S30 •	Purdue	35	14
O7 •	at Michigan State	16	0
O14 •	Pittsburgh	42	16
O21 •	Missouri	26	30
O28 •	TCU	21	0
N4 •	Navy PHIL	42	23
N11 •	at Air Force	21	7
N18 •	Miami, Fla.	20	17
D2 •	at Southern Cal	23	45
ORANGE BOWL			
J1	Nebraska	6	40

1973 — 11-0-0
Date	Opponent		
S22 •	Northwestern	44	0
S29 •	at Purdue	20	7
O6 •	Michigan State	14	10
O13 •	at Rice	28	0
O20 •	at Army	62	3
O27 •	Southern Cal	23	14
N3 •	Navy	44	7
N10 •	at Pittsburgh	31	10
N22 •	Air Force	48	15
D1 •	at Miami, Fla.	44	0
SUGAR BOWL			
D31 •	Alabama	24	23

1974 — 10-2-0
Date	Opponent		
S9 •	at Georgia Tech	31	7
S21 •	at Northwestern	49	3
S28 •	Purdue	20	31
O5 •	at Michigan State	19	14
O12 •	Rice	10	3
O19 •	Army	48	0
O26 •	Miami, Fla.	38	7
N2 •	Navy PHIL	14	6
N16 •	Pittsburgh	14	10
N23 •	Air Force	38	0
N30 •	at Southern Cal	24	55
ORANGE BOWL			
J1 •	Alabama	13	11

DAN DEVINE
1975-80 (.764)   53-16-1

1975 — 8-3-0
Date	Opponent		
S15 •	Boston College FOX	17	3
S20 •	at Purdue	17	0
S27 •	Northwestern	31	7
O4 •	Michigan State	3	10
O11 •	at North Carolina	21	14
O18 •	at Air Force	31	30
O25 •	Southern Cal	17	24
N1 •	Navy	31	10
N8 •	Georgia Tech	24	3
N15 •	at Pittsburgh	20	34
N22 •	at Miami, Fla.	32	9

1976 — 9-3-0
Date	Opponent		
S11 •	Pittsburgh	10	31
S18 •	Purdue	23	0
S25 •	at Northwestern	48	0
O2 •	at Michigan State	24	6
O16 •	Oregon	41	0
O23 •	at South Carolina	13	6
O30 •	Navy CLEV	27	21
N6 •	at Georgia Tech	14	23
N13 •	Alabama	21	18
N20 •	Miami, Fla.	40	27
N27 •	at Southern Cal	13	17
GATOR BOWL			
D27 •	Penn State	20	9

1977 — 11-1-0
Date	Opponent		
S10 •	at Pittsburgh	19	9
S17 •	Mississippi JAM	13	20
S24 •	at Purdue	31	24
O1 •	Michigan State	16	6
O15 •	Army ERUT	24	0
O22 •	Southern Cal	49	19
O29 •	Navy	43	10
N5 •	Georgia Tech	69	14
N12 •	at Clemson	21	17
N19 •	Air Force	49	0
D3 •	at Miami, Fla.	48	10
COTTON BOWL			
J2 •	Texas	38	10

1978 — 9-3-0
Date	Opponent		
S9 •	Missouri	0	3
S23 •	Michigan	14	28
S30 •	Purdue	10	6
O7 •	at Michigan State	29	25
O14 •	Pittsburgh	26	17
O21 •	at Air Force	38	15
O28 •	Miami, Fla.	20	0
N4 •	Navy CLEV	27	7
N11 •	Tennessee	31	14
N18 •	at Georgia Tech	38	21
N25 •	at Southern Cal	25	27
COTTON BOWL			
J1 •	Houston	35	34

1979 — 7-4-0
Date	Opponent		
S15 •	at Michigan	12	10
S22 •	at Purdue	22	28
S29 •	Michigan State	27	3
O6 •	Georgia Tech	21	13
O13 •	at Air Force	38	13
O20 •	Southern Cal	23	42
O27 •	South Carolina	18	17
N3 •	Navy	14	0
N10 •	at Tennessee	18	40
N17 •	Clemson	10	16
N24 •	Miami, Fla. TOK	40	15

1980 — 9-2-1
Date	Opponent		
S6 •	Purdue	31	10
S20 •	Michigan	29	27
O4 •	at Michigan State	26	21
O11 •	Miami, Fla.	32	14
O18 •	Army	30	3
O25 •	at Arizona	20	3
N1 •	Navy ERUT	33	0
N8 =	at Georgia Tech	3	3
N15 •	Alabama BIRM	7	0
N22 •	Air Force	24	10
D6 •	at Southern Cal	3	20
SUGAR BOWL			
J1	Georgia	10	17

GERRY FAUST
1981-85 (.535)   30-26-1

1981 — 5-6-0
	Opponent		
S12	•	LSU	27 9
S19		at Michigan	7 25
S26		at Purdue	14 15
O3	•	Michigan State	20 7
O10		Florida State	13 19
O24		Southern Cal	7 14
O31	•	Navy	38 0
N7		Georgia Tech	35 3
N14	•	at Air Force	35 7
N21		at Penn State	21 24
N27		at Miami, Fla.	15 37

1982 — 6-4-1
	Opponent		
S18	•	Michigan	23 17
S25	•	Purdue	28 14
O2	•	at Michigan State	11 3
O9	•	Miami, Fla.	16 14
O16		Arizona	13 16
O23	=	at Oregon	13 13
O30	•	Navy *ERut*	27 10
N6	•	at Pittsburgh	31 16
N13		Penn State	14 24
N20		at Air Force	17 30
N27		at Southern Cal	13 17

1983 — 7-5-0
	Opponent		
S10	•	at Purdue	52 6
S17	•	Michigan State	23 28
S24		at Miami, Fla.	0 20
O1	•	at Colorado	27 3
O8	•	at South Carolina	30 6
O15		Army *ERut*	42 0
O22	•	Southern Cal	27 6
O29	•	Navy	28 12
N5		Pittsburgh	16 21
N12		at Penn State	30 34
N19		Air Force	22 23
LIBERTY BOWL			
D29	•	Boston College	19 18

1984 — 7-5-0
	Opponent		
S8		Purdue *IND*	21 23
S15	•	at Michigan State	24 20
S22	•	Colorado	55 14
S29	•	at Missouri	16 14
O6		Miami, Fla.	13 31
O13		Air Force	7 21
O20		South Carolina	32 36
O27		at LSU	30 22
N3	•	Navy *ERut*	18 17
N17		Penn State	44 7
N24		at Southern Cal	19 7
ALOHA BOWL			
D29		SMU	20 27

1985 — 5-6-0
	Opponent		
S14		at Michigan	12 20
S21	•	Michigan State	27 10
S28		at Purdue	17 35
O5		at Air Force	15 21
O19	•	Army	24 10
O26	•	Southern Cal	37 3
N2	•	Navy	41 17
N9	•	Mississippi	37 14
N16		at Penn State	6 36
N23		LSU	7 10
N30		at Miami, Fla.	7 58

LOU HOLTZ
1986-96 (.765)   100-30-2

1986 — 5-6-0
	Opponent		
S13		Michigan	23 24
S20		at Michigan State	15 20
S27	•	Purdue	41 9
O4		Alabama *BIRM*	10 28
O11		Pittsburgh	9 10
O18	•	Air Force	31 3
N1	•	Navy *BALT*	33 14
N8	•	SMU	61 29
N15		Penn State	19 24
N22		at LSU	19 21
N29	•	at Southern Cal	38 37

1987 — 8-4-0
	Opponent		
S12	•	at Michigan	26 7
S19	•	Michigan State	31 8
S26	•	Purdue	44 20
O10		at Pittsburgh	22 30
O17	•	at Air Force	35 14
O24	•	Southern Cal	26 15
O31	•	Navy	56 13
N7	•	Boston College	32 25
N14	•	Alabama	37 6
N21		at Penn State	20 21
N28	•	at Miami, Fla.	0 24
COTTON BOWL			
J1		Texas A&M	10 35

1988 — 12-0-0
	Opponent		
S10	•	Michigan	19 17
S17	•	at Michigan State	20 3
S24	•	Purdue	52 7
O1	•	Stanford	42 14
O8	•	at Pittsburgh	30 20
O15	•	Miami, Fla.	31 30
O22	•	Air Force	41 13
O29	•	Navy *BALT*	22 7
N5	•	Rice	54 11
N19	•	Penn State	21 3
N26	•	at Southern Cal	27 10
FIESTA BOWL			
J2	•	West Virginia	34 21

1989 — 12-1-0
	Opponent		
A31	•	Virginia *ERut*	36 13
S16	•	at Michigan	24 19
S23	•	Michigan State	21 13
S30	•	at Purdue	40 7
O7	•	at Stanford	27 17
O14	•	at Air Force	41 27
O21	•	Southern Cal	28 24
O28	•	Pittsburgh	45 7
N4	•	Navy	41 0
N11	•	SMU	59 6
N18	•	at Penn State	34 23
N25	•	at Miami, Fla.	10 27
ORANGE BOWL			
J1	•	Colorado	21 6

1990 — 9-3-0
	Opponent		
S15	•	Michigan	28 24
S22	•	at Michigan State	20 19
S29	•	Purdue	37 11
O6	•	Stanford	31 36
O13	•	Air Force	57 27
O20	•	Miami, Fla.	29 20
O27	•	at Pittsburgh	31 22
N3	•	Navy *ERut*	52 31
N10	•	at Tennessee	34 29
N17	•	Penn State	21 24
N24	•	at Southern Cal	10 6
ORANGE BOWL			
J1		Colorado	9 10

1991 — 10-3-0
	Opponent		
S7	•	Indiana	49 27
S14	•	at Michigan	14 24
S21	•	Michigan State	49 10
S28	•	at Purdue	45 20
O5	•	at Stanford	42 26
O12	•	Pittsburgh	42 7
O19	•	at Air Force	28 15
O26	•	Southern Cal	24 20
N2	•	Navy	38 0
N9		Tennessee	34 35
N16		at Penn State	13 35
N30		at Hawaii	48 42
SUGAR BOWL			
J1	•	Florida	39 28

1992 — 10-1-1
	Opponent		
S5	•	Northwestern *CHI*	42 7
S12	= •	Michigan	17 17
S19	•	at Michigan State	52 31
S26	•	Purdue	48 0
O3		Stanford	16 33
O10	•	at Pittsburgh	52 21
O24	•	Brigham Young	42 16
O31	•	Navy *ERut*	38 7
N7	•	Boston College	54 7
N14	•	Penn State	17 16
N28	•	at Southern Cal	31 23
COTTON BOWL			
J1	•	Texas A&M	28 3

1993 — 11-1-0
	Opponent		
S4	•	Northwestern	27 12
S11	•	at Michigan	27 23
S18	•	Michigan State	36 14
S25	•	at Purdue	17 0
O2	•	at Stanford	48 20
O9	•	Pittsburgh	44 0
O16	•	at Brigham Young	45 20
O23	•	Southern Cal	31 13
O30	•	Navy *PHIL*	58 27
N13	•	Florida State	31 24
N20	•	Boston College	39 41
COTTON BOWL			
J1	•	Texas A&M	24 21

1994 — 6-5-1
	Opponent		
S3	•	Northwestern *CHI*	42 15
S10	•	Michigan	24 26
S17	•	at Michigan State	21 20
S24	•	Purdue	39 21
O1	•	Stanford	34 15
O8	•	at Boston College	11 30
O15	•	Brigham Young	14 21
O29	•	Navy	58 21
N12	•	Florida State *ORL*	16 23
N19	•	Air Force	42 30
N26	=	at Southern Cal	17 17
FIESTA BOWL			
J2	•	Colorado	24 41

1995 — 9-3-0
	Opponent		
S2	•	Northwestern	15 17
S9	•	at Purdue	35 28
S16	•	Vanderbilt	41 0
S23	•	Texas	55 27
S30	•	at Ohio State	26 45
O7	•	at Washington	29 21
O14	•	Army *ERut*	28 27
O21	•	Southern Cal	38 10
O28	•	Boston College	20 10
N4	•	Navy	35 17
N18	•	at Air Force	44 14
ORANGE BOWL			
J1		Florida State	26 31

1996 — 8-3
	Opponent		
S5	•	at Vanderbilt	14 7
S14	•	Purdue	35 0
S21	•	at Texas	27 24
S28	•	Ohio State	16 29
O12	•	Washington	54 20
O19	•	Air Force	17 20
N2	•	Navy *DUB*	54 21
N9	•	at Boston College	48 21
N16	•	Pittsburgh	60 6
N23	•	Rutgers	62 0
N30	•	at Southern Cal	20 27

BOB DAVIE
1997-2001 (.583)   35-25

1997 — 7-6
	Opponent		
S6	•	Georgia Tech	17 13
S13	•	at Purdue	17 28
S20	•	Michigan State	7 23
S27	•	at Michigan	14 21
O4	•	at Stanford	15 33
O11	•	at Pittsburgh	45 21
O18	•	Southern Cal	17 20
O25	•	Boston College	52 20
N1	•	Navy	21 17
N15	•	at LSU	24 6
N22	•	West Virginia	21 14
INDEPENDENCE BOWL			
N29	•	at Hawaii	23 22
D28	•	LSU	9 27

1998 — 9-3
	Opponent		
S5	•	Michigan	36 20
S12	•	at Michigan State	23 45
S26	•	Purdue	31 30
O3	•	Stanford	35 17
O10	•	at Arizona State	28 9
O24	•	Army	20 17
O31	•	Baylor	27 3
N7	•	at Boston College	31 26
N14	•	Navy *RAJ*	30 0
N21	•	LSU	39 36
N28	•	at Southern Cal	0 10
GATOR BOWL			
J1	•	Georgia Tech	28 35

1999 — 5-7
	Opponent		
A28	•	Kansas	48 13
S4	•	at Michigan	22 26
S11	•	at Purdue	23 28
S18	•	Michigan State	13 23
O2	•	Oklahoma	34 30
O9	•	Arizona State	48 17
O16	•	Southern Cal	25 24
O30	•	Navy	28 24
N6	•	at Tennessee	14 38
N13	•	at Pittsburgh	27 37
N20	•	Boston College	29 31
N27	•	at Stanford	37 40

2000 — 9-3
	Opponent		
S2	•	Texas A&M	24 10
S9	•	Nebraska	24 27
S16	•	Purdue	23 21
S23	•	at Michigan State	21 27
O7	•	Stanford	20 14
O14	•	Navy *ORL*	45 14
O21	•	at West Virginia	42 28
O28	•	Air Force	34 31
N11	•	Boston College	28 16
N18	•	at Rutgers	45 17
N25	•	at Southern Cal	38 21
FIESTA BOWL			
J1		Oregon State	9 41

2001 — 5-6
	Opponent		
S8	•	at Nebraska	10 27
S22	•	Michigan State	10 17
S29	•	at Texas A&M	3 24
O6	•	Pittsburgh	24 7
O13	•	West Virginia	34 24
O20	•	Southern Cal	27 16
O27	•	at Boston College	17 21
N3		Tennessee	18 28
N17	•	Navy	34 16
N24	•	at Stanford	13 17
D1	•	at Purdue	24 18

TYRONE WILLINGHAM
2002-04 (.583)   21-15

2002 — 10-3
	Opponent		
A31	•	Maryland *ERut*	22 0
S7	•	Purdue	24 17
S14	•	Michigan	25 23
S21	•	at Michigan State	21 17
O5	•	Stanford	31 7
O12	•	Pittsburgh	14 6
O19	•	at Air Force	21 14
O26	•	at Florida State	34 24
N2	•	Boston College	7 14
N9	•	Navy *BALT*	30 23
N23	•	Rutgers	42 0
N30	•	at Southern Cal	13 44
GATOR BOWL			
J1	•	North Carolina St.	6 28

2003 — 5-7
	Opponent		
S6	•	Washington State	29 26
S13	•	at Michigan	0 38
S20	•	Michigan State	16 22
S27	•	at Purdue	10 23
O11	•	at Pittsburgh	20 14
O18	•	Southern Cal	14 45
O25	•	at Boston College	25 27
N1	•	Florida State	0 37
N8	•	Navy	27 24
N15	•	Brigham Young	33 14
N29	•	at Stanford	57 7
D6	•	at Syracuse	12 38

KENT BAER
2004 (.000)   0-1

2004 — 6-6
	Opponent		
S4	•	at Brigham Young	17 20
S11	•	Michigan	28 20
S18	•	at Michigan State	31 24
S25	•	Washington	38 3
O2		Purdue	16 41
O9	•	Stanford	23 15
O16	•	Navy *ERut*	27 9
O23		Boston College	23 24
N6	•	at Tennessee	17 13
N13		Pittsburgh	38 41
N27		at Southern Cal	10 41
INSIGHT BOWL			
D28	•	Oregon State	21 38

OHIO

BY ED KRZEMIENSKI

LIKE EVERY COLLEGE IN THE STATE, Ohio University looks with a degree of envy at the football monster in Columbus. For Ohio U., though, there is a bit of spite added to the envy, since the Ohio State University not only drains the state of recruits, but hijacked the name Ohio itself—both for its stadium and as its band's halftime signature. While it may not be the seat of Western civilization, or hold the best football team in the state, the university at Athens still does have a fairly rich football tradition. From the late 1920s through World War II, the Bobcats dominated the Buckeye conference, going undefeated three times. In the 1960s, Ohio frequently stood atop the MAC, winning or sharing the conference title four times in that decade. After four separate consecutive losing seasons, things look more promising as the school hired former Nebraska coach Frank Solich after the 2004 season.

TRADITION The team plays Marshall University annually in the Battle for the Bell. Playing for a mounted bell from an Ohio River steamboat, the teams first met in 1905. Played off and on until Marshall's admission into the MAC, the rivalry marked its 50th meeting in 2002.

BEST PLAYER Vince Costello certainly became the greatest Ohio football alum, playing 12 years as a linebacker in the NFL, but his collegiate accolades include only a second-team All-MAC selection at center in his 1952 senior season. But for accomplishments as a Bobcat, no one surpasses Todd Snyder, who set school records for receptions and yards in each of his varsity seasons, 1967 to 1969: 33 catches for 629 yards, 46 for 777 and 62 for 835, respectively. He also led the team in scoring his senior season and remains at or near the top of every school receiving record.

BEST COACH No one comes close to Don Peden. An Ohio alum (class of 1914), Peden compiled a 121–46–11 record from 1924 to 1946, with the 1943 and 1944 seasons canceled. That is a .711 winning percentage (Bear Bryant's, in comparison, is .780). His teams went undefeated three times, and his only losing season was in 1945. Peden's accomplishments are legendary, and who can argue with having a stadium named after him?

BEST TEAM The competition was a lesser caliber, the players were smaller, the ball was rounder and the stock market crashed midseason. Still, it's difficult to overlook the accomplishment of Ohio's 1929 squad. That season, Don Peden's team won the Buckeye A.A. championship with a 9–0 record, including a victory over the Big Ten's Indiana. Most amazingly, though, the team gave up only seven points all season. Only Ohio Wesleyan scored on the Bobcats, who

---

PROFILE

Ohio University
Athens, Ohio
Founded: 1804
Enrollment: 16,854
Colors: Hunter Green and White
Nickname: Bobcats
Stadium: Peden Stadium
 Opened in 1929
 FieldTurf; 24,000 capacity
First football game: 1894
All-time record: 467–486–48 (.491)
Bowl record: 0–2
Mid-American Conference championships:
5 (4 outright)
First-round NFL draftees: 1
Website: www.ohiobobcats.com

THE BEST OF TIMES

1959-68: a 62–36–2 cumulative record, four MAC championships and two bowl appearances.

THE WORST OF TIMES

1985 to 1995: a 19–97–5 cumulative record, a 15-game losing streak and three 12-game losing streaks.

CONFERENCE

Ohio was a charter member of the Mid-American Conference in 1946 (the conference began play in 1947) and has remained there since.

DISTINGUISHED ALUMNI

Matt Lauer; Paul Newman; Clarence Page, journalist; Mike Schmidt, baseball Hall of Famer; George Voinovich, U.S. senator and Ohio governor

FIGHT SONG

STAND UP AND CHEER
Stand up and cheer,
Cheer loud and long for old Ohio,
For today we raise The Green and White above the rest.
Our team is fighting
And we are bound to win the fray.
We've got the team,
We've got the steam,
For this is old Ohio's day!
Rah! Rah! Rah!

finished the season with a 305–7 scoring margin. From 1929 to 1931, Ohio went 24–1–1, outscoring its opponents 704 to 53. In the modern era, the 1968 squad stands out. That team won the MAC with an undefeated regular season before losing to Richmond by seven points in the Tangerine Bowl. While defense set the 1929 team apart, offense made the 1968 Bobcats go. Dave LeVeck ran for 850 yards, Cleve Bryant passed for 1,524, Todd Snyder caught 46 passes for 777 yards and Bob Houmard scored 19 touchdowns, each school records at the time. Houmard's mark of 114 points still stands.

Marshall judges Ohio as its greatest rival and the two schools play annually in the Battle for the Bell, but Ohio vs. Miami (Ohio) has a more consistent history.

Gophers ended the 1999 season ranked No. 18 and Ohio had not defeated a Big Ten opponent since it beat Northwestern in 1973, the Bobcats upset Minnesota 23-17. Halfback Chad Brinker served as the hero. Brinker ran for 119 yards and had a 50-yard touchdown reception, and passed for another touchdown. Ohio completed three passes all game. Minnesota was not especially down in 2000, either. The Gophers ended the season in a bowl game.

BIGGEST GAME On Nov. 12, 1960, the Bobcats traveled to Bowling Green for a MAC clash of titans. Both teams were undefeated for the year, and the Falcons were riding an 18-game winning streak that included an undefeated 1959 season. In a thriller, Ohio won the game 14-7 and dethroned Bowling Green as MAC and National College Division champions.

BIGGEST UPSET In the second game of the 2000 season, Ohio played at Minnesota. Despite the facts that the

HEARTBREAKER After riding the most powerful offense in school history to an undefeated regular season and Top 20 rankings in AP and UPI polls, the 1968 Bobcats faced the Richmond Spiders in a Tangerine Bowl that promised to be a shootout. It was. Cleve Bryant threw four touchdown passes, including three to Todd Snyder, who caught 11 passes for 214 yards. In the end, the Bobcats put up 42 points on the scoreboard. But, Richmond put up 49 to end Ohio's undefeated season.

BEST COMEBACK With the clock winding down, Ohio trailed Bowling Green 27-14; it looked as if Ohio's 1968

RECORDS

RUSHING YARDS

	GAME
282	Kareem Wilson vs. Bowling Green, Oct. 26, 1996 (19 att.)
	SEASON
1,315	Steveland Hookfin, 1998 (273 att.)
	CAREER
3,972	Steveland Hookfin, 1995-98 (767 att.)

PASSING YARDS

	GAME
409	Donny Harrison vs. Kent State, Oct. 22, 1983 (29 of 45)
	SEASON
2,366	Sammy Shon, 1981 (175 of 320)
	CAREER
5,412	Sammy Shon, 1978-81 (452 of 805)

RECEIVING YARDS

	GAME
214	Todd Snyder vs. Richmond, Dec. 27, 1968 (11 rec.)
	SEASON
866	Eddie Washington, 1983 (68 rec.)
	CAREER
2,241	Todd Snyder, 1967-69 (141 rec.)

POINTS

	GAME
33	Eller Armbrust vs. Rio Grande, Sept. 18, 1937
	SEASON
114	Bob Houmard, 1968 (19 TDs)
	CAREER
302	Kareem Wilson, 1995-98 (49 TDs, 4 two-pt. conv.)

CONSENSUS ALL-AMERICANS

1935	Art Lewis, T
1960	Dick Grecni, C

unbeaten season would end. Destiny sided with Ohio that Saturday. Ohio scored two touchdowns in the game's final 4:20, winning 28-27.

WILDEST FINISH In 1968, Ohio defeated Cincinnati 60-48. Combined, the teams produced 1,175 total yards and 67 first downs. In fact, though, the teams accomplished these feats in 59 minutes and 46 seconds of game time. With 14 seconds left, a massive fight between the Bobcats and Bearcats broke out and officials stopped the game.

STADIUM In its 74th season hosting the Bobcats, Peden Stadium stands as one of college football's bucolic jewels. The 24,000 capacity makes Ohio's home field cozy, but recent renovations added state-of-the-art practice and training facilities to the old house.

RIVAL Although Marshall judges Ohio as its greatest rival and the two schools play annually in the Battle for the Bell, Ohio vs. Miami (Ohio) has a more consistent history. The Bobcats and RedHawks, née Redskins, first played in 1908 and began a series of uninterrupted annual meetings beginning in 1928 (with a break for two years during World War II). Ohio trails the series against Miami by a 29–50–2 margin.

NICKNAME In 1925, Hal Rowland won $10 for proposing Bobcats as the new Ohio nickname. The animal was chosen due to its reputation as a sly, wily and scrappy animal. Any animal would have been an improvement: prior to that year, the team was known as the Green and White.

MASCOT In addition to the costumed Bobcat, Ohio introduced Sir Winsalot to its family in 1983. Owned by an Ohio alum and kept at his house, Sir Winsalot was joined by Paws and moved to the Columbus Zoo in 1986. Sir Winsalot died in 1999 and Paws died in 2002. There have been no official replacements, athough the plaque commemorating the cats still stands at the zoo.

UNIFORMS Hunter green home jerseys with white numbers and player's name on the back over white pants with a double green stripe up the side mark the Bobcats on their home field. On the road, the colors are flipped: white jerseys and green or white pants. The team wears white helmets with an arched Ohio across the side. In years past, the helmets sported a paw print and an outline of the state of Ohio with the namesake within.

QUIRK Which side are you on? Two of the greatest players in Ohio Bobcats history, Vince Costello and Dick Grecni, played both ways in college, and each made all-MAC squads at center. Both spent their entire professional careers as linebackers—Costello with the Cleveland Browns and New York Giants, and Grecni with the Minnesota Vikings.

LORE The man given credit for introducing the first football—not just football, but the first football—to the Ohio campus is John Brough, who, in 1826, was fond of kicking the ball over the campus' Center Building, now Cutler Hall. Kicking a ball over a building is impressive enough, but Brough added something else to his resume: on Jan. 11, 1864, he was inaugurated as governor of Ohio.

QUOTE "That will be enough of that s---! We're going after their asses!"—Coach Bill Hess, shouting at staff members in 1959 after 15 winless years against Miami. It worked. Ohio won in 1960, kickstarting a five-year winning streak versus its rival

OHIO ANNUAL STATISTICAL LEADERS

YR	RUSHING	YDS	ATT	AVG	PASSING	ATT	CMP	PCT	YDS	RECEIVING	REC	YDS	AVG
1962	Jim Albert	397	88	4.5	Bob Babbitt	113	57	.50	1,010	Jim Albert	14	304	21.7
1963	Jim Albert	707	122	5.8	Wes Dayno	108	42	.39	635	Jim Albert	13	186	14.3
1964	Wash Lyons	835	192	4.3	Larry Bainter	79	30	.38	443	Jim Dorna	15	162	10.8
1965	Sam Bogan	308	75	4.1	Sam Fornsaglio	51	26	.51	305	Dick Conley	15	305	20.3
1966	Bob Houmard	641	189	3.4	Ron DeLucca	111	44	.40	655	Jay Maupin	26	447	17.2
1967	Dick Conley	841	226	3.7	Cleve Bryant	180	68	.38	1,157	Todd Snyder	33	629	19.1
1968	Dave LeVeck	850	175	4.9	Cleve Bryant	200	98	.49	1,524	Todd Snyder	46	777	16.9
1969	Dave LeVeck	464	106	4.4	Steve Skiver	109	47	.43	749	Todd Snyder	62	835	13.5
1970	Bill Gary	1,064	265	4.0	Steve Skiver	229	107	.47	1,417	Bob Allen	48	699	14.6
1971	Dave Juenger	646	211	3.1	Dave Juenger	163	80	.49	922	Bob Allen	37	485	13.1
1972	L.C. Lyons	554	161	3.4	Rich Bevly	132	56	.42	865	Dave Juenger	32	508	15.9
1973	Dave Houseton	731	209	3.5	Rich Bevly	147	62	.42	1,007	Mike Green	22	425	19.3
1974	L.C. Lyons	928	231	4.0	Rich Bevly	173	71	.41	1,001	Rick Lilienthal	22	315	14.3
1975	Arnold Welcher	1,175	236	5.0	Rick Lilienthal	215	84	.39	982	Mike Green	50	642	12.8
1976	Arnold Welcher	1,034	213	4.9	Andy Vetter	135	71	.53	877	Phil Buckner	12	226	18.8
1977	Kevin Babcock	585	147	4.0	Andy Vetter	202	116	.57	1,548	Nigel Turpin	46	624	13.6
1978	Kevin Babcock	866	232	3.7	Mike Scimeca	93	40	.43	483	Mark Geisler	25	244	9.8
1979	Tony Carifa	727	156	4.7	Sammy Shon	220	133	.60	1,336	Tony Carifa	45	380	8.4
1980	Tony Carifa	853	198	4.3	Sammy Shon	235	131	.56	1,527	Mark Green	30	489	16.3
1981	Todd Yoho	500	113	4.4	Sammy Shon	320	175	.55	2,366	Shawn Silcott	39	573	14.7
1982	Orvell Johns	451	130	3.5	Donny Harrison	198	114	.58	1,308	Eddie Washington	37	524	14.2
1983	Glenn Hunter	338	92	3.7	Donny Harrison	357	203	.57	2,309	Eddie Washington	68	866	12.7
1984	Glenn Hunter	800	228	3.5	Dennis Swearingen	185	117	.63	1,211	Tom Compernolle	36	459	12.8
1985	Jesse Owens	709	209	3.4	Dennis Swearingen	383	195	.51	2,056	Tom Compernolle	46	524	11.4
1986	Jesse Owens	557	161	3.5	Bruce Porter	383	216	.56	2,281	Tom Compernolle	61	626	10.3
1987	John Caldwell	950	238	4.0	Anthony Thornton	180	75	.42	949	Cyle Feldman	21	302	14.4
1988	Andrew Greer	863	193	4.5	Anthony Thornton	187	78	.42	1,162	Byron Cross	20	342	17.1
1989	Andrew Greer	905	192	4.7	Anthony Thornton	234	120	.51	1,502	Jim Swanson	37	503	13.6
1990	Rickey Howell	832	192	4.3	Anthony Thornton	228	125	.55	1,586	Gerald Harris	33	497	15.1
1991	Tim Curtis	1,085	271	4.0	Tom Dubs	264	144	.55	1,835	Richard Hill	49	863	17.6
1992	Tim Curtis	825	213	3.9	Tom Dubs	139	57	.41	712	Chris Jenkins	38	550	14.5
1993	Tim Curtis	829	217	3.9	D.R. Robinson	148	81	.55	844	Courtney Burton	31	366	11.8
1994	Lakarlos Townsend	676	199	3.4	Sam Vink	195	90	.46	944	Jason Goss	23	357	15.5
1995	Kareem Wilson	893	244	3.7	Kareem Wilson	130	48	.37	657	Shawn Smith	8	192	24.0
1996	Steveland Hookfin	1,125	195	5.8	Kareem Wilson	90	38	.42	567	Damion Maxwell	17	184	10.8
1997	Steveland Hookfin	864	159	5.4	Kareem Wilson	54	14	.26	369	Damion Maxwell	7	180	18.0
1998	Steveland Hookfin	1,315	273	4.8	Kareem Wilson	71	26	.37	512	Damion Maxwell	14	194	13.9
1999	Chad Brinker	600	121	5.0	Dontrell Jackson	113	52	.46	745	Raynald Ray	22	466	21.2
2000	Dontrell Jackson	864	155	5.6	Dontrell Jackson	119	54	.45	881	Raynald Ray	15	308	20.5
2001	Jamel Patterson	638	117	5.5	Dontrell Jackson	83	44	.53	559	Joe Mohler	21	269	12.8
2002	Chad Brinker	1,099	228	4.8	Fred Ray	100	56	.56	712	Stafford Owens	17	259	15.2
2003	Fred Ray	382	77	5.0	Ryan Hawk	100	49	.49	765	Anthony Hackett	26	452	17.4
2004	Kalvin McRae	559	142	3.9	Ryan Hawk	262	137	.52	1,585	Chris Jackson	39	390	10.0

Receiving leaders by receptions
The NCAA began including postseason stats in 2002

THE SCHOOLS

OHIO ALL-TIME SCORES

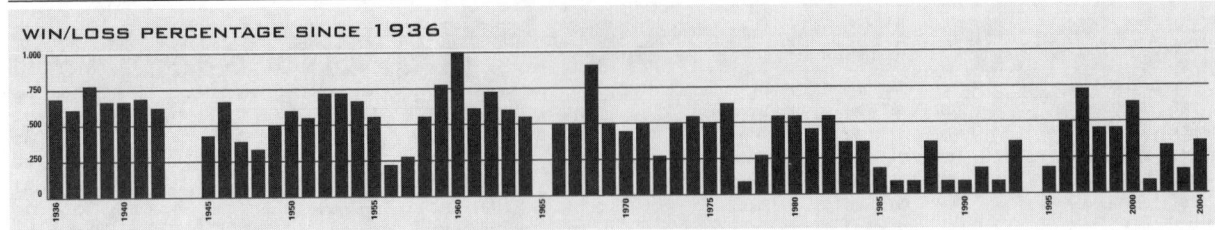

WIN/LOSS PERCENTAGE SINCE 1936

NO HEAD COACH

1894　　0-1-0
U	Marietta *Unk*	0	8

HARVEY DEME
1895 (.400)　　2-3

1895　　2-3-0
U	Parker HS *Unk*	18	0
U	Ohio Wesleyan *Unk*	0	38
U	Marietta *Unk*	0	24
U	Marietta *Unk*	0	66
U ●	Lancaster *Unk*	60	0

FRANK REMSBURG
1896 (.643)　　4-2-1

1896　　4-2-1
U	Marietta *Unk*	10	22
U ●	Chillicothe *Unk*	12	6
U	Cincinnati *Unk*	0	52
U =	Parker HS *Unk*	0	0
U ●	Portsmouth *Unk*	18	0
U ●	Denison *Unk*	18	12
U ●	Chillicothe YMCA *Unk*	22	8

WARWICK FORD
1897 (.778)　　7-2

1897　　7-2-0
U	Cincinnati *Unk*	0	12
U	Marietta *Unk*	0	4
U ●	Muskingum *Unk*	32	0
U ●	Denison *Unk*	28	0
U ●	Ohio Medical *Unk*	12	0
U ●	Otterbein *Unk*	24	0
U ●	Marietta *Unk*	6	4
N5	West Virginia *Unk*	12	0
U ●	D&D Institute *Unk*	36	6

PETER McLAREN
1898 (.375)　　1-2-1

1898　　1-2-1
U =	Cincinnati *Unk*	12	12
U ●	Dayton YMCA *Unk*	11	5
U	Ohio Medical *Unk*	0	12
N15	West Virginia *Unk*	0	16

FRED SULLIVAN
1899, 1903 (.400)　　4-6

1899　　2-2-0
U ●	Muskingum *Unk*	33	0
U	Ohio Medical *Unk*	0	36
O21	Ohio State *Unk*	0	41
U ●	Nelsonville *Unk*	45	0

KARL CORE
1900 (.438)　　3-4-1

1900　　3-4-1
U ●	Nelsonville *Unk*	45	0
U	Parkersburg AC *Unk*	0	5
O6	at Ohio State	0	20
U ●	Otterbein *Unk*	12	0
U ●	Ohio Wesleyan *Unk*	17	0
U ●	Wash. & Jeff. *Unk*	0	49
U =	Wittenberg *Unk*	5	5
U	Ohio Wesleyan *Unk*	5	6

ART JONES
1901 (.778)　　6-1-2

1901　　6-1-2
U ●	Ohio Wesleyan *Unk*	6	5
U ●	Parkersburg HS *Unk*	35	0
O12	at Ohio State	0	17
U ●	Denison *Unk*	12	0
U ●	Marietta *Unk*	11	5
U ●	Cincinnati *Unk*	16	0
U =	Otterbein *Unk*	0	0
U ●	Muskingum *Unk*	17	5
U =	Marietta *Unk*	11	11

HAROLD MONOSMITH
1902 (.083)　　0-5-1

1902　　0-5-1
U =	at Pittsburgh	0	0
O4	at Ohio State	0	17
U	Parkersburg AC *Unk*	0	31
U	W. Pennsylvania *Unk*	0	34
U	Bethany *Unk*	0	11
U	Marietta *Unk*	0	50

FRED SULLIVAN

1903　　2-4-0
U ●	Gallipolis *Unk*	28	0
U ●	Mercer Bus. Coll. *Unk*	5	0
U	Marietta *Unk*	5	28
U	Wittenberg *Unk*	0	40
U	Otterbein *Unk*	0	22
U	Marietta *Unk*	0	54

HENRY HART
1904 (.357)　　2-4-1

1904　　2-4-1
U ●	Mercer Bus. Coll. *Unk*	34	0
U	Marietta *Unk*	0	31
U	Wittenberg *Unk*	5	10
U	Otterbein *Unk*	0	18
U	Buckhannon *Unk*	0	18
U ●	Athens HS *Unk*	12	0
U =	Bethany *Unk*	6	6

JOSEPH RAILSBACK
1905 (.333)　　2-5-2

1905　　2-5-2
U =	Marietta *Unk*	0	0
O7	at Wash. & Jeff.	0	57
O14	West Virginia *Unk*	0	28
U	Otterbein *Unk*	5	6
U	Ohio Northern *Unk*	0	44
U =	Muskingum *Unk*	0	0
N11	at Marshall	5	6
U ●	Marietta *Unk*	6	0
U ●	Muskingum *Unk*	32	0

ARTHUR McFARLAND
1906-08 (.563)　　13-10-1

1906　　7-1-0
U ●	Columbus East HS *Unk*	20	0
S29 ●	at West Virginia	9	6
U ●	Otterbein *Unk*	10	0
U ●	Buckhannon *Unk*	65	0
U ●	Muskingum *Unk*	16	5
U ●	Cincinnati *Unk*	16	5
U ●	Denison *Unk*	20	0
U	Marietta *Unk*	2	12

1907　　3-4-1
U =	Parkersburg YMCA *Unk*	6	6
S28 ●	at West Virginia	5	35
U ●	D&D Inst. *Unk*	47	0
U	Ohio Wesleyan *Unk*	0	6
U ●	Parkersburg YMCA *Unk*	10	0
U	Mount Union *Unk*	0	30
U ●	Ohio Northern *Unk*	8	0
U	Marietta *Unk*	0	60

1908　　3-5-0
O3 ●	Marshall	59	0
U	Ohio Northern *Unk*	0	10
O17	Miami, Ohio	0	5
U	Denison *Unk*	0	12
U ●	Mount Union *Unk*	14	11
U ●	Wittenberg *Unk*	25	5
U	Otterbein *Unk*	5	6
U	Parkersburg HS *Unk*	0	15

ROBERT WOODS
1909-10 (.233)　　2-10-3

1909　　2-4-2
U	W.V. Wesleyan *Unk*	0	11
U	Otterbein *Unk*	3	18
O16	at Miami, Ohio	0	45
U =	Ohio Northern *Unk*	0	0
U ●	Willmington *Unk*	17	3
U ●	Muskingum *Unk*	6	0
U	Ohio Northern *Unk*	0	29
U =	Heidelberg *Unk*	0	0

1910　　0-6-1
S24	at Kentucky	0	10
U	Denison *Unk*	0	12
U	Marietta *Unk*	0	12
U	Wilmington *Unk*	0	6
O29	Pittsburgh *Unk*	0	71
U =	Muskingum *Unk*	0	0
U	Otterbein *Unk*	0	12

ARTHUR HINAMAN
1911-12 (.324)　　4-10-3

1911　　3-3-2
O7	at Ohio Wesleyan	0	10
O14	at West Virginia	0	3
O21 =	Marshall	5	5
O28 =	at Otterbein	11	11
U ●	Kenyon *Unk*	16	0
U ●	Muskingum *Unk*	50	0
U	Wittenberg *Unk*	0	10
N30	at Marietta	6	5

1912　　1-7-1
U =	Kenyon *Unk*	7	7
U	Ohio Wesleyan *Unk*	6	8
U	Wittenberg *Unk*	12	27
O26	at West Virgina	0	6
U	Buchtel *Unk*	0	27
N9	Miami, Ohio *Unk*	6	18
U ●	Otterbein *Unk*	10	7
U	West Reston *Unk*	7	41
U	Marietta *Unk*	0	27

MARK BANKS
1913-17 (.561)　　22-17-2

1913　　2-5-1
U ●	Wilmington *Unk*	30	0
U	Cincinnati *Unk*	2	20
U =	Muskingum *Unk*	3	3
U	Otterbein *Unk*	0	21
U	Denison *Unk*	0	52
N8	at Miami, Ohio	6	44
U ●	Wooster *Unk*	7	6
U	Marietta *Unk*	7	13

1914　　4-4-0
U ●	Otterbein *Unk*	36	0
O10 ●	Miami, Ohio	6	0
U	Denison *Unk*	0	20
U ●	Ohio Wesleyan *Unk*	16	7
U	Marietta *Unk*	19	23
U ●	Wooster *Unk*	36	6
U	Mount Union *Unk*	6	28
U	Cincinnati *Unk*	0	15

1915　　8-1-0
U ●	Transylvania *Unk*	5	0
O2 ●	Ohio Northern	16	0
O9 ●	at Cincinnati	15	0
U ●	Muskingum *Unk*	36	0
U ●	Otterbein *Unk*	48	7
U ●	Marietta *Unk*	16	6
U ●	Wittenberg *Unk*	12	0
N13	Miami, Ohio *Unk*	7	13 *
N20 ●	Marshall	18	7

1916　　5-2-1
U =	Ohio Wesleyan *Unk*	0	0
O7	at Syracuse	0	73
U ●	Otterbein *Unk*	13	7
U ●	Kenyon *Unk*	6	0
U ●	Wittenberg *Unk*	89	3
U ●	Cincinnati *Unk*	33	10
U	Wooster *Unk*	0	9
U ●	Oberlin *Unk*	13	7

1917　　3-5-0
U	Wooster *Unk*	0	20
U	Ohio Wesleyan *Unk*	0	14
U	Carnegie Tech *Unk*	0	21
U ●	Cincinnati *Unk*	22	0
U ●	Baldwin Wallace *Unk*	43	0
U ●	Kenyon *Unk*	20	0
U	Oberlin *Unk*	0	46
U	Marietta *Unk*	0	6

FRANK GULLUM
1918-19 (.577)　　7-5-1

1918　　4-0-1
U ●	Ohio State JV *Unk*	13	6
N9 =	Cincinnati	6	6
U ●	Denison *Unk*	7	0
U ●	Camp Sherman *Unk*	62	0
U ●	Marietta *Unk*	52	7

1919　　3-5-0
U ●	Muskingum *Unk*	13	6
U ●	Akron *Unk*	6	10
U	Heidelberg *Unk*	6	7
U ●	Kenyon *Unk*	19	7
U	Ohio Wesleyan *Unk*	0	6
U ●	Baldwin Wallace *Unk*	80	0
U	Wittenberg *Unk*	7	33
U	Denison *Unk*	16	32

RUSS FINSTERWALD
1920-22 (.563)　　13-10-1

1920　　4-3-0
U ●	Bethany *Unk*	7	0
O9	at Cincinnati	0	6
O16 ●	at Marshall	55	0
U ●	Otterbein *Unk*	54	14
U	Denison *Unk*	0	17
U	Heidelberg *Unk*	0	7
U ●	Akron *Unk*	39	0

1921　　4-4-1
S24	Morris-Harvey	40	0
O1	at Syracuse	0	38
O8	Bethany *Unk*	0	13
O15	at West Virginia	0	7
O22	at Denison	7	14
O29 ●	Baldwin Wallace	35	0
N5	Cincinnati	7	6
N12	at Columbia	23	21
N19 =	Marietta	0	0

1922　　5-3-0
U ●	Baldwin Wallace *Unk*	28	0
U ●	Marietta *Unk*	3	0
N25	at West Virginia	0	28
U	Bethany *Unk*	0	7
U	Xavier *Unk*	7	13
U ●	Western Reserve *Unk*	35	0
U ●	Denison *Unk*	7	0
U ●	Otterbein *Unk*	20	0

F.B. HELDT
1923 (.389) 3-5-1

1923 3-5-1
S29	●	Rio Grande	20	0
O6		at Oberlin	0	6
O13		at Xavier	7	15
O20		Cincinnati	6	13 *
O26	●	Western Reserve	7	0
N3	●	Kenyon	14	0
N10		at Ohio Wesleyan	0	40
N17	=	at Denison	7	7
N29		Marietta	3	7

DON PEDEN
1924-46 (.711) 121-46-11

1924 4-4-0
S27	●	Rio Grande	10	0
O4		at Wittenberg	0	3
O11		Oberlin	7	13
O24	●	Kenyon	6	0
U		Ohio Northern UNK	7	12
N8	●	at Marietta	21	17
N15		Denison	7	14
N22	●	at Ohio Wesleyan	6	0

1925 6-2-0
O3	●	Rio Grande	19	6
O10	●	at Denison	26	0
O17	●	at Toledo	7	0
O24		Ohio Wesleyan	0	26
O31		at Ohio Northern	0	6
N7	●	Marietta	10	0
N14	●	at Cincinnati	13	2
U	●	Wittenberg UNK	20	0

1926 5-2-1
O2	●	Rio Grande	40	0
O9		Akron	0	3
O16	●	at Denison	6	0
O23	●	Cincinnati	38	7
O30	=	at Ohio Wesleyan	0	0
N6	●	Ohio Northern	9	0
N12	●	at Marietta	12	0
N20		at Wittenberg	6	7

1927 4-2-2
S24	●	Rio Grande	21	0
O1		at Michigan State	0	27
O8	●	Ohio Northern	25	0
O15	●	Marietta	20	0
O22		Wittenberg	0	28
N5	●	at Denison	12	7
N12	=	at Cincinnati	7	7
N18	=	Ohio Wesleyan	0	0

1928 6-3-0
S29	●	Rio Grande	45	7
U	●	West Liberty	14	6
O13		at Wittenberg	12	13
O20	●	Cincinnati	65	0 *
O27	●	at Ohio Northern	39	0
N3		at Miami, Ohio	13	20
N10	●	Marietta	40	0
N17		at Ohio Wesleyan	0	7
N24	●	Denison	27	13

1929 9-0-0
S28	●	at Indiana	18	0
O5	●	West Liberty	26	0
O12	●	Ohio Wesleyan	21	7
O19	●	at Muskingum	59	0
O26	●	at Cincinnati	35	0
N2	●	Miami, Ohio	14	0
N9	●	at Denison	54	0
N16	●	at Marietta	45	0
N22	●	Wittenberg	33	0

1930 8-0-1
S27	●	Wilmington	27	0
O3	●	at Butler	12	7
O11	=	West Liberty	13	13
O18	●	at Western Reserve	47	0
O25	●	at Miami, Ohio	27	6
N1	●	at Cincinnati	48	0
N8	●	Denison	36	0
N15	●	Dayton	10	6
N22	●	at Ohio Wesleyan	7	0

1931 7-1-0
S26		at Indiana	6	7
O3	●	Butler	40	0
O10	●	at Denison	33	0
O17	●	Simpson	22	0
O24	●	at Cincinnati	13	7
O31	●	Ohio Wesleyan	18	0
N7	●	at DePauw	27	0
N14	●	Miami, Ohio	13	0

1932 7-2-0
S24	●	Rio Grande	19	0
O1		at Indiana	6	7
O8	●	Franklin	39	0
O15	●	at Navy	14	0
O22		at Miami, Ohio	0	16
O28	●	Georgetown	27	0
N5	●	Wittenberg	19	6
N12	●	Cincinnati	23	0
N19	●	at Ohio Wesleyan	25	0

1933 6-2-1
S30	●	Morris-Harvey	61	0
O7		at Purdue	6	13
O14	●	Franklin	78	0
O21	●	Miami, Ohio	6	0
O28	●	Transylvania	68	0
N4	●	at Wittenberg	39	0
N11	=	at Marshall	0	0
N18		at Cincinnati	0	2
N25	●	Ohio Wesleyan	19	13

1934 4-4-1
S22	●	Rio Grande	53	0
S29		at Indiana	0	27
O13	●	Georgetown	36	6
O20		at Miami, Ohio	0	7
O27	●	Marshall	8	0
N3		at West Virginia	2	7
N10	=	Cincinnati	0	0
N17	●	at Dayton	17	0
N24		at Ohio Wesleyan	0	20

1935 8-0-0
S28	●	at Illinois	6	0
O11	●	at John Carroll	49	0
O19	●	Marshall	20	13
O26	●	Dayton	26	0
N2	●	Miami, Ohio	20	0
N9	●	Muskingum	20	17
N16	●	Cincinnati	16	6
N23	●	Ohio Wesleyan	13	0

1936 5-2-1
S26		at Purdue	0	47
O10	=	Marshall	13	13
O17	●	Kent State	6	0
O24		at Miami, Ohio	0	3
O31	●	Cincinnati	10	7
U	●	Muskingum	32	0
N14	●	Ohio Wesleyan	20	0
N21	●	John Carroll	21	0

1937 5-3-1
S18	●	Rio Grande	80	0
S25		at Illinois	6	20
O9		at Western Reserve	0	7
O16	●	Miami, Ohio	19	0
O23		Dayton	0	6
O30	=	at Marshall	13	13
N6	●	at Cincinnati	17	0
N13	●	at Rutgers	13	0
N20	●	Ohio Wesleyan	20	6

1938 7-2-0
S24	●	at Illinois	6	0
O1	●	at Xavier	14	12
O8		at Western Reserve	14	26
O15	●	at Ohio Wesleyan	28	0
O22	●	Wayne St.	52	7
O29	●	Cincinnati	13	12
N5	●	Miami, Ohio	20	12
N12		at Dayton	0	13
N19	●	Marshall	14	7

1939 6-3-0
S23		Western Kentucky	7	14
S30		at Butler	7	12
O7	●	Western Reserve	14	12
O14		Ohio Wesleyan	7	12
O21	●	at Xavier	20	6
O28	●	Dayton	14	0
N4	●	at Morris-Harvey	14	13
N11	●	Miami, Ohio	20	7
N18	●	at Western Michigan	13	6

1940 5-2-2
S28	●	Youngstown St.	13	0
O5	=	Butler	7	7
O12	●	Western Michigan	20	7
O19	●	Furman	15	6
O26	=	at Ohio Wesleyan	0	0
N2	●	at Miami, Ohio	27	0
N9		at Western Reserve	0	6
N16	●	at Dayton	7	0
N21		at Xavier	0	6

1941 5-2-1
S26		at Youngstown St.	0	14
O4		Western Reserve	0	7
O11	●	Western Kentucky	20	7
O18	=	at Akron	0	0
O25	●	at Butler	20	7
N1	●	Miami, Ohio	26	0
N8	●	Ohio Wesleyan	21	0
N20	●	at Dayton	21	7

1942 5-3-0
O3	●	Akron	39	0
O10	●	Butler	6	0
O17		at Cincinnati	7	26
O24	●	Ohio Wesleyan	26	14
O31	●	at Miami, Ohio	39	13
N7		at Western Reserve	7	20
N14	●	Xavier	20	14
N26		at Dayton	0	20

1943-44
NO TEAM

1945 3-4-0
S29		Bowling Green	0	6
O6		Western Michigan	20	21
O13	●	Cincinnati	20	19
N20		at Miami, Ohio	0	34
U		Murray St.	13	19
U	●	Baldwin Wallace	33	7
N17	●	at West Virginia	14	0

1946 6-3-0
S28	●	Murray St.	27	7
O5	●	at Western Michigan	25	7
O12	●	Muskingum	38	0
O19		at Cincinnati	0	19
O26		Miami, Ohio	14	23
N2	●	at Ohio Wesleyan	49	7
N9	●	Baldwin Wallace	21	14
N16		Dayton	7	14
N23	●	at Xavier	25	6

1947-PRESENT
MAC

HAROLD WISE
1947-48 (.361) 6-11-1

1947 3-5-1 (1-3-0)
S27	●	Ohio Northern	34	0
O4	● │	Butler	14	7
O11	│	at Western Reserve	7	20
O18		at Bowling Green	0	2
O25	│	at Miami, Ohio	0	21
N1	│	Cincinnati	0	34
N8	=	Ohio Wesleyan	7	7
N15		at Dayton	6	18
N22	●	Xavier	12	7

1948 3-6-0 (2-3-0)
S25		Bowling Green	7	13
O2		at Wash. & Lee	0	13
O9	│	at Cincinnati	13	18
O16	● │	at Western Reserve	37	7
O23	│	Miami, Ohio	0	21
O30	●	Duquesne	14	13
N6		at West Virginia	6	48
N13	● │	at Butler	14	6
N20	│	Western Michigan	7	40

CARROLL WIDDOES
1949-57 (.536) 42-36-5

1949 4-4-1 (2-2-1)
S24	●	West Virginia	17	7
O1	● │	at Western Michigan	16	6
O7	●	at Kent State	34	6
O15	= │	at Western Reserve	7	7
O22	│	at Miami, Ohio	0	26
O29		at Marshall	6	14
N5	│	Cincinnati	13	34
N12	● │	Butler	14	0
N19		Buffalo	7	20

1950 6-4-0 (2-2-0)
S23	●	at Akron	28	6
S30		at Illinois	2	28
O7	●	at Butler	21	14
O14	● │	Western Reserve	35	0
O21		at Kent State	13	35
O28	│	at Miami, Ohio	20	28
N4	│	at Cincinnati	0	23
N11	●	at Buffalo	22	14
N18	● │	Western Michigan	10	7
N23	●	Marshall	14	6

1951 5-4-1 (2-2-0)
S22	●	at Morris-Harvey	26	0
S29	●	Akron	40	7
O6	● │	at Western Michigan	13	0
O13	●	Bowling Green	28	7
O20	│	at Miami, Ohio	0	7
O27	● │	Kent State	28	27
N3		at Toledo	6	13
N10	│	Cincinnati	0	40
N17		Eastern Kentucky	13	27
N22	=	at Marshall	13	13

1952 6-2-1 (5-2-0)
S25	●	at Morris-Harvey	20	6
O4	● │	Toledo	22	20
O11	● │	at Western Reserve	22	7
O18	● │	at Kent State	27	18
O25	│	Miami, Ohio	0	20
N1	● │	Western Michigan	28	13
N8	│	at Cincinnati	7	41 *
N15	● │	at Bowling Green	33	14
N22	=	Marshall	21	21

1953 6-2-1 (5-0-1)
S19	● │	at Toledo	26	0
O3		at Harvard	0	16
O10	● │	Western Reserve	39	0
O17	● │	Kent State	40	21
O24	= │	at Miami, Ohio	7	7
O31	● │	at Western Michigan	67	12
N7	●	Morris-Harvey	38	7
N14	● │	Bowling Green	22	14
N21		at Marshall	6	9

1954 6-3-0 (5-2-0)
S25	●	Xavier	12	0
O2	● │	Toledo	28	20
O9	● │	at Western Reserve	37	0
O16	● │	at Kent State	14	7
O23	│	Miami, Ohio	13	46
O30		at Harvard	13	27
N6	│	at Western Michigan	6	19
N13	● │	at Bowling Green	26	14
N20	● │	Marshall	26	25

1955 5-4-0 (3-3-0)
S15	●	at Youngstown St.	6	0
S24	● │	Marshall	13	6
O1	● │	at Toledo	34	13 *
O15	│	Kent State	14	20
O22	│	at Miami, Ohio	7	34
O29		at Indiana	14	21
N5	● │	Western Michigan	40	14
N12	│	Bowling Green	0	13
N19	●	Morris-Harvey	32	13

1956 2-7-0 (2-4-0)
S22		at Florida State	7	47
S29	│	Toledo	13	19
O6		at Xavier	7	31
O13	│	at Kent State	13	32
O20	│	Miami, Ohio	7	16
O27		Louisville	19	25
N3	● │	at Western Michigan	27	0
N10	│	at Bowling Green	27	41
N17	● │	Marshall	16	0

1957 2-6-1 (1-4-1)
S21	●	at Indiana, Pa.	50	0
S28	│	at Toledo	6	14
O5	│	Kent State	9	14
O12		at Harvard	7	14
O19	│	at Miami, Ohio	0	26
O26	│	at Marshall	28	34
N2	● │	Western Michigan	20	7
N9	= │	Bowling Green	7	7
N16		at Louisville	7	40

BILL HESS
1958-77 (.537) 107-92-4

1958 5-4-0 (2-4-0)
S20	●	Youngstown St.	38	0
S27	● │	Toledo	13	6
O4	│	at Kent State	6	14
O11	●	at Dayton	27	8
O18	│	Miami, Ohio	10	14
O25	● │	Marshall	22	0
N1	│	at Western Michigan	14	21
N8	│	at Bowling Green	6	33
N15	●	Louisville	23	6

1959 7-2-0 (4-2-0)
S26	● │	at Toledo	36	7
O3	● │	Kent State	46	0
O10	●	Xavier	25	7
O17	●	at Youngstown St.	44	12
O24	│	Miami, Ohio	0	24
O31	● │	Western Michigan	12	9
N7	● │	Marshall	21	14
N14	●	at Louisville	22	15
N21	│	Bowling Green	9	13

652 OHIO

THE SCHOOLS

1960 — 10-0-0 (6-0-0)

S17	●	at Dayton	28	0
S24	● |	Toledo	48	7
O1	● |	at Kent State	25	8
O8	●	at Boston U.	36	6
O15	●	at Xavier	6	0
O22	● |	Miami, Ohio	21	0
O29	● |	at Western Michigan	24	0
N5	● |	Marshall	19	0
N12	● |	at Bowling Green	14	7
N19	●	So. Illinois	48	6

1961 — 5-3-1 (3-2-1)

S23	● |	at Toledo	10	6
S30	|	Kent State	17	23
O7	●	at Dayton	14	13
O14		Xavier	3	6
O21	● |	at Miami, Ohio	28	18
O28	●	at Delaware	17	16
N4	● |	at Marshall	14	7
N11	|	Bowling Green	6	7
N18	= |	Western Michigan	20	20

1962 — 8-3-0 (5-1-0)

S22	● |	Toledo	31	0
S29	● |	at Kent State	21	0
O6	●	Dayton	27	25
O13	●	Xavier	20	6
O20	● |	Miami, Ohio	12	6
O27	●	at Buffalo	41	6
N3	● |	Marshall	35	0
N10	|	at Bowling Green	6	7
N17	● |	at Western Michigan	32	16
N24		at Iowa State	22	31
		SUN BOWL		
D31		West Texas St.	14	15

1963 — 6-4-0 (5-1-0)

S21		Buffalo	0	7
S28	●	at Dayton	13	6
O5	● |	Kent State	20	0
O12	|	at Toledo	17	18
O19		Delaware	12	29
O26	● |	at Miami, Ohio	13	10
N2		at Xavier	0	20
N9	● |	Western Michigan	27	13
N16	● |	Bowling Green	16	0
N23	● |	at Marshall	17	0

1964 — 5-4-1 (3-2-1)

S19	●	at West Texas St.	16	14
S26		at Purdue	0	17
O3	= |	at Kent State	3	3
O10	● |	Toledo	21	12
O17		Xavier	19	23
O24	● |	Miami, Ohio	10	7
O31	●	Dayton	24	0
N7	|	at Western Michigan	8	13
N14	● |	at Bowling Green	21	0
N21	|	Marshall	0	10

1965 — 0-10-0 (0-6-0)

S18		at West Texas St.	0	7
S25		at Maryland	7	24
O2	|	Kent State	10	27
O9	|	at Toledo	7	21
O16		Xavier	19	21
O23	|	at Miami, Ohio	0	34
O30		at Dayton	7	13
N6	|	Western Michigan	6	17
N13	|	at Bowling Green	7	17
N20	|	at Marshall	14	29

1966 — 5-5-0 (3-3-0)

S17		at Purdue	3	42
S24	●	at Boston College	23	14
O1	● |	at Kent State	12	10
O8	● |	Toledo	21	6
O15	●	Xavier	24	10
O22	|	Miami, Ohio	13	33
O29		Dayton	12	20
N5	|	at Western Michigan	13	20
N12	|	at Bowling Green	0	28
N19	● |	Marshall	28	6

1967 — 5-5-0 (4-2-0)

S16	● |	at Toledo	20	14
S23	● |	at Marshall	48	14
S30	|	at Kent State	14	21 †
O7	●	at Kansas	30	15
O14		William & Mary	22	25
O21	|	at Miami, Ohio	15	22
O28		at Dayton	9	10
N4	● |	Western Michigan	20	10
N11	● |	Bowling Green	31	7
N18		at Penn State	14	35

1968 — 10-1-0 (6-0-0)

S21	● |	at Marshall	48	8
S28	● |	at Kent State	31	7
O5	● |	Toledo	40	31
O12	●	at William & Mary	41	0
O19	● |	Miami, Ohio	24	7
O26	●	Dayton	42	12
N2	● |	at Western Michigan	34	27
N9	● |	at Bowling Green	28	27
N16	●	at Cincinnati	60	48
N23	●	Northern Illinois	28	12
		TANGERINE BOWL		
D27		Richmond	42	49

1969 — 5-4-1 (2-3-0)

S20	● |	Kent State	35	0
S27	=	at Minnesota	35	35
O4	|	at Toledo	9	34
O11	●	Xavier	31	6
O18	|	Miami, Ohio	21	24
O25		at Penn State	3	42
N1	● |	Western Michigan	22	17
N8	|	Bowling Green	16	23
N15	●	Cincinnati	46	6
N22	●	at Marshall	38	35

1970 — 4-5-0 (3-2-0)

S19	● |	at Kent State	24	14
S26		at Minnesota	7	49
O3	|	Toledo	7	42
O10	●	Dayton	17	14
O17	● |	Miami, Ohio	23	22
O24		at Cincinnati	21	29
O31	|	at Western Michigan-	23	52
N7	● |	at Bowling Green	34	7
N14		at Penn State	22	32

1971 — 5-5-0 (2-3-0)

S18	|	Bowling Green	19	20
S25	● |	Kent State	37	21
O2	|	at Toledo	28	31
O9	●	at Kentucky	35	6
O16	● |	at Miami, Ohio	3	0
O23		at Virginia Tech	29	37
O30	|	Western Michigan	14	28
N6	●	at Tulane	30	7
N13		Cincinnati	15	23
N20	●	at Marshall	30	0

1972 — 3-8-0 (1-4-0)

S9	●	Central Michigan	26	21
S16		at Idaho	14	17
S23	|	at Kent State	14	37
S30	● |	Toledo	38	22
O7	●	at Cincinnati	28	14
O14	|	at Miami, Ohio	7	31
O21		Virginia Tech	21	53
O28	|	at Western Michigan	17	34
N4	|	at Bowling Green	0	17
N11		at Tulane	6	44
N18		Marshall	14	31

1973 — 5-5-0 (2-3-0)

S22	|	Kent State	7	35
S29	|	at Toledo	8	35
O6	●	at Northwestern	14	12
O13	|	at Miami, Ohio	6	10
O20		at South Carolina	22	38
O27	● |	Western Michigan	16	0
N3	● |	Bowling Green	24	23
N10	●	Cincinnati	14	8
N17		at Penn State	10	49
N22	●	at Marshall	35	21

1974 — 6-5-0 (3-2-0)

S14		at North Carolina	7	42
S21	● |	at Kent State	20	0
S28	|	Toledo	16	19
O5	●	Northern Illinois	31	14
O12	|	Miami, Ohio	3	31
O19	●	Morehead St.	49	10
O26	● |	at Western Michigan	26	3
N2	● |	at Bowling Green	33	22
N9		at Cincinnati	13	35
N16		at Penn State	16	35
N23	●	Marshall	35	0

1975 — 5-5-1 (3-3-1)

S13	= |	at Central Michigan	6	6
S20	● |	Ball State	10	0
S27	● |	Kent State	23	21
O4		at Minnesota	0	21
O11	●	at William & Mary	22	8
O18	|	at Miami, Ohio	9	17
O25	|	at Toledo	10	14
N1	● |	Western Michigan	24	10
N8	|	Bowling Green	17	19
N15		Cincinnati	5	6
N22	●	at Marshall	38	21

1976 — 7-4-0 (6-2-0)

S4	● |	at Eastern Michigan	23	7
S18	● |	at Kent State	14	12
S25	●	Idaho	35	0
O2	● |	Toledo	34	8
O9	|	at Central Michigan	15	17
O16	● |	Miami, Ohio	28	14
O23		William & Mary	0	20
O30	|	at Western Michigan	10	21
N6	● |	at Bowling Green	31	26
N13		at Cincinnati	0	35
N20	● |	Northern Illinois	63	15

1977 — 1-10-0 (0-8-0)

S10	●	at Marshall	49	27
S17		at Purdue	7	44
S24	|	Central Michigan	14	31
O1	|	Kent State	23	44
O8	|	at Eastern Michigan	14	31
O15	|	at Miami, Ohio	24	28
O22	|	at Toledo	29	31
O29	|	Western Michigan	22	28
N5		Cincinnati	26	38
N12	|	Bowling Green	27	39
N19	|	at Northern Illinois	6	20

BOB KAPPES
1978 (.273) 3-8

1978 — 3-8-0 (3-5-0)

S9	● |	Eastern Michigan	23	22
S23		at Purdue	0	24
S30	|	at Kent State	14	20
O7	|	Central Michigan	3	17
O14		at South Carolina	7	24
O21	|	Toledo	14	28
O28	● |	at Western Michigan	10	7
N4	|	Miami, Ohio	16	31
N11		at Cincinnati	0	35
N18	● |	at Bowling Green	19	15
N25	|	Northern Illinois	14	23

BRIAN BURKE
1979-84 (.477) 31-34-1

1979 — 6-5-0 (4-4-0)

S8		at Minnesota	10	24
S15	● |	Eastern Michigan	20	7
S22	●	Marshall	35	0
S29	● |	Kent State	43	13
O6	|	at Central Michigan	0	26
O13	● |	at Miami, Ohio	9	7
O20	|	at Toledo	13	21
O27	|	Western MIchigan	6	20
N10	●	at Cincinnati	27	7
N17	● |	Bowling Green	48	21
N24	|	at Northern Illinois	27	28

1980 — 6-5-0 (5-4-0)

S13		at Minnesota	14	38
S20	● |	Eastern Michigan	34	6
S27	|	Northern Illinois	21	22
O4	|	at Kent State	14	15
O11	● |	Central Michigan	24	9
O18	● |	Miami, Ohio	17	7
O25	● |	Toledo	24	9
N1	|	at Western Michigan	7	13
N8	●	Marshall	28	20
N15	|	at Ball State	18	37
N22	● |	at Bowling Green	21	20

1981 — 5-6-0 (5-4-0)

S12		at Minnesota	17	19
S19	● |	Bowling Green	23	21
S26	● |	Ball State	30	27
O3	|	at Toledo	14	21
O10		Cincinnati	9	19
O17	● |	Eastern Michigan	29	7
O24	|	at Miami, Ohio	14	40
O31	|	Central Michigan	21	38
N7	|	at Northern Illinois	14	38
N14	● |	Western Michigan	37	20
N21	● |	at Kent State	20	7

1982 — 6-5-0 (5-4-0)

S4	|	at Bowling Green	0	40
S11		at Minnesota	3	57
S18	●	Richmond ColO	23	14
O2	● |	Toledo	17	14
O9	● |	at Ball State	34	7
O16	● |	at Eastern Michigan	14	13
O23	● |	Miami, Ohio	20	0
O30	|	at Central Michigan	18	42
N6	|	Northern Illinois	0	36
N13	|	at Western Michigan	7	16
N20	● |	Kent State	24	20

1983 — 4-7-0 (3-6-0)

S3		at West Virginia	3	55
S10	●	at Richmond	17	10
S17	|	Ball State	14	31
S24	● |	Eastern Michigan	31	14
O1	|	at Toledo	0	31
O15	|	Central Michigan	9	14
O22	● |	at Kent State	21	20
O29	|	Western Michigan	14	16
N5	● |	at Miami, Ohio	17	14
N12	|	Bowling Green	20	24
N19	|	at Northern Illinois	17	41

1984 — 4-6-1 (4-4-1)

S1		at West Virginia	0	38
S8		at North Carolina St.	6	43
S15	● |	at Ball State	31	17
S22	● |	at Eastern Michigan	16	13
S29	= |	Toledo	16	16
O13	|	at Central Michigan	3	35
O20	|	Kent State	7	19
O27	|	at Western Michigan	14	33
N3	● |	Miami, Ohio	24	19
N10	|	at Bowling Green	7	28
N17	● |	Northern Illinois	10	3

CLEVE BRYANT
1985-89 (.182) 9-44-2

1985 — 2-9-0 (2-7-0)

S14		at Marshall	7	31
S21		at Duke	13	34
S28	|	Central Michigan	7	13
O5	|	at Miami, Ohio	22	29
O12	|	Ball State	23	36
O19	|	Eastern Michigan	21	27
O26	|	at Toledo	10	24
N2	● |	at Kent State	33	23
N9	● |	Western Michigan	21	15
N16	|	at Northern Illinois	7	35
N23	|	Bowling Green	17	38

1986 — 1-10-0 (0-8-0)

S6	|	at Bowling Green	16	21
S13		Marshall	7	21
S20		at Duke	7	22
S27	|	at Central Michigan	27	56
O4	|	Miami, Ohio	14	34
O11	|	at Ball State	9	30
O18	|	at Eastern Michigan	31	33
O25	|	Toledo	21	24
N1	|	Kent State	13	17
N8	|	at Western Michigan	17	45
N15	●	Northern Illinois	34	26

1987 — 1-10-0 (0-8-0)

S5		at West Virginia	3	23
S12	●	Marshall	23	15
S19	|	at Toledo	12	17
O3		at Kentucky	0	28
O10	|	Bowling Green	7	28
O17	|	at Miami, Ohio	9	10
O24	|	Kent State	10	24
O31	|	at Eastern Michigan	16	34
N7	|	Central Michigan	17	31
N14	|	at Ball State	17	30
N21	|	Western Michigan	13	31

1988 — 4-6-1 (4-3-1)

S10		at Marshall	14	31
S17		at Purdue	10	33
S24		at Nevada-Las Vegas	18	26
O1	● |	Toledo	24	14
O8	|	at Bowling Green	0	42
O15	● |	Miami, Ohio	38	21
O22	● |	at Kent State	21	14
O29	= |	Eastern Michigan	17	17
N5	|	at Central Michigan	10	42
N12	● |	Ball State	27	25
N19	|	at Western Michigan	16	23

1989 — 1-9-1 (1-6-1)

S2	|	at Toledo	18	27
S9		at Iowa State	3	28
S16	|	Eastern Michigan	25	30
S23		at Vanderbilt	10	54
S30		at LSU	6	57
O7	|	Bowling Green	28	31
O14	= |	at Miami, Ohio	22	22
O21	● |	Kent State	37	14
O28	|	at Western Michigan	13	28
N11	|	at Central Michigan	15	24
N18	|	Ball State	14	33

THE SCHOOLS

TOM LICHTENBERG
1990-94 (.164)   8-45-2

1990   1-9-1 (0-7-1)
S1		at Pittsburgh	3 35
S15		at Eastern Michigan	18 21
S22	●	Tennessee Tech	42 32
S29		Toledo	20 27
O6	=	at Bowling Green	10 10
O13		Miami, Ohio	18 40
O20		at Kent State	15 44
O27		Western Michigan	23 31
N3		at Youngstown St.	0 27
N10		Central Michigan	7 52
N17		at Ball State	6 23

1991   2-8-1 (1-6-1)
A31	=	Central Michigan	17 17
S14	●	Tenn. Tech	35 14
S21		at Mississippi	14 38
S28		at Western Michigan	9 35
O5		at Toledo	13 17
O12		Bowling Green	14 45
O19		at Miami, Ohio	0 34
O26	●	Kent State	45 40
N2		at Ball State	6 10
N9		Eastern Michigan	10 13
N23		at Tulsa	13 45

1992   1-10-0 (1-7-0)
S5		at Iowa State	9 35
S12	●	at Kent State	27 14
S19		at Central Michigan	0 24
S26		Western Michigan	3 19
O3		Akron	0 13
O10		at Bowling Green	14 31
O17		Miami, Ohio	21 23
O24		at Eastern Michigan	6 7
O31		Ball State	21 24
N7		Youngstown St.	20 28
N14		at Colorado State	24 35

1993   4-7-0 (4-5-0)
S4		at North Carolina	3 44
S11		at Central Michigan	0 38
S18		Ball State	16 24
S25		at Toledo	10 28
O2		at Virginia	7 41
O9		Bowling Green	0 20
O16	●	Kent State	15 10
O23	●	at Miami, Ohio	22 20
O30	●	Akron	21 13
N6		Western Michigan	28 34
N13	●	at Eastern Michigan	12 10

1994   0-11-0 (0-9-0)
S10		at Pittsburgh	16 30
S17		Utah State	0 5
S24		at Ball State	14 21
O1		Toledo	6 31
O8		at Bowling Green	0 32
O15		Miami, Ohio	10 31
O22		at Kent State	0 24
O29		Central Michigan	10 22
N5		at Western Michigan	3 15
N12		Eastern Michigan	13 24
N19		at Akron	10 24

JIM GROBE
1995-2000 (.500)   33-33-1

1995   2-8-1 (1-6-1)
A31		at Iowa State	21 36
S9	●	Illinois St.	14 6
S16	=	Kent State	28 28
S23		at Eastern Michigan	20 31
S30		at North Carolina	0 62
O14		Western Michigan	17 34
O21	●	at Akron	29 23
O28		Ball State	3 6
N4		at Bowling Green	7 33
N11		Miami, Ohio	2 30
N18		at Toledo	20 31

1996   6-6 (5-3)
A29	●	Akron	44 14
S7	●	at Hawaii	21 10
S14		at Army	20 37
S21		at Northwestern	7 28
O5	●	Eastern Michigan	7 0
O12		at Ball State	27 30
O19	●	at Kent State	24 15
O26	●	Bowling Green	38 0
N2	●	at Western Michigan	38 0
N9		at Miami, Ohio	8 24
N16		at East Carolina	45 55
N23		Toledo	23 24

1997   8-3 (6-2)
A28	●	Kent State	31 7
S6		at Maryland	21 14
S13		at Kansas State	20 23
S20	●	Buffalo	50 0
S27	●	Western Michigan	31 7
O4	●	at Eastern Michigan	47 7
O18	●	Bowling Green	24 0
O25	●	at Akron	21 17
N1	●	at Northern Illinois	35 30
N8		Miami, Ohio	21 45
N15		at Marshall	0 27

1998   5-6 (5-3)
S3		at North Carolina St.	31 34
S12		at Wisconsin	0 45
S19		East Carolina	14 21
S26	●	at Western Michigan	37 35
O3		at Bowling Green	7 35
O10		Marshall	23 30
O17	●	Akron	28 14
O31		at Miami, Ohio	21 35
N7	●	Eastern Michigan	49 21
N14	●	Northern Illinois	28 12
N21	●	at Kent State	31 21

1999   5-6 (5-3)
S4		at Minnesota	7 33
S11		No. Iowa	21 36
S18		at Ohio State	16 40
S25	●	Buffalo	45 6
O2	●	Kent State	31 3
O9		at Akron	28 41
O16		at Eastern Michigan	26 27
O23	●	Bowling Green	17 14
O30	●	at Ball State	37 25
N13	●	Miami, Ohio	40 28
N26	●	at Marshall	3 34

2000   7-4 (5-3)
S2		at Iowa State	15 25
S9	●	at Minnesota	23 17
S16	●	Tenn. Tech	52 14
S23		Akron	20 23
S30		at Western Michigan	10 23
O7	●	Buffalo	42 20
O14	●	at Kent State	44 7
O21	●	Central Michigan	52 3
N4		at Miami, Ohio	24 27
N11	●	at Bowling Green	23 21
N18	●	Marshall	38 28

BRIAN KNORR
2001-04 (.239)   11-35

2001   1-10 (1-7)
A30		at Akron	29 31
S8		at West Virginia	3 20
S22		Iowa State	28 31
O6		Toledo	41 48
O13	●	at Central Michigan	34 3
O20		Miami, Ohio	24 36
O27		Kent State	14 24
N3		at Buffalo	0 44
N10		Bowling Green	0 17
N17		at Marshall	18 42
N24		at North Carolina St.	20 27

2002   4-8 (4-4)
A31		at Pittsburgh	14 27
S7		Northeastern	0 31
S14		at Florida	6 34
S21		at Connecticut	19 37
S28	●	Buffalo	34 32
O5		at Bowling Green	21 72
O12	●	Eastern Michigan	55 27
O19	●	at Kent State	50 0
N2		at Miami, Ohio	20 38
N9	●	Akron	27 10
N23		Marshall	21 24
N30		at Central Florida	32 42

2003   2-10 (1-7)
A28	●	S.E. Missouri St.	17 3
S6		at Iowa State	20 48
S13		Minnesota	20 42
S27		Western Michigan	32 39
O4		at Northern Illinois	23 30
O11	●	Central Florida	28 0
O18		at Kentucky	14 35
O25		at Buffalo	17 26
N8		Kent State	33 37
N15		at Akron	28 35
N22		Miami, Ohio	31 49
N28		at Marshall	0 28

2004   4-7 (2-6)
S4	●	VMI	42 14
S11		at Pittsburgh	3 24
S18		at Miami, Ohio	20 40
S25	●	Buffalo	34 0
O2	●	at Kentucky	28 16
O9		Marshall	13 16
O16		at Toledo	13 31
O23		Bowling Green	16 41
O30		at Kent State	16 42
N6	●	at Central Florida	17 16
N13		Akron	19 31

ƒ Forfeit † Game Later Forfieted # Disputed Victor * Disputed Score || Designated Conference Game |2 Counted Twice in Conference Standings

OHIO STATE

BY TODD JONES

TWO WEEKS AFTER OHIO STATE upset Miami in the 2003 Fiesta Bowl, a crowd of nearly 60,000 attended a ceremony at Ohio Stadium to honor the national champions. The people stood and cheered their 14–0 team during a 50-minute ceremony in 10° weather.

Such is the love for the Buckeyes. There is actually a man in Columbus who earns money by dressing up like Woody Hayes and imitating the coaching icon. Calendars for the 1.5 million residents in central Ohio are marked by the annual Michigan grudge match as much as by birthdays and anniversaries. The state capital is a place where, as the nation struggled with a beef shortage in August 1973, locals were reassured by a newspaper's front-page headline: "OSU Gridders Will Get Meat."

There is always something to chew on about the Buckeyes.

TRADITION Dotting the "i" as the marching band performs its "Script Ohio" formation has occurred since 1936 and is one of sport's mesmerizing moments. The drum major of "The Best Damn Band in the Land" high-steps toward the "i" and points to a spot, and the sousaphone player steps up, doffs his hat and bows to each side of the roaring 100,000 fans crammed into Ohio Stadium. Bob Hope once dotted the "i." So did Woody Hayes. The 225-member band conducts a "Skull Session" for 13,276 fans in St. John Arena, 90 minutes before kickoff. The band then files due south, enters the north tunnel of Ohio Stadium and is greeted like a conquering army. Since 1954, victories are celebrated with the ringing of the 2,420-pound Victory Bell, which hangs 150 feet up in the stadium's southeast tower. Win or lose, the team gathers behind head coach Jim Tressel and sings "Carmen Ohio" to the band at game's end, and the song concludes with everyone doing the "O-H-I-O" chant. "Senior Tackle" has been conducted since 1913, and it calls for senior players to hit the tackling sled once in the final practice prior to the Michigan game. Some years, Senior Tackle is a public event; in 1996, over 20,000 came to Ohio Stadium to watch. A victory over Michigan earns every player a pair of miniature gold pants.

BEST PLAYER Only Notre Dame has more Heisman Trophy winners than USC's and Ohio State's six each. A

PROFILE

Ohio State University
Columbus, Ohio
Founded: 1870
Enrollment: 37,509
Colors: Scarlet and Gray
Nickname: Buckeyes
Stadium: Ohio Stadium
Opened in 1922
Prescription Athletic Turf; 101,568 capacity
First football game: 1890
All-time record: 765–298–53 (.709)
Bowl record: 17–19
Consensus national championship, 1936-present: 6 (1942, 1954, 1957, 1961, 1968, 2002)
Big Ten Conference championships: 29 (15 outright)
Heisman Trophy: Les Horvath, 1944; Vic Janowicz, 1950; Howard Cassady, 1955; Archie Griffin, 1974-75; Eddie George, 1995
Outland Trophy: Jim Parker, 1956; Jim Stillwagon, 1970; John Hicks, 1973; Orlando Pace, 1996
First-round NFL draftees: 56
Website: www.ohiostatebuckeyes.com

THE BEST OF TIMES

Woody Hayes' iconic powers peaked from 1968 to 1977, when he went 91–16–2, including a 68–8 Big Ten record that produced nine league titles (three outright) and a national championship in 1968.

THE WORST OF TIMES

Three consecutive losing seasons and a 12–14–5 record in a four-year span from 1922 to 1925 under coach John W. Wilce.

CONFERENCE

Ohio State joined the Western Conference in 1913 and has remained in the league since. The Western Conference was popularly known as the Big Ten since 1917, but didn't officially change its name to the Big Ten Conference until 1987.

DISTINGUISHED ALUMNI

Jesse Owens; Jack Nicklaus; Bobby Knight; Jack Buck, baseball announcer; John Havlicek, 13-time NBA All-Star; Richard Lewis, comedian; R.L. Stine, author; Leslie H. Wexner, founder and president, The Limited, Inc.; Mal Whitfield, Olympic track and field

FIGHT SONGS

BUCKEYE BATTLE CRY
In old Ohio there's a team
That's known thru-out the land;
Eleven warriors, brave and bold,
Whose fame will ever stand.
And when the ball goes over,
Our cheers will reach the sky,
Ohio fields will hear again
The Buckeye Battle Cry -
Drive!
Drive on down the field,
Men of the scarlet and gray;
Don't let them thru that line,
We have to win this game today,
Come on, Ohio!
Smash through to Victory.
We cheer you as you go:
Our honor defend
We will fight to the end for O-hi-o.

Bob Hope once dotted the "i" at halftime.

Buckeye, however, is the only player to win the award twice. Archie Griffin did so, despite playing at 5'9", 180 pounds. The Columbus native gained 239 yards against North Carolina in his second game as a freshman, and four Rose Bowl appearances later he had a permanent place in the sport's history. Griffin used his quickness to blast out of the Power-I formation and cut back against pursuing defenders. He piled up 5,589 rushing yards, including at least 100 in an NCAA-record 31 consecutive games. Teammates called him Duckfoot for his self-described running style. Hayes called him "a better young man than he is a football player, and he's the best football player I've ever seen." As a senior in 1975, Griffin cast the deciding vote among teammates to name QB Cornelius Greene the team's MVP. Ohio State retired Griffin's No. 45, an unprecedented honor. He later worked 18 years in OSU's athletic department before resigning as associate athletic director to become president and CEO of the Ohio State Alumni Association.

BEST COACH Wayne Woodrow "Woody" Hayes is a caricature for many outside of his native Ohio. He's the stompin', snortin', fire-breathin' bully who ran a caveman "three yards and a cloud of dust" offense, tormented game officials, tore up yard markers, smashed his wrist watches and went down swinging. For Buckeyes fans, Hayes was the diabetic, sentimental, emotional, charming soul who quoted philosophers and generals, worked his entire career on one-year contracts, preached discipline to his players and urged them to "pay forward" to others. Hayes last coached the Buckeyes in 1978 and died in 1987, but he remains a larger-than-life figure and a measuring stick for everything about Ohio State. He won 205 games, 13 Big Ten championships and three national titles in 28 seasons. He did so with a complex combination—as tough, irascible, colloquial, brilliant and polarizing autocrat. "All good commanders want to die in the field," said Hayes, a former lieutenant commander in the Navy. In essence, he did so at the 1978 Gator Bowl. He punched Clemson noseguard Charlie Bauman after his interception sealed Ohio State's 17-15 loss. OSU president Harold Enarson fired Hayes the next day. Hayes cleaned out his office Monday morning.

BEST TEAM While the nation seemed unhinged by social

RECORDS		
RUSHING YARDS		
	GAME	
314	Eddie George vs. Illinois, Nov. 11, 1995 (36 att.)	
	SEASON	
1,927	Eddie George, 1995 (328 att.)	
	CAREER	
5,589	Archie Griffin, 1972-75 (924 att.)	
PASSING YARDS		
	GAME	
458	Art Schlichter vs. Florida State, Oct. 3, 1981 (31 of 52)	
	SEASON	
3,330	Joe Germaine, 1998 (230 of 384)	
	CAREER	
7,547	Art Schlichter, 1978-81 (497 of 951)	

RECEIVING YARDS	
GAME	
253	Terry Glenn vs. Pittsburgh, Sept. 23, 1995 (9 rec.)
SEASON	
1,435	David Boston, 1998 (85 rec.)
CAREER	
2,855	David Boston, 1996-98 (191 rec.)
POINTS	
GAME	
30	Keith Byars vs. Illinois, Oct. 13, 1984 (5 TDs); Pete Johnson vs. North Carolina, Sept. 27, 1975 (5 TDs)
SEASON	
156	Pete Johnson, 1975 (26 TDs)
CAREER	
356	Mike Nugent, 2001-04 (72 FGs, 140 PATs)

CONSENSUS ALL-AMERICANS	
1916-17, 1919	Charles Harley, B
1917	Charles Bolen, E
1920-21	Iolas Huffman, G/T
1920	Gaylord Stinchcomb, B
1925	Ed Hess, G
1928-30	Wes Fesler, E
1935	Gomer Jones, C
1939	Esco Sarkkinen, E
1944	Jack Dugger, E
1944	Les Horvath, B
1944	Bill Hackett, G
1945-46	Warren Amling, G/T
1950	Vic Janowicz, B
1954-55	Howard Cassady, B
1956	Jim Parker, G
1958	Bob White, B
1960-61	Bob Ferguson, B
1968	David Foley, T
1969	Jim Otis, RB
1969-70	Jack Tatum, DB
1969-70	Jim Stillwagon, MG
1973	John Hicks, OT
1972-73	Randy Gradishar, LB

(Continued on next page)

unrest in 1968, the conservative Hayes put together a monster team devoid of individualism and fueled by old-fashioned values. He also went against his nature and started five sophomores on offense and six on defense. The "Super Sophomores"—including quarterback Rex Kern, defensive back Jack Tatum and defensive lineman Jim Stillwagon—powered an offense that averaged 32 points and 440 yards per game and a defense that yielded an average of 15 points and 292 yards. The Buckeyes, spurred by an early-season upset of No. 1 Purdue, rolled 9–0 through the regular season and capped the national championship with a 27-16 win over USC in the Rose Bowl. Eleven players from that team, including seven of the sophomores, earned All-America honors during their careers. Six became first-round NFL draft picks. At a 20th reunion in 1988, members of the 1968 team presented Ohio State with a $1.2 million endowment in memory of Hayes.

BIGGEST GAME The 2003 Fiesta Bowl between Ohio State and Miami was arguably the greatest college football game ever played—a long, jazzy riff of controversy, breathless moments, bone-jarring hits and clutch performances. Ohio State's 31-24 double-overtime victory earned the school its fifth national championship, and its first since 1970. Freshman tailback Maurice Clarett ran five yards for the decisive TD in the second OT, then the Buckeyes' defense held on four downs from inside its own 2. The Hurricanes forced OT when Todd Sievers made a 40-yard field goal on the final play of regulation, tying the game at 17. The clutch kick was set up by Roscoe Parrish's 50-yard punt return. Trailing 24-17 in the first OT, Ohio State QB Craig Krenzel converted a fourth-and-14 play with a pass to Michael Jenkins. The Buckeyes then faced fourth and three at the Miami 5. Krenzel threw incomplete to Chris Gamble in the right corner of the end zone. Fireworks went off. The Hurricanes celebrated—prematurely. Field judge Terry Porter, a Big

CONSENSUS ALL-AMERICANS (CONT.)	
1974	Steve Myers, C
1974	Kurt Schumacher, OT
1974-75	Archie Griffin, RB
1975	Ted Smith, G
1975	Tim Fox, DB
1976	Bob Brudzinski, DE
1976-77	Chris Ward, T
1977-78	Tom Cousineau, LB
1979	Ken Fritz, G
1982	Marcus Marek, LB
1984	Keith Byars, RB
1984	Jim Lachey, OG
1986	Cris Carter, WR
1986-87	Chris Spielman, LB
1987	Tom Tupa, P
1993	Dan Wilkinson, DL
1994	Korey Stringer, OL
1995	Eddie George, RB
1995	Terry Glenn, WR
1995-96	Orlando Pace, OL
1996	Mike Vrabel, DL
1996	Shawn Springs, DB
1997	Andy Katzenmoyer, LB
1998	Rob Murphy, OL
1998	Antoine Winfield, DB
2001	LeCharles Bentley, C
2002	Mike Nugent, PK
2002	Matt Wilhelm, LB
2002	Mike Doss, DB
2003	Will Allen, DB
2004	Mike Nugent, PK
2004	A.J. Hawk, LB

12 official, called pass interference on Miami's Glenn Sharpe, who was covering Gamble. Three plays later, Krenzel dove in from the 1 to force a second OT. "We've always had the best damn band in the land," Tressel said. "Now we've got the best damn team in the land."

BIGGEST UPSET Purdue was ranked No. 1 and was a 14-point favorite against an OSU team it had smashed 41-6 the previous year. The Boilermakers were averaging 41.3 points when they entered Ohio Stadium on Oct. 12, 1968, to face the No. 4-ranked Buckeyes. A then-stadium-record crowd of 84,834 saw a scoreless first half turn into a 13-0 OSU victory. "It was the greatest effort I've ever seen," Hayes said. Ted Provost intercepted Purdue QB Mike Phipps on the fourth play of the second half and returned the ball 35 yards for a touchdown. Jim Stillwagon's interception later in the third quarter set up the second Ohio State TD. The Buckeyes sacked Phipps four times and held him to 106 passing yards. Ohio State's ferocious defensive play allowed it to overcome its own three missed field goals. Purdue star tailback Leroy Keyes gained just 18 yards while OSU fullback Jim Otis ground out 144 yards. The victory catapulted the Buckeyes to No. 2 in the polls and sent them on their way to the national championship.

HALLOWED GROUND Buckeye Grove sits on the east side of Ohio Stadium, and since 1934, a Buckeye tree has been planted in the spring to honor each Ohio State All-America from the previous season.

HEARTBREAKER Defending national champion Ohio State took a 22-game winning streak and a No. 1 ranking to Ann Arbor, Mich., on Nov. 22, 1969. The Buckeyes had won a conference-record 17 consecutive Big Ten games, had outscored eight opponents 371-69 and had won each game that season by at least 27 points. They hadn't

trailed in a game and were averaging 46 points and 512 yards of offense. Michigan's rookie coach, Bo Schembechler, a former Ohio State assistant, devised a way to defeat what some consider the greatest Buckeyes team. The Wolverines intercepted six passes and outrushed Ohio State 266-22. Michigan won 24-12, with all scoring coming in the first half. The "Ten Year War" was on.

WILDEST FINISH Buckeyes QB Pandel Savic had a pass from the Northwestern 12-yard line intercepted on the apparent final play of a 1947 game. The Ohio State band, figuring the home team had lost, took the field. Northwestern, however, was penalized for having 12 men on the field. The Buckeyes then tried a reverse, but Rodney Swinehart was tackled at the 2-yard line. Northwestern was penalized for being offside. Savic then threw a TD pass to Jimmy Clark to tie the score. The Wildcats blocked Emil Moldea's point-after kick, but they were again called for offsides. Head linesman E.C. Curtis called all three penalties with time expired. Moldea's second PAT was good for a 7-6 Ohio State win.

BEST COMEBACK Embattled coach John Cooper, 8–8–1 in his first 17 games at Ohio State, saw his 1989 team trailing Minnesota 31-0 late in the second quarter. The visiting Buckeyes, however, scored 41 of the game's last 47 points to pull out a 41-37 victory. QB Greg Frey capped a 73-yard drive by throwing a 15-yard TD pass to flanker Jeff Graham with 51 seconds remaining.

STADIUM Ohio Stadium was feared to be too large with a capacity of 66,210 when it opened in 1922. Instead, so many fans consistently filled the concrete horseshoe that increasingly larger temporary bleachers were constructed over the years in the open south end. Permanent seats now fill that area, but people still refer to the stadium on the east bank of the Olentangy River as The Horseshoe. The stadium, on the National Register of Historic Places,

ALL-CENTURY TEAM	
In February 2002, the Columbus Touchdown Club selected these players to the team.	
OFFENSE	
1954-56	Jim Parker, OL
1970, 1972-73	John Hicks, OL
1994-96	Orlando Pace, OL
1928-30	Wes Fesler, E
1984-86	Cris Carter, WR
1996-98	David Boston, WR
1968-70	Rex Kern, QB
1978-81	Art Schlichter, QB
1996-98	Joe Germaine, QB
1916-17, 1919	Chic Harley, RB
1940-42, 1944	Les Horvath, RB
1949-51	Vic Janowicz, RB
1952-55	Howard "Hopalong" Cassady, RB
1972-75	Archie Griffin, RB
1992-95	Eddie George, RB
1977-80	Vlade Janakievski, PK
DEFENSE	
1942-44	Bill Willis, DL
1968-70	Jim Stillwagon, DL
1971-73	Randy Gradishar, LB
1984-87	Chris Spielman, LB
1996-98	Andy Katzenmoyer, LB
1968-70	Jack Tatum, DB
1972-74	Neal Colzie, DB
1995-98	Antoine Winfield, DB
1973-76	Tom Skladany, P

is also called "the house that Harley built," in honor of Chic Harley, who became Ohio State's first three-time All-America in 1919. He was so popular that Ohio Field became too small for the crowds, causing a 1920 fund drive to build the $1.3 million Ohio Stadium. Prior to the 2001 season, a three-year, $210 million renovation project added the permanent south-end seats, along with 81 private luxury suites and over 2,600 club seats. The project lowered the field and raised capacity to 101,568.

RIVAL There are urinals throughout Columbus with a Michigan "M" painted in them. "They brainwash you into hating those suckers, and then you really believe it," Ohio State linebacker Steve Tovar said. Some people won't refer to Michigan by name, instead calling it "that school up north." Hayes started that, and he's responsible for turning the annual season-ending game, first played in 1897, into pigskin Armageddon. Legend has it that Hayes once pushed his car across the state border rather than buy gasoline in Michigan. In 1974, the Ohio State coach greeted then-president Gerald Ford, a Michigan alum, at the Columbus airport. A photo of the two ran in the next day's newspaper under the caption: "Woody Hayes and Friend." Hayes tried a two-point conversion with his team leading the Wolverines 50-14 in 1968. The play failed. Asked why he'd gone for two, Hayes said: "Because they wouldn't let me go for three." Hayes' hatred and paranoia of Michigan stemmed in part from Ohio State being known as "the graveyard of coaches" because of the Wolverines' dominance. Ohio State had 18 head coaches—including Pro Football Hall of Fame inductee Paul Brown—in the 60 years before Hayes' arrival in 1951. Cooper went 111–43–4 at Ohio State, but was fired after the 2000 season with a 2–10–1 record against the Wolverines.

DUBIOUS DISTINCTION His career began with over 100,000 fans chanting "Maur-ice" during his first Ohio

State game and ended in controversy after just one season, with fans in Columbus wearing T-shirts that read "Maurice Who?" Maurice Clarett helped the Buckeyes win one national championship and prompted two NCAA investigations of the program. The mercurial tailback from Youngstown, Ohio, ran for 1,237 yards and 16 touchdowns as a freshman in 2002. Clarett scored the winning touchdown, a five-yard run in the Fiesta Bowl's second overtime, as the Buckeyes upset Miami 31-24 in the BCS championship game to earn the school's first national title in 34 years. It was Clarett's last carry at Ohio State. He was suspended for his sophomore season for violating 14 NCAA rules, 12 of them pertaining to receiving improper benefits and two for lying to investigators. Clarett left school and sued the NFL, challenging the league's rules on early entry to the draft. After he originally won his case, U.S. district judge Shira A. Scheindlin overturned the decision. In a November 2004 *ESPN The Magazine* story, Clarett accused Ohio State coach Jim Tressel, some members of his staff and school boosters of a series of improprieties, including the arranging of loaner cars, no-show jobs and academic fraud. Tressel and Ohio State denied the charges. The NCAA returned to Columbus and is investigating the matter. One month after Clarett's public accusations, Ohio State suspended quarterback Troy Smith from the 2004 Alamo Bowl for accepting cash from a booster. A "bone-weary" and "burned-out" Andy Geiger announced on Jan. 5, 2005, that he was retiring as Ohio State athletic director on June 30, one year prior to his contract's expiration.

CONTROVERSY Ohio State fans still contend Brian Baschnagel scored from one yard out on the final play at Michigan State in 1974. The game officials ruled otherwise, and the Buckeyes suffered a 16-13 loss. The frantic, final play occurred after Champ Henson had carried the ball six yards to within inches of the goal line with 29 seconds remaining. Michigan State's players were slow getting off the pile. Ohio State scrambled and snapped the ball, but it went through QB Cornelius Greene's legs. Baschnagel picked it up and ran into the end zone. The head linesman signaled touchdown, but the back judge and field judge ruled that time had run out before the play began. Fans of each school climbed atop the goalposts, uncertain which team had won. Forty-six minutes later, the public address announcer told the half-empty stadium that Big Ten commissioner

Wayne Duke decided the officials were correct in ruling time had expired.

NICKNAME For years, Ohio State athletic teams called themselves Buckeyes, after Ohio's state tree, the buckeye. The school made it the official moniker in 1950.

MASCOT Brutus Buckeye, a student dressed in a big head shaped like a buckeye nut, first appeared in 1965. He wears a scarlet-and-gray shirt with BRUTUS across the chest. On at least two occasions before Michigan games, the mascot's head has been stolen, later retrieved and paid for with rewards.

UNIFORMS Three Ohio State students formed a selection committee in 1878 and chose orange and black as the school's colors. They later learned Princeton already used those colors, so scarlet and gray was settled on for no significant reason. In 1968, Hayes began awarding buckeye leaves to players who made good plays in games. These decal leaves are still placed on helmets today.

NUMBERS Other Buckeyes besides Griffin (45) to have their jersey numerals retired by Ohio State include Eddie George (27), Vic Janowicz (31), Howard "Hopalong" Cassady (40) and Les Horvath (22) … George rushed for a school-record 1,927 yards while winning the Heisman Trophy in 1995 … The Buckeyes have had 56 players selected in the first round of the NFL draft, including 12 from 1991 through 1997 … ABC television affiliate WSYX reported that 79% of the TVs turned on in Columbus on the night of the 2003 Fiesta Bowl were tuned into that game … Chris Gamble played 120 snaps in the Fiesta Bowl at cornerback, wide receiver and kick returner.

QUIRK The Buckeyes won the 1961 Big Ten championship with an 8–0–1 record, but the school's faculty committee voted 28-25 against accepting a Rose Bowl invitation. It reasoned that there was too much emphasis on football at Ohio State. Hayes and supporters went berserk, but the coach later helped keep peace in the streets by ordering co-captains Tom Perdue and Mike Ingram to tell protesting groups on campus to accept the school's decision.

LORE The game-time temperature was 10° for the Michigan game in Columbus on Nov. 25, 1950. Winds up to 40 mph blew snow horizontally. Ohio State AD Dick Larkins and Michigan AD Fritz Crisler discussed before kickoff the idea of postponing the game. "We're here and we're not coming

back down next week," Crisler said. Some in the crowd of 50,535 covered their heads with cardboard boxes. Officials used brooms to find yard lines. The teams combined for 68 total yards and booted 45 punts (some on first down) for 1,408 yards. Michigan won 9-3, scoring a touchdown and a safety on blocked punts. Ohio State then fired coach Wes Fesler (0–3–1 against the Wolverines) and hired Hayes.

QUOTE "You win with people."

— Woody Hayes

OHIO STATE ANNUAL STATISTICAL LEADERS

YR	RUSHING	YDS	ATT	AVG	PASSING	ATT	CMP	PCT	YDS	RECEIVING	REC	YDS	AVG
1944	Les Horvath	924	163	5.7	Les Horvath	32	14	.44	344		NA	NA	NA
1945	Ollie Cline	936	181	5.2	Dick Fisher	28	9	.32	245		NA	NA	NA
1946	Joseph Whisler	544	129	4.2	George Spencer	51	25	.49	398	Cecil Soudere	9	157	17.4
1947	Ollie Cline	332	80	4.2	Dick Slager	69	19	.28	236	Fred Morrison	7	113	16.1
1948	Joseph Whisler	579	132	4.4	Pandel Savic	69	36	.52	486	Alex Verdova	12	117	9.8
1949	Gerald Krall	606	128	4.7	Pandel Savic	84	35	.42	581	Ray Hamilton	15	347	23.1
1950	Walt Klevay	520	66	7.9	Vic Janowicz	77	32	.42	561	Thomas Watson	23	461	20.0
1951	Vic Janowicz	376	106	3.5	Tony Curcillo	133	58	.44	912	Bob Joslin	18	281	15.6
1952	John Hlay	535	133	4.0	John Borton	196	115	.59	1,555	Bob Grimes	39	534	13.7
1953	Bob Watkins	875	153	5.7	John Borton	86	45	.52	522	Thomas Hague	19	275	14.5
1954	Howard Cassady	609	102	6.0	Bill Leggett	95	46	.48	578	Howard Cassady	12	137	11.4
1955	Howard Cassady	958	161	6.0	Frank Ellwood	23	9	.39	60	Paul Michael	4	50	12.5
1956	Don Clark	797	139	5.7	Don Clark	7	3	.43	88	Leo Brown	8	151	18.9
1957	Don Clark	737	132	5.6	Frank Kremblas	47	20	.43	337	Dick LeBeau	7	91	13.0
1958	Bob White	859	218	3.9	Frank Kremblas	42	16	.38	281	Dick LeBeau/Donald Clark	8	110	13.8
1959	Bob Ferguson	371	61	6.1	Tom Matte	51	28	.55	439	James Houston	11	214	19.5
1960	Bob Ferguson	853	160	5.3	Tom Matte	95	50	.53	737	Charles Bryant	17	336	19.8
1961	Bob Ferguson	938	202	4.6	Joe Sparma	38	16	.42	341	Charles Bryant	15	270	18.0
1962	David Francis	624	119	5.2	Joe Sparma	71	30	.42	288	Paul Warfield	8	139	17.4
1963	Matt Snell	491	134	3.7	Don Unverferth	117	48	.41	586	Paul Warfield	22	266	12.1
1964	Willard Sander	626	147	4.3	Don Unverferth	160	73	.46	871	Bo Rein	22	320	14.5
1965	Tom Barrington	554	139	4.0	Don Unverferth	191	91	.48	1,061	Bo Rein	29	328	11.3
1966	Bo Rein	456	139	3.3	Bill Long	192	106	.55	1,180	Billy Anders	55	671	12.2
1967	Jim Otis	530	103	5.1	Bill Long	102	44	.43	563	Billy Anders	28	403	14.4
1968	Jim Otis	985	141	7.0	Rex Kern	131	75	.57	972	Bruce Jankowski	31	328	10.6
1969	Jim Otis	1,027	219	4.7	Rex Kern	135	68	.50	1,002	Bruce Jankowski	23	404	17.6
1970	John Brockington	1,142	261	4.4	Rex Kern	98	45	.46	470	Jan White	17	171	10.1
1971	Rick Galbos	540	141	3.8	Don Lamka	107	54	.50	718	Dick Wakefield	31	432	13.9
1972	Archie Griffin	867	159	5.5	Greg Hare	111	55	.50	815	Rick Galbos	11	235	21.4
1973	Archie Griffin	1,577	247	6.4	Cornelius Greene	46	20	.43	343	Fred Pagac	9	159	17.7
1974	Archie Griffin	1,695	256	6.6	Cornelius Greene	97	58	.60	939	Brian Baschnagel	19	244	12.8
1975	Archie Griffin	1,450	262	5.5	Cornelius Greene	121	68	.56	1,066	Brian Baschnagel	24	362	15.1
1976	Jeff Logan	1,248	218	5.7	Jim Pacenta	54	28	.52	404	James Harrell	14	288	20.6
1977	Ron Springs	1,166	200	5.8	Rod Gerald	114	67	.59	1,016	Ron Springs	16	90	5.6
1978	Paul Campbell	591	142	4.2	Art Schlichter	175	87	.50	1,250	Doug Donley	24	510	21.3
1979	Calvin Murray	872	173	5.0	Art Schlichter	200	105	.53	1,816	Doug Donley	37	800	21.6
1980	Calvin Murray	1,267	195	6.5	Art Schlichter	226	122	.54	1,930	Doug Donley	43	887	20.6
1981	Tim Spencer	1,217	226	5.4	Art Schlichter	350	183	.52	2,551	Gary Williams	50	941	18.8
1982	Tim Spencer	1,538	273	5.6	Mike Tomczak	187	96	.51	1,602	Gary Williams	40	690	17.3
1983	Keith Byars	1,199	222	5.4	Mike Tomczak	237	131	.55	1,942	John Frank	45	641	14.2
1984	Keith Byars	1,764	336	5.3	Mike Tomczak	244	145	.59	1,952	Keith Byars	42	479	11.4
1985	John Wooldridge	820	174	4.7	Jim Karsatos	289	177	.61	2,311	Cris Carter	58	950	16.4
1986	Vince Workman	1,030	210	4.9	Jim Karsatos	272	145	.53	2,122	Cris Carter	69	1,127	16.3
1987	Vince Workman	470	118	4.0	Tom Tupa	242	134	.55	1,786	Everett Ross	29	585	20.2
1988	Carlos Snow	775	152	5.1	Greg Frey	293	152	.52	2,028	Jeff Ellis	40	492	12.3
1989	Carlos Snow	990	190	5.2	Greg Frey	246	144	.59	2,132	Jeff Graham	32	608	19.0
1990	Robert Smith	1,126	177	6.4	Greg Frey	276	139	.50	2,062	Bobby Olive	41	652	15.9
1991	Carlos Snow	828	169	4.9	Kent Graham	153	79	.52	1,018	Bernard Edwards	27	381	14.1
1992	Robert Smith	819	147	5.6	Kirk Herbstreit	264	155	.59	1,904	Brian Stablein	53	643	12.1
1993	Raymont Harris	1,344	273	4.9	Bobby Hoying	202	109	.54	1,570	Joey Galloway	47	946	20.1
1994	Eddie George	1,442	276	5.2	Bobby Hoying	301	170	.56	2,335	Joey Galloway	44	669	15.2
1995	Eddie George	1,927	328	5.9	Bobby Hoying	341	211	.62	3,269	Terry Glenn	64	1,411	22.0
1996	Pepe Pearson	1,484	299	5.0	Stanley Jackson	165	87	.53	1,298	Dimitrious Stanley	43	829	19.3
1997	Pepe Pearson	869	192	4.5	Joe Germaine	210	129	.61	1,847	David Boston	73	970	13.3
1998	Michael Wiley	1,235	198	6.2	Joe Germaine	384	230	.60	3,330	David Boston	85	1,435	16.9
1999	Michael Wiley	952	183	5.2	Steve Bellisari	224	101	.45	1,616	Reggie Germany	43	656	15.3
2000	Derek Combs	888	175	5.1	Steve Bellisari	310	163	.53	2,319	Ken-Yon Rambo	53	794	15.0
2001	Jonathan Wells	1,294	251	5.2	Steve Bellisari	220	119	.54	1,919	Michael Jenkins	49	988	20.2
2002	Maurice Clarett	1,237	222	5.6	Craig Krenzel	249	148	.59	2,110	Michael Jenkins	61	1,076	17.6
2003	Lydell Ross	826	193	4.3	Craig Krenzel	278	153	.55	2,040	Michael Jenkins	55	834	15.2
2004	Lydell Ross	475	117	4.1	Justin Zwick	187	93	.50	1,209	Santonio Holmes	55	769	14.0

Receiving leaders by receptions
All statistics include postseason

OHIO STATE ALL-TIME SCORES

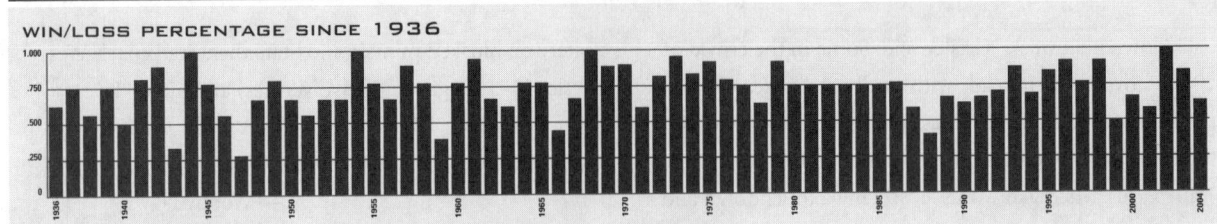

WIN/LOSS PERCENTAGE SINCE 1936

THE SCHOOLS

ALEXANDER S. LILLEY
1890-91 (.375)   3-5

1890   1-3-0
M3 •	at Ohio Wesleyan	20	14
N1	Wooster	0	64
N14	at Denison	0	14
N27	Kenyon	0	18

1891   2-2-0
N11	Western Reserve	6	50
N14	at Kenyon	0	26
N28 •	Denison	8	4
D5 •	at Akron	6	0

JACK RYDER
1892-95, '98 (.500)   22-22-2

1892   5-3-0
O15	at Oberlin	4	40
O22 •	at Akron	62	0
O29 •	Marietta	80	0
N5 •	at Denison	32	0
N7	Oberlin	0	50
N12	Dayton YMCA	42	4
N19 •	at Western Reserve	18	40
N24 •	Kenyon	26	10

1893   4-5-0
S30	at Otterbein	16	22
O14 •	Wittenberg	36	10
O21	Oberlin	10	38
O28	at Kenyon	6	42
N4	Western Reserve	16	30
N11 •	Akron	32	18
N18 •	Cincinnati	38	0
N25 •	Marietta	40	8
N30	Kenyon	8	10

1894   6-5-0
S15	at Akron	6	12
S17	at Wittenberg	0	6
O6 •	Antioch	32	0
O13	at Wittenberg	6	18
O20 •	at Columbus Barracks	30	0
O27 •	Western Reserve	4	24
N3 •	Marietta	10	4
N10	at Case	0	38
N17 •	at Cincinnati	6	4
N24 •	17th Regiment	46	4
N29 •	Kenyon	20	4

1895   4-4-2
O5 •	Akron	14	6
O12	at Otterbein	6	14
O19	Oberlin	0	12
O26 =	at Denison	4	4
N2 •	Ohio Wesleyan	8	8
N9 •	at Cincinnati	4	0
N15 •	at Kentucky	8	6
N16	at Central Kentucky	0	18
N23	at Marietta	0	24
N28 •	Kenyon	12	10

CHARLES A. HICKEY
1896 (.500)   5-5-1

1896   5-5-1
O3 •	Ohio Medical	24	0
O10	at Cincinnati	6	8
O17 •	at Otterbein	12	0
O23 •	at Oberlin	0	16
O30 •	Case	30	10
N5	Ohio Wesleyan	4	10
N7 •	Columbus Barracks	10	2
N11 =	Ohio Medical	0	0
N14 •	Wittenberg	6	24
N21 •	Ohio Medical	12	0
N26	Kenyon	18	34

DAVID F. EDWARDS
1897 (.167)   1-7-1

1897   1-7-1
O6 •	Ohio Medical	6	0
O9	Case	0	14
O16	at Michigan	0	34 *
O23 =	Otterbein	12	12
O26	Columbus Barracks	0	6
O30	Oberlin	0	44
N6	at West Virginia	0	24 *
N13	at Cincinnati	0	24 *
N25	Ohio Wesleyan	0	6

JACK RYDER

1898   3-5-0
O1 •	Heidelberg	17	0
O8	Ohio Medical	0	10
O15 •	Denison	34	0
O22	Marietta	0	10
N5 •	at Western Reserve	0	49
N12	Case	5	23
N19	Kenyon	0	29
N24 •	Ohio Wesleyan	24	0

JOHN B. ECKSTORM
1899-1901 (.810)   22-4-3

1899   9-0-1
S30 •	Otterbein	30	0
O7 •	Wittenberg	28	0
O14 =	at Case	5	5
O21 •	Ohio U.	41	0
O28 •	at Oberlin	6	0
N4 •	Western Reserve	6	0
N11 •	Marietta	17	0
N18 •	Ohio Medical	12	0
N25 •	at Muskingum	34	0
N30 •	Kenyon	5	0

1900   8-1-1
S29 •	Otterbein	20	0
O6 •	Ohio U.	20	0
O13 •	at Cincinnati	29	0
O20 •	Ohio Wesleyan	47	0
O27 •	Oberlin	17	0
N3 •	West Virginia	27	0
N10 •	Case	24	10
N17 •	Ohio Medical	6	11
N24 =	at Michigan	0	0
N29 •	Kenyon	23	5

1901   5-3-1
S28 =	Otterbein	0	0
O5 •	Wittenberg	30	0
O12 •	Ohio U.	17	0
O19 •	Marietta	24	0
O26 •	Western Reserve	6	5
N9	Michigan	0	21
N16	at Oberlin	0	6
N23	Indiana	6	18
N28 •	Kenyon	11	6

PERRY HALE
1902-03 (.714)   14-5-2

1902   6-2-2
S27 •	Otterbein	5	0
O4 •	Ohio U.	17	0
O11 •	West Virginia	30	0
O18 •	Marietta	34	0
O25	at Michigan	0	86
N1 •	Kenyon	51	5
N8 •	Case	12	23
N15 =	Illinois	0	0
N22 •	at Ohio Wesleyan	17	16
N27 =	Indiana	6	6

1903   8-3-0
S26 •	Otterbein	18	0
O3 •	Wittenberg	28	0
O10 •	Denison	24	5
O14 •	Muskingum	30	0
O17 •	Kenyon	59	0
O24 •	at Case	0	12
O31 •	West Virginia	34	6
N7 •	at Michigan	0	36
N14 •	Oberlin	27	5
N21 •	Ohio Wesleyan	29	6
N28 •	Indiana	16	17

E.R. SWEETLAND
1904-05 (.652)   14-7-2

1904   6-5-0
S24 •	Otterbein	34	0
O1 •	Miami, Ohio	80	0
O5 •	Denison	24	0
O8 •	Muskingum	46	0
O15 •	Michigan	6	31
O22 •	Case	16	6
O29 •	at Indiana	0	8
N5 •	Illinois	0	46
N12 •	at Oberlin	2	4
N19 •	Kenyon	11	5
N24 •	Carlisle	0	23

1905   8-2-2
S23 =	Otterbein	6	6
S30 •	Heildelberg	28	0
O4 •	Muskingum	40	0
O7 •	Wittenberg	17	0
O14 •	Denison	2	0
O21 •	DePauw	32	6
O28 =	Case	0	0
N4 •	Kenyon	23	0
N11 •	at Michigan	0	40
N18 •	Oberlin	36	0
N25 •	Wooster	15	0
N30 •	Indiana	0	11

A.E. HERRNSTEIN
1906-09 (.731)   28-10-1

1906   8-1-0
S29 •	Otterbein	41	0
O6 •	Wittenberg	52	0
O10 •	Muskingum	16	0
O20 •	Michigan	0	6
N3 •	at Oberlin	6	0
N10 •	Kenyon	6	0
N17 •	at Case	9	0
N24 •	Wooster	12	0
N29 •	Ohio Medical	11	8

1907   7-2-1
S28 •	Otterbein	28	0
O5 •	Muskingum	16	0
O12 •	Denison	28	0
O19 =	Wooster	6	6
O26 •	at Michigan	0	22
N2 •	Kenyon	12	0
N9 •	Oberlin	22	10
N16 •	Case	9	11
N23 •	Heidelburg	23	0
N28 •	Ohio Wesleyan	16	0

1908   6-4-0
S26 •	Otterbein	18	0
O3 •	Wooster	0	8
O10 •	Denison	16	2
O17 •	Western Reserve	0	18
O24 •	Michigan	6	10
O31 •	Ohio Wesleyan	20	9
N7 •	at Case	8	18
N14 •	at Vanderbilt	17	6
N21 •	Oberlin	14	12
N26 •	Kenyon	19	9

1909   7-3-0
S25 •	Otterbein	14	0
O2 •	Wittenberg	39	0
O9 •	Wooster	74	0
O16 •	at Michigan	6	33
O23 •	Denison	29	0
O30 •	Ohio Wesleyan	21	6
N6 •	Case	3	11
N13 •	Vanderbilt	5	0
N20 •	at Oberlin	6	26
N25 •	Kenyon	22	0

HOWARD JONES
1910 (.750)   6-1-3

1910   6-1-3
S24 •	Otterbein	14	5
O1 •	Wittenberg	62	0
O8 •	Cinncinnati	23	0
O15 •	Western Reserve	6	0
O22 =	Michigan	3	3
O29 •	Denison	5	5
N5	at Case	10	14
N12 •	Ohio Wesleyan	6	0
N19 •	Oberlin	0	0
N24 •	Kenyon	53	0

HARRY VAUGHN
1911 (.600)   5-3-2

1911   5-3-2
S30 •	Otterbein	6	0
O7 •	Miami, Ohio	3	0
O14 •	Western Reserve	0	0
O21 •	at Michigan	0	19
O28 •	Ohio Wesleyan	3	0
N4 •	Case	0	9
N11 •	Kenyon	24	0
N18 •	at Oberlin	0	0
N25 •	Syracuse	0	6
N30 •	at Cincinnati	11	6

JOHN R. RICHARDS
1912 (.667)   6-3

1912   6-3-0
O5 •	at Otterbein	55	0
O12 •	Denison	34	0
O19 •	Michigan	0	14
O26 •	Cincinnati	47	7 *
N2 •	at Case	31	6
N9 •	Oberlin	23	17
N16 •	Penn State	0	37
N23 •	at Ohio Wesleyan	36	6
N28 •	Michigan State	20	35

JOHN W. WILCE
1913-28 (.688)   78-33-9

1913-PRESENT
BIG 10

1913   4-2-1 (1-2-0)
O4 •	Ohio Wesleyan	58	0
O11 •	Western Reserve	14	8
O18 •	Oberlin	0	0
N1 |	Indiana	6	7
N8 |	at Wisconsin	0	12
N15 •	Case	18	0
N22 • |	Northwestern	58	0

1914   5-2-0 (2-2-0)
O3 •	Ohio Wesleyan	16	2
O10 •	at Case	7	6
O17 |	at Illinois	0	37
O24 |	Wisconsin	6	7
N7 • |	at Indiana	13	3
N14 •	Oberlin	39	0
N21 • |	Northwestern	27	0

1915 — 5-1-1 (2-1-1)
O2	●	Ohio Wesleyan	19 6
O9	●	Case	14 0
O16	|	Illinois	3 3
O23		at Wisconsin	0 21
N6	●	Indiana	10 9
N13	●	Oberlin	25 0
N20	|	at Northwestern	34 0

1916 — 7-0-0 (4-0-0)
O7	●	Ohio Wesleyan	12 0
O14	●	Oberlin	128 0
O21	|	at Illinois	7 6
N4	●	Wisconsin	14 13
N11	●	Indiana	46 7
N18		at Case	28 0
N25	|	Northwestern	23 3

1917 — 8-0-1 (4-0-0)
S29	●	Case	49 0
O6	●	Ohio Wesleyan	53 0
O13	|	Northwestern	40 0
O27	●	Denison	67 0
N3	●	at Indiana	26 3
N10	|	at Wisconsin	16 3
N17	●	Illinois	13 0
N24	|	Auburn MONT	0 0
N29	●	Camp Sherman	28 0

1918 — 3-3-0 (0-3-0)
O5	●	Ohio Wesleyan	41 0
O12	●	Denison	34 0
N9	●	Case	56 0
N16		at Illinois	0 13
N23	|	Wisconsin	3 14
N30	|	at Michigan	0 14

1919 — 6-1-0 (3-1-0)
O4	●	Ohio Wesleyan	38 0
O11	●	Cincinnati	46 0
O18	●	Kentucky	49 0
O25	●	at Michigan	13 3
N8	●	Purdue	20 0
N15		at Wisconsin	3 0
N22	|	Illinois	7 9

1920 — 7-1-0 (5-0-0)
O2	●	Ohio Wesleyan	55 0
O9	●	Oberlin	37 0
O16	●	Purdue	17 0
O23	●	Wisconsin	13 7
O30	●	at Chicago	7 6
N6	●	Michigan	14 7
N20	●	at Illinois	7 0
ROSE BOWL			
J1		California	0 28

1921 — 5-2-0 (4-1-0)
O1	●	Ohio Wesleyan	28 0
O8	●	Oberlin	6 7
O15	●	Minnesota	27 0
O22	●	at Michigan	14 0
N5	●	at Chicago	7 0
N12	●	Purdue	28 0
N19	|	Illinois	0 7

1922 — 3-4-0 (1-4-0)
O7	●	Ohio Wesleyan	5 0
O14	●	Oberlin	14 0
O21	|	Michigan	0 19
O28		at Minnesota	0 9
N11	●	Chicago	9 14
N18	●	Iowa	9 12
N25	●	at Illinois	6 3

1923 — 3-4-1 (1-4-0)
O6	●	Ohio Wesleyan	24 7
O13	=	Colgate	23 23
O20	|	at Michigan	0 23
O27	|	Iowa	0 20
N3	●	Denison	42 0
N10	●	at Purdue	32 0
N17	|	at Chicago	3 17
N24	|	Illinois	0 9

1924 — 2-3-3 (1-3-2)
O4	|	Purdue	7 0
O11	=	at Iowa	0 0
O18	●	Ohio Wesleyan	10 0
O25	=	Chicago	3 3
N1	●	Wooster	7 7
N8	|	Indiana	7 12
N15	|	Michigan	6 16
N22	|	at Illinois	0 7

1925 — 4-3-1 (1-3-1)
O3	●	Ohio Wesleyan	10 3
O10	●	Columbia	9 0
O17	=	at Chicago	3 3
O24	|	Iowa	0 15
O31	●	Wooster	17 0
N7	|	Indiana	7 0
N14	|	at Michigan	0 10
N21	|	Illinois	9 14

1926 — 7-1-0 (3-1-0)
O2	●	Wittenberg	40 0
O9	●	Ohio Wesleyan	47 0
O16	●	Columbia NYC	32 7
O23	●	Iowa	23 6
O30	●	at Chicago	18 0
N6	●	Wilmington	13 7
N13	|	Michigan	16 17
N20	●	at Illinois	7 6

1927 — 4-4-0 (2-3-0)
O1	●	Wittenberg	31 0
O8	●	at Iowa	13 6
O15	|	Northwestern	13 19
O22	|	at Michigan	0 21
O29	●	Chicago	13 7
N5		at Princeton	0 20
N12	●	Denison	61 6
N19	|	Illinois	0 13

1928 — 5-2-1 (3-2-0)
O6	●	Wittenberg	41 0
O13	●	at Northwestern	10 0
O20	|	Michigan	19 7
O27	●	at Indiana	13 0
N3	|	Princeton	6 6
N10	|	Iowa	7 14
N17	●	Muskingum	39 0
N24	|	at Illinois	0 8

SAM S. WILLAMAN
1929-33 (.695) — 26-10-5

1929 — 4-3-1 (2-2-1)
O5	●	Wittenberg	19 0
O12	|	Iowa	7 6
O19		at Michigan	7 0
O26	=	Indiana	0 0
N2		at Pittsburgh	2 18
N9	|	Northwestern	6 18
N16	●	Kenyon	54 0
N23	|	Illinois	0 27

1930 — 5-2-1 (2-2-1)
S27	●	Mt. Union	59 0
O4	●	Indiana	23 0
O11	|	at Northwestern	2 19
O18	|	Michigan	0 13
N1	=	Wisconsin	0 0
N8	●	Navy BALT	27 0
N15	●	Pittsburgh	16 7
N22	●	at Illinois	12 9

1931 — 6-3-0 (4-2-0)
O3	●	Cincinnati	67 6
O10	●	Vanderbilt	21 26
O17	●	at Michigan	20 7
O24	|	Northwestern	0 10
O31	●	at Indiana	13 6 *
N7	●	Navy	20 0
N14	●	at Wisconsin	6 0
N21	●	Illinois	40 0
N28	|	at Minnesota	7 19

1932 — 4-1-3 (2-1-2)
O1	●	Ohio Wesleyan	34 7
O8	|	Indiana	7 7
O15	|	Michigan	0 14
O22		at Pittsburgh	0 0
O29	|	Wisconsin	7 7
N5	|	at Northwestern	20 6
N12	●	Pennsylvania	19 0
N19	●	at Illinois	3 0

1933 — 7-1-0 (4-1-0)
O7	●	Virginia	75 0
O14	●	Vanderbilt	20 0
O21	|	at Michigan	0 13
O28	●	Northwestern	12 0
N4	●	Indiana	21 0
N11	●	at Pennsylvania	20 7
N18	●	at Wisconsin	6 0
N25	●	Illinois	7 6

FRANCIS A. SCHMIDT
1934-40 (.705) — 39-16-1

1934 — 7-1-0 (5-1-0)
O6	●	Indiana	33 0
O13	|	at Illinois	13 14
O20	●	Colgate	10 7
O27	●	at Northwestern	28 6
N3	●	at Western Reserve	76 0
N10	●	Chicago	33 0
N17	●	Michigan	34 0
N24	|	Iowa	40 7

1935 — 7-1-0 (5-0-0)
O5	●	Kentucky	19 6
O12	●	Drake	85 7
O19	●	Northwestern	28 7
O26	●	at Indiana	28 6
N2	|	Notre Dame	13 18
N9	|	at Chicago	20 13
N16	●	Illinois	6 0
N23	●	at Michigan	38 0

1936 — 5-3-0 (4-1-0)
O3	●	NYU	60 0
O10	|	Pittsburgh	0 6
O17	●	at Northwestern	13 14
O24	●	Indiana	7 0
O31	|	at Notre Dame	2 7
N7	●	Chicago	44 0
N14	●	at Illinois	13 0
N21	●	Michigan	21 0

1937 — 6-2-0 (5-1-0)
S25	●	TCU	14 0
O2	●	Purdue	13 0
O9	|	at Southern Cal	12 13
O23	●	Northwestern	7 0
O30	●	at Chicago	39 0
N6	|	Indiana	0 10
N13	●	Illinois	19 0
N20	●	at Michigan	21 0

1938 — 4-3-1 (3-2-1)
O1	●	Indiana	6 0
O8	|	Southern Cal	7 14
O15	=	at Northwestern	0 0
O22	●	Chicago	42 7
O29	●	NYU NYC	32 0
N5	|	Purdue	0 12
N12	●	at Illinois	32 14
N19	|	Michigan	0 18

1939 — 6-2-0 (5-1-0)
O7	●	Missouri	19 0
O14	●	Northwestern	13 0
O21	●	at Minnesota	23 20
O28	|	Cornell	14 23
N4	●	Indiana	24 0
N11	●	at Chicago	61 0
N18	●	Illinois	21 0
N25	|	at Michigan	14 21

1940 — 4-4-0 (3-3-0)
S28	●	Pittsburgh	30 7
O5	|	Purdue	17 14
O12	|	at Northwestern	3 6
O19	●	Minnesota	7 13
O26	●	at Cornell	7 21
N2	●	Indiana	21 6
N16	|	at Illinois	14 6
N23	|	at Michigan	0 40

PAUL E. BROWN
1941-43 (.685) — 18-8-1

1941 — 6-1-1 (3-1-1)
S27	●	Missouri	12 7
O4	●	at Southern Cal	33 0
O18	●	Purdue	16 14
O25	●	Northwestern	7 14
N1	●	at Pittsburgh	21 14
N8	●	Wisconsin	46 34
N15	●	Illinois	12 7
N22	=	at Michigan	20 20

1942 — 9-1-0 (5-1-0)
S26	●	Fort Knox	59 0
O3	|	Indiana	32 21
O10	●	Southern Cal	28 12
O17	●	Purdue	26 0
O24	●	at Northwestern	20 6
O31	●	at Wisconsin	7 17
N7	●	Pittsburgh	59 19
N14	●	Illinois CLEV	44 20
N21	●	Michigan	21 7
N28	●	Iowa Pre-Flight	41 12

1943 — 3-6-0 (1-4-0)
S25	●	Iowa Pre-Flight	13 28
O2	●	Missouri	27 6
O9	●	at Great Lakes NAS	6 13
O16	●	Purdue CLEV	7 30
O23	|	Northwestern	0 13
O30	●	Indiana	14 20
N6	●	at Pittsburgh	46 6
N13	●	Illinois	29 26
N20	|	at Michigan	7 45

CARROLL C. WIDDOES
1944-45 (.889) — 16-2

1944 — 9-0-0 (6-0-0)
S30	●	Missouri	54 0
O7	|	Iowa	34 0
O14	●	at Wisconsin	20 7
O21	●	Great Lakes NAS	26 6
O28	●	Minnesota	34 14
N4	●	Indiana	21 7
N11	●	Pittsburgh	54 19
N18	●	Illinois CLEV	26 12
N25	●	Michigan	18 14

1945 — 7-2-0 (5-2-0)
S29	●	at Missouri	47 6
O6	●	Iowa	42 0
O13	●	Wisconsin	12 0
O20	|	Purdue	13 35
O27	●	at Minnesota	20 7
N3	●	Northwestern	16 14
N10	●	at Pittsburgh	14 0
N17	●	Illinois	27 2
N24	|	at Michigan	3 7

PAUL O. BIXLER
1946 (.556) — 4-3-2

1946 — 4-3-2 (2-3-1)
S28	=	Missouri	13 13
O5	●	at Southern Cal	21 0
O12	|	at Wisconsin	7 20
O19	|	Purdue	14 14
O26	●	Minnesota	39 9
N2	|	at Northwestern	39 27
N9	●	Pittsburgh	20 13
N16	|	at Illinois	7 16
N23	|	Michigan	6 58

WESLEY E. FESLER
1947-50 (.608) — 21-13-3

1947 — 2-6-1 (1-4-1)
S27	●	Missouri	13 7
O4	|	at Purdue	20 24
O11	|	Southern Cal	0 32
O18	=	Iowa	13 13
O25	|	at Pittsburgh	0 12
N1	|	Indiana	0 7
N8	●	Northwestern	7 6
N15	|	Illinois	7 28
N22	|	at Michigan	0 21

1948 — 6-3-0 (3-3-0)
S25	●	Missouri	21 7
O2	●	Southern Cal	20 0
O9	|	Iowa	7 14
O16	●	at Indiana	17 0
O23	●	Wisconsin	34 32
O30	|	at Northwestern	7 21
N6	●	Pittsburgh	41 0
N13	●	at Illinois	34 7
N20	|	Michigan	3 13

1949 — 7-1-2 (4-1-1)
S24	●	Missouri	35 34
O1	●	Indiana	46 7
O8	=	at Southern Cal	13 13
O15	|	Minnesota	0 27
O22	●	at Wisconsin	21 0
O29	|	Northwestern	24 7
N5	●	at Pittsburgh	14 10
N12	●	Illinois	30 17
N19	=	at Michigan	7 7
ROSE BOWL			
J2	●	California	17 14

662 OHIO STATE

THE SCHOOLS

1950 6-3-0 (5-2-0)

S30		SMU	27	32
O7	●	Pittsburgh	41	7
O14	●	at Indiana	26	14
O21	●	at Minnesota	48	0
O28	●	Iowa	83	21
N4	●	at Northwestern	32	0
N11	●	Wisconsin	19	14
N18		at Illinois	7	14
N25		Michigan	3	9

W.W. "WOODY" HAYES
1951-78 (.761) 205-61-10

1951 4-3-2 (2-2-2)

S29	●	SMU	7	0
O6		Michigan State	20	24
O13	=	at Wisconsin	6	6
O20		Indiana	10	32
O27	●	Iowa	47	21
N3	●	Northwestern	3	0
N10	●	at Pittsburgh	16	14
N17	=	Illinois	0	0
N24		at Michigan	0	7

1952 6-3-0 (5-2-0)

S27	●	Indiana	33	13
O4		Purdue	14	21
O11	●	Wisconsin	23	14
O18	●	Washington State	35	7
O25		at Iowa	0	8
N1	●	at Northwestern	24	21
N8		Pittsburgh	14	21
N15	●	at Illinois	27	7
N22	●	Michigan	27	7

1953 6-3-0 (4-3-0)

S26	●	Indiana	36	12
O3	●	at California	33	19
O10		Illinois	20	41
O17	●	at Pennsylvania	12	6
O24	●	at Wisconsin	20	19
O31	●	Northwestern	27	13
N7		Michigan State	13	28
N14	●	Purdue	21	6
N21		at Michigan	0	20

1954 10-0-0 (7-0-0)

S25	●	Indiana	28	0
O2	●	California	21	13
O9	●	at Illinois	40	7
O16	●	Iowa	20	14
O23	●	Wisconsin	31	14
O30	●	at Northwestern	14	7
N6	●	Pittsburgh	26	0
N13	●	at Purdue	28	6
N20	●	Michigan	21	7
		ROSE BOWL		
J1	●	Southern Cal	20	7

1955 7-2-0 (6-0-0)

S24	●	Nebraska	28	20
O1		at Stanford	0	6
O8	●	Illinois	27	12
O15		Duke	14	20
O22	●	at Wisconsin	26	16
O29	●	Northwestern	49	0
N5	●	Indiana	20	13
N12	●	Iowa	20	10
N19	●	at Michigan	17	0

1956 6-3-0 (4-2-0)

S29	●	Nebraska	34	7
O6	●	Stanford	32	20
O13	●	at Illinois	26	6
O20		Penn State	6	7
O27	●	Wisconsin	21	0
N3	●	at Northwestern	6	2
N10	●	Indiana	35	14
N17		at Iowa	0	6
N24		Michigan	0	19

1957 9-1-0 (7-0-0)

S28		TCU	14	18
O5	●	at Washington	35	7
O12	●	Illinois	21	7
O19	●	Indiana	56	0
O26	●	at Wisconsin	16	13
N2	●	Northwestern	47	6
N9	●	Purdue	20	7
N16	●	Iowa	17	13
N23	●	at Michigan	31	14
		ROSE BOWL		
J1	●	Oregon	10	7

1958 6-1-2 (4-1-2)

S27	●	SMU	23	20
O4	●	Washington	12	7
O11	●	at Illinois	19	13
O18	●	Indiana	49	8
O25	=	Wisconsin	7	7
N1		at Northwestern	0	21
N8	=	Purdue	14	14
N15	●	at Iowa	38	28
N22	●	Michigan	20	14

1959 3-5-1 (2-4-1)

S26	●	Duke	14	13
O2		at Southern Cal	0	17
O10		Illinois	0	9
O17	●	Purdue	15	0
O24		at Wisconsin	3	12
O31	●	Michigan State	30	24
N7	=	Indiana	0	0
N14		Iowa	7	16
N21		at Michigan	14	23

1960 7-2-0 (5-2-0)

S24	●	SMU	24	0
O1	●	Southern Cal	20	0
O8	●	at Illinois	34	7
O15		at Purdue	21	24
O22	●	Wisconsin	34	7
O29	●	at Michigan State	21	10
N5	●	Indiana	36	7
N12		at Iowa	12	35
N19	●	Michigan	7	0

1961 8-0-1 (6-0-0)

S30	=	TCU	7	7
O7	●	UCLA	13	3
O14	●	Illinois	44	0
O21	●	at Northwestern	10	0
O28	●	at Wisconsin	30	21
N4	●	Iowa	29	13
N11	●	at Indiana	16	7
N18	●	Oregon	22	12
N25	●	at Michigan	50	20

1962 6-3-0 (4-2-0)

S29	●	North Carolina	41	7
O6		at UCLA	7	9
O13	●	at Illinois	51	15
O20		Northwestern	14	18
O27	●	Wisconsin	14	7
N3		at Iowa	14	28
N10	●	Indiana	10	7
N17	●	Oregon	26	7
N24	●	Michigan	28	0

1963 5-3-1 (4-1-1)

S28	●	Texas A&M	17	0
O5	●	at Indiana	21	0
O12	=	Illinois	20	20
O19		at Southern Cal	3	32
O26	●	at Wisconsin	13	10
N2	●	Iowa	7	3
N9		Penn State	7	10
N16		Northwestern	8	17
N23	●	at Michigan	14	10

1964 7-2-0 (5-1-0)

S26	●	SMU	27	8
O3	●	Indiana	17	9
O10	●	at Illinois	26	0
O17	●	Southern Cal	17	0
O24	●	Wisconsin	28	3
O31	●	at Iowa	21	19
N7		Penn State	0	27
N14	●	Northwestern	10	0
N21		Michigan	0	10

1965 7-2-0 (6-1-0)

S25		North Carolina	3	14
O2	●	at Washington	23	21
O9	●	Illinois	28	14
O16		at Michigan State	7	32
O23	●	at Wisconsin	20	10
O30	●	Minnesota	11	10
N6	●	Indiana	17	10
N13	●	Iowa	38	0
N20	●	at Michigan	9	7

1966 4-5-0 (3-4-0)

S24	●	TCU	14	7
O1		Washington	22	38
O8		at Illinois	9	10
O15		Michigan State	8	11
O22	●	Wisconsin	24	13
O29		at Minnesota	7	17
N5	●	Indiana	7	0
N12	●	at Iowa	14	10
N19		Michigan	3	17

1967 6-3-0 (5-2-0)

S30		Arizona	7	14
O7	●	at Oregon	30	0
O14		Purdue	6	41
O21	●	at Northwestern	6	2
O28		Illinois	13	17
N4	●	at Michigan State	21	7
N11	●	Wisconsin	17	15
N18	●	Iowa	21	10
N25	●	at Michigan	24	14

1968 10-0-0 (7-0-0)

S28	●	SMU	35	14
O5	●	Oregon	21	6
O12	●	Purdue	13	0
O19	●	Northwestern	45	21
O26	●	at Illinois	31	24
N2	●	Michigan State	25	20
N9	●	at Wisconsin	43	8
N16	●	at Iowa	33	27
N23	●	Michigan	50	14
		ROSE BOWL		
J1	●	Southern Cal	27	16

1969 8-1-0 (6-1-0)

S27	●	TCU	62	0
O4	●	at Washington	41	14
O11	●	Michigan State	54	21
O18	●	at Minnesota	34	7
O25	●	Illinois	41	0
N1	●	at Northwestern	35	6
N8	●	Wisconsin	62	7
N15	●	Purdue	42	14
N22		at Michigan	12	24

1970 9-1-0 (7-0-0)

S26	●	Texas A&M	56	13
O3	●	Duke	34	10
O10	●	at Michigan State	29	0
O17	●	Minnesota	28	8
O24	●	at Illinois	48	29
O31	●	Northwestern	24	10
N7	●	at Wisconsin	24	7
N14	●	at Purdue	10	7
N21	●	Michigan	20	9
		ROSE BOWL		
J1		Stanford	17	27

1971 6-4-0 (5-3-0)

S11	●	Iowa	52	21
S25		Colorado	14	20
O2	●	California	35	3
O9	●	at Illinois	24	10
O16	●	at Indiana	27	7
O23	●	Wisconsin	31	6
O30	●	at Minnesota	14	12
N6		Michigan State	10	17
N13		Northwestern	10	14
N20		at Michigan	7	10

1972 9-2-0 (7-1-0)

S16	●	Iowa	21	0
S30	●	North Carolina	29	14
O7	●	at California	35	18
O14	●	Illinois	26	7
O21	●	Indiana	44	7
O28	●	at Wisconsin	28	20
N4	●	Minnesota	27	19
N11		at Michigan State	12	19
N18	●	at Northwestern	27	14
N25	●	Michigan	14	11
		ROSE BOWL		
J1		Southern Cal	17	42

1973 10-0-1 (7-0-1)

S15	●	Minnesota	56	7
S29	●	TCU	37	3
O6	●	Washington State	27	3
O13	●	at Wisconsin	24	0
O20	●	at Indiana	37	7
O27	●	Northwestern	60	0
N3	●	at Illinois	30	0
N10	●	Michigan State	35	0
N17	●	Iowa	55	13
N24	=	at Michigan	10	10
		ROSE BOWL		
J1	●	Southern Cal	42	21

1974 10-2-0 (7-1-0)

S14	●	at Minnesota	34	19
S21	●	Oregon State	51	10
S28	●	SMU	28	9
O5	●	Washington State[SEA]	42	7
O12	●	Wisconsin	52	7
O19	●	Indiana	49	9
O26	●	at Northwestern	55	7
N2	●	Illinois	49	7
N9		at Michigan State	13	16
N16	●	at Iowa	35	10
N23	●	Michigan	12	10
		ROSE BOWL		
J1		Southern Cal	17	18

1975 11-1-0 (8-0-0)

S13	●	at Michigan State	21	0
S20	●	Penn State	17	9
S27	●	North Carolina	32	7
O4	●	at UCLA	41	20
O11	●	Iowa	49	0
O18	●	Wisconsin	56	0
O25	●	at Purdue	35	6
N1	●	Indiana	24	14
N8	●	at Illinois	40	3
N15	●	Minnesota	38	6
N22	●	at Michigan	21	14
		ROSE BOWL		
J1		UCLA	10	23

1976 9-2-1 (7-1-0)

S11	●	Michigan State	49	21
S18	●	at Penn State	12	7
S25		Missouri	21	22
O2	=	UCLA	10	10
O9	●	at Iowa	34	14
O16	●	at Wisconsin	30	20
O23	●	Purdue	24	3
O30	●	at Indiana	47	7
N6	●	Illinois	42	10
N13	●	at Minnesota	9	3
N20		Michigan	0	22
		ORANGE BOWL		
J1	●	Colorado	27	10

1977 9-3-0 (7-1-0)

S10	●	Miami, Fla.	10	0
S17	●	Minnesota	38	7
S24		Oklahoma	28	29
O1	●	at SMU	35	7
O8	●	Purdue	46	0
O15	●	at Iowa	27	6
O22	●	at Northwestern	35	15
O29	●	Wisconsin	42	0
N5	●	at Illinois	35	0
N12	●	Indiana	35	7
N19		at Michigan	6	14
		SUGAR BOWL		
J1		Alabama	6	35

1978 7-4-1 (6-2-0)

S16		Penn State	0	19
S23	●	at Minnesota	27	10
S30	●	Baylor	34	28
O7	=	SMU	35	35
O14		at Purdue	16	27
O21	●	Iowa	31	7
O28	●	Northwestern	63	20
N4	●	at Wisconsin	49	14
N11	●	Illinois	45	7
N18	●	at Indiana	21	18
N25		Michigan	3	14
		GATOR BOWL		
D29		Clemson	15	17

EARLE BRUCE
1979-87 (.755) 81-26-1

1979 11-1-0 (8-0-0)

S8	●	Syracuse	31	8
S15	●	at Minnesota	21	17
S22	●	Washington State	45	29
S29	●	at UCLA	17	13
O6	●	Northwestern	16	7
O13	●	Indiana	47	6
O20	●	Wisconsin	59	0
O27	●	Michigan State	42	0
N3	●	at Illinois	44	7
N10	●	Iowa	34	7
N17	●	at Michigan	18	15
		ROSE BOWL		
J1		Southern Cal	16	17

1980 9-3-0 (7-1-0)

S13	●	Syracuse	31	21
S20	●	Minnesota	47	0
S27	●	Arizona State	38	21
O4		UCLA	0	17
O11	●	at Northwestern	63	0
O18	●	Indiana	27	17
O25	●	at Wisconsin	21	0
N1	●	at Michigan State	48	16
N8	●	Illinois	49	42
N15	●	at Iowa	41	7
N22		Michigan	3	9
		FIESTA BOWL		
D26		Penn State	19	31

1981 · 9-3-0 (6-2-0)

S12	●	Duke	34 13
S19	†	Michigan State	27 13
S26		at Stanford	24 19
O3		Florida State	27 36
O10	●	at Wisconsin	21 24
O17	●	Illinois	34 27
O24	●	Indiana	29 10
O31	●	at Purdue	45 33
N7		at Minnesota	31 35
N14	●	Northwestern	70 6
N21	●	at Michigan	14 9
		LIBERTY BOWL	
D30		Navy	31 28

1982 · 9-3-0 (7-1-0)

S11	●	Baylor	21 14
S18	†	at Michigan State	31 10
S25		Stanford	20 23
O2		Florida State	17 34
O9		Wisconsin	0 6
O16	●	at Illinois	26 21
O23	●	at Indiana	49 25
O30	●	Purdue	38 6
N6	●	Minnesota	35 10
N13	●	at Northwestern	40 28
N20	●	Michigan	24 14
		HOLIDAY BOWL	
D17	●	Brigham Young	47 17

1983 · 9-3-0 (6-3-0)

S10	●	Oregon	31 6
S17	●	at Oklahoma	24 14
S24		at Iowa	14 20
O1	●	Minnesota	69 18
O8	●	Purdue	33 22
O15		at Illinois	13 17
O22	●	Michigan State	21 11
O29	●	Wisconsin	45 27
N5	●	at Indiana	56 17
N12	●	Northwestern	55 7
N19		at Michigan	21 24
		FIESTA BOWL	
J2	●	Pittsburgh	28 23

1984 · 9-3-0 (7-2-0)

S8	●	Oregon State	22 14
S15	●	Washington State	44 0
S22	●	Iowa	45 26
S29	●	at Minnesota	35 22
O6		at Purdue	23 28
O13	●	Illinois	45 38
O20	●	at Michigan State	23 20
O27		at Wisconsin	14 16
N3	●	Indiana	50 7
N10	●	at Northwestern	52 3
N17	●	Michigan	21 6
		ROSE BOWL	
J1		Southern Cal	17 20

1985 · 9-3-0 (5-3-0)

S14	●	Pittsburgh	10 7
S21	●	at Colorado	36 13
S28	●	Washington State	48 32
O5		at Illinois	28 31
O12	●	Indiana	48 7
O19	●	Purdue	41 27
O26	●	at Minnesota	23 19
N2		Iowa	22 13
N9	●	at Northwestern	35 17
N16		Wisconsin	7 12
N23		at Michigan	17 27
		CITRUS BOWL	
D28	●	Brigham Young	10 7

1986 · 10-3-0 (7-1-0)

A27		Alabama _ERuT_	10 16
S13		at Washington	7 40
S20	●	Colorado	13 10
S27	●	Utah	64 6
O4	●	at Indiana	14 0
O11	●	at Indiana	24 22
O18	●	at Purdue	39 11
O25	●	Minnesota	33 0
N1	●	at Iowa	31 10
N8	●	Northwestern	30 9
N15	●	at Wisconsin	30 17
N22		Michigan	24 26
		COTTON BOWL	
J1	●	Texas A&M	28 12

1987 · 6-4-1 (4-4-0)

S12	●	West Virginia	24 3
S19	●	Oregon	24 14
S26	=	at LSU	13 13
O3	●	at Illinois	10 6
O10		Indiana	10 31
O17	●	at Purdue	20 17
O24	●	Minnesota	42 9
O31		Michigan State	7 13
N7		at Wisconsin	24 26
N14		Iowa	27 29
N21	●	at Michigan	23 20

1988 · 4-6-1 (2-5-1)

S10	●	Syracuse	26 9
S17		at Pittsburgh	10 42
S24	●	LSU	36 33
O1		Illinois	12 31
O8		at Indiana	7 41
O15	●	Purdue	26 31
O22	●	at Minnesota	13 6
O29		at Michigan State	10 20
N5	●	Wisconsin	34 12
N12	=	at Iowa	24 24
N19		Michigan	31 34

1989 · 8-4-0 (6-2-0)

S16	●	Oklahoma State	37 13
S23		at Southern Cal	3 42
S30	●	Boston College	34 29
O7		at Illinois	14 34
O14	●	Indiana	35 31
O21	●	Purdue	21 3
O28	●	at Minnesota	41 37
N4	●	at Northwestern	52 27
N11	●	Iowa	28 0
N18	●	Wisconsin	42 22
N25		at Michigan	18 28
		HALL OF FAME BOWL	
J1		Auburn	14 31

1990 · 7-4-1 (5-2-1)

S8	●	Texas Tech	17 10
S15		at Boston College	31 10
S29	●	Southern Cal	26 35
O6		Illinois	20 31
O13	=	at Indiana	27 27
O20	●	at Purdue	42 2
O27	●	Minnesota	52 23
N3	●	Northwestern	48 7
N10	●	at Iowa	27 26
N17	●	at Wisconsin	35 10
N24		Michigan	13 16
		LIBERTY BOWL	
D27		Air Force	11 23

1991 · 8-4-0 (5-3-0)

S7	●	Arizona	38 14
S14	●	Louisville	23 15
S21	●	Washington State	33 19
O5	●	Wisconsin	31 16
O12		at Illinois	7 10
O19	●	Northwestern _CLEV_	34 3
O26	●	Michigan State	27 17
N2		Iowa	9 16
N9	●	at Minnesota	35 6
N16	●	Indiana	20 16
N23		at Michigan	3 31
		HALL OF FAME BOWL	
J1		Syracuse	17 24

1992 · 8-3-1 (5-2-1)

S5	●	Louisville	20 19
S12	●	Bowling Green	17 6
S19	●	at Syracuse	35 12
O3		at Wisconsin	16 20
O10		Illinois	16 18
O17	●	Northwestern	31 7
O24	●	at Michigan State	27 17
O31	●	at Iowa	38 15
N7	●	Minnesota	17 0
N14	●	at Indiana	27 10
N21	=	Michigan	13 13
		CITRUS BOWL	
J1		Georgia	14 21

1993 · 10-1-1 (6-1-1)

S4	●	Rice	34 7
S11	●	Washington	21 12
S18	●	at Pittsburgh	63 28
O2	●	Northwestern	51 3
O9	●	at Illinois	20 12
O16	●	Michigan State	28 21
O23	●	at Purdue	45 24
O30	●	Penn State	24 6
N6	=	at Wisconsin	14 14
N13	●	Indiana	23 17
N20		at Michigan	0 28
		HOLIDAY BOWL	
D30	●	Brigham Young	28 21

1994 · 9-4-0 (6-2-0)

A29	●	Fresno State _ANA_	34 10
S10		at Washington	16 25
S17	●	Pittsburgh	27 3
S24	●	Houston	52 0
O1	●	at Northwestern	17 15
O8		Illinois	10 24
O15	●	at Michigan State	23 7
O22	●	Purdue	48 14
O29		at Penn State	14 63
N5	●	Wisconsin	24 3
N12	●	at Indiana	32 17
N19		Michigan	22 6
		CITRUS BOWL	
J2		Alabama	17 24

1995 · 11-2-0 (7-1-0)

A27	●	Boston College _ERut_	38 6
S16	●	Washington	30 20
S23	●	at Pittsburgh	54 14
S30	●	Notre Dame	45 26
O7	●	at Penn State	28 25
O14	●	at Wisconsin	27 16
O21	●	Purdue	28 0
O28	●	Iowa	56 35
N4	●	at Minnesota	49 21
N11	●	Illinois	41 3
N18	●	Indiana	42 3
N25		at Michigan	23 31
		CITRUS BOWL	
J1		Tennessee	14 20

1996 · 11-1 (7-1)

S7	●	Rice	70 7
S21	●	Pittsburgh	72 0
S28	●	at Notre Dame	29 16
O5	●	Penn State	38 7
O12	●	Wisconsin	17 14
O19	●	at Purdue	42 14
O26	●	at Iowa	38 26
N2	●	Minnesota	45 0
N9	●	at Illinois	48 0
N16	●	at Indiana	27 17
N23		Michigan	9 13
		ROSE BOWL	
J1	●	Arizona State	20 17

1997 · 10-3 (6-2)

A28	●	Wyoming	24 10
S13	●	Bowling Green	44 13
S20	●	Arizona	28 20
S27	●	at Missouri	31 10
O4	●	Iowa	23 7
O11		at Penn State	27 31
O18	●	Indiana	31 0
O25	●	Northwestern	49 6
N1	●	at Michigan State	37 13
N8	●	at Minnesota	31 3
N15	●	Illinois	41 6
N22		Michigan	14 20
		SUGAR BOWL	
J1		Florida State	14 31

1998 · 11-1 (7-1)

S5	●	at West Virginia	34 17
S12	●	Toledo	49 0
S19	●	Missouri	35 14
O3	●	Penn State	28 9
O10	●	at Illinois	41 0
O17	●	Minnesota	45 15
O24	●	at Northwestern	36 10
O31	●	at Indiana	38 7
N7		Michigan State	24 28
N14	●	at Iowa	45 14
N21	●	Michigan	31 16
		SUGAR BOWL	
J1	●	Texas A&M	24 14

1999 · 6-6 (3-5)

A29		Miami, Fla. _ERuT_	12 23
S11	●	UCLA	42 20
S18	●	Ohio U.	40 16
S25	●	Cincinnati	34 20
O2		Wisconsin	17 42
O9	●	Purdue	25 22
O16		at Penn State	10 23
O23	●	at Minnesota	20 17
O30	●	Iowa	41 11
N6		at Michigan State	7 23
N13		Illinois	20 46
N20		at Michigan	17 24

2000 · 8-4 (5-3)

S2	●	Fresno State	43 10
S9		at Arizona	27 17
S16	●	Miami, Ohio	27 16
S23	●	Penn State	45 6
O7		at Wisconsin	23 7
O14		Minnesota	17 29
O21	●	at Iowa	38 10
O28		at Purdue	27 31
N4		Michigan State	27 13
N11	●	at Illinois	24 21
N18		Michigan	26 38
		OUTBACK BOWL	
J1		South Carolina	7 24

2001 · 7-5 (5-3)

S8	●	Akron	28 14
S22		at UCLA	6 13
S29	●	at Indiana	27 14
O6	●	Northwestern	38 20
O13		Wisconsin	17 20
O20	●	San Diego State	27 12
O27	●	at Penn State	27 9
N3	●	at Minnesota	31 28
N10	●	Purdue	35 9
N17		Illinois	22 34
N24	●	at Michigan	26 20
		OUTBACK BOWL	
J1		South Carolina	28 31

2002 · 14-0 (8-0)

A24	●	Texas Tech	45 21
S7	●	Kent State	51 17
S14	●	Washington State	25 7
S21	●	at Cincinnati	23 19
S28	●	Indiana	45 17
O5	●	at Northwestern	27 16
O12	●	San Jose State	50 7
O19	●	at Wisconsin	19 14
O26	●	Penn State	13 7
N2	●	Minnesota	34 3
N9	●	at Purdue	10 6
N16	●	at Illinois	23 16
N23	●	Michigan	14 9
		FIESTA BOWL	
J3	●	Miami, Fla.	31 24

2003 · 11-2 (6-2)

A30	●	Washington	28 9
S6	●	San Diego State	16 13
S13	●	North Carolina St.	44 38
S20	●	Bowling Green	24 17
S27	●	Northwestern	20 0
O11		at Wisconsin	10 17
O18	●	Iowa	19 10
O25	●	at Indiana	35 6
N1	●	at Penn State	21 20
N8	●	Michigan State	33 23
N15	●	Purdue	16 13
N22		at Michigan	21 35
		FIESTA BOWL	
J2	●	Kansas State	35 28

2004 · 8-4 (4-4)

S4	●	Cincinnati	27 6
S11	●	Marshall	24 21
S18		at North Carolina St.	22 14
O2		at Northwestern	27 33
O9		Wisconsin	13 24
O16		at Iowa	7 33
O23	●	Indiana	30 7
O30	●	Penn State	21 10
N6	●	at Michigan State	32 19
N13		at Purdue	17 24
N20	●	Michigan	37 21
		ALAMO BOWL	
D29	●	Oklahoma State	33 7

OKLAHOMA

BY MARK WANGRIN

THE SCHOOLS

LONG AFTER OKLAHOMA BECAME the 46th state in 1907, the territory was still perceived as rough and wild. In the middle of the 20th century, Oklahoma was known for dust storms and as the home of John Steinbeck's fictional protagonist, Tom Joad, an ex-con whose life was hard and future bleak—like the widespread image of the state itself. That changed when Charles Burnham "Bud" Wilkinson became head coach of the football team in 1947. A sharp dresser with an even sharper football mind, Wilkinson took a team loaded with World War II veterans and began what would become one of college football's greatest dynasties. The crimson-clad Sooners won three national championships and were the perfect jolt of pride to a state whose name is formed by the joining of the Choctaw words "okla" (people) and "humma" (red). "His teams dispelled the Dust Bowl *Grapes of Wrath* image of the Depression years," said former Oklahoma president George L. Cross, who hired Wilkinson. "They made Oklahoma proud and called

national attention to the state's potential." Wilkinson's success begat a tradition that was later reinvigorated by Chuck Fairbanks and then by a young, hip, wisecracking assistant named Barry Switzer, who added national titles in 1974, 1975 and 1985. But Switzer's reign came apart in a flurry of off-field scandals and the Sooners seemed to come full circle back to a barren existence with the decline of the program in the late 1980s and 1990s. Again the school turned to a young assistant coach, picking Bob Stoops in late 1998 to oversee a turnaround that proved so rapid it surprised even those clinging to the Wilkinson gold standard. It resulted in the school's seventh national title in 2000 and a feeling in the state that the Sooners were back where they belonged.

TRADITION Many of the Sooners' game-day traditions center around the Ruf/Neks, a spirit group with roots back to 1915, when a rowdy group of football players were cheering so enthusiastically at an OU basketball game that a fan yelled, "Sit down and be quiet, you roughnecks." Today the 36-member group fires modified 12-gauge single-round shotguns and carries red-and-white paddles, which became a tradition in the 1920s when it was suggested paddles would

---

PROFILE

Oklahoma University
Norman, Okla.
Founded in 1890
Enrollment: 20,966
Colors: Crimson and Cream
Nickname: Sooners
Stadium: Gaylord Family-Oklahoma Memorial Stadium
    Opened in 1923
    Grass; 82,112 capacity
First football game: 1895
All-time record: 749–285–53 (.713)
Bowl record: 23–14–1
Consensus national championships, 1936-present: 7 (1950, 1955, 1956, 1974, 1975, 1985, 2000)
Big 12 Conference championships: 3
Heisman Trophy: Billy Vessels, 1952; Steve Owens, 1969; Billy Sims, 1978; Jason White, 2003
Outland Trophy: Jim Weatherall, 1951; J.D. Roberts, 1953; Lee Roy Selmon, 1975; Greg Roberts, 1978; Jammal Brown, 2004
First-round NFL draftees: 35
Website: www.soonersports.com

THE BEST OF TIMES

Bud Wilkinson had the Sooners at their heyday in the 1950s, with three national titles (1950, 1955 and 1956), nine conference championships and a 48-game unbeaten streak from 1953 to 1957.

THE WORST OF TIMES

1990s. A program spiraling downward marked the only decade since the 1920s when the Sooners won no conference titles.

CONFERENCE

A charter member of the Southwest Conference when it was formed in 1915, the Sooners moved to the Missouri Valley Conference in 1920. In 1928, OU and five other schools (Iowa State, Kansas, Kansas State, Missouri and Nebraska) withdrew from the Valley to form the Big Six Conference. The league became the Big Seven in 1948 with the addition of Colorado and the Big Eight in 1960 when Oklahoma State—formerly Oklahoma A&M—joined. Along with fellow Big Eight members, the Sooners joined Southwest Conference expatriates Baylor, Texas, Texas A&M and Texas Tech to form the Big 12 in 1996.

DISTINGUISHED ALUMNI

Carl Albert, U.S. congressman; Admiral William S. Crowe, chair of U.S. Joint Chiefs of Staff; James Garner, actor; Ed Harris, actor; Tony Hillerman, author; Shannon Miller, Olympic gymnast

FIGHT SONG

BOOMER SOONER
Boomer Sooner, Boomer Sooner
Boomer Sooner, Boomer Sooner
Boomer Sooner, Boomer Sooner
Boomer Sooner, OK U!
Oklahoma, Oklahoma
Oklahoma, Oklahoma
Oklahoma, Oklahoma
Oklahoma, OK U!
I'm a Sooner born and Sooner bred
and when I die, I'll be Sooner dead
Rah Oklahoma, Rah Oklahoma
Rah Oklahoma, OK U!

intimidate the OU fans into cheering more loudly. The group also takes care of the Big Red Rocket, a 1923 Model-T Ford that was once driven by the Sooners' biggest fan, Cecil Samara. At every home game the Ruf/Neks accompany the team as it runs on the field, sprinting with OU flags to the far goalpost, where they slide to the turf and repeat a chant called "FADADA."

Fifteen years after the three brothers left, OU fans would still punctuate the pregame prayer with, "God Bless Mrs. Selmon."

BEST PLAYER As the youngest of nine children, Lee Roy Selmon spent his formative years following footsteps. As arguably the greatest player in OU history, the two-time All-America and winner of the Outland Trophy and Lombardi Award had few peers in a rich history of Sooner players. Lee Roy, the most accomplished of the three Selmons who played together at OU, was the first pick of the 1976 NFL draft, by Tampa Bay. By 1995, he became the first Sooner in the Pro Football Hall of Fame. Two-time All-America and 1978 Heisman Trophy winner Billy Sims gives Selmon a run for the title. Sims, inducted

into the College Football Hall of Fame in 1995, finished with 4,118 yards (first all-time at OU) and 53 touchdowns.

BEST COACH After World War II, Bud Wilkinson reluctantly entered the family mortgage-trading business, but found the pace too slow. To the dismay of his father, Wilkinson joined Jim Tatum's staff at Oklahoma in 1946. Good thing for the Sooners, who the next year promoted the then-31-year-old former aircraft-carrier deck officer to replace Tatum and unleash his modified split-T formation on an unsuspecting nation. The Minnesota native went 145–29–4 in 17 seasons in Norman, including national championship years in 1950, 1955 and 1956. His Sooners won 31 straight games from 1948 to 1950 and then topped that, winning a major-college-record 47 consecutive from 1953 to 1957. Wilkinson retired at 47 and spent less than two seasons coaching the NFL's St. Louis Cardinals.

RECORDS

RUSHING YARDS
GAME
294 — Greg Pruitt vs. Kansas State, Oct. 23, 1971 (19 att.)
SEASON
1,925 — Adrian Peterson, 2004 (339 att.)
CAREER
4,118 — Billy Sims, 1975-79 (593 att.)

PASSING YARDS
GAME
429 — Josh Heupel vs. Louisville, Sept. 25, 1999 (29 of 42)
SEASON
3,850 — Josh Heupel, 1999 (349 of 553)
CAREER
7,922 — Jason White, 1999-2004 (622 of 990)

RECEIVING YARDS
GAME
190 — Mark Clayton vs. Texas, Oct. 11, 2003 (8 rec.)
SEASON
1,425 — Mark Clayton, 2003 (83 rec.)
CAREER
3.241 — Mark Clayton, 2001-2004 (221 rec.)

POINTS
GAME
36 — Quentin Griffin vs. Texas, Oct. 7, 2000 (6 TDs)
SEASON
138 — Billy Sims, 1979 (23 TDs)
CAREER
342 — Steve Owens, 1967-69 (57 TDs)

CONSENSUS ALL-AMERICANS

1938	Waddy Young, E
1948	Buddy Burris, G
1950	Leon Heath, B
1950-51	Jim Weatherall, T
1952	Billy Vessels, B
1953	J.D. Roberts, G
1954	Max Boydston, E
1954	Kurt Burris, C
1955	Bo Bolinger, G
1956	Jerry Tubbs, C
1956	Tommy McDonald, B
1957	Bill Krisher, G
1957	Clendon Thomas, B
1958	Bob Harrison, C
1963	Jim Grisham, B
1964	Ralph Neely, T
1965	Carl McAdams, LB
1967	Granville Liggins, MG
1969	Steve Owens, B
1971-72	Greg Pruitt, B
1971-72	Tom Brahaney, C
1973	Lucious Selmon, DL
1973-74	Rod Shoate, LB
1974	John Roush, G

(Continued on next page)

BEST TEAM As great as the 1955 national championship team was, the 1956 team, which returned nearly all its key players, was even better. Led by HB/DB Tommy McDonald, who won the Maxwell Trophy, and C/LB Jerry Tubbs, who captured the Walter Camp Trophy, the Sooners rolled through the season. They finished with a 54-6 win over Nebraska in Norman and a 53-0 victory over Oklahoma State to secure their second straight national championship.

BIGGEST GAME At the time, it was widely billed as the Game of the Century II, but the 1987 Oklahoma-Nebraska game was no simple remake. NU was No. 1; OU No. 2. They met in Lincoln, with OU the decided underdog, and the Huskers uncharacteristically providing bulletin board fodder in the form of linebacker Broderick Thomas' vow that the Sooners wouldn't have a happy visit to "our house." OU quarterback Jamelle Holieway was out with a knee injury suffered two weeks earlier, leaving the offense in the hands of redshirt freshman Charles Thompson. "You will shock the nation," Coach Barry Switzer told Thompson, and he did just that. Overcoming early fumbles, the OU offense clicked and the Sooners outgained NU 444-235 to win 17-7. They earned a trip to the Orange Bowl, but lost to Miami for the third time in three seasons, the only team to beat them during a 36-game span.

BIGGEST UPSET Despite being the nation's only unbeaten team, the 2000 Sooners didn't get much respect. Oddsmakers made the No.1 Sooners a 10-point underdog to No. 3 Florida State in the 2001 Orange Bowl. Miami groused that it belonged in the title game because it had defeated FSU earlier in the season. Still, the Sooners believed that their ensemble cast, led by sore-armed quarterback Josh Heupel and a stout defense, could contain the speedy Seminoles and breach their defense. A pair of Tim Duncan field goals gave the workmanlike Sooners a 6-0 lead heading into the fourth quarter before Quentin Griffin's 10-yard touchdown run on a worn-out FSU defense clinched the game. FSU

CONSENSUS ALL-AMERICANS (CONT.)	
1974	Joe Washington, RB
1975	Lee Roy Selmon, DT
1975	Dewey Selmon, MG
1975	Jimbo Elrod, DE
1976	Mike Vaughan, OT
1977	Zac Henderson, DB
1978	Greg Roberts, G
1978-79	Billy Sims, RB
1979	George Cumby, LB
1980	Louis Oubre, OL
1981	Terry Crouch, OL
1982-83	Rick Bryan, DL
1984-85	Tony Casillas, DL
1985-86	Brian Bosworth, LB
1986-87	Keith Jackson, TE
1987	Mark Hutson, OL
1987	Dante Jones, LB
1987	Rickey Dixon, DB
1988	Anthony Phillips, OL
2000	Josh Heupel, QB
2000	J.T. Thatcher, DB
2000-01	Rocky Calmus, LB
2001	Roy Williams, DB
2002-03	Tommie Harris, DL
2002-03	Teddy Lehman, LB
2003	Jason White, QB
2003	Antonio Perkins, ALL-PURPOSE/KR
2003	Derrick Strait, DB
2004	Jammal Brown, OL
2004	Adrian Peterson, RB

avoided its first shutout in 12 seasons only when OU punter Jeff Ferguson was tackled for a safety with 55 seconds left.

HEARTBREAKER More than three decades after it was played, it's still known as the Game of the Century—even in Oklahoma. "That was the game of the lifetime," said OU quarterback Jack Mildren. Nebraska was No. 1; OU was No. 2. They met on Thanksgiving Day 1971 at Owen Field with the national title at stake. Nebraska struck first, with a 72-yard punt return by Johnny Rodgers—some OU fans still claim a clip should have called it back. NU aimed to prevent OU star halfback Greg Pruitt from making the same kind of difference, loading up on the outside. That opened holes for Mildren, who finished with 130 yards. OU rallied from a 28-17 deficit to take a 31-28 lead with 7:10 left, but the Cornhuskers responded with a 12-play, 74-yard drive for the winning touchdown. "It was a case of who had it last," OU coach Chuck Fairbanks said. "If we'd have had enough time, I'm certain we would have scored." OU finished the season ranked No. 2.

WILDEST FINISH OU had built up a 20-0 lead on Ohio State in the third quarter of their 1977 game and it appeared the Sooners could relax. But OU's fortunes quickly turned. Thomas Lott and Billy Sims were knocked out of the game and the Buckeyes scored 28 unanswered points to take a 28-20 lead. OU scored, but the Buckeyes stuffed the two-point try with 1:29 left and the stunned Sooners appeared beaten. But OU recovered kicker Uwe von Schamann's onside kick and drove to the OSU 24-yard line with three seconds left. The Buckeyes called time to try to ice von Schamann and the home crowd began chanting "Block that kick." Defiantly, von Schamann raised his hands like an orchestra conductor and led the chants. Seconds later, he drilled the game-winning 41-yarder. "I don't know why," von Schamann said years later when asked why he did that. "It's something I didn't plan to do. Something I haven't done since. Because if you miss it, you look pretty stupid." The miracle ending led coach Barry Switzer to coin the

phrase Sooner Magic to describe the program's knack for improbable victories. "Sooner Magic," Switzer said, "is great players making great plays."

BEST COMEBACK Claude Arnold knew what patience was. The Sooner quarterback made his first start in 1950, eight years after he arrived on campus, because of the interruption created by World War II and by the emergence of Darrell Royal. That patience came in handy against Texas A&M, when the Sooners found themselves trailing 28-21 in the fourth quarter. Arnold's passing led the Sooners on a 69-yard scoring drive. After the two-point conversion failed, he led them on another with 1:09 remaining to keep alive the winning streak that would eventually reach 31 games and spur the Sooners to their first national title.

STADIUM What began as a movement to build a student union in 1921 turned into a push by the student body to make it a combination union and football stadium. The first game was played at the site in 1923, even before construction began, and the field was named after coach Bennie Owen. By 1925, the 16,000-seat west-side grandstands were completed at Oklahoma Memorial Stadium, named in honor of OU personnel who died in World War I, and erected at a cost of $293,000. Stands were added on the east side of the stadium in 1929, doubling capacity. In 1949, the field was lowered, the track removed and the north end closed in. An upper deck was added in 1975. Beginning in 1994, the stadium began a series of renovations, including a $65 million project that remodeled the press box and added 8,000 seats. In 2003, the Sooners averaged 83,202 fans a game, 1,995 more than capacity.

RIVAL The first Saturday in October means two things in Dallas: eating corndogs at the Texas State Fair and watching the annual Red River Shootout between the school that pioneered the wishbone attack and the school that perfected it: Texas and Oklahoma. It is regarded as one of the top rivalries in college football. The stakes are consistently high,

ALL-CENTURY TEAM		
Selected by the Tulsa World *in 1999.*		
OFFENSE		
1946-49	Stan West,	OL
1950-52	Tom Catlin,	OL
1970-72	Tom Brahaney,	OL
1974-76	Mike Vaughan ,	OL
1975-78	Greg Roberts,	OL
1984-87	Keith Jackson,	TE
1966-68	Eddie Hinton,	WR
1969-71	Jack Mildren,	QB
1950-52	Billy Vessels,	RB
1967-69	Steve Owens,	RB
1975, 1977-79	Billy Sims,	RB
1976-78	Uwe von Schamann,	PK
DEFENSE		
1951-54	Max Boydston,	DL
1972-75	Lee Roy Selmon,	DL
1980-83	Ricky Bryan,	DL
1982-85	Tony Casillas,	DL
1954-56	Tommy McDonald,	DB
1954-56	Jerry Tubbs,	LB
1972-74	Rod Shoate,	LB
1984-86	Brian Bosworth,	LB
1955-57	Clendon Thomas,	DB
1972-74	Randy Hughes,	DB
1984-87	Rickey Dixon,	DB

and the game has frequently been a midseason elimination game for the national-title race. Texas leads the series by a fairly wide margin, but it has been one of ebb and flow for both teams. The Longhorns dominated in the late 1950s and 1960s, winning 12 of 13, but the Sooners had the upper hand in the mid-1970s, late 1980s and early part of the 21st century. Some of the most colorful games came during the tenure of Barry Switzer, including the 15-15 tie on a rain-soaked Cotton Bowl turf in 1984 that introduced the world to The Boz. Blond and mohawked OU linebacker Brian Bosworth, a native Texan, ripped the Longhorns for settling for a tying field goal and later said that UT's predominant school color, burnt orange, "makes me puke."

DUBIOUS DISTINCTION In 1989, one Sooner would shoot another, three others would be charged with rape and starting quarterback Charles Thompson would be arrested for selling cocaine. A photo of Thompson in a prison-orange jumpsuit and handcuffs filled the cover of *Sports Illustrated*, branding the program as being out of control before a national audience. Under pressure around the nation and within the university—including a plea from Bosworth for him to quit—Switzer resigned in June 1989.

CONTROVERSY In 1976, Texas Coach Darrell Royal, a former Sooners quarterback/punter, was singing a new school song, but he was more concerned with the eyes of Oklahoma than "The Eyes of Texas." Acting on a report he received that an OU operative had been spying on UT practices, Royal offered Switzer and assistant Larry Lacewell $10,000 each if they could pass a lie-detector test about the alleged spy. Both declined. Several years later, Lacewell admitted that OU did spy in 1972, but Switzer continues to say it didn't occur when he was head coach. OU was on the other end of a covert op at the end of the 1949 season, when Sooners fans discovered a man identified as Piggy Barnes, a former LSU tackle, watching practice with binoculars from under a blanket. Police rousted Barnes, whose alleged espionage didn't help LSU in a 35-0 OU rout in the Sugar Bowl.

NICKNAME At the turn of the 20th century, the OU teams were known as the Rough Riders or Boomers, but school officials grew to like the name of a school pep club, "The Sooner Rooters," and decided in 1908 to adopt the nickname. The term originally was less than complimentary, referring to settlers who jumped the gun and moved into the Oklahoma Territory in the Land Run of 1889. "Boomers" were the settlers who waited for the firing of the cannon; "Sooners" were those who left early. Over the years, the term evolved into a synonym of progressivism, now described in the school media guide as an "energetic individual who travels ahead of the human procession."

MASCOT Though the original Conestoga wagon and its two Shetland ponies, Boomer and Sooner, were donated in 1964 by Dr. Merrill S. Bartlett and his brother Charles "Buzz" Bartlett, the Sooner Schooner didn't become the official mascot until 1980. The wagon still circles the field on game days, though its forays have been curtailed over the years to passes before and after the game and brief trips around the goalpost after scores. During a 28-17 loss to Washington in the 1985 Orange Bowl, the Sooners drew a 15-yard unsportsmanlike conduct penalty when the Schooner rolled onto the field to celebrate an apparent 22-yard Tim Lashar field goal that had been nullified by a penalty. Lashar's subsequent attempt from 42 yards was blocked. "Those ponies," Switzer said, "didn't know what that yellow flag meant."

UNIFORMS It was autumn 1895 and, as the only female faculty member, Miss May Overstreet was asked to chair a committee to select the school colors. The group selected crimson and cream, and although the colors have evolved to red and white, Sooners fans still proudly refer to them as crimson and cream. Early teams sported solid jerseys with white stripes circling the sleeves. In the 1930s and 1940s, OU used a variety of looks, including jerseys with a big "O" on the front and all-crimson uniforms. Legend has it that when OU replaced its leather helmets with hard-shell models in the late 1940s, university president George Cross rode atop the vehicle that took them to the practice field and passed out the new headgear. In 1966, the helmets were changed from white to crimson and an interlocking "OU" was added to the sides of the helmets. A year later, the logo was changed to the familiar block-letter look used today.

LORE When Lucious Selmon went on his recruiting trip to OU in the winter of 1969-70, his two little brothers tagged along. Barry Switzer caught sight of Lee Roy and Dewey piling food on their plates and asked Lacewell, "Who's that?" Lacewell told him, and soon the entire football nation would know the Selmon brothers. They played side by side on the defensive line in 1973 on what was likely the Sooners' best defense. The brothers from Eufala, Okla., were named All-America a total of five times. Fifteen years after the brothers left, OU fans would still punctuate the pregame prayer with, "God Bless Mrs. Selmon."

QUOTE "I would like to build a university which the football team could be proud of." —University president George Cross (1943-68) to a state legislative committee on why the school needed increased funding

OKLAHOMA ANNUAL STATISTICAL LEADERS

YR	RUSHING	YDS	ATT	AVG	PASSING	ATT	CMP	PCT	YDS	RECEIVING	REC	YDS	AVG
1946	Joe Golding	890	122	7.3	Dave Wallace	58	18	.31	262	Jim Owens	19	262	13.8
1947	Jack Mitchell	573	125	4.6	Jack Mitchell	22	14	.64	169	Jim Tyree	10	138	13.8
1948	George Thomas	835	126	6.6	Darrell Royal	37	18	.49	302	Frankie Anderson	9	210	23.3
1949	George Thomas	859	133	6.5	Darrell Royal	63	34	.54	509	Jim Owens	15	207	13.8
1950	Billy Vessels	870	135	6.4	Claude Arnold	114	57	.50	1,048	Billy Vessels	11	229	20.8
1951	Buck McPhail	865	101	8.6	Eddie Crowder	57	30	.53	475	John Reddell	13	362	27.8
1952	Billy Vessels	1,072	67	16.0	Eddie Crowder	52	30	.58	704	Max Boydston	13	334	25.7
1953	Larry Grigg	792	130	6.1	Buddy Leake	21	9	.43	138	Larry Grigg	3	102	34.0
1954	Bob Herndon	588	98	6.0	Buddy Leake	26	12	.46	249	Max Boydston	11	276	25.1
1955	Tommy McDonald	702	103	6.8	Tommy McDonald	24	17	.71	265	Joe Mobra	6	126	21.0
1956	Tommy McDonald	853	119	7.2	Jimmy Harris	37	23	.62	482	Tommy McDonald	12	282	23.5
1957	Clendon Thomas	816	130	6.3	David Baker	18	12	.67	261	Dick Carpenter	8	90	11.3
1958	Prentice Gautt	627	105	6.0	Bobby Boyd	50	24	.48	353	Dick Carpenter	11	103	9.4
1959	Prentice Gautt	674	130	5.2	Bobby Boyd	54	19	.35	256	Brewster Hobby	10	143	14.3
1960	Ronnie Hartline	688	138	5.0	Jimmy Carpenter	40	25	.63	357	Jerry Payne	6	140	23.3
1961	Mike McClellan	508	82	6.2	Bobby Page	40	17	.43	233	Jimmy Carpenter	12	143	11.9
1962	Joe Don Looney	852	137	6.2	Monte Deere	65	38	.58	789	John Flynn	10	247	24.7
1963	Jim Grisham	861	153	5.6	Bobby Page	45	13	.29	198	John Flynn	8	115	14.4
1964	Jim Grisham	535	146	3.7	John Hammond	38	16	.42	284	Lance Rentzel	18	268	14.9
1965	Larry Brown	344	102	3.4	Gene Cagle	80	34	.43	382	Gordon Brown	35	413	11.8
1966	Ron Shotts	535	149	3.6	Bobby Warmack	103	57	.55	843	Ben Hart	33	565	17.1
1967	Steve Owens	808	190	4.3	Bobby Warmack	151	80	.53	1,136	Eddie Hinton	28	427	15.3
1968	Steve Owens	1,536	357	4.3	Bobby Warmack	186	106	.57	1,548	Eddie Hinton	60	967	16.1
1969	Steve Owens	1,523	358	4.3	Jack Mildren	172	79	.46	1,319	Steve Zabel	22	203	9.2
1970	Joe Wylie	984	159	6.2	Jack Mildren	110	54	.49	1,818	Greg Pruitt	19	240	12.6
1971	Greg Pruitt	1,665	178	9.4	Jack Mildren	64	31	.48	878	Jon Harrison	17	494	29.1
1972	Greg Pruitt	938	152	6.2	Dave Robertson	110	56	.51	1,054	John Carroll	17	343	20.2
1973	Joe Washington	1,173	176	6.7	Steve Davis	92	38	.41	934	Tinker Owens	18	472	26.2
1974	Joe Washington	1,321	194	6.8	Steve Davis	63	26	.41	601	Tinker Owens	18	413	22.9
1975	Joe Washington	871	171	5.1	Steve Davis	56	19	.34	438	Tinker Owens	9	241	26.8
1976	Kenny King	791	141	5.6	Dean Blevins	44	18	.41	370	Steve Rhodes	6	160	26.7
1977	Thomas Lott	760	139	5.5	Dean Blevins	29	16	.55	347	Steve Rhodes	12	226	18.8
1978	Billy Sims	1,762	231	7.6	Thomas Lott	55	21	.38	440	Bobby Kimball	12	198	16.5
1979	Billy Sims	1,506	224	6.7	J.C. Watts	81	39	.48	785	Fred Nixon	13	257	19.8
1980	David Overstreet	678	96	7.1	J.C. Watts	78	35	.45	905	Bobby Grayson	14	389	27.8
1981	Stanley Wilson	1,008	156	6.5	Darrell Shepard	56	26	.46	371	Bobby Grayson	12	249	20.8
1982	Marcus Dupree	905	129	7.0	Kelly Phelps	91	33	.36	492	David Carter	11	218	19.8
1983	Spencer Tillman	1,047	188	5.6	Danny Bradley	143	61	.43	1,125	Buster Rhymes	32	747	23.3
1984	Lydell Carr	625	138	4.5	Danny Bradley	130	67	.52	971	Steve Sewell	16	315	19.7
1985	Jamelle Holieway	861	161	5.3	Jamelle Holieway	58	24	.41	517	Keith Jackson	20	486	24.3
1986	Jamelle Holieway	811	139	5.8	Jamelle Holieway	63	30	.48	541	Keith Jackson	14	403	28.8
1987	Jamelle Holieway	860	142	6.1	Jamelle Holieway	62	21	.34	548	Keith Jackson	13	358	27.5
1988	Charles Thompson	829	145	5.7	Jamelle Holieway	41	27	.66	548	Eric Bross	14	279	19.9
1989	Mike Gaddis	829	110	7.5	Steve Collins	49	18	.37	442	Arthur Guess	9	357	39.7
1990	Dewell Brewer	872	154	5.7	Cale Gundy	109	54	.50	904	Adrian Cooper	13	301	23.2
1991	Mike Gaddis	1,240	221	5.6	Cale Gundy	172	91	.53	1,228	Corey Warren	26	366	14.1
1992	Dewell Brewer	561	120	4.7	Cale Gundy	227	131	.58	1,914	Corey Warren	35	659	18.8
1993	James Allen	788	153	5.2	Cale Gundy	243	144	.59	2,096	Rickey Brady	35	536	15.3
1994	Jerald Moore	659	129	5.1	Garrick McGee	284	149	.52	1,909	Albert Hall	36	515	14.3
1995	Jerald Moore	1,001	165	6.1	Eric Moore	200	90	.45	1,375	Stephen Alexander	43	580	13.5
1996	De'Mond Parker	1,184	180	6.6	Justin Fuente	196	91	.46	1,271	Michael McDaniel	28	553	19.8
1997	De'Mond Parker	1,143	194	5.9	Justin Fuente	129	69	.53	1,018	Stephen Alexander	29	450	15.5
1998	De'Mond Parker	1,077	204	5.3	Jake Sills	83	39	.47	502	Jarrail Jackson	12	218	18.2
1999	Michael Thornton	383	78	4.9	Josh Heupel	553	349	.63	3,850	Brandon Daniels	50	572	11.4
2000	Quentin Griffin	783	189	4.1	Josh Heupel	433	280	.65	3,392	Antwone Savage	48	598	12.5
2001	Quentin Griffin	804	182	4.4	Nate Hybl	380	222	.58	2,234	Trent Smith	61	564	9.2
2002	Quentin Griffin	1,884	287	6.6	Nate Hybl	363	209	.58	2,538	Trent Smith	46	396	8.6
2003	Kejuan Jones	925	225	4.1	Jason White	451	278	.62	3,846	Mark Clayton	83	1,425	17.2
2004	Adrian Peterson	1,925	339	5.7	Jason White	390	255	.65	3,205	Mark Clayton	66	876	13.3

Receiving leaders by receptions
All statistics include postseason

OKLAHOMA ALL-TIME SCORES

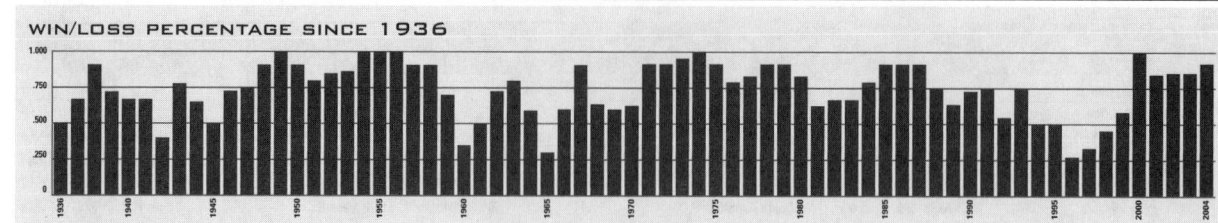

WIN/LOSS PERCENTAGE SINCE 1936

JOHN A. HARTS
1895 (.000) — **0-1**

1895 — 0-1-0
N7	Oklahoma City	0	34

NO HEAD COACH

1896 — 2-0-0
O28 ●	Norman HS	12	0
N11 ●	Norman HS	16	4

V. L. PARRINGTON
1897-1900 (.792) — **9-2-1**

1897 — 2-0-0
D1 ●	Oklahoma City	16	0
D31 ●	Kingfisher Coll.	17	8

1898 — 2-0-0
N17 ●	Arkansas City	5	0
N28 ●	at Fort Worth	24	0

1899 — 2-1-0
O12 ●	Kingfisher Coll.	39	6
N4 ●	Arkansas *SHA*	11	5
N9	at Arkansas City	11	17

1900 — 3-1-1
O10 ●	at Texas	2	28
O17 ●	Chilocco	27	0
O24 ●	Fort Reno	79	0
N6 =	at Kingfisher Coll.	0	0
N20 ●	Arkansas City	10	0

FRED ROBERTS
1901 (.600) — **3-2**

1901 — 3-2-0
O19 ●	at Texas	6	12
O26 ●	Baylor	17	6 *
N6 ●	at Wichita St.	42	0
N13 ●	Kingfisher Coll.	28	6
N25 ●	Texas	0	11

MARK McMAHON
1902-03 (.595) — **11-7-3**

1902 — 6-3-0
O1 ●	Guthrie	62	0
O4 ●	at Texas	6	22
O15 ●	at Dallas AC	6	11
O22 ●	at Arkansas	28	0
O29 ●	Oklahoma City	30	0
N5 ●	Kingfisher Coll.	15	0
N12 ●	at Missouri	5	22
N19 ●	Emporia St.	6	5
N24 ●	Kingfisher Coll.	17	0

1903 — 5-4-3
O3 ●	at Chilocco	38	5
O10 =	Kingfisher Coll.	0	0
O17 =	at Texas	6	6
O24 ●	at Texas A&M	6	6
O31 ●	Wichita St.	11	5
N4 =	Emporia St.	6	6
N7 ●	at Kansas	5	17
N13 ●	Texas	5	11
N21 ●	Arkansas	0	12
N30 ●	at Missouri Mines	12	6
D3 ●	at Bethany	10	12
D10 ●	Lawton	27	5

FRED EWING
1904 (.563) — **4-3-1**

1904 — 4-3-1
O10 =	Kingfisher Coll.	0	0
O17 ●	at Pauls Valley	33	0
O21 ●	Kansas	0	16
O31 ●	at Lawton	6	0
N6 ●	Oklahoma State *GUT*	75	0
N16 ●	at Texas	10	40
N20 ●	OKC Military	71	4
N25 ●	Bethany	9	36

BENNIE OWEN
1905-26 (.677) — **122-54-16**

1905 — 7-2-0
O9 ●	at Central Oklahoma	28	0
O16 ●	Haskell	18	12
O21 ●	at Kansas	0	34
O23 ●	KC Medics	33	0
O30 ●	Washburn	6	9
N3 ●	Texas	2	0
N12 ●	at Kingfisher Coll.	55	0
N19 ●	Central Oklahoma	58	0
N24 ●	Bethany	29	0

1906 — 5-2-2
O6 ●	Central Oklahoma	12	0
O13 ●	Kingfisher Coll.	11	6
O19 ●	at Oklahoma State	23	0
O20 ●	at Kansas	4	20
N2 ●	Texas	9	10
N9 ●	at Central Oklahoma	17	0
N16 =	Pawhuska	0	0
N23 ●	Sulphur	48	0
N28 =	at Washburn	0	0

1907 — 4-4-0
O4 ●	at Kingfisher Coll.	32	0
O11 ●	Chilocco	43	0
O19 ●	Kansas	0	15
O25 ●	Epworth	29	0
N9 ●	Oklahoma State	67	0
N12 ●	at Texas A&M	0	19
N15 ●	at Texas	10	29
N28 ●	Washburn	0	12

1908 — 8-1-1
S25 ●	at Central Oklahoma	51	5
O3 ●	at Oklahoma State	18	0
O10 ●	Kingfisher Coll.	51	0
O17 ●	at Kansas	0	11
O23 ●	at Kansas State	33	4
O31 ●	Arkansas	27	5
N5 ●	Epworth	24	0
N13 ●	Texas	50	0
N19 ●	Wichita St.	12	4
N24 =	at Washburn	6	6

1909 — 6-4-0
S23 ●	Central Oklahoma	55	0
O2 ●	Kingfisher Coll.	46	5
O9 ●	at Kansas	0	11
O13 ●	N.W. Oklahoma	23	2
O23 ●	at Arkansas	6	21 *
N5 ●	Washburn	11	5
N12 ●	at Washington, Mo.	11	5
N17 ●	Texas A&M *DAL*	8	14
N19 ●	at Texas	0	30
N29 ●	Epworth	12	11

1910 — 4-2-1
O7 ●	at Kingfisher Coll.	66	0
O17 ●	at Central Oklahoma	79	0
O21 ●	Oklahoma State	12	0
O28 ●	Missouri	0	26
N12 ●	Kansas	0	2
N24 ●	at Texas	3	0
D2 =	Epworth	3	3

1911 — 8-0-0
O7 ●	Kingfisher Coll.	104	0
O14 ●	Oklahoma Christian	62	0
O20 ●	at Oklahoma State	22	0
O27 ●	Washburn	37	0
N4 ●	at Missouri	14	6
N11 ●	at Kansas	3	0
N22 ●	N.W. Oklahoma	34	6
N25 ●	Texas *DAL*	6	3

1912 — 5-4-0
O5 ●	at Kingfisher Coll.	40	0
O11 ●	Central Oklahoma	87	0
O19 ●	Texas *DAL*	21	6
O25 ●	Missouri	0	14
N2 ●	at Kansas	6	5
N9 ●	Texas A&M *HOU*	6	28
N16 ●	Oklahoma State	16	0
N23 ●	at Nebraska	9	13
N28 ●	Colorado *DEN*	12	14

1913 — 6-2-0
S27 ●	Kingfisher Coll.	74	0
O4 ●	at Central Oklahoma	83	0
O11 ●	N.W. Oklahoma	101	0
O18 ●	at Missouri	17	20
N1 ●	Kansas	21	7
N10 ●	Texas *HOU*	6	14
N21 ●	at Oklahoma State	7	0
N27 ●	Colorado	14	3

1914 — 9-1-1
S26 ●	Central Oklahoma	67	0
O3 ●	at Kingfisher Coll.	67	0
O9 ●	East Central Ok.	96	6
O17 ●	Missouri	13	0
O24 ●	Texas *DAL*	7	32
O31 =	at Kansas	16	16
N6 ●	Oklahoma State	23	6 *
N13 ●	at Kansas State	52	10
N21 ●	Arkansas *OKC*	35	7
N26 ●	Haskell *KC*	33	12
N30 ●	at Tulsa	26	7

1915-1919
SWC

1915 — 10-0-0 (3-0-0)
S25 ●	Kingfisher Coll.	67	0
O2 ●	at S.W. Oklahoma	55	0
O9 ●	N.W. Oklahoma	102	0
O16 ●	at Missouri	24	0
O23 ●	Texas *DAL*	14	13
O30 ●	Kansas	23	14
N6 ●	at Tulsa	14	13
N14 ●	at Arkansas	24	0
N19 ●	at Kansas State	21	7
N25 ●	Oklahoma State *OKC*	26	7

1916 — 6-5-0 (2-1-0)
S23 ●	Central Oklahoma	27	0
S30 ●	at Oklahoma Baptist	107	0
O7 ●	S.W. Oklahoma	140	0
O14 ●	Tulsa	0	16
O21 ●	Texas *DAL*	7	21
O28 ●	Missouri	14	23
N4 ●	at Kansas	13	21
N11 ●	at Kingfisher Coll.	96	0
N17 ●	Kansas State	13	14
N23 ●	Arkansas *FTS*	14	13
N30 ●	Oklahoma State *OKC*	41	7

1917 — 6-4-1 (1-1-1)
S22 ●	at Central Oklahoma	99	0
S29 ●	Kingfisher Coll.	179	0
O6 ●	Phillips *OKC*	52	9
O13 ●	at Illinois	0	44
O20 ●	Texas *DAL*	14	0
N3 ●	at Missouri	14	7
N10 ●	Kansas	6	13
N17 ●	Arkansas *FTS*	0	0
N24 ●	Tulsa	80	0
N29 ●	Oklahoma State *OKC*	0	9
D15 ●	at Camp Doniphan	7	21

1918 — 6-0-0 (2-0-0)
O19 ●	Arkansas	103	0
O26 ●	Central Oklahoma	44	0
N2 ●	Post Field	58	0
N9 ●	at Kansas	33	0
N23 ●	Phillips *OKC*	13	7
N28 ●	Oklahoma State *OKC*	27	0

1919 — 5-2-3 (2-1-0)
S27 ●	at Central Oklahoma	40	0
O4 ●	Kingfisher Coll.	157	0
O11 ●	Tulsa	0	27
O18 ●	Texas *DAL*	12	7
O25 =	Nebraska *OMA*	7	7
N1 ●	Missouri	6	6
N8 ●	at Kansas	0	0
N15 ●	at Arkansas	6	7
N22 ●	at Kansas State	14	3
N27 ●	Oklahoma State *OKC*	33	6

1920-1927
MISSOURI VALLEY

1920 — 6-0-1 (4-0-1)
O9 ●	Central Oklahoma	16	7
O23 ●	Washington, Mo.	24	14
O30 ●	at Missouri	28	7
N6 ●	Kansas	21	9
N13 ●	at Oklahoma State	36	0
N19 ●	at Kansas State	7	7
N25 ●	Drake	44	7

1921 — 5-3-0 (2-3-0)
O8 ●	at Central Oklahoma	21	0
O15 ●	Oklahoma State	6	0
O22 ●	Washington, Mo.	28	13
O29 ●	at Nebraska	0	44
N5 ●	Kansas	24	7
N12 ●	at Missouri	14	24
N19 ●	at Kansas State	7	14
N24 ●	Rice	27	0

1922 — 2-3-3 (1-2-2)
O14 ●	Central Oklahoma	21	0
O21 =	Kansas State	7	7
O28 ●	Nebraska	7	39
N4 ●	at Kansas	3	19
N11 ●	Missouri	18	14
N18 ●	Texas	7	32
N25 =	at Oklahoma State	3	3
D2 ●	at Washington, Mo.	0	0

1923 — 3-5-0 (2-4-0)
O13 ●	at Nebraska	0	24
O20 ●	Washington, Mo.	62	7
O27 ●	Oklahoma State	12	0 *
N3 ●	Kansas	3	7
N10 ●	at Missouri	13	0
N17 ●	at Texas	14	26
N23 ●	at Kansas State	20	21
N29 ●	Drake	20	26

1924 — 2-5-1 (2-3-1)
O4 ●	Central Oklahoma	0	2
O11 ●	Nebraska	14	7
O25 ●	at Drake	0	28
N1 ●	at Oklahoma State	0	6
N8 ●	Missouri	0	10
N15 ●	at Kansas	0	20 *
N22 ●	at Washington, Mo.	7	0
N26 =	Kansas State	7	7

1925 — 4-3-1 (3-3-1)
O3 ●	at Kansas State	0	16
O17 ●	Drake	7	0
O24 ●	at SMU	9	0
O31 ●	at Nebraska	0	12
N7 ●	Kansas	0	0
N14 ●	at Missouri	14	16
N21 ●	Washington, Mo.	28	0
N26 ●	Oklahoma State	35	0

1926 5-2-1 (3-2-1)
O9 ● Arkansas 13 6
O16 ● | at Drake 11 0
O23 | Kansas State 12 15
O30 ● | at Washington, Mo. 21 0
N6 ● | Missouri 10 7
N11 | at Kansas 9 10
N20 ● St. Louis 47 0
N25 = | at Oklahoma State 14 14

ADRIAN LINDSEY
1927-31 (.500) 19-19-6

1927 3-3-2 (2-3-0)
O1 ● at Chicago 13 7
O15 = Creighton 13 13
O22 | at Kansas State 14 20
O29 = at Central Oklahoma 14 14
N5 ● | Washington, Mo. 23 7
N12 ● | Kansas 26 7
N19 | Oklahoma State 7 13
N24 | at Missouri 7 20

1928-1995
BIG 8

1928 5-3-0 (3-2-0)
O6 at Indiana 7 10
O20 ● at Creighton 7 0
O27 ● | Kansas State 33 21
N3 | at Iowa State 0 13
N10 | Nebraska 6 44
N17 ● | at Kansas 7 0
N24 ● at Oklahoma State 46 0
N29 ● | Missouri 14 0

1929 3-3-2 (2-2-1)
O12 ● Creighton 26 0
O19 Texas DAL 0 21
O26 ● | at Kansas State 14 13
N2 ● | Iowa State 21 7
N9 | Kansas 0 7
N16 = | at Nebraska 13 13
N23 = Oklahoma State 7 7
N28 | at Missouri 0 13

1930 4-3-1 (3-1-1)
O4 ● New Mexico 47 0
O11 ● | Nebraska 20 7
O18 Texas DAL 7 17
O25 ● | Kansas State 7 0
N1 ● | at Iowa State 19 13
N15 | at Kansas 0 13
N22 at Oklahoma State 0 7
N27 = | Missouri 0 0

1931 4-7-1 (1-4-0)
O3 ● Rice 19 6
O10 | at Nebraska 0 13
O17 Texas DAL 0 3
O24 | at Kansas State 0 14
O31 | Iowa State 12 13
N7 ● | Kansas 10 0
N14 | at Missouri 0 7
N26 = Oklahoma State 0 0
D5 Oklahoma City 0 6
D12 ● at Tulsa 20 7
D25 at Hawaii All Stars 20 39
J1 ● at Hawaii 7 0

LEWIE HARDAGE
1932-34 (.481) 11-12-4

1932 4-4-1 (3-2-0)
O1 ● Tulsa 7 0
O8 ● | at Kansas 21 6
O15 Texas DAL 10 17
O22 ● | Kansas State 20 13
O29 at Oklahoma State 0 7
N5 | Missouri 6 14
N12 ● | at Iowa State 19 12
N19 | Nebraska 0 5
N24 = at George Washington 7 7

1933 4-4-1 (3-2-0)
S30 = Vanderbilt 0 0
O7 at Tulsa 6 20
O14 ● Texas DAL 9 0
O21 ● | Iowa State 19 7
O28 | at Nebraska 7 16
N4 ● | Kansas 20 0
N11 ● | at Missouri 21 0
N18 | at Kansas State 0 14
N23 Oklahoma State 0 13

1934 3-4-2 (2-2-1)
O6 ● Centenary 7 0
O13 Texas DAL 0 19
O20 | Nebraska 0 6
O27 = | at Kansas 7 7
N3 ● | Missouri 31 0
N10 ● | Iowa State 12 0
N17 | Kansas State 7 8
N22 = at Oklahoma State 0 0
D1 at George Washington 0 3

LAWRENCE "BIFF" JONES
1935-36 (.583) 9-6-3

1935 6-3-0 (3-2-0)
S28 ● Colorado 3 0
O5 ● New Mexico 25 0
O12 Texas DAL 7 12
O19 ● | Iowa State 16 0
O26 | at Nebraska 0 19
N2 | Kansas 0 7
N9 ● | at Missouri 20 6
N16 ● | at Kansas State 3 0
N28 ● Oklahoma State 25 0

1936 3-3-3 (1-2-2)
S26 = Tulsa 0 0
O3 ● at Colorado 8 0
O10 Texas DAL 0 6
O17 ● | at Kansas 14 0
O24 | Nebraska 0 14
O31 = | at Iowa State 7 7
N7 = | Kansas State 6 6
N14 | Missouri 14 21
N26 ● at Oklahoma State 35 3

TOM STIDHAM
1937-40 (.750) 27-8-3

1937 5-2-2 (3-1-1)
S25 at Tulsa 7 19
O2 ● Rice 6 0
O9 = Texas DAL 7 7
O16 = | at Nebraska 0 0
O23 Kansas 3 6
O30 ● | at Kansas State 19 0
N6 ● | Iowa State 33 7
N13 ● | at Missouri 7 0
N25 ● Oklahoma State 16 0

1938 10-1-0 (5-0-0)
O1 ● at Rice 7 6
O8 ● Texas DAL 13 0
O15 ● | at Kansas 19 0
O22 ● | Nebraska 14 0
O29 ● Tulsa 28 6
N5 ● | Kansas State 26 0
N12 ● | Missouri 21 0
N19 ● | at Iowa State 10 0
N24 ● at Oklahoma State 19 0
D3 ● Washington State 28 0
ORANGE BOWL
J2 Tennessee 0 17

1939 6-2-1 (3-2-0)
S30 = SMU 7 7
O7 ● at Northwestern 23 0
O14 ● Texas DAL 24 12
O21 ● | Kansas 27 7
O28 ● Oklahoma State 41 0
N4 ● | Iowa State 38 6
N11 ● | at Kansas State 13 10
N18 | at Missouri 6 7
N25 | at Nebraska 7 13

1940 6-3-0 (4-1-0)
O5 ● Oklahoma State 29 27
O12 Texas DAL 16 19
O19 ● | Kansas State 14 0
O26 ● | at Iowa State 20 7
N2 | Nebraska 0 13
N9 ● | at Kansas 13 0
N16 ● | Missouri 7 0
N23 ● Temple 9 6
N30 at Santa Clara 13 33

DEWEY "SNORTER" LUSTER
1941-45 (.594) 27-18-3

1941 6-3-0 (3-2-0)
S27 ● Oklahoma State 19 0
O11 Texas DAL 7 40
O18 ● | at Kansas State 16 0
O25 ● Santa Clara 16 6
N1 ● | Kansas 38 0
N8 ● | Iowa State 55 0
N15 | at Missouri 0 28
N22 ● Marquette 61 14
N29 | at Nebraska 6 7

1942 3-5-2 (3-1-1)
S26 = at Oklahoma State 0 0
O3 at Tulsa 0 23
O10 Texas DAL 0 7
O17 ● | at Kansas 25 0
O24 | Nebraska 0 7
O31 ● | at Iowa State 14 7
N7 ● | Kansas State 76 0
N14 = | Missouri 6 6
N21 at Temple 7 14
N28 William & Mary 7 14

1943 7-2-0 (5-0-0)
S25 ● Norman NAS 22 6
O2 ● Oklahoma State OKC 22 13
O9 Texas DAL 7 13
O16 Tulsa OKC 6 20
O23 ● | at Kansas State 37 0
O30 ● | Iowa State 21 7
N6 ● | Kansas 26 13
N13 ● | at Missouri 20 13
N27 ● | at Nebraska 26 7

1944 6-3-1 (4-0-1)
S30 Norman NAS 14 28
O7 ● Texas A&M OKC 21 14
O14 Texas DAL 0 20
O21 ● | Kansas State 68 0
O28 ● TCU OKC 34 19
N4 ● | at Iowa State 12 7
N11 = | Missouri 21 21
N18 ● | at Kansas 20 0
N25 Oklahoma State OKC 6 28
D2 ● | Nebraska OKC 31 12

1945 5-5-0 (4-1-0)
S22 ● at Hondo AAF 21 6
S29 ● | at Nebraska 20 0
O6 Texas A&M 14 19
O13 Texas DAL 7 12
O20 ● | Kansas 39 7
O27 ● | at Kansas State 41 13
N3 TCU 7 13
N10 ● | Iowa State 14 7
N17 | at Missouri 6 14
N24 Oklahoma State 0 47

JIM TATUM
1946 (.727) 8-3

1946 8-3-0 (4-1-0)
S28 at Army 7 21
O5 ● Texas A&M 10 7
O12 Texas DAL 13 20
O19 ● | Kansas State 28 7
O26 ● | at Iowa State 63 0
N2 ● at TCU 14 12
N9 | at Kansas 13 16
N16 ● | Missouri 27 6
N23 ● | Nebraska 27 6
N30 ● at Oklahoma State 73 12
GATOR BOWL
J1 ● North Carolina St. 34 13

BUD WILKINSON
1947-63 (.826) 145-29-4

1947 7-2-1 (4-0-1)
S26 ● at Detroit 24 20
O4 ● Texas A&M 26 14
O11 Texas DAL 14 34
O18 = | Kansas 13 13
O25 TCU 7 20
N1 ● | Iowa State 27 9
N8 ● | at Kansas State 27 13
N15 ● | at Missouri 21 12
N22 ● | at Nebraska 14 13
N29 ● Oklahoma State 21 13

1948 10-1-0 (5-0-0)
S25 at Santa Clara 17 20
O2 ● Texas A&M 42 14
O9 ● Texas DAL 20 14
O16 ● | Kansas State 42 0
O23 ● at TCU 21 18
O30 ● | at Iowa State 33 6
N6 ● | Missouri 41 7
N13 ● | Nebraska 41 14
N20 ● | at Kansas 60 7
N27 ● at Oklahoma State 19 15
SUGAR BOWL
J1 ● North Carolina 14 6

1949 11-0-0 (5-0-0)
S23 ● at Boston College 46 0
O1 ● Texas A&M 33 13
O8 ● Texas DAL 20 14
O15 ● | Kansas 48 26
O22 ● | at Nebraska 48 0
O29 ● | Iowa State 34 7
N5 ● | at Kansas State 39 0
N12 ● | at Missouri 27 7
N19 ● Santa Clara 28 21
N26 ● Oklahoma State 41 0
SUGAR BOWL
J2 ● LSU 35 0

1950 10-1-0 (6-0-0)
S30 ● Boston College 28 0
O7 ● Texas A&M 34 28
O14 ● Texas DAL 14 13
O21 ● | Kansas State 58 0
O28 ● | at Iowa State 20 7
N4 ● | at Colorado 27 18
N11 ● | at Kansas 33 13
N18 ● | Missouri 41 7
N25 ● | Nebraska 49 35
D2 ● at Oklahoma State 41 14
SUGAR BOWL
J1 Kentucky 7 13

1951 8-2-0 (6-0-0)
S29 ● William & Mary 49 7
O6 at Texas A&M 7 14
O13 Texas DAL 7 9
O20 ● | Kansas 33 21
O27 ● | Colorado 55 14
N3 ● | at Kansas State 33 0
N10 ● | at Missouri 34 20
N17 ● | Iowa State 35 6
N24 ● | at Nebraska 27 0
D1 ● Oklahoma State 41 6

1952 8-1-1 (5-0-1)
S27 = | at Colorado 21 21
O4 ● Pittsburgh 49 20
O11 ● Texas DAL 49 20
O18 ● | at Kansas 42 20
O25 ● | Kansas State 49 6
N1 ● | at Iowa State 41 0
N8 at Notre Dame 21 27
N15 ● | Missouri 47 7
N22 ● | Nebraska 34 13
N29 ● at Oklahoma State 54 7

1953 9-1-1 (6-0-0)
S26 Notre Dame 21 28
O3 = at Pittsburgh 7 7
O10 ● Texas DAL 19 14
O17 ● | Kansas 45 0
O24 ● | Colorado 27 20
O31 ● | at Kansas State 34 0
N7 ● | at Missouri 14 7 *
N14 ● | Iowa State 47 0
N21 ● | at Nebraska 30 7
N28 ● Oklahoma State 42 7
ORANGE BOWL
J1 ● Maryland 7 0

1954 10-0-0 (6-0-0)
S18 ● at California 27 13
S25 ● TCU 21 16
O9 ● Texas DAL 14 7
O16 ● | at Kansas 65 0
O23 ● | Kansas State 21 0
O30 ● | at Colorado 13 6
N6 ● | at Iowa State 40 0
N13 ● | Missouri 34 13
N20 ● | Nebraska 55 7
N27 ● at Oklahoma State 14 0

1955 11-0-0 (6-0-0)
S24 ● at North Carolina 13 6
O1 ● Pittsburgh 26 14
O8 ● Texas DAL 20 0
O15 ● | Kansas 44 6
O22 ● | Colorado 56 21
O29 ● | at Kansas State 40 7
N5 ● | at Missouri 20 0
N12 ● | Iowa State 52 0
N19 ● | at Nebraska 41 0
N26 ● Oklahoma State 53 0
ORANGE BOWL
J2 ● Maryland 20 6

THE SCHOOLS

1956 — 10-0-0 (6-0-0)
Date	Opponent	OU	Opp
S29	North Carolina	36	0
O6	Kansas State	66	0
O13	Texas DAL	45	0
O20	at Kansas	34	12
O27	at Notre Dame	40	0
N3	at Colorado	27	19
N10	at Iowa State	44	0
N17	Missouri	67	14
N24	Nebraska	54	6
D1	at Oklahoma State	53	0

1957 — 10-1-0 (6-0-0)
Date	Opponent	OU	Opp
S21	at Pittsburgh	26	0
O5	Iowa State	40	14
O12	Texas DAL	21	7
O19	Kansas	47	0
O26	Colorado	14	13
N2	at Kansas State	13	0
N9	at Missouri	39	14
N16	Notre Dame	0	7
N23	at Nebraska	32	7
N30	Oklahoma State	53	6
ORANGE BOWL			
J1	Duke	48	21

1958 — 10-1-0 (6-0-0)
Date	Opponent	OU	Opp
S27	West Virginia	47	14
O4	Oregon	6	0
O11	Texas DAL	14	15
O18	at Kansas	43	0
O25	Kansas State	40	6
N1	at Colorado	23	7
N8	at Iowa State	20	0
N15	Missouri	39	0
N22	Nebraska	40	7
N29	at Oklahoma State	7	0
ORANGE BOWL			
J1	Syracuse	21	6

1959 — 7-3-0 (5-1-0)
Date	Opponent	OU	Opp
S26	at Northwestern	13	45
O3	Colorado	42	12
O10	Texas DAL	12	19
O17	at Missouri	23	0
O24	Kansas	7	6
O31	at Nebraska	21	25
N7	at Kansas State	36	0
N14	Army	28	20
N21	Iowa State	35	12
N28	Oklahoma State	17	7

1960 — 3-6-1 (2-4-1)
Date	Opponent	OU	Opp
S24	Northwestern	3	19
O1	Pittsburgh	15	14
O8	Texas DAL	0	24
O15 =	at Kansas	13	13
O22	Kansas State	49	7
O29	at Colorado	0	7
N5	at Iowa State	6	10
N12	Missouri	19	41
N19	Nebraska	14	17
N26	at Oklahoma State	17	6

1961 — 5-5-0 (4-3-0)
Date	Opponent	OU	Opp
S30	at Notre Dame	6	19
O7	Iowa State	15	21
O14	Texas DAL	7	28
O21	Kansas	0	10
O28	Colorado	14	22
N4	at Kansas State	17	6
N11	at Missouri	7	0
N18	Army BRNX	14	8
N25	at Nebraska	21	14
D2	Oklahoma State	21	13

1962 — 8-3-0 (7-0-0)
Date	Opponent	OU	Opp
S22	Syracuse	7	3
S29	Notre Dame	7	13
O13	Texas DAL	6	9
O20	at Kansas	13	7
O27	Kansas State	47	0
N3	at Colorado	62	0
N10	at Iowa State	41	0
N17	Missouri	13	0
N24	Nebraska	34	6
D1	at Oklahoma State	37	6
ORANGE BOWL			
J1	Alabama	0	17

1963 — 8-2-0 (6-1-0)
Date	Opponent	OU	Opp
S21	Clemson	31	14
S28	at Southern Cal	17	12
O12	Texas DAL	7	28
O19	Kansas	21	18
O26	at Kansas State	34	9
N2	Colorado	35	0
N9	Iowa State	24	14
N16	at Missouri	13	3
N23	at Nebraska	20	29
N30	Oklahoma State	34	10

GOMER JONES
1964-65 (.452)   9-11-1

1964 — 6-4-1 (5-1-1)
Date	Opponent	OU	Opp
S19	at Maryland	13	3
S26	Southern Cal	14	40
O10	Texas DAL	7	28
O17	at Kansas	14	15
O24	Kansas State	44	0
O31	at Colorado	14	11
N7	Iowa State	30	0
N14 =	Missouri	14	14
N21	Nebraska	17	7
N28	at Oklahoma State	21	16
GATOR BOWL			
J2	Florida State	19	36

1965 — 3-7-0 (3-4-0)
Date	Opponent	OU	Opp
S25	at Pittsburgh	9	13
O2	Navy	0	10
O9	Texas DAL	0	19
O16	Kansas	21	7
O23	at Kansas State	27	0
O30	Colorado	0	13
N6	Iowa State	24	20
N13	at Missouri	0	30
N25	at Nebraska	9	21
D4	Oklahoma State	16	17

JIM MacKENZIE
1966 (.600)   6-4

1966 — 6-4-0 (4-3-0)
Date	Opponent	OU	Opp
S17	Oregon	17	0
S24	at Iowa State	33	11
O8	Texas DAL	18	9
O15	at Kansas	35	0
O22	Notre Dame	0	38
O29	at Colorado	21	24
N5	Kansas State	37	6
N12	Missouri	7	10
N24	Nebraska	10	9
D3	at Oklahoma State	14	15

CHUCK FAIRBANKS
1967-72 (.772)   52-15-1

1967 — 10-1-0 (7-0-0)
Date	Opponent	OU	Opp
S23	Washington State	21	0
S30	Maryland	35	0
O14	Texas DAL	7	9
O21	at Kansas State	46	7
O28	at Missouri	7	0
N4	Colorado	23	0
N11	at Iowa State	52	14
N18	Kansas	14	10
N25	at Nebraska	21	14
D2	Oklahoma State	38	14
ORANGE BOWL			
J1	Tennessee	26	24

1968 — 7-4-0 (6-1-0)
Date	Opponent	OU	Opp
S21	at Notre Dame	21	45
S28	North Carolina St.	28	14
O12	Texas DAL	20	26
O19	Iowa State	42	7
O26	at Colorado	27	41
N2	Kansas State	35	20
N9	at Kansas	27	23
N16	Missouri	28	14
N23	Nebraska	47	0
N30	at Oklahoma State	41	7
BLUEBONNET BOWL			
D31	SMU	27	28

1969 — 6-4-0 (4-3-0)
Date	Opponent	OU	Opp
S20	at Wisconsin	48	21
S27	Pittsburgh	37	8
O11	Texas DAL	17	27
O18	Colorado	42	30
O25	at Kansas State	21	59
N1	Iowa State	37	14
N8	at Missouri	10	44
N15	Kansas	31	15
N22	Nebraska	14	44
N29	at Oklahoma State	28	27

1970 — 7-4-1 (5-2-0)
Date	Opponent	OU	Opp
S12	at SMU	28	11
S19	Wisconsin	21	7
S26	Oregon State	14	23
O10	Texas DAL	9	41
O17	at Colorado	23	15
O24	Kansas State	14	19
O31	at Iowa State	29	28
N7	Missouri	28	13
N14	at Kansas	28	24
N21	at Nebraska	21	28
N28	Oklahoma State	66	6
BLUEBONNET BOWL			
D31 =	Alabama	24	24

1971 — 11-1-0 (6-1-0)
Date	Opponent	OU	Opp
S18	SMU	30	0
S25	at Pittsburgh	55	29
O2	Southern Cal	33	20
O9	Texas DAL	48	27
O16	Colorado	45	17
O23	at Kansas State	75	28
O30	Iowa State	43	12
N6	at Missouri	20	3
N13	Kansas	56	10
N25	Nebraska	31	35
D4	at Oklahoma State	58	14
SUGAR BOWL			
J1	Auburn	40	22

1972 — 11-1-0 (6-1-0)
Date	Opponent	OU	Opp
S16	Utah State	49	0
S23	Oregon	68	3
S30	Clemson	52	3
O14	Texas DAL	27	0
O21	at Colorado	14	20
O28	Kansas State	52	0
N4	at Iowa State	20	6
N11	Missouri	17	6 †
N18	at Kansas	31	7 †
N23	at Nebraska	17	14
D2	Oklahoma State	38	15 †
SUGAR BOWL			
D31	Penn State	14	0

BARRY SWITZER
1973-88 (.837)   157-29-4

1973 — 10-0-1 (7-0-0)
Date	Opponent	OU	Opp
S15	at Baylor	42	14
S29 =	at Southern Cal	7	7
O6	Miami, Fla.	24	20
O13	Texas DAL	52	13
O20	Colorado	34	7
O27	at Kansas State	56	14
N3	Iowa State	34	17
N10	at Missouri	31	3
N17	Kansas	48	20
N23	Nebraska	27	0
D1	at Oklahoma State	45	18

1974 — 11-0-0 (7-0-0)
Date	Opponent	OU	Opp
S14	Baylor	28	11
S28	Utah State	72	3
O5	Wake Forest	63	0
O12	Texas DAL	16	13
O19	at Colorado	49	14
O26	Kansas State	63	0 †
N2	at Iowa State	28	10 †
N9	Missouri	37	0
N16	at Kansas	45	14 †
N23	at Nebraska	28	14
N30	Oklahoma State	44	13

1975 — 11-1-0 (6-1-0)
Date	Opponent	OU	Opp
S13	Oregon	62	7
S20	Pittsburgh	46	10
S26	at Miami, Fla.	20	17
O4	Colorado	21	20
O11	Texas DAL	24	17
O18	at Kansas State	25	3
O25	Iowa State	39	7
N1	at Oklahoma State	27	7
N8	Kansas	3	23
N15	at Missouri	28	27
N22	Nebraska	35	10
ORANGE BOWL			
J1	Michigan	14	6

1976 — 9-2-1 (5-2-0)
Date	Opponent	OU	Opp
S11	at Vanderbilt	24	3
S18	California	28	17
S25	Florida State	24	9
O2	at Iowa State	24	10
O9 =	Texas DAL	6	6
O16	at Kansas	28	10
O23	Oklahoma State	24	31
O30	at Colorado	31	42
N6	Kansas State	49	20
N13	Missouri	27	20
N26	at Nebraska	20	17
FIESTA BOWL			
D25	Wyoming	41	7

1977 — 10-2-0 (7-0-0)
Date	Opponent	OU	Opp
S10	Vanderbilt	25	23
S17	Utah	62	24
S24	at Ohio State	29	28
O1	Kansas	24	9
O8	Texas DAL	6	13
O15	at Missouri	21	17
O22	Iowa State	35	16
O29	at Kansas State	42	7
N5	at Oklahoma State	61	28
N12	Colorado	52	14
N25	Nebraska	38	7
ORANGE BOWL			
J2	Arkansas	6	31

1978 — 11-1-0 (6-1-0)
Date	Opponent	OU	Opp
S9	at Stanford	35	29
S16	West Virginia	52	10
S23	Rice	66	7
S30	Missouri	45	23
O7	Texas	31	10
O14	at Kansas	17	16
O21	at Iowa State	34	6
O28	Kansas State	56	19
N4	at Colorado	28	7
N11	at Nebraska	14	17
N18	Oklahoma State	62	7
ORANGE BOWL			
J1	Nebraska	31	24

1979 — 11-1-0 (7-0-0)
Date	Opponent	OU	Opp
S15	Iowa	21	6
S22	Tulsa	49	13
S29	at Rice	63	21
O6	Colorado	49	24
O13	Texas DAL	7	16
O20	at Kansas State	38	6
O27	Iowa State	38	9
N3	at Oklahoma State	38	7
N10	Kansas	38	0
N17	at Missouri	24	22
N24	Nebraska	17	14
ORANGE BOWL			
J1	Florida State	24	7

1980 — 10-2-0 (7-0-0)
Date	Opponent	OU	Opp
S13	Kentucky	29	7
S27	Stanford	14	31
O4	at Colorado	82	42
O11	Texas DAL	13	20
O18	Kansas State	35	21
O25	at Iowa State	42	7
N1	North Carolina	41	7
N8	at Kansas	21	19
N15	Missouri	17	7
N22	at Nebraska	21	17
N29	Oklahoma State	63	14
ORANGE BOWL			
J1	Florida State	18	17

1981 — 7-4-1 (4-2-1)
Date	Opponent	OU	Opp
S12	Wyoming	37	20
S26	at Southern Cal	24	28
O3 =	Iowa State	7	7
O10	Texas DAL	14	34
O17	Kansas	45	7
O24	Oregon State	42	3
O31	Colorado	49	0
N7	at Kansas State	28	21
N14	at Missouri	14	19
N21	Nebraska	14	37
N28	at Oklahoma State	27	3
SUN BOWL			
D26	Houston	40	14

1982   8-4-0 (6-1-0)

S11	●	West Virginia	27	41
S18	●	at Kentucky	29	8
S25		Southern Cal	0	12
O2	●	at Iowa State	13	3
O9		Texas DAL	28	22
O16	●	at Kansas	38	14
O23	●	Oklahoma State	27	9
O30	●	at Colorado	45	10
N6		Kansas State	24	10
N13	●	Missouri	41	14
N26	●	at Nebraska	24	28

FIESTA BOWL

J1		Arizona State	21	32

1983   8-4-0 (5-2-0)

S10	●	at Stanford	27	14
S17		Ohio State	14	24
S24	●	Tulsa	28	18
O1	●	at Kansas State	29	10
O8		Texas DAL	16	28
O15	●	at Oklahoma State	21	20
O22	●	Iowa State	49	11
O29	●	Kansas	45	14
N5		at Missouri	0	10
N12	●	Colorado	41	28
N26		Nebraska	21	28
D3		at Hawaii	21	17

1984   9-2-1 (6-1-0)

S8	●	Stanford	19	7
S15	●	at Pittsburgh	42	10
S22	●	Baylor	34	15
S29	●	Kansas State	24	6
O13	=	Texas DAL	15	15
O20	●	at Iowa State	12	10
O27		at Kansas	11	28
N3	●	Missouri	49	7
N10	●	at Colorado	42	17
N17	●	at Nebraska	17	7
N24	●	Oklahoma State	24	14

ORANGE BOWL

J1		Washington	17	28

1985   11-1-0 (7-0-0)

S28	●	at Minnesota	13	7
O5	●	at Kansas State	41	6
O12	●	Texas DAL	14	7
O19		Miami, Fla.	14	27
O26	●	Iowa State	59	14
N2	●	Kansas	48	6
N9	●	at Missouri	51	6
N16	●	Colorado	31	0
N23	●	Nebraska	27	7
N30	●	at Oklahoma State	13	0
D7	●	SMU	35	13

ORANGE BOWL

J1	●	Penn State	25	10

1986   11-1-0 (7-0-0)

S6	●	UCLA	38	3
S20	●	Minnesota	63	0
S27	●	at Miami, Fla.	16	28
O4	●	Kansas State	56	10
O11	●	Texas	47	12
O18	●	Oklahoma State	19	0
O25	●	at Iowa State	38	0
N1	●	at Kansas	64	3
N8	●	Missouri	77	0
N15	●	at Colorado	28	0
N22	●	at Nebraska	20	17

ORANGE BOWL

J1	●	Arkansas	42	8

1987   11-1-0 (7-0-0)

S5	●	North Texas	69	14
S12	●	North Carolina	28	0
S26	●	at Tulsa	65	0
O3	●	at Iowa State	56	3
O10	●	Texas DAL	44	9
O17	●	at Kansas State	59	10
O24	●	Colorado	24	6
O31	●	at Kansas	71	10
N7	●	Oklahoma State	29	10
N14	●	Missouri	17	13
N21	●	at Nebraska	17	7

ORANGE BOWL

J1	●	Miami, Fla.	14	20

1988   9-3-0 (6-1-0)

S10	●	at North Carolina	28	0
S17	●	Arizona	28	10
S24	●	at Southern Cal	7	23
O1	●	Iowa State	35	7
O8	●	Texas DAL	28	13
O15	●	Kansas State	70	24
O22	●	at Colorado	17	14
O29	●	Kansas	63	14
N5	●	at Oklahoma State	31	28
N12	●	at Missouri	16	7
N19		Nebraska	3	7

CITRUS BOWL

J2		Clemson	6	13

1989   7-4-0 (5-2-0)

S2	●	New Mexico St.	73	3
S9	●	Baylor	33	7
S16	●	at Arizona	3	6
S30	●	at Kansas	45	6
O7	●	Oklahoma State	37	15
O14	●	Texas DAL	24	28
O21	●	at Iowa State	43	40
O28		Colorado	3	20
N4	●	Missouri	52	14
N11	●	Kansas State	42	19
N18		at Nebraska	25	42

1990   8-3-0 (5-2-0)

S8	●	at UCLA	34	14
S15	●	Pittsburgh	52	10
S22	●	Tulsa	52	10
S29	●	Kansas	31	17
O6	●	at Oklahoma State	31	17
O13	●	Texas DAL	13	14
O20		Iowa State	31	33
O27	●	at Colorado	23	32
N3	●	at Missouri	55	10
N10	●	Kansas State	34	7
N23		Nebraska	45	10

1991   9-3-0 (5-2-0)

S14	●	North Texas	40	2
S21	●	Utah State	55	21
S28	●	Virginia Tech	27	17
O5	●	at Iowa State	29	8
O12	●	Texas DAL	7	10
O19		Colorado	17	34
O26	●	Kansas	41	3
N2	●	Kansas State	28	7
N9	●	at Missouri	56	16
N16	●	Oklahoma State	21	6
N29		at Nebraska	14	19

GATOR BOWL

D29		Virginia	48	14

1992   5-4-2 (3-2-2)

S3	●	at Texas Tech	34	9
S12	●	Arkansas State	61	0
S19	●	Southern Cal	10	20
O3	●	Iowa State	17	3
O10		Texas DAL	24	34
O17	=	at Colorado	24	24
O24	●	Kansas	10	27
O31	●	Kansas State	16	14
N7	●	Missouri	51	17
N14	=	at Oklahoma State	15	15
N27		Nebraska	9	33

1993   9-3-0 (4-3-0)

S4	●	at TCU	35	3
S11	●	Texas A&M	44	14
S25	●	Tulsa	41	20
O2	●	at Iowa State	24	7
O9	●	Texas DAL	38	17
O16	●	Colorado	10	27
O23	●	Kansas	38	23
O30	●	at Kansas State	7	21
N6	●	at Missouri	42	23
N13	●	Oklahoma State	31	0
N26	●	at Nebraska	7	21

SUN BOWL

D24	●	Texas Tech	41	10

1994   6-6-0 (4-3-0)

S3	●	at Syracuse	30	29
S10	●	at Texas A&M	14	36
S17	●	Texas Tech	17	11
O1	●	Iowa State	34	6
O8	●	Texas DAL	10	17
O15	●	at Colorado	7	45
O22	●	at Kansas	20	17
O29	●	Kansas State	20	37
N5	●	Missouri	30	13
N12	●	at Oklahoma State	33	14
N25		Nebraska	3	13

COPPER BOWL

D29		Brigham Young	6	31

1995   5-5-1 (2-5-0)

S9	●	San Diego State	38	22
S16	●	SMU	24	10
S23	●	North Texas	51	10
S30		Colorado	17	38
O7	●	at Iowa State	39	26
O14	=	Texas DAL	24	24
O21		Kansas	17	38
O28	●	at Missouri	13	9
N4		at Kansas State	10	49
N11		Oklahoma State	0	12
N24		Nebraska	0	37

1996   3-8 (3-5)

S7	●	TCU	7	20
S21		at San Diego State	31	51
S28	●	Tulsa	24	31
O5		Kansas	24	52
O12	●	Texas DAL	30	27
O19	●	at Baylor	28	24
O26	●	Kansas State	35	42
N2	●	Nebraska	21	73
N9	●	at Oklahoma State	27	17
N16	●	at Texas A&M	16	33
N23		Texas Tech	12	22

1997   4-8 (2-6)

A23		Northwestern CHI	0	24
S6	●	Syracuse	36	34
S20	●	at California	36	40
S27	●	Louisville	35	14
O4		at Kansas	17	20
O11		Texas DAL	24	27
O18	●	Baylor	24	23
O25		Kansas State	7	26
N1		Nebraska	7	69
N8	●	Oklahoma State	7	30
N15		Texas A&M	7	51
N22	●	at Texas Tech	32	21

1998   5-6 (3-5)

S5	●	North Texas	37	9
S12	●	at TCU	10	9
S19	●	California	12	13
O3		Colorado	25	27
O10	●	Texas DAL	3	34
O17	●	at Missouri	6	20
O24	●	at Oklahoma State	26	41
O31	●	Iowa State	17	14
N7		at Texas A&M	0	29
N14	●	at Baylor	28	16
N21		Texas Tech	20	17

1999   7-5 (5-3)

S11	●	Indiana St.	49	0
S18	●	Baylor	41	10
S25	●	at Louisville	42	21
O2		at Notre Dame	30	34
O9		Texas DAL	28	38
O23	●	Texas A&M	51	6
O30	●	at Colorado	24	38
N6	●	Missouri	37	0
N13	●	at Iowa State	31	10
N20	●	at Texas Tech	28	38
N27	●	Oklahoma State	44	7

INDEPENDENCE BOWL

D31		Mississippi	25	27

2000   13-0 (8-0)

S2	●	Texas El Paso	55	14
S9	●	Arkansas State	45	7
S23	●	Rice	42	14
S30	●	Kansas	34	16
O7	●	Texas DAL	63	14
O14	●	at Kansas State	41	31
O28	●	Nebraska	31	14
N4	●	at Baylor	56	7
N11	●	at Texas A&M	35	31
N18	●	Texas Tech	27	13
N25	●	at Oklahoma State	12	7

BIG 12 CHAMPIONSHIP

D2		Kansas State KC	27	24

ORANGE BOWL

J3	●	Florida State	13	2

2001   11-2 (6-2)

A25	●	North Carolina	41	27
S1	●	at Air Force	44	3
S8	●	North Texas	37	10
S29	●	Kansas State	38	37
O6	●	Texas DAL	14	3
O13	●	at Kansas	38	10
O20	●	Baylor	33	17
O27	●	at Nebraska	10	20
N3	●	Tulsa	58	0
N10	●	Texas A&M	31	10
N17	●	at Texas Tech	30	13
N24	●	Oklahoma State	13	16

COTTON BOWL

J1	●	Arkansas	10	3

2002   12-2 (6-2)

A30	●	at Tulsa	37	0
S7	●	Alabama	37	27
S14	●	Texas-El Paso	68	0
S28	●	South Florida	31	14
O5	●	at Missouri	31	24
O12	●	Texas DAL	35	24
O19	●	Iowa State	49	3
N2	●	Colorado	27	11
N9	●	at Texas A&M	26	30
N16	●	at Baylor	49	9
N23	●	Texas Tech	60	15
N30	●	at Oklahoma State	28	38

BIG 12 CHAMPIONSHIP

D7	●	Colorado HOU	29	7

ROSE BOWL

J1	●	Washington State	34	14

2003   12-2 (8-0)

A30	●	North Texas	37	3
S6	●	at Alabama	20	13
S13	●	Fresno State	52	28
S20	●	UCLA	59	24
O4	●	at Iowa State	53	7
O11	●	Texas DAL	65	13
O18	●	Missouri	34	13
O25	●	at Colorado	34	20
N1	●	Oklahoma State	52	9
N8	●	Texas A&M	77	0
N15	●	Baylor	41	3
N22	●	at Texas Tech	56	25

BIG 12 CHAMPIONSHIP

D6		Kansas State KC	7	35

SUGAR BOWL

J4		LSU	14	21

2004   12-1 (8-0)

S4	●	Bowling Green	40	24
S11	●	Houston	63	13
S18	●	Oregon	31	7
O2	●	Texas Tech	28	13
O9	●	Texas DAL	12	0
O16	●	at Kansas State	31	21
O23	●	Kansas	41	10
O30	●	at Oklahoma State	38	35
N6	●	at Texas A&M	42	35
N13	●	Nebraska	30	3
N20	●	at Baylor	35	0

BIG 12 CHAMPIONSHIP

D4	●	Colorado KC	42	3

ORANGE BOWL

J4		Southern Cal	19	55

Neutral Site key: *Hou* Houston, TX / *KC* Kansas City, MO / *Den* Denver, CO / *KC* Kansas City, MO / *FtS* Fort Smith, AR / *Gut* Guthrie, OK / *Oma* Omaha, NE / *Sha* Shawnee, OK / *OkC* Oklahoma City, OK / *Chi* Chicago, IL / *Dal* Dallas, TX / *Brnx* Bronx, NY
f Forfeit   † Game Later Forfeited   # Disputed Victor   * Disputed Score || Designated Conference Game |2 Counted Twice in Conference Standings

OKLAHOMA STATE

BY MARK WANGRIN

IT RECEIVES NO MENTION IN THE school's media guide, whether through oversight or ignominy, but in 1889, the game students of Oklahoma A&M ventured to nearby Guthrie to take on territorial power Kingfisher College. Without a coach, wearing home-sewn uniforms and with their ranks swelled by some town residents, they were sent packing by a 22-0 score. The account in the *Kingfisher Free Press* detailed the slaughter: "The Kingfisher College football team ... proceeded to wipe the face of the earth with the clodhoppers and blacksmiths of the Agricultural college, and left their carcasses to bleach and blister on the barren plains of Stillwater. It was a full grown skunk, and its stifling odor drives the turkey buzzards crazy." It would get better—in time. Oklahoma A&M won only three of its first 20 games, but the Cowboys would have their day. Under inspired coaching from Pappy Waldorf to E.M. "Smiling Jim" Lookabaugh and Jim Stanley, they won 10 conference titles. Though the conference titles haven't been coming too often recently, the

Cowboys have had the welcome consolation prize of playing spoiler to the school that replaced Kingfisher as their powerful in-state rival, twice knocking the Oklahoma Sooners out of a shot at the national title in the early 21st century.

TRADITION Before games and after touchdowns, the Spirit Rider, a student in an orange shirt and black hat, vest and pants, rides up and down the field on Bullet, a black quarterhorse. In 1984, OSU band director Richard Kastendieck and student John Beall, the president of the OSU Rodeo Association at the time, came up with the idea of Beall riding his own quarterhorse, Della, to celebrate Cowboy touchdowns. Four years later, the school bought a horse and the student newspaper, *The Daily O'Collegian*, held a contest to pick a nickname.

In 2001, coach Les Miles introduced The Walk, which he hoped would stick as a tradition. Two hours and fifteen minutes before home-game kickoffs, the team, led by the coach and accompanied by the OSU marching band and several spirit groups, walks down Hester Street to Lewis Field.

BEST PLAYER Thurman Thomas wrapped up a sparkling four-year career in 1987 as the school's all-time leading

PROFILE

Oklahoma State University
Stillwater, Okla.
Founded: 1890
Enrollment: 17,493
Colors: Orange and Black
Nickname: Cowboys
Stadium: Boone Pickens Stadium/Lewis Field
　　Opened in 1920
　　AstroPlay; 48,500 capacity
First football game: 1901
All-time record: 470–492–49 (.489)
Bowl record: 10–6
Heisman Trophy: Barry Sanders, 1988
First-round NFL draftees: 15
Website: www.okstate.com

THE BEST OF TIMES

A real power in the war years, the Cowboys went 17–1 in 1944 and 1945, winning the Cotton Bowl and Sugar Bowl in the process.

THE WORST OF TIMES

OSU did not post a winning record in any of its first 12 seasons as a member of the Big Eight.

CONFERENCE

A charter member of the Southwest Conference in 1915, Oklahoma State bolted to the Missouri Valley Conference in 1925. The Cowboys left to become an independent in 1957, then joined the Big Eight in 1960. In 1996, they would be reunited with some old SWC foes when the Big Eight absorbed four Texas schools to form the Big 12.

DISTINGUISHED ALUMNI

Brent Ashabranner, children's author, Peace Corps director; Henry Bellmon, Oklahoma governor and U.S. senator; Garth Brooks, country music singer/songwriter; Tim DuBois, president of Arista Nashville Records; Chester Gould, cartoonist/creator of "Dick Tracy"; Scott Hendricks, president of Virgin Records; Dr. H. Edward Roberts, personal computer pioneer

FIGHT SONG

RIDE 'EM COWBOYS
Cowboys a riding,
Lassoes a-flying,
Under the western sky.
And as they ride,
We rise to sing and shout our battle cry!
Ride, ride, ride, ride,
Ride 'em Cowboys,
Right down the field;
Fight! Fight! Fight! Fight!
Fight 'em Cowboys, and never yield.
Ride, ride, ride, ride,
Ride on, Cowboys, to victory;
Cross [opponent]'s goal;
Then we'll sing.
Oklahoma State!

After touchdowns, the Spirit Rider rides up and down the Lewis Field sideline on Bullet, a black quarterhorse.

rusher, but replacing him was easier than it first appeared. Barry Sanders, a diminutive junior who had been Thomas' backup, inherited the job. Despite being far off the Heisman Trophy radar when the season began, the 5'8", 190-pounder crammed a career into one season, rushing for 2,628 yards and 39 touchdowns, both Division I-A records that have not been remotely challenged. Raised by a hardworking father, who had his sons help him roof houses and would not tolerate any showing off, Sanders was a quiet superstar. "They are get-up early, hardworking, go-do-your-job people," Sanders said of his parents. "They don't want anything from anybody. They want to take care of their own. That was exactly my approach to football. I wasn't necessarily looking for fame and fortune." In Tokyo for the Cowboys' regular-season finale, Sanders insisted his offensive linemen join him when he accepted the 1988 Heisman Trophy via television hookup. Sanders went on to have an outstanding professional career with the Detroit Lions, winning four NFL rushing titles, but retired suddenly after the 1999 season within 1,500 yards of becoming the NFL's all-time leading rusher. "He was a Picasso," fellow NFL Hall of Famer Marcus Allen said of Sanders. "He was one of the few that would make other athletes' jaws drop. You'd call up another top running back and go, 'Yo, Dickerson, did you check that out?'"

BEST COACH When Lookabaugh became coach in February 1939, he faced a daunting task. The Cowboys hadn't had a winning season since 1933, and some questioned whether A&M should even have a football program. "Money used in hiring football coaches ought to be spent in improving livestock," said Joe C. Scott, president of the state's Board of Agriculture. "You ought to be able to buy a dozen dandy bulls for what one coaching staff costs, and A&M would be better off if football was abolished." Lookabaugh was worth his modest salary, guiding the program to a 58–41–6 record in 11 seasons with players

RECORDS

RUSHING
GAME
332 Barry Sanders vs. Texas Tech, Dec. 4, 1988 (44 att.)
SEASON
2,628 Barry Sanders, 1988 (344 att.)
CAREER
4,595 Thurman Thomas, 1984-87 (898 att.)

PASSING
GAME
429 Mike Gundy vs. Kansas, Nov. 4, 1989 (27 of 35)
SEASON
3,145 Josh Fields, 2002 (226 of 408)
CAREER
7,997 Mike Gundy, 1986-89 (604 of 1,035)

RECEIVING
GAME
232 Rashaun Woods vs. SMU, Sept. 20, 2003 (13 rec.)
SEASON
1,695 Rashaun Woods, 2002 (107 rec.)
CAREER
4,414 Rashaun Woods, 2000-03 (216 rec.)

POINTS
GAME
42 Rashaun Woods vs. SMU, Sept. 20, 2003 (7 TDs)
SEASON
234 Barry Sanders, 1988 (39 TDs)
CAREER
330 Barry Sanders, 1986-88 (55 TDs)

CONSENSUS ALL-AMERICANS

1945	Bob Fenimore	B
1969	John Ward	T
1976	Derrel Gofourth	C
1977	Terry Miller	RB
1984	Rod Brown	DB
1985	Thurman Thomas	RB
1985	Leslie O'Neal	DL
1988	Hart Lee Dykes	WR
1988	Barry Sanders	RB
1997	Alonzo Mayes	TE
2002	Rashaun Woods	WR

such as All-Americas Bob Fenimore and Neill Armstrong. The Cowboys' appearances in the Cotton, Sugar and Delta bowls increased the school's profile. In 1949, Lookabaugh was so stung by criticism following a 55-14 loss to Kansas that he abruptly resigned.

BEST TEAM The mid-1940s were the salad days of OSU sports, with the basketball team winning back-to-back NCAA titles and the wrestlers getting their 14th national title. It was not much different on the football field, where Lookabaugh's 1945 team went unbeaten in nine games, never allowing an opponent more than 14 points. Behind standout players such as halfback Fenimore, who led them in passing, rushing and interceptions, and ends Armstrong and Glenn Moore, the Cowboys crushed Oklahoma 47-0, the worst loss in Sooners history up to that point. OSU finished the season ranked fifth, its highest finish ever.

BIGGEST GAME OSU hadn't beaten the Sooners in 19 seasons when the teams met in Norman in 1965, and there was little to convince even the most diehard Cowboys fan that that year would be any different. OU's Ron Shotts made up for an earlier missed extra point when he kicked a field goal with four minutes left to put OU up 16-14. Glenn Baxter came out passing, including a key completion to Lynn Chadwick, who wrested the ball away from two Sooners at the OU 26. On fourth and two at the OU 18, Charles "Mickey" Durkee kicked the game-winning field goal. OU turned over two bell clappers, the rivalry's trophy. The Sooners had lost one over those 19 years and had another made before they found the original. A bonfire raged, classes were canceled on Monday and Durkee's kicking shoe was bronzed and put on permanent display.

BIGGEST UPSET Things appeared to be going true to form heading into the annual Bedlam game with Oklahoma in 2001. OSU had won only three games; OU was coming off a national championship season, and was 10–1 and ranked No. 4 in the nation. The Cowboys' defense was weak

ALL-CENTURY TEAM	
Selected by the staff of the Tulsa World in August 1999.	
OFFENSE	
1943-45	Jake Colhouer, OL
1958-60	Frank Parker, OL
1966-68	Jon Kolb, OL
1967-69	John Ward, OL
1974-76	Derrel Gofourth, OL
1994-97	Alonzo Mayes, TE
1985-88	Hart Lee Dykes, WR
1986-89	Mike Gundy, QB
1943-45	Bob Fenimore, RB
1984-87	Thurman Thomas, RB
1986-88	Barry Sanders, RB
1987-90	Cary Blanchard, PK
1995-97	R.W. McQuarters, KR
DEFENSE	
1951-54	Dale Meinert, DL
1968-69	Jerry Sherk, DL
1972-75	James White, DL
1973-75	Phillip Dokes, DL
1982-85	Leslie O'Neal, DL
1928-30	Jack Baker, LB
1976-79	John Corker, LB
1943-46	Neill Armstrong, DB
1951-53	Bill Bredde, DB
1957-60	Tony Banfield, DB
1983-86	Mark Moore, DB
1970-71	Jim Benien, P

and its offense inconsistent, facts reflected in the oddsmakers' 27-point spread. But the Cowboys' defense stiffened, sacking Nate Hybl seven times, and the offense came through in the clutch, getting a 65-yard scoring drive from freshman quarterback Josh Fields that was capped by a 14-yard touchdown pass to Rashaun Woods with 1:36 left. The 16-13 win knocked OU out of the Big 12 championship game and a shot at the national title, sending the Sooners to the Cotton Bowl. Offensive lineman Jeff Machado put it in proper Cowboys perspective when he said, "It's probably the biggest win in OSU history. We aren't going to the Rose Bowl. But I guess OU isn't either."

HEARTBREAKER The state of Oklahoma had never known a football matchup like the one that loomed on Nov. 24, 1984, when the 9–1, No. 3 Cowboys went to Norman to face the 9–1, No. 2 Sooners. The victor would win the Big Eight and earn a berth in the Orange Bowl. Rusty Hilger threw a 77-yard touchdown pass to Malcolm Lewis to give the Cowboys a 14-7 lead early in the third quarter. But OU came back to tie the score on a 72-yard drive that ended with Spencer Tillman's three-yard touchdown run, and a pair of late OSU fumbles—including a controversial call against the Cowboys—made the difference for the Sooners in a 24-14 win.

WILDEST FINISH OSU did what it set out to do against Kansas in 1964 by holding Jayhawks star Gale Sayers to 67 yards. But the Cowboys will forever claim that what Sayers couldn't do the game officials did. An apparent mistake in explaining the options on a punt penalty led to a 38-yard shift in field position and a six-minute delay as coach Phil Cutchin, KU coach Jack Mitchell and the officials argued. Up 14-7 in the closing seconds, KU tried a field goal that was blocked by Jerry Gill and returned 60 yards for a touchdown. Cutchin chose to go for two points, and Baxter threw to Tony Sellari, who made a leaping grab at the goal line and was sandwiched by two Jayhawks defenders as he came down. The official signaled that he didn't cross the

plane, but a photo in the local paper the next day showed Sellari straddling the goal line. KU won 14-13.

BEST COMEBACK South Carolina had wiped out a 13-0 OSU lead in the 1984 Gator Bowl with two long touchdown passes in the third quarter. Just when it appeared a wide extra-point attempt by Larry Roach would cost them the game, the Cowboys rallied. Taking over at its own 12-yard line midway through the fourth quarter, OSU moved downfield, converting a fourth and six at midfield with a 13-yard pass from Hilger to tight end Barry Hanna. With just over a minute left and the ball at the South Carolina 25, Hilger found Hanna near the sideline. The burly tight end bounced off two tacklers and carried three more into the end zone, all while tightroping the sideline, for his only touchdown of the season. OSU won 21-14 and finished the season ranked No. 7.

STADIUM For its first six years, Lewis Field, named in 1914 by the student body after popular dean Dr. Laymon Lowery Lewis, was simply that. In 1920, an 8,000-seat grandstand was erected. Four years later, the first steel and concrete addition was made. In 1929, the school spent $37,000 to install lights. The ball was painted white, for better night visibility, and called a "ghost ball." By 1947, capacity was increased to almost 30,000. A series of five expansion projects from 1950 to 1985 included the lowering of the field and the first artificial turf surface (1971). In 2003, a $70 million gift from 1951 alumnus Boone Pickens helped kick off a proposed $110 million renovation of the stadium. Unlike most football fields, which run north-south in deference to the glare of the sun, Lewis Field—renamed Boone Pickens Stadium in 2003—was set up east-west to allow the teams to better deal with the region's prevailing winds.

RIVAL The OSU-Oklahoma Bedlam rivalry is so contentious that the schools can't even agree on the series record. The sticking point is the 1972 game, won by OU 38-15, but later ordered forfeited by the NCAA because the Sooners used an ineligible player. The Bedlam nickname was coined in 1948 by OU sports information director Harold Keith to describe a basketball game between the schools, but it quickly spread to all sporting contests. In 1917, A&M beat OU for the first time after 11 losses, 9-0, setting off a celebration the school newspaper described thusly: "Whistles, bells and gunshots made the Battle of Verdun seem like a small boy's Fourth of July." In the late 1940s, the Sooners tried to end the series unless the game was permanently moved to Norman, a ploy

successfully thwarted by OSU athletic director Henry Iba. Despite OU's domination, the Cowboys have made the most of their wins. Three times—in 1976, 2001 and 2002—the Sooners came into the game ranked in the Top 5 only to be upset by the unranked Cowboys.

LORE OSU students would celebrate wins over Oklahoma by ringing the bell in the campus bell tower, Old Central. After a 7-0 Cowboys victory in 1930, Sooners students stole the clapper from the bell. A&M players launched a recovery mission to an OU fraternity house and returned with a clapper. OU students claimed the recovered clapper was taken from a nearby church that the Cowboys had mistakenly raided. Beginning in 2001, the clapper was awarded to the school that won the annual all-sports competition between the teams.

DUBIOUS DISTINCTION Making ends meet was always a major concern in the early days of the athletic program, so when in 1932 Jefferson Law School of Dallas offered a $3,000 guarantee for Oklahoma A&M to add a 12th game, the school jumped at the chance. Facing no eligibility requirements, Jefferson cherry-picked ringers from other schools and beat the Cowboys 12-6. It was the only defeat in a 9–1–2 season, which otherwise would have marked the first unbeaten record in school history, and only the second ever. To make it worse, the man who offered the $3,000 ducked out of the game early and the Cowboys were never paid.

TRAGEDY The football program had some scarce momentum in 1901, coming off a 2–3 record. But during a pickup game on an off weekend, Joe Houska led the flying wedge into the opposing tacklers. Trying to break up the wedge, the opponents dog-piled Houska, whose chest was crushed. The next day the freshman from Kremlin, Okla., died. The faculty immediately canceled the 1902 season. When play resumed in 1903, the program had lost direction, and the team was shut out in 11 of 15 games over the next three seasons.

NICKNAME Oklahoma A&M's first nickname in the 1890s was accurate, but it was not guaranteed to strike fear in even the most lily-livered opponents. Thankfully for the school, Agriculturalists quickly gave way to Aggies and Farmers and, for a brief and unpopular spell, Tigers. By 1924, Charles Saulsberry, sports editor of the *Oklahoma City Times*, first began to call the teams Cowboys, a term that

also gave rise to a series of synonyms, including Cowpokes, Waddies and Cowpunchers. School officials liked the image of Cowboys, and when the athletic council okayed the printing of 2,000 balloons with "Oklahoma Aggies—Ride 'Em Cowboy," the nickname took root.

MASCOT Around 1923, school officials began looking for something original to replace the tiger mascot that had been unabashedly copied, along with the school colors, from Princeton. A group of students saw legendary Oklahoma gunslinger Frank Eaton leading an Armistice Day parade and grew inspired. They asked Eaton if they could model a new mascot on him and he agreed. The likeness was used on apparel and other merchandise, and for the next 35 years Eaton would represent the school at a variety of events, signing autographs and telling stories. A cartoonlike version of Eaton, featuring chaps, a leather vest, an oversize head and a pair of loaded six-guns, ultimately evolved into Pistol Pete, the school's current mascot. Eaton was 8 years old when he watched his father, who fought for the Union army in the Civil War, get shot and killed by a renegade group of former Confederate soldiers in 1868. Challenged by a family friend to avenge his father's death, Eaton quickly became a deadeye shot, reputed to have been able to shoot off a snake's head with either hand. When he was 15 he set off in search of the killers, stopping to polish his skills at a cavalry outpost. In no time he was beating the Army's best marksmen and Colonel Copinger, the commander of the fort, dubbed him Pistol Pete. Over the next six years, he tracked down and shot five of the six

killers—the other was killed the day before Eaton caught up to him—and earned a commission as a U.S. Deputy.

UNIFORMS The small agricultural college's early infatuation with Princeton influenced them to adopt copycat black jerseys with orange-striped sleeves. OSU switched to orange home jerseys in the early 1970s. In the late 1980s, the block-letter Cowboys on the jerseys gave way to Oklahoma State, which was later shortened to State when Les Miles became head coach in 2001. The Cowboys' helmets have gone back and forth between black, orange and white. A logo featuring a cowboy on a bucking horse replaced the uniform number on the side of the helmets in 1967 and 1968. The school's initials first appeared in 1969, with the large-serifed S flanked by a smaller O and U first appearing in 1973. OSU in orange letters outlined in black on a white helmet debuted in 2001.

NUMBERS Sanders' name may never be erased from the NCAA record book. His 2,628 yards rushing in 1988 are 286 more than the next closest player, USC's Marcus Allen, ran for in 1981. His 39 rushing touchdowns in 1988 are seven more than the runner-up, Boise State's Brock Forsey, had in 2002. His 21.3 points per game are more than a field goal better than Nebraska halfback Bobby Reynolds' 17.4 in 1950.

QUOTE "When you're at Notre Dame or Alabama, as soon as you win one game people say you're great. At Oklahoma State, it takes six wins before anybody notices."—OSU coach Jimmy Johnson, 1981

OKLAHOMA STATE ANNUAL STATISTICAL LEADERS

YR	RUSHING	YDS	ATT	AVG	PASSING	ATT	CMP	PCT	YDS	RECEIVING	REC	YDS	AVG
1940	Jim Reynolds	685			Jim Reynolds				568	Ed Moore		207	
1941	Al Scanland	465	121	3.8	Al Scanland	78	26	.33	327	George Darrow	12	188	15.7
1942	Ralph Tate	562	117	4.8	Al Scanland	75	35	.47	413	Curtis Myers	12	152	12.7
1943	Bob Fenimore	286	58	4.9	Bob Fenimore	81	37	.46	364	Neill Armstrong	39	317	8.1
1944	Bob Fenimore	897	162	5.5	Bob Fenimore	79	49	.62	861	Cecil Hankins	19	474	24.9
1945	Bob Fenimore	1,048	142	7.4	Bob Fenimore	61	31	.51	593	Neill Armstrong	18	312	17.3
1946	Bob Meinert	344	69	5.0	Bob Fenimore	78	39	.50	497	Neill Armstrong	32	479	15.0
1947	Jim Spavital	411	89	4.6	Bob Cook	37	13	.35	188	Don Van Pool	8	92	11.5
1948	Bob Meinert	571	93	6.1	Jack Hartman	74	32	.43	469	Bill Long	14	234	16.7
1949	Ken Roof	466	91	5.1	Jack Hartman	177	86	.49	1,278	Alex Loyd	47	657	14.0
1950	Bob Cook	411	205	2.0	Bob Cook	138	56	.41	654	Arlen McNeil	20	263	13.2
1951	Rob Bennett	385	75	5.1	Don Babers	247	121	.49	1,352	George Wooden	40	502	12.6
1952	Ron Bennett	393	90	4.4	Don Babers	82	37	.45	493	John Weigle	25	314	12.6
1953	Earl Lunsford	748	147	5.1	Bobby Green	35	16	.46	219	Bob LaRue	12	122	10.2
1954	Earl Lunsford	761	140	5.4	Fred Duvall	28	8	.29	195	Chester Spencer	8	119	14.9
1955	Earl Lunsford	596	140	4.3	Tom Pontius	95	39	.41	764	Chester Spencer	18	319	17.7
1956	Jim Wiggins	473	90	5.3	Johnny Allen	55	23	.42	380	Jim Wood	9	190	21.1
1957	Jim Wiggins	418	108	3.9	Dick Soergel	85	34	.40	587	Jim Wood	16	316	19.8
1958	Duane Wood	492	83	5.9	Dick Soergel	79	36	.46	539	Jim Wood	20	273	13.7
1959	Jim Dillard	582	111	5.2	Dick Soergel	155	93	.60	1,100	Bill Dodson	21	286	13.6
1960	Jim Dillard	631	153	4.1	Jim Elliott	30	10	.33	90	Tommy Jackson	6	110	18.3
1961	Jim Dillard	627	126	5.0	Mike Miller	86	37	.43	371	Don Brewington	14	215	15.4
1962	Don Derrick	539	110	4.9	Mike Miller	180	81	.45	1,056	Don Karns	21	328	15.6
1963	George Thomas	399	88	4.5	Mike Miller	127	64	.50	674	Jack Jacobson	22	282	12.8
1964	Walt Garrison	730	176	4.1	Glenn Baxter	136	55	.40	845	Tony Sellari	17	238	14.0
1965	Walt Garrison	924	217	4.3	Glenn Baxter	112	43	.38	574	Tony Sellari	21	226	10.8
1966	Jack Reynolds	585	153	3.8	Ronnie Johnson	127	60	.47	659	Jerry Philpott	28	312	11.1
1967	Jack Reynolds	643	134	4.8	Ronnie Johnson	91	42	.46	494	Terry Brown	34	425	12.5
1968	Duane Porter	307	75	4.1	Ronnie Johnson	247	121	.49	1,438	Terry Brown	54	688	12.7
1969	Bub Deerinwater	587	135	4.3	Bob Cutburth	275	111	.40	1,593	Herman Eben	41	733	17.9
1970	Bobby Cole	685	167	4.1	Tony Pounds	269	133	.49	1,871	Herman Eben	48	937	19.5
1971	Bobby Cole	631	176	3.6	Tony Pounds	133	56	.42	792	Dick Graham	41	631	15.4
1972	George Palmer	937	193	4.9	Brent Blackman	102	30	.29	572	Steve Pettes	9	194	21.6
1973	Brent Blackman	809	175	4.6	Brent Blackman	110	40	.36	602	Reuben Gant	19	447	23.5
1974	George Palmer	516	99	5.2	Charlie Weatherbie	113	42	.37	622	Gerald Bain	16	336	21.0
1975	Terry Miller	1,026	179	5.7	Charlie Weatherbie	46	23	.50	563	Sam Lisle	16	384	24.0
1976	Terry Miller	1,541	268	5.8	Charlie Weatherbie	99	40	.40	752	Sam Lisle	21	360	17.1
1977	Terry Miller	1,680	314	5.4	Randy Stephenson	61	22	.36	386	Gerald Bain	16	349	21.8
1978	Worley Taylor	807	176	4.6	Scott Burk	134	50	.37	722	Ron Ingram	7	239	34.1
1979	Worley Taylor	994	216	4.6	Harold Bailey	210	94	.45	1,301	Ron Ingram	19	323	17.0
1980	Ed Smith	613	158	3.9	Jim Traber	99	46	.46	619	Mel Campbell	39	536	13.7
1981	Shawn Jones	788	209	3.8	John Doerner	145	79	.54	877	John Chesley	26	350	13.5
1982	Ernest Anderson	1,877	353	5.3	Ike Jackson	198	100	.51	1,254	Terry Young	35	507	14.5
1983	Shawn Jones	923	212	4.4	Rusty Hilger	154	82	.53	1,110	Jamie Harris	42	549	13.1
1984	Thurman Thomas	688	173	4.0	Rusty Hilger	240	141	.59	1,843	Jamie Harris	28	413	14.8
1985	Thurman Thomas	1,553	301	5.2	Ronnie Williams	248	120	.48	1,506	Bobby Riley	33	610	18.5
1986	Thurman Thomas	741	173	4.3	Mike Gundy	225	117	.52	1,525	Hart Lee Dykes	60	814	13.6
1987	Thurman Thomas	1,613	251	6.4	Mike Gundy	287	170	.59	2,106	Hart Lee Dykes	61	978	16.0
1988	Barry Sanders	2,628	344	7.6	Mike Gundy	236	153	.65	2,163	Hart Lee Dykes	74	1,278	17.3
1989	Gerald Hudson	910	187	4.9	Mike Gundy	287	164	.57	2,203	Curtis Mayfield	49	879	17.9
1990	Gerald Hudson	1,642	279	5.9	Earl Wheeler	112	53	.47	727	Robert Kirksey	29	486	16.8
1991	Rafael Denson	568	150	3.8	Kenny Ford	238	111	.47	1,377	Bert Milliner	47	631	13.4
1992	Rafael Denson	435	99	4.4	Gary Porter	188	96	.51	1,280	Shannon Culver	41	629	15.3
1993	David Thompson	466	111	4.2	Tone Jones	111	54	.49	608	Rafael Denson	27	356	13.2
1994	David Thompson	819	186	4.4	Tone Jones	256	114	.45	1,486	Rafael Denson	40	713	17.8
1995	David Thompson	1,509	256	5.9	Tone Jones	218	104	.48	1,185	Alonzo Mayes	32	421	13.2
1996	David Thompson	1,595	293	5.4	Tone Jones	234	130	.56	1,551	Alonzo Mayes	30	512	17.1
1997	Jamaal Fobbs	846	161	5.3	Tony Lindsay	123	76	.62	1,172	Alonzo Mayes	29	424	14.6
1998	Nathan Simmons	937	204	4.6	Tony Lindsay	196	97	.49	1,442	Terance Richardson	25	337	13.5
1999	Jamaal Fobbs	544	110	4.9	Tony Lindsay	116	61	.53	767	Ethan Howell	32	496	15.5
2000	Reggie White	1,049	210	5.0	Aso Pogi	247	139	.56	1,550	Jamaal Fobbs	31	334	10.8
2001	Tatum Bell	781	197	4.0	Aso Pogi	296	179	.60	1,854	Rashaun Woods	80	914	11.4
2002	Tatum Bell	1,096	175	6.3	Josh Fields	408	226	.55	3,145	Rashaun Woods	107	1,695	15.8
2003	Tatum Bell	1,286	213	6.0	Josh Fields	338	184	.54	2,494	Rashaun Woods	77	1,367	17.8
2004	Vernand Morency	1,474	258	5.7	Donovan Woods	187	97	.52	1,628	D'Juan Woods	33	690	20.1

The NCAA began including postseason stats in 2002

OKLAHOMA STATE ALL-TIME SCORES

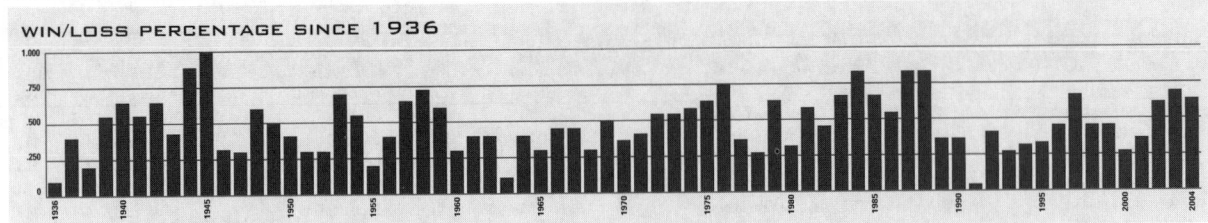

WIN/LOSS PERCENTAGE SINCE 1936

NO HEAD COACH

1901   2-3-0
U		at Kingfisher Coll.	0	12
U	●	at N.W. Oklahoma	17	0
U		Chilocco	5	6
U		Kingfisher Coll.	5	11
U	●	Pawnee	12	0

1902
NO TEAM

1903   0-2-2
U		at Oklahoma City	0	5
U	=	Tonkawa Prep	0	0
U	=	at Ok. City Military	0	5
U	=	Ok. City Military	6	6

1904   0-4-1
U		at Chilocco	0	23
U	=	Chilocco	0	0
U		at Tonkawa Prep	0	6
U		at Kingfisher Coll.	0	11
N6		Oklahoma *Gut*	0	75

1905   1-3-2
U	=	Chilocco	0	0
U	=	at Oklahoma City	0	0
U	●	Central St.	5	0
U		at Central St.	0	6
U		Tulsa Business Men	5	6
U		Logan HS *Gut*	11	17

BOYD A. HILL
1906 (.286)

1906   1-4-2
U		Central St.	0	10
O19		Oklahoma	0	23
U		Chilocco	5	26
U		at Central St.	2	23
U	=	Oklahoma City	6	6
U	●	at Tonkawa Prep	11	4
U	=	Kingfisher Coll.	0	0

ED PARRY
1907-08 (.458)   5-6-1

1907   1-3-1
U	●	Tonkawa Prep	10	0
U		at S.W. Kansas	2	6
U	=	Central St.	6	6
N9		at Oklahoma	0	67
U		at Oklahoma City	6	16

1908   4-3-0
U		at Central St.	5	8
U	●	Oklahoma City	18	0
O3		Oklahoma	0	18
U	●	at S.W. Kansas	6	0
N14		at Kansas State	10	40
U	●	Central St.	17	0
U	●	Chilocco	30	0

PAUL J. DAVIS
1909-14 (.641)   29-16-1

1909   5-3-0
U		Ok.City HS	0	5
U	●	Phillips	6	0
O23		at Kansas State	0	9
U	●	at S.E. Oklahoma	6	0
U	●	Kingfisher Coll.	5	0
U	●	at N.W. Oklahoma	5	0
U		S.W. Oklahoma	0	2
U	●	at Central Okla. St.	27	0

1910   3-4-0
U	●	Kingfisher Coll.	35	0
O21		at Oklahoma	0	12
U		at S.W. Kansas	0	5
U		at Phillips	0	12
U	●	S.W. Oklahoma	42	0
U		at Oklahoma City	0	15
U	●	Central St.	52	0

1911   5-2-0
U	●	Blackwell Coll.	35	5
U	●	at Central St.	46	5
O20		Oklahoma	0	22
U	●	at Kingfisher Coll.	84	0
U	●	OKC Military	30	0
U	●	S.W. Kansas	61	16
N24		Kansas State	0	11

1912   6-2-0
U	●	Central St.	81	0
U	●	Blackwell Coll.	79	0
O12		at Arkansas	13	7
U	●	Baker	37	13
U	●	Oklahoma Methodist	90	0
N16		at Oklahoma	0	16
U		at Missouri Mines	7	13
U	●	Emporia Coll.	28	7

1913   4-3-0
U	●	Phillips	112	3
O18		at Arkansas	0	3
U	●	Washburn	3	0
N15		at Texas A&M	3	0
U	●	Tonkawa Preps	47	0
N21		Oklahoma	0	7
U		Missouri Mines *Mus*	0	14

1914   6-2-1
O3	●	Phillips	134	0
O10	●	at Tonkawa Prep	48	0
O16	●	Tulsa	13	6
O24	●	Baylor	60	0
O31	●	Arkansas	46	0
N6		at Oklahoma	6	23 *
N14	=	at Rice	13	13
N21		at Texas A&M	0	24
N26	●	Colorado State *OkC*	7	0

1915-1924 SWC

JOHN G. GRIFFITH
1915-16 (.472)   8-9-1

1915   4-5-1 (0-3-0)
O2		at Missouri	6	13
O9	●	Friends	6	0
O15	=	Tulsa	0	0
O23		Arkansas *FrS*	9	14
O30	●	Baker	30	7
N6	●	at N.W. Oklahoma	77	0
N13		at Baylor	6	12
N16	●	at TCU	13	0
N20		at Haskell	7	21
N25		Oklahoma *OkC*	7	26

1916   4-4-0 (0-3-0)
O7	●	N.W. Oklahoma	90	0
O13		Texas *SA*	7	14 *
O21	●	S.W. Oklahoma	117	0
O28	●	Central Mo. St.	16	7
N4		at Tulsa	13	17
N11	●	at Central St.	34	6
N18		Baylor	7	10
N30		Oklahoma *OkC*	7	41

EARL A. PRITCHARD
1917-18 (.533)   8-7

1917   4-5-0 (1-2-0)
O6		at Kansas State	0	23
O13		at Phillips	0	6
O20		at Baylor	0	17
O27	●	Central Mo. St.	27	0
N3	●	Central Ok. St.	13	0
N10		at Texas	3	7
N17		Tulsa	41	2
N24		Camp MacArthur	0	39
N29	●	Oklahoma *OkC*	9	0

1918   4-2-0 (0-2-0)
O12	●	Haskell Indians	19	6
O19	●	at Central St.	26	6
N10		at Texas	5	27
N16	●	Wichita St.	26	7
N23	●	at Tulsa	33	0
N28		Oklahoma *OkC*	0	27

JAMES E. PIXLEE
1919-20 (.281)   3-10-3

1919   3-3-2 (0-2-0)
O4	●	S.W. Oklahoma	37	0
O11		at Haskell	3	12
O18		at TCU	14	7
N1		at Texas A&M	0	28
N8	●	Central St.	52	0
N15	=	Phillips	7	7
N21	=	Tulsa	7	7
N27		Oklahoma *OkC*	6	33

1920   0-7-1 (0-3-0)
O2		at Baylor	0	7
O9		at Tulsa	14	20 *
O16		Texas *Dal*	0	21
O23		S.W. Kansas	7	7
O30		Texas A&M	0	35
N13		Oklahoma	0	36
N20		Haskell	7	33
N25		Colorado *OkC*	7	40

JOHN F. MAULBETSCH
1921-28 (.429)   27-37-6

1921   5-4-1 (1-1-0)
S24	●	S.W. Oklahoma	53	0
O1		at Missouri	0	36
O8	●	TCU	28	21
O15		at Oklahoma	0	6
O22		Arkansas	7	0
O29		at Texas A&M	7	23
N5		at Creighton	13	26
N12	=	Emporia Coll.	7	7
N19		at Phillips	7	6
N26	●	Washburn	13	0

1922   4-4-1 (2-3-0)
S30	●	N.W. Oklahoma	49	0
O7	●	Central St.	17	0
O14		at Texas	7	19
O21	●	Rice	21	0
O28		at SMU	6	32
N11		at TCU	14	22
N18		Baylor	0	10
N25	=	Oklahoma	3	3
N30	●	Arkansas *FrS*	13	0

1923   2-8-0 (1-3-0)
S29		at Iowa	0	20
O6		TCU	6	7
O13		at Kansas	0	9
O20	●	at Rice	13	0
O27		at Oklahoma	0	12 *
N3		Phillips	13	0
N10		Central St.	6	14
N17		at SMU	0	9
N24		Creighton	2	13
D1		Arkansas *FrS*	0	13

1924   6-1-2 (1-1-1)
S27	●	S.W. Oklahoma	9	0
O4	●	at Kansas	3	0
O11		at TCU	10	17
O18	●	Missouri Mines	23	0
O25	●	Phillips	13	0
N1	●	Oklahoma	6	0
N8	=	at Creighton	20	20
N21	●	Arkansas	20	0
N29	=	at SMU	13	13

1925-1956 MISSOURI VALLEY

1925   2-5-1 (0-3-1)
O3		at Kansas	3	13
O10		Emporia St.	0	21
O17	=	at Washington, Mo.	0	0
O24	●	TCU	22	7
O31		Grinnell	0	28
N7	●	S.W. Oklahoma	9	2
N21		at Arkansas	7	9
N26		at Oklahoma	0	35

1926   3-4-1 (3-0-1)
O2		at Michigan	3	42
O9		at Iowa State	13	0
O16		at Tulsa	0	28
O23		at TCU	0	3
N6	●	Washington, Mo.	37	3
N13		Grinnell	10	0
N19	●	Arkansas	2	24
N25	=	Oklahoma	14	14

1927   4-4-0 (2-1-0)
O1		at Washington, Mo.	0	6
O8		at Minnesota	0	40
O15	●	Marquette	8	0
O22		Tulsa	26	28
O29		Creighton	18	6
N12		at Arkansas	20	33
N19	●	at Oklahoma	13	7
N24	●	at Kansas State	25	18

1928   1-7-0 (0-1-0)
S29	●	St. Regis	13	6
O6		Kansas State	6	13
O13		at Creighton	0	37
O27		at Marquette	0	26
N3		Oklahoma City	0	9
N10		at West Virginia	6	32
N24		Oklahoma	0	46
N29		at Tulsa	0	31

LYNN O. WALDORF
1929-33 (.735)   34-10-7

1929   4-3-2 (1-1-0)
S28	●	N.W. Oklahoma	12	0
O5		at Drake	6	18
O12		at Oklahoma City	18	0
O19		Creighton	32	13
O26		West Virginia	6	9
N2	●	Tulsa	20	0
N16	=	St. Louis	0	0
N23	=	at Oklahoma	7	7
N28		Arkansas	6	32

1930   7-2-1 (2-0-0)
S27	●	Wichita St.	12	0
O4	●	at Iowa	6	0
O11		at Indiana	7	7
O18		at Oklahoma City	0	6
O25	●	Washington, Mo.	28	7
N1		Haskell	12	13
N8	●	at Arkansas	26	0
N22	●	Oklahoma	7	0
N27		at Creighton	13	0
D13	●	at Tulsa	13	7

1931 — 8-2-1 (1-0-0)

S19	●	Bethany	34	9
S26	●	N.E. Oklahoma	25	0
O3		at Minnesota	0	20
O10	●	Arizona	31	0
O17	●	Haskell	39	0
O24		at Oklahoma City	0	13
O31	●	at Kansas	13	7
N7	● |	Creighton	20	0
N14	●	at Tulsa	7	6
N21	●	Wichita St.	14	6
N26	=	at Oklahoma	0	0

1932 — 9-1-2 (3-0-0)

S17	●	Phillips	13	0
S24	=	Central St.	0	0
O1	●	S.W. Oklahoma	33	3
O8	● |	at Drake	27	7
O14	● |	Creighton	18	7
O22	●	at Oklahoma City	14	6
O29	●	Oklahoma	7	0
N5	=	at Tulsa	0	0
N12		at Jefferson	6	12
N19	● |	Grinnell	27	0
N26	●	at Arizona	13	6
D3	●	at Texas El Paso	20	7

1933 — 6-2-1 (2-0-0)

S30	●	Central St.	20	12
O6		Colorado	0	6
O14		at Oklahoma City	13	19
O21	=	at SMU	7	7
O28	●	Haskell	18	0
N4	●	at Tulsa	7	0
N11	● |	Drake	21	0
N18	● |	at Creighton	33	13
N23	●	at Oklahoma	13	0

ALBERT A. EXENDINE
1934-35 (.375) 7-12-1

1934 — 4-5-1 (1-1-0)

S29	●	Oklahoma Baptist	12	0
O6	● |	at Drake	7	0
O13	●	Haskell	9	6
O20		at SMU	0	41
O26	|	Creighton	7	13
N3	●	at Detroit	19	6
N10		at Duquesne	0	32
N17		at Tulsa	0	19
N22	=	Oklahoma	0	0
D1		at Oklahoma City	0	13

1935 — 3-7-0 (0-3-0)

S28	●	Oklahoma City	6	0
O5	|	at Creighton	0	16
O11		at Detroit	0	13
O19	●	Haskell	20	0
O26	|	at Tulsa	0	12
N2		at Texas Tech	0	14
N9		Duquesne	7	20
N16	●	S.E. Oklahoma	20	13
N28		at Oklahoma	0	25
D7	|	at Washington, Mo.	13	39

TED COX
1936-38 (.233) 7-23

1936 — 1-9-0 (1-2-0)

S26		at Oklahoma City	6	9
O3		Kansas State	0	31
O9		at Detroit	12	46
O17	● |	Washburn	6	0
O24	|	at Tulsa	0	13
O31	|	at Washington, Mo.	6	39
N6		at Texas Tech	0	12
N14		Baylor	0	13
N26		Oklahoma	13	35
D5		at Centenary	0	7

1937 — 4-6-0 (2-2-0)

S25	●	at Wichita St.	14	8
O2	● |	Creighton	16	13
O9		at Arizona	13	22
O16	● |	at Washburn	25	3
O23	|	at Tulsa	0	27
O30		Texas Tech	6	14
N6	|	at Washington, Mo.	0	12
N13	●	Oklahoma City	27	7
N25		at Oklahoma	0	16
D4		Centenary	0	19

1938 — 2-8-0 (0-4-0)

S17	●	Central St.	23	12
S24		at Arkansas	7	27
O1		Baylor WiFi	6	20
O8	|	at Creighton	7	16
O22	|	at Tulsa	7	20
O29	|	Washburn	0	14
N5	|	Washington, Mo.	0	24
N12		Wichita St.	6	14
N19	●	at Oklahoma City	19	12
N24		Oklahoma	0	19

JIM LOOKABAUGH
1939-49 (.581) 58-41-6

1939 — 5-4-1 (3-1-0)

S23		Texas A&M	0	32
S30	●	N.W. Oklahoma	52	0
O7		Baylor	0	13
O14	● |	at Tulsa	9	7
O21	● |	at Washburn	27	6
O28		at Oklahoma	0	41
N4	●	New Mexico St.	20	0
N11	|	at Washington, Mo.	0	7
N18	=	at Wichita St.	0	0
N25	● |	Creighton	20	9

1940 — 6-3-1 (4-1-0)

S21	●	Central St.	25	6
S27	=	at Texas Tech	6	6
O5		at Oklahoma	27	29
O12	●	Wichita St.	26	6
O19	● |	Washington, Mo.	53	12
O26		at Arizona	0	24
N2	● |	at Creighton	20	14
N9	● |	Washburn	33	14
N16	● |	St. Louis	14	7
N23	|	at Tulsa	6	19

1941 — 5-4-0 (3-1-0)

S27		at Oklahoma	0	19
O3		Texas Tech	6	16
O11	● |	at Washington, Mo.	41	12
O18		Detroit	14	20
O25	|	Tulsa	0	16
N1	● |	Creighton	13	6
N8	● |	at St. Louis	13	7
N22	●	Arizona	41	14
N27	●	at Wichita St.	33	13

1942 — 6-3-1 (4-1-0)

S26	=	Oklahoma	0	0
O3		Baylor OkC	12	18
O10	●	at Texas Tech	9	6
O17		at Arizona	6	20
O24	● |	Washington, Mo.	40	7
O31	● |	at Creighton	20	6
N7	|	at Tulsa	6	34
N14	● |	St. Louis	54	7
N21	● |	Drake	55	12
N28	●	at Detroit	33	6

1943 — 3-4-0 (0-1-0)

S24	●	Texas Tech OkC	21	13
O2		Oklahoma OkC	13	22
O16		Norman NAS	0	20
O23		TCU OkC	0	25
N6	|	at Tulsa	6	55
N19	●	Arkansas FtS	19	13
N27	●	at Denver	7	6

1944 — 8-1-0 (1-0-0)

S23	●	West Texas	41	6
S29	●	Arkansas OkC	19	0
O7	●	at Texas Tech	14	7
O14	●	at Denver	33	21
O28	● |	at Tulsa	46	40
N4		Norman NAS	0	15
N11	●	at Texas	13	8
N25	●	Oklahoma	28	6
		COTTON BOWL		
J1	●	TCU	34	0

1945 — 9-0-0 (1-0-0)

S29	●	at Arkansas	19	14
O6	●	at Denver	31	7
O12	●	SMU OkC	26	12
O20	●	at Utah	46	6
O27	●	at TCU	25	12
N10	● |	Tulsa	12	6
N17	●	Texas Tech	46	6
N24	●	at Oklahoma	47	0
		SUGAR BOWL		
J1	●	Saint Mary's-Cal	33	13

1946 — 3-7-1 (1-1-0)

S21	●	Denver	40	7
S28	=	Arkansas	21	21
O5		at Texas	6	54
O11		at SMU	6	15
O19		at Georgia	13	33
O26	●	TCU OkC	7	6
N2		at Kansas	13	14
N9	|	at Tulsa	18	20
N16		at Texas Tech	7	14
N23	● |	Drake	59	7
N30		Oklahoma	12	73

1947 — 3-7-0 (0-2-0)

S20	●	at Kansas State	12	0
S27	●	at TCU	14	7
O4		at Denver	14	26
O11		SMU	14	21
O18		Georgia	7	20
O25	|	at Drake	9	13
N1	●	at Temple	26	0
N8	|	Tulsa	0	13
N15		Kansas	7	13
N29		at Oklahoma	13	21

1948 — 6-4-0 (1-0-0)

S18	● |	at Wichita St.	27	14
S25		TCU	14	21
O9	●	Denver	27	7
O16	●	at San Francisco	27	20
O23	●	Temple	41	7
O30		at Kansas	7	13
N6	● |	at Tulsa	19	0
N20	●	Kansas State	42	6
N27		Oklahoma	15	19
		DELTA BOWL		
J1		William & Mary	0	20

1949 — 4-4-2 (2-1-1)

S24	=	at TCU	33	33
O1	●	at Denver	48	2
O8		at Missouri	7	21
O15	● |	Drake	28	0
O22		Kansas	14	55
O28	|	at Detroit	7	13
N5	= |	Tulsa	13	13
N12	●	at Kansas State	26	14
N19	● |	Wichita St.	47	20
N26		at Oklahoma	0	41

J.B. WHITWORTH
1950-54 (.451) 22-27-2

1950 — 4-6-1 (1-2-1)

S23	●	Arkansas LR	12	7
S30	●	TCU	18	7 *
O7	= |	at Drake	14	14
O14		at SMU	0	56
O21		at Kansas	7	40
O28		Missouri	0	27
N4	|	at Tulsa	13	27
N11	● |	at Wichita St.	32	20
N18	|	Detroit	13	20
N25	●	Kansas State	41	0
D2		Oklahoma	14	41

1951 — 3-7-0 (3-2-0)

S22		Arkansas	7	42
S29		at Missouri	26	27
O5		Washington State SpO	13	27
O13	● |	Wichita St.	43	0
O20	● |	Drake	27	14
O26	● |	at Detroit	20	7
N3	|	Tulsa	7	35
N17		Kansas	12	27
N24	|	at Houston	7	31
D1		at Oklahoma	6	41

1952 — 3-7-0 (2-2-0)

S20		Arkansas LR	20	22
S27		Texas A&M DAL	7	14
O4	|	Houston	7	10
O11	● |	at Wichita St.	35	21
O18	●	Missouri	14	7
O25	● |	Detroit	21	6
N1	|	at Tulsa	21	23
N15		at Kansas	7	12
N22		Washington State	7	9
N29		Oklahoma	7	54

1953 — 7-3-0 (3-1-0)

S19	●	Hardin Simmons	20	0
S26	●	Arkansas LR	7	6
O3		Texas Tech	13	27
O10	● |	Wichita St.	14	7
O17	● |	at Houston	14	7
O24	|	at Detroit	14	18
O31	● |	Tulsa	28	14
N7	●	Wyoming	20	14
N14	●	at Kansas	41	14
N28		at Oklahoma	7	42

1954 — 5-4-1 (2-2-0)

S18	●	at Wyoming	14	6
S25	●	Texas A&M DAL	14	6
O2	=	at Texas Tech	13	13
O9	|	at Wichita St.	13	22
O16	|	Houston	7	14
O23		at Hardin Simmons	7	13
O30	● |	at Tulsa	12	0
N6	● |	Detroit	34	19
N13	●	Kansas	47	12
N27		Oklahoma	0	14

CLIFF SPEEGLE
1955-62 (.463) 36-42-3

1955 — 2-8-0 (1-3-0)

S24		Arkansas LR	0	21
O1		Texas Tech	6	24
O8	|	Wichita St.	7	14
O15	|	at Houston	13	21
O21	|	at Detroit	0	7
O29	● |	Tulsa	14	0
N5		Colorado State	13	20
N12		at Kansas	7	12
N19	●	Kansas State	28	0
N26		at Oklahoma	0	53

1956 — 3-5-2 (2-1-1)

S22	●	at Kansas State	27	7
S29		Arkansas LR	7	19
O6	● |	at Wichita St.	32	6
O13	= |	at Tulsa	14	14
O20	|	Houston	0	13
O27		Kansas	13	21
N3	=	at Texas Tech	13	13
N10		at LSU	0	13
N17	● |	Detroit	25	7
D1		Oklahoma	0	53

1957-1959
INDEPENDENT

1957 — 6-3-1

S21		Arkansas LR	0	12
S28	●	at North Texas	25	19
O5	●	Wichita St.	26	0
O12	●	Tulsa	28	13
O19	=	at Houston	6	6
N2	●	Texas Tech	13	0
N9	●	Wyoming	39	6
N16		at Kansas	7	13
N23	●	at Hardin Simmons	32	7
N30		at Oklahoma	6	53

1958 — 8-3-0

S19	●	at Denver	31	14
S27	●	North Texas	21	14
O4	●	at Wichita St.	43	12
O11		at Tulsa	6	24
O18	●	at Houston	7	0
O25	●	at Cincinnati	19	14
N1		Air Force	29	33
N8	●	Kansas State	14	7
N15	●	Kansas	6	3
N29		Oklahoma	0	7
		BLUEGRASS BOWL		
D13	●	Florida State	15	6

1959 — 6-4-0

S19		Cincinnati	9	22
S26		Arkansas LR	7	13
O3	●	at Kansas State	27	21
O10	●	Tulsa	26	0
O17	●	Houston	19	12
O24	●	Wichita St.	34	14
O31	●	at Marquette	18	12
N7	●	Denver	20	12
N14		at Kansas	14	28
N28		at Oklahoma	7	17

1960-1995
BIG 8

1960 3-7-0 (2-5-0)

S17			Arkansas LR	0	9
S24		|	at Missouri	7	28
O8	●		at Tulsa	28	7
O15			at Houston	7	12
O22		|	Kansas	7	14
O29		|	Iowa State	6	13
N5	●	|	at Kansas State	28	7
N12	●	|	at Nebraska	7	6
N19		|	Colorado	6	13
N26		|	Oklahoma	6	17

1961 4-6-0 (2-5-0)

S23		|	at Iowa State	7	14
S30		|	at Colorado	0	24
O7	●		Tulsa	26	0
O14		|	Missouri	0	10
O21	●	|	Nebraska	14	6
O28		|	at Kansas	8	42
N4			at Wichita St.	13	25
N18	●		Houston	28	24
N25	●	|	Kansas State	45	0
D2		|	at Oklahoma	13	21

1962 4-6-0 (2-5-0)

S22			Arkansas LR	7	34
O6	●		at Tulsa	17	7
O13	●	|	Colorado	36	16
O20		|	at Missouri	6	23
O27		|	Kansas	17	36
N3		|	Iowa State	7	34
N10	●		at Army	12	7
N17		|	at Nebraska	0	14
N24	●	|	at Kansas State	30	6
D1		|	Oklahoma	6	37

PHIL CUTCHIN
1963-68 (.339) 19-38-2

1963 1-8-0 (0-6-0)

S21			Arkansas LR	0	21
O5			at Texas	7	34
O12		|	at Colorado	0	25
O19		|	Missouri	6	28
O26		|	at Kansas	7	41
N2		|	at Iowa State	28	33
N9	●		Tulsa	33	24
N16		|	Nebraska	16	20
N30		|	at Oklahoma	10	34

1964 4-6-0 (3-4-0)

S19			Arkansas LR	10	14
S26	●	|	Iowa State	29	14
O3	●	|	at Missouri	10	7
O10	●	|	Colorado	14	10
O24		|	Kansas	13	14
O31			at Tulsa	14	61
N7	●		Wichita St.	31	7
N14		|	at Nebraska	14	27
N21		|	at Kansas State	14	17
N28		|	Oklahoma	16	21

1965 3-7-0 (2-5-0)

S18			Arkansas LR	14	28
S25		|	Missouri	0	13
O2	●		Tulsa	17	14
O9		|	at Colorado	11	34
O16			at Texas Tech	14	17
O23		|	at Kansas	0	9
O30		|	at Iowa State	10	14
N13		|	Nebraska	17	21
N20	●	|	Kansas State	31	7
D4	●	|	at Oklahoma	17	16

1966 4-5-1 (4-2-1)

S17			Arkansas LR	10	14
O1			at Houston	9	35
O8	●	|	Colorado	11	10
O15		|	at Missouri	0	7
O22	●	|	Kansas	10	7
O29	=	|	Iowa State	14	14
N5			at Texas Tech	7	10
N12		|	at Nebraska	6	21
N19	●	|	at Kansas State	21	6
D3	●	|	Oklahoma	15	14

1967 4-5-1 (3-4-0)

S16	=		Air Force	0	0
S23	●		Arkansas LR	7	6
O7			at Texas	0	19
O21		|	Kansas	15	26
O28	●	|	at Colorado	10	7
N4		|	Missouri	0	7
N11		|	at Nebraska	0	9
N18	●	|	at Iowa State	28	14
N25	●	|	Kansas State	49	14
D2		|	at Oklahoma	14	38

1968 3-7-0 (2-5-0)

S21			Arkansas LR	15	32
O5			at Texas	3	31
O12	●		at Houston	21	17
O19		|	at Kansas	14	49
O26		|	Nebraska	20	21
N2		|	at Missouri	7	42
N9	●	|	Colorado	34	17
N16	●	|	Iowa State	26	17
N23		|	at Kansas State	14	21
N30		|	Oklahoma	7	41

FLOYD GASS
1969-71 (.422) 13-18-1

1969 5-5-0 (3-4-0)

S20			Arkansas LR	0	39
S27	●		Houston	24	18
O4	●		Texas Tech	17	10
O18		|	at Missouri	21	31
O25		|	at Nebraska	3	13
N1	●	|	at Kansas	28	25
N8	●	|	Kansas State	28	19
N15		|	at Colorado	14	17
N22	●	|	at Iowa State	35	0
N29		|	Oklahoma	27	28

1970 4-7-0 (2-5-0)

S12			Mississippi State JaM	13	14
S19			Arkansas LR	7	23
S26	●		Houston	26	17
O3		|	Missouri	20	40
O10	●		TCU	34	20
O24		|	at Nebraska	31	65
O31	●	|	Kansas	19	7
N7		|	at Kansas State	15	28
N14		|	Colorado	6	30
N21	●	|	Iowa State	36	27
N28		|	at Oklahoma	6	66

1971 4-6-1 (2-5-0)

S11	●		Mississippi State	26	7
S18			Arkansas LR	10	31
S25	●		Virginia Tech	24	16
O9	=		at TCU	14	14
O16	●	|	at Missouri	37	16
O23		|	Nebraska	13	41
O30	●	|	at Kansas	17	10
N6		|	Kansas State	23	35
N13		|	at Colorado	6	40
N20		|	at Iowa State	0	54
D4		|	Oklahoma	14	58

DAVE SMITH
1972 (.545) 6-5

1972 6-5-0 (4-3-0)

S16	●		Texas Arlington	21	3
S23			Arkansas LR	23	24
S30	●	|	Colorado	31	6
O7	●	|	Missouri	17	16
O14			at Virginia Tech	32	34
O21	●	|	Baylor	20	7
O28		|	at Nebraska	0	34
N4		|	Kansas	10	13
N11	●	|	at Kansas State	45	14
N25	●	|	Iowa State	45	14
D2		|	at Oklahoma	15	38 †

JIM STANLEY
1973-78 (.529) 35-31-2

1973 5-4-2 (2-3-2)

S15	●		Texas Arlington	56	7
S22	●		Arkansas LR	38	6
S29	●		So. Illinois	70	7
O6			Texas Tech	7	20
O20		|	at Missouri	9	13
O27	=	|	Nebraska	17	17
N3	=	|	at Kansas	10	10
N10	●	|	Kansas State	28	9
N17	●	|	at Colorado	38	24
N24		|	at Iowa State	12	28
D1		|	Oklahoma	18	45

1974 7-5-0 (4-3-0)

S14	●		Wichita St.	59	0
S21	●		Arkansas LR	26	7
S28			at Baylor	14	31
O5			at Texas Tech	13	14
O19	●	|	Missouri	31	7
O26		|	at Nebraska	3	7
N2	●	|	Kansas	24	13
N9	●	|	at Kansas State	29	5
N16		|	Colorado	20	37
N23	●	|	Iowa State	14	12
N30		|	at Oklahoma	13	44
			FIESTA BOWL		
D28	●		Brigham Young	16	6

1975 7-4-0 (3-4-0)

S13	●		Wichita St.	34	0
S20	●		Arkansas	20	13
S27	●		North Texas	61	7
O4	●		Texas Tech	17	16
O11		|	at Missouri	14	41
O18		|	Nebraska	20	28
O25	●	|	at Kansas	35	19
N1		|	Oklahoma	7	27
N8		|	at Colorado	7	17
N15	●	|	Kansas State	56	3
N22	●	|	at Iowa State	14	7

1976 9-3-0 (5-2-0)

S11	●		Tulsa	33	21
S18			Arkansas LR	10	16
O2	●		North Texas	16	10
O9	●	|	Kansas	21	14
O16		|	Colorado	10	20
O23	●	|	at Oklahoma	31	24
O30	●	|	Missouri	20	19
N6		|	at Nebraska	10	14
N13	●	|	at Kansas State	45	21
N20	●	|	Iowa State	42	21
N27	●		at Texas El Paso	42	13
			TABGERINE BOWL		
D18	●		Brigham Young	49	21

1977 4-7-0 (2-5-0)

S10	●		at Tulsa	34	17
S17			Arkansas LR	6	28
S24	●		Texas El Paso	54	0
O1			Florida State	17	25
O8		|	at Colorado	13	29
O15	●	|	Kansas State	21	14
O22	●	|	at Kansas	21	0
O29		|	Nebraska	14	31
N5		|	Oklahoma	28	61
N12		|	at Missouri	14	41
N19		|	at Iowa State	13	21

1978 3-8-0 (3-4-0)

S9			at Wichita St.	10	20
S16			at Florida State	20	38
S23			Arkansas	7	19
S30			North Texas Irv	7	12
O7		|	at Kansas State	7	18
O14	●	|	Colorado	24	20
O21	●	|	Kansas	21	7
O28		|	at Nebraska	14	22
N4	●	|	Missouri	35	20
N11		|	Iowa State	15	28
N18		|	at Oklahoma	7	62

JIMMY JOHNSON
1979-83 (.535) 29-25-3

1979 7-4-0 (5-2-0)

S8	●		North Texas	25	7
S15	●		Wichita St.	16	6
S22			Arkansas LR	7	27
O6			at South Carolina	16	23
O13	●	|	at Missouri	14	13
O20		|	Nebraska	0	36
O27	●	|	at Kansas	30	17
N3		|	Oklahoma	7	38
N10	●	|	at Colorado	21	20
N17	●	|	Kansas State	42	15
N24	●	|	at Iowa State	13	10

1980 3-7-1 (2-4-1)

S13			West Texas St.	19	20
S20			Arkansas LR	20	33
O4			Washington	18	24
O11		|	Missouri	7	30
O18		|	at Nebraska	7	48
O25	=	|	Kansas	14	14 †
N1	●		San Diego State	15	6
N8	●	|	Colorado	42	7
N15	●	|	at Kansas State	10	0
N22		|	Iowa State	21	23
N29		|	at Oklahoma	14	63

1981 7-5-0 (4-3-0)

S19	●		Tulsa	23	21
S26			San Diego State	16	23
O3	●		North Texas Irv	9	0
O10	●	|	at Kansas	20	7
O17		|	at Colorado	10	11
O24	●		Louisville	19	11
O31	●	|	at Missouri	16	12
N7		|	Nebraska	7	54
N14	●	|	Kansas State	31	10
N21	●	|	at Iowa State	27	7
N28		|	Oklahoma	3	27
			INDEPENDENCE BOWL		
D12			Texas A&M	16	33

1982 4-5-2 (3-2-2)

S11	●		North Texas	27	6
S19			at Tulsa	15	25
S25			at Louisville	22	28
O9	=	|	Kansas	24	24
O16	=	|	Colorado	25	25
O23		|	at Oklahoma	9	27
O30	●	|	Missouri	30	20
N6		|	at Nebraska	10	48
N13	●	|	at Kansas State	24	16
N20	●	|	Iowa State	49	13
N27			at San Diego State	6	35

1983 8-4-0 (3-4-0)

S10	●		North Texas	20	13
S17	●		at Cincinnati	27	17
S23	●		at Texas A&M	34	15
O1	●		Tulsa	9	0
O8		|	Nebraska	10	14
O15		|	Oklahoma	20	21
O22	●	|	at Kansas	27	10
O29	●	|	at Colorado	40	14
N5		|	Kansas State	20	21
N12		|	at Missouri	10	16
N19	●	|	at Iowa State	30	7
			BLUEBONNET BOWL		
D31	●		Baylor	24	14

PAT JONES
1984-94 (.508) 62-60-3

1984 10-2-0 (5-2-0)

S8	●		at Arizona State	45	3
S15	●		Bowling Green	31	14
S22	●		San Diego State	19	16
S29	●		at Tulsa	31	7
O6		|	at Nebraska	3	17
O20	●	|	Kansas	47	10
O27	●	|	Colorado	20	14
N3	●	|	at Kansas State	34	6
N10	●	|	Missouri	31	13
N17	●	|	Iowa State	16	10
N24		|	at Oklahoma	14	24
			GATOR BOWL		
D28	●		South Carolina	21	14

1985 8-4-0 (4-3-0)

S7	●		at Washington	31	17
S14	●		North Texas	10	9
S28	●		Miami, Ohio	45	10
O5	●		Tulsa	25	13
O12		|	Nebraska	24	34
O26	●	|	at Kansas	17	10
N2	●	|	at Colorado	14	11
N9	●	|	Kansas State	35	3
N16	●	|	at Missouri	21	19
N23		|	at Iowa State	10	15
N30		|	Oklahoma	0	13
			GATOR BOWL		
D30			Florida State	23	34

1986 6-5-0 (4-3-0)

S6	●		at La. Lafayette	21	20
S13			at Tulsa	23	27
S20			Houston	12	28
S27	●		Illinois St.	23	7
O11		|	at Nebraska	10	30
O18		|	at Oklahoma	0	19
O25	●	|	Kansas	24	6
N1		|	Colorado	14	31
N8	●	|	at Kansas State	23	3
N22	●	|	Iowa State	21	14
D4	●	|	Missouri	10	6

1987 10-2-0 (5-2-0)

S5	●		Tulsa	39	28
S12	●		at Houston	35	0
S19	●		at Wyoming	35	29
S26	●		La. Lafayette	36	0
O10	●	|	Colorado	42	17
O17		|	Nebraska	0	35
O24	●	|	at Missouri	24	20
O31	●	|	Kansas State	56	7
N7		|	at Oklahoma	10	29
N14	●	|	at Kansas	49	17
N21	●	|	Iowa State	48	27
			SUN BOWL		
D25	●		West Virginia	35	33

1988
10-2-0 (5-2-0)

S10	●	Miami, Ohio	52 20
S24	●	Texas A&M	52 15
O1	●	Tulsa	56 35
O8	●	at Colorado	41 21
O15		at Nebraska	42 63
O22	●	Missouri	49 21
O29	●	at Kansas State	45 27
N5		Oklahoma	28 31
N12	●	Kansas	63 24
N19	●	at Iowa State	49 28
D4	●	Texas Tech Tok	45 42
		HOLIDAY BOWL	
D30		Wyoming	62 14

1989
4-7-0 (3-4-0)

S9		at Tulsa	10 20
S16		at Ohio State	13 37
S23		Texas Tech	15 31
S30	●	Wyoming	27 7
O7		at Oklahoma	15 37
O14	●	Kansas State	17 13
O21		Nebraska	23 48
O28	●	at Missouri	31 30
N4	●	at Kansas	37 24
N11		Colorado	17 41
N18		Iowa State	21 31

1990
4-7-0 (2-5-0)

S1	●	Tulsa	10 3
S8		at Florida	7 50
S15	●	Northern Iowa	33 23
S22		at TCU	21 31
O6		Oklahoma	17 31
O13		at Kansas State	17 23
O20		at Nebraska	3 31
O27	●	Missouri	48 28
N3		Kansas	30 31
N10		at Colorado	22 41
N17	●	at Iowa State	25 17

1991
0-10-1 (0-6-1)

S7		at Tulsa	7 13
S14		Arizona State	3 30
S21		TCU	21 24
O5		at Miami, Fla.	3 40
O12		Nebraska	15 49
O19		at Missouri	7 41
O26	=	at Iowa State	6 6
N2		Kansas	0 31
N9		Colorado	12 16
N16		at Oklahoma	6 21
N23		Kansas State	26 36

1992
4-6-1 (2-4-1)

S5	●	Indiana St.	35 3
S19		at Michigan	3 35
S26	●	Tulsa	24 19
O3		at TCU	11 13
O10		at Nebraska	0 55
O17	●	Missouri	28 26
O24	●	Iowa State	27 21
O31		at Kansas	18 26
N7		at Colorado	0 28
N14	=	Oklahoma	15 15
N21		at Kansas State	0 10

1993
3-8-0 (0-7-0)

S11	●	S.W. Missouri St.	45 7
S18	●	at Tulsa	16 10
S25		at Arizona State	10 12
O2	●	TCU	27 22
O7		Nebraska	13 27
O16		at Missouri	9 42
O23		at Iowa State	17 20
O30		Kansas	6 13
N6		Colorado	14 31
N13		at Oklahoma	0 31
N20		Kansas State	17 21

1994
3-7-1 (0-6-1)

S1	●	at Northern Illinois	31 14
S17		at Baylor	10 14
S24	●	Tulsa	17 10
O1	●	North Texas	36 34
O8		at Nebraska	3 32
O15		Missouri	15 24
O22	=	Iowa State	31 31
O29		at Kansas	14 24
N5		at Colorado	3 17
N12		Oklahoma	14 33
N19		at Kansas State	6 23

BOB SIMMONS
1995-2000 (.441)   30-38

1995
4-8-0 (2-5-0)

A31		Nebraska	21 64
S9		at Tulsa	23 24
S16	●	S.W. Missouri St.	35 7
S23	●	at Wyoming	25 45
S30		at Tennessee	0 31
O14		Kansas State	17 23
O21	●	at Missouri	30 26
O28		at Iowa State	14 38
N4		Colorado	32 45
N11	●	at Oklahoma	12 0
N18		Kansas	17 22
D2		at Hawaii	24 20

1996-PRESENT
BIG 12

1996
5-6 (2-6)

A31	●	S.W. Missouri	23 20
S7		Texas Tech Inv	3 31
S14	●	Tulsa	30 9
S21	●	Utah State	31 17
O5		at Texas	14 71
O12		at Colorado	13 35
O19	●	Iowa State	28 27
O26		at Missouri	28 35
N2		Texas A&M	19 38
N9		Oklahoma	17 27
N23	●	Baylor	37 17

1997
8-4 (5-3)

A30	●	at Iowa State	21 14
S6	●	at La. Lafayette	31 7
S13	●	Fresno State	35 0
S27	●	La. Monroe	38 7
O4	●	Texas	42 16
O11	●	Colorado	33 29
O25		Missouri	50 51
N1		at Texas A&M	25 28
N8		at Oklahoma	30 7
N15		Texas Tech	3 27
N22	●	at Baylor	24 14
		ALAMO BOWL	
D30		Purdue	20 33

1998
5-6 (3-5)

S5	●	at Kansas	38 28
S12	●	at Tulsa	20 35
S19	●	Mississippi State	42 23
O3		Nebraska KC	17 24
O10		at Texas Tech	17 24
O17		at Kansas State	20 52
O24	●	Oklahoma	41 26
O31	●	Texas A&M	6 17
N7		at Texas	34 37
N14	●	La. Lafayette	44 20
N21	●	Baylor	24 10

1999
5-6 (3-5)

S4	●	La. Lafayette	24 7
S11	●	Tulsa	46 9
S18	●	at Mississippi State	11 29
O2		at Nebraska	14 38
O9	●	Texas Tech	41 21
O23		Kansas State	21 44
O30		at Texas A&M	3 21
N6		Texas	21 34
N13		Kansas	45 13
N20	●	at Baylor	34 14
N27		at Oklahoma	7 44

2000
3-8 (1-7)

S9	●	at Tulsa	36 26
S16	●	Texas St.	23 0
S23		Southern Miss	6 28
S30		at Texas	7 42
O7		at Missouri	10 24
O14		Iowa State	26 33
O28		at Colorado	21 37
N4		Texas A&M	16 21
N11		at Texas Tech	0 58
N18	●	Baylor	50 22
N25		Oklahoma	7 12

LES MILES
2001-04 (.571)   28-21

2001
4-7 (2-6)

S1		at Southern Miss	9 17
S8	●	Louisiana Tech	30 23
S22		at Texas A&M	7 21
S29	●	Northwestern St.	24 0
O6		Missouri	38 41
O13		Texas	17 45
O20		at Iowa State	14 28
O27		Colorado	19 22
N10		Texas Tech	30 49
N17	●	at Baylor	38 22
N24		at Oklahoma	16 13

2002
8-5 (5-3)

A31		Louisiana Tech Shre	36 39
S7	●	No. Iowa	45 10
S14		UCLA	24 38
S21	●	SMU	52 16
O5		at Texas	15 17
O12		at Kansas State	9 44
O19	●	Nebraska	24 21
N2	●	Texas A&M	28 23
N9		at Texas Tech	24 49
N16	●	at Kansas	55 20
N23	●	Baylor	63 28
N30	●	Oklahoma	38 28
		HOUSTON BOWL	
D27		Southern Miss	33 23

2003
9-4 (5-3)

A30		at Nebraska	7 17
S6	●	Wyoming	48 24
S13	●	S.W. Missouri St.	35 3
S20	●	at SMU	52 6
O4	●	La. Lafayette	56 3
O11	●	Kansas State	38 34
O18	●	Texas Tech	51 49
O25	●	at Texas A&M	38 10
N1		at Oklahoma	9 52
N8	●	Texas	16 55
N15	●	Kansas	44 21
N22	●	at Baylor	38 21
		COTTON BOWL	
J2		Mississippi	28 31

2004
7-5 (4-4)

S4	●	at UCLA	31 20
S11	●	Tulsa	38 21
S18	●	SMU	59 7
O2	●	Iowa State	36 7
O9	●	at Colorado	42 14
O16		Texas A&M	20 36
O23	●	at Missouri	20 17
O30		Oklahoma	35 38
N6		at Texas	35 56
N13	●	Baylor	49 21
N27		at Texas Tech	15 31
		ALAMO BOWL	
D29		Ohio State	7 33

OREGON

By Bud Withers

Few college football programs have known a sharper delineation between mediocrity and excellence than Oregon. For most of their first century, the Ducks had the occasional success or the extraordinary player, but there never was any sustained glory. That all began to change in the late 1980s with the recruitment of an understated but efficient quarterback, Bill Musgrave. In 1989, he led the Ducks to their first bowl game in 26 years. Oregon began improving its facilities, and by the mid-1990s, Nike co-founder Phil Knight was dropping millions into the program. Parlaying Knight's largesse with a run of astute coaches, Oregon has become a perennial player in the Top 25.

TRADITION Without a rich football history, Oregon doesn't have a wealth of traditions, and at least one of them has had a desultory life span. In 1959, Warren Spady, an art student at the school, was commissioned to design a trophy commemorating the Civil War football game with Oregon State. He carved a platypus—half duck, half beaver—from a slab of maple. The trophy was stolen repeatedly before it disappeared in the early 1960s. Spady then discovered it in a trophy case at the UO swimming pool in 1986, but when the facility was renovated in 2000, the contents of the trophy case were put into storage. At last word, nobody is sure where the platypus now calls home. In recent years, Oregon players have walked from their buses—deemed the March to Victory—through the Moshofsky Center indoor facility through a phalanx of fans on their way to their locker room.

BEST PLAYER This is a distinction that could be debated for hours in Eugene's bistros and bars. Mel Renfro led the Ducks in rushing for three years (1961-63) and never averaged less than 5.5 yards a carry, validating his athleticism at the 1962 NCAA track championships with a second-place finish in the high hurdles. He then played 14 seasons with the Dallas Cowboys—appearing in the Pro Bowl the first 10—and was elected into both the College and Pro Football halls of fame. Before Renfro there was George Shaw, who had a nation-leading 13 interceptions at defensive back in 1951 and was the No. 1 pick in the 1955 NFL draft as a quarterback. But in Oregon's most successful era, the emotional leader was a gregarious, piano-playing college kid who sometimes joined the face-painted rabble-rousers at basketball games, wearing a pom-pom hairdo. Joey Harrington was 25–3 as a starting quarterback for the Ducks from 1999 to 2001, led successful fourth-quarter comebacks four times as a senior and was the first of several Oregon players depicted on the side of a building eight stories high in New York's Times Square as a school promotion.

BEST COACH Through a generally tepid history, Oregon's most compelling figure on the sideline was Hugo Bezdek, an Amos Alonzo Stagg protégé who led three different teams to the Rose Bowl in seven years: Oregon (1917), Mare Island (1918) and Penn State (1923). Then along came Mike Bellotti,

---

PROFILE

University of Oregon
Eugene, Ore.
Founded: 1876
Enrollment: 16,358
Colors: Green and Yellow
Nickname: Ducks
Stadium: Autzen Stadium
    Opened in 1967
    FieldTurf; 54,000 capacity
First football game: 1894
All-time record: 522–449–46 (.536)
Bowl record: 7–11
Pac-10 championships: 7 (2 outright)
First-round NFL draftees: 10
Website: www.goducks.com

THE BEST OF TIMES

Starting with a surprise run to the Rose Bowl in 1994, the Ducks amassed an 84–38 record over a decade that included three BCS bowl appearances.

THE WORST OF TIMES

The Ducks went 15–51 in a six-season stretch from 1973 to 1978, changing head coaches twice.

CONFERENCE

UO became a charter member of the Pacific Coast Conference—the forerunner to the Pac-10—when it was founded in 1916. They've remained in the different incarnations of the conference since then, save for a brief stint as an independent, from 1959-1963.

DISTINGUISHED ALUMNI

Edwin L. Artzt, Procter & Gamble CEO; Ann Bancroft, first woman to cross both North and South poles; Ken Kesey, author; Phil Knight, Nike CEO and co-founder; Lila Wallace, *Reader's Digest* co-founder and philanthropist

FIGHT SONG

MIGHTY OREGON
Oregon, our alma mater
We will guard thee on and on
Let us gather round and cheer her
Chant her glory Oregon
Roar the praises of her warriors
Sing the story Oregon
On to victory urge the heroes
Of our mighty Oregon

so collected and laid-back he would sometimes show up at the team's media day festivities wearing shorts and sandals. First schooled as an offensive coordinator under longtime Ducks coach Rich Brooks, Bellotti turned out extremely sophisticated passing teams and assembled an 80–40 record in his first 10 seasons (1995-2004) as Oregon's head coach. He was courted by more prestigious schools like Southern California and Ohio State, but said his family preferred the cozier atmosphere in Eugene.

The Ducks are closer to their natural rival than most schools. But proximity is far different from perception.

BEST TEAM The 2001 Ducks were hardly a dominant team. It wasn't Oregon's best offensive unit ever, nor—at 400 yards allowed per game—its best defense. But it was a team that knew how to win, prevailing five times by seven points or fewer, starting with a Harrington-led comeback victory over Wisconsin in an opener featuring six lead changes. With Harrington throwing for 27 touchdowns and only six interceptions, Oregon won the Pac-10 title and posted a No. 2 national finish with an 11–1 record. The climactic victory was a 38-16 lacing of Colorado, which threw more fuel on a controversy involving the Bowl Championship Series. At the end of the regular season, Oregon was No. 2 in the human polls of the BCS standings but only fourth overall, thanks to low ratings by four of the eight computers. Colorado was third overall and Nebraska was No. 2, despite being trounced in late November by the Buffaloes and failing to make the Big 12 title game. The Huskers thus gained

the national championship berth opposite Miami and were routed 37-14, giving Oregon fans reason to claim they were robbed. Alas, the Ducks had let an undefeated regular season slip away by losing to Stanford at home in a game they led by two touchdowns with 10 minutes left.

BEST GAME On balance, the 2002 Fiesta Bowl seemed like a stiff test for the Ducks, the finesse team from the Pac-10 against bruising, burgeoning power Colorado, which had punished mighty Nebraska 62-36. But the game provided testimony for Oregon's savvy coaching staff, and served as a national coming-out party for the Ducks. Oregon stacked the line of scrimmage against the Colorado run, forced the Buffalo quarterbacks into an out-of-whack 47 pass attempts and bedazzled the Buffs with a 500-yard attack, including 350 by Harrington in Oregon's slick passing game. "We dominated," said linebacker Kevin Mitchell. "It's not a secret, it's not a fairy tale, it's a fact."

BIGGEST UPSET The betting line on the 1994 Oregon-Washington game was only eight points, but the magnitude of the Ducks' 31-20 victory made it the most apocalyptic day in the program's history. With less than a minute left, Washington was at the Oregon 8-yard line, poised to overcome a 24-20 deficit. But Huskies coaches called for a deep out route, and as quarterback Damon Huard threw it, Oregon cornerback Kenny Wheaton stepped in front of the

RECORDS

RUSHING YARDS

GAME	
285	Onterrio Smith vs. Washington State, Oct. 27, 2001 (26 att.)
SEASON	
1,343	Saladin McCullough, 1997 (267 att.)
CAREER	
3,296	Derek Loville, 1986-89 (814 att.)

PASSING YARDS

GAME	
489	Bill Musgrave vs. Brigham Young, Nov. 4, 1989 (26 of 44)
SEASON	
3,763	Akili Smith, 1998 (215 of 371)
CAREER	
8,343	Bill Musgrave, 1987-90 (634 of 1,104)

RECEIVING YARDS

GAME	
242	Tony Hartley vs. Washington, Nov. 7, 1998 (9 rec.)
SEASON	
1,123	Bob Newland, 1970 (67 rec.)
CAREER	
2,744	Tony Hartley, 1996-99 (160 rec.)

POINTS

GAME	
56	Charles Taylor vs. Puget Sound, Oct. 22, 1910
SEASON	
117	Nathan Villegas, 1998 (22 FGs, 57 PATs)
CAREER	
323	Jared Siegel, 2001-04 (49 FGs, 176 PATs)

CONSENSUS ALL-AMERICANS

1962	Mel Renfro, HB

receiver, intercepted and ran 97 yards for a touchdown. Shown before every game on Oregon's video board, that play is the program's biggest moment. The Ducks built on that October victory for their first Rose Bowl trip in 37 years, the first of three post-New Year's Eve bowls in an eight-season span.

TRAGEDY Oregon carried an eight-game losing streak against Oregon State into its 1972 Civil War game. On the sideline, coach Dick Enright held up the jersey of defensive end Alan Eustace, who'd had a promising sophomore season in 1971 before being sidelined by leukemia. "I looked around that huddle," said teammate Greg Lindsey, "and all I saw were a lot of narrow eyes." The Ducks won 30-3 and gave Eustace the game ball. He died at age 20, five months later.

WILDEST FINISH At Arizona State in 2000, the Pac-10-leading Ducks trailed 49-35 inside the four-minute mark. They scored to get within a touchdown, but a second thrust fell short at the ASU 1-yard line. Attempting to run out the clock on third down, Sun Devils back Mike Williams fumbled at the 17, which set up a tying touchdown pass from Harrington to Justin Peelle with 27 seconds left. Oregon then prevailed 56-55 in double overtime.

BEST COMEBACK With several minutes remaining in Oregon's 1970 game against UCLA at the Los Angeles Coliseum, most writers did what they always do when the outcome is decided: they left the press box for the field level and the postgame interviews. It was 40-21, UCLA, with less than five minutes left, and the scribes headed for the elevator. When some of them arrived at the field, they discovered they had missed a 15-yard touchdown pass from Tom Blanchard to Bobby Moore (later Ahmad Rashad), a UCLA fumble and another Blanchard-to-Moore score. The Bruins now led 40-35. Oregon recovered an onside kick, but Blanchard injured his shoulder and had to turn the game back over to sophomore Dan Fouts, who had been benched earlier. Fouts

hit receiver Greg Specht for a 15-yard touchdown with 21 seconds left to give the Ducks a 41-40 win.

STADIUM Built in 1967 for a frugal $2.5 million, Autzen Stadium replaced Hayward Field—the Ducks' storied track facility—as the venue for football. It originally seated 41,698, and when Oregon began turning out winning teams with consistency in the 1990s, it was expanded to 54,000 before the 2002 season at a cost of $90 million, which included 32 skyboxes and a new press box.

RIVAL Separated from Oregon State by only 40 miles of farmland, the Ducks are closer to their natural rival than most schools. But proximity is far different from perception: the Beavers tag Oregon with a label of front-runners whose expectations are rarely achieved, while the Ducks pelt OSU with the requisite cow-college insults. But Oregon has significant distaste for Washington, as well, dating at least to the 1948 season, when the Huskies' vote helped break a tie in the old Pacific Coast Conference, sending California to the Rose Bowl and consigning the Ducks to the Cotton Bowl.

NICKNAME Oregon teams in the school's first half-century were referred to as Webfoots, a sobriquet that fit the drizzly climate in Eugene. In the 1940s, athletic director Leo Harris capitalized on a personal friendship with Walt Disney to use Donald Duck as the school mascot, and that reference gradually overtook Webfoots in common usage.

MASCOT In the 1920s, fraternity students brought Puddles, a white duck, from the nearby Millrace—a bordering campus—for football and basketball games. In the late 1960s, a student was designated to wear an oversize duck outfit. That "traditional" duck was joined in 2002 by a more streamlined, striated, 21st-century version.

UNIFORMS Few of college football's ensembles are more distinctive than the Ducks'. In 1999, they began wearing Nike-

ALL-TIME TEAM	
Selected by the Eugene Register-Guard *in 1995.*	
OFFENSE	
1917-20	Bill Steers, OG
1980-83	Gary Zimmerman, OG
1928-30	George Christensen, OT
1960-62	Steve Barnett, OT
1946-48	Brad Ecklund, C
1946-48	Dan Garza, TE
1969-71	Ahmad Rashad, WR
1992-95	Cristin McLemore, WR
1947-48	Norm Van Brocklin, QB
1928-30	Johnny Kitzmiller, TB
1916, 1918-19	Hollis Huntington, FB
1908-09	F.C. Moullen, PK
DEFENSE	
1913-16	John Beckett, DL
1934-35	Ross Carter, DL
1934-36	Del Bjork, DL
1977-80	Vince Goldsmith, DL
1931-33	Mike Mikulak, LB
1962-63	Dave Wilcox, LB
1969-71	Tom Graham, LB
1951-54	George Shaw, CB
1965-67	Jim Smith, CB
1914-16	Shy Huntington, S
1961-63	Mel Renfro, S

inspired home uniforms officially described as mallard green, dark spruce and lightning yellow. Road uniforms are white. Both helmets are mallard green, inscribed with a blocky O. In 2003, they debuted a shocking yellow-with-green-trim uniform, which was derided nationally—except, insisted Bellotti, by Oregon players and recruits: "I think you have to put yourself in the mind-set of a 17-year-old young man."

QUOTE "I'd rather be whipped in a public square than watch a football game like that."—Newly installed school president William Boyd, when asked to assess the team's performance after a 5-0 home loss to San Jose State in 1975

OREGON ANNUAL STATISTICAL LEADERS

YR	RUSHING	YDS	ATT	AVG	PASSING	ATT	CMP	PCT	YDS	RECEIVING	REC	YDS	AVG
1945	Jake Leicht	411	NA	NA	Jake Leicht	NA	NA	NA	376		NA	NA	NA
1946	James Newquist	289	90	3.2	James Newquist	NA	NA	NA	281		NA	NA	NA
1947	Jake Leicht	630	119	5.3	Norm Van Brocklin	168	76	.45	939	Dan Garza	21	365	17.4
1948	George Bell	648	139	4.7	Norm Van Brocklin	139	68	.49	1,010	Dick Wilkins	27	520	19.3
1949	Robert Sanders	726	153	4.7	Earl Stelle	119	59	.50	687	Darrell Robinson	31	404	13.0
1950	James Edwards	264	NA	NA	Earl Stelle	NA	NA	NA	506	Monte Brethauer	33	279	8.5
1951	Tom Novikoff	322	80	4.0	Hal Dunham	189	82	.43	918	Monte Brethauer	33	292	8.8
1952	Tom Novikoff	486	123	4.0	George Shaw	116	55	.47	666	Monte Brethauer	41	486	11.9
1953	Dick James	479	106	4.5	George Shaw	119	49	.41	652	John Reed	15	152	10.1
1954	Jasper McGee	380	88	4.3	George Shaw	196	91	.46	1,358	Dick James	24	394	16.4
1955	Jim Shanley	711	100	7.1	Tom Crabtree	63	24	.38	335	Jim Shanley	8	139	17.4
1956	Jack Morris	519	137	3.8	Tom Crabtree	65	28	.43	366	Phil McHugh	11	139	12.6
1957	Jim Shanley	664	168	4.0	Jack Crabtree	99	55	.56	624	Ron Stover	24	247	10.3
1958	Willie West	470	101	4.7	Dave Grosz	91	42	.46	468	Willie West	18	140	7.8
1959	Dave Powell	495	126	3.9	Dave Grosz	139	67	.48	865	Cleveland Jones	17	205	12.1
1960	Dave Grayson	631	117	5.4	Dave Grosz	141	57	.40	910	Cleveland Jones	25	402	16.1
1961	Mel Renfro	335	61	5.5	Doug Post	NA	NA	NA	662	Kent Petersen	18	209	11.6
1962	Mel Renfro	753	126	6.0	Bob Berry	115	62	.54	995	Greg Willener	19	263	13.8
1963	Mel Renfro	452	82	5.5	Bob Berry	171	101	.59	1,675	Dick Imwalle	23	401	17.4
1964	Dick Winn	345	103	3.3	Bob Berry	208	108	.52	1,478	Ray Palm	42	570	13.6
1965	Dick Winn	423	96	4.4	Mike Brundage	180	85	.47	1,127	Steve Bunker	51	838	16.4
1966	Steve Jones	542	158	3.4	Mike Barnes	128	49	.38	710	Scott Cress	28	402	14.4
1967	Claxton Welch	474	130	3.6	Eric Olson	123	51	.41	840	Roger Smith	26	402	15.5
1968	Claxton Welch	505	141	3.6	Eric Olson	90	48	.53	796	Denny Schuler	30	351	11.7
1969	Pat Verutti	682	151	4.5	Tom Blanchard	184	106	.58	1,488	Bobby Moore*	54	786	14.6
1970	Bobby Moore*	924	203	4.6	Dan Fouts	361	188	.52	2,390	Bob Newland	67	1,123	16.8
1971	Bobby Moore*	1,211	249	4.9	Dan Fouts	247	123	.50	1,564	Leland Glass	46	584	12.7
1972	Don Reynolds	421	52	8.1	Dan Fouts	348	171	.49	2,041	Greg Specht	52	710	13.7
1973	Don Reynolds	1,002	226	4.4	Herb Singleton	234	109	.47	1,333	Russ Francis	31	495	16.0
1974	Don Reynolds	787	165	4.8	Norval Turner	202	99	.49	1,261	Bob Palm	31	466	15.0
1975	George Bennett	805	175	4.6	Jack Henderson	321	151	.47	1,492	Greg Bauer	52	616	11.8
1976	Jim Johnson	356	89	4.0	Jack Henderson	298	157	.53	1,582	Greg Bauer	53	632	11.9
1977	Kim Nutting	359	101	3.6	Jack Henderson	223	108	.48	1,286	Ken Page	40	591	14.8
1978	Vince Williams	842	183	4.6	Michael Kennedy	136	58	.43	683	Curt Jackson	21	237	11.3
1979	Reggie Ogburn	644	156	4.1	Reggie Ogburn	139	71	.51	905	Ricky Ward	16	217	13.6
1980	Reggie Brown	775	171	4.5	Reggie Ogburn	183	99	.54	1,257	Greg Moser	32	611	19.1
1981	Reggie Brown	690	177	3.9	Kevin Lusk	174	86	.49	864	Greg Moser	29	605	20.9
1982	Terrance Jones	715	165	4.3	Mike Jorgensen	74	33	.45	393	Osborn Thomas	30	369	12.3
1983	Ladaria Johnson	294	85	3.5	Mike Jorgensen	174	72	.41	938	Lew Barnes	30	625	20.8
1984	Tony Cherry	569	87	6.5	Chris Miller	289	145	.50	1,712	Kevin McCall	39	317	8.1
1985	Tony Cherry	1,006	211	4.8	Chris Miller	329	182	.55	2,237	Lew Barnes	50	789	15.8
1986	Derek Loville	544	140	3.9	Chris Miller	356	216	.61	2,503	Bobby DeBisschop	40	500	12.5
1987	Derek Loville	591	165	3.6	Bill Musgrave	234	139	.59	1,936	Terry Obee	33	640	19.4
1988	Derek Loville	1,202	265	4.5	Pete Nelson	140	66	.47	897	Terry Obee	33	596	18.1
1989	Derek Loville	959	244	3.9	Bill Musgrave	401	231	.58	3,081	Terry Obee	46	741	16.1
1990	Sean Burwell	969	223	4.3	Bill Musgrave	348	202	.58	2,611	Joe Reitzug	40	639	16.0
1991	Sean Burwell	510	139	3.7	Danny O'Neil	115	55	.48	713	Anthony Jones	34	435	12.8
1992	Sean Burwell	822	193	4.3	Danny O'Neil	316	176	.56	2,152	Sean Burwell	35	293	8.4
1993	Sean Burwell	457	113	4.0	Danny O'Neil	360	223	.62	3,224	Derrick Deadwiler	52	811	15.6
1994	Dino Philyaw	716	181	4.0	Danny O'Neil	341	182	.53	2,212	Cristin McLemore	42	564	13.4
1995	Ricky Whittle	1,021	260	3.9	Tony Graziani	426	231	.54	2,604	Cristin McLemore	64	1,036	16.2
1996	Saladin McCullough	685	122	5.6	Ryan Perry-Smith	241	125	.52	1,874	Damon Griffin	43	711	16.5
1997	Saladin McCullough	1,343	267	5.0	Jason Maas	187	104	.56	1,631	Pat Johnson	55	1,072	19.5
1998	Reuben Droughns	824	112	7.4	Akili Smith	371	215	.58	3,763	Damon Griffin	58	1,038	17.9
1999	Reuben Droughns	1,234	277	4.5	A.J. Feeley	259	136	.53	1,951	Tony Hartley	56	881	15.7
2000	Maurice Morris	1,106	260	4.3	Joey Harrington	405	214	.53	2,967	Keenan Howry	52	780	15.0
2001	Onterrio Smith	1,058	175	6.0	Joey Harrington	364	214	.59	2,764	Keenan Howry	52	682	13.1
2002	Onterrio Smith	1,141	244	4.7	Jason Fife	367	190	.52	2,752	Samie Parker	49	724	14.8
2003	Terrence Whitehead	737	192	3.8	Kellen Clemens	304	182	.60	2,400	Samie Parker	77	1,088	14.1
2004	Terrence Whitehead	1,144	200	5.7	Kellen Clemens	372	223	.60	2,548	Demetrius Williams	47	593	12.6

Later Ahmad Rashad

Receiving leaders by receptions
All statistics include postseason

OREGON ALL-TIME SCORES

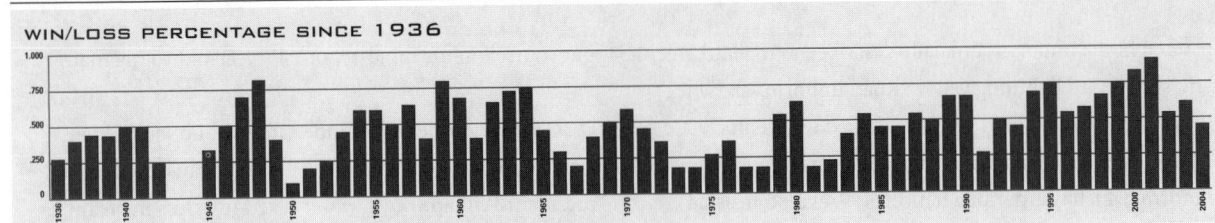

WIN/LOSS PERCENTAGE SINCE 1936

CAL YOUNG/ J.A. CHURCH
1894 (.375)   1-2-1

1894   1-2-1
U	●	Albany Coll. *U*	44	2
U		at Oregon State	0	16
U		Portland *U*	0	12
U	=	Pacific *U*		

PERCY BENSON
1895 (1.000)   4-0

1895   4-0-0
U	●	at Oregon State	46	0 *
U	●	Willamette *U*	8	4
U	●	Portland *U*	6	4
U	●	Willamette *U*	6	0

J.F. FRICK
1896 (.667)   2-1

1896   2-1-0
U	●	Oregon State	2	0 *
U	●	at Oregon State	12	8
U		Multnomah AC *U*	6	12

JOE SMITH
1897 (.500)   1-1

1897   1-1-0
U	●	Chemawa Ind. *U*	10	0
U		Oregon State	8	26 *

FRANK SIMPSON
1898-99 (.650)   6-3-1

1898   3-1-0
U	●	Chemawa Ind. *U*	34	0
U	●	Portland *U*	95	0
U		Multnomah AC. *U*	0	21
U	●	at Oregon State	38	0

1899   3-2-1
N4	●	Chemawa Ind. *U*	29	0
N11		Multnomah AC. *U*	0	5
N18		at California	0	12
N21	●	Southern Oregon *U*	35	0
N25	=	Multnomah AC. *U*	0	0
N30	●	Oregon St	38	0

LAWRENCE KAARSBERG
1900 (.500)   3-3-1

1900   3-3-1
O27	●	Capital AC *U*	0	5
N3	●	Multnomah AC *U*	0	5
N10		at Stanford	0	34
N17		at California	2	0
N19	●	Southern Oregon *U*	21	0
N29	=	Multnomah AC *U*	0	0
D1	●	Washington	43	0

WARREN SMITH
1901, '03 (.533)   7-6-2

1901   3-4-1
O26	●	Chemawa Ind. *U*	11	0
N2		Multnomah AC *U*	0	5
N6	=	Idaho *U*	0	0
N9		at Washington State	0	16
N12		Whitman *U*	0	6
N13	●	Pendleton H.S. *U*	12	0
N28		Multnomah AC *U*	0	17
N30	●	Pacific *U*	10	0

MARION DOLPH
1902 (.643)   3-1-3

1902   3-1-3
O18	=	Albany *U*	0	0
O22	●	Whitman *U*	6	0
N1	●	Oregon Medical *U*	11	0
N8	=	at Oregon State	0	0
N15	=	Albany *U*	0	0
N21	●	Pacific *U*	70	0
N27		Multnomah AC *U*	0	16

WARREN SMITH

1903   4-2-1
O17	●	Oregon Alumni *U*	6	0
O24	●	Albany Coll. *U*	22	0
O31	●	Willamette *U*	37	0
N7		Washington State		
N14		at Washington	5	6
N21	●	Oregon State	5	0
N26		Multnomah AC *U*	0	12

R.S. SMITH
1904, '25 (.433)   6-8-1

1904   5-3-0
O8	●	Oregon Alumni *U*	20	0
O12	●	Albany *U*	4	0
O15	●	Willamette *U*	16	0
O22		at California	0	12
O29		at Stanford	0	35
N12	●	Washington	18	0
N19	●	at Oregon State	6	5
N24		Multnomah AC *U*	0	7

BRUCE SHORTS
1905 (.625)   4-2-2

1905   4-2-2
O8	●	Oregon Alumni *U*	15	5
O12	=	at California	0	0
O18		at Stanford	4	10
O29	●	Chemawa *U*	17	0
N4	●	Wilamette *U*	11	6
N11	●	Oregon State	6	0
N18	●	Washington	12	12
N30		Multnomah AC *U*	0	6

HUGO BEZDEK
1906, '13-17 (.727)   30-10-4

1906   5-0-1
O26	●	Idaho *U*	12	0
N3	●	Willamette *U*	4	0
N20	●	Washington	16	6 *
N24	=	at Oregon State	0	0
N30	●	Multnomah AC *U*	8	4
D7	●	Whitworth *U*	10	0

GORDON FROST
1907 (.833)   5-1

1907   5-1-0
O19	●	Pacific *U*	52	0
O26	●	Idaho *U*	21	5
N2	●	Willamette *U*	11	0
N9		Oregon State	0	4
N16	●	at Washington	6	0
N28	●	Multnomah AC *U*	10	5

ROBERT FORBES
1908-09 (.667)   8-4

1908   5-2-0
O17	●	Oregon Alumni *U*	4	0
O24	●	Willamette *U*	15	0
O31	●	Idaho *U*	27	21
N7	●	Whitman *U*	10	16
N14		Washington	0	15
N21	●	Oregon State *PORT*	8	0
N26	●	Multnomah AC *U*	10	0

1909   3-2-0
O30	●	Willamette *U*	29	0
N6		Multnomah AC *U*	0	3
N13	●	Idaho *U*	22	6
N19	●	Oregon State	12	0
N20		at Washington	6	20

BILL WARNER
1910-11 (.700)   7-3

1910   4-1-0
O15	●	Alumni *U*	16	6
O22	●	Puget Sound *U*	115	0
O29	●	Idaho *U*	29	0
N12	●	at Oregon State	12	0
N24		Multnomah AC *U*	0	5

1911   3-2-0
O20	●	Vancouver Barracks *U*	36	0
O27	●	at Washington State	6	0
N4	●	Whitman *U*	8	5
N18		Washington *PORT*	3	29
N30		Multnomah AC *U*	6	17

LOUIS PINKHAM
1912 (.429)   3-4

1912   3-4-0
O12	●	Willamette *U*	12	0
O19	●	Whitman *U*	0	20
O26		Washington State	0	7
N2	●	Idaho *U*	3	0
N16		at Washington	14	30
N23	●	Oregon State *ALB*	3	0
N28		Multnomah AC *U*	7	20

HUGO BEZDEK

1913   3-3-1
O4	●	Alumni *U*	42	3
O18	●	Bremerton *U*	43	6
O25	●	Idaho *U*	27	0
N1	●	Willamette *U*	3	6
N8	=	Oregon State *ALB*	10	10
N15		Washington *PORT*	7	10
N27		Multnomah AC *U*	0	19

1914   4-2-1
O10	●	Whitman *U*	29	3
O17	●	Washington State *PORT*	7	0
O24	●	Idaho *U*	13	0
O30	●	Willamette *U*	61	0
N14		at Washington	0	10
N21	=	at Oregon State	3	3
N26		Multnomah AC *U*	0	14

1915   7-2-0
O2	●	Multnomah AC *U*	7	16
O9		at Washington State	3	28
O16	●	Idaho *U*	19	7
O23	●	Whitman *U*	21	0
O30	●	Willamette *U*	49	0
N2	●	Pacific *U*	47	0
N8	●	at Southern Cal	34	0
N20	●	Oregon State	9	0
N25	●	Multnomah AC *U*	15	2

1916-1958
PACIFIC COAST

1916   7-0-1 (2-0-1)
O7	●	Willamette *U*	97	0
O14	●	Multnomah AC	28	0
O21	│	at California	39	14
N4	=	Washington	0	0
N11	●	Washington State *PORT*	12	3 *
N25	●	at Oregon State	27	0
N29	●	at Multnomah AC	27	0
		ROSE BOWL		
J1	●	Pennsylvania	14	0

1917   4-3-0 (1-2-0)
O13	●	at Multnomah AC	14	7
O20	│	at Washington State	3	26
O27	●	Idaho	14	0
N3	●	Willamette	14	0
N10	●	at Mare Island Marines	0	27
N17	│	California	21	0
N29	│	Oregon State *PORT*	7	14

SHY HUNTINGTON
1918-23 (.659)   26-12-6

1918   4-2-0 (2-1-0)
O12	│	Multnomah AC	0	20
N2	●	Foundation	41	0
N9	●	at Camp Lewis	20	3
N16	│	at Oregon State	13	6
N23	│	at California	0	6
D1	│	Washington	7	0

1919   5-2-0 (2-1-0)
O11	●	Multnomah AC	23	0
O18	●	Idaho	26	6
N1	│	at Washington	24	13
N8	│	Washington State *PORT*	0	7
N15	│	Oregon State	9	0
N27	●	at Multnomah AC	15	7
		ROSE BOWL		
J1		Harvard	6	7

1920   3-2-1 (1-1-1)
O9	●	Multnomah AC	7	0
O23	●	Idaho	13	7
O30	●	at Stanford	0	10
N13	●	Washington	17	0
N20	=	at Oregon State	0	0
N25	●	Southern Cal *PAS*	0	21

1921   5-1-3 (0-1-2)
O1	●	Willmette	7	3
O8	●	at Pacific	21	7
O15	=	at Idaho	7	7
O22	│	at California	0	39
N5	=	at Washington State	7	7
N12	●	Multnomah AC	21	7
N19	=	Oregon State	0	0
D26	●	at Hawaii	47	0
J1	●	at Pearl Harbor	35	5

1922   6-1-1 (3-0-1)
O7	●	Willamette	37	0
O14	●	at Multnomah AC	0	20
O20	●	at Whitman	6	3
O28	●	│ Idaho	6	3
N4	│	Pacific	27	0
N11	●	│ Washington State	13	0
N18	●	│ at Oregon State	10	0
N30	●	│ at Washington	3	3

1923   3-4-1 (0-4-1)
S30	●	Willamette	40	0
O13	●	Pacific	35	7
O18	●	at Whitman	21	0
O27	=	│ at Idaho	0	0
N3	│	at Washington State	7	13
N10	│	Stanford	3	14
N25	│	Oregon State	0	6
D1	│	at Washington	7	26

JOE MADDOCK
1924 (.555)   4-3-2

1924   4-3-2 (2-2-1)
S27	●	at Willamette	0	0
O11	●	Pacific	20	0
O18	│	at Stanford	13	28
O25	●	Whitman	40	6
N1	│	Washington	7	3
N8	│	Idaho	0	13
N15	=	│ Washington State *PORT*	7	7
N22	●	at Oregon State	7	3
N29	│	at Multnomah AC	0	6

R.S. SMITH

1925 1-5-1 (0-5-0)

O3	=	Multnomah AC	0	0	
O10	|	Idaho	0	6	
O17	●	at Pacific	13	0	
O24	|	California PORT	0	28	
O31	|	at Stanford	13	35	
N14	|	Oregon State	13	24	
N28	|	at Washington	14	15	

JOHN McEWAN
1926-29 (.600) 20-13-2

1926 2-4-1 (1-4-0)

S25	●	at Willamette	44	0	
O2	=	Pacific	0	0	
O9	|	Washington PORT	9	23	
O23	|	Stanford	12	19	*
O30	● |	at California	21	13	
N13	|	at Washington State	0	7	
N20	|	at Oregon State	0	16	

1927 2-4-1 (0-4-1)

S25	●	Linfield	7	0	
O1	●	Pacific	31	6	
O8	= |	Idaho	0	0	
O15	|	California PORT	0	16	
O29	|	at Stanford	0	19	
N12	|	Oregon State	7	21	
N24	|	at Washington	0	7	

1928 9-2-0 (4-2-0)

S30	●	Pacific	45	0	
O6	|	Stanford	12	26	*
O13	●	Willamette	38	6	
O20	● |	Washington PORT	27	0	
O27	●	Western Oregon	24	0	
N3	|	at California	0	13	
N17	● |	at Oregon State	12	0	
N24	● |	Montana	31	6	
N29	● |	at UCLA	26	6	
D25	●	at Hawaii All Stars	13	2	
J1	●	at Hawaii	6	0	

1929 7-3-0 (4-1-0)

S29	●	Pacific	58	0	
O5	|	at Stanford	7	33	
O12	●	Willamette	34	0	
O19	● |	Idaho PORT	34	7	
O26	● |	at Washington	14	0	
N2	● |	UCLA	27	0	
N16	● |	Oregon State	16	0	
N23	●	Hawaii	7	0	
N28		at Saint Mary's-Cal	6	31	
D7		Florida MIA	6	20	

W. SPEARS
1930-31 (.736) 13-4-2

1930 7-2-0 (3-1-0)

S15	●	Pacific	20	0	
S22	●	Willamette	51	0	
S29	●	Linfield	6	0	
O4	●	Drake CHI	14	7	
O18	● |	Washington PORT	7	0	
O25	● |	Idaho	20	6	
N8	● |	UCLA	7	0	
N15	|	at Oregon State	0	15	
N27		at Saint Mary's-Cal	6	7	

1931 6-2-2 (3-1-1)

S20	●	Western Oregon	21	6	
S27	●	Willamette	20	0	
O3	● |	Idaho PORT	9	0	
O10	● |	at Washington	13	0	
O17	|	at Southern Cal	0	53	
O24	=	at North Dakota	0	0	
O31	●	NYU BRNX	14	6	
N14	= |	Oregon State	0	0	
N21	● |	at UCLA	13	6	
N26		at Saint Mary's-Cal	0	16	

PRINK CALLISON
1932-37 (.586) 33-23-2

1932 6-3-1 (2-2-1)

S23	●	Pacific	26	6	
O1	●	Santa Clara	7	0	
O8	= |	Washington PORT	0	0	
O15	|	UCLA PORT	7	12	
O22	● |	at Idaho	32	0	
O29	●	Gonzaga	13	0	
N5	● |	at Oregon State	12	6	
N12	|	at Southern Cal	0	33	
N24		at Saint Mary's-Cal	0	7	
D17	●	at LSU	12	0	

1933 9-1-0 (4-1-0)

S23	●	Linfield	53	0	
S30	●	at Gonzaga	14	0	
O7	●	Portland	14	7	
O14	● |	at Washington	6	0	
O20	● |	Idaho	19	0	
O28	● |	at UCLA	7	0	
N4	●	Utah	23	7	*
N11	● |	Oregon State PORT	13	3	
N18	|	at Southern Cal	0	26	
N30	●	at Saint Mary's-Cal	13	7	

1934 6-4-0 (4-2-0)

S23	●	Gonzaga	13	0	
S30	● |	UCLA PORT	26	3	
O13	|	Washington PORT	6	16	
O20	● |	at Idaho	13	6	
O27	●	at Utah	8	7	
N3	● |	Montana	13	0	
N10	● |	Oregon State PORT	9	6	
N17	|	at Southern Cal	0	33	
N29		at Saint Mary's-Cal	7	13	
D15		at LSU	13	14	

1935 6-3-0 (3-2-0)

S28	●	Gonzaga PORT	18	0	
O5	●	Utah	6	0	
O12	|	California PORT	0	6	
O19	● |	Idaho	14	0	
O26	|	at UCLA	6	33	
N9	● |	Oregon State	13	0	
N16	●	at Portland	6	0	
N23	● |	at Washington	7	6	*
D7		at Saint Mary's-Cal	0	18	

1936 2-6-1 (1-6-1)

S25	●	Portland	14	0	
O3	|	at Southern Cal	0	26	
O10	= |	at Stanford	7	7	
O17	● |	Idaho PORT	13	0	
O24	|	at Washington State	0	3	
O31	|	Washington PORT	0	7	
N7	|	UCLA PORT	0	7	
N14	|	at California	0	28	
N21	|	at Oregon State	0	18	

1937 4-6-0 (2-5-0)

S24	|	at UCLA	13	26	
O2	● |	Stanford	7	6	
O9	●	at Gonzaga	40	6	
O16	|	at Southern Cal	14	34	
O23	|	Oregon State	0	14	
N6	● |	Washington State PORT	10	6	
N13	|	California PORT	0	26	
N20	|	at Washington	0	14	
N27	●	at U.S. Marines	24	6	
D4		at Arizona	6	20	

TEX OLIVER
1938-41, '45-46 (.454) 23-28-3

1938 4-5-0 (4-4-0)

S24	● |	at Washington State	10	2	
O1	● |	UCLA	14	12	
O15	|	at Stanford	16	27	
O22		Fordham NYC	0	26	
O29	|	Southern Cal PORT	7	31	
N5	● |	Idaho	19	6	
N12	|	at California	0	20	
N19	● |	Washington PORT	3	0	
N26	|	Oregon State PORT	0	14	

1939 3-4-1 (3-3-1)

S30	= |	at Southern Cal	7	7	
O7	● |	Stanford PORT	10	0	
O14	● |	at California	6	0	
O21		Gonzaga	7	12	
O28	|	at UCLA	6	16	
N4	●	Washington State	38	0	*
N11	|	Oregon State	14	19	
N25	|	at Washington	13	20	

1940 4-4-1 (3-4-1)

S27	●	U.S. Marines	12	2	
O5	|	at Stanford	0	13	
O12	|	Washington PORT	0	10	
O19	|	at Southern Cal	0	13	
O26	= |	at Washington State	6	6	
N2	● |	Montana	38	0	
N9	● |	UCLA	18	0	
N16	|	at California	6	14	
N30	● |	at Oregon State	20	0	

1941 5-5-0 (4-4-0)

S27	|	at Stanford	15	19	
O3	● |	Idaho	21	7	
O11	● |	at Southern Cal	20	6	
O18	● |	California PORT	19	7	
O25	|	at UCLA	7	14	
N1	|	Washington State	0	13	
N11	●	Santa Clara PORT	21	19	
N22	● |	at Washington	19	16	
N29	|	Oregon State	7	12	
D6		at Texas	7	71	

JOHN WARREN
1942 (.250) 2-6

1942 2-6-0 (2-5-0)

S26		Saint Mary's, Pre-Flight PORT	9	10	
O3	|	at Washington State	0	7	
O10	|	Washington PORT	7	15	
O24	● |	Idaho	28	0	
O31	|	at California	7	20	
N7	● |	UCLA	14	7	
N14	|	at Southern Cal	0	40	
N21	|	at Oregon State	2	39	

1943-1944
NO TEAM WWII

TEX OLIVER

1945 3-6-0 (3-6-0)

S29	|	at Washington	6	20	
O6	● |	Idaho	33	7	
O13	|	at Oregon State	6	19	
O20	● |	Washington State	26	13	
O27	|	at UCLA	0	12	
N3	|	Washington PORT	0	7	
N10	|	at Washington State	13	20	
N17	● |	at California	20	13	
D1	|	Oregon State	12	13	

1946 4-4-1 (3-4-1)

S28	●	Pacific	7	6	
O5	● |	at California	14	13	
O12	●	Montana	34	0	
O19	= |	Washington State	0	0	
O26	● |	at Idaho	26	13	
N2	|	at Southern Cal	0	43	
N9	|	UCLA PORT	0	14	
N16	|	at Washington	0	16	
N23	|	at Oregon State	0	13	

JIM AIKEN
1947-50 (.512) 21-20

1947 7-3-0 (5-1-0)

S20	●	Montana State	27	14	
S27		Texas PORT	13	38	
O4		Nevada	6	13	
O11	|	at UCLA	7	24	
O18	● |	Washington PORT	6	0	
O25	●	San Francisco	34	7	
N1	● |	Idaho	34	7	
N8	● |	at Washington State	12	6	
N15	● |	at Stanford	21	6	
N22	● |	Oregon State	14	6	

1948 9-2-0 (7-0-0)

S18	●	Santa Barbara	55	7	
S25	● |	at Stanford	20	12	
O2		at Michigan	0	14	
O9	● |	at Idaho	15	8	
O16	● |	Southern Cal PORT	8	7	
O23	● |	Washington State	33	7	
O30	●	Saint Mary's-Cal	14	13	
N6	● |	at Washington	13	7	
N12	● |	at UCLA	26	7	
N20	● |	at Oregon State	10	0	
		COTTON BOWL			
J1		SMU	13	21	

1949 4-6-0 (2-5-0)

S16	●	at Saint Mary's-Cal	24	7	
S24	● |	Idaho	41	0	
S30	|	at UCLA	27	35	
O8	● |	at Washington State	21	0	
O15	●	Colorado	42	14	
O22	|	at Southern Cal	13	40	
O29		at Iowa	31	34	
N5	|	Washington PORT	27	28	
N12	|	at California	14	41	
N19	|	Oregon State	10	20	

1950 1-9-0 (0-7-0)

S23	|	at UCLA	0	28	
S30	|	California PORT	7	28	
O7	●	Montana	21	13	
O14	|	at Idaho	0	14	
O21		Saint Mary's-Cal	13	18	
O28	|	at Southern Cal	21	30	
N4	|	Washington State	13	21	*
N11	|	at Washington	13	27	*
N18		at Colorado	7	21	
N25	|	Oregon State PORT	2	14	

LEN CASANOVA
1951-66 (.528) 82-73-8

1951 2-8-0 (1-6-0)

S22	|	Stanford PORT	20	27	
S29	●	Arizona	39	21	
O6		at Pacific	6	34	
O13	|	Washington PORT	6	63	
O20	|	at UCLA	0	41	
O27	|	at Washington State	6	41	
N3	● |	Idaho	14	13	
N10		at Boston U.	6	35	
N17	|	at California	26	28	
N24	|	Oregon State	7	14	

1952 2-7-1 (2-5-0)

S20	|	at UCLA	6	13	
S27		Nebraska PORT	13	28	
O4	● |	at Idaho	20	14	
O11	|	California PORT	7	41	
O18	|	at Washington	0	49	
O25	=	Montana	14	14	
N1		Pacific	6	14	
N8	|	Washington State	6	19	
N15	● |	at Stanford	21	20	
N22	|	Oregon State PORT	19	22	

1953 4-5-1 (2-5-1)

S19	●	at Nebraska	20	12	
S26	|	at Stanford	0	7	
O3	|	UCLA	0	12	
O10	|	at Washington State	0	7	
O17	|	Washington PORT	6	14	
O24	●	San Jose State	26	13	
O31	● |	Southern Cal PORT	13	7	
N7	● |	Idaho	26	6	
N14	= |	at California	0	0	
N21	|	Oregon State	0	7	

1954 6-4-0 (5-3-0)

S18	● |	at Idaho	41	0	
S25	|	Stanford PORT	13	18	
O2		Utah	6	7	
O9	● |	at California	33	27	
O16	|	Southern Cal PORT	14	24	
O23	●	San Jose State	26	7	
O30	● |	at Washington	26	7	
N6	|	at UCLA	0	41	
N13	● |	Washington State	26	14	
N20	● |	at Oregon State	33	14	

1955 6-4-0 (4-3-0)

S17	●	at Utah	14	13	
S23	|	at Southern Cal	15	42	
O1	|	Washington PORT	7	19	
O8		Colorado	6	13	
O15	● |	California PORT	21	0	
O22	●	at Arizona	46	27	
O29	● |	Idaho	25	0	
N5	● |	at Washington State	35	0	
N12	|	at Stanford	7	44	
N19	● |	Oregon State	28	0	

1956 4-4-2 (3-3-2)

S22	●	at Colorado	35	0	
S29	● |	Idaho	21	14	
O6	|	at UCLA	0	6	
O13	|	at Washington	7	20	
O20	|	Stanford	7	21	
O27		at Pittsburgh	7	14	
N3	● |	at California	28	6	
N10	= |	Washington State	7	7	
N17	● |	Southern Cal PORT	7	0	
N24	= |	at Oregon State	14	14	

1957 7-4-0 (6-2-0)

S21	● |	at Idaho	9	6	
S28		Pittsburgh PORT	3	6	
O5	● |	UCLA PORT	21	0	
O12	●	San Jose State	26	0	
O19	● |	at Washington State	14	13	
O26	● |	California	24	6	
N2	● |	at Stanford	27	26	
N9	|	Washington PORT	6	13	
N16	● |	at Southern Cal	16	7	
N23	|	Oregon State	7	10	
		ROSE BOWL			
J1		Ohio State	7	10	

THE SCHOOLS

1958 — 4-6-0 (4-4-0)

S20 •	Idaho	27	0
O4	at Oklahoma	0	6
O11 •	Southern Cal *PORT*	25	0
O18	Washington State	0	6
O25	at California	6	23
N1	at Washington	0	6
N8 •	Stanford	12	0
N15	at UCLA	3	7
N22 •	at Oregon State	20	0
D5	at Miami, Fla.	0	2

1959-1963 INDEPENDENT

1959 — 8-2-0

S19 •	at Stanford	28	27
S26 •	Utah	21	6
O3	Washington State	14	6
O9 •	at San Jose State	35	12
O17 •	Air Force	20	3
O24	Washington *PORT*	12	13
O31 •	at Idaho	45	7
N7 •	California *PORT*	20	18
N14 •	at Washington State	7	6
N21	Oregon State	7	15

1960 — 7-3-1

S17 •	Idaho	33	6
S24	at Michigan	0	21
O1	at Utah	20	17
O8	San Jose State	33	0
O15 •	Washington State	21	12
O22	at California	20	0
O29	at Washington	6	7
N5 •	Stanford *PORT*	27	6
N12 •	West Virginia *PORT*	20	6
N19 =	at Oregon State	14	14

LIBERTY BOWL

D17	Penn State	12	41

1961 — 4-6-0

S23 •	Idaho	51	0
S30	at Utah	6	14
O7	at Minnesota	7	14
O14	Arizona *PORT*	6	15
O21 •	San Jose State	21	6
O28 •	Washington *PORT*	7	6
N4	at Stanford	19	7
N11	at Washington State	21	22
N18	at Ohio State	12	22
N25	Oregon State	2	6

1962 — 6-3-1

S22	at Texas	13	25
S29	Utah	35	8
O6	San Jose State	14	0
O13 •	at Rice	31	12
O20	at Air Force	35	20
O27 =	at Washington	21	21
N3 •	Stanford *PORT*	28	14
N10 •	Washington State	28	10
N17	at Ohio State	7	26
N24	at Oregon State	17	20

1963 — 8-3-0

S21	Penn State *PORT*	7	17
S28 •	at Stanford	36	7
O5 •	at West Virginia	35	0
O12 •	Idaho	41	21
O19 •	at Arizona	28	12
O26	Washington *PORT*	19	26
N2	San Jose State	7	13
N9 •	at Washington State	21	7
N16 •	Indiana *PORT*	28	22
N30 •	Oregon State	31	14

SUN BOWL

D31 •	SMU	21	14

1964-1967 AAWU

1964 — 7-2-1 (1-2-1)

S19 •	Brigham Young	20	13
S26 •	Pittsburgh *PORT*	22	13
O3 •	at Penn State	22	14
O10 •	at Idaho	14	8
O17 •	Arizona	21	0
O24 •	at Washington	7	0
O31	Stanford *PORT*	8	10
N7 =	Washington State	21	21
N14 •	at Indiana	29	21
N21	at Oregon State	6	7

1965 — 4-5-1 (0-5-0)

S18 •	at Pittsburgh	17	15
S25 •	at Utah	31	14
O2	Brigham Young	27	14
O9	at Stanford	14	17
O16 =	Air Force *PORT*	18	18
O23	Washington *PORT*	20	24
O30 •	Idaho	17	14
N6	at Washington State	7	24
N13	California *PORT*	0	24
N20	Oregon State	14	19

1966 — 3-7-0 (1-3-0)

S17	at Oklahoma	0	17
S24	Utah	14	17
O1	San Jose State	7	21
O8 •	Stanford *PORT*	7	3
O15 •	at Air Force	17	6
O22	at Washington	7	10
O29 •	Idaho *BOI*	28	7
N5	Washington State	13	14
N12	at Arizona State	10	14
N19	at Oregon State	15	20

JERRY FREI
1967-71 (.434)   22-29-2

1967 — 2-8-0 (1-5-0)

S16	at California	13	21
S23	Colorado	13	17
S30	at Utah	0	21
O7	Ohio State	0	30
O14	Washington	0	26
O21 •	Idaho	31	6
O28	at Southern Cal	6	28
N4 •	at Washington State	17	13
N11	at Stanford	14	17
N18	Oregon State	10	14

1968-PRESENT PAC 10

1968 — 4-6-0 (2-4-0)

S21	at Colorado	7	28
S28	Stanford	12	28
O5	at Ohio State	6	21
O12 •	at Washington	3	0
O19 •	Idaho	23	8
O26 •	Utah	14	6
N2	Southern Cal	13	20
N9 •	Washington State	27	13
N16	at California	8	36
N23	at Oregon State	19	41

1969 — 5-5-1 (2-3-0)

S20 •	at Utah	28	17
S27	at Stanford	0	28
O4 •	at Washington State	25	24
O11	San Jose State	34	36
O18	at Air Force	13	60
O25 •	Washington	22	7
N1 •	Idaho	58	14
N8 =	Army	17	17
N15	UCLA	10	13
N22	Oregon State	7	10
N29 •	at Hawaii	57	16

1970 — 6-4-1 (4-3-0)

S12 •	California *PORT*	31	24
S19	at Illinois	16	20
S26	Stanford	10	33
O3	Washington State	28	13
O10 •	at UCLA	41	40
O17 •	Idaho	49	13
O24 •	Southern Cal	10	7
O31	at Washington	23	25
N7 •	Air Force	46	35
N14 =	at Army	22	22
N21	at Oregon State	9	24

1971 — 5-6-0 (2-4-0)

S11	at Nebraska	7	34
S18 •	Utah	36	29
S25	at Stanford	17	38
O2	at Texas	7	35
O9 •	at Southern Cal	28	23
O16 •	Washington	23	21
O23	San Jose State	34	14
O30	Washington State *SPO*	21	31
N6 •	at Air Force	23	14
N13	California	10	17
N20	Oregon State	29	30

DICK ENRIGHT
1972-73 (.273)   6-16

1972 — 4-7-0 (2-5-0)

S9	at Missouri	22	24
S16 •	Arizona	34	7
S23	at Oklahoma	3	68
S29	at UCLA	20	65
O7	at Washington	17	23
O14	Washington State	14	31
O21 •	Stanford	15	13
O28	Southern Cal	0	18
N4	at California	12	31
N11 •	San Jose State	27	2
N18 •	at Oregon State	30	3

1973 — 2-9-0 (2-5-0)

S15	Arizona State	20	26
S22	at Air Force	17	24
S29	Utah	17	35
O6	at Michigan	0	24
O13 •	California	41	10
O20	at Southern Cal	10	31
O27 •	Washington	58	0
N3	at Washington State	14	21
N10	UCLA	7	27
N17	at Stanford	7	24
N24	Oregon State	14	17

DON REID
1974-76 (.273)   9-24

1974 — 2-9-0 (0-7-0)

S14	at Nebraska	7	61
S21 •	Air Force	27	23
S28 •	at Utah	23	16
O5	at Northwestern	10	14
O12	at California	10	40
O19	Southern Cal	7	16
O26	at Washington	0	66
N2	Washington State	16	21
N9	at UCLA	0	21
N16	Stanford	0	17
N23	at Oregon State	16	35

1975 — 3-8-0 (2-5-0)

S13	at Oklahoma	7	62
S20	San Jose State	0	5
S27	at Minnesota	7	10
O4	Washington	17	27
O11	California	7	34
O18	at Southern Cal	3	17
O25 •	Utah	18	7
N1 •	at Washington State	26	14
N8	UCLA	17	50
N15	at Stanford	30	33
N22 •	Oregon State	14	7

1976 — 4-7-0 (1-6-0)

S11 •	Colorado State	17	3
S18	Southern Cal	0	53
S25 •	at Utah	21	13
O2	Utah State	27	9
O9	at California	10	27
O16	at Notre Dame	0	41
O23	at Washington	7	14
O30	Washington State	22	23
N6	at UCLA	0	46
N13	Stanford	17	28
N20 •	at Oregon State	23	14

RICH BROOKS
1977-94 (.456)   91-109-4

1977 — 2-9-0 (1-6-0)

S10	at Georgia	16	27
S17 •	at TCU	29	24
S24	Wisconsin	10	22
O1	at Stanford	10	20
O8	Washington	0	54
O15 •	at Southern Cal	15	33
O22	at LSU	17	56
O29	at Washington State	20	56
N5	UCLA	3	21
N12	California	16	48
N19 •	Oregon State	28	16

1978 — 2-9-0 (2-5-0)

S9	at Colorado	7	24
S16	Southern Cal	10	37
S23	TCU	10	14
S30	at Wisconsin	19	22
O7	at California	18	21
O14	Brigham Young	16	17
O21	at Washington	14	20
O28 •	Washington State	31	7
N4	at UCLA	21	23
N11	Arizona	3	24
N25 •	at Oregon State	24	3

1979 — 6-5-0 (4-3-0)

S8 •	at Colorado	33	19
S15	at Michigan State	17	41
S22	Washington	17	21
S29	at Purdue	7	13
O6 •	California	19	14
O13	at Arizona	13	24
O20	Air Force	17	9
O27 •	at Washington State	37	26
N10 •	at UCLA	16	7
N17	UCLA	0	35
N29 •	Oregon State	24	3

1980 — 6-3-2 (4-3-1)

S6	Stanford	25	35
S13 •	Kansas	7	7
S20 •	Michigan State	35	7
S27 •	at Washington	34	10
O11	at California	6	31
O18 =	Southern Cal	7	7
O25 •	Nevada-Las Vegas	32	9
N1 •	Washington State	20	10
N8 •	at UCLA	20	14
N15 •	at Oregon State	40	21
N22 •	at Arizona State	37	42

1981 — 2-9-0 (1-6-0)

S5	at Fresno State	16	23
S12	at Kansas	10	19
S19 •	Pacific	34	0
S26 •	Washington	3	17
O10	at Arizona State	0	24
O17	Arizona	14	18
O24	Air Force	10	20
O31 •	UCLA	11	28
N7	at Washington State	7	39
N14	at Stanford	3	42
N21 •	Oregon State	47	17

1982 — 2-8-1 (2-6-0)

S4	Arizona State	3	34
S11	San Jose State	13	18
S18	Fresno State	4	10
S25	at Washington	21	37
O2	at Southern Cal	7	38
O16	at California	7	10
O23 =	Notre Dame	13	13
O30	at UCLA	12	40
N6	Washington State	3	10
N20 •	Arizona	13	7
N27 •	at Oregon State	7	6

1983 — 4-6-1 (3-3-1)

S3	Pacific	15	21
S10	at Ohio State	6	31
S24 •	Houston	15	14
O1	at San Jose State	34	44
O8 •	California	24	17
O15 •	at Arizona	19	10
O22	Washington	3	32
O29	at Washington State	7	24
N5	UCLA	13	24
N12 •	at Stanford	16	7
N19 =	Oregon State	0	0

1984 — 6-5-0 (3-5-0)

S8 •	Long Beach State	28	17
S15 •	Colorado	27	20
S22 •	at California	21	14
S29 •	Pacific	30	14
O6	at Arizona	14	28
O13 •	Southern Cal	9	19
O20 •	at Washington	10	17
O27 •	Washington State	41	50
N3 •	at UCLA	20	18
N10 •	Arizona State	10	44
N17 •	at Oregon State	31	6

1985   5-6-0 (3-4-0)

A31	●	at Washington State	42 39
S14		at Colorado	17 21
S21	●	Stanford	45 28
S28		at Nebraska	0 63
O5		Washington	13 19
O19		California	24 27
O26	●	at San Diego State	49 37
N2	●	San Jose State	35 13
N16		at Arizona	8 20
N23	●	Oregon State	34 13
N30		Southern Cal *Tok*	6 20

1986   5-6-0 (3-5-0)

S6	●	at San Jose State	21 14
S13	●	Colorado	32 30
S20		Arizona	17 41
S27		at Nebraska	14 48
O4		at Southern Cal	21 35
O11		Arizona State	17 37
O18		Stanford	7 41
O25		at Washington	3 38
N1	●	at California	27 9
N15		Washington State	27 17
N22		at Oregon State	49 28

1987   6-5-0 (4-4-0)

S12	●	at Colorado	10 7
S19		at Ohio State	14 24
S26	●	San Diego State	25 20
O3		Washington	29 22
O10		Southern Cal	34 27
O17		at UCLA	10 41
O24		at Stanford	10 13
O31		California	6 20
N7		at Arizona State	17 37
N14		at Washington State	31 17
N21		Oregon State	44 0

1988   6-6-0 (3-5-0)

S10	●	Long Beach State	49 0
S17	●	at Washington State	43 28
S24		Stanford	7 3
O1		at San Diego State	34 13
O8		at Southern Cal	14 42
O15	●	Idaho	52 7
O22	●	Washington	17 14
O29		Arizona State	20 21
N5		UCLA	6 16
N12		at Arizona	27 41
N19		at Oregon State	10 21
D3		at Hawaii	17 41

1989   8-4-0 (5-3-0)

S9		California	35 19
S16		at Iowa	44 6
S23		at Stanford	17 18
S30	●	Arizona	16 10
O7		Washington State	38 51
O14		at Washington	14 20
O21	●	at Arizona State	27 7
O28	●	Long Beach State	52 10
N4		at Brigham Young	41 45
N11	●	at UCLA	38 20
N18	●	Oregon State	30 21
		INDEPENDENCE BOWL	
D16	●	Tulsa	27 24

1990   8-4-0 (4-3-0)

S8	●	San Diego State	42 21
S15	●	Idaho	55 23
S22		at Arizona	17 22
S29	●	Brigham Young	32 16
O6		Utah State	52 7
O13		at Washington	17 38
O20	●	Arizona State	27 7
O27		Stanford	31 0
N3	●	UCLA	28 24
N10		at California	3 28
N17	●	at Oregon State	6 3
		FREEDOM BOWL	
D29		Colorado State	31 32

1991   3-8-0 (1-7-0)

S7	●	Washington State	40 14
S14	●	at Texas Tech	28 13
S21		at Utah	17 24
S28		Southern Cal	14 30
O5	●	New Mexico State	29 6
O12		at California	7 45
O26		at Washington	7 29
N2		Stanford	13 33
N9		at Arizona State	21 24
N16		at UCLA	7 16
N23		Oregon State	3 14

1992   6-6-0 (4-4-0)

S5	●	Hawaii	21 24
S12		at Stanford	7 21
S19	●	Texas Tech	16 13
S26	●	Nevada-Las Vegas	59 6
O3	●	Arizona State	30 20
O10		at Southern Cal	10 32
O17		Washington	3 24
O31	●	at Washington State	34 17
N7	●	California	37 17
N14		UCLA	6 9
N21	●	at Oregon State	7 0
		INDEPENDENCE BOWL	
D31		Wake Forest	35 39

1993   5-6-0 (2-6-0)

S4	●	at Colorado State	23 9
S11	●	Montana	35 30
S25	●	at Illinois	13 7
O2		at California	41 42
O9		Southern Cal	13 24
O16	●	at Arizona State	45 36
O23		at Washington	6 21
O30	●	Washington State	46 23
N6		at Arizona	10 31
N13		Stanford	34 38
N20		Oregon State	12 15

1994   9-4-0 (7-1-0)

S3	●	Portland State	58 16
S10	●	at Hawaii	16 36
S17	●	Utah	16 34
S24	●	Iowa	40 18
O1		at Southern Cal	22 7
O8		at Washington State	7 21
O15	●	California	23 7
O22	●	Washington	31 20
O29		Arizona	10 9
N5		Arizona State	34 10
N12		at Stanford	55 21
N19	●	at Oregon State	17 13
		ROSE BOWL	
J2		Penn State	20 38

MIKE BELLOTTI
1995-PRESENT (.667)   80-40

1995   9-3-0 (6-2-0)

S2	●	at Utah	27 20
S9	●	Illinois	34 31
S16	●	at UCLA	38 31
S23		Stanford	21 28
O7		Pacific	45 7
O14	●	at California	52 30
O21	●	Washington State	26 7
O28		Arizona State	24 35
N4	●	at Washington	24 22
N11		at Arizona	17 13
N18	●	Oregon State	12 10
		COTTON BOWL	
J1		Colorado	6 38

1996   6-5 (3-5)

A31	●	at Fresno State	30 27
S7	●	Nevada	44 30
S14	●	Colorado State	35 28
S21		at Washington State	44 55
S28		at Arizona State	27 48
O5		UCLA	22 41
O12		at Stanford	24 27
O26		Washington	14 33
N9	●	Arizona	49 31
N16	●	California	40 23
N23	●	at Oregon State	49 13

1997   7-5 (3-5)

S4		Arizona	16 9
S13	●	at Nevada	24 20
S20	●	Fresno State	43 40
S27	●	at Stanford	49 58
O4		Washington State	13 24
O11		UCLA	31 39
O18		Utah	31 13
O25		at Southern Cal	22 24
N8	●	at Washington	31 28
N15		at Arizona State	31 52
N22	●	Oregon State	48 30
		LAS VEGAS BOWL	
D20	●	Air Force	41 13

1998   8-4 (5-3)

S5	●	Michigan State	48 14
S12	●	at Texas El Paso	33 26
S19	●	San Jose State	58 3
S26		Stanford	63 28
O10	●	at Washington State	51 29
O17		at UCLA	38 41
O24		Southern Cal	17 13
O31		at Arizona	3 38
N7	●	Washington	27 22
N14	●	Arizona State	51 19
N21		at Oregon State	41 44
		ALOHA BOWL	
D25		Colorado	43 51

1999   9-3 (6-2)

S2		at Michigan State	20 27
S11	●	Texas El Paso	47 28
S18	●	Nevada	72 10
S25		Southern Cal	33 30
O2		at Washington	20 34
O9		at UCLA	29 34
O23	●	at Arizona	44 41
O30	●	Arizona State	20 17
N6	●	Washington State	52 10
N13		at California	24 19
N20	●	Oregon State	25 14
		SUN BOWL	
D31	●	Minnesota	24 20

2000   10-2 (7-1)

S2	●	Nevada	36 7
S9		at Wisconsin	23 27
S16	●	Idaho	42 13
S23	●	UCLA	29 10
S30		Washington	23 16
O14		at Southern Cal	28 17
O21		Arizona	14 10
O28		at Arizona State	56 55
N4	●	at Washington State	27 24
N11	●	California	25 17
N18	●	at Oregon State	13 23
		HOLIDAY BOWL	
D29	●	Texas	35 30

2001   11-1 (7-1)

S1	●	Wisconsin	31 28
S8	●	Utah	24 10
S22	●	Southern Cal	24 22
S29	●	at Utah State	38 21
O6		at Arizona	63 28
O13	●	at California	48 7
O20		Stanford	42 49
O27	●	at Washington State	24 17
N3		Arizona State	42 24
N10	●	at UCLA	21 20
D1		Oregon State	17 14
		FIESTA BOWL	
J1	●	Colorado	38 16

2002   7-6 (3-5)

A31	●	Mississippi State	36 13
S7	●	Fresno State	28 24
S14	●	Idaho	58 21
S21	●	Portland State	41 0
O5		at Arizona	31 14
O12		at UCLA	31 30
O19		Arizona State	42 45
O26		Southern Cal	33 44
N2	●	Stanford	41 14
N9		at Washington State	21 32
N16		Washington	14 42
N23		at Oregon State	24 45
		SEATTLE BOWL	
D30		Wake Forest	17 38

2003   8-5 (5-3)

A30	●	at Mississippi State	42 34
S6	●	Nevada	31 23
S13	●	at Arizona	48 10
S20	●	Michigan	31 27
S27		Washington State	16 55
O3		at Utah	13 17
O11		at Arizona State	14 59
O25	●	Stanford	35 0
N1		at Washington	10 42
N8	●	California	21 17
N15	●	at UCLA	31 13
N22	●	Oregon State	34 20
		SUN BOWL	
D31		Minnesota	30 31

2004   5-6 (4-4)

S11		Indiana	24 30
S18		at Oklahoma	7 31
S25	●	Idaho	48 10
O2		Arizona State	13 28
O9	●	at Washington State	41 38
O16		Arizona	28 14
O23	●	at Stanford	16 13
O30	●	Washington	31 6
N6		at California	27 28
N13		UCLA	26 34
N20		at Oregon State	21 50

OREGON STATE

BY BUD WITHERS

IN THE LAST QUARTER OF THE 20TH century, Oregon State became a venue where the experience of the game was about all the Beavers could offer their fans, who suffered almost relentlessly. But that began to change with the hiring of Mike Riley and then Dennis Erickson as successive head coaches. Both were subsequently lost to the NFL, but during their tenures—particularly Erickson's four years as coach—the Beavers became known for a brash, penalty-laced, in-your-face style. Riley and Erickson changed the program's persona, and OSU became a player both competitively and in the facilities race, giving the Beavers their first real whiff of euphoria since the days of Tommy Prothro and Dee Andros in the 1950s and 1960s.

TRADITION Jerry Pettibone's attempt at generating a tradition during his coaching regime (1991-96) only served to magnify OSU's futility. Pettibone had a bronze beaver installed at the top of a ramp leading to the playing field, and players would rub it for good luck on their way to battle. But when Pettibone exited—with a 13–52–1 record—the beaver was removed as well. In 2002, a Beavers baseball player brought the critter out of storage and stuck it in the OSU dugout for good luck.

BEST PLAYER Terry Baker holds the distinction of winning a Heisman Trophy and playing on a Final Four basketball team in the same 1962-63 school year. In the 1962 Liberty Bowl against Villanova, on a 25° day with snow on the ground, Baker raced 99 yards early in the first quarter for the only points in a 6-0 OSU victory. That season, Beavers sports information director John Eggers unwittingly ushered in an era of extravagant promotion of honors candidates by merely mailing weekly statistics to voters, who made Baker the first Heisman winner from the West.

BEST COACH Tommy Prothro was an expert chess player, a master's-level bridge player and a football coach always looking for an edge. From 1955 to 1964, he led OSU to a record of 63–37–2 and their last two Rose Bowl appearances. When he moved on to UCLA in 1965, he devised a system of communication—soon outlawed—by which a coach in the press box would watch video replays and relay information to the quarterback via radio headset.

BEST TEAM There was little to suggest imminent superlatives for the 2000 Beavers. The quarterback,

---

PROFILE

Oregon State University
Corvallis, Ore.
Founded: 1868
Enrollment: 15,713
Colors: Orange and Black
Nickname: Beavers
Stadium: Reser Stadium
Opened in 1953
FieldTurf; 35,362 capacity
First football game: 1893
All-time record: 454–508–50 (.473)
Bowl record: 6–4
Pac-10 Conference championships:
5 (2 outright)
Heisman Trophy winners: Terry Baker, 1962
First-round NFL draftees: 5
Website: www.osubeavers.com

THE BEST OF TIMES

From 1955 through 1970 under Tommy Prothro and Dee Andros, OSU went 101–59–3, had a single losing season and went to two Rose Bowls.

THE WORST OF TIMES

Beginning in 1971 and lasting through 1998, Oregon State had losing records an NCAA-record 28 straight seasons, going a combined 65–239–6. The deepest abyss was Joe Avezzano's 1980-84 tenure, during which OSU was 6–47–2.

CONFERENCE

OSU became a charter member of the Pacific Coast Conference—the forerunner to the Pac-10—when it was founded in 1916, though the Beavers played as an independent from 1959 to 1963.

DISTINGUISHED ALUMNI

M. Lowell Edwards, co-inventor of the artificial heart valve, inventor of Lande-Edwards artificial lung; Dick Fosbury, Olympic gold medalist in high jump, pioneer of the Fosbury Flop; Linus Pauling, chemist, two-time Nobel Prize winner

FIGHT SONG

HAIL TO OSU
OSU our hats are off to you
Beavers, Beavers fighters thru and thru
We'll cheer for every man
We'll root for every plan
That's made for OSU

Watch our team goes tearin' down the field
Men of iron, our strength will never yield
Hail, hail, hail, hail,
Hail to old OSU

Riley and Erickson gave OSU its first real whiff of euphoria since the 1960s.

Jonathan Smith, was a 5'10" walk-on. The tailback, Ken Simonton, was a 5'8" reject of most recruiting coordinators, but he was a runner of such instinct that he finished his career ranked No. 2 in Pac-10 career rushing with 5,044 yards. The offense also had All-America center Chris Gibson and gifted receivers, particularly NFL second-round draft choice Chad Johnson. LaDairis Jackson and DeLawrence Grant, a quick pair of truculent ends, headed the defense. OSU shrugged off its only loss of the season, a 33-30 thriller at Washington in early October, improved steadily and climaxed an 11–1 season with a 41-9 lacing of 10th-ranked Notre Dame in the Fiesta Bowl to earn a No. 4 ranking, its highest ever.

BIGGEST GAME In 1967, OSU beat second-ranked Purdue on the road and then tied No. 2-ranked UCLA in Los Angeles. The team known as the Giant Killers then hosted top-rated USC on a muddy field in Corvallis and edged the Trojans 3-0 on a 30-yard field goal in the second quarter by Mike Haggard. USC's O.J. Simpson ran for 188 yards on 33 carries as the elements rendered passing attacks irrelevant. USC's Steve Sogge had four completions in 10 attempts for six yards, while OSU's Steve Preece—later an NFL safety—hit a single completion in four tries

for just eight yards. As usual when Andros' teams prevailed, the fullback was the key; Bill "Earthquake" Enyart rushed 24 times for 135 yards. OSU finished 7–2–1.

BIGGEST UPSET Almost nobody, including Las Vegas oddsmakers, gave the Beavers much chance against a 4–2 Washington team in 1985. But when they arrived in Seattle the day before the Oct. 19 game, the 37-point underdog Beavers were greeted by the mocking words of a Seattle columnist, who wrote that they "play football like Barney Fife plays deputy." An inspired OSU team hung in the game until the waning moments, when cornerback Andre Todd blocked a Washington punt and Lavance Northington fell on it in the end zone for the tying touchdown. The extra point gave OSU a 21-20 victory, one of just three that year.

HEARTBREAKER In its 2004 season opener, the Beavers ventured to Louisiana State, which had claimed the BCS national title the previous year. An expected blowout was delayed by a thunderstorm that made footing treacherous and offense sporadic. The Beavers actually had a 15-7 lead in the fourth quarter, and it was that close only because of blown extra points by

RECORDS		
RUSHING YARDS		
	GAME	
299	Bill Enyart vs. Utah, Sept. 28, 1968 (50 att.)	
	SEASON	
1,690	Steven Jackson, 2002 (319 att.)	
	CAREER	
5,044	Ken Simonton, 1998-2001 (1,041 att.)	
PASSING YARDS		
	GAME	
485	Derek Anderson vs. USC, Dec. 6, 2003 (34 of 60)	
	SEASON	
4,058	Derek Anderson, 2003 (261 of 510)	
	CAREER	
11,249	Derek Anderson, 2001-04 (768 of 1,515)	

RECEIVING YARDS		
	GAME	
293	Mike Hass vs. Boise State, Sept. 10, 2004 (12 rec.)	
	SEASON	
1,379	Mike Hass, 2004 (86 rec.)	
	CAREER	
3,572	James Newson, 2000-03 (213 rec.)	
POINTS		
	GAME	
24	Five players; most recently by Ken Simonton vs. Georgia Southern, Sept. 18, 1999 (4 TDs)	
	SEASON	
118	Ken Simonton, 1999 (19 TDs, 2 two-pt. conv.)	
	CAREER	
366	Ken Simonton, 1998-2001 (60 TDs, 3 two-pt. conv.)	

CONSENSUS ALL-AMERICANS		
1956	John Witte, T	
1958	Ted Bates, T	
1962	Terry Baker, QB	
1963	Vern Burke, SE	
1968	John Didion, C	

placekicker Alexis Serna. The Tigers sent the game to overtime with a late touchdown and two-point conversion, and survived 22-21 when the extra period ended abruptly with Serna's third missed conversion.

BEST COMEBACK Highlights of the Joe Avezzano coaching regime were sparse—his teams went 6–47–2 in five years—but the Beavers generated an improbable one on Sept. 12, 1981. After they fell behind 28-0 to visiting Fresno State early in the third quarter, the turnaround began with an 80-yard scoring drive. With 5:54 to play, OSU tied it at 28 on a short pass from Ed Singler to Victor Simmons, and after an interception by monster back Tony Fuller at the FSU 36, Chris Mangold kicked the winning 36-yard field goal with 1:57 remaining.

STADIUM Built in 1953, it was first called Parker Stadium and seated 28,000. It became known as Reser Stadium in 1999 when food magnate Al Reser pledged $10 million, and he ensured in 2002 that the facility will bear his family name through 2038 by pledging another $12.5 million. Another expansion began in 2004.

RIVAL Nothing makes a Beaver's blood boil like Oregon, partly because the schools, which began playing each other in 1894, are only 37 miles apart. Newspaper articles before their 1929 game began referring to the rivalry as the Civil War. During OSU's long spell of ineptitude in the last decades of the 1900s, Oregon was often toothless as well, seemingly adding to the importance of the internecine competition. The Ducks' resurgence in the 1990s, however, helped prod OSU to upgrade its football program. Since the university offers strong courses in agriculture, forestry and engineering, it draws barbs from Oregon as the "hick" school, while the Ducks' liberal arts

bent—and campus unrest during the turbulent 1960s—earns them a "hippie" label.

DUBIOUS DISTINCTION Beginning in 1971, OSU strung together 28 consecutive losing seasons, an NCAA record. The bleak years included a series of questionable coaching hires, until OSU was able to attract Oregon native Riley from the USC staff. During one year of the Pettibone regime, the Beavers posted a 95% graduation rate—tops in the NCAA—but that didn't soothe their long-suffering supporters. Said Bert Babb, a prominent donor, "I'd trade a few of those points for a few more football victories."

NICKNAME In its earliest years, OSU was known as the Aggies. When orange uniforms replaced a dingy gray-and-tan ensemble, the Beavers became the Orangemen. In 1916, the school yearbook was named *The Beaver*, which is the state animal, and that moniker became associated with the school.

MASCOT Benny the Beaver, a student in a six-foot costume, has served as the OSU mascot since 1952. Before that, the school had at least three mascots, including a coyote.

UNIFORMS Orange has been the official, and predominant, color since the earliest days of OSU football, though Prothro helped popularize the use of all-black uniforms during his 10 years at the school. The helmet has evolved from orange to white to black. The logo is a beaver likeness over the script "Beavers."

QUOTE "I'm tired of playing these No. 2 teams. Bring on No. 1!"—OSU coach Dee Andros, looking forward in 1967 to top-ranked USC after beating second-ranked Purdue and tying No. 2 UCLA on the road

OREGON STATE ANNUAL STATISTICAL LEADERS

YR	RUSHING	YDS	ATT	AVG	PASSING	ATT	CMP	PCT	YDS	RECEIVING	REC	YDS	AVG
1952	Sam Baker	517	160	3.2	James Withrow	92	41	.45	601	Jack Gotta	29	351	12.1
1953	Ralph Carr	352	116	3.0	James Withrow	97	43	.44	504	Wes Ediger	16	186	11.6
1954	Dick Mason	283	67	4.2	James Withrow	94	37	.39	432	Leon Hittner	22	222	10.1
1955	Tom Berry	378	71	5.3	Joe Francis	42	20	.48	337	Sam Wesley	11	235	21.4
1956	Don Durden	508	71	7.2	Joe Francis	48	27	.56	377	Bob DeGrant	10	105	10.5
1957	Nub Beamer	760	172	4.4	Joe Francis	54	32	.59	456	Bob DeGrant	19	239	12.6
1958	Nub Beamer	434	108	4.0	Dainard Paulson	27	10	.37	146	Aaron Thomas	9	172	19.1
1959	Don Kasso	345	94	3.7	Sonny Sanchez	45	19	.42	305	Aaron Thomas	11	150	13.6
1960		NA	NA	NA		NA	NA	NA	NA		NA	NA	NA
1961	Leroy Whittle	364	81	4.5	Terry Baker	134	61	.46	875	Don Kasso	20	258	12.9
1962	Terry Baker	538	115	4.7	Terry Baker	203	112	.55	1,738	Vern Burke	69	1,007	14.6
1963	Charlie Shaw	459	75	6.1	Gordon Queen	183	84	.46	1,281	Vern Burke	48	792	16.5
1964	Paul Brothers	451	151	3.0	Paul Brothers	144	75	.52	1,036	Olvin Moreland	35	428	12.2
1965	Pete Pifer	1,095	234	4.7	Paul Brothers	121	45	.37	416	Fred Schweer Sr.	15	127	8.5
1966	Pete Pifer	1,088	230	4.7	Paul Brothers	122	55	.45	610	Bob Grim	25	289	11.6
1967	Bill Enyart	851	201	4.2	Steve Preece	129	47	.36	737	Roger Cantlon	14	214	15.3
1968	Bill Enyart	1,304	293	4.5	Steve Preece	126	55	.44	881	Roger Cantlon	23	409	17.8
1969	Dave Schilling	635	173	3.7	Steve Endicott	190	93	.49	1,251	Billy Main	21	282	13.4
1970	Dave Schilling	1,084	254	4.3	Jim Kilmartin	90	39	.43	463	Jeff Kolberg	39	534	13.7
1971	Dave Schilling	833	214	3.9	Steve Endicott	203	105	.52	1,334	Jeff Kolberg	35	525	15.0
1972	Mike Davenport	538	120	4.5	Scott Spiegelberg	56	22	.39	278	Rod Petersen	17	232	13.6
1973	Dick Maurer	393	95	4.1	Alvin White	301	130	.43	1,437	Dick Maurer	33	326	9.9
1974	Elvin Momon	479	120	4.0	Alvin White	256	120	.47	1,662	Dave Brown	26	383	14.7
1975	Rich Dodge	558	126	4.4	Kyle Grossart	185	89	.48	969	Phil Wroblicky	27	370	13.7
1976	James Fields	649	163	4.0	Dave White	100	47	.47	552	Lee Overton	30	382	12.7
1977	James Fields	740	191	3.9	John Norman	200	90	.45	929	Steve Coury	36	458	12.7
1978	Willie Johnson	324	100	3.2	Steve Smith	196	96	.49	1,182	Steve Coury	31	502	16.2
1979	Tony Robinson	525	143	3.7	Scott Richardson	291	145	.50	1,645	Steve Coury	66	842	12.8
1980	Tony Robinson	882	213	4.1	Ed Singler	180	106	.59	1,166	Tony Robinson	38	291	7.7
1981	Randy Holmes	637	148	4.3	Ed Singler	220	118	.54	1,500	Victor Simmons	43	703	16.3
1982	Bryce Oglesby	676	126	5.4	Jeff Seay	147	69	.47	888	Ron Vogel	27	280	10.4
1983	Bryce Oglesby	878	171	5.1	Ladd McKittrick	191	74	.39	1,106	Reggie Bynum	24	580	24.2
1984	Donald Beavers	392	99	4.0	Ricky Greene	140	69	.49	927	Reggie Bynum	51	711	13.9
1985	Darvin Malone	554	134	4.1	Rich Gonzales	181	94	.52	986	Reggie Bynum	61	703	11.5
1986	Pat Chaffey	232	47	4.9	Erik Wilhelm	470	283	.60	2,871	Dave Montagne	78	862	11.1
1987	Brian Taylor	411	97	4.2	Erik Wilhelm	423	226	.53	2,736	Robb Thomas	58	891	15.4
1988	Pat Chaffey	475	113	4.2	Erik Wilhelm	442	275	.62	2,896	Robb Thomas	58	763	13.2
1989	Pat Chaffey	714	205	3.5	Nick Schichtle	187	93	.50	1,378	Pat Chaffey	46	457	9.9
1990	Dwayne Owens	364	87	4.2	Matt Booher	183	100	.55	892	Maurice Wilson	41	425	10.4
1991	Chad Paulson	490	79	6.2	Ed Browning	43	13	.30	171	Maurice Wilson	10	155	15.5
1992	Mark Olford	525	167	3.1	Mark Olford	64	22	.34	331	Kenyan Branscomb	11	174	15.8
1993	J.J. Young	955	136	7.0	Rahim Muhammad	29	7	.24	124	Chris Cross	8	92	11.5
1994	J.J. Young	891	148	6.0	Don Shanklin	73	29	.40	560	Cameron Reynolds	10	231	23.1
1995	Tim Alexander	439	109	4.0	Tim Alexander	76	25	.33	400	Cameron Reynolds	13	219	16.8
1996	Akili King	740	182	4.1	Tim Alexander	94	34	.36	328	DeShawn Williams	18	173	9.6
1997	Tim Alexander	288	127	2.3	Tim Alexander	327	157	.48	1,745	Greg Ainsworth	49	600	12.2
1998	Ken Simonton	1,028	224	4.6	Terrance Bryant	272	136	.50	1,362	Greg Ainsworth	58	749	12.9
1999	Ken Simonton	1,486	294	5.1	Jonathan Smith	425	207	.49	3,053	Imani Percoats	51	816	16.0
2000	Ken Simonton	1,559	284	5.5	Jonathan Smith	338	170	.50	2,773	T.J. Houshmandzadeh	48	730	15.2
2001	Ken Simonton	971	239	4.1	Jonathan Smith	317	180	.57	2,427	James Newson	57	968	17.0
2002	Steven Jackson	1,690	319	5.3	Derek Anderson	449	211	.47	3,313	James Newson	74	1,284	17.4
2003	Steven Jackson	1,545	350	4.4	Derek Anderson	510	261	.51	4,058	James Newson	81	1,306	16.1
2004	Dwight Wright	784	209	3.8	Derek Anderson	515	279	.54	3,615	Mike Hass	86	1,379	16.0

Receiving leaders by receptions
All statistics include postseason

THE SCHOOLS

OREGON STATE ALL-TIME SCORES

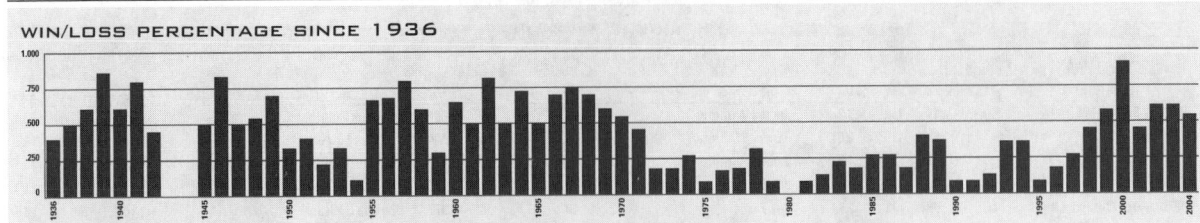

WIN/LOSS PERCENTAGE SINCE 1936

BILL BLOSS
1893, '97 (.857)   6-1

1893   4-1-0
U	● Albany Coll.	62	0
U	● at Monmouth Coll.	36	22
U	● Monmouth Coll.	28	0
U	● Multnomah AC	6	0
U	Portland	12	26

GUY KENNEDY
1894 (.667)   2-1

1894   2-1-0
U	● Oregon	16	0
U	Portland	0	22
U	● at Monmouth Club	36	6

PAUL DOWNING
1895 (.167)   0-2-1

1895   0-2-1
U	= Forest Grove	0	0
U	at Willamette	6	36
U	Oregon	0	46 *

TOMMY CODE
1896 (.333)   1-2

1896   1-2-0
U	● Fort Vancouver	18	0
U	at Oregon	0	2
U	Oregon	8	12 *

BILL BLOSS

1897   2-0-0
U	● at Oregon	26	8 *
D4	● Washington	16	0

NO HEAD COACH

1898   1-2-1
U	● Albany College	25	6
U	= Forest Grove	5	5
U	Chemawa Ind.	6	29
U	Oregon	0	38

HIGHLAND STICKNEY
1899 (.600)   3-2

1899   3-2-0
U	● Willamette	10	0
U	● Albany Coll.	47	0
U	Multnomah AC	0	5
N30	at Oregon	0	38
U	● Chemawa	18	17

1900-1901
NO TEAM

FRANK HERBOLD
1902 (.750)   4-1-1

1902   4-1-1
U	● Willamette	67	0
O25	at Washington	6	16 *
N8	● Oregon	0	0
U	● at Willamette	21	0
U	● Mc Minnville	33	0
U	● Pacific	31	0

McFADDEN
1903 (.357)   2-4-1

1903   2-4-1
U	Washington	0	5
U	Multnomah AC *Port*	0	16
U	at Albany Coll.	0	6
U	= Pacific	0	0
N11	● Washington State	6	0
N21	at Oregon	0	5
N26	● Nevada	15	0

ALLEN STECKLE
1904-05 (.667)   10-5

1904   4-2-0
U	● Alumni	11	0
U	● Portland Medics	22	0
O15	● at Washington	26	5
U	● Utah State	45	0
N19	● Oregon	5	6
U	Multnomah AC *Port*	10	11

1905   6-3-0
U	● Alumni	10	6
U	● Chemawa	18	0
U	● Whitman	58	0
O21	● Washington State	29	0
O28	at California	0	10
N11	● Oregon	0	6
U	● Willamette *SAL*	28	0
N30	● Washington	16	0 *
U	Multnomah AC *Port*	5	6

F.S. NORCROSS
1906-08 (.738)   14-4-3

1906   4-1-2
U	● Albany AC	24	0
U	● Alumni	16	0
O27	= at Washington	0	0
U	● Pacific	28	0
U	● Columbia AC	9	0
N24	● Oregon	0	0
U	at Willamette	0	4

1907   6-0-0
U	● Astoria AC	26	0
U	● Whitman	6	0
U	● Pacific	49	0
N9	● at Oregon	4	0
U	● Willamette	42	0
U	● at State Vincent Coll.	10	0

1908   4-3-1
U	= Alumni	0	0
U	● Puget Sound	26	0
U	● Columbia AC	10	0
U	● Willamette	28	0
U	● Whitman	9	0
N21	Oregon *Port*	0	8
N28	at Washington	0	32
U	Multnomah AC *Port*	10	11

SOL S. METZGER
1909 (.643)   4-2-1

1909   4-2-1
U	● Alumni	0	0
U	● Pacific	21	0
U	● Catholic YMCA	12	0
U	● at Whitman	10	0
N13	Washington	0	21
N19	at Oregon	0	12
U	● Multnomah AC *Port*	11	8

GEORGE SCHILDMILLER
1910 (.583)   3-2-1

1910   3-2-1
U	= Alumni	0	0
U	● at Willamette	9	6
O29	● Washington State *Port*	9	3
U	● Whitman	9	0
N12	Oregon	0	12
N24	at Washington	0	22

SAM DOLAN
1911-12 (.571)   8-6

1911   5-2-0
U	Alumni	2	3
U	● Pacific	26	0
U	● Chemawa	75	6
N4	at Washington	0	34
N11	● Washington State	6	0
U	● Willamette	5	3
U	● at Whitman	5	3

1912   3-4-0
U	● Alumni	2	0
U	Multnomah AC *Port*	0	9
N1	at Washington State	9	10
N9	Washington *Port*	3	9
U	● Whitman	20	3
N23	Oregon *ALB*	0	3
U	● at Occidental	23	6

E.J. STEWART
1913-15 (.700)   15-5-5

1913   3-2-3
U	= Alumni	0	0
U	Multnomah AC *Port*	0	6
U	= Multnomah AC	7	7
U	● at Whitman	29	3
O25	at Washington	0	47
N8	● Oregon *ALB*	10	10
N15	● Washington State	10	2
U	● Idaho	3	0

1914   7-0-2
U	● Alumni	12	0
U	● Rooks	12	0
U	● at Multnomah AC	10	6
U	● Willamette	64	0
O24	● at Washington State	7	0
O31	● Washington *ALB*	0	0
U	● Idaho *Port*	26	0
N21	= Oregon	3	3
N26	● Southern Cal *TAC*	38	6

1915   5-3-0
U	● Alumni	3	0
O2	● Willamette	69	0
U	● Whitman	34	7
O16	● Washington State	0	29
O30	● at Michigan State	20	0
U	● Idaho	40	0
N20	at Oregon	0	9
D1	Syracuse *Port*	0	28

1916-1958
PACIFIC COAST

JOSEPH PIPALL
1916-17 (.531)   8-7-1

1916   4-5-0 (0-2-0)
S23	Alumni	7	13
S30	Multnomah AC	0	3
O7	● at Idaho	26	0
O14	● at Washington State	13	10
O21	Nebraska *Port*	7	17
N4	● Whitman	23	0
N11	at Washington	0	35
N25	Oregon	0	27
N30	● at Southern Cal	16	7

1917   4-2-1 (1-2-1)
O13	● Vancouver Barracks	34	0
O20	● Idaho *Pen*	26	6
O27	● at California	3	14
N3	● Multnomah AC	6	0
N10	Washington State	0	6
N17	= at Washington	0	0
N29	● Oregon *Port*	14	7

W.H. HARGISS
1918-19 (.433)   6-8-1

1918   2-4-0 (0-2-0)
O26	● at Vancouver Barracks	7	0
N2	Camp Lewis	6	21
N9	● Stand. Ship Builders	14	0
N16	Oregon	6	13
N23	at Washington	0	6
N28	Multnomah AC *Port*	0	6

1919   4-4-1 (1-3-0)
O4	= Alumni	0	0
O11	● Rooks	21	0
O18	● Pacific	46	6
O25	● Stanford	6	14
N1	at California	14	21
N8	Multnomah AC	0	14
N15	at Oregon	0	9
N22	● Washington State *Port*	6	0
N27	● Gonzaga		500

R.B. RUTHERFORD
1920-23 (.485)   13-14-6

1920   2-2-2 (1-2-1)
O16	= Multnomah AC	0	0
O23	● at Washington	3	0
O30	California	7	17
N13	at Washington State	0	28
N20	= Oregon	0	0
N27	● Multnomah AC *Port*	10	7

1921   4-3-2 (1-2-1)
S24	● Rooks	68	7
O1	● Chemawa	68	0
O8	= Multnomah AC	7	7
O15	● at Willamette	54	0
O22	● Washington	24	0
O29	at Stanford	7	14
N12	Washington State	3	7
N19	= at Oregon	0	0
N26	Southern Cal *PAS*	0	7

1922   3-4-0 (1-3-0)
O7	● Alumni	22	6
O14	● Pacific	3	0
O21	at Washington	3	14
O28	Stanford	0	6
N4	Multnomah AC *Port*	0	6
N18	Oregon	0	10
N25	● Washington State *Port*	16	0

1923   4-5-2 (1-3-1)
S29	Pacific	12	0
O6	= Multnomah AC	0	0
O13	● Alumni	13	0
O20	at California	0	26
N3	Washington	0	14
N10	at Idaho	0	0
N17	= Washington State *Tac*	3	3
N25	● at Oregon	6	0
D1	Multnomah AC *Port*	12	0
D25	at Hawaii All Stars	9	14
J1	at Hawaii	0	7

PAUL SCHISSLER
1924-32 (.613) 48-30-2

1924 3-5-0 (1-4-0)

O4	●	Whitman PEN	41	0
O11	●	Multnomah AC	7	6
O18	|	Southern Cal PORT	3	17
O25	|	at Washington	3	6
N1	|	Idaho	0	22
N8	● |	Washington State PORT	14	13
N22	|	Oregon	3	7
N27		at Nebraska	0	14

1925 7-2-0 (3-2-0)

O3	●	Willamette	51	0
O10	●	Gonzaga	22	0
O17	●	Whitman PORT	62	0
O24	|	at Stanford	10	26
O31	● |	Montana	27	7
N7	●	Pacific	56	0
N14	● |	at Oregon	24	13
N21	● |	Idaho BOI	16	7
D5	|	at Southern Cal	0	28

1926 7-1-0 (4-1-0)

S25	●	Multnomah AC	67	0
O2	● |	at Montana	49	0
O8	●	Gonzaga	23	6
O16	● |	at California	27	7
O30	● |	Idaho PORT	3	0
N11	|	Southern Cal PORT	7	17
N20	● |	Oregon	16	0
N26	●	at Marquette	29	0

1927 3-3-1 (2-3-0)

O1	●	Cal State	25	6
O8	|	at Southern Cal	12	13
O22	|	Stanford PORT	6	20
O29	● |	Washington State	13	6
N12	● |	at Oregon	21	7
N19	|	Idaho PORT	7	12
N26	=	Carnegie Tech PORT	14	14

1928 6-3-0 (2-3-0)

S29	●	Cal State	14	0
O6	|	at Southern Cal	0	19
O13	●	Portland PORT	41	0
O13	●	Pacific PORT	46	0
O20	|	at Washington State	7	9
O27	● |	at Washington	9	0 *
N3	● |	Montana	44	0
N17	|	Oregon	0	12
N29	●	NYU BRNX	25	13

1929 5-4-0 (1-4-0)

S21	●	Willamette	37	6
S28	●	Cal State	19	0
O5	|	at Southern Cal	7	21
O12	●	Portland	71	7
O19	|	at Stanford	7	40
O26	● |	Idaho	27	0
N2	|	Washington State PORT	0	9
N16	|	at Oregon	0	16
N23	●	at Detroit	14	7

1930 7-3-0 (2-3-0)

S20	●	Willamette	48	0
S27	●	Gonzaga	16	0
O4	|	at Southern Cal	7	27
O10	●	Cal State	20	0
O18	|	at Stanford	7	13
O25	●	Pacific	57	0
N1	|	Washington State	7	14
N15	● |	Oregon	15	0
N21	● |	at UCLA	19	0
N27	●	West Virginia CHI	12	0

1931 6-3-1 (1-3-1)

S19	●	Willamette	76	0
S26	●	Colorado PORT	16	0
O3	|	at Southern Cal	0	30
O9	●	Linfield	25	0
O17	|	at Stanford	7	25
O23	●	Oregon Coll.	37	0
O31	|	Washington State PORT	6	7
N7	● |	Montana	19	0
N14	= |	at Oregon	0	0
D5	● |	Utah PORT	12	0

1932 4-6-0 (1-4-0)

S17	●	at Gonzaga	19	16
S24	●	Willamette	32	0
O1	|	Stanford PORT	0	27
O8	|	at Southern Cal	0	10
O22	|	Washington State	6	7
O28	●	West Coast Army	20	9
N5	|	Oregon	6	12
N12	● |	at Montana	35	6
N19		Fordham NYC	6	8
N24		at Detroit	6	14

LON STINER
1933-48 (.589) 74-49-17

1933 6-2-2 (2-1-1)

S23	●	So. Oregon	21	0
S23	●	Willamette	21	0
S30	● |	Montana	20	0
O7	=	Gonzaga PORT	0	0
O14	●	at San Francisco	12	7
O21	= |	Southern Cal PORT	0	0
O28	● |	Washington State PORT	2	0
N11	|	Oregon PORT	3	13
N18	●	Fordham NYC	9	6
N30		at Nebraska	0	22

1934 3-6-2 (0-5-2)

S22	●	Willamette	13	0
S22	●	Pacific	19	0
S28		San Francisco	0	10
O6	|	Stanford PORT	0	17
O12	●	Portland	39	12
O20	= |	at Southern Cal	6	6
O27	|	at Washington State	0	31
N3	|	at Washington	7	14
N10	|	Oregon PORT	6	9
N17	= |	Montana	7	7
N24	|	at UCLA	7	25

1935 6-4-1 (2-3-1)

S21	●	Linfield	31	0
S28	●	Willamette	26	0
O5	|	UCLA PORT	7	20
O11	●	Gonzaga	33	6
O19	● |	at Southern Cal	13	7
O26	|	Washington State PORT	13	26
N2	●	Portland	19	2
N9	|	at Oregon	0	13
N16	● |	Idaho	13	0
N23	= |	at Montana	0	0
N28		at Nebraska	20	26

1936 4-6-0 (3-5-0)

S26	|	at Southern Cal	7	38
O3	●	Willamette	13	0
O10	|	California PORT	0	7
O17	|	at Washington	7	19
O24	|	at UCLA	13	22
O31	● |	Montana	11	7
N7	● |	at Washington State	16	6
N14	|	Stanford PORT	14	20
N21	● |	Oregon	18	0
N28		Nebraska PORT	14	32

1937 3-3-3 (2-3-3)

S25	|	at Idaho	6	7
O2	|	at California	6	24
O9	● |	at Washington	6	3
O16	= |	UCLA	7	7
O23	● |	at Oregon	14	0
O30	= |	at Stanford	0	0
N6	●	Willamette	18	0
N13	= |	at Southern Cal	12	12
N20	|	Washington State	0	7

1938 5-3-1 (4-3-1)

S24	|	Idaho	0	13
O1	|	at Southern Cal	0	7
O8	●	Portland	19	0
O15	● |	at Washington	13	6
O22	● |	Washington State PORT	7	6
O29	|	at California	7	13
N12	● |	Stanford	6	0
N26	● |	Oregon PORT	14	0
D10	= |	at UCLA	6	6

1939 9-1-1 (6-1-1)

S30	● |	at Stanford	12	0
O7	● |	Idaho	7	6
O14	● |	Portland PORT	14	12
O21	● |	at Washington	13	7
O28	● |	Washington State	13	0
N4	|	Southern Cal PORT	7	19
N11	● |	at Oregon	19	14
N18	● |	California	21	0
N25	= |	at UCLA	13	13
D30	●	at Hawaii All Stars	28	0
J1	●	at Hawaii	39	6

1940 5-3-1 (4-3-1)

S28	● |	Idaho	41	0
O5	= |	at Southern Cal	0	0
O11	●	Portland	26	0
O19	|	at Washington	0	19
O26	● |	at UCLA	7	0
N2	● |	at California	19	13
N9	● |	Washington State	21	0
N16	|	at Stanford	14	28
N30	|	Oregon	0	20

1941 8-2-0 (7-2-0)

S27	|	at Southern Cal	7	13
O4	● |	Washington PORT	9	6
O11	● |	Stanford	10	0
O25		at Washington St	0	7
N1	● |	Idaho	33	0
N8	● |	UCLA	19	0
N15	● |	at California	6	0
N22	● |	Montana PORT	27	0
N29	● |	at Oregon	12	7
		ROSE BOWL		
J1	●	Duke	20	16

1942 4-5-1 (4-4-0)

S26	● |	at Idaho	32	0
O3	● |	California	13	8
O10	|	at UCLA	7	30
O17		Santa Clara PORT	0	7
O24	|	Washington State PORT	13	26
O31	|	at Washington	0	13
N7	● |	Montana	33	0
N14	|	at Stanford	13	49
N21	● |	Oregon	39	2
N28	=	at Michigan State	7	7

1943-1944
NO TEAM WWII

1945 4-4-1 (4-4-0)

S29	=	Camp Beale	14	14
O6	|	at Washington State	0	33
O13	● |	Oregon	19	6
O20	|	Washington PORT	0	13
N3	● |	Idaho	34	0
N10	● |	at Washington	7	6
N17	|	Washington State	6	13
N24	|	at Southern Cal	7	34
D1	● |	at Oregon	13	12

1946 7-1-1 (6-1-1)

S28	|	at UCLA	7	50
O5	●	Portland	35	0
O12	● |	Southern Cal PORT	6	0
O26	● |	at Washington State	13	12
N2	= |	Stanford	0	0
N9	● |	Idaho	34	0
N16	● |	at California	28	7
N23	● |	Oregon	13	0
N30	● |	Washington PORT	21	12

1947 5-5-0 (3-4-0)

S27		at Utah	6	7
O4	● |	at Washington	14	7
O11	● |	at Idaho	33	6
O18	|	at Southern Cal	6	48
O25	●	Portland	46	0
N1	● |	at Stanford	13	7
N8	|	UCLA PORT	7	27
N15	|	Washington State	13	14
N22	|	at Oregon	6	14
N29	●	at Nebraska	27	6

1948 5-4-3 (2-3-2)

S18	● |	Idaho	27	12
S24	|	at Southern Cal	6	21
O2	= |	Washington PORT	14	14
O9	●	Portland	32	6
O16	|	at California	0	42
O23	● |	at UCLA	28	0
O30		Michigan State	21	46
N6	= |	at Washington State	26	26
N13	=	Utah	20	20
N20	|	Oregon	0	10
N27	●	Nebraska PORT	28	12
		PINEAPPLE BOWL		
J1	●	Hawaii	47	27

KIP TAYLOR
1949-54 (.357) 20-36

1949 7-3-0 (5-3-0)

S16	|	at UCLA	13	35
S24	●	Utah PORT	27	7
O1	|	California PORT	0	41
O8	● |	at Washington	7	3
O15	● |	Montana	63	14
O22	|	at Stanford	7	27
O29	● |	Washington State	35	6
N5	● |	at Idaho	35	25
N12	●	Michigan State PORT	25	20
N19	● |	at Oregon	20	10

1950 3-6-0 (2-5-0)

S23		at Michigan State	13	38
O7	|	Stanford PORT	7	21 *
O14	|	Washington PORT	6	35
O21	|	California PORT	0	27
O28	●	Montana	20	0
N4	|	at UCLA	13	20
N11	● |	Idaho	34	19
N18	|	at Washington State	7	21
N25	● |	Oregon PORT	14	2

1951 4-6-0 (3-5-0)

S22		at Michigan State	0	6
S29	●	Utah	61	28
O6	● |	Idaho SPO	34	6
O13	|	at Southern Cal	14	16
O20	|	Washington State	13	26
O27	|	at California	14	35
N3	● |	at Washington	40	14
N10	|	UCLA PORT	0	7
N17	|	at Stanford	14	35
N24	● |	at Oregon	14	7

1952 2-7-0 (1-6-0)

S20	●	at Utah	14	7
O4		Michigan State PORT	14	17
O11	|	at Stanford	28	41
O18	|	Southern Cal PORT	6	28
O25	|	at Washington State	20	33
N1	|	Washington PORT	13	38
N8	|	at UCLA	0	57
N15	|	Idaho	6	27
N22	● |	Oregon PORT	22	19

1953 3-6-0 (3-5-0)

S18	|	at UCLA	0	41
S26	|	California PORT	0	26
O3	|	at Washington	0	28
O10	|	Stanford PORT	0	21
O17	|	at Southern Cal	0	37
O24	● |	at Idaho	19	0
O31		at Michigan State	6	34
N14	● |	Washington State	7	0
N21	● |	at Oregon	7	0

1954 1-8-0 (1-6-0)

S25	● |	Idaho	13	0
O2	|	Washington PORT	7	17
O9	|	at Washington State	6	34
O16		at Nebraska	7	27
O23	|	UCLA	0	61
O30	|	at Southern Cal	0	34
N6		at Minnesota	6	44
N13	|	at California	7	46
N20	|	Oregon	14	33

TOMMY PROTHRO
1955-64 (.627) 63-37-2

1955 6-3-0 (5-2-0)

S17	●	Brigham Young	33	0
S24	● |	Stanford PORT	10	0
O8	|	at UCLA	0	38
O15		at Pacific	7	13
O22	● |	Washington State	14	6
O29	● |	at Washington	13	7
N5	● |	Idaho	33	14
N12	● |	at California	16	14
N19	|	at Oregon	0	28

1956 7-3-1 (6-1-1)

S22	●	at Missouri	19	13
S28	|	at Southern Cal	13	21
O6		at Iowa	13	14
O13	● |	California	21	13
O20	● |	at Washington State	21	0
O27	● |	UCLA	21	7
N3	● |	Washington	28	20
N10	● |	at Stanford	20	19
N17	● |	at Idaho	14	10
N24	= |	Oregon	14	14
		ROSE BOWL		
J1		Iowa	19	35

1957 8-2-0 (6-2-0)

S21	● |	Southern Cal PORT	20	0
S28	●	at Kansas	34	6
O5	●	at Northwestern	22	13
O12	● |	Idaho	20	0
O19	|	at UCLA	7	26
O26	|	at Washington	6	19
N2	● |	Washington State	39	25
N9	● |	at California	21	19
N16	● |	Stanford	24	14
N23	● |	at Oregon	10	7

THE SCHOOLS

1958 — 6-4-0 (5-3-0)

S19		at Southern Cal	0	21
S27	●	Kansas *Port*	12	0
O4	●	UCLA	14	0
O11		at Wyoming	0	28
O18	●	at Idaho	20	6
O25	●	Washington *Port*	14	12
N1	●	California	14	8
N8	●	at Washington State	0	7
N15		at Stanford	24	16
N22		Oregon	0	20

1959-1963
INDEPENDENT

1959 — 3-7-0

S19		Southern Cal *Port*	6	27
S26		at Texas Tech	14	15
O3		at Nebraska	6	7
O10		at Michigan	7	18
O17	●	Idaho	66	18
O24	●	at California	24	20
O31		Washington State	0	14
N7		at Washington	6	13
N14		Stanford	22	39
N21	●	at Oregon	15	7

1960 — 6-3-1

S16	●	at Southern Cal	14	0
S24		at Iowa	12	22
O1	●	Houston *Port*	29	20
O8	●	at Indiana	20	6
O15	●	at Idaho	28	8
O22	●	Washington *Port*	29	30
O29	●	California	6	14
N5	●	at Washington State	20	10
N12	●	at Stanford	25	21
N19	=	Oregon	14	14

1961 — 5-5-0

S23		Syracuse *Port*	8	19
S30		Stanford	0	34
O7	●	Idaho	44	6
O14		at Wisconsin	20	23
O21		at Arizona State	23	24
N4	●	Washington State	14	6
N11	●	at Washington	3	0
N18	●	Brigham Young	35	0
N25	●	at Oregon	6	2
D2		at Houston	12	23

1962 — 9-2-0

S22	●	Iowa State *Port*	39	35
S29		at Iowa	8	28
O6	●	at Stanford	27	0
O13	●	Washington *Port*	13	14
O20	●	Pacific	40	6
O27	●	West Virginia *Port*	51	22
N3	●	at Washington State	18	12
N10	●	at Idaho	32	0
N17	●	Colorado State	25	14
N24	●	Oregon	20	17

LIBERTY BOWL

| D15 | ● | Villanova | 6 | 0 |

1963 — 5-5-0

S21	●	at Utah	29	14
S28	●	Colorado *Port*	41	6
O3	●	Baylor *Port*	22	15
O12		at Washington	7	34
O19	●	Washington State	30	6
O26		at Syracuse	8	31
N2	●	Stanford	10	7
N9		at Indiana	15	20
N15		at Southern Cal	22	28
N30		at Oregon	14	31

1964-1967
AAWU

1964 — 8-3-0 (3-1-0)

S19		at Northwestern	3	7
S26	●	at Colorado	14	7
O3	●	at Baylor	13	6
O10		Washington *Port*	9	7
O17	●	Idaho	10	7
O24	●	Syracuse *Port*	31	13
O31	●	at Washington State	24	7
N7	●	Indiana	24	14
N14		at Stanford	7	16
N21	●	Oregon	7	6

ROSE BOWL

| J1 | | Michigan | 7 | 34 |

1965 — 5-5-0 (1-3-0)

S18	●	at Illinois	12	10
S25		Iowa *Port*	7	27
O1		at Southern Cal	12	26
O9		at Northwestern	7	15
O16		Idaho *Boi*	16	14
O23	●	Utah	10	6
O30		Washington State	8	10
N6	●	at Syracuse	13	12
N13		at Washington	21	28
N20	●	at Oregon	19	14

1966 — 7-3-0 (3-1-0)

S17		at Michigan	0	41
S24	●	at Iowa	17	3
O1		Southern Cal *Port*	0	21
O8		Northwestern	6	14
O15	●	Idaho	14	7
O22	●	at Arizona State	18	17
O29	●	at Washington State	41	13
N5	●	Arizona *Port*	31	12
N12	●	Washington	24	13
N19	●	Oregon	20	15

1967 — 7-2-1 (4-1-1)

S16	●	Stanford *Port*	13	7
S23	●	at Arizona State	27	21
S30	●	at Iowa	38	18
O7		at Washington	6	13
O14		Brigham Young	13	31
O21	●	at Purdue	22	14
O28	●	Washington State	35	7
N4	=	at UCLA	16	16
N11	●	Southern Cal	3	0
N18	●	at Oregon	14	10

1968-Present
PAC 10

1968 — 7-3-0 (5-1-0)

S21		at Iowa	20	21
S28	●	at Utah	24	21
O5	●	Washington	35	21
O12		at Kentucky	34	35
O19	●	Arizona State *Port*	28	9
O26	●	at Washington State	16	8
N2	●	at Stanford	29	7
N9		UCLA	45	21
N16		at Southern Cal	13	17
N23	●	Oregon	41	19

1969 — 6-4-0 (4-3-0)

S13		at UCLA	0	37
S20	●	at Iowa	42	14
S27	●	at Arizona State	30	7
O4		Southern Cal	7	31
O18	●	at Washington	10	6
O25		Utah *Port*	3	7
N1		Stanford	0	33
N8	●	at California	35	3
N15	●	Washington State	38	3
N22	●	at Oregon	10	7

1970 — 6-5-0 (3-4-0)

S12	●	UCLA	9	14
S19	●	Iowa *Port*	21	14
S26	●	at Oklahoma	23	14
O3		at Southern Cal	13	45
O10	●	Utah	31	21
O17		at Houston	16	19
O24		Washington	20	29
O31		at Stanford	10	48
N7	●	California	16	10
N14	●	Washington State *Spo*	28	16
N21	●	Oregon		249

1971 — 5-6-0 (3-3-0)

S11		at Georgia	25	56
S18	●	Iowa	33	19
S25		at Michigan State	14	31
O2	●	at UCLA	34	17
O9		at California	27	30
O16		Arizona State *Port*	24	18
O23		at Washington	14	38
O30		Stanford	24	31
N6		at Arizona	22	34
N13	●	Washington State	21	14
N20	●	at Oregon	30	29

1972 — 2-9-0 (1-6-0)

S8		at San Diego State	8	17
S16		at Southern Cal	6	51
S23		at Iowa	11	19
S30	●	Brigham Young	29	3
O7		at Arizona State	7	38
O14		UCLA	7	37
O21		at Washington State	7	37
O28		at Stanford	11	17
N4		Washington	16	23
N11	●	California *Port*	26	23
N18		Oregon	3	30

1973 — 2-9-0 (2-5-0)

S15		Auburn *Birm*	9	18
S22		SMU	16	35
S29		at Brigham Young	14	37
O6		Southern Cal	7	21
O13	●	at Washington	31	7
O20		at California	14	24
O27		Arizona State *Port*	14	44
N3		Stanford	23	24
N10		Washington State	7	13
N17		at UCLA	14	56
N24	●	at Oregon	17	14

1974 — 3-8-0 (3-4-0)

S7		at Syracuse	15	23
S14		at Georgia	35	48
S21		at Ohio State	10	51
O5		at SMU	30	37
O12	●	Washington	23	9
O19		California	14	17
O26		at Southern Cal	10	31
N2		at Stanford	13	17
N9	●	at Washington State	17	3
N16		UCLA	14	33
N23	●	Oregon	35	16

1975 — 1-10-0 (1-6-0)

S13		San Diego State *Port*	0	25
S19		at Southern Cal	7	24
S27		at Kansas	0	20
O4		Grambling	12	19
O11		Colorado State	8	17
O18		at California	24	51
O25		at Washington	7	35
N1		Stanford	22	28
N8	●	Washington State	7	0
N15		at UCLA	9	31
N22		at Oregon	7	14

1976 — 2-10-0 (1-6-0)

S4		Kansas	16	28
S11		at Kentucky	13	38
S18		at LSU	11	28
O2		at Syracuse	3	21
O9		Washington	12	24
O16	●	California	10	9
O23		at Southern Cal	0	56
O30		at Stanford	3	24
N6		at Washington State	24	29
N13		UCLA	14	45
N20		Oregon	14	23
N27	●	at Hawaii	59	0

1977 — 2-9-0 (0-7-0)

S10	●	Syracuse	24	12
S17		Southern Cal	10	17
S24		at Arizona State	31	33
O1		at Tennessee	10	41
O8		Brigham Young	24	19
O15		at California	17	41
O22		at Washington	6	14
O29		Stanford	7	26
N5		Washington State	10	24
N12		at UCLA	18	48
N19		at Oregon	16	28

1978 — 3-7-1 (2-6-0)

S9		Brigham Young	6	10
S16		at Arizona	7	21
S23	=	at Tennessee	13	13
S30		Washington	0	34
O7	●	at Minnesota	17	14
O21		at Southern Cal	7	38
O28		at Stanford	6	24
N4	●	at Washington State	32	31
N11	●	UCLA	15	13
N18		Arizona State	22	44
N25		Oregon	3	24

1979 — 1-10-0 (1-7-0)

S8		at New Mexico	16	35
S15		Southern Cal	5	42
S22		at Kansas State	16	22
S29		Arizona State	0	45
O6		at Washington	0	41
O13		at California	0	45
O20		San Jose State	14	24	†
O27	●	Stanford	33	31
N3		Washington State	42	45
N17		at Arizona	18	42
N29		at Oregon	3	24

1980 — 0-11-0 (0-8-0)

S13		at Wyoming	10	30
S20		at Arizona State	14	42
S27		at Texas	0	35
O11		Washington	6	41
O18		at California	6	27
O25		Long Beach State	21	31
N1		at Stanford	13	54
N8		at Washington State	7	28
N15		Oregon	21	40
N22		Arizona	7	24
N30		UCLA *Tok*	3	34

1981 — 1-10-0 (0-7-0)

S12	●	Fresno State	31	28
S19		at LSU	24	27
S26		at Minnesota	12	42
O3		Southern Cal	22	56
O10		Washington State	0	23
O17		at Washington	17	56
O24		at Oklahoma	3	42
O31		at California	3	45
N7		Stanford	9	63
N14		Arizona	7	40
N21		at Oregon	17	47

1982 — 1-9-1 (0-7-1)

S11		at Arizona	12	38
S18		at LSU	7	45
S25		San Jose State	13	17
O2		at Stanford	5	45
O9	=	at Washington State	14	14
O16		Washington	17	34
O23		at Southern Cal	0	38
O30		California	14	28
N6		at Arizona State	16	30
N20	●	Montana	30	10
N27		Oregon	6	7

1983 — 2-8-1 (1-6-1)

S3		at Arizona	6	50
S10	●	Portland State *Port*	51	14
S17		Southern Cal	10	33
S24		at Colorado	14	38
O1		Nevada-Las Vegas	21	35
O8		at Washington	7	34
O15		at California	19	45
O29	●	Stanford	31	18
N5		Washington State	9	27
N12		at Arizona State	3	38
N19	=	at Oregon	0	0

1984 — 2-9-0 (1-7-0)

S8		at Ohio State	14	22
S15		Arizona *Port*	8	27
S22	●	Wyoming	41	14
S29		at Idaho	22	41
O6		Washington	7	19
O13	●	California	9	6
O20		at Arizona State	10	45
O27		Stanford	21	28
N3		at Washington State	3	20
N10		at UCLA	17	26
N17		Oregon	6	31

1985 — 3-8-0 (2-6-0)

S7	●	Idaho	43	28
S14	●	California *Port*	23	20
S21		Fresno State	24	33
S28	●	at Grambling	6	23
O5		at Southern Cal	0	63
O12		Washington State	0	34
O19	●	at Washington	21	20
N2		Arizona	6	27
N9		at Stanford	24	39
N16		at UCLA	0	41
N23		at Oregon	13	34

1986 — 3-8-0 (1-6-0)

Date		Opponent		
S13		at Fresno State	0	27
S20		at Michigan	12	31
S27		Stanford	7	17
O4		at Washington State	14	24
O11	●	at California	14	12
O18		at Arizona	12	23
O25	●	Boise State	34	3
N1		UCLA *Port*	0	49
N8		Washington	12	28
N15	●	at Brigham Young	10	7
N22		Oregon	28	49

1987 — 2-9-0 (0-7-0)

Date		Opponent		
S12		at Georgia	7	41
S19	●	San Jose State	36	34
S26		at Texas	16	61
O3		at Southern Cal	14	48
O10	●	Akron	42	26
O17		at Arizona	17	31
O24		Arizona State	21	30
O31		at Washington	12	28
N7		UCLA	17	52
N14		Stanford	7	38
N21		at Oregon	0	44

1988 — 4-6-1 (2-5-1)

Date		Opponent		
S3		Arizona	13	24
S10	●	at San Jose State	41	27
S17	●	California	17	16
S24		at Colorado	21	28
O1		Fresno State	21	10
O8		at UCLA	21	38
O22	=	at Stanford	20	20
O29		Southern Cal	20	41
N5		at Arizona State	24	30
N12		at Washington State	27	36
N19	●	Oregon	21	10

1989 — 4-7-1 (3-4-1)

Date		Opponent		
S9	●	Stanford	20	16
S16		at Washington State	3	41
S23	●	at Boise State	37	30
S30		at Nebraska	7	35
O7		at Fresno State	18	35
O14	=	Arizona State	17	17
O21		UCLA	18	17
O28	●	at California	25	14
N4		at Southern Cal	6	48
N11		Washington	14	51
N18		at Oregon	21	30
N25		at Hawaii	21	23

1990 — 1-10-0 (1-6-0)

Date		Opponent		
S1		Montana	15	22
S8		at Kansas	12	38
S15		Nevada-Las Vegas	20	45
S22		at Stanford	3	37
S29		at Nebraska	7	31
O13	●	Arizona	35	21
O20		Washington State	24	55
O27		at UCLA	17	26
N3		at Arizona State	9	34
N10		Southern Cal	7	56
N17		Oregon	3	6

1991 — 1-10-0 (1-7-0)

Date		Opponent		
S7		Utah	10	22
S14		at Nevada-Las Vegas	9	23
S21		Fresno State	20	24
O5		at Washington State	7	55
O12		Arizona State	7	24
O19		UCLA	7	44
O26		at Stanford	10	40
N2		at Arizona	21	45
N9		California	14	27
N16		Washington	6	58
N23	●	at Oregon	14	3

1992 — 1-9-1 (0-7-1)\

Date		Opponent		
S5		Kansas	20	49
S12	●	Fresno State	46	36
S19	=	Arizona	14	14
S26		at Utah	9	42
O3		at California	0	42
O10		Washington State	10	35
O17		at Arizona State	13	40
O24		Stanford	21	27
N7		at UCLA	14	26
N14		at Washington	16	45
N21		Oregon	0	7

1993 — 4-7-0 (2-6-0)

Date		Opponent		
S4	●	at Wyoming	27	16
S11		at Fresno State	30	48
S18		at Washington State	6	51
S25		Arizona	0	33
O2	●	Arizona State	30	14
O9	●	Pacific	42	7
O16		at Southern Cal	9	34
O23		UCLA	17	20
O30		at Stanford	27	31
N6		Washington	21	28
N20	●	at Oregon	15	12

1994 — 4-7-0 (2-6-0)

Date		Opponent		
S3		at Arizona State	16	22
S10	●	Wyoming	44	31
S17		at Fresno State	14	24
O1		at Arizona	10	30
O8		Southern Cal	19	27
O15	●	at UCLA	23	14
O22		Stanford	29	35
O29		at Washington	10	24
N5		Pacific	24	12
N12	●	Washington State	21	3
N19		Oregon	13	17

1995 — 1-10-0 (0-8-0)

Date		Opponent		
S2	●	Idaho	14	7
S9		at Pacific	10	23
S16		at North Texas	27	30
S23		at Arizona State	11	20
S30		Washington	16	26
O7		at Washington State	14	40
O21		California	12	13
O28		at Stanford	3	14
N4		Arizona	9	14
N11		Southern Cal	10	28
N18		at Oregon	10	12

1996 — 2-9 (1-7)

Date		Opponent		
S7		Montana	14	35
S14		at Southern Cal	17	46
S21		at Baylor	10	42
S28		at California	42	48
O12		Washington State	3	24
O19	●	Stanford	26	12
O26		at Arizona	7	33
N2		Arizona State	14	29
N9		at Washington	3	42
N16	●	Northern Illinois	67	28
N23		Oregon	13	49

1997 — 3-8 (0-8)

Date		Opponent		
S6	●	North Texas	33	7
S20		Stanford	24	27
S27		Arizona State	10	13
O4		San Jose State	26	12
O11	●	Utah State	24	16
O18		at UCLA	10	34
O25		Washington	17	45
N1		at California	14	33
N8		at Arizona	7	27
N15		Southern Cal	0	23
N22		at Oregon	30	48

1998 — 5-6 (2-6)

Date		Opponent		
S5	●	Nevada	48	6
S12	●	Baylor	27	17
S19		at Southern Cal	20	40
S26		at Arizona State	3	24
O3	●	at Utah State	20	6
O10	●	at Stanford	30	23
O17		Arizona	7	28
O24		at Washington	34	35
O31		California	19	20
N7		UCLA	34	41
N21	●	Oregon	44	41

1999 — 7-5 (4-4)

Date		Opponent		
S4	●	at Nevada	28	13
S11	●	Fresno State	46	23
S18	●	Georgia Southern	48	41
O2		at Southern Cal	29	37
O9		Washington	21	47
O16		at Stanford	17	21
O23	●	UCLA	55	7
O30	●	at Washington State	27	13
N6	●	California	17	7
N13	●	Arizona	28	20
N20		at Oregon	14	25

OAHU BOWL

Date		Opponent		
D25		Hawaii	17	23

2000 — 11-1 (7-1)

Date		Opponent		
S2	●	Ea. Washington	21	19
S9	●	at New Mexico	28	20
S23	●	San Diego State	35	3
S30	●	Southern Cal	31	21
O7		at Washington	30	33
O14	●	Stanford	38	6
O21	●	at UCLA	44	38
O28	●	Washington State	38	9
N4	●	at California	38	32
N11	●	at Arizona	33	9
N18	●	Oregon	23	13

FIESTA BOWL

Date		Opponent		
J1	●	Notre Dame	41	9

2001 — 5-6 (3-5)

Date		Opponent		
S2		at Fresno State	24	44
S8	●	at New Mexico State	27	22
S29		UCLA	7	38
O6		at Washington State	27	34
O13	●	Arizona	38	3
O20		at Arizona State	24	41
O27	●	California	19	10
N3		at Southern Cal	13	16
N10		Washington	49	24
N17	●	No. Arizona	45	10
D1		at Oregon	14	17

2002 — 8-5 (4-4)

Date		Opponent		
A29	●	Eastern Kentucky	49	10
S7	●	at Temple	35	3
S14	●	Nevada-Las Vegas	47	17
S21	●	Fresno State	59	19
S28		at Southern Cal	0	22
O5		UCLA	35	43
O12		at Arizona State	9	13
O26	●	California	24	13
N2	●	Arizona	38	3
N9		at Washington	29	41
N16	●	at Stanford	31	21
N23	●	Oregon	45	24

INSIGHT BOWL

Date		Opponent		
D26		Pittsburgh	13	38

2003 — 8-5 (4-4)

Date		Opponent		
A28	●	Sacremento State	40	7
S5		at Fresno State	14	16
S13	●	New Mexico State	28	16
S20		Boise State	26	24
S27		Arizona State	45	17
O4	●	at California	35	21
O18		Washington	17	38
O25		at Washington State	30	36
N1		Arizona	52	23
N15	●	Stanford	43	3
N22	●	at Oregon	20	34
D6	●	at Southern Cal	28	52

LAS VEGAS BOWL

Date		Opponent		
D24	●	New Mexico	55	14

2004 — 7-5 (5-3)

Date		Opponent		
S4		at LSU	21	22
S10		at Boise State	34	53
S18	●	New Mexico	17	7
S25		at Arizona State	14	27
O2		California	7	49
O16	●	at Washington	29	14
O23		Washington State	38	19
O30	●	at Arizona	28	14
N6		Southern Cal	20	28
N13	●	at Stanford	24	19
N20	●	Oregon	50	21

INSIGHT BOWL

Date		Opponent		
D28	●	Notre Dame	38	21

PENN STATE

BY TODD JONES

LOCATING PENN STATE CAN BE A trying task for outsiders. The TCU football team flew into Harrisburg in 1953, mistakenly thinking the school was there. But State College is 90 miles away, nestled in the state's central valley, in the shadow of Mount Nittany. Though difficult to find on a map, Penn State is much easier to locate in the landscape of college football history, where Happy Valley is a national landmark of stability and gridiron excellence. The Nittany Lions recorded 49 consecutive nonlosing seasons (from 1939 to 1987), have had just two coaches since 1950 and have enjoyed five undefeated seasons and two national championships since 1968. Penn State is where over 100,000 fans turn out to see old-fashioned football, with the home team in generic uniforms and its players helping opponents up, handing the ball to officials after scores and providing pride for an entire region.

TRADITION Only one school is known as Linebacker U. Penn State has churned out top linebackers in assembly-line fashion. Seven of them—LaVar Arrington, Greg Buttle, Shane Conlan, Jack Ham, Dennis Onkotz, Brandon Short and John Skorupan—have been named All-America by The Associated Press. Many others have contributed to that position's legacy at Penn State. Since 1928, their exploits have been dissected and discussed every Wednesday during the season. That year, fans began gathering midweek at the Nittany Lion Inn to rehash the previous game and talk about the upcoming opponent. The gatherings became known as the State College Quarterback Club, and coach Joe Paterno still attends the weekly meetings. He also brings along players, providing fans a better connection to the men who inspire "We Are Penn State" cheers. That chant is accompanied by the Blue Band, and blasts of a lion's roar from the public address speakers add to the atmosphere at home games. Fans often pass the Lion mascot overhead up the Beaver Stadium grandstand through the student section to the top of the seats.

BEST PLAYER While Lydell Mitchell gained more yards in college and Franco Harris was among the career leading ground-gainers in the NFL, it was another Penn State back, Lenny Moore, whom Paterno would call the best player he ever coached. Moore, who played tailback and

PROFILE

Pennsylvania State University
University Park, Pa.
Founded: 1855
Enrollment: 35,000
Colors: Blue and White
Nickname: Nittany Lions
Stadium: Beaver Stadium
    Opened in 1960
    FieldTurf; 107,282 capacity
First football game: 1887
All-time record: 760–338–42 (.685)
Bowl record: 23–12–2
Consensus national championships,
1936-present: 2 (1982, 1986)
Big Ten Conference championships:
1 (outright)
Heisman Trophy: John Cappelletti, 1973
Outland Trophy: Mike Reid, 1969
First-round NFL draftees: 32
Website: www.gopsusports.com

THE BEST OF TIMES

Two Joe Paterno eras stand out. Penn State went 76–19–1 from 1980 to 1987, including a two-season 23–1 mark ending with an undefeated national championship team in 1986. From 1967 to 1974, his teams went 80–10–1, including a 31-game unbeaten streak. The Nittany Lions were undefeated in 1968, 1969 and 1973, but were not national champions.

THE WORST OF TIMES

The Nittany Lions went seven straight seasons without a winning record while going 21–33–3 from 1930 to 1936 under Bob Higgins. Penn State was shut out 17 times during that span.

CONFERENCE

Penn State joined the Big Ten Conference in 1993 after playing as an independent for 106 seasons.

DISTINGUISHED ALUMNI

Guion Bluford, first African-American astronaut in space; Margaret Carlson, political commentator; Mary Ellen Clark, two-time Olympic bronze medalist diver; Tom Ridge, governor; Rick Santorum, U.S. senator

FIGHT SONG

FIGHT ON STATE
Fight on State, Fight on State,
Strike your gait and win,
Victory we predict for thee,
We're ever true to you,
Dear old White and Blue.
Onward State, Onward State
Roar Lions roar,
We'll hit that line, roll up the score,
Fight on to victory evermore,
Fight on, on
On, on, on!
Fight on, on,
Penn State!

> *JoePa, a brooding perfectionist decked out in huge trifocals, rolled-up trousers, white athletic socks and black shoes, is synonymous with Penn State football.*

defensive back, wasn't huge at six feet and 185 pounds, and he never made first-team All-America (thanks to Syracuse's Jim Brown). But the Pennsylvania native could work magic on both sides of the ball. The Reading Rambler averaged 6.2 yards per rush from 1953 to 1955. He also intercepted 10 passes, six as a senior, and was a special-teams star. Moore still ranks fourth at Penn State in punt return average (15.8 yards) and ninth in kickoff return average (24.3). In 1954, a national TV audience saw him run for 143 yards and 2 TDs, then clinch a 35-13 win at Pennsylvania by intercepting a fourth-quarter pass and returning it 53 yards for his third score. Moore went on to a Hall of Fame career in pro football, scoring 113 TDs and gaining more than 12,000 yards over 12 seasons with the Baltimore Colts.

BEST COACH Critics labeled him pious and self-righteous when he spoke in the late 1960s of a "grand experiment" to prove a school could win football games and educate players. Joe Paterno has done that. Entering the 2005 season, he's coached 69 first-team All-Americas and 23 first-team academic All-Americas. The 2000 NCAA graduation report showed 75% of Penn State's football players earned a degree in four years, compared to the national rate of 50%. And entering 2005, Paterno had the second-most Division I-A victories (343), two national championships, four other undefeated seasons and a record 20 bowl victories. He's the only coach to win the Orange, Cotton, Sugar, Fiesta and Rose bowls. Not bad for a Brown University English major who said he never wanted to coach football. Paterno spent 16 years as a Penn State assistant and was in his 40th season as head coach in 2005. JoePa, a brooding perfectionist decked out in huge trifocals, rolled-up trousers, white athletic socks and black shoes, is synonymous with Penn State football.

RECORDS

RUSHING YARDS

	GAME
327	Larry Johnson vs. Indiana, Nov. 16, 2002 (28 att.)

	SEASON
2,087	Larry Johnson, 2002 (271 att.)

	CAREER
3,398	Curt Warner, 1979-82 (649 att.)

PASSING YARDS

	GAME
399	Zack Mills vs. Iowa, Sept. 28, 2002 (23 of 44)

	SEASON
2,679	Kerry Collins, 1994 (176 of 264)

	CAREER
7,212	Zack Mills, 2001-04 (606 of 1,082)

RECEIVING YARDS

	GAME
212	O.J. McDuffie vs. Boston College, Oct. 17, 1992 (11 rec.)

	SEASON
1,084	Bobby Engram, 1995 (63 rec.)

	CAREER
3,026	Bobby Engram, 1991, 1993-95 (167 rec.)

POINTS

	GAME
36	Harry Robb vs. Gettysburg, Oct. 6, 1917 (6 TDs)

	SEASON
174	Lydell Mitchell, 1971 (29 TDs)

	CAREER
282	Craig Fayak, 1990-93 (132 PATs, 50 FGs)

CONSENSUS ALL-AMERICANS

1906	Mother Dunn, C
1919	Bob Higgins, E
1920	Charles Way, B
1921	Glenn Killinger, B
1923	Harry Wilson, B
1959	Rich Lucas, B
1964	Glenn Ressler, G
1968	Ted Kwalick, E
1968-69	Dennis Onkotz, LB
1969	Mike Reid, DT
1970	Jack Ham, LB
1971	Dave Joyner, T
1972	Bruce Bannon, DE
1972	John Skorupan, LB
1973	John Cappelletti, B
1974	Mike Hartenstine, DL
1975	Greg Buttle, LB
1978	Keith Dorney, OT
1978	Chuck Fusina, QB
1978-79	Bruce Clark, DL
1981	Sean Farrell, OL
1986	D.J. Dozier, RB
1986	Shane Conlan, LB

(Continued on next page)

BEST TEAM Paterno has coached in more than a third of the football games in Penn State's history, so he should know. He says his 1968 Nittany Lions were the school's marquee team. They weren't big on defense, but they were quick, aggressive and tenacious. Junior tackles Mike Reid and Steve Smear set the tone up front, and linebacker Jack Ham and the other "Rover Boys" cleaned up the rest. Much-maligned QB Chuck Burkart—"He can't run and he can't pass. All he does is think and win," Paterno said—and halfbacks Charlie Pittman and Bob Campbell powered Penn State to a then school-record 4,025 total yards of offense, including a school-record 2,739 rushing yards. The Nittany Lions went 10–0 in the regular season and beat Kansas in the Orange Bowl, but finished No. 2 behind Ohio State in the final poll. Penn State went 11–0 a year later, including an Orange Bowl win over Missouri, but again finished second in the final polls, behind Texas.

BIGGEST GAME Like a heavyweight title fight, the 1987 Fiesta Bowl was prepackaged as both a sports event and a battle of Good vs. Evil. Clean-cut Penn State (11–0) and rowdy Miami (11–0) staged a morality play in the Arizona desert to decide the national championship. Miami arrived in Tempe wearing combat fatigues, and the No. 1 Hurricanes walked out of a steak dinner they were sharing with No. 2 Penn State. "Did the Japanese sit down and eat with Pearl Harbor before they bombed them?" asked Miami defensive lineman Jerome Brown. The coat-and-tie-clad Nittany Lions kept their mouths shut and gained confidence in a defensive game plan designed to confuse Heisman-winning QB Vinny Testaverde. A college football-record 70 million people watching the game on NBC saw Penn State's

defense intercept five Testaverde passes—two by linebacker Shane Conlan—and sack him five times. The turnovers offset Miami's otherwise dominating performance; the Canes held a 445-162 advantage in total offense, including 22 first downs to Penn State's eight. The Nittany Lions' 14-10 win gave them their second national championship in five years.

BIGGEST UPSET Channels were being switched all over the country early in Penn State's nationally televised game against No. 1-ranked Pittsburgh on Nov. 28, 1981. Led by QB Dan Marino, Pitt was ahead 14-0 and threatening to score again with less than a minute remaining in the first quarter. Marino, who had completed nine of his first 10 passes, tried to hit Dwight Collins for a third TD, but Penn State DB Roger Jackson intercepted. The Nittany Lions promptly drove 80 yards and scored to make it a 14-7 game. And they kept scoring. Penn State rang up 48 consecutive points against the nation's No. 1-ranked defense. The 48-14 upset cost the Panthers a chance for a national title.

HEARTBREAKER Alabama fans at the 1979 Sugar Bowl held up a sign reading "Remember Gettysburg." All Penn State could remember after the game was how a national championship was lost after a remarkable defensive stand. The Nittany Lions were top-ranked and had six first-team All-Americas. But Bear Bryant's Crimson Tide, ranked No. 2, pulled off a 14-7 upset after Penn State failed to score on first down from the Bama 8 with about seven minutes left in the game. The final two plays in that stand began two feet from the end zone. Mike Guman tried to score over left tackle on fourth down, but was smashed short by Alabama linebacker Barry Krauss.

CONSENSUS ALL-AMERICAS (CONT.)		
1992	O.J. McDuffie,	WR
1994	Ki-Jana Carter,	RB
1994	Kerry Collins,	QB
1995	Jeff Hartings,	OL
1997	Curtis Enis,	RB
1999	LaVar Arrington,	LB
1999	Brandon Short,	LB
1999	Courtney Brown,	DL
2002	Larry Johnson,	RB

ALL-CENTURY TEAM

Lou Prato, author of the Penn State Football Encyclopedia and director of the Penn State All-Sports Museum, selected the players from the 1900-1999 era.

OFFENSE

1921-23	Joe Bedenk,	G
1962-64	Glenn Ressler,	G
1979-81	Sean Farrell,	G
1979, 1981	Mike Munchak,	G
1914-17, 1919	Bob Higgins,	TE
1966-68	Ted Kwalick,	TE
1918, 1920-21	Glenn Killinger,	QB
1992-94	Kerry Collins,	QB
1980-83	Kenny Jackson,	WR
1991, 1993-95	Bobby Engram,	WR
1921-23	Harry Wilson,	RB
1953-55	Lenny Moore,	RB/KR
1979-82	Curt Warner,	RB/KR
1976-79	Matt Suhey,	FB
1909-12	Pete Mauthe,	PK/FB

DEFENSE

1945-48	Sam Tamburo,	DE
1960-62	Dave Robinson,	DE
1976-79	Bruce Clark,	DT
1966, 1968-69	Mike Reid,	DT
1903-06	Mother Dunn,	LB
1967-69	Dennis Onkotz,	LB
1967-69	Neal Smith,	DB
1968-70	Jack Ham,	LB
1997-99	LaVar Arrington,	LB
1921-23	Harry Wilson,	DB
1953-55	Lenny Moore,	DB
1957-59	Rich Lucas,	DB
1980-83	Mark Robinson,	DB
1942, 1946-48	Joe Colone,	P

WILDEST FINISH Trailing 14-7 in the 1969 Orange Bowl, the Nittany Lions blocked a Kansas punt and recovered the ball at the 50 with 1:16 remaining. Burkhart completed a 47-yard pass to Campbell as the PA announcer told the crowd that Kansas running back Donnie Shanklin was the game's MVP. Three plays later, Burkhart scored around left end. Paterno decided to go for two points. A pass to WR Bob Campbell fell incomplete, and Kansas' band and fans took the field in celebration. The Jayhawks, however, were penalized for having 12 men on the field. (Game films showed they used 12 on four consecutive plays.) Paterno gambled again. Campbell ran around left end and dived into the end zone for a 15-14 victory that Paterno later said put Penn State on the national map.

CONFERENCE CALL Penn State spurred extreme upheaval in conference makeups when it ceased being an independent and gained membership to the Big Ten Conference in June 1990. The move had seismic implications, indirectly prompting the SEC to add new members and split into two divisions, leading the Big Eight to follow suit (thereby contributing to the demise of the Southwest Conference) and creating resulting jolts in almost every major conference in big-time college football. In 1993, the Nittany Lions played their first league game, ending 106 years of independence. They went 12–0 in 1994, claimed the Big Ten championship outright and won the Rose Bowl. Success in the league fueled $55 million in construction and renovation projects for sports facilities at Penn State, and it led to increases in booster membership and alumni donations.

STADIUM What began as a 30,000-seat horseshoe is now the nation's second-largest stadium, an intimidating 107,282-seat monstrosity distinguished by a hodgepodge of designs borne out of repeated expansions. Beaver Stadium actually sat on the west side of campus for 50 years, but was moved to the east side in 1960, when the school president wanted to make room for an academic building. The entire stadium was dismantled into 700 pieces and moved one mile to its permanent location. While reassembling the stadium, school officials added 16,000 seats, which began five decades of capacity growth. A $93 million expansion that included 12,000 new seats and 60 sky boxes was finished before the 2001 season.

RIVAL Ohio State is probably Penn State's biggest current rival, but that series does not come close to matching the ferocity that defined the Nittany Lions' annual in-state grudge matches with Pittsburgh. The Penn State-Pitt series began in 1893 and, from 1900, was played every season (except 1932-34) until 1993, when Penn State joined the Big Ten. It resumed in 1997, but ended in acrimony after the 2000 game. The rivalry between the schools, separated by 140 miles, reached a zenith in the late 1970s and early 1980s, when Paterno and Pitt coach Jackie Sherrill met five times. The coaches squabbled as their teams battled with Eastern supremacy and national rankings on the line. Paterno went 3–2 against his nemesis. JoePa ended the series after Pitt refused a deal to play twice at State College and once at home. Critics say Paterno dropped Pitt as payback for the betrayal he still felt from the Panthers' joining the Big East in 1982 rather than helping Penn State form a proposed all-sports Eastern league.

INSPIRATION John Cappelletti won the 1973 Heisman Trophy after running for more than 200 yards in three consecutive late-season games to finish the year with 1,522 yards. The tailback is best remembered, however, for his Heisman acceptance speech. Cappelletti mesmerized the crowd, which included U.S. vice president Gerald Ford. He spoke of how the rigors of football were nothing compared to the leukemia battle being fought by his 11-year-old brother, Joey. "This trophy is more his than mine because of the inspiration he has been to me," Cappelletti said. Joey Cappelletti died of leukemia on April 8, 1976. A year later, the brothers' relationship was depicted in a CBS-TV movie, *Something for Joey* … On Sept. 23, 2000, Penn State cornerback Adam Taliaferro was lying on the soggy Ohio Stadium field without movement in his fingers or legs. The freshman from Voorhees, N.J., had just attempted to tackle Ohio State running back Jerry Westbrooks. Taliaferro's C-5 vertebra was fractured and his spinal cord bruised. Two days later, doctors at the Ohio State Medical Center inserted a metal pin and grafted bone to stabilize Taliaferro's spine at the neck in place of broken vertebra pieces. Doctors said this type of spinal injury results in permanent paralysis of the legs in most cases, but in January 2001, Taliaferro walked out of a rehabilitation center on crutches. And on Sept. 1, 2001, Taliaferro led the Penn State team onto the field for its season-opening game against Miami. Although he couldn't play again, Taliaferro smiled as he jogged out to midfield. The Beaver Stadium crowd erupted. "We believe" flashed on the scoreboard.

CONTROVERSY Nebraska fans still howl that Penn State's Mike McCloskey was out of bounds when he caught a crucial pass in No. 8-ranked Penn State's 27-24 upset over the No. 3 Cornhuskers at Beaver Stadium on Sept. 25, 1982. Both teams won the rest of their games, so this contest in effect decided the national championship. The winning score came two plays after McCloskey's controversial 15-yard reception put Penn State on the Nebraska 2. The Cornhuskers argued furiously that McCloskey failed to get a foot inbounds while making his catch, and TV replays seemed to support Nebraska's argument. In 1998, McCloskey appeared at a banquet in Omaha, Neb. After viewing a video of the play, he admitted he appeared to be out of bounds.

> *Sixteen years later, even McCloskey admitted that he was probably out-of-bounds.*

NICKNAME Legend has it that Mount Nittany, which overlooks Beaver Stadium, was named after Indian princess Nita-Nee by the Great Spirit. H.D. "Joe" Mason, a member of the Penn State Class of 1907, had seen the Princeton Tigers at a baseball game in 1906 and liked their moniker. With a Penn State publication asking people to select a mascot for the school, Mason pushed for the use of Lions. His campaign was so strong, the students settled on Nittany Lions.

MASCOT The Nittany Lion made its first appearance when a student donned a lion suit and roamed the sideline at a 1922 Penn State game at the Polo Grounds in New York City. Today, the Lion remains a fixture on the road and at home.

UNIFORMS A three-member student committee decided in October 1887 that Penn State's teams should wear dark pink and black. However, the pink in the baseball team's striped blazers and caps faded to white over time. So the students instead picked blue and white. Those were named the school's official colors on March 18, 1890. Today, Penn State's uniforms are simple. Helmets are solid white with a single blue stripe in the middle. Players wear plain white pants and socks. Cleats are black. Jerseys have no names, only numerals—although the school was the first to allow Nike to move its swoosh from the sleeve to the chest, as part of a wide-ranging deal that included all of Penn State's athletic teams in 1994.

NUMBERS Penn State has won the Lambert Trophy, signifying Eastern football supremacy, 25 times … Charles A. "Rip" Engle, a member of the College Football Hall of Fame, served as Penn State's football coach for 16 years. He retired after the 1965 season with a 104–48–4 record … Defensive lineman Courtney Brown and linebacker LaVar Arrington were the top two picks, respectively, in the 2000 NFL draft, making Penn State the first school since Nebraska in 1984 to have players selected 1-2 … Jerry Sandusky, a former Penn State linebacker, served 32 years as an assistant coach on Paterno's staff, including 23 years as defensive coordinator … Penn State has had five players inducted into the Pro Football Hall of Fame: Lenny Moore, Jack Ham, Franco Harris, Mike Munchak and August Michalske.

QUIRK Paterno broke Bear Bryant's Division I-A record for most wins, but JoePa went 0–4 against Bear's Alabama teams. The Crimson Tide beat Penn State 13-6 in the 1975 Sugar Bowl and again three years later in the same bowl, 14-7. In 1981, Alabama won at Penn State 31-16. Penn State won the 1982 national title despite a 42-21 regular-season loss to Alabama at Birmingham's Legion Field.

LORE 31-6 win over Navy in 1968 showed why Penn State eventually finished the season 11–0 and ranked No. 2. The Nittany Lions not only intercepted five Navy passes and recovered four fumbles, they also found a lucky item. Penn State cheerleaders discovered a small bamboo horseshoe in the end zone after the game. The team took it everywhere the rest of the season. The horseshoe hung on the goalpost crossbar during home games. On the road, it was placed near the bench.

QUOTE "How could Nixon know so little about Watergate and so much about football?"—Joe Paterno, some years after the president gave Texas his mythical national championship, even though Penn State had a 30-game unbeaten streak after defeating Missouri in the 1970 Orange Bowl

PENN STATE ANNUAL STATISTICAL LEADERS

YR	RUSHING	YDS	ATT	AVG	PASSING	ATT	CMP	PCT	YDS	RECEIVING	REC	YDS	AVG
1946	Elwood Petchel	373	71	5.3	Elwood Petchel	37	16	.43	287	Sam Tamburo	7	126	18.0
1947	Fran Rogel	499	110	4.5	Elwood Petchel	38	18	.47	353	Jeff Durkota	6	110	18.3
1948	Fran Rogel	602	152	4.0	Elwood Petchel	100	48	.48	628	Sam Tamburo	17	301	17.7
1949	Fran Rogel	395	110	3.6	Owen Dougherty	28	12	.43	281	Robert Hicks	10	196	19.6
1950	Tony Orsini	563	146	3.9	Vince O'Bara	103	38	.37	640	John Smidansky	23	383	16.7
1951	Ted Shattuck	579	135	4.3	Bob Szajna	86	41	.48	528	Don Malinak	14	138	9.9
1952	Bob Pollard	341	110	3.1	Tony Rados	186	93	.50	937	Jesse Arnelle	33	291	8.8
1953	Lenny Moore	601	108	5.6	Tony Rados	171	81	.47	1,025	Jim Garrity	30	349	11.6
1954	Lenny Moore	1,082	136	8.0	Don Bailey	80	33	.41	393	Jack Sherry	11	160	14.5
1955	Lenny Moore	697	138	5.1	Bobby Hoffman	53	25	.47	355	Billy Kane	9	184	20.4
1956	Billy Kane	544	105	5.2	Milt Plum	75	40	.53	675	Billy Kane	16	232	14.5
1957	Dave Kasperian	469	122	3.8	Al Jacks	103	53	.51	673	Les Walters	24	440	18.3
1958	Dave Kasperian	381	98	3.9	Rich Lucas	80	36	.45	483	Maurice Schleicher	9	127	14.1
1959	Rich Lucas	325	99	3.3	Rich Lucas	117	58	.50	913	Dick Hoak	14	167	11.9
1960	Jim Kerr	389	93	4.2	Galen Hall	89	39	.44	448	Jim Kerr	13	163	12.5
1961	Roger Kochman	666	129	5.2	Galen Hall	97	50	.52	951	Jim Schwab	16	257	16.1
1962	Roger Kochman	652	120	5.4	Pete Liske	162	91	.56	1,037	Junior Powell	32	303	9.5
1963	Gary Klingensmith	450	102	4.4	Pete Liske	161	87	.54	1,117	Dick Anderson	21	229	10.9
1964	Tom Urbanik	625	134	4.7	Gary Wydman	149	70	.47	832	Bill Huber	25	347	13.9
1965	Dave McNaughton	884	193	4.6	Jack White	205	98	.48	1,275	Jack Curry	42	572	13.6
1966	Bob Campbell	482	79	6.1	Tom Sherman	135	58	.43	943	Jack Curry	34	584	17.2
1967	Charlie Pittman	580	119	4.9	Tom Sherman	205	104	.51	1,616	Jack Curry	41	681	16.6
1968	Charlie Pittman	950	186	5.1	Chuck Burkhart	177	87	.49	1,170	Ted Kwalick	31	403	13.0
1969	Charlie Pittman	706	149	4.7	Chuck Burkhart	114	59	.52	805	Greg Edmonds	20	246	12.3
1970	Lydell Mitchell	751	134	5.6	Mike Cooper	64	32	.50	429	Greg Edmonds	38	506	13.3
1971	Lydell Mitchell	1,567	254	6.2	John Hufnagel	136	86	.63	1,185	Bob Parsons	30	489	16.3
1972	John Cappelletti	1,117	233	4.8	John Hufnagel	216	115	.53	2,039	Dan Natale	30	460	15.3
1973	John Cappelletti	1,522	286	5.3	Tom Shuman	161	83	.52	1,375	Gary Hayman	30	525	17.5
1974	Tony Donchez	880	195	4.5	Tom Shuman	183	97	.53	1,355	Jerry Jeram	17	259	15.2
1975	Woody Petchel	621	148	4.2	John Andress	149	71	.48	991	Dick Barvinchak	17	327	19.2
1976	Steve Geise	560	116	4.8	Chuck Fusina	168	88	.52	1,260	Mickey Shuler	21	281	13.4
1977	Matt Suhey	638	139	4.6	Chuck Fusina	246	142	.58	2,221	Mickey Shuler	33	600	18.2
1978	Matt Suhey	720	184	3.9	Chuck Fusina	242	137	.57	1,859	Scott Fitzkee	37	630	17.0
1979	Matt Suhey	973	185	5.3	Dayle Tate	176	92	.52	1,179	Brad Scovill	26	331	12.7
1980	Curt Warner	922	196	4.7	Todd Blackledge	159	76	.48	1,037	Kenny Jackson	21	386	18.4
1981	Curt Warner	1,044	171	6.1	Todd Blackledge	207	104	.50	2,218	Gregg Garrity	23	415	18.0
1982	Curt Warner	1,041	198	5.3	Todd Blackledge	292	161	.55	1,557	Kenny Jackson	41	697	17.0
1983	D.J. Dozier	1,002	174	5.8	Doug Strang	259	134	.52	1,944	Kevin Baugh	36	547	15.2
1984	D.J. Dozier	691	125	5.5	Doug Strang	148	57	.39	840	Herb Bellamy	16	306	19.1
1985	D.J. Dozier	723	154	4.7	John Shaffer	228	103	.45	1,366	Ray Roundtree	15	285	19.0
1986	D.J. Dozier	811	171	4.7	John Shaffer	204	114	.56	1,510	D.J. Dozier	26	287	11.0
1987	Blair Thomas	1,414	268	5.3	Matt Knizner	223	113	.51	1,478	Blair Thomas	23	300	13.0
1988	Gary Brown	689	136	5.1	Tony Sacca	146	54	.37	821	Michael Timpson	22	342	15.5
1989	Blair Thomas	1,341	264	5.1	Tony Sacca	137	56	.41	694	David Daniels	22	362	16.5
1990	Leroy Thompson	573	152	3.8	Tony Sacca	249	122	.49	1,866	David Daniels	31	538	17.4
1991	Richie Anderson	779	152	5.1	Tony Sacca	292	169	.58	2,488	Terry Smith	55	846	15.4
1992	Richie Anderson	900	195	4.6	John Sacca	155	81	.52	1,118	O.J. McDuffie	63	977	15.5
1993	Ki-Jana Carter	1,026	155	6.6	Kerry Collins	250	127	.51	1,605	Bobby Engram	48	873	18.2
1994	Ki-Jana Carter	1,539	198	7.8	Kerry Collins	264	176	.67	2,679	Bobby Engram	52	1,029	19.8
1995	Curtis Enis	683	113	6.0	Wally Richardson	335	193	.58	2,198	Bobby Engram	63	1,084	17.2
1996	Curtis Enis	1,210	224	5.4	Wally Richardson	279	145	.52	1,732	Joe Jurevicius	41	869	21.2
1997	Curtis Enis	1,363	228	6.0	Mike McQueary	255	146	.57	2,211	Joe Jurevicius	39	817	20.9
1998	Eric McCoo	822	127	6.5	Kevin Thompson	226	121	.54	1,691	Corey Jones	27	368	13.6
1999	Eric McCoo	739	148	5.0	Kevin Thompson	242	133	.55	1,916	Chafie Fields	39	692	17.7
2000	Eric McCoo	692	140	4.9	Rashard Casey	309	163	.53	2,001	Tony Stewart	38	451	11.9
2001	Larry Johnson	337	71	4.7	Zack Mills	230	127	.55	1,669	Bryant Johnson	51	866	17.0
2002	Larry Johnson	2,087	271	7.7	Zack Mills	333	188	.56	2,417	Bryant Johnson	48	917	19.1
2003	Austin Scott	436	100	4.4	Zack Mills	251	136	.54	1,404	Tony Johnson	32	445	13.9
2004	Tony Hunt	777	169	4.6	Zack Mills	268	155	.58	1,722	Tony Hunt	39	334	8.6

Receiving leaders by receptions
All statistics include postseason

THE SCHOOLS

PENN STATE ALL-TIME SCORES

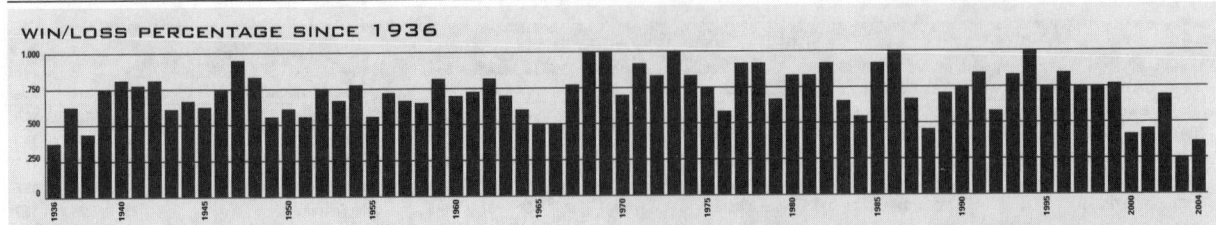

WIN/LOSS PERCENTAGE SINCE 1936

NO HEAD COACH

1887   2-0-0
N5	●	at Bucknell	54 0
N19	●	Bucknell	24 0

1888   0-2-1
O31	=	Dickinson	6 6
N7		at Dickinson	0 16
N10		Lehigh	0 30

1889   2-2-0
N2	●	Swarthmore	20 6
N9		at Lafayette	0 26
N11		at Lehigh	0 106
N25	●	Bucknell	12 0

1890   2-2-0
O10		at Pennsylvania	0 20
O12		at Franklin & Marshall	0 10
N15		Altoona	68 0
N22		at Bellefonte	23 0

1891   6-2-0
O2	●	at Lafayette	14 4
O3		at Lehigh	2 24
O17		at Swarthmore	44 0
O24	●	at Franklin & Marshall	26 6
O27	●	at Gettysburg	18 0
N7	●	at Bucknell	10 12
N26	●	Dickinson	1 0 f
D5	●	at Haverford	58 0

GEORGE HOSKINS
1892-95 (.760)   17-4-4

1892   5-1-0
O1		at Pennsylvania	0 20
O27	●	at Wyoming Seminary	40 0
N5	●	at Pittsburgh AC	16 0
N12	●	Bucknell	18 0
N23	●	Lafayette *WB*	18 0
N25	●	Dickinson *HARR*	16 0

1893   4-1-0
O14	●	at Virginia	6 0
O25		at Pennsylvania	6 18
N6	●	Pittsburgh	32 0
N11	●	at Bucknell	36 18
N30	●	at Pittsburgh AC	12 0

1894   6-0-1
O13	●	Gettysburg	60 0
O20	●	Lafayette	72 0
N10	●	at Navy	6 4
N17	●	Bucknell *WLM*	12 6
N23	●	at Wash. & Jeff	6 0
N24	=	at Oberlin	9 6
N29	●	at Pittsburg AC	14 0

1895   2-2-3
S25	●	Gettysburg	48 0
O5	=	at Cornell	0 0
O26	●	Bucknell *WLM*	16 0
N9		at Pennsylvania	4 35
N16	●	at Pittsburgh AC	10 11
N18	=	at Wash. & Jeff.	6 6
N28	●	at Western Reserve	8 8

DR. SAMUEL NEWTON
1896-98 (.462)   12-14

1896   3-4-0
S26	●	Gettysburg	40 0
O3	●	Pittsburgh	10 4
O10	●	Dickinson	8 0
O24		at Princeton	0 39
O31	●	Bucknell *WLM*	0 10
N14		at Pennsylvania	0 27
N28		Carlisle Indians	5 48

1897   3-6-0
S25	●	Gettysburg	32 0
O2		at Lafayette	0 24
O13		at Princeton	0 34
O20		at Pennsylvania	0 24
O23		at Navy	0 4
O30		at Cornell	0 45
N13	●	Bucknell *WLM*	27 4
N20	●	Bloomsburg	10 0
N25	●	Dickinson *SUN*	0 6

1898   6-4-0
S24	●	Gettysburg	47 0
O1		at Pennsylvania	0 40
O8	●	at Lafayette	5 0
O15	●	Susquehanna	45 6
O22		at Navy	11 16
O26		at Princeton	0 5
O29	●	Duquesne AC *PIT*	5 18
N5	●	Bucknell *WLM*	16 0
N19	●	at Wash. & Jeff.	11 6
O28	●	Dickinson *WLM*	34 0

SAM BOYLE
1899 (.409)   4-6-1

1899   4-6-1
S23	●	Mansfield	38 0
S30	●	Gettysburg	40 0
O7	●	at Army	6 0
O13	=	Wash. & Jeff.	0 0
O18		at Princeton	0 12
O21		at Navy	0 6
O28	●	Dickinson	15 0
N4	●	Bucknell *WLM*	0 5
N11		at Yale	0 42
N17		at Pennsylvania	0 47
N25	●	Duquesne AC *WLM*	5 64

POP GOLDEN
1900-02 (.569)   16-12-1

1900   4-6-1
S23	●	Susquehanna	17 0
S30	●	Pittsburgh *BEL*	12 0
O6	=	at Army	0 0
O10		at Princeton	0 26
O17		at Pennsylvania	6 17 *
O20		at Dickinson	0 18
O27		Duquesne AC *PIT*	0 29
N3	●	Bucknell *WLM*	6 0
N10		at Navy	0 44
N17	●	at Gettysburg	44 0
N29		at Buffalo	0 10

1901   5-3-0
S22	●	Susquehanna	17 0
S29	●	Pittsburgh *BEL*	33 0 *
O5		at Pennsylvania	6 23
O19		at Yale	0 22
O26	●	at Navy	11 6
N2		Homestead AC *PIT*	0 39
N16	●	Lehigh *WLM*	38 0
N23	●	Dickinson	12 0

1902   7-3-0
S20	●	Dickinson Seminary	27 0
S27	●	Pittsburgh	27 0
O4		at Pennsylvania	0 17
O11	●	Villanova	32 0
O18		at Yale	0 11
O25	●	Susquehanna	55 0
N1	●	at Navy	6 0
N8	●	Gettysburg	37 0
N22	●	at Dickinson	23 0
N27		at Steelton YMCA	5 6

DAN REED
1903 (.625)   5-3

1903   5-3-0
S19	●	Dickinson Seminary	60 0
O3	●	Allegheny	24 5
O10		at Pennsylvania	0 39
O17		at Yale	0 27
O24	●	at Pittsburgh	59 0
O31	●	at Navy	17 0
N14		Dickinson *WLM*	0 6
N26	●	Wash. & Jeff. *PIT*	22 0

TOM FENNELL
1904-08 (.657)   33-17-1

1904   6-4-0
S24		at Pennsylvania	0 6
O1	●	Allegheny	50 0
O8		at Yale	0 24
O15	●	West Virginia	34 0
O22	●	Wash. & Jeff. *PIT*	12 0
O29	●	Jersey Shore	30 0
N5		at Navy	9 20
N12	●	Dickinson *WLM*	11 0
N19	●	Geneva	44 0
N24		at Pittsburgh	5 22 *

1905   8-3-0
S16	●	Lebanon Valley	23 0
S30	●	California St.	29 0
O7		Carlisle Indians *HARR*	0 11
O14	●	Gettysburg	18 0
O21		at Yale	0 12
O28	●	Villanova	29 0
N4		at Navy	5 11
N11	●	Geneva	73 0
N18	●	Dickinson *WLM*	6 0
N25	●	West Virginia	6 0
N30	●	at Pittsburgh	6 0

1906   8-1-1
S22	●	Lebanon Valley	24 0
S29	●	Allegheny	26 0
O6	●	Carlisle Indians *WLM*	4 0
O13	=	Gettysburg	0 0
O20		at Yale	0 10
N3	●	at Navy	5 0
N12	●	Bellefonte Aca.	12 0
N17	●	Dickinson *WLM*	6 0
N23	●	West Virginia	10 0 *
N29	●	at Pittsburgh	6 0

1907   6-4-0
S21	●	Altoona AA	27 0
S28	●	Geneva	34 0
O5	●	Carlisle Indians *WLM*	5 18
O12	●	Grove City	46 0
O19		at Cornell	8 6
O26	●	Lebanon Valley	75 0
N2	●	Dickinson *WLM*	52 0
N9		at Pennsylvania	0 28
N16		at Navy	4 6
N28		at Pittsburgh	0 6

1908   5-5-0
S19	●	Bellefonte Aca.	5 6
S26	●	Grove City	31 0
O3	●	Carlisle Indians *WB*	5 12
O10		at Pennsylvania	0 6
O17	●	Geneva	51 0
O24	●	West Virginia	12 0
O31		at Cornell	4 10
N7	●	Bucknell	33 6
N14		at Navy	0 5
N26	●	at Pittsburgh	12 6

BILL HOLLENBACK
1909, '11-14 (.732)   28-9-4

1909   5-0-2
O2	●	Grove City	31 0
O9	=	Carlisle Indians *WB*	8 8
O16	●	Geneva	46 0
O23	=	at Pennsylvania	3 3
N6	●	at Bucknell	33 0
N13	●	West Virginia	40 0
N25	●	at Pittsburgh	5 0

JACK HOLLENBACK
1910 (.688)   5-2-1

1910   5-2-1
O1	●	Harrisburg AC	58 0
O8	●	Carnegie Tech	61 0
O15	●	Sterling AC	45 0
O22		at Pennsylvania	0 10
O29	=	Villanova	0 0
N5	●	St. Bonaventure	34 0
N12	●	Bucknell	45 3
N24		at Pittsburgh	0 11

BILL HOLLENBACK

1911   8-0-1
S30	●	Geneva	57 0
O7	●	Gettysburg	31 0
O14	●	at Cornell	5 0
O21	●	Villanova	18 0
O28	●	at Pennsylvania	22 6
N4	●	St. Bonaventure	46 0
N11	●	Colgate	17 9
N18	=	at Navy	0 0
N30	●	at Pittsburgh	3 0

1912   8-0-0
O5	●	Carnegie Tech	41 0
O12	●	Wash. & Jeff.	30 0
O19	●	at Cornell	29 6
O26	●	Gettysburg	25 0
N2	●	at Pennsylvania	14 0
N9	●	Villanova	71 0
N16	●	at Ohio State	37 0
N28	●	at Pittsburgh	38 0

1913   2-6-0
O4	●	Carnegie Tech	49 0
O11	●	Gettysburg	16 0
O18		at Wash. & Jeff.	0 17
O25		at Harvard	0 29
N1		at Pennsylvania	0 17
N7		Notre Dame	7 14
N15		at Navy	0 10
N27		at Pittsburgh	6 7

1914   5-3-1
S26	●	Westminster	13 0
O3	●	Muhlenberg	22 0
O10	●	Gettysburg	13 0
O17	●	Ursinus	30 0
O24	=	at Harvard	13 13
O31	●	at Lafayette	17 0
N7		at Lehigh	7 20
N13		Michigan State	3 6
N26		at Pittsburgh	3 13

DICK HARLOW
1915-17 (.714)   20-8

1915   7-2-0
S25	●	Westminster	26 0
O2	●	Lebanon Valley	13 0
O9		at Pennsylvania	13 3
O16	●	Gettysburg	27 12
O23	●	W. V. Wesleyan	28 0
O30		at Harvard	0 13
N5	●	Lehigh	7 0
N13	●	at Lafayette	33 3
N25		at Pittsburgh	0 20

THE SCHOOLS

1916 — 8-2-0
S23 • Susquehanna 27 0
S30 • Westminster 55 0
O7 • Bucknell 50 7
O14 • W. V. Wesleyan 39 0
O21 at Pennsylvania 0 15
O28 • Gettysburg 48 2
N4 • Geneva 79 0
N11 at Lehigh 10 7
N17 • Lafayette 40 0
N30 at Pittsburgh 0 31

1917 — 5-4-0
S29 • Army Amb. Corp ALL 10 0
O6 • Gettysburg 80 0
O13 • St. Bonaventure 99 0
O20 at Wash. & Jeff. 0 7
O27 • W. V. Wesleyan 8 7
N3 at Dartmouth 7 10
N10 • Lehigh 0 9
N17 • Maryland 57 0
N29 at Pittsburgh 6 28

HUGO BEZDEK
1918-29 (.665) 65-30-11

1918 — 1-2-1
N2 = Wissahickon Barracks 6 6
N9 • Rutgers 3 26
N16 at Lehigh 7 6
N28 at Pittsburgh 6 28

1919 — 7-1-0
O4 • Gettysburg 33 0
O11 • Bucknell 9 0
O18 at Dartmouth 13 19
O25 • Ursinus 48 7
N1 at Pennsylvania 10 0
N8 • Lehigh 20 7
N15 at Cornell 20 0
N27 at Pittsburgh 20 0

1920 — 7-0-2
S25 • Muhlenburg 27 7
O2 • Gettysburg 13 0
O9 • Dartmouth 14 7
O16 • North Carolina St. 41 0
O23 • Lebanon Valley 109 7
O30 at Pennsylvania 28 7
N6 • Nebraska 20 0
N13 at Lehigh 7 7
N25 = at Pittsburgh 0 0

1921 — 8-0-2
S24 • Lebanon Valley 53 0
O1 • Gettysburg 24 0
O8 • North Carolina St. 35 0
O15 • Lehigh 28 7
O22 at Harvard 21 21
O29 • Georgia Tech NYC 28 7
N5 • Carnegie Tech 28 7
N12 • Navy PHIL 13 7
N24 at Pittsburgh 0 0
D3 at Washington 21 7

1922 — 6-4-1
S23 • St. Bonaventure 54 0
S30 • William & Mary 27 7
O7 • Gettysburg 20 0
O14 • Lebanon Valley 32 6
O21 • Middlebury 33 0
O28 • Syracuse NYC 0 0
N3 • Navy DC 0 14
N11 • Carnegie Tech 10 0
N18 at Pennsylvania 6 7
N30 at Pittsburgh 0 14

ROSE BOWL
J1 Southern Cal 3 14

1923 — 6-2-1
S29 • Lebanon Valley 58 0
O6 • North Carolina St. 16 0
O13 • Gettysburg 20 0
O20 • Navy 21 3
O27 = West Virginia BRNX 13 13
N3 at Syracuse 0 10
N10 • Georgia Tech 7 0
N17 at Pennsylvania 21 0
N29 at Pittsburgh 3 20

1924 — 6-3-1
S27 • Lebanon Valley 47 3
O4 • North Carolina St. 51 6
O11 • Gettysburg 26 0
O18 at Georgia Tech 13 15
O25 • Syracuse 6 10
N1 • at Navy 6 0
N8 • Carnegie Tech 22 7
N15 = at Pennsylvania 0 0
N22 • Marietta 28 0
N27 at Pittsburgh 3 24

1925 — 4-4-1
S26 • Lebanon Valley 14 0
O3 • Franklin & Marshall 13 0
O10 • Georgia Tech BRNX 7 16
O17 • Marietta 13 0
O24 • Michigan State 13 6
O31 at Syracuse 0 7
N7 = Notre Dame 0 0
N14 at West Virginia 0 14
N26 at Pittsburgh 7 23

1926 — 5-4-0
S25 • Susquehanna 82 0
O2 • Lebanon Valley 35 0
O9 • Marietta 48 6
O16 at Notre Dame 0 28
O23 • Syracuse 0 10
O30 • George Washington 20 12
N6 at Pennsylvania 0 3
N13 • Bucknell 9 0
N25 at Pittsburgh 6 24

1927 — 6-2-1
S24 • Lebanon Valley 27 0
O1 • Gettysburg 34 13
O8 • Bucknell 7 13
O15 • at Pennsylvania 20 0
O22 • at Syracuse 9 6
O29 • Lafayette 40 6
N5 • George Washington 13 0
N12 = NYU 13 13
N24 at Pittsburgh 0 30

1928 — 3-5-1
S29 • Lebanon Valley 25 0
O6 • Gettysburg 12 0
O12 • Bucknell 0 6
O20 • at Pennsylvania 0 14
O26 = Syracuse 6 6
N3 • Notre Dame PHIL 0 9
N9 • George Washington 50 0
N16 • at Lafayette 0 7
N29 • at Pittsburgh 0 26

1929 — 6-3-0
S28 • Niagara 16 0
O5 • Lebanon Valley 15 0
O12 • Marshall 26 7
O19 • NYU BRNX 0 7
O26 = Lafayette 6 3
N2 • at Syracuse 6 4
N9 • at Pennsylvania 19 7
N16 • Bucknell 6 27
N28 • at Pittsburgh 7 20

BOB HIGGINS
1930-48 (.607) 91-57-11

1930 — 3-4-2
S27 • Niagara 31 14
O4 • Lebanon Valley 27 0
O11 • Marshall 65 0
O18 at Lafayette 0 0
O25 • Colgate 0 40
N1 • at Bucknell 7 19
N8 = Syracuse 0 0
N15 • at Iowa 0 19
N26 at Pittsburgh 12 19

1931 — 2-8-0
S26 • Waynesburg 0 7
O3 • Lebanon Valley 19 6
O10 at Temple 0 12
O17 • Dickinson 6 10
O24 at Syracuse 0 7
O31 • Pittsburgh 6 41
N8 • Colgate 7 32
N14 at Lafayette 0 33
N21 at West Virginia 0 19
N28 • Lehigh PHIL 31 0

1932 — 2-5-0
O1 • Lebanon Valley 27 0
O8 • Waynesburg 6 7
O15 • at Harvard 13 46
O22 • Syracuse 6 12 *
O29 • at Colgate 0 31
N3 • Sewanee 18 6
N12 • at Temple 12 13

1933 — 3-3-1
O7 • Lebanon Valley 32 6
O14 • Muhlenburg 0 3
O21 • Lehigh 33 0
O28 • at Columbia 0 33
N4 • at Syracuse 6 12
N11 • Johns Hopkins 40 6
N18 = at Pennsylvania 6 6

1934 — 4-4-0
O6 • Lebanon Valley 13 0
O13 • Gettysburg 32 6
O20 • at Lehigh 31 0
O27 • at Columbia 7 14
N3 • Syracuse 0 16
N10 • at Pennsylvania 0 3
N17 • Lafayette 25 6
N24 • Bucknell 7 13

1935 — 4-4-0
O5 • Lebanon Valley 12 6
O12 • Western Maryland 2 0
O19 • Lehigh 26 0
O26 • at Pittsburgh 0 9
N2 • at Syracuse 3 7
N9 • Villanova 27 13
N16 • at Pennsylvania 6 33
N23 • at Bucknell 0 2

1936 — 3-5-0
O3 • Muhlenburg 45 0
O10 • Villanova 0 13
O17 • at Lehigh 6 7
O24 • at Cornell 7 13
O31 • at Syracuse 18 0
N7 • at Pittsburgh 7 34
N14 • at Pennsylvania 12 19
N21 • Bucknell 14 0

1937 — 5-3-0
S25 • at Cornell 19 26
O2 • Gettysburg 32 6
O9 • Bucknell 30 14
O16 • Lehigh 14 7
O30 • at Syracuse 13 19
N6 • at Pennsylvania 7 0
N13 • Maryland 21 14
N20 • at Pittsburgh 7 28

1938 — 3-4-1
O1 • Maryland 33 0
O8 • Bucknell 0 14
O15 • at Lehigh 59 6
O22 • at Cornell 6 21
O29 • Syracuse 33 6
N5 • Lafayette 0 7
N12 • at Pennsylvania 7 7
N19 • at Pittsburgh 0 26

1939 — 5-1-2
O7 • Bucknell 13 3
O14 • Lehigh 49 7
O21 • at Cornell 0 47
O28 = at Syracuse 6 6
N4 • Maryland 12 0
N11 • at Pennsylvania 10 0
N18 = at Army 14 14
N25 • Pittsburgh 10 0

1940 — 6-1-1
O5 • Bucknell 9 0
O12 • West Virginia 17 13
O19 • at Lehigh 34 0
O26 • at Temple 18 0
N2 • South Carolina 12 0
N9 = at Syracuse 13 13
N16 • NYU 25 0
N23 • Pittsburgh 7 20

1941 — 7-2-0
O4 • Colgate BUF 0 7
O11 • Bucknell 27 13
O18 • at Temple 0 14
O25 • Lehigh 40 6
O31 • NYU NYC 42 0
N8 • Syracuse 34 19
N15 • West Virginia 7 0
N22 • at Pittsburgh 31 7
N29 • at South Carolina 19 12

1942 — 6-1-1
O3 • Bucknell 14 7
O10 • at Lehigh 19 3
O17 = at Cornell 0 0
O24 • Colgate 13 10
O31 • at West Virginia 0 24
N7 • Syracuse 18 13
N14 • at Pennsylvania 13 7
N21 • Pittsburgh 14 6

1943 — 5-3-0
S25 • Bucknell 14 0
O2 at North Carolina 0 19
O9 • Colgate 0 0
O16 at Navy 6 14
O23 • at Maryland 45 0
O30 • West Virginia 32 7
N6 at Cornell 0 13
N13 • Temple 13 0
N20 • at Pittsburgh 14 0

1944 — 6-3-0
S30 • Muhlenburg 58 13
O7 at Navy 14 55
O14 • Bucknell 20 6
O21 at Colgate 6 0
O28 • West Virginia 27 28
N4 at Syracuse 41 0
N11 at Temple 7 6
N18 • Maryland 34 19
N25 at Pittsburgh 0 14

1945 — 5-3-0
S29 • Muhlenberg 47 7
O6 • Colgate 27 7
O13 at Navy 0 28
O20 at Bucknell 46 7
N3 • Syracuse 26 0
N10 • Temple 27 0
N17 at Michigan State 0 33
N24 at Pittsburgh 0 7

1946 — 6-2-0
O5 • Bucknell 48 6
O12 at Syracuse 9 0
O19 • Michigan State 16 19
O26 • at Colgate 6 2
N2 • Fordham 68 0
N9 • Temple 26 0
N16 at Navy 12 7
N23 at Pittsburgh 7 14

1947 — 9-0-1
S20 • Washington State HER 27 6
O4 • Bucknell 54 0
O11 • Fordham NYC 75 0
O18 • Syracuse 40 0
O25 • West Virginia 21 14
N1 • Colgate 46 0
N8 • at Temple 7 0
N15 • Navy BALT 20 7
N22 • at Pittsburgh 29 0

COTTON BOWL
J1 = SMU 13 13

1948 — 7-1-1
O2 • Bucknell 35 0
O8 • at Syracuse 34 14
O16 • West Virginia 37 7
O23 = Michigan State 14 14
O30 • at Colgate 32 13
N6 • at Pennsylvania 13 0
N13 • Temple 47 0
N20 at Pittsburgh 0 7
N27 • Washington State TAC 7 0

JOE BEDENK
1949 (.556) 5-4

1949 — 5-4-0
S24 • Villanova 6 27
O1 at Army 7 42
O8 • Boston College 32 14
O15 • Nebraska 22 7
O22 at Michigan State 0 24
O29 • Syracuse 33 21
N5 • at West Virginia 34 14
N12 • at Temple 28 7
N19 • at Pittsburgh 0 19

RIP ENGLE
1950-65 (.679) 104-48-4

1950 — 5-3-1
S30 • Georgetown 34 14
O7 at Army 7 41
O14 at Syracuse 7 27
O21 at Nebraska 0 19
O28 = Temple 7 7
N4 • at Boston College 20 13
N11 • West Virginia 27 0
N18 • Rutgers 18 14
N25 • at Pittsburgh 21 20

1951 — 5-4-0
S29 • Boston U. 40 34
O6 • Villanova ALL 14 20
O13 at Nebraska 15 7
O20 • Michigan State 21 32
O27 • West Virginia 13 7
N3 at Purdue 0 28
N10 • Syracuse 32 13
N17 at Rutgers 13 7
N24 at Pittsburgh 7 13

1952 7-2-1

S20	●	Temple	20	13
S27	=	Purdue	20	20
O4	●	William & Mary	35	23
O11	●	at West Virginia	35	21
O18	●	Nebraska	10	0
O25		at Michigan State	7	34
N1	●	at Pennsylvania	14	7
N8		at Syracuse	7	25
N15	●	Rutgers	7	6
N22	●	at Pittsburgh	17	0

1953 6-3-0

S26		at Wisconsin	0	20
O3		at Pennsylvania	7	13
O10	●	at Boston U.	35	13
O17	●	Syracuse	20	14
O24	●	TCU	27	21
O31		West Virginia	19	20
N7	●	Fordham	28	21
N14	●	at Rutgers	54	26
N21	●	at Pittsburgh	17	0

1954 7-2-0

S25	●	at Illinois	14	12
O2	●	at Syracuse	13	0
O9	●	Virginia	34	7
O16		West Virginia	14	19
O23		at TCU	7	20
O30	●	at Pennsylvania	35	13
N6	●	Holy Cross	39	7
N13	●	Rutgers	37	14
N20	●	at Pittsburgh	13	0

1955 5-4-0

S24	●	Boston U.	35	0
O1		at Army	6	35
O8	●	Virginia RICH	26	7
O15		Navy	14	34
O22		at West Virginia	7	21
O29	●	at Pennsylvania	20	0
N5	●	Syracuse	21	20
N12	●	at Rutgers	34	13
N19		Pittsburgh	0	20

1956 6-2-1

S29	●	at Pennsylvania	34	0
O6		at Army	7	14
O13	●	Holy Cross	43	0
O20	●	at Ohio State	7	6
O27	●	West Virginia	16	6
N3		at Syracuse	9	13
N10	●	Boston U.	40	7
N17	●	North Carolina St.	14	7
N24	=	at Pittsburgh	7	7

1957 6-3-0

S28	●	at Pennsylvania	19	14
O5		Army	13	27
O12	●	William & Mary	21	13
O19		Vanderbilt	20	32
O26	●	at Syracuse	20	12
N2	●	West Virginia	27	6
N9	●	at Marquette	20	7
N16	●	at Holy Cross	14	10
N23		at Pittsburgh	13	14

1958 6-3-1

S20		at Nebraska	7	14
S27	●	at Pennsylvania	43	0
O4		at Army	0	26
O11	●	Marquette	40	8
O18	●	at Boston U.	34	0
O25		Syracuse	6	14
N1	●	Furman	36	0
N8	=	at West Virginia	14	14
N15	●	Holy Cross	32	0
N27	●	at Pittsburgh	25	21

1959 9-2-0

S19	●	at Missouri	19	8
S26	●	VMI	21	0
O3	●	Colgate	58	20
O10	●	at Army	17	11
O17	●	Boston U.	21	12
O24	●	Illinois CLEV	20	9
O31	●	at West Virginia	28	10
N7		Syracuse	18	20
N14	●	Holy Cross	46	0
N21		at Pittsburgh	7	22
		LIBERTY BOWL		
D19	●	Alabama	7	0

1960 7-3-0

S17	●	Boston U.	20	0
O1		Missouri	8	21
O8	●	at Army	27	16
O15		at Syracuse	15	21
O22		at Illinois	8	10
O29	●	West Virginia	34	13
N5	●	Maryland	28	9
N12	●	at Holy Cross	33	8
N19	●	at Pittsburgh	14	3
		LIBERTY BOWL		
D17	●	Oregon	41	12

1961 8-3-0

S23	●	Navy	20	10
S29		at Miami, Fla.	8	25
O6	●	at Boston U.	32	0
O14		Army	6	10
O21	●	Syracuse	14	0
O28	●	California	33	16
N4		at Maryland	17	21
N11	●	at West Virginia	20	6
N18	●	Holy Cross	34	14
N25	●	at Pittsburgh	47	26
		GATOR BOWL		
D30	●	Georgia Tech	30	15

1962 9-2-0

S22	●	Navy	41	7
S29	●	Air Force	20	6
O6	●	at Rice	18	7
O13		at Army	6	9
O20	●	Syracuse	20	19
O27	●	at California	23	21
N3	●	Maryland	23	7
N10	●	West Virginia	34	6
N17	●	at Holy Cross	48	20
N24	●	at Pittsburgh	16	0
		GATOR BOWL		
D29		Florida	7	17

1963 7-3-0

S21	●	Oregon PORT	17	7
S28	●	UCLA	17	14
O5	●	Rice	28	7
O12		Army	7	10
O19		at Syracuse	0	9
O26	●	West Virginia	20	9
N2	●	at Maryland	17	15
N9	●	at Ohio State	10	7
N16	●	Holy Cross	28	14
D7		at Pittsburgh	21	22

1964 6-4-0

S19		Navy	8	21
S26		at UCLA	14	21
O3		Oregon	14	22
O10	●	at Army	6	2
O17		Syracuse	14	21
O24	●	at West Virginia	37	8
O31	●	Maryland	17	9
N7	●	at Ohio State	27	0
N14	●	at Houston	24	7
N21	●	at Pittsburgh	28	0

1965 5-5-0

S25		Michigan State	0	23
O2		UCLA	22	24
O9	●	at Boston College	17	0
O16		at Syracuse	21	28
O23	●	West Virginia	44	6
O30		at California	17	21
N6	●	Kent	21	6
N13	●	Navy	14	6
N20		at Pittsburgh	27	30
D4	●	at Maryland	19	7

JOE PATERNO
1966-PRESENT (.742) 343-116-3

1966 5-5-0

S17	●	Maryland	15	7
S24		at Michigan State	8	42
O1		at Army	0	11
O8	●	Boston College	30	21
O15		at UCLA	11	49
O22	●	at West Virginia	38	6
O29	●	California	33	15
N5		Syracuse	10	12
N12		at Georgia Tech	0	21
N19	●	at Pittsburgh	48	24

1967 8-2-1

S23		at Navy	22	23
S29	●	at Miami, Fla.	17	8
O7		UCLA	15	17
O14	●	at Boston College	50	28
O21	●	West Virginia	21	14
O28	●	at Syracuse	29	20
N4	●	at Maryland	38	3
N11	●	North Carolina St.	13	8
N18	●	Ohio U.	35	14
N25	●	Pittsburgh	42	6
		GATOR BOWL		
D30	=	Florida State	17	17

1968 11-0-0

S21	●	Navy	31	6
S28	●	Kansas State	25	9
O5	●	at West Virginia	31	20
O12	●	at UCLA	21	6
O26	●	at Boston College	29	0
N2	●	Army	28	24
N9	●	Miami, Fla.	22	7
N16	●	at Maryland	57	13
N23	●	at Pittsburgh	65	9
D7	●	Syracuse	30	12
		ORANGE BOWL		
J1	●	Kansas	15	14

1969 11-0-0

S20	●	at Navy	45	22
S27	●	Colorado	27	3
O4	●	at Kansas State	17	14
O11	●	West Virginia	20	0
O18	●	at Syracuse	15	14
O25	●	Ohio U.	42	3
N1	●	Boston College	38	16
N15	●	Maryland	48	0
N22	●	at Pittsburgh	27	7
N29	●	at North Carolina St.	33	8
		ORANGE BOWL		
J1	●	Missouri	10	3

1970 7-3-0

S19	●	Navy	55	7
S26		at Colorado	13	41
O3		at Wisconsin	16	29
O10	●	at Boston College	28	3
O17		Syracuse	7	24
O24	●	at Army	38	14
O31	●	West Virginia	42	8
N7	●	at Maryland	34	0
N14	●	Ohio U.	32	22
N21	●	Pittsburgh	35	15

1971 11-1-0

S18	●	at Navy	56	3
S25	●	at Iowa	44	14
O2	●	Air Force	16	14
O9	●	Army	42	0
O16	●	at Syracuse	31	0
O23	●	TCU	66	14
O30	●	at West Virginia	35	7
N6	●	Maryland	63	27
N13	●	North Carolina St.	35	3
N20	●	at Pittsburgh	55	18
D4		at Tennessee	11	31
		COTTON BOWL		
J1	●	Texas	30	6

1972 10-2-0

S16		at Tennessee	21	28
S23	●	Navy	21	10
S30	●	Iowa	14	10
O7	●	at Illinois	35	17
O14	●	at Army	45	0
O21	●	Syracuse	17	0
O28	●	at West Virginia	28	19
N4	●	Maryland	46	16
N11	●	North Carolina St.	37	22
N18	●	at Boston College	45	26
N25	●	Pittsburgh	49	27
		SUGAR BOWL		
D31		Oklahoma	0	14

1973 12-0-0

S15	●	at Stanford	20	6
S22	●	at Navy	39	0
S29	●	Iowa	27	8
O6	●	at Air Force	19	9
O13	●	Army	54	3
O20	●	at Syracuse	49	6
O27	●	West Virginia	62	14
N3	●	at Maryland	42	22
N10	●	North Carolina St.	35	29
N17	●	Ohio U.	49	10
N24	●	Pittsburgh	35	13
		ORANGE BOWL		
J1	●	LSU	16	9

1974 10-2-0

S14	●	Stanford	24	20
S21		Navy	6	7
S28	●	at Iowa	27	0
O5	●	at Army	21	14
O12	●	Wake Forest	55	0
O19	●	Syracuse	30	14
O26	●	at West Virginia	21	12
N2	●	Maryland	24	17
N9		at North Carolina St.	7	12
N16	●	Ohio U.	35	16
N28	●	at Pittsburgh	31	10
		COTTON BOWL		
J1	●	Baylor	41	20

1975 9-3-0

S6	●	Temple PHIL	26	25
S13	●	Stanford	34	14
S20		at Ohio State	9	17
S27	●	at Iowa	30	10
O4	●	Kentucky	10	3
O11	●	West Virginia	39	0
O18	●	at Syracuse	19	7
O25	●	Army	31	0
N1	●	at Maryland	15	13
N8		North Carolina St.	14	15
N22	●	at Pittsburgh	7	6
		SUGAR BOWL		
D31		Alabama	6	13

1976 7-5-0

S11	●	Stanford	15	12
S18		Ohio State	7	12
S25		Iowa	6	7
O2		at Kentucky	6	22
O9	●	Army	38	16
O16	●	Syracuse	27	3
O23	●	at West Virginia	33	0
O30	●	at Temple	31	30
N6	●	North Carolina St.	41	20
N13	●	at Miami, Fla.	21	7
N26		at Pittsburgh	7	24
		GATOR BOWL		
D27		Notre Dame	9	20

1977 11-1-0

S2	●	Rutgers ERUT	45	7
S17	●	Houston	31	14
S24	●	Maryland	27	9
O1		Kentucky	20	24
O8	●	Utah State	16	7
O15	●	at Syracuse	31	24
O22	●	West Virginia	49	28
O29	●	Miami, Fla.	49	7
N5	●	at North Carolina St.	21	17
N12	●	Temple	44	7
N19	●	at Pittsburgh	15	13
		FIESTA BOWL		
D25	●	Arizona State	42	30

1978 11-1-0

S1	●	at Temple	10	7
S9	●	Rutgers	26	10
S16	●	at Ohio State	19	0
S23	●	SMU	26	21
S30	●	TCU	58	0
O7	●	at Kentucky	30	0
O21	●	Syracuse	45	15
O28	●	at West Virginia	49	21
N4	●	Maryland	27	3
N11	●	North Carolina St.	19	10
N25	●	Pittsburgh	17	10
		SUGAR BOWL		
J1		Alabama	7	14

1979 8-4-0

S15	●	Rutgers	45	10
S22		Texas A&M	14	27
S29		at Nebraska	17	42
O6	●	at Maryland	27	7
O13	●	Army	24	3
O20	●	Syracuse ERUT	35	7
O27	●	West Virginia	31	6
N3		Miami, Fla.	10	26
N10	●	at North Carolina St.	9	7
N17	●	Temple	22	7
D1		at Pittsburgh	14	29
		LIBERTY BOWL		
D22	●	Tulane	9	6

1980 10-2-0
S6 ● Colgate 54 10
S20 ● at Texas A&M 25 9
S27 Nebraska 7 21
O4 ● at Missouri 29 21
O11 ● at Maryland 24 10
O18 ● Syracuse 24 7
O25 ● at West Virginia 20 15
N1 ● Miami, Fla. 27 12
N8 ● North Carolina St. 21 13
N15 ● at Temple 50 7
N29 Pittsburgh 9 14
FIESTA BOWL
D26 ● Ohio State 31 19

1981 10-2-0
S12 ● Cincinnati 52 0
S26 ● at Nebraska 30 24
O3 ● Temple 30 0
O10 ● Boston College 38 7
O17 ● at Syracuse 41 16
O24 ● West Virginia 30 7
O31 at Miami, Fla. 14 17
N7 ● at North Carolina St. 22 15
N14 Alabama 16 31
N21 ● Notre Dame 24 21
N28 ● at Pittsburgh 48 14
FIESTA BOWL
J1 ● Southern Cal 26 10

1982 11-1-0
S4 ● Temple 31 14
S11 ● Maryland 39 31
S18 ● Rutgers 49 14
S25 ● Nebraska 27 24
O9 Alabama *Birm* 21 42
O16 ● Syracuse 28 7
O23 ● at West Virginia 24 0
O30 ● at Boston College 52 17
N6 ● North Carolina St. 54 0
N13 ● at Notre Dame 24 14
N27 ● Pittsburgh 19 10
SUGAR BOWL
J1 ● Georgia 27 23

1983 8-4-1
A29 Nebraska *ERut* 6 44
S10 Cincinnati 3 14
S17 Iowa 34 42
S24 ● Temple *Phil* 23 18
O1 ● Rutgers *ERut* 36 25
O8 ● Alabama 34 28
O15 ● at Syracuse 17 6
O22 ● West Virginia 41 23
O29 Boston College *Fox* 17 27
N5 ● Brown 38 21
N12 ● Notre Dame 34 30
N19 = at Pittsburgh 24 24
ALOHA BOWL
D26 ● Washington 13 10

1984 6-5-0
S8 ● Rutgers 15 12
S15 ● at Iowa 20 17
S22 ● William & Mary 56 18
S29 Texas *ERut* 3 28
O6 ● Maryland 25 24
O13 at Alabama 0 6
O20 ● Syracuse 21 3
O27 at West Virginia 14 17
N3 ● Boston College 37 30
N17 at Notre Dame 7 44
N24 Pittsburgh 11 31

1985 11-1-0
S7 ● at Maryland 20 18
S14 ● Temple 27 25
S21 ● East Carolina 17 10
S28 ● Rutgers *ERut* 17 10
O12 ● Alabama 19 17
O19 ● at Syracuse 24 20
O26 ● West Virginia 27 0
N2 ● Boston College 16 12
N9 ● at Cincinnati 31 10
N16 ● Notre Dame 36 6
N23 ● at Pittsburgh 31 0
ORANGE BOWL
J1 Oklahoma 10 25

1986 12-0-0
S6 ● Temple 45 15
S20 ● Boston College *Fox* 26 14
S27 ● East Carolina 42 17
O4 ● Rutgers 31 6
O11 ● Cincinnati 23 17
O18 ● Syracuse 42 3
O25 ● at Alabama 23 3
N1 ● at West Virginia 19 0
N8 ● Maryland 17 15
N15 ● at Notre Dame 24 19
N22 ● Pittsburgh 34 14
FIESTA BOWL
J2 ● Miami, Fla. 14 10

1987 8-4-0
S5 ● Bowling Green 45 19
S12 Alabama 13 24
S19 ● Cincinnati 41 0
S26 ● Boston College *Fox* 27 17
O3 ● Temple 27 13
O10 ● Rutgers 35 21
O17 at Syracuse 21 48
O31 ● West Virginia 25 21
N7 ● Maryland *Balt* 21 16
N14 at Pittsburgh 0 10
N21 ● Notre Dame 21 20
CITRUS BOWL
J1 Clemson 10 35

1988 5-6-0
S10 ● at Virginia 42 14
S17 ● Boston College 23 20
S24 Rutgers 16 21
O1 ● Temple *Phil* 45 9
O8 ● Cincinnati 35 9
O15 Syracuse 10 24
O22 Alabama *Birm* 3 8
O29 at West Virginia 30 51
N5 ● Maryland 17 10
N12 Pittsburgh 7 14
N19 at Notre Dame 3 21

1989 8-3-1
S9 Virginia 6 14
S16 ● Temple 42 3
S23 ● Boston College 7 3
S30 ● at Texas 16 12
O7 ● Rutgers *ERut* 17 0
O14 ● at Syracuse 34 12
O28 Alabama 16 17
N4 ● West Virginia 19 9
N11 = Maryland *Balt* 13 13
N18 Notre Dame 23 34
N25 ● at Pittsburgh 16 13
HOLIDAY BOWL
D29 ● Brigham Young 50 39

1990 9-3-0
S8 Texas 13 17
S15 at Southern Cal 14 19
S22 ● Rutgers 28 0
O6 ● Temple 48 10
O13 ● Syracuse 27 21
O20 ● at Boston College 40 21
O27 ● at Alabama 9 0
N3 ● at West Virginia 31 19
N10 ● Maryland 24 10
N17 ● at Notre Dame 24 21
N24 ● Pittsburgh 22 17
BLOCKBUSTER BOWL
D28 Florida State 17 24

1991 11-2-0
A28 ● Georgia Tech *ERut* 34 22
S7 ● Cincinnati 81 0
S14 at Southern Cal 10 21
S21 ● Brigham Young 33 7
S28 ● Boston College 28 21
O5 ● Temple *Phil* 24 7
O12 at Miami, Fla. 20 26
O19 ● Rutgers 37 17
O26 ● West Virginia 51 6
N9 ● Maryland *Balt* 47 7
N16 ● Notre Dame 35 13
N30 ● at Pittsburgh 32 20
FIESTA BOWL
J1 ● Tennessee 42 17

1992 7-5-0
S5 ● at Cincinnati 24 20
S12 ● Temple 49 8
S19 ● Eastern Michigan 52 7
S26 ● Maryland 49 13
O3 ● Rutgers *ERut* 38 24
O10 Miami, Fla. 14 17
O17 Boston College 32 35
O24 ● at West Virginia 40 26
O31 at Brigham Young 17 30
N14 at Notre Dame 16 17
N21 ● Pittsburgh 57 13
BLOCKBUSTER BOWL
J1 Stanford 3 24

1993-PRESENT
BIG 10

1993 10-2-0 (6-2-0)
S4 ● | Minnesota 38 20
S11 ● Southern Cal 21 20
S18 ● | at Iowa 31 0
S25 ● Rutgers 31 7
O2 ● at Maryland 70 7
O16 | Michigan 13 21
O30 | at Ohio State 6 24
N6 ● | Indiana 38 31
N13 ● | Illinois 28 14
N20 ● | at Northwestern 43 21
N27 ● | at Michigan State 38 37
CITRUS BOWL
J1 ● Tennessee 31 13

1994 12-0-0 (8-0-0)
S3 ● | at Minnesota 56 3
S10 ● Southern Cal 38 14
S17 ● | Iowa 61 21
S24 ● Rutgers 55 27
O1 ● at Temple 48 21
O15 ● | at Michigan 31 24
O29 ● | Ohio State 63 14
N5 ● | at Indiana 35 29
N12 ● | at Illinois 35 31
N19 ● | Northwestern 45 17
N26 ● | Michigan State 59 31
ROSE BOWL
J2 ● Oregon 38 20

1995 9-3-0 (5-3-0)
S9 ● Texas Tech 24 23
S16 ● Temple 66 14
S23 ● Rutgers *ERut* 59 34
S30 | Wisconsin 9 17
O7 | Ohio State 25 28
O14 ● | at Purdue 26 23
O21 ● | at Iowa 41 27
O28 ● | Indiana 45 21
N4 | at Northwestern 10 21
N18 ● | Michigan 27 17
N25 ● | at Michigan State 24 20
HALL OF FAME BOWL
J1 ● Auburn 43 14

1996 11-2 (6-2)
A25 ● Southern Cal *ERut* 24 7
S7 ● Louisville 24 7
S14 ● Northern Illinois 49 0
S21 ● Temple *ERut* 41 0
S28 ● | at Wisconsin 23 20
O5 | at Ohio State 7 38
O12 ● | Purdue 31 14
O19 | Iowa 20 21
O26 ● | at Indiana 48 26
N2 ● | Northwestern 34 9
N16 ● | at Michigan 29 17
N23 ● | Michigan State 32 29
FIESTA BOWL
J1 ● Texas 38 15

1997 9-3 (6-2)
S6 ● Pittsburgh 34 17
S13 ● Temple 52 10
S20 ● at Louisville 57 21
O4 ● | at Illinois 41 6
O11 ● | Ohio State 31 27
O18 ● | Minnesota 16 15
N1 ● | at Northwestern 30 27
N8 | Michigan 8 34
N15 ● | at Purdue 42 17
N22 ● | Wisconsin 35 10
N29 | at Michigan State 14 49
CITRUS BOWL
J1 Florida 6 21

1998 9-3 (5-3)
S5 ● So. Mississippi 34 6
S12 ● Bowling Green 48 3
S19 ● at Pittsburgh 20 13
O3 | at Ohio State 9 28
O10 ● | at Minnesota 27 17
O17 ● | Purdue 31 13
O31 ● | Illinois 27 0
N7 | at Michigan 0 27
N14 ● | Northwestern 41 10
N21 | at Wisconsin 3 24
N28 ● | Michigan State 51 28
OUTBACK BOWL
J1 ● Kentucky 26 14

1999 10-3 (5-3)
A28 ● Arizona 41 7
S4 ● Akron 70 24
S11 ● Pittsburgh 20 17
S18 ● at Miami, Fla. 27 23
S25 ● | Indiana 45 24
O9 ● | at Iowa 31 7
O16 ● | Ohio State 23 10
O23 ● | at Purdue 31 25
O30 ● | at Illinois 27 7
N6 | Minnesota 23 24
N13 | Michigan 27 31
N20 | at Michigan State 28 35
ALAMO BOWL
D28 ● Texas A&M 24 0

2000 5-7 (4-4)
A27 Southern Cal *ERut* 5 29
S2 Toledo 6 24
S9 ● Louisiana Tech 67 7
S16 at Pittsburgh 0 12
S23 | at Ohio State 6 45
S30 ● | Purdue 22 20
O7 | at Minnesota 16 25
O21 ● | Illinois 39 25
O28 ● | Indiana *Ind* 27 24
N4 | Iowa 23 26
N11 | at Michigan 11 33
N18 ● | Michigan State 42 23

2001 5-6 (4-4)
S1 Miami, Fla. 7 33
S22 | Wisconsin 6 18
S29 | at Iowa 18 24
O6 | Michigan 0 20
O20 ● | at Northwestern 38 35
O27 ● | Ohio State 29 27
N3 ● So. Mississippi 38 20
N10 | at Illinois 28 33
N17 ● | Indiana 28 14
N24 ● | at Michigan State 42 37
D1 at Virginia 14 20

2002 9-4 (5-3)
A31 ● Central Florida 27 24
S14 ● Nebraska 40 7
S21 ● Louisiana Tech 49 17
S28 | Iowa 35 42
O5 ● | at Wisconsin 34 31
O12 | at Michigan 24 27
O19 ● | Northwestern 49 0
O26 | at Ohio State 7 13
N2 ● | Illinois 18 7
N9 ● Virginia 35 14
N16 ● | at Indiana 58 25
N23 ● | Michigan State 61 7
CAPITAL ONE BOWL
J1 Auburn 9 13

2003 3-9 (1-7)
A30 ● Temple 23 10
S6 Boston College 14 27
S13 at Nebraska 10 18
S20 ● Kent State 32 10
S27 | Minnesota 14 20
O4 | Wisconsin 23 30
O11 | at Purdue 14 28
O25 | at Iowa 14 26
N1 | Ohio State 20 21
N8 | at Northwestern 7 17
N15 ● | Indiana 52 7
N22 | at Michigan State 10 41

2004 4-7 (2-6)
S4 ● Akron 48 10
S11 at Boston College 7 21
S18 ● Central Florida 37 13
S25 | at Wisconsin 3 16
O2 | at Minnesota 7 16
O9 | Purdue 13 20
O23 | Iowa 4 6
O30 | at Ohio State 10 21
N6 | Northwestern 7 14
N13 ● | at Indiana 22 18
N20 ● | Michigan State 37 13

Neutral Site key: *Her* Hershey, Pa. / *Balt* Baltimore, Md. / *Tac* Tacoma, Wash. / *All* Allentown, Pa. / *Rich* Richmond, Va. / *Clev* Cleveland, Ohio / *Phil* Philadelphia, Pa. / *Port* Portland, Ore. / *Wlm* Williamsport, Pa. / *ERut* East Rutherford, N.J. / *Birm* Birmingham, Ala. / *Fox* Foxboro, Mass. *Sun* Sunbury, Pa. / *Brnx* Bronx. N.Y. / *Ind* Indianapolis, Ind. / *Pit* Pittsburgh, Pa. / *Bel* Bellefonte, Pa. / *Harr* Harrisburg, Pa. / *WB* Wilkes-Barre, Pa. / *Buf* Buffalo, N.Y. / *NYC* New York, N.Y.

f **Forfeit** † **Game Later Forfieted** # **Disputed Victor** * **Disputed Score** || **Designated Conference Game** |2 **Counted Twice in Conference Standings**

PITTSBURGH

BY MIKE VACCARO

IN THE BEGINNING, THERE WAS western Pennsylvania. Many other football constituencies have grown through the years: Florida, Texas, California. All are hot pockets of talent, hotbeds and feeder systems to the game's grandest programs, places where football players grow into superstars. But once there was only one place that mattered, one place practically bursting with blue-chip talent.

No place embodied the football-as-life perspective of the Keystone State more than the University of Pittsburgh, whose proud tradition stretches across much of the history of the sport. The Panthers staked a claim to the first of four national championships in 1916 and achieved the last one in 1976. Their tradition of talent brims with names such as Ditka, Dorsett, Marino, Green, McLaren, Martin, May, Schmidt.

Pittsburgh's first national champions were guided by Pop Warner, whose identity is synonymous with the development of football players everywhere. Warner was 60–12–4 before heading for Stanford and leaving the program in the capable hands of Jock Sutherland, who added one official national title and went 111–20–12 in 15 years. Later, Johnny Majors would resume that legacy, elevating Pitt back to prominence by pushing the Panthers to the 1976 national title.

And even after Walt Harris helped revive Pittsburgh's program in the new century, he was reminded of the school's exacting standards. Though he led the Panthers to a BCS bowl berth by winning the Big East in 2004, Harris' departure to Stanford prior to a Fiesta Bowl loss to Utah was met with little resistance. Pitt quickly responded by turning to one of its own: Class of '76 alumnus Dave Wannstedt.

TRADITION One of the most lasting game day events is the Panthers Prowl, which is held before each home game. Fans form a gauntlet for the Panthers to walk through as they exit the bus and head for the locker room. The crowd often chants the familiar cheer "Pitt is it!" If all goes well, the university's Cathedral of Learning—the second-tallest educational building in the world—is bathed in a gold light, as it has been on every Saturday night following a Panthers

PROFILE

University of Pittsburgh
Pittsburgh, Pa.
Founded: 1787
Enrollment: 17,181
Colors: Blue and Gold
Nickname: Panthers
Stadium: Heinz Field
   Opened in 2001
   FieldTurf; 65,000 capacity
First football game: 1890
All-time record: 628–452–42 (.578)
Bowl record: 10–14
Consensus national championships, 1936-present: 2 (1937, 1976)
Big East Conference championships: 1 (shared)
Heisman Trophy: Tony Dorsett, 1976
Outland Trophy: Mark May, 1980
First-round NFL draftees: 21
Website: www.pittsburghpanthers.com

THE BEST OF TIMES

With Glenn Scobey "Pop" Warner at the helm, Pittsburgh enjoyed one of the most dominant stretches in the history of college football. Warner's first three teams, from 1915 to 1917, went undefeated (26–0), outscoring opponents 762-72, and won the school's first national title in 1916.

THE WORST OF TIMES

Under the three-year stewardship of David Hart (1966 -1968), Pittsburgh was 3–27 and was outscored 1,014-277.

CONFERENCE

From 1890 to 1990, Pittsburgh was one of the strongest independents in all of college football. It became a charter member of the Big East Football Conference in 1991.

DISTINGUISHED ALUMNI

Myron Cope, voice of the Pittsburgh Steelers; Pat Croce, president of the Philadelphia 76ers; Mike Ditka, NFL coach; Dee Kantner, one of the first female NBA referees; Gene Kelly, actor/dancer/director; Lorin Maazel, conductor; Dave Wannstedt, Panthers head coach; Vladimir Zworykin, an inventor of television

FIGHT SONG

PITT VICTORY SONG
Let's go Pitt, we're set for victory
So lend a hand, strike up the band!
Let's go Pitt, we're making history
We'll never yield out on the field.
The whistle blows, we're on our toes
The ball is in the air.
It may be rough the going tough
But always fighting fair so …
Fight on for dear old Pittsburgh
And for the glory of the game
Show our worthy foe that the Panther's on the go
Pitt must win today! Rah! Rah! Rah!
Cheer loyal sons of Pittsburgh
Cheer on to victory and fame
For the Blue and Gold shall conquer as of old
So fight, Pitt, fight!
Da da da da da-da. Fight, Pitt, fight!
Da da da da da-da. Fight, Pitt, fight!
V-I-C-T-O-R-Y!

football victory since 1937. Pittsburgh is also believed to be the first football team to add numbers to their jerseys, in 1908. One of the school's oldest traditions—the shortening of the school name to "Pitt"—was phased out in 1997. The official reason was "marketing," since the school wanted its full name prominently displayed. The fact that opposing teams—notably West Virginia—had long used derogatory rhymes for Pitt didn't hurt either.

BEST PLAYER The Panthers' roster of distinguished alumni is vast, but no player had the immediate and lasting impact of Tony Dorsett. He was the cornerstone of Johnny Majors' first recruiting class, arriving on campus late in the summer of 1973, just after the return of freshman eligibility. By the time he left four years later, Dorsett and his classmates had transformed the Panthers from a languishing program of the late 1960s-early 1970s into national champions (1976). Dorsett, from Aliquippa, Pa., is Pitt's only

> *Tony Dorsett and his teammates transformed Pitt from a languishing program into a national champion.*

Heisman Trophy winner and is the only man besides Marcus Allen to win the Heisman, a college national championship and a Super Bowl, and be named to both the college and pro football halls of fame. In 46 games as a Panther, Dorsett gained 100 yards in 36 games, including in 20 straight. In the last seven games of the 1976 season, he averaged 212 yards rushing, pushing the Panthers toward the national title. His 6,526 career rushing yards was a record that stood for 22 years, until Texas' Ricky Williams surpassed him in 1998. Penn State coach Joe Paterno, at a time when Penn State-Pitt was one of the sport's most bitter rivalries, gushed in 1976: "I look at him with a football, and it's about as beautiful as football is ever supposed to look. I think that's part of why it's hard to tackle him. He's so elegant, it would be like tackling Fred Astaire." Dorsett's son, Anthony Jr., was a four-year letterman for the Panthers from 1992 to 1995.

BEST COACH Jock Sutherland was a native of Scotland who,

RECORDS

RUSHING YARDS

GAME

303 Tony Dorsett vs. Notre Dame, Nov. 15, 1975 (23 att.)

SEASON

2,150 Tony Dorsett, 1976 (370 att.)

CAREER

6,526 Tony Dorsett, 1973-76 (1,163 att.)

PASSING YARDS

GAME

470 Pete Gonzalez vs. Rutgers, Oct. 25, 1997 (27 of 42)

SEASON

3,679 Rod Rutherford, 2003 (247 of 413)

CAREER

11,267 Alex Van Pelt, 1989-92 (867 of 1,503)

RECEIVING YARDS

GAME

225 Dietrich Jells vs. West Virginia, Oct. 15, 1994 (5 rec.)

SEASON

1,672 Larry Fitzgerald, 2003 (92 rec.)

CAREER

3,061 Antonio Bryant, 1999-2001 (173 rec.)

POINTS

GAME

36 Norman Bill Budd vs. Ohio, Oct. 29, 1910 (6 TDs)

SEASON

140 Tony Dorsett, 1976 (23 TDs, 1 two-pt. conv.)

CAREER

380 Tony Dorsett (63 TDs; 1 two-pt. conv.)

CONSENSUS ALL-AMERICANS

1915-16	Robert Peck	C
1916	James Herron	E
1917	Jock Sutherland	G
1917	Dale Sies	G
1918	Leonard Hilty	T
1918	Tom Davies	B
1918	George McLaren	B
1920-21	Herb Stein	C
1925	Ralph Chase	T
1927	Gibby Welch	B
1928	Mike Getto	T
1929	Joe Donchess	E
1929	Ray Montgomery	G
1931	Jesse Quatse	T
1932-33	Joe Skladany	E
1932	Warren Heller	B
1934	Charles Hartwig	G
1934	George Shotwell	C
1936	Averell Daniell	T
1937	Tony Matisi	T
1937-38	Marshall Goldberg	B
1956	Joe Walton	E
1958	John Guzik	G
1960	Mike Ditka	E
1963	Paul Martha	B
1976	Tony Dorsett	RB

(Continued on next page)

according to legend, played in the first football game he ever saw, and then became an All-America guard at Pitt playing for Pop Warner. After five years coaching at Lafayette, Sutherland replaced Warner in 1924. His 1937 team went 9–0–1 and won the school's first consensus national title. When he died suddenly in 1948 of a brain tumor while coaching the Steelers, the *Pittsburgh Post-Gazette* editorialized: "There is nothing anybody can say about the passing of Jock Sutherland that isn't felt in the heart of every man and woman in Pittsburgh. In any list of the district's assets, he was close to the top."

BEST TEAM Pittsburgh hadn't won a national title in 39 years when the Panthers gathered in the fall of 1976 to begin practice. Majors had been hired in December 1972 to help salvage a program that had lost 56 of its previous 72 games dating to 1966, and he rapidly changed Pitt's fortunes by earning bids to the Fiesta and Sun bowls in two of his first three years. Part of his plan was to recruit hordes of players, which later precipitated NCAA legislation limiting scholarships. With 18 of 22 starters returning for 1976, Pitt was poised to do something special; just how special was emphasized in a 31-10 opening victory over Notre Dame. Its 10 other regular-season games featured a resounding 24-7 victory at Penn State, Pitt's first win over its archrival since 1965, and Majors' only win against Joe Paterno. Prior to the Sugar Bowl against Georgia, Majors announced he would leave Pitt for Tennessee, his alma mater. Pitt won the Sugar Bowl 27-3 and secured the No. 1 spot in both season-ending wire-service polls.

BIGGEST GAME Pittsburgh came into the first Sugar Bowl game ever played indoors with a No. 1 national ranking, but because of decades-long biases against Northeast schools, the Panthers still had plenty to prove against Georgia, champion of the Southeastern Conference, on New Year's Day 1977. Just how good were the Panthers that day? With the Bulldogs' defense geared to stop him, freshly crowned Heisman Trophy-winner Dorsett rushed for a Sugar Bowl-record 202 yards–and didn't even win the MVP award. That honor went to quarterback Matt Cavanaugh, who was 10-for-18 for 192 yards, and whose six-yard first-quarter run gave Pitt its first touchdown, igniting the 27-3 rout, which *Sports Illustrated* amplified with an exclamation point to its headline: "PITT IS

CONSENSUS ALL-AMERICANS (CONT.)		
1976	Al Romano,	MG
1977	Randy Holloway,	DL
1977	Bob Jury,	DB
1977	Tom Brzoza,	C
1978-80	Hugh Green,	DL
1980	Mark May,	OL
1981	Sal Sunseri,	LB
1982	Jimbo Covert,	OL
1983-84	Bill Fralic,	OL/OT
1986	Randy Dixon,	OL
1986	Tony Woods,	DL
1987	Craig Heyward,	RB
1988	Mark Stepnoski,	OL
1990	Brian Greenfield,	P
2000	Antonio Bryant,	WR
2003	Larry Fitzgerald,	WR

IT!" The Panthers' defense caused six turnovers, limited the Bulldogs to 181 yards and actually caught more Georgia passes than Georgia's receivers did (four Pitt interceptions, three Georgia receptions). The performance moved Georgia coach Vince Dooley to proclaim, "They proved today they are the best team in the country. They have amazing balance. They are the best defensive team we've seen. I think that's obvious. They're also the best offensive team we've faced."

BIGGEST UPSET Sutherland left after the 1938 season, and Pittsburgh was in the midst of one of the most dismal stretches of its football history on the afternoon of Nov. 8, 1941. The Panthers were 0–5 heading into the game against Fordham, ranked No. 5 in the country. But the Panthers stunned the Sugar Bowl-bound Rams 13-0, which remains, all these years later, the clear-cut biggest upset in Pitt history.

HEARTBREAKER The Panthers were ranked No. 1 in the country and riding a 17-game winning streak when they welcomed Penn State to Pitt Stadium on Nov. 28, 1981. Already slated to play Georgia in the upcoming Sugar Bowl, the Panthers were eyeing their second national title in six years. Pitt dashed to a 14-0 lead and appeared on its way to a blowout. But Penn State sophomore quarterback Todd Blackledge upstaged Pitt junior Dan Marino, throwing for two touchdowns and running for another as the Nittany Lions scored 48 unanswered points to stun 60,260 fans into silence with a 48-14 thrashing. Marino seemed to be driving Pitt to a third touchdown early in the second quarter but was intercepted in the end zone by Roger Jackson, the first of four interceptions. "We had the locomotive going against us the wrong way," Pitt coach Jackie Sherrill said, "and nothing to stop it with."

DISPUTE An ugly shroud continues to shadow the memory of the 1956 Sugar Bowl, Pitt's first bowl appearance in 19 years. John Michelosen's team had compiled a 7–3 record, the program's best since 1938, earning a bid to play Georgia Tech. Pitt's roster included defensive back Bobby Grier, the first black man to ever play in the Sugar Bowl. This was an emotionally charged issue in 1950s New Orleans, and it resulted in a series of firestorms. For one thing, Georgia's

segregationist governor, Marvin Griffin, attempted to bar his team from competing against Pitt, and relented only after 2,000 Tech students protested and Pitt's chancellor, Charles Nutting, uttered a famous four-word rebuttal: "No Grier, no game." (Griffin's request was voted down by the University of Georgia Board of Regents after these protests.) For another, after Tech's 7-0 victory, Louisiana would outlaw integrated sports competition until 1963. It would not be until a Floyd Little-and Jim Nance-led Syracuse team played in the 1965 game that another black face would appear in the Sugar Bowl. And lastly, amid the simmering tension, Grier was whistled for a pass interference penalty in the end zone in the first quarter, a call that Pitt fans continue to howl about nearly 50 years later, and which set up the game's only touchdown. Was the call racially motivated? All Grier would say when asked about the play 36 years later was: "It was a bad call. The receiver pushed me, and I was on the ground, and the ball was five yards over his head. The next thing I knew, the referee says that I had pushed the receiver. How could I, on the ground? No, the referee definitely missed that one."

STADIUM For 75 years, Pittsburgh played its home games in one of the most intimidating facilities in college football, Pitt Stadium, a 56,150-seat bandbox whose history was capped on Nov. 13, 1999, when Pitt throttled Notre Dame, 37-27. But after a year in Three Rivers Stadium, the Panthers moved, with the Pittsburgh Steelers, into one of the country's state-of-the-art facilities, the 65,000-seat Heinz Field. Though it lacks Pitt Stadium's history, it does boast every imaginable amenity, from a heated grass playing surface to the Duratz Locker Room—named after longtime university benefactor James J. Duratz—a private, expansive area solely for the Panthers' use.

RIVAL Pittsburgh and Penn State. There was a time when it wasn't only one of the longest rivalries in college football, but one of the most heated. Families were divided over it. Neighborhoods were split. And every few years, it seemed, the winner of their annual season finale would catapult itself into the national title picture. That happened for Pitt in 1976 and for Penn State in 1982, and delirious Pennsylvania football fans believed the series—and bad blood—would last forever. Turns out they were only half right. A combination of Pittsburgh's entry into the Big East, Penn State's subsequent entry into the Big Ten and simmering bad blood led to the series' discontinuation after 1992, save for a four-year resumption in the late 1990s. The schools aren't scheduled to meet again. Paterno says Pitt made it all but impossible to keep the series going by not making concessions to the teams'

new conference affiliations. But ESPN's Beano Cook, formerly the sports information director at Pitt and a longtime Pitt observer, puts it more bluntly: "I think Joe Paterno is like the little boy with the baseball, and if he doesn't get to pitch he's going to take it home. And that's what happened here. If it isn't Joe Paterno's way, he's going to cry and go home to mama." For the record, Penn State leads the series 50–42–4. That isn't a good subject to broach on the Pittsburgh campus.

NICKNAME Student and alumni leaders adopted the Panther as Pittsburgh's mascot in 1909. The name was chosen because the panther is the most formidable creature once indigenous to the Pittsburgh region, because it has an ancient heritage as a noble animal, because of the happy accident of alliteration and because the university's gold color closely resembled the panther's. One other factor: at the time, no other college team was called Panthers.

MASCOT Since its creation in 1909, there have been at least six versions of the Pitt Panther. They range from a leopardlike spotted creature in 1920, the oldest known photograph of the mascot, to a raggedy specimen from the 1970s that troubled many alumni, to the cartoon character of today. In between, there even was what appears to be a panther costume created from an actual lion's hide. "From the mid-'30s to the mid-'60s, I think it's a female lion," Pitt archivist Rebecca Abromitis said of the costume. "It would be totally not politically correct at all right now. I am sure it's real fur."

UNIFORMS Blue and gold have been Pittsburgh's colors from the very start, although the tones of the colors have varied through the years. The most recent uniform changes, in 1997, were the most dramatic. After utilizing the "Pitt" logo script since 1970, the school unveiled a new gold helmet, featuring a blue Panther. The jersey now has the name "Pittsburgh" emblazoned across the chest. The only diversion from traditional blue and gold came during the World War II era, when the team wore red and white because head coach Clark Shaughnessy thought it made the players look bigger.

QUOTE "Jock had the finest running attack football has ever known, and this doesn't bar Knute Rockne, Lou Little, Percy Haughton, Hurry Up Yost, Howard Jones, Pop Warner and anyone you can mention. Jock's great Pitt teams rumbled and blasted out their yardage in the single-wing, unbalanced line attack. When Jock had the horses, which was his custom, the Panthers' attack was something to behold." — Grantland Rice, describing Jock Sutherland's squads

PITTSBURGH ALL-TIME SCORES

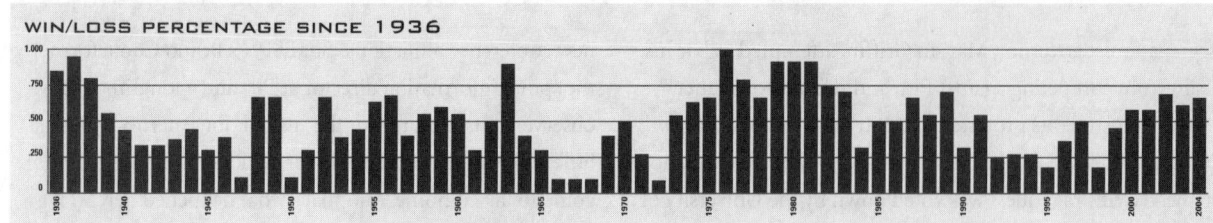

WIN/LOSS PERCENTAGE SINCE 1936

NO HEAD COACH

1890   1-2-0
U	Allegheny	0	38
U	Wash. & Jeff.	0	32
U	Geneva	10	4

1891   2-5-0
U	Wash. & Jeff.	6	40
U •	Geneva	6	0
U •	W.Penn Med.	54	0
U	Geneva	4	12
U	E E Gymnastics	0	24
U	Geneva	4	6
U	Indiana Teachers	0	16

1892   4-2-0
U	E E Gymnastics	0	16
U •	Geneva	6	4
U •	Kiski	12	0
U •	Indiana Teachers	8	6
U •	Greensburg AA	6	2
U	Wash. & Jeff.	6	18

ANSON F. HARROLD
1893 (.200)   1-4

1893   1-4-0
U	Pittsburgh AC	0	10
U •	Allegheny AA	4	0
U	Pittsburgh AC	10	16
N6	Penn State *Bel*	0	32
U	Wash. & Jeff.	0	12

NO HEAD COACH

1894   1-1-0
U •	Sewickley AC	6	0
U	Indiana Teachers	0	44

J.P. LINN
1895 (.143)   1-6

1895   1-6-0
U	Duquesne AC	0	36
U	Greenburg AC	2	42
O26	at West Virginia	0	8
U •	Emerald AA	22	0
N2	Wash. & Jeff.	0	28
U	Carnegie AC	6	10
U	Wheeling T.I.G.	0	12

GEORGE W. HOSKINS
1896 (.333)   3-6

1896   3-6-0
U	Pittsburgh AC	4	6
O3	at Penn State	4	10
U	Latrobe	0	4
U	Duquesne AC	0	26
U •	West Theol	4	0
U •	at Geneva	1	0 *f*
U •	Sewickley AA	18	0
U	Wheeling Tig	6	11
U	Grove City	0	12

THOMAS GAWTHROP TRENCHARD
1897 (.250)   1-3

1897   1-3-0
U •	Pittsburgh HS	8	0
U	Latrobe	0	30
U	Greensburg AC	0	47
U	Waynesburg	5	14

DR. FRED A. ROBINSON
1898-99 (.692)   8-3-2

1898   5-2-1
U •	Duquesne AC	6	5
U •	Pittsburgh Acad.	24	5
U •	Westminster	5	0
N4	at West Virginia	0	6 *
U	Grove City	10	12
U	Notrona AC	17	0
U •	New Castle T.	6	6
U •	Cal Teachers	6	0

1899   3-1-1
U =	Westminster	11	11
U •	Grove City	16	0
U •	Swissvale AC	11	0
U •	Bethany	5	0
U	J.F.Lalus	0	12

DR. M. ROY JACKSON
1900 (.556)   5-4

1900   5-4-0
S30	Penn State *Bel*	0	12
O6	at West Virginia	5	6
U	DC & AC	0	5
U •	Grove City	12	0
U •	Cal Teachers	12	0
U •	Akron Buchtel	17	0
U •	Theil	47	0
U •	Westminster	17	5
U	Shady Side A	0	5

WILBUR D. HOCKENSMITH
1901 (.750)   7-2-1

1901   7-2-1
S29	Penn State *Bel*	0	33 *
O5 •	at West Virginia	12	0
U =	Ind. Teachers	0	0
U •	Allegheny	11	0
U •	Duquesne	18	0
U •	Cal Teachers	15	0
U •	Geneva	12	5
U •	Thiel	17	0
U •	Westminster	11	0
U	Allegheny	0	15

FREDERICK JOSEPH CROLIUS
1902 (.458)   5-6-1

1902   5-6-1
U	Aleghany AA	5	15
S27	at Penn State	0	27
U •	Grove City	16	0
U =	Westminster	6	6
O18	Bucknell	24	0
O22	West Virginia	6	23
U	Geneva	2	22
U •	Ohio U.	34	0
U	Aleghany	0	6
U	Geneva	0	30
U •	Alegheny AC	29	0
U •	Mt. Union	6	0

ARTHUR ST. LEDGER MOSSE
1903-05 (.661)   20-10-1

1903   0-8-1
O3	at West Virginia	6	24
U	Geneva	0	57
U	Manchester AC	6	11
U	Bellvue OC	2	6
O24	Penn State	0	59
U	Geneva	0	32
U	East Side AA	0	28
U =	Grove City	0	0
U	Marietta	6	45

1904   10-0-0
U •	Grove City	12	0
U •	Mt. Union	67	0
U •	Westminster	38	0
U •	Geneva	30	0
U •	Susquehanna	40	0
U •	California, Pa	40	0
U •	Waynesburg	83	0
N8 •	West Virginia	53	0
U •	Bethany	21	0
N24 •	Penn State	22	5 *

1905   10-2-0
S23 •	Westminster	11	0 *
S27 •	California, Pa.	71	0
O7 •	Mt Union	57	0
O14 •	Bethany	48	0
O21 •	at Cornell	0	30
O28 •	Dickinson	24	10
N4 •	Franklin & Marshall	53	0
N11 •	Wash. & Jeff.	11	0
N15 •	Butler YMCA	67	0
N18 •	Ohio Med.	51	0
N25 •	at Geneva	12	0
N30 •	Penn State	0	6

E.R. WINGARD
1906 (.600)   6-4

1906   6-4-0
S29 •	Westminster	17	0
O6 •	Hiram	66	0
O13 •	Allegheny	74	0
O20 •	Carlisle	0	22
O27 •	Carnegie Tech	31	0
N3 •	at Cornell	0	23
N10 •	West Virginia	17	0
N17 •	Grove City	24	0
N24 •	Wash. & Jeff.	0	4
N29 •	Penn State	0	6

JOHN A. MOORHEAD
1907 (.800)   8-2

1907   8-2-0
O5 •	Marietta	6	0
O12 •	Carnigie Tech	6	0
O19 •	Muskingum	33	0
O26 •	Bucknell	12	0
N2 •	at Cornell	5	18
N6 •	Ohio Northern	16	0
N9 •	West Virginia	10	0
N16 •	Wash. & Jeff.	2	9
N23 •	Wooster	51	0
N28 •	Penn State	6	0

JOSEPH H. THOMPSON
1908-12 (.674)   30-14-2

1908   8-3-0
S26 •	Mt. Union	26	4
O3 •	Bethany	27	0
O10 •	Marietta	7	0
O17 •	Carnegie Tech	22	0
O24 •	Bucknell	22	0
O31 •	at St. Louis	13	0
N7 •	West Virginia	11	0
N14 •	Carlisle	0	6
N21 •	Gettysburg	6	0
N26 •	Penn State	6	12
D5 •	Wash. & Jeff.	0	14

1909   6-2-1
O2 •	Ohio Northern	16	0
O9 •	Marietta	12	0
O16 •	Bucknell	18	6
O23 •	Carlisle	14	3
O30 •	Notre Dame	0	6
N6 =	at West Virginia	0	0
N13 •	Wash. & Jeff.	17	3
N20 •	Mt. Union	17	3
N25 •	Penn State	0	5

1910   9-0-0
O1 •	Ohio Northern	36	0
O8 •	Westminster *Wlk*	18	0
O15 •	Waynesburg	42	0
O22 •	Georgetown	17	0
O29 •	Ohio U.	71	0
N5 •	West Virginia	38	0
N12 •	Wash. & Jeff.	14	0
N19 •	Carnegie Tech	35	0
N24 •	Penn State	11	0

1911   4-3-1
O7 •	Westminster	23	0
O14 •	Ohio Northern	22	0
O21 •	Carlisle	0	17
O28 •	at Cornell	3	9
N4 =	Notre Dame	0	0
N11 •	Villanova	12	0
N18 •	Wash. & Jeff.	12	0
N30 •	Penn State	0	3

1912   3-6-0
S28 •	Ohio Northern	22	0
O5 •	Westminster	13	3
O12 •	Bucknell	0	6
O19 •	Carlisle	8	45
O26 •	at Navy	6	13
N2 •	Notre Dame	0	3
N9 •	Maryland U.	64	0
N16 •	Wash. & Jeff.	0	13
N28 •	Penn State	0	38

JOSEPH M. DUFF, JR.
1913-14 (.806)   14-3-1

1913   6-2-1
S27 •	Ohio Northern	67	0
O4 =	at Navy	0	0
O11 •	West Virginia	40	0
O18 •	Carlisle	12	6
O25 •	at Cornell	20	7
N1 •	Bucknell	0	9
N8 •	Lafayette	13	0
N15 •	Wash. & Jeff.	6	18
N27 •	Penn State	7	6

1914   8-1-0
S30 •	at Cornell	9	3
O3 •	at Westminster	21	0
O10 •	at Navy	13	6
O17 •	Carlisle	10	3
O24 •	Georgetown	21	0
O31 •	Dickinson	96	0
N7 •	Wash. & Jeff.	10	13
N14 •	Carnegie Tech	14	0
N26 •	Penn State	13	3

GLENN "POP" WARNER
1915-23 (.816)   60-12-4

1915   8-0-0
O2 •	Westminster	32	0
O9 •	at Navy	47	12
O16 •	Carlisle	45	0
O23 •	at Pennsylvania	14	7
O30 •	Allegheny	42	7
N6 •	Wash. & Jeff.	19	0
N13 •	Carnegie Tech	28	0
N25 •	Penn. St.	20	0

1916   8-0-0
O7 •	Westminster	57	0
O14 •	at Navy	20	19
O21 •	at Syracuse	30	0
O28 •	Pennsylvania	20	0
N4 •	Allegheny	46	0
N11 •	Wash. & Jeff.	37	0
N18 •	Carnegie Tech	14	6
N30 •	Penn State	31	0

1917 — 10-0-0

S29	●	at West Virginia	14	9
O6	●	Bethany	40	0
O13	●	Lehigh	41	0
O20	●	Syracuse	28	0
O27	●	at Pennsylvania	14	6
N3	●	Westminster	25	0
N10	●	Wash. & Jeff.	13	0
N17	●	Carnegie Tech	27	0
N29	●	Penn State	28	6
D1	●	Camp Lee All Stars	30	0

1918 — 4-1-0

N9	●	Wash. & Jeff.	34	0
N16	●	Pennsylvania	37	0
N23	●	Georgia Tech	32	0
N28	●	Penn State	28	6
N30		at Cleveland Navy	9	10

1919 — 6-2-1

O4	●	at Geneva	33	0
O11	●	West Virginia	26	0
O18		at Syracuse	3	24
O25	●	Georgia Tech	16	6
N1	●	at Lehigh	14	0
N8	●	Wash. & Jeff.	7	6
N15	=	at Pennsylvania	3	3
N22	●	Carnegie Tech	17	7
N27		Penn State	0	20

1920 — 6-0-2

O2	●	at Geneva	47	0
O9	●	West Virginia	34	13
O16	=	at Syracuse	7	7
O23	●	Georgia Tech	10	3
O30	●	Lafayette	14	0
N6	●	at Pennsylvania	27	21
N13	●	Wash. & Jeff.	7	0
N25	=	Penn State	0	0

1921 — 5-3-1

S24	●	at Geneva	28	0	
O1		at Lafayette	0	6	
O8	●	West Virginia	21	14	*
O15	●	Cincinnati	21	14	
O22	●	Syracuse	30	0	*
O29	●	at Pennsylvania	28	0	
N5		Nebraska	0	10	
N12		Wash. & Jeff.	0	7	
N24	=	Penn State	0	0	

1922 — 8-2-0

S30	●	at Cincinnati	38	0	*
O7		Lafayette	0	7	
O14		West Virginia	6	9	
O21	●	at Syracuse	21	14	
O28	●	Bucknell	7	0	
N4	●	at Pennsylvania	7	6	
N11	●	Geneva	62	0	
N18	●	Wash. & Jeff.	19	0	
N30	●	Penn State	14	0	
D30	●	at Stanford	16	7	

1923 — 5-4-0

S29	●	at Bucknell	21	0
O6	●	Lafayette	7	0
O13		West Virginia	7	13
O20		Syracuse BRNX	0	3
O27		Carnegie Tech	2	7
N3		at Pennsylvania	0	6
N10	●	Grove City	13	7
N17	●	Wash. & Jeff.	13	6
N29	●	Penn State	20	3

DR. JOHN B. "JOCK" SUTHERLAND
1924-38 (.818) 111-20-12

1924 — 5-3-1

S27	●	Grove City	14	0
O4		Lafayette	0	10
O11	●	West Virginia	14	7
O18	●	at Johns Hopkins	26	0
O25		Carnegie Tech	0	6
N1	=	at Syracuse	7	7
N8	●	Geneva	13	0
N15		Wash. & Jeff.	0	10
N27	●	Penn State	24	3

1925 — 8-1-0

S26	●	Wash. & Jeff.	28	0
O3		Lafayette	9	20
O10	●	Gettysburg	13	0
O17	●	West Virginia	15	7
O24	●	Carnegie Tech	12	0
O31	●	Wash. & Jeff.	6	0
N7	●	Pennsylvania	14	0
N14	●	at Penn State	23	7
N26	●	Johns Hopkins	31	0

1926 — 5-2-2

S25	●	Allegheny	9	7
O2	=	Georgetown	6	6
O9		Lafayette	7	17
O16	●	Colgate	19	16
O23		Carnegie Tech	0	14
O30	●	Westminster	88	0
N6	●	West Virginia	17	7
N13	=	Wash. & Jeff.	0	0
N25	●	Penn State	24	6

1927 — 8-1-1

S24	●	Thiel	42	0
O1	●	Grove City	33	0
O8	●	West Virginia	40	0
O15	●	at Drake	32	0
O22	●	Carnegie Tech	23	7
O29	●	Allegheny	62	0
N5	=	Wash. & Jeff.	0	0
N12	●	Nebraska	21	13
N24	●	Penn State	30	0
		ROSE BOWL		
J2		Stanford	6	7

1928 — 6-2-1

S29	●	Thiel	20	0
O6	●	Bethany	53	0
O13		West Virginia	6	9
O20	●	Allegheny	29	0
O27		Carnegie Tech	0	6
N3	●	Syracuse	18	0
N10	●	Wash. & Jeff.	25	0
N17	=	at Nebraska	0	0
N29	●	Penn State	26	0

1929 — 9-1-0

S28	●	Waynesburg	53	0
O5	●	at Duke	52	7
O12	●	West Virginia	27	7
O19	●	at Nebraska	12	7
O26	●	at Allegheny	40	0
N2	●	Ohio State	18	2
N9	●	Wash. & Jeff.	21	0
N16	●	Penn State	20	7
N28	●	Carnegie Tech	34	13
		ROSE BOWL		
J1		Southern Cal	14	47

1930 — 6-2-1

S27	●	Waynesburg	52	0
O4	●	at West Virginia	16	0
O11	●	at West Reserve	52	0
O18	●	at Syracuse	14	0
O25		Notre Dame	19	35
N1	=	at Nebraska	0	0
N8	●	Carnegie Tech	7	6
N15		at Ohio State	7	16
N26	●	Penn State	19	12

1931 — 8-1-0

S26	●	Miami, Ohio	61	0
O3	●	at Iowa	20	0
O10	●	West Virginia	34	0
O17	●	Western Reserve	32	0
O24		at Notre Dame	12	25
O31	●	at Penn State	41	6
N7	●	Carnegie Tech	14	6
N14	●	Army	26	0
N26	●	Nebraska	40	0

1932 — 8-1-2

S24	●	Ohio Northern	47	0
O1	●	at West Virginia	40	0
O8	●	Duquesne	33	0
O15	●	at Army	18	13
O22	=	Ohio State	0	0
O29	●	Notre Dame	12	0
N5	●	at Pennsylvania	19	12
N12	=	at Nebraska	0	0
N19	●	Carnegie Tech	6	0
N26	●	Stanford	7	0
		ROSE BOWL		
J2		Southern Cal	0	35

1933 — 8-1-0

S30	●	Wash. & Jeff.	9	0
O7	●	West Virginia	21	0
O14	●	Centre	37	0
O21	●	Navy	34	6
O28		at Minnesota	3	7
N4	●	at Notre Dame	14	0
N11	●	Duquesne	7	0
N18	●	Nebraska	6	0
N30	●	Carnegie Tech	16	0

1934 — 8-1-0

S29	●	Wash. & Jeff.	26	6
O6	●	at West Virginia	27	6
O13	●	Southern Cal	20	6
O20		Minnesota	7	13
O27	●	at Westminster	30	0
N3	●	Notre Dame	19	0
N10	●	at Nebraska	25	6
N17	●	at Navy	31	7
N29	●	Carnegie Tech	20	0

1935 — 7-1-2

S28	●	Waynesburg	14	0
O5	●	at Wash. & Jeff.	35	0
O12	●	West Virginia	24	6
O19		at Notre Dame	6	9
O26	●	Penn State	9	0
N2	=	Fordham NYC	0	0
N9	●	Army	29	6
N16	●	Nebraska	6	0
N28	=	Carnegie Tech	0	0
D14	●	at Southern Cal	12	7

1936 — 8-1-1

S26	●	Ohio Wesleyan	53	0
O3	●	West Virginia	34	0
O10	●	at Ohio State	6	0
O17		Duquesne	0	7
O24	●	Notre Dame	26	0
O31	=	Fordham NYC	0	0
N7	●	Penn State	24	7
N14	●	at Nebraska	19	6
N26	●	Carnegie Tech	31	14
		ROSE BOWL		
J1	●	Washington	21	0

1937 — 9-0-1

S24	●	Ohio Wesleyan	59	0
O2	●	at West Virginia	20	0
O9	●	Duquesne	6	0
O16	=	Fordham NYC	0	0
O23	●	Wisconsin	21	0
O30	●	Carnegie Tech	25	14
N6	●	at Notre Dame	21	6
N13	●	Nebraska	13	7
N20	●	Penn State	28	7
N27	●	at Duke	10	0

1938 — 8-2-0

S24	●	West Virginia	19	0
O1	●	at Temple	28	6
O8	●	Duquesne	27	0
O15	●	at Wisconsin	26	6
O22	●	SMU	34	7
O29	●	Fordham	24	13
N5		Carnegie Tech	10	20
N12	●	at Nebraska	19	0
N19	●	Penn State	26	0
N26		at Duke	0	7

CHARLES W. BOWSER
1939-42 (.414) 14-20-1

1939 — 5-4-0

S30	●	at Washington	27	6
O7	●	West Virginia	20	0
O14	●	Duke	14	13
O21		Duquesne	13	21
O28		Fordham NYC	13	27
N4	●	at Temple	13	7
N11	●	Carnegie Tech	6	0
N18		Nebraska	13	14
N25		at Penn State	0	10

1940 — 3-4-1

S28		at Ohio State	7	30
O5	●	Missouri	19	13
O12	=	SMU	7	7
O19		Fordham	12	24
N9	●	Carnegie Tech	6	0
N16		Nebraska	7	9
N23	●	Penn State	20	7
N30		at Duke	7	12

1941 — 3-6-0

O4		Purdue	0	6
O11		at Michigan	0	40
O18		at Minnesota	0	39
O25		Duke	7	27
N1		Ohio State	14	21
N8	●	Fordham	13	0
N15	●	at Nebraska	14	7
N22		Penn State	7	31
N29	●	Carnegie Tech	27	0

1942 — 3-6-0

S26		at Minnesota	7	50
O3	●	SMU	20	7
O10		Great Lakes NAS CLEV	6	7
O17		Indiana	7	19
O24		Duke	0	28
O31	●	Carnegie Tech	19	6
N7		at Ohio State	19	59
N14	●	Nebraska	6	0
N21		at Penn State	6	14

CLARK D. SHAUGHNESSY
1943-45 (.370) 10-17

1943 — 3-5-0

S25		Notre Dame	0	41
O2		at Great Lakes NAS	0	40
O9	●	West Virginia	20	0
O16		at Illinois	25	33
O23	●	Bethany	18	0
O30	●	Carnegie Tech	45	0
N6		Ohio State	6	46
N20		Penn State	0	14

1944 — 4-5-0

S23	●	West Virginia	26	13
S30		Notre Dame	0	58
O7	●	Bethany	50	13
O14		at Army	7	69
O21		Illinois	5	39
O28	●	Chatham Field	26	0
N11		at Ohio State	19	54
N18		at Indiana	0	47
N25	●	Penn State	14	0

1945 — 3-7-0

S22		at Illinois	6	23
S29	●	West Virginia	20	0
O6	●	Bucknell	38	0
O13		Michigan State	7	12
O20		Notre Dame	9	39
O27		Temple	0	6
N3		at Purdue	0	28
N10		Ohio State	0	14
N17		Indiana	0	19
N24	●	Penn State	7	0

WESLEY E. FESLER
1946 (.389) 3-5-1

1946 — 3-5-1

S21		Illinois	7	33
S28	●	West Virginia	33	7
O5		at Notre Dame	0	33
O12	=	Temple	0	0
O19	●	Marquette	7	6
O26		Purdue	8	10
N2		at Indiana	6	20
N9		at Ohio State	13	20
N23	●	Penn State	14	7

WALTER S. MILLIGAN
1947-49 (.481) 13-14

1947 — 1-8-0

S27		at Illinois	0	14
O4		Notre Dame	6	40
O11		at Michigan	0	69
O18		at Indiana	6	41
O25	●	Ohio State	12	0
N1		at Minnesota	0	29
N15		at Purdue	0	28
N22		Penn State	0	29
N29		West Virginia	2	17

1948 — 6-3-0

S25		SMU	14	33
O2		Notre Dame	0	40
O9	●	West Virginia	16	6
O16	●	Marquette	21	7
O23	●	Indiana	21	14
O30	●	at Western Reserve	20	0
N6		at Ohio State	0	41
N13	●	at Purdue	20	13
N20	●	Penn State	7	0

1949 — 6-3-0

S24	●	William & Mary	13	7
O1	●	at Northwestern	16	7
O8	●	at West Virginia	20	7
O15	●	Miami, Ohio	35	26
O22		at Indiana	14	48
O29	●	at Pennsylvania	22	21
N5		Ohio State	10	14
N12		Minnesota	7	24
N19	●	Penn State	19	0

LEONARD J. CASANOVA
1950 (.111)   1-8

1950
S30	at Duke	14	28
O7	at Ohio State	7	41
O14	Rice	7	14
O21	at Northwestern	23	28
O28	Miami, Fla.	0	28
N4	West Virginia	21	7
N11	at Notre Dame	7	18
N18	Michigan State	0	19
N25	Penn State	20	21

TOM HAMILTON
1951, '54 (.438)   7-9

1951   3-7-0
S29	Duke	14	19
O6	at Indiana	6	13
O13	at Iowa	17	34
O20	Notre Dame	0	33
O27	at Michigan State	26	53
N3	at Rice	13	21
N10	Ohio State	14	16
N17 ●	West Virginia	32	12
N24 ●	Penn State	13	7
D7 ●	at Miami, Fla.	21	7

LOWELL P. "RED" DAWSON
1952-54 (.452)   9-11-1

1952   6-3-0
S27 ●	Iowa	26	14
O4	at Oklahoma	20	49
O11 ●	at Notre Dame	22	19
O18 ●	at Army	22	14
O25	West Virginia	0	16
N1 ●	Indiana	28	7
N8 ●	at Ohio State	21	14
N15 ●	North Carolina St.	48	6
N22	Penn State	0	17

1953   3-5-1
S26	West Virginia	7	17
O3 =	Oklahoma	7	7
O10 ●	Nebraska	14	6
O17	at Notre Dame	14	23
O24	at Northwestern	21	27
O31	at Minnesota	14	35
N7 ●	at Virginia	26	0
N14 ●	North Carolina St.	40	6
N21	Penn State	0	17

TOM HAMILTON

1954   4-5-0
S24	at Southern Cal	7	27
O2	Minnesota	7	46
O9	Notre Dame	0	33
O16 ●	Navy	21	19
O23 ●	Northwestern	14	7
O30 ●	at West Virginia	13	10
N6	at Ohio State	0	26
N13 ●	at Nebraska	21	7
N20	Penn State	0	13

JOHN P. MICHELOSEN
1955-65 (.531)   56-49-7

1955   7-4-0
S17 ●	California	27	7
S24 ●	at Syracuse	22	12
O1	at Oklahoma	14	26
O8	Navy BALT	0	21
O15 ●	Nebraska	21	7
O22 ●	at Duke	26	7
O29	Miami, Fla.	7	21
N5 ●	Virginia	18	7
N12 ●	West Virginia	26	7
N19 ●	at Penn State	20	0
	SUGAR BOWL		
J2	Georgia Tech	0	7

1956   7-3-1
S22 ●	at West Virginia	14	13
S29 ●	Syracuse	14	7
O6	at California	0	14
O20 ●	Duke NOR	27	14
O27 ●	Oregon	14	7
N3	at Minnesota	6	9
N10 ●	Notre Dame	26	13
N17 ●	Army	20	7
N24 =	Penn State	7	7
D8 ●	at Miami, Fla.	14	7
	GATOR BOWL		
D29	Georgia Tech	14	21

1957   4-6-0
S21	Oklahoma	0	26
S28 ●	Oregon PORT	6	3
O4	at Southern Cal	20	14
O12 ●	Nebraska	34	0
O19	at Army	13	29
O26	at Notre Dame	7	13
N2	Syracuse	21	24
N9	West Virginia	6	7
N23 ●	Penn State	14	13
D7	at Miami, Fla.	13	28

1958   5-4-1
S20 ●	at UCLA	27	6
S27 ●	Holy Cross	17	0
O4 ●	at Minnesota	13	7
O11	at Michigan State	8	22
O18 ●	West Virginia	15	8
O25 =	Army	14	14
N1	at Syracuse	13	16
N8 ●	at Notre Dame	29	26
N15	at Nebraska	6	14
N27	Penn State	21	25

1959   6-4-0
S19 ●	at Marquette	21	15
S25	at Southern Cal	0	23
O3 ●	UCLA	25	21
O10 ●	Duke	12	0
O17 ●	at West Virginia	15	23
O24	TCU	3	13
O31	Syracuse	0	35
N7 ●	at Boston College	22	14
N14 ●	Notre Dame	28	13
N21 ●	Penn State	22	7

1960   4-3-3
S17 ●	at UCLA	7	8
S24 =	Michigan State	7	7
O1	at Oklahoma	14	15
O8 ●	Miami, Fla.	17	6
O15 ●	West Virginia	42	0
O22	at TCU	7	7
O29 ●	at Syracuse	10	0
N5 ●	at Notre Dame	20	13
N12 ●	Army	7	7
N19	Penn State	3	14

1961   3-7-0
S16 ●	at Miami, Fla.	10	7
S30	Baylor	13	16
O7	at Washington	17	22
O14	West Virginia	6	20
O21	at UCLA	6	20
O28	Navy	28	14
N4	at Syracuse	9	28
N11	Notre Dame	20	26
N18 ●	Southern Cal	10	9
N25	Penn State	26	47

1962   5-5-0
S15 ●	Miami, Fla.	14	23
S29 ●	at Baylor	24	14
O6 ●	at California	26	24
O13 ●	West Virginia	8	15
O20 ●	UCLA	8	6
O27 ●	Navy NOR	9	32
N3 ●	Syracuse	24	6
N10 ●	at Notre Dame	22	43
N17 ●	Army BRNX	7	6
N24	Penn State	0	16

1963   9-1-0
S20 ●	at UCLA	20	0
S28 ●	Washington	13	6
O5 ●	California	35	15
O19 ●	at West Virginia	13	10
O26 ●	at Navy	12	24
N2 ●	Syracuse	35	27
N9 ●	at Notre Dame	27	7
N16 ●	Army	28	0
N30 ●	at Miami, Fla.	31	20
D7 ●	Penn State	22	21

1964   3-5-2
S12 ●	UCLA	12	17
S26 ●	Oregon PORT	13	22
O3 ●	William & Mary	34	7
O10 ●	West Virginia	14	0
O17 =	at Miami, Fla.	20	20
O24 =	Navy	14	14
O31 ●	at Syracuse	6	21
N7	Notre Dame	15	17
N14 ●	at Army	24	8
N21	Penn State	0	28

1965   3-7-0
S18 ●	Oregon	15	17
S25 ●	Oklahoma	13	9
O2	at West Virginia	48	63
O9	at Duke	13	21
O16	Navy DC	0	12
O23 ●	Miami, Fla.	28	14
O30	Syracuse FLU	13	51
N6	Notre Dame	13	69
N13	at Southern Cal	0	28
N20 ●	Penn State	30	27

DAVID R. HART
1966-68 (.100)   3-27

1966   1-9-0
S17	at UCLA	14	57
S24	Duke	7	14
O1	at California	15	30
O8 ●	West Virginia	17	14
O15	Navy	7	24
O22	at Army	0	28
O29	at Syracuse	7	33
N5	at Notre Dame	0	40
N11	at Miami, Fla.	14	38
N19	Penn State	24	48

1967   1-9-0
S23	UCLA	8	40
S30	at Illinois	6	34
O7	at West Virginia	0	15
O14 =	at Wisconsin	13	11
O21	Miami, Fla.	0	58
O28	Navy	21	22
N4	Syracuse	7	14
N11	Notre Dame	0	38
N18	Army	12	21
N25	at Penn State	6	42

1968   1-9-0
S21	at UCLA	7	63
S28	West Virginia	15	38
O5 ●	William & Mary	14	3
O12	at Syracuse	17	50
O19	at Navy	16	17
O26	Air Force	14	27
N1	at Miami, Fla.	0	48
N9	at Notre Dame	7	56
N16	Army	0	26
N23	Penn State	9	65

CARL A. DePASQUA
1969-72 (.310)   13-29

1969   4-6-0
S20	at UCLA	8	42
S27	at Oklahoma	8	37
O4 ●	at Duke	14	12
O11 ●	Navy	46	19
O18	Tulane	22	26
O25	at West Virginia	18	49
N1 ●	Syracuse	21	20
N8	Notre Dame	7	49
N15 ●	at Army	15	6
N22	Penn State	7	27

1970   5-5-0
S19 ●	UCLA	15	24
S26 ●	at Baylor	15	10
O3 ●	Kent	27	6
O10 ●	at Navy	10	8
O17 ●	West Virginia	36	35
O24 ●	Miami, Fla.	28	17
O31 ●	at Syracuse	13	43
N7 ●	at Notre Dame	14	46
N14 ●	Boston College	6	21
N21 ●	at Penn State	15	35

1971   3-8-0
S11 ●	at UCLA	29	25
S25 ●	Oklahoma	29	55
O2 ●	at West Virginia	9	20
O9 ●	Navy	36	35
O16 ●	at Tulane	8	33
O23 ●	at Boston College	22	40
O30 ●	Syracuse	31	21
N6 ●	Notre Dame	7	56
N13 ●	at Army	14	17
N20 ●	Penn State	18	55
N27 ●	at Florida State	13	31

1972   1-10-0
S9 ●	Florida State	7	19
S16 ●	UCLA	28	38
S23 ●	at Air Force	13	41
S30 ●	Northwestern	22	27
O7 ●	at Tulane	6	38
O14 ●	at Notre Dame	16	42
O21 ●	Boston College	35	20
O28 ●	at Syracuse	6	10
N4 ●	West Virginia	20	38
N11 ●	at Navy	13	28
N25 ●	at Penn State	27	49

JOHN MAJORS
1973-76 '93-96 (.500) 45-45-1

1973   6-5-1
S15 =	at Georgia	7	7
S22 ●	Baylor	14	20
S29 ●	at Northwestern	21	14
O6 ●	Tulane	6	24
O13 ●	at West Virginia	35	7
O20 ●	at Boston College	28	14
O27 ●	Navy	22	17
N3 ●	Syracuse	28	14
N10 ●	Notre Dame	10	31
N17 ●	at Army	34	0
N24 ●	at Penn State	13	35
	FIESTA BOWL		
D21	Arizona State	7	28

1974   7-4-0
S14 ●	at Florida State	9	6
S21 ●	at Georgia Tech	27	17
S28 ●	Southern Cal	7	16
O5	at North Carolina	29	45
O12 ●	West Virginia	31	14
O19 ●	Boston College	35	11
O26 ●	at Navy	13	11
N2 ●	at Syracuse	21	13
N9 ●	Temple	35	24
N16 ●	at Notre Dame	10	14
N28 ●	Penn State	10	31

1975   8-4-0
S13 ●	at Georgia	19	9
S20 ●	at Oklahoma	10	46
S27 ●	William & Mary	47	0
O4 ●	Duke	14	0
O11 ●	at Temple	55	6
O18 ●	at Army	52	20
O25 ●	Navy	0	17
N1 ●	at Syracuse	38	0
N8	at West Virginia	14	17
N15 ●	Notre Dame	34	20
N22 ●	Penn State	6	7
	SUN BOWL		
D26 ●	Kansas	33	19

1976   12-0-0
S11 ●	at Notre Dame	31	10
S18 ●	at Georgia Tech	42	14
S25 ●	Temple	21	7
O2 ●	at Duke	44	31
O9 ●	Louisville	27	6
O16 ●	Miami, Fla.	36	19
O23 ●	at Navy	45	0
O30 ●	Syracuse	23	13
N6 ●	Army	37	7
N13 ●	West Virginia	24	16
N26 ●	Penn State	24	7
	SUGAR BOWL		
J1 ●	Georgia	27	3

JACKIE SHERRILL
1977-81 (.842)   50-9-1

1977   9-2-1
S10	Notre Dame	9	19
S17 ●	William & Mary	28	6
S24 ●	at Temple	76	0
O1 ●	at Boston College	45	7
O8 =	at Florida	17	17
O15 ●	Navy	34	17
O22 ●	Syracuse	28	21
O29 ●	Tulane	48	0
N5 ●	at West Virginia	44	3
N12 ●	Army ERUT	52	26
N19	Penn State	13	15
	GATOR BOWL		
D30 ●	Clemson	34	3

1978   8-4-0

S16	●	at Tulane	24	6
S23	●	Temple	20	12
S30	●	North Carolina	20	16
O7	●	at Boston College	32	15
O14	●	at Notre Dame	17	26
O21	●	Florida State	7	3
O28	●	at Navy	11	21
N4	●	at Syracuse	18	17
N11	●	West Virginia	52	7
N18	●	Army	35	17
N25		at Penn State	10	17
		TANGERINE BOWL		
D23		North Carolina St.	17	30

1979   11-1-0

S15	●	Kansas	24	0
S22	●	at North Carolina	7	17
S29	●	at Temple	10	9
O6	●	Boston College	28	7
O13	●	Cincinnati	35	0
O20	●	at Washington	26	14
O27	●	Navy	24	7
N3	●	Syracuse	28	21
N10	●	at West Virginia	24	17
N17	●	at Army	40	0
D1	●	Penn State	29	14
		FIESTA BOWL		
D25	●	Arizona	16	10

1980   11-1-0

S13	●	Boston College	14	6
S20	●	at Kansas	18	3
S27	●	Temple	36	2
O4	●	Maryland	38	9
O11	●	at Florida State	22	36
O18	●	West Virginia	42	14
O25	●	at Tennessee	30	6
N1	●	at Syracuse	43	6
N8	●	Louisville	41	23
N15	●	at Army	45	7
N29	●	at Penn State	14	9
		GATOR BOWL		
D29	●	South Carolina	37	9

1981   11-1-0

S5	●	Illinois	26	6
S19	●	Cincinnati	38	7
O3	●	at South Carolina	42	28
O10	●	at West Virginia	17	0
O17	●	Florida State	42	14
O24	●	Syracuse	23	10
O31	●	at Boston College	29	24
N7	●	Rutgers ERUT	47	3
N14	●	Army	48	0
N21	●	at Temple	35	0
N28		Penn State	14	48
		SUGAR BOWL		
J1	●	Georgia	24	20

SERAFINO "FOGE" FAZIO
1982-85 (.576)   25-18-3

1982   9-3-0

S9	●	North Carolina	7	6
S18	●	at Florida State	37	17
S25	●	at Illinois	20	3
O2	●	West Virginia	16	13
O16	●	Temple	38	7
O23	●	at Syracuse	14	0
O30	●	Louisville	63	14
N6		Notre Dame	16	31
N13	●	at Army	24	6
N20	●	Rutgers	52	6
N26		at Penn State	10	19
		COTTON BOWL		
J1		SMU	3	7

1983   8-3-1

S3	●	at Tennessee	13	3
S10	●	Temple	35	0
S24	●	at Maryland	7	13
O1	●	at West Virginia	21	24
O8	●	Florida State	17	16
O15	●	at Louisville	55	10
O22	●	at Navy	21	14
O29	●	Syracuse	23	10
N5	●	at Notre Dame	21	16
N12	●	Army	38	7
N19	=	Penn State	24	24
		FIESTA BOWL		
J2		Ohio State	23	28

1984   3-7-1

S1		Brigham Young	14	20
S15	●	Oklahoma	10	42
S22	●	at Temple	12	13
S29	●	West Virginia	10	28
O6	●	East Carolina	17	10
O13	●	at South Carolina	21	45
O20	●	at Miami, Fla.	7	27
O27	=	Navy	28	28
N3		at Syracuse	7	13
N10	●	Tulane	21	10
N24	●	at Penn State	31	11

1985   5-5-1

A31	●	Purdue	31	30
S14		at Ohio State	7	10
S21		Boston College	22	29
S28	=	at West Virginia	10	10
O5	●	South Carolina	42	7
O12	●	North Carolina St.	24	10
O19	●	Rutgers ERUT	38	10
O26		at Navy	7	21
N2		Syracuse	0	12
N9	●	at Temple	21	17
N23		Penn State	0	31

MIKE GOTTFRIED
1986-89 (.600)   26-17-2

1986   5-5-1

S1		Maryland	7	10
S13	=	at North Carolina St.	14	14
S20	●	at Purdue	41	26
S27	●	West Virginia	48	16
O4		Temple	13	19 †
O11	●	at Notre Dame	10	9
O25	●	Navy	56	14
N1		at Syracuse	20	24
N8		Miami, Fla.	10	37
N15	●	Rutgers	20	6
N22		at Penn State	14	34

1987   8-4-0

S2	●	at Brigham Young	27	17
S12	●	North Carolina St.	34	0
S19	●	Temple	21	24
S26	●	at West Virginia	6	3
O3		Boston College	10	13
O10	●	Notre Dame	30	22
O24	●	at Navy	10	6
O31		Syracuse	10	24
N7	●	Rutgers ERUT	17	0
N14		Penn State	10	0
N21	●	Kent	28	5
		BLUEBONNET BOWL		
D31		Texas	27	32

1988   6-5-0

S3	●	No. Iowa	59	10
S17	●	Ohio State	42	10
S24	●	West Virginia	10	31
O1		at Boston College	31	34
O8		Notre Dame	20	30
O15	●	Temple	42	7
O22	●	Navy	52	6
N5	●	Rutgers	20	10
N12	●	at Penn State	14	7
N19	●	at North Carolina St.	3	14
D3		at Syracuse	7	24

1989   8-3-1

S2	●	Pacific	38	3
S9	●	at Boston College	29	10
S23	●	Syracuse	30	23
S30	=	at West Virginia	31	31
O7	●	at Temple	27	3
O14	●	Navy	31	14
O28	●	at Notre Dame	7	45
N11	●	Miami, Fla.	3	24
N18	●	East Carolina	47	42
N25		Penn State	13	16
D2	●	Rutgers DUB	46	29
		SUN BOWL		
D30	●	Texas A&M	31	28

PAUL HACKETT
1989-92 (.397)   13-20-1

1990   3-7-1

S1	●	Ohio U.	35	3
S8	●	Boston College	29	6
S15	●	at Oklahoma	10	52
S22	=	at Syracuse	20	20
S29	●	West Virginia	24	38
O13	●	Rutgers	45	21
O20		Louisville	20	27
O27		Notre Dame	22	31
N3		at Miami, Fla.	0	45
N10		Temple	18	28
N24		at Penn State	17	22

1991-PRESENT
BIG EAST

1991   6-5-0 (3-2-0)

A31	●	at West Virginia	34	3
S7	●	Southern Miss	35	14
S14	●	Temple	26	7
S28	●	at Minnesota	14	13
O5	●	Maryland	24	20
O12		at Notre Dame	7	42
O19		Syracuse	27	31
O26		at East Carolina	23	24
N2		at Boston College	12	38
N9	●	Rutgers	22	17
N28		Penn State	20	32

SAL SUNSERI
1992 (.000)   0-1

1992   3-9-0 (1-3-0)

S5	●	Kent	51	10
S12		West Virginia	6	44
S17		at Rutgers	16	21
S26	●	Minnesota	41	33
O3		at Maryland	34	47
O10		Notre Dame	21	52
O17	●	at Temple	27	20
O24		East Carolina	31	37
O31		at Syracuse	10	41
N14		Louisville	16	31
N21		at Penn State	13	57
D5		at Hawaii	23	36

JOHN MAJORS

1993   3-8-0 (2-5-0)

S4	●	at Southern Miss	14	10
S11		Virginia Tech	21	63
S18		Ohio State	28	63
O2		Louisville	7	29
O9		at Notre Dame	0	44
O16		Syracuse	21	24
O23		at West Virginia	21	42
O28	●	Rutgers ERUT	21	10
N6		Miami, Fla.	7	35
N13		Boston College	0	33
N20	●	at Temple	28	18

1994   3-8-0 (2-5-0)

S3		Texas	28	30
S10		Ohio U.	30	16
S17		at Ohio State	3	27
S24		Boston College	9	21
O1		at Louisville	29	33
O8		at Syracuse	7	31
O15		West Virginia	41	47
O22		at Virginia Tech	7	45
O29	●	Temple	45	19
N12		at Miami, Fla.	12	17
N19	●	Rutgers	35	21

1995   2-9-0 (0-7-0)

S2	●	Washington St.	17	13
S9	●	Eastern Michigan	66	30
S16		at Texas	27	38
S23		Ohio State	14	54
S30		Virginia Tech	16	26
O7		at Boston College	0	17
O14		at Temple	27	29
O21		Miami, Fla.	16	17
O28		at Rutgers	24	42
N11		Syracuse	10	42
N24		at West Virginia	0	21

1996   4-7 (3-4)

A31		West Virginia	0	34
S7	●	Kent	52	14
S14		Houston	35	42
S21		at Ohio State	0	72
S28		at Miami, Fla.	0	45
O5	●	Temple	53	52
O12		at Syracuse	7	55
O26		at Virginia Tech	17	34
O31	●	Boston College	20	13
N16		at Notre Dame	6	60
N30	●	Rutgers	24	9

WALT HARRIS
1997-2004 (.542)   52-44

1997   6-6 (4-3)

A30	●	La. Lafayette	45	13
S6		at Penn State	17	34
S13		at Houston	35	24
S18	●	Miami, Fla.	21	17
O4		at Temple	13	17
O11		Notre Dame	21	45
O25	●	at Rutgers	55	48
N1		at Boston College	21	22
N15		Syracuse	27	32
N22	●	Virginia Tech	30	23
N28	●	at West Virginia	41	38
		LIBERTY BOWL		
D31		Southern Miss	7	41

1998   2-9 (0-7)

S5	●	Villanova	48	41
S19		Penn State	13	20
S26		at Virginia Tech	7	27
O3	●	Akron	35	0
O10		at North Carolina	10	29
O17		Rutgers	21	25
O31		at Syracuse	28	45
N7		Temple	33	34
N14		Boston College	15	23
N19		at Miami, Fla.	10	38
N27		West Virginia	14	52

1999   5-6 (2-5)

S4	●	Bowling Green	30	10
S11		at Penn State	17	20
S18	●	Kent	30	23
O2	●	Temple	55	24
O7		Syracuse	17	24
O16		at Boston College	16	20
O23	●	at Rutgers	38	15
O30		Virginia Tech	17	30
N6		Miami, Fla.	3	33
N13		Notre Dame	37	27
N27		West Virginia	21	52

2000   7-5 (4-3)

S2	●	Kent	30	7
S9	●	at Bowling Green	34	16
S16	●	Penn State	12	0
S23	●	Rutgers	29	17
O7		at Syracuse	17	24
O21	●	Boston College	42	26
O28		at Virginia Tech	34	37
N4		North Carolina	17	20
N11		at Miami, Fla.	7	35
N18	●	at Temple	7	0
N24	●	West Virginia	38	28
		INSIGHT.COM BOWL		
D28		Iowa State	29	37

2001   7-5 (4-3)

S1	●	East Tenn. St.	31	0
S8	●	South Florida	26	35
S27		Miami, Fla.	21	43
O6		at Notre Dame	7	24
O13		Syracuse	10	42
O20		at Boston College	7	45
O27	●	at Temple	33	7
N3		Virginia Tech	38	7
N10	●	at Rutgers	42	0
N24	●	at West Virginia	23	17
D1	●	UAB	24	6
		FLORIDA TANGERINE BOWL		
D20	●	North Carolina St.	34	19

2002 9-4 (5-2)

A31	●	Ohio U.	27 14
S7		Texas A&M	12 14
S14	●	at UAB	26 20
S21	●	Rutgers	23 3
S28	●	Toledo	37 19
O5	●	at Syracuse	48 24
O12		at Notre Dame	6 14
O26	●	Boston College	19 16
N2	●	at Virginia Tech	28 21
N9	●	Temple	29 22
N21		at Miami, Fla.	21 28
N30		West Virginia	17 24
		INSIGHT BOWL	
D26	●	Oregon State	38 13

2003 8-5 (5-2)

S6	●	Kent State	43 3
S13	●	Ball State	42 21
S20		at Toledo	31 35
S27	●	at Texas A&M	37 26
O11		Notre Dame	14 20
O18	●	at Rutgers	42 32
O25	●	Syracuse	34 14
N1	●	at Boston College	24 13
N8	●	Virginia Tech	31 28
N15		at West Virginia	31 52
N22	●	at Temple	30 16
N29		Miami, Fla.	14 28
		CONTINENTAL TIRE BOWL	
D27		Virginia	16 23

2004 8-4 (4-2)

S11	●	Ohio U.	24 3
S18		Nebraska	17 24
S25	●	Furman	41 38
S30		at Connecticut	17 29
O9	●	at Temple	27 22
O16	●	Boston College	20 17
O23	●	Rutgers	41 17
N6		at Syracuse	31 38
N13	●	at Notre Dame	41 38
N25	●	West Virginia	16 13
D4	●	at South Florida	43 14
		FIESTA BOWL	
J1	●	Utah	7 35

Neutral Site key: *Balt* Baltimore, MD / *Bel* Bellefonte, PA / *Brnx* Bronx, NY / *Clev* Cleveland, OH / *Dub* Dublin, Ireland / *ERut* East Rutherford, NJ / *Flu* Flushing, NY / *NYC* New York, NY / *Nor* Norfolk, VA / *Port* Portland, OR / *DC* Washington, DC / *Wlk* Wilkinsburg, PA
f Forfeit   † Game Later Forfieted   # Disputed Victor   * Disputed Score || Designated Conference Game |2 Counted Twice in Conference Standings

PITTSBURGH ANNUAL STATISTICAL LEADERS

YR	RUSHING	YDS	ATT	AVG	PASSING	ATT	CMP	PCT	YDS	RECEIVING	REC	YDS	AVG
1914	Andy Hastings	252	NA	NA	George Kenneth Fry	20	8	.40	176	Philip Dillon	NA	101	NA
1915	Andy Hastings	503	NA	NA	Guy Williamson	10	6	.60	117	James DeHart	NA	74	NA
1916	James DeHart	786	NA	NA	Andy Hastings	16	7	.44	132	James Herron	NA	64	NA
1917	George McLaren	782	NA	NA	George McLaren	24	11	.46	136	Ralph Gougler	NA	130	NA
1918	Tom Davies	361	NA	NA	Tom Davies	14	7	.50	114	Tom Davies	NA	102	NA
1919	Tom Davies	650	NA	NA	Tom Davies	19	5	.26	80	James DeHart	NA	64	NA
1920	Tom Davies	413	NA	NA	Tom Davies	19	11	.58	171	Thomas Holleran	NA	115	NA
1921	Orville Hewitt	454	NA	NA	Tom Davies	36	15	.42	146	Thomas Holleran	NA	181	NA
1922	Orville Hewitt	609	NA	NA	W.H. Flanagan	34	17	.50	187	John Anderson	NA	79	NA
1923	Andrew Gustafson	493	NA	NA	W.H. Flanagan	67	30	.45	406	Karl Bohren	NA	216	NA
1924	Andrew Gustafson	432	NA	NA	Jesse Brown	29	16	.55	180	Jack Harding	NA	81	NA
1925	Gibby Welch	589	NA	NA	Gibby Welch	26	11	.42	182	John Kifer	NA	109	NA
1926	Gibby Welch	815	NA	NA	Gibby Welch	56	25	.45	357	Gibby Welch	NA	118	NA
1927	Allan Booth	659	NA	NA	Gibby Welch	55	27	.49	439	Albert Guarino	NA	198	NA
1928	Josh Williams	777	NA	NA	Toby Uansa	16	8	.50	82	Joseph Donchess	NA	49	NA
1929	Toby Uansa	964	NA	NA	James Rooney	15	5	.33	149	Joseph Donchess	NA	65	NA
1930	Warren Heller	491	NA	NA	Warren Heller	17	11	.65	198	Edward Baker	NA	234	NA
1931	Warren Heller	744	NA	NA	Warren Heller	53	23	.43	594	Paul Reider	NA	379	NA
1932	Warren Heller	684	NA	NA	Warren Heller	69	16	.23	450	Joseph Skladany	NA	162	NA
1933	Henry Weisenbaugh	427	NA	NA	Howard Odell	47	22	.47	302	Mike Nicksick	NA	119	NA
1934	Mike Nicksick	779	NA	NA	Mike Nicksick	27	9	.33	151	Harvey Rooker	NA	106	NA
1935	Herbert Randour	569	NA	NA	Herbert Randour	38	11	.29	133	Frank Souchak	NA	68	NA
1936	Marshall Goldberg	886	NA	NA	Marshall Goldberg	19	7	.37	92	Fabian Hoffman	NA	132	NA
1937	Marshall Goldberg	698	NA	NA	Marshall Goldberg	11	6	.55	76	Lawrence Peace	NA	58	NA
1938	Dick Cassiano	739	NA	NA	Emil Narick	10	4	.40	114	Robert Thurbon	NA	82	NA
1939	Dick Cassiano	492	NA	NA	Emil Narick	41	22	.54	280	Robert Thurbon	NA	165	NA
1940	Edgar Jones	447	104	4.3	Edgar Jones	37	11	.30	171	Jack Goodridge	6	117	19.5
1941	Edgar Jones	500	131	3.8	Edgar Jones	23	7	.30	116	Walt West	4	16	4.0
1942	William Dutton	575	209	2.8	William Dutton	95	32	.34	610	Walt West	9	116	12.9
1943	Thomas Kalmanir	301	41	7.3	Joseph Mocha	80	34	.43	506	James Maloney	14	181	12.9
1944	Donald Matthews	284	49	5.8	Paul Rickards	178	84	.47	897	Donald Matthews	16	136	8.5
1945	Jimmy Joe Robinson	273	83	3.3	William Wolff	83	32	.39	499	Jimmy Joe Robinson	11	160	14.5
1946	William Abraham	295	71	4.2	Carl DePasqua	41	13	.32	247	Bill McPeak	13	235	18.1
1947	Lou Cecconi	114	55	2.1	Robert Lee	25	10	.40	121	Lou Cecconi	8	90	11.3
1948	Lou Cecconi	292	104	2.8	Lou Cecconi	87	30	.34	542	Leo Skladany	11	159	14.5
1949	Lou Cecconi	397	113	3.5	Lou Cecconi	91	35	.38	656	Nick DeRosa	11	238	21.6
1950	Joe Capp	258	62	4.2	Bob Bestwick	113	62	.55	757	Billy Reynolds	11	130	11.8
1951	Louis Cimarolli	399	89	4.5	Bob Bestwick	178	99	.56	1,165	Chris Warriner	37	502	13.6
1952	Billy Reynolds	748	133	5.6	Rudy Mattiola	122	52	.43	534	Billy Reynolds	14	132	9.4
1953	Bobby Epps	424	100	4.2	Henry Ford	80	33	.41	305	Dick Deitrick	13	139	10.7
1954	Henry Ford	322	95	3.4	Corny Salvaterra	57	19	.33	286	Henry Ford	5	103	20.6
1955	Louis Cimarolli	339	57	5.9	Corny Salvaterra	54	25	.46	329	Joe Walton	16	241	15.1
1956	Corny Salvaterra	504	123	4.1	Corny Salvaterra	88	33	.38	500	Joe Walton	21	360	17.1
1957	Fred Riddle	407	76	5.4	Bill Kaliden	93	40	.43	519	Dick Scherer	20	403	20.2
1958	Dick Haley	311	93	3.3	Ivan Toncic	69	49	.71	641	Mike Ditka	18	252	14.0
1959	Fred Cox	392	47	8.3	Ivan Toncic	133	56	.42	667	Mike Ditka	16	249	15.6
1960	Bob Clemens	349	74	4.7	Jim Traficant	57	29	.51	407	Mike Ditka	11	229	20.8
1961	Rick Leeson	452	103	4.4	Jim Traficant	67	32	.48	437	John Kuprok	18	247	13.7
1962	Rick Leeson	481	104	4.6	Jim Traficant	88	39	.44	611	Paul Martha	12	246	20.5
1963	Fred Mazurek	646	132	4.9	Fred Mazurek	127	74	.58	949	Joe Kuzneski	21	258	12.3
1964	Barry McKnight	551	129	4.3	Fred Mazurek	93	53	.57	686	Eric Crabtree	14	255	18.2
1965	Barry McKnight	406	124	3.3	Ken Lucas	268	144	.54	1,921	Eric Crabtree	45	724	16.1

YR	RUSHING	YDS	ATT	AVG	PASSING	ATT	CMP	PCT	YDS	RECEIVING	REC	YDS	AVG
1966	Mike Raklewicz	324	110	2.9	Ed James	193	91	.47	1,162	Bob Longo	46	732	15.9
1967	Gary Cramer	312	78	4.0	Bob Bazylak	124	55	.44	679	Bob Longo	40	548	13.7
1968	Dennis Ferris	472	120	3.9	Dave Havern	287	140	.49	1,810	Harry Orszulak	50	725	14.5
1969	Tony Esposito	743	201	3.7	Jim Friedl	263	128	.49	1,277	Steve Moyer	48	437	9.1
1970	Tony Esposito	623	160	3.9	John Hogan	140	72	.51	801	Dennis Ferris	35	506	14.5
1971	Lou Julian	368	101	3.6	Dave Havern	207	108	.52	1,197	Joel Klimek	39	452	11.6
1972	Stan Ostrowski	493	140	3.5	John Hogan	192	91	.47	1,250	Todd Toerper	34	531	15.6
1973	Tony Dorsett	1,686	318	5.3	Bill Daniels	176	84	.48	1,170	Bruce Murphy	20	325	16.3
1974	Tony Dorsett	1,004	220	4.6	Bill Daniels	127	71	.56	919	Bruce Murphy	25	400	16.0
1975	Tony Dorsett	1,686	255	6.6	Robert Haygood	78	42	.54	687	Jim Corbett	24	322	13.4
1976	Tony Dorsett	2,150	370	5.8	Matt Cavanaugh	110	65	.59	1,046	Jim Corbett	34	538	15.8
1977	Elliott Walker	1,025	172	6.0	Matt Cavanaugh	187	110	.59	1,844	Gordon Jones	45	793	17.6
1978	Freddie Jacobs	634	152	4.2	Rick Trocano	283	138	.49	1,648	Gordon Jones	45	666	14.8
1979	Randy McMillan	802	184	4.4	Dan Marino	222	130	.59	1,680	Benjie Pryor	45	588	13.1
1980	Randy McMillan	692	147	4.7	Dan Marino	224	116	.52	1,609	Benjie Pryor	47	574	12.2
1981	Bryan Thomas	1,132	217	5.2	Dan Marino	380	226	.59	2,876	Julius Dawkins	46	767	16.7
1982	Bryan Thomas	955	219	4.4	Dan Marino	378	221	.58	2,432	Bryan Thomas	54	404	7.5
1983	Joe McCall	961	197	4.9	John Congemi	286	170	.59	1,940	Bill Wallace	45	727	16.2
1984	Craig Heyward	539	123	4.4	John Congemi	174	93	.53	1,102	Bill Wallace	43	610	14.2
1985	Charles Gladman	1,085	194	5.6	John Congemi	241	122	.51	1,377	Chuck Scales	34	446	13.1
1986	Craig Heyward	756	171	4.4	John Congemi	293	165	.56	2,048	Bill Osborn	33	414	12.5
1987	Craig Heyward	1,791	387	4.6	Sal Genilla	145	80	.55	1,051	Reggie Williams	31	535	17.3
1988	Curvin Richards	1,228	207	5.9	Darnell Dickerson	213	104	.49	1,599	Henry Tuten	37	571	15.4
1989	Curvin Richards	1,282	232	5.5	Alex Van Pelt	347	192	.55	2,881	Henry Tuten	41	975	23.8
1990	Curvin Richards	682	145	4.7	Alex Van Pelt	351	201	.57	2,427	Olanda Truitt	49	895	18.3
1991	Jermaine Williams	682	137	5.0	Alex Van Pelt	398	227	.57	2,796	Dave Moore	51	505	9.9
1992	Tim Colicchio	743	139	5.3	Alex Van Pelt	407	245	.60	3,163	Dietrich Jells	55	1,091	19.8
1993	Curtis Martin	1,075	210	5.1	John Ryan	203	115	.57	1,282	Curtis Martin	33	249	7.5
1994	Billy West	1,358	252	5.4	John Ryan	144	87	.60	1,294	Billy Davis	51	731	14.3
1995	Demetrius Harris	610	137	4.5	John Ryan	232	115	.50	1,439	Dietrich Jells	48	789	16.4
1996	Billy West	687	145	4.7	Matt Lytle	214	105	.49	1,249	Jake Hoffart	39	667	17.1
1997	Dwayne Schulters	861	169	5.1	Pete Gonzalez	374	211	.56	2,829	Jake Hoffart	69	852	12.3
1998	Kevan Barlow	533	121	4.4	Matt Lytle	306	159	.52	2,092	Latef Grim	60	906	15.1
1999	Kevan Barlow	630	141	4.5	David Priestley	158	92	.58	1,305	Latef Grim	75	1,106	14.7
2000	Kevan Barlow	1,167	219	5.3	John Turman	269	148	.55	2,482	Antonio Bryant	73	1,457	20.0
2001	Raymond Kirkley	672	166	4.0	David Priestley	312	183	.59	2,399	Antonio Bryant	49	760	15.5
2002	Brandon Miree	943	214	4.4	Rod Rutherford	367	192	.52	2,783	Larry Fitzgerald	69	1,005	14.6
2003	Brandon Miree	573	115	5.0	Rod Rutherford	413	247	.60	3,679	Larry Fitzgerald	92	1,672	18.2
2004	Raymond Kirkley	560	154	3.6	Tyler Palko	409	230	.56	3,067	Greg Lee	68	1,297	19.1

Receiving leaders by receptions
All statistics include postseason

PURDUE

BY TODD JONES

THERE MIGHT NEVER HAVE BEEN A Big Ten Conference without the Purdue Boilermakers. On Jan. 11, 1895, Purdue president James H. Smart invited six other university presidents to the Palmer House in Chicago. He wanted to discuss possible solutions to the problems plaguing collegiate athletics.

The meeting between Purdue, Michigan, Minnesota, Wisconsin, Illinois, Chicago and Northwestern created an Intercollegiate Conference of Faculty Representatives and led to an affiliation later known as the Big Ten. Pride and passion for that league, and its football, has remained alive in northwestern Indiana through various levels of success and failure at Purdue. Joe Tiller added to the spirit, and rekindled the glory days of Jack Mollenkopf, by coaching a wide-open offense and stout defense. The combination has again made every fall Saturday an event near the Wabash River in West Lafayette.

TRADITION A home game at Purdue doesn't begin until "I Am an American" is read over the public-address system.

Throughout the game, the school's "All-American" Band, 340 members strong, entertains the crowd with the Big Bass Drum, built in 1921, and the Golden Girl twirling group. The Gimlets line the north end zone and, after every Purdue score, do push-ups for each of the team's points. If the Boilermakers win, the "W" flag is raised atop the stadium's south scoreboard. Big Ten wins at home are celebrated by the ringing of the Victory Bell, which hung in the school's bell tower in the 1870s and is now mounted on a four-wheel carriage near the north end zone. Purdue and Notre Dame play for The Shillelagh, donated in 1957 by merchant seaman Joe McLaughlin. Illinois plays the Boilermakers for ownership of The Cannon. Purdue students took the cannon to Champaign, Ill., in 1905 to fire it after an expected win, but Illinois fraternity brothers from Delta Upsilon confiscated the weapon until 1943, when Illinois fan Quincy A. Hall suggested the schools use it as a trophy. The oldest trophy Purdue plays for is the Old Oaken Bucket, which goes to the winner of the Indiana game. Chicago alumni groups from both schools decided in 1925 that the rivalry needed a trophy. Fritz Ernst of Purdue and Whiley J. Huddle of Indiana found an old bucket—supposedly used during the Civil War—on a southern Indiana farm, and

---

His glasses made him look like a librarian, but foes knew Jack Mollenkopf as Jack the Ripper.

the schools agreed to make it the game's trophy. A "P" or an "I" link on the bucket signifies the winner.

BEST PLAYER The multiple skills of Leroy Keyes bubbled forth early. In his second game at Notre Dame in 1966, the sophomore defensive back from Newport News, Va., returned a fumble 95 yards for a touchdown. He finished the season with four interceptions, a kickoff-return average of 26 yards and bursts of promise on a few carries as running back. Purdue coach Jack Mollenkopf figured he had to get the football into Keyes' hands more often, so his talent was switched primarily to offense in 1967, although occasional defensive stints continued when necessity beckoned. Keyes won MVP of the Big Ten and finished third in the Heisman Trophy balloting as a junior, after rushing for 986 yards, with a school-record average of 6.6 yards per carry, and 19 touchdowns, including six receiving TDs. His senior year in 1968 was better, prompting Mollenkopf to refer to his beloved sweep play as "Leroy left and Leroy right." Keyes set Purdue records with 1,003 rushing yards and 14 rushing

TDs. He capped his career in magnificent fashion, running for 140 yards, catching six passes for 149 yards, and scoring four TDs in a 38-35 win over Indiana. Keyes was runner-up for the 1968 Heisman. He ended his three seasons with numerous Purdue records for scoring, rushing and receiving and also completed 12 passes in his career, eight for touchdowns.

BEST COACH His glasses made him look like a librarian, but opponents knew him as Jack the Ripper. Jack Mollenkopf earned a deadly reputation in big games by going 11–2–1 against Indiana and 10–4 against Notre Dame, and by leading Purdue to its only Rose Bowl victory, in its first appearance at the end of the 1966 season. The Ohio native was a football and baseball star at Bowling Green and later coached high school football in Toledo. He left the prep ranks to become one of Stuart Holcomb's assistant coaches at Purdue in 1947. Mollenkopf replaced the man who had hired him in 1956, and promptly suffered his only losing season as Purdue coach. That memory was buried by a slew of victories before

RECORDS

RUSHING YARDS

	GAME
276	Otis Armstrong vs. Indiana, Nov. 25, 1972 (32 att.)
	SEASON
1,436	Mike Alstott, 1995 (243 att.)
	CAREER
3,635	Mike Alstott, 1992-95 (644 att.)

PASSING YARDS

	GAME
522	Drew Brees vs. Minnesota, Oct. 3, 1998 (31 of 36)
	SEASON
3,983	Drew Brees, 1998 (361 of 569)
	CAREER
11,792	Drew Brees, 1997-2000 (1,026 of 1,678)

RECEIVING YARDS

	GAME
301	Chris Daniels vs. Michigan State, Oct. 16, 1999 (21 rec.)
	SEASON
1,307	John Standeford, 2002 (75 rec.)
	CAREER
3,788	John Standeford, 2000-03 (266 rec.)

POINTS

	GAME
43	Elmer Oliphant vs. Rose Poly, Nov. 17, 1912
	SEASON
114	Leroy Keyes, 1967 (19 TDs)
	CAREER
355	Travis Dorsch, 1998-2001 (68 FGs, 151 PATs)

CONSENSUS ALL-AMERICANS

1929	Elmer Sleight, T
1929	Ralph Welch, B
1932	Paul Moss, E
1933	Duane Purvis, B
1940	Dave Rankin, E
1943	Alex Agase, G
1952	Bernie Flowers, E
1965	Bob Griese, QB
1967-68	Leroy Keyes, B
1968	Chuck Kyle, MG
1969	Mike Phipps, QB
1972	Otis Armstrong, B
1972	Dave Butz, DT
1980	Dave Young, TE
1980	Mark Herrmann, QB
1986	Rod Woodson, DB
2001	Travis Dorsch, P
2004	Taylor Stubblefield, WR

Mollenkopf retired after the 1969 season. In the final six seasons of his 14-year tenure, the Boilermakers went 46–13–1 and never finished below third in the Big Ten. The high-water mark of Mollenkopf's career came in 1968 when he had Purdue ranked No. 1 in October. He ended up with a school-record 84 wins, 39 defeats and nine ties. When he died in 1975, *The Indianapolis Star* wrote: "What Purdue got from Mollenkopf was 24 hours of loyalty each and every day."

BEST TEAM Purdue went 9–0 in 1943, shared the Big Ten title with Michigan and ended the season ranked No. 5 in the nation. Those Boilermakers, however, can't quite match a team that set Purdue's all-time standard for success 14 years earlier. Jimmy Phelan put together an undefeated (8–0) season in his final one as coach of the Boilermakers. A pair of All-Americas—halfback Ralph "Pest" Welch and tackle Elmer Sleight—anchored the 1929 team. Welch, quarterback John White and running backs Glen Harmeson and Alex Yunevich served as the heart. Together, the Four Riveters, as they were called, averaged 4.5 yards per carry for an offense that outscored opponents 187-44. The season's highlight was a 30-16 win over Michigan, the school's first victory against the Wolverines since 1892. Purdue ended the year with a 32-0 win over Indiana that earned the Boilermakers their first Big Ten championship, which is still the school's only outright conference title.

BIGGEST GAME Purdue's 41-20 loss to Michigan State on Oct. 22, 1966, ended up costing the Boilermakers the Big Ten championship. However, a Big Ten rule at the time kept league members from going to the Rose Bowl in consecutive years. So it was second-place Purdue—instead of repeat conference champ Michigan State—who headed to Pasadena. The Boilermakers were 8–2 and rolling, having ended the season with four consecutive victories, the final three by a total of 90-6. Purdue then found a way

ALL-TIME TEAM

As part of the celebration of the 100-year anniversary of Purdue football during the 1987 season, an all-time team was selected on the basis of ballots tabulated from game programs, the Purdue Alumnus and John Purdue Club mailings. Leroy Keyes was named the all-time greatest player.

OFFENSE

1943	Alex Agase,	OG
1951-54	Tom Bettis,	OG
1927-29	Elmer Sleight,	OT
1963-65	Karl Singer,	OT
1977-80	Pete Quinn,	C
1977-80	Dave Young,	TE
1965-67	Jim Beirne,	WR
1964-66	Bob Griese,	QB
1932-34	Duane Purvis,	RB
1966-68	Leroy Keyes,	RB
1970-72	Otis Armstrong,	RB
1976-78	Scott Sovereen,	PK

DEFENSE

1945-47	Ned Maloney,	DE
1954-56	Lamar Lundy,	DE
1966-68	Chuck Kyle,	MG
1970-72	Dave Butz,	DT
1973-75	Ken Novak,	DT
1970-72	Gregg Bingham,	LB
1976-79	Keena Turner,	LB
1964-66	John Charles,	DB
1966-68	Leroy Keyes,	DB
1967-69	Tim Foley,	DB
1983-86	Rod Woodson,	DB
1981-83	Matt Kinzer,	P

to win in its first Rose Bowl despite Southern California gaining more yards (323-244) and producing more first downs (18-11). Sophomore fullback Perry Williams scored on a 1-yard run in the second quarter and a 2-yard run in the third quarter to give the Boilermakers a 14-7 lead. USC dominated the fourth quarter, running 26 offensive plays to just eight for Purdue. The trailing Trojans scored their second TD with 2:28 remaining in the game on a 19-yard pass from Troy Winslow to Rod Sherman. Southern California coach John McKay ordered a two-point conversion attempt. Winslow tried to hit Jim Lawrence with a pass, but Purdue senior defensive back George Catavolos stepped in front for the interception. "I could almost feel the ball in my hands, it was so close," Lawrence said. Purdue senior defensive back John Charles was named Rose Bowl MVP, but the difference in the game was two extra-point conversions, both kicked by Boilermakers quarterback Bob Griese.

BIGGEST UPSET Nothing suggested hope for Purdue when it traveled to South Bend, Ind., on Oct. 7, 1950. The 0–1 Boilermakers were facing defending national champion Notre Dame, a team that hadn't lost in 39 games. During that span, which stretched back to the 1946 season, the Irish only suffered two ties, to Army and USC. Notre Dame hadn't lost a home game in eight years and was 61–3–5 under coach Frank Leahy. Purdue entered the game a 20-point underdog but dominated play while building a 21-0 halftime lead. Fullback John Kerestes ran for a TD in the first and second quarters and QB Dale Samuels added a 30-yard scoring pass to halfback Neil Schmidt. In that first half, the Boilermakers had another TD called back because of a penalty and had an 85-yard drive stall at Notre Dame's 1-yard line. The Fighting Irish rallied after Purdue lost a fumble on its own 10-yard line in the third quarter. The turnover set up a 4-yard TD pass from Bob Williams to Jim Mutscheller. Notre Dame's John Petitbon added a six-yard scoring run

early in the fourth quarter to cut the deficit to 21-14. The Boilermakers immediately answered with a TD pass from Samuels to halfback Mike Maccioli. Coach Stu Holcomb's "Spoilermakers" won 28-14.

HEARTBREAKER Purdue was ranked No. 1 and expected to win its second consecutive Big Ten championship in 1968—the Boilers had shared the 1967 Big Ten title with Indiana—when it traveled to Ohio State as a 14-point favorite on Oct. 12. The odds reflected the Boilermakers' 41-6 thrashing of the Buckeyes the previous season. Ohio State's class of "super sophomores" made this a different team and game. It showed when the Boilermakers, averaging 41.3 points, found themselves in a scoreless tie at halftime. On the fourth play of the second half, the Buckeyes put a heavy rush on Boilermakers QB Mike Phipps. His pass was intercepted by Ted Provost and returned 35 yards for a touchdown. Jim Stillwagon intercepted another Phipps pass later in the third quarter. He returned it to the Purdue 25-yard line, leading to a 14-yard TD run by Ohio State quarterback Bill Long, who was briefly subbing for a shaken-up Rex Kern. The No. 4-ranked Buckeyes held on for a 13-0 upset, despite missing three field goal attempts. A then-record Ohio Stadium crowd of 84,834 saw the home team total 411 yards of offense, led by fullback Jim Otis' 144 on the ground. The Boilermakers were held to just 186 total yards, with running back Leroy Keyes rushing for only 18. "We just got clobbered, that's all," Mollenkopf said.

BEST COMEBACK On Nov. 8, 1997, Michigan State led 21-10 with less than three minutes to play when the Spartans attempted a 39-yard field goal. Purdue blocked the kick and returned it 62 yards for a touchdown. A failed two-point conversion left the Boilermakers trailing 21-16. Chris Daniels then recovered an onside kick for Purdue at its 45-yard line. Boilermakers QB Billy Dicken completed four passes and Edwin Watson capped the drive by carrying two Michigan State defenders into the end zone on a three-yard TD run. The extra point kick gave Purdue a 22-21 lead with 40 seconds remaining. The Spartans had one final chance to win but Chris Gardner missed a 43-yard field goal attempt with three seconds left. One year later, Purdue erased an 11-point deficit in the fourth quarter and won 25-24 at Michigan State.

STADIUM Purdue alum David E. Ross, president of the school's board of trustees, figured new athletic facilities would create more successful teams, leading to more alumni donations. So he decided in the early 1920s that the Boilermakers needed to move out of dinky Stuart Field. Ross and George Ade—an alum, author, playwright, and humorist—paid $40,000 for a 65-acre dairy farm north of campus and donated it to Purdue. The Ross-Ade Foundation raised money for the construction of a stadium on that site. Purdue dedicated Ross-Ade Stadium on Nov. 22, 1924, with a 26-7 homecoming win over Indiana. Various expansions over the years took the original capacity of 13,500 to a high of 69,357 in 1970. A $70 million renovation program began after the 2000 season. A new press box, 34 luxury suites and a brick-and-limestone façade were added to Ross-Ade Stadium, which now seats 62,500.

RIVAL Indiana has historically served as Purdue's main rival, with their first meeting dating back to 1891. The Boilermakers, however, have dominated the series, which hasn't had much national pizzazz. Only once, in 1945, have Purdue and Indiana both been ranked when they played. No wonder Purdue fans get more heated about a different in-state foe, tradition-laden Notre Dame. "The way you were measured around here is the way you fared against Notre Dame," said Brock Spack, a Purdue linebacker from 1980 to 1983. The Boilermakers and Fighting Irish first played in 1896, and have met every year since 1946. Notre Dame leads the series 49–25–2, but Purdue has been an occasional thorn for the Irish. The Boilermakers actually dominated the series from 1954 through 1969, winning 11 of 16 games. Since then, Notre Dame has given Purdue fans plenty of reason to further scorn the Golden Dome. The Irish won 11 of 14 against the Boilermakers from 1970 to 1983 and enjoyed 11 consecutive victories over Purdue from 1986 to 1996.

NICKNAME "Slaughter of Innocents," screamed the headline in the *Daily Argus News* in Crawfordsville, Ind., after Purdue beat Wabash College 44–0 in 1891. The smaller headline referred to the visiting team as "Burly Boiler Makers." The term Boilermakers was the latest in slurs aimed at Purdue, a land-grant university. Other nonflattering monikers were Pumpkin Shuckers, Rail Splitters, Cornfield Sailors, Foundry Hands, G Rangers and Blacksmiths. Newspapers that liked Purdue, however, took the term "Boilermakers" and turned in into a positive image, and the school adopted the name for its sports teams.

MASCOT A Purdue student in 1930 decided to honor the school's engineering and agrarian heritage by creating a mascot using a replica Victorian-era locomotive. Ten years later, Purdue alumni provided the first Special mascot train. The Reamer Club, a spirit group, was picked by school president Edward Elliott to maintain and operate the train. There have been four versions of the Special, although the latest, debuted in 1993, was dubbed Special V. Since 1956, mascot Purdue Pete has been played by a student outfitted with a huge head and a hammer. Purdue Pete actually began as advertising for the university bookstore in 1940. His sidekick, Rowdy, inflated to 10 feet by a battery-powered blower strapped to a student, was created in 1997.

UNIFORM Purdue's first football team in 1887 wanted to use Princeton's colors, but instead of that school's orange and black, the Boilermakers settled on old gold and black. The Boilers' helmets have been gold since 1962, except for two seasons (1989 and 1990), when they were black. Purdue has had an elongated "P" on the side of its helmet since 1971.

NUMBERS The 1943 Boilermakers, who went 9–0 and were co-champs of the Big Ten with Michigan, had a roster made up of 26 Marines, nine Navy men and nine civilians ... RB Otis Armstrong rushed for 3,315 yards from 1970 to 1972. He ran for 276 yards and 3 TDs in the final game of his career, a 42-7 win over Indiana ... Mike Pruitt gained 179 yards on 10 carries in a 1974 game against Iowa in which the Boilermakers rushed for 501 yards ... Although Purdue is known for QBs, Mike Alstott scored 39 touchdowns and ran for 3,635 yards from 1992 to 1995 ... Purdue has not been ranked No. 1 since Oct. 7, 1968 ... The Boilermakers upset No. 1 Michigan 16-14 on Nov. 6, 1976 ... Purdue beat Minnesota 35-28 in overtime in 2001 despite trailing by three with 19 seconds remaining in regulation and having the ball on its own 3-yard line with no timeouts.

LORE Purdue was known for throwing the football long before Joe Tiller brought his "Basketball on Grass" offense to West Lafayette in 1997. Bob DeMoss started the "Cradle of Quarterbacks" tradition by throwing for 2,790 yards and 20 touchdowns from 1945 to 1948. Dale Samuels and NFL Hall of Famers Len Dawson and Bob Griese added to Purdue's reputation for passing. Mike Phipps followed Griese and set numerous school records from 1967 to 1969, including passing yards (5,423) and passing TDs (37). Other top QBs kept up the tradition: Gary Danielson, Mark Herrmann, Scott Campbell, Jim Everett, Eric Hunter, Rick Trefzger and Billy Dicken. The best passer was Drew Brees. From 1997 to 2000, he set two NCAA records, 13 Big Ten records and 19 Purdue records, including career school marks for pass attempts (1,678), completions (1,026), completion percentage (.611), passing yards (11,792) and passing TDs (90).

QUOTE "Beat the little man."—Joe Tiller

PURDUE ANNUAL STATISTICAL LEADERS

YR	RUSHING	YDS	ATT	AVG	PASSING	ATT	CMP	PCT	YDS	RECEIVING	REC	YDS	AVG
1946	Ed Cody	378	80	4.7	Bob DeMoss	122	59	.48	814	Ned Maloney	22	269	12.2
1947	Harry Szulborski	851	136	6.3	Bob DeMoss	88	37	.42	509	Clyde Grimenstein	9	107	11.9
1948	Harry Szulborski	989	183	5.4	Bob DeMoss	105	40	.38	694	Bob Heck	12	119	9.9
1949	John Kerestes	647	146	4.4	Ken Grogal	75	33	.44	503	Bob Whitmer	13	214	16.5
1950	John Kerestes	477	145	3.3	Dale Samuels	172	77	.45	1,076	Neil Schmidt	22	282	12.8
1951	Phil Klezek	441	72	6.1	Dale Samuels	160	79	.49	954	Bernie Flowers	24	222	9.3
1952	Max Schmaling	593	147	4.0	Dale Samuels	185	104	.56	1,131	Bernie Flowers	43	603	14.0
1953	Ed Neves	245	55	4.5	Roy Evans	76	30	.39	514	Rex Brock	9	187	20.8
1954	Bill Murakowski	404	93	4.3	Len Dawson	167	87	.52	1,464	John Kerr	20	337	16.9
1955	Bill Murakowski	493	125	3.9	Len Dawson	155	87	.56	1,005	Bob Khoenle	18	162	9.0
1956	Mel Dillard	873	193	4.5	Len Dawson	130	69	.53	856	Lamar Lundy	15	248	16.5
1957	Bob Jarus	278	72	3.9	Ross Fichtner	58	23	.40	355	Tom Franckhauser	12	228	19.0
1958	Bob Jarus	396	115	3.4	Ross Fichtner	67	25	.37	414	Tom Franckhauser	13	300	23.1
1959	Jack Laraway	281	65	4.3	Bernie Allen	86	33	.38	416	Len Wilson	8	75	9.4
1960	Willie Jones	575	124	4.6	Bernie Allen	103	61	.59	765	Jim Tiller	21	237	11.3
1961	Roy Walker	491	123	4.0	Ron DiGravio	100	52	.52	861	Jack Elwell	16	343	21.4
1962	Roy Walker	427	97	4.4	Ron DiGravio	92	34	.37	629	Tom Bloom	13	217	16.7
1963	John Kuzniewski	242	62	3.9	Ron DiGravio	161	88	.55	1,108	Bob Hadrick	29	388	13.4
1964	Gordon Teter	614	152	4.0	Bob Griese	156	76	.49	934	Bob Hadrick	37	441	11.9
1965	Gordon Teter	490	123	4.0	Bob Griese	238	142	.60	1,719	Bob Hadrick	47	562	12.0
1966	Perry Williams	750	199	3.8	Bob Griese	233	140	.60	1,888	Jim Beirne	68	837	12.3
1967	Leroy Keyes	986	149	6.6	Mike Phipps	243	118	.49	1,800	Leroy Keyes	45	758	16.8
1968	Leroy Keyes	1,003	193	5.2	Mike Phipps	169	88	.52	1,096	Bob Dillingham	35	456	13.0
1969	Randy Cooper	697	171	4.1	Mike Phipps	321	169	.53	2,527	Ashley Bell	49	669	13.7
1970	Otis Armstrong	1,009	213	4.7	Gary Danielson	98	39	.40	546	Darryl Stingley	23	286	12.4
1971	Otis Armstrong	945	214	4.4	Gary Danielson	154	89	.58	1,467	Rick Sayers	39	573	14.7
1972	Otis Armstrong	1,361	243	5.6	Gary Danielson	138	50	.36	735	Rick Sayers	16	196	12.3
1973	Pete Gross	560	133	4.2	Bo Bobrowski	135	57	.42	849	Larry Burton	15	271	18.1
1974	Scott Dierking	779	164	4.8	Mark Vitali	145	68	.47	1,006	Larry Burton	38	702	18.5
1975	Scott Dierking	914	180	5.1	Mark Vitali	127	46	.36	728	Paul Beery	27	454	16.8
1976	Scott Dierking	1,000	201	5.0	Mark Vitali	172	73	.42	1,184	Reggie Arnold	16	287	17.9
1977	John Skibinski	665	147	4.5	Mark Herrmann	319	175	.55	2,453	Reggie Arnold	44	840	19.1
1978	John Macon	913	225	4.1	Mark Herrmann	274	152	.55	1,904	Russell Pope	35	292	8.3
1979	Wally Jones	754	183	4.1	Mark Herrmann	348	203	.58	2,377	Dave Young	55	584	10.6
1980	Jimmy Smith	657	139	4.7	Mark Herrmann	368	242	.66	3,212	Bart Burrell	66	1,001	15.2
1981	Jimmy Smith	540	152	3.6	Scott Campbell	321	185	.58	2,686	Steve Bryant	60	971	16.2
1982	Mel Gray	916	195	4.7	Scott Campbell	399	218	.55	2,626	Cliff Benson	50	762	15.2
1983	Mel Gray	849	190	4.5	Scott Campbell	305	183	.60	2,031	Jeff Price	40	633	15.8
1984	Ray Wallace	587	145	4.0	Jim Everett	431	249	.58	3,256	Steve Griffin	64	1,060	16.5
1985	Ray Wallace	522	100	5.2	Jim Everett	450	285	.63	3,651	Rodney Carter	98	1,099	11.2
1986	James Medlock	488	137	3.6	Jeff George	227	122	.54	1,217	Jerry Chaney	46	257	5.6
1987	James Medlock	634	175	3.6	Shawn McCarthy	177	98	.55	1,088	Anthony Hardy	58	723	12.5
1988	Jarrett Scales	362	112	3.2	Brian Fox	235	121	.51	1,250	Calvin Williams	37	479	12.9
1989	Jerome Sparkman	451	118	3.8	Eric Hunter	178	91	.51	1,368	Calvin Williams	51	630	12.4
1990	Tony Vinson	198	49	4.0	Eric Hunter	366	200	.55	2,355	Ernest Calloway	47	541	11.5
1991	Jeff Hill	678	116	5.8	Eric Hunter	162	77	.48	1,018	Ernest Calloway	24	475	19.8
1992	Arlee Conners	676	154	4.4	Eric Hunter	112	54	.48	857	Jermaine Ross	26	579	22.3
1993	Mike Alstott	816	153	5.3	Rick Trefzger	154	90	.58	1,247	Jeff Hill	35	559	16.0
1994	Mike Alstott	1,188	202	5.9	Rick Trefzger	131	74	.56	1,137	Burt Thornton	45	726	16.1
1995	Mike Alstott	1,436	243	5.9	Rick Trefzger	208	123	.59	1,521	Brian Alford	34	686	20.2
1996	Edwin Watson	768	194	4.0	Rick Trefzger	170	96	.56	1,158	Brian Alford	63	1,057	16.8
1997	Edwin Watson	927	175	5.3	Billy Dicken	407	224	.55	3,136	Brian Alford	63	1,228	19.5
1998	J. Crabtree	648	152	4.3	Drew Brees	569	361	.63	3,983	Randall Lane	67	940	14.0
1999	Montrell Lowe	841	173	4.9	Drew Brees	554	337	.61	3,909	Chris Daniels	121	1,236	10.2
2000	Montrell Lowe	998	226	4.4	Drew Brees	512	309	.60	3,668	Vinny Sutherland	72	1,014	14.1
2001	Montrell Lowe	640	183	3.5	Brandon Hance	258	136	.53	1,529	Taylor Stubblefield	73	910	12.5
2002	Joey Harris	1,115	250	4.5	Kyle Orton	317	192	.61	2,257	Taylor Stubblefield	77	789	10.2
2003	Jerod Void	952	235	4.1	Kyle Orton	414	251	.61	2,885	Taylor Stubblefield	86	835	9.7
2004	Jerod Void	625	159	3.9	Kyle Orton	389	236	.61	3,090	Taylor Stubblefield	89	1,095	12.3

Receiving leaders by receptions
All statistics include postseason

PURDUE ALL-TIME SCORES

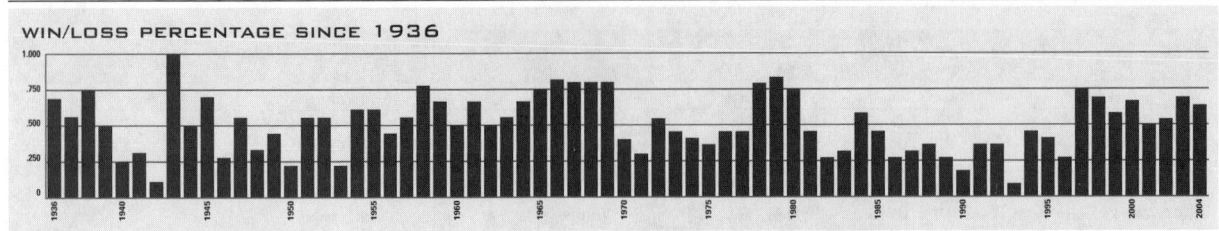

WIN/LOSS PERCENTAGE SINCE 1936

ALBERT BERG
1887 (.000)   0-1

1887   0-1-0
| O29 | at Butler | 6 | 48 |

1888
NO TEAM

G.A. REISNER
1889 (.667)   2-1

1889   2-1-0
N16	●	DePauw	34	10
N23		at Wabash	18	4
N29		at Butler	0	14

C.L. HARE
1890 (.500)   3-3

1890   3-3-0
O18	●	Chicago Stars	6	10
O25	●	Wabash	54	0
N1		at Michigan	6	34
N15	●	at DePauw	32	0
N22	●	Illinois	62	0
N27	●	at Butler	10	12

KNOWLTON AMES
1891-92 (1.000)   12-0

1891   4-0-0
O24	●	at Wabash	44	0
N9	●	DePauw	30	0
N14	●	Indiana	60	0
N26	●	Butler	58	0

1892   8-0-0
O8	●	at Illinois	12	6
O15	●	at Wabash	72	0
O19	●	Wisconsin	32	4	*
O24	●	Michigan	24	0
O29	●	Butler	40	6
N5	●	Indiana	68	0
N19	●	Chicago	38	0
N24	●	at DePauw	32	6

D.M. BALLIET
1893-95,1901 (.667) 21-10-2

1893   5-2-1
O14	●	Indiana	64	0
O21	●	Butler	96	0
O25	●	Chicago	20	10
N4	●	Wabash	48	8
N11		Michigan	8	46
N18		at Wisconsin	30	36	†
N25	=	Illinois	26	26
N30		DePauw _IND_	42	18

1894   9-1-0
O6	●	Light Artillery	6	4
O13	●	at Butler	30	0
O15	●	at Wisconsin	1	0	f
O20	●	Armour	36	0
O27	●	at Minnesota	0	24
N3	●	at Chicago	10	6
N17	●	at Illinois	22	2
N22	●	at Wabash	44	0
N24	●	at Indiana	1	0	f
N29	●	at DePauw	28	0

1895   3-3-0
O12	●	Kentucky	32	0
O19	●	Missouri _StL_	6	16
O29	●	Minnesota	16	4	*
N2		Northwestern	6	24
N16		at Michigan	10	12
N28		Illinois	6	2

1896-Present
BIG 10

S.M. HAMMOND
1896 (.643)   4-2-1

1896   4-2-1 (0-2-1)
O3	●	Greer	36	0
O10	●	Rush Medical	32	4
O17		at Minnesota	0	14
O24		Michigan	0	16
N7	●	at DePauw	22	0
N14	●	at Notre Dame	28	22
N25	=	Illinois	4	4

WILLIAM S. CHURCH
1897 (.611)   5-3-1

1897   5-3-1 (1-2-0)
O2	●	Illinois St.	28	0
O9		Oberlin	6	22
O16	●	at DePauw	8	0
O23		at Illinois	4	34
O30	●	Indiana	20	6
N6		at Michigan	4	34
N13	●	Missouri	30	12
N20	●	Minnesota	6	0
N25	=	Alumni	0	0

ALPHA P. JAMISON
1898-1900 (.500)   11-11-1

1898   3-3-0 (0-1-0)
O8	●	Alumni	0	6
O18	●	at Haskell	5	0
O22	●	Haskell	15	0
N5		at Chicago	0	17
N12	●	Indiana	14	0
N24		Oberlin	0	10

1899   4-4-1 (1-2-0)
S30	●	Alumni	10	5
O7	●	Earlham	30	5
O14		at Oberlin	0	12
O28	●	DePauw	40	0
N4		at Chicago	0	44
N18	=	Notre Dame	10	10
N22	●	at Illinois	5	0
N25		at Northwestern	0	29
N30		Indiana	5	17

1900   4-4-0 (0-4-0)
S29	●	Illinois Wesleyan	39	0
O6		at Chicago	5	17
O13	●	DePauw	28	7
O20		at Michigan	6	11
O27	●	Rose Poly	46	5
N3		at Illinois	5	17
N17	●	Earlham	38	0
N29		Indiana	5	24

D.M. BALLIET

1901   4-4-1 (0-3-1)
S28	●	Franklin	24	0
O5	●	Wabash	45	0
O12	=	at Chicago	5	5
O19	●	DePauw	19	0
O26		at Indiana	6	11
N2	●	Case	22	0
N9		at Notre Dame	6	12
N16		Illinois	6	28
N28		Northwestern	5	10

C.M. BEST
1902 (.750)   7-2-1

1902   7-2-1 (2-2-0)
S27	●	Franklin	56	0
O4	●	DePauw	39	0
O11		at Chicago	0	33
O18	●	at Illinois	5	29
O25	●	Case	5	0
N1	●	at Northwestern	5	0
N8	●	at Greer	73	0
N15	●	Indiana	39	0
N22	●	Butler	87	0
N27		Notre Dame	6	6

OLIVER F. CUTTS
1903-04 (.722)   13-5

1903   4-2-0 (0-2-0)
S26	●	Englewood HS	34	0
O1	●	at Wabash	18	0
O3	●	Beloit	17	0
O10		at Chicago	0	22
O17		Illinois	0	24
O24	●	Oberlin	18	2

1904   9-3-0 (1-2-0)
S17		Alumni	2	6
S24	●	North Division HS	5	0
S28	●	Beloit	11	0
O1		at Earlham	28	11
O8		at Chicago	0	20
O15	●	Wabash	6	0
O22		Illinois	6	24
O28	●	Missouri _StL_	11	0
N5	●	Indiana Medical	34	5
N12	●	Indiana _IND_	27	0
N19	●	at Culver	10	0
N24	●	Notre Dame	36	0

A.E. HERNSTEIN
1905 (.813)   6-1-1

1905   6-1-1 (1-1-1)
S23	●	Wendell Phillips HS	33	0
S30	●	Beloit	36	0
O14	●	at Wabash	12	0
O21	●	at Illinois	29	0
O28	=	Indiana _IND_	11	11
N4	●	Missouri	24	0
N11		at Chicago	0	19
N24	●	Notre Dame	32	0

M.E. WITHAM
1906 (.000)   0-5

1906   0-5-0 (0-3-0)
O20		at Chicago	0	39
O27		Wabash	0	11
N3		Notre Dame	0	2
N17		at Wisconsin	5	29
N25		Illinois	0	5

L.C. TURNER
1907 (.000)   0-5

1907   0-5-0 (0-3-0)
O12		Wabash	0	2
N2		at Illinois	4	21
N9		at Chicago	0	56
N16		Wisconsin	6	12
N23		Notre Dame	0	17

FREDERICK. SPEIK
1908-09 (.429)   6-8

1908   4-3-0 (1-3-0)
O3		at Chicago	0	39
O10	●	Earlham	40	0
O17	●	Monmouth	30	0
O31	●	DePauw	28	4
N7	●	at Northwestern	16	10
N14		Illinois	6	15
N21		Indiana	4	10

1909   2-5-0 (0-4-0)
O2		at Chicago	0	40
O9		Northwestern	5	14
O16	●	DePauw	15	12
O30		at Illinois	6	24
N6		Wabash	17	18
N13		Rose Poly	26	3
N20		Indiana	3	36

M.BILL. HORR
1910-12 (.425)   8-11-1

1910   1-5-0 (0-4-0)
O8		Wabash	0	3
O22		at Iowa	0	16
O29		Illinois	0	11
N5		at Chicago	5	14
N12	●	DePauw	14	6
N19		Indiana	0	15

1911   3-4-0 (1-3-0)
O8		Wabash	0	3
O14		at Chicago	3	11
O28	●	DePauw	5	0
N4		at Illinois	3	12
N11		Iowa	0	11
N18	●	Rose Poly	35	6
N25	●	at Indiana	12	5

1912   4-2-1 (2-2-1)
O5	●	DePauw	21	0
O19		at Wisconsin	0	41
O26		at Chicago	0	7
N2	●	at Northwestern	21	6
N9	=	Illinois	9	9
N17	●	Rose Poly	91	0
N24	●	Indiana	34	7

ANDREW L. SMITH
1913-15 (.643)   12-6-3

1913   4-1-2 (2-1-2)
O4	●	Wabash	26	0
O11	●	Northwestern	34	0
O18		Wisconsin	7	7
O25		at Chicago	0	6
N8	●	Rose Poly	62	0
N15	=	at Illinois	0	0
N23	●	at Indiana	42	7

1914   5-2-0 (2-2-0)
O3	●	Wabash	27	3
O10	●	Western Reserve	26	0
O17		at Wisconsin	7	14
O24		at Chicago	0	21
N7	●	Kentucky	40	6
N14	●	at Northwestern	34	6
N21	●	Indiana	23	13

1915   3-3-1 (2-2-0)
O2	=	Wabash	7	7
O9	●	Beloit	26	0
O16		Wisconsin	3	28
O23		at Chicago	0	7
N6	●	Iowa	19	13
N13		at Kentucky	0	7
N20	●	at Indiana	7	0

CLEO O'DONNELL 1916-17 (.393) — 5-8-1

1916 — 2-4-1 (0-4-1)
O7	●	DePauw	13	0
O14	●	Wabash	28	7
O21		at Iowa	6	24
O28		Illinois	7	14
N4		at Chicago	7	16
N18	●	at Northwestern	6	38
N25	=	Indiana	0	0

1917 — 3-4-0 (0-4-0)
O6	●	Franklin	54	0
O13	●	DePauw	7	6
O20		at Chicago	0	27
O27		at Illinois	0	27
N3		Northwestern	6	12
N17	●	Wabash	28	0
N24		Indiana	0	37

A. BUTCH SCANLON 1918-20 (.375) — 7-12-1

1918 — 3-3-0 (1-0-0)
O26		DePauw	7	9
N2	●	Chicago	7	3
N9		at Michigan State	14	6
N16	●	Wabash IND	53	6
N23		Notre Dame	6	26
N30		at Great Lakes NAS	0	28

1919 — 2-4-1 (0-3-0)
O4	=	Franklin	14	14
O11		Illinois	7	14
O18		at Chicago	0	16
N1	●	Michigan State	13	7
N8		at Ohio State	0	20
N17	●	DePauw	24	0
N22		Notre Dame	13	33

1920 — 2-5-0 (0-4-0)
O2	●	DePauw	10	0
O9		at Chicago	0	20
O16		at Ohio State	0	17
O30	●	Wabash	19	14
N6		at Notre Dame	0	28
N13		at Northwestern	0	14
N20		Indiana	7	10

WILLIAM H. DEITZ 1921 (.143) — 1-6

1921 — 1-6-0 (1-4-0)
O1		Wabash	0	9
O8		at Chicago	0	9
O15		Notre Dame	0	33
O29		Iowa	6	13
N5	●	Northwestern	3	0
N12		at Ohio State	0	28
N19		at Indiana	0	3

JAMES PHELAN 1922-29 (.605) — 35-22-5

1922 — 1-5-1 (0-3-1)
O7	●	James Milliken	10	0
O14		Notre Dame	0	20
O21		at Chicago	0	12
O28		at Iowa	0	56
N4		Wabash	6	7
N11		at Northwestern	13	24
N25	=	Indiana	7	7

1923 — 2-5-1 (1-4-0)
O6	●	Willmington	39	0
O13		at Iowa	0	7
O20		Wabash	7	7
O27		at Chicago	6	20
N3		at Notre Dame	7	34
N10		Ohio State	0	32
N17	●	Northwestern	6	3
N24		at Indiana	0	3

1924 — 5-2-0 (2-2-0)
S27	●	Wabash	21	7
O4		at Ohio State	0	7
O11	●	Rose Poly	41	3
O18	●	at Northwestern	7	3
N1		at Chicago	6	19
N8	●	DePauw	36	0
N22	●	Indiana	26	7

1925 — 3-4-1 (0-3-1)
O3		Wabash	7	13
O10	●	DePauw	39	0
O17	●	Rose Poly	44	0
O24		at Wisconsin	0	7
O31		at Chicago	0	6
N7		Franklin	20	0
N14		Northwestern	9	13
N21	=	at Indiana	0	0

1926 — 5-2-1 (2-1-1)
O2		at Navy	13	17
O9	●	Wabash	21	14
O16	=	Wisconsin	0	0
O23	●	at Chicago	6	0
O30	●	Indiana St.	38	0
N6		at Northwestern	0	22
N13	●	Franklin	44	0
N20	●	Indiana	24	14

1927 — 6-2-0 (2-2-0)
O1	●	DePauw	15	0
O8	●	at Harvard	19	0
O15		at Chicago	6	7
O22		at Wisconsin	6	12
O29	●	Montana St.	39	7
N5	●	Northwestern	18	6
N12	●	Franklin	46	0
N19	●	at Indiana	21	6

1928 — 5-2-1 (2-2-1)
O6	●	DePauw	31	0
O13		at Minnesota	0	15
O20	=	Wisconsin	19	19
O27	●	at Chicago	40	0
N3		Case	19	0
N10		at Northwestern	6	7
N17	●	Wabash	14	0
N24	●	Indiana	14	0

1929 — 8-0-0 (5-0-0)
O5	●	Kansas State	26	14
O12		Michigan	30	16
O19	●	DePauw	26	7
O26	●	at Chicago	26	0
N2	●	at Wisconsin	13	0
N9	●	Mississippi	27	7
N16	●	Iowa	7	0
N23	●	at Indiana	32	0

NOBLE KIZER 1930-36 (.724) — 42-13-3

1930 — 6-2-0 (4-2-0)
O4	●	Baylor	20	7
O11		at Michigan	13	14
O18	●	at Iowa	20	0
O25	●	Wisconsin	7	6
N1	●	at Illinois	25	0
N8	●	at Chicago	26	7
N15	●	Butler	33	0
N22		Indiana	6	7

1931 — 9-1-0 (5-1-0)
O3	●	Western Reserve	28	0
O3	●	Coe	19	0
O10	●	Illinois	7	0
O17		Wisconsin	14	21
O24	●	at Carnegie Tech	13	6
O31	●	at Chicago	14	6
N7	●	Centenary	49	6
N14	●	Iowa	22	0
N21	●	at Indiana	19	0
N28	●	Northwestern CHI	7	0

1932 — 7-0-1 (5-0-1)
O1	●	Kansas State	29	13
O8	●	at Minnesota	7	0
O15	●	Wisconsin	7	6
O22	=	at Northwestern	7	7
O29	●	NYU BRNX	34	9
N5	●	at Chicago	37	0
N12	●	at Iowa	18	0
N19	●	Indiana	25	0

1933 — 6-1-1 (3-1-1)
O7	●	Ohio U.	13	6
O14	●	at Minnesota	7	7
O21	●	at Chicago	14	0
O28	●	at Wisconsin	14	0
N4	●	Carnegie Tech	17	7
N11	●	at Notre Dame	19	0
N18		Iowa	6	14
N25	●	at Indiana	19	3

1934 — 5-3-0 (3-1-0)
O6		Rice	0	14
O13		at Notre Dame	7	18
O20	●	Wisconsin	14	0
O27	●	at Carnegie Tech	20	0
N3		at Chicago	26	20
N10	●	at Iowa	13	6
N17	●	Fordham NYC	7	0
N24		Indiana	6	17

1935 — 4-4-0 (3-3-0)
O5	●	at Northwestern	7	0
O12	●	Fordham NYC	20	0
O19	●	at Chicago	19	0
O26		Carnegie Tech	0	7
N2		at Minnesota	7	29
N9		at Wisconsin	0	8
N16	●	Iowa	12	6
N23		at Indiana	0	7

1936 — 5-2-1 (3-1-1)
S26	●	Ohio U.	47	0
O10	●	Wisconsin	35	14
O17	●	at Chicago	35	7
O24		at Minnesota	0	33
O31	●	at Carnegie Tech	7	6
N7		Fordham NYC	0	15
N14	●	at Iowa	13	0
N21	=	Indiana	20	20

MAL ELWARD 1937-41 (.475) — 16-18-6

1937 — 4-3-1 (2-2-1)
S25	●	Butler	33	7
O2		at Ohio State	0	13
O9	●	Carnegie Tech	7	0
O16	●	at Northwestern	7	14
O30	●	Iowa	13	0
N6		Fordham NYC	3	21
N13	=	at Wisconsin	7	7
N20	●	at Indiana	13	7

1938 — 5-1-2 (3-1-1)
S24	●	Detroit	19	6
O1	●	at Butler	21	6
O8		at Minnesota	0	7
O15	=	Fordham NYC	6	6
O22	●	Wisconsin	13	7
O29		at Iowa	0	0
N5		at Ohio State	12	0
N19		Indiana	13	6

1939 — 3-3-2 (2-1-2)
S30		at Notre Dame	0	3
O14	=	at Minnesota	13	13
O21	●	Michigan State	20	7
O28		at Santa Clara	6	13
N4		Iowa	0	4
N11	●	at Northwestern	3	0
N18	=	at Wisconsin	7	7
N25	●	at Indiana	7	6

1940 — 2-6-0 (1-4-0)
S28	●	Butler	28	0
O5		at Ohio State	14	17
O12		at Michigan State	7	20
O26		Wisconsin	13	14
N2	●	at Iowa	21	6
N9		Fordham NYC	7	13
N16		at Minnesota	6	33
N23		Indiana	0	3

1941 — 2-5-1 (1-3-0)
S27		Vanderbilt	0	3
O4	●	at Pittsburgh	6	0
O18		at Ohio State	14	16
O25	=	Iowa	7	6
N1		Fordham NYC	0	17
N8	=	Michigan State	0	0
N15		at Wisconsin	0	13
N22		at Indiana	0	7

ELMER BURNHAM 1942-43 (.556) — 10-8

1942 — 1-8-0 (1-4-0)
S26		Fordham	7	14
O3		at Vanderbilt	0	26
O10	●	at Northwestern	7	6
O17		at Ohio State	0	26
O24		Wisconsin	0	13
O31		at Iowa	7	13
N7		Great Lakes NAS	0	42
N14		at Michigan State	6	19
N21		Indiana	0	20

1943 — 9-0-0 (6-0-0)
S18	●	at Great Lakes NAS	23	13
S25	●	at Marquette	21	0
O2		Illinois	40	21
O9	●	Camp Grant	19	0
O16	●	Ohio State CLEV	30	7
O23	●	Iowa	28	7
O30	●	at Wisconsin	32	0
N6	●	at Minnesota	14	7
N20	●	at Indiana	7	0

CECIL ISBELL 1944-46 (.500) — 14-14-1

1944 — 5-5-0 (4-2-0)
S23	●	at Great Lakes NAS	18	27
S30	●	Marquette	40	0
O7	●	at Illinois	35	19
O14	●	Iowa Pre-Flight	6	13
O21	●	at Iowa	26	7
O28		at Michigan	14	40
N4	●	Wisconsin	35	0
N11	●	at Northwestern	27	7
N18		Navy BALT	0	32
N25	●	Indiana	6	14

1945 — 7-3-0 (3-3-0)
S22	●	Marquette	14	13
S29		at Great Lakes NAS	20	6
O6	●	at Wisconsin	13	7
O13	●	Iowa	40	0
O20	●	at Ohio State	35	13
O27		at Northwestern	14	26
N3	●	Pittsburgh	28	0
N10	●	Miami, Ohio	21	7
N17		at Michigan	13	27
N24	●	at Indiana	0	26

1946 — 2-6-1 (0-5-1)
S21	●	Miami, Ohio	13	7
S28		at Iowa	0	16
O5		at Illinois	7	43
O12		at Notre Dame	6	49
O19	=	at Ohio State	14	14
O26	●	at Pittsburgh	10	8
N2		Wisconsin	20	24
N9		at Minnesota	7	13
N23		Indiana	20	34

STUART HOLCOMB 1947-55 (.457) — 35-42-4

1947 — 5-4-0 (3-3-0)
S27		at Wisconsin	14	32
O4	●	Ohio State	24	20
O11		Notre Dame	7	22
O18	●	Boston U. BOS	62	7
O25	●	Illinois	14	7
N1	●	Iowa	21	0
N8		at Minnesota	21	26
N15	●	Pittsburgh	28	0
N22		at Indiana	14	16

1948 — 3-6-0 (2-4-0)
S25		at Notre Dame	27	28
O2		at Northwestern	0	21
O9		Michigan	0	40
O16	●	at Iowa	20	13
O23		at Illinois	6	10
O30	●	Marquette	14	9
N6		at Minnesota	7	34
N13		Pittsburgh	13	20
N20	●	Indiana	39	0

1949 — 4-5-0 (2-4-0)
S24		at Northwestern	6	20
O1		Iowa	7	21
O8		Notre Dame	12	35
O14	●	at Miami, Fla.	14	0
O22		Illinois	0	19
O29	●	at Minnesota	13	7
N5	●	at Michigan	12	20
N12	●	Marquette	41	7
N19	●	at Indiana	14	6

1950 — 2-7-0 (1-4-0)
S30		at Texas	26	34
O7	●	at Notre Dame	28	14
O14		Miami, Fla.	14	20
O21		at Iowa	21	33
O28		UCLA	6	20
N4		at Wisconsin	7	33
N11	●	Northwestern	14	19
N18		at Minnesota	14	27
N25	●	Indiana	13	0

1951 — 5-4-0 (4-1-0)

S29			Texas	0	14
O6	●	|	Iowa	34	30
O12			at Miami, Fla.	0	7
O20		|	Wisconsin	7	31
O27			at Notre Dame	9	30
N3	●		Penn State	28	0
N10	●	|	at Northwestern	35	14
N17	●	|	Minnesota	19	13
N24	●	|	at Indiana	21	13

1952 — 4-3-2 (4-1-1)

S27	=		at Penn State	20	20
O4	●	|	at Ohio State	21	14
O11	●	|	Iowa	41	14
O18			Notre Dame	14	26
O25	●	|	at Illinois	40	12
N1			Michigan State	7	14
N8	=	|	at Minnesota	14	14
N15		|	at Michigan	10	21
N22	●	|	Indiana	21	16

1953 — 2-7-0 (2-4-0)

S26			at Missouri	7	14
O3			Notre Dame	7	37
O10			at Duke	14	20
O17		|	Wisconsin	19	28
O24	●	|	Michigan State	6	0
O31		|	at Illinois	0	21
N7		|	Iowa	0	26
N14		|	at Ohio State	6	21
N21	●	|	at Indiana	30	0

1954 — 5-3-1 (3-3-0)

S25	●		Missouri	31	0
O2	●		at Notre Dame	27	14
O9	=		Duke	13	13
O16		|	at Wisconsin	6	20
O23	●	|	at Michigan State	27	13
O30	●	|	Illinois	28	14
N6		|	at Iowa	14	25
N13		|	Ohio State	6	28
N20	●	|	Indiana	13	7

1955 — 5-3-1 (4-2-1)

S24	●		Pacific	14	7
O1	●	|	at Minnesota	7	6
O8		|	Wisconsin	0	9
O15	=	|	at Iowa	20	20
O22			Notre Dame	7	22
O29	●	|	at Illinois	13	0
N5		|	Michigan State	0	27
N12	●	|	Northwestern	46	8
N19	●	|	at Indiana	6	4

JACK MOLLENKOPF
1956-69 (.670) 84-39-9

1956 — 3-4-2 (1-4-2)

S29	●		Missouri	16	7
O6		|	at Minnesota	14	21
O13	●		at Notre Dame	28	14
O20	=	|	at Wisconsin	6	6
O27		|	Iowa	20	21
N3	=	|	Illinois	7	7
N10		|	at Michigan State	9	12
N17		|	at Northwestern	0	14
N24	●	|	Indiana	39	20

1957 — 5-4-0 (4-3-0)

S28			Notre Dame	0	12
O5		|	at Minnesota	17	21
O12		|	Wisconsin	14	23
O19	●	|	at Michigan State	20	13
O26	●		Miami, Ohio	37	6
N2	●	|	at Illinois	21	6
N9		|	at Ohio State	7	20
N16	●	|	Northwestern	27	0
N23	●	|	at Indiana	35	13

1958 — 6-1-2 (3-1-2)

S27	●		Nebraska	28	0
O4	●		at Rice	24	0
O11		|	at Wisconsin	6	31
O18	●	|	Michigan State	14	6
O25	●		at Notre Dame	29	22
N1	●	|	Illinois	31	8
N8	=	|	at Ohio State	14	14
N15	●	|	at Northwestern	23	6
N22	=	|	Indiana	15	15

1959 — 5-2-2 (4-2-1)

S18	=		at UCLA	0	0
O3	●		Notre Dame	28	7
O10	●	|	Wisconsin	21	0
O17		|	at Ohio State	0	15
O24	●	|	Iowa	14	7
O31	=	|	at Illinois	7	7
N7		|	at Michigan State	0	15
N14	●	|	Minnesota	29	23
N21	●	|	at Indiana	10	7

1960 — 4-4-1 (3-4-0)

S24	=		UCLA	27	27
O1	●		at Notre Dame	51	19
O8		|	at Wisconsin	13	24
O15	●	|	Ohio State	24	21
O22		|	at Iowa	14	21
O29		|	Illinois	12	14
N5		|	Michigan State	13	17
N12	●	|	at Minnesota	23	14
N19	●	|	Indiana	35	6

1961 — 6-3-0 (4-2-0)

S23	●		at Washington	13	6
O7			Notre Dame	20	22
O14	●		Miami, Ohio	19	6
O21		|	at Michigan	14	16
O28	●	|	Iowa	9	0
N4	●	|	at Illinois	23	9
N11	●	|	Michigan State	7	6
N18		|	at Minnesota	7	10
N25	●	|	at Indiana	34	12

1962 — 4-4-1 (3-3-0)

S22	=		at Washington	7	7
O6	●		at Notre Dame	24	6
O13			Miami, Ohio	7	10
O20	●	|	Michigan	37	0
O27	●	|	at Iowa	26	3
N3		|	Illinois	10	14
N10	●	|	at Michigan State	17	9
N17		|	at Minnesota	6	7
N24		|	Indiana	7	12

1963 — 5-4-0 (4-3-0)

S28			at Miami, Fla.	0	3
O5	●		Notre Dame	7	6
O12		|	at Wisconsin	20	38
O19	●	|	at Michigan	23	12
O26	●	|	Iowa	14	0
N2		|	at Illinois	21	41
N9		|	Michigan State	0	23
N16	●	|	Minnesota	13	11
N30	●	|	at Indiana	21	15

1964 — 6-3-0 (5-2-0)

S26	●		Ohio U.	17	0
O3			at Notre Dame	15	34
O10	●	|	Wisconsin	28	7
O17	●	|	at Michigan	21	20
O24	●	|	at Iowa	19	14
O31	●	|	Illinois	26	14
N7		|	at Michigan State	7	21
N14		|	at Minnesota	7	14
N21	●	|	Indiana	28	22

1965 — 7-2-1 (5-2-0)

S18	●		Miami, Ohio	38	0
S25	●		Notre Dame	25	21
O2	=		SMU DAL	14	14
O9	●	|	at Iowa	17	14
O16	●	|	at Michigan	17	15
O23		|	Michigan State	10	14
O30		|	at Illinois	0	21
N6	●	|	Wisconsin	45	7
N13	●	|	Minnesota	35	0
N20	●	|	at Indiana	26	21

1966 — 9-2-0 (6-1-0)

S17	●		Ohio U.	42	3
S24			at Notre Dame	14	26
O1	●		SMU	35	23
O8	●	|	Iowa	35	0
O15	●	|	at Michigan	22	21
O22		|	at Michigan State	20	41
O29	●	|	Illinois	25	21
N5	●	|	at Wisconsin	23	0
N12	●	|	at Minnesota	16	0
N19	●	|	Indiana	51	6
			ROSE BOWL		
J2	●		Southern Cal	14	13

1967 — 8-2-0 (6-1-0)

S23	●		Texas A&M DAL	24	20
S30	●		Notre Dame	28	21
O7	●	|	Northwestern	25	16
O14	●	|	at Ohio State	41	6
O21			Oregon State	14	22
O28	●	|	at Iowa	41	22
N4	●	|	at Illinois	42	9
N11	●	|	Minnesota	41	12
N18	●	|	Michigan State	21	7
N25		|	at Indiana	14	19

1968 — 8-2-0 (5-2-0)

S21	●		Virginia	44	6
S28	●		at Notre Dame	37	22
O5	●	|	at Northwestern	43	6
O12		|	at Ohio State	0	13
O19	●		Wake Forest	28	27
O26	●	|	Iowa	44	14
N2	●	|	Illinois	35	17
N9		|	at Minnesota	13	27
N16	●	|	at Michigan State	9	0
N23	●	|	Indiana	38	35

1969 — 8-2-0 (5-2-0)

S20	●		at TCU	42	35
S27	●		Notre Dame	28	14
O4	●		Stanford	36	35
O11		|	at Michigan	20	31
O18	●	|	Iowa	35	31
O25	●	|	Northwestern	45	20
N1	●	|	at Illinois	49	22
N8	●	|	Michigan State	41	13
N15		|	at Ohio State	14	42
N22	●	|	at Indiana	44	21

BOB DEMOSS
1970-72 (.419) 13-18

1970 — 4-6-0 (2-5-0)

S19	●		TCU	15	0
S26			at Notre Dame	0	48
O3	●		at Stanford	26	14
O10		|	Michigan	0	29
O17	●	|	at Iowa	24	3
O24		|	at Northwestern	14	38
O31		|	Illinois	21	23
N7		|	at Michigan State	14	24
N14		|	Ohio State	7	10
N21	●	|	Indiana	40	0

1971 — 3-7-0 (3-5-0)

S18			at Washington	35	38
S25			Notre Dame	7	8
O2	●	|	Iowa	45	13
O9	●	|	Minnesota	27	13
O16	●	|	at Northwestern	21	20
O23		|	at Illinois	7	21
O30		|	Michigan State	10	43
N6		|	at Wisconsin	10	14
N13		|	Michigan	17	20
N20		|	at Indiana	31	38

1972 — 6-5-0 (6-2-0)

S16			Bowling Green	14	17
S23			Washington	21	22
S30			at Notre Dame	14	35
O7	●	|	at Iowa	24	0
O14	●	|	at Minnesota	28	3
O21	●	|	Northwestern	37	0
O28	●	|	Illinois	20	14
N4		|	at Michigan State	12	22
N11	●	|	Wisconsin	27	6
N18		|	at Michigan	6	9
N25	●	|	Indiana	42	7

ALEX AGASE
1973-76 (.420) 18-25-1

1973 — 5-6-0 (4-4-0)

S15	●	|	at Wisconsin	14	13
S22			Miami, Ohio	19	24
S29			Notre Dame	7	20
O6	●		Duke	27	7
O13		|	at Illinois	13	15
O20	●	|	Northwestern	21	10
O27		|	Michigan State	7	10
N3	●	|	at Iowa	48	23
N10		|	at Minnesota	7	34
N17		|	Michigan	9	34
N24	●	|	at Indiana	28	23

1974 — 4-6-1 (3-5-0)

S14		|	Wisconsin	14	28
S21	=		Miami, Ohio	7	7
S28	●		at Notre Dame	31	20
O5			at Duke	14	16
O12		|	Illinois	23	27
O19	●	|	at Northwestern	31	26
O26		|	at Michigan State	7	31
N2	●	|	Iowa	38	14
N9		|	Minnesota	20	24
N16		|	at Michigan	0	51
N23	●	|	Indiana	38	17

1975 — 4-7-0 (4-4-0)

S13		|	at Northwestern	25	31
S20			Notre Dame	0	17
S27			at Southern Cal	6	19
O4			Miami, Ohio	3	14
O11		|	Wisconsin	14	17
O18	●	|	at Illinois	26	24
O25		|	Ohio State	6	35
N1	●	|	Michigan State	20	10
N8		|	at Michigan	0	28
N15	●	|	Iowa	19	18
N22	●	|	at Indiana	9	7

1976 — 5-6-0 (4-4-0)

S11	●	|	Northwestern	31	19
S18			at Notre Dame	0	23
S25			Southern Cal	13	31
O2	●		Miami, Ohio	42	20
O9	●	|	at Wisconsin	18	16
O16		|	Illinois	17	21
O23		|	at Ohio State	3	24
O30		|	at Michigan State	13	45
N6	●	|	Michigan	16	14
N13	●	|	at Iowa	21	0
N20		|	Indiana	14	20

JIM YOUNG
1977-81 (.664) 38-19-1

1977 — 5-6-0 (3-5-0)

S10		|	at Michigan State	14	19
S17	●		Ohio U.	44	7
S24			Notre Dame	24	31
O1	●		Wake Forest	26	17
O8		|	at Ohio State	0	46
O15		|	Illinois	22	29
O22	●	|	Iowa	34	21
O29	●	|	at Northwestern	28	16
N5	●	|	at Wisconsin	22	0
N12		|	Michigan	7	40
N19		|	at Indiana	10	21

1978 — 9-2-1 (6-1-1)

S16	●	|	Michigan State	21	14
S23	●		Ohio U.	24	0
S30			at Notre Dame	6	10
O7	●		Wake Forest	14	7
O14	●	|	Ohio State	27	16
O21	●	|	at Illinois	13	0
O28	●	|	at Iowa	34	7
N4	●	|	Northwestern	31	0
N11	=	|	at Wisconsin	24	24
N18		|	at Michigan	6	24
N25	●	|	Indiana	20	7
			PEACH BOWL		
D25	●		Georgia Tech	41	21

1979 — 10-2-0 (7-1-0)

S8	●	|	Wisconsin	41	20
S15			at UCLA	21	31
S22	●		Notre Dame	28	22
S29	●		Oregon	13	7
O6		|	at Minnesota	14	31
O13	●	|	Illinois	28	14
O20	●	|	at Michigan State	14	7
O27	●	|	Northwestern	20	16
N3	●	|	at Iowa	20	14
N10	●	|	Michigan	24	21
N17	●	|	at Indiana	37	21
			BLUEBONNET BOWL		
D31	●		Tennessee	27	22

1980 — 9-3-0 (7-1-0)

S6			at Notre Dame	10	31
S13	●	|	at Wisconsin	12	6
S20			UCLA	14	23
O4	●		Miami, Ohio	28	3
O11	●	|	Minnesota	21	7
O18	●	|	at Illinois	45	20
O25	●	|	Michigan State	36	25
N1	●	|	at Northwestern	52	31
N8	●	|	Iowa	58	13
N15		|	at Michigan	0	26
N22	●	|	Indiana	24	23
			LIBERTY BOWL		
D27	●		Missouri	28	25

1981 — 5-6-0 (3-6-0)

S12	●		Stanford	27	19
S19		|	at Minnesota	13	16
S26	●		Notre Dame	15	14
O3		|	at Wisconsin	14	20
O10	●	|	Illinois	44	20
O17	●	|	at Northwestern	35	0
O24	●	|	Michigan State	27	26
O31		|	Ohio State	33	45
N7		|	at Iowa	7	33
N14		|	Michigan	10	28
N21		|	at Indiana	17	20

LEON BURTNETT
1982-86 (.384)   **21-34-1**

1982   3-8-0 (3-6-0)
S11		Stanford	14 35
S18		Minnesota	10 36
S25		at Notre Dame	14 28
O2		Wisconsin	31 35
O9		at Illinois	34 38
O16	●	Northwestern	34 21
O23	●	at Michigan State	24 21
O30		at Ohio State	6 38
N6	●	Iowa	16 7
N13		at Michigan	21 52
N20		Indiana	7 13

1983   3-7-1 (3-5-1)
S10		Notre Dame	6 52
S17		at Miami, Fla.	0 35
S24	●	at Minnesota	32 20
O1	=	Michigan State	29 29
O8		at Ohio State	22 33
O15		at Iowa	14 31
O22		Illinois	21 35
O29	●	Northwestern	48 17
N5		at Michigan	10 42
N12		Wisconsin	38 42
N19		at Indiana	31 30

1984   7-5-0 (6-3-0)
S8	●	Notre Dame _IND_	23 21
S15		Miami, Fla.	17 28
S22	●	Minnesota	34 10
S29	●	at Michigan State	13 10
O6		Ohio State	28 23
O13		Iowa	3 40
O20		at Illinois	20 34
O27	●	at Northwestern	49 7
N3	●	Michigan	31 29
N10		at Wisconsin	13 30
N17	●	Indiana	31 24
		PEACH BOWL	
D31		Virginia	24 27

1985   5-6-0 (3-5-0)
A31		at Pittsburgh	30 31
S21	●	Ball State	37 18
S28	●	Notre Dame	35 17
O5		at Minnesota	15 45
O12	●	Illinois	30 24
O19		at Ohio State	27 41
O26		Michigan State	24 28
N2	●	Northwestern	31 7
N9		at Michigan	0 47
N16		Iowa	24 27
N23	●	at Indiana	34 21

1986   3-8-0 (2-6-0)
S13	●	Ball State	20 3
S20		Pittsburgh	26 41
S27		at Notre Dame	9 41
O4		Minnesota	9 36
O11		at Illinois	27 34
O18		Ohio State	11 39
O25		at Michigan State	3 37
N1	●	at Northwestern	17 16
N8		Michigan	7 31
N15		at Iowa	14 42
N22		Indiana	17 15

FRED AKERS
1987-90 (.284)   **12-31-1**

1987   3-7-1 (3-5-0)
S12		at Washington	10 28
S19	=	Louisville	22 22
S26		Notre Dame	20 44
O3		at Minnesota	19 21
O10	●	Illinois	9 3
O17		Ohio State	17 20
O24		at Iowa	14 38
O31	●	Wisconsin	49 14
N7		at Michigan State	3 45
N14	●	Northwestern	20 15
N21		at Indiana	14 35

1988   4-7-0 (3-5-0)
S10		Washington	6 20
S17		Ohio U.	33 10
S24		at Notre Dame	7 52
O1	●	Minnesota	14 10
O8		at Illinois	0 20
O15	●	at Ohio State	31 26
O22		Iowa	7 31
O29	●	at Wisconsin	9 6
N5		Michigan State	3 48
N12		at Northwestern	7 28
N19		Indiana	7 52

1989   3-8-0 (2-6-0)
S9	●	Miami, Ohio	27 10
S16		at Washington	9 38
S30		Notre Dame	7 40
O7		at Minnesota	15 35
O14		Illinois	2 14
O21		at Ohio State	3 21
O28		Michigan State	21 28
N4		at Michigan	27 42
N11	●	Northwestern	46 15
N18		Iowa	0 24
N25	●	at Indiana	15 14

1990   2-9-0 (1-7-0)
S15		Washington	14 20
S22	●	Indiana St.	41 13
S29		at Notre Dame	11 37
O6		Minnesota	7 19
O13		at Illinois	0 34
O20		Ohio State	2 42
O27		at Michigan State	33 55
N3		Michigan	13 38
N10	●	at Northwestern	33 13
N17		at Iowa	9 38
N24		Indiana	14 28

JIM COLLETTO
1991-96 (.326)   **20-43-3**

1991   4-7-0 (3-5-0)
S7	●	Eastern Michigan	49 3
S14		at California	18 42
S28		Notre Dame	20 45
O5	●	at Northwestern	17 14
O12		at Minnesota	3 6
O19	●	Wisconsin	28 7
O26		Iowa	21 31
N2		at Michigan	0 42
N9		Illinois	14 41
N16	●	Michigan State	27 17
N23		at Indiana	22 24

1992   4-7-0 (3-5-0)
S12	●	California	41 14
S19		Toledo	29 33
S26		at Notre Dame	0 48
O3		Northwestern	14 28
O10	●	Minnesota	24 20
O17		at Wisconsin	16 19
O24	●	at Iowa	27 16
O31		Michigan	17 24
N7		at Illinois	17 20
N14		at Michigan State	13 35
N21	●	Indiana	13 10

1993   1-10-0 (0-8-0)
S4		at North Carolina St.	7 20
S11	●	Western Michigan	28 13
S25		Notre Dame	0 17
O2		Illinois	10 28
O9		at Minnesota	56 59
O16		Wisconsin	28 42
O23		Ohio State	24 45
O30		at Iowa	17 26
N6		at Michigan	10 25
N13		Michigan State	24 27
N20		at Indiana	17 24

1994   4-5-2 (2-4-2)
S10	●	Toledo	51 17
S17	●	Ball State	49 21
S24		at Notre Dame	21 39
O1	●	at Illinois	22 16
O8	●	Minnesota	49 37
O15	=	at Wisconsin	27 27
O22		at Ohio State	14 48
O29	=	Iowa	21 21
N5		Michigan	23 45
N12		at Michigan State	30 42 †
N19		Indiana	29 33

1995   4-6-1 (2-5-1)
S2	●	at West Virginia	26 24
S9		Notre Dame	28 35
S23	●	Michigan State	35 35
S30	●	Ball State	35 13
O7		at Minnesota	38 39
O14		Penn State	23 26
O21		at Ohio State	0 28
N4	●	Wisconsin	38 27
N11		at Michigan	0 5
N18		Northwestern	8 23
N24	●	at Indiana	51 14

1996   3-8 (2-6)
A31		at Michigan State	14 52
S14		at Notre Dame	0 35
S21		West Virginia	6 20
S28	●	North Carolina St.	42 21
O5	●	Minnesota	30 27
O12		at Penn State	14 31
O19		Ohio State	14 42
N2		at Wisconsin	25 33
N9	●	Michigan	9 3
N16		at Northwestern	24 27
N23		Indiana	16 33

JOE TILLER
1997-Present (.626)   **62-37**

1997   9-3 (6-2)
S6		at Toledo	22 36
S13		Notre Dame	28 17
S20	●	Ball State	28 14
S27	●	Northwestern	21 9
O11	●	at Minnesota	59 43
O18	●	Wisconsin	45 20
O25	●	at Illinois	48 3
N1		at Iowa	17 35
N8	●	Michigan State	22 21
N15		Penn State	17 42
N22	●	at Indiana	56 7
		ALAMO BOWL	
D30	●	Oklahoma State	33 20

1998   9-4 (6-2)
A30		at Southern Cal	17 27
S12	●	Rice	21 19
S19	●	Central Florida	35 7
S26		at Notre Dame	30 31
O3	●	Minnesota	56 21
O10		at Wisconsin	24 31
O17		at Penn State	13 31
O24	●	Illinois	42 9
O31	●	Iowa	36 14
N7	●	at Northwestern	56 21
N14	●	at Michigan State	25 24
N21	●	Indiana	52 7
		ALAMO BOWL	
D29	●	Kansas Kansas State	37 34

1999   7-5 (4-4)
S4	●	at Central Florida	47 13
S11	●	Notre Dame	28 23
S18	●	Central Michigan	58 16
S25	●	Northwestern	31 23
O2		at Michigan	12 38
O9		at Ohio State	22 25
O16	●	Michigan State	52 28
O23		Penn State	25 31
O30	●	at Minnesota	33 28
N6		Wisconsin	21 28
N20	●	at Indiana	30 24
		OUTBACK BOWL	
J1		Georgia	25 28

2000   8-4 (6-2)
S2	●	Central Michigan	48 0
S9	●	Kent	45 10
S16		at Notre Dame	21 23
S23	●	Minnesota	38 24
S30		at Penn State	20 22
O7	●	Michigan	32 31
O14	●	at Northwestern	41 28
O21	●	at Wisconsin	30 24
O28	●	Ohio State	31 27
N11		at Michigan State	10 30
N18	●	Indiana	41 13
		ROSE BOWL	
J1		Washington	24 34

2001   6-6 (4-4)
S2	●	at Cincinnati	19 14
S22	●	Akron	33 14
S29	●	at Minnesota	35 28
O6	●	Iowa	23 14
O13		at Michigan	10 24
O27	●	Northwestern	32 27
N3		Illinois	13 38
N10		at Ohio State	9 35
N17	●	Michigan State	24 14
N24		at Indiana	7 13
D1		Notre Dame	18 24
		SUN BOWL	
D31		Washington State	27 33

2002   7-6 (4-4)
A31	●	Illinois St.	51 10
S7		at Notre Dame	17 24
S14	●	Western Michigan	28 24
S21		Wake Forest	21 24
S28	●	Minnesota	28 15
O5		at Iowa	28 31
O12		at Illinois	31 38
O19		Michigan	21 23
O26	●	at Northwestern	42 13
N9		Ohio State	6 10
N16	●	at Michigan State	45 42
N23	●	Indiana	34 10
		SUN BOWL	
D31	●	Washington	34 24

2003   9-4 (6-2)
S6		Bowling Green	26 27
S13	●	at Wake Forest	16 10
S20	●	Arizona	59 7
S27	●	Notre Dame	23 10
O4	●	Illinois	43 10
O11	●	Penn State	28 14
O18	●	at Wisconsin	26 23
O25		at Michigan	3 31
N1	●	Northwestern	34 14
N8	●	Iowa	27 14
N15		at Ohio State	13 16
N22	●	at Indiana	24 16
		CAPITAL ONE BOWL	
J1		Georgia	27 34

2004   7-5 (4-4)
S5	●	Syracuse	51 0
S11	●	Ball State	59 7
S25	●	at Illinois	38 30
O2	●	at Notre Dame	41 16
O9	●	at Penn State	20 13
O16	●	Wisconsin	17 20
O23	●	Michigan	14 16
O30	●	at Northwestern	10 13
N6		at Iowa	21 23
N13	●	Ohio State	24 17
N20	●	Indiana	63 24
		SUN BOWL	
D31		Arizona State	23 27

Neutral Site key: _CHI_ Chicago, Ill. / _BRNX_ Bronx, N.Y. / _IND_ Indianapolis, Ind. / _STL_ St. Louis, Mo. / _NYC_ New York, N.Y. / _CLEV_ Cleveland, Ohio / _BALT_ Baltimore, Md. / _BOS_ Boston, Mass. / _DAL_ Dallas, Texas
_f_ Forfeit † Game Later Forfeited # Disputed Victor * Disputed Score ‖ Designated Conference Game |2 Counted Twice in Conference Standings

RICE

BY DAVE REARDON

IN THE SPRING OF 2004, SOME faculty members at Rice University wondered aloud whether football—and all intercollegiate sports—still had a place at the school. A long tradition of football mediocrity would seem to have augured little interest, but a letter and e-mail campaign generated 2,000 responses from Rice alumni around the nation. The alumni raged: it didn't matter whether the Owls had lost more games than they'd won in their 90-plus seasons of football. Nor did it matter that the program didn't generate huge crowds or huge profits. What mattered was how the sport built character in its participants, how it fostered camaraderie and tradition among the student body. Rice hadn't been to a bowl game since 1961, but its fans weren't ready to flush away their beloved team.

TRADITION Not many football teams encourage people to come out of the stands and onto the playing field before games, but such things occur regularly at Rice. Fans cheer the players onto the field as part of the Spirit Line before every home game. And the MOB truly rules; that's the Marching Owl Band, known as much for its skits and humorous antics as for the high quality of its music. You don't have to be a great musician to be part of the MOB since some members also assist in show production. Rice has also recently restored an old tradition, the coaches table. Rice head coaches, opposing coaches and All-America Owls engrave their names on a table at Rice Stadium's Owl Club. The original coaches table was at Ye Olde College Inn, a Houston restaurant where the Rice staff convened during breaks from the 1940s to the 1960s. The table was lost for a time, but was recovered in 1990.

BEST PLAYER Two-time All-Southwest Conference guard Weldon Humble starred on teams in 1941, 1942 and 1946 that went a combined 22–7–2. He co-captained the 1946 team, which tied for the SWC championship and beat Tennessee 8-0 in the Orange Bowl on its way to a 9–2 overall record and No. 10 final ranking in the Associated Press poll. Humble was a consensus All-American on the football field and a war hero off of it; he served in the Marines during World War II and again later in the Korean conflict, receiving the Bronze Star for action on Okinawa and Saipan. As a pro, he was a standout for the Cleveland Browns and played in the Pro Bowl in 1951.

PROFILE

Rice University
Houston, Texas
Founded in 1912
Enrollment: 2,857
Colors: Blue and Gray
Nickname: Owls
Stadium: Rice Stadium
   Opened in 1950
   AstroTurf; 70,000 capacity
First football game: 1912
All-time record: 404–511–32 (.444)
Bowl record: 4–3
First-round NFL draftees: 7
Website: www.riceowls.com

THE BEST OF TIMES

From 1946 to 1954, Rice went nine years without a losing season and captured at least a share of four Southwest Conference titles.

THE WORST OF TIMES

The Owls did not have a winning season from 1964 through 1991, and weathered an 18-game losing streak and two winless seasons during that span.

CONFERENCE

Rice was a charter member of the Southwest Conference, formed in 1915, and remained in the SWC until it dissolved in 1995. After spending nine seasons in the Western Athletic Conference, the Owls join Conference USA in 2005.

DISTINGUISHED ALUMNI

Lance Berkman, baseball player; William Broyles Jr., founding editor, *Texas Monthly*, and screenwriter; Fred Hansen, Olympic pole vault gold medalist; Howard Hughes, aviator and famed recluse; Larry McMurtry, author

FIGHT SONG

FIGHT FOR RICE
Fight for Rice, Rice fight on
Loyal sons arise!
The Blue and Gray of Rice today,
Comes breaking through the skies
Stand and cheer!
Victory's near!
Sammy leads the way,
Onward go, to crush the foe,
We'll fight for the Blue and Gray.

> *It's huge any time tiny Rice can beat gargantuan Texas, and it has happened only 21 times in the schools' 87 meetings.*

Humble was a 1961 inductee into the College Hall of Fame and was enshrined in the Texas Sports Hall of Fame in 1969.

BEST COACH Jess Neely guided Rice to four SWC championships and six bowl games while compiling a 144–124–10 record over 27 seasons. As a player, he had captained a Vanderbilt team that went 8–0–1 in 1922; he later took the Rice job after coaching Clemson from 1931 to 1939. After leaving Rice in 1966, he returned to Vanderbilt, where he was athletic director until 1970. Neely was inducted into the College Football Hall of Fame in 1971 and died in 1985 at the age of 83.

BEST TEAM Neely was known as a conservative coach, but in 1949 he adjusted to the team's surfeit of talent and loosened up a bit. With quarterback Tobin Rote throwing the ball and end Froggy Williams catching it, Rice was one of the nation's best passing teams that year; the Owls went 10–1, won the SWC title and defeated North Carolina 27-13 in the Cotton Bowl. Linemen Joe Watson, Gerald Weatherly and Ralph Murphy were other top players. Rice ended the season ranked fifth in the Associated Press poll.

BIGGEST GAME It's huge any time tiny Rice can beat gargantuan Texas, and it has happened only 21 times in the schools' 87 meetings. The most recent was Oct. 16, 1994; the Owls, with a defense led by all-conference performers Larry Izzo at linebacker, Ndukwe Kalu at end, Brynton Goynes at tackle and Jeff Sowells and Bobby Dixon in the secondary, edged the Longhorns 19-17 in rainy Rice Stadium. The victory ended a 28-game losing streak that Rice had experienced against the boys from Austin. Even though the Owls ultimately went on to finish coach Ken Hatfield's first season 5–6, the upset still carried significance, as Rice went 4–3 to tie for first in a balanced Southwest Conference. It was Rice's first SWC title since 1957, and its last; the league broke up after the 1995 season, and Rice joined the WAC.

RECORDS

RUSHING YARDS

	GAME
265	Dicky Maegle vs. Alabama, Jan. 1, 1954 (11 att.)
	SEASON
1,692	Trevor Cobb, 1991 (360 att.)
	CAREER
4,948	Trevor Cobb, 1989-92 (1,091 att.)

PASSING YARDS

	GAME
409	Tommy Kramer vs. Houston, Nov. 27, 1976 (27 of 51)
	SEASON
3,317	Tommy Kramer, 1976 (269 of 501)
	CAREER
6,197	Tommy Kramer, 1973-76 (507 of 1,036)

RECEIVING YARDS

	GAME
196	David Houser vs. Florida, Nov. 20, 1976 (14 rec.)
	SEASON
931	David Houser, 1976 (52 rec.)
	CAREER
2,358	David Houser, 1974, 1976-78 (152 rec.)

POINTS

	GAME
36	Griff Vance vs. Southern Methodist, Nov. 17, 1916 (6 TDs)
	SEASON
96	Benji Wood, 1997 (16 TDs)
	CAREER
260	Trevor Cobb, 1989-92 (43 TDs, 2 PATs)

CONSENSUS ALL-AMERICANS

1946	Weldon Humble, G
1949	James Williams, E
1954	Dicky Maegle, B
1958	Buddy Dial, E
1976	Tommy Kramer, QB
1991	Trevor Cobb, RB

BIGGEST UPSET Rice went into its 1957 game against Texas A&M with a 4–3 record and a possible Southwest Conference championship on the line. No one gave the Owls much of a chance against the top-ranked Aggies, who boasted coach Paul "Bear" Bryant and star player John David Crow. Somehow, though, Rice held off high-powered A&M, winning 7-6. The Owls rode the momentum to close the season with shutout wins over TCU and Baylor, securing the SWC title.

HEARTBREAKER In 1955, Rice led Texas A&M 12-0 with 4:12 to play, and figured to end a four-game losing streak. The visiting Aggies had other ideas, scoring three touchdowns in less than three minutes to stun the Owls 20-12. The Owls lost their last seven games of the season, finishing 2–7–1, their worst record since 1939.

STADIUM Rice Stadium seats 70,000, though in recent years it has rarely been more than a third full for Owls games. Nonetheless, it has been the site of some major events, including Super Bowl VIII and a 1962 speech by president John F. Kennedy in which he promised that the U.S. would put a man on the moon by the end of the decade. At various times, the stadium has served as the home for the Bluebonnet Bowl, the University of Houston, Texas Southern University and the NFL's Houston Oilers. It was built in 1950 when the previous stadium of the same name, with its 37,000-capacity, was deemed too small for the Owls crowds. Unaware of the irony that would become clear in later years, Rice beat Santa Clara 27-7 when the stadium opened on Sept. 30, 1950.

RIVAL When Rice and Houston tangle, city bragging rights are at stake, as is the Bayou Bucket. Houston leads the series 22–9. In 1974, former Rice guard Fred Curry, president of the Houston Touchdown Club, came up with the idea of a trophy for the Rice-Houston winner. He found a weathered bucket at an antique shop and took it to a trophy shop to be designed into the Bayou Bucket—an investment of $310.

NICKNAME In Rice's case, the school logo preceded the nickname. Back around 1900, the creator of the crest for the Rice Institute (as the school was known before 1960) used in his design the Owls of Athena, which were featured on an ancient Greek coin. When the school began competing in sports in 1912, the nickname Owls was a natural.

MASCOT Sammy the Owl got his name from a private detective in 1917. The large canvas owl was kidnapped by Texas A&M students that year; the gumshoe recovered the owl and sent a telegram to Rice that read, "Sammy is fairly well and would like to see his parents at 11 o'clock." The canvas Sammy still keeps his perch in Rice Stadium. There is also a student-costumed Sammy, and several live owls have served as Sammies over the years as well.

UNIFORMS The Owls uniforms resemble those of the Philadelphia Eagles, except that navy blue complements their silver instead of green. The home set consists of navy tops and pants with white and silver trim. The road uniforms are the opposite. Formerly, the uniforms were blue and gray, which remain the official school colors.

NUMBERS Tommy Kramer was fifth in the 1976 Heisman Trophy voting, the year in which he passed for an NCAA-best 3,317 yards. Kramer is one of only two players to lead the Owls in passing for four consecutive seasons. Trevor Cobb, winner of the 1991 Doak Walker Award as the nation's top running back, led Rice in rushing for four consecutive years. He left Rice as the Owls' all-time leading rusher (4,948 yards) and scorer (260 points).

QUIRK No Rice player has won the Heisman Trophy, but the award is named for a man who coached at the school. John W. Heisman was Rice's first full-time football coach. He compiled a record of 14–18–3 from 1924 to 1927. Heisman would go on to become athletic director of the Downtown Athletic Club in New York, and his name was later attached to the trophy given annually to the nation's best college football player.

QUOTE "Why does Rice play Texas? We choose to go to the Moon. We choose to go to the Moon in this decade and do the other things, not because they are easy, but because they are hard."—John F. Kennedy, at Rice Stadium, Sept. 12, 1962

RICE ANNUAL STATISTICAL LEADERS

YR	RUSHING	YDS	ATT	AVG	PASSING	ATT	CMP	PCT	YDS	RECEIVING	REC	YDS	AVG
1951	Teddy Riggs	639	114	5.6	Dan Drake	109	51	.49	859	Bill Howton	33	747	22.6
1952	Kosse Johnson	592	108	5.5	Dan Drake	129	49	.38	630	Jack Day	20	301	15.0
1953	Kosse Johnson	944	187	5.1	Leroy Fenstemaker	58	21	.36	328	Dan Hart	15	239	15.9
1954	Dicky Maegle	905	144	6.3	Pinky Nisbet	62	37	.60	419	Dicky Maegle	18	198	11.0
1955	Jerry Hall	255	55	4.6	Pinky Nisbet	49	25	.51	339	Marshall Crawford	11	172	15.6
1956	Raymond Chilton	405	92	4.4	Frank Ryan	109	60	.55	704	Buddy Dial	21	357	17.0
1957	King Hill	466	90	5.0	King Hill	82	44	.54	798	Buddy Dial	21	508	24.2
1958	Pat Bailey	342	63	5.4	Alvin Hartman	51	22	.43	429	Buddy Dial	19	264	13.9
1959	Bill Bucek	511	117	4.3	Bill Bucek	55	20	.36	259	Thomas Stellman	7	108	15.4
1960	Robert Wayt	392	83	4.7	Billy Cox	80	45	.56	510	Johnny Burrell	20	266	13.3
1961	Roland Jackson	415	88	4.4	Randall Kerbow	79	37	.47	505	Johnny Burrell	7	133	19.0
1962	Paul Piper	387	85	4.5	Randall Kerbow	143	53	.37	703	Gene Raesz	29	363	12.5
1963	Paul Piper	475	128	3.7	Walter McReynolds	117	53	.45	728	Jerry Kelley	17	225	13.2
1964	Gene Fleming	395	103	3.8	Walter McReynolds	111	58	.52	675	Billy Hale	14	170	12.1
1965	Lester Lehman	422	101	4.2	David Ferguson	109	44	.40	584	Tommy Tyner	27	295	10.9
1966	Robby Shelton	607	150	4.1	Robert Hailey	149	72	.48	859	Glen Hine	29	323	11.1
1967	Terry Shelton	651	133	4.9	Robert Hailey	222	111	.50	1,437	Larry Davis	54	708	13.1
1968	Terry Conley	681	182	3.8	Robby Shelton	109	53	.49	594	Larry Davis	31	410	13.2
1969	Mike Spruill	440	101	4.4	Stahle Vincent	100	51	.51	556	Bob Brown	35	375	10.7
1970	Stahle Vincent	453	91	5.0	Philip Wood	112	39	.35	489	Macon Hughes	13	116	8.9
1971	Stahle Vincent	945	243	3.9	Bruce Gadd	180	87	.48	1,061	Gary Butler	27	397	14.7
1972	Gary Ferguson	639	160	4.0	Bruce Gadd	323	171	.53	2,075	Gary Butler	45	708	15.7
1973	Gary Ferguson	385	99	3.9	Tommy Kramer	139	58	.42	705	Ed Lofton	39	534	13.7
1974	Gary Ferguson	417	117	3.8	Tommy Kramer	170	67	.39	847	Ed Lofton	42	483	11.5
1975	John Coleman	782	172	4.6	Tommy Kramer	226	113	.50	1,328	Ed Lofton	31	261	8.4
1976	James Sykes	435	100	4.4	Tommy Kramer	501	269	.54	3,317	James Sykes	76	653	8.6
1977	Earl Cooper	598	135	4.4	Randy Hertel	356	156	.44	1,620	David Houser	55	795	14.5
1978	Earl Cooper	350	95	3.7	Randy Hertel	279	156	.56	1,677	Doug Cunningham	39	430	11.0
1979	Earl Cooper	536	146	3.7	Randy Hertel	294	147	.50	1,652	Earl Cooper	47	463	9.9
1980	Calvin Fance	730	192	3.8	Randy Hertel	192	102	.53	1,212	Robert Hubble	38	482	12.7
1981	Tim Sanders	408	116	3.5	Michael Calhoun	233	98	.42	1,480	Hosea Fortune	29	489	16.9
1982	Tim Sanders	379	111	3.4	Doug Johnson	162	79	.49	936	Melvin Robinson	34	584	17.2
1983	Kevin Trigg	579	198	2.9	Philip Money	197	97	.49	1,131	Ricky Askew	25	337	13.5
1984	Larry Collins	358	88	4.1	Kerry Overton	271	117	.43	1,593	Melvin Robinson	46	593	12.9
1985	Antonio Brinkley	860	168	5.1	Mark Comalander	182	100	.55	1,232	Darrick Wells	36	612	17.0
1986	Marc Scott	325	94	3.5	Mark Comalander	219	116	.53	1,430	Kenny Major	38	409	10.8
1987	Lorenzo Cyphers	751	170	4.4	Mark Comalander	214	102	.48	1,191	Lorenzo Cyphers	31	187	6.0
1988	Lorenzo Cyphers	516	163	3.2	Quentis Roper	271	135	.50	1,607	Mike Boudousquie	38	657	17.3
1989	Trevor Cobb	545	169	3.2	Donald Hollas	276	156	.57	1,815	Eric Henley	81	900	11.1
1990	Trevor Cobb	1,325	283	4.7	Donald Hollas	265	151	.57	1,808	Eric Henley	48	607	12.7
1991	Trevor Cobb	1,692	360	4.7	Greg Willig	141	75	.53	974	Eric Henley	31	410	13.2
1992	Trevor Cobb	1,386	279	5.0	Bert Emanuel	180	94	.52	1,558	Louis Balady	31	552	17.8
1993	Yoncy Edmonds	941	199	4.7	Bert Emanuel	204	118	.58	1,521	Jimmy Lee	36	365	10.1
1994	Spencer George	804	185	4.3	Josh LaRocca	130	65	.50	806	Ed Howard	19	315	16.6
1995	Yoncy Edmonds	490	84	5.8	Josh LaRocca	118	59	.50	807	Jeff Venghaus	22	371	16.9
1996	Chad Nelson	801	128	6.3	Chad Richardson	43	9	.21	259	Thad Bridges	15	103	6.9
1997	Michael Perry	1,034	162	6.4	Chad Nelson	50	20	.40	526	Jason Blackwell	14	210	15.0
1998	Chad Richardson	746	181	4.1	Chad Richardson	91	34	.37	598	Jason Blackwell	22	422	19.2
1999	Chad Richardson	831	203	4.1	Chad Richardson	88	36	.42	563	Raphael Tillman	14	218	15.6
2000	Jamie Tyler	400	95	4.2	Ben Wulf	66	30	.46	449	Gavin Boothe	18	313	17.4
2001	Kyle Herm	897	205	4.4	Kyle Herm	142	72	.51	1,121	Gilbert Okoronkwo	23	439	19.1
2002	Robbie Beck	601	120	5.0	Kyle Herm	86	42	.49	685	Marcus Battle	26	430	16.5
2003	Thomas Lott	714	98	7.3	Greg Henderson	81	37	.46	485	Marcus Battle	19	333	17.5
2004	Ed Bailey	1,021	208	4.9	Greg Henderson	76	33	.43	487	Marcus Battle	15	213	14.2

Receiving leaders by receptions

The NCAA began including postseason stats in 2002

RICE ALL-TIME SCORES

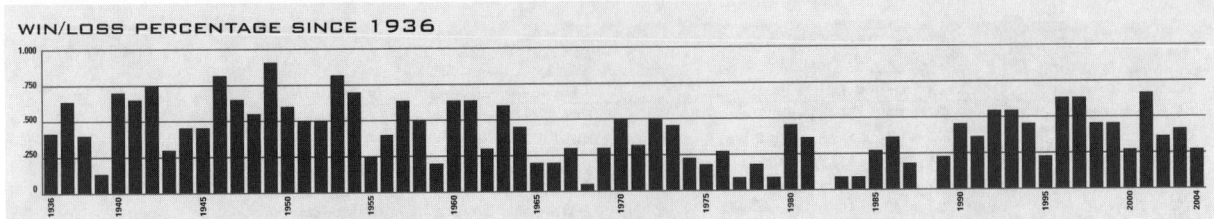

WIN/LOSS PERCENTAGE SINCE 1936

PHIL ARBUCKLE
1912-17, '19-23 (.655) 51-25-8

1912 3-2-0
O26	●	at Houston HS	7	6
O30	●	at Orange HS	13	0
N9	●	at Sam Houston St.	20	6
N15		at Southwestern	0	32
N28		at Austin Coll.	0	81

1913 4-0-0
O17	●	Signal Corps	14	0
O25	●	Houston HS	7	0
N18	●	Southwestern	53	14
N27		at Trinity	7	0

1914 3-2-3
O10	●	Southwestern	12	7
O17		at Texas	0	41
O24	=	TCU	0	0
O31	●	Daniel Baker	13	7
N9		Texas A&M	7	32
N14	●	Oklahoma State	13	13
N20	●	Baylor	14	13
N26		at Austin Coll.	0	0

1915-1995
SWC

1915 5-3-0 (1-2-0)
O2	●	Trinity	46	0
O8		Baylor	0	26
O16		at Texas	0	59
O23		Daniel Baker	28	0
O30	●	TCU	33	3 *
N8	●	Texas A&M	7	0
N17	●	LSU	6	0
N27		Notre Dame	2	55

1916 6-1-2 (2-1-0)
O7		at Texas	2	16
O13	●	Austin Coll.	40	0
O21	●	Southwestern	54	0
O27	=	at TCU	7	7
N4	●	Texas A&M	20	0
N11		Tulane	23	13
N17	●	SMU	146	3
N24	=	at LSU	7	7
N30	●	Arizona	47	16 *

1917 7-1-0 (1-1-0)
O6		Illinois Medics	31	0
O13	●	TCU	26	0
O19	●	Austin Coll.	53	13
O27	●	at Texas	13	0
N3	●	Haskell	55	13
N10	●	Southwestern	34	13
N17	●	at Tulane	16	0
N29		Texas A&M	0	10

JOHN ANDERSON
1918 (.214) 1-5-1

1918 1-5-1 (1-1-0)
O5		Camp Logan	0	10
O19		Park Place Flyers	0	7
O26	=	Camp Logan	0	0
N2		Kelly Field	0	28
N9		Park Place Flyers	0	3
N16		Texas	0	14
N30	●	SMU	13	0

PHIL ARBUCKLE

1919 8-1-0 (3-1-0)
O4	●	Trinity	12	0
O11	●	at Baylor	8	0
O18	●	Southwestern	22	0
O24	●	Austin Coll.	54	0
N1		at Texas	7	32
N8		SMU	21	14
N15		Sewanee	19	7
N21		Howard Payne	7	0
N27		Arkansas	40	7

1920 4-2-2 (2-2-1)
O9	●	Baylor	28	0
O16	=	at Tulane	0	0
O23	●	Southwestern	19	0
O30		Texas	0	21
N6	●	at SMU	10	0
N15		at Texas A&M	0	7
N19	●	SW. Texas	48	0
N25		Arkansas	0	0

1921 4-4-1 (1-2-1)
O1	●	La. Lafayette	54	0
O8		at Baylor	14	17
O15		Tulane	6	7
O22	●	Southwestern	28	0
O29		at Texas	0	56
N5	●	SMU	7	0
N11	=	Texas A&M	7	7
N18	●	at Trinity	28	14
N24		at Oklahoma	0	27

1922 4-4-0 (1-4-0)
O7	●	Sam Houston St.	23	3
O14		Baylor	0	31
O21		at Oklahoma State	0	21
O28	●	Southwestern	28	6
N4		Texas	0	29
N11	●	Arkansas	31	7
N18		at Texas A&M	0	24
N25	●	Arizona	14	7

1923 3-5-0 (1-4-0)
O6	●	Sam Houston St.	10	0
O13		Arkansas *LR*	0	23
O20		Oklahoma State	0	13
O27		SW. Texas St.	6	19
N3		at Texas	0	27
N10	●	Southwestern	12	0
N17	●	Texas A&M	7	6
N29		TCU	0	6

JOHN HEISMAN
1924-27 (.443) 14-18-3

1924 4-4-0 (2-2-0)
O4	●	Sam Houston St.	22	6
O11	●	Southwestern	20	6
O18		LSU	0	12
O25	●	at TCU	7	3
N1	●	Texas	19	6
N7		Austin Coll.	2	6
N15		at Texas A&M	6	13
N27		Baylor	9	17

1925 4-4-1 (1-2-1)
S26	●	Stephen F. Austin	33	0
O3	●	Sam Houston St.	7	0
O10		Trinity	0	13
O17	●	Arkansas	13	9
O24		at Texas	6	27
O31	●	Southwestern	19	0
N7		at LSU	0	6
N14		Texas A&M	0	17
N28	=	Baylor	7	7

1926 4-4-1 (0-4-0)
S25	●	Stephen F. Austin	25	0
O2	●	Sam Houston St.	20	0
O9	=	Trinity	6	6
O16	●	St. Edwards	19	0
O23		Texas	0	20
O30	●	Southwestern	7	6
N6		at SMU	0	20
N12		at Texas A&M	0	20
N25		at Baylor	7	9

1927 2-6-1 (1-3-0)
S24		at Loyola-New Orleans	0	13
O1	●	Sam Houston St.	20	13
O8	●	St. Edwards	0	0
O14		at SMU	6	34
O22		at Texas	0	27
O29		Southwestern	12	14
N5		Centenary	7	33
N11		Texas A&M	0	14
N24	●	Baylor	19	12

CLAUDE ROTHGEB
1928 (.222) 2-7

1928 2-7-0 (0-5-0)
S29	●	Sam Houston St.	24	6
O6		St. Edwards	0	31
O13	●	Trinity	20	6
O20		at SMU	13	53
O27		Texas	6	13
N3		Southwestern	6	14
N10		TCU	0	7
N16		at Texas A&M	0	19
N29	●	Baylor	14	25

JACK MEAGHER
1929-33 (.500) 26-26

1929 2-7-0 (0-5-0)
S28		Loyola-New Orleans	0	33
O5	●	Sam Houston St.	7	2
O12	●	Southwestern	14	7
O26		at Texas	0	39
N2		St. Edwards	7	20
N9		at TCU	0	24
N16		Texas A&M	6	26
N23		at SMU	0	34 *
N30		Baylor	0	19

1930 8-4-0 (2-4-0)
S20	●	Southwestern	32	6
S27	●	Sam Houston St.	13	12
O4	●	St. Edwards	20	0
O11	●	Arizona	21	0
O18		at Arkansas	6	7
O25	●	Texas	6	0
N1	●	Southern U.	12	0
N8		TCU	0	20
N15	●	at Texas A&M	7	0
N22		SMU	0	32
N29		at Baylor	4	7 *
D6	●	Iowa State	14	7

1931 6-4-0 (3-3-0)
S19	●	Texas A&I	37	0
S26	●	Sam Houston St.	32	0
O3		at Oklahoma	6	19
O10	●	at Texas	7	0
O17		SMU	12	21
O23	●	at Arizona	32	0
N7		at TCU	6	7
N14		Texas A&M	0	7
N21	●	Arkansas	26	12
N28	●	Baylor	20	0

1932 7-3-0 (3-3-0)
S24	●	Texas A&I	20	0
O1	●	LSU	10	8
O8		at SMU	13	0
O15	●	Loyola-New Orleans	14	7
O22		Texas	6	18
O29	●	Creighton	41	7
N5	●	at Arkansas	12	7
N11	●	at Texas A&M	7	14
N19		TCU	6	16
N26	●	at Baylor	12	0

1933 3-8-0 (1-5-0)
S23	●	Texas A&I	7	0
S30		at LSU	0	13
O7	●	Loyola-New Orleans	13	0
O14		SMU	7	13
O21		at Creighton	13	14
O28		at Texas	0	18
N4		at Santa Clara	0	13
N11	●	Arkansas	7	6
N18		Texas A&M	0	27
N25		at TCU	3	26
D2		at Baylor	6	7

JIMMY KITTS
1934-39 (.530) 33-29-4

1934 9-1-1 (5-1-0)
S22	●	Loyola-New Orleans	12	0
S29	=	LSU	9	9
O6		at Purdue	14	0
O13		SMU	9	0
O20	●	at Creighton	47	13
O27	●	Texas	20	9
N3		Texas A&I	27	0
N10		at Arkansas	7	0
N17		at Texas A&M	25	6
N24		TCU	2	7
D1		at Baylor	32	0

1935 8-3-0 (3-3-0)
S21	●	at St. Mary's, Texas	38	0
S28	●	at LSU	10	7
O5		Duquesne	27	7
O12		Creighton	14	0
O19		at SMU	0	10
O26		at Texas	28	19
N2		at George Washington	41	6
N9	●	Arkansas	20	7
N16	●	Texas A&M	17	10
N23		at TCU	6	27
N30		Baylor	0	6 *

1936 5-7-0 (1-5-0)
S19	●	at Texas A&I	33	0
S26	●	at LSU	7	20
O2		at Duquesne	0	14
O10		Texas A&M	0	3
O17	●	at Georgia	13	6
O24	●	Texas	7	0
O31	●	George Washington	12	6
N7		at Arkansas	14	20
N14	●	Sam Houston St.	34	7
N21		TCU	0	13
N28	●	Baylor	7	10
D5		SMU	0	9
*				

1937 6-3-2 (4-1-1)
O2		at Oklahoma	0	6
O9		LSU	0	13
O16	=	Tulsa	0	0
O23	●	at Texas	14	7
O30	●	Auburn	13	7
N6	=	Arkansas	26	20
N13	●	Texas A&M	6	6
N20		at TCU	2	7
N27	●	Baylor	13	7
D4	●	at SMU	15	7

COTTON BOWL
| J1 | ● | Colorado | 28 | 14 |

1938 4-6-0 (3-3-0)

Date		Opponent		
O1		Oklahoma	6	7
O8		at LSU	0	3
O15		at Tulane	17	26
O22	•	Texas	13	7 *
O29	•	Auburn	14	0
N5		at Arkansas	3	0
N12		at Texas A&M	0	27
N19		TCU	7	29
N26		Baylor	6	21 *
D3	•	SMU	25	14

1939 1-9-1 (0-5-1)

Date		Opponent		
S30		Vanderbilt	12	13
O7	•	Centenary	13	0
O14		at LSU	0	7
O21		Sam Houston St.	8	9
O28		at Texas	12	26
N4		Fordham NYC	7	13
N11	=	Arkansas	12	12
N18		Texas A&M	0	19
N25		at TCU	0	21
D2		Baylor	7	10
D9		at SMU	6	13

JESS NEELY
1940-66 (.536)   144-124-10

1940 7-3-0 (4-2-0)

Date		Opponent		
O5	•	Centenary	25	0
O12	•	LSU	23	0
O19		at Tulane	6	15
O26	•	Texas	13	0
N2	•	Texas A&I	9	6
N9	•	at Arkansas	14	7
N16	•	at Texas A&M	0	25
N23	•	TCU	14	6
N30	•	Baylor	21	12
D7		SMU	6	7

1941 6-3-1 (3-2-1)

Date		Opponent		
O4	•	Sam Houston St.	42	0
O11	•	Tulane	10	9
O18		at LSU	0	27
O25		at Texas	0	40
N1	•	Centenary	54	0
N8		Arkansas	21	12
N15		Texas A&M	6	19
N22	=	at TCU	0	0
N29		Baylor	28	14
D6		at SMU	6	0

1942 7-2-1 (4-1-1)

Date		Opponent		
S26	•	Corpus Christi NAS	18	7
O3	•	LSU	27	14
O10		at Tulane	7	18
O24		Texas	7	12
O31		Texas Tech	19	7
N7	•	at Arkansas	40	9
N14	=	Texas A&M	0	0
N21		TCU	21	0 *
N28		at Baylor	20	0
D5		SMU	13	7

1943 3-7-0 (2-3-0)

Date		Opponent		
S25		Randolph AFB	0	6
O2		at LSU	7	20
O9		Tulane	0	33
O16		at SMU	0	12
O23		at Texas	0	58
O30	•	Texas Tech	13	0
N6	•	Arkansas	20	7
N13		Texas A&M	0	7
N20		at TCU	13	6
N27		Southwestern	7	21

1944 5-6-0 (2-3-0)

Date		Opponent		
S23	•	Galveston AAF	57	0
S30		Randolph AFB	0	59
O7	•	LSU	14	13
O14		at Tulane	0	21
O21	•	SMU	21	10 *
O28	•	Texas	7	0
N4		Texas Tech	7	13
N11		at Arkansas	7	12
N18		Texas A&M	7	19 *
N25		TCU	6	9
D2	•	Southwestern	18	7

1945 5-6-0 (3-3-0)

Date		Opponent		
S22		Corpus Christi NAS	13	26
S29		at LSU	0	42
O6		Southwestern	7	13
O13	•	Tulane	13	7
O20		at SMU	18	21
O27	•	at Texas	7	6
N3	•	Texas Tech	13	0
N10	•	Arkansas	26	7
N17	•	Texas A&M	6	0
N24		at TCU	13	14
D1		Baylor	14	17

1946 9-2-0 (5-1-0)

Date		Opponent		
S28	•	LSU	6	7
O5	•	Southwestern	48	0
O12	•	at Tulane	25	6
O19	•	SMU	21	7
O26	•	Texas	18	13
N2	•	Texas Tech	41	6
N9	•	Arkansas LR	0	7
N16	•	at Texas A&M	27	10
N23	•	TCU	13	0
N30	•	Baylor	38	6
		ORANGE BOWL		
J1	•	Tennessee	8	0

1947 6-3-1 (4-2-0)

Date		Opponent		
S27		at LSU	14	21
O4	=	at Southern Cal	7	7
O11	•	Tulane	33	0
O18		at SMU	0	14
O25		at Texas	0	12
N1	•	Texas Tech	40	7
N8	•	Arkansas	26	0
N15	•	Texas A&M	41	7
N22	•	at TCU	7	0
N29	•	Baylor	34	6

1948 5-4-1 (3-2-1)

Date		Opponent		
S25	•	Sam Houston St.	46	0
O2	•	LSU	13	26
O9		at Southern Cal	0	7
O16		SMU	7	33
O23		Texas	7	20
O30	•	at Texas Tech	14	7
N6	•	Arkansas LR	25	6
N13	•	at Texas A&M	28	6
N20	•	TCU	21	7
N27	=	at Baylor	7	7

1949 10-1-0 (6-0-0)

Date		Opponent		
S24	•	Clemson	33	7
O1	•	at LSU	7	14
O8	•	New Mexico	55	0
O15		at SMU	41	27
O22		at Texas	17	15
O29	•	Texas Tech	28	0
N5	•	Arkansas	14	0
N12	•	Texas A&M	13	0
N19	•	at TCU	20	14
N26	•	Baylor	21	7
		COTTON BOWL		
J2	•	North Carolina	27	13

1950 6-4-0 (2-4-0)

Date		Opponent		
S30	•	Santa Clara	27	7
O7	•	LSU	35	20
O14	•	at Pittsburgh	14	7
O21	•	SMU	21	42
O28		Texas	7	35
N4	•	Texas Tech	13	7
N11	•	at Arkansas	9	6
N18	•	at Texas A&M	21	13
N25		TCU	14	26
D2	•	at Baylor	7	33

1951 5-5-0 (3-3-0)

Date		Opponent		
S29		Clemson	14	20
O6	•	at LSU	6	7 *
O13	•	Navy	21	14
O20	•	at SMU	28	7
O27		at Texas	6	14
N3	•	Pittsburgh	21	13
N10	•	Arkansas	6	0 *
N17	•	Texas A&M	28	13 *
N24		at TCU	6	22
D1		Baylor	13	34

1952 5-5-0 (4-2-0)

Date		Opponent		
S27	•	Texas Tech	34	7
O4		LSU	7	27
O11		at UCLA	0	20
O18		SMU	14	21
O25		Texas	5	20
N1		Wisconsin	7	21
N8	•	at Arkansas	35	33
N15	•	at Texas A&M	16	6 *
N22		TCU	12	6
N29	•	at Baylor	20	14

1953 9-2-0 (5-1-0)

Date		Opponent		
S19	•	Florida	20	16
O3	•	at Cornell	28	7
O10	•	Hardin-Simmons	40	0
O17		at SMU	7	12
O24	•	Texas	18	13
O31		Kentucky	13	19
N7		Arkansas	47	0
N14	•	Texas A&M	34	7
N21	•	at TCU	19	6
N28	•	Baylor	41	19
		COTTON BOWL		
J1		Alabama	28	6

1954 7-3-0 (4-2-0)

Date		Opponent		
S18	•	Florida	34	14
O2	•	Cornell	41	20
O9	•	at Wisconsin	7	13
O16		SMU	6	20
O23	•	Texas	13	7
O30	•	Vanderbilt	34	13
N6	•	Arkansas LR	15	28
N13	•	at Texas A&M	29	19
N20	•	TCU	6	0
N27	•	at Baylor	20	14

1955 2-7-1 (0-6-0)

Date		Opponent		
S24	•	Alabama	20	0
O1	=	LSU	20	20
O8	•	Clemson	21	7
O15		at SMU	0	20
O22		at Texas	14	32
O29		at Kentucky	16	20
N5		Arkansas	0	10
N12		Texas A&M	12	20
N19		at TCU	0	35
N26		Baylor	7	15

1956 4-6-0 (1-5-0)

Date		Opponent		
S22	•	Alabama	20	13
O6	•	LSU	23	14
O13	•	at Florida	0	7
O20		SMU	13	14
O27	•	Texas	28	7
N3	•	Utah	27	0
N10		at Arkansas	12	27
N17	•	at Texas A&M	7	21
N24		TCU	17	20
D1		at Baylor	13	46

1957 7-4-0 (5-1-0)

Date		Opponent		
S21	•	at LSU	20	14
O5	•	Stanford	34	7
O12		Duke	6	7
O19	•	at SMU	27	21
O26		at Texas	14	19
N2		Clemson	7	20
N9	•	Arkansas	13	7
N16	•	Texas A&M	7	6
N23	•	at TCU	20	0
N30	•	Baylor	20	0
		COTTON BOWL		
J1		Navy	7	20

1958 5-5-0 (4-2-0)

Date		Opponent		
S20	•	LSU	6	26
S27	•	at Stanford	30	7
O4	•	Purdue	0	24
O11	•	at Arkansas	24	0
O18	•	at SMU	13	7
O25		Texas	34	7
N8		Army	7	14
N15	•	Texas A&M	21	28
N22		TCU	10	21
N29	•	at Baylor	33	21

1959 1-7-2 (1-4-1)

Date		Opponent		
S19		at LSU	3	26
O3	•	at Duke	7	24
O10	=	Florida	13	13
O17	=	SMU	13	13
O24		at Texas	6	28
O31		Clemson	0	19
N7		Arkansas	10	14
N14	•	Texas A&M	7	2
N21	•	at TCU	6	35
N28	•	Baylor	21	23

1960 7-4-0 (5-2-0)

Date		Opponent		
S24	•	Georgia Tech	13	16
O1	•	Tulane	10	7
O8	•	Florida Mia	10	0
O15	•	at SMU	47	0
O22	•	Texas	7	0
O29	•	Texas Tech	30	6
N5	•	Arkansas LR	0	3
N12	•	Texas A&M	21	14
N19	•	TCU	23	0
N26	•	at Baylor	7	12
		SUGAR BOWL		
J2		Mississippi	6	14

1961 7-4-0 (5-2-0)

Date		Opponent		
S23	•	LSU	16	3
S30	•	at Georgia Tech	0	24
O14	•	Florida	19	10
O21	•	SMU	10	0
O28		at Texas	7	34
N4	•	at Texas Tech	42	7
N11		Arkansas	0	10
N18	•	Texas A&M	21	7
N25	•	at TCU	35	16
D2	•	Baylor	26	14
		BLUEBONNET BOWL		
D16		Kansas	7	33

1962 2-6-2 (2-4-1)

Date		Opponent		
S29	=	at LSU	6	6
O6		Penn State	7	18
O13		Oregon	12	31
O20		at SMU	7	15
O27	=	Texas	14	14
N3	•	Texas Tech	14	0
N10		at Arkansas	14	28
N17	•	Texas A&M	23	3
N24		TCU	7	30
D1		at Baylor	15	28

1963 6-4-0 (4-3-0)

Date		Opponent		
S28	•	LSU	21	12
O5	•	at Penn State	7	28
O12	•	Stanford	23	13
O19	•	SMU	13	7
O26		at Texas	6	10
N2	•	at Texas Tech	17	3
N9	•	Arkansas	7	0
N16	•	Texas A&M	6	13
N30	•	Baylor	12	21
D7	•	at TCU	33	7

1964 4-5-1 (3-3-1)

Date		Opponent		
S26		LSU	0	3
O3	•	West Virginia	24	0
O10	•	at Stanford	7	34
O17	•	at SMU	7	6
O24		Texas	3	6
O31	=	Texas Tech	6	6
N7	•	at Arkansas	0	21
N14	•	Texas A&M	19	8
N21	•	TCU	31	0
N28	•	at Baylor	20	27

1965 2-8-0 (1-6-0)

Date		Opponent		
S18	•	Louisiana Tech	14	0
S25	•	at LSU	14	42
O2	•	Duke	21	41
O16		SMU	14	17
O23	•	at Texas	20	17
O30		at Texas Tech	0	27
N6	•	Arkansas	0	31
N13	•	Texas A&M	13	14
N20	•	at TCU	14	42
N27		Baylor	13	17

THE SCHOOLS

1966 2-8-0 (1-6-0)

S24	●	LSU	17	15
O1		at Tennessee	3	23
O8		UCLA	24	27
O15		at SMU	24	28
O22		Texas	6	14
O29		Texas Tech	19	35
N5		Arkansas LR	20	31
N12		Texas A&M	6	7
N19	●	TCU	21	10
N26		at Baylor	14	21

HAROLD "BO" HAGAN
1967-70 (.313) 12-27-1

1967 4-6-0 (2-5-0)

S23		at LSU	14	20
S30	●	Navy	21	7
O14	●	Northwestern	50	6
O21	●	SMU	14	10
O28		at Texas	6	28
N4		at Texas Tech	10	24
N11		Arkansas	9	23
N18		Texas A&M	3	18
N25		at TCU	10	14
D2	●	Baylor	27	25

1968 0-9-1 (0-7-0)

S21	=	at Washington	35	35
S28		LSU	7	21
O5		Tennessee	0	52
O19		at SMU	24	32
O26		Texas	14	38
N2		Texas Tech	15	38
N9		at Arkansas	21	46
N16		at Texas A&M	14	24
N23		TCU	14	24
N30		at Baylor	7	16

1969 3-7-0 (2-5-0)

S20	●	VMI	55	0
S27		LSU	0	42
O4		at California	21	31
O18		SMU	14	34
O25		at Texas	0	31
N1		at Texas Tech	14	24
N8		Arkansas	6	30
N15	●	Texas A&M	7	6
N22		at TCU	17	21
N29	●	Baylor	34	6

1970 5-5-0 (3-4-0)

S19	●	VMI	42	0
S26		at LSU	0	24
O3	●	California	28	0
O17		at SMU	0	10
O24		Texas	21	45
O31		Texas Tech	0	3
N7		at Arkansas	14	38
N14	●	at Texas A&M	18	17
N21	●	TCU	17	15
N28	●	at Baylor	28	23

BILL PETERSON
1971 (.318) 3-7-1

1971 3-7-1 (2-4-1)

S11		Houston	21	23
S18		Southern Cal	0	24
S25	●	Tulane	14	11
O2		at LSU	3	38
O16		SMU	10	16
O23		at Texas	10	39
O30	●	at Texas Tech	9	7
N6	=	Arkansas	24	24
N13		Texas A&M	13	18
N20		at TCU	19	20
N27	●	Baylor	23	0

AL CONOVER
1972-75 (.341) 14-28-2

1972 5-5-1 (3-4-0)

S9	●	Houston	14	13
S23	●	Clemson	29	10
S30	=	at Georgia Tech	36	36
O7		LSU	6	12
O21		at SMU	14	29
O28		Texas	9	45
N4		Texas Tech	6	10
N11	●	Arkansas LR	23	20
N18	●	at Texas A&M	20	14
N25	●	TCU	25	21
D2		at Baylor	14	28

1973 5-6-0 (4-3-0)

S15		at Houston	6	24
S22	●	Montana	21	10
S29		at LSU	9	24
O13		Notre Dame	0	28
O20		SMU	16	27
O27		at Texas	13	55
N3		at Texas Tech	6	19
N10	●	Arkansas	17	7
N17	●	Texas A&M	24	20
N24	●	at TCU	14	9
D1	●	Baylor	27	0

1974 2-8-1 (2-5-0)

S14		Houston	0	21
S21		Cincinnati	21	28
S28	=	LSU	10	10
O12		at Notre Dame	3	10
O19		at SMU	14	19
O26		Texas	6	27
N2	●	Texas Tech	21	7
N9		at Arkansas	6	25
N16		at Texas A&M	7	37
N23	●	TCU	26	14
N30		at Baylor	3	24

1975 2-9-0 (1-6-0)

S13	●	at Houston	24	7
S20		Vanderbilt	6	9
S27		LSU Shre	13	16
O11		Mississippi State	14	28
O18	●	SMU	28	17
O25		at Texas	9	41
N1		at Texas Tech	24	28
N8		Arkansas	16	20
N15		Texas A&M	14	33
N22		at TCU	21	28
N29		Baylor	7	25

HOMER RICE
1976-77 (.182) 4-18

1976 3-8-0 (2-6-0)

S18	●	Utah	43	22
S25		at LSU	0	31
O2		Texas	15	42
O9	●	at TCU	26	23
O16		Texas Tech	13	37
O23		at Texas A&M	34	57
O30		at Arkansas	16	41
N6	●	SMU	41	34
N13		Baylor	6	38
N20		at Florida	22	50
N27		Houston	20	42

1977 1-10-0 (0-8-0)

S10	●	Idaho	31	10
S17		Florida	3	48
S24		at LSU	0	77
O1		at Texas	15	72
O8		TCU	15	35
O15		at Texas Tech	7	42
O22		Texas A&M	14	28
O29		Arkansas	7	30
N5		at SMU	24	41
N12		at Baylor	14	24
N26		Houston	21	51

RAY ALBORN
1978-83 (.197) 13-53

1978 2-9-0 (2-6-0)

S9		Iowa State	19	23
S16		Texas	0	34
S23		at Oklahoma	7	66
S30		LSU	7	37
O14	●	at TCU	21	14
O21		Texas Tech	28	42
O28		at Texas A&M	21	38
N4		at Arkansas	7	37
N11		SMU	0	58
N18	●	Baylor	24	10
D2		at Houston	25	49

1979 1-10-0 (0-8-0)

S8		at SMU	17	35
S15	●	Tulane	21	17
S22		at LSU	3	47
S29		Oklahoma	21	63
O6		at Texas	9	26
O13		TCU	7	17
O20		at Texas Tech	7	30
O27		Texas A&M	15	41
N3		Arkansas	7	34
N17		at Baylor	14	45
D1		Houston	0	63

1980 5-6-0 (4-4-0)

S13		at Clemson	3	19
S20		at Tulane	14	35
S27	●	LSU	17	7
O4		Texas	28	41
O11	●	at TCU	28	24
O18		Texas Tech	3	10
O25	●	at Texas A&M	10	6
N1	●	Arkansas LR	17	16
N8		SMU	14	34
N15		Baylor	6	16
N29	●	at Houston	35	7

1981 4-7-0 (3-5-0)

S12		at Texas	3	31
S19		at Missouri	10	42
S26		at LSU	14	28
O3	●	Tulane	20	16
O10	●	TCU	41	28
O17	●	at Texas Tech	30	23
O24		Texas A&M	26	51
O31		Arkansas	7	41
N7		at SMU	12	33
N14	●	at Baylor	17	14
N28		Houston	3	40

1982 0-11-0 (0-8-0)

S11		La. Lafayette	14	21
S18		at Tulane	6	30
S25		at LSU	13	52
O2		Texas	7	34
O9		at TCU	16	24
O16		Texas Tech	21	23
O23		at Texas A&M	7	49
O30		at Arkansas	6	24
N6		SMU	14	41
N13		Baylor	13	35
N27		at Houston	21	28

1983 1-10-0 (0-8-0)

S1		Houston	14	45
S10		Minnesota	17	21
S17		LSU	10	24
S24	●	La. Lafayette	22	21
O1		at Texas	6	42
O8		TCU	3	34
O15		at Texas Tech	3	14
O22		Texas A&M	10	29
O29		Arkansas LR	0	35
N5		at SMU	6	20
N12		at Baylor	14	48

WATSON BROWN
1984-85 (.182) 4-18

1984 1-10-0 (0-8-0)

S8		at Minnesota	24	31
S22	●	Lamar	36	19
S29		at Miami, Fla.	3	38
O6		Texas	13	38
O13		at TCU	24	45
O20		Texas Tech	10	30
O27		at Texas A&M	14	38
N3		Arkansas LR	6	28
N10		SMU	17	31
N17		Baylor	40	46
D1		at Houston	26	38

1985 3-8-0 (2-6-0)

S14		Miami, Fla.	20	48
S21		at Air Force	17	59
S28	●	Lamar	29	28
O5		at Texas	16	44
O12	●	TCU	34	27
O19	●	at Texas Tech	29	27
O26		Texas A&M	28	43
N2		Arkansas	15	30
N9		at SMU	15	40
N16		at Baylor	10	34
N30		Houston	20	24

JERRY BERNDT
1986-88 (.182) 6-27

1986 4-7-0 (2-6-0)

S6	●	Lamar	28	14
S13		SMU	3	45
S20		SW. Texas St.	6	31
O4		Texas	14	17
O11	●	at TCU	37	31
O18		Texas Tech	21	49
O25		at Texas A&M	10	45
N1		at Arkansas	14	45
N15		Baylor	17	23
N22	●	Air Force	21	17
N29	●	at Houston	14	13

1987 2-9-0 (0-7-0)

S5	●	Lamar	34	30
S12		at Indiana	13	35
S19		at LSU	16	49
S26	●	SW. Texas St.	38	28
O3		at Texas	26	45
O10		TCU	16	30
O17		at Texas Tech	7	59
O24		Texas A&M	21	34
O31		Arkansas	14	38
N14		at Baylor	31	34
N28		Houston	21	45

1988 0-11-0 (0-7-0)

S10		Indiana	14	41
S24		at La. Lafayette	16	41
O1		Texas	13	20
O8		at TCU	10	21
O15		Texas Tech	36	38
O22		at Texas A&M	10	24
O29		Arkansas LR	14	21
N5		at Notre Dame	11	54
N12		Baylor	10	20
N19		North Texas	17	33
N26		at Houston	14	45

FRED GOLDSMITH
1989-93 (.427) 23-31-1

1989 2-8-1 (2-6-0)

S2	●	at SMU	35	6
S9		at Tulane	19	20
S23		La. Lafayette	3	18
S30	=	at Wake Forest	17	17
O7		at Texas	30	31
O14		TCU	16	30
O21		at Texas Tech	25	41
O28		Texas A&M	7	45
N4		Arkansas	17	38
N18	●	at Baylor	6	3
D2		Houston	0	64

1990 5-6-0 (3-5-0)

S1	●	Wake Forest	33	17
S8		Tulane	10	21
S22	●	Northwestern	31	14
S29		at Houston	22	24
O6		Texas	10	26
O13		at TCU	28	38
O20	●	Texas Tech	42	21
O27		at Texas A&M	15	41
N3	●	Arkansas LR	19	11
N10	●	SMU	30	28
N17		Baylor	16	17

1991 4-7-0 (2-6-0)

S14	●	at Northwestern	36	7
S21	●	at Tulane	28	19
S28		Iowa State	27	28
O5		at Texas	7	28
O12	●	at Baylor	20	17
O19		TCU	28	39
O26		at Texas Tech	20	40
N2		Texas A&M	21	38
N9	●	at SMU	31	10
N16		Houston	21	41
N23		Arkansas LR	0	20

1992 6-5-0 (4-3-0)

S5		at Air Force	21	30
S19		at Duke	12	17
S26	●	Sam Houston St.	45	14
O3		Texas	21	23
O10	●	SMU	28	13
O17		at Texas A&M	9	35
O24	●	at TCU	29	12
N7	●	Texas Tech	34	3
N14	●	Baylor	34	31
N21	●	Navy	27	22
N28		at Houston	34	61

1993 6-5-0 (3-4-0)

S4		at Ohio State	7	34
S11	●	Tulane	34	0
S18	●	Sam Houston St.	14	13
S25	●	Iowa State	49	21
O2		at Texas	38	55
O9	●	TCU	34	19
O16		at Texas Tech	16	45
O23		Texas A&M	10	38
N6	●	at SMU	31	24
N13		at Baylor	14	38
N26	●	Houston	37	7

THE SCHOOLS

KEN HATFIELD
1994-Present (.443) 54-68-1

1994
5-6-0 (4-3-0)

S10		Tulane	13	15
S17		at Kansas State	18	27
S24	●	at Iowa State	28	18
O8	●	Texas Tech	24	21
O16	●	Texas	19	17
O22		at Texas A&M	0	7
O29		at TCU	25	27
N5	●	SMU	17	10
N12		Baylor	14	19
N19		at Navy	17	29
N26	●	at Houston	31	13

1995
2-8-1 (1-6-0)

S2	●	Nevada-Las Vegas	38	0
S16		Tulane	15	17
S23		at LSU	7	52
S30	=	at Army	21	21
O7		at Texas	13	37
O14		TCU	28	33
O21		at Texas Tech	26	31
O28	●	at SMU	34	24
N9		Texas A&M	10	17
N18		at Baylor	6	34
D2		Houston	17	18

1996-2004
WAC

1996
7-4 (6-2)

S7		at Ohio State	7	70
S14	●	at Tulane	21	14
S21		Kansas State	7	34
S28		at Air Force	17	45
O5	●	New Mexico	38	21
O19	●	SMU	35	17
O26	●	at Texas-El Paso	48	21
N2	●	Utah	51	10
N9		at Brigham Young	0	49
N16	●	at TCU	30	17
N23	●	Tulsa	42	14

1997
7-4 (5-3)

S6		Air Force	12	41
S13	●	at Tulane	30	24
S20	●	at Northwestern	40	34
S27		Texas	31	38
O4	●	at Tulsa	42	24
O11	●	Brigham Young	27	14
O18	●	at New Mexico	35	23
N1		at SMU	6	24
N8	●	TCU	38	19
N15		at Utah	14	31
N22	●	Texas-El Paso	31	13

1998
5-6 (5-3)

S5	●	SMU	23	17
S12		at Purdue	19	21
S19		Northwestern	14	23
S26		at Texas	21	59
O10		at San Jose State	17	20
O17	●	Tulsa	14	10
O24		at Wyoming	24	34
O31	●	Colorado State	35	23
N7	●	at TCU	14	12
N14	●	Nevada-Las Vegas	38	16
N21		at Air Force	16	22

1999
5-6 (4-3)

S4		at Houston	3	28
S11		at Michigan	3	37
S18		at Texas	13	18
S25	●	Navy	20	17
O2	●	at Tulsa	20	10
O9	●	at Hawaii	38	19
O16	●	San Jose State	49	7
O23	●	TCU	42	21
O30		at SMU	2	27
N6		at Fresno State	18	47
N13		Texas-El Paso	29	30

2000
3-8 (2-6)

S2	●	Houston	30	27
S9		at Michigan	7	38
S16		Tulsa	16	23
S23		at Oklahoma	14	42
S30		at San Jose State	16	29
O5		Fresno State	24	27
O21	●	Hawaii	38	13
O28		at TCU	0	37
N4	●	SMU	43	14
N11		at Texas-El Paso	21	38
N18		Nevada	28	34

2001
8-4 (5-3)

S1	●	at Houston	21	14
S8	●	Duke	15	13
S20		at Nebraska	3	48
S29	●	at Hawaii	27	24
O6	●	Boise State	45	14
O13	●	at Navy	21	13
O20	●	Nevada	33	30
O27		at Louisiana Tech	38	41
N3		at Fresno State	24	52
N10	●	Tulsa	59	32
N17	●	Texas-El Paso	27	17
N24		at SMU	20	37

2002
4-7 (3-5)

A31		Houston	10	24
S7		at Michigan State	10	27
S21		at Nevada	21	31
S28		Fresno State	28	31
O5	●	Louisiana Tech	37	20
O12	●	at Navy	17	10
O19		at Texas-El Paso	35	38
O26	●	SMU	27	15
N2	●	at Tulsa	33	18
N9		at Boise State	7	49
N16		Hawaii	28	33

2003
5-7 (5-3)

A30		at Houston	14	48
S13		at Duke	24	27
S20		Texas	7	48
S27		at Hawaii	21	41
O4	●	San Jose State	28	24
O18		Navy	6	38
O25		at Fresno State	28	31
N1	●	Nevada	52	42
N8		Tulsa	28	31
N15	●	at SMU	41	20
N22	●	Texas-El Paso	45	14
N29	●	at Louisiana Tech	49	14

2004
3-8 (2-6)

S5	●	Houston	10	7
S18	●	Hawaii	41	29
S25		at Texas	13	35
O2		at San Jose State	63	70
O9	●	SMU	44	10
O16		at Nevada	10	35
O23		at Navy	13	14
O30		at Tulsa	22	39
N6		Fresno State	21	52
N13		at Texas-El Paso	28	35
N29		Louisiana Tech	14	51

RUTGERS

BY MIKE VACCARO

THERE HAVE BEEN SO MANY JOKES over the years. So many long seasons that seemed to stretch into infinity. New Jersey has been a fertile recruiting ground for years and years, and yet, across most of those years, the indigenous talent has seen fit to bypass the state university—named in honor of Colonel Henry Rutgers, a Revolutionary War veteran and trustee of the formerly named Queen's College—to play instead for … well, everyone else.

Penn State has made a living off Jersey kids for years. Notre Dame, too. Two-thirds of Nebraska's Triplets offense in 1983—All-Americas Mike Rozier and Irving Fryar—were from New Jersey. Year after year, you heard the familiar cry: why don't Jersey kids stay in Jersey? And the familiar rationale: New Jersey isn't a football state, and Rutgers has absolutely no football tradition. And that's pretty ironic, because on Nov. 6, 1869, at 3 o'clock in the afternoon, the first intercollegiate football game was contested on a plot of land in New Brunswick, N.J., featuring two New Jersey universities and dozens of New Jersey's sons. William J. Leggett, later a high-ranking clergyman in the Dutch Reformed Church, captained Rutgers. William Gunmere, later chief justice of the New Jersey Supreme Court, helmed the visitors from Princeton University, who'd trekked 20 miles to play the game. Then, as now, it wasn't easy to win on the road. Final score: Rutgers 6, Princeton 4.

TRADITION Rutgers Stadium as it now stands is a relatively new structure, dedicated Sept. 3, 1994, and the teams that have played there since have been something less than championship quality. Still, the Scarlet Knights take their game-day routine seriously. When the team arrives at the stadium, it proceeds directly off the bus and begins the Scarlet Walk on the way to the Hale Center, the building adjoining the stadium containing the football offices, locker rooms, weight rooms and training facilities. As part of the Scarlet Walk, each member of the team touches the statue that memorializes Rutgers as the "Birthplace of College Football."

BEST PLAYER Paul Robeson lived one of the great American lives of the 20th century. As an actor, law clerk and activist, Robeson's deep voice became an eloquent symbol of African-American struggles and progress. His rich basso singing voice gave eternal life to his signature song, "Ol' Man River," and he starred on Broadway in *The Emperor Jones*, *Othello* and *Showboat*. But before any of that, from 1915 through 1918, he established himself as the greatest football

---

PROFILE

Rutgers University
New Brunswick, N.J.
Founded: 1766
Enrollment: 26,813
Colors: Scarlet, White and Black
Nickname: Scarlet Knights
Stadium: Rutgers Stadium
   Opened in 1938
   FieldTurf; 41,500 capacity
First football game: 1869
All-time record: 562–573–43 (.495)
Bowl record: 0–1
Website: www.scarletknights.com

THE BEST OF TIMES

From 1975 to 1979, Frank Burns led the Scarlet Knights to their lone period of prosperity, piling up a 45–11 (.804) record that included a perfect 11–0 mark in 1976.

THE WORST OF TIMES

Rutgers keeps rewriting that dubious distinction, but it is clear the program is in the midst of its greatest nadir. From 1991 to 2004, the Knights went 18–75–1 in the Big East. Entering 2005, they were 7–56 in their last 63 conference games.

CONFERENCE

Rutgers joined the Big East when it was formed in 1991, ending 30 years as a major independent. From 1946 to 1951, Rutgers was a member of the Middle Three Conference, and from 1958 to 1961, the Knights played in the Middle Atlantic States Collegiate Athletic Conference.

DISTINGUISHED ALUMNI

Jim Valvano; David Stern; Janet Evanovich, author; Calista Flockhart, actress; Louis Freeh, director of the FBI; James Gandolfini, actor; Paul Robeson, actor/social activist; Michael Shaara, author; Sonny Werblin, sports impresario

FIGHT SONG

R-U RAH, RAH
R-U, Rah, Rah
R-U, Rah, Rah
Hoo-Raa, Hoo-Raa
Rutgers Rah
Up-Stream Red Team
Red Team Up-Stream
Rah, Rah
Rutgers Rah

Rutgers has played football longer than all but one college, yet it has never left New Jersey to compete in the postseason.

player in Rutgers history. Robeson's father had escaped slavery in North Carolina, and Robeson himself was only the third black man given an academic scholarship to attend Rutgers. By the time he graduated Phi Beta Kappa he had twice been named All-America (the first Rutgers player so honored), and when Walter Camp named Robeson to his team in 1918, he called Robeson "the greatest end to ever trod the gridiron." During his playing days, the Scarlet Knights compiled a record of 22–6–3 and outscored opponents 944-191, and he earned 12 varsity letters—four in football, three each in basketball and baseball and two in track and field.

BEST COACH Frank Burns has the most wins in Rutgers history, compiling a 78–43–1 record from 1973 through 1983. Burns was the engineer of the 1976 team that went 11–0 and ended up with a No. 17 national ranking in the final Associated Press poll, the team's loftiest mark ever. Two years later, his 9–3 Scarlet Knights earned the only bowl bid in school history, gaining a berth in the first-ever Garden State Bowl, where Rutgers lost 34-18 to Arizona State before 33,402 fans at Giants Stadium.

"Flinging Frank" had also been an honorable mention All-America quarterback for Rutgers in the 1940s, and in 1949 he was named MVP of the College All-Star Game by registering 17 tackles against the New York Giants. Among his finest hours as a coach was guiding the Knights to a 13-7 win at Tennessee in 1979, and a near-miss 17-13 loss to Alabama at Giants Stadium in 1980.

BEST TEAM For a program that has earned only one bowl bid in more than 130 years, it doesn't take long to compile a list of its most glorious teams. At the top stands the 1976 team, which stormed to an 11–0 record, shutting out four opponents, including a 34-0 stomping of Louisville. The team was spearheaded by defensive end Nate Toran and led the nation in total defense, permitting just 179.2 yards per game, and was also tops against the run (83.9 yards per game). The Scarlet Knights were tied with Michigan in points allowed, yielding just 7.4 per game; only Cornell, Lehigh and Colgate came within a touchdown of Rutgers. Still, due to their perceived "soft" schedule, the Knights were left out of the bowl picture that year, and thanks to Pittsburgh winning the national title, Rutgers couldn't even cop a Lambert Trophy, given to the best team in the East.

RECORDS

RUSHING YARDS
	GAME
232	Terrell Willis vs. Temple, Nov. 5, 1994 (35 att.)

	SEASON
1,353	JJ Jennings, 1973 (303 att.)

	CAREER
3,114	Terrell Willis, 1993-95 (588 att.)

PASSING YARDS
	GAME
436	Scott Erney vs. Vanderbilt, Sept. 17, 1988 (35 of 55)

	SEASON
3,154	Ryan Hart, 2004 (295 of 453)

	CAREER
7,188	Scott Erney, 1986-89 (614 of 1,128)

RECEIVING YARDS
	GAME
237	Jack Emmer vs. Holy Cross, Nov. 12, 1966 (13 rec.)

	SEASON
1,056	Tres Moses, 2004 (81 rec.)

	CAREER
2,268	Andrew Baker, 1981-84 (127 rec.)

POINTS
	GAME
48	Howard Talman vs. Rensselaer, Oct. 9, 1915 (6 TDs, 12 PATs)

	SEASON
135	Howard Talman, 1915

	CAREER
261	Kennan Starzell, 1976-79 (46 FGs, 123 PATs)

CONSENSUS ALL-AMERICANS

1917-18	Paul Robeson, E
1961	Alex Kroll, C
1995	Marco Battaglia, TE

BIGGEST GAME Of all the indignities that a string of Rutgers coaches has suffered through the years, the most consistently aggravating has been watching a parade of blue-chip talent leave the state. Few programs have benefited more from this annual exodus than Penn State, and in a game against the Scarlet Knights on Sept. 24, 1988, the Nittany Lions used two quarterbacks, Tom Bill and Tony Sacca, who had both been top Jersey schoolboys and spurned their home school. Penn State was ranked 15th in the country, but in front of 85,531 of its fans, Rutgers burst out to a 21-10 lead thanks to a pair of touchdown runs by running back Mike Botti. But Sacca led the Nittany Lions back and drove Penn State to first and goal at the Rutgers 3-yard line with 53 seconds to play. Rutgers caught a break when PSU tight end Dave Jakob, all alone in the end zone, couldn't gather in a Sacca pass on third down. Then, on fourth down, cornerback Darrin Czellecz tightly covered intended receiver Michael Timpson, and one last Sacca pass fell incomplete. Rutgers had an unfathomable 21-16 win, its first over Penn State in 13 games since 1918. "The first thing that went through my mind was that I was looking for penalty flags," safety Derek Baker said afterward. "Then I looked at the scoreboard to make sure we were still leading. Then I fell to the ground and starting kissing everyone."

BIGGEST UPSET Tennessee was 4–2, ranked 17th in the country, a 21-point favorite, in front of 84,265 at Neyland Stadium, and hadn't lost to a team from the Northeast in 39 years. The morning of Nov. 3, 1979, a local newspaper columnist, when surmising what exactly "Rutgers" were, had written, "Some people seem to think they are something like mathematics or physics. Others say that they always come in groups, and that it is impossible to find just one Rutger by itself. One housewife told me she bought a pound of them at the supermarket last week for 59 cents … This one man who has been up East told me that he doesn't know exactly what Rutgers are, but he's pretty sure that they are quite a bit like Yonkers. Now, if I just knew what Yonkers were …"

Final score: Rutgers 13, Tennessee 7. "Well," Rutgers lineman Kevin Kurdyla said afterward, "I guess they know what a Rutgers is. They know we come higher than 59 cents a pound."

HEARTBREAKER Rutgers has never beaten a team ranked in the Associated Press poll at home. Maybe the closest call of all came on Oct. 11, 1980, at Giants Stadium, when the Scarlet Knights hosted top-ranked Alabama. Trailing by four points with less than eight minutes to go, Rutgers had a first down at the Crimson Tide 33, but the threat was stymied when quarterback Ed McMichael was sacked for a 13-yard loss. After Bama's 17-13 victory, Crimson Tide coach Bear Bryant gave perhaps the most glowing compliment in Rutgers football history: "There's a big difference between winning and beating someone," Bryant said. "We won. But we didn't beat them. We were as lucky as a three-legged dog."

NICKNAME Dating to the school's origin as Queen's College, athletes were commonly known as Queensmen. Beginning in 1925, the Rutgers mascot was a chanticleer, a fighting bird. In the 1950s, in the hope of spurring both Rutgers' as yet-untapped athletic potential and a collegial fighting spirit, a campus-wide vote changed the nickname to Knights, which evolved into Scarlet Knights.

MASCOT Since 1955, the Scarlet Knight has ridden atop a spirited white charger and brandished a sword. During one memorable game against Army in 1994, the knight was responsible for a 15-yard unsportsmanlike penalty for rushing the field on horseback after a Rutgers touchdown.

UNIFORMS Rutgers pioneered the use of color in college football uniforms, going all the way back to 1869 when the student newspaper suggested scarlet as the team color, because scarlet ribbons were easily obtainable. In the first college football game played, against Princeton, Rutgers donned scarlet turbans and kerchiefs as a manner of identification. The color scheme has changed little in more than a century, although the helmet design has, mirroring the program's own instability. When coach Greg Schiano commissioned a new design in 2001—white capital R against a scarlet background—it was no less than the eighth different helmet design since 1965.

STADIUM When Rutgers at last made its official commitment to big-time football by joining the Big East in 1991, one of the things school officials understood was the need for a credible football stadium, preferably on-campus. Past Rutgers teams had called Giants Stadium in East Rutherford home, but that venue sits nearly an hour from campus and in its history of hosting college football, only Notre Dame has ever been able to regularly fill its 76,000 seats. But the on-campus stadium that Rutgers had used since 1938 needed serious renovations. Governor Jim Florio agreed, and he approved a construction and renovation project in January 1992. Fourteen months later ground was broken,

with Florio stating: "There is no doubt that what is good for Rutgers is good for New Jersey." The $418 million athletic facilities project expanded the stadium's capacity to 41,500, added light towers and generally upgraded the entire spectra of Rutgers football—just in time for the 125th anniversary of the Rutgers-Princeton game. Rutgers christened the stadium in fine fashion, defeating Kent State 28-6.

RIVAL Once Rutgers joined the Big East, it left behind its longest and, for a time, most detested rival. Princeton was a natural foe for Rutgers, since the campuses were located less than 20 miles apart, and because, for the first half of the century, Rutgers could muster only a 17–53–1 record before the series was discontinued after 1980. But Rutgers won the two most symbolic games in the series, including, of course, the first college football game ever played. That game bore little resemblance to modern football, since teams were 25 men to a side and the game lasted more than five hours. The game started as a grudge match, as the previous spring Princeton had defeated Rutgers in baseball by a most ungentlemanly score of 40-2. Rutgers seethed, plotted revenge and got it the following fall on the gridiron. Exactly 100 years later, Rutgers repeated the trick, blanking the Tigers 29-0 during the centennial celebration.

LORE Rutgers will surely know when it has truly arrived as a football team worth discussing when someone tries to steal—or simply ring—The Bell. It has hung in an old cupola on campus since 1826—a gift from Colonel Henry Rutgers himself—and is rung only on special occasions, including those of prized athletic success. Most recently, it was struck by the women's basketball team when it reached the 2000 Final Four, and by the 1990 men's soccer team, which reached the finals of the NCAA tournament.

QUIRK Rutgers has played football longer than all but one college program in the country, yet it has never left New Jersey to compete in a postseason game. The only bowl the Scarlet Knights were ever invited to was the short-lived Garden State Bowl. On Dec. 16, 1978, Arizona State topped Rutgers 34-18 at Giants Stadium.

QUOTE "They ran the first couple of plays right at me. After the third one, I was stretched out on the ground with my hand extended palm up. One of the players walked by me and deliberately stepped on it. I thought all the bones were broken. They weren't. But a couple of fingernails came off. Later, after all that, the coach had a simple message: 'Hey, Robey, you just made the varsity.'" —Paul Robeson, on gaining acceptance from his teammates in 1915

RUTGERS ALL-TIME SCORES

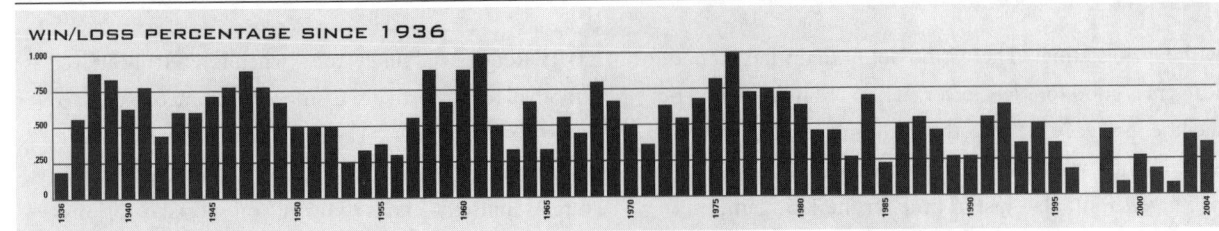

WIN/LOSS PERCENTAGE SINCE 1936

NO HEAD COACH

1869   1-1-0
N6	●	Princeton	6	4
N13		at Princeton	0	8

1870   1-1-0
N5	●	Columbia	6	3
N12		at Princeton	2	6

1871
NO FOOTBALL

1872   1-1-1
N2	=	at Columbia	0	0
N9	●	Columbia	7	5
N16		at Princeton	1	4

1873   1-2-0
O25		at Yale	1	3
N1	●	Columbia	5	4
N8		at Columbia	3	4

1874   2-2-0
O24	●	Columbia	6	1
N1		Stevens	6	0
N14		at Columbia	1	4
N18		at Princeton	0	6

1875   1-1-1
O24		Stevens	6	0
N2	=	Columbia	1	1
N6		at Yale	1	4

1876   1-0-0
N1	●	Stevens	3	2

1877   0-3-0
O27		at Stevens	1	2
N6		at Columbia	0	6
N14		Stevens	0	1

1878   1-2-1
O29	=	Stevens	0	0
N2		at Princeton	0	5
N9		at Stevens	0	1
D7	●	CCNY	6	0

1879   1-2-3
N11	●	at Stevens	1	0
N15		at Yale	0	5
N20	=	at Columbia	0	0
N23		Stevens	3	3
N25		Stevens	1	3
D13	=	at Stevens	0	0

1880   2-2-0
O9	●	Stevens	5	1
O16	●	at Stevens	1	0
N2		at Princeton	0	8
N13		at Columbia	0	3

1881   2-4-1
O15		at Princeton	0	3
N3		at Stevens	0	1
N8	=	Columbia	0	0
N10		Princeton	0	1
N17	●	CCNY	3	0
N19	●	at Pennsylvania	2	1
N23		at Columbia	0	1

1882   6-4-0
O14		at Princeton	0	5
O20	●	CCNY	3	0
O21		at Yale	0	9
O28		Yale	0	5
N4	●	at Pennsylvania	3	1
N7	●	Lafayette	3	0
N9	●	Columbia	2	1
N14		Princeton	0	3
N18	●	Pennsylvania	1	0
N24		at Stevens	2	0

1883   1-6-0
O17		Princeton	0	20
O20		at Wesleyan	0	37
O27		Princeton	0	61
O31	●	CCNY	54	2
N6		Yale *BKLN*	0	92
N10		at Lafayette	0	25
N17		at Pennsylvania	0	18

1884   3-4-0
O10		Princeton	5	23
O15	●	Columbia	35	5
O18		at Princeton	0	35
O22		Yale	10	76
N1	●	Lehigh	61	0
N8	●	Lafayette	26	0
N15		Wesleyan	0	31

1885   0-1-0
N4		at Lehigh	5	10

1886   1-3-0
O16		at Lafayette	2	28
N6	●	Vineland	58	0
N10		at Pennsylvania	0	65
N17		Lafayette	10	26

1887   2-6-0
O8	●	Stevens	26	0
O12		Princeton	0	30
O15	●	at Lafayette	0	20
O19	=	at Stevens	5	2
O29		at Williams	6	12
N2		Pennsylvania	10	13
N5		at Yale	0	74
N12		Lafayette	0	36

1888   1-6-1
O6		at Yale	0	65
O20		Lafayette	0	4
O24		at Princeton	0	80
O27		Princeton	0	82
N1	●	Stevens	18	18
N2		Williams	0	48
N5	●	at Ridgefield AC	18	6
N7		at Lehigh	0	30

1889   1-4-0
O12		Pennsylvania	0	4
O16		Lafayette	0	16
O19		at Wesleyan	4	58
N1	●	Ridgefield AC	18	0
N16		at Pennsylvania	0	14

1890   5-5-1
O4		at Pennsylvania	4	16
O8		at Princeton	0	27
O18	●	at New York AC	30	0
O25	●	at Orange AC	6	4
N1	●	Crescent AC	68	0
N3		Lehigh	2	4
N8		Yale	0	70
N14	●	NYU	62	0
N15	=	at Columbia	6	6
N22	●	Manhattan AC	32	0
D13		at Pennsylvania	10	13

WILLIAM A. REYNOLDS
1891 (.571)   8-6

1891   8-6-0
O3		at Princeton	0	12
O10		at Orange AC	6	10
O13	●	at Schuylkill Navy	24	0
O17		at Lehigh	0	22
O21		at Pennsylvania	6	32
O24		Stevens	12	10
O28		Columbia	44	0
O31		at Navy	12	20	*
N2	●	at Columbia AC	4	0
N3		at New York AC	12	21
N7	●	NYU	70	4
N14	●	at Army	27	6
N18	●	N.Y. Law	14	0
N24	●	Manhattan AC	34	0

NO HEAD COACH

1892   3-5-1
O1		at Princeton	0	30
O15		at Orange AC	10	22
O19		at Lafayette	16	8
O22	●	New York AC	18	0
O26	●	at Manhattan AC	30	0
O29		Lafayette	10	24
N2		at Stevens	6	22
N5		at Navy	12	48
N7	=	at Columbia AC	6	6

1893   0-4-0
O14		at New York AC	0	14
O21		Stevens	8	39
O28		at Orange AC	0	34
N4		Lafayette	0	1	*f*

1894   4-6-0
S29		at Lehigh	0	24
O6	●	Lafayette	12	10
O10		at Princeton	0	48
O17		at Stevens	20	0
O20	●	at New Jersey AC	8	0
O27		at Crescent AC	4	20
N1	●	North Carolina	5	0
N3		at Virginia	4	20
N24		at Columbia AC	0	20
D1		at Franklin & Marshall	4	68

H.W. AMBRUSTER
1895 (.429)   3-4

1895   3-4-0
S28		Lehigh	0	25
N5		at Princeton	0	22
N19	●	Roseville AC	38	4
N23	●	Swarthmore	26	12
N26	●	NYU	16	0
N30		at Lafayette	0	52
N6		at Elizabeth AC	6	14

JOHN C.B. PENDLETON
1896-97 (.400)   8-12

1896   6-6-0
O3		at Princeton	0	44
O7	●	Ursinus	20	0
O10		at Elizabeth AC	0	28
O14		at Lehigh	0	44
O17	●	Haverford	6	2
O21	●	Stevens	10	0
O24	●	at Swarthmore	16	10
O31		at Navy	6	40
N3		at Irvington AC	0	20
N7		at Union	0	10
N11	●	at Stevens	12	0
N14	●	Newark AC	4	0

1897   2-6-0
O2	●	Newark FC	12	6
O6		at Princeton	0	53
O10		Swarthmore	6	8
O27		at Haverford	0	26
O30		at Union	0	10
N3		Stevens	0	14
N10		Navy	0	1	*f*
N17	●	at Stevens	16	0

WILLIAM V.B. VAN DYCK, JR.
1898-99 (.184)   3-15-1

1898   1-6-1
S28		at Lehigh	0	12
O8		at Swarthmore	0	6
O12		at Stevens	0	11
O15	●	at NYU	11	5
O22	=	Haverford	0	0
O29		at Union	0	17
N5		Stevens	0	5
N12		at Wesleyan	0	59

1899   2-9-0
S30		Columbia	0	26
O7		Lehigh	0	10
O14		at Lafayette	0	57
O21		at Haverford	0	36
O25		at Swarthmore	0	34
O28		Ursinus	6	53
N4	●	at Stevens	39	0
N11		NYU	5	6
N22	●	CCNY	59	0
N29		Stevens	5	12
D2		Knickerbocker AC	0	11

MICHAEL F. DALY
1900 (.500)   4-4

1900   4-4-0
S26		CCNY	5	0
O3		Columbia	0	11
O13	●	Haverford	11	0
O20		at Lehigh	0	21
O27	●	Ursinus	17	0
N7		at Army	0	23
N17	●	at NYU	11	0
N24		Union	6	11

ARTHUR P. ROBINSON
1901 (.000)   0-7

1901   0-7-0
O2		Columbia	0	27
O5		Manhattan	0	10
O12		at Ursinus	0	30
O19		at Swarthmore	0	27
O26		NYU	0	16
N2		Delaware	5	6
N9		at Haverford	0	17

HARRY W. VAN HOVENBERG
1902 (.300)   3-7

1902   3-7-0
S28		at Manhattan	0	6
O4		Columbia	0	43
O12		at Lehigh	0	34
O19		Ursinus	0	16
O22		Swarthmore	6	12
O25		at Haverford	5	43
N1	●	at Stevens	10	0
N8		at NYU	0	22
N15	●	Delaware	15	12
N22	●	Stevens	6	0

OLIVER D. MANN
1903 (.500) 4-4-1

1903 — 4-4-1

S26		at Fordham	0	15
O3		at Delaware	0	5
O10	●	Manhattan	8	6
O17		at Ursinus	0	40
O24		Haverford	6	18
O31	●	Stevens	36	6
N7	●	at Stevens	26	5
N14	●	NYU	18	5
N24	=	Franklin & Marshall	0	0

A.E. HITCHENS
1904 (.222) 1-6-2

1904 — 1-6-2

O1	●	at Stevens	4	0
O8		at Haverford	0	40
O15		Ursinus	0	37
O22		at Wesleyan	0	39
O29		at Union	0	35
N5	=	Delaware	6	6
N8		at NYU	6	35
N12		Maryland U.	0	10
N19	=	Stevens	0	0

OLIVER D. MANN
1905 (.333) 3-6

1905 — 3-6-0

O3	●	Stevens	6	0
O7		at Trinity	0	11
O10		at Union	0	11
O17		Seton Hall	10	22
O24	●	at Delaware	10	0
N10		at NYU	7	10
N14	●	at Stevens	5	0
N21		at Haverford	0	28
N28		at Fordham	6	17

F.H. GORTON
1906-07 (.528) 8-7-3

1906 — 5-2-2

S28	●	at Fordham	6	0
O6	=	at Stevens	0	0
O13		at Villanova	0	17
O20	=	at Haverford	0	0
O27		Delaware	0	4
N6	●	at NYU	15	0
N10	●	CCNY	55	0
N17	●	Stevens	18	4
N24	●	Ursinus	29	5

1907 — 3-5-1

S28	=	Fordham	5	5
O5		at Swarthmore	5	29
O12		Lehigh	6	16
O19	●	at Union	12	5
O26	●	at Delaware	39	0
N5		at NYU	0	11
N9		Haverford	5	6
N16		at Jefferson MS	0	27
N23	●	Stevens	4	0

JOSEPH SMITH
1908 (.389) 3-5-1

1908 — 3-5-1

O3		at Navy	0	18
O10		at Lehigh	0	12
O24		at Haverford	5	9
O31	●	Hamilton	5	4
N3	●	Franklin & Marshall	9	0
N7	=	Delaware	6	6
N10		Ursinus	0	35
N14	●	Muhlenberg	15	5
N21		at Stevens	13	16

HERMAN PRITCHARD
1909 (.389) 3-5-1

1909 — 3-5-1

O2		Fordham	0	9
O9		at Navy	3	12
O16		at Franklin & Marshall	0	15
O23	=	Penn. Medical	0	0
O30	●	at Hamilton	8	5
N6		at NYU	0	11
N10	●	Muhlenberg	35	5
N13	●	Haverford	11	0
N20		at Stevens	5	17

HOWARD GARGAN
1910-12 (.538) 12-10-4

1910 — 3-2-3

O1	=	Franklin & Marshall	0	0
O8	=	at Navy	0	0
O15	●	Swarthmore	21	6
O22	=	at Haverford	0	0
O29		at NYU	8	15
N8	●	St. Lawrence	17	0
N12		at Wash. Maryland	5	6
N19	●	at Stevens	8	6

1911 — 4-4-1

O3		at Princeton	0	37
O7	●	Haverford	10	6
O14		at Army	0	18
O21	●	Union	6	0
O28		Swarthmore	0	21
N4	●	Rensselaer	6	0
N11	=	at NYU	0	0
N18		Ursinus	0	17
N25	●	at Stevens	3	0

1912 — 5-4-0

S28		Fanklin & Marshall	0	20
O2		at Princeton	6	41
O12		at Army	0	19
O19	●	Hobart	16	7
O26		at Union	0	3
N2	●	Hamilton	25	6
N9	●	Rensselaer	21	0
N16	●	at Haverford	18	0
N23	●	at Stevens	26	6

GEORGE FOSTER SANFORD
1913-23 (.629) 56-32-5

1913 — 6-3-0

S27		at Princeton	3	14
O4	●	Union	39	6
O11		at Army	0	29
O18	●	Hobart	71	0
O25	●	at Rensselaer	13	0
N1		Wesleyan	9	20
N8	●	at Hamilton	38	0
N15	●	Trinity	37	7
N22	●	at Stevens	37	0

1914 — 5-3-1

S26		at Princeton	0	12
O3	●	Rensselaer	32	0
O10		at Army	0	13
O17	●	Muhlenberg	17	7
O24	●	Tufts NWK	16	7
N7	=	at Syracuse	14	14
N21	●	at Stevens	83	0
N26	●	at NYU	33	0
N28		Wash. & Jeff. NYC	13	20

1915 — 7-1-0

S25	●	Albright	53	0
O2		at Princeton	0	10
O9	●	Rensselaer	96	0
O16	●	Muhlenberg	21	0
O30	●	Springfield	44	13
N13	●	Hamilton Fish A.S.	28	7
N20	●	at Stevens	39	3
N25	●	at NYU	70	0

1916 — 3-2-2

O7	●	Villanova	33	0
O14	=	Wash. & Lee	13	13
O28		at Brown	3	21
N4	●	Holy Cross NWK	14	6
N11	=	West Virginia	0	0
N25	●	Dickinson	34	0
N30		Wash. & Jeff. NYC	9	12

1917 — 7-1-1

S29	●	Ursinus	25	0
O6	●	Fort Wadsworth	90	0
O13		at Syracuse	10	14
O20	●	at Lafayette	33	7
O27	●	at Fordham	28	0
N3	=	West Virginia	7	7
N10	●	Springfield	61	0
N17	●	League Navy	27	0
N24	●	Newport Navy BKLN	14	0

1918 — 5-2-0

S28	●	Ursinus	66	0
O19	●	Pelham Bay NTS	7	0
O26	●	at Lehigh	39	0
N2	●	Port Hoboken NTS	40	0
N9	●	at Penn State	26	3
N16		Great Lakes NAS BKLN	14	54
N30		Syracuse NYC	0	21

1919 — 5-3-0

S27	●	Ursinus	34	0
O4	●	North Carolina	19	0
O11		at Lehigh	0	19
O25	●	New York St.	14	0
N4		Syracuse NYC	6	14
N8	●	at Boston College	13	7
N15		West Virginia	7	30
N27	●	Northwestern NWK	28	0

1920 — 2-7-0

S25		Ursinus	7	14
O2	●	Maryland	6	0
O9		at Lehigh	0	9
O16	●	Virginia Tech	19	6
O23		Virginia	0	7
O30		at Cornell	0	24
N2		Nebraska NYC	0	28
N13		at West Virginia	0	17
N25		at Detroit	0	27

1921 — 4-5-0

S24	●	at Ursinus	33	0
O1		Maryland	0	3
O8		Lehigh	0	7
O15	●	Wash. & Lee	14	13
O22		at Georgia Tech	14	48
O29		at Lafayette	0	35
N8		Notre Dame NYC	0	48
N12	●	at NYU	21	7
N19	●	West Virginia	17	7

1922 — 5-4-0

S30	●	Penn. Military Coll.	13	0
O7	●	Fordham	20	15
O14	●	at Lehigh	13	7
O21		Bethany	7	14
O28		at West Virginia	0	28
N7	●	LSU NYC	25	0
N11		Lafayette	6	33
N18	●	NYU E&O	37	0
N25		Bucknell	13	20

1923 — 7-1-1

S29	●	Penn. Military Coll.	27	0
O6	●	Villanova	44	0
O13	●	Lehigh	10	0
O20	●	NYU	7	3
O27	=	at Lafayette	6	6
N6		West Virginia NYC	7	27
N10	●	Richmond	56	0
N17	●	Boston U.	61	0
N24	●	Fordham E&O	42	0

JOHN H. WALLACE
1924-26 (.463) 12-14-1

1924 — 7-1-1

S27	●	Villanova	14	0
O4	●	Lebanon Valley	56	0
O11	●	St. Bonaventure	36	7
O18	●	at Cornell	10	0
O25	=	at Lehigh	13	13
N1	●	Franklin & Marshall	30	6
N8	●	Lafayette UNK	43	7
N15	●	at NYU	41	3
N22		Bucknell UNK	7	12

1925 — 2-7-0

S26	●	Alfred	19	3
O3		Villanova	0	20
O10		Maryland UNK	0	16
O17		at Cornell	0	41
O24		Lehigh	0	7
O31		Penn. Military Coll.	12	13
N7		at Lafayette	0	34
N14		at Holy Cross	0	6
N21	●	NYU	7	6

1926 — 3-6-0

S25	●	Manhattan	8	0
O2	●	Ursinus	14	0
O9		at Wash. & Jeff.	6	19
O16		Holy Cross UNK	0	21
O23		at NYU	0	30
O30	●	Delaware	21	0
N6		Lafayette	0	38
N13		at Lehigh	0	14
N20		Swarthmore	0	13

HARRY J. ROCKAFELLER
1927-30, '42-45 (.558) 33-26-1

1927 — 4-4-0

O1	●	Manhattan	24	6
O8		at Lafayette	0	56
O15		George Washington	0	6
O22		NYU UNK	6	60
O29		Holy Cross UNK	0	39
N5	●	Alfred	42	0
N12	●	at Swarthmore	19	6
N17	●	Lehigh	12	6

1928 — 6-3-0

S29	●	St. John's	12	0
O6	●	Albright	19	0
O13		Holy Cross UNK	0	46
O20		NYU UNK	0	48
O27	●	Delaware	34	0
N3	●	Catholic U.	12	0
N10		Lafayette	0	17
N17	●	at Lehigh	7	3
N24	●	Swarthmore	13	2

1929 — 5-4-0

S28	●	Providence	17	0
O5	●	Delaware	19	0
O12		at Holy Cross	3	20
O19	●	St. John's	14	7
O26		Catholic U.	10	14
N2	●	Ursinus	19	13
N9		at Lafayette	6	20
N16	●	Lehigh	14	0
N23		NYU UNK	7	20

1930 — 4-5-0

S27		Providence	6	12
O4	●	George Washington	20	6
O11		at Syracuse	0	27
O18	●	Johns Hopkins	33	0
O25	●	Delaware	40	0
N1		Holy Cross	20	32
N8		Lafayette	26	31
N15	●	at Lehigh	14	13
N22		NYU UNK	0	33

J. WILDER TASKER
1931-37 (.532) 31-27-5

1931 — 4-3-1

S26	●	Providence	19	0
O3	●	Drexel	27	6
O10	●	Springfield	26	0
O17		NYU UNK	7	27
O24		at Holy Cross	0	27
O31	=	Delaware	6	6
N7		at Lafayette	0	22
N14	●	Lehigh	26	12

1932 — 6-3-1

S24	=	Providence	6	6
O1	●	Penn. Military Coll.	20	6
O8		NYU UNK	0	21
O15	●	Delaware	32	0
O22		Holy Cross	0	6
O29	●	Johns Hopkins	33	0
N5	●	Lafayette	7	6
N12	●	at Lehigh	37	6
N23	●	at Springfield	18	0
D3	●	Manhattan	6	7

1933 — 6-3-1

S30	●	Franklin & Marshall	10	0
O7	●	Providence	21	0
O14		at Colgate	2	25
O21	●	Penn. Military Coll.	10	0
O28	●	Lehigh	27	0
N4	●	Springfield	31	6
N11	●	at Lafayette	20	13
N18	=	NYU UNK	6	6
N25		at Princeton	6	26
D2		Villanova	13	18

1934 — 5-3-1

S29	=	Penn. Medical	0	0
O6		at Franklin & Marshall	0	7
O13	●	Springfield	19	7
O20		at Pennsylvania	19	27
O27	●	at Lehigh	45	0
N3	●	Boston U.	52	0
N10	●	Lafayette	27	6
N17	●	NYU	22	7
N24		Colgate	0	27

THE SCHOOLS

1935 4-5-0
S28   West Chester   7 19
O5 •   Marietta   26 9
O12   at Columbia   6 20
O19   at Princeton   6 29
O26 •   Lehigh   27 6
N2   at Lafayette   31 6
N9   at Boston U.   12 6
N15   at NYU   0 48
N22   Colgate   0 27

1936 1-6-1
O3 •   Marietta   13 0
O10   at Princeton   0 20
O17   Springfield   0 6
O24   at Yale   0 28
O31   at Lehigh   0 19
N7   Boston U.   0 7
N14   NYU *Unk*   0 46
N21 =   at Wesleyan   7 7

1937 5-4-0
S25 •   Susquehanna   9 0
O2 •   Hampden Sydney   20 0
O9 •   Delaware   27 0
O16 •   at Springfield   26 0
O23   at Princeton   0 6
O30 •   Lehigh   34 0
N7   at Lafayette   6 13
N13   Ohio U.   0 13
N25   Brown   6 7

HARVEY J. HARMAN
1938-41 '46-55 (.625)74-44-2

1938 7-1-0
S24 •   Marietta   20 0
O1 •   Vermont   15 14
O8 •   NYU   6 25
O15 •   Springfield   6 0
O22 •   Hampden Sydney   32 0
O29 •   at Lehigh   13 0
N5 •   Princeton   20 18
N12 •   Lafayette   6 0

1939 7-1-1
S30 •   Wesleyan   13 7
O7 •   Wooster   20 0
O14 =   Richmond   6 6
O21 •   Maryland   25 12
O28 •   Lehigh   20 6
N4 •   New Hampshire   32 13
N11 •   at Lafayette   13 6
N18 •   Springfield   17 7
N30   at Brown   0 13

1940 5-3-0
O5 •   Springfield   33 0
O12 •   at Lehigh   34 0
O19 •   Marietta   53 0
O26 •   at Princeton   13 28
N2 •   Connecticut   45 7
N9 •   Lafayette   6 7
N16 •   St. Lawrence   20 0
N23   at Maryland   7 14

1941 7-2-0
S27 •   Alfred   34 0
O4 •   Springfield   26 0
O11 •   Lehigh   16 6
O18 •   Fort Monmouth   26 0
O25   at Syracuse   7 49
N1 •   Maryland   20 0
N8   at Lafayette   0 16
N15 •   Connecticut   32 7
N22 •   at Brown   13 7

HARRY J. ROCKAFELLER

1942 3-4-1
O3 •   Vermont   27 20
O10   at Maryland   13 27
O17   Bucknell   9 7
O24   at Lehigh   10 28
O31   Springfield   21 0
N7   Lafayette   13 19
N14 =   Fort Monmouth   0 0
N21   Syracuse   7 12

1943 3-2-0
O23   at Lehigh   26 0
N6 •   at Lafayette   13 0
N13 •   Lehigh   20 0
N20   Lafayette   2 9
N27   Brooklyn   6 12

1944 3-2-0
S30   at Lafayette   6 19
O7 •   at Lehigh   19 6
O14   Lafayette   0 39
O28 •   ASTP   18 12
N4 •   Lehigh   15 6

1945 5-2-0
O6   Swarthmore   6 13
O13 •   at Muhlenberg   19 6
O20 •   Rhode Island St.   39 7
O27   at Princeton   6 14
N3 •   Lehigh   25 0
N10 •   at Lafayette   32 14
N17 •   NYU   13 7

HARVEY J. HARMAN

1946 7-2-0
S28   at Columbia   7 13
O5 •   Johns Hopkins   53 0
O12 •   NYU *NYC*   26 0
O19 •   at Princeton   7 14
O26 •   George Washington   25 13
N2 •   at Harvard   13 0
N9 •   Lafayette   41 2
N16 •   at Lehigh   55 6
N23 •   Bucknell   25 0

1947 8-1-0
S27 •   at Columbia   28 40
O4 •   Western Reserve   21 6
O11 •   Princeton   13 7
O18 •   Fordham   36 6
O25 •   Lehigh   46 13
N1 •   at Harvard   31 7
N8 •   at Lafayette   20 0
N15 •   NYU   40 0
N27 •   at Brown   27 20

1948 7-2-0
S25 •   at Columbia   6 27
O2 •   Colgate   35 19
O9 •   Temple   34 20
O16 •   at Princeton   22 6
O23 •   at Lehigh   20 6
O30 •   Brown   6 20
N6 •   Lafayette   34 13
N13 •   NYU *Bronx*   40 0
N20 •   Fordham   28 19

1949 6-3-0
S24 •   USMM   79 6
O1 •   at Temple   7 14
O8 •   Lehigh   40 27
O15 •   Syracuse   9 21
O22 •   at Colgate   35 13
O29 •   at Princeton   14 34
N5 •   at Lafayette   14 0
N12 •   NYU   33 9
N19 •   Fordham   35 14

1950 4-4-0
S23   at Syracuse   12 42
O7 •   at Princeton   28 34
O14 •   Temple   26 20
O21 •   NYU   42 0
O28 •   at Lehigh   18 21
N4 •   Brown   15 12
N11 •   Lafayette   31 7
N18 •   at Penn State   14 18

1951 4-4-0
S29 •   at Lafayette   47 12
O6 •   at Temple   7 14
O13 •   NYU *NYC*   55 0
O20 •   Lehigh   6 21
N3 •   Fordham   13 7
N10 •   at Brown   28 21
N17 •   Penn State   7 13
N24 •   Colgate   21 26

1952 4-4-1
S27 =   Muhlenberg   19 19
O4 •   at Princeton   19 61
O11 •   at Colgate   7 13
O18 •   at Dartmouth   20 29
O25 •   at Brown   19 7
N1 •   Temple   40 28
N8 •   Lafayette   21 6
N15 •   at Penn State   6 7
N22 •   NYU   27 14

1953 2-6-0
O3 •   Virginia Tech   20 13
O10 •   at Princeton   7 9
O17 •   Brown   20 27
O24 •   Fordham   13 40
O31 •   Colgate   13 33
N7 •   at Lafayette   14 13
N14 •   Penn State   26 54
N21 •   at Columbia   13 27

1954 3-6-0
S25 •   at Princeton   8 10
O2 •   Fordham   7 13
O9 •   at Colgate   14 26
O16 •   William & Mary   7 14
O23 •   at Lehigh   13 3
O30 •   Temple   25 0
N6 •   Lafayette   7 0
N13 •   at Penn State   14 37
N20 •   at Columbia   45 12

1955 3-5-0
S24 •   at Princeton   7 41
O8 •   Muhlenberg   21 0
O15 •   at Brown   14 12
O22 •   Lehigh   14 21
O29 •   Delaware   7 33
N5 •   at Lafayette   7 16
N12 •   Penn State   13 34
N19 •   at Columbia   12 6

JOHN R. STEIGMAN
1956-59 (.595)   22-15

1956 3-7-0
S22 •   Ohio Wesleyan   33 13
S29 •   at Princeton   6 28
O6 •   at Connecticut   7 27
O13 •   Colgate   6 48
O20 •   Boston College   0 32
O27 •   at Lehigh   13 27
N3 •   Lafayette   20 19
N10 •   at Delaware   0 22
N17 •   William & Mary   20 6
N24 •   Columbia   12 13

1957 5-4-0
S28 •   at Princeton   0 7
O5 •   Connecticut   14 7
O12 •   at Colgate   48 6
O19 •   Lehigh   7 13
O26 •   Richmond   26 13
N2 •   Delaware   19 23
N9 •   at Lafayette   34 19
N16 •   at William & Mary   7 38
N23 •   at Columbia   26 7

1958 8-1-0
S27 •   at Princeton   28 0
O4 •   at Colgate   21 7
O11 •   Richmond   23 12
O18 •   Bucknell   57 12
O25 •   at Lehigh   44 13
N1 •   at Delaware   37 20
N8 •   Lafayette   18 0
N15 •   Quantico Marines   12 13
N22 •   Columbia   61 0

1959 6-3-0
S26 •   at Princeton   8 6
O3 •   Connecticut   20 8
O10 •   Colgate   15 12
O17 •   at Bucknell   8 15
O24 •   Lehigh   23 0
O31 •   Delaware   14 34
N7 •   at Lafayette   16 14
N14 •   Villanova   12 6
N21 •   at Columbia   16 26

JOHN F. BATEMAN
1960-72 (.589)   73-51

1960 8-1-0
S24 •   at Princeton   13 8
O1 •   at Connecticut   19 6
O8 •   Colgate   49 12
O15 •   Bucknell   23 19
O22 •   at Lehigh   8 0
O29 •   Villanova   12 14
N5 •   Lafayette   36 8
N12 •   at Delaware   22 0
N19 •   at Columbia   43 2

1961 9-0-0
S30 •   at Princeton   16 13
O7 •   Connecticut   35 12
O14 •   at Bucknell   21 6
O21 •   Lehigh   32 15
O28 •   at Pennsylvania   20 6
N4 •   at Lafayette   37 6
N11 •   Delaware   27 19
N18 •   at Colgate   26 6
N25 •   Columbia   32 9

1962 5-5-0
S29 •   at Princeton   7 15
O6 •   at Connecticut   9 15
O13 •   Colgate   27 15
O20 •   at Lehigh   29 13
O27 •   at Pennsylvania   12 7
N3 •   Lafayette   40 0
N10 •   at Delaware   6 23
N17 •   Villanova   12 34
N24 •   at Columbia   22 6
D1 •   Virginia   0 41

1963 3-6-0
S28 •   at Princeton   0 24
O5 •   at Harvard   0 28
O12 •   at Colgate   8 28
O19 •   Lehigh   30 6
O26 •   at Pennsylvania   6 7
N2 •   Boston U.   21 6
N9 •   at Lafayette   49 0
N16 •   Delaware   3 14
N23 •   Columbia   28 35

1964 6-3-0
S26 •   at Princeton   7 10
O3 •   Connecticut   9 3
O10 •   at Lehigh   20 7
O17 •   at Pennsylvania   10 7
O24 •   at Columbia   38 35
O31 •   Boston U.   9 0
N7 •   Lafayette   31 6
N14 •   at Delaware   18 27
N21 •   Colgate   7 20

1965 3-6-0
S25 •   at Princeton   6 32
O2 •   at Connecticut   17 8
O9 •   Lehigh   6 0
O16 •   at Army   6 23
O23 •   Columbia   7 12
O30 •   at Boston U.   0 30
N6 •   at Lafayette   18 23
N13 •   Holy Cross   14 0
N20 •   Colgate   10 24

1966 5-4-0
S24 •   at Princeton   12 16
O1 •   at Yale   17 14
O8 •   at Lehigh   42 14
O15 •   Army   9 14
O22 •   Columbia   37 34
O29 •   Boston U.   16 7
N5 •   Lafayette   32 28
N12 •   at Holy Cross   12 24
N19 •   Colgate   7 26

1967 4-5-0
S30 •   at Princeton   21 22
O7 •   Lehigh   14 7
O14 •   Delaware   29 21
O21 •   at Army   3 14
O28 •   at Columbia   13 24
N4 •   at Lafayette   27 3
N11 •   at Massachusetts   7 30
N18 •   Holy Cross   10 21
N25 •   Colgate   31 28

1968 8-2-0
S21 •   Lafayette   37 7
S28 •   at Princeton   20 14
O5   at Cornell   16 17
O12 •   at Lehigh   29 26
O19 •   Army   0 24
O26 •   at Columbia   28 17
N2 •   Delaware   23 14
N9 •   Connecticut   27 15
N16 •   Holy Cross   41 14
N23 •   Colgate   55 34

1969 — 6-3-0

S20	●	at Lafayette	44 22
S27	●	Princeton	29 0
O4	●	Cornell	21 7
O11		Lehigh	7 17
O18	●	Navy	20 6
O25	●	Columbia	21 14
N1		at Delaware	0 44
N8		at Connecticut	22 28
N22	●	Colgate	48 12

1970 — 5-5-0

S19	●	Lafayette	41 16
S26		at Princeton	14 41
O3		at Harvard	9 39
O10		at Lehigh	0 7
O17		Delaware	21 51
O24		at Columbia	14 30
O31	●	Bucknell	21 7
N7		at Boston U.	6 3
N14	●	Holy Cross	37 7
N21	●	Colgate	30 14

1971 — 4-7-0

S18		at Lafayette	7 13
S25	●	at Princeton	33 18
O2		Cornell	17 31
O9		Lehigh	14 35
O16		at Delaware	7 48
O23		Columbia	16 17
O30		at Bucknell	13 14
N6		at Army	17 30
N13	●	Holy Cross	14 13
N20	●	Colgate	28 16
N27	●	Morgan St.	27 8

1972 — 7-4-0

S16		at Holy Cross	14 24
S23	●	Lehigh	41 13
S30		at Princeton	6 7
O7		at Cornell	22 36
O14	●	at Lafayette	21 7
O21		Army	28 35
O28	●	at Columbia	6 3
N4	●	Connecticut	21 13
N11	●	Boston U.	51 7
N18	●	Morgan St.	37 14
N25	●	Colgate	43 13

FRANK R. BURNS
1973-83 (.643)   78-43-1

1973 — 6-5-0

S22	●	at Lehigh	31 13
S29	●	at Princeton	39 14
O6		Massachusetts	22 25
O13	●	Lafayette	35 6
O20	●	Delaware	24 7
O27	●	Columbia	28 2
N3		at Connecticut	19 27
N10		at Air Force	14 31
N17	●	at Holy Cross	27 7
N24	●	Colgate	0 42
D1		at Tampa	6 34

1974 — 7-3-1

S21	●	at Bucknell	16 14
S28	=	at Princeton	6 6
O5	●	at Harvard	24 21
O12	●	Lehigh	37 16
O19		at William & Mary	15 28
O26	●	Air Force	20 3
N2		Connecticut	7 9
N9	●	at Lafayette	35 0
N16		Boston U.	6 0
N23	●	Colgate	62 21
N30		at Hawaii	16 28

1975 — 9-2-0

S20	●	Bucknell	47 3
S27	●	at Princeton	7 10
O4	●	Hawaii	7 3
O11		at Lehigh	20 34
O18	●	William & Mary	24 0
O25	●	Columbia	41 0
N1		at Connecticut	35 8
N8	●	Lafayette	48 6
N15		at Boston U.	41 3
N22	●	Colgate	56 14
N29	●	Syracuse	21 10

1976 — 11-0-0

S11	●	at Navy	13 3
S18	●	at Bucknell	19 7
S25	●	at Princeton	17 0
O2	●	Cornell	21 14
O9	●	Connecticut	38 0
O16	●	at Lehigh	28 21
O23	●	Columbia _ERut_	47 0
O30	●	Massachusetts	24 7
N6	●	Louisville	34 0
N13	●	at Tulane	29 20
N18	●	Colgate _ERut_	17 9

1977 — 8-3-0

S2	●	Penn State _ERut_	7 45
S10	●	at Colgate	0 23
S17	●	Bucknell	36 14
S24	●	at Princeton	10 6
O1	●	at Cornell	30 14
O8	●	at Connecticut	42 18
O15	●	Lehigh	20 0
O29	●	at William & Mary	22 21
N5	●	at Temple	14 24
N12	●	Tulane	47 8
N19	●	Boston U.	63 8

1978 — 9-3-0

S9	●	at Penn State	10 26
S23	●	at Bucknell	27 13
S30	●	Princeton _ERut_	24 0
O7	●	at Yale	28 27
O14	●	Connecticut	10 0
O21	●	Villanova	24 9
O28	●	Columbia _ERut_	69 0
N4	●	at Massachusetts	21 11
N11	●	Temple	13 10
N18	●	at Holy Cross	31 21
N25	●	Colgate	9 14

GARDEN STATE BOWL

D16	●	Arizona State	18 34

1979 — 8-3-0

S8	●	Holy Cross	28 0
S15	●	at Penn State	10 45
S22	●	Bucknell	16 14
S29	●	at Princeton	38 14
O6	●	Temple	20 41
O13	●	at Connecticut	26 14
O20	●	at William & Mary	24 0
N3	●	at Tennessee	13 7
N10	●	Army _ERut_	20 0
N17	●	Villanova	17 32
N25	●	at Louisville	31 7

1980 — 7-4-0

S13	●	at Temple	21 3
S20	●	Cincinnati	24 7
S27	●	Princeton	44 13
O4	●	at Cornell	44 3
O11	●	Alabama _ERut_	13 17
O18	●	William & Mary	18 21
O25	●	at Syracuse	9 17
N1	●	at Army	37 21
N8	●	at Virginia	19 17
N15	●	West Virginia	15 24
N22	●	Colgate	35 13

1981 — 5-6-0

S5	●	at Syracuse	29 27
S12	●	Colgate	13 5
S18	●	Virginia _ERut_	3 0
S26	●	at Cincinnati	0 10
O3	●	Cornell	31 17
O10	●	at Army	17 0
O17	●	Temple	12 24
O24	●	at Alabama	7 31
N7	●	Pittsburgh _ERut_	3 47
N14	●	at West Virginia	3 20
N21	●	at Boston College	21 27

1982 — 5-6-0

S4	●	Syracuse _ERut_	8 31
S18	●	at Penn State	14 49
S25	●	at Temple	10 7
O2	●	William & Mary	27 17
O9	●	Army _ERut_	24 3
O16	●	at Boston College	13 14
O23	●	Colgate	34 17
O30	●	at Richmond	20 14
N6	●	at Auburn	7 30
N11	●	West Virginia _ERut_	17 44
N20	●	at Pittsburgh	6 52

1983 — 3-8-0

S10	●	Connecticut	22 5
S17	●	Boston College _ERut_	22 42
S24	●	at Syracuse	13 17
O1	●	Penn State _ERut_	25 36
O8	●	at Army	12 20
O15	●	Colgate	29 26
O22	●	at William & Mary	35 28
O29	●	Tennessee	0 7
N5	●	at Cincinnati	7 18
N12	●	at West Virginia	7 35
N19	●	Temple	23 24

DICK ANDERSON
1984-89 (.446)   27-34-4

1984 — 7-3-0

S8	●	at Penn State	12 15
S15	●	Temple	10 9
S22	●	at Syracuse	19 0
S29	●	Cincinnati	43 15
O6	●	at Kentucky	14 27
O13	●	Army _ERut_	14 7
O20	●	Louisville	38 21
O27	●	at Boston College	23 35
N10	●	West Virginia _ERut_	23 19
N17	●	Colgate	17 7

1985 — 2-8-1

S14	=	at Florida	28 28
S21	●	at Army	16 20
S28	●	Penn State _ERut_	10 17
O5	●	Boston College _ERut_	10 20
O12	●	at Temple	13 14
O19	●	Pittsburgh _ERut_	10 38
O26	●	Richmond	20 17
N2	●	at Tennessee	0 40
N9	●	at West Virginia	0 27
N16	●	Colgate	28 14
N23	●	Syracuse	14 31

1986 — 5-5-1

S6	●	at Boston College	11 9
S13	=	at Kentucky	16 16
S20	●	Cincinnati	48 28
S27	●	at Syracuse	16 10
O4	●	at Penn State	6 31
O18	●	Florida _ERut_	3 15
O25	●	Army _ERut_	35 7
N1	●	at Louisville	41 0
N8	●	West Virginia _ERut_	17 24
N15	●	at Pittsburgh	6 20
N22	●	Temple	22 29 †

1987 — 6-5-0

S5	●	at Cincinnati	10 7
S12	●	Syracuse	3 20
S26	●	Kentucky _ERut_	19 18
O3	●	Duke _ERut_	7 0
O10	●	at Penn State	21 35
O17	●	Boston College	38 24
O24	●	at Army	27 14
O31	●	at Vanderbilt	13 27
N7	●	Pittsburgh _ERut_	0 17
N14	●	at West Virginia	13 37
N21	●	at Temple	17 14

1988 — 5-6-0

S10	●	at Michigan State	17 13
S17	●	Vanderbilt _ERut_	30 31
S24	●	at Penn State	21 16
O1	●	Cincinnati	38 9
O8	●	at Syracuse	20 34
O15	●	at Boston College	17 6
O22	●	Army _ERut_	24 34
O29	●	Temple	30 35
N5	●	at Pittsburgh	10 20
N12	●	West Virginia _ERut_	25 35
N19	●	Colgate	41 22

1989 — 2-7-2

S2	=	at Cincinnati	17 17
S9	=	Ball State	31 31
S16	●	Boston College _ERut_	9 7
S23	●	at Northwestern	38 27
O7	●	Penn State _ERut_	0 17
O14	●	at Kentucky	26 33
O21	●	Syracuse	28 49
O28	●	at Army	14 35
N11	●	at West Virginia	20 21
N18	●	at Temple	33 36
D2	●	Pittsburgh _Dub_	29 46

DOUG GRABER
1990-95 (.447)   29-36-1

1990 — 3-8-0

S8	●	Kentucky _ERut_	24 8
S15	●	Colgate	28 17
S22	●	at Penn State	0 28
S29	●	Michigan State _ERut_	10 34
O6	●	at Boston College	14 19
O13	●	at Pittsburgh	21 45
O20	●	at Syracuse	0 42
O27	●	Akron	20 17
N3	●	at Army	31 35
N10	●	West Virginia _ERut_	3 28
N17	●	at Temple	22 29

1991-PRESENT
BIG EAST

1991 — 6-5-0 (2-3-0)

A31	● |	Boston College	20 13
S14	|	at Duke	22 42
S21	●	Northwestern	22 18
S28	●	at Michigan State	14 7
O5	●	Army _ERut_	14 12
O12	●	Maine	40 17
O19	●	at Penn State	17 37
O26	|	Syracuse _ERut_	7 21
N2	|	at West Virginia	3 28
N9	|	at Pittsburgh	17 22
N16	● |	Temple	41 0

1992 — 7-4-0 (4-2-0)

S5	●	at Boston College	20 37
S12	●	Colgate	41 0
S17	● |	Pittsburgh	21 16
S26	●	at Navy	40 0
O3	|	Penn State _ERut_	24 38
O10	|	at Syracuse	28 50
O17	● |	Army _ERut_	45 10
O31	● |	Virginia Tech	50 49
N7	|	at Cincinnati	24 26
N14	● |	West Virginia	13 9
N21	● |	at Temple	35 10

1993 — 4-7-0 (1-6-0)

S4	●	Colgate _ERut_	68 6
S11	●	Duke _ERut_	39 38
S25	●	at Penn State	7 31
O2	|	Temple _ERut_	62 0
O9	|	Boston College _ERut_	21 31
O16	● |	at Army	45 38
O23	|	at Virginia Tech	42 49
O28	|	Pittsburgh _ERut_	10 21
N6	|	at West Virginia	22 58
N13	|	at Miami, Fla.	17 31
N26	|	Syracuse _ERut_	18 31

1994 — 5-5-1 (2-4-1)

S3	●	Kent	28 6
S10	● |	West Virginia	17 12
S17	|	at Syracuse	36 37
S24	|	at Penn State	27 55
O1	|	Miami, Fla.	3 24
O8	● |	Army _ERut_	16 14
O15	|	Cincinnati	14 9
O22	= |	at Boston College	7 7
N5	● |	Temple	38 21
N12	|	at Virginia Tech	34 41
N19	|	at Pittsburgh	21 35

1995 — 4-7-0 (2-5-0)

S9	●	at Duke	14 24
S16	●	Navy	27 17
S23	●	Penn State _ERut_	34 59
S30	●	Syracuse	17 27
O14	|	at Miami, Fla.	21 56
O21	|	Virginia Tech	17 45
O28	● |	Pittsburgh	42 24
N4	|	at West Virginia	26 59
N11	● |	at Tulane	45 40
N18	● |	at Temple	23 20
N24	|	Boston College	38 41

TERRY SHEA
1996-2000 (.200)   11-44

1996 — 2-9 (1-6)

A31	●	Villanova	38 28
S7	|	Navy	6 10
S12	|	Miami, Fla.	0 33
S21	|	at Virginia Tech	14 30
O5	|	at Syracuse	0 42
O12	|	Army _ERut_	21 42
O19	|	at Boston College	13 37
O26	● |	Temple	28 17
N9	|	West Virginia	14 55
N23	|	at Notre Dame	0 62
N30	|	at Pittsburgh	9 24

1997   0-11   (0-7)

A30	Virginia Tech	19	59
S6	at Texas	14	48
S13	at Navy	7	36
S20	Boston College	21	35
O4	at West Virginia	0	48
O9	Syracuse	3	50
O18	at Army	35	37
O25	Pittsburgh	48	55
N1	at Temple	7	49
N8	Wake Forest	14	28
N15	at Miami, Fla.	23	51

1998   5-6   (2-5)

S5	●	Richmond	7	6
S12		at Boston College	14	41
S19		at Syracuse	14	70
S26	●	Army	27	15
O3		Miami, Fla.	17	53
O17	●	at Pittsburgh	25	21
O24		Tulane	24	52
O31	●	Temple	21	10
N7		at Navy	36	33
N14		West Virginia	14	28
N21		at Virginia Tech	7	47

1999   1-10   (1-6)

S4		at California	7	21
S11		Texas	21	38
S25		Boston College	7	27
O2		at Wake Forest	10	17
O9		Virginia Tech	20	58
O16		at West Virginia	16	62
O23		Pittsburgh	15	38
O30		at Temple	28	56
N6		Navy	7	34
N13	●	Syracuse	24	21
N20		at Miami, Fla.	0	55

2000   3-8   (0-7)

S2	●	Villanova	34	21
S9	●	Buffalo	59	0
S16		at Virginia Tech	0	49
S23		at Pittsburgh	17	29
S30		Miami, Fla.	6	64
O14		Temple	14	48
O21	●	at Navy	28	21
O28		at Boston College	13	42
N11		West Virginia	24	31
N18		Notre Dame	17	45
N25		at Syracuse	21	49

GREG SCHIANO
2001-Present (.261)   12-34

2001   2-9   (0-7)

S1	●	at Buffalo	31	15
S8		at Miami, Fla.	0	61
S22		Virginia Tech	0	50
S29		Connecticut	19	20
O6		Syracuse	17	24
O13		at Temple	5	30
O20	●	Navy	23	17
N3		at West Virginia	7	80
N10		Pittsburgh	0	42
N17		Boston College	7	38
N24		California	10	20

2002   1-11   (0-7)

A31		Villanova	19	37
S7		Buffalo	11	34
S14	●	Army	44	0
S21		at Pittsburgh	3	23
S28		at Tennessee	14	35
O12		West Virginia	0	40
O19		at Virginia Tech	14	35
O26		at Syracuse	14	45
N2		Miami, Fla.	17	42
N16		Temple	17	20
N23		at Notre Dame	0	42
N30		at Boston College	14	44

2003   5-7   (2-5)

A30	●	Buffalo	24	10
S6		at Michigan State	28	44
S13	●	at Army	36	21
S27	●	Navy	48	27
O4		Virginia Tech	22	48
O11		at West Virginia	19	34
O18		Pittsburgh	32	42
O25	●	at Temple	30	14
N8		at Connecticut	31	38
N15		Boston College	25	35
N22		at Miami, Fla.	10	34
N29	●	Syracuse	24	7

2004   4-7   (1-5)

S4	●	Michigan State	19	14
S11		New Hampshire	24	35
S18	●	Kent State	29	21
O2		at Syracuse	31	41
O9	●	at Vanderbilt	37	34
O16	●	Temple	16	6
O23		at Pittsburgh	17	41
O30		West Virginia	30	35
N6		at Boston College	10	21
N20		at Navy	21	54
N25		Connecticut	35	41

RUTGERS ANNUAL STATISTICAL LEADERS

YR	RUSHING	YDS	ATT	AVG	PASSING	ATT	CMP	PCT	YDS	RECEIVING	REC	YDS	AVG
1957	Bill Austin	946	193	4.9	Bill Austin	80	38	.48	479	Bob Simms	12	180	15.0
1958	Bill Austin	747	145	5.2	Bruce Webster	74	40	.54	513	Bob Simms	33	468	14.2
1959	Jim Rogers	161	54	3.0	Sam Mudie	50	20	.40	339	Bob Simms	19	345	18.2
1960	Steve Simms	613	102	6.0	Sam Mudie	77	34	.44	452	Arny Byrd	18	269	14.9
1961	Steve Simms	614	103	6.0	Bill Speranza	46	15	.33	318	Lee Curley	12	274	22.8
1962	Bill Thompson	405	99	4.1	Bob Yaksick	87	36	.41	502	Bill Craft	23	426	18.5
1963	Don Viggiano	404	86	4.7	Dave Stout	120	58	.48	634	Paul Strelick	27	242	9.0
1964	Bob Brendel	464	125	3.7	Roger Kalinger	158	84	.53	916	Jack Emmer	22	306	13.9
1965	Rich Capria	242	58	4.2	Jack Callaghan	73	38	.52	456	Charley Mudie	18	243	13.5
1966	Bryant Mitchell	540	133	4.1	Fred Eckert	94	44	.47	756	Jack Emmer	41	701	17.1
1967	Bryant Mitchell	542	124	4.4	Bruce Van Ness	104	44	.42	524	Jim Baker	20	242	12.1
1968	Bryant Mitchell	1,204	238	5.1	Rich Policastro	122	68	.56	994	Bob Stonebreaker	31	448	14.5
1969	Steve Ferrughelli	564	131	4.3	Rich Policastro	258	149	.58	1,690	Jim Benedict	48	650	13.5
1970	Larry Robertson	397	101	3.9	Mike Yanchef	185	93	.50	974	Al Fenstemacher	27	254	9.4
1971	Larry Robertson	405	133	3.0	Leo Gasiencia	197	98	.50	1,148	Bob Carney	30	351	11.7
1972	JJ Jennings	1,262	287	4.4	Leo Gasiencia	198	107	.54	1,409	Tom Sweeney	23	369	16.0
1973	JJ Jennings	1,353	303	4.5	John Piccirillo	63	26	.41	415	Tom Sweeney	28	479	17.1
1974	Curt Edwards	889	189	4.7	Bert Kosup	150	63	.42	1,070	Mark Twitty	9	314	34.9
1975	Curt Edwards	1,157	236	4.9	Jeff Rebholz	69	33	.48	715	Mark Twitty	24	544	22.7
1976	Glen Kehler	764	151	5.1	Bert Kosup	141	69	.49	1,098	Mark Twitty	29	514	17.7
1977	Glen Kehler	866	164	5.3	Bert Kosup	157	82	.52	1,445	George Carter	17	391	23.0
1978	Glen Kehler	883	212	4.2	Bob Hering	193	88	.46	1,193	Dave Dorn	27	535	19.8
1979	Albert Ray	567	107	5.3	Ed McMichael	211	124	.59	1,529	Dave Dorn	27	468	17.3
1980	Albert Ray	778	187	4.2	Ed McMichael	229	146	.64	1,761	Tim Odell	49	718	14.7
1981	Albert Ray	679	180	3.8	Ralph Leek	167	80	.48	926	Andrew Baker	18	356	19.8
1982	Albert Smith	466	130	3.6	Jacque LaPrarie	186	100	.54	1,164	Andrew Baker	30	472	15.7
1983	Albert Smith	572	122	4.7	Jacque LaPrarie	203	104	.51	1,275	Andrew Baker	37	857	23.2
1984	Albert Smith	869	178	4.9	Eric Hochberg	305	162	.53	1,905	Andrew Baker	42	583	13.9
1985	Albert Smith	362	112	3.2	Joe Gagliardi	220	128	.58	1,273	Albert Smith	36	244	6.8
1986	Matt Prescott	606	155	3.9	Scott Erney	190	96	.51	1,160	Brian Cobb	21	368	17.5
1987	Henry Henderson	846	158	5.4	Scott Erney	225	122	.54	1,369	Eric Young	25	364	14.6
1988	Mike Botti	715	161	4.4	Scott Erney	339	188	.55	2,123	Eric Young	48	592	12.3
1989	James Cann	429	117	3.7	Scott Erney	374	208	.56	2,536	James Cann	42	507	12.1
1990	Tekay Dorsey	505	131	3.9	Tom Tarver	188	107	.57	1,348	James Guarantano	26	386	14.8
1991	Antoine Moore	627	145	4.3	Tom Tarver	307	164	.53	1,969	James Guarantano	62	740	11.9
1992	Bruce Presley	817	148	5.5	Bryan Fortay	230	115	.50	1,608	James Guarantano	56	755	13.5
1993	Terrell Willis	1,261	195	6.5	Ray Lucas	188	109	.58	1,011	Chris Brantley	56	589	10.5
1994	Terrell Willis	1,080	216	5.0	Ray Lucas	268	156	.58	1,869	Marco Battaglia	58	779	13.4
1995	Terrell Willis	773	177	4.4	Ray Lucas	347	188	.54	2,180	Marco Battaglia	69	894	13.0
1996	Chad Bosch	523	111	4.7	Mike Stephans	172	73	.42	918	Steven Harper	25	321	12.8
1997	Jacki Crooks	758	174	4.4	Mike McMahon	212	104	.49	1,259	Walter King	18	445	24.7
1998	Jacki Crooks	821	159	5.2	Mike McMahon	276	143	.52	2,203	Bill Powell	37	730	19.7
1999	Jacki Crooks	587	161	3.6	Mike McMahon	146	66	.45	989	Errol Johnson	35	507	14.5
2000	Dennis Thomas	587	137	4.3	Mike McMahon	340	169	.50	2,157	Errol Johnson	46	555	12.1
2001	Dennis Thomas	372	97	3.8	Ryan Cubit	268	120	.45	1,433	Aaron Martin	25	523	20.9
2002	Markis Facyson	398	124	3.2	Ted Trump	155	71	.46	740	L.J. Smith	32	384	12.0
2003	Brian Leonard	880	213	4.1	Ryan Hart	398	234	.59	2,714	Brian Leonard	53	488	9.2
2004	Brian Leonard	732	199	3.7	Ryan Hart	453	295	.65	3,154	Tres Moses	81	1,056	13.0

Receiving leaders by receptions
All statistics include postseason

THE SCHOOLS

SAN DIEGO STATE

BY DERRICK GOOLD

AN EARLY LAUNCHPAD FOR THE popularity of today's pass-powered offenses was Montezuma Mesa, where a little-known coach turned San Diego State into a high-scoring, fan-jazzing juggernaut. Between Oct. 23, 1965, and Nov. 14, 1970, coach Don Coryell's Aztecs won 55 of 57 games, losing just once and averaging 35.4 points per contest. In the 1968 and 1969 seasons, Coryell's team went 20–0–1 and outscored opponents 869 to 349. The Coryell teams, particularly the offense nicknamed Air Coryell, sent the Aztecs' fan base soaring and helped conjure a tradition. St. Louis Rams coach Mike Martz, who grew up in San Diego watching Coryell's Aztecs, used what he saw there as the basis for his own high-wire offense that produced three consecutive NFL MVPs from 1999 to 2001. His prime weapon comes from San Diego State stock—2000 NFL MVP Marshall Faulk.

TRADITION During the height of Air Coryell, Saturday nights in San Diego electrified when the Aztecs took the field wearing The Look. The team's all-black uniform with a red helmet has become the program's calling card, even, according to booster scripture, cursing those San Diego State squads that haven't worn it. Coryell replaced the Aztecs' black and silver with The Look in 1963, debuting with a 33-8 win over Long Beach State on Oct. 12. Night games had been a San Diego staple since 1930, and the pitch-black uniforms fit perfectly. In 1980, the team donned red jerseys. The Aztecs lost eight of their first nine games before pulling out the black jerseys and winning the next three. In 1983, home games were switched to day kickoffs, and the team shed the sizzling black pants for cool white ones. SDSU won one home game that season. Lesson learned. Black was back.

BEST PLAYER Deemed a defensive back by every other recruiter who came to New Orleans, Marshall Faulk chose faraway San Diego State because coach Al Luginbill offered a spot in the offensive backfield. Why he wanted to stay at tailback was immediately clear as Faulk made perhaps the best first impression in college football history. Two games into Faulk's freshman season, senior running back T.C. Wright left with a thigh bruise. Faulk got his first carry

10 minutes into the game against Pacific on Sept. 14, 1991. By the end of the third quarter, he had 323 yards rushing. He set a then-NCAA all-divisions record with 386 yards and scored a Division I-A freshman-record seven touchdowns. Due to team policy regarding injuries, Faulk was not the starter the next week, but he did end the season leading the nation in rushing with 1,429 yards. It was the lowest sum of his three seasons. He was the third freshman first-team AP All-America ever and a consensus All-American in 1992 and 1993. Faulk finished as high as second in the Heisman voting.

BEST COACH In Coryell's first season with the Aztecs, 1961, he guided the program to as many victories (seven) as they had had in the four seasons before he arrived. Coryell, a member of the College Football Hall of Fame, led the Aztecs to wins in 104 of 125 games and two national college division titles in 12 seasons. The average score of those games was Aztecs 32, opponents 13. In four

> *The Look—the Aztecs' all-black uniforms and red helmets—is one of football's most distinctive calling cards.*

seasons from 1966 to 1969, the Aztecs had three without a loss. He had 42 players drafted by the NFL before he followed them there. Coryell went on to coach the San Diego Chargers and St. Louis Cardinals and became the only coach to win 100 games in both college and the NFL.

BEST TEAM In 1969, the school's first season in what would become Division I-A, the Aztecs completed their second 11–0 season in four years and averaged 44.7 points per game. Despite the gaudy debut, the Aztecs did not crack the AP Top 25 during the season, probably because their schedule lacked national-names oomph. Quarterback Dennis Shaw finished with 3,185 yards—the most of any of Coryell's quarterbacks—and 39 touchdowns. The Aztecs finished the season with a 28-7 victory against Boston University in the Pasadena Bowl.

BIGGEST GAME It was 12 games into the 25-game winning streak, but the Aztecs' 36-0 victory against North

RECORDS

RUSHING YARDS

GAME
386 — Marshall Faulk vs. Pacific, Sept. 14, 1991 (37 att.)

SEASON
1,842 — George Jones, 1995 (305 att.)

CAREER
4,589 — Marshall Faulk, 1991-93 (766 att.)

PASSING YARDS

GAME
568 — Dave Lowery vs. BYU, Nov. 16, 1991 (26 of 39)

SEASON
3,932 — Todd Santos, 1987 (306 of 492)

CAREER
11,425 — Todd Santos, 1984-87 (910 of 1,484)

RECEIVING YARDS

GAME
363 — Tom Nettles vs. Southern Miss, Nov. 9, 1968 (11 rec.)

SEASON
1,785 — J.R. Tolver, 2002 (128 rec.)

CAREER
3,572 — J.R. Tolver, 1999-2002 (262 rec.)

POINTS

GAME
44 — Marshall Faulk vs. Pacific, Sept. 14, 1991 (7 TDs; 1 two-pt. conv.)

SEASON
144 — Paul Hewitt, 1987; Marshall Faulk, 1993 (24 TDs)

CAREER
376 — Marshall Faulk, 1991-93 (62 TDs, 2 two-pt. conv.)

CONSENSUS ALL-AMERICANS

1935	John Butler	G
1966	Don Horn	QB
1967	Steve Duich	OT
1967	Haven Moses	WR
1968	Fred Dryer	DE
1968	Lloyd Edwards	B
1992-93	Marshall Faulk	RB
1997	Kyle Turley	OL

Dakota State on Nov. 5, 1966, is considered the win that launched Air Coryell. North Dakota State came in as the nation's top-ranked small college, and San Diego State wanted a crack at the rank. Coryell remembers the team was hushed by its nervousness as the bus approached a record crowd at Balboa Stadium. Running back Teddy Washington hopped up from his seat and yelled, "What's the problem here? There's 100 million in China that don't even know we're playing tonight." The mood unknotted and the Aztecs cruised. A late, shutout-threatening drive by North Dakota State was thwarted by Bob Jones' interception and 98-yard return.

BIGGEST UPSET Bobby Bowden was in his second season with Florida State when he took his Seminoles way west for the first time in 1977. San Diego State was an unheralded independent, on its way to a second consecutive 10–1 season without a bowl invitation. It has been argued that the 1977 team—with coach Claude Gilbert, quarterback Joe Davis and running back David Turner—was the Aztecs' best ever. The next season they joined the Western Athletic Conference, and the upset of Florida State has long been considered the breakthrough game for post-Coryell SDSU. The 13th-ranked Seminoles, at 8–1, spent the day before the game at the San Diego Zoo, and later would rationalize the Aztecs' 41–16 upset with their exhaustion from visiting the animals. Florida State finished the season ranked 14th; San Diego State finished No. 16 with no bowl.

HEARTBREAKER Needing a win to stay in the hunt for the WAC Pacific Division title and a Holiday Bowl berth in 1996, San Diego State, at 6–2, traveled to face UNLV, winless in 10 games that season and owner of the nation's longest active losing streak. A 27-point favorite, SDSU lost in a game that included 86 points, seven touchdowns of 35 yards or longer and a missed field goal in the final seconds. With 13 seconds remaining, SDSU kicker Peter Holt, the team's leading scorer that season with 15 field goals and 41 points after, shanked a 35-yard field goal, and UNLV had a 44-42 win. The Aztecs won their final two games to finish 8–3 but were still that field goal shy of a potential bowl invite.

STADIUM On its third name since opening, Qualcomm Stadium has been the Aztecs' home since 1967, when the $27 million multipurpose stadium opened as San Diego Stadium. Located less than five miles from campus,

Qualcomm is also the home of the San Diego Chargers and the Holiday Bowl and was the home of the San Diego Padres. It hosted its third Super Bowl in 2003 and has also been the site of the World Series. In between being called Qualcomm and San Diego Stadium, the edifice was named Jack Murphy Stadium for *The San Diego Union* columnist who was instrumental in bringing the Chargers south from Los Angeles. Capacity at Qualcomm is 59,000 for San Diego State games, and on Sept. 4, 2004, against Idaho State, the Aztecs broke a 13-year-old record with a crowd of 57,216, largest in school history. Before playing there, SDSU played at the Aztec Bowl, a 13,000-seat facility on campus, and Balboa Stadium in downtown San Diego.

RIVAL Fresno State is the Aztecs' oldest and closest-fought rivalry, although it's been muted, since the schools no longer play in the same conference. San Diego State first played Fresno in 1923, and played every season from 1940 to 1979 (the 1943 and '44 seasons were canceled because of World War II). The Aztecs lead the series 26–20–4, the last game being played in 2002. The teams do have four games scheduled from 2007 to 2010.

NICKNAME Overcoming a strong lobby during the 1923-24 school year by the student newspaper for the nickname Wampus Cats, student leaders selected Aztecs in 1925. Before 1925, teams were known as Staters or Professors, and the newspaper presented other options such as Panthers, Thoroughbreds and Balboans. Student officials thought Aztecs was the most appropriate moniker, as it evoked the university's Southwest environment.

MASCOT In 1941, Monty Montezuma—based on Montezuma II, ruler of the Aztec Empire—made his debut during a halftime skit. With the exception of 1983, when the mascot struck what the school felt was a more "regal" presence atop a pyramid during games, Monty patrolled the field. In 2001, Monty Montezuma was abandoned as the school's mascot upon pressure from Native American and Latino students who found the mascot degrading and offensive. In 2003, a vote of students and alumni overwhelmingly approved an Aztec warrior as mascot. The generalized warrior carries a spear and wears a headdress.

UNIFORMS The red helmet has been blank and, for the longest time, had just Aztecs written on the side in

various fonts. In 2002, the school switched to a solitary, encircled A pierced with a spear on the helmet. While black has been the rule, the home jerseys have undergone several design changes, including a jersey with black sleeves and a red "bib." At the start of 2004, players pushed to wear red jerseys trimmed in black. The jerseys were believed to be vintage 1980 and did not have the players' names on the back. The apparent hex on previous teams not wearing black didn't kick in since the team won that night, and the athletic director promised that the team would wear other nontraditional jerseys.

QUOTE "The country is full of good coaches. What it takes to win is a bunch of interested players." —Don Coryell

SAN DIEGO STATE ANNUAL STATISTICAL LEADERS

YR	RUSHING	YDS	ATT	AVG	PASSING	ATT	CMP	PCT	YDS	RECEIVING	REC	YDS	AVG
1947	Joe Riccobono	405	101	4.0	Art Filson	49	19	.39	363	Jack Kaiser	12	216	18.0
1948	Murry Callan	528	95	5.6	John Simcox	103	49	.48	665	Leo Heaton	17	229	13.5
1949	Jim Simmons	523	87	6.0	Leon Parma	87	40	.46	603	Bud Milke	16	192	12.0
1950	Art Preston	780	114	6.8	Leon Parma	103	49	.48	732	Bud Milke	25	315	12.6
1951	Art Preston	588	118	5.0	Jesse Thompson	155	86	.55	1,304	Chet Nicholson	30	510	17.0
1952	Norm Nygaard	1,016	153	6.6	Paul Held	194	82	.42	1,062	Don Jurk	21	383	18.2
1953	Norm Nygaard	889	126	7.1	Paul Held	98	39	.40	603	Bob Lyon	19	312	16.4
1954	Norm Nygaard	714	128	5.6	Bill Richardson	60	27	.45	251	Claude Lewis	11	120	10.9
1955	Jim Pyles	326	54	6.0	Don Magee	123	66	.54	792	Braxton Pinkins	13	214	16.5
1956	Claude Lewis	470	87	5.4	Bob Moneymaker	65	25	.38	433	Braxton Pinkins	14	294	21.0
1957	Cecil McGehee	218	75	2.9	Joe Duke	121	49	.40	719	Braxton Pinkins	15	288	19.2
1958	Bob Ball	344	77	4.5	Joe Duke	150	62	.41	787	Bob Ball	20	264	13.2
1959	Dick Morris	313	68	4.6	Joe Duke	132	63	.48	698	Dick Morris	28	283	10.1
1960	Dick Morris	306	83	3.7	Russ Boehmke	74	37	.50	293	Dick Morris	13	118	9.1
1961	Kern Carson	560	87	6.4	Harry Korsmeier	72	35	.49	547	Neal Petties	19	428	22.5
1962	Kern Carson	796	114	7.0	Wayne Sevier	62	40	.65	578	Neal Petties	22	384	17.5
1963	Kern Carson	555	115	4.8	Rod Dowhower	120	58	.48	1,136	Neal Petties	22	465	21.1
1964	Jim Allison	1,186	174	6.8	Rod Dowhower	193	101	.52	1,728	Gary Garrison	78	1,272	16.3
1965	Nate Johns	921	115	8.0	Don Horn	206	123	.60	1,688	Gary Garrison	70	916	13.1
1966	Ted Washington	591	97	6.1	Don Horn	253	134	.53	2,234	Craig Scoggins	81	1,212	15.0
1967	Ted Washington	608	147	4.1	Thom Williams	103	59	.57	945	Haven Moses	54	958	17.7
1968	Lloyd Edwards	809	178	4.5	Dennis Shaw	240	134	.56	2,139	Tom Nettles	62	1,227	19.8
1969	George Brown	558	134	4.2	Dennis Shaw	335	199	.59	3,185	Tim Delaney	85	1,259	14.8
1970	Eddie Steward	580	84	6.9	Brian Sipe	337	195	.58	2,618	Tim Delaney	62	794	12.8
1971	Adam Victoria	483	147	3.3	Brian Sipe	369	196	.53	2,532	Tom Reynolds	67	1,070	16.0
1972	Dennis Haughn	301	90	3.3	Jesse Freitas	171	97	.57	1,200	Isaac Curtis	44	832	18.9
1973	Frank Geary	479	106	4.5	Jesse Freitas	347	227	.65	2,993	Darold Nogle	59	945	16.0
1974	Bill Kramer	905	148	6.1	Craig Penrose	235	132	.56	1,683	Dwight McDonald	86	1,157	13.5
1975	Monty Reedy	617	144	4.3	Craig Penrose	349	198	.57	2,660	Duke Fergerson	57	886	15.5
1976	David Turner	982	193	5.1	Tom Craft	109	75	.69	809	Ronnie Smith	27	416	15.4
1977	David Turner	1,252	240	5.2	Joe Davis	290	174	.60	2,360	Dennis Pearson	49	864	17.6
1978	Phil DuBois	705	153	4.6	Mark Halda	358	205	.57	2,262	Don Warren	39	483	12.4
1979	Tony Allen	1,094	226	4.8	Mark Halda	234	123	.53	1,684	Steve Stapler	37	794	21.5
1980	Derrick Harvey	338	71	4.8	Matt Kofler	179	99	.55	1,139	Bobby Taylor	40	656	16.4
1981	Bull Williams	256	65	3.9	Matt Kofler	436	262	.60	3,337	Darius Durham	65	988	15.2
1982	Derrick Harvey	558	155	3.6	Mark McKay	250	142	.57	1,985	Don Roberts	53	380	7.2
1983	Mike Waters	562	132	4.3	Mark McKay	337	187	.55	2,490	Jim Sandusky	69	1,171	17.0
1984	Mike Waters	704	180	3.9	Todd Santos	285	160	.56	2,063	Webster Slaughter	40	576	14.4
1985	Chris Hardy	1,150	158	7.3	Todd Santos	357	226	.62	2,877	Webster Slaughter	82	1,071	13.1
1986	Chris Hardy	947	237	4.0	Todd Santos	350	218	.62	2,553	Corey Gilmore	48	325	6.8
1987	Paul Hewitt	1,001	233	4.3	Todd Santos	492	306	.62	3,932	Kerry Reed-Martin	49	719	14.7
1988	Paul Hewitt	1,055	240	4.4	Brad Platt	226	130	.58	1,466	Monty Gilbreath	60	799	13.3
1989	Ron Slack	914	220	4.2	Dan McGwire	440	258	.59	3,651	Monty Gilbreath	80	903	11.3
1990	T.C. Wright	730	116	6.3	Dan McGwire	449	270	.60	3,833	Patrick Rowe	71	1,392	19.6
1991	Marshall Faulk	1,429	201	7.1	David Lowery	311	176	.57	2,575	Patrick Rowe	57	822	14.4
1992	Marshall Faulk	1,630	265	6.2	David Lowery	366	191	.52	2,632	Darnay Scott	68	1,150	16.9
1993	Marshall Faulk	1,530	300	5.1	Tim Gutierrez	341	208	.61	3,033	Darnay Scott	75	1,262	16.8
1994	Wayne Pittman	1,136	274	4.1	Billy Blanton	178	112	.63	1,586	Curtis Shearer	55	737	13.4
1995	George Jones	1,842	305	6.0	Billy Blanton	389	243	.62	3,300	Will Blackwell	86	1,207	14.0
1996	George Jones	968	181	5.3	Billy Blanton	344	227	.66	3,221	Will Blackwell	60	1,000	16.7
1997	Jonas Lewis	1,021	227	4.5	Kevin McKechnie	179	107	.60	1,449	Taj Johnson	44	802	18.2
1998	Jonas Lewis	897	181	5.0	Brian Russell	230	123	.53	1,438	Damon Gourdine	55	649	11.8
1999	Larry Ned	894	162	5.5	Jack Hawley	266	145	.55	1,942	Damon Gourdine	38	439	11.6
2000	Larry Ned	357	139	2.6	Lon Sheriff	290	155	.53	2,163	J.R. Tolver	62	808	13.0
2001	Larry Ned	1,549	311	5.0	Lon Sheriff	236	111	.47	1,295	J.R. Tolver	63	878	13.9
2002	James Truvillion	392	120	3.3	Adam Hall	452	272	.60	3,253	J.R. Tolver	128	1,785	13.9
2003	Lynell Hamilton	1,087	234	4.6	Adam Hall	206	105	.51	1,320	Jeff Webb	55	706	12.8
2004	Brandon Bornes	578	133	4.3	Matt Dlugolecki	203	123	.61	1,349	Jeff Webb	71	863	12.2

Receiving leaders by receptions
The NCAA began including postseason stats in 2002

SAN DIEGO STATE ALL-TIME SCORES

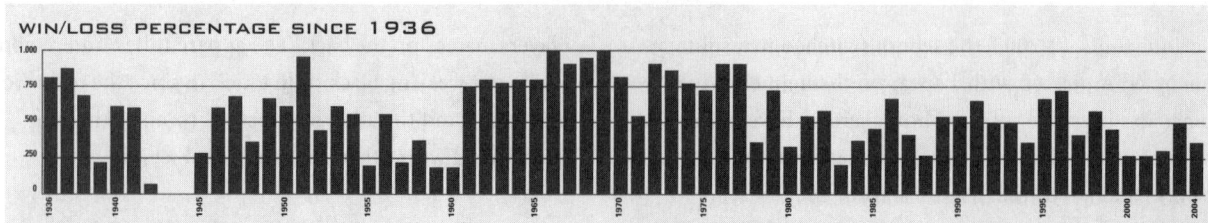

WIN/LOSS PERCENTAGE SINCE 1936

C.E. PETERSON
1921-29 (.577)   43-31-4

1921   4-6-0
O1	●	Army-Navy Acad.	6	0
O6		Reserve Destroyers	0	3
O13		USS Birmingham	0	14
O15		Naval Air	7	12
O19	●	USS Birmingham	14	6
O21	●	Army-Navy Acad.	12	0
O28		at Santa Ana JC	0	26
N4		at Fullerton JC	0	20
N19	●	Chaffey JC	14	0
N21		at Riverside JC	7	19

1922   6-4-0
S19	●	San Diego Marines	18	0
S22		Coronado HS	39	0
S26		Fleet Air	6	7
S30		Occidental	7	33
O7		UCLA	6	24 *
O21		Whittier College	7	33
N4	●	at Santa Ana JC	50	0
N10	●	at Fullerton JC	31	0
N24	●	Riverside JC	20	6
N30	●	at Chaffey JC	6	0

1923   8-2-0
S29	●	USS Melville	10	3
O6		Occidental	7	33
O13		at UCLA	0	12
O19	●	San Diego Marines	14	3
O27	●	at Riverside JC	39	3
N3	●	UC Santa Barbara	38	13
N12	●	Santa Ana JC	26	6
N17	●	San Diego Marines	34	7
N24	●	La Verne	27	0
N29	●	Fresno State	12	2

1924   7-1-2
O4	●	San Diego Marines	30	0
O11	●	California Christian	54	6
O18	●	Redlands	13	0
O25	=	at La Verne	7	7
N1	●	Riverside JC	6	0
N5	●	at El Centro JC	58	0
N8	●	at UC Santa Barbara	42	6
N15	=	UCLA	13	13
N22	●	Santa Ana JC	26	14
N27		at Fresno State	0	7

1925   5-3-1
S26		at UCLA	0	7
O3	●	at Redlands	10	0
O17	●	Cal Tech	10	6
O24	●	Whittier	24	0
O31		Loyola-Marymount	9	13
N7	●	at UC Santa Barbara	10	0
N14	=	San Diego Marines	14	14
N21	●	California Christian	14	6
N26		La Verne	7	13

1926   3-4-1
O2		at Pomona	6	20
O9		at UCLA	7	42
O16	●	Redlands	14	9
O23	●	California Christian	21	16
O30		Fresno State	7	28
N6	●	UC Santa Barbara	16	0
N13	=	La Verne	7	7
N25		Whittier	0	28

1927   4-3-0
O1	●	California Christian	71	0
O8		at Redlands	32	0
O15	●	Cal Tech	13	17
O29		Pomona	12	18
N5		at Whittier	7	25
N12	●	at UC Santa Barbara	16	13
N24	●	La Verne	39	6

1928   3-3-0
O13		Occidental	7	20
O27		Whittier	34	12
N3	●	at California Christian	18	13
N10	●	La Verne	40	0
N17		at Pomona	0	27
N29		Cal Tech	12	33

1929   3-5-0
S28	●	California Christian	26	18
O5		at Whittier	7	13
O12		at Redlands	0	7
O19	●	UC Santa Barbara	7	6
N2		Occidental	0	20
N9	●	La Verne	35	0
N16		Pomona	0	13
N28		Cal Tech	6	19

W.B. HERREID
1930-34 (.489)   20-21-5

1930   5-4-0
S25	●	San Diego Marines JV	39	0
O3		at Pomona	6	0
O11	●	California Christian	19	0
O17	●	at Occidental	14	7
O25	●	La Verne	14	6
N1		Whittier	13	19
N8		Redlands	0	6
N15		Submarines Pacific	7	13
N27		Cal Tech	0	20

1931   5-3-2
S19	=	Alumni	0	0
S26	●	at Arizona	8	0
O2	●	at California Christian	27	0
O9		Occidental	2	13
O16	=	Redlands	6	6
O23	●	at Whittier	7	0
O31	●	at Pomona	6	0
N11		San Diego Marines	0	13
N26		Cal Tech	0	13
D5	●	at Fresno State	15	0

1932   3-5-1
S23		UC Santa Barbara	2	6
O1	●	at Pomona	13	0
O8		La Verne	12	15
O22	=	Occidental	0	0
O28	●	at Redlands	6	19
N5		Whittier	14	19
N11		San Diego Marines	0	14
N19	●	Arizona	13	0
N26	●	Cal Tech	20	0

1933   4-4-1
S23		at UCLA	0	13
S30		San Diego Marines	0	34
O6	=	at Whittier	0	0
O14	●	Pomona	10	0
O20	●	at La Verne	6	0
O27		Redlands	0	13
N10	●	at UC Santa Barbara	6	0
N18		at Occidental	0	12
N25	●	Cal Tech	37	0

1934   3-5-1
S22		at UCLA	0	20
S29		at Arizona	0	7
O6	●	Army-Navy Acad.	19	7
O13	●	Occidental	20	7
O19	=	at La Verne	0	0
N3		Whittier	6	26
N10		Loyola-Marymount	3	19
N17	●	at Redlands	7	6
N29		Arizona State	6	14

LEO CALLAND
1935-41 (.600)   34-22-4

1935   3-4-1
O5	=	UC Santa Barbara	7	7
O12		Occidental	0	7
O19	●	La Verne	14	6
O25		at Whittier	0	13
N9	●	Loyola-Marymount	6	0
N16	●	Redlands	13	7
N28		at San Jose State	9	24
D7		Pacific	6	19

1936   6-1-1
O3	●	Occidental	7	0
O10	●	La Verne	35	6
O17	●	at Redlands	27	7
O24	●	San Jose State	14	6
O31	=	at New Mexico State	7	7
N11	●	San Diego Marines	0	14
N21	●	UC Santa Barbara	9	8
N28	●	at Whittier	19	14

1937   7-1-0
O2	●	Occidental	3	0
O9	●	Whittier	6	0
O16	●	La Verne	26	0
O23	●	New Mexico State	20	0
N6		Redlands	9	10
N11	●	San Diego Marines	6	0
N20	●	at UC Santa Barbara	13	0
N25	●	at San Jose State	7	6

1938   5-2-1
S24	●	USS New Mexico	29	20
O1	●	Occidental	8	0
O8	=	at Whittier	6	6
O15		Pomona	0	9
O22	●	at Redlands	14	7
O29		San Diego State	0	14
N11	●	San Diego Marines	9	0
N19	●	at UC Santa Barbara	16	13

1939   2-7-0
S21		Arizona State	0	20
S29	●	Redlands	26	0
O6		Occidental	10	6
O13		at San Jose State	0	42
O28		Pomona	6	12
N4		Whittier	12	23
N11		San Diego Marines	6	13
N15		Hawaii	0	13
N25		UC Santa Barbara	0	19

1940   5-3-1
S27	●	Pomona	33	3
O4	●	Occidental	20	0
O11		at San Jose State	0	10
O19	●	Redlands	20	14
O25	=	Fresno State	0	0
N8		San Diego Marines	6	20
N16	●	at Whittier	33	6
N23	●	at UC Santa Barbara	9	7
D7		at Hawaii	7	33

1941   6-4-0
S26	●	Pomona	6	0
O4	●	Occidental	7	6
O10		San Jose State	0	20
O18	●	Redlands	12	3
O25		Fresno State	0	26
N7		Camp Haan	0	6
N14	●	Cal Tech	44	6
N21	●	at Whittier	18	7
N28	●	UC Santa Barbara	6	7
D5	●	Pacific	12	6

LEO CALLAND
1935-41 (.600)   34-22-4

JOHN EUBANK
1942 (.071)   0-6-1

1942   0-6-1
O3	=	Pomona	6	6
O11		Fresno State	0	66
O17		Redlands	12	14
O25		March Field Flyers	6	39
O31		at Cal Poly SLO	13	32
N8		at San Jose State	0	26
N14		Whittier	13	28

1943-44
NO TEAM

BOB BREITBARD
1945 (.286)   2-5

1945   2-5-0
S29		at Redlands	6	7
O6		Cal Tech	20	32
O20		at Arizona	0	46
O27		at Fresno State	7	0
N3	●	Pomona	26	6
N11		at Nevada	6	44
N17		at Arizona	0	28

BILL TERRY
1946 (.600)   6-4

1946   6-4-0
S28	●	Pomona	34	0
O5		Cal Poly	13	21
O12	●	at Whittier	35	7
O19	●	Nevada	0	26
O26	●	Fresno State	7	0
N2	●	Occidental	21	12
N8	●	at Loyola-Marymount	20	7
N16		San Jose State	0	6
N23	●	at UC Santa Barbara	9	7
N30	●	at Pacific	13	19

BILL SCHUTTE
1947-55 (.568)   48-36-4

1947   7-3-1
S19	●	at Utah State	24	19
O4	●	Cal Poly SLO	56	13
O11		at Pacific	0	13
O18	●	Occidental	14	0
O25		San Jose State	7	32
N1	=	at Fresno State	7	7
N8	●	Loyola-Marymount	13	12
N15	●	Whittier	19	0
N22	●	Brigham Young	32	7
N29	●	UC Santa Barbara	19	0
HARBOR BOWL				
J1		Hardin-Simmons	0	53

1948   4-7-0
S18		at Brigham Young	6	14
S25		at Arizona	6	14
O2	●	Redlands	38	7
O9		Pacific	14	41
O16	●	Pepperdine	7	6
O30		Loyola-Marymount	6	20
N6		Fresno State	6	7
N12		at San Jose State	13	21
N20	●	at Cal Poly	28	14
N27		at UC Santa Barbara	6	27
D4	●	Utah State	28	19

1949   6-3-0
O1	●	at Pepperdine	9	7
O8	●	Pomona	33	13
O15	●	New Mexico State	39	18
O22		Pacific	14	62
O29		Loyola-Marymount	20	34
N5	●	at Fresno State	18	7
N12		San Jose State	0	40
N19	●	Cal Poly	40	19
N24	●	UC Santa Barbara	22	0

1950 5-3-1

S20	●	at Hawaii	49	27
S29		at San Jose State	0	26
O7		San Diego Marines	14	28
O14	●	Pepperdine	28	14
O21	=	Fresno State	20	20
O28	●	Pomona	49	20
N4		at Arizona State	13	31
N18	●	at Cal Poly	12	8
N25	●	at UC Santa Barbara	28	12

1951 10-0-1

S21	●	at San Francisco State	32	14
S29	●	Submarines Pacific	37	21
O6	●	Cal Poly SLO	32	13
O13	●	San Diego Marines	34	18
O20	=	Arizona State	27	27
O27	●	Cal State LA	64	0
N3	●	at Fresno State	13	7
N10	●	at Redlands	46	14
N16	●	at Pepperdine	27	6
N22	●	UC Santa Barbara	40	0
		PINEAPPLE BOWL		
J1	●	Hawaii	34	13

1952 4-5-0

S27		San Jose State	6	47
O4		at Cal Poly SLO	18	20
O11	●	Pepperdine	33	13
O18	●	Redlands	27	12
O25	●	Cal State LA	41	26
N1		Fresno State	33	49
N8	●	San Francisco State	39	28
N17		San Diego Marines	21	51
N21		at UC Santa Barbara	20	21

1953 5-3-1

S26	●	Hawaii	40	7
O3		Cal Poly SLO	12	33
O10	●	at Pepperdine	6	0
O17		at New Mexico	12	41
O23	●	at Cal State LA	40	13
O31	=	at Fresno State	27	27
N7	●	Occidental	14	7
N14		San Diego Marines	7	14
N21	●	UC Santa Barbara	72	0

1954 5-4-0

S25		New Mexico	7	28
O2		at Cal Poly SLO	14	26
O8		at San Francisco State	10	12
O16	●	San Diego Marines	14	0
O23	●	Cal State LA	38	0
O30		Fresno State	0	20
N13	●	Pepperdine	20	12
N20	●	at UC Santa Barbara	33	14
N27	●	Whittier	41	28

1955 2-8-0

S25		at Pepperdine	0	21
O1		Cal Poly SLO	6	12
O8		at Pomona	20	28
O15		Arizona State	0	46
O22	●	San Diego NTC	14	12
O29	●	San Francisco State	7	6
N5		at Fresno State	6	20
N12		at New Mexico State	6	26
N19		San Diego Marines	0	32
N26		at Whittier	6	28

PAUL GOVERNALI
1956-60 (.310) 11-27-4

1956 4-3-2

S29	●	Pepperdine	27	7
O5	●	at San Francisco State	26	6
O13	●	at Cal Poly SLO	7	6
O20	=	San Jose State	27	27
O27	=	San Diego Marines	19	19
N3		at Arizona State	0	61
N10	●	at UC Santa Barbara	30	7
N17		Fresno State	7	50
N24		at New Mexico	6	34

1957 2-7-0

S21		Pacific	6	32
S28	●	San Francisco State	14	13
O5	●	at La Verne	38	0
O12		San Diego Marines	7	20
O19		at San Jose State	0	46
O26		Arizona State	0	66
N2		at Fresno State	0	27
N9		Hawaii Marines	0	25
N15		at Pepperdine	12	14

1958 3-5-0

S20		at UC Santa Barbara	0	25
S27	●	Pepperdine	6	0
O3	●	at Long Beach State	20	12
O18	●	Cal State LA	7	0
N1		Fresno State	20	22
N8		San Diego Marines	0	25
N15		at Cal Poly SLO	14	48
N22		Pacific	17	68

1959 1-6-1

S26		Cal State LA	3	21
O3		Cal Poly SLO	6	13
O10		at Long Beach State	6	14
O17	●	at Redlands	19	15
O31		at Fresno State	13	38
N7		UC Santa Barbara	7	29
N14	=	at Pepperdine	14	14
N21		San Diego Marines	6	64

1960 1-6-1

S24		Cal State LA	14	24
O1		at Cal Poly SLO	6	34
O8		at Long Beach State	0	28
O15	=	Redlands	0	0
O22		at UC Santa Barbara	6	8
O29		Fresno State	0	60
N5	●	Pepperdine	27	20
N12		San Diego Marines	0	33

DON CORYELL
1961-72 (.840) 104-19-2

1961 7-2-1

S23	=	at Cal State LA	13	13
S30	●	Cal Poly SLO	9	6
O7		Long Beach State	15	17
O14	●	at Redlands	32	20
O21	●	UC Santa Barbara	21	6
O28		at Fresno State	6	27
N4	●	at Pepperdine	21	6
N11	●	Cal Western	54	34
N18	●	San Diego University	42	12
N27	●	San Diego Marines	18	13

1962 8-2-0

S15		Cal Poly Pomona	6	13
S22	●	Cal State LA	26	14
S29	●	at Cal Poly SLO	35	14
O6	●	at Long Beach State	36	8
O13	●	Redlands	39	0
O19	●	at UC Santa Barbara	46	8
O27	●	Fresno State	29	26
N3	●	San Fernando Valley St.	39	0
N10	●	Pacific	32	18
N17		San Diego Marines	6	34

1963 7-2-0

S28	●	Cal Poly Pomona	42	7
O5	●	Cal Poly SLO	69	0
O12	●	Long Beach State	33	8
O19		at Cal State LA	30	43
O26	●	UC Santa Barbara	42	14
N9	●	at Fresno State	34	6
N16	●	at Pacific	34	18
N23	●	at San Fernando Valley St.	21	6
N30		San Diego Marines	12	16

1964 8-2-0

S19	●	at Cal Poly Pomona	53	8
S26	●	San Francisco State	54	0
O3	●	at Cal Poly SLO	59	7
O10	●	at Long Beach State	45	8
O17		Cal State LA	0	7
O24	●	at UC Santa Barbara	50	9
O31	●	Fresno State	44	6
N14	●	San Fernando Valley St.	53	0
N21	●	Cal Western	50	6
N28		at San Jose State	15	20

1965 8-2-0

S18	●	Pacific	46	6
S25	●	Akron	41	0
O2	●	Cal Poly SLO	41	0
O9		Long Beach State	32	35
O16		at Cal State LA	12	26
O23	●	Cal Poly Pomona	41	13
O30	●	at Fresno State	26	7
N13	●	at San Fernando Valley St.	50	0
N20	●	at Northern Arizona	20	0
N27	●	Cal Western	44	0

1966 11-0-0

S17	●	Mexico Polytechnic	45	0
S24	●	at Weber State	38	34
O1	●	at Cal Poly SLO	14	13
O8	●	at Long Beach State	21	18
O15	●	at San Jose State	25	0
O29	●	Fresno State	34	13
N5	●	North Dakota State	36	0
N12	●	San Fernando Valley St.	21	0
N19	●	Northern Arizona	16	8
N26	●	Cal State LA	39	12
		CAMELLIA BOWL		
D10	●	Montana State	28	7

1967 10-1-0

S15	●	Tennessee State	16	8
S23	●	Weber State	58	12
S30	●	Cal Poly SLO	26	20
O7	●	Long Beach State	20	7
O14	●	at Cal State LA	28	0
O21	●	at Northern Illinois	47	6
O28	●	at Fresno State	28	21
N11	●	at San Fernando Valley St.	30	21
N18	●	Montana State	14	3
N25		Utah State	25	31
		CAMELLIA BOWL		
D9	●	San Francisco State	27	6

1968 9-0-1

S14	●	Texas-Arlington	23	18
S20	●	Northern Illinois	40	21
S28	●	at Montana State	34	22
O12	●	Texas Southern	42	23
O19	●	Cal State LA	37	14
O26	●	San Jose State	48	6
N2	●	Fresno State	42	12
N9	●	Southern Miss	68	7
N23	=	Tennessee State	13	13
N30	●	Utah State	30	19

1969-1975
PCAA

1969 11-0-0 (6-0-0)

S27	● |	Cal State LA	49	0
O4	● |	at San Jose State	55	21
O11	●	at West Texas State	24	14
O18	●	at Texas-Arlington	27	10
O25	● |	UC Santa Barbara	55	13
N1	● |	at Fresno State	48	20
N8	● |	Pacific	58	32
N15	●	New Mexico State	70	21
N22	●	North Texas	42	24
N29	● |	Long Beach State	36	32
		PASADENA BOWL		
D6	●	Boston University	28	7

1970 9-2-0 (5-1-0)

S12	●	at Northern Illinois	35	3
S19	●	at North Texas	23	0
S26	● |	Cal State LA	35	0
O3	●	Brigham Young	31	11
O10	●	Southern Miss	41	14
O17	● |	San Jose State	32	6
O31	● |	Fresno State	56	14
N7	● |	at Pacific	14	13
N14	● |	UC Santa Barbara	64	7
N20	|	Long Beach State	11	27
N28		Iowa State	22	28

1971 6-5-0 (2-3-0)

S25		at Southern Miss	0	10
O2	●	Northern Illinois	30	10
O9	● |	Pacific	14	7
O16	● |	at UC Santa Barbara	27	23
O22	●	Utah State	36	20
O30	|	at Fresno State	10	17
N6	|	at San Jose State	7	45
N13	|	Long Beach State	7	12
N20	●	Arizona	39	10
N27		Iowa State	31	48
D4	●	North Texas	44	28

1972 10-1-0 (4-0-0)

S8	●	Oregon State	17	8
S23	●	North Texas IRV	25	0
S30	●	at Kent State	14	0
O7	● |	San Jose State	23	12
O14		at Houston	14	49
O21	●	Bowling Green	35	19
O28	● |	Fresno State	21	14
N4	●	West Texas State	37	6
N11	● |	Pacific	20	7
N25	● |	at Long Beach State	33	14
D2	●	Iowa State	27	14

CLAUDE GILBERT
1973-80 (.697) 61-26-2

1973 9-1-1 (3-0-1)

S22	●	at Utah State	35	7
S30	●	Kent State	17	9
O6		Houston	9	14
O13	●	New Mexico State	27	0
O20	● |	at Pacific	13	10
O27	●	Florida State	38	17
N3	= |	at San Jose State	27	27
N10	● |	Long Beach State	17	2
N17	● |	at Fresno State	41	6
N24	●	North Texas	56	9
D1	●	Iowa State	41	28

1974 8-2-1 (4-0-0)

S14		at Arizona	10	17
S21	●	Tampa	28	25
S28	●	at Texas-El Paso	26	12
O12	● |	at Fresno State	24	21
O19	● |	San Jose State	40	14
O26	● |	Long Beach State	27	17
N2		at North Texas	9	14
N9	● |	Pacific	37	9
N16	●	New Mexico State	35	14
N23	=	Bowling Green	21	21
N30	●	Utah State	34	6

1975 8-3-0 (3-2-0)

S6	●	Texas-El Paso	31	10
S13	●	Oregon State PORT	25	0
S20	●	North Texas	30	12
S27	●	at Utah State	19	10
O4	● |	Fullerton St.	59	14
O11	● |	at Fresno State	29	0
O18	●	New Mexico State	48	3
N1	● |	at Pacific	31	13
N8		Arizona	24	31
N15	|	at San Jose State	7	31
N22	|	Long Beach State	17	21

1976-1977
INDEPENDENT

1976 10-1-0

S12	●	Arkansas State	24	14
S18	●	Fresno State	7	3
S25	●	at Bowling Green	27	15
O2		Brigham Young	0	8
O16	●	Pacific	21	15
O23	●	Fullerton St.	27	14
O30	●	at Texas-El Paso	27	16
N6	●	San Jose State	30	17
N13	●	Utah State	7	6
N20	●	at Long Beach State	10	3
N27	●	New Mexico	17	14

1977 10-1-0

S10	●	Fullerton St.	34	17
S17	●	at Arizona	21	14
O1	●	Utah State	19	0
O8		at Fresno State	14	34
O15	●	Texas-El Paso	49	7
O22	●	Nevada-Las Vegas	31	7
O29	●	Tulsa	41	7
N5	●	at Pacific	29	7
N12	●	Long Beach State	33	22
N19	●	Florida State	41	16
D3	●	at San Jose State	37	34

1978-1998
WAC

1978 4-7-0 (2-4-0)

S16		at Iowa State	13	14
S23	|	at Texas-El Paso	24	31
O7	● |	Fresno State	31	14
O14	|	at Wyoming	22	31
O21	●	Pacific	31	28
O28		at Long Beach St.	25	27
N4	● |	Colorado State	34	31
N11	|	at Brigham Young	3	21
N18		at Miami, Fla.	14	16
N25	● |	New Mexico	27	24
D2	|	Utah	18	20

1979 8-3-0 (5-2-0)

S8		at Missouri	15	45
S22	●	at Fresno State	32	23
S29	●	Wisconsin	24	17
O6	● |	at New Mexico	35	7
O13	●	Miami, Fla.	31	20
O20	|	at Colorado State	3	37
O27	● |	at Utah	17	13
N3	● |	Wyoming	31	21
N10	● ||	Arizona	42	10
N17	● |	Texas-El Paso	42	20
N24	|	Brigham Young	14	63

THE SCHOOLS

1980 — 4-8-0 (4-4-0)

S13		at Brigham Young	11 35
S20 ●		at Air Force	13 10
S27		Missouri	7 31
O4		at Wisconsin	12 35
O11		Nevada-Las Vegas	17 28
O18		Colorado State	7 26
O25		at Wyoming	9 34
N1		at Oklahoma State	6 15
N8		at Hawaii	6 31
N15 ●		at Texas-El Paso	28 7
N22 ●		New Mexico	24 22
N29 ●		Utah	21 20

DOUG SCOVIL 1981-85 (.432) 24-32-3

1981 — 6-5-0 (3-5-0)

S12 ●		at Colorado State	30 14
S26 ●		at Oklahoma State	23 16
O3 ●		at New Mexico	17 15
O10 ●		Iowa State	52 31
O17 ●		Brigham Young	7 27
O24 ●		Hawaii	10 28
O31 ●		at Utah	14 17
N7 ●		Wyoming	13 24
N14 ●		at Nevada-Las Vegas	38 20
N21 ●		Texas-El Paso	59 14
N28		Air Force *Tok*	16 21

1982 — 7-5-0 (4-3-0)

S11		at Air Force	32 44
S18		at California	0 28
S25 ●		Nevada-Las Vegas	26 23
O2		at Washington	25 46
O9 ●		at Wyoming	24 21
O16		New Mexico	17 22
O23 ●		Long Beach St.	51 17
O30 ●		Utah	21 17
N6 ●		at Hawaii	31 28
N13		at Brigham Young	8 58
N20 ●		Colorado State	38 10
N27		Oklahoma State	35 6

1983 — 2-9-1 (1-6-1)

S3		at Tulsa	9 34
S10 ●		California	28 14
S17		at Utah	24 27
S24 ●		at Texas-El Paso	41 33
O1 =		at Hawaii	27 27
O8 ●		at Long Beach St.	13 20
O15 ●		at Colorado State	15 17
O22 ●		Brigham Young	12 47
O29 ●		at Nevada-Las Vegas	10 28
N12 ●		Wyoming	21 33
N19 ●		at New Mexico	14 34
N26		Air Force	7 38

1984 — 4-7-1 (4-3-1)

S1		at Air Force	16 34
S8		UCLA	15 18
S15 ●		Texas-El Paso	51 2
S22		at Oklahoma State	16 19
O6 ●		at Wyoming	21 0
O13 =		Utah	24 24
O20 ●		Colorado State	41 24
O27 ●		at Hawaii	10 16
N3		Nevada-Las Vegas	14 30 †
N10 ●		at Brigham Young	3 34
N17 ●		New Mexico	37 31
N24 ●		Long Beach St.	17 18

1985 — 5-6-1 (3-4-1)

S14 ●		at Long Beach St.	34 14
S21 ●		at UCLA	16 34
S28 ●		Colorado State	48 23
O5 ●		Stanford	41 22
O12 ●		at Brigham Young	0 28
O19 ●		Utah	37 39
O26 ●		Oregon	37 49
N2 ●		at Air Force	10 31
N9 ●		at Wyoming	20 41
N16 ●		at Texas-El Paso	34 6
N23 ●		at New Mexico	55 20
N30 =		at Hawaii	10 10

DENNY STOLZ 1986-88 (.457) 16-19

1986 — 8-4-0 (7-1-0)

S6 ●		Long Beach St.	27 24
S13 ●		at Utah	37 30
S20		UCLA	14 45
S27 ●		at New Mexico	38 34
O4		at Stanford	10 17
O18 ●		at Texas-El Paso	15 10
O25		Air Force	10 22
N1 ●		at Colorado State	27 26
N15 ●		Wyoming	31 24
N22 ●		Hawaii	35 5
N29 ●		Brigham Young	10 3
HOLIDAY BOWL			
D30		Iowa	38 39

1987 — 5-7-0 (4-4-0)

S5		at UCLA	14 47
S12 ●		Utah	52 34
S19		at Air Force	7 49
S26		at Oregon	20 25
O3 ●		at Wyoming	10 52
O10 ●		Texas-El Paso	33 34
O17		Stanford	40 44
O24 ●		at Long Beach St.	52 42
O31 ●		at Hawaii	29 21
N7		at Brigham Young	21 38
N14 ●		Colorado State	26 12
N21 ●		New Mexico	53 30

1988 — 3-8-0 (3-5-0)

S3		at UCLA	6 59
S11 ●		Air Force	39 36
S17		at Stanford	10 31
O1		Oregon	13 34
O8 ●		Wyoming	27 55
O15 ●		Hawaii	30 32
O22 ●		at Colorado State	7 13
O29 ●		at Utah	20 41
N5 ●		Brigham Young	27 15
N12 ●		at Texas-El Paso	7 58
N19 ●		at New Mexico	18 10

AL LUGINBILL 1989-93 (.551) 31-25-3

1989 — 6-5-1 (4-3-0)

S2		at Air Force	36 52
S16		UCLA	25 28
S23 =		Fullerton St.	41 41
S30 ●		at Utah	38 27
O7		at Hawaii	30 31
O14 ●		Long Beach St.	30 26
O21 ●		Pacific	35 7
O28 ●		at Texas-El Paso	34 31
N4 ●		New Mexico	45 28
N11 ●		Wyoming	27 17
N18 ●		at Miami, Fla.	6 42
N25 ●		Brigham Young	27 48

1990 — 6-5-0 (5-2-0)

S8		at Oregon	21 42
S15 ●		Long Beach St.	38 20
S22 ●		at Brigham Young	34 62
S29 ●		Air Force	48 18
O6 ●		at Wyoming	51 52
O13 ●		at UCLA	31 45
N3 ●		Utah	66 14
N10 ●		Hawaii	44 38
N17 ●		at New Mexico	40 34
N24 ●		Texas-El Paso	58 31
D1		Miami, Fla.	28 30

1991 — 8-4-1 (6-1-1)

S7 ●		Long Beach St.	49 13
S14 ●		Pacific	55 34
S21 ●		at Air Force	20 21
S26		UCLA	12 37
O5 ●		at Hawaii	47 21
O12 ●		New Mexico	38 24
O19 ●		at Texas-El Paso	28 21
O26 ●		at Utah	24 21
N2 ●		Wyoming	24 22
N9 ●		Colorado State	42 32
N16 =		Brigham Young	52 52
N30 ●		at Miami, Fla.	12 39
FREEDOM BOWL			
D30		Tulsa	17 28

1992 — 5-5-1 (5-3-0)

S5 =		Southern Cal	31 31
S10 ●		at Brigham Young	45 38
S26		at UCLA	7 35
O3 ●		at New Mexico	49 21
O17 ●		Texas-El Paso	49 27
O24		Air Force	17 20
O31 ●		at Colorado State	20 13
N7		at Wyoming	6 17
N14 ●		Hawaii	52 28
N21		Fresno State	41 45
N28		Miami, Fla.	17 63

1993 — 6-6-0 (4-4-0)

S4 ●		Northridge St.	34 17
S11		at California	25 45
S18 ●		at Air Force	38 31
S25 ●		Minnesota	48 17
S30		UCLA	13 52
O9 ●		at Hawaii	45 14
O16 ●		Colorado State	30 3
O23 ●		New Mexico	20 17
O30 ●		at Utah	41 45
N11 ●		Brigham Young	44 45
N20 ●		at Fresno State	37 63
N27 ●		Wyoming	38 43

TED TOLLNER 1994-2001 (.473) 43-48

1994 — 4-7-0 (2-6-0)

S3 ●		Navy	56 14
S10 ●		California	22 20
S17		at Minnesota	17 40
S24		at Colorado State	17 19
O1		Air Force	35 36
O8		Utah	22 38
O15 ●		at New Mexico	20 13
O22 ●		at Wyoming	35 52
O29 ●		Hawaii	38 23
N10 ●		at Brigham Young	28 35
N26		Fresno State	42 49

1995 — 8-4-0 (5-3-0)

S2 ●		California	33 9
S9 ●		at Oklahoma	22 38
S16 ●		at Brigham Young	19 31
S28 ●		Nevada	30 27
O7 ●		at Utah	24 21
O14 ●		Fresno State	48 24
O21 ●		San Jose State	49 20
O28 ●		at Texas-El Paso	45 16
N4 ●		New Mexico	38 29
N11 ●		Wyoming	31 34
N18 ●		at Hawaii	49 10
N25		Colorado State	13 24

1996 — 8-3 (6-2)

S7 ●		Idaho	40 21
S14		at California	37 42
S21 ●		Oklahoma	51 31
O11		Hawaii	56 8
O19 ●		at New Mexico	48 42
O26		at Colorado State	18 27
N2 ●		at San Jose State	49 20
N7 ●		Wyoming	28 24
N16 ●		at Nevada-Las Vegas	42 44
N23 ●		Fresno State	31 21
N28 ●		Air Force	28 23

1997 — 5-7 (4-4)

S5 ●		Navy	45 31
S13		at Washington	3 36
S20		at Wisconsin	10 36
S27		at Air Force	18 24
O4		at Arizona	28 31
O11		New Mexico	21 36
O18 ●		Nevada-Las Vegas	20 17
O25 ●		at Hawaii	10 3
N1		at Wyoming	17 41
N8 ●		San Jose State	48 21
N15 ●		at Fresno State	20 19
N22		Colorado State	17 38

1998 — 7-5 (7-1)

S5		Wisconsin	14 26
S12		at Southern Cal	6 35
S24		Arizona	16 35
O3 ●		at Tulsa	24 14
O9 ●		Hawaii	35 13
O17 ●		at New Mexico	36 33
O24 ●		Utah	21 20
O29 ●		at Brigham Young	0 13
N7 ●		Fresno State	10 0
N14 ●		at San Jose State	34 6
N21		Texas-El Paso	34 29
LAS VEGAS BOWL			
D19		North Carolina	13 20

1999-PRESENT MOUNTAIN WEST

1999 — 5-6 (3-4)

S4 ●		South Florida	41 12
S11		at Illinois	10 38
S18		at Southern Cal	21 24
S25 ●		at Kansas	41 13
O2		Air Force	22 23
O9		New Mexico	21 24
O16 ●		at Colorado State	17 10
O23		at Utah	16 38
N6		Brigham Young	7 30
N20 ●		at Nevada-Las Vegas	37 7
N27 ●		Wyoming	39 7

2000 — 3-8 (3-4)

A31		Arizona State	7 10
S9		Illinois	13 49
S16		at Arizona	3 17
S23		at Oregon State	3 35
O7 ●		at Wyoming	34 0
O14		Utah	7 21
O21 ●		at Brigham Young	16 15
O28 ●		Colorado State	22 34
N4 ●		at New Mexico	17 16
N18 ●		at Air Force	24 45
N25 ●		Nevada-Las Vegas	24 31

2001 — 3-8 (2-5)

A30		Arizona	10 23
S8		at Arizona State	7 38
S22 ●		at Colorado State	14 7
S29		Air Force	21 45
O6 ●		Eastern Illinois	40 7
O13 ●		at Nevada-Las Vegas	3 31
O20		at Ohio State	12 27
O27		Brigham Young	21 59
N3		New Mexico	15 20
N10		at Utah	3 17
N17 ●		Wyoming	38 16

TOM CRAFT 2002-PRESENT (.389) 14-22

2002 — 4-9 (4-3)

A29		at Fresno State	14 16
S7		at Colorado	14 34
S14		Arizona State	28 39
S21		at Idaho	38 48
S28		UCLA	7 43
O12 ●		Utah	36 17
O19		at Wyoming	24 20
O26 ●		Nevada-Las Vegas	31 21
N2		at Brigham Young	10 34
N9		at New Mexico	8 15
N16		Colorado State	21 49
N23 ●		at Air Force	38 34
D7		at Hawaii	40 41

2003 — 6-6 (3-4)

A30 ●		Ea. Washington	19 9
S6		at Ohio State	13 16
S13 ●		at Texas-El Paso	34 0
S20 ●		Samford	37 17
S27 ●		at UCLA	10 20
O4		Brigham Young	36 44
O11		at Utah	6 27
O18		New Mexico	7 30
O25 ●		Wyoming	25 20
N8 ●		at Nevada-Las Vegas	7 0
N15		at Colorado State	6 21
N22 ●		Air Force	24 3

2004 — 4-7 (2-5)

S4 ●		Idaho State	38 21
S18		at Michigan	21 24
S25 ●		Nevada	27 10
O2		at UCLA	10 33
O9		at Wyoming	10 20
O16		Colorado State	17 21
O23		at New Mexico	9 19
O30		Utah	28 51
N6		at Brigham Young	16 49
N13 ●		at Air Force	37 31
N20 ●		Nevada-Las Vegas	21 3

SAN JOSE STATE

BY DAVE REARDON

SAN JOSE STATE FOOTBALL HAS the misfortune of being an afterthought for most Bay Area sports fans—if it's a thought at all. Despite having a football program dating back to 1893, the Spartans must vie for fans with two major Division I-A programs, Stanford and Cal, as well as with major league franchises in football, baseball, basketball and hockey, all within an hour's drive of the San Jose State campus. The Cardinal and the Golden Bears also make recruiting a tough task, forcing the Spartans to rely on junior college talent. At times, dwindling game attendance and familiar questions about the team's relevance have threatened the program's existence. Hard-core loyalists—and there are some, if you know where to look—swear they'll someday look back at late December 2004 as the turning point in San Jose State's fortunes. That was when Dick Tomey, the all-time leader in coaching victories at both Hawaii and Arizona, was named Spartans head coach.

TRADITION For a program that's over a century old, San Jose State doesn't have many traditions. For the past several years, the team has sung "The Spartan Fight Song" to fans after victories. Recently, San Jose State started a Ring of Honor to recognize legends of the program like Jack Elway, Jeff Garcia and Bill Walsh. That's it, at least until the Tomey era is in full blossom.

BEST PLAYER Middle linebacker Dave Chaney holds the San Jose State career record for total tackles (527), as well as marks for primary tackles in a game (21), season (125) and career (297). He also led the Spartans to one of their biggest wins, 13-12 at Stanford in 1971. His 24 tackles in that game helped him earn a first-team All-America nod from The Associated Press. Chaney went on to become a high school teacher and tennis coach.

BEST COACH Under Dudley S. DeGroot, the Spartans went 59–19–8 from 1932 to 1939. His last team went 13–0, San Jose State's only undefeated season. The former four-sport athlete from Stanford (basketball, football, swimming and water polo) also won an Olympic gold medal in rugby, then went to coach at the University of Rochester for four years before going on to lead the Washington Redskins.

PROFILE

San Jose State University
San Jose, Calif.
Founded: 1857
Enrollment: 21,396
Colors: Gold, White and Blue
Nickname: Spartans
Stadium: Spartan Stadium
    Opened in 1933
    Grass; 30,456 capacity
First football game: 1893
All-time record: 421–403–38 (.510)
Bowl record: 4–3
First-round NFL draftees: 6
Website: www.sjsuspartans.com

THE BEST OF TIMES

From 1937 to 1940, the Spartans went 46–4–1, including a 13–0 season in 1939.

THE WORST OF TIMES

From 1965 to 1972, San Jose State was 26–56–1 under three different head coaches.

CONFERENCE

San Jose State joined the Western Athletic Conference in 1996. It played in the Pacific Coast Athletic Conference starting in 1969. The PCAC was renamed the Big West Conference in 1988.

DISTINGUISHED ALUMNI

Ben Nighthorse Campbell, U.S. senator; Christopher Darden, prosecuting attorney, O.J. Simpson murder trial; Lee Evans, 1968 Olympic gold medalist in track; Dr. Harry Edwards, sports sociologist; Juli Inkster, LPGA player/Hall of Famer; Jenny Ming, Old Navy president; Stevie Nicks, singer, Fleetwood Mac; Peter Ueberroth, baseball commissioner

FIGHT SONG

THE SPARTAN FIGHT SONG
Fight on for dear old San Jose State
Fight on for victory!
We are with you in every way
No matter what the price may be!
Onward for Sparta noble and true
Fight hard in everything you do!
And so we'll Fight! (RAH!) Win! (RAH!)
March onward down the field
and we will win the day!

When San Jose State lost a 13-10 squeaker to Hawaii in 2003, the Spartans felt like they were playing against two teams: the Warriors and the Zebras.

BEST TEAM The 1939 squad—one of the nation's first racially integrated teams—outscored the competition 324-29, including eight shutouts, and no opponent scored more than seven points. The team was a turnover-forcing machine, picking off 32 passes and recovering 12 fumbles for what still stands as a school record for turnovers forced. Back and punter Leroy Zimmerman was the team's best player, and he became the first Spartan to be chosen in the NFL draft. Other standouts were future San Jose State head coaches Robert Titchenal and Bob Bronzan.

BIGGEST GAME After San Jose State played Fresno State on Oct. 4, 1986, *Sports Illustrated* tagged it the Game of the Year. It was a dramatic seesaw; after the Spartans took a 24-0 lead, the Bulldogs came back to score the next 31 and led 41-31 with a minute left. However, San Jose State quarterback Mike Perez connected with Guy Liggins for a five-yard TD pass—and after the Spartans recovered the onside kick, Perez found Lafo Malauulu for a long score for the final points of the 4½-hour game. By the end, San Jose State had racked up 555 yards to Fresno State's 517. The 45-41 homecoming victory was the second of nine consecutive wins, propelling the Spartans to the PCAA championship and a 37-7 trouncing of Miami (Ohio) in the California Bowl.

BIGGEST UPSET When San Jose State visited Baylor in 1980, the Spartans went in as 27½ point underdogs—no surprise, since the Top 10-ranked Bears featured Mike Singletary on defense and Walter Abercrombie on offense, and would later represent the Southwest Conference in the Cotton Bowl. But the Spartans had a few weapons of their own, including Gerald Willhite at tailback, Stacey Bailey at receiver and Gill Byrd at cornerback. Baylor lived up to its hype early, leading 15-0 as the Spartans couldn't get their offense going, especially with fourth-string

RECORDS

RUSHING YARDS

GAME	
286	Nathan DuPree vs. Nevada-Las Vegas, Oct. 31, 1992 (43 att.)
SEASON	
1,577	Deoncé Whitaker, 2000 (224 att.)
CAREER	
3,515	Deoncé Whitaker, 1998-2001 (602 att.)

PASSING YARDS

GAME	
543	Scott Rislov vs. UTEP, Nov. 8, 2003 (28 of 39)
SEASON	
3,260	Mike Perez, 1987 (243 of 408)
CAREER	
7,190	Ed Luther, 1976-79 (600 of 1,118)

RECEIVING YARDS

GAME	
269	Edell Shepherd vs. Nevada, Nov. 10, 2001 (9 rec.)
SEASON	
1,500	Edell Shepherd, 2001 (83 rec.)
CAREER	
2,223	Stacey Bailey, 1978-81 (123 rec.)

POINTS

GAME	
30	Deoncé Whitaker vs. Saint Mary's-Cal., Sept. 18, 1999 (5 TDs)
SEASON	
116	Johnny Johnson Jr., 1988 (19 TDs, 1 two-pt. conv.)
CAREER	
236	Joe Nedney, 1991-94 (119 PATs, 39 FGs)

CONSENSUS ALL-AMERICANS

1938	Lloyd Thomas, E
1939	Leroy Zimmerman, B

quarterback Jack Overstreet making his first start. After three Overstreet interceptions, Baylor coach Grant Teaff began to empty his bench. Elway put in his No. 1 quarterback, Steve Clarkson, who had missed several games with a dislocated shoulder, and Clarkson drove the Spartans 91 yards for a TD near the end of the first half. Later, Singletary unwittingly contributed to a San Jose State touchdown by knocking a pass out of Rick Parma's hands and into Willhite's, cutting the deficit to 15-13, and a field goal put San Jose ahead. Baylor scored again, but Willhite found the end zone twice more in the fourth quarter as the Spartans took advantage of four interceptions and two fumble recoveries to win 30-22.

HEARTBREAKER Elway left San Jose State for Stanford before the 1984 season. In a Sept. 22 game against their erstwhile coach, the Spartans—after twice falling behind by 11 points—went ahead of the Cardinal 27-21 on a one-yard run by quarterback Bob Frasco in the fourth quarter. Thomas Henley's second TD put Stanford back ahead by one, but with 30 seconds left and the Spartans in field goal range, tailback Randy Walker mishandled a handoff from Frasco. Stanford recovered, icing the victory—its first against San Jose State after three consecutive losses.

STADIUM Spartan Stadium has been home to San Jose State football since 1933. Two expansions in the 1980s increased seating from 18,000 to its current capacity of 28,867. The largest attendance at a San Jose State home football game was a sellout crowd of 31,681 on Aug. 23, 2003, against Grambling. Spartan Stadium is also a popular soccer venue, playing host to the 1999 Women's World Cup and the 1999 NCI Women's College Cup.

RIVAL Sometimes geography means a lot more than parity. Through 2004, Fresno State had defeated San Jose State in 11 straight meetings, but both schools still consider the series a bitter rivalry. It's about history. "We had some real wars in the 1980s, when every year it seemed like the winner of the game won the conference," Fresno State coach Pat Hill said. "And a lot of people in the [San Joaquin] Valley feel very passionately about this game, just like the people over there, which makes it even more fun to be involved in." Even with the Bulldogs' long run of success, the Spartans trail the series by just two games, with Fresno leading 34–32–3.

DISPUTE When San Jose State lost a 13-10 squeaker to Hawaii in 2003, the Spartans felt like they were playing against two teams: the Warriors and the Zebras. According to the Western Athletic Conference office, the Spartans were justified in their feelings against the referees; after a review, WAC commissioner Karl Benson handed the officials a single-game suspension for errors on the game's final play. Spartans quarterback Scott Rislov had appeared to spike the ball at the Hawaii 1-yard line before time expired, but the officials mistakenly ruled the game over. Benson ruled time had not expired, and San Jose State should have been allowed to run one more play.

MASCOT Sammy the Spartan has filled the role of mascot. Although he has a fearsome appearance and carries an ancient warrior's sword, Sammy also wears a permanent grin and mingles with fans throughout games. Sometimes he enhances his costume armor by decorating it according to the opponent or current events.

UNIFORMS In 1925, a campus debate raged over whether to change the school colors from gold and white to purple and white. The effort failed. In 1946, gold and white prevailed yet again over another failed purple movement. Finally, during the 1970s, blue found its way into the mix, and since then uniform pants have been some combination of yellow, gold, white and blue. No purple, though.

LORE Neil Parry's determination and perseverance was the feel-good story of the college football year in 2003. On Oct. 14, 2000, the safety's right leg was fractured in San Jose State's game against Texas-El Paso. Nine days later, the leg was amputated below the knee. After 25 surgeries, Parry returned to the field on Sept. 18, 2003, against Nevada on punt coverage, and went on to play the remainder of the season, including the 2004 East-West Shrine Game.

QUOTE "I'm a microwave guy. But now I'm gonna make popcorn the old-fashioned way. The grease is hot."—San Jose State coach Fitz Hill, on switching from a passing offense to a run-first attack

THE SCHOOLS

SAN JOSE STATE ANNUAL STATISTICAL LEADERS

YR	RUSHING	YDS	ATT	AVG	PASSING	ATT	CMP	PCT	YDS	RECEIVING	REC	YDS	AVG
1938	Leroy Zimmerman	422	88	4.8	Leroy Zimmerman	85	51	.60	689	Herm Zetterquist	14	136	9.7
1939	Carlton Peregoy	514	153	3.4	Leroy Zimmerman	84	35	.42	459	Johnny Allen	11	206	18.7
1940	Bud Nygren	624	100	6.2	Deward Tornell	89	45	.51	501	Johnny Allen	21	373	17.8
1941	Allen Hardisty	499	147	3.4	Allen Hardisty	81	30	.37	281		NA	NA	NA
1942	NA	NA	NA		NA	NA	NA	NA		NA	NA	NA
1943	No team due to WWII				No team due to WWII					No team due to WWII			
1944	No team due to WWII				No team due to WWII					No team due to WWII			
1945	No team due to WWII				No team due to WWII					No team due to WWII			
1946		NA	NA	NA		NA	NA	NA	NA		NA	NA	NA
1947	Jack Donaldson	609	89	6.8	Jim Jackson	122	49	.40	799	Junior Morgan	18	218	12.1
1948	Fred Mangini	521	85	6.1	Chuck Hughes	115	47	.41	757	Billy Wilson	11	251	22.8
1949	Harry Russell	688	95	7.2	Gene Menges	182	99	.54	1,490	Junior Morgan	25	468	18.7
1950	Harry Beck	830	119	7.0	Gene Menges	126	56	.44	999	Billy Wilson	21	369	17.6
1951	Gibby Mendosa	312	60	5.2	Lynn Aplanalp	95	55	.58	592	Bob Osborne	14	282	20.1
1952	Dick Stults	801	118	6.8	Lynn Aplanalp	139	71	.51	1,157	Bob Amaral	18	369	20.5
1953	Larry Matthews	461	67	6.9	Larry Rice	78	33	.42	446	Larry Matthews	8	126	15.8
1954	Roy Hiram	395	61	6.5	Ben Pierce	85	42	.49	577	Clarence Wessman	13	227	17.5
1955	Stan Beasley	522	107	4.9	Tony Teresa	89	39	.44	709	Mel Powell	12	288	24.0
1956	Harvel Pollard	320	65	4.9	Bob Reinhart	172	90	.52	1,138	Art Powell	40	583	14.6
1957	Harvel Pollard	313	76	4.1	Dick Vermeil	84	43	.51	580	Dan Colchico	13	245	18.8
1958	Sam Dawson	339	57	5.9	Emmett Lee	116	63	.54	580	Dan Colchico	23	277	12.0
1959	Oneal Cuterry	491	100	4.9	Emmett Lee	150	86	.57	973	Oneal Cuterry	29	378	13.0
1960	Johnny Johnson	523	92	5.7	Mike Jones	152	71	.47	1,049	Mark Burton	23	376	16.3
1961	Johnny Johnson	597	124	4.8	Chon Gallegos	197	117	.59	1,480	Oscar Donahue	35	527	15.1
1962	Johnny Johnson	579	151	3.8	Rand Carter	168	90	.54	902	Dave Johnson	23	352	15.3
1963	Herb Engel	280	95	2.9	Rand Carter	135	74	.55	920	Walt Roberts	23	477	20.7
1964	Charlie Harraway	270	69	3.9	Ken Berry	188	94	.50	1,101	Bob Bonds	17	239	14.1
1965	Charlie Harraway	792	159	5.0	Ken Berry	202	94	.47	1,593	Steve Cox	38	513	13.5
1966	Jamie Townsend	156	58	2.7	Danny Holman	260	160	.62	1,925	Steve Cox	54	653	12.1
1967	Walt Shockley	341	85	4.0	Danny Holman	221	110	.50	1,403	Dwight Tucker	20	354	17.7
1968	Frank Slaton	287	59	4.9	Russ Munson	110	54	.49	701	John Crivello	17	257	15.1
1969	Larry Merlini	423	109	3.9	Ivan Lippi	301	105	.35	1,395	Butch Ellis	46	691	15.0
1970	Dale Knott	409	136	3.0	Ivan Lippi	241	109	.45	1,499	Al Ghysels	22	329	15.0
1971	Lawrence Brice	592	135	4.4	Dave Ellis	159	73	.46	977	Eric Dahl	27	563	20.9
1972	Dale Knott	271	122	2.2	Craig Kimball	323	145	.45	1,798	Chris Moyneur	46	559	12.2
1973	Larry Lloyd	764	237	3.2	Craig Kimball	305	165	.54	1,940	Ike McBee	43	712	16.6
1974	Walt Robinson	617	174	3.5	Craig Kimball	355	175	.49	2,401	Ike McBee	33	466	14.1
1975	Rick Kane	823	161	5.1	Roger Profitt	258	113	.44	1,661	Gary Maddocks	28	452	16.1
1976	Rick Kane	1,144	210	5.4	Steve DeBerg	262	141	.54	2,084	Gary Maddocks	32	557	17.4
1977	Kevin Cole	775	200	3.9	Ed Luther	268	126	.47	1,527	Steve Joyce	29	444	15.3
1978	Kevin Cole	1,154	204	5.7	Ed Luther	386	205	.53	2,275	Rick Parma	31	374	12.1
1979	Jewerl Thomas	859	154	5.6	Ed Luther	415	241	.58	3,049	Stacey Bailey	45	296	6.6
1980	Gerald Willhite	1,239	245	5.1	Steve Clarkson	213	103	.48	1,365	Gerald Willhite	55	492	8.9
1981	Gerald Willhite	1,255	297	4.2	Steve Clarkson	464	249	.54	3,373	Tim Kearse	71	946	13.3
1982	Bobby Johnson	674	142	4.7	Steve Clarkson	340	196	.58	2,485	Tim Kearse	51	799	15.7
1983	Bobby Johnson	942	214	4.4	Jon Carlson	290	153	.53	1,961	Eric Richardson	54	911	16.9
1984	Frank Robinson	582	129	4.5	Bob Frasco	387	221	.57	2,688	Kevin Bowman	54	652	12.1
1985	K.C. Clark	462	89	5.2	Doug Allen	290	142	.49	1,717	Randy Walker	32	253	7.9
1986	Kenny Jackson	1,184	268	4.4	Mike Perez	421	249	.59	3,225	Guy Liggins	80	1,116	14.0
1987	Kenny Jackson	917	200	4.6	Mike Perez	408	243	.60	3,260	Guy Liggins	81	1,262	15.6
1988	Johnny Johnson	1,285	233	5.5	Ken Lutz	321	199	.62	2,547	Kevin Evans	61	887	14.5
1989	Sheldon Canley	1,289	258	5.0	Matt Veatch	234	123	.53	1,722	Sheldon Canley	42	353	8.4
1990	Sheldon Canley	1,338	296	4.5	Ralph Martini	362	204	.56	2,928	Bobby Blackmon	39	599	15.4
1991	Maceo Barbosa	1,073	207	5.2	Matt Veatch	206	110	.53	1,752	Bobby Blackmon	38	590	15.5
1992	Nathan DuPree	1,297	236	5.5	Jeff Garcia	371	209	.56	2,418	Brian Lundy	38	679	17.9
1993	Nathan DuPree	789	136	5.8	Jeff Garcia	356	196	.55	2,608	Brian Lundy	46	712	15.5
1994	Patrick Walsh	532	119	4.5	Alli Abrew	270	135	.50	1,743	Jacobbi Williams	34	575	16.9
1995	Donald Lindsey	845	164	5.2	Carl Dean	302	182	.60	2,214	Brian Roche	66	729	11.0
1996	Patrick Walsh	406	104	3.9	Carl Dean	369	191	.52	2,449	Windrell Hayes	58	848	14.6
1997	Carlos Meeks	535	105	5.1	Dan O'Dell	180	87	.48	1,130	Oliver Newell	58	942	16.2
1998	Deoncé Whitaker	762	133	5.7	Chris Kasteler	221	115	.52	1,505	Oliver Newell	39	583	14.9
1999	Deoncé Whitaker	822	137	6.0	Chris Kasteler	350	193	.55	2,239	Steven Pulley	54	772	14.3
2000	Deoncé Whitaker	1,577	224	7.0	Marcus Arroyo	326	166	.54	2,334	Edell Sheperd	42	707	16.8
2001	Jarmar Julien	897	174	5.2	Marcus Arroyo	261	141	.54	1,905	Edell Sheperd	83	1,500	18.1
2002	Lamar Ferguson	634	128	5.0	Scott Rislov	449	275	.61	3,251	Jamall Broussard	62	681	11.0
2003	Lance Martin	520	119	4.4	Scott Rislov	437	261	.60	3,016	Tuati Wooden	61	780	12.8
2004	Tyson Thompson	811	151	5.4	Dale Rogers	181	96	.53	1,389	Rufus Skillern	40	588	14.7

Receiving leaders by receptions
The NCAA began including postseason stats in 2002

SAN JOSE STATE ALL-TIME SCORES

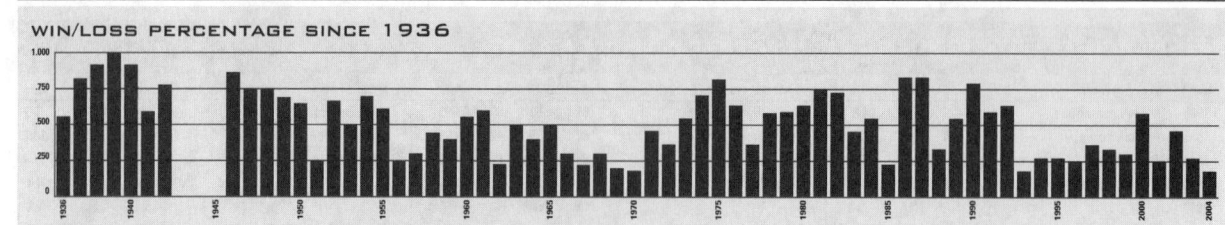

WIN/LOSS PERCENTAGE SINCE 1936

JAMES E. ADDICOTT
1893-98, 1900 (.536)   6-5-3

1893   0-1-0
U		San Jose YMCA *Unk*	0	18

1894
NO TEAM

1895   0-0-1
| U | = | Pacific *Unk* | 6 | 6 |

1896-1897
NO TEAM

1898   4-1-1
U	●	Pacific *Unk*	18	0
U	●	Alameda HS *Unk*	29	5
U	=	San Jose HS *Unk*	6	6
U	●	Stockton HS *Unk*	6	0
U	●	Oakland HS *Unk*	16	0
U		Lowell HS *Unk*	6	11

JESS WOODS
1899 (.688)   5-2-1

1899   5-2-1
U	●	Pacific *Unk*	6	0
U	●	Santa Clara HS *Unk*	23	0
U	●	Palo Alto HS *Unk*	17	0
U	●	Hoitts School *Unk*	28	0
U	●	St. Matthews *Unk*	35	12
N22		California *Unk*	0	44
N30		Nevada *Unk*	0	6
U	=	Santa Clara College *Unk*	6	6

JAMES E. ADDICOTT

FIELDING H. YOST
1900 (1.000)   1-0

1900   3-3-1
U		Stanford *Unk*	0	35
U		Stanford *Unk*	0	24
U	=	Nevada *Unk*	0	0
U	●	California JC *Unk*	6	0
N22		California *Unk*	0	5
U	●	Chico *Unk*	5	0
U	●	Chico *Unk*	12	0

1901-20
NO TEAM

DAVID WOOSTER
1921-22 (.250)   3-10-1

1921   1-5-0
U		San Jose HS *Unk*	7	20
U		Santa Clara HS *Unk*	0	48
U		Pacific *Unk*	0	34
U		San Jose HS *Unk*	0	7
U	●	at Fresno State	14	2
U		Hollister JC. *Unk*	14	30

1922   2-5-1
U	=	San Jose HS *Unk*	6	6
U	●	San Mateo JC *Unk*	3	6
U	●	Santa Clara Prep *Unk*	12	7
U	●	Hollister JC *Unk*	13	0
U		Chico State *Unk*	0	21
N11		UC Davis *Unk*	0	58
U		Modesto JC *Unk*	0	6
U		Pacific *Unk*	0	23

H.C. McDONALD
1923 (.000)   0-6

1923   0-6-0
U		Modesto JC *Unk*	0	28
U		Stanford JV *Unk*	0	79
O27		Cal Poly SLO *Unk*	0	14
U		Pacific *Unk*	0	46
U		San Mateo JC *Unk*	0	45
U		Chico State *Unk*	3	50

E.R. KNOLLIN
1924-28 (.389)   13-21-2

1924   1-4-0
U	●	Hollister JC *Unk*	13	0
U		San Mateo JC *Unk*	0	28
U		Modesto JC *Unk*	6	26
U		Santa Rosa JC *Unk*	6	7
U		Chico State *Unk*	0	26

1925   2-5-0
U	●	Santa Rosa JC *Unk*	21	0
U		Modesto JC *Unk*	0	16
U		at Fresno State	7	23
U		Chico State *Unk*	0	53
U		San Mateo JC *Unk*	14	44
N20	●	Cal Poly SLO *Unk*	20	9
U		Sacramento JC *Unk*	7	13

1926   1-5-1
U	=	Modesto JC *Unk*	0	0
U	●	Bakersfield JC *Unk*	14	0
U	●	San Mateo JC *Unk*	6	14
U		Santa Rosa JC *Unk*	6	12
O23		Cal Poly SLO *Unk*	0	13
N6		at Fresno State	0	34
U		Chico State *Unk*	0	21

1927   4-5-0
U	●	Marin JC *Unk*	44	0
U		Sacramento JC *Unk*	7	13
U	●	Santa Barbara JC *Unk*	7	13
U	●	Santa Rosa JC *Unk*	25	0
U	●	San Mateo JC *Unk*	12	0
N5		at Fresno State	7	10
U		Chico State *Unk*	0	19
N18	●	Cal Poly SLO *Unk*	12	0
U		Modesto JC *Unk*	7	12

1928   5-2-1
U	●	Marin JC *Unk*	26	0
U	●	Santa Rosa JC *Unk*	32	6
O20	●	Cal Poly SLO *Unk*	6	0
U	●	Modesto JC *Unk*	6	13
U	●	Chico State *Unk*	6	0
U	●	Santa Barbara JC *Unk*	6	0
U	●	San Mateo JC *Unk*	14	24
U	=	San Mateo JC *Unk*	21	21

WALTER CRAWFORD
1929-31 (.348)   6-13-4

1929   3-3-1
O12		UC Davis	0	13
O19		at Sacramento JC	6	20
U	=	Pacific *Unk*	6	6
U		Stanford Grays *Unk*	6	25
U		Chico State *Unk*	6	0
N16		at Fresno State	26	14
N22	●	Cal Poly SLO *Unk*	54	0

1930   2-3-3
O4	=	at UC Davis	0	0
U		Fireman's AC *Unk*	0	19
U	=	Sacramento JC *Unk*	0	0
O24		at Pacific *Unk*	0	27
U	●	Chico State *Unk*	19	0
U	=	San Mateo JC *Unk*	0	0
N15		Fresno State	12	27
U	●	Modesto JC *Unk*	19	6

1931   1-7-0
U		San Diego Marines *Unk*	0	8
U	●	San Mateo JC *Unk*	20	0
O17		at Fresno State	0	32
U		Chico State *Unk*	0	7
O31		Nevada *Unk*	0	18
N14		UC Davis *Unk*	3	13
U		Modesto JC *Unk*	0	9
N20		Pacific *Unk*	0	27

DUDLEY S. DeGROOT
1932-39 (.733)   59-19-8

1932   7-0-2
O1	●	S.F. State	19	0
O8	●	at Pacific	7	0
O15	●	Sacramento JC	13	6
O22	=	Fresno State	0	0
O29	●	Chico State	14	7
N5	=	Nevada	0	0
N11	●	Marin JC	24	7
N19	●	UC Davis	19	7
N24	●	Weber State	20	0

1933   4-4-0
S23		at Stanford	0	27
S30		at Sacramento JC	8	20
O7	●	S.F. State	44	6
O16	●	Pacific	12	6
O21		California JV	0	12
N11	●	at UC Davis	20	0
N18		at Fresno State	18	7 *
N30		at Chico State	0	7

1934   3-3-4
S22		at Stanford	0	48
S29		Santa Barbara AC	28	19
O6		at S.F. Olympic Club	13	19
O13	=	Chico State	6	6
O20	=	at UC Davis	0	0
O27		Nevada	10	0
N3	=	Fresno State	7	7
N12		Willamette	7	21
N17	●	at Pacific	13	0
N29	=	at Whittier	6	6

1935   5-5-1
S21		at Willamette	0	14
S28		at Stanford	0	35
O12	●	McKinley-Honolulu	19	0
O18	=	at Pacific	0	0
O26		Antioch Legion Coll.	0	3
N1		Whittier	6	14
N11		at Redlands	0	7
N16	●	at Nevada	20	6
N22	●	Humboldt State	25	6
N28	●	San Diego State	24	9
D7	●	at Kamehameha	22	7

1936   5-4-0
S5	●	San Francisco	0	13
S10	●	Pacific	8	0
S17		Santa Clara	0	20
S24	●	at San Diego State	6	14
N7		Humboldt State	0	20
N11	●	Redlands	40	6
N26	●	Arizona State	33	6
D4	●	at Kamehameha	36	6
D11	●	at Hawaii	13	8

1937   11-2-1
S20	●	Coll. of Idaho	59	0
S25	●	La Verne Coll.	40	0
O1	●	at Pacific	12	7
O8	●	Northern Arizona	21	6
O16	●	Willamette	8	7
O22	●	Cal Tech	48	6
O30	=	at San Diego Marines	7	7
N7		Santa Clara	2	25
N11	●	Redlands	12	0
N13	●	at Humboldt State	13	2
N20	●	at Arizona State	25	6
N25	●	San Diego State	6	7
D4	●	at Hawaii	7	6
D11	●	at Honolulu Town	13	0

1938   11-1-0
S19	●	at Arizona State	18	7
S23	●	California JV	39	12
S30	●	Cal Tech	52	0
O7	●	Humboldt State	48	0
O14	●	at Pacific (Ore.)	39	0
O21	●	Pacific	19	6
O29	●	at San Diego State	14	0
N5	●	at UC Santa Barbara	20	0
N11	●	Redlands	21	6
N20	●	at San Diego MC	6	0
N27	●	Northern Arizona	34	12
D3		at Hawaii	12	13

1939   13-0-0
S15	●	Montana State	35	0
S18	●	Texas A&I	9	0
S24	●	at San Francisco	16	6
O1	●	California JV	27	0
O7	●	Nevada	28	0
O13	●	San Diego State	42	0
O20	●	Pacific	13	3
O27	●	UC Santa Barbara	23	7
N3	●	at Willamette	15	0
N10	●	Redlands	52	6
N17	●	at Loyola-Marymount	10	0
N24	●	Fresno State	42	7
N30	●	Drake	12	0

BEN WINKLEMAN
1940-41 (.761)   16-4-3

1940   11-1-0
S16		Texas A&I	0	10
S23	●	at Montana State	34	0
S30	●	at Utah State	19	0
O4	●	at Willamette	21	0
O11	●	San Diego State	10	0
O18	●	at San Francisco	7	6
O25	●	at UC Santa Barbara	33	6
N1	●	at Loyola-Marymount	27	12
N8	●	Pacific	28	7
N16	●	at Fresno State	14	7
N21	●	South Dakota	40	7
N30	●	Nevada	30	7

1941   5-3-3
S19	●	Texas A&I	14	7
S26	●	Utah State	30	0
O3	=	Fort Ord	6	6
O10	●	San Diego State	20	0
O17		Hardin-Simmons	7	7
O24	●	at Pacific	7	0
O31	●	UC Santa Barbara	33	14
N8		Nevada	19	20
N14		at Fresno State	0	0
N22		at San Francisco	0	20
N26		Moffett Field	13	22

GLENN HARTRANFT
1942 (.778) 7-2

1942 7-2-0

S26	•	Cal Poly SLO-Pomona	33	6
O3	•	at Whittier	20	0
O10	•	Occidental	26	7
O17	•	Pacific	29	0
O25		at San Francisco	13	20
N1	•	US Coast Guard	9	0
N8	•	San Diego State	26	0
D11	•	McClelland Field	27	7
D26		at Fresno State	0	6

1943-45

NO TEAM WWII

WILBUR "BILL" HUBBARD
1946-49 (.760) 36-11-1

1946 9-1-1

S28	•	Willamette	44	6
O5		at Hardin-Simmons	7	34
O10	=	Hawaii All-Stars	19	19
O19	•	at Idaho	26	14
O25	•	Brigham Young	14	0
N1	•	at UC Santa Barbara	20	0
N8	•	at Pacific	32	0
N16	•	at San Diego State	6	0
N22	•	Fresno State	13	2
N29	•	Portland	26	19
		RAISIN BOWL		
D6	•	Utah State	20	0

1947 9-3-0

S19		San Francisco	6	20
S26	•	Hawaii All-Stars	35	19
O3	•	Hardin-Simmons	19	12
O11	•	at Puget Sound	18	0
O17	•	UC Santa Barbara	39	0
O25	•	at San Diego State	32	7
O31		Pacific	0	14
N8	•	at Brigham Young	28	19
N22	•	Cal Poly SLO	47	0
N27		Fresno State	20	21
D3	•	at Molili Bears	53	0
D10	•	at Leihuhua	20	14

1948 9-3-0

S18		at Stanford	20	26
S24		Nevada	0	39
O1	•	Puget Sound	20	7
O9	•	at Pepperdine	61	6
O16	•	at Cal Poly SLO	47	7
O22	•	at UC Santa Barbara	43	13
O30	•	at Pacific	14	7
N5	•	Brigham Young	21	6
N12	•	San Diego State	21	13
N19	•	Fresno State	41	6
N26		Saint Mary's-Cal	14	19
D4	•	U. of Mexico	71	19

1949 9-4-0

S10	•	U. of Mexico	103	0
S17		at Stanford	0	49
S24		Santa Clara	13	14
O1	•	at Brigham Young	40	21
O7	•	Pepperdine	49	12
O14		San Francisco	20	27
O21	•	UC Santa Barbara	55	14
O28		Pacific	7	45
N4	•	at Cal Poly SLO	47	0
N12	•	at San Diego State	40	0
N18	•	Saint Mary's-Cal	40	13
N24	•	at Fresno State	43	7
		RAISIN BOWL		
D31	•	Texas Tech	20	13

ROBERT T. BRONZAN
1950-56 (.515) 32-30-5

1950 6-3-1

S23		at Stanford	16	33
S29	•	San Diego State	26	0
O7	•	Santa Clara	14	10
O13		Loyola-Marymount	7	14
O20		at San Francisco	0	27
O28	•	at Pepperdine	48	7
N3	•	Fresno State	33	7
N10	•	Saint Mary's-Cal	18	6
N18	=	at Pacific	7	7
N24	•	Montana Hon	32	7

1951 2-7-1

S21		at San Francisco	2	39
S29		at Stanford	13	26
O6	•	at Fresno State	32	6
O12		San Francisco	7	42
O20		at Idaho	7	40
O26		Loyola-Marymount	12	13
N3		at San Diego NTC	12	28
N17	=	Santa Clara	7	7
N23	•	Pacific	7	0
D1		Marquette	7	21

1952 6-3-0

S20		at Colorado	14	20
S27	•	at San Diego State	47	6
O4	•	at Arizona State	21	14
O10	•	Fresno State	40	6
O18	•	at Pacific	26	21
N1		at Stanford	13	35
N7	•	Brigham Young	44	27
N14	•	Montana State	39	20
N27		Santa Clara	7	15

1953 4-4-1

S18	•	Idaho	34	6
S25	•	at Brigham Young	28	25
O3	•	at Fresno State	27	21
O10		Arizona State	20	35
O17		at California	14	34
O24		at Oregon	13	26
O31	=	North Texas	13	13
N7	•	Pacific	7	6
N14		at Stanford	0	54

1954 7-3-0

S18	•	Utah State	20	0
S25		at California	0	45
O2	•	at Idaho	38	7
O9	•	at Arizona State	19	12
O23		at Oregon	7	26
O30	•	at North Texas	27	20
N6		at Pacific	7	13
N13	•	at Stanford	19	14
N19	•	Fresno State	28	0
N27	•	New Mexico	26	14

1955 5-3-1

S16	•	at Utah State	13	0
S23	•	Hawaii	34	0
O8	•	Arizona State	27	20
O15	•	at New Mexico	14	0
O22		Pacific	7	14
O29		at Stanford	18	34
N5	•	Cal Poly SLO	20	14
N12	=	at Washington State	13	13
N18		at Fresno State	13	19

1956 2-7-1

S22	•	Drake	26	7
S29		at Washington State	18	33
O13		at Stanford	20	40
O20	=	at San Diego State	27	27
O27		at Arizona State	13	47
N3		Denver	26	35
N10		at Pacific	7	34
N17	•	Cal Poly SLO	35	28
N22		Fresno State	14	30
N30		at Hawaii	0	20

ROBERT TITCHENAL
1957-64 (.424) 33-45-1

1957 3-7-0

S21		at Stanford	7	47
S27	•	at Denver	27	20
O5		Arizona State	6	44
O12		at Oregon	0	26
O19	•	San Diego State	46	0
O26		North Texas	6	12
N2		at Cal Poly SLO	7	14
N9		Pacific	6	21
N16		at Fresno State	6	13
N30	•	at Hawaii	12	0

1958 4-5-0

S20		at Washington	6	14
S27		Hawaii	6	8
O11		Cal Poly SLO	6	10
O18	•	at Arizona State	21	20
O25	•	Denver	27	7
N1	•	at Idaho	41	6
N8		at Pacific	13	26
N15	•	Fresno State	48	6
N21		Iowa State	6	9

1959 4-6-0

S18	•	at Denver	14	13
S25		Washington State	6	30
O3	•	Hawaii	44	14
O9		Oregon	12	35
O17	•	at Fresno State	40	14
O24	•	Arizona State	24	15
O31		at Stanford	38	54
N7		Wyoming	7	28
N14		at Iowa State	0	55
N20		at Pacific	7	20

1960 5-4-0

S23	•	Brigham Young	21	8
O8		at Oregon	0	33
O15	•	at Stanford	34	20
O22	•	at Arizona State	12	7
O29		Washington State	6	29
N5		at Pacific	20	26
N11		Fresno State	12	27
N18	•	Idaho	22	20
D2	•	at Hawaii	48	6

1961 6-4-0

S16	•	at Brigham Young	14	13
S22	•	Pacific	16	0
S30		at Idaho	18	27
O7	•	Colorado State	14	0
O14		at Stanford	6	17
O21		at Oregon	6	21
O28	•	at Washington State	21	19
N4	•	Arizona State	32	26
N11	•	at Pacific	29	26
N18		at Fresno State	27	36

1962 2-8-1

S15		Utah State	18	29
S22		at Washington State	8	49
S29		at California	8	25
O6		at Oregon	0	14
O13	=	Idaho	12	12
O20		at Arizona State	8	44
O27		New Mexico	13	25
N3	•	at Pacific	24	22
N10		Fresno State	14	20
N17		at Stanford	9	21
N30	•	at Hawaii	19	0

1963 5-5-0

S21		at Stanford	13	29
S28	•	Kansas State	16	0
O5		at Utah State	0	20
O12	•	at Washington State	13	8
O19		at California	13	34
O26		at Idaho	12	28
N2	•	at Oregon	13	7
N9		Arizona State	19	21
N16	•	Fresno State	56	27
N30	•	Pacific	32	20

1964 4-6-0

S19		Idaho	0	3
S26		at Stanford	8	10
O3	•	at Montana State	20	14
O17		Washington State	14	16
O24	•	at Pacific	37	13
O31		at West Texas State	7	18
N7		at Colorado State	3	14
N14		at Arizona State	16	28
N21	•	Fresno State	26	14
N28	•	San Diego State	20	15

HARRY ANDERSON
1965-68 (.333) 13-26

1965 5-5-0

S17		at Stanford	6	26
S25		at Idaho	7	17
O2		Utah State	8	35
O8		at Brigham Young	7	34
O16	•	Arizona State	21	14
O23	•	at Arizona	13	7
O30	•	at New Mexico	27	7
N6	•	Pacific	52	21
N13	•	Montana State	25	7
N20		at Fresno State	18	24

1966 3-7-0

S17		at Stanford	21	25
S24		Brigham Young	9	19
O1	•	at Oregon	21	7
O8	•	California	24	0
O15		San Diego State	0	25
O22		at Texas-El Paso	0	35
O29		at Pacific	35	38
N5	•	Idaho	21	7
N12		at Utah State	7	27
N19		Fresno State	13	15

1967 2-7-0

S16		at Arizona State	16	27
S30		at Stanford	14	28
O14		at West Texas State	14	28
O21	•	New Mexico	52	14
O28		Pacific	14	34
N4		Wyoming	7	28
N11		at California	6	30
N18	•	at Fresno State	35	30
N25		at Brigham Young	8	67

1968 3-7-0

S21		at Stanford	20	68
S28	•	Fresno State	25	21
O5		at California	0	46
O19	•	at New Mexico	55	24
O26		at San Diego State	6	48
N2		at Pacific	0	28
N9		Idaho	17	35
N16		Washington State	0	46
N23		at Arizona State	0	66
N30	•	Brigham Young	25	21

1969-1995
BIG WEST

JOE McMULLEN
1969-70 (.231) 3-10

1969 2-8-0 (1-1-0)

S20		at Stanford	21	63
S27		at Utah	7	42
O4	|	San Diego State	21	55
O11	•	at Oregon	36	34
O18		Arizona State	11	45
O25		at Wyoming	7	16
N1		New Mexico	24	27
N8		at Brigham Young	3	21
N15		at California	7	31
N22	• |	Pacific	15	12

DeWAYNE "DEWEY" KING
1970-72 (.339) 10-20-1

1970 2-9-0 (2-3-0)

S12	• |	UC Santa Barbara	28	14
S19		at Stanford	3	34
S26		at Arizona	29	30
O3	|	Long Beach St.	3	7
O10		at New Mexico	25	48
O17	|	at San Diego State	6	32
O24	• |	at Pacific	48	7
O31		Utah	9	13
N7		at Arizona State	10	46
N14		at California	28	35
N21	|	Fresno State	19	27

1971 5-6-1 (4-1-0)

S18	|	at Fresno State	7	14
S25		at California	10	34
O2		at Houston	20	34
O8	• |	Long Beach St.	30	28
O16	=	New Mexico	21	21
O23		at Oregon	14	34
O30	• |	Pacific	28	18
N6	• |	San Diego State	45	7
N13	•	at Stanford	13	12
N20		Arizona State	6	49
N27	• |	at UC Santa Barbara	55	10
		PASADENA BOWL		
D18		Memphis	9	28

1972 4-7-0 (1-3-0)

S9	•	Santa Clara	33	28
S16		at Stanford	0	44
S23	•	at California	17	10
S30	|	Fresno State	21	23
O7	|	at San Diego State	12	23
O21	|	at Pacific	2	38
O28	• |	Long Beach St.	35	8
N4	•	New Mexico	14	7
N11		at Oregon	2	27
N18		at Arizona State	21	51
N25		at Hawaii	14	28

DARRYL ROGERS
1973-75 (.691) 22-9-3

1973 5-4-2 (2-0-2)

S8	•	Santa Clara	14	12
S15	• |	at Fresno State	24	6
S21	• |	at Long Beach St.	24	6
S29		Stanford	12	23
O6	= |	Pacific	21	21
O13		at Arizona State	3	28
O20		Utah	21	28
O27	•	New Mexico	15	0
N3	= |	San Diego State	27	27
N10		at California	9	19
N24	•	at Hawaii	23	3

1974 8-3-1 (2-2-0)

S7	•	Santa Clara	47	10
S14	• |	Fresno State	28	7
S21		at California	16	17
S28	=	at Stanford	21	21
O5	• |	Long Beach St.	27	17
O12	•	at New Mexico	13	11
O19	|	at San Diego State	14	40
O26	|	Pacific	27	29
N2	•	at Utah	24	6
N9	•	at Hawaii	32	11
N16	•	at Fullerton St.	49	8
N22	•	at La. Lafayette	25	22

1975 9-2-0 (5-0-0)

S13	•	Santa Clara	13	0
S20	•	at Oregon	5	0
S27	•	at Stanford	36	34
O4		at California	24	27
O11	• |	at Long Beach St.	30	7
O18	• |	Pacific	41	13
O25	• |	Fullerton St.	41	7
N1	• |	at Fresno State	21	7
N8	•	New Mexico	29	20
N15	• |	San Diego State	31	7
N29		at Hawaii	20	30

LYNN STILES 1976-78 (.529) 18-16

1976 7-4-0 (4-0-0)

S4	•	Utah State	45	10
S11	•	Hawaii	48	7
S18	• |	at Fullerton St.	20	0
S25		at Stanford	23	28
O2		at California	16	43
O9		at New Mexico	30	36
O16	• |	Long Beach St.	34	7
O23	• |	Fresno State	21	7
O30	•	Santa Clara	50	15
N6		at San Diego State	17	30
N13	• |	at Pacific	50	30

1977 4-7-0 (2-2-0)

S10		at Utah State	10	22
S17		at Washington	3	24
S24	• |	Fullerton St.	23	12
O1		at California	3	52
O8	•	Santa Clara	44	22
O15	• |	at Long Beach St.	33	16
O22	|	at Fresno State	24	45
O29	|	Pacific	7	24
N5	•	Hawaii	24	14
N12		at Stanford	26	31
D3		San Diego State	34	37

1978 7-5-0 (4-1-0)

S9	•	Idaho	31	14
S16		at Stanford	9	38
S23		at Colorado	7	22
S30	•	Santa Clara	17	7
O7		at Hawaii	11	25
O14		at Boise State	15	30
O21	• |	Fresno State	26	16
O28	|	at Utah State	21	31
N4	• |	Fullerton St.	30	21
N11	• |	at Pacific	33	31
N18	•	Montana	35	7
D2	• |	Long Beach St.	24	6

JACK ELWAY 1979-83 (.634) 35-20-1

1979 6-4-1 (4-0-1)

S8	= |	Utah State	48	48 †
S15		at Stanford	29	45
S22		at California	10	13
S29		at Arizona	18	38
O6	• |	Fullerton St.	23	0 †
O13	• |	at Fresno State	35	22 †
O20	•	at Oregon State	24	14 †
O27	• |	Long Beach St.	53	42
N10	• |	Pacific	32	31
N17	•	Santa Clara	23	14
N24		Central Michigan	32	34

1980 7-4-0 (3-2-0)

S6	•	Santa Clara	28	14
S13	•	Washington State SPO	31	26
S20		at Iowa State	6	27
O4		at Stanford	21	35
O11	• |	Fresno State	26	14
O18	|	Long Beach St.	21	23
O25	•	Idaho	32	10
N1	•	at Baylor	30	22
N8	• |	at Pacific	28	23
N15	• |	Fullerton St.	33	21
N22	|	Utah State	38	44

1981 9-3-0 (5-0-0)

S5		Nevada-Las Vegas	6	16
S12	•	Santa Clara	41	7
S19	•	at Stanford	28	6
S26	•	at California	27	24
O3	• |	at Fresno State	65	33
O17	• |	Fullerton St.	45	23
O24	• |	at Utah State	27	24
O31		at Arizona State	24	31
N14	• |	Pacific	40	25
N21	• |	at Long Beach St.	24	22
N28	•	North Texas	28	16
		CALIFORNIA BOWL		
D19		Toledo	25	27

1982 8-3-0 (4-2-0)

S11	•	at Oregon	18	13
S18	•	at Stanford	35	31
S25	•	at Oregon State	17	13
O2		at California	7	26
O9	• |	at Fullerton St.	38	15
O16	|	Long Beach St.	21	22
O23	|	Fresno State	27	39
O30	• |	at Nevada-Las Vegas	48	14
N6	•	Santa Clara	40	0
N13	• |	at Pacific	31	0
N20	• |	Utah State	49	26

1983 5-6-0 (3-3-0)

S10	• |	Nevada-Las Vegas	31	26
S17		at California	9	30
S24	•	at Stanford	23	10
O1	•	Oregon	44	34
O8	• |	at Fresno State	41	23
O15	|	Fullerton St.	11	20
O22	• |	at Long Beach St.	18	9
N5	|	at Utah State	15	22
N12	|	Pacific	26	30
N19		at Arizona State	17	24
N26		La. Lafayette	21	25

CLAUDE GILBERT 1984-89 (.558) 38-30-1

1984 6-5-0 (5-2-0)

S1	• |	New Mexico State	14	0
S8	|	at Nevada-Las Vegas	15	30 †
S15		at Arizona State	0	48
S22		at Stanford	27	28
S29	•	at California	33	18
O6	• |	Utah State	38	21
O13	|	at Fullerton St.	12	21
O20		La. Lafayette	28	35
O27	• |	Fresno State	18	17
N10	• |	Long Beach St.	42	7
N17	• |	at Pacific	33	0

1985 2-8-1 (2-4-1)

A31		at California	21	48
S7	• |	New Mexico State	32	3
S14		at Stanford	7	41
S21	|	at Utah State	32	35
O3	|	Fullerton St.	18	20
O12	|	at Fresno State	17	37
O19		at Arizona	0	41
O26	• |	Pacific	34	26
N2		at Oregon	13	35
N7	|	at Long Beach St.	22	37
N16	= |	Nevada-Las Vegas	16	16

1986 10-2-0 (7-0-0)

S6		Oregon	14	21
S13	•	at Washington State	20	13
S20		at Stanford	10	28
S27	•	at California	35	14
O4	• |	Fresno State	45	41
O11	• |	Utah State	38	28
O18	• |	at Nevada-Las Vegas	23	20
O25	• |	at Pacific	44	15
N1	• |	at New Mexico State	45	7
N8	• |	at Fullerton St.	48	24
N15	• |	Long Beach St.	38	14
		CALIFORNIA BOWL		
D13	•	Miami, Ohio	37	7

1987 10-2-0 (7-0-0)

S5	•	Eastern Illinois	24	3
S12	•	at California	27	25
S19		at Oregon State	34	36
S26	•	at Stanford	24	17
O3	• |	Fullerton St.	46	19
O10	• |	New Mexico State	57	6
O17	• |	at Fresno State	20	16
O24	• |	Nevada-Las Vegas	48	24
O31	• |	at Utah State	24	14
N7	• |	Pacific	42	17
N14	• |	Long Beach St.	44	16
		CALIFORNIA BOWL		
D12		Eastern Michigan	27	30

1988 4-8-0 (4-3-0)

S3	• |	at New Mexico State	51	0
S10		Oregon State	27	41
S17		at Hawaii	27	36
S24		at Washington	31	35
O1		at California	14	21
O8		at Stanford	12	44
O15	• |	at Pacific	35	17
O22	• |	Utah State	36	31
O29	|	Fresno State	15	17
N5	|	Long Beach St.	13	34
N12	|	at Fullerton St.	13	58
N19	• |	at Nevada-Las Vegas	42	0

1989 6-5-0 (5-2-0)

S16		at Arizona State	21	28
S23	• |	Pacific	41	32
S30	•	at Stanford	40	33
O7		at California	21	26
O14		at Miami, Fla.	16	48
O21	• |	at Long Beach St.	21	10
O28	• |	New Mexico State	34	6
N4	|	at Fresno State	30	31
N11	• |	at Utah State	33	7
N18	|	Fullerton St.	14	28
N25	• |	Nevada-Las Vegas	38	28

TERRY SHEA 1990-91 (.696) 15-6-2

1990 9-2-1 (7-0-0)

S1	=	Louisville	10	10
S8		at Washington	17	20
S15	• |	at Pacific	28	14
S22	• |	at Nevada-Las Vegas	47	13
S29	•	at Stanford	29	23
O6		at California	34	35
O13	• |	Long Beach St.	46	29
O20	• |	Utah State	34	27
N3	• |	at Fullerton St.	44	6
N10	• |	at New Mexico State	56	20
N17	• |	Fresno State	42	7
		RAISIN BOWL		
D8	•	Central Michigan	48	24

1991 6-4-1 (6-1-0)

S7		at Florida	21	59
S14		at Minnesota	20	26
S21	• |	at Long Beach St.	32	20
S28	• |	at Utah State	23	7
O12	• |	at New Mexico State	39	13
O19	• |	Pacific	64	47
O26		at California	20	41
N2	• |	Nevada-Las Vegas	55	12
N9	• |	Fullerton St.	35	7
N16	=	Hawaii	35	35
N23	|	at Fresno State	28	31

RON TURNER 1992 (.636) 7-4

1992 7-4-0 (4-2-0)

S5		at California	16	46
S12	•	at Minnesota	39	30
S19	•	La. Lafayette	38	13
S26		at Stanford	13	37
O3	•	at Wyoming	26	24
O10	• |	Fullerton St.	49	3
O24	• |	at Utah State	27	25
O31	|	at Nevada-Las Vegas	31	35
N7	• |	Nevada	39	35
N14	• |	at Pacific	28	27
N21	|	New Mexico State	24	34

JOHN RALSTON 1993-96 (.244) 11-34

1993 2-9-0 (2-4-0)

S4		at Louisville	24	31
S11		at Stanford	28	31
S18		Wyoming	25	36
S25		at California	13	46
O2		at Washington	17	52
O16	• |	at New Mexico State	52	13
O23	• |	Louisiana Tech	31	6
O30	|	at La. Lafayette	13	24
N6	|	at Nevada	45	46
N13	|	Nevada-Las Vegas	14	28
N20	|	Pacific	20	24

1994 3-8-0 (3-3-0)

S3		at Fresno State	13	45
S10		Baylor	20	54
S17		at Stanford	20	51
S24	• |	La. Lafayette	31	28
O1		at California	0	55
O8		at Washington	20	34
O22	|	Nevada	10	42
O29	|	at Nevada-Las Vegas	10	23
N5	|	New Mexico State	21	24
N12	• |	at Louisiana Tech	27	6
N19	• |	at Pacific	28	15

1995 3-8-0 (3-4-0)

S2		Stanford	33	47
S9		at Southern Cal	7	45
S16	|	Northern Illinois	17	18
S23		at California	7	40
S30	• |	Utah State	32	30
O14	• |	Nevada-Las Vegas	52	14
O21		at San Diego State	20	49
O28	|	Pacific	30	32
N4	|	at Arkansas State	7	21
N11	• |	at New Mexico State	38	37
N18	|	at Nevada	28	45

1996-PRESENT
WAC

1996 3-9 (3-5)

A31	|	at Air Force	0	45
S7		California	25	45
S14		at Stanford	2	25
S21	• |	Texas-El Paso	26	25
S28		at Washington State	16	52
O5	|	Wyoming	22	45
O12	|	at Fresno State	18	28
O19	|	at Colorado State	13	36
N2	|	San Diego State	20	49
N9	• |	at Hawaii	38	17
N16		at Washington	10	53
N23	• |	Nevada-Las Vegas	31	28

DAVE BALDWIN 1997-2000 (.400) 18-27

1997 4-7 (4-4)

S6		at Stanford	12	28
S13		Wisconsin	10	56
S20	|	at Wyoming	10	30
O4		at Oregon State	12	26
O11	|	Colorado State	20	55
O18	• |	at Texas-El Paso	10	7
O25	• |	Air Force	25	22
N1	|	Fresno State	12	53
N8	|	at San Diego State	21	48
N15	• |	Hawaii	38	14
N22	• |	at Nevada-Las Vegas	55	48

1998 4-8 (3-5)

S5	•	at Stanford	35	23
S12		Idaho	12	17
S19		at Oregon	3	58
S26	• |	New Mexico	37	20
O3		at Virginia	14	52
O10	• |	Rice	20	17
O17	|	at Texas-El Paso	21	28
O24	|	at Brigham Young	43	46
O31	|	Utah	17	49
N7	• |	at Hawaii	45	17
N14	|	San Diego State	6	34
N21	|	at Fresno State	21	24

1999 3-7 (1-5)

S4		at LSU	21	29
S11		at Colorado	35	63
S18	•	Saint Mary's-Cal	38	3
S25	• |	Tulsa	34	10
O2	•	at Stanford	44	39
O9	|	at TCU	0	42
O16	|	at Rice	7	49
O30	|	at Texas-El Paso	26	42
N6	|	Hawaii	41	62
N20	|	at Fresno State	12	63

2000 7-5 (5-3)

S2		at Nebraska	13	49
S9	•	at Stanford	40	27
S16	•	So. Utah	47	7
S23		at Southern Cal	24	34
S30	• |	Rice	29	16
O7	• |	at SMU	35	10
O14	|	Texas-El Paso	30	47
O21	• |	at Nevada	49	30
O28	• |	at Hawaii	57	48
N4	• |	TCU	27	24
N18	|	at Tulsa	17	28
N25	|	Fresno State	6	37

THE SCHOOLS

DR. FITZ HILL
2000-04 (.298)   1 4 - 3 3

2001   3-9   (3-5)

S1		at Southern Cal	10	21
S8		at Colorado	15	51
S29		at Arizona State	15	53
O6	|	at Louisiana Tech	20	41
O13	|	SMU	17	24
O20	● |	at Texas-El Paso	40	28
O27	● |	Tulsa	63	27
N3	|	at Hawaii	10	34
N10	● |	Nevada	65	45
N17	|	at Boise State	6	56
N23	|	at Fresno State	21	40
D1	|	Stanford	14	41

2002   6-7   (4-4)

A31	●	at Arkansas State *LR*	33	14
S7		at Washington	10	34
S14		at Stanford	26	63
S21	●	at Illinois	38	35
S28	● |	Texas-El Paso	58	24
O5	● |	at SMU	34	23
O12		at Ohio State	7	50
O19	|	at Nevada	24	52
O26	|	Boise State	8	45
N2	|	at Hawaii	31	40
N9	● |	Louisiana Tech	42	30
N16	● |	at Tulsa	49	38
N23	|	Fresno State	16	19

2003   3-8   (2-6)

A23	●	Grambling	29	0
A30		at Florida	3	65
S6		at Stanford	10	31
S18	|	Nevada	30	42
O4	|	at Rice	24	28
O11	● |	SMU	31	14
O25	|	at Boise State	14	77
N1	|	Hawaii	10	13
N8	● |	at Texas-El Paso	69	41
N15	|	at Fresno State	7	41
N22	|	Tulsa	32	34

2004   2-9   (1-7)

S4		at Stanford	3	43
S18	●	Morgan St.	47	28
S25		at SMU	13	36
O2	● |	Rice	70	63
O9		at Washington	6	21
O23	|	at Hawaii	28	46
O30	|	Texas-El Paso	20	38
N6	|	at Nevada	24	42
N13	|	Boise State	49	56
N20	|	at Tulsa	24	34
N27	|	Fresno State	28	62

SMU

BY DAVE REARDON

FROM A NATIONAL CHAMPIONSHIP (1935) to abolishment of the football program (1987) for NCAA violations, SMU experienced highs and lows last century rivaling those of any school in the country. But recovering from the one-two punch of the "death penalty" and the dissolution of the Southwest Conference (SMU was shunned by the Big 12 and wound up in the WAC) has been an arduous, uphill climb—with no end in sight. The only way even the most rabid Mustang can take solace from their 3–8 mark in 2004 is by looking back in horror at 0–12 in 2003.

TRADITION Singing the alma mater before games, SMU students raise their right hands in a victory salute. What makes it special—and distinct from the dreaded Hook 'Em, Horns gesture—is that when a Mustang makes the V sign while crimping his fingers slightly, the result actually resembles the ear of a pony. (Sort of.) That pony, of course, would be SMU's mascot, Peruna.

BEST PLAYER A three-time All-America and Heisman Trophy winner (1948) with Homecoming King good looks, Doak Walker to this day symbolizes the archetypal college football hero. The 5'11", 170-pound tailback became so popular that a second deck was added to the Cotton Bowl to hold the crowds that flocked to watch him. Some old-timers still argue that he was the greatest all-round player ever: elusive runner, electric kick returner, accurate kicker, strong punter, sneaky-good passer—and topflight defensive back. Walker played for the Mustangs in 1945 and from 1947 to 1949. "Some called it luck, others called it destiny," said his coach, Matty Bell. "But Doak had a natural knack for pulling off great deeds." Walker led SMU to Southwest Conference championships in 1947 and 1948. He is tied with Eric Dickerson in career points (288) and leads in punt-return yards (750). He rushed for 1,954 yards, passed for 1,638 yards and served as both kicker and punter. As a pro, he (along with former high school teammate Bobby Layne) led the Detroit Lions to two NFL championships. Walker is one of a select group of players inducted to both the College and Pro Football halls of fame. Since 1990, the Doak Walker Award has been given to college football's best running back. Walker died in 1998 after a skiing accident.

BEST COACH Any discussion of SMU's greatest coach comes down to Ray Morrison and Matty Bell. Morrison is the winningest (84–44–22) coach in SMU history. But Bell

---

PROFILE

Southern Methodist University
Dallas, Texas
Founded: 1911
Enrollment: 6,299
Colors: Red and Blue
Nickname: Mustangs
Stadium: Gerald J. Ford Stadium
    Opened in 2000
    A-Turf; 32,000 capacity
First football game: 1915
All-time record: 426–442–54 (.491)
Bowl record: 4–6–1
First-round NFL draftees: 7
Heisman Trophy: Doak Walker, 1948
Website: www.smumustangs.com

THE BEST OF TIMES

From 1981 through 1984, SMU went 41–5–1, won the Southwest Conference Championship outright the first two years, placed second in 1983 and tied for first in 1984.

THE WORST OF TIMES

Tough call. Is it not playing at all for two years, or going 0–12? The Mustangs' 1987 and 1988 seasons were canceled because of NCAA violations, but in 2003 SMU matched the WAC record for losses in a season with 12.

CONFERENCE

The Mustangs had been Southwest Conference members since 1918. SMU joined the WAC after the Southwest Conference dissolved in 1996. They became members of Conference USA in 2005.

DISTINGUISHED ALUMNI

Kathy Bates, actress; Laura Bush, First Lady; James Cronin, Nobel prize winning physicist; Robert Dennard, computing pioneer/inventor; Aaron Spelling, TV/film producer

FIGHT SONG

PONY BATTLE CRY
Hail to the Red and the Blue
We're the Mustangs from SMU
Give a cheer, show your might
Get the victory in sight
for our battle cry will be
Fight! Fight! Fight!
Spirits the best in the land
And right to the end we'll stand
For the M-U-S-T-A-N-G-S
Fight! Fight! Fight!

One key indicator of a program in flux is a constantly changing uniform—and in the past 40 years, SMU has sported at least 11 distinct helmet designs.

gets the nod for outdoing Morrison in conference titles, 4-3, and for capturing the 1935 national championship—in his first season. In two Cotton Bowls under Bell after winning the 1947 and 1948 Southwest Conference champions, SMU tied Penn State 13-13 and beat Oregon 21-13. After the 1949 season Bell retired from coaching—Doak Walker was leaving, after all—but remained at SMU as athletic director until 1964.

BEST TEAM The 1935 team—led by All-America tailback Bobby Wilson, tackle Truman Spain, guard J.C. Wetsel and fullback Harry Shuford—went unbeaten in the regular season and suffered its only loss, 7-0, to Stanford in the Rose Bowl. But in that last year before the advent of the Associated Press writers poll, SMU was still the national champion, according to one of the most respected barometers of the day, the Dickinson System. And then there was the Pony Express team of 1982 that went 11–0–1 and featured one of the greatest running back combinations ever in Eric Dickerson and Craig James. It was the second of three Southwest Conference championship squads in four years.

BIGGEST GAME In 1935, No. 1 SMU and No. 2 TCU squared off in what became known as the Game of the First Half of the Century. The Mustangs and Horned Frogs were both 10–0. Both featured star players: running back Bobby Wilson for SMU, quarterback Sammy Baugh for TCU. Wilson scored two touchdowns to give the Mustangs a 14-0 lead, but Baugh's TD pass in the fourth quarter tied the game. Facing fourth-and-four at TCU's 37, SMU went into deep punt formation, from which quarterback Bob Finley threw long to Wilson, who made a marvelous over-the-shoulder catch at the 4-yard line and raced into the end zone. Wilson's catch became known as "the $85,000 touchdown," since that was the payout for the Rose Bowl berth the victory helped clinch. (The money, conveniently, went to pay off the note on the then-new SMU Stadium.)

BIGGEST UPSET On Oct. 11, 1963, in the midst of an otherwise undistinguished 4–7 season, SMU hosted fourth-ranked Navy and quarterback Roger Staubach. John Roderick rushed for 146 yards, including two touchdowns,

RECORDS

RUSHING

GAME

244	Mike Richardson vs. Texas A&M, Nov. 9, 1968 (39 att.)

SEASON

1,617	Eric Dickerson, 1982 (232 att.)

CAREER

4,450	Eric Dickerson, 1979-82 (790 att.)

PASSING

GAME

450	Mike Romo vs. North Texas, Oct. 28, 1989 (32 of 47)

SEASON

3,103	Chuck Hixson, 1968 (265 of 468)

CAREER

7,179	Chuck Hixson, 1968-70 (642 of 1,115)

RECEIVING

GAME

213	Jerry LeVias vs. North Carolina State, Oct. 5, 1968 (9 rec.)

SEASON

1,131	Jerry LeVias, 1968 (80 rec.)

CAREER

2,784	Emanuel Tolbert, 1976-79 (171 rec.)

POINTS

GAME

	11 tied; most recently by ShanDerrick Charles vs. UTEP, Oct. 27, 2001 (4 TDs)

SEASON

114	Eric Dickerson, 1981 (19 TDs)

CAREER

288	Eric Dickerson, 1979-82 (48 TDs); Doak Walker, 1945, 1947-49 (38 TDs, 57 PATs, 1 FG)

CONSENSUS ALL-AMERICANS

1935	J.C. Wetsel,	G
1935	Bobby Wilson,	B
1947-49	Doak Walker,	B
1950	Kyle Rote,	B
1951	Dick Hightower,	C
1966	John LaGrone,	MG
1968	Jerry LeVias,	E
1972	Robert Popelka,	DB
1974	Louie Kelcher,	G
1978	Emanuel Tolbert,	WR
1980	John Simmons,	DB
1982	Eric Dickerson,	TB
1983	Russell Carter,	CB
1985	Reggie Dupard,	TB

for the Mustangs. Meanwhile, a hard-hitting defense pounded Staubach, sidelining him twice with a dislocated left shoulder. SMU trailed late in the game, but Billy Gannon's one-yard run with 2:05 left on the clock provided the winning margin in a 32–28 victory.

HEARTBREAKER The 1980 Holiday Bowl began auspiciously for SMU, with Eric Dickerson's 15-yard touchdown run. In fact, the Ponies led Brigham Young the entire way, and with 2:33 left in the game were ahead 45-25. Somehow, though, quarterback Jim McMahon led BYU to three unanswered touchdowns—the third a 41-yard pass to Clay Brown in the end zone as time expired—and the Cougars won, 46-45. The teams combined for 890 yards of offense, including 225 yards rushing and three touchdowns by Craig James and 446 yards passing by McMahon.

DUBIOUS DISTINCTION SMU became the only school to receive the so-called death penalty, for recruiting violations in the early 1980s; players had allegedly received more than $60,000 from boosters. The Mustangs' 1987 season was canceled by the NCAA, the 1988 season by the university itself. SMU was banned from bowl games and TV appearances until the 1990 season, and the school lost 60 football scholarships over the course of four years.

STADIUM True or false: SMU's Gerald J. Ford Stadium is named after a former president. (Warning: this is a trick question.) The stadium namesake Ford is an SMU alumnus and bank CEO who donated $20 million to help build a new stadium—and is not related to former president Gerald *R.* Ford. Half the stadium seats lie below ground level in order to be less obtrusive to the surrounding neighborhood and campus. The smallish stadium (32,000 seats, convertible to 45,000) and adjoining sports center were completed in 2000. Prior to that, the Mustangs played either in Ownby Stadium or in the Cotton Bowl, which was the school's homefield from 1948 to 1978 and again from 1995 to 1999.

RIVAL SMU and TCU have battled for local, regional and denominational supremacy since long before the Dallas-

Fort Worth area came to be known as the Metroplex. The series dates to 1915; since then, the game has been played every year but five. SMU won 15 times in a row from 1972 to 1986. Overall, TCU holds a 40–38–7 edge in the series.

NICKNAME In the early 20th century, a sportswriter called the SMU football team the Parsons because many of the players were theology students. The name didn't stick. On Oct. 17, 1917, a student vote was held at a pep rally and Mustangs was selected over Bisons and Greyhounds.

MASCOT Peruna VIII, a miniature horse, represents the Mustangs. On Nov. 5, 1932, Peruna I (named after a alcohol-charged tonic of the prohibition era) made his first appearance at an SMU football game, against Texas A&M. He was struck and killed by a car during a 1934 Halloween celebration. All the Perunas since then have been donated by the Culwell family, which owns a 500-acre ranch in nearby Grapevine. C.W. "Cully" Culwell, a 1954 graduate, continues a tradition begun by his father, W.E. Culwell.

UNIFORMS One key indicator of a program in flux is a constantly changing uniform—and in the past 40 years, SMU has sported at least 11 distinct helmet designs. The shifting appearance is a far cry from SMU's glory days in the 1930s, when their uniforms were among the most glamorous in the college game—red helmets, red jerseys with blue numerals and two-tone pants that were khaki in front and red in the back.

LORE Jerry LeVias, the first African-American football scholarship player in the Southwest Conference, played for SMU from 1966 to 1968. He was an athletic and academic All-America and an All-SWC player three times. As a pro, he was an exciting receiver and kick returner for the Houston Oilers and the San Diego Chargers. LeVias was enshrined in the College Football Hall of Fame in 2004.

QUOTE "What I should have done was to have banned banquets, abolished autographs and taken the team into the desert until the day of the game."—Coach Matty Bell, after the Mustangs' loss to Stanford in the 1936 Rose Bowl

SMU ANNUAL STATISTICAL LEADERS

YR	RUSHING	YDS	ATT	AVG	PASSING	ATT	CMP	PCT	YDS	RECEIVING	REC	YDS	AVG
1945	Paul Page	355	23	15.4	Doak Walker	65	38	.58	387	Gene Wilson	31	311	10.0
1946	Paul Page	209	48	4.4	Frank Payne	107	50	.47	585	Gene Wilson	19	260	13.7
1947	Doak Walker	684	163	4.2	Gil Johnson	78	43	.55	565	Sid Halliday	14	131	9.4
1948	Doak Walker	532	108	4.9	Gil Johnson	128	78	.61	1,026	Kyle Rote	19	215	11.3
1949	Kyle Rote	777	142	5.5	Fred Benners	85	47	.55	1,069	Zohn Miliam	20	362	18.1
1950	Kyle Rote	762	152	5.0	Fred Benners	192	109	.57	1,361	J. Champion	31	454	14.6
1951	Jerry Norton	438	128	3.4	Fred Benners	204	110	.54	1,306	B. Musslewhite	36	532	14.8
1952	Jerry Norton	383	148	2.6	Jerry Norton	62	29	.47	431	Don Miller	16	202	12.6
1953	Frank Eidom	273	63	4.3	Duane Nutt	91	39	.43	581	Ed Bernet	17	227	13.4
1954	Frank Eidom	677	126	5.4	Duane Nutt	105	58	.55	783	Frank Eidom	19	246	12.9
1955	Don McIlhenny	544	104	5.2	John Roach	141	64	.45	907	Tommy Gentry	10	145	14.5
1956	Charlie Jackson	571	97	5.9	Charlie Arnold	157	71	.45	912	Tommy Gentry	23	255	11.1
1957	Charlie Jackson	234	42	5.6	Don Meredith	102	71	.70	912	Lon Slaughter	21	203	9.7
1958	Tirey Wilemon	350	48	7.3	Don Meredith	112	65	.58	952	Henry Christopher	17	286	16.8
1959	Glynn Gregory	269	50	5.4	Don Meredith	181	105	.58	1,266	G. Gregory	30	369	12.3
1960	Frank Jackson	269	80	3.4	Frank Jackson	54	25	.46	298	Tommy Brennan	11	117	10.6
1961	Billy Gannon	187	57	3.3	Jerry Rhome	129	74	.57	683	Billy Gannon	17	155	9.1
1962	Don Campbell	299	76	3.9	Don Campbell	89	43	.48	450	Billy Gannon	23	235	10.2
1963	John Roderick	345	60	5.8	Danny Thomas	138	55	.40	846	Tom Hillary	25	306	12.2
1964	Floyd Burke	174	51	3.4	Danny Thomas	121	49	.40	491	Don Crowder	18	150	8.3
1965	Mac White	486	176	2.8	Mac White	130	52	.40	658	John Roderick	24	248	10.3
1966	Mac White	606	135	4.5	Mike Livingston	81	37	.46	475	Jerry LeVias	18	420	23.3
1967	Daryl Doggett	172	33	5.2	Mike Livingston	250	152	.61	1,750	Jerry LeVias	57	724	12.7
1968	Mike Richardson	1,034	207	5.0	Chuck Hixson	468	265	.57	3,103	Jerry LeVias	80	1,131	14.1
1969	Daryl Doggett	809	189	4.3	Chuck Hixson	362	217	.60	2,313	Gary Hammond	51	722	14.2
1970	Gary Hammond	891	228	3.9	Chuck Hixson	285	160	.56	1,763	Gary Hammond	50	489	9.8
1971	Alvin Maxson	1,012	219	4.6	Gary Hammond	160	75	.47	787	Alvin Maxson	25	224	9.0
1972	Alvin Maxson	1,005	224	4.5	Keith Bobo	120	65	.54	1,003	Kenny Harrison	29	542	18.7
1973	Alvin Maxson	717	115	6.2	Keith Bobo	57	27	.47	541	Oscar Roan	16	331	20.7
1974	Ricky Wesson	885	181	4.9	Ricky Wesson	88	37	.42	688	Oscar Roan	19	351	18.5
1975	Wayne Morris	800	163	4.9	Ricky Wesson	84	35	.42	672	Freeman Johns	22	452	20.5
1976	Arthur Whittington	789	161	4.9	Ricky Wesson	154	69	.45	1,011	Robert Fisher	23	369	16.0
1977	Arthur Whittington	824	205	4.0	Mike Ford	301	153	.51	2,064	Emanuel Tolbert	64	996	15.6
1978	Derrek Shelton	332	98	3.4	Mike Ford	389	224	.58	3,007	Emanuel Tolbert	62	1,041	16.8
1979	Craig James	761	168	4.5	Jim Bob Taylor	148	73	.49	1,001	Emanuel Tolbert	28	376	13.4
1980	Eric Dickerson	928	188	4.9	Mike Ford	158	75	.47	951	Anthony Smith	25	329	13.2
1981	Eric Dickerson	1,428	255	5.6	Lance McIlhenny	155	67	.43	1,066	Jackie Wilson	20	397	19.9
1982	Eric Dickerson	1,617	232	7.0	Lance McIlhenny	120	57	.48	910	Gary Smith	21	154	7.3
1983	Reggie Dupard	1,249	197	6.3	Lance McIlhenny	162	77	.48	1,233	Ron Morris	41	688	16.8
1984	Reggie Dupard	1,160	196	5.9	Don King	177	93	.53	1,598	Ron Morris	27	554	20.5
1985	Reggie Dupard	1,278	229	5.6	Don King	209	107	.51	1,386	Ron Morris	31	411	13.3
1986	Jeff Atkins	796	201	4.0	Bobby Watters	285	154	.54	2,041	Jeffrey Jacobs	52	692	13.3
1987	*Season canceled*												
1988	*Season canceled*												
1989	Kevin Love	423	112	3.8	Mike Romo	503	282	.56	2,927	Jason Wolf	61	676	11.1
1990	Kevin Love	469	131	3.6	Mike Romo	412	250	.61	2,434	Michael Bowen	60	528	8.8
1991	Rongea Hill	663	168	3.9	Todd Ritz	202	103	.51	1,053	Jason Wolf	59	565	9.6
1992	Rongea Hill	512	128	4.0	Dan Freiburger	390	229	.59	2,580	Korey Beard	64	813	12.7
1993	Kevin Shepard	463	112	4.1	Ramon Flanigan	199	111	.56	1,334	Mick Rossley	46	468	10.2
1994	Ramon Flanigan	502	182	2.8	Ramon Flanigan	312	168	.54	1,869	Mick Rossley	83	857	10.3
1995	Donte Womack	758	208	3.6	Derek Canine	179	100	.56	1,019	Kevin Thornal	44	531	12.1
1996	Donte Womack	887	160	5.5	Ramon Flanigan	212	106	.50	1,715	Kevin Thornal	37	501	13.5
1997	Donte Womack	775	181	4.3	Chris Sanders	128	57	.45	678	Jack Brewer	19	352	18.5
1998	Rodnick Phillips	1,115	239	4.7	Chris Sanders	181	99	.55	1,050	Albert Johnson	39	536	13.7
1999	Kris Briggs	522	102	5.1	Josh McCown	234	125	.53	1,434	Chris Cunningham	39	570	14.6
2000	Kris Briggs	828	231	3.6	Josh McCown	331	169	.51	1,969	John Hampton	46	572	12.4
2001	ShanDerrick Charles	860	134	6.4	David Page	193	104	.54	1,209	Chris Cunningham	45	516	11.5
2002	Keylon Kincade	1,279	327	3.9	Richard Bartel	148	89	.60	1,078	Cody Cardwell	47	659	14.0
2003	Keylon Kincade	1,280	317	4.0	Richard Bartel	151	68	.45	797	Matt Rushbrook	30	359	12.0
2004	Jerad Rome	434	87	5.0	Tony Eckert	203	111	.55	1,406	Bobby Chase	31	483	15.6

The NCAA began including postseason stats in 2002

SMU ALL-TIME SCORES

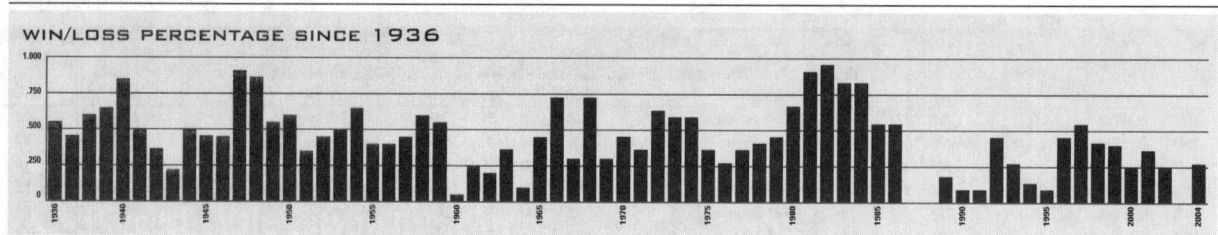

WIN/LOSS PERCENTAGE SINCE 1936

RAY MORRISON
1915-16, '22-34 (.633) 84-44-22

1915 — 2-5-0
O8	●	at TCU	0 43
O14	●	Hendrix	13 2
U		Austin Coll.	0 21
N4	●	Dallas U.	7 0
U		Daniel Baker	0 30
U		Southwestern	0 21
U		Trinity	0 14

1916 — 0-8-2
S30		at Texas	0 74
O7		at Baylor	0 61
O14		TCU	3 48
O21		at Texas A&M	0 62
O30		Dallas U.	6 14
N4	=	Austin Coll.	0 0
N10		Daniel Baker	0 27
N17		at Rice	3 146
N24		Trinity	6 14
D1	=	at Southwestern	9 9

J. BURTON RIX
1917-21 (.464) 16-19-7

1917 — 3-2-3
O6	●	Meridian	20 7
O13	●	at Austin Coll.	20 0
O20		at TCU	0 21
O27	●	Dallas U.	7 7
N3	●	Trinity	20 0
N10		Howard Payne	7 14
N17	=	Baylor	0 0
N29		Southwestern	0 0

1918-1995 SWC

1918 — 4-2-0 (1-2-0)
O19	●	Austin Coll.	19 0
O26	●	TCU	1 0 *f*
N2	●	Love Field	14 0
N9		Baylor	14 0
N23		at Texas	0 32
N30		at Rice	0 13

1919 — 5-4-1 (0-2-1)
S27	●	Burleson Coll.	26 6
O4	●	Wesley Coll.	7 6
O11		Texas A&M	0 16
O18	●	Daniel Baker	6 0
O25		Howard Payne	9 14
N1	●	Austin Coll.	41 0
N8	●	at Rice	14 21
N15	●	Trinity	46 6
N22	=	at Baylor	7 7
N27		at Southwestern	6 10

1920 — 3-5-2 (0-4-1)
S25	●	Daniel Baker	70 0
O2	=	Hardin-Simmons	0 0
O9		Texas A&M	0 3
O15	●	Howard Payne	14 0
O22		Arkansas	0 6
O30	●	Trinity	38 7
N6		Rice	0 10
N13		Texas	3 21
N20		Austin Coll.	0 43
N27		Baylor	0 0

1921 — 1-6-1 (0-4-0)
O1	●	Howard Payne	3 0
O12		Texas A&M	0 13
O21		Austin Coll.	6 17
O29		Arkansas *FrS*	0 14
N5		at Rice	0 7
N12		TCU	6 13
N19	=	Southwestern	0 0
N26		at Baylor	0 28

RAY MORRISON

1922 — 6-3-1 (2-2-0)
S30	●	SMU JV	16 0
O7	●	North Texas	66 0
O14	●	LSU	51 0
O20		Austin Coll.	7 10
O28	●	Oklahoma State	32 6
N4	●	Southwestern	46 14
N11	●	Texas A&M	17 6
N18		at Arkansas	0 9
N30		Baylor	0 24
D2	=	at TCU	0 0

1923 — 9-0-0 (5-0-0)
S29	●	North Texas	41 0
O6	●	Henderson-Brown	33 0
O10	●	Austin Coll.	10 3
O16	●	Missouri Mines	35 0
O26	●	at Texas A&M	10 0
N4	●	TCU	40 0
N10	●	Arkansas	13 6
N17	●	Oklahoma State	9 0
N29	●	Baylor	16 0

1924 — 5-1-4 (2-0-4)
S27	●	North Texas	7 0
O4	●	Trinity	14 3
O10	●	Austin Coll.	7 0
O17	●	Texas	10 6
O25	=	Texas A&M	7 7
N1	●	at TCU	6 0
N8	●	at Arkansas	14 14
N15		Baylor	7 7
N29		Oklahoma State	13 13
		DIXIE CLASSIC	
J1		W.V. Wesleyan	7 9

1925 — 5-2-2 (1-1-2)
S26	●	North Texas	48 0
O3	●	Abilene Christian	52 0
O9	●	Washington, Mo.	20 6
O16		at Texas A&M	0 7
O24		Oklahoma	0 9
O31		Texas	0 0
N7	=	Arkansas	0 0
N14		Baylor	7 6
N26	●	Drake	21 6

1926 — 8-0-1 (5-0-0)
S24	●	North Texas	42 0
O2	●	Trinity	48 0
O8	●	Centenary	37 0
O16		at Missouri	7 7
O23		Texas A&M	9 7
O30		at Texas	21 17
N6		Rice	20 0
N13	●	Baylor	31 3
N25		TCU	14 13

1927 — 7-2-0 (4-1-0)
S24	●	North Texas	68 0
O1	●	Howard Payne	32 0
O8		at Centenary	12 21
O14		Rice	34 6
O22	●	Missouri	32 9
O28		Texas	14 0
N5		Texas A&M	13 39
N12	●	Baylor	34 0
N19	●	at TCU	28 6

1928 — 6-3-1 (2-2-1)
S22	●	North Texas	60 6
S29	●	Howard Payne	31 0
O6		at Army	13 14
O13		Hardin-Simmons *WiFL*	6 0
O20		Rice	53 13
O27		Trinity	60 7
N3	●	at Texas	6 2
N10	=	Texas A&M	19 19
N17		at Baylor	0 2
N24		TCU	6 15

1929 — 6-0-4 (3-0-2)
S21	●	North Texas	13 3
S28	=	Howard Payne	13 13
O5	=	at Nebraska	0 0
O11	●	Austin Coll.	16 0
O26	●	Mississippi	52 0
N2		Texas	0 0
N9	●	at Texas A&M	12 7
N16		Baylor	25 6
N23	●	Rice	34 0 *
N30	=	at TCU	7 7

1930 — 6-3-1 (2-2-1)
S27	●	Howard Payne	26 0
O4	●	at Notre Dame	14 20
O10	●	Austin Coll.	34 0
O18	=	at Baylor	14 14
O25	●	Indiana	27 0
N1		at Texas	7 25
N8	●	Texas A&M	13 7
N15	●	Navy *BALT*	20 7
N22	●	at Rice	32 0
N29		TCU	0 13

1931 — 9-1-1 (5-0-1)
S26	●	North Texas	13 0
O3	●	Hardin-Simmons	27 10
O10	●	at Arkansas	42 6
O17	●	at Rice	21 12
O24	●	Centenary	19 0
N1		Texas	9 7
N7	●	at Texas A&M	8 0
N14	●	Baylor	6 0
N21	●	Navy	13 7 *
N28	=	at TCU	0 0
D5		at Saint Mary's-Cal	2 7

1932 — 3-7-2 (1-4-1)
S24	=	North Texas	0 0
O1		at Texas Tech	0 6
O8		Rice	0 13
O15		at Syracuse	16 6
O22		Centenary	7 18
O29		at Texas	6 14
N5	=	Texas A&M	0 0
N12	●	Arkansas	13 7
N19		at Baylor	0 19
N26		TCU	0 8
D3		Nebraska	14 21
J2		at Texas-El Paso	26 0

1933 — 4-7-1 (2-4-0)
S23		North Texas	0 7
S29	●	Texas Tech	14 0
O7	●	Texas-El Paso	27 6
O14	●	at Rice	13 7
O21	=	Oklahoma State	7 7
O28		at Arkansas	0 3
N4		Texas	0 10
N11	●	at Texas A&M	19 0
N18		Centenary	0 7
N25		Baylor	7 13
D2		at TCU	6 26
D9		Saint Mary's-Cal	6 18

1934 — 8-2-2 (3-2-1)
S22	●	North Texas	33 0
S29	●	Austin Coll.	33 0
O6	=	at LSU	14 14
O13		at Rice	0 9
O20	●	Oklahoma State	41 0
O27	●	Fordham *NYC*	26 14
N3	=	at Texas	7 7
N10	●	Texas A&M	28 0
N17	●	Arkansas	10 6
N24		at Baylor	6 13
D1	●	TCU	19 0
D8	●	at Washington, Mo.	7 0

MADISON BELL
1935-41, '45-49 (.654) 79-40-8

1935 — 12-1-0 (6-0-0)
S21	●	North Texas	29 0 *
S28	●	Austin Coll.	60 0
O5	●	Tulsa	14 0
O12	●	at Washington, Mo.	35 6
O19	●	Rice	10 0
O26	●	Hardin-Simmons	18 6
N2		Texas	20 0
N9		at UCLA	21 0
N16		at Arkansas	17 6
N23		Baylor	10 0
N30		at TCU	20 14
D7	●	at Texas A&M	24 0
		ROSE BOWL	
J1		Stanford	0 7

1936 — 5-4-1 (2-3-1)
S26	●	North Texas	6 0
O3	●	Texas A&I	60 0
O10		Fordham *NYC*	0 7
O17	●	Vanderbilt	16 0
O31		at Texas	14 7
N7		Texas A&M	6 22
N14		Arkansas	0 17
N21		at Baylor	7 13
N28	=	TCU	0 0
D5	●	at Rice	9 0

1937 — 5-6-0 (2-4-0) *
S25	●	North Texas	14 3 *
O2		Centenary	6 7
O9	●	at Washington, Mo.	14 0
O13		Vanderbilt	0 6
O23		Arkansas *FrS*	0 13
O30	●	Texas	13 2
N6		at Texas A&M	0 14
N13		Baylor	13 7
N20	●	at UCLA	26 13
N27		at TCU	0 3
D4		Rice	7 15

1938 — 6-4-0 (4-2-0)
S24	●	North Texas	34 7
O1	●	Arizona	29 7
O7		Marquette *CHI*	0 7
O22		at Pittsburgh	7 34
O30	●	Texas	7 6
N5	●	Texas A&M	10 7
N12	●	Arkansas	19 6
N19		at Baylor	21 6
N26		TCU	7 20
D3		at Rice	14 25

1939 — 6-3-1 (4-2-0)
S30	=	at Oklahoma	7 7
O7	●	North Texas	16 0
O14		at Notre Dame	19 20
O21	●	Marquette	16 0
N4		Texas	10 0
N11		at Texas A&M	2 6
N17		Arkansas *LR*	0 14
N25	●	Baylor	21 0
D2	●	at TCU	14 7
D9		Rice	13 6

1940 — 8-1-1 (5-1-0)

Date	Opponent		
S28 •	at UCLA	9	6
O5 •	North Texas	20	7
O12 =	at Pittsburgh	7	7
O19 •	Auburn	20	13
N2 •	at Texas	21	13
N9	Texas A&M	7	19
N16 •	Arkansas	28	0
N23 •	at Baylor	7	4
N30 •	TCU	16	0
D7 •	at Rice	7	6

1941 — 5-5-0 (2-4-0)

Date	Opponent		
S27	North Texas	54	0
O4	Fordham NYC	10	16
O11 =	Pacific TYL	34	0
O18 •	Auburn BIRM	20	7
N1	Texas	0	34
N8	at Texas A&M	10	21
N15	at Arkansas	14	7
N22 •	Baylor	14	0
N29	at TCU	13	15
D6	Rice	0	6

JAMES H. STEWART
1942-44 (.367) — 10-18-2

1942 — 3-6-2 (1-4-1)

Date	Opponent		
S26 •	North Texas	26	7
O3	at Pittsburgh	7	20
O10	Hardin-Simmons SA	6	7
O17 =	Temple	6	6
O24 •	Corpus Christi NAS	21	6
O31	at Texas	7	21
N7	Texas A&M	20	27
N14 •	Arkansas	14	6
N20 =	at Baylor	6	6
N28	TCU	6	14
D5	at Rice	7	13

1943 — 2-7-0 (2-3-0)

Date	Opponent		
S25	Tulsa	7	20
O9	NTAC	6	20
O16 •	Rice	12	0
O23	at Tulane	6	12
O30	Texas	0	20
N6	at Texas A&M	0	22
N13	Arkansas SA	12	14
N20	Texas Tech	6	7
N27 •	at TCU	20	0

1944 — 5-5-0 (2-3-0)

Date	Opponent		
S30 •	Memphis Navy	49	0
O7 •	Southwestern	16	15
O14	at Randolph AFB	0	41
O21	at Rice	10	21 *
O28	at Tulane	7	27
N4	at Texas	7	34
N11	Texas A&M	6	39
N18 •	Arkansas	20	12
N25 •	at Texas Tech	7	6
D2 •	TCU	9	6

MADISON BELL

1945 — 5-6-0 (4-2-0)

Date	Opponent		
S22 •	Lackland AFB	51	0
S29	at Corpus Christi NAS	7	22
O6	Missouri	7	10
O12	Oklahoma State OkC	12	26
O20 •	Rice	21	18
O27	at Tulane	7	19
N3	Texas	7	12
N10	at Texas A&M	0	3
N17 •	Arkansas	21	0
N24 •	Baylor	34	0
D1 •	at TCU	34	0

1946 — 4-5-1 (2-4-0)

Date	Opponent		
S30 =	at Temple	7	7
O5	Texas Tech	0	7
O11 •	Oklahoma State	15	6
O19	at Rice	7	21
O26 •	at Missouri	17	0
N2	at Texas	3	19
N8	Texas A&M	0	14
N16	at Arkansas	0	13
N23 •	at Baylor	35	0
N30 •	TCU	30	13

1947 — 9-0-2 (5-0-1)

Date	Opponent		
S9 •	at Santa Clara	22	6
O4 •	Missouri	35	19
O11 •	at Oklahoma State	21	14
O18 •	Rice	14	0
O25 •	at UCLA	7	0
N1 •	Texas	14	13
N8 •	at Texas A&M	13	0
N15 •	Arkansas	14	6
N22 •	at Baylor	10	0
N29 •	at TCU	19	19

COTTON BOWL

Date	Opponent		
J1 =	Penn State	13	13

1948 — 9-1-1 (5-0-1)

Date	Opponent		
S25 •	at Pittsburgh	33	14
O2 •	Texas Tech	41	6
O9 •	at Missouri	14	20
O16 •	at Rice	33	7
O23 •	Santa Clara	33	0
O30 •	at Texas	21	6
N6 •	Texas A&M	20	14
N13 •	at Arkansas	14	12
N20 •	Baylor	13	6
N27 =	TCU	7	7

COTTON BOWL

Date	Opponent		
J1 •	Oregon	21	13

1949 — 5-4-1 (2-3-1)

Date	Opponent		
S24 •	Wake Forest	13	7
O1 •	Missouri	28	27
O15	Rice	27	41
O22	Kentucky	20	7
O29 =	Texas	7	6
N5 •	at Texas A&M	27	27
N12 •	Arkansas	34	6
N19	Baylor	26	35
N26	at TCU	13	21
D3	Notre Dame	20	27

H.N. RUSSELL
1950-52 (.467) — 13-15-2

1950 — 6-4-0 (2-4-0)

Date	Opponent		
S23 •	Georgia Tech	33	13
S30 •	at Ohio State	32	27
O7 •	at Missouri	21	0
O14 •	Oklahoma State	56	0
O21 •	at Rice	42	21
N4	at Texas	20	23
N11	Texas A&M	20	25
N18 •	Arkansas	14	7
N25	Baylor	0	3
D2	TCU	13	27

1951 — 3-6-1 (1-4-1)

Date	Opponent		
S22 •	at Georgia Tech	7	21
S29 •	at Ohio State	0	7
O6 •	Missouri	34	0
O13 •	at Notre Dame	27	20
O20	Rice	7	28
N3	Texas	13	20
N10 =	at Texas A&M	14	14
N17 •	Arkansas	47	7
N24	at Baylor	13	14
D1	at TCU	2	13

1952 — 4-5-1 (3-2-1)

Date	Opponent		
S26	Duke	7	14
O4	Georgia Tech	7	20
O11 •	at Missouri	25	7
O18 •	at Rice	21	14
O25	Kansas	0	26
N1	at Texas	14	31
N8 •	Texas A&M	21	13
N15	at Arkansas	27	17
N22 •	Baylor	7	7
N29	TCU	7	14

CHALMER WOODARD
1953-56 (.488) — 19-20-1

1953 — 5-5-0 (3-3-0)

Date	Opponent		
O3	at Georgia Tech	4	6
O9 •	Missouri	20	7
O17 •	Rice	12	7
O24 •	at Kansas	14	6
O31	Texas	7	16
N7	at Texas A&M	23	0
N14 •	Arkansas	13	7
N21	at Baylor	21	27
N28	at TCU	0	13
D5	at Notre Dame	14	40

1954 — 6-3-1 (4-1-0)

Date	Opponent		
O2	Georgia Tech	7	10
O9 •	at Missouri	25	6
O16 •	at Rice	20	6
O23 •	Kansas	36	18
O30 =	at Texas	13	13
N6 •	Texas A&M	6	3
N13 •	at Arkansas	21	14
N20	Baylor	21	33
N27 •	TCU	21	6
D4	Notre Dame	14	26

1955 — 4-6-0 (2-4-0)

Date	Opponent		
S24	at Notre Dame	0	17
O1	at Georgia Tech	7	20
O7 •	Missouri	13	6
O15 •	Rice	20	0
O22 •	at Kansas	33	14
O29	Texas	18	19
N5	at Texas A&M	2	13
N12	Arkansas	0	6
N19 •	at Baylor	12	0
N26	at TCU	13	20

1956 — 4-6-0 (2-4-0)

Date	Opponent		
S22 •	Notre Dame	19	13
S29	Georgia Tech	7	9
O6 •	at Missouri	33	27
O13	at Duke	6	14
O20 •	at Rice	14	13
N3 •	at Texas	19	19
N10	Texas A&M	7	33
N17	Arkansas LR	13	27
N24	Baylor	0	26
D1	TCU	6	21

BILL MEEK
1957-61 (.380) — 17-29-4

1957 — 4-5-1 (3-3-0)

Date	Opponent		
S21 •	at California	13	6
S28 =	at Georgia Tech	0	0
O11	Missouri	6	7
O19 •	Rice	21	27
N2 •	Texas	19	12
N9	at Texas A&M	6	19
N16 •	Arkansas	27	22
N23 •	at Baylor	14	7
N30	at TCU	0	21
D7	Notre Dame	21	54

1958 — 6-4-0 (4-2-0)

Date	Opponent		
S27 •	at Ohio State	20	23
O4 •	Notre Dame	6	14
O11 •	at Missouri	32	19
O18 •	Rice	7	13
O25 •	Georgia Tech	20	0
N1 •	at Texas	26	10
N8 •	Texas A&M	33	0
N15 •	at Arkansas	6	13
N22 •	Baylor	33	29
N29 •	TCU	20	13

1959 — 5-4-1 (2-3-1)

Date	Opponent		
S26 •	at Georgia Tech	12	16
O3 •	Navy	20	7
O9 •	Missouri	23	2
O17 =	at Rice	13	13
O24 •	Texas Tech	21	13
O31	Texas	0	21
N7 •	at Texas A&M	14	11
N14	Arkansas	14	17
N21 •	at Baylor	30	14
N28	at TCU	0	19

1960 — 0-9-1 (0-6-1)

Date	Opponent		
S17	at Missouri	0	20
S24	at Ohio State	0	24
O8	Navy NOR	7	26
O15	Rice	0	47
O22	at Texas	7	28
O29	at Texas	7	17
N5 =	Texas A&M	0	0
N12	at Arkansas	3	26
N19	Baylor	7	20
N26	TCU	0	13

1961 — 2-7-1 (1-5-1)

Date	Opponent		
S23	Maryland	6	14
S29	at Southern Cal	16	21
O7 •	Air Force	9	7
O21 •	at Rice	0	10
O28 •	Texas Tech	8	7
N4	Texas	0	27
N11	at Texas A&M	12	25
N18	Arkansas	7	21
N25	at Baylor	6	31
D2 =	at TCU	28	28

HAYDEN FRY
1962-72 (.427) — 49-66-1

1962 — 2-8-0 (2-5-0)

Date	Opponent		
S22	at Maryland	0	7
S29	Southern Cal	3	33
O6	Air Force	20	25
O20 •	Rice	15	7
O27 •	at Texas Tech	14	0
N3	at Texas	0	6
N10	Texas A&M	7	12
N17	Arkansas LR	7	9
N24	Baylor	13	17
D1	TCU	9	14

1963 — 4-7-0 (2-5-0)

Date	Opponent		
S28 •	at Michigan	16	27
O5 •	Air Force	10	0
O11 •	Navy	32	28
O19	at Rice	7	13
O26	Texas Tech	6	13
N2	Texas	12	17
N9 •	at Texas A&M	9	7
N16 •	Arkansas	14	7
N23	at TCU	15	22
D7	at Baylor	6	20

SUN BOWL

Date	Opponent		
D31	Oregon	14	21

1964 — 1-9-0 (0-7-0)

Date	Opponent		
S19	at Florida	8	24
S26	at Ohio State	8	27
O3 •	Texas Arlington	14	0
O17	Rice	6	7
O24	at Texas Tech	0	12
O31	at Texas	0	7
N7	Texas A&M	0	23
N14	at Arkansas	0	44
N21	Baylor	13	16
N28	TCU	6	17

1965 — 4-5-1 (3-4-0)

Date	Opponent		
S18 •	at Miami, Fla.	7	3
S25	at Illinois	0	42
O2 =	Purdue	14	14
O16 •	at Rice	17	14
O23	Texas Tech	24	26
O30 •	Texas	31	14
N6 •	at Texas A&M	10	0
N13	Arkansas	3	24
N20	at Baylor	10	20
N27	TCU	7	10

1966 — 8-3-0 (6-1-0)

Date	Opponent		
S17 •	Illinois	26	7
S24	Navy	21	3
O1	at Purdue	23	35
O15 •	Rice	28	24
O22 •	at Texas Tech	24	7
O29 •	at Texas	13	12
N5 •	at Texas A&M	21	14
N12	at Arkansas	0	22
N19 •	Baylor	24	22
N26 •	TCU	21	0

COTTON BOWL

Date	Opponent		
D31	Georgia	9	24

1967 — 3-7-0 (3-4-0)

Date	Opponent		
S16 •	at Texas A&M	20	17
S23 •	at Missouri	0	21
O7	at Minnesota	3	23
O13	Army	6	24
O21 •	at Rice	10	14
O28	Texas Tech	7	21
N4	Texas	28	35
N18 •	Arkansas	17	35
N25 •	at Baylor	16	10
D2 •	TCU	28	14

1968   8-3-0 (5-2-0)

S21	●	at Auburn	37	28
S28		at Ohio State	14	35
O5	●	North Carolina St.	35	14
O12		at TCU	21	14
O19		Rice	32	24
O26	●	at Texas Tech	39	18
N2		at Texas	7	38
N9	●	Texas A&M	36	23
N16		Arkansas *LR*	29	35
N23	●	Baylor	33	17
		BLUEBONNET BOWL		
D31	●	Oklahoma	28	27

1969   3-7-0 (3-4-0)

S13	●	Air Force	22	26
S20		at Georgia Tech	21	24
S27		at Michigan State	15	23
O10		TCU	19	17
O18		at Rice	34	14
O25		Texas Tech	24	27
N1		Texas	14	45
N8		at Texas A&M	10	20
N15		Arkansas	15	28
N22	●	at Baylor	12	6

1970   5-6-0 (3-4-0)

S12	●	Oklahoma	11	28
S19		at Tennessee	3	28
S26	●	New Mexico State	34	21
O3	●	at Northwestern	21	20
O17		Rice	10	0
O24		at Texas Tech	10	14
O31		at Texas	15	42
N7	●	Texas A&M	6	3
N14		at Arkansas	3	36
N21	●	Baylor	23	10
N28		at TCU	17	26

1971   4-7-0 (3-4-0)

S18		at Oklahoma	0	30
S25		at Missouri	12	24
O2	●	New Mexico State	28	25
O9		at Air Force	0	30
O16	●	at Rice	16	10
O23	●	Texas Tech	18	17
O30		Texas	18	22
N6		at Texas A&M	10	27
N13		Arkansas	13	18
N20	●	at Baylor	20	6
N27		TCU	16	18

1972   7-4-0 (4-3-0)

S16	●	Wake Forest	56	10
S23	●	Florida *TAM*	21	14
S30		at Virginia Tech	10	13
O7	●	New Mexico State	55	6
O21	●	Rice	29	14
O28		Texas Tech	3	17
N4		at Texas	9	17
N11		Texas A&M	17	27
N18	●	at Arkansas	22	7
N25	●	Baylor	12	7
D2	●	at TCU	35	22

1973   6-4-1 (3-3-1)

S15	●	Santa Clara	49	7
S22	●	at Oregon State	35	16
S29	●	Virginia Tech	37	6
O6		Missouri	7	17
O20	●	at Rice	27	16
O27		at Texas Tech	14	31
N3		Texas	14	42
N10		at Texas A&M	10	45
N17	=	Arkansas	7	7
N24	●	at Baylor	38	22
D1	●	TCU	21	19

1974   6-4-1 (3-3-1)

S14	●	North Texas	7	6
S21	●	Virginia Tech	28	25
S28		at Ohio State	9	28
O5	●	Oregon State	37	30
O12		at TCU	33	13
O19		Rice	19	14
O26		Texas Tech	17	20
N2		at Texas	15	35
N9	●	Texas A&M	18	14
N16	=	Arkansas *LR*	24	24
N23		Baylor	14	31

1975   4-7-0 (2-5-0)

S6	●	at Wake Forest	14	7
S13		at Florida	14	40
S27		at Houston	26	16
O4		West Virginia	22	28
O10	●	TCU	28	13
O18		at Rice	17	28
O25		at Texas Tech	20	37
N1		Texas	22	30
N8		at Texas A&M	3	36
N15		Arkansas	7	35
N22	●	at Baylor	34	31

1976   3-8-0 (2-6-0)

S11	●	TCU	34	14
S18	●	Alabama *BIRM*	3	56
S25	●	North Texas	38	31
O2		at Memphis	13	27
O9		at Baylor	20	27
O16		Houston	6	29
O23		at Texas	12	13
O30		Texas A&M	0	36
N6		at Rice	34	41
N13		at Texas Tech	7	34
N20	●	Arkansas *SHRE*	35	31

1977   4-7-0 (3-5-0)

S10	●	at TCU	45	21
S17		North Texas	13	24
S24	●	Tulane	28	23
O1		Ohio State	7	35
O8		at Baylor	6	9
O15	●	at Houston	37	23
O22		Texas	14	30
O29		at Texas A&M	21	38
N5	●	Rice	41	24
N12		Texas Tech	7	45
N19		at Arkansas	7	47

1978   4-6-1 (3-5-0)

S9	●	TCU	45	14
S16	●	Florida *ORL*	35	25
S23		at Penn State	21	26
O7	=	at Ohio State	35	35
O14	●	at Baylor	28	21
O21		Houston	28	42
O28		at Texas	3	22
N4		Texas A&M	17	20
N11	●	at Rice	58	0
N18	●	at Texas Tech	16	19
N25		Arkansas	14	27

1979   5-6-0 (3-5-0)

S8	●	Rice	35	17
S15	●	at TCU	27	7
S22	●	North Texas	20	9
S29		at Tulane	17	24
O13		Baylor	21	24
O20		at Houston	10	37
O27		Texas	6	30
N3		at Texas A&M	14	47
N10	●	at Wichita St.	34	0
N17	●	Texas Tech	35	10
N24		Arkansas *LR*	7	31

1980   8-4-0 (5-3-0)

S13	●	North Texas	28	9
S20	●	TCU	17	14
S27	●	Texas Arlington	52	16
O4	●	at Tulane	31	21
O11		at Baylor	28	32
O18		Houston	11	13
O25	●	at Texas	20	6
N1		Texas A&M	27	0
N8	●	at Rice	34	14
N15		at Texas Tech	0	14
N22	●	Arkansas	31	7
		HOLIDAY BOWL		
D19		Brigham Young	45	46

1981   10-1-0 (7-1-0)

S5	●	Texas Arlington	48	0
S12	●	North Texas	34	7
S19	●	Grambling	59	27
S26	●	at TCU	20	9
O10	●	Baylor	37	20
O17	●	at Houston	38	22
O24		Texas	7	9
O31	●	at Texas A&M	27	7
N7	●	Rice	33	12
N14	●	Texas Tech	30	6
N21	●	at Arkansas	32	18

1982   11-0-1 (7-0-1)

S11	●	Tulane	51	7
S18	●	at Texas-El Paso	31	10
S25	●	TCU	16	13
O2	●	North Texas	38	10
O9	●	at Baylor	22	19
O16	●	Houston	20	14
O23	●	at Texas	30	17
O30	●	Texas A&M	47	9
N6	●	at Rice	41	14
N13	●	at Texas Tech	34	27
N20	=	Arkansas	17	17
		COTTON BOWL		
J1	●	Pittsburgh	7	3

1983   10-2-0 (7-1-0)

S3	●	Louisville	24	6
S10	●	Grambling *SHRE*	20	13
S24	●	at TCU	21	17
O1	●	Texas Arlington	34	0
O8	●	Baylor	42	26
O22		Texas	12	15
O29	●	at Texas A&M	10	7
N5	●	Rice	20	6
N12	●	Texas Tech	33	7
N19	●	Arkansas *LR*	17	0
N26	●	Houston *TOK*	34	12
		SUN BOWL		
D24		Alabama	7	28

1984   10-2-0 (6-2-0)

S15	●	at Louisville	41	7
S22	●	North Texas	24	6
S29	●	TCU	26	17
O13	●	at Baylor	24	20
O20		Houston	20	29
O27		at Texas	7	13
N3	●	Texas A&M	28	20
N10	●	at Rice	31	17
N17	●	at Texas Tech	31	0
N24		Arkansas	31	28
D1	●	at Nevada-Las Vegas	38	21
		ALOHA BOWL		
D29	●	Notre Dame	27	20

1985   6-5-0 (5-3-0)

S7	●	Texas-El Paso	35	23
S28		at TCU	56	21
O5		at Arizona	6	28
O12		Baylor	14	21
O19	●	at Houston	37	13
O26	●	Texas	44	14
N2		at Texas A&M	17	19
N9	●	Rice	40	15
N16	●	Texas Tech	9	7
N23		at Arkansas	9	15
D7		at Oklahoma	13	35

1986   6-5-0 (5-3-0)

S13	●	at Rice	45	3
S20		at Arizona State	0	30
S27	●	TCU	31	21
O4		Boston College	31	29
O11	●	at Baylor	27	21
O18	●	Houston	10	3
O25		at Texas	24	27
N1		Texas A&M	35	39
N8		at Notre Dame	29	61
N15	●	at Texas Tech	13	7
N22		Arkansas	0	41

1987-1988   0-0-0
NO TEAM

1989   2-9-0 (0-8-0)

S2		Rice	6	35
S16	●	Connecticut	31	30
S23		Texas	13	45
S30		at TCU	10	28
O14		Baylor	3	49
O21		at Houston	21	95
O28	●	North Texas	35	9
N4		at Texas A&M	14	63
N11		at Notre Dame	6	59
N18		Texas Tech	24	48
D2		Arkansas *LR*	24	38

1990   1-10-0 (0-8-0)

S8	●	Vanderbilt	44	7
S15		at Tulane	7	43
S29		TCU	21	42
O6		at North Texas	7	14
O13		at Baylor	17	52
O20		Houston	17	44
O27		at Texas	3	52
N3		Texas A&M	17	38
N10		at Rice	28	30
N17		at Texas Tech	7	62
N24		Arkansas	29	42

1991   1-10-0 (0-8-0)

S7		Arkansas *LR*	6	17
S14		at Vanderbilt	11	14
S28		Baylor	7	45
O5	●	at Tulane	31	17
O12		Texas Tech	14	38
O19		at Houston	20	49
O26		Texas	0	34
N2		at TCU	10	18
N9		Rice	10	31
N23		at Texas A&M	6	65
N30		Tulsa	26	31

1992   5-6-0 (2-5-0)

S5		Tulane	12	13
S12	●	North Texas	28	14
S19		at New Mexico	20	13
S26	●	TCU	21	9
O3		at Baylor	7	49
O10		at Rice	13	28
O24		at Texas Tech	25	39
O31		Texas A&M	7	41
N7	●	Houston	41	16
N14		at Texas	14	35
N21	●	Arkansas *LR*	24	19

1993   2-7-2 (1-5-1)

S4		Arkansas	6	10
S11		Wisconsin	16	24
S25	●	at TCU	21	15
O2	=	at Missouri	10	10
O9		Baylor	12	31
O16	=	at Houston	28	28
O23		Texas *SA*	10	37
O30		at Texas A&M	13	37
N6		Rice	24	31
N13		Texas Tech	24	41
N20	●	at Navy	42	13

1994   1-9-1 (0-6-1)

S3		Arkansas *LR*	14	34
S10		at UCLA	10	17
S17	●	New Mexico	34	31
S24		at Texas Tech	7	35
O1		North Carolina	24	28
O8		at Baylor	10	44
O15		Houston	33	39
O22		Texas	20	42
O29	=	Texas A&M *SA*	21	21
N5		at Rice	10	17
N12		TCU	14	35

1995   1-10-0 (0-7-0)

S2	●	Arkansas	17	14
S9		Navy	2	33
S16		at Oklahoma	10	24
S23		at Wisconsin	0	42
S30		Texas	10	35
O14		at Texas A&M	17	20
O21		at Houston	15	38
O28		Rice	24	34
N4		at TCU	16	19
N11		Baylor	7	48
N18		Texas Tech	14	45

1996-2004   WAC

1996   5-6 (4-4)

A31	●	Tulsa	17	10
S7	●	at Arkansas	23	10
S14		Utah	17	21
S21		at Navy	17	19
S28		at Brigham Young	3	31
O5		Missouri	26	27
O19		at Rice	17	35
O26	●	New Mexico	52	31
N2		at Wyoming	17	59
N9	●	at Texas-El Paso	30	0
N21	●	TCU	27	24

MIKE CAVAN
1997-2001 (.393)   22-34

1997   6-5   (5-3)
S6		at Mississippi	15	23
S13	●	Arkansas *Shre*	31	9
S20		Navy	16	46
S27		Brigham Young	16	19
O4		at New Mexico	15	22
O11	●	at Utah	20	19
O25	●	Wyoming	22	17
N1	●	Rice	24	6
N8	●	Texas-El Paso	28	14
N15	●	at Tulsa	42	41
N20		at TCU	18	21

1998   5-7   (4-4)
S5		at Rice	17	23
S12		Tulane	21	31
S19		Arkansas *LR*	17	44
S26		Mississippi	41	48
O3	●	at Hawaii	28	0
O10		at Wyoming	7	12
O17	●	TCU	10	6
O24	●	Nevada-Las Vegas	10	7
O31		at Air Force	7	31
N7	●	Tulsa	33	3
N14		Colorado State	10	32
N21	●	at Navy	24	11

1999   4-6   (3-3)
S4		Arkansas	0	26
S11		at Tulane	19	53
S25		Hawaii	0	20
O2		at Kansas	9	27
O9		at Texas-El Paso	28	42
O14	●	Fresno State	24	14
O30	●	Rice	27	2
N13	●	Cal St. Northridge	58	16
N20	●	at Tulsa	28	14
N26		at TCU	0	21

2000   3-9   (2-6)
S2	●	Kansas	31	17
S9		at Texas-El Paso	20	37
S16		at North Carolina St.	0	41
S23		Tulane	17	29
S30		at Houston	15	17
O7		San Jose State	10	35
O14		at Hawaii	15	30
O28	●	Nevada	21	7
N4		at Rice	14	43
N11	●	Tulsa	24	20
N18		at Fresno State	7	14
N24		TCU	7	62

2001   4-7   (4-4)
S1		Louisiana Tech *Shre*	6	36
S8		TCU	10	38
S22		North Carolina St.	17	26
O6		Hawaii	31	38
O13	●	at San Jose State	24	17
O27	●	Texas-El Paso	40	14
N3		at Nevada	14	35
N10		Fresno State	13	38
N17	●	at Tulsa	24	14
N24	●	Rice	37	20
D1		at North Carolina	10	19

PHIL BENNETT
2002-Present (.171)   6-29

2002   3-9   (3-5)
A31		Navy	7	38
S7		Texas Tech	14	24
S14		at TCU	6	17
S21		Oklahoma State	16	52
S28		at Hawaii	10	42
O5		San Jose State	23	34
O12		at Fresno State	7	30
O19	●	Louisiana Tech	37	34
O26		at Rice	15	27
N2		Nevada	6	24
N16	●	at Texas-El Paso	42	35
N23	●	Tulsa	24	21

2003   0-12   (0-8)
A30		at Texas Tech	10	58
S13		at Baylor	7	10
S20		Oklahoma State	6	52
S27		at Nevada	9	12
O4		Texas-El Paso	19	21
O11		at San Jose State	14	31
O18		Boise State	3	45
O25		at Tulsa	16	35
N1		Fresno State	11	20
N8		at Louisiana Tech	6	41
N15		Rice	20	41
N29		TCU	13	20

2004   3-8   (3-5)
S4		Texas Tech	13	27
S11		at TCU	0	44
S18		at Oklahoma State	7	59
S25	●	San Jose State	36	13
O2		at Boise State	20	38
O9		at Rice	10	44
O16		Louisiana Tech	10	41
O30		at Fresno State	0	42
N6	●	Tulsa	41	35
N13	●	Nevada	38	20
N20		at Texas-El Paso	27	57

SOUTH CAROLINA

BY GEOFFREY NORMAN

LOYALTY IN THE FACE OF ADVERSITY is plainly the virtue that best characterizes the University of South Carolina's football program. There is nothing exceptional about a school that routinely wins—or contends for—national and conference championships, packing its stadium on Saturdays with fervent fans even in years when the team is struggling. Fans of the perennial powers understand—sort of—that you can't win them all and you can't be on top every year.

But the South Carolina Gamecocks have never won a national championship. They've never been ranked No. 1. Nor have they finished on top of the SEC since joining in 1992. Before that year, the Gamecocks had been to eight bowl games and lost all of them.

And yet, at every home game, Williams-Brice Stadium in Columbia is packed with more than 80,000 of the most loyal, long-suffering fans in all of college football. South Carolina, like its neighboring states, is passionate about football. But it is also a small state; thus, homegrown talent is in short supply. The Gamecocks must compete with in-state archrival Clemson and with raiding big-name recruiters from Tennessee, Georgia and Alabama.

The Gamecocks have brought in head coaches who had won national titles elsewhere—Paul Dietzel, who did it at LSU, and Lou Holtz, who'd been No. 1 at Notre Dame. And in 2005, the Gamecocks will try again with Steve Spurrier, who certainly knows a thing or two about how to win in the SEC, and who also owns a national championship. One thing for sure that Spurrier will not have to do in Columbia is energize the fans. Their loyalty is solid.

TRADITION The sense of gravity is palpable before home games. The Gamecocks take the field through a tunnel constructed by the school's marching band, which plays Richard Strauss' "Thus Spake Zarathustra" (the theme to *2001: A Space Odyssey*) as the players pour onto the field. The band, the Mighty Sound of the Southeast, travels to all away games.

BEST PLAYER George Rogers (1977 to 1980) was the nation's second-leading rusher in 1979 and topped that in 1980 when he finished first with 1,894 yards and won the Heisman Trophy. Rogers conclusively established his

---

PROFILE

University of South Carolina
Columbia, S.C.
Founded: 1801
Enrollment: 17,689
Colors: Garnet and Black
Nickname: Gamecocks
Stadium: Williams-Brice Stadium
     Opened in 1934
     Grass; 80,250 capacity
First football game: 1892
All-time record: 499–508–44 (.496)
Bowl record: 3–8
Heisman Trophy: George Rogers, 1980
First-round NFL draftees: 8
Website: www.uscsports.com

THE BEST OF TIMES

It's hard to argue with the second and third year of the Lou Holtz era. After an 0–11 first season, South Carolina went 8–4 and 9–3, landing two New Year's bowl berths and establishing the Gamecocks for the first time as a force to be reckoned with in the SEC.

THE WORST OF TIMES

During one span over the 1963 and 1964 seasons, the Gamecocks went winless in 15 straight games.

CONFERENCE

Few schools are as well traveled as the Gamecocks, who played in the Southern Conference from 1922 to 1952, then spent nearly two decades in the ACC (1953-71), before spending the next 20 years as an independent. In 1992, they joined the SEC.

DISTINGUISHED ALUMNI

Alex English, NBA player; Leeza Gibbons, TV personality; Ernest "Fritz" Hollings, U.S. senator; Robert McNair, owner, Houston Texans; Darius Rucker, Dean Felber, Jim "Soni" Sonefeld and Mark Bryan of Hootie & the Blowfish

FIGHT SONG

THE FIGHTING GAMECOCKS LEAD THE WAY
Hey, Let's give a cheer, Carolina is here,
The Fighting Gamecocks lead the way.

Who gives a care, If the going gets tough,
And when it is rough, that's when the Cocks get going.

Hail to our colors of Garnet and Black,
In Carolina pride have we.

So, Go Gamecocks Go—FIGHT!
Drive for the goal—FIGHT!
USC will win today—GO COCKS!
So, let's give a cheer, Carolina is here.
The Fighting Gamecocks All The Way!

Unlike many other states, in South Carolina, the "aggie school" gets favorable political treatment.

Heisman bona fides by gaining more than 140 yards in back-to-back performances on the road against national powers Southern California and Michigan. He carried the Gamecocks to a rare national television appearance in that year's Gator Bowl against Pittsburgh and fellow Heisman candidate Hugh Green. Rogers rushed for over 100 yards in 22 consecutive games, and the New Orleans Saints made him the first player selected in the 1981 NFL draft.

BEST COACH A tough call. Glory has eluded South Carolina coaches and, in fact, none has ever gone on to another Division I-A head coaching job. Lou Holtz has the gaudiest lifetime résumé. Gamecocks fans expected big things from Holtz when he arrived in 1999, inheriting a program that had gone 1–10 the previous season. The turnaround did not occur immediately, as Holtz's first team lost every game. Then things got decidedly better, and the Gamecocks accomplished the following firsts under Holtz's leadership: 17 wins, back-to-back New Year's Day bowl victories and Top 20 finishes in 2000 and

2001, and Holtz winning SEC Coach of the Year honors in 2000.

But, like most USC coaches, Holtz finished with a mediocre overall record (33–34) and earned only one win in six tries over archrival Clemson.

In the affections of longtime Gamecocks fans, Holtz's nearest rival would be Rex Enright, who also finished his career with a losing record (64–69–7). But Enright was revered so much that the offices of the athletic department and the adjacent practice facilities are named for him. Enright took over as head coach in 1938 and stayed until 1955, with three years off to serve in the Navy during World War II. He made his legend where Holtz struggled, against Clemson, beating the Tigers seven times in his last 10 seasons—a span when Clemson was a national power.

BEST TEAM Expectations were not especially high before the 1984 season. Then Joe Morrison's team won nine straight, including a victory over Notre Dame in South Bend. The Gamecocks had also beaten Georgia, Pitt, Kansas State and Florida State, and were ranked No.

RECORDS

RUSHING YARDS

GAME
278	Brandon Bennett vs. East Tennessee State, Oct. 5, 1991 (31 att.)

SEASON
1,894	George Rogers, 1980 (324 att.)

CAREER
5,204	George Rogers, 1977-80 (954 att.)

PASSING YARDS

GAME
473	Steve Taneyhill vs. Mississippi State, Oct. 14, 1995 (38 of 44)

SEASON
3,206	Todd Ellis, 1987 (241 of 432)

CAREER
9,953	Todd Ellis, 1986-89 (747 of 1,350)

RECEIVING YARDS

GAME
206	Zola Davis vs. Vanderbilt, Oct. 24, 1998 (14 rec.)

SEASON
1,106	Sterling Sharpe, 1986 (74 rec.)

CAREER
2,497	Sterling Sharpe, 1983, 1985-87 (169 rec.)

POINTS

GAME
24	Stanley Pritchett vs. Mississippi State, Oct. 14, 1995 (6 TDs); Mike Dingle vs. Virginia Tech, Sept. 22, 1990 (6 TDs)

SEASON
113	Collin Mackie, 1987 (25 FGs, 38 PATs)

CAREER
330	Collin Mackie, 1987-90 (72 FGs, 114 PATs)

CONSENSUS ALL-AMERICANS

1980	George Rogers,	RB
1984	Del Wilkes,	OG

2 in the nation, behind Washington, with Navy coming up. The game had been scheduled for Columbia but was switched to Annapolis so South Carolina could get an additional home game the following year. Perhaps because they were on the road, or maybe because the high national ranking made them dizzy, the Gamecocks were upset by the Midshipmen. Hard as the defeat was to accept, it was made even worse when Washington also lost that weekend. If the Gamecocks had beaten Navy, they would have been No. 1. The team bounced back against Clemson, rallying from a 21-3 deficit to win 22-21, but went on to lose to Oklahoma State in the Gator Bowl and finish No.11 in the final AP rankings.

BIGGEST GAME The Gamecocks were an unranked and much-overlooked independent when they played mighty Michigan in Ann Arbor on Sept. 27, 1980. Michigan was aware of George Rogers and stacked its defense to stop him. Still, Rogers ran the ball 36 times for 142 yards. Ahead 14-3, Michigan opened the second half by marching to the Gamecocks 8, then fumbling into the end zone. South Carolina recovered and drove 80 yards to score on a two-yard run by Rogers. Later, the Gamecocks sniffed out a fake punt by Michigan and scored on a short drive for a win that put South Carolina on the map and made Rogers the leading Heisman candidate.

BIGGEST UPSET North Carolina was ranked No. 3 in the nation on Oct. 24, 1981, when South Carolina QB Gordon Beckham completed 16 of 17 passes and led the Gamecocks to a 31-13 blowout. USC's loss two weeks later to the

University of the Pacific made the win even more remarkable. Pacific couldn't afford a charter flight to South Carolina and stayed in one of the cheapest motels in Columbia. The Gamecocks had improved to 5–3 after upsetting the Tar Heels but finished their first season after Rogers' departure with a 6–6 mark.

TRAGEDY Steve "The Cadillac" Wadiak did not play football in high school. He learned the game in the Navy during World War II and was playing sandlot ball in Chicago after the war when a Gamecock loyalist saw that he had talent and alerted coach Rex Enright. Wadiak's 2,878 yards rushing made him the Gamecocks' all-time leading rusher for 28 years, until George Rogers broke his record. After graduating in 1951, Wadiak was drafted by the Pittsburgh Steelers and also had an offer from Montreal in the Canadian Football League. He was working his way toward a decision when he was killed in an automobile accident on March 9, 1952. Wadiak was much loved by Gamecock fans for his enthusiasm and for the spark he provided, especially against Clemson, and the team's MVP award is named after him.

WILDEST FINISH In a 1952 game in Norfolk, Va., that was sponsored by the Shriners and called The Oyster Bowl, South Carolina was trailing a heavily favored Virginia team 14-0 midway through the fourth quarter. Dick Balka, a Notre Dame transfer, came in as quarterback and with three quick completions moved the Gamecocks more than 70 yards. With the score 14-7, Virginia fumbled away the kickoff inside its own 5-yard line. The Gamecocks quickly scored and tied the game. A clip on the next kickoff put Virginia deep in

ALL-TIME TEAMS

In 1992, South Carolina celebrated its football centennial by selecting two all-time teams— 12 players from the pre-World War II era (when players went both ways) and 29 from the modern (postwar) era.

Pre-World War II (1892-1945)

1920-21	Tatum Gressette, B
1928-30	Bru Boineau, B
1931-33	Earl Clay, B
1931-33	Fred Hambright, B
1911-15	Luke Hill, L
1920-23	Joe Wheeler, L
1927-29	Julian Beall, L
1940-42	Lou Sossamon, L
1935-38	Larry Craig, L
1938-40	Alex Urban, L
1942-43	Dominic Fusci, L
1942-44	Skimp Harrison, L

Modern Era (1946-92)
OFFENSE

1973-76	Steve Courson, G
1980-81, 1983-84	Del Wilkes, G
1968-70	Dave DeCamilla, T
1978, 1981	Chuck Slaughter, T
1945-46	Bryant Meeks, C
1973-75	Mike McCabe, C
1973, 1975	Jay Saldi, TE
1977-80	Willie Scott, TE
1967-69	Fred Zeigler, WR
1983, 1985-87	Sterling Sharpe, WR
1973-75	Jeff Grantz, QB
1948-51	Steve Wadiak, RB
1977-80	George Rogers, RB
1986-89	Harold Green, RB
1987-90	Collin Mackie, PK
1988-91	Robert Brooks, KR

DEFENSE

1970-72	John LeHeup, L
1980-81	Emmanuel Weaver, L
1980-82	Andrew Provence, L
1983-84, 1986-87	Roy Hart, L
1985-88	Kevin Hendrix, L
1979-80	Ed Baxley, LB
1981-84	James Seawright, LB
1988-90	Corey Miller, LB
1964-66	Bobby Bryant, DB
1969-71	Dick Harris, DB
1975-78	Rick Sanford, DB
1984-87	Brad Edwards, DB
1974, 1976-78	Max Runager, P

the hole. The Gamecocks recovered a fumble in the end zone to make it three touchdowns in less than two minutes and a 21-14 final.

BEST GOAL-LINE STAND

South Carolina was leading Tennessee 24-17 late in the fourth quarter in 1992 when the Vols scored a touchdown. In the days before overtime, UT went for two points and the win. The Vols' QB faked a pass and had what looked like clear sailing to the end zone—except for Hank Campbell. The walk-on linebacker made the stop, saved the game and was named SEC defensive player of the week for his effort.

South Carolina-Clemson is the fourth-oldest uninterrupted series in college football.

BEST COMEBACK The Gamecocks were struggling at Clemson in 1964. Quarterback Dan Reeves struggled on a badly injured foot, and the game turned into a long defensive battle after Clemson kicked a field goal on its first possession. Down 3-0 late in the fourth quarter, the Gamecocks replaced Reeves with backup Jim Rogers. A 45-yard completion to J.R. Wilburn put the ball on the Clemson 15. On third down, Rogers rolled out to pass but couldn't find an open receiver. So he scrambled for the crucial first down, then kept going, all the way to the end zone. South Carolina won 7-3 in Death Valley.

STADIUM Williams-Brice Stadium took life in 1934. Constructed under the New Deal's Works Progress Administration, the original structure was called Carolina Stadium and seated some 17,600 fans. There have been several improvements and additions over the years, including one in 1972 that enlarged capacity to more than 53,000. This project was financed by a bequest from the estate of Mrs. Martha Williams Brice, whose husband was a Gamecocks letterman from 1922 to 1924. The facility was dedicated as Williams-Brice Stadium at the season opener in 1972. The most recent improvements, completed prior to the 1996 season, raised capacity to its present 80,250. Those seats are routinely filled, consistently making the Gamecocks among the top 12 in the nation in home attendance.

RIVAL Clemson and South Carolina played in 96

straight seasons (and a total of 102 times) through 2004, making theirs the fourth-longest uninterrupted series in all of college football. And that's only the beginning of the story. College football fans were appalled when players from both squads fought on the field at the 2004 game—behavior that cost both schools bowl trips for which they were otherwise eligible. Unfortunate as this episode was, it was not without precedent. In 1902, when the game was still played on the fairgrounds of Columbia on what was called Big Thursday, South Carolina won 12-6. The Clemson cadets, who had bivouacked on the fairgrounds, were so unhappy with the result that they marched, with fixed bayonets, on the South Carolina campus and a riot followed. The series was suspended until 1909, when Clemson got its revenge, 6-0. Unlike many other states, in South Carolina, the "aggie school" receives favorable political treatment and, thus, has a decided advantage in football.

DISPUTE When Thomas Hill fell on Derek Watson's fumble in the end zone with less than a minute to go, the Gamecocks went ahead of Clemson, 14-13, on Nov. 18, 2000. It looked like the end of a three-game losing streak to the Tigers until, with only 10 seconds left, Woody Dantzler completed a 50-yard pass to Rod Gardner, whom Gamecocks fans swear to this day pushed a South Carolina defender out of the way. Gardner wasn't called for a penalty, and Clemson won on a 25-yard field goal.

NICKNAME The South Carolina football players were described in a 1902 newspaper story as having "fought like gamecocks." The simile stuck. But modern non-Carolinians might ask, "What does that mean?"

The gamecock is a pugnacious rooster, bred for fighting. The fights go to the death of one bird and bring in lots of passionate wagering. Though it has long been outlawed in the United States, cockfighting is still hugely popular in some parts of the world. Cockfighting was commonplace and accepted in the Colonies, however, and one able Revolutionary War figure from South Carolina, General Thomas Sumter, was nicknamed The Gamecock. Another American general—one considerably less esteemed in South

Carolina—went on to the White House and kept fighting cocks there. He was Ulysses S. Grant.

UNIFORMS Garnet and black have been South Carolina's colors for a century, and coach Joe Morrison famously dressed entirely in black during his tenure.

LORE During the early 1980s, the Gamecocks came to be known as Fire Ants and Black Magic, after defensive coordinator Tom Gadd described the defense as looking like "a bunch of fire ants getting after the football." The Black Magic nickname was the result of Morrison's trademark black coaching attire.

QUOTE "The chicken curse is on South Carolina and they'll never win big." —Doug Nye, sports editor of *The Columbia Record*, remarking in 1963 on South Carolina's football misfortunes

SOUTH CAROLINA ANNUAL STATISTICAL LEADERS

YR	RUSHING	YDS	ATT	AVG	PASSING	ATT	CMP	PCT	YDS	RECEIVING	REC	YDS	AVG
1947	Bishop Strickland	510	94	5.4		NA	NA	NA	NA		NA	NA	NA
1948	Steve Wadiak	420	51	8.2		NA	NA	NA	NA		NA	NA	NA
1949	Steve Wadiak	775	152	5.1	John Boyle	84	29	.35	383	Jim Pinkerton	18	333	18.5
1950	Steve Wadiak	998	164	6.1	Ed Pasky	52	21	.40	196	Steve Wadiak	12	83	6.9
1951	Steve Wadiak	685	176	3.9	Dick Balka	57	26	.46	401	W.A. Skelton	13	204	15.7
1952	Gene Wilson	403	130	3.1	Johnny Gramling	144	61	.42	709	Clyde Bennett	34	502	14.8
1953	Gene Wilson	502	77	6.5	Johnny Gramling	132	68	.52	1,045	Clyde Bennett	23	413	18.0
1954	Mike Caskey	556	83	6.7	Mackie Prickett	116	68	.59	682	Carl Brazell	29	241	8.3
1955	Carl Brazell	305	46	6.6	Mackie Prickett	73	35	.48	513	Carl Brazell	11	162	14.7
1956	King Dixon	655	136	4.8	Mackie Prickett	44	15	.34	193	Alex Hawkins	10	91	9.1
1957	Alex Hawkins	450	110	4.1	Alex Hawkins	12	9	.75	153	Julius Derrick	6	126	21.0
1958	John Saunders	653	128	5.1	Bobby Bunch	23	13	.57	177	King Dixon	10	189	18.9
1959	Phil Lavoie	522	121	4.3	Steve Satterfield	44	17	.39	180	Jimmy Hunter	9	60	6.7
1960	Buddy Bennett	401	79	5.1	Dave Sowell	38	17	.45	190	Billy Gambrell	12	106	8.8
1961	Dick Day	400	100	4.0	Jim Costen	146	61	.42	764	Billy Gambrell	24	243	10.1
1962	Billy Gambrell	582	106	5.5	Dan Reeves	131	66	.50	930	Billy Gambrell	21	226	10.8
1963	Marty Rosen	382	87	4.4	Dan Reeves	146	62	.42	657	Larry Gill	14	188	13.4
1964	Phil Branson	276	86	3.2	Dan Reeves	164	83	.51	974	J.R. Wilburn	21	236	11.2
1965	Ben Garnto	437	89	4.9	Mike Fair	175	89	.51	1,049	J.R. Wilburn	38	562	14.8
1966	Benny Galloway	580	129	4.5	Mike Fair	82	31	.38	467	Ben Garnto	19	243	12.8
1967	Warren Muir	805	187	4.3	Mike Fair	165	79	.48	970	Fred Zeigler	35	370	10.6
1968	Rudy Holloman	530	110	4.8	Tommy Suggs	207	110	.53	1,544	Fred Zeigler	59	848	14.4
1969	Warren Muir	969	225	4.3	Tommy Suggs	196	109	.56	1,342	Fred Zeigler	52	658	12.7
1970	Tommy Simmons	572	163	3.5	Tommy Suggs	269	136	.51	2,030	Jim Mitchell	41	842	20.5
1971	Tommy Simmons	430	126	3.4	Glenn Morris	229	104	.45	1,313	Jim Mitchell	47	618	13.1
1972	Jay Lynn Hodgin	675	188	3.6	Dobby Grossman	117	61	.52	874	Mike Haggard	46	639	13.9
1973	Jay Lynn Hodgin	862	172	5.0	Jeff Grantz	121	62	.51	864	Marty Woolbright	23	347	15.1
1974	Jay Lynn Hodgin	941	154	6.1	Jeff Grantz	95	39	.41	642	Mike Farrell	18	258	14.3
1975	Kevin Long	1,133	189	6.0	Jeff Grantz	216	120	.56	1,815	Philip Logan	39	716	18.4
1976	Clarence Williams	873	175	5.0	Ron Bass	199	110	.55	1,320	Philip Logan	41	678	16.5
1977	Spencer Clark	777	134	5.8	Ron Bass	176	82	.47	1,140	Philip Logan	21	415	19.8
1978	George Rogers	1,006	176	5.7	Garry Harper	135	62	.46	776	Zion McKinney	19	281	14.8
1979	George Rogers	1,681	311	5.4	Garry Harper	143	73	.51	929	Zion McKinney	23	387	16.8
1980	George Rogers	1,894	324	5.8	Garry Harper	177	90	.51	1,266	Willie Scott	34	469	13.8
1981	Johnnie Wright	834	214	3.9	Gordon Beckham	180	92	.51	1,221	Horace Smith	27	451	16.7
1982	Thomas Dendy	848	139	6.1	Gordon Beckham	146	63	.43	725	Chris Corley	24	163	6.8
1983	Thomas Dendy	725	132	5.5	Allen Mitchell	172	80	.47	1,142	Ira Hillary	30	422	14.1
1984	Thomas Dendy	634	102	6.2	Mike Hold	137	64	.47	1,385	Ira Hillary	27	564	20.9
1985	Thomas Dendy	560	119	4.7	Mike Hold	208	107	.51	1,596	Sterling Sharpe	32	471	14.7
1986	Anthony Smith	469	96	4.9	Todd Ellis	340	205	.60	3,020	Sterling Sharpe	74	1,106	14.9
1987	Harold Green	1,022	227	4.5	Todd Ellis	432	241	.56	3,206	Sterling Sharpe	62	915	14.8
1988	Harold Green	606	164	3.7	Todd Ellis	391	198	.51	2,353	Harold Green	36	315	8.8
1989	Harold Green	989	202	4.9	Todd Ellis	187	103	.55	1,374	Robert Brooks	34	471	13.9
1990	Mike Dingle	746	187	4.0	Bobby Fuller	294	171	.58	2,372	Robert Brooks	33	548	16.6
1991	Brandon Bennett	702	153	4.6	Bobby Fuller	340	202	.59	2,524	Robert Brooks	55	684	12.4
1992	Brandon Bennett	646	150	4.3	Steve Taneyhill	162	86	.53	1,272	Brandon Bennett	22	194	8.8
1993	Brandon Bennett	853	194	4.4	Steve Taneyhill	291	149	.51	1,930	Toby Cates	27	541	20.0
1994	Brandon Bennett	854	190	4.5	Steve Taneyhill	403	257	.64	2,486	Brandon Bennett	47	340	7.2
1995	Duce Staley	736	127	5.8	Steve Taneyhill	389	261	.67	3,094	Stanley Pritchett	62	664	10.7
1996	Duce Staley	1,116	219	5.1	Anthony Wright	244	131	.54	1,850	Corey Bridges	28	399	14.3
1997	Troy Hambrick	604	114	5.3	Anthony Wright	252	139	.55	1,685	Jermale Kelly	43	618	14.4
1998	Troy Hambrick	701	143	4.9	Anthony Wright	273	145	.53	1,899	Zola Davis	48	733	15.3
1999	Derek Watson	394	113	3.5	Phil Petty	146	65	.45	803	Jermale Kelly	24	366	15.3
2000	Derek Watson	1,066	187	5.7	Phil Petty	315	170	.54	2,285	Jermale Kelly	42	640	15.2
2001	Andrew Pinnock	622	115	5.4	Phil Petty	288	164	.57	1,926	Brian Scott	47	730	15.5
2002	Corey Jenkins	655	160	4.1	Corey Jenkins	180	100	.56	1,334	Ryan Brewer	28	299	10.7
2003	Daccus Turman	646	132	4.9	Dondrial Pinkins	322	162	.50	2,127	Troy Williamson	31	428	13.8
2004	Demetris Summers	487	88	5.5	Syvelle Newton	131	70	.53	1,093	Troy Williamson	43	835	19.4

Receiving leaders by receptions
All statistics include postseason

SOUTH CAROLINA ALL-TIME SCORES

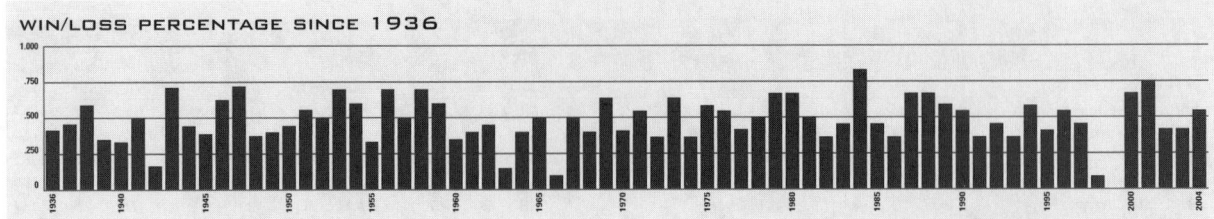

WIN/LOSS PERCENTAGE SINCE 1936

NO HEAD COACH

1892 0-1-0
D24	Furman ChSC	0	44

1893
NO TEAM

1894 0-2-0
N3	Georgia	0	40
N11	Augusta YMCA	4	16

1895 2-1-0
N2 ●	Columbia AA	20	0
N8 ●	Furman	14	10
N14	Wofford	0	10

W.H. WHALEY
1896 (.250) 1-3

1896 1-3-0
O31	at Charleston Y	4	6
N12 ●	Clemson	12	6
N19	Wofford	4	6
N26	at Furman	0	12

W.P. MURPHY
1897 (.000) 0-3

1897 0-3-0
O23	at Charleston YMCA	0	4
N10 ●	Clemson	6	18 *
N26	Charleston YMCA	0	6

W. WERTENBAKER
1898 (.333) 1-2

1898 1-2-0
O18 ●	Bingham	16	5
N17	Clemson	0	24
N24	at Davidson	0	6

I.O. HUNT
1899-1900 (.500) 6-6

1899 2-3-0
O15 ●	Columbia YMCA	5	0
N9	Clemson	0	34
N15 ●	Bingham	11	5
N22	at Bingham	6	18
N30	at Davidson	0	5

1900 4-3-0
O20	at Georgia	0	5
O25 ●	Guilford	10	0
N1	Clemson	0	51
N10 ●	North Carolina St.	12	0
N17 ●	at Furman	27	0
N22	at Davidson	0	5
N29 ●	at North Carolina St.	17	5

B.W. DICKSON
1901 (.429) 3-4

1901 3-4-0
O12	Georgia Aug	5	10
O22 ●	Furman	12	0
O24 ●	at Bingham	11	6
O30 ●	Davidson	5	12
N9	at Georgia Tech	0	13
N12 ●	N.C. MA.	47	0
N18	at Wofford	5	11

C.R. WILLIAMS
1902-03 (.824) 14-3

1902 6-1-0
O15 ●	Guilford	10	0
O21 ●	N.C. M.A.	60	0
O25 ●	Bingham	28	0
O30 ●	Clemson	12	6
N6 ●	St. Albans	5	0
N14	at Furman	0	10
N28 ●	Charleston M.C.	80	0

1903 8-2-0
O2 ●	Columbia YMCA	24	0
O6 ●	Welsh Neck	89	0
O10	North Carolina	0	17
O17 ●	at Georgia	17	0
O23 ●	Guilford	29	0
O29 ●	Tennessee	24	0
N8 ●	at Davidson	29	12
N14	at North Carolina St.	5	6
N21	at Charleston	6	0
N26	at Georgia Tech	16	0

CHRISTIE BENET
1904-05, '08-09 (.453) 13-16-3

1904 4-3-1
O7 ●	Welsh Neck	14	0
O15	at North Carolina	0	27
O20 ●	Guilford	21	4
O26 ●	Georgia	2	0
N5 =	at North Carolina St.	0	0
N12	Davidson	0	6
N19	at Charleston AC	0	6
N24 ●	at Wash. & Lee	25	0

1905 4-2-1
O13 ●	Welsh Neck	14	0
O20 ●	Bingham	19	6
O26	North Carolina St.	0	29
N4 ●	at Davidson	6	4
N11 =	at Bingham	5	5
N18 ●	Virginia Tech Roa	0	34
N30 ●	at Citadel	47	0

1906
NO TEAM

DOUGLAS McKAY
1907 (1.000) 3-0

1907 3-0-0
N16 ●	Charleston	14	4
N21 ●	Georgia Coll.	4	0
N28	at Citadel	12	0

CHRISTIE BENET

1908 3-5-1
O3 =	Ridgewood	0	0
O10 ●	Charleston	17	0
O17	at Georgia	6	29
O22 ●	Charleston AA	4	15
O29	Davidson	0	22
N4 ●	at Georgia MS	19	5
N7 ●	Bingham	6	10
N14	at North Carolina	0	22
N26 ●	at Citadel	12	0

1909 2-6-0
O9	N.C. Medical Coll.	0	5
O16 ●	at Georgia Tech	0	59
O23 ●	Wake Forest	0	8
O28 ●	Charleston	17	11
N4 ●	Clemson	0	6
N13	Davidson Char	5	29
N20 ●	at Mercer	3	5
N25 ●	at Citadel	11	5

JOHN H. NEFF
1910-11 (.400) 5-8-2

1910 4-4-0
O8 ●	Charleston	8	0
O15 ●	Georgia MS Aug	14	0
O22 ●	Lenoir	33	0
O27 ●	Wake Forest	6	0
N3	Clemson	0	24
N12	at Davidson	0	53
N19	North Carolina Dur	6	23 *
N24	at Citadel	0	5

1911 1-4-2
O7	at Georgia	0	38
O14 ●	at Charleston	16	0
O21 =	Florida	6	6
N2	Clemson	0	27
N11	at North Carolina	0	21
N18	Davidson	0	10
N30 =	at Citadel	0	0

N.B. EDGERTON
1912-15 (.586) 19-13-3

1912 5-2-1
O5 ●	Wake Forest	10	3
O14	at Virginia	0	19
O19	at Florida	6	10
O26 ●	at Charleston	68	0
O31 ●	Clemson	22	7
N9 =	at North Carolina	6	6
N16 ●	Porter	66	0
N28 ●	Citadel	26	2

1913 4-3-0
O4	at Virginia	0	54
O11 ●	Wake Forest	27	10
O18	North Carolina	3	13
O30	Clemson	0	32
N8 ●	Florida	13	0
N15	at Davidson	10	0
N26 ●	Citadel	42	13

1914 5-5-1
S30 ●	Mach. Mates	30	7
O3	at Georgia Tech	0	20
O12	at North Carolina	0	48
O17	at Virginia	7	49
O24 =	Newberry	13	13
O29 ●	Clemson	6	29
N4 ●	at Wofford	25	0
N7 ●	Wake Forest	26	0
N14	Davidson	7	13
N19 ●	at Newberry	47	6
N26 ●	Citadel	7	6

1915 5-3-1
O2 ●	Newberry	29	0
O9 ●	Presbyterian	41	0
O21 ●	at North Carolina St.	19	10
O28 =	Clemson	0	0
N4 ●	at Wofford	33	6
N6 ●	Cumberland	68	0
N13	Virginia	0	13
N20	at Georgetown	0	61
N25	Citadel	0	3

RICE WARREN
1916 (.222) 2-7

1916 2-7-0
O7	Newberry	0	10
O14 ●	Wofford	23	3
O21	at Tennessee	0	26
O26	Clemson	0	27
N4 ●	Wake Forest	7	33
N11	at Virginia	6	35
N18 ●	Mercer	47	0
N23	at Furman	0	14
N30	Citadel	2	20

DIXON FOSTER
1917, '19 (.265) 4-12-1

1917 3-5-0
O6 ●	Newberry	38	0
O13	at Florida	13	21
O25	Clemson	13	21
N3	Erskine	13	14
N8 ●	Furman Flo	26	0
N17	at Wofford	0	20
N24	Presbyterian	14	20
N29 ●	Citadel	20	0

FRANK DOBSON
1918 (.625) 2-1-1

1918 2-1-1
N2	Clemson	0	39
N16 ●	at Furman	20	12
N23	Wofford	13	0
N28 ●	Citadel Ora	0	0

DIXON FOSTER

1919 1-7-1
S27	Presbyterian	0	6
O4 ●	Erskine	6	0
O11	at Georgia	0	14
O18	Davidson	0	7
O30	Clemson	6	19
N8 =	Tennessee	6	6
N15	at Wash. & Lee	0	26
N22	Florida	0	13
N27	Citadel	7	14

SOL METZGER
1920-24 (.587) 26-18-2

1920 5-4-0
O2 ●	Wofford	10	0
O9	Georgia	0	37
O16	at North Carolina	0	7
O21 ●	Presbyterian Aug	14	0
O28 ●	Clemson	3	0
N6	at Davidson	0	27
N13	at Navy	0	63
N20 ●	Newberry	48	0
N25 ●	at Citadel	7	6

1921 5-1-2
O1 ●	Erskine	13	7
O8 ●	Newberry	7	0
O15 =	North Carolina	7	7
O22 ●	Presbyterian	48	0
O27 ●	Clemson	21	0
N5 =	Florida Tam	7	7
N12	at Furman	0	7
N19 ●	Citadel	13	0

1922-1952
SOUTHERN

1922 5-4-0 (0-3-0)
S29 ●	Erskine	13	0
O7 ●	Presbyterian	7	0
O14	at North Carolina	7	10
O20 ●	Wofford	20	0
O26	Clemson	0	3
N4	Sewanee	6	7
N11 ●	Furman	27	7
N16 ●	Citadel Ora	13	0
N30	at Centre	0	42

1923 4-6-0 (0-4-0)
S29 ●	Erskine	35	0
O6	Presbyterian	3	7
O13	at North Carolina St.	0	7
O19 ●	Newberry	24	0
O25	Clemson	6	7
N3	North Carolina	0	13
N10	at Furman	3	23
N15 ●	Citadel Ora	12	0
N17	Wash. & Lee	7	13
N29 ●	Wake Forest	14	7

1924 7-3-0 (3-2-0)
S27 ●	Erskine	47	0
O4	at Georgia	0	18
O11 ●	North Carolina St.	10	0
O17 ●	Presbyterian	29	0
O23	Clemson	3	0
O29 ●	Citadel Ora	14	3
N1	at North Carolina	10	7
N8	Furman	0	10
N15	Sewanee	0	10
N27	Wake Forest	7	0

BRANCH BOCOCK
1925-26 (.650) 13-7

1925 7-3-0 (2-2-0)

S26	●		Erskine	33	0
O3		|	North Carolina	0	7
O11	●	|	at North Carolina St.	7	6
O16	●		Wofford	6	0
O22	●	|	Clemson	33	0
O28	●		Citadel ORA	30	6
O31		|	Virginia Tech RICH	0	6
N14			at Furman	0	2
N20	●		Presbyterian	21	0
N28	●		Centre	20	0

1926 6-4-0 (4-2-0)

S25	●		Erskine	41	0
O2	●	|	Maryland	12	0
O9		|	at North Carolina	0	7
O15	●		Wofford	27	13
O21	●	|	Clemson	24	0
O28			Citadel ORA	9	12
O30		|	Virginia	0	6
N6	●	|	Virginia Tech RICH	19	0
N13			Furman	7	10
N20	●	|	North Carolina St.	20	14

HARRY LIGHTSEY
1927 (.444) 4-5

1927 4-5-0 (2-4-0)

S24	●		Erskine	13	6
O1		|	at Maryland	0	26
O8	●	|	at Virginia	13	12
O15	●	|	North Carolina	14	6
O20		|	Clemson	0	20
O27	●		Citadel ORA	6	0
N5		|	Virginia Tech RICH	0	35
N12			at Furman	0	33
N24		|	North Carolina St.	0	34

BILLY LAVAL
1928-34 (.592) 39-26-6

1928 6-2-2 (2-2-1)

S22	●		Erskine	19	0
S29	●		at Chicago	6	0
O6	●	|	at Virginia	24	13
O13	●	|	Maryland	21	7
O19	●		Presbyterian	13	0
O25		|	Clemson	0	32
N1	=		Citadel ORA	0	0
N10	=	|	at North Carolina	0	0
N17	●		Furman	6	0
N29		|	at North Carolina St.	7	18

1929 6-5-0 (2-5-0)

S28	●		Erskine	26	7
O5		|	Virginia	0	6
O12	●	|	at Maryland	26	6
O18	●		Presbyterian	41	0
O24		|	Clemson	14	21
O31	●		Citadel ORA	27	14
N9		|	North Carolina	0	40
N16	●		at Furman	2	0
N23		|	Florida	7	20
N30	●	|	at North Carolina St.	20	6
D7		|	at Tennessee	0	54

1930 6-4-0 (4-3-0)

S20	●		Erskine	19	0
S27	●	|	at Duke	22	0
O4		|	at Georgia Tech	0	45
O11	●	|	LSU	7	6
O23		|	Clemson	7	20
O30	●		Citadel ORA	13	0
N8			at Furman	0	14
N15	●	|	Sewanee	14	13
N22	●	|	North Carolina St.	19	0
N27		|	Auburn COLGA	7	25

1931 5-4-1 (3-3-1)

S26	●	|	Duke	7	0
O3		|	at Georgia Tech	13	25
O10		|	at LSU	12	19
O22	●	|	Clemson	21	0
O29	●		Citadel ORA	26	7
N7	●		Furman	27	0
N14	=	|	Florida JACF	6	6
N21	●	|	North Carolina St.	21	0
N26		|	Auburn MONT	6	13
D5			Centre	7	9

1932 5-4-2 (2-2-2)

S24	●	|	Sewanee	7	3
O1	●		at Villanova	7	6
O8			Wake Forest CHAR	0	6
O14	●		Wofford	19	0
O20	●	|	Clemson	14	0
O29		|	at Tulane	0	6
N5		|	LSU	0	6
N12			at Furman	0	14
N19	●		Citadel	19	0
N24	=	|	at North Carolina St.	7	7
D3	=	|	Auburn BIRM	20	20

1933 6-3-1 (3-0-0)

S23	●		Wofford	31	0
S29			at Temple	6	26
O7			Villanova	6	15
O19	●	|	Clemson	7	0
O26	●		Citadel ORA	12	6
O28	●	|	at Virginia Tech	12	0
N4			at LSU	7	30
N11	●	|	North Carolina St.	14	0
N19	=		Furman	0	0
D2	●		Auburn BIRM	16	14

1934 5-4-0 (2-3-0)

S29	●		Erskine	25	0
O6	●	|	VMI	22	6
O13		|	at North Carolina St.	0	6
O18	●		Citadel ORA	20	6
O25		|	Clemson	0	19
N3	●	|	Virginia Tech	20	0
N10			at Villanova	0	20
N17	●		at Furman	2	0
N29		|	Wash. & Lee	7	14

DON McCALLISTER
1935-37 (.397) 13-20-1

1935 3-7-0 (1-4-0)

S21	●		Erskine	33	0
S28		|	at Duke	0	47
O5		|	North Carolina St.	0	14
O12			at Davidson	6	13
O17	●		Citadel ORA	25	0
O24		|	Clemson	0	44
N2		|	at Virginia Tech	0	27
N16			Furman	7	20
N23	●	|	Wash. & Lee	2	0
D7			Florida TAM	0	22

1936 5-7-0 (2-5-0)

S19	●		Erskine	38	0
S26		|	at VMI	7	24
O3		|	Duke	0	21
O10	●		Florida	7	0
O17	●	|	Virginia Tech	14	0
O22		|	Clemson	0	19
O30	●	|	Citadel ORA	9	0
N7			Villanova	0	14
N14		|	at Furman	6	23
N21		|	North Carolina	0	14
N26			at Xavier	13	21
D11	●		at Miami, Fla.	6	3

1937 5-6-1 (2-2-1)

S18	●		Emory & Henry	45	7
S25	=	|	at North Carolina	13	13
O2			Georgia	7	13
O9			at Alabama	0	20
O16	●	|	Davidson	12	7
O21		|	Clemson	6	34
O29	●	|	Citadel ORA	21	6
N6			at Kentucky	7	27
N13		|	Furman	0	12
N20	●		Presbyterian	64	0
D3	●		at Miami, Fla.	3	0
D25			at Catholic U.	14	27

REX ENRIGHT
1938-42, '46-55 (.482) 64-69-7

1938 6-4-1 (2-2-0)

S19	●		Erskine	53	0
S24	●		at Xavier	6	0
O1			Georgia	6	7
O8		|	Wake Forest	19	20
O14	●	|	Davidson SUM	25	0
O20		|	Clemson	12	34
O28	=		Villanova ORA	6	6
N5	●		Duquesne	7	0
N12	●	|	at Furman	27	6
N19			Fordham NYC	0	13
N28	●		at Catholic U.	7	0

1939 3-6-1 (1-3-0)

S23		|	at Wake Forest	7	19
S29			Catholic U.	0	12
O6			Villanova PHIL	0	40
O13	●	|	Davidson SUM	7	0
O19		|	Clemson	0	27
O27	=		West Virginia ORA	6	6
N4	●		Florida	6	0 *
N11		|	Furman	0	20
N18			at Georgia	7	33
N25	●		Miami, Fla.	7	6

1940 3-6-0 (1-3-0)

O5			Georgia	2	33
O11			at Duquesne	21	27
O24		|	Clemson	13	21
N2			at Penn State	0	12
N9	●		Kansas State	20	13
N16		|	at Furman	7	25
N22	●		Miami, Fla.	7	2
N28		|	Wake Forest CHAR	6	7
D7	●	|	at Citadel	31	6

1941 4-4-1 (4-0-1)

S27	●	|	at North Carolina	13	7
O4			at Georgia	6	34
O11	=	|	Wake Forest	6	6
O23	●	|	Clemson	18	14
O31	●	|	Citadel ORA	13	6
N8			at Kansas State	0	3
N15	●	|	Furman	26	7
N21			at Miami, Fla.	6	7
N29			Penn State	12	19

1942 1-7-1 (1-4-0)

S26	=		Tennessee	0	0
O3		|	at North Carolina	6	18
O10			at West Virginia	0	13
O22		|	Clemson	6	18
O30	●	|	Citadel ORA	14	0
N7			at Alabama	0	29
N14		|	Furman	0	6
N21			at Miami, Fla.	6	13
D5		|	Wake Forest CHAR	14	33

J.P. MORAN
1943 (.714) 5-2

1943 5-2-0 (2-1-0)

S25	●		Newberry	19	7
O2			176th Infantry	7	13
O9	●		Presbyterian	20	7
O21	●	|	Clemson	33	6
O30	●		Charleston CG ORA	20	0
N6		|	North Carolina	6	21
N25	●	|	Wake Forest CHAR	13	2

WILLIAM NEWTON
1944 (.444) 3-4-2

1944 3-4-2 (1-3-0)

S23	●		Newberry	48	0
S30			Georgia Pre-Flight	14	20
O7	=		at Miami, Fla.	0	0
O19		|	Clemson	13	20
O27	=		Charleston CG ORA	6	6
N4	●	|	at North Carolina	6	0
N11	●		Presbyterian	28	7
N18		|	Duke	7	34
N23		|	Wake Forest CHAR	13	19

JOHNNIE McMILLAN
1945 (.389) 2-4-3

1945 2-4-3 (0-2-2)

S22		|	at Duke	0	60
S29	●		Presbyterian	40	0
O6	●		Camp Blandind	20	6
O13			Alabama MONT	0	55
O25	=	|	Clemson	0	0
N9	=		at Miami, Fla.	13	13
N22	=	|	Wake Forest CHAR	13	13
D1		|	Maryland	13	19
			GATOR BOWL		
J1			Wake Forest	14	26

REX ENRIGHT

1946 5-3-0 (4-2-0)

S29	●		Newberry	21	0
O5			Alabama	6	14
O11	●	|	at Furman	14	7
O24	●	|	Clemson	26	14
N1	●	|	Citadel ORA	19	7
N9	●	|	at Maryland	21	17
N16		|	Duke	0	39
N28		|	Wake Forest CHAR	0	35

1947 6-2-1 (4-1-1)

S20	●		Newberry	27	6
S27		|	Maryland	13	19
O4			Mississippi MEM	0	33
O11	●	|	Furman	26	8
O23	●	|	Clemson	21	19
O31	●		at Miami, Fla.	8	0
N7	●	|	Citadel ORA	12	0
N15	=	|	at Duke	0	0
N27	●	|	Wake Forest CHAR	6	0

1948 3-5-0 (1-3-0)

S24	●		Newberry	46	0
O1	●	|	at Furman	7	0
O9			at Tulane	0	14
O21		|	Clemson	7	13
O30			at West Virginia	12	35
N6		|	Maryland	7	19
N13	●		at Tulsa	27	7
N25		|	Wake Forest	0	38

1949 4-6-0 (3-3-0)

S24			at Baylor	6	20
S30		|	Furman	7	14
O8		|	North Carolina	13	28
O20	●	|	Clemson	27	13
O29		|	at Maryland	7	44
N5	●		at Marquette	6	3
N11			at Miami, Fla.	7	13
N19			at Georgia Tech	3	13
N26	●	|	Wake Forest	27	20
D3	●	|	Citadel	42	0

1950 3-4-2 (2-4-1)

S23		|	Duke	0	14
S30	●		at Georgia Tech	7	0
O6	●	|	at Furman	21	6
O19	=	|	Clemson	14	14
O27	●	|	at George Washington	34	20
N3	=		Marquette	13	13
N11		|	at Citadel	7	19
N18		|	North Carolina	7	14
N25		|	Wake Forest	7	14

1951 5-4-0 (5-3-0)

S22		|	Duke	6	34
S29	●	|	Citadel	26	7
O6	●	|	Furman	21	6
O13		|	at North Carolina	6	21
O25	●	|	Clemson	20	0
N3		|	George Washington	14	20
N10	●	|	at West Virginia	34	13
N17		|	at Virginia	27	28
N24	●	|	Wake Forest	21	6 *

1952 5-5-0 (3-4-0)

S20	●		Wofford	33	0
S27			at Army	7	28
O4	●	|	at Furman	27	7
O11		|	Duke	7	33
O23	●	|	Clemson	6	0
N1	●		Virginia NOR	21	14
N8	●	|	at Citadel	35	0
N15			North Carolina	19	27
N22		|	West Virginia	6	13
N29		|	Wake Forest W-S	14	39

1953-1971
ACC

1953 7-3-0 (2-3-0)

S19		|	Duke	7	20
S26	●		Citadel	25	0
O3	●		at Virginia	19	0
O10	●		Furman	27	13
O22	●	|	Clemson	14	7
O31		|	at Maryland	6	24
N7	●	|	North Carolina	18	0
N14	●		at West Virginia	20	14
N21	●		Wofford	49	0
N26		|	Wake Forest CHAR	13	19

1954 6-4-0 (3-3-0)

S25	●		at Army	34	20
O2			West Virginia	6	26
O9	●		at Furman	27	7
O21	●	|	Clemson	13	8
O30		|	Maryland	0	20
N6		|	at North Carolina	19	21
N13	●	|	Virginia	27	0
N20		|	at Duke	7	26
N27	●	|	Wake Forest	20	19
D4	●		at Citadel	19	6

1955 — 3-6-0 (1-5-0)

S17	●	Wofford	26	7
S24	|	Wake Forest W-S	19	34
O1		Navy	0	26
O8	●	Furman	19	0
O20	|	Clemson	14	28
O29	|	at Maryland	0	27
N5	|	North Carolina Nor	14	32
N12	|	Duke	7	41
N26	● |	at Virginia	21	14

WARREN GIESE
1956-60 (.570) 28-21-1

1956 — 7-3-0 (5-2-0)

S15	●	Wofford	26	13
S22	● |	Duke	7	0
S28		at Miami, Fla.	6	14
O6	● |	North Carolina	14	0
O13	● |	Virginia Rich	27	13
O25	|	Clemson	0	7
N3	●	at Furman	13	6
N10	|	at North Carolina St.	7	14
N17	● |	Maryland	13	0
N22	● |	Wake Forest Char	13	0

1957 — 5-5-0 (2-5-0)

S21	|	Duke	14	26
S28	●	Wofford	26	0
O5	●	at Texas	27	21
O12	●	Furman	58	13
O24	|	Clemson	0	13
N2	|	Maryland	6	10
N9	|	at North Carolina	6	28
N16	● |	at Virginia	13	0
N23	|	North Carolina	26	29
N30	● |	at Wake Forest	26	7

1958 — 7-3-0 (5-2-0)

S20	● |	Duke	8	0
S27		at Army	8	45
O4	●	at Georgia	24	14
O11	|	at North Carolina	0	6
O23	● |	Clemson	26	6
N1	|	at Maryland	6	10
N8	●	at Furman	32	7
N15	● |	Virginia	28	14
N22	● |	North Carolina St.	12	7
N27	● |	Wake Forest	24	7

1959 — 6-4-0 (4-3-0)

S19	● |	Duke	12	7
S26	●	Furman	30	0
O3	●	Georgia	30	14
O10	|	at North Carolina	6	19
O22	|	Clemson	0	27
O31	● |	Maryland	22	6
N7	● |	at Virginia	32	20
N13		at Miami, Fla.	6	26
N21	● |	North Carolina St.	12	7
N28	|	Wake Forest Char	20	43

1960 — 3-6-1 (3-3-1)

S24	|	Duke	0	31
O1		at Georgia	6	38
O14		at Miami, Fla.	6	21
O22	● |	North Carolina	22	6
O29	|	at Maryland	0	15
N5		at LSU	6	35
N12	|	at Clemson	2	12
N19	= |	North Carolina St.	8	8
N26	● |	Wake Forest	41	20
D3	● |	Virginia	26	0

MARVIN BASS
1961-65 (.380) 17-29-4

1961 — 4-6-0 (3-4-0)

S23	|	Duke	6	7
S30	● |	at Wake Forest	10	7
O7		at Georgia	14	17
O14		LSU	0	42
O21	|	North Carolina	0	17
O28	● |	Maryland	20	10
N4	|	at Virginia	20	28
N11	● |	Clemson	21	14
N18	|	at North Carolina St.	14	38
N25	●	at Vanderbilt	23	7

1962 — 4-5-1 (3-4-0)

S22		at Northwestern	20	37
S29	|	at Duke	8	21
O6	=	Georgia	7	7
O13	● |	Wake Forest	27	6
O20	|	at North Carolina	14	19
O27	|	at Maryland	11	13
N3	● |	Virginia	40	6
N10	● |	North Carolina St.	17	6
N17	●	at Detroit	26	13
N24	|	at Clemson	17	20

1963 — 1-8-1 (1-5-1)

S21	|	at Duke	14	22
S28	● |	Maryland	21	13
O5		at Georgia	7	27
O12	|	North Carolina St.	6	18
O19	= |	at Virginia	10	10
O26	|	North Carolina	0	7
N2		Tulane	7	20
N9		at Memphis	0	9
N16	|	at Wake Forest	19	20
N28	|	Clemson	20	24

1964 — 3-5-2 (2-3-1)

S19	= |	Duke	9	9
S26	|	at Maryland	6	24
O3	=	Georgia	7	7
O10		at Nebraska	6	28
O17		at Florida	0	37
O24	|	at North Carolina	6	24
O31	|	at North Carolina St.	14	17
N7	●	Citadel	17	14
N14	● |	Wake Forest	23	13
N28	● |	at Clemson	7	3

1965 — 5-5-0 (4-2-0)

S18	●	at Citadel	13	3
S25	|	Duke	15	20
O2	● |	North Carolina St.	13	7
O9		at Tennessee	3	24
O16	● |	Wake Forest	38	7
O23		at LSU	7	21
O30	|	Maryland	14	27
N6	● |	at Virginia	17	7 †
N13		at Alabama	14	35
N20	● |	Clemson	17	16

PAUL DIETZEL
1966-74 (.443) 42-53-1

1966 — 1-9-0 (1-3-0)

S17		at LSU	12	28
S24		Memphis	7	16
O1		Georgia	0	7
O8	● |	at North Carolina St.	31	21
O15	|	Wake Forest	6	10
O22		at Tennessee	17	29
O29	|	at Maryland	2	14
N5		Florida State	10	32
N12		at Alabama	0	24
N26	|	at Clemson	10	35

1967 — 5-5-0 (4-2-0)

S16	●	Iowa State	34	3
S23	● |	North Carolina	16	10
S30	● |	at Duke	21	17
O7		at Georgia	0	21
O14		at Florida State	0	17
O21	● |	Virginia	24	23
O28	● |	Maryland	31	0
N4	|	at Wake Forest	21	35
N18		at Alabama	0	17
N25	|	Clemson	12	23

1968 — 4-6-0 (4-3-0)

S21	|	Duke	7	14
S28	● |	at North Carolina	32	27
O5		Georgia	20	21
O12	|	at North Carolina St.	12	36
O19	|	at Maryland	19	21
O26		Florida State	28	35
N2	● |	at Virginia	49	28
N9	● |	at Wake Forest	34	21
N16		Virginia Tech	6	17
N23	● |	at Clemson	7	3

1969 — 7-4-0 (6-0-0)

S20	● |	Duke	27	20
S27	● |	North Carolina	14	6
O4		at Georgia	16	41
O11	● |	North Carolina St.	21	16
O18	●	at Virginia Tech	17	16
O25	● |	Maryland	17	0
N1		at Florida State	9	34
N8		at Tennessee	14	29
N15	● |	at Wake Forest	24	6
N22	● |	Clemson	27	13
		PEACH BOWL		
D30		West Virginia	3	14

1970 — 4-6-1 (3-2-1)

S12		at Georgia Tech	20	23
S19	● |	Wake Forest	43	7
S26	= |	at North Carolina St.	7	7
O3	●	Virginia Tech	24	7
O10	● |	at North Carolina	35	21
O17	|	at Maryland	15	21
O24		Florida State	13	21
O31		at Georgia	34	52
N7		Tennessee	18	20
N14	|	Duke	38	42
N21	● |	at Clemson	38	32

1971 — 6-5-0 (4-2-0)

S11	●	Georgia Tech	24	7
S18	|	at Duke	12	28
S25	● |	North Carolina St.	24	6
O2	●	at Memphis	7	3
O9	● |	Virginia	34	14
O16	● |	Maryland	35	6
O23		at Florida State	18	49
O30		Georgia	0	24
N6		at Tennessee	6	35
N20	● |	Wake Forest	24	7
N27	|	Clemson	7	17

1972-1991
INDEPENDENT

1972 — 4-7-0

S9		Virginia	16	24
S16		at Georgia Tech	6	34
S23		Mississippi	0	21
S30	●	Memphis	34	7
O14	●	Appalachian St.	41	7
O21		Miami, Ohio	8	21
O28		at North Carolina St.	24	42
N4	●	Wake Forest	35	3
N11		at Virginia Tech	20	45
N18	●	Florida State	24	21
N25		at Clemson	6	7

1973 — 7-4-0

S15	●	Georgia Tech	41	28
S21		at Houston	19	27
S29		Miami, Ohio	11	13
O6	●	at Virginia Tech	27	24
O13	●	at Wake Forest	28	12
O20	●	Ohio U.	38	22
O27		LSU	29	33
N3		North Carolina St.	35	56
N10	●	Appalachian St.	35	14
N17	●	at Florida State	52	12
N24	●	Clemson	32	20

1974 — 4-7-0

S14		at Georgia Tech	20	35
S21		Duke	14	20
S28		at Georgia	14	52
O5		Houston	14	24
O12		Virginia Tech	17	31
O19	●	at Mississippi	10	7
O26	●	North Carolina	31	23
N2		at North Carolina St.	27	42
N9	●	Appalachian St.	21	18
N16	●	Wake Forest	34	21
N23		at Clemson	21	39

JIM CARLEN
1975-81 (.555) 45-36-1

1975 — 7-5-0

S13	●	Georgia Tech	23	17
S20	●	at Duke	24	16
S27		Georgia	20	28
O4	●	Baylor	24	13
O11	●	Virginia	41	14
O18	●	Mississippi JaM	35	29
O25		at LSU	6	24
N1		at North Carolina St.	21	28
N8		Appalachian St.	34	39
N15	●	Wake Forest	37	26
N22	●	Clemson	56	20
		TANGERINE BOWL		
D20		Miami, Ohio	7	20

1976 — 6-5-0

S4	●	Appalachian St.	21	10
S11	●	at Georgia Tech	27	17
S18	●	Duke	24	6
S25		at Georgia	12	20
O2		at Baylor	17	18
O9	●	Virginia	35	7
O16	●	Mississippi	10	7
O23		Notre Dame	6	13
O30	●	North Carolina St.	27	7
N13		Wake Forest	7	10
N20		at Clemson	9	28

1977 — 5-7-0

S3	●	Appalachian St.	32	17
S10	●	Georgia Tech	17	0
S17	●	Miami, Ohio	42	19
S24		Georgia	13	15
O1	●	East Carolina	19	16
O8		Duke	21	25
O15		at Mississippi	10	17
O22		at North Carolina	0	17
O29		at North Carolina St.	3	7
N12	●	at Wake Forest	24	14
N19		Clemson	27	31
N26		at Hawaii	7	24

1978 — 5-5-1

S9	●	Furman	45	10
S16	=	Kentucky	14	14
S23		at Duke	12	16
S30	●	Georgia	27	10
O7		at Georgia Tech	3	6
O14	●	Ohio U.	24	7
O21	●	Mississippi	18	17
O28		North Carolina	22	24
N4		at North Carolina St.	13	22
N18	●	Wake Forest	37	14
N25		at Clemson	23	41

1979 — 8-4-0

S8		at North Carolina	0	28
S15	●	Western Michigan	24	7
S22	●	Duke	35	0
S29	●	at Georgia	27	20
O6	●	Oklahoma State	23	16
O20	●	Mississippi	21	14
O27		at Notre Dame	17	18
N3	●	North Carolina St.	30	28
N10		at Florida State	7	27
N17	●	Wake Forest	35	14
N24	●	Clemson	13	9
		HALL OF FAME CLASSIC		
D29		Missouri	14	24

1980 — 8-4-0

S6	●	Pacific	37	0
S13	●	Wichita St.	73	0
S20		at Southern Cal	13	23
S27	●	at Michigan	17	14
O4	●	North Carolina St.	30	10
O11	●	Duke	20	7
O18	●	Cincinnati	49	7
N1		at Georgia	10	13
N8	●	Citadel	45	24
N15	●	Wake Forest	39	38
N22		at Clemson	6	27
		GATOR BOWL		
D29		Pittsburgh	9	37

1981 — 6-6-0

S5	●	at Wake Forest	23	6
S12		Mississippi	13	20
S19	●	Duke	17	3
S26		at Georgia	0	24
O3		Pittsburgh	28	42
O10	●	at Kentucky	28	14
O17	●	Virginia	21	3
O24	●	at North Carolina	31	13
O31	●	North Carolina St.	20	12
N7		Pacific	21	23
N21		Clemson	13	29
D5		at Hawaii	10	33

RICHARD BELL
1982 (.364) 4-7

1982 — 4-7-0

S4	●	Pacific	41	6
S11	●	Richmond	30	10
S18		Duke	17	30
S25		Georgia	18	34
O2	●	Cincinnati	37	10
O16		Furman	23	28
O23		at LSU	6	14
O30		at North Carolina St.	3	33
N6		Florida State	26	56
N13	●	Navy	17	14
N20		at Clemson	6	24

JOE MORRISON
1983-88 (.580)   39-28-2

1983   5-6-0
S3		North Carolina	8 24
S10	•	Miami, Ohio	24 3
S17	•	at Duke	31 24
S24	•	at Georgia	13 31
O1	•	Southern Cal	38 14
O8	•	Notre Dame	6 30
O22	•	at LSU	6 20
O29	•	North Carolina St.	31 17
N5	•	at Florida State	30 45
N12	•	Navy	31 7
N19	•	Clemson	13 22

1984   10-2-0
S8	•	Citadel	31 24
S22	•	Duke	21 0
S29	•	Georgia	17 10
O6	•	Kansas State	49 17
O13	•	Pittsburgh	45 21
O20	•	at Notre Dame	36 32
O27	•	East Carolina	42 20
N3	•	at North Carolina St.	35 28
N10	•	Florida State	38 26
N17	•	at Navy	21 38
N24	•	at Clemson	22 21
GATOR BOWL			
D28		Oklahoma State	14 21

1985   5-6-0
A31	•	Citadel	56 17
S7	•	Appalachian St.	20 13
S21	•	Michigan	3 34
S28	•	at Georgia	21 35
O5	•	at Pittsburgh	7 42
O12	•	Duke	28 7
O26	•	at East Carolina	52 10
N2	•	North Carolina St.	17 21
N9	•	at Florida State	14 56
N16	•	Navy	34 31
N23	•	Clemson	17 24

1986   3-6-2
A30	•	Miami, Fla.	14 34
S6	•	at Virginia	20 30
S13	•	Western Carolina	45 24
S27	•	Georgia	26 31
O4	•	Nebraska	24 27
O11	=	at Virginia Tech	27 27
O25	•	East Carolina	38 3
N1	•	at North Carolina St.	22 23
N8	•	Florida State	28 45
N15	•	Wake Forest	48 21
N22	=	at Clemson	21 21

1987   8-4-0
S5	•	Appalachian St.	24 3
S12	•	Western Carolina	31 6
S26	•	at Georgia	6 13
O3	•	at Nebraska	21 30
O10	•	Virginia Tech	40 10
O17	•	Virginia	58 10
O24	•	East Carolina	34 12
O31	•	North Carolina St.	48 0
N14	•	at Wake Forest	30 0
N21	•	Clemson	20 7
D5	•	at Miami, Fla.	16 20
GATOR BOWL			
D31		LSU	13 30

1988   8-4-0
S3	•	North Carolina	31 10
S10	•	Western Carolina	38 0
S17	•	East Carolina	17 0
S24	•	Georgia	23 10
O1	•	Appalachian St.	35 9
O8	•	at Virginia Tech	26 24
O15	•	at Georgia Tech	0 34
O29	•	at North Carolina St.	23 7
N5	•	Florida State	0 59
N12	•	Maryland	19 8
N19	•	at Clemson	10 29
LIBERTY BOWL			
D28		Indiana	10 34

SPARKY WOODS
1989-93 (.464)   24-28-3

1989   6-4-1
S2	•	Duke	27 21
S9	=	Virginia Tech	17 17
S16	•	at West Virginia	21 45
S23	•	Georgia Tech	21 10
S30	•	at Georgia	24 20
O7	•	East Carolina	47 14
O21	•	Western Carolina	24 3
O28	•	North Carolina St.	10 20
N4	•	at Florida State	10 35
N11	•	at North Carolina	27 20
N18	•	Clemson	0 45

1990   6-5-0
S1	•	Duke	21 10
S8	•	North Carolina	27 5
S22	•	at Virginia Tech	35 24
S29	•	at Georgia Tech	6 27
O13	•	East Carolina	37 7
O20	•	Citadel	35 38
O27	•	at North Carolina St.	29 38
N3	•	Florida State	10 41
N10	•	So. Illinois	38 13
N17	•	at Clemson	15 24
N22	•	West Virginia	29 10

1991   3-6-2
S7	=	Duke	24 24
S14	•	at West Virginia	16 21
S21	•	Virginia Tech	28 21
S28	•	at East Carolina	20 31
O5	•	East Tenn. St.	55 7
O12	=	Louisiana Tech	12 12
O19	•	Georgia Tech	23 14
N2	•	North Carolina St.	21 38
N9	•	at Florida State	10 38
N16	•	at North Carolina	17 21
N23	•	Clemson	24 41

1992-PRESENT
SEC

1992   5-6-0 (3-5-0)
S5		Georgia	6 28
S12		Arkansas	7 45
S19		East Carolina	18 20
S26		at Kentucky	9 13
O3		at Alabama	7 48
O17	•	Mississippi State	21 6
O24	•	at Vanderbilt	21 17
O31		Tennessee	24 23
N7	•	Louisiana Tech	14 13
N14		at Florida	9 14
N21	•	at Clemson	24 13

1993   4-7-0 (2-6-0)
S4	•	at Georgia	23 21
S11		at Arkansas	17 18
S18	•	Louisiana Tech	34 3
S23		Kentucky	17 21
O2		Alabama	6 17 †
O9	•	East Carolina	27 3
O16		at Mississippi State	0 23
O23	•	Vanderbilt	22 0
O30		at Tennessee	3 55
N13		Florida	26 37
N20	•	Clemson	13 16

BRAD SCOTT
1994-98 (.420)   23-32-1

1994   7-5-0 (4-4-0)
S3		Georgia	21 24
S10	•	Arkansas	14 0
S17	•	Louisiana Tech	31 6
S24	•	at Kentucky	23 9
O1		at LSU	18 17
O8		East Carolina	42 56
O15		Mississippi State	36 41
O22	•	at Vanderbilt	19 16
O29		Tennessee	22 31
N12		at Florida	17 48
N19	•	at Clemson	33 7
CARQUEST BOWL			
J2	•	West Virginia	24 21

1995   4-6-1 (2-5-1)
S2		at Georgia	23 42
S9		at Arkansas	21 51
S16	•	Louisiana Tech	68 21
S23		Kentucky	30 35
S30	=	LSU	20 20
O7		Kent State	77 14
O14		at Mississippi State	65 39
O21	•	Vanderbilt	52 14
O28		at Tennessee	21 56
N11		Florida	7 63
N18		Clemson	17 38

1996   6-5 (4-4)
S7	•	Central Florida	33 14
S14	•	Georgia	23 14
S21		East Carolina	7 23
S28		Mississippi State	10 14
O5		at Auburn	24 28
O12	•	at Kentucky	25 14
O19	•	Arkansas	23 17
O26	•	at Vanderbilt	27 0
N2		Tennessee	14 31
N16	•	at Florida	25 52
N23	•	at Clemson	34 31

1997   5-6 (3-5)
S6	•	Central Florida	33 31
S13		at Georgia	15 31
S20	•	at East Carolina	26 0
S27		at Mississippi State	17 37
O4		Auburn	6 23
O11	•	Kentucky	38 24
O18	•	Arkansas LR	39 13
O25	•	Vanderbilt	35 3
N1		at Tennessee	7 22
N15		Florida	21 48
N22		Clemson	21 47

1998   1-10 (0-8)
S5	•	Ball State	38 20
S12		Georgia	3 17
S19		Marshall	21 24
S26		Mississippi State	0 38
O3		at Mississippi	28 30
O10		at Kentucky	28 33
O17		Arkansas	28 41
O24		at Vanderbilt	14 17
O31		Tennessee	14 49
N14		at Florida	14 33
N21		at Clemson	19 28

LOU HOLTZ
1999-2004 (.471)   33-37

1999   0-11 (0-8)
S4		at North Carolina St.	0 10
S11		at Georgia	9 24
S18		East Carolina	3 21
S25		at Mississippi State	0 17
O2		Mississippi	10 36
O9		Kentucky	10 30
O16		Arkansas LR	14 48
O23		Vanderbilt	10 11
O30		at Tennessee	7 30
N13		Florida	3 20
N20		Clemson	21 31

2000   8-4 (5-3)
S2	•	New Mexico St.	31 0
S9	•	Georgia	21 10
S16	•	Eastern Michigan	41 6
S23	•	Mississippi State	23 19
S30		at Alabama	17 27
O7	•	at Kentucky	20 17
O14	•	Arkansas	27 7
O21	•	at Vanderbilt	30 14
O28	•	Tennessee	14 17
N11	•	at Florida	21 41
N18		at Clemson	14 16
OUTBACK BOWL			
J1	•	Ohio State	24 7

2001   9-3 (5-3)
S1		Boise State	32 13
S8	•	at Georgia	14 9
S20	•	at Mississippi State	16 14
S29	•	Alabama	37 36
O6	•	Kentucky	42 6
O13	•	Arkansas LR	7 10
O20	•	Vanderbilt	46 14
O27		at Tennessee	10 17
N3	•	Wofford	38 14
N10	•	Florida	17 54
N17	•	Clemson	20 15
OUTBACK BOWL			
J1	•	Ohio State	31 28

2002   5-7 (3-5)
A31	•	New Mexico State	34 24
S7		at Virginia	21 34
S14		Georgia	7 13
S21	•	Temple	42 21
S28	•	at Vanderbilt	20 14
O5	•	Mississippi State	34 10
O12	•	at Kentucky	16 12
O19		at LSU	14 38
N2		Tennessee	10 18
N9		Arkansas	0 23
N16		at Florida	7 28
N23		at Clemson	20 27

2003   5-7 (2-6)
A30	•	La. Lafayette	14 7
S6	•	Virginia	31 7
S13		at Georgia	7 31
S20	•	UAB	42 10
S27		at Tennessee	20 23
O9	•	Kentucky	27 21
O18		LSU	7 33
O25	•	Vanderbilt	35 24
N1		at Mississippi	40 43
N6	•	Arkansas LR	6 28
N15		Florida	22 24
N22		Clemson	17 63

2004   6-5 (4-4)
S4	•	at Vanderbilt	31 6
S11		Georgia	16 20
S18	•	South Florida	34 3
S25	•	Troy	17 7
O2	•	at Alabama	20 3
O9		Mississippi	28 31
O16	•	at Kentucky	12 7
O30		Tennessee	29 43
N6	•	Arkansas	35 32
N13		at Florida	14 48
N20		at Clemson	7 29

THE SCHOOLS

Neutral Site key: *Nor* Norfolk, VA / *W-S* Winston-Salem, NC / *Rich* Richmond, VA / *JaM* Jackson, MS / *Birm* Birmingham, AL / *LR* Little Rock, AR / *Tam* Tampa, FL / *ChSC* Charleston, SC / *Dur* Durham, NC / *Flo* Florence, SC / *ColGa* Columbus, GA / *Sum* Sumter, SC / *NYC* New York, NY *Phil* Philadelphia, PA / *Aug* Augusta, GA / *Roa* Roanoke, VA / *Char* Charlotte, NC / *Ora* Orangeburg, SC / *Mont* Montgomery, AL / *JacF* Jacksonville, FL / *Mem* Memphis, TN
ƒ Forfeit † Game Later Forfieted # Disputed Victor * Disputed Score || Designated Conference Game |2 Counted Twice in Conference Standings

SOUTH FLORIDA

BY KEVIN GLEASON

FEW PROGRAMS IN THE HISTORY OF college football have become successful as quickly as South Florida's. The team began Division I-AA play in 1997 and by 2001 had recorded an 8–3 season in its D1-A debut. The school won nine games in 2002 while gaining national attention with a win over Bowling Green, which was then ranked 25th in the ESPN/*USA Today* poll. South Florida became a player in Conference USA soon after joining the league in 2003, going 5–3 and 7–4 overall. Shortly thereafter, South Florida was accepting a bid into the Big East (to start in 2005). In 2004, the program nabbed four of the top 68 prospects in the state, according to *The Orlando Sentinel*, at times beating out state superpowers Florida and Florida State.

Coach Jim Leavitt has the school thinking big. "Florida, Florida State and Miami have always been the big three," Leavitt said. "I graduated from high school in 1974, and in 1974 they weren't very good, they weren't real strong. But over the years they built three awfully good programs. You have to win, that's all there is to it."

TRADITION As it says on the front page of South Florida's football website, "We Don't Follow Tradition, We Create It." South Florida obviously doesn't have an attic full of archives, but it has begun to create one under Leavitt. South Florida opened a $15 million on-campus athletic facility in May 2004. Finally coaches and players had one place for offices, meeting rooms, locker rooms, film-editing suites and academic services. There is a 10,000-square-foot strength and conditioning center. Already three South Florida alumni own Super Bowl rings: long-snapper Ryan Benjamin for the 2002 Bucs and tackle Kenyatta Jones and receiver Scott McCready for the 2001 Patriots. "Now the other schools—Florida, Florida State, Miami—they'll probably hit [recruits] with 'tradition,'" Leavitt said. "They've won national championships; they've won conference championships. I guess we're going to hit them with 'opportunity': be a part of history, go where no man has gone before."

BEST PLAYER Quarterback Marquel Blackwell—who comes from nearby St. Petersburg—owns just about every passing record in the South Florida book. Blackwell, who played from 1999 to 2002, was named the Bulls' most valuable offensive player three straight seasons, 2000-02. He had

---

PROFILE

University of South Florida
Tampa, Fla.
Founded: 1956
Enrollment: 32,442
Colors: Green and Gold
Nickname: Bulls
Stadium: Raymond James Stadium
  Opened in 1998
  Grass; 41,441 capacity
First football game: 1997
All-time record: 55–33 (.625)
Website: www.gousfbulls.com

THE BEST OF TIMES

Through 2004, the Bulls were 28–16 since gaining full-time Division I-A status in 2001. South Florida went 7–4 (5–3 league) in its Conference USA debut in 2003.

THE WORST OF TIMES

South Florida lost its first-ever football game, 80-3 to Kentucky Wesleyan at home, on Sept. 6, 1997. The Bulls went 5–6 that year, their only sub-.500 season until they went 4–7 in 2004.

CONFERENCE

South Florida competed in Conference USA for the 2003 and 2004 seasons after playing its first six seasons as an independent. The Bulls joined the Big East in 2005.

DISTINGUISHED ALUMNI

Mark Consuelos, actor; Terry Bollea, a.k.a. wrestler/actor Hulk Hogan; Leo Gallagher, comedian; Lauren Hutton, model/actress; Tony La Russa, baseball manager

FIGHT SONG

USF FIGHT SONG
USF Bulls are we,
We hold our standard upright and free.
For green and gold we stand united,
Our beacon lighted and noble to see.
USF Bulls are we,
For USF will always be.
With all our might
We fight the battle here and now,
And we will win the victory.
S-O-U-T-H F-L-O-R-I-D-A! South Florida!
South Florida!
Go Bulls

Few programs in the history of college football have become successful as quickly as South Florida's.

been recruited by Miami and USC as a defensive back but wanted to play quarterback. Leavitt recruited him as a quarterback and Blackwell was on his way. He threw for 9,108 yards and 57 touchdowns but wasn't taken in the 2003 NFL draft. He was signed as a free agent by the New York Jets and later released.

BEST COACH Jim Leavitt gets a unanimous vote as top coach, and not just because he's been South Florida's only coach. Leavitt has recruited well in Florida's football hotbed. "When we started our program, it was always [Florida, Florida State, Miami] and then it was everybody else," Leavitt said. He's changing that perception.

Leavitt's words give a hint of the passion he shows on the field. Players respect his in-your-face approach. Unhappy with South Florida's play against Army in 2003, Leavitt cut his right hand open during a tirade at halftime. South Florida broke open the 13-0 lead to win 28-0.

BEST TEAM The 2002 team finished 9–2 and seriously contended for a bowl game, no small feat for an

independent. But South Florida didn't get a bid, despite going 4–0 against C-USA teams. Its losses came against Arkansas (42-3) and Oklahoma (31-14).

BIGGEST GAME South Florida soothed concerns over whether it could compete in Conference USA one year before entering the league. Hugh Smith scored on a seven-yard reverse with 9:31 left to give South Florida a 16-13 win over perennial C-USA power Southern Miss on Oct. 12, 2002.

BIGGEST UPSET On Nov. 16, 2002, South Florida beat 8–1 Bowling Green, the first ranked Division I-A team to come into Raymond James Stadium, 29-7. The following day South Florida attracted poll attention for the first time, receiving four votes in the Associated Press poll and two in the ESPN/*USA Today* poll.

RIVAL South Florida hasn't had much time to forge any deep-rooted rivalries. In its short Conference USA history, the biggest nemesis was probably Southern Mississippi,

---

RECORDS

RUSHING YARDS

	GAME
275	Andre Hall vs. UAB, Nov. 6, 2004 (29 att.)
	SEASON
1,357	Andre Hall, 2004 (210 att.)
	CAREER
2,253	Rafael Williams, 1997-2000 (462 att.)

PASSING YARDS

	GAME
360	Marquel Blackwell vs. Western Kentucky, Nov. 4, 2000 (27 of 39)
	SEASON
2,882	Marquel Blackwell, 2001 (258 of 456)
	CAREER
9,108	Marquel Blackwell, 1999-2002 (795 of 1,417)

RECEIVING YARDS

	GAME
149	Clif Dell vs. Kentucky Wesleyan, Sept. 6, 1997 (5 rec.)
	SEASON
661	Hugh Smith, 2002 (62 rec.)
	CAREER
1,823	Hugh Smith, 1999-2002 (131 rec.)

POINTS

	GAME
24	Three tied; most recently by Andre Hall vs. TCU, Sept. 25, 2004 (4 TDs)
	SEASON
94	Bill Gramatica, 1998 (16 FGs, 46 PATs)
	CAREER
246	Santiago Gramatica, 2001-04 (38 FGs, 132 PATs)

CONSENSUS ALL-AMERICANS

1998	Bill Gramatica, PK

which won three of four encounters between 2000 and 2004. With the team moving to the Big East, a new rival will surely emerge. In a perfect world, it would be one of the big Florida schools, but the three most prominent Florida schools have historically shown little interest in playing the upstart Bulls. That changes in 2005, when South Florida travels to the Orange Bowl to face Miami in the first game of a home-and-home series. It will mark the Bulls' first-ever road game in the state of Florida.

STADIUM After playing its first season at Tampa Stadium, South Florida moved to Raymond James Stadium, home of the Tampa Bay Buccaneers, in 1998. The Bulls won 21 straight games at home before losing to TCU 13-10 in 2003. The lower half of the stadium creates a capacity of 41,441 for South Florida fans.

HEARTBREAKER TCU came into Tampa in 2003 with a 5–0 record and tied for the No. 18 ranking. At 3–1, South Florida was looking to continue a home winning streak and upset the top team in Conference USA. But TCU snapped the Bulls' streak at 21 with a 13-10 win. Brian Fisher hit Elgin Hicks with a 19-yard pass with 9:27 remaining to pull South Florida to within 13-10, but the Bulls couldn't break through again. TCU had 10 sacks.

DISPUTE South Florida's 38-37 overtime win over East Carolina in 2003 brought its share of controversy. South Florida's Ronnie Banks hit Elgin Hicks with a 22-yard touchdown pass that gave the Bulls a 38-31 lead in the second overtime. Replays showed that the ball hit the ground first and that Hicks trapped it. The play stood and East Carolina pulled to within 38-37 on a three-yard run by Vonta Leach. But Cam Broadwell missed the extra point to give South Florida the win.

NICKNAME South Florida's team originally was called the Brahman Bulls in recognition of cattle farming in the state. But in the mid-1980s newspapers started referring to South Florida as the Bulls in headlines. Soon the school decided for good to go with just the Bulls.

MASCOT Picture a bull with two yellow horns wearing a tank top. That's your South Florida mascot, Rocky. The story of Rocky's roots goes back almost as far as the day

South Florida opened its doors in 1960. Chickens, Roosters, Camels, even Desert Rats were among the early nickname possibilities. Golden Brahmans eventually joined the list of finalists (Buccaneers, Olympians, Cougars and Golden Eagles). A 12-member judiciary committee decided on Buccaneers, at which point students expressed displeasure. A heavily signed petition brought a runoff between the Buccaneers and the Golden Brahmans, and on Nov. 17, 1962, the Golden Brahman was introduced as South Florida's official mascot. The South Florida Golden Brahmans, though, became extinct in the early 1980s. The school athletic department made the switch to Bulls for promotional purposes.

UNIFORMS South Florida's uniforms have been the same since the football team's inception. The helmets are still gold and feature a stylized bull's head logo in the shape of a U, a not-so-modest presumption that USF might compete with another school whose helmet features a U, perennial power Miami University. The home jerseys are green with white numerals outlined in gold, with white jerseys and green numerals on the road.

NUMBERS In 2002, only its second year of Division I-A competition, South Florida finished No. 18 in the final *New York Times* computer ranking, then one of the factors used in determining the Bowl Championship Series rankings.

QUIRK Lee Roy Selmon, the very first draftee of the Tampa Bay Buccaneers in 1976, has spent over a decade at South Florida, including three years as athletic director. Selmon took over as president of the USF Foundation Partnership for Athletics in 2004 and is responsible for building financial support for South Florida's move into the Big East. His son, Lee Roy Jr., was a captain and sixth-year senior on South Florida's 2004 team, having earned the sixth year because of a series of knee injuries. The younger Selmon, a 5'11", 280-pound defensive tackle, was named third-team All-Conference USA in 2003. The elder Salmon was inducted into the Pro Football Hall of Fame in 1995.

QUOTE "I can see myself coaching at South Florida until I retire. Then I can buy season tickets and sit and watch the Bulls play on Saturdays." —Jim Leavitt

SOUTH FLORIDA ANNUAL STATISTICAL LEADERS

YR	RUSHING	YDS	ATT	AVG	PASSING	ATT	CMP	PCT	YDS	RECEIVING	REC	YDS	AVG
2001	Clenton Crossley	380	88	4.3	Marquel Blackwell	456	258	.57	2,882	Huey Whittaker	52	548	10.5
2002	Clenton Crossley	415	92	4.5	Marquel Blackwell	403	230	.57	2,590	Hugh Smith	62	661	10.7
2003	DeJuan Green	490	113	4.3	Ronnie Banks	261	127	.49	1,448	Huey Whittaker	39	516	13.2
2004	Andre Hall	1,357	210	6.5	Pat Julmiste	247	118	.48	1,570	Johnny Peyton	22	469	21.3

Receiving leaders by receptions
All statistics include postseason

SOUTH FLORIDA ALL-TIME SCORES

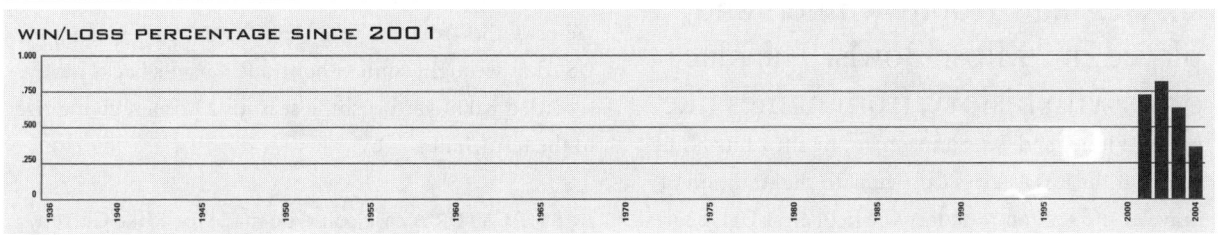

WIN/LOSS PERCENTAGE SINCE 2001

JIM LEAVITT
1997-PRESENT (.625)   55-33

2001   8-3
A30	at Northern Illinois	17	20
S8 ●	at Pittsburgh	35	26
S22	at Memphis	9	17
S29 ●	North Texas	28	10
O6	at Utah	21	52
O13 ●	Connecticut	40	21
O20 ●	So. Utah	42	12
O27 ●	Liberty	68	37
N3 ●	Houston	45	6
N10 ●	Western Illinois	48	17
N24 ●	Utah State	34	13

2002   9-2
A29 ●	Florida Atlantic	51	10
S7 ●	Northern Illinois	37	6
S14	at Arkansas *LR*	3	42
S28	at Oklahoma	14	31
O5 ●	at North Texas	24	17
O12 ●	Southern Miss	16	13
O19 ●	at East Carolina	46	30
N2 ●	Charleston So.	56	6
N9 ●	Memphis	31	28
N16 ●	Bowling Green	29	7
N23 ●	at Houston	32	14

2003-2004
C-USA

2003   7-4   (5-3)
A30 ●	Alabama *BIRM*	17	40
S6 ●	Nicholls St.	27	17
S27 ●	at Army	28	0
O4 ●	Louisville	31	28
O10	TCU	10	13
O18 ●	Charleston So.	55	7
O25	at Southern Miss	6	27
N1 ●	Cincinnati	24	17
N8 ●	at East Carolina	38	37
N22	UAB	19	22
N29 ●	at Memphis	21	16

2004   4-7   (3-5)
S11 ●	Tenn. Tech	21	7
S18	at South Carolina	3	34
S25 ●	at TCU	45	44
O2	Southern Miss	20	27
O16	Army	35	42
O22	at Louisville	9	41
N6 ●	at UAB	45	20
N13 ●	East Carolina	41	17
N20	at Cincinnati	23	45
N27	Memphis	15	31
D4	Pittsburgh	14	43

f Forfeit † Game Later Forfeited # Disputed Victor * Disputed Score || Designated Conference Game |2 Counted Twice in Conference Standings

SOUTHERN CAL

BY BUD WITHERS

Few programs in the nation, and none in the West, embody the notion of big-time football like Southern California. The school has won 11 national championships, had six Heisman Trophy winners and played in 29 Rose Bowls. The place drips with history, from names like Howard Jones and O.J. Simpson, to the site of its home games at the Los Angeles Coliseum, to the tradition of Traveler the stallion rounding the field after USC scores.

Not surprisingly, game day at USC seems more like a celebration of the history of the program than of any collective concern about victory or the opponent. It's traditionally been almost a given that the Trojans will win—even though during most of the 1980s and 1990s it was not exactly a sure thing.

And then, before the 2001 season, Pete Carroll turned up, bringing with him a boundless enthusiasm, NFL head coaching experience and—very soon thereafter—national championships. From 2002 to 2004, Carroll's Trojans went 36–3, won the AP national championship in 2003 and received both the coaches' and media vote in 2004.

TRADITION They're in abundance at USC. On campus is a bronze Trojan warrior, popularly named Tommy Trojan, a composite of 1930 Rose Bowl player of the game Russ Saunders and All-America Erny Pinckert, among other players. The 295-pound Victory Bell goes back and forth between winners in the USC-UCLA rivalry, and a bejeweled shillelagh—a Gaelic war club—awaits the victor of the Trojans-Notre Dame game. On the field, USC has wrought some other traditions: its backs have recorded 1,000-yard rushing seasons 23 times, giving rise to the term Tailback U.

BEST PLAYER A case could be made for Mike Garrett, whose 1,440 yards in 1965 was a rare total in that era. Or one could argue for Charles White, who had the astronomical number of 6,245 yards rushing in his four years. Then there was Marcus Allen, whose 2,427 yards on the ground in 1981 was not surpassed until 1988, when Oklahoma State's Barry Sanders gained 2,628. When USC finally had a Heisman Trophy winner who wasn't a running back, it was a most worthy quarterback, Carson Palmer.

But the best USC player was its most notorious, 1968 Heisman winner O.J. Simpson. With a devastating combination of speed and fluidity, Simpson amassed 3,423

PROFILE

University of Southern California
Los Angeles, Calif.
Founded: 1880
Enrollment: 16,500
Colors: Cardinal and Gold
Nickname: Trojans
Stadium: Los Angeles Memorial Coliseum
Opened in 1923
FieldTurf; 92,000 capacity
First football game: 1888
All-time record: 719–297–54 (.697)
Bowl record: 28–15
Consensus national championships,
1936-present: 7 (1962, 1967, 1972, 1974, 1978, 2003, 2004)
Pac-10 Conference championships: 34 (26 outright)
Heisman Trophy: Mike Garrett, 1965; O.J. Simpson, 1968; Charles White, 1979; Marcus Allen, 1981; Carson Palmer, 2002; Matt Leinart, 2004
Outland Trophy: Ron Yary, 1967
First-round NFL draftees: 65
Website: www.usctrojans.com

THE BEST OF TIMES

In the 16-season reign of coach John McKay (1960-75), the Trojans captured four national championships.

THE WORST OF TIMES

In 1982, USC was slapped with a three-year probation by the NCAA. Players had profited from sales of complimentary tickets, primarily through longtime assistant coach Marv Goux. The probation included a ban from TV and bowl games for two years.

CONFERENCE

A longtime member of the Pac-10 Conference, USC joined the Pac-10's forerunner, the Pacific Coast Conference, in 1922, six years after its inception.

DISTINGUISHED ALUMNI

John Wayne; Ron Howard; George Lucas; Art Buchwald, syndicated columnist; Will Ferrell, actor; Macy Gray, singer; Marilyn Horne, opera star; Warren Christopher, U.S. secretary of state; David L. Wolper, television producer

FIGHT SONG

FIGHT ON
Fight on for ol' SC
Our men fight on to victory.
Our alma mater dear,
Looks up to you
Fight on and win
For ol' SC
Fight on to victory
Fight on!

yards in only two seasons, rushing for 23 touchdowns his senior year. He then validated his college career at Buffalo in 1973 by becoming the first NFL running back to gain more than 2,000 yards in a season. Simpson became a broadcaster and actor before his fame came crashing down in 1994. Accused of the stabbing deaths of Nicole Brown Simpson, his former wife, and Ronald Goldman, Simpson stood trial on murder charges. He was acquitted in a controversial verdict but was later held liable in a civil trial.

BEST COACH John McKay was renowned for his withering sense of humor, but he earned his greatest acclaim for a dominating 16-year (1960-75) tenure with the Trojans. When a writer wondered how one of his tailbacks could flourish getting so many carries, McKay sniffed, "The ball's not that heavy." When Mike Hunter, a smallish defensive back, slipped and fell on a kickoff return in the hostile environs of Notre Dame in 1965, McKay said in amazement, "My god, they shot him." But he could motivate. "He knew when to loosen a team up,

> *Twenty-three times, Trojan backs have recorded 1,000-yard rushing seasons, giving rise to the term Tailback U.*

and he knew how to get after you," said former USC quarterback Craig Fertig. "You'd never have to worry about him slapping a player. He could do it with his tongue."

On the field, the Trojans were overpowering through much of the McKay era, winning national titles in 1962, 1967, 1972 and 1974. His teams finished in the Top 10 on nine occasions and won or shared conference titles nine times. Early in his tenure, he began employing the I-formation, using a shifty tailback behind big, mauling offensive lines. He combined that with the Arkansas defense he borrowed from the Razorbacks' Frank Broyles. Well before McKay, USC had another dominating era under Howard Jones (1925-40). With a succession of Trojans greats like Cotton Warburton, Morley Drury and Doyle Nave, Jones' teams rang up national championships in 1928, 1931 and 1932, allowing 13 points in the 1932 title season.

BEST TEAM Old-timers might cast a vote for Jones' 1932 national championship squad, which blew through 10 opponents by the composite score of 201-13, including a

---

RECORDS

RUSHING YARDS

	GAME
347	Ricky Bell vs. Washington State, Oct. 9, 1976 (51 att.)
	SEASON
2,427	Marcus Allen, 1981 (433 att.)
	CAREER
6,245	Charles White, 1976-79 (1,147 att.)

PASSING YARDS

	GAME
448	Carson Palmer vs. Oregon, Oct. 26, 2002 (31 of 42)
	SEASON
3,942	Carson Palmer, 2002 (309 of 489)
	CAREER
11,818	Carson Palmer, 1998-2002 (927 of 1,569)

RECEIVING YARDS

	GAME
260	R. Jay Soward vs. UCLA, Nov. 23, 1996 (6 rec.)
	SEASON
1,520	Johnnie Morton, 1993 (88 rec.)
	CAREER
3,201	Johnnie Morton, 1990-93 (201 rec.)

POINTS

	GAME
36	Anthony Davis vs. Notre Dame, Dec. 2, 1972 (6 TDs)
	SEASON
138	O.J. Simpson, 1968 (23 TDs); Marcus Allen, 1981 (23 TDs)
	CAREER
329	Ryan Killeen, 2002-04 (176 PATs, 51 FGs)

CONSENSUS ALL-AMERICANS

1926	Mort Kaer, B
1927	Jesse Hibbs, T
1927	Morley Drury, B
1930	Erny Pinckert, B
1931	John Baker, G
1931	Gus Shaver, B
1932	Ernie Smith, T
1933	Aaron Rosenberg, G
1933	Cotton Warburton, B
1939	Harry Smith, G
1943	Ralph Heywood, E
1944	John Ferraro, T
1947	Paul Cleary, E
1952	Elmer Willhoite, G
1952	Jim Sears, DB
1962	Hal Bedsole, E
1965	Mike Garrett, TB
1966-67	Ron Yary, T
1966	Nate Shaw, DB
1967-68	O.J. Simpson, B
1967	Tim Rossovich, DE
1967	Adrian Young, LB

(Continued on next page)

THE SCHOOLS

35-0 thrashing of Pittsburgh in the Rose Bowl. But the 1972 McKay-coached team ranks as one of the greatest in college football history. It had a dizzying array of talent, including sophomore tailback Anthony Davis, fullback Sam Cunningham, offensive tackle Pete Adams, tight end Charles Young, wide receivers Lynn Swann and Edesel Garrison, defensive tackles Jeff Winans and John Grant and linebacker Richard Wood. Five of those players were All-Americas that year; another six were likewise honored during the next two seasons. "I've never seen any team that could beat them," said McKay. USC began 1972 ranked No. 8 and quickly established its superiority, throttling fourth-rated Arkansas on the road. Then it breezed. Its only victory by single digits was a 30-21 decision at Stanford against a 15th-ranked team. The final two games were illustrative of USC's dominance. Behind Davis' six touchdowns, including two kickoff returns for scores, the Trojans swamped Notre Dame 45-23, and in the Rose Bowl, USC battered Ohio State 42-17 as Davis ran for 157 yards, Cunningham dove for four touchdowns and quarterback Mike Rae completed 18 of 25 passes for 229 yards. USC gained every first-place ballot in both the Associated Press and United Press International polls, a first.

CONSENSUS ALL-AMERICANS (CONT.)	
1969	Jim Gunn, DE
1970	Charlie Weaver, DE
1972	Charles Young, TE
1973	Lynn Swann, WR
1973	Booker Brown, OT
1973-74	Richard Wood, LB
1973	Artimus Parker, DB
1974	Anthony Davis, RB
1975-76	Ricky Bell, RB
1976	Gary Jeter, DT
1976-77	Dennis Thurman, DB
1978	Pat Howell, G
1978-79	Charles White, RB
1979	Brad Budde, G
1980	Keith Van Horne, OL
1980	Ronnie Lott, DB
1981	Roy Foster, OL
1981	Marcus Allen, RB
1982	Don Mosebar, OL
1982	Bruce Matthews, OL
1982	George Achica, NG
1983	Tony Slaton, C
1984	Jack Del Rio, LB
1985-86	Jeff Bregel, OL
1986	Tim McDonald, DB
1987	Dave Cadigan, OL
1989	Mark Carrier, DB
1989	Tim Ryan, DL
1993	Johnnie Morton, WR
1994	Tony Boselli, OL
1995	Keyshawn Johnson, WR
1998	Chris Claiborne, LB
2002	Carson Palmer, QB
2002	Troy Polamalu, DB
2003	Mike Williams, WR
2003	Jacob Rogers, OL
2003	Kenechi Udeze, DL
2004	Reggie Bush, AP/KR
2004	Shaun Cody, DL
2004	Matt Grootegoed, LB
2004	Matt Leinart, QB

helped them win the national championship. Another big game came in the 2005 Orange Bowl against Oklahoma. In what was billed as a near-even matchup, the Trojans destroyed the Sooners 55-19 behind Heisman Trophy winner Matt Leinart.

BIGGEST UPSET In 1964, Notre Dame came to Los Angeles with a roster that included Heisman Trophy winner John Huarte at quarterback and end Jack Snow, a first-round NFL draft pick in 1965. The Irish were top-ranked, 9–0, and, in an era when they didn't accept bowl invitations, found themselves on the threshold of a national title with a 17-0 halftime lead. That's when McKay delivered one of his most understated, but effective, halftime speeches. He told his team: "If we don't score more than 17 points in the second half, you'll lose." Then he walked out of the locker room. The Trojans, who that day finished a pedestrian 7–3 season, proceeded to stun Notre Dame with a second-half comeback capped by Fertig's touchdown pass to Rod Sherman with 1:33 left and won 20-17.

BEST COMEBACK There have been comebacks from bigger deficits. But perhaps none is as renowned as USC's cataclysmic rebound from a 24-0 deficit to shock Notre Dame 55-24 in Los Angeles in 1974. The Irish entered the game 9–1 and had eight

BIGGEST GAME The 1967 USC-UCLA game seemed to have something for everyone. It had the 1967 Heisman Trophy winner, UCLA quarterback Gary Beban, against the 1968 honoree, O.J. Simpson. It featured the nation's No. 1 team in the Bruins, who came in at 7–0–1, while USC (8–1) was No. 4 only because it had lost at Oregon State, 3-0, the previous week. And of course, it matched intracity rivals. Beban's 20-yard touchdown pass to Dave Nuttall early in the final quarter put the Bruins ahead 20-14, but with 10:38 remaining, Simpson unspooled a winding, 64-yard touchdown to give the Trojans a 21-20 victory, one that

NFL draft picks in 1975. They had an imposing defense, keyed by two future first-round linemen, Mike Fanning and Steve Niehaus, which was underscored by the hole USC found itself in when trailing 24-0 late in the first half. The Trojans, however, took a kernel of momentum into the dressing room with a touchdown 10 seconds before the half, making it 24-6. Then the floodgates flew open. Anthony Davis took the second-half kickoff and bolted 102 yards and, suddenly, the Coliseum was alive. "We turned into madmen," Davis would say later. That touchdown ignited a 35-point third quarter for USC, with quarterback Pat Haden throwing

for two scores to J.K. McKay and Davis scoring twice on the ground. In staccato fashion, USC scored another two touchdowns early in the fourth quarter, the second on safety Charles Phillips' 58-yard interception return. That made it a 55-point barrage in less than 17 minutes. Said a dumbfounded McKay, son of the USC coach: "Against Notre Dame? Maybe against Kent State . . . but Notre Dame?"

STADIUM USC first played football at the Los Angeles Memorial Coliseum in 1923 and is the one constant at a facility that has also hosted six pro football teams, two Olympic Summer Games, baseball's Dodgers and the Trojans' archrival, UCLA. Built at a cost of $800,000, the structure was renovated in 1993, including an 11-foot lowering of the floor and removal of the running track. That had just been finished when a massive earthquake in early 1994 brought about the need for $93 million in repairs.

RIVAL The Trojans have two, both on different levels. Their intersectional rivalry with Notre Dame is considered the greatest in the sport on a national level. Begun in 1926, it is an unbroken series except for a 1943-45 hiatus owing to World War II. The game was played in November at both Los Angeles and South Bend sites until 1959, when the Trojans performed so miserably in a cold-weather 16-6 loss at Notre Dame that athletic director Jess Hill proposed October home dates for the Irish and late November dates for Notre Dame to visit USC. The UCLA rivalry is its own rarity, pitting two schools in a major metropolis that both boast big-time football. In this one, the Trojans are the long-standing program with a thick pedigree, appealing more naturally to athletes in the area with a hardscrabble background. UCLA is seen as the nouveau riche school, reflected in its upscale Westwood locale compared to USC's comparatively gritty neighborhood.

NICKNAME USC's earliest teams were known as the Methodists or Wesleyans. In 1912, athletic director Warren Bovard asked *Los Angeles Times* sports editor Owen Bird to come up with a nickname more favorable to university officials, and Bird, seeking one which befitted a fighting spirit, settled on Trojans.

MASCOT It began when USC director of special events Bob Jani saw a fellow named Richard Saukko riding his white horse, Traveler I, in the 1961 Rose Parade. Saukko was persuaded to appear with his steed at USC games, and a tradition began. There have been several successors to the original Traveler, but the horse has always been white, and always ridden by an alumnus or student. It appears annually at the Rose Parade and has also been on stage and screen.

UNIFORMS At home, USC wears cardinal jerseys with gold crescent stripes and numerals on the sleeves, a style reminiscent of the jerseys the team wore during the glory years of the 1960s. Road jerseys are white with cardinal numerals and crescent stripes and numerals on the sleeves. Pants and helmets are the same at home and away. Pants are gold with double-cardinal piping, and helmets are cardinal with the Trojan warrior symbol on the sides.

LORE The Notre Dame-USC series never would have happened if not for a woman's touch. With the hope of talking Irish coach Knute Rockne into a series with the Trojans, USC graduate manager Gwynn Wilson traveled in 1925 with his bride Marion to Lincoln, where Notre Dame was playing Nebraska. As the Wilsons joined Knute and Bonnie Rockne on the train from Lincoln to Chicago, Gwynn Wilson quickly became pessimistic, discovering that Rockne felt his team was traveling too extensively. But in another compartment, Mrs. Wilson spoke eloquently about the weather and the wonders of Southern California to Mrs. Rockne, who then persuaded her husband. In 1926, the teams began a memorable series, one that Gwynn Wilson credited to his wife.

QUOTE "USC's not the No. 1 team in the country. The Miami Dolphins are better."—Washington State coach Jim Sweeney, on the 1972 national champion Trojans, widely recognized as one of the greatest college teams of all time

SOUTHERN CAL ALL-TIME SCORES

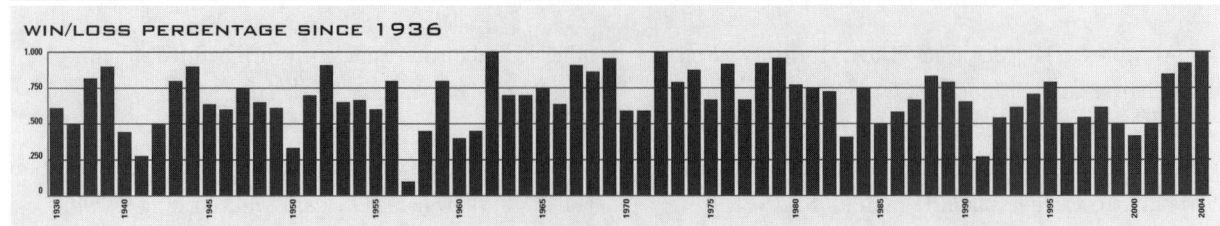

WIN/LOSS PERCENTAGE SINCE 1936

HENRY GODDARD/FRANK SUFFEL
1888 (1.000)   2-0

1888   2-0-0
N14	●	Alliance AC	16	0
J19	●	Alliance AC	4	0

NO HEAD COACH

1889   2-0-0
U	●	Loyola, Marymount	40	0
N28	●	Pasadena	26	0

1890
NO TEAM   0-0-0

1891   1-2-0
N26		Olive Club	12	16
J23	●	S.C. Academy	34	0
F22		Loyola, Marymount	2	10

1892
NO TEAM

1893   3-1-0
J14	●	Chaw-sir Club	14	2
N18	●	Cal Tech	22	12
D11		Chaffey Coll.	6	32
D22	●	Cal Tech	14	4

1894   1-0-0
U	●	Cal Tech	12	0

1895   0-1-1
N18		Occidental	0	10
D7	=	Cal Tech	4	4

1896   0-3-0
O24		Whittier	0	30
O31		Los Angeles AC	0	22
N14		Cal Tech	0	22

LEWIS R. FREEMAN
1897 (.833)   5-1

1897   5-1-0
U	●	Loyola, Marymount	34	0
N6	●	Los Angeles HS	10	0
N13	●	Chaffey College	38	0
N25	●	Pomona	6	0
D25		San Diego YMCA	0	18
J1	●	Ventura	12	0

NO HEAD COACH

1898   5-1-1
O15	=	Los Angeles HS	0	0
O22	●	Pasadena AC	17	0
N19	●	Los Angeles HS	0	6
N24	●	Pomona	14	11
N26	●	7 TH Regiment	34	0
D3	●	Phoenix Indians	27	11
J2	●	Santa Barbra AC	5	0

1899   2-3-1
O21	●	Whittier	11	0
N4		at Santa Anna HS	0	11
N8	●	Occidental	11	0
N15	●	Occidental	0	0
N30		at Pomona	0	12
J1		at Santa Barbra AC	0	10

1900   1-1-1
N10	●	at Occidental	5	0
N24	=	Los Angeles HS *FIE*	0	0
N29		Pomona *FIE*	0	11

CLAIR S. TAPPAAN
1901 (.000)   0-1

1901   0-1-0
D7		at Pomona	0	6

NO HEAD COACH

1902   2-3-0
O11		Loyola, Marymount *FIE*	5	6
O25		Santa Anna	2	5
N7		Santa Anna *FIE*	6	0
N15	●	Pomona	16	5
N22		at Sherman	0	8

JOHN WALKER
1903 (.667)   4-2

1903   4-2-0
O10	●	Cal Tech	5	0
O17	●	Los Angeles HS	10	0
O24		Occidental	0	5
O31	●	Loyola, Marymount	12	5
N7	●	Orange AC	31	5
N14		Sherman	0	12

HARVEY R. HOLMES
1904-07 (.759)   19-5-3

1904   6-1-0
O15	●	Los Angeles HS *FIE*	42	0
O22	●	Cal Tech	35	0
O29	●	Occidental	36	4
N5	●	Loyola, Marymount	1	0 *f*
N5	●	USC Prep	26	0
N12		Sherman Institute *LB*	0	17
N19	●	at Whittier	60	6

1905   6-3-1
O4	●	Nat'l Guard	28	0
O10	●	Harvard Sch.	12	0
O16	●	L. A. Poly HS	27	0
O18	●	Whittier R.	75	0
N1	●	Alumni	63	0
N4		at Stanford	0	16
N11		at Occidental	0	10
N25		Sherman *FIE*	0	15
D2		Loyola, Marymount	0	0
D9	●	Pomona *FIE*	6	4

1906   2-0-2
O6	=	Los Angeles HS *FIE*	0	0
O13	●	Occidental	22	0
N17	●	at Pomona	14	0
N29	=	Sherman *FIE*	0	0

1907   5-1-0
O12	●	Los Angeles HS *FIE*	6	0
O16	●	Whittier R.	57	0
O26	●	at Santa Ana HS	51	0
N9	●	Whitter	46	0
N15	●	USS Colorado	16	4
D25		Los Angeles HS *FIE*	6	16

WILLIAM I. TRAEGER
1908 (.700)   3-1-1

1908   3-1-1
O10		Los Angeles HS *FIE*	0	12
O17	●	Whittier	15	0
O24	●	at Arrowhead AC	28	0
N7	●	Occidental	14	0
N14	=	at Pomona	6	6

DEAN B. CROMWELL
1909-10, '16-18 (.686)   21-8-6

1909   3-1-2
O9	●	at Cal Poly SLO	51	0
O16	●	at Whittier	22	2
O23		Loyola, Marymount	6	8
O30	●	Orange AC	51	0
N6	=	at Occidental	3	3
N13	=	Pomona	0	0

1910   7-0-1
O5	●	Long Beach HS	22	6
O8	●	Chaffey HS	65	6
O15	●	at Throop Acad.	9	0
O22	●	at San Diego HS	32	0
O29	●	at Redlands	35	0
N5	●	Occidental	6	0
N12	●	at Whittier	11	3
N19	=	at Pomona	9	9

1911-1913
PLAYED RUGBY

RALPH GLAZE
1914-15 (.500)   7-7

1914   4-3-0
S26	●	Los Angeles AC	20	0
O10	●	Redlands	41	0
O24	●	Whittier	17	14
O31		Occidental	13	20
N7	●	at Redlands	13	6
N14		at Pomona	6	10
N26		Oregon State *TAC*	6	38

1915   3-4-0
O2	●	Los Angeles AC	21	9
O16	●	Saint Mary's-Cal	47	3
O23	●	at California	28	10
N8		Oregon	0	34
N20		at Utah	13	20
N25		California	21	23
D11		Whittier	2	20

DEAN B. CROMWELL

1916   5-3-0
O7	●	Sherman Ind.	14	0
O14	●	at Sante Fe AC	14	0
O21		Utah	12	27
N4		California	0	27
N11	●	Los Angeles AC	34	0
N25	●	Pomona	28	3
N30		Oregon State	7	16
D9	●	Arizona *PHO*	20	7

1917   4-2-1
O20	●	Arizona	31	6
O27		Saint Mary's-Cal	0	7
N3	●	at 21st Infantry	3	0
N10	●	Fort MacArthur	42	0
N17	●	at Utah	51	0
N24		Mare Is. Marines	0	34
N29	=	California	0	0

1918   2-2-2
N23		Stanford	25	8
N30	=	at Whittier	13	13
D7	=	at Pomona	0	0
D14		California	7	33
D21	●	Occidental	6	7
D25	●	Redlands	10	0

ELMER C. HENDERSON
1919-24 (.865)   45-7

1919   4-1-0
O25	●	Pomona	6	0
N1	●	Occidental	27	0
N8		California	13	14
N15	●	Utah	28	7
N27	●	Stanford	13	0

1920   6-0-0
O9	●	Cal Tech	46	7
O16	●	Stanford	10	0
O23	●	Occidental	48	7
O30	●	at Pomona	7	0
N13	●	Nevada	38	7
N25	●	Oregon	21	0

1921   10-1-0
O1	●	USS Arizona	62	0
O1	●	USS New York	35	0
O8	●	Cal Tech	70	0
O12	●	Sub Base	34	0
O15	●	at Occidental	42	0
O19	●	at Sub Base	28	0
O29	●	Pomona	35	7
N5		at California	7	38
N19	●	Whittier	14	0
N26	●	Oregon State	7	0
D3	●	Washington State	28	7

1922-1958
PACIFIC COAST

1922   10-1-0 (3-1-0)
S30	●	USS Mississippi	20	0
S30	●	Alumni	20	0
O7	●	at Pomona	54	13
O14	●	Arizona	15	0
O21	●	Nevada	6	0
O28		California *PAS*	0	12
N4	●	Occidental	46	0
N11	●	at Stanford	6	0
N18	●	Idaho *PAS*	14	0
N30	●	Washington State *PAS*	41	3

ROSE BOWL
J1	●	Penn State	14	3

1923   6-2-0 (2-2-0)
S29	●	Cal Tech	18	7
O6	●	Pomona	23	7
O13	●	Nevada	33	0
O20		at Washington	0	22
O27	●	at Stanford	14	7
N10		California	7	13
N17	●	Arizona	69	6
N24		Idaho	9	0

1924   9-2-0 (2-1-0)
S27	●	Cal Tech	78	6
O4	●	Pomona	14	0
O11	●	Arizona	29	0
O18	●	Oregon State *PORT*	17	3
O25	●	Nevada	21	7
N1		at California	0	7
N8		Saint Mary's-Cal	10	14
N15	●	Whittier	51	0
N22	●	Idaho	13	0
D6	●	Syracuse	16	0

CHRISTMAS FESTIVAL
D25	●	Missouri	20	7

HOWARD H. JONES
1925-40 (.750) 121-36-13

1925 11-2-0 (3-2-0)

S26	●	Whittier	74	0
S26	●	Cal Tech	32	0
O3	●	Pomona	80	0
O10	●	Utah	28	2
O17	|	Stanford	9	13
O24	●	Arizona	56	0
O30	● |	at Idaho	51	7
N7	●	Santa Clara	29	9
N14	● |	Montana	27	7
N21	●	Iowa	18	0
N28	|	Washington State	12	17
D5	● |	Oregon State	28	0
D12	●	Saint Mary's-Cal	12	0

1926 8-2-0 (5-1-0)

S25	●	Whittier	74	0
O2	●	Santa Clara	42	0
O9	● |	Washington State	16	7
O16	●	Occidental	28	6
O23	● |	at California	27	0
O30	|	Stanford	12	13
N11	● |	Oregon State PORT	17	7
N20	● |	Idaho	28	6
N25	● |	Montana	61	0
D4		Notre Dame	12	13

1927 8-1-1 (4-0-1)

S24	●	Occidental	33	0
O1	●	Santa Clara	52	12
O8	● |	Oregon State	13	12
O15	= |	at Stanford	13	13
O22	●	Cal Tech	51	0
O29	● |	California	13	0
N12	●	Colorado	46	7
N19	● |	Washington State	27	0
N26		Notre Dame CHI	6	7
D3	● |	Washington	33	13 *

1928 9-0-1 (4-0-1)

S29	●	Utah State	40	12
O6	● |	Oregon State	19	0
O13	●	Saint Mary's-Cal	19	6
O20	= |	at California	0	0
O27	●	Occidental	19	0
N3	● |	Stanford	10	0
N10	●	Arizona	78	7
N17	● |	Washington State	27	13
N24	● |	Idaho	28	7
D1	●	Notre Dame	27	14

1929 10-2-0 (6-1-0)

S28	● |	UCLA	76	0
O5	● |	Oregon State	21	7
O12	● |	at Washington	48	0
O19	● |	Occidental	64	0
O26	● |	at Stanford	7	0
N2	|	California	7	15
N9	●	Nevada	66	0
N16		Notre Dame CHI	12	13
N23	● |	Idaho	72	0
N30	● |	Washington State	27	7
D14	●	Carnegie Tech	45	13
		ROSE BOWL		
J1	●	Pittsburgh	47	14

1930 8-2-0 (5-1-0)

S27	● |	at UCLA	52	0
O4	● |	Oregon State	27	7
O11	|	at Washington State	6	7
O18	●	Utah State	65	0
O25	● |	at Stanford	41	12
N1	●	Denver	33	13
N8	● |	California	74	0
N15	●	Hawaii	52	0
N27	● |	Washington	32	0
D6		Notre Dame	0	27

1931 10-1-0 (7-0-0)

S26		Saint Mary's-Cal	7	13
O3	● |	Oregon State	30	0
O10	● |	Washington State	38	6
O17	● |	Oregon	53	0
O24	● |	at California	6	0
N7	● |	at Stanford	19	0
N14	● |	Montana	69	0
N21	●	at Notre Dame	16	14
D5	● |	Washington	44	7
D12	●	Georgia	60	0
		ROSE BOWL		
J1	●	Tulane	21	12

1932 10-0-0 (6-0-0)

S24	●	Utah	35	0
O1	● |	Washington State	20	0
O8	● |	Oregon State	10	0
O15	●	Loyola, Marymount	6	0
O22	● |	at Stanford	13	0
N5	● |	California	27	7
N12	● |	Oregon	33	0
N24	● |	at Washington	9	6
D10	●	Notre Dame	13	0
		ROSE BOWL		
J2	●	Pittsburgh	35	0

1933 10-1-1 (4-1-1)

S23	●	Occidental	39	0
S23	●	Whittier	51	0
S30	●	Loyola, Marymount	18	0
O7	● |	Washington State	33	0
O14	●	Saint Mary's-Cal	14	7
O21	= |	Oregon State PORT	0	0
O28	● |	at California	6	3
N11	|	Stanford	7	13
N18	● |	Oregon	26	0
N25	●	at Notre Dame	19	0
D2	●	Georgia	31	0
D9	● |	Washington	13	7

1934 4-6-1 (1-4-1)

S21	●	Occidental	20	0
S22	●	Whittier	40	14
S29	●	Pacific	6	0
O6	|	Washington State	0	19
O13		at Pittsburgh	6	20
O20	= |	Oregon State	6	6
O27	|	at Stanford	0	16
N10	|	California	2	7
N17	● |	Oregon	33	0
D1	|	Washington	7	14
D8		Notre Dame	0	14

1935 5-7-0 (2-4-0)

S28	● |	Montana	9	0
O5	●	Pacific	19	7
O12		Illinois	0	19
O19	|	Oregon State	7	13
O26	|	at California	7	21
N9	|	Stanford	0	3
N16	● |	Washington State	20	10
N23		at Notre Dame	13	20
D7	|	Washington	2	6
D14		Pittsburgh	7	12
D25	●	at Kamehameha Alumni	33	7
J1	●	at Hawaii	38	6

1936 4-2-3 (3-2-2)

S26	● |	Oregon State	38	7
O3	● |	Oregon	26	0
O10	●	at Illinois	24	6
O17	= |	Washington State	0	0
O24	● |	at Stanford	14	7
N7	|	California	7	13
N14	|	at Washington	0	12
N26	= |	UCLA	7	7
D5	=	Notre Dame	13	13

1937 4-4-2 (2-3-2)

S25	●	Pacific	40	0
O2	|	Washington	0	7
O9	●	Ohio State	13	12
O16	● |	Oregon	34	14
O23	|	at California	6	20
O30	= |	at Washington State	0	0
N6	|	Stanford	6	7
N13	= |	Oregon State	12	12
N27		at Notre Dame	6	13
D4	● |	at UCLA	19	13

1938 9-2-0 (6-1-0)

S24		Alabama	7	19
O1	● |	Oregon State	7	0
O8	●	at Ohio State	14	7
O15	● |	Washington State	19	6
O22	● |	at Stanford	13	2
O29	● |	Oregon	31	7
N5	● |	California	13	7
N12	|	at Washington	6	7
N24	● |	UCLA	42	7
D3	●	Notre Dame	13	0
		ROSE BOWL		
J2	●	Duke	7	3

1939 8-0-2 (5-0-2)

S30	= |	Oregon	7	7
O7	● |	Washington State	27	0
O14	●	Illinois	26	0
O28	● |	at California	26	0
N4	● |	Oregon State PORT	19	7
N11	● |	Stanford	33	0
N25	●	at Notre Dame	20	12
D2	● |	Washington	9	7
D9	= |	at UCLA	0	0
		ROSE BOWL		
J1	●	Tennessee	14	0

1940 3-4-2 (2-3-2)

S28	= |	Washington State	14	14
O5	= |	Oregon State	0	0
O12	●	at Illinois	13	7
O19	● |	Oregon	13	0
O26	|	at Stanford	7	21
N9	|	California	7	20
N16	|	at Washington	0	14
N30	● |	UCLA	28	12
D7		Notre Dame	6	10

JUSTIN M. BARRY
1941 (.278) 2-6-1

1941 2-6-1 (2-4-1)

S27	● |	Oregon State	13	7
O4		Ohio State	0	33
O11	|	Oregon	6	20
O18	● |	Washington State	7	6
O25	|	at California	0	14
N8	|	Stanford	0	13
N22		at Notre Dame	18	20
N29	|	Washington	13	14
D6	= |	at UCLA	7	7

NEWELL J. CRAVATH
1942-50 (.644) 54-28-8

1942 5-5-1 (4-2-1)

S26		Tulane	13	27
O3	= |	at Washington	0	0
O10		at Ohio State	12	28
O17	● |	Washington State	26	12
O24	|	Stanford SF	6	14
N7	● |	California	21	7
N14	● |	Oregon	40	0
N28		Notre Dame	0	13
D5	● |	Montana	38	0
D12	|	UCLA	7	14
D19	●	Saint Mary's-Cal Pre-Flight	21	13

1943 8-2-0 (4-0-0)

S25	● |	at UCLA	20	0
O2	● |	at California	7	0
O9	●	State Marys Pre-Flight	13	0
O16	●	at San Francisco	34	0
O23	●	Pacific	6	0
O30	● |	California	13	0
N6		at San Diego Naval	7	10
N13		March Field	0	35
N27	● |	UCLA	26	13
		ROSE BOWL		
J1	●	Washington	29	0

1944 8-0-2 (3-0-2)

S23	= |	UCLA	13	13
S30	●	Pacific	18	6
O7	= |	California	6	6
O14	●	Saint Mary's-Cal Pre-Flight FRE	6	0
O23	● |	Washington	38	7
O28	●	Saint Mary's-Cal	34	7
N4	●	San Diego Navy	28	21
N18	● |	at California	32	0
N25	● |	at UCLA	40	13
		ROSE BOWL		
J1	●	Tennessee	25	0

1945 7-4-0 (5-1-0)

S21	● |	at UCLA	13	6
S29	● |	at California	13	2
O6	●	State Marys P-F	26	14
O13		at San Diego Navy	6	33
O20	●	Pacific	52	0
O27	|	at Washington	7	13
N3		Saint Mary's-Cal	0	26
N10	● |	California	14	0
N24	● |	Oregon State	34	7
D1	● |	UCLA	26	15
		ROSE BOWL		
J1		Alabama	14	34

1946 6-4-0 (5-2-0)

S27	● |	Washington State	13	7
O5		Ohio State	0	21
O12	|	Oregon State PORT	0	6
O19	● |	Washington	28	0
O26	● |	at Stanford	28	20
N2	● |	Oregon	43	0
N9	● |	California	14	0
N23	|	at UCLA	6	13
N30		at Notre Dame	6	26
D21	●	at Tulane	20	13

1947 7-2-1 (6-0-0)

S27	● |	Washington State	21	0
O4	=	Rice	7	7
O11	●	at Ohio State	32	0
O18	● |	Oregon State	48	6
O25	● |	at California	39	14
N1	● |	at Washington	19	0
N8	● |	Stanford	14	0
N22	● |	UCLA	6	0
D6		Notre Dame	7	38
		ROSE BOWL		
J1		Michigan	0	49

1948 6-3-1 (4-2-0)

S17	●	Utah	27	0
S24	● |	Oregon State	21	6
O2		at Ohio State	0	20
O9	●	Rice	7	0
O16	|	Oregon PORT	7	8
O23	● |	at Stanford	7	6
O30	|	California	7	13
N13	● |	Washington	32	7
N20	● |	at UCLA	20	13
D4	=	Notre Dame	14	14

1949 5-3-1 (4-2-0)

S24	●	Navy	42	20
O1	● |	Washington State	35	7
O8	=	Ohio State	13	13
O15	|	at California	10	16
O22	● |	Oregon	40	13
O29	● |	at Washington	40	28
N5	|	Stanford	13	34
N19	● |	UCLA	21	7
N26		at Notre Dame	0	32

1950 2-5-2 (1-3-2)

S29		Iowa	14	20
O7	= |	at Washington State	20	20
O14	|	California	7	13
O21		Navy BALT	14	27
O28	● |	Oregon	30	21
N4	= |	at Stanford	7	7
N18	|	Washington	13	28
N25	|	at UCLA	0	39
D2	●	Notre Dame	9	7

JESSE T. HILL
1951-56 (.722) 45-17-1

1951 7-3-0 (4-2-0)

S22	● |	Washington State	31	21
S29	●	San Diego Navy	41	7
O6	● |	at Washington	20	13
O13	● |	Oregon State	16	14
O20	● |	at California	21	14
O27	●	TCU	28	26
N3	●	Army BRNX	28	6
N10	|	Stanford	20	27
N24	|	UCLA	7	21
D1		Notre Dame	12	19

1952 10-1-0 (6-0-0)

S19	● |	Washington State	35	7
S26	●	Northwestern	31	0
O4	●	Army	22	0
O10	●	San Diego Navy	20	6
O18	● |	Oregon State PORT	28	6
O25	● |	California	10	0
N8	● |	at Stanford	54	7
N15	● |	Washington	33	0
N22	● |	at UCLA	14	12
N29		at Notre Dame	0	9
		ROSE BOWL		
J1	●	Wisconsin	7	0

THE SCHOOLS

1953 6-3-1 (4-2-1)

S19	●	at Washington State	29	13
S26	●	Minnesota	17	7
)2	●	Indiana	27	14
O10	=	at Washington	13	13
O17	●	Oregon State	37	0
O24	●	at California	32	20
O31	●	Oregon *Port*	7	13
N7	●	Stanford	23	20
N21		UCLA	0	13
N28		Notre Dame	14	48

1954 8-4-0 (6-1-0)

S17	●	Washington State	39	0
S24	●	Pittsburgh	27	7
O2	●	at Northwestern	12	7
O8		TCU	7	20
O16	●	Oregon *Port*	24	14
O23	●	California	29	27
O30	●	Oregon State	34	0
N6	●	at Stanford	21	7
N13	●	Washington	41	0
N20	●	at UCLA	0	34
N27		at Notre Dame	17	23
ROSE BOWL				
J1		Ohio State	7	20

1955 6-4-0 (3-3-0)

S17	●	Washington State	50	12
S23	●	Oregon	42	15
S30	●	Texas	19	7
O8	●	at Washington	0	7
O14	●	Wisconsin	33	21
O22	●	at California	33	6
O29	●	at Minnesota	19	25
N5	●	Stanford	20	28
N19	●	UCLA	7	17
N26	●	Notre Dame	42	20

1956 8-2-0 (5-2-0)

S22	●	at Texas	44	20
S28	●	Oregon State	21	13
O6	●	at Wisconsin	13	6
O20	●	Washington	35	7
O27	●	at Stanford	19	27
N3	●	at Washington State	28	12
N10	●	California	20	7
N17	●	Oregon *Port*	0	7
N24	●	at UCLA	10	7
D1	●	Notre Dame	28	20

DON R. CLARK
1957-59 (.450)   13-16-1

1957 1-9-0 (1-6-0)

S21		Oregon State *Port*	0	20
S28		Michigan	6	16
O4		Pittsburgh	14	20
O19		at California	0	12
O26		Washington State	12	13
N2	●	at Washington	19	12
N9		Stanford	7	35
N16		Oregon	7	16
N23		UCLA	9	20
N30		at Notre Dame	12	40

1958 4-5-1 (4-2-1)

S19	●	Oregon State	21	0
S27	●	at Michigan	19	20
O3		North Carolina	7	8
O11		Oregon *Port*	0	25
O18		California	12	14
O25	●	Washington State *Spo*	14	6
N1	●	at Stanford	29	6
N8	●	Washington	21	6
N22	=	at UCLA	15	15
N29		Notre Dame	13	20

1959-1967 AAWU

1959 8-2-0 (3-1-0)

S19	●	Oregon State *Port*	27	6
S25	●	Pittsburgh	23	0
O2	●	Ohio State	17	0
O17	●	at Washington	22	15
O24	●	Stanford	30	28
O31	●	at California	14	7
N7	●	West Virgini	36	0
N14	●	Baylor	17	8
N21		UCLA	3	10
N28		at Notre Dame	6	16

JOHN McKAY
1960-75 (.749)   127-40-8

1960 4-6-0 (3-1-0)

S16		Oregon State	0	14
S24		TCU	6	7
O1		at Ohio State	0	20
O7	●	Georgia	10	3
O15	●	California	27	10
O29	●	at Stanford	21	6
N5		Washington	0	34
N12		at Baylor	14	35
N19	●	at UCLA	17	6
N26		Notre Dame	0	17

1961 4-5-1 (2-1-1)

S22		Georgia Tech	7	27
S29	●	SMU	21	16
O7		Iowa	34	35
O14	●	at Notre Dame	0	30
O21	●	at California	28	14
O28	●	Illinois	14	10
N4	=	at Washington	0	0
N11	●	Stanford	30	15
N18	●	at Pittsburgh	9	10
N25		UCLA	7	10

1962 11-0-0 (4-0-0)

S22	●	Duke	14	7
S29	●	at SMU	33	3
O6	●	at Iowa	7	0
O20	●	California	32	6
O27	●	at Illinois	28	16
N3	●	Washington	14	0
N10	●	at Stanford	39	14
N17	●	Navy	13	6
N24	●	at UCLA	14	3
D1	●	Notre Dame	25	0
ROSE BOWL				
J1	●	Wisconsin	42	37

1963 7-3-0 (3-1-0)

S21	●	at Colorado	14	0
S28	●	Oklahoma	12	17
O4	●	Michigan State	13	10
O12	●	at Notre Dame	14	17
O19	●	Ohio State	32	3
O26	●	at California	36	6
N2	●	at Washington	7	22
N9	●	Stanford	25	11
N15	●	Oregon State	28	22
N30	●	UCLA	26	6

1964 7-3-0 (3-1-0)

S18	●	Colorado	21	0
S26	●	at Oklahoma	40	14
O3		at Michigan State	7	17
O10	●	Texas A&M	31	7
O17		at Ohio State	0	17
O24	●	California	26	21
O31	●	Washington	13	14
N7	●	at Stanford	15	10
N21	●	at UCLA	34	13
N28	●	Notre Dame	20	17

1965 7-2-1 (4-1-0)

S17	=	Minnesota	20	20
S25	●	at Wisconsin	26	6
O1	●	Oregon State	26	12
O9	●	at Washington	34	0
O16	●	Stanford	14	0
O23	●	at Notre Dame	7	28
N6	●	at California	35	0
N13	●	Pittsburgh	28	0
N20	●	UCLA	16	20
N27	●	Wyoming	56	6

1966 7-4-0 (4-1-0)

S17	●	at Texas	10	6
S24	●	Wisconsin	38	3
O1	●	Oregon State *Port*	21	0
O8	●	Washington	17	14
O15	●	at Stanford	21	7
O22	●	Clemson	30	0
O28	●	at Miami, Fla.	7	10
N5	●	California	35	9
N19	●	at UCLA	7	14
N26	●	Notre Dame	0	51
ROSE BOWL				
J2	●	Purdue	13	14

1967 10-1-0 (6-1-0)

S15	●	Washington State	49	0
S23	●	Texas	17	13
S30	●	at Michigan State	21	17
O7	●	Stanford	30	0
O14	●	at Notre Dame	24	7
O21	●	at Washington	23	6
O28	●	Oregon	28	6
N4	●	at California	31	12
N11	●	at Oregon State	0	3
N18	●	UCLA	21	20
ROSE BOWL				
J1	●	Indiana	14	3

1968-PRESENT PAC 10

1968 9-1-1 (6-0-0)

S21	●	at Minnesota	29	20
S28	●	at Northwestern	24	7
O5	●	Miami, Fla.	28	3
O12	●	at Stanford	27	24
O19	●	Washington	14	7
N2	●	at Oregon	20	13
N9	●	California	35	17
N16	●	Oregon State	17	13
N23	●	at UCLA	28	16
N30	=	Notre Dame	21	21
ROSE BOWL				
J1		Ohio State	16	27

1969 10-0-1 (6-0-0)

S20	●	at Nebraska	31	21
S27	●	Northwestern	48	6
O4	●	at Oregon State	31	7
O11	●	Stanford	26	24
O18	=	at Notre Dame	14	14
O25	●	Georgia Tech	29	18
N1	●	at California	14	9
N8	●	Washington State	28	7
N15	●	at Washington	16	7
N22	●	UCLA	14	12
ROSE BOWL				
J1	●	Michigan	10	3

1970 6-4-1 (3-4-0)

S12	●	Alabama *Birm*	42	21
S19	=	Nebraska	21	21
S26	●	at Iowa	48	0
O3	●	Oregon State	45	13
O10	●	at Stanford	14	24
O17	●	Washington	28	25
O24	●	at Oregon	7	10
O31	●	California	10	13
N7	●	Washington State *Spo*	70	33
N21	●	at UCLA	20	45
N28	●	Notre Dame	38	28

1971 6-4-1 (3-2-1)

S10	●	Alabama	10	17
S18	●	at Rice	24	0
S25	●	Illinois	28	0
O2		at Oklahoma	20	33
O9		Oregon	23	28
O16		Stanford	18	33
O23	●	at Notre Dame	28	14
O30		at California	28	0
N6		Washington State	30	20
N13		at Washington	13	12
N20	=	UCLA	7	7

1972 12-0-0 (7-0-0)

S9	●	Arkansas *LR*	31	10
S16	●	Oregon State	51	6
S23	●	at Illinois	55	20
S30	●	Michigan State	51	6
O7	●	at Stanford	30	21
O14	●	California	42	14
O21	●	Washington	34	7
O28	●	at Oregon	18	0
N4	●	Washington State *Sea*	44	3
N18	●	at UCLA	24	7
D2	●	Notre Dame	45	23
ROSE BOWL				
J1	●	Ohio State	42	17

1973 9-2-1 (7-0-0)

S15	●	Arkansas	17	0
S22	●	at Georgia Tech	23	6
S29	=	Oklahoma	7	7
O6	●	at Oregon State	21	7
O13	●	Washington State	46	35
O20	●	Oregon	31	10
O27	●	at Notre Dame	14	23
N3	●	at California	50	14
N10	●	Stanford	27	26
N17	●	at Washington	42	19
N24	●	UCLA	23	13
ROSE BOWL				
J1		Ohio State	21	42

1974 10-1-1 (6-0-1)

S14	●	Arkansas *LR*	7	22
S28	●	at Pittsburgh	16	7
O5	●	Iowa	41	3
O12	●	Washington State *Spo*	54	7
O19	●	at Oregon	16	7
O26	●	Oregon State	31	10
N2	=	California	15	15
N9	●	at Stanford	34	10
N16	●	Washington	42	11
N23	●	at UCLA	34	9
N30	●	Notre Dame	55	24
ROSE BOWL				
J1	●	Ohio State	18	17

1975 8-4-0 (3-4-0)

S12	●	Duke	35	7
S19	●	Oregon State	24	7
S27	●	Purdue	19	6
O4	●	at Iowa	27	16
O11	●	Washington State	28	10
O18	●	Oregon	17	3
O25	●	at Notre Dame	24	17
N1	●	at California	14	28
N8	●	Stanford	10	13
N15	●	at Washington	7	8
N28	●	UCLA	22	25
LIBERTY BOWL				
D22	●	Texas A&M	20	0

JOHN ROBINSON
1976-82, '93-97 (.741)   104-35-4

1976 11-1-0 (7-0-0)

S11		Missouri	25	46
S18	●	at Oregon	53	0
S25	●	at Purdue	31	13
O2		Iowa	55	0
O9		Washington State *Sea*	23	14
O23		Oregon State	56	0
O30		California	20	6
N6	●	at Stanford	48	24
N13		Washington	20	3
N20	●	at UCLA	24	14
N27		Notre Dame	17	13
ROSE BOWL				
J1	●	Michigan	14	6

1977 8-4-0 (5-2-0)

S10	●	at Missouri	27	10
S17	●	at Oregon State	17	10
S24		TCU	51	0
S30		Washington State	41	7
O8		Alabama	20	21
O15	●	Oregon	33	15
O22		at Notre Dame	19	49
O29		at California	14	17
N5		Stanford	49	0
N12		at Washington	10	28
N25		UCLA	29	27
BLUEBONNET BOWL				
D31	●	Texas A&M	47	28

1978 12-1-0 (6-1-0)

S9		Texas Tech	17	9
S16	●	at Oregon	37	10
S23	●	Alabama *Birm*	24	14
S29		Michigan State	30	9
O14		at Arizona State	7	20
O21	●	Oregon State	38	7
O28		California	42	17
N4	●	at Stanford	13	7
N11		Washington	28	10
N18	●	at UCLA	17	10
N25		Notre Dame	27	25
D2	●	at Hawaii	21	5
ROSE BOWL				
J1	●	Michigan	17	10

1979   11-0-1 (6-0-1)

S8 ●	Texas Tech	21	7
S15 ● |	at Oregon State	42	5
S22 ●	at Minnesota	48	14
S29 ●	at LSU	17	12
O6 = |	Washington State	50	21
O13 =	Stanford	21	21
O20 ●	at Notre Dame	42	23
O27 ● |	at California	24	14
N3 ●	Arizona	34	7
N10 ● |	at Washington	24	17
N24 ● |	UCLA	49	14
ROSE BOWL			
J1	Ohio State	17	16

1980   8-2-1 (4-2-1)

S13 ●	at Tennessee	20	17
S20 ●	South Carolina	23	13
S27 ●	at Minnesota	24	7
O4 ● |	Arizona State	23	21
O11 ● |	at Arizona	27	10
O18 = |	at Oregon	7	7
N1 ● |	California	60	7
N8 ● |	at Stanford	34	9
N15 ●	Washington	10	20
N22 ●	at UCLA	17	20
D6 ●	Notre Dame	20	3

1981   9-3-0 (5-2-0)

S12 ●	Tennessee	43	7
S19 ●	at Indiana	21	0
S26 ●	Oklahoma	28	24
O3 ● |	at Oregon State	56	22
O10 ●	Arizona	10	13
O17 ● |	at Stanford	25	17
O24 ●	Notre Dame	14	7
O31 ● |	Washington State	41	17
N7 ● |	at California	21	3
N14 ●	at Washington	3	13
N21 ● |	UCLA	22	21
FIESTA BOWL			
J1	Penn State	10	26

1982   8-3-0 (5-2-0)

S11 ●	at Florida	9	17
S18 ●	Indiana	28	7
S25 ●	at Oklahoma	12	0
O2 ● |	Oregon	38	7
O16 ● |	at Stanford	41	21
O23 ● |	Oregon State	38	0
O30 ●	at Arizona State	10	17
N6 ● |	California	42	0
N13 ● |	at Arizona	48	41
N20 ●	at UCLA	19	20
N27 ● |	Notre Dame	17	13

1983   4-6-1 (4-3-0)

S10 =	Florida	19	19
S17 ● |	at Oregon State	33	10
S24 ●	Kansas	20	26
O1 ●	at South Carolina	14	38
O8 ● |	Washington State	38	17
O15 ●	Arizona State	14	34
O22 ●	at Notre Dame	6	27
O29 ● |	at California	19	9
N5 ● |	Stanford	30	7
N12 ●	at Washington	0	24
N19 ● |	UCLA	17	27

1984   9-3-0 (7-1-0)

S8 ●	Utah State	42	7
S22 ● |	at Arizona State	6	3
S29 ●	LSU	3	23
O6 ● |	at Washington State	29	27
O13 ● |	at Oregon	19	9
O20 ●	Arizona	17	14
O27 ● |	California	31	7
N3 ● |	at Stanford	20	11
N10 ● |	Washington	16	7
N17 ● |	at UCLA	10	29
N24 ●	Notre Dame	7	19
ROSE BOWL			
J1 ●	Ohio State	20	17

1985   6-6-0 (5-3-0)

S7 ●	at Illinois	20	10
S21 ● |	Baylor	13	20
S28 ●	at Arizona State	0	24
O5 ● |	Oregon State	63	0
O19 ● |	Stanford	30	6
O26 ●	at Notre Dame	3	37
N2 ● |	Washington State	31	13
N9 ●	at California	6	14
N16 ●	at Washington	17	20
N23 ● |	UCLA	17	13
N30 ●	Oregon TOK	20	6
ALOHA BOWL			
D28	Alabama	3	24

1986   7-5-0 (5-3-0)

S13 ●	Illinois	31	16
S20 ●	at Baylor	17	14
S27 ● |	Washington	20	10
O4 ● |	Oregon	35	21
O11 ● |	at Washington State	14	34
O18 ● |	Arizona State	20	29
O25 ● |	at Stanford	10	0
N1 ● |	at Arizona	20	13
N15 ● |	California	28	3
N22 ● |	at UCLA	25	45
N29 ●	Notre Dame	37	38
CITRUS BOWL			
J1	Auburn	7	16

1987   8-4-0 (7-1-0)

S5 ●	at Michigan State	13	27
S19 ●	Boston College	23	17
S26 ● |	at California	31	14
O3 ● |	Oregon State	48	14
O10 ● |	at Oregon	27	34
O17 ● |	at Washington	37	23
O24 ●	at Notre Dame	15	26
O31 ● |	Washington State	42	7
N7 ● |	Stanford	39	24
N14 ●	Arizona	12	10
N21 ● |	UCLA	17	13
ROSE BOWL			
J1	Michigan State	17	20

1988   10-2-0 (8-0-0)

S1 ●	at Boston College	34	7
S10 ● |	at Stanford	24	20
S24 ● |	Oklahoma	23	7
O1 ● |	at Arizona	38	15
O8 ● |	Oregon	42	14
O15 ● |	Washington	28	27
O29 ● |	at Oregon State	41	20
N5 ● |	California	35	3
N12 ● |	at Arizona State	50	0
N19 ● |	at UCLA	31	22
N26 ●	Notre Dame	10	27
ROSE BOWL			
J2 ●	Michigan	14	22

1989   9-2-1 (6-0-1)

S4 ●	Illinois	13	14
S16 ● |	Utah State	66	10
S23 ● |	Ohio State	42	3
S30 ● |	at Washington State	18	17
O7 ● |	Washington	24	16
O14 ● |	at California	31	15
O21 ● |	at Notre Dame	24	28
O28 ● |	Stanford	19	0
N4 ● |	Oregon State	48	6
N11 ● |	at Arizona	24	3
N18 = |	UCLA	10	10
ROSE BOWL			
J1 ●	Michigan	17	10

1990   8-4-1 (5-2-1)

A31 ●	Syracuse ERUT	34	16
S15 ●	Penn State	19	14
S22 ●	at Washington	0	31
S29 ● |	at Ohio State	35	26
O6 ● |	Washington State	30	17
O13 ● |	at Stanford	37	22
O20 ● |	Arizona	26	35
O27 ● |	at Arizona State	13	6
N3 = |	California	31	31
N10 ● |	at Oregon State	56	7
N17 ● |	at UCLA	45	42
N24 ●	Notre Dame	6	10
SUN BOWL			
D31	Michigan State	16	17

1991   3-8-0 (2-6-0)

S2 ●	Memphis	10	24
S14 ●	Penn State	21	10
S21 ● |	Arizona State	25	32
S28 ●	at Oregon	30	14
O12 ● |	at Washington State	34	27
O19 ● |	Stanford	21	24
O26 ●	at Notre Dame	20	24
N2 ● |	at California	30	52
N9 ● |	Washington	3	14
N16 ● |	at Arizona	14	31
N23 ● |	UCLA	21	24

1992   6-5-1 (5-3-0)

S5 =	at San Diego State	31	31
S19 ●	at Oklahoma	20	10
O3 ● |	at Washington	10	17
O10 ● |	Oregon	32	10
O17 ● |	California	27	24
O24 ● |	Washington State	31	21
O31 ● |	at Arizona State	23	13
N7 ● |	at Stanford	9	23
N14 ● |	Arizona	14	7
N21 ● |	at UCLA	37	38
N28 ●	Notre Dame	23	31
FREEDOM BOWL			
D29	Fresno State	7	24

1993   8-5-0 (6-2-0)

A29 ●	North Carolina ANA	9	31
S4 ●	Houston	49	7
S11 ●	at Penn State	20	21
S25 ● |	Washington State	34	3
O2 ● |	at Arizona	7	38
O9 ● |	at Oregon	24	13
O16 ● |	Oregon State	34	9
O23 ●	at Notre Dame	13	31
O30 ● |	at California	42	14
N6 ● |	Stanford	45	20
N13 ● |	at Washington	22	17
N20 ● |	UCLA	21	27
FREEDOM BOWL			
D30 ●	Utah	28	21

1994   8-3-1 (6-2-0)

S3 ● |	Washington	24	17
S10 ● |	at Penn State	14	38
S24 ● |	Baylor	37	27
O1 ● |	Oregon	7	22
O8 ● |	at Oregon State	27	19
O15 ● |	at Stanford	27	20
O22 ● |	California	61	0
N5 ● |	at Washington State	23	10
N12 ● |	Arizona	45	28
N19 ● |	at UCLA	19	31
N26 = |	Notre Dame	17	17
COTTON BOWL			
J2 ●	Texas Tech	55	14

1995   9-2-1 (6-1-1)

S9 ●	San Jose St	45	7
S16 ● |	Houston	45	10
S23 ● |	at Arizona	31	10
S30 ● |	Arizona State	31	0
O7 ● |	at California	26	16
O14 ● |	Washington State	26	14
O21 ● |	at Notre Dame	10	38
O28 = |	at Washington	21	21
N4 ● |	Stanford	31	30
N11 ● |	at Oregon State	28	10
N18 ● |	UCLA	20	24
ROSE BOWL			
J1 ●	Northwestern	41	32

1996   6-6 (3-5)

A25 ●	Penn State ERUT	7	24
S7 ●	at Illinois	55	3
S14 ● |	Oregon State	46	17
S21 ●	at Houston	26	9
O5 ●	California	15	22
O12 ● |	Arizona	14	7
O19 ● |	at Arizona State	35	48
O26 ●	at Washington State	29	24
N2 ● |	Washington	10	21
N9 ● |	at Stanford	20	24
N23 ● |	at UCLA	41	48
N30 ●	Notre Dame	27	20

1997   6-5 (4-4)

S6 ●	Florida State	7	14
S13 ● |	Washington State	21	28
S27 ● |	at California	27	17
O4 ●	Nevada-Las Vegas	35	21
O11 ●	at Arizona State	7	35
O18 ●	at Notre Dame	20	17
O25 ● |	Oregon	24	22
N1 ●	at Washington	0	27
N8 ● |	Stanford	45	21
N15 ● |	at Oregon State	23	0
N22 ● |	UCLA	24	31

1998   8-5 (5-3)

A30 ●	Purdue	27	17
S12 ● |	San Diego State	35	6
S19 ● |	Oregon State	40	20
S26 ●	at Florida State	10	30
O3 ● |	Arizona State	35	24
O10 ● |	California	31	32
O17 ● |	at Washington State	42	14
O24 ●	at Oregon	13	17
O31 ● |	Washington	33	10
N7 ● |	at Stanford	34	9
N21 ● |	at UCLA	17	34
N28 ● |	Notre Dame	10	0
SUN BOWL			
D31	TCU	19	28

1999   6-6 (3-5)

S4 ●	at Hawaii	62	7
S18 ● |	San Diego State	24	21
S25 ●	at Oregon	30	33
O2 ● |	Oregon State	37	29
O9 ●	at Arizona	24	31
O16 ●	at Notre Dame	24	25
O23 ●	Stanford	31	35
O30 ● |	at California	7	17
N6 ●	Arizona State	16	26
N13 ● |	at Washington State	31	28
N20 ● |	UCLA	17	7
N26 ● |	Louisiana Tech	45	19

2000   5-7 (2-6)

A27 ●	Penn State ERUT	29	5
S9 ●	Colorado	17	14
S23 ●	San Jose State	34	24
S30 ●	at Oregon State	21	31
O7 ●	Arizona	15	31
O14 ●	Oregon	17	28
O21 ●	at Stanford	30	32
O28 ●	California	16	28
N4 ●	at Arizona State	44	38
N11 ●	Washington State	27	33
N18 ● |	at UCLA	38	35
N25 ●	Notre Dame	21	38

2001   6-6 (5-3)

S1 ●	San Jose State	21	10
S8 ●	Kansas State	6	10
S22 ● |	at Oregon	22	24
S29 ● |	Stanford	16	21
O6 ●	at Washington	24	27
O13 ● |	Arizona State	48	17
O20 ● |	at Notre Dame	16	27
O27 ● |	at Arizona	41	34
N3 ● |	Oregon State	16	13
N10 ● |	at California	55	14
N17 ● |	UCLA	27	0
LAS VEGAS BOWL			
D25	Utah	6	10

2002   11-2 (7-1)

S2 ●	Auburn	24	17
S14 ●	at Colorado	40	3
S21 ●	at Kansas State	20	27
S28 ● |	Oregon State	22	0
O5 ●	at Washington State	27	30
O12 ● |	California	30	28
O19 ● |	Washington	41	21
O26 ● |	at Oregon	44	33
N9 ● |	at Stanford	49	17
N16 ● |	Arizona State	34	13
N23 ● |	at UCLA	52	21
N30 ●	Notre Dame	44	13
ORANGE BOWL			
J2 ●	Iowa	38	17

2003   12-1   (7-1)

A30	●	at Auburn	23	0
S6	●	Brigham Young	35	18
S13	●	Hawaii	61	32
S27	|	at California	31	34
O4	● |	at Arizona State	37	17
O11	● |	Stanford	44	21
O18	● |	at Notre Dame	45	14
O25	● |	at Washington	43	23
N1	● |	Washington State	43	16
N15	● |	at Arizona	45	0
N22	● |	UCLA	47	22
D6	● |	Oregon State	52	28

ROSE BOWL

J1	●	Michigan	28	14

2004   13-0   (8-0)

A28	●	Virginia Tech *LAN*	24	13
S11	●	Colorado State	49	0
S18	●	at Brigham Young	42	10
S25	● |	at Stanford	31	28
O9	● |	California	23	17
O16	● |	Arizona State	45	7
O23	● |	Washington	38	0
O30	● |	at Washington State	42	12
N6	● |	at Oregon State	28	20
N13	● |	Arizona	49	9
N27	●	Notre Dame	41	10
D4	● |	at UCLA	29	24

ORANGE BOWL

J4	●	Oklahoma	55	19

SOUTHERN CAL ANNUAL STATISTICAL LEADERS

YR	RUSHING	YDS	ATT	AVG	PASSING	ATT	CMP	PCT	YDS	RECEIVING	REC	YDS	AVG
1925	Mort Kaer	576	105	5.5		NA	NA	NA	NA		NA	NA	NA
1926	Mort Kaer	852	155	5.5		NA	NA	NA	NA		NA	NA	NA
1927	Morley Drury	1,163	223	5.2		NA	NA	NA	NA		NA	NA	NA
1928	Don Williams	681	173	3.9		NA	NA	NA	NA		NA	NA	NA
1929	Russ Saunders	972	185	5.3		NA	NA	NA	NA		NA	NA	NA
1930	Orv Mohler	983	145	6.8		NA	NA	NA	NA		NA	NA	NA
1931	Gus Shaver	936	199	4.7		NA	NA	NA	NA		NA	NA	NA
1932	Cotton Warburton	420	115	3.7		NA	NA	NA	NA		NA	NA	NA
1933	Cotton Warburton	885	149	5.9		NA	NA	NA	NA		NA	NA	NA
1934	Inky Wotkyns	588	133	4.4		NA	NA	NA	NA		NA	NA	NA
1935	Nick Pappas	414	102	4.1		NA	NA	NA	NA		NA	NA	NA
1936	Davie Davis	501	141	3.6		NA	NA	NA	NA		NA	NA	NA
1937	Amby Schindler	599	134	4.5	Grenny Lansdell	63	28	.44	310	Bill Sangster	10	125	12.5
1938	Grenny Lansdell	462	118	3.9	Grenny Lansdell	112	44	.39	458	Bob Hoffman	11	112	10.2
1939	Grenny Lansdell	742	154	4.8	Grenny Lansdell	85	42	.49	479	Bob Peoples	16	128	8.0
1940	Bobby Robertson	667	146	4.6	Bob Peoples	63	21	.33	479	Al Krueger	9	98	10.9
1941	Bobby Robertson	483	120	4.0	Bobby Robertson	73	33	.45	530	Paul Taylor	10	149	14.9
1942	Mickey McCardle	413	96	4.3	Mickey McCardle	55	24	.44	395	Ralph Heywood	12	205	17.1
1943	Eddie Saenz	445	71	6.3	Jim Hardy	71	33	.46	516	Ralph Heywood	11	196	17.8
1944	Don Burnside*	428	70	6.1	Jim Hardy	117	58	.50	739	Gordon Gray	12	181	15.1
1945	Ted Tannehill	574	99	5.8	Jerry Bowman	64	29	.45	401	Harry Adelman	12	127	10.6
1946	Art Battle	296	69	4.3	Mickey McCardle	74	39	.53	490	Gordon Gray	13	168	12.9
1947	Don Doll	246	57	4.3	Jim Powers	94	50	.53	603	Mickey McCardle	17	115	6.8
1948	Don Doll	265	67	4.0	Jim Powers	106	49	.46	511	Don Doll	15	157	10.5
1949	Bill Martin	357	128	2.8	Jim Powers	148	87	.59	1,215	Pat Duff	21	183	8.7
1950	Al Carmichael	514	103	5.0	Wilbur Robertson	106	50	.47	481	Hal Hatfield	22	192	8.7
1951	Frank Gifford	841	195	4.3	Dean Schneider	106	48	.45	606	Dean Schneider	13	161	12.4
1952	Leon Sellers	386	103	3.7	Jim Sears	102	48	.47	712	Tom Nickoloff	25	372	14.9
1953	Aramis Dandoy	578	113	5.1	Aramis Dandoy	55	24	.44	242	Tom Nickoloff	16	214	13.4
1954	Jon Arnett	601	96	6.3	Jim Contratto	79	32	.41	702	Leon Clarke	13	232	17.8
1955	Jon Arnett	672	141	4.8	Jim Contratto	52	22	.42	406	Leon Clarke	15	215	14.3
1956	C. R. Roberts	775	140	5.5	Frank Hall	23	10	.43	196	Tony Ortega	7	223	31.9
1957	Rex Johnston	304	74	4.1	Tom Maudlin	100	48	.48	552	Larry Boies	14	144	10.3
1958	Don Buford	306	64	4.8	Tom Maudlin	95	41	.43	535	Hillard Hill	11	319	29.0
1959	Jerry Traynham	583	123	4.7	Ben Charles	46	20	.43	348	Luther Hayes	9	179	19.9
1960	Hal Tobin	318	61	5.2	Bill-Nelsen	72	29	.40	446	Marlin McKeever	15	218	14.5
1961	Ben Wilson	619	139	4.5	Bill Nelsen	86	39	.45	683	Hal Bedsole	27	525	19.4
1962	Willie Brown	574	88	6.5	Pete Beathard	107	54	.50	948	Hal Bedsole	33	827	25.1
1963	Mike Garrett	833	128	6.5	Pete Beathard	140	66	.47	944	Willie Brown	34	448	13.2
1964	Mike Garrett	948	217	4.4	Craig Fertig	209	109	.52	1,671	Fred Hill	33	436	13.2
1965	Mike Garrett	1,440	267	5.4	Troy Winslow	127	78	.61	1,019	Dave Moton	29	493	17.0
1966	Don McCall	560	127	4.4	Troy Winslow	138	82	.59	1,023	Ron Drake	52	607	11.7
1967	O.J. Simpson	1,543	291	5.3	Steve Sogge	151	75	.50	1,032	Earl McCullouch	30	540	18.0
1968	O.J. Simpson	1,880	383	4.9	Steve Sogge	207	122	.59	1,454	Jim Lawrence	26	386	14.8
1969	Clarence Davis	1,351	297	4.5	Jimmy Jones	209	88	.42	1,220	Sam Dickerson	24	473	19.7
1970	Clarence Davis	972	214	4.5	Jimmy Jones	234	121	.52	1,877	Bob Chandler	41	590	14.4
1971	Lou Harris	801	167	4.8	Jimmy Jones	161	89	.55	995	Lynn Swann	27	305	11.3
1972	Anthony Davis	1,191	207	5.8	Mike Rae	199	114	.57	1,754	Charles Young	29	470	16.2
1973	Anthony Davis	1,112	276	4.0	Pat Haden	247	137	.55	1,832	Lynn Swann	42	714	17.0
1974	Anthony Davis	1,421	301	4.7	Pat Haden	149	70	.47	988	Johnny McKay	34	550	16.2
1975	Ricky Bell	1,957	385	5.1	Vince Evans	112	35	.31	695	Randy Simmrin	26	478	18.4
1976	Ricky Bell	1,433	280	5.1	Vince Evans	177	95	.54	1,440	Shelton Diggs	37	655	17.7
1977	Charles White	1,478	285	5.2	Rob Hertel	245	132	.54	2,145	Randy Simmrin	41	840	20.5
1978	Charles White	1,859	374	5.0	Paul McDonald	203	115	.57	1,690	Calvin Sweeney	32	644	20.1
1979	Charles White	2,050	332	6.2	Paul McDonald	264	164	.62	2,223	Danny Garcia	29	492	17.0
1980	Marcus Allen	1,563	354	4.4	Gordon Adams	179	104	.58	1,237	Marcus Allen	30	231	7.7
1981	Marcus Allen	2,427	433	5.6	John Mazur	194	93	.48	1,128	Marcus Allen	34	256	7.5
1982	Todd Spencer	596	141	4.2	Sean Salisbury	142	82	.58	1,062	Jeff Simmons	56	973	17.4
1983	Michael Harper	685	151	4.5	Sean Salisbury	248	142	.57	1,882	Hank Norman	31	407	13.1
1984	Fred Crutcher	1,155	307	3.8	Tim Green	224	116	.52	1,448	Hank Norman	39	643	16.5
1985	Ryan Knight	732	195	3.8	Sean Salisbury	172	98	.57	1,180	Joe Cormier	44	409	9.3
1986	Ryan Knight	536	148	3.6	Rodney Peete	305	160	.52	2,138	Ken Henry	43	807	18.8
1987	Steven Webster	1,109	239	4.6	Rodney Peete	332	197	.59	2,709	Erik Affholter	44	649	14.8
1988	Aaron Emanuel	545	108	5.0	Rodney Peete	359	223	.62	2,812	Erik Affholter	68	952	14.0
1989	Ricky Ervins	1,395	269	5.2	Todd Marinovich	352	219	.62	2,578	John Jackson	62	964	15.5
1990	Mazio Royster	1,168	235	5.0	Todd Marinovich	322	196	.61	2,423	Gary Wellman	66	1,015	15.4
1991	Deon Strother	614	129	4.8	Reggie Perry	255	131	.51	1,574	Johnnie Morton	49	662	13.5
1992	Estrus Crayton	700	183	3.8	Rob Johnson	285	163	.57	2,118	Curtis Conway	49	764	15.6
1993	Shawn Walters	711	156	4.6	Rob Johnson	449	308	.69	3,630	Johnnie Morton	88	1,520	17.3
1994	Shawn Walters	976	193	5.1	Rob Johnson	276	186	.67	2,499	Keyshawn Johnson	66	1,362	20.6
1995	Delon Washington	1,109	236	4.7	Brad Otton	256	159	.62	1,923	Keyshawn Johnson	102	1,434	14.1
1996	LaVale Woods	601	119	5.1	Brad Otton	370	196	.53	2,649	Chris Miller	43	793	18.4
1997	Delon Washington	444	125	3.6	John Fox	280	153	.55	1,940	Billy Miller	56	649	11.6
1998	Chad Morton	985	199	4.9	Carson Palmer	235	130	.55	1,755	Billy Miller	49	623	12.7
1999	Chad Morton	1,141	262	4.4	Mike Van Raaphorst	258	139	.54	1,758	Windrell Hayes	55	720	13.1
2000	Sultan McCullough	1,163	227	5.1	Carson Palmer	415	228	.55	2,914	Kareem Kelly	55	796	14.5
2001	Sultan McCullough	410	115	3.6	Carson Palmer	377	221	.59	2,717	Kareem Kelly	49	801	16.3
2002	Sultan McCullough	814	179	4.5	Carson Palmer	489	309	.63	3,942	Mike Williams	81	1,265	15.6
2003	LenDale White	754	141	5.3	Matt Leinart	402	255	.63	3,556	Mike Williams	95	1,314	13.8
2004	LenDale White	1,103	203	5.4	Matt Leinart	412	269	.65	3,322	Dwayne Jarrett	55	849	15.4

* Later Don Doll

Receiving leaders by receptions
All statistics include postseason

SOUTHERN MISS

BY KEVIN GLEASON

So WHERE DOES SOUTHERN MISSISSIPPI stand with the tradition-rich football schools of the South? The Golden Eagles may not be in the class of giants such as Alabama, Georgia and Tennessee, but they have carved a niche in the gridiron nobility nonetheless. Football at the Hattiesburg school dates back to 1912, and Southern Miss has produced one of the best quarterbacks in the sport's history in Brett Favre, who was the Golden Eagles' gunslinger from 1987 to 1990. Southern Miss has won four Conference USA titles and appeared in seven bowl games since joining the league in 1996. In 2003, undefeated TCU was threatening to bust up the BCS system until Southern Miss beat the Horned Frogs 40-28 in the next-to-last week of the season. The team went on to win the C-USA title that year under Jeff Bower, whose first full season was in 1991. He has proceeded to turn Southern Miss into a conference power that is respected across the nation.

TRADITION They call it the Eagle Walk: players stroll from campus to the locker room at M.M. Roberts Stadium as fans line both sides of the route. Then they walk under the stands on the east side of the stadium, through an area decorated with plaques honoring former standouts and bowl teams. Members of the school's ROTC shoot off a cannon as the players take the field.

BEST PLAYER Kiln, Miss., native Favre was recruited by Southern Miss as a defensive back and started his freshman year in 1987 seventh on the quarterback depth chart. He became the Eagles' starter by Game 3 of that season, and his exploits made him a folk hero in Hattiesburg long before he achieved such status in Green Bay. Favre led the Golden Eagles to 29 wins from 1987 to 1990 and set school career records for passing yards (7,695), pass attempts (1,169), completions (613) and completions in a season (206) and tied for most touchdowns (52). He evolved into one of the best quarterbacks in NFL history with the Packers, leading them to victory in Super Bowl XXXI. Favre is the only three-time NFL MVP (1995-97). He still owns a 460-acre home in Hattiesburg, where he spends much of the off-season fishing and hunting.

BEST COACH Bower's expansive list of achievements at Southern Miss includes a 96–67–1 record and three C-USA Coach of the Year honors (1997, 1999, 2003). Southern Miss was ranked among the nation's top 11 teams in total defense from 2001 to 2003. The Golden Eagles went to four straight bowl games (1997-2000) under Bower, who began his tenure in the 1990 All-

---

PROFILE

University of Southern Mississippi
Hattiesburg, Miss.
Founded in 1910
Enrollment: 12,371
Colors: Black and Gold
Nickname: Golden Eagles
Stadium: M.M. Roberts Stadium
    Opened in 1938
    Momentum Turf; 33,000 capacity
First football game: 1912
All-time record: 503–337–27 (.596)
Bowl record: 6–7
Conference USA championships: 4 (3 outright)
First-round NFL draftees: 4
Website: www.southernmiss.com

THE BEST OF TIMES

Southern Miss has won four Conference USA titles under Jeff Bower since joining the league in 1996.

THE WORST OF TIMES

From 1925 to 1931, the program endured seven straight losing seasons and went 17–35–4.

CONFERENCE

Southern Miss was a charter member of Conference USA in 1996 and has won four league titles. The Golden Eagles were independent from 1952 to 1995.

DISTINGUISHED ALUMNI

Jimmy Buffett, singer/songwriter, author; Jim "Peanuts" Davenport, San Francisco Giants manager; Gary Grubbs, actor

FIGHT SONG

SOUTHERN TO THE TOP
Southern Mississippi to the top, to the top!
So lift your voices high,
Show them the reason why,
The Southern Spirit will never stop.
Fight! Fight! Fight!
Southern Mississippi all the way,
banners high
And we will Fight! Fight! Fight! to victory,
Hear our battle cry!

Brett Favre started his freshman year seventh on the quarterback depth chart.

American Bowl, and was nationally ranked for 21 straight weeks during 1999 and 2000. The school had begun to have success in the 1980s, but Bower has taken the program to a level worthy of national attention.

BEST TEAM Led by quarterback Reggie Collier, the 1981 squad was ranked as high as No. 9 in the nation and finished the year 9–2–1. The Golden Eagles beat Florida State and Mississippi State and tied Alabama during the regular season. Coached by Bobby Collins, the team fell to Missouri 19-17 in the Tangerine Bowl.

BIGGEST GAME Southern Miss beat No. 4 Mississippi and quarterback Archie Manning 30-14 on Oct. 17, 1970. The stunner put Southern Miss on the map, derailed the Rebels' national title hopes and put a blemish on Manning's Heisman campaign (Jim Plunkett of Stanford won the award). The Rebels remain the highest-ranked opponent Southern Miss has defeated.

BIGGEST UPSET Southern Miss shocked Alabama 38-29 in Tuscaloosa on Nov. 13, 1982, to end the Crimson Tide's 56-game home winning streak. Equally memorable is the fact that it served as Bear Bryant's final loss. Southern Miss

finished 7–4 that year under Jim Carmody, now a scout for the Arizona Cardinals.

HEARTBREAKER On Sept. 15, 1990, in front of 79,812 fans in Athens, Ga., Georgia beat Southern Miss 18-17 when Jim Taylor's potential game-winning 42-yard field goal in the final minute bounced off the right upright.

STADIUM Affectionately known as The Rock at Southern Miss, cozy M.M. Roberts Stadium has a seating capacity of 33,000, with plans to expand it to 41,300. The stadium history dates back to Oct. 29, 1932, when State Teachers College beat Spring Hill College 12-0 in front of 4,000 fans plopped on wooden bleachers. The first version of the current stadium opened in 1938. In 1976, Southern Miss named its new $6.3 million football stadium after M.M. Roberts, a former member of the Board of Trustees of State Institutions of Higher Learning. In 1989, the playing field had a new irrigation system installed. The Robert "Ace" Cleveland Press Box has been renovated, chair-back seating has been added to the west side of the stadium and a state-of-the-art Daktronics scoreboard was added prior to the 1998 season.

DISPUTE Trailing East Carolina 21-20 with eight seconds left on Nov. 1, 1986, Southern Miss got possession of the

RECORDS

RUSHING YARDS

GAME	
304	Sam Dejarnette vs. Florida State, Sept. 25, 1982 (43 att.)
SEASON	
1,545	Sam Dejarnette, 1982 (311 att.)
CAREER	
3,595	Ben Garry, 1974-77 (723 att.)

PASSING YARDS

GAME	
400	Jeff Kelly vs. Tulane, Nov. 17, 2001 (23 of 31)
SEASON	
2,680	Lee Roberts, 1998 (185 of 325)
CAREER	
7,695	Brett Favre, 1987-90 (613 of 1,169)

RECEIVING YARDS

GAME	
260	Kendrick Lee vs. Houston, Nov. 9, 1996 (10 rec.)
SEASON	
1,186	Sherrod Gideon, 1998 (66 rec.)
CAREER	
3,214	Sherrod Gideon, 1996-99 (193 rec.)

POINTS

GAME	
24	Seven different players; most recently by Derrick Nix vs. Memphis, Nov. 14, 1998 (4 TDs)
SEASON	
120	Sammy Winder, 1980 (20 TDs)
CAREER	
234	Sammy Winder, 1978-81 (39 TDs)

CONSENSUS ALL-AMERICANS

1953	Hugh Pepper, B
1956	Don Owens, T
1958	Robert Yencho, E
1959	Hugh McInnis, E

ball on its 18-yard line. Quarterback Andrew Anderson threw a pass that was caught by Lyneal Austin at the Southern Miss 40. He ran the ball to East Carolina's 10 and lateralled to fullback Randolph Brown, who ran it in for a touchdown. Southern Miss was flagged for an illegal forward lateral and penalized from the point of the foul. Rex Banks kicked a 31-yard field goal to give the Golden Eagles a 23-21 win.

NICKNAME Southern Miss sported several different nicknames before undergoing an identity change in November 1972. Some 400 suggestions were made during a five-month campaign to determine a new mascot. An ad hoc committee of alumni, students and friends of Southern Miss narrowed the suggestions to five: Golden Eagles, Golden Raiders, Southerners, Timber Wolves and War Lords—all of which appeared on a ballot. After two schoolwide votes, Golden Eagles won by a 60% majority.

MASCOT A student leads Southern Miss into action wearing a Golden Eagles costume complete with beak and tail. The Golden Eagle often wears a straw hat and dons a No. 1 jersey.

ALL-CENTURY TEAM

Selected in 2001 by fans and a committee of players, administrators and coaches.

OFFENSE

1952-54	Hamp Cook,	OG
1975-77	Amos Fowler,	OG
1953-56	Don Owens,	OT
1980-83	Glen Howe,	OT
1956-58	Richard Johnston,	C
1977-80	Marvin Harvey,	TE
1948-49	Cliff Coggin,	E
1955-58	Bob Yencho,	E
1980-83	Louis Lipps,	WR
1996-99	Sherrod Gideon,	WR
1979-82	Reggie Collier,	QB
1987-90	Brett Favre,	QB
1951-53	Bucky McElroy,	FB
1947-50	Bubba Phillips,	RB
1952-53	Hugh Laurin Pepper,	RB
1978-81	Sammy Winder,	RB
1998-2002	Derrick Nix,	RB
1981-83	Steve Clark,	PK
1986-88	James Henry,	PR
1989-91	Tony Smith,	KR

DEFENSE

1971-73	Fred Cook,	DE
1996-99	Adalius Thomas,	DE
1954-56	P.W. Underwood,	DL
1960-62	Don Hultz,	DL
1980-83	Jerald Baylis,	DL
1981-84	Richard Byrd,	DL
1960-62	Harold Hays,	LB
1963-65	Doug Satcher,	LB
1964-66	Ken Avery,	LB
1976-79	Ronald "Clump" Taylor,	LB
1962-63	Tommy Walters,	DB
1977-80	Hanford Dixon,	DB
1980-83	Bud Brown,	DB
1994-97	Patrick Surtain,	DB
1970-72	Ray Guy,	P

UNIFORMS Southern Miss has worn uniforms with oversize numbers on the front and back since 1998. The helmets are black with Southern Miss written in gold. The colors have always been black and gold, but styles have varied from plain uniforms in the 1960s to jerseys with numbers on the tops of the shoulders from 1970 to 1997.

QUOTE "If it weren't for Jeff Bower, people wouldn't know if it were Southern Miss or Northern Miss. There's a reason why Jeff Bower's name is on every athletic director's short list of job candidates. The guy knows how to win and does it the right way."
—Gene Wojciechowski, *ESPN The Magazine*

SOUTHERN MISS ANNUAL STATISTICAL LEADERS

YR	RUSHING	YDS	ATT	AVG	PASSING	ATT	CMP	PCT	YDS	RECEIVING	REC	YDS	AVG
1947	Bubba Phillips	659	78	8.4	Vernon Wells	54	18	.33	208	Hindu Reynolds	12	230	19.2
1948	Bubba Phillips	831	79	10.5	Vernon Wells	76	27	.36	464	Cliff Coggin	19	455	23.9
1949	Bubba Phillips	492	63	7.8	Bobby Holmes	99	56	.57	903	Cliff Coggin	53	1,087	20.5
1950	Bubba Phillips	545	92	5.9	Bobby Holmes	90	52	.58	660	Ivan Rosamond	20	309	15.5
1951	Bucky McElroy	854	155	5.5	Tom LeGros	125	46	.37	698	Bob McKellar	23	385	16.7
1952	Hugh Laurin Pepper	1,227	144	8.5	Billy Jarrell	71	36	.51	653	Bob McKellar	22	379	17.2
1953	Hugh Laurin Pepper	677	83	8.2	Jim Davenport	79	35	.44	503	Hub Waters	21	350	16.7
1954	Fred Smallwood	579	88	6.6	George Herring	88	33	.38	498	Hub Waters	13	220	16.9
1955	Eddie Cardenas	321	59	5.4	George Herring	68	31	.46	457	Ted Trenton	9	101	11.2
1956	Bo Dickinson	670	93	7.2	Bobby Hughes	102	50	.49	825	Jerry Taylor	17	284	16.7
1957	Bo Dickinson	461	73	6.3	George Sekul	58	21	.36	478	J.C. Arban	6	124	20.7
1958	Buddy Supple	551	87	6.3	George Sekul	61	28	.46	592	Bob Yencho	11	230	20.9
1959	Buddy Supple	413	100	4.1	Don Fuell	41	21	.51	356	Andin McLeod	12	164	13.7
1960	Don Fuell	385	69	5.6	Don Fuell	80	42	.53	652	Tommy Morrow	15	246	16.4
1961	Don Fuell	417	104	4.0	Don Fuell	101	56	.55	678	Charley Dedwyler	30	276	9.2
1962	John Sklopan	511	80	6.4	Bobby Coleman	98	46	.47	848	Billy Lyons	16	272	17.0
1963	Harmon Brannon	583	108	5.4	Vic Purvis	94	41	.44	460	Robert Brown	12	102	8.5
1964	Vic Purvis	422	117	3.6	Vic Purvis	114	55	.48	802	Bill Gorney	14	246	17.6
1965	Vic Purvis	663	144	4.6	Vic Purvis	109	33	.30	465	Robert Brown	17	262	15.4
1966	Milo McCarthy	685	164	4.2	Mike McClellan	77	36	.47	525	Clyde Dowd	17	329	19.4
1967	Johnny Johnson	422	117	3.6	Tommy Boutwell	104	55	.53	510	Danny Haley	23	278	12.1
1968	Johnny Johnson	663	144	4.6	Tommy Boutwell	285	151	.53	1,583	Danny Haley	40	504	12.6
1969	Larry Moulton	604	157	3.8	Rick Donegan	177	94	.53	1,093	Billy Mikel	47	774	16.5
1970	Larry Moulton	685	164	4.2	Rick Donegan	311	165	.53	1,593	Billy Mikel	26	299	11.5
1971	Doyle Orange	505	146	3.5	Rick Donegan	204	99	.49	1,121	Steve Broussard	26	463	17.8
1972	Doyle Orange	905	221	4.1	Buddy Palazzo	291	160	.55	1,888	Doug Parker	41	534	13.0
1973	Doyle Orange	539	109	4.9	Jeff Bower	199	116	.58	1,495	Harvey McGee	28	359	12.8
1974	David Hosemann	413	79	5.2	Jeff Bower	162	87	.54	1,189	John Sawyer	26	390	15.0
1975	Ben Garry	846	178	4.8	Jeff Bower	145	75	.52	905	Greg Pieper	29	446	15.4
1976	Ben Garry	1,236	236	5.2	Ken Alderman	141	71	.50	800	John Cannon	19	258	13.6
1977	Ben Garry	1,134	219	5.2	Dane McDaniel	73	38	.52	473	John Cannon	19	295	15.5
1978	Tiko Beal	698	179	3.9	Dane McDaniel	82	45	.55	528	Chuck Brown	27	357	13.2
1979	Sammy Winder	749	173	4.3	Dane McDaniel	114	54	.47	806	Larry Taylor	18	325	18.1
1980	Sammy Winder	996	237	4.2	Reggie Collier	199	97	.49	1,268	Marvin Harvey	28	359	12.8
1981	Sammy Winder	1,029	228	4.5	Reggie Collier	139	81	.58	1,004	Raymond Powell	20	254	12.7
1982	Sam Dejarnette	1,545	311	5.0	Reggie Collier	219	98	.45	1,265	Louis Lipps	38	468	12.3
1983	Sam Dejarnette	795	178	4.5	Robert Ducksworth	141	71	.50	1,201	Louis Lipps	42	800	19.0
1984	Vincent Alexander	572	105	5.4	Robert Ducksworth	126	56	.44	745	Lyneal Alston	18	256	14.2
1985	Vincent Alexander	837	188	4.5	Andrew Anderson	174	84	.48	1,319	Robert Ray Stallings	20	259	13.0
1986	Vincent Alexander	688	160	4.3	Andrew Anderson	164	87	.53	1,137	Lyneal Alston	22	463	21.0
1987	Shelton Gandy	1,025	225	4.6	Brett Favre	194	79	.41	1,264	Darryl Tillman	25	548	21.9
1988	Rickey Bradley	665	144	4.6	Brett Favre	319	178	.56	2,271	Alfred Williams	39	601	15.4
1989	Rickey Bradley	496	129	3.8	Brett Favre	381	206	.54	2,588	Darryl Tillman	30	468	15.6
1990	Tony Smith	657	158	4.2	Brett Favre	275	150	.55	1,572	Michael Jackson	25	358	14.3
1991	Tony Smith	998	194	5.1	Tommy Waters	250	135	.54	1,606	Greg Reed	23	434	18.9
1992	Michael Welch	759	200	3.8	Tommy Waters	212	110	.52	1,159	Greg Reed	36	526	14.6
1993	Barry Boyd	805	176	4.6	Kevin Bentley	192	77	.40	911	Fred Brock	20	309	15.5
1994	Chris Buckhalter	814	182	4.5	Heath Graham	208	121	.58	1,603	Mark Montgomery	42	523	12.5
1995	Chris Buckhalter	664	160	4.2	Heath Graham	329	161	.49	1,816	Fred Brock	42	624	14.9
1996	Eric Booth	699	160	4.4	Lee Roberts	142	86	.61	1,296	Kendrick Lee	33	669	20.3
1997	Harold Shaw	1,045	245	4.3	Lee Roberts	350	194	.55	2,248	Sherrod Gideon	54	1,008	18.7
1998	Derrick Nix	1,180	226	5.2	Lee Roberts	325	185	.57	2,680	Sherrod Gideon	66	1,186	18.0
1999	Derrick Nix	1,054	255	4.1	Jeff Kelly	260	153	.59	2,062	Todd Pinkston	48	977	20.4
2000	Dawayne Woods	631	146	4.3	Jeff Kelly	341	198	.58	2,381	Shawn Mills	55	713	13.0
2001	Dawayne Woods	594	140	4.2	Jeff Kelly	362	214	.59	2,613	LeRoy Handy	59	823	13.9
2002	Derrick Nix	1,194	219	5.5	Micky D'Angelo	232	122	.53	1,647	Chris Johnson	50	673	13.5
2003	Anthony Harris	671	158	4.2	Dustin Almond	251	121	.48	1,877	Marvin Young	42	703	16.7
2004	Anthony Harris	714	175	4.1	Dustin Almond	269	138	.51	1,848	Antwon Courington	47	659	14.0

Receiving leaders by receptions
The NCAA began including postseason stats in 2002

THE SCHOOLS

SOUTHERN MISS ALL-TIME SCORES

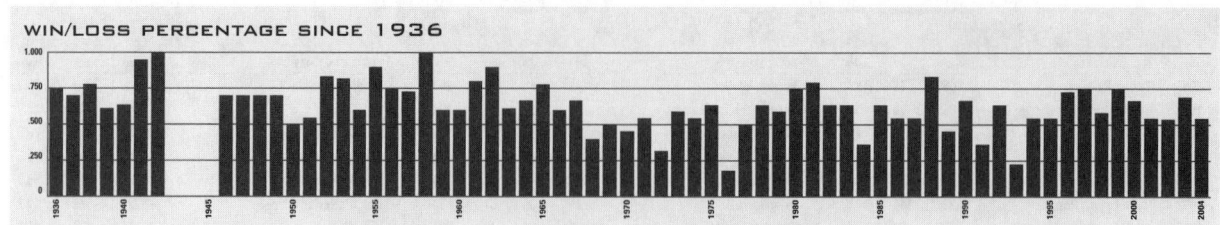

WIN/LOSS PERCENTAGE SINCE 1936

RONALD J. SLAY
1912 (.667)   2-1

1912   2-1-0
O13	●	Hattiesburg Scouts	30	0
O19	●	Gulf Coast Acad.	0	6
N5	●	Mobile Acad.	6	0

M.J. "BLONDIE" WILLIAMS
1913 (.214)   1-5-1

1913   1-5-1
S27		at Poplarville HS	0	25
O11		at Gulf Coast Acad.	0	19
O18	●	Mobile Acad.	11	0
O25		Gulf Coast Acad	6	11
N8		at Mobile Acad.	0	14
N22	=	Poplarville HS	0	0
N27		Mississippi	7	13

A.B. DILLIE
1914-16 (.382)   6-10-1

1914   2-3-1
O2		at Mississippi Coll.	0	39
O17		at Spring Hill	13	24
O24	●	Mobile Acad.	24	0
O31		Gulf Coast Acad.	0	9
N7	●	Perkinston HS	9	0
N14	=	Poplarville HS	0	0

1915   4-4-0
O9		Poplarville HS	0	6
O16		at Gulf Coast Acad.	0	3
O30	●	Perkinston HS	26	0
N6		at Spring Hill	7	33
N13	●	Copiah-Lincoln HS	55	0
N20	●	Poplarville HS	12	0
N25	●	Gulf Coast Acad.	7	6
U		Mississippi Coll. *Unk*	7	55

1916   0-3-0
O16		at Meridian HS	0	31
N7		Mississippi Coll.	0	75
N11		Spring Hill	0	87

1917-18
NO TEAM

CEPHUS ANDERSON
1919 (.714)   4-1-2

1919   4-1-2
O4	●	Perkinston HS	12	0
O18	●	Poplarville HS	2	0
O25	=	at Meridian Coll.	6	6
N1	●	Gulf Coast Acad.	6	6
N8	●	Chamberlain Acad.	20	0
N17	●	Mississippi Coll.	7	19
N27	●	Meridian Coll.	47	0

B.B. O'MARA
1920 (.688)   5-2-1

1920   5-2-1
O2	●	Perkinston HS	64	0
O9		Mississippi	0	54
O16	=	Milsaps	7	7
O23	●	at Spring Hill	12	2
N6	●	Spring Hill	32	0
N11	●	Tlane JV	0	19
N20	●	Columbia TS	27	0
N25	●	Gulf Coast Acad.	40	0

O.V. "SPOUT" AUSTIN
1921-23 (.381)   8-13

1921   3-4-0
O7	●	at Ellisville HS	20	0
O15	●	Smith County HS	113	0
O21		at Milsaps	0	27
O29	●	Jones County HS	37	0
N5		at St. Stanislaus Coll.	0	49
N11	●	Poplarville HS	0	40
N26		Loyola, New Orleans	13	25

1922   2-6-0
S29	●	at Jones County HS	31	0
O7		Purvis HS	0	6
O10		at Milsaps	7	10
O28		at St. Stranislaus	0	10
N4	●	Gulf Coast Acad.	0	20
N11	●	at Loyola, New Orleans	6	20
N18		at Marion Inst.	0	44
N25	●	Mississippi State JV	19	12

1923   3-3-0
O5	●	Purvis HS	26	0
O12		at Milsaps	0	31
N3	●	Seashore Camp Ground	52	0
N10		Gulf Coast Acad.	6	7
N17		at La. Lafayette	0	66
N23	●	Mississippi Coll. JV	6	0

WILLIAM HERSCHEL BOBO
1924-27 (.367)   9-17-4

1924   3-3-2
O4	●	Clarke Coll.	27	0
O18		at Loyola, New Orleans	7	32
O24	=	at Gulf Coast Acad.	14	14
N1	●	Pearl River JC	6	26
N7	=	at Mississippi State JV	14	14
N17		at Stetson	6	48
N24	●	Marion Inst.	7	6
N27	●	Louisiana Coll.	13	12

1925   0-6-0
O1	●	Clarke Coll.	0	32
O10		Mississippi JV	6	38
O15		at Navy All Stars	6	32
O24	=	at La. Lafayette	0	40 *
N7	●	at Pearl River JC	7	13
N14		at Spring Hill	0	40

1926   3-4-1
S25		at La. Lafayette	6	33
O2	●	Clarke Coll.	12	7
O9		at Spring Hill	6	27
O16	●	Louisiana Coll.	14	7
O22	●	at Perkinston JC	26	3
O30	=	Gulf Coast Acad.	6	6
N13		Pearl River JC	0	20
N27		at Mississippi State JV	7	26

1927   3-4-1
S24		at La. Lafayette	0	6
O1	=	Perkinston JC	0	0
O8	●	Hinds JC	12	0
O21		Mississippi State JV	0	24
O29		at Clarke Coll.	0	18
N5		at Spring Hill	0	37
N11	●	Pearl River JC	15	0
N18	●	at St. Stranislaus	25	13

WILLIAM B. SAUNDERS
1928-29 (.361)   6-11-1

1928   4-5-0
S29		at Mississippi Coll.	0	83
O5	●	at Perkinston JC	12	2
O13	●	Newton JC	7	0
O17	●	Pearl River JC	6	0
O27		at La. Lafayette	7	37
N9	●	Mississippi Coll. JV	12	6
N16		at Marion Inst.	6	53
N24	●	Copiah-Lincoln JC	6	13
N29	●	Clarke Coll.	6	40

1929   2-6-1
S28		at La. Lafayette	0	7
O5		at Mississippi Coll.	0	20
O12	●	Marion Inst.	31	0
O18	=	S.W. Mississippi JC	6	6
N2		at Spring Hill	6	25
N9		Pearl River JC	7	14
N16		at Louisiana Coll.	6	12
N22		at Delta St.	6	14
N29	●	Clarke Coll.	12	7

JOHN LUMPKIN
1930 (.389)   3-5-1

1930   3-5-1
S27	●	Clarke Coll.	45	0
O4		at Milsaps	0	26
O11		at Mississippi Coll.	6	18
O18		at La. Lafayette	0	14
O25	●	Louisiana Coll.	47	20
N1		Spring Hill	6	7
N14		at Northwestern St.	12	32
N22	●	Delta St.	46	0
N27	=	Union U.	0	0

ALLISON "POOLEY" HUBERT
1931-36 (.518)   26-24-5

1931   2-5-0
O3		Milsaps	0	19
O10	●	at Mississippi Coll.	13	46
O17		at Spring Hill	2	12
O24		at Louisiana Coll.	0	13
N7	●	La. Lafayette	13	7
N14	●	Northwestern St.	32	0
N21		at Delta St.	7	27

1932   5-4-0
S24		at Mississippi	0	49
O1		at Milsaps	0	27
O7	●	at La. Lafayette	12	7
O22		at Southwestern	0	19
O29	●	Spring Hill	12	0
N5	●	Louisiana Coll.	12	0
N12		at Northwestern St.	6	31
N19	●	Delta St.	33	25
N24	●	Union U.	6	0

1933   3-5-2
S22		at Loyola, New Orleans	0	47
S30		at Mississippi	0	45
O7		at Mississippi Coll.	7	33
O14	=	at Milsaps	0	0
O21	●	La. Lafayette	6	0
O28	●	at Louisiana Coll.	21	6
N4	=	at Spring Hill	0	0
N11	●	Northwestern St.	0	13
N25	●	Delta St.	33	6
D1		at Murray St.	0	30

1934   3-4-2
S28	●	Poplarville JC	20	12
O6		at Mississippi Coll.	0	12
O12	●	at Delta St.	13	13
O20	●	La. Lafayette	12	6
O27	=	Milsaps	0	0
N2		Spring Hill	0	7
N9		at Northwestern St.	0	31
N17		Union U.	6	26
N29	●	Murray St.	12	2

1935   6-4-0
S20	●	at Jones County JC	7	0
O5	●	Louisiana Coll.	12	0
O12		Troy	13	14
O18	●	Northwestern St.	26	12
O26		at Memphis	12	0
N1		at Spring Hill	0	19
N8		at La. Lafayette	19	7
N15		Mississippi State	0	27
N28		at Louisiana Tech	0	27
D7	●	Union U.	12	6

1936   7-2-1
S26	●	at Louisiana Coll.	7	0
O3		at Union U.	0	7
O9	=	Milsaps	7	7
O16	●	at Louisiana Tech	12	7
O23	●	Memphis	25	0
O29	●	Spring Hill	12	7
N6	●	Troy	24	0
N13	●	La. Lafayette	44	14
N21		at Northwestern St.	0	13
N26	●	East Texas St.	13	6

REED GREEN
1937-48 (.735)   59-20-4

1937   7-3-0
S24	●	Louisiana Coll.	19	0
O1	●	at Spring Hill	33	0
O8	●	at La. Lafayette	13	0
O15		at Louisiana Tech	0	7
O22	●	Alabama St. Teachers	58	0
O29	●	Troy	53	0
N5	●	Union U.	34	0
N13		Northwestern St.	0	3
N25	●	East Texas St.	6	14
D3	●	Appalachian St. *Gul*	7	0

1938   7-2-0
S23	●	Arkansas A&M	39	0
O1	●	at Troy	19	0
O8		at Mississippi	0	14
O15	●	Delta St.	44	0
O28	●	Milsaps	47	0
N5	●	at Louisiana Coll.	7	0
N11	●	La. Lafayette	15	6
N18		at Northwestern St.	0	6
N24	●	Union U.	32	0

1939   4-2-3
S29	●	Troy	13	6
O6	=	at Sam Houston St.	7	7
O13	=	at Milsaps	0	0
O20	●	at Delta St.	21	0
N4	●	Louisiana Coll.	7	0
N11		Mississippi	7	27
N18	●	at La. Lafayette	9	7
N23		Northwestern St.	0	7
D1	=	St. Mary's, Texas	13	13

1940 — 7-4-0

S27	●	Troy	25	0
O4		Sam Houston St.	16	18
O11	●	at S.E. Louisiana	13	6
O19		at Milsaps	7	14
O26	●	Spring Hill	38	6
N1		at Louisiana Coll.	0	7
N8		at Northwestern St.	6	9
N15	●	La. Lafayette	21	14
N22	●	Delta St.	41	0
D5	●	at St. Mary's, Texas	27	6
D14	●	37th Division	26	0

1941 — 9-0-1

S26	●	Georgia St. Teachers	70	0
O3	●	at Louisiana Tech	19	7
O10	●	S.E. Louisiana	43	6
O17	●	Milsaps	20	0
O24	●	at Spring Hill	26	7
N1	●	Louisiana Coll.	13	6
N7	●	Northwestern St.	21	7
N14	=	at La. Lafayette	0	0
N21	●	at Delta St.	27	7 *
N29	●	at St. Mary's, Texas	7	0

1942 — 4-0-0

O23	●	6th Squad	41	0
O31	●	at Mobile Shipbuilders	26	7
N20	●	Mobile Shipbuilders	42	0
D4	●	Brookley Field	33	0

1943-45

NO TEAM

1946 — 7-3-0

S21	●	Louisiana Tech	7	0 *
S27		Auburn MONT	12	13
O4	●	Jacksonville St.	65	0
O18	●	La. Lafayette	6	0
O25	●	Oklahoma City	20	6
N1	●	at S. F. Austin	7	0
N11		at Northwestern St.	6	7
N15	●	Louisiana Coll.	65	0
N22		S.E. Louisiana	0	20
		CIGAR BOWL		
D7	●	at Havana U.	55	0

1947 — 7-3-0

S20		Alabama BIRM	7	34
S26	●	Auburn MONT	19	13
O11	●	at Louisiana Tech	7	6
O18	●	at La. Lafayette	15	7
O25		at Oklahoma City	6	21
N1	●	S. F. Austin	20	7
N7	●	Northwestern St.	20	0
N14	●	Union U.	18	0
N22		at Mississippi State	7	14
N27	●	at S.E. Louisiana	35	0

1948 — 7-3-0

S24		Auburn MONT	14	20
O1	●	S. F. Austin	41	0
O8		Trinity	9	26
O15	●	La. Lafayette	26	6
O23	●	at Oklahoma City	55	20
O30	●	at Northwestern St.	38	14
N6		at Alabama	0	27
N13	●	Louisiana Tech	20	6
N19	●	S.E. Louisiana	27	0
N24	●	Union U.	47	8

THAD "PIE" VANN
1949-68 (.700) 139-59-2

1949 — 7-3-0

S17		at Kentucky	7	71
S24	●	Delta St.	20	13
O8	●	Mc Murray	55	32
O15	●	at La. Lafayette	25	0
O21	●	at U.T. Chattanooga	33	20
O29	●	Northwestern St.	67	28
N5	●	Oklahoma City	27	21
N12		at Louisiana Tech	13	34
N19		at Alabama	26	34
N25	●	Louisville	26	21

1950 — 5-5-0

S23		at Tennessee	0	56
S30		Delta St.	13	19
O7		at Mc Murray	19	37
O14	●	La. Lafayette	6	0
O21		at S.E. Louisiana	0	7
O27	●	U.T. Chattanooga MBL	14	13
N4	●	at Northwestern St.	7	0
N11		at Alabama	0	53
N18	●	Louisiana Tech	41	20
N25	●	Louisville	34	28

1951 — 6-5-0

S15	●	East Carolina	40	0
S22		at LSU	0	13
S29		Carswell AFB	0	26
O6	●	Mc Murray	54	7
O13	●	at La. Lafayette	41	0
O20	●	S.E. Louisiana	35	6
O26		at U.T. Chattanooga	7	19
N3	●	Northwestern St.	76	0
N10		at Alabama	7	40
N17	●	at Louisiana Tech	33	7 *
N23		at Louisville	13	14

1952 — 10-2-0

S19		Alabama MONT	6	20
S27	●	Memphis	27	20
O4	●	at Tampa	52	25
O11	●	at La. Lafayette	32	12
O18	●	S.E. Louisiana	20	12
O25	●	at U.T. Chattanooga	27	14
N1	●	Northwestern St.	39	13
N8	●	at Florida State	50	21
N15	●	Louisiana Tech	52	0
N22	●	Louisville JAM	55	26
N29	●	Stetson	42	0
		SUN BOWL		
J1		Pacific	7	26

1953 — 9-2-0

S18	●	Alabama MONT	25	19
S26	●	Parris Island Marines	40	0
O3	●	Tampa	42	6
O10	●	at La. Lafayette	41	14
O17	●	S.E. Louisiana	7	0
O31		at Memphis	13	27
N7	●	Florida State	21	0
N14	●	at Louisiana Tech	30	0
N21	●	Georgia JAM	14	0
N26	●	at U.T. Chattanooga	33	19
		SUN BOWL		
J1		Texas-El Paso	14	37

1954 — 6-4-0

S17	●	Alabama MONT	7	2
S25	●	Louisiana Tech	28	0
O2		at North Texas	7	15
O9	●	Abilene Christian	23	7
O16		S.E. Louisiana	7	13
O23	●	U.T. Chattanooga	14	7
N6		at Dayton	7	20
N13	●	Villanova MBL	27	0
N20	●	Memphis	34	21
N27		at Florida State	18	19

1955 — 9-1-0

S17	●	Elon	39	0
S24	●	at Louisiana Tech	7	6
S30		at U.T. Chattanooga	0	10
O8	●	North Texas	26	0
O15	●	at S.E. Louisiana	33	0
O21	●	at Memphis	34	14
N5	●	at Abilene Christian	40	0
N12	●	North Dakota St.	58	0
N19	●	Dayton JAM	19	13
N25	●	Florida State	21	6

1956 — 7-2-1

S22	●	Louisiana Tech	14	0
O6	●	at Dayton	23	6
O13	●	S.E. Louisiana	21	14
O20	●	Memphis	27	0
O27	●	U.T. Chattanooga	33	0
N3	●	Abilene Christian	36	6
N10	●	at Trinity	20	13
N17		at Florida State	19	20
N24	=	at Alabama	13	13
		TANGERINE BOWL		
J1		West Texas St.	13	20

1957 — 8-3-0

S21	●	at Louisiana Tech	7	0
S28	●	Trinity	13	0
O5	●	at West Texas St.	34	0
O12	●	at S.E. Louisiana	14	0
O19	●	at Memphis	14	6
O25	●	at U.T. Chattanooga	20	0
N2	●	Abilene Christian	7	0
N9		Houston JAM	12	27
N16	●	Florida State	20	0
N23		at Alabama	2	29
		TANGERINE BOWL		
J1		East Texas St.	9	10

1958 — 9-0-0

S20	●	Louisiana Tech	14	0
S27	●	at Trinity	15	0
O4	●	Memphis	24	22
O11	●	S.E. Louisiana	33	6
O25	●	West Texas St.	15	0
N1	●	at Abilene Christian	22	0
N8	●	North Carolina St. MBL	26	14
N15	●	Virginia Tech	41	0
N27	●	at U.T. Chattanooga	20	13

1959 — 6-4-0

S26	●	Trinity	29	8
O3		Texas A&M MBL	3	7
O10	●	S.E. Louisiana	26	6
O17	●	at West Texas St.	37	6
O24	●	Abilene Christian	30	10
O31		at Memphis	6	21
N7	●	North Carolina St. MBL	19	14
N14	●	U.T. Chattanooga	14	6
N21		at Auburn	7	28
N28		at Louisiana Tech	0	16

1960 — 6-4-0

S23	●	Hardin Simmons MBL	27	0
O1	●	West Texas St.	28	18
O8	●	at Trinity	16	0
O15	●	Florida State MBL	15	13
O22		North Carolina St.	13	20
O29	●	at Abilene Christian	34	8
N5		at Arkansas State	13	14
N12		Louisiana Tech	7	10
N18		Memphis	6	7
N24	●	at U.T. Chattanooga	30	6

1961 — 8-2-0

S16	●	Texas Arlington	30	7
S30	●	at La. Lafayette	22	6
O7	●	U.T. Chattanooga	24	7
O14		at Memphis	7	21
O21	●	Arkansas State	20	0
O28	●	Abilene Christian	33	6
N4		North Carolina St. MBL	6	7
N11	●	at Louisiana Tech	7	0
N18	●	at Florida State	12	0
N25	●	Trinity	22	14

1962 — 9-1-0

S15	●	at Texas Arlington	28	7
S22	●	Richmond	29	8
S29	●	La. Lafayette	29	0
O6	●	at U.T. Chattanooga	31	13
O13		at Memphis	6	8
O20	●	North Carolina St. MBL	30	0
O27	●	Abilene Christian	30	0
N3	●	at Arkansas State	20	7
N10	●	Trinity	33	6
N17	●	Louisiana Tech	22	14 *

1963 — 5-3-1

S14		Memphis JAM	7	28
S28		North Carolina St.	0	14
O12	●	Richmond	7	0
O19	=	Florida State MBL	0	0
O26	●	Arkansas State	25	0
N2	●	at La. Lafayette	28	0
N16		at Louisiana Tech	0	10
N23	●	Citadel	37	12
N28	●	at U.T. Chattanooga	24	0

1964 — 6-3-0

S26	●	La. Lafayette	30	0
O3	●	Richmond	14	9
O10	●	at Memphis	20	14
O17		at Mississippi State	7	48
O24		at Auburn	7	14
O31		at Florida State	0	34
N7	●	U.T. Chattanooga	31	0
N14	●	Louisiana Tech	14	7
N21	●	Memphis JAM	20	18

1965 — 7-2-0

S18	●	S.E. Louisiana	15	0
S25	●	Memphis JAM	21	16
O2	●	Richmond	28	7
O9		at Mississippi State	9	27
O16	●	VMI	3	0
O23	●	at Auburn	3	0
O30		William & Mary NOR	0	3
N6	●	at U.T. Chattanooga	17	0
N13	●	at Louisiana Tech	31	7

1966 — 6-4-0

S17	●	Louisiana Tech	14	0
S24	●	at S.E. Louisiana	15	13
O1		at Memphis	0	6
O8		at Mississippi State	9	10
O15		at Mississippi	7	14
O29	●	Richmond	27	0
N5	●	VMI	42	6
N12	●	North Carolina St. NOR	7	6
N19	●	at East Carolina	35	14
N26		Alabama MBL	0	34

1967 — 6-3-0

S16	●	at Citadel	10	7
S23	●	S.E. Louisiana	20	7
S30		Alabama MBL	3	25
O7	●	Tampa	48	0
O14	●	at Mississippi State	21	14
O21		at Mississippi	14	23
O28		Memphis JAM	8	24
N4	●	Richmond	19	7
N23	●	Louisiana Tech SHRE	58	7

1968 — 4-6-0

S21	●	at S.E. Louisiana	27	15
S28		Alabama MBL	14	17
O5	●	East Carolina	65	0
O12	●	at Mississippi State	47	14
O19		at Mississippi	13	21
O26		at Memphis	7	29
N2		Louisiana Tech	20	27
N9		at San Diego State	7	68
N16		Richmond	7	33
N23	●	at Tampa	21	7

P.W. "BEAR" UNDERWOOD
1969-74 (.492) 31-32-2

1969 — 5-5-0

S20	●	S.E. Louisiana	14	6
S27		at Alabama	14	63
O3		Idaho MBL	21	31
O11		at Mississippi State	20	34
O18		at Mississippi	7	69
O25	●	Richmond	31	28
N1	●	at Louisiana Tech	24	23
N8		at Memphis	7	37
N22	●	at East Carolina	14	7
N29	●	West Texas St.	10	9

1970 — 5-6-0

S12	●	at La. Lafayette	16	14
S19		at Auburn	14	33
S26	●	Texas Arlington	26	20
O3	●	Richmond	43	21
O10		at San Diego State	14	41
O17	●	at Mississippi	30	14
O24		at Mississippi State	15	51
O31		at Memphis	0	33
N14		Louisiana Tech	6	27
N21		at West Texas St.	11	14
N28	●	Trinity	53	31

1971 — 6-5-0

S11		Florida State MB	9	24
S18		at Alabama	6	42
S25	●	San Diego State JAM	10	0
O9		at Auburn	14	27
O16		at Mississippi	6	20
O23		at Memphis	12	27
O30	●	Richmond	31	24
N6	●	VMI	38	0
N13	●	at Louisiana Tech	24	20
N20	●	at Virginia Tech	17	8
N27	●	West Texas St.	35	0

1972 — 3-7-1

S9	●	Texas Arlington	38	17
S16		Louisiana Tech	14	33
S30		at Mississippi	9	13
O7	●	West Texas St.	14	7
O14	●	at Richmond	34	9
O21		at Mississippi State	7	26
O28		Alabama IRM	11	48
N4		at Virginia Tech	14	27
N11		U.T. Chattanooga	6	10
N18		at Utah State	21	27
D2	=	Memphis JAM	14	14

1973 — 6-4-1

S15		East Carolina	0	13
S22		Florida TAM	13	14
S29		at Mississippi	0	41
O6	●	at U.T. Chattanooga	42	7
O13		at Richmond	20	42
O20	●	at Texas Arlington	41	14
O27	=	at Mississippi State	10	10
N3	●	Weber St.	28	7
N10	●	at Memphis	13	10
N17	●	at West Texas St.	28	0
N22	●	Utah State	32	8

1974 6-5-0

S14	●	at Memphis	6	0
S21		Alabama [Birm]	0	52
S28		at Mississippi	14	20
O5		at West Texas St.	0	31
O12	●	Texas Arlington [JaM]	39	10
O19	●	VMI [MBL]	15	14
O26		at Lamar	7	10
N2	●	at La. Lafayette	41	7
N9	●	at Utah State	7	3
N16		Bowling Green [MBL]	20	38
N23	●	at Tampa	11	10

BOBBY COLLINS
1975-81 (.588) 46-32-2

1975 7-4-0

S13	●	at Weber St.	14	0
S20		at Bowling Green	14	16
S27		at Mississippi	8	24
O4		at Mississippi State	3	7 †
O11	●	at Memphis	21	7
O18	●	at Texas Arlington	34	7
O25	●	at Louisiana Tech	24	14
N1	●	Lamar [NO]	43	3
N15		at Alabama	6	27
N22	●	Fullerton St. [BiL]	70	0
N29	●	Brigham Young [JaM]	42	14

1976 2-9-0

S11		at East Carolina	0	48
S18		at Virginia Tech	7	16
S25		Mississippi	0	28
O2		Cincinnati	21	28
O9		Alabama [Birm]	8	24
O16		at Brigham Young	19	63
O23		Mississippi State	6	14 †
N6		at Florida State	27	30
N13		at Louisiana Tech	22	23
N20	●	Memphis	14	12
N27	●	Texas Arlington	21	10

1977 6-6-0

S3	●	Troy [Mont]	42	19
S10		Florida State	6	35
S17	●	at Auburn	24	13
S24	●	at Mississippi	27	19
O1		at Cincinnati	6	17
O8		North Texas	14	27
O15	●	at Hawaii	28	26
O22	●	at Mississippi State	14	7
O29		at Memphis	14	42
N5	●	at Texas Arlington	20	3
N12		Louisiana Tech	10	28
N19		Arkansas State	10	14

1978 7-4-0

S2	●	at Richmond	10	7
S9	●	Arkansas State [LR]	21	6
S16		at Cincinnati	14	26
S30		Mississippi [JaM]	13	16
O7	●	Mississippi State	22	17
O14	●	East Carolina	17	16
O21	●	at Memphis	13	10
O28		Florida State	16	38
N4		at North Texas	12	25
N11	●	Bowling Green	38	21
N18	●	Louisville	37	3

1979 6-4-1

S8		at Florida State	14	17
S15	●	Cincinnati	24	6
S22		at Auburn	9	31
S29	●	Mississippi [JaM]	38	8
O6	●	North Texas	30	10
O13		Tulane	19	20
O20	●	Memphis	22	0
O27	●	at Mississippi State	21	7
N3	=	at Louisville	10	10
N10		at Bowling Green	27	31
N17	●	Arkansas State	14	6

1980 9-3-0

S6	●	at Tulane	17	14
S20	●	Louisiana Tech	38	11
S27	●	at East Carolina	35	7
O4	●	Mississippi [JaM]	28	22
O11	●	at Mississippi State	42	14
O18	●	Arkansas State	35	0
O25		at Alabama	7	42
N1	●	Lamar	36	10
N8		at Auburn	0	31
N15	●	Richmond	33	12
N22		Louisville	3	6
		INDEPENDENCE BOWL		
D13	●	McNeese St.	16	14

1981 9-2-1

S5	●	La. Lafayette	33	7
S19	●	Tulane	21	3
S26	●	at Richmond	17	10
O3	●	Texas Arlington	52	9
O10	=	Alabama [Birm]	13	13
O17	●	at Memphis	10	0
O31	●	at North Texas	22	0
N7	●	Mississippi State [JaM]	7	6
N14	●	at Florida State	58	14
N21		at Louisville	10	13
N28	●	Lamar	45	14
		TANGERINE BOWL		
D19		Missouri	17	19

JIM CARMODY
1982-87 (.561) 37-29

1982 7-4-0

S4	●	La. Monroe	45	27
S11		at Mississippi	19	28
S18		at Auburn	19	21
S25		Florida State	17	24
O2	●	Memphis	34	14
O9	●	Mississippi State [JaM]	20	14
O16	●	at Tulane	22	10
O23	●	Louisville	48	0
O30	●	La. Lafayette	36	0
N13	●	at Alabama	38	29
N20		Louisiana Tech	6	13

1983 7-4-0

S3	●	Richmond	32	3
S10		at Auburn	3	24
S17	●	Louisiana Tech	28	10
O1	●	at Mississippi	27	7
O8	●	Mississippi State [JaM]	31	6
O15	●	at Memphis	27	20
O22		Tulane	7	14
O29	●	La. Lafayette	31	3
N5	●	at Louisville	27	3
N12		Alabama [Birm]	16	28
N19		East Carolina	6	10

1984 4-7-0

S8		at Georgia	19	26
S15	●	Louisiana Tech	34	0
S22		at Auburn	12	35
S29		at Memphis	13	23
O6		Mississippi State [JaM]	18	27
O13		at Tulane	7	35
O20	●	Mississippi [JaM]	13	10
O27		at La. Lafayette	7	13
N3		Northwestern St.	0	22
N10	●	at East Carolina	31	27
N17	●	Louisville	34	25

1985 7-4-0

S7	●	Louisiana Tech	28	0
S14		at Auburn	18	29
S21		Mississippi State [JaM]	20	23
S28	●	Northwestern St.	14	7
O5	●	La. Lafayette	38	16
O12	●	at Louisville	42	12
O19	●	at Memphis	14	7
N2	●	East Carolina	27	0
N9		at Colorado State	17	35
N16		at Alabama	13	24
N23	●	Tulane	24	6

1986 6-5-0

S6	●	La. Monroe	28	19
S13		Alabama [Birm]	17	31
S20	●	Mississippi State [JaM]	28	24
S27		at Texas A&M	7	16
O4		at Kentucky	0	32
O18	●	Memphis	14	9
O25		at Tulane	20	35
N1	●	at East Carolina	23	21
N8	●	La. Lafayette	17	0
N15		at Florida State	13	49
N22	●	Louisville	31	16

1987 6-5-0

S5		Alabama [Birm]	6	38
S19	●	Tulane	31	24
S26		Texas A&M [JaM]	14	27
O3	●	at Louisville	65	6
O10		Florida State	10	61
O17	●	Mississippi State [JaM]	18	14
O24	●	at Memphis	17	14
O31	●	Jackson St.	17	7
N7		La. Monroe	24	34
N14	●	East Carolina	38	34
N28		at La. Lafayette	30	37

CURLEY HALLMAN
1988-90 (.676) 23-11

1988 10-2-0

S3	●	S. F. Austin	21	7
S10		at Florida State	13	49
S17	●	Virginia Tech	35	13
S24	●	at East Carolina	45	42
O1	●	Louisville	30	23
O8	●	at Tulane	38	13
O15	●	Mississippi State [JaM]	38	21
O22	●	at La. Lafayette	27	14
O29	●	Memphis	34	27
N5		at Auburn	8	38
N12	●	at Louisiana Tech	26	19
		INDEPENDENCE BOWL		
D23	●	Texas-El Paso	38	18

1989 5-6-0

S2	●	Florida State [JacF]	30	26
S9		Mississippi State	23	26
S16		at Auburn	3	24
S23		at TCU	17	19
S30		at Texas A&M	14	31
O7	●	Tulane	30	21
O14	●	at Louisville	16	10
O21		La. Lafayette	21	24
O28	●	at Memphis	31	7
N18		at Alabama	14	37
N25	●	East Carolina	41	27

1990 8-4-0

S1	●	Delta St.	12	0
S8	●	Alabama [Birm]	27	24
S15		at Georgia	17	18
S22		at Mississippi State	10	13
S29	●	Louisville	25	13
O6	●	at East Carolina	16	7
O13	●	at Tulane	20	14
O20	●	Memphis	23	7
O27		at Virginia Tech	16	20
N3	●	at La. Lafayette	14	13
N10	●	at Auburn	13	12
		ALL-AMERICAN BOWL		
D28		North Carolina St.	27	31

JEFF BOWER
1990-PRESENT (.582) 95-68-1

1991 4-7-0

A31	●	Delta St.	25	7
S7		at Pittsburgh	14	35
S21	●	Colorado State	39	7
S28		at Louisville	14	28
O5	●	at Auburn	10	9
O12		at Memphis	12	17
O19	●	Tulane	47	14
O26		at Cincinnati	7	17
N2		at Tulsa	10	13
N9		East Carolina	20	48
N16		at Louisiana Tech	14	30

1992 7-4-0

S4	●	Memphis	23	21
S12		Alabama [Birm]	10	17
S19	●	Louisiana Tech	16	13
S26		at Auburn	8	16
O3	●	Tulsa	33	24
O10		at Northern Illinois	10	23
O15	●	at Tulane	17	7
O24	●	Cincinnati	31	17
O29	●	at East Carolina	38	21
N7		at Florida	20	24
N14	●	at Virginia Tech	13	12

1993 2-8-1

S4		Pittsburgh	10	14
S18	●	La. Monroe	44	37
S25		at Auburn	24	35
O2		at La. Lafayette	7	13
O9		at Georgia	24	54
O16		at Louisville	27	35
O23	●	East Carolina	24	16
O30		at Alabama	0	40 †
N6		Tulane	15	17
N13		at Memphis	9	20
N20	=	at Tulsa	30	30

1994 6-5-0

S3	●	at Tulane	25	10
S10		Virginia Tech	14	24
S17	●	Memphis	20	3
S24		at Texas A&M	17	41
O1		at East Carolina	10	31
O8		at Alabama	6	14
O15	●	La. Lafayette	43	20
O22	●	Samford	59	16
O29	●	Tulsa	47	29
N5		at Florida	17	55
N12	●	at LSU	20	18

1995 6-5-0

A31	●	Northern Illinois	45	13
S9		Alabama [Birm]	20	24
S16	●	at Utah State	24	21
S23		at Indiana	26	27
S30	●	Tulane	45	0
O7	●	Louisville	25	21
O14		at Cincinnati	13	16
O28		East Carolina	34	36
N4		at Tennessee	0	42
N11	●	at Memphis	17	9
N18	●	at La. Lafayette	35	32

1996-PRESENT
C-USA

1996 8-3 (4-1)

A31	●	at Georgia	11	7
S7		Alabama [Birm]	10	20
S14	●	Utah State	31	24
S21	●	La. Lafayette	52	27
S28	● |	at Louisville	24	7
O10	● |	at East Carolina	28	7
O19	● |	Memphis	16	0
O26	● |	at Tulane	31	28
N2	● |	Cincinnati	21	17
N9	|	at Houston	49	56
N16		at Florida State	14	54

1997 9-3 (6-0)

A30		at Florida	6	21
S6	●	at Illinois	24	7
S20	●	Nevada	35	19
S27		Alabama [Birm]	13	27
O4	● |	Louisville	42	24
O11	● |	at East Carolina	23	13
O25	● |	Tulane	34	13
N1	● |	at Cincinnati	24	17
N8		at Tennessee	20	44
N15	● |	Houston	33	0
N22	● |	at Memphis	42	18
		LIBERTY BOWL		
D31	●	Pittsburgh	41	7

1998 7-5 (5-1)

S5		at Penn State	6	34
S19		Texas A&M	6	24
S26	●	La. Lafayette	55	0
O3	|	at Tulane	7	21
O10	● |	Louisville	56	21
O17	● |	at Army	37	13
O24	● |	East Carolina	41	7
O31		at Alabama	20	30
N7	● |	at Houston	21	15
N14	● |	Memphis	45	3
N21	●	at Nevada	55	28
		HUMANITARIAN BOWL		
D30		Idaho	35	42

1999 9-3 (6-0)

S6	● |	Tulane	48	14
S11	●	Northwestern St.	40	6
S18		at Nebraska	13	20
S25		at Texas A&M	6	23
O9	● |	at East Carolina	39	22
O16	● |	Army	24	0
O23	● |	Cincinnati	28	20
O30		at Alabama	14	35
N6	● |	at Memphis	20	5
N13	●	La. Lafayette	48	0
N20	● |	at Louisville	30	27
		LIBERTY BOWL		
D31	●	Colorado State	23	17

2000 8-4 (4-3)

S2		at Tennessee	16	19
S16	●	Alabama [Birm]	21	0
S23	●	at Oklahoma State	28	6
S30	● |	Memphis	24	3
O7	●	South Florida	41	7
O14	● |	at Tulane	56	24
O28	● |	at Houston	6	3
N4	|	Louisville	28	49
N11	● |	at UAB	33	30
N18	|	at Cincinnati	24	27
N24	|	East Carolina	9	14
		MOBILE BOWL		
D20	●	TCU	28	21

2001   6-5   (4-3)

S1	●		Oklahoma State	17	9
S22	●		at La. Lafayette	35	10
S29	●	|	UAB	3	0
O6		|	at Memphis	17	22
O16		|	at Louisville	14	24
O27	●	|	Houston	58	14
N3			at Penn State	20	38
N17	●	|	Tulane	59	6
N23	●	|	at East Carolina	28	21
N29			Alabama *BIRM*	15	28
D7		|	TCU	12	14

2002   7-6   (5-3)

A31	●		Jackson St.	55	7
S7	●		Illinois	23	20
S14	●	|	Memphis	33	14
S21			at Alabama	7	20
S28	●	|	at Army	27	6
O12		|	at South Florida	13	16
O19	●	|	Cincinnati	23	14
N2		|	at TCU	7	37
N9	●	|	at UAB	20	13
N14		|	Louisville	17	20
N23		|	at Tulane	10	31
N30	●	|	East Carolina	24	7
			HOUSTON BOWL		
D27			Oklahoma State	23	33

2003   9-4   (8-0)

A30			at California	2	34
S4	●	|	at UAB	17	12
S13	●	|	Memphis	23	6
S25			Nebraska	14	38
O4	●	|	at Cincinnati	22	20
O11		|	at Alabama	3	17
O25	●	|	South Florida	27	6
N1	●	|	La. Lafayette	48	3
N8	●	|	at Houston	31	10
N15	●	|	Tulane	28	14
N20	●	|	TCU	40	28
N29	●	|	at East Carolina	38	21
			LIBERTY BOWL		
D31			Utah	0	17

2004   7-5   (5-3)

S11	●		at Nebraska	21	17
S25	●	|	at Tulane	32	14
O2	●	|	at South Florida	27	20
O7	●	|	Houston	35	29
O16		|	at Alabama	3	27
O23	●	|	East Carolina	51	10
N6		|	Cincinnati	24	52
N13		|	at Memphis	26	30
N20		|	at TCU	17	42
N27	●	|	UAB	26	21
D4		|	California	16	26
			NEW ORLEANS BOWL		
D14	●		North Texas	31	10

THE SCHOOLS

STANFORD

BY BUD WITHERS

NOTHING IS QUITE LIKE A FOOTBALL game at Stanford—for better or worse. Saturday afternoons at 85,500-seat Stanford Stadium usually have an easy ambience to them, in marked contrast to the hard-edged urgency of games in the South and Midwest. Leland Stanford, a California governor and U.S. senator, founded the university on 650 acres that had served as breeding and training grounds for his trotting horses. On game day, the routine for many on the sprawling Farm is a wine-and-cheese tailgate among the eucalyptus trees, followed by a football game in a milieu where the term "student-athlete" is still a cherished concept. But don't make the leap that football here is a feckless enterprise. Stanford has played in 12 Rose Bowls, and its decorated history includes innovation as well as a list of coaching luminaries that is perhaps unparalleled.

TRADITION On game day, Stanford players take part in The Walk along Sam McDonald Road, a quarter-mile stretch that leads from their dressing quarters to Stanford Stadium. But outsiders know Stanford better for its zany marching band that twits the establishment and occasionally embarrasses and infuriates those associated with the school. Stanford had a conventional marching band through 1963, but budget cuts forced the change to a more ad hoc group, which then evolved into the free-spirited outfit seen today. Band members wear black pants and red sport jackets—and anything else that might suit their mood. The group has elicited disgust not only from other schools but also from Stanford itself, for performing irreverent skits on a wide variety of subjects.

BEST PLAYER There was no Heisman Trophy in the mid-1920s, but if there had been, Ernie Nevers likely would have won it. Nevers, a Minnesota native, moved to Santa Rosa, Calif., before his senior year of high school and excelled at Stanford as a fullback, being named by *Sports Illustrated* in 1962 as its greatest football player ever. Against Notre Dame and the Four Horsemen in the 1925 Rose Bowl, Nevers played on two heavily braced ankles fractured earlier in the season, rushing for 114 yards on 34 carries in a losing effort. Nevers is popularly viewed as Stanford's

PROFILE

Stanford University
Stanford, Calif.
Founded: 1885
Enrollment: 6,753
Colors: Cardinal and White
Nickname: Cardinal
Stadium: Stanford Stadium
    Opened in 1921
    Grass; 85,500 capacity
First football game: 1891
All-time record: 535–399–49 (.569)
Bowl record: 9–10–1
Consensus national championships, 1936-present: 1 (1940)
Pac-10 championships: 12 (8 outright)
Heisman Trophy: Jim Plunkett, 1970
First-round NFL draftees: 19
Website: www.gostanford.com

THE BEST OF TIMES

Stanford interrupted USC's conference stranglehold with consecutive Rose Bowl victories in 1971 and 1972.

THE WORST OF TIMES

From 1958 to 1964, Stanford went 22–48 and had seven consecutive nonwinning seasons. The low point was an 0-10 record in 1960.

CONFERENCE

A longtime member of the Pac-10 Conference, Stanford joined the Pac-10's forerunner, the Pacific Coast Conference, in 1918.

DISTINGUISHED ALUMNI

Tiger Woods; Herbert Hoover; Sandra Day O'Connor; William Rehnquist; John Steinbeck; William Hewlett and David Packard, co-founders, Hewlett-Packard; Sally Ride, first U.S. woman in space; Sigourney Weaver, actress

FIGHT SONG

ALL RIGHT NOW
There she stood in the street
Smiling from her head to her feet
I said a hey, what is this now baby, maybe,
Maybe, she's in need of a kiss
I said hey, what's your name baby
Maybe we can see things the same
Now don't you wait or hesitate
Let's move before they raise the parking rate

All right now, baby it'sa all right now
All right now, baby it'sa all right now

I took her home, to my place
Watching every move on her face
She said "look, what's your game baby,
Are you trying put me in shame"
I said "slow … don't go so fast,
Don't you think that love can last?"
She said, "Love … Lord above,
Now you're trying to trick me in love"

All right now, baby it'sa all right now
All right now, baby it'sa all right now

greatest player, but quarterback Jim Plunkett won the school's only Heisman in 1970, part of a storybook college career. Plunkett had been raised by Mexican-American parents who met at a school for the blind, and his early performance at Stanford was so undistinguished there was talk about moving him to defensive end. He went on to set school passing records and become MVP of both the Rose Bowl and Super Bowl.

BEST COACH Stanford's coaching roster is littered with illustrious names: Walter Camp (1892, 1894-95), Fielding "Hurry Up" Yost (1900), Glenn "Pop" Warner (1924-32), Clark Shaughnessy (1940-41), John Ralston (1963-71), Bill Walsh (1977-78, 1992-94) and Tyrone Willingham (1995-2001). Warner belongs at the top of the list for compiling a 71–17–8 record at Stanford and, even more important, for authoring imaginative offenses with the single- and double-wing attacks. The double-wing meant halfbacks aligned outside the ends, leading to an intricate series of reverses, passes and other plays that were deceptive in their

Stanford plays its games in a milieu where the term "student-athlete" still represents a cherished concept.

time. He also introduced the huddle and a numbering system for plays. Shaughnessy was also an innovator of note: in his T-formation, quarterback Frankie Albert lined up directly behind the center with the backs abreast behind him. Shaughnessy's 1940 team, the Wow Boys, swept to a 10–0 record, including a 21-13 victory over Nebraska in the Rose Bowl that certified the T formation as a burgeoning new force in the game. Shaughnessy was the classic mad scientist, forgetting names, becoming lost in thought and once having to confess to a Los Angeles police officer that his weaving down a major thoroughfare was caused by his diagramming a play in the condensation on his windshield.

BEST TEAM The 1926 Stanford team won the school's first national championship and the only title the school claims—awarded on the basis of rankings compiled by a University of Illinois economics professor, Frank Dickinson. Led by All-America end Ted Shipkey and sophomore fullback Clifford "Biff" Hoffman, the 1926

RECORDS

RUSHING YARDS
GAME
220   Jon Volpe vs. Washington, Oct. 29, 1988 (29 att.)
SEASON
1,084   Tommy Vardell, 1991 (226 att.)
CAREER
4,033   Darrin Nelson, 1977-81 (703 att.)

PASSING YARDS
GAME
450   Todd Husak vs. Oregon State, Oct. 10, 1998 (26 of 48)
SEASON
3,627   Steve Stenstrom, 1993 (300 of 455)
CAREER
10,531   Steve Stenstrom, 1991-94 (833 of 1,320)

RECEIVING YARDS
GAME
278   Troy Walters vs. UCLA, Sept. 25, 1999 (9 rec.)
SEASON
1,456   Troy Walters, 1999 (74 rec.)
CAREER
3,986   Troy Walters, 1996-99 (244 rec.)

POINTS
GAME
30   Darrin Nelson vs. Oregon State, Nov. 7, 1981 (5 TDs)
SEASON
120   Tommy Vardell, 1991 (20 TDs)
CAREER
282   Eric Abrams, 1992-95 (52 FGs, 126 PATs)

CONSENSUS ALL-AMERICANS

1924	Jim Lawson	E
1925	Ernie Nevers	RB
1928	Seraphim Post	G
1928	Don Robesky	G
1932-33	Bill Corbus	G
1934	Bob Reynolds	T
1934-35	Bobby Grayson	B
1935	Monk Moscrip	E
1940-41	Frank Albert	B
1942	Chuck Taylor	G
1950-51	Bill McColl	E
1956	John Brodie	QB
1970	Jim Plunkett	QB
1971	Jeff Siemon	LB
1974	Pat Donovan	DL
1977	Guy Benjamin	QB
1979-80	Ken Margerum	WR
1982	John Elway	QB
1986	Brad Muster	RB
1991	Bob Whitfield	OL
1999	Troy Walters	WR

team went 10–0–1; its only blemish was a 7-7 tie in the Rose Bowl against Alabama. In Pasadena, Stanford used the fakes and reverses of Warner's offense to dominate the Crimson Tide statistically—gaining 311 yards to Alabama's 92—but surrendered a blocked punt deep in its territory late in the game and allowed the tying touchdown.

Though it played many close games, Shaughnessy's 1940 team also deserves candidacy as the program's best. It featured the magical Albert, halfbacks Pete Kmetovic and Hugh Gallarneau and fullback Norm Standlee, a backfield Shaughnessy described as among the dozen greatest of all time.

BIGGEST GAME Appearing in the Rose Bowl for a second straight year in 1972, Stanford faced the classic offensive challenge of West Coast teams of that era: a pass-oriented attack versus the crunching running game of Michigan. The Indians—Stanford's nickname then—were led by senior quarterback Don Bunce and a defensive line dubbed the Thunderchickens by Pete Lazetich, a tackle who likened its recklessness to a motorcycle gang in his Billings, Mont., hometown. The 11–0 Wolverines ground out 264 yards on an astonishing 74 carries, but Stanford prevailed 13-12 with a stirring rally from a 10-3 fourth-quarter deficit that was capped by Rod Garcia's 31-yard field goal with 12 seconds left.

BIGGEST UPSET Stanford has always been associated with passing offense, and that was the key element in the 1971 Rose Bowl against Ohio State. The Buckeyes were ranked second and were favored by as many as 13 points in some quarters—owing partly to Stanford's up-and-down play that season, including losses to Air Force and California in its previous two games. But Plunkett completed 20 passes in 30 attempts for 265 yards, and Stanford drove 80 yards for the winning score in the fourth quarter for a 27-17 victory. The go-ahead touchdown came after a key defensive stop on fourth and one at the Stanford 20.

ALL-CENTENNIAL TEAM		
The team, which was announced in conjunction with the university's centennial celebration in 1991, was selected by a vote of fans for Stanford players and coaches from 1891 to 1991.		
1963-71	John Ralston, COACH	
OFFENSE		
1940-42	Chuck Taylor, OG	
1966-68	George Buehler, OG	
1933-35	Bob Reynolds, OT	
1965-67	Blaine Nye, OT	
1940-41	Vic Lindskog, C	
1949-51	Bill McColl, TE	
1966-68	Gene Washington, WR	
1975-77	James Lofton, WR	
1968-70	Jim Plunkett, QB	
1923-25	Ernie Nevers, RB	
1977-81	Darrin Nelson, RB	
1971-73	Rod Garcia, PK	
DEFENSE		
1954-56	Paul Wiggin, DL	
1969-71	Pete Lazetich, DL	
1972-74	Pat Donovan, DL	
1981-84	Garin Veris, DL	
1969-71	Jeff Siemon, LB	
1975-78	Gordy Ceresino, LB	
1982-84, 1986	David Wyman, LB	
1949-51	Dick Horn, DB	
1970-71	Benny Barnes, DB	
1971-73	Randy Poltl, DB	
1984-86	Toi Cook, DB	
1939-41	Frankie Albert, P	

STADIUM Completed in 1921, sprawling Stanford Stadium has hosted some of the world's greatest events, including World Cup soccer in 1994 and Super Bowl XIX in 1985. The U.S.-Soviet track meet in 1962 that drew 150,000 fans over two days also took place there.

RIVAL Stanford and California engage in a kind of erudite joust with the common aim of proving which of the two prestigious schools is superior. The rivalry began with a thud in 1891 in front of more than 15,000 spectators in San Francisco, when nobody brought a ball; the game was delayed an hour as a sporting-goods store owner had to ride a horse into town to fetch one. In 1902 and 1924, the teams turned each other in for ineligible players. And then there's the Axe, an imposing 10-pound, 15-inch blade for which the programs annually vie. It was first bought by Stanford rooters in 1899 but pirated by Golden Bears supporters to Berkeley, where it stayed until 1930. At that time, a Stanford delegation, with some in the group posing as newspaper photographers, heisted the trophy as it was being returned to its sanctuary in a bank after a Cal pep rally. There have been multiple thefts of the Axe.

DUBIOUS DISTINCTION It was Stanford that played unwitting foil to California's famous five-lateral extravaganza on the last play of the game in 1982. Indelibly stamped on fans' minds is the sight of Cal's Kevin Moen completing the touchdown by running into trombonist Gary Tyrrell as the Stanford band waited in the end zone for a celebration that never happened.

NICKNAME In 1930, Stanford officially adopted Indians as its nickname, but that was dropped in 1972 after a vote of the student senate was made in response to dissent among the school's Native Americans. In 1975, a move to reinstate the nickname failed, but not until—in typical freethinking Stanford fashion—other suggestions went down as well,

including Robber Barons, Railroaders, Sequoias and Huns. In 1981, university president Donald Kennedy declared that the operative nickname would be the singular description "Cardinal."

MASCOT Officially, the Cardinal doesn't have one. But the Tree is its most recognizable entity—a loopy, oversized, green-felt creation with distended eyes. It originates from the tree on the official Stanford seal.

UNIFORMS Stanford plays in a rather traditional outfit: at home, cardinal jerseys with white pants and double red piping; on the road, exactly the opposite. All helmets are white with a cardinal stripe and a block-S logo on the sides.

QUOTE "The football players there have almost no contact with the rest of the student body. They have an athletic department compound, and that's where they spend their time. When they use up their eligibility and are expected to return to society, they have none of the skills you are supposed to gain in college." — Bill Walsh, differentiating between the University of Washington and the Cardinal program at a controversial 1993 Sacramento booster engagement

STANFORD ANNUAL STATISTICAL LEADERS

YR	RUSHING	YDS	ATT	AVG	PASSING	ATT	CMP	PCT	YDS	RECEIVING	REC	YDS	AVG
1963	Steve Thurlow	495	92	5.4	Dick Berg	62	29	.47	301	Bob Howard	11	174	15.8
1964	Ray Handley	936	197	4.8	Terry DeSylvia	71	39	.55	451	John Mason	22	250	11.4
1965	Ray Handley	654	163	4.0	Dave Lewis	183	94	.51	1,257	Mike Connelly	29	366	12.6
1966	Jack Root	571	136	4.2	Gene Washington	102	35	.34	479	Bob Conrad	45	555	12.3
1967	Nate Kirtman	573	130	4.4	Chuck Williams	153	76	.50	923	Gene Washington	48	575	12.0
1968	Howie Williams	499	105	4.8	Jim Plunkett	268	142	.53	2,156	Gene Washington	71	1,117	15.7
1969	Bubba Brown	588	127	4.6	Jim Plunkett	336	197	.59	2,673	Bob Moore	38	476	12.5
1970	Hillary Shockley	622	171	3.6	Jim Plunkett	358	191	.53	2,715	Randy Vataha	48	844	17.6
1971	Jackie Brown	479	124	3.9	Don Bunce	297	162	.55	2,265	Miles Moore	38	816	21.5
1972	John Winesberry	536	125	4.3	Mike Boryla	350	183	.52	2,284	Eric Cross	53	730	13.8
1973	Scott Laidlaw	639	145	4.4	Mike Boryla	256	140	.55	1,629	Bill Singler	31	501	16.2
1974	Scott Laidlaw	636	156	4.1	Mike Cordova	295	128	.43	1,569	Tony Hill	34	542	15.9
1975	Don Stevenson	650	138	4.7	Mike Cordova	231	106	.46	1,311	Tony Hill	55	916	16.7
1976	Don Stevenson	452	121	3.7	Guy Benjamin	295	170	.58	1,982	Tony Hill	44	696	15.8
1977	Darrin Nelson	1,069	183	5.8	Guy Benjamin	330	208	.63	2,521	James Lofton	53	931	17.6
1978	Darrin Nelson	1,061	167	6.4	Steve Dils	391	247	.63	2,943	Ken Margerum	53	942	17.8
1979	Vincent White	475	104	4.6	Turk Schonert	221	148	.67	1,927	Andre Tyler	45	652	14.5
1980	Darrin Nelson	889	161	5.5	John Elway	379	248	.65	2,889	Andre Tyler	53	737	13.9
1981	Darrin Nelson	1,014	192	5.3	John Elway	366	214	.58	2,674	Darrin Nelson	67	846	12.6
1982	Mike Dotterer	535	113	4.7	John Elway	405	262	.65	3,242	Vincent White	68	677	10.0
1983	Thomas Henley	228	66	3.5	John Paye	297	150	.51	1,971	Mike Tolliver	58	656	11.3
1984	Brad Muster	823	184	4.5	Fred Buckley	166	81	.49	940	Brad Muster	31	228	7.4
1985	Brad Muster	521	140	3.7	John Paye	405	271	.67	2,589	Brad Muster	78	654	8.4
1986	Brad Muster	1,053	243	4.3	John Paye	349	217	.62	2,261	Brad Muster	61	565	9.3
1987	Brad Muster	543	119	4.6	Brian Johnson	203	112	.55	1,510	Jeff James	42	516	12.3
1988	Jon Volpe	1,027	228	4.5	Jason Palumbis	228	128	.56	1,569	Charlie Young	43	560	13.0
1989	Scott Eschelman	334	77	4.3	Steve Smith	270	150	.56	1,502	Ed McCaffrey	53	871	16.4
1990	Glyn Milburn	729	152	4.8	Jason Palumbis	341	234	.69	2,579	Glyn Milburn	64	632	9.9
1991	Tommy Vardell	1,084	226	4.8	Steve Stenstrom	197	119	.60	1,683	Chris Walsh	66	934	14.2
1992	Glyn Milburn	851	177	4.8	Steve Stenstrom	335	197	.59	2,399	Mike Cook	51	649	12.7
1993	Ellery Roberts	419	111	3.8	Steve Stenstrom	455	300	.66	3,627	Ethan Allen	52	313	6.0
1994	Anthony Bookman	577	129	4.5	Steve Stenstrom	333	217	.65	2,822	Justin Armour	67	1,092	16.3
1995	Anthony Bookman	872	181	4.8	Mark Butterfield	333	194	.58	2,533	Mark Harris	57	984	17.3
1996	Mike Mitchell	809	164	4.9	Chad Hutchinson	312	190	.61	2,134	Brian Manning	37	383	10.4
1997	Anthony Bookman	800	122	6.6	Chad Hutchinson	315	189	.60	2,101	Troy Walters	86	1,206	14.0
1998	Coy Wire	298	85	3.5	Todd Husak	447	233	.52	3,092	DeRonnie Pitts	74	1,012	13.7
1999	Brian Allen	604	115	5.3	Todd Husak	308	176	.57	2,688	Troy Walters	74	1,456	19.7
2000	Kerry Carter	729	179	4.1	Randy Fasani	180	93	.52	1,400	DeRonnie Pitts	77	882	11.5
2001	Brian Allen	899	174	5.2	Randy Fasani	167	86	.51	1,479	Luke Powell	40	790	19.8
2002	Kerry Carter	524	149	3.5	Kyle Matter	214	116	.54	1,219	Teyo Johnson	41	467	11.4
2003	Kenneth Tolon	522	150	3.5	Chris Lewis	207	100	.48	1,178	Luke Powell	45	520	11.6
2004	J.R. Lemon	440	93	4.7	Trent Edwards	271	148	.55	1,718	Alex Smith	52	706	13.6

Receiving leaders by receptions
All statistics include postseason

STANFORD ALL-TIME SCORES

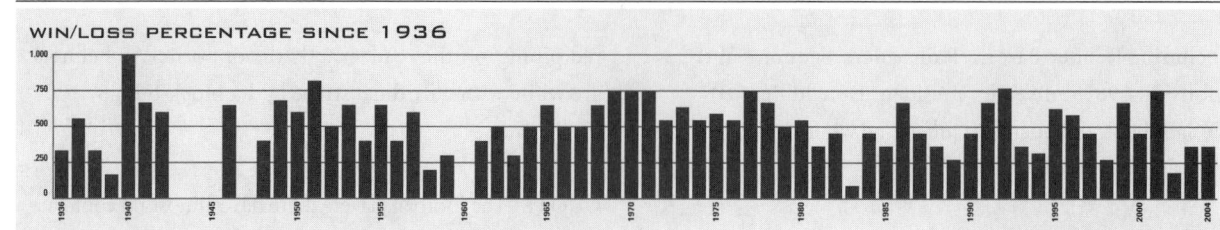

WIN/LOSS PERCENTAGE SINCE 1936

NO HEAD COACH

1891 — 3-1-0
U	●	Hopkins Acad.	10	6
U	●	Berkely Gym *SJ*	22	0
U		Olympic Club	6	10
M19	●	California *SF*	14	10

WALTER CAMP
1892, '94-95 (.735) — 11-3-3

1892 — 1-0-2
U	●	Olympic Club	20	5
U	=	Olympic Club *SF*	14	14
D17	=	California *SF*	10	10

POP BLISS
1893 (.944) — 8-0-1

1893 — 8-0-1
U	●	Olympic Club *SF*	46	0
U	●	Reliance Club *SJ*	34	0
U	●	Olympic Club *SF*	24	11
N30	=	California *SF*	6	6
U	●	Reliance Club *SF*	18	0
U	●	at Tacoma	48	0
U	●	at Port Townsend	50	0
D29	●	at Washington	40	0
U	●	Multnomah AC *Port*	18	0

WALTER CAMP

1894 — 6-3-0
U	●	Reliance Club *SF*	4	12
U	●	at Santa Cruz	14	4
U	●	Reliance Club *SF*	6	12
U	●	at Sacramento	6	0
U	●	Reliance Club	20	0
N29	●	California *SF*	6	0
D15	●	Chicago *SF*	4	24
D17	●	Chicago *LA*	12	0
U	●	at Los Angeles AC	28	0

1895 — 4-0-1
O19	●	Olympic Club	4	0
O23	●	Reliance Club	8	0
N5	●	Olympic Club *SF*	10	2
N16	●	Olympic Club	6	0
N28	=	California	6	6

H.P. CROSS
1896, '98 (.615) — 7-4-2

1896 — 2-1-1
U	=	Olympic Club *SF*	0	0
U	●	Reliance Club *SF*	10	0
U	●	Olympic Club *SF*	0	4
N26	●	California *SF*	20	0

G.H. BROOKE
1897 (.800) — 4-1

1897 — 4-1-0
U	●	Reliance Club *SF*	6	4
U	●	Reliance Club *SF*	8	6
U	●	Reliance club *SJ*	12	6
U	●	Reliance Club *SF*	0	10
N25	●	California *SF*	28	0

H.P. CROSS

1898 — 5-3-1
U	●	Wash. Vol.	22	0
U	●	Kansas Vol.	10	0
U	●	Olympic Club *SF*	22	0
U	●	Kansas Vol.	15	11
U		Iowa Vol.	0	6
U	●	League of the Cross	18	5
U	=	Olympic Club *SF*	6	6
U	●	Olympic Club *SF*	0	12
N24	●	California *SF*	0	22

BURR CHAMBERLAIN
1899 (.222) — 2-5-2

1899 — 2-5-2
U	=	Olympic Club *SF*	0	0
U	=	Olympic Club *SF*	0	0
U	●	Olympic Club *SF*	5	6
U	●	Olympic Club	5	16
N11	●	Nevada	17	5
U	●	Olympic Club *SF*	0	10
N30	●	California *SF*	0	30
U	●	Multnomah AC *Port*	6	11
U	●	All-Seattle	28	0

FIELDING H. YOST
1900 (.750) — 7-2-1

1900 — 7-2-1
U	●	Reliance Club	6	0
U	●	at San Jose State	35	0
U	●	Reliance Club *SF*	6	0
U	●	San Jose State	24	0
U	●	Stanford A.L.	0	14
U	●	Reliance Club	44	0
N10	●	Oregon	34	0
N17	●	Nevada	0	6
N29	●	California *SF*	5	0
U	=	Multnomah AC *Port*	0	0

C.M. FICKERT
1901 (.571) — 3-2-2

1901 — 3-2-2
U	●	Olympic Club	6	0
U	●	Reliance Club *SF*	0	0
U	=	Olympic Club *SF*	6	6
U	●	Reliance Club	10	0
N2	●	Nevada	12	0
N9	●	California *SF*	0	2
		ROSE BOWL		
J1		Michigan	0	49

C.L. CLEMANS
1902 (.857) — 6-1

1902 — 6-1-0
U	●	Reliance Club	12	0
U	●	Alumni	18	0
U	●	Reliance Club	12	0
O25	●	Nevada	11	5
U	●	Reliance Club	23	5
N8	●	California *SF*	0	16
N27	●	at Utah	33	11

JAMES F. LANAGAN
1903-05 (.862) — 23-2-4

1903 — 8-0-3
U	=	Reliance Club	0	0
U	●	Pensacola	17	0
U	●	Reliance Club	34	0
U	●	Pensacola	34	0
U	●	Fort Baker	57	0
O24	=	Nevada	0	0
U	●	Chemawa	33	0
U	●	Reliance Club	17	0
U	●	Multnomah AC	11	0
N14	=	California *SF*	6	6
U	●	Sherman *LA*	18	0

1904 — 7-2-1
U	●	Olympic Club	0	5
U	●	Pensacola	34	0
U	●	Olympic Club	12	0
U		Sherman	0	5
U	●	Multnomah AC *U*	0	0
O22	●	Nevada	17	0
O29	●	Oregon	35	0
U	●	Utah State	57	0
N12	●	at California	18	0
N24	●	Colorado	33	0

1905 — 8-0-0
U	●	State Vincent	10	0
U	●	Willamette	12	0
U	●	15th Infantry	51	0
O18	●	Oregon	10	4
O26	●	Nevada	21	0
U	●	Sherman	6	4
N4	●	Southern Cal	16	0
N11	●	California	12	5

1906-1917
NO TEAM-PLAYED RUGBY

1918-1958
PACIFIC COAST

A.H. BADENOCH
1918 (.000) — 0-4

1918 — 0-4-0 (0-1-0)
N2		Mare Island	0	80
N9		Mather Field	0	70
N23		Southern Cal *Pas*	8	25
N30		at California	0	67

BOB EVANS
1919 (.571) — 4-3

1919 — 4-3-0 (1-1-0)
O11	●	USS Boston	59	0
O18	●	Olympic Club	0	13
O25	●	at Oregon State	14	6
N1	●	Saint Mary's-Cal	34	0
N8	●	Santa Clara	13	0
N22		California	10	14
N27	●	at Southern Cal	0	13

WALTER POWELL
1920 (.571) — 4-3

1920 — 4-3-0 (2-1-0)
O2	●	Saint Mary's-Cal	41	0
O9	●	Olympic Club	7	10
O16	●	at Southern Cal	0	10
O23	●	at Santa Clara	21	7
O30		Oregon	10	0
N6		at Washington	3	0
N20		at California	0	38

C.E. VAN GENT
1921 (.625) — 4-2-2

1921 — 4-2-2 (1-1-1)
O1	●	US Marines	41	0
O8	●	Saint Mary's-Cal	10	7
O15	●	Olympic Club	7	0
O22	●	Pacific Fleet	7	27
O29		Oregon State	14	7
N5	=	at Washington	0	0
N12	=	Nevada	14	14
N19		California	7	42

ANDREW KERR
1922-23 (.611) — 11-7

1922 — 4-5-0 (1-3-0)
O7	●	Olympic Club	9	27
O14	●	Santa Clara	7	0
O21	●	Saint Mary's-Cal	9	0
O28	●	at Oregon State	6	0
N4	●	Nevada	17	7
N11	●	Southern Cal	0	6
N18	●	Washington	8	12
N25	●	California	0	28
D30	●	Pittsburgh	7	16

1923 — 7-2-0 (2-2-0)
S29	●	Mare Island	82	0
O6	●	Nevada	27	0
O13	●	Santa Clara	55	6
O20	●	at Occidental	42	0
O27	●	Southern Cal	7	14
N3	●	Olympic Club	40	7
N10	●	at Oregon	14	3
N17	●	Idaho	17	7
N24	●	at California	0	9

GLENN "POP" WARNER
1924-32 (.781) — 71-17-8

1924 — 7-1-1 (3-0-1)
O4	●	Occidental	20	6
O11	●	Olympic Club	7	0
O18	●	Oregon	28	13
O25	●	Idaho *Port*	3	0
N1	●	Santa Clara	20	0
N8	●	Utah *Berk*	30	0
N15	●	Montana	41	3
N22	=	at California	20	20
		ROSE BOWL		
J1		Notre Dame	10	27

1925 — 7-2-0 (4-1-0)
S26	●	Olympic Club	0	9
O3	●	Santa Clara	20	3
O10	●	Occidental	28	0
O17	●	at Southern Cal	13	9
O24	●	Oregon State	26	10
O31	●	Oregon	35	13
N7	●	at Washington	0	13
N14	●	UCLA	82	0
N21	●	California	27	14

1926 — 10-0-1 (4-0-1)
S18	●	Fresno State	44	0
S25	●	Cal Tech	13	0
O2	●	Occidental	19	0
O9	●	Olympic Club	7	3
O16	●	Nevada	33	9
O23	●	at Oregon	19	12 *
O30	●	at Southern Cal	13	12
N6	●	Santa Clara	33	14
N13	●	Washington	29	10
N20	●	at California	41	6
		ROSE BOWL		
J1	=	Alabama	7	7

1927 — 8-2-1 (4-0-1)
S17	●	Fresno State	44	7
S24	●	Olympic Club	7	6
O1	●	Saint Mary's-Cal	0	16
O8	●	Nevada	20	2
O15	=	Southern Cal	13	13
O22	●	Oregon State *Port*	20	6
O29	●	Oregon	19	0
N5	●	at Washington	13	7
N12	●	Santa Clara	6	13
N19	●	California	13	6
		ROSE BOWL		
J2		Pittsburgh	7	6

THE SCHOOLS

1928 — 8-3-1 (4-1-1)

	Opponent		
S15	YMI	0	7
S22 ●	West Coast Army	21	8
S29	Olympic Club	6	12
O6 ●	at Oregon	26	12 *
O13 ●	UCLA	45	7
O20 ●	Idaho SF	47	0
O27 ●	Fresno State	47	0
N3	at Southern Cal	0	10
N10 ●	Santa Clara	31	0
N17 ●	Washington	12	0
N24 =	at California	13	13
D1 ●	Army BRNX	26	0

1929 — 9-2-0 (5-1-0)

	Opponent		
S21 ●	West Coast Army	45	0
S28 ●	Olympic Club	6	0
O5 ●	Oregon	33	7
O12 ●	at UCLA	57	0
O19 ●	Oregon State	40	7
O26 ●	Southern Cal	0	7
N2 ●	Cal Tech	39	0
N9 ●	at Washington	6	0
N16 ●	Santa Clara	7	13
N23 ●	California	21	6
D28 ●	Army	34	13

1930 — 9-1-1 (4-1-0)

	Opponent		
S20 ●	West Coast Army	32	0
S27 ●	Olympic Club	18	0
O4 ●	Santa Clara	20	0
O11 =	at Minnesota	0	0
O18 ●	Oregon State	13	7
O25	Southern Cal	12	41
O31	UCLA	20	0
N8 ●	Washington	25	7
N15 ●	Cal Tech	57	7
N22 ●	at California	41	0
N29 ●	Dartmouth	14	7

1931 — 7-2-2 (2-2-1)

	Opponent		
S19 ●	West Coast Army	46	0
S26 ●	Olympic Club	0	0
O3 ●	Santa Clara	6	0
O10 ●	Minnesota	13	0
O17 ●	Oregon State	25	7
O24 =	at Washington	0	0
O31 ●	UCLA	12	6
N7	at Southern Cal	0	19
N14 ●	Nevada	26	0
N21	California	0	6
N28 ●	Dartmouth BOS	32	6

1932 — 6-4-1 (1-3-1)

	Opponent		
S17 ●	Olympic Club	6	0
S24 ●	at San Francisco	20	7
O1 ●	Oregon State PORT	27	0
O8 ●	Santa Clara	14	0
O15 ●	West Coast Army	26	0
O22	Southern Cal	0	13
O29	at UCLA	6	13
N5	Washington	13	18
N12 ●	Cal State	59	0
N19 =	at California	0	0
N26	at Pittsburgh	0	7

C.E. THORNHILL
1933-39 (.575) — 35-25-7

1933 — 8-2-1 (4-1-0)

	Opponent		
S23 ●	San Jose State	27	0
S30 ●	UCLA	3	0
O7 ●	Santa Clara	7	0
O14 =	Northwestern CHI	0	0
O21 ●	at San Francisco	20	13
O28	at Washington	0	6
N4 ●	Olympic Club	21	0
N11 ●	at Southern Cal	13	7
N18 ●	Montana	33	7
N25 ●	California	7	3
	ROSE BOWL		
J1	Columbia	0	7

1934 — 9-1-1 (5-0-0)

	Opponent		
S22 ●	San Jose State	48	0
S29 =	Santa Clara	7	7
O6 ●	Oregon State PORT	17	0
O13 ●	Northwestern	20	0
O20 ●	at San Francisco	3	0
O27 ●	Southern Cal	16	0
N3 ●	at UCLA	27	0
N10	Washington	24	0
N17 ●	Olympic Club	40	0
N24 ●	at California	9	7
	ROSE BOWL		
J1	Alabama	13	29

1935 — 8-1-0 (4-1-0)

	Opponent		
S28 ●	San Jose State	35	0
O5 ●	at San Francisco	10	0
O19	UCLA	6	7
O26 ●	at Washington	6	0
N2 ●	Santa Clara	9	6
N9 ●	at Southern Cal	3	0
N16 ●	Montana	32	0
N23 ●	California	13	0
	ROSE BOWL		
J1	SMU	7	0

1936 — 2-5-2 (2-3-2)

	Opponent		
S26	Santa Clara	0	13
O3	at Washington State	13	14
O10 =	Oregon	7	7
O24	Southern Cal	7	14
O31 ●	at UCLA	19	6
N7	Washington	14	14
N14 ●	Oregon State PORT	20	14
N21	at California	0	20
N28	Columbia NYC	0	7

1937 — 4-3-2 (4-2-1)

	Opponent		
S25	Santa Clara	7	13
O2	at Oregon	6	7
O9 ●	UCLA	12	7
O23 ●	at Washington	13	7
O30 =	Oregon State	0	0
N6	at Southern Cal	7	6
N13 ●	Washington State	23	0
N20	California	0	13
N27 =	at Columbia	0	0

1938 — 3-6-0 (2-5-0)

	Opponent		
O1 ●	Santa Clara	0	22
O8 ●	Washington State	8	0
O15 ●	Oregon	27	16
O22	Southern Cal	2	13
O29 ●	at UCLA	0	6
N5	Washington	7	10
N12 ●	at Oregon State	0	6
N19 ●	at California	0	6
N26 ●	Dartmouth	23	13

1939 — 1-7-1 (0-6-1)

	Opponent		
S30	Oregon State	0	12
O7	Oregon PORT	0	10
O14 =	UCLA	14	14
O28	at Washington	5	8
N4	Santa Clara	7	27
N11	at Southern Cal	0	33
N18	Washington State	0	7
N25	California	14	32
D2	Dartmouth NYC	14	13

CLARK SHAUGHNESSY
1940-41 (.842) — 16-3

1940 — 10-0-0 (7-0-0)

	Opponent		
S28 ●	at San Francisco	27	0
O5	Oregon	13	0
O12	Santa Clara	7	6
O19 ●	at Washington State	26	14
O26	Southern Cal	21	7
N2	at UCLA	20	14
N9	Washington	20	10
N16 ●	Oregon State	28	14
N30 ●	at California	13	7
	ROSE BOWL		
J1	Nebraska	21	13

1941 — 6-3-0 (4-3-0)

	Opponent		
S27	Oregon	19	15
O4 ●	UCLA	33	0
O11	at Oregon State	0	10
O18 ●	San Francisco	42	26
O25 ●	at Washington	13	7
N1 ●	Santa Clar	27	7
N8	at Southern Cal	13	0
N15	Washington State	13	14
N29	California	0	16

MARCHMONT SCHWARTZ
1942-50 (.500) — 28-28-4

1942 — 6-4-0 (5-2-0)

	Opponent		
S26	Washington State	0	6
O3	Santa Clara SF	6	14
O10	at Notre Dame	0	27
O17 ●	Idaho	54	7
O24 ●	Southern Cal SF	14	6
O31 ●	at UCLA	7	20 *
N7 ●	Washington SF	20	7
N14 ●	Oregon State	49	13
N21 ●	at California	26	7
N28 ●	Saint Mary's-Cal Pre-Flight	28	13

1943-1945
NO TEAM WWII

1946 — 6-3-1 (3-3-1)

	Opponent		
S28 ●	Idaho	45	0
O5 ●	San Francisco	33	7
O12 ●	at UCLA	6	26
O19 ●	Santa Clara	33	27
O26 ●	Southern Cal	20	28
N2	at Oregon State	0	0
N9	Washington	15	21
N16 ●	Washington State	27	26
N23 ●	at California	25	6
D23 ●	at Hawaii	18	7

1947 — 0-9-0 (0-7-0)

	Opponent		
S27	Idaho	16	19
O4	at Michigan	13	49
O11	Santa Clara	7	13
O18	UCLA	6	39
O25	at Washington	0	25
N1	Oregon State	7	13
N8	at Southern Cal	0	14
N15	Oregon	6	21
N22	California	18	21

1948 — 4-6-0 (3-4-0)

	Opponent		
S18 ●	San Jose State	26	20
S25	Oregon	12	20
O2	at Washington State	7	14
O9	Santa Clara	14	27
O16 ●	at UCLA	34	14
O23	Southern Cal	6	7
O30 ●	Washington	20	0
N6	Army BRNX	0	43
N13 ●	Montana	39	7
N20	at California	6	7

1949 — 7-3-1 (4-2-0)

	Opponent		
S17 ●	San Jose State	49	0
S24 ●	Harvard	44	0
O1	Michigan	7	27
O8	UCLA	7	14
O15 ●	at Washington	40	0
O22 ●	Oregon State	27	7
O29 =	Santa Clara	7	7
N5 ●	at Southern Cal	34	13
N12 ●	Idaho	63	0
N19	California	14	33
J2 ●	at Hawaii	74	20

1950 — 5-3-2 (2-2-2)

	Opponent		
S23 ●	San Jose State	33	16
S30 ●	San Francisco	55	7
O7	Oregon State PORT	21	7 *
O14 ●	Santa Clara	23	13
O21	at UCLA	7	21
O28	Washington	7	21
N4 =	Southern Cal	7	7
N11 ●	Washington State	26	17 *
N18	Army	0	7
N25 =	at California	7	7

CHARLES A. TAYLOR
1951-57 (.577) — 40-29-2

1951 — 9-2-0 (6-1-0)

	Opponent		
S22 ●	Oregon PORT	27	20
S29 ●	San Jose State	26	13
O6	at Michigan	23	13
O13 ●	UCLA	21	7
O20 ●	Santa Clara	21	14
O27 ●	at Washington	14	7
N3 ●	Washington State	21	13
N10 ●	at Southern Cal	27	20
N17 ●	Oregon State	35	14
N24	California	7	20
	ROSE BOWL		
J1	Illinois	7	40

1952 — 5-5-0 (2-5-0)

	Opponent		
S20 ●	Santa Clara	28	13
S27	at Washington State	14	13
O4 ●	Michigan	14	7
O11 ●	Oregon State	41	28
O18	at UCLA	14	24
O25	Washington	14	27
N1 ●	San Jose State	35	13
N8	Southern Cal	7	54
N15 ●	Oregon	20	21
N22	at California	0	26

1953 — 6-3-1 (5-1-1)

	Opponent		
S19	Pacific	20	25
S26 ●	Oregon	7	0
O3	at Illinois	21	33
O10 ●	Oregon State PORT	21	0
O17 ●	UCLA	21	20
O24	at Washington	13	7
O31 ●	Washington State	48	19
N7	at Southern Cal	20	23
N14 ●	San Jose State	54	0
N21 =	California	21	21

1954 — 4-6-0 (2-4-0)

	Opponent		
S17	at Pacific	13	12
S25 ●	Oregon State PORT	18	13
O2	Illinois	12	2
O9	Navy	0	25
O16	at UCLA	0	72
O23 ●	Washington	13	7
O30	Washington State	26	30
N6	Southern Cal	7	21
N13 ●	San Jose State	14	19
N20	at California	20	28

1955 — 6-3-1 (3-2-1)

	Opponent		
S17 ●	Pacific	33	14
S24	Oregon State PORT	0	10
O1 ●	Ohio State	6	0
O8	at Michigan State	14	38
O15 ●	UCLA	13	21
O22 =	at Washington	7	7
O29 ●	San Jose State	34	18
N5	at Southern Cal	28	20
N12	Oregon	44	7
N19	California	19	0

1956 — 4-6-0 (3-4-0)

	Opponent		
S22	Washington State SPO	40	26
S29	Michigan State	7	21
O6	at Ohio State	20	32
O13 ●	San Jose State	40	20
O20 ●	at Oregon	21	7
O27 ●	Southern Cal	27	19
N3	at UCLA	13	14
N10	Oregon State	19	20
N17	Washington	13	34
N24	at California	18	20

1957 — 6-4-0 (4-3-0)

	Opponent		
S21 ●	San Jose State	46	7
S28 ●	Northwestern	26	6
O5	at Rice	7	34
O12	Washington State	18	21
O19 ●	at Washington	21	14
O26	UCLA	20	6
N2	Oregon	26	27
N9 ●	at Southern Cal	35	7
N16	at Oregon State	14	24
N23	California	14	12

JACK C. CURTICE
1958-62 (.280) — 14-36

1958 — 2-8-0 (2-5-0)

	Opponent		
S20	at Washington State	6	40
S27	Rice	7	30
O4	at Northwestern	0	28
O11 ●	Washington	22	12
O18	Air Force	0	16
O25 ●	at UCLA	21	19
N1	Southern Cal	6	29
N8	at Oregon	0	12
N15	Oregon State	16	24
N22	at California	15	16

1959-1967
AAWU

1959 — 3-7-0 (0-4-0)

	Opponent		
S19	Oregon	27	28
S26	at Wisconsin	14	16
O3 ●	Pacific	21	6
O10	at Washington	0	10
O17	Washington State	19	36
O24	at Southern Cal	28	30
O31 ●	San Jose State	54	38
N7	UCLA	13	55
N14	at Oregon State	39	22
N21	California	17	20

1960 0-10-0 (0-4-0)

S17		Washington State [Spo]	14	15
S24		Wisconsin	7	24
O1		Air Force	9	32
O8	|	Washington	10	29
O15		San Jose State	20	34
O22	|	at UCLA	8	26
O29	|	Southern Cal	6	21
N5		Oregon [Port]	6	27
N12		Oregon State	21	25
N19	|	at California	10	21

1961 4-6-0 (1-3-0)

S23	●	Tulane	9	7
S30	●	at Oregon State	34	0
O7		at Michigan State	3	31
O14	●	San Jose State	17	6
O21	|	at Washington	0	13
O28	|	UCLA	0	20
N4		Oregon	7	19
N11	|	at Southern Cal	15	30
N18		Washington State	0	30
N25	● |	California	20	7

1962 5-5-0 (2-3-0)

S21	●	at Tulane	6	3
S29	●	Michigan State	16	13
O6		Oregon State	0	27
O13	|	Washington State [Spo]	6	21
O20	|	Washington	0	14
O27	● |	at UCLA	17	7
N3		Oregon [Port]	14	28
N10	|	Southern Cal	14	39
N17	●	San Jose State	21	9
N24	● |	at California	30	13

JOHN RALSTON
1963-71 (.601) 55-36-3

1963 3-7-0 (1-4-0)

S21	●	San Jose State	29	13
S28		Oregon	7	36
O5	|	UCLA	9	10
O12		at Rice	13	23
O19	|	at Washington	11	19
O26	●	Notre Dame	24	14
N2		at Oregon State	7	10
N9	|	at Southern Cal	11	25
N16	|	Washington State	15	32
N30	● |	California	28	17

1964 5-5-0 (3-4-0)

S19	|	Washington State [Spo]	23	29
S26	●	San Jose State	10	8
O3	|	at UCLA	20	27
O10	●	Rice	34	7
O17	|	Washington	0	6
O24		at Notre Dame	6	28
O31	● |	Oregon [Port]	10	8
N7	|	Southern Cal	10	15
N14	● |	Oregon State	16	7
N21	● |	at California	21	3

1965 6-3-1 (2-3-0)

S17	●	San Jose State	26	6
S25	=	Navy	7	7
O2	●	at Air Force	17	16
O9	● |	Oregon	17	14
O16	|	at Southern Cal	0	14
O23	●	Army	31	14
O30	|	at Washington	8	41
N6	●	at Tulane	16	0
N13	|	UCLA	13	30
N20	● |	California	9	7

1966 5-5-0 (1-4-0)

S17	●	San Jose State	25	21
S24		at Minnesota	21	35
O1	●	Tulane	33	14
O8	|	Oregon [Port]	3	7
O15	|	Southern Cal	7	21
O22	●	at Illinois	6	3
O29	|	Washington	20	22
N5	●	Air Force	21	6
N12	|	at UCLA	0	10
N19	● |	at California	13	7

1967 5-5-0 (3-4-0)

S16	|	Oregon State [Port]	7	13
S23	●	Kansas	21	20
S30	●	San Jose State	28	14
O7	|	at Southern Cal	0	30
O14	● |	Washington State	31	10
O21	|	UCLA	16	21
O28		at Army	20	24
N4	● |	at Washington	14	7
N11	● |	Oregon	17	14
N18	|	California	3	26

1968-PRESENT
PAC 10

1968 6-3-1 (3-3-1)

S21	●	San Jose State	68	20
S28	● |	at Oregon	28	12
O5	●	Air Force	24	13
O12	|	Southern Cal	24	27
O19	= |	Washington State [Spo]	21	21
O26	|	at UCLA	17	20
N2	|	Oregon State	7	29
N9	● |	Washington	35	20
N16	●	at Pacific	24	0
N23	● |	at California	20	0

1969 7-2-1 (5-1-1)

S20	●	San Jose State	63	21
S27	● |	Oregon	28	0
O4		at Purdue	35	36
O11	|	at Southern Cal	24	26
O18	● |	Washington State	49	0
O25	= |	UCLA	20	20
N1	● |	at Oregon State	33	0
N8	● |	at Washington	21	7
N15	●	Air Force	47	34
N22	● |	California	29	28

1970 9-3-0 (6-1-0)

S12	●	Arkansas [LR]	34	28
S19	●	San Jose State	34	3
S26	● |	at Oregon	33	10
O3		Purdue	14	26
O10	● |	Southern Cal	24	14
O17	● |	Washington State [Spo]	63	16
O24	● |	at UCLA	9	7
O31	● |	Oregon State	48	10
N7	● |	Washington	29	22
N14		at Air Force	14	31
N21	|	at California	14	22
		ROSE BOWL		
J1	●	Ohio State	27	17

1971 9-3-0 (6-1-0)

S11	●	at Missouri	19	0
S18	●	at Army	38	3
S25	● |	Oregon	38	17
O2		Duke	3	9
O9	● |	at Washington	17	6
O16	● |	at Southern Cal	33	18
O23	|	Washington State	23	24
O30	● |	at Oregon State	31	24
N6	● |	UCLA	20	9
N13		San Jose State	12	13
N20	● |	California	14	0
		ROSE BOWL		
J1	●	Michigan	13	12

JACK CHRISTIANSEN
1972-76 (.573) 30-22-3

1972 6-5-0 (2-5-0)

S16	●	San Jose State	44	0
S23	●	at Duke	10	6
S30	●	West Virginia	41	35
O7	|	Southern Cal	21	30
O14	● |	Washington	24	0
O21	|	at Oregon	13	15
O28	● |	Oregon State	17	11
N4	|	at UCLA	23	28
N11	|	at Washington State	13	27
N18	|	at California	21	24
D2	●	at Hawaii	39	7

1973 7-4-0 (5-2-0)

S15		Penn State	6	20
S22		at Michigan	10	47
S29	●	San Jose State	23	12
O6	●	at Illinois	24	0
O13	|	UCLA	13	59
O20	● |	at Washington	23	14
O27	● |	Washington State	45	14
N3	● |	at Oregon State	24	23
N10	|	at Southern Cal	26	27
N17	● |	Oregon	24	7
N24	● |	California	26	17

1974 5-4-2 (5-1-1)

S14		at Penn State	20	24
S21		Illinois	7	41
S28	=	San Jose State	21	21
O5		Michigan	16	27
O12	= |	at UCLA	13	13
O19	● |	Washington	34	17
O26	● |	at Washington State	20	18
N2	● |	Oregon State	17	13
N9	|	Southern Cal	10	34
N16	● |	at Oregon	17	0
N23	● |	at California	22	20

1975 6-4-1 (5-2-0)

S13		at Penn State	14	34
S20	=	at Michigan	19	19
S27		San Jose State	34	36
O4	●	Army	67	14
O11	|	UCLA	21	31
O18	● |	at Washington	24	21
O25	● |	Washington State	54	14
N1	● |	at Oregon State	28	22
N8	● |	at Southern Cal	13	10
N15	● |	Oregon	33	30
N22	|	California	15	48

1976 6-5-0 (5-2-0)

S11		at Penn State	12	15
S18		at Michigan	0	51
S25	●	San Jose State	28	23
O2		at Army	20	21
O9	|	at UCLA	20	38
O16	● |	Washington	34	28
O23	● |	at Washington State	22	16
O30	● |	Oregon State	24	3
N6	|	Southern Cal	24	48
N13	● |	at Oregon	28	17
N20	● |	at California	27	24

BILL WALSH
1977-78, '92-94 (.585) 34-24-1

1977 9-3-0 (5-2-0)

S10		at Colorado	21	27
S17	●	at Tulane	21	17
S24	●	Illinois	37	24
O1	● |	Oregon	20	10
O8	● |	UCLA	32	28
O15	|	at Washington	21	45
O22	● |	Washington State	31	29
O29	● |	at Oregon State	26	7
N5	|	at Southern Cal	0	49
N12	●	San Jose State	31	26
N19	● |	California	21	3
		SUN BOWL		
D31	●	LSU	24	14

1978 8-4-0 (4-3-0)

S9		Oklahoma	29	35
S16	●	San Jose State	38	9
S23	●	at Illinois	35	10
S30	●	Tulane	17	14
O7	|	at UCLA	26	27
O14	|	Washington	31	34
O21	● |	at Washington State	43	27
O28	● |	Oregon State	24	6
N4	|	Southern Cal	7	13
N11	● |	at Arizona State	21	14
N18	● |	at California	30	10
		BLUEBONNET BOWL		
D31	●	Georgia	25	22

ROD DOWHOWER
1979 (.500) 5-5-1

1979 5-5-1 (3-3-1)

S8		at Tulane	10	33
S15	●	San Jose State	45	29
S22		Army	13	17
S29	●	Boston College	33	14
O6	● |	UCLA	27	24
O13	= |	at Southern Cal	21	21
O20	● |	at Arizona	30	10
O27	|	at Oregon State	31	33
N3	● |	Arizona State	28	21
N10	|	Oregon	7	16
N17	|	California	14	21

PAUL WIGGIN
1980-83 (.364) 16-28

1980 6-5-0 (3-4-0)

S6	● |	at Oregon	35	25
S13	●	Tulane	19	14
S20		at Boston College	13	30
S27	●	at Oklahoma	31	14
O4	●	San Jose State	35	21
O11	|	at UCLA	21	35
O18	|	Washington	24	27
O25	● |	at Washington State	48	34
N1	● |	Oregon State	54	13
N8	|	Southern Cal	9	34
N22	|	at California	23	28

1981 4-7-0 (4-4-0)

S12		at Purdue	19	27
S19		San Jose State	6	28
S26		Ohio State	19	24
O3	|	at Arizona	13	17
O10	● |	UCLA	26	23
O17	|	at Southern Cal	17	25
O24	|	Arizona State	36	62
O31	|	at Washington	31	42
N7	● |	at Oregon State	63	9
N14	● |	Oregon	42	3
N21	● |	California	42	21

1982 5-6-0 (3-5-0)

S11	●	at Purdue	35	14
S18		San Jose State	31	35
S25	●	at Ohio State	23	20
O2	● |	Oregon State	45	5
O9	|	at Arizona State	17	21
O16	|	Southern Cal	21	41
O23	● |	at Washington State	31	26
O30	● |	Washington	43	31
N6	|	Arizona	26	41
N13	|	at UCLA	35	38
N20	|	at California	20	25

1983 1-10-0 (1-7-0)

S10		Oklahoma	14	27
S17		at Illinois	7	17
S24		San Jose State	10	23
O1	|	at Arizona State	11	29
O8	|	UCLA	21	39
O15	|	at Washington	15	32
O22	● |	Arizona	31	22
O29	|	at Oregon State	18	31
N5	|	at Southern Cal	7	30
N12	|	Oregon	7	16
N27	|	California	18	27

JACK ELWAY
1984-88 (.464) 25-29-2

1984 5-6-0 (3-5-0)

S8		at Oklahoma	7	19
S15	●	Illinois	34	19
S22	●	San Jose State	28	27
S29	|	Arizona State	10	28
O6	● |	at UCLA	23	21
O13	|	Washington	15	37
O20	|	Washington State	42	49
O27	● |	at Oregon State	28	21
N3	|	Southern Cal	11	20
N10	|	at Arizona	14	28
N17	● |	at California	27	10

1985 4-7-0 (3-5-0)

S14	●	San Jose State	41	7
S21	|	at Oregon	28	45
S28		Texas	34	38
O5		at San Diego State	22	41
O12	|	UCLA	9	34
O19	|	at Southern Cal	6	30
O26	● |	Arizona	28	17
N2	|	at Washington	0	34
N9	● |	Oregon State	39	24
N16	|	at Arizona State	14	21
N23	|	California	24	22

1986 8-4-0 (5-3-0)

S13	●	at Texas	31	20
S20	●	San Jose State	28	10
S27	● |	at Oregon State	17	7
O4	●	San Diego State	17	10
O11	|	Washington	14	24
O18	● |	at Oregon	41	7
O25	|	Southern Cal	0	10
N1	● |	Washington State	42	12
N8	● |	at UCLA	28	23
N22	|	at California	11	17
N29	● |	Arizona [Tok]	29	24
		GATOR BOWL		
D27		Clemson	21	27

1987 5-6-0 (4-4-0)

S5	|	at Washington	21	31
S19		at Colorado	17	31
S26		San Jose State	17	24
O3	|	UCLA	0	49
O10	● |	at Washington State	44	7
O17	●	at San Diego State	44	40
O24	● |	Oregon	13	10
O31	|	Arizona	13	23
N7	|	at Southern Cal	24	39
N14	● |	at Oregon State	38	7
N21	● |	California	31	7

1988   3-6-2 (1-5-2)

Date		Opponent		
S10		Southern Cal	20	24
S17	●	San Diego State	31	10
S24		at Oregon	3	7
O1		at Notre Dame	14	42
O8	●	San Jose State	44	12
O15	●	Arizona State	24	3
O22	=	Oregon State	20	20
O29		at Washington	25	28
N5		Washington State	21	24
N12		at UCLA	17	27
N19	=	at California	19	19

DENNIS GREEN
1989-91 (.471)   16-18

1989   3-8-0 (3-5-0)

Date		Opponent		
S2		at Arizona	3	19
S9		at Oregon State	16	20
S23	●	Oregon	18	17
S30		San Jose State	33	40
O7		Notre Dame	17	27
O14		at Washington State	13	31
O21		Utah	24	27
O28		at Southern Cal	0	19
N4	●	UCLA	17	14
N11		at Arizona State	22	30
N18	●	California	24	14

1990   5-6-0 (4-4-0)

Date		Opponent		
S6		at Colorado	17	21
S15		at UCLA	31	32
S22	●	Oregon State	37	3
S29		San Jose State	23	29
O6	●	at Notre Dame	36	31
O13		Southern Cal	22	37
O20		Washington	16	52
O27		at Oregon	0	31
N3	●	Washington State	31	13
N10	●	at Arizona	23	10
N17	●	at California	27	25

1991   8-4-0 (6-2-0)

Date		Opponent		
S7		Washington	7	42
S14		at Arizona	23	28
S28	●	Colorado	28	21
O5		Notre Dame	26	42
O12	●	Cornell	56	6
O19	●	at Southern Cal	24	21
O26	●	Oregon State	40	10
N2	●	at Oregon	33	13
N9	●	UCLA	27	10
N16	●	at Washington State	49	14
N23	●	California	38	21

ALOHA BOWL

D25		Georgia Tech	17	18

BILL WALSH

1992   10-3-0 (6-2-0)

Date		Opponent		
A26		Texas A&M ᴬᴺᴬ	7	10
S12	●	Oregon	21	7
S19	●	Northwestern	35	24
S26	●	San Jose State	37	13
O3		at Notre Dame	33	16
O10	●	at UCLA	19	7
O17		Arizona	6	21
O24	●	at Oregon State	27	21
O31		at Washington	7	41
N7	●	Southern Cal	23	9
N14	●	Washington State	40	3
N21	●	at California	41	21

BLOCKBUSTER BOWL

J1	●	Penn State	24	3

1993   4-7-0 (2-6-0)

Date		Opponent		
S4		at Washington	14	31
S11	●	San Jose State	31	28
S18	●	Colorado	41	37
S25		UCLA	25	28
O2		Notre Dame	20	48
O16		at Arizona	24	27
O23		Arizona State	30	38
O30	●	Oregon State	31	27
N6		at Southern Cal	20	45
N13	●	at Oregon	38	34
N20		California	17	46

1994   3-7-1 (2-6-0)

Date		Opponent		
S10	=	at Northwestern	41	41
S17	●	San Jose State	51	20
S24		Arizona	10	34
O1		at Notre Dame	15	34
O8		at Arizona State	35	36
O15		Southern Cal	20	27
O22	●	at Oregon State	35	29
O29		at UCLA	30	31
N5	●	Washington	46	28
N12		Oregon	21	55
N19		at California	23	24

TYRONE WILLINGHAM
1995-2001 (.549)   44-36-1

1995   7-4-1 (5-3-0)

Date		Opponent		
S2	●	at San Jose State	47	33
S9	●	at Utah	27	20
S16	=	Wisconsin	24	24
S23	●	at Oregon	28	21
O7	●	at Arizona State	30	28
O14		Washington	28	38
O21		UCLA	28	42
O28	●	Oregon State	24	3
N4		at Southern Cal	30	31
N11	●	at Washington State	36	24
N18	●	California	29	24

LIBERTY BOWL

D30		East Carolina	13	19

1996   7-5 (5-3)

Date		Opponent		
S7		Utah	10	17
S14	●	San Jose State	25	2
S21		at Wisconsin	0	14
O5		at Washington	6	27
O12	●	Oregon	27	24
O19		at Oregon State	12	26
O26		Arizona State	9	41
N2	●	at UCLA	21	20
N9	●	Southern Cal	24	20
N16	●	Washington State	33	17
N23	●	at California	42	21

SUN BOWL

D31	●	Michigan State	38	0

1997   5-6 (3-5)

Date		Opponent		
S6	●	San Jose State	28	12
S13		at North Carolina	17	28
S20	●	at Oregon State	27	24
S27	●	Oregon	58	49
O4	●	Notre Dame	33	15
O11		at Arizona	22	28
O18		Arizona State	14	31
N1		UCLA	7	27
N8		at Southern Cal	21	45
N15		at Washington State	28	38
N22	●	California	21	20

1998   3-8 (2-6)

Date		Opponent		
S5		San Jose State	23	35
S12		Arizona	14	31
S19	●	North Carolina	37	34
S26		at Oregon	28	63
O3		at Notre Dame	17	35
O10		Oregon State	23	30
O22		at Arizona State	38	44
O31		at UCLA	24	28
N7		Southern Cal	9	34
N14	●	Washington State	38	28
N21	●	at California	10	3

1999   8-4 (7-1)

Date		Opponent		
S4		at Texas	17	69
S11	●	Washington State	54	17
S18	●	at Arizona	50	22
S25	●	UCLA	42	32
O2		San Jose State	39	44
O16	●	Oregon State	21	17
O23	●	at Southern Cal	35	31
O30		at Washington	30	35
N13	●	at Arizona State	50	30
N20	●	California	31	13
N27	●	Notre Dame	40	37

ROSE BOWL

J1		Wisconsin	9	17

2000   5-6 (4-4)

Date		Opponent		
S2	●	at Washington State	24	10
S9		San Jose State	27	40
S16	●	Texas	27	24
S30		Arizona	3	27
O7		at Notre Dame	14	20
O14		at Oregon State	6	38
O21	●	Southern Cal	32	30
O28		Washington	28	31
N4		at UCLA	35	37
N11	●	Arizona State	29	7
N18	●	at California	36	30

2001   9-3 (6-2)

Date		Opponent		
S8	●	Boston College	38	22
S22	●	Arizona State	51	28
S29	●	at Southern Cal	21	16
O13		Washington State	39	45
O20	●	at Oregon	49	42
O27	●	UCLA	38	28
N3		at Washington	28	42
N10	●	at Arizona	51	37
N17	●	California	35	28
N24	●	Notre Dame	17	13
D1	●	at San Jose State	41	14

SEATTLE BOWL

D27		Georgia Tech	14	24

BUDDY TEEVENS
2002-04 (.303)   10-23

2002   2-9 (1-7)

Date		Opponent		
S7		at Boston College	27	34
S14	●	San Jose State	63	26
S28		at Arizona State	24	65
O5		at Notre Dame	7	31
O12		Washington State	11	36
O19	●	Arizona	16	6
O26		at UCLA	18	28
N2		at Oregon	14	41
N9		Southern Cal	17	49
N16		Oregon State	21	31
N23		at California	7	30

2003   4-7 (2-6)

Date		Opponent		
S6	●	San Jose State	31	10
S20	●	at Brigham Young	18	14
S27		at Washington	17	28
O11		at Southern Cal	21	44
O18		Washington State	14	24
O25		at Oregon	0	35
N1	●	UCLA	21	14
N8	●	Arizona State	38	27
N15		at Oregon State	3	43
N22		California	16	28
N29		Notre Dame	7	57

2004   4-7 (2-6)

Date		Opponent		
S4	●	San Jose State	43	3
S11	●	Brigham Young	37	10
S25		Southern Cal	28	31
O2	●	Washington	27	13
O9		at Notre Dame	15	23
O16	●	at Washington State	23	17
O23		Oregon	13	16
O30		at UCLA	0	21
N6		at Arizona State	31	34
N13		Oregon State	19	24
N20		at California	6	41

SYRACUSE

BY MIKE VACCARO

TODAY, SYRACUSE UNIVERSITY IS regarded as a basketball school. But a full decade before Dave Bing would arrive on campus and plant the seeds for a hoops powerhouse, a kid from Long Island named Jim Brown arrived in central New York, was issued a No. 44 jersey and took his first steps toward revolutionizing the position of running back. Long before the Big East brought Syracuse basketball games into living rooms from Maine to California, another No. 44, Ernie Davis, was leading the football Orangemen to the 1959 national championship as a sophomore, winning the 1961 Heisman Trophy as a senior.

And long before Jim Boeheim's basketball team made regular trips to the Final Four, Ben Schwartzwalder ran a football factory in upstate New York.

From 1950 through 1971, the Orangemen (as they were known until 2004, when they changed their nickname to the Orange) were the class of Eastern football, going 22 years without a losing season, winning four Lambert trophies (given to the best team in the East) and finishing in the Top 20

11 times. Then, after a spell of mediocrity through the 1970s, an outgoing, jovial coach named Dick MacPherson guided the Orangemen back to prominence, capped by an unbeaten season in 1987 and an ascension right to the top of the newly formed Big East Conference at the dawn of the 1990s.

"All I know," says Boeheim, Syracuse Class of 1966, "is that when I was in school in the '60s, basketball was a nice little diversion. You know how they say at the football factories that basketball is what keeps people from jumping off buildings between fall football and spring football? That's what it was like here. Man, people never stopped talking about the football team."

In 2004, after a spell of subpar seasons, SU said goodbye to head coach Paul Pasqualoni after 14 years, and hired Texas Longhorns co-defensive coordinator Greg Robinson in the hope that he'll return the program to glory.

TRADITION There is nothing quite like it anywhere in the country. Other schools may have famous graduates who shared the same uniform numbers, as a matter of coincidence or circumstance. But at Syracuse, there is nothing accidental about No. 44. If you are issued No. 44, it's because someone deems you worthy of a fabled lineage of running backs. And that's as serious a responsibility as it sounds.

PROFILE

Syracuse University
Syracuse, N.Y.
Founded: 1870
Enrollment: 11,448
Colors: Orange, Blue and White
Nickname: Orange
Stadium: Carrier Dome
    Opened in 1980
    AstroTurf; 50,000 capacity
First football game: 1889
All-time record: 664–435–49 (.600)
Bowl record: 12–9–1
Consensus national championships, 1936-present: 1 (1959)
Big East championships: 4 (2 outright)
Heisman Trophy: Ernie Davis, 1961
First-round NFL draftees: 18
Website: www.suathletics.com

THE BEST OF TIMES

From 1950 through 1971, the Orange enjoyed 22 consecutive .500 or better seasons, won four Lambert Trophies, finished in the Top 20 nine times and won the 1959 national championship.

THE WORST OF TIMES

From 1973 to 1982, the Orangemen went 40–70–1, an era in which three different coaches (Ben Schwartzwalder, Frank Maloney, Dick MacPherson) endured 2–9 seasons. In 1979, the Orangemen played all of their games away from home while the Carrier Dome was being built, playing "home" games in Buffalo, Ithaca and New Jersey. Ironically, they finished 7–5.

CONFERENCE

Syracuse was a charter member of the Big East when it formed as a basketball-only league in 1979; it added football in 1991, ending SU's 102 years as a major independent.

DISTINGUISHED ALUMNI

Marv Albert; Bob Costas; Ted Koppel; Stephen Crane, author; Peter Falk, actor; F. Story Musgrave, astronaut; S.I. Newhouse Jr., magazine publisher; Aaron Sorkin, screen/TV writer; Jerry Stiller, actor, comedian; Vanessa Williams, singer, actress

FIGHT SONG

DOWN, DOWN THE FIELD
Down, down the field goes
Old Syracuse,
Just see those backs hit the line
And go thro'
Down, down the field they go
Marching, Fighting for the Orange
Staunch and true.
Rah! Rah! Rah!
Vict'ry's in sight for old Syracuse,
Each loyal son knows she
Ne'er more will lose,
For We'll fight, yes. We'll fight,
And with all our might
For the glory of Syracuse.

THE SCHOOLS

THE SCHOOLS

At Syracuse, if you are issued No. 44, it's because someone deems you worthy of a fabled lineage.

BEST PLAYER As great as Jim Brown was as a pro football player, even he isn't spoken of as reverently as Davis, who as a sophomore in 1959 led Syracuse to its only national championship game and turned in a brilliant performance in the Cotton Bowl against Texas. Syracuse won 23-14, with Davis scoring two touchdowns— one on an 87-yard reception—and adding two two-point conversions and an interception on defense. Two years later, he would become the first black player to win the Heisman Trophy. The Elmira Express ran for 823 yards and 12 touchdowns as a senior, breaking Brown's school records for career rushing yards, total offense, touchdowns and scoring along the way. Unfortunately, part of the Davis saga—and one of the reasons he's remembered so wistfully—was his shocking death from leukemia on May 18, 1963. Davis never did get to play pro ball for the Cleveland Browns, who had traded for his rights with the idea of playing Davis and Brown in the same backfield.

BEST COACH When Ben Schwartzwalder arrived at Syracuse at age 40 in the spring of 1949, he inherited a program that had won only nine games in the previous four seasons. Schwartzwalder's coaching résumé consisted of three years at Muhlenberg College and didn't exactly possess the sexy name that success-starved alumni were looking for. "The alumni wanted a big-name coach," he said many years later, in an interview with the *Syracuse Post-Standard*. "What they got was a long-name coach." What they also got was the man who would permanently plant Syracuse on the map of big-time college football. By the time he retired at the conclusion of the 1973 season, Schwartzwalder had compiled a record of 153–91–3, highlighted by the 11–0 national championship season of 1959. Schwartzwalder's secrets of success were simple: for one thing, he recruited the likes of Brown, Davis, Little, Csonka and Jim Nance; for another, as his wife once explained, "he simply refuses to clutter up his mind with anything but football."

BEST TEAM In 1959, exactly 70 years after first fielding a team, the Orangemen strung together a dream season for the ages, ripping through a 10-game regular-season

RECORDS

RUSHING YARDS

	GAME
252	Joe Morris vs. Kansas, Oct. 6, 1979 (23 att.)
	SEASON
1,372	Joe Morris, 1979 (238 att.)
	CAREER
4,299	Joe Morris, 1978-81 (813 att.)

PASSING YARDS

	GAME
425	Marvin Graves vs. Rutgers, Oct. 10, 1992 (18 of 28)
	SEASON
2,547	Marvin Graves, 1993 (171 of 280)
	CAREER
8,466	Marvin Graves, 1990-93 (563 of 943)

RECEIVING YARDS

	GAME
249	Scott Schwedes vs. Boston College, Nov. 16, 1985 (8 rec.)
	SEASON
1,131	Marvin Harrison, 1995 (56 rec.)
	CAREER
2,728	Marvin Harrison, 1992-95 (133 rec.)

POINTS

	GAME
43	Jim Brown vs. Colgate, Nov. 17, 1956 (6 TDs, 7 PATs)
	SEASON
128	Walter Reyes, 2003 (21 TDs, 1 two-pt. conv.)
	CAREER
334	Nate Trout, 1996-99 (49 FGs, 187 PATs)

CONSENSUS ALL-AMERICANS

1908	Bill Horr, T
1915	Harold White, G
1917	Alfred Cobb, T
1918	Lou Usher, T
1918-19	Joe Alexander, G
1923	Pete McRae, E
1926	Vic Hanson, E
1956	Jim Brown, B
1959	Roger Davis, G
1960-61	Ernie Davis, B
1967	Larry Csonka, B
1985	Tim Green, DL
1987	Ted Gregory, DL
1987	Don McPherson, QB
1990	John Flannery, C
1992	Chris Gedney, TE
2001	Dwight Freeney, DL

schedule before winning the Cotton Bowl and securing their first—and, to date, only—national championship. Syracuse won its games by an average score of 39-5 during the regular season, leading the nation in both total offense and total defense, and surviving only one scare the whole year, a 20-18 win over perennial nemesis Penn State in the season's seventh week. The Orangemen took the No.1 ranking into the Cotton Bowl and held off No. 4 Texas before a raucous partisan crowd of 75,504. "And every second since," former coach Dick MacPherson said a few years ago, "the people have been waiting for the successor to that team."

BIGGEST GAME Syracuse had never won a bowl game in its history, and by the time it arrived for the Cotton Bowl on Jan. 1, 1960, the Orangemen had already been anointed the AP's national champion. Still, a nation of cynics, always skeptical of a Northeast school's championship credentials, watched intently as Syracuse took on 9–1 Texas, playing in its home state. Davis gave the Orangemen a much-needed early boost on the third play from scrimmage, gathering in a pass from Ger Schwedes and motoring 87 yards for a touchdown. Davis scored a second touchdown on a fourth-down one-yard plunge later in the half, and then added the two-point conversion. After Texas trimmed the score to 15-6 early in the third quarter, Davis intercepted a pass, returning it to the Texas 24. Schwedes then scored on a three-yard run and Davis, capping a 16-point day, caught another two-pointer. That wrapped up the Orangemen's 23-14 victory, sealed an 11–0 season and solidified Syracuse's status as champion.

BIGGEST UPSET A week before, the Orangemen had looked overmatched in a 19-0 loss to Rutgers. A year before, they'd

ALL-TIME TEAM	
Top 44 players of the 20th century, picked by fans in athletics department poll in 2000.	
OFFENSE	
1905-08	Bill Horr, OL
1916-20	Joe Alexander, OL
1957-59	Roger Davis, OL
1958-59	Bob Yates, OL
1960-62	Walt Sweeney, OL
1965-66	Gary Bugenhagen, OL
1970-71	Stan Walters, OL
1976-79	Craig Wolfley, OL
1950-52	Jim Ringo, C
1987-90	John Flannery, C
1960-62	John Mackey, TE
1989-92	Chris Gedney , TE
1976-79	Art Monk, WR
1987-89	Rob Moore, WR
1992-95	Marvin Harrison, WR
1985-87	Don McPherson, QB
1990-93	Marvin Graves, QB
1995-98	Donovan McNabb, QB
1965-67	Larry Csonka, FB
1985-88	Daryl Johnston, FB
1954-56	Jim Brown, RB
1959-61	Ernie Davis, RB
1964-66	Floyd Little, RB
1978-81	Joe Morris, RB
1978-81	Gary Anderson, PK
1996-98	Kevin Johnson, KR
DEFENSE	
1924-26	Vic Hanson, DL
1951-53	Bob Fleck, DL
1966-68	Arthur Thoms, DL
1969-70, 1972	Joe Ehrmann, DL
1982-85	Tim Green, DL
1984-87	Paul Frase, DL
1984-87	Ted Gregory, DL
1987-89	Rob Burnett, DL
1976, 1978-80	Jim Collins, LB
1986-89	Terry Wooden, LB
1990-93	Kevin Mitchell, LB
1990-94	Dan Conley, LB
1954-56	Jim Ridlon, DB
1969-71	Tommy Myers, DB
1985-88	Markus Paul, DB
1994-96	Kevin Abrams, DB
1994-97	Donovan Darius, DB
1990-93	Pat O'Neill, P

looked overwhelmed when they'd gotten steamrolled by Nebraska, 63-7. But something clicked inside the Carrier Dome on Sept. 29, 1984, when Nebraska came into Syracuse with a 24-game regular-season winning streak and the nation's No. 1 ranking. Maybe it was the presence of 30 members of the 1959 Syracuse national championship team, honored at halftime on the silver anniversary of that golden season. Maybe it was the delirious crowd of 47,280 that jammed the Dome. Perhaps it was the dreaded *Sports Illustrated* cover jinx, which had spotlighted the Cornhuskers after their blowout of UCLA a week earlier. Whatever the reason, the Corn-huskers left on the wrong end of a humbling 17-9 score that sounded the official return of Syracuse to national legitimacy in coach Dick MacPherson's fourth year on the job (it would finish the season 6-5). Trailing 7-3 at halftime, Syracuse received second-half scores from Mike Siano (on a 40-yard pass from Todd Norley) and a one-yard sweep around right end by fullback Harold Gayden. The defense did the rest, squashing a Nebraska team that had averaged 40.7 points.

HEARTBREAKER Penn State came into Archbold Stadium on Oct. 18, 1969, carrying a 23-game winning streak, but Syracuse sent a rabid crowd of 42,491 into a tizzy by seizing a 14-0 lead at the half. But two controversial penalties and one ill-fated bouncing ball doomed the Orangemen's upset bid. The first questionable call, an interference flag, came early in the fourth quarter, after Syracuse had apparently stopped Penn State on fourth and six, extending a Nittany Lions drive. The second came a few moments later, after Penn State capped the drive with a touchdown. Lions coach Joe Paterno opted to go for two, and Syracuse stuffed the run; however, a holding penalty on Syracuse gave Penn State a second

chance, and this time the gamble worked. Even more disheartening, with just over four minutes left in the game, Franco Harris picked up his own fumble and raced for the winning score.

STADIUM Long before the Carrier Dome, there was Archbold Stadium, billed as "a modern adaptation of the Roman Coliseum," home on windblown football afternoons to the Orangemen, who proved to a disbelieving nation that you could, indeed, play championship-level college football in the Northeast at someplace other than West Point.

As beloved as Archbold Stadium was, it was completely inadequate by the late 1970s, and its 30,000-seat capacity simply wasn't enough to maintain Syracuse's place among Eastern football powers. So, between April 1979 and September 1980, a $26.85 million dome began to rise over the Syracuse campus. A $2.75 million gift from the Carrier Corporation provided a name that is now among the most recognizable in college sports. The Orangemen christened their new building with a 36-24 victory over Miami of Ohio on Sept. 20, 1980, in front of 50,564 fans. Ever since, the Orange have won just under 70 percent of their games inside one of college football's loudest facilities. As then-Miami coach Butch Davis said in 1999: "Playing inside the Carrier Dome is like playing inside the amplifier at a rock 'n roll concert."

RIVAL Although its arrival in the Big East changed the face of Syracuse's favored rivalries, Penn State remains the most frequent Syracuse opponent; the two teams have played 68 times, with the Nittany Lions owning a 40–23–5 record. The two teams haven't played since 1990; in the 40 years before, Syracuse and Penn State had combined to win 23 Lambert trophies (Syracuse won five times, second only to PSU in that span). In the 1960s, this was one of the nation's fiercest rivalries, thanks largely to the public rivalry between the coaches, Syracuse's Schwartzwalder and Penn State's Rip Engle. Floyd Little recalls that prior to a game in Beaver Stadium in 1964, Schwartzwalder, a war hero not immune to a little hyperbole, told him that Engle was a communist and a personal friend of Nikita Khrushchev.

NICKNAME Syracuse had worn pink and blue prior to the fall of 1890; that April, Syracuse accepted a challenge from Hamilton College to hold a track meet. Fans took the train to the meet, carrying canes festooned with the school colors. But after Syracuse won the meet, and a celebration broke out on the train home, the students wanted to cheer for teams wearing colors more imposing than pink and blue (though at the time pink was a popular color among college football squads). That Monday, a group of students visited the chancellor to see about changing the colors, and he agreed. A committee was formed, unanimously changing the school colors to orange and blue. Orangemen was the nickname that soon followed, and it held until 2004, when the moniker was trimmed to simply the Orange.

MASCOT Though the fuzzy orange mascot is a ubiquitous presence on *SportsCenter* commercials and other public forums, the Saltine Warrior, a Native American figure named Big Chief Bill Orange, became the school's unofficial symbol starting in 1931. For 40 years, members of the Lambda Chi Alpha fraternity wore the Saltine Warrior costume. By 1978, though, Native American students began to publicly denounce the school's choice of mascot, and a contest to find a successor ensued. A Roman-style gladiator was used briefly, but was soon being laughed and booed off fields and courts. A string of possibilities didn't yield a permanent solution until 1995, when the fuzzy orange figure dubbed Otto emerged as the unlikely winner, and now anywhere from two to six students per year inhabit the warm, woolly costume.

UNIFORMS On Nov. 23, 1889, Syracuse played its first football game, losing 36-0 to Rochester wearing pink-and-blue uniforms. One year later, orange was adopted as the prominent school color and has remained that way since—with the exception of 1947-48, when the jerseys were white, the pants khaki moleskins and there wasn't a drop of orange in sight. Since 1978, the Syracuse helmet has remained virtually unchanged: a plain orange surface with blue-and-white piping down the middle.

QUOTE "The biggest thing was already done before I got here. It was called the Carrier Dome."—Dick MacPherson, on revitalizing Syracuse football in the 1980s

SYRACUSE ALL-TIME SCORES

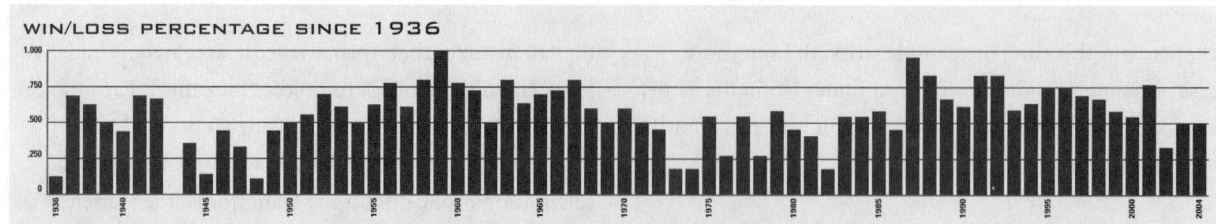

WIN/LOSS PERCENTAGE SINCE 1936

NO HEAD COACH

1889   0-1-0
| N23 | | at Rochester | 0 | 36 |

BOBBY WINSTON
1890 (.636)   7-4

1890   7-4-0
S26	●	at Syracuse AA	14	0
O2	●	at Syracuse AA	32	0
O18	●	at St. John's MA	26	6
O27		at Union	0	26
N1	●	at Hamilton	14	12
N8		at Union	0	28
N15	●	at Rochester	4	0
N22		at Rochester	0	1 f
U		at Hamilton	4	6
N27	●	at Syracuse AA	16	4
U	●	at St. John's MA	18	4

WILLIAM GALBRAITH
1891 (.364)   4-7

1891   4-7
O3		at Cornell	0	68
O17		Cornell JV	6	12
O22	●	at Syracuse AA	22	0
O24		at St. John's MA	0	4
O30		at Hamilton	4	22
N7		Colgate	16	22
N11		at Union	0	75
N12	●	at Syracuse AA	0	22
N21	●	at Rochester	18	16
N26	●	at Syracuse AA	22	10
U	●	at St. John's MA	22	4

JORDAN C. WELLS
1892 (.056)   0-8-1

1892   0-8-1
O1		at Cornell	0	58
O12	=	at Syracuse AA	0	24
O21	●	at Syracuse AA	4	18
O29		at Union	0	52
N5		at Hamilton	0	12
N9		at Syracuse AA	0	0
N12		at Rochester	0	22
N15		at Syracuse AA	0	4
U		at St. John's MA	0	28

NO HEAD COACH

1893   4-9-1
S21		at Syracuse AA	0	22
S27		at Cornell JV	0	44
O7		at St. John's MA	16	24
O14	●	at Syracuse AA	0	28
O21		at St. John's MA	4	18
O26		at Colgate	0	58
O31	●	at Syracuse HS	20	0
N4		at Hamilton	16	14
N11		at Union	0	66
N15		at Syracuse AA	4	28
N18	=	at Rochester	10	10
N30		at Rochester	0	6
U	●	at Onondaga Acad.	30	0
U	●	at Cazenovia	24	0

GEORGE H. BOND
1894 (.545)   6-5

1894   6-5-0
S26		at Cornell	0	39
S29	●	at Hobart	18	4
O6		Colgate	8	32
O13	●	Cornell JV	22	0
U		at Syracuse AA	6	10
N3	●	at Cazenovia	20	0
N6	●	at St. Johns MA	20	12
N10	●	at Rochester	28	18
N17	●	at Hamilton	50	0
N21	●	at Union	10	20
N24	●	at St. Johns MA	6	22

GEORGE O. REDINGTON
1895-96 (.650)   11-5-4

1895   6-2-2
S26		at Cornell	0	8
O5	●	at Scranton AA	12	0
O10	●	at Syracuse AA	24	0
O19		at Williams	10	28
O26	=	at St. Johns MA	6	6
N2	●	Hobart	46	0
N9	●	Colgate	4	0
N13	●	at Syracuse AA	18	0
N16	●	at Rochester	30	0
N23	=	at St. John's MA	4	4

1896   5-3-2
U	●	at Syracuse HS	24	0
O3		at Cornell	0	22
O10	●	at Elmira AA	20	6
O17		Williams	6	24
O24		at Colgate	0	6
O27	●	at Rochester	62	4
O31	●	at Syracuse AA	26	0
N7	=	at Buffalo	6	6
N14	●	at St.John's MA	40	0
N26	=	at Clyde AA	10	10

FRANK E. WADE
1897-99 (.643)   17-9-2

1897   5-3-1
S25	●	at Cazenovia	36	0
O3		at Cornell	0	16
O7	●	at Hobart	18	0
O16	=	at Colgate	6	6
O23	●	at Union	40	0
O30	●	at Cortland St.	24	0
N3	●	at Rochester	36	0
N6		at Buffalo	0	16
N13		at Buffalo	0	10

1898   8-2-1
S21	●	at Cornell	0	28
O1	●	at Rochester	35	0
O5		Cornell	0	30
O12	●	at Hobart	46	5
O22	●	at Case	10	0
O26	●	at Syracuse AA	28	0
O29	●	at Ogdenburg	17	6
N5	●	at NYU	17	0
N9	●	at Syracuse AA	28	0
N12	●	at Wyoming Seminary	11	0
N19	=	Trinity	0	0

1899   4-4-0
S27		at Cornell	0	17
O7	●	Syracuse AA *Unk*	6	0
O14	●	NYU	10	5
O28		Williams	0	6
N4		Buffalo	0	16
N11	●	at Rochester	23	0
N18		at Army	6	12
N22	●	at Dickinson	18	7

EDWIN R. SWEETLAND
1900-02 (.778)   20-5-2

1900   7-2-1
S22	●	Cortland St.	35	0
S29		at Cornell	0	6
O6	●	St. Lawrence	70	0
O13	●	NYU	12	0
O17		at Princeton	0	43
O20	●	Amherst	5	0
N3	●	at Oberlin	6	0
N10	●	Dickinson	6	0
N17	●	Rochester	68	5
N24	=	at Brown	6	6

1901   7-1-0
S21	●	Cortland St.	35	0
S28	●	Rensselaer	26	0
O5	●	Brown	20	0
O12	●	Lafayette	0	5
O19	●	Clarkson	27	0
O26	●	Amherst	28	17
N9	●	Columbia	11	5
N20	●	Vermont	38	0

1902   6-2-1
S20	●	Cortland St.	21	0
S27	●	Onondaga Indians	34	0
O4	●	Clarkson	47	0
O11	●	Colgate	23	0
O18	●	Amherst	15	0
O25	●	at Yale	0	24
N1	●	Willaims	26	17
N15		Army	0	46
N27	=	at Columbia	6	6

ANCIL D. BROWN / JASON B. PARISH
1903 (.556)   5-4

1903   5-4-0
S19	●	at Cortland St.	23	0
S26	●	at Onondaga Indians	35	0
O3	●	at Clarkson	47	0
O10	●	at Rensselaer	33	0
O17		Colgate	5	10
O24		Williams	5	17
O31	●	at Niagara	47	0
N7		at Yale	0	30
N14		Brown	5	12

DR. CHARLES P. HUTCHINS
1904-05 (.700)   14-6

1904   6-3-0
S24	●	at Cortland St.	27	0
O1	●	at Clarkson	69	0
O8		Colgate	0	11
O15		at Yale	9	17
O22	●	at Niagara	52	4
O29	●	at Allegheny	69	0
N5	●	Manhattan	144	0
N12	●	at Lehigh	30	4
N19		at Army	5	21

1905   8-3-0
S22	●	Alfred	52	0
S27	●	Hobart	24	0
S30	●	Rochester	16	0
O7		at Yale	0	16
O14	●	at Hamilton	27	0
O21	●	Colgate	11	5
O28	●	Lehigh	17	0
N4		at Brown	0	27
N11	●	Holy Cross	16	4
N18	●	Rensselaer	62	0
N25		at Army	0	17

FRANK J. O'NEILL
1906-07, '13-15, '17-19 (.714)   52-19-6

1906   6-3-0
S26	●	Hobart	28	6
S29	●	Rochester	38	0
O6		at Yale	0	51
O13	●	Hamilton	36	0
O20		Colgate	0	5
N3		Carlisle *Buf*	4	9
N10	●	Niagara	46	0
N17	●	at Lafayette	12	4
N24		at Army	4	0

1907   5-3-1
S25	●	Hobart	28	0
S28	●	Rochester	40	6
O5		at Yale	0	11
O12		Carlisle *Buf*	6	14
O19	●	Williams	9	0
O26	●	Hamilton	22	0
N2	●	Bucknell	20	6
N16	=	Lafayette	4	4
N23		Army	4	23

HOWARD H. JONES
1908 (.650)   6-3-1

1908   6-3-1
S23	●	Hobart	51	0
S26	●	Hamilton	18	0
O3		at Yale	0	5
O10		Carlisle *Buf*	0	12
O17	●	Rochester	23	12
O25	=	at Princeton	0	0
O31	●	Williams	23	0
N7		Colgate	0	5
N14	●	Tufts	28	0
N21	●	Michigan	28	4

T.A.D. JONES
1909-10 (.500)   9-9-2

1909   4-5-1
S25	●	Hamilton	20	0
O2		at Yale	0	15
O9	●	Rochester	17	0
O16		CarlisleNYC	11	14
O23	●	Niagara	39	0
O30		at Michigan	0	43
N6	●	Tufts	5	0
N13		Colgate	5	6
N20		Illinois	8	17
N25		at Fordham	5	5

1910   5-4-1
S24	=	St. Bonaventure	0	0
O1		at Yale	6	12
O8	●	Rochester	6	0
O15	●	Carlisle	14	0
O22	●	Hobart	12	5
O29		Michigan	0	11
N5	●	Vermont	3	0
N12		Colgate	6	11
N19		at Illinois	0	3
N24	●	at St. Louis	6	0

C.D. CUMMINGS
1911-12 (.526)   9-8-2

1911   5-3-2
S30	●	Hobart	6	0
O7		at Yale	0	12
O14	●	at Rochester	6	5
O21		Lafayette	0	10
O28		Springfield	5	9
N4	=	at Michigan	6	6
N11	●	Vermont	16	0
N18	●	Carlisle	12	11
N25		at Ohio State	6	0
N30	=	at St. Louis	6	6

Helmets

There are few symbols in American sports as distinctive as the helmets of the nation's most storied college football teams. From Notre Dame's golden dome to Michigan's wings of victory to Nebraska's elegantly minimalist 'N,' they are icons of modern culture. What follows is not a comprehensive record, but rather a few glimpses of how each school's helmet design has evolved over the past five decades.

Air Force

| 1959-73 | 1974-79 | 1999-Present |

Akron

| Mid '60s | Mid '70s-1980 | 2003-Present |

Alabama

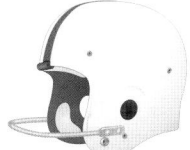  

| 1950s | 1960s | 1970-Present |

Arizona

| 1973-76 | 1977-79 | 2004-Present |

Arizona State

| Early '70s | 1974-75 | 1996-Present |

Arkansas

| 1958-63 | 1967-Mid '70s | 2001-Present |

Arkansas State

| 1969-79 | 1980 | 1999-Present |

ARMY

1957-71

1981-82

1983-Present

1961-65

1966-78

1984-Present

AUBURN

BALL STATE

1957-60

1971-84

1990-Present

1967-68

1969-71

2003-Present

BAYLOR

BOISE STATE

1974-75

1997-2001

2002-Present

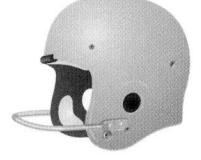
1960s

1980s-1990

1991-Present

BOSTON COLLEGE

BOWLING GREEN

1964-67

1971-75

2004-Present

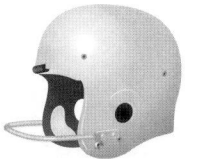
1955-60

1999-2004

Present

BRIGHAM YOUNG

BROWN

Late 1960s-'71

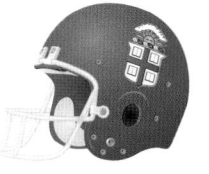

1984-89

2004-Present

1960-62

1984-89

2001-Present

BUFFALO

CALIFORNIA

1966-71

1972-75

1987-Present

1979-80

1985-94

2003-Present

CENTRAL FLORIDA

CENTRAL MICHIGAN

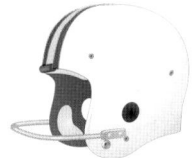

Early '70s

1973-80

1997-Present

1970-72

1984

1993-Present

CINCINNATI

CLEMSON

Early '60s

1967-68

1977-Present

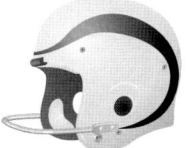

1960-62

1969-Late '70s

1985-Present

COLORADO

COLORADO STATE

 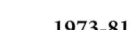 

1965-68   1973-81   1995-Present

COLUMBIA

1971-76   Late 1980s-1997   2003-Present

CONNECTICUT

1964   1978-82   2003-Present

CORNELL

Mid '60s   1967-75   2002-Present

DARTMOUTH

 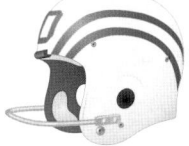  

1965-82   1987-98   1999-Present

DUKE

1961-64   1966-69   2004-Present

EAST CAROLINA

1963-68   1977-88   1999-Present

EASTERN MICHIGAN

1967-75   1979-83   2004-Present

FLORIDA

1964-65

1971-75

1979-Present

FAU/2001-Present

FIU/2002-Present

FLORIDA ATLANTIC & FLORIDA INTERNATIONAL

FLORIDA STATE

1964

1971-74

1976-Present

1970s

1980s-Mid '90s

1997-Present

FRESNO STATE

GEORGIA

1962

1964-77

2001-Present

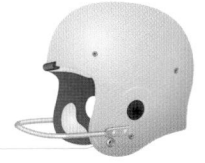

Early '60s

1969-71

Late '70s-Present

GEORGIA TECH

GRAMBLING

1960s

Mid 1990s

2004

1961-63

1982-93

2004-Present

HARVARD

HAWAII

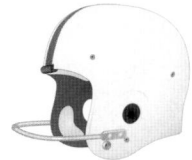

1960s

1982-88

2000-Present

1966-78

1987-94

2000-Present

HOUSTON

IDAHO

Early '60s

1980s

Early 1990s-Present

Early 1960s-1970

1971-76

1989-Present

ILLINOIS

INDIANA

1965-66

1973-75

2002-Present

1960-64

1972-73

1979-Present

IOWA

IOWA STATE

1962-66

1968-74

2003-Present

1962

1970-76

2002-Present

KANSAS

KANSAS STATE

Mid 1950s-1963

1975-77

1989-Present

1960-63

1974-75

2000-Present

KENT STATE

KENTUCKY

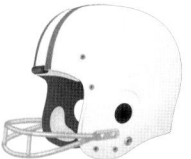

1970-71

1975-81

2001-Present

1960s-1971

1972-76

1980-Present

LSU

LOUISIANA TECH

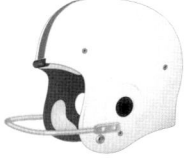

1960s

1968-Early '80s

Early 1990s-Present

1960s-1973

1992-95

2002-Present

LOUISIANA-LAFAYETTE

LOUISIANA-MONROE

1960-63

1972-77

2004-Present

1966-67

1981-82

2003-Present

LOUISVILLE

MARSHALL

Early '60s

1972-74

1993-Present

1959-62

1972-78

2001-Present

MARYLAND

MEMPHIS

1973-79

1986-87

1999-Present

1960-64

1972-75

1984-Present

MIAMI (FLA.)

MIAMI (OHIO)

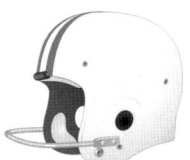

1960

1974-77

1998-Present

1959-68

1969-75

1976-Present

MICHIGAN

MICHIGAN STATE

1960-64

1966-68

2003-Present

1964

1971-73

2000-Present

MIDDLE TENNESSEE

MINNESOTA

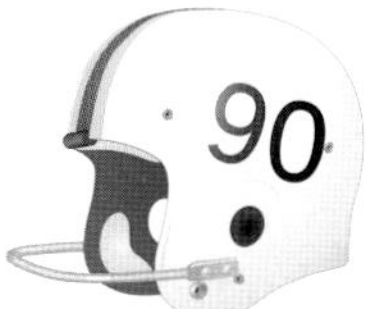

1967

1972-75

1999-Present

MISSISSIPPI

1960s

1970

1995-Present

MISSISSIPPI STATE

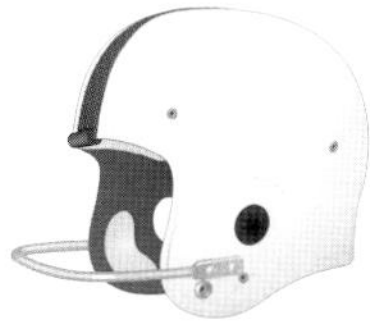

1951-62

1973-77

2004-Present

MISSOURI

1970

1971-77

1996-Present

NAVY

1961

Early '60s

2004-Present

NEBRASKA

1961-65

1967-68

1982-Present

NEVADA

Early '70s

1986

2002-Present

NEW MEXICO

Mid-'60s

1974-79

2004-Present

NEW MEXICO STATE

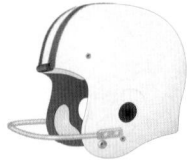
1966-68

1974-77

Present

1963-66

1967-77

2001-Present

NORTH CAROLINA

NORTH CAROLINA STATE

1964-67

1972-77

2000-Present

1968-71

1979-82

2003-Present

NORTH TEXAS

NORTHERN ILLINOIS

Late '60s

1970-Mid '70s

2002-Present

Early '60s-1967

1968

1994-Present

NORTHWESTERN

NOTRE DAME

1959-62

1963

1964-Present

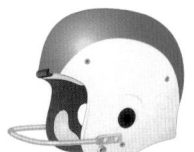
1964-65

1973-76

2004-Present

OHIO

Ohio State

1962-63

1966-67

1968-Present

Late '50s-1965

1967-76

1977-Present

Oklahoma

Oklahoma State

1961-66

1973-75

2001-Present

1969-71

1978-83

1999-Present

Oregon

Oregon State

1965-72

1986-90

1999-Present

1968-74

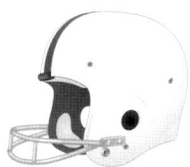

1975-86

1987-Present

Penn State

Pennsylvania

1970-78

1981-91

2004-Present

1970-72

1973-80

1997-2004

Pittsburgh

PRINCETON

1968

1970-72

1998-Present

1962-68

1972-79

1997-Present

PURDUE

RICE

Mid 1950s-1964

1971-75

1997-Present

1965

1975-78

2001-Present

RUTGERS

SAN DIEGO STATE

Early '60s

1974-79

2004-Present

1974-75

1999

2001-Present

SAN JOSE STATE

SMU

1966

1976-86

2004-Present

1966-67

1975-81

2004-Present

SOUTH CAROLINA

SOUTH FLORIDA

1997-2002

2003-Present

1964-68

1993-2000

2001-Present

SOUTHERN CAL

SOUTHERN MISS

1982-87

1990-2002

2003-Present

1968-76

1980-91

2002-Present

STANFORD

SYRACUSE

Mid '60s-1973

1974-77

1983-Present

Early '60s

1977-80

1998-Present

TCU

TEMPLE

1966

1972-79

2004-Present

1964-66

1967-76

1983-Present

TENNESSEE

TEXAS

 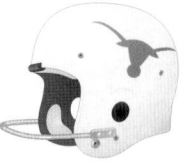 

1960-62   1970-76   1977-Present

TEXAS A&M

Early '60s   1972-77   2004-Present

TEXAS TECH

Mid '60s   1970-73   2000-Present

TOLEDO

1964-66   1977-80   1997-Present

TROY

1978-82   1983-88   2004-Present

TULANE

1976-80   1989-91   1998-Present

TULSA

1964   1990   2003-Present

UAB

1991   1993   2003-Present

UCLA

Mid '60s-1972

1973-95

2004-Present

UNLV

1976

1983-86

1999-Present

UTAH

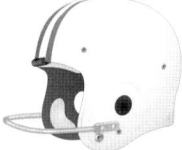
1968-73

1977-85

2004-Present

UTAH STATE

1964-67

1973-75

1995-Present

UTEP

1967-69

1992-98

2000-Present

VANDERBILT

1966-68

1976-78

2002-Present

VIRGINIA

1968-75

1978-81

2001-Present

VIRGINIA TECH

1974-77

1978-82

1999-Present

WAKE FOREST

1964

1979-86

2001-Present

WASHINGTON

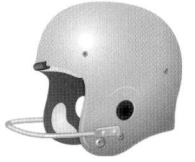
1960-71

1996-98

1999-Present

WASHINGTON STATE

1970-75

1976-77

1999-Present

WEST VIRGINIA

Mid '50s-1964

1971-72

1980-Present

WESTERN MICHIGAN

1964-68

1978-83

1998-Present

WISCONSIN

1961-66

1972-74

1991-Present

WYOMING

1962-64

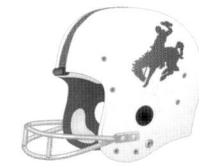
1973-74

2000-Present

YALE

Late '50s-1963

1970-71

1997-Present

1912   4-5-0
S28	•	Hobart	12	0
O5		at Yale	0	21
O12		Carlisle	0	33
O19		at Princeton	0	62
O26	•	Michigan	18	7
N2	•	Rochester	28	0
N9		at Lafayette	30	7
N16		Colgate	0	7
N23		at Army	7	23

FRANK J. O'NEILL

1913   6-4-0
S27	•	Hobart	41	0
O4	•	Hamilton	18	0
O11		at Rochester	6	0
O18		at Princeton	0	13
O25	•	Western Reserve	36	0
N1		at Michigan	7	43
N8	•	NYU	48	0
N15	•	Colgate	13	35
N22	•	Carlisle	27	35
N27		at St. Louis	75	0

1914   5-3-2
S26	•	Hobart	37	0
O3	•	Hamilton	81	0
O10		at Princeton	9	12 *
O17	•	Rochester	19	0
O24	•	Michigan	20	6
O31	•	Carlisle _BUF_	24	3
N7	•	Rutgers	14	14
N14	•	Colgate	0	0
N21		at Dartmouth	0	40
N26	•	Notre Dame	0	20

1915   9-1-2
S25	•	Alumni	43	0
O2	•	Bucknell	6	0
O9		at Princeton	0	3
O16	•	Rochester	82	0
O23	•	Brown	6	0
O30	•	at Michigan	14	7
N6	•	Mt. Union	73	0
N13	•	Colgate	38	0
N20	=	Dartmouth	0	0
N25	=	at Montana	6	6
D1	•	Oregon State _PORT_	28	0
D6	•	at Occidental	35	0

W.M. HOLLENBACK
1916 (.556)   5-4

1916   5-4-0
S30	•	Alumni	57	0
O7	•	Ohio U.	73	0
O14	•	Franklin & Marshall	60	0
O21	•	Pittsburgh	0	30
O28		at Michigan	13	14
N4	•	Dartmouth _SPR_	10	15
N11	•	Susquehanna	42	0
N18	•	Colgate	0	15
N25	•	at Tufts	20	13

FRANK J. O'NEILL

1917   8-1-1
S29	=	47th Infantry	0	0
O6	=	47th Infantry	19	0
O13	•	Rutgers	14	10
O20		at Pittsburgh	0	28
O27	•	Tufts	58	0
N3		at Brown	6	0
N10	•	Bucknell	42	0
N17	•	Colgate	27	7
N24		at Michigan State	21	7
N29		at Nebraska	10	9

1918   5-1-0
O26	•	USN Transport	13	0
N3		at Dartmouth	34	6
N10	•	Brown	53	0
N16		at Michigan	0	15
N28	•	Columbia	20	0
N30	•	Rutgers _NYC_	21	0

1919   8-3-0
S27	•	All Syracuse	10	0
O4	•	Vermont	27	0
O11		at Army	7	3
O18	•	Pittsburgh	24	3
O25	•	Wash. & Jeff.	0	13
N1	•	at Brown	13	0
N4	•	Rutgers _NYC_	14	6
N8	•	Bucknell	9	0
N15	•	Colgate	13	7
N22		at Indiana	6	12
N27		at Nebraska	0	3

JOHN F. MEEHAN
1920-24 (.787)   35-8-4

1920   6-2-1
S25	•	Hobart	55	7
O2	•	Vermont	49	0
O9	•	Johns Hopkins	45	0
O16	•	Pittsburgh	7	7
O23		at Dartmouth	10	0
O30		at Holy Cross	0	3
N6	•	Wash. & Jeff.	14	0
N13	•	Maryland	7	10 *
N20	•	Colgate	14	0

1921   7-2-0
S24	•	Hobart	35	0
O1	•	Ohio U.	38	0
O8	•	Maryland	42	0
O15	•	Brown	28	0
O22		at Pittsburgh	0	30 *
O29	•	Wash. & Jeff.	10	17
N5	•	McGill _MTL_	13	0
N12	•	Colgate	14	0
N19	•	Dartmouth _NYC_	14	7

1922   6-1-2
S23	•	Hobart	28	7
S30	•	Muhlenberg	47	0
O7	•	NYU	34	0
O14	=	at Brown	0	0
O21	•	Pittsburgh	14	21
O28		at Penn State _NYC_	0	0
N4	•	Nebraska	9	6
N11	•	McGill	32	0
N18	•	Colgate	14	7

1923   8-1-0
S29	•	Hobart	33	0
O6	•	William & Mary	61	3
O13	•	Alabama	23	0
O20	•	Pittsburgh _BRNX_	3	0
O27	•	Penn State	10	0
N3	•	Springfield	44	0
N10	•	Boston U.	49	0
N17	•	Colgate	7	16
N24		at Nebraska	7	0

1924   8-2-1
S27	•	Hobart	35	0
O4	•	Mercer _BUF_	26	0
O11	•	William & Mary	24	7
O18	•	Boston College	10	0
O25		at Penn State	10	6
N1	•	Pittsburgh	7	7
N8	•	W.V. Wesleyan	3	7
N15	•	Niagara	23	6
N22	•	Colgate	7	3
N27	•	Columbia _NYC_	9	6
D6		at Southern Cal	0	16

C.W.P. REYNOLDS
1925-26 (.800)   15-3-2

1925   8-1-1
S26	•	Hobart	32	0
O3	•	Vermont	26	0
O10	•	William & Mary	33	0
O17	•	Niagara	17	0
O24	•	Providence	48	0
O31		at Indiana	14	0
N7	•	Penn State	7	0
N14	•	Ohio Wesleyan	3	3
N21	•	Colgate	6	19
N26	•	Columbia _NYC_	16	5

1926   7-2-1
S25	•	Hobart	18	0
O2	•	Vermont	64	0
O9	•	William & Mary	35	0
O16		at Army	21	27
O23		at Penn State	10	0
O30	•	Johns Hopkins	31	0
N6		Georgetown	7	13
N13	•	Colgate	10	10
N20	•	Niagara	12	6
N25	•	Columbia _NYC_	19	2

LEWIS P. ANDREAS
1927-29 (.589)   15-10-3

1927   5-3-2
S26	•	Hobart	13	0
O1	•	William & Mary	18	0
O8	•	Johns Hopkins	21	6
O15	•	Georgetown	19	6
O22	•	Penn State	6	9
O29		at Nebraska	0	21
N5	•	Ohio Wesleyan	6	6
N12	=	Colgate	13	13
N19	•	Niagara	13	6
N24	•	Columbia _NYC_	7	14

1928   4-4-1
S29	•	Hobart	14	6
O6	•	William & Mary	38	0
O13	•	Johns Hopkins	58	0
O20		at Nebraska	6	7
O26	=	at Penn State	6	6
N3		at Pittsburgh	0	18
N10	•	Ohio Wesleyan	0	6
N17	•	Colgate	6	30
N29	•	at Columbia	14	6

1929   6-3-0
S28	•	Hobart	77	0
O5	•	St. Lawrence	55	0
O12	•	Nebraska	6	13
O19	•	Johns Hopkins	85	6
O26		at Brown	6	0
N2	•	Penn State	4	6
N9	•	Niagara	20	0
N16	•	Colgate	7	36
N28	•	at Columbia	6	0

VICTOR A. HANSON
1930-36 (.602)   33-21-5

1930   5-2-2
S27	•	Rensselaer	55	0
O4	•	Hobart	49	0
O11	•	Rutgers	27	0
O18	•	Pittsburgh	0	14
O25	•	St. Lawrence	34	6
N1	•	Brown	16	16
N8	=	at Penn State	0	0
N15	•	Colgate	7	36
N27	•	at Columbia	19	7

1931   7-1-1
S26	•	St. Lawrence	46	6
O3	•	Hobart	49	0
O10	•	Ohio Wesleyan	48	7
O17	•	Florida	33	12
O24	•	Penn State	7	0
O31		at Michigan State	15	10
N7	•	Western Reserve	33	0
N14	•	Colgate	7	21
N21	•	at Columbia	0	0

1932   4-4-1
S24	•	Clarkson	13	6
O1	•	St. Lawrence	54	0
O8	•	Ohio Wesleyan	12	19
O15	•	SMU	6	16
O22		at Penn State	12	6 *
O29	•	Michigan State	13	27
N5	•	Oglethorpe	27	6
N12	•	Colgate	0	16
N19	=	at Columbia	0	0

1933   4-4-0
O7	•	Clarkson	52	0
O14	•	Ohio Wesleyan	40	0
O21		at Cornell	14	7
O28		at Michigan State	3	27
N4	•	Penn State	12	6
N11	•	Brown	7	10
N18	•	Colgate	3	13
N25		at Columbia	0	16

1934   6-2-0
O6	•	Clarkson	28	0
O13		at Cornell	20	7
O20	•	Ohio Wesleyan	32	10
O27		at Brown	33	0
N3		at Penn State	16	0
N10	•	Michigan State	10	0
N17	•	Colgate	2	13
N25		at Columbia	0	12

1935   6-1-1
O5	•	Clarkson	33	0
O12	•	Cornell	21	14
O19	•	Ohio Wesleyan	18	10
O26	•	Brown	19	0
N2	•	Penn State	7	3
N9		at Columbia	14	2
N16	•	Colgate	0	27
N28	=	Maryland _BALT_	0	0

1936   1-7-0
O3	•	Clarkson	31	0
O10	•	Baldwin Wallace	0	19
O17		at Cornell	7	20
O24	•	Maryland _NYC_	0	20
O31	•	Penn State	0	18
N7		at Indiana	7	9
N14		at Columbia	0	17
N21		at Colgate	0	13

OSSIE SOLEM
1937-45 (.524)   30-27-6

1937   5-2-1
O1	•	Clarkson	26	6
O9	•	St. Lawrence	40	0
O16		at Cornell	14	6
O23	•	Maryland _BALT_	0	13
O30	•	Penn State	19	13
N6	•	Western Reserve	27	6
N13	=	at Columbia	6	6
N20	•	Colgate	0	7

1938   5-3-0
S30	•	Clarkson	27	0
O8	•	Maryland	53	0
O15	•	Cornell	19	17
O22		at Michigan State	12	19
O29		at Penn State	6	33
N5	•	Colgate	7	0
N12	•	Duke	0	21
N19		at Columbia	13	12

1939   3-3-2
S29	•	Clarkson	12	0
O7		at Cornell	6	19
O14	=	Georgetown	13	13
O21		at Duke	6	33
O28	•	Penn State	6	6
N4	•	Michigan State	3	14
N18	=	Colgate	7	0
N30		at Maryland	10	7

1940   3-4-1
S27	•	Clarkson	33	0
O5	•	Northwestern	0	40
O12	•	NYU _BRNX_	47	13
O19		at Cornell	6	33
O26		at Columbia	3	0
N2	•	Georgetown	6	28
N9	•	Penn State	13	13
N16	•	Colgate	6	7

1941   5-2-1
S26	•	Clarkson	39	0
O4		at Cornell	0	6
O11	•	Holy Cross	6	0
O18	•	NYU _BRNX_	31	0
O25	•	Rutgers	49	7
N1		at Wisconsin	27	20
N8		at Penn State	19	34
N15	•	Colgate	19	19

1942   6-3-0
S25	•	Clarkson	58	6
O3	•	Boston U.	25	0
O9	•	Western Reserve	13	0
O17		at Holy Cross	19	0
O24	•	Cornell	12	7
O31	•	N.C. Pre-Flight	0	9
N7		at Penn State	13	18
N14	•	Colgate	0	14
N21		at Rutgers	12	7

1943
NO TEAM WWII

1944   2-4-1
S23	•	Cornell	6	39
O7	•	Columbia	2	26
O14	•	Lafayette	32	7
O21	=	at Temple	7	7
O28		at Boston College	12	19
N4	•	Penn State	0	41
N18	•	Colgate	43	13

1945   1-6-0
S24	•	Cornell	14	26
S28		at Temple	6	7
O6		at Columbia	0	32
O12	•	West Virginia	12	0
O27	•	Dartmouth	0	8
N3		at Penn State	0	26
N17	•	Colgate	6	7

CLARENCE L. MUNN
1946 (.444)   4-5

1946   4-5-0
S28	•	Boston U.	41	6
O5		at Dartmouth	14	20
O12	•	Penn State	0	9
O19	•	at Holy Cross	21	12
O26		at West Virginia	0	13
N2	•	Temple	28	7
N9		at Cornell	14	7
N16	•	Colgate	7	25
N23		at Columbia	21	59

REAVES H. BAYSINGER
1947-48 (.222) 4-14

1947 — 3-6-0
S26	●	Niagara	14	7
O4		Dartmouth	7	28
O11	●	Temple	28	12
O18		at Penn State	0	40
O25		Holy Cross	0	26
N1		at Lafayette	7	14
N8		at Cornell	6	12
N15	●	Colgate	7	0
N22		at Columbia	8	28

1948 — 1-8-0
S28	●	Niagara	13	9
O2		at Holy Cross	7	33
O8		Penn State	14	34
O16		Cornell	7	34
O23		at Northwestern	0	48
O30		Boston U. *Bos*	7	12
N6		at Temple	0	20
N13		Colgate	13	20
N20		at Columbia	28	34

BEN SCHWARTZWALDER
1949-73 (.626) 153-91-3

1949 — 4-5-0
S23		Boston U.	21	33
O1	●	Lafayette	20	13
O7		Temple	14	27
O15	●	at Rutgers	21	9
O22		Fordham *NYC*	21	47
O29		at Penn State	21	33
N5		at Cornell	7	33
N12	●	Holy Cross	47	13
N15	●	Colgate	35	7

1950 — 5-5-0
S23	●	Rutgers	42	12
S29		at Temple	6	7
O7		Cornell	7	26
O14	●	Penn State	27	7
O21	●	at Holy Cross	34	27
O28	●	Boston U. *Bos*	13	7
N4	●	at Lafayette	34	0
N10		John Carroll *Clev*	16	21
N18		Colgate	14	19
D2		Fordham *NYC*	6	13

1951 — 5-4-0
S21	●	Temple	19	0
S29		at Cornell	14	21
O6	●	Lafayette	46	0
O13		Illinois	20	41
O20		at Dartmouth	0	14
O27	●	Fordham	33	20
N10		at Penn State	13	32
N17	●	Colgate	9	0
N24	●	at Boston U.	26	19

1952 — 7-3-0
S20		Bolling Field	12	13
S27	●	Boston U.	34	21
O3	●	at Temple	27	0
O11	●	Cornell	26	6
O18		at Michigan State	7	48
N1	●	Holy Cross	20	19
N8	●	Penn State	25	7
N15	●	Colgate	20	14
N22	●	at Fordham	26	13
		ORANGE BOWL		
J1		Alabama	6	61

1953 — 5-3-1
S26	●	Temple	42	0
O2	=	Boston U.	14	14
O10	●	Fordham	20	13
O17		at Penn State	14	20
O24		at Illinois	13	20
O31	●	at Holy Cross	21	0
N7	●	at Cornell	26	0
N14	●	Colgate	34	18
N21		Villanova *Phil*	13	14

1954 — 4-4-0
S25	●	Villanova	28	6
O2		Penn State	0	13
O16		at Boston U.	19	41
O23		at Illinois	6	34
O30	●	Holy Cross	25	20
N6		at Cornell	6	14
N13	●	Colgate	31	12
N20	●	Fordham *NYC*	20	7

1955 — 5-3-0
S24		Pittsburgh	12	22
O8	●	Boston U.	27	12
O15	●	at Army	13	0
O22		Maryland	13	34
O29	●	at Holy Cross	49	9
N5		at Penn State	20	21
N12	●	Colgate	26	19
N19	●	at West Virginia	20	13

1956 — 7-2-0
S22	●	at Maryland	26	12
S29		at Pittsburgh	7	14
O13	●	West Virginia	27	20
O20	●	Army	7	0
O27	●	at Boston U.	21	7
N3	●	Penn State	13	9
N10	●	Holy Cross	41	20
N17	●	Colgate	61	7
		COTTON BOWL		
J1		TCU	27	28

1957 — 5-3-1
S28	=	Iowa State	7	7
O5	●	Boston U.	27	7
O12	●	at Cornell	34	0
O19	●	at Nebraska	26	9
O26		Penn State	12	20
N2	●	at Pittsburgh	24	21
N9		Holy Cross	19	20
N16	●	Colgate	34	6
N23		at West Virginia	0	7

1958 — 8-2-0
S27	●	Boston College	24	14
O4		at Holy Cross	13	14
O11	●	Cornell	55	0
O18	●	Nebraska	38	0
O25	●	at Penn State	14	6
N1	●	Pittsburgh	16	13
N7	●	at Boston U.	42	0
N15	●	Colgate	47	0
N22	●	at West Virginia	15	12
		ORANGE BOWL		
J1		Oklahoma	6	21

1959 — 11-0-0
S26	●	Kansas	35	21
O3	●	Maryland	29	0
O10	●	Navy *Nor*	32	6
O17	●	Holy Cross	42	6
O24	●	West Virginia	44	0
O31	●	at Pittsburgh	35	0
N7	●	at Penn State	20	18
N14	●	Colgate	71	0
N21	●	at Boston U.	46	0
D5	●	at UCLA	36	8
		COTTON BOWL		
J1	●	Texas	23	14

1960 — 7-2-0
S24	●	Boston U.	35	7
O1	●	at Kansas	14	7
O8	●	at Holy Cross	15	6
O15	●	Penn State	21	15
O22	●	at West Virginia	45	0
O29		Pittsburgh	0	10
N5		Army *Brnx*	6	9
N12	●	Colgate	46	6
N18	●	at Miami, Fla.	21	14

1961 — 8-3-0
S23	●	Oregon State *Port*	19	8
S30	●	West Virginia	29	14
O7		at Maryland	21	22
O14	●	at Nebraska	28	6
O21		at Penn State	0	14
O28	●	Holy Cross	34	6
N4	●	Pittsburgh	28	9
N11	●	Colgate	51	8
N18		at Notre Dame	15	17
N25	●	at Boston College	28	13
		LIBERTY BOWL		
D16	●	Miami, Fla.	15	14

1962 — 5-5-0
S22		at Oklahoma	3	7
S29		Army *NYC*	2	9
O13	●	Boston College	12	0
O20		at Penn State	19	20
O27	●	at Holy Cross	30	20
N3		at Pittsburgh	6	24
N10	●	Navy	34	6
N17	●	George Washington	35	0
N24		West Virginia	6	17
D8	●	at UCLA	12	7

1963 — 8-2-0
S21	●	Boston College	32	21
S28		at Kansas	0	10
O5	●	Holy Cross	48	0
O11	●	at UCLA	29	7
O19	●	Penn State	9	0
O26	●	Oregon State	31	8
N2		at Pittsburgh	27	35
N9	●	West Virginia	15	13
N16	●	Richmond	50	0
N28	●	Notre Dame *Brnx*	14	7

1964 — 7-4-0
S19		at Boston College	14	21
S26	●	Kansas	38	6
O3	●	at Holy Cross	34	8
O10	●	UCLA	39	0
O17	●	at Penn State	21	14
O24		Oregon State *Port*	13	31
O31	●	Pittsburgh	21	6
N7	●	Army *Brnx*	27	15
N14	●	Virginia Tech	20	15
N21		at West Virginia	27	28
		SUGAR BOWL		
J1		LSU	10	13

1965 — 7-3-0
S18	●	at Navy	14	6
S25		Miami, Fla.	0	24
O2	●	at Maryland	24	7
O9		at UCLA	14	24
O16	●	Penn State	28	21
O23	●	Holy Cross	32	6
O30	●	Pittsburgh *Flu*	51	13
N6		Oregon State	12	13
N13	●	at West Virginia	41	19
N20	●	Boston College	21	13

1966 — 8-3-0
S10		at Baylor	12	35
S24		UCLA	12	31
O1	●	Maryland	28	7
O8	●	Navy	28	14
O15	●	at Boston College	30	0
O22	●	at Holy Cross	28	6
O29	●	Pittsburgh	33	7
N5	●	at Penn State	12	10
N12	●	Florida State	37	21
N19	●	at West Virginia	34	7
		GATOR BOWL		
D31		Tennessee	12	18

1967 — 8-2-0
S23	●	Baylor	7	0
S30	●	West Virginia	23	6
O7	●	at Maryland	7	3
O14		at Navy	14	27
O21	●	California	20	14
O28		Penn State	20	29
N4	●	at Pittsburgh	14	7
N11	●	Holy Cross	41	7
N18	●	at Boston College	32	20
N25	●	at UCLA	32	14

1968 — 6-4-0
S21		at Michigan State	10	14
S28	●	Maryland	32	14
O5	●	UCLA	20	7
O12	●	Pittsburgh	50	17
O26		at California	0	43
N2	●	at Holy Cross	47	0
N9	●	William & Mary	31	0
N16	●	Navy	44	6
N23		at West Virginia	6	23
D7		at Penn State	12	30

1969 — 5-5-0
S20	●	Iowa State	14	13
S27		at Kansas	0	13
O4	●	at Wisconsin	43	7
O11	●	at Maryland	20	9
O18		Penn State	14	15
N1		at Pittsburgh	20	21
N8	●	Arizona	23	0
N15	●	at Navy	15	0
N22		West Virginia	10	13
N29		Boston College	10	35

1970 — 6-4-0
S19		at Houston	15	42
S26		Kansas	14	31
O3		at Illinois	0	27
O10	●	Maryland	23	7
O17	●	at Penn State	24	7
O24	●	Navy	23	8
O31	●	Pittsburgh	43	13
N7	●	at Army	31	29
N14		at West Virginia	19	28
N21	●	Miami, Fla.	56	16

1971 — 5-5-1
S18	=	Wisconsin	20	20
S25		at Northwestern	6	12
O2	●	at Indiana	7	0
O9	●	at Maryland	21	13
O16		Penn State	0	31
O23	●	Holy Cross	63	21
O30		at Pittsburgh	21	31
N6		Boston College	3	10
N13		at Navy	14	17
N20	●	West Virginia	28	24
D4	●	at Miami, Fla.	14	0

1972 — 5-6-0
S9	●	Temple	17	10
S16		at North Carolina St.	20	43
S23		at Wisconsin	7	31
S30	●	Maryland	16	12
O7		Indiana	2	10
O14	●	Navy	30	14
O21		at Penn State	0	17
O28	●	Pittsburgh	10	6
N4		at Boston College	0	37
N11	●	Army	27	6
N18		at West Virginia	12	43

1973 — 2-9-0
S15		Bowling Green	14	41
S22		Michigan State	8	14
S29		at Washington	7	21
O6		at Maryland	0	38
O13		at Navy	14	23
O20		Penn State	6	49
O27		Miami, Fla.	23	34
N3		at Pittsburgh	14	28
N10	●	at Holy Cross	5	3
N17	●	Boston College	24	13
N24		West Virginia	14	24

FRANK MALONEY
1974-80 (.410) 32-46

1974 — 2-9-0
S7	●	Oregon State	23	15
S14		Kent State	14	20
S21		at Michigan State	0	19
S28		North Carolina St.	22	28
O5		Maryland	0	31
O12	●	Navy	17	9
O19		at Penn State	14	30
N2		Pittsburgh	13	21
N9		at West Virginia	11	39
N16		at Boston College	0	45
N22		at Miami, Fla.	7	14

1975 — 6-5-0
S13	●	Villanova	24	17
S20	●	Iowa	10	7
S27	●	at Tulane	31	13
O4		at Maryland	7	24
O11		at Navy	6	10
O18		Penn State	7	19
O25	●	Boston College	22	14
N1		Pittsburgh	0	38
N15	●	at Virginia	37	0
N22	●	West Virginia	20	19
N29		at Rutgers	10	21

1976 — 3-8-0
S11		Bowling Green	7	22
S18		at Iowa	3	41
S25		Maryland	28	42
O2	●	Oregon State	21	3
O9	●	Tulane	3	0
O16		at Penn State	3	27
O23	●	Temple	24	16
O30		at Pittsburgh	13	23
N6		Navy	10	27
N13		at Boston College	14	28
N20		at West Virginia	28	34

1977 — 6-5-0
S10		at Oregon State	12	24
S17		North Carolina St.	0	38
S24	●	Washington	22	20
O1	●	at Illinois	30	20
O8		at Maryland	10	24
O15		Penn State	24	31
O22		at Pittsburgh	21	28
O29	●	Virginia	6	3
N5	●	at Navy	45	34
N12	●	Boston College	20	3
N19	●	West Virginia	28	9

1978 — 3-8-0

S9		Florida State	0	28
S16		at North Carolina St.	19	27
S23		at Michigan State	21	49
S30		Illinois	14	28
O7	●	at West Virginia	31	15
O14		Maryland	9	24
O21		at Penn State	15	45
N4		Pittsburgh	17	18
N11	●	Navy	20	17
N18	●	at Boston College	37	23
N25		at Miami, Fla.	9	21

1979 — 7-5-0

S8		at Ohio State	8	31
S15	●	West Virginia ERUT	24	14
S22	●	at Northwestern	54	21
S29	●	Washington State BUF	52	25
O6	●	at Kansas	45	27
O13		Temple PHIL	17	49
O20		Penn State ERUT	7	35
O27	●	Miami, Fla. BUF	25	15
N3		at Pittsburgh	21	28
N10	●	at Navy	30	14
N17		Boston College ITH	10	27
		INDEPENDENCE BOWL		
D15	●	McNeese St.	31	7

1980 — 5-6-0

S13		at Ohio State	21	31
S20	●	Miami, Ohio	36	24
S27	●	Northwestern	42	21
O4		Kansas	8	23
O11	●	Temple	31	7
O18		at Penn State	7	24
O25	●	Rutgers	17	9
N1		Pittsburgh	6	43
N8		Navy	3	6
N15		at Boston College	16	27
N22	●	at West Virginia	20	7

RICHARD F. MACPHERSON
1981-90 (.586) 66-46-4

1981 — 4-6-1

S5		Rutgers	27	29
S12		Temple PHIL	19	31
S19		at Illinois	14	17
S26	●	Indiana	21	7
O3	=	at Maryland	17	17
O17		Penn State	16	41
O24		at Pittsburgh	10	23
O31	●	Colgate	47	24
N7		at Navy	23	35
N14	●	Boston College	27	17
N21	●	West Virginia	27	24

1982 — 2-9-0

S4	●	Rutgers ERUT	31	8
S11		Temple	18	23
S18		Illinois	10	47
S25		at Indiana	10	17
O2		Maryland	3	26
O16		at Penn State	7	28
O23		Pittsburgh	0	14
O30	●	Colgate	49	15
N6		Navy	18	20
N13		at Boston College	13	20
N20		at West Virginia	0	26

1983 — 6-5-0

S2		Temple PHIL	6	17
S10	●	Kent State	22	10
S17	●	Northwestern	35	0
S24	●	Rutgers	17	13
O1		Nebraska	7	63
O8		at Maryland	13	34
O15		at Penn State	6	17
O29		at Pittsburgh	10	13
N5	●	at Navy	14	7
N12	●	Boston College	21	10
N19	●	West Virginia	27	16

1984 — 6-5-0

S8	●	at Maryland	23	7
S15	●	at Northwestern	13	12
S22		Rutgers	0	19
S29	●	Nebraska	17	9
O6		at Florida	0	16
O13		at West Virginia	10	20
O20		at Penn State	3	21
O27	●	Army	27	16
N3	●	Pittsburgh	13	7
N10	●	Navy	29	0
N17		Boston College FOX	16	24

1985 — 7-5-0

S14		at Mississippi State	3	30
S21	●	Kent State	34	0
S28		at Virginia Tech	14	24
O5	●	Louisville	48	0
O19		Penn State	20	24
O26	●	Temple	29	14
N2	●	at Pittsburgh	12	0
N9	●	at Navy	24	20
N16	●	Boston College	41	21
N23	●	at Rutgers	31	14
N30		West Virginia	10	13
		CHERRY BOWL		
D21		Maryland	18	35

1986 — 5-6-0

S6		Mississippi State	17	24
S13		at Army	28	33
S20		Virginia Tech	17	26
S27		Rutgers	10	16
O4	●	Missouri	41	9
O18		at Penn State	3	42
O25	●	Temple PHIL	27	24
N1	●	Pittsburgh	24	20
N8	●	Navy	31	22
N15		at Boston College	9	27
N22	●	at West Virginia	34	23

1987 — 11-0-1

S5	●	Maryland	25	11
S12	●	at Rutgers	20	3
S19	●	Miami, Ohio	24	10
S26	●	at Virginia Tech	35	21
O3	●	at Missouri	24	13
O17	●	Penn State	48	21
O24	●	Colgate	52	6
O31	●	at Pittsburgh	24	10
N7	●	at Navy	34	10
N14	●	Boston College	45	17
N21	●	West Virginia	32	31
		SUGAR BOWL		
J1	=	Auburn	16	16

1988 — 10-2-0

S3	●	Temple	31	21
S10		at Ohio State	9	26
S24	●	Virginia Tech	35	0
O1	●	Maryland	20	9
O8	●	Rutgers	34	20
O15	●	at Penn State	24	10
O22	●	at East Carolina	38	14
N5	●	Navy	49	21
N12	●	at Boston College	45	20
N19		at West Virginia	9	31
D3	●	Pittsburgh	24	7
		HALL OF FAME BOWL		
J2	●	LSU	23	10

1989 — 8-4-0

S9	●	Temple PHIL	43	3
S16	●	Army	10	7
S23		at Pittsburgh	23	30
O7		Florida State	10	41
O14		Penn State	12	34
O21	●	at Rutgers	49	28
O28	●	East Carolina	18	16
N4	●	Boston College	23	11
N11	●	at Navy	38	17
N23		West Virginia	17	24
D4	●	Louisville TOK	24	13
		PEACH BOWL		
D30	●	Georgia	19	18

1990 — 7-4-2

A31		Southern Cal ERUT	16	34
S8	●	Temple	19	9
S15	=	Michigan State	23	23
S22	=	Pittsburgh	20	20
O6	●	at Vanderbilt	49	14
O13		at Penn State	21	27
O20	●	Rutgers	42	0
O27	●	at Army	26	14
N3	●	at Boston College	35	6
N10		Tulane	24	26
N17	●	at West Virginia	31	7
N24		at Miami, Fla.	7	33
		ALOHA BOWL		
D25	●	Arizona	28	0

1991-PRESENT
BIG EAST

PAUL L. PASQUALONI
1991-2004 (.644) 107-59-1

1991 — 10-2-0 (5-0-0)

S7	●	Vanderbilt	37	10
S14	●	at Maryland	31	17
S21	●	Florida	38	21
S28	●	at Tulane	24	0
O5		at Florida State	14	46
O12		East Carolina	20	23
O19	● |	at Pittsburgh	31	27
O26	● |	Rutgers ERUT	21	7
N2	● |	Temple	27	6
N16	● |	Boston College	38	16
N23	● |	West Virginia	16	10
		HALL OF FAME BOWL		
J1	●	Ohio State	24	17

1992 — 10-2-0 (6-1-0)

S5	●	at East Carolina	42	21
S12	●	Texas	31	21
S19		Ohio State	12	35
O3	●	at Louisville	15	9
O10	● |	Rutgers	50	28
O17	● |	at West Virginia	20	17
O24	● |	Temple PHIL	38	7
O31	● |	Pittsburgh	41	10
N7	● |	Virginia Tech	28	9
N14	● |	at Boston College	27	10
N21	|	Miami, Fla.	10	16
		FIESTA BOWL		
J1	●	Colorado	26	22

1993 — 6-4-1 (3-4-0)

S4	●	Ball State	35	12
S9	●	at East Carolina	41	22
S18	=	at Texas	21	21
S25	●	Cincinnati	24	21
O2	|	Boston College	29	33
O16	● |	at Pittsburgh	24	21
O23	|	at Miami, Fla.	0	49
O30	|	West Virginia	0	43
N6	● |	Temple	52	3
N13	|	at Virginia Tech	24	45
N26	● |	Rutgers ERUT	31	18

1994 — 7-4-0 (4-3-0)

S3		Oklahoma	29	30
S10	●	at Cincinnati	34	19
S17	● |	Rutgers	37	36
S24	●	at East Carolina	21	18
O1	● |	Virginia Tech	28	20
O8	● |	Pittsburgh	31	7
O22	● |	Temple PHIL	49	42
N5	|	Miami, Fla.	6	27
N12	|	at Boston College	0	31
N19	●	Maryland	21	16
N24	|	at West Virginia	0	13

1995 — 9-3-0 (5-2-0)

S2	●	at North Carolina	20	9
S9		East Carolina	24	27
S23	●	Minnesota	27	17
S30	● |	at Rutgers	27	17
O7	● |	Temple	31	14
O14	●	Eastern Michigan	52	24
O21	● |	West Virginia	22	0
N4	|	at Virginia Tech	7	31
N11	● |	at Pittsburgh	42	10
N18	● |	Boston College	58	29
N25	|	at Miami, Fla.	24	35
		GATOR BOWL		
J1	●	Clemson	41	0

1996 — 9-3 (6-1)

S7		North Carolina	10	27
S21		at Minnesota	33	35
S28	● |	Virginia Tech	52	21
O5	● |	Rutgers	42	0
O12	● |	Pittsburgh	55	7
O26	● |	at Boston College	45	17
N2	● |	at West Virginia	30	7
N9	●	at Tulane	31	7
N16	●	Army	42	17
N23	● |	Temple PHIL	36	15
N30	|	Miami, Fla.	31	38
		LIBERTY BOWL		
D27	●	Houston	30	17

1997 — 9-4 (6-1)

A24	●	Wisconsin ERUT	34	0
A30		North Carolina St.	31	32
S6		at Oklahoma	34	36
S13	|	at Virginia Tech	3	31
S20	●	Tulane	30	19
O4	●	East Carolina	56	0
O9	● |	at Rutgers	50	3
O18	● |	Temple	60	7
N1	● |	West Virginia	40	10
N8	● |	Boston College	20	13
N15	● |	at Pittsburgh	32	27
N29	● |	at Miami, Fla.	33	13
		FIESTA BOWL		
D31		Kansas State	18	35

1998 — 8-4 (6-1)

S5		Tennessee	33	34
S12	●	at Michigan	38	28
S19	● |	Rutgers	70	14
O1		at North Carolina St.	17	38
O10	●	Cincinnati	63	21
O17	● |	at Boston College	42	25
O31	● |	Pittsburgh	45	28
N7	|	at West Virginia	28	35
N14	● |	Virginia Tech	28	26
N21	● |	Temple PHIL	38	7
N28	● |	Miami, Fla.	66	13
		ORANGE BOWL		
J2		Florida	10	31

1999 — 7-5 (3-4)

S2	●	at Toledo	35	12
S11	●	Central Michigan	47	7
S18		Michigan	13	18
S25	● |	West Virginia	30	7
O2	●	Tulane	47	17
O7	● |	at Pittsburgh	24	17
O16	|	at Virginia Tech	0	62
O30	|	Boston College	23	24
N6	● |	Temple	27	10
N13	|	at Rutgers	21	24
N27	|	at Miami, Fla.	13	45
		MUSIC CITY BOWL		
D29	●	Kentucky	20	13

2000 — 6-5 (4-3)

S2	●	Buffalo	63	7
S9		at Cincinnati	10	12
S23		at East Carolina	17	34
S30	●	Brigham Young	42	14
O7	● |	Pittsburgh	24	17
O14	|	at Boston College	13	20
O21	|	Virginia Tech	14	22
N4	● |	at West Virginia	31	27
N11	● |	at Temple	31	12
N18	|	Miami, Fla.	0	26
N25	● |	Rutgers	49	21

2001 — 10-3 (6-1)

A25		Georgia Tech ERUT	7	13
S1		at Tennessee	9	33
S8	●	Central Florida	21	10
S22	●	Auburn	31	14
S29	●	East Carolina	44	30
O6	● |	at Rutgers	24	17
O13	● |	at Pittsburgh	42	10
O20	● |	Temple	45	3
O27	● |	at Virginia Tech	22	14
N10	● |	West Virginia	24	13
N17	|	at Miami, Fla.	0	59
N24	● |	Boston College	39	28
		INSIGHT.COM BOWL		
D29	●	Kansas State	26	3

2002   4-8   (2-5)

A29		at Brigham Young	21	42
S7		North Carolina	22	30
S14	●	Rhode Island	63	17
S28		at Auburn	34	37
O5	│	Pittsburgh	24	48
O12	│	at Temple	16	17
O19	│	at West Virginia	7	34
O26	● │	Rutgers	45	14
N2	●	at Central Florida	38	35
N9	● │	Virginia Tech	50	42
N16	│	at Boston College	20	41
N30	│	Miami, Fla.	7	49

2003   6-6   (2-5)

S6	●	at North Carolina	49	47
S13		Louisville	20	30
S20	●	Central Florida	38	14
S27	●	Toledo	34	7
O11	│	at Virginia Tech	7	51
O18	● │	Boston College	39	14
O25	│	at Pittsburgh	14	34
N8	● │	Temple	41	17
N15	│	at Miami, Fla.	10	17
N22	│	West Virginia	23	34
N29	│	at Rutgers	7	24
D6	●	Notre Dame	38	12

2004   6-6   (4-2)

S5		at Purdue	0	51
S11	●	at Buffalo	37	17
S18	●	Cincinnati	19	7
S25		at Virginia	10	31
O2	● │	Rutgers	41	31
O9		Florida State	13	17
O21	│	at West Virginia	6	27
O30	● │	Connecticut	42	30
N6	● │	Pittsburgh	38	31
N13	│	at Temple	24	34
N27	● │	at Boston College	43	17
		CHAMPS SPORTS BOWL		
D21		Georgia Tech	14	51

THE SCHOOLS

SYRACUSE ANNUAL STATISTICAL LEADERS

YR	RUSHING	YDS	ATT	AVG	PASSING	ATT	CMP	PCT	YDS	RECEIVING	REC	YDS	AVG
1945	Robert Ferri	179	67	2.7	Roger Robinson	55	29	.53	434		NA	NA	NA
1946	John Manderino	395	134	2.9	Walt Slovenski	17	9	.53	199	Paul McKee	12	245	20.4
1947	Ed Dolan	337	97	3.5	Ed Dolan	48	15	.31	168	Angelo Acocella	8	100	12.5
1948	George Davis	208	66	3.2	Bernie Custis	131	52	.40	721	George Urban	13	207	15.9
1949	George Davis	805	159	5.1	Bernie Custis	134	70	.52	1,121	Jim Dragotta	14	194	13.9
1950	Bob Young	709	122	5.8	Bernie Custis	159	74	.47	775	Joe Szombathy	20	257	12.9
1951	John Donati	477	114	4.2	Avatus Stone	55	18	.33	358	Joe Szombathy	11	223	20.3
1952	Bill Wetzel	670	132	5.1	Pat Stark	151	78	.52	1,035	Joe Szombathy	21	178	8.5
1953	Bob Leberman	513	110	4.7	Pat Stark	141	73	.52	1,045	Ray Perkins	18	212	11.8
1954	Ray Perkins	499	98	5.1	Mickey Rich	52	17	.33	234	Tom Richardson	6	107	17.8
1955	Jim Brown	666	128	5.2	Ed Albright	34	19	.56	324	Don Althouse	10	173	17.3
1956	Jim Brown	986	158	6.2	Chuck Zimmerman	42	18	.43	272	Jim Ridlon	8	153	19.1
1957	Ed Coffin	448	106	4.2	Chuck Zimmerman	96	53	.55	770	Dick Lasse	16	202	12.6
1958	Ger Schwedes	360	83	4.3	Chuck Zimmerman	76	46	.61	645	Ger Schwedes	13	117	9.0
1959	Ernie Davis	686	98	7.0	Dave Sarette	83	49	.59	763	Fred Mautino	17	215	12.6
1960	Ernie Davis	877	112	7.8	Dave Sarette	65	30	.46	327	Fred Mautino	14	171	12.2
1961	Ernie Davis	823	150	5.5	Dave Sarette	106	55	.52	813	Ernie Davis	16	157	9.8
1962	Jim Nance	417	84	5.0	Walley Mahle	71	33	.46	455	John Mackey	8	131	16.4
1963	Walley Mahle	457	78	5.9	Rich King	80	37	.46	675	Dick Bowman	10	190	19.0
1964	Jim Nance	951	190	5.0	Walley Mahle	80	31	.39	324	Floyd Little	16	248	15.5
1965	Floyd Little	1,065	193	5.5	Rick Cassata	104	47	.45	525	Floyd Little	21	248	11.8
1966	Larry Csonka	1,012	197	5.1	Rick Cassata	85	41	.48	472	Ed Schreck	14	175	12.5
1967	Larry Csonka	1,127	261	4.3	Rick Cassata	176	92	.52	992	Tom Coughlin	26	257	9.9
1968	Al Newton	618	125	4.9	Paul Paolisso	164	87	.53	939	John Massis	29	400	13.8
1969	Al Newton	689	154	4.5	Randy Zur	148	73	.49	816	Tony Gabriel	30	419	14.0
1970	Marty Januszkiewicz	769	199	3.9	Paul Paolisso	71	33	.46	370	Tony Gabriel	28	402	14.4
1971	Roger Praetorius	705	169	4.2	Bob Woodruff	132	74	.56	910	Rick Steiner	24	310	12.9
1972	Marty Januszkiewicz	618	126	4.9	Bob Woodruff	136	63	.46	649	Brian Hambleton	15	156	10.4
1973	Bob Mitch	448	139	3.2	Bob Mitch	139	58	.42	722	Bob Petchel	22	183	8.3
1974	Ken Kinsey	610	152	4.0	Jim Donoghue	136	68	.50	938	Lonnie Allgood	22	477	21.7
1975	Earl Vaughn	470	118	4.0	Jim Donoghue	118	52	.44	832	Lonnie Allgood	27	477	17.7
1976	Bill Hurley	716	185	3.9	Bill Hurley	95	38	.40	638	Mike Jones	16	240	15.0
1977	Bill Hurley	625	200	3.1	Bill Hurley	201	108	.54	1,455	Art Monk	41	590	14.4
1978	Joe Morris	1,001	170	5.9	Tim Wilson	68	22	.32	345	Art Monk	19	293	15.4
1979	Joe Morris	1,372	238	5.8	Bill Hurley	158	79	.50	1,276	Art Monk	40	716	17.9
1980	Joe Morris	732	144	5.1	Dave Warner	167	81	.49	1,008	Tony Sidor	23	288	12.5
1981	Joe Morris	1,194	261	4.6	Dave Warner	223	120	.54	1,445	Willie Sydnor	29	418	14.4
1982	Jaime Covington	774	171	4.5	Todd Norley	134	70	.52	833	Nick Bruckner	24	374	15.6
1983	Jaime Covington	606	143	4.2	Todd Norley	177	87	.49	999	Scott Schwedes	21	261	12.4
1984	Jaime Covington	745	201	3.7	Todd Norley	171	93	.54	829	Scott Schwedes	37	506	13.7
1985	Don McPherson	489	157	3.1	Don McPherson	159	85	.53	1,469	Mike Siano	46	852	18.5
1986	Don McPherson	523	191	2.7	Don McPherson	269	142	.53	1,827	Scott Schwedes	47	652	13.9
1987	Robert Drummond	746	124	6.0	Don McPherson	229	129	.56	2,341	Tommy Kane	44	968	22.0
1988	Robert Drummond	747	124	6.0	Todd Philcox	234	141	.60	2,076	Rob Moore	44	797	18.1
1989	Michael Owens	1,018	211	4.8	Bill Scharr	169	107	.63	1,625	Rob Moore	53	1,064	20.1
1990	David Walker	730	150	4.9	Marvin Graves	200	115	.58	1,711	Rob Carpenter	52	895	17.2
1991	David Walker	969	169	5.7	Marvin Graves	221	131	.59	1,912	Qadry Ismail	37	693	18.7
1992	David Walker	855	168	5.1	Marvin Graves	242	146	.60	2,296	Qadry Ismail	36	625	17.4
1993	Terry Richardson	526	104	5.1	Marvin Graves	280	171	.61	2,547	Shelby Hill	56	937	16.7
1994	Kirby Dar Dar	853	188	4.5	Kevin Mason	187	105	.56	1,627	Marvin Harrison	36	761	21.1
1995	Malcolm Thomas	603	124	4.9	Donovan McNabb	207	128	.62	1,991	Marvin Harrison	56	1,131	20.2
1996	Malcolm Thomas	891	166	5.4	Donovan McNabb	215	118	.55	1,776	Deon Maddox	23	344	15.0
1997	Kyle McIntosh	898	181	5.0	Donovan McNabb	265	145	.55	2,488	Quinton Spotwood	41	797	19.4
1998	Kyle McIntosh	742	137	5.4	Donovan McNabb	251	157	.63	2,134	Kevin Johnson	60	894	14.9
1999	Dee Brown	741	145	5.1	Troy Nunes	161	95	.59	1,141	Quinton Spotwood	32	380	11.9
2000	Dee Brown	1,031	172	6.0	Troy Nunes	154	94	.61	1,366	Pat Woodcock	29	453	15.6
2001	James Mungro	1,170	248	4.7	R.J. Anderson	144	72	.50	1,123	Maurice Jackson	19	254	13.4
2002	Walter Reyes	1,135	182	6.2	Troy Nunes	198	115	.58	1,337	Jamel Riddle	41	626	15.3
2003	Walter Reyes	1,347	253	5.3	R.J. Anderson	310	186	.60	2,164	Johnnie Morant	46	799	17.4
2004	Damien Rhodes	870	153	5.7	Perry Patterson	289	168	.58	1,851	Jared Jones	43	621	14.4

Receiving leaders by receptions
The NCAA began including postseason stats in 2002

TCU

BY KEVIN GLEASON

A FEW YEARS AFTER THE CIVIL WAR had ended, brothers Addison and Randolph Clark gathered 13 students in a one-room schoolhouse. The first college in the Southwest to educate both genders was born. Over the next 12 decades, Texas Christian University has experienced all the highs and lows of major college football, from a national championship, major bowl games and Heisman-winning superstars to years of futility, collapsing conference affiliations and the sting of probation. In the past 10 years, the revived TCU football program has enjoyed one of its two or three greatest eras, a period of prosperity that promises to continue despite the Horned Frogs' six-year bowl streak being snapped in 2004.

TRADITION Opponents must love the train horn—yes, an actual train horn, a 120-decibel "frog horn" to be exact—which is blown after every home score. But head coach Gary Patterson has a greater affinity for the sounds of grunts and screeches from the weight room. Patterson created the Iron Frog Award upon his arrival as defensive coordinator in 1998. The honor goes to players who exhibit top weight-lifting prowess on the team's annual Night of Champions.

BEST PLAYER Sammy Baugh played at TCU. So did Bob Lilly. But quarterback Davey O'Brien, at just 5'7" and 150 pounds, is regarded as the school's premier player. In 1938, he became the first player to win the Heisman, Walter Camp Award and Maxwell trophies in the same year. The impact of O'Brien's career is evident at the end of each season, when the nation's top quarterback earns the Davey O'Brien Award. The Frogs ranked first in the country in passing and second in total offense in 1938, as O'Brien completed 93 of 166 passes for 1,457 yards and 20 touchdowns.

BEST COACH L.R. "Dutch" Meyer led TCU to a school-record 109 victories against 79 losses with 13 ties from 1934 to 1952. Meyer delivered TCU both its national championships, in 1935—according to the Williamson System—and 1938, and three Southwest Conference titles while introducing the spread offense to college football. "Dutch was almost a cartoon character of a football coach, a tough little man in a baseball cap with a whistle

---

PROFILE

Texas Christian University
Fort Worth, Texas
Founded: 1873
Enrollment: 7,154
Colors: Purple and White
Nickname: Horned Frogs
Stadium: Amon G. Carter Stadium
    Opened in 1930
    Grass; 46,000 capacity
First football game: 1896
All-time record: 515–502–57 (.506)
Bowl record: 7–13–1
Consensus national championships, 1936-present: 1 (1938)
Heisman Trophy: Davey O'Brien, 1938
First-round NFL draftees: 10
Website: www.gofrogs.com

THE BEST OF TIMES

Credit L.R. "Dutch" Meyer with leading the Horned Frogs to one of the greatest decades in college football history. Meyer took over in 1934 and brought TCU two national championships (1935 by the Williamson System and 1938 by AP, among others) in his first five seasons. Meyer's teams went 109–79–13, for a .575 winning percentage.

THE WORST OF TIMES

TCU had a rough go of it in the 1970s. The decade included just one winning season, 6–4–1 in 1971, a year marred by coach Jim Pittman's collapsing during the Baylor game and dying afterward. Jim Shofner took over in 1974 and led TCU to two wins in three years. Another winning season didn't come until 1984.

CONFERENCE

In 1923, TCU joined the Southwest Conference, where it remained until becoming a member of the Western Athletic Conference in 1996. The Frogs then moved to Conference USA in 2001 for four seasons before bouncing to the Mountain West in 2005.

DISTINGUISHED ALUMNI

Betty Buckley, actor and singer; Eddie Berniece Johnson, U.S. congresswoman; Sue Monk Kidd, author; Chuck LaMar, general manager, Tampa Bay Devil Rays; Kate Staples Lehrer, author; Bob Schieffer, CBS News broadcaster

FIGHT SONG

TCU FIGHT SONG
We'll raise a song, both loud and long
To cheer our team to victory.
For TCU, so tried and true,
We pledge eternal loyalty.
Fight on boys,
Fight with all your might,
Roll up the scores for TCU.
Hail white and purple flag,
Whose heroes never lag,
Horned Frogs, we are all for you.

Dennis Franchione began a resurrection project that included bowl berths and WAC championships.

around his neck," wrote the famed TCU alum Dan Jenkins. "When he spoke the word 'football,' it sounded like a volcano erupting, and all the words that followed in a sentence came out like the scratching of cleats on a sheet of rusty tin." Meyer was also versatile, posting an 85–71 record as TCU's baseball coach. TCU's most recent slide preceded the arrival of Dennis Franchione in 1998. The Frogs had won 24 games the previous six seasons under Pat Sullivan when Franchione began a resurrection project that eventually yielded a three-season run that included three bowl berths (with two wins), a 25–10 record (16–7 in the Western Athletic Conference) and WAC co-championship in 1999 and 2000. Carrying the torch after Franchione left for Alabama was TCU defensive coordinator Gary Patterson, who kept the team in the national spotlight, winning 27 games and going to three bowls in his first three seasons. Under Patterson, the Frogs enjoyed consecutive Top-25 finishes (2002-03) for the first time since the 1950s.

BEST TEAM The Horned Frogs won the 1938 national championship with an 11–0 finish—the school's only unbeaten and untied record—spearheaded by the Heisman-winning quarterback O'Brien (who was also a star defensive back) and two-way terror Ki Aldrich, who played center and linebacker. The key regular-season game saw TCU rout previously unbeaten Baylor 39-7 to move up to No. 2 in the polls. At the Sugar Bowl, after trailing at the half for the first time all season (7-6 to Carnegie Tech), TCU marched 80 yards with the first possession of the second half to go ahead for good, winning 15-7. They won with a lineup that included three All-Americas and six all-conference players.

BIGGEST GAME Of the 1935 showdown between unbeatens SMU and TCU, *New York Times* sports columnist Allison Danzig once remarked, "All my life, I had dreamed of covering the Harvard-Yale game. And there I was, covering the Harvard-Yale game, but longing to be in

RECORDS

RUSHING YARDS

	GAME
406	LaDainian Tomlinson vs. UTEP, Nov. 20, 1999 (43 att.)
	SEASON
2,158	LaDainian Tomlinson, 2000 (369 att.)
	CAREER
5,263	LaDainian Tomlinson, 1997-2000 (907 att.)

PASSING YARDS

	GAME
690	Matt Vogler vs. Houston, Nov. 3, 1990 (44 of 79)
	SEASON
2,624	Max Knake, 1994 (184 of 316)
	CAREER
7,370	Max Knake, 1992-95 (622 of 1115)

RECEIVING YARDS

	GAME
206	Jimmy Oliver vs. Texas Tech, Nov. 25, 1994 (7 rec.)
	SEASON
1,012	Reggie Harrell, 2003 (58 rec.)
	CAREER
2,739	Mike Renfro, 1974-77 (162 rec.)

POINTS

	GAME
36	LaDainian Tomlinson vs. UTEP, Nov. 20, 1999 (6 TDs)
	SEASON
132	LaDainian Tomlinson, 2000 (22 TDs)
	CAREER
324	LaDainian Tomlinson, 1997-2000 (54 TDs)

CONSENSUS ALL-AMERICANS

1934-35	Darrell Lester	C
1936	Sammy Baugh	B
1938	Davey O'Brien	B
1938	Ki Aldrich	C
1955	Jim Swink	HB
1959	Don Floyd	T
1960	Bob Lilly	T
1984	Kenneth Davis	RB
1991	Kelly Blackwell	TE
1995	Michael Reeder	PK
2000	LaDainian Tomlinson	RB
2003	Nick Browne	PK

Fort Worth for the TCU-SMU game." The school added 3,500 temporary seats to Amon G. Carter Stadium to bring the capacity for the game to 31,000, and managed to shoehorn 40,000 people into the stadium for the Nov. 30 battle of the unbeatens. It was 14-all in the fourth quarter when SMU lined up in punt formation at TCU's 37, only to have quarterback Bob Finley connect with Wilson down the left sideline for the touchdown and an eventual 20-14 victory. No less an authority than Grantland Rice, who was there, called it "one of the greatest football games ever played in the 67-year history of the nation's finest college sport." In the Sugar Bowl, however, TCU recovered to beat LSU 3-2, earning a national championship nod from the Williamson System (the only ranking system of the era to publish a ranking after the bowl games).

BIGGEST UPSET Unbeaten Texas was No. 1 ranked and fresh off a cover appearance on *Life* magazine in 1941 when the Horned Frogs traveled to Austin and played the Longhorns dead-even for nearly 60 minutes. With the game tied 7-7, TCU stopped Texas at fourth and one on its own 27, then mounted a final drive, which featured quarterback Emery Nix running for 35 yards early, then converting on fourth down with a run to the Longhorns' 24. With eight seconds left in the game, Nix hit Van Hall with a 19-yard touchdown pass to silence the Memorial Stadium crowd and vanquish the Longhorns' dreams of an undefeated season.

STADIUM It's not often that a newspaperman gets a stadium named for him, but Amon G. Carter, late publisher of the *Fort Worth Star-Telegram*, is an exception. Amon G. Carter Stadium began as a 22,000-seat facility and has grown to 46,000 capacity, though a school-record 47,280 tucked in to see Texas beat TCU 44-23 in 1984.

HEARTBREAKER Oklahoma was No. 1 and on its way to

ALL-TIME TEAM	
Sportswriter Dan Jenkins, TCU Class of 1953, selected the finest of the Horned Frogs in 2004.	
OFFENSE	
1927-29	Mike Brumbelow, G
1930-32	Johnny Vaught, G
1933-35	Darrell Lester, C
1936-38	I.B. Hale, T
1940-42	Derrell Palmer, T
1957-59	Don Floyd, T
1934-36	Walter Roach, E
1937-39	Don Looney, E
1988-91	Kelly Blackwell, E
1934-36	Sammy Baugh, QB
1936-38	Davey O'Brien, QB
1954-56	Jim Swink, HB
1997-00	LaDainian Tomlinson, RB
1928-30	Cy Leland, KR
2001-03	Nick Browne, PK
DEFENSE	
1925-27	Rags Matthews, DL
1942-44	Clyde Flowers, DL
1954-56	Norm Hamilton, DL
1958-60	Bob Lilly, DL
1997-00	Aaron Schobel, DL
1936-38	Ki Aldrich, LB
1953-55	Hugh Pitts, LB
2000-02	LaMarcus McDonald, LB
1933-35	Jimmy Lawrence, DB
1946-49	Lindy Berry, DB
1955-57	Jim Shofner, DB
1971-72	Lyle Blackwood, DB
1934-36	Sammy Baugh, P

the longest winning streak in college football history. TCU was headed for an otherwise nondescript 4–6 season. Yet early in the fourth quarter of their game on Sept. 25, 1954, the scoreboard shone TCU 16, Oklahoma 7. But Oklahoma used a 50-yard punt return with six minutes left to take a 21-16 lead. The Frogs had one last run in them. They went 84 yards on 14 plays to reach Oklahoma's 7-yard line. But that's where TCU was stranded as time expired.

RIVAL TCU's rivalry with SMU began in 1915. The winner of their games takes home the Iron Skillet. The schools are located 40 miles apart and played together in the Southwest Conference and in the Western Athletic Conference from 1996 to 2000. But in the early 2000s, SMU's program began sputtering, and the rivalry has suffered.

DISPUTE LaDainian Tomlinson couldn't hide his bitterness upon finishing fourth in the 2000 Heisman Trophy balloting. Having run for 2,158 yards to lead the country a second straight season, Tomlinson said, "It lets me know that it's almost impossible for a guy from TCU to win the Heisman." Florida State's Chris Weinke won the award, followed by Oklahoma's Josh Heupel and Purdue's Drew Brees. A year earlier, Tomlinson didn't even finish in the top 10 despite going for 1,850 yards and a Division I-A record 406 against UTEP.

NICKNAME Four students put their heads together in 1897 (five years before the school became TCU) to arrive at one of the most distinctive nicknames in college sports, the Horned Frogs. The nickname is said to derive from a time when the practice field was overrun by the fierce-looking reptiles, technically known as Texas Horned Lizards. Others say TCU and the lizard simply share a certain feistiness.

MASCOT SuperFrog candidates must come up with a 60-second skit and are judged on several criteria, including

rhythm and coordination. ESPN named the Horned Frog the nation's No. 1 mascot in 1980.

UNIFORMS For much of the 1970s, TCU's dominant football colors were purple and silver, but with the arrival of Dennis Franchione in 1998, the team adopted a bolder, more muscular purple-and-black look. After the helmet design changed 13 times in 30 years, the school settled on a purple shell with TCU in white block letters over a gray horned frog, the first appearance of the school's mascot on the helmet since 1965.

NUMBERS TCU won its 500th game with a 17-3 victory

over Mountain West champion Colorado State in the 2002 Liberty Bowl … The 34 victories from 1999 to 2002 were the most in any four-year period at TCU since 1935-38, and the 2002 team didn't trail at halftime all season on its way to a 10–2 finish … In the classroom, TCU was among 32 Division I-A schools to graduate at least 70% of its footsball players who entered as freshmen in 1997 … In 1961, TCU turned in the best 3–5–2 record you'll find. The Frogs ruined two perfect seasons by tying No. 3 Ohio State 7-7 and beating No. 1 Texas 6-0.

QUOTE "Fight 'em 'til hell freezes over … then fight 'em on the ice."—Dutch Meyer

TCU ANNUAL STATISTICAL LEADERS

YR	RUSHING	YDS	ATT	AVG	PASSING	ATT	CMP	PCT	YDS	RECEIVING	REC	YDS	AVG
1956	Jim Swink	669	157	4.3	Chuck Curtis	119	53	.45	867	Jim Swink	19	390	20.5
1957	Jim Shofner	682	131	5.2	Dick Finney	37	14	.38	230	Marvin Lasater	6	124	20.7
1958	Jack Spikes	580	124	4.7	Hunter Enis	103	51	.50	585	Marshall Harris	19	265	13.9
1959	Jack Spikes	660	140	4.7	Donald George	62	24	.39	315	Bubba Meyer	8	88	11.0
1960	R.E. Dodson	276	70	3.9	Sonny Gibbs	111	47	.42	473	Buddy Iles	24	237	9.9
1961	Tommy Crutcher	577	148	3.9	Sonny Gibbs	137	71	.52	999	Buddy Iles	31	479	15.5
1962	Tommy Crutcher	533	106	5.0	Sonny Gibbs	169	89	.53	1,013	Tom Magoffin	32	430	13.4
1963	Tommy Crutcher	473	108	4.4	Gray Mills	93	45	.48	526	Jim Fauver	11	167	15.2
1964	Jim Fauver	789	154	5.1	Kent Nix	117	51	.44	624	Sonny Campbell	35	502	14.3
1965	Kenny Post	555	150	3.7	Kent Nix	106	50	.47	634	Sonny Campbell	32	437	13.7
1966	Ross Montgomery	467	109	4.3	Rick Bridges	86	42	.49	520	Sonny Campbell	33	442	13.4
1967	Ross Montgomery	700	198	3.5	P.D. Shabay	99	50	.51	689	Bill Ferguson	27	419	15.5
1968	Ross Montgomery	645	170	3.8	Ted Fay	144	70	.49	978	Linzy Cole	21	368	17.5
1969	Marty Whelan	657	153	4.3	Steve Judy	283	144	.51	1,677	Jerry Miller	41	569	13.9
1970	Raymond Rhodes	786	176	4.5	Steve Judy	247	113	.46	1,327	Frankie Grimmett	27	286	10.6
1971	Bobby Davis	701	130	5.4	Steve Judy	139	60	.43	882	Ronnie Peoples	15	185	12.3
1972	Mike Luttrell	906	178	5.1	Terry Drennan	47	26	.55	310	Steve Patterson	22	255	11.6
1973	Mike Luttrell	865	208	4.2	Kent Marshall	110	47	.43	575	Steve Patterson	19	248	13.1
1974	Mike Luttrell	541	161	3.4	Lee Cook	237	106	.45	1,191	Mike Luttrell	35	252	7.2
1975	Ronnie Littleton	232	88	2.6	Lee Cook	226	105	.46	1,307	Mike Renfro	49	810	16.5
1976	Tony Accomando	283	88	3.2	Jimmy Elzner	233	100	.43	1,354	Mike Renfro	42	773	18.4
1977	Jimmy Allen	445	125	3.6	Steve Bayuk	250	114	.46	1,474	Mike Renfro	50	794	15.9
1978	Jimmy Allen	502	151	3.3	Steve Bayuk	241	114	.47	1,118	Craig Richardson	46	360	7.8
1979	Jimmy Allen	498	147	3.4	Steve Stamp	137	64	.47	777	Bobby Stewart	20	274	13.7
1980	Marcus Gilbert	350	90	3.9	Steve Stamp	247	127	.51	1,830	Bobby Stewart	46	688	15.0
1981	Marcus Gilbert	498	117	4.3	Steve Stamp	235	130	.55	2,013	Stanley Washington	49	854	17.4
1982	Marcus Gilbert	849	166	5.1	Rueben Jones	136	65	.48	1,036	Stanley Washington	32	617	19.3
1983	Kenneth Davis	682	145	4.7	Anthony Sciaraffa	183	95	.52	1,423	James Maness	37	690	18.6
1984	Kenneth Davis	1,611	211	7.6	Anthony Gulley	131	71	.54	1,022	James Maness	40	871	21.8
1985	Tony Jeffery	695	176	3.9	David Rascoe	165	71	.43	941	Ricky Stone	22	281	12.8
1986	Tony Jeffery	861	122	7.1	David Rascoe	180	89	.49	985	Jarrod Delaney	26	382	14.7
1987	Tony Jeffery	1,353	202	6.7	David Rascoe	173	88	.51	1,110	Jarrod Delaney	23	284	12.3
1988	Tony Darthard	854	192	4.4	David Rascoe	137	58	.42	660	Jarrod Delaney	30	440	14.7
1989	Tommy Palmer	642	118	5.4	Ron Jiles	286	145	.51	1,763	Michael Jackson	42	411	9.8
1990	Curtis Modkins	893	209	4.3	Matt Vogler	261	136	.52	1,646	Kelly Blackwell	64	832	13.0
1991	Curtis Modkins	659	181	3.6	Tim Schade	168	101	.60	1,253	Kelly Blackwell	64	762	11.9
1992	Curtis Modkins	689	162	4.3	Leon Clay	287	143	.50	1,526	Stephen Shipley	36	500	13.9
1993	Andre Davis	867	189	4.6	Max Knake	357	207	.58	2,130	John Oglesby	47	404	8.6
1994	Andre Davis	1,492	260	5.7	Max Knake	316	184	.58	2,624	Andre Davis	47	522	11.1
1995	Andre Davis	820	186	4.4	Max Knake	369	199	.54	2,237	John Washington	52	699	13.4
1996	Basil Mitchell	953	221	4.3	Jeff Dover	221	129	.58	1,456	Basil Mitchell	40	344	8.6
1997	Basil Mitchell	719	159	4.5	Jeff Dover	199	97	.49	1,063	Patrick Batteaux	27	396	14.7
1998	Basil Mitchell	1,111	166	6.7	Pat Batteaux	114	55	.48	519	Mike Scarborough	19	223	11.7
1999	LaDainian Tomlinson	1,850	268	6.9	Casey Printers	150	86	.57	1,213	Mike Scarborough	35	524	15.0
2000	LaDainian Tomlinson	2,158	369	5.8	Casey Printers	176	102	.58	1,584	Tim Maiden	19	348	18.3
2001	Ricky Madison	611	174	3.5	Casey Printers	252	136	.54	1,824	Adrian Madise	50	819	16.4
2002	Lonta Hobbs	952	137	6.9	Sean Stilley	204	114	.56	1,371	Adrian Madise	30	506	16.9
2003	Robert Merrill	1,107	201	5.5	Brandon Hassell	240	136	.57	2,039	Reggie Harrell	58	1,012	17.4
2004	Robert Merrill	753	179	4.2	Brandon Hassell	217	123	.57	1,724	Cory Rodgers	61	836	13.7

The NCAA began including postseason stats in 2002

TCU ALL-TIME SCORES

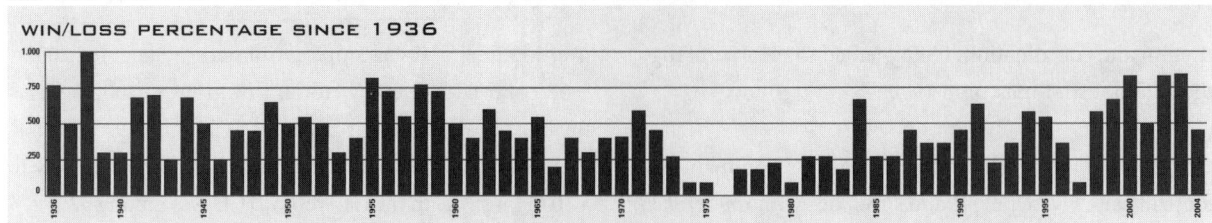

WIN/LOSS PERCENTAGE SINCE 1936

NO HEAD COACH

1896   1-1-1

U	●	Toby's BC *WAC*	8	6
U		at Houston HW	0	22
U	=	Houston HW *WAC*	0	0

JOE FIELD
1897 (.750)   3-1

1897   3-1-0

U	●	at Dallas U.	6	0
N3		Texas *WAC*	10	18
U	●	at Texas A&M	30	6
U	●	at Fort Worth U.	32	0

JAMES MORRISON
1898 (.300)   1-3-1

1898   1-3-1

O15		Texas *WAC*	0	16 *
U	●	at Toby's BC	41	0
U	=	Fort Worth U. *WAC*	0	0
N5		at Texas	0	29
U		Texas A&M *WAC*	0	16

NO HEAD COACH

1899   0-0-1

U	=	at Baylor	0	0

1900

NO TEAM

1901   1-2-1

U	=	Trinity	0	0
U		Baylor *WAC*	9	42 *
U	●	Taylor	5	0
N23		Baylor *WAC*	0	36 *

H.E. HILDEBRAND
1902 (.083)   0-5-1

1902   0-5-1

U		Trinity *WAC*	0	28
N1		at Baylor	0	0
U		Texas A&M *WAC*	0	22
N22		Baylor *WAC*	0	6
U		at Trinity	0	17
D1		Baylor *WAC*	0	20

NO HEAD COACH

1903   0-7-0

O3		Baylor *UNK*	0	12
O10		Texas A&M *UNK*	0	11
O17		at Daniel Baker	5	10
O24		at Trinity	0	30
O31		Baylor *UNK*	0	5
N14		at Texas A&M	0	16
N28		at Texas A&M	6	14

C.E. CRONK
1904 (.250)   1-4-1

1904   1-4-1

O1	=	Baylor *UNK*	0	0
O8		at Texas	0	40
O15		at Fort Worth U.	0	4
O22		at Texas A&M	0	29
O29		Baylor *UNK*	0	17
N24	●	at Baylor	5	0

E.J. HYDE
1905-07 (.478)   10-11-2

1905   4-4-0

S23	●	Baylor *UNK*	16	0
S30		at Texas A&M	0	20
O7		at Texas	0	11
O14	●	at Austin Coll.	21	0
O21	●	Trinity *UNK*	6	0
O28	●	Baylor *UNK*	6	10
N4		Texas A&M *UNK*	11	24
N11	●	Baylor *UNK*	17	0

1906   2-5-0

O6		Fort Worth U. *UNK*	0	6
O13		at Texas	0	22
O20		at Daniel Baker	0	4
O27		at Texas A&M	0	42
N10		Texas A&M *UNK*	0	22
N17	●	Deaf & Dumb *UNK*	17	6
N29	●	Fort Worth U. *UNK*	9	6

1907   4-2-2

S28	=	at Fort Worth U.	0	0
O5	●	at Baylor	6	6
O12	●	at Austin Coll.	27	0
O19	●	at Trinity	27	0
O26	●	at Baylor	11	10
N5		at Texas A&M	5	32
N16	●	at Trinity	6	5
N23		at Baylor	8	16

J.R. LANGLEY
1908-09 (.676)   11-5-1

1908   6-3-0

S26	●	Deaf School *UNK*	59	0
O3	●	Baylor *UNK*	15	0
O10		at Texas	6	11
O17	●	at Trinity	11	10
O24	●	Baylor *UNK*	10	6
O31		Texas A&M *UNK*	10	13
N7	●	Trinity *UNK*	22	0
N14		at Southwestern	14	5
N26		Baylor *UNK*	8	23

1909   5-2-1

O9	●	at Fort Worth U.	42	0
O16	=	at Texas A&M	0	0
O23	●	at Baylor	9	0
O30		at Texas	0	24
N6	●	at Austin Coll.	18	3
N13	●	at Baylor	11	0
N20	●	at Southwestern	12	0
N25		at Baylor	3	6

KEMP LEWIS
1910 (.277)   2-6-1

1910   2-6-1

O1	=	Fort Worth Poly	6	6
O8		at Texas A&M	0	35
O15		at Baylor	0	52
O22	●	Trinity	18	6
O29		Texas A&M	6	23
N5	●	at Trinity	9	0
N12		at Southwestern	3	25
N19		Baylor	3	10
D3		Epworth	0	30

HENRY W. LEVER
1911 (.444)   4-5

1911   4-5-0

U	●	Trinity	30	0
U		at Southwestern	0	21
U		at Austin Coll.	0	39
U		at Baylor	0	12
U		Austin Coll.	8	18
U		Fort Worth Poly	3	16
U	●	Fort Worth HS	24	0
U	●	at SW. Oklahoma	25	0
U	●	at SW. Oklahoma	24	0

W.T. STEWART
1912 (.889)   8-1

1912   8-1-0

U	●	at Britten TS	16	0
O5		at Texas	10	30
U	●	at Southwestern	20	0
U	●	Baylor	22	0
U	●	at Austin Coll.	7	0
U	●	Fort Worth Poly	33	3
U	●	Howard Payne	53	0
U	●	at Trinity	48	13
U	●	Fort Worth Poly	21	7

FRED CAHOON
1913 (.667)   3-1-2

1913   3-1-2

U	=	at SW. Oklahoma	0	0
U	=	Dallas U.	0	0
U	●	at Howard Payne	6	0
U	●	at Burleson Coll.	25	0
U	●	at North Texas	40	0
U		at Dallas U.	0	6

S.A. BOLES
1914 (.500)   4-4-2

1914   4-4-2

S26	●	North Texas *UNK*	40	0
O3	●	Oklahoma Mines	20	0
O10	●	at Southwestern	9	10
O17		at Texas A&M	0	40
O24	=	at Rice	0	0
N7		at Baylor	14	28
N14	●	Austin Coll.	13	0
N21		at Daniel Baker	0	33
N26	●	at Howard Payne	14	0
D3	●	Trinity	7	7

E.Y. FREELAND
1915 (.444)   4-5

1915   4-5-0

O2		at Texas	0	72
O8	●	SMU	43	0
O16		Texas A&M	10	13
O23	●	at Austin Coll.	28	0
O30		at Rice	3	33 *
N6	●	at Trinity	25	0
N13	●	Southwestern	21	0
N16		Oklahoma State	0	13
N25		at Baylor	0	51

MILTON DANIEL
1916-17 (.763)   14-4-1

1916   6-2-1

S30	●	at Meridian	7	0
O7	●	Austin Coll.	28	2
O14	●	at SMU	48	3
O27	=	Rice	7	7
N4	●	Trinity	35	0
N11		at Southwestern	13	41
N18	●	at Daniel Baker	23	0
N25	●	at Howard Payne	42	0
N30		Baylor	14	32

1917   8-2-0

S29	●	Meridian	20	0
O6	●	1st Texas Aty.	14	7
O13		at Rice	0	26
O20	●	SMU	21	0
O27	●	at Trinity	20	6
N3	●	Southwestern	20	6
N10	●	at Austin Coll.	59	0
N17		2nd Texas 132nd Inf.	7	14
N24	●	at 111th Ambulance	6	0
N29	●	Baylor	34	0

E.M. TIPTON
1918 (.571)   4-3

1918   4-3-0

S28		at Texas	0	19
O5		Carruthers Field	6	7
O12		SMU	0	1 *f*
O19	●	at Southwestern	14	6
N2	●	North Texas	39	0
N9	●	Austin Coll.	25	0
N28	●	at Baylor	12	7

T.D. HACKNEY
1919 (.125)   1-7

1919   1-7-0

O4		North Texas	6	14
O11		at Decatur Baptist	0	20
O18		Oklahoma State	7	14
O25		Southwestern	0	10
N1	●	at Trinity	7	0
N8		at Austin Coll.	0	6
N15		at Texas A&M	0	48
N27		Baylor	0	7

W.L. DRIVER
1920-21 (.775)   15-4-1

1920   9-1-0

O2	●	SE. Oklahoma	20	0
O9	●	Austin Coll.	9	7
O16	●	at Arkansas	19	2
O23	●	at Trinity	20	7
O30	●	Phillips	3	0
N6	●	Missouri O's	19	3
N13	●	at Baylor	21	9
N20	●	Hardin Simmons	31	2
N27	●	Southwestern	21	16

FORT WORTH CLASSIC

J1		Centre	7	63

1921   6-3-1

S24	●	at West Texas St.	30	0
O1		at Hardin Simmons	7	10
O8		at Oklahoma State	21	28
O15	●	Trinity	19	3
O21	●	Tulsa	16	0
O29	=	at Phillips	0	0
N5	●	Missouri O's	7	0
N12	●	at SMU	13	6
N19		Haskell	0	14
N24	●	Arkansas	19	14

JOHN McKNIGHT
1922 (.350)   2-5-3

1922   2-5-3

S23	●	at Dallas U.	21	6
O7		at Daniel Baker	13	21
O14		at Austin Coll.	7	20
O21		at Howard Payne	14	26
O28		at Tulsa	0	21
O30	=	at Hardin Simmons	7	7
N11	●	Oklahoma State	22	14
N18	=	at Trinity	7	7
N30		at Kansas State	0	45
D2	=	SMU	0	0

1923-1995
SWC

MADISON BELL
1923-28 (.645)   33-17-5

1923   4-5-0 (2-1-0)
O6	●	at Oklahoma State	7 6
O13	●	Hardin Simmons	16 0
O20	●	Daniel Baker	47 6
O27		Centenary	0 23
N4		at SMU	0 40
N10		Austin Coll.	0 26
N17		at Howard Payne	7 20
N24		Trinity	10 16
N29	●	at Rice	6 0

1924   4-5-0 (1-5-0)
S27	●	East Texas St.	43 0
O4	●	Daniel Baker	13 12
O11	●	Oklahoma State	17 10
O18	●	at Hardin Simmons	7 0
O25		Rice	3 7
N1		SMU	0 6
N8		at Texas A&M	0 28
N15		Texas	0 13
N27		at Arkansas	0 20

1925   7-1-1 (2-0-1)
S26	●	East Texas St.	31 0
O3	●	Daniel Baker	12 0
O10	=	Baylor *DAL*	7 7
O17	●	Hardin Simmons	28 16
O24	●	at Oklahoma State	7 22
O31	●	Abilene Christian	21 9
N7	●	Texas A&M	3 0
N14	●	Arkansas	3 0
N21	●	Austin Coll.	21 0

1926   6-1-2 (1-1-2)
S25	●	Daniel Baker	5 3
O2	●	Centenary	24 14
O9	=	Baylor *DAL*	7 7
O16	●	Austin Coll.	7 0
O23	●	Oklahoma State	3 0
O30	●	Texas Tech	28 16
N6	=	at Texas A&M	13 13
N12	●	at Arkansas	10 7
N25		at SMU	13 14

1927   4-3-2 (1-2-2)
S24	●	Daniel Baker	27 0
O1	=	at Texas	0 0
O8	●	Texas Tech	16 6
O15	●	Austin Coll.	20 13
O22	=	Texas A&M	0 0
O29	●	at Baylor	14 0
N5		Arkansas	3 10
N12		at Centenary	3 7
N19		SMU	6 28

1928   8-2-0 (3-2-0)
S22	●	East Texas St.	21 0
S29	●	Daniel Baker	19 0
O6	●	at Hardin Simmons	19 3
O13	●	Austin Coll.	21 0
O20	●	at Texas A&M	6 0
O27	●	Texas Tech	28 6
N3		Baylor	6 7
N10	●	at Rice	7 0
N17		Texas	0 6
N24	●	at SMU	15 6

FRANCIS A. SCHMIDT
1929-33 (.851)   46-6-5

1929   9-0-1 (4-0-1)
S28	●	Daniel Baker	61 0
O5	●	at Hardin Simmons	20 0
O12	●	at Centenary	28 0
O19	●	Texas A&M	13 7
O26	●	at Texas Tech	22 0
N2	●	North Texas	25 0
N9	●	Rice	24 0
N16	●	at Texas	15 12
N23	●	at Baylor	34 7
N30	=	SMU	7 7

1930   9-2-1 (4-2-0)
S13	●	East Texas St.	40 0
S20	●	at North Texas	47 0
S27	●	Austin Coll.	33 7
O4	=	at Hardin Simmons	0 0
O11	●	Arkansas	40 0
O18	●	at Texas A&M	3 0
O25	●	Texas Tech	26 0
N1	●	Abilene Christian	62 0
N8	●	at Rice	20 0
N15		Texas	0 7
N22		Baylor	14 35
N29	●	at SMU	13 0

1931   9-2-1 (4-1-1)
S12	●	at Texas Military	40 0
S19	●	North Texas	33 6
S26	●	LSU	3 0
O3		at Tulsa	0 13
O10	●	Austin Coll.	38 0
O17	●	Texas A&M	6 0
O24	●	at Hardin Simmons	6 0
O31	●	at Arkansas	7 0
N7	●	Rice	7 6
N14		at Texas	0 10
N21	●	at Baylor	19 6
N28	=	SMU	0 0

1932   10-0-1 (6-0-0)
S17	●	North Texas	14 2
S24	=	at LSU	3 3
O1	●	Daniel Baker	55 0
O8	●	Arkansas	34 12
O15	●	at Texas A&M	17 0
O22	●	Austin Coll.	68 0
O29	●	Baylor	27 0
N5	●	at Hardin Simmons	27 0
N11	●	Texas	14 0
N19	●	at Rice	16 6
N26	●	at SMU	8 0

1933   9-2-1 (4-2-0)
S16	●	at Austin Coll.	33 0
S23	●	at Daniel Baker	28 6
S30	●	at North Texas	13 0
O7		at Arkansas	0 13
O14	●	Hardin Simmons	20 0
O21	●	Texas A&M	13 7
O28	=	at Centenary	0 0
N4		at Baylor	0 7
N11	●	North Dakota	19 7
N18	●	at Texas	30 0
N25	●	Rice	26 3
D2	●	SMU	26 6

DUTCH MEYER
1934-52 (.575)   109-79-13

1934   8-4-0 (3-3-0)
S22	●	at Daniel Baker	33 7
S29	●	North Texas	27 0
O6		Arkansas	10 24
O13	●	at Tulsa	14 12
O20	●	at Texas A&M	13 0
O27		at Centenary	0 13
N3	●	Baylor	34 12
N10	●	at Loyola-New Orleans	7 0
N17		Texas	19 20
N24	●	at Rice	7 2
D1		at SMU	0 19
D8	●	at Santa Clara	9 7

1935   12-1-0 (5-1-0)
S21	●	Howard Payne	41 0
S28	●	North Texas	28 11
O5	●	at Arkansas	13 7
O12	●	at Tulsa	13 0
O19	●	Texas A&M	19 14
O26	●	at Centenary	27 7
N2	●	at Baylor	28 0
N8	●	at Loyola-New Orleans	14 0
N16	●	at Texas	28 0
N23	●	Rice	27 6
N30		SMU	14 20
D7	●	at Santa Clara	10 6
		SUGAR BOWL	
J1	●	LSU	3 2

1936   9-2-2 (4-1-1)
S19	●	at Howard Payne	6 0
S26		at Texas Tech	0 7
O3	●	Arkansas	18 14
O10	●	at Tulsa	10 7 *
O17		at Texas A&M	7 18
O24	=	Mississippi State *DAL*	0 0
O31	●	Baylor	28 0
N7	●	Texas	27 6
N14	●	Centenary	26 0
N21	●	at Rice	13 0
N28	=	at SMU	0 0
D5	●	at Santa Clara	9 0
		COTTON BOWL	
J1	●	Marquette	16 6

1937   4-4-2 (3-1-2)
S25		at Ohio State	0 14
O2	=	at Arkansas	7 7
O9	●	Tulsa	20 13
O16	=	Texas A&M	7 7
O23	●	Fordham *NYC*	6 7
O30		at Baylor	0 6
N6		at Centenary	9 10
N13	●	at Texas	14 0
N20	●	Rice	7 2
N27	●	SMU	3 0

1938   11-0-0 (6-0-0)
S24	●	Centenary	13 0
O1	●	Arkansas	21 14
O8	●	at Temple	28 6
O15	●	at Texas A&M	34 6
O22	●	at Marquette	21 0
O29	●	Baylor	39 7
N5	●	at Tulsa	21 0
N12	●	Texas	28 6
N19	●	at Rice	29 7
N26	●	at SMU	20 7
		SUGAR BOWL	
J2	●	Carnegie Tech	15 7

1939   3-7-0 (1-5-0)
S29		at UCLA	2 6
O7		at Arkansas	13 14
O14		at Temple	11 13
O21		Texas A&M	6 20
O28	●	at Centenary	21 0
N4		at Baylor	0 27
N11	●	Tulsa	16 0
N18		at Texas	19 25
N25	●	Rice	21 0
D2		SMU	7 14

1940   3-7-0 (2-4-0)
S28	●	Centenary	41 6
O5	●	Arkansas	20 0
O12		at North Carolina	14 21
O19		at Texas A&M	7 21
O26		at Tulsa	0 7
N2		Baylor	12 14
N9		at Detroit	0 3
N16		Texas	14 21
N23		at Rice	6 14
N30		at SMU	0 16

1941   7-3-1 (4-1-1)
S27	●	Tulsa	6 0
O4	●	at Arkansas	9 0
O11		at Indiana	20 14
O18		Texas A&M	0 14
O25		Fordham *NYC*	14 28
N1	●	at Baylor	23 12
N8	●	Centenary	35 7
N15	●	at Texas	14 7
N22	=	Rice	0 0
N29	●	SMU	15 13
		ORANGE BOWL	
J1		Georgia	26 40

1942   7-3-0 (4-2-0)
S25	●	at UCLA	7 6
O3	●	Arkansas	13 6
O10	●	Kansas	41 6
O17	●	at Texas A&M	7 2
O24	●	at Pensacola NAS	21 0
O31		Baylor	7 10
N7		at Texas Tech	6 13
N14	●	Texas	13 7
N21		at Rice	0 21 *
N28	●	at SMU	14 6

1943   2-6-0 (1-4-0)
O2	●	Arkansas *LR*	13 0
O16		Texas A&M	0 13
O23	●	Oklahoma State *OKC*	25 0
O30		at LSU	0 14
N6		Texas Tech	20 40
N13		at Texas	7 46
N20	●	Rice	6 13
N27		SMU	0 20

1944   7-3-1 (3-1-1)
S23	●	Kansas *KC*	7 0
S30	●	So. Plains Field	34 0
O7		Arkansas	6 6
O21	●	at Texas A&M	13 7
O28		Oklahoma *OKC*	19 34
N4	●	at Chatham AFB	19 7
N11	●	Texas Tech	14 0
N18	●	Texas	7 6
N25	●	at Rice	9 6
D2		at SMU	6 9
		COTTON BOWL	
J1		Oklahoma State	0 34

1945   5-5-0 (3-3-0)
S22	●	Kansas *KC*	18 0
S29	●	at Baylor	7 6
O6		Arkansas	14 27
O20	●	Texas A&M	13 12
O27		Oklahoma State	12 25
N3	●	at Oklahoma	13 7
N10		at Texas Tech	0 12
N17		at Texas	0 20
N24	●	Rice	14 13
D1		SMU	0 34

1946   2-7-1 (2-4-0)
S21	●	Kansas *KC*	0 0
S28	●	Baylor	19 16
O5		Arkansas	14 34
O11		at Miami, Fla.	12 20
O19		at Texas A&M	0 14
O26		Oklahoma State *OKC*	6 7
N2		Oklahoma	12 14
N16	●	Texas	14 0
N23		at Rice	0 13
N30	●	at SMU	13 30

1947   4-5-2 (2-3-1)
S20	=	Kansas *KC*	0 0
S27		Oklahoma State	7 14
O4		at Arkansas	0 6
O10	●	at Miami, Fla.	19 6
O18	●	Texas A&M	26 0
O25	●	at Oklahoma	20 7
N1	●	at Baylor	14 7
N15		at Texas	0 20
N22		Rice	0 7
N29	●	SMU	19 19
		DELTA BOWL	
J1		Mississippi	9 13

1948   4-5-1 (1-4-1)
S18	●	at Kansas	14 13
S25	●	at Oklahoma State	21 14
O2		Arkansas	14 27
O9	●	at Indiana	7 6
O16	●	at Texas A&M	27 14
O23		Oklahoma	18 21
O30		Baylor	3 6
N13		Texas	7 14
N20	●	at Rice	7 21
N27	=	at SMU	7 7

1949   6-3-1 (3-3-0)
S17	●	at Kansas	28 0
S24	=	Oklahoma State	33 33
O1		at Arkansas	7 27
O8	●	at Indiana	13 6
O15		Texas A&M	28 6
O22	●	Mississippi	33 27
O29	●	at Baylor	14 40
N12	●	at Texas	14 13
N19		Rice	14 20
N26	●	SMU	21 13

1950   5-5-0 (3-3-0)
S23	●	at Kansas	14 7
S30		at Oklahoma State	7 18 *
O7	●	Arkansas	13 6
O14	●	Texas Tech	19 6
O21		at Texas A&M	23 42
O28	●	Mississippi *MEM*	7 19
N4		Baylor	14 20
N18		Texas	7 21
N25	●	at Rice	26 14
D2	●	at SMU	27 14

1951　6-5-0 (5-1-0)

S22	Kansas	13	27
S29 ●	at Nebraska	28	7
O6 ●	Arkansas LR	17	7
O13	at Texas Tech	19	33
O20 ●	Texas A&M	20	14
O27	at Southern Cal	26	28
N3 ●	at Baylor	20	7
N17	at Texas	21	32
N24 ●	Rice	22	6
D1 ●	SMU	13	2
	COTTON BOWL		
J1	Kentucky	7	20

1952　4-4-2 (2-2-2)

S20	at Kansas	0	13
S27	at UCLA	0	14
O4 ●	Arkansas	13	7
O11 ●	at Trinity	47	0
O18 =	at Texas A&M	7	7
N1 =	Baylor	20	20
N8 ●	Wake Forest	27	9
N15	Texas	7	14
N22	at Rice	6	12
N29	at SMU	14	7

ABE MARTIN		
1953-66 (.534)		74-64-7

1953　3-7-0 (1-5-0)

S19 ●	Kansas	13	0
O3	at Arkansas	6	13
O10	at Michigan State	19	26
O17	Texas A&M	7	20
O24	at Penn State	21	27
O31	at Baylor	7	25
N7	Washington State SPO	21	7
N14	at Texas	3	13
N21	Rice	6	19
N28	SMU	13	0

1954　4-6-0 (1-5-0)

S18 ●	at Kansas	27	6
S25	at Oklahoma	16	21
O2	Arkansas	13	20
O8 ●	at Southern Cal	20	7
O16	at Texas A&M	21	7
O23	Penn State	20	7
O30	Baylor	7	12
N13	Texas	34	35
N20	at Rice	0	6
N27	at SMU	6	21

1955　9-2-0 (5-1-0)

S17 ●	Kansas	47	14
S24 ●	at Texas Tech	32	0
O1	at Arkansas	26	0
O8 ●	at Alabama	21	0
O15	Texas A&M	16	19
O21 ●	at Miami, Fla.	21	19
O29 ●	at Baylor	28	6
N12 ●	at Texas	47	20
N19	Rice	35	0
N26	SMU	20	13
	COTTON BOWL		
J2	Mississippi	13	14

1956　8-3-0 (5-1-0)

S22 ●	at Kansas	32	0
O6 ●	Arkansas	41	6
O13 ●	at Alabama	23	6
O20 ●	at Texas A&M	6	7
O27	Miami, Fla.	0	14
N3 ●	Baylor	7	6
N10	at Texas Tech	7	21
N17 ●	Texas	46	0
N24 ●	at Rice	20	17
D1 ●	at SMU	21	6
	COTTON BOWL		
J1 ●	Syracuse	28	27

1957　5-4-1 (2-4-0)

S21 =	Kansas	13	13
S28 ●	at Ohio State	18	14
O5 ●	Arkansas LR	7	20
O12 ●	Alabama	28	0
O19	Texas A&M	0	7
O26 ●	at Marquette	26	7
N2 ●	at Baylor	19	6
N16	at Texas	2	14
N23	Rice	0	20
N30 ●	SMU	21	0

1958　8-2-1 (5-1-0)

S20 ●	at Kansas	42	0
S27	at Iowa	0	17
O4 ●	Arkansas	12	7
O11 ●	Texas Tech	26	0
O18 ●	at Texas A&M	24	8
N1 ●	Baylor	22	0
N8 ●	Marquette	36	8
N15 ●	Texas	22	8
N22 ●	at Rice	21	10
N29	at SMU	13	20
	COTTON BOWL		
J1 ●	Air Force	0	0

1959　8-3-0 (5-1-0)

S19 ●	Kansas	14	7
S26	at LSU	0	10
O3	at Arkansas	0	3
O10 ●	at Texas Tech	14	8
O17 ●	Texas A&M	39	6
O24	at Pittsburgh	13	3
O31 ●	at Baylor	14	0
N14 ●	at Texas	14	9
N21 ●	Rice	35	6
N28 ●	SMU	14	7
	BLUEBONNET BOWL		
D19	Clemson	7	23

1960　4-4-2 (3-3-1)

S17	at Kansas	7	21
S24 =	at Southern Cal	7	6
O1	Arkansas	0	7
O8 ●	Texas Tech	21	7
O15 =	at Texas A&M	14	14
O22 =	Pittsburgh	7	7
O29 ●	Baylor	14	6
N12	Texas	2	3
N19	at Rice	0	23
N26 ●	at SMU	13	0

1961　3-5-2 (2-4-1)

S23 ●	Kansas	17	16
S30 =	at Ohio State	7	7
O7	Arkansas LR	3	28
O14	at Texas Tech	0	10
O21 ●	Texas A&M	15	14
N4	at Baylor	14	28
N10	at UCLA	7	28
N18 ●	at Texas	6	0
N25 ●	Rice	16	35
D2 =	SMU	28	28

1962　6-4-0 (5-2-0)

S22 ●	at Kansas	6	3
S29 ●	at Miami, Fla.	20	21
O6	Arkansas	14	42
O13 ●	Texas Tech	35	13
O20 ●	at Texas A&M	20	14
N3 ●	Baylor	28	26
N10	at LSU	0	5
N17	Texas	0	14
N24 ●	at Rice	30	7
D1 ●	at SMU	14	9

1963　4-5-1 (2-4-1)

S21 ●	Kansas	10	6
S28 ●	at Florida State	13	0
O5	at Arkansas	3	18
O12 ●	at Texas Tech	35	3
O19 =	Texas A&M	14	14
N2	at Baylor	13	32
N9	at LSU	14	28
N16	at Texas	0	17
N23 ●	SMU	22	15
D7	Rice	7	33

1964　4-6-0 (3-4-0)

S19	at Kansas	3	7
S26	Florida State	0	10
O3	Arkansas	6	29
O10	Texas Tech	10	25
O17 ●	at Texas A&M	14	9
O24	Clemson	14	10
O31 ●	Baylor	17	14
N14	Texas	13	28
N21	at Rice	0	31
N28 ●	at SMU	17	6

1965　6-5-0 (5-2-0)

S18	at Nebraska	14	34
S25 ●	Florida State	7	3
O2	Arkansas LR	0	28
O9	at Texas Tech	24	28
O16 ●	Texas A&M	17	9
O23	at Clemson	0	3
O30 ●	at Baylor	10	7
N13 ●	at Texas	25	10
N20 ●	Rice	42	14
N27 ●	at SMU	10	7
	SUN BOWL		
D31	Texas-El Paso	12	13

1966　2-8-0 (2-5-0)

S17	at Nebraska	10	14
S24	at Ohio State	7	14
O1	Arkansas	0	21
O8 ●	Texas Tech	6	3
O15	at Texas A&M	7	35
O22	at Auburn	6	7
O29 ●	Baylor	6	0
N12 ●	Texas	3	13
N19 ●	at Rice	10	21
N26 ●	at SMU	0	21

FRED TAYLOR		
1967-70 (.378)		15-25-1

1967　4-6-0 (4-3-0)

S23	at Iowa	9	24
S30	at Georgia Tech	7	24
O7	at Arkansas	0	26
O21	Texas A&M	0	20
O28	Nebraska	0	29
N4 ●	at Baylor	29	7
N11 ●	Texas Tech	16	0
N18 ●	at Texas	24	17
N25 ●	Rice	14	10
D2	at SMU	14	28

1968　3-7-0 (2-5-0)

S21	at Georgia Tech	7	17
S28 ●	Iowa	28	17
O5	Arkansas	7	17
O12	SMU	14	21
O19	at Texas A&M	7	27
O26	at LSU	7	10
N2 ●	Baylor	47	14
N9	at Texas Tech	14	31
N16	Texas	21	47
N23 ●	at Rice	24	14

1969　4-6-0 (4-3-0)

S20	Purdue	35	42
S27	at Ohio State	0	62
O4	Arkansas LR	6	24
O10	at SMU	17	19
O18 ●	Texas A&M	16	6
O25	at Miami, Fla.	9	14
N1 ●	at Baylor	31	14
N8 ●	Texas Tech	35	26
N15	at Texas	7	69
N22	Rice	21	17

1970　4-6-1 (3-4-0)

S12	Texas Arlington	31	7
S19	at Purdue	0	15
S26 =	at Wisconsin	14	14
O3	Arkansas	14	49
O10	at Oklahoma State	20	34
O17 ●	at Texas A&M	31	15
O31 ●	Baylor	24	17
N7	at Texas Tech	14	22
N14	Texas	0	58
N21	at Rice	15	17
N28 ●	SMU	26	17

JIM PITTMAN		
1971 (.500)		3-3-1

BILLY TOHILL		
1971-73 (.423)		11-15

1971　6-4-1 (5-2-0)

S18 ●	Texas Arlington	42	0
S25	at Washington	26	44
O2	at Arkansas	15	49
O9 =	Oklahoma State	14	14
O16	Texas A&M	14	3
O23	at Penn State	14	66
O30 ●	at Baylor	34	27
N6	Texas Tech	17	6
N13	at Texas	0	31
N20 ●	Rice	20	19
N27 ●	at SMU	18	16

1972　5-6-0 (2-5-0)

S23 ●	at Indiana	31	28
S30 ●	Texas Arlington	38	14
O7	Arkansas	13	27
O14	at Tulsa	35	9
O21 ●	at Texas A&M	13	10
O28	at Notre Dame	0	21
N4	Baylor	9	42
N11 ●	at Texas Tech	31	7
N18	Texas	0	27
N25	at Rice	21	25
D2	SMU	22	35

1973　3-8-0 (1-6-0)

S22 ●	Texas Arlington	49	13
S29	at Ohio State	3	37
O6	Arkansas LR	5	13
O13	Idaho	30	14
O20	Texas A&M	16	35
O27	at Tennessee	7	39
N3 ●	at Baylor	34	28
N10	Texas Tech	10	24
N17	at Texas	7	52
N24	Rice	9	14
D1	at SMU	19	13

JIM SHOFNER		
1974-76 (.061)		2-31

1974　1-10-0 (0-7-0)

S14 ●	Texas Arlington	12	3
S21	at Arizona State	7	37
S28	at Minnesota	7	9
O5	Arkansas	0	49
O12	SMU	13	33
O19	at Texas A&M	0	17
O26	Alabama BIRM	3	41
N2	Baylor	7	21
N9	at Texas Tech	0	28
N16	Texas	16	81
N23	at Rice	14	26

1975　1-10-0 (1-6-0)

S13	Texas Arlington	7	24
S20	Arizona State	10	33
S27	at Nebraska	14	56
O4	Arkansas LR	8	19
O10	at SMU	13	28
O18	Texas A&M	6	14
O25	Alabama BIRM	0	45
N1	at Baylor	6	24
N8	Texas Tech	0	34
N15	at Texas	11	27
N22 ●	Rice	28	21

1976　0-11-0 (0-8-0)

S11	at SMU	14	34
S18	at Tennessee	0	31
S25	at Nebraska	10	64
O2	at Arkansas	14	46
O9	Rice	23	26
O23	at Miami, Fla.	0	49
O30	at Houston	21	49
N6	Texas Tech	10	14
N13	Texas	7	34
N20	at Texas A&M	10	59
N27	Baylor	19	24

F.A. DRY		
1977-82 (.205)		12-51-3

1977　2-9-0 (1-7-0)

S10	SMU	21	45
S17	Oregon	24	29
S24	at Southern Cal	0	51
O1	Arkansas	6	42
O8 ●	at Rice	35	15
O22	Miami, Fla.	21	17
O29	Houston	14	42
N5	at Texas Tech	17	49
N12	at Texas	14	44
N19	Texas A&M	23	52
N26	at Baylor	9	48

1978　2-9-0 (0-8-0)

S9	at SMU	14	45
S23 ●	at Oregon	14	10
S30	at Penn State	0	58
O7	Arkansas LR	3	42
O14	Rice	14	21
O21 ●	at Tulane	13	7
O28	Baylor	21	28
N4	at Houston	6	63
N11	Texas Tech	17	27
N18	Texas	0	41
N25	at Texas A&M	7	15

1979 2-8-1 (1-6-1)

S15	|	SMU	7	27
S22		Tulane	19	33
S29		Texas Arlington	14	21
O6	|	Arkansas	13	16
O13	• |	at Rice	17	7
O20	•	at Tulsa	24	17
O27	|	at Baylor	3	16
N3	|	Houston	10	21
N10	= |	at Texas Tech	3	3
N17	|	at Texas	10	35
N24	|	Texas A&M	7	30

1980 1-10-0 (1-7-0)

S13		Auburn	7	10
S20	|	at SMU	14	17
S27		at Georgia	3	34
O4	|	at Arkansas	7	44
O11	|	Rice	24	28
O18		Tulsa	17	23
O25	|	Baylor	6	21
N1	|	at Houston	5	37
N8	• |	Texas Tech	24	17
N15	|	Texas	26	51
N22	|	at Texas A&M	10	13

1981 2-7-2 (1-6-1)

S5		at Auburn	16	24
S19	•	Texas Arlington	38	16
S26	|	SMU	9	20
O3	• |	Arkansas	28	24
O10	|	at Rice	28	41
O17	=	Utah State	13	13
O24	|	at Baylor	21	34
O31	|	Houston	16	20
N7	= |	at Texas Tech	39	39
N14	|	at Texas	15	31
N21	|	Texas A&M	7	37

1982 3-8-0 (2-6-0)

S11	•	Utah State	24	9
S18		at Kansas	19	30
S25	|	at SMU	13	16
O2	|	Arkansas *LR*	0	35
O9	• |	Rice	24	16
O16		at Mississippi	9	27
O23	• |	Baylor	38	14
O30	|	at Houston	27	31
N6	|	Texas Tech	14	16
N13	|	Texas	21	38
N20	|	at Texas A&M	14	34

JIM WACKER
1983-91 (.410) 40-58-2

1983 1-8-2 (1-6-1)

S10	=	Kansas	16	16
S17		at Kansas State	3	20
S24	|	SMU	17	21
O1	|	Arkansas	21	38
O8	• |	at Rice	34	3
O15		Mississippi	7	20
O22	|	at Baylor	21	56
O29	|	Houston	21	28
N5	= |	at Texas Tech	10	10
N12	|	at Texas	14	20
N19	|	Texas A&M	10	20

1984 8-4-0 (5-3-0)

S15	•	at Utah State	62	18
S22	•	Kansas State	42	10
S29	|	at SMU	17	26
O6	• |	at Arkansas	32	31
O13	• |	Rice	45	24
O20	•	North Texas	34	3
O27	• |	Baylor	38	28
N3	• |	at Houston	21	14
N10	• |	Texas Tech	27	16
N17	|	Texas	23	44
N24	|	at Texas A&M	21	35
		BLUEBONNET BOWL		
D31		West Virginia	14	31

1985 3-8-0 (0-8-0)

S14	•	Tulane	30	13
S21	•	at Kansas State	24	22
S28	|	SMU	21	56
O5	|	Arkansas	0	41
O12	|	at Rice	27	34
O19	•	North Texas	14	10
O26	|	at Baylor	0	45
N2	|	Houston	21	26
N9	|	at Texas Tech	7	63
N16	|	at Texas	0	20
N23	|	Texas A&M	6	53

1986 3-8-0 (1-7-0)

S13	•	at Tulane	48	31
S20	•	Kansas State	35	22
S27	|	at SMU	21	31
O4	|	at Arkansas	17	34
O11	|	Rice	31	37
O18		North Texas	20	24
O25	|	Baylor	17	28
N1	• |	at Houston	30	14
N8	|	Texas Tech	14	36
N15	|	Texas	16	45
N22	|	at Texas A&M	10	74

1987 5-6-0 (3-4-0)

S5		at Boston College	20	38
S12		at Air Force	10	21
S19	•	Brigham Young	33	12
O3	|	Arkansas	10	20
O10	• |	at Rice	30	16
O17	•	North Texas	19	10
O24	• |	at Baylor	24	0
O31	• |	Houston	35	7
N7	|	at Texas Tech	35	36
N14	|	at Texas	21	24
N21	|	Texas A&M	24	42

1988 4-7-0 (2-5-0)

S10		at Georgia	10	38
S17	•	Bowling Green	49	12
S24	•	Boston College	31	17
O1	|	at Arkansas	10	53
O8	• |	Rice	21	10
O15		at Brigham Young	18	31
O22	• |	Baylor	24	14
O29	|	at Houston	12	40
N5	|	Texas Tech	10	23
N12	|	Texas	21	30
N19	|	at Texas A&M	0	18

1989 4-7-0 (2-6-0)

S9		at Missouri	10	14
S16	|	Texas A&M	7	44
S23	•	Southern Miss	19	17
S30	• |	SMU	28	10
O7	|	Arkansas	19	41
O14	• |	at Rice	30	16
O21	•	Air Force	27	9
O28	|	at Baylor	9	27
N4	|	Houston	10	55
N11	|	at Texas Tech	7	37
N18	|	at Texas	17	31

1990 5-6-0 (3-5-0)

S1		Washington State	3	21
S8	•	at Missouri	20	19
S22	•	Oklahoma State	31	21
S29	• |	at SMU	42	21
O6	• |	Arkansas *LR*	54	26
O13	• |	Rice	38	28
O27	|	Baylor	21	27
N3	|	at Houston	35	56
N10	|	Texas Tech	28	40
N17	|	Texas	10	38
N24	|	at Texas A&M	10	56

1991 7-4-0 (4-4-0)

S7	•	New Mexico	60	7
S14	•	Ball State	22	16
S21	•	at Oklahoma State	24	21
S28	• |	at Texas Tech	30	16
O5	|	Arkansas	21	22
O19	• |	at Rice	39	28
O26	|	at Baylor	9	26
N2	• |	SMU	18	10
N9	|	Texas A&M	7	44
N16	|	at Texas	0	32
N23	• |	Houston	49	45

PAT SULLIVAN
1992-97 (.366) 24-42-1

1992 2-8-1 (1-6-0)

S5		at New Mexico	7	24
S12	=	Western Michigan	17	17
S26	|	at SMU	9	21
O3	•	Oklahoma State	13	11
O10	|	Baylor	20	41
O17		at Miami, Fla.	10	45
O24	|	Rice	12	29
O31	|	at Houston	46	49
N7	• |	Texas	23	14
N14	|	Texas Tech	28	31
N21	|	at Texas A&M	10	37

1993 4-7-0 (2-5-0)

S4		Oklahoma	3	35
S11	•	New Mexico	35	34
S25	|	SMU	15	21
O2		at Oklahoma State	22	27
O9	|	at Rice	19	34
O16	•	Tulane	14	7
O23	• |	at Baylor	38	13
O30	• |	Houston	28	10
N6	|	at Texas Tech	21	49
N13	|	at Texas	3	24
N20	|	Texas A&M	3	59

1994 7-5-0 (4-3-0)

S3		at North Carolina	17	27
S10	•	at New Mexico	44	29
S17	•	Kansas	31	21
S24	|	Texas	18	34
O1	|	Baylor	18	42
O15	•	at Tulane	30	28
O22	• |	at Houston	31	10
O29	• |	Rice	27	25
N12	• |	at SMU	35	14
N19	|	at Texas A&M	17	34
N25	• |	Texas Tech	24	17
		INDEPENDENCE BOWL		
D28		Virginia	10	20

1995 6-5-0 (3-4-0)

S9	•	Iowa State	27	10
S14		at Kansas	20	38
S23	•	at Vanderbilt	16	3
O7	• |	Houston	31	21
O14	• |	at Rice	33	28
O21	•	Tulane	16	11
O28	|	at Baylor	24	27
N4	• |	SMU	19	16
N11	|	at Texas Tech	6	27
N18	|	at Texas	19	27
N25	|	Texas A&M	6	38

1996-2000
WAC

1996 4-7 (3-5)

S7	•	at Oklahoma	20	7
S14		Kansas	17	52
S28	|	at New Mexico	7	27
O5		at Tulane	7	35
O12	• |	Texas-El Paso	18	0
O19	|	at Utah	7	21
O26	|	Brigham Young	21	45
N2	• |	Nevada-Las Vegas	42	34
N9	• |	at Tulsa	31	24
N16	|	Rice	17	30
N21	|	at SMU	24	27

1997 1-10 (1-7)

S6		at Kansas	10	17
S13	|	Utah	18	32
S20		at Vanderbilt	16	40
O4		North Carolina	10	31
O11	|	at Nevada-Las Vegas	19	21
O18	|	Tulsa	22	33
O25	|	at Brigham Young	10	31
N1	|	New Mexico	10	40
N8	|	at Rice	19	38
N15	|	at Texas-El Paso	17	24
N20	• |	SMU	21	18

DENNIS FRANCHIONE
1998-2000 (.714) 25-10

1998 7-5 (4-4)

S5	•	at Iowa State	31	21
S12		Oklahoma	9	10
S26	• |	Air Force	35	34
O3	•	Vanderbilt	19	16
O10	• |	Fresno State	21	10
O17	|	at SMU	6	10
O24	|	at Colorado State	21	42
O31	|	Wyoming	27	34
N7	|	Rice	12	14
N14	• |	at Tulsa	17	7
N21	• |	at Nevada-Las Vegas	41	18
		SUN BOWL		
D31	•	Southern Cal	28	19

1999 8-4 (5-2)

S5		Arizona	31	35
S11		at Northwestern	7	17
S25	•	at Arkansas State	24	21
O2	|	at Fresno State	19	26
O9	• |	San Jose State	42	0
O16	• |	Tulsa	56	17
O23	|	at Rice	21	42
O30	• |	at Hawaii	34	14
N13	•	North Texas	27	3
N20	• |	Texas-El Paso	52	24
N26	• |	SMU	21	0
		MOBILE BOWL		
D22	•	East Carolina	28	14

2000 10-2 (7-1)

S9	• |	at Nevada	41	10
S16	•	Northwestern	41	14
S23	•	Arkansas State	52	3
S30	•	at Navy	24	0
O7	• |	Hawaii	41	21
O21	• |	at Tulsa	17	3
O28	• |	Rice	37	0
N4	|	at San Jose State	24	27
N11	• |	Fresno State	24	7
N18	• |	Texas-El Paso	47	14
N24	• |	at SMU	62	7
		MOBILE BOWL		
D20		Southern Miss	21	28

2001-2004
C-USA

GARY PATTERSON
2000-PRESENT (.653) 32-17

2001 6-6 (4-3)

A25		at Nebraska	7	21
S1	•	at North Texas	19	5
S8	•	at SMU	38	10
S22		Northwestern St.	24	27
S29	• |	at Houston	34	17
O13	|	at Tulane	22	48
O20	• |	Army	38	20
O30	|	East Carolina	30	37
N10	|	at UAB	17	38
N23	• |	Louisville	37	22
D7	• |	at Southern Miss	14	12
		GALLERYFURNITURE.COM BOWL		
D28		Texas A&M	9	28

2002 10-2 (6-2)

S2	|	at Cincinnati	29	36
S7	•	at Northwestern	48	24
S14	•	SMU	17	6
S21	•	North Texas	16	10
O5	• |	Houston	34	17
O12	• |	at Army	46	27
O19	• |	at Louisville	45	31
O30	• |	Southern Miss	37	7
N9	• |	Tulane	17	10
N23	|	at East Carolina	28	31
N30	• |	Memphis	27	20
		LIBERTY BOWL		
D31	•	Colorado State	17	3

2003 11-2 (7-1)

S1	• |	at Tulane	38	35
S6	•	Navy	17	3
S20	•	Vanderbilt	30	14
S27	•	at Arizona	13	10
O4	• |	Army	27	0
O10	• |	at South Florida	13	10
O18	• |	UAB	27	24
O25	• |	at Houston	62	55
N5	• |	Louisville	31	28
N15	• |	Cincinnati	43	10
N20	|	at Southern Miss	28	40
N29	•	at SMU	20	13
		FORT WORTH BOWL		
D23		Boise State	31	34

2004 5-6 (3-5)

S2	•	Northwestern	48	45
S11	•	SMU	44	0
S18		at Texas Tech	35	70
S25	|	South Florida	44	45
O2	• |	at Army	21	17
O15	|	at UAB	25	41
O23	• |	Houston	34	27
O30	|	at Cincinnati	10	21
N9	|	at Louisville	28	55
N20	• |	Southern Miss	42	17
N27	|	Tulane	31	35

Neutral Site Key: ***Birm*** Birmingham, AL / ***Dal*** Dallas, TX / ***KC*** Kansas City, MO / ***LR*** Little Rock, AR / ***Mem*** Memphis, TN / ***NYC*** New York, NY / ***OkC*** Oklahoma City, OK / ***Spo*** Spokane, WA / ***Unk*** Unknown, Unknown / ***Wac*** Waco, TX
f **Forfeit** † **Game Later Forfieted** # **Disputed Victor** * **Disputed Score** || **Designated Conference Game** |2 **Counted Twice in Conference Standings**

TEMPLE

BY MIKE VACCARO

PHILADELPHIA IS A FOOTBALL TOWN. Ask the thousands of rabid Eagles fans who fill Lincoln Financial Field on fall Sundays. Ask the thousands more on the waiting list for seats. An edge for Temple, right? For more than two decades, ever since Villanova's football program dropped to Division I-AA, Temple's had a lock on college football in Philadelphia.

Except it hasn't helped. The Owls haven't had a winning season since 1990. They haven't played in a bowl game since 1979. And they were kicked out of the Big East in 2004 for their lack of success on the field and in the business office.

But Temple remains committed to Division I-A football. After playing in 2005 as an independent, the Owls plan to join the Mid-American Conference. There they'll seek to alter the balance of a bipolar football legacy: namely, the knack of attracting some fine football players over the years—notably Paul Palmer, an All-America in 1986, as well as the Kleckos, Joe and Dan, father and son—coupled with an unfortunate habit of collecting 10-loss seasons (six in less than two decades).

TRADITION Temple believes walk-ons should be an integral part of the overall football program, and the results have been fruitful. Russell Newman walked onto the program in 1998, was an all-conference defensive tackle two years later and made the Denver Broncos' roster as a rookie. Sean Dillard walked onto the team in 1999; by 2001, he was an All-Big East wide receiver who would go on to play for the Washington Redskins. "Recruiting will never be an exact science," Temple coach Bobby Wallace said. "We figure we owe it to certain kids who may be overlooked in the recruiting process to give them a look. More often than you might imagine, it works out wonderfully for everyone."

BEST PLAYER Bill Cosby, ol' No. 39, may be the most famous running back ever to wear the cherry and white, but Paul Palmer rules the Owls' record book. Considered too small and too slight coming out of high school in 1983, Palmer nevertheless jumped at the chance to come to Philadelphia and play for coach Bruce Arians, who figured Palmer as "a guy who could carry the ball eight, 10 times a game, a solid guy who could be a contributor." In the fourth game of Palmer's freshman year, the kid got his shot against Boston College, carrying 11 times for 98 yards. He was off and running. In 1986, Palmer rushed for a team-record 349 yards against East Carolina; over his career, he

---

PROFILE

Temple University
Philadelphia, Pa.
Founded: 1884
Enrollment: 22,982
Colors: Cherry and White
Nickname: Owls
Stadium: Lincoln Financial Field
    Opened in 2003
    Grass; 68,532 capacity
First football game: 1894
All-time record: 388–493–52 (.444)
Bowl record: 1–1
First-round NFL draftees: 2
Website: www.owlsports.com

THE BEST OF TIMES

Temple's positive football history can be summed up in two names: Glenn "Pop" Warner and Wayne Hardin. Warner finished his legendary career at Temple, going 31–18–9 from 1933 to 1938, guiding the Owls to their first-ever bowl appearance, a 20-14 loss to Tulane in the inaugural Sugar Bowl in 1935. Hardin, 80–52–3 from 1970 to 1982, led the Owls to their only 10-win season and their only bowl victory (28-17 over Cal in the Garden State Bowl) in 1979.

THE WORST OF TIMES

From 1989 to 1999, covering the coaching tenures of Jerry Berndt and Ron Dickerson and the first two years of Bobby Wallace, the Owls went 23–98—including 8–58 from 1991 to 1996—losing 27 straight Big East games at one point.

CONFERENCE

From the program's inception in 1894 through 1957, Temple played as an independent. From 1957 through 1970, while playing in the NCAA's small-college division, the Owls were a member of the Middle Atlantic States Collegiate Athletic Conference. After moving up to Division I in 1970, the Owls again played as an independent for 20 years. In 1991 they joined the Big East, which expelled them after the 2004 season.

DISTINGUISHED ALUMNI

Bill Cosby; Norman Braman, owner, Philadelphia Eagles; David Brenner, comedian; Robert Merton, sociologist; Bob Saget, actor; Patricia Wettig, actress

FIGHT SONG

T FOR TEMPLE U
U-ni-versity!
Fight, fight fight!
For the Cherry and the White,
For the Cherry and the White,
We'll fight, fight, fight!

Bill Cosby is the most famous running back ever to wear the cherry and white, but Paul Palmer rules the Owls' record book.

gained 4,895 yards—over 1,500 more than any other Owl. "I never imagined this," Palmer said following his senior year, in which he finished second to Vinny Testaverde for the Heisman Trophy. "I wanted to leave a mark. But I never dreamed it would be this kind of impression."

BEST COACH Glenn "Pop" Warner was already a legend, having built powerhouses at Pittsburgh and Stanford, when Temple lured the Old Fox to Philadelphia to breathe life into the Owls program. Warner did just that, leading Temple to a 31–18–9 record from 1933 to 1938. In 1934, a 7–1–2 record earned Temple an invitation to the first Sugar Bowl, where the Owls battled Tulane's Green Wave even for three quarters before a late touchdown gave Tulane a 20-14 win. Warner's tenure came to an end on Dec. 3, 1938, when the Owls upset Florida 20-12 in the heat and humidity of Gainesville. It was the last of Pop's 319 career coaching victories.

BEST TEAM Temple hadn't received a bowl bid of any kind in more than 40 years, but when Wayne Hardin's team bolted out of the gate 8–1 in 1979, the Owls seemed intent on ending those four decades of futility. Penn State put a dent into those dreams, beating Temple 22-7. But the Owls bounced back with a 42-10 rout of Villanova in the season finale, earning a spot in the Garden State Bowl on Dec. 15, 1979, against California. Temple jumped out to a 21-0 lead in the first quarter, but the Golden Bears came roaring back to score 17 unanswered points. Then, in a fitting conclusion to the best season in Owls history, quarterback Brian Broomell engineered a 14-play, 78-yard scoring drive late in the game, cementing a 10–2 season and No. 17 final ranking in both polls, the high-water mark in school history on both counts.

BIGGEST GAME The Mid-Winter Sports Association of New Orleans was created in 1934 to craft plans for an annual New Year's Day football game. On Dec. 2 of that year, the association selected Tulane—9–1 and fresh off a 13-12 win over LSU—and Temple, 7–0–2 under Warner. Some 28,000 people jammed into the first Sugar Bowl and saw Temple's Danny Testa score the first touchdown in Sugar Bowl history,

RECORDS

RUSHING YARDS

GAME
349	Paul Palmer vs. East Carolina, Oct. 11, 1986 (43 att.)

SEASON
1,866	Paul Palmer, 1986 (346 att.)

CAREER
4,895	Paul Palmer, 1983-86 (935 att.)

PASSING YARDS

GAME
445	Henry Burris vs. Pittsburgh, Oct. 5, 1996 (25 of 41)

SEASON
2,716	Henry Burris, 1994 (215 of 409)

CAREER
7,495	Henry Burris, 1993-96 (558 of 1,136)

RECEIVING YARDS

GAME
214	Van Johnson vs. Pittsburgh, Oct. 5, 1996 (7 rec.)

SEASON
964	Gerald Lucear, 1979 (45 rec.)

CAREER
2,272	Willie Marshall, 1983-86 (111 rec.)

POINTS

GAME
30	Sherman Myers vs. Syracuse, Oct. 13, 1979 (5 TDs)

SEASON
95	Don Bitterlich, 1975 (21 FGs, 32 PATs)

CAREER
264	Paul Palmer, 1983-86 (43 TDs, 3 two-pt. conv.)

CONSENSUS ALL-AMERICANS

1985	John Rienstra, OL
1986	Paul Palmer, RB

gathering in a Glenn Frey pass. The Owls' Dave Smukler (who played all 60 minutes) later added a 25-yard touchdown run to give the Owls a 14-0 lead. Tulane battled back to a 20-14 victory, but Temple earned the lasting admiration of its legendary coach: "This is a game that people will remember for many, many years, and this is a team that Temple University will be proud of forever."

BIGGEST UPSET Bobby Wallace had lost his first six games as Temple coach to start the 1998 season, and Temple had lost every one of the 25 conference road games it had played since joining the Big East in 1991. Before a homecoming crowd, Virginia Tech, ranked No. 14, seized a 17-7 halftime lead and seemed perfectly safe. But Temple refused to roll over and play dead. Midway through the fourth quarter, Carlos Johnson hauled in an 80-yard pass from Devin Scott to give the Owls a 21-17 lead. Later, a one-yard plunge by Scott made the score 28-24. But the Hokies still had time and drove to the Temple 3, where they had second and two with less than a minute to play. But somehow, Temple's defense stiffened, Tech turned the ball over on downs and the Owls had their stunner.

HEARTBREAKER Temple was in the midst of another long, awful (1–8, 0–4 in Big East play) season when it welcomed 12th-ranked Virginia Tech to Lincoln Financial Field on Nov. 15, 2003. The Hokies had looked far from sharp, but still led 17-0 with 14:23 to go. But then the afternoon took a strange twist. Temple quarterback Walter Washington led the Owls on drives of 82 and 80 yards, narrowing the gap to 17-14. The suddenly revitalized Owls defense kept stopping Tech, and a 37-yard field goal by Temple kicker Jared Davis tied the game with 40 seconds left. Remarkably, after an interception, Davis had a chance to win the game as time expired, but he missed a 50-yard attempt. In overtime, Tech jumped out to a 24-17 lead, but Temple answered right back with a 22-yard hookup from Washington to Zamir Cobb that should have sent the game into double overtime—except that Davis missed the extra point. Game over: Virginia Tech 24, Temple 23. "They didn't play like a team that's won just one ball game," Hokies coach Frank Beamer said. "I've never felt so bad about winning a game in my life."

STADIUM Temple moved into Lincoln Financial Field to start the 2003 season, signing a 15-year lease to play its games at the 68,532-seat, natural-grass, state-of-the-art home of the Philadelphia Eagles—a giant step in the right direction for the program. Prior to that, Temple had been a co-tenant at Veterans Stadium since 1975. The Owls had their own on-campus stadium, Temple Stadium, which they called home from 1928 to 1975.

RIVAL Temple used to battle Bucknell every year for the Old Shoe, but that game was discontinued in 1971, after Temple jumped to Division I-A status. Temple and Villanova also used to play an annual game for intracity bragging rights, but after Villanova dropped to I-AA in 1980, that also dissolved. (From Temple's point of view, it should have stayed dissolved: Villanova beat the Owls in Temple's 2003 home opener, the first game between the schools in 23 years and the first nonexhibition football game ever played at Lincoln Financial.) Since the advent of Big East play in 1991, Rutgers has emerged as Temple's closest rival. Through 2004, Rutgers held a 9-5 edge.

NICKNAME Temple was the first school to adopt an owl as its official mascot, something it did shortly after opening its doors in 1884. Only Rice University and Florida Atlantic share the nickname among Division I-A football competitors. Legend has it that the owl, a nocturnal hunter, was originally proposed as the school mascot because Temple was founded as a night school, and its founder, Russell Conwell, urged his students on with the remark, "The owl of the night makes the eagle of the day."

UNIFORMS Temple was also the first school in the nation to officially adopt the color cherry as its primary hue. The combination of red and white for football uniforms is quite common, but only one other school (Rensselaer Polytechnic Institute in Troy, N.Y.) uses cherry and white as its official designation. The helmet has undergone many changes through the years.

QUOTE "Football at Temple—Division I-A football—is as important in maintaining a national institution as things like our health system, as our Research I status. You're in a select group of about 110 institutions out of several thousand. It gives you identity. In the 1920s, there were the same issues at Temple. They brought in Pop Warner as the coach. The academics here said, 'You're killing Temple. You're making it a sports factory.' Well, we went to the first Sugar Bowl. Anybody who lived in that period said it was the greatest period that Temple ever had, because you're doing national things."

— Temple president Peter Liacouras, 2000

TEMPLE ANNUAL STATISTICAL LEADERS

YR	RUSHING	YDS	ATT	AVG	PASSING	ATT	CMP	PCT	YDS	RECEIVING	REC	YDS	AVG
1971	Paul Loughran	468	108	4.3	Doug Shobert	191	120	.63	1,513	Randy Grossman	27	473	17.5
1972	Paul Loughran	593	125	4.7	Doug Shobert	238	130	.55	1,416	Clint Graves	63	707	11.2
1973	Tom Sloan	1,036	173	6.0	Steve Joachim	159	80	.50	1,312	Randy Grossman	39	683	17.5
1974	Henry Hynoski	1,006	206	4.9	Steve Joachim	221	128	.58	1,950	Pete Righi	35	608	17.4
1975	Tom Duff	752	146	5.2	Pat Carey	198	103	.52	1,304	Jeff Stempel	30	510	17.0
1976	Anthony Anderson	803	176	4.6	Pat Carey	126	62	.49	839	Ken Williams	35	580	16.6
1977	Anthony Anderson	756	195	3.9	Pat Carey	163	77	.47	1,074	Steve Watson	31	573	18.5
1978	Zachary Dixon	1,153	223	5.2	Brian Broomell	209	112	.54	1,362	Steve Watson	41	637	15.5
1979	Mark Bright	1,036	193	5.4	Brian Broomell	214	120	.56	2,103	Gerald Lucear	45	964	21.4
1980	Kevin Duckett	651	129	5.0	Tink Murphy	191	90	.47	1,097	Gerald Lucear	29	387	13.3
1981	Jim Brown	883	163	5.4	Tink Murphy	245	128	.52	1,589	Gerald Lucear	47	493	10.5
1982	Harold Harmon	883	165	5.4	Tim Riordan	247	157	.64	1,840	Reggie Brown	43	591	13.7
1983	Paul Palmer	628	141	4.5	Tim Riordan	277	143	.52	1,732	Russell Carter	31	482	15.5
1984	Paul Palmer	885	182	4.9	Lee Saltz	184	97	.53	1,337	Willie Marshall	22	503	22.9
1985	Paul Palmer	1,516	275	5.5	Lee Saltz	229	107	.47	1,875	Willie Marshall	40	893	22.3
1986	Paul Palmer	1,866	346	5.4	Lee Saltz	203	117	.58	1,729	Willie Marshall	30	514	17.1
1987	Todd McNair	1,058	249	4.2	James Thompson	153	66	.43	985	Rich Drayton	18	286	15.9
1988	Todd McNair	761	197	3.9	Matt Baker	193	101	.52	1,539	Rich Drayton	26	460	17.7
1989	Ventres Stevenson	841	173	4.9	Anthony Richardson	126	68	.54	812	Maurice Johnson	31	290	9.4
1990	Scott McNair	623	116	5.4	Matt Baker	222	134	.60	1,462	Rich Drayton	48	564	11.8
1991	Scott McNair	605	152	4.0	Trent Thompson	172	79	.46	927	Leslie Shepherd	26	436	16.8
1992	Sam Jenkins	524	146	3.6	Chris Paliscak	137	65	.47	691	Wilbur Washington	22	285	13.0
1993	Ralphiel Mack	570	107	5.3	Henry Burris	149	62	.42	691	Ramondo Davidson	25	266	10.6
1994	Juan Gaddy	285	103	2.8	Henry Burris	409	215	.53	2,716	Sidney Morse	39	261	6.7
1995	Eugene Culbreath	451	103	4.4	Henry Burris	300	139	.46	2,004	Troy Kersey	20	469	23.5
1996	Ramod Lee	526	130	4.0	Henry Burris	280	142	.51	2,084	Van Johnson	50	902	18.0
1997	Stacey Mack	842	173	4.9	Pat Bonner	202	107	.53	1,561	Kevin Walker	34	688	20.2
1998	Stacey Mack	749	125	6.0	Devin Scott	69	25	.36	459	Carlos Johnson	18	378	21.0
1999	Marcus Godfrey	332	84	4.0	Devin Scott	369	222	.60	1,815	Carlos Johnson	51	520	10.2
2000	Tanardo Sharps	1,038	201	5.2	Devin Scott	216	136	.63	1,456	Greg Muckerson	41	487	11.9
2001	Tanardo Sharps	771	150	5.1	Mike McGann	190	87	.46	934	Sean Dillard	51	747	14.6
2002	Tanardo Sharps	1,267	311	4.1	Mike McGann	353	173	.49	1,994	Zamir Cobb	45	483	10.7
2003	Walter Washington	579	156	3.7	Mike McGann	234	123	.52	1,405	Zamir Cobb	74	866	11.7
2004	Walter Washington	889	222	4.0	Walter Washington	332	187	.56	2,207	Phil Goodman	47	677	14.4

Receiving leaders by receptions

The NCAA began including postseason stats in 2002

TEMPLE ALL-TIME SCORES

WIN/LOSS PERCENTAGE SINCE 1936

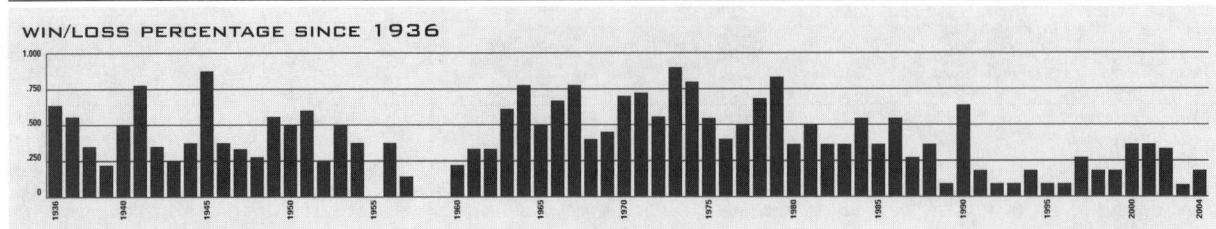

CHARLES M. WILLIAMS
1894-98 (.466)   13-15-1

1894 — 4-1-0
U	●	Phil. Dental Coll. Unk	14	6
U		First Regiment Unk	26	0
U		Ursinus Unk	0	16
U	●	Crescent AC Unk	12	10
U	●	Central Pa. Coll. Unk	18	0

1895 — 1-4-1
U	=	Schuylkill Navy Unk	0	0
U		Trenton Unk	0	8
U	●	Central Pa. Coll. Unk	30	0
U		Stevens Unk	0	10
U		Pratt Inst. Unk	0	15
U		Ursinus Unk	0	56

1896 — 3-2-0
U		Brooklyn Poly Unk	8	16
U		Loyola-Baltimore Unk	6	14
U	●	Trenton Unk	4	2
U	●	Phil. Dental Coll. Unk	6	0
U	●	Central Pa. Coll. Unk	26	0

1897 — 3-3-0
U	●	Eastburn Acad. Unk	18	3
U	●	Phil. Dental Canisius Unk	22	0
U		Loyola-Baltimore Unk	6	22
U	●	Central Pa. Coll. Unk	54	10
U		St. Francis Unk	0	30
U		Phil. Pharmacy Unk	0	20

1898 — 2-5-0
U		Oak Lane AC Unk	0	12
U		West Chester Unk	6	20
U	●	U. of Phil. Unk	3	0
U	●	Schuylkill Navy Unk	12	8
U		Widener Unk	8	15
U		Trenton Unk	3	40
U		Beverly AC Unk	0	38

JOHN T. ROGERS
1899-1900 (.357)   4-8-2

1899 — 1-4-1
U		St. Joseph's Unk	0	10
U		Phil. Pharmacy Unk	0	15
U		Ursinus Unk	0	1 f
U	●	Eastburn Acad. Unk	22	0
U	=	U. of Phil. Unk	5	5
U		Franklin & Marshall Unk	0	96

1900 — 3-4-1
U	=	St. Joseph's Unk	0	0
U		W. Chester Teachers Unk	0	5
U	●	U. of Phil. Unk	40	3
U	●	La Salle Unk	12	3
U	●	Eastburn Acad. Unk	25	6
U		Medico Unk	0	5
U		Jefferson Unk	6	11
U		Widener Unk	12	36

H. SHINDLE WINGERT
1901-05 (.583)   13-9-2

1901 — 3-2-0
U		Trenton Unk	0	15
U	●	La Salle Unk	6	5
U		St. Joseph's Unk	0	32
U	●	Phil. Dental Coll. Unk	10	0
U	●	Central Pa. Coll. Unk	21	13

1902 — 1-4-1
U		Phil. Pharmacy Unk	6	11
U		Trenton Unk	0	12
U	=	St. Joseph's Unk	0	0
U	●	Phil. Dental Coll. Unk	18	12
U		Pratt Inst. Unk	0	21
U		Medico Unk	5	6

1903 — 4-1-0
U	●	Tioga AC Unk	13	6
U	●	Medico Unk	13	6
U		Trenton Unk	0	6
U	●	St. Joseph's Unk	12	0
U	●	La Salle Unk	18	6

1904 — 3-2-0
U	●	Phil. Dental Coll. Unk	21	0
U	●	Medico Unk	30	6
O22	●	La Salle Unk	14	0
U		Widener Unk	0	3
U		Pratt Inst. Unk	0	14

1905 — 2-0-1
U	=	La Salle Unk	12	12
U	●	Phil. Dental Coll. Unk	30	0
U	●	Medico Unk	6	0

1906
NO TEAM

HORACE BUTTERWORTH
1907 (.833)   4-0-2

1907 — 4-0-2
U	●	Schuylkill Navy Unk	21	5
U	●	Widener Unk	17	6
U	●	Girard Coll. Unk	14	0
U	=	St. Joseph's Unk	5	5
U	●	Loyola-Baltimore Unk	13	12
U	=	Phil. Pharmacy Unk	12	12

DR. FRANK W. WHITE
1908 (.583)   3-2-1

1908 — 3-2-1
U		Widener Unk	0	22
U	=	La Salle Unk	12	12
U	●	Phil. Pharmacy Unk	6	5
U	●	Girard Coll. Unk	25	12
U	●	Loyola-Baltimore Unk	12	10
U		Villanova Unk	0	12

WILLIAM J. SCHATZ
1909-13 (.500)   13-13-3

1909 — 0-4-1
U		Lebanon Unk	0	45
U		Widener Unk	0	12
U		Muhlenberg Unk	0	24
U		Phil. Pharmacy Unk	0	18
U	=	Schuylkill Navy Unk	0	0

1910 — 3-3-0
U		Ursinus Unk	0	53
U	●	Widener Unk	6	18
U	●	St. Joseph's Unk	9	6
U	●	Girard Coll. Unk	21	13
U		Phil. Osteopathy Unk	22	6
U		Wenonah Military Unk	6	27

1911 — 6-1-0
U	●	Phil. Osteopathy Unk	21	6
U	●	La Salle Unk	25	0
U		Widener Unk	0	30
U	●	New York Aggies Unk	18	12
U	●	Pratt Inst. Unk	6	0
U	●	Phil. Navy Unk	13	6
U	●	West Chester Unk	7	0

1912 — 3-2-0
U		Widener Unk	0	28
U	●	New York Aggies Unk	6	0
U	●	Phil. Normal Unk	18	0
U	●	Pratt Inst. Unk	7	13
U	●	La Salle Unk	6	0

1913 — 1-3-2
U		Widener Unk	0	18
O18		at Delaware	0	28
U	=	Albright Unk	0	0
U	●	Camden BC Unk	12	0
U	=	St. Joseph's Unk	13	13
U		La Salle Unk	6	22

WILLIAM NICHOLAI
1914-16 (.618)   9-5-3

1914 — 3-3-0
U	●	Phil. Normal Unk	24	12
U		La Salle Unk	6	0
U	●	Bloomsburg Unk	13	6
O17		Delaware	7	20
U	●	St. Joseph's Unk	7	14
U		Albright Unk	12	28

1915 — 3-1-1
U		Schuylkill Navy Unk	0	21
U	●	Phil. Navy Unk	6	0
U	●	La Salle Unk	13	12
U	=	Phil. Normal Unk	0	0
U	●	St. Joseph's Unk	13	7

1916 — 3-1-2
U	=	La Salle Unk	0	0
U	=	Millersville Unk	0	0
U		Bryn Athyn Unk	0	7
U	●	Coatesville Unk	20	7
U	●	Phil. Normal Unk	35	0
U	●	Phil. Navy Unk	6	0

ELWOOD GEIGES
1917 (.071)   0-6-1

1917 — 0-6-1
U		Widener Unk	0	1 f
U		Franklin & Marshall Unk	0	1 f
U		Albright Unk	0	1 f
U		Moravian Unk	0	1 f
U		Susquehanna Unk	0	1 f
U		Lebanon Valley Unk	0	1 f
U	=	Temple Prep Unk	6	6

1918-1919
NO TEAM WWI

1920-1921
NO TEAM

FRANCOIS M. D'ELISCU
1922-23 (.136)   1-9-1

1922 — 1-4-1
U	●	East Stroudsburg Unk	14	0
U	=	Trenton Unk	0	0
U		New York Aggies Unk	0	40
U		Millersville Unk	0	31
U		Gallaudet Unk	6	31
U		St. Joseph's Unk	6	20

1923 — 0-5-0
O6		at Haverford	0	3
O20		at Juniata	6	14
O27		at Ursinus	0	52
N10		at Susquehanna	7	25
N17		Drexel	0	7

ALBERT BARRON
1924 (.200)   1-4

1924 — 1-4-0
O4		at East Stroudsburg	6	40
O18		at St. Thomas	0	19
N1		at Wyoming Seminary	0	34
N8		at West Chester	3	13
N22	●	Drexel	6	0

HENRY J. MILLER
1925-32 (.740)   50-15-8

1925 — 5-2-2
O2	●	Upsala	19	0
O10		at Schuylkill	3	0
O17		at St. John's	18	0
O24		at Widener	0	13
O31	=	Lebanon Valley	0	0
N7	=	at George Washington	0	0
N14	●	St. Joseph's	32	0
N21		at Susquehanna	26	10
N25		at Schuylkill Navy	6	16

1926 — 5-3-0
S25	●	at Ursinus	12	0
O9	●	Lebanon Valley	13	3
O16	●	Susquehanna	14	0
O23	●	Schuylkill Navy	12	0
O30	●	Albright	0	19
N6	●	at Muhlenberg	12	29
N11	●	Quantico Marines	12	42
N20	●	Washington Coll.	13	0

1927 — 7-1-0
O1	●	Blue Ridge	110	0
O8	●	Juniata	58	0
O15		at Dartmouth	7	47
O22	●	Gallaudet	62	0
O29		at Brown	7	0
N5	●	Albright	13	0
N12	●	Washington Coll.	75	0
N19	●	Bucknell	19	13

1928 — 7-1-2
S29	●	St. Thomas	12	0
O6	●	Gallaudet	39	0
O13	●	W. Maryland	7	0
O20	●	Albright	32	0
O27	●	Providence	41	0
N3		at Schuylkill Navy	7	10
N10	=	Villanova	0	0
N17	●	Geneva	6	0
N24	●	Washington Coll.	73	6
N29	●	Bucknell	7	7

1929 — 6-3-1
S28	●	Thiel	25	0
O5	●	St. Thomas	20	0
O12	●	St. Bonaventure	28	0
O19	●	W. Maryland	0	23
O26	=	Wash. & Jeff.	0	0
N2	●	Bucknell	0	13
N9	●	Gallaudet	31	0
N16	●	Lafayette	13	0
N23	●	Drake	16	14
N30	●	Villanova	0	15

1930 — 7-3-0
S26	●	Thiel	13	6
O3	●	St. Thomas	28	2
O10	●	Bucknell	7	6
O18	●	Wash. & Jeff.	20	7
O25	●	Villanova Phil	7	8
N1	●	Wake Forest	36	0
N8	●	Miami, Fla.	34	0
N15	●	Lafayette	46	0
N22	●	Carnegie Tech	13	32
N29	●	Drake	20	49

1931 — 8-1-1
S25	●	Mt. St. Mary's	33	0
O2	●	Albright	19	7
O10	●	Penn State	12	0
O16	●	Bucknell	0	0
O23	●	Haskell	6	0
O30	●	Wash. & Jeff.	6	3
N7	●	Villanova	13	7
N14	●	Carnegie Tech	13	19
N21	●	at Denver	18	0
N28	●	Missouri KC	38	6

THE SCHOOLS

1932 — 5-1-2

S30	• Thiel	31	0
O7	West Virginia	14	13
O14	Bucknell	12	0
O21	Denver	14	0
O28	= Carnegie Tech	7	7
N4	Haskell	14	14
N12	Penn State	13	12
N19	Villanova	0	7

GLENN "POP" WARNER
1933-38 (.612) 31-18-9

1933 — 5-3-0

S29	• South Carolina	26	6
O7	at Carnegie Tech	0	25
O13	• Haskell	31	0
O20	• West Virginia	13	7
O28	at Bucknell	7	20
N4	• Drake	20	14
N18	• Wash. & Jeff.	13	0
N25	Villanova	0	24

1934 — 7-1-2

S29	• Virginia Tech	34	0
O6	• Texas A&M	40	6
O13	= Indiana	6	6
O19	• West Virginia	28	13
O27	at Marquette	28	6
N3	• Holy Cross	14	0
N10	• at Carnegie Tech	34	6
N24	• Villanova	22	0
D1	= Bucknell	0	0
	SUGAR BOWL		
J1	Tulane	14	20

1935 — 7-3-0

S20	• St. Joseph's	51	0
S27	• Centre	25	13
O5	• at Texas A&M	14	0
O12	• Vanderbilt	6	3
O19	• at Carnegie Tech	13	0
O26	• at West Virginia	19	6
N2	• Michigan State	7	12
N16	• Marquette	26	6
N23	• Villanova	14	21
N30	• Bucknell	6	7

1936 — 6-3-2

S19	• at St. Joseph's	18	0
S26	• Centre	50	7
O2	• Mississippi	12	7
O12	• at Boston Collge	14	0
O17	at Carnegie Tech	0	7
O31	• Holy Cross	3	0
N7	• Michigan State	7	7
N14	• Villanova	6	0
N21	• Iowa	0	25
N28	• Bucknell	0	0
D5	at Saint Mary's-Cal	7	13

1937 — 3-2-4

S25	• VMI	18	7
O1	• Mississippi	0	0
O8	• Florida	7	6
O12	• at Boston College	0	0
O23	• Carnegie Tech	7	0
O30	• at Holy Cross	0	0
N6	• Michigan State	6	13
N13	• at Bucknell	0	0
N20	Villanova	0	33

1938 — 3-6-1

S24	• Albright	6	0
O1	• Pittsburgh	6	28
O8	• TCU	6	28
O15	• Bucknell	26	0
O21	= Boston College	26	26
O29	• Georgetown	0	13
N5	at Holy Cross	0	33
N12	• Villanova	7	20
N19	at Michigan State	0	10
D3	• at Florida	20	12

FRED H. SWAN
1939 (.222) 2-7

1939 — 2-7-0

S29	• Georgetown	2	3
O7	• Carnegie Tech	0	6
O14	• TCU	13	11
O21	at Boston College	0	19
O27	• Bucknell	16	0
N4	Pittsburgh	7	13
N11	at Holy Cross	0	14
N18	Villanova	6	12
N25	at Michigan State	7	18

RAY MORRISON
1940-48 (.455) 31-38-9

1940 — 4-4-1

S27	• Muhlenberg	64	7
O4	Georgetown	0	14
O12	at Boston College	20	33
O18	• Michigan State	21	19
O26	Penn State	0	18
N2	at Bucknell	10	7
N9	• Villanova	28	0
N16	at Holy Cross	6	6
N23	at Oklahoma	6	9

1941 — 7-2-0

S26	• Kansas	31	9
O4	• VMI	28	13
O10	• Georgetown	17	7
O18	• Penn State	14	0
O25	• Bucknell	41	14
N1	at Boston College	0	31
N8	• Villanova	14	13
N15	at Michigan State	0	46
N22	at Holy Cross	31	13

1942 — 2-5-3

S25	Georgetown	0	7
O2	• VMI	7	6
O9	• Bucknell	7	7
O16	= at SMU	6	6
O23	• N.C. Pre-Flight	0	34
O31	= Michigan State	7	7
N7	at Boston College	0	28
N14	Holy Cross	0	13
N21	• Oklahoma	14	7
N28	Villanova	7	20

1943 — 2-6-0

S24	• VMI	27	0
O1	• Swarthmore	13	6
O9	at Army	0	51
O15	• Ursinus	6	10
O22	Bucknell	6	7
N6	at Holy Cross	6	42
N13	at Penn State	0	13
N20	Villanova	7	34

1944 — 2-4-2

S29	• Swarthmore	34	12
O6	• Holy Cross	0	30
O14	• at NYU	25	0
O20	= Syracuse	7	7
O27	• Bucknell	7	7
N4	at West Virginia	0	6
N11	• Penn State	6	7
N18	at Tennessee	14	27

1945 — 7-1-0

S28	• Syracuse	7	6
O5	• NYU	59	0
O12	• Bucknell	64	0
O19	• West Virginia	28	12
O27	at Pittsburgh	6	0
N3	• Lafayette	20	0
N10	at Penn State	0	27
N17	• at Holy Cross	14	6

1946 — 2-4-2

S27	= SMU	7	7
O4	• Georgia	7	35
O12	= at Pittsburgh	0	0
O18	• West Virginia	6	0
N2	at Syracuse	7	28
N9	at Penn State	0	26
N16	• Bucknell	27	6
N23	Holy Cross	7	12

1947 — 3-6-0

S26	• NYU	32	7
O4	at Holy Cross	13	19
O11	at Syracuse	12	28
O17	• Muhlenberg	7	6
O25	• at Bucknell	21	0
N1	Oklahoma State	0	26
N8	Penn State	0	7
N15	at Michigan State	6	14
N22	at West Virginia	0	21

1948 — 2-6-1

S24	= Lebanon Valley	7	7
O2	• West Virginia *Her*	7	27
O9	• at Rutgers	20	34
O15	• Boston U.	7	13
O23	• at Oklahoma State	7	41
O29	• Bucknell	20	0
N6	• Syracuse	20	0
N13	at Penn State	0	47
N20	Holy Cross	7	13

ALBERT P. KAWAL
1949-54 (.464) 24-28-3

1949 — 5-4-0

S24	Texas	0	54
O1	• Rutgers	14	7
O7	• at Syracuse	27	14
O14	• Bucknell	20	19
O21	• Rhode Island	47	6
O29	• at Michigan State	14	62
N5	• at Boston U.	7	28
N19	• at Holy Cross	20	7
N28	Penn State	7	28

1950 — 4-4-1

S22	• Albright	32	6
S29	• Syracuse	7	6
O14	• at Rutgers	20	26
O21	• Wayne St.	26	0
O28	= at Penn State	7	7
N4	• Delaware	39	0
N11	• Bucknell	0	35
N18	• Fordham	21	26
N25	• at Holy Cross	21	26

1951 — 6-4-0

S21	• at Syracuse	0	19
S29	• at Brown	20	4
O6	• Rutgers	14	7
O12	• Albright	47	6
O20	• at Delaware	13	7
O26	• Boston U.	20	13
N3	• at Bucknell	7	28
N10	• NYU	34	6
N17	• Fordham	6	35
N24	• at Holy Cross	7	41

1952 — 2-7-1

S20	• at Penn State	13	20
S26	• Albright	21	0
O3	• Syracuse	0	27
O10	• Bucknell	12	19
O18	• at Indiana	0	33
O25	• NYU	34	7
N1	• at Rutgers	28	40
N6	= at Boston U.	14	14
N15	• Fordham	6	33
N22	• Holy Cross	0	28

1953 — 4-4-1

S18	• Albright	34	0
S26	• at Syracuse	0	42
O3	• Bowling Green	27	0
O17	• at Bucknell	27	21
O24	• Scranton	33	7
O31	• Bainbridge	7	7
N7	• at Yale	6	32
N14	• at Fordham	0	28
N21	• Boston U.	0	20

1954 — 3-5-0

O2	• Boston College	9	21
O9	• at Delaware	13	51
O16	• Bucknell	0	27
O23	• at Brown	19	14
O30	• at Rutgers	0	25
N6	• Brandeis	27	0
N13	• at Scranton	20	0
N20	• Boston U.	7	19

JOSH CODY
1955 (.000) 0-8

1955 — 0-8-0

S24	• at Holy Cross	7	42
O1	• Scranton	6	20
O15	• at Bucknell	0	38
O22	• at Carnegie Tech	16	18
O29	• at Lehigh	14	27
N5	• Muhlenberg	6	7
N12	• Delaware	0	46
N19	• at Boston U.	0	25

PETER P. STEVENS
1956-59 (.125) 4-28

1956 — 3-5-0

S29	• at Lafayette	0	20
O6	• at Muhlenberg	19	14
O13	• Scranton	28	20
O20	• Carnegie Tech	27	12
O27	• Bucknell	6	12
N3	• Lehigh	0	21
N10	• Gettysburg	7	13
N17	• at Delaware	7	14

1957 — 1-6-0

O5	• at Bucknell	6	19
O12	• at Hofstra	7	13
O19	• Lafayette	13	12
N2	• Muhlenberg	16	40
N9	• at Delaware	7	71
N16	• at Gettysburg	7	42
N23	• Buffalo	6	13

1958 — 0-8-0

O4	• Delaware	14	35
O11	• at Muhlenberg	18	21
O18	• at Lafayette	0	35
O25	• at Scranton	0	6
N1	• at Buffalo	6	54
N8	• Bucknell	6	44
N15	• Gettysburg	6	22
N22	• Hofstra	6	34

1959 — 0-9-0

S26	• Buffalo	14	28
O3	• Scranton	12	26
O10	• Muhlenberg	13	14
O17	• Lafayette	20	52
O24	• Hofstra	0	15
O31	• at Drexel	8	12
N7	• at Delaware	0	62
N14	• at Bucknell	6	26
N21	• at Gettysburg	0	35

GEORGE MAKRIS
1960-69 (.505) 45-44-4

1960 — 2-7-0

S24	• Kings Point	26	13
O1	• Buffalo	12	21
O8	• at Muhlenberg	14	17
O15	• at Lafayette	7	9
O22	• at Hofstra	4	6
O29	• Drexel	30	8
N5	• Delaware	12	26
N12	• at Bucknell	0	23
N19	• Gettysburg	8	14

1961 — 2-5-2

S23	• at Kings Point	0	12
S30	• Bucknell	7	8
O7	• Muhlenberg	36	12
O14	• Lafayette	12	12
O21	• at Buffalo	3	30
O28	• Hofstra	14	12
N4	• at Delaware	0	28
N11	= at Gettysburg	0	0
N18	• Toledo	14	15

1962 — 3-6-0

S22	• Kings Point	14	3
S29	• Bucknell	14	15
O6	• at Muhlenberg	38	7
O13	• at Lafayette	21	0
O20	• Buffalo	13	16
O27	• at Hofstra	10	19
N3	• Delaware	8	20
N10	• at Toledo	0	13
N17	• Gettysburg	15	22

1963 — 5-3-1

S21	• Ithaca	30	21
S28	= at Kings Point	20	20
O5	• Connecticut	9	7
O12	• Muhlenberg	29	0
O19	• Lafayette	31	0
O26	• Hofstra	46	13
N2	• at Bucknell	3	14
N9	• at Delaware	23	32
N16	• at Susquehanna	18	22

1964 — 7-2-0

S26	• Kings Point	34	9
O3	• So. Connecticut	22	6
O10	• at Boston U.	44	13
O17	• at Lafayette	38	18
O24	• at Connecticut	7	25
O31	• Bucknell	28	31
N7	• at Delaware	21	0
N14	• Gettysburg	32	20
N21	• Hofstra	21	6

1965 — 5-5-0

S18	• George Washington	13	21
S25	• at Kings Point	21	27
O2	• Boston U.	7	14
O9	• at Bucknell	14	40
O16	• Lafayette	27	12
O23	• at Connecticut	12	11
O30	• Delaware	31	22
N6	• Rhode Island	28	0
N13	• Gettysburg	22	21
N20	• Hofstra	28	42

836 TEMPLE
THE SCHOOLS

1966 6-3-0

S24	•	at Kings Point	48	8
O1	•	Boston U.	9	6
O8	•	Bucknell	82	28
O15	•	at Hofstra	18	7
O22	•	Connecticut	35	25
O29		Delaware	14	20
N5	•	at Rhode Island	21	19
N12		at Gettysburg	19	21
N19		Bowling Green	20	62

1967 7-2-0

S23	•	at Kings Point	18	12
S30	•	Boston U.	22	16
O7		at Buffalo	14	44
O14	•	Hofstra	35	23
O21		at Dayton	6	56
O28	•	at Delaware	26	17
N4	•	at Bucknell	13	8
N11	•	Gettysburg	45	27
N18	•	Akron	22	21

1968 4-6-0

S21	•	Rhode Island	28	0
S28	•	at Wayne St.	26	6
O5		at Boston U.	0	7
O12		Bucknell	26	29
O19	•	at Hofstra	20	12
O26		Delaware	27	50
N2		Buffalo	40	50
N9	•	at Gettysburg	30	11
N16		Northeastern	26	41
N23		Dayton	17	35

1969 4-5-1

S20	•	at Rhode Island	47	3
S27		William & Mary	6	7
O4	•	Wayne St.	34	0
O11	=	at Bucknell	7	7
O18	•	Hofstra	34	7
O25		at Delaware	0	33
N1		at Buffalo	0	33
N8		Gettsburg	14	16
N15	•	at Northeastern	35	17
N22		Boston U.	3	21

WAYNE HARDIN
1970-82 (.604) 80-52-3

1970 7-3-0

S12		Akron	0	21
S19	•	at Bucknell	10	3
S26	•	at Holy Cross	23	13
O3	•	at Boston U.	10	7
O10	•	Connecticut	41	23
O17	•	at Xavier	28	15
O31		Delaware	13	15
N7	•	Rhode Island	18	15
N14	•	Buffalo	21	8
N26		Villanova	26	31

1971 6-2-1

S18		Boston College	3	17
O2	•	Boston U.	34	10
O9	•	at Connecticut	38	0
O16	•	Xavier	38	0
O23		at West Virginia	33	43
O30	•	at Delaware	32	27
N6	•	Rhode Island	40	13
N13	•	William & Mary	17	13
N20	=	Villanova	13	13

1972 5-4-0

S9		at Syracuse	10	17
S16	•	at Xavier	16	12
S23		at Boston College	27	49
S30	•	Holy Cross	15	7
O14	•	West Virginia	39	36
O20		at Boston U.	14	17
O28		Delaware	9	28
N11	•	Rhode Island	22	0
N18	•	at Villanova	12	10

1973 9-1-0

S8	•	Xavier	49	7
S15		at Boston College	0	45
S22	•	Akron	47	33
S29	•	at Holy Cross	63	34
O6	•	Cincinnati	16	15
O13	•	Boston U.	35	15
O27	•	at Delaware	31	8
N3	•	Rhode Island	43	0
N17	•	at Drake	35	10
N24	•	at Villanova	34	0

1974 8-2-0

S14	•	Rhode Island	38	7
S28	•	Boston College	34	7
O5	•	Marshall	31	10
O12	•	So. Illinois	59	16
O19	•	Holy Cross	56	0
O26	•	Delaware	21	17
N2		at Cincinnati	20	22
N9		at Pittsburgh	24	35
N16	•	at West Virginia	35	21
N23	•	Villanova PHIL	17	7

1975 6-5-0

S6		Penn State PHIL	25	26
S13		at West Virginia	7	50
S20		Boston College	9	27
O4	•	Cincinnati	21	17
O11		Pittsburgh	6	55
O18		Akron	23	24
O25	•	at Delaware	45	0
N1	•	Dayton	23	10
N8	•	Rhode Island	45	6
N22	•	Drake	44	7
N29	•	Villanova PHIL	41	3

1976 4-6-0

S11	•	at Akron	23	13
S18	•	Grambling	31	30
S25		at Pittsburgh	7	21
O2		Delaware	16	18
O9		West Virginia	0	42
O23		at Syracuse	16	24
O30		Penn State	30	31
N6	•	at Drake	31	7
N13	•	at Dayton	35	6
N20		Villanova PHIL	7	24

1977 5-5-1

S10		So. Illinois	20	24
S17	•	Drake	42	0
S24		Pittsburgh	0	76
O1	•	at Delaware	6	3
O8		at West Virginia	16	38
O22	•	La. Lafayette	27	20
O29	=	at Cincinnati	17	17
N5	•	Rutgers	24	14
N12		at Penn State	7	44
N19	•	at Villanova	38	15
D11		Grambling TOK	32	35

1978 7-3-1

S1		Penn State	7	10
S16	•	at Drake	36	29
S23		at Pittsburgh	12	20
S30	•	Delaware	38	7
O7	=	at William & Mary	22	22
O14	•	Cincinnati	16	13
O21	•	West Virginia	28	27
O28	•	at Akron	56	21
N11		at Rutgers	10	13
N18	•	Villanova PHIL	27	17
D9	•	Boston College TOK	28	24

1979 10-2-0

S8	•	at West Virginia	38	16
S15	•	Drake	43	21
S22	•	at Delaware	31	14
S29		Pittsburgh	9	10
O6	•	at Rutgers	41	20
O13	•	Syracuse PHIL	49	17
O20	•	Cincinnati	35	14
N3	•	at Hawaii	34	31
N10	•	Akron	42	6
N17		at Penn State	7	22
N24	•	at Villanova	42	10
		GARDEN STATE BOWL		
D15	•	California	28	17

1980 4-7-0

S13		Rutgers	3	21
S20		Delaware	7	28
S27		at Pittsburgh	2	36
O4	•	Boston U.	53	6
O11		at Syracuse	7	31
O18	•	Akron	16	7
O25	•	Cincinnati	23	7
N1	•	at Louisville	17	12
N8		West Virginia	28	41
N15		Penn State	7	50
N22		at Villanova	7	23

1981 5-5-0

S5	•	William & Mary	42	0
S12	•	Syracuse PHIL	31	19
S19		at Delaware	7	13
O3		at Penn State	0	30
O10	•	Colgate PHIL	31	0
O17	•	at Rutgers	24	12
O24	•	at Cincinnati	24	13
O31		at Georgia	3	49
N7		at West Virginia	19	24
N21		Pittsburgh	0	35

1982 4-7-0

S4		at Penn State	14	31
S11	•	at Syracuse	23	18
S18	•	Delaware	22	0
S25		Rutgers	7	10
O2		at Boston College	7	17
O9	•	at Louisville	55	14
O16		at Pittsburgh	7	38
O30	•	Cincinnati	41	7
N6		West Virginia	17	20
N13		at Colgate	17	24
N20		East Carolina	10	23

BRUCE ARIANS
1983-88 (.409) 27-39

1983 4-7-0

S2	•	Syracuse PHIL	17	6
S10		at Pittsburgh	0	35
S24		Penn State PHIL	18	23
O1		Boston College	15	18
O8		at Cincinnati	16	31
O15		East Carolina	11	24
O22	•	at Delaware	23	16
O29		at Georgia	14	31
N5		at West Virginia	9	27
N12	•	Louisville	24	7
N19	•	at Rutgers	24	23

1984 6-5-0

S8	•	East Carolina	17	0
S15		at Rutgers	9	10
S22	•	Pittsburgh	13	12
S29		at Florida State	27	44
O6	•	at William & Mary	28	14
O13		at Boston College	10	24
O20		Delaware	19	34
O27		Virginia Tech	7	9
N3	•	Cincinnati	42	10
N17	•	West Virginia	19	17
N30	•	Toledo	35	6

1985 4-7-0

S7		at Boston College	25	28
S14		at Penn State	25	27
S21		Brigham Young	24	26
S28	•	at East Carolina	21	7
O5	•	at Cincinnati	28	16
O12	•	Rutgers	14	13
O19	•	William & Mary	45	16
O26		at Syracuse	14	29
N2		at Delaware	10	17
N9		Pittsburgh	17	21
N16		at West Virginia	10	23

1986 6-5-0

S6		at Penn State	15	45
S13	•	at Western Michigan	49	17 †
S20	•	Florida A&M	38	17 †
S27		at Brigham Young	17	27
O4	•	at Pittsburgh	19	13 †
O11	•	East Carolina	45	28 †
O18	•	Virginia Tech NOR	29	13 †
O25		Syracuse PHIL	24	27
N8		Boston College	29	38
N15		at Alabama	14	24
N22	•	at Rutgers	29	22 †

1987 3-8-0

S5	•	at Toledo	13	12
S12		at Boston College	7	28
S19	•	at Pittsburgh	24	21
S26	•	Akron	23	3
O3		at Penn State	13	27
O10		Tulsa	17	24
O17		at Florida	3	34
O31		at Army	7	17
N7		at East Carolina	26	31
N14		Houston	7	37 †
N21		Rutgers	14	17

1988 4-7-0

S3		at Syracuse	21	31
S10		Alabama	0	37
S17	•	at Navy	12	7
O1		Penn State PHIL	9	45
O15		at Pittsburgh	7	42
O22		at California	14	31
O29	•	at Rutgers	35	30
N5		East Carolina	17	34
N12	•	at Akron	37	17
N19		at Tulsa	10	15
N26	•	Boston College	45	28

JERRY BERNDT
1989-92 (.250) 11-33

1989 1-10-0

S2		at Western Michigan	24	31
S9		Syracuse PHIL	3	43
S16		at Penn State	3	42
S23		at Virginia Tech	0	23
S30		at Houston	7	65
O7		Pittsburgh	3	27
O14		at Boston College	14	35
O28		Northern Illinois	17	20
N4		at Georgia	10	37
N11		at East Carolina	24	31
N18	•	Rutgers	36	33

1990 7-4-0

S1		at Wyoming	23	38
S8		at Syracuse	9	19
S15	•	Austin Peay	28	0
S22	•	at Wisconsin	24	18
O6		at Penn State	10	48
O20	•	Virginia Tech	31	28
O27	•	East Carolina	30	27
N3		at Tennessee	20	41
N10	•	at Pittsburgh	28	18
N17	•	Rutgers	29	22
N24	•	at Boston College	29	10

1991-2004
BIG EAST

1991 2-9-0 (0-5-0)

S7		Alabama BIRM	3	41
S14	|	at Pittsburgh	7	26
S21		at Clemson	7	37
S28	•	Samford	40	0
O5		Penn State PHIL	7	24
O12	|	at West Virginia	9	10
O19	•	Navy	21	14
N2	|	at Syracuse	6	27
N9	|	Boston College	13	33
N16	|	at Rutgers	0	41
N23		Akron	32	37

1992 1-10-0 (0-6-0)

S5	•	Boston U.	35	0
S12		at Penn State	8	49
S19	|	Virginia Tech	7	26
S26		at Kansas State	14	35
O3		at Washington State	10	51
O17	|	Pittsburgh	20	27
O24	|	Syracuse PHIL	7	38
O31	|	at Boston College	6	45
N7		at Akron	15	29
N14	|	at Miami, Fla.	0	48
N21	|	Rutgers	10	35

RON DICKERSON
1993-97 (.145) 8-47

1993 1-10-0 (0-7-0)

S9	•	at Eastern Michigan	31	28
S18		California	0	58
S25	|	at Boston College	14	66
O2	|	Rutgers ERUT	0	62
O9		Army	21	56
O16	|	at Virginia Tech	7	55
O23		Akron	7	31
O30	|	at Miami, Fla.	7	42
N6	|	at Syracuse	3	52
N13	|	West Virginia	7	49
N20	|	Pittsburgh	18	28

1994 2-9-0 (0-7-0)

S3	•	at Akron	32	7
S17		East Carolina	14	31
S24	•	at Army	23	20
O1		Penn State	21	48
O8	|	at Virginia Tech	13	41
O15	|	at Boston College	28	45
O22	|	Syracuse PHIL	42	49
O29	|	at Pittsburgh	19	45
N5	|	at Rutgers	21	38
N12	|	West Virginia	17	55
N19	|	Miami, Fla.	14	38

1995   1-10-0 (1-6-0)

S2		at Kansas State	7	34
S9	|	at West Virginia	13	24
S16	|	at Penn State	14	66
S30		Bowling Green	31	37
O7	|	at Syracuse	14	31
O14	● |	Pittsburgh	29	27
O21		at East Carolina	22	32
O28	|	at Miami, Fla.	12	36
N4	|	Boston College	9	10
N11	|	Virginia Tech *DC*	16	38
N18	|	Rutgers	20	23

1996   1-10 (0-7)

A31	●	at Eastern Michigan	28	24
S7		Washington State	34	38
S14		at Bowling Green	16	20
S21		Penn State *ERut*	0	41
O5	|	at Pittsburgh	52	53
O12	|	at Virginia Tech	0	38
O19	|	West Virginia	10	30
O26	|	at Rutgers	17	28
N2	|	Miami, Fla.	26	57
N16	|	at Boston College	20	21
N23	|	Syracuse *PHIL*	15	36

1997   3-8 (3-4)

A28		at Western Michigan	14	34
S6	● |	Boston College	28	21
S13		at Penn State	10	52
S20	|	Virginia Tech	13	23
S27		Maryland *PHIL*	21	24
O4	● |	Pittsburgh	17	13
O18	|	at Syracuse	7	60
O25	|	at Miami, Fla.	15	47
N1	● |	Rutgers	49	7
N8		at Navy	17	49
N15	|	at West Virginia	21	41

BOBBY WALLACE
1998-Present (.241)   **19-60**

1998   2-9 (2-5)

S5		at Toledo	12	24
S12		Akron *PHIL*	28	35
S19	|	at Boston College	7	31
S26	|	at Maryland	20	30
O3		William & Mary	38	45
O10	|	West Virginia	7	37
O17	● |	at Virginia Tech	28	24
O31	|	at Rutgers	10	21
N7	● |	at Pittsburgh	34	33
N14	|	Miami, Fla.	7	42
N21	|	Syracuse *PHIL*	7	38

1999   2-9 (2-5)

S2		Maryland	0	6
S11		at Kansas State	0	40
S18		at Akron	15	25
S25		at Marshall	0	34
O2	|	at Pittsburgh	24	55
O9	● |	Boston College	24	14
O23	|	at West Virginia	17	20
O30	● |	Rutgers	56	28
N6	|	at Syracuse	10	27
N20	|	Virginia Tech	7	62
D4	|	at Miami, Fla.	0	55

2000   4-7 (1-6)

S2	●	at Navy	17	6
S9		at Maryland	10	17
S16	●	Bowling Green	31	14
S23	●	Eastern Michigan	49	40
S28	|	West Virginia	24	29
O7	|	at Virginia Tech	13	35
O14	● |	at Rutgers	48	14
O21	|	Miami, Fla.	17	45
N4	|	at Boston College	3	31
N11	|	Syracuse	12	31
N18	|	Pittsburgh	0	7

2001   4-7 (2-5)

A30	●	Navy	45	26
S8		Toledo	7	33
S22		at Bowling Green	23	42
O6	|	at Boston College	10	23
O13	● |	Rutgers	30	5
O20	|	at Syracuse	3	45
O27	|	Pittsburgh	7	33
N3	|	at Miami, Fla.	0	38
N10	|	Virginia Tech	0	35
N17	● |	at West Virginia	17	14
N24	●	Connecticut	56	7

2002   4-8 (2-5)

A29	●	Richmond	34	7
S7		Oregon State	3	35
S14	|	Miami, Fla.	21	44
S21	|	at South Carolina	21	42
S28		Cincinnati	22	35
O12	● |	Syracuse	17	16
O19	● |	at Connecticut	38	24
O26	|	at Virginia Tech	10	20
N2	|	West Virginia	20	46
N9	|	at Pittsburgh	22	29
N16	● |	at Rutgers	20	17
N23	|	Boston College	14	36

2003   1-11 (0-7)

A30		at Penn State	10	23
S6		Villanova	20	23
S20		at Cincinnati	24	30
S27		at Louisville	12	21
O4	●	at Middle Tennessee	44	36
O11	|	Boston College	13	38
O18	|	at Miami, Fla.	14	52
O25	|	Rutgers	14	30
N8	|	at Syracuse	17	41
N15	|	Virginia Tech	23	24
N22	|	Pittsburgh	16	30
N29	|	at West Virginia	28	45

2004   2-9 (1-5)

S4		Virginia	14	44
S11		at Maryland	22	45
S18	●	Florida A&M	38	7
S25		at Toledo	17	45
O2		Bowling Green	16	70
O9		Pittsburgh	22	27
O16	|	at Rutgers	6	16
O23	|	at Connecticut	31	45
N6	|	at West Virginia	21	42
N13	● |	Syracuse	34	24
N20	|	Boston College	17	34

THE SCHOOLS

TENNESSEE

BY GEOFFREY NORMAN

THE IDENTITY AND PERSONALITY of the Tennessee Volunteers are instantly recognizable to any fan of the game. Just try to imagine college football without orange jerseys, blue tick hounds, that Promethean stadium on the river, checkered end zones and Saturday crowds the size of a small city.

This is, in short, one of the major brands. One of only 10 football programs with 700 wins at the end of the 2004 season, Tennessee has produced several national champions, a few legends and one mythic coach. The Vols are, without doubt, among college football's elite.

TRADITION Since Tennessee plays its home games in a stadium that sits on the banks of the Tennessee River, it was probably inevitable that some fan would decide to beat the traffic by getting to the game by boat. Former Volunteers broadcaster George Mooney is credited as the first to try it, in 1962. Others followed his example, and soon there was a fairly substantial flotilla consisting of all manner of vessels out on the river on game day. This became the Volunteer Navy, and today the crews of more than 200 boats join up for a floating tailgate party whenever Tennessee plays at home. "Rocky Top" is not the official Vols fight song, though it might as well be. The song was first played at a 1972 game as part of a county music show and has been part of the Tennessee football personality ever since.

BEST PLAYER Archie Manning, patriarch of the famous quarterback clan, is still known by his first name in Mississippi. His son Peyton could have gone to Ole Miss and been welcomed as the prince of destiny. But football fortunes were on the wane in Oxford, so Peyton chose Tennessee and became a legend himself among the Volunteers faithful. He came in for injured starting quarterback Jerry Colquitt in the first game of his freshman year and went on a mythic four-year quest for an ever-elusive national championship. But he did just about everything else a quarterback could do. In his Tennessee career, Manning set 33 school, seven SEC and two NCAA records. He threw 89 touchdown passes and passed for a total of more than 11,000 yards. In 1,381 attempts, he was intercepted 33 times. That's why there's a road today leading to Neyland Stadium called Peyton Manning Pass.

PROFILE

University of Tennessee
Knoxville, Tenn.
Founded: 1794
Enrollment: 19,639
Colors: Orange and White
Nickname: Volunteers
Stadium: Neyland Stadium
    Opened in 1921
    Grass; 104,079 capacity
First football game: 1891
All-time record: 745–306–54 (.699)
Bowl record: 24–21
Consensus national championships, 1936-present: 3 (1938, 1951, 1998)
Southeastern Conference championships: 13 (9 outright)
Outland Trophy: Steve DeLong, 1964; John Henderson, 2000
First-round NFL draftees: 35
Website: utsports.collegesports.com

THE BEST OF TIMES

It's got to be Phillip Fulmer and the Vols' run from 1995 to 1998. They posted a 45–5 mark, culminating in the 1998 national title.

THE WORST OF TIMES

From 1958 to 1964, Tennessee was unable to win more than six games in any season and didn't make a single bowl appearance.

CONFERENCE

After 12 years in the Southern Conference, Tennessee became a charter member of the SEC in 1933.

DISTINGUISHED ALUMNI

Deanna Carter, singer; Cormac McCarthy, writer; Todd Helton, baseball player; Chamique Holdsclaw, WNBA player; Chad Holliday, CEO of DuPont; Allan Houston, NBA player; Ali Hussein Abu Ragheb, prime minister of Jordan; Chris Moneymaker, World Series of Poker winner; Kevin Nash, pro wrestler; Ron Rice, CEO, Hawaiian Tropic

FIGHT SONG

DOWN THE FIELD
(Here's to Old Tennessee)
Here's to old Tennessee
Never we'll sever
We pledge our loyalty
Forever and ever
Backing our football team
Faltering never
Cheer and fight with all of your might
For Tennessee.

The orange-and-white checkerboarding is one of the most recognizable end zone paint jobs.

Manning could have gone pro after his third year of eligibility—he had already graduated—but he came back to school for one more shot at a national title and a Heisman. Neither was meant to be. The Vols came up short, and Manning was second to Michigan's Charles Woodson in 1997 Heisman balloting. When he did leave for the NFL, Manning's record with the Vols was 39–6 as a starter, with four of those losses coming against nemesis Florida. Close runners-up to Manning would be a couple of defensive giants: Doug Atkins, who helped Tennessee to a 29–4–1 record during his three varsity years (1950-52), and Reggie White (1980-83), who holds all the Tennessee sack records: single game (four), season (15) and career (32).

BEST COACH When he first took the job in 1926, Robert Neyland—a West Point graduate who served in France during World War I—was an ROTC instructor, and Tennessee had to share him with the Army, first for a peacetime tour in Panama and then for duty in the China-Burma-India theater, where he served as a brigadier general during World War II. In his tours as head football coach at Tennessee, the Vols were a national power, running off undefeated streaks of 33 and 28 games and appearing in the Orange, Rose and Sugar bowls. Neyland's 1939 team shut out 10 consecutive opponents. When he returned from World War II in 1946, Neyland's team went to the Orange Bowl. But the following two seasons produced mediocre records (5–5 and 4–4–2) and predictable murmurings that the game had passed The General by. He was a single-wing man, and this was the age of the T-formation.

But Neyland proved the whisperers wrong, going 7–2–1 in 1949 and 11–1 in 1950, with, according to two rating services, a national title. He followed that up in 1951 with an undefeated regular season and a consensus national championship. In Neyland's last season, 1952, the Vols were 8–2–1, making his record in his third stint as head coach 54–17–4. Overall, The General went 173–31–12.

The record doesn't tell the story of the man, though. Neyland's approach to the game reflected his military

RECORDS

RUSHING YARDS
GAME
294 Chuck Webb vs. Mississippi, Nov. 18, 1989 (35 att.)
SEASON
1,464 Travis Stephens, 2001 (291 att.)
CAREER
3,078 Travis Henry, 1997-2000 (556 att.)

PASSING YARDS
GAME
523 Peyton Manning vs. Kentucky, Nov. 22, 1997 (25 of 35)
SEASON
3,819 Peyton Manning, 1997 (287 of 477)
CAREER
11,201 Peyton Manning, 1994-97 (863 of 1,381)

RECEIVING YARDS
GAME
256 Kelley Washington vs. LSU, Sept. 29, 2001 (11 rec.)
SEASON
1,170 Marcus Nash, 1997 (76 rec.)
CAREER
2,814 Joey Kent, 1993-96 (183 rec.)

POINTS
GAME
24 Six tied; most recently by Jamal Lewis vs. Kentucky, Nov. 22, 1997 (4 TDs)
SEASON
130 Gene McEver, 1929 (21 TDs, 4 PATs)
CAREER
371 Jeff Hall, 1995-98 (61 FGs, 188 PATs)

CONSENSUS ALL-AMERICANS

1929	Gene McEver, B
1933	Beattie Feathers, B
1938	Bowden Wyatt, E
1939	Ed Molinski, G
1939	George Cafego, B
1940	Bob Suffridge, G
1946	Dick Huffman, T
1951	Hank Lauricella, B
1952	John Michels, G
1956	John Majors, B
1965	Frank Emanuel, LB
1966	Paul Naumoff, LB
1967	Bob Johnson, C
1968	Charles Rosenfelder, G
1968-69	Steve Kiner, LB
1969-70	Chip Kell, G
1971	Bobby Majors, DB
1975-76	Larry Seivers, E/SE
1979	Roland James, DB
1983	Reggie White, DL
1984	Bill Mayo, OG
1985	Tim McGee, WR
1989	Eric Still, OL
1990	Antone Davis, OL

(Continued on next page)

roots. He preached organization, discipline and teamwork. He stressed, above all, defense and the kicking game. In his 216 games as head coach, an astonishing 112 of Tennessee's opponents failed to score. The 71 consecutive scoreless quarters against Tennessee during his tenure still stands as an NCAA record.

BEST TEAM The 1939 Vols were 10–0 during the regular season and outscored their opponents 212-0. It seems inexplicable that they could lose to Southern Cal 14–0 in the Rose Bowl. But because of that single loss, the choice for best-ever Vols team is the 1998 national championship squad that went 13–0, defeating Florida State 23-16 in the Fiesta Bowl. What made that season especially sweet for Vols fans is that it came on the heels of the Peyton Manning era. Besides winning it all, this Tennessee team did something no Manning-led UT team had ever done—beat Florida. The Vols did it in overtime at home in September, in front of more than 107,000 fans. It doesn't get any better than that in Knoxville.

BIGGEST GAME 1998 was the first year of the Bowl Championship Series (BCS), which had been devised to preserve the existing bowl game arrangements in college football and arrange an official national title game. It was a new—and controversial, to say the very least—alternative to a playoff system. In its first season, the BCS system matched Tennessee and Florida State in the Fiesta Bowl for the crown on January 4, 1999. Tennessee was undefeated and ranked No. 1 going in. The Seminoles had lost once during the regular season. The Vols jumped ahead on an interception returned for a touchdown by Dwayne Goodrich. And though Florida State stayed close through three quarters, the Vols regained a decisive edge when Tee Martin hit Peerless Price on a 79-yard touchdown pass

CONSENSUS ALL-AMERICANS (CONT.)	
1991	Dale Carter, DB
1997	Peyton Manning, QB
1998	Al Wilson, LB
1999	Cosey Coleman, OL
1999	Deon Grant, DB
2000-01	John Henderson, DL
2003	Dustin Colquitt, P
2004	Michael Munoz, OL

ALL-CENTENNIAL TEAM

Players from 1891 to 1990 were selected by a fan vote and a panel of school officials.

OFFENSE

1984-87	Harry Galbreath, OG
1986-89	Eric Still, OG
1978-80	Tim Irwin, OT
1983-86	Bruce Wilkerson, OT
1965-67	Bob Johnson, C
1973-76	Stanley Morgan, WR
1974-76	Larry Seivers, WR
1979-82	Willie Gault, WR
1972-74	Condredge Holloway, QB
1949-51	Hank Lauricella, B
1954-56	Johnny Majors, B
1969-71	Curt Watson, RB
1987-88	Reggie Cobb, RB
1981-84	Fuad Reveiz, PK

DEFENSE

1950-52	Doug Atkins, DE
1983-86	Dale Jones, DE
1980-83	Reggie White, DT
1986-89	Marion Hobby, DT
1962-64	Steve DeLong, MG
1967-69	Steve Kiner, LB
1967-69	Jack Reynolds, LB
1985-88	Keith DeLong, LB
1969-71	Bobby Majors, DB
1971-73	Eddie Brown, DB
1976-79	Roland James, DB
1979-82	Bill Bates, DB
1975-77	Craig Colquitt, P

with just 9:17 remaining, making the score 20-9. Florida State battled back to within a touchdown, then recovered a late Tennessee fumble to give itself a chance to tie. UT would have none of that. The Vols' defense forced another turnover, sealing a 23-16 win and the national championship.

BIGGEST UPSET On Oct. 20, 1928, the Vols played Alabama in Tuscaloosa. So heavily favored was Alabama that before the game, Neyland asked Bama coach Wallace Wade if they could end it early if the score got out of hand. This was pure gamesmanship—before the word had even been invented. It was a statement game for Neyland's team, and the Vols made their statement early. Halfback Gene McEver returned the opening kickoff 98 yards for a touchdown, whereupon Tennessee settled in and played Neyland football. Final score: Tennessee 15, Alabama 13. This game, more than any other, established the Neyland dynasty and secured Tennessee's place at the head table of college football.

HEARTBREAKER Tennessee entered the SEC championship game on Dec. 8, 2001, with a No. 2 ranking and a trip to the national title game on the line. But the uninspired Vols fell 31-20 to 21st-ranked LSU and had to settle for the Citrus Bowl, which turned out to be Michigan's misfortune as well. The Vols took out their frustrations on the Wolverines in a 45-17 beating.

BEST COMEBACK Down 31-7 to Notre Dame in the second quarter. Bad enough. But this game, on Nov. 9, 1991, was in South Bend, making Tennessee's chances look dire—until an unexpected twist just before the half as the Irish lined up for a field goal. The Vols blocked the kick and ran the ball back 85 yards for a touchdown. Tennessee headed to the locker room inspired and with

new life. The Vols rode that momentum all the way to an improbable, nail-biting 35-34 victory sealed by a missed 27-yard Notre Dame field goal as time expired.

STADIUM Officially, it is Neyland Stadium at Shields-Watkins Field. The seating capacity is 104,079 and change—though 108,768 fans packed Neyland for the 2004 game with rival Florida. The stadium is the third largest in all of college football and one of only two (the other is at Washington) that can be accessed by water. The Vols play their home games on natural grass—Tifway 419 hybrid-Bermuda, to be precise—that features one of the most recognizable end zone paint jobs. The orange-and-white checkerboard pattern first appeared on Oct. 10, 1964, when Boston College came to town, and lasted until an artificial surface was installed in 1968. The memory lingered, however, and the checkerboarding, and grass, returned in 1989.

RIVAL The Vols' traditional rival is Alabama, the only SEC team with a better overall record. Bear Bryant is said to have relished a victory over Tennessee even more than beating Auburn, though he couldn't say so out loud. But he remembered the Tennessee rivalry from his own playing days at Alabama. The game was traditionally played on the third Saturday in October, but recently the vicissitudes of modern scheduling have changed that. Still, the winning team lights up cigars to celebrate—a tradition established by Bryant during his time at Alabama and picked up by Tennessee in the 1990s. As close and intense as the series has been, it is oddly characterized by streaks. Alabama won seven straight from 1986 to 1992. Then Tennessee turned the Tide, so to speak, and took nine of 10 from 1995 to 2004.

The more contemporary, but equally intense, rivalry between Tennessee and Florida is the product of Steve Spurrier's ride to glory in the SEC. From 1992 to 2004, the SEC East was won by either Florida or Tennessee 11 times. And in those years, both teams were routinely considered contenders for the national championship. The game is played in September and usually is both teams' first major test of the season.

NICKNAME Tennessee began officially calling itself the Volunteer State in 1905. The name is a reflection on the way Tennesseans historically responded when they heard the call to arms. It started during the American Revolution, when virtually all 1,000 of the men living in the settlements that eventually became the state of Tennessee volunteered

to fight the British. In the War of 1812, when 3,500 troops from Tennessee were needed, 25,000 volunteered. During the Mexican War, the War Department established a quota of 2,800 from the state and 30,000 stepped forward. The name was first attached to the football team in 1902 in a story that appeared in *The Atlanta Constitution*. Three years later, the *Knoxville Journal* reported that the school had officially taken the name Volunteers. "The name sounds good," the story concluded, "and it is likely that it will stick." Right they were.

MASCOT During halftime of the 1953 Mississippi State game, a competition was held to determine which of several coonhounds would serve as the official mascot of the Tennessee football team. As each dog was introduced, fans "voted" with their cheers. The last dog introduced was a blue tick named Blue Smokey, who, when he heard the cheers, let out with a distinctive, musical bark. The fans cheered again, the dog sang once more and soon there was a chorus of cheering followed by Blue Smokey's barking. He got the job. The current Smokey is ninth in this distinguished line, and his predecessors have led interesting lives. One was dognapped by some Kentucky students and also got into it with the Baylor Bear. Smokey VI suffered heat exhaustion in a game with UCLA and was carried on the Vols' injury report until he made it back to the sideline later in the 1991 season.

UNIFORMS Tennessee's famous orange was copied from the common American daisy, a flower that grew abundantly on a little elevated piece of ground near the stadium known as The Hill. The color became official in 1891, but the team didn't appear in the distinctive burnt-orange jerseys until the first game of the 1922 season, when the Vols beat Emory & Henry 50-0. That was good enough reason to keep them. The distinctive capital "T" with the clipped serifs has been a staple of Tennessee helmets since 1967, replacing a block-letter "T" after three years of use. In the early 1970s, when Condredge Holloway was running the option for the Vols, they briefly wore white road jerseys with orange shoulders—a look that made a comeback in 2004.

QUOTE "If Neyland could score a touchdown against you, he had you beat. If he could score two, he had you in a rout."—Herman Hickman, one of Neyland's stars and later part of *Sports Illustrated*'s original staff, on The General's passion for defensive football.

TENNESSEE ALL-TIME SCORES

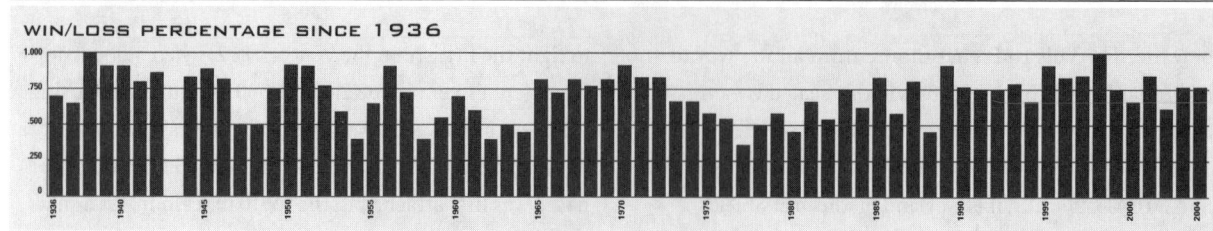

WIN/LOSS PERCENTAGE SINCE 1936

NO HEAD COACH

1891   0-1-0
N21		Sewanee *Chat*	0	24

1892   2-5-0
O15	●	at Maryville	25	0
O21		at Vanderbilt	0	12 *
O24		at Sewanee	0	54
N2		Sewanee	0	10
N12		Chattanooga AC *Chat*	16	6
N17		Vanderbilt	0	10
N24		Wake Forest	6	10

1893   2-4-0
O21	●	Kentucky	0	56
N3		at Wake Forest	0	64
N4		at Duke	0	70
N7		at North Carolina	0	60
N18	●	Maryville	32	0
N30		Asheville AA	12	6

1894-1895
NO TEAM

1896   4-0-0
O22	●	Williamsburg	10	6
O24	●	Chattanooga AC *Chat*	4	0
N14	●	Virginia Tech	6	4
N26	●	Central U.	30	0

1897   4-1-0
O15	●	King	28	0
O23	●	Williamsburg	6	0
N8		North Carolina	0	16
N25	●	Virginia Tech *Roa*	18	0
N26	●	at Bristol AC	12	0

1898
NO TEAM

J.A. PIERCE
1899-1900 (.654)   8-4-1

1899   5-2-0
O11	●	King	11	5
O21		Virginia Tech	0	5
O28		at Sewanee	0	51
N4	●	Kentucky	12	0
N11	●	Georgia	5	0
N23	●	Wash. & Lee	11	0
N30	●	Transylvania, Ky	41	0

1900   3-2-1
O10	●	King	22	0
O22	=	at Vanderbilt	0	0
N1		North Carolina	5	22
N10		Auburn *Birm*	0	23
N27	●	U.T. Chattanooga	28	0
D1	●	Georgetown	12	6

GEORGE KELLEY
1901 (.500)   3-3-2

1901   3-3-2
O12	●	King	8	0
O19	●	Clemson	6	6
O26		at Nashville	5	16
N2		Transylvania, Ky	0	6
N9		at Vanderbilt	0	22
N16	●	Georgetown	12	0
N23	●	Kentucky	5	0
N28	=	Alabama *Birm*	6	6

H.F. FISHER
1902-03 (.588)   10-7

1902   6-2-0
O11	●	King	12	0
O21	●	Maryville	34	0
O25		Vanderbilt	5	12
N1	●	Sewanee	6	0
N7	●	at Nashville	10	0
N15		Mississippi *Mem*	11	10
N22	●	at Georgia Tech	10	6
N27		Clemson	0	11

1903   4-5-0
O3	●	Maryville	17	0
O10	●	Carson-Newman	38	0
O17		at Vanderbilt	0	40
O29		at South Carolina	0	24
O31		at Nashville	10	0
N7		Georgia	0	5
N14		Sewanee	0	17
N21	●	Georgia Tech	11	0
N26		Alabama *Birm*	0	24

S.D. CRAWFORD
1904 (.389)   3-5-1

1904   3-5-1
O1	●	Maryville	17	0
O15	=	Nashville	0	0
O22		at Georgia Tech	0	2
O29		Sewanee	0	12
N5		at Vanderbilt	0	22
N12		Clemson	0	6
N16		Cincinnati	0	35
N19	●	at U.T. Chattanooga	23	0
N24	●	Alabama *Birm*	5	0

J.D. DePREE
1905-06 (.306)   4-11-3

1905   3-5-1
S30	●	Deaf School	16	6
O7	●	American U.	104	0
O14	=	at Clemson	5	5
O21		Vanderbilt	0	45
O28	●	at Sewanee	6	11
N4		at Georgia Tech	0	45
N18	●	Centre	31	5
N30		Alabama *Birm*	0	29
D3		at U.T. Chattanooga	0	5

1906   1-6-2
O6	●	American U.	10	0
O13		Maryville	0	11
O20		Centre	0	6
O25	=	at American U.	5	5
N3		Sewanee	0	17
N10		at Kentucky	0	21
N19		at Clemson	0	16
N21	=	at Georgia	0	0
N29		Alabama *Birm*	0	51

GEORGE LEVENE
1907-09 (.589)   15-10-3

1907   7-2-1
O5	●	Tenn. Military	30	0
O12	●	at Georgia	15	0
O19	●	at Georgia Tech	4	6
O21	●	at Clemson	4	0
O26	●	Maryville	34	0
N2	●	U.T. Chattanooga	57	0
N9	=	Kentucky	0	0
N16	●	Mississippi State *Mem*	11	4
N18	●	Arkansas *Mem*	14	2
N28		Alabama *Birm*	0	5

1908   7-2-0
O3	●	North Carolina	12	0
O10	●	Maryville	39	5
O17	●	Kentucky	7	0
O24	●	Georgia	10	0
O31	●	at Georgia Tech	6	5
N7		at Vanderbilt	9	16
N14	●	Clemson	6	5
N21	●	U.T. Chattanooga	35	6
N26		Alabama *Birm*	0	4

1909   1-6-2
O2	=	Centre	0	0
O9		North Carolina	0	3
O16		at Kentucky	0	17
O23		Georgia	0	3
O30		Georgia Tech	0	29
N6		at Vanderbilt	0	51
N13		Alabama	0	10
N20	=	at U.T. Chattanooga	0	0
N25	●	Transylvania, Ky	11	0

ANDREW A. STONE
1910 (.389)   3-5-1

1910   3-5-1
O1		Centre	2	17
O8	●	Mooney	7	0
O15		at Vanderbilt	0	18
O22		at Georgia	5	35
O29	●	at Samford	17	0
O31		at Mississippi State	0	48
N5		Kentucky	0	10
N12	●	Maryville	13	0
N19	●	U.T. Chattanooga	6	6

Z.G. CLEVENGER
1911-15 (.628)   26-15-2

1911   3-4-2
O7	●	Mooney School	27	0
O14		at Georgia Tech	0	24
O21	●	Maryville	22	5
O28		at North Carolina St.	0	16
N4		Centre	0	0
N11		at Virginia Tech	11	36
N18	●	Southwestern	22	0
N25	=	at UT Med. School	0	0
N30		at Kentucky	0	12

1912   4-4-0
O5	●	King	101	0
O12	●	Maryville	38	0
O19	●	at Tenn. Med. Coll.	62	0
O26	●	Sewanee *Chat*	6	33
N2	●	Centre	67	0
N9		at Mercer	14	27
N16		Kentucky	6	13
N28		Alabama *Birm*	0	7

1913   6-3-0
S27	●	Carson-Newman	58	0
O4	●	Athens	95	0
O11	●	Maryville	75	0
O18	●	Sewanee *Chat*	6	17
O26	●	Davidson	9	0
N1	●	U.T. Chattanooga	21	0
N8		at Vanderbilt	6	7
N14		at Alabama	0	6
N27		at Kentucky	13	7

1914   9-0-0
S26	●	Carson-Newman	89	0
O3	●	King	55	3
O10	●	Clemson	27	0
O17	●	at Louisville	66	0
O24	●	Alabama	17	7
O31	●	U.T. Chattanooga	67	0
N7	●	at Vanderbilt	16	14
N14	●	Sewanee *Chat*	14	7
N26	●	Kentucky	23	6

1915   4-4-0
S25	●	Carson-Newman	101	0
O2	●	Tusculm	21	0
O9		Clemson	0	3
O16	●	Centre	80	0
O23	●	Cumberland	101	0
O30		at Vanderbilt	0	35
N13		at Mississippi State	0	14
N25		at Kentucky	0	6

JOHN R. BENDER
1916-20 (.741)   18-5-4

1916   8-0-1
S30	●	Tusculum	33	0
O7	●	Maryville	32	6
O14		at Clemson	14	0
O21	●	South Carolina	26	0
O28	●	Florida *Tam*	24	0
N4	●	at U.T. Chattanooga	12	7
N11	●	Vanderbilt	10	6
N18	●	Sewanee *Chat*	17	0
N30	=	Kentucky	0	0

1917-1918
NO TEAM WWI

1919   3-3-3
S27	●	Tusculum	29	6
O3	●	Maryville	32	2
O11	=	at Vanderbilt	3	3
O18		Mississippi State	0	6
O25		at Clemson	0	14
N1	=	North Carolina	0	0
N8	=	at South Carolina	6	6
N15	●	Cincinnati	33	12
N27		at Kentucky	0	13

1920   7-2-0
S25	●	Emory & Henry	45	0
O2	●	Maryville	47	0
O9		Vanderbilt	0	20
O16	●	at U.T. Chattanooga	35	0
O23	●	Clemson	26	0
O30		at Mississippi State	7	13
N6	●	Transylvania, Ky	49	0
N13	●	at Sewanee	20	0
N25	●	Kentucky	14	7

1921-1932 SOUTHERN

M.B. BANKS
1921-25 (.633)   27-15-3

1921   6-2-1 (1-0-1)
S24	●	Emory & Henry	27	0
O1	●	at Maryville	7	0
O8	●	U.T. Chattanooga	21	0
O15		at Dartmouth	3	14
O22	●	Florida	9	0
O29		at Vanderbilt	0	14
N5		Mississippi State *Mem*	14	7
N12	●	Sewanee	21	0
N24		at Kentucky	0	0

1922   8-2-0 (4-2-0)
S23	●	Emory & Henry	50	0
S30	●	Carson-Newman	32	7
O7	●	Maryville	21	0
O14		at Fort Benning	15	0
O21		at Georgia	3	7
O28		Mississippi	49	0
N4		Vanderbilt	6	14
N11		Mississippi State *Mem*	31	3
N18	●	Sewanee *Chat*	18	7
N30	●	Kentucky	14	7

1923 — 5-4-1 (4-2-0)

S29		at Army	0	41
O6	=	Maryville	14	14
O13	●	Georgetown	13	6
O20	|	Georgia	0	17
O27	● |	Mississippi State Mem	7	3
N3	● |	Tulane	13	2
N10	|	at Vanderbilt	7	51
N17		VMI	0	33
N24	● |	Mississippi	10	0
N29	● |	at Kentucky	18	0

1924 — 3-5-0 (0-4-0)

O4	●	Emory & Henry	27	0
O11	●	Maryville	28	10
O18	●	Carson-Newman	13	0
O25	|	Mississippi State Mem	2	7
N1	|	at Georgia	0	33
N8		Centre	0	32
N15	|	at Tulane	7	26
N27	|	Kentucky	6	27

1925 — 5-2-1 (2-2-1)

O3	●	Emory & Henry	51	0
O10	●	Maryville	13	0
O17	|	at Vanderbilt	7	34
O24	= |	LSU	0	0
O31	● |	Georgia	12	7
N7	●	at Centre	12	0
N14	● |	Mississippi State	14	9
N26	|	at Kentucky	20	23

ROBERT R. NEYLAND
1926-34, '36-40, '46-52 (.829) 173-31-12

1926 — 8-1-0 (5-1-0)

S25	●	Carson-Newman	13	0
O2	● |	North Carolina	34	0
O9	● |	at LSU	14	7
O15	●	Maryville	6	0
O23	●	Centre	30	7
O30	● |	at Mississippi State	33	0
N6	● |	Sewanee	12	0
N13	|	at Vanderbilt	3	20
N25	● |	Kentucky	6	0

1927 — 8-0-1 (5-0-1)

S24	●	Carson-Newman	33	0
O1	● |	at North Carolina	26	0
O8	●	Maryville	7	0
O15	● |	Mississippi	21	7
O22	●	Transylvania, Ky	57	0
O29	● |	Virginia	42	0
N5	● |	Sewanee	32	12
N12	= |	Vanderbilt	7	7
N24	● |	at Kentucky	20	0

1928 — 9-0-1 (6-0-1)

S29	●	Maryville	41	0
O6	●	Centre	41	7
O13	● |	Mississippi	13	12
O20	● |	at Alabama	15	13
O27	● |	Wash. & Lee	26	7
N3	●	Carson-Newman	57	0
N10	● |	Sewanee	37	0
N17	● |	at Vanderbilt	6	0
N29	= |	Kentucky	0	0
D8	● |	Florida	13	12

1929 — 9-0-1 (6-0-1)

S28	●	Centre	40	6
O5	●	at U.T. Chattanooga	20	0
O12	● |	Mississippi	52	7
O19	● |	Alabama	6	0
O26	● |	Wash. & Lee Roa	30	0
N2	● |	Auburn	27	0
N9	●	Carson-Newman	73	0
N16	● |	Vanderbilt	13	0
N28	= |	at Kentucky	6	6
D7	● |	South Carolina	54	0

1930 — 9-1-0 (6-1-0)

S27	●	Maryville	54	0
O4	●	at Centre	18	0
O11	● |	Mississippi	27	0
O18	|	at Alabama	6	18
O25	● |	North Carolina	9	7
N1	● |	Clemson	27	0
N8	●	Carson-Newman	34	0
N15	● |	at Vanderbilt	13	0
N27	● |	Kentucky	8	0
D6	● |	Florida JacF	13	6

1931 — 9-0-1 (6-0-1)

S26	● |	Maryville	33	0
O3	● |	Clemson	44	0
O10	● |	Mississippi	38	0
O17	● |	Alabama	25	0
O24	● |	at North Carolina	7	0
O31	● |	Duke	25	2
N7	●	Carson-Newman	31	0
N14	● |	Vanderbilt	21	7
N26	= |	at Kentucky	6	6
D6	●	NYU Brnx	13	0

1932 — 9-0-1 (7-0-1)

S24	●	at U.T. Chattanooga	13	0
O1	● |	Mississippi	33	0
O8	● |	North Carolina	20	7
O15	● |	Alabama Birm	7	3
O22	●	Maryville	60	0
O29	● |	Duke	16	13
N5	● |	Mississippi State	31	0
N12	= |	at Vanderbilt	0	0
N24	● |	Kentucky	26	0
D3	● |	Florida JacF	32	13

1933-PRESENT
SOUTHEASTERN

1933 — 7-3-0

S30	●	Virginia Tech	27	0
O7	● |	Mississippi State	20	0
O14		at Duke	2	10
O21	|	Alabama	6	12
O28	● |	Florida	13	6
N4	●	at George Washington	13	0
N11	● |	Mississippi	35	6
N18	● |	Vanderbilt	33	6
N30	● |	at Kentucky	27	0
D9	|	at LSU	0	7

1934 — 8-2-0 (5-1-0)

S29	●	Centre	32	0
O6	●	at North Carolina	19	7
O13	● |	Mississippi	27	0
O20	|	Alabama Birm	6	13
O27	●	Duke	14	6
N3		Fordham NYC	12	13
N10	● |	Mississippi State	14	0
N17	● |	at Vanderbilt	13	6
N29	● |	Kentucky	19	0
D8	● |	LSU	19	13

W.H. BRITTON
1935 (.444) 4-5

1935 — 4-5-0 (2-3-0)

S28	●	Southwestern	20	0
O5		North Carolina	13	38
O12	● |	Auburn Birm	13	6
O19	|	Alabama	0	25
O26	●	Centre	25	14
N2		at Duke	6	19
N9	● |	Mississippi Mem	14	13
N16	|	Vanderbilt	7	13
N28	|	at Kentucky	0	27

ROBERT R. NEYLAND

1936 — 6-2-2 (3-1-2)

S26	●	U.T. Chattanooga	13	0
O3		at North Carolina	6	14
O10	|	Auburn	0	6
O17	= |	Alabama Birm	0	0
O24	●	Duke	15	13
O31	● |	at Georgia	46	0
N7	●	Maryville	34	0
N14	● |	at Vanderbilt	26	13
N26	● |	Kentucky	7	6
D5	= |	Mississippi Mem	0	0

1937 — 6-3-1 (4-3-0)

S25	●	Wake Forest	32	0
O2	●	Virginia Tech	27	0
O9	=	at Duke	0	0
O16	|	Alabama	7	14
O23	● |	Sewanee	32	0
O30	● |	Georgia	32	0
N6	|	Auburn Birm	7	20
N13	|	Vanderbilt	7	13
N25	● |	at Kentucky	13	0
D4	● |	Mississippi Mem	32	0

1938 — 11-0-0 (7-0-0)

S24	● |	Sewanee	26	3
O1	●	Clemson	20	7
O8	● |	Auburn	7	0
O15	● |	Alabama Birm	13	0
O22	●	Citadel	44	0
O29	● |	LSU	14	6
N5	●	U.T. Chattanooga	45	0
N12	● |	at Vanderbilt	14	0
N24	● |	Kentucky	46	0
D3	● |	Mississippi Mem	47	0
		ORANGE BOWL		
J2	●	Oklahoma	17	0

1939 — 10-1-0 (6-0-0)

S29	●	at North Carolina St.	13	0
O7	● |	Sewanee	40	0
O14	●	at U.T. Chattanooga	28	0
O21	● |	Alabama	21	0
O28	●	Mercer	17	0
N4	● |	at LSU	20	0
N11	●	Citadel	34	0
N18	● |	Vanderbilt	13	0
N30	● |	at Kentucky	19	0
D9	● |	Auburn	7	0
		ROSE BOWL		
J1		Southern Cal	0	14

1940 — 10-1-0 (5-0-0)

S28	●	Mercer	49	0
O5	●	Duke	13	0
O12	●	U.T. Chattanooga	53	0
O19	● |	Alabama Birm	27	12
O26	● |	Florida	14	0
N2	● |	LSU	28	0
N9	●	at Southwestern	41	0
N16	●	Virginia	41	14
N23	● |	Kentucky	33	0
N30	● |	at Vanderbilt	20	0
		SUGAR BOWL		
J1		Boston College	13	19

JOHN BARNHILL
1941-45 (.846) 32-5-2

1941 — 8-2-0 (3-1-0)

S20	●	Furman	32	6
O4		at Duke	0	19
O11	●	Dayton	26	0
O18	|	Alabama	2	9
O25	●	Cincinnati	21	6
N1	● |	at LSU	13	6
N8	●	Samford	28	6
N15	●	at Boston College	14	7
N22	● |	at Kentucky	20	7
N29	● |	Vanderbilt	26	7

1942 — 9-1-1 (4-1-0)

S26	=	at South Carolina	0	0
O3	●	Fordham	0	14
O10	●	Dayton	34	6
O17	|	Alabama Birm	0	8
O24	●	Furman	52	7
O31	● |	LSU	26	0
N7	●	Cincinnati	34	12
N14	● |	Mississippi Mem	14	0
N21	● |	Kentucky	26	0
N28	● |	at Vanderbilt	19	7
		SUGAR BOWL		
J1	●	Tulsa	14	7

1943

NO TEAM WWII

1944 — 7-1-1 (5-0-1)

S30	● |	Kentucky	26	13
O7	● |	Mississippi Mem	20	7
O14	● |	Florida	40	0
O21	= |	Alabama	0	0
O28	●	Clemson	26	7
N4	● |	at LSU	13	0
N18	●	Temple	27	14
N25	● |	at Kentucky	21	7
		ROSE BOWL		
J1		Southern Cal	0	25

1945 — 8-1-0 (3-1-0)

S29	●	Wake Forest	7	6
O6	●	William & Mary	48	13
O13	●	U.T. Chattanooga	30	0
O20	|	Alabama Birm	7	25
O27	●	Villanova	33	2
N3	●	North Carolina	20	6
N10	● |	Mississippi Mem	34	0
N24	● |	at Kentucky	14	0
D1	● |	Vanderbilt	45	0

ROBERT R. NEYLAND

1946 — 9-2-0 (5-0-0)

S28	● |	Georgia Tech	13	9
O5	●	at Duke	12	7
O12	●	U.T. Chattanooga	47	7
O19	● |	Alabama	12	0
O26		Wake Forest	6	19
N2	●	North Carolina	20	14
N9	● |	Mississippi Mem	18	14
N16	●	at Boston College	33	13
N23	● |	Kentucky	7	0
N30	● |	at Vanderbilt	7	6
		ORANGE BOWL		
J1		Rice	0	8

1947 — 5-5-0 (2-3-0)

S27	|	at Georgia Tech	0	27
O4		Duke	7	19
O11	●	U.T. Chattanooga	26	7
O18	|	Alabama Birm	0	10
O25	●	Tennessee Tech	49	0
N1		at North Carolina	6	20
N8	|	Mississippi Mem	13	43
N15	●	Boston College	38	13
N22	● |	at Kentucky	13	6
N29	● |	Vanderbilt	12	7

1948 — 4-4-2 (2-3-1)

S25	|	Mississippi State	6	21
O2	=	at Duke	7	7
O9	●	U.T. Chattanooga	26	0
O16	● |	Alabama	21	6
O23	●	Tennessee Tech	41	0
O30		North Carolina	7	14
N6	● |	at Georgia Tech	13	6
N13	|	Mississippi Mem	13	16
N20	= |	Kentucky	0	0
N27	|	at Vanderbilt	6	28

1949 — 7-2-1 (4-1-1)

S24	● |	Mississippi State	10	0
O1		Duke	7	21
O8	●	U.T. Chattanooga	39	7
O15	= |	Alabama Birm	7	7
O22	●	Tennessee Tech	36	6
O29	●	at North Carolina	35	6
N5	|	Georgia Tech	13	30
N12	● |	Mississippi Mem	35	7
N19	● |	at Kentucky	6	0
N26	● |	Vanderbilt	26	20

1950 — 11-1-0 (4-1-0)

S23	●	Southern Miss	56	0
S30	|	at Mississippi State	0	7
O7	●	at Duke	28	7
O14	●	U.T. Chattanooga	41	0
O21	● |	Alabama	14	9
O28	●	Wash. & Lee	27	20
N4	●	North Carolina	16	0
N11	●	Tennessee Tech	48	14
N18	● |	Mississippi	35	0
N25	● |	Kentucky	7	0
D2	● |	at Vanderbilt	43	0
		COTTON BOWL		
J1	●	Texas	20	14

1951 — 10-1-0 (5-0-0)

S29	● |	Mississippi State	14	0
O6	●	Duke	26	0
O13	●	U.T. Chattanooga	42	13
O20	● |	Alabama Birm	27	13
O27	●	Tennessee Tech	68	0
N3	●	at North Carolina	27	0
N10	●	Wash. & Lee	60	14
N17	● |	at Mississippi	46	21
N24	● |	at Kentucky	28	0
D1	● |	Vanderbilt	35	27
		SUGAR BOWL		
J1		Maryland	13	28

1952 — 8-2-1 (5-0-1)

S27	● |	Mississippi State Mem	14	7
O4		at Duke	0	7
O11	●	U.T. Chattanooga	26	6
O18	● |	Alabama	20	0
O25	●	Wofford	50	0
N1	●	North Carolina	41	14
N8	● |	at LSU	22	3
N15	● |	Florida	26	12
N22	= |	Kentucky	14	14
N29	● |	at Vanderbilt	46	0
		COTTON BOWL		
J1		Texas	0	16

THE SCHOOLS

HARVEY ROBINSON
1953-54 (.500)   10-10-1

1953   6-4-1 (3-2-1)
S26		Mississippi State	0 26
O3		Duke	7 21
O10	●	U.T. Chattanooga	40 7
O17	=	Alabama *Birm*	0 0
O24	●	Louisville	59 6
O31	●	at North Carolina	20 6
N7	●	LSU	32 14
N14	●	at Florida	9 7
N21		at Kentucky	21 27
N28	●	Vanderbilt	33 6
D5		at Houston	19 33

1954   4-6-0 (1-5-0)
S25	●	Mississippi State *Mem*	19 7
O2		at Duke	6 7
O9	●	U.T. Chattanooga	20 14
O16		Alabama	0 27
O23	●	Dayton	14 7
O30	●	North Carolina	26 20
N6		at Georgia Tech	7 28
N13		Florida	0 14
N20		Kentucky	13 14
N27		at Vanderbilt	0 26

BOWDEN WYATT
1955-62 (.622)   49-29-4

1955   6-3-1 (3-2-1)
S24		Mississippi State	7 13
O1		Duke	0 21
O8	●	U.T. Chattanooga	13 0
O15	●	Alabama *Birm*	20 0
O22	●	Dayton	53 7
O29	●	at North Carolina	48 7
N5	=	Georgia Tech	7 7
N12	●	at Florida	20 0
N19		at Kentucky	0 23
N26	●	Vanderbilt	20 14

1956   10-1-0 (6-0-0)
S29	●	Auburn *Birm*	35 7
O6	●	at Duke	33 20
O13	●	U.T. Chattanooga	42 20
O20	●	Alabama	24 0
O27	●	Maryland	34 7
N3	●	North Carolina	20 0
N10	●	at Georgia Tech	6 0
N17	●	Mississippi	27 7
N24	●	Kentucky	20 7
D1	●	at Vanderbilt	27 7
	SUGAR BOWL		
J1		Baylor	7 13

1957   8-3-0 (4-3-0)
S28		Auburn	0 7
O5	●	Tennessee State	14 9
O12	●	U.T. Chattanooga	28 13
O19		Alabama *Birm*	14 0
O26	●	at Maryland	16 0
N2	●	at North Carolina	35 0
N9	●	Georgia Tech	21 6
N16		Mississippi *Mem*	7 14
N23		at Kentucky	6 20
N30	●	Vanderbilt	20 6
	GATOR BOWL		
D28	●	Texas A&M	3 0

1958   4-6-0 (4-3-0)
S27		Auburn *Birm*	0 13
O4	●	Mississippi State *Mem*	13 8
O11		at Georgia Tech	7 21
O18	●	Alabama	14 7
O25		Florida State	0 10
N1		North Carolina	7 21
N8		U.T. Chattanooga	6 14
N15	●	Mississippi	18 16
N22		Kentucky	2 6
N29	●	at Vanderbilt	10 6

1959   5-4-1 (3-4-1)
S26	●	Auburn	3 0
O3	●	Mississippi State	22 6
O10		Georgia Tech	7 14
O17	=	Alabama *Birm*	7 7
O24	●	U.T. Chattanooga	23 0
O31	●	at North Carolina	29 7
N7	●	LSU	14 13
N14		Mississippi *Mem*	7 37
N21		at Kentucky	0 20
N28		Vanderbilt	0 14

1960   6-2-2 (3-2-2)
S24	●	Auburn *Birm*	10 3
O1	=	Mississippi State *Mem*	0 0
O8	●	Tampa	62 7
O15	●	Alabama	20 7
O22	●	U.T. Chattanooga	35 0
O29	●	North Carolina	27 14
N5		at Georgia Tech	7 14
N12		Mississippi	3 24
N19	●	Kentucky	10 10
N26	●	at Vanderbilt	35 0

1961   6-4-0 (4-3-0)
S30		Auburn	21 24
O7	●	Mississippi State	17 3
O14	●	Tulsa	52 6
O21		Alabama *Birm*	3 34
O28	●	U.T. Chattanooga	20 7
N4		at North Carolina	21 22
N11	●	Georgia Tech	10 6
N18		Mississippi *Mem*	10 24
N25	●	at Kentucky	26 16
D2	●	Vanderbilt	41 7

1962   4-6-0 (2-6-0)
S29		Auburn *Birm*	21 22
O6		Mississippi State *Mem*	6 7
O13		at Georgia Tech	0 17
O20		Alabama	7 27
O27	●	U.T. Chattanooga	48 14
N3	●	Wake Forest	23 0
N10	●	Tulane	28 16
N17		Mississippi	6 19
N24		Kentucky	10 12
D1	●	at Vanderbilt	30 0

JIM McDONALD
1963 (.500)   5-5

1963   5-5-0 (3-5-0)
S21		Richmond	34 6
S28		Auburn	19 23
O5		Mississippi State	0 7
O12		Georgia Tech	7 23
O19		Alabama *Birm*	0 35
O26	●	U.T. Chattanooga	49 7
N9	●	at Tulane	26 0
N16		Mississippi *Mem*	0 20
N23		at Kentucky	19 0
N30	●	Vanderbilt	14 0

DOUG DICKEY
1964-69 (.738)   46-15-4

1964   4-5-1 (1-5-1)
S19	●	U.T. Chattanooga	10 6
S26		Auburn *Birm*	0 3
O3	●	Mississippi State *Mem*	14 13
O10	●	Boston College	16 14
O17		Alabama	8 19
O24	=	at LSU	3 3
N7	●	at Georgia Tech	22 14
N14		Mississippi	0 30
N21	●	Kentucky	7 12
N28		at Vanderbilt	0 7

1965   8-1-2 (3-1-2)
S18	●	Army	21 0
S25	●	Auburn	13 13
O9	‖	South Carolina	24 3
O16	=	Alabama *Birm*	7 7
O23	●	Houston	17 8
N6	●	Georgia Tech	21 7
N13		Mississippi *Mem*	13 14
N20	●	at LSU	19 3
N27	●	Vanderbilt	21 3
D4	●	UCLA *Mem*	37 34
	BLUEBONNET BOWL		
D18	●	Tulsa	27 6

1966   8-3-0 (4-2-0)
S24	●	Auburn *Birm*	28 0
O1	●	Rice	23 3
O8		at Georgia Tech	3 6
O15		Alabama	10 11
O22	‖	South Carolina	29 17
O29	●	Army	38 7
N5	●	U.T. Chattanooga	28 10
N12		Mississippi	7 14
N19	●	Kentucky	28 19
N26	●	at Vanderbilt	28 0
	GATOR BOWL		
D31	●	Syracuse	18 12

1967   9-2-0 (6-0-0)
S16		at UCLA	16 20
S30	●	Auburn	27 13
O14	●	Georgia Tech	24 13
O21	●	Alabama *Birm*	24 13
O28	●	LSU	17 14
N4	●	at Tampa	38 0
N11	●	Tulane	35 14
N18	●	Mississippi *Mem*	20 7
N25	●	at Kentucky	17 7
D2	●	Vanderbilt	41 14
	ORANGE BOWL		
J1		Oklahoma	24 26

1968   8-2-1 (4-1-1)
S14	=	Georgia	17 17
S28	●	Memphis	24 17
O5	●	at Rice	52 0
O12	●	at Georgia Tech	24 7
O19	●	Alabama	10 9
N2	●	UCLA	42 18
N9	●	Auburn *Birm*	14 28
N16	●	Mississippi	31 0
N23	●	Kentucky	24 7
N30	●	at Vanderbilt	10 7
	COTTON BOWL		
J1		Texas	13 36

1969   9-2-0 (5-1-0)
S20	●	U.T. Chattanooga	31 0
S27	●	Auburn	45 19
O4	●	at Memphis	55 16
O11	●	Georgia Tech	26 8
O18	●	Alabama *Birm*	41 14
N1	●	at Georgia	17 3
N8	●	South Carolina	29 14
N15		Mississippi *JaM*	0 38
N22	●	at Kentucky	31 26
N29	●	Vanderbilt	40 27
	GATOR BOWL		
D27		Florida	13 14

BILL BATTLE
1970-76 (.723)   59-22-2

1970   11-1-0 (4-1-0)
S19	●	SMU	28 3
S26		Auburn *Birm*	23 36
O3	●	Army	48 3
O10	●	at Georgia Tech	17 6
O17	●	Alabama	24 0
O24	●	Florida	38 7
O31	●	Wake Forest *Mem*	41 7
N7	●	at South Carolina	20 18
N21	●	Kentucky	45 0
N28	●	at Vanderbilt	24 6
D5	●	UCLA	28 17
	SUGAR BOWL		
J1	●	Air Force	34 13

1971   10-2-0 (4-2-0)
S18	●	Santa Barbara	48 6
S25	●	Auburn	9 10
O2	●	at Florida	20 13
O9	●	Georgia Tech	10 6
O16	●	Alabama *Birm*	15 32
O23	●	Mississippi State *Mem*	10 7
O30	●	Tulsa	38 3
N6	●	South Carolina	35 6
N20	●	at Kentucky	21 7
N27	●	Vanderbilt	19 7
D4	●	Penn State	31 11
	LIBERTY BOWL		
D20	●	Arkansas	14 13

1972   10-2-0 (4-2-0)
S9	●	at Georgia Tech	34 3
S16	●	Penn State	28 21
S23	●	Wake Forest	45 6
S30		Auburn *Birm*	6 10
O7	●	at Memphis	38 7
O21	●	Alabama	10 17
O28	●	Hawaii	34 2
N4	●	at Georgia	14 0
N18	●	Mississippi	17 0
N25	●	Kentucky	17 7
D2	●	at Vanderbilt	30 10
	BLUEBONNET BOWL		
D30	●	LSU	24 17

1973   8-4-0 (3-3-0)
S15	●	Duke	21 17
S22	●	at Army	37 18
S29	●	Auburn	21 0
O6		Kansas *Mem*	28 27
O13	●	Georgia Tech	20 14
O20		Alabama *Birm*	21 42
O27	●	TCU	39 7
N3		Georgia	31 35
N17	●	Mississippi *JaM*	18 28
N24	●	at Kentucky	16 14
D1	●	Vanderbilt	20 17
	GATOR BOWL		
D29		Texas Tech	19 28

1974   7-3-2 (2-3-1)
S7	=	UCLA	17 17
S21	●	Kansas	17 3
S28		at Auburn	0 21
O5	●	Tulsa	17 10
O12		at LSU	10 20
O19		Alabama	6 28
O26	=	Clemson	29 28
N9	●	Memphis	34 6
N16	●	Mississippi *Mem*	29 17
N23	●	Kentucky	24 7
N30	=	at Vanderbilt	21 21
	LIBERTY BOWL		
D16	●	Maryland	7 3

1975   7-5-0 (3-3-0)
S13	●	Maryland	26 8
S20	●	at UCLA	28 34
S27	●	Auburn	21 17
O11	●	LSU	24 10
O18	●	Alabama *Birm*	7 30
O25	●	North Texas	14 21
N1	●	Colorado State	28 5
N8	●	Utah	40 7
N15		Mississippi *Mem*	6 23
N22	●	at Kentucky	17 13
N29	●	Vanderbilt	14 17
D6	●	at Hawaii	28 6

1976   6-5-0 (2-4-0)
S11	●	Duke	18 21
S18	●	TCU	31 0
S25	●	Auburn *Birm*	28 38
O2	●	Clemson	21 19
O9	●	at Georgia Tech	42 7
O16	●	Alabama	13 20
O23	●	Florida	18 20
N6	●	at Memphis	21 14
N13	●	Mississippi	32 6
N20	●	Kentucky	0 7
N27	●	at Vanderbilt	13 10

JOHNNY MAJORS
1977-92 (.645)   116-62-8

1977   4-7-0 (1-5-0)
S10		California	17 27
S17	●	Boston College	24 18
S24	●	Auburn	12 14
O1	●	Oregon State	41 10
O8	●	Georgia Tech	8 24
O15	●	Alabama *Birm*	10 24
O22	●	at Florida	17 27
N5	●	Memphis	27 14
N12		Mississippi *Mem*	14 43
N19	●	at Kentucky	17 21
N26	●	Vanderbilt	42 7

1978   5-5-1 (3-3-0)
S16		UCLA	0 13
S23	=	Oregon State	13 13
S30	●	Auburn *Birm*	10 29
O7	●	Army	31 13
O21	●	Alabama	17 30
O28	●	Mississippi State *Mem*	21 34
N4	●	Duke	34 0
N11	●	at Notre Dame	14 31
N18	●	Mississippi	41 17
N25	●	Kentucky	29 14
D2	●	at Vanderbilt	41 15

1979   7-5-0 (3-3-0)
S15	●	at Boston College	28 16
S22	●	Utah	51 18
S29	●	Auburn	35 17
O6		Mississippi State *Mem*	9 28
O13		Georgia Tech	31 0
O20		Alabama *Birm*	17 27
N3		Rutgers	7 13
N10	●	Notre Dame	40 18
N17	●	Mississippi *JaM*	20 44
N24	●	at Kentucky	20 17
D1	●	Vanderbilt	31 10
	BLUEBONNET BOWL		
D31	●	Purdue	22 27

1980   5-6-0 (3-3-0)

S6	Georgia	15	16
S13	Southern Cal	17	20
S20	Washington State	35	23
S27 ●	at Auburn	42	0
O11 ●	at Georgia Tech	23	10
O18	Alabama	0	27
O25	Pittsburgh	6	30
N1	Virginia	13	16
N15 ●	Mississippi *Mem*	9	20
N22 ●	Kentucky	45	14
N29 ●	at Vanderbilt	51	13

1981   8-4-0 (3-3-0)

S5	at Georgia	0	44
S12	at Southern Cal	7	43
S19	Colorado State	42	0
S26 ●	Auburn	10	7
O10	Georgia Tech	10	7
O17	Alabama *Birm*	19	38
O24 ●	at Memphis	28	9
N7	Wichita St.	24	21
N14 ●	Mississippi	28	20
N21 ●	at Kentucky	10	21
N28 ●	Vanderbilt	38	34
GARDEN STATE BOWL			
D13 ●	Wisconsin	28	21

1982   6-5-1 (3-2-1)

S4	Duke	24	25
S11	Iowa State	23	21
S25	at Auburn	14	24
O2 ●	Washington State	10	3
O9 =	at LSU	24	24
O16 ●	Alabama	35	28
O23	at Georgia Tech	21	31
N6 ●	Memphis	29	3
N13 ●	Mississippi *JaM*	30	17
N20 ●	Kentucky	28	7
N27 ●	at Vanderbilt	21	28
PEACH BOWL			
D31	Iowa	22	28

1983   9-3-0 (4-2-0)

S3	Pittsburgh	3	13
S10 ●	New Mexico	31	6
S24 ●	Auburn	14	37
O1 ●	Citadel *Mem*	45	6
O8 ●	LSU	20	6
O15 ●	Alabama *Birm*	41	34
O22 ●	Georgia Tech	37	3
O29 ●	Rutgers *ERut*	7	0
N12	Mississippi	10	13
N19 ●	at Kentucky	10	0
N26 ●	Vanderbilt	34	24
CITRUS BOWL			
D17 ●	Maryland	30	23

1984   7-4-1 (3-3-0)

S1 ●	Washington State	34	27
S15 ●	Utah	27	21
S22 =	Army	24	24
S29 ●	at Auburn	10	29
O13 ●	Florida	30	43
O20 ●	Alabama	28	27
O27 ●	at Georgia Tech	24	21
N10 ●	Memphis	41	9
N17 ●	Mississippi *JaM*	41	17
N24	Kentucky	12	17
D1 ●	at Vanderbilt	29	13
SUN BOWL			
D22 ●	Maryland	27	28

1985   9-1-2 (5-1-0)

S14 =	UCLA	26	26
S28 ●	Auburn	38	20
O5 ●	Wake Forest	31	29
O12 ●	at Florida	10	17
O19 ●	Alabama *Birm*	16	14
O26 ●	Georgia Tech	6	6
N2 ●	Rutgers	40	0
N9 ●	at Memphis	17	7
N16 ●	Mississippi	34	14
N23 ●	at Kentucky	42	0
N30 ●	Vanderbilt	30	0
SUGAR BOWL			
J1 ●	Miami, Fla.	35	7

1986   7-5-0 (3-3-0)

S6 ●	New Mexico	35	21
S13 ●	Mississippi State	23	27
S27 ●	at Auburn	8	34
O4 ●	Texas-El Paso	26	16
O11 ●	Army	21	25
O18 ●	Alabama	28	56
O25 ●	at Georgia Tech	13	14
N8 ●	Memphis	33	3
N15 ●	Mississippi *JaM*	22	10
N22 ●	Kentucky	28	9
N29 ●	at Vanderbilt	35	20
LIBERTY BOWL			
D29 ●	Minnesota	21	14

1987   10-2-1 (4-1-1)

A30 ●	Iowa *ERut*	23	22
S5 ●	Colorado State	49	3
S12 ●	at Mississippi State	38	10
S26 =	Auburn	20	20
O3 ●	California	38	12
O17 ●	Alabama *Birm*	22	41
O24 ●	Georgia Tech	29	15
O31 ●	at Boston College	18	20
N7 ●	Louisville	41	10
N14 ●	Mississippi	55	13
N21 ●	at Kentucky	24	22
N28 ●	Vanderbilt	38	36
PEACH BOWL			
J2 ●	Indiana	27	22

1988   5-6-0 (3-4-0)

S3 ●	at Georgia	17	28
S10 ●	Duke	26	31
S17 ●	LSU	9	34
S24 ●	at Auburn	6	38
O1 ●	Washington State	24	52
O15 ●	Alabama	20	28
O22 ●	at Memphis	38	25
N5 ●	Boston College	10	7
N12 ●	at Mississippi	20	12
N19 ●	Kentucky	28	24
N26 ●	at Vanderbilt	14	7

1989   11-1-0 (6-1-0)

S2 ●	Colorado State	17	14
S9 ●	at UCLA	24	6
S16 ●	Duke	28	6
S30 ●	Auburn	21	14
O7 ●	Georgia	17	14
O21 ●	Alabama *Birm*	30	47
O28 ●	at LSU	45	39
N11 ●	Akron	52	9
N18 ●	Mississippi	33	21
N25 ●	at Kentucky	31	10
D2 ●	Vanderbilt	17	10
COTTON BOWL			
J1 ●	Arkansas	31	27

1990   9-2-2 (5-1-1)

A26 =	Colorado *ANA*	31	31
S1 ●	Pacific	55	7
S8 ●	at Mississippi State	40	7
S15 ●	Texas-El Paso	56	0
S29 =	at Auburn	26	26
O13 ●	Florida	45	3
O20 ●	Alabama	6	9
N3 ●	Temple	41	20
N10 ●	Notre Dame	29	34
N17 ●	Mississippi	22	13
N24 ●	Kentucky	42	28
D1 ●	at Vanderbilt	49	20
SUGAR BOWL			
J1 ●	Virginia	23	22

1991   9-3-0 (5-2-0)

S5 ●	at Louisville	28	11
S14 ●	UCLA	30	16
S21 ●	Mississippi State	26	24
S28 ●	Auburn	30	21
O12 ●	at Florida	18	35
O19 ●	Alabama *Birm*	19	24
N2 ●	Memphis	52	24
N9 ●	at Notre Dame	35	34
N16 ●	Mississippi	36	25
N23 ●	at Kentucky	16	7
N30 ●	Vanderbilt	45	0
FIESTA BOWL			
J1	Penn State	17	42

PHILLIP FULMER
1992–Present (.795) 122-31-1

1992   9-3-0 (5-3-0)

S5 ●	La. Lafayette	38	3
S12 ●	at Georgia	34	31
S19 ●	Florida	31	14
S26 ●	Cincinnati	40	0
O3 ●	at LSU	20	0
O10 ●	Arkansas	24	25
O17 ●	Alabama	10	17
O31 ●	at South Carolina	23	24
N14 ●	at Memphis	26	21
N21 ●	Kentucky	34	13
N28 ●	at Vanderbilt	29	25
HALL OF FAME BOWL			
J1 ●	Boston College	38	23

1993   9-2-1 (6-1-1)

S4 ●	Louisiana Tech	50	0
S11 ●	Georgia	38	6
S18 ●	at Florida	34	41
S25 ●	LSU	42	20
O2 ●	Duke	52	19
O9 ●	Arkansas *LR*	28	14
O16 =	Alabama *Birm*	17	17 †
O30 ●	South Carolina	55	3
N6 ●	Louisville	45	10
N20 ●	at Kentucky	48	0
N27 ●	Vanderbilt	62	14
CITRUS BOWL			
J1	Penn State	13	31

1994   8-4-0 (5-3-0)

S3 ●	at UCLA	23	25
S10 ●	at Georgia	41	23
S17 ●	Florida	0	31
S24 ●	at Mississippi State	21	24
O1 ●	Washington State	10	9
O8 ●	Arkansas	38	21
O15 ●	Alabama	13	17
O29 ●	at South Carolina	31	22
N12 ●	Memphis	24	13
N19 ●	Kentucky	52	0
N26 ●	at Vanderbilt	65	0
GATOR BOWL			
D30 ●	Virginia Tech	45	23

1995   11-1-0 (7-1-0)

S2 ●	East Carolina	27	7
S9 ●	Georgia	30	27
S16 ●	at Florida	37	62
S23 ●	Mississippi State	52	14
S30 ●	Oklahoma State	31	0
O7 ●	at Arkansas	49	31
O14 ●	Alabama *Birm*	41	14
O28 ●	South Carolina	56	21
N4 ●	Southern Miss	42	0
N18 ●	at Kentucky	34	31
N25 ●	Vanderbilt	12	7
CITRUS BOWL			
J1 ●	Ohio State	20	14

1996   10-2 (7-1)

A31 ●	Nevada-Las Vegas	62	3
S7 ●	UCLA	35	20
S21 ●	Florida	29	35
O3 ●	Mississippi *Mem*	41	3
O12 ●	at Georgia	29	17
O26 ●	Alabama	20	13
N2 ●	at South Carolina	31	14
N9 ●	at Memphis	17	21
N16 ●	Arkansas	55	14
N23 ●	Kentucky	56	10
N30 ●	Vanderbilt	14	7
CITRUS BOWL			
J1 ●	Northwestern	48	28

1997   11-2 (7-1)

A30 ●	Texas Tech	52	17
S6 ●	at UCLA	30	24
S20 ●	at Florida	20	33
O4 ●	Mississippi	31	17
O11 ●	Georgia	38	13
O18 ●	Alabama *Birm*	38	21
N1 ●	South Carolina	22	7
N8 ●	Southern Miss	44	20
N15 ●	Arkansas *LR*	30	22
N22 ●	at Kentucky	59	31
N29 ●	Vanderbilt	17	10
SEC CHAMPIONSHIP GAME			
D6 ●	Auburn *Atl*	30	29
ORANGE BOWL			
J2	Nebraska	17	42

1998   13-0 (8-0)

S5 ●	at Syracuse	34	33
S19 ●	Florida	20	17
S26 ●	Houston	42	7
O3 ●	at Auburn	17	9
O10 ●	at Georgia	22	3
O24 ●	Alabama	35	18
O31 ●	at South Carolina	49	14
N7 ●	UAB	37	13
N14 ●	Arkansas	28	24
N21 ●	Kentucky	59	21
N28 ●	at Vanderbilt	41	0
SEC CHAMPIONSHIP GAME			
D5 ●	Mississippi State *Atl*	24	14
FIESTA BOWL			
J4 ●	Florida State	23	16

1999   9-3 (6-2)

S4 ●	Wyoming	42	17
S18 ●	at Florida	21	23
S25 ●	Memphis	17	16
O2 ●	Auburn	24	0
O9 ●	Georgia	37	20
O23 ●	at Alabama	21	7
O30 ●	South Carolina	30	7
N6 ●	Notre Dame	38	14
N13 ●	at Arkansas	24	28
N20 ●	at Kentucky	56	21
N27 ●	Vanderbilt	38	10
FIESTA BOWL			
J2 ●	Nebraska	21	31

2000   8-4 (5-3)

S2 ●	Southern Miss	19	16
S16 ●	Florida	23	27
S23 ●	La. Monroe	70	3
S30 ●	at LSU	31	38
O7 ●	at Georgia	10	21
O21 ●	Alabama	20	10
O28 ●	at South Carolina	17	14
N4 ●	at Memphis	19	17
N11 ●	Arkansas	63	20
N18 ●	Kentucky	59	20
N25 ●	at Vanderbilt	28	26
COTTON BOWL			
J1 ●	Kansas State	21	35

2001   11-2 (7-1)

S1 ●	Syracuse	33	9
S8 ●	at Arkansas	13	3
S29 ●	LSU	26	18
O6 ●	Georgia	24	26
O20 ●	at Alabama	35	24
O27 ●	South Carolina	17	10
N3 ●	at Notre Dame	28	18
N10 ●	Memphis	49	28
N17 ●	at Kentucky	38	35
N24 ●	Vanderbilt	38	0
D1 ●	at Florida	34	32
SEC CHAMPIONSHIP GAME			
D8 ●	LSU *Atl*	20	31
CITRUS BOWL			
J1 ●	Michigan	45	17

2002   8-5 (5-3)

A31 ●	Wyoming *Nash*	47	7
S7 ●	Middle Tennessee	26	3
S21 ●	Florida	13	30
S28 ●	Rutgers	35	14
O5 ●	Arkansas	41	38
O12 ●	at Georgia	13	18
O26 ●	Alabama	14	34
N2 ●	at South Carolina	18	10
N9 ●	Miami, Fla.	3	26
N16 ●	at Mississippi State	35	17
N23 ●	at Vanderbilt	24	0
N30 ●	Kentucky	24	0
PEACH BOWL			
D31 ●	Maryland	3	30

2003   10-3 (6-2)

A30 ●	Fresno State	24	6
S6 ●	Marshall	34	24
S20 ●	at Florida	24	10
S27 ●	South Carolina	23	20
O4 ●	at Auburn	21	28
O11 ●	Georgia	14	41
O25 ●	at Alabama	51	43
N1 ●	Duke	23	6
N8 ●	at Miami, Fla.	10	6
N15 ●	Mississippi State	59	21
N22 ●	Vanderbilt	48	0
N29 ●	at Kentucky	20	7
PEACH BOWL			
J2 ●	Clemson	14	27

2004   10-3 (7-1)

S5	●	Nevada-Las Vegas	42	17
S18	● |	Florida	30	28
S25	●	Louisiana Tech	42	17
O2	|	Auburn	10	34
O9	● |	at Georgia	19	14
O16	● |	at Mississippi	21	17
O23	● |	Alabama	17	13
O30	● |	at South Carolina	43	29
N6		Notre Dame	13	17
N20	● |	at Vanderbilt	38	33
N27	● |	Kentucky	37	31
		SEC CHAMPIONSHIP GAME		
D4		Auburn *Atl*	28	38
		COTTON BOWL		
J1	●	Texas A&M	38	7

THE SCHOOLS

TENNESSEE ANNUAL STATISTICAL LEADERS

YR	RUSHING	YDS	ATT	AVG	PASSING	ATT	CMP	PCT	YDS	RECEIVING	REC	YDS	AVG
1950	Andy Kozar	648	126	5.1	Hank Lauricella	72	23	.32	364	Bert Rechichar	9	205	22.8
1951	Hank Lauricella	881	111	7.9	Hank Lauricella	51	24	.47	352	John Davis	8	160	20.0
1952	Andy Kozar	660	122	5.4	Pat Shires	38	15	.39	252	John Davis	14	297	21.2
1953	Jimmy Wade	675	158	4.3	Jimmy Wade	63	25	.40	451	Jerry Hyde	8	173	21.6
1954	Tom Tracy	794	116	6.8	Johnny Majors	24	8	.33	107	Hugh Garner	5	57	11.4
1955	Johnny Majors	657	183	3.6	Johnny Majors	65	36	.55	476	Buddy Cruze	12	232	19.3
1956	Tommy Bronson	562	105	5.4	Johnny Majors	59	36	.61	552	Buddy Cruze	20	357	17.9
1957	Bobby Gordon	526	167	3.2	Bobby Gordon	40	20	.50	260	Tommy Potts	10	123	12.3
1958	Bill Majors	294	148	1.9	Bill Majors	25	17	.68	215	Murray Armstrong	14	195	13.9
1959	Glenn Glass	261	75	3.5	Gene Etter	36	22	.61	298	Cotton Letner	8	92	11.5
1960	Glenn Glass	478	90	5.3	Glenn Glass	26	11	.42	167	Ken Waddell	8	60	7.5
1961	Mallon Faircloth	475	123	3.9	Mallon Faircloth	52	31	.60	460	Hubert McClain	11	149	13.5
1962	George Canale	455	79	5.8	Bobby Morton	40	20	.50	305	John Bill Hudson	15	259	17.3
1963	Mallon Faircloth	652	137	4.8	Mallon Faircloth	75	31	.41	509	Buddy Fisher	12	242	20.2
1964	Stan Mitchell	325	94	3.5	Art Galiffa	59	29	.49	338	Hal Wantland	21	284	13.5
1965	Walter Chadwick	470	101	4.7	Dewey Warren	79	44	.56	588	Johnny Mills	23	328	14.3
1966	Charlie Fulton	463	109	4.2	Dewey Warren	229	136	.59	1,716	Johnny Mills	48	725	15.1
1967	Walter Chadwick	645	144	4.5	Dewey Warren	132	78	.59	1,053	Richmond Flowers	41	585	14.3
1968	Richard Pickens	736	133	5.5	Bubba Wyche	237	134	.57	1,539	Ken DeLong	34	393	11.6
1969	Curt Watson	807	146	5.5	Bobby Scott	191	92	.48	1,352	Gary Kreis	38	609	16.0
1970	Curt Watson	791	190	4.3	Bobby Scott	252	118	.47	1,697	Joe Thompson	37	502	13.6
1971	Curt Watson	766	193	4.0	Jim Maxwell	102	46	.45	544	Joe Thompson	15	247	16.5
1972	Haskel Stanback	890	183	4.9	Condredge Holloway	120	73	.61	807	Emmon Love	20	280	14.0
1973	Haskel Stanback	682	165	4.1	Condredge Holloway	154	89	.58	1,149	Stanley Morgan	22	511	23.2
1974	Stanley Morgan	723	128	5.6	Condredge Holloway	133	76	.57	1,146	Larry Seivers	25	347	13.9
1975	Stanley Morgan	809	133	6.1	Randy Wallace	145	72	.50	1,318	Larry Seivers	41	840	20.5
1976	Bobby Emmons	462	75	6.2	Randy Wallace	130	68	.52	1,046	Larry Seivers	51	737	14.5
1977	Kelsey Finch	770	154	5.0	Jimmy Streater	105	59	.56	742	Reggie Harper	30	331	11.0
1978	Jimmy Streater	593	146	4.1	Jimmy Streater	198	101	.51	1,418	Reggie Harper	31	356	11.5
1979	Hubert Simpson	792	157	5.0	Jimmy Streater	161	80	.50	1,256	Anthony Hancock	34	687	20.2
1980	James Berry	543	131	4.1	Steve Alatorre	119	58	.49	747	Anthony Hancock	33	580	17.6
1981	James Berry	500	129	3.9	Steve Alatorre	154	81	.53	1,171	Anthony Hancock	32	437	13.7
1982	Chuck Coleman	600	113	5.3	Alan Cockrell	294	174	.59	2,021	Willie Gault	50	668	13.4
1983	Johnnie Jones	1,116	191	5.8	Alan Cockrell	243	128	.53	1,683	Clyde Duncan	33	640	19.4
1984	Johnnie Jones	1,290	229	5.6	Tony Robinson	253	156	.62	1,963	Tim McGee	54	809	15.0
1985	Keith Davis	684	141	4.9	Tony Robinson	143	91	.64	1,246	Tim McGee	50	947	18.9
1986	William Howard	787	177	4.4	Jeff Francis	233	150	.64	1,946	Joey Clinkscales	37	511	13.8
1987	Reggie Cobb	1,197	237	5.1	Jeff Francis	201	121	.60	1,512	Thomas Woods	26	335	12.9
1988	Reggie Cobb	547	118	4.6	Jeff Francis	314	191	.61	2,237	Thomas Woods	58	689	11.9
1989	Chuck Webb	1,236	209	5.9	Andy Kelly	156	92	.59	1,299	Thomas Woods	34	511	15.0
1990	Tony Thompson	1,261	219	5.8	Andy Kelly	304	179	.59	2,241	Carl Pickens	53	917	17.3
1991	James Stewart	939	190	4.9	Andy Kelly	361	228	.63	2,759	Carl Pickens	49	877	17.9
1992	Charlie Garner	928	154	6.0	Heath Shuler	224	130	.58	1,712	Cory Fleming	40	490	12.3
1993	Charlie Garner	1,161	159	7.3	Heath Shuler	285	184	.65	2,353	Craig Faulkner	40	680	17.0
1994	James Stewart	1,028	170	6.1	Peyton Manning	144	89	.62	1,141	Joey Kent	36	470	13.1
1995	Jay Graham	1,438	272	5.3	Peyton Manning	380	244	.64	2,954	Joey Kent	69	1,055	15.3
1996	Jay Graham	797	179	4.6	Peyton Manning	380	243	.64	3,287	Joey Kent	68	1,080	15.9
1997	Jamal Lewis	1,364	232	5.9	Peyton Manning	477	287	.60	3,819	Marcus Nash	76	1,170	15.4
1998	Travis Henry	970	176	5.5	Tee Martin	267	153	.57	2,164	Peerless Price	61	920	15.1
1999	Jamal Lewis	816	182	4.5	Tee Martin	305	165	.54	2,317	Cedrick Wilson	57	827	14.5
2000	Travis Henry	1,314	253	5.2	Casey Clausen	194	121	.62	1,473	Cedrick Wilson	62	681	11.0
2001	Travis Stephens	1,464	291	5.0	Casey Clausen	354	227	.64	2,969	Kelley Washington	64	1,010	15.8
2002	Cedric Houston	779	153	5.1	Casey Clausen	310	194	.63	2,297	Jason Witten	39	493	12.6
2003	Cedric Houston	744	149	5.0	Casey Clausen	412	233	.57	2,968	James Banks	42	621	14.8
2004	Gerald Riggs	1,107	193	5.7	Erik Ainge	198	109	.55	1,452	Tony Brown	31	388	12.5

Receiving leaders by receptions

NCAA began including postseason stats in 2002

THE SCHOOLS

Texas

BY MARK WANGRIN

IN 1998, THE UNIVERSITY OF TEXAS kicked off a $1 billion fund-raising effort with a series of commercials featuring a voice-over by former student Walter Cronkite. At the end of each ad, the famous Cronkite voice would solemnly intone, "We're Texas."

The ads, according to the university, were designed to reflect "humor and humanity." Fine, but they also reflected the pride, even arrogance, that somehow always seems to kick in when Texans get to talking about their state's flagship university—and especially about its football team.

Problem is, since the 1976 retirement of resident deity and coaching legend Darrell Royal, who brought the school its only three national championships (in 1963, 1969 and 1970), the Longhorns spent almost three decades falling short of state expectations.

But in 2004, the Longhorns earned their first Bowl Championship Series berth after a string of cruel near misses. And on New Year's Day, UT scored 17 fourth-quarter points to beat Michigan 38-37 in one of the most thrilling Rose Bowls in history.

They're Texas.

TRADITION It might get you punched out in Italy, where extending the pinkie and index fingers from a closed fist is considered a particularly personal insult, but at Texas the Hook 'Em Horns signal is sacrosanct. Created by UT cheerleader Harley Clark in 1955, it signifies a steer's horns and is raised before and after games as 85,000 fans at Royal Memorial Stadium stand and sing "The Eyes of Texas." Game days are filled with pageantry, ranging from Smokey the Cannon, which fires two blank 10-gauge shotgun shells after each UT score, to performances featuring the Longhorn Band and Big Bertha, at 500 pounds and 54 inches in diameter the largest bass drum in the world.

BEST PLAYER After Royal retired in 1976, new coach Fred Akers installed an offense called the I-formation to showcase the talents of wishbone fullback Earl Campbell, who responded by running for 1,744 yards and 19 touchdowns in winning the 1977 Heisman Trophy. "A long time ago someone said to me, 'A person is not measured by

PROFILE

University of Texas
Austin, Texas
Founded: 1883
Enrollment: 39,916
Colors: Burnt Orange and White
Nickname: Longhorns
Stadium: Darrell K Royal-
Texas Memorial Stadium
    Opened in 1924
    TifSport Bermuda grass; 80,082 capacity
First football game: 1893
All-time record: 787–310–33 (.711)
Bowl record: 21–21–2
Consensus national championships, 1936-present: 3 (1963, 1969, 1970)
Big 12 Conference championships: 1 (outright)
Heisman Trophy: Earl Campbell, 1977; Ricky Williams, 1998
Outland Trophy: Scott Appleton, 1963; Tommy Nobis, 1965; Brad Shearer, 1977
First-round NFL draftees: 36
Website: www.texassports.com

THE BEST OF TIMES

From 1961 to 1970, Hall of Fame coach Darrell Royal guided Texas to an 89–17–2 record and three national titles.

THE WORST OF TIMES

1935-38. A school-record four straight losing seasons, three of two or fewer wins.

CONFERENCE

Texas was a charter member of the Southwest Conference in 1915. The Longhorns won 25 SWC titles between 1915 and 1994. Texas and fellow Southwest Conference members Texas A&M, Texas Tech and Baylor joined with the Big Eight to form the Big 12 in February 1994. In 1996, the Big 12's inaugural season, the Horns upset heavily favored Nebraska 37-27 to win the first conference title game.

DISTINGUISHED ALUMNI

Walter Cronkite; Tom Landry; Bill Moyers; James Baker, U.S. secretary of state; Marcia Gay Harden, actress; Matthew McConaughey, actor; Renee Zellweger, actress

FIGHT SONG

TEXAS FIGHT
Texas fight! Texas fight!
And it's goodbye to A&M
Texas fight! Texas fight!
And we'll put over one more win
Texas fight! Texas fight!
For it's Texas that we love best

Give 'em hell! Give 'em hell!
Go, Horns, Go!
And it's goodbye to all the rest

Yea orange, yea white,
Yea Longhorns, Fight-fight-fight!
Texas fight, Texas fight,
Yea, Texas fight
Texas fight, Texas fight,
Yea, Texas fight

the breaths he takes, but by the breathless moments he creates,'" said Akers. "And he has created more breathless moments than anybody I have ever been around."

BEST COACH In retrospect it sounded like the unthinkable: hire a hated Oklahoma Sooner to guide UT's football fortunes. But that's just what Texas did in December 1956 when it lured a 32-year-old former All-America quarterback (OU, 1946-49) away from Washington, where he was head coach. Folksy but tough, Darrell Royal turned out to be a pretty good fit. His teams won 76% of their games and captured three national titles. The key to his best years was the wishbone offense that he and offensive coordinator Emory Bellard unveiled in 1968. Royal retired after the 1976 season at the age of 52, young for a legend that's as large today as the stadium that now bears his name. "I didn't need to have my picture taken again, and I didn't need another trophy. Life's been good to me."

BEST TEAM The 1969 Longhorns, after a year of perfecting the nuances of the triple option, used it to roll to their second

> *It might get you punched in Italy, but in Texas the Hook 'Em Horns signal is sacrosanct.*

national title. Quarterback James Street, nicknamed Slick as much for his glib personality as his deft handling of the offense, spearheaded a powerful attack featuring three All-Americas—halfback Steve Worster, offensive tackle Bobby Wuensch and receiver Cotton Speyrer—that ran and ran and ran to a 10–0 record. In the Cotton Bowl, a Street-to-Speyrer pass on fourth-and-two at the Notre Dame 10-yard line on the game's last drive set up the winning touchdown. Final score: Texas 21, Notre Dame 17.

BIGGEST GAME Before the 1969 season, which marked the 100th anniversary of college football, ABC television executives approached administrators from Texas and Arkansas about moving their Oct. 18 game to the end of the season. At the time it was just a move to get a game for Dec. 6. By the end of November, it looked like pure genius. Texas was No. 1 in both polls; Arkansas was No. 2 in AP and No. 3 in UPI. "It makes them look wiser than a tree full of owls," said Royal, who in an off-the-cuff comment dubbed the game the Big Shootout. In front of a sellout crowd in

RECORDS

RUSHING YARDS
GAME
350   Ricky Williams vs. Iowa State, Oct. 3, 1998 (37 att.)
SEASON
2,124   Ricky Williams, 1998 (361 att.)
CAREER
6,279   Ricky Williams, 1995-98 (1,011 att.)

PASSING YARDS
GAME
419   Chris Simms vs. Nebraska, Nov. 2, 2002 (29 of 47)
SEASON
3,357   Major Applewhite, 1999 (271 of 467)
CAREER
8,353   Major Applewhite, 1998-2001 (611 of 1,065)

RECEIVING YARDS
GAME
198   Johnny "Lam" Jones, vs. Baylor, Nov. 24, 1979 (8 rec.)
SEASON
1,188   Kwame Cavil, 1999 (100 rec.)
CAREER
3,866   Roy Williams, 2000-03 (241 rec.)

POINTS
GAME
36   Ricky Williams vs. Rice, Sept. 26, 1998 (6 TDs); Williams vs. New Mexico State, Sept. 5, 1998 (6 TDs)
SEASON
168   Ricky Williams, 1998 (28 TDs)
CAREER
452   Ricky Williams, 1995-98 (75 TDs, 1 2-pt. conv.)

CONSENSUS ALL-AMERICANS

1945-46	Hub Bechtol, E
1947	Bobby Layne, B
1950	Bud McFadin, G
1953	Carlton Massey, E
1961	Jimmy Saxton, B
1962	Johnny Treadwell, G
1963	Scott Appleton, T
1965	Tommy Nobis, LB
1968	Chris Gilbert, B
1969	Bob McKay, T
1970	Bobby Wuensch, T
1970	Steve Worster, B
1970	Bill Atessis, DE
1971-72	Jerry Sisemore, T
1973	Bill Wyman, C
1973	Roosevelt Leaks, B
1975	Bob Simmons, T
1977	Earl Campbell, RB
1977	Brad Shearer, DL
1978-79	Johnnie Johnson, DB
1979	Steve McMichael, DL
1980-81	Kenneth Sims, DL
1981	Terry Tausch, OL
1983	Doug Dawson, OL

(Continued on next page)

Fayetteville that included President Richard Nixon and evangelist Billy Graham, the host Razorbacks held a 14-0 lead heading into the fourth quarter. But Street broke a 42-yard touchdown run and a two-point conversion, the Horns' first of the season. Later, facing fourth and three at the Texas 43 with 4:47 left, Royal had a hunch and called a pass. Street hit tight end Randy Peschel, who was double covered, with a 44-yarder. Two plays later halfback Jim Bertlesen scored the game-winner in the 15-14 comeback.

BIGGEST UPSET Exasperated by a reporter's question about No. 3 Nebraska being a 21-point favorite heading into the first Big 12 championship game, UT quarterback James Brown cracked, "I think we're going to win by three touchdowns." A group of Nebraska coeds sent Brown a funereal bouquet of tulips with a card that read, "Thanks for keeping us focused."

Late in the game on Dec. 7, 1996, focus was never more important. Facing fourth and inches at their own 28-yard line and clinging to a 30-27 lead over the Cornhuskers, the Longhorns' logical call would have been to punt the ball and then take their chances with an option team's passing attack. Instead, coach John Mackovic gambled. With the Huskers stacking the middle against the Longhorns' triple-I, Brown rolled left and found tight end Derek Lewis wide open. Lewis' 61-yard ramble set up an insurance touchdown, and the unranked Longhorns beat Nebraska 37-27.

HEARTBREAKER Following a legend is an unenviable task, but Akers nearly won the ultimate get-out-of-jail card in his first season, going 11–0 before Notre Dame foiled hopes for a national title by dominating the top-ranked Longhorns in the 1978 Cotton Bowl. Akers would get another chance, in 1983, and the outcome was even more heartbreaking. The No. 2 Longhorns went into the Cotton Bowl against No. 7 Georgia with one of the most dominant defenses in recent college football history and an offense that did enough to win. But not on Jan. 2, 1984, when a string of UT mistakes and letdowns limited them to only three field goals on seven penetrations inside the Bulldogs' 33-yard line. UT's defense forced Georgia into a fourth and 17 at its own 34 with less than five minutes left. Fearing a fake, Akers kept his defense in, a move that backfired when safety Craig Curry muffed Chip Andrews' punt and Georgia recovered at

the UT 23. Three plays later Georgia scored the winning touchdown. "The sad part is that no one will remember the 11 games we won," UT defensive tackle Tony Degrate said later. Later that night, Miami got the last word, stunning No. 1 Nebraska 31-30 in the Orange Bowl to win the national title.

CONSENSUS ALL-AMERICANS (CONT.)	
1983	Jeff Leiding, LB
1983-84	Jerry Gray, DB
1984	Tony Degrate, DL
1995	Tony Brackens, DL
1996	Dan Neil, OL
1997-98	Ricky Williams, RB
2000	Leonard Davis, OL
2000	Casey Hampton, DL
2001	Mike Williams, OL
2001	Quentin Jammer, DB
2002	Derrick Dockery, G
2003-04	Derrick Johnson, LB

BEST COMEBACK Mack Brown rarely completes an interview without invoking the name of his idol, Darrell Royal, so it was little surprise he borrowed a motivational technique from the legendary coach. In 1965 Royal's Longhorns were down 17-0 to rival Texas A&M at halftime. Royal entered the locker room, wrote "21-17" on the blackboard, then turned on his heel and left. UT came back to win 21-17. Thirty-nine years later, Brown found his Longhorns in a tighter spot, down 28 points at home to Oklahoma State. Brown told his players, "They don't know who we are. We're going to go out and score on our first drive and we're going to win 42-35." Brown didn't have Royal's skill for precise prognostication, but he didn't mind. With running back Cedric Benson rushing for five touchdowns and quarterback Vince Young completing a school-record 12 straight passes, the No. 6 Longhorns came back to win 56-35, the biggest comeback in UT's history. After the game a chagrined Brown delivered another message to his team: "I apologized for underestimating them." The come-from-behind victory, one of three the Longhorns had over their last five games from deficits of at least 10 points, propelled UT into its first BCS berth. True to form, UT came back from a 10-point deficit in the third quarter against Michigan to win the Rose Bowl.

WILDEST FINISH UT was on a seemingly unstoppable roll early in the 1970 season, riding the wishbone offense to a winning streak that had reached 22 games, tied with Arkansas for the longest in Southwest Conference history. Then, on Oct. 3, UCLA came to Austin with two weapons ready for the Longhorns: quarterback Dennis Dummitt and a defensive scheme that shot an outside linebacker or cornerback toward the Longhorns' pitch man. The wishbone was shut down, and Dummitt threw for 340 yards and two touchdowns. With 20 seconds to play and the Horns down 17-13, UT's winning streak appeared to be over. Then split end Cotton Speyrer showed why he's considered the best clutch receiver in Texas history. On

third-and-19 at the Bruin 45, quarterback Eddie Phillips hit Speyrer with a 45-yard TD pass that gave the Horns a 20-17 win. The streak reached 30 before the Longhorns, who had already been named national champions by United Press International, were upset 24-11 by Notre Dame in the Cotton Bowl.

DUBIOUS DISTINCTION The 1969 Longhorns were the last all-white team to win the national championship. Guard Julius Whittier became the first African-American to letter at Texas in 1970, paving the way two years later for star fullback Roosevelt Leaks and, ultimately, Earl Campbell in 1974.

TRAGEDY Three days after beating Arkansas in the Big Shootout to win the school's second national title, bone cancer was diagnosed in safety Freddie Steinmark. Two days later his left leg was amputated. "They said there was just muscle holding the bone together," defensive coordinator Mike Campbell said. Steinmark recovered from the surgery in 1969 in time to be on the sideline for the Horns' Jan. 1 Cotton Bowl win over Notre Dame, and he made light of his predicament. When chemotherapy threatened his full head of hair, he shaved his scalp, got a gold hoop earring and pretended he was a one-legged pirate. But the cancer spread to his lungs, and on June 6, 1971, he died at age 22.

NICKNAME In 1903 D.A. Frank, a writer for the school paper, *The Daily Texan*, labeled the team the Longhorns and it stuck. In the 1920s it was recognized as their official name.

MASCOT Legend has it that Bevo was named, at least indirectly, by a bunch of Aggies. In 1916 former UT team manager Stephen Pinckney proposed that the team get a live mascot, and he collected $1 from more than 100 fans to buy an orange-and-white steer. It had seemed like a good idea, but the steer was wild and ornery. While the students were trying to figure out what to do with the rambunctious animal, some Texas A&M students stole onto his home turf and branded

him with the score of the 1915 game, a 13-0 Aggie win. His handlers doctored the brand, turning the 13 into a B and adding an E and V before the O to give the beast his name, which was also the name of a nonalcoholic beer. Bevo I never calmed down and was eventually the guest of honor—and main course—at a barbecue for fans of both schools. In 1936, the tradition was restored, and the student group the Silver Spurs now tend to Bevo XIV, who joined the lineage of UT mascots in fall 2004.

UNIFORMS On May 10, 1900, the board of regents approved orange and white as the official school colors. In the past 50 years, the uniforms have remained fairly constant, with burnt orange home jerseys and white road jerseys, both over white pants. In 1978, the school added the word "Texas" to the front of its home jersey, a move that upset some hard-core fans who felt an explanation was unnecessary. Coach Royal had earlier defended tradition when he responded to a suggestion that the UT uniforms be jazzed up with stripes: "Hell, no! I'm not going to candy this thing up. These are work clothes."

ALL-CENTURY TEAM	
Selected by UT fans in a 17-day Internet survey in December 1999.	
OFFENSE	
1961-63	Scott Appleton, OL
1970-72	Jerry Sisemore, OL
1980-83	Doug Dawson, OL
1992-94	Blake Brockermeyer, OL
1993-96	Dan Neil, OL
1994-96	Pat Fitzgerald, TE
1976-79	Johnny "Lam" Jones, WR
1979-82	Anthony Carter, WR
1995-96, 1998	Wane McGarity, WR
1944-47	Bobby Layne, QB
1974-77	Earl Campbell, RB
1995-98	Ricky Williams, RB
1994-97	Phil Dawson, K
DEFENSE	
1972-74	Doug English, DL
1976-79	Steve McMichael, DL
1978-81	Kenneth Sims, DL
1993-95	Tony Brackens, DL
1963-65	Tommy Nobis, LB
1984-85, 1987-88	Britt Hager, LB
1989-90, 1992-93	Winfred Tubbs, LB
1973-76	Raymond Clayborn, DB
1976-79	Johnnie Johnson, DB
1981-84	Jerry Gray, DB
1993-96	Bryant Westbrook, DB
1975-78	Russell Erxleben, P

STADIUM Some 10,000 students, alumni and fans donated $275,000 to build the original 27,000-seat stadium, which opened on Nov. 8, 1924. Dedicated to the Texans who died in World War I—including 1914 team captain Louis Jordan—the facility was expanded six times during the century. In 1996, the name was changed to Darrell K Royal-Texas Memorial Stadium.

RIVAL In 1912, UT athletics chairman W.T. Mather sent a letter to Texas A&M officials saying that the game between the two teams would be canceled—in part because of bad blood stemming from a 1908 brawl in which one UT fan was stabbed three times in the head. In 1915, after coach Charley Moran, whom Texas fans accused of coaching "dirty" football, left A&M, the teams revived the rivalry. Both schools single out the other in their fight songs. Mascots on both sides have been kidnapped. In 1996, an A&M fan filed a request under the state Open Records law

to obtain the Texas playbook. Texas president Robert Berdahl, a historian by trade, responded by quoting the inscription on the battle flag the Texicans took into the Battle of Gonzales in 1835 during the Texas War of Independence: "Come and take it." The rivalry softened in 1999, when 12 current and former A&M students were killed when the bonfire the Aggies light before the Longhorns game collapsed. At the game eight days later at A&M's Kyle Field, A&M won an emotional game, during which the Longhorns band paid tribute to the fallen by playing "Amazing Grace."

The Texas-Texas A&M rivalry softened after the death of 12 Aggies in 1999.

LORE Bobby Layne was known as the greatest Longhorns quarterback, but it was on the baseball field that he cemented his reputation for, ah, eccentric behavior. Horsing around the night before he was to pitch against A&M on May 4, 1946, Layne put his foot through a plate glass window, cutting it severely. More afraid of coach Bibb Falk than the pain, Layne taped up the foot and—aided by 18 cans of Falstaff beer guzzled between innings to kill the pain—he pitched a no-hitter over the Aggies, winning 2-1.

COACH KNOWS BEST Whenever Darrell Royal spoke, Longhorns listened. On the passing game: "Only three things can happen when you throw the ball, and two of them are bad." On optimism: "You've got to think lucky. If you fall into a mud hole, check your back pocket—you might have caught a fish." On good fortune: "Luck is what happens when preparation meets opportunity." On how to behave: "When you get to the end zone, act like you've been there before."

NUMBERS In 1998, halfback Ricky Williams broke Tony Dorsett's 22-year-old NCAA Division I-A record for most career rushing yards, finishing with 6,279. (The record lasted one year before it was broken by Wisconsin's Ron Dayne, who ran for 6,397.) Williams' No. 34 and Earl Campbell's No. 20 are the only football jersey numbers UT has retired.

QUOTE "Dance with the one that brung ya."—Darrell Royal, on sticking with the ground-bound wishbone attack over a trendier passing attack

TEXAS ALL-TIME SCORES

WIN/LOSS PERCENTAGE SINCE 1936

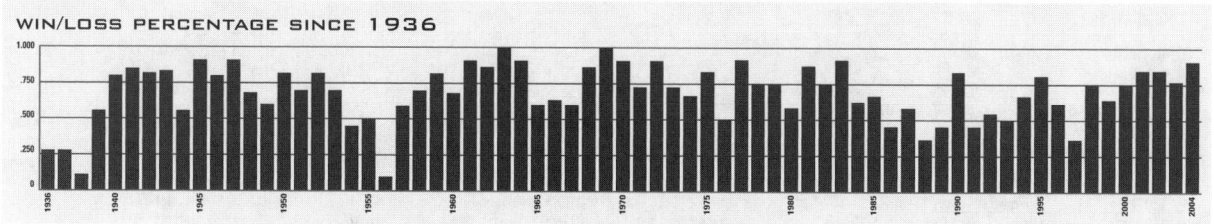

NO HEAD COACH

1893   4-0-0
N30 •	at Dallas	18	16
D16 •	San Antonio	30	0
F3 •	at San Antonio	34	0
F22 •	Dallas	16	0

R.D. WENTWORTH
1894 (.857)   6-1

1894   6-1-0
O19 •	Texas A&M	38	0
O27 •	Tulane	12	0
N9 •	Austin YMCA	6	0
N16 •	Austin YMCA	24	0
N29 •	Arkansas	54	0
D8 •	at San Antonio	57	0
D14 •	Missouri	0	28

FRANK CRAWFORD
1895 (1.000)   5-0

1895   5-0-0
N11 •	at Dallas U	10	0
N18 •	Austin YMCA	24	0
N23 •	Tulane	16	0
N28 •	San Antonio	38	0
D6 •	Galveston	8	0

HARRY ROBINSON
1896 (.643)   4-2-1

1896   4-2-1
O17 •	Galveston	42	0
O24 =	at Dallas	0	0
N7 •	San Antonio	12	4
N14 •	at Tulane	12	4
N16 •	at LSU	0	14
N26 •	Dallas U.	22	4
D14 •	Missouri	0	10

W.F. KELLY
1897 (.750)   6-2

1897   6-2-0
O23 •	San Antonio	10	0
O30 •	at Dallas	4	22
N1 •	at Fort Worth	0	6
N3 •	TCU *WAC*	18	10
N13 •	Houston Town Team	42	6
N20 •	at San Antonio	12	0
N25 •	Fort Worth	38	0
D11 •	Dallas	26	16

D.F. EDWARDS
1898 (.833)   5-1

1898   5-1-0
O15 •	TCU *WAC*	16	0 *
O22 •	Texas A&M	48	0
O29 •	Galveston	17	0
N5 •	TCU	29	0
N10 •	Sewanee	0	4
N24 •	Dallas	26	0

M.G. CLARKE
1899 (.750)   6-2

1899   6-2-0
O21 •	at Dallas	11	6
O31 •	San Antonio	28	0
N4 •	Texas A&M *SA*	6	0
N9 •	Sewanee	0	12
N18 •	at Vanderbilt	0	6
N20 •	at Tulane	11	0
N25 •	Tulane	32	0
N30 •	LSU	29	0

S.H. THOMPSON
1900-01 (.853)   14-2-1

1900   6-0-0
O10 •	Oklahoma	28	2
O13 •	Vanderbilt	22	0
O27 •	Texas A&M *SA*	5	0
N17 •	Missouri	17	11 *
N24 •	K.C. Medics	30	0
N29 •	Texas A&M	11	0

1901   8-2-1
O7 •	Houston Town Team	32	0
O12 =	Nashville U. *DAL*	5	5
O19 •	Oklahoma	12	6
O26 •	Texas A&M *SA*	17	0
O29 •	at Baylor	23	0
N9 •	Dallas AC	12	0
N16 •	at Missouri	10	0
N19 •	at American Osteopath	0	48
N23 •	at Kansas	0	12
N25 •	at Oklahoma	11	0
N28 •	Texas A&M	32	0

J.B. HART
1902 (.650)   6-3-1

1902   6-3-1
O4 •	Oklahoma	22	6
O10 •	Sewanee *DAL*	11	0
O18 •	LSU *SA*	0	5
O25 =	Texas A&M *SA*	0	0
N1 •	Trinity	27	0
N8 •	Haskell	0	12
N15 •	at Nashville U.	11	5
N19 •	at Alabama	10	0
N24 •	at Tulane	6	0
N27 •	Texas A&M	0	12 *

RALPH HUTCHINSON
1903-05 (.680)   16-7-2

1903   5-1-2
O3 •	Deaf School	17	0
O9 •	Haskell *DAL*	0	6
O17 =	Oklahoma	6	6
O24 •	Baylor *SA*	48	0
O30 •	Arkansas	15	0
N6 •	Vanderbilt	5	5
N13 •	at Oklahoma	11	5
N29 •	Texas A&M	29	6

1904   6-2-0
O8 •	TCU	40	0
O15 •	Trinity	24	0
O21 •	Haskell	0	4
O29 •	at Washington, Mo.	23	0
N5 •	at Chicago	0	68
N16 •	Oklahoma	40	10
N19 •	Baylor	58	0
N24 •	Texas A&M	34	6

1905   5-4-0
O7 •	TCU	11	0
O13 •	Haskell	0	17
O21 •	Baylor	39	0
O28 •	at Vanderbilt	0	33
O31 •	at Arkansas	4	0
N3 •	Oklahoma *OKC*	0	2
N10 •	Transylvania, Ky	0	6
N17 •	Sewanee	17	10
N22 •	Texas A&M	27	0

H.R. SCHENKER
1906 (.900)   9-1

1906   9-1-0
O5 •	26th Infantry	21	0
O13 •	TCU	22	0
O20 •	WTMA	28	0
O27 •	at Vanderbilt	0	45
O30 •	Arkansas	11	0
N2 •	Oklahoma *OKC*	10	9
N9 •	Haskell	28	0
N16 •	Daniel Baker	40	0
N23 •	Washington, Mo.	17	6
N29 •	Texas A&M	24	0

W.E. METZENTHIN
1907-08 (.676)   11-5-1

1907   6-1-1
O12 =	Texas A&M *DAL*	0	0
O19 •	LSU	12	5
O25 •	Haskell	45	10
O30 •	at Arkansas	26	6
N2 •	at Missouri	4	5
N9 •	Baylor	27	11
N15 •	Oklahoma	29	10
N28 •	Texas A&M	11	6

1908   5-4-0
O10 •	TCU	11	6
O17 •	Baylor	27	5
O24 •	Colorado College	0	15
N5 •	Southwestern	9	11
N7 •	Arkansas	21	0
N9 •	Texas A&M *HOU*	24	8
N13 •	at Oklahoma	0	50
N18 •	Tulane	15	28
N29 •	Texas A&M	28	12

DEXTER DRAPER
1909 (.563)   4-3-1

1909   4-3-1
O9 •	Southwestern	12	0
O16 •	Haskell *DAL*	11	12
O23 •	Trinity	18	0
O30 •	TCU	24	0
N8 •	Texas A&M *HOU*	0	23
N13 •	at Tulane	10	10
N19 •	Oklahoma	30	0
N25 •	Texas A&M	0	5

W.S. WASMUND
1910 (.750)   6-2

1910   6-2-0
O8 •	Southwestern	11	6
O15 •	Haskell	68	3
O22 •	Transylvania, Ky	48	0
O29 •	Auburn	9	0
N5 •	at Baylor	1	0 f
N14 •	Texas A&M *HOU*	8	14
N19 •	LSU	12	0
N24 •	Oklahoma	0	3

DAVE ALLERDICE
1911-15 (.825)   33-7

1911   5-2-0
O13 •	Southwestern	11	2
O24 •	Baylor	11	0
O28 •	Arkansas	12	0
N2 •	Sewanee	5	6
N13 •	Texas A&M *HOU*	6	0
N17 •	Auburn	18	5
N25 •	Oklahoma *DAL*	3	6

1912   7-1-0
O5 •	TCU	30	10
O12 •	Austin Coll.	3	0
O19 •	Oklahoma *DAL*	6	21
O26 •	Haskell	14	7
N4 •	at Baylor	19	7
N13 •	Mississippi *HOU*	53	14
N23 •	Southwestern	28	3
N28 •	Arkansas	48	0

1913   7-1-0
O3 •	Fort Worth Poly	14	7
O10 •	Austin Coll.	27	6
O16 •	Baylor	77	0
O25 •	Sewanee *DAL*	13	7
N3 •	Southwestern	52	0
N10 •	Oklahoma *HOU*	14	6
N18 •	Kansas State	46	0
N27 •	Notre Dame	7	30

1914   8-0-0
O3 •	Trinity	30	0
O10 •	at Baylor	57	0
O17 •	Rice	41	0
O24 •	Oklahoma *DAL*	32	7
O31 •	Southwestern	70	0
N7 •	Haskell *HOU*	23	7
N17 •	Mississippi	66	7
N26 •	Wabash	39	0

1915-1995 SWC

1915   6-3-0 (2-2-0)
O2 •	TCU	72	0
O9 •	Daniel Baker	92	0
O16 |	Rice	59	0
O23 •	Oklahoma *DAL*	13	14
O30 |	Southwestern	45	0
N6 |	Sewanee *HOU*	27	6
N13 •	Alabama	20	0
N19 |	at Texas A&M	0	13
N25 |	Notre Dame	7	36

EUGENE VAN GENT
1916 (.778)   7-2

1916   7-2-0   6-1-0
S30 •	SMU	74	0
O7 |	Rice	16	2
O13 •	Oklahoma State *SA*	14	7 *
O21 •	Oklahoma *DAL*	21	7
O28 |	Baylor	3	7
N4 |	at Missouri	0	3
N14 •	Arkansas	52	0
N21 |	Southwestern	17	3
N30 |	Texas A&M	21	7

BILL JUNEAU
1917-19 (.731)   19-7

1917   4-4-0 (2-4-0)
O6 •	Trinity	27	0
O13 •	Southwestern	35	0
O20 |	Oklahoma *DAL*	0	14
O27 |	Rice	0	13
N3 |	at Baylor	0	3
N10 •	Oklahoma State	7	3
N20 |	at Texas A&M	0	7
N29 • |	Arkansas	20	0

1918   9-0-0 (4-0-0)
S28 •	TCU	19	0
O13 •	Radio School	25	0
O27 •	Radio School	22	7
N3 •	Ream Fly Sch.	26	2
N10 •	Oklahoma State	27	5
N13 •	Auto Mech. Sch.	22	0
N16 •	at Rice	14	0
N23 • |	SMU	32	0
N28 • |	Texas A&M	7	0

854 TEXAS

THE SCHOOLS

1919 6-3-0 (3-2-0)

S27	●		Howard Payne	26	0
O4	●		Southwestern	39	0
O11			Phillips	0	10
O18		│	Oklahoma [DAL]	7	12
O25	●	│	at Baylor	29	13
N1	●	│	Rice	32	7
N8	●	│	Arkansas	35	7
N13	●		Haskell	13	7
N27		│	at Texas A&M	0	7

BERRY WHITAKER
1920-22 (.865) 22-3-1

1920 9-0-0 (5-0-0)

S25	●		Hardin Simmons	63	0
O2	●		Southwestern	27	0
O9	●		Howard Payne	41	7
O16	●	│	Oklahoma State [DAL]	21	0
O22	●		Austin Coll. [DAL]	54	0
O30	●	│	at Rice	21	0
N5	●	│	Phillips	27	0
N13	●	│	at SMU	21	3
N25	●	│	Texas A&M	7	3

1921 6-1-1 (1-0-1)

O1	●		St. Edwards	33	0
O8	●		Austin Coll.	60	0
O15	●		Howard Payne	21	0
O21			Vanderbilt [DAL]	0	20
O29	●	│	Rice	56	0
N5	●		Southwestern	44	0
N11	●		Mississippi State	54	7
N24	=	│	at Texas A&M	0	0

1922 7-2-0 (2-1-0)

S29	●		Austin Coll.	19	0
O7	●		Phillips	41	10
O14	●	│	Oklahoma State	19	7
O21			Vanderbilt [DAL]	10	20
O28	●		Alabama	19	10
N4	●	│	at Rice	29	0
N11	●		Southwestern	26	0
N18	●		at Oklahoma	32	7
N30		│	Texas A&M	7	14

E.J. STEWART
1923-26 (.708) 24-9-3

1923 8-0-1 (2-0-1)

S28	●		Austin Coll.	31	0
O68	●		at Phillips	51	0
O13	●		Tulane [BEAU]	33	0
O20	●		Vanderbilt [DAL]	16	0
O27	●		Southwestern	44	0
N3	●	│	Rice	27	0
N10	=	│	at Baylor	7	7
N17	●		Oklahoma	26	14
N29	●	│	at Texas A&M	6	0

1924 5-3-1 (2-3-0)

S27	●		Southwestern	27	0
O4	●		Phillips	27	0
O11	●		Howard Payne	6	0
O17		│	at SMU	6	10
O25	=		Florida	7	7
N1		│	at Rice	6	19
N8		│	Baylor	10	28
N15	●	│	at TCU	13	0
N27	●	│	Texas A&M	7	0

1925 6-2-1 (2-1-1)

S26	●		Southwestern	33	0
O3	●		Mississippi	25	0
O10			at Vanderbilt	6	14
O17	●		Auburn [DAL]	33	0
O24	●	│	Rice	27	6
O31	=	│	at SMU	0	0
N7	●	│	Baylor	13	3
N14	●		Arizona	20	0
N26		│	at Texas A&M	0	28

1926 5-4-0 (2-2-0)

S25	●		S.W. Okla. St.	31	7
O2			at Kansas State	3	13
O9	●		Phillips	27	0
O16			Vanderbilt [DAL]	0	7
O23	●	│	at Rice	20	0
O30		│	SMU	17	21
N6		│	at Baylor	7	10
N13	●		Southwestern	27	6
N25	●	│	Texas A&M	14	5

CLYDE LITTLEFIELD
1927-33 (.691) 44-18-6

1927 6-2-1 (2-2-1)

S24	●		S.W. Okla. St.	43	0
O1	=	│	TCU	0	0
O8	●		Trinity	20	6
O15	●		Vanderbilt [DAL]	13	6
O22	●	│	Rice	27	0
O28		│	at SMU	0	14
N5	●	│	Baylor	13	12
N12	●		Kansas State	41	7
N24		│	at Texas A&M	7	28

1928 7-2-0 (5-1-0)

S29	●		St. Edwards	32	0
O6	●		Texas Tech	12	0
O13			Vanderbilt [DAL]	12	13
O20	●	│	Arkansas	20	7
O27	●	│	at Rice	13	6
N3		│	SMU	2	6
N10	●	│	at Baylor	6	0
N17	●	│	at TCU	6	0
N29	●	│	Texas A&M	19	0

1929 5-2-2 (2-2-2)

S29	●		St. Edwards	13	0
O5	●		Centenary	20	0
O12	●	│	at Arkansas	27	0
O19	●		Oklahoma [DAL]	21	0
O26	●	│	Rice	39	0
N2	=	│	at SMU	0	0
N9	=	│	Baylor	0	0
N16		│	TCU	12	15
N28		│	at Texas A&M	0	13

1930 8-1-1 (4-1-0)

S21	●		Southwestern, Tex.	36	0
S28	●		Texas-El Paso	28	0
O4	=		Centenary	0	0
O11	●		Howard Payne	26	0
O18	●		Oklahoma [DAL]	17	7
O25		│	at Rice	0	6
N1	●	│	SMU	25	7
N8	●	│	at Baylor	14	0
N15	●	│	at TCU	7	0
N27	●	│	Texas A&M	44	260

1931 6-4-0 (2-3-0)

S27	●		Hardin Simmons	36	0
O3	●		Missouri	31	0
O10		│	Rice	0	7
O17	●		Oklahoma [DAL]	3	0
O24			at Harvard	7	35
N1		│	at SMU	7	9
N7	●	│	Baylor	25	0
N14	●	│	TCU	10	0
N20	●		at Centenary	6	0
N26		│	at Texas A&M	6	7

1932 8-2-0 (5-1-0)

S24	●		Daniel Baker	26	0
O1			Centenary	6	13
O8	●		at Missouri	65	0
O15	●		Oklahoma [DAL]	17	10
O22	●	│	at Rice	18	6
O29	●	│	SMU	14	6
N5	●	│	at Baylor	19	0
N11		│	at TCU	0	14
N18	●	│	at Arkansas	34	0
N24	●	│	Texas A&M	21	0

1933 4-5-2 (2-3-1)

S23	●		at Southwestern	46	0
S30	●		Texas-El Paso	22	6
O7			at Nebraska	0	26
O14			Oklahoma [DAL]	0	9
O21	=		Centenary [SA]	0	0
O28	●	│	Rice	18	0
N4	●	│	at SMU	10	0
N12		│	Baylor	0	3
N18		│	TCU	0	30
N24		│	Arkansas	6	20
N30	=	│	at Texas A&M	10	10

JACK CHEVIGNY
1934-36 (.483) 13-14-2

1934 7-2-1 (4-1-1)

S22	●		at Texas Tech	12	6
O6	●		at Notre Dame	7	6
O13	●		Oklahoma [DAL]	19	0
O20			Centenary	6	9
O27		│	at Rice	9	20
N3	=	│	SMU	7	7
N10	●	│	Baylor	25	6
N17	●	│	at TCU	20	19
N23	●	│	at Arkansas	19	12
N28	●	│	Texas A&M	13	0

1935 4-6-0 (1-5-0)

S28	●		Texas A&I	38	6
O5			at LSU	6	18
O12	●		Oklahoma [DAL]	12	7
O19	●		Centenary	19	13
O26		│	Rice	19	28
N2		│	at SMU	0	20
N9	●	│	at Baylor	25	6
N16		│	TCU	0	28
N22		│	Arkansas	13	28
N28		│	at Texas A&M	6	20

1936 2-6-1 (1-5-0)

O3	=		LSU	6	6
O10	●		Oklahoma [DAL]	6	0
O17		│	Baylor	18	21
O24		│	at Rice	0	7
O31		│	SMU	7	14
N7		│	at TCU	6	27
N14			at Minnesota	19	47
N26	●	│	Texas A&M	7	0
D3		│	Arkansas [LR]	0	6

D.X. BIBLE
1937-46 (.665) 63-31-3

1937 2-6-1 (1-5-0)

S25	●		Texas Tech	25	12
O2			at LSU	0	9
O9	=		Oklahoma [DAL]	7	7
O16		│	Arkansas	10	21
O23		│	Rice	7	14
O30		│	at SMU	2	13
N6	●	│	at Baylor	9	6
N13		│	TCU	0	14
N25		│	at Texas A&M	0	7

1938 1-8-0 (1-5-0)

S24			at Kansas	18	19
O1			LSU	0	20
O8			Oklahoma [DAL]	0	13
O15		│	Arkansas [LR]	6	42
O22		│	at Rice	7	13 *
O30		│	at SMU	6	7
N5		│	Baylor	3	14
N12		│	at TCU	6	28
N24	●	│	Texas A&M	7	6

1939 5-4-0 (3-3-0)

S30	●		Florida	12	0
O7	●		at Wisconsin	17	7
O14			Oklahoma [DAL]	12	24
O21	●	│	Arkansas	14	13
O28	●	│	Rice	26	12
N4		│	at SMU	0	10
N11		│	at Baylor	0	20
N18	●	│	TCU	25	19
N30		│	at Texas A&M	0	20

1940 8-2-0 (4-2-0)

S28	●		Colorado	39	7
O5	●		at Indiana	13	6
O12	●		Oklahoma [DAL]	19	16
O19	●	│	Arkansas [LR]	21	0
O26		│	at Rice	0	13
N2		│	SMU	13	21
N9	●	│	Baylor	13	0
N16	●	│	at TCU	21	14
N28	●	│	Texas A&M	7	0
D7	●		at Florida	26	0

1941 8-1-1 (4-1-1)

S27	●		at Colorado	34	6
O4	●		LSU	34	0
O11	●		Oklahoma [DAL]	40	7
O18	●	│	Arkansas	48	14
O25	●	│	Rice	40	0
N1	●	│	at SMU	34	0
N8	=	│	at Baylor	7	7
N15		│	TCU	7	14
N27	●	│	at Texas A&M	23	0
D6	●		Oregon	71	7

1942 9-2-0 (5-1-0)

S19	●		Corpus Christi NAS	40	0
S26	●		Kansas State	64	0
O3			at Northwestern	0	3
O10	●		Oklahoma [DAL]	7	0
O17	●	│	Arkansas [LR]	47	6
O24	●	│	at Rice	12	7
O31	●	│	SMU	21	7
N7	●	│	Baylor	20	0
N14		│	at TCU	7	13
N26	●	│	Texas A&M	12	6
			COTTON BOWL		
J1	●		Georgia Tech	14	7

1943 7-1-1 (5-0-0)

S25	●		Blackland AAF	65	6
O2			Southwestern	7	14
O9	●		Oklahoma [DAL]	13	7
O16	●	│	Arkansas	34	0
O23	●	│	Rice	58	0
O30	●	│	at SMU	20	0
N13	●	│	TCU	46	7
N25	●	│	at Texas A&M	27	13
			COTTON BOWL		
J1	=		Randolph Field	7	7

1944 5-4-0 (3-2-0)

S30	●		Southwestern	20	0
O7			Randolph Field	6	42
O14	●		Oklahoma [DAL]	20	0
O21	●	│	Arkansas [LR]	19	0
O28		│	at Rice	0	7
N4	●	│	SMU	34	7
N11			Oklahoma State	8	13
N18		│	at TCU	6	7
N30	●	│	Texas A&M	6	0

1945 10-1-0 (5-1-0)

S22	●		Bergstrom Field	13	7
S29	●		Southwestern	46	0
O6	●		Texas Tech	33	0
O13	●		Oklahoma [DAL]	12	7
O20	●	│	Arkansas [LR]	34	7
O27		│	Rice	6	7
N3	●	│	at SMU	12	7
N10	●	│	Baylor	21	14
N17	●	│	TCU	20	0
N29	●	│	at Texas A&M	20	10
			COTTON BOWL		
J1	●		Missouri	40	27

1946 8-2-0 (4-2-0)

S21	●		Missouri	42	0
S28	●		Colorado	76	0
O5	●		Oklahoma State	54	6
O12	●		Oklahoma [DAL]	20	13
O19	●	│	Arkansas	20	0
O26		│	at Rice	13	18
N2	●	│	SMU	19	3
N9	●	│	at Baylor	22	7
N16		│	at TCU	0	14
N28	●	│	Texas A&M	24	7

BLAIR CHERRY
1947-50 (.756) 32-10-1

1947 10-1-0 (5-1-0)

S20	●		Texas Tech	33	0
S27	●		Oregon [PORT]	38	13
O4	●		North Carolina	34	0
O11	●		Oklahoma [DAL]	34	14
O18	●	│	Arkansas [MEM]	21	6
O25	●	│	Rice	12	0
N1		│	at SMU	13	14
N8	●	│	Baylor	28	7
N15	●	│	TCU	20	0
N27	●	│	at Texas A&M	32	13
			SUGAR BOWL		
J1	●		Alabama	27	7

1948 7-3-1 (4-1-1)

S18	●		LSU	33	0
S25			at North Carolina	7	34
O2	●		New Mexico	47	0
O9			Oklahoma [DAL]	14	20
O16	●	│	Arkansas	14	6
O23	●	│	at Rice	20	7
O30		│	SMU	6	21
N6	●	│	at Baylor	13	10
N13	●	│	at TCU	14	7
N25	=	│	Texas A&M	14	14
			ORANGE BOWL		
J1	●		Georgia	41	28

1949 6-4-0 (3-3-0)

S17	●		Texas Tech	43	0
S24	●		at Temple	54	0
O1	●		Idaho	56	7
O8			Oklahoma [DAL]	14	20
O15	●	│	Arkansas [LR]	27	14
O22		│	Rice	15	17
O29		│	at SMU	6	7
N5	●	│	Baylor	20	0
N12		│	TCU	13	14
N24	●	│	at Texas A&M	42	14

1950   9-2-0 (6-0-0)

S23	●	at Texas Tech	28	14
S30	●	Purdue	34	26
O14		Oklahoma *DAL*	13	14
O21	●	Arkansas	19	14
O28	●	at Rice	35	7
N4	●	SMU	23	20
N11	●	at Baylor	27	20
N18	●	at TCU	21	7
N30	●	Texas A&M	17	0
D9	●	LSU	21	6
COTTON BOWL				
J1		Tennessee	14	20

ED PRICE
1951-56 (.549)   33-27-1

1951   7-3-0 (3-3-0)

S22	●	Kentucky	7	6
S29	●	at Purdue	14	0
O6	●	North Carolina	45	20
O13	●	Oklahoma *DAL*	9	7
O20		at Arkansas	14	16
O27	●	Rice	14	6
N3	●	at SMU	20	13
N10		Baylor	6	18
N17		TCU	32	21
N29	●	at Texas A&M	21	22

1952   9-2-0 (6-0-0)

S20	●	at LSU	35	14
S27	●	at North Carolina	28	7
O4		Notre Dame	3	14
O11	●	Oklahoma *DAL*	20	49
O18	●	Arkansas	44	7
O25	●	at Rice	20	7
N1		SMU	31	14
N8		at Baylor	35	33
N15	●	at TCU	14	7
N27	●	Texas A&M	32	12
COTTON BOWL				
J1	●	Tennessee	16	0

1953   7-3-0 (5-1-0)

S19	●	at LSU	7	20
S26	●	Villanova	41	12
O3	●	Houston	28	7
O10	●	Oklahoma *DAL*	14	19
O17		at Arkansas	16	7
O24		Rice	13	18
O31		at SMU	16	7
N7	●	Baylor	21	20
N14	●	TCU	13	3
N26	●	at Texas A&M	21	12

1954   4-5-1 (2-3-1)

S18	●	LSU	20	6
S25		at Notre Dame	0	21
O2	●	Washington State	40	14
O9	●	Oklahoma *DAL*	7	14
O16		Arkansas	7	20
O23		at Rice	7	13
O30	=	SMU	13	13
N6		at Baylor	7	13
N13	●	at TCU	35	34
N25		Texas A&M	22	13

1955   5-5-0 (4-2-0)

S17		Texas Tech	14	20
S24	●	Tulane	35	21
S30		at Southern Cal	7	19
O8	●	Oklahoma *DAL*	0	20
O15		Arkansas *LR*	20	27
O22	●	Rice	32	14
O29	●	at SMU	19	18
N5	●	Baylor	21	20
N12		TCU	20	47
N24	●	at Texas A&M	21	6

1956   1-9-0 (0-6-0)

S22	●	Southern Cal	20	44
S29	●	at Tulane	7	6
O6	●	West Virginia	6	7
O13		Oklahoma *DAL*	0	45
O20		Arkansas	14	32
O27		at Rice	7	28
N3		SMU	19	20
N10		at Baylor	7	10
N17		at TCU	0	46
N29		Texas A&M	21	34

DARRELL ROYAL
1957-76 (.774)   167-47-5

1957   6-4-1 (4-1-1)

S21	●	Georgia *ATL*	26	7
S28	●	Tulane	20	6
O5		South Carolina	21	27
O12		Oklahoma *DAL*	7	21
O19	●	at Arkansas	17	0
O26	●	Rice	19	14
N2		SMU	12	19
N9	=	Baylor	7	7
N16	●	TCU	14	2
N28		at Texas A&M	9	7
SUGAR BOWL				
J1		Mississippi	7	39

1958   7-3-0 (3-3-0)

S20	●	Georgia	13	8
S26	●	at Tulane	21	20
O4	●	Texas Tech	12	7
O11	●	Oklahoma *DAL*	15	14
O18	●	Arkansas *LR*	24	6
O25		at Rice	7	34
N1		SMU	10	26
N8	●	at Baylor	20	15
N15		at TCU	8	22
N27	●	Texas A&M	27	0

1959   9-2-0 (5-1-0)

S19	●	at Nebraska	20	0
S26	●	Maryland	26	0
O3	●	California	33	0
O10	●	Oklahoma *DAL*	19	12
O17	●	Arkansas	13	12
O24		Rice	28	6
O31		at SMU	21	0
N7		Baylor	13	12
N14		TCU	9	14
N26	●	at Texas A&M	20	17
COTTON BOWL				
J1		Syracuse	14	23

1960   7-3-1 (5-2-0)

S17	●	Nebraska	13	14
S24	●	at Maryland	34	0
O1	●	Texas Tech	17	0
O8	●	Oklahoma *DAL*	24	0
O15		Arkansas	23	24
O22		at Rice	0	7
O29	●	SMU	17	7
N5		at Baylor	12	7
N12	●	at TCU	3	2
N24	●	Texas A&M	21	14
BLUEBONNET BOWL				
D17	=	Alabama	3	3

1961   10-1-0 (6-1-0)

S23	●	at California	28	3
S30	●	Texas Tech	42	14
O7	●	Washington State	41	8
O14	●	Oklahoma *DAL*	28	7
O21	●	at Arkansas	33	7
O28	●	Rice	34	7
N4	●	at SMU	27	0
N11	●	Baylor	33	7
N18		TCU	0	6
N23	●	at Texas A&M	25	0
COTTON BOWL				
J1	●	Mississippi	12	7

1962   9-1-1 (6-0-1)

S22	●	Oregon	25	13
S29	●	at Texas Tech	34	0
O6	●	Tulane	35	8
O13	●	Oklahoma *DAL*	9	6
O20	●	Arkansas	7	3
O27	=	at Rice	14	14
N3	●	SMU	6	0
N10	●	at Baylor	27	12
N17	●	at TCU	14	0
N22	●	Texas A&M	13	3
COTTON BOWL				
J1		LSU	0	13

1963   11-0-0 (7-0-0)

S20	●	at Tulane	21	0
S28		Texas Tech	49	7
O5		Oklahoma State	34	7
O12	●	Oklahoma *DAL*	28	7
O19		Arkansas *LR*	17	13
O26		Rice	10	6
N2		at SMU	17	12
N9		Baylor	7	0
N16		TCU	17	0
N28	●	at Texas A&M	15	13
COTTON BOWL				
J1	●	Navy	28	6

1964   10-1-0 (6-1-0)

S19	●	Tulane	31	0
S26	●	at Texas Tech	23	0
O3		Army	17	6
O10	●	Oklahoma *DAL*	28	7
O17		Arkansas	13	14
O24	●	at Rice	6	3
O31		SMU	7	0
N7	●	at Baylor	20	14
N14	●	at TCU	28	13
N26	●	Texas A&M	26	7
ORANGE BOWL				
J1	●	Alabama	21	17

1965   6-4-0 (3-4-0)

S18	●	Tulane	31	0
S25	●	Texas Tech	33	7
O2	●	Indiana	27	12
O9	●	Oklahoma *DAL*	19	0
O16		at Arkansas	24	27
O23		Rice	17	20
O30		at SMU	14	31
N6		Baylor	35	14
N13		TCU	10	25
N25	●	at Texas A&M	21	17

1966   7-4-0 (5-2-0)

S17		Southern Cal	6	10
S24	●	at Texas Tech	31	21
O1	●	Indiana	35	0
O8		Oklahoma *DAL*	9	18
O15		Arkansas	7	12
O22	●	at Rice	14	6
O29		SMU	12	13
N5		at Baylor	26	14
N12	●	at TCU	13	3
N24	●	Texas A&M	22	14
BLUEBONNET BOWL				
D17	●	Mississippi	19	0

1967   6-4-0 (4-3-0)

S23		at Southern Cal	13	17
S30		Texas Tech	13	19
O7	●	Oklahoma State	19	0
O14	●	Oklahoma *DAL*	9	7
O21	●	Arkansas *LR*	21	12
O28	●	Rice	28	6
N4	●	at SMU	35	28
N11	●	Baylor	24	0
N18		TCU	17	24
N23		at Texas A&M	7	10

1968   9-1-1 (6-1-0)

S21	=	Houston	20	20
S28		at Texas Tech	22	31
O5	●	Oklahoma State	31	3
O12	●	Oklahoma *DAL*	26	20
O19	●	Arkansas	39	29
O26	●	at Rice	38	14
N2	●	SMU	38	7
N9	●	at Baylor	47	26
N16	●	at TCU	47	21
N28	●	Texas A&M	35	14
COTTON BOWL				
J1	●	Tennessee	36	13

1969   11-0-0 (7-0-0)

S20	●	at California	17	0
S27	●	Texas Tech	49	7
O4	●	Navy	56	17
O11	●	Oklahoma *DAL*	27	17
O25	●	Rice	31	0
N1	●	at SMU	45	14
N8	●	Baylor	56	14
N15	●	TCU	69	7
N27	●	at Texas A&M	49	12
D6	●	at Arkansas	15	14
COTTON BOWL				
J1	●	Notre Dame	21	17

1970   10-1-0 (7-0-0)

S19	●	California	56	15
S26	●	at Texas Tech	35	13
O3	●	UCLA	20	17
O10	●	Oklahoma *DAL*	41	9
O24	●	at Rice	45	21
O31	●	SMU	42	15
N7	●	at Baylor	21	14
N14	●	at TCU	58	0
N26	●	Texas A&M	52	14
D5	●	Arkansas	42	7
COTTON BOWL				
J1		Notre Dame	11	24

1971   8-3-0 (6-1-0)

S18	●	at UCLA	28	10
S25	●	Texas Tech	28	0
O2	●	Oregon	35	7
O9		Oklahoma *DAL*	27	48
O16		Arkansas *LR*	7	31
O23	●	Rice	39	10
O30	●	at SMU	22	18
N6	●	Baylor	24	0
N13	●	TCU	31	0
N25	●	at Texas A&M	34	14
COTTON BOWL				
J1		Penn State	6	30

1972   10-1-0 (7-0-0)

S23	●	Miami, Fla.	23	10
S30	●	at Texas Tech	25	20
O7	●	Utah State	27	12
O14		Oklahoma *DAL*	0	27
O21	●	Arkansas	35	15
O28	●	at Rice	45	9
N4	●	SMU	17	9
N11	●	at Baylor	17	3
N18	●	at TCU	27	0
N23	●	Texas A&M	38	3
COTTON BOWL				
J1	●	Alabama	17	13

1973   8-3-0 (7-0-0)

S21	●	at Miami, Fla.	15	20
S29		Texas Tech	28	12
O6	●	Wake Forest	41	0
O13	●	Oklahoma *DAL*	13	52
O20	●	at Arkansas	34	6
O27	●	Rice	55	13
N3	●	at SMU	42	14
N10	●	Baylor	42	6
N17	●	TCU	52	7
N22	●	at Texas A&M	42	13
COTTON BOWL				
J1		Nebraska	3	19

1974   8-4-0 (5-2-0)

S14	●	at Boston College	42	19
S21	●	Wyoming	34	7
S28	●	at Texas Tech	3	26
O5	●	Washington	35	21
O12	●	Oklahoma *DAL*	13	16
O19	●	Arkansas	38	7
O26	●	at Rice	27	6
N2	●	SMU	35	15
N9		at Baylor	24	34
N16	●	at TCU	81	16
N29	●	Texas A&M	32	3
GATOR BOWL				
D30		Auburn	3	27

1975   10-2-0 (6-1-0)

S13	●	Colorado State	46	0
S20	●	at Washington	28	10
S27	●	Texas Tech	42	18
O4	●	Utah State	61	7
O11	●	Oklahoma *DAL*	17	24
O18	●	at Arkansas	24	18
O25		Rice	41	9
N1	●	at SMU	30	22
N8	●	Baylor	37	21
N15	●	TCU	27	11
N28	●	at Texas A&M	10	20
BLUEBONNET BOWL				
D27	●	Colorado	38	21

1976   5-5-1 (4-4-0)

S11	●	at Boston College	13	14
S18	●	North Texas	17	14
O2	●	at Rice	42	15
O9	=	Oklahoma *DAL*	6	6
O23	●	SMU	13	12
O30	●	at Texas Tech	28	31
N6		Houston	0	30
N13	●	at TCU	34	7
N20	●	at Baylor	10	20
N25	●	Texas A&M	3	27
D4	●	Arkansas	29	12

FRED AKERS
1977-86 (.731)   86-31-2

1977   11-1-0 (8-0-0)
S10	●	Boston College	44 0
S17	●	Virginia	68 0
O1	●	Rice	72 15
O8	●	Oklahoma *DAL*	13 6
O15	●	at Arkansas	13 9
O22	●	at SMU	30 14
O29		Texas Tech	26 0
N5	●	at Houston	35 21
N12		TCU	44 14
N19		Baylor	29 7
N26	●	at Texas A&M	57 28
COTTON BOWL			
J2		Notre Dame	10 38

1978   9-3-0 (6-2-0)
S16	●	at Rice	34 0
S23	●	Wyoming	17 3
S30	●	at Texas Tech	24 7
O7		Oklahoma *DAL*	10 31
O14	●	North Texas	26 16
O21	●	Arkansas	28 21
O28		SMU	22 3
N11		Houston	7 10
N18	●	at TCU	41 0
N25	●	at Baylor	14 38
D2	●	Texas A&M	22 7
SUN BOWL			
D23	●	Maryland	42 0

1979   9-3-0 (6-2-0)
S22	●	Iowa St.	17 9
S29	●	at Missouri	21 0
O6	●	Rice	26 9
O13		Oklahoma *DAL*	16 7
O20	●	Arkansas *LR*	14 17
O27	●	at SMU	30 6
N3	●	Texas Tech	14 6
N10	●	at Houston	21 13
N17	●	TCU	35 10
N24	●	Baylor	13 0
D1		at Texas A&M	7 13
SUN BOWL			
D22	●	Washington	7 14

1980   7-5-0 (4-4-0)
S1	●	Arkansas	23 17
S20	●	Utah State	35 17
S27	●	Oregon State	35 0
O4	●	at Rice	41 28
O11		Oklahoma *DAL*	20 13
O25		SMU	6 20
N1		at Texas Tech	20 24
N8	●	Houston	15 13
N15	●	at TCU	51 26
N22	●	at Baylor	0 16
N29	●	Texas A&M	14 24
BLUEBONNET BOWL			
D31		North Carolina	7 16

1981   10-1-1 (6-1-1)
S12		Rice	31 3
S19	●	North Texas	23 10
S26	●	Miami, Fla.	14 7
O10		Oklahoma *DAL*	34 14
O17	●	at Arkansas	11 42
O24	●	at SMU	9 7
O31	●	Texas Tech	26 9
N7	=	at Houston	14 14
N14	●	TCU	31 15
N21	●	Baylor	34 12
N26	●	at Texas A&M	21 13
COTTON BOWL			
J1	●	Alabama	14 12

1982   9-3-0 (7-1-0)
S18	●	Utah	21 12
S25	●	Missouri	21 0
O2	●	at Rice	34 7
O9		Oklahoma *DAL*	22 28
O23		SMU	17 30
O30	●	at Texas Tech	27 0
N6	●	Houston	50 0
N13	●	at TCU	38 21
N20	●	at Baylor	31 23
N25	●	Texas A&M	53 16
D4	●	Arkansas	33 7
SUN BOWL			
D25	●	North Carolina	10 26

1983   11-1-0 (8-0-0)
S17		at Auburn	20 7
S24	●	North Texas	26 6
O1		Rice	42 6
O8	●	Oklahoma *DAL*	28 16
O15	●	Arkansas *LR*	31 3
O22	●	at SMU	15 12
O29	●	Texas Tech	20 3
N5	●	at Houston	9 3
N12	●	TCU	20 14
N19	●	Baylor	24 21
N26	●	at Texas A&M	45 13
COTTON BOWL			
J2		Georgia	9 10

1984   7-4-1 (5-3-0)
S15	●	Auburn	35 27
S29	●	Penn State *ERUT*	28 3
O6	●	at Rice	38 13
O13	=	Oklahoma *DAL*	15 15
O20	●	Arkansas	24 18
O27	●	SMU	13 7
N3	●	at Texas Tech	13 10
N10		Houston	15 29
N17	●	at TCU	44 23
N24		at Baylor	10 24
D1		Texas A&M	12 37
FREEDOM BOWL			
D26		Iowa	17 55

1985   8-4-0 (6-2-0)
S21	●	Missouri	21 17
S28	●	at Stanford	38 34
O5	●	Rice	44 16
O12	●	Oklahoma *DAL*	7 14
O19	●	at Arkansas	15 13
O26		at SMU	14 44
N2	●	Texas Tech	34 21
N9	●	at Houston	34 24
N16	●	TCU	20 0
N23	●	Baylor	17 10
N28	●	at Texas A&M	10 42
BLUEBONNET BOWL			
D31		Air Force	16 24

1986   5-6-0 (4-4-0)
S13		Stanford	20 31
S20	●	at Missouri	27 25
O4	●	at Rice	17 14
O11		Oklahoma *DAL*	12 47
O18		Arkansas	14 21
O25	●	SMU	27 24
N1		at Texas Tech	21 23
N8	●	Houston	30 10
N15	●	at TCU	45 16
N22	●	at Baylor	13 18
N27		Texas A&M	3 16

DAVID McWILLIAMS
1987-91 (.544)   31-26

1987   7-5-0 (5-2-0)
S5		at Auburn	3 31
S12		Brigham Young	17 22
S26	●	Oregon State	61 16
O3	●	Rice	45 26
O10		Oklahoma *DAL*	9 44
O17	●	Arkansas *LR*	16 14
O31	●	Texas Tech	41 27
N7	●	at Houston	40 60
N14	●	TCU	24 21
N21	●	Baylor	34 16
N26	●	at Texas A&M	13 20
BLUEBONNET BOWL			
D31	●	Pittsburgh	32 27

1988   4-7-0 (2-5-0)
S8		at Brigham Young	6 47
S17	●	New Mexico	47 0
S24	●	North Texas	27 24
O1		at Rice	20 13
O8		Oklahoma *DAL*	13 28
O15		Arkansas	24 27
O29	●	at Texas Tech	32 33
N5		Houston	15 66
N12	●	at TCU	30 21
N19	●	at Baylor	14 17
N24		Texas A&M	24 28

1989   5-6-0 (4-4-0)
S4		at Colorado	6 27
S23	●	at SMU	45 13
S30	●	Penn State	12 16
O7	●	Rice	31 30
O14	●	Oklahoma *DAL*	28 24
O21	●	at Arkansas	24 20
N4		Texas Tech	17 24
N11		at Houston	9 47
N18	●	TCU	31 17
N25		Baylor	7 50
D2		at Texas A&M	10 21

1990   10-2-0 (8-0-0)
S8		at Penn State	17 13
S22		Colorado	22 29
O6	●	at Rice	26 10
O13	●	Oklahoma *DAL*	14 13
O20	●	Arkansas	49 17
O27	●	SMU	52 3
N3	●	at Texas Tech	41 22
N10	●	Houston	45 24
N17	●	at TCU	38 10
N24	●	at Baylor	23 13
D1	●	Texas A&M	28 27
COTTON BOWL			
J1		Miami, Fla.	3 46

1991   5-6-0 (4-4-0)
S7	●	at Mississippi State	6 13
S21		Auburn	10 14
O5	●	Rice	28 7
O12	●	Oklahoma *DAL*	10 7
O19	●	Arkansas *LR*	13 14
O26	●	at SMU	34 0
N2		Texas Tech	23 15
N9		at Houston	14 23
N16	●	TCU	32 0
N23		Baylor	11 21
N28		at Texas A&M	14 31

JOHN MACKOVIC
1992-97 (.592)   41-28-2

1992   6-5-0 (4-3-0)
S5	●	Mississippi State	10 28
S12		at Syracuse	21 31
S26	●	North Texas	33 15
O3	●	at Rice	23 21
O10	●	Oklahoma *DAL*	34 24
O24	●	Houston	45 38
O31	●	at Texas Tech	44 33
N7	●	at TCU	14 23
N14	●	SMU	35 14
N21	●	at Baylor	20 21
N26	●	Texas Tech	13 34

1993   5-5-1 (5-2-0)
S4	●	at Colorado	14 36
S18	=	Syracuse	21 21
S25	●	at Louisville	10 41
O2	●	Rice	55 38
O9		Oklahoma *DAL*	17 38
O23	●	SMU *SA*	37 10
O30	●	Texas Tech	22 31
N4	●	at Houston	34 16
N13	●	TCU	24 3
N20	●	Baylor	38 17
N25	●	at Texas A&M	9 18

1994   8-4-0 (4-3-0)
S3	●	at Pittsburgh	30 28
S10	●	Louisville	30 16
S24	●	at TCU	34 18
O1		Colorado	31 34
O8	●	Oklahoma *DAL*	17 10
O16		at Rice	17 19
O22	●	SMU	42 20
O29	●	at Texas Tech	9 33
N5	●	Texas A&M	10 34
N12	●	Houston	48 13
N24	●	at Baylor	63 35
SUN BOWL			
D30	●	North Carolina	35 31

1995   10-2-1 (7-0-0)
S2	●	at Hawaii	38 17
S16	●	Pittsburgh	38 27
S23		at Notre Dame	27 55
S30	●	at SMU	35 10
O7	●	Rice	37 13
O14	=	Oklahoma *DAL*	24 24
O21	●	Virginia	17 16
N4	●	Texas Tech	48 7
N11	●	at Houston	52 20
N18	●	TCU	27 19
N23	●	Baylor	21 13
D2	●	at Texas A&M	16 6
SUGAR BOWL			
D31		Virginia Tech	10 28

1996   8-5 (6-2)
A31	●	Missouri	40 10
S7	●	New Mexico St.	41 7
S21	●	Notre Dame	24 27
S28	●	at Virginia	13 37
O5	●	Oklahoma State	71 14
O12	●	Oklahoma *DAL*	27 30
O26	●	at Colorado	24 28
N2	●	Baylor	28 23
N9	●	at Texas Tech	38 32
N16	●	at Kansas	38 17
N29	●	Texas A&M	51 15
BIG 12 CHAMPIONSHIP			
D7	●	Nebraska *StL*	37 27
FIESTA BOWL			
J1		Penn State	15 38

1997   4-7 (2-6)
S6		Rutgers	48 14
S13		UCLA	3 66
S27	●	at Rice	38 31
O4		at Oklahoma State	16 42
O11	●	Oklahoma *DAL*	27 24
O18	●	at Missouri	29 37
O25		Colorado	30 47
N1	●	at Baylor	21 23
N8		Texas Tech	10 24
N15	●	Kansas	45 31
N28	●	at Texas A&M	16 27

MACK BROWN
1998-Present (.787)   70-19

1998   9-3 (6-2)
S5	●	New Mexico St.	66 36
S12		at UCLA	31 49
S19		at Kansas State	7 48
S26	●	Rice	59 21
O3		Iowa St.	54 33
O10	●	Oklahoma *DAL*	34 3
O24	●	Baylor	30 20
O31		at Nebraska	20 16
N7	●	Oklahoma State	37 34
N14	●	at Texas Tech	35 42
N27	●	Texas A&M	26 24
COTTON BOWL			
J1	●	Mississippi State	38 11

1999   9-5 (6-2)
A28		North Carolina St.	20 23
S4	●	Stanford	69 17
S11	●	at Rutgers	38 21
S18	●	Rice	18 13
S25	●	at Baylor	62 0
O2		Kansas State	17 35
O9	●	Oklahoma *DAL*	38 28
O23	●	Nebraska	24 20
O30	●	at Iowa St.	44 41
N6	●	at Oklahoma State	34 21
N13	●	Texas Tech	58 7
N26	●	at Texas A&M	20 16
BIG 12 CHAMPIONSHIP			
D4		Nebraska *SA*	6 22
COTTON BOWL			
J1		Arkansas	6 27

2000   9-3 (7-1)
S9	●	La. Lafayette	52 10
S16		at Stanford	24 27
S23	●	Houston	48 0
S30	●	Oklahoma State	42 7
O7		Oklahoma *DAL*	14 63
O14	●	at Colorado	28 14
O21	●	Missouri	46 12
O28	●	Baylor	48 14
N4	●	at Texas Tech	29 17
N11	●	at Kansas	51 16
N24	●	Texas A&M	43 17
HOLIDAY BOWL			
D29	●	Oregon	30 35

2001   11-2 (7-1)
S1	●	New Mexico St.	41 7
S8	●	North Carolina	44 14
S22	●	at Houston	53 26
S29	●	Texas Tech	42 7
O6		Oklahoma *DAL*	3 14
O13	●	at Oklahoma State	45 17
O20	●	Colorado	41 7
O27	●	at Missouri	35 16
N3	●	at Baylor	49 10
N10	●	Kansas	59 0
N23	●	at Texas A&M	21 7
BIG 12 CHAMPIONSHIP			
D1		Colorado *DAL*	37 39
HOLIDAY BOWL			
D28	●	Washington	47 43

1996-Present
BIG 12

2002 11-2 (6-2)

A31	●	North Texas	27	0
S14	●	at North Carolina	52	21
S21	●	Houston	41	11
S28	●	at Tulane	49	0
O5	● |	Oklahoma State	17	15
O12	● |	Oklahoma DAL	24	35
O19	● |	at Kansas State	17	14
O26	● |	Iowa State	21	10
N2	● |	at Nebraska	27	24
N9	● |	Baylor	41	0
N16	● |	at Texas Tech	38	42
N29	● |	Texas A&M	50	20
		COTTON BOWL		
J1	●	LSU	35	20

2003 10-3 (7-1)

A31	●	New Mexico State	66	7
S13	●	Arkansas	28	38
S20	●	at Rice	48	7
S27	●	Tulane	63	18
O4	● |	Kansas State	24	20
O11	● |	Oklahoma DAL	13	65
O18	● |	at Iowa State	40	19
O25	● |	at Baylor	56	0
N1	● |	Nebraska	31	7
N8	● |	at Oklahoma State	55	16
N15	● |	Texas Tech	43	40
N28	● |	at Texas A&M	46	15
		HOLIDAY BOWL		
D30	●	Washington State	20	28

2004 11-1 (7-1)

S4	●	North Texas	65	0
S11	●	at Arkansas	22	20
S25	●	Rice	35	13
O2	● |	Baylor	44	14
O9	● |	Oklahoma DAL	0	12
O16	● |	Missouri	28	20
O23	● |	at Texas Tech	51	21
O30	● |	at Colorado	31	7
N6	● |	Oklahoma State	56	35
N13	● |	at Kansas	27	23
N26	● |	Texas A&M	26	13
		ROSE BOWL		
J1	●	Michigan	38	37

Neutral Site key: *Mem* Memphis, TN / *Atl* Atlanta, GA / *ERut* East Rutherford, NJ / *StL* St. Louis, MO / *Dal* Dallas, TX / *Beau* Beaumont, TX / *SA* San Antonio, TX / *Wac* Waco, TX / *OkC* Oklahoma City, OK / *Hou* Houston, TX / *LR* Little Rock, AR / *Port* Portland, OR
f Forfeit † Game Later Forfieted # Disputed Victor * Disputed Score || Designated Conference Game 2 Counted Twice in Conference Standings

TEXAS ANNUAL STATISTICAL LEADERS

YR	RUSHING	YDS	ATT	AVG	PASSING	ATT	CMP	PCT	YDS	RECEIVING	REC	YDS	AVG
1944	Bobby Layne	264	78	3.4	Bobby Layne	91	50	.55	662	Hub Bechtol	14	220	15.7
1945	George Graham	268	84	3.2	Bobby Layne	54	20	.37	396	Hub Bechtol	25	289	11.6
1946	Bobby Layne	305	82	3.7	Bobby Layne	140	77	.55	1,115	Jim Canady	17	420	24.7
1947	Jim Canady	383	207	1.9	Bobby Layne	115	63	.55	965	Max Bumgardner	15	234	15.6
1948	Ray Borneman	704	111	6.3	Paul Campbell	135	59	.44	893	Ben Procter	15	205	13.7
1949	Byron Townsend	543	111	4.9	Paul Campbell	182	91	.50	1,372	Ben Procter	43	724	16.8
1950	Byron Townsend	946	251	3.8	Ben Tompkins	118	65	.55	956	Ben Procter	24	453	18.9
1951	Gib Dawson	671	94	7.1	Dan Page	33	15	.45	402	Gib Dawson	8	170	21.3
1952	Dick Ochoa	927	220	4.2	James "T" Jones	132	63	.48	1,018	Tom Stohlandske	30	519	17.3
1953	Dougal Cameron	518	136	3.8	Charles Brewer	68	33	.49	533	Carlton Massey	11	165	15.0
1954	Billy Quinn	442	83	5.3	Charles Brewer	71	28	.39	473	Menan Schriewer	17	306	18.0
1955	Walter Fondren	577	108	5.3	Joe Clements	128	65	.51	818	Menan Schriewer	21	301	14.3
1956	Walter Fondren	493	115	4.3	Joe Clements	151	74	.49	793	Bob Bryant	24	301	12.5
1957	Mike Dowdle	429	99	4.3	Walter Fondren	49	33	.67	428	George Blanch	10	152	15.2
1958	Mike Dowdle	345	85	4.1	Vince Matthews	32	16	.50	183	Bob Bryant	14	233	16.6
1959	Jack Collins	450	89	5.1	Bobby Lackey	23	11	.48	142	Jack Collins	8	134	16.8
1960	James Saxton	407	76	5.4	Mike Cotten	58	32	.55	539	James Saxton	9	185	20.6
1961	James Saxton	846	107	7.9	Mike Cotten	77	44	.57	500	Bob Moses	14	177	12.6
1962	Ray Poage	452	141	3.2	Tommy Wade	78	33	.42	434	Sandy Sands	12	148	12.3
1963	Tommy Ford	738	160	4.6	Duke Carlisle	79	33	.42	416	Charles Talbert	14	188	13.4
1964	Ernie Koy	574	154	3.7	Marvin Kristynik	99	41	.41	563	Pete Lammons	13	204	15.7
1965	Tom Stockton	517	127	4.1	Marvin Kristynik	148	72	.49	1,005	Pete Lammons	27	405	15.0
1966	Chris Gilbert	1,080	206	5.2	Bill Bradley	76	36	.47	535	Ragan Gennusa	19	243	12.8
1967	Chris Gilbert	1,019	205	5.0	Bill Bradley	153	72	.47	1,181	Ragan Gennusa	19	310	16.3
1968	Chris Gilbert	1,132	184	6.2	James Street	135	67	.50	1,099	Cotton Speyrer	26	449	17.3
1969	Jim Bertelsen	740	104	7.1	James Street	81	40	.49	699	Cotton Speyrer	30	492	16.4
1970	Steve Worster	898	160	5.6	Eddie Phillips	96	39	.41	695	Danny Lester	17	365	21.5
1971	Jim Bertelsen	879	160	5.5	Donnie Wigginton	67	35	.52	544	Pat Kelly	17	226	13.3
1972	Roosevelt Leaks	1,099	230	4.8	Alan Lowry	117	46	.39	766	Jim Moore	23	413	18.0
1973	Roosevelt Leaks	1,415	229	6.2	Marty Akins	70	35	.50	475	Pat Kelly	19	268	14.1
1974	Earl Campbell	928	162	5.7	Marty Akins	47	19	.40	250	Pat Padgett	12	141	11.8
1975	Earl Campbell	1,118	198	5.6	Marty Akins	56	31	.55	463	Alfred Jackson	32	596	18.6
1976	Earl Campbell	653	138	4.7	Mike Cordaro	49	22	.45	407	Alfred Jackson	19	364	19.2
1977	Earl Campbell	1,744	267	6.5	Randy McEachern	89	45	.51	906	Johnny "Lam" Jones	21	543	25.9
1978	A.J. "Jam" Jones	465	121	3.8	Randy McEachern	96	40	.42	658	Johnny "Lam" Jones	25	446	17.8
1979	A.J. "Jam" Jones	918	188	4.9	Donnie Little	113	56	.50	750	Johnny "Lam" Jones	36	535	14.9
1980	A.J. "Jam" Jones	657	146	4.5	Donnie Little	155	82	.53	1,098	Les Koenning	27	401	14.9
1981	A.J. "Jam" Jones	834	190	4.4	Rick McIvor	139	56	.40	918	Donnie Little	18	338	18.8
1982	Darryl Clark	1,049	198	5.3	Robert Brewer	193	91	.47	1,415	Herkie Walls	25	702	28.1
1983	Ronnie Robinson	479	81	5.9	Rob Moerschell	110	44	.40	871	Brent Duhon	13	344	26.5
1984	Terry Orr	580	125	4.6	Todd Dodge	210	100	.48	1,599	William Harris	34	637	18.7
1985	Charles Hunter	717	154	4.7	Bret Stafford	108	60	.56	943	Everett Gay	22	431	19.6
1986	Darron Norris	496	130	3.8	Bret Stafford	329	176	.53	2,233	Eric Metcalf	42	556	13.2
1987	Eric Metcalf	1,161	223	5.2	Bret Stafford	245	127	.52	1,321	Gabriel Johnson	40	466	11.7
1988	Eric Metcalf	932	218	4.3	Mark Murdock	202	98	.49	1,189	Tony Jones	42	838	20.0
1989	Adrian Walker	814	193	4.2	Peter Gardere	186	107	.58	1,511	Johnny Walker	55	785	14.3
1990	Butch Hadnot	541	99	5.5	Peter Gardere	282	159	.56	2,131	Johnny Walker	40	565	14.1
1991	Butch Hadnot	501	109	4.6	Peter Gardere	228	114	.50	1,390	Darrick Duke	35	497	14.2
1992	Adrian Walker	852	129	6.6	Peter Gardere	329	181	.55	2,364	Phil Brown	31	361	11.6
1993	Phil Brown	770	126	6.1	Shea Morenz	335	183	.55	2,341	Mike Adams	52	908	17.5
1994	Rodrick Walker	598	129	4.6	Shea Morenz	235	124	.53	1,368	Eric Jackson	43	762	17.7
1995	Shon Mitchell	1,099	176	6.2	James Brown	322	163	.51	2,447	Mike Adams	53	876	16.5
1996	Ricky Williams	1,272	205	6.2	James Brown	299	170	.57	2,468	Mike Adams	56	942	16.8
1997	Ricky Williams	1,893	279	6.8	James Brown	267	133	.50	1,676	Kwame Cavil	23	316	13.7
1998	Ricky Williams	2,124	361	5.9	Major Applewhite	273	159	.58	2,453	Wane McGarity	58	1,087	18.7
1999	Hodges Mitchell	1,343	256	5.2	Major Applewhite	467	271	.58	3,357	Kwame Cavil	100	1,188	11.9
2000	Hodges Mitchell	1,118	224	5.0	Major Applewhite	279	152	.54	2,164	B.J. Johnson	41	698	17.0
2001	Cedric Benson	1,053	223	4.7	Chris Simms	362	214	.59	2,603	Roy Williams	67	836	12.5
2002	Cedric Benson	1,293	305	4.2	Chris Simms	396	235	.59	3,207	Roy Williams	64	1,142	17.8
2003	Cedric Benson	1,360	258	5.3	Chance Mock	184	100	.54	1,469	Roy Williams	70	1,079	15.4
2004	Cedric Benson	1,834	326	5.6	Vince Young	250	148	.59	1,849	Tony Jeffery	33	437	13.2

Receiving leaders by receptions
The NCAA began including postseason stats in 2002

TEXAS A&M

BY MARK WANGRIN

TUCKED AWAY IN THE LAND OF PINE trees and pickup trucks is a place of starched military khakis, buzz cuts and leather riding boots. College Station was named after its reason for existence, Texas A&M University, and it's a quiet, bucolic setting for a football program that forever chafed at existing in the shadow of the University of Texas.

A&M was founded in 1876, seven years before Texas, but the land grant agricultural school that originally made military training compulsory and didn't turn coed until 1963 has always been the stepchild who's been shoved to the rear. In the 1880s there was talk of phasing the school out, and the Texas Constitution has always considered A&M an arm of the UT system, much to the Aggies' chagrin. When oil was discovered on UT land in 1923, A&M reluctantly agreed to become part of the state university system so it could claim a one-third share of the revenue that bloated the Permanent University Fund.

While the Longhorns felt entitled, the Aggies sought vindication. Football was a clear avenue to that, and A&M prospered under Homer Norton and Bear Bryant in the late 1930s, early 1940s and mid-1950s. But A&M beat its rival only once from 1957 through 1974, and that stuck in the Aggies' craw so pointedly that they hired Jackie Sherrill away from Pittsburgh in 1982 for an unheard-of annual salary of $267,000. Under Sherrill and his successor, R.C. Slocum, the Aggies won seven conference titles and lifted A&M back into the national elite.

TRADITION Founded on flat land in the Brazos Valley in East Texas, A&M was built as much with tradition as with bricks. Detailing all the Aggie traditions would fill a book of its own, ranging from the close marching of the Aggie Band to the kisses the Corps of Cadets get from their girlfriends after A&M scores. Among the most notable are Silver Taps, Muster and Yell Practice. Silver Taps is a solemn ceremony that honors an Aggie who has died. The campus lights are dimmed, chimes are rung, three rifle volleys are fired and buglers play "Silver Taps" three times. Each year the Aggies hold Muster, in which all the Aggies who died in the past year are honored. Midnight Yell Practice is held the night before home games and features as many as 20,000

PROFILE

Texas Agricultural & Mechanical University
College Station, Texas
Founded: 1876
Enrollment: 35,732
Colors: Maroon and White
Nickname: Aggies
Stadium: Kyle Field
  Opened in 1929
  Grass; 82,600 capacity
First football game: 1894
All-time record: 634–409–49 (.603)
Bowl record: 13–15
Consenus national championships, 1936-present: 1 (1939)
Big 12 Conference championships:
1 (outright)
Heisman Trophy: John David Crow, 1957
First-round NFL draftees: 26
Website: www.aggieathletics.com

THE BEST OF TIMES

In the first five years of the 1990s, R.C. Slocum's Aggies won 51 games and posted two unbeaten regular seasons.

THE WORST OF TIMES

Bear Bryant's exit hurt. In the first nine years after he left, 1958 to 1966, the Aggies went 25–59–6, never winning more than four games in any of those seasons.

CONFERENCE

A charter member of the Southwest Conference, Texas A&M remained in the league throughout its history before joining the Big 12 in 1996.

DISTINGUISHED ALUMNI

Lyle Lovett, singer/songwriter; Rick Perry, Texas governor; Jeff Maggert, golfer; Stacy Sykora, volleyball player; Martin Torrijos, president of Panama; Jorge Quiroga Ramirez, president of Bolivia

FIGHT SONG

THE AGGIE WAR HYMN
Hullabaloo, Caneck! Caneck!
Hullabaloo, Caneck! Caneck!
First Verse
All hail to dear old Texas A&M,
Rally around Maroon and White,
Good luck to the dear old Texas Aggies,
They are the boys who show the fight.
That good old Aggie spirit thrills us.
And makes us yell and yell and yell;
So let's fight for dear old Texas A&M,
We're goin' to beat you all to
Chig-gar-roo-gar-rem!
Chig-gar-roo-gar-rem!
Rough! Tough!
Real stuff! Texas A&M!
Second Verse
Good-bye to Texas University.
So long to the Orange and White.
Good luck to the dear old Texas Aggies,
They are the boys who show the real old fight.
The eyes of Texas are upon you.
That is the song they sing so well,
So, good-bye to Texas University,
We're goin' to beat you all to
Chig-gar-roo-gar-rem!

Founded in 1876 on flat land in the Brazos Valley in East Texas, A&M was built as much with tradition as with bricks.

students. During Yell Practice the students assume a position known as "humping it," in which they bend over with hands placed just above the knees to "properly align the back, mouth and throat for maximum volume."

BEST PLAYER Popular acclaim pins this title on John David Crow, the 1957 Heisman Trophy winner. But Crow rushed for only 562 yards that season, and many around Aggieland believe Crow won the award because of a push from head coach Bear Bryant as much as for his accomplishments. "If they don't give the Heisman Trophy to John Crow they should stop handing out the award," Bryant said. But a better case can be made for fullback "Jarrin'" John Kimbrough, whose heroics in 1939 helped A&M win its only national title and established the program. Kimbrough, who originally attended Tulane only to be cut after an unsuccessful position switch to tackle, used his hard-running style to propel the Aggies to an 11–0 record. He finished as the Heisman runner-up in 1940. "He's the greatest football

player in the world, and you can put my name on that with a picture," Aggie coach Homer Norton said.

BEST COACH Paul "Bear" Bryant was the most high-profile of the Aggie coaches, but it was Homer Norton who set the standard to which Bryant and every A&M coach has aspired. Hoping to restore the early glory days under Dana X. Bible, who won six conference titles and a claim to a national championship in 1919, A&M lured Norton from Centenary in 1934. Norton had an unremarkable 22–23–6 record in his first five seasons, but everything clicked in 1939, when the Aggies shut out six opponents and allowed only one—Tulane in the Sugar Bowl—to score in double digits. Norton added SWC championships in 1940 and 1941.

BEST TEAM Norton knew that he needed a great recruiting class to fulfill the trust placed in him to restore the A&M program, so he told trainer Lilburn Dimmitt to come up with a list of the best players in the state in 1936. A&M

RECORDS	
RUSHING YARDS	
GAME	
297	Bob Smith vs. SMU, Nov. 11, 1950 (29 att.)
SEASON	
1,692	Darren Lewis, 1988 (306 att.)
CAREER	
5,012	Darren Lewis, 1987-90 (909 att.)
PASSING YARDS	
GAME	
399	Dustin Long vs. Kansas, Oct. 19, 2002 (18 of 32)
SEASON	
2,791	Reggie McNeal, 2004 (200 of 344)
CAREER	
6,846	Corey Pullig, 1992-95 (533 of 945)

RECEIVING YARDS	
GAME	
250	Ken McLean vs. Texas, Nov. 25, 1965 (13 rec.)
SEASON	
885	Robert Ferguson, 2000 (58 rec.)
CAREER	
2,600	Terrence Murphy, 2001-04 (172 rec.)
POINTS	
GAME	
44	Jelly Woodman vs. New Mexico, Oct. 16, 1926 (7 TDs, 2 PATs)
SEASON	
128	Joel Hunt, 1927 (19 TDs; complete scoring breakdown unavailable)
CAREER	
325	Kyle Bryant, 1994-97 (60 FGs, 145 PATs)

CONSENSUS ALL-AMERICANS	
1937	Joe Routt, G
1939-40	John Kimbrough, B
1940	Marshall Robnett, G
1957	John David Crow, B
1970	Dave Elmendorf, DB
1974-75	Pat Thomas, DB
1975	Ed Simonini, LB
1976	Tony Franklin, PK
1976	Robert Jackson, LB
1985	Johnny Holland, LB
1987	John Roper, DL
1990	Darren Lewis, RB
1991	Kevin Smith, DB
1992	Marcus Buckley, LB
1993	Aaron Glenn, DB
1993	Sam Adams, DL
1994	Leeland McElroy, KR
1998	Dat Nguyen, LB

enrolled 37 of the "Wanted 40," and after the cash-strapped Aggies administration got an alumnus to strong-arm his bank for a $25,000 loan to pay their scholarship costs, they were set. Two years after they arrived, the Aggies, led by quarterback Marion Pugh, center Tommie Vaughn and Kimbrough, rolled through the regular season—allowing only 18 points in 10 games—and then came from behind to edge Tulane 14-13 in the Sugar Bowl to secure the national title.

BIGGEST GAME Few people outside of Texas knew of A&M's football prowess, or even gave the Aggies much credit in 1939 despite an unbeaten regular season. That changed in the 1940 Sugar Bowl, when the Aggies took on Tulane in the Green Wave's home stadium. Kimbrough pounded Tulane early and led A&M to a quick 7-0 lead. But the Green Wave rallied to take a 13-7 lead. In the fourth quarter Kimbrough capped a 70-yard drive with a touchdown and the ensuing extra point gave the Aggies a 14-13 victory.

BIGGEST UPSET Oklahoma came into College Station in 2002 at 8–0, ranked No. 1 and apparently on its way to a second national title in three years. The Aggies, meanwhile, were coming off a 28-23 loss at Oklahoma State and were beset by injuries to key starters, including leading rusher Derrick Farmer. After OU did the expected, jumping to a quick 10-0 lead, Slocum put in freshman Reggie McNeal. Mixing elusive runs with deep balls, McNeal rallied A&M to a 13-13 tie at the half. He continued to burn OU deep, with the last of his four touchdown passes giving the Aggies a 27-23 lead. A key fourth-down stop and an interception sealed the 30-26 victory.

STADIUM E.J. Kyle, the first dean of A&M's School of Agriculture, had been put in charge of a significant parcel of land, with the mandate to use it for horticulture. Kyle used it to grow a football program, fencing in the land in 1905 to preserve its use for the school's fledgling athletic programs.

ALL-TIME TEAM		
Selected by the editors of 12th Man Magazine *in 1999.*		
OFFENSE		
1935-37	Joe Routt, OL	
1937-39	Joe Boyd, OL	
1955-57	Charlie Krueger, OL	
1985-88	Jerry Fontenot, OL	
1986-89	Richmond Webb, OL	
1987-90	Mike Arthur, OL	
1983-86	Rod Bernstine, TE	
1999-02	Bethel Johnson, WR	
2001-04	Terrence Murphy, WR	
1983-86	Kevin Murray, QB	
1938-40	John Kimbrough, RB	
1955-57	John David Crow, RB	
1987-90	Darren Lewis, RB	
1975-78	Tony Franklin, PK	
1993-95	Leeland McElroy, KR	
1936-38	Dick Todd, PR	
DEFENSE		
1977-79	Jacob Green, DL	
1981-84	Ray Childress, DL	
1991-93	Sam Adams, DL	
1993-96	Brandon Mitchell, DL	
1972-75	Ed Simonini, LB	
1983-86	Johnny Holland, LB	
1986-89	Aaron Wallace, LB	
1995-98	Dat Nguyen, LB	
1966-68	Tommy Maxwell, DB	
1968-70	Dave Elmendorf, DB	
1972-75	Pat Thomas, DB	
1973-76	Lester Hayes, DB	
1988-91	Kevin Smith, DB	
1992-93	Aaron Glenn, DB	
1996-99	Shane Lechler, P	

In 1906, the field was named after him. Slowly it was expanded, with a $365,000 concrete stadium completed in 1929 to replace the ramshackle wooden bleachers. A horseshoe-shape grandstand wrapped around the end zone, and double and triple decks were erected on each side of the field. In 1999, a triple deck was completed in the north end zone at a cost of $32.9 million to increase capacity to 82,600.

HEARTBREAKER In 1975, the Aggies had just come off a 20-10 win at Texas, their first over the Longhorns since 1967 and only their second in 18 years. Unbeaten and untied, the Aggies needed only to beat Arkansas in Little Rock to win their first conference title since 1967. But the No. 18 Razorbacks took a 7-0 lead late in the first half and then steamrolled the second-ranked Aggies in the second half on their way to a 31-6 victory. The Aggies were unable to regroup in time for the Liberty Bowl, where USC trounced them 20-0.

BEST GOAL-LINE STAND In the 1986 Cotton Bowl, the Wrecking Crew defense stopped Heisman Trophy winner Bo Jackson four times inside the A&M 10-yard line. Down 23-16, Auburn drove 93 yards to the A&M 6, where the Tigers had a first down. The first carry by Jackson gained four, but he couldn't get any closer on the next two. On fourth down linebackers Larry Kelm and Basil Jackson tackled Jackson for a one-yard loss on the Aggies' 3-yard line. Jackson, who accounted for 202 yards from scrimmage and earned game Most Outstanding Offensive Player honors, second-guessed coach Pat Dye after the game, saying they should have run outside rather than off tackle. Then Bo second-guessed Bo. "They probably would have stopped us on the outside play, too," he said.

BEST COMEBACK In what's generally accepted as the wildest finish in A&M football history, the Aggies stunned Kansas State, then No. 1 in the ESPN/*USA Today* Coaches

Poll, in the 1998 Big 12 championship game. KSU came in unbeaten behind a suffocating defense and the run-pass threat of Heisman Trophy runner-up Michael Bishop. A&M was coming off a disappointing loss at Texas, starting quarterback Randy McCown's arm was in a sling and the offensive line was in disarray. In the first quarter McCown's replacement, Branndon Stewart, hyperextended his knee, and the Aggies looked like they would have to press punter Shane Lechler into emergency signal-calling duties. KSU led 27-12 at the start of the fourth quarter but Stewart, who had miraculously returned, began picking apart the KSU secondary. His nine-yard touchdown pass and ensuing two-point conversion pass, both to Sirr Parker, tied the game. KSU nearly won it on a Hail Mary pass by Bishop at the final gun, but Toya Jones made a game-saving tackle of Everett Burnett at the A&M 1 to send the game into overtime. The teams swapped field goals in the first overtime, but after KSU settled for a field goal in the second period, Stewart threw a slant to Parker, who just managed to get inside the right pylon for the winning touchdown. The final score: 36-33.

DUBIOUS DISTINCTION In 2002, Oklahoma came into Kyle Field undefeated and ranked No. 1 and left on the short end of a 30-26 upset. On Nov. 8, 2003, the Aggies traveled to Norman prepared to shock the college football world one more time. They did, but not in the way that they had hoped. A&M had only three first downs and 54 yards of total offense. OU scored 35 points in the second quarter and, even though it pulled many of its starters in the third quarter, kept piling on the points. The Sooners didn't throw a pass in the final five minutes and took a knee at the A&M 5-yard line with eight minutes left. The result was a 77-0 blowout and the cruelest Aggie joke since Texas beat them 48-0 in 1898.

RIVAL They refer to the school only as "t.u." and have a chant that implores the Aggies to "saw Varsity's horns off." This, of course, refers to Texas. The Aggies have kidnapped Bevo, the UT mascot, three times. The Longhorns dognapped a retired Reveille, the Aggies mascot, once. One year, some Aggies sneaked into Memorial Stadium and cut the horns off the Longhorn logo on the artificial turf in the end zone. As the 21st century began, A&M also found itself more agitated by Texas Tech, particularly after a 12-0 Tech win in Lubbock in 2001 that culminated with Red Raider fans tearing down the goalposts and trying to carry them into the A&M fans section at Jones Stadium.

TRAGEDY In 1909, a group of Aggies gathered around a burning fir tree days before the annual game with Texas, giving birth to one of the Aggies' most treasured traditions. Over the years, The Bonfire grew to as high as 109 feet and burned every year—save 1963, when the stack was dismantled out of respect for assassinated president John F. Kennedy—until 1999. In the early morning hours of Nov. 18, 1999, wire holding the stack together snapped, sending the giant logs down on the workers stacking them. The football team canceled practice to help look for survivors. Twelve current or former students were killed. Seven days later, 50,000 people surrounded the collapse site for a candlelight vigil. The next day the Aggies, playing on emotion, came from behind and beat the No. 5 Longhorns 20-16. "We put our hearts and soul into this game," said linebacker Brian Gamble. "I know God and those Aggies were looking down on us." The Bonfire has not burned since. School officials continue to search for a way to make the practice safe.

NICKNAME Aggies is derived from the school's agricultural background, harkening back to the university's original name, the Agricultural and Mechanical College of Texas.

MASCOT Driving down a street near campus in 1931, some Aggies students accidentally struck a dog with their Model T. They picked up the injured collie and brought her back to their dorm. When the bugler sounded the military song "Reveille" the next morning, the dog began barking wildly. Reveille had her name. The dog was soon adopted by the Corps and joined the cadets on marches. She became the official mascot when she accompanied the Aggie band on the field at the first home football game the following fall. Reveille VII, introduced in 2001, is as revered as all her predecessors, with a commission as a five-star general, making her the highest ranking member of the Corps.

UNIFORMS Red and white were the school colors from the early 1900s, but in the 1920s a uniform supplier erroneously sent maroon jerseys. An athletic department official decided to use the jerseys, figuring the color set the Aggies apart from the scores of other schools that used red. A&M's jerseys have featured a variety of stripes on the sleeves and trunk. Early in his tenure, Sherrill adopted a solid jersey with two stripes on the sleeves from the cuff to the neckline before reverting to horizontal stripes on the sleeves. Slocum returned the school's name above the front number when he became coach. The Aggies' helmet has been maroon, with the notable exception of 1972 to 1978, when it was

white. In the mid-1960s the numbers on the sides of the helmet were dropped in favor of the now familiar logo with a small "A" and "M" flanking a large "T."

QUIRK It sends a tingle down the spine of anyone who's ever lived near an earthquake fault—and even those who haven't. When the verse of the Aggie War Hymn that lights into UT is played during games, the fans and students lock arms and sway in unison, causing the upper decks to noticeably sway. The school's weekly press release issues this prominent warning: "Welcome to Kyle Field. For those of you visiting for the first time, please do not be alarmed. The press box will move during the Aggie War Hymn." To assuage fears, structural engineers routinely examine the decks and have declared them safe. The singing and swaying help make A&M one of the most intimidating stadiums. Coach Bear Bryant claimed that "10 Aggies can yell louder than a hundred of anybody else." Former safety Patrick Bates said the influence of the home crowd is worth "at least a touchdown and a couple of sacks."

QUOTE "We will get to the point where we will be very awesome. And it won't be very long. So all the people better get their licks in while they can." —Jackie Sherrill, after a 47-9 loss to SMU in 1982

TEXAS A&M ANNUAL STATISTICAL LEADERS

YR	RUSHING	YDS	ATT	AVG	PASSING	ATT	CMP	PCT	YDS	RECEIVING	REC	YDS	AVG
1949	Bob Smith	694	145	4.8	Don Nicholas	58	28	.48	311	Wray Whittaker	26	291	11.2
1950	Bob Smith	1,302	199	6.5	Dick Gardemal	66	39	.59	559	Andy Hillhouse	24	398	16.6
1951	Glenn Lippman	801	118	6.8	Ray Graves	98	45	.46	621	Billy Tidwell	13	256	19.7
1952	Don Ellis	377	156	2.4	Ray Graves	164	93	.57	989	Don Ellis	33	273	8.3
1953	Connie Magouirk	283	52	5.4	Don Ellis	171	76	.44	960	Bennie Sinclair	19	287	15.1
1954	Elwood Kettler	446	149	3.0	Elwood Kettler	72	36	.50	471	Bennie Sinclair	22	293	13.3
1955	Jack Pardee	452	83	5.4	James Wright	67	24	.36	368	Bobby Marks	7	94	13.4
1956	Roddy Osborne	568	141	4.0	Roddy Osborne	23	14	.61	258	John David Crow	7	125	17.9
1957	John David Crow	562	129	4.4	Charles Milstead	35	14	.40	185	John Tracey	8	103	12.9
1958	Luther Hall	238	70	3.4	Charles Milstead	167	88	.53	1,135	John Tracey	37	466	12.6
1959	Gordon LeBoeuf	351	113	3.1	Charles Milstead	117	62	.53	752	Russell Hill	19	341	17.9
1960	Sam Byer	381	105	3.6	Daryle Keeling	50	18	.36	204	Randy Sims	5	66	13.2
1961	Lee Roy Caffey	371	85	4.4	John Erickson	73	34	.47	468	Travis Reagan	10	201	20.1
1962	Jim Linnstaedter	167	36	4.6	Jim Keller	80	30	.38	343	George Hargett	14	194	13.9
1963	Budgie Ford	234	62	3.8	Charles LaGrange	73	28	.38	393	George Hargett	12	162	13.5
1964	Lloyd Curington	287	99	2.9	Dan McIlhany	111	47	.42	598	Billy Uzzell	22	246	11.2
1965	Bill Sallee	272	84	3.2	Harry Ledbetter	182	83	.46	940	Ken McLean	60	835	13.9
1966	Wendell Housley	548	155	3.5	Edd Hargett	265	132	.50	1,532	Tommy Maxwell	27	445	16.5
1967	Larry Stegent	568	161	3.5	Edd Hargett	208	99	.48	1,526	Bob Long	24	541	22.5
1968	Larry Stegent	527	105	5.0	Edd Hargett	348	169	.49	2,321	Barney Harris	49	745	15.2
1969	Larry Stegent	676	197	3.4	Rocky Self	199	87	.44	1,136	Barney Harris	34	191	5.6
1970	Doug Neill	426	107	4.0	Lex James	225	111	.49	1,662	Homer May	26	479	18.4
1971	Mark Green	593	181	3.3	Joe Mac King	87	36	.41	559	Robert Murski	17	212	12.5
1972	Brad Dusek	549	124	4.4	Don Dean	113	57	.50	820	Richard Osborne	31	440	14.2
1973	Bubba Bean	711	112	6.3	Mike Jay	86	36	.42	682	Richard Osborne	29	405	14.0
1974	Bubba Bean	938	158	5.9	David Walker	102	46	.45	666	Richard Osborne	13	145	11.2
1975	Bubba Bean	944	144	6.6	David Shipman	60	24	.40	422	Richard Osborne	13	191	14.7
1976	George Woodard	1,153	239	4.8	David Walker	90	51	.57	675	Gary Haack	21	265	12.6
1977	George Woodard	1,107	245	4.5	David Walker	107	49	.46	750	Curtis Dickey	17	231	13.6
1978	Curtis Dickey	1,146	205	5.6	Mike Mosley	139	80	.58	1,157	Russell Mikeska	29	429	14.8
1979	Curtis Dickey	894	172	5.2	Mike Mosley	142	82	.58	938	Gerald Carter	39	528	13.5
1980	Johnny Hector	928	173	5.4	David Beal	94	45	.48	671	Mike Whitwell	30	603	20.1
1981	Earnest Jackson	887	153	5.8	Gary Kubiak	209	111	.53	1,808	Mike Whitwell	27	731	27.1
1982	Johnny Hector	554	140	4.0	Gary Kubiak	324	181	.56	1,948	Don Jones	32	461	14.4
1983	Roger Vick	425	91	4.7	Kevin Murray	249	132	.53	1,544	Rich Siler	40	465	11.6
1984	Thomas Sanders	738	167	4.4	Craig Stump	189	94	.50	1,135	Jimmy Teal	35	631	18.0
1985	Anthony Toney	845	208	4.1	Kevin Murray	251	147	.59	1,965	Jeff Nelson	51	651	12.8
1986	Roger Vick	960	220	4.4	Kevin Murray	349	212	.61	2,463	Rod Bernstine	65	710	10.9
1987	Darren Lewis	668	127	5.3	Craig Stump	98	41	.42	524	Keith Woodside	25	237	9.5
1988	Darren Lewis	1,692	306	5.5	Chris Osgood	112	54	.48	656	Rod Harris	37	592	16.0
1989	Darren Lewis	961	185	5.2	Lance Pavlas	227	134	.59	1,681	Percy Waddle	36	600	16.7
1990	Darren Lewis	1,691	291	5.8	Lance Pavlas	89	56	.63	871	Gary Oliver	28	455	16.3
1991	Greg Hill	1,216	240	5.1	Bucky Richardson	156	79	.51	1,492	Tony Harrison	31	577	18.6
1992	Greg Hill	1,339	267	5.0	Corey Pullig	126	63	.50	953	Greg Schorp	24	280	11.7
1993	Rodney Thomas	996	191	5.2	Corey Pullig	243	144	.59	1,732	Tony Harrison	31	481	15.5
1994	Rodney Thomas	868	199	4.4	Corey Pullig	269	161	.60	2,056	Ryan Mathews	29	395	13.6
1995	Leeland McElroy	1,122	246	4.6	Corey Pullig	307	165	.54	2,105	Albert Connell	41	653	15.9
1996	Sirr Parker	704	149	4.7	Branndon Stewart	299	146	.49	1,904	Albert Connell	57	872	15.3
1997	Dante Hall	973	134	7.3	Branndon Stewart	196	111	.57	1,429	Derrick Spiller	25	436	17.4
1998	Dante Hall	1,024	243	4.2	Randy McCown	130	66	.51	1,025	Chris Cole	38	667	17.6
1999	Ja'Mar Toombs	583	147	4.0	Randy McCown	295	152	.52	2,374	Chris Taylor	33	591	17.9
2000	Richard Whitaker	455	84	5.4	Mark Farris	347	208	.60	2,551	Robert Ferguson	58	885	15.3
2001	Derek Farmer	503	110	4.6	Mark Farris	347	203	.59	2,094	Jamaar Taylor	39	489	12.5
2002	Derek Farmer	739	172	4.3	Dustin Long	333	177	.53	2,509	Greg Porter	48	669	13.9
2003	Courtney Lewis	1,024	186	5.5	Reggie McNeal	221	113	.51	1,782	Terrence Murphy	44	762	17.3
2004	Courtney Lewis	742	175	4.2	Reggie McNeal	344	200	.58	2,791	Terrence Murphy	56	721	12.9

Receiving leaders by receptions
The NCAA began including postseason stats in 2002

TEXAS A&M ALL-TIME SCORES

WIN/LOSS PERCENTAGE SINCE 1936

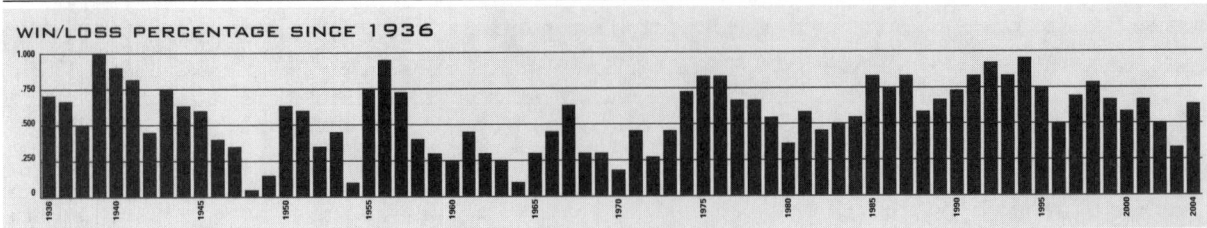

F.D. PERKINS
1894 (.500)   1-1

1894   1-1-0
U	● Galveston HS	14	6
O19	at Texas	0	38

1895
NO TEAM

A.M. SOULE / H.W. SOUTH
1896 (.833)   2-0-1

1896   2-0-1
U	= Galveston HS	0	0
U	● Austin Coll.	22	4
U	● Houston HS	28	0

C.W. TAYLOR
1897 (.333)   1-2

1897   1-2-0
U	Houston HS	0	10
U	TCU	6	30
U	● Austin Coll.	4	0

H.W. WILLIAMS
1898 (.667)   4-2

1898   4-2-0
U	● Houston HS	51	0
O22	at Texas	0	48
U	Houston HS	0	6
U	● TCU *WAC*	16	0
U	● Austin Coll.	22	6
U	● Fort Worth	28	0

W.A. MURRAY
1899-1901 (.469)   7-8-1

1899   4-2-0
U	● Houston HS	43	0
N4	Texas *SA*	0	6
N10	Sewanee	0	10
U	● Baylor	33	0
N27	● Tulane	22	0
D2	● LSU	52	0

1900   2-2-1
U	K.C. Med. Coll.	6	6
O27	Texas *SA*	0	5
U	Waxahachie AC	11	0
U	● Henry Coll.	44	0
N29	at Texas	0	11

1901   1-4-0
U	Baylor	6	17
O26	Texas *SA*	0	17
N5	● Baylor	6	0
U	Baylor	0	46 *
N28	at Texas	0	32

J.E. PLATT
1902-04 (.750)   18-5-2

1902   7-0-2
U	● St.Edwards	11	0
U	= Trinity	0	0
O10	● Baylor	11	6
O14	● Baylor	22	0
O25	Texas *SA*	0	0
N8	Tulane	17	5
U	● TCU *WAC*	22	0
U	● Trinity	34	0
N27	at Texas	12	0 *

1903   7-3-1
O3	● Trinity	16	0
O10	● TCU *UNK*	11	0
O17	= at Baylor	0	0
O24	● Oklahoma	0	6
O31	● Arkansas	6	0
N7	● Baylor	16	0 *
N14	● TCU	16	0
N18	Trinity	0	18
N21	● Baylor	5	0
N28	at TCU	14	6
N29	at Texas	6	29

1904   4-2-0
O8	● Deaf & Dumb	49	0
O15	● at Baylor	5	0
O22	● TCU	29	0
N5	Sewanee *DAL*	5	17
N12	● Baylor	10	0
N24	at Texas	6	34

W.E. BACHMAN
1905-06 (.813)   13-3

1905   7-2-0
S23	● Houston YMCA	29	0
S30	● TCU	20	0
O14	● at Baylor	42	0
O21	● Austin Coll.	18	11
O28	● Trinity	24	0
N4	● TCU *UNK*	24	11
N11	Transylvania, Ky	6	29
N18	● Baylor	17	5
N22	at Texas	0	27

1906   6-1-0
O27	● TCU	42	0
N3	● Daniel Baker	34	0
N10	● TCU *UNK*	22	0
N17	at Tulane	18	0
N19	at LSU	22	12
N24	● Haskell	32	6
N29	at Texas	0	24

L.L. LARSON
1907 (.813)   6-1-1

1907   6-1-1
O5	● Fort Worth	34	0
O12	= Texas *DAL*	0	0
O21	● LSU	11	5
O28	● Haskell	5	0
N5	● TCU	32	5
N12	● Oklahoma	19	0
N16	at Tulane	18	6
N28	at Texas	6	11

N.A. MERRIAM
1908 (.375)   3-5

1908   3-5-0
O3	● Trinity	6	0
O10	Baylor	5	6
O17	LSU *NO*	0	26
O31	● TCU *UNK*	13	10
N9	Texas *HOU*	8	24
N13	Haskell	0	23
N21	● Southwestern	32	0
N29	at Texas	12	28

CHARLES B. MORAN
1909-14 (.800)   38-8-4

1909   7-0-1
O9	● Austin Coll.	17	0
O16	● TCU	0	0
O23	● Haskell	15	0
O30	● at Baylor	9	6
N8	● Texas *HOU*	23	0
N13	● Trinity	47	0
N17	● Oklahoma *DAL*	14	8
N25	● at Texas	5	0

1910   8-1-0
S24	● Marshall School	48	0
O1	● Austin Coll.	27	5
O8	● TCU	35	0
O15	● Transylvania, Ky	33	0
O29	at Arkansas	0	5
N5	● at TCU	23	6
N14	● Texas *HOU*	14	8
N19	● Southwestern	6	0
N24	● Tulane *HOU*	17	0

1911   6-1-0
O7	● Southwestern	22	0
O14	● Austin Coll.	33	0
O21	● Auburn *DAL*	16	0
O27	● Mississippi	17	0
N13	Texas *HOU*	0	6
N18	● Baylor	22	11
N25	● Dallas U.	24	0

1912   8-1-0
O5	● Daniel Baker	50	0
O12	● Trinity	59	0
O18	● Arkansas *DAL*	27	0
O26	● Austin Coll.	57	0
N9	● Oklahoma *HOU*	28	6
N16	● Mississippi State *HOU*	41	7
N19	● Tulane	41	0
N20	● Kansas State	10	13
N28	● Baylor *DAL*	53	0

1913   3-4-2
O11	● Trinity	7	0
O18	● Austin Coll.	6	0
O25	● Fort Worth Poly	19	6
N1	● Mississippi State	0	6
N8	at Kansas State	0	12
N15	● Oklahoma State	0	3
N19	● Haskell	0	28
N22	● Baylor	14	14
N27	● LSU *HOU*	7	7

1914   6-1-1
O3	● Austin Coll.	32	0
O10	● Trinity	0	0
O17	● TCU	40	0
O23	● Haskell *FrW*	0	10
O31	● LSU *DAL*	63	9
N9	at Rice	32	7
N21	● Oklahoma State	24	0
N26	● Mississippi *BEAU*	14	7

1915-1995
SWC

E.H. HARLAN
1915-16 (.706)   12-5

1915   6-2-0 (1-1-0)
O2	● Austin Coll.	40	0
O9	● Trinity	62	0
O16	at TCU	13	10
O23	● Missouri Rolla	33	3
O30	● Haskell *DAL*	21	7
N8	at Rice	0	7
N19	| Texas	13	0
N25	Mississippi State *DAL*	0	7

1916   6-3-0 (2-2-0)
S30	| Southwestern	6	0
O7	| Dallas U.	20	6
O14	LSU *GAL*	0	13
O21	| SMU	62	0
O28	| Haskell *DAL*	13	6
N4	| at Rice	0	20
N11	| at Baylor	3	0
N18	| Missouri Rolla	77	0
N30	| at Texas	7	21

D.X. BIBLE
1917, '19-28 (.765)   72-19-9

1917   8-0-0 (3-0-0)
O6	● Austin Coll.	66	0
O13	● Dallas U.	98	0
O20	● Southwestern	20	0
O27	● LSU *SA*	27	0
N2	● Tulane	35	0
N10	| at Baylor	7	0
N20	| Texas	7	0
N29	| at Rice	10	0

D.V. GRAVES
1918 (.857)   6-1

1918   6-1-0 (1-1-0)
O12	● Ream. Field	6	0
O19	● Camp Travis	12	6
N2	● at Baylor	19	0
N9	● Southwestern	7	0
N16	● Camp Mabry	19	6
N28	| at Texas	0	7
D7	● Camp Travis	60	0

D.X. BIBLE

1919   10-0-0 (4-0-0)
S27	● Sam Houston St.	77	0
O4	● Texas St.	28	0
O11	● at SMU	16	0
O18	● Howard Payne	12	0
O25	● Trinity	42	0
N1	● Oklahoma State	28	0
N8	● at Baylor	10	0
N15	● TCU	48	0
N22	● Southwestern	7	0
N27	● Texas	7	0

1920   6-1-1 (5-1-0)
O2	● Daniel Baker	110	0
O9	● at SMU	3	0
O16	= LSU	0	0
O23	| Phillips	47	0
O30	● at Oklahoma State	35	0
N6	| at Baylor	24	0
N15	| Rice	7	0
N25	| at Texas	3	7

1921   6-1-2 (3-0-2)
O8	● Howard Payne	14	7
O12	● at SMU	13	0
O15	at LSU	0	6
O22	● Arizona	17	13
O29	| Oklahoma State	23	7
N5	| at Baylor	14	3
N11	= at Rice	7	7
N24	| Texas	0	0

DIXIE CLASSIC
J2	● Centre	22	14

1922   5-4-0 (2-2-0)
S30	● Howard Payne	7	13
O10	● Tulsa *DAL*	10	13
O14	● Southwestern	33	0
O20	● LSU	46	0
O28	● Ouachita	19	6
N4	| at Baylor	7	13
N11	| at SMU	6	17
N18	| Rice	24	0
N30	● at Texas	14	7

1923   5-3-1 (0-3-1)
S22	● Sam Houston St.	53	0
S29	● Howard Payne	21	0
O6	● Southwestern	13	0
O13	● Sewanee *DAL*	14	0
O20	at LSU	28	0
O26	| SMU	0	10
N3	= at Baylor	0	0
N17	| at Rice	6	7
N29	| Texas	0	6

1924 7-2-1 (2-2-1)

S20	•	Tarleton St.	40	0
S27	•	Trinity	33	0
O4	•	Southwestern	54	0
O11	•	Sewanee *DAL*	7	0
O18	•	Arkansas State	40	0
O25	=	at SMU	7	7
N1	•	at Baylor	7	15
N8	•	TCU	28	0
N15	•	Rice	13	6
N27			at Texas	0	7

1925 7-1-1 (4-1-0)

S26	•	Trinity	20	10
O3	•	Southwestern	23	6
O10	=	Sewanee *DAL*	6	6
O16	•	SMU	7	0
O24	•	Sam Houston St.	77	0
O31	•	at Baylor	13	0
N7			at TCU	0	3
N14	•	at Rice	17	0
N26	•	Texas	28	0

1926 5-3-1 (1-3-1)

S25	•	Trinity	26	0
O2	•	Southwestern	35	0
O9	•	Sewanee *DAL*	6	3
O16	•	New Mexico	63	0
O23			at SMU	7	9
O30			at Baylor	9	20
N6	=	TCU	13	13
N12	•	Rice	20	0
N25			at Texas	5	14

1927 8-0-1 (4-0-1)

S24	•	Trinity	45	0
O1	•	Southwestern	31	0
O8	•	Sewanee *DAL*	18	0
O15			Arkansas	40	6
O22	=	at TCU	0	0
O28	•	Texas Tech	47	6
N5	•	at SMU	39	13
N11	•	at Rice	14	0
N24			Texas	28	7

1928 5-4-1 (1-3-1)

S22	•	Trinity	21	0
S29	•	Southwestern	21	0
O6	•	Sewanee *DAL*	69	0
O13	•	Centenary	0	6
O20			TCU	0	6
O29			at Arkansas	12	27
N3	•	North Texas	44	0
N10	•	at SMU	19	19
N16	•	Rice	19	0
N29			at Texas	0	19

MADISON BELL
1929-33 (.531)   24-21-3

1929 5-4-0 (2-3-0)

S28	•	Southwestern	54	7
O5	•	at Tulane	10	13
O12	•	Kansas State *DAL*	19	0
O19			at TCU	7	13
O26	•	Arkansas	13	14
N2	•	S.F. Austin	54	0
N9			SMU	7	12
N16	•	at Rice	26	6
N28	•	Texas	13	0

1930 2-7-0 (0-5-0)

S27	•	Southwestern	43	0
O4	•	at Nebraska	0	13
O11	•	Tulane *DAL*	9	19
O18	•	TCU	0	3
O25			Arkansas *LR*	0	13
N1	•	Centenary	7	6
N8	•	at SMU	7	13
N15			Rice	0	7
N27			at Texas	0	26

1931 7-3-0 (3-2-0)

S19	•	Southwestern	33	0
S26	•	Tarleton St.	21	0
O3			at Tulane	0	7
O10	•	Iowa *DAL*	29	0
O17			at TCU	0	6
O24			Baylor	33	7
O31	•	at Centenary	7	0
N7			SMU	0	8
N14	•	at Rice	7	0
N26	•	Texas	7	6

1932 4-4-2 (1-2-2)

S24	•	Texas Tech *AMAR*	7	0
O1	•	at Tulane	14	26
O8	•	Sam Houston St.	26	0
O12	•	Texas A&I	14	0
O15			TCU	0	17
O22	=	at Baylor	0	0
O29			at Centenary	0	7
N5	=	at SMU	0	0
N11	•	Rice	14	7
N24			at Texas	0	21

1933 6-3-1 (2-2-1)

S23	•	Trinity	38	0
S30	•	at Tulane	13	6
O7	•	Sam Houston St.	34	14
O14	•	Texas A&I	17	0
O21			at TCU	7	13
O28	•	Baylor	14	7
N4			at Centenary	0	20
N11			SMU	0	19
N18	•	at Rice	27	0
N30	=	Texas	10	10

HOMER NORTON
1934-47 (.601)   82-53-9

1934 2-7-2 (1-4-1)

S22	•	Sam Houston St.	28	0
S29	=	Texas A&I	14	14
O6			at Temple	6	40
O13			Centenary *BEAU*	0	13
O20			TCU	0	13
O27	c	at Baylor	10	7
N3	=	Arkansas	7	7
N10			at SMU	0	28
N17			Rice	6	25
N28			at Texas	0	13
D8			Michigan State *SA*	13	26

1935 3-7-0 (1-5-0)

S21	•	S.F. Austin	37	6
S28	•	at Sam Houston St.	25	0
O5			Temple	0	14
O12	•	at Centenary	6	7
O19			at TCU	14	19
O26			Baylor	6	14
N2			Arkansas *LR*	7	14
N16			at Rice	10	17
N28	•	Texas	20	6
D7			SMU	0	24

1936 8-3-1 (3-2-1)

S26	•	Sam Houston St.	39	6
O3	•	at Hardin Simmons	3	0
O10	•	at Rice	3	0
O17			TCU	18	7
O24	=	at Baylor	0	0
O31			Arkansas	0	18
N7	•	at SMU	22	6
N14	•	at Utah	20	7
N21	•	at Centenary	0	3
N26			Texas	7	0
D5	•	Manhattan	13	6
D12	•	at San Francisco	38	14

1937 5-2-2 (2-2-2)

O2	•	Manhattan *NYC*	14	7
O9	•	Mississippi State *TYL*	14	0
O16			at TCU	7	7
O23			Baylor	0	13
O30			at Arkansas	13	26
N6	•	SMU	14	0
N13	=	at Rice	6	6
N25	•	Texas	7	0
D4	•	at San Francisco	42	0

1938 4-4-1 (2-3-1)

S24	•	Texas A&I	52	0
O1	•	Tulsa *TYL*	20	0
O8			Santa Clara	0	7
O15			TCU	6	34
O22	=	at Baylor	6	6
O29	•	Arkansas	13	7
N5			at SMU	7	10
N12	•	Rice	27	0
N24			at Texas	6	7

1939 11-0-0 (6-0-0)

S23	•	at Oklahoma State	32	0
S30	•	Centenary	14	0
O7	•	at Santa Clara	7	3
O14	•	Villanova *TYL*	33	7
O21	•	at TCU	20	6
O28	•	Baylor	20	0
N4	•	at Arkansas	27	0
N11	•	SMU	6	2
N18	•	at Rice	19	0
N30			Texas	20	0

SUGAR BOWL

J1	•	Tulane	14	13

1940 9-1-0 (5-1-0)

S28	•	Texas A&I	26	0
O5	•	Tulsa *SA*	41	6
O12	•	at UCLA	7	0
O19	•	TCU	21	7
O26	•	at Baylor	14	7
N2	•	Arkansas	17	0
N9	•	at SMU	19	7
N16	•	Rice	25	0
N28			at Texas	0	7

COTTON BOWL

J1	•	Fordham	13	12

1941 9-2-0 (5-1-0)

S27	•	Sam Houston St.	54	0
O4	•	Texas A&I	41	0
O11	•	NYU *BRNX*	49	7
O18	•	at TCU	14	0
O25	•	Baylor	48	0
N1			Arkansas	7	0
N8	•	SMU	21	10
N15	•	at Rice	19	6
N27			Texas	0	23
D6	•	Washington State *TAC*	7	0

COTTON BOWL

J1	•	Alabama	21	29

1942 4-5-1 (2-3-1)

S26	•	at LSU	7	16
O3	•	Texas Tech	19	0
O10	•	at Corpus Christi NAS	7	18
O17			TCU	2	7
O24	•	at Baylor	0	6
O31	•	Arkansas	41	0
N7	•	at SMU	27	20
N14	=	at Rice	0	0
N26			at Texas	6	12
D5	•	Washington State *SA*	21	0

1943 7-2-1 (4-1-0)

S25	•	Bryan AFB	48	6
O2	•	Texas Tech *SA*	13	0
O9	•	at LSU	28	13
O16	•	at TCU	13	0
O23	=	North Texas AC	0	0
O30	•	at Arkansas	13	0
N6			SMU	22	0
N13	•	at Rice	20	0
N25			Texas	13	27

ORANGE BOWL

J1	•	LSU	14	19

1944 7-4-0 (2-3-0)

S23	•	Bryan AFB	39	0
S30	•	Texas Tech *SA*	27	14
O7	•	Oklahoma *OKC*	14	21
O14	•	at LSU	7	0
O21			TCU	7	13
O28	•	North Texas AC	61	0
N4			Arkansas	6	7
N11	•	at SMU	39	6
N18	•	at Rice	19	7 *
N30			at Texas	0	6
D8	•	at Miami, Fla.	70	14

1945 6-4-0 (3-3-0)

S22	•	Ellington Field	54	0
S29	•	Texas Tech *SA*	16	6
O6	•	at Oklahoma	19	14
O13			at LSU	12	31
O20			at TCU	12	13
O27	•	Baylor	19	13
N3	•	at Arkansas	34	0
N10	•	SMU	3	0
N17	•	at Rice	0	6
N29			Texas	10	20

1946 4-6-0 (3-3-0)

S21	•	North Texas	47	0
S28	•	Texas Tech *SA*	0	6
O5	•	at Oklahoma	7	10
O12	•	at LSU	9	33
O19	•	TCU	14	0
O26	•	at Baylor	17	0
N2			Arkansas	0	7
N8	•	at SMU	14	0
N16	•	Rice	10	27
N28			at Texas	7	24

1947 3-6-1 (1-4-1)

S20	•	Southwestern	48	0
S27	•	Texas Tech *SA*	29	7
O4	•	at Oklahoma	14	26
O11	•	at LSU	13	19
O18	•	at TCU	0	26
O25	•	Baylor	24	0
N1	=	at Arkansas	21	21
N8			SMU	0	13
N15	•	at Rice	7	41
N27			Texas	13	32

HARRY STITELER
1948-50 (.290)   8-21-2

1948 0-9-1 (0-5-1)

S18	•	Villanova *PHIL*	14	34
S25	•	Texas Tech *SA*	14	20
O2	•	at Oklahoma	14	42
O9	•	at LSU	13	14
O16			TCU	14	27
O23			at Baylor	14	20
O30			Arkansas	6	28
N6			at SMU	14	20
N13			Rice	6	28
N25	•	at Texas	14	14

1949 1-8-1 (0-5-1)

S17	•	Villanova	0	35
S24	•	Texas Tech *SA*	26	7
O1	•	at Oklahoma	13	33
O8			at LSU	0	34
O15			at TCU	6	28
O22			Baylor	0	21
O29			at Arkansas	6	27
N5	=	SMU	27	27
N12			at Rice	0	13
N24			Texas	14	42

1950 7-4-0 (3-3-0)

S23	•	Nevada *SA*	48	18
S30	•	Texas Tech *SA*	34	13
O7	•	at Oklahoma	28	34
O14	•	VMI	52	0
O21			TCU	42	23
O28			at Baylor	20	27
N4	•	Arkansas	42	13
N11	•	at SMU	25	20
N18	•	Rice	13	21
N30			at Texas	0	17

PRESIDENTIAL CUP

D9	•	Georgia	40	20

RAYMOND GEORGE
1951-53 (.467)   12-14-4

1951 5-3-2 (1-3-2)

S21	•	at UCLA	21	14
S29	•	Texas Tech *SA*	20	7
O6	•	Oklahoma	14	7
O13	•	at Trinity	53	14
O20			at TCU	14	20
O27	=	Baylor	21	21
N3			at Arkansas	21	33
N10	=	SMU	14	14
N17			at Rice	13	28 *
N29	•	Texas	22	21

1952 3-6-1 (1-4-1)

S20	•	at Houston	21	13
S27	•	Oklahoma State *DAL*	14	7
O4	•	Kentucky	7	10
O11	•	at Michigan State	6	48
O18	=	TCU	7	7
O25			at Baylor	20	21
N1	•	Arkansas	31	12
N8			at SMU	13	21
N15			Rice	6	16 *
N27			at Texas	12	32

THE SCHOOLS

1953 — 4-5-1 (1-5-0)

S19 •	at Kentucky	7	6
S26 =	Houston	14	14
O3 •	Georgia *DAL*	14	12
O10 •	at Texas Tech	27	14
O17		at TCU	20	7
O24		Baylor	13	14
O31		Arkansas *LR*	14	41
N7		SMU	0	23
N14		at Rice	7	34
N26		Texas	12	21

PAUL "BEAR" BRYANT
1954-57 (.634)   25-14-2

1954 — 1-9-0 (0-6-0)

S18	Texas Tech	9	41
S25	Oklahoma State *DAL*	6	14
O2 •	at Georgia	6	0
O9 •	at Houston	7	10
O16		TCU	20	21
O23		at Baylor	7	20
O30		Arkansas	7	14
N6 •	at SMU	3	6
N13		Rice	19	29
N25		at Texas	13	22

1955 — 7-2-1 (4-1-1)

S16 •	at UCLA	0	21
S24 •	LSU *DAL*	28	0
O1 •	Houston	21	3
O8 •	at Nebraska	27	0
O15		at TCU	19	16
O22		Baylor	19	7
O29 =	at Arkansas	7	7
N5		SMU	13	2
N12		at Rice	20	12
N24		Texas	6	21

1956 — 9-0-1 (6-0-0)

S22 •	Villanova	19	0
S29 •	at LSU	9	6
O6 •	Texas Tech *DAL*	40	7
O13 •	at Houston	14	14
O20		TCU	7	6
O27 •	at Baylor	19	13
N3		Arkansas	27	0
N10 •	at SMU	33	7
N17		Rice	21	7
N29 •	at Texas	34	21

1957 — 8-3-0 (4-2-0)

S21 •	Maryland *DAL*	21	13
S28 •	at Texas Tech	21	0
O5 •	at Missouri	28	0
O12 •	Houston	28	6
O19		at TCU	7	0
O26 •	Baylor	14	0
N2 •	at Arkansas	7	6
N9 •	at SMU	19	6
N16		Rice	6	7
N28		Texas	7	9
GATOR BOWL			
D28 •	Tennessee	0	3

JIM MYERS
1958-61 (.350)   12-24-4

1958 — 4-6-0 (2-4-0)

S20	Texas Tech *DAL*	14	15
S27	at Houston	14	39
O4 •	Missouri	12	0
O11 •	at Maryland	14	10
O18		TCU	8	24
O25 •	at Baylor	33	27
N1		Arkansas	8	21
N8		at SMU	0	33
N15 •	at Rice	28	21
N27		at Texas	0	27

1959 — 3-7-0 (0-6-0)

S19	Texas Tech *DAL*	14	20
S26 •	at Michigan State	9	7
O3 •	Southern Miss *MOB*	7	3
O10 •	Houston	28	6
O17		at TCU	6	39
O24		Baylor	0	13
O31		at Arkansas	7	12
N7		SMU	11	14
N14 •	at Rice	2	7
N26		Texas	17	20

1960 — 1-6-3 (0-4-3)

S17	at LSU	0	9
S24 =	Texas Tech	14	14
O1 =	at Trinity	14	0
O8	at Houston	0	17
O15 =	TCU	14	14
O22	at Baylor	0	14
O29	Arkansas	3	7
N5 =	at SMU	0	0
N12	at Rice	14	21
N24	at Texas	14	21

1961 — 4-5-1 (3-4-0)

S23 =	Houston	7	7
S30	at LSU	7	16
O7 •	at Texas Tech	38	7
O14 •	at Trinity	55	0
O21		at TCU	14	15
O28 •	Baylor	23	0
N4 •	at Arkansas	8	15
N11 •	SMU	25	12
N18 •	at Rice	7	21
N23 •	Texas	0	25

HANK FOLDBERG
1962-64 (.217)   6-23-1

1962 — 3-7-0 (3-4-0)

S22 •	at LSU	0	21
S29 •	at Houston	3	6
O6 •	Texas Tech	7	3
O13 •	at Florida	6	42
O20		TCU	14	20
O27 •	at Baylor	6	3
N3		Arkansas	7	17
N10 •	at SMU	12	7
N17 •	at Rice	3	23
N22 •	at Texas	3	13

1963 — 2-7-1 (1-5-1)

S21 •	at LSU	6	14
S28 •	at Ohio State	0	17
O5 •	at Texas Tech	0	10
O12 •	Houston	23	13
O19 =	at TCU	14	14
O26		Baylor	7	34
N2 •	Arkansas *LR*	7	21
N9		SMU	7	9
N16 •	at Rice	13	6
N28		Texas	13	15

1964 — 1-9-0 (1-6-0)

S19 •	at LSU	6	9
S25 •	at Houston	0	10
O3		Texas Tech	12	16
O10 •	at Southern Cal	7	31
O17		TCU	9	14
O24		at Baylor	16	20
O31		Arkansas	0	17
N7 •	at SMU	23	0
N14 •	at Rice	8	19
N26		at Texas	7	26

GENE STALLINGS
1965-71 (.377)   27-45-1

1965 — 3-7-0 (1-6-0)

S18 •	at LSU	0	10
S25 •	at Georgia Tech	14	10
O2		at Texas Tech	16	20
O9 •	Houston	10	7
O16		at TCU	9	17
O23		Baylor	0	31
O30		Arkansas *LR*	0	31
N6		SMU	0	10
N13 •	at Rice	14	13
N25		Texas	17	21

1966 — 4-5-1 (4-3-0)

S17	at Georgia Tech	3	38
S24 •	at Tulane	13	21
O1 •	Texas Tech	35	14
O8 =	at LSU	7	7
O15		TCU	35	7
O22 •	at Baylor	17	13
O29		Arkansas	0	34
N5		at SMU	14	21
N12 •	at Rice	7	6
N24		at Texas	14	22

1967 — 7-4-0 (6-1-0)

S16		SMU	17	20
S23 •	Purdue *DAL*	20	24
S30 •	at LSU	6	17
O7 •	Florida State	18	19
O12 •	at Texas Tech	28	24
O21 •	at TCU	20	0
O28 •	Baylor	21	3
N4 •	at Arkansas	33	21
N18 •	at Rice	18	3
N23 •	Texas	10	7
COTTON BOWL			
J1 •	Alabama	20	16

1968 — 3-7-0 (2-5-0)

S21 •	at LSU	12	13
S28 •	at Tulane	35	3
O5	at Florida State	14	20
O12		Texas Tech	16	21
O19 •	TCU	27	7
O26		at Baylor	9	10
N2		Arkansas	22	25
N9		at SMU	23	36
N16 •	Rice	24	14
N28		at Texas	14	35

1969 — 3-7-0 (2-5-0)

S20 •	at LSU	6	35
S27 •	at Nebraska	0	14
O4 •	at Army	20	13
O11 •	at Texas Tech	9	13
O18 •	at TCU	6	16
O25 •	Baylor	24	0
N1 •	at Arkansas	13	35
N8 •	SMU	20	10
N15		at Rice	6	7
N27		Texas	12	49

1970 — 2-9-0 (0-7-0)

S12 •	Wichita St.	41	14
S19 •	at LSU	20	18
S26 •	at Ohio State	13	56
O3 •	at Michigan	10	14
O10 •	Texas Tech	7	21
O17		TCU	15	31
O24 •	at Baylor	24	29
O31 •	Arkansas	6	45
N7 •	at SMU	3	6
N14 •	Rice	17	18
N26 •	at Texas	14	52

1971 — 5-6-0 (4-3-0)

S11 •	Wichita St.	41	7
S18 •	at LSU	0	37
S25 •	at Nebraska	7	34
O2 •	Cincinnati	0	17
O9 •	at Texas Tech	7	28
O16 •	at TCU	3	14
O23 •	Baylor	10	9
O30 •	Arkansas *LR*	17	9
N6 •	SMU	27	10
N13 •	at Rice	18	13
N25		Texas	14	34

EMORY BELLARD
1972-78 (.640)   48-27

1972 — 3-8-0 (2-5-0)

S9 •	at Wichita St.	36	13
S16 •	at Nebraska	7	37
S23 •	at LSU	17	42
S30 •	Army	14	24
O14 •	Texas Tech	14	17
O21 •	TCU	10	13
O28 •	at Baylor	13	15
N4 •	Arkansas	10	7
N11 •	at SMU	27	17
N18		Rice	14	20
N23		at Texas	3	38

1973 — 5-6-0 (3-4-0)

S15 •	Wichita St.	48	0
S22 •	at LSU	23	28
S29 •	Boston College	24	32
O6 •	at Clemson	30	15
O13 •	at Texas Tech	16	28
O20 •	at TCU	35	16
O27 •	Baylor	28	22
N3 •	at Arkansas	10	14
N10 •	SMU	45	10
N17 •	at Rice	20	24
N22 •	Texas	13	42

1974 — 8-3-0 (5-2-0)

S14 •	Clemson	24	0
S21 •	at LSU	21	14
S28 •	at Washington	28	15
O5 •	at Kansas	10	28
O12		Texas Tech	28	7
O19 •	TCU	17	0
O26 •	at Baylor	20	0
N2 •	Arkansas	20	10
N9 •	at SMU	14	18
N16 •	Rice	37	7
N29		at Texas	3	32

1975 — 10-2-0 (6-1-0)

S13 •	Mississippi	7	0
S20 •	at LSU	39	8
S27 •	Illinois	43	13
O4 •	at Kansas State	10	0
O11 •	at Texas Tech	38	9
O18 •	at TCU	14	6
O25 •	Baylor	19	10
N8 •	SMU	36	3
N15 •	at Rice	33	14
N28 •	Texas	20	10
D6 •	Arkansas *LR*	6	31
LIBERTY BOWL			
D22 •	Southern Cal	0	20

1976 — 10-2-0 (6-2-0)

S11 •	Virginia Tech	19	0
S18 •	Kansas State	34	14
S25 •	at Houston	10	21
O2 •	at Illinois	14	7
O9 •	Texas Tech	16	27
O16 •	Baylor	24	0
O23 •	Rice	57	34
O30 •	at SMU	36	0
N13 •	Arkansas *LR*	31	10
N20 •	TCU	59	10
N25 •	at Texas	27	3
SUN BOWL			
J2 •	Florida	37	14

1977 — 8-4-0 (6-2-0)

S10 •	Kansas	28	14
S17 •	at Virginia Tech	27	6
S24 •	at Texas Tech	33	17
O1 •	at Michigan	3	41
O15 •	at Baylor	38	31
O22 •	at Rice	28	14
O29 •	SMU	38	21
N12 •	Arkansas	20	26
N19 •	at TCU	52	23
N26		Texas	28	57
D3 •	Houston	27	7
BLUEBONNET BOWL			
D31 •	Southern Cal	28	47

TOM WILSON
1978-81 (.525)   21-19

1978 — 8-4-0 (4-4-0)

S9 •	at Kansas	37	10
S23 •	at Boston College	37	2
S30 •	Memphis	58	0
O7		Texas Tech	38	9
O14		at Houston	0	33
O21 •	Baylor	6	24
O28 •	Rice	38	21
N4 •	at SMU	20	17
N18 •	Arkansas	7	26
N25 •	TCU	15	7
D2 •	at Texas	7	22
HALL OF FAME CLASSIC			
D20 •	Iowa St.	28	12

1979 — 6-5-0 (4-4-0)

S8 •	Brigham Young *HOU*	17	18
S15 •	at Baylor	7	17
S22 •	at Penn State	27	14
S29 •	at Memphis	17	7
O6		at Texas Tech	20	21
O13 •	Houston	14	17
O27 •	at Rice	41	15
N3 •	SMU	47	14
N17 •	Arkansas	10	22
N24 •	at TCU	30	7
D1 •	Texas	3	7

1980 4-7-0 (3-5-0)

S6	●	Mississippi JaM	23	20
S13		at Georgia	0	42
S20		Penn State	9	25
O4	● |	Texas Tech	41	21
O11	|	at Houston	13	17
O18	|	Baylor	7	46
O25	|	Rice	6	10
N1	|	at SMU	0	27
N15	|	at Arkansas	24	27
N22	● |	TCU	13	10
N29	● |	at Texas	24	14

1981 7-5-0 (4-4-0)

S5	●	at California	29	28
S19		at Boston College	12	13
S26	●	Louisiana Tech	43	7
O3	● |	at Texas Tech	24	23
O10	● |	Houston	7	6
O17	|	at Baylor	17	19
O24	● |	at Rice	51	26
O31	|	SMU	7	27
N14	|	Arkansas	7	10
N21	● |	at TCU	37	7
N26	|	Texas	13	21
		INDEPENDENCE BOWL		
D12	●	Oklahoma State	33	16

JACKIE SHERRILL
1982-88 (.648) 52-28-1

1982 5-6-0 (3-5-0)

S4		Boston College	16	38
S18	●	Texas Arlington	61	22
S25	●	Louisiana Tech	38	27
O2	|	Texas Tech	15	24
O9	|	at Houston	20	24
O16	● |	Baylor	28	23
O23	● |	Rice	49	7
O30	|	at SMU	9	47
N13	|	Arkansas LR	0	35
N20	● |	TCU	34	14
N25	|	at Texas	16	53

1983 5-5-1 (4-3-1)

S3		California	17	19
S17	●	Arkansas State	38	0
S23		Oklahoma State	15	34
O1	|	at Texas Tech	0	3
O8	● |	Houston	30	7
O15	= |	at Baylor	13	13
O22	● |	at Rice	29	10
O29	|	SMU	7	10
N12	● |	Arkansas	36	23
N19	● |	at TCU	20	10
N26	|	Texas	13	45

1984 6-5-0 (3-5-0)

S1	●	Texas-El Paso	20	17
S22	●	Iowa St.	38	17
S29	●	Arkansas State	22	21
O6	|	Texas Tech	12	30
O13	|	at Houston	7	9
O20	|	Baylor	16	20
O27	● |	Rice	38	14
N3	|	at SMU	20	28
N17	|	at Arkansas	0	28
N24	● |	TCU	35	21
D1	● |	at Texas	37	12

1985 10-2-0 (7-1-0)

S14		Alabama BIRM	10	23
S21	●	La. Monroe	31	17
S28	●	Tulsa	45	10
O5	● |	at Texas Tech	28	27
O12	● |	Houston	43	16
O19	|	at Baylor	15	20
O26	● |	at Rice	43	28
N2	● |	SMU	19	17
N16	● |	Arkansas	10	6
N23	● |	at TCU	53	6
N28	● |	Texas	42	10
		COTTON BOWL		
J1	●	Auburn	36	16

1986 9-3-0 (7-1-0)

S13		at LSU	17	35
S20	●	North Texas	48	28
S27	●	Southern Miss	16	7
O4	● |	Texas Tech	45	8
O11	● |	at Houston	19	7
O18	● |	Baylor	31	30
O25	● |	Rice	45	10
N1	● |	at SMU	39	35
N15	|	Arkansas LR	10	14
N22	● |	TCU	74	10
N27	● |	at Texas	16	3
		COTTON BOWL		
J1		Ohio State	12	28

1987 10-2-0 (6-1-0)

S5		LSU	3	17
S19	●	Washington	29	12
S26	●	Southern Miss JaM	27	14
O3	|	at Texas Tech	21	27
O10	● |	Houston	22	17
O17	● |	at Baylor	34	10
O24	● |	at Rice	34	21
O31	●	Louisiana Tech	32	3
N14	● |	Arkansas	14	0
N21	● |	at TCU	42	24
N26	● |	Texas	20	13
		COTTON BOWL		
J1	●	Notre Dame	35	10

1988 7-5-0 (6-1-0)

A27		Nebraska ERut	14	23
S3		at LSU	0	27
S24		at Oklahoma State	15	52
O1	● |	Texas Tech	50	15
O8	● |	at Houston	30	16
O15	● |	Baylor	28	14
O22	● |	Rice	24	10
N5	●	Louisiana Tech	56	17
N12	|	at Arkansas	20	25
N19	● |	TCU	18	0
N24	● |	at Texas	28	24
D1		Alabama	10	30

R.C. SLOCUM
1989-2002 (.721) 123-47-2

1989 8-4-0 (6-2-0)

S2	●	LSU	28	16
S9		at Washington	6	19
S16	● |	at TCU	44	7
S30	●	Southern Miss	31	14
O7	|	at Texas Tech	24	27
O14	● |	Houston	17	13
O21	● |	at Baylor	14	11
O28	● |	at Rice	45	7
N4	● |	SMU	63	14
N24	|	Arkansas	22	23
D2	● |	Texas	21	10
		SUN BOWL		
D30		Pittsburgh	28	31

1990 9-3-1 (5-2-1)

S1	●	at Hawaii	28	13
S15	●	La. Lafayette	63	14
S22	●	North Texas	40	8
S29		at LSU	8	17
O6	● |	Texas Tech	28	24
O13	|	at Houston	31	36
O20	= |	Baylor	20	20
O27	● |	Rice	41	15
N3	● |	at SMU	38	17
N17	● |	at Arkansas	20	16
N24	● |	TCU	56	10
D1	|	at Texas	27	28
		HOLIDAY BOWL		
D29	●	Brigham Young	65	14

1991 10-2-0 (8-0-0)

S14	●	LSU	45	7
S21		at Tulsa	34	35
S28	●	La. Lafayette	34	7
O5	● |	at Texas Tech	37	14
O19	● |	at Baylor	34	12
O26	● |	Houston	27	18
N2	● |	at Rice	38	21
N9	● |	at TCU	44	7
N16	● |	Arkansas	13	3
N23	● |	SMU	65	6
N28	● |	Texas	31	14
		COTTON BOWL		
J1		Florida State	2	10

1992 12-1-0 (7-0-0)

A26	●	Stanford ANA	10	7
S5	●	at LSU	31	22
S12	●	Tulsa	19	9
S19	●	at Missouri	26	13
O3	● |	Texas Tech	19	17
O17	● |	Rice	35	9
O24	● |	Baylor	19	13
O31	● |	at SMU	41	7
N7	●	Louisville	40	18
N12	● |	at Houston	38	30
N21	● |	TCU	37	10
N26	● |	at Texas	34	13
		COTTON BOWL		
J1		Notre Dame	3	28

1993 10-2-0 (7-0-0)

S4	●	LSU	24	0
S11		at Oklahoma	14	44
S18	●	Missouri	73	0
O2	● |	at Texas Tech	31	6
O9	● |	Houston	34	10
O16	● |	at Baylor	34	17
O23	● |	at Rice	38	10
O30	● |	SMU	37	13
N13	●	Louisville	42	7
N20	● |	at TCU	59	3
N25	● |	Texas	18	9
		COTTON BOWL		
J1		Notre Dame	21	24

1994 10-0-1 (6-0-1)

S3	●	at LSU	18	13
S10	●	Oklahoma	36	14
S24	●	Southern Miss	41	17
O1	● |	Texas Tech	23	17
O8	● |	at Houston	38	7
O15	● |	Baylor	41	21
O22	● |	Rice	7	0
O29	= |	SMU SA	21	21
N5	● |	at Texas	34	10
N12	●	at Louisville	26	10
N19	● |	TCU	34	17

1995 9-3-0 (5-2-0)

S2	●	LSU	33	17
S16	●	Tulsa	52	9
S23		at Colorado	21	29
O7	|	at Texas Tech	7	14
O14	● |	SMU	20	17
O21	● |	at Baylor	24	9
O28	● |	Houston	31	7
N9	● |	at Rice	17	10
N18	●	Middle Tennessee	56	14
N25	● |	at TCU	38	6
D2	|	Texas	6	16
		ALAMO BOWL		
D28	●	Michigan	22	20

1996-PRESENT
BIG 12

1996 6-6 (4-4)

A24		at Brigham Young	37	41
S14		at La. Lafayette	22	29
S21	●	North Texas	55	0
S28	|	Colorado	10	24
O5	●	Louisiana Tech	63	13
O12	● |	at Iowa St.	24	21
O19	|	Kansas State	20	23
O26	|	Texas Tech	10	13
N2	● |	at Oklahoma State	38	19
N9	● |	at Baylor	24	7
N16	● |	Oklahoma	33	16
N29	|	at Texas	15	51

1997 9-4 (6-2)

S6	●	Sam Houston St.	59	6
S20	●	La. Lafayette	66	0
S27	●	North Texas Irv	36	10
O4	● |	at Colorado	16	10
O11	● |	Iowa St.	56	17
O18	|	at Kansas State	17	36
O25	|	at Texas Tech	13	16
N1	● |	Oklahoma State	28	25
N8	● |	Baylor	38	10
N15	● |	at Oklahoma	51	7
N28	● |	Texas	27	16
		BIG 12 CHAMPIONSHIP		
D6		Nebraska SA	15	54
		COTTON BOWL		
J1		UCLA	23	29

1998 11-3 (7-1)

A31		Florida State ERut	14	23
S12	●	Louisiana Tech	28	7
S19	●	at Southern Miss	24	6
S26	●	North Texas	28	9
O3	● |	at Kansas	24	21
O10	● |	Nebraska	28	21
O17	● |	at Baylor	35	14
O24	● |	Texas Tech	17	10
O31	● |	at Oklahoma State	17	6
N7	● |	Oklahoma	29	0
N14	● |	Missouri	17	14
N27	|	at Texas	24	26
		BIG 12 CHAMPIONSHIP		
D5	●	Kansas State StL	36	33
		SUGAR BOWL		
J1		Ohio State	14	24

1999 8-4 (5-3)

S4	●	at Louisiana Tech	37	17
S18	●	Tulsa	62	13
S25	●	Southern Miss	23	6
O2	|	at Texas Tech	19	21
O9	● |	Baylor	45	13
O16	● |	Kansas	34	17
O23	|	at Oklahoma	6	51
O30	● |	Oklahoma State	21	3
N6	|	at Nebraska	0	37
N13	● |	at Missouri	51	14
N26	● |	Texas	20	16
		ALAMO BOWL		
D28		Penn State	0	24

2000 7-5 (5-3)

S2		at Notre Dame	10	24
S9	●	Wyoming	51	3
S16	●	Texas-El Paso	45	17
S30	● |	Texas Tech	33	15
O7	|	Colorado	19	26
O14	● |	at Baylor	24	0
O21	● |	at Iowa St.	30	7
O28	● |	Kansas State	26	10
N4	● |	at Oklahoma State	21	16
N11	|	Oklahoma	31	35
N24	|	at Texas	17	43
		INDEPENDENCE BOWL		
D31		Mississippi State	41	43

2001 8-4 (4-4)

S1	●	McNeese St.	38	24
S6	●	at Wyoming	28	20
S22	● |	Oklahoma State	21	7
S29	●	Notre Dame	24	3
O6	● |	Baylor	16	10
O13	|	at Colorado	21	31
O20	●	at Kansas State	31	24
O27	● |	Iowa St.	24	21
N3	|	at Texas Tech	0	12
N10	|	at Oklahoma	10	31
N23	|	Texas	7	21
		GALLERYFURNITURE.COM BOWL		
D28	●	TCU	28	9

2002 6-6 (3-5)

A31	●	La. Lafayette	31	7
S7	●	at Pittsburgh	14	12
S21		Virginia Tech	3	13
S28	●	Louisiana Tech	31	3
O5	|	Texas Tech	47	48
O12	● |	at Baylor	41	0
O19	● |	at Kansas	47	22
O26	|	Nebraska	31	38
N2	|	at Oklahoma State	23	28
N9	● |	Oklahoma	30	26
N16	|	Missouri	27	33
N29	|	at Texas	20	50

DENNIS FRANCHIONE
2003-PRESENT (.458) 11-13

2003 4-8 (2-6)

A30	●	Arkansas State	26	11
S6	●	Utah	28	26
S18		at Virginia Tech	19	35
S27		Pittsburgh	26	37
O4	|	at Texas Tech	28	59
O11	● |	Baylor	73	10
O18	|	at Nebraska	12	48
O25	|	Oklahoma State	10	38
N1	● |	Kansas	45	33
N8	|	at Oklahoma	0	77
N15	|	at Missouri	22	45
N28	|	Texas	15	46

2004 7-5 (5-3)

S2		at Utah	21	41
S11	●	Wyoming	31	0
S18	●	Clemson	27	6
O2	● |	Kansas State	42	30
O9	● |	at Iowa State	34	3
O16	● |	at Oklahoma State	36	20
O23	● |	Colorado	29	26
O30	|	at Baylor	34	35
N6	|	Oklahoma	35	42
N13	● |	Texas Tech	32	25
N26	|	at Texas	13	26
		COTTON BOWL		
J1		Tennessee	7	38

THE SCHOOLS

Neutral Site key: *Unk* Unknown, Unknown / *OkC* Oklahoma City, OK / *Phil* Philadelphia, PA / *Mob* Mobile, AL / *Birm* Birmingham, AL / *JaM* Jackson, MS / *Wac* Waco, TX / *ERut* East Rutherford, NJ / *Ana* Anaheim, CA / *Irv* Irving, TX / *StL* St. Louis, MO / *Beau* Beaumont, TX / *FtW* Fort Worth, TX / *Gal* Galveston, TX / *Amar* Amarillo, TX / *SA* San Antonio, TX / *NYC* New York, NY / *Tyl* Tyler, TX / *Dal* Dallas, TX / *Hou* Houston, TX / *NO* New Orleans, LA / *Brnx* Bronx, NY / *LR* Little Rock, AR / *Tac* Tacoma, WA

f **Forfeit** † **Game Later Forfieted** # **Disputed Victor** * **Disputed Score** || **Designated Conference Game** |2 **Counted Twice in Conference Standings**

TEXAS TECH

BY MARK WANGRIN

TEXAS TECH OPENED THE 21ST century in coach Mike Leach's fast-paced spread offense much as it began its football history—in one hell of a hurry. When Texas governor Pat Neff finally signed the bill that created Texas Technological College in Lubbock on Feb. 10, 1923, the school was already decades behind its in-state rivals in creating a football program. Pete Cawthon, a Knute Rockne disciple who became the school's third coach, wanted to put Tech on the football map, so he scheduled the powers on both coasts. Cawthon even had a recruiting brochure printed that read, "Join the Raiders and see the U.S.A." Cawthon's dream of national prominence never materialized, and the Red Raiders assumed a bit role in the history of the Southwest Conference, often playing in the shadow of Texas and Texas A&M. That didn't mean they had to like it. The Red Raiders had some stellar moments and frequently got the better of the Longhorns and Aggies in the 1990s and early 2000s, proving it's not when you start, it's how you finish.

TRADITION Students flash a "guns up" hand signal formed by extending the thumb and index finger. Originated by a Tech alum, the gesture represents the Red Raider's ability to shoot down his opponents. The Class of 1936 donated two bells, one large and one small, which hang in the east tower of the administration building. Known as the Victory Bells, they ring on special occasions and for 30 minutes after the school's athletic victories. The Saddle Tramps, an all-male spirit group formed in 1936, "paint the campus red" with crepe paper the night before games and ring Bangin' Bertha, a large bell donated by the Santa Fe Railroad. During the mid-1990s students began flinging tortillas—often frozen to improve distance—onto the field after Red Raider scores. University officials banned the practice after the Red Raiders were called for two unsportsmanlike conduct penalties in a home victory over Missouri in October 2002.

BEST PLAYER Donny Anderson's statistics don't hold up in the current video game era of bloated numbers, but the the Golden Palomino more than made up for that with his tremendous versatility. A three-year starter at halfback, the 6'3", 210-pound Anderson was a nifty runner with great hands. A two-time first-team All-America, Anderson gave the Tech program legitimacy at a time (1963-65) when it was struggling to make a name for itself.

BEST COACH Tech was just another program trying to scrape out a reputation when JT King became head coach after the 1960 season. New to the Southwest Conference, the Red Raiders were looked down on as a refugee from the Border Conference, with a budget so minor league that approval was required from the athletic director to make a

---

PROFILE

Texas Tech University
Lubbock, Texas
Founded: 1923
Enrollment: 23,595
Colors: Scarlet and Black
Nickname: Red Raiders
Stadium: Jones SBC Stadium
    Opened in 1947
    AstroTurf; capacity 52,702
First football game: 1925
All-time record: 465–375–32 (.552)
Bowl record: 8–19–1
First-round NFL draftees: 5
Website: www.texastech.com

THE BEST OF TIMES

1993-present. Under Spike Dykes and Mike Leach, Red Raiders were bowl eligible for 12 straight seasons, the only Big 12 team to earn that distinction every year of the league's existence.

THE WORST OF TIMES

1956-62. Only three years removed from 11–1 mark under DeWitt Weaver, the program nosedived to seven straight losing seasons and a 19–49–2 record.

CONFERENCE

Texas Tech joined fellow former Southwest Conference members Texas, Texas A&M and Baylor in merging with the Big Eight (Oklahoma, Iowa State, Oklahoma State, Nebraska, Missouri, Kansas, Kansas State and Colorado) to form the Big 12 in 1996.

DISTINGUISHED ALUMNI

George Eads, actor; Pat Green, musician; Rick Husband, astronaut; Sheryl Swoopes, WNBA player; Edward Whitacre Jr., chairman/CEO SBC Communications

FIGHT SONG

FIGHT, RAIDERS, FIGHT!
Fight, Raiders, Fight! Fight, Raiders, Fight!
Fight for the school we love so dearly.
You'll hit 'em high, you'll hit 'em low.
You'll push the ball across the goal,
Tech, Fight! Fight!
We'll praise your name, boost you to fame.
Fight for the Scarlet and Black.
You will hit 'em, you will wreck 'em.
Hit 'em! Wreck 'em, Texas Tech!
And the Victory Bells will ring out

long-distance phone call. After opening with two straight losing seasons under King, Tech broke through in 1963 and made back-to-back bowl trips in 1964 and 1965. King's 1966 team beat Arkansas and his 1967 and 1968 teams beat Texas. His overall record was only 44–45–3, but his value to Tech was immeasurable.

Texas Tech has had some stellar moments and frequently has gotten the better of the Longhorns and Aggies.

Red Raiders hooked the Horns 19-13. Tech's Kenny Vinyard kicked a pair of field goals, including a game-clinching 54-yarder with 4:33 to play. "I'm sick of hearing about Texas and the Texas jinx," King said in a raucous postgame locker room. A crowd estimated at 7,500 rushed the Lubbock International Airport runway, forcing the Red Raiders' plane to divert to Amarillo, where it waited until police got the crowd under control.

BEST TEAM The 1973 Red Raiders came within an early-season loss to Texas of going undefeated, and notched big wins against unbeaten Oklahoma State and Arizona. The team's strength was its option offense, led by quarterback Joe Barnes and running back Larry Isaac. Tight end Andre Tillman was named the Red Raiders' ninth All-America. All-SWC picks tackle Ecomet Burley and backs Kenneth Wallace and Danny Willis led the defense. Tech earned a berth in the Gator Bowl, where a 79-yard touchdown pass from Barnes to Lawrence Williams keyed a 28-19 victory over Tennessee and capped an 11–1 season.

BIGGEST GAME Tech hadn't beaten Texas since 1955, the last year the Red Raiders were in the Border Conference, and reporters wrote freely about the Texas Jinx heading into the 1967 meeting in Dallas. Quarterback John Scovell had other plans, running for a then-school-record 175 yards and a touchdown and throwing for another score as the

BIGGEST UPSET Before the three-touchdown-underdog Red Raiders took the field at Jones Stadium against No. 6 Arkansas on Nov. 19, 1966, assistant coach Berl Huffman tossed a funeral wreath into the locker room and read a purported letter of condolence from the Razorbacks. "The more he read," said tackle Phil Tucker, "the madder we got." Then they did something about it. With Arkansas up 10-7 in the second quarter, the Red Raiders twice stopped the Razorbacks from the 1-yard line, the best goal-line stand in school history. Tech's 21-16 victory spoiled the plans of the Cotton Bowl, which had hoped to invite the Razorbacks. After the game, Scovell ran up to his father, John Scovell Sr., who was chairman of the bowl's selection committee. "Pop, sure sorry about messing up your Cotton Bowl thing," the son said. Shot back John Sr., "Yeah? Well y'all sure … weren't playing like you were trying to keep from messing it up."

RECORDS

RUSHING YARDS

	GAME
287	Byron Hanspard vs. Baylor, Oct. 5, 1996 (35 att.)

	SEASON
2,084	Byron Hanspard, 1996 (339 att.)

	CAREER
4,219	Byron Hanspard, 1994-96 (760 att.)

PASSING YARDS

	GAME
661	B.J. Symons vs. Mississippi, Sept. 27, 2003 (44 of 64)

	SEASON
5,833	B.J. Symons, 2003 (470 of 719)

	CAREER
12,429	Kliff Kingsbury, 1999-2002 (1,231 of 1,883)

RECEIVING YARDS

	GAME
251	Rodney Blackshear vs. Houston, Nov. 30, 1991 (5 rec.)

	SEASON
1,261	Lloyd Hill, 1992 (76 rec.)

	CAREER
3,069	Wes Welker, 2000-03 (259 rec.)

POINTS

	GAME
30	Three tied; most recently by Byron Hanspard vs. SMU, Nov. 18, 1995 (5 TDs)

	SEASON
134	Byron Morris, 1993 (22 TDs, 1 two-pt. conv.)

	CAREER
312	James Gray, 1986-89 (52 TDs)

CONSENSUS ALL-AMERICANS

1935	Herschel Ramsey, E
1945	Walter Schlinkman, B
1960	E.J. Holub, C
1965	Donny Anderson, B
1977	Dan Irons, T
1982	Gabriel Rivera, DL
1991	Mark Bounds, P
1995	Zach Thomas, LB
1996	Byron Hanspard, RB
1998	Montae Reagor, DL

LANDMARK Will Rogers endeared himself to Tech when he put up $200 to get the Red Raiders band to play at a road game at TCU on Oct. 30, 1926, saying he wanted people to hear "a real band." Rogers also donated $1,500 for new uniforms. In 1948, 13 years after Rogers' death in a plane crash, the Amon G. Carter Foundation presented Tech with a sculpture of Rogers and his horse, Soapsuds, called *Riding Into the Sunset*. The statue was erected in what was known as Soapsuds Pavilion and, in a dig at rival Texas A&M, it was set up looking 23° north of true west—so that the horse's rump faced College Station, home of the Aggies.

HEARTBREAKER Jerry Moore was looking to build some momentum early in his tenure as Red Raiders coach, and it appeared he might have some with time running out against 9–0 and No. 2 SMU on Nov. 13, 1982. Kicker Ricky Gann had just kicked a 28-yard field goal to tie the mighty Mustangs 27-27 with only 17 seconds left. But SMU resorted to trickery, using a one-hop lateral from Blaine Smith to Bobby Leach to get outside Tech's kickoff contain. Leach ran 91 yards down the sideline for the winning score and earned the nickname Miracle Man. "This is one of the hardest experiences I've ever had to go through," a dejected Moore said afterward.

BEST COMEBACK "Extra points are guaranteed," Tech kicker Robert Treece said after the Red Raiders' 48-47 overtime victory at Texas A&M on Oct. 5, 2002. "JV and varsity players make them all the time." Not all the time. Treece's Aggie counterpart, John Pierson, missed a PAT in regulation and another in overtime. A&M led 35-17 midway through the third quarter when Tech quarterback Kliff Kingsbury got hot. Kingsbury, who would complete an NCAA-record 49 of 59 passes for 474 yards and five touchdowns, led the Red Raiders back to take a 38-35 lead. A&M rallied on the sixth of Dustin Long's seven touchdown passes but Pierson missed the PAT, allowing Treece to send the game into overtime with a 42-yard field goal with two seconds left. In OT, A&M scored a go-ahead touchdown, but Pierson missed the PAT. That left the door open for Tech, which matched A&M's TD. Treece's PAT attempt was perfect.

ALL-TIME TEAM		
Selected by the sports staff of the Lubbock Avalanche-Journal *in 1999.*		
OFFENSE		
1958-60	E.J. Holub,	OL
1965-67	Phil Tucker,	OL
1971-73	Dennis Allen,	OL
1975-77	Dan Irons,	OL
1986-89	Charles Odiorne,	OL
1971-73	Andre Tillman,	TE
1961-63	Dave Parks,	WR
1990-93	Lloyd Hill,	WR
1990-93	Robert Hall,	QB
1963-65	Donny Anderson,	RB
1994-96	Byron Hanspard,	RB
1989-91	Lin Elliot,	PK
1972-74	Lawrence Williams,	KR
1985-88	Tyrone Thurman,	PR
DEFENSE		
1966, 1968-69	Richard Campbell,	DL
1972-75	Ecomet Burley,	DL
1979-82	Gabriel Rivera,	DL
1995-98	Montae Reagor,	DL
1974-76	Thomas Howard,	LB
1983-86	Brad Hastings,	LB
1992-95	Zach Thomas,	LB
1967-69	Denton Fox,	DB
1973-75	Curtis Jordan,	DB
1978-80	Ted Watts,	DB
1989-92	Tracy Saul,	DB
1978-81	Maury Buford,	P

STADIUM After playing its early games at Tech Field, the Red Raiders moved into 18,000-seat Jones Stadium in 1947. The field was lowered 28 feet and new grandstands were built on the east side in 1959. Renovations in 1969 and 1972 expanded capacity to 50,050. A new press box, club seats and luxury suites were added in 2003, swelling capacity to 52,702.

RIVAL Take your pick. In even-number years, Texas comes to Lubbock. In odd years, it's Texas A&M. Tech fans hate both schools, but they appear to have a special place in their hearts for the Aggies. A&M leads the series 34–28–1, winning the first six games between the schools. The rivalry started smoldering in 1994, when Texas A&M basketball players got into a fistfight with Tech fans while leaving the court after a one-point win. Since joining the Big 12, Tech has gone 6–3 against the Aggies, including the infamous 2001 game at Jones Stadium when Tech students tore down the goalposts and tried to toss them into the A&M fan section, setting off a minor melee. Amid protests from the Aggies, Tech coach Mike Leach said, "It is interesting to me that all these Aggies … sit around with these halos over their head with some divine expertise on fanmanship. I just don't believe that's the case. For the record, I think that our fans are better than the Aggie fans." That summer the A&M media fired back, including an article in the school's *12th Man Magazine* that described Lubbock as "a barren stretch of dirt some West Texans call a city."

CONTROVERSY Tech's first football game, played against McMurry on Oct. 3, 1925, ended in a disputed 0-0 tie. Tech's Elson Archibald appeared to dropkick a 20-yard field goal as time expired. Even as the fans carried Archibald off the field on their shoulders, the umpire told the referee that time had

expired before the kick, and the referee waved off the points. One of the team members, P.C. Callaway, later claimed that the referee—whose name escaped historians—had applied for the coaching job and was turned down, giving him a strong motive for revenge.

TRAGEDY Defensive tackle Stoney Garland was riding in a truck with three friends when it was involved in an accident with another car just after midnight on Thanksgiving Day 1997. Garland, who wasn't wearing a seatbelt, was thrown against the windshield, breaking his clavicle, fracturing two vertebrae and crushing his trachea. He was paralyzed from the chest down. Tech made Garland an honorary captain in 1998 and he went out for the coin toss in five of six home games. Stricken with a kidney infection, he missed only one game that season, a loss to Missouri—the only home game the Red Raiders lost. Garland, who lives in a specially outfitted home in nearby Plains that was paid for by donations from fans and Lubbock residents, still regularly attends Tech home games.

NICKNAME In September 1925, new coach Eking Y. Freeland announced that the school would adopt "Matadors" as its nickname, in homage to the campus' prevalent Spanish architecture, and scarlet and black as its colors. In the early 1930s, the team's early coast-to-coast scheduling and its predominant color inspired Lubbock *Avalanche-Journal* sportswriter Collier Parish to call the team the "Red Raiders." Coach Pete Cawthon liked the name, and in 1932 the school changed nicknames.

MASCOT The original mascot was a black calf, donated after the Red Raiders' first win, a 30-0 rout of Montezuma in the third game of the 1925 season. No opposing fan was able to ride the calf, which became a regular feature of halftime shows. Branded with the score, the calf was later slaughtered and fed to the team. The Masked Rider made his debut on Sept. 26, 1935. Masked to hide his true identity, the rider wore a scarlet satin cape and rode a palomino stallion. In 1971, the Southwest Conference passed a rule preventing its schools from taking live animal mascots to nonhome games. Instead, the school created Raider Red, a mascot based on a drawing by Lubbock cartoonist Dirk West. Raider Red shoots two modified 12-gauge shotguns after every Tech touchdown and field goal.

UNIFORMS Early jerseys were scarlet, with white-trimmed black patches over the shoulders and a long

stripe down the sleeves. In the late 1930s, the Double-T logo on the chest was replaced with a white number trimmed in black. The socks were black with a series of scarlet-and-white horizontal stripes. The school's name was added to the front of the jersey in the early 1960s. Tech went to black jerseys when David McWilliams became head coach in 1986. The Red Raiders' first hard-shell helmets were silver, then black with a white numeral on the side in the early 1960s. In 1963, the school's Double-T logo first appeared on a black helmet and, with the exception of going with a white shell from 1970 to 1974, it's remained fairly constant since.

NUMBERS Given Coach Mike Leach's proclivity for the forward pass, it should come as little surprise that Tech quarterbacks Kliff Kingsbury and B.J. Symons combined to set or tie 32 NCAA passing records in their careers. But Tech also holds the individual record for most punts and punting yards in a game. In 1939, the Red Raiders played at Centenary in heavy rains, with puddles lapping over the tops of the players' shoes. With both coaches waiting on the other to make a mistake, they had their teams punt a combined 77 times—67 times on first down. Charlie Calhoun kicked 36 of them for 1,318 yards. The game ended a 0-0 tie.

QUIRK The fourth quarter of the 1965 game between Tech and Kansas was only 56 seconds old when game officials got word of a tornado warning in the area. Tech was leading 26-7 and a driving rain was already making visibility nil and play hazardous, so the officials summoned the head coaches. KU's Jack Mitchell agreed to call the game. Tech's J.T. King, however, told the officials he wanted to continue to get his backups more playing time. King would agree to call the game only after Kansas conceded defeat.

LORE One of the most colorful boosters in Tech history was Robert Walker. Nicknamed Daddy Warbucks, he was a fun-loving, hard-partying man whose fortune came from inventing a way to quickly review videotape. His innovation— later to gain fame as "Instant Replay"—allowed King to immediately review plays on the sideline of Tech's 26-7 victory over Kansas in 1965. Two years later the NCAA banned its use by teams during games, saying that the technology was cost-prohibitive for most schools.

QUOTE "I dress you like Notre Dame, I feed you like Notre Dame and you play like Canyon Normal." —Pete Cawthon, Tech coach and legendary Rocknephile, to his team in 1937

TEXAS TECH ALL-TIME SCORES

WIN/LOSS PERCENTAGE SINCE 1936

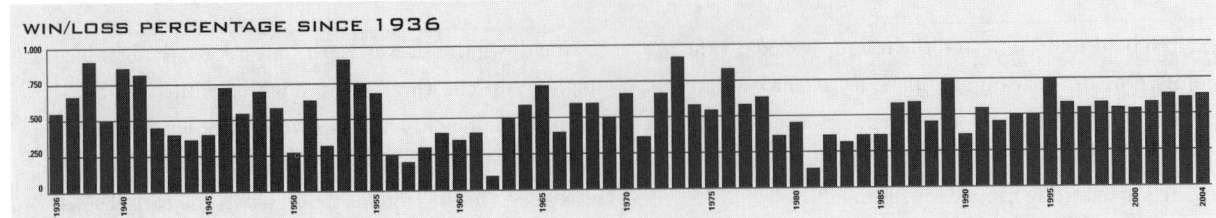

E.Y. FREELAND
1925-28 (.649)   21-10-6

1925   6-1-2
Date		Opponent		
O3	=	Mc Murry	0	0
O9	●	Austin Coll.	3	3
O17	●	Montezuma	30	0
O24	●	Clarendon	13	7
O31	●	at Sul Ross	21	7
N5	●	Wayland	120	0
N11	●	at Abilene Christian	10	7
N18		at Howard Payne	0	29
N26	●	West Texas A&M	13	12

1926   6-1-3
O				
S21	●	at Mc Murry	7	0
O2	=	Schreiner	0	0
O8	●	St. Edwards	7	6
O15	●	at Hardin-Simmons	0	0
O23	●	Clarendon	14	0
O30		at TCU	16	28
N5		at Daniel Baker	0	0
N11	●	Abilene Christian	28	7
N18	●	Howard Payne	27	6
N25		at West Texas A&M	7	2

1927   5-4-0
O				
S24	●	Panhandle A&M	62	0
O1	●	St. Edwards	13	6
O8		at TCU	6	16
O15	●	Hardin-Simmons	10	6
O22	●	Sul Ross	6	0
O28		Texas A&M	6	47
N5	●	Daniel Baker	19	7
N11		at Abilene Christian	3	6
N24		West Texas A&M	9	12

1928   4-4-1
O				
S29	●	Schriener	7	0
O2		at Texas	0	12
O13	●	St. Edwards	13	6
O20	=	at Mc Murray	3	0
O27		at TCU	6	28
N2	=	at Daniel Baker	0	0
N10	●	Abilene Christian	0	7
N17	●	Hardin-Simmons	0	19
N29	●	at West Texas A&M	18	7

GRADY HIGGENBOTHAM
1929 (.200)   1-7-2

1929   1-7-2
O				
S27	●	Wayland	19	0
O5	●	Sul Ross	7	7
O12		at Daniel Baker	2	6
O19	●	at Mc Murray	0	0
O26		TCU	0	22
N2		at Baylor	0	34
N11	●	Abilene Christian	3	7
N19	●	Howard Payne	0	24
N28		at Hardin-Simmons	0	21
D6		at West Texas A&M	0	20

PETE CAWTHON
1930-40 (.693)   76-32-6

1930   3-6-0
O				
S27		Wayland	0	6
O3	●	New Mexico St.	14	0
O11	●	Mc Murry	10	0
O17		Texas-El Paso	0	31
O25		at TCU	0	26
N1		at West Texas A&M	0	6
N11	●	Abilene Christian	53	7
N19		at Howard Payne	7	26
N27		Hardin-Simmons	6	20

1931   6-3-0
O				
S25	●	at West Texas A&M	21	0
O3		at New Mexico St.	7	0
O13		at Haskell Indians	0	8
O23	●	Colorado Mines	46	0
O31		at Baylor	0	32
N6	●	Abilene Christian	26	6
N11		at Texas-El Paso	12	14
N20	●	New Mexico	32	6
N26		at Hardin-Simmons	6	0

1932-1955
BORDER

1932   10-2-0 (2-0-0)
O				
S17	●	Panhandle A&M	44	0
S24		Texas A&M *Amar*	0	7
O1	●	SMU	6	0
O7	●	Austin Coll.	64	0
O14	●	Arizona	21	0
O15		at N.M. Highlands	43	7
O22	●	at Colorado Mines	21	0
O28		Notre Dame J.V.	39	0
N4	●	Trinity	79	0
N11	●	Baylor	14	2
N19	●	at New Mexico	39	6
N24		Hardin-Simmons	12	13

1933   8-1-0 (1-0-0)
O				
S29	●	at SMU	0	14
O6	●	at Dixie U.	33	0
O14	●	at Arizona	7	0
O20	●	Louisiana Tech	40	10
O28	●	at Texas-El Paso	12	0
N4	●	at Haskell	26	6
N11	●	Hardin-Simmons	7	0
N17	●	Baylor	13	0
N30	●	Kansas State	6	0

1934   7-2-1 (1-0-0)
O				
S22		Texas	6	12
S29	●	Mc Murry	24	7
O5	●	Baylor	14	7
O12		at Oklahoma City	20	0
O26		at Loyola Marymount	7	12
N2	●	Texas-El Paso	27	0
N9	●	Hardin-Simmons	13	0
N16	●	DePaul	48	19
N23	=	North Dakota St.	20	20
N29	●	at Arizona	13	7 *

1935   5-3-2 (0-1-0)
O				
S20	●	at Hardin-Simmons	9	0
S27	●	Daniel Baker	27	6
O4	●	Wichita St.	13	7
O12		at DePaul	0	0
O25		at Loyola Marymount	0	16
N2	●	Oklahoma State	14	0
N11		Arizona	6	7
N23	●	at St. Mary's, Texas	27	0
N28		Detroit	7	12
D7	●	at Oklahoma City	7	7

1936   5-4-1 (0-0-1)
O				
S19	●	at Texas Wesleyan	26	7
S26	●	TCU	7	0
O3	●	Oklahoma City	34	6
O9		Wichita St.	0	6
O24	●	Centenary	12	6
N6	●	Oklahoma State	12	0
N12		at Loyola Marymount	7	26
N20	●	DePaul	6	13
N26		at Loyola, La.	0	14
D5	=	at Arizona	7	7

1937   8-4-0 (3-0-0)
O				
S18	●	No. Arizona	6	0
S25		at Texas	12	25
O2	●	Montana	6	13
O9		at Detroit	0	34
O16	●	Arizona	20	0
O23	●	New Mexico	27	0
O30		at Oklahoma State	14	6
N5	●	at Loyola-New Orleans	25	6
N11	●	Duquesne	13	0
N20		at Centenary	7	2
N25	●	Creighton	27	0

SUN BOWL
J1		West Virginia	6	7

1938   10-1-0 (2-0-0)
O				
S17	●	Montana St.	35	0
S24	●	Wyoming	35	0 *
S30	●	Duquesne *Buf*	7	6
O8		at Oklahoma City	60	0
O15		at Montana	19	13
O22	●	at Texas-El Paso	14	7
N5	●	Loyola-New Orleans.	55	0
N11	●	Gonzaga	7	0
N19	●	at New Mexico	17	7
N26	●	Marquette	21	2

COTTON BOWL
J2		Saint Mary's-Cal	3	20

1939   5-5-1 (1-1-0)
O				
S23	●	at Texas-El Paso	2	7
S30	●	Texas Wesleyan	30	0
O7		Gonzaga	0	6
O14	●	Arizona St. JV	54	0
O21	●	New Mexico	19	7
O27		at Duquesne	0	13
N3		at Miami, Fla.	0	19
N11	=	at Centenary	0	0
N18		Marquette	19	22
N25		Montana St.	13	0
N30		at Loyola-New Orleans	13	0

1940   9-1-1 (0-1-0)
O				
S27	=	Oklahoma State	6	6
O5	●	Loyola Marymount	19	0
O12	●	at Montana	32	19
O18	●	Brigham Young	21	20
O26	●	at Marquette	20	13
N1	●	Miami, Fla.	61	14
N11	●	Centenary	26	6
N16	●	Wake Forest	12	7
N21	●	at St. Louis	7	6
N30		at New Mexico	14	19
D7	●	at San Francisco	23	21

DELL MORGAN
1941-50 (.528)   55-49-3

1941   9-2-0 (2-0-0)
O				
S21	●	Abilene Christian	34	0
O3		at Oklahoma State	16	6
O10	●	at Loyola Marymount	14	0
O18	●	Centenary	25	0
O24	●	New Mexico	36	0
O31		at Miami, Fla.	0	6
N8	●	Creighton	13	6
N15	●	St. Louis	46	6
N21	●	Hardin-Simmons	7	0
N29	●	Wake Forest *Char*	25	6 *

SUN BOWL
J1		Tulsa	0	6

1942   4-5-1 (3-0-1)
O				
S26	●	West Texas St.	39	0
O3		at Texas A&M	0	19
O10		Oklahoma State	6	9
O17		Baylor	7	14
O24	●	at New Mexico	20	0 *
O31		at Rice		
N7	●	TCU	13	6
N14		at Creighton	6	13
N21	=	Hardin-Simmons	0	0
N26	●	at Arizona	13	7

1943   4-6-0 (0-0-0)
O				
S18	●	Lubbock AAF	26	14
S24		Oklahoma State *OkC*	13	21
O2		Texas A&M *SA*	0	13
O9		at Tulsa	7	34
O16	●	South Plains AAF	14	12
O23	●	Lubbock AAF	7	10
O30		at Rice	0	13
N6		at TCU	40	20
N13		Texas-Arlington	14	34
N20		at SMU	7	6

1944   4-7-0 (2-0-0)
O				
S23		Lubbock AAF	13	27
S30		Texas A&M *SA*	14	27
O7		Oklahoma State	7	14
O14		at Tulsa	7	34
O21		Southwestern	19	21
O27		at West Texas St.	35	6
N4	●	at Rice	13	7
N11		at TCU	0	14
N18	●	New Mexico	13	7
N25		SMU	6	7
D2		at South Plains AAF	7	6

1945   3-5-2 (1-0-1)
O				
S22	●	Southwestern	7	0
S29		Texas A&M *SA*	6	16
O6		at Texas	0	33
O13		Tulsa	7	18
O20	=	Baylor	7	7
O27		West Texas St.	12	6
N3		at Rice	0	13
N10	●	TCU	12	0
N17		at Oklahoma State	6	46
N24		at New Mexico	6	6

1946   8-3-0 (3-1-0)
O				
S21		West Texas St.	26	14
S28	●	Texas A&M *SA*	6	0
O5	●	at SMU	7	0
O12		at Tulsa	6	21
O19	●	Baylor	13	6 *
O26	●	Denver	21	6
N2	●	at Rice	6	41
N9		at New Mexico	27	0
N16		Oklahoma State	14	7
N23		at Arizona	16	0
N30		at Hardin-Simmons	6	21

1947   6-5-0 (4-0-0)
O				
S20		at Texas	0	33
S27		Texas A&M *SA*	7	39
O4		West Texas St.	21	13
O11		Tulsa	14	7
O18		Baylor	6	32
O25		at Denver	36	7
N1		at Rice	7	40
N8	●	Arizona	41	28
N22	●	at New Mexico	26	20
N29	●	Hardin-Simmons	14	6

SUN BOWL
J1		Miami, Ohio	12	13

1948   7-3-0 (5-0-0)
O				
S18		West Texas St.	19	0
S25		Texas A&M *SA*	20	14
O2		at SMU	6	41
O9		at Tulsa	41	20
O16		at Baylor	0	13
O23	●	at Arizona	31	0
O30		Rice	7	14
N6	●	Texas-El Paso	46	6
N20	●	New Mexico	14	7
N27		at Hardin-Simmons	28	20

1949   7-5-0 (5-0-0)

S10	●	Abilene Christian	20	0
S17		at Texas	0	43
S24		Texas A&M SA	7	26
O1	●	West Texas St.	35	19
O8	●	Tulsa	15	0
O15		Baylor	7	28
O22	●	Arizona	27	7
O29		at Rice	0	28
N5	●	at Texas-El Paso	13	0
N19		at New Mexico	27	0
N26	●	Hardin-Simmons	23	13
		RAISIN BOWL		
D31		San Jose State	13	20

1950   3-8-0 (3-1-0)

S23		Texas	14	28
S30		Texas A&M SA	13	34
O7		West Texas St.	13	28
O14		at TCU	6	19
O21		at Baylor	12	26
O28	●	Texas-El Paso	61	7
N4		at Rice	7	13
N11		Tulsa	7	39
N18	●	at Arizona	39	7
N25	●	New Mexico	37	12
D2		at Hardin-Simmons	13	28

DeWITT WEAVER   1951-60 (.490)   49-51-5

1951   7-4-0 (5-0-0)

S22	●	West Texas St.	46	7
S29		Texas A&M SA	7	20
O6		at Houston	0	6
O13	●	TCU	33	19
O20		at Baylor	20	40
O27	●	Arizona	41	0
N3	●	at Texas-El Paso	27	7
N17		at Tulsa	14	21
N24	●	at New Mexico	60	14
D1	●	Hardin-Simmons	28	21
		SUN BOWL		
J1	●	Pacific	25	14

1952   3-7-1 (2-1-1)

S20	●	West Texas St.	48	7
S27		at Rice	7	34
O4		at Pacific	21	42
O11		Texas-El Paso	14	20
O18		Baylor	10	21
N1		Houston	7	20
N8		at North Texas	19	34
N15	=	at Hardin-Simmons	14	14
N22	=	at Arizona	19	14
N29		North Carolina St.	54	7
D6		Tulsa	20	26

1953   11-1-0 (5-0-0)

S19	●	West Texas St.	40	14
S26	●	at Texas-El Paso	27	6
O3	●	at Oklahoma State	27	13
O10	●	Texas A&M	14	27
O17	●	Pacific	34	7
O24	●	New Mexico St.	71	0
O31	●	Mississippi State JAM	27	20
N7	●	Arizona	52	27
N14	●	at Tulsa	49	7
N21	●	at Houston	41	21
N28	●	Hardin-Simmons	46	12
		GATOR BOWL		
J1	●	Auburn	35	13

1954   7-2-1 (4-0-0)

S18	●	at Texas A&M	41	9
S25	●	West Texas St.	33	7
O2	=	Oklahoma State	13	13
O9	●	Texas-El Paso	55	28
O16		at LSU	13	20
O23		at Pacific	7	20
N6	●	at Arizona	28	14
N13	●	Tulsa	55	13
N20	●	Houston	61	14
N27	●	at Hardin-Simmons	61	19

1955   7-3-1 (3-0-1)

S17	●	at Texas	20	14
S24		TCU	0	32
O1	●	at Oklahoma State	24	6
O8	=	at Texas-El Paso	27	27
O22		at Houston	0	7
O29	●	West Texas St.	27	24
N5	●	Arizona	27	7
N12	●	at Tulsa	34	7
N19	●	Pacific	13	7
N26	●	Hardin-Simmons	16	14
		SUN BOWL		
J2	●	Wyoming	14	21

1956   2-7-1 (0-0-0)

S22		Texas-El Paso	13	17
S29		at Baylor	0	27
O6		Texas A&M DAL	7	40
O13		West Texas St.	14	34
O27	●	at Arizona	21	7
N3	=	Oklahoma State	13	13
N10	●	TCU	21	7
N17		at Tulsa	7	10
N24		Houston	7	20
D1		at Hardin-Simmons	14	41

1957   2-8-0 (0-0-0)

S21	●	West Texas St.	0	19
S28	●	Texas A&M	0	21
O5		LSU	14	19
O12		at Texas-El Paso	14	26
O19		Baylor	12	15
O26	●	at Arizona	28	6
N2		at Oklahoma State	0	13
N9		Tulsa	0	3
N16	●	Hardin-Simmons	26	21
N23		Arkansas LR	26	47

1958   3-7-0 (0-0-0)

S20	●	Texas A&M DAL	15	14
S27	●	West Texas St.	32	7
O4		at Texas	7	12
O11		at TCU	0	26
O18		Baylor	7	26
O31		at Tulane	0	27
N8	●	Arizona	33	6
N15		at Tulsa	7	9
N22		Arkansas	8	14
N29		at Houston	17	22

1959   4-6-0 (0-0-0)

S19	●	Texas A&M DAL	20	14
S26	●	Oregon State	15	14
O3	●	Tulsa	8	7
O10		TCU	8	14
O17		at Baylor	7	14
O24		at SMU	13	21
O30		at Tulane	7	17
N7		at Arizona	26	30
N14	●	Houston	27	0
N21		Arkansas LR	8	27

1960   3-6-1 (1-5-1)

S17	●	West Texas St.	38	14
S24	=	at Texas A&M	14	14
O1		at Texas	0	17
O8		at TCU	7	21
O15		Baylor	7	14
O22	●	SMU	28	7
O29		at Rice	6	30
N5	●	Tulane	35	21
N12		Wyoming	7	10
N19		Arkansas	6	34

JT KING   1961-69 (.495)   44-45-3

1961   4-6-0 (2-5-0)

S23		Mississippi State JAM	0	6
S30		at Texas	14	42
O7		Texas A&M	7	38
O14	●	TCU	10	0
O21	●	Baylor	19	17
O28	●	at SMU	7	8
N4		Rice	7	42
N11	●	Boston College	14	6
N25	●	Arkansas LR	0	28
D2	●	West Texas St.	16	14

1962   1-9-0 (0-7-0)

S22		West Texas St.	27	30
S29		Texas	0	34
O6		at Texas A&M	3	7
O13		at TCU	13	35
O20		at Baylor	6	28
O27		SMU	0	14
N3		at Rice	0	14
N10		at Boston College	13	42
N17	●	Colorado	21	12
N24		Arkansas	0	34

1963   5-5-0 (2-5-0)

S21	●	Washington State	16	7
S28		at Texas	7	49
O5		Texas A&M	10	0
O12		TCU	3	35
O19		Baylor	17	21
O26	●	at SMU	13	6
N2		Rice	3	17
N9		Kansas State	51	13
N16	●	at Texas-El Paso	7	3
N23		at Arkansas	20	27

1964   6-4-1 (3-3-1)

S19	●	Mississippi State	21	7
S26		Texas	0	23
O3	●	at Texas A&M	16	12
O10	●	at TCU	25	10
O17		at Baylor	0	28
O24	●	SMU	12	0
O31	=	at Rice	6	6
N7	●	West Texas St.	48	0
N14	●	Washington State	28	10
N21		Arkansas	0	17
		SUN BOWL		
D26		Georgia	0	7

1965   8-3-0 (5-2-0)

S18	●	Kansas	26	7
S25		at Texas	7	33
O2	●	Texas A&M	20	16
O9	●	TCU	28	24
O16	●	Oklahoma State	17	14
O23	●	at SMU	26	24
O30	●	Rice	27	0
N6	●	New Mexico St.	48	9
N13	●	Baylor	34	22
N20		at Arkansas	24	42
		GATOR BOWL		
D31		Georgia Tech	21	31

1966   4-6-0 (2-5-0)

S17	●	at Kansas	23	7
S24		Texas	21	31
O1		at Texas A&M	14	35
O8		at TCU	3	6
O15		Florida State	33	42
O22		SMU	7	24
O29	●	at Rice	35	19
N5	●	Oklahoma State	10	7
N12	●	Baylor	14	29
N19	●	Arkansas	21	16

1967   6-4-0 (5-2-0)

S23	●	Iowa St.	52	0
S30	●	at Texas	19	13
O7		Mississippi State	3	7
O12		Texas A&M	24	28
O21		at Florida State	12	28
O28	●	at SMU	21	7
N4	●	Rice	24	10
N11	●	at TCU	0	16
N18	●	Baylor	31	29
N25	●	Arkansas LR	31	27

1968   5-3-2 (4-3-0)

S21	=	Cincinnati	10	10
S28	●	Texas	31	22
O5		Colorado State	43	13
O12	●	at Texas A&M	21	16
O19	●	Mississippi State JAM	28	28
O26		SMU	18	39
N2	●	at Rice	38	15
N9	●	TCU	31	14
N16		at Baylor	28	42
N23		Arkansas	7	42

1969   5-5-0 (4-3-0)

S20	●	Kansas	38	22
S27	●	at Texas	7	49
O4		at Oklahoma State	10	17
O11	●	Texas A&M	13	9
O18		Mississippi State	26	30
O25	●	at SMU	27	24
N1	●	Rice	24	14
N8		at TCU	26	35
N15	●	Baylor	41	7
N27		Arkansas LR	0	33

JIM CARLEN   1970-74 (.644)   37-20-2

1970   8-4-0 (5-2-0)

S12	●	Tulane	21	14
S19	●	Kansas	23	0
S26		at Texas	13	35
O3		Santa Barbara	63	21
O10	●	at Texas A&M	21	7
O17		Mississippi State JAM	16	20
O24		SMU	14	10
O31	●	at Rice	3	0
N7		TCU	22	14
N14		at Baylor	7	3
N21		Arkansas	10	24
		SUN BOWL		
D19		Georgia Tech	9	17

1971   4-7-0 (2-5-0)

S11		at Tulane	9	15
S18		New Mexico	10	13
S25		at Texas	0	28
O2	●	at Arizona	13	10
O9	●	Texas A&M	28	7
O16	●	Boston College	14	6
O23		at SMU	17	18
O30		Rice	7	9
N6		at TCU	6	17
N13	●	Baylor	27	0
N20		at Arkansas	0	15

1972   8-4-0 (4-3-0)

S16	●	Utah	45	2
S23	●	at New Mexico	41	16
S30		Texas	20	25
O7	●	Tulsa	35	18
O14	●	at Texas A&M	17	14
O21	●	Arizona	35	10
O28	●	at SMU	17	3
N4	●	at Rice	10	6
N11	●	TCU	7	31
N18	●	at Baylor	13	7
N25		Arkansas	14	24
		SUN BOWL		
D30		North Carolina	28	32

1973   11-1-0 (6-1-0)

S15	●	Utah	29	22
S22	●	New Mexico	41	7
S29		at Texas	12	28
O6		at Oklahoma State	20	7
O13	●	Texas A&M	28	16
O20	●	at Arizona	31	17
O27	●	SMU	31	14
N3	●	Rice	19	6
N10	●	at TCU	24	10
N17	●	Baylor	55	24
N24	●	Arkansas	24	17
		GATOR BOWL		
D29	●	Tennessee	28	19

1974   6-4-2 (3-4-0)

S14	●	Iowa St.	24	3
S21	●	at New Mexico	21	21
S28	●	Texas	26	3
O5	●	Oklahoma State	14	13
O12		at Texas A&M	7	28
O19	●	Arizona	17	8
O26	●	at SMU	20	17
N2		at Rice	7	21
N9	●	TCU	28	0
N16		at Baylor	10	17
		PEACH BOWL		
N23		Arkansas	13	21
D28	●	Vanderbilt	6	6

STEVE SLOAN   1975-77 (.657)   23-12

1975   6-5-0 (4-3-0)

S13	●	Florida State	31	20
S20	●	New Mexico	24	17
S27		at Texas	18	42
O4		at Oklahoma State	16	17
O11		Texas A&M	9	38
O18		at Arizona	28	32
O25	●	SMU	37	20
N1	●	Rice	28	24
N8	●	at TCU	34	0
N15	●	Baylor	33	10
N22		at Arkansas	14	31

THE SCHOOLS

1976 — 10-2-0 (7-1-0)

S11	●	Colorado	24 7
S25	●	at New Mexico	20 16
O9	●	at Texas A&M	27 16
O16	●	at Rice	37 13
O23	●	Arizona	52 27
O30	●	Texas	31 28
N6	●	at TCU	14 10
N13	●	SMU	34 7
N20		Houston	19 27
N27	●	Arkansas LR	30 7
D4	●	Baylor	24 21
BLUEBONNET BOWL			
D31		Nebraska	24 27

1977 — 7-5-0 (4-4-0)

S10	●	at Baylor	17 7
S17	●	New Mexico	49 14
S24		Texas A&M	17 33
O1	●	at North Carolina	10 7
O8	●	at Arizona	32 26
O15	●	Rice	42 7
O29		at Texas	0 26
N5	●	TCU	49 17
N12	●	at SMU	45 7
N19		at Houston	7 45
N26		Arkansas	14 17
TANGERINE BOWL			
D23		Florida State	17 40

REX DOCKERY
1978-80 (.485)   15-16-2

1978 — 7-4-0 (5-3-0)

S9		at Southern Cal	9 17
S23	●	Arizona	41 26
S30		Texas	7 24
O7		at Texas A&M	9 38
O14	●	at New Mexico	36 23
O21	●	at Rice	42 28
N4	●	Baylor	27 9
N11	●	at TCU	27 17
N18	●	SMU	19 16
N25	●	Houston	22 21
D2		at Arkansas	7 49

1979 — 3-6-2 (2-5-1)

S8		Southern Cal	7 21
S15	●	New Mexico	17 7
S22	=	at Arizona	14 14
S29		at Baylor	17 27
O6	●	Texas A&M	21 20
O13		Arkansas	6 20
O20	●	Rice	30 7
N3		at Texas	6 14
N10	=	TCU	3 3
N17		at SMU	10 35
N24		at Houston	10 14

1980 — 5-6-0 (3-5-0)

S6	●	Texas-El Paso	35 7
S13		North Carolina	3 9
S20	●	New Mexico	28 17
S27		Baylor	3 11
O4		at Texas A&M	21 41
O18	●	at Rice	10 3
N1	●	Texas	24 20
N8		at TCU	17 24
N15	●	SMU	14 0
N22		Houston	7 34
N29	●	Arkansas LR	16 22

JERRY MOORE
1981-85 (.309)   16-37-2

1981 — 1-9-1 (0-7-1)

S12		at Colorado	27 45
S19	●	New Mexico	28 21
S26		at Baylor	15 28
O3		Texas A&M	23 24
O10		Arkansas	14 26
O17		Rice	23 30
O24		Washington	7 14
O31		at Texas	9 26
N7	=	TCU	39 39
N14		at SMU	6 30
N21		at Houston	7 15

1982 — 4-7-0 (3-5-0)

S11		at New Mexico	0 14
S18	●	Air Force	31 30
S25		Baylor	23 24
O2	●	at Texas A&M	24 15
O9		at Arkansas	3 21
O16	●	at Rice	23 21
O23		at Washington	3 10
O30		Texas	0 27
N6	●	at TCU	16 14
N13		SMU	27 34
N20		Houston	7 24

1983 — 3-7-1 (3-4-1)

S10		at Air Force	13 28
S24	●	at Baylor	26 11
O1	●	Texas A&M	3 0
O8		New Mexico	10 30
O15	●	Rice	14 3
O22		Tulsa	20 59
O29		at Texas	3 20
N5	=	TCU	10 10
N12	●	at SMU	7 33
N19		at Houston	41 43
N26		Arkansas	13 16

1984 — 4-7-0 (2-6-0)

S15	●	Texas Arlington	44 7
S22		at New Mexico	24 29
S29		Baylor	9 18
O6	●	at Texas A&M	30 12
O13		Arkansas LR	0 24
O20	●	at Rice	30 10
O27		Tulsa	20 17
N3		Texas	10 13
N10	●	at TCU	16 27
N17		SMU	0 31
N24		Houston	17 24

1985 — 4-7-0 (1-7-0)

S7	●	New Mexico	32 31
S14	●	at Tulsa	21 17
S21	●	North Texas	28 7
S28		at Baylor	0 31
O5		Texas A&M	27 28
O12		Arkansas	7 30
O19		Rice	27 29
N2		at Texas	21 34
N9	●	TCU	63 7
N16		at SMU	7 9
N23		at Houston	16 17

DAVID McWILLIAMS
1986 (.636)   7-4

1986 — 7-5-0 (5-3-0)

S6	●	Kansas State	41 7
S13		at Miami, Fla.	11 61
S20	●	New Mexico	14 7
S27		Baylor	14 45
O4		at Texas A&M	8 45
O11	●	at Arkansas	17 7
O18	●	at Rice	49 21
N1	●	Texas	23 21
N8	●	at TCU	36 14
N15		SMU	7 13
N22	●	Houston	34 7
INDEPENDENCE BOWL			
D20		Mississippi	17 20

SPIKE DYKES
1986-99 (.550)   82-67-1

1987 — 6-4-1 (3-3-1)

S5		at Florida State	16 40
S12	●	Colorado State	33 24
S19	●	Lamar	43 14
S26		at Baylor	22 36
O3	●	Texas A&M	27 21
O10		Arkansas	0 31
O17	●	Rice	59 7
O24	●	Tulsa	42 7
O31		at Texas	27 41
N7	●	TCU	36 35
N21	=	at Houston	10 10

1988 — 5-6-0 (4-3-0)

S3		North Texas	24 29
S10		at Arizona	19 35
S24	●	Baylor	36 6
O1		at Texas A&M	15 50
O8	●	Arkansas LR	10 31
O15	●	at Rice	38 36
O29	●	Texas	33 32
N5		at TCU	23 10
N12	●	Lamar	59 28
N19		Houston	29 30
D3		Oklahoma State TOK	42 45

1989 — 9-3-0 (5-3-0)

S9	●	Arizona	24 14
S16	●	New Mexico	27 20
S23	●	at Oklahoma State	31 15
S30		at Baylor	15 29
O7		Texas A&M	27 24
O14	●	Arkansas	13 45
O21	●	Rice	41 25
N4	●	at Texas	24 17
N11	●	TCU	37 7
N18	●	at SMU	48 24
N25		at Houston	24 40
ALL-AMERICAN BOWL			
D28	●	Duke	49 21

1990 — 4-7-0 (3-5-0)

S8		at Ohio State	10 17
S13		Houston	35 51
S22	●	at New Mexico	34 32
S29		Baylor	15 21
O6	●	at Texas A&M	24 28
O13	●	at Arkansas	49 44
O20		at Rice	21 42
O27		Miami, Fla.	10 45
N3		Texas	22 41
N10	●	at TCU	40 28
N17	●	SMU	62 7

1991 — 6-5-0 (5-3-0)

S7	●	Fullerton St.	41 7
S14		Oregon	13 28
S21		at Wyoming	17 22
S28		TCU	16 30
O5		Texas A&M	14 37
O12	●	at SMU	38 14
O26	●	Rice	40 20
N2		at Texas	15 23
N9	●	Arkansas	38 21
N16	●	at Baylor	31 24
N30	●	at Houston	52 46

1992 — 5-6-0 (4-3-0)

S3		Oklahoma	9 34
S12	●	Wyoming	49 32
S19		at Oregon	13 16
S26	●	Baylor	36 17
O3		at Texas A&M	17 19
O10		at North Carolina St.	13 48
O24	●	SMU	39 25
O31		Texas	33 44
N7		at Rice	3 34
N14	●	at TCU	31 28
N21	●	Houston	44 35

1993 — 6-6-0 (5-2-0)

S4	●	Pacific	55 7
S11	●	at Nebraska	27 50
S18		at Georgia	37 52
S25		at Baylor	26 28
O2		Texas A&M	6 31
O9		North Carolina St.	34 36
O16	●	Rice	45 16
O30	●	at Texas	31 22
N6		TCU	49 21
N13	●	at SMU	41 24
N20		Houston SA	58 7
SUN BOWL			
D24		Oklahoma	10 41

1994 — 6-6-0 (4-3-0)

S3	●	New Mexico	37 31
S8		Nebraska	16 42
S17		at Oklahoma	11 17
S24	●	SMU	35 7
O1		at Texas A&M	17 23
O8		at Rice	21 24
O22	●	Baylor	38 7
O29	●	Texas	33 9
N12	●	La. Lafayette	39 7
N19	●	Houston SA	34 0
N25		at TCU	17 24
COTTON BOWL			
J2		Southern Cal	14 55

1995 — 9-3-0 (5-2-0)

S9		at Penn State	23 24
S16	●	Missouri	41 14
S30		at Baylor	7 9
O7		Texas A&M	14 7
O14	●	Arkansas State	63 25
O21	●	Rice	31 26
O28		at New Mexico	34 7
N4		at Texas	7 48
N11	●	TCU	27 6
N18	●	at SMU	45 14
N25	●	at Houston	38 26
COPPER BOWL			
D27	●	Air Force	55 41

1996-PRESENT
BIG 12

1996 — 7-5 (5-3)

A31		at Kansas State	14 21
S7	●	Oklahoma State Inv	31 3
S21		at Georgia	12 15
S28	●	Utah State	58 20
O5		Baylor	45 24
O12	●	at Kansas	30 17
O19		Nebraska	10 24
O26	●	at Texas A&M	13 10
N9		Texas	32 38
N16	●	La. Lafayette	56 21
N23		at Oklahoma	22 12
ALAMO BOWL			
D29		Iowa	0 27

1997 — 6-5 (5-3)

A30		at Tennessee	17 52
S13	●	La. Lafayette	59 14
S20		North Texas	27 30
O4	●	at Baylor	35 14
O11	●	Kansas	7 7
O18		at Nebraska	0 29
O25	●	Texas A&M	16 13
N1		Kansas State	2 13
N8	●	at Texas	24 10
N15	●	at Oklahoma State	27 3
N22		Oklahoma	21 32

1998 — 7-5 (4-4)

S5	●	Texas-El Paso	35 3
S12	●	North Texas Inv	30 0
S19	●	Fresno State	34 28
S26	●	at Iowa St.	31 24
O3		Baylor	31 29
O10	●	Oklahoma State	24 17
O17		at Colorado	17 19
O24		at Texas A&M	10 17
O31		Missouri	26 28
N14	●	Texas	42 35
N21		at Oklahoma	17 20
INDEPENDENCE BOWL			
D31		Mississippi	18 35

1999 — 6-5 (5-3)

S6		at Arizona State	13 31
S11	●	at La. Lafayette	38 17
S18	●	North Texas	14 21
O2	●	Texas A&M	21 19
O9		at Oklahoma State	21 41
O16	●	Colorado	31 10
O23	●	at Baylor	35 7
O30		at Missouri	7 34
N6	●	Iowa St.	28 16
N13		at Texas	7 58
N20	●	Oklahoma	38 28

MIKE LEACH
2000-PRESENT (.609)   39-25

2000 — 7-6 (3-5)

A26	●	New Mexico	24 3
S2	●	Utah State	38 16
S9	●	North Texas	13 7
S16	●	La. Lafayette	26 0
S30		at Texas A&M	15 33
O7	●	Baylor	28 0
O14		Nebraska	3 56
O21	●	at Kansas State	23 28
O28	●	at Kansas	45 39
N4		Texas	17 29
N11	●	Oklahoma State	58 0
N18		at Oklahoma	13 27
GALLERYFURNITURE.COM BOWL			
D27		East Carolina	27 40

2001 — 7-5 (4-4)

S8		New Mexico	42 30
S22	●	North Texas Inv	42 14
S29		at Texas	7 42
O6		Kansas	31 34
O13	●	Kansas State	38 19
O20		at Nebraska	31 41
O27	●	at Baylor	63 19
N3		Texas A&M	12 0
N10	●	at Oklahoma State	49 30
N17		Oklahoma	13 30
N24	●	Stephen F. Austin	58 3
ALAMO BOWL			
D29		Iowa	16 19

2002		9-5	(5-3)
A24	at Ohio State	21	45
S7 ●	at SMU	24	14
S14 ●	Mississippi	42	28
S21	North Carolina St.	48	51
S27 ●	at New Mexico	49	0
O5 ●	at Texas A&M	48	47
O12	at Iowa State	17	31
O19 ●	Missouri	52	38
O26	at Colorado	13	37
N2 ●	Baylor	62	11
N9 ●	Oklahoma State	49	24
N16 ●	Texas	42	38
N23	at Oklahoma	15	60
TANGERINE BOWL			
D23 ●	Clemson	55	15

2003		8-5	(4-4)
A30 ●	SMU	58	10
S6 ●	New Mexico	42	28
S20	at North Carolina St.	21	49
S27 ●	at Mississippi	49	45
O4 ●	Texas A&M	59	20
O11 ●	Iowa State	52	21
O18 ●	at Oklahoma State	49	51
O25	at Missouri	31	62
N1 ●	Colorado	26	21
N8 ●	at Baylor	62	14
N15	at Texas	40	43
N22	Oklahoma	25	56
HOUSTON BOWL			
D30 ●	Navy	38	14

2004		8-4	(5-3)
S4 ●	at SMU	27	13
S11 ●	at New Mexico	24	27
S18 ●	TCU	70	35
S25 ●	at Kansas	31	30
O2	at Oklahoma	13	28
O9 ●	Nebraska	70	10
O23	Texas	21	51
O30 ●	at Kansas State	35	25
N6 ●	Baylor	42	17
N13	at Texas A&M	25	32
N27 ●	Oklahoma State	31	15
HOLIDAY BOWL			
D30 ●	California	45	31

Neutral Site key: *LR* Little Rock, AR / *Tok* Tokyo, Japan / *Inv* Irving, TX / *Amar* Amarillo, TX / *Buf* Buffalo, NY / *Char* Charlotte, NC / *Dal* Dallas, TX / *OkC* Oklahoma City, OK / *SA* San Antonio, TX / *JaM* Jackson, MS
ƒ Forfeit † Game Later Forfieted # Disputed Victor * Disputed Score || Designated Conference Game |2 Counted Twice in Conference Standings

TEXAS TECH ANNUAL STATISTICAL LEADERS

YR	RUSHING	YDS	ATT	AVG	PASSING	ATT	CMP	PCT	YDS	RECEIVING	REC	YDS	AVG
1951	Bobby Cavazos	705	138	5.1	Junior Arterburn	87	39	.45	622	Jim Turner	13	197	15.2
1952	Bobby Cavazos	674	124	5.4	Jerry Johnson	109	48	.44	702	Don Lewis	11	165	15.0
1953	Bobby Cavazos	747	97	7.7	Jack Kirkpatrick	46	22	.48	343	Bobby Cavazos	9	116	12.9
1954	Lonnie Graham	457	50	9.1	Jerry Johnson	61	27	.44	569	Dean White	10	252	25.2
1955	Don Schmidt	508	105	4.8	Buddy Hill	60	33	.55	481	Ken Vakey	13	186	14.3
1956	Doug Duncan	360	67	5.4	Buddy Hill	52	24	.46	326	Ken Vakey	14	180	12.9
1957	Ronnie Rice	426	67	6.4	Jerry Bell	77	37	.48	489	Jimmy Knox	14	201	14.4
1958	Ronnie Rice	263	67	3.9	Jerry Bell	99	48	.48	435	Floyd Dellinger	20	213	10.7
1959	Carl Gatlin	211	49	4.3	Ken Talkington	116	65	.56	603	Bake Turner	22	444	20.2
1960	Coolidge Hunt	527	127	4.1	Glen Amerson	88	33	.38	464	Dick Polson	13	155	11.9
1961	Coolidge Hunt	486	128	3.8	Doug Cannon	77	37	.48	442	Bob Witucki	26	335	12.9
1962	Roger Gill	379	61	6.2	Richard Mahan	67	26	.39	260	David Parks	32	399	12.5
1963	Donny Anderson	609	146	4.2	James Ellis	69	39	.57	536	David Parks	32	499	15.6
1964	Donny Anderson	966	211	4.6	Tom Wilson	119	65	.55	777	Donny Anderson	32	396	12.4
1965	Donny Anderson	705	169	4.2	Tom Wilson	283	172	.61	2,119	Donny Anderson	60	797	13.3
1966	Mike Leinert	495	102	4.9	John Scovell	232	107	.46	1,323	Larry Gilbert	52	767	14.8
1967	Mike Leinert	689	163	4.2	John Scovell	114	44	.39	470	Larry Gilbert	35	491	14.0
1968	Roger Freeman	471	129	3.7	Joe Matulich	125	73	.58	864	Bobby Allen	35	546	15.6
1969	Danny Hardaway	483	159	3.0	Charles Napper	153	65	.42	901	Johnny Odom	23	320	13.9
1970	Doug McCutchen	1,068	227	4.7	Charles Napper	155	86	.55	979	Johnny Odom	26	331	12.7
1971	Doug McCutchen	548	131	4.2	Jimmy Carmichael	80	38	.48	423	Johnny Odom	20	242	12.1
1972	George Smith	740	107	6.9	Joe Barnes	168	86	.51	1,142	Andre Tillman	21	285	13.6
1973	Joe Barnes	568	135	4.2	Joe Barnes	125	73	.58	978	Andre Tillman	26	428	16.5
1974	Larry Isaac	671	155	4.3	Tommy Duniven	82	43	.52	552	Lawrence Williams	27	477	17.7
1975	Larry Isaac	751	151	5.0	Tommy Duniven	125	72	.58	1,038	Sammy Williams	32	601	18.8
1976	Larry Isaac	685	145	4.7	Rodney Allison	139	83	.60	1,458	Sammy Williams	32	601	18.8
1977	Billy Taylor	931	209	4.5	Rodney Allison	83	50	.60	589	Billy Taylor	30	186	6.2
1978	James Hadnot	1,369	251	5.5	Ron Reeves	161	77	.48	1,195	Brian Nelson	26	443	17.0
1979	James Hadnot	1,371	273	5.0	Ron Reeves	120	51	.43	656	Howie Lewis	24	317	13.2
1980	Wes Hightower	515	126	4.1	Ron Reeves	228	115	.50	1,461	Renie Baker	40	625	15.6
1981	Anthony Hutchison	545	100	5.5	Ron Reeves	254	109	.43	1,376	Renie Baker	28	453	16.2
1982	Anthony Hutchison	796	204	3.9	Jim Hart	227	107	.47	1,081	Leonard Harris	30	366	12.2
1983	Robert Lewis	750	175	4.3	Jim Hart	216	108	.50	1,216	Leonard Harris	35	506	14.5
1984	Timmy Smith	711	164	4.3	Aaron Keesee	140	70	.50	755	Buzz Tatom	20	312	15.6
1985	James McGowen	479	107	4.5	Billy Joe Tolliver	124	61	.49	863	Wayne Walker	26	447	17.2
1986	James Gray	613	108	5.7	Billy Joe Tolliver	333	145	.44	1,602	Wayne Walker	38	717	18.9
1987	James Gray	1,006	199	5.1	Billy Joe Tolliver	196	97	.49	1,422	Wayne Walker	32	659	20.6
1988	James Gray	938	172	5.5	Billy Joe Tolliver	354	190	.54	2,869	Tyrone Thurman	48	726	15.1
1989	James Gray	1,509	263	5.7	Jamie Gill	186	105	.56	1,464	Travis Price	23	389	16.9
1990	Anthony Lynn	884	224	3.9	Robert Hall	217	110	.51	1,581	Rodney Blackshear	44	973	22.1
1991	Byron Morris	514	98	5.2	Robert Hall	220	111	.50	1,788	Rodney Blackshear	30	649	21.6
1992	Byron Morris	1,279	242	5.3	Robert Hall	219	111	.51	1,645	Lloyd Hill	76	1,261	16.6
1993	Byron Morris	1,752	298	5.9	Robert Hall	341	216	.63	2,894	Lloyd Hill	57	794	13.9
1994	Byron Hanspard	761	173	4.4	Zebbie Lethridge	261	132	.51	1,596	Sheldon Bass	34	400	11.8
1995	Byron Hanspard	1,374	248	5.5	Zebbie Lethridge	281	136	.48	1,885	Byron Hanspard	35	474	13.5
1996	Byron Hanspard	2,084	339	6.1	Zebbie Lethridge	267	117	.44	1,686	Donnie Hart	22	494	22.5
1997	Ricky Williams	894	201	4.4	Zebbie Lethridge	261	134	.51	1,622	Malcolm McKenzie	42	462	11.0
1998	Ricky Williams	1,582	306	5.2	Rob Peters	183	96	.52	1,269	Donnie Hart	48	871	18.1
1999	Shaud Williams	658	112	5.9	Rob Peters	211	105	.50	1,437	Sammy Morris	23	386	16.8
2000	Ricky Williams	421	127	3.3	Kliff Kingsbury	585	362	.62	3,418	Tim Baker	69	765	11.1
2001	Ricky Williams	726	142	5.1	Kliff Kingsbury	529	365	.69	3,502	Ricky Williams	92	617	6.7
2002	Taurean Henderson	793	153	5.2	Kliff Kingsbury	712	479	.67	5,017	Taurean Henderson	98	633	6.5
2003	Taurean Henderson	736	124	5.9	B.J. Symons	719	470	.65	5,833	Wes Welker	97	1,099	11.3
2004	Taurean Henderson	840	162	5.2	Sonny Cumbie	642	421	.67	4,742	Jarrett Hicks	76	1,177	15.5

The NCAA began including postseason stats in 2002

TOLEDO

BY ED KRZEMIENSKI

ALTHOUGH BEST KNOWN FOR ITS minor league baseball team, the Mud Hens, and its fictional son, Max Klinger, the city of Toledo also boasts an excellent football team. Along with fellow Mid-American Conference members Miami and Marshall, the University of Toledo stands as one of the giants of the MAC—nationally ranked eight times in the polls and the owner of the second-longest winning streak in Division I-A history, a 35-game run that encompassed three entire seasons from 1969 through 1971. In 2001, Toledo hired alum and hometown boy Tom Amstutz as head coach. In four years, Amstutz led Toledo to a 36–15 overall record, two MAC championships, three bowl berths and four wins over Top 25 teams.

TRADITION Every time the Rockets score, the Phi Kappa Phi fraternity fires a cannon. It was fired off the northeast stone tower in the Glass Bowl until 1989, when the cannon needed to be moved to the field due to structural concerns. Not to be outdone by a cannon, Toledo players bang their helmets on the doorway when entering or leaving any locker room. No word as to whether the players have to be wearing their helmets when adhering to this tradition. Students, meanwhile, gather around the Spirit Rock for pep rallies; on campus since 1968, the rock has been burned, painted and tarred and feathered hundreds of times. Tradition holds, however, that it is proper to paint the Spirit Rock only during twilight hours.

BEST PLAYER In 1968, Toledo recruited a quarterback named Chuck Ealey from Portsmouth, Ohio, a small town on the Kentucky border. Ealey had an impressive résumé, to say the least, having gone 30–0 in his prep career. In college, Ealey got better. Continuing his unbeaten streak in the first game of his sophomore season at Toledo, Ealey proceeded to lead the Rockets to wins in all 35 of his college games from 1969 to 1971. Dubbed the Wizard of Oohs and Ahs, Ealey led the Rockets to a 35-game winning streak, bested only by Oklahoma's 47-game streak from 1953 to 1957. Ealey won MAC Back of the Year in each of his three varsity seasons and was the first MAC player to place in the top 10 in Heisman Trophy voting, when he finished eighth in 1971. One of Ealey's performances against Western Michigan was so amazing that WMU's coach Bill Doolittle remarked, "I think God was throwing some of those passes. I know he [Ealey] had to have some help, somehow." Part of a generation of gifted black quarterbacks ignored by the NFL, Ealey went on to a seven-year career in the Canadian Football League, where he led the Hamilton Tiger-Cats to the Grey Cup championship in his rookie season.

BEST COACH Gary Pinkel holds Toledo records for victories (73) and years served (10). Before taking over at Missouri in

---

PROFILE

University of Toledo
Toledo, Ohio
Founded: 1872
Enrollment: 16,366
Colors: Midnight Blue and Gold
Nickname: Rockets
Stadium: Glass Bowl
 Opened in 1937
 NeXturf; 26,248 capacity
First football game: 1917
All-time record: 438-359-24 (.548)
Bowl record: 6-3
Mid-American Conference championships:
10 (8 outright)
First-round NFL draftees: 1
Website: www.utrockets.com

THE BEST OF TIMES

From 1969 to 1971, the Rockets went 35–0, winning three consecutive MAC championships and Tangerine Bowls.

THE WORST OF TIMES

From 1956 to 1964, UT won only 24 games while losing 57 and tying two. UT also had one of the worst beginnings in the history of the game, losing the first three of its inaugural season's games by a combined 262-0.

CONFERENCE

Toledo joined the Mid-American Conference in 1952, and has remained there since. Previously, UT played as an independent from 1917 to 1920, 1936 to 1937 and 1948 to 1951; in the Northwestern Ohio Intercollegiate Athletic Association from 1921 to 1930; and in the Ohio Athletic Conference from 1932 to 1935 and 1938 to 1947.

DISTINGUISHED ALUMNI

Seth Abraham, president, Madison Square Garden/Radio City Entertainment; Jon Hendricks, jazz singer; John Neff, investment legend; Karl Ronn, inventor of the Swiffer; Mildred Taylor, children's author

FIGHT SONG

U OF TOLEDO
U of Toledo, we'll fight for you
(Fight! Fight! Fight!)
U of Toledo, we love the gold and blue
(Let's go blue!)
Men of the varsity, the enemy must yield,
We'll fight just like our ancestors
And march right down the field!
T-O-L-E-D-O, Toledo!

Toledo and Bowling Green play for the Peace Pipe, but they rarely choose to smoke it.

2001, Pinkel coached the Rockets to eight winning seasons in his decade at Toledo, including an 11–0–1 mark in 1995 and a 10–1 record in 2000. In the 1995 season, Toledo won the MAC, defeated Nevada in the Las Vegas Bowl and ended up ranked No. 24 in the nation. Pinkel's Rockets finished their 2000 season ranked No. 25.

BEST TEAM An argument could be made for any of the three consecutive undefeated teams from 1969 to 1971, but the 1970 squad deserves the nod. Led by junior quarterback Ealey, who threw for 1,898 yards and 16 touchdowns, the 1970 Rockets outscored their opponents 344-76 in their 12–0–0 season. Most impressive was the fact that except for a 14-13 thriller against a strong Miami (Ohio) team, no one even challenged this Toledo squad; Colorado State put up the next-best effort against Toledo, losing by 10 points. Overall, the Rockets' average margin of victory was more than 24 points per game. Included in that garish total was a 40-12 rout of William & Mary in the Tangerine Bowl. Four players from this team ended up in the NFL, and one of those, defensive tackle Mel Long, was a consensus All-American. Toledo was No. 12 in the final AP poll.

BIGGEST GAME On Dec. 14, 1995, in the Las Vegas Bowl, Toledo and Nevada played the first overtime game in Division I history. It looked dark for the Rockets late in the game, when Nevada recovered a fumble at the Toledo 4-yard line. Leading 34-31, the Toledo defense held the Wolf Pack to a field goal, and did the same in overtime, as Nevada took its first—very fragile—lead of the game. Running back Wasean Tait proved to be the Toledo hero when he scored on his third consecutive carry of the overtime to give the Rockets a 40-37 victory. It was fitting that Tait won the game: he ran for 185 yards, accounted for 238 all-purpose yards and ran for four touchdowns, all then-Las Vegas Bowl records. (In a rare regular-season meeting earlier in the year, Tait ran for 176 yards against the Wolf Pack on his way to a season total of 1,905 yards.)

BIGGEST UPSET In its fourth game of the 2003 season, Toledo faced a home game against Pitt—a rare visit to the MAC from a major power, and by a team that had spanked the Rockets 37-19 the previous season. Toledo entered the late-September game with little hope, and the chances of an upset seemed even more remote by the fourth quarter, with Pitt leading 31-21 and the Rockets on their own 2-yard line. Toledo quarterback Bruce Gradkowski, however, led the team on a 98-yard touchdown drive that cut the lead to 31-28 with 6:45 left. With 43 seconds to go, Gradkowski finished the comeback with a nine-yard touchdown pass to Lance Moore

RECORDS

RUSHING YARDS

	GAME	
304	Casey McBeth, at Akron, Oct. 22, 1994 (36 att.)	
	SEASON	
2,090	Wasean Tait, 1995 (370 att.)	
	CAREER	
4,849	Chester Taylor, 1998-2001 (837 att.)	

PASSING YARDS

	GAME	
461	Bruce Gradkowski vs. Pittsburgh, Sept. 20, 2003 (49 of 62)	
	SEASON	
3,518	Bruce Gradkowski, 2004 (280 of 399)	
	CAREER	
7,266	Gene Swick, 1972-75 (556 of 938)	

RECEIVING YARDS

	GAME	
233	Kenny Higgins vs. Ball State, Oct. 2, 2004 (10 rec.)	
	SEASON	
1,194	Lance Moore, 2003 (103 rec.)	
	CAREER	
2,776	Lance Moore, 2001-04 (222 rec.)	

POINTS

	GAME	
32	Casey McBeth vs. Akron, Oct. 22, 1994 (5 TDs, 1 two-pt. conv.)	
	SEASON	
144	Chester Taylor, 2001 (24 TDs)	
	CAREER	
366	Chester Taylor, 1998-2001 (61 TDs)	

CONSENSUS ALL-AMERICANS

1938	Dan Buckwick, G
1971	Mel Long, DT

that gave Toledo a stunning 35-31 victory. Toledo's win comprised part of one of the greatest days in MAC football history: along with the Rockets win, Marshall upset No. 6 Kansas State, Northern Illinois beat No. 21 Alabama and Bowling Green played No. 5 Ohio State close in Columbus, losing by a touchdown.

BIGGEST COMEBACK In the 2001 MAC championship, it looked like Toledo would waste its opportunity to impress a national television audience. Midway through the second quarter, the Rockets trailed the Byron Leftwich-led Marshall Thundering Herd 23-0 in front of a discouraged home crowd. But Toledo scored 10 quick points before the half and another 25 in the third, and led Marshall 35-29 at the start of the final quarter. Marshall took back the lead by a point when Leftwich threw an 18-yard touchdown pass to Denero Marriott early in the fourth quarter. But Toledo running back Chester Taylor, who ran for 152 of his 188 yards in the second half, answered back, scoring the game's final touchdown to give the Rockets a 41-36 victory and end Marshall's four-year run of MAC championships.

STADIUM Toledo's Glass Bowl is widely regarded as the best football stadium in the MAC. It was constructed almost entirely with federal funds made available by FDR's Works Progress Administration and completed in 1937. In honor of the local companies that donated glass for the stadium's towers and press box, the school officially named it the Glass Bowl. Unfortunately, Toledo attempted to christen the Glass Bowl during a heavy rainstorm. With no grass yet planted around the stadium, the deluge flooded the area and mud blocked the gates. The school was forced to postpone its opening game to the following Monday, Sept. 27, 1937. Despite the fact that the listed capacity for the Glass Bowl is 26,248, a crowd of 36,852 jammed in to watch the Rockets play host to Navy in 2001.

RIVAL Without question, Toledo's greatest rival is Bowling Green. The teams play annually for the Peace Pipe, but they rarely choose to smoke it. The week of the game is known as BG week in Toledo, since it is considered in bad taste to utter the words Bowling Green. Diehard Rocket fans refrain from uttering so much as their rival's initials, preferring "that school down the road." Making matters even more intense is the Nike-Ajax missile that the school received from the U.S. Army in 1961. Known simply as The Rocket, the missile resides

on the northeast corner of the Glass Bowl. It is pointed on a trajectory 25 miles to the south of Toledo. Were it to be fired, The Rocket would land directly on the 50-yard line of Bowling Green's Doyt L. Perry Stadium. Despite the continuing possibility of a preemptive missile attack, Toledo trails the series 29–36–4.

NICKNAME In 1923, Carnegie Tech played against a Toledo team without a nickname. Pressed by Pittsburgh sportswriters to come up with one, James Neal, a UT student working in the press box, labeled the team Skyrockets in honor of their high-flying performance against the stronger Techsters. The sportswriters shortened the name to Rockets, which has been used ever since. Prior to 1923, writers referred to the team variously as the Blue and Gold, Munies (for municipal university) and Dwyer's boys (for coach Joseph Dwyer).

MASCOT Rocky the Rocket's career began in 1966 when the student government's spirit and traditions committee began selecting students to periodically dress up. In 1968, the "uniform" consisted of a wastepaper basket with a pointed top. In 1977, U.S. senator and former astronaut John Glenn helped the school upgrade to an authentic spacesuit, helmet and boots from the NASA Space Center in Houston. Beginning in 1998, Rocky the Rocket appeared in a blue-and-gold rocket-man costume with jet pack and helmet.

UNIFORMS At an organizational meeting of the Varsity T booster club on Dec. 1, 1919, 10 of Toledo's varsity football lettermen chose midnight blue and gold as the school's official colors. Ever since, the Rockets have appeared in a combination of these two colors, as well as white. Currently, the team wears midnight blue jerseys with matching pants at home and white jerseys on the road. Except for a period in the mid-1960s, when the helmets were white with a rocket on the side, Toledo's headgear has been blue with gold or white lettering—spelling either UT or the word Toledo. Since 1997, the helmets have been blue with Toledo written across the side in white and a gold rocket in flight overhead.

NUMBERS Two years after Ealey ended his career at Toledo, the Rockets put another sensation behind center. Although Gene Swick never matched Ealey's winning ways, he put up some gaudy numbers when it came to throwing the ball. In his final game at Toledo, against Kent State in

1975, Swick passed for 283 yards to send his career mark for total offense to 8,074, surpassing the NCAA 1A record held previously by Stanford's Jim Plunkett. Swick was the first to break the 8,000-yard mark.

QUOTE "Nobody else wanted the job."—Team member Charles Morgan, on how John Brandeberry became Toledo's first head coach. The Rockets failed to score in their 1917 debut season, losing their first game to Detroit 145-0

TOLEDO ALL-TIME SCORES

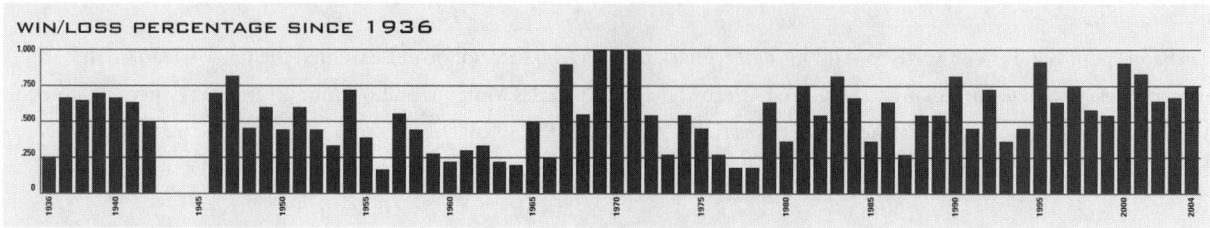

WIN/LOSS PERCENTAGE SINCE 1936

JOHN BRANDEBERRY
1917 (.000) — 0-3-0

1917 — 0-3-0
O10	at Detroit	0	145
O20	at Ohio Northern	0	90
U	at Findlay	0	27

JAMES BAXTER
1918 (.500) — 1-1

1918 — 1-1-0
U ●	Defiance *Unk*	19	12
U	Hillsdale *Unk*	18	31

WALT HOBT
1919-20 (.222) — 2-7

1919 — 2-4-0
S27	Ohio Northern *Unk*	0	13
O3 ●	at Bowling Green	6	0
U	Western Reserve *Unk*	0	19
O19	Adrian *Unk*	6	27
U	Defiance *Unk*	12	6
U	Wayne St.	7	8

1920 — 0-3-0
S25	at Western Reserve	7	17
O1	Wooster	0	36
O7	at Wayne St.	0	14

JOSEPH DWYER
1921-22 (.433) — 5-7-3

1921 — 3-5-0
S24	at Cincinnati	0	20
O8 ●	at Findlay	46	0
O15 ●	Defiance	40	0
O22 ●	at Adrian	0	1*
O29 ●	Bowling Green	7	20
N5 ●	Baldwin-Wallace	1	0*
N11 ●	at Bluffton	0	14
N19 ●	Wayne St.	0	13

1922 — 2-2-3
O7 ●	at Defiance	0	7
O14 =	Alma	0	0
O20 ●	Hillsdale	6	0
N4 =	at Bowling Green	6	6
N11 ●	Muskingum	3	0
N18 ●	at Wayne St.	2	6
N24 =	Baldwin-Wallace	0	0

JAMES DWYER
1923-25 (.444) — 12-15

1923 — 6-4-0
S29 ●	at Carnegie Tech	12	32
O6 ●	Eastern Michigan	13	0
O13 ●	at Akron	3	10
O19 ●	Defiance	26	0
O27 ●	Bowling Green	27	0
N3 ●	Findlay	87	0
N10 ●	Grand Rapids	32	0
N17 ●	Wayne St.	38	0
N24 ●	at Hillsdale	19	32
D1	Notre Dame JV	0	31

1924 — 5-3-0
O4 ●	at Eastern Michigan	7	0
O11 ●	at Carnegie Tech	0	54
O25 ●	at Bowling Green	12	7
U ●	Hillsdale	19	0
N1 ●	Assumption	6	0
N8 ●	at Dayton	6	52
N15 ●	at Wayne St.	27	0
N22 ●	at Akron	7	14

1925 — 1-8-0
S6	Western Reserve	0	14
O3	at Buffalo	0	2
O10	Dayton	6	29
O17	Ohio U.	0	7
O31	at Assumption	2	6
N7	at Michigan State	0	58
N11 ●	at Findlay	20	0
N14	Wayne St.	0	23
N21	at Louisville	0	33 *

BONI PETCOFF
1926-29 (.466) — 13-15-1

1926 — 3-5-0
O2	at Alma	0	19
O9	Hillsdale	14	26
O16	at Defiance	0	12
O23	Bluffton	7	13
O30 ●	Findlay	7	0
N6	at Xavier	6	69
N13 ●	at Wayne St.	14	7
N20 ●	Bufflao	33	7

1927 — 5-2-0
O1	Alma	0	30
O8 ●	Hillsdale	19	0
O15 ●	Wayne St.	13	0
O22 ●	at Bluffton	6	0
N4 ●	Defiance	16	7
N11 ●	at Findlay	34	0
N18 ●	at Wittenberg	0	25

1928 — 1-6-0
O5 ●	Findlay	31	9
O13	at Central Michigan	0	13
O20 ●	at Bowling Green	0	14
O27 ●	at Defiance	0	15
N3	at Wayne St.	6	13
N9	Bluffton	9	33
N17	Michigan JV	0	33

1929 — 4-2-1
S28	Akron	0	26
O12 ●	at Findlay	7	0
O26 =	Bowling Green	0	0
N2 ●	at Bluffton	7	0
N9 ●	Wayne St.	17	0
N16 ●	at Central Michigan	12	31
N23 ●	Defiance	25	13

JIM NICHOLSON
1930-35 (.550) — 20-16-4

1930 — 2-5-1
S27	at Akron	0	41
O4	at Ohio Northern	0	6
O11 ●	at Defiance	12	13
O17 ●	at Findlay	6	20
O24 ●	Heidelberg	0	58
N1 =	at Bowling Green	0	0
N8 ●	Bluffton	14	0
N22 ●	at Wayne St.	18	0

1931
NO TEAM

1932 — 3-4-0
O1 ●	Capital	18	0
O8 ●	Wayne St.	0	3
O15 ●	at Heidelberg	0	12
O22 ●	Marietta	6	0
O28 ●	Ohio State JV	0	6
N5 ●	at Bowling Green	6	12
N12 ●	Otterbein	12	7

1933 — 4-2-2
S30 ●	at Capital	2	27
O7 =	at Wayne St.	0	0
O14 ●	Defiance	29	6
O21 ●	at Kenyon	12	0
O28 ●	Bowling Green	25	7
N4 =	Heidelberg	6	6
N11 ●	John Carroll	13	33
N18 ●	Otterbein	12	7

1934 — 5-3-0
S29 ●	Capital	20	0
O6 ●	Western Reserve	0	7
O13 ●	Louisville	19	7
O20 ●	Kenyon	40	0
O27 ●	at Buffalo	0	8
N3 ●	at Bowling Green	22	0
N10 ●	at Muskingum	9	0
N23 ●	Case	13	33

1935 — 6-2-1
S28 ●	Capital	0	6
O5 ●	at Boston U.	0	6
O12 =	Haskell	0	0
O19 ●	at Case	18	7
O26 ●	Denison	13	0
N1 ●	Bowling Green	63	0
N9 ●	at Louisville	41	7
N16 ●	Buffalo	19	6
N23 ●	Heidelberg	31	0

DOC SPEARS
1936-42 (.591) — 38-26-2

1936 — 2-6-0
O3 ●	Findlay	32	0
O10 ●	Boston U.	0	6
O17 ●	at Denison	6	9
O24 ●	Western Reserve	0	14
O31 ●	Wayne St.	6	9
N7 ●	at Miami, Ohio	0	13
N14 ●	at Heidelberg	0	7
N21 ●	Otterbein	50	0

1937 — 6-3-0
S27 ●	Bluffton	26	0
O2 ●	Georgetown, Ky.	19	0
O9 ●	at Ohio Wesleyan	6	0
O16 ●	Akron	7	21
O23 ●	Miami, Ohio	13	7
O30 ●	at Wayne St.	39	19
N6 ●	Dayton	12	7
N13 ●	at West Virginia	0	34
N20 ●	at Xavier	6	8

1938 — 6-3-1
S24 ●	West Liberty	13	0
O1 ●	St. Joseph	26	0
O8 ●	Ohio Wesleyan	26	0
O15 ●	at Dayton	13	17
O22 ●	Marshall	13	7
O29 ●	at Wayne St.	39	20
N5 ●	John Carroll	6	6
N12 ●	at Akron	7	13
N24 ●	at Xavier	0	13
D2 ●	at St. Mary's, Texas	13	7

1939 — 7-3-0
S23 ●	Valparaiso	39	0
S30 ●	Detroit Tech	19	6
O7 ●	St. Mary's, Texas	20	12
O14 ●	North Dakota	26	7
O20 ●	at Scranton	6	7
O28 ●	Western Michigan	6	0
N4 ●	at John Carroll	20	0
N11 ●	at Marshall	12	14
N18 ●	Long Island	12	13
N23 ●	at Xavier	20	0

1940 — 6-3-0
S28 ●	Detroit Tech	21	3
O5 ●	Davis & Elkins	34	12
O12 ●	Marshall	7	6
O19 ●	Scranton	26	0
O26 ●	at Western Michigan	12	0
N2 ●	John Carroll	33	12
N8 ●	at Baldwin-Wallace	12	14
N16 ●	at Butler	20	6
N23 ●	at Long Island	7	19

1941 — 7-4-0
S27 ●	St. Joseph	0	3
O4 ●	Detroit Tech	55	0
O11 ●	at Marshall	7	33
O18 ●	at John Carroll	20	0
O25 ●	at Western Michigan	0	34
N2 ●	at Illinois Wesleyan	9	0
U ●	Camp Shelby	39	0
N8 ●	Butler	2	18
N15 ●	Baldwin-Wallace	27	7
N22 ●	at Bradley	14	6
N27 ●	at Jefferson Barracks	22	21

1942 — 4-4-1
S26 ●	Kent State	26	14
O3 ●	Illinois Wesleyan	26	0
O10 ●	Western Michigan	0	13
O16 =	at John Carroll	6	6
O24 ●	Marshall	7	0
O31 ●	US Coast Guard	0	26
N7 ●	at Butler	0	12
N14 ●	at Youngstown St.	12	30
N21 ●	Bradley	14	13

1943-45
NO TEAM – WWII

BILL ORWIG
1946-47 (.762) — 15-4-2

1946 — 6-2-2
S28 =	Western Reserve	14	14
O5 ●	Case	42	14
O12 =	at Marshall	14	14
O19 ●	Dayton	13	20
O26 ●	at Akron	33	19
N2 ●	John Carroll	28	19
N11 ●	Wayne St.	14	6
N16 ●	at Baldwin-Wallace	14	7
N23 ●	at Wichita St.	7	13
	GLASS BOWL		
D7 ●	Bates	21	12

1947 — 9-2-0
S20 ●	Great Lakes NAS	40	0
S27 ●	Case	41	0
O4 ●	John Carroll	14	35
O11 ●	Youngtown St.	21	7
O18 ●	at Dayton	14	13
O25 ●	Akron	38	7
N1 ●	Baldwin-Wallace	14	6
N8 ●	at Wayne St.	7	0
N15 ●	South Dakota St.	33	12
N22 ●	at Canisius	13	21
	GLASS BOWL		
D6 ●	Hampshire	20	14

J.N. STAHLEY
1948-49 (.524) — 11-10

1948 — 5-6-0
S18 ●	Bates	42	0
S24 ●	at Detroit	0	36
O2 ●	John Carroll	20	46
O9 ●	Bowling Green	6	21
O16 ●	Dayton	0	20
O23 ●	at Springfield	21	14
O30 ●	Baldwin-Wallace	14	20
N6 ●	Wayne St.	27	14
N13 ●	Canisius	21	26
N20 ●	at New Hampshire	28	14
	GLASS BOWL		
D4 ●	Oklahoma City	27	14

1949 — 6-4-0

S25		Loras	26	35
O1		JohnCarroll	14	28
O8	●	Bowling Green	20	19
O15		at Dayton	14	47
O22	●	Springfield	42	14
O29	●	Oklahoma City	48	7
N5	●	at Wayne St.	37	7
N12	●	North Dakota	56	6
N19	●	at New Hampshire	48	14
		GLASS BOWL		
D3		Cincinnati	13	33

ROBERT SNYDER
1950 (.444) 4-5

1950 — 4-5-0

S24	●	Pittsburgh, Kansas	32	14
S30		John Carroll	0	41
O7		at Western Michigan	19	54
O14		Dayton	13	14
O21	●	at Bradley	32	20
O28		Bowling Green	14	39
N4	●	Western Reserve	27	7
N10		at St. Bonaventure	7	38
N17	●	Wayne St.	56	7

DON GREENWOOD
1951 (.571) 4-3

CLAIR DUNN
1951-53 (.429) 9-12

1951 — 6-4-0

S15	●	Davis & Elkins	88	0
S22		at Detroit	32	34
S29		Western Michigan	6	14
O6	●	John Carroll	26	12
O13		at Dayton	7	47
O20	●	Marshall	32	14
O27	●	at Bowling Green	12	6
N3	●	Ohio U.	13	6
N10	●	Bradley	38	13
N22		at Xavier	6	32

1952-PRESENT
MAC

1952 — 4-5-0 (1-4-0)

S20		Eastern Kentucky	6	7
S27	● |	Western Reserve	10	9
O4	|	at Ohio U.	20	22
O11	●	John Carroll	6	3
O18	|	at Western Michigan	14	19
O25	|	Bowling Green	19	29
N1	|	at Miami, Ohio	13	27
N8	●	Bradley	20	14
N15	●	at Youngstown St.	24	21

1953 — 3-6-0 (2-3-0)

S19	|	Ohio U.	0	26
S26	|	at Western Reserve	20	21
O3		Fort Belvoir	13	62
O10		at Cincinnati	7	41
O17	● |	Western Michigan	19	7
O24	● |	at Bowling Green	20	19
O31	|	Miami, Ohio	0	81
N7	●	at Bradley	27	12
N14		John Carroll	7	36

FORREST ENGLAND
1954-55 (.556) 9-7-2

1954 — 6-2-1 (3-2-0)

S18	●	Muskingum	27	6
S25	|	Western Reserve	7	12
O2	|	at Ohio U.	20	28
O9	●	John Carroll	7	6
O16	● |	at Western Michigan	19	7
O23	● |	Bowling Green	38	7
O30	=	at Eastern Kentucky	13	13
N6	●	Baldwin-Wallace	47	13
N12	● |	at Marshall	27	21

1955 — 3-5-1 (2-4-0)

S17	=	Eastern Kentucky	6	6
S23	●	at Detroit	12	7
O1	|	Ohio U.	13	34 *
O8	|	at Miami, Ohio	0	47
O15	● |	Western Michigan	6	0
O22	|	at Bowling Green	0	39
N5	|	Kent State	0	27
N12	● |	Marshall	27	13
N19		at Louisville	13	33

JACK MORTON
1956 (.167) 1-7-1

1956 — 1-7-1 (1-5-0)

S15		Eastern Kentucky	6	12
S22		Louisville	12	27
S29	● |	at Ohio U.	19	13
O6	|	Miami, Ohio	14	33
O13	|	at Western Michigan	15	26
O20	|	Bowling Green	12	34
N3	|	at Kent State	6	52
N9	|	at Marshall	13	32
N17	=	Brandeis	21	21

HARRY LARCHE
1957-59 (.426) 11-15-1

1957 — 5-4-0 (3-2-0)

S21	●	at Eastern Kentucky	7	0
S28	● |	Ohio U.	14	6
O5		at Louisville	20	48
O12	|	Marshall	7	14
O19	|	at Bowling Green	0	29
O26	● |	Western Michigan	27	16 *
N2	● |	Kent State	21	7
N9		at Xavier	7	20
N16	●	Muskingum	33	7

1958 — 4-5-0 (1-4-0)

S20	●	Eastern Kentucky	19	2
S27	|	at Ohio U.	6	13
O4	●	Louisville	13	7
O11	|	at Marshall	12	35
O18	|	Bowling Green	16	31
O25	● |	at Western Michigan	21	6
N1	|	at Kent State	6	32 *
N8		Xavier	8	34
N15	●	Youngtown St.	21	8

1959 — 2-6-1 (0-6-0)

S19	●	Eastern Kentucky	20	2
S26	|	Ohio U.	7	36
O3	●	Baldwin-Wallace	26	20
O10	|	Marshall	13	20
O17	|	at Bowling Green	21	51
O24	|	Western Michigan	14	24
O31	|	Kent State	7	14
N7	|	at Miami, Ohio	7	25
N12	=	at Youngstown St.	8	8

CLIVE RUSH
1960-62 (.286) 8-20

1960 — 2-7-0 (0-6-0)

S17	●	Youngstown St.	34	30
S24	|	at Ohio U.	7	48
O1	|	at Marshall	0	14
O8		Hillsdale	25	31
O15	|	Bowling Green	3	14
O22	|	at Western Michigan	3	7
O29	|	at Kent State	13	18
N5	|	Miami, Ohio	13	30
N12	●	Bradley	28	0

1961 — 3-7-0 (2-4-0)

S16		Wichita St.	7	12
S23	|	Ohio U.	6	10
S30		at Youngstown St.	12	14
O7	● |	Marshall	33	6
O14	|	at Bowling Green	6	17
O21	|	Western Michigan	0	7
O28	● |	Kent State	31	22
N4	|	at Miami, Ohio	14	40
N11		at Bradley	22	28
N18	●	at Temple	15	14

1962 — 3-6-0 (1-5-0)

S15		South Dakota St.	14	25
S22	|	at Ohio U.	0	31
O6	● |	at Marshall	42	12
O13	|	Bowling Green	13	28
O20	|	at Western Michigan	0	21
O27	|	at Kent State	18	20
N3	|	Miami, Ohio	12	21
N10	●	Temple	13	0
N17	●	at Tulsa	21	18

FRANK LAUTERBUR
1963-70 (.598) 48-32-2

1963 — 2-7-0 (1-5-0)

S21		at Dayton	19	22
S28		Villanova	14	18
O5	|	at Marshall	18	19
O12	● |	Ohio U.	18	17
O19	|	at Bowling Green	20	22
O26	|	Western Michigan	7	18
N2	|	Kent State	0	20
N9	|	at Miami, Ohio	8	40
N16	●	So. Illinois	14	0

1964 — 2-8-0 (1-5-0)

S19		Villanova	6	22
S25		at Detroit	6	22
O3	|	Marshall	0	13
O10	|	at Ohio U.	12	21
O17	|	Bowling Green	14	31
O24	● |	at Western Michigan	21	13
O31	|	at Kent State	11	14
N7	|	Miami, Ohio	14	35
N14	●	at So. Illinois	27	8
N21		Tulsa	16	39

1965 — 5-5-0 (2-4-0)

S18	●	at Villanova	9	7
S25	●	Quantico Marines	9	0
O2	|	at Marshall	0	14
O9	● |	Ohio U.	21	7
O16	|	at Bowling Green	14	21
O23	|	Western Michigan	0	3
O30	● |	Kent State	7	3
N6	|	at Miami, Ohio	16	20
N13		at Xavier	7	14
N20	●	Dayton	21	7

1966 — 2-7-1 (1-5-0)

S17	●	Xavier	9	0
S24		at Villanova	11	20
O1	● |	Marshall	23	7
O8	|	at Ohio U.	6	21
O15	|	Bowling Green	13	14
O22	|	at Western Michigan	13	14
O29	|	at Kent State	20	28
N5	|	Miami, Ohio	12	24
N12	=	Quantico Marines	14	14
N19		at Dayton	16	20

1967 — 9-1-0 (5-1-0)

S16	|	Ohio U.	14	20
S23	●	at Xavier	24	7
S30	● |	at Marshall	14	7
O14	● |	at Bowling Green	33	0
O21	● |	Western Michigan	35	9
O28	● |	Kent State	14	13
N4	● |	at Miami, Ohio	24	14
N11	●	Northern Illinois	35	0
N18	●	Dayton	21	7
N23	●	Villanova	52	6

1968 — 5-4-1 (3-2-1)

S14	●	Richmond	31	14
S21	●	at Villanova	45	21
S28	● |	Marshall	35	12
O5	|	at Ohio U.	31	40
O12	= |	Bowling Green	0	0
O19	● |	at Western Michigan	30	6
O26	● |	at Kent State	28	12
N2	|	Miami, Ohio	17	21
N9		Xavier	10	20
N16		at Dayton	3	10

1969 — 11-0-0 (5-0-0)

S20	●	Villanova	45	18
S27	●	at Marshall	38	13
O4	● |	Ohio U.	34	9
O11	● |	at Bowling Green	27	26
O18	● |	Western Michigan	38	13
O25	● |	Kent State	43	17
N1	● |	at Miami, Ohio	14	10
N8	●	at Northern Illinois	35	21
N15	●	Dayton	20	0
N22	●	at Xavier	35	0
		TANGERINE BOWL		
D26	●	Davidson	56	33

1970 — 12-0-0 (5-0-0)

S12	●	East Carolina	35	2
S19	●	at Buffalo	27	6
S26	●	Marshall	52	3
O3	● |	at Ohio U.	42	7
O10	● |	Bowling Green	20	0
O17	● |	at Western Michigan	20	0
O24	● |	at Kent State	34	17
O31	● |	Miami, Ohio	14	13
N7	●	Northern Illinois	45	7
N14	●	at Dayton	31	7
N21	●	Colorado State	24	14
		TANGERINE BOWL		
D28	●	William & Mary	40	12

JOHN MURPHY
1971-76 (.522) 35-32

1971 — 12-0-0 (5-0-0)

S11	●	at East Carolina	45	0
S18	●	Villanova	10	7
S25	●	at Texas- Arlington	23	0
O2	● |	Ohio U.	31	28
O9	● |	at Bowling Green	24	7
O16	● |	Western Michigan	35	24
O23	●	Dayton	35	7
O30	● |	at Miami, Ohio	45	6
N6	●	at Northern Illinois	23	8
N13	●	at Marshall	43	0
N20	● |	Kent State	41	6
		TANGERINE BOWL		
D28	●	Richmond	28	3

1972 — 6-5-0 (2-3-0)

S9		at Tampa	0	21
S16	●	at Eastern Michigan	16	0
S23	●	Texas- Arlington	38	24
S30	|	at Ohio U.	22	38
O7	|	Bowling Green	8	19
O14	● |	at Western Michigan	20	13
O21	●	at Dayton	20	17
O28	● |	Miami, Ohio	35	21
N4		Northern Illinois	7	30
N11	●	Marshall	21	0
N18	|	at Kent State	9	27

1973 — 3-8-0 (1-4-0)

S15		at Tampa	25	35
S22	●	Central Michigan	23	21
S29	● |	Ohio U.	35	8
O6	|	at Bowling Green	35	49
O13	|	Western Michigan	22	24
O20	●	Dayton	14	10
O27	|	at Miami, Ohio	0	16
N3		at Colorado State	14	21
N10		at Marshall	14	17
N17	|	Kent State	16	52
N24		at Xavier	31	35

1974 — 6-5-0 (3-2-0)

S14		at Tampa	13	47
S21		Villanova	0	7
S28	● |	at Ohio U.	19	16
O5	● |	Bowling Green	24	19
O12	● |	at Western Michigan	31	24
O19	●	at Dayton	38	27
O26	|	Miami, Ohio	22	38
N2	●	Northern Illinois	44	14
N9	●	Marshall	45	14
N16	|	at Kent State	14	35
N23		Eastern Michigan	12	28

1975 — 5-6-0 (4-4-0)

S6	●	Western Carolina	32	31
S13	|	at Ball State	28	38
S20		at Villanova	10	14
S27	|	Central Michigan	27	34
O4		Dayton	13	24
O11	|	at Bowling Green	17	34
O18	● |	Western Michigan CLEV	25	7
O25	● |	Ohio U.	14	10
N1	|	at Miami, Ohio	21	35
N8	● |	at Northern Illinois	24	22
N22	● |	Kent State	33	28

1976 — 3-8-0 (2-6-0)

S11		at Massachusetts	14	28
S18	|	at Central Michigan	7	9
S25	|	Ball State	14	27
O2	|	at Ohio U.	8	34
O9	|	Bowling Green	28	29
O16	|	at Western Michigan	21	34
O23		at Dayton	14	17
O30	● |	Miami, Ohio	24	9
N6	● |	Northern Illinois	17	2
N13	●	Marshall	39	8
N20	|	at Kent State	9	35

CHUCK STOBART
1977-81 (.438) 24-31-1

1977 — 2-9-0 (2-7-0)

S10	|	Ball State	3	43
S17		East Carolina	9	22
S24		at Marshall	0	24
O1	|	at Eastern Michigan	7	17
O8	|	at Bowling Green	13	21
O15	|	Western Michigan	7	28
O22	● |	Ohio U.	31	29
O29	|	at Miami, Ohio	3	27
N5	● |	at Northern Illinois	27	9
N12	|	Central Michigan	0	44
N19	|	Kent State	12	23

THE SCHOOLS

1978 2-9-0 (2-7-0)

S9		Marshall	0	17
S16		at Minnesota	12	38
S23	|	at Ball State	0	20
S30	|	Eastern Michigan	12	17
O7	|	Bowling Green	27	45
O14	|	at Western Michigan	7	17
O21	● |	at Ohio U.	28	14
O28	|	Miami, Ohio	7	28
N4	|	at Central Michigan	3	27
N11	● |	Northern Illinois	35	16
N18	|	at Kent State	13	17

1979 7-3-1 (7-1-1)

S8		at Marshall	14	31
S15	● |	Ball State	31	14
S22		at Arizona State	0	49
S29	● |	at Eastern Michigan	37	7
O6	● |	at Bowling Green	23	17
O13	● |	Western Michigan	17	0
O20	● |	Ohio U.	21	13
O27	● |	at Miami, Ohio	24	21
N3	= |	Central Michigan	7	7
N10	|	at Northern Illinois	10	28
N17	● |	Kent State	29	3

1980 4-7-0 (3-6-0)

S13		McNeese St.	17	20
S20	|	at Ball State	7	27
S27	● |	Eastern Michigan	49	7
O4	|	at Central Michigan	10	14
O11	|	Bowling Green	6	17
O18	|	at Western Michigan	7	17
O25	|	at Ohio U.	9	24
N1	● |	Miami, Ohio	17	14
N8	● |	Northern Illinois	13	6
N15	●	at Marshall	38	10
N22	|	at Kent State	14	34

1981 9-3-0 (8-1-0)

S12		at Louisville	6	31
S19	● |	Ball State	40	0
S26		at East Carolina	24	28
O3	● |	Ohio U.	21	14
O10	● |	at Eastern Michigan	42	7
O17	● |	Central Michigan	17	3
O24	|	at Bowling Green	0	38
O31	● |	Miami, Ohio	17	10
N7	● |	at Western Michigan	28	14
N14	● |	Kent State	17	0
N21	● |	at Northern Illinois	31	0
		CALIFORNIA BOWL		
D19	●	San Jose State	27	25

DAN SIMRELL
1982-89 (.562) 49-38-2

1982 6-5-0 (5-4-0)

S4	● |	Northern Illinois	9	3
S11	● |	at Ball State	31	14
S18	●	Marshall	17	9
S25		at Wisconsin	27	36
O2	|	at Ohio U.	14	17
O9	● |	Eastern Michigan	20	19
O16	|	at Central Michigan	12	16
O23	● |	Bowling Green	24	10
O30	|	at Miami, Ohio	17	21
N6	|	Western Michigan	10	17
N13	● |	at Kent State	3	0

1983 9-2-0 (7-2-0)

S10	●	Massachusetts	45	13
S17	●	at Richmond	31	6
S24	● |	Ball State	43	7
O1	● |	Ohio U.	31	0
O8	● |	at Bowling Green	6	3
O15	● |	Miami, Ohio	10	9
O22	● |	at Eastern Michigan	37	9
O29	● |	Kent State	37	34
N5	● |	at Western MIchigan	20	16
N12	|	at Northern Illinois	10	26
N19	|	Central Michigan	8	34

1984 8-3-1 (7-1-1)

S8	● |	at Ball State	20	2
S22	●	Ea. Illinois	38	17
S29	= |	at Ohio U.	16	16
O6	● |	Bowling Green	17	6
O13	● |	at Miami, Ohio	10	7
O20	● |	Eastern Michigan	17	7
O27	|	at Kent State	6	17
N3	● |	Western Michigan	17	13
N10	● |	Northern Illinois	13	7
N17	● |	at Central Michigan	14	7
N30		at Temple	6	35
		CALIFORNIA BOWL		
D15		Nevada-Las Vegas	13	30 †

1985 4-7-0 (3-6-0)

S7		at Arizona	10	23
S21	●	at Wichita St.	22	15
S28	|	Ball State	19	23
O5	|	at Eastern Michigan	10	21
O12	|	Miami, Ohio	14	26
O19	|	at Northern Illinois	3	16
O26	● |	Ohio U.	24	10
N2	|	at Western Michigan	13	18
N9	● |	Central Michigan	10	7
N16	|	at Bowling Green	0	21
N23	● |	Kent State	10	7

1986 7-4-0 (5-3-0)

A30		at Florida State	0	24
S6	|	at Kent State	16	18
S13	●	Wichita St.	30	13
S27	|	at Ball State	10	27
O4	● |	Eastern Michigan	23	18
O11	|	at Miami, Ohio	8	24
O18	●	Northern Illinois	29	28
O25	● |	at Ohio U.	24	21
N1	● |	Western Michigan	28	7
N8	● |	at Central Michigan	26	14
N15	● |	Bowling Green	22	3

1987 3-7-1 (3-4-1)

S5		Temple	12	13
S12	● |	Ball State	21	17
S19	● |	Ohio U.	17	12
O3	|	at Western Michigan	14	21
O10		at Northern Illinois	5	41
O17	|	at Bowling Green	6	20
O24	● |	Miami, Ohio	37	25
O31	|	at Kent State	13	17
N5	|	Eastern Michigan	9	38
N14	= |	at Central Michigan	17	17
N21		at Miami, Fla.	14	24

1988 6-5-0 (4-4-0)

S3	|	at Ball State	3	13
S10	|	Western Michigan	9	31
S17		at McNeese St.	19	46
S24	● |	Bowling Green	34	5
O1	|	at Ohio U.	14	24
O8	●	Northern Illinois	33	20
O15	●	Austin Peay	38	14
O22	● |	at Miami, Ohio	20	7
O29	● |	Kent State	35	28
N5	|	at Eastern Michigan	19	20
N12	● |	Central Michigan	20	13

1989 6-5-0 (6-2-0)

S2	● |	Ohio U.	27	18
S16		at Wisconsin	10	23
S23	● |	Ball State	29	22
S30		at Indiana	12	32
O7	|	at Eastern Michigan	14	31
O14	|	at Bowling Green	23	27
O21	● |	Miami, Ohio	17	14
O28	● |	at Kent State	47	42
N4	● |	Western Michigan	19	18
N11		at Northern Illinois	27	39
N18	● |	Central Michigan	29	6

NICK SABAN
1990 (.818) 9-2

1990 9-2-0 (7-1-0)

S8	● |	at Miami, Ohio	20	14
S15	●	Northern Illinois	23	14
S22	● |	at Ball State	28	16
S29	● |	at Ohio U.	27	20
O6	● |	Eastern Michigan	37	23
O13	● |	Bowling Green	19	13
O20	|	at Central Michigan	12	13
O27	● |	Kent State	28	14
N3	● |	at Western Michigan	37	9
N10		Navy	10	14
N17	●	Arkansas State	43	28

GARY PINKEL
1991-2000 (.659) 73-37-3

1991 5-5-1 (4-3-1)

S7		Kansas	7	30
S21	● |	at Western Michigan	23	13
S28	= |	Central Michigan	16	16
O5	● |	Ohio U.	17	13
O12		at Washington	0	48
O19	|	at Bowling Green	21	24
O26	● |	Miami, Ohio	24	7
N2	|	at Kent State	13	14
N9	|	Ball State	3	9
N16	● |	at Eastern Michigan	21	14
N23	●	Northern Illinois	42	21

1992 8-3-0 (5-3-0)

S5	●	Arkansas State	49	0
S12	|	at Akron	20	23
S19	●	at Purdue	33	29
S26	|	at Central Michigan	9	28
O10	● |	Western Michigan	21	12
O17	|	Bowling Green	9	10
O24	● |	at Miami, Ohio	20	17
O31	●	Kent State	32	17
N7	● |	at Ball State	10	9
N14	● |	Eastern Michigan	41	0
N21	●	at Northern Illinois	25	8

1993 4-7-0 (3-5-0)

S4		at Indiana	0	27
S18	●	So. Illinois	49	28
S25	● |	Ohio U.	28	10
O2	|	at Bowling Green	10	17
O9	|	at Ball State	30	31
O16	|	Miami, Ohio	19	22
O23		Cincinnati	24	31
O30	● |	at Kent State	45	27
N6	|	Central Michigan	7	38
N13	|	at Western Michigan	26	39
N19	● |	Eastern Michigan	14	0

1994 6-4-1 (4-3-1)

S3	●	Indiana St.	20	17
S10		at Purdue	17	51
S17	●	Liberty	47	37
O1	● |	at Ohio U.	31	6
O8	= |	Ball State	24	24
O15	|	Bowling Green	16	31
O22	● |	at Akron	48	25
O29	● |	Kent State	48	14
N5	|	at Central Michigan	27	45
N12	● |	Western Michigan	37	34
N19	|	at Eastern Michigan	37	40

1995 11-0-1 (7-0-1)

S9	●	East Tenn. St.	41	20
S14	● |	at Western Michigan	31	21
S23	●	at Nevada	49	35
S30	●	at Cincinnati	45	31
O7	● |	Ball State	17	14
O14	= |	at Miami, Ohio	28	28
O21	● |	at Bowling Green	35	16
O28	● |	Eastern Michigan	34	28
N4	● |	at Central Michigan	19	7
N11	● |	Akron	41	7
N18	● |	Ohio U.	31	20
		LAS VEGAS BOWL		
D14	●	Nevada	40	37

1996 7-4 (6-2)

S7		Indiana	6	40
S14	● |	at Akron	27	10
S21	● |	at Eastern Michigan	24	7
S28	●	Weber St.	31	24
O5	● |	Bowling Green	24	16
O19		at Louisiana Tech	20	61
O26	● |	Western Michigan	10	7
N2	|	Miami, Ohio	7	27
N9	● |	Central Michigan	23	20
N16	|	at Ball State	14	24
N23	● |	at Ohio U.	24	23

1997 9-3 (7-1)

S6	●	Purdue	36	22
S13	● |	Eastern Michigan	38	35
S20	● |	at Western Michigan	23	13
S27	●	Nevada	31	13
O11	● |	at Central Michigan	41	10
O18	●	Northern Illinois	41	14
O25	● |	at Bowling Green	35	20
N1	● |	Miami, Ohio	35	28
N8	|	at Ball State	3	35
N15	● |	Akron	42	10
N22		at Central Florida	17	34
		MAC CHAMPIONSHIP GAME		
D5		at Marshall	14	34

1998 7-5 (6-2)

S5	●	Temple	24	12
S12		at Ohio State	0	49
S19	● |	Western Michigan	35	7
S26	|	at Miami, Ohio	14	28
O3		Central Florida	24	31
O10	● |	Ball State	27	6
O17	● |	Bowling Green	24	16
O24	● |	at Akron	24	17
O31	● |	at Northern Illinois	16	3
N14	● |	Central Michigan	17	14
N21	|	at Eastern Michigan	7	10
		MAC CHAMPIONSHIP GAME		
D4		at Marshall	17	23

1999 6-5 (5-3)

S2		Syracuse	12	35
S18	● |	at Ball State	23	10
S25	●	Massachusetts	24	3
O2	|	at Bowling Green	23	34
O9	● |	Kent State	47	7
O14	|	at Marshall	13	38
O23	|	Eastern Michigan	13	20
O30		Louisiana Tech	17	34
N6	● |	at Central Michigan	32	13
N13	● |	Northern Illinois	44	14
N20	● |	Western Michigan	45	21

2000 10-1 (6-1)

S2	●	at Penn State	24	6
S9	●	Weber St.	51	0
S16	●	Eastern Ill.	31	26
S23	|	at Western Michigan	14	21
S30	● |	Central Michigan	41	0
O7	● |	at Eastern Michigan	42	14
O14	● |	Marshall	42	0
O28	●	at Navy	35	14
N4	● |	at Northern Illinois	38	24
N11	● |	Ball State	31	3
N22	● |	Bowling Green	51	17

TOM AMSTUTZ
2001-PRESENT (.706) 36-15

2001 10-2 (5-2)

A30	●	Minnesota	38	7
S8	●	at Temple	33	7
S22	● |	at Central Michigan	52	28
S29	● |	Northern Illinois	41	20
O6	● |	at Ohio U.	48	41
O20	|	at Ball State	20	24
O27	●	Navy	21	20
N6	● |	Western Michigan	41	35
N17	● |	Eastern Michigan	28	7
N23	|	at Bowling Green	21	56
		MAC CHAMPIONSHIP GAME		
N30	●	Marshall	41	36
		MOTOR CITY BOWL		
D29	●	Cincinnati	23	16

2002 9-5 (7-1)

A29	●	Cal Poly SLO	44	16
S7	● |	at Eastern Michigan	65	13
S14		at Minnesota	21	31
S21	●	Nevada-Las Vegas	38	21
S28		at Pittsburgh	19	37
O12	● |	Ball State	37	17
O19	● |	at Central Florida	27	24
O26	|	Miami, Ohio	13	27
N9	● |	Central Michigan	44	17
N16	● |	at Western Michigan	42	21
N23	● |	at Northern Illinois	33	30
N30	● |	Bowling Green	42	24
		MAC CHAMPIONSHIP GAME		
D7		at Marshall	45	49
		MOTOR CITY BOWL		
D26		Boston College	25	51

2003 8-4 (6-2)

A29		at Nevada-Las Vegas	18	28
S6	●	Liberty	49	3
S12	● |	at Marshall	24	17
S20	●	Pittsburgh	35	31
S27		at Syracuse	7	34
O11	● |	Eastern Michigan	49	14
O18	● |	at Central Michigan	31	13
O25	|	at Ball State	13	38
N1	● |	Buffalo	56	29
N15	● |	Northern Illinois	49	30
N22	● |	Western Michigan	34	17
N29	|	at Bowling Green	23	31

2004 9-4 (7-1)

S4		at Minnesota	21	63
S11		at Kansas	14	63
S18	● |	at Eastern Michigan	42	32
S25	●	Temple	45	17
O2	● |	Ball State	52	14
O9	● |	at Western Michigan	59	33
O16	● |	Ohio U.	31	13
O23	● |	Central Michigan	27	22
N3	|	at Miami, Ohio	16	23
N10	● |	at Northern Illinois	31	17
N23	● |	Bowling Green	49	41
		MAC CHAMPIONSHIP GAME		
D2	●	Miami, Ohio DET	35	27
		MOTOR CITY BOWL		
D27		Connecticut	10	39

f Forfeit † Game Later Forfieted # Disputed Victor * Disputed Score || Designated Conference Game |2 Counted Twice in Conference Standings

TOLEDO ANNUAL STATISTICAL LEADERS

YR	RUSHING	YDS	ATT	AVG	PASSING	ATT	CMP	PCT	YDS	RECEIVING	REC	YDS	AVG
1951	A.C. Jenkins	899	116	7.8	Steve Piskach	86	27	.31	493		NA	NA	NA
1952	Bob Carson	322	110	2.9	Dave Andrzejewski	106	41	.39	582	Bob Carson	18	428	23.8
1953	Mel Triplett	479	81	5.9	Dave Andrzejewski	84	28	.33	403	Rick Kaser	11	189	17.2
1954	Mel Triplett	803	149	5.4	Jerry Nowak	53	25	.47	393	Dick Basich	14	255	18.2
1955	Julius Taormina	449	83	5.4	Sam Tisci	58	22	.38	404	Gene Cook	10	230	23.0
1956	Don Wright	498	112	4.4	Sam Tisci	64	22	.34	354	Dan Howell	13	218	16.8
1957	Norm Billingslea	565	104	5.4	Sam Tisci	131	56	.43	760	Gene Cook	30	495	16.5
1958	Occie Burt	618	124	5.0	Jerry Stoltz	75	29	.39	403	Jack Campbell	16	214	13.4
1959	Occie Burt	437	91	4.8	Dennis Wilkie	122	47	.39	723	Bob Smith	18	455	25.3
1960	John Murray	608	142	4.3	Jerry Stoltz	50	16	.32	277	Bob Smith	14	268	19.1
1961	Frank Baker	739	169	4.4	Phil Yenrick	95	37	.39	563	Pete Jolliff	18	330	18.3
1962	Frank Baker	613	147	4.2	Phil Yenrick	97	37	.38	552	Jim Thibert	11	198	18.0
1963	Jim Gray	645	114	5.7	Dan Simrell	118	48	.41	608	Jim Gray	15	168	11.2
1964	Jim Berkey	408	103	4.0	Dan Simrell	215	115	.53	1,239	Henry Burch	47	412	8.8
1965	Jim Berkey	440	142	3.1	John Schneider	108	54	.50	598	Henry Burch	36	325	9.0
1966	Roland Moss	443	175	2.5	John Schneider	273	130	.48	1,537	Henry Burch	38	480	12.6
1967	Roland Moss	833	213	3.9	John Schneider	245	127	.52	1,650	Pete Kramer	34	556	16.4
1968	Roland Moss	1,145	267	4.3	Steve Jones	243	98	.40	1,197	Dennis Tobias	27	294	10.9
1969	Tony Harris	889	153	5.8	Chuck Ealey	175	98	.56	1,428	Don Fair	33	469	14.2
1970	Charles Cole	774	196	3.9	Chuck Ealey	285	161	.56	2,026	Don Fair	81	949	11.7
1971	Joe Schwartz	1,130	226	5.0	Chuck Ealey	237	126	.53	1,821	Don Fair	57	773	13.6
1972	Joe Schwartz	776	223	3.5	Bruce Arthur	171	83	.49	1,168	Jeff Calabrese	62	886	14.3
1973	Herman Price	595	168	3.5	Gene Swick	301	165	.55	2,234	Don Seymour	44	773	17.6
1974	Mike Taormina	609	161	3.8	Gene Swick	287	178	.62	2,234	John Ross	77	866	11.2
1975	Tim Zimmerman	496	126	3.9	Gene Swick	308	190	.62	2,487	Scott Resseguie	39	683	17.5
1976	Skip McCulley	578	102	5.7	Jeff Hepinstall	198	89	.45	1,299	Scott Resseguie	32	530	16.6
1977	Mike Alston	772	154	5.0	Jeff Hepinstall	72	26	.36	359	Frank Jarm	12	204	17.0
1978	Mike Alston	460	101	4.6	Maurice Hall	110	39	.35	610	Butch Hunyadi	19	494	26.0
1979	Mike Alston	806	166	4.9	Maurice Hall	122	53	.43	648	Butch Hunyadi	29	500	17.2
1980	Melvin Tucker	563	120	4.7	Jim Kelso	82	41	.50	589	Rod Achter	10	269	26.9
1981	Arnold Smiley	1,013	197	5.1	Jim Kelso	121	58	.48	875	Rod Achter	14	361	25.8
1982	Steve Morgan	598	143	4.2	Jim Kelso	281	149	.53	1,963	Capus Robinson	43	709	16.5
1983	Steve Morgan	630	145	4.3	Jim Kelso	197	106	.54	1,346	Capus Robinson	31	499	16.1
1984	Steve Morgan	1,271	336	3.8	A.J. Sager	290	156	.54	1,647	Eric Hutchinson	26	451	17.3
1985	Kelvin Farmer	748	229	3.3	A.J. Sager	253	130	.51	1,335	Jay Walsh	27	284	10.5
1986	Kelvin Farmer	1,532	299	5.1	A.J. Sager	189	96	.51	1,107	Eric Hutchinson	33	504	15.3
1987	David Rohrs	681	178	3.8	Bill Bergan	130	72	.55	908	Eric Hutchinson	29	431	14.9
1988	Neil Trotter	783	163	4.8	Steve Keene	128	66	.52	793	Rick Isaiah	25	389	15.6
1989	Wayne Goodwin	859	196	4.4	Mark Melfi	237	131	.55	1,632	Rick Isaiah	46	743	16.2
1990	Troy Parker	879	233	3.8	Kevin Meger	257	139	.54	1,861	Rick Isaiah	49	717	14.6
1991	Steve Cowan	748	162	4.6	Kevin Meger	276	147	.53	1,787	Marcus Goodwin	42	600	14.3
1992	Casey McBeth	1,037	223	4.7	Kevin Meger	285	139	.49	1,727	Marcus Goodwin	58	738	12.7
1993	Wasean Tait	680	139	4.9	Tim Kubiak	146	70	.48	970	Scott Brunswick	41	571	13.9
1994	Casey McBeth	1,053	180	5.9	Ryan Huzjak	289	170	.59	1,928	Scott Brunswick	44	572	13.0
1995	Wasean Tait	2,090	370	5.6	Ryan Huzjak	314	179	.57	2,134	Steve Rosi	44	546	12.4
1996	Kevin Kidd	453	127	3.6	Ryan Huzjak	332	183	.55	2,058	James Spriggs	53	754	14.2
1997	Dwayne Harris	1,278	254	5.0	Chris Wallace	433	232	.54	2,955	Mel Long	47	556	11.8
1998	Wasean Tait	625	151	4.1	Chris Wallace	400	219	.55	2,476	Ray Curry	45	513	11.4
1999	Chester Taylor	1,176	182	6.5	Tavares Bolden	229	123	.54	1,354	Mel Long	47	599	12.7
2000	Chester Taylor	1,470	250	5.9	Tavares Bolden	283	161	.57	1,597	Mel Long	50	587	11.7
2001	Chester Taylor	1,620	299	5.4	Tavares Bolden	319	214	.67	2,466	Donta Greene	64	643	10.0
2002	Astin Martin	785	135	5.8	Brian Jones	423	297	.70	3,446	Carl Ford	79	1,062	13.4
2003	Trinity Dawson	999	199	5.0	Bruce Gradkowski	389	277	.71	3,210	Lance Moore	103	1,194	11.6
2004	Scooter McDougle	620	146	4.2	Bruce Gradkowski	399	280	.70	3,518	Lance Moore	90	1,189	13.2

Receiving leaders by receptions
All statistics include postseason

THE SCHOOLS

TROY

BY SETH WICKERSHAM

TROY UNIVERSITY IS OL' SCHOOL, and not just because it's played football since 1909. For most of those years, through three small school national championships and 15 titles in three different conferences, the icing on the cake of any Trojans season was lifting the Ol' School Bell, the prize for winning the annual game against Jacksonville State.

But even while it held the bell, fans in south-central Alabama had visions of greater prizes, and in 2001 Troy moved up to Division I-A. After going 4–8 in 2002 and 6–6 in 2003, it was clear that transition to college football's top division wouldn't be easy. But in 2004 the Trojans went 7–5, easing local anxiety about the step up in class.

Whatever happens in new-school football, though, Troy gets to keep the Bell. With Jacksonville State staying in I-AA, no future games between the schools are planned.

TRADITION The Ol' School Bell, perhaps a silly name for a bell, holds a certain logic as a prize. Both Troy and Jacksonville State started in the 1800s as teachers colleges, so it seemed only fitting that they would play for a school bell.

Now that the two schools won't meet for a while, Troy University has new traditions. Fans line up on campus two hours before home games for the Trojan Walk, during which the players stroll from their dorms to Movie Gallery Veterans Stadium. Adding formality to tradition, the players are required to wear neckties.

BEST PLAYER Success has rarely come to Troy without Mike Turk being involved. As a four-year starter at quarterback, he led the Trojans to a pair of Division II national championships (1984, 1987). Turk rushed for 2,533 yards—the Trojan record for a quarterback—and scored 32 touchdowns. In a 31-17 Division II national title win over Portland State in 1987, Turk capped an All-America season with a then-championship-game record 190 rushing yards. After Turk graduated, he would join the coaching staff. As a player or coach, Turk has participated in 20 of Troy's 23 postseason games.

BEST COACH In 1966, Billy Atkins took over a team that had won two or fewer games five of the previous six years. Atkins lost five games his first year—and only lost 11 more in his next five seasons as coach. In 1968, he helped guide one of the most balanced teams in Troy history, with QB Sim Byrd throwing for 30 touchdowns and the

---

PROFILE

Troy University
Troy, Ala.
Founded: 1887
Enrollment: 5,205
Colors: Cardinal, Silver and Black
Nickname: Trojans
Stadium: Movie Gallery Veterans Stadium
   Opened in 1950
   AstroPlay; 30,000 capacity
First football game: 1909
All-time record: 442–327–27 (.572)
Bowl record: 0–1
Website: www.troystate.com

THE BEST OF TIMES

In 1984 and 1987, Troy State won Division II national championships.

THE WORST OF TIMES

From 1953 through 1965, the Trojans won more than three games only once.

CONFERENCE

Troy State began competing in the Sun Belt Conference in 2004. Prior to becoming D1-A in 2001, the Trojans' last affiliation was with the Southland Football League (1996-2000). From 1991 to 1995 and 2001 to 2003, Troy State was independent. Some of its other conference memberships include the Gulf South (1970-90) and the Alabama Intercollegiate (1938-69).

DISTINGUISHED ALUMNI

James Byron Huggins, author; Dr. William Novick, founding doctor of the International Children's Heart Foundation

FIGHT SONG

TROJANS, ONE AND ALL
Here's to the school we love
We are Trojans one and all
We will always cheer for VICTORY,
And you'll never let us fall—GO, GO, GO
Cheers to old Troy State
We are with you all the way
So get out there, Team, and FIGHT, FIGHT,
FIGHT, FIGHT, FIGHT!
And WIN today.

Larry Blakeney, the school's winningest coach, is building his own legend at Troy.

defense recording four shutouts. That Troy team went 11–1 and beat Texas A&M-Kingsville 43-35 for the NAIA championship. Atkins finished his career with a 44–16–2 record. Atkins' position may only be temporary however, as Larry Blakeney, the coach who ushered the Trojans into Division I-A, now holds the school record for wins and is building his own legend at Troy.

BEST TEAM Pick a national champion: 1968, 1984 or 1987? Each only lost once. The 1984 Trojans won 12 games, but some were close victories. The 1987 squad lost its first game and tied its second. So that leaves the 1968 version, which beat opponents by scores of 47-7, 31-0, 41-0, 52-0, 76-0 and 63-10. That team featured Byrd's 3,569 passing yards and receiver Danny Grant's 72 catches for 1,002 yards and 14 touchdowns. Safety Ronnie Shelley picked off 15 passes and Byrd was named All-America that year.

BIGGEST GAME It's the 1984 Division II national championship game, 1:30 left, Troy trailing North Dakota State 17-15, on its own 10, relying on a backup quarterback

with an injured foot. So what did Carey Christensen do? He drove the Trojans to the Bison 30-yard line and, with the clock running, Troy sent its field goal unit on. The ball was snapped with just seconds to go, and Ted Clem's 50-yard field goal gave the Trojans an 18-17 win and a national championship. It was the last game for head coach Chan Gailey, who was hired as a defensive assistant by the Denver Broncos following the season and went on to coach the Dallas Cowboys.

BIGGEST UPSET Missouri seemed a little arrogant in 2004 coming into Movie Gallery Veterans Stadium, ranked No. 19 and leading 14-0 after its first two drives. But Troy, which had never beaten a ranked Division I-A team, called for wide receiver Jason Samples to throw deep off a lateral, and he hit running back Jermaine Richardson wide-open in the end zone. From there, the field tilted the Trojans' way. On Troy's next possession, tailback DeWhitt Betterson ran up the middle for 10 yards and was hit hard, and the ball squirted right into the arms of Trojans guard Junior Louissaint. Smoothly, Louissaint picked the ball out of the air, tucked it away and sprinted. Somehow, the 6'1", 276-pounder outran

RECORDS

RUSHING YARDS
GAME
230 — DeWhitt Betterson vs. Utah State, Nov. 15, 2003 (46 att.)
SEASON
1,339 — Arrid Gregory, 1996 (212 att.)
CAREER
3,441 — DeWhitt Betterson, 2001-04 (653 att.)

PASSING YARDS
GAME
454 — Sim Byrd vs. Samford, Sept. 14, 1968 (23 of 33)
SEASON
3,569 — Sim Byrd, 1968 (260 of 414)
CAREER
7,791 — Brock Nutter, 1998-2001 (581 of 1,037)

RECEIVING YARDS
GAME
205 — Danny Grant vs. McNeese State, Nov. 2, 1968 (16 rec.)
SEASON
1,169 — Rufus Cox, 1984 (56 rec.)
CAREER
2,907 — Danny Grant, 1967-69 (215 rec.)

POINTS
GAME
24 — Twelve tied; most recently by Thad Buttone vs. Sam Houston State, Oct. 23, 1999 (4 TDs)
SEASON
105 — Ted Clem, 1987 (16 FGs, 57 PATs)
CAREER
310 — Ted Clem, 1984-87 (166 PATs, 48 FGs)

CONSENSUS ALL-AMERICANS

1939	Sherrill Busby	E
1973-74	Mark King	C
1976	Perry Griggs	OE
1978	Tim Tucker	LB
1980	Willie Tullis	QB
1984	Mitch Geier	OG
1986-87	Freddie Thomas	DB
1987	Mike Turk	QB
1994-95	Bob Hall	OL
1996	Pratt Lyons	DL
1996	Kerry Jenkins	OL
1997	Clifford Ivory	DB
1997	Andy Swafford	KR
1998	Marcus Spriggs	DL
1998	Cleve Roberts	OL
1998-99	Al Lucas	DT
1999	Michael Moore	OT
1999	Anthony Rabb	LB
2000	Lawrence Tynes	PK

every Tiger defensive back and scored from 63 yards out. Missouri quarterback Brad Smith completed only 16 of 36 passes after the first two drives and was picked off twice, leaving nothing but the goalposts to be torn down after a 24-14 win.

HEARTBREAKER In its 2002 season finale, with a last chance to beat a D1-A opponent that season, Troy led Utah State 16-13 with 38 seconds left, and Utah State had the ball at its own 20-yard line. The Trojans went into a prevent defense that allowed Aggies quarterback Jose Fuentes to complete four of six passes and set up a game-tying field goal as time expired. Then, down 19-16 in overtime, Troy receiver Andrew Amerson broke open on a post route and quarterback Hansell Bearden found him—but Amerson dropped the ball. The Trojans didn't recover, failing to move the ball on the next three plays and losing the game.

STADIUM Movie Gallery Veterans Stadium is a curious name at a school that's not known for show business. But Movie Gallery purchased the naming rights in 2003 for $5 million. The company bought a field that opened as Memorial Stadium in 1950 in honor of the school's students who died in World War II, and has grown in seating from 5,000, to 12,500, to 17,500, to 30,000 in 2002, when it also unveiled 27 luxury suites.

RIVAL Troy University fans have a rival in Jacksonville State, even if they aren't very original when coming up with daunting chants. Still, when the Gamecocks come to town, Trojans fans shout "Whup Jax State," a takeoff from the "Whup Troy" that Jacksonville State fans stomped to in the 1970s. The good news is that the Trojans had been doing most of the whupping, as Troy beat Jacksonville State every year from 1995 to 2001. With the move to Division I, however, Troy University will have to find a new rival.

NICKNAME Troy's had four nicknames since its first game in 1909. The team was called the Bulldogs, then the Teachers and finally, in 1922, the Trojans. But that only lasted until coach Albert Elmore arrived and changed the name to the Red Wave, a spin-off of the Crimson Tide, Elmore's alma mater. The Red Wave stuck until 1973, when a student vote sent the team back to the future and picked Trojans as the permanent name.

MASCOT A Trojan mascot had roamed the field and stands since 1973, but no one really knew what to call it. That changed in the mid-1980s, when Troy let students vote on a name for the mascot. T-Roy won, and he's been a staple of Troy games since.

UNIFORMS Troy wore cardinal and black at home until the 1940s, when the team began to wear white. In the 1960s, the Trojans wore white jerseys with cardinal-and-black stripes, and cardinal helmets with a T on the side. In the late 1970s, they switched to cardinal home jerseys and Troy, in cursive, on the side of the helmet. The national championship teams of the 1980s wore red helmets with a Trojan decal on the side, similar to Southern Cal. In the 1990s, they switched their cardinal helmets to black, with an emblem comprised of the letters TSU and a Trojan. In 2004, the Trojans changed to a cardinal helmet with the Troy logo and the word Trojans on the front of their jerseys.

QUOTE "I just thank God."—Kicker Ted Clem, after his 50-yard field goal sailed through as time expired in the 1984 Division II championship game, which Troy won 18-17

THE SCHOOLS

TROY ANNUAL STATISTICAL LEADERS

YR	RUSHING	YDS	ATT	AVG	PASSING	ATT	CMP	PCT	YDS	RECEIVING	REC	YDS	AVG
2001	LeBarron Black	757	210	3.6	Hansell Bearden	288	125	.43	1,462	Jason Samples	45	552	12.3
2002	LeBarron Black	757	210	3.6	Hansell Bearden	288	125	.43	1,462	Jason Samples	45	552	12.3
2003	DeWhitt Betterson	1,164	244	4.8	Aaron Leak	259	110	.42	1,427	Jason Samples	48	620	12.9
2004	DeWhitt Betterson	1,340	256	5.0	Aaron Leak	118	54	.46	756	Jason Samples	38	687	18.1

Receiving leaders by receptions
The NCAA began including postseason stats in 2002

TROY ALL-TIME SCORES

WIN/LOSS PERCENTAGE SINCE 2001

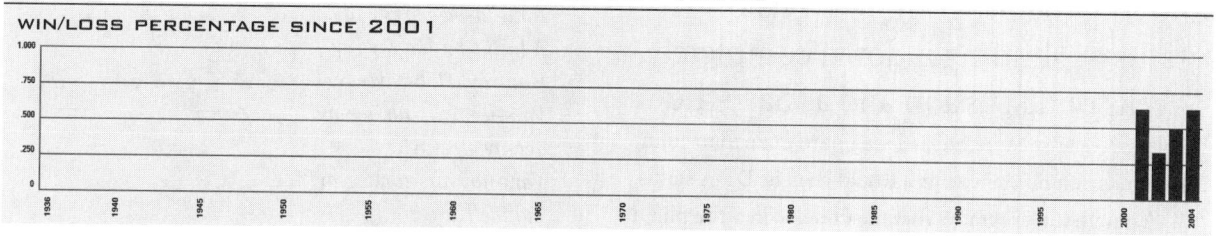

2001-2003 INDEPENDENT

LARRY BLAKENEY
1991-PRESENT (.689) 116-52-1

2001   7-4
S1		at Nebraska	14	42
S8		at Middle Tennessee	17	54
S22	●	Nicholls St.	26	0
O6		at Miami, Fla.	7	38
O13	●	at Mississippi State	21	9
O20	●	Cal St. Northridge	44	31
O27	●	So. Utah	20	17
N3		at Maryland	14	47
N10	●	at La. Monroe	44	12
N17	●	Jacksonville St.	21	3
D1	●	North Texas	18	16

2002   4-8
A31		at Nebraska	16	31
S7		at UAB	26	27
S14	●	So. Utah	40	15
S21		at Iowa State	12	42
S28		at Missouri	7	44
O5	●	Austin Peay	41	3
O12		at Mississippi State	8	11
O19		at Marshall	7	24
O26	●	Fla. Atl.	21	6
N2		Arkansas *LR*	0	23
N9	●	Florida A&M *MBL*	24	7
N16		Utah State	16	19

2003   6-6
A30		at Kansas State	5	41
S6		at Minnesota	7	48
S13	●	at UAB	20	9
S20	●	S.E. Louisiana	28	0
S27	●	Marshall	33	24
O4		at Nebraska	0	30
O18	●	Florida Intl.	21	10
O25		at Virginia	0	24
N1		at North Texas	0	21
N8		at Middle Tennessee	20	27
N15	●	at Utah State	23	14
N22	●	La. Monroe	28	24

2004-PRESENT SUN BELT

2004   7-5 (4-2)
S4	●	at Marshall	17	15
S9	●	Missouri	24	14
S18	|	at New Mexico State	18	22
S25		at South Carolina	7	17
O2	|	Utah State	49	21
O16		at Arkansas State	9	13
O23		at LSU	20	24
O30	●	Idaho	47	7
N6	●	Florida Atlantic	24	6
N13	● |	at La. Lafayette	13	10
N20	● |	Middle Tennessee	37	17
		SILICON VALLEY BOWL		
D30		Northern Illinois	21	34

f Forfeit † Game Later Forfieted # Disputed Victor * Disputed Score || Designated Conference Game |2 Counted Twice in Conference Standings

TULANE

BY KEVIN GLEASON

JUST SIX MONTHS AFTER AN 8–5 season and a win in the 2002 Hawaii Bowl, the Tulane football team was jolted by news that budget-pinching school administrators were considering moving the program to Division II status or shutting it down completely. Weeks of discussion and a "Save the Wave" drive ensued before Tulane board chairman John Koernor announced the school would keep its D1-A status.

Though the program's fortune underscored the plight of many mid-major conference schools locked out of BCS riches, Tulane certainly didn't play as if it deserved the fate. The Green Wave went 12–0 and finished ranked No. 7 in 1998, and has sent three quarterbacks—Shaun King, Patrick Ramsey and J.P. Losman—to the NFL since that season.

The school's proud football heritage dates all the way back to 1893, and includes an epic early era when football mastermind Clark Shaughnessy was head coach, along with a 33-year stint as a member of the Southeastern Conference, from 1933 to 1965. Competing in the modern SEC proved a tough task for the private school, and Tulane left the SEC after nine straight losing seasons, including an 0–10 mark in 1962. The Green Wave played as an independent from 1966 to 1995 before joining Conference USA as a charter member in 1996.

TRADITION In addition to the fight song played before and after every Tulane athletic event, Tulane has one of the most distinctive cheers in college athletics, "The Hullabaloo." With its origins going back to the 1800s, it can be heard after every Tulane score:

A one, a two
A helluva hullabaloo
A hu-la-ba-loo ray ray!
A hu-la-ba-loo ray ray!
Hoo-ray! Hoo-ray!
Vars-uh, vars-uh, tee-ay!
Tee-ay! Tee-ay!
Vars-uh, vars-uh, tee-ay!
Tulane!!

BEST COACH Clark Shaughnessy was just 23 years old when he took his first head-coaching job, at Tulane in 1915. Over the next 12 seasons (with a year off in 1921), he'd develop a regional powerhouse, compiling a 59–28–7 record. The father of the T-formation was still running a single-wing offense in the 1910s and 1920s at Tulane, but his missionary zeal helped transform both the program and the school's image. After compiling a 17–1–1 record over the 1924 and 1925 seasons, Tulane earned an invitation to the Rose Bowl (school president Dr. A. B. Dinwiddie wouldn't approve the trip). Because of the 1925 football team's success, it took Shaughnessy just five days to raise $300,000 to help pay for Tulane Stadium,

PROFILE

Tulane University
New Orleans, La.
Founded: 1834
Enrollment: 7,862
Colors: Olive Green and Sky Blue
Nickname: Green Wave
Stadium: Louisiana Superdome
   Opened in 1975
   Momentum Turf; 69,767 capacity
First football game: 1893
All-time record: 473–528–38 (.474)
Bowl record: 4–6
Conference USA championships: 1 (outright)
First-round NFL draftees: 5
Website: www.tulanegreenwave.com

THE BEST OF TIMES

From 1929 to 1931, Tulane went 28–2 over three seasons under coach Bernie Bierman.

THE WORST OF TIMES

In 1962, Tulane went 0–10, scoring just 76 points.

CONFERENCE

Tulane was a charter member of Conference USA in 1996. From 1966 to 1995, the Green Wave were an independent. They competed in the SEC from 1933 to 1965 and in the Southern Conference from 1922 to 1932.

DISTINGUISHED ALUMNI

Neil Bush, brother of president George W. Bush; Newt Gingrich, politician; Bruce Paltrow, television and movie producer; Jerry Springer, talk-show host; D.B. Sweeney, actor; David Filo, co-founder of Yahoo!

FIGHT SONG

TULANE FIGHT SONG
Green wave green wave
Hats off to thee.
We're out to
Fight fight fight
For our victory.
Shout to the skies
Our Green Wave war cries.
The bravest we'll defy.
Hold that line for
Olive and blue.
We will cheer for you.
So fight, fight, fight, old Tulane
Fight on to victory.

which served as the home of Tulane football for the next half-century. After the 1926 season, Shaughnessy left for crosstown rival Loyola University—where he convinced that institution's leaders to change the school's name to the more grandiose Loyola of the South. He was succeeded by two more University of Minnesota alums, Bernie Bierman (who coached Tulane in the 1932 Rose Bowl) and Ted Cox (who coached Tulane in the 1935 Sugar Bowl).

BEST PLAYER Some would point to two-time All-America Gerald "Jerry" Dalrymple, the cornerstone of the 1931 squad that went to the Rose Bowl. But it's hard to argue with the prolific running back Mewelde Moore, who gained 6,505 yards from 2000 to 2003 to become Tulane's career all-purpose yardage leader. The total was almost 2,000 yards more than runner-up Michael Pierce (4,627 from 1987 to 1989). The Baton Rouge native wasn't heavily recruited out of high school (former LSU coach Nick Saban later admitted that the school went after him too late) and was never a burner, but from early in his freshman year, he showed himself to be a scrappy runner and an agile receiver. The two-sport star (he played in the San Diego Padres organization from 2001 to 2003) eventually gave up baseball and was chosen by

Tulane's "Hullabaloo" cheer is one of the most unique in college football.

the Minnesota Vikings in the 2004 NFL draft.

BEST TEAM The 1998 squad was the first Tulane team to win 12 games in a season and the third unbeaten, untied squad in school history (5–0 in 1900 and 9–0 in 1929). Only one opponent, Louisville, came within a touchdown of Tulane. Still, the question will always remain: how good was the 1998 Tulane team? Thanks to the Bowl Alliance, now called the BCS, Tulane didn't get to play in a major bowl game against one of the big boys of college football. That Green Wave team was loaded with talent. King threw 38 touchdowns on the season, including three in a 49-35 win over Army. He became the first Tulane player to run for 100 yards and throw for 300 in the same game.

The only sore spot in the season came when Tommy Bowden accepted the coaching job at Clemson and departed prior to the Liberty Bowl. Bowden was succeeded by Chris Scelfo, the current Green Wave coach. "We had something to prove today," King said after Tulane defeated BYU in the Liberty Bowl. "Hopefully, we answered some of our doubters. We've always been confident in our ability and our character. We've got a great group of guys who work hard and know what it takes to be successful."

RECORDS

RUSHING YARDS

GAME

249	Mewelde Moore vs. Cincinnati, Oct. 6, 2001 (28 att.)

SEASON

1,421	Mewelde Moore, 2001 (262 att.)

CAREER

4,364	Mewelde Moore, 2000-03 (909 att.)

PASSING YARDS

GAME

447	Patrick Ramsey vs. Army, Sept. 18, 1999 (34 of 49)

SEASON

3,410	Patrick Ramsey, 1999 (310 of 513)

CAREER

9,205	Patrick Ramsey, 1998-01 (798 of 1,355)

RECEIVING YARDS

GAME

271	Jerome McIntosh vs. Vanderbilt, Nov. 18, 1989 (11 rec.)

SEASON

1,206	Marc Zeno, 1987 (77 rec.)

CAREER

3,725	Marc Zeno, 1984-87 (236 rec.)

POINTS

GAME

31	Charles Flournoy vs. Louisiana Tech, Nov. 7, 1925 (4 TDs, 4 PATs, 1 FG)

SEASON

128	Bill Banker, 1928 (breakdown unknown); Charles Flournoy, 1925 (19 TDs, 11 PATs, 1 FG)

CAREER

333	Seth Marler, 1999-2002 (66 FGs, 135 PATs)

CONSENSUS ALL-AMERICANS

1931	Jerry Dalrymple, E
1932	Don Zimmerman, B
1939	Harley McCollum, T
1941	Ernie Blandin, T

BIGGEST GAME There was plenty at stake when Tulane finished the 1998 season 11–0 to earn a bid in the Liberty Bowl against BYU. But the stakes went up in the wake of Bowden's departure for Clemson. The Green Wave and its green head coach faced a stern challenge in BYU, which went 9–4 in 1998 and was the nation's fifth-ranked defensive team. But King ran for a game-high 109 yards and passed for 276 yards and two scores to lead Tulane to a 41-27 rout of the Cougars, Tulane's first bowl victory in 28 years.

BIGGEST UPSET Tulane came in with a 3–7 record. LSU came in ranked No. 12 in the nation and bound for the Orange Bowl. None of it kept Tulane from recording a 31-28 upset on Nov. 27, 1982, in Baton Rouge. Tulane won it when Mike McKay tossed a 31-yard touchdown pass to Reggie Reginelli on fourth down with 5:15 left.

DISPUTE Tulane lost to Miami 24-21 on Oct. 14, 1972, after the Hurricanes were mistakenly awarded a fifth-down play with 1:03 left. Miami promptly scored the winning touchdown to beat the Green Wave 24-21.

HEARTBREAKER Tulane took an 18-game win streak into the 1932 Rose Bowl, with a team that had shut out eight of its 11 opponents in the 1931 regular season. But Southern California jumped out to a 21-0 lead before Tulane's two second-half scores narrowed the gap to 21-12. But there would be no more scoring. The loss was particularly frustrating, since Tulane outgained USC 341 yards to 218. The loss not only ended Tulane's quest for a perfect season, but probably cost Tulane the mythical national championship, as the Dickinson System declared the Trojans the national champions.

STADIUM For years, Tulane played its home games on campus at Tulane Stadium in New Orleans, the site of Super Bowls IV, VI and IX. The stadium was demolished in 1980 and is now the site of an athletic and recreation center. Tulane had long since vacated it, moving into the Louisiana Superdome in 1975, the year it opened. The Superdome is also renowned, having hosted six Super Bowls, four men's Final Fours and 30 Sugar Bowls. What's been lost in the transition, of course, is the sense of intimacy and homefield advantage offered by Tulane Stadium.

RIVAL Tulane's rival has always been LSU. The rivalry began in 1893. From 1893 to 1938, passion between the schools increased, going from harmless pranks to a riot in Tiger Stadium when raging fans from both teams took the field kicking and swinging after the Wave defeated the Tigers on Nov. 26, 1938. LSU leads the all-time series 64-23-7. They last met in 2001, with LSU winning 48-17. LSU has won 14 straight meetings against the Green Wave, dating back to 1983.

NICKNAME From 1893 to 1919, Tulane teams were known as the Olive and Blue, the official school colors. One of the school's student newspapers, *The Tulane Weekly*, began calling the football team the Greenbacks in 1919. Tulane has been called the Green Wave for more than eight decades thanks to a journalist named Earl Sparling. Sparling was editor of the *Tulane Hullabaloo* when he wrote a football song and had it printed in the paper. That was 1920. The title was "The Rolling Green Wave." The paper began using the nickname to describe Tulane athletic teams.

MASCOT Mascots come in all shapes and sizes, but a pelican riding shotgun on a surfboard is clearly of the unique variety. Such was the picture of Tulane's mascot for more than 50 years. The pelican was turned into a mischievous little boy in 1945, the product of John Chase, a local cartoonist who drew the cover of Tulane game programs. The boy was called Greenie.

In the 1960s, athletic director Dr. Rix Yard wanted a more masculine symbol for the teams. Yard called upon Art Evans, who had created the Purdue Boilermaker and USC Trojan. Evans designed a determined looking Green Wave that was adopted in 1964 and became an athletic department staple for more than 20 years. In 1998, Tulane introduced a new set of icons, featuring the return of the pelican, dubbed Riptide after a student vote.

UNIFORMS Tulane's uniforms bear a resemblance to Michigan State's. The jerseys and pants are green with solid white numbers. The helmets have changed dramatically over the years. Today's design shows a dark green background with a white T outlined in blue, and a green-blue wave wrapped around the T. White helmets were worn until 1997. A green-lettered T showed up in 1971.

LORE Tulane played its first football game on Nov. 18, 1893, losing to the Southern Athletic Club 12-0. Tulane coach T.L. Bayne played for the opponent.

QUOTE "Spring practice is necessary for perfection." —Jerry Dalrymple, Tulane's two-time All-America end and leader of the team that played in the 1932 Rose Bowl

TULANE ANNUAL STATISTICAL LEADERS

YR	RUSHING	YDS	ATT	AVG	PASSING	ATT	CMP	PCT	YDS	RECEIVING	REC	YDS	AVG
1937	William Mattis	460	120	3.8		NA	NA	NA	NA		NA	NA	NA
1938	Warren Brunner	662	136	4.9		NA	NA	NA	NA		NA	NA	NA
1939	Bobby Kellogg	473	111	4.3	Bobby Kellogg	21	NA	NA	75		NA	NA	NA
1940	Lou Thomas	385	86	4.5	Jim Ely	19	12	.63	138	Bill Brinkman	6	NA	NA
1941	Bobby Glass	583	119	4.9	Bobby Glass	33	18	.55	264	Walter McDonald	27	437	16.2
1942	Lou Thomas	338	87	3.9	Lou Thomas	55	32	.58	479	Walter McDonald	10	155	15.5
1943	Joe Renfroe	267	54	4.9	Dub Jones	40	13	.33	253	Leonard Finley	11	197	17.9
1944	Dub Jones	700	140	5.0	Bennie Ellender	NA	9	NA	163	Jim Randall	6	95	15.8
1945	Richard Hoot	238	48	5.0	Ernest Crouch	78	31	.40	487	Richard Hoot	11	195	17.7
1946	Eddie Price	309	49	6.3	Jim Keeton	51	21	.41	282	Ed Heider	16	193	12.1
1947	Eddie Price	471	106	4.4	Bennie Ellender	62	29	.47	286	Kenneth Tarzetti	8	89	11.1
1948	Eddie Price	1,178	188	6.3	Joe Ernst	123	57	.46	809	Dick Sheffield	17	316	18.6
1949	Eddie Price	1,137	171	6.6	Joe Ernst	88	49	.56	575	Dick Sheffield	24	376	15.7
1950	Harold Waggoner	663	98	6.8	Joe Ernst	128	69	.54	990	Joe Shinn	24	358	14.9
1951	Max McGee	537	123	4.4	Fred Dempsey	101	48	.48	575	W.C. McElhannon	33	484	14.7
1952	Max McGee	428	109	3.9	Peter Clement	129	59	.46	664	W.C. McElhannon	27	387	14.3
1953	Max McGee	430	82	5.2	Peter Clement	93	46	.49	472	Eddie Bravo	14	137	9.8
1954	Bobby Saia	422	99	4.3	Fred Wilcox	41	19	.46	193	Harry Duvigneaud	11	103	9.4
1955	Ronny Quillian	685	150	4.6	Gene Newton	49	21	.43	312	Otis Gilmore	9	124	13.8
1956	Ronny Quillian	625	156	4.0	Gene Newton	48	21	.44	280	Will Billon	10	143	14.3
1957	Claude Mason	338	61	5.5	Carleton Sweeney	48	22	.46	306	Claude Mason	9	132	14.7
1958	Percy Colon	288	64	4.5	Ritchie Petitbon	125	66	.53	728	Pete Abadie	21	266	12.7
1959	Terry Terrebonne	407	103	4.0	Phil Nugent	102	41	.40	411	Pete Abadie	14	188	13.4
1960	Tommy Mason	663	120	5.5	Phil Nugent	139	67	.48	880	Tommy Mason	28	376	13.4
1961	Gordon Rush	191	42	4.5	Jack Domingue	97	41	.42	338	Thomas Emerson	11	116	10.5
1962	Jerry Graves	200	48	4.2	Ted Miller	103	54	.52	548	Clem Dellenger	39	375	9.6
1963	George Smith	217	60	3.6	Al Burguieres	147	58	.39	664	Ron Chapoton	14	130	9.3
1964	George Smith	307	77	4.0	David East	192	85	.44	846	Lanis O'Steen	24	232	9.7
1965	Carl Crowder	301	90	3.3	Bobby Duhon	151	64	.42	807	Jerry Colquette	36	466	12.9
1966	Bobby Duhon	748	151	5.0	Bobby Duhon	126	56	.44	577	Lanis O'Steen	21	240	11.4
1967	Warren Bankston	473	121	3.9	Bobby Duhon	144	67	.47	753	Nick Pizzolatto	22	282	12.8
1968	Warren Bankston	473	102	4.6	Wayne Francingues	162	66	.41	938	Sonny Pisarich	18	279	15.5
1969	Jimmy Batey	320	59	5.4	Rusty Lachaussee	199	90	.45	1,291	Steve Barrios	23	353	15.3
1970	David Abercrombie	993	219	4.5	Mike Walker	133	56	.42	1,038	Steve Barrios	20	505	25.3
1971	Ricky Hebert	819	210	3.9	Mike Walker	162	64	.40	995	Maxie LeBlanc	25	423	16.9
1972	Doug Bynum	507	108	4.7	Steve Foley	147	74	.50	914	Frank Anderson	17	186	10.9
1973	Steve Foley	601	124	4.8	Steve Foley	112	58	.52	824	Jaime Garza	21	261	12.4
1974	Steve Treuting	523	136	3.8	Terry Looney	128	57	.45	829	Jaime Garza	24	457	19.0
1975	Don Lemon	420	102	4.1	Buddy Gilbert	264	108	.41	1,559	Jaime Garza	27	539	20.0
1976	Bill Kramer	467	121	3.9	Roch Hontas	114	61	.54	697	Zack Mitchell	18	212	11.8
1977	Marvin Christian	691	170	4.1	Roch Hontas	186	118	.63	1,277	Alton Alexis	30	357	11.9
1978	Marvin Christian	879	185	4.8	Roch Hontas	190	108	.57	1,350	Alton Alexis	28	384	13.7
1979	Marvin Christian	582	120	4.9	Roch Hontas	367	215	.59	2,345	Alton Alexis	47	557	11.9
1980	Marvin Lewis	424	80	5.3	Nickie Hall	322	159	.49	2,039	Robert Griffin	45	801	17.8
1981	Marvin Lewis	860	198	4.3	Mike McKay	124	78	.63	927	Nolan Franz	35	611	17.5
1982	Kelvin Robinson	334	70	4.8	Mike McKay	260	152	.58	1,903	Robert Griffin	56	784	14.0
1983	Elton Veals	471	99	4.8	Jon English	184	97	.53	1,258	Larry Route	38	421	11.1
1984	Mike Jones	573	129	4.4	Ken Karcher	230	112	.49	1,341	Larry Route	46	478	10.4
1985	Terrence Jones	377	118	3.2	Ken Karcher	306	175	.57	1,991	Marc Zeno	73	1,137	15.6
1986	Rodney Hunter	657	153	4.3	Terrence Jones	284	159	.56	2,124	Marc Zeno	68	1,033	15.2
1987	Melvin Adams	421	83	5.1	Terrence Jones	319	192	.60	2,551	Marc Zeno	77	1,206	15.7
1988	Terrence Jones	454	164	2.8	Terrence Jones	329	162	.49	2,305	Jerome McIntosh	52	908	17.5
1989	Stanley Barre	418	118	3.5	Deron Smith	423	237	.56	2,613	Jerome McIntosh	55	899	16.3
1990	Chance Miller	805	190	4.2	Deron Smith	361	193	.53	2,282	Melvin Ferdinand	57	757	13.3
1991	Chance Miller	580	163	3.6	Jerome Woods	192	115	.60	1,238	Wil Ursin	70	969	13.8
1992	Joey Perry	429	98	4.4	Shawn Meadows	146	66	.45	752	Wil Ursin	55	755	13.7
1993	Jerald Sowell	403	79	5.1	Craig Randall	305	151	.50	1,565	Wil Ursin	50	565	11.3
1994	Jerald Sowell	609	156	3.9	Tracey Watts	204	91	.45	916	Derrick Franklin	45	450	10.0
1995	Jamaican Dartez	544	150	3.6	Shaun King	199	92	.46	1,046	Derrick Franklin	29	462	15.9
1996	Jerald Sowell	595	154	3.9	Shaun King	273	132	.48	1,574	Jeff Liggon	26	348	13.4
1997	Toney Converse	777	137	5.7	Shaun King	363	199	.55	2,567	P.J. Franklin	58	703	12.1
1998	Toney Converse	871	156	5.6	Shaun King	328	223	.68	3,232	P.J. Franklin	74	1,174	15.9
1999	Toney Converse	366	89	4.1	Patrick Ramsey	513	310	.60	3,410	JaJuan Dawson	96	1,051	10.9
2000	Mewelde Moore	890	174	5.1	Patrick Ramsey	389	229	.59	2,833	Adrian Burnette	74	1,075	14.5
2001	Mewelde Moore	1,421	262	5.4	Patrick Ramsey	448	256	.57	2,935	Mewelde Moore	65	756	11.6
2002	Mewelde Moore	1,138	288	4.0	J.P. Losman	401	230	.57	2,468	Mewelde Moore	52	545	10.5
2003	Mewelde Moore	915	185	5.0	J.P. Losman	422	251	.60	3,077	Roydell Williams	66	1,006	15.2
2004	Matt Forte	624	110	4.5	Lester Ricard	231	143	.62	1,881	Roydell Williams	52	826	15.9

Receiving leaders by receptions
The NCAA began including postseason stats in 2002

TULANE ALL-TIME SCORES

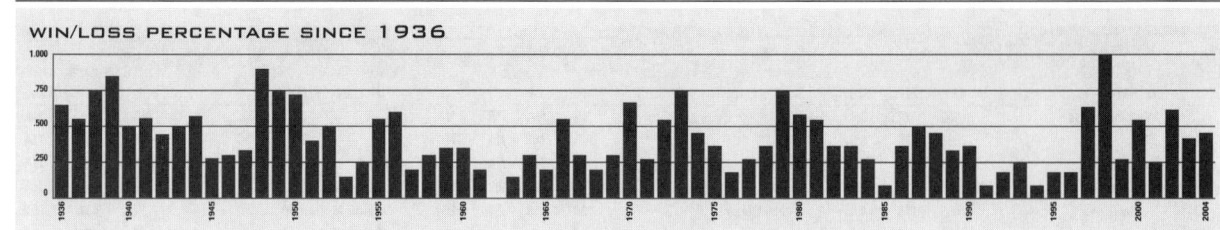

WIN/LOSS PERCENTAGE SINCE 1936

T.L. BAYNE
1893, '95 (.500)　　　4-4

1893　　1-2-0
N18	Southern AC	0	12
N25	LSU	34	0
D2	Mississippi	4	12

FRED SWEET
1894 (.000)　　　0-4

1894　　0-4-0
O27	at Texas	0	12
N3	Alabama	6	18
N17	Sewanee	6	12
N29	Mississippi	2	8

T.L. BAYNE

1895　　3-2-0
O26	at LSU	4	8
N9 ●	Southern AC	12	0
N16 ●	Alabama	22	0
N23	at Texas	0	16
N28 ●	Mississippi	28	4

HARRY BAUM
1896 (.600)　　　3-2

1896　　3-2-0
O17 ●	Alumni	12	0
O24 ●	LSU	0	1 f
N9	at Vicksburg AC	48	0
N14 ●	Texas	4	12
N26 ●	Mississippi	10	0

1897
NO TEAM

JOHN LOMBARD
1898 (.500)　　　1-1

1898　　1-1-0
D12 ●	Mississippi	14	9
D14	at LSU	0	37

H.H. COLLIER
1899 (.071)　　　0-6-1

1899　　0-6-1
N11	Sewanee	0	23
N18 =	Southern AC	0	0
N20	Texas	0	11
N25	at Texas	0	32
N27	Texas A&M *Hou*	0	22
N30	Mississippi	0	15
D8	at LSU	0	38

H.T. SUMMERSGILL
1900-01 (.818)　　　9-2

1900　　5-0-0
O27 ●	Southern AC	23	0
N3	at Alabama	6	0
N10 ●	Milsaps	35	0
N17 ●	LSU	29	0
N29 ●	Mississippi	12	0

1901　　4-2-0
O16 ●	at Meridian	15	0
O26	at Mobile YMCA	0	2
N2 ●	YMCA	23	0
N9 ●	Mississippi State	24	6
N16 ●	LSU	0	11 #
N28 ●	Mississippi	25	11

VIRGINIUS DABNEY
1902 (.286)　　　1-4-2

1902　　1-4-2
O18 ●	Alumni	26	0
O25 =	Auburn	0	0
N1 =	Mississippi State	11	11
N8	at Texas A&M	5	17
N15	Vanderbilt	5	23
N24	Texas	0	6
N27	Mississippi	0	10

CHARLES ESHELMAN
1903 (.500)　　　2-2-1

1903　　2-2-1
O31 ●	Meridian AA	46	0
N7	Shreveport AA	0	23
N18 ●	Cumberland	0	28
N26 ●	Richmond	8	5
D5 =	Mississippi State	0	0

T. BARRY / J. JANVIER
1904 (.714)　　　5-2

1904　　5-2-0
23 ●	Louisiana Tech	11	0
O29 ●	Mississippi State	10	0
N5 ●	at Marion	10	0
N12 ●	Sewanee	0	18
N19 ●	LSU	5	0
N24 ●	Mississippi	22	0
D3 ●	Alabama	0	6

J. TOBIN / H. LUDLOW
1905 (.000)　　　0-1

1905　　0-1-0
N25	LSU		5

JOHN RUSS
1906 (.100)　　　0-4-1

1906　　0-4-1
O27 ●	Samford	0	0
N3	Mississippi	0	17
N10	Sewanee	0	35
N17	Texas A&M	0	18
N24	Arkansas	0	22

JOE CURTIS
1907-08 (.769)　　　10-3

1907　　3-2-0
O26 ●	Samford	13	0
N2 ●	Drury	12	0
N5 ●	Centre	28	9
N9	Arkansas Coll.	12	17
N16	Texas A&M	6	18

1908　　7-1-0
O10 ●	N.O. Gym Club	11	0
O24 ●	Centre	10	0
O31 ●	Mississippi	10	0
N7 ●	Baylor	10	2
N14 ●	Mississippi State	23	0
N18 ●	at Texas	28	15
N21	at Baylor	0	6
N26 ●	Washington, Mo.	11	0

BUSTER BROWN
1909 (.556)　　　4-3-2

1909　　4-3-2
O9 ●	N.O. Gym Club	12	0
O16 ●	Mississippi	5	0
O23 ●	Centre	0	6
O30 ●	Mississippi State	2	0
N6 ●	Cincinnati	6	0
N13 =	Texas	10	10
N20 =	Alabama	5	5
N25	Southwestern, Tex	0	18
J1	at Havana AC	0	11

A.A. MASON
1910-12 (.438)　　　10-13-1

1910　　0-7-0
O13	Mississippi	0	16
O26	at Centre	0	35
O29	at Kentucky	3	10
N5	Mississippi State	0	10
N12	Auburn *Gul*	0	33
N19	Alabama	3	5
N24	Texas A&M *Hou*	0	17

1911　　5-3-1
O12 ●	Mississippi Coll.	10	0
O18 ●	La. Lafayette	27	0
O21 ●	Louisiana Tech	45	0
O28 ●	Samford	10	0
N4 ●	Sewanee	3	9
N18	at Alabama	0	22
N20 ●	at Mississippi State	5	4
N30 =	Wash. & Lee	5	5
D9	at LSU	0	6

1912　　5-3-0
O8 ●	Jefferson	37	0
O12 ●	La. Lafayette	95	0 *
O19 ●	Mississippi Coll.	19	6
O26 ●	Samford	35	0
N2 ●	Alabama	0	7
N9 ●	Mississippi State	27	24
N19 ●	at Texas A&M	0	41
N28 ●	LSU	3	21

A.C. HOFFMAN
1913 (.375)　　　3-5

1913　　3-5-0
O11 ●	Jefferson	13	0
O18 ●	Mississippi Coll.	3	32
O25	Alabama	0	26
N1 ●	at St. Louis	12	6
N8	at Mississippi State	0	32
N15 ●	Southwestern	31	9
N22	at LSU	0	40
N27	Arkansas	0	14

E.R. SWEETLAND
1914 (.500)　　　3-3-1

1914　　3-3-1
O17 ●	La. Lafayette	33	0
O24 ●	Centenary	82	0
O27 ●	Jefferson	24	7
O31	at Alabama	0	58
N7	Mississippi	6	20
N14	Mississippi State *JaM*	0	61
N26 =	LSU	0	0

CLARK SHAUGHNESSY
1915-20, '22-26 (.665)　　59-28-7

1915　　4-4-0
S25 ●	at St. Paul	24	0
O9 ●	La. Lafayette	13	0
O16 ●	Spring Hill	36	13
O23	at Alabama	0	16
O30 ●	Mississippi Coll.	6	20
N13 ●	Samford	32	3
N18	at Florida	7	14
N25	at LSU	0	12

1916　　4-3-1
O14 ●	Spring Hill	14	0
O21 ●	Jefferson	39	3
O27 ●	Mississippi Coll. *JaM*	13	3
N4	at Georgia Tech	0	45
N11	at Rice	13	23
N18 ●	Alabama	33	0
N30 =	LSU	14	14
D9	Georgetown	0	61

1917　　5-3-0
O6 ●	Jefferson	32	0
O13 ●	Spring Hill	28	0
O20 ●	at Florida	52	0
O27 ●	Wash. Aty.	19	0
N2	at Texas A&M	0	35
N10	Georgia Tech	0	48
N17	Rice	0	16
N29 ●	at LSU	28	6

1918　　4-1-1
N2 ●	Camp Shelby	7	0
N9 ●	Camp Beauregard	13	6
N13 ●	Spring Hill	32	0
N16	Camp Pike	7	10
N23 =	Pensacola NAS	0	0
N28 ●	La. Lafayette	74	0

1919　　6-2-1
O4 ●	Jefferson	27	0
O11 ●	La. Lafayette	73	0
O18 ●	at Spring Hill	21	0
O25 ●	Mississippi	27	12
N1 ●	Mississippi Coll.	49	0
N8 ●	Florida	14	2
N15 =	Georgia *Aug*	7	7
N22	LSU	6	27
N27	Wash. & Lee	0	7

1920　　6-2-1
O2 ●	La. Lafayette	79	0 *
O9 ●	Mississippi Coll.	29	0
O16 =	Rice	0	0
O23 ●	at Mississippi	32	0
O30	at Michigan	0	21
N6 ●	Florida *Tam*	14	0
N13 ●	Mississippi State	6	0
N25 ●	at LSU	21	0
D4	Detroit	0	7

MYRON FULLER
1921 (.400)　　　4-6

1921　　4-6-0
O1 ●	Mississippi Coll.	0	14
O8 ●	Mississippi	26	0
O15 ●	at Rice	7	6
O22 ●	Mississippi State	7	0
O29	at Detroit	10	14
N5	Auburn	0	14
N12	at Washington, Mo.	6	14
N19 ●	LSU	21	0
N24	Centre	0	21
D3	Alabama	7	14

1922-1932
SOUTHERN

CLARK SHAUGHNESSY

1922 4-4-0 (1-4-0)
O7 ● Mississippi Coll. 30 0
O14 ● Spring Hill 30 10
O21 ● Fort Benning 18 0
O28 ● | Mississippi State 26 0
N4 | North Carolina 12 19
N11 | Auburn MONT 0 19
N18 | Florida 6 27
N30 | at LSU 14 25

1923 6-3-1 (2-2-1)
S29 ● La. Lafayette 20 2
O6 ● Mississippi Coll. 18 3
O13 Texas BEAU 0 33
O20 ● Louisiana Tech 13 7
O27 | at Vanderbilt 0 17
N3 | at Tennessee 2 13
N10 = | Auburn MONT 6 6
N17 ● | Mississippi 19 0
N24 ● | LSU 20 0
N29 ● Washington, Mo. 19 8

1924 8-1-0 (4-1-0)
S27 ● La. Lafayette 14 0
O4 ● Mississippi Coll. 32 7
O11 ● Louisiana Tech 42 12
O18 ● | Vanderbilt 21 13
O25 ● Spring Hill 33 0
N1 | Mississippi State 6 14
N8 ● | Auburn MONT 14 6
N15 ● | Tennessee 26 7
N27 ● | at LSU 13 0

1925 9-0-1 (5-0-0)
S26 ● Louisiana Coll. 77 0
O3 = Missouri 6 6
O10 ● | Mississippi 26 7
O17 ● | Mississippi State 25 3
O24 ● | Northwestern CHI 18 7
O31 ● | Auburn MONT 13 0
N7 ● Louisiana Tech 37 9 *
N14 ● | Sewanee 14 0
N21 ● | at LSU 16 0
N26 ● at Centenary 14 0

1926 3-5-1 (2-4-0)
S25 ● Louisiana Tech 40 0
O2 = at Missouri 0 0
O9 | at Georgia Tech 6 9
O16 at NYU 0 21
O23 | Auburn 0 2
O30 ● | Mississippi 6 0
N6 | Mississippi State 0 14
N13 ● | Sewanee 19 7
N25 | LSU 0 7

BERNIE BIERMAN
1927-31 (.771) 36-10-2

1927 2-5-1 (2-5-1)
O1 ● | Mississippi 19 7
O8 | at Georgia Tech 6 13
O15 | Mississippi State 6 13
O22 | at Vanderbilt 0 32
O29 | Georgia 0 31
N5 = | Auburn 6 6
N12 | Sewanee 6 12
N24 ● | at LSU 13 6

1928 6-3-1 (3-3-1)
S29 ● at Northwestern St. 65 0
O6 ● | Mississippi State JAM 51 6
O13 | Georgia Tech 0 12
O20 | Vanderbilt 6 13
O27 | at Georgia 14 20
N3 ● Milsaps 27 0
N10 ● | Auburn 13 12
N17 ● | Sewanee 41 6
N24 ● Louisiana Coll. 47 7
N29 = | LSU 0 0

1929 9-0-0 (6-0-0)
S28 ● Northwestern St. 40 6
O5 ● Texas A&M 13 10
O12 ● | Mississippi State 34 0
O19 ● La. Lafayette 60 0
O26 ● | Georgia Tech 20 14
N2 ● | Georgia OLGA 21 15
N9 ● | Auburn 52 0
N16 ● | Sewanee 18 0
N28 ● | at LSU 21 0

1930 8-1-0 (5-0-0)
S27 ● La. Lafayette 84 0
O4 at Northwestern 0 14
O11 ● Texas A&M DAL 19 9
O18 ● B'ham Southern 21 0
O25 ● | at Georgia Tech 28 0
N1 ● | Mississippi State 53 0
N8 ● | Auburn 21 0
N15 ● | Georgia 25 0
N27 ● | LSU 12 7

1931 11-1-0 (8-0-0)
S26 ● | Mississippi 31 0
O3 ● Texas A&M 7 0
O10 ● Spring Hill 40 0
O17 ● | at Vanderbilt 19 0
O24 ● | Georgia Tech 33 0
O31 ● | Mississippi State 59 7
N7 ● | Auburn MONT 27 0
N14 ● | at Georgia 20 0
N21 ● | Sewanee 40 0
N28 ● | LSU 34 7
D5 ● Washington State 28 14
ROSE BOWL
J1 Southern Cal 12 21

TED COX
1932-35 (.725) 28-10-2

1932 6-2-1 (5-2-1)
O1 ● Texas A&M 26 14
O8 ● | Georgia 34 25
O15 = | Vanderbilt 6 6
O22 | Auburn 7 19
O29 ● | South Carolina 6 0
N5 ● | at Georgia Tech 20 14
N12 ● | at Kentucky 6 3
N19 ● | Sewanee 26 0
N26 | at LSU 0 14

1933-1965
SEC

1933 6-3-1 (4-2-1)
S30 Texas A&M 6 13
O7 | at Georgia 13 26
O14 ● Maryland 20 0
O21 ● | at Georgia Tech 7 0
O28 | Auburn 7 13
N4 ● Colgate BNX 7 0
N11 ● | Mississippi 33 0
N18 ● | Kentucky 34 0
N25 ● | Sewanee 26 9
D2 = | LSU 7 7

1934 10-1-0 (8-0-0)
S29 ● U.T. Chattanooga 41 0
O6 ● | Auburn 13 0
O13 ● | at Florida 28 12
O20 ● | Georgia 7 6
O27 ● | Georgia Tech 20 12
N3 ● | Mississippi 15 0
N10 Colgate 6 20
N17 ● | at Kentucky 20 7
N24 ● | Sewanee 32 0
D1 ● | at LSU 13 12
SUGAR BOWL
J1 ● Temple 20 14

1935 6-4-0 (3-3-0)
S28 ● VMI 44 0
O5 | Auburn 0 10
O12 ● | Florida 19 7
O19 at Minnesota 0 20
O26 ● | Sewanee 33 0
N2 ● Colgate 14 6
N9 | Georgia 13 26
N16 ● | Kentucky 20 13
N23 ● Northwestern St. 13 0
N30 | LSU 0 41

LOWELL "RED" DAWSON
1936-41 (.644) 36-19-4

1936 6-3-1 (2-3-1)
S26 ● | Mississippi 7 6
O3 = | Auburn 0 0
O10 ● Centenary 19 0
O17 ● Colgate NYC 28 6
O24 ● North Carolina 21 7
O31 ● Louisiana Tech 22 13
N7 | Alabama BIRM 7 34
N14 | Georgia 6 12
N21 ● | Sewanee 53 6
N28 | at LSU 0 33

1937 5-4-1 (2-3-1)
S25 ● Clemson 7 0
O2 = | Auburn 0 0
O9 ● Mississippi Coll. 84 0
O16 ● Colgate BUF 7 6
O23 at North Carolina 0 13
O30 ● | Mississippi 14 7
N6 | Alabama 6 9
N13 | at Georgia 6 7
N20 ● | Sewanee 13 7
N27 | LSU 7 20

1938 7-2-1 (4-1-1)
S24 Clemson 10 13
O1 = | Auburn 0 0
O8 ● at North Carolina 17 14
O15 ● Rice 26 17
O22 ● Mercer 51 0
O29 ● | Mississippi State 27 0
N5 | Alabama BIRM 0 3
N12 ● | Georgia 28 6
N19 ● | Sewanee 38 0
N26 ● | at LSU 14 0

1939 8-1-1 (5-0-0)
S30 ● Clemson 7 6
O7 ● | Auburn 12 0
O14 ● Fordham 7 0
O21 = North Carolina 14 14
O28 ● | Mississippi 18 6
N11 ● | Alabama 13 0
N18 ● at Columbia 25 0
N25 ● | Sewanee 52 0
D2 ● | LSU 33 20
SUGAR BOWL
J1 Texas A&M 13 14

1940 5-5-0 (1-3-0)
S28 Boston College 7 27
O5 | Auburn 14 20
O12 Fordham NYC 7 20
O19 ● Rice 15 6
O26 ● at North Carolina 14 13
N2 ● Clemson 13 0
N9 | Alabama BIRM 6 13
N16 ● | Georgia 21 13
N23 ● Northwestern St. 47 0
N30 | at LSU 0 14

1941 5-4-0 (2-3-0)
S27 ● Boston College 21 7
O4 ● | Auburn 32 0
O11 at Rice 9 10
O18 ● North Carolina 52 6
O25 | Mississippi 13 20
N1 ● | at Vanderbilt 34 14
N8 | Alabama 14 19
N15 ● NYU BNX 45 0
N29 | LSU 0 19

CLAUDE SIMONS, JR.
1942-45 (.435) 13-17-1

1942 4-5-0 (1-4-0)
S26 ● at Southern Cal 27 13
O3 | Auburn 13 27
O10 ● Rice 18 7
O17 | at Georgia 0 40
O24 ● North Carolina 29 14
O31 ● | Vanderbilt 28 21
N7 | Mississippi State 0 7
N14 Georgia Pre-Flight 0 7
N26 | at LSU 6 18

1943 3-3-0 (1-1-0)
O2 Memphis Navy 7 41
O9 ● at Rice 33 0
O23 ● SMU 12 6
O30 Georgia Pre-Flight 13 14
N13 | Georgia Tech 0 33
N20 ● | LSU 27 0

1944 4-3-0 (1-2-0)
O7 at Notre Dame 0 26
O14 ● Rice 21 0
O21 ● | Auburn 16 13
O28 ● SMU 27 7
N11 | at Georgia Tech 7 34
N18 ● Clemson 36 20
N25 | at LSU 6 25

1945 2-6-1 (1-3-1)
O6 = | Florida 6 6
O13 at Rice 7 13
O20 | Auburn 14 20
O27 ● SMU 19 7
N3 ● | Mississippi State 14 13
N10 | Georgia Tech 7 41
N17 Clemson 20 47
N24 Notre Dame 6 32
D1 | LSU 0 33

HENRY E. FRNKA
1946-51 (.569) 31-23-4

1946 3-7-0 (2-4-0)
S28 | Alabama 6 7
O5 ● | Florida 27 13
O12 Rice 6 25
O19 ● | Auburn 32 0
O26 | Mississippi State 7 14
N9 ● Clemson 54 13
N16 | at Georgia Tech 7 35
N23 Notre Dame 0 41
N30 | at LSU 27 41
D21 Southern Cal 13 20

1947 2-5-2 (2-3-2)
S27 ● | Alabama 21 20
O4 | Georgia Tech 6 20 *
O11 at Rice 0 33
O18 | Mississippi 14 27
O25 ● | Auburn 40 0
N1 | Mississippi State 0 20
N15 = | Florida 7 7
N22 at Notre Dame 6 59
D6 = | LSU 6 6

1948 9-1-0 (5-1-0)
S25 ● | Alabama 21 14
O2 | at Georgia Tech 7 13
O9 ● South Carolina 14 0
O16 ● | Mississippi 20 7
O23 ● | Auburn 21 6
O30 ● | Mississippi State 9 0
N6 ● VMI 28 7
N13 ● Baylor 35 13
N20 ● at Cincinnati 6 0
N27 ● | at LSU 46 0

1949 7-2-1 (5-1-0)
S24 ● | Alabama MBL 28 14
O1 ● | Georgia Tech 18 0
O8 ● SE. Louisiana 40 0
O15 at Notre Dame 7 46
O22 ● | Auburn 14 6
O29 ● | Mississippi State 54 6
N5 = Navy 21 21
N12 ● | at Vanderbilt 41 14
N19 ● at Virginia 28 14
N26 | LSU 0 21

1950 6-2-1 (3-1-1)
S30 | Alabama 14 26
O7 ● Louisiana Coll. 64 0
O14 Notre Dame 9 13
O21 ● | Mississippi 27 20
O28 ● | at Auburn 28 0
N11 ● Navy BALT 27 0
N18 ● Virginia 42 18
N25 ● | Vanderbilt 35 6
D2 = | LSU 14 14

1951 4-6-0 (1-5-0)
S29 ● Miami, Fla. 21 7
O6 Baylor 14 27
O13 ● Holy Cross 20 14
O20 | at Mississippi 6 25
O27 | Auburn 0 21
N3 | Mississippi State 7 10
N10 | Kentucky 0 37
N17 ● | at Vanderbilt 14 10
N24 ● SE. Louisiana 48 7
D1 | at LSU 13 14

RAYMOND WOLF
1952-53 (.325) 6-13-1

1952 5-5-0 (3-5-0)
S27 | Georgia 16 21
O4 ● Santa Clara 35 0
O11 | at Georgia Tech 0 14
O18 | Mississippi 14 20
O25 ● | Auburn MBL 21 6
N1 ● | Mississippi State 34 21
N8 | at Kentucky 6 27
N15 ● | Vanderbilt 16 7
N22 ● Louisiana Coll. 46 14
N29 | LSU 0 16

1953 1-8-1 (0-7-0)

S19	●	Citadel	54	6
S26	|	at Georgia	14	16
O3		at Michigan	7	26
O10	|	Georgia Tech	13	27
O17	|	Mississippi	14	45
O24	|	Auburn MBL	7	34
O31	=	Army	0	0
N7	|	Mississippi State	0	21
N14	|	Vanderbilt	7	21
N28	|	at LSU	13	32

ANDY PILNEY
1954-61 (.350) 25-49-6

1954 1-6-3 (1-6-1)

S18	|	at Georgia Tech	0	28
S25	=	Memphis	13	13
O2	=	North Carolina	7	7
O9	|	Mississippi State	0	14
O16	|	at Mississippi	7	34
O23	|	Georgia	0	7
O30	|	Auburn MBL	0	27
N6	= |	Alabama	0	0
N13	● |	at Vanderbilt	6	0
N27	|	LSU	13	14

1955 5-4-1 (3-3-1)

S17	●	VMI	20	7
S24		at Texas	21	35
O1	●	Northwestern	21	0
O8	|	at Mississippi State	0	14
O15	|	Mississippi	13	27
O22	● |	at Georgia	14	0
O29	● |	Auburn	27	13
N5	● |	Alabama MBL	27	7
N12	|	Vanderbilt	7	20
N26	= |	at LSU	13	13

1956 6-4-0 (3-3-0)

S22	●	Virginia Tech	21	14
S29		Texas	6	7
O6	●	at Northwestern	20	13
O13	●	Navy	21	6
O20	● |	Mississippi JAM	10	3
O27	|	at Georgia Tech	0	40
N3	● |	Mississippi State	20	14
N10	|	Alabama	7	13
N17	● |	at Vanderbilt	13	6
D1	|	LSU	6	7

1957 2-8-0 (1-5-0)

S20		Virginia Tech	13	14
S28		at Texas	6	20
O5	●	at Marquette	20	6
O11	|	Georgia	6	13
O18	|	Mississippi	0	50
O26	|	Georgia Tech	13	20
N2	|	Mississippi State JAM	6	27
N9	● |	Alabama MBL	7	0
N16		at Army	14	20
N30	|	at LSU	6	25

1958 3-7-0 (1-5-0)

S20	|	at Florida	14	34
S26		Texas	20	21
O4	|	at Georgia Tech	0	14
O11	|	Mississippi	8	19
O18	●	Navy NOR	14	6
O25		at Kansas	9	14
O31	●	Texas Tech	27	0
N7	● |	Alabama	13	7
N15	|	at Vanderbilt	0	12
N22	|	LSU	0	62

1959 3-6-1 (0-5-1)

S18	|	Florida	0	30
S25		at Miami, Fla.	7	26
O3	●	Wake Forest	6	0
O9	●	Detroit	25	0
O17	|	at Mississippi	7	53
O24	|	Georgia Tech	13	21
O30	●	Texas Tech	17	7
N7	|	Alabama MBL	7	19
N14	= |	Vanderbilt	6	6
N21	|	at LSU	6	14

1960 3-6-1 (1-4-1)

S17	●	at California	7	3
S24	= |	Alabama	6	6
O1		at Rice	7	10
O15	|	Mississippi	13	26
O22	|	at Georgia Tech	6	14
O28	●	William & Mary	40	8
N5		at Texas Tech	21	35
N12	|	at Florida	6	21
N19	● |	at Vanderbilt	20	0
N26	|	LSU	6	17

1961 2-8-0 (1-5-0)

S23		at Stanford	7	9
S30	|	Alabama MBL	0	9
O6	|	Florida	3	14
O14	●	Virginia Tech	27	14
O21	|	Mississippi JAM	0	41
O28	|	Georgia Tech	0	35
N4		at Clemson	6	21
N11		Miami, Fla.	0	6
N17	● |	Vanderbilt	17	14
N25	|	at LSU	0	62

TOMMY O'BOYLE
1962-65 (.163) 6-33-1

1962 0-10-0 (0-7-0)

S21		Stanford	3	6
S28	|	Alabama	6	44
O6		at Texas	8	35
O12	|	Mississippi State	6	35
O20	|	Mississippi JAM	0	21
O27	|	at Georgia Tech	12	42
N3		Virginia Tech	22	24
N10	|	at Tennessee	16	28
N17	|	at Vanderbilt	0	20
N24	|	LSU	3	38

1963 1-8-1 (0-6-1)

S20		Texas	0	21
S28	|	Alabama MBL	0	28
O4		Miami, Fla.	0	10
O12	|	Mississippi State JAM	10	31
O19	|	Mississippi	0	21
O26	|	Georgia Tech	3	17
N2	●	at South Carolina	20	7
N9	|	Tennessee	0	26
N16	= |	Vanderbilt	10	10
N23	|	at LSU	0	20

1964 3-7-0 (1-5-0)

S19		at Texas	0	31
S26	|	Alabama MBL	6	36
O10	|	at Mississippi State	6	17
O17	|	Mississippi	9	14
O24		at Georgia Tech	6	7
O31	●	VMI	25	6
N6	||	at Miami, Fla.	0	21
N14	● |	at Vanderbilt	7	2
N21	|	LSU	3	13
N28	●	Duke	17	0

1965 2-8-0 (1-5-0)

S18		at Texas	0	31
S25	|	Alabama MBL	0	27
O2	●	Miami, Fla.	24	16
O9		Georgia Tech	10	13
O16	|	Mississippi JAM	7	24
O22	● |	Mississippi State	17	15
O30	|	Vanderbilt	0	13
N6		Stanford	0	16
N13	|	at Florida	13	51
N20	|	at LSU	0	62

1966-1995
INDEPENDENT

JIM PITTMAN
1966-70 (.413) 21-30-1

1966 5-4-1

S17	●	Virginia Tech	13	0
S24	●	Texas A&M	21	13
O1		at Stanford	14	33
O8	●	at Virginia	20	6
O15	●	Cincinnati	28	21
O22		at Georgia Tech	17	35
O29	●	at Vanderbilt	13	12
N5	=	Miami, Fla.	10	10
N12		at Florida	10	31
N19		LSU	7	21

1967 3-7-0

S23		Miami, Ohio	3	14
S30	●	at North Carolina	36	11
O6		at Miami, Fla.	14	34
O14		Florida	0	35
O21		Air Force	10	13
O28	●	Georgia Tech	23	12
N4	●	Vanderbilt	27	14
N11		at Tennessee	14	35
N18		Virginia	10	14
N25		at LSU	27	41

1968 2-8-0

S14		at Houston	7	54
S28		Texas A&M	3	35
O5		Tampa	14	17
O12		at Florida	3	24
O19	●	Boston College	28	14
O26		at Georgia Tech	19	23
N2		at Vanderbilt	7	21
N9	●	Tulsa	25	15
N16		at Virginia	47	63
N23		at LSU	10	34

1969 3-7-0

S20		at Georgia	0	35
S27		West Virginia	17	35
O4		at Boston College	24	28
O11		Florida TAM	17	18
O18	●	at Pittsburgh	26	22
O25		Notre Dame	0	37
N1		Vanderbilt	23	26
N8	●	Georgia Tech	14	7
N15	●	Virginia	31	0
N22		at LSU	0	27

1970 8-4-0

S12		at Texas Tech	14	21
S19	●	Georgia	17	14
S26	●	at Illinois	23	9
O3	●	at Cincinnati	6	3
O10		at Air Force	3	24
O17	●	North Carolina	24	17
O24		at Georgia Tech	6	20
O31	●	at Vanderbilt	10	7
N7	●	Miami, Fla.	31	16
N21	●	North Carolina St.	31	0
N28		LSU	14	26
		LIBERTY BOWL		
D12	●	Colorado	17	3

BENNIE ELLENDER
1971-75 (.482) 27-29

1971 3-8-0

S11	●	Texas Tech	15	9
S18		at Georgia	7	17
S25		at Rice	11	14
O2		William & Mary	3	14
O9	●	at North Carolina	37	29
O16	●	Pittsburgh	33	8
O23		Georgia Tech	16	24
O30		Vanderbilt	9	13
N6		Ohio U.	7	30
N13		at Notre Dame	7	21
N27		at LSU	7	36

1972 6-5-0

S16	●	at Boston College	10	0
S23	●	Georgia	24	13
S30		at Michigan	7	41
O7	●	Pittsburgh	38	6
O14		at Miami, Fla.	21	24
O21		at West Virginia	19	31
O28		at Georgia Tech	7	21
N4	●	Kentucky	18	7
N11	●	Ohio U.	44	6
N18	●	at Vanderbilt	21	7
D2		LSU	3	9

1973 9-3-0

S22	●	Boston College	21	16
S29	●	VMI	42	0
O6	●	at Pittsburgh	24	6
O13	●	at Duke	24	17
O20	●	North Carolina	16	0
O27	●	Georgia Tech	23	14
N3		at Kentucky	7	34
N10	●	Navy	17	15
N17	●	Vanderbilt	24	3
N24		at Maryland	9	42
D1	●	LSU	14	0
		BLUEBONNET BOWL		
D29		Houston	7	47

1974 5-6-0

S14	●	La. Lafayette	17	16
S21	●	at Army	31	14
S28	●	West Virginia	17	14
O12	●	at Air Force	10	3
O19	●	Citadel	30	3
O26		at Georgia Tech	7	27
N2		Kentucky	7	30
N9		at Boston College	3	27
N16		at Vanderbilt	22	30
N23		at LSU	22	24
N30		Mississippi	10	26

1975 4-7-0

S13	●	at Clemson	17	13
S20	●	Mississippi	14	3
S27		Syracuse	13	31
O4		Vanderbilt	3	6
O11	●	at Boston College	17	7
O18	●	at West Virginia	16	14
O25		Georgia Tech	0	23
N1		at Kentucky	10	23
N8		Air Force	12	13
N15		North Carolina	15	17
N22		LSU	6	42

LARRY SMITH
1976-79 (.400) 18-27

1976 2-9-0

S11		Cincinnati	14	21
S18		at Mississippi	7	34
S25		Boston College	3	27
O2	●	at Vanderbilt	24	13
O9		at Syracuse	0	3
O16	●	Army	23	10
O23		at Georgia Tech	16	28
O30		Memphis	7	14
N6		West Virginia	28	32
N13		Rutgers	20	29
N20		at LSU	7	17

1977 3-8-0

S10		at Memphis	9	27
S17		Stanford	17	21
S24		at SMU	23	28
O1	●	Vanderbilt	36	7
O8		at Boston College	28	30
O15	●	Cincinnati	16	13
O22		Georgia Tech	14	38
O29		at Pittsburgh	0	48
N5	●	at Miami, Fla.	13	10
N12		at Rutgers	8	47
N19		LSU	17	20

1978 4-7-0

S9		at Maryland	7	31
S16		Pittsburgh	6	24
S23		at Georgia Tech	17	27
S30		at Stanford	14	17
O7	●	at Vanderbilt	38	3
O14	●	Boston College	9	3
O21		TCU	7	13
O28	●	Memphis	41	24
N4	●	Miami, Fla.	20	16
N11		at Mississippi	3	13
N25		at LSU	21	40

1979 9-3-0

S8	●	Stanford	33	10
S15		at Rice	17	21
S22	●	at TCU	33	19
S29	●	SMU	24	17
O6	●	Vanderbilt	42	14
O13	●	at Southern Miss	20	19
O20		at West Virginia	17	27
O27	●	Georgia Tech	12	7
N3	●	at Boston College	43	8
N10	●	Mississippi	49	15
N24	●	LSU	24	13
		LIBERTY BOWL		
D22		Penn State	6	9

VINCE GIBSON
1980-82 (.500) 17-17

1980 7-5-0

S6		Southern Miss	14	17
S13		at Stanford	14	19
S20	●	Rice	35	14
S27	●	at Mississippi	26	24
O4		SMU	21	31
O11	●	at Vanderbilt	43	21
O18	●	Air Force	28	7
O25	●	at Georgia Tech	31	14
N1	●	Kentucky	24	22
N15	●	Memphis	21	16
N22		at LSU	7	24
		HALL OF FAME CLASSIC		
D27		Arkansas	15	34

1981 6-5-0

S5		Mississippi	18	19
S12		Clemson	5	13
S19		at Southern Miss	3	21
O3		at Rice	16	20
O10	●	Vanderbilt	14	10
O17	●	at Air Force	31	13
O24	●	Georgia Tech	27	10
O31		at Cincinnati	13	17
N7	●	Maryland	14	7
N14	●	at Memphis	24	7
N28	●	LSU	48	7

1982 4-7-0

S4		Mississippi State	21	30
S11		at SMU	7	51
S18	●	Rice	30	6
O2		at Vanderbilt	21	24
O9		Georgia Tech	13	19
O16		Southern Miss	10	22
O23	●	Memphis	17	10
O30	●	Baylor	30	15
N6		Mississippi	14	45
N20		Florida	7	21
N27		at LSU	31	28

WALLY ENGLISH
1983-84 (.318) 7-15

1983 4-7-0

S3		at Mississippi State	9	14
S10	●	Mississippi JAM	27	23 †
S17	●	Florida State	34	28 †
S24		at Kentucky	14	26
O1		Vanderbilt	17	30
O8		at Memphis	25	28
O15	●	La. Lafayette	17	15
O22	●	at Southern Miss	14	7
O29		at Baylor	18	24
N5		Virginia Tech	10	26
N19		LSU	7	20

1984 3-8-0

S1		Mississippi State	3	30
S15		at Florida	21	63
S22		Kentucky	26	30
S29		at Mississippi	14	19
O6	●	at Vanderbilt	27	23
O13	●	Southern Miss	35	7
O20		at Florida State	6	27
N3		at Virginia Tech	6	13
N10		at Pittsburgh	10	21
N17	●	Memphis	14	9
N24		at LSU	15	33

MACK BROWN
1985-87 (.324) 11-23

1985 1-10-0

A31		Florida State	12	38
S14		at TCU	13	30
S21		at Kentucky	11	16
S28		Mississippi	10	27
O5		Vanderbilt	17	24
O12		at Memphis	21	38
O19		at Mississippi State	27	31
N2		at Georgia	3	58
N9	●	La. Lafayette	27	17
N23		at Southern Miss	6	24
N30		LSU	19	31

1986 4-7-0

S13		TCU	31	48
S20	●	at Vanderbilt	35	17
S27		at Mississippi	10	35
O4		Wichita St.	20	21
O11		at Florida State	21	54
O18		Mississippi State	27	34
O25	●	Southern Miss	35	20
N1		La. Lafayette	42	39
N8		Louisville	12	23
N15	●	Memphis	15	6
N29		at LSU	17	37

1987 6-6-0

S5		at Louisville	40	42
S12	●	Iowa State	25	12
S19		at Southern Miss	24	31
S26	●	Mississippi	31	24
O3	●	Vanderbilt	27	17
O17		at Memphis	36	45
O24		Virginia Tech	57	38
O31		at Florida State	14	73
N7		at Mississippi State	30	19
N14		La. Lafayette	38	10
N21		LSU	36	41

INDEPENDENCE BOWL

D19		Washington	12	24

GREG DAVIS
1988-91 (.311) 14-31

1988 5-6-0

S3	●	U.T. Chattanooga	33	19
S10		at Iowa State	13	30
S17	●	Kansas State	20	16
S24	●	Memphis	20	19
O1		Florida State	28	48
O8		Southern Miss	13	38
O22		Louisville	35	38
O29		La. Lafayette	34	51
N5	●	at Mississippi	14	9
N19	●	Mississippi State	27	22
N26		at LSU	14	44

1989 4-8-0

S2		at Hawaii	26	31
S9	●	Rice	20	19
S16	●	La. Lafayette	17	10
S23		at Florida State	9	59
S30		Iowa State	24	25
O7		at Southern Miss	21	30
O21		Mississippi	28	32
O28		at Virginia Tech	13	30
N4	●	Memphis	38	34
N11		at Mississippi State	7	27
N18	●	at Vanderbilt	37	13
N25		LSU	7	27

1990 4-7-0

S1		La. Lafayette	6	48
S8	●	at Rice	21	10
S15	●	SMU	43	7
S22		Florida State	13	31
S29		at Mississippi	21	31
O6	●	at Memphis	14	21
O13		Southern Miss	14	20
O20		Mississippi State	17	38
O27	●	Cincinnati	49	7
N10	●	at Syracuse	26	24
N24		at LSU	13	16

1991 1-10-0

A31		Mississippi	3	22
S7		at Florida State	11	38
S14		at Mississippi State	0	48
S21		Rice	19	28
S28		Syracuse	0	24
O5		SMU	17	31
O12		at Alabama	0	62
O19		at Southern Miss	14	47
N2		at East Carolina	28	38
N9	●	Navy	34	7
N23		LSU	20	39

BUDDY TEEVENS
1992-96 (.179) 10-46

1992 2-9-0

S5	●	at SMU	13	12
S12		at Mississippi	9	35
S19		at Iowa State	14	38
S26	●	Nevada	34	17
O10		Alabama	0	37
O15		Southern Miss	7	17
O24		Boston College	3	17
O31		Memphis	20	62
N7		at Navy	17	20
N14		at Florida State	7	70
N21		at LSU	12	24

1993 3-9-0

S4		Alabama BIRM	17	31 †
S11		at Rice	0	34
S18	●	William & Mary	10	0
S25		Mississippi State	10	36
O2	●	Navy	27	25
O9		La. Lafayette	15	36
O16		at TCU	7	14
O30		at Boston College	14	42
N6	●	at Southern Miss	17	15
N13		North Carolina	10	42
N20		at LSU	10	24
D4		at Hawaii	17	56

1994 1-10-0

S3		Southern Miss	10	25
S10	●	at Rice	15	13
S17		at North Carolina	0	49
S24		Alabama BIRM	10	20
O8		at Memphis	0	13
O15		TCU	28	30
O22		at Mississippi State	22	66
O29		at Maryland	10	38
N5		Navy	15	17
N12		Mississippi	0	38
N19		LSU	25	49

1995 2-9-0

S2		Maryland	10	29
S9	●	Wake Forest	35	9
S16	●	at Rice	17	15
S30		at Southern Miss	0	45
O7		at Mississippi	17	20
O14		Memphis	8	23
O21		at TCU	11	16
O28		La. Lafayette	28	32
N4		at Louisville	14	34
N11		Rutgers	40	45
N18		at Navy	7	35

1996-PRESENT
C-USA

1996 2-9 (1-4)

A30	●	at Cincinnati	34	14
S14		Rice	14	21
S21		at Memphis	10	17
O5	●	TCU	35	7
O12		Louisville	20	23
O19		at Army	10	34
O26		Southern Miss	28	31
N2		Houston	17	20
N9		Syracuse	7	31
N16		at Navy	21	35
N23		at LSU	17	35

TOMMY BOWDEN
1997-98 (.818) 18-4

1997 7-4 (5-1)

S6	●	Cincinnati	31	17
S13		Rice	24	30
S20		at Syracuse	19	30
O4		Army	41	0
O11	●	at Louisville	64	33
O18	●	East Carolina	33	16
O25		at Southern Miss	13	34
N1		at La. Lafayette	56	0
N8	●	Memphis	26	14
N15		Mississippi	24	41
N22	●	at Houston	44	10

1998 12-0 (6-0)

S5	●	at Cincinnati	52	34
S12	●	at SMU	31	21
S26	●	Navy	42	24
O3	●	Southern Miss	21	7
O17	●	Louisville	28	22
O24	●	at Rutgers	52	24
O31	●	La. Lafayette	72	20
N7	●	at Memphis	41	31
N14	●	at Army	49	35
N21	●	Houston	48	20
N26	●	Louisiana Tech	63	30

LIBERTY BOWL

D31	●	Brigham Young	41	27

CHRIS SCELFO
1998-PRESENT (.437) 31-40

1999 3-8 (1-5)

S6	●	at Southern Miss	14	48
S11	●	SMU	53	19
S18	●	Army	48	28
O2		at Syracuse	17	47
O9		at Mississippi	13	20
O16	●	La. Lafayette	48	32
O23		at East Carolina	7	52
O30		Memphis	7	49
N6		at Houston	31	36
N13		at Navy	21	45
N20		UAB	20	23

2000 6-5 (3-4)

S2		at Mississippi	20	49
S16		at East Carolina	17	37
S23	●	at SMU	29	17
S30		Cincinnati	24	19
O7		at La. Lafayette	38	37
O14		Southern Miss	24	56
O21		at Army	17	21
O28		at Louisville	32	35
N4	●	Houston	41	23
N11		Navy	50	38
N18	●	Memphis	37	14

2001 3-9 (1-6)

A25		at Brigham Young	35	70
S1		at LSU	17	48
S8		East Carolina	24	51
S22		Central Florida	29	36
S29	●	Southern U.	41	7
O6		at Cincinnati	33	46
O13	●	TCU	48	22
O20		at UAB	27	34
O27		at Army	35	42
N3		Louisville	7	52
N10	●	at Navy	42	28
N17		at Southern Miss	6	59

2002 8-5 (4-4)

A31		Southern U.	37	19
S7	●	at Houston	34	13
S14		at East Carolina	20	24
S21		at Memphis	10	38
S28		Texas	0	49
O5	●	at La. Monroe	52	9
O12	●	Cincinnati	35	17
O19	●	UAB	35	14
O26	●	Navy	51	30
N9		at TCU	10	17
N16		Army	10	14
N23	●	Southern Miss	31	10

HAWAII BOWL

D25	●	Hawaii	36	28

2003 5-7 (3-5)

S1		TCU	35	38
S6	●	Northwestern St.	27	24
S13		Mississippi State	31	28
S20	●	at Army	50	33
S27		at Texas	18	63
O11		Houston	42	45
O17		at Louisville	28	47
O25		Memphis	9	41
N1		at Navy	17	35
N8	●	at UAB	38	24
N15		at Southern Miss	14	28
N22	●	East Carolina	28	18

2004 5-6 (3-5)

S4		at Mississippi State	7	28
S11	●	Florida A&M	39	19
S25		Southern Miss	14	32
O9		at East Carolina	25	27
O16		at Memphis	24	49
O23	●	UAB	59	55
O30		at Houston	3	24
N6	●	Navy	42	10
N13	●	Army	45	31
N27	●	at TCU	35	31
D4		Louisville	7	55

THE SCHOOLS

TULSA

BY DAVE REARDON

Hard though it may be for some younger folks to believe, Tulsa was in many ways the cradle of the modern passing game. The Golden Hurricane led the nation in passing for five consecutive years in the 1960s, and in 1964, quarterback Jerry Rhome and wide receiver Howard Twilley broke 20 NCAA records for total offense, passing, receiving and scoring. Their connection led to back-to-back Heisman Trophy runner-up finishes for Rhome in 1964 and for Twilley in 1965.

College football had never seen anything like it before, and yet it was Tulsa's *second* heyday. Back in the 1940s, Tulsa became the first school to play in five consecutive New Year's Day bowl games.

Sixty years later, first-year coach Steve Kragthorpe began to resurrect a program that had won only two games in two years. In 2003, the Hurricane landed a Humanitarian Bowl berth. Fans now hope another renaissance is brewing in Tulsa, where, during the last two decades of the 20th century, basketball overshadowed football.

TRADITION For a school with such a storied past, Tulsa is surprisingly bereft of long-standing ritual. In 1988, coach Dave Rader started one with an old mechanical siren that blares loudly after Hurricane touchdowns—a late "bad weather" warning to opponents.

BEST PLAYER Glenn Dobbs was perhaps the best all-around player of his era, a tailback who was an outstanding passer and punter. From 1940 to 1942, he led Tulsa to a 25–6 record and two bowl games. In 1942, his All-America year, the Golden Hurricane charged to a 10–1 record and finished No. 4 in the final AP poll, despite a 14-7 loss to Tennessee in the Sugar Bowl. After a pro career, Dobbs coached Tulsa from 1961 to 1968. In 2000, the section of Eighth Street running in front of Skelly Stadium was renamed Glenn Dobbs Drive. Dobbs died Nov. 12, 2002.

BEST COACH After coaching Greenville (Texas) High School to a 51–5–6 record that included an undefeated state championship season in 1933, Henry Frnka needed new challenges. He found them at Tulsa, where his teams compiled a 40–9–1 record from 1941 to 1945 and played in bowl games every year. Frnka's first

PROFILE

University of Tulsa
Tulsa, Okla.
Founded: 1894
Enrollment: 2,756
Colors: Old Gold, Royal Blue and Crimson
Nickname: Golden Hurricane
Stadium: Skelly Stadium
Opened in 1930
FieldTurf; 40,385 capacity
First football game: 1895
All-time record: 521–420–27 (.552)
Bowl record: 4–8
First-round NFL draftees: 2
Website: www.tulsahurricane.com

THE BEST OF TIMES

Tulsa football made its best run during World War II. From the 1941 to 1945 seasons, the Golden Hurricane won two of the five bowl games they played in, beating Texas Tech 6-0 in the 1942 Sun Bowl and Georgia Tech 26-12 in the 1945 Orange Bowl. The 1942 team began the season with six shutouts, outscoring opponents 296-0. Tulsa was 10–0 at the end of the regular season, but lost 14-7 to Tennessee in the Sugar Bowl.

THE WORST OF TIMES

In 2001 and 2002, Tulsa won a total of two games. The Golden Hurricane went 1–15 in the Western Athletic Conference and 2–21 overall. At one point Tulsa lost 17 in a row, with only one defeat by less than a touchdown. Coach Keith Burns resigned after the 2002 season ended with the Golden Hurricane going 1–11 and tying Bernie Witucki's 0–11 team in 1954 for the most losses in school history.

CONFERENCE

Tulsa played in the Western Athletic Conference from 1996 to 2004 before joining Conference USA in 2005. Prior, TU competed in the Missouri Valley Conference (1935-85), the Big Four Conference (1929-32) and the Oklahoma Collegiate Conference (1914-28).

DISTINGUISHED ALUMNI

S.E. Hinton, author; Nancy Lopez, golfer; Rue McClanahan, actress; Mary Kay Place, actress

FIGHT SONG

HURRICANE FIGHT SONG
Down the field to victory,
On Tulsa on,
Fight on University, battle on and on.
March to the goal line, oh Tulsa,
Score on mounting score,
March to the goal line, oh Tulsa,
Let that Hurricane roar!
Drive those [opponent's name] back and back,
Onward, Tulsa, on,
Gold, Blue and Red, go right ahead
Down the field to victory!

The Golden Hurricane had been known at various times as the Kendallites, Presbyterians, Tigers, Tulsans and Orange and Black.

squad was also the first Tulsa team to go to a bowl game; the 1941 team went 8–2, won the Missouri Valley Conference with a 4–0 record and beat Texas Tech 6-0 in the Sun Bowl. That squad was enshrined in the Tulsa Hall of Fame in 2001. Frnka left Tulsa after the 1945 season to be head coach at Tulane.

BEST TEAM In 1942, Tulsa finished the regular season with the nation's only perfect record, going 10–0 and shutting out its opponents 296-0 in the first six games. Tulsa's only loss was 14-7 to Tennessee in the Sugar Bowl; the Hurricane drove to the Volunteers' 11-yard line late in the game, but faltered with an interception. Tulsa finished the season ranked fourth in the nation.

BIGGEST GAME On Jan. 1, 1942, Tulsa played in its first bowl game, coming away with a 6-0 upset of Texas Tech at the Sun Bowl. Tulsa held Texas Tech to 104 yards and four first downs, and Glenn Dobbs connected with Sax Judd for a 32-yard touchdown pass late in the game. The victory served as the springboard for the Hurricane's great 1942 season.

BIGGEST UPSET The Golden Hurricane beat heavily favored Villanova 21-19 in Philadelphia on Oct. 14, 1949. Villanova was ranked 17th and finished the season ranked 13th, its only blemish being the loss to Tulsa.

HEARTBREAKER On Jan. 1, 1953, Florida held a 14-0 lead against Tulsa in the Gator Bowl. But drives of 73 and 46 yards got the Hurricane back into the contest in the second half. Jake Roberts rushed for a three-yard touchdown and Tom Miner made the extra point to cut it to 14-7; Howard Waugh then scored on another three-yard run in the fourth quarter, but afterward Miner missed the point that would have tied the game.

RECORDS

RUSHING YARDS

GAME
312 — Mark Brus vs. New Mexico State, Oct. 27, 1990 (43 att.)

SEASON
1,464 — Michael Gunter, 1982 (195 att.)

CAREER
3,536 — Michael Gunter, 1980-83 (568 att.)

PASSING YARDS

GAME
502 — Billy Guy Anderson vs. Colorado State, Nov. 25, 1965 (37 of 57)

SEASON
3,464 — Billy Guy Anderson, 1965 (296 of 509)

CAREER
9,324 — T.J. Rubley, 1987-91 (682 of 1,336)

RECEIVING YARDS

GAME
322 — Rick Eber vs. Idaho State, Oct. 7, 1967 (20 rec.)

SEASON
1,779 — Howard Twilley, 1965 (134 rec.)

CAREER
3,343 — Howard Twilley, 1963-65 (261 rec.)

POINTS

GAME
36 — Howard Twilley vs. Louisville, Nov. 6, 1965 (5 TDs, 4 PATs, 1 two-pt. conv.)

SEASON
127 — Howard Twilley, 1965 (16 TDs, 23 PATs, 4 two-pt. conv.)

CAREER
281 — Jason Staurovsky, 1981, 1983-85 (53 FGs, 122 PATs)

CONSENSUS ALL-AMERICANS

1934	Rudy Prochaska	C
1965	Howard Twilley	E
1991	Jerry Ostroski	OL

STADIUM Skelly Field opened on Oct. 4, 1930, with an initial capacity of 14,500. That April, William Skelly had donated $125,000, and other Tulsa businessmen came up with $150,000 more to build the facility. In 1947, 5,000 seats were added and Skelly Field became Skelly Stadium. In 1987, after subsequent expansions, the largest crowd in stadium history—47,350—saw Tulsa lose to the No.1-ranked Oklahoma Sooners 65-0.

RIVAL Although it's abated a bit in recent years, the Tulsa-Oklahoma State rivalry has historically been as intense as a Saturday night in an oil patch boomtown. In the 1930s, Tulsa beat Oklahoma State in four consecutive homecoming games; the Cowboys didn't even score in any of them until the final game of the stretch (1938). The teams squared off nine times in the 1990s, with Oklahoma State winning six of the meetings. Overall, Tulsa is 28–37–5 in the series.

NICKNAME In 1922, new coach Howard Acher inherited a team known as the Yellow Jackets for the color of their uniforms. Previously, they had been called the Orange and Black, Kendallites, Presbyterians, Tigers and Tulsans. A chance remark in practice about "roaring through opponents" gave Acher the idea of renaming the team the Golden Tornadoes, but that was one of Georgia Tech's nicknames at the time. So Acher had the team vote on Golden Hurricane instead. Good call.

MASCOT Captain Cane, a colorfully costumed student with a funnel-shaped head, is the current mascot. He is a descendent of Huffy the Hurricane, who was designed by an art class in 1978; the nine-foot Huffy gave way to Captain Cane in the mid-1990s.

UNIFORMS In 1941, the team colors changed from yellow and black to blue, gold and crimson. In 2003, the Golden Hurricane unveiled a new look with gold pants and gold helmets, blue home jerseys and white road jerseys.

LORE Ellis Jones became an All-America lineman despite having just one arm. When he was 11, his right arm was amputated eight inches below the shoulder after an accident. Jones helped Tulsa to bowl game appearances in 1942, 1943 and 1944. He made three tackles for loss in a single series against the Chicago Bears in the 1944 College All-Star Game. Drafted by the NFL's Boston Yanks, he played one year for them. Jones died in 2002 at age 80.

QUOTE "It's like I've told our team on a couple of occasions. There has been a legacy that has been left for us and a torch we need to bear, because there have been some great, great football players and some great, great football teams here."—Coach Steve Kragthorpe, evoking the Golden Hurricane's past to light the way to the future

---

ALL-CENTURY TEAM

Selected by The Tulsa World *in 1999.*

OFFENSE

1942-44	Ellis Jones, OG
1988-91	Jerry Ostroski, OG
1973-76	Steve August, OT
1943-45	Bob Hellinghausen, C
1943-45	Felto Prewitt, C
1963-65	Howard Twilley, WR
1973-75	Steve Largent, WR
1987-89, 1991	Dan Bitson, WR
1963-64	Jerry Rhome, QB
1940-42	Glenn Dobbs, RB
1980-83	Michael Gunter, RB
1981, 1983-85	Jason Staurovsky, PK
1994-97	Jason Jacoby, KR

DEFENSE

1978-80	Don Blackmon, DE
1952	Bob St. Clair, DT
1964-65	Willie Townes, DT
1951-52	Marvin Matuszak, LB
1970-73	Al Humphrey, LB
1987, 1989-91	Michael White, MLB
1945-47	Hardy Brown, DB
1961-64	Jeff Jordan, DB
1966-69	Doug Wyatt, S
1976-79	Lovie Smith, S
1976-78	Eddie Hare, P

TULSA ANNUAL STATISTICAL LEADERS

YR	RUSHING	YDS	ATT	AVG	PASSING	ATT	CMP	PCT	YDS	RECEIVING	REC	YDS	AVG
1941	N.A. Keithley	297	83	3.6	Glenn Dobbs	69	34	.49	507	Cal Purdin	13	217	16.7
1942	N.A. Keithley	497	87	5.7	Glenn Dobbs	107	67	.63	1,066	Sax Judd	35	509	14.5
1943	Clyde LeForce	290	56	5.2	Clyde LeForce	90	43	.48	557	Barney White	16	188	11.8
1944	Camp Wilson	662	103	6.4	Perry Moss	77	45	.58	789	Barney White	29	531	18.3
1945	Camp Wilson	662	138	4.8	Bob Smith	42	17	.40	307	Dick Moseley	8	77	9.6
1946	Paul Barry	548	85	6.4	Clyde LeForce	125	61	.49	797	Jimmy Ford	13	186	14.3
1947	J.R. Boone	661	125	5.3	Jim Finks	136	59	.43	1,041	Jimmy Ford	17	276	16.2
1948	Paul Barry	342	90	3.8	Jim Finks	209	112	.54	1,363	Jimmy Ford	35	403	11.5
1949	Paul Barry	406	100	4.1	Pete Annex	128	65	.51	980	Fred Smith	31	441	14.2
1950	Jake Roberts	954	138	6.9	Ronnie Morris	128	61	.48	1,014	Fred Smith	34	425	12.5
1951	Howard Waugh	1,118	165	6.8	Ronnie Morris	136	74	.54	1,268	Tom Miner	31	459	14.8
1952	Howard Waugh	1,372	164	8.4	Ronnie Morris	139	78	.56	1,442	Willie Roberts	39	691	17.7
1953	Bob Decker	302	72	4.2	Bob Bohn	73	31	.42	445	Tom Miner	18	363	20.2
1954	Dick Scholtz	339	74	4.6	Mack Warren	104	39	.38	667	Kenny Kmet	16	271	16.9
1955	Dick Scholtz	395	119	3.3	Charlie Wynes	71	39	.55	476	Al Backus	11	156	14.2
1956	Dick Hughes	618	128	4.8	George Cagiola	48	25	.52	394	Ronnie Morris	9	150	16.7
1957	Ronnie Morris	569	125	4.6	George Cagiola	43	14	.33	239	Dick Brown	6	104	17.3
1958	Ronnie Morris	624	128	4.9	Jerry Keeling	99	50	.51	698	Billy Neal	14	200	14.3
1959	Bob Brumble	599	151	4.0	Jerry Keeling	144	58	.40	752	Buddy Kelly	21	270	12.9
1960	David White	444	85	5.2	Jerry Keeling	161	81	.50	1,018	Buddy Kelly	19	178	9.4
1961	David White	293	74	4.0	Ronnie Sine	94	44	.47	512	Max Letterman	21	277	13.2
1962	Henry Dorsch	250	56	4.5	Stu McBirnie	177	87	.49	1,169	John Simmons	65	860	13.2
1963	Henry Dorsch	211	48	4.4	Jerry Rhome	258	150	.58	1,909	John Simmons	39	543	13.9
1964	Bob Daugherty	456	77	5.9	Jerry Rhome	326	224	.69	2,870	Howard Twilley	95	1,178	12.4
1965	Gene Lakusiak	351	70	5.0	Billy Guy Anderson	509	296	.58	3,464	Howard Twilley	134	1,779	13.3
1966	Gene Lakusiak	330	65	5.1	Greg Barton	235	133	.57	1,673	Neal Sweeney	56	740	13.2
1967	Cee Ellison	661	153	4.3	Mike Stripling	185	86	.46	1,271	Rick Eber	78	1,168	15.0
1968	Mike Stripling	307	118	2.6	Mike Stripling	347	164	.47	1,968	Harry Wood	65	988	15.2
1969	Josh Ashton	851	231	3.7	Rick Arrington	288	141	.49	1,641	Jim Butler	46	593	12.9
1970	Josh Ashton	685	196	3.5	John Dobbs	114	44	.39	664	Jim Butler	28	245	8.8
1971	Mike Ridley	311	90	3.5	Todd Starks	263	156	.59	1,687	Jim Butler	50	484	9.7
1972	Ed White	675	160	4.2	Todd Starks	170	78	.46	1,201	Drew Pearson	33	690	20.9
1973	Freddie Carolina	540	137	3.9	Joe McCulley	227	132	.58	1,579	Freddie Carolina	38	271	7.1
1974	Thomas Bailey	456	85	5.4	Jeb Blount	260	142	.55	1,831	Steve Largent	52	884	17.0
1975	Carlisle Cantrell	914	157	5.8	Jeb Blount	218	116	.53	1,663	Steve Largent	51	1,000	19.6
1976	Rickey Watts	464	99	4.7	Ron Hickerson	247	114	.46	1,554	Cornell Webster	38	622	16.4
1977	Rickey Watts	423	108	3.9	Bill Blankenship	211	93	.44	1,293	Rickey Watts	40	639	16.0
1978	Sherman Johnson	826	169	4.9	Dave Rader	184	90	.49	1,683	Rickey Watts	34	730	21.5
1979	Paul Roberson	546	117	4.7	Bill Blankenship	84	38	.45	627	Paul Johns	20	408	20.4
1980	Ken Session	662	164	4.0	Kenny Jackson	174	80	.46	1,208	Paul Johns	29	420	14.5
1981	Brett White	740	119	6.2	Kenny Jackson	111	61	.55	806	John Green	16	252	15.8
1982	Micheal Gunter	1,464	195	7.5	Skip Ast	102	45	.44	596	Kirk Phillips	18	374	20.8
1983	Micheal Gunter	1,198	226	5.3	Steve Gage	126	66	.52	876	John Green	22	365	16.6
1984	Gordon Brown	995	159	6.3	Richie Stephenson	138	70	.51	1,134	Ronnie Kelley	27	675	25.0
1985	Gordon Brown	1,201	169	7.1	Steve Gage	141	78	.55	1,069	Ronnie Kelley	34	379	11.1
1986	Derrick Ellison	1,064	170	6.3	Steve Gage	137	57	.42	1,090	Ronnie Kelley	25	533	21.3
1987	Derrick Ellison	593	126	4.7	T.J. Rubley	313	159	.51	2,058	Dan Bitson	29	608	21.0
1988	Brett Adams	602	142	4.2	T.J. Rubley	374	182	.49	2,497	Dan Bitson	52	1,138	21.9
1989	Brett Adams	1,071	224	4.8	T.J. Rubley	308	155	.50	2,292	Dan Bitson	73	1,425	19.5
1990	Chris Hughley	700	126	5.6	Gus Frerotte	216	97	.45	1,066	Frank Cassano	31	464	15.0
1991	Chris Hughley	1,326	267	5.0	T.J. Rubley	260	148	.57	2,054	Chris Penn	37	792	21.4
1992	Lamont Headd	827	171	4.8	Gus Frerotte	249	116	.47	1,467	Gary Brown	36	560	15.6
1993	Lamont Headd	969	227	4.3	Gus Frerotte	383	214	.56	2,871	Chris Penn	105	1,578	15.0
1994	Solomon White	1,003	230	4.4	John Fitzgerald	255	136	.53	1,409	Wes Caswell	74	893	12.1
1995	Reggie Williams	729	144	5.1	Troy DeGar	245	120	.49	1,304	Michael Kedzior	44	620	14.1
1996	Reggie Williams	759	152	5.0	Troy DeGar	219	97	.44	1,336	Wes Caswell	49	817	16.7
1997	Charlie Higgins	1,043	202	5.2	John Fitzgerald	256	139	.54	2,003	Damon Savage	66	1,084	16.4
1998	Charlie Higgins	447	79	5.7	John Fitzgerald	226	131	.58	1,457	Wes Caswell	52	598	11.5
1999	John Mosley	873	160	5.5	Josh Blankenship	235	119	.51	1,416	Damon Savage	67	752	11.2
2000	Ken Bohanon	802	202	4.0	Josh Blankenship	379	196	.52	2,507	Donald Shoals	80	1,195	14.9
2001	Eric Richardson	469	131	3.6	Josh Blankenship	230	128	.56	1,350	Donald Shoals	75	908	12.1
2002	Eric Richardson	957	182	5.3	Tyler Gooch	348	190	.55	2,100	Romby Bryant	49	593	12.1
2003	Eric Richardson	811	181	4.5	James Kilian	331	188	.57	2,217	Romby Bryant	47	748	15.9
2004	Uril Parrish	1,064	210	5.1	James Kilian	337	184	.55	2,247	Garrett Mills	51	560	11.0

All statistics include postseason

TULSA ALL-TIME SCORES

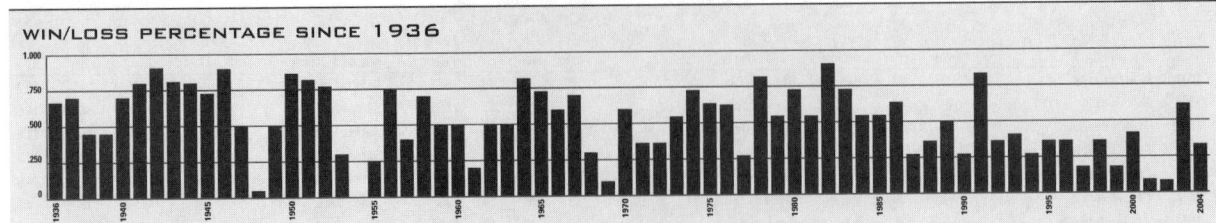

WIN/LOSS PERCENTAGE SINCE 1936

NORMAN LEARD
1895-97 (.714) — 5-2

1895 — 1-0-0
U	●	Bacone JC	NA	NA

1896 — 2-1-0
U	●	Bacone JC	NA	NA
U	●	Northeastern St.	NA	NA
U		Northeastern St.	0	6

1897 — 2-1-0
U	●	Bacone JC	NA	NA
U	●	Northeastern St.	NA	NA
U	●	Northeastern St.	NA	NA

FRED TAYLOR
1898-99 (.500) — 1-1-1

1898 — 1-0-0
U	●	Arkansas Coll.	NA	NA

1899 — 0-1-1
O28		at Arkansas	0	11
N3	=	Arkansas *Mus*	0	0

NO HEAD COACH

1900 — 2-1-0
U	●	Bacone Jr Coll. *Mus*	33	0
U	●	Krebs HS *Mus*	11	5
U	●	NE. Oklahoma *Tah*	0	18

1901 — 0-1-0
N9		at Arkansas	0	48

1902 — 0-1-0
O28		Arkansas *Mus*	0	33

1903-1904
NO TEAM

1905 — 1-2-0
U		at NE. Oklahoma	5	18
U	●	Fort Smith HS *Mus*	5	0
U		Epworth *Mus*	0	6

1906-1907
NO TEAM

SAM McBIRNEY
1908, '14-16 (.790) — 24-6-1

1908 — 2-3-0
O30		at Muskogee HS	5	10
N7		Muskogee HS	0	10
N13		at Osage Indians	11	23
N20	●	at Claremore HS	48	0
N26	●	Tulsa HS	16	0

NO HEAD COACH

1909 — 2-1-0
O8		at NE. Oklahoma	6	22
O11	●	at Claremore HS	1	0 *f*
O30	●	Claremore HS	16	11

1910 — 1-1-0
O14		at Broken Arrow HS	6	11
N11	●	at Claremore HS	3	0

1911
NO TEAM

HARVEY ALLEN
1912 (.250) — 1-3

1912 — 1-3-0
S27		at Oklahoma City	6	39
N1		at NE. Oklahoma	6	32
N18	●	at Euchee Indians	57	0
N28		Tulsa HS	6	32

GEORGE EVANS
1913 (.714) — 5-2

1913 — 5-2-0
S27	●	at Euchee Indians	92	0
O3	●	at Haskell	58	0
O10	●	Claremore HS	43	0
O24	●	NE. Oklahoma	28	0
O31	●	Oklahoma City	18	0
N14		at Pittsburg St.	25	32
N27		Tulsa HS	7	27

SAM McBIRNEY

1914 — 6-2-0
O3	●	NW. Oklahoma	33	0
O6	●	No. Okla. Jr. Coll.	47	0
O16		at Oklahoma State	6	13
O23	●	at Ea. Cent. Okla.	12	0
O31	●	at Pittsburg St.	63	0
N6	●	at Claremore HS	54	0
N13	●	at Oklahoma City	39	9
N30		Oklahoma	7	26

1915 — 6-1-1
O1	●	Ea. Okla. Jr. Coll.	62	0
O8	●	at NE. Oklahoma	55	0
O15	=	at Oklahoma State	0	0
O29	●	at NW. Oklahoma	26	6
N6		Oklahoma	13	14
N13	●	Ea. Cent. Okla.	49	3
N20	●	at SE. Oklahoma	45	7
N25	●	Haskell	7	3

1916 — 10-0-0
S30	●	Cumberland	81	0
O6	●	at Phillips	50	7
O14	●	at Oklahoma	16	0
O21	●	NW. Oklahoma	60	7
O28	●	Pittsburg St.	49	3
N4	●	Oklahoma State	17	13
N11	●	at K.C. Vet Coll.	48	10
N18	●	Haskell	46	0
N25	●	St. Gregory	82	0
N30	●	Missouri Rolla	117	0

HAL MEDFORD
1917 (.056) — 0-8-1

1917 — 0-8-1
O6		Drury Coll.	13	14
O13		Haskell	7	12
O20	=	Pittsburg St.	0	0
O27		at Arkansas	7	19
N3		at Camp Funston	6	15
N10		Denver	19	20
N17		at Oklahoma State	2	41
N24		at Oklahoma	0	80
N29		Phillips	7	20

ARTHUR SMITH
1918 (.333) — 1-2

1918 — 1-2-0
O26		at Arkansas	6	23
N2		at Ea. Cent. Okla.	3	0
N23		Oklahoma State	0	33

FRANCIS SCHMIDT
1919-21 (.862) — 24-3-2

1919 — 8-0-1
S27	●	Oklahoma Baptist	152	0
O4	●	Ea. Cent. Okla.	60	0
O11	●	at Oklahoma	27	0
O18	●	Central Okla. St.	67	6
O25	●	NW. Oklahoma	75	0
N1	●	at Arkansas	63	7
N8	●	Trinity	70	0
N15	●	Burleson Coll.	70	7
N21	=	at Oklahoma State	7	7

1920 — 10-0-1
S25	●	St. Gregory	121	0
S29	●	NE. Oklahoma	151	0
O2	●	Chilocco	88	0
O9	●	Oklahoma State	20	14 *
O16	●	at Ea. Cent. Okla.	10	0
O23	●	at Central Okla. St.	3	0
O30	●	NW. Oklahoma	14	7
N6	●	Oklahoma Baptist	81	0
N11	●	Kingfisher Coll.	88	0
N19	=	at Phillips	0	0
N26	●	Missouri Rolla	45	0

1921 — 6-3-0
O1	●	Ea. Cent. Okla.	92	0
O8	●	Chilocco	75	13
O15	●	NW. Oklahoma	17	7
O21		at TCU	0	16
O29		at Haskell	0	21
N4	●	at Oklahoma Baptist	28	0
N11		Central Okla. St.	0	21
N19	●	Kingfisher Coll.	24	7
N24	●	Phillips	21	10

HOWARD ACHER
1922-24 (.500) — 11-11-2

1922 — 8-0-0
S29	●	at Arkansas Tech	14	12
O7	●	SE. Oklahoma	26	9
O10	●	Texas A&M *DAL*	13	10
O20	●	Oklahoma Baptist	34	9
O28	●	TCU	21	0
N4	●	at Arkansas	13	6
N18	●	at SW. Oklahoma	21	14
N30	●	Central Okla. St.	14	0

1923 — 2-5-1
O11		Arkansas Tech	7	50
O27		St. Edwards	7	35
N3	=	at Tenn. Med. Coll.	6	6
N10	●	St. John's	60	0
N16		at Austin Coll.	7	13
N24		at Georgetown	0	26
D1	●	Des Moines U.	20	0
D8		Haskell	0	35

1924 — 1-6-1
O4		Haskell	3	26
O11	●	Coll. of Ozarks	7	0
O25		Central Okla. St.	0	20
N1		at Tenn. Med. Coll.	0	43
N7		at St. Edwards	7	35
N15	=	NW. Oklahoma	0	0
N22		Austin Coll.	0	9
N27		Arkansas Tech	7	24

ELMER HENDERSON
1925-35 (.725) — 70-25-5

1925 — 6-2-0
S26	●	No. Ok. JC	7	3
O3		Haskell	0	33
O10	●	Tenn. Med. Coll.	27	7
O30	●	NW. Oklahoma	42	13
N7		at Phillips	6	0
N11	●	Central Okla. St.	20	8
N20	●	at SE. Oklahoma	19	7
N28		Arkansas	7	20

1926 — 7-2-0
S25	●	SE. Oklahoma	33	10
O1	●	NW. Oklahoma	35	0
O16	●	Oklahoma State	28	0
O23	●	Phillips	19	0
O30	●	at NE. Oklahoma	17	0
N6		Oklahoma Baptist	3	12
N18	●	at Oklahoma City	13	0
N25	●	Arkansas	14	7
D4		Haskell	7	27

1927 — 8-1-0
O1	●	Parsons	19	6
O8	●	South Dakota	33	12
O15	●	at DePaul	30	6
O22	●	at Oklahoma State	28	26
O29	●	Phillips	7	13
N5	●	Oklahoma City	7	0
N11	●	Oklahoma Baptist	21	7
N19	●	SE. Oklahoma	32	0
D3	●	Haskell	24	14

1928 — 7-2-1
S29	●	NW. Oklahoma	19	0
O6		Detroit	14	19
O13	●	DePaul	27	0
O20	●	Wichita St.	46	0
O27		Phillips	26	27
N10	●	Oklahoma City	13	8
N17	=	at Oklahoma Baptist	13	13
N24	●	SE. Oklahoma	51	0
N29	●	at Oklahoma State	31	0
D8	●	Haskell	33	6

1929 — 6-3-1
S28	●	at Wichita St.	19	0
O5	●	Phillips	14	0
O12		at Detroit	6	21
O19	●	Oklahoma City	15	0
O26	=	at Phillips	7	7
N2		at Oklahoma State	0	20
N9	●	Oklahoma Baptist	7	3
N16	●	Washburn	19	7
N28	●	Oklahoma City	6	3
D7		Haskell	14	20

1930 — 7-2-0
O4	●	Arkansas	26	6
O17	●	Hendrix	27	0
O25	●	Phillips	25	0
O31	●	George Washington	14	7
N8	●	at Oklahoma Baptist	14	6
N15	●	Missouri Rolla	18	0
N27	●	Oklahoma City	33	13
D6		Haskell	7	34
D13		Oklahoma State	7	13

TULSA 901

THE SCHOOLS

1931 — 8-3-0

S25	●	Hendrix	26	0
O3	●	TCU	13	0
O9	●	Oklahoma Baptist	25	0
O16	●	at George Washington	24	7
O23	●	Creighton	28	0
O30	●	at Phillips	31	7
N7	●	U. of Mexico	89	0
N14		Oklahoma State	6	7
N26		Oklahoma City	0	14
D5	●	Haskell	6	0
D12		Oklahoma	7	20

1932 — 7-1-1

O1		at Oklahoma	0	7
O7	●	Washburn	20	0
O15	●	Phillips	21	2
O22	●	George Washington	29	14
O29	●	Oklahoma Baptist	39	13
N5	=	Oklahoma State	0	0
N11	●	Missouri Rolla	26	0
N24	●	at Oklahoma City	14	0
D3	●	Mississippi	26	0

1933 — 6-1-0

O7	●	Oklahoma	20	6
O12	●	at Washburn	7	0
O21	●	Kansas	7	0
N4		Oklahoma State	0	7
N11	●	Oklahoma City	39	0
N17	●	at George Washington	13	6
N30	●	Arkansas	7	0

1934 — 5-2-1

S21	●	Central St.	26	0
O6	●	Kansas	7	0
O13		TCU	12	14
O19		at George Washington	0	10
O27	●	Kansas State	21	0
N10	●	Centenary	14	8
N17	●	Oklahoma State	19	0
N29	=	Arkansas	7	7

1935-1985
MISSOURI VALLEY

1935 — 3-6-1 (3-0-0)

S27		Central Oklahoma	0	9
O5		at SMU	0	14
O12		TCU	0	13
O18	● |	at Washburn	19	6
O26	● |	Oklahoma State	12	0
N2	=	Kansas State	13	13
N9		at Centenary	0	22
N16		at George Washington	0	3
N23	● |	Drake	7	0
N28		Arkansas	7	14

VIC HURT
1936-38 (.603) 15-9-5

1936 — 5-2-2 (3-0-0)

S26	=	at Oklahoma	0	0
O3	●	Central Oklahoma	40	7
O10		TCU	7	10 *
O24	● |	Oklahoma State	13	0
O31	●	Kansas State	10	7
N7	=	Centenary	3	3
N14	● |	at Drake	21	6
N21	● |	Washburn	47	0
N26		Arkansas	13	23

1937 — 6-2-2 (3-0-0)

S25	●	Oklahoma	19	7
O2	●	Central Oklahoma	42	6
O9		at TCU	13	20
O16	=	at Rice	0	0
O23	● |	Oklahoma State	27	0
O29	●	at George Washington	14	13
N6	● |	Drake	41	9
N13	● |	at Washington, Mo.	32	7
N25		Arkansas	7	28
D4	=	Manhattan	0	0

1938 — 4-5-1 (3-1-0)

S24	●	Central St.	20	0
O1		Texas A&M TYL	0	20
O8	● |	Washington, Mo.	14	0
O14	● |	at St. Louis	28	0
O22	● |	Oklahoma State	20	7
O29		at Oklahoma	6	28
N5		TCU	0	21
N12	|	at Drake	7	27
N19		at Detroit	14	39
N24	=	Arkansas	6	6

CHET BENEFIEL
1939-40 (.575) 11-8-1

1939 — 4-5-1 (2-1-1)

S30	●	Wichita St.	23	6
O7	● |	at Creighton	21	14
O14	|	Oklahoma State	7	9
O21	●	Centenary	15	7
O28		Detroit	7	16
N4		at Catholic U.	7	13
N11		at TCU	0	16
N18	= |	St. Louis	0	0
N25	● |	Drake	14	0
N30		Arkansas	0	23

1940 — 7-3-0 (4-0-0)

S28	● |	Washburn	37	6
O5		Texas A&M SA	6	41
O12	● |	Creighton	32	0
O18	● |	at St. Louis	19	6
O26	●	TCU	7	0
N2	●	at Detroit	7	0
N9	●	Catholic U.	12	6
N16		at Baylor	6	20
N23	● |	Oklahoma State	19	6
N28		Arkansas	21	27

HENRY FRNKA
1941-45 (.810) 40-9-1

1941 — 8-2-0 (4-0-0)

S27		at TCU	0	6
O11	● |	Creighton	19	7
O18	● |	St. Louis	33	7
O25	● |	at Oklahoma State	16	0
N1	●	at Wichita St.	13	7
N8	●	North Dakota St.	61	6
N15	●	Baylor	20	13
N22	● |	Drake	20	6
N27		Arkansas	6	13
		SUN BOWL		
J1	●	Texas Tech	6	0

1942 — 10-1-0 (5-0-0)

S27	●	Waco AFB	84	0
O3	●	Oklahoma	23	0
O11	●	Randolph AFB	68	0
O17	● |	Washington, Mo.	40	0
O23	● |	at St. Louis	41	0
O30	● |	at Drake	40	0
N7	● |	Oklahoma State	34	6
N14	●	Baylor	24	0
N21	● |	at Creighton	33	19
N26	●	Arkansas	40	7
		SUGAR BOWL		
J1		Tennessee	7	14

1943 — 6-1-1 (1-0-0)

S25	●	at SMU	20	7
O9	●	Texas Tech	34	7
O16	●	Oklahoma OKC	20	6
O23	●	Utah	55	0
O30	=	Southwestern	6	6
N6	● |	Oklahoma State	55	6
N25	●	Arkansas	61	0
		SUGAR BOWL		
J1		Georgia Tech	18	20

1944 — 8-2-0 (0-1-0)

S23	●	Texas Arlington	47	6
O7	●	Kansas	27	0
O14	●	Texas Tech	34	7
O21	●	Mississippi MEM	47	0
O28	|	Oklahoma State	40	46
N4		Iowa Pre-Flight	27	47
N11	●	Southwestern	51	6
N23	●	Arkansas	33	2
D1	●	at Miami, Fla.	48	2
		ORANGE BOWL		
J1	●	Georgia Tech	26	12

1945 — 8-3-0 (1-1-0)

S22	●	Wichita St.	61	0
S29	●	West Texas St.	32	0
O6	● |	Drake	19	0
O13	●	at Texas Tech	18	7
O20	●	Nevada	40	0
O27		at Indiana	2	7
N10	|	at Oklahoma State	6	12
N17	●	at Baylor	26	7
N23	●	Arkansas	45	13
D1	●	Hondo AAF	20	18
		OIL BOWL		
J1		Georgia	6	20

J.O. BROTHERS
1946-52 (.635) 45-25-4

1946 — 9-1-0 (2-0-0)

S21	●	at Wichita St.	33	13
S28	●	New Mexico State	52	0
O5	● |	at Drake	48	13
O12	●	Texas Tech	21	6
O18		at Detroit	14	20
O26	●	Kansas	56	0
N2	●	Cincinnati	20	0
N9	● |	Oklahoma State	20	18
N16	●	Baylor	17	0
N28	●	Arkansas	14	13

1947 — 5-5-0 (3-0-0)

S20	●	West Texas St.	26	13
O4	● |	Drake	28	14
O11		at Texas Tech	7	14
O18		Georgetown	0	12
O25		at Nevada	13	21
N1	● |	Wichita St.	7	0
N8	● |	at Oklahoma State	13	0
N15		Baylor	6	7
N22	●	Detroit	30	20
N27		Arkansas	13	27

1948 — 0-9-1 (0-1-1)

S25		at Baylor	19	42
O2		at Florida	14	28
O9		Texas Tech	20	41
O16		Georgetown	7	13
O23		Nevada	14	65
O30	= |	at Wichita St.	14	14
N6	|	Oklahoma State	0	19
N13		South Carolina	7	27
N20		Arkansas LR	18	55
N27		Detroit	22	26

1949 — 5-5-1 (1-2-1)

S17	●	McMurry	27	26
S23	|	at Detroit	14	20
O1		Florida	7	40
O8		at Texas Tech	0	15
O14	●	at Villanova	21	19
O22	● |	Bradley	55	6
O29	|	Wichita St.	21	27
N5	= |	at Oklahoma State	13	13
N12	●	San Francisco	10	0
N19	●	Kansas State	48	27
N26		at Arkansas	7	40

1950 — 9-1-1 (3-0-1)

S16	●	McMurry	20	13
S23		at San Francisco	14	23
O7	●	at Georgetown	21	7
O14	●	Villanova	27	7
O21	= |	Detroit	13	13
O28	● |	at Bradley	74	7
N4	● |	Oklahoma State	27	13
N11	●	at Texas Tech	39	7
N18	● |	Wichita St.	48	0
N23	●	Arkansas	28	13
D2	●	at Houston	28	21

1951 — 9-2-0 (4-0-0)

S22	●	Hawaii	58	0
S29		at Cincinnati	35	47
O13	● |	Houston	46	27
O20	●	Marquette	27	21
O27	● |	at Wichita St.	33	0
N3	● |	at Oklahoma State	35	7
N10	●	Kansas State	42	26
N17	●	Texas Tech	21	14
N24		Arkansas LR	7	24
D1	● |	Detroit	34	20
D8	●	Hardin-Simmons	33	14

1952 — 8-2-1 (3-1-0)

S27	●	Hardin-Simmons	56	27
O4	=	Cincinnati	14	14
O11	|	at Houston	7	33
O18	●	Kansas State	26	7
O25	● |	Wichita St.	28	0
N1	● |	Oklahoma State	23	21
N8	●	Villanova	42	6
N14	● |	at Detroit	62	21
N22	●	Arkansas	44	34
D6	●	at Texas Tech	26	20
		GATOR BOWL		
J1		Florida	13	14

BERNIE WITUCKI
1953-54 (.143) 3-18

1953 — 3-7-0 (1-3-0)

S19		Cincinnati	7	14
S26	|	at Wichita St.	10	19
O3	●	at Pacific	22	13
O10		at Alabama	13	41
O17	●	Hardin-Simmons	14	13
O31	|	at Oklahoma State	14	28
N7	● |	Houston	23	21
N14		Texas Tech	7	49
N21	|	Detroit	0	33
N28		at Arkansas	7	27

1954 — 0-11-0 (0-4-0)

S18		Hardin-Simmons	14	21
S25		at Arkansas	0	41
O2		at Cincinnati	7	40
O9		at Alabama	0	40
O16		Kansas State	13	20
O22	|	at Detroit	18	28
O30	|	Oklahoma State	0	12
N6	|	at Houston	7	20
N13		at Texas Tech	13	55
N20		Wyoming	27	28
N25	|	Wichita St.	19	33

BOBBY DOBBS
1955-60 (.517) 30-28-2

1955 — 2-7-1 (1-3-0)

S17		at Arkansas	6	21
S24	●	Hardin-Simmons	41	19
O1		at Marquette	0	13
O15		at Wyoming	19	33
O22	=	Cincinnati	21	21
O29	|	at Oklahoma State	0	14
N5	● |	Houston	17	14
N12		Texas Tech	7	34
N19	|	Detroit	13	19
N24	|	at Wichita St.	0	54

1956 — 7-2-1 (2-1-1)

S15	●	New Mexico State	27	6
S29		at Cincinnati	6	7
O6	●	Marquette	54	0
O13	= |	Oklahoma State	14	14
O20	● |	at Detroit	3	0
O27	●	Hardin-Simmons	27	9
N3	●	Pacific	14	13
N10	|	at Houston	0	14
N17	●	Texas Tech	10	7
N24	● |	Wichita St.	14	6

1957 — 4-6-0 (2-2-0)

S21		Hardin-Simmons	0	14
S28		at Arkansas	14	41
O5		at Pacific	13	21
O12		at Oklahoma State	13	28
O19	|	North Texas	12	14
O26	●	Air Force	12	7
N9	●	at Texas Tech	3	0
N16	● |	Cincinnati	12	7
N23	|	Houston	7	13
N30	● |	at Wichita St.	24	0

1958 — 7-3-0 (2-2-0)

S20		Hardin-Simmons	0	14
S27	●	at Arkansas	27	14
O4	●	Arizona	34	0
O11	●	Oklahoma State	24	16
O18	●	Drake	59	0
O25	|	at North Texas	7	8
N1	● |	at Houston	25	20
N8	|	at Cincinnati	6	15
N15	●	Texas Tech	9	7
N27	● |	Wichita St.	25	6

1959 — 5-5-0 (2-2-0)

S19		at Arkansas	0	28
S26	●	New Mexico State	28	27
O3		at Texas Tech	7	8
O10		at Oklahoma State	0	26
O17	●	Hardin-Simmons	16	8
O24	●	Detroit	21	6
O31	|	Houston	13	22
N7	● |	Cincinnati	14	7
N14	● |	North Texas	17	6
N26	|	at Wichita St.	21	26

902 TULSA

THE SCHOOLS

1960 5-5-0 (2-1-0)

S17		New Mexico State	18	38
S24		at Arkansas	7	48
O1	●	Hardin-Simmons	21	7
O8		Oklahoma State	7	28
O15	●	at Arizona	17	16
O22	● |	at Cincinnati	34	3
O29		at Georgia	7	45
N5	|	Wichita St.	20	21
N12	● |	North Texas	12	8
N26	●	at Houston	26	16

GLENN DOBBS
1961-68 (.549) 45-37

1961 2-8-0 (1-2-0)

S16	●	Hardin-Simmons	27	0
S23		Memphis	12	48
S30		at Arkansas	0	6
O7		at Oklahoma State	0	26
O14		at Tennessee	6	52
O21	|	at North Texas	12	23
O28	|	at Wichita St.	7	9
N4	● |	Cincinnati	19	0
N11		Houston	2	14
N18		Iowa State	6	27

1962 5-5-0 (3-0-0)

S15	●	Hardin-Simmons	39	0
S29		at Arkansas	14	42
O6		Oklahoma State	7	17
O13	● |	North Texas	34	0
O20	●	Louisville	25	7
O27		at Alabama	6	35
N3	● |	at Cincinnati	24	18
N10		at Houston	31	35
N17		Toledo	18	21
N22	● |	Wichita St.	21	6

1963 5-5-0 (2-2-0)

S21	●	Montana St.	23	13
O5		at Memphis	15	28
O12	|	Cincinnati	15	21
O19	● |	at North Texas	22	21
O26		at Arkansas	7	56
N2	●	So. Illinois	49	6
N9		at Oklahoma State	24	33
N16	●	Houston	22	21
N30	|	at Wichita St.	15	26
D7	● |	Louisville	22	16

1964 9-2-0 (3-1-0)

S26		at Arkansas	22	31
O3	●	So. Illinois	63	7
O10	●	at Houston	31	23
O17	● |	at Louisville	58	0
O24	|	at Cincinnati	23	28
O31	●	Oklahoma State	61	14
N7	●	Memphis	19	7
N14	● |	North Texas	47	0
N21	●	at Toledo	39	16
N26	● |	Wichita St.	21	7
		BLUEBONNET BOWL		
D19	●	Mississippi	14	7

1965 8-3-0 (4-0-0)

S11	●	at Houston	14	0
S25		at Arkansas	12	20
O2		at Oklahoma State	14	17
O9	●	Memphis	32	28
O16	● |	at North Texas	27	20
O23	● |	Cincinnati	49	6
O30	●	at So. Illinois	55	12
N6	● |	Louisville	51	18
N20	● |	at Wichita St.	13	3
N25	●	Colorado State	48	20
		BLUEBONNET BOWL		
D18		Tennessee	6	27

1966 6-4-0 (3-1-0)

S17	●	Tampa	57	11
S24		at Arkansas	8	27
O8	●	at Colorado State	20	6
O15	● |	North Texas	30	27
O22		at Memphis	0	6
O29	● |	at Cincinnati	13	0
N5		at Houston	14	73
N12	●	Montana St.	13	10
N19	|	at Louisville	18	29
N24	● |	Wichita St.	47	14

1967 7-3-0 (3-1-0)

S30	●	at Arkansas	14	12
O7	●	Idaho St.	58	0
O14	●	Tampa	77	0
O21	● |	Cincinnati	35	6
O28		at So. Illinois	13	16
N4	● |	at Wichita St.	14	0
N11		Wake Forest	24	31
N18	|	at North Texas	12	54
N25	●	Houston	22	13
D2	● |	Louisville	35	23

1968 3-7-0 (2-3-0)

S28		at Arkansas	13	56
O5	●	So. Illinois	20	3
O12	|	at Louisville	7	16
O19	|	North Texas	17	20
O26	● |	at Cincinnati	34	27
N2	|	Memphis	6	32
N9		at Tulane	15	25
N16		at Air Force	8	28
N23		at Houston	6	100
N28	● |	Wichita St.	23	7

VINCE CARILLOT
1969 (.100) 1-9

1969 1-9-0 (1-4-0)

S20		at Colorado	14	35
S27		at Arkansas	0	55
O11		at Tampa	14	31
O18		Florida State	20	38
O25	● |	Cincinnati	40	24
N1	|	at Memphis	24	42
N8		Houston	14	47
N15	|	at North Texas	16	42
N22	|	at Wichita St.	12	28
N27	|	Louisville	29	35

CLAUDE GIBSON
1970-72 (.407) 11-16

1970 6-4-0 (3-1-0)

S12	●	Cincinnati	7	3
S19	●	Idaho St.	38	13
S26		at Arkansas	7	49
O3	● |	Memphis	27	12
O10	|	at Louisville	8	14
O17		at Virginia Tech	14	17
O31		at Houston	9	21
N7	● |	Wichita St.	21	12
N21	●	Idaho	30	17
D5	● |	North Texas	26	20

1971 4-7-0 (1-1-0)

S18		Kansas State	10	19
S25	●	at Arkansas	21	20
O2	●	at West Texas St.	17	13
O9	●	Virginia Tech	46	39
O16		at Wake Forest	21	51
O23		Brigham Young	7	25
O30		at Tennessee	3	38
N6	|	Louisville	0	17
N13		Air Force	7	17
N20		at Florida State	10	45
N27	● |	at Wichita St.	31	13

F.A. DRY
1972-76 (.630) 31-18-1

1972 4-7-0 (3-1-0)

S9		at Kansas State	13	21
S16	● |	Wichita St.	10	9
S23		Houston	0	21
S30		at Arkansas	20	21
O7		at Texas Tech	18	35
O14		TCU	9	35
O28	|	at Memphis	21	49
N4	● |	at Louisville	28	26
N11		at Florida State	21	23
N18	●	Montana	10	7
N25	● |	North Texas	45	22

1973 6-5-0 (5-1-0)

S15	● |	West Texas St.	48	3
S22		at Kansas State	0	21
S29	●	Cincinnati	16	13
O6	● |	Drake	44	7
O13		at Memphis	16	28
O20	● |	New Mexico State	52	14
O27		Arkansas [LR]	6	20
N3	● |	Louisville	17	9
N17	● |	at North Texas	24	15
N24	|	at Wichita St.	19	28
D1		at Houston	16	35

1974 8-3-0 (6-0-0)

S14		at Kansas State	14	31
S21	● |	North Texas	31	6
S28		at Arkansas	0	60
O5		at Tennessee	10	17
O12	● |	Wichita St.	35	13
O19	● |	West Texas St.	17	14
O26	●	at Tampa	31	21
N2	● |	at Louisville	37	7
N9	● |	New Mexico State	28	7
N16	● |	at Drake	52	14
N30	●	Houston	30	14

1975 7-4-0 (4-0-0)

S13		Kansas State	16	17
S20	● |	at West Texas St.	23	14
S27		at Arkansas	15	31
O4	● |	at New Mexico State	35	7
O11	●	Cincinnati	24	16
O18	● |	at Wichita St.	41	10
O25		Memphis	14	16
N1	●	Louisville	38	14
N8	● |	Drake	70	7
N15	●	Indiana St.	62	7
N29		at Houston	30	42

1976 7-4-1 (2-1-1)

S4	●	Richmond	22	7
S11		at Oklahoma State	21	33
S18	●	Memphis	16	14
S25	●	at Arkansas	9	3
O2	● |	New Mexico State	32	7
O16		at Cincinnati	7	16
O30	●	at Louisville	20	10
N6	●	at Virginia Tech	35	31
N13	● |	at Drake	45	20
N20	|	Wichita St.	13	30
N27	= |	West Texas St.	17	17
		INDEPENDENCE BOWL		
D13		McNeese St.	16	20

JOHN COOPER
1977-84 (.636) 56-32

1977 3-8-0 (2-2-0)

S3		at La. Lafayette	21	48
S10		Oklahoma State	17	34
S17	●	La. Monroe	37	35
S24		at Arkansas	3	37
O1	|	Wichita St.	26	38
O8		at Louisville	0	33
O22		at Cincinnati	0	28
O29		at San Diego State	7	41
N5	● |	at Drake	33	23
N12	● |	New Mexico State	27	24
N19	|	at West Texas St.	21	57

1978 9-2-0 (3-1-0)

S2	●	Arkansas State	21	20
S9	●	at Virginia Tech	35	33
S16	●	La. Lafayette	10	3
S23	●	Kansas State	24	14
S30		at Arkansas	13	21
O7	●	Louisville	24	7
O14	|	at New Mexico State	20	23
O21	●	at Cincinnati	27	26
O28	● |	Drake	44	20
N4	● |	West Texas St.	44	23
N11	● |	at Wichita St.	27	13

1979 6-5-0 (2-0-0)

S1		McNeese St.	3	6
S8	●	at Air Force	24	7
S15	●	La. Lafayette	28	20
S22		at Oklahoma	13	49
S29		at Arkansas	8	33
O6	●	at Kansas State	9	6
O13		at Louisville	7	24
O20		TCU	17	24
O27	●	at Florida	20	10
N3	● |	Wichita St.	28	26
N10	● |	New Mexico State	38	16

1980 8-3-0 (2-1-0)

S13	●	Cincinnati	31	13
S20	|	at Wichita St.	10	23
S27		at Arkansas	10	13
O4	●	Kansas State	3	0
O11	●	North Texas	28	27
O18	●	at TCU	23	17
O25	● |	West Texas St.	44	24
N1		at Florida State	2	45
N8	●	Indiana St.	30	7
N15	●	at So. Illinois	41	7
N22	● |	at New Mexico State	21	20

1981 6-5-0 (4-0-0)

S5		Kansas	11	15 †
S12		at Arkansas	10	14
S19		at Oklahoma State	21	23
S26		So. Illinois	34	36
O3	●	Kansas State	35	21
O17	●	at Indiana St.	20	19
O24	● |	Wichita St.	52	21
O31	● |	Drake	59	6
N7	● |	New Mexico State	31	0
N14	● |	at West Texas St.	24	10
N21		at Arkansas State	7	31

1982 10-1-0 (4-0-0)

S4	●	Air Force	35	17
S11		at Arkansas	0	38
S19	●	Oklahoma State	25	15
O2	●	at Kansas	20	15
O9	● |	at New Mexico State	31	14
O16	●	So. Illinois	22	3
O23	● |	at Drake	34	18
O30	● |	at Wichita St.	30	21
N6	● |	West Texas St.	59	21
N13	●	Indiana St.	48	14
N20	●	at North Texas	38	20

1983 8-3-0 (4-0-0)

S3	●	San Diego State	34	9
S10		at Arkansas	14	17
S17	●	Northwestern St.	26	19
S24		at Oklahoma	18	28
O1		at Oklahoma State	0	9
O8	● ||	New Mexico State	24	10
O15	●	Illinois St.	39	25
O22	●	at Texas Tech	59	20
O29	● |	Wichita St.	30	19
N5	● |	at Drake	22	13
N12	● |	West Texas St.	31	16

1984 6-5-0 (2-0-0)

S1	●	So. Illinois	23	10
S15		at Brigham Young	15	38
S22		at Arkansas	9	18
S29		Oklahoma State	7	31
O5	● |	at West Texas St.	35	7
O13		East Carolina	31	20
O20	● |	Wichita St.	55	20
O27		Texas Tech	17	20
N3	●	at Illinois St.	28	7
N10	●	at Indiana St.	24	17
N17		La. Lafayette	17	18

DON MORTON
1985-86 (.591) 13-9

1985 6-5-0 (3-0-0)

S7	●	Houston	31	24
S14		Texas Tech	17	21
S21		Arkansas [LR]	0	24
S28		at Texas A&M	10	45
O5		at Oklahoma State	13	25
O12	●	Long Beach St.	37	35
O19		at Florida State	14	76
O26	● |	West Texas St.	44	17
N2	● |	at Wichita St.	42	26
N9	● |	Drake	45	15
N16	●	at East Carolina	21	20

1986-1995
INDEPENDENT

1986 7-4-0

A30		Louisiana Tech	17	22
S6	●	Tennessee Tech	51	0
S13	●	Oklahoma State	27	23
S20		at Arkansas	17	34
S27	●	at Houston	24	14
O2	●	Fullerton St.	20	10
O11		at La. Lafayette	13	17
O18	●	Central Michigan	42	6
N1	●	Wichita St.	38	10
N8	●	at New Mexico	34	27
N15		at Miami, Fla.	10	23

GEORGE HENSHAW
1987 (.273) 3-8

1987 3-8-0

S5		at Oklahoma State	28	39
S12		at Florida	0	52
S19		at Arkansas	15	30
S26		Oklahoma	0	65
O3	●	at Kansas State	37	25
O10	●	at Temple	24	17
O17		at Central Michigan	18	41
O24		at Texas Tech	7	42
O31	●	Louisville	26	22
N7		No. Arizona	20	24
N21		Memphis	0	14

DAVID RADER
1988-99 (.381)   49-80-1

1988   4-7-0
S3	•	Kansas State	35 9
S10		at Arkansas	26 30
S24		Texas-El Paso	24 27
O1		at Oklahoma State	35 56
O8		at Louisville	3 9
O15		at Houston	28 82
O29	•	at Nevada-Las Vegas	33 7
N5		at Miami, Fla.	3 34
N12		at Memphis	20 26
N19	•	Temple	15 10
N26	•	Colorado State	32 28

1989   6-6-0
S2	•	at Texas-El Paso	23 14
S9	•	Oklahoma State	20 10
S16		at Arkansas	7 26
S23	•	New Mexico	35 33
S30		at Iowa	22 30
O7		at La. Lafayette	13 21
O14	•	New Mexico State	34 13
O21	•	Louisville	31 24
O28		at Louisiana Tech	31 34
N11		at Wake Forest	17 29
N18	•	Bowling Green	45 10
		INDEPENDENCE BOWL	
D16		Oregon	24 27

1990   3-8-0
S1		at Oklahoma State	3 10
S8	•	SW. Missouri St.	41 28
S15		at Arkansas	3 28
S22		at Oklahoma	10 52
S29		Memphis	10 22
O6		at Louisville	14 38
O13		Louisiana Tech	21 35
O20		La. Lafayette	13 25
O27	•	at New Mexico State	35 10
N10		at Colorado State	13 31
N17		Montana St.	20 2

1991   10-2-0
A31	•	SW. Missouri St.	34 13
S7	•	Oklahoma State	13 7
S14		at Kansas	17 23
S21	•	Texas A&M	35 34
S28		Miami, Fla.	10 34
O12	•	at La. Lafayette	34 20
O26		at Memphis	33 28
N2	•	Southern Miss	13 10
N16	•	Louisville	40 0
N23	•	Ohio U.	45 13
N30	•	at SMU	31 26
		FREEDOM BOWL	
D30	•	San Diego State	28 17

1992   4-7-0
S5	•	Houston	28 25
S12		at Texas A&M	9 19
S19		Kansas	7 40
S26		at Oklahoma State	19 24
O3		at Southern Miss	24 33
O10	•	SW. Missouri St.	17 14
O17		at Louisville	27 32
O24		Memphis	25 30
O31	•	La. Lafayette	27 9
N7		Texas-El Paso	48 39
N28		at Hawaii	9 38

1993   4-6-1
S4	•	at Iowa	25 26
S11	•	at Houston	38 24
S18		Oklahoma State	10 16
S25		at Oklahoma	20 41
O2		Cincinnati	15 22
O16		at Memphis	23 19
O30	•	Middle Tennessee	38 17
N6	•	at East Carolina	52 26
N13		at Arkansas	11 24
N20	=	Southern Miss	30 30
N25		Louisville	0 28

1994   3-8-0
S3	•	at Missouri	20 17
S10		Memphis	18 42
S17		at Wyoming	7 17
S24		at Oklahoma State	10 17
O8		Texas-El Paso	17 24
O15	•	Nevada-Las Vegas	44 22
O22		East Carolina	21 28
O29		at Southern Miss	29 47
N12	•	SW. Missouri St.	38 28
N19		at Cincinnati	13 28
N26		at Louisville	27 34

1995   4-7-0
S2		Baylor	5 37
S9	•	Oklahoma State	24 23
S16		at Texas A&M	9 52
S23	•	East Tenn. St.	45 20
S30		at Louisiana Tech	23 27
O7	•	Wyoming	35 6
O14	•	at Texas-El Paso	38 28
O28		at Memphis	7 10
N4		at Brigham Young	35 45
N11		at East Carolina	7 28
N18		Cincinnati	5 24

1996-2004
WAC

1996   4-7 (2-6)
A31	|	at SMU	10 17
S14	|	at Oklahoma State	9 30
S21	• |	Iowa	27 20
S28	• |	at Oklahoma	31 24
O12	• |	Colorado State	20 14
O19	|	Brigham Young	30 55
O26	|	at Utah	19 45
N2	|	New Mexico	23 34
N9	|	TCU	24 31
N16	• |	at Texas-El Paso	38 21
N23	|	at Rice	14 42

1997   2-9 (2-6)
A28	|	at Cincinnati	24 34
S13	|	at Iowa	16 54
S20	|	Missouri	21 42
O4	|	Rice	24 42
O11	|	Texas-El Paso	18 33
O18	• |	at TCU	33 22
O26	|	at Colorado State	8 44
N1	• |	Utah	21 13
N8	|	at Brigham Young	39 49
N15	|	SMU	41 42
N22	|	at New Mexico	13 51

1998   4-7 (2-6)
S5	• |	SW. Missouri St.	49 14
S12	• |	Oklahoma State	35 20
S26	|	at West Virginia	21 44
O3	|	San Diego State	14 24
O10	|	at Colorado State	7 34
O17	|	at Rice	10 14
O24	|	Air Force	21 42
O31	• |	at Nevada-Las Vegas	20 16
N7	|	at SMU	3 33
N14	|	TCU	7 17
N21	• |	Wyoming	35 0

PAT HENDERSON
1999 (.250)   1-3

1999   2-9 (1-6)
S4	• |	SW. Missouri St.	45 21
S11	|	at Oklahoma State	9 46
S18	|	at Texas A&M	13 62
S25	|	at San Jose State	10 34
O2	|	Rice	10 20
O16	|	at TCU	17 56
O23	|	Hawaii	21 35
O30	|	Fresno State	14 28
N6	• |	at Texas-El Paso	43 19
N13	|	La. Monroe	34 37
N20	|	SMU	14 28

KEITH BURNS
2000-02 (.200)   7-28

2000   5-7 (4-4)
S2	|	at North Carolina	9 30
S9	|	Oklahoma State	26 36
S16	• |	at Rice	23 16
S23	• |	Louisiana Tech	22 10
S30	• |	at Hawaii	24 14
O7	|	Texas-El Paso	7 40
O14	|	at New Mexico State	28 42
O21	|	TCU	3 17
O28	|	at Fresno State	12 34
N11	|	at SMU	20 24
N18	• |	San Jose State	28 17
N25	• |	Nevada	38 3

2001   1-10 (0-8)
A30	• |	Indiana St.	51 0
S22	|	Fresno State	18 37
S29	|	at Texas-El Paso	10 26
O6	|	New Mexico State	7 24
O13	|	at Boise State	10 41
O20	|	Hawaii	15 36
O27	|	at San Jose State	27 63
N3	|	at Oklahoma	0 58
N10	|	at Rice	32 59
N17	|	SMU	14 24
N24	|	Louisiana Tech	7 19

2002   1-11 (1-7)
A30	|	Oklahoma	0 37
S7	• |	at Arkansas State	19 21
S14	|	at Louisiana Tech	9 53
S21	|	at Baylor	25 37
S28	|	Kansas	33 43
O12	|	Boise State	24 52
O19	|	at Hawaii	14 37
O26	• |	Texas-El Paso	20 0
N2	|	Rice	18 33
N9	|	at Fresno State	12 31
N16	|	San Jose State	38 49
N23	|	at SMU	21 24

STEVE KRAGTHROPE
2003-Present (.480)   12-13

2003   8-5 (6-2)
A30	|	at Minnesota	10 49
S6	|	at Arkansas	13 45
S13	• |	Texas St.	41 15
S20	• |	Arkansas State	54 7
O4	• |	Hawaii	27 16
O11	|	at Boise State	20 27
O18	|	Nevada	21 28
O25	• |	SMU	35 16
N1	• |	at Texas-El Paso	56 28
N8	• |	at Rice	31 28
N15	• |	Louisiana Tech	48 18
N22	• |	at San Jose State	34 32
		HUMANITARIAN BOWL	
J3		Georgia Tech	10 52

2004   4-8 (3-5)
S4	|	at Kansas	3 21
S11	|	at Oklahoma State	21 38
S18	|	Navy	0 29
S25	• |	S.W. Missouri St.	49 7
O2	• |	at Hawaii	16 44
O16	|	Boise State	42 45
O23	|	at Nevada	48 54
O30	• |	Rice	39 22
N6	|	at SMU	35 41
N13	|	at Louisiana Tech	21 38
N20	• |	San Jose State	34 24
N27	• |	Texas-El Paso	37 35

THE SCHOOLS

UAB

BY KEVIN GLEASON

IT'S HARD TO BELIEVE THAT IT WASN'T until 1991 that UAB played its first varsity football game, losing 28-0 to Millsaps College in a Division III contest in Jackson, Miss. Two years later, UAB moved to Division I-AA, and in 1996, became a Division 1-A football program. Too far, too fast? Hardly. The Blazers have proved they belong, as both a Division 1-A team and a member of Conference USA.

UAB beat Houston 29-10 in its first conference game in 1999 and finished tied for second place in the league. In 2001, UAB came within a 3-0 loss to Southern Mississippi of winning a share of the C-USA title. Through the 2004 season the Blazers had the third-best league record since 1999. Only Louisville (34–10) and Southern Mississippi (32–12) fared better than UAB (25–19).

"We've not had any bad teams," head coach Watson Brown said before the 2004 season. "We've always had good teams. Now we want that great team." Brown can take credit for much of the success. A former head coach at Vanderbilt, Cincinnati and Rice, he took over in 1995 as the school's second football coach (Dr. Jim Hilyer was

27–12–2 in four seasons), and immediately started scouring the state for players turned away or ignored completely by Alabama and Auburn. Since those players generally feel that they have something to prove, Brown sounded like the coach of an underdog when he said, "I think the program has been very consistent and we're proud of that, but I think somewhat, what we have done has been underappreciated."

TRADITION Tradition? We're talking about a program that didn't celebrate perhaps the greatest of all college football traditions, homecoming day, until 1994. Before that, homecoming activities took place during basketball season. To its credit, UAB won nine of its first 11 homecoming games. But just as impressive has been its knack for spoiling opponent homecomings. A shocking upset of LSU in 2000 is the best example. UAB is 4–4–1 in road homecoming games, including a 19-14 win at North Texas in 1995, the school's biggest D1-A win to that point.

BEST PLAYER Defensive end Bryan Thomas may have been a better talent. Linebacker Zac Woodfin was a Butkus Award nominee. But nobody made an impact at UAB quite like defensive tackle Josh Evans. Evans has a special place in the hearts of UAB fans as one of 16 players to participate on each of the first four teams in program history (1991-94).

PROFILE

University of Alabama at Birmingham
Birmingham, Ala.
Founded: 1969
Enrollment: 11,441
Colors: Forest Green and Old Gold
Nickname: Blazers
Stadium: Legion Field
  Opened in 1927
  Grass; 83,091 capacity
First football game: 1991
All-time record: 81–71–2 (.532)
Bowl record: 0–1
First-round NFL draftees: 2
Website: www.uabsports.com

THE BEST OF TIMES

UAB finished 5–3, tied for second place in Conference USA and received its first bowl berth in 2004.

THE WORST OF TIMES

This is a program that hasn't been worse than its 4–7 record in 1998.

CONFERENCE

UAB played Division III ball its first two seasons before moving into D1-AA in 1993. The Blazers were a D1-A independent from 1996 to 1998, then joined Conference USA to start the 1999 season. UAB has responded by twice finishing tied for second.

DISTINGUISHED ALUMNI

Murry Bartow, college basketball coach; Deidre Downs, 2004 Miss America; Vonetta Flowers, 2002 Olympic bobsled gold medalist

FIGHT SONG

UAB FIGHT SONG
At UAB in Birmingham
All hail our players bold
They are the mighty Blazers
Who wear the Green and Gold.
Tonight let's fire their golden blaze
The flame of victory
Go Blazers! Go Blazers! Win for UAB! WIN FOR UAB!

Evans stuffed the run and rushed the quarterback with similar fervor, recording 72 tackles and five sacks his senior season. In 2002, Thomas became UAB's first player taken in the first round of the NFL draft, 22nd by the Jets.

BEST COACH UAB still has nowhere near the facilities of most Division I-A schools. But it has Watson Brown, and that counts for a lot. Brown has been the brains behind UAB's remarkable ascension, and his specialty is offense. He was offensive coordinator for Oklahoma in 1993-94 and at Mississippi State in 1991-92, when the Bulldogs went 14–10, played in two bowl games and upset two nationally ranked teams. Brown, a star quarterback for Vanderbilt from 1969 to 1972, continues to raise the bar. "We're hungry right now and I think the kids are anxious," he said before the 2004 season. "We want to get back up to seven or eight wins or more and [we] have the goal of a conference championship."

BEST TEAM The 2001 squad stands above the rest. The Blazers went 5–2 in Conference USA—earning a three-way tie for second place—and 6–5 overall, spearheaded by one of the best defenses in the country. UAB allowed 57 yards

> ## UAB has struggled to draw fan support in a state divided by loyalties to Alabama and Auburn.

rushing a game, and held Houston to minus-6 yards rushing in a 43-21 win. The offense wasn't bad either, as Army learned in UAB's 55-3 rout of the Black Knights just 11 days after 9/11.

BIGGEST GAME Blazers fans still talk about the 13-10 upset of LSU before 83,000 fans in Death Valley in 2000. Rhett Gallego made two field goals, including a 32-yarder as time expired, and quarterback Daniel Dixon came off the bench and hit Leron Little with a 24-yard touchdown pass. UAB intercepted four passes from heralded quarterback Josh Booty, including Chris Brown's pick that helped set up the game-winning kick.

BIGGEST UPSET UAB stunned No. 18 East Carolina 36-17 in 1999—just its fifth C-USA contest—to win its first game over a nationally ranked team.

HEARTBREAKER UAB was coming off a 55-3 rout of Army 11 days after Sept. 11, 2001—the day of the terrorist attacks. But the Blazers followed it up with a 3-0 loss at Southern Mississippi. The Blazers lost to Cincinnati 31-17 two weeks later, but the Southern Miss loss stayed with

RECORDS

RUSHING YARDS

	GAME
240	Carl Sanders vs. Charleston Southern, Nov. 21, 1996 (20 att.)
	SEASON
1,154	Carl Sanders, 1996 (168 att.)
	CAREER
2,817	Pat Green, 1991-94 (630 att.)

PASSING YARDS

	GAME
539	John Whitcomb vs. Prairie View A&M, Nov. 19, 1994 (33 of 42)
	SEASON
3,070	Darrell Hackney, 2004 (197 of 358)
	CAREER
7,420	John Whitcomb, 1992-94 (560 of 947)

RECEIVING YARDS

	GAME
289	Derrick Ingram vs. Prairie View A&M, Nov. 19, 1994 (12 rec.)
	SEASON
1,457	Derrick Ingram, 1994 (83 rec.)
	CAREER
3,379	Derrick Ingram, 1991-94 (207 rec.)

POINTS

	GAME
24	Keith Roland vs. Louisiana-Lafayette, Oct. 19, 1996 (4 TDs)
	SEASON
86	Kevin Thomason, 1993 (15 FGs, 41 PATs)
	CAREER
288	Nick Hayes, 2001-04 (57 FGs, 117 PATs)

CONSENSUS ALL-AMERICANS

1994	Derrick Ingram, WR

UAB. They finished 5–2 in Conference USA and missed a share of the league title by one game.

RIVAL Yes, teams can be rivals when one dominates the series. UAB exited the 2004 season with an 0–5 record against Southern Mississippi. But losing the five games by a combined 23 points has only refined the Blazers' determination. Consider that Southern Miss won 26-21 in 2004, 17-12 in 2003 and 20-13 in 2002 at Legion Field, 3-0 in 2001 in Hattiesburg and 33-30 in two overtimes in 2000 at Legion Field. In 2003, 44,669 people came out to Legion Field for the ESPN2 game, at the time the largest crowd in C-USA history for a game involving conference schools. Of course, UAB spent weeks trying to drum up fan support for the Southern Miss game, going so far as to partner with *The Birmingham News* on a promotion that gave away tickets. UAB's closest neighbors, Auburn and Alabama, have shunned the Blazers. In fact, they are the Blazers' principal rivals: UAB has always struggled to draw fan support in a state divided by loyalties to the Crimson Tide and the Tigers.

STADIUM Legion Field got its name in 1927 in honor of the American Legion. But the lasting memory of the 83,091-seat football shrine is of Paul "Bear" Bryant roaming the sideline as Alabama's coach. Legion Field has also served as the home of the Birmingham Americans and Birmingham Vulcans of the World Football League, Birmingham Stallions of the United States Football League, Birmingham Fire of the World League of American Football, Birmingham Barracudas of the Canadian Football League and Birmingham Bolts of the XFL. UAB is 52–23–1 in 14 seasons at Legion Field.

NICKNAME The Portland Trail Blazers actually helped UAB come up with the Blazers nickname. The NBA team was enjoying unprecedented popularity in the late-1970s, highlighted by its 1977 championship led by shaggy-haired center Bill Walton. The summer of 1977 brought UAB's first athletics director and basketball coach, Gene Bartow, and the following fall, in 1978, UAB played its first sports season. The name had a particular resonance, with UAB blazing a new trail in college sports.

MASCOT Before UAB ever had a mascot, it had a symbol, a stylized arrow that looked a little like a stealth bomber and a little like a badminton shuttlecock. What the arrow stood for is anybody's guess. As one former sports information employee put it, the arrow "really didn't look like anything." In the late 1980s, UAB tried a crazy looking mascot named Reinegard D. Rooster, which looked more like the San Diego Chicken than anything else. In the early 1990s the school went to its first dragon, a menacing creature that drew criticism for being too fierce looking, to the point where it scared some children. Then came Blaze, the friendly dragon that has become UAB's dominant logo in the new millennium.

UNIFORMS After sporting green helmets for its first four years of football, UAB went to a Notre Dame-like gold helmet bearing "UAB" in 1995. In 1996, the school added the dragon logo to both sides of its helmets, which are still gold with green face masks and a green stripe extending front to back.

LORE Head coach Watson Brown's brother, Mack, is head coach at Texas. Their grandfather, Eddie "Jelly" Watson, was a well-known high school coach in Tennessee for 30 years.

QUOTE "This team should have been playing in bowls two and three seasons ago. I don't mind talking about that. We want to get one of those bowl bids and the next step is trying to win a conference championship."—Watson Brown

UAB ANNUAL STATISTICAL LEADERS

YR	RUSHING	YDS	ATT	AVG	PASSING	ATT	CMP	PCT	YDS	RECEIVING	REC	YDS	AVG
1996	Carl Sanders	1,154	168	6.9	Rodney Hudson	194	77	.40	1,176	Kenny Causey	24	482	20.1
1997	Lucious Foster	737	149	4.9	Lee Jolly	209	108	.52	1,530	Kevin Drake	38	823	21.7
1998	Lucious Foster	568	100	5.7	Daniel Dixon	139	69	.50	870	Darrius Malone	24	530	22.1
1999	Percy Coleman	689	122	5.6	Daniel Dixon	245	127	.52	1,347	Darrius Malone	33	551	16.7
2000	Jegil Dugger	852	177	4.8	Jeff Aaron	182	100	.55	1,135	Percy Coleman	34	256	7.5
2001	Jegil Dugger	839	218	3.8	Jeff Aaron	148	77	.52	828	Willie Quinnie	36	460	12.8
2002	Dan Burks	554	124	4.5	Darrell Hackney	293	149	.51	1,977	Roddy White	39	580	14.9
2003	Trey Chaney	479	136	3.5	Darrell Hackney	209	106	.51	1,659	Roddy White	39	844	21.6
2004	Dan Burks	880	164	5.4	Darrell Hackney	358	197	.55	3,070	Roddy White	71	1,452	20.5

Receiving leaders by receptions
The NCAA began including postseason stats in 2002

UAB ALL-TIME SCORES

WIN/LOSS PERCENTAGE SINCE 1996

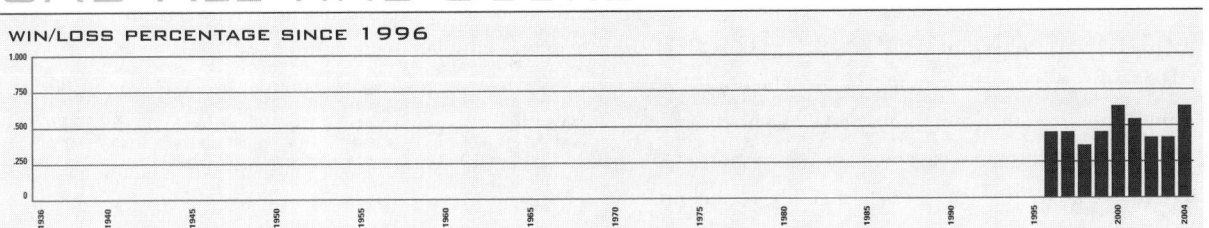

WATSON BROWN		
1995-PRESENT (.478)		54-59

1996 5-6
A31	at Auburn	0	29
S7	at Maryland	15	39
S14 ●	Arkansas State	42	17
S21 ●	Jacksonville St.	24	17
O5 ●	Western Kentucky	24	0
O19 ●	La. Lafayette	39	29
O26	at Louisiana Tech	31	35
N2	at Vanderbilt	15	31
N9	Central Florida	13	35
N16	Cincinnati	14	34
N21 ●	Charleston So.	49	13

1997 5-6
A28	at Kansas	0	24
S6	at Memphis	7	28
S13	at Arizona	10	24
S20 ●	Jacksonville St.	34	16
S27 ●	at La. Lafayette	42	7
O4 ●	Western Kentucky	20	16
O11	at Cincinnati	29	33
N1	at Virginia Tech	0	37
N8	Louisiana Tech	29	32
N15 ●	Tennessee Tech	38	14
N22 ●	at Arkansas State	13	7

1998 4-7
S5	at Nebraska	7	38
S19 ●	Tennessee Tech	38	6
S26	Kansas	37	39
O3 ●	La. Lafayette	24	13
O10	at East Carolina	7	26
O17	at Louisiana Tech	23	54
O24	Virginia Tech	0	41
O31	at La. Monroe	14	20
N7	at Tennessee	13	37
N14 ●	Middle Tennessee	26	17
N21 ●	Tenn. Martin	48	17

1999-PRESENT		
C-USA		

1999 5-6 (4-2)
S4	at Missouri	28	31
S11	at Virginia Tech	10	31
S25 ●	Houston	29	10
O2 ●	La. Monroe	47	0
O9	Memphis	14	38
O16 ●	at Cincinnati	24	21
O23	at Wake Forest	3	47
O30	at Louisville	14	23
N6 ●	East Carolina	36	17
N13	Louisiana Tech	20	41
N20 ●	at Tulane	23	20

2000 7-4 (3-3)
S7 ●	U.T. Chattanooga	20	15
S16	at Kansas	20	23
S23 ●	at LSU	13	10
S30 ●	La. Lafayette	47	2
O7	Louisville	17	38
O14 ●	Memphis	13	9
O21 ●	Middle Tennessee	14	9
O28 ●	at East Carolina	16	13
N4	at Cincinnati	21	33
N11	Southern Miss	30	33
N18 ●	at Army	27	7

2001 6-5 (5 2)
A30 ●	Montana St.	41	13
S8	at Florida State	7	29
S22 ●	Army	55	3
S29	at Southern Miss	0	3
O6	at Central Florida	7	24
O13	Cincinnati	17	31
O20 ●	Tulane	34	27
O27 ●	at Memphis	17	14
N10 ●	TCU	38	17
N17 ●	at Houston	43	21
D1	at Pittsburgh	6	24

2002 5-7 (4-4)
A31	at Florida	3	51
S7 ●	Troy State	27	26
S14	Pittsburgh	20	26
S21	at La. Lafayette	0	34
S28 ●	Memphis	31	17
O12 ●	Houston	51	34
O19	at Tulane	14	35
O26 ●	at Army	29	26
N9	Southern Miss	13	20
N16 ●	East Carolina	36	29
N23	at Louisville	21	41
N30	at Cincinnati	23	31

2003 5-7 (4-4)
A30 ●	at Baylor	24	19
S4	Southern Miss	12	17
S13	Troy State	9	20
S20	at South Carolina	10	42
O4 ●	at Memphis	24	10
O11 ●	Cincinnati	31	14
O18	at TCU	24	27
O25	at Georgia	13	16
N1 ●	Army	24	9
N8	Tulane	24	38
N22 ●	at South Florida	22	19
N29	at Houston	28	56

2004 7-5 (5-3)
S4 ●	Baylor	56	14
S18	at Florida State	7	34
S25 ●	Memphis	35	28
O2 ●	at Cincinnati	30	27
O9 ●	at Mississippi State	27	13
O15 ●	TCU	41	25
O23	at Tulane	55	59
N6	South Florida	20	45
N13	Houston	20	7
N20 ●	at Army	20	14
N27	at Southern Miss	21	26
	HAWAII BOWL		
D24	Hawaii	40	59

---

f Forfeit † Game Later Forfieted # Disputed Victor * Disputed Score || Designated Conference Game |2 Counted Twice in Conference Standings

UCLA

BY BUD WITHERS

NO PROGRAM SYMBOLIZES THE national perception of West Coast football more than UCLA, a place where the players always seem faster, the sun brighter and the cheerleaders prettier. In reality, the Bruins are a distant second to USC in conference championships among Pac-10 teams.

Pretty good for a team that didn't exist before 1919, a much later start than most of its West Coast brethren. But UCLA's performance has sometimes fallen short of the promise of bountiful high school talent in the region. Brian Bosworth, the notorious Oklahoma linebacker, accused the Bruins of playing "girls football," and while that's a rude way to say it, UCLA has had to work at living down its soft image.

TRADITION On game day at the Rose Bowl, the team walks through fans in the main tailgate area to the dressing room. Fans wave "12th Bruin" towels sold by vendors.

BEST PLAYER The son of a San Francisco longshoreman, Gary Beban was a high school single-wing tailback who chose UCLA over Oregon State. When he arrived in Westwood, his coach, Tommy Prothro, was also the man who had recruited him for OSU. Beban became a T-formation quarterback for the Bruins and, with his running and passing skills, led the team to a 24–5–2 record from 1965 to 1967. He won a Heisman Trophy in 1967. His only 300-yard passing day was a 16-for-24, 301-yard effort in a 21-20 loss to USC in 1967 in one of history's most heralded games.

BEST COACH Vanderbilt's Henry R. "Red" Sanders was tapped to lead the Bruins in 1949. Sanders, who drew his nickname from the color of a sweater he favored as a kid, liked jazz, reading about Andrew Jackson and the single-wing attack. Although widely panned when he was hired,

PROFILE

University of California, Los Angeles
Founded: 1919
Enrollment: 25,715
Colors: Blue and Gold
Nickname: Bruins
Stadium: Rose Bowl
 Opened in 1922
 Grass; 91,136 capacity
First football game: 1919
All-time record: 511–336–37 (.599)
Bowl record: 12–13–1
Consensus national championships 1936-present: 1 (1954)
Pac-10 championships: 17 (11 outright)
Heisman Trophy: Gary Beban, 1967
Outland Trophy: Jonathan Ogden, 1995; Kris Farris, 1998
First-round NFL draftees: 28
Website: www.uclabruins.com

THE BEST OF TIMES

In a six-year run under Red Sanders that included the 1954 national title, the Bruins went 49–10. Three decades later under Terry Donahue, the winningest coach in Pac-10 history, UCLA won an NCAA-record seven consecutive bowl games from 1982 to 1988.

THE WORST OF TIMES

Between the Rose Bowl seasons of 1961 and 1965, UCLA had three losing records and won 10 games.

CONFERENCE

A longtime member of the Pac-10 Conference, UCLA joined the Pac-10's forerunner, the Pacific Coast Conference, in 1928, 12 years after the league's inception.

DISTINGUISHED ALUMNI

Arthur Ashe; Jackie Robinson; Carol Burnett; Francis Ford Coppola; Jackie Joyner-Kersee; Tom Bradley, Los Angeles mayor; Ralph Bunche, 1950 Nobel Peace Prize winner; Randy Newman, singer/composer; Donna de Varona, Olympic swimming gold medalist, co-founder of Women's Sports Foundation

FIGHT SONG

SONS OF WESTWOOD
We are sons of Westwood,
And we hail the blue and gold.
True to thee our hearts will be,
Our love will not grow old,
Fight, fight, fight.
Bruins roam the hills of Westwood,
By the blue Pacific shore,
And if by chance you see,
A man from USC,
Ev'ry Bruin starts to roar.
U… C… L… A… UCLA,
Fight, fight, fight!

Sanders led the Bruins to a 66–19–1 record and the 1954 national title, and was named No. 1 citizen of Los Angeles in a newspaper poll conducted in the early 1950s. No one since has been able to match a national title, but Sanders' successors have included a string of talented coaches, including Prothro, Dick Vermeil and Terry Donahue, the winningest coach in Pac-10 history, with a 151–74–8 (.665) record in 20 years (1976-95) at UCLA. From 1982 to 1988, Donahue's Bruins set an NCAA record by winning seven straight bowl games.

BEST TEAM The 1954 Bruins led the nation in scoring and scoring defense and blew through nine successive opponents to win UPI's national championship. Led by three All-America selections—tackle Jack Ellena, guard Jim

> *UCLA seems a place where the players are faster, the sun is brighter, the cheerleaders are prettier.*

Salsbury and fullback Bob Davenport—the Bruins eked out a 12-7 victory over defending national champion Maryland early in the season, then flattened everybody else. Sanders was named consensus coach of the year for a team that was prevented from playing in the Rose Bowl by the Pacific Coast Conference's no-repeat rule.

BIGGEST GAME UCLA's 20-16 victory over rival USC in 1965 set up a Rose Bowl confrontation with Michigan State that featured one of the golden moments in the program's history. The Bruins trailed the Trojans 16-6 with four minutes left, but the sophomore Beban rolled out and hit Dick Witcher for a 34-yard touchdown, and a two-point conversion made it 16-14. Linebacker Dallas Grider recovered Kurt Zimmerman's onside kick, and Beban fired a

RECORDS

RUSHING YARDS

	GAME
322	Maurice Drew vs. Washington, Sept. 18, 2004 (26 att.)
	SEASON
1,571	Karim Abdul-Jabbar, 1995 (296 att.)
	CAREER
3,731	Gaston Green, 1984-87 (708 att.)

PASSING YARDS

	GAME
513	Cade McNown vs. Miami, Fla., Dec. 5, 1998 (26 of 35)
	SEASON
3,470	Cade McNown, 1998 (207 of 357)
	CAREER
10,708	Cade McNown, 1995-98 (694 of 1,250)

RECEIVING YARDS

	GAME
263	J.J. Stokes vs. USC, Nov. 21, 1992 (6 rec.)
	SEASON
1,494	Freddie Mitchell, 2000 (77 rec.)
	CAREER
3,020	Danny Farmer, 1996-99 (159 rec.)

POINTS

	GAME
30	Maurice Drew vs. Washington, Sept. 18, 2004 (5 TDs)
	SEASON
156	Skip Hicks, 1997 (26 TDs)
	CAREER
390	John Lee, 1982-85 (85 FGs, 135 PATs)

CONSENSUS ALL-AMERICANS

1946	Burr Baldwin, E
1952	Donn Moomaw, C
1953	Paul Cameron, TB
1954	Jack Ellena, T
1955	Hardiman Cureton, G
1957	Dick Wallen, E
1966	Mel Farr, B
1967	Gary Beban, B
1967	Don Manning, LB
1969	Mike Ballou, LB
1973	Kermit Johnson, B
1975	John Sciarra, QB
1976-78	Jerry Robinson, LB
1978-80	Kenny Easley, DB
1981	Tim Wrightman, TE
1983	Don Rogers, DB
1985	John Lee, PK
1988	Troy Aikman, QB
1988	Darryl Henley, DB
1992	Carlton Gray, DB
1993	J.J. Stokes, WR
1993	Bjorn Merten, PK
1993	Jamir Miller, LB
1995	Jonathan Ogden, OL
1997	Chad Overhauser, OL
1998	Cade McNown, QB
1998	Kris Farris, OL
2000	Fred Mitchell, WR
2001	Robert Thomas, LB
2003	Dave Ball, DL

52-yard strike to Kurt Altenberg for the winning score with 2:39 remaining.

BIGGEST UPSET When the 1965 Bruins qualified for the Rose Bowl against top-ranked Michigan State, renowned columnist Jim Murray wrote: "Playing Michigan State is a job that calls for volunteers, not victors. It's like winning a ticket to a hemorrhage, as good a break as getting a stateroom on the Titanic." Fourteen-point underdogs, the Bruins took a 14-0 lead before Michigan State got within 14-12 inside the final minute and called on fullback Bob Apisa to run the ball on a would-be two-point conversion. Apisa was stopped on the 4-yard line by Grider and safety Bob Stiles, who knocked himself out on the play.

BEST COMEBACK UCLA was the 12th-ranked team and Michigan 20th when they met in Ann Arbor in September of 1982, but the Wolverines took a 21-0 lead early in the second quarter. Then the Bruins came alive behind quarterback Tom Ramsey, who completed 22 of 36 passes for 311 yards and two touchdowns. In a third-and-25 predicament, he hit Dokie Williams on a 46-yard touchdown pass late in the first half, and Ramsey's sneak made it 24-14 at halftime. Safety Don Rogers intercepted a pass early in the second half to inspire the UCLA defense, which held Michigan to a field goal after intermission in a 31-27 victory. Running back Kevin Nelson scored the go-ahead touchdown late in the third quarter, and the Bruins' defense had the final word as the clock ran out on the Wolverines at the UCLA 8-yard line.

WILDEST FINISH The Bruins seemed headed for a home loss to Washington State in 1984 as WSU's John Traut measured a 45-yard field goal for the Cougars, who had tied the game at 24 with 2:25 left. But the snap went through the hands of holder Ed Blount and bounced from the 34 to midfield. From there, the Bruins launched a short drive that ended with a 47-yard field goal by John Lee for a 27-24 victory.

STADIUM Since 1982, the Bruins have played at one of the nation's most fabled stadiums, the Rose Bowl in Pasadena. Before 1982, UCLA shared the Los Angeles Coliseum with USC.

RIVAL The Bruins save most of their vitriol for USC, whose Tommy Trojan campus statue is a mere half-hour away. The earliest recorded blue-and-gold painting of

Tommy was in 1941, but an attempted prank against him in 1958 misfired badly. UCLA students plotted to fly a helicopter over the statue and drop manure on it, but they didn't account for the aerodynamics and some of the stuff was sucked back into the copter.

HEARTBREAKER It was all set up for UCLA on Dec. 5, 1998: defeat Miami, and the unbeaten Bruins would secure a top-two spot in the Bowl Championship Series standings and play in the national title game. When the Cade McNown-led offense began clicking early, staking the Bruins to a 38-21 lead late in the third quarter, UCLA seemed a cinch. McNown would account for six touchdowns, throwing for 513 yards and five scores. But the defense, a liability all year long, finally collapsed. Miami back Edgerrin James rushed 39 times for a Big East-record 299 yards and the Hurricanes scored with 50 seconds left to win 49-45.

NICKNAME In its first years of football, UCLA was known as the southern branch of the University of California, giving rise to the nickname Cubs, a logical extension of Cal's Golden Bears. In 1923, Cubs was changed to Grizzlies, but that lasted only until 1928, when UCLA joined the Pacific Coast Conference to find that Montana already had that nickname. UCLA then adopted the Bruins handle.

MASCOT UCLA has had at least three live bears as mascots, first in the 1930s and again in the 1950s and 1960s. Upkeep-related problems led to costumed students posing as Joe and Josephine Bruin. The female bear is identifiable by her skirt and hair bow.

UNIFORMS At home, the Bruins wear light-blue jerseys with gold numerals, gold-and-white shoulder striping and gold pants. On the road, white jerseys are accented by blue numerals and blue-and-gold shoulder striping. Both helmets are gold with a "UCLA" script. To shed an image of finesse football, the Bruins in 2001 switched from a powder-blue jersey to a darker shade.

LORE Before he broke baseball's color barrier, Jackie Robinson was the first four-sport letter-winner at UCLA, honored in football, basketball, track and baseball. He led the nation in punt returns in both 1939 and 1940, and his 18.8-yard career average is fourth in NCAA history.

And then there are the intertwined stories of two walk-on quarterbacks, one of whom coached the other.

In the late 1970s, lightly recruited Rick Neuheisel

picked UCLA partly on the basis of the passing stats in his Sunday newspaper; the poorest ones offered him the best chance of playing. In 1983, his fifth season, Neuheisel took over for an injured Steve Bono and not only led the Bruins to the Rose Bowl, but overcame food poisoning to throw four TD passes in a 45-9 victory over Illinois.

UCLA was John Barnes' fourth school, and in fall camp of 1992 he was a fifth-string quarterback. While he was awaiting admission, he slept in his car for a week. He crashed the 1991 UCLA-USC game with a student ID card passed through a fence by his girlfriend. None of that mattered when Barnes, whose position coach was Neuheisel, faced a 31-17 deficit against USC in 1992. He led the Bruins to three fourth-quarter TDs, completing the game with 385 passing yards. UCLA survived USC's late two-point conversion attempt to win 38-37.

QUOTE "Yes, I'm prejudiced—in favor of the player who can block, tackle and run fast."—Red Sanders, responding to the notion that he favored white players over blacks

UCLA ANNUAL STATISTICAL LEADERS

YR	RUSHING	YDS	ATT	AVG	PASSING	ATT	CMP	PCT	YDS	RECEIVING	REC	YDS	AVG
1952	Ted Narleski	206	96	2.1	Paul Cameron	96	36	.38	518	Ike Jones	25	270	10.8
1953	Paul Cameron	665	146	4.6	Paul Cameron	106	39	.37	478	Bill Stits	9	208	23.1
1954	Jim Decker	508	47	10.8	Primo Villanueva	49	23	.47	400	Rommie Loudd	13	157	12.1
1955	Sam Brown	892	144	6.2	Ronnie Knox	63	36	.57	526	Chuck Holoway	10	184	18.4
1956	Barry Billington	396	106	3.7	Doug Bradley	48	22	.46	293	Dick Wallen	23	308	13.4
1957	Chuck Kendall	388	98	4.0	Don Long	56	35	.63	479	Dick Wallen	20	303	15.2
1958	Ray Smith	307	79	3.9	Don Long	64	36	.56	395	Dick Wallen	19	211	11.1
1959	Ray Smith	417	132	3.2	Bill Kilmer	101	41	.41	702	Marv Luster	22	366	16.6
1960	Bill Kilmer	803	163	4.9	Bill Kilmer	129	64	.50	1,086	Marv Luster	17	250	14.7
1961	Mike Haffner	703	112	6.3	Bob Smith	33	16	.48	305	Kermit Alexander	14	297	21.2
1962	Kermit Alexander	472	82	5.8	Larry Zeno	62	25	.40	458	Mel Profit	12	229	19.1
1963	Jim Colletto	179	47	3.8	Larry Zeno	154	77	.50	1,036	Mel Profit	28	393	14.0
1964	Larry Zeno	325	113	2.9	Larry Zeno	196	97	.49	1,363	Mike Haffner	31	515	16.6
1965	Mel Farr	821	122	6.7	Gary Beban	152	78	.51	1,483	Kurt Altenberg	32	599	18.7
1966	Mel Farr	809	138	5.9	Gary Beban	157	78	.50	1,245	Harold Busby	29	474	16.3
1967	Greg Jones	662	111	6.0	Gary Beban	156	87	.56	1,359	Dave Nuttall	37	612	16.5
1968	Greg Jones	476	121	3.9	Jim Nader	163	72	.44	1,008	Ron Copeland	21	372	17.7
1969	Greg Jones	761	158	4.8	Dennis Dummit	208	114	.55	1,963	Gwen Cooper	38	734	19.3
1970	Marv Kendricks	573	107	5.4	Dennis Dummit	344	175	.51	2,393	Rick Wilkes	43	595	13.8
1971	Marv Kendricks	556	131	4.2	Mike Flores	111	51	.46	671	Terry Vernoy	21	281	13.4
1972	Kermit Johnson	952	140	6.8	Mark Harmon	70	30	.43	574	Brad Lyman	13	211	16.2
1973	Kermit Johnson	1,129	150	7.5	John Sciarra	62	27	.44	503	Norm Andersen	19	315	16.6
1974	Russel Charles	763	132	5.8	John Sciarra	92	47	.51	835	Norm Andersen	27	480	17.8
1975	Wendell Tyler	1,388	208	6.7	John Sciarra	145	74	.51	1,313	Wally Henry	17	287	16.9
1976	Theotis Brown	1,092	200	5.5	Jeff Dankworth	120	66	.55	866	Wally Henry	22	370	16.8
1977	James Owens	938	176	5.3	Rick Bashore	149	74	.50	1,015	Homer Butler	25	584	23.4
1978	Theotis Brown	1,283	211	6.1	Rick Bashore	129	62	.48	811	Severn Reece	15	340	22.7
1979	Freeman McNeil	1,396	271	5.2	Rick Bashore	122	60	.49	964	Tim Wrightman	22	321	14.6
1980	Freeman McNeil	1,105	203	5.4	Tom Ramsey	148	82	.55	1,116	Cormac Carney	33	581	17.6
1981	Kevin Nelson	883	195	4.5	Tom Ramsey	230	134	.58	1,793	Cormac Carney	29	539	18.6
1982	Danny Andrews	482	97	5.0	Tom Ramsey	336	209	.62	2,986	Cormac Carney	46	779	16.9
1983	Kevin Nelson	898	188	4.8	Rick Neuheisel	267	185	.69	2,245	Mike Sherrard	48	709	14.8
1984	Danny Andrews	605	158	3.8	Steve Bono	245	136	.56	1,576	Mike Sherrard	43	729	17.0
1985	Gaston Green	712	158	4.5	David Norrie	214	136	.64	1,819	Karl Dorrell	39	565	14.5
1986	Gaston Green	1,405	253	5.6	Matt Stevens	280	150	.54	1,869	Willie Anderson	36	675	18.8
1987	Gaston Green	1,098	206	5.3	Troy Aikman	273	178	.65	2,527	Willie Anderson	48	903	18.8
1988	Eric Ball	784	166	4.7	Troy Aikman	354	228	.64	2,771	Mike Farr	66	700	10.6
1989	Brian Brown	463	130	3.6	Bret Johnson	252	145	.58	1,791	Charles Arbuckle	33	309	9.4
1990	Brian Brown	798	154	5.2	Tommy Maddox	327	182	.56	2,682	Reggie Moore	40	643	16.1
1991	Kevin Williams	1,141	191	6.0	Tommy Maddox	343	209	.61	2,681	Sean LaChapelle	73	1,056	14.5
1992	Kevin Williams	582	115	5.1	John Barnes	117	61	.52	957	J.J. Stokes	41	728	17.8
1993	Skip Hicks	563	100	5.6	Wayne Cook	297	165	.56	2,067	J.J. Stokes	82	1,181	14.4
1994	Karim Abdul-Jabbar	1,227	210	5.8	Wayne Cook	302	179	.59	2,501	Kevin Jordan	73	1,228	16.8
1995	Karim Abdul-Jabbar	1,571	296	5.3	Cade McNown	245	122	.50	1,698	Kevin Jordan	43	558	13.0
1996	Skip Hicks	1,034	224	4.6	Cade McNown	336	176	.52	2,424	Danny Farmer	31	524	16.9
1997	Skip Hicks	1,282	258	5.0	Cade McNown	312	189	.61	3,116	Jim McElroy	47	988	21.0
1998	DeShaun Foster	673	126	5.3	Cade McNown	357	207	.58	3,470	Danny Farmer	58	1,274	22.0
1999	Keith Brown	421	98	4.3	Cory Paus	197	95	.48	1,336	Freddie Mitchell	38	533	14.0
2000	DeShaun Foster	1,037	269	3.9	Cory Paus	241	134	.56	2,154	Freddie Mitchell	77	1,494	19.4
2001	DeShaun Foster	1,109	216	5.1	Cory Paus	194	101	.52	1,740	Craig Bragg	29	408	14.1
2002	Tyler Ebell	994	234	4.2	Cory Paus	184	109	.59	1,647	Craig Bragg	55	889	16.2
2003	Maurice Drew	582	135	4.3	Drew Olson	325	173	.53	2,067	Craig Bragg	73	1,065	14.6
2004	Maurice Drew	1,007	160	6.3	Drew Olson	341	196	.58	2,565	Craig Bragg	36	483	13.4

Receiving leaders by receptions
All statistics include postseason

UCLA ALL-TIME SCORES

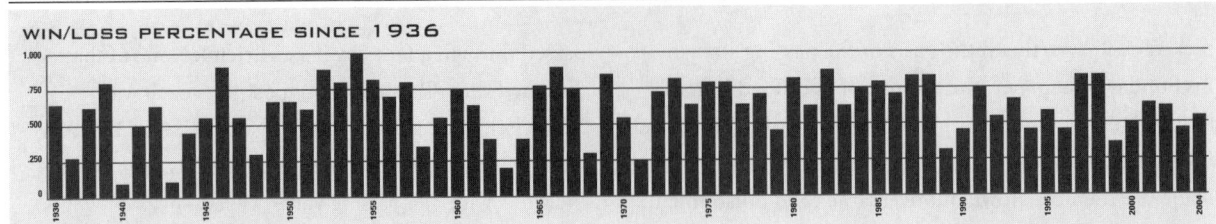

WIN/LOSS PERCENTAGE SINCE 1936

FRED COZENS
1919 (.250)   2-6

1919   2-6-0
O3		at Manual Arts HS	0 74
O10		at Hollywood HS	6 19
O17		at Bakersfield HS	12 27
O24	●	Occidental JV	7 2
O30	●	Los Angeles JC	7 0
N7		USS Idaho	0 20
N14		Los Angeles JC	7 21
N21		Occidental JV	13 30

HARRY TROTTER
1920-22 (.156)   2-13-1

1920   0-5-0
O2	Pomona	0 41
O9	Occidental	0 21
O30	at Redlands	21 27
N13	Cal Tech	0 32
N20	at Whittier	0 103

1921   0-5-0
O8	Redlands	7 35
O15	Pomona	7 55
O29	at Occidental	0 35
N5	Whittier	0 62
N11	at Cal Tech	0 27

1922   2-3-1
O7	●	at San Diego State	24 6 *
O14	●	at Redlands	34 9
O21		Occidental	7 14
N4	=	at Whittier	6 6
N18		at Pomona	6 20
N25		Cal Tech	6 7

JAMES CLINE
1923-24 (.233)   2-10-3

1923   2-5-0
O13	●	San Diego State	12 0
O20	●	Loyola, Marymount	6 0
O27		Whittier	12 14
N3		Pomona	6 27
N12		Redlands	6 12
N17		at Occidental	6 20
N24		Cal Tech *Pas*	6 59

1924   0-5-3
O4	=	Loyola, Marymount	0 0
O11		La Verne	13 14
O18		at Whittier	0 6
O25		Occidental	7 20
N1		at Pomona	7 50
N11		at Redlands	0 0
N15	=	at San Diego State	13 13
N22		Cal Tech	0 0

WILLIAM SPAULDING
1925-38 (.580)   72-51-8

1925   5-3-1
S26	●	San Diego State	7 0
O3	●	La Verne	16 3
O10	●	Pomona	26 0
O16		Whittier	0 7
O24	●	at Occidental	9 0
O31		at Saint Mary's-Cal	0 28
N7	●	Redlands	23 0
N14		at Stanford	0 82
N21	=	at Cal Tech	10 10

1926   5-3-0
S25	●	Santa Barbra State	25 0
O9	●	San Diego State	42 7
O16		at Whittier	6 16
O23	●	at Pomona	27 7
N6	●	Occidental	24 7
N13	●	at Redlands	26 3
N20		Cal Tech	3 7
N27		Iowa State	0 20

1927   6-2-1
S24	●	Santa Barbra State	33 0
O1		Fresno State	7 0
O8	●	Whittier	25 6
O15	●	Occidental	8 0
O28	●	Redlands	32 0
N5		Pomona	7 7
N12		at Cal Tech	13 0
N19		at Arizona	13 16
N26		Drake	6 25

1928-1958
PACIFIC COAST

1928   4-4-1 (0-4-0)
S22	●	Santa Barbra State	19 0
S29	=	Arizona	7 7
O6	●	at Cal Tech	32 0
O13		at Stanford	7 45
O20	●	Pomona	29 0
O27		at Idaho	6 20
N10		Washington State *Port*	0 38
N17		Laverne	65 0
N29		Oregon	6 26

1929   4-4-0 (1-3-0)
S28		at Southern Cal	0 76
O5	●	Fresno State	56 6
O12		Stanford	0 57
O19	●	at Cal Tech	31 0
O26	●	Pomona	20 0
N2		at Oregon	0 27
N16		Saint Mary's-Cal	0 24
N28	●	Montana	14 0

1930   3-5-0 (1-4-0)
S27		Southern Cal	0 52
O11	●	Pomona	21 0
O17	●	Saint Mary's-Cal	6 21
O24	●	Cal Tech	30 0
O31		at Stanford	0 20
N8		Oregon	0 7
N21		Oregon State	0 19
N29	●	Idaho	20 6

1931   3-4-1 (0-3-0)
S25	=	Occidental	0 0
O3		at Washington State	0 13
O17		at Northwestern	0 19
O24	●	Pomona	46 0
O31		at Stanford	6 12
N11	●	Saint Mary's-Cal	12 0
N21		Oregon	6 13
N26	●	Florida	13 0

1932   6-4-0 (4-2-0)
S23	●	Cal-Davis	26 0
S30		Idaho	6 0
O15		Oregon *Port*	12 7
O22	●	Cal Tech	51 0
O29		Stanford	13 6
N11		Saint Mary's-Cal	7 14
N19	●	Montana	32 0
N24		Washington State	0 3
D3		Washington	0 19
D17		at Florida	2 12

1933   6-4-1 (1-3-1)
S23	●	Los Angeles JC	34 0
S23	●	San Diego State	13 0
S30		at Stanford	0 3
O6	●	Utah	21 0 *
O21	●	Loyola, Marymount	20 7
O28		Oregon	0 7
N4	=	California	0 0
N11	●	at San Diego Marines	14 13
N18		at Washington	0 10
N25		Saint Mary's-Cal	14 22
N30		Washington State	7 0

1934   7-3-0 (2-3-0)
S22	●	Pomona	14 0
S22	●	San Diego State	20 0
S30		Oregon *Port*	3 26
O13	●	Montana	16 0
O20		at California	0 3
O27	●	Cal-Davis	49 0
N3		Stanford	0 27
N12	●	Saint Mary's-Cal	6 0
N24	●	Oregon State	25 7
N29	●	Loyola, Marymount	13 6

1935   8-2-0 (4-1-0)
S28	●	Utah State	39 0
O5	●	Oregon State *Port*	20 7
O19	●	at Stanford	7 6
O26	●	Oregon	33 6
N2		California	2 14
N9		SMU	0 21
N15	●	Hawaii	19 6
N23	●	Loyola, Marymount	14 6
D7	●	Idaho	13 6
D14	●	at Saint Mary's-Cal	13 7

1936   6-3-1 (4-3-1)
S26	●	Occidental	21 0
S26	●	Pomona	26 0
O2		Montana	30 0
O10		Washington	0 14
O17	●	at California	17 6
O24	●	Oregon State	22 13
O31	●	Stanford	6 19
N7	●	Oregon *Port*	7 0
N14		Washington State	7 32
N26		at Southern Cal	7 7

1937   2-6-1 (1-5-1)
S24		Oregon	26 13
O9		at Stanford	7 12
O16		at Oregon State	7 7
O23		Washington State	0 3
O30		California	14 27
N13		at Washington	0 26
N20		SMU	13 26
N27		Missouri	13 0
D4		Southern Cal	13 19

1938   7-4-1 (4-3-1)
S23	●	Iowa	27 3
O1		at Oregon	12 14
O8		at Washington	13 0
O15		at California	7 20
O22	●	Idaho	33 0
O29		Stanford	6 0
N5		at Washington State	21 0
N12		Wisconsin	7 14
N24		at Southern Cal	7 42
D10		Oregon State	6 6
D26		at Hawaii All Stars	46 0
J2		Hawaii *Hon*	32 7

EDWIN HORRELL
1939-44 (.443)   24-31-6

1939   6-0-4 (5-0-3)
S29	●	TCU	6 2
O7	●	at Washington	14 7
O14	=	at Stanford	14 14
O21	●	Montana	20 6
O28	●	Oregon	16 6
N4	●	at Oregon State	20 7
N18	=	Santa Clara	0 0
N25	=	Oregon State	13 13
N30	●	Washington State	24 7
D9	=	Southern Cal	0 0

1940   1-9-0 (1-6-0)
S28		SMU	6 9
O4		Santa Clara	6 9
O12		Texas A&M	0 7
O19		at California	7 9
O26		Oregon State	0 7
N2		Stanford	14 20
N9		at Oregon	0 18
N16	●	Washington State	34 26
N23		Washington	0 41
N30		at Southern Cal	12 28

1941   5-5-1 (3-4-1)
S26	●	Washington State	7 6
O4		at Stanford	0 33
O10	●	Montana	14 7
O18		at Washington	7 14
O25	●	Oregon	14 7
N1		California	7 27
N8		at Oregon State	0 19
N15	●	Camp Haan	29 0
N22		Santa Clara	13 31
D6	=	Southern Cal	7 7
D20	●	Florida *JacF*	30 27

1942   7-4-0 (6-1-0)
S25	●	TCU	6 7
O3		Saint Mary's Pre-Flight	7 18
O10	●	Oregon State	30 7
O17	●	at California	21 0
O24	●	Santa Clara	14 6
O31	●	Stanford	20 7 *
N7		at Oregon	7 14
N21	●	Washington	14 10
D5	●	Idaho	40 13
D12	●	at Southern Cal	14 7

ROSE BOWL
J1	Georgia	0 9

1943   1-8-0 (0-4-0)
S25	Southern Cal	0 20
O2	Pacific	7 19
O9	at March Field	7 47
O16	California	0 13
O30	at San Diego Naval	0 28
N6	Del Monte Pre-Flight	7 26
N13	at California	6 13
N20	●	Saint Mary's-Cal	19 7
N27		at Southern Cal	13 26

1944   4-5-1 (1-2-1)
S23	=	at Southern Cal	13 13
S30		at California	0 6
O7		at San Diego Navy	12 14
O14	●	Saint Mary's-Cal	39 0
O21		Saint Mary's Pre-Flight	12 21
O27	●	Alameda CG	26 13
N4		at March Field	13 35
N11	●	California	7 0
N18	●	Pacific	54 7
N25		Southern Cal	13 40

BERT LABRUCHERIE 1945-48 (.590)   23-16

1945   5-4-0 (2-3-0)

S21		Southern Cal	6	13
S29	•	San Diego Navy	20	14
O5	•	Pacific	50	0
O13	•	California	13	0
O19		State Marys Pre-Flight	6	13
O27	•	Oregon	12	0
N17		Saint Mary's-Cal	13	7
N24		at California	0	6
D1		at Southern Cal	15	26

1946   10-1-0 (7-0-0)

S28	•	Oregon State	50	7
O5		at Washington	39	13
O12		Stanford	26	6
O19	•	at California	13	6
O26	•	Santa Clara	33	7
N1	•	Saint Mary's-Cal	46	20
N9	•	Oregon Port	14	0
N16	•	Montana	61	7
N23		Southern Cal	13	6
N30	•	Nebraska	18	0
ROSE BOWL				
J1		Illinois	14	45

1947   5-4-0 (4-2-0)

S26	•	Iowa	22	7
O4		at Northwestern	26	27
O11	•	Oregon	24	7
O18	•	at Stanford	39	6
O25		SMU	0	7
N1		California	0	6
N8		Oregon State Port	27	7
N15		Washington	34	7
N22		at Southern Cal	0	6

1948   3-7-0 (2-6-0)

S18	•	Washington State	48	26
S25		Northwestern	0	19
O2	•	Idaho	28	12
O9		at Washington	6	27
O16		Stanford	14	34
O23		Oregon State	0	28
O30	•	at Nebraska	27	15
N6		at California	13	28
N12		Oregon	7	26
N20		Southern Cal	13	20

HENRY "RED" SANDERS 1949-57 (.773)   66-19-1

1949   6-3-0 (5-2-0)

S16	•	Oregon State	35	13
S24	•	at Iowa	41	25
S30	•	Oregon	35	27
O8		at Stanford	14	7
O15		Santa Clara	0	14
O22	•	at Washington State	27	20
O29		California	21	35
N12		Washington	47	26
N19		at Southern Cal	7	21

1950   6-3-0 (5-2-0)

S23	•	Oregon	28	0
S30	•	Washington State	42	0
O7		at Washington	20	21
O13		Illinois	6	14
O21		Stanford	21	7
O28	•	at Purdue	20	6
N4	•	Oregon State	20	13
N11	•	at California	0	35
N25	•	Southern Cal	39	0

1951   5-3-1 (4-1-1)

S21	•	Texas A&M	14	21
S29	•	at Illinois	13	27
O6	•	Santa Clara	44	17
O13		at Stanford	7	21
O20	•	Oregon	41	0
N3	•	California	21	7
N10	•	Oregon State Port	7	0
N17	=	Washington	20	20
N24	•	at Southern Cal	21	7

1952   8-1-0 (5-1-0)

S20	•	Oregon	13	6
S27	•	TCU	14	0
O4		at Washington	32	7
O11	•	Rice	20	0
O18		Stanford	24	14
O25	•	at Wisconsin	20	7
N1	•	at California	28	7
N8		Oregon State	57	0
N22		Southern Cal	12	14

1953   8-2-0 (6-1-0)

S18	•	Oregon State	41	0
S25	•	Kansas	19	7
O3	•	at Oregon	12	0
O9		Wisconsin	13	0
O17		at Stanford	20	21
O24	•	Washington State	44	7
O31	•	California	20	7
N14	•	Washington	22	6
N21	•	at Southern Cal	13	0
ROSE BOWL				
J1		Michigan State	20	28

1954   9-0-0 (6-0-0)

S18	•	San Diego NTC	67	0
S25	•	at Kansas	32	7
O1	•	Maryland	12	7
O9		at Washington	21	20
O16		Stanford	72	0
O23	•	at Oregon State	61	0
O30		at California	27	6
N6		Oregon	41	0
N20		Southern Cal	34	0

1955   9-2-0 (6-0-0)

S16	•	Texas A&M	21	0
S24		at Maryland	0	7
O1	•	at Washington State	55	0
O8	•	Oregon State	38	0
O15	•	at Stanford	21	13
O21	•	Iowa	33	13
O29		California	47	0
N5		at Pacific	34	0
N12		Washington	19	17
N19		at Southern Cal	17	7
ROSE BOWL				
J2		Michigan State	14	17

1956   7-3-0 (5-2-0)

S21	•	Utah	13	7
S29	•	at Michigan	13	42
O6	•	Oregon	6	0
O13	•	Washington State	28	0
O20	•	at California	34	20
O27		at Oregon State	7	21
N3	•	Stanford	14	13
N10	•	at Washington	13	9
N17	•	Kansas	13	0
N24		Southern Cal	7	10

1957   8-2-0 (5-2-0)

S20	•	Air Force	47	0
S27	•	Illinois	16	6
O5		Oregon Port	0	21
O12	•	Washington	19	0
O19	•	Oregon State	26	7
O26		at Stanford	6	20
N2	•	California	16	14
N9		Washington State Spo	19	13
N16	•	at Pacific	21	0
N23	•	at Southern Cal	20	9

GEORGE DICKERSON 1958 (.333)   1-2

BILL BARNES 1958-64 (.478)   31-34-3

1958   3-6-1 (2-4-1)

S20	•	Pittsburgh	6	27
S27	•	at Illinois	18	14
O4		at Oregon State	0	14
O10		Florida	14	21
O18	•	at Washington	20	0
O25		Stanford	19	21
N1		Washington State	20	38
N8		at California	17	20
N15	•	Oregon	7	3
N22	=	Southern Cal	15	15

1959-1967 AAWU

1959   5-4-1 (3-1-0)

S18	=	Purdue	0	0
O3		at Pittsburgh	21	25
O17	•	California	19	12
O23		Air Force	7	20
O31		Washington	7	23
N7	•	at Stanford	55	13
N13	•	North Carolina State	21	12
N21		at Southern Cal	10	3
N28	•	Utah	21	6
D5	•	Syracuse	8	36

1960   7-2-1 (2-2-0)

S17	•	Pittsburgh	8	7
S24	=	at Purdue	27	27
O15		at Washington	8	10
O22		Stanford	26	8
O29		North Carolina State	7	0
N5		at California	28	0
N12		Air Force	22	0
N19		Southern Cal	6	17
N26	•	at Utah	16	9
D3	•	Duke	27	6

1961   7-4-0 (3-1-0)

S23	•	Air Force Den	19	6
S30	•	at Michigan	6	29
O7		at Ohio State	3	13
O14	•	Vanderbilt	28	21
O21	•	Pittsburgh	20	6
O28	•	at Stanford	20	0
N4	•	California	35	15
N10	•	TCU	28	7
N18	•	Washington	13	17
N25	•	at Southern Cal	10	7
ROSE BOWL				
J1		Minnesota	3	21

1962   4-6-0 (1-3-0)

O6	•	Ohio State	9	7
O12	•	Colorado State	35	7
O20	•	at Pittsburgh	6	8
O27		Stanford	7	17
N3	•	at California	26	16
N10	•	Air Force	11	17
N17		at Washington	0	30
N24		Southern Cal	3	14
D1	•	at Utah	14	11
D8	•	Syracuse	7	12

1963   2-8-0 (2-2-0)

S20	•	Pittsburgh	0	20
S28	•	at Penn State	14	17
O5	•	at Stanford	10	9
O11	•	Syracuse	7	29
O19	•	at Notre Dame	12	27
O25		Illinois	12	18
N2		California	0	25
N9		at Air Force	21	48
N16	•	Washington	14	0
N30		at Southern Cal	6	26

1964   4-6-0 (2-2-0)

S12	•	at Pittsburgh	17	12
S26	•	Penn State	21	14
O3	•	Stanford	27	20
O10		at Syracuse	0	39
O17	•	at Notre Dame	0	24
O24		at Illinois	7	26
O31	•	at California	25	21
N7		Air Force	15	24
N14		at Washington	20	22
N21		Southern Cal	13	34

TOMMY PROTHRO 1965-70 (.685)   41-18-3

1965   8-2-1 (4-0-0)

S18	•	at Michigan State	3	13
O2	•	at Penn State	24	22
O9	•	Syracuse	24	14
O16	=	at Missouri	14	14
O23	•	California	56	3
O30	•	at Air Force	10	0
N6		Washington	28	24
N13	•	at Stanford	30	13
N20	•	at Southern Cal	20	16
D4		Tennessee Mem	34	37
ROSE BOWL				
J1	•	Michigan State	14	12

1966   9-1-0 (3-1-0)

S17	•	Pittsburgh	57	14
S24	•	at Syracuse	31	12
O1	•	Missouri	24	15
O8	•	at Rice	27	24
O15	•	Penn State	49	11
O22	•	at California	28	15
O29	•	Air Force	38	13
N5		at Washington	3	16
N12	•	Stanford	10	0
N19		Southern Cal	14	7

1967   7-2-1 (4-1-1)

S16	•	Tennessee	20	16
S23	•	at Pittsburgh	40	8
S30	•	Washington State Spo	51	23
O7	•	at Penn State	17	15
O14	•	California	37	14
O21	•	at Stanford	21	16
N4	=	Oregon State	16	16
N11	•	Washington	48	0
N18		at Southern Cal	20	21
N25		Syracuse	14	32

1968-PRESENT PAC 10

1968   3-7-0 (2-4-0)

S21	•	Pittsburgh	63	7
S28	•	Washington State	31	21
O5	•	at Syracuse	7	20
O12		Penn State	6	21
O19	•	at California	15	39
O26	•	Stanford	20	17
N2	•	at Tennessee	18	42
N9	•	at Oregon State	21	45
N16	•	at Washington	0	6
N23		Southern Cal	16	28

1969   8-1-1 (5-1-1)

S13	•	Oregon State	37	0
S20	•	Pittsburgh	42	8
S27	•	at Wisconsin	34	23
O4	•	at Northwestern	36	0
O11	•	Washington State Spo	46	14
O18	•	California	32	0
O25	=	at Stanford	20	20
N1	•	Washington	57	14
N15	•	at Oregon	13	10
N22	•	at Southern Cal	12	14

1970   6-5-0 (4-3-0)

S12	•	at Oregon State	14	9
S19	•	at Pittsburgh	24	15
S26	•	Northwestern	12	7
O3		at Texas	17	20
O10		Oregon	40	41
O17	•	at California	24	21
O24		Stanford	7	9
O30	•	Washington State	54	9
N14		at Washington	20	61
N21	•	Southern Cal	45	20
D5		at Tennessee	17	28

PEPPER RODGERS 1971-73 (.609)   19-12-1

1971   2-7-1 (1-4-1)

S11		Pittsburgh	25	29
S18		Texas	10	28
S25		at Michigan	0	38
O2		Oregon State	17	34
O9	•	Washington State Spo	34	21
O16	•	at Arizona	28	12
O23		California	24	31
O30		Washington	12	23
N6		at Stanford	9	20
N20	=	at Southern Cal	7	7

1972   8-3-0 (5-2-0)

S9	•	Nebraska	20	17
S16	•	at Pittsburgh	38	28
S23	•	Michigan	9	26
S29	•	Oregon	65	20
O7	•	Arizona	42	31
O14	•	at Oregon State	37	7
O21	•	at California	49	13
O28	•	Washington State	35	20
N4	•	Stanford	28	23
N11	•	at Washington	21	30
N18		Southern Cal	7	24

1973   9-2-0 (6-1-0)

S8	•	at Nebraska	13	40
S22	•	Iowa	55	18
S29	•	at Michigan State	34	21
O6	•	Utah	66	16
O13	•	at Stanford	59	13
O20	•	Washington State Spo	24	13
O27	•	California	61	21
N3	•	Washington	62	13
N10	•	at Oregon	27	7
N17	•	Oregon State	56	14
N24		at Southern Cal	13	23

THE SCHOOLS

914 UCLA

THE SCHOOLS

DICK VERMEIL
1974-75 (.717) 15-5-3

1974 6-3-2 (4-2-1)

S7	=	at Tennessee	17	17
S21		at Iowa	10	21
S28	●	Michigan State	56	14
O5	●	at Utah	27	14
O12	= │	Stanford	13	13
O19	● │	Washington State	17	13
O26	● │	at California	28	3
N2	│	at Washington	9	31
N9	● │	Oregon	21	0
N16	● │	at Oregon State	33	14
N23	│	Southern Cal	9	34

1975 9-2-1 (6-1-0)

S13	●	Iowa State	37	21
S20	●	Tennessee	34	28
S27	=	at Air Force	20	20
O4		Ohio State	20	41
O11	● │	at Stanford	31	21
O18	● │	Washington State *Spo*	37	23
O25	● │	California	28	14
N1	│	Washington	13	17
N8	● │	at Oregon	50	17
N15	● │	Oregon State	31	9
N28	● │	at Southern Cal	25	22
		ROSE BOWL		
J1	●	Ohio State	23	10

TERRY DONAHUE
1976-95 (.665) 151-74-8

1976 9-2-1 (6-1-0)

S9	●	at Arizona State	28	10
S18	●	Arizona	37	9
S25	●	Air Force	40	7
O2	=	at Ohio State	10	10
O9	● │	Stanford	38	20
O16	● │	Washington State	62	3
O23	● │	at California	35	19
O30	● │	at Washington	30	21
N6	● │	Oregon	46	0
N13	● │	at Oregon State	45	14
N20	│	Southern Cal	14	24
		LIBERTY BOWL		
D20		Alabama	6	36

1977 7-4-0 (5-2-0)

S12		at Houston	13	17
S17	●	Kansas	17	7 †
S24		at Minnesota	13	27
O1	●	Iowa	34	16 †
O8	│	at Stanford	28	32
O15	● │	Washington State *Spo*	27	16 †
O22	● │	California	21	19 †
O29	● │	Washington	20	12 †
N5	● │	at Oregon	21	3
N12	● │	Oregon State	48	18
N25	│	at Southern Cal	27	29

1978 8-3-1 (6-2-0)

S9	● │	at Washington	10	7
S16	●	at Tennessee	13	0
S23		at Kansas	24	28
S30	●	Minnesota	17	3
O7	● │	Stanford	27	26
O14	● │	Washington State	45	31
O21	● │	at California	45	0
O27	● │	Arizona	24	14
N4	● │	Oregon	23	21
N11	│	at Oregon State	13	15
N18	│	Southern Cal	10	17
		FIESTA BOWL		
D25	=	Arkansas	10	10

1979 5-6-0 (3-4-0)

S8		Houston	16	24
S15	●	Purdue	31	21
S22	●	at Wisconsin	37	12
S29		Ohio State	13	17
O6	│	at Stanford	24	27
O13	│	at Washington State	14	17
O20	● │	California	28	27
O27	│	Washington	14	34
N10	● │	Arizona State	31	28
N17	● │	at Oregon	35	0
N24	│	at Southern Cal	14	49

1980 9-2-0 (5-2-0)

S13	●	Colorado	56	14
S20	●	at Purdue	23	14
S27	●	Wisconsin	35	0
O4	●	at Ohio State	17	0
O11	● │	Stanford	35	21
O25	● │	at California	32	9
N1	│	at Arizona	17	23
N8	│	Oregon	14	20
N15	● │	at Arizona State	23	14
N22	● │	Southern Cal	20	17
N30	● │	Oregon State *Tok*	34	3

1981 7-4-1 (5-2-1)

S12	● │	at Arizona	35	18
S19	●	at Wisconsin	31	13
S26		at Iowa	7	20
O3	●	Colorado	27	7
O10	│	at Stanford	23	26
O17	= │	at Washington State	17	17
O24	● │	California	34	6
O31	● │	at Oregon	28	11
N7	● │	Washington	31	0
N14	● │	Arizona State	34	24
N21	│	at Southern Cal	21	22
		BLUEBONNET BOWL		
D31		Michigan	14	33

1982 10-1-1 (5-1-1)

S11	●	Long Beach State	41	10
S18	●	at Wisconsin	51	26
S25	●	at Michigan	31	27
O2	●	at Colorado	34	6
O9	= │	Arizona	24	24
O16	● │	Washington State	42	17
O23	● │	at California	47	31
O30	● │	Oregon	40	12
N6	│	at Washington	7	10
N13	● │	Stanford	38	35
N20	● │	Southern Cal	20	19
		ROSE BOWL		
J1	●	Michigan	24	14

1983 7-4-1 (6-1-1)

S3		at Georgia	8	19
S17	= │	Arizona State	26	26
S24		at Nebraska	10	42
O1		Brigham Young	35	37
O8	● │	at Stanford	39	21
O15	● │	at Washington State	24	14
O22	● │	California	20	16
O29	● │	Washington	27	24
N5	● │	at Oregon	24	13
N12	│	at Arizona	24	27
N19	● │	at Southern Cal	27	17
		ROSE BOWL		
J2	●	Illinois	45	9

1984 9-3-0 (5-2-0)

S8	●	at San Diego State	18	15
S15	●	Long Beach State	23	17
S22		Nebraska	3	42
S29	●	at Colorado	33	16
O6	│	Stanford	21	23
O13	● │	Washington State	27	24
O20	● │	at California	17	14
O27	● │	at Arizona State	21	13
N3	│	Oregon	18	20
N10	● │	Oregon State	26	17
N17	● │	Southern Cal	29	10
		FIESTA BOWL		
J1	●	Miami, Fla.	39	37

1985 9-2-1 (6-2-0)

S7	●	at Brigham Young	27	24
S14	=	at Tennessee	26	26
S21	●	San Diego State	34	16
S28	│	at Washington	14	21
O5	● │	Arizona State	40	17
O12	● │	at Stanford	34	9
O19	● │	at Washington State	31	30
O26	● │	California	34	7
N9	● │	at Arizona	24	19
N16	● │	Oregon State	41	0
N23	│	at Southern Cal	13	17
		ROSE BOWL		
J1	●	Iowa	45	28

1986 8-3-1 (5-2-1)

S6		at Oklahoma	3	38
S20	●	at San Diego State	45	14
S27	●	Long Beach State	41	23
O4	│	Arizona State	9	16
O11	● │	Arizona	32	25
O18	● │	at California	36	10
O25	● │	Washington State	54	16
N1	● │	Oregon State *Port*	49	0
N8	│	Stanford	23	28
N15	= │	at Washington	17	17
N22	● │	Southern Cal	45	25
		FREEDOM BOWL		
D30	●	Brigham Young	31	10

1987 10-2-0 (7-1-0)

S5	●	San Diego State	47	14
S12		at Nebraska	33	42
S19	●	Fresno State	17	0
S26	● │	Arizona	34	24
O3	● │	at Stanford	49	0
O17	● │	Oregon	41	10
O24	● │	California	42	18
O31	● │	at Arizona State	31	23
N7	● │	at Oregon State	52	17
N14	● │	Washington	47	14
N21	│	at Southern Cal	13	17
		ALOHA BOWL		
D25	●	Florida	20	16

1988 10-2-0 (6-2-0)

S3	●	San Diego State	59	6
S10	●	Nebraska	41	28
S17	●	Long Beach State	56	3
O1	● │	at Washington	24	17
O8	● │	Oregon State	38	21
O15	● │	at California	38	21
O22	● │	at Arizona	24	3
O29	│	Washington State	30	34
N5	● │	at Oregon	16	6
N12	● │	Stanford	27	17
N19	│	Southern Cal	22	31
		COTTON BOWL		
J2	●	Arkansas	17	3

1989 3-7-1 (2-5-1)

S9		Tennessee	6	24
S16	●	at San Diego State	28	25
S23		Michigan	23	24
S30	● │	California	24	6
O7	● │	Arizona State	33	14
O14	│	at Arizona	7	42
O21	│	at Oregon State	17	18
O28	│	Washington	27	28
N4	│	at Stanford	14	17
N11	│	Oregon	20	38
N18	= │	at Southern Cal	10	10

1990 5-6-0 (4-4-0)

S8		Oklahoma	14	34
S15	● │	Stanford	32	31
S22		at Michigan	15	38
S29	● │	at Washington State	30	20
O6	│	Arizona	21	28
O13	●	San Diego State	45	31
O20	│	at California	31	38
O27	● │	Oregon State	26	17
N3	│	at Oregon	24	28
N10	● │	at Washington	25	22
N17	│	Southern Cal	42	45

1991 9-3-0 (6-2-0)

S7	●	Brigham Young	27	23
S14		at Tennessee	16	30
S26	●	at San Diego State	37	12
O5	│	California	24	27
O12	● │	Arizona	54	14
O19	● │	at Oregon State	44	7
O26	● │	at Arizona State	21	16
N2	● │	Washington State	44	3
N9	│	at Stanford	10	27
N16	● │	Oregon	16	7
N23	● │	at Southern Cal	24	21
		SUN BOWL		
D31	●	Illinois	6	3

1992 6-5-0 (3-5-0)

S12	●	Fullerton State	37	14
S19	●	at Brigham Young	17	10
S26	●	San Diego State	35	7
O3	│	at Arizona	3	23
O10	│	Stanford	7	19
O17	│	at Washington State	17	30
O24	│	Arizona State	0	20
O31	│	at California	12	48
N7	● │	Oregon State	26	14
N14	● │	at Oregon	9	6
N21	● │	Southern Cal	38	37

1993 8-4-0 (6-2-0)

S4	│	California	25	27
S18		Nebraska	13	14
S25	● │	at Stanford	28	25
S30	●	at San Diego State	52	13
O9	●	Brigham Young	68	14
O16	● │	Washington	39	25
O23	● │	at Oregon State	20	17
O30	● │	Arizona	37	17
N6	● │	at Washington State	40	27
N13	│	Arizona State	3	9
N20	● │	at Southern Cal	27	21
		ROSE BOWL		
J1		Wisconsin	16	21

1994 5-6-0 (3-5-0)

S3	●	Tennessee	25	23
S10	●	SMU	17	10
S17		at Nebraska	21	49
S24	│	Washington State	0	21
O1	│	at Washington	10	37
O8	│	at California	7	26
O15	│	Oregon State	14	23
O22	│	at Arizona	24	34
O29	● │	Stanford	31	30
N12	● │	at Arizona State	59	23
N19	● │	Southern Cal	31	19

1995 7-5-0 (4-4-0)

S2	●	Miami, Fla.	31	8
S9	●	at Brigham Young	23	9
S16	│	Oregon	31	38
S23	│	at Washington State	15	24
S30	●	Fresno State	45	21
O14	● │	Arizona	17	10
O21	● │	at Stanford	42	28
O28	● │	California	33	16
N4	│	at Arizona State	33	37
N11	│	Washington	14	38
N18	● │	at Southern Cal	24	20
		ALOHA BOWL		
D25		Kansas	30	51

BOB TOLEDO
1996-2002 (.605) 49-32

1996 5-6 (4-4)

S7		at Tennessee	20	35
S14	●	La. Monroe	44	0
S28		at Michigan	9	38
O5	● │	at Oregon	41	22
O12	│	Arizona State	34	42
O19	│	at Washington	21	41
O26	● │	at California	38	29
N2	│	Stanford	20	21
N9	● │	Washington State	38	14
N16	│	at Arizona	17	35
N23	● │	Southern Cal	48	41

1997 10-2 (7-1)

A30	│	at Washington State	34	37
S6		Tennessee	24	30
S13	●	at Texas	66	3
S27	● │	Arizona	40	27
O4	●	Houston	66	10
O11	● │	at Oregon	39	31
O18	● │	Oregon State	34	10
O25	● │	California	35	17
N1	● │	at Stanford	27	7
N15	● │	Washington	52	28
N22	● │	at Southern Cal	31	24
		COTTON BOWL		
J1	●	Texas A&M	29	23

1998 10-2 (8-0)

S12	●	Texas	49	31
S19	●	at Houston	42	24
O3	● │	Washington State	49	17
O10	● │	at Arizona	52	28
O17	● │	Oregon	41	38
O24	● │	at California	28	16
O31	● │	Stanford	28	24
N7	● │	at Oregon State	41	34
N14	● │	at Washington	36	24
N21	● │	Southern Cal	34	17
D5		at Miami, Fla.	45	49
		ROSE BOWL		
J1		Wisconsin	31	38

1999 4-7 (2-6)

S4	●	Boise State	38 7
S11		at Ohio State	20 42
S18	●	Fresno State	35 21
S25	|	at Stanford	32 42
O2		at Arizona State	27 28
O9	● |	Oregon	34 29
O16	|	California	0 17
O23	|	at Oregon State	7 55
O30	|	Arizona	7 33
N13	● |	Washington	23 20
N20	|	at Southern Cal	7 17

2000 6-6 (3-5)

S2	●	Alabama	35 24
S9	●	Fresno State	24 21
S16	●	Michigan	23 20
S23	|	at Oregon	10 29
S30	● |	Arizona State	38 31
O14	|	at California	38 46
O21	|	Oregon State	38 44
O28	● |	at Arizona	27 24
N4	● |	Stanford	37 35
N11	|	at Washington	28 35
N18	|	Southern Cal	35 38
SUN BOWL			
D29		Wisconsin	20 21

2001 7-4 (4-4)

S1	●	at Alabama	20 17
S8	●	at Kansas	41 17
S22	●	Ohio State	13 6
S29	● |	at Oregon State	38 7
O13	● |	Washington	35 13
O20	● |	California	56 17
O27	|	at Stanford	28 38
N3	|	at Washington State	14 20
N10	|	Oregon	20 21
N17	|	at Southern Cal	0 27
D1	● |	Arizona State	52 42

ED KEZIRIAN
2002 (1.000) 1-0

2002 8-5 (4-4)

S7	●	Colorado State	30 19
S14	●	at Oklahoma State	38 24
S21		Colorado	17 31
S28	●	at San Diego State	43 7
O5	● |	at Oregon State	43 35
O12	|	Oregon	30 31
O19	|	at California	12 17
O26	● |	Stanford	28 18
N2	|	at Washington	34 24
N9	● |	at Arizona	37 7
N23	|	Southern Cal	21 52
D7	|	Washington State	27 48
LAS VEGAS BOWL			
D25	●	New Mexico	27 13

KARL DORRELL
2003-PRESENT (.480) 12-13

2003 6-7 (4-4)

S6		at Colorado	14 16
S13	●	Illinois	6 3
S20		at Oklahoma	24 59
S27	●	San Diego State	20 10
O4	● |	Washington	46 16
O11	● |	at Arizona	24 21
O18	● |	California	23 20
O25	● |	Arizona State	20 13
N1	|	at Stanford	14 21
N8	|	at Washington State	13 31
N15	|	Oregon	13 31
N22	|	at Southern Cal	22 47
SILICON VALLEY BOWL			
D30		Fresno State	9 17

2004 6-6 (4-4)

S4		Oklahoma State	20 31
S11	●	at Illinois	35 17
S18	● |	at Washington	37 31
O2	● |	San Diego State	33 10
O9	● |	Arizona	37 17
O16	|	at California	28 45
O23	|	at Arizona State	42 48
O30	● |	Stanford	21 0
N6	|	Washington State	29 31
N13	● |	at Oregon	34 26
D4	|	Southern Cal	24 29
LAS VEGAS BOWL			
D23		Wyoming	21 24

Neutral Site key: *Hon* Honolulu, HI / *Pas* Pasadena, CA / *JacF* Jacksonville, FL / *Port* Portland, OR / *Spo* Spokane, WA / *Den* Denver, CO / *Mem* Memphis, TN / *Tok* Tokyo, Japan
f Forfeit † Game Later Forfieted # Disputed Victor * Disputed Score || Designated Conference Game |2 Counted Twice in Conference Standings

UNLV

BY STU DURANDO

GETTING COLLEGE FOOTBALL TO take root in the Southern Nevada desert was not the most daunting task at Nevada-Las Vegas. Keeping it entrenched and flourishing has been a greater challenge for an athletic department that has made its name and its money in basketball. As one of the youngest football programs in the country, UNLV has displayed flashes: the Rebels quickly became a Division II power, were an immediate success in Division I-A and have been perfect in three bowl games. But since the program's birth in 1968, UNLV has struggled to achieve consistency under frequently changing leadership.

By the time football was launched, the basketball program had been growing for 10 years and women's club sports had sprouted on campus. The football program has been playing catch-up ever since. UNLV posted a 126–70–4 record in its first 18 seasons, thanks to the presence of NFL-caliber players such as Mike Thomas in the 1970s and Randall Cunningham and Ickey Woods in the early 1980s. Over the next 19 years, however, the team only managed a 77–138 record even though it featured the receiving talents of Keenan McCardell in the late 1980s and early 1990s.

Nine coaches have already walked the sideline and none for more than six years. The most prominent hire came when former USC and NFL coach John Robinson was lured out of retirement in December 1998. He arrived on the heels of UNLV's least successful period and led the Rebels to a 28–42 record before retiring at the end of the 2004 season. Mike Sanford was hired in December 2004. It was his first head coaching position; previously he was the offensive coordinator at Utah.

TRADITION UNLV has developed little in the way of tradition during the program's short life. The Star of Nevada Marching Band, however, has etched itself a nice spot in the school's lore, thanks to a helping hand from Wayne Newton, who headlined a 1978 fund-raiser—which also included Sammy Davis Jr. and Glen Campbell—for uniforms and instruments. Other Vegas-style fund-raisers ensued over the years with help coming from the likes of Frank Sinatra.

BEST PLAYER Randall Cunningham was known for his work at quarterback, but his skills as a punter made him a double threat. He remains UNLV's career passing leader with 8,020 yards and 59 touchdown passes, but he earned first-team All-America honors as a punter in 1983 and was second team in 1984. His 1984 punting average of 47.5 yards and career average of 45.6 are school records. In 1985, Cunningham became the highest drafted UNLV

PROFILE

University of Nevada, Las Vegas
Las Vegas, Nev.
Founded: 1957
Enrollment: 20,842
Colors: Scarlet and Gray
Nickname: Rebels
Stadium: Sam Boyd Stadium
    Opened in 1971
    TurfTech; 36,800 capacity
First football game: 1968
All-time record: 203–208–4 (.494)
Bowl record: 3–0
Website: www.unlvrebels.com

THE BEST OF TIMES

The Rebels were 27–8 during coach Ron Meyer's tenure from 1973 to 1975 and had their only undefeated regular season in 1974 before losing in the Division II semifinals.

THE WORST OF TIMES

Jeff Horton left rival Nevada to become the head coach in 1994, but kept UNLV buried in the Big West and then the WAC with a 13–44 mark that included a 0–11 finale in 1998.

CONFERENCE

UNLV became a charter member of the Mountain West in 1999 after spending three years in the Western Athletic Conference. The school's first conference affiliation was with the Big West from 1982 to 1995. The Big West was called the Pacific Coast Athletic Association through 1987 and changed its name to Big West in 1988.

DISTINGUISHED ALUMNI

Lori Harrigan, Olympic gold medal-winning softball player; Larry Johnson, NBA player; George Maloof Jr., executive VP, Maloof Companies (family-owned Sacramento Kings, casinos); Anthony Zuiker, TV producer, creator, *CSI*

FIGHT SONG

WIN WITH THE REBELS
Win with the Rebels
A victory today
Win with the Rebels
The scarlet and grey
From mountains that surround you
To far across the sea,
We'll win with the Rebels of UNLV!
U ... N ... L ... V ...
UNLV, Go, Fight, Win!
We'll win with the Rebels of UNLV!

player at that point, going No. 37 overall to Philadelphia.

BEST COACH He was around for only six seasons, from 1976 to 1981, but Tony Knap ranks as the program's winningest coach and he helped the Rebels make a successful transition to Division I-A. Knap led UNLV to the Division II playoffs in 1976, and the Rebels went 7–4 in their first D1-A season, against a schedule consisting largely of Western Athletic Conference programs. He finished 47–20–2, the biggest win being an upset of No. 8 Brigham Young in 1981.

BEST TEAM The 1984 squad featured future NFL stars Cunningham and Woods and became the first team in the Pacific Coast Athletic Association (later the Big West) to win seven conference games. The Rebels clinched the title in the PCAA finale with a 27-13 win over visiting Fresno State. They were 11–2 overall, losing at Hawaii and against No. 10 Southern Methodist. The season ended with the school's first bowl win, a 30-13 victory against Toledo.

BIGGEST GAME UNLV had lost five consecutive meetings with rival Nevada when they met to decide

> *Randall Cunningham was known as a quarterback, but he was also an All-America punter.*

which team would play in the 1994 Las Vegas Bowl. UNLV pulled off a 32-27 upset that gave the Rebels a share of the Big West championship. They defeated Central Michigan 52-24 in the bowl game.

BIGGEST UPSET In the midst of what would become the program's first mediocre season at the Division I-A level, the Rebels went to Provo, Utah, in 1981 and beat No. 8-ranked Brigham Young, 45-41. UNLV quarterback Sam King threw for 473 yards and connected with Jim Sandusky for a 20-yard touchdown with 19 seconds left to complete a comeback from a 41-24 deficit. Steve Young threw for 269 yards and had four interceptions for BYU. UNLV followed the victory with four consecutive losses and finished 6–6.

HEARTBREAKER UNLV was leading Arkansas 10-0 at War Memorial Stadium in Little Rock in the 2001 season opener, and they were dominating statistically. The Rebels held Arkansas to 114 total yards, and the Razorbacks went 0-for-15 on third down. But Arkansas scored on an interception return in the third quarter and took advantage of a botched punt late in the fourth to set up the decisive score in a 14-10 victory. UNLV went on to lose its next three games.

RECORDS

RUSHING YARDS
GAME
314 Mike Thomas vs. Santa Clara, Nov. 3, 1973 (30 att.)
SEASON
1,741 Mike Thomas, 1973 (274 att.)
CAREER
3,149 Mike Thomas, 1973-74 (475 att.)

PASSING YARDS
GAME
503 Jon Denton vs. San Diego State, Nov. 16, 1996 (27 of 53)
SEASON
3,778 Sam King, 1981 (255 of 433)
CAREER
8,020 Randall Cunningham, 1982-84 (596 of 1,029)

RECEIVING YARDS
GAME
363 Randy Gatewood vs. Idaho, Sept. 17, 1994 (23 rec.)
SEASON
1,346 Jim Sandusky, 1981 (68 rec.)
CAREER
2,604 Earvin Johnson, 2001-04 (183 rec.)

POINTS
GAME
26 Mike Thomas vs. Santa Clara, Oct. 5, 1974 (4 TDs, 1 two-pt. conv.)
SEASON
128 Mike Thomas, 1973 (21 TDs, 1 two-pt. conv.)
CAREER
244 Mike Thomas, 1973-74 (40 TDs, 2 two-pt. conv.)

CONSENSUS ALL-AMERICANS

1973-74	Mike Thomas, RB
1975	Joseph Ingersoll, DL
1998	Joe Kristosik, P

WILDEST FINISH Pro football has its Miracle at the Meadowlands, and the college game has its Brain Lock at Baylor. In 1999, UNLV became the first college team to win a game on the last play while trailing and not possessing the ball. The Rebels had a coaching decision by Baylor's Kevin Steele to thank. Leading 24-21, Baylor had the ball at UNLV's 8-yard line with eight seconds left, but instead of having his quarterback take a knee, Steele called for a handoff. Darrell Bush fumbled and UNLV defensive back Kevin Thomas picked up the ball in the end zone and returned it more than 100 yards for the winning touchdown.

STADIUM Las Vegas Stadium rose from an open expanse of desert seven miles from the UNLV campus in 1971 and has undergone various renovations. The stadium was renamed the Las Vegas Silver Bowl in 1978 and the Sam Boyd Silver Bowl in 1984 in honor of a local gaming pioneer. Since 1994, it has been known simply as Sam Boyd Stadium. The facility was long known for its retractable playing surface, which was removed in favor of grass in 1999 and then TurfTech in 2003. End zone seating has occasionally been added to the horseshoe stadium to handle crowds in excess of 40,000.

RIVAL UNLV's relationship with its only in-state Division I foe is so feisty that the school refuses to recognize the name used by its rival. The series is about even. The school to the north has asked to be called Nevada since the early 1990s, but to most in Las Vegas, it's still Nevada-Reno. The schools play each year for the Fremont Cannon, a replica of the cannon used by John C. Fremont during his westward trek in 1843 that has been valued at more than $10,000.

DUBIOUS DISTINCTION The program's best team (1984) will go down in history as winless in the eyes of the Pacific Coast Athletic Association, which later became the Big West. The PCAA made the Rebels forfeit their wins from an 11–2 season because of the use of several academically ineligible players.

NICKNAME Teams were dubbed the Rebels to represent the school stepping out of the shadow of Nevada-Reno and rebelling against the older university to the north. Runnin' Rebels (always spelled without a "g") was coined in 1974 by a sports information director, and it is used only in reference to the men's basketball team.

MASCOT Hey Reb is a more muscular version of the longstanding, mustached cartoon soldier who became widely recognized during the school's basketball heyday. The new version, created in 1997, features a more menacing look and no musket. The original mascot was a winking cartoon wolf named Beauregard, who wore a Confederate cap. He was replaced after a group of African-American athletes voiced their displeasure in the early 1970s.

UNIFORMS UNLV has had an abundance of helmet designs for a program so young. The first change came after one season, when a Confederate flag inserted in a football was removed in favor of lettering. Coach Jim Strong, who arrived after a stint at Notre Dame, brought the program an Irish-inspired look from 1990-93 (except the helmets were solid silver instead of gold). The helmets now are silver with UNLV in block lettering.

LORE To help launch the program, UNLV solicited 100 people to make $1,000 contributions. The financial commitments came in exchange for a promise that the donors would receive two seasons tickets for football and basketball games in perpetuity.

QUOTE "We're not going to make predictions. We are going to be on the move. We are going to be second to none." —John Robinson, at the press conference to announce his hiring in December 1998

UNLV ANNUAL STATISTICAL LEADERS

YR	RUSHING	YDS	ATT	AVG	PASSING	ATT	CMP	PCT	YDS	RECEIVING	REC	YDS	AVG
1968	Larry Hodges	568	128	4.4	Bill Casey	168	95	.57	1,423	Mark Larson	27	391	14.5
1969	Mack Gilchrist	765	153	5.0	Don Kennedy	141	64	.45	966	Nathaniel Hawkins	21	370	17.6
1970	Mack Gilchrist	764	175	4.4	Jim Starkes	113	59	.52	1,097	Greg Brown	44	741	16.8
1971	Charles Cooper	402	116	3.5	Jim Starkes	202	87	.43	1,059	Greg Brown	38	626	16.5
1972	Steve Matousek	389	103	3.8	Sonny Brasile	146	68	.47	807	Jack Hansen	38	459	12.1
1973	Mike Thomas	1,741	274	6.4	Mike Pry	69	28	.41	481	Jesse Roberts	12	225	18.8
1974	Mike Thomas	1,408	201	7.0	Glenn Carano	106	49	.46	839	Mike Haverty	15	251	16.7
1975	Darall Moore	547	105	5.2	Glenn Carano	226	128	.57	2,039	Kurt Schnabel	32	690	21.6
1976	Raymond Strong	907	125	7.3	Glenn Carano	277	148	.53	2,024	Mike Haverty	51	738	14.5
1977	Raymond Strong	843	143	5.9	Greg Van Ness	251	122	.49	1,736	Brian Harris	45	663	14.7
1978	Leon Walker	922	130	7.1	Doug Robertson	173	72	.42	1,104	Brian Harris	20	380	19.0
1979	Michael Morton	881	143	6.2	Sam King	188	103	.55	1,594	Sam Greene	40	821	20.5
1980	Michael Morton	552	79	7.0	Larry Gentry	209	113	.54	1,691	Sam Greene	43	859	20.0
1981	Michael Morton	692	123	5.6	Sam King	433	255	.59	3,778	Jim Sandusky	68	1,346	19.8
1982	Lloyd Henderson	239	54	4.4	Randall Cunningham	381	200	.52	2,847	Darral Hambrick	60	1,060	17.7
1983	Keyvan Jenkins	456	87	5.2	Randall Cunningham	316	189	.60	2,545	Michael McDade	46	526	11.4
1984	Kirk Jones	1,007	154	6.5	Randall Cunningham	332	207	.62	2,628	Tony Gladney	38	641	16.9
1985	Kirk Jones	790	156	5.1	Steve Stallworth	292	158	.54	1,920	Tony Lewis	37	400	10.8
1986	Rod Emery	584	117	5.0	Steve Stallworth	256	135	.53	1,869	George Thomas	34	808	23.8
1987	Ickey Woods	1,658	259	6.4	Scott Sims	180	76	.42	809	George Thomas	45	586	13.0
1988	Tommy Jackson	894	179	5.0	Charles Price	200	96	.48	1,200	Tommy Jackson	26	254	9.8
1989	Kyle Toomer	736	134	5.5	Derek Stott	222	114	.51	1,701	Keenan McCardell	54	883	16.4
1990	Marvin Eastman	731	141	5.2	Derek Stott	254	143	.56	1,877	Keenan McCardell	68	1,046	15.4
1991	Derek Black	588	147	4.0	Derek Stott	168	78	.46	1,147	Henry Bailey	37	595	16.1
1992	Shannon Wilson	650	143	4.5	John Ma'ae	176	75	.43	1,179	Demond Thompkins	54	919	17.0
1993	Omar Love	545	129	4.2	Bob Stockham	373	179	.48	2,490	Demond Thompkins	62	1,068	17.2
1994	Omar Love	548	150	3.7	Jason Davis	267	130	.49	1,539	Randy Gatewood	88	1,203	13.7
1995	Tony Burton	880	163	5.4	Jared Brown	304	147	.48	1,783	Damon Williams	41	515	12.6
1996	Omar Love	356	91	3.9	Jon Denton	506	277	.55	3,591	Carlos Baker	71	887	12.5
1997	Coury Hankins	641	127	5.0	Jon Denton	374	199	.53	2,586	Damon Williams	61	770	12.6
1998	James Wofford	816	173	4.7	Kevin Crook	115	50	.43	688	Len Ware	39	500	12.8
1999	Jeremi Rudolph	693	155	4.5	Jason Vaughan	195	104	.53	1,043	Nate Turner	45	627	13.9
2000	Jeremi Rudolph	1,005	178	5.6	Jason Thomas	201	106	.53	1,708	Nate Turner	66	947	14.3
2001	Joe Haro	1,107	218	5.1	Jason Thomas	194	83	.43	1,353	Michael Johnson	25	435	17.4
2002	Joe Haro	841	159	5.3	Jason Thomas	274	134	.49	1,936	Earvin Johnson	51	793	15.5
2003	Larry Croom	932	208	4.5	Kurt Nantkes	323	167	.52	1,883	Earvin Johnson	60	834	13.9
2004	Dominique Dorsey	1,260	226	5.6	Shane Steichen	187	92	.49	1,011	Earvin Johnson	60	795	13.3

Receiving leaders by receptions
The NCAA began including postseason stats in 2002

THE SCHOOLS

UNLV All-Time Scores

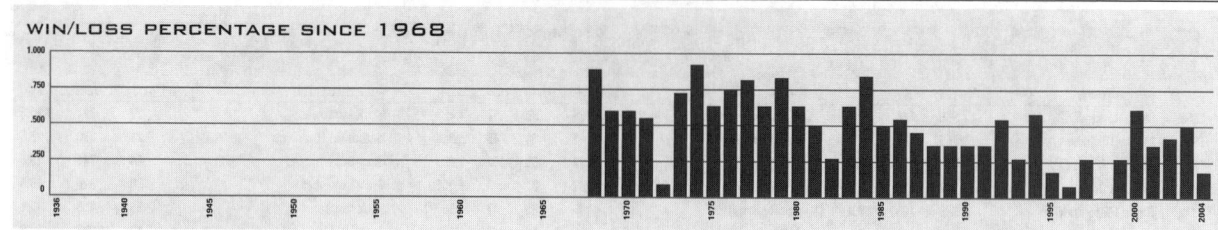

WIN/LOSS PERCENTAGE SINCE 1968

BILL IRELAND
1968-72 (.530)   26-23-1

1968   8-1-0
S14	●	Saint Mary's-Cal	27 20
S21	●	at Azusa Pacific	29 8
S28	●	at San Francisco	23 7
O5	●	Westminster	27 7
O19	●	Southern Colorado	25 21
O26	●	Cal Tech	69 0
N2	●	Southern Utah State	26 17
N16	●	UC San Diego	27 6
N23		Cal Lutheran	13 17

1969   6-4-0
S20		Cal Lutheran	0 26
S27	●	LaVerne	39 26
O4	●	at Southern Utah State	30 12
O11		Santa Clara	13 26
O18	●	at Azusa Pacific	35 13
O25		at Hawaii	19 57
N1	●	UC Riverside	36 6
N8	●	Idaho State	35 31
N15	●	Hiram Scott College	36 28
N22		at Nevada	28 30

1970   6-4-0
S19	●	Southern Utah State	28 6
S26	●	at Idaho State	34 64
O3	●	Oregon Tech	56 0
O10		at UC Riverside	19 21
O17		Cal St. LA	20 21
O22	●	at Fullerton St.	20 10
O31	●	at Santa Clara	35 25
N7		Hawaii	21 28
N14	●	Montana State	38 36
N26	●	Nevada	42 30

1971   5-4-1
S18	●	Adams State College	38 0
S25		at Utah State	7 27
O9	●	Santa Clara	23 14
O16		at Northern Arizona	7 20
O23		Weber State	17 30
O30	●	N.M. Highlands	55 31
N6		Cal Poly-SLO	3 13
N13	=	North Dakota	17 17
N20	●	at Nevada	24 13
N27	●	U. of Mexico	63 6

1972   1-10-0
S9		Western Illinois	28 35
S16		at Boise State	16 36
S23	●	Cal St. LA	31 0
S30		UC Riverside	7 14
O7		Missouri Southern	0 7
O14		at Santa Clara	14 28
O21		Fullerton St.	20 30
O28		at Weber State	0 30
N4		at Miami, Fla.	7 51
N11		North Dakota	13 17
N18		Nevada	13 41

RON MEYER
1973-75 (.771)   27-8

1973   8-3-0
S8	●	Arkansas Coll.	38 6
S15	●	Cal St. LA	42 7
S21	●	Marshall	31 9
S29		Utah State	3 7
O6	●	La. Monroe	26 0
O13	●	Boise State	24 19
O20	●	Wisconsin-Milwaukee	35 24
O27		at Hawaii	29 31
N3	●	at Santa Clara	31 15
N10	●	Northern Arizona	42 14
N17		at Nevada	3 19

1974   12-1-0
S14	●	at Weber State	28 10
S21	●	at Northern Arizona	31 14
S28	●	Montana	20 17
O5	●	Santa Clara	51 19
O12	●	Prairie View A&M	63 28
O19	●	Boise State	37 35
O26	●	Hawaii	33 8
N2	●	N.M. Highlands	52 14
N9	●	South Dakota State	24 21
N16	●	Nevada	28 7
N23	●	Idaho State	31 7
	D-II PLAYOFFS		
N30	●	Alcorn State	35 22
	GRANTLAND RICE BOWL		
D7		Delaware	11 49

1975   7-4-0
S13	●	Northern Iowa	48 10
S20		at Idaho State	7 15
S27		at Montana	20 21
O4	●	Jackson State	39 2
O11	●	Nebraska-Omaha	35 6
O18		at Boise State	21 34
O25		Idaho	7 39
N1	●	Northern Arizona	34 21
N8	●	South Dakota State	38 23
N15	●	Weber State	38 14
N22	●	at Nevada	45 7

TONY KNAP
1976-81 (.696)   47-20-2

1976   9-3-0
S11	●	Montana	21 19
S18	●	South Dakota	28 26
S25	●	at Weber State	33 16
O2	●	Idaho State	31 17
O9		at Pacific	13 38
O16	●	Nebraska-Omaha	63 42
O23		at Northern Arizona	28 31
O30	●	Cal Poly-SLO	28 10
N6	●	Boise State	31 26
N13	●	Missouri Southern	28 3
N20	●	Nevada	49 33
	D-II PLAYOFFS		
N27		at Akron	6 27

1977   9-2-0
S10	●	at Montana	15 13
S17	●	Troy State	35 28
S24		at Boise State	14 45
O1	●	Northern Arizona	20 16
O8	●	Western Illinois	59 29
O15	●	Weber State	26 13
O22		at San Diego State	7 31
O29	●	Fullerton St.	24 21
N5	●	at Idaho	35 14
N12	●	North Dakota	38 14
N19	●	at Nevada	27 12

1978   7-4-0
S9	●	Washington State *Spo*	7 34
S16	●	Nevada	14 23
S23	●	at New Mexico	0 24
O7	●	Idaho	53 14
O14	●	Hawaii	30 20
O21	●	at Colorado State	33 6
O28	●	at Montana	25 16
N11	●	Wyoming	12 10
N18	●	Texas-El Paso	27 0
N25	●	Fullerton St.	24 7
D2		Brigham Young *Yox*	24 28

1979   9-1-2
S8	●	at Fullerton St.	35 14
S15	●	at Nevada	26 21
S22	●	at Texas-El Paso	15 17
S29	●	at Hawaii	48 31
O6	●	No. Colorado	35 31
O13	●	New Mexico	28 20
O20	●	Utah	43 41
O27	●	at Wyoming	28 24
N3	●	at Fresno State	31 28
N10	●	at Tennessee St.	36 28
N17	=	Colorado State	21 21
N24	=	Lamar	24 24

1980   7-4-0
S13	●	Fresno State	35 6
S20		at Utah	29 45
S27	●	at Colorado State	56 15
O4	●	Fullerton St.	36 17
O11	●	at San Diego State	28 17
O18	●	Texas-El Paso	53 14
O25		at Oregon	9 32
N1	●	at New Mexico	72 7
N8	●	Wyoming	33 26
N15		Hawaii	19 24
N29		Brigham Young	14 54

1981   6-6-0
S5	●	at San Jose State	16 6
S12	●	New Mexico	49 42
S19	●	West Texas St.	17 21
S26	●	Long Beach St.	32 31
O3		at Wyoming	21 45
O10	●	at Brigham Young	45 41
O24		Utah	28 69
O31		at Hawaii	21 57
N7		at Fresno State	26 42
N14		San Diego State	20 38
N21	●	Air Force	24 21
N28	●	at Texas-El Paso	27 20

**1982-1995
BIG WEST**

HARVEY HYDE
1982-85 (.576)   26-19-1

1982   3-8-0 (1-5-0)
S2		Brigham Young	0 27
S18		at New Mexico	21 49
S25		at San Diego State	23 26
O2		at Pacific	27 29
O9		Texas-El Paso	28 21
O16	‖	at Utah	14 24
O30		San Jose State	14 48
N6		at Colorado State	36 31
N13		at Long Beach St.	13 24
N20		Fresno State	28 30
N27		Fullerton St.	42 23

1983   7-4-0 (4-2-0)
S3	●	Nevada	28 18
S10		at San Jose State	26 31
S17	●	at Pacific	28 7
S24		Washington State *Spo*	28 41
O1	●	at Oregon State	35 21
O15		Hawaii	0 23
O22	●	Utah State	28 10
O29	●	San Diego State	28 10
N5	●	at Fresno State	20 7
N12	●	at Fullerton St.	13 0
N19		Long Beach St.	21 24

1984   11-2-0 (7-0-0)
S8	●	San Jose State	30 15 †
S15	●	at New Mexico State	28 21 †
S22	●	Wichita St.	38 21 †
S29	●	at Hawaii	12 16
O6	●	at Long Beach St.	41 23 †
O13	●	Idaho St.	33 20 †
O20	●	at Pacific	35 21 †
N3	●	at San Diego State	30 14 †
N10	●	Fullerton St.	26 20 †
N17	●	at Utah State	36 20 †
N24	●	Fresno State	27 13 †
D1		SMU	21 38
	CALIFORNIA BOWL		
D15	●	Toledo	30 13 †

1985   5-5-1 (4-2-1)
S7	●	Tenn. Tech	35 7
S14		at Fresno State	6 26
S21		at Wisconsin	23 26
S28		Long Beach St.	24 28
O5	●	Utah State	14 7
O12	●	Pacific	24 14
O19	●	at Fullerton St.	10 6
O26		at La. Lafayette	13 20
O31	●	New Mexico State	17 12
N9		at Nevada	7 48
N16	=	at San Jose State	16 16

WAYNE NUNNELY
1986-89 (.432)   19-25

1986   6-5-0 (3-4-0)
S6		at Washington State	14 34
S13		at Portland St.	51 14
S20	●	Wisconsin	17 7
S27		Fullerton St.	40 23
O11		at Pacific	15 21
O18		San Jose State	20 23
O25		at Utah State	6 7
N1	●	North Texas	27 26
N8		Fresno State	7 36
N15	●	at New Mexico State	58 42
N22	●	at Long Beach St.	31 8

1987   5-6-0 (4-3-0)
S12		at La. Lafayette	10 21
S19		Baylor	14 21
O3		Nevada	24 19
O10		Utah State	28 27
O17		Fullerton St.	14 28
O24		San Jose State	24 48
O31		at Fresno State	10 45
N7	●	Long Beach St.	30 17
N14		at New Mexico State	29 6
N21	●	Pacific	30 24
N28		Northern Illinois	31 34

1988   4-7-0 (3-4-0)
S3		at Baylor	3 27
S17		Fullerton St.	10 20
S24	●	Ohio U.	26 18
O1		at Nebraska	6 48
O8	●	at Pacific	30 16
O15		New Mexico State	28 20
O29		Tulsa	7 33
N5		at Utah State	10 17
N12		Fresno State	14 31
N19		San Jose State	0 42
N26	●	at Long Beach St.	42 41

1989   4-7-0 (3-4-0)
S2		Houston	0 69
S9		Weber St.	16 12
S23	●	New Mexico State	26 14
S30	●	at Fullerton St.	20 34
O7	●	Pacific	30 7
O21		at Northern Illinois	24 42
O28		at Fresno State	17 31
N4	●	Long Beach St.	43 21
N11		at Nevada	7 45
N18		Utah State	22 27
N25		at San Jose State	28 38

JIM STRONG
1990-93 (.386)   17-27

1990   4-7-0 (3-4-0)
S1		S.W. Missouri St.	24	31
S8		at Houston	9	37
S15	•	at Oregon State	45	20
S22		San Jose State	13	47
S29	•	at Pacific	37	28
O6	•	Fullerton St.	29	10
O13	•	at New Mexico State	24	20
O20		Nevada	14	26
O27		at Utah State	6	31
N3		Fresno State	18	45
N17		at Long Beach St.	20	29

1991   4-7-0 (2-5-0)
S7		at Nevada	8	50
S14	•	Oregon State	23	9
S21	•	at New Mexico	23	22
S28		Washington State	13	40
O5		Long Beach St.	19	31
O12	•	at Fullerton St.	25	3
O26		at Fresno State	22	48
N2		at San Jose State	12	55
N9		Utah State	14	27
N16	•	New Mexico State	38	28
N23		Pacific	23	44

1992   6-5-0 (3-3-0)
S12	•	Texas-El Paso	19	17
S19	•	No. Arizona	40	7
S26		at Oregon	6	59
O3	•	at Pacific	21	17
O10		at New Mexico State	10	40
O17		Nevada	10	14
O24		at Hawaii	25	55
O31	•	San Jose State	35	31
N7		at Utah State	8	48
N21	•	Montana St.	36	7
N28	•	Fullerton St.	33	16

1993   3-8-0 (2-4-0)
S4		at Clemson	14	24
S11		at Texas-El Paso	24	41
S18	•	Central Michigan	33	20
S25		at Kansas State	20	36
O2		at Nevada	14	49
O9		Northridge St.	18	24
O23		Utah State	26	33
O30		New Mexico State	40	52
N6	•	at Louisiana Tech	28	23
N13	•	at San Jose State	28	14
N20		La. Lafayette	14	31

JEFF HORTON
1994-98 (.228)   13-44

1994   7-5-0 (5-1-0)
S3	•	Eastern Michigan	17	3
S10		at Central Michigan	23	35
S17		Idaho	38	48
S24	•	at Utah State	23	21
O1	•	at New Mexico State	31	27
O8	•	Louisiana Tech	24	20
O15		at Tulsa	22	44
O29	•	San Jose State	23	10
N5		at La. Lafayette	27	28
N19	•	Nevada	32	27
N26		Kansas State	3	42

LAS VEGAS BOWL
D15	•	Central Michigan	52	24

1995   2-9-0 (1-5-0)
S2		at Rice	0	38
S9	•	Arkansas State	28	23
S16		at Eastern Michigan	6	51
S23		at Iowa State	30	57
S30		Hawaii	30	58
O7		at Northern Illinois	14	62
O14		at San Jose State	14	52
O28		at Nevada	32	55
N4	•	North Texas	34	24
N11		Utah State	0	42
N18		New Mexico State	34	58

1996-1998
WAC

1996   1-11 (1-8)
A31		at Tennessee	3	62
S7	•	Air Force	17	65
S14		Wisconsin	17	52
S21		at Colorado State	16	35
S28		Wyoming	21	33
O5		Nevada	17	54
O12		at Brigham Young	28	63
O19		at Hawaii	28	38
O26		Fresno State	23	34
N2		at TCU	34	42
N16	•	San Diego State	44	42
N23		at San Jose State	28	31

1997   3-8 (2-6)
S6		at Nevada	14	31
S13		at Air Force	24	25
S20	•	Hawaii	25	15
S27	•	Illinois St.	41	6
O4		at Southern Cal	21	35
O11	•	TCU	21	19
O18		at San Diego State	17	20
O25		at Fresno State	28	46
N1		Colorado State	19	45
N8		at Wyoming	23	35
N22		San Jose State	48	55

1998   0-11 (0-8)
S5		at Northwestern	7	41
S12		Air Force	10	52
S19		at Wisconsin	7	52
S26		at Colorado State	16	38
O3		Nevada	20	31
O10		at Brigham Young	14	38
O17		Wyoming	25	28
O24		at SMU	7	10
O31		Tulsa	16	20
N14		at Rice	16	38
N21		TCU	18	41

1999-Present
MOUNTAIN WEST

JOHN ROBINSON
1999-2004 (.400)   28-42

1999   3-8 (1-6)
S4	•	at North Texas	26	3
S11	•	at Baylor	27	24
S18		Iowa State	0	24
S25		Utah	14	52
O2		at Nevada	12	26
O9	•	at Wyoming	35	32
O23		Brigham Young	0	29
O30		at New Mexico	6	27
N13		at Air Force	16	35
N20		San Diego State	7	37
N27		Colorado State	17	35

2000   8-5 (4-3)
S9		at Iowa State	22	37
S16	•	North Texas	38	0
S23		at Brigham Young	7	10
S30	•	Air Force	34	13
O7	•	Nevada	38	7
O14		at Colorado State	19	20
O21	•	Wyoming	42	23
O28		at Mississippi	40	43
N4		at Utah	16	38
N11	•	New Mexico	18	14
N25	•	at San Diego State	31	24
D2	•	at Hawaii	34	32

LAS VEGAS BOWL
D21	•	Arkansas	31	14

2001   4-7 (3-4)
A30		Arkansas LR	10	14
S7	•	Northwestern	28	37
S22		at Arizona	21	38
S29		Brigham Young	31	35
O6	•	at Nevada	27	12
O13	•	San Diego State	31	3
O20		Colorado State	24	26
O27	•	at Wyoming	47	26
N3		Utah	14	42
N10		at New Mexico	17	27
N17	•	at Air Force	34	10

2002   5-7 (3-4)
A31		Wisconsin	7	27
S7	•	Kansas	31	20
S14		at Oregon State	17	47
S21		at Toledo	21	38
O5	•	Nevada	21	17
O12		New Mexico	16	25
O19	•	at Brigham Young	24	3
O26		at San Diego State	21	31
N2	•	Wyoming	49	48
N9		at Utah	17	28
N16		Air Force	32	49
N30	•	at Colorado State	36	33

2003   6-6 (2-5)
A29	•	Toledo	28	18
S6		at Kansas	24	46
S13	•	at Wisconsin	23	5
S19	•	Hawaii	33	22
O4		at Nevada	16	12
O11		at Air Force	7	24
O18		Utah	10	28
O25		Brigham Young	20	27
N1	•	at New Mexico	37	35
N8		San Diego State	0	7
N22		Colorado State	23	24
N29	•	at Wyoming	35	24

2004   2-9 (1-6)
S5		at Tennessee	17	42
S11		at Wisconsin	3	18
S18		Air Force	10	27
S25		Utah State	21	31
O2	•	Nevada	48	13
O8	•	at Brigham Young	24	20
O16		New Mexico	20	24
O23		at Utah	28	63
N6		Wyoming	45	53
N13		at Colorado State	10	45
N20		at San Diego State	3	21

THE SCHOOLS

UTAH

BY STU DURANDO

THE UNIVERSITY OF UTAH HAS NEVER been a menacing football power, but the Utes have been consistently strong since they first took the field in 1892. Under legendary coach Ike Armstrong, the university enjoyed its longest period of success from 1925 to 1949. But Utah failed to make a major national impact until the 1990s, when it finally started to climb out of Brigham Young's shadow. Coach Ron McBride raised expectations so dramatically that not even a run of six bowl appearances between 1992 and 2001 could save him from being replaced in 2002 by Urban Meyer, who led the Utes back into the national polls in 2003.

The big breakout came in 2004, of course, when the Utes went 12–0, became the first non-BCS team to play in a BCS bowl game and were ranked No. 4 in the final Associated Press poll.

You win that big, you reap big rewards: even before the Utes finished the season, Meyer had agreed to become head coach at Florida. Goodbye, Salt Lake City. Hello, Gainseville.

TRADITION Sitting 5,300 feet above sea level and looming 700 feet above the campus, the Block U has been displayed on Mount Van Cott since 1907. The design was changed and 124 lights were placed around the border of the U in 1969. It is lit during athletic events and flashes after a Utah win.

BEST PLAYER Longtime fans lean toward Larry Wilson (1957-59), who went on to become an NFL Hall of Famer. A defensive back and halfback at Utah, Wilson holds the school record of five touchdowns in a game. With the St. Louis Cardinals, he made the safety blitz famous and played in eight Pro Bowls. Younger fans favor defensive tackle Luther Elliss, a consensus All-America on the 1994 team, considered by many the best player in school history. He was a first-round pick of the Detroit Lions in 1995.

BEST COACH Ike Armstrong coached Utah for 25 seasons and posted a 141–55–15 record. He didn't have a

PROFILE

University of Utah
Salt Lake City, Utah
Founded: 1850
Enrollment: 22,421
Colors: Crimson and White
Nickname: Utes
Stadium: Rice-Eccles Stadium
   Opened in 1998
   FieldTurf; 45,017 capacity
First football game: 1892
All-time record: 560–405–31 (.578)
Bowl record: 7–3
Mountain West Conference championships:
3 (2 outright)
First-round NFL draftees: 6
Website: www.utahhutes.com

THE BEST OF TIMES

Urban Meyer went 22–2 in 2003-04 and won Utah's first outright conference title in his first season. Utah went undefeated in 2004 and finished No. 4 in the AP rankings.

THE WORST OF TIMES

From 1974 to 1977, Utah had four consecutive losing seasons for the first time, including a 2–20 mark in 1974 and 1975.

CONFERENCE

A charter member of the Mountain West Conference in 1999, Utah was previously in the Rocky Mountain Conference (1910-37) and the Mountain States (1938-47). Utah then played in the Skyline Conference for 14 seasons and the Western Athletic Conference for 36.

DISTINGUISHED ALUMNI

Nolan Bushnell, inventor of Pong; Stephen Covey, business consultant, author of *7 Habits of Highly Effective People*; Wilbert (Bill) Gore, inventor of Gore-Tex; Robert Jarvik, inventor of Jarvik-7 artificial heart; J. Willard Marriott Sr. and J. Willard Marriott Jr., hoteliers; Evelyn Wood, speed-reading innovator

FIGHT SONG

UTAH MAN

I am a Utah man, sir, and I live across the green.
Our gang, it is the jolliest that you have ever seen.
Our coeds are the fairest and each one's a shining star.
Our yell, you hear it ringing through the mountains near and far.

Who am I, sir? A Utah man am I, A Utah man, sir, and will be till I die; Ki!Yi!
We're up to snuff; we never bluff,
We're game for any fuss,
No other gang of college men
dare meet us in the muss.
So fill your lungs and sing it out and shout it to the sky,
We'll fight for dear old Crimson,
for a Utah man am I.

And when we prom the avenue, all lined up in a row,
And arm-in-arm and step in time as down the street we go.
No matter if a freshman green, or in a senior's gown,
The people all admit we are the warmest gang in town.

We may not live forever on this jolly good old sphere,
But while we do we'll live a life of merriment and cheer,
And when our college days are o'er and night is drawing nigh,
With parting breath we'll sing that song:
"A Utah Man Am I."

losing record until his 19th campaign. The Utes had 21 winning seasons under Armstrong and went unbeaten five times. He won championships in three conferences—seven in the Rocky Mountain, four in the Big Seven, one in the Skyline. His teams were 18–1–3 against BYU.

In 2004, the Utes became the first non-BCS school to play in a BCS game.

Arizona 5-yard line, quarterback Mike McCoy connected with Kevin Dyson on fourth and goal for the game-winning touchdown with 3:34 left. It capped the program's first 10-win season.

BEST TEAM Think about those 2004 highlights again: 12–0, No. 4 in the nation, first non-BCS team to appear in a BCS bowl game. Quarterback Alex Smith led a high-powered offense that ranked fifth nationally in total offense. The Utes averaged 45.3 points and were rarely challenged; their smallest margin of victory was 14 points. To top a can-you-believe-it season, they routed Pittsburgh 35-7 in the Fiesta Bowl.

BIGGEST GAME The Utes won their first bowl game in 30 years when they pulled out a 16-13 squeaker over heavily favored Arizona in the 1994 Freedom Bowl. After freshman Cal Beck returned a kickoff 72 yards to the

BIGGEST UPSET After starting the 1988 season 2–5, Utah needed to win its final four games to post a winning record. The Utes pulled off the first three before encountering bowl-bound BYU in the finale. They handed the Cougars their worst loss of the season with a 57-28 thrashing to finish 6–5 overall and 4–4 in the WAC. Utah quarterback Scott Mitchell passed for 384 yards as the Utes had their biggest offensive day in the 79-game history of the series and snapped a nine-game losing streak against the Cougars.

HEARTBREAKER The second-largest crowd (45,634) in the history of Rice-Eccles Stadium was ready to explode, but Ryan Kaneshiro's 32-yard field goal attempt smacked the right upright and fell harmlessly to the ground,

RECORDS

RUSHING YARDS

GAME
254   Mike Anderson vs. Fresno State, Dec. 18, 1999 (34 att.)

SEASON
1,507   Carl Monroe, 1982 (309 att.)

CAREER
3,219   Eddie Johnson, 1984-88 (564 att.)

PASSING YARDS

GAME
631   Scott Mitchell vs. Air Force, Oct. 15, 1988 (36 of 60)

SEASON
4,322   Scott Mitchell, 1988 (323 of 533)

CAREER
8,981   Scott Mitchell, 1987-89 (669 of 1,165)

RECEIVING YARDS

GAME
255   Carl Harry vs. Idaho State, Sept. 10, 1988 (8 rec.)

SEASON
1,145   Carl Harry, 1988 (65 rec.)

CAREER
3,143   Bryan Rowley, 1989-93 (177 rec.)

POINTS

GAME
32   Larry Wilson vs. Arizona, Oct. 31, 1959 (5 TDs, 1 two-pt. conv.)

SEASON
110   Dennis Smith, 1989 (18 TDs, 1 two-pt. conv.)

CAREER
235   Frank Christensen, 1930-32

CONSENSUS ALL-AMERICANS

| 1994 | Luther Elliss, DT |
| 2002 | Jordan Gross, OL |

preserving BYU's 26-24 win in 1998. The win allowed BYU to take the WAC Pacific Division title.

BEST COMEBACK Despite throwing four interceptions, quarterback Don Van Galder led the biggest fourth-quarter comeback in NCAA Division I-A history on Nov. 4, 1972. Trailing Arizona 27-0, Utah stormed back. Van Galder threw two touchdown passes to start the rally, and Steve Marshall pulled the Utes within a touchdown when he returned an interception 68 yards for a score. Then, with Utah at the 3-yard line and out of timeouts, Van Galder dropped back to pass, scrambled and dived into the end zone with 10 seconds left. Fleming Jensen added the extra point: Utah 28, Arizona 27.

STADIUM Two days after Utah's last home game of the season on Nov. 15, 1997, much of Rice Stadium, the Utes' home for 70 years, was demolished, with only the south end zone escaping the wrecking ball. The original structure, christened Ute Stadium when it opened in 1927, was made of timber and concrete. Ten months and $50 million later, Rice-Eccles Stadium, an imposing steel, concrete and glass edifice, was completed. Rice-Eccles, which seats 45,017, retains the name of the philanthropist Robert Rice, who donated $1 million to renovate the old stadium in 1972, and honors the George and Dolores Eccles Foundation, the major private donor ($20 million) for the new facility.

RIVAL Utah's athletic rivalry with BYU started in 1895 with a baseball game that is the earliest recorded sporting event between the schools. The scoreless tie, marked by a bench-clearing brawl, set the tone for years

of contentious games. In football, the annual Utah-BYU meeting—a.k.a. the Holy War—has been played every year since 1922 with the exception of three years during World War II. Utah dominated the series through 1971, boasting a 38–5–4 record, including 20 consecutive years without a loss. BYU then won 19 of the next 21 meetings before Utah leveled the playing field in the 1990s, winning eight of 12 games from 1993 to 2004.

NICKNAME The team remains named after a Native American tribe that first settled in Utah, but the school long ago dropped a second name that was commonly used. Athletic teams were called the Utes and Redskins during the university's early days, but in 1972 the latter name was officially dropped. The school retained the use of Utes with the blessing of the Ute Tribal Council.

MASCOT The use of Swoop, a mascot representing a red-tailed hawk, began in 1996, again with permission from the Ute Tribal Council. The red-tailed hawk is indigenous to the state of Utah.

UNIFORMS The drum-and-feather logo on the Utah helmet first appeared in 1975 and has undergone alterations several times. The uniforms were changed every two years for more than two decades until the arrival of coach Urban Meyer in 2003. The Utes' red home jerseys and white road jerseys both have black inserts on the sides.

NUMBERS The Utes went 46 years without an outright conference championship until first-year coach Urban Meyer led the Utes to the Mountain West title in 2003.

ALL-TIME TEAM

A university committee selected one team for the first 50 years and a second for the next 50 in 1992.

FIRST 50 YEARS

1936-37	Paul McDonough,	E
1939-41	Max Speedie,	E
1928-30	George Watkins,	E
1935-37	Karl Schleckman,	T
1930-32	Denoil "Jack" Johnson,	T
1936-38	Bernard "Barney" McGarry,	T
1939-41	Floyd Spendlove,	T
1938-40	Rex Geary,	G
1932-34	Don Savich,	G
1928-29	Dean Olsen,	G
1894	David McKay,	G
1928-30	Marwin "Marv" Jonas,	C
1940-42	Burt Davis,	C
1932-33	Roland Sleater,	QB
1933-35	Delmar "Swede" Larson,	QB
1930-32	Frank Christensen,	HB
1924-27	John "Jack" Howells,	HB
1939-41	Isadore "Izzy" Spector,	HB
1942, 1946-47	Frank Nelson,	HB
1927-29	Earl "Powerhouse" Pomeroy,	FB
1928-30	Raymond Price,	FB
1902, 1904-06	Fred Bennion,	K
1936-38	Paul Snow,	P

SECOND 50 YEARS

1960-62	Marvin Fleming,	TE
1958-60	Thorton Petersen,	OT
1968-70	Gordon Jolley,	T
1970-72	Bob Peterson,	T
1965-67	Norm Chow,	G
1978-80	Dean Miraldi,	G
1959-61	Ed Pine,	C
1971-73	Chuck Johanson,	C
1962-64	Roy Jefferson,	WR
1971-73	Steve Odom,	WR
1989-91, 1993	Bryan Rowley,	WR
1957-58	Lee Grosscup,	QB
1987-89	Scott Mitchell,	QB
1963-64	Allen Jacobs,	RB
1978-81	Del Rodgers,	RB
1984-86, 1988	Eddie Johnson,	RB
1980-81	Gilbert Alvarez,	K
1962-64	Roy Jefferson,	DE
1982-85	Filipo Mokofisi,	DE
1957, 1959-60	Tony Polychronis,	DL
1961-62	Dave Costa,	DL
1964-66	John Stipech,	DL
1970-72	Bob Fratto,	DL
1971-73	Ron Rydalch,	DL
1978-81	Steve Clark,	DL
1973-75	John Huddleston,	LB
1990-91	Anthony Davis,	LB
1957-59	Larry Wilson,	DB
1969-70	Norm Thompson,	DB
1971-73	Steve Marshall,	DB
1984-85	Erroll Tucker,	DB
1988-91	LaVon Edwards,	DB
1969-71	Marv Bateman,	P
1980-81	Gilbert Alvarez,	K

LORE Coach Jack Curtice (1950-57) was known for his innovations, and in his final season his ball-control passing attack featured what is known today as the shovel pass. Although the play had been seen previously, Curtice made it his signature in a season that saw the Utes win the Skyline Conference championship. Utah didn't win another outright title until 2003, when Meyer implemented his own version of the shovel pass.

QUOTE "A word of warning to the Pennsylvania governor. Don't make a wager—uh, what is it, a 'friendly gift exchange'?— without knowing the point spread."
—Utah coach Kyle Whittingham, joking about the Fiesta Bowl bet Pennsylvania governor Ed Rendell lost to former Utah governor Olene Walker. Since Mormons frown on gambling, Walker had referred to the wager as a "traditional gift exchange event"

UTAH ANNUAL STATISTICAL LEADERS

YR	RUSHING	YDS	ATT	AVG	PASSING	ATT	CMP	PCT	YDS	RECEIVING	REC	YDS	AVG
1951	Jack Cross	483	109	4.4	Tom Dublinski	239	124	.52	1,418	Sandy Morris	31	308	9.9
1952	George Bean	594	94	6.3	Don Rydalch	145	80	.55	974	Jack Cross	12	213	17.8
1953	Don Peterson	720	138	5.2	Don Rydalch	128	77	.60	980	Paul Cook	9	190	21.1
1954	Herb Makken	769	160	4.8	David Dungan	128	74	.58	862	Max Pierce	25	457	18.3
1955		NA	NA	NA		NA	NA	NA	NA		NA	NA	NA
1956		NA	NA	NA		NA	NA	NA	NA		NA	NA	NA
1957	Merrill Douglas	646	97	6.7	Lee Grosscup	137	94	.69	1,398	Stuart Vaughan	53	756	14.3
1958	Monk Bailey	564	113	5.0	Lee Grosscup	124	68	.55	828	Larry Wilson	13	256	19.7
1959	Monk Bailey	640	138	4.6	Ken Vierra	115	63	.55	854	Bob Mastelotto	15	290	19.3
1960	Stan Uyeshiro	388	44	8.8	Terry Nofsinger	96	47	.49	614	Marv Fleming	9	237	26.3
1961	Dennis Zito	374	76	4.9	Gary Hertzfeldt	107	52	.49	701	Joe Borich	29	489	16.9
1962	Doug Wasko	454	103	4.4	Gary Hertzfeldt	122	61	.50	889	Roy Jefferson	17	336	19.8
1963	Allen Jacobs	564	124	4.5	Gary Hertzfeldt	130	64	.49	945	Roy Jefferson	29	435	15.0
1964	Allen Jacobs	752	175	4.3	Richard Groth	107	50	.47	785	John Pease	23	406	17.7
1965	Marv Lowery	554	121	4.6	Richard Groth	164	66	.40	967	Mike Butera	29	469	16.2
1966	Robert Woodson	683	180	3.8	Jack Gehrke	127	54	.43	715	Terry Baker	17	195	11.5
1967	Charles Smith	588	154	3.8	Jack Gehrke	171	81	.47	1,029	Jack Andrews	38	452	11.9
1968	Steve Molnar	438	127	3.5	Ray Groth	203	84	.41	1,181	Speedy Thomas	60	1,006	16.8
1969	David Smith	695	140	5.0	Ray Groth	151	56	.37	714	James Brown	19	280	14.7
1970	William Hunter	484	120	4.0	Scooter Longmire	158	64	.41	674	James Brown	27	342	12.7
1971	Gene Belczyk	514	101	5.1	Scooter Longmire	212	103	.49	1,078	Fred Graves	45	511	11.4
1972	Gene Belczyk	777	140	5.6	Don Van Galder	178	85	.48	1,425	Steve Odom	30	663	22.1
1973	Ike Spencer	761	179	4.3	Don Van Galder	254	121	.48	2,012	Steve Odom	38	723	19.0
1974	Ike Spencer	632	130	4.9	Jim Miller	133	59	.44	773	Willie Armstead	34	520	15.3
1975	Steve Peake	418	103	4.1	Pat Degnan	289	140	.48	1,621	Dick Graham	34	463	13.6
1976	Steve Peake	502	133	3.8	Dan Hagemann	222	117	.53	1,585	Jack Steptoe	38	752	19.8
1977	Tony Lindsay	467	117	4.0	Randy Gomez	315	155	.49	2,015	Jack Steptoe	42	724	17.2
1978	Tony Lindsay	803	209	3.8	Randy Gomez	266	138	.52	2,027	Frank Henry	45	771	17.1
1979	Tony Lindsay	816	132	6.2	Floyd Hodge	138	62	.45	1,006	Jim Teahan	33	560	17.0
1980	Tony Lindsay	909	190	4.8	Ricky Hardin	290	179	.62	2,458	Floyd Hodge	44	829	18.8
1981	Del Rodgers	1,127	170	6.6	Tyce Ferguson	177	102	.58	1,235	Tony Graham	29	476	16.4
1982	Carl Monroe	1,507	309	4.9	Kenny Vierra	166	85	.51	1,315	Tony Graham	30	473	15.8
1983	Eddie Lewis	734	112	6.6	Mark Stevens	268	149	.56	1,986	Joe Tarver	51	757	14.8
1984	Eddie Johnson	1,021	156	6.5	Mark Stevens	216	117	.54	1,889	Danny Huey	52	869	16.7
1985	Eddie Lewis	1,018	195	5.2	Larry Egger	417	237	.57	2,988	Loren Richey	73	971	13.3
1986	Eddie Johnson	1,046	166	6.3	Larry Egger	382	232	.61	2,761	Loren Richey	67	775	11.6
1987	Martell Black	520	103	5.0	Chris Mendonca	332	194	.58	2,389	Carl Harry	63	826	13.1
1988	Eddie Johnson	748	157	4.8	Scott Mitchell	533	323	.61	4,322	Carl Harry	65	1,145	17.6
1989	Clifton Smith	681	142	4.8	Scott Mitchell	444	237	.53	3,211	Dennis Smith	73	1,091	14.9
1990	Steve Abrams	551	151	3.6	Mike Richmond	287	156	.54	1,976	Bryan Rowley	28	762	27.2
1991	Keith Williams	1,076	207	5.2	Frank Dolce	314	177	.56	2,444	Bryan Rowley	60	1,011	16.9
1992	Pierre Jones	715	136	5.3	Frank Dolce	322	188	.58	2,369	Sean Williams	51	734	14.4
1993	Jamal Anderson	958	168	5.7	Mike McCoy	430	276	.64	3,860	Bryan Rowley	55	838	15.2
1994	Charlie Brown	839	144	5.8	Mike McCoy	381	247	.65	3,035	Curtis Marsh	61	859	14.1
1995	Chris Fuamatu-Ma'afala	834	141	5.9	Mike Fouts	323	179	.55	2,581	Rocky Henry	55	866	15.7
1996	Chris Fuamatu-Ma'afala	982	168	5.8	Mike Fouts	302	177	.59	2,526	Kevin Dyson	53	812	15.3
1997	Juan Johnson	838	181	4.6	Jonathan Crosswhite	222	130	.59	1,588	Kevin Dyson	60	824	13.7
1998	Mike Anderson	1,173	244	4.8	Jonathan Crosswhite	221	128	.58	1,615	Daniel Jones	57	809	14.2
1999	Mike Anderson	977	195	5.0	Darnell Arceneaux	165	83	.50	1,342	Steve Smith	43	860	20.0
2000	Adam Tate	660	160	4.1	Darnell Arceneaux	169	93	.55	1,375	Cliff Russell	37	517	14.0
2001	Dameon Hunter	1,396	257	5.4	Lance Rice	302	169	.56	2,086	Cliff Russell	53	744	14.0
2002	Brandon Warfield	919	201	4.6	Brett Elliott	221	130	.59	1,529	Josh Lyman	44	590	13.4
2003	Brandon Warfield	976	237	4.1	Alex Smith	266	173	.65	2,247	Paris Warren	76	809	10.6
2004	Marty Johnson	802	165	4.9	Alex Smith	317	214	.68	2,952	Paris Warren	80	1,076	13.5

Receiving leaders by receptions
The NCAA began including postseason stats in 2002

UTAH ALL-TIME SCORES

WIN/LOSS PERCENTAGE SINCE 1936

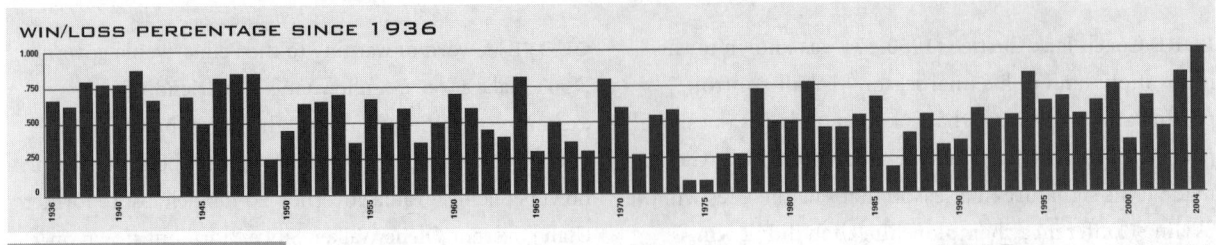

NO HEAD COACH

1892
0-1-0

N25	Utah State	0	12

1893
NO TEAM

1894
1-2-0

O4	at Salt Lake HS	4	20
N3	at YMCA	0	14
N29	at Salt Lake HS	14	6

1895
0-1-0

N28	at YMCA	0	20

C.B. FERRIS
1896 (.600)   3-2

1896
3-2-0

A6	Brigham Young Acad.	12	4
N14	at Brigham Young Acad.	6	0
N26	at Crescent AC	0	4
D5	at Brigham Young Acad.	6	8
D25	at Salt Lake HS	6	4

MR. CUMMINGS
1897 (.167)   1-5

1897
1-5-0

O23	at YMCA	0	8
N1	at LDS Coll.	8	0
N5	Westminster Coll.	4	6
N25	at YMCA	0	16
D4	Brigham Young Acad.	0	14
D18	at Brigham Young Acad.	0	22

MR. WILSON
1898 (.667)   2-1

1898
2-1-0

N14	at Salt Lake HS	0	6
N24 ●	Brigham Young Acad.	6	0
D12 ●	All Hallows Coll.	1	0 f

NO HEAD COACH

1899
2-1-0

N3 ●	9th Calvary	18	0
N13 =	9th Calvary	5	0
N25 ●	Salt Lake HS	0	34

HARVEY R. HOLMES
1900-03 (.563)   13-10-1

1900
2-2-0

N10 ●	at All Hallows	36	6
N17 ●	at Utah State	21	0
N24 ●	at YMCA	0	6
D8 ●	Carlisle	0	22

1901
3-1-0

O19 ●	at Ogden HS	12	0
O26 ●	at All Hallows	17	0
N9 ●	Utah State	16	0 *
N28 ●	Nevada	2	6

1902-1937
ROCKY MOUNTAIN

1902
5-2-1 (1-0-1)

S26 ●	at Fort Douglas	5	0
O4 ●	at Ogden Acad.	29	5
O11 ●	at Salt Lake HS	42	0
O18 ●	Fort Douglas	35	0
O25 =	at Colorado State	0	0
N1	at National Guard	0	11
N15 ●	Utah State	18	0
N27	at Stanford	11	33

1903
3-5-0 (0-4-0)

S26 ●	at Ogden HS	11	0
O3	at Colorado	0	22
O10 ●	at Fort Douglas	63	0
O17	at Utah State	0	17
O31	Denver	0	10
N14 ●	12th Infantry	46	0
N26	at Colorado State	6	16 *
D19	Carlisle	0	22

JOSEPH H. MADDOCK
1904-09 (.744)   30-10-1

1904
7-1-0 (3-1-0)

O1	Colorado	6	32
O15 ●	at Montana	17	0
O22 ●	Oregon Short Line	50	0
O29 ●	at Denver	12	0
O31 ●	at Wyoming	23	0
N5 ●	at Fort Douglas	107	0
N19 ●	Utah State	43	0
N24 ●	Colorado College	43	0

1905
6-2-0 (4-2-0)

O7 ●	Wyoming	31	0
O14 ●	at Montana	42	0
O21 ●	at Denver	24	6
O28 ●	at Fort Douglas	129	0
N4	at Colorado	5	46
N11	Colorado Mines	0	22
N25 ●	at Utah State	5	0
N30 ●	Colorado State	24	0

1906
4-1-0 (3-1-0)

O13	at Colorado College	0	6
O20 ●	at Denver	24	0
N3 ●	Montana	42	0
N17 ●	Colorado	10	0
N29 ●	Utah State	35	0

1907
6-3-0 (4-1-0)

S28 ●	Ogden HS	19	0
O5 ●	Salt Lake HS	39	0
O12 ●	Denver	24	4
O19 ●	Old Timers	11	7
O26 ●	Colorado Mines	11	10
N2	St. Vincent LA	5	11
N9	Utah State	10	24
N16	at Colorado	10	24
N28 ●	Colorado College	13	10

1908
3-2-1 (2-2-0)

O10	at Denver	15	17
O17	at Colorado College	4	18
O24 ●	Fort Douglas	11	0
N7 ●	Wyoming	75	0
N14 ●	Colorado	21	14
N26 =	Idaho	0	0

1909
4-1-0 (2-1-0)

O9	at Utah State	28	0
O23	Colorado Mines DEN	8	14
O30 ●	at Fort Douglas	21	5
N13 ●	at Montana St.	46	0
N25 ●	Utah State	22	0

FRED BENNION
1910-13 (.648)   16-8-3

1910
4-2-0 (4-2-0)

O8 ●	at Utah State	21	12
O15 ●	Colorado Mines	6	0
O22 ●	Colorado College	17	21
O29 ●	at Colorado	0	11
N12 ●	Denver	20	0
N24 ●	Utah State	6	0

1911
5-1-1 (3-1-1)

O7 ●	Colorado State	51	0
O14 =	at Denver	0	0
O28 ●	Montana St.	97	0
N4 ●	Colorado Mines	15	0
N11 ●	at Colorado College	18	0
N18 ●	Colorado	0	9
N30 ●	Idaho	19	0

1912
5-1-1 (4-1-1)

O5 ●	Wyoming	9	0
O19 ●	Denver	66	0
O26 ●	Colorado Mines DEN	18	3
N2 ●	Montana St.	10	3
N9	Colorado DEN	0	3
N16 ●	Colorado College	42	0
N28	Utah State	7	7

1913
2-4-1 (1-3-0)

O11 ●	Fort Douglas	89	6
O18 ●	Colorado College	7	6
O25 ●	Colorado Mines	0	7
N8	Colorado	12	30
N15	Occidental	14	26
N19 ●	Cal Poly Pomona CLA	7	7
N27	Utah State	0	21

NELSON H. NORGREN
1914-17 (.542)   13-11

1914
3-3-0 (2-3-0)

O10 ●	Wyoming	20	0
O17	Colorado College	7	46
O24	Colorado Mines DEN	6	13
N7	at Colorado	0	33
N14 ●	Occidental	34	14
N26 ●	Utah State	20	2 *

1915
5-2-0 (4-2-0)

O9 ●	Wyoming	70	7
O16	Colorado State	9	21
O23 ●	Colorado Mines	7	0
O30 ●	Colorado	35	3
N6	at Colorado College	7	27
N20 ●	Southern Cal	20	13
N25 ●	Utah State	14	0

1916
3-2-0 (2-2-0)

O21 ●	at Southern Cal	27	12
O28 ●	Colorado	28	0
N11 ●	Utah State	46	0
N18 ●	at Colorado State	6	12
N30	Colorado College	6	21

1917
2-4-0 (2-3-0)

O20 ●	at Wyoming	14	0
O27 ●	at Colorado College	0	21
N3 ●	Colorado State	25	12
N10 ●	at Colorado	9	18
N17 ●	Southern Cal	0	51
N29 ●	Utah State	0	14

1918
NO TEAM WWI

THOMAS FITZPATRICK
1919-24 (.570)   23-17-3

1919
5-2-0 (4-1-0)

O11 ●	Colorado College	20	0
O18 ●	at Colorado State	21	34
O25 ●	Idaho	20	0
N1 ●	Montana St.	66	0
N8 ●	Colorado	7	0
N15	at Southern Cal	7	28
N29 ●	Utah State	10	0

1920
1-5-1 (1-2-1)

O23	at Colorado College	2	20
O30	at California	0	63
N6	Nevada	7	14
N11 ●	at Colorado	7	0
N20	Idaho BOI	0	10
N25 =	Wyoming	0	0
N25	Utah State	3	9

1921
3-2-1 (2-1-1)

O15 ●	Wyoming	14	3
O22 ●	at Colorado College	14	3
O29 ●	Idaho	17	7
N5	at Nevada	7	28
N12 =	Colorado	0	0
N24	Utah State	3	14

1922
7-1-0 (5-0-0)

O7 ●	Albertson	16	12
O14 ●	Brigham Young	49	0
O21 ●	at Colorado	3	0
O25 ●	at Wyoming	27	0
N4 ●	Colorado College	20	6
N11 ●	Idaho BOI	0	16
N18 ●	Whitman	24	0
N30 ●	Utah State	14	0

1923
4-3-0 (2-3-0)

O6 ●	at Whitman	16	0
O13 ●	at Wyoming	79	0
O27 ●	Brigham Young	15	0
N3 ●	Albertson	105	3
N10 ●	at Colorado College	6	7
N17 ●	Colorado	7	17
N29 ●	Utah State	13	21

1924
3-4-1 (2-2-1)

O4 ●	Drake	14	33
O11 ●	Colorado College	0	9
O18 ●	Arizona	32	7
O25 ●	Brigham Young	35	6
N1 ●	at Colorado	0	3
N8 ●	Stanford BERK	0	30
N15 ●	Wyoming	28	0
N27 =	Utah State	7	7

IKE ARMSTRONG
1925-49 (.704)   141-55-15

1925
6-2-0 (5-1-0)

O10 ●	at Southern Cal	2	28
O16 ●	at Arizona	9	0
O24 ●	Colorado	12	7
O31 ●	Denver	27	0
N7 ●	at Brigham Young	27	0
N14 ●	at Colorado College	20	0
N18 ●	at Wyoming	7	6
N26 ●	Utah State	6	10

1926
7-0-0 (5-0-0)

O9 ●	South Dakota	13	0
O23 ●	at Colorado	37	3
O30 ●	Colorado State	10	6
N6 ●	at Denver	13	0
N13 ●	Brigham Young	40	7
N25 ●	Utah State	34	0
D18 ●	at Hawaii	17	7

1927
3-3-1 (3-1-1)

O1 ●	Colorado Mines	44	6
O8 ●	at Northwestern	6	13
O22 ●	Colorado	20	13
O29 ●	at Colorado State	0	12
N5 ●	Creighton	7	16
N12 ●	at Brigham Young	20	0
N24 =	Utah State	0	0

1928 5-0-2 (4-0-1)

O6	●		at Nevada	32	7
O20	●	|	Colorado State	6	0
O27	●	|	at Colorado	25	6
N3	●	|	Colorado College	27	21
N10	=		at Creighton	7	7
N17	=	|	Brigham Young	0	0
N29	●	|	Utah State	20	0

1929 7-0-0 (6-0-0)

O5	●		Nevada	31	0
O19	●	|	Colorado	40	0
O26	●	|	at Colorado State	21	0
N2	●	|	Brigham Young	45	13
N9	●	|	at Colorado College	12	0
N16	●	|	at Wyoming	44	0
N28	●	|	Utah State	26	7

1930 8-0-0 (7-0-0)

S27	●		at Nevada	20	7
O4	●	|	Wyoming	72	0
O18	●	|	Brigham Young	34	7 *
O25	●	|	Denver	59	0
N1	●	|	at Colorado State	39	0
N8	●	|	Colorado College	41	6
N15	●	|	at Colorado	34	0
N27	●	|	Utah State	41	0

1931 7-2-0 (6-0-0)

S26			at Washington	6	7
O3	●		Albertson	52	0
O17	●	|	Brigham Young	43	0
O24	●	|	at Denver	46	0
O31	●	|	Colorado State	60	6
N7	●	|	at Colorado College	28	6
N14	●	|	Colorado	32	0
N26	●	|	Utah State	34	0
D5			Oregon State *Port*	0	12

1932 6-1-1 (6-0-0)

S24			Southern Cal	0	35
O1	●	|	Colorado College	54	6
O8	=		Nevada	6	6
O15	●	|	Brigham Young	29	0
O29	●	|	Utah State	16	0
N5	●	|	Colorado	14	0
N12	●	|	Denver	27	0
N19	●	|	Colorado State	16	0

1933 5-3-0 (5-1-0)

S23	●	|	Montana St.	61	0
O6			at UCLA	0	21 *
O14	●	|	Brigham Young	21	6
O28	●	|	Utah State	14	6
N4			at Oregon	7	23 *
N11	●	|	Colorado	13	6
N18		|	at Denver	0	13
N30	●	|	Colorado State	13	0

1934 5-3-0 (4-2-0)

S28	●		at Drake	6	0
O6	●	|	Colorado College	61	6
O13	●	|	Brigham Young	43	0
O20	●	|	at Denver	7	0
O27			Oregon	7	8
N10		|	at Colorado	6	7
N17		|	at Colorado State	6	14
N29	●	|	Utah State	14	7

1935 4-3-1 (4-1-1)

O5			at Oregon	0	6
O12	●	|	Montana St.	47	0
O26	●	|	Denver	39	14
N2	●	|	at Brigham Young	32	0
N9		|	Colorado	0	14
N16	●	|	at Colorado State	14	0
N28	=	|	Utah State	14	14
D14			at Hawaii	20	21

1936 6-3-0 (5-2-0)

S26	●	|	No. Colorado	26	0
O3	●		Arizona	14	6
O10	●	|	Western St.	26	0
O17	●	|	at Denver	31	6
O24		|	at Utah State	0	12
O31	●	|	Brigham Young	18	0
N7		|	at Colorado	7	31
N14			Texas A&M	7	20
N26	●	|	Colorado State	13	0

1937 5-3-0 (5-2-0)

S25	●	|	at Montana St.	19	7
O2	●	|	Brigham Young	14	0
O9			Idaho	7	9
O16	●	|	at No. Colorado	7	6
O23		|	Denver	7	13
N6		|	Colorado	7	17
N13	●	|	at Colorado State	45	0
N25	●	|	Utah State	27	0

1938-1947 Mountain States

1938 7-1-2 (4-0-2)

O1	●		Montana St.	34	0
O15	=	|	Brigham Young	7	7
O22	●	|	at Utah State	33	0
O29	●	|	Denver	21	0
N5	=	|	at Colorado	0	0
N12	●	|	Colorado State	13	0
N19	●	|	at Wyoming	39	0
N24			Idaho	6	16
D17	●		at Hawaii	14	13
			SUN BOWL		
J2	●		New Mexico	26	0

1939 6-1-2 (4-1-1)

S30	=		Santa Clara	7	7
O7	●	|	Wyoming	60	0
O14	●	|	at Brigham Young	35	13
O21	●		Idaho *Boi*	35	0
O28	=	|	at Denver	7	7
N4		|	Colorado	14	21
N11	●		Hawaii	34	18
N18	●	|	at Colorado State	42	7
N23	●	|	Utah State	27	0

1940 7-2-0 (5-1-0)

S28			Santa Clara *SF*	13	34
O5	●	|	Brigham Young	12	6
O12	●		Arizona	24	0
O19		|	at Utah State	0	7
O26	●	|	Denver	25	14
N2	●	|	at Colorado	21	13
N9	●	|	at Wyoming	34	7
N16	●	|	Colorado State	27	0
N21	●		Idaho	13	6

1941 6-0-2 (4-0-2)

S27	●		at Idaho	26	7
O11	●	|	Wyoming	60	6
O18	=	|	Brigham Young	6	6
O25	=	|	at Denver	0	0
N1	●	|	Colorado	46	6
N15	●	|	at Colorado State	26	13
N26	●	|	Utah State	33	21
D6	●		at Arizona	12	6

1942 6-3-0 (5-1-0)

S26			Santa Clara	0	12
O3			at Arizona	0	14
O10		|	Brigham Young	7	12
O17	●	|	at Utah State	34	7 *
O24	●	|	Denver	21	12
O31	●	|	Colorado State	33	14
N7	●	|	at Colorado	13	0
N14	●	|	at Wyoming	34	7
N26	●		Idaho	13	7

1943 0-7-0 (0-2-0)

O2			Fort Warren	0	60
O9		|	at Colorado	0	35
O16			Nevada	19	27
O23			at Tulsa	0	55
N6		|	Colorado	19	22
N13			at Colorado College	0	64
N25			Saint Mary's-Cal	0	34

1944 5-2-1 (1-2-1)

S30	●		Idaho St.	24	0
O6		|	at Denver	12	28
O14		|	Colorado	0	26
O21	●		at Idaho St.	38	12
O28	●		at Nevada	19	14
N4	=	|	Denver	0	0
N11	●		at Colorado College	21	6
N23	●	|	Utah State	47	0

1945 4-4-0 (3-2-0)

S29			Nevada	14	33
O6		|	at Colorado	13	18
O12		|	at Denver	7	21
O20			Oklahoma State	6	46
O27	●	|	at Colorado State	28	0
N3	●	|	Denver	33	21
N10	●		at New Mexico	21	20
N22	●	|	Utah State	24	6

1946 8-3-0 (4-2-0)

S28	●		New Mexico	56	14
O5	●		Arizona	14	7
O12	●	|	at Brigham Young	35	6
O19		|	at Denver	14	20
O26	●	|	Wyoming	27	7
N2	●	|	Colorado	7	0
N9	●	|	at Colorado State	13	0
N16	●		at San Francisco	21	13
N28		|	Utah State	14	22
D25	●		at Hawaii All Stars	40	6
J1			Hawaii *Hon*	16	19

1947 8-1-1 (6-0-0)

S27	●		Oregon State	7	6
O4	●		Hawaii	35	0
O11	●	|	Brigham Young	28	6
O18	●	|	Denver	13	7
O25	●	|	at Wyoming	26	7
N1	●	|	at Colorado	13	7
N8	●	|	Colorado State	19	0
N15			Idaho *Boi*	6	7
N27	●	|	Utah State	40	14
D6	=		at Arizona	20	20

1948-1961 Skyline

1948 8-1-1 (5-0-0)

S17			at Southern Cal	0	27
S25	●		Idaho	21	6
O2	●		Arizona	47	14
O9	●	|	at Brigham Young	30	0
O16	●	|	at Denver	17	0
O23	●	|	Wyoming	19	7
O30	●		Colorado	14	12
N6	●	|	at Colorado State	12	3
N13	=		at Oregon State	20	20
N25	●	|	Utah State	41	7

1949 2-7-1 (2-3-0)

S17			at Washington	7	14
S24			Oregon State *Port*	7	27
O1	=		at Arizona	12	12
O8	●	|	Brigham Young	38	0
O15		|	Denver	18	20
O22		|	at Wyoming	0	13
O29			at Colorado	7	14
N5		|	Colorado State	12	21
N12			Pacific *Lod*	6	45
N24	●	|	Utah State	34	0

JACK CURTICE
1950-57 (.580) 45-32-4

1950 3-4-3 (1-2-2)

S23			Idaho *Boi*	19	26
S30	●		Arizona	27	14
O7	=	|	at Brigham Young	28	28
O14	=	|	at Denver	14	14
O21		|	Wyoming	13	53
O28	=		Colorado	20	20
N4			Kansas	26	39
N11		|	at Colorado State	7	32
N23	●	|	Utah State	46	0
D16	●		at Hawaii	40	28

1951 7-4-0 (4-1-0)

S15	●		Montana St.	55	6
S22	●		at Arizona	27	7
S29			at Oregon State	28	61
O6	●	|	Brigham Young	7	6
O13			at Kansas	7	26
O20	●	|	Denver	17	14
O27		|	Wyoming	0	13
N3	●	|	at Utah State	28	20
N10			at Colorado	0	54
N17	●	|	Colorado State	27	21
N22	●		Idaho	40	19

1952 6-3-1 (5-0-0)

S20			Oregon State	7	14
S27	=		Idaho *Boi*	21	21
O4			Arizona	0	27
O11	●	|	Brigham Young	34	6
O18	●	|	at Denver	35	0
O25	●	|	at Wyoming	27	21
N1			Colorado	14	20
N8	●	|	at Colorado State	14	6
N15	●		Santa Clara *Sac*	16	13
N27	●	|	Utah State	20	0

1953 8-2-0 (5-0-0)

S19	●		at Arizona	28	7
S26	●		Idaho	21	0
O3	●		Hawaii	47	24
O10	●	|	at Utah State	33	13
O17	●	|	Denver	40	6
O24	●	|	Wyoming	13	12
O31			at Washington	14	21
N7			at Colorado	0	21
N14	●	|	Colorado State	35	14
N26	●	|	Brigham Young	33	32

1954 4-7-0 (3-3-0)

S18			at Washington	6	7
S25			Arizona	20	54
O2	●		at Oregon	7	6
O9	●	|	at Brigham Young	12	7
O16		|	Denver	20	28
O23	●	|	at Wyoming	14	7
O30			Idaho	13	14
N6		|	at Colorado State	13	14
N13			Colorado	7	20
N20	●	|	at Montana	41	20
N25		|	Utah State	19	35

1955 6-3-0 (4-1-0)

S17			Oregon	13	14
S24	●		Idaho *Boi*	20	13
O1	●		at Missouri	20	14
O8	●	|	Brigham Young	41	9
O14	●	|	at Denver	27	7
O22		|	Wyoming	13	23
N5			at Colorado	7	37
N12	●	|	Colorado State	27	6
N24	●	|	Utah State	14	13

1956 5-5-0 (5-1-0)

S21			at UCLA	7	13
S29	●	|	Montana	26	6
O5	●	|	at Brigham Young	41	6
O13	●	|	Denver	27	13
O20		|	at Wyoming	20	30
O27			Idaho	21	27
N3			at Rice	0	27
N10	●	|	at Colorado State	49	27
N17			Colorado	7	21
N22	●	|	Utah State	29	7

1957 6-4-0 (5-1-0)

S21	●	|	Montana	32	13
S28			at Colorado	24	30
O5			Idaho *Boi*	6	21
O12	●	|	Brigham Young	27	0
O19		|	at Denver	7	12
O26	●	|	Wyoming	23	15
N3	●	|	Colorado State	55	0
N9			at Army	33	39
N16	●		Air Force	34	0
N28	●	|	Utah State	21	6

RAY NAGEL
1958-65 (.518) 42-39-1

1958 4-7-0 (3-3-0)

S20	●	|	Montana	20	6
S27		|	Brigham Young	7	14
O4			Idaho	0	20
O11			at California	21	36
O18	●	|	Denver	20	16
O25			at Air Force	14	16
N1		|	at Wyoming	20	25
N8		|	at Colorado State	0	20
N15			Colorado	0	7
N27	●	|	Utah State	12	7
D6	●		at Hawaii	47	20

1959 5-5-0 (3-2-0)

S26			at Oregon	6	21
O3			at Washington	6	51
O9	●	|	Brigham Young	20	8
O16	●	|	at Denver	26	12
O24		|	Wyoming	7	21
O31	●		Arizona	54	6
N7	●		Idaho *Boi*	47	13
N14		|	Colorado State	17	21
N21	●	|	Utah State	35	21
N28			at UCLA	6	21

1960 7-3-0 (5-1-0)

S17	●		Hawaii	33	6
S24	●		at Arizona	13	3
O1			Oregon	17	20
O7	●	|	Brigham Young	17	0
O22	●	|	Denver	49	16
O29		|	at Wyoming	7	17
N5	●	|	at Colorado State	27	6
N12	●	|	Montana	16	6
N19	●	|	Utah State	6	0
N26			UCLA	9	16

1961 6-4-0 (3-3-0)

S16	● |	Colorado State	40	0
S23		at Wisconsin	0	7
S30	●	Oregon	14	6
O7	●	at Arizona State	28	26
O14	● |	Brigham Young	21	20
O21	● |	at Montana	24	12
O28	|	Wyoming	6	13
N4	|	at New Mexico	16	21
N11	●	at Colorado	21	12
N18	|	at Utah State	6	17

1962-1998
WAC

1962 4-5-1 (1-2-1)

S22	●	Colorado	37	21
S29		at Oregon	8	35
O6	|	at Wyoming	7	16
O13	● |	Brigham Young	35	20
O20	= |	New Mexico	7	7
O27	●	Idaho	25	21
N3	●	at Colorado State	26	8
N10	|	at Arizona State	7	35
N17		Utah State	6	19
D1		UCLA	11	14

1963 4-6-0 (2-2-0)

S21		Oregon State	14	29
S28		Idaho BOI	9	10
O5	● |	at New Mexico	19	6
O12	● |	Brigham Young	15	6
O19	●	Colorado State	48	14
O26	|	Wyoming	23	26
N2	|	at Arizona State	22	30
N9		at Army	7	8
N16		California	22	35
N23	●	at Utah State	25	23

1964 9-2-0 (3-1-0)

S19	● |	New Mexico	16	0
S26		at Missouri	6	23
O3	●	Idaho	22	0
O10	|	at Wyoming	13	14
O17	●	at Colorado State	13	3
O24	● |	Arizona State	16	3
O31	●	at Texas-El Paso	41	0
N7	● |	Brigham Young	47	13
N14	●	at California	14	0
N21	●	Utah State	14	6
		LIBERTY BOWL		
D19	●	West Virginia	32	6

1965 3-7-0 (1-3-0)

S11	●	Montana	28	13
S18	|	Arizona	9	16
S25		Oregon	14	31
O9	● |	Wyoming	42	3
O16	|	at New Mexico	10	13
O23		at Oregon State	6	10
O30	●	Colorado State	22	19
N6	|	at Brigham Young	20	25
N13		Texas-El Paso	19	20
N20		Utah State	7	14

MIKE GIDDINGS
1966-67 (.429) 9-12

1966 5-5-0 (3-2-0)

S24	●	at Oregon	17	14
O8	|	at Wyoming	7	40
O15	●	Washington State	26	15
O22	● |	at Arizona	24	19
O29	● |	New Mexico	27	0
N5	● |	at Arizona State	21	6
N12	|	Brigham Young	13	35
N19		Utah State	7	13
N26		at Texas-El Paso	20	27
D3		at Houston	14	34

1967 4-7-0 (2-3-0)

S23		at Minnesota	12	13
S30	●	Oregon	21	0
O7	● |	at New Mexico	42	27
O14	|	Wyoming	0	28
O21	● |	at Arizona	33	29
O28	|	at Brigham Young	13	17
N4	|	Arizona State	32	49
N11		at Army	0	22
N18		Utah State	18	19
N25		Texas-El Paso	8	28
D2	●	at Hawaii	25	20

BILL MEEK
1968-73 (.516) 33-31

1968 3-7-0 (2-3-0)

S21		at Nebraska	0	31
S28		Oregon State	21	24
O5	●	at Washington State	17	14
O12	● |	New Mexico	30	7
O19	|	at Wyoming	9	20
O26		at Oregon	6	14
N2	● |	Brigham Young	30	21
N9	|	at Arizona State	21	59
N16	|	Arizona	15	16
N23		at Utah State	13	28

1969 8-2-0 (5-1-0)

S20		Oregon	17	28
S27	●	San Jose State	42	7
O4	● |	at Texas-El Paso	24	6
O11	● |	Arizona State	24	23
O18	● |	at New Mexico	24	0
O25	●	Oregon State PORT	7	3
N1	●	Utah State	27	7
N8	● |	Wyoming	34	10
N15	|	at Arizona	16	17
N22	● |	at Brigham Young	16	6

1970 6-4-0 (4-2-0)

S19	● |	Texas-El Paso	44	20
S26	|	New Mexico	28	34
O3		Iowa State	13	16
O10		at Oregon State	21	31
O17	● |	at Wyoming	20	16
O24	● |	Arizona	24	0
O31	●	at San Jose State	13	9
N7	●	at Utah State	17	0
N14	|	at Arizona State	14	37
N21	● |	Brigham Young	14	13

1971 3-8-0 (3-4-0)

S18		at Oregon	29	36
S25	|	Arizona State	21	41
O2		Washington State	12	34
O9	● |	at Texas-El Paso	32	10
O16	● |	Colorado State	42	16
O23	|	at Arizona	3	14
O30	|	Wyoming	16	29
N6	|	at New Mexico	39	57
N13		Utah State	17	21
N20	● |	at Brigham Young	17	15
N27		at Houston	16	42

1972 6-5-0 (5-2-0)

S16		at Texas Tech	2	45
S23		at Iowa State	22	44
S30	●	at Washington State	44	25
O7	● |	Texas-El Paso	39	20
O14	|	at Arizona State	48	59
O21	● |	at Wyoming	27	6
O28	● |	New Mexico	59	14
N4	● |	Arizona	28	27
N11		at Utah State	16	44
N18	|	Brigham Young	7	16
N25	● |	Colorado State	62	36

1973 7-5-0 (4-2-0)

S15		at Texas Tech	22	29
S22	● |	Texas-El Paso	82	6
S29	●	at Oregon	35	17
O6		at UCLA	16	66
O13	● |	Wyoming	50	16
O20	●	at San Jose State	28	21
O27	|	at Arizona	21	42
N3	● |	Arizona State	36	31
N10	● |	at New Mexico	36	35
N17	●	Utah State	31	28
N24	|	Brigham Young	22	46
D1		at Hawaii	6	7

TOM LOVAT
1974-76 (.152) 5-28

1974 1-10-0 (1-5-0)

S21	|	at Texas-El Paso	7	34
S28		Oregon	16	23
O5		UCLA	14	27
O12	|	Arizona	8	41
O19	|	at Arizona State	0	32
O26	|	at Wyoming	13	31
N2		San Jose State	6	24
N9	● |	New Mexico	21	10
N16		at Utah State	0	34
N23	|	at Brigham Young	20	48
N30		at LSU	10	35

1975 1-10-0 (1-4-0)

S13		Utah State	7	13
S20		Washington State	14	30
S27		at Indiana	7	31
O4		Iowa State	3	31
O11	● |	Wyoming	16	13
O18	|	at New Mexico	23	27
O25		at Oregon	7	18
N1	|	Arizona State	14	40
N8		at Tennessee	7	40
N15	|	at Brigham Young	20	51
N22	|	at Arizona	14	38

1976 3-8-0 (3-3-0)

S18		at Rice	22	43
S25		Oregon	13	21
O2	● |	Texas-El Paso	38	14
O9		at Iowa State	14	44
O16		at Utah State	17	28
O23	|	at Wyoming	22	45
O30	|	Arizona	35	38
N6	● |	New Mexico	34	31
N13	● |	at Arizona State	31	28
N20	|	Brigham Young	12	34
N27		at LSU	7	35

WAYNE HOWARD
1977-81 (.554) 30-24-2

1977 3-8-0 (2-5-0)

S17		at Oklahoma	24	62
S24		Houston	16	34
O1	|	at Colorado State	3	44
O8	● |	Wyoming	23	13
O15	●	Utah State	20	0
O22	|	at Arizona	17	45
O29	|	Arizona State	19	47
N5	|	at Brigham Young	8	38
N12	● |	Texas-El Paso	29	17
N19		at Florida	29	38
N26	|	at New Mexico	24	41

1978 8-3-0 (4-2-0)

S9	●	Idaho St.	56	0
S23		at Houston	25	42
S30	● |	Colorado State	30	6
O7	●	at Iowa	13	9
O14	●	Weber St.	30	7
O21	|	at Wyoming	21	34
N4	|	New Mexico	12	24
N11	● |	at Texas-El Paso	38	0
N18	● |	Brigham Young	23	22
N25	●	at Utah State	23	20
D2	● |	at San Diego State	20	18

1979 6-6-0 (5-2-0)

S1	●	Long Beach St.	34	10
S8	● |	at Hawaii	27	23
S15		at Washington	7	41
S22		at Tennessee	18	51
S29		Utah State	21	47
O6	● |	at Colorado State	21	16
O13	● |	Wyoming	24	14
O20		at Nevada-Las Vegas	41	43
O27	|	San Diego State	13	17
N3	● |	at New Mexico	26	7
N10	● |	Texas-El Paso	35	0
N17	|	at Brigham Young	0	27

1980 5-5-1 (3-3-1)

S6		Boise State	7	28
S13		at Nebraska	9	55
S20	● ||	Nevada-Las Vegas	45	29
S27	●	Fresno State	27	12
O4	●	at Utah State	23	19
O11	● |	at Texas-El Paso	31	7
O18	|	at Wyoming	21	24
O25	= |	Colorado State	21	21
N8	● |	New Mexico	49	21
N22	|	Brigham Young	6	56
N29	|	at San Diego State	20	21

1981 8-2-1 (5-1-1)

S5	●	Utah State	10	0
S12		at Arizona State	10	52
S19	●	Portland St.	46	0
S26	●	at Northwestern	42	0
O2	● |	Texas-El Paso	38	10
O17	● |	at Colorado State	24	13
O24	● ||	at Nevada-Las Vegas	69	28
O31	● |	San Diego State	17	14
N7	= |	at New Mexico	7	7
N14	● |	Wyoming	30	27
N21	|	at Brigham Young	28	56

CHUCK STOBART
1982-84 (.485) 16-17-1

1982 5-6-0 (3-4-0)

S4	●	Montana St.	30	12
S11		at Arizona State	10	23
S18		at Texas	12	21
O1	● |	Colorado State	35	14
O9	|	at Hawaii	7	10
O16	● ||	Nevada-Las Vegas	24	14
O23	|	at Wyoming	13	16
O30	|	at San Diego State	17	21
N6	●	Utah State	42	10
N13	● |	at Texas-El Paso	45	30
N20	|	Brigham Young	12	17

1983 5-6-0 (4-4-0)

S3	|	at New Mexico	7	17
S10		at Arizona	0	38
S17	● |	San Diego State	27	24
S24	● |	Hawaii	28	25
O1	|	at Colorado State	28	31
O8	● |	Texas-El Paso	35	11
O15	● |	Wyoming	69	14
O22	|	at Air Force	31	33
N5	●	Fullerton St.	47	20
N12		at Utah State	17	21
N19	|	at Brigham Young	7	55

1984 6-5-1 (4-3-1)

S1	●	Weber St.	52	16
S8		at Washington State	40	42
S15		at Tennessee	21	27
S22	● |	Air Force	28	17
S29	|	at Wyoming	14	21
O5	● |	New Mexico	38	14
O13	= |	at San Diego State	24	24
O20	|	at Hawaii	17	20
O27	● |	Texas-El Paso	43	15
N3	● |	Colorado State	35	23
N10	●	at Utah State	21	10
N17	|	Brigham Young	14	24

JIM FASSEL
1985-89 (.431) 25-33

1985 8-4-0 (5-3-0)

S7	●	Boise State	20	17
S14	● |	at Hawaii	29	27
S21	●	Washington State	44	37
S28	● |	Texas-El Paso	55	19
O4	● |	Wyoming	37	20
O12		at Arizona State	27	34
O19	● |	at San Diego State	39	37
O26	|	at Air Force	15	37
N2	●	Utah State	34	7
N9	● |	New Mexico	58	49
N16	|	at Colorado State	19	21
N23	|	at Brigham Young	28	38

1986 2-9-0 (1-7-0)

S13	|	San Diego State	30	37
S27		at Ohio State	6	64
O3	|	Air Force	35	45
O11	|	at Wyoming	14	38
O18	|	at New Mexico	43	47
O25		at Arizona State	7	52
N1	|	Hawaii	13	33
N8	● |	Colorado State	38	28
N15	●	at Utah State	27	10
N22	|	Brigham Young	21	35
N29	|	at Texas-El Paso	44	55

1987 5-7-0 (2-6-0)

S5	● |	New Mexico	24	20
S12	|	at San Diego State	34	52
S19	●	at Wisconsin	31	28
S26	●	Idaho St.	51	16
O3	|	at Air Force	27	48
O10	● |	at Colorado State	24	23
O17	|	at Hawaii	14	25
O24		Utah State	36	41
O31	●	at Boise State	31	27
N7	|	Texas-El Paso	24	30
N14	|	Wyoming	7	31
N21	|	at Brigham Young	18	21

1988 6-5-0 (4-4-0)

S10	●	Idaho St.	41	16
S17		at Illinois	24	35
S24	|	Hawaii	20	48
O1	|	at Texas-El Paso	28	38
O8	● |	at New Mexico	33	27
O15	|	Air Force	49	56
O22	|	at Wyoming	18	61
O29	● |	San Diego State	41	20
N5	● |	Colorado State	46	7
N12	●	at Utah State	42	21
N19	● |	Brigham Young	57	28

1989   4-8-0 (2-6-0)

S2		at Fresno State	22	52
S9	●	Utah State	45	10
S16		at Nebraska	30	42
S23	‖	at Hawaii	20	67
S30		San Diego State	27	38
O7	● ‖	at Texas-El Paso	50	45
O14	‖	at Wyoming	24	45
O21	● ‖	at Stanford	27	24
O28	‖	Colorado State	10	50
N11	● ‖	New Mexico	41	39
N18	‖	at Brigham Young	31	70
N25	‖	Air Force	38	42

RON McBRIDE
1990-2002 (.583)   88-63

1990   4-7-0 (2-6-0)

S1	●	at Utah State	19	0
S8	●	at Minnesota	35	29
S15	●	Fresno State	7	31
S22		Hawaii	7	19
S29	‖	Wyoming	10	28
O6	‖	at Colorado State	13	22
O20	● ‖	Texas-El Paso	37	23
O27	‖	at Air Force	21	52
N3	‖	at San Diego State	14	66
N10	● ‖	at New Mexico	29	27
N17	‖	Brigham Young	22	45

1991   7-5-0 (4-4-0)

A31	●	Utah State	12	7
S7	●	at Oregon State	22	10
S14		Air Force	21	24
S21	●	Oregon	24	17
O5		at Arizona State	15	21
O12	● ‖	at Wyoming	57	42
O19	● ‖	Colorado State	21	16
O26	‖	San Diego State	21	24
N2	‖	at Hawaii	26	52
N9	● ‖	New Mexico	30	7
N16	● ‖	at Texas-El Paso	10	9
N23	‖	at Brigham Young	17	48

1992   6-6-0 (4-4-0)

S5		at Nebraska	22	49
S12	●	at Utah State	42	18
S26	●	Oregon State	42	9
O3	● ‖	at Colorado State	33	29
O10	● ‖	Hawaii	38	17
O17	‖	at New Mexico	7	24
O24	‖	Texas-El Paso	13	20
O31	● ‖	at Air Force	20	13
N7	‖	at Fresno State	15	41
N14	● ‖	Wyoming	38	7
N21	‖	Brigham Young	22	31
		COPPER BOWL		
D29	●	Washington State	28	31

1993   7-6-0 (5-3-0)

S4		at Arizona State	0	38
S11	●	Utah State	31	29
S18	●	at Kansas	41	16
S25	●	at Wyoming	12	28
O2		Idaho	17	28
O9		New Mexico	35	42
O16	● ‖	at Texas-El Paso	45	29
O23	● ‖	Colorado State	38	21
O30	● ‖	San Diego State	45	41
N6	‖	at Hawaii	30	41
N13	● ‖	Air Force	41	24
N20	‖	at Brigham Young	34	31
		FREEDOM BOWL		
D30	●	Southern Cal	21	28

1994   10-2-0 (6-2-0)

S3	●	at Utah State	32	17
S10	●	Idaho St.	66	0
S17	●	at Oregon	34	16
S24	●	Wyoming	41	7
O8	● ‖	at San Diego State	38	22
O15	● ‖	Hawaii	14	3
O22	● ‖	at Colorado State	45	31
O29	● ‖	Texas-El Paso	52	7
N5	‖	at New Mexico	21	23
N12	‖	at Air Force	33	40
N19	‖	Brigham Young	34	31
		FREEDOM BOWL		
D27	●	Arizona	16	13

1995   7-4-0 (6-2-0)

S2		Oregon	20	27
S9		Stanford	20	27
S16	● ‖	at New Mexico	36	9
S23	‖	Fresno State	25	21
S30	● ‖	at Texas-El Paso	34	21
O7	‖	San Diego State	21	24
O14	‖	Colorado State	14	19
O21	● ‖	Air Force	22	21
O28	● ‖	Utah State	40	20
N4	● ‖	at Wyoming	30	24
N18	● ‖	at Brigham Young	34	17

1996   8-4 (6-2)

A31	●	at Utah State	17	20
S7	●	at Stanford	17	10
S14	●	at SMU	21	17
S21	●	Fresno State	45	17
S28	●	Kansas	45	42
O5	● ‖	at Texas-El Paso	34	27
O19	● ‖	TCU	21	7
O26	● ‖	Tulsa	45	19
N2	‖	at Rice	10	51
N9	● ‖	at New Mexico	31	24
N23	‖	Brigham Young	17	37
		COPPER BOWL		
D27		Wisconsin	10	38

1997   6-5 (5-3)

A30	●	Utah State	14	21
S6	●	at Louisville	27	21
S13	● ‖	at TCU	32	18
S20	● ‖	Texas-El Paso	56	3
O2	‖	at Fresno State	13	27
O11	‖	SMU	19	20
O18	‖	at Oregon	13	31
O25	● ‖	New Mexico	15	10
N1	‖	at Tulsa	13	21
N15	● ‖	Rice	31	14
N22	● ‖	at Brigham Young	20	14

1998   7-4 (5-3)

S5	●	at Utah State	20	12
S12	●	Louisville	45	22
S19	●	Hawaii	30	21
S26		Boise State	28	31
O3	‖	at Wyoming	24	27
O17	● ‖	Fresno State	24	16
O24	‖	at San Diego State	20	21
O31	● ‖	at San Jose State	49	17
N7	● ‖	Texas-El Paso	34	27
N14	● ‖	at New Mexico	41	7
N21	‖	Brigham Young	24	26

1999-Present
MOUNTAIN WEST

1999   9-3 (5-2)

S4	●	at Washington State	27	7
S18	●	Utah State	38	18
S25	● ‖	at Nevada-Las Vegas	52	14
O2	●	at Boise State	20	26
O9	●	La. Monroe	42	0
O16	● ‖	at Air Force	21	15
O23	● ‖	San Diego State	38	16
O28	● ‖	at Colorado State	24	31
N6	‖	Wyoming	29	43
N13	● ‖	New Mexico	52	7
N20	● ‖	at Brigham Young	20	17
		LAS VEGAS BOWL		
D18	●	Fresno State	17	16

2000   4-7 (3-4)

S2	●	Arizona	3	17
S9		at California	21	24
S16		Washington State	21	38
S23	‖	Air Force	14	23
S30	●	at Utah State	35	14
O14	● ‖	at San Diego State	21	7
O21	‖	Colorado State	17	24
O28	‖	at New Mexico	3	10
N4	● ‖	Nevada-Las Vegas	38	16
N11	● ‖	at Wyoming	34	0
N24	‖	Brigham Young	27	34

2001   8-4 (4-3)

S1	●	Utah State	23	19
S8	●	at Oregon	10	24
S22	●	at Indiana	28	26
S29	●	New Mexico	37	16
O6	●	South Florida	52	21
O20	● ‖	Wyoming	35	0
O27	● ‖	at Colorado State	17	19
N3	● ‖	at Nevada-Las Vegas	42	14
N10	● ‖	San Diego State	17	3
N17	‖	at Brigham Young	21	24
D1	‖	at Air Force	37	38
		LAS VEGAS BOWL		
D25	●	Southern Cal	10	6

2002   5-6 (3-4)

A31	●	at Utah State	23	3
S7	●	Indiana	40	13
S14		at Arizona	17	23
S21		at Michigan	7	10
S28	●	Air Force	26	30
O12	● ‖	at San Diego State	17	36
O19	● ‖	Colorado State	20	28
O26	‖	at New Mexico	35	42
N9	● ‖	Nevada-Las Vegas	28	17
N16	● ‖	at Wyoming	23	18
N23	● ‖	Brigham Young	13	6

URBAN MEYER
2003-04 (.917)   22-2

2003   10-2 (6-1)

A28	●	Utah State	40	20
S6		at Texas A&M	26	28
S11	●	California	31	24
S27	● ‖	at Colorado State	28	21
O3	●	Oregon	17	13
O11	● ‖	San Diego State	27	6
O18	● ‖	at Nevada-Las Vegas	28	10
O25	‖	New Mexico	35	47
N1	● ‖	at Air Force	45	43
N15	● ‖	Wyoming	47	17
N22	● ‖	at Brigham Young	3	0
		LIBERTY BOWL		
D31	●	Southern Miss	17	0

2004   12-0 (7-0)

S2	●	Texas A&M	41	21
S11	●	at Arizona	23	6
S18	●	at Utah State	48	6
S25	●	Air Force	49	35
O2	●	at New Mexico	28	7
O16	●	North Carolina	46	16
O23	● ‖	Nevada-Las Vegas	63	28
O30	● ‖	at San Diego State	51	28
N6	● ‖	Colorado State	63	31
N13	● ‖	at Wyoming	45	28
N20	● ‖	Brigham Young	52	21
		FIESTA BOWL		
J1	●	Pittsburgh	35	7

UTAH STATE

BY RYAN HOCKENSMITH

BEFORE EVERY GAME, ROAD OR home, Utah State players run onto the field and slap a sign that reads, "Aggie Pride." The inscription isn't really about wins and losses or Heismans and BCS crystals. You won't find any of those things in the Aggies' trophy case. But there's pride. Fans claim as their own model student-athlete Merlin Olsen, a born-and-bred Logan product, fraternity brother, ROTC enlistee and, oh yeah, inductee to both the College and Pro Football halls of fame. Or they can forever tell the story of how running back Jack Hill returned in 1955 from a two-year Mormon mission, boarded a train to Wyoming, learned the playbook on the way to the game, then rushed for more than 200 yards. But the Aggies didn't win. In the record books that game counts as a 21–13 loss. In the collective memory of Aggies fans, it's one of many wins that never looked that way on the scoreboard.

TRADITION Utah State has its fight song, "Hail the Utah Aggies," but "The Scotsman" is a close second in popularity. Legend has it that the song began decades ago when a huge town water pump broke and a local plumber, a Scotsman, was called. He climbed the 30-foot water pump and stared at it for five minutes. Then he raised his sledgehammer and slammed the pump, which immediately started up again. Soon after, a bill arrived for $1,000. The stunned local superintendent asked how he could charge that much for five minutes of work and requested an itemized bill. The Scotsman replied with a note that read: "For hitting the wheel with the hammer: 50 cents. For knowing where to hit the wheel: $999.50." Now he is remembered by alumni and students every time the song is played.

BEST PLAYER It's hard to imagine a more complete college football player than Olsen, an All-America and Outland Trophy-winning defensive lineman at Utah State. The Los Angeles Rams took him third overall in the 1962 NFL draft, and Olsen became a 14-time Pro Bowler and a crucial member of LA's Fearsome Foursome. Olsen visits campus at least once every August to offer words of encouragement to the latest batch of Aggies.

BEST COACH John Ralston spent only four seasons in

PROFILE

Utah State University
Logan, Utah
Founded: 1888
Enrollment: 13,985
Colors: Navy Blue and White
Nickname: Aggies
Stadium: Romney Stadium
   Opened in 1968
   Sprinturf; 30,257 capacity
First football game: 1892
All-time record: 468–447–31 (.511)
Bowl record: 1–5
Outland Trophy: Merlin Olsen, 1961
First-round NFL draftees: 4
Website: www.utahstateaggies.com

THE BEST OF TIMES

From 1960 to 1963, Utah State went 34–7–1 and won two conference championships. With Outland Trophy-winner Merlin Olsen, the Aggies went to two of their six all-time bowl games during this period, though they lost both games.

THE WORST OF TIMES

After losing 76 games in the 1960s and 1970s combined, Utah State racked up 68 defeats during the 1980s, the low point in the football program's history. The Aggies didn't have a winning season from 1981 through 1992 and went through three coaches: Bruce Snyder, Chris Pella, Chuck Shelton.

CONFERENCE

The Aggies left the Sun Belt Conference after two seasons (2003-04) to join the WAC in 2005. Twice an independent (1962-67 and 2001-02), Utah State was previously affiliated with the Big West Conference/PCAA (1978-2000) and the Mountain States Conference/Skyline Conference (1938-61).

DISTINGUISHED ALUMNI

Rick Bass, writer; Kathleen Clarke, director, Bureau of Land Management; Robert List, Nevada governor; Deanna Tanner Okun, Chairman of the U.S. International Trade Commission; Harry Reid, U.S. senator

FIGHT SONG

HAIL THE UTAH AGGIES
Hail the Utah Aggies,
we'll play the game with all our might
See the colors flying
The Aggies blue and fighting white
How they stir us onward;
We'll win the victory all right
Hail the Utah Aggies;
We're out to win, so fight, fight, fight!
Utah State, Hey!
Aggies all the way!
Go Aggies! Go Aggies!
Hey! Hey! Hey!

Logan, but they might have been the four most important years in the program's history. After a rocky 5–6 debut in 1959, Ralston spearheaded the best three-year run in school history (26–5–1). He constructed the powerhouse 1960 and 1961 teams, which went 18–3–1, reached No. 10 in the polls and went to two bowl games, with some of the top talents to ever wear Aggies jerseys. A total of 15 Utah State players were drafted during Ralston's tenure, including two of the program's four first-round picks.

Utah State may not be a national powerhouse, but it's got pride and Merlin Olsen on its side.

arriving at 2–5 Utah State, which had lost 10 straight times to BYU (average score: 41-11). Not a promising Saturday matchup, any way you looked at it. But that day, the 26,328 fans in attendance got their money's worth. In a manic, seesaw battle, Utah State took a 20-14 halftime lead and clung to it for the entire second half as BYU made push after push to reclaim the game. BYU quarterback John Walsh threw for 619 yards and five touchdowns to lead a late charge, but Utah State recovered an onside kick to seal a 58-56 victory. (That's right: 58-56.) BYU went on to finish 6–6 (including a loss to Ohio State in the Holiday Bowl) while the win resuscitated Utah State. The Aggies rallied to 7–5, with their first and only bowl win: 42-33 over Ball State in the Las Vegas Bowl.

BEST TEAM The 1961 squad went 9–1–1 and to their second straight postseason game, the Gotham Bowl (New York City's first and only bowl). Led by Olsen and a shutdown defense, the Aggies outscored opponents 396–102. "Those Aggies just punished people," says sports information director Mike Strauss.

BIGGEST GAME In 1993, BYU came to Logan after starting the season with four victories and a No. 19 ranking. The Cougars lost three straight games before

BIGGEST UPSET The entire West Coast was abuzz on Nov. 2, 1991, as unheralded and undefeated Fresno State, led by rocket-armed quarterback Trent Dilfer, stormed into the Top 25. The Bulldogs traveled to Logan to take on the woeful Aggies, who were 1–6 with just a win over

RECORDS

RUSHING YARDS
GAME
322 Emmett White vs. New Mexico State, Nov. 4, 2000 (34 att.)
SEASON
1,536 Demario Brown, 1999 (279 att.)
CAREER
4,053 Demario Brown, 1996-99 (792 att.)

PASSING YARDS
GAME
561 Tony Adams vs. Utah, Nov. 11, 1972 (30 of 43)
SEASON
3,268 Jose Fuentes, 2002 (246 of 454)
CAREER
9,168 Jose Fuentes, 1999-2002 (704 of 1,270)

RECEIVING YARDS
GAME
297 Aaron Jones vs. Boise State, Sept. 28, 2002 (10 rec.)
SEASON
1,531 Kevin Curtis, 2001 (100 rec.)
CAREER
2,943 Kendal Smith, 1985-88 (169 rec.)

POINTS
GAME
33 Jack Hill vs. Drake, Sept. 15, 1956 (5 TDs, 3 FGs)
SEASON
105 Jack Hill, 1956 (15 TDs, 15 PATs)
CAREER
284 Brad Bohn, 1997-2000 (59 FGs, 107 PATs)

CONSENSUS ALL-AMERICANS

1961	Merlin Olsen	T
1969	Phil Olsen	DE

Cal State Fullerton under their belts. With 13 All-Big West players, Fresno State looked like a lock. But in a Fresno State-controlled contest, Utah State broke loose with 28 seconds left in the third quarter, when defensive back Damon Smith took a Lorenzo Neal fumble 37 yards for a touchdown. The Aggies had their first lead of the day and began to believe. Then kicker Sean Jones booted a 45-yard field goal with 51 seconds left and defensive back Donald Toomer intercepted a Dilfer pass as time expired to preserve the 20-19 win, Utah State's first and only upset of a ranked team. Fresno State finished that season 10–2.

HEARTBREAKER Utah State hoped to win a Sun Belt Conference invite with a strong showing against intrastate rival BYU on Oct. 4, 2002. On the last play before halftime, cornerback Jerome Dennis intercepted a BYU pass and went 75 yards for a touchdown with no time remaining, good for a 34-7 lead. But the Aggies mustered only 80 yards on five second-half drives as BYU rallied for a 35-34 win. The Sun Belt welcomed Utah State anyway, but that loss still stings Aggies fans.

STADIUM The school built its first football complex in 1927 and named it in honor of longtime athletics director and coach Dick Romney. A tunnel connected the stadium to a nearby dorm building, where many players lived, so Romney's charges had only a 30-second hike from bed to bench on game days. But in 1968, with the school and sports department expanding, Romney Stadium was relocated across campus and enlarged.

RIVAL The school's series with BYU has been passionate, but lopsided. Before 1975, Utah State led 30–17–3, including 18 wins by 14 points or more. But since then, BYU has been extremely dominant. That's only fueled the rivalry for Utah State fans. "The game is so huge for our fans because we're kind of looked down upon," says

Strauss. That David vs. Goliath feel has provided eight of the top 15 gates in school history, all since 1979.

NICKNAME School officials changed the Utah State nickname to the Highlanders in the early 1970s. When the name change was announced at halftime of a football game, students booed into the second half of the game, then kept booing for two weeks until Utah State elected to keep Aggies as the team name.

MASCOT Since as far back as 1916, the Aggies used a bull costume for their mascot. In the 1960s, the school actually used a live bull, but found postgame cleanup wasn't worth the hassle. Ever since, the school has dressed a student in a Navy blue outfit with a bull head.

UNIFORMS *The Logan Journal* started calling Utah State teams Big Blue in 1916, an apparent reference to Paul Bunyan's Blue Ox. Since then, the school has stuck with blue for its uniforms and helmets. The Aggies' home jerseys have always been simple, with a white number below the school name on a blue background. The school switched its helmets in 1995, from a bull jumping through a large U to just a solid blue U.

NUMBERS In one of college football's amazing all-time outbursts, Utah State tailback Emmett White exploded on New Mexico State in 2000 for 578 all-purpose yards, obliterating the previous NCAA record of 435. White carried 34 times for 322 yards (a school record), caught seven passes for 134 yards, returned four kickoffs for 120 yards and had one punt return for two yards. His most important carry was his last, when he bounded into the end zone with two minutes left for a nine-yard touchdown, his fourth of the day, which gave Utah State a 44-37 win.

QUOTE "Those guys think we play in a pasture."
—John Ralston to his players before the Utah State-Utah grudge match in 1961

CENTENNIAL TEAM

Selected by fans and announced in 1993. The voting was sponsored by The Herald Journal of Logan, Utah.

OFFENSE

1974–77	Jim Hough,	OG
1981–84	Dave Kuresa,	OG
1951–54	Dave Kragthorpe,	OT
1957–59	Len Rohde,	OT
1941–42, 1946–47	Ralph Maughan,	C
1946–49	Norvel "Nog" Hansen,	TE
1970–72	Tom Forzani,	WR
1985–88	Kendal Smith,	WR
1976–79	Eric Hipple,	QB
1934–36	Kent Ryan,	RB
1973–75	Louie Giammona,	RB
1981–84	Willie Beecher,	PK

DEFENSE

1959–61	Merlin Olsen,	DL
1960–62	Lionel Aldridge,	DL
1967–69	Phil Olsen,	DL
1976–79	Rulon Jones,	DL
1980–83	Greg Kragen,	DL
1949–51	LaVell Edwards,	LB
1980, 1982–84	Hal Garner,	LB
1984–86	Al Smith,	LB
1966–68	Chuck Detwiler,	DB
1978–79	Donnie Henderson,	DB
1980–83	Patrick "Doc" Allen,	DB
1978–81	Guy McClure,	P

UTAH STATE ANNUAL STATISTICAL LEADERS

YR	RUSHING	YDS	ATT	AVG	PASSING	ATT	CMP	PCT	YDS	RECEIVING	REC	YDS	AVG
1956	Jack Hill	920	140	6.6	Bob Winters	130	65	.50	943	John Whatcott	23	400	17.4
1957	Overton Curtis	616	146	4.2	Bob Winters	179	92	.51	1,139	Gary Kapp	45	635	14.1
1958	Buddy Allen	509	88	5.8	Rick Dobbins	95	39	.41	539	Jerry Pelovsky	17	243	14.3
1959	Buddy Allen	553	79	7.0	Mel Montalbo	66	29	.44	543	Tom Larscheid	8	258	32.3
1960	Tom Larscheid	1,044	124	8.4	Dolph Camilli	35	15	.43	281	Doug Mayberry	6	74	12.3
1961	Tom Larscheid	773	121	6.4	Mel Montalbo	46	23	.50	478	Tom Larscheid	10	178	17.8
1962	Roger Leonard	349	66	5.3	Jim Turner	56	30	.54	414	John Matthews	13	223	17.2
1963	Larry Campbell	585	82	7.1	Bill Munson	201	120	.60	1,699	John Matthews	16	212	13.3
1964	Craig Murray	455	85	5.4	Ron Edwards	105	50	.48	798	Jack Hannum	18	296	16.4
1965	Roy Shivers	1,138	189	6.0	Ron Edwards	160	86	.54	1,095	Dave Clark	35	579	16.5
1966	Eric Maughan	574	117	4.9	John Pappas	97	38	.39	535	Dave Clark	20	251	12.6
1967	Altie Taylor	717	159	4.5	John Pappas	205	106	.52	1,424	Mike O'Shea	41	599	14.6
1968	Altie Taylor	929	203	4.6	John Pappas	203	98	.48	1,647	Mike O'Shea	56	1,077	19.2
1969	George Tribble	469	124	3.8	Dave Holman	226	110	.49	1,511	Paul Reuter	22	261	11.9
1970	John Strycula	644	157	4.1	Tony Adams	232	108	.47	1,394	Bob Wicks	47	642	13.7
1971	Ed Giles	510	128	4.0	Tony Adams	284	144	.51	2,035	Bob Wicks	58	862	14.9
1972	Jerry Hughes	679	171	4.0	Tony Adams	351	204	.58	2,797	Tom Forzani	85	1,169	13.8
1973	Archie Gibson	1,150	216	5.3	Tom Wilson	159	80	.50	1,177	Craig Clark	27	495	18.3
1974	Louie Giammona	1,534	329	4.7	Bill Swanson	99	44	.44	614	Cory Coles	16	225	14.1
1975	Louie Giammona	1,454	303	4.8	Greg Van Ness	166	82	.49	1,281	Paul Tippets	24	360	15.0
1976	Dan Cox	410	123	3.3	Keith Myers	145	82	.57	1,042	Greg Daly	37	498	13.5
1977	Rick Parros	1,135	261	4.3	Eric Hipple	173	91	.53	1,301	Jimmy Bryant	41	561	13.7
1978	Rick Parros	966	221	4.4	Eric Hipple	287	150	.52	2,088	Jimmy Bryant	48	696	14.5
1979	Rick Parros	1,236	259	4.8	Eric Hipple	239	144	.60	1,924	James Murphy	63	1,067	16.9
1980	Marvin Jackson	418	76	5.5	Bob Gagliano	345	184	.53	2,365	James Murphy	66	996	15.1
1981	Maurice Turner	641	163	3.9	Doug Samuels	168	78	.46	1,127	Eric McPherson	31	566	18.3
1982	Maurice Turner	485	121	4.0	Doug Samuels	265	135	.51	1,764	James Samuels	30	462	15.4
1983	Marc White	672	159	4.2	Chico Canales	214	117	.55	1,343	Andre Bynum	31	239	7.7
1984	Marc White	431	96	4.5	Gym Kimball	308	152	.49	1,913	Mickey Bell	29	439	15.1
1985	Glen Crawford	495	105	4.7	Brett Stevens	151	75	.50	909	Derek McPherson	25	331	13.2
1986	Demetrius Brown	289	97	3.0	Tom Ponich	259	107	.41	1,230	Kendal Smith	25	474	19.0
1987	Brett Payne	412	77	5.4	Brent Snyder	427	226	.53	2,887	Kendal Smith	67	1,048	15.6
1988	Timo Tagaloa	330	91	3.6	Brent Snyder	447	246	.55	3,218	Kendal Smith	65	1,196	18.4
1989	Demetrius Brown	615	171	3.6	Kirk Johnson	286	127	.44	1,862	Patrick Newman	45	791	17.6
1990	Roger Grant	1,370	266	5.2	Ron Lopez	260	138	.53	1,961	Tracey Jenkins	52	842	16.2
1991	Roger Grant	1,017	218	4.7	Ron Lopez	314	153	.49	2,221	Rod Moore	60	944	15.7
1992	Abu Wilson	795	164	4.8	Anthony Calvillo	360	201	.56	2,494	Greg Watts	42	448	10.7
1993	Profail Grier	947	190	5.0	Anthony Calvillo	469	247	.53	3,148	Mike Lee	70	715	10.2
1994	Abu Wilson	822	158	5.2	Matt Wells	311	153	.49	1,812	Shawn Turner	43	563	13.1
1995	Abu Wilson	1,476	275	5.4	Patrick Mullins	383	209	.55	2,774	Kevin Alexander	92	1,400	15.2
1996	Abu Wilson	840	195	4.3	Matt Sauk	286	154	.54	2,489	Nakia Jenkins	82	1,397	17.0
1997	Demario Brown	971	184	5.3	Matt Sauk	378	190	.50	2,896	Nakia Jenkins	73	1,086	14.9
1998	Demario Brown	846	210	4.0	Riley Jensen	194	93	.48	1,231	Robert Scott	55	808	14.7
1999	Demario Brown	1,536	279	5.5	Jeff Crosbie	361	169	.47	2,007	Aaron Jones	54	653	12.1
2000	Emmett White	1,322	242	5.5	Jose Fuentes	368	194	.53	2,709	Aaron Jones	63	1,159	18.4
2001	Emmett White	1,361	250	5.4	Jose Fuentes	437	260	.59	3,100	Kevin Curtis	100	1,531	15.3
2002	James Samuel	633	120	5.3	Jose Fuentes	454	246	.54	3,268	Kevin Curtis	74	1,258	17.0
2003	David Fiefia	997	205	4.9	Travis Cox	415	235	.57	2,791	Chris Cooley	62	732	11.8
2004	Chris Forbes	396	108	3.7	Travis Cox	306	179	.58	1,908	Kevin Robinson	44	602	13.7

Receiving leaders by receptions
The NCAA began including postseason stats in 2002

THE SCHOOLS

UTAH STATE ALL-TIME SCORES

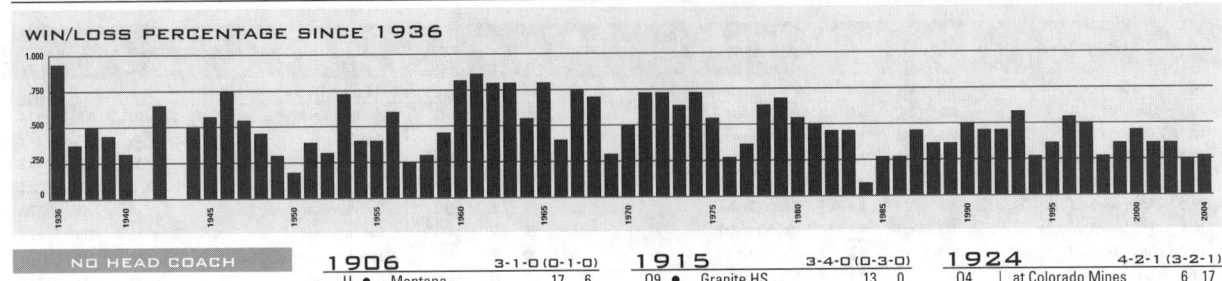

WIN/LOSS PERCENTAGE SINCE 1936

NO HEAD COACH

1892 1-0-0
U ●	Utah	12	0

1893-1895
NO TEAM

PROFESSOR MAYO 1896 (.000) 0-1

1896 0-1-0
U	Brigham Young Acad.	0	6

1897
NO TEAM

LT. DUNNING 1898 (.000) 0-1

1898 0-1-0
U	Brigham Young Acad.	5	12

WILLARD LANGTON 1899-1900 (.500) 1-1

1899 1-0-0
U ●	Brigham Young Acad.	10	6

1900 0-1-0
N17	Utah	0	21

DICK RICHARDS 1901 (.500) 3-2-1

1901 3-2-1
U ●	Ogden Mutes	15	5
U ●	Ogden HS	15	6
N9	at Utah	0	16 *
U	Brigham Young Acad.	NA	NA
U	National Guard	NA	NA
U =	Salt Lake HS	0	0

1902-1937 Rocky Mountain

GEORGE P. CAMPBELL 1902-06 (.420) 10-14-1

1902 0-4-0 (0-2-0)
O11	Colorado State	5	24
N15	at Utah	0	18
U	at National Guard	0	21
U ●	Fort Douglas	5	10

1903 3-0-0 (1-0-0)
O17 ●	Utah	17	0
N21 ●	Wyoming	46	0
U ●	Salt Lake HS	15	0

1904 4-8-0 (0-1-0)
U	at Montana St.	0	5
U ●	Idaho St.	22	0
U	at Oregon State	0	45
U	at Stanford	0	57
O22	at Washington	0	45
U	Montana	0	5
U ●	Idaho St.	10	0
N9	at Nevada	5	24
N19	at Utah	0	43
U ●	Ogden HS	21	0
U ●	Salt Lake HS	5	0
U ●	at Multnomah AC	0	29

1905 2-2-1 (0-1-0)
U =	at Montana St.	5	5
U	at Montana St.	0	23
N25	Utah *Unk*	0	5
U ●	Ogden HS *Unk*	21	0
U ●	Salt Lake HS *Unk*	5	0

1906 3-1-0 (0-1-0)
U ●	Montana	17	6
N29	at Utah	0	35
U ●	Fort Douglas	16	10
U ●	Ogden HS	5	0

FRED M. WALKER 1907-08 (.846) 11-2

1907 7-0-0 (1-0-0)
U ●	Ogden HS	6	0
U ●	Brigham Young Coll.	NA	NA
U ●	Salt Lake HS	21	5
N9	at Utah	24	10
U ●	Logan All Stars	11	5
U ●	All Hallows	45	6
U ●	Crimsons	100	0

1908 4-2-0 (0-1-0)
U ●	Salt Lake HS	52	0
U ●	All Hallows	33	6
U ●	Ogden HS	29	0
U ●	Logan All Stars	24	0
O24	Colorado Mines	4	22
U	at St. Vincent	0	11

CLAYTON T. TEETZEL 1909-15 (.568) 24-18-2

1909 2-2-1 (0-2-0)
O9	Utah	0	28
U ●	Logan All Stars	22	5
U ●	Fort Douglas	12	0
U =	Montana St.	0	0
N25	Utah	0	22

1910 5-2-0 (0-2-0)
O8	Utah	12	21
U ●	Ogden HS	18	3
U ●	Idaho Acad.	45	0
U	at Montana	5	3
U ●	at Montana Tech	5	0
U ●	Montana St.	19	0
N24	at Utah	0	6

1911 5-0-0 (1-0-0)
U ●	Logan All Stars	10	0
O14	Colorado State	29	0
U ●	Idaho Acad.	88	0
N4 ●	at Montana St.	29	0
N11 ●	at Montana	8	0

1912 4-2-1 (1-2-1)
O5	at Colorado	3	16
O12	at Colorado Mines	0	9
O26	Montana	17	0
N2	Wyoming	53	0
N9	Alumni	30	0
N16	Logan All Stars *Unk*	44	7
N28 =	at Utah	7	7

1913 3-3-0 (1-1-0)
U ●	at Salt Lake HS	60	26
U	Logan All Stars	0	3
U ●	at Montana	9	7
U	at Montana St.	0	13
N8	at Colorado State	7	20
N27 ●	Utah	21	0

1914 2-5-0 (1-2-0)
O10 ●	Alumni	20	0
O17	Montana St.	3	52
O24	at Gonzaga	0	60
O31	at Montana	0	32
N7 ●	Wyoming	24	3
N14	Colorado State	7	41
N26 ●	at Utah	2	20 *

1915 3-4-0 (0-3-0)
O9	Granite HS	13	0
O16	Nevada	26	0
O23	at Colorado State	0	59
O27	at Wyoming	7	13
N6 ●	Montana Tech	10	6
N13	Montana St.	0	7
N25	at Utah	0	14

JACK WATSON 1916-17 (.600) 8-5-2

1916 1-5-1 (0-3-0)
O7 ●	West Logan HS	20	3
O14	Colorado State	0	53
O21	Wyoming	10	23
O28	at Nevada	7	9
N11	Utah	0	46
N18 =	Montana St.	17	17
N25	Idaho	15	27

1917 7-0-1 (4-0-1)
O6	Granite HS	77	0
O13	Utah Field Aty.	21	6
O20 ●	at Montana	21	6
O24	Wyoming	57	0
N3 ●	Colorado State	47	7
N10 =	at Montana St.	7	7
N17 ●	Colorado	23	0
N29 ●	at Utah	14	0

1918
NO TEAM WWI

E. LOWELL ROMNEY 1919-48 (.579) 128-91-16

1919 5-2-0 (3-2-0)
O11 ●	Idaho St.	136	0
O18 ●	Montana	47	0
O25 ●	Montana St.	19	0
N8 ●	at Colorado State	7	27
N15 ●	at Colorado	19	7
N20 ●	at Wyoming	6	0
N29	at Utah	0	10

1920 4-2-1 (2-1-1)
O9 ●	at Ogden AC	16	0
O16 ●	Colorado Mines	27	3
O23 =	at Montana St.	0	0
O30	Colorado State	0	21
N6	at Nevada	0	21
N13 ●	Montana Tech	21	0
N25 ●	at Utah	9	3

1921 7-1-0 (4-0-0)
O8 ●	Ogden AC	47	21
O11 ●	Wyoming	14	3 *
O15 ●	Montana St.	30	7
O22	Nevada	0	41
A29 ●	Montana Tech	3	0
A5 ●	Colorado Mines	23	7
N12 ●	Albertson	20	0
N24 ●	at Utah	14	3

1922 5-4-0 (3-3-0)
S30 ●	at Montana Wesleyan	6	0
O7 ●	at Brigham Young	41	3 *
O13 ●	at Montana St.	39	6
O21	Colorado Mines	0	19
O28	at Colorado State	6	34
N4 ●	Montana Tech	7	0
N11 ●	Wyoming	25	0 *
N30	at Utah	0	14
D9	Arizona *Pho*	6	7

1923 5-2-0 (4-2-0)
O6 ●	at Montana Tech	26	0
O13	Denver	7	14
O20 ●	at Colorado Mines	26	0
O27	Colorado State	7	26
N12 ●	Brigham Young	40	0
N16 ●	at Wyoming	20	6
N29 ●	at Utah	21	13

1924 4-2-1 (3-2-1)
O4	at Colorado Mines	6	17
O18	Montana Tech	47	0
O25 ●	at Denver	16	0
N1	at Colorado State	13	17
N7 ●	at Brigham Young	13	9
N19 ●	Wyoming	25	2
N27 =	at Utah	7	7

1925 6-1-0 (5-1-0)
O10 ●	at Denver	13	0
O24 ●	Brigham Young	14	0
O31	Colorado State	0	13
N5 ●	Wyoming	26	13
N14 ●	Montana St.	10	7
N21 ●	at Montana Tech	38	0
N26 ●	at Utah	10	6

1926 5-1-2 (4-1-2)
O2 ●	Montana Tech	29	0
O9 =	Colorado College *Ogd*	7	0
O15 =	at Brigham Young	0	0
O23 =	at Wyoming	6	6
O30 ●	at Denver	7	3
N6 ●	at Colorado State	13	0
N13 ●	Western St.	31	0
N25 ●	at Utah	0	34

1927 3-4-1 (3-3-1)
O8	Western St.	39	0
O15	Montana St. *Ogd*	6	13
O22 ●	Wyoming	42	0
O29 ●	Brigham Young	22	0
N5	Denver	0	13
N11 ●	at Colorado State	0	6
N24 =	at Utah	0	0
D17	at Hawaii	20	21

1928 5-3-1 (4-2-1)
S29	at Southern Cal	12	40
O6 ●	Montana Tech	54	0
O13 =	at Denver	7	7
O19 ●	at Wyoming	24	6
O27 ●	at Brigham Young	10	0
N3	at Colorado State	6	7
N10 ●	Western St.	54	0
N17 ●	Montana St.	15	7
N29	at Utah	0	20

1929 3-4-0 (3-4-0)
O5 ●	at Montana St.	9	0
O19 ●	Brigham Young *Unk*	6	7
O26 ●	at Wyoming	12	7
N2 ●	Colorado College	10	0
N9	Colorado State	6	7
N16	at Denver	0	13
N28	at Utah	7	26

1930 3-5-1 (3-4-1)
S27 ●	Western St.	31	0
O4 ●	at Colorado College	8	7
O11 =	Colorado	0	0
O18	at Southern Cal	0	65
O25 ●	Wyoming	13	8
N1	Brigham Young *Unk*	14	39
N8	at Denver	7	32
N15	Colorado State	0	13
N27	at Utah	0	41

1931 6-2-0 (5-2-0)
S26 ●	Montana Tech	58	0
O3 ●	Montana St.	21	6
O10 ●	Western St.	58	20
O17 ●	Denver	12	6
O24 ●	at Wyoming	12	0
N7 ●	Brigham Young *Unk*	0	6
N14 ●	at Colorado State	6	0
N26	at Utah	0	34

1932 4-4-0 (3-3-0)

S24	●	Idaho St.	32	0
O1	● |	Montana St.	26	0
O8	|	at Colorado	7	26
O15	● |	Western St.	39	0
O29	|	at Utah	0	16
N5	● |	Colorado State	13	12
N19	|	at Brigham Young	6	18
N26		at Idaho	0	33

1933 4-4-0 (4-3-0)

S30	● |	Western St.	28	0
O7	● |	at Montana St.	40	6
O21	|	at Denver	0	12
O28	|	at Utah	6	14
N4	● |	Wyoming	27	0
N11	|	at Colorado State	0	3
N18	● |	Brigham Young	14	0
N25		at Montana	0	26

1934 5-1-1 (4-1-1)

S29	● |	at Denver	26	7
O6	●	Montana	6	0
O20	● |	at Wyoming	19	0
N3	● |	at Brigham Young	15	0
N10	= |	Colorado State	21	21
N17	● |	Colorado Mines	37	0
N29	|	at Utah	7	14

1935 5-2-1 (5-1-1)

S21	● |	Montana St.	33	7
S28		at UCLA	0	39
O19	|	at Denver	7	13
O26	● |	Colorado Mines	53	0
N2	● |	Colorado State	13	0
N9	● |	Wyoming	16	0 *
N16	● |	Brigham Young	27	0
N28	= |	at Utah	14	14

1936 7-0-1 (6-0-1)

S26	● |	Montana St.	12	0
O10	● |	at Wyoming	25	0
O17	● |	at Brigham Young	13	0
O24	● |	Utah	12	0
O31	= |	at Denver	0	0
N7	● |	at Colorado State	13	0
N14	● |	Colorado	14	13
N21	●	at Idaho	10	0

1937 2-4-2 (2-4-1)

O2	= |	Montana St.	6	6
O9	|	at Colorado	0	33
O16	=	at Idaho	0	0
O23	● |	Wyoming	34	7
O30	● |	Colorado State	7	0
N6	|	at Denver	0	25
N13	|	Brigham Young	0	54
N25	|	at Utah	0	27

1938-1947
MOUNTAIN STATES

1938 4-4-0 (3-3-0)

O1	●	Albertson	44	6
O8	● |	Colorado	20	0
O15	|	at Denver	0	7
O22	|	Utah	0	33
O29	● |	at Colorado State	6	0
N5	● |	at Brigham Young	3	0
N12	|	Wyoming	13	27 *
N19		at Idaho	0	14

1939 3-4-1 (2-3-1)

S30	●	Albertson	33	0
O7	● |	at Colorado	16	6
O21	|	Denver	0	7
O28	|	Colorado State	0	9
N4		at Idaho	7	19
N11	= |	Brigham Young	0	0
N18	● |	at Wyoming	20	13
N23	|	at Utah	0	27

1940 2-5-1 (2-4-0)

S30		San Jose State	0	19
O12	|	Colorado	0	26
O19	● |	Utah	7	0
O26	=	Idaho Boi	0	0
N2	|	at Brigham Young	7	12
N9	|	at Colorado State	12	13
N16	|	at Denver	6	34
N23	● |	Wyoming	16	0

1941 0-8-0 (0-6-0)

S26		at San Jose State	0	30
O11	|	at Colorado	7	13
O18		Idaho	0	16
O25	|	Colorado State	6	7
N1	|	Brigham Young	0	28
N8	|	Denver	6	14
N15	|	at Wyoming	6	12
N26	|	at Utah	21	33

1942 6-3-1 (2-3-1)

S26	●	at Idaho Marines	47	0
O3	●	Regis	28	2
O9	|	at Colorado	14	31
O17	|	Utah	7	34 *
O23	●	Fort Douglas	49	7
O31	● |	at Brigham Young	9	6
N7	|	at Colorado State	0	25
N14	= |	at Denver	13	13
N21	● |	Wyoming	14	6
N26	●	at Wichita St.	21	13

1943
NO TEAM WWII

1944 3-3-0 (0-2-0)

O14	●	Idaho Marines	40	0
O21		Nevada	7	13
O28	|	at Denver	6	36
N4	●	at Idaho Marines	27	6
N11	●	Idaho St.	8	7
N23	|	at Utah	0	47

1945 4-3-0 (1-3-0)

S29	●	Idaho Marines	45	0
O13	●	Montana	44	13
O20	● |	Colorado State	13	0
O27	|	at Denver	6	41
N3	●	at Idaho Marines	52	0
N10	|	at Colorado	7	14
N22	|	at Utah	6	24

1946 7-2-1 (4-1-1)

S28	●	Idaho St.	47	0
O5	|	at Colorado	0	6
O12	●	Montana St.	28	14
O19	● |	Colorado State	47	0 *
N2	●	at Montana	26	0
N9	= |	Brigham Young	0	0
N16	● |	Wyoming	21	7
N28	● |	at Utah	22	14
D7	● |	at Denver	28	14
		RAISIN BOWL		
J1		San Jose State	0	20

1947 6-5-0 (3-3-0)

S20		San Diego State	19	24
S27	●	Wichita St.	21	6
O4	● |	at Colorado State	26	13
O11	●	Montana	13	7
O18	|	at Wyoming	19	33
O25	|	at Brigham Young	12	20 *
N1	●	at Montana St.	28	13
N8	● |	Colorado	35	12
N15	● |	Denver	20	0
N27	|	at Utah	14	40
		GRAPE BOWL		
D13		Pacific	21	35

1948-1961
SKYLINE

1948 5-6-0 (2-3-0)

S17	●	Montana St.	31	6
S25	●	at Montana	18	7
O2	|	Colorado State	7	9
O9	●	Arizona State	22	17
O16		at Wichita St.	7	20
O23	● |	Brigham Young	20	7
O30	● |	Wyoming	45	34
N6		at Colorado	14	28
N13	|	at Denver	6	41
N25	|	at Utah	7	41
D4		at San Diego State	19	28

GEORGE MELINKOVICH
1949-50 (.238) 5-16

1949 3-7-0 (1-3-0)

S17		at Washington State	0	33
S24	●	Pacific Fleet	26	7
O1		Montana	13	18
O15	|	at Wyoming	0	27
O22		Colorado	7	20
O29	|	at Colorado State	6	28
N5	● |	at Brigham Young	22	3
N12	●	Montana St.	19	14
N24	|	at Utah	0	34
D3		at Arizona State	12	27

1950 2-9-0 (0-5-0)

S16	●	Nevada	7	6
S23		Washington State	6	46
S30		at Wichita St.	20	49
O7	●	at Montana St.	34	6
O14	|	Wyoming	7	40
O21		at Arizona State	0	28
O28	|	Colorado State	13	33
N4	|	Brigham Young	13	34
N11	|	at Denver	0	48
N18		at Montana	7	38
N23	|	at Utah	0	46

JOHN O. RONING
1951-54 (.463) 18-21-2

1951 3-5-1 (2-3-1)

S22		Arizona State	27	33
S28	●	Wichita St.	21	7
O6	|	at Wyoming	0	37
O20	= |	at Colorado State	20	20
O27	● |	Montana	19	6
N3	|	Utah	20	28
N10	|	at Brigham Young	27	28
N17	● |	at Denver	14	7
D1		at New Mexico	13	17

1952 3-7-1 (3-4-0)

S20	● |	at Montana	7	0
S27		Pacific	7	34
O4	|	Wyoming	0	14
O11		Idaho	3	6
O18		at Fresno State	21	27
O25	|	Colorado State	7	21
N1	=	at Wichita St.	20	20
N15	● |	Brigham Young	27	26
N22	● |	Denver	29	13
N27	|	at Utah	0	20
D6	|	at New Mexico	0	28

1953 8-3-0 (5-2-0)

S19	●	Wichita St.	14	7
S26	● |	New Mexico	6	0
O3	|	at Wyoming	13	20
O10	|	Utah	13	33
O16	● |	at Brigham Young	14	7
O24	● |	at Colorado State	14	13
O31	● |	Montana	33	14
N7	●	Fresno State	46	6
N14	● |	at Denver	21	12
N21	●	Idaho Boi	19	7
N26		at Pacific	14	20

1954 4-6-0 (4-3-0)

S18		at San Jose State	0	20
S25		at Wichita St.	7	32
O2	● |	at New Mexico	6	0
O9		at Fresno State	13	23
O16	|	at Montana	13	20
O23	● |	Colorado State	20	14
O30	● |	Brigham Young	45	13
N6	|	Wyoming	12	21
N13	|	Denver	7	25
N25	● |	at Utah	35	19

EV FAUNCE
1955-58 (.388) 15-24-1

1955 4-6-0 (3-4-0)

S16		San Jose State	0	13
S24		at Wichita St.	0	19
O1	|	at Wyoming	13	21
O8	● |	New Mexico	18	0
O15	● |	Montana	32	6
O22	|	at Colorado State	9	26
O29	●	Fresno State	39	14
N5	● |	at Brigham Young	47	21
N12	|	at Denver	6	39
N24	|	at Utah	13	14

1956 6-4-0 (4-3-0)

S15	●	at Drake	39	33
S22	● |	Denver	18	13
S29	|	at New Mexico	19	27
O6	●	at Arizona	12	7
O13	● |	at Montana	27	13
O20	● |	Colorado State	46	7
O27	● |	Brigham Young	33	7
N3	|	Wyoming	0	21
N10		at Idaho	20	42
N22	|	at Utah	7	29

1957 2-7-1 (1-5-1)

S14	●	Hawaii	26	12
S28		at Iowa	14	70
O5	= |	at Wyoming	19	19
O12	|	New Mexico	10	14
O19	|	Montana	25	35
O26	● |	at Colorado State	27	14
N2	|	at Brigham Young	0	14
N9		Idaho	7	35
N16	|	at Denver	19	21
N28	|	at Utah	6	21

1958 3-7-0 (1-5-0)

S20		at Arizona	6	7
S26	|	Denver	8	20
O4	●	at Kansas State	20	13
O11	|	at New Mexico	14	34
O18	● |	at Montana	27	14
O25	● |	Colorado State	15	0
N1	|	Brigham Young	6	13
N8	|	Wyoming	13	41
N15		at Idaho	7	34
N27	|	at Utah	7	12

JOHN RALSTON
1959-62 (.733) 31-11-1

1959 5-6-0 (2-5-0)

S19	●	Idaho	14	0
S26		at Arizona State	12	34
O3	|	at Wyoming	2	27
O10	|	New Mexico	6	28
O17	● |	Montana	28	0
O24	●	Montana St.	22	13
O31	|	at Brigham Young	0	18
N7	|	at Colorado State	7	10
N14	● |	at Denver	21	14
N21	|	at Utah	21	35
D11	●	at Hawaii	48	6

1960 9-2-0 (6-1-0)

S17	●	at Texas-El Paso	20	7
S24	● |	at Montana	14	12
O1	● |	Denver	31	8
O8	●	Idaho Boi	33	6
O15	● |	at New Mexico	46	7
O22	● |	Colorado State	21	0
O29	● |	Brigham Young	34	0
N5	● |	Wyoming	17	13
N12	●	at Pacific	45	6
N19	|	at Utah	0	6
		SUN BOWL		
D31		New Mexico State	13	20

1961 9-1-1 (5-0-1)

S16	●	Texas-El Paso	21	6
S23	● |	Montana	54	6
S30	●	Washington State Spo	34	14
O7	= |	at Wyoming	6	6
O14	● |	New Mexico	41	7
O21	● |	at Colorado State	49	3
O28	● |	Idaho	69	0
N4	● |	at Brigham Young	31	8
N11	● |	at Western Michigan	65	22
N18	● |	at Utah	17	6
		GOTHAM BOWL		
D9		Baylor	9	24

1962-1977
INDEPENDENT

1962 8-2-0

S15	●	at San Jose State	29	18
S22	●	Idaho Boi	45	7
S29	●	Montana	43	20
O6	●	at Montana St.	41	13
O13		at New Mexico	13	14
O20	●	Colorado State	21	0
O27	●	Brigham Young	27	21
N3		at Arizona State	15	34
N10	●	Wyoming	20	6
N17	●	at Utah	19	6

TONY KNAP
1963-66 (.638) 25-14-1

1963 8-2-0

S21	●	at Arizona	42	0 *
S30		at Wyoming	14	21
O5	●	San Jose State	20	0
O12	●	New Mexico	47	14
O19	●	at Montana	62	6
O26	●	Pacific	40	14
N2	●	at Brigham Young	26	0
N9	●	at Colorado State	36	13
N16	●	at New Mexico State	7	6
N23		Utah	23	25

1964 5-4-1

S19		at Arizona State	8	24
S26	●	New Mexico State	76	0
O3	●	at Montana	41	0
O10	●	Wichita St.	51	7
O17	●	at New Mexico	14	3
O24	●	Colorado State	42	13
O31		at Brigham Young	14	28
N7	=	Wyoming	20	20
N14		Idaho Boi	22	27
N21		at Utah	6	14

1965 8-2-0

S11	●	Hawaii	31	12
S25	●	at Arizona State	13	0
O2	●	at San Jose State	35	8
O9	●	Idaho	30	19
O16	●	Montana	54	21
O23	●	at Colorado State	41	20
O30	●	Brigham Young	34	21
N6		at Memphis	0	7
N13		at Wichita St.	19	21
N20	●	at Utah	14	7

1966 4-6-0

S17		at New Mexico	8	17
S24		at Nebraska	7	28
O1		New Mexico State	7	23
O8		at Brigham Young	7	27
O15		Colorado State	7	10
O22		at Wyoming	10	35
N5	●	at Pacific	47	9
N12	●	San Jose State	27	7
N19	●	at Utah	13	7
N26	●	at Hawaii	48	0

CHUCK MILLS
1967-72 (.621) 38-23-1

1967 7-2-1

S16	=	at Wichita St.	3	3
S23	●	at West Texas St.	44	27
S30		at New Mexico State	9	10
O7	●	Memphis SLC	28	14
O14	●	Pacific	7	6
O21		at Colorado State	14	17
N4	●	Brigham Young	30	9
N11	●	Montana	20	14
N18	●	at Utah	19	18
N25	●	at San Diego State	31	25

1968 7-3-0

S14	●	New Mexico State	28	12
S21		Wyoming	3	48
S28	●	Wichita St.	38	0
O5	●	Montana	50	3
O12	●	Wisconsin	20	0
O19		Pacific	7	18
O26	●	West Texas St.	20	10
N9	●	Brigham Young	34	8
N23	●	Utah	28	13
N30		at San Diego State	19	30

1969 3-7-0

S13		at Wichita St.	7	17
S20	●	at Bowling Green	14	6
S27		Pacific	3	36
O11		Colorado State	33	37
O18	●	at Army	23	7
O25		Memphis	0	40
N1		at Utah	7	27
N8		at Air Force	13	38
N15		Brigham Young	3	21
N22	●	at Idaho	31	21

1970 5-5-0

S12		Kansas State	0	37
S19	●	Bowling Green	33	14
S26	●	at Wyoming	42	29
O10	●	at Kentucky	35	6
O24		at Brigham Young	20	27
O31		at Colorado State	13	20
N7		Utah	0	17
N14		Idaho	14	42
N21	●	at Memphis	15	12
N28	●	at New Mexico State	45	21

1971 8-3-0

S11	●	at Kansas State	10	7
S18	●	New Mexico State	34	0
S25	●	Nevada-Las Vegas	27	7
O2		at Nebraska	6	42
O9	●	Brigham Young	29	7
O16	●	Memphis	7	6
O22		at San Diego State	20	36
O30	●	at Colorado State	18	17
N6		Wyoming	29	31
N13	●	at Utah	21	17
N20	●	at Idaho	42	13

1972 8-3-0

S9	●	at New Mexico State	48	14
S16		at Oklahoma	0	49
S23	●	at Brigham Young	42	19
S30	●	Colorado State	21	0
O7		at Texas	12	27
O14		at Memphis	29	38
O28	●	at Wyoming	35	23
N4	●	Idaho	51	7
N11	●	Utah	44	16
N18	●	Southern Miss	27	21
N23	●	Weber St.	20	16

PHIL KRUEGER
1973-75 (.636) 21-12

1973 7-4-0

S15	●	at Weber St.	10	3
S22		San Diego State	7	35
S29	●	at Nevada-Las Vegas	7	3
O6	●	Brigham Young	13	7
O13	●	at Colorado State	34	18
O20	●	at West Texas St.	36	14
O27		Kent State	16	27
N3	●	Wyoming	31	20
N10	●	at New Mexico State	40	12
N17		at Utah	28	31
N22		at Southern Miss	8	32

1974 8-3-0

S14	●	at Wyoming	17	7
S21	●	at Brigham Young	9	6
S28		at Oklahoma	3	72
O12	●	Colorado State	24	23
O19	●	at Kent State	27	24
O26	●	West Texas St.	21	16
N2	●	at Idaho	17	3
N9		Southern Miss	3	7
N16	●	Utah	34	0
N23	●	Weber St.	20	7
N30		at San Diego State	6	34

1975 6-5-0

S13	●	at Utah	13	7
S20		at Florida State	8	17
S27		San Diego State	10	19
O4		at Texas	7	61
O11	●	West Texas St.	21	17
O18	●	at Weber St.	30	7
O25		Arkansas LR	0	31
N1	●	Wyoming	27	21
N8		Brigham Young	7	24
N15	●	at Boise State	42	19
N22	●	at Colorado State	28	17

BRUCE SNYDER
1976-82 (.494) 37-38-2

1976 3-8-0

S4		at San Jose State	10	45
S11		Arkansas LR	16	33
S18		Long Beach St.	10	32
S25		at Wyoming	3	20
O2		at Oregon	9	27
O9		Colorado State	7	10
O16	●	Utah	28	17
O23		at Brigham Young	14	45
N6	●	Weber St.	36	10
N13		at San Diego State	6	7
N20	●	Pacific	31	17

1977 4-7-0

S10	●	San Jose State	22	10
S17		at Memphis	26	31
S24		Brigham Young	6	65
O1		at San Diego State	0	19
O8		at Penn State	7	16
O15		at Utah	0	20
O29		Boise State	16	23
N5	●	at Weber St.	23	14
N12	●	Wyoming	32	31
N19	●	at Idaho St.	35	7
N26		at Colorado State	10	13

1978-2000
Big West

1978 7-4-0

S3	●	Idaho St. OSA	10	0
S16	●	at Colorado State	21	20
S23	● |	Fresno State	45	22
S30	● ||	at Wyoming	20	13
O7	●	at Brigham Young	24	7
O14	|	Long Beach St.	17	33
O21		at Miami, Fla.	16	17
O28	● |	San Jose State	31	21
N4	● |	Pacific	40	14
N11		Weber St.	25	44
N25		Utah	20	23

1979 7-3-1 4-0-1

S8	= |	at San Jose State	48	48 †
S15		at Nebraska	14	35
S22	●	Colorado State	24	0
S29	●	at Utah	47	21
O6	● |	Long Beach St.	51	28
O13		Brigham Young	24	48
O20	● |	at Pacific	15	14
O27		at Arizona State	14	28
N3	● |	Fullerton St.	35	7
N17	●	at Weber St.	34	10
N24	● |	at Fresno State	41	31

1980 6-5-0 (4-1-0)

S6		at Kentucky	10	17
S13	●	Idaho St.	14	7
S20		at Texas	17	35
O4		Utah	19	23
O11	● |	at Fullerton St.	28	17
O18		Brigham Young	46	70
O25	● |	at Fresno State	14	0
N1	● |	Pacific	21	7
N8	●	at Weber St.	50	13
N15	|	at Long Beach St.	27	28
N22	● |	at San Jose State	44	38

1981 5-5-1 (4-1-0)

S5		at Utah	0	10
S12	● |	Fullerton St.	14	9
S19	●	Weber St.	31	18
S26		at Houston	7	35
O2		at Brigham Young	26	32
O10	● |	at Pacific	17	14
O17	=	at TCU	13	13
O24	|	San Jose State	24	27
O31	● |	Fresno State	20	0
N7	● |	at Long Beach St.	28	2
N14		at Idaho St.	24	50

1982 5-6-0 (2-3-0)

S11		at TCU	9	24
S18	●	Weber St.	31	10
S25	● |	at Fullerton St.	19	0
O2	|	at Fresno State	6	31
O9	●	Idaho St.	30	3
O16	● |	Pacific	14	12
O30	●	Brigham Young	20	17
N6		at Utah	10	42
N13		at Boise State	10	30
N20	|	at San Jose State	26	49
N27	|	at Long Beach St.	17	44

CHRIS PELLA
1983-85 (.273) 9-24

1983 5-6-0 (3-3-0)

S10		at Arizona State	12	39
S17	|	Fullerton St.	24	25
S24		at Missouri	10	17
O1	● |	Fresno State	20	12
O8	● |	at Pacific	27	10
O15	●	Boise State	10	7
O22	|	at Nevada-Las Vegas	10	28
O29		at Brigham Young	34	38
N5	● |	San Jose State	22	15
N12	●	Utah	21	17
N25	|	at Long Beach St.	3	6

1984 1-10-0 (1-5-0)

S8		at Southern Cal	7	42
S15		TCU	18	62
S29	|	at Fullerton St.	16	27
O6	|	at San Jose State	21	38
O13	|	Long Beach St.	22	24
O20	|	at Fresno State	18	43
O27	● |	Pacific	41	14
N3		at Arizona	10	45
N10	||	Utah	10	21
N17	|	Nevada-Las Vegas	20	36 †
N24		at Brigham Young	13	38

1985 3-8-0 (3-4-0)

S7	● |	at Long Beach St.	19	17
S14		at Iowa State	3	10
S21	● |	San Jose State	35	32
S28	|	at Pacific	7	33
O5	|	at Nevada-Las Vegas	7	14
O12	|	Fullerton St.	30	32
O19		at Arizona State	10	42
O26	|	Fresno State	19	38
N2		at Utah	7	34
N9		Brigham Young	0	44
N23	● |	at New Mexico State	40	23

CHUCK SHELTON
1986-91 (.402) 26-39-1

1986 3-8-0 (3-4-0)

S6		at Brigham Young	0	52
S13		at Missouri	10	24
S20		at Kansas	13	16
O4	● |	New Mexico State	42	9
O11	|	at San Jose State	28	38
O18	|	at Fullerton St.	0	33
O25	● |	Nevada-Las Vegas	7	6
N1	|	Long Beach St.	3	14
N8	● |	at Pacific	14	10
N15		Utah	10	27
N22	|	at Fresno State	7	14

1987 5-6-0 (4-3-0)

S5		at Nebraska	12	56
S12		at Kentucky	0	41
S26	|	Fullerton St.	11	30
O2		at Brigham Young	24	45
O10	|	at Nevada-Las Vegas	27	28
O17	● |	Pacific	17	13
O24	●	at Utah	41	36
O31	|	San Jose State	14	24
N7	● |	at New Mexico State	25	6
N14	● |	Fresno State	17	13
N21	● |	at Long Beach St.	17	14

1988 4-7-0 (4-3-0)

S3		at Nebraska	13	63
S10		at Missouri	21	35
S24	● |	New Mexico State	32	20
S30		at Brigham Young	3	38
O8	● |	Long Beach St.	31	24
O15	|	at Fresno State	10	51
O22	|	at San Jose State	31	36
O29	● |	Pacific	23	20
N5	● |	Nevada-Las Vegas	17	10
N12		Utah	21	42
N19	|	at Fullerton St.	13	23

1989 4-7-0 (4-3-0)

S9		at Utah	10	45
S16		at Southern Cal	10	66
S23		at Illinois	2	41
S30		Brigham Young	10	37
O7	● |	Fullerton St.	34	23
O14	|	Fresno State	7	34
O21	● |	at New Mexico State	28	13
N4	● |	at Pacific	38	10
N11	|	San Jose State	7	33
N18	● |	at Nevada-Las Vegas	27	22
N25	|	at Long Beach St.	18	31

1990 5-5-1 (5-1-1)

S1		Utah	0	19
S8	● |	Long Beach St.	27	13
S15		at Missouri	10	45
O6		at Oregon	7	52
O13	= |	at Fresno State	24	24
O20	|	at San Jose State	27	34
O27	● |	Nevada-Las Vegas	31	6
N3	● |	New Mexico State	55	10
N10	● |	at Fullerton St.	45	17
N17	● |	Pacific	51	45
N24		at Brigham Young	10	45

1991 5-6-0 (5-2-0)

A31		at Utah	7	12
S7		at Nebraska	28	59
S21		at Oklahoma	21	55
S28	|	San Jose State	7	23
O4		at Brigham Young	10	38
O19	● |	Fullerton St.	26	3
O26	|	at Long Beach St.	6	7
N2	● |	Fresno State	20	19
N9	● |	at Nevada-Las Vegas	27	14
N16	● |	Pacific	21	14
N23	● |	at New Mexico State	46	21

CHARLIE WEATHERBIE
1992-94 (.441) 15-19

1992 5-6-0 (4-2-0)

S5		at Arizona	3	49
S12		Utah	18	42
S19		at Baylor	10	45
S26	● |	New Mexico State	48	21
O2		at Brigham Young	9	30
O17	●	Kansas State	28	16
O24	|	San Jose State	25	27
O31	● |	at Fullerton St.	26	7
N7	● |	Nevada-Las Vegas	48	8
N14	|	at Nevada	47	48
N21	● |	at Pacific	38	35

1993   7-5-0 (5-1-0)

S4	●	at La. Lafayette	34 13
S11		at Utah	29 31
S18		Baylor	24 28
S25		at Fresno State	14 30
O2		at LSU	17 38
O16		Nevada	44 48
O23	●	at Nevada-Las Vegas	33 26
O30	●	Brigham Young	58 56
N6	●	Pacific	24 21
N13	●	Louisiana Tech	24 13
N20	●	at New Mexico State	20 17
		LAS VEGAS BOWL	
D17	●	Ball State	42 33

1994   3-8-0 (2-4-0)

S3		Utah	17 32
S10		at Colorado State	16 41
S17	●	at Ohio U.	5 0
S24		Nevada-Las Vegas	21 23
S30		at Brigham Young	6 34
O15	●	at Louisiana Tech	7 3
O22		La. Lafayette	25 27
O29		at Pacific	6 28
N5		Ea. Washington	31 49
N12		at Nevada	28 56
N19	●	New Mexico State	47 20

JOHN L. SMITH
1995-97 (.471)   16-18

1995   4-7-0 (4-3-0)

S2		at Arkansas State	17 21
S9		Boise State	14 38
S16		Southern Miss	21 24
S30		at San Jose State	30 32
O7		Colorado State	17 59
O14	●	Northern Illinois	42 7
O21	●	at New Mexico State	27 14
O28		at Utah	20 40
N4		Nevada	25 30
N11	●	at Nevada-Las Vegas	42 0
N18	●	Pacific	38 22

1996   6-5 (4-1)

A31	●	Utah	20 17
S7	●	Cal St. Northridge	57 27
S14		at Southern Miss	24 31
S21		at Oklahoma State	17 31
S28		at Texas Tech	20 58
O4		Brigham Young	17 45
O12	●	at New Mexico State	53 21
O19	●	at Boise State	39 14
O26	●	Idaho	35 28
N2	●	North Texas	21 13
N9		Nevada	27 54

1997   6-6 (4-1)

A30	●	at Utah	21 14
S6	●	Idaho St.	41 7
S13		Colorado State	24 35
S20		New Mexico	22 25
O3		at Brigham Young	35 42
O11		at Oregon State	16 24
O18	●	New Mexico State	38 7
O25	●	at Idaho	63 17
N1	●	Boise State	24 20
N15	●	at Nevada	38 19
N22		at North Texas	48 51
		HUMANITARIAN BOWL	
D29		Cincinnati	19 35

DAVE ARSLANIAN
1998-99 (.318)   7-15

1998   3-8 (2-3)

S5		Utah	12 20
S12		at New Mexico	36 39
S19		at Colorado	6 25
S26	●	Sam Houston St.	47 17
O3		Oregon State	16 20
O10		at Washington	12 53
O17		Idaho	14 26
O24		at Boise State	16 30
O31	●	at New Mexico State	29 26
N7		Nevada	21 26
N14	●	North Texas	28 27

1999   4-7 (3-3)

S4		at Georgia	7 38
S11	●	Stephen F. Austin	51 17
S18		at Utah	18 38
O1		Brigham Young	31 34
O9	●	Arkansas State	20 14
O16		at Kansas State	0 40
O23		Idaho *Pull*	3 31
O30		Boise State	27 33
N6		New Mexico State	6 14
N20	●	at Nevada	37 35
N27	●	at North Texas	34 7

MICK DENNEHY
2000-04 (.339)   19-37

2000   5-6 (4-1)

S2		at Texas Tech	16 38
S9	●	So. Utah	30 14
S23		at Arizona State	20 44
S30		Utah	14 35
O6		at Brigham Young	14 38
O14	●	at North Texas	17 12
O21	●	Idaho	31 14
O28	●	Arkansas State	44 31
N4	●	at New Mexico State	44 37
N11		at Boise State	38 66
N18		Idaho St.	24 27

2001-2002
INDEPENDENT

2001   4-7-0

S1		at Utah	19 23
S8		at LSU	14 31
S22		Wyoming	42 43
S29		Oregon	21 38
O5		at Brigham Young	34 54
O20	●	Idaho St.	28 27
O27	●	Central Florida	30 27
N10	●	at Connecticut	38 31
N17	●	Weber St.	56 43
N24		at South Florida	13 34
D1		at Fresno State	21 70

2002   4-7 (0-0)

A31		Utah	3 23
S7		at Nebraska	13 44
S14	●	Idaho St.	38 33
S21		at Iowa	7 48
S28		at Boise State	38 63
O4		Brigham Young	34 35
O19	●	New Mexico	45 44
O26		at La. Monroe	48 51
N9	●	New Mexico State	32 30
N16	●	at Troy State	19 16
N30		at Middle Tennessee	28 45

2003-2004
SUN BELT

2003   3-9 (3-3)

A28		at Utah	20 40
S6		at Nebraska	7 31
S13		at Arizona State	16 26
S27	●	La. Monroe	28 10
O4		at New Mexico	7 34
O11		Wyoming	21 48
O18		at North Texas	27 37
O25	●	Arkansas State	49 0
N1	●	Middle Tennessee	41 20
N6		at New Mexico State	21 26
N15		Troy State	14 23
N22		at Idaho	13 20

2004   3-8 (2-5)

S4		at Alabama	17 48
S11	●	Idaho	14 7
S18		Utah	6 48
S25	●	at Nevada-Las Vegas	31 21
O2		at Troy State	21 49
O9		North Texas	23 31
O16		at Clemson	6 35
O30		at Middle Tennessee	0 21
N6		at La. Monroe	25 32
N11		at Arkansas State	7 16
N20	●	New Mexico State	34 25

Neutral Site Key: *Boi* Boise, ID / *LR* Little Rock, AR / *Ogd* Ogden, UT / *Osa* Osaka, Japan / *Pho* Phoenix, AZ / *Pull* Pullman, WA / *SLC* Salt Lake City, UT / *Spo* Spokane, WA / *Unk* Unknown, Unknown
f Forfeit † Game Later Forfieted # Disputed Victor * Disputed Score || Designated Conference Game |2 Counted Twice in Conference Standings

UTEP

BY DAVE REARDON

TEXAS-EL PASO ISN'T WHAT YOU'D call a perennial football powerhouse; far from it. But even before current coach Mike Price came in to lead the team to an 8–4 season in 2004, the Miners had some of the most loyal, patient and passionate fans in the land. Make that two lands: UTEP benefits not only from 700,000 residents on the Texas side of the Rio Grande, but also from another 1.2 million in Ciudad Juarez, Mexico. They haven't had a whole lot to cheer about—in English or Spanish—over the decades, but the Sun Bowl is also host to the oldest independent bowl game, and every now and then the home team manages to sneak in.

TRADITION The UTEP-New Mexico State rivalry is so established that the winner gets two trophies: the Silver Spade and the Brass Spittoon. The original spade was a prospector's shovel found in 1947 in the Organ Mountains near Las Cruces, N.M. It was later replaced with a silver spade that has each year's winner engraved on it. In 1982, El Paso mayor Jonathan Rogers and Las Cruces mayor David Steinberg added the brass spittoon—officially known as the Mayor's Cup—to the victor's spoils.

BEST PLAYER Old-timers have a soft spot for Ken Heineman, while relative youngsters side with Billy Stevens; both were multitalented quarterbacks. Heineman made All-America three times, from 1937 to 1939. He led the Miners in rushing, passing and punting all three years and intercepted nine passes in 1939. Stevens (1965-67) became an instant legend when he passed for 500 yards in his first game. He still holds school records for most passes in a season (432) and career (910), career passing yards (6,495) and longest TD pass (92 yards to Bob Wallace on the last play of the game against Utah in 1965).

BEST COACH Bobby Dobbs wasn't much better than .500 for his career, with a 42–38–2 record from 1965 to 1972. But he took over a team that went 0–8–2 in 1964 and turned UTEP into a Sun Bowl champion with an 8–3 record. His teams finished in the nation's top five in passing every year from 1965 to 1969.

BEST TEAM In 1988, the Miners went 10–3, including a run of six consecutive wins, four of which were road

PROFILE
University of Texas at El Paso
El Paso, Texas
Founded: 1914
Enrollment: 15,085
Colors: Dark Blue and Orange
Nickname: Miners
Stadium: Sun Bowl
     Opened in 1963
     AstroPlay; 52,000 capacity
First football game: 1914
All-time record: 335–489–28 (.410)
Bowl record: 5–6
First-round NFL draftees: 2
Website: www.utepathletics.com

THE BEST OF TIMES
Bobby Dobbs turned it around for the Miners in 1965 after UTEP had seven straight losing seasons, including an 0–8–2 record in 1964. From 1965 to 1967, Texas-El Paso, under Dobbs, went 21–9–1 and captured Sun Bowl victories over TCU and Mississippi.

THE WORST OF TIMES
From 1975 to 1985, the Miners never won more than two games in a season. Texas-El Paso was a miserable 15–110 overall and 6–72 in the WAC during that span.

CONFERENCE
UTEP has been an independent (1914-34), a member of the Border Conference (1935-61), an independent again (1962-67) and in the WAC (1968-2004), where the Miners were co-champs with TCU in 2000. UTEP joined Conference USA in 2005.

DISTINGUISHED ALUMNI
Nate Archibald, Basketball Hall of Famer; Bob Beamon, 1968 Olympic gold medalist in long jump; Sam Donaldson, TV newscaster; Jaime Oaxaca, chairman of the board, Space Foundation; Nolan Richardson, college basketball coach

FIGHT SONG
Out in the west Texas town of El Paso
Home of the river they call Rio Grande
Down on the border the town of El Paso
Home of the Miners the best in the land.

Fighting to win the Miners of UTEP
long live the College of Mines! (men)
GO COLLEGE OF MINES! (women)
Loyal forever we're standing together
Onward to victory orange and blue!
WE WILL BE TRUE!

MINERS FIGHT
Miners Fight!
Miners Fight!
Miners Fight!
And it's goodbye to (opponent)
Miners Fight!
Miners Fight!
For we'll put over one more win
Miners Fight!
Miners Fight!
For it's Miners that we love best
Hail! Hail!
The gang's all here
And it's goodbye to all the rest!

The UTEP-New Mexico State rivalry is so established that the winner gets two trophies: the Silver Spade and the Brass Spittoon.

games. UTEP scored the most points in school history (445) behind quarterback Pat Hegarty and Chris Jacke, one of the best kickers in the nation. The Miners finished second in the WAC at 6–2, and went on to lose 38-18 to Southern Miss in the Independence Bowl.

BIGGEST GAME Not many games are immortalized on canvas, but Tom Lea's painting *The Turning Point* captures UTEP's 20-19 win at Utah in 1965. On the last play of the game (and in the painting), Stevens completed a pass to secondary receiver Wallace for a 92-yard touchdown—and the victory. On the other side of the ball, Fred Carr led the UTEP defense with 15 tackles. The victory ended a three-game slide and was the start of a four-game winning streak to close the season for the Miners, who went 8–3 in the first of three consecutive winning seasons.

BIGGEST UPSET The Miners' only win in 1985 came against seventh-ranked and defending national champion Brigham Young. UTEP used only two pass-rushers, dropping nine men into coverage; one of those nine was Danny Taylor, who ran an interception back 103 yards to help the Miners beat the Cougars 23-16.

STADIUM The Sun Bowl opened with a bang on Sept. 21, 1963, as UTEP's Larry Durham ran for a 54-yard touchdown on the stadium's first play from scrimmage; the Miners went on to defeat North Texas State 34-7. On Nov. 1, 1997, UTEP fans tore down the south goalposts after the Miners beat No. 25 Brigham Young 14-3. Three years later, on Nov. 11, 2000, some fans in the crowd of 53,304 (the largest in Sun Bowl history) went further, taking down both sets of goalposts as the Miners won a share of the WAC champion-ship by beating Rice 38-21.

HEARTBREAKER In 2000, LaDainian Tomlinson ran all over UTEP's hopes of a national ranking. The Texas Christian running back rambled for 305 yards in the Horned Frogs' 47-14 win, a game that forced the Miners to settle for a tie with TCU for the WAC championship. Tomlinson's

RECORDS

RUSHING YARDS
	GAME
326	Fred Wendt vs. New Mexico State, Nov. 25, 1948 (25 att.)
	SEASON
1,570	Fred Wendt, 1948 (184 att.)
	CAREER
3,576	John Harvey, 1985-88 (678 att.)

PASSING YARDS
	GAME
507	Bill Craigo at Colorado State, Oct. 17, 1970 (26 of 59)
	SEASON
3,140	Sammy Garza, 1986 (258 of 410)
	CAREER
6,485	Billy Stevens, 1965-67 (426 of 943)

RECEIVING YARDS
	GAME
349	Chuck Hughes vs. North Texas, Sept. 18, 1965 (10 rec.)
	SEASON
1,519	Chuck Hughes, 1965 (80 rec.)
	CAREER
2,908	Lee Mays, 1998-2001 (200 rec.)

POINTS
	GAME
42	Fred Wendt vs. New Mexico State, Nov. 25, 1948 (6 TDS, 6 PATs)
	SEASON
152	Fred Wendt, 1948 (20 TDs, 32 PATs)
	CAREER
306	John Harvey, 1985-88 (51 TDs)

CONSENSUS ALL-AMERICANS
2000	Brian Natkin, TE

numbers couldn't have come as much of a surprise—he ran for 406 yards against UTEP in 1999 in a 52-24 TCU win.

RIVAL Forty miles of Interstate 10 and a state line separate UTEP and New Mexico State. The Miners are 47–33–2 against the Aggies, and through 2004 had won five of the past seven meetings.

DISPUTE On Nov. 18, 1967, a 5–1–1 UTEP team hosted No. 6 Wyoming at the Sun Bowl. The Cowboys led 21-19 late in the game, but Stevens led the Miners on a nine-play, 70-yard drive that stalled deep in Wyoming territory. Jerry Waddles' 44-yard field goal try was good—at least according to one official. The other signaled that it was wide, and his ruling stood. UTEP lost 21-19.

NICKNAME The school was founded as the State School of Mines and Metallurgy, and its team was known early on as Ore Diggers and Muckers. While there is no conclusive proof, many believe the name Miners was the brainchild of John W.

"Cap" Kidd, a faculty member and booster. Considering he donated $800 to equip the football team when funds were short in 1915, how could anyone deny the man his wish?

MASCOT The school's first mascot was a burro named Clyde, but UTEP president Dr. Joseph Ray didn't like Clyde's appearance—so in 1966, Ray replaced Clyde with Henry, an ostensibly more handsome burro. The cartoon mascot Paydirt Pete arrived in 1974. The school unveiled a tougher looking Paydirt Pete in 1999; the new Pete was also politically correct, having ditched his cigar.

QUIRK The team is escorted by a band of Harley-Davidson motorcycles before each home game.

QUOTE "He walks into his first team meeting with a hard hat and a pickax. He marches in with a strut and tells us we're going to be more enthusiastic. We all started going crazy, yelling and screaming like we were at a concert."—Linebacker Robert Rodriguez, on the first time he met coach Mike Price

UTEP ANNUAL STATISTICAL LEADERS

YR	RUSHING	YDS	ATT	AVG	PASSING	ATT	CMP	PCT	YDS	RECEIVING	REC	YDS	AVG
1937	Ken Heineman	827	128	6.5	Ken Heineman	175	75	.43	1,282	Red Andrews	31	480	15.5
1938	Ken Heineman	589	122	4.8	Ken Heineman	125	57	.46	787	Morris Raney	17	281	16.5
1939	Ken Heineman	585	97	6.0	Ken Heineman	184	82	.45	804	Charles Dean	20	316	15.8
1940	Owen Price	596	118	5.1	Gil Salcedo	66	27	.41	542	Jack Telford	23	318	13.8
1941	Owen Price	475	139	3.4	Owen Price	208	94	.45	997	Jack Telford	28	418	14.9
1942	Raymond Evans	624	120	5.2	Vic Clark	136	71	.52	846	Albert Salem	36	401	11.1
1943	No team due to WWII												
1944	No team due to WWII												
1945	No team due to WWII												
1946	Ed Smith	415	63	6.6	Vic Clark	64	38	.59	369	Albert Salem	23	169	7.3
1947	Ed Smith	742	135	5.5	Jim Bowden	93	53	.57	574	Ed Smith	11	159	14.5
1948	Fred Wendt	1,570	184	8.5	Jim Bowden	38	26	.68	357	Robert Grounds	11	119	10.8
1949	Pug Gabrel	886	145	6.1	Ralph Brewster	57	23	.40	419	Robert Grounds	12	108	9.0
1950	Lee Cargile	573	101	5.7	Ralph Brewster	47	22	.47	410	Jimmy Walker	9	179	19.9
1951	Clovis Riley	481	97	5.0	Billy Bob Plumbley	122	65	.53	780	Jimmy Walker	40	440	11.0
1952	Clovis Riley	670	140	4.8	Dick Shinaut	208	102	.49	1,520	Gene Odell	26	462	17.8
1953	Clovis Riley	552	86	6.4	Dick Shinaut	92	53	.58	720	Gene Odell	25	391	15.6
1954	Reeves Tevis	676	134	5.0	Jesse Whittenton	111	45	.41	577	John Howle	27	339	12.6
1955	Rusty Rutledge	374	77	4.9	Jesse Whittenton	97	47	.48	780	Dick Forrest	18	338	18.8
1956	Jimmy Bevers	606	98	6.2	Bob Laraba	75	26	.35	568	Don Maynard	7	165	23.6
1957	Bob Forrest	365	60	6.1	Bob Laraba	55	28	.51	412	Don Maynard	11	309	28.1
1958	Charles Bradshaw	435	105	4.1	John Furman	70	29	.41	355	Don Maynard	13	333	25.6
1959	Charles Bradshaw	547	115	4.8	John Furman	187	89	.48	1,132	Jackie Meeks	24	235	9.8
1960	Charles Bradshaw	585	131	4.5	John Furman	192	94	.49	1,094	Paul Paxon	15	160	10.7
1961	Don Boyce	611	158	3.9	John Furman	180	85	.47	1,026	Ralph Kennedy	18	349	19.4
1962	Larry Durham	218	72	3.0	Jerry Tucker	156	59	.38	480	Jim Evans	21	242	11.5
1963	Larry Durham	305	72	4.2	Jerry Tucker	181	70	.39	865	Jim Evans	36	480	13.3
1964	Dick Weeks	539	98	5.5	Mario Lopez	55	23	.42	296	Chuck Hughes	34	616	18.1
1965	Dick Weeks	403	95	4.2	Billy Stevens	432	196	.45	3,032	Chuck Hughes	80	1,519	19.0
1966	Leroy Johnson	467	110	4.2	Billy Stevens	305	140	.46	2,088	Chuck Hughes	48	747	15.6
1967	Larry McHenry	366	94	3.9	Billy Stevens	206	90	.44	1,365	Volley Murphy	40	876	21.9
1968	Gene Childs	534	118	4.5	Brooks Dawson	279	125	.45	1,711	David Karns	34	419	12.3
1969	Gene Childs	653	151	4.3	Bill Craigo	285	111	.39	1,560	Ed Puishes	55	899	16.3
1970	Phil Hatch	785	151	5.2	Bill Craigo	309	138	.45	2,123	Ed Puishes	57	1,000	17.5
1971	James Berry	550	154	3.6	Gary Keithley	218	123	.56	1,375	Mike Anderson	33	500	15.2
1972	Al Barnett	585	119	4.9	Gary Keithley	252	144	.57	1,870	Greg Taylor	53	878	16.6
1973	Don Willis	608	121	5.0	Frank Duncan	225	107	.48	1,370	Lonnie Crittenden	40	650	16.3
1974	Mike Belew	600	141	4.3	Bobby McKinley	195	95	.49	1,512	Mike Walker	23	438	19.0
1975	Robert Elliott	896	189	4.7	Bobby McKinley	153	51	.33	673	Bill Avery	18	271	15.1
1976	Robert Elliott	861	204	4.2	Steve Smith	122	45	.37	690	Harold Johnson	16	314	19.6
1977	Robert Elliott	1,011	200	5.1	Oscar Ramirez	179	74	.41	1,127	Bubba Garcia	53	826	15.6
1978	Ray Holt	671	119	5.6	Oscar Ramirez	278	118	.42	1,460	Bubba Garcia	40	451	11.3
1979	James Copeland	638	121	5.3	Keith Castle	67	28	.42	308	David Logston	19	190	10.0
1980	Delbert Thompson	923	213	4.3	Keith Castle	90	42	.47	471	Delbert Thompson	22	172	7.8
1981	Delbert Thompson	560	102	5.5	Brad McEachern	124	71	.57	690	Delbert Thompson	26	272	10.5
1982	Kevin Ward	813	187	4.3	Kevin Ward	208	84	.40	1,141	Jerry Jones	21	322	15.3
1983	Kevin Ward	496	119	4.2	Jay Cleveland	146	71	.49	834	Larry Linne	24	378	15.8
1984	Tony George	555	105	5.3	Sammy Garza	141	60	.43	899	Eric Anderson	21	390	18.6
1985	John Harvey	777	147	5.3	Sammy Garza	200	120	.60	1,654	Larry Linne	30	481	16.0
1986	John Harvey	878	165	5.3	Sammy Garza	410	258	.63	3,140	Bob Keseday	47	620	13.2
1987	John Harvey	1,170	235	5.0	Pat Hegarty	273	153	.56	2,064	John Harvey	35	250	7.1
1988	John Harvey	751	131	5.7	Pat Hegarty	330	181	.55	2,586	Reggie Barrett	50	781	15.6
1989	Scooter Menifee	533	124	4.3	Howard Gasser	359	189	.53	2,586	Reggie Barrett	58	1,042	18.0
1990	Kevin Bogan	532	137	3.9	Mike Perez	211	100	.47	1,220	Reggie Barrett	43	710	16.5
1991	Kenny Brown	454	77	5.9	Mike Perez	265	131	.49	1,913	Glenn Bishop	38	676	17.8
1992	Shawn Gray	563	117	4.8	Shawn Gray	197	100	.51	1,297	J.J. Rowlett	33	442	13.4
1993	Kaio Aumua	642	129	5.0	Corey Tucker	143	64	.45	889	J.J. Rowlett	32	508	15.9
1994	Toraino Singleton	1,277	289	4.4	Shawn Gray	260	110	.42	1,662	J.J. Rowlett	35	664	19.0
1995	Toraino Singleton	1,358	268	5.1	John Rayborn	295	156	.53	1,913	Alvin Black	39	349	8.9
1996	Joseph Polk	569	154	3.7	Leonard Lilja	220	106	.48	1,193	Cedric Johnson	52	634	12.2
1997	Elzie Johnson	526	127	4.1	Rocky Perez	114	58	.51	728	Jimmy Carpenter	47	767	16.3
1998	Joseph Polk	676	155	4.4	John Rayborn	258	139	.54	1,641	Jimmy Carpenter	52	691	13.3
1999	Paul Smith	1,258	272	4.6	Jay Stuckey	225	145	.64	1,918	Lee Mays	60	881	14.7
2000	Chris Porter	681	142	4.8	Rocky Perez	338	200	.59	2,661	Lee Mays	70	1,098	15.7
2001	Chris Porter	454	79	5.7	Wesley Phillips	257	143	.56	1,839	Lee Mays	53	733	13.8
2002	Howard Jackson	844	173	4.9	Omar Duarte	161	79	.49	1,000	Terrance Minor	41	630	15.4
2003	Howard Jackson	1,146	208	5.5	Orlando Cruz	203	103	.51	1,360	Chris Marrow	34	467	13.7
2004	Howard Jackson	1,187	239	5.0	Jordan Palmer	366	213	.58	2,818	Johnnie Higgins	34	700	20.6

Receiving leaders by receptions
The NCAA began including postseason stats in 2002

UTEP All-Time Scores

WIN/LOSS PERCENTAGE SINCE 1936

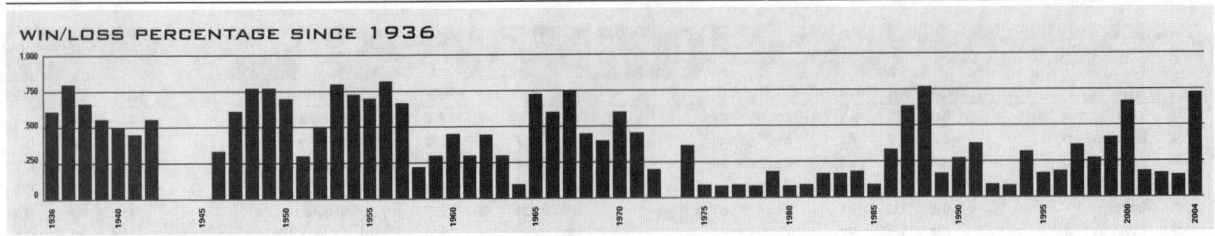

TOMMY DWYER
1914-19 (.432)   9-12-1

1914   2-3-0
O24 ●	El Paso YMCA	7	6
O31 ●	at New Mexico State	0	19
N7 ●	at New Mexico Military	0	19
N14 ●	20th Infantry	27	0
N26 ●	at El Paso HS	0	20

1915   3-2-0
O7 ●	20th Infantry	42	6
O21 ●	4th Artillery	13	6
O30 ●	at New Mexico State	0	34 *
N11 ●	2nd Artillery	0	14
N24 ●	at El Paso HS	10	0

1916   2-3-0
O21 ●	El Paso HS	3	14
N4 ●	at Arizona	0	41
N20 ●	at El Paso HS	19	0
N25 ●	at New Mexico State	6	3
N30 ●	New Mexico Military	0	79

1917   0-0-1
U =	at El Paso HS	0	0

1918
NO TEAM WWI

1919   2-4-0
O24 ●	Motor Transport	32	0
N1 ●	at El Paso HS	13	6
N8 ●	New Mexico Military	7	12
N15 ●	New Mexico	13	57
N24 ●	at Arizona	0	46
N27 ●	Fort Bliss All Star	0	10

H.E. VAN SURDAM
1920 (.333)   2-4

1920   2-4-0
O30 ●	Arizona	7	60
N6 ●	at New Mexico	0	67
N11 ●	New Mexico State	7	12
N19 ●	at New Mexico Military	0	41
N25 ●	Base Hospital	28	0
N30 ●	Aviation Corps	3	0

THOMAS C. HOLIDAY
1921 (.000)   0-5

1921   0-5-0
O21 ●	Calamus Club	0	21
O29 ●	at Arizona	0	74
N11 ●	New Mexico State	0	13
N19 ●	at N.M. Military	7	27
N24 ●	Fort Bliss All Stars	7	14

JACK C. VOWELL
1922-23 (.500)   8-8

1922   5-4-0
S30 ●	Arizona	0	18
O6 ●	Commercial Club	6	7
O14 ●	El Paso JC	58	0
O21 ●	Lower Valley	40	0
O28 ●	at New Mexico	0	13
N4 ●	New Mexico Military	12	0
N11 ●	at New Mexico State	0	64
N18 ●	8th Cavalry	38	0
N23 ●	Daniel Baker	3	0

1923   3-4-0
O13 ●	8th Cavalry	20	0
O20 ●	at Arizona	7	12
O27 ●	New Mexico	0	3
N3 ●	at N.M. Military	7	19
N10 ●	New Mexico State	2	23
N22 ●	Sul Ross	45	2
D8 ●	at 1st Division	25	6

GEORGE B. POWELL
1924-26 (.600)   11-7-2

1924   3-2-1
O18 ●	Sul Ross	30	6
O25 ●	at New Mexico	0	18
N1 =	N.M. Military	6	6
N8 ●	New Mexico State	0	19
N15 ●	at El Paso JC	26	0
N27 ●	at Wayland	6	2

1925   5-1-1
O17 ●	at Sul Ross	7	31
O24 ●	New Mexico	19	2
O31 ●	N.M. Military	28	0
N7 ●	New Mexico State	6	6
N13 ●	El Paso JC	12	6
N21 ●	at Western New Mexico	21	0
N26 ●	Arizona State	21	12 *

1926   3-4-0
O16 ●	Western New Mexico	25	3
O23 ●	at New Mexico	7	19
O30 ●	at N.M. Military	20	7
N6 ●	New Mexico State	8	10
N13 ●	at Sul Ross	0	21
N20 ●	N.M. Mines	40	0
N25 ●	at St. Edwards	6	32

E.J. STEWART
1927-28 (.464)   5-6-3

1927   2-2-2
O6 ●	Arizona	6	19
O22 =	New Mexico	6	6
O29 ●	N.M. Military	19	3
N11 ●	New Mexico State	19	7
N19 ●	at Hardin-Simmons	19	34
N24 =	Arizona State	0	0

1928   3-4-1
O5 ●	Western New Mexico	68	0
O13 ●	at Southwestern, Texas	7	33
U =	Arizona State	0	0
O27 ●	Arizona	6	12
N3 ●	Sul Ross	0	18
N9 ●	New Mexico State	6	0
N17 ●	at New Mexico	0	33
N29 ●	Hardin-Simmons	13	7

MACK SAXON
1929-41 (.597)   66-43-9

1929   6-1-2
S28 ●	New Mexico Mines	46	0
O5 ●	Arizona State	31	7
O19 ●	Arizona	0	19
O25 ●	Wayland	9	6
N2 =	Sul Ross	0	0
N9 ●	New Mexico State	8	0
N16 ●	New Mexico Military	20	14
N23 ●	Gila JC	40	0
N30 ●	St. Edwards	0	0

1930   7-1-1
S28 ●	Texas	0	28
O4 ●	Arizona State	19	6
O11 ●	Gila JC	36	6
O17 ●	at Texas Tech	31	0
O24 ●	New Mexico Military	27	7
N1 ●	at New Mexico	20	13
N8 =	Arizona	0	0
N15 ●	at New Mexico State	25	0
N27 ●	at Sul Ross	25	7

1931   7-1-0
S26 ●	at Wayland	10	0
O3 ●	Arizona State	27	13 *
O9 ●	Sul Ross	26	0
O17 ●	at Hardin-Simmons	0	45
O24 ●	at N.M. Military	31	6
O31 ●	McMurry	18	7
N11 ●	Texas Tech	14	12
N21 ●	New Mexico State	20	0

1932   7-3-0
O1 ●	Wayland	38	7
O8 ●	Howard Payne	9	7
O14 ●	at Hardin-Simmons	13	2
O22 ●	N.M. Military	14	12
O29 ●	at New Mexico State	31	6
N11 ●	at Arizona State	14	15
N19 ●	at Army All Stars	44	7
N24 ●	St. Edwards	27	13
D3 ●	Oklahoma State	7	20
J2 ●	SMU	0	26

1933   3-5-1
S30 ●	at Texas	6	22
O7 ●	at SMU	6	27
O14 ●	at Howard Payne	0	6
O21 =	at New Mexico Military	6	6
O28 ●	Texas Tech	0	12
N4 ●	New Mexico State	9	0
N11 ●	Sul Ross	34	0
N18 ●	at Hardin-Simmons	10	6
N24 ●	St. Edwards	0	6

1934   4-4-0
S29 ●	Daniel Baker	34	7
O5 ●	at West Texas St.	7	20
O13 ●	New Mexico	15	21
O20 ●	N.M. Military	24	0
N2 ●	at Texas Tech	0	27
N10 ●	at Sul Ross	12	13
N17 ●	Hardin-Simmons	13	3
N29 ●	at St. Edwards	27	13

1935-1961
BORDER

1935   1-8-0 (0-3-0)
S28 ●	at New Mexico	0	20
O5 ●	at St. Mary's, Texas	0	38
O12 ●	Sul Ross	7	19
O19 ●	West Texas St.	0	14
O26 ●	at Arizona State	0	14
N9 ●	N.M. Military	7	13
N16 ●	Western New Mexico	9	7
N23 ●	at Hardin-Simmons	0	46
N28 ●	at New Mexico State	0	7

1936   5-3-1 (2-1-1)
O3	West Texas St.	7	13
O10 ●	at N.M. Military	13	6
O17 ●	New Mexico	12	7
O24 ●	at Sul Ross	6	0
O31 ●	at Western New Mexico	21	0
N7 =	at No. Arizona	0	0
N14	Arizona State	0	19
N26 ●	New Mexico State	27	7

SUN BOWL
J1	Hardin-Simmons	6	34

1937   7-1-2 (2-1-1)
S24	at New Mexico State	0	4
O1 ●	at N.M. Military	19	13
O9	West Texas St.	16	14
O16 =	at New Mexico	7	7
O23	at Santa Barbara	13	13
O30	No. Colorado	10	0
N6 ●	No. Arizona	53	15
N11 ●	at Arizona State	19	0
N20 ●	Sul Ross	34	0
N27 ●	St. Edwards	34	7

1938   6-3-0 (3-2-0)
O1 ●	N.M. Military	26	0
O8 ●	at No. Colorado	32	0
O15 ●	New Mexico	7	6
O22 ●	Texas Tech	7	14
O29 ●	at St. Mary's, Texas	6	13
N12 ●	at Arizona	26	14
N19 ●	New Mexico State	9	13
N24 ●	Arizona State	14	6
D3 ●	at Fresno State	26	6

1939   5-4-0 (3-2-0)
S23 ●	Texas Tech	7	2
S30 ●	at Fresno State	7	10
O7 ●	Hardin-Simmons	0	12
O12 ●	at New Mexico	0	14
O21 ●	at Wichita St.	17	0
O28 ●	at Arizona State	7	27
N11 ●	Arizona	14	6
N18 ●	Louisiana Tech	27	0
N25 ●	at New Mexico State	34	0

1940   4-4-1 (3-1-1)
S21 ●	at No. Arizona	28	7
S28 ●	North Dakota	20	6
O5	at Louisiana Tech	7	19
O12	at Hardin-Simmons	6	20
O19 ●	New Mexico	9	7
O26 =	Arizona State	0	0
N2	Arizona	13	20
N9	at Fresno State	6	16
N28 ●	New Mexico State	40	26

1941   4-5-1 (3-4-0)
S27 =	Louisiana Tech	0	0
O4	New Mexico	14	16
O18	Loyola-Marymount	6	20
O25	Hardin-Simmons	14	44
N1	Arizona	14	33
N8 ●	Arizona State	28	0
N15	West Texas St.	7	40
N22 ●	New Mexico State	24	13 *
N29 ●	No. Arizona	23	20
D6	260th Coast Aty.	54	6

WALTER MILNER
1942 (.556)   5-4

1942   5-4-0 (4-3-0)
S25	at Louisiana Tech	0	20
O2 ●	New Mexico	7	0
O17	at Abilene Christian	20	14
O24	at West Texas St.	0	7
O31	at Hardin-Simmons	0	39
N7	No. Arizona	20	0
N14 ●	Arizona State	40	6
N21	Arizona	7	19 *
N26	New Mexico State	61	6

1943-1945
NO TEAM WWII

JACK CURTICE
1946-49 (.638)   24-13-3

1946   3-6-0 (2-4-0)
S27	Drake	2	7
O12	at Arizona	13	27
O19 ●	West Texas St.	26	20
O26 ●	Houston	21	7
N2	at New Mexico	13	21
N9 ●	at Arizona State	34	20
N16	Hardin-Simmons	7	20
N23	Brigham Young	13	14
N28	New Mexico State	7	14

UTEP 943

1947 5-3-1 (3-3-1)

S19	●		at Drake	19	7
S26	●		Kansas State	20	6
O4	●	│	No. Arizona	40	0
O11		│	at West Texas St.	0	14
O18		│	Arizona	13	14
N1	=	│	New Mexico	20	20
N8	●	│	Arizona State	21	0
N15		│	at Hardin-Simmons	0	18
N22	●	│	New Mexico State	26	0

1948 8-2-1 (4-1-1)

S18	●		McMurry ODE	33	14
S25	●		Houston	35	7
O9	●	│	West Texas St.	21	7
O15	●		Brigham Young	34	20
O23	●		at New Mexico	27	13
O30	=	│	Hardin-Simmons	27	27
N6		│	at Texas Tech	6	46
N13	●	│	at Arizona	25	14
N25	●	│	New Mexico State	92	7
D4	●		at Hawaii	49	6
			SUN BOWL		
J1			West Virginia	12	21

1949 8-2-1 (4-2-0)

S17	●		at Brigham Young	47	6
S24	●		John Carroll	33	7
O1	●		Hawaii	14	7
O8	●	│	at West Texas St.	34	7
O15	●	│	at Arizona	28	0
O22	●	│	New Mexico	7	0
O29		│	at Hardin-Simmons	14	33
N5		│	Texas Tech	0	13
N12	=		at West Virginia	13	13
N26	●	│	New Mexico State	69	7
			SUN BOWL		
J2	●		Georgetown	33	20

MIKE BRUMBELOW
1950-56 (.651) 46-24-3

1950 7-3-0 (4-2-0)

S16			at Cincinnati	0	32
S23	●	│	New Mexico State	40	26
O7	●		Idaho	43	33
O14	●	│	Arizona	14	13
O21	●	│	at New Mexico	41	13
O28		│	at Texas Tech	7	61
N4		│	West Texas St.	12	40
N11	●	│	Hardin-Simmons	21	20
N25	●	│	West Virginia	48	7
D1	●		at Hawaii	46	13

1951 3-7-0 (3-4-0)

S22			North Texas	0	33
S29	●	│	New Mexico State	41	7
O6			at Abilene Christian	13	20
O13		│	at Arizona	15	19
O20	●	│	New Mexico	32	7
O27			at Cincinnati	18	53
N3		│	Texas Tech	7	27
N9		│	at Hardin-Simmons	0	46
N17		│	Arizona State	13	23
N24	●	│	at West Texas St.	13	6

1952 5-5-1 (2-3-1)

S20			North Texas ODE	14	27
S27	●		Sul Ross	42	0
O4	●		Hawaii	42	25
O11	●	│	at Texas Tech	20	14
O18	=	│	at New Mexico State	20	20
O25			New Mexico	13	14
N1	●		at Midwestern Texas	13	7
N8		│	Hardin-Simmons	26	27
N15		│	Arizona	7	55
N22		│	at Arizona State	0	39
N27	●	│	West Texas St.	7	3

1953 8-2-0 (4-2-0)

S19	●		Sul Ross	26	7
S26		│	Texas Tech	6	27
O3	●	│	Arizona State	28	27
O17	●	│	New Mexico State	39	0
O24	●		North Texas	26	21
O31	●		Midwestern Texas	27	7
N7		│	at Hardin-Simmons	13	14
N14	●	│	at Arizona	28	20
N28	●	│	at West Texas St.	27	7
			SUN BOWL		
J1	●		Southern Miss	37	14

1954 8-3-0 (4-2-0)

S18	●		Sul Ross	35	14
S25	●		McMurry	27	6
O2		│	at Arizona State	27	34
O9		│	at Texas Tech	28	55
O16			Trinity	14	20
O23	●		at North Texas	6	0
O30	●	│	at New Mexico State	12	7
N6	●	│	Hardin-Simmons	20	7
N13	●	│	Arizona	41	21
N25	●	│	West Texas St.	33	13
			SUN BOWL		
J1	●		Florida State	47	20

1955 6-2-2 (3-2-1)

S24	=		North Texas	7	7
O1	●		at New Mexico	34	0
O8	=	│	Texas Tech	27	27
O15	●	│	at Arizona	29	0
O22	●		at Wichita St.	28	12
O29	●	│	New Mexico State	41	6
N4		│	at Hardin-Simmons	21	23
N12		│	Arizona State	13	20
N19	●	│	West Texas St.	13	7
N26	●		at Trinity	14	13

1956 9-2-0 (5-0-0)

S22	●		at Texas Tech	17	13
S29	●		Abilene Christian	20	0
O6	●		New Mexico	34	0
O13	●	│	Arizona	28	6
O20			at North Texas	6	13
O27	●	│	at New Mexico State	51	7
N3	●	│	Hardin-Simmons	51	13
N10	●	│	at Arizona State	28	0
N17	●	│	at West Texas St.	16	13
N24	●		Trinity	54	0
			SUN BOWL		
J1			George Washington	0	13

BEN COLLINS
1957-61 (.385) 18-29-1

1957 6-3-0 (3-2-0)

S21	●		North Texas	14	13
S28	●	│	West Texas St.	20	12
O5	●		at New Mexico	15	13
O12	●		Texas Tech	26	14
O26	●	│	New Mexico State	42	12
N2		│	at Hardin-Simmons	20	33
N9		│	Arizona State	7	43
N16	●	│	at Arizona	51	14
N23			at Trinity	7	14

1958 2-7-0 (1-4-0)

S20			at North Texas	8	26
S27	●		New Mexico	15	6
O4			Abilene Christian	6	14
O11	●	│	at West Texas St.	29	12
O25		│	at New Mexico State	16	17
N1		│	Hardin-Simmons	6	14
N8		│	at Arizona State	0	27
N15		│	Arizona	12	14
N22			Trinity	0	49

1959 3-7-0 (2-3-0)

S19	●		U. of Mexico	43	8
S26			North Texas	7	31
O3			at New Mexico	7	17
O10	●	│	West Texas St.	13	12
O17			at Trinity	20	21
O24	●	│	New Mexico State	20	15
O31		│	at Hardin-Simmons	14	25
N7		│	Arizona State	7	20
N14			Abilene Christian	22	28
N21		│	at Arizona	10	14

1960 4-5-1 (2-3-0)

S17			Utah State	7	20
S24	=		at North Texas	16	16
O1	●		New Mexico	23	17
O8	●	│	at West Texas St.	6	3
O15	●		Trinity	41	14
O29	●	│	Hardin-Simmons	45	6
N5		│	at Arizona State	0	24
N12		│	Arizona	14	28
N19			Bowling Green	0	21
N26		│	at New Mexico State	15	27

1961 3-7-0 (1-3-0)

S16			at Utah State	6	21
S30		│	West Texas St.	27	56
O7			at New Mexico	6	7
O14	●		McMurry	20	16
O21	●		at Trinity	19	14
O28		│	New Mexico State	6	42
N4	●	│	at Hardin-Simmons	35	7
N11		│	Arizona State	28	48
N18			at Arizona	15	48
N25			North Texas	14	24

1962-1967
INDEPENDENT

BUM PHILLIPS
1962 (.444) 4-5

1962 4-5-0

S22			at North Texas	6	19
S29			at West Texas St.	0	49
O6	●		New Mexico	16	14
O13			Wyoming	6	14
O27			at Arizona State	7	35
N3	●		Hardin-Simmons	7	6
N10	●		at New Mexico State	21	0
N17			Arizona	0	7
N22	●		Trinity	21	0

WARREN HARPER
1963-64 (.200) 3-15-2

1963 3-7-0

S21	●		North Texas	34	7
S28			at New Mexico	7	23
O5	●		New Mexico State	14	13
O12			at Arizona	7	13
O19			Arizona State	0	27
O26			at Colorado State	14	21
N9			at Xavier	0	24
N16			Texas Tech	3	7
N30	●		West Texas St.	13	0
D7			Wyoming	6	7

1964 0-8-2

S19	=		at North Texas	0	0
O3			at West Texas St.	0	14
O10			at Arizona State	13	42
O17			at Wyoming	6	20
O24	=		Brigham Young	18	18
O31			Utah	0	41
N7			New Mexico	12	20
N14			Arizona	0	14
N21			at New Mexico State	7	13
N26			Colorado State	8	35

BOBBY DOBBS
1965-72 (.524) 42-38-2

1965 8-3-0

S18	●		North Texas	61	15
S25	●		at New Mexico	35	14
O2	●		New Mexico State	21	6
O9	●		Colorado State	35	10
O16			at Wyoming	14	38
O30			Arizona State	20	28
N6			at Arizona	3	10
N13	●		at Utah	20	19
N20	●		Xavier	57	33
N27	●		West Texas St.	38	21
			SUN BOWL		
D31	●		TCU	13	12

1966 6-4-0

S17			at Arizona State	26	30
S24			at North Texas	9	12
O1	●		New Mexico	51	3
O8	●		at West Texas St.	9	3
O15	●		Texas Arlington	68	21
O22	●		San Jose State	35	0
N5			at Brigham Young	33	53
N12			Wyoming	7	31
N19	●		New Mexico State	28	14
N26	●		Utah	27	20

1967 7-2-1

S16	●		Santa Barbara	50	14
O7			at Arizona State	32	33
O14	=		at Arizona	9	9
O21	●		Brigham Young	47	17
O28	●		at New Mexico	75	12
N4	●		New Mexico State	46	24
N11	●		Colorado State	17	0
N18			Wyoming	19	21
N25	●		at Utah	28	8
			SUN BOWL		
D30	●		Mississippi	14	7

1968-2004
WAC

1968 4-5-1 (3-3-0)

S14	=		Santa Barbara	14	14
S21	●	│	New Mexico	44	15
S28		│	at Arizona State	19	31
O5		│	at Arizona	0	25
O12			Long Beach St.	21	22
O19	●		at New Mexico State	30	14
O26	●	│	at Brigham Young	31	25
N9			North Texas	31	34
N16		│	Wyoming	19	26
N30	●	│	Colorado State	23	19

1969 4-6-0 (2-5-0)

S13	●		Pacific	14	10
S27	●	│	at New Mexico	21	6
O4		│	Utah	6	24
O11		│	at Wyoming	9	37
O18		│	at Arizona	10	26
O25		│	Brigham Young	7	30
N1	●	│	at Colorado State	17	16
N8			New Mexico State	38	41
N15		│	Arizona State	19	42
N29	●		Xavier	17	10

1970 6-4-0 (4-3-0)

S12			Pacific	18	24
S19		│	at Utah	20	44
S26	●	│	at Brigham Young	17	0
O3	●		New Mexico State	21	14
O17	●	│	at Colorado State	41	37
O24		│	Arizona State	13	42
O31		│	New Mexico	16	35
N7	●	│	Wyoming	47	7
N14	●	│	Arizona	33	17
N19	●		at Trinity	37	16

1971 5-6-0 (1-6-0)

S11	●		Texas Arlington	38	9
S18	●		Pacific	21	3
S25		│	Arizona	6	14
O2		│	at Arizona State	7	24
O9		│	Utah	10	32
O16	●		at New Mexico State	14	7
O23	●	│	at Wyoming	12	7
O30		│	Brigham Young	0	16
N13		│	at New Mexico	13	49
N20		│	Colorado State	7	24
N27	●		Long Beach St.	38	32

1972 2-8-0 (1-6-0)

S16			Lamar	18	42
S23			Pacific	14	19
S30	●		New Mexico State	21	20
O7		│	at Utah	20	39
O14		│	at Brigham Young	14	21
O21		│	New Mexico	7	56
O28		│	at Arizona	22	45
N4		│	Arizona State	14	55
N11	●	│	Wyoming	20	13
N18		│	at Colorado State	22	35

TOMMY HUDSPETH
1973 (.000) 0-11

1973 0-11-0 (0-7-0)

S8			at Idaho	14	62
S15			Pacific	9	34
S22		│	at Utah	6	82
S29		│	at Wyoming	8	31
O6			New Mexico State	23	27
O13			Lamar	27	31
O20		│	at New Mexico	0	49
O27		│	Colorado State	24	76
N3		│	Arizona	18	35
N17		│	Arizona State	13	54
D1		│	Brigham Young	0	63

GILL BARTOSH
1974-76 (.176) 6-28

1974 4-7-0 (3-4-0)

S14			Pacific	14	17
S21	●	│	Utah	34	7
S28			San Diego State	12	26
O5		│	at Arizona	13	42
O12			at New Mexico State	13	14
O19		│	at Brigham Young	21	45
O26	●		at Texas Arlington	28	14
N2	●	│	at Arizona State	31	27
N9	●	│	Wyoming	35	13
N16		│	at Colorado State	24	56
N23		│	New Mexico	21	37

THE SCHOOLS

1975 — 1-10-0 (0-6-0)

S6	at San Diego State	10	31
S13	New Mexico State	24	31
S20 ●	East Tenn. St.	6	3
O4	at Pacific	10	40
O11	Arizona	0	36
O18	at Wyoming	14	31
O25	at Arizona State	6	24
N1	at New Mexico	3	23
N8	Colorado State	17	21
N15	at Hawaii	9	21
N22	Brigham Young	10	20

1976 — 1-11-0 (0-7-0)

S4	Texas Arlington	38	15
S11	at New Mexico State	10	13
S18	New Mexico	7	25
O2	at Utah	14	38
O9	at Arizona	12	63
O16	Arizona State	6	23
O23	at Colorado State	7	28
O30	San Diego State	16	27
N6	at Brigham Young	27	40
N13	Wyoming	10	14
N20	at Hawaii	12	28
N27	Oklahoma State	13	42

BILL MICHAEL
1977-81 (.104)   5-43

1977 — 1-10-0 (0-7-0)

S10	North Texas	10	41
S17	at Wyoming	17	27
S24	at Oklahoma State	0	54
O1 ●	New Mexico State	23	21
O8	Colorado State	14	31
O15	at San Diego State	7	49
O22	at Arizona State	3	66
N5	at New Mexico	17	33
N12	at Utah	17	29
N19	Arizona	24	41
N26	Brigham Young	19	68

1978 — 1-11-0 (1-5-0)

S2	at North Texas	0	49
S9	Air Force	25	34
S16	at New Mexico State	32	35
S23 ●	San Diego State	31	24
S30	at Arizona State	0	27
O7	at Colorado State	29	39
O21	at Brigham Young	0	44
O28	New Mexico	0	21
N4	at Hawaii	13	35
N11	Utah	0	38
N18	at Nevada-Las Vegas	0	27
N25	Wyoming	21	51

1979 — 2-9-0 (0-7-0)

S1	at North Texas	0	35
S8 ●	Pacific	31	7
S15	New Mexico State	13	14
S22 ●	Nevada-Las Vegas	17	15
S29	at Brigham Young	7	31
O6	at Wyoming	3	23
O13	Colorado State	3	17
O20	at New Mexico	0	20
O27	Hawaii	12	27
N10	at Utah	0	35
N17	at San Diego State	20	42

1980 — 1-11-0 (1-6-0)

S6	at Texas Tech	7	35
S13	at New Mexico State	3	6
S20	North Texas	15	35
S27	at Pacific	14	28
O4 ●	at Hawaii	34	14
O11	Utah	7	31
O18	at Nevada-Las Vegas	14	53
O25	New Mexico	21	22
N1	at Brigham Young	7	83
N8	at Colorado State	7	37
N15	San Diego State	7	28
N22	Wyoming	7	52

BILL ALTON
1981 (.111)   1-8

1981 — 1-10-0 (1-6-0)

S5	New Mexico State	7	14
S12	Texas A&I	15	37
S19	Brigham Young	8	65
O2	at Utah	10	38
O10	at New Mexico	3	26
O17	at Wyoming	12	63
O24 ●	Colorado State	35	29
O31	at Arizona	15	48
N7	Hawaii	7	35
N21	at San Diego State	14	59
N28	Nevada-Las Vegas	20	27

BILL YUNG
1982-85 (.152)   7-39

1982 — 2-10-0 (1-6-0)

S4	at New Mexico State	20	17
S11	at Washington	0	55
S18	SMU	10	31
S25	at Hawaii	10	17
O2	Brigham Young	3	51
O9	at Nevada-Las Vegas	21	28
O16	at Arizona State	6	37
O23	Air Force	7	35
O30	at Colorado State	13	38
N6	New Mexico	18	31
N13	Utah	30	45
N20 ●	Wyoming	39	32

1983 — 2-10-0 (0-8-0)

S3 ●	New Mexico State	20	9
S10	Idaho St.	10	12
S17	Baylor	6	20
S24	San Diego State	33	41
O1	at Wyoming	17	49
O8	at Utah	11	35
O15	at Air Force	25	37
O22	Colorado State	15	31
O29	at Hawaii	24	25
N5	Brigham Young	9	31
N12	at New Mexico	0	35
N19 ●	Weber St.	40	34

1984 — 2-9-0 (1-7-0)

S1	at Texas A&M	17	20
S8 ●	Idaho St.	16	14
S15	at San Diego State	2	51
S29	New Mexico	7	34
O6	at New Mexico State	16	27
O13	Hawaii	20	24
O27	at Utah	15	43
N3	at Brigham Young	9	42
N10	at Colorado State	31	59
N17 ●	Wyoming	35	22
N24	Air Force	12	38

1985 — 1-10-0 (1-7-0)

A31	at Air Force	6	48
S7	at SMU	23	35
S14	at Colorado State	24	41
S21	New Mexico State	20	22
S28	at Utah	19	55
O12	at Kent State	24	51
O26 ●	Brigham Young	23	16
N2	New Mexico	23	27
N9	Hawaii	7	23
N16	San Diego State	6	34
D6	Wyoming *Mel*	21	24

BOB STULL
1986-88 (.583)   21-15

1986 — 4-8-0 (2-6-0)

A30 ●	No. Michigan	64	29
S6	Air Force	21	23
S13 ●	at New Mexico State	47	33
S20	at Hawaii	21	31
S27	at Iowa	7	69
O4	at Tennessee	16	26
O11 ●	at New Mexico	22	24
O18	San Diego State	10	15
O25	at Brigham Young	13	37
N8	at Wyoming	12	41
N22 ●	Colorado State	21	19
N29 ●	Utah	55	44

1987 — 7-4-0 (5-3-0)

S5	New Mexico State	31	0
S19 ●	at Colorado State	45	6
S26 ●	Hawaii	37	13
O3	at Arizona State	16	35
O10 ●	at San Diego State	34	33
O17	Lamar	38	14
O24	at Air Force	7	35
O31 ●	New Mexico	34	0
N7 ●	at Utah	30	24
N14	Brigham Young	24	37
N21	Wyoming	13	37

1988 — 10-3-0 (6-2-0)

S3 ●	Mankato St.	37	3
S10	Weber St.	48	21
S17	at Brigham Young	27	31
S24 ●	at Tulsa	27	24
O1	Utah	38	28
O8	at Hawaii	42	25
O15	Colorado State	34	14
O22 ●	at New Mexico	37	0
O29 ●	at New Mexico State	42	9
N5	at Wyoming	6	51
N12 ●	San Diego State	58	7
N19	Air Force	31	24

INDEPENDENCE BOWL

D23	Southern Miss	18	38

DAVID LEE
1989-93 (.217)   11-41-1

1989 — 2-10-0 (1-7-0)

S2	Tulsa	14	23
S9	Lamar	19	21
S16 ●	at New Mexico State	29	27
S23	at Air Force	26	43
S30	Arkansas *LR*	7	39
O7	Utah	45	50
O14 ●	New Mexico	26	7
O21	at Brigham Young	24	49
O28	San Diego State	31	34
N4	at Hawaii	7	26
N11	Colorado State	0	52
N18	at Wyoming	10	41

1990 — 3-8-0 (1-7-0)

S1	Brigham Young	10	30
S8 ●	New Mexico State	27	24
S15	at Tennessee	0	56
S22	at Colorado State	20	38
S29 ●	Sam Houston St.	17	10
O6	at New Mexico	28	48
O13 ●	Hawaii	12	10
O20	at Utah	23	37
O27	Wyoming	10	17
N17	Air Force	13	14
N24	at San Diego State	31	58

1991 — 4-7-1 (2-5-1)

A31 ●	New Mexico	35	19
S7	at Baylor	7	27
S14 ●	at New Mexico State	22	21
S21 ●	Northwestern St.	14	0
S28 =	at Wyoming	28	28
O5	Colorado State	18	23
O12	at Brigham Young	29	31
O19	San Diego State	21	28
O26	at Air Force	13	20
N9 ●	at Hawaii	41	24
N16	Utah	9	10
N23	Louisiana Tech	17	21

1992 — 1-10-0 (1-7-0)

S5	Brigham Young	28	38
S12	at Nevada-Las Vegas	17	19
S19	New Mexico State	24	30
O3	Air Force	22	28
O10	at Colorado State	24	42
O17	at San Diego State	27	49
O24 ●	at Utah	20	13
O31	Hawaii	21	41
N7	at Tulsa	39	48
N14	at New Mexico	14	35
N28	Fresno State	18	43

CHARLIE BAILEY
1993-99 (.267)   19-53-1

1993 — 1-11-0 (0-8-0)

S4	at Arizona	6	24
S11 ●	Nevada-Las Vegas	41	24
S18	at New Mexico State	14	31
S25	at Hawaii	0	52
O2	at North Carolina	39	45
O9	Wyoming	26	33
O16	Colorado State	29	45
O30	at Air Force	10	31
N6	at Fresno State	10	30
N13	Colorado State	0	52
N20	New Mexico	29	35
N27	at Brigham Young	16	47

1994 — 3-7-1 (1-6-1)

S3	at Wyoming	13	36
S10 ●	Ea. Illinois	22	20
S17	New Mexico State	22	23
S24	Air Force *SA*	7	47
O1 ●	Hawaii	34	28
O8 ●	at Tulsa	24	17
O15	at Colorado State	9	47
O22	Brigham Young	28	34
O29	at Utah	7	52
N12 =	Fresno State	30	30
N19	at Utah	21	25

1995 — 2-10-0 (1-7-0)

S2	at New Mexico State	17	45
S9	at Arizona State	20	45
S16 ●	Valdosta St.	34	24
S23 ●	at Hawaii	21	42
S30	Utah	21	34
O8	at Air Force	46	56
O14	Tulsa	28	38
O28	San Diego State	16	45
N4	at Colorado State	10	56
N11	at Fresno State	14	47
N18 ●	New Mexico	17	12
N25	Wyoming	19	42

1996 — 2-9 (0-8)

A31	at Arizona	3	23
S14 ●	New Mexico State	14	7
S21	at San Jose State	25	26
S28 ●	at Northern Illinois	37	6
O5	Utah	27	34
O12	at TCU	0	18
O26	Rice	21	48
N2	at Brigham Young	18	40
N9	SMU	0	30
N16	Tulsa	21	38
N23	at New Mexico	17	44

1997 — 4-7 (3-5)

S6	at LSU	3	55
S13	New Mexico	20	38
S20	at Utah	3	56
S27 ●	New Mexico State	24	16
O4	at Clemson	7	39
O11 ●	at Tulsa	33	18
O18	San Jose State	7	10
N1 ●	Brigham Young	13	3
N8	at SMU	14	28
N15 ●	TCU	24	17
N22	at Rice	13	31

1998 — 3-8 (3-5)

S5	at Texas Tech	3	35
S12	Oregon	26	33
S26	at New Mexico State	24	33
O3	Colorado State	17	20
O10 ●	at New Mexico	22	19
O17 ●	San Jose State	28	21
O24	at Fresno State	6	32
O31 ●	Hawaii	30	13
N7	at Utah	27	34
N14	Brigham Young	14	31
N21 ●	at San Diego State	29	34

1999 — 5-7 (3-4)

S4	New Mexico	13	10
S11	at Oregon	28	47
S18	at Kansas State	7	40
S25 ●	New Mexico State	54	23
O2	at Hawaii	3	33
O9 ●	SMU	42	28
O16	at Arizona	21	34
O23	at Fresno State	23	24
O30 ●	San Jose State	42	26
N6	Tulsa	19	43
N13 ●	at Rice	30	29
N20	at TCU	24	52

GARY NORD
2000-03 (.292)   14-34

2000 — 8-4 (7-1)

S2	at Oklahoma	14	55
S9 ●	SMU	37	20
S16	at Texas A&M	17	45
S23 ●	Hawaii	39	7
S30 ●	New Mexico State	41	31
O7 ●	at Tulsa	40	7
O14 ●	at San Jose State	47	30
O21 ●	Fresno State	23	13
N4 ●	at Nevada	45	22
N11 ●	Rice	38	21
N18	at TCU	14	47

HUMANITARIAN BOWL

D28	Boise State	23	38

2001   2-9   (1-7)

S1	at New Mexico	6	26
S8 ●	Texas Southern	52	6
S22 |	at Boise State	17	42
S29 ● |	Tulsa	26	10
O6	Alabama *Birm*	7	56
O13 |	at Hawaii	7	66
O20 |	San Jose State	28	40
O27 |	at SMU	14	40
N10 |	Louisiana Tech	30	53
N17 |	at Rice	17	27
N24 |	Nevada	31	48

2002   2-10   (1-7)

A31 ●	Sacremento St.	42	12
S7	at Kentucky	17	77
S14	at Oklahoma	0	68
S21 |	Hawaii	6	31
S28 |	at San Jose State	24	58
O5	at New Mexico State	14	49
O19 ● |	Rice	38	35
O26 |	at Tulsa	0	20
N2 |	Boise State	3	58
N9 |	at Nevada	17	23
N16 |	SMU	35	42
N23 |	at Louisiana Tech *Shre*	24	38

2003   2-11   (1-7)

A30	at Arizona	7	42
S6	at Cal Poly SLO	13	34
S13	San Diego State	0	34
S20	at Louisville	14	42
S27 ●	Sam Houston St.	59	14
O4 ● |	at SMU	21	19
O11 |	Louisiana Tech	35	38
O25 |	at Hawaii	15	31
N1 |	Tulsa	28	56
N8 |	San Jose State	41	69
N15 |	at Boise State	21	51
N22 |	at Rice	14	45
N29 |	Fresno State	20	23

MIKE PRICE
2004-Present (.667)   8-4

2004   8-4   (6-2)

S2	at Arizona State	9	41
S11 ●	Weber St.	32	0
S18 |	Boise State	31	47
O2 ●	New Mexico State	45	0
O9 ● |	at Fresno State	24	21
O16 ● |	Hawaii	51	20
O23 ● |	at Louisiana Tech	44	27
O30 ● |	at San Jose State	38	20
N13 ● |	Rice	35	28
N20 ● |	SMU	57	27
N27 |	at Tulsa	35	37
HOUSTON BOWL			
D29	Colorado	28	33

Neutral Site Key: *Birm* Birmingham, AL / *LR* Little Rock, AR / *Mel* Melbourne, Australia / *Ode* Odessa, TX / *SA* San Antonio, TX
f Forfeit † Game Later Forfieted # Disputed Victor * Disputed Score ‖ Designated Conference Game |2 Counted Twice in Conference Standings

VANDERBILT

BY GEOFFREY NORMAN

VANDERBILT HAS TO TRAVEL A HARD football road. The university is one of elite standards, possessively watchful of its academic standards. Yet it plays in the SEC, perhaps the toughest football neighborhood of all. Vanderbilt, then, is the nerd at a party full of jocks. The best comparison might be to Northwestern in the Big Ten—but even the Wildcats experienced bowl games and a football renaissance around the close of the last century. Meanwhile the Commodores continue to struggle. Vanderbilt fans believe in their university and are exceedingly proud of it. They are sympathetic to the challenges of the football team and still believe that the right combination of motivated recruits will, one day, give them what has become the grail of Vanderbilt football. Not a national championship. Not even an SEC championship— though one can dream. But a simple winning season, and an invitation to play in a bowl game. That would suffice. Their last postseason trip was 1982.

Still, the spirit of another era in Vanderbilt football, one long since passed, lives on. In those days, the Commodores ran off winning seasons as effortlessly as the university now produces Rhodes scholars. There once was a time when they beat archrival Tennessee so routinely that when the Vols hired their legendary coach, Robert Neyland, his first order was to beat Vandy. For now, Vanderbilt boosters have to settle for the occasional upset of one conference behemoth or another, and some measure of hope for the future.

TRADITION It's not an old tradition but it is certainly unique. In sync with the program's squeaky-clean image, the team instituted a no-cursing policy on the football field in 2002, policing its own language as a step toward discipline. That's one helluva commitment.

BEST PLAYER Quarterback Bill Wade was SEC Player of the Year in 1951. He completed 111 of 223 passes that season and 13 went for touchdowns. Wade was the first-round pick of the Los Angeles Rams, who traded him to Chicago. In 1963 he scored two touchdowns in the Bears' 14-10 win over the New York Giants in the NFL championship game.

BEST COACH Dan McGugin guided the Commodores for three decades—1904 to 1934—with one year, 1918, off for military duty. His first squad outscored opponents 474-4 and finished 9–0. McGugin finished his career 197–55–19 and has more than four times as many wins as any other coach in school history. He's also a member of the College Football Hall of Fame.

BEST TEAM McGugin's 1904 team would probably get the nod, though some Commodores fans hold a special affection for the 1922 team that outscored opponents 177-16 and ran

up a record of 8–0–1. There were three Hall of Famers associated with that team: McGugin; assistant Wallace Wade, who went on to glory at Alabama; and team captain Jess Neely, whose career at Rice was equally impressive. In the modern era, the distinction of best team belongs to the 1955 squad. Under coach Art Guepe (1953-62), the Commodores finished 8–3 and received an invitation to the Gator Bowl, a first in team history. There Vandy beat No. 8 Auburn 25-13.

STORYBOOK SEASON The Commodores started the 1982 season 1–2. But coach George MacIntyre got things turned around and Vandy took seven of its next eight, including wins over powerhouse Florida and archrival Tennessee. Vandy was invited to the Hall of Fame Bowl and lost a 36-28 shoot-out to Air Force.

BIGGEST GAME The inaugural game in the new Dudley Field, on Oct. 14, 1922, was played against Michigan in a coaching battle of wits that matched McGugin with his brother-in-law, Michigan's Fielding "Hurry-Up" Yost. McGugin played at Michigan in the early 1900s under Yost, adding to the drama. The crucial moment came on a fourth-and-goal play at the 1 when

> *For now, Vanderbilt boosters have to settle for the occasional upset of one conference behemoth or another.*

a Vandy defender got an extra burst by pushing off the goalpost to stop a Michigan runner, preserving the 0-0 tie. Though not a win, it was a statement game. As one impressed Detroit reporter wrote, "Michigan was lucky to escape with their lives."

BIGGEST UPSET Playing No. 12 Alabama in Mobile on Oct. 7, 1950, the Commodores spoiled the Tide's season with a 27-22 win that no one saw coming. Another victory over Alabama also merits mention. On Nov. 22, 1941, Vandy topped the Tide 7-0 in Nashville. Bama finished that season 9–2 and, with a victory over Texas A&M in the Cotton Bowl, was named national champion by Deke Houlgate's popular mathematical system syndicated in newspapers at the time. The Commodores wound up 8–2, but did not play in a bowl game.

HEARTBREAKER A 25-23 loss to No. 1 Oklahoma on Sept. 10, 1977, was particularly stinging, and not just because of the close margin. An official ruled—incorrectly, according to the faithful—that the Commodores had not recovered a fumble in the end zone that would've made the difference. At Vandy, you live for upsets like this, especially in a season that ran to a doleful 2–9 conclusion.

RECORDS

RUSHING

	GAME
321	Frank Mordica vs. Air Force, Nov. 18, 1978 (22 att.)
	SEASON
1,103	Corey Harris, 1991 (229 att.)
	CAREER
2,632	Frank Mordica, 1976-79 (546 att.)

PASSING

	GAME
464	Whit Taylor vs. Tennessee, Nov. 28, 1981 (29 of 53)
	SEASON
3,178	Kurt Page, 1983 (286 of 493)
	CAREER
7,981	Greg Zolman, 1998-2001 (596 of 1,156)

RECEIVING

	GAME
222	Clarence Sevillian vs. Tennessee, Nov. 28, 1992 (6 rec.)
	SEASON
1,213	Boo Mitchell, 1988 (78 rec.)
	CAREER
2,964	Boo Mitchell, 1985-88 (188 rec.)

POINTS

	GAME
30	Frank Mordica vs. Air Force, Nov. 18, 1978 (5 TDs)
	SEASON
90	Jack Jenkins, 1941 (15 PATs, 12 TDs, 1 FG)
	CAREER
209	John Markham, 1997-2000 (68 PATs, 47 FGs)

CONSENSUS ALL-AMERICANS

1923	Lynn Bomar,	E
1924	Henry Wakefield,	E
1932	Pete Gracey,	C
1958	George Deiderich,	G
1982	Jim Arnold,	P
1984	Ricky Anderson,	P

WILDEST FINISH The Sept. 18, 1999, 37-34 overtime win against Mississippi was Vandy's first SEC road victory in five seasons. The Commodores came back and tied the game on a Greg Zolman-to-Todd Yoder touchdown pass with 49 seconds left in regulation. On Mississippi's first overtime possession, the Commodores held and forced a field goal. Then, on a third and goal, Zolman hit his tight end, Elliott Carson, for the touchdown and the win.

BEST COMEBACK On Sept. 11, 1999, trailing Northern Illinois 28-3 in the second half, the Commodores rallied for three touchdowns, including a 61-yard touchdown pass from Greg Zolman to M.J. Garrett on a short slant pattern. After an exchange of field goals, the score stood at 31-26 when Jimmy Williams returned a punt 65 yards for the go-ahead touchdown with 1:41 remaining. After the two-point conversion, Vandy held on for a 34-31 win.

STADIUM Old Dudley Field was the Commodores' home from 1892 until 1922, when it was replaced by a facility of the same name, in honor of Dr. William Dudley, dean of the Vanderbilt Medical College from 1885 to 1914. The new Dudley Field stood until 1980, when a booster-financed rebuilding effort called for a serious remodeling. With the exception of a section of metal bleachers seating 12,088, the entire stadium was demolished and replaced by Vanderbilt Stadium in 1981 at a cost of $10.1 million. The entire project was completed in just nine months. When the NFL's Tennessee Oilers moved to Nashville from Memphis in 1998, they played their home games at Vanderbilt Stadium. Seating capacity stands at 39,773.

RIVAL Before Tennessee hired General Robert R. Neyland in 1925, Vandy had the Vols' number. Since 1915, Vanderbilt had regularly beaten UT, but that soon changed and Tennessee has dominated the rivalry ever since. One notable exception came in 1982, when the Commodores were playing for a rare bowl bid and quarterback Whit Taylor rose to the occasion, completing 24 of 41 passes for 391 yards. With the score tied 21-21 late in the fourth quarter, Taylor took the Commodores on an 84-yard drive, finishing it with a 1-yard touchdown run with 2:53 remaining. Any win against Tennessee is sweet; this one was pure nectar.

TRAGEDY Irby Rice "Rabbit" Curry was the Commodores' team captain, starring at both running back and quarterback from 1914 to 1916 . He went to war after graduation and was killed while flying a combat mission over France. When the Commodores began playing at the new Dudley Field in 1922, the old facility, now used for practices, was renamed in his honor. More recently, running back Kwane Doster was shot and killed not far from his home in Ybor City, Fla., over the 2004 Christmas holiday.

NICKNAME *Nashville Banner* writer William Beard first used the nickname in an 1897 story. Beard himself had played quarterback for Vandy in 1892. The university's founder, Cornelius Vanderbilt, was nicknamed "Commodore" in homage to his business acumen and success.

MASCOT First there was George, the basset hound that belonged to halfback Toby Wilt. During the 1964 Tennessee game, George chased a Tennessee Walking Horse—a sort of unofficial Vol mascot—out of the stadium to the delight of Vanderbilt fans. The Commodores defeated Tennessee that day, 7-0. George was crowned mascot for life, which didn't last very long. He died in 1966, and was succeeded by a female bassett named Samantha, who remained on campus until 1970. Since then the school has been content with a costumed Commodore as mascot.

UNIFORMS Opinions vary on the origins of the black and gold colors. Some say that the original colors were orange and black, a present from Judge W.L. Granbery of Princeton. Others credit various Princeton alums with the choice. When members of the 1890 team were asked in the 1930s how the colors came to be black and gold, they said they couldn't remember. And there, after numerous uniform changes, it stands.

QUOTE "There is no way you can be Harvard Monday through Friday, and try to be Alabama on Saturday."

—Art Guepe

VANDERBILT ANNUAL STATISTICAL LEADERS

YR	RUSHING	YDS	ATT	AVG	PASSING	ATT	CMP	PCT	YDS	RECEIVING	REC	YDS	AVG
1946	J.P. Moore	263	73	3.6	Jamie Wade	44	12	.27	222	John North	11	100	9.1
1947	Dean Davidson	461	90	5.1	Jamie Wade	70	27	.39	506	John North	11	197	17.9
1948	Herb Rich	514	95	5.4	Bob Berry	27	15	.56	360	Bucky Curtis	12	259	21.6
1949	Herb Rich	668	177	3.8	Jamie Wade	143	62	.43	1,021	Bucky Curtis	22	446	20.3
1950	Jim Tabor	654	111	5.9	Bill Wade	177	76	.43	1,596	Bucky Curtis	27	791	29.3
1951	R.C. Allen	321	74	4.3	Bill Wade	223	110	.49	1,609	Ben Roderick	40	627	15.7
1952	R.C. Allen	397	106	3.7	Bill Krietemeyer	153	69	.45	999	Ben Roderick	29	384	13.2
1953	Charles Horton	461	75	6.1	Jim Looney	82	61	.74	362	Charles Hawkins	19	269	14.2
1954	Don Hunt	474	95	5.0	Jim Looney	132	54	.41	813	Joe Stephenson	16	352	22.0
1955	Phil King	628	98	6.4	Don Orr	80	30	.38	486	Joe Stephenson	11	204	18.5
1956	Phil King	651	129	5.0	Boyce Smith	57	27	.47	361	Bob Taylor	12	187	15.6
1957	Phil King	438	115	3.8	Boyce Smith	98	49	.50	664	Phil King	14	172	12.3
1958	Tom Moore	584	145	4.0	Boyce Smith	105	49	.47	638	Tom Moore	12	135	11.3
1959	Tom Moore	676	125	5.4	Russ Morris	92	44	.48	579	Tom Moore	14	170	12.1
1960	Jim Johnson	312	77	4.1	Hank Lesesne	130	54	.42	620	Jeff Starling	14	127	9.1
1961	Hank Lesesne	325	112	2.9	Hank Lesesne	126	50	.40	607	Jeff Starling	25	273	10.9
1962	Hank Lesesne	214	105	2.0	Hank Lesesne	157	65	.41	741	Jeff Starling	34	494	14.5
1963	Bill Waldrup	244	67	3.6	Jon Cleveland	94	39	.41	512	Bennett Baldwin	15	176	11.7
1964	Bob Sullins	512	133	3.8	David Waller	141	61	.43	646	Bennett Baldwin	20	261	13.1
1965	Jim Whiteside	297	103	2.9	Bob Kerr	82	33	.40	346	Toby Wilt	13	171	13.2
1966	Jim Whiteside	267	94	2.8	Gary Davis	153	62	.41	777	Rusty Cantwell	17	157	9.2
1967	Jim Whiteside	255	105	2.4	Roger May	149	82	.55	929	Bob Goodridge	79	1,114	14.1
1968	Allan Spear	438	142	3.1	John Miller	201	99	.49	1,164	Curt Chesley	48	543	11.3
1969	Doug Mathews	849	167	5.1	Watson Brown	111	69	.62	696	Curt Chesley	44	516	11.7
1970	Steve Burger	552	162	3.4	Denny Painter	106	43	.41	563	Curt Chesley	33	393	11.9
1971	Jamie O'Rourke	677	165	4.1	Steve Burger	134	57	.43	671	Gary Chesley	19	253	13.3
1972	Lonnie Sadler	423	122	3.5	Steve Lainhart	89	34	.38	524	Walter Overton	20	317	15.9
1973	Jamie O'Rourke	592	132	4.5	Fred Fisher	234	128	.55	1,450	Jesse Mathers	34	423	12.4
1974	Jamie O'Rourke	933	201	4.6	David Lee	159	85	.53	1,173	Jesse Mathers	23	369	16.0
1975	Lonnie Sadler	536	175	3.1	Fred Fisher	106	51	.48	552	Barry Burton	31	306	9.9
1976	Adolph Groves	347	96	3.6	Randy Hampton	107	53	.50	805	Martin Cox	38	738	19.4
1977	Frank Mordica	449	133	3.4	Mike Wright	211	106	.50	1,383	Martin Cox	48	783	16.3
1978	Frank Mordica	1,065	173	6.2	Van Heflin	155	76	.49	984	Martin Cox	40	674	16.9
1979	Frank Mordica	830	162	5.1	Van Heflin	124	64	.52	748	Preston Brown	52	786	15.1
1980	Terry Potter	579	149	3.9	Whit Taylor	173	72	.42	899	Wamon Buggs	37	448	12.1
1981	Van Heflin	374	105	3.6	Whit Taylor	357	209	.59	2,318	Wamon Buggs	54	778	14.4
1982	Keith Edwards	340	88	3.9	Whit Taylor	406	228	.56	2,481	Allama Matthews	43	797	13.1
1983	Carl Woods	644	160	4.0	Kurt Page	493	286	.58	3,178	Keith Edwards	97	909	9.4
1984	Carl Woods	688	192	3.6	Kurt Page	350	203	.58	2,405	Keith Edwards	60	576	9.6
1985	Carl Woods	615	160	3.8	John Gromos	224	124	.55	1,483	Everett Crawford	50	533	10.7
1986	Carl Woods	552	107	5.2	Mark Wracher	134	75	.56	827	Everett Crawford	40	517	12.9
1987	Eric Jones	665	179	3.7	Eric Jones	229	139	.61	1,954	Carl Parker	42	806	19.2
1988	Eric Jones	305	144	2.1	Eric Jones	360	196	.54	2,548	Boo Mitchell	78	1,213	15.6
1989	Carlos Thomas	254	61	4.2	John Gromos	320	154	.48	1,744	Brad Gaines	67	634	9.5
1990	Carlos Thomas	680	113	6.0	Mike Healy	130	75	.58	1,041	Clarence Sevillian	29	536	18.5
1991	Corey Harris	1,103	229	4.8	Marcus Wilson	63	32	.51	491	Corey Harris	23	283	12.3
1992	Tony Jackson	652	114	5.7	Marcus Wilson	164	75	.46	1,030	Clarence Sevillian	33	701	21.2
1993	Tony Jackson	607	120	5.1	Ronnie Gordon	98	40	.41	400	Kenny Simon	15	166	11.1
1994	Jermaine Johnson	877	167	5.3	Ronnie Gordon	203	86	.42	991	Kenny Simon	20	271	13.6
1995	Jermaine Johnson	1,072	267	4.0	Damian Allen	136	62	.46	728	Sanford Ware	34	402	11.8
1996	Jason Dunnavant	374	131	2.9	Damian Allen	279	118	.42	1,472	Todd Yoder	21	471	22.4
1997	Jimmy Williams	527	98	5.4	Damian Allen	283	128	.45	1,544	Jimmy Williams	24	183	7.6
1998	Rodney Williams	608	126	4.8	Greg Zolman	145	69	.48	969	Tavarus Hogans	28	366	13.1
1999	Rodney Williams	644	148	4.4	Greg Zolman	300	154	.51	2,059	Tavarus Hogans	53	837	15.8
2000	Jared McGrath	527	133	4.0	Greg Zolman	354	187	.53	2,441	Dan Stricker	61	994	16.3
2001	Lew Thomas	675	105	6.4	Greg Zolman	357	186	.52	2,512	Dan Stricker	65	1,079	16.6
2002	Kwane Doster	798	160	5.0	Jay Cutler	212	103	.49	1,433	Dan Stricker	44	620	14.1
2003	Norval McKenzie	639	162	3.9	Jay Cutler	327	187	.57	1,347	Erik Davis	41	638	15.6
2004	Norval McKenzie	446	102	4.4	Jay Cutler	241	147	.61	1,544	Brandon Smith	41	553	13.5

Receiving leaders by receptions
The NCAA began including postseason stats in 2002

VANDERBILT ALL-TIME SCORES

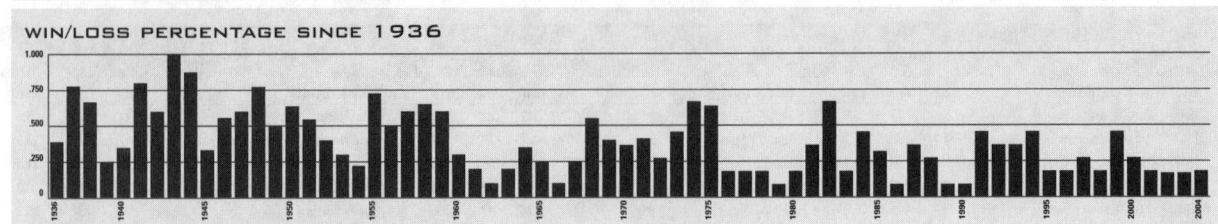

WIN/LOSS PERCENTAGE SINCE 1936

ELLIOTT H. JONES
1890-92 (.615)   8-5

1890   1-0-0
N27	●	Nashville	40	0

1891   3-1-0
N7	●	at Sewanee	22	0
N14		Washington, Mo.	6	24
N26	●	Sewanee	26	4
D4	●	at Washington, Mo.	4	0

1892   4-4-0
O15	●	at Sewanee	4	22
O21	●	Tennessee	12	0 *
O28	●	Nashville	40	0
N5		Washington, Mo.	4	14
N12		Sewanee	14	28
N17	●	at Tennessee	10	0
N19	●	at Georgia Tech	20	10
N24		North Carolina	0	24

W.J. KELLER
1893 (.857)   6-1

1893   6-1-0
U	●	Memphis AC	68	0
U	●	at Sewanee	10	8
N6	●	Auburn *Mont*	10	30
N7	●	Georgia	35	10 *
N19	●	at Louisville AC	36	12
N23	●	Sewanee	10	0
D1	●	Central Kentucky	12	0

HENRY THORNTON
1894 (.875)   7-1

1894   7-1-0
O6	●	at Memphis AC	64	0
O20	●	Centre	6	0
O27	●	at Louisville AC	8	10
N4	●	Auburn *Mont*	20	4
N10	●	Mississippi	40	0
N21	●	Central Kentucky	34	6
N24	●	at Cumberland	62	0
N29	●	Sewanee	12	0

C.L. UPTON
1895 (.611)   5-3-1

1895   5-3-1
O12	●	at Missouri	0	16
O19	●	at Central Kentucky	10	0
O28	●	North Carolina	0	12
N2	=	Centre	0	0
N7	●	at Nashville AC	20	4
N9	●	Auburn	9	6
N16	●	Virginia *Atl*	4	6
N23	●	Georgia	6	0
N28	●	at Sewanee	18	6

R.G. ACTON
1896-98 (.575)   10-7-3

1896   3-2-2
O10	●	Kentucky	6	0
O17	●	at Centre	0	46
N7	●	Missouri *StL*	6	26
U	●	at Central Kentucky	0	0
U	●	at Southwestern	36	0
U	=	Nashville	0	0
N27	●	at Sewanee	10	4

1897   6-0-1
U	●	at Kentucky St. Coll.	24	0
U	●	Central Kentucky	14	0
O19	●	VMI	12	0
O30	●	at Kentucky	50	0
N6	●	at North Carolina	31	0
N26	●	Sewanee	10	0
D6	=	Virginia	0	0

1898   1-5-0
O22	●	Cincinnati	0	10 *
O29	●	at Georgia	0	4
N5	●	Nashville	5	0
N12	●	at Virginia	0	18
N19	●	Central Kentucky	0	10
N25	●	Sewanee	4	19

J.L. CRANE
1899-1900 (.639)   11-6-1

1899   7-2-0
O6	●	at Cumberland	32	0
O13	●	Miami, Ohio	12	0
O20	●	Cincinnati	0	6
O28	●	Indiana	0	20
N4	●	at Mississippi	11	0
N11	●	Bethel	22	0
N18	●	Texas	6	0
N25	●	Central Kentucky	21	16
U	●	at Nashville	5	0

1900   4-4-1
O6	●	Mississippi	6	0
O13	●	at Texas	0	22
O22	=	Tennessee	0	0
U	●	Central Kentucky	0	11
N3	●	North Carolina	0	48
U	●	Central Ky	27	0
U	●	Sewanee	10	11
U	●	Bethel	29	0
U	●	Nashville	18	0

W.H. WATKINS
1901-02 (.853)   14-2-1

1901   6-1-1
O5	●	Kentucky	22	0
O12	●	Central Kentucky	25	0
O19	●	Georgia	47	0
N2	●	at Washington, Mo.	11	12
N8	●	Auburn *Mont*	41	0 *
N9	●	Tennessee	22	0
N16	=	Sewanee	0	0
N28	●	at Nashville	10	0

1902   8-1-0
S27	●	at Cumberland	45	0
O11	●	Mississippi	29	0
O18	●	at Centre	24	17
O25	●	at Tennessee	12	5
N1	●	Washington, Mo.	33	12
N8	●	Transylvania, Ky	16	5
N15	●	at Tulane	23	5
N17	●	at LSU	27	5
N27	●	Sewanee	5	11

J.H. HENRY
1903 (.813)   6-1-1

1903   6-1-1
O3		Cumberland	0	6
O10	●	Alabama	30	0
O17	●	Tennessee	40	0
O24	●	Mississippi	33	0
O31	●	at Georgia	33	0
N6	●	at Texas	5	5
N14	●	Washington, Mo.	41	0
N21	●	Sewanee	10	5

DAN McGUGIN
1904-17, '19-34 (.762)   197-55-19

1904   9-0-0
O1	●	Mississippi State *ColMs*	61	0
O8	●	Georgetown, Ky	66	0
O15	●	Mississippi	69	0
O22	●	Missouri Mines	29	4
O29	●	at Centre	97	0
N5	●	Tennessee	22	0
N12	●	Nashville	81	0
N19	●	at Centre	22	0
N24	●	Sewanee	27	0

1905   7-1-0
S30	●	Maryville	97	0
O7	●	Alabama	34	0
O14	●	at Michigan	0	18
O21	●	at Tennessee	45	0
O28	●	Texas	33	0
N4	●	Auburn	54	0
N18	●	Clemson	41	0
N30	●	Sewanee	68	4

1906   8-1-0
O6	●	Kentucky	28	0
O13	●	Mississippi	29	0
O20	●	Alabama	78	0
O27	●	Texas	45	0
N3	●	at Michigan	4	10
N10	●	Rose Poly	33	0
N17	●	at Georgia Tech	37	6
N24	●	Carlisle	4	0
N29	●	Sewanee	20	0

1907   5-1-1
O5	●	Kentucky	40	0
O12	=	at Navy	6	6
O19	●	Rose Poly	65	10
N2	●	Michigan	0	8
N9	●	Mississippi *Mem*	60	0
N16	●	Georgia Tech	54	0
N23	●	Sewanee	17	12

1908   7-2-1
S26	●	Southwestern	11	5
O3	●	Maryville	32	0
O10	●	Rose Poly	32	0
O17	●	Clemson	41	0
O24	●	Mississippi	29	0
O31	●	at Michigan	6	24
N7	●	Tennessee	16	9
N14	●	Ohio State	6	17
N21	●	at Washington, Mo.	28	0
N26	=	Sewanee	6	6

1909   7-3-0
S25	●	Southwestern	52	0
O2	●	Mercer	28	5
O9	●	Rose Poly	28	3
O16	●	Alumni	0	3
O23	●	Auburn	17	0
O30	●	Mississippi	17	0
N6	●	Tennessee	51	0
N13	●	at Ohio State	0	5
N20	●	at Washington, Mo.	12	0
N25	●	Sewanee	5	16

1910   8-0-1
S24	●	Mooney	34	0
O1	●	Rose Poly	23	0
O8	●	Castle Heights	14	0
O15	●	Tennessee	18	0
O22	=	at Yale	0	0
O29	●	Mississippi	9	2
N5	●	LSU	22	0
N12	●	at Georgia Tech	23	0
N24	●	Sewanee	23	6

1911   8-1-0
S30	●	B'Ham Southern	40	0
O7	●	Maryville	46	0
O14	●	Rose Poly	33	0
O21	●	Centre	45	0
O28	●	at Michigan	8	9
N4	●	Georgia	17	0
N11	●	Kentucky	18	0
N18	●	Mississippi	21	0
N30	●	Sewanee	31	0

1912   8-1-1
S28	●	Bethel	105	0
O5	●	Maryville	100	3
O12	●	Rose Poly	54	0
O19	●	Georgia *Atl*	46	0
O26	●	Mississippi	24	0
N2	●	Virginia	13	0
N9	●	at Harvard	3	9
N16	●	Centre	23	0
N23	●	Auburn *Mont*	7	7
N28	●	Sewanee	16	0

1913   5-3-0
O4	●	Maryville	59	0
O11	●	Centre	48	0
O18	●	Henderson - Brown	33	0
O25	●	Michigan	2	33
N1	●	at Virginia	0	34
N8	●	Tennessee	7	6
N15	●	Auburn *Mont*	6	14
N22	●	Sewanee	63	13

1914   2-6-0
O3	●	Henderson-Brown	42	6
O10	●	at Michigan	3	23
O17	●	Centre	59	0
O24	●	North Carolina	9	10
O31	●	Virginia	7	20
N7	●	Tennessee	14	16
N14	●	Auburn *Mont*	0	6
N21	●	Sewanee	13	14

1915   9-1-0
S25	●	Middle Tennessee	51	0
O2	●	Southwestern	47	0
O9	●	Georgetown Ky.	75	0
O13	●	Cumberland	60	0
O16	●	Henderson-Brown	100	0
O23	●	Mississippi *Mem*	91	0
O30	●	Tennessee	35	0
N6	●	at Virginia	10	35
N13	●	Auburn *Mont*	17	0
N20	●	Sewanee	27	3

1916   7-1-1
S30	●	Southwestern	86	0
O7	●	Transylvania, Ky	42	0
O14	●	at Kentucky	45	0
O21	●	Mississippi	35	0
O28	●	Virginia	27	6
N4	●	Rose Poly	67	0
N11	●	at Tennessee	6	10
N18	●	Auburn *Mont*	20	9
N25	=	Sewanee	0	0

1917   5-3-0
O6	●	Transylvania, Ky	41	0
O13	●	at Chicago	0	48
O20	●	at Kentucky	5	0
O27	●	Samford	69	0
N3	●	at Georgia Tech	0	83
N10	●	Alabama *Mont*	7	2
N17	●	Auburn	7	31
N29	●	Sewanee	13	6

RAY MORRISON
1918, '35-39 (.566)   29-22-2

1918   4-2-0
O19	●	Camp Greenleaf	0	6
O26	●	Camp Hancock	6	25
N2	●	Kentucky	33	0
N9	●	Tennessee JV	76	0
N16	●	Auburn *Mont*	21	0
N28	●	Sewanee	40	0

VANDERBILT 951

DAN McGUGIN

1919 — 5-1-2

O4	●		Union	41	0
O11	=		Tennessee	3	3
O18			at Georgia Tech	0	20
O25	●		Auburn	7	6
N1	=		at Kentucky	0	0
N8	●		Alabama	16	12
N15	●		at Virginia	10	6
N27	●		Sewanee	33	21

1920 — 5-3-1

O2	●		B'ham Southern	54	0
O9	●		at Tennessee	20	0
O16			Georgia Tech	0	44
O23			Auburn MONT	6	56
O30	●		Kentucky	20	0
N6			Alabama MONT	7	14
N13	●		at Middle Tennessee	34	0
N20	=		Virginia	7	7
N27	●		Sewanee	21	3

1921 — 7-0-1

O1	●		Middle Tennessee	34	0
O8	●		Mercer	42	0
O15	●		at Kentucky	21	14
O21	●		Texas DAL	20	0
O29	●		Tennessee	14	0
N5	●		Alabama MONT	14	0
N13	=		Georgia	7	7
N19	●		Sewanee	9	0

1922-1932
SOUTHERN

1922 — 8-0-1 (4-0-0)

S30	●		Middle Tennessee	38	0
O7	●		Henderson-Brown	33	0
O14	=		Michigan	0	0
O21	●		Texas DAL	20	10
O28	●		Mercer	25	0
N4	●	|	at Tennessee	14	6
N11	●	|	Kentucky	9	0
N18	●	|	at Georgia	12	0
N25	●	|	Sewanee	26	0

1923 — 5-2-1 (4-0-1)

O6	●		Samford	27	0
O13			at Michigan	0	3
O20			Texas DAL	0	16
O27	●	|	Tulane	17	0
N3	=	|	Mississippi State	0	0
N10	●	|	Tennessee	51	7
N17	●	|	Georgia	35	7
N24	●	|	Sewanee	77	0

1924 — 6-3-1 (3-3-0)

S27	●		Henderson-Brown	13	0
O4	●		B'ham Southern	61	0
O11	=		at Quantico Marines	13	13
O18		|	at Tulane	13	21
O25		|	Georgia	0	3
N1	●	|	Auburn	13	0
N8	●	|	Mississippi State	18	0
N15	●	|	at Georgia Tech	3	0
N22	●		at Minnesota	16	0
N29		|	Sewanee	0	16

1925 — 6-3-0 (3-3-0)

S26	●		Middle Tennessee	27	0
O3	●		Henderson-Brown	41	0
O10	●		Texas	14	6
O17	●	|	Tennessee	34	7
O24		|	at Georgia	7	26
O31	●	|	Mississippi	7	0
N7		|	Georgia Tech	0	7
N14		|	Auburn MONT	9	10
N21	●	|	Sewanee	19	7

1926 — 8-1-0 (4-1-0)

S25	●		Middle Tennessee	69	0
O2		|	Alabama	7	19
O9	●		Bryson	48	0
O16	●		Texas DAL	7	0
O23	●	|	Georgia	14	13
O30	●		Southwestern	50	0
N6	●	|	at Georgia Tech	13	7
N13	●	|	Tennessee	20	3
N20	●	|	Sewanee	13	0

1927 — 8-1-2 (5-0-2)

S24	●		at U.T. Chattanooga	45	18
O1	●		Ouachita	39	10
O8	●		at Centre	53	6
O15			Texas DAL	6	13
O22	●	|	Tulane	32	0
O29	●	|	Kentucky	34	6
N6	=	|	Georgia Tech	0	0
N12	=	|	at Tennessee	7	7
N19	●	|	Maryland	39	20
N26	●	|	Sewanee	26	6
D3	●	|	Alabama MONT	14	7

1928 — 8-2-0 (4-2-0)

S29	●		at U.T. Chattanooga	20	0
O6	●		Colgate	12	7
O13	●		Texas AL	13	12
O20	●	|	at Tulane	13	6
O27	●	|	Virginia	34	0
N3	●	|	Kentucky	14	7
N10		|	at Georgia Tech	7	19
N17		|	Tennessee	0	6
N24	●		Centre	26	0
D1	●	|	Sewanee	13	0

1929 — 7-2-0 (5-1-0)

S28	●	|	Mississippi	19	7
O5	●		Ouachita	26	6
O12			at Minnesota	6	15
O19	●	|	Auburn MONT	41	2
O26	●		Maryville	33	0
N2	●	|	Alabama	13	0
N9	●	|	Georgia Tech	23	7
N16		|	at Tennessee	0	13
N23	●	|	Sewanee	26	6

1930 — 8-2-0 (5-2-0)

S27	●		U.T. Chattanooga	39	0
O4	●		at Minnesota	33	7
O11	●	|	Virginia Tech	40	0
O18	●		Spring Hill	27	6
O25		|	Alabama MONT	7	12
N1	●	|	Mississippi	24	0
N8	●	|	at Georgia Tech	6	0
N15		|	Tennessee	0	13
N22	●	|	Auburn	27	0
D1	●	|	Maryland	22	7

1931 — 5-4-0 (3-4-0)

S26	●		Western Kentucky	52	0
O3	●	|	North Carolina	13	0
O10	●		at Ohio State	26	21
O17		|	Tulane	0	19
O24		|	at Georgia	0	9
O31	●	|	at Georgia Tech	49	7
N7	●	|	Maryland	39	12
N14		|	at Tennessee	7	21
N26		|	Alabama	6	14

1932 — 6-1-2 (4-1-2)

S24	●		Mercer	20	7
O1	●	|	at North Carolina	39	7
O8	●		Western Kentucky	26	0
O15	=	|	at Tulane	6	6
O22	●	|	Georgia	12	6
O29	●	|	Georgia Tech	12	0
N5	●	|	Maryland DC	13	0
N12	=	|	Tennessee	0	0
N24		|	Alabama MONT	0	20

1933-PRESENT
SEC

1933 — 4-3-3 (2-2-2)

S23	●		Cumberland	50	0
S30	=		at Oklahoma	0	0
O7	●		North Carolina	20	13
O14			at Ohio State	0	20
O21	=	|	Mississippi State	7	7
O28	=	|	at LSU	7	7
N4	●	|	at Georgia Tech	9	6
N11	●	|	Sewanee	27	14
N18		|	at Tennessee	6	33
N30		|	Alabama	0	7

1934 — 6-3-0 (4-3-0)

S29	●	|	Mississippi State	7	0
O6	●	|	at Georgia Tech	27	12
O13	●		Cincinnati	32	0
O20	●	|	Auburn	7	6
O27		|	LSU	0	29
N3	●		at George Washington	7	6
N10	●	|	Sewanee	19	0
N17		|	Tennessee	6	13
N29		|	Alabama MONT	0	34

RAY MORRISON

1935 — 7-3-0 (5-1-0)

S21	●		Union	34	0
S28	●	|	Mississippi State	14	9
O5	●		Cumberland	32	7
O12			at Temple	3	6
O19			Fordham NYC	7	13
O26		|	LSU	2	7
N2	●	|	at Georgia Tech	14	13
N9	●	|	Sewanee	46	0
N16	●	|	at Tennessee	13	7
N28	●	|	Alabama	14	6

1936 — 3-5-1 (1-3-1)

S26	●		Middle Tennessee	45	0
O3	●		at Chicago	37	0
O10			Southwestern	0	12
O17			at SMU	0	16
O24	=	|	Georgia Tech	0	0
O31		|	LSU	0	19
N7	●	|	Sewanee	14	0
N14		|	Tennessee	13	26
N25		|	Alabama MONT	6	14

1937 — 7-2-0 (4-2-0)

S25	●	|	Kentucky	12	0
O2	●		Chicago	18	0
O8	●		at Southwestern	17	6
O13	●		at SMU	6	0
O23	●	|	LSU	7	6
O30		|	at Georgia Tech	0	14
N6	●	|	Sewanee	41	0
N13	●	|	at Tennessee	13	7
N25		|	Alabama	7	9

1938 — 6-3-0 (4-3-0)

S24	●		at Washington, Mo.	20	0
O1	●		Western Kentucky	12	0
O8	●	|	at Kentucky	14	7
O15	●	|	Mississippi	13	7
O22		|	at LSU	0	7
O29	●	|	Georgia Tech	13	7
N5	●	|	Sewanee	14	0
N12		|	Tennessee	0	14
N24		|	Alabama MONT	0	7

1939 — 2-7-1 (1-6-0)

S23	=		Tennessee Tech	13	13
S30	●		at Rice	13	12
O7		|	Kentucky	13	21
O14			VMI	13	20
O21		|	at Georgia Tech	6	14
O28		|	LSU	6	12
N4		|	Mississippi MEM	7	14
N11	●	|	Sewanee	25	7
N18		|	at Tennessee	0	13
N30		|	Alabama	0	39

RED SANDERS

1940-42, '46-48 (.617) 36-22-2

1940 — 3-6-1 (0-5-1)

S28	●		Wash. & Lee	19	0
O5			at Princeton	6	7
O12	=	|	Kentucky	7	7
O19		|	at Georgia Tech	0	19
O26		|	at LSU	0	7
N2		|	Mississippi	7	13
N9	●		Sewanee	20	0
N16	●		Tennessee Tech	21	0
N23		|	Alabama MONT	21	25
N30		|	Tennessee	0	20

1941 — 8-2-0 (3-2-0)

S27	●		at Purdue	3	0
O4	●		Tennessee Tech	42	0
O11	●	|	at Kentucky	39	15
O18	●	|	Georgia Tech	14	7
O25	●		Princeton	46	7
N1		|	Tulane	14	34
N8	●		Sewanee	20	0
N15	●		at Louisville	68	0
N22	●	|	Alabama	7	0
N29		|	at Tennessee	7	26

1942 — 6-4-0 (2-4-0)

S26	●		Tennessee Tech	52	0
O3	●		Purdue	26	0
O10	●	|	at Kentucky	7	6
O17		|	Mississippi State	0	33
O24	●		Centre	66	0
O31		|	at Tulane	21	28
N7	●	|	Mississippi MEM	19	0
N14	●		at Union	27	0
N21		|	Alabama MONT	7	27
N28		|	Tennessee	7	19

E.H. ALLEY

1943 (1.000) 5-0

1943 — 5-0-0 (0-0-0)

S25	●		at Tennessee Tech	30	0
O9	●		at Camp Campbell	40	14
O16	●		Milligan	26	6
O30	●		Carson-Newman	12	6
N13	●		Tennessee Tech	47	7

DOBY BARTLING

1944-45 (.500) 6-6-1

1944 — 3-0-1 (0-0-0)

O7	=		at Sewanee	0	0
O14	●		Tennessee Tech	19	7
O21	●		at Tennessee Tech	20	9
O28	●		Sewanee	28	7

1945 — 3-6-0 (2-4-0)

S29	●		Tennessee Tech	12	0
O6		|	Mississippi	7	14
O13	●	|	at Florida	7	0
O20	●	|	Kentucky	19	6
O27		|	at LSU	7	39
N3			VMI	13	27
N10			U.T. Chattanooga	6	13
N17		|	Alabama	0	71
D1		|	at Tennessee	0	45

RED SANDERS

1946 — 5-4-0 (3-4-0)

S28	●		Tennessee Tech	35	0
O5	●	|	Mississippi MEM	7	0
O12	●	|	Florida	20	0
O19		|	at Kentucky	7	10
O26		|	LSU	0	14
N2	●	|	Auburn	19	0
N9	●		North Carolina St. MONT	7	0
N16		|	Alabama MONT	7	12
N30		|	Tennessee	6	7

1947 — 6-4-0 (3-3-0)

S27	●		at Northwestern	3	0
O4	●	|	Alabama	14	7
O11	●	|	Mississippi	10	6
O18		|	Kentucky	0	14
O25		|	at LSU	13	19
N1	●	|	Auburn	28	0
N8	●		Tennessee Tech	68	0
N14	●		at Miami, Fla.	33	7
N22			Maryland	6	20
N29		|	at Tennessee	7	12

1948 — 8-2-1 (4-2-1)

S25		|	Georgia Tech	0	13
O2	=	|	Alabama MBL	14	14
O9		|	at Mississippi	7	20
O16	●	|	at Kentucky	26	7
O23	●		at Yale	35	0
O29	●	|	Auburn MONT	47	0
N6	●	|	LSU	48	7
N13	●		Marshall	56	0
N20	●		Maryland DC	34	0
N27	●	|	Tennessee	28	6
D3	●		at Miami, Fla.	33	6

BILL EDWARDS

1949-52 (.524) 21-19-2

1949 — 5-5-0 (4-4-0)

S24		|	at Georgia Tech	7	12
O1	●	|	Alabama	14	7
O8	●	|	Mississippi	28	27
O15	●	|	Florida JACF	22	17
O22			Arkansas	6	7
O29	●	|	Auburn	26	7
N5		|	at LSU	13	33
N12		|	Tulane	14	41
N19	●		Marshall	27	6
N26		|	at Tennessee	20	26

1950 — 7-4-0 (3-4-0)

S23	●		Middle Tennessee	47	0
S30	●	|	Auburn	41	0
O7	●	|	Alabama MBL	27	22
O14	●	|	Mississippi	20	14
O21		|	Florida	27	31
O28	●		Arkansas LR	14	13
N3	●		at U.T. Chattanooga	34	12
N11		|	LSU	7	33
N18	●		at Memphis	29	13
N25		|	at Tulane	6	35
D2		|	Tennessee	0	43

THE SCHOOLS

952 VANDERBILT

THE SCHOOLS

1951 6-5-0 (3-5-0)

S22	•	Middle Tennessee	22	7
S29	|	at Auburn	14	24
O6	• |	Alabama	22	20
O13	• |	Mississippi MEM	34	20
O20	|	at Florida	13	33
O27	|	Georgia Tech	7	8
N3	•	U.T. Chattanooga	19	14
N10	• |	at LSU	20	13
N17	|	Tulane	10	14
N24	•	Memphis	13	7
D1	|	at Tennessee	27	35

1952 3-5-2 (1-4-1)

S20	|	Georgia	7	19
S27		at Virginia	0	27
O4	=	at Northwestern	20	20
O11	= |	Mississippi	21	21
O18	• |	Florida	20	13
O25	|	at Georgia Tech	0	30
N1	•	Wash. & Lee	67	7
N7	•	at Miami, Fla.	9	0
N15	|	at Tulane	7	16
N29	|	Tennessee	0	46

ART GUEPE
1953-62 (.425) 39-54-7

1953 3-7-0 (1-5-0)

S26		at Pennsylvania	7	13
O3	|	Alabama	12	21
O10	|	at Mississippi	6	28
O17		at Baylor	6	47
O24	•	Virginia	28	13
O31	|	Georgia Tech	0	43
N7	|	Kentucky	14	40
N14	• |	at Tulane	21	7
N21	•	Middle Tennessee	31	13
N28	|	at Tennessee	6	33

1954 2-7-0 (1-5-0)

S25		Baylor	19	25
O2	|	Alabama MBL	14	28
O9	|	Mississippi	7	22
O16	|	at Georgia	14	16
O30		at Rice	13	34
N6	|	at Kentucky	7	19
N13	|	Tulane	0	6
N20	•	Villanova	34	19
N27	• |	Tennessee	26	0

1955 8-3-0 (4-3-0)

S24	|	at Georgia	13	14
O1	• |	Alabama	21	6
O8	|	Mississippi MEM	0	13
O14	•	at U.T. Chattanooga	12	0
O22	•	Middle Tennessee	46	0
O29	•	Virginia	34	7
N5	• |	Kentucky	34	0
N12	• |	at Tulane	20	7
N19	• |	Florida	21	6
N26	|	at Tennessee	14	20
		GATOR BOWL		
D31	•	Auburn	25	13

1956 5-5-0 (2-5-0)

S22	• |	Georgia	14	0
S29	•	U.T. Chattanooga	46	7
O6	• |	Alabama MBL	32	7
O13	|	at Mississippi	0	16
O20	|	Florida	7	21
O27	•	at Middle Tennessee	23	13
N3	•	at Virginia	6	2
N10	|	at Kentucky	6	7
N17	|	Tulane	6	13
D1	|	Tennessee	7	27

1957 5-3-2 (3-3-1)

S21	=	Missouri	7	7
S28	• |	at Georgia	9	6
O5	= |	Alabama	6	6
O12	|	Mississippi	0	28
O19	•	at Penn State	32	20
N2	• |	LSU	7	0
N9	• |	Kentucky	12	7
N16	|	at Florida	7	14
N23	•	Citadel	27	0
N30	|	at Tennessee	6	20

1958 5-2-3 (2-1-3)

S20	•	at Missouri	12	8
S27	• |	Georgia	21	14
O4	= |	Alabama MONT	0	0
O11		Clemson	7	12
O18	= |	at Florida	6	6
O25	•	Virginia	39	6
O31	•	at Miami, Fla.	28	15
N8	= |	at Kentucky	0	0
N15	• |	Tulane	12	0
N29	|	Tennessee	6	10

1959 5-3-2 (3-2-2)

S26	|	at Georgia	6	21
O3	= |	Alabama	7	7
O10	|	Mississippi	0	33
O17	• |	Florida	13	6
O24	•	at Virginia	33	0
O31		at Minnesota	6	20
N7	• |	Kentucky	11	6
N14	= |	at Tulane	6	6
N21	•	Florence St.	42	7
N28	• |	at Tennessee	14	0

1960 3-7-0 (0-7-0)

S24	|	Georgia	7	18
O1	|	Alabama MONT	0	21
O8	|	Mississippi	0	26
O15	|	at Florida	0	12
O22	•	at Marquette	23	6
O29	•	Clemson	22	20
N5	|	at Kentucky	0	27
N12	•	William & Mary	22	8
N19	|	Tulane	0	20
N26	|	Tennessee	0	35

1961 2-8-0 (1-6-0)

S23	•	West Virginia	16	6
S30	• |	at Georgia	21	0
O7	|	Alabama	6	35
O14		at UCLA	21	28
O21	|	Florida	0	7
O28	|	at Mississippi	0	47
N11	|	Kentucky	3	16
N17	|	at Tulane	14	17
N25		South Carolina	7	23
D2	|	at Tennessee	7	41

1962 1-9-0 (1-6-0)

S22		at West Virginia	0	26
S29	|	Georgia	0	10
O6	|	Alabama MONT	7	17
O13		Citadel	6	21
O20	|	at Florida	7	42
O27	|	Mississippi MEM	0	35
N3		Boston College	22	27
N10	|	at Kentucky	0	7
N17	• |	Tulane	20	0
D1	|	Tennessee	0	30

JACK GREEN
1963-66 (.225) 7-29-4

1963 1-7-2 (0-5-2)

S21		Furman	13	14
S28	|	at Georgia	0	20
O5	|	Alabama	6	21
O19	|	Florida	0	21
O26	|	at Mississippi	7	27
N2		at Boston College	6	19
N9	= |	Kentucky	0	0
N16	= |	at Tulane	10	10
N23	•	George Washington	31	0
N30	|	at Tennessee	0	14

1964 3-6-1 (1-4-1)

S19		at Georgia Tech	2	14
S26	|	Georgia	0	7
O3	|	Alabama MONT	0	24
O10	•	Wake Forest	9	6
O17	•	at George Washington	14	0
O24	= |	Mississippi	7	7
N7	|	at Kentucky	21	22
N14	|	Tulane	2	7
N20		at Miami, Fla.	17	35
N28	• |	Tennessee	7	0

1965 2-7-1 (1-5-0)

S18	=	Georgia Tech	10	10
S25	|	at Georgia	10	24
O2		at Wake Forest	0	7
O9	|	Alabama	7	22
O16	•	Virginia Tech	21	10
O23	|	at Mississippi	7	24
O30	• |	at Tulane	13	0
N6	|	Kentucky	0	34
N13		Miami, Fla.	14	28
N27	|	at Tennessee	3	21

1966 1-9-0 (0-6-0)

S17	•	Citadel	24	0
S24		at Georgia Tech	0	42
O1	|	Florida	0	13
O15		Virginia Tech RICH	6	21
O22	|	Alabama MONT	6	42
O29	||	Tulane	12	13
N5	|	at Kentucky	10	14
N12		Navy	14	30
N19	|	Mississippi JAM	0	34
N26	|	Tennessee	0	28

BILL PACE
1967-72 (.373) 22-38-3

1967 2-7-1 (0-6-0)

S23		Georgia Tech	10	17
S30	•	William & Mary	14	12
O7	•	at North Carolina	21	7
O14	|	Alabama	21	35
O28	|	at Florida	22	27
N4	||	at Tulane	14	27
N11	|	Kentucky	7	12
N18	=	at Navy	35	35
N25	|	Mississippi	7	28
D2	|	at Tennessee	14	41

1968 5-4-1 (2-3-1)

S21	•	VMI	25	12
S28	•	at Army	17	13
O5		North Carolina	7	8
O12	|	at Alabama	7	31
O19	|	at Georgia	6	32
O26	= |	Florida	14	14
N2	• ||	Tulane	21	7
N9	• |	at Kentucky	6	0
N23	•	at Davidson	53	20
N30	|	Tennessee	7	10

1969 4-6-0 (2-3-0)

S20		at Michigan	14	42
S27		Army	6	16
O4		at North Carolina	22	38
O11	• |	Alabama	14	10
O18	|	Georgia	8	40
O25	|	at Florida	20	41
N1	•	at Tulane	26	23
N8	• |	Kentucky	42	6
N22	•	Davidson	63	8
N29	|	at Tennessee	27	40

1970 4-7-0 (1-5-0)

S12	•	U.T. Chattanooga	39	6
S19	•	Citadel	52	0
S26	|	Mississippi State MEM	6	20
O3		North Carolina	7	10
O10	|	at Alabama	11	35
O17	|	at Georgia	3	7
O24	|	Mississippi	16	26
O31		Tulane	7	10
N7	• |	at Kentucky	18	17
N21	•	at Tampa	36	28
N28	|	Tennessee	6	24

1971 4-6-1 (1-5-0)

S11	•	U.T. Chattanooga	20	19
S18	=	Louisville	0	0
S25	• |	at Mississippi State	49	19
O2		at Virginia	23	27
O9	|	Alabama	0	42
O16	|	Georgia	0	24
O23	|	at Mississippi	7	28
O30	•	at Tulane	13	9
N6	|	Kentucky	7	14
N20	•	Tampa	10	7
N27	|	at Tennessee	7	19

1972 3-8-0 (0-6-0)

S9	•	U.T. Chattanooga	24	7
S23	|	Mississippi State	6	10
S30	|	at Alabama	21	48
O7	•	Virginia	10	7
O14	•	at William & Mary	21	17
O21	|	at Georgia	3	28
O28	|	Mississippi	7	31
N11	|	at Kentucky	13	14
N18		Tulane	7	21
N25		at Tampa	7	30
D2	|	Tennessee	10	30

STEVE SLOAN
1973-74 (.565) 12-9-2

1973 5-6-0 (1-5-0)

S15	•	U.T. Chattanooga	14	12
S22	|	at Mississippi State	21	52
S29	|	Alabama	0	44
O6	•	at Virginia	39	22
O13	•	William & Mary	20	7
O20	• |	Georgia	18	14
O27	|	at Mississippi	14	24
N10	|	Kentucky	17	27
N17		at Tulane	3	24
N24	•	Tampa	18	16
D1	|	at Tennessee	17	20

1974 7-3-2 (2-3-1)

S14	•	U.T. Chattanooga	28	6
S21	•	VMI	45	7
S28	|	at Alabama	10	23
O12	• |	Florida	24	10
O19	|	at Georgia	31	38
O26	• |	Mississippi	24	14
N2	•	at Army	38	14
N9	|	at Kentucky	12	38
N16	•	Tulane	30	22
N23	•	at Louisville	44	0
N30	= |	Tennessee	21	21
		PEACH BOWL		
D28	=	Texas Tech	6	6

FRED PANCOAST
1975-78 (.295) 13-31

1975 7-4-0 (2-4-0)

S13	•	U.T. Chattanooga	17	7
S20	•	at Rice	9	6
S27	|	Alabama	7	40
O4	•	at Tulane	6	3
O11	|	at Florida	0	35
O18	|	Georgia	3	47
O25	|	at Mississippi	7	17
N1	•	Virginia	17	14
N8	• |	Kentucky	13	3
N15	•	Army	23	14
N29	• |	at Tennessee	17	14

1976 2-9-0 (0-6-0)

S11		Oklahoma	3	24
S18	•	Wake Forest	27	24
S25	|	at Alabama	14	42
O2		Tulane	13	24
O9	|	at LSU	20	33
O16	|	at Georgia	0	45
O23	|	Mississippi	3	20
N6	|	at Kentucky	0	14
N13	•	Air Force	34	10
N20		at Cincinnati	7	33
N27	|	Tennessee	10	13

1977 2-9-0 (0-6-0)

S10		at Oklahoma	23	25
S17	•	at Wake Forest	3	0
S24	|	Alabama	12	24
O1		at Tulane	7	36
O8	|	LSU	15	28
O15	|	Georgia	13	24
O22	|	at Mississippi	14	26
N5	|	Kentucky	6	28
N12		at Air Force	28	34
N19	•	Cincinnati	13	9
N26	|	at Tennessee	7	42

1978 2-9-0 (0-6-0)

S16		Arkansas LR	17	48
S23	•	Furman	17	10
S30	|	at Alabama	28	51
O7		Tulane	3	38
O14	|	Auburn	7	49
O21	|	at Georgia	10	31
O28	|	Mississippi	10	35
N4		at Memphis	14	35
N11	|	at Kentucky	2	53
N18	•	Air Force	41	27
D2	|	Tennessee	15	41

GEORGE MacINTYRE
1979-85 (.327) 25-52-1

1979 1-10-0 (0-6-0)

S15		at Indiana	13	44
S22		Citadel	14	27
S29	|	Alabama	3	66
O6		at Tulane	14	42
O13	|	at Auburn	35	52
O20	|	Georgia	10	31
O27	|	at Mississippi	28	63
N3	•	Memphis	13	3
N10	|	Kentucky	10	29
N17		at Air Force	29	30
D1	|	at Tennessee	10	31

1980 2-9-0 (0-6-0)

S13		at Maryland	6	31
S20	|	Mississippi State	14	24
S27	|	at Alabama	0	41
O11		Tulane	21	43
O18	|	at Georgia	0	41
O25	|	Mississippi	14	27
N1	•	at Memphis	14	10
N8	|	at Kentucky	10	31
N15		Miami, Fla.	17	24
N22	•	U.T. Chattanooga	31	29
N29	|	Tennessee	13	51

1981   4-7-0 (1-5-0)

S12	●	Maryland	23	17
S19		at Mississippi State	9	29
S26		Alabama	7	28
O3		at Miami, Fla.	16	48
O10		at Tulane	10	14
O17		Georgia	21	53
O24	●	at Mississippi	27	23
O31	●	Memphis	26	0
N7		Kentucky	10	17
N21	●	U.T. Chattanooga	28	14
N28		at Tennessee	34	38

1982   8-4-0 (4-2-0)

S11	●	at Memphis	24	14
S18		at North Carolina	10	34
S25		at Alabama	21	24
O2	●	Tulane	24	21
O9	●	Florida	31	29
O16		at Georgia	13	27
O23	●	Mississippi	19	10
N6		at Kentucky	23	10
N13		Virginia Tech	45	0
N20	●	U.T. Chattanooga	27	16
N27		Tennessee	28	21

HALL OF FAME BOWL

D31		Air Force	28	36

1983   2-9-0 (0-6-0)

S10		Maryland	14	21
S17		Iowa State	29	26
S24		Alabama	24	44
O1	●	at Tulane	30	17
O8		at Florida	10	29
O15		Georgia	13	20
O22		at Mississippi	14	21
O29		Memphis	7	24
N5		Kentucky	8	17
N12		at Virginia Tech	10	21
N26		at Tennessee	24	34

1984   5-6-0 (2-4-0)

S8	●	Kansas State	26	14
S15		at Maryland	23	14
S22	●	Kansas	41	6
S29	●	at Alabama	30	21
O6		Tulane	23	27
O13		at LSU	27	34
O20		at Georgia	35	62
O27	●	Mississippi	37	20
N10		at Kentucky	18	27
N17		Virginia Tech	3	23
D1		Tennessee	13	29

1985   3-7-1 (1-4-1)

S7	●	U.T. Chattanooga	7	0
S14		at Kansas	16	42
S21		at Iowa State	17	20
S28		Alabama	20	40
O5	●	at Tulane	24	17
O12		LSU	7	49
O19	=	Georgia	13	13
O26		at Mississippi	7	35
N9	●	Kentucky	31	24
N16		Virginia Tech	24	38
N30		at Tennessee	0	30

WATSON BROWN
1986-90 (.162)   10-45

1986   1-10-0 (0-6-0)

S6		at Alabama	10	42
S13		at Maryland	21	35
S20		Tulane	17	35
O4	●	Duke	24	18
O11		Auburn	9	31
O18		at Georgia	16	38
O25		Mississippi	12	28
N1		Memphis	21	22
N8		at Kentucky	22	34
N15		at Virginia Tech	21	29
N29		Tennessee	20	35

1987   4-7-0 (1-5-0)

S12	●	Memphis	27	17
S19		at Duke	31	35
S26		Alabama	23	30
O3		at Tulane	17	27
O10		at Auburn	15	48
O17		Georgia	24	52
O24		at Mississippi	14	42
O31	●	Rutgers	27	13
N7	●	Kentucky	38	29
N21	●	Maryland	34	24
N28		at Tennessee	36	38

1988   3-8-0 (2-5-0)

S10	●	Mississippi State	24	20
S17		Rutgers *ERut*	31	30
S24		at Alabama	10	44
O1		Duke	15	17
O8		at Georgia	22	41
O15	●	Florida	24	9
O22		Mississippi	28	36
N5		at Kentucky	13	14
N12		at Army	19	24
N19		at Memphis	9	28
N26		Tennessee	7	14

1989   1-10-0 (0-7-0)

S2		at Mississippi State	7	42
S23	●	Ohio U.	54	10
S30		Alabama	14	20
O7		at Memphis	10	13
O14		at Florida	11	34
O21		Georgia	16	35
O28		at Mississippi	16	21
N4		at Virginia Tech	0	18
N11		Kentucky	11	15
N18		Tulane	13	37
D2		at Tennessee	10	17

1990   1-10-0 (1-6-0)

S8		at SMU	7	44
S22	●	LSU	24	21
S29		at Alabama	28	59
O6		Syracuse	14	49
O13		at Auburn	6	56
O20		at Georgia	28	39
O27		Mississippi	13	14
N10		at Kentucky	21	28
N17		Army	38	42
N24		Wake Forest	28	56
D1		Tennessee	20	49

GERRY DiNARDO
1991-94 (.409)   18-26

1991   5-6-0 (3-4-0)

S7		at Syracuse	10	37
S14	●	SMU	14	11
S21		at LSU	14	16
S28		Alabama	17	48
O5		at Duke	13	17
O12		Auburn	22	24
O19	●	Georgia	27	25
O26	●	at Mississippi	30	27
N2		at Army	41	10
N9	●	Kentucky	17	7
N30		at Tennessee	0	45

1992   4-7-0 (2-6-0)

S5		at Alabama	8	25
S12	●	Duke	42	37
S19	●	Mississippi	31	9
O3		at Auburn	7	31
O10		Wake Forest	6	40
O17		at Georgia	20	30
O24		South Carolina	17	21
N7		at Kentucky	20	7
N14	●	at Navy	27	7
N21		Florida	21	41
N28		Tennessee	25	29

1993   4-7-0 (1-7-0)

S4	●	at Wake Forest	27	12
S11		Alabama	6	17 †
S18		at Mississippi	7	49
O2		Auburn	10	14
O9	●	Cincinnati	17	7
O16		Georgia	3	41
O23		at South Carolina	0	22
N6	●	Kentucky	12	7
N13	●	Navy	41	7
N20		at Florida	0	52
N27		at Tennessee	14	62

1994   5-6-0 (2-6-0)

S3	●	Wake Forest	35	14
S10		at Alabama	7	17
S17		Mississippi	14	20
O1		Arkansas *LR*	6	42
O8	●	at Cincinnati	34	24
O15	●	at Georgia	43	30
O22		South Carolina	16	19
O29	●	Northern Illinois	17	16
N5	●	at Kentucky	24	6
N19		Florida	7	24
N26		Tennessee	0	65

ROD DOWHOWER
1995-96 (.182)   4-18

1995   2-9-0 (1-7-0)

S2		Alabama	25	33
S16		at Notre Dame	0	41
S23		TCU	3	16
S30		Arkansas	7	35
O14		Georgia	6	17
O21		at South Carolina	14	52
O28		at Mississippi	10	21
N4	●	Kentucky	14	10
N11	●	Louisiana Tech	29	6
N18		at Florida	7	38
N25		at Tennessee	7	12

1996   2-9 (0-8)

S5		Notre Dame	7	14
S14		at Alabama	26	36
S21		Mississippi	9	20
O5		at LSU	0	35
O12		at North Texas	19	7
O19		at Georgia	2	13
O26		South Carolina	0	27
N2	●	UAB	31	15
N9		Florida	21	28
N16		at Kentucky	0	25
N30		Tennessee	7	14

WOODY WIDENHOFER
1997-2001 (.273)   15-40

1997   3-8 (0-8)

A30		North Texas	29	12
S11		Alabama	0	20
S20		TCU	40	16
S27		at Mississippi	3	15
O4		LSU	6	7
O11	●	at Northern Illinois	17	7
O18		Georgia	13	34
O25		at South Carolina	3	35
N8		at Florida	13	21
N15		Kentucky	10	21
N29		at Tennessee	10	17

1998   2-9 (1-7)

S5		at Mississippi State	0	42
S12		Alabama *Mont*	7	32
S19		Mississippi	6	30
O3		at TCU	16	19
O10		Western Michigan	24	27
O17		at Georgia	6	31
O24	●	South Carolina	17	14
O31	●	Duke	36	33
N7		Florida	13	45
N14		at Kentucky	17	55
N28		Tennessee	0	41

1999   5-6 (2-6)

S4		Alabama	17	28
S11	●	Northern Illinois	34	31
S18	●	at Mississippi	37	34
S25	●	at Duke	31	14
O2		Mississippi State	14	42
O9	●	Citadel	58	0
O16		Georgia	17	27
O23	●	at South Carolina	11	10
N6		at Florida	6	13
N13		Kentucky	17	19
N27		at Tennessee	10	38

2000   3-8 (1-7)

S2		Miami, Ohio	30	33
S9		Alabama *Mont*	10	28
S16		Mississippi	7	12
S23	●	Duke	26	7
S30		at Auburn	0	33
O7	●	at Wake Forest	17	10
O14		at Georgia	19	29
O21		South Carolina	14	30
N4		Florida	20	43
N11	●	at Kentucky	24	20
N25		Tennessee	26	28

2001   2-9 (0-8)

A30		Middle Tennessee	28	37
S8		Alabama	9	12
S22	●	Richmond	28	22
S29		Auburn	21	24
O13		Georgia	14	30
O20		at South Carolina	14	46
O27	●	at Duke	42	28
N3		at Florida	13	71
N10		Kentucky	30	56
N24		at Tennessee	0	38
D1		at Mississippi	27	38

BOBBY JOHNSON
2002-Present (.171)   6-29

2002   2-10 (0-8)

A31		at Georgia Tech	3	45
S7	●	Furman	49	18
S14		at Auburn	6	31
S21		at Mississippi	38	45
S28		South Carolina	14	20
O12		Middle Tennessee	20	21
O19		at Georgia	17	48
O26	●	Connecticut	28	24
N2		Alabama	8	30
N9		Florida	17	21
N16		at Kentucky	21	41
N23		Tennessee	0	24

2003   2-10 (1-7)

A30		Mississippi	21	24
S6	●	U.T. Chattanooga	51	6
S13		Auburn	7	45
S20		at TCU	14	30
S27		Georgia Tech	17	24
O4		at Mississippi State	21	30
O11		Navy	27	37
O18		Georgia	8	27
O25		at South Carolina	24	35
N8		at Florida	17	35
N15	●	Kentucky	28	17
N22		at Tennessee	0	48

2004   2-9 (1-7)

S4		South Carolina	6	31
S18		at Mississippi	23	26
S25		at Navy	26	29
O2	●	Mississippi State	31	13
O9		Rutgers	34	37
O16		at Georgia	3	33
O23	●	Eastern Kentucky	19	7
O30		at LSU	7	24
N6		Florida	17	34
N13		at Kentucky	13	14
N20		Tennessee	33	38

VIRGINIA

BY BOB HARIG

NEAR THE END OF HIS LIFE, A decade after his presidency, Thomas Jefferson founded the University of Virginia. He never saw the Cavaliers play a football game, though the program seems to go back almost as far—more than 115 years. Among UVa's memorable players have been "Bullet Bill" Dudley, John Papit, Herman Moore and twins Tiki and Ronde Barber. The 8,000-seat Lambeth Stadium opened in 1913; as football became more popular, Lambeth gave way to Scott Stadium, still in use today. The school didn't experience its first losing season until 1916, but despite their early success, the Cavs didn't play a postseason game until 1984, when they defeated Purdue in the Peach Bowl.

TRADITION Before each home game, a video is produced specifically for the team's entrance onto the field and designed for that week's opponent. Students have been known to dress up for games—men in jacket and tie, women in cocktail dress—although current coach Al Groh has tried to create an atmosphere more about fervor and football. The UVa alum has actively shunned the social tradition he knew when attending the school in the early 1960s, encouraging students to wear orange T-shirts and stand for the entire game.

BEST PLAYER Bill Dudley is widely considered the greatest ever to wear a Virginia uniform. From 1939 to 1941, he ran, passed, kicked, blocked, tackled and intercepted his way to All-America honors. Nicknamed Bullet Bill, Dudley led Virginia to an 8–1 record in 1941 as a 19-year-old senior, having a hand in 206 of the team's 279 points. He led the nation that year in points (134) and finished second nationally in total offense (1,824 yards). In the final game of his career, against North Carolina, Dudley ran for 215 yards, passed for 117, scored three touchdowns, passed for a fourth and made all four extra points to lead the Cavaliers to a 28-7 victory. He became the first Virginia player to have his number (35) retired. He finished fifth in the 1941 Heisman Trophy balloting, joined the Air Force and later went on to a Pro Football Hall of Fame career.

BEST COACH Before George Welsh's arrival in 1982, the Cavaliers had managed just two winning seasons in 29 years. Welsh instilled discipline befitting his military background—he led the nation in passing and total

PROFILE

University of Virginia
Charlottesville, Va.
Founded: 1819
Enrollment: 13,829
Colors: Orange and Blue
Nickname: Cavaliers
Stadium: Harrison Field at Scott Stadium
   Opened in 1931
   Prescription Athletic Turf; 61,500 capacity
First football game: 1888
All-time record: 585–510–48 (.533)
Bowl record: 6–9
Atlantic Coast Conference championships:
2 (shared)
First-round NFL draftees: 12
Website: www.virginiasports.com

THE BEST OF TIMES

From 1987 to 1999, the Cavaliers were consistently ranked, won at least seven games every year, went to 10 bowl games and won two ACC titles.

THE WORST OF TIMES

From 1958 to 1960, the Cavaliers lost 28 consecutive games, then an NCAA record.

CONFERENCE

Virginia joined the Atlantic Coast Conference in 1954, a year after the ACC's inception, and has been a member ever since.

DISTINGUISHED ALUMNI

Edgar Allan Poe; Woodrow Wilson; Katie Couric; Paul Ereng, Olympic gold medalist (track and field) ; Samuel J. Goldwyn Jr., MGM president; Dawn Staley, Olympic gold medalist (basketball); Claudio Renya, captain, U.S. national soccer team

FIGHT SONG

GOOD OLD SONG
That good old song of
Wah-hoo-wah
We'll sing it o'er and o'er
It cheers our hearts and
Warms our blood
To hear them shout and roar.
We come from Old Virginia,
Where all is bright and gay.
Let's all join hands and give a yell
For the dear old UVa
Wah-hoo-wah,
Wah-hoo-wah.
Uni-v, Virginia,
Hoo-rah-ray,
Hoo-rah-ray,
Ray! Ray! U-V-a

Before George Welsh's arrival, the Cavaliers managed just two winning seasons in 29 years.

offense in 1955 at Navy, where he would go on to coach (1973-81) before taking over at Virginia—and changed the prevailing opinion that the Cavaliers could not win in football. He went 134–86–3 from 1982 to 2000 to become the winningest coach in Virginia history, as well as the winningest ACC coach ever. (He would later be surpassed by Bobby Bowden.) Welsh guided the Cavs to two ACC championships and 12 bowl games, including Virginia's first bowl appearance. In 1990, his Cavs were briefly ranked No. 1 in the nation before a midseason loss to Georgia Tech.

BEST TEAM The 1995 UVa squad lost four games but defeated nationally ranked Florida State, dealing the Seminoles their first conference loss (FSU joined the ACC in 1992) and forcing them to share the conference title. The Cavaliers finished 9–4 overall and 7–1 in the ACC behind quarterback Mike Groh, who set a school single-season passing yardage record. The Cavaliers then capped their season with a 34-27 victory over Georgia in the Peach Bowl.

BIGGEST GAME A 33-28 home victory over Florida State in 1995. FSU had won 29 straight conference games since joining the ACC in 1992 and was ranked No. 2 in the nation. It was the first-ever Thursday night game in Charlottesville and was played before a national television audience and 44,300 fans, who sweated out FSU's final drive from its own 20-yard line with 1:37 to play. Danny Kanell led FSU to the UVa 6-yard line with four seconds remaining, but the Cavaliers stopped FSU tailback Warrick Dunn—who had taken a direct snap from center—inches from the goal line to preserve the victory.

BIGGEST UPSET Virginia's 20-7 victory over Clemson at home in 1990 not only snapped a 29-game losing streak (the nation's longest) against the Tigers, it also was the Cavs' first-ever victory over Clemson—or any other Top 10 team.

HEARTBREAKER Virginia, with All-America wide receiver Herman Moore leading the offensive attack, came into its 1990 homecoming game in an unusual position: undefeated

RECORDS

RUSHING YARDS

	GAME	
224	John Papit vs. Washington and Lee, Oct. 16, 1948 (16 att.)	
	SEASON	
1,798	Thomas Jones, 1999 (334 att.)	
	CAREER	
3,998	Thomas Jones, 1996-99 (809 att.)	

PASSING YARDS

	GAME	
393	Matt Schaub vs. NC State, Nov. 1, 2003 (41 of 55)	
	SEASON	
2,976	Matt Schaub, 2002 (288 of 418)	
	CAREER	
7,502	Matt Schaub, 2000-03 (716 of 1,069)	

RECEIVING YARDS

	GAME	
241	Ken Shelton vs. William & Mary, Sept. 21, 1974 (9 rec.)	
	SEASON	
1,190	Herman Moore, 1990 (54 rec.)	
	CAREER	
2,978	Billy McMullen, 1999-2002 (210 rec.)	

POINTS

	GAME	
36	Gene Mayer vs. Richmond, Oct. 9, 1915 (5 TDs, 6 PATs)	
	SEASON	
134	Bill Dudley, 1941 (18 TDs, 23 PATs, 1 FG)	
	CAREER	
293	Gene Mayer, 1912-15 (46 TDs, 17 PATs)	

CONSENSUS ALL-AMERICANS

1915	Eugene Mayer, B
1941	Bill Dudley, B
1985	Jim Dombrowski, OL
1990	Herman Moore, WR
1992	Chris Slade, DL
1993	Mark Dixon, OL
1998	Anthony Poindexter, DB
1999	Thomas Jones, RB
2004	Heath Miller, TE
2004	Elton Brown, OL

and ranked No. 1 in the nation. It was the first time in school history the Cavaliers had attained that spot, and it didn't last long. Virginia took a 28-14 halftime lead over unbeaten Georgia Tech in the nationally televised ACC showdown, but the Yellow Jackets fought back to tie, then won on a 37-yard field goal by Scott Sisson with seven seconds remaining. That spelled the difference in Tech's 41-38 win, and proved decisive for both teams. Georgia Tech won out, earning a share of the national championship, while the devastated Cavaliers won just once more all season, finishing the year with an 8–4 record.

DISPUTE Virginia's 28-27 victory over rival Virginia Tech in 1974 came when the Hokies failed to score on a two-point conversion with no time on the clock. Tech coach Jimmy Sharpe decided to try for two, and quarterback Bruce Arians seemingly was stopped at the goal line on an option play. Or was he? Arians contended that he had scored, as did many on the sideline. The officials did not agree, however, and Virginia emerged with the win.

STADIUM Scott Stadium opened in 1931 with a capacity of nearly 22,000. It was the gift of Frederic William Scott and Elisabeth Strother Scott, and was dedicated in the memory of their parents, Frederic Robert Scott and Frances Branch Scott. The stadium underwent a major renovation in 1974, including the installation of new aluminum seating and artificial turf. In 1980, another 12,000 seats were added, and three years later, a permanent lighting system was installed. By 2000, seating capacity had increased to 61,500.

RIVAL Virginia and Virginia Tech are the only two Division I-A schools in the state. The rivalry promises to only grow more intense, as the schools are now conference rivals as well. The series dates to 1895 and has been played every year since 1923, save for two years(1943-44) during World War II and a three-year break (1967-1969).

NICKNAME The school has had a wide, and sometimes confusing, array of nicknames. The most prominent and widely accepted are Cavaliers, Wahoos and Hoos. Virginia athletic teams have also been called V-men, Virginians and Old Dominion. Cavaliers is the nickname most used

by the media, while students and fans frequently go with Wahoos and Hoos. Washington and Lee baseball fans first dubbed Virginia players Wahoos during a fierce rivalry in the 1890s, according to a school legend. By 1940, Wahoos was in general use as a reference to students or events relating to them. In 1923, the student newspaper, *College Topics*, ran a contest to choose the official alma mater and fight song. "Virginia, Hail All Hail" became the alma mater, while "The Cavalier Song" won best fight song. Although both songs failed to become part of university tradition, "The Cavalier Song" inspired the school's primary nickname.

> *Scott Stadium opened in 1931 seating 22,000, but has nearly tripled in size over the past 70 years.*

MASCOT A costumed Cavalier with a large character head debuted during the 1984 football season and has remained the school's official mascot. The Cavalier performs with the UVa cheerleaders at all football and basketball games, as well as at other events. The Cavalier is selected from the student body through open tryouts. The school's previous mascot, a barefaced horseback rider in Cavalier garb, stopped appearing when turf was installed at Scott Stadium in 1974. The mounted Cavalier made his return at the Florida Citrus Bowl at the end of the 1989 season. Since then, he leads the team onto the field at the start of all home games.

UNIFORMS Orange and blue were adopted as Virginia's official athletic colors in 1888. UVa athletic teams had previously worn silver gray and cardinal red, but the colors didn't stand out well on muddy football fields, prompting a student movement to change them. Virginia's navy-blue helmet, introduced in 1994, has crossed sabers beneath a strong "V." At the same time, Virginia's home jerseys went from orange to navy blue.

LORE On Sept. 30, 1944, Virginia held NC State to zero first downs in a driving rainstorm—and lost 13-0. The Wolfpack did it by recovering two fourth-quarter Virginia fumbles in the end zone for touchdowns at Foreman Field in Norfolk, Va. It was Virginia's only loss in a 6–1–2 season.

QUOTE "Will you stick your face in the fan today?"
— A quote in the locker room popularized by Al Groh

VIRGINIA ANNUAL STATISTICAL LEADERS

YR	RUSHING	YDS	ATT	AVG	PASSING	ATT	CMP	PCT	YDS	RECEIVING	REC	YDS	AVG
1940	Bill Dudley	469	106	4.4	Bill Dudley	140	67	.48	722	Eddie Bryant	30	222	7.4
1941	Bill Dudley	968	155	6.2	Bill Dudley	107	57	.53	856	Bill Preston	22	377	17.1
1942	Herb Munhall	117	46	2.5	Tabb Gillette	144	82	.57	920	Ed Kreich	10	140	14.0
1943		NA	NA	NA		NA	NA	NA	NA		NA	NA	NA
1944	John Duda	716	125	5.7	Lucien Burnett	37	14	.38	133	Ward Speer	9	70	7.8
1945		NA	NA	NA		NA	NA	NA	NA		NA	NA	NA
1946	Ray Brown	387	60	6.5	Ray Brown	35	17	.49	301	Sam Fray	10	161	16.1
1947	Grover Jones	446	89	5.0	Joe McCary	35	19	.54	299	Ed Bessell	10	226	22.6
1948	John Papit	885	134	6.6	Joe McCary	44	23	.52	300	Carlton Elliott	9	76	8.4
1949	John Papit	1,214	197	6.2	Whitey Michels	79	36	.46	529	Myron Mausteller	12	177	14.8
1950	John Papit	949	167	5.7	Rufus Barkley	111	59	.53	911	Gene Schroeder	33	552	16.7
1951	Bobby Pate	440	100	4.4	Rufus Barkley	80	43	.54	468	Bill Chisolm	21	241	11.5
1952	Gerry Furst	699	115	6.1	Charlie Harding	115	48	.42	686	Bobby Pate/Bob Tata	9	118	13.1
1953	Henry Strempek	315	93	3.4	Rives Bailey	88	41	.47	517	Ray Quillen	12	117	9.8
1954	Herb Hartwell	390	93	4.2	Rives Bailey	63	23	.37	309	Herb Hartwell	8	104	13.0
1955	Jim Bakhtiar	733	158	4.6	Whitey Clarke	81	37	.46	372	Jesse Hagy	17	173	10.2
1956	Jim Bakhtiar	879	203	4.3	Nelson Yarbrough	91	43	.47	626	Fred Polzer	24	231	9.6
1957	Jim Bakhtiar	822	194	4.2	Reece Whitley	99	42	.42	501	Fred Polzer	25	232	9.3
1958	Tom Gravins	258	56	4.6	Sandy Dempsey	152	74	.49	697	Sonny Randle	47	642	13.7
1959	Tom Gravins	359	86	4.2	Stan Fischer	119	58	.49	603	Brerry Jones	20	207	10.4
1960	Fred Shepherd	529	126	4.2	Gary Cuozzo	103	40	.39	397	Joe Kehoe	34	378	11.1
1961	Doug Thomson	294	70	4.2	Gary Cuozzo	93	42	.45	382	Tony Ulehla	9	85	9.4
1962	Ted Rzempoluch	347	77	4.5	Gary Cuozzo	181	98	.54	1,136	Terry Sieg	27	281	10.4
1963	John Pincavage	256	61	4.2	Tom Hodges	90	39	.43	440	John Pincavage	15	136	9.1
1964	Bob Davis	427	84	5.1	Bob Davis	156	80	.51	1,054	John Pincavage	30	331	11.0
1965	Carroll Jarvis	385	106	3.6	Tom Hodges	196	103	.53	1,299	John Pincavage	44	566	12.9
1966	Frank Quayle	727	162	4.5	Bob Davis	222	107	.48	1,461	Ed Carrington	32	411	12.8
1967	Jeff Anderson	774	183	4.2	Gene Arnette	147	73	.50	984	Frank Quayle	25	299	12.0
1968	Frank Quayle	1,213	175	6.9	Gene Arnette	206	106	.51	1,463	Frank Quayle	30	426	14.2
1969	Gary Helman	851	229	3.7	Danny Fassio	150	67	.45	828	Bob Bischoff	35	498	14.2
1970	Gary Helman	743	172	4.3	Bill Troup	184	93	.51	1,289	Dave Sullivan	37	523	14.1
1971	Kent Merritt	828	189	4.4	Harrison Davis	176	63	.36	806	Bill Davis	49	617	12.6
1972	Kent Merritt	575	118	4.9	George Allen	115	55	.48	650	Dave Sullivan	51	662	13.0
1973	Billy Copeland	700	130	5.4	Scott Gardner	234	99	.42	1,687	Harrison Davis	44	773	17.6
1974	Joe Sroba	632	167	3.8	Scott Gardner	195	110	.56	1,344	Tom Fadden	34	416	12.2
1975	David Sloan	848	176	4.8	Scott Gardner	272	133	.49	1,547	Tom Fadden	48	620	12.9
1976	Raymond Keys	505	120	4.2	Andy Hitt	220	98	.45	1,222	Jim Wicks	29	297	10.2
1977	Bill Harris	339	119	2.8	Chip Mark	124	65	.52	720	Jim Theiling	16	170	10.6
1978	Tommy Vigorito	800	168	4.8	Chip Mark	71	37	.52	458	Jim Theiling	16	239	14.9
1979	Tommy Vigorito	1,045	184	5.7	Todd Kirtley	178	88	.49	1,159	Mike Newhall	20	196	9.8
1980	Tommy Vigorito	742	201	3.7	Todd Kirtley	183	94	.51	1,156	Tommy Vigorito	29	239	8.2
1981	Derek Jenkins	412	118	3.5	Gordie Whitehead	178	95	.53	1,116	Kevin Riccio	32	351	11.0
1982	Antonio Rice	764	196	3.9	Wayne Schuchts	176	72	.41	1,243	Henry Johnson	21	377	18.0
1983	Howard Petty	835	169	4.9	Wayne Schuchts	261	129	.49	1,881	Billy Smith	42	777	18.5
1984	Howard Petty	811	170	4.8	Don Majkowski	168	83	.49	1,235	Geno Zimmerlink	22	350	15.9
1985	Barry Word	1,224	207	5.9	Don Majkowski	199	95	.48	1,233	Geno Zimmerlink	24	412	17.2
1986	Durwin Greggs	404	83	4.9	Don Majkowski	199	104	.52	1,375	Keith Mattioli	44	717	16.3
1987	Marcus Wilson	692	172	4.0	Scott Secules	296	174	.59	2,311	John Ford	48	855	17.8
1988	Marcus Wilson	429	89	4.8	Shawn Moore	282	141	.50	2,158	John Ford	29	444	15.3
1989	Marcus Wilson	1,098	223	4.9	Shawn Moore	221	125	.57	2,078	Bruce McGonnigal	42	634	15.1
1990	Terry Kirby	1,020	165	6.2	Shawn Moore	241	144	.60	2,262	Herman Moore	54	1,190	22.0
1991	Terry Kirby	887	164	5.4	Matt Blundin	224	135	.60	1,902	Terry Kirby	37	406	11.0
1992	Terry Kirby	1,130	175	6.5	Bobby Goodman	232	130	.56	1,707	Terry Kirby	28	241	8.6
1993	Jerrod Washington	871	162	5.4	Symmion Willis	276	165	.60	2,347	Patrick Jeffers	32	580	18.1
1994	Kevin Brooks	741	173	4.3	Mike Groh	216	138	.64	1,711	Tyrone Davis	38	691	18.2
1995	Tiki Barber	1,397	265	5.3	Mike Groh	330	182	.55	2,510	Patrick Jeffers	34	517	15.2
1996	Tiki Barber	1,360	250	5.4	Tim Sherman	203	102	.50	1,572	Germane Crowell	33	687	20.8
1997	Thomas Jones	692	201	3.4	Aaron Brooks	270	164	.61	2,282	Germane Crowell	53	969	18.3
1998	Thomas Jones	1,303	238	5.5	Aaron Brooks	290	156	.54	2,319	Terrence Wilkins	45	811	18.0
1999	Thomas Jones	1,798	334	5.4	Dan Ellis	258	156	.60	2,050	Billy McMullen	28	483	17.3
2000	Antwoine Womack	1,028	210	4.9	Dan Ellis	210	116	.55	1,642	Billy McMullen	30	541	18.0
2001	Alvin Pearman	371	88	4.2	Matt Schaub	240	140	.58	1,524	Billy McMullen	83	1,060	12.8
2002	Wali Lundy	826	196	4.2	Matt Schaub	418	288	.69	2,976	Billy McMullen	69	894	13.0
2003	Wali Lundy	929	227	4.1	Matt Schaub	403	281	.70	2,952	Heath Miller	70	835	11.9
2004	Alvin Pearman	1,037	195	5.3	Marques Hagans	261	164	.63	2,024	Heath Miller	41	541	13.2

Receiving leaders by receptions
The NCAA began including postseason stats in 2002

THE SCHOOLS

VIRGINIA ALL-TIME SCORES

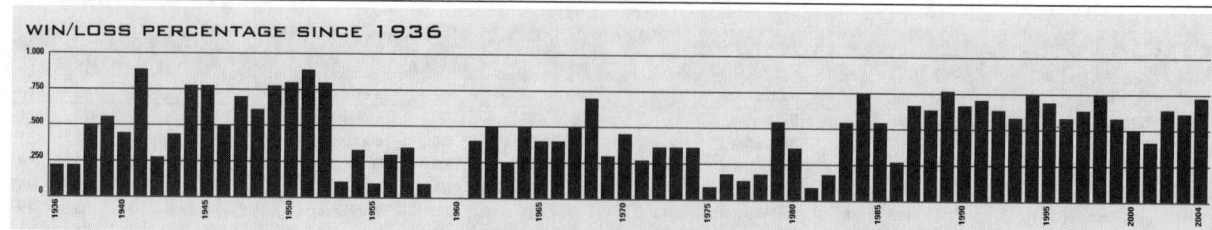

WIN/LOSS PERCENTAGE SINCE 1936

NO HEAD COACH

1888　　2-1-0
N20	●	Pantops	20	0
N24	●	Episcopal HS	16	0
D8		Johns Hopkins	0	26

1889　　4-2-0
O8	●	Pantops	44	0
O15	●	Georgetown	32	0
O22	●	Johns Hopkins	58	0
D2		Lehigh	12	24
D7		at Navy	12	22 *
D9	●	Wake Forest *RICH*	46	4

1890　　5-2-0
O31		Pennsylvania *UNK*	0	72
N1		Princeton *BALT*	0	115
N8	●	Randolph Macon	136	0
N10	●	Dickinson *DC*	12	0
N15	●	at Wash. & Lee	46	0
N21	●	Lafayette	20	6
N29	●	Duke *RICH*	10	4

1891　　2-1-2
N14	●	St. John's	34	0
N16	=	Schuylkill Navy	16	16
N20	=	Lafayette	6	6
N23	●	Princeton J.V.	12	0
N28		Duke *RICH*	0	20

1892　　3-2-1
O11		Pennsylvania	0	32
O22	●	North Carolina	30	18
O29	●	Sewanee *RICH*	30	0
U	=	Georgetown	4	4
N24	●	Duke *ATL*	46	4
N26		North Carolina *ATL*	0	26

JOHN POE
1893-94 (.762)　　16-5

1893　　8-3-0
O7	●	Richmond	34	4
O14		Penn State	0	6
O19	●	Washington YMCA	20	0
O21		at Navy	0	28
O28	●	Johns Hopkins	28	12
N4		Georgetown	24	28
N11	●	Duke *LYN*	30	0
N18	●	at Georgetown	58	0
N22	●	at Navy	12	0
N25	●	at VMI	22	0
N30	●	North Carolina *RICH*	16	0

1894　　8-2-0
O2	●	Richmond	48	0
O6	●	Baltimore City Coll.	36	0
O13		Princeton *BALT*	0	12
O18	●	at Richmond	28	0
O20	●	Johns Hopkins	76	0
O26		Pennsylvania *DC*	6	14
N3	●	Rutgers	20	0
N13	●	Fort Monroe	102	0
N20	●	West Philadelphia AC	64	0
N22	●	North Carolina *RICH*	34	0

HARRY MACKEY
1895 (.818)　　9-2

1895　　9-2-0
O2	●	Miller School	30	0
O5	●	Virginia Tech	38	0
O9		Princeton *BALT*	0	36
O12	●	Maryland AC	20	0
O19		at Pennsylvania	0	54
O26	●	Gallaudet	16	6
O29	●	Roanoke Coll.	14	0
N11	●	St. Albans	14	4
N12	●	Richmond	62	0
N16	●	Vanderbilt *ATL*	6	4
N28	●	North Carolina *RICH*	6	0

MARTIN BERGEN
1896-97 (.725)　　13-4-3

1896　　7-2-2
O3	=	Hampton AC	10	10
O10	●	Miller School	26	2
O14		at Pennsylvania	0	20
O17	●	St.Johns	48	0
O21		at Princeton	0	48
O31	●	Virginia Tech	44	0
N2	●	St. Albans	6	0
N11	●	VMI *LYN*	46	0
N14	=	at Hampton AC	6	6
N21	●	Gallaudet	6	0
N26	●	North Carolina *RICH*	46	0

1897　　6-2-1
O2	●	Franklin & Marshall	38	0
U	●	St. Albans	14	0
O13		at Pennsylvania	0	42
O30	●	at Georgia	17	4
U	●	Gallaudet	20	4
N6		at Navy	0	4
N18	●	George Washington	10	0
N22	●	North Carolina *RICH*	12	0
D6	=	at Vanderbilt	0	0

JOSEPH MASSIE
1898 (.546)　　6-5

1898　　6-5-0
O1	●	St. Albans	16	0
O12		at Pennsylvania	0	34 *
O15	●	Gallaudet	16	0
O29	●	George Washington	47	0
N2		at Princeton	0	12
N5	●	Maryland Medical	6	0
N8	●	at Georgetown	12	0
N12	●	Vanderbilt	18	0
N14		West Virginia *CHWV*	0	6
N19		Navy	0	6
N24		North Carolina *RICH*	2	6

ARCHIE HOXTON
1899-1900 (.658)　　11-5-3

1899　　4-3-2
S30	●	St.Albans	10	0
O7	●	Episcopal HS	33	6
O11		at Pennsylvania	6	33
O14		Maryland Medical	0	0
O21	●	Gallaudet *UNK*	5	11
N4		Michigan *DET*	0	38
N11	●	Virginia Tech	28	0
N18	=	at Georgetown	0	0
N30	●	Lehigh *RICH*	10	0

1900　　7-2-1
O5	●	Wash. & Lee	28	0
O10	●	Richmond	51	0
O13	●	Carlisle *DC*	2	17
O20	●	Johns Hopkins	20	0
O24		at VMI	0	0
N10	●	Gallaudet	34	0
N14	●	Virginia Tech	17	5
N17		at Georgetown	0	10
N24	●	North Carolina *NOR*	17	0
N29	●	Sewanee *RICH*	17	5

WESLEY ABBOTT
1901 (.800)　　8-2

1901　　8-2-0
O2	●	Wash. & Lee	28	0
O5	●	Roanoke Coll.	68	0
O9	●	St. Albans	39	0
O12	●	Gallaudet	24	0
O16		at Pennsylvania	5	20
O26	●	at Virginia Tech	16	0
N11	●	VMI *LYN*	28	0
N16		at Georgetown	16	17
N23	●	North Carolina *NOR*	23	6
N28	●	Sewanee *RICH*	23	5

JOHN DE SAULLES
1902 (.850)　　8-1-1

1902　　8-1-1
S27	●	Wash.& Lee	16	0
O4	●	St. Albans	15	0
O11	●	at Nashville	27	0
O18	●	at Transylvania, Ky	12	0
O25	●	St.Johns	22	0
N1	●	Davidson	35	0
N8		Lehigh *DC*	6	34
N15	●	Virginia Tech	6	0
N22	●	Carlisle *NOR*	6	5
N27	=	North Carolina *RICH*	12	12

GRESHAM POE
1903 (.750)　　7-2-1

1903　　7-2-1
S26	●	St. Albans	16	0
O3	●	Wash. & Lee	16	0
O10	●	Randolph Macon	37	0
O14		at Navy	5	6
O21	●	Transylvania, Ky	6	0
O24	●	Virginia Tech *RICH*	21	0
N7	●	Davidson *CHAR*	22	0
N14	●	St. John's	48	6
N21	=	Carlisle *NOR*	6	6
N25		North Carolina *RICH*	0	16

FOSTER SANFORD
1904 (.667)　　6-3

1904　　6-3-0
S24	●	Randolph Macon	16	0
S28	●	Wash. & Lee	17	0
O1		at Pennsylvania	0	24
O15	●	VMI	17	0
O22	●	North Carolina St.	5	0
N5	●	Virginia Tech *RICH*	5	0
N9		Carlisle *NOR*	6	14
N12		Navy	0	5
N24	●	North Carolina *RICH*	12	11

WILLIAM COLE
1905-06 (.650)　　12-6-2

1905　　5-4-0
S23	●	Randolph Macon	59	0
S30	●	St.Johns	30	5
O7	●	North Carolina St.	10	0
O14		Carlisle *RICH*	0	12
O21	●	Bucknell *RICH*	15	11
N4		Virginia Tech	0	11
N11	●	George Wash. *DC*	55	0
N18		at Navy	0	22
N30		North Carolina *NOR*	0	17

1906　　7-2-2
S29	●	St. John's	11	0
O3	●	Richmond	22	0
O6	=	North Carolina St.	0	0
O10	●	Randolph Macon	38	0
O13	●	Hampden-Syd.	38	5
O20	●	VMI	4	0
O27	●	Richmond	12	6
N3		Bucknell *RICH*	5	12
N10	●	at Georgetown	12	0
N17	=	at George Washington	0	0
N29		Carlisle *NOR*	17	18

HAMMOND JOHNSON
1907 (.650)　　6-3-1

1907　　6-3-1
S28	=	Davidson	5	5
O2	●	Richmond	38	0
O9	●	St. John's	22	4
O12	●	Gallaudet	40	0
O19	=	VMI	18	17
O26	●	North Carolina *RICH*	9	4
N2		Sewanee *NOR*	0	12
N9		Wash. & Lee	5	6
N16	●	at Georgetown	28	6
N23		North Carolina St. *NOR*	4	10

MERRITT COOKE, JR.
1908 (.938)　　7-0-1

1908　　7-0-1
O3	●	William & Mary	11	0
O10	●	St. John's	18	9
O17	=	Sewanee *NOR*	0	0
O24	●	Davidson	12	0
N7	●	Randolph Macon	22	0
N14	●	North Carolina St. *NOR*	6	0
N21	●	at Georgetown	6	0
N26	●	North Carolina *RICH*	31	0

JOHN NEFF
1909 (.875)　　7-1

1909　　7-1-0
S18	●	William & Mary	30	0
S25	●	Hampden-Sydney	37	0
O2	●	Davidson	11	0
O9	●	St. John's	12	0
O16		Lehigh *NOR*	7	11
O23	●	at Navy	5	0
O30	●	VMI	32	0
N6	●	at Georgetown	21	0

CHARLES CRAWFORD
1910 (.750)　　6-2

1910　　6-2-0
O1	●	William & Mary	10	0
O8	●	Randolph Macon	17	0
O15	●	Roanoke Coll.	21	0
O22	●	St. John's	29	0
O29	●	VMI	28	0
N5		Carlisle *DC*	5	22
N12		at Georgetown	0	15
N24	●	North Carolina *RICH*	7	0

KEMPER YANCEY
1911 (.800)　　8-2

1911　　8-2-0
S23	●	Hampden-Sydney	23	0
S30	●	William & Mary	81	0
O7	●	Randolph Macon	31	0
O14		Swarthmore	8	9
O21	●	St. John's	6	0
O28	●	VMI	22	6
N2	●	Wake Forest	29	6
N11	●	at Johns Hopkins	34	0
N18		at Georgetown	0	9
N30	●	North Carolina *RICH*	28	0

JOHN "SPEED" ELLIOTT
1912 (.667)   6-3

1912   6-3-0
S28	• William & Mary	60	0
O5	• Randolph Macon	45	0
O12	• Hampden-Sydney	10	0
O14	• South Carolina	19	0
O19	• VMI	0	19
O26	• Norfolk Blues	7	0
N2	at Vanderbilt	0	13
N16	at Georgetown	13	16
N26	North Carolina RICH	66	0

RICE WARREN
1913, '20-21 (.692)   17-7-2

1913   7-1-0
S27	• Randolph Macon	49	0
O4	• South Carolina	54	0
O11	• Hampden-Sydney	53	0
O18	• VMI	38	7
O25	• Georgia Atl	13	6
N1	• Vanderbilt	34	0
N15	at Georgetown	7	8
N27	• North Carolina RICH	26	7

JOSEPH WOOD
1914 (.889)   8-1

1914   8-1-0
S26	• Randolph Macon	39	0
O3	at Yale	0	21
O10	• Richmond	62	0
O17	• South Carolina	49	7
O24	• Georgia	28	0
O31	at Vanderbilt	20	7
N7	• St. John's	88	0
N14	at Swarthmore	47	0
N26	North Carolina RICH	20	3

HARRY VARNER
1915 (.889)   8-1

1915   8-1-0
S25	• Randolph Macon	20	0
O2	at Yale	10	0
O9	• Richmond	74	0
O16	at Harvard	0	9
O23	at Georgia	9	7
O30	• VMI	44	0
N6	• Vanderbilt	35	10
N13	at South Carolina	13	0
N25	• North Carolina RICH	14	0

PEYTON EVANS
1916 (.444)   4-5

1916   4-5-0
S30	• Davidson	14	0
O7	at Yale	3	61
O14	• Richmond	21	0
O21	Georgia	7	13
O28	at Vanderbilt	6	27
N4	at Harvard	0	51
N11	• South Carolina	35	6
N18	• VMI	20	7
N30	North Carolina RICH	0	7

1917-1918
NO TEAM WWI

HARRIS COLEMAN
1919 (.333)   2-5-2

1919   2-5-2
S27	• Randolph Macon	12	2
O4	• Richmond	0	0
O11	Maryland	0	13
O18	• VMI	7	0
O25	at Harvard	0	47
N1	Centre	7	49
N7	= at Georgia	7	7
N15	Vanderbilt	6	10
N27	at North Carolina	0	6

RICE WARREN

1920   5-2-2
S25	• William & Mary	27	0
O2	• Randolph Macon	65	0
O9	VMI	6	22
O16	at Johns Hopkins	14	0
O23	at Rutgers	7	0
O30	at Harvard	0	24
N6	= Georgia	0	0
N20	• at Vanderbilt	7	7
N25	• North Carolina	14	0

1921-1935
SOUTHERN CONFERENCE

1921   5-4-0 (0-2-0)
S24	• Davidson	28	0
O1	• George Washington	28	0
O8	• Richmond	14	0
O15	at VMI	14	7
O22	• Johns Hopkins	14	7
O29	at Princeton	0	34
N6	at Georgia	0	21
N12	West Virginia	0	7
N24	at North Carolina	3	7

THOMAS CAMPBELL
1922 (.500)   4-4-1

1922   4-4-1 (1-1-1)
S30	• George Washington	34	0
O7	at Princeton	0	5
O14	• Richmond	14	6
O21	VMI	0	14
O28	• at Johns Hopkins	19	0
N4	• Wash. & Lee	22	6
N11	= Georgia	6	6
N18	at West Virginia	0	13
N30	North Carolina	7	10

EARLE NEALE
1923-28 (.555)   28-22-5

1923   3-5-1 (0-3-1)
S29	Furman	10	13
O6	• Richmond	9	0
O13	• St. John's	32	7
O20	VMI	0	35
O27	• Duke	33	0
N3	at Wash. & Lee	0	7
N10	at Georgia	0	13
N17	Virginia Tech	3	6
N29	= at North Carolina	0	0

1924   5-4-0 (3-2-0)
S27	• Hampden-Sydney	13	9
O4	at Harvard	0	14
O11	• Randolph Macon	26	6
O18	VMI	13	0
O25	at Pennsylvania	0	27
N1	• Wash. & Lee	7	20
N8	Georgia	0	7
N15	• at Virginia Tech	6	0
N27	• North Carolina	7	0

1925   7-1-1 (4-1-1)
S26	• Hampden-Sydney	40	0
O3	• at Georgia	7	6
O10	• Richmond	19	0
O17	• VMI	18	10
O24	Maryland	6	0
N7	• at Wash. & Lee	0	12
N14	• Virginia Tech	10	0
N21	• Randolph Macon	41	0
N26	= at North Carolina	3	3

1926   6-2-2 (4-2-1)
S25	= Hampden-Sydney	0	0
O2	Georgia	7	27 *
O9	• Lynchburg	38	0
O16	• at VMI	14	7
O23	• at Virginia Tech	0	6
O30	• at South Carolina	6	0
N6	• Wash. & Lee	30	7
N13	= at Maryland	6	6
N20	• Randolph Macon	57	0
N23	North Carolina	3	0

1927   5-4-0 (4-4-0)
S24	• Hampden-Sydney	38	6
O1	at Georgia	0	32
O8	South Carolina	12	13
O15	• VMI	13	8
O22	Virginia Tech	7	0
O29	at Tennessee	0	42
N5	• at Wash. & Lee	13	7
N12	• Maryland	21	0
N24	at North Carolina	13	14

1928   2-6-1 (1-6-0)
S29	• Randolph Macon	66	0
O6	South Carolina	13	24
O13	= at Princeton	0	0
O20	at VMI	0	9
O27	at Vanderbilt	0	34
N3	• Wash. & Lee	20	13
N10	at Virginia Tech	0	20
N17	at Maryland	2	18
N29	North Carolina	20	24

EARL ABELL
1929-30 (.474)   8-9-2

1929   4-3-2 (1-3-2)
S28	• Randolph Macon	27	6
O5	at South Carolina	6	0
O12	Swarthmore	12	7
O19	VMI	7	20
O26	St. John's	32	7
N2	at Maryland	13	13
N9	Virginia Tech	12	32
N16	at Wash. & Lee	13	13
N28	North Carolina	7	41

1930   4-6-0 (2-5-0)
S20	• Roanoke Coll.	37	0
S27	• Randolph Macon	48	0
O4	at Duke	0	32
O11	at Pennsylvania	6	40
O18	at VMI	13	0
O25	at Kentucky	0	47
N1	Maryland	6	14
N8	at Virginia Tech	13	31 *
N15	• Wash. & Lee	21	7
N27	North Carolina	0	41

FRED DAWSON
1931-33 (.345)   8-17-4

1931   1-7-2 (0-5-1)
S19	• Roanoke Coll.	18	0
S26	= Randolph Macon	7	7
O3	at Maryland	6	7
O10	Sewanee	0	3
O17	VMI	3	18
O24	at Wash. & Lee	0	18
O31	at Harvard	0	19
N7	at Columbia	0	27
N14	= Virginia Tech	0	0
N26	at North Carolina	6	13

1932   5-4-0 (2-3-0)
S24	• Hampden-Sydney	32	0
O1	Maryland	7	6
O8	Roanoke Coll.	12	0
O15	at Columbia	6	22
O22	at VMI	4	6
O29	• St. John's	20	6
N5	Wash. & Lee	0	7
N12	at Virginia Tech	0	13
N24	• North Carolina	14	7

1933   2-6-2 (1-3-1)
S23	= Hampden-Sydney	7	7
S30	• Randolph Macon	39	0
O7	at Ohio State	0	75
O14	at Columbia	6	15
O21	at Navy	7	13
O28	VMI	12	13
N4	• Maryland	6	0
N11	• at Wash. & Lee	0	6
N18	= Virginia Tech	6	6
N30	at North Carolina	0	14

GUS TEBELL
1934-36 (.286)   6-18-4

1934   3-6-0 (1-4-0)
S29	• Hampden-Sydney	8	0
O6	Navy DC	6	21
O13	• St. John's	27	6
O20	at Dartmouth	0	27
O27	• at VMI	17	13
N3	at Maryland	0	20
N10	Wash. & Lee	0	20
N17	at Virginia Tech	6	19
N24	North Carolina	6	25

1935   1-5-4 (0-3-2)
S21	= at William & Mary	0	0
S28	• Hampden-Sydney	7	12
O5	Davidson	0	0
O10	at Navy	7	26
O19	• St. John's	18	0
O26	VMI	0	0
N2	Maryland	7	14
N9	at Wash. & Lee	0	20
N16	= Virginia Tech	0	0
N28	at North Carolina	0	61

1936-1953
INDEPENDENT

1936   2-7-0
S26	• Hampden-Sydney	26	10
O3	William & Mary Nor	7	0
O10	at Navy	14	35
O17	Maryland	0	21
O24	• Wash. & Lee	0	13
O31	at VMI	6	12
N7	at Harvard	0	65
N14	at Virginia Tech	6	7
N26	North Carolina	14	59

FRANK MURRAY
1937-45 (.544)   41-34-5

1937   2-7-0
S25	• Hampden-Sydney	13	7
O2	at Princeton	0	26
O9	at Navy	13	40
O16	Maryland	0	3
O23	VMI	7	26
O30	• William & Mary	6	0
N6	at Wash. & Lee	6	13
N13	Virginia Tech	7	14
N27	at North Carolina	0	40

1938   4-4-1
S24	= VMI	12	12
O1	• Wash. & Lee	13	0
O8	at Navy	0	33
O15	• at Virginia Tech	14	6
O22	• at Maryland	27	19
O29	• William & Mary	34	0
N5	at Columbia	0	39
N12	at Harvard	13	40
N24	North Carolina	0	20

1939   5-4-0
S23	• Hampden-Sydney	26	0
O7	at Navy	12	14
O14	Maryland	12	7
O21	at VMI	13	16
O28	• William & Mary Nor	26	6
N4	Chicago	47	0
N10	• at Wash. & Lee	7	0
N18	Virginia Tech	0	13
N30	at North Carolina	0	19

1940   4-5-0
S28	• Lehigh	32	0
O5	• at Yale	19	14
O12	• at Maryland	19	6
O19	VMI	0	7
O26	• at William & Mary	6	13
N2	Virginia Tech Nor	0	6
N9	• Wash. & Lee	20	6
N16	at Tennessee	14	41
N23	North Carolina	7	10

1941   8-1-0
S20	• Hampden-Sydney	41	0
S27	• Lafayette	25	0
O4	at Yale	19	21
O11	• Richmond	44	0
O18	• at VMI	27	7
N1	Virginia Tech Nor	34	0
N8	• Wash. & Lee	27	7
N15	• Lehigh	34	0
N20	• at North Carolina	28	7

1942   2-6-1
S26	• Hampden-Sydney	12	0
O3	at Navy	0	35
O10	VMI	18	38
O17	= at Richmond	7	7
O24	at Lafayette	13	19
O31	Virginia Tech Nor	14	20
N7	• at Wash. & Lee	34	7
N14	Maryland	12	7
N21	North Carolina	13	28

1943   3-4-1
S25	= Richmond Air Base	7	7
O2	• West Virginia ChWV	6	0
O9	Richmond	7	16
O16	at Newport News	6	7
O30	• at VMI	34	0
N6	• Maryland	39	0
N13	at Duke	0	49
N27	at North Carolina	7	54

960 VIRGINIA

THE SCHOOLS

1944 6-1-2

S23	●	Hampden Sydney	37	0
S30		North Carolina St. [Nor]	0	13
O7	●	West Virginia [ChWV]	24	6
O14	=	N.C. Pre-Flight	13	13
O21	●	VMI [Lyn]	34	0
N4	●	Maryland [DC]	18	7
N11	●	at Richmond	39	0
N25	=	at Yale	6	6
D2	●	North Carolina [Nor]	26	7

1945 7-2-0

S22	●	Coast Guard	39	0
S29	●	North Carolina St. [Nor]	26	6
O20	●	VMI [Lyn]	40	7
O27	●	Virginia Tech [Roa]	31	13
N3	●	West Virginia [ChWV]	13	7
N11	●	Richmond	45	0
N17	●	Oceana	40	0
N24		Maryland [DC]	13	19
D1		at North Carolina	18	27

ARTHUR GUEPE
1946-52 (.727) 47-17-2

1946 4-4-1

S28	●	Hampden-Sydney	71	0
O5	=	Virginia Tech [Roa]	21	21
O12	●	VMI	19	8
O19		at Pennsylvania	0	40
N2		at Richmond	7	19
N9	●	at Princeton	20	6
N16		at North Carolina St.	7	27
N23	●	West Virginia	21	0
N30		North Carolina	14	49

1947 7-3-0

S27	●	George Washington	33	13
O4	●	Virginia Tech [Roa]	41	7
O11	●	Harvard	47	0
O18	●	Wash. & Lee	32	7
O25	●	VMI [Lex]	35	6
N1	●	Richmond	34	0
N8		at Pennsylvania	7	19
N15	●	at West Virginia	6	0
N22		North Carolina St.	2	7
N29		at North Carolina	7	40

1948 5-3-1

S25	=	Miami, Ohio	14	14
O2	●	Virginia Tech [Roa]	28	0
O9		George Washington	12	20
O16	●	at Wash. & Lee	41	6
O23	●	VMI	26	14
O30		at Princeton	14	55
N6	●	at North Carolina St.	21	14
N13	●	West Virginia	7	0
N27		North Carolina	12	34

1949 7-2-0

S24	●	George Washington	27	13
O1	●	Miami, Ohio	21	18
O8	●	Virginia Tech [Roa]	26	0
O15	●	Wash. & Lee	27	7
O22	●	VMI [Lyn]	32	13
O29	●	West Virginia	19	14
N5	●	at Pennsylvania	26	14
N19		Tulane	14	28
N26		at North Carolina	7	14

1950 8-2-0

S23	●	George Washington	19	0
S30		at Pennsylvania	7	21
O7	●	Virginia Tech [Roa]	45	6
O14	●	Wash. & Lee [Rich]	26	21
O21	●	VMI	26	13
O28	●	at West Virginia	28	21
N4	●	at Citadel	34	14
N11	●	William & Mary	13	0
N18		at Tulane	18	42
D2	●	North Carolina	44	13

1951 8-1-0

S29	●	George Washington	20	0
O6	●	Virginia Tech [Roa]	33	0
O13		at Wash. & Lee	14	42
O20	●	VMI	34	14
O27	●	at Duke	30	7
N3	●	Citadel	39	0
N10	●	North Carolina	34	14
N17	●	South Carolina	28	27
N24	●	William & Mary	46	0

1952 8-2-0

S27	●	Vanderbilt	27	0
O4	●	Virginia Tech [Roa]	42	0
O11	●	George Washington	50	0
O18	●	VMI [Rich]	33	14
O25		Duke	7	21
N1		South Carolina [Nor]	14	21
N8	●	at North Carolina	34	7
N15	●	Richmond	49	0
N22	●	Wash. & Lee	21	14
N29	●	at William & Mary	20	13

NED McDONALD
1953-55 (.179) 5-23

1953 1-8-0

S26		Virginia Tech	6	20
O3		South Carolina	0	19
O10	●	George Washington [AlexV]	24	20
O17		VMI	6	21
O24		at Vanderbilt	13	28
O31		Duke [Nor]	6	48
N7		Pittsburgh	0	26
N14		at Wash. & Lee	13	27
N21		North Carolina	7	33

1954-PRESENT
ACC

1954 3-6-0 (0-2-0)

S25	●	Lehigh	27	21
O2	●	George Washington	14	13
O9		at Penn State	7	34
O16	●	VMI	21	0
O23		Virginia Tech [Roa]	0	6
O30		at Army	20	21
N13	│	at South Carolina	0	27
N20	│	North Carolina	14	26
N27		West Virginia	10	14

1955 1-9-0 (0-4-0)

S24	│	Clemson	7	20
O1		George Washington	0	13
O8		Penn State [Rich]	7	26
O15	●	VMI	20	13
O22		Virginia Tech [Roa]	13	17
O29		at Vanderbilt	7	34
N5		at Pittsburgh	7	18
N12	│	Wake Forest	7	13
N19	│	at North Carolina	14	26
N26	│	South Carolina	14	21

BEN MARTIN
1956-57 (.325) 6-13-1

1956 3-7-0 (1-4-0)

S22	●	VMI	18	0
S29	│	Duke	7	40
O6	● │	Wake Forest	7	6
O13	│	South Carolina [Rich]	13	27
O20	●	at Lehigh	24	12
O27		Virginia Tech [Roa]	7	14
N3		Vanderbilt	2	6
N10	│	North Carolina	7	21 †
N17		Navy [Balt]	7	34
N24	│	at Clemson	0	7

1957 3-6-1 (2-4-0)

S21	=	at West Virginia	6	6
S28	│	at Duke	0	40
O5	● │	at Wake Forest	28	20
O12	│	Clemson	6	20
O19	●	Virginia Tech [Rich]	38	7
O26		Army	12	20
N2		VMI	7	20
N16	│	South Carolina	0	13
N23	│	at Maryland	0	12
N30	● │	at North Carolina	20	13

RICHARD VORIS
1958-60 (.033) 1-29

1958 1-9-0 (1-5-0)

S20	│	at Clemson	15	20
S27	● │	Duke	15	12
O4	│	North Carolina St.	14	26
O11		Virginia Tech [Roa]	13	22
O18		at Army	6	35
O25		at Vanderbilt	6	39
N1		VMI [Nor]	0	33
N8	│	North Carolina	0	42
N15	│	at South Carolina	14	28
N22	│	Maryland	6	44

1959 0-10-0 (0-5-0)

S19		William & Mary	0	37
S26	│	Clemson	0	47
O3		at Florida	10	55
O10		VMI [Lyn]	12	19
O17		Virginia Tech [Rich]	14	40
O24		Vanderbilt	0	33
O31	│	at Wake Forest	12	34
N7	│	South Carolina	20	32
N14	│	at North Carolina	0	41
N21	│	at Maryland	12	55

1960 0-10-0 (0-6-0)

S24		William & Mary [Nor]	21	41
O1	│	at North Carolina St.	7	26
O8	│	at Clemson	7	21
O15		VMI	16	30
O22		Virginia Tech [Roa]	6	40
O29	│	Wake Forest	20	28
N12		at Navy	6	41
N19	│	Maryland	12	44
N26	│	North Carolina	8	35
D3	│	at South Carolina	0	26

BILL ELIAS
1961-64 (.413) 16-23-1

1961 4-6-0 (2-4-0)

S23	●	William & Mary	21	6
S30	│	Duke [Rich]	0	42
O7	│	North Carolina St.	14	21
O14	●	VMI [Nor]	14	7
O21		Virginia Tech [Roa]	0	20
O28	│	at Wake Forest	15	21
N4	● │	South Carolina	28	20
N18		at Navy	3	13
N25	● │	Maryland	28	16
D2	│	at North Carolina	0	24

1962 5-5-0 (1-4-0)

S22	●	William & Mary	19	7
O6		Virginia Tech [Roa]	15	20
O13	●	VMI	28	6
O20	● │	Wake Forest	14	12
O27	●	Davidson	34	7
N3	│	at South Carolina	6	40
N10	│	North Carolina	7	11
N17	│	at North Carolina St.	12	24
N24	│	at Maryland	18	40
D1	●	at Rutgers	41	0

1963 2-7-1 (0-5-1)

S21	│	at North Carolina	7	11
S28	│	Duke	8	30
O5		Virginia Tech [Roa]	0	10
O12	●	VMI [Rich]	6	0
O19	= │	South Carolina	10	10
O26	│	Clemson	0	35
N2	│	North Carolina St. [Nor]	9	15
N9	●	William & Mary	9	7
N16		at Boston College	21	30
N23	│	at Maryland	6	21

1964 5-5-0 (1-5-0)

S19	│	Wake Forest	21	31
S26	│	at Duke	0	30
O3	●	Virginia Tech	20	17
O11	●	VMI [Rich]	20	19
O17	●	Army	35	14
O24	│	North Carolina St.	15	24
O31	│	at Clemson	7	29
N7	●	at William & Mary	14	13
N14	● │	North Carolina	31	27
N21	│	Maryland	0	10

GEORGE BLACKBURN
1965-70 (.459) 28-33

1965 4-6-0 (2-4-0)

S18	│	Duke	7	21
S25	│	Clemson	14	20
O2	● │	at North Carolina	21	17
O9	●	VMI	14	10
O16	●	West Virginia [Rich]	41	0
O23		at Virginia Tech	14	22
O30	│	North Carolina St.	0	13
N6	│	South Carolina	7	17 †
N13		at Georgia Tech	19	42
N20	● │	at Maryland	33	27

1966 4-6-0 (3-3-0)

S17	● │	Wake Forest	24	10
S24	│	at Clemson	35	40
O1	│	at Duke	8	27
O8		Tulane	6	20
O15	●	VMI	38	27
O22		Virginia Tech	7	24
O29	│	at North Carolina St.	21	42
N5		at Georgia Tech	13	14
N19	● │	Maryland	41	17
N26	● │	at North Carolina	21	14

1967 5-5-0 (3-3-0)

S23		at Army	7	26
S30	●	Buffalo	35	12
O7	● │	at Wake Forest	14	12
O14	│	Duke	6	13
O21	│	at South Carolina	23	24
O28		VMI	13	18
N4	│	North Carolina St.	8	30
N11	● │	North Carolina	40	17
N18	●	at Tulane	14	10
N25	● │	at Maryland	12	7

1968 7-3-0 (3-2-0)

S21		at Purdue	6	44
S28	●	VMI	47	0
O5	●	Davidson	41	14
O12	● │	at Duke	50	20
O19	│	at North Carolina St.	0	19
O26	●	at Navy	24	0
N2	│	South Carolina	28	49
N9	● │	at North Carolina	41	6
N16	●	Tulane	63	47
N23	● │	Maryland	28	23

1969 3-7-0 (1-5-0)

S20	│	Clemson	14	21
S27	● │	Duke	10	0
O4	●	at William & Mary	28	15
O11	●	VMI [Rich]	28	10
O18	│	North Carolina St.	0	31
O25		at Navy	0	10
N1	│	North Carolina	0	12
N8	│	Wake Forest	21	23
N15		at Tulane	0	31
N22	│	at Maryland	14	17

1970 5-6-0 (0-6-0)

S12	●	at Virginia Tech	7	0
S19	│	at Clemson	17	27
S26	│	at Duke	7	17
O3	│	Wake Forest	7	27
O10	●	VMI	49	10
O17	●	Army	21	20
O24	●	William & Mary	33	6
O31	│	at North Carolina	15	30
N7	│	at North Carolina St.	16	21
N14	●	Colgate	54	12
N21	│	Maryland	14	17

DON LAWRENCE
1971-73 (.333) 11-22

1971 3-8-0 (2-4-0)

S11		Navy	6	10
S18		at Michigan	0	56
S25	│	Duke	0	28
O2	●	Vanderbilt	27	23
O9	│	at South Carolina	14	34
O16	│	Clemson [Rich]	15	32
O23		at Army	9	14
O30	● │	at North Carolina St.	14	10
N6		Virginia Tech	0	6
N13	│	North Carolina	20	32
N20	● │	at Maryland	29	27

1972 4-7-0 (1-5-0)

S9	●	at South Carolina	24	16
S16	●	Virginia Tech	24	20
S23		West Virginia	10	48
S30	│	at Duke	13	37
O7		at Vanderbilt	7	10
O14	●	VMI	45	14
O21	│	at Clemson	21	37
O28	│	Maryland	23	24
N4	│	North Carolina St.	14	35
N11	│	at North Carolina	3	23
N18	● │	at Wake Forest	15	12

1973 4-7-0 3-3-0

S8	●	VMI	16	0
S15	│	at North Carolina St.	23	43
S22		at Missouri	7	31
S29	● │	Duke	7	3
O6		Vanderbilt	22	39
O13	│	at Clemson	27	32
O20		at Virginia Tech	15	27
O27	● │	Wake Forest	21	10
N3	● │	North Carolina	44	40
N10	│	at Maryland	0	33
N17		at West Virginia	17	42

SONNY RANDLE
1974-75 (.227) 5-17

1974 — 4-7-0 (1-5-0)

S14		at Navy	28	35
S21	●	William & Mary	38	28
S28	|	at Duke	7	27
O5		at Georgia Tech	24	28
O12	|	North Carolina St.	21	22
O19	●	Virginia Tech	28	27
O26	● |	at Wake Forest	14	0
N2	|	at North Carolina	10	24
N9	●	VMI	28	10
N16	|	at Clemson	9	28
N23	|	Maryland	0	10

1975 — 1-10-0 (0-4-0)

S13		Navy	14	42
S20	●	VMI	22	21
S27	|	at Duke	11	26
O4	|	North Carolina	28	31
O11		at South Carolina	14	41
O18		at Virginia Tech	17	24
O25	|	Wake Forest	21	66
N1		at Vanderbilt	14	17
N8		East Carolina	10	61
N15		Syracuse	0	37
N22	|	at Maryland	24	62

DICK BESTWICK
1976-81 (.246) 16-49-1

1976 — 2-9-0 (1-3-0)

S11		at Washington	17	38
S18		William & Mary	0	14
S25	|	Duke	6	21
O2		at Georgia Tech	14	35
O9		at South Carolina	7	35
O16		Virginia Tech	10	14
O23	● |	at Wake Forest	18	17
O30		VMI NOR	7	13
N6	●	Lehigh	21	20
N13	|	at North Carolina	6	31
N20	|	Maryland	0	28

1977 — 1-9-1 (1-5-0)

S10	|	at North Carolina St.	0	14
S17		at Texas	0	68
S24	|	Duke	7	31
O1		West Virginia	0	13
O8	|	at Clemson	0	31
O15	=	at Virginia Tech	14	14
O22	● |	Wake Forest	12	10
O29		at Syracuse	3	6
N5		VMI	6	30
N12	|	North Carolina	14	35
N19	|	at Maryland	0	28

1978 — 2-9-0 (0-6-0)

S9	|	at Wake Forest	0	14
S16		Navy	0	32
S23	●	at Army	21	17
S30		VMI	9	17
O7	|	at Duke	13	20
O14	|	Clemson	14	30
O21	●	Virginia Tech	17	7
N4		at West Virginia	17	20
N11	|	Maryland	7	17
N18	|	at North Carolina	20	38
N25	|	North Carolina St.	21	24

1979 — 6-5-0 (1-4-0)

S8	●	Richmond	31	0
S15	|	at North Carolina St.	27	31
S22	●	VMI	19	0
S29	● |	Duke	30	12
O6	|	at Clemson	7	17
O13	●	James Madison	69	9
O20		at Navy	10	17
N3	●	at Georgia	31	0
N10	●	Virginia Tech	20	18
N17	|	North Carolina	7	13
N24	|	at Maryland	7	17

1980 — 4-7-0 (2-4-0)

S13	●	Navy	6	3
S20	|	North Carolina St.	13	27
S27	● |	at Duke	20	17
O4		at West Virginia	21	45
O11	|	Clemson	24	27
O18		at Virginia Tech	0	30
O25	● |	at Wake Forest	24	21
N1	●	at Tennessee	16	13
N8		Rutgers	17	19
N15	|	at North Carolina	3	26
N22	|	Maryland	0	31

1981 — 1-10-0 (0-6-0)

S12		West Virginia	18	32
S18		Rutgers ERUT	0	3
S26	|	Duke	24	29
O3	|	at North Carolina St.	24	30
O10	|	at Clemson	0	27
O17		at South Carolina	3	21
O24	|	Wake Forest	21	24
O31	●	VMI	13	10
N14	|	North Carolina	14	17
N21	|	at Maryland	7	48
N28		Virginia Tech	3	20

GEORGE WELSH
1982-2000 (.608) 134-86-3

1982 — 2-9-0 (1-5-0)

S11		at Navy	16	20
S18		James Madison	17	21
S25	|	at Duke	17	51
O2	|	North Carolina St.	13	16
O9	|	Clemson	0	48
O23	● |	Wake Forest	34	27
O30	●	VMI	37	6
N6		at Georgia Tech	32	38
N13	|	at North Carolina	14	27
N20	|	Maryland	14	45
N25		at Virginia Tech	14	21

1983 — 6-5-0 (3-4-0)

S3	● |	Duke	38	30
S10	●	Navy	27	16
S17	●	James Madison	21	14
S24	● |	at North Carolina St.	26	14
O1	|	at Maryland	3	23
O8	|	at Clemson	21	42
O15	●	VMI	38	10
O22	|	at Wake Forest	34	38
N3	|	at Georgia Tech	27	31
N12	● |	North Carolina	17	14
N19		Virginia Tech	0	48

1984 — 8-2-2 (3-2-2)

S8	|	Clemson	0	55
S15	●	VMI	35	7
S22	●	Navy	21	9
S29	●	Virginia Tech	26	23
O6	● |	Duke	38	10
O13	= |	Georgia Tech	20	20
O20	● |	Wake Forest	28	9
N3	●	West Virginia	27	7
N10	● |	North Carolina St.	45	0
N17	= |	North Carolina	24	24
N24	|	Maryland	34	45
		PEACH BOWL		
D31	●	Purdue	27	24

1985 — 6-5-0 (4-3-0)

S14	●	VMI	40	15
S21	● |	at Georgia Tech	24	13
S28		Navy	13	17
O5	● |	Duke	37	14
O12	|	at Clemson	24	27
O19		Virginia Tech	10	28
O26	● |	at Wake Forest	20	18
N2	●	West Virginia	27	7
N9	|	at North Carolina St.	22	23
N16	● |	North Carolina	24	22
N29	|	at Maryland	21	33

1986 — 3-8-0 (2-5-0)

S6	●	South Carolina	30	20
S13		at Navy	10	20
S20	|	Georgia Tech	14	28
S27	|	at Duke	13	20
O4	● |	at Wake Forest	30	28
O11	|	Clemson	17	31
O25		at Virginia Tech	10	42
N1		William & Mary	37	41
N8	● |	North Carolina St.	20	16
N15	|	at North Carolina	7	27
N28	|	Maryland	10	42

1987 — 8-4-0 (5-2-0)

S5		at Georgia	22	30
S12	|	at Maryland	19	21
S19	●	Virginia Tech	14	13
S26	● |	Duke	42	17
O3	●	VMI	30	0
O10	|	at Clemson	21	38
O17		at South Carolina	10	58
O24	● |	Wake Forest	35	21
N7	● |	at Georgia Tech	23	14
N14	● |	North Carolina	20	17
N21	● |	at North Carolina St.	34	31
		ALL-AMERICAN BOWL		
D22	●	Brigham Young	22	16

1988 — 7-4-0 (5-2-0)

S3	●	William & Mary	31	23
S10		Penn State	14	42
S17	● |	Georgia Tech	17	16
S24	|	at Duke	34	38
O8	|	Clemson	7	10
O15		at Louisville	28	30
O22	● |	at Wake Forest	34	14
O29	●	at Virginia Tech	16	10
N5	● |	North Carolina St.	19	14
N12	● |	at North Carolina	27	24
N19	● |	Maryland	24	23

1989 — 10-3-0 (6-1-0)

A31		Notre Dame ERUT	13	36
S9	●	at Penn State	14	6
S16	● |	at Georgia Tech	17	10
S23	● |	Duke	49	28
S30	●	William & Mary	24	12
O7	|	at Clemson	20	34
O14	● |	North Carolina	50	17
O21	● |	Wake Forest	47	28
O28	●	Louisville	16	15
N4	● |	at North Carolina St.	20	9
N11	●	Virginia Tech	32	25
N18	● |	at Maryland	48	21
		CITRUS BOWL		
J1		Illinois	21	31

1990 — 8-4-0 (5-2-0)

S1	●	at Kansas	59	10
S8	● |	Clemson	20	7
S15	●	Navy	56	14
S22	● |	at Duke	59	0
S29	●	William & Mary	63	35
O13	● |	North Carolina St.	31	0
O20	● |	at Wake Forest	49	14
N3	|	Georgia Tech	38	41
N10	● |	at North Carolina	24	10
N17	|	Maryland	30	35
N24		at Virginia Tech	13	38
		SUGAR BOWL		
J1		Tennessee	22	23

1991 — 8-3-1 (4-2-1)

S7	|	at Maryland	6	17
S14	●	Navy	17	10
S19	|	at Georgia Tech	21	24
S28	● |	Duke	34	3
O5	●	Kansas	31	19
O12	= |	at Clemson	20	20
O19	● |	North Carolina	14	9
O26	● |	Wake Forest	48	7
N2	●	VMI	42	0
N9	● |	at North Carolina St.	42	10
N23	●	Virginia Tech	38	0
		GATOR BOWL		
D29		Oklahoma	14	48

1992 — 7-4-0 (4-4-0)

S5	● |	Maryland	28	15
S12	●	at Navy	53	0
S19	● |	Georgia Tech	55	24
S26	● |	at Duke	55	28
O3	● |	at Wake Forest	31	17
O10	|	Clemson	28	29
O17	|	at North Carolina	7	27
O24	●	William & Mary	33	7
O31	|	Florida State	3	13
N7	|	North Carolina St.	7	31
N21	●	at Virginia Tech	41	38

1993 — 7-5-0 (5-3-0)

S4	● |	at Maryland	43	29
S11	●	Navy	38	0
S16	● |	at Georgia Tech	35	14
S25	● |	Duke	35	0
O2	●	Ohio U.	41	7
O16	|	at Florida State	14	40
O23	● |	North Carolina	17	10
O30	|	at North Carolina St.	29	34
N6	● |	Wake Forest	21	9
N13	|	at Clemson	14	23
N20		Virginia Tech	17	20
		BLOCKBUSTER BOWL		
J1		Boston College	13	31

1994 — 9-3-0 (5-3-0)

S3	|	at Florida State	17	41
S10	●	at Navy	47	10
S17	● |	Clemson	9	6
O1	●	William & Mary	37	3
O8	● |	at Wake Forest	42	6
O15	● |	at Georgia Tech	24	7
O22	● |	North Carolina	34	10
N5	|	at Duke	25	28
N12	● |	Maryland	46	21
N19	●	at Virginia Tech	42	23
N25	|	North Carolina St.	27	30
		INDEPENDENCE BOWL		
D28	●	TCU	20	10

1995 — 9-4-0 (7-1-0)

A26		Michigan	17	18
S2	●	William & Mary	40	16
S9	● |	North Carolina St.	29	24
S16	● |	Georgia Tech	41	14
S23	● |	Clemson	22	3
S30	● |	Wake Forest	35	17
O7	|	North Carolina	17	22
O14	● |	Duke	44	30
O21		Texas	16	17
N2	● |	Florida State	33	28
N11	● |	Maryland	21	18
N18		Virginia Tech	29	36
		PEACH BOWL		
D30	●	Georgia	34	27

1996 — 7-5 (5-3)

S7	●	Central Michigan	55	21
S14	● |	Maryland	21	3
S21	● |	at Wake Forest	42	7
S28	●	Texas	37	13
O5	|	at Georgia Tech	7	13
O19	● |	North Carolina St.	62	14
O26	|	at Florida State	24	31
N2	● |	at Duke	27	3
N9	|	Clemson	16	24
N16	● |	North Carolina	20	17
N29		at Virginia Tech	9	26
		CARQUEST BOWL		
D27		Miami, Fla.	21	31

1997 — 7-4 (5-3)

S4		Auburn	17	28
S13	●	Richmond	26	7
S27	|	at North Carolina	20	48
O4	● |	Wake Forest	21	13
O11	● |	at Clemson	21	7
O18	● |	Duke	13	10
O25	|	Florida State	21	47
N1	● |	at Maryland	45	0
N8	● |	Georgia Tech	35	31
N15	|	at North Carolina St.	24	31
N29	●	Virginia Tech	34	20

1998 — 9-3 (6-2)

S3	●	at Auburn	19	0
S12	● |	Maryland	31	19
S19	● |	Clemson	20	18
S26	● |	at Duke	24	0
O3	●	San Jose State	52	14
O17	|	at Georgia Tech	38	41
O24	● |	North Carolina St.	23	13
O31	● |	at Wake Forest	38	17
N7	|	at Florida State	14	45
N14	● |	North Carolina	30	13
N28	●	at Virginia Tech	36	32
		PEACH BOWL		
D31		Georgia	33	35

1999 — 7-5 (5-3)

S4	● |	at North Carolina	20	17
S11	|	at Clemson	14	33
S18	● |	Wake Forest	35	7
S25	●	at Brigham Young	45	40
O2		Virginia Tech	7	31
O9	|	Duke	17	24
O16	● |	at North Carolina St.	47	26
O30	|	Florida State	10	35
N6	● |	Georgia Tech	45	38
N13	●	Buffalo	50	21
N20	● |	at Maryland	34	30
		MICRON PC BOWL		
D30		Illinois	21	63

2000 — 6-6 (5-3)

S2		Brigham Young	35	38
S9	●	Richmond	34	6
S16	● |	at Duke	26	10
S23	|	Clemson	10	31
S30	● |	at Wake Forest	27	10
O7	● |	Maryland	31	23
O21	|	at Florida State	3	37
O28	● |	North Carolina	17	6
N9	|	at Georgia Tech	0	35
N18	● |	North Carolina St.	24	17
N25		at Virginia Tech	21	42
		OAHU BOWL		
D24		Georgia	14	37

THE SCHOOLS

AL GROH
2001-Present (.588)   30-21

2001   5-7   (3-5)

A25		at Wisconsin	17	26
S1	●	Richmond	17	16
S22	● |	at Clemson	26	24
S29	● |	Duke	31	10
O6	|	at Maryland	21	41
O13	|	at North Carolina	24	30
O20	|	Florida State	7	43
O27	|	at North Carolina St.	0	24
N3	|	Wake Forest	30	34
N10	● |	Georgia Tech	39	38
N17	|	Virginia Tech	17	31
D1	●	Penn State	20	14

2002   9-5   (6-2)

A22		Colorado State	29	35
A31	|	at Florida State	19	40
S7	● |	South Carolina	34	21
S21	●	Akron	48	29
S28	● |	at Wake Forest	38	34
O5	● |	at Duke	27	22
O12	● |	Clemson	22	17
O19	● |	North Carolina	37	27
O26	|	at Georgia Tech	15	23
N9		at Penn State	14	35
N16	● |	North Carolina St.	14	9
N23	● |	Maryland	48	13
N30	|	at Virginia Tech	9	21

CONTINENTAL TIRE BOWL

D28	●	West Virginia	48	22

2003   8-5   (4-4)

A30	● |	Duke	27	0
S6	|	at South Carolina	7	31
S13	● |	at Western Michigan	59	16
S27	● |	Wake Forest	27	24
O4	● |	at North Carolina	38	13
O11	|	at Clemson	27	30
O18	|	Florida State	14	19
O25	●	Troy State	24	0
N1	|	at North Carolina St.	37	51
N13	|	at Maryland	17	27
N22	● |	Georgia Tech	29	17
N29	● |	Virginia Tech	35	21

CONTINENTAL TIRE BOWL

D27	●	Pittsburgh	23	16

2004   8-4   (5-3)

S4	● |	at Temple	44	14
S11	● |	North Carolina	56	24
S18	|	Akron	51	0
S25	●	Syracuse	31	10
O7	● |	Clemson	30	10
O16	|	at Florida State	3	36
O23	● |	at Duke	37	16
N6	● |	Maryland	16	0
N13	|	Miami, Fla.	21	31
N20	● |	at Georgia Tech	30	10
N27	|	at Virginia Tech	10	24

MPC COMPUTERS BOWL

D27		Fresno State	34	37

Neutral Site key: *AlexV* Alexandria, Va. / *Atl* Atlanta, Ga. / *Balt* Baltimore, Md. / *Char* Charlotte, N.C. / *ChWV* Charleston, W. Va. / *DC* Washington, D.C. / *Det* Detroit, Mich. / *ERut* East Rutherford, N.J. / *Lex* Lexington, Va. / *Lyn* Lynchburg, Va. / *Nor* Norfolk, Va. / *Rich* Richmond, Va. / *Roa* Roanoke, Va. / *Unk* Unknown Unknown

f Forfeit   † Game Later Forfieted   # Disputed Victor   * Disputed Score || Designated Conference Game |2 Counted Twice in Conference Standings

VIRGINIA TECH

BY MIKE VACCARO

F RANK BEAMER DIDN'T INVENT Virginia Tech football; it only seems that way. Michael Vick wasn't the first Hokie to make a deep impact on the NFL; it just feels that way. And Virginia Tech didn't just tumble out of the sky in the last decade, asserting itself as one of college football's dominant programs.

It just appears that way to those who haven't experienced the football life in Blacksburg, Va., a college town in the purest sense of the word, described by ESPN football analyst Kirk Herbstreit as "a place that has an absolute love affair with its football program. It's a 100% crazy, loud stadium environment. You can go places with 100,000 people and Tech's stadium is just as loud, or louder."

Five Hokies—Hunter Carpenter, Carroll Dale, Frank Loria, Andy Gustafson and Jerry Claiborne—are in the College Football Hall of Fame. Still, it wasn't until the arrival of Beamer as coach in 1987 and Vick as a do-everything quarterback a decade later that Virginia Tech finally lodged itself in the national consciousness.

And it was the 1999 team that stormed to an 11–0 record, outscoring opponents 455-116, that nearly scaled the mountaintop. That team's dream ride ended in the

Sugar Bowl, where it was vanquished 46-29 by Florida State. But the team's legacy lives, in a program that remains a perennial Top 10 and BCS bowl contender.

TRADITION Two cadets from the Class of 1964 made a pact following a traditional Thanksgiving Day game with then-rival VMI that they would build a cannon for Virginia Tech (then known as VPI) to outgun VMI's own cannon, "Little John." The cadets, Butch Harper and Sonny Hickam, were tired of hearing VMI's Keydets chant "Where's your cannon?" after firing their own. Harper and Hickam collected brass from fellow cadets, added it to metal donated by Hickam's father, collected donations from the corps to purchase other supplies and used a mold created in one of the engineering departments from Civil War-style plans to make their cannon. They derived its name—"Skipper"—from recently assassinated President John F. Kennedy's role as skipper of PT-109 during World War II. On its first firing at the next game with VMI, they tripled the charge, which blew the hats off half the Keydets and shook the glass in the press-box windows of VMI's Victory Stadium in Roanoke.

BEST PLAYER Virginia Tech has enjoyed the services of two players who would receive unanimous All-America acclaim: center Jim Pyne (1993) and defensive end Corey

---

PROFILE

Virginia Polytechnic Institute and State University
Blacksburg, Va.
Founded: 1872
Enrollment: 21,348
Colors: Chicago Maroon and Burnt Orange
Nickname: Hokies
Stadium: Lane Stadium/Worsham Field
    Opened in 1965
    Green Tech ITM grass; 65,115 capacity
First football game: 1892
All-time record: 615–414–46 (.593)
Bowl record: 6–12
Atlantic Coast Conference championships:
1 (outright)
Outland Trophy: Bruce Smith, 1984
First-round NFL draftees: 6
Website: www.hokiesports.com

THE BEST OF TIMES

Frank Beamer led the Hokies to unprecedented heights as the century turned. From 1998 to 2000, the Hokies went 31–5.

THE WORST OF TIMES

Tech's football history bottomed out from 1948 to 1951, when the Hokies went 3–33–3.

CONFERENCE

The Hokies joined the Atlantic Coast Conference in 2004 after 13 seasons in the Big East. Previously, Virginia Tech had been an independent since 1965.

DISTINGUISHED ALUMNI

J. Wade Gilley, president, University of Tennessee; Christopher Kraft Jr., director, Lyndon B. Johnson Space Center; Robert Richardson, Nobel Prize winner in physics; Thomas Richards, four-star general, Air Force

FIGHT SONG

TECH TRIUMPH
Techmen, we're Techmen, with spirit true and faithful,
Backing up our teams with hopes undying;
Techmen, oh, Techmen, we're out to win today,
Showing pep and life with which we're trying;
VP, old VP, you know our hearts are with you
In our luck which never seems to die;
Win or lose, we'll greet you with a glad returning,
You're the pride of VPI.
Just watch our men so big and active
Support the Orange and Maroon.
Let's go Techs.
We know our ends and backs are stronger,
With winning hopes, we fear defeat no longer.
To see our team plow through the line, boys.
Determined now to win or die:
So give a Hokie, Hokie, Hokie, Hi,
Rae, Ri, old VPI

Moore (1998, 1999). Tech's also the place where Bruce Smith, one of the greatest defensive linemen in NFL history, first came to the attention of football fans. But no single player left the permanent imprint on the program that Michael Vick did. As a redshirt freshman in 1999, the darting, quicksilver quarterback led the Hokies to an 11–0 regular season and a spot in the Sugar Bowl, finishing third in the Heisman voting along the way. In two seasons, Vick threw for 3,074 yards and 20 touchdowns, and while his fame may have grown exponentially since entering the NFL in 2001, his legacy at Virginia Tech lives on.

BEST COACH Frank Beamer suffered through an inauspicious beginning at his alma mater after taking over for Bill Dooley in 1987. Dooley's last team had gone 9–2–1 and won a thrilling Peach Bowl game against NC State, while Beamer's first two teams amassed back-to-back 2–9 and 3–8 records. There were many Tech fans who had grown weary of Beamer's tenure after his sixth team was 2–8–1 during Tech's first full season as a member of the Big East. But his squad went 9–3 in 1993, and it was then that the Hokies finally, and permanently,

The question most asked about Virginia Tech is a simple one: what the heck is a Hokie?

turned the corner, peaking with the 1999-2000 teams that went 22–2 over two seasons. Then, in the Hokies' first year as an ACC member in 2004, Beamer led his team to the conference championship and a spot in the BCS, securing a spot in the Sugar Bowl, where Tech gave undefeated Auburn everything it could ask for before losing 16-13. Despite his slow start at Tech, Beamer (Class of 1968) won close to two-thirds of his games at his alma mater through the 2004 season. One of the most relevant trademarks of the Beamer era has been an incredible run of special-teams excellence, especially in the area of blocking kicks. In the 1990s, no Division I-A team blocked more kicks than Virginia Tech, which blocked a total of 63 kicks during the decade—31 punts, 18 PATs and 14 field goals.

BEST TEAM Few people expected Virginia Tech to make a huge national splash in 1999, but in Blacksburg the faithful understood one thing: the Hokies had a very special player on each side of the ball. Corey Moore anchored the defense, while Michael Vick took control of the offense and fueled one of the most exciting attacks in the nation. Tech earned its reputation the hard way, throttling Clemson 31-11 in a

RECORDS

RUSHING YARDS

	GAME
223	Kenny Lewis vs. VMI, Nov. 18, 1978 (26 att.)
	SEASON
1,647	Kevin Jones, 2003 (281 att.)
	CAREER
3,767	Cyrus Lawrence, 1979-82 (843 att.)

PASSING YARDS

	GAME
527	Don Strock vs. Houston, Oct. 7, 1972 (34 of 53)
	SEASON
3,243	Don Strock, 1972 (228 of 427)
	CAREER
6,009	Don Strock, 1970-72 (440 of 829)

RECEIVING YARDS

	GAME
279	Ernest Wilford vs. Syracuse, Nov. 9, 2002 (8 rec.)
	SEASON
962	Andre Davis, 1999 (35 rec.)
	CAREER
2,272	Ricky Scales, 1972-74 (113 rec.)

POINTS

	GAME
36	Tommy Francisco vs. VMI, Nov. 24, 1966 (6 TDs)
	SEASON
168	Lee Suggs, 2000 (28 TDs)
	CAREER
371	Shayne Graham, 1996-99 (68 FGs, 167 PATs)

CONSENSUS ALL-AMERICANS

1967	Frank Loria, DB
1984	Bruce Smith, DL
1993	Jim Pyne, C
1995	Cornell Brown, DL
1999	Corey Moore, DL
2003	Jake Grove, C
2003	Kevin Jones, RB

nationally televised Thursday night game, obliterating conference favorite Syracuse 62-0 and humbling Miami 43-10. The Hokies eventually rose to No. 2 in the national polls, and after routing Boston College 38-14 in the regular-season finale, they earned a spot in the national championship game against Florida State. Before 79,280 Superdome fans, the glass slipper finally cracked, though not before Tech sneaked to a 29-28 lead at the end of the third quarter. Florida State ended the game with 18 straight points, but Tech earned a greater national profile for its efforts.

BIGGEST GAME It is the one game that stands out in an otherwise dominant 1999 campaign. In Tech's other 10 regular-season games, the Hokies won by at least 13 points. But on Nov. 6, facing an unimpressive West Virginia team, the Hokies found themselves trailing at Morgantown 20-19 with 1:11 remaining. Second-ranked Penn State had lost that day, meaning the Hokies were in position to sneak into the national title game picture. This looked like it would be one of the all-time heartbreakers in school history, as the Hokies held a 19-7 lead with less than five minutes left in the fourth quarter before West Virginia struck for two scores in under three minutes. But Michael Vick completed three key passes and added a critical 26-yard run and Shayne Graham nailed a 44-yard field goal as time ran out, keeping Tech's title hopes alive.

BIGGEST UPSET West Virginia had played in the Fiesta Bowl for the national title only nine months earlier. Virginia Tech was still trying to get a foothold under third-year coach Beamer. West Virginia entered the game ranked ninth in the country and harboring hopes of a New Year's Day bowl game, but Tech put an end to that on Oct. 7, 1989, with a 12-10 victory at Morgantown that many believe was a turning point in the Beamer era. Tech quarterback Cam Young, making his first career start, passed for 167 yards and outplayed West Virginia's highly regarded Major Harris. It was West Virginia's first regular-season loss since the last game of the 1987 season.

HEARTBREAKER Virginia Tech was 8–0 and enjoying a lofty No. 3 ranking in the national polls, positioning itself for a BCS title game berth, when the Pittsburgh Panthers came to Blacksburg on Nov. 2, 2002. Tech raced to a 21-7 lead early in the third quarter, and it seemed the Hokies were primed to keep the pressure on the BCS formula, much to the delight of 64,971 partisans. But the Hokies never scored again, and Pittsburgh wide receiver Larry

Fitzgerald gathered in a pair of touchdown catches from quarterback Rod Rutherford. Then, with 4:11 left in the game, Tech's normally reliable run defense allowed Brandon Miree to scamper 53 yards with the winning touchdown to clinch a stunning 28-21 Pitt win.

STADIUM Lane Stadium was officially dedicated on Oct. 23, 1965, before a 22-14 victory over Virginia. The facility was renamed Lane Stadium/Worsham Field on Sept. 5, 1992.

RIVAL Although Virginia Tech and VMI used to have one of the fiercest rivalries in the nation, given both schools' roots as military institutions, the teams haven't played since 1984. Tech holds a commanding 49–25–5 mark in that series. Currently, and for the foreseeable future, the No. 1 game on Tech's schedule every year is Virginia, especially now that both teams reside in the ACC. The winner of the annual Hokies-Hoos showdown is awarded the Commonwealth Cup, made of marble and cherrywood, which stands four feet high and weighs more than 100 pounds. The top of the cup is silver-plated and lists the scores of every game played, going back to Virginia's 38-0 win in 1895.

NICKNAME The question most asked about Virginia Tech is a simple one: what the heck is a Hokie? The answer traces back to 1896, when the Virginia Agricultural and Mechanical College changed its name to Virginia Polytechnic Institute, necessitating a fresh nickname. Senior O.M. Stull won the student competition by authoring the "Hokie" yell, which is still used today, explaining the word was solely a product of his imagination and was strictly used as an attention-getter for his catchy yell. Though he may not have known it, Hokie had been around at least since 1842. According to Johann Norstedt, now a retired Virginia Tech English professor, Hokie "was a word that people used to express feeling, approval, excitement, surprise. Hokie, then, is a word like 'hooray' or 'yeah' or 'rah.'"

MASCOT In the early 1900s, Tech football players were supposedly notorious for "gobbling" up huge servings of food, and in 1909 coach Branch Bocock founded an impromptu and informal Gobbler Club. Four years later, Fred Meade, a local resident chosen by the student body to serve as the school's mascot, piled into a cart pulled by a large turkey. The school's president halted the practice after one game because he thought it was cruel to the turkey, but Meade continued to parade his mascot, and the use of

a live gobbler mascot continued into the 1950s. The first permanent costumed Gobbler took the field in the fall of 1962. In 1982, the costume was changed to look like a maroon cardinal with a snood, and the character began being referred to as the Hokie mascot, the Hokie and the Hokie bird. The costume worn by today's Hokie Bird made its initial appearance in 1987.

UNIFORMS In 1896, a committee was formed to find a suitable combination of colors to replace the original colors of black and gray, which appeared in stripes on hats, books, athletic uniforms and other paraphernalia, and bore an unlucky resemblance to prison uniforms. The committee selected burnt orange and Chicago maroon after discovering that no other college utilized this particular combination. Burnt orange and Chicago maroon were officially adopted and were first worn during a football game against nearby Roanoke College on Oct. 20, 1896, and have remained the school colors ever since.

QUOTE "No one can tell this team any longer that it doesn't belong. This team belongs in the same conversation as any team in America right now. Just try to tell them differently."—Frank Beamer, after the Hokies completed an undefeated regular season with a 38-14 thrashing of Boston College in 1999

VIRGINIA TECH ANNUAL STATISTICAL LEADERS

YR	RUSHING	YDS	ATT	AVG	PASSING	ATT	CMP	PCT	YDS	RECEIVING	REC	YDS	AVG
1965	Bobby Owens	526	146	3.6	Bobby Owens	122	68	.56	891	Gene Fisher	30	387	12.9
1966	Tommy Francisco	753	203	3.7	Tommy Stafford	113	53	.47	610	Ken Barefoot	22	267	12.1
1967	Terry Smoot	356	68	5.2	Al Kincaid	132	64	.48	556	Ken Barefoot	26	225	8.7
1968	Terry Smoot	820	196	4.2	Al Kincaid	97	47	.48	537	Danny Cupp	21	323	15.4
1969	Terry Smoot	940	246	3.8	Bob German	105	51	.49	743	Terry Smoot	18	161	8.9
1970	Perry Tiberio	764	184	4.2	Gil Schwabe	126	61	.48	815	Jimmy Quinn	30	481	16.0
1971	James Barber	501	93	5.4	Don Strock	356	195	.55	2,577	Mike Burnop	46	558	12.1
1972	James Barber	624	186	3.4	Don Strock	427	228	.53	3,243	Ricky Scales	43	826	19.2
1973	Phil Rogers	1,036	175	5.9	Rick Popp	131	70	.53	784	Ricky Scales	36	772	21.4
1974	Phil Rogers	663	153	4.3	Bruce Arians	118	53	.45	952	Ricky Scales	34	674	19.8
1975	Roscoe Coles	1,045	194	5.4	Phil Rogers	53	25	.47	379	Steve Galloway	18	378	21.0
1976	Roscoe Coles	1,119	209	5.4	Mitcheal Barnes	72	39	.54	589	Moses Foster	20	429	21.5
1977	Roscoe Coles	672	158	4.3	David Lamie	107	43	.40	752	Ellis Savage	23	416	18.1
1978	Kenny Lewis	1,020	184	5.5	Steve Casey	118	61	.52	678	Dennis Scott	21	300	14.3
1979	Cyrus Lawrence	791	177	4.5	Steve Casey	190	105	.55	1,419	Sidney Snell	43	706	16.4
1980	Cyrus Lawrence	1,221	271	4.5	Steve Casey	176	97	.55	1,119	Sidney Snell	43	568	13.2
1981	Cyrus Lawrence	1,403	325	4.3	Steve Casey	163	79	.48	1,083	Mike Giacolone	28	514	18.4
1982	Billy Hite	622	145	4.3	Todd Greenwood	148	82	.55	987	Mike Giacolone	37	405	10.9
1983	Otis Copeland	709	158	4.5	Mark Cox	156	86	.55	1,188	Mike Shaw	23	357	15.5
1984	Maurice Williams	574	149	3.9	Mark Cox	164	86	.52	983	Joe Jones	39	452	11.6
1985	Maurice Williams	936	167	5.6	Todd Greenwood	169	85	.50	919	Donald Snell	31	369	11.9
1986	Maurice Williams	1,029	166	6.2	Erik Chapman	222	113	.51	1,627	Donald Snell	34	661	19.4
1987	Jon Jeffries	599	125	4.8	Erik Chapman	231	119	.52	1,340	Steve Johnson	38	475	12.5
1988	Ralph Brown	514	140	3.7	Will Furrer	279	128	.46	1,384	Myron Richardson	36	583	16.2
1989	Vaughn Hebron	584	134	4.4	Will Furrer	88	45	.51	589	Myron Richardson	27	450	16.7
1990	Vaughn Hebron	640	133	4.8	Will Furrer	296	173	.58	2,122	Marcus Mickel	38	409	10.8
1991	Tony Kennedy	684	143	4.8	Will Furrer	257	148	.58	1,820	Bo Campbell	29	494	17.0
1992	Vaughn Hebron	579	105	5.5	Maurice DeShazo	215	101	.47	1,504	Antonio Freeman	32	703	22.0
1993	Dwayne Thomas	1,130	214	5.3	Maurice DeShazo	230	129	.56	2,080	Antonio Freeman	32	644	20.1
1994	Dwayne Thomas	655	142	4.6	Maurice DeShazo	296	164	.55	2,110	Antonio Freeman	38	586	15.4
1995	Dwayne Thomas	673	167	4.0	Jim Druckenmiller	294	151	.51	2,103	Bryan Still	32	628	19.6
1996	Ken Oxendine	890	150	5.9	Jim Druckenmiller	250	142	.57	2,071	Shawn Scales	30	510	17.0
1997	Ken Oxendine	904	237	3.8	Al Clark	192	110	.57	1,476	Marcus Parker	20	212	10.6
1998	Lamont Pegues	745	178	4.2	Al Clark	148	72	.49	1,050	Ricky Hall	37	650	17.6
1999	Shyrone Stith	1,119	226	5.0	Michael Vick	152	90	.59	1,840	Andre Davis	35	962	27.4
2000	Lee Suggs	1,207	222	5.4	Michael Vick	161	87	.54	1,234	Emmett Johnson	34	574	16.9
2001	Kevin Jones	957	175	5.5	Grant Noel	254	146	.57	1,826	Andre Davis	39	623	16.0
2002	Lee Suggs	1,325	257	5.2	Bryan Randall	248	158	.64	2,134	Ernest Wilford	51	925	18.1
2003	Kevin Jones	1,647	281	5.9	Bryan Randall	245	150	.61	1,996	Ernest Wilford	55	886	16.1
2004	Mike Imoh	720	158	4.6	Bryan Randall	306	170	.56	2,264	Eddie Royal	28	470	16.8

Receiving leaders by receptions
All statistics include postseason

VIRGINIA TECH ALL-TIME SCORES

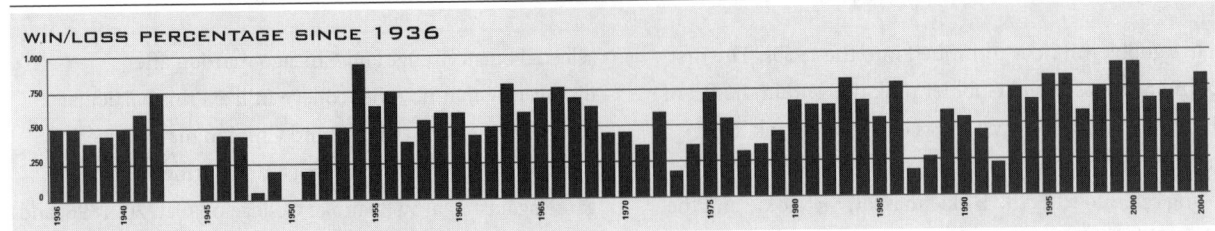

WIN/LOSS PERCENTAGE SINCE 1936

E.A. SMYTH
1892-93 (.250)   1-3

1892   1-1-0
O21	●	St. Albans	14	10
O29		at St. Albans	0	10

1893   0-2-0
O21		at Emory & Henry	0	6
N11		Randolph Macon *BED*	6	34

JOSEPH A. MASSIE
1894 (.800)   4-1

1894   4-1-0
O20	●	Emory & Henry	16	0
O29	●	Roanoke Coll.	36	0
N10	●	St. Albans	42	0
N17	●	at St.Albans	12	0
N30		VMI *StV*	6	10

AC JONES
1895-96 (.679)   9-4-1

1895   4-2-0
O5		at Virginia	0	38
O12	●	St.Albans	12	0
O26	●	at Washington & Lincoln	30	0
N9	●	at Roanoke YMCA	16	2
N16	●	North Carolina *CHAR*	5	32
N28	●	VMI *LYN*	6	4

1896   5-2-1
O10	●	Allegheny Inst.	20	0
O20	●	Roanoke Coll.	12	0
O24	=	North Carolina *DAN*	0	0
O31	●	at Virginia	0	44
N2	●	Hampton-Sydney *LYN*	46	0
N14	●	at Tennessee	4	6
N16	●	Maryville College *KNOX*	52	0
N26	●	VMI *ROA*	24	0

CHARLES FIRTH
1897 (.714)   5-2

1897   5-2-0
O16	●	King College	54	0
O30	●	North Carolina *DAN*	4	0
N2	●	Roanoke Coll.	41	0
N6	●	Maryland U. *NOR*	4	18
N13	●	at Richmond	36	0
N15	●	at Hampden-Sydney	10	0
N25	●	Tennessee *ROA*	0	18

J. LEWIS INGLES
1898 (.600)   3-2

1898   3-2-0
N4	●	North Carolina *W-S*	6	28
N5	●	at Guilford	17	0
N7	●	Maryland U. *LYN*	0	23
N11	●	King College	58	0
N12	●	Bellvue	29	0

JAMES MORRISON
1899 (.800)   4-1

1899   4-1-0
O13	●	St. Alban	21	0
O21	●	at Tennessee	5	0
N11	●	at Virginia	0	28
N18	●	Roanoke Coll. *ROA*	45	0
N25	●	Wash. & Lee *ROA*	35	0

DR. DAVIS
1900 (.500)   3-3-1

1900   3-3-1
O6	●	St.Albans	21	0
O20	●	at St.Albans	16	6
O25	●	at North Carolina St.	18	2
O27	=	at North Carolina	0	0
N14	●	at Virginia	5	17
N24	●	Clemson *CHAR*	5	12
N25	●	VMI *ROA*	0	5

A.B. MORRISON, JR.
1901 (.857)   6-1

1901   6-1-0
S28	●	at Roanoke	16	0
O12	●	Wash. & Lee	11	0
O19	●	at Georgetown	32	6
O26	●	Virginia	0	16
O31	●	Clemson *COLU*	17	11
N16	●	Maryland U. *RICH*	18	0
N28	●	VMI *NOR*	21	0

R.R. BROWN
1902 (.583)   3-2-1

1902   3-2-1
O11	●	Wash. & Lee *LYN*	0	6
O18	●	North Carolina St.	10	6 *
O25	=	North Carolina *ROA*	0	0
N8	●	Georgetown	28	0
N15	●	at Virginia	0	6
N27	●	VMI *NOR*	50	5

C.A. LUEDER
1903 (.833)   5-1

1903   5-1-0
O14	●	St. Albans	29	0
O17	●	North Carolina St.	21	0
O24	●	Virginia *RICH*	0	21
N7	●	North Carolina *NOR*	21	0
N21	●	at Navy	11	0
N25	●	Davidson *ROA*	26	0

JOHN O'CONNOR
1904 (.625)   5-3

1904   5-3-0
O1	●	Richmond	18	0
O7	●	Wash. & Lee	24	0
O12	●	Nashville	32	0
O22	●	William & Mary	30	0
O29	●	North Carolina	0	5
N5		Virginia *RICH*	0	5
N19	●	at Navy	0	11
N24	●	VMI *RICH*	17	5

C.P. MILES
1905-06 (.789)   14-3-2

1905   9-1-0
S30	●	Roanoke Coll.	86	0
O6	●	Cumberland	12	0
O14	●	at Army	16	6
O21	●	Gallaudet	56	0
O28	●	North Carolina *RICH*	35	6
N4	●	at Virginia	11	0
N11	●	Wash. & Lee	15	0
N18	●	South Carolina *ROA*	34	0
N25	●	at Navy	6	12
N30	●	VMI *RICH*	34	0

1906   5-2-2
O6	●	William & Mary	12	0
O8	●	William & Mary *ROA*	28	0
O13	●	at Clemson	0	0
O27	=	North Carolina *RICH*	0	0
N3	●	Roanoke	18	0
N10	●	Bucknell *NOR*	0	10
N17	●	Davidson	10	0
N24	●	at Navy	0	5
N29	●	North Carolina St. *RICH*	6	0

C.R. WILLIAMS
1907 (.778)   7-2

1907   7-2-0
O5	●	Roanoke	33	0
O12	●	Hampden-Sydney	18	0
O19	●	Wash. & Lee *LYN*	5	0
O20	●	Davidson *ROA*	5	12
N2	●	Georgetown *RICH*	20	0
N9	●	VMI *ROA*	22	0
N16	●	George Washington	34	0
N23	●	at Navy	0	12
N28	●	North Carolina *RICH*	20	6

R.M. BROWN
1908 (.556)   5-4

1908   5-4-0
O3	●	Hampden-Sydney	50	0
O10	●	at Clemson	6	0
O17	●	at Princeton	4	10
O24	●	VMI *ROA*	10	0
O31	●	Wash. & Lee *LYN*	15	4
N7	●	North Carolina *RICH*	10	0
N14	●	George Washington	0	6
N21	●	at Navy	4	15
N26	●	North Carolina St. *NOR*	5	6

BRANCH BOCOCK
1909-10, '12-15 (.680) 34-14-2

1909   6-1-0
O2	●	Clemson	6	0
O13	●	at Princeton	6	8
O23	●	at Richmond	52	0
O30	●	Wash. & Lee *LYN*	34	6
N6	●	North Carolina *RICH*	15	0
N13	●	at George Washington	17	8
N25	●	North Carolina St. *NOR*	18	5

1910   6-2-0
O1	●	Hampden-Sydney	18	0
O5	●	Davidson	16	5
O15	●	Western Maryland	13	0
O22	●	at Navy	0	3
O29	●	Wash. & Lee *ROA*	23	0
N5	●	North Carolina *RICH*	20	0
N12	●	George Washington *LYN*	15	5
N24	●	North Carolina St. *NOR*	3	5

L.W. REISS
1911 (.778)   6-1-2

1911   6-1-2
S30	●	Hampden-Sydney	16	0
O6	●	Maryland U. *NOR*	12	0
O14	●	at Yale	0	33
O24	●	Roanoke	94	0
O28	●	Wash. & Lee *ROA*	5	5
N4	=	North Carolina *RICH*	0	0
N11	●	Tennesse	36	11
N18	●	Morris-Harvey	10	3
N30	●	North Carolina St. *NOR*	3	0

BRANCH BOCOCK

1912   5-4-0
S30	●	Roanoke Coll.	40	0
O5	●	Hampden - Sydney	42	7
O12	●	at Princeton	0	31
O19	●	Western Maryland	44	0
O26	●	North Carolina *RAL*	26	0
N2	●	Virginia Med.	0	10
N9	●	Wash. & Lee *ROA*	6	20
N16	●	West Virginia	41	0
N28	●	at Georgetown	3	24

1913   7-1-1
S27	●	Roanoke	26	0
O4	●	Hampden-Sydney	14	0
O11	●	Mississippi	35	14 *
O18	●	VPI Stars	20	12
O25	●	North Carolina *W-S*	14	7
N1	●	Wash. & Lee *ROA*	0	21
N8	●	Marshall	47	0
N15	●	Morris-Harvey	14	0
N27	=	VMI *ROA*	6	6

1914   6-2-1
S26	●	King	35	0
O3	●	Randolph Macon	13	0
O10	●	Hampden-Sydney	22	0
O17	●	W.V. Wesleyan *CHWV*	0	13
O24	=	Roanoke	7	7
O31	●	Wash. & Lee *ROA*	6	7
N7	●	Marshall	54	6
N14	●	North Carolina St. *ROA*	3	0
N26	●	VMI *ROA*	3	0

1915   4-4-0
S26	●	Roanoke	26	0
O2	●	Randolph Macon	19	3
O9	●	Hampden-Sydney	19	0
O16	●	Wash. & Lee *ROA*	0	14
O23	●	at Navy	0	20
O30	●	at Cornell	0	45
N13	●	at West Virginia	0	19
N25	●	VMI *ROA*	27	9

JACK INGERSEL
1916 (.778)   7-2

1916   7-2-0
S30	●	Richmond	13	0
O7	●	Hampden-Sydney	10	0
O14	●	West Virginia *CHWV*	0	20
O20	●	at Yale	0	19
O28	●	North Carolina St. *NOR*	40	0
N4	●	North Carolina *ROA*	14	7
N11	●	Wake Forest	52	0
N18	●	Roanoke	41	0
N30	●	VMI *ROA*	23	14

CHARLES BERNIER
1917-19 (.740)   18-6-1

1917   6-2-1
O6	●	Hampden-Sydney	12	0
O13	●	Emory & Henry	59	6
O20	●	Davidson	13	7
O27	●	at Georgetown	0	28
N3	●	Wake Forest	50	0
N10	●	West Virginia *HUN*	3	27
N17	=	North Carolina St. *NOR*	7	7
N24	●	Roanoke	70	0
N29	●	VMI *ROA*	6	0

1918   7-0-0
O19	●	Belmont	30	0
O26	●	Camp Humphreys	33	6
N2	●	Wash. & Lee *ROA*	13	0
N9	●	Wake Forest	27	0
N16	●	North Carolina St. *NOR*	25	0
N23	●	at North Carolina JV	18	7
N28	●	VMI *ROA*	6	0

1919 — 5-4-0

O4	●	Hampden-Sydney	13	0
O11	●	Richmond	21	0
O18		at Georgetown	7	33
O25	●	at Maryland	6	0
N1		Wash. & Lee LYN	0	3
N8	●	Wake Forest	40	0
N15		North Carolina St. NOR	0	3
N22	●	Emory & Henry	99	0
N27		VMI ROA	0	13

STANLEY SUTTON 1920 (.400) 4-6

1920 — 4-6-0

S25	●	Hampden-Sydney	35	0
O2	●	William & Mary	21	0
O9	●	Emory & Henry	75	6
O16		at Rutgers	6	19
O23		Maryland	0	7
O30		Wash. & Lee LYN	0	13
N6	●	at Richmond	21	0
N11		North Carolina St. NOR	6	14
N20		Centre LOU	0	28
N25		VMI ROA	7	24

1921-1964
SOUTHERN

BEN CUBBAGE 1921-25 (.688) 30-12-6

1921 — 7-3-0 (1-2-0)

S24	●	Hampden-Sydney	14	6
O1	●	Wm .& Mary	14	0
O8		at Centre	0	14
O15	●	at Richmond	34	0
O22	|	Maryland DC	7	10
O29	|	Wash. & Lee LYN	0	3
N5	●	Morris-Harvey	54	7
N11	● |	North Carolina St. NOR	7	3
N19	●	Roanoke	35	0
N24	●	VMI ROA	26	7

1922 — 8-1-1 (3-0-0)

S23	●	Hampden-Sydney	38	0
S30	●	King Coll.	25	0
O7	●	William & Mary	20	6
O14		Centre RICH	6	10
O21	=	at Davidson	7	7
O28	●	Catholic U.	73	0
N4	● |	Maryland	21	0
N11	● |	North Carolina St. NOR	24	0
N18	● |	Wash. & Lee LYN	41	6
N30	●	VMI ROA	7	3

1923 — 6-3-0 (4-1-0)

S29	●	Hampden-Sydney	29	0
O6	●	Davidson	7	0
O13		at 3rd Army Corps	17	21
O20	● |	Maryland DC	16	9 *
O27	|	Wash. & Lee LYN	0	12
N3	● |	Clemson	25	6
N10	● |	North Carolina St. NOR	16	0
N17	● |	at Virginia	6	3
N29		VMI ROA	0	6

1924 — 4-2-3 (2-2-3)

S27	●	Richmond	28	0
O4	●	Hampden-Sydney	10	0
O11	= |	Auburn RICH	0	0
O18	● |	Maryland DC	12	0
O25	= |	Wash. & Lee LYN	0	0
N1	● |	at Clemson	50	6
N8	|	at North Carolina St.	3	6
N15	|	Virginia	0	6
N27	= |	VMI ROA	0	0

1925 — 5-3-2 (3-3-1)

S19	●	Lynchburg	10	0
S26	=	Roanoke	0	0
O3	●	Hampden-Sydney	13	3
O10	|	at Auburn	0	19
O17	● |	Maryland DC	3	0
O24	|	Wash. & Lee LYN	0	20
O31	● |	South Carolina RICH	6	0
N7	= |	North Carolina St.	0	0
N14	|	at Virginia	0	10
N26	● |	VMI ROA	7	0

ANDY GUSTAFSON 1926-29 (.625) 22-13-1

1926 — 5-3-1 (3-2-1)

S25	●	Roanoke Coll.	47	0
O2	●	Hampden-Sydney	30	0
O9		at Dartmouth	0	21
O16	● |	Maryland NOR	24	8
O23	● |	Virginia	6	0
O30	= |	at Kentucky	13	13
N6	|	South Carolina RICH	0	19
N13	|	Wash. & Lee LYN	0	13
N25	● |	VMI ROA	14	7

1927 — 5-4-0 (2-3-0)

S24	●	Roanoke	21	2
O1	●	Hampden-Sydney	13	0
O8	●	at Colgate	6	0
O15	|	Maryland NOR	7	13
O22	|	at Virginia	0	7
O29		at U.T. Chattanooga	13	14
N5	● |	South Carolina RICH	35	0
N12	● |	Wash. & Lee	21	0
N24	|	VMI ROA	9	12

1928 — 7-2-0 (4-1-0)

S29	●	Roanoke	34	7
O6	●	Hampden-Sydney	32	7
O13		at Colgate	14	35
O20	● |	at North Carolina	16	14
O27	● |	King Coll.	54	0
N3	● |	Maryland NOR	9	6
N10	● |	Virginia	20	0
N17	● |	at Wash. & Lee	13	7
N29	|	VMI ROA	6	16

1929 — 5-4-0 (2-3-0)

S28	●	Roanoke	19	0
O5	●	Hampden-Sydney	37	6
O12		at Pennsylvania	8	14
O19	●	William & Mary RICH	25	14
O26	|	at North Carolina	13	38
N2	● |	Wash. & Lee LYN	36	6
N9	● |	at Virginia	32	12
N16	|	Maryland NOR	0	24
N28	|	VMI ROA	0	14

O.E. NEALE 1930-31 (.528) 8-7-3

1930 — 5-3-1 (2-3-1)

S27	●	Roanoke	9	0
O4	|	North Carolina	21	39
O11	|	at Vanderbilt	0	40
O18	● |	William & Mary RICH	7	6
O25	●	at Davidson	20	19
N1	= |	at Wash. & Lee	0	0
N8	● |	Virginia	31	13 *
N15	|	Maryland NOR	7	13
N27	● |	VMI ROA	24	0

1931 — 3-4-2 (1-4-1)

S26	●	King Coll.	33	0
O3	|	at Georgia	0	40
O10	●	Davidson	18	6
O17	=	William & Mary RICH	6	6
O24	|	at Kentucky	6	20
O31	|	Maryland	0	20
N6	|	Wash. & Lee ROA	0	7
N14	= |	at Virginia	0	0
N26	● |	VMI ROA	13	6

HENRY B. REDD 1932-40 (.534) 43-37-8

1932 — 8-1-0 (6-1-0)

S24	●	Roanoke	32	7
O1	● |	at Georgia	7	6
O8	●	at Maryland	23	0
O15	● |	William & Mary RICH	7	0
O22	● |	Kentucky	7	0
O29	● |	at Wash. & Lee	32	6
N5	|	at Alabama	6	9
N12	● |	Virginia	13	0
N24	● |	VMI ROA	26	0

1933 — 4-3-3 (1-1-3)

S23	●	Roanoke	7	0
S30		at Tennessee	0	27
O7	● |	Maryland NOR	14	0 *
O14	● |	William & Mary RICH	13	7
O21	●	at Richmond	7	0
O28	|	South Carolina	0	12
N4	= |	Wash. & Lee	7	7
N11		at Alabama	0	27
N18	= |	at Virginia	6	6
N30	= |	VMI ROA	0	0

1934 — 5-5-0 (3-3-0)

S22	●	Roanoke	21	0
S29		at Temple	0	34
O6		Florida	13	20
O13	●	William & Mary RICH	6	0
O20	|	Maryland NOR	9	14
O27	|	at Wash. & Lee	7	13
N3	|	at South Carolina	0	20
N10	● |	North Carolina St. PTS	7	6
N17	● |	Virginia	19	6
N29	● |	VMI ROA	13	0

1935 — 4-3-2 (3-3-1)

S21	●	Roanoke	7	0
S28	|	Clemson	7	28
O5	|	Maryland	0	7
O12	= |	William & Mary BALT	0	0
O26	● |	Wash. & Lee RICH	15	0
N2	● |	South Carolina BLU	27	0
N9	|	North Carolina St. PTS	0	6
N16	= |	at Virginia	0	0
N28	● |	VMI ROA	12	6

1936 — 5-5-0 (3-5-0)

S17	●	Roanoke	16	7
S26	|	at Clemson	0	20
O3	|	Maryland ROA	0	6
O10	● |	William & Mary RICH	14	0
O17	|	at South Carolina	0	14
O24	|	at North Carolina St.	0	13
O31	● |	Richmond	20	7
N7	|	at Wash. & Lee	0	27
N14	●	Virginia	7	6
N26	● |	VMI ROA	6	0

1937 — 5-5-0 (2-4-0)

S18	●	Roanoke	27	7
S25	|	Duke GRO	0	25
O2		at Tennessee	0	27
O9	|	William & Mary RICH	0	12
O16	|	at North Carolina St.	7	13
O23	● |	Wash. & Lee	19	7
O30	●	Hampden-Sydney	31	0
N6	|	at Richmond	7	12
N13	● |	at Virginia	14	7
N25	● |	VMI ROA	12	6

1938 — 3-5-2 (2-3-2)

S17	●	Emory & Henry	33	0
S24	|	Duke GRO	0	18
O1		at Army	0	39
O8	● |	William & Mary RICH	27	0
O15		Virginia	6	14
O22	|	at Wash. & Lee	0	6
O29	● |	North Carolina St.	7	0
N5	|	at North Carolina	0	7
N11	= |	at Richmond	0	0
N24	= |	VMI ROA	2	2

1939 — 4-5-1 (1-4-1)

S23	●	Randolph Macon	26	0
S30		at Marshall	0	20
O7	|	North Carolina NOR	6	13
O17	= |	William & Mary RICH	6	6
O27	●	Centre	28	0
O28	|	Wash. & Lee LYN	0	6
N4	●	Furman	20	7
N11	|	at Richmond	0	13
N18	●	at Virginia	13	0
N30	|	VMI ROA	7	19

1940 — 5-5-0 (2-3-0)

S21	●	Catawba	34	12
S28		at Marshall	7	13
O5	|	Richmond	7	13
O12	|	William & Mary RICH	13	20
O19		at Georgetown	4	46
O26	● |	Wash. & Lee LYN	21	0
N2	●	Virginia NOR	6	0
N9	● |	Furman ROA	38	21
N16	●	at Centre	10	6
N21	|	VMI	0	14

JAMES KITTS 1941, '46-47 (.500) 13-13-3

1941 — 6-4-0 (4-2-0)

S20	●	Catawba	22	2
S27		Kentucky LOU	14	37
O4	●	Georgetown	3	0
O11	|	William & Mary RICH	7	16
O18	● |	at Davidson	16	0
O25	● |	Wash. & Lee LYN	13	3
N1		Virginia NOR	0	34
N8	● |	North Carolina St. W-S	14	13
N20	|	VMI LYN	10	15
N29	● |	Richmond	13	0

H.M. McEVER / S.D. TILSON 1942 (.750) 7-2-1

1942 — 7-2-1 (5-1-0)

S19	●	Catawba	28	14
S26	● |	at Furman	7	6
O3	|	William & Mary	7	21
O10	● |	Davidson	16	0
O17	=	Kentucky ROA	21	21
O24	● |	Wash. & Lee LYN	19	6
O31	●	Virginia NOR	20	14
N7	● |	at Richmond	16	7
N14		at Army	7	19
N26	● |	VMI ROA	20	6

1943-1944

NO TEAM WWII

H.M. McEVER 1945 (.250) 2-6

1945 — 2-6-0 (2-5-0)

O6	|	North Carolina ROA	0	14
O13	|	William & Mary RICH	0	38
O20	● |	Maryland	21	13
O27		Virginia ROA	13	31
N3	|	at North Carolina St.	0	6
N10	|	at Clemson	0	35
N17	● |	Richmond	44	6
N22	|	VMI ROA	0	7

JAMES KITTS

1946 — 3-4-3 (3-3-2)

S28	= |	at North Carolina	14	14
O5	=	Virginia ROA	21	21
O12	|	William & Mary	0	49
O18	|	at Maryland	0	6
O26	● |	North Carolina St.	14	6
N2	|	Clemson	7	14
N9	● |	Wash. & Lee LYN	13	7
N16	= |	at Richmond	7	7
N28	● |	VMI ROA	20	7
		SUN BOWL		
J1		Cincinnati	6	18

1947 — 4-5-0 (4-3-0)

S27	● |	Furman	20	6
O4		Virginia ROA	7	41
O11	|	William & Mary RICH	7	21
O18		at Army	0	40
O25	|	Maryland	19	21
O31	●	at George Washington	42	6
N8	● |	Wash. & Lee LYN	27	14
N15	● |	Richmond	26	14
N27	|	VMI ROA	14	28

ROBERT McNEISH 1948-50 (.086) 1-25-3

1948 — 0-8-1 (0-6-1)

S25	|	George Washington	0	13
O2		Virginia ROA	0	28
O9	|	Maryland DC	0	28
O16	|	William & Mary	0	30
O23	|	Duke ROA	0	7
O30		at Army	7	49
N6	|	Wash. & Lee LYN	7	14
N13	= |	at Richmond	7	7
N25	|	VMI ROA	7	33

1949 — 1-7-2 (1-5-2)

S17		Quantico Marines ALEXV	14	33
S24	|	Maryland	7	34
O1	|	at William & Mary	13	39
O8		Virginia ROA	0	26
O15	|	George Washington	14	24
O22	|	at Duke	7	55
O29	|	North Carolina St. NOR	13	14
N5	= |	Wash. & Lee LYN	6	6
N12	● |	at Richmond	28	13
N24	= |	VMI ROA	28	28

1950 — 0-10-0 (0-8-0)

S30		Quantico	21	61
O7		Virginia ROA	6	45
O13	|	at George Washington	7	42
O21	|	William & Mary	0	54
O28	|	at North Carolina St.	6	34
N4	|	at Wash. & Lee	7	25
N11	|	Richmond	12	32
N18	|	Duke W-S	6	47
N23	|	VMI ROA	0	27
D2	|	at Maryland	7	63

FRANK MOSELEY
1951-60 (.560) 54-42-4

1951 2-8-0 (1-7-0)
S15	●	Marshall *Blu*	18 12
S29		Davidson	20 32
O6		Virginia *Roa*	0 33
O12		George Washington *AlexV*	13 38
O20		Duke *Nor*	6 55
O27		North Carolina St.	14 19
N3		Wash. & Lee *Rich*	0 60
N10		at William & Mary	7 28
N17		Richmond	20 14
N22		VMI *Roa*	7 20

1952 5-6-0 (4-4-0)
S13	●	Marshall *Blu*	19 14
S20		at Davidson	27 14
S27		at Citadel	14 7
O4		Virginia *Roa*	0 42
O11		at Alabama	0 33
O18		George Washington	0 6
O25		at Wash. & Lee	27 34
N1	●	at Richmond	20 2
N8		William & Mary	15 35
N15		at West Virginia	7 27
N27	●	VMI *Roa*	26 7

1953 5-5-0 (3-3-0)
S19	●	Marshall *Blu*	7 0
S26	●	at Virginia	20 6
O3		at Rutgers	13 20
O10	●	Richmond	21 7
O17		at William & Mary	7 13
O24	●	Wash. & Lee	32 12
O30	●	Citadel *Roa*	22 0
N7		West Virginia *Blu*	7 12
N13		at Miami, Fla.	0 26
N26	●	VMI *Roa*	13 28

1954 8-0-1 (3-0-1)
S18	●	North Carolina St.	30 21
S25	●	Wake Forest *Rich*	32 0
O2		at Clemson	18 7
O16	●	at Richmond	19 12
O23	●	Virginia	6 0
O30	=	William & Mary	7 7
N5	●	at George Washington	20 13
N13		Waynesburg	20 6
N25	●	VMI *Roa*	46 9

1955 6-3-1 (2-1-1)
S17		at Wake Forest	0 13
S24	●	at Pennsylvania	33 0
O1	●	at William & Mary	14 7
O8	●	at Florida State	24 20
O15	=	Richmond	7 7
O22	●	Virginia *Roa*	17 13
O29		George Washington	7 13
N5		Clemson *Roa*	16 21
N12	●	North Carolina St. *Blu*	34 26
N24	●	VMI *Roa*	39 13

1956 7-2-1 (3-0-0)
S15	●	East Carolina *Blu*	37 2
S22		at Tulane	14 21
S29	●	North Carolina St. *Nor*	35 6
O6		at Florida State	20 7
O13	●	William & Mary	34 7
O20	●	at Richmond	46 14
O27	●	Virginia *Roa*	14 7
N3		at Clemson	6 21
N10	=	Wake Forest	13 13
N22	●	VMI *Roa*	45 0

1957 4-6-0 (1-3-0)
S20	●	at Tulane	14 13
S28		at West Virginia	0 14
O5		at William & Mary	7 13
O12	●	Villanova	21 14
O19		Virginia *Rich*	7 38
O26		at Florida State	7 20
N2	●	Richmond	42 7
N9		at Wake Forest	10 3
N16		North Carolina St. *Roa*	0 12
N28		VMI *Roa*	6 14

1958 5-4-1 (3-1-0)
S20	●	West Texas St. *Roa*	28 12
S27		Wake Forest *Nor*	6 13
O4	●	William & Mary	27 15
O11	●	Virginia *Roa*	22 13
O18		at Florida State	0 28
O25		West Virginia *Rich*	20 21
N1	=	at North Carolina St.	14 14
N8	●	Richmond	27 23
N15		at Southern Miss	0 41
N27	●	VMI *Roa*	21 16

1959 6-4-0 (3-1-0)
S19		North Carolina St. *Nor*	13 15
S26		at Wake Forest	18 27
O3	●	William & Mary *Roa*	20 14
O10		Florida State	6 7
O17	●	Virginia *Rich*	40 14
O24	●	at Villanova	24 14
O31	●	Richmond	51 29
N7	●	at West Texas St.	26 21
N14	●	at West Virginia	12 0
N26		VMI *Roa*	12 37

1960 6-4-0 (4-2-0)
S17		North Carolina St.	14 29
S24	●	Virginia *Rich*	15 0
O1		at Clemson	7 13
O8	●	Wake Forest	22 13
O15	●	at William & Mary	27 0
O22	●	Virginia *Roa*	40 6
O29	●	at Richmond	20 0
N5		Davidson	7 9
N11	●	at George Washington	8 21
N24	●	VMI *Roa*	13 2

JERRY CLAIBORNE
1961-70 (.608) 61-39-2

1961 4-5-0 (2-3-0)
S16	●	William & Mary *Roa*	20 6
O7		at West Virginia	0 28
O14		at Tulane	14 27
O21	●	Virginia *Roa*	20 0
O28	●	Florida State	10 7
N4		at Richmond	0 11
N11		at Wake Forest	15 24
N17	●	George Washington	14 3
N23		VMI *Roa*	0 6

1962 5-5-0 (2-3-0)
S15		at William & Mary	0 3
S22	●	George Washington *Roa*	15 14
S29		West Virginia *Rich*	0 14
O6		Virginia *Roa*	20 15
O13	●	Richmond	13 7
O20		at Army	12 20
O27		at Florida State	7 20
N3		at Tulane	24 22
N10	●	Wake Forest	37 8
N22		VMI *Roa*	9 14

1963 8-2-0 (5-0-0)
S21		at Kentucky	14 33
S28	●	at Wake Forest	27 0
O5	●	Virginia *Roa*	10 0
O11	●	at George Washington	22 8
O19		William & Mary	28 13
O26	●	at Florida State	31 23
N2	●	at Richmond	14 13
N9		at North Carolina St.	7 13
N16	●	at West Virginia	28 3
N28	●	VMI *Roa*	35 20

1964 6-4-0 (3-1-0)
S19	●	at Tampa	18 14
S26		Wake Forest *Roa*	21 38
O3		at Virginia	17 20
O10	●	George Washington	33 0
O17		West Virginia	10 23
O24	●	Florida State	20 11
O31	●	at William & Mary	27 20
N7		North Carolina St.	28 19
N14		at Syracuse	15 20
N26	●	VMI *Roa*	35 13

1965-1990 INDEPENDENT

1965 7-3-0
S18	●	Wake Forest *Roa*	12 3
S25	●	at Richmond	25 7
O2	●	William & Mary	9 7
O9	●	at George Washington	17 12
O16		at Vanderbilt	10 21
O23	●	Virginia	22 14
O30		at Florida State	6 7
N6		at West Virginia	22 31
N13		Villanova	21 19
N25	●	VMI *Roa*	44 13

1966 8-2-1
S17		at Tulane	0 13
S24	●	George Washington	49 0
O1	=	West Virginia	13 13
O8	●	at Kentucky	7 0
O15	●	Vanderbilt *Rich*	21 6
O22	●	at Virginia	24 7
O29	●	Florida State	23 21
N5	●	at Wake Forest	11 0
N12	●	at William & Mary	20 18
N24	●	VMI *Roa*	70 12

LIBERTY BOWL
D10		Miami, Fla.	7 14

1967 7-3-0
S16	●	at Tampa	13 3
S23	●	William & Mary	31 7
S30	●	at Kansas State	15 3
O7	●	Villanova	3 0
O14	●	at Kentucky	24 14
O21	●	Richmond	45 14
O28	●	at West Virginia	20 7
N4		Miami, Fla.	7 14
N11	●	at Florida State	15 38
N23		VMI *Roa*	10 12

1968 7-4-0
S21	●	Alabama *Birm*	7 14
S28	●	at William & Mary	12 0
O5		Kansas State	19 34
O12	●	Wake Forest	7 6
O18	●	at Miami, Fla.	8 13
O26	●	West Virginia	27 12
N2	●	at Florida State	40 22
N9	●	Richmond	31 18
N16	●	at South Carolina	17 6
N28	●	VMI *Roa*	55 6

LIBERTY BOWL
D14		Mississippi	17 34

1969 4-5-1
S20		Alabama	13 17
S27		at Wake Forest	10 16
O4		at Richmond	10 17
O11		Kentucky	6 7
O18		South Carolina	16 17
O25	●	at Buffalo	21 7
N1		William & Mary *Roa*	48 7
N8	=	Florida State	10 10
N15	●	Duke *Nor*	48 12
N27	●	VMI *Roa*	52 0

1970 5-6-0
S12		Virginia	0 7
S19		Alabama *Birm*	18 51
S26		Memphis	20 21
O3		South Carolina	7 24
O10		Wake Forest	9 28
O17	●	Tulsa	17 14
O24	●	Buffalo	31 14
O31	●	William & Mary	35 14
N7	●	Villanova	34 7
N14		Florida State	8 34
N21	●	VMI *Roa*	20 14

CHARLIE COFFEY
1971-73 (.379) 12-20-1

1971 4-7-0
S18		Wake Forest	9 20
S25		at Oklahoma State	16 24
O2		Florida State	3 17
O9		at Tulsa	39 46
O16	●	William & Mary	41 30
O23	●	Ohio U.	37 29
O30		at Kentucky	27 33
N6		at Virginia	6 0
N13		at Houston	29 56
N20		Southern Miss	8 17
N27	●	VMI *Roa*	34 0

1972 6-4-1
S16		at Virginia	20 24
S23		at Florida State	15 27
S30	●	SMU	13 10
O7	=	Houston	27 27
O14	●	Oklahoma State	34 32
O21	●	at Ohio U.	53 21
O28		William & Mary *Rich*	16 17
N4	●	Southern Miss	27 14
N11	●	South Carolina	45 20
N18		at Alabama	13 52
N25	●	at Wake Forest	44 9

FRANK MOSELEY (cont'd columns)
1973 2-9-0
S8	●	William & Mary	24 31
S15	●	at Kentucky	26 31
S22		at West Virginia	10 24
S29	●	SMU *Inv*	6 37
O6		South Carolina	24 27
O12		at Houston	27 54
O20	●	Virginia	27 15
O27	●	at Alabama	6 77
N3		at Memphis	16 49
N10	●	Florida State	36 13
N17		VMI	21 22

JIMMY SHARPE
1974-77 (.489) 21-22-1

1974 4-7-0
S14		Kentucky	7 38
S21		at SMU	25 28
S28		Houston	12 49
O5		VMI *Rich*	17 22
O12	●	at South Carolina	31 17
O19		at Virginia	27 28
O26	●	Richmond	41 7
N1		at Miami, Fla.	7 14
N9	●	at William & Mary	34 15
N16	●	at Florida State	56 21
N23		West Virginia	21 22

1975 8-3-0
S13		at Kentucky	8 27
S20		at Kent	11 17
S27	●	Richmond	21 9
O4		at Auburn	23 16
O11		Florida State	13 10
O18	●	Virginia	24 17
O24		at West Virginia	7 10
N1	●	William & Mary *Nor*	24 7
N8	●	at Houston	34 28
N15		VMI	33 0
N22	●	Wake Forest	40 10

1976 6-5-0
S4	●	at Wake Forest	23 6
S11		at Texas A&M	0 19
S18	●	Southern Miss	16 7
O2		William & Mary	15 21
O9	●	VMI *Rich*	37 7
O16	●	at Virginia	14 10
O23	●	Kent	42 14
O30	●	West Virginia	24 7
N6		Tulsa	31 35
N13		at Richmond	0 16
N20		at Florida State	21 28

1977 3-7-1
S17		Texas A&M	6 27
S24		at Memphis	20 21
O1		Clemson	13 31
O8	●	William & Mary *Rich*	17 8
O15	=	Virginia	14 14
O22		at Richmond	14 17
O29		at Kentucky	0 32
N5		Florida State	21 23
N12		at West Virginia	14 20
N19	●	Wake Forest	28 10
N26	●	VMI	27 7

BILL DOOLEY
1978-86 (.623) 63-38-1

1978 4-7-0
S9	●	Tulsa	33 35
S16	●	at Wake Forest	28 6
S23		Auburn	7 18
S30	●	William & Mary	22 19
O7		at Clemson	7 38
O14	●	West Virginia	16 3
O21		at Virginia	7 17
O28		at Alabama	0 35
N4		Kentucky	0 28
N11		at Florida State	14 24
N18	●	VMI	28 2

1979 5-6-0
S8	●	at Louisville	15 14
S15	●	Appalachian St.	41 32
S22	●	William & Mary	35 14
S29	●	Florida State	10 17
O6		Wake Forest	14 19
O13		Clemson	0 21
O20	●	Richmond	34 0
O27		at Alabama	7 31
N3		at West Virginia	23 34
N10		at Virginia	18 20
N17	●	VMI	27 20

1980 — 8-4-0

S6	●	at Wake Forest	16	7
S13	●	East Tenn. St.	35	7
S20	●	William & Mary	7	3
S27	●	James Madison	38	6
O4		at Clemson	10	13
O11	●	Rhode Island	34	7
O18	●	Virginia	30	0
O25		at Richmond	7	18
N1	●	West Virginia	34	11
N8		at Florida State	7	31
N15	●	VMI *Roa*	21	6
		PEACH BOWL		
J2		Miami, Fla.	10	20

1981 — 7-4-0

S12	●	Richmond	28	12
S19	●	William & Mary	47	3
S26	●	Wake Forest	30	14
O3	●	Memphis	17	13
O10		at Duke	7	14
O17		at West Virginia	6	27
O24	●	Appalachian St.	34	12
O31	●	at Kentucky	29	3
N14		at Miami, Fla.	14	21
N21		VMI	0	6
N28	●	at Virginia	20	3

1982 — 7-4-0

S4	●	at Richmond	20	9
S18		Miami, Fla.	8	14
S25	●	William & Mary	47	3
O2		Wake Forest	10	13
O9	●	at Duke	22	21
O16		West Virginia	6	16
O23	●	Appalachian St.	34	0
O30	●	Kentucky	29	3
N13		at Vanderbilt	0	45
N20	●	VMI *Nor*	14	3
N25	●	Virginia	21	14

1983 — 9-2-0

S10		Wake Forest	6	13
S17	●	at Memphis	17	10
S24	●	VMI	28	0
O1	●	Louisville	31	0
O8	●	Duke	27	14
O15		at West Virginia	0	13
O22	●	Richmond	38	0
O29	●	William & Mary	59	21
N5	●	at Tulane	26	10
N12	●	Vanderbilt	21	10
N19	●	at Virginia	48	0

1984 — 8-4-0

S8	●	at Wake Forest	21	20
S15		West Virginia	7	14
S22	●	Richmond	21	13
S29		Virginia	23	26
O6	●	VMI *Nor*	54	7
O13	●	Duke	27	0
O20	●	William & Mary	38	14
O27	●	at Temple	9	7
N3	●	Tulane	13	6
N10		at Clemson	10	17
N17	●	at Vanderbilt	23	3
		INDEPENDENCE BOWL		
D15		Air Force	7	23

1985 — 6-5-0

A31		at Cincinnati	14	31
S7		Richmond	14	24
S14		Clemson	17	20
S28	●	Syracuse	24	14
O5		at West Virginia	9	24
O12	●	William & Mary	40	10
O19	●	at Virginia	28	10
O26		at Florida	18	35
N2	●	Memphis	31	10
N9	●	Louisville	41	17
N16	●	at Vanderbilt	38	24

1986 — 9-2-1

S6		Cincinnati	20	24
S13	●	at Clemson	20	14
S20	●	at Syracuse	26	17
S27	●	East Tenn. St.	37	10
O4	●	West Virginia	13	7
O11	=	South Carolina	27	27
O18		Temple *Nor*	13	29 †
O25	●	Virginia	42	10
N1	●	Kentucky	17	15
N8	●	at Richmond	17	10
N15	●	Vanderbilt	29	21
		PEACH BOWL		
D31	●	North Carolina St.	25	24

FRANK BEAMER
1987-Present (.636) 135-77-2

1987 — 2-9-0

S12		Clemson	10	22
S19		at Virginia	13	14
S26		Syracuse	21	35
O3	●	Navy	31	11
O10		at South Carolina	10	40
O17		East Carolina	23	32
O24		at Tulane	38	57
O31		at Kentucky	7	14
N7		at West Virginia	16	28
N14		at Miami, Fla.	13	27
N21	●	Cincinnati	21	20

1988 — 3-8-0

S3		at Clemson	7	40
S10	●	East Carolina	27	16
S17		at Southern Miss	13	35
S24		at Syracuse	0	35
O1		West Virginia	10	22
O8		South Carolina	24	26
O15	●	at Cincinnati	41	14
O29		Virginia	10	16
N5		at Louisville	3	13
N12		at Florida State	14	41
N19	●	James Madison	27	6

1989 — 6-4-1

S2	●	Akron	29	3
S9	=	at South Carolina	17	17
S16		Clemson	7	27
S23	●	Temple	23	0
O7	●	at West Virginia	12	10
O14		Florida State	7	41
O21		at East Carolina	10	14
O28	●	Tulane	30	13
N4	●	Vanderbilt	18	0
N11		at Virginia	25	32
N18	●	at North Carolina St.	25	23

1990 — 6-5-0

S1		at Maryland	13	20
S8	●	Bowling Green	21	7
S15	●	at East Carolina	24	23
S22		South Carolina	24	35
S29		at Florida State	28	39
O6	●	West Virginia	26	21
O20		at Temple	28	31
O27	●	Southern Miss	20	16
N3	●	North Carolina St.	20	16
N10		at Georgia Tech	3	6
N24	●	Virginia	38	13

1991-2003
Big East

1991 — 5-6-0 (1-0-0)

A31	●	James Madison	41	12
S7		at North Carolina St.	0	7
S21		at South Carolina	21	28
S28		at Oklahoma	17	27
O5	● |	at West Virginia	20	14
O12		Florida State *Orl*	20	33
O19	●	Cincinnati	56	9
O26	●	Louisville	41	13
N9	●	Akron	42	24
N16		East Carolina	17	24
N23		at Virginia	0	38

1992 — 2-8-1 (1-4-0)

S5	●	James Madison	49	20
S12		at East Carolina	27	30
S19	● |	at Temple	26	7
S26	|	West Virginia	7	16
O10		at Louisville	17	21
O17	=	North Carolina St.	13	13
O24	|	Miami, Fla.	23	43
O31	|	at Rutgers	49	50
N7	|	at Syracuse	9	28
N14		Southern Miss	12	13
N21		Virginia	38	41

1993 — 9-3-0 (4-3-0)

S4	●	Bowling Green	33	16
S11	● |	at Pittsburgh	63	21
S18	|	at Miami, Fla.	2	21
S25	●	Maryland	55	28
O2	|	at West Virginia	13	14
O16	● |	Temple	55	7
O23	● |	Rutgers	49	42
O30	●	East Carolina	31	12
N6	|	at Boston College	34	48
N13	● |	Syracuse	45	24
N20	●	at Virginia	20	17
		INDEPENDENCE BOWL		
D31	●	Indiana	45	20

1994 — 8-4-0 (5-2-0)

S3	●	ArKansas State	34	7
S10	●	at Southern Miss	24	14
S17	● |	at Boston College	12	7
S22	● |	West Virginia	34	6
O1	|	at Syracuse	20	28
O8	● |	Temple	41	13
O15	●	at East Carolina	27	20
O22	● |	Pittsburgh	45	7
O29	|	at Miami, Fla.	3	24
N12	● |	Rutgers	41	34
N19		Virginia	23	42
		GATOR BOWL		
D30		Tennessee	23	45

1995 — 10-2-0 (6-1-0)

S7	|	Boston College	14	20
S16		Cincinnati	0	16
S23	● |	Miami, Fla.	13	7
S30	● |	at Pittsburgh	26	16
O7	●	at Navy	14	0
O14	●	Akron	77	27
O21	● |	at Rutgers	45	17
O28	● |	at West Virginia	27	0
N4	● |	Syracuse	31	7
N11	● |	Temple *DC*	38	16
N18	●	at Virginia	36	29
		SUGAR BOWL		
D31	●	Texas	28	10

1996 — 10-2 (6-1)

S7	●	at Akron	21	18
S14	● |	at Boston College	45	7
S21	● |	Rutgers	30	14
S28	|	at Syracuse	21	52
O12	● |	Temple	38	0
O26	● |	Pittsburgh	34	17
N2	●	La. Lafayette	47	16
N9	●	East Carolina	35	14
N16	● |	at Miami, Fla.	21	7
N23	● |	West Virginia	31	14
N29	●	Virginia	26	9
		ORANGE BOWL		
D31		Nebraska	21	41

1997 — 7-5 (5-2)

A30	● |	at Rutgers	59	19
S13	● |	Syracuse	31	3
S20	● |	at Temple	23	13
S27	●	ArKansas State	50	0
O4		Miami, Ohio	17	24
O11	● |	Boston College	17	7
O25	|	at West Virginia	17	30
N1	●	UAB	37	0
N8	● |	Miami, Fla.	27	25
N22	|	at Pittsburgh	23	30
N29		at Virginia	20	34
		GATOR BOWL		
J1		North Carolina	3	42

1998 — 9-3 (5-2)

S5	●	East Carolina	38	3
S12	●	at Clemson	37	0
S19	● |	at Miami, Fla.	27	20
S26	● |	Pittsburgh	27	7
O8	● |	at Boston College	17	0
O17	|	Temple	24	28
O24	●	at UAB	41	0
O31	● |	West Virginia	27	13
N14	|	at Syracuse	26	28
N21	● |	Rutgers	47	7
N28		Virginia	32	36
		MUSIC CITY BOWL		
D29	●	Alabama	38	7

1999 — 11-1 (7-0)

S4	●	James Madison	47	0
S11	●	UAB	31	10
S23	●	Clemson	31	11
O2	●	at Virginia	31	7
O9	● |	at Rutgers	58	20
O16	● |	Syracuse	62	0
O30	● |	at Pittsburgh	30	17
N6	● |	at West Virginia	22	20
N13	● |	Miami, Fla.	43	10
N20	● |	at Temple	62	7
N26	● |	Boston College	38	14
		SUGAR BOWL		
J4		Florida State	29	46

2000 — 11-1 (6-1)

S2	●	Akron	52	23
S9	●	at East Carolina	45	28
S16	● |	Rutgers	49	0
S30	● |	at Boston College	48	34
O7	● |	Temple	35	13
O12	● |	West Virginia	48	20
O21	● |	at Syracuse	22	14
O28	● |	Pittsburgh	37	34
N4	|	at Miami, Fla.	21	41
N11	●	at Central Florida	44	21
N25	●	Virginia	42	21
		GATOR BOWL		
J1	●	Clemson	41	20

2001 — 8-4 (4-3)

S1	●	Connecticut	52	10
S8	●	Western Michigan	31	0
S22	● |	at Rutgers	50	0
S29	●	Central Florida	46	14
O6	● |	at West Virginia	35	0
O13	● |	Boston College	34	20
O27	|	Syracuse	14	22
N3	|	at Pittsburgh	7	38
N10	● |	at Temple	35	0
N17	●	at Virginia	31	17
D1	|	Miami, Fla.	24	26
		GATOR BOWL		
J1		Florida State	17	30

2002 — 10-4 (3-4)

A25	●	Arkansas State	63	7
S1	●	LSU	26	8
S12	●	Marshall	47	21
S21	●	at Texas A&M	13	3
S28	●	at Western Michigan	30	0
O10	● |	at Boston College	28	23
O19	● |	Rutgers	35	14
O26	● |	Temple	20	10
N2	|	Pittsburgh	21	28
N9	|	at Syracuse	42	50
N20	|	West Virginia	18	21
N30	●	Virginia	21	9
D7	|	at Miami, Fla.	45	56
		SAN FRANCISCO BOWL		
D31	●	Air Force	20	13

2003 — 8-5 (4-3)

A31	●	Central Florida	49	28
S6	●	James Madison	43	0
S18	●	Texas A&M	35	19
S27	●	Connecticut	47	13
O4	● |	at Rutgers	48	22
O11	● |	Syracuse	51	7
O22	|	at West Virginia	7	28
N1	● |	Miami, Fla.	31	7
N8	|	at Pittsburgh	28	31
N15	● |	at Temple	24	23
N22	|	Boston College	27	34
N29		at Virginia	21	35
		INSIGHT BOWL		
D26		California	49	52

2004-Present
ACC

2004 — 10-3 (7-1)

A28		Southern Cal *LAN*	13	24
S11	●	Western Michigan	63	0
S18	● |	Duke	41	17
S25	|	North Carolina St.	16	17
O2	●	West Virginia	19	13
O9	● |	at Wake Forest	17	10
O16	●	Florida A&M	62	0
O28	● |	at Georgia Tech	34	20
N6	● |	at North Carolina	27	24
N18	● |	Maryland	55	6
N27	● |	Virginia	24	10
D4	● |	at Miami, Fla.	16	10
		SUGAR BOWL		
J3		Auburn	13	16

Neutral Site key: *AlexV* Alexandria, VA / *Balt* Baltimore, MD / *Bed* Bedford, VA / *Birm* Birmingham, AL / *Blu* Bluefield, WV / *ChWV* Charleston, WV / *Char* Charlotte, NC / *Colu* Columbia, SC / *Dan* Danville, VA / *ElP* El Paso, TX / *Gro* Greensboro, NC / *Hun* Huntington, WV / *Irv* Irving, TX / *Knox* Knoxville, TN / *Lou* Louisville, KY / *Lyn* Lynchburg, VA / *Mem* Memphis, TN / *Nor* Norfolk, VA / *Orl* Orlando, FL / *Pts* Portsmouth, VA / *Ral* Raleigh, NC / *Rich* Richmond, VA / *Roa* Roanoke, VA / *StV* Staunton, VA / *DC* Washington, DC / *W-S* Winston-Salem, NC

f **Forfeit** † **Game Later Forfieted** # **Disputed Victor** * **Disputed Score** || **Designated Conference Game** |2 **Counted Twice in Conference Standings**

WAKE FOREST

BY BOB HARIG

I T SEEMS EASY TO CHUCKLE AT WAKE Forest's gridiron "history," but consider the circumstances. This is a private university with fewer than 4,000 undergraduates trying to compete at the highest echelon of college football. Stringent academic requirements and a small pool of eligible talent make the task a daunting one, and the school has not always made the necessary commitments. Thus, winning seasons have been rare, championships all but impossible. That's why the school lists among its greatest achievements a 1992 Independence Bowl victory; why its lone ACC title in 1970 was achieved despite an overall record of 6–5; and why latest head coach Jim Grobe, after opening his tenure with two winning seasons, was rewarded with a 10-year contract extension in 2003.

TRADITION Because there have been so few opportunities over the years, players and coaches take seriously the singing of the school fight song, "O Here's to Wake Forest," in the locker room after a victory. Each year, incoming freshmen are taught the tune in the hopes that they'll have a chance to use it often. Lately, the Demon Deacons have taken to singing their alma mater, "Dear Old Wake Forest," in front of students after wins. Students have also developed their own postvictory tradition, known as "Rolling the Quad"—covering everything on campus with toilet paper.

BEST PLAYER Bill George was the first Demon Deacon ever named to an All-America team, earning the honor as a sophomore in 1949. George, a defensive tackle, was named All-Southern Conference three times and went on to stardom in the NFL with the Chicago Bears and Los Angeles Rams. An eight-time All-Pro linebacker, he was inducted into the Pro Football Hall of Fame in 1974. "Bill was also Wake's one-man wrestling team," said Skeeter Francis, a former Wake Forest student and sports information director. "He would show up at the Southern Conference meet as Wake's lone rep."

BEST COACH D.C. "Peahead" Walker has had the longest tenure, the most victories and the best winning percentage of any coach in Wake Forest history. He led the Demon Deacons to 10 winning seasons in 14 years, 1937-50, and finished with a record of 77–51–6 (.597). Douglas Clyde Walker's nickname stuck with him from

PROFILE

Wake Forest University
Winston-Salem, N.C.
Founded: 1834
Enrollment: 4,128
Colors: Old Gold and Black
Nickname: Demon Deacons
Stadium: Groves Stadium
    Opened in 1968
    FieldTurf; 31,500 capacity
First football game: 1888
All-time record: 374–568–33 (.401)
Bowl record: 4–2
Atlantic Coast Conference championships: 1 (outright)
First-round NFL draftees: 3
Website: www.wakeforestsports.com

THE BEST OF TIMES

From 1944 to 1950, coach D.C. Walker had just one losing season and won 41 games.

THE WORST OF TIMES

The 1962-63 seasons saw the Demon Deacons win only one game under coach Billy Hildebrand, who went 0–10 in 1962, including a 50-0 loss to Duke.

CONFERENCE

Wake Forest was a charter member of the Atlantic Coast Conference in 1953 and has remained in the ACC since. Previously, Wake joined the Southern Conference in 1936.

DISTINGUISHED ALUMNI

Arnold Palmer; Tim Duncan; Billy Packer; Curtis Strange; Lanny Wadkins

FIGHT SONG

O HERE'S TO WAKE FOREST
O here's to Wake Forest
A glass of the finest
Red Ruddy, Rhenish filled up to the brim.
Her sons, they are many
Unrivaled by any
With hearts o'erflowing, we will sing a hymn.

Rah! Rah! Wake Forest, Rah!
Old Alma Mater's sons are we
We'll herald the story
and die for her glory
Old Gold and Black is ever waving high.

As frosh we adore her
As sophs we explore her
And carve our names upon her ancient walls.
As juniors patrol her
As seniors extol her
And weep to leave fore'er her sacred halls.

the age of 11—but once he attended Yale, no one could rightfully call him Peahead anymore. Walker left Wake in 1950 due to a contract dispute that was said to be a matter of $500. He took an assistant coaching position at Yale, and a year later became the head coach for the Montreal Alouettes of the Canadian Football League.

BEST TEAM The 1992 Deacs won six straight games after a 1–3 start and eventually came away with a 39-35 Independence Bowl victory over Oregon, finishing 25th in the Associated Press poll. Nonetheless, the 1970 team is regarded as the best in school history; it claimed the school's only ACC title after rebounding from an 0–3 start. Picked by many to finish last in the ACC that year, Wake toughened itself with a brutal nonconference schedule (they opened with a 36-12 loss to eventual national champion Nebraska and also visited No. 9 Tennessee and Houston). Quarterback Larry Russell won All-ACC honors as a junior, and Win Headley, a three-year starter at defensive tackle, anchored the Deacons' defense. Coach Cal Stoll was named ACC Coach of the Year.

In 1973, Chuck Ramsey set dubious ACC records for punting yardage in a game and in a season.

BIGGEST GAME After the 1970 squad knocked off Duke—previously unbeaten in the ACC—on the road on Nov. 7, the Deacons returned home the next week, needing a win over NC State to give themselves a chance for the conference title. Wake rallied for a 16-13 win over the Wolfpack and finished the season with a 4–0 home record. However, because Duke played one more conference game in 1970, the Blue Devils could have won the title outright by beating North Carolina a week later. But the Tar Heels routed Duke, 59-34, and Wake Forest had its first—and as yet only—ACC title.

BIGGEST UPSET In 1946, the Deacs traveled to fourth-ranked Tennessee and won 19-6. That remains the highest-ranked opponent Wake has ever defeated. Wake finished the season 6–3.

HEARTBREAKER Needing a victory to gain a rare bowl berth, Wake could manage only a 34-34 tie against Division I-AA Appalachian State in the last game of the 1988 season. Independence Bowl representatives were on hand to extend

RECORDS

RUSHING YARDS
GAME — 329 John Leach vs. Maryland, Nov. 20, 1993 (46 att.)
SEASON — 1,228 Larry Hopkins, 1971 (249 att.)
CAREER — 3,811 James McDougald, 1976-79 (880 att.)

PASSING YARDS
GAME — 545 Rusty LaRue vs. NC State, Nov. 18, 1995 (50 of 67)
SEASON — 2,775 Rusty LaRue, 1995 (264 of 421)
CAREER — 8,017 Brian Kuklick, 1994-98 (665 of 1,230)

RECEIVING YARDS
GAME — 271 Wayne Baumgardner vs. South Carolina, Nov. 15, 1980 (12 rec.)
SEASON — 1,053 Ricky Proehl, 1989 (65 rec.)
CAREER — 2,949 Ricky Proehl, 1986-89 (188 rec.)

POINTS
GAME — 28 John Polanski vs. Davidson, Nov. 30, 1939 (4 TDs, 4 PATs)
SEASON — 111 Brian Piccolo, 1964 (17 TDs, 9 PATs)
CAREER — 230 Wilson Hoyle, 1986-89 (37 FGs, 119 PATs)

CONSENSUS ALL-AMERICANS
1976 Bill Armstrong, DB

the Deacs an invitation to their game in Shreveport, La., but could not do so after the tie.

DISPUTE When Wake Forest defeated Clemson 18-15 in 1992, the Tigers claimed that Wake's Todd Dixon was out of the end zone when he made a touchdown reception. However, a photo later showed that the touchdown was valid and that Dixon was indeed inbounds.

STADIUM Groves Stadium was dedicated in 1968, but its name is older. When the school was located in Wake Forest, N.C., it played its games beginning in 1940 in a different version of Groves Stadium, a 20,000-seat facility named in honor of Henry H. Groves, the original stadium's primary benefactor. The Deacs played their final game at the original site in 1955, before the entire school relocated to Winston-Salem for economic and growth reasons. (Land was made available in Winston-Salem, where it was easier for the school to expand.) Once in Winston-Salem, the Deacs played in Bowman Gray Stadium from 1956 to 1967, when a fund-raising campaign made possible the new 31,500-seat Groves Stadium—and continued membership in the ACC.

RIVAL The Deacs consider North Carolina their biggest rival, although the feeling is not likely reciprocated. After all, the Tar Heels have won more than twice as many games in the series as Wake Forest has. Wake has played North Carolina more than any other school—and lost to them more times than to any other school—since their first meeting in 1888. Before moving to Winston-Salem, though, Wake regarded NC State as its main rival, as the two schools were then located in the same county; that series dates to 1895 and has a similarly one-sided history.

NICKNAME After Wake Forest defeated rival Trinity (now Duke) in coach Hank Garrity's inaugural 1923 season, school newspaper editor Mayon Parker referred to the team as Demon Deacons because of what he called their "devilish" play and fighting spirit. Garrity liked the title, as did Wake's news director, Henry Belk; they began using it extensively soon after. Previously, the most common nicknames for the school had been Baptists or the Old Gold & Black.

MASCOT The school mascot comes directly from the nickname; in a Deacon costume that features top hat and tails, a student leads Wake into action. Jack Baldwin, Wake

Forest 1943, was the original student mascot. Donning a tuxedo and a worn top hat, he led the Wake Forest football team onto the field as a stunt in 1941. Over time, the spectacle turned into a tradition, and now tryouts are held annually to fill the position. Over the years, some of the Deacons have taken on a personality of their own. Jeff Dobbs (1977) was an acrobatic dancer who has returned to inspire Wake crowds.

UNIFORMS As early as 1895, the school began using its gold and black colors in athletic competition. The helmets have always been solid gold, white or black. The letters WF appeared in 1978, and have remained, though for a time, numbers were also placed on helmets. The jerseys have been white or black with gold numbers, and the uniform pants have rotated among those three colors.

NUMBERS Despite a modest bowl history, Wake does have one distinction: it played in the first Gator Bowl in 1946, defeating South Carolina 26-14 … On Oct. 20, 1973, punter Chuck Ramsey set a rather dubious ACC record, with 601 punting yards in a 37-0 loss against Maryland. He also holds the season punting record for that 1973 season, with 3,896 yards … Wake Forest is the only ACC school with an all-time record under .500.

LORE Although he was a lightly recruited running back who played on Wake Forest teams that won just once in 20 games, Brian Piccolo merits a full page in the Wake Forest media guide. In 1964, Piccolo carried the ball 252 times and gained 1,044 yards, both ACC records at the time. His rushing total and 111 points scored (he also kicked nine extra points) led the country. Piccolo was not drafted, but he signed a free agent contract with the Chicago Bears. In 1965, he became a friend, roommate and backfield mate to a more celebrated rookie, future Hall of Famer Gale Sayers. In 1970, Piccolo died of cancer at the age of 26. The story of their friendship inspired the 1971 tearjerker *Brian's Song*, starring James Caan as Piccolo and Billy Dee Williams as Sayers. Film critic Leonard Maltin has called it "a milestone of excellence in made-for-TV movies."

QUOTE "Oh, that was the West Campus. You have to stay here at the East Campus as a freshman." —D.C. "Peahead" Walker, greeting a student he'd recruited the previous summer by showing off the magnificent Duke University campus in nearby Durham

WAKE FOREST ANNUAL STATISTICAL LEADERS

YR	RUSHING	YDS	ATT	AVG	PASSING	ATT	CMP	PCT	YDS	RECEIVING	REC	YDS	AVG
1948	Bill Gregus	628	122	5.1	Carroll Blackerby	78	38	.49	598	Red O'Quinn	39	605	15.5
1949	Nub Smith	572	108	5.3	Carroll Blackerby	131	65	.50	837	Red O'Quinn	34	490	14.4
1950	Bill Miller	721	178	4.1	Ed Kissell	70	36	.51	436	Jack Lewis	15	195	13.0
1951	Guido Scarton	507	106	4.8	Ed Kissell	120	56	.47	593	Jack Lewis	32	488	15.3
1952	Bruce Hillenbrand	413	89	4.6	Sonny George	142	66	.46	868	Jack Lewis	30	438	14.6
1953	Johnny Parham	304	96	3.2	Joe White	87	32	.37	486	Bob Ondilla	21	294	14.0
1954	Nick Maravic	430	98	4.4	Nick Consoles	115	54	.47	743	Ed Stowers	22	277	12.6
1955	Bill Barnes	401	116	3.5	Nick Consoles	123	66	.54	787	Bill Barnes	31	349	11.3
1956	Bill Barnes	1,010	168	6.0	Charlie Carpenter	91	34	.37	495	Jack Ladner	12	125	10.4
1957	Neil MacLean	542	108	5.0	Jim Dalrymple	61	21	.34	261	Aubrey Currie	9	97	10.8
1958	Neil MacLean	624	139	4.5	Norman Snead	151	67	.44	1,003	Pete Manning	25	307	12.3
1959	Neil MacLean	373	105	3.6	Norman Snead	191	82	.43	1,361	Bobby Allen	25	462	18.5
1960	Bobby Robinson	232	57	4.1	Norman Snead	259	123	.47	1,676	Bobby Allen	23	391	17.0
1961	Alan White	586	93	6.3	Chuck Reiley	88	32	.36	516	Donnie Frederick	11	237	21.5
1962	Brian Piccolo	324	77	4.2	John Mackovic	130	57	.44	594	Henry Newton	19	265	13.9
1963	Brian Piccolo	367	84	4.4	Karl Sweetan	218	79	.36	674	Wayne Welborn	17	102	6.0
1964	Brian Piccolo	1,044	252	4.1	John Mackovic	195	89	.46	1,340	Richard Cameron	29	410	14.1
1965	Andy Heck	497	151	3.3	Jon Wilson	104	44	.42	513	Ken Henry	30	367	12.2
1966	Andy Heck	608	127	4.8	Ken Erickson	126	57	.45	787	Ken Henry	20	279	14.0
1967	Freddie Summers	510	179	2.8	Freddie Summers	159	77	.48	909	Rick Decker	29	352	12.1
1968	Freddie Summers	439	159	2.8	Freddie Summers	250	125	.50	1,664	Ron Jurewicz/Rick White	28	451	16.1
1969	Larry Russell	471	187	2.5	Larry Russell	153	70	.46	794	Gary Winrow	27	277	10.3
1970	Larry Hopkins	984	203	4.8	Larry Russell	109	55	.50	671	Gary Winrow	20	253	12.7
1971	Larry Hopkins	1,228	249	4.9	Larry Russell	73	29	.40	290	Dave Doda	6	31	5.2
1972	Frank Harsh	663	157	4.2	Andy Carlton	70	24	.34	268	Gary Johnson	9	135	15.0
1973	Clayton Heath	616	178	3.5	Andy Carlton	141	51	.36	605	Walter Sims	12	143	11.9
1974	Clark Gaines	329	98	3.4	Mike McGlamry	115	50	.43	585	Tom Fehring	17	234	13.8
1975	Clark Gaines	929	238	3.9	Jerry McManus	152	77	.51	950	Bill Millner	28	327	11.7
1976	James McDougald	1,018	232	4.4	Mike McGlamry	183	91	.50	1,066	Steve Young	36	414	11.5
1977	James McDougald	987	242	4.1	Mike McGlamry	252	133	.53	1,532	Steve Young	51	483	9.5
1978	James McDougald	629	146	4.3	David Webber	182	101	.55	1,070	Mike Mullen	22	307	14.0
1979	James McDougald	1,177	260	4.5	Jay Venuto	363	198	.55	2,432	Wayne Baumgardner	55	1,000	18.2
1980	Wayne McMillan	694	152	4.6	Jay Venuto	413	214	.52	2,624	Kenny Duckett	50	656	13.1
1981	Wayne McMillan	407	90	4.5	Gary Schofield	404	241	.60	2,572	Phil Denfeld	51	461	9.0
1982	Michael Ramseur	966	245	3.9	Gary Schofield	376	212	.56	2,380	Phil Denfeld	42	424	10.1
1983	Michael Ramseur	629	125	5.0	Gary Schofield	333	187	.56	2,253	Duane Owens	46	447	9.7
1984	Michael Ramseur	961	214	4.5	Foy White	252	143	.57	1,544	Duane Owens	30	420	14.0
1985	Topper Clemons	916	164	5.6	Foy White	210	132	.63	1,322	Michael Ramseur	54	450	8.3
1986	Darryl McGill	859	184	4.7	Mike Elkins	380	205	.54	2,541	James Brim	66	930	14.1
1987	Mark Young	795	179	4.4	Mike Elkins	317	169	.53	1,915	Ricky Proehl	54	788	14.6
1988	Mark Young	711	165	4.3	Mike Elkins	280	165	.59	2,205	Ricky Proehl	51	845	16.6
1989	Anthony Williams	430	119	3.6	Phil Barnhill	377	182	.48	2,454	Ricky Proehl	65	1,053	16.2
1990	Anthony Williams	866	181	4.8	Phil Barnhill	276	125	.45	1,443	John Henry Mills	46	623	13.5
1991	Anthony Williams	523	139	3.8	Keith West	296	153	.52	1,969	John Henry Mills	51	559	11.0
1992	Ned Moultrie	717	156	4.6	Keith West	281	159	.57	2,039	Todd Dixon	51	750	14.7
1993	John Leach	1,089	215	5.1	Jim Kemp	217	126	.58	1,488	John Leach	41	340	8.3
1994	Sherron Gudger	261	78	3.3	Rusty LaRue	230	132	.57	1,303	Roger Pettus	30	312	10.4
1995	John Lewis	304	110	2.8	Rusty LaRue	421	264	.63	2,775	Marlon Estes	68	833	12.3
1996	Morgan Kane	490	135	3.6	Brian Kuklick	396	205	.52	2,526	Desmond Clark	61	782	12.8
1997	Herman Lewis	491	114	4.3	Brian Kuklick	312	190	.61	2,180	Desmond Clark	72	950	13.2
1998	Morgan Kane	454	128	3.5	Brian Kuklick	396	216	.55	2,683	Jammie Deese	68	826	12.1
1999	Morgan Kane	1,161	275	4.2	Ben Sankey	224	133	.59	1,496	Jammie Deese	32	444	13.9
2000	Tarence Williams	661	130	5.1	James MacPherson	207	113	.55	1,324	Ira Williams	45	495	11.0
2001	Tarence Williams	1,018	249	4.1	James MacPherson	209	113	.54	1,555	Jason Anderson	28	472	16.9
2002	Tarence Williams	852	186	4.6	James MacPherson	223	123	.55	1,837	Jax Landfried	38	533	14.0
2003	Chris Barclay	1,192	235	5.1	Cory Randolph	246	144	.59	1,773	Jason Anderson	44	751	17.1
2004	Chris Barclay	1,010	243	4.2	Cory Randolph	147	78	.53	972	Nate Morton	26	391	15.0

Receiving leaders by receptions
The NCAA began including postseason stats in 2002

WAKE FOREST ALL-TIME SCORES

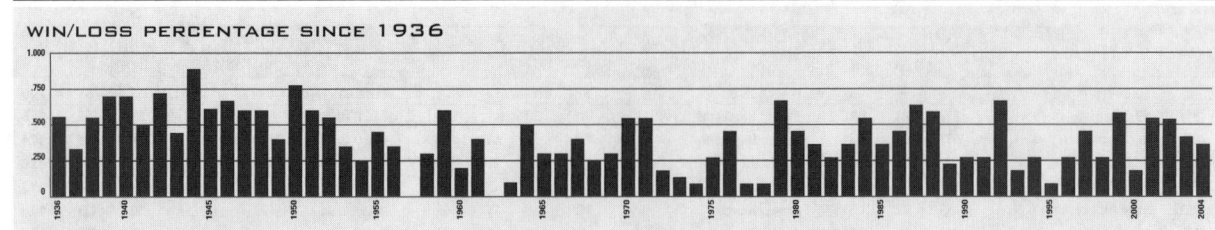

WIN/LOSS PERCENTAGE SINCE 1936

W.C. DOWD
1888 (1.000)   1-0

1888   1-0-0
O18	●	North Carolina *RAL*	6 4

W.C. RIDDICK
1889 (.500)   3-3

1889   3-3-0
M1	●	North Carolina *RAL*	0 33
M29	●	Duke *RAL*	32 0
N22	●	North Carolina *RAL*	18 8
N27	●	Duke	4 8
D9	●	Virginia *RICH*	4 46
D10	●	Richmond *UNK*	32 14

1890
NO TEAM

W.E. SIKES
1891-93 (.722)   6-2-1

1891   1-0-0
N10	●	North Carolina *RAL*	1 0 f

1892   4-0-1
U	●	Ashville Ath. *UNK*	40 0
O21	=	VMI *UNK*	12 12
O22	●	Wash.& Lee *UNK*	16 0
O24	●	Richmond *UNK*	16 0
N24	●	at Tennessee	10 6

1893   1-2-0
O18	●	Duke	6 12
N3	●	Tennessee	64 0
N18	●	North Carolina *RAL*	0 40

1894
NO TEAM

NO HEAD COACH

1895   0-0-1
O19	=	at North Carolina St.	4 4

1896-1907
NO TEAM

A.P. HALL, JR.
1908 (.167)   1-5

1908   1-5-0
S26		at North Carolina	0 17
S30		at North Carolina St.	0 76
O3	●	Warrenton Prep	21 0
O10	●	Davidson *CHAR*	0 34
N14	●	Davidson *CHAR*	0 31
N21		North Carolina St.	0 25

A.T. MYERS
1909 (.333)   2-4

1909   2-4-0
O2		at North Carolina	0 18
O4	●	Maryville	3 0
O16		at Wash. & Lee	0 17
O23	●	at South Carolina	8 0
N5		Richmond	0 5
N12		N.C. Med. Coll.	0 5

REDDY ROWE
1910 (.222)   2-7

1910   2-7-0
S24	●	Warrenton Prep	17 0
O8	●	Horner	28 0
O22		at North Carolina	0 37
O27		at South Carolina	0 6
O29		at Citadel	5 9
N12		USS Franklin	0 11
N19		at North Carolina St.	3 28
N24		Davidson *CHAR*	0 32
D3		Norfolk Blues	0 31

FRANK THOMPSON
1911-13 (.208)   5-19

1911   3-5-0
S30	●	Warrenton Prep	52 0
O7		at North Carolina	3 12
O14	●	Roanoke Coll.	62 0
O21		at Wash.& Lee	5 18
N2		at Virginia	6 29
N11	●	Davidson *GRO*	0 9
N18		North Carolina St.	6 13 *
N23	●	USS Franklin *DUR*	26 0

1912   2-6-0
S28	●	N.C. Medical Coll.	33 0
O5		at South Carolina	3 10
O12		at North Carolina	2 9
O26		at Wash. & Lee	0 20
N2		North Carolina St.	0 12
N9	●	Horner	49 0
N16		VA. Medical Coll.	14 23
N28		Davidson *CHAR*	7 13

1913   0-8-0
S27		at North Carolina	0 7
O11		at South Carolina	10 27
O18		Richmond	13 14
O25		at Wash. & Lee	0 33
N1		North Carolina St.	0 37
N8		Gallaudet	7 47
N15		North Carolina *UNK*	0 29
N27		Davidson *CHAR*	0 6

DR. W.C. SMITH
1914-15 (.375)   6-10

1914   3-6-0
O3		at North Carolina St.	0 51
O8		North Carolina *UNK*	0 53
O10	●	USS Franklin	13 0
O24		at Wash. & Lee	0 72
O31	●	Roanoke Coll.	19 0
N7		at South Carolina	0 26
N14		North Carolina	7 12
N26		at Davidson	6 7
D5	●	Wofford	41 0

1915   3-4-0
S25	●	Florence YMCA	80 0
O9		at North Carolina	0 35
O16		North Carolina St.	0 7
O30	●	Richmond Blues	40 0
N6		at VMI	6 21
N11	●	Gallaudet	28 6
N25		Davidson *CHAR*	7 21

C.M. BILLINGS
1916 (.500)   3-3

1916   3-3-0
S30		at North Carolina	0 20
O7	●	Guilford	33 0
O19		North Carolina St.	0 6
N4	●	at South Carolina	33 7
N11		at Virginia Tech	0 52
N18	●	Wofford	41 0

E.T. MacDONNELL
1917 (.188)   1-6-1

1917   1-6-1 (0-0-0)
S29		at Georgia Tech	0 33
O6		at Furman	6 7
O13	●	Guilford	20 0
O18		at North Carolina St.	6 17
O27		at Maryland	13 29
N3		at Virginia Tech	0 50
N17		at Davidson	7 72
N29	=	Hampden-Sydney	7 7

HARRY RABENHORST
1918-19 (.273)   3-8

1918   1-2-0
N9		at Virginia Tech	0 27
N16		at Wash. & Lee	7 20
N23	●	at North Carolina St.	21 0

1919   2-6-0
S26		Davidson	0 21
O4		Georgia Tech	0 14
O18		at North Carolina	0 6
O25		at Furman	0 6
N1		at Sewanee Club	39 3
N8		at Virginia Tech	0 40
N15	●	Guilford	65 0
N27		at North Carolina St.	7 21

J.L. WHITE
1920-21 (.211)   4-15

1920   2-7-0
S25		at Georgia Tech	0 44
O2		at North Carolina	0 6
O9		at Wash. & Lee	0 27
O16		Davidson *CHAR*	7 27
O23		at Furman	0 17
O30	●	Guilford	40 0
N6	●	Elon	29 0
N13		at Richmond	7 20
N25		North Carolina St.	7 49

1921   2-8-0
S24		at Georgia Tech	0 42
O1		at North Carolina	0 21
O8		at VMI	0 20
O15	●	Davidson *CHAR*	10 7
O22		at William & Mary	14 21
O29	●	Guilford	28 0
N5		at Richmond	0 41
N11		Duke	0 17
N19		North Carolina St.	0 14
N24		at Hampden-Sydney	14 39

GEORGE LEVENE
1922 (.400)   3-5-2

1922   3-5-2
S23		Atlantic Christian	34 0
S30		North Carolina *UNK*	3 62
O7	●	Elon	3 0
O14	=	Davidson *CHAR*	6 6
O21		at Lynchburg	7 20
O27	=	at Guilford	0 0
N4		William & Mary	0 18
N11		Duke	0 3
N25		North Carolina St.	0 32
D2	●	Hampden & Sydney	9 3

HANK GARRITY
1923-25 (.722)   19-7-1

1923   6-3-0
S29		at North Carolina	0 22
O6	●	Guilford	41 0
O13	●	Lynchburg	25 0
O20	●	Davidson *CHAR*	6 0
O27		Florida *TAM*	7 16
N10	●	Duke	16 6
N17	●	Elon	9 6
N24	●	North Carolina St.	14 0
N29		at South Carolina	7 14

1924   7-2-0
S27	●	North Carolina	7 6
O11	●	at Wash. & Lee	10 8
O18	●	Florida *TAM*	0 34
O25	●	at Lynchburg	37 7
N1	●	Guilford	67 0
N11	●	at Duke	32 0
N22	●	at North Carolina St.	12 0
N27		at South Carolina	0 7
D6	●	Elon	41 0

1925   6-2-1
S26	●	North Carolina	6 0
O3	=	Davidson *CHAR*	7 7
O10	●	Lenior Rhyne	49 0
O24		at Florida	3 24
O31	●	Guilford	25 0
N7	●	at Duke	21 3
N14		at North Carolina St.	0 6
N20	●	Furman *ASHE*	9 0
N26	●	at Elon	65 0

JAMES BALDWIN
1926-27 (.425)   7-10-3

1926   5-4-1
S25	●	North Carolina	13 0
O2	●	at Wofford	27 0
O9		at Furman	0 10
O16		at Presbyterian	0 13
O23	=	Davidson *CHAR*	3 3
O30	●	Duke *GOL*	21 0
N6	●	Elon	53 0
N13		at William & Mary	6 13
N20	●	Guilford	60 0
N27		at North Carolina St.	3 7

1927   2-6-2
S24		at North Carolina	9 8
O1	=	Elon	0 0
O7		at Presbyterian	7 14
O13		at North Carolina St.	7 30
O22	=	Davidson	13 13
O29		Duke	6 32
N5		Furman	0 53
N11		at Quantico Marines	10 39
N19	●	High Point	13 0
N24		at Mercer	0 34

STANLEY B. COFALL
1928 (.300)   2-6-2

1928   2-6-2
S29		at North Carolina	0 65
O6		Presbyterian	7 12
O13	=	at William & Mary	0 0
O18		at North Carolina St.	0 37
O27	●	Davidson *CHAR*	25 6
N3		Furman *CHAR*	0 18
N10		at Duke	0 38
N16	=	Wofford	7 7
N29		at Mercer	12 14
D25	●	at Miami, Fla.	13 6

F.S. MILLER
1929-32 (.541) 18-15-4

1929 6-5-1

S21	●	Catawba	20	0
S28		at North Carolina	0	48
O5	●	at Richmond	19	0
O11	●	Elon	25	6
O17		at North Carolina St.	6	8
O26	●	Davidson *Gro*	6	0
N2		Furman	0	12
N9	●	at Wofford	18	0
N16		at Navy	0	61
N19	=	Presbyterian *Gro*	0	0
N23		at Duke	0	20
N28	●	Mercer *Ashe*	13	0

1930 5-3-1

S27		at North Carolina	7	13
O4	●	Guilford	20	0
O10	●	Baltimore	44	0
O16	●	at North Carolina St.	7	0
O25	●	Mercer	21	0
N1		at Temple	0	36
N8		Presbyterian *Ashe*	0	13
N22	=	Duke	13	13
N27	●	Davidson *Char*	13	2

1931 4-4-0

S26		at North Carolina	0	37
O3		Furman *Gas*	6	36
O16	●	at North Carolina St.	6	0
O23		at Duke	0	28
O31	●	Erskine	13	0
N7	●	Presbyterian *Gro*	12	0
N14		at Oglethorpe	0	37
N26	●	Davidson *Char*	7	0

1932 3-3-2

S24	=	at North Carolina	0	0
O8	●	South Carolina *Char*	6	0
O15	=	at North Carolina St.	0	0
O21		at Duke	0	9
O29	●	at Delaware	7	0
N5		at Catholic U.	6	14
N11	●	Carson-Newman	20	6
N24		at Davidson	0	7

JAMES H. WEAVER
1933-36 (.309) 10-23-1

1933 0-5-1

O7		at Duke	0	22
O21	=	at North Carolina St.	0	0
O28		Catholic U.	0	12
N4		Clemson *Char*	0	13
N11		at North Carolina	0	26
N30		Davidson *Char*	13	20

1934 3-7-0

S22	●	Guilford	62	0
S29		at North Carolina	0	21
O6	●	at North Carolina St.	13	12
O11		Furman *Flo*	2	3
O20	●	Presbyterian	14	6
O26		at George Washington	2	6
N3		Emory & Henry	0	13
N10		at Duke	7	28
N17		Richmond *Char*	6	39
N29		at Davidson	12	13

1935 2-7-0

S21		Duke *Gro*	7	26
S28		at North Carolina	0	14
O5		at Clemson	7	13
O12		at North Carolina St.	6	21
O18		Furman *Char*	0	9
O26	●	George Washington	7	6
N1	●	Presbyterian	18	0
N15		at Miami, Fla.	0	3
N28		Davidson	7	14

1936-1952
SOUTHERN

1936 5-4-0 (2-3-0)

S26	|	North Carolina *Char*	7	14
O3	● |	at North Carolina St.	9	0
O10	●	Wofford	32	0
O16	● |	Clemson	6	0
O23		at George Washington	12	13
O31	●	Presbyterian	19	0
N7	|	Duke	0	20
N13	●	Erskine	19	6
N26	|	at Davidson	6	19

D.C. WALKER
1937-50 (.597) 77-51-6

1937 3-6-0 (1-4-0)

S25		at Tennessee	0	32
O1		at George Washington	6	34
O8	●	Erskine	19	0
O16	|	North Carolina	0	28
O23	|	North Carolina St.	0	20
O30	|	at Clemson	0	32
N6	|	at Duke	0	67
N12	●	at Wofford	24	0
N25	● |	Davidson *Char*	19	7

1938 4-5-1 (3-4-1)

S17	●	Randolph Macon	57	6
S24	|	at North Carolina	6	14
S30	● |	Citadel *Char*	31	0
O8	● |	at South Carolina	20	19
O15	|	at North Carolina St.	7	19
O22	|	Duke *W-S*	0	7
O28	|	Clemson	0	7
N5	= |	at VMI	6	6
N12		Western Maryland	13	20
N24	● |	Davidson *Char*	21	0

1939 7-3-0 (3-3-0)

S16	●	Elon *Gro*	34	0
S23	● |	South Carolina	19	7
S30	|	at North Carolina	6	36
O6	●	at Miami, Fla.	33	0
O14	● |	at North Carolina St.	32	0
O21	●	Western Maryland	66	0
O28	|	at Duke	0	6
N4	●	at Marshall	14	13
N11	|	at Clemson	7	20
N30	● |	Davidson *Char*	46	7

1940 7-3-0 (4-2-0)

S21	●	William Jewell	79	0
S28	● |	at North Carolina	12	0
O5	● |	Furman	19	0
O12	|	at Clemson	0	39
O19	●	Marshall	31	19
O26	|	Duke	0	23
N1	●	at George Washington	18	0
N9	● |	at North Carolina St.	20	14
N16		at Texas Tech	7	12
N28	● |	South Carolina *Char*	7	6

1941 5-5-1 (4-2-1)

S20	●	at Camp Davis	66	0
S27	|	at Duke	14	43
O4	● |	at Furman	52	13
O11	= |	at South Carolina	6	6
O18	● |	at North Carolina St.	7	0
O25	● |	North Carolina	13	0
N1		at Marshall	6	16
N8		at Boston College	6	26
N15	|	at Clemson	0	29
N20	● |	at George Washington	42	0
N29		Texas Tech *Char*	6	25 *

1942 6-2-1 (6-1-1)

S26	|	at North Carolina	0	6
O3	● |	Duke	20	7
O10	● |	at Furman	14	6
O17	= |	at North Carolina St.	0	0
O25		at Boston College	0	27
O31	● |	Clemson	19	6
N7	● |	VMI *W-S*	28	0
N13	● |	at George Washington	20	0
D5	● |	South Carolina *Char*	33	14

1943 4-5-0 (3-2-0)

S25		at Camp Davis	20	24
O2	|	at Maryland	7	13
O8		at Georgia	0	7
O16	● |	at North Carolina St.	54	6
O23	● |	VMI *Lyn*	21	0
O30	● |	at Clemson	41	12
N6	●	N.C. Pre-Flight	20	12
N13		at Greensboro AAB	0	14
N25	|	South Carolina *Char*	2	13

1944 8-1-0 (6-1-0)

S23	● |	at North Carolina	7	0
S29	●	at Georgia	14	7
O7	● |	Maryland	39	0
O14	● |	VMI *Gro*	38	7
O21	● |	at North Carolina St.	21	7
O27	●	at Miami, Fla.	27	0
N4	● |	Clemson	13	7
N11	|	at Duke	0	34
N23	● |	South Carolina *Char*	19	13

1945 5-3-1 (3-1-1)

S29		at Tennessee	6	7
O6		at Army	0	54
O13	|	Duke	19	26
O20	● |	at North Carolina St.	19	18
N3	●	Presbyterian	53	9
N17	● |	at North Carolina	14	13
N22	= |	South Carolina	13	13
D1	● |	at Clemson	13	6
		GATOR BOWL		
J1	●	South Carolina	26	14

1946 6-3-0 (2-3-0)

S27	●	at Boston College	12	6
O4	●	at Georgetown	19	6
O12	● |	Clemson	19	7
O19	|	North Carolina St.	6	14
O26	●	at Tennessee	19	6
N1	●	at U.T. Chattanooga	32	14
N9	|	at Duke	0	13
N16	|	at North Carolina	14	26
N28	● |	South Carolina *Char*	35	0

1947 6-4-0 (3-4-0)

S27	●	Georgetown	6	0
O4	● |	at Clemson	16	14
O11	● |	at North Carolina	19	7
O18	● |	at George Washington	39	7
O25	|	Duke	6	13
N1	|	at William & Mary	0	21
N8	●	at Boston College	14	13
N15	|	at North Carolina St.	0	20
N21	●	Duquesne *W-S*	33	0
N27	|	South Carolina *Char*	0	6

1948 6-4-0 (5-2-0)

S18	● |	at George Washington	27	13
S24		at Boston College	9	26
O2	● |	at William & Mary	21	12
O9	|	North Carolina	6	28
O16	●	at Duquesne	41	15
O30	● |	North Carolina St.	34	13
N6	● |	at Duke	27	20
N13	|	Clemson *W-S*	14	21
N25	● |	at South Carolina	38	0
		DIXIE BOWL		
J1		Baylor	7	20

1949 4-6-0 (3-3-0)

S17	●	Duquesne	22	7
S24		at SMU	7	13
S30		at Boston College	7	13
O8		Georgetown	6	12
O15	|	at North Carolina	14	28
O22	● |	William & Mary	55	28
O29	● |	at Clemson	35	2
N5	● |	at Duke	27	7
N12	|	at North Carolina St.	14	27
N26	|	at South Carolina	20	27

1950 6-1-2 (6-1-1)

S22	=	at Boston College	7	7
S30	● |	Richmond	43	0
O7	● |	at William & Mary	47	0
O14	● |	at North Carolina	13	7
O21	● |	George Washington	13	7
O28	|	Clemson	12	13
N11	● |	at Duke	13	7
N18	= |	North Carolina St.	6	6
N25	● |	at South Carolina	14	7

TOM ROGERS
1951-55 (.460) 21-25-4

1951 6-4-0 (5-3-0)

S21	●	at Boston College	20	6
S29	● |	at North Carolina St.	21	6
O6	● |	Richmond	56	6
O13	|	William & Mary *Rich*	6	7
O19	● |	at George Washington	27	13
O27	● |	North Carolina	39	7
N3	|	at Clemson	6	21
N10	● |	at Duke	19	13
N17		at Baylor	0	42
N24	|	at South Carolina	6	21 *

1952 5-4-1 (5-1-0)

S20		at Baylor	14	17
S27	● |	at William & Mary	28	21
O4	=	Boston College *W-S*	7	7
O11		Villanova *Phil*	0	20
O18	● |	at North Carolina	9	7
N1	● |	North Carolina St.	21	6
N8		at TCU	9	27
N15	|	Duke	7	14
N22	● |	at Furman	28	0
N29	● |	South Carolina *W-S*	39	14

1953-PRESENT
ACC

1953 3-6-1 (2-3-0)

S19		William & Mary *Rich*	14	16
S26	|	at Duke	0	19
O3	●	Villanova *W-S*	18	12
O10	|	North Carolina	13	18
O17	● |	at North Carolina St.	20	7
O24	=	at Richmond	13	13
O31	|	at Clemson	0	18
N7		at Boston College	7	20
N21		Furman	10	21
N26	● |	South Carolina *Char*	19	13

1954 2-7-1 (1-4-1)

S18	●	George Washington	14	0
S25		Virginia Tech *Rich*	0	32
O2	● |	North Carolina St.	26	0
O9	= |	Maryland *W-S*	13	13
O23	|	at North Carolina	7	14
O30	|	Clemson *Char*	20	32
N6		at Richmond	0	13
N13	|	Duke	21	28
N20		at William & Mary	9	13
N27	|	at South Carolina	19	20

1955 5-4-1 (3-3-1)

S17	●	Virginia Tech	13	0
S24	● |	South Carolina *W-S*	34	19
O1		at West Virginia	0	46
O8	|	at Maryland	7	28
O15	= |	at North Carolina St.	13	13
O22	● |	North Carolina	25	0
O29	|	at Clemson	13	19
N5	●	William & Mary	13	7
N12	● |	at Virginia	13	7
N19	|	at Duke	0	14

PAUL AMEN
1956-59 (.313) 11-26-3

1956 2-5-3 (1-5-1)

S22	●	at William & Mary	39	0
S29	|	Maryland	0	6
O6	|	at Virginia	6	7
O13	|	Clemson	0	17
O20	=	at Florida State	14	14
O27	= |	at North Carolina	6	6
N3	● |	North Carolina St.	13	0
N10	=	at Virginia Tech	13	13
N17	|	Duke	0	26
N22	|	South Carolina *Char*	0	13

1957 0-10-0 (0-7-0)

S28		at Florida	0	27
O5	|	Virginia	20	28
O12	|	at Maryland	0	27
O19	|	at Duke	7	34
O26	|	North Carolina	7	14
N2	|	at North Carolina st.	0	19
N9		Virginia Tech	3	10
N16		West Virginia	14	27
N23	|	at Clemson	6	13
N30	|	South Carolina	7	26

1958 3-7-0 (2-4-0)

S20	● |	Maryland	34	0
S27	●	Virginia Tech *Nor*	13	6
O4		at Florida State	24	27
O11	● |	North Carolina St.	13	7
O18		at Villanova	7	9
O25	|	at North Carolina	7	26
N1	|	at Clemson	12	14
N15	|	Duke	0	29
N22		at Auburn	7	21
N27	|	at South Carolina	7	24

1959 6-4-0 (4-3-0)

S19	●	at Florida State	22	20
S26	●	Virginia Tech	27	18
O3		at Tulane	0	6
O10	● |	at Maryland	10	7
O17	● |	at North Carolina St.	17	14
O24	|	North Carolina	19	21
O31	● |	Virginia	34	12
N14	|	at Duke	15	27
N21	|	at Clemson	31	33
N28	● |	South Carolina *Char*	43	20

BILLY HILDEBRAND
1960-63 (.175) 7-33

1960 2-8-0 (2-5-0)

S24		Clemson	7	28
O1		at Florida State	6	14
O8		at Virginia Tech	13	22
O15	●	at North Carolina	13	12
O22		Maryland	13	14
O29	●	at Virginia	28	20
N5		North Carolina St.	12	14
N12		Duke	7	34
N19		at LSU	0	16
N26		at South Carolina	20	41

1961 4-6-0 (3-4-0)

S23		at Baylor	0	31
S30		South Carolina	7	10
O7		at Duke	3	23
O14	●	at Clemson	17	13
O21		at North Carolina St.	0	7
O28	●	Virginia	21	15
N4		at Auburn	7	21
N11	●	Virginia Tech	24	15
N18		at Maryland	7	10
N25	●	North Carolina	17	14

1962 0-10-0 (0-7-0)

S22		at Army	14	40
S29		at Maryland	2	13
O6		Clemson	7	24
O13		at South Carolina	6	27
O20		at Virginia	12	14
O27		at North Carolina	14	23
N3		at Tennessee	0	23
N10		at Virginia Tech	8	37
N17		Duke	0	50
N22		North Carolina St.	3	27

1963 1-9-0 (1-5-0)

S21		at East Carolina	10	20
S28		Virginia Tech	0	27
O5		North Carolina	0	21
O12		at Florida State	0	35
O19		at Army	0	47
O26		Maryland	0	32
N2		at Clemson	0	3
N9		at Duke	7	39
N16	●	South Carolina	20	19
N22		at North Carolina St.	0	42

BILL TATE
1964-68 (.350) 17-32-1

1964 5-5-0 (4-3-0)

S19	●	at Virginia	31	21
S26	●	Virginia Tech *ROA*	38	21
O3		at North Carolina	0	23
O10		at Vanderbilt	6	9
O17		Clemson	2	21
O24	●	at Maryland	21	17
O31		at Memphis	14	23
N7	●	Duke	20	7
N14		at South Carolina	13	23
N20	●	North Carolina St.	27	13

1965 3-7-0 (1-5-0)

S18		Virginia Tech *ROA*	3	12
S25		at North Carolina St.	11	13
O2	●	Vanderbilt	7	0
O9		Maryland	7	10
O16		at South Carolina	7	38
O23	●	North Carolina	12	10
O30		at Clemson	13	26
N6		at Florida State	0	35
N13		at Duke	7	40
N20	●	at Memphis	21	20

1966 3-7-0 (2-4-0)

S17		at Virginia	10	24
S24		at Maryland	7	34
O1		North Carolina St.	12	15
O8		at Auburn	6	14
O15	●	at South Carolina	10	6
O22	●	at North Carolina	3	0
O29		Clemson	21	23
N5		Virginia Tech	0	11
N12	●	Memphis	21	7
N19		at Florida State	0	28

1967 4-6-0 (3-4-0)

S16		Duke *RAL*	13	31
S23		at Clemson	6	23
S29		at Houston	6	50
O7		Virginia	12	14
O14		at Memphis	10	42
O21		at North Carolina St.	7	24
O28	●	at North Carolina	20	10
N4	●	South Carolina	35	21
N11	●	at Tulsa	31	24
N17	●	Maryland	35	17

1968 2-7-1 (2-3-1)

S14		North Carolina St.	6	10
S21	=	Clemson	20	20
O5		at Minnesota	19	24
O12		at Virginia Tech	6	7
O19		at Purdue	27	28
O26	●	North Carolina	48	31
N2	●	Maryland	38	14
N9		South Carolina	21	34
N16		at Duke	3	18
N23		at Florida State	24	42

CAL STOLL
1969-71 (.469) 15-17

1969 3-7-0 (2-5-0)

S13	●	at North Carolina St.	22	21
S20		at Auburn	0	57
S27	●	Virginia Tech	16	10
O4		Maryland	14	19
O11		Duke	20	27
O18		at Clemson	14	28
O25		at North Carolina	3	23
N8	●	at Virginia	23	21
N15		South Carolina	6	24
N21		at Miami, Fla.	7	49

1970 6-5-0 5-1-0

S12		at Nebraska	12	36
S19		at South Carolina	7	43
S26		at Florida State	14	19
O3	●	at Virginia	27	7
O10	●	Virginia Tech	28	9
O17	●	Clemson	36	20
O24	●	North Carolina	14	13
O31		Tennessee *MEM*	7	41
N7	●	at Duke	28	14
N14	●	North Carolina St.	16	13
N21		at Houston	2	26

1971 6-5-0 2-4-0

S11	●	Davidson	27	7
S18	●	at Virginia Tech	20	9
S25		Miami, Fla.	10	29
O2	●	at Maryland	18	14
O9		at North Carolina St.	14	21
O16	●	Tulsa	51	21
O23		at North Carolina	3	7
O30		at Clemson	9	10
N6	●	William & Mary	36	29
N13	●	Duke	23	7
N20		at South Carolina	7	24

TOM HARPER
1972 (.182) 2-9

1972 2-9-0 (1-5-0)

S9	●	Davidson	26	20
S16		SMU *IRV*	10	56
S23		at Tennessee	6	45
O7		at Maryland	0	23
O14		North Carolina St.	13	42
O21		North Carolina	0	21
O28		Clemson	0	31
N4		at South Carolina	3	35
N11	●	at Duke	9	7
N18		Virginia	12	15
N25		Virginia Tech	9	44

CHUCK MILLS
1973-77 (.209) 11-43-1

1973 1-9-1 (0-5-1)

S15	●	Florida State	9	7
S22		William & Mary	14	15
S29		at Richmond	0	41
O6		at Texas	0	41
O13		South Carolina	12	28
O20		Maryland	0	37
O27		at Virginia	10	21
N3		at Clemson	8	35
N10	=	Duke	7	7
N17		at North Carolina	0	42
N24		at North Carolina St.	13	52

1974 1-10-0 (0-6-0)

S7		North Carolina St.	15	33
S14		William & Mary	6	17
S21		North Carolina	0	31
O5		at Oklahoma	0	63
O12		at Penn State	0	55
O19		at Maryland	0	47
O26		Virginia	0	14
N2		Clemson	9	21
N9		at Duke	7	23
N16		at South Carolina	21	34
N23	●	Furman	16	10

1975 3-8-0 (3-3-0)

S6		SMU	7	14
S13	●	at North Carolina St.	30	22
S20		Appalachian St.	17	19
S27		Kansas State	16	17
O11		at Clemson	14	16
O18		Maryland	0	27
O25	●	at Virginia	66	21
N1	●	at North Carolina	21	9
N8		Duke	14	42
N15		at South Carolina	26	37
N22		at Virginia Tech	10	40

1976 5-6-0 (3-3-0)

S4		Virginia Tech	6	23
S11	●	North Carolina St.	20	18
S18		at Vanderbilt	24	27
S25	●	at Kansas State	13	0
O2		at Michigan	0	31
O9	●	Clemson	20	14
O16		at Maryland	15	17
O23		Virginia	17	18
O30		North Carolina	14	34
N6	●	at Duke	38	17
N13	●	at South Carolina	10	7

1977 1-10-0 (0-6-0)

S10	●	Furman	24	13
S17		Vanderbilt	0	3
S24		at North Carolina St.	14	41
O1		at Purdue	17	26
O8		at North Carolina	3	24
O15		Maryland	7	35
O22		at Virginia	10	12
O29		at Clemson	0	26
N5		Duke	14	38
N12		South Carolina	14	24
N19		at Virginia Tech	10	28

JOHN MACKOVIC
1978-80 (.412) 14-20

1978 1-10-0 (1-5-0)

S9	●	Virginia	14	0
S16		Virginia Tech	6	28
S23		at LSU	11	13
S30		North Carolina St.	10	34
O7		at Purdue	7	14
O14		North Carolina	29	34
O21		at Maryland	0	39
O28		at Auburn	7	21
N4		Clemson	6	51
N11		at Duke	0	3
N18		at South Carolina	14	37

1979 8-4-0 (3-2-0)

S8	●	Appalachian St.	30	23
S15	●	at Georgia	22	21
S22	●	East Carolina	23	20
S29		at North Carolina St.	14	17
O6	●	at Virginia Tech	19	14
O13	●	at North Carolina	24	19
O20	●	Maryland	25	17
O27	●	Auburn	42	38
N3		at Clemson	0	31
N10	●	Duke	17	14
N17		at South Carolina	14	35
		TANGERINE BOWL		
D22		LSU	10	34

1980 5-6-0 (2-4-0)

S6		Virginia Tech	7	16
S20	●	Citadel	24	7
S27	●	at North Carolina St.	27	7
O4	●	at William & Mary	27	7
O11		North Carolina	9	27
O18		at Maryland	10	11
O25		Virginia	21	24
N1		Clemson	33	35
N8	●	at Duke	27	24
N15		at South Carolina	38	39
N22	●	Appalachian St.	28	16

AL GROH
1981-86 (.394) 26-40

1981 4-7-0 (1-5-0)

S5		South Carolina	6	23
S12		North Carolina St.	23	28
S19	●	at Auburn	24	21
S26		at Virginia Tech	14	30
O3	●	Appalachian St.	15	14
O10		at North Carolina	10	48
O17		Maryland	33	45
O24	●	at Virginia	24	21
O31		at Clemson	24	82
N7		Duke	10	31
N14	●	at Richmond	34	22

1982 3-8-0 (0-6-0)

S4	●	Western Carolina	31	10
S11		at Auburn	10	28
S18		at North Carolina St.	0	30
S25	●	Appalachian St.	31	22
O2	●	at Virginia Tech	13	10
O9		North Carolina	7	24
O16		at Maryland	31	52
O23		at Virginia	27	34
N6		at Duke	26	46
N13		Georgia Tech	7	45
N27		Clemson *TOK*	17	21

1983 4-7-0 (1-6-0)

S3		Appalachian St.	25	27
S10	●	at Virginia Tech	13	6
S17	●	Western Carolina	21	0
S24	●	at Richmond	31	6
O1		North Carolina St.	15	38
O8		at North Carolina	10	30
O15		Maryland	33	36
O22	●	Virginia	38	34
O29		at Clemson	17	24
N5		Duke	21	31
N12		at Georgia Tech	33	49

1984 6-5-0 (3-4-0)

S8		Virginia Tech	20	21
S15	●	Appalachian St.	17	13
S22	●	at North Carolina St.	24	15
S29		at Maryland	17	38
O6	●	at Richmond	29	16
O13	●	North Carolina	14	3
O20		at Virginia	9	28
O27	●	William & Mary	34	21
N3		at Clemson	14	37
N10	●	at Duke	20	16
N17		Georgia Tech	7	24

1985 4-7-0 (1-6-0)

S7	●	William & Mary	30	23
S14	●	at Boston U.	30	0
S21		North Carolina St.	17	20
S28	●	Appalachian St.	24	21
O5		at Tennessee	29	31
O12		at North Carolina	14	34
O19		Maryland	3	26
O26		Virginia	18	20
N2		at Clemson	10	26
N9	●	Duke	27	7
N16		at Georgia Tech	10	41

1986 5-6-0 (2-5-0)

S6	●	Appalachian St.	21	13
S13	●	Boston U.	31	0
S20		at North Carolina St.	38	42
S27	●	at Army	49	14
O4		Virginia	28	30
O11		North Carolina	30	40
O18	●	at Maryland	27	21
N1		Clemson	20	28
N8		at Duke	36	38
N15		at South Carolina	21	48
N22	●	Georgia Tech	24	21

BILL DOOLEY
1987-92 (.448) 29-36-2

1987 7-4-0 (4-3-0)

S12	●	Richmond	24	0
S19	●	North Carolina St.	21	3
S26	●	Appalachian St.	16	12
O3	●	at Army	17	13
O10	●	at North Carolina	22	14
O17		Maryland	0	14
O24		at Virginia	21	35
O31		at Clemson	17	31
N7	●	Duke	30	27
N14		South Carolina	0	30
N21	●	at Georgia Tech	33	6

1988 6-4-1 (4-3-0)

S3	●	at Villanova	31	11
S10	●	Illinois St.	35	0
S17		at North Carolina St.	6	14
S24		at Michigan	9	19
O8	●	North Carolina	42	24
O15	●	at Maryland	27	24
O22		Virginia	14	34
O29		Clemson	21	38
N5	●	at Duke	35	16
N12	●	Georgia Tech	28	24
N19	=	Appalachian St.	34	34

1989   2-8-1 (1-6-0)

S9		Appalachian St.	10	15
S16		North Carolina St.	17	27
S23		at Army	10	14
S30	=	Rice	17	17
O7	●	at North Carolina	17	16
O14		Maryland	7	27
O21		at Virginia	28	47
O28		at Clemson	10	44
N4		Duke	35	52
N11	●	Tulsa	29	17
N18		at Georgia Tech	14	43

1990   3-8-0 (0-7-0)

S1		at Rice	17	33
S8	●	Appalachian St.	23	12
S15		at North Carolina St.	15	20
S29	●	Army	52	14
O6		North Carolina	24	31
O13		at Maryland	13	41
O20		Virginia	14	49
O27		Clemson	6	24
N3		at Duke	20	57
N17		Georgia Tech	7	42
N24		at Vanderbilt	56	28

1991   3-8-0 (1-6-0)

S14	●	Western Carolina	40	24
S21		North Carolina St.	3	30
S28		at Northwestern	14	41
O5		Appalachian St.	3	17
O12		at North Carolina	10	24
O19		Maryland	22	23
O26		at Virginia	7	48
N2		at Clemson	10	28
N9	●	Duke	31	14
N16		at Georgia Tech	3	27
N23	●	at Navy	52	24

1992   8-4-0 (4-4-0)

S5	●	North Carolina	17	35
S12	●	Appalachian St.	10	7
S26		at Florida State	7	35
O3		Virginia	17	31
O10	●	at Vanderbilt	40	6
O17	●	at Maryland	30	23
O24	●	Army	23	7
O31	●	Clemson	18	15
N7	●	at Duke	28	14
N14	●	at Georgia Tech	23	10
N21		at North Carolina St.	14	42
		INDEPENDENCE BOWL		
D31	●	Oregon	39	35

JIM CALDWELL
1993-2000 (.292)   26-63

1993   2-9-0 (1-7-0)

S4		Vanderbilt	12	27
S11		North Carolina St.	16	34
S18	●	Appalachian St.	20	3
S25		at Northwestern	14	26
O9		at North Carolina	35	45
O16	●	at Clemson	20	16
O23		Duke	13	21
O30		at Florida State	0	54
N6		at Virginia	9	21
N13		Georgia Tech	28	38
N20		Maryland	32	33

1994   3-8-0 (1-7-0)

S3		at Vanderbilt	14	35
S10	●	Appalachian St.	12	10
S17		Florida State	14	56
S23		at Maryland	7	31
O1	●	Army	33	27
O8		Virginia	6	42
O15		at North Carolina St.	3	34
O22		Duke	26	51
O29		at Clemson	8	24
N12		North Carolina	0	50
N19	●	at Georgia Tech	20	13

1995   1-10-0 (0-8-0)

A31		Appalachian St.	22	24
S9		at Tulane	9	35
S16		Clemson	14	29
S23	●	at Navy	30	7
S30		at Virginia	17	35
O7		Maryland	6	9
O14		at Florida State	13	72
O21		at North Carolina	7	31
O28		at Duke	26	42
N4		Georgia Tech	23	24
N18		North Carolina St.	23	52

1996   3-8 (1-7)

A29	●	Appalachian St.	19	13
S7	●	Northwestern	28	27
S14		at Georgia Tech	10	30
S21		Virginia	7	42
S28		at Clemson	10	21
O5		North Carolina	6	45
O19		at Maryland	0	52
O26		Navy	18	47
N9		Florida State ORL	7	44
N16	●	Duke	17	16
N23		at North Carolina St.	22	37

1997   5-6 (3-5)

S6		Northwestern	27	20
S13		at East Carolina	24	25
S20		Georgia Tech	26	28
S25	●	North Carolina St.	19	18
O4		at Virginia	13	21
O11		at North Carolina	12	30
O18	●	Maryland	35	17
O25	●	at Duke	38	24
N1		Clemson	16	33
N8	●	at Rutgers	28	14
N15		at Florida State	7	58

1998   3-8 (2-6)

S5		at Air Force	0	42
S10	●	Navy	26	14
S26	●	at Clemson	29	19
O3		Appalachian St.	27	30
O10		Duke	16	19
O17	●	at Maryland	20	10
O24		North Carolina	31	38
O31		Virginia	17	38
N7		at North Carolina St.	27	38
N14		Florida State	7	24
N21		at Georgia Tech	35	63

1999   7-5 (3-5)

S11	●	at Army	34	15
S18	●	at Virginia	7	35
S25	●	North Carolina St.	31	7
O2	●	Rutgers	17	10
O9		Maryland	14	17
O16		at Florida State	10	33
O23	●	UAB	47	3
O30		Clemson	3	12
N6	●	at North Carolina	19	3
N13		at Duke	35	48
N20	●	Georgia Tech	26	23
		ALOHA BOWL		
D25	●	Arizona State	23	3

2000   2-9 (1-7)

A31		Appalachian St.	16	20
S9		North Carolina	14	35
S16		at Clemson	7	55
S30		Virginia	10	27
O7		Vanderbilt	10	17
O14		at Georgia Tech	20	52
O21		at Maryland	7	37
N4	●	Duke	28	26
N11		Florida State	6	35
N18	●	at Navy	49	26
N25		at North Carolina St.	14	32

JIM GROBE
2001-Present (.469)   22-25

2001   6-5 (3-5)

S1	●	at East Carolina	21	19
S8	●	Appalachian St.	20	10
S22		Maryland	20	27
S29		at Florida State	24	48
O6		North Carolina St.	14	17
O13	●	at Duke	42	35
O27		Clemson	14	21
N3	●	at Virginia	34	30
N10	●	at North Carolina	32	31
N17		Georgia Tech	33	38
N24	●	Northern Illinois	38	35

2002   7-6 (3-5)

A29		at Northern Illinois	41	42
S7	●	/East Carolina	27	22
S14		at North Carolina St.	13	32
S21	●	at Purdue	24	21
S28		Virginia	34	38
O5	●	at Georgia Tech	24	21
O12	●	Duke	36	10
O19		at Clemson	23	31
O26	●	North Carolina	31	0
N2		Florida State	21	34
N23	●	Navy	30	27
N30		at Maryland	14	32
		SEATTLE BOWL		
D30	●	Oregon	38	17

2003   5-7 (3-5)

A30	●	at Boston College	32	28
S6	●	North Carolina St.	38	24
S13		Purdue	10	16
S20	●	East Carolina	34	16
O11		Georgia Tech	7	24
O18	●	at Duke	42	13
O25		at Florida State	24	48
N1	●	Clemson	45	17
N8	●	at North Carolina	34	42
N15		Connecticut	17	51
N29		Maryland	28	41

2004   4-7 (1-7)

S4		at Clemson	30	37
S11	●	at East Carolina	31	17
S18	●	North Carolina A&T	42	3
S25	●	Boston College	17	14
O2		at North Carolina St.	21	27
O9		Virginia Tech	10	17
O23		Florida State	17	20
O30	●	Duke	24	22
N13		North Carolina	24	31
N20		at Miami, Fla.	7	52
N27		at Maryland	7	13

WASHINGTON

BY BUD WITHERS

Tucked in the far northwest is a football program that can reasonably claim to be unique. More than any other Division I-A school in a metropolitan area, Washington has prospered alongside professional teams, even dominated the spotlight at times. Before there were Seahawks, Sonics or Mariners, there were Huskies. Of Seattle's sporting entities, they represent the most history and the oldest money in town. Elsewhere, college football teams have been dwarfed in public consciousness by their pro neighbors. Not in Seattle. The Huskies have 63,000 season ticket-holders and annually lead the Pac-10 in attendance by a wide margin. Unlike the ambience that much of the country attaches to West Coast football—shirt sleeves, sunshine, insouciance about the actual game—an autumn Saturday at Washington is apt to be chilly, maybe a bit gloomy, always pulsating with passion for the Huskies.

In sum, an atmosphere more evocative of the college football-crazy Midwest or South.

TRADITION The 139-foot-long tunnel from the locker rooms to the field is an edifice that houses UW's poster-size bowl plaques, and when the Huskies and their opponents happen to converge in these close quarters, visitors have been known to be intimidated. If that doesn't annoy them, then an air-raid siren marking Washington scores likely will. At homecoming, UW football lettermen line the field from the tunnel to the Huskies' sideline after halftime and hold up "W" blankets.

BEST PLAYER A small-town farm kid from the East Side of the state, he was pursued only by Washington and Washington State. But defensive tackle Steve Emtman was truly a man among boys, finishing fourth in the 1991 Heisman Trophy balloting, a vote he might have won against a tepid field the next year if he hadn't chosen to enter the NFL draft. Until Emtman, the consensus best players in UW history were running backs: George Wilson (1923-25), whom famed sportswriter Grantland Rice put in an All-America backfield alongside Red Grange and Ernie Nevers, and The King, Hugh McElhenny (1949-51).

BEST COACH The oldest of the old-timers would make a case for Gil Dobie, who coached the Huskies to a

---

PROFILE

**University of Washington
Seattle, Wash.**
Founded: 1861
Enrollment: 29,028
Colors: Purple and Gold
Nickname: Huskies
Stadium: Husky Stadium
Opened in 1920
FieldTurf; 72,500 capacity
First football game: 1889
All-time record: 638–364–50 (.630)
Bowl record: 15–14–1
Consensus national championships, 1936-present: 1 (1991)
Pac-10 championships: 15 (12 outright)
Outland Trophy: Steve Emtman, 1991
First-round NFL draftees: 18
Website: www.gohuskies.com

THE BEST OF TIMES

From 1990 to 1992, Washington went 31–5, went to three straight Rose Bowls and shared the 1991 national championship with Miami.

THE WORST OF TIMES

In 1969, the Huskies had a 1–9 record and were wracked internally by black players' demands that they receive better treatment from the staff of coach Jim Owens. At the height of the controversy, black players boycotted a game at UCLA, which the Bruins won 57-14.

CONFERENCE

UW was a charter member of the Pacific Coast Conference—the forerunner to the Pac-10—when it was founded in 1916.

DISTINGUISHED ALUMNI

Dyan Cannon, actress; Kenny Gorelick, saxophonist Kenny G; Kitty Kelley, author; Hank Ketcham, creator of "Dennis the Menace" cartoon; Bruce Lee, actor and martial artist; Ann Rule, author

FIGHT SONG

BOW DOWN TO WASHINGTON
Bow down to Washington,
Bow down to Washington,
Mighty are the men
Who wear the Purple and the Gold,
Joyfully we welcome them
Within the victors' fold.
We will carve their names
In the hall of fame
To preserve the memory of our devotion.
Heaven help the foes of Washington;
They're trembling at the feet
Of mighty Washington,
The boys are there with bells,
Their fighting blood excels
It's harder to push them over the line
Than pass the Dardanelles.
Victory's the cry of Washington . . .
Leather lungs together
With a Rah! Rah! Rah!
And o'er the land
Our loyal band
Will sing the glory
Of Washington forever.

58–0–3 record from 1908 to 1916 and was so dour he once berated his team, a 90-0 victor, for not scoring 100. But the consensus cream of UW coaches was Don James, a spare, detail-driven man who coached from a tower. In his 18 years (1975-92), he went 150–60–2 and took the Huskies to six Rose Bowls. James restored a program that had grown stagnant and also hired several assistants who went on to head coaching positions. Among them: Nick Saban (Miami Dolphins) and Gary Pinkel (Missouri).

BEST TEAM Led by Emtman, a voracious defense and a devil-may-care quarterback named Billy Joe Hobert, the 1991 Huskies not only won the coaches' vote for the national championship—Associated Press poll voters sided with Miami—but some experts believe they deserve mention among the game's finest teams. The 1991 team went 12–0 and stated its case with a 34-14 victory over Michigan in the Rose Bowl, where the Huskies held

Elsewhere, college football teams have been dwarfed in public consciousness by their pro neighbors.

Heisman Trophy winner Desmond Howard to a single catch. The team's closest call was a 24-17 victory over seventh-ranked California on the road.

Washington's 1977 team went a timely 8-4—two wins were added later as a result of forfeits awarded by the NCAA—after coming off a 5–6 season. Attendance was flagging and the Seahawks, born in 1976, were the talk of the town. A Warren Moon-led club overcame a 1–3 start and upset two-touchdown favorite Michigan in the Rose Bowl, helping to re-establish Washington as a darling in its hometown.

BIGGEST GAME In 1994, the 19th-ranked Huskies went to No. 6 Miami playing for little else but pride; they were in the second year of a Pac-10-ordered bowl sanction and would wind up the season 7–4. Underdogs by 14 points, they fell behind 14-3 at halftime. Then the floodgates flew open, and Washington scored 22 points in the first five minutes of the second half on the way to a 38-20 upset that broke the

---

RECORDS

RUSHING YARDS
GAME
296 Hugh McElhenny vs. Washington State, Nov. 25, 1950 (20 att.)
SEASON
1,695 Corey Dillon, 1996 (301 att.)
CAREER
4,106 Napoleon Kaufman, 1991-94 (735 att.)

PASSING YARDS
GAME
455 Cody Pickett vs. Arizona, Oct. 20, 2001 (29 of 49)
SEASON
4,458 Cody Pickett, 2002 (365 of 612)
CAREER
10,220 Cody Pickett, 1999-2003 (821 of 1,429)

RECEIVING YARDS
GAME
257 Dave Williams vs. UCLA, Nov. 6, 1965 (10 rec.)
SEASON
1,454 Reggie Williams, 2002 (94 rec.)
CAREER
3,598 Reggie Williams, 2001-03 (243 rec.)

POINTS
GAME
42 Ervin Daily vs. Whitman, Oct. 25, 1919 (7 TDs)
SEASON
138 Corey Dillon, 1996 (22 TDs)
CAREER
380 Jeff Jaeger, 1983-86 (85 FGs, 125 PATs)

CONSENSUS ALL-AMERICANS

1925	George Wilson	HB
1928	Chuck Carroll	HB
1936	Max Starcevich	G
1940	Rudy Mucha	C
1941	Ray Frankowski	G
1963-64	Rick Redman	G
1966	Tom Greenlee	DT
1968	Al Worley	DB
1982	Chuck Nelson	PK
1984	Ron Holmes	DL
1986	Jeff Jaeger	PK
1986	Reggie Rogers	DL
1991	Mario Bailey	WR
1991	Steve Emtman	DL
1992	Lincoln Kennedy	OL
1995	Lawyer Milloy	DB
1996	Benji Olson	OL
1997	Olin Kreutz	C
2002	Reggie Williams	WR

Hurricanes' NCAA-record 58-game home winning streak. Afterward, in front of TV cameras, euphoric guard Bob Sapp dubbed it "the whammy in Miami."

BIGGEST UPSET No game is more symbolic of both the Huskies' and West Coast football's rise to prominence than the 1960 Rose Bowl. Coached by hardened Oklahoma-bred Jim Owens and quarterbacked by one-eyed Bob Schloredt, the eighth-ranked Huskies flattened No. 6 Wisconsin 44-8. Until that game, the Big Ten had won 11 of the previous 12 Rose Bowls. The Pac-10 won 21 of the next 28.

TRAGEDY Under most circumstances, the afternoon of Oct. 28, 2000, would have been cause for great celebration by the Huskies. After they allowed Stanford 22 straight points in the last six minutes, Washington stormed 80 yards in 30 seconds on three precision passes by quarterback Marques Tuiasosopo to win 31-28. But there would be no exuberance afterward. Late in the third quarter, on a seemingly innocent four-yard plunge by Stanford back Kerry Carter, Washington safety Curtis Williams was knocked backward on a helmet-to-helmet collision and was paralyzed from the neck down. Eighteen months later, he returned to Husky Stadium for the first time to watch UW's annual spring game. Williams, 24, died at his brother's house in central California a week later.

WILDEST FINISH Pour it on or take the safe field goal? In 1975, ahead 27-14 and facing fourth and one at the UW 14-yard line with three minutes left, Washington State coach Jim Sweeney unwisely listened to his players—who were only too ready to rub it in to their lordly cross-state neighbor—and called for a pass. But Al Burleson returned an interception 93 yards for a touchdown, Robert "Spider" Gaines took a tipped pass another 78 yards for a score, and Washington had an improbable 28-27 victory. The next week, Sweeney resigned.

DUBIOUS DISTINCTION McElhenny, probably the greatest running back in Washington history, once said only half-jokingly that he took about a $3,000 pay cut when he began a distinguished NFL career. That sort of largesse from boosters to McElhenny and a score of other Huskies caused a two-year bowl ban and probation from the old Pacific Coast Conference in 1956. Washington's second major blemish came in 1992, after *The Seattle Times* discovered that Hobert had accepted an improper $50,000 loan from an Idaho benefactor. When the NCAA came calling, it found the Huskies had also been guilty of bookkeeping errors in overseeing expense money for recruits, as well as

handing out some cushy summer jobs. That prompted a two-year bowl ban from the Pac-10, as well as a loss of 20 scholarships and a year's worth of TV revenue (about $1.4 million)—and triggered the resignation of James in protest of the severity of the penalties.

STADIUM More than the facility, it's the setting, which ranks among the most stunning in the game. Built in 1920, Husky Stadium sits hard by the western shore of Lake Washington, so close that some fans arrive by boat. On a clear day, those in the north upper deck can glimpse Mount Rainier, 65 miles to the southeast. But this is hardly a place of dreamy reveries: the noise level created by the double decks caused one Army player in 1995 to compare it to a C-130 transport plane. The last of four stadium expansions was the most eventful. In February of 1987, a northside upper-deck addition collapsed ignominiously, but was rebuilt for the opener that year.

RIVAL Washington fans have, by turns, considered Washington State and Oregon the Huskies' most distasteful adversaries. The WSU series is best captured by the two games in 1981 and 1982, when Washington won in Seattle to claim the Rose Bowl berth the Cinderella Cougars would have captured, only to have a 2–7–1 WSU team rob the Huskies of a repeat bid the next year in Pullman. In recent years, dislike of Oregon has spiked around Seattle in one of the nation's most underrated rivalries. The temperature grew much hotter in 1995, when UW coach Jim Lambright, campaigning against the Ducks for a Cotton Bowl bid, labored through a litany of reasons why the Huskies were the better choice—no matter that Oregon won head-to-head in Seattle. Despite Lambright's efforts, the Ducks got the nod.

NICKNAME In the early 1900s, Washington's teams were known as the Sun Dodgers. When alumni and administration realized that wasn't exactly a chamber of commerce endorsement, a committee settled on the nickname Huskies in 1922.

CONTROVERSY After only four seasons on the job, and despite a 33–16 record and four bowl appearances, coach Rick Neuheisel was booted in 2003. Neuheisel admitted to having won several thousand dollars in an auction-style pool on the 2002 and 2003 NCAA men's basketball tournaments. The Huskies fired him, alleging he had at first lied to NCAA investigators about his participation, and replaced him with offensive coordinator Keith Gilbertson, whose 6–6 season in 2003 was followed by a complete collapse in 2004.

With three games left in Washington's 1–10 campaign, Gilbertson announced that he would not return as coach in 2005. Neuheisel gained a measure of vindication when it was learned that a misguided compliance memo had authorized participation in pools outside the athletic department. Tyrone Willingham, whose firing at Notre Dame after a 21–15 record in three seasons had created its own stir, became Huskies coach in late 2004.

MASCOT "Spirit" is the 10th Alaskan Malamute to serve as Huskies mascot, leading the team out of the tunnel and patrolling the sideline. The first was Frosty I (1922-29).

UNIFORMS James introduced the current style in 1975. At home: purple jerseys, gold pants, gold helmets. On the road: white jerseys, purple pants, gold helmets. In 1995, Lambright unveiled purple helmets, much to the dismay of fans and players. When Neuheisel, in his introductory talk to the team after being named coach in 1999, promised to reinstate gold helmets, he drew a lusty cheer.

QUOTE "If it were up to me, I'd dog the Rose Bowl. Go find Florida State or Miami and play for No. 1. I wouldn't care if they'd put us on probation for 100 years."—Billy Joe Hobert, as the debate over No. 1 heated up in 1991

WASHINGTON ANNUAL STATISTICAL LEADERS

YR	RUSHING	YDS	ATT	AVG	PASSING	ATT	CMP	PCT	YDS	RECEIVING	REC	YDS	AVG
1960	Ray Jackson	500	108	4.6	Bob Hivner	58	31	.53	580	Pat Claridge	13	252	19.4
1961	Jim Stiger	582	130	4.5	Pete Ohler	59	17	.29	394	Lee Bernhardi	5	137	27.4
1962	Junior Coffey	581	98	5.9	Bill Siler	27	15	.56	294	Charlie Mitchell	9	108	12.0
1963	Ron Medved	431	75	5.7	Bill Douglas	113	64	.57	952	Dave Kopay	13	190	14.6
1964	Junior Coffey	638	147	4.3	Bill Douglas	64	33	.52	360	Gary Carr	14	190	13.6
1965	Don Moore	637	144	4.4	Tod Hullin	168	90	.54	1,318	Dave Williams	38	795	20.9
1966	Don Moore	447	88	5.1	Tom Sparlin	165	68	.41	954	Jim Cope	25	379	15.2
1967	Tom Manke	483	139	3.5	Tom Manke	81	32	.40	613	Jim Cope	20	284	14.2
1968	Carl Wojciechowski	651	138	4.7	Jerry Kaloper	115	43	.37	595	Harrison Wood	17	250	14.7
1969	Bo Cornell	613	136	4.5	Gene Willis	99	33	.33	568	Ralph Bayard	13	290	22.3
1970	Bo Cornell	340	97	3.5	Sonny Sixkiller	362	186	.51	2,303	Jim Krieg	54	738	13.7
1971	Pete Taggares	401	102	3.9	Sonny Sixkiller	297	126	.42	2,068	Tom Scott	35	820	23.4
1972	Pete Taggares	450	127	3.5	Sonny Sixkiller	152	73	.48	1,125	John Brady	30	450	15.0
1973	Pete Taggares	342	93	3.7	Chris Rowland	234	97	.41	1,521	Walter Oldes	27	450	16.7
1974	Dennis Fitzpatrick	697	137	5.1	Chris Rowland	124	59	.48	848	Scott Phillips	34	716	21.1
1975	Robin Earl	782	167	4.7	Chris Rowland	117	45	.38	597	Scott Phillips	33	433	13.1
1976	Ron Rowland	1,002	203	4.9	Warren Moon	175	81	.46	1,106	Scott Phillips	26	348	13.4
1977	Joe Steele	942	211	4.5	Warren Moon	222	125	.56	1,772	Spider Gaines	34	782	23.0
1978	Joe Steele	1,111	237	4.7	Tom Porras	176	84	.48	1,151	Keith Richardson	24	330	13.8
1979	Joe Steele	694	151	4.6	Tom Flick	122	71	.58	852	Paul Skansi	31	378	12.2
1980	Kyle Stevens	765	165	4.6	Tom Flick	319	191	.60	2,460	David Bayle	42	360	8.6
1981	Ron Jackson	647	167	3.9	Steve Pelluer	263	125	.48	1,280	Anthony Allen	34	457	13.4
1982	Jacque Robinson	976	238	4.1	Steve Pelluer	200	113	.57	1,248	Paul Skansi	60	718	12.0
1983	Sterling Hinds	859	168	5.1	Steve Pelluer	357	232	.65	2,365	Mark Pattison	44	455	10.3
1984	Jacque Robinson	1,036	223	4.6	Hugh Millen	175	91	.52	1,092	Danny Greene	33	492	14.9
1985	Vince Weathersby	523	134	3.9	Hugh Millen	264	158	.60	1,565	Lonzell Hill	50	744	14.9
1986	Vince Weathersby	908	169	5.4	Chris Chandler	318	180	.57	2,193	Lonzell Hill	48	798	16.6
1987	Vince Weathersby	766	160	4.8	Chris Chandler	279	143	.51	1,973	Darryl Franklin	47	773	16.4
1988	Aaron Jenkins	691	138	5.0	Cary Conklin	302	153	.51	1,833	Brian Slater	38	737	19.4
1989	Greg Lewis	1,197	266	4.5	Cary Conklin	404	229	.57	2,786	Andre Riley	57	1,071	18.8
1990	Greg Lewis	1,407	248	5.7	Mark Brunell	275	132	.48	1,895	Mario Bailey	42	720	17.1
1991	Beno Bryant	981	173	5.7	Billy Joe Hobert	319	191	.60	2,463	Mario Bailey	68	1,163	17.1
1992	Napoleon Kaufman	1,084	182	6.0	Mark Brunell	219	127	.58	1,612	Joe Kralik	35	503	14.4
1993	Napoleon Kaufman	1,299	226	5.7	Damon Huard	197	116	.59	1,282	Mark Bruener	30	414	13.8
1994	Napoleon Kaufman	1,390	255	5.5	Damon Huard	275	153	.56	1,887	Eric Bjornson	49	770	15.7
1995	Rashaan Shehee	995	174	5.7	Damon Huard	313	198	.64	2,609	Dave Janoski	40	657	16.4
1996	Corey Dillon	1,695	301	5.6	Brock Huard	254	129	.51	1,881	Jerome Pathon	46	714	15.5
1997	Rashaan Shehee	1,055	168	6.3	Brock Huard	274	164	.60	2,319	Jerome Pathon	73	1,299	17.8
1998	Willie Hurst	604	158	3.8	Brock Huard	347	191	.56	2,191	Dane Looker	72	762	10.6
1999	M. Tuiasosopo	571	149	3.8	M. Tuiasosopo	322	189	.59	2,418	Chris Juergens	45	539	12.0
2000	Rich Alexis	816	128	6.4	M. Tuiasosopo	345	186	.54	2,284	Todd Elstrom	51	707	13.9
2001	Willie Hurst	744	154	4.8	Cody Pickett	355	196	.55	2,696	Reggie Williams	60	1,035	17.3
2002	Rich Alexis	688	202	3.4	Cody Pickett	612	365	.60	4,458	Reggie Williams	94	1,454	15.5
2003	Rich Alexis	566	138	4.1	Cody Pickett	454	257	.57	3,043	Reggie Williams	89	1,109	12.5
2004	Kenny James	702	172	4.1	Casey Paus	274	116	.42	1,476	Sonny Shackelford	21	298	14.2

Receiving leaders by receptions
All statistics include postseason

WASHINGTON ALL-TIME SCORES

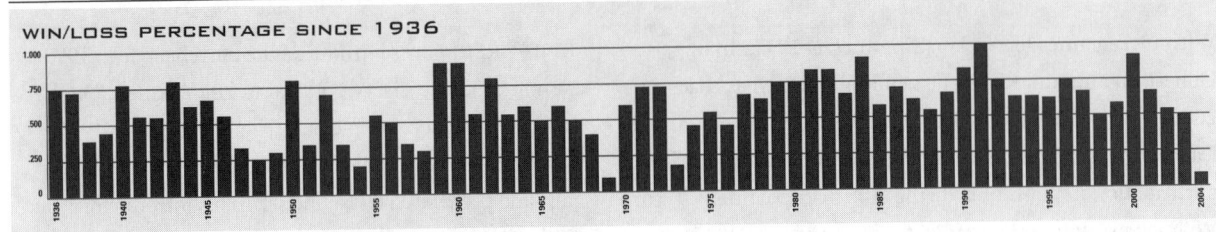

WIN/LOSS PERCENTAGE SINCE 1936

NO HEAD COACH

1889   0-1-0
| N28 | | Ea. Coll. Alumni | 0 | 20 |

1890   0-0-1
| N27 | | at Wash. Coll. | 0 | 0 |

1891
NO TEAM

W.B. GOODWIN
1892-93 (.357)   2-4-1

1892   1-1-0
| O16 | | Seattle AC | 0 | 28 |
| D17 | ● | Seattle AC | 14 | 0 |

1893   1-3-1
N11	●	at Viciendas	8	4
N18		Tacoma AC **WS**	4	6
N25	=	at Port Townsend	6	6
N30		at Multnomah AC	0	30
D29		Stanford **WS**	0	40

C. COBB
1894 (.500)   1-1-1

1894   1-1-1
O13	=	at Port Townsend	14	14
O27		Seattle AC	0	24
N22	●	at Whitman	46	0

RALPH NICHOLS
1895-96, '98 (.625)   7-4-1

1895   4-0-1
O19	●	Seattle AC	12	0
O26	=	Seattle AC	0	0
N9	●	Vashon College	44	4
N21	●	at Tacoma	8	4
D7	●	Vashon College	34	0

1896   2-3-0
O24		Seattle AC	4	6
N14		at Port Townsend	0	18
D12		at Multnomah AC	0	10
D15	●	YMCA	4	0
D19	●	Seattle AC	12	6

CARL CLEMANS
1897 (.333)   1-2

1897   1-2-0
O9	●	YMCA	10	0
N18		Seattle AC	6	10
D4		at Oregon State	0	16

RALPH NICHOLS

1898   1-1-0
| D17 | | Puyallup Indians | 11 | 18 |
| D24 | ● | Puyallup Indians | 13 | 0 |

A.S. JEFFS
1899 (.750)   4-1-1

1899   4-1-1
O14	●	Port. Townsend HS	16	0
O28	●	Port. Townsend HS	0	11
N4	●	at Everett AC	33	0
N7	=	All Seattle	5	5
N18	●	Wilson B.C.	11	0
N25	●	Whitman	6	5

J.S. DODGE
1900 (.400)   1-2-2

1900   1-2-2
S29	●	Seattle HS	5	0
O24		at Whitman	11	11
O27	●	Idaho **Spo**	6	12
N30	=	Washington State	5	5
D1		at Oregon	0	43

JACK WRIGHT
1901 (.500)   3-3

1901   3-3-0
O26		Whitman	0	10
N1		at Washington State	0	10
N9	●	Port Townsend	10	0
N12		Multnomah AC	6	17
N16	●	Vashon Coll.	17	5
N21	●	Idaho	10	0

JAMES KNIGHT
1902-04 (.775)   15-4-1

1902   5-1-0
O18	●	All Seattle	12	0
O25	●	Oregon State	16	6	*
N3	●	at Idaho	10	0
N8	●	at Whitman	11	5
N15		Multnomah AC	0	7
N27	●	Washington State	16	0

1903   6-1-0
O17	●	at Oregon State	5	0
O24	●	Whitman	35	0
O30	●	at Washington State	10	0
N14	●	Oregon	6	5
N20	●	Nevada	2	0
N26	●	Idaho	5	0
D5		at Multnomah AC	0	6

1904   4-2-1
O8	●	Whitman	33	0
O15		Oregon State	5	26
O22	●	at Utah State	45	0
O29	●	Washington State	12	6
N5	●	Idaho	12	10
N12		at Oregon	0	18
N24	=	California	6	6

OLIVER CUTTS
1905 (.625)   4-2-2

1905   4-2-2
O4	●	USS Chicago	11	0
O7	●	Whitworth **Tac**	10	4
O14	=	Whitman	6	6
O21	●	Chemawa	11	6
O30		at Idaho	0	8
N11	●	Sherman Indians	29	0
N18	=	at Oregon	12	12
N30		at Oregon State	0	16	*

VICTOR PLACE
1906-07 (.579)   8-5-6

1906   4-1-4
O10	●	USS Philadelphia	5	0
O13	●	Whitworth	8	0
O20	●	Seattle HS	4	0
O20		Seattle AC	10	10
O27	=	Oregon State	0	0
N3		Whitman	0	0
N10	=	Willamette	0	0
N20		at Oregon	6	16	*
N29	●	Idaho	16	9

1907   4-4-2
O5	=	Seattle HS	0	0
O12	●	at Multnomah AC	10	0
O14	=	at Willamette	21	0
O19	●	Whitworth **Tac**	5	0
O26	●	Chemawa	40	0
N2		USS Nebraska	6	19
N8	●	at Whitman	8	12
N16		Oregon	0	6
N21		Washington State	5	11
N28	=	Idaho	0	0

GIL DOBIE
1908-16 (.975)   58-0-3

1908   6-0-1
S26	●	Lincoln HS	22	0
O3	●	Washington HS	23	5
O17	●	Whitworth	24	4
O24	●	Whitman	6	0
N7	=	Washington State	6	6
N14	●	at Oregon	15	0
N28	●	Oregon State	32	0

1909   7-0-0
O2	●	USS Milwaukee	52	0
O9	●	Queen Anne HS	34	0
O23	●	Lincoln HS	20	0
O30	●	at Idaho	50	0
N6	●	Whitman	17	0
N13	●	at Oregon State	21	0
N20	●	Oregon	20	6

1910   6-0-0
O8	●	Lincoln HS	20	0
O15	●	Coll. Puget Sound	51	0
O22	●	Whitman	12	8
N5	●	Idaho	29	0
N12	●	Washington State **Spo**	16	0
N24	●	Oregon State	22	0

1911   7-0-0
O2	●	Lincoln H. S.	42	0
O14	●	Fort Worden	90	0
O21	●	Coll. Puget Sound	35	0
O28	●	Idaho **Spo**	17	0
N4	●	Oregon State	34	0
N18	●	Oregon **Port**	29	3
N30	●	Washington State	30	6

1912   6-0-0
O12	●	Coll. Puget Sound	53	0
O19	●	Bremerton	55	0
O26	●	Idaho	24	0
N9	●	Oregon State **Port**	9	3
N16	●	Oregon	30	14
N28	●	Washington State	19	0

1913   7-0-0
S27	●	Everette HS	26	0
O11	●	ALL Navy	23	7
O18	●	Whitworth	100	0
O25	●	Oregon State	47	0
N1	●	Whitman	40	6
N15	●	Oregon **Port**	10	7
N27	●	Washington State	20	0

1914   6-0-1
S26	●	Aberdeen AC	33	6
O3	●	Wash. Park AC	45	0
O10	●	Rainier Valley AC	81	0
O24	●	Whitman	28	7
O31	=	at Oregon State	0	0
N14	●	Oregon	10	0
N26	●	Washington State	45	0

1915   7-0-0
O2	●	Ballard Meteors	31	0
O9	●	Wash. Park AC	64	0
O23	●	at Gonzaga	21	7
O30	●	Whitman	27	0
N6	●	at California	72	0
N13	●	California	13	7
N26	●	Colorado	46	0

1916-1958
PACIFIC COAST

1916   6-0-1 (3-0-1)
O14	●	Ballard Meteors	28	0
O21	●	Bremerton	62	0
O28	●	Whitman	37	6
N4			at Oregon	0	0
N11			Oregon State	35	0
N18			at California	13	3
N30			California	14	7

CLAUDE J. HUNT
1917, '19 (.650)   6-3-1

1917   1-2-1 (0-2-1)
O20	●	Whitman	14	6
N3			at California	0	27
N17	=		Oregon State	0	0
N29			Washington State	0	14

TONY SAVAGE
1918 (.500)   1-1

1918   1-1-0 (1-1-0)
| N23 | ● | Oregon State | 6 | 0 |
| D1 | | | at Oregon | 0 | 7 |

CLAUDE J. HUNT

1919   5-1-0 (2-1-0)
O18	●	USS New York	35	0
O25	●	Whitman	120	0
N1			Oregon	13	24
N15	●	at Washington State	13	7
N22	●	Pacific Fleet	14	0
N27			California	7	0

LEONARD ALLISON
1920 (.167)   1-5

1920   1-5-0 (0-3-0)
O9	●	Whitman	33	14
O16			Montana	14	18
O23			Oregon State	0	3
N6			Stanford	0	3
N13			at Oregon	0	17
N27			Dartmouth	7	28	*

ENOCH BAGSHAW
1921-29 (.725)   63-22-6

1921   3-4-1 (0-3-1)
O1	●	9th Army Corps	24	7
O8	●	Whitman	7	0
O15	●	Montana	28	7
O22			at Oregon State	0	24
N5	=		Stanford	0	0
N12			at California	3	72
N24			Washington State	0	14
D3			Penn State	7	21

1922　6-1-1 (4-1-1)

		Opponent		
S30	●	USS Idaho	49	0
O7		Montana	26	0
O14	●	Idaho	2	0
O21	●	Oregon State	14	3
O28	●	at Washington State	16	13
N11		California	7	45
N18	●	at Stanford	12	8
N30	=	Oregon	3	3

1923　10-1-1 (4-1-0)

S22	●	USS Mississippi	33	0
S29	●	USS New York	42	7
O6	●	Willamette	54	0
O13	●	Whitman	19	0
O20	●	Southern Cal	22	0
O27	●	at Puget Sound	24	0
N3	●	at Oregon State	14	0
N10	●	Montana	26	14
N17		at California	0	9
N24	●	Washington State	24	7
D1	●	Oregon	26	7
		ROSE BOWL		
J1	=	Navy	14	14

1924　8-1-1 (3-1-1)

S20	●	West Seattle AC	32	0
S27	●	USS Maryland	33	0
O4	●	Willamette	57	0
O11	●	Whitman	55	0
O18	●	Montana	52	7
O25	●	Oregon State	6	3
N1		at Oregon	3	7
N8	●	California	7	7
N15	●	at Puget Sound	96	0
N22	●	Washington State	14	0

1925　10-1-1 (5-0-0)

S19	●	Willamette	108	0
S26	●	USS Oklahoma	59	0
O3	●	West Seattle AC	56	0
O10	●	Montana	30	10
O17		at Nebraska	6	6
O24	●	Whitman	64	2
O31	●	at Washington State	23	0
N7	●	Stanford	13	0
N14		at California	7	0
N21	●	at Puget Sound	80	7
N28	●	Oregon	15	14
		ROSE BOWL		
J1		Alabama	19	20

1926　8-2-0 (3-2-0)

S18	●	USS New Mexico	20	0
S25	●	Willamette	28	0
O2	●	Puget Sound	33	0
O9	●	Oregon _Port_	23	9
O16	●	Idaho	26	0
O23		Washington State	6	9
O30	●	at Whitman	44	0
N6	●	California	13	7
N13	●	at Stanford	10	29
N25	●	Nebraska	10	6

1927　9-2-0 (4-2-0)

S17	●	Willamette	32	6
S24	●	USS Idaho	27	0
O1	●	USS Idaho	48	0
O8	●	at Puget Sound	40	0
O15	●	at Montana	32	0
O22	●	Washington State	14	0
O29	●	Whitman	61	7
N5		Stanford	7	13
N12	●	at California	6	0
N24	●	Oregon	7	0
D3	●	at Southern Cal	13	33 *

1928　7-4-0 (2-4-0)

S15	●	Willamette	26	0
S22	●	USS Tennessee	41	0
S29	●	Pacific	43	0
O6	●	Whitman	7	0
O13	●	Montana	25	0
O20	●	Oregon _Port_	0	27
O27		Oregon State	0	9 *
N3	●	at Puget Sound	40	0
N10	●	California	0	6
N17	●	at Stanford	0	12
N29	●	Washington State	6	0

1929　2-6-1 (0-5-1)

S28	●	Whitman	47	0
O5	=	Montana	6	6
O12		Southern Cal	0	48
O19		at Washington State	13	20
O26		Oregon	0	14
N2	●	at Puget Sound	73	0
N9		Stanford	0	6
N16	●	at California	0	7
N23	●	at Chicago	6	26

1930　5-4-0 (3-4-0)

S27	●	Whitman	48	0
O4	●	Montana	27	0
O11	●	Idaho	27	0
O18	●	Oregon _Port_	0	7
O25	●	California	13	0
N1	●	Puget Sound	60	0
N8		at Stanford	7	25
N15		Washington State	0	3
N27		at Southern Cal	0	32

1931　5-3-1 (3-3-1)

S26	●	Utah	7	6
O3	●	Montana	25	0
O10	●	Oregon	0	13
O17	●	Idaho	38	7
O24	=	Stanford	0	0
O31	●	Whitman	77	0
N7		at California	0	13
N14	●	Washington State	12	0
D5	●	at Southern Cal	7	44

1932　6-2-2 (3-2-2)

S24	●	Gonzaga	19	7
O1	●	Montana	26	13
O8	●	Oregon _Port_	0	0
O22	●	California	6	7
O29	●	Whitman	33	7
N5	●	at Stanford	18	13
N12	=	Washington State	0	0
N24	●	Southern Cal	6	9
D3	●	at UCLA	19	0
D10	●	West Seattle AC	66	0

1933　5-4-0 (3-4-0)

S23	●	Gonzaga	13	0
S30	●	Idaho	32	6
O14		Oregon	6	0
O21	●	at Puget Sound	14	6
O28	●	Stanford	6	0
N11		at California	0	33
N18	●	UCLA	10	0
N25		at Washington State	6	17
D9		at Southern Cal	7	13

1934　6-1-1 (5-1-1)

S29	●	Idaho	13	0
O13	●	Oregon _Port_	16	6
O27	●	California	13	7
N3	●	Oregon State	14	7
N10		at Stanford	0	24
N17	●	Puget Sound	34	0
N24	=	Washington State	0	0
D1	●	at Southern Cal	14	7

1935　5-3-0 (4-3-0)

S28	●	Idaho	14	0
O12	●	Santa Clara	13	6
O19	●	at Washington State	21	0
O26		Stanford	0	6
N2	●	Montana	33	7
N9		at California	0	14
N23	●	Oregon	6	7 *
D7	●	at Southern Cal	6	2

1936　7-2-1 (7-0-1)

S26	●	Minnesota	7	14
O3	●	Idaho	22	0
O10		at UCLA	14	0
O17	●	Oregon State	19	7
O24	●	California	13	0
O31	●	Oregon _Port_	7	0
N7	=	at Stanford	14	14
N14	●	Southern Cal	12	0
N26	●	Washington State	40	0
		ROSE BOWL		
J1		Pittsburgh	0	21

1937　7-2-2 (4-2-2)

S25	●	Iowa	14	0
O2	●	at Southern Cal	7	0
O9		Oregon State	3	6
O16	=	at Washington State	7	7
O23		Stanford	7	13
O30	●	Idaho	21	7
N6	●	at California	0	0
N13		UCLA	26	0
N20	●	Oregon	14	0
D8	●	at Hawaii All Stars	35	6
		PINEAPPLE BOWL		
J1		Hawaii	53	13

1938　3-5-1 (3-4-1)

S24		at Minnesota	0	15
O1	=	Idaho	12	12
O8		at UCLA	0	13
O15		Oregon State	6	13
O22		California	7	14
N5	●	at Stanford	10	7
N12		Southern Cal	7	6
N19		Oregon _Port_	0	3
N26	●	Washington State	26	0

1939　4-5-0 (4-4-0)

S30	●	Pittsburgh	6	27
O7		UCLA	7	14
O14		at Washington State	0	6
O21		Oregon State	7	13
O28	●	Stanford	8	5
N4	●	Montana	9	0
N11	●	at California	13	6
N25	●	Oregon	20	13
D2		at Southern Cal	7	9

1940　7-2-0 (7-1-0)

S28		at Minnesota	14	19
O5	●	Idaho	21	0
O12	●	Oregon _Port_	10	0
O19	●	Oregon State	19	0
O26	●	California	7	6
N9		at Stanford	10	20
N16	●	Southern Cal	14	0
N23	●	at UCLA	41	0
N30	●	Washington State	33	9

1941　5-4-0 (5-3-0)

S27		Minnesota	6	14
O4		Oregon State _Port_	6	9
O11	●	at Washington State	23	13
O18	●	UCLA	14	7
O25		Stanford	7	13
N1	●	Montana	21	0
N8	●	at California	13	6
N22		Oregon	16	19
N29		at Southern Cal	14	13

1942　4-3-3 (3-3-2)

S26	●	Pacific	27	0
O3	=	Southern Cal	0	0
O10		Oregon _Port_	15	7
O17	●	Montana	35	0
O24		California	6	19
O31	●	Oregon State	13	0
N7		Stanford _SF_	7	20
N14		Saint Mary's-Cal Pre-Flight	0	0
N21		at UCLA	10	14
N28	=	Washington State	0	0

1943　4-1-0 (0-1-0)

S25	●	Whitman	35	6
O9		at Spokane Air Comm.	47	12
O23	●	March Field	27	7
O30	●	Spokane Air comm.	41	7
		ROSE BOWL		
J1		Southern Cal	0	29

1944　5-3-0 (1-1-0)

S23	●	Willamette	71	0
S30	●	Whitman	65	6
O7	●	at Willamette	40	6
O14	●	at Whitman	71	0
O23		at Southern Cal	7	38
O28	●	at California	33	7
N11		March Field	0	28
N18		Second Air Force _Spo_	6	47

1945　6-3-0 (6-3-0)

S29	●	Oregon	20	6
O6		at California	14	27
O13	●	Washington State	6	0
O20	●	Oregon State _Port_	13	0
O27	●	Southern Cal	13	7
N3	●	Oregon _Port_	7	0
N10	●	Oregon State	6	7
N17	●	Idaho	12	0
N24		at Washington State	0	7

1946　5-4-0 (5-3-0)

S28	●	Saint Mary's-Cal	20	24
O5		UCLA	13	39
O12	●	at Washington State	21	7
O19		at Southern Cal	0	28
O26	●	California	20	6
N9	●	at Stanford	21	15
N16	●	Oregon	16	0
N23	●	Montana	21	0
N30	●	Oregon State _Port_	12	21

1947　3-6-0 (2-5-0)

S27	●	at Minnesota	6	7
O4		Oregon State	7	14
O11	●	Saint Mary's-Cal	26	6
O18		Oregon _Port_	0	6
O25	●	Stanford	25	0
N1		Southern Cal	0	19
N8		at California	7	13
N15		at UCLA	7	34
N22	●	Washington State	20	0

1948　2-7-1 (2-5-1)

S25	●	Minnesota	0	20
O2	=	Oregon State _Port_	14	14
O9	●	UCLA	27	0
O16		at Washington State	0	10
O23		California	0	21
O30		at Stanford	0	20
N6		Oregon	7	13
N13		at Southern Cal	7	32
N20	●	Idaho	34	7
N27		at Notre Dame	0	46

1949　3-7-0 (2-5-0)

S17	●	Utah	14	7
S24		at Minnesota	20	48
O1		Notre Dame	7	27
O8		Oregon State	3	7
O15		Stanford	0	40
O22		at California	7	21
O29		Southern Cal	28	40
N5	●	Oregon _Port_	28	27
N12		at UCLA	26	47
N19	●	Washington State	34	21

1950　8-2-0 (6-1-0)

S23	●	Kansas State	33	7
S30	●	Minnesota	28	13
O7	●	UCLA	21	20
O14	●	Oregon State _Port_	35	6
O21	●	at Illinois	13	20
O28	●	at Stanford	21	7
N4	●	California	7	14
N11	●	Oregon	27	13 *
N18	●	at Southern Cal	28	13
N25	●	Washington State _Spo_	52	21

1951　3-6-1 (1-5-1)

S22	●	Montana	58	7
S29	●	at Minnesota	25	20
O6		Southern Cal	13	20
O13	●	Oregon _Port_	63	6
O20		Illinois	20	27
O27		Stanford	7	14
N3		Oregon State	14	40
N10		at California	28	37
N17	=	at UCLA	20	20
N24		Washington State	25	27

1952　7-3-0 (6-2-0)

S20	●	Idaho	39	14
S27	●	Minnesota	19	13
O4		UCLA	7	32
O11		at Illinois	14	48
O18	●	Oregon	49	0
O25	●	at Stanford	27	14
N1	●	Oregon State _Port_	38	13
N8	●	California	22	7
N15		at Southern Cal	0	33
N29	●	Washington State _Spo_	33	27

JOHN CHERBERG
1953-55 (.367) 10-18-2

1953 3-6-1 (2-4-1)

S19		Colorado	20	21
S26		at Michigan	0	50
O3	● |	Oregon State	28	0
O10	= |	Southern Cal	13	13
O17	● |	Oregon *Port*	14	6
O24	|	Stanford	7	13
O31	●	Utah	21	14
N7	|	at California	25	53
N14	|	at UCLA	6	22
N21	|	Washington State	20	25

1954 2-8-0 (1-6-0)

S18	●	Utah	7	6
S25		Michigan	0	14
O2	● |	Oregon State *Port*	17	7
O9	|	UCLA	20	21
O16		at Baylor	7	34
O23	|	at Stanford	7	13
O30	|	Oregon	7	26
N6	|	California	6	27
N13	|	at Southern Cal	0	41
N20	|	at Washington State	7	26

1955 5-4-1 (4-3-1)

S17	● |	Idaho	14	7
S24	●	at Minnesota	30	0
O1	● |	Oregon *Port*	19	7
O8	● |	Southern Cal	7	0
O15		Baylor	7	13
O22	= |	Stanford	7	7
O29	|	Oregon State	7	13
N5	|	at California	6	20
N12	|	at UCLA	17	19
N19	● |	Washington State	27	7

DARRELL ROYAL
1956 (.500) 5-5

1956 5-5-0 (4-4-0)

S22	● |	Idaho	53	21
S29		Minnesota	14	34
O6	●	Illinois	28	13
O13	● |	Oregon	20	7
O20	|	at Southern Cal	7	35
O27	|	California	7	16
N3	|	Oregon State *Port*	20	28
N10	|	UCLA	9	13
N17	● |	at Stanford	34	13
N24	● |	Washington State *Spo*	40	26

JIM OWENS
1957-74 (.545) 99-82-6

1957 3-6-1 (3-4-0)

S21	=	Colorado	6	6
S28		at Minnesota	7	46
O5		Ohio State	7	35
O12	|	at UCLA	0	19
O19	|	Stanford	14	21
O26	● |	Oregon State	19	6
N2	|	Southern Cal	12	19
N9	● |	Oregon *Port*	13	6
N16	● |	at California	35	27
N23	|	Washington State	7	27

1958 3-7-0 (1-6-0)

S20	●	San Jose State	14	6
S27	●	Minnesota	24	21
O4		at Ohio State	7	12
O11	|	at Stanford	12	22
O18	|	UCLA	0	20
O25	|	Oregon State *Port*	12	14
N1	● |	Oregon	6	0
N8	|	at Southern Cal	6	21
N15	|	California	7	12
N22	|	Washington State *Spo*	14	18

1959-1967
AAWU

1959 10-1-0 (3-1-0)

S19	●	at Colorado	21	12
S26	●	Idaho	23	0
O3	●	Utah	51	6
O10	● |	Stanford	10	0
O17	|	Southern Cal	15	22
O24	●	Oregon *Port*	13	12
O31	● |	at UCLA	23	7
N7	●	Oregon State	13	6
N14	● |	at California	20	0
N21	●	Washington State	20	0
ROSE BOWL				
J1	●	Wisconsin	44	8

1960 10-1-0 (4-0-0)

S17	●	Pacific	55	6
S24	●	Idaho	41	12
O1		Navy	14	15
O8	● |	at Stanford	29	10
O15	● |	UCLA	10	8
O22	●	Oregon State *Port*	30	29
O29	●	Oregon	7	6
N5	● |	at Southern Cal	34	0
N12	● |	California	27	7
N19	●	Washington State *Spo*	8	7
ROSE BOWL				
J2	●	Minnesota	17	7

1961 5-4-1 (2-1-1)

S23		Purdue	6	13
S30	●	at Illinois	20	7
O7	●	Pittsburgh	22	17
O14	|	at California	14	21
O21	● |	Stanford	13	0
O28		Oregon *Port*	6	7
N4	= |	Southern Cal	0	0
N11		Oregon State	0	3
N18	● |	at UCLA	17	13
N25	●	Washington State	21	17

1962 7-1-2 (4-1-0)

S22	=	Purdue	7	7
S29	●	Illinois	28	7
O6	●	Kansas State	41	0
O13	●	Oregon State *Port*	14	13
O20	● |	at Stanford	14	0
O27	=	Oregon	21	21
N3	|	at Southern Cal	0	14
N10	● |	California	27	0
N17	● |	UCLA	30	0
N24	● |	Washington State *Spo*	26	21

1963 6-5-0 (4-1-0)

S21		at Air Force	7	10
S28		at Pittsburgh	6	13
O5		Iowa	7	17
O12	●	Oregon State	34	7
O19	● |	Stanford	19	11
O26	●	Oregon *Port*	26	19
N2	● |	Southern Cal	22	7
N9	● |	at California	39	26
N16		at UCLA	0	14
N23	● |	Washington State	16	0
ROSE BOWL				
J1		Illinois	7	17

1964 6-4-0 (5-2-0)

S19		Air Force	2	3
S26	●	Baylor	35	14
O3		at Iowa	18	28
O10	|	Oregon State *Port*	7	9
O17	● |	at Stanford	6	0
O24	|	Oregon	0	7
O31	● |	at Southern Cal	14	13
N7	● |	California	21	16
N14	● |	UCLA	22	20
N21	● |	Washington State *Spo*	14	0

1965 5-5-0 (4-3-0)

S18	●	Idaho	14	9
S25		at Baylor	14	17
O2		Ohio State	21	23
O9	|	Southern Cal	0	34
O16	|	at California	12	16
O23	●	Oregon *Port*	24	20
O30	● |	Stanford	41	8
N6	|	at UCLA	24	28
N13	● |	Oregon State	28	21
N20	● |	Washington State	27	9

1966 6-4-0 (4-3-0)

S17	●	Idaho	19	7
S24		Air Force	0	10
O1	●	at Ohio State	38	22
O8	|	at Southern Cal	14	17
O15	|	California	20	24
O22	● |	Oregon	10	7
O29	● |	at Stanford	22	20
N5	● |	UCLA	16	3
N12		at Oregon State	13	24
N19	● |	Washington State *Spo*	19	7

1967 5-5-0 (3-4-0)

S16		Nebraska	7	17
S23	●	Wisconsin	17	0
S30	●	at Air Force	30	7
O7	● |	Oregon State	13	6
O14	● |	at Oregon	26	0
O21	|	Southern Cal	6	23
O28	● |	at California	23	6
N4	|	Stanford	7	14
N11	|	at UCLA	0	48
N18	|	Washington State	7	9

1968-PRESENT
PAC 10

1968 3-5-2 (1-5-1)

S21	=	Rice	35	35
S28	●	at Wisconsin	21	17
O5	|	at Oregon State	21	35
O12	|	Oregon	0	3
O19	|	at Southern Cal	7	14
O26	●	Idaho	37	7
N2	= |	California	7	7
N9	|	at Stanford	20	35
N16	● |	UCLA	6	0
N23	|	Washington State *Spo*	0	24

1969 1-9-0 (1-6-0)

S20		at Michigan State	11	27
S27		at Michigan	7	45
O4		Ohio State	14	41
O11	|	at California	13	44
O18	|	Oregon State	6	10
O25	|	at Oregon	7	22
N1	|	at UCLA	14	57
N8	|	Stanford	7	21
N15	|	Southern Cal	7	16
N22	● |	Washington State	30	21

1970 6-4-0 (4-3-0)

S19	●	Michigan State	42	16
S26		Michigan	3	17
O3	●	Navy	56	7
O10	|	California	28	31
O17	|	at Southern Cal	25	28
O24	● |	at Oregon State	29	20
O31	● |	Oregon	25	23
N7	|	at Stanford	22	29
N14	● |	UCLA	61	20
N21	● |	Washington State *Spo*	43	25

1971 8-3-0 (4-3-0)

S11	●	Santa Barbara	65	7
S18	●	Purdue	38	35
S25	●	TCU	44	26
O2	●	at Illinois	52	14
O9	|	Stanford	6	17
O16	|	at Oregon	21	23
O23	● |	Oregon State	38	14
O30	● |	at UCLA	23	12
N6	● |	at California	30	7
N13	|	Southern Cal	12	13
N20	● |	Washington State	28	20

1972 8-3-0 (4-3-0)

S9	●	Pacific	13	6
S16	●	Duke	14	6
S23	●	at Purdue	22	21
S30	●	Illinois	31	11
O7	● |	Oregon	23	17
O14	|	at Stanford	0	24
O21	|	at Southern Cal	7	34
O28	● |	California	35	21
N4	● |	at Oregon State	23	16
N11	● |	UCLA	30	21
N18	|	Washington State *Spo*	10	27

1973 2-9-0 (0-7-0)

S15		Hawaii	7	10
S22		at Duke	21	23
S29	●	Syracuse	21	7
O6	|	at California	49	54
O13	|	Oregon State	7	31
O20	|	Stanford	14	23
O27	|	at Oregon	0	58
N3	|	at UCLA	13	62
N10	●	Idaho	41	14
N17	|	Southern Cal	19	42
N24	|	Washington State	26	52

1974 5-6-0 (3-4-0)

S14	●	Cincinnati	21	17
S21	●	Iowa State	31	28
S28		Texas A&M	15	28
O5		at Texas	21	35
O12	|	at Oregon State	9	23
O19	|	at Stanford	17	34
O26	● |	Oregon	66	0
N2	● |	UCLA	31	9
N9	|	California	26	52
N16	|	at Southern Cal	11	42
N23	● |	Washington State *Spo*	24	17

DON JAMES
1975-92 (.712) 150-60-2

1975 6-5-0 (5-2-0)

S13		at Arizona State	12	35
S20		Texas	10	28
S27	●	Navy	14	13
O4	● |	at Oregon	27	17
O11		at Alabama	0	52
O18	|	Stanford	21	24
O25	● |	Oregon State	35	7
N1	● |	at UCLA	17	13
N8	|	at California	24	27
N15	● |	Southern Cal	8	7
N22	● |	Washington State	28	27

1976 5-6-0 (3-4-0)

S11	●	Virginia	38	17
S18		Colorado	7	21
S25		Indiana	13	20
O2	●	Minnesota	38	7
O9	● |	at Oregon State	24	12
O16	|	at Stanford	28	34
O23	● |	Oregon	14	7
O30	|	UCLA	21	30
N6	|	California	0	7
N13	|	at Southern Cal	3	20
N20	● |	Washington State *Spo*	51	32

1977 8-4-0 (6-1-0)

S10		Mississippi State	18	27 †
S17	●	San Jose State	24	3
S24		at Syracuse	20	22
O1		at Minnesota	17	19
O8	● |	at Oregon	54	0
O15	● |	Stanford	45	21
O22	● |	Oregon State	14	6
O29	|	at UCLA	12	20 †
N5	● |	at California	50	31
N12	● |	Southern Cal	28	10
N19	● |	Washington State	35	15
ROSE BOWL				
J2	●	Michigan	27	20

1978 7-4-0 (6-2-0)

S9	|	UCLA	7	10
S16	●	Kansas	31	2
S23		at Indiana	7	14
S30	● |	at Oregon State	34	0
O7		Alabama	17	20
O14	● |	at Stanford	34	31
O21	● |	Oregon	20	14
O28	● |	Arizona State	41	7
N4	● |	Arizona	31	21
N11	|	at Southern Cal	10	28
N25	● |	Washington State *Spo*	38	8

1979 9-3-0 (5-2-0)

S8	●	Wyoming	38	2
S15	●	Utah	41	7
S22	● |	at Oregon	21	17
S29	●	Fresno State	49	14
O6	● |	Oregon State	41	0
O13	|	at Arizona State	7	12 †
O20		Pittsburgh	14	26
O27	● |	at UCLA	34	14
N3	● |	at California	28	24
N10	|	Southern Cal	17	24
N17	● |	Washington State	17	7
SUN BOWL				
D22	●	Texas	14	7

1980 9-3-0 (6-1-0)

S13	●	Air Force	50	7
S20	●	Northwestern	45	7
S27	|	Oregon	10	34
O4	●	at Oklahoma State	24	18
O11	● |	at Oregon State	41	6
O18	● |	at Stanford	27	24
O25		Navy	10	24
N1	● |	Arizona State	25	0
N8	● |	Arizona	45	22
N15	● |	at Southern Cal	20	10
N22	● |	Washington State *Spo*	30	23
ROSE BOWL				
J1		Michigan	6	23

1981 10-2-0 (6-2-0)

S12	●	Pacific	34	14
S19	●	Kansas State	20	3
S26	● |	at Oregon	17	3
O3	|	Arizona State	7	26
O10	● |	at California	27	26
O17	● |	Oregon State	56	17
O24	●	at Texas Tech	14	7
O31	● |	Stanford	42	31
N7	|	at UCLA	0	31
N14	● |	Southern Cal	13	3
N21	● |	Washington State	23	10
ROSE BOWL				
J1	●	Iowa	28	0

1982 — 10-2-0 (6-2-0)

Date		Opponent		
S11	•	Texas El Paso	55	0
S18	•	at Arizona	23	13
S25	•	Oregon	37	21
O2	•	San Diego State	46	25
O9	•	California	50	7
O16	•	at Oregon State	34	17
O23	•	Texas Tech	10	3
O30	•	at Stanford	31	43
N6	•	UCLA	10	7
N13	•	at Arizona State	17	13
N20	•	at Washington State	20	24
ALOHA BOWL				
D25	•	Maryland	21	20

1983 — 8-4-0 (5-2-0)

Date		Opponent		
S10	•	at Northwestern	34	0
S17	•	Michigan	25	24
S24	•	at LSU	14	40
O1	•	Navy	27	10
O8	•	Oregon State	34	7
O15	•	Stanford	32	15
O22	•	at Oregon	32	3
O29	•	at UCLA	24	27
N5	•	at Arizona	23	22
N12		Southern Cal	24	0
N19		Washington State	6	17
ALOHA BOWL				
D26	•	Penn State	10	13

1984 — 11-1-0 (6-1-0)

Date		Opponent		
S8	•	Northwestern	26	0
S15	•	at Michigan	20	11
S22	•	Houston	35	7
S29	•	Miami, Ohio	53	7
O6	•	at Oregon State	19	7
O13	•	at Stanford	37	15
O20	•	Oregon	17	10
O27	•	Arizona	28	12
N3	•	California	44	14
N10	•	at Southern Cal	7	16
N17	•	at Washington State	38	29
ORANGE BOWL				
J1	•	Oklahoma	28	17

1985 — 7-5-0 (5-3-0)

Date		Opponent		
S7	•	Oklahoma State	17	31
S14	•	at Brigham Young	3	31
S21	•	at Houston	29	12
S28	•	UCLA	21	14
O5	•	at Oregon	19	13
O12	•	at California	28	12
O19	•	Oregon State	20	21
N2	•	Stanford	34	0
N9	•	at Arizona State	7	36
N16	•	Southern Cal	20	17
N23	•	Washington State	20	21
FREEDOM BOWL				
D30	•	Colorado	20	17 ǀ

1986 — 8-3-1 (5-2-1)

Date		Opponent		
S13	•	Ohio State	40	7
S20	•	Brigham Young	52	21
S27	•	at Southern Cal	10	20
O4	•	California	50	18
O11	•	at Stanford	24	14
O18	•	Bowling Green	48	0
O25	•	Oregon	38	3
N1	•	at Arizona State	21	34
N8	•	at Oregon State	28	12
N15	=	UCLA	17	17
N22	•	at Washington State	44	23
SUN BOWL				
D25	•	Alabama	6	28

1987 — 7-4-1 (4-3-1)

Date		Opponent		
S5	•	Stanford	31	21
S12	•	Purdue	28	10
S19	•	at Texas A&M	12	29
S26	•	Pacific	31	3
O3		at Oregon	22	29
O10	•	Arizona State	27	14
O17		Southern Cal	23	37
O31	•	Oregon State	28	12
N7	=	at Arizona	21	21
N14	•	at UCLA	14	47
N21	•	Washington State	34	19
INDEPENDENCE BOWL				
D19	•	Tulane	24	12

1988 — 6-5-0 (3-5-0)

Date		Opponent		
S10	•	at Purdue	20	6
S17	•	Army	31	17
S24	•	San Jose State	35	31
O1		UCLA	17	24
O8	•	at Arizona State	10	0
O15	•	at Southern Cal	27	28
O22		at Oregon	14	17
O29	•	Stanford	28	25
N5		Arizona	13	16
N12	•	California	28	27
N19		at Washington State	31	32

1989 — 8-4-0 (5-3-0)

Date		Opponent		
S9	•	Texas A&M	19	6
S16	•	Purdue	38	9
S23	•	at Arizona	17	20
S30		Colorado	28	45
O7		at Southern Cal	16	24
O14	•	Oregon	20	14
O21	•	at California	29	16
O28	•	at UCLA	28	27
N4		Arizona State	32	34
N11	•	at Oregon State	51	14
N18	•	Washington State	20	9
FREEDOM BOWL				
D30	•	Florida	34	7

1990 — 10-2-0 (7-1-0)

Date		Opponent		
S8	•	San Jose State	20	17
S15	•	at Purdue	20	14
S22		Southern Cal	31	0
S29		at Colorado	14	20
O6	•	at Arizona State	42	14
O13	•	Oregon	38	17
O20	•	at Stanford	52	16
O27	•	California	46	7
N3	•	Arizona	54	10
N10	•	UCLA	22	25
N17	•	at Washington State	55	10
ROSE BOWL				
J1	•	Iowa	46	34

1991 — 12-0-0 (8-0-0)

Date		Opponent		
S7	•	at Stanford	42	7
S21	•	at Nebraska	36	21
S28	•	Kansas State	56	3
O5	•	Arizona	54	0
O12	•	Toledo	48	0
O19	•	at California	24	17
O26	•	Oregon	29	7
N2	•	Arizona State	44	16
N9	•	at Southern Cal	14	3
N16	•	at Oregon State	58	6
N23	•	Washington State	56	21
ROSE BOWL				
J1	•	Michigan	34	14

1992 — 9-3-0 (6-2-0)

Date		Opponent		
S5	•	at Arizona State	31	7
S12	•	Wisconsin	27	10
S19	•	Nebraska	29	14
O3	•	Southern Cal	17	10
O10	•	California	35	16
O17	•	at Oregon	24	3
O24	•	Pacific	31	7
O31	•	Stanford	41	7
N7	•	at Arizona	3	16
N14	•	Oregon State	45	16
N21	•	at Washington State	23	42
ROSE BOWL				
J1	•	Michigan	31	38

JIM LAMBRIGHT
1993-98 (.636)   44-25-1

1993 — 7-4-0 (5-3-0)

Date		Opponent		
S4	• ǀ	Stanford	31	14
S11		at Ohio State	12	21
S25	•	East Carolina	35	0
O2	•	San Jose State	52	17
O9	•	at California	24	23
O16		at UCLA	25	39
O23		Oregon	21	6
O30		at Arizona State	17	32
N6	•	at Oregon State	28	21
N13		Southern Cal	17	22
N20	•	Washington State	26	3

1994 — 7-4-0 (4-4-0)

Date		Opponent		
S3	•	at Southern Cal	17	24
S10	•	Ohio State	25	16
S24	•	at Miami, Fla.	38	20
O1	•	UCLA	37	10
O8	•	San Jose State	34	20
O15	•	Arizona State	35	14
O22	•	at Oregon	20	31
O29	•	Oregon State	24	10
N5	•	at Stanford	28	46
N12	•	California	31	19
N19		at Washington State	6	23

1995 — 7-4-1 (6-1-1)

Date		Opponent		
S2	•	Arizona State	23	20
S16	•	at Ohio State	20	30
S23	•	Army	21	13
S30	•	at Oregon State	26	16
O7		Notre Dame	21	29
O14	•	at Stanford	38	28
O21	•	at Arizona	31	17
O28	=	Southern Cal	21	21
N4		Oregon	22	24
N11	•	at UCLA	38	14
N18	•	Washington State	33	30
SUN BOWL				
D29	•	Iowa	18	38

1996 — 9-3 (7-1)

Date		Opponent		
S7	•	at Arizona State	42	45
S14	•	Brigham Young	29	17
S21	•	Arizona	31	17
O5	•	Stanford	27	6
O12		at Notre Dame	20	54
O19	•	UCLA	41	21
O26	•	at Oregon	33	14
N2	•	at Southern Cal	21	10
N9	•	Oregon State	42	3
N16	•	San Jose State	53	10
N23	•	at Washington State	31	24
HOLIDAY BOWL				
D30	•	Colorado	21	33

1997 — 8-4 (5-3)

Date		Opponent		
S6	•	at Brigham Young	42	20
S13	•	San Diego State	36	3
S20	•	Nebraska	14	27
O4	•	Arizona State	26	14
O11	•	at California	30	3
O18	•	at Arizona	58	28
O25	•	at Oregon State	45	17
N1		Southern Cal	27	0
N8		Oregon	28	31
N15	•	at UCLA	28	52
N22		Washington State	35	41
ALOHA BOWL				
D25	•	Michigan State	51	23

1998 — 6-6 (4-4)

Date		Opponent		
S5	•	at Arizona State	42	38
S19	•	Brigham Young	20	10
S26	•	at Nebraska	7	55
O3		Arizona	28	31
O10		Utah State	53	12
O17	•	California	21	13
O24	•	Oregon State	35	34
O31		at Southern Cal	10	33
N7	•	at Oregon	22	27
N14	•	UCLA	24	36
N21	•	at Washington State	16	9
OAHU BOWL				
D25	•	Air Force	25	45

RICK NEUHEISEL
1999-2002 (.673)   33-16

1999 — 7-5 (6-2)

Date		Opponent		
S9	•	at Brigham Young	28	35
S18	•	Air Force	21	31
S25	•	Colorado	31	24
O2	•	Oregon	34	20
O9	•	at Oregon State	47	21
O16		Arizona State	7	28
O23	•	at California	31	27
O30		Stanford	35	30
N6	•	at Arizona	33	25
N13	•	at UCLA	20	23
N20		Washington State	24	14
HOLIDAY BOWL				
D29	•	Kansas State	20	24

2000 — 11-1 (7-1)

Date		Opponent		
S2	•	Idaho	44	20
S9	•	Miami, Fla.	34	29
S16	•	at Colorado	17	14
S30	•	at Oregon	16	23
O7	•	Oregon State	33	30
O14	•	at Arizona State	21	15
O21	•	California	36	24
O28	•	at Stanford	31	28
N4	•	Arizona	35	32
N11	•	UCLA	35	28
N18	•	at Washington State	51	3
ROSE BOWL				
J1	•	Purdue	34	24

2001 — 8-4 (6-2)

Date		Opponent		
S8	•	Michigan	23	18
S22	•	Idaho	53	3
S29	•	at California	31	28
O6	•	Southern Cal	27	24
O13	•	at UCLA	13	35
O20	•	Arizona	31	28
O27	•	at Arizona State	33	31
N3	•	Stanford	42	28
N10	•	at Oregon State	24	49
N17	•	Washington State	26	14
N24	•	at Miami, Fla.	7	65
HOLIDAY BOWL				
D28	•	Texas	43	47

2002 — 7-6 (4-4)

Date		Opponent		
A31	•	at Michigan	29	31
S7	•	San Jose State	34	10
S21	•	Wyoming	38	7
S28	•	Idaho	41	27
O5	•	California	27	34
O12	•	Arizona	32	28
O19	•	at Southern Cal	21	41
O26	•	at Arizona State	16	27
N2	•	UCLA	24	34
N9	•	Oregon State	41	29
N16	•	at Oregon	42	14
N23	•	at Washington State	29	26
SUN BOWL				
D31	•	Purdue	24	34

KEITH GILBERTSON
2003-04 (.304)   7-16

2003 — 6-6 (4-4)

Date		Opponent		
A30		at Ohio State	9	28
S6	•	Indiana	38	13
S20	•	Idaho	45	14
S27	•	Stanford	28	17
O4	•	at UCLA	16	46
O11	•	Nevada	17	28
O18	•	at Oregon State	38	17
O25	•	Southern Cal	23	43
N1	•	Oregon	42	10
N8	•	at Arizona	22	27
N15	•	at California	7	54
N22	•	Washington State	27	19

2004 — 1-10 (0-8)

Date		Opponent		
S5		Fresno State	16	35
S18	•	UCLA	31	37
S25	•	at Notre Dame	3	38
O2	•	at Stanford	13	27
O9	•	San Jose State	21	6
O16		Oregon State	14	29
O23	•	at Southern Cal	0	38
O30	•	at Oregon	6	31
N6	•	Arizona	13	23
N13	•	California	12	42
N20	•	at Washington State	25	28

WASHINGTON STATE

BY BUD WITHERS

BASED IN A RURAL OUTPOST surrounded by rolling wheat and lentil fields, Washington State is a stark contrast to the Pac-10 schools in the West's cosmopolitan cities. WSU students make up 85 percent of the town's population of 25,000, and the remoteness of the campus in south-eastern Washington tends to have polar effects on those football prospects who might consider matriculating: either they're aghast at its isolation or they're enchanted by the camaraderie they often find there.

On the field, the Cougars' success has been sporadic. Their Holiday Bowl appearance in 1981 ended a 50-year postseason drought, and when the 1997 team broke through to the Rose Bowl, it halted a 67-year absence in Pasadena.

TRADITION In 1892, the Victory Bell was installed at College Hall, at first used to signal the start and finish of class periods, later to celebrate Cougars athletic victories. In 1938, the Palouse Walk began, as Idaho students walked the eight miles home after losing to rival Washington State. That trek became less cause for Cougar gloating after 1966 as the series became dominated by WSU.

BEST PLAYER Mel Hein's dad ran a power plant on Clayton Bay near the northwest Washington town of Bellingham, and the younger Hein spent much of his time in a rowboat there, building up his arms and legs to fulfill his intention of competing in crew at Washington. After he decided to join brother Lloyd at WSU, he would become a 6'3", 223-pound center, an All-America on the Cougars team that played in the 1931 Rose Bowl and a charter member of both the college and professional football halls of fame. Hein is often called the finest center in college football history.

BEST COACH Orin Ercel "Babe" Hollingbery came to WSU in 1926 from San Francisco, where he drew acclaim coaching the Olympic Club. Hollingbery, who never attended college himself, compiled a 93–53–14 record over 17 years at WSU, building on a foundation of tough defense and the running game. His Cougars team of 1929 won 10 games and the 1930 squad went to the Rose Bowl. Also worth noting is Mike Price. In his 14-year run (1989-2002), Price didn't threaten Hollingbery's record, but he did do something most Cougars fans would have deemed impossible: he took the team to two Rose Bowls in six seasons. He was named head coach at Alabama before the second one, staying on to direct a losing effort in Pasadena against Oklahoma.

BEST TEAM Not much was expected of the 1997 Cougars, who were coming off a 5–6 season. But, led by

---

PROFILE

Washington State University
Pullman, Wash.
Founded: 1890
Enrollment: 18,609
Colors: Crimson and Gray
Nickname: Cougars
Stadium: Martin Stadium
   Opened in 1936
   FieldTurf; 37,600 capacity
First football game: 1894
All-time record: 473–457–45 (.508)
Bowl record: 6–4
Pac-10 championships: 3 (2 outright)
Outland Trophy: Rien Long, 2002
First-round NFL draftees: 8
Website: www.wsucougars.com

THE BEST OF TIMES

From 2001 to 2003, the Cougars strung together an unprecedented three straight 10-victory seasons, made their second Rose Bowl appearance in six years and won the Sun and Holiday bowls.

THE WORST OF TIMES

In the middle of a 16-game conference losing streak, the 1970 Cougars went 1–10 and in one four-game stretch allowed 63, 45, 54 and 70 points.

CONFERENCE

A longtime member of the Pac-10 Conference, Washington State joined the Pac-10's forerunner, the Pacific Coast Conference, in 1917, just one year after the league was formed.

DISTINGUISHED ALUMNI

Keith Jackson; Edward R. Murrow; Philip Abelson, father of the atomic submarine; Paul Allen, co-founder of Microsoft; Gary Larson, "The Far Side" cartoonist; Patty Murray, state's first female U.S. senator

FIGHT SONG

WSU FIGHT SONG
Fight, fight, fight for Washington State!
Win the victory!
Win the day for Crimson and Gray!
Best in the West, we know you'll all do your best, so
On, on, on, on! Fight to the end!
Honor and glory you must win! So
Fight, fight, fight for Washington State and victory!

quarterback Ryan Leaf, they opened with victories over UCLA and USC, gathered confidence and didn't stop until they had earned their first Rose Bowl berth in 67 years. They lost to national champion Michigan 21-16, but went 10–2 and made a huge impact on the WSU record book, setting standards for points (483), yards (5,922) and touchdowns (64). If not for the 1930 squad's 24-0 loss to Alabama in the Rose Bowl, that WSU team would have been rated the consensus best in school history. Anchored by the great Hein, the Cougars ran up nine straight victories before the setback in Pasadena, shutting out five opponents.

BIGGEST GAME It wasn't as though they came unannounced to play their archrival on Nov. 22, 1997. The Cougars roared in 9–1 and 11th-ranked, with wide receiver Chris Jackson vowing brashly that WSU would "kill" Washington. Although Jackson's pronouncement regarding the nature of the victory proved to be just a bit overstated, he surely did his part. He caught eight passes for 185 yards and two touchdowns from Leaf, who was 22-for-38 for 358

> *Some WSU fans are so passionate about the Apple Cup—the game trophy honoring one of the state's chief crops—that they would take a victory over Washington over a winning season.*

yards as the Cougars ended their Rose Bowl drought with a 41-35 victory over the Huskies.

BIGGEST UPSET On Oct. 29, 1988, UCLA was undefeated and ranked No. 1 with Troy Aikman at quarterback. WSU was 4–3 and had just surrendered 76 points in two weeks. At the Rose Bowl, the Cougars fell behind 27-6 early in the third quarter before flooding the Bruins with three straight touchdowns, the last when Timm Rosenbach hit Tim Stallworth on a short pass route and Stallworth ran most of the way for an 81-yard score. After WSU took a 34-30 lead, the Bruins were at the WSU 6 inside the last minute before the Cougars, blitzing Aikman, denied his last passes to complete the stunner.

WILDEST FINISH At Iowa in 1963, the Cougars scored a pair of touchdowns to tie the game at 14 and were driving to win it. They were positioned for a field goal at the Iowa 24 late in the game, but head linesman Gus Skibbee mistakenly flipped the down marker ahead on an Iowa penalty, denying WSU fourth down. The game ended in a deadlock.

RECORDS

RUSHING YARDS

GAME
357 — Rueben Mayes vs. Oregon, Oct. 27, 1984 (39 att.)

SEASON
1,632 — Rueben Mayes, 1984 (258 att.)

CAREER
3,519 — Rueben Mayes, 1982-85 (636 att.)

PASSING YARDS

GAME
476 — Drew Bledsoe vs. Utah, Dec. 29, 1992 (30 of 46)

SEASON
3,968 — Ryan Leaf, 1997 (227 of 410)

CAREER
8,830 — Jason Gesser, 1999-2002 (611 of 1,118)

RECEIVING YARDS

GAME
255 — Deron Pointer vs. Arizona State, Oct. 9, 1993 (10 rec.)

SEASON
1,163 — Nakoa McElrath, 2001 (72 rec.)

CAREER
2,452 — Hugh Campbell, 1960-62 (176 rec.)

POINTS

GAME
30 — Rueben Mayes vs. Stanford, Oct. 20, 1984; James Matthews vs. Idaho, Sept. 11, 1982 (5 TDs)

SEASON
116 — Drew Dunning, 2003 (27 FGs, 35 PATs)

CAREER
336 — Drew Dunning, 2000-03 (68 FGs, 132 PATs)

CONSENSUS ALL-AMERICANS

1984	Rueben Mayes	RB
1988	Mike Utley	OL
1989	Jason Hanson	PK
2002	Rien Long	DL

BEST GOAL-LINE STAND Ahead 37-34 in the last minute against UCLA on Aug. 30, 1997, the Cougars expected a fourth-down run by Skip Hicks from the WSU 1-yard line in what would have added to a 27-carry, 190-yard workload. But Hicks opted out of the last play due to fatigue and the Bruins replaced him with a freshman back 40 pounds lighter, Jermaine Lewis. WSU stoned him before the goal line, launching the drive to the Rose Bowl.

BEST COMEBACK On Oct. 20, 1984, WSU trailed at Stanford 42-14 with under six minutes remaining in the third quarter. Then WSU's Rueben Mayes, a remarkable running back from the unlikely spawning ground of North Battleford, Saskatchewan, took over. With 3:20 left in the third, Mayes began an unanswered 35-point avalanche in a span of 15:14. His contribution to those five touchdowns? Scoring runs of 39, 5 and 22 yards and a 53-yard TD pass from quarterback Mark Rypien. The explosion gave the Cougars a 49-42 victory. Mayes rushed for 216 yards on 29 carries, but he was only getting started. The next week at Oregon, he exploded for 357 yards rushing, setting what were then NCAA records for both one and two games (573 yards).

STADIUM The second incarnation of Rogers Field was partially destroyed by fire in 1970. When Los Angeles businessman Dan Martin donated $250,000 for the rebuilding in honor of his father, Clarence D. Martin, governor from 1933 to 1940, it reopened as Martin Stadium in 1972.

RIVAL While Washington has by turns divided its disgust for others between schools like Oregon and USC, WSU trains all its enmity on the Huskies. The small-town Cougars think the Huskies are arrogant. The cosmopolitan Huskies believe the Cougars to be paranoid. Two coaches during the 1980s said it best. "Nothing in my

ALL-TIME TEAM	
Selected by The Spokane Spokesman-Review in 1995.	
1926-42	O.E. "Babe" Hollingbery, coach
OFFENSE	
1972-74	Steve Ostermann, OG
1985-88	Mike Utley, OG
1929-31	Turk Edwards, OT
1946-48	Laurie Niemi, OT
1928-30	Mel Hein, C
1957-59	Gail Cogdill, WR
1960-62	Hugh Campbell, WR
1975-77	Mike Levenseller, WR
1990-92	Drew Bledsoe, QB
1958-60	Keith Lincoln, RB
1982-85	Rueben Mayes, RB
1987-89	Steve Broussard, RB
1988-91	Jason Hanson, PK
1946-48	Jerry Williams, RET
DEFENSE	
1938, 1940-41	Dale Gentry, DE
1981-83	Keith Millard, DL
1982-85	Erik Howard, DL
1991-94	DeWayne Patterson, DE
1948-50	LaVern Torgeson, LB
1985-87	Brian Forde, LB
1992, 1994	Mark Fields, LB
1947-49	Don Paul, DB
1962-64	Clancy Williams, DB
1963-65	Bill Gaskins, DB
1974-76	Ken Greene, DB
1974-77	Gavin Hedrick, P

job—not the Rose Bowls, not the Holiday Bowls, nothing—is more important than beating Washington," Jim Walden once observed. In 1987, his successor, Dennis Erickson, grated over a defeat to UW and said, "Every night when I go to bed for the next year, I'm going to ask myself, 'What did I do today to beat the Huskies?'" Some WSU fans are so passionate about the Apple Cup— the game trophy honoring one of the state's chief crops—that they would take a victory over Washington over a winning season.

NICKNAME The earliest WSU teams were Warriors or Indians. That changed in 1919, when WSU upended a powerful California team 14-0, and a Bay Area journalist noted that the team played like cougars. A few days later, the WSU student body officially adopted the nickname.

MASCOT Two stuffed cougars served as mascots in the early days after the nickname designation, but in 1927, WSU got the real thing, presented at the Idaho homecoming game during halftime by Washington governor Roland Hartley. The animal was quickly named Butch, after Herbert "Butch" Meeker, a 5'4" quarterback of the late 1920s. WSU students voted to end the tradition of a live mascot after the sixth Butch died at the age of 15 in 1978.

UNIFORMS At home, WSU wears crimson jerseys and pants with broad gray piping on the side, flaring to the chest—a design inspired by the Denver Broncos. Road uniforms are white with crimson trim in the same style. WSU helmets—gray at home, crimson on the road—are affixed with the cougar's-head logo designed in 1936 by student Randall Johnson.

LORE In their early days, the Cougars had four different Native American coaches, all of them products of Carlisle Indian School in Pennsylvania. The most successful— and, doubtless, the most colorful—was William "Lone

Star" Dietz, son of a German engineer father and a half-blood Oglala Sioux mother. Dietz had an elaborate wardrobe, ranging from formal clothes to Native American wear, complete with headdress, which he would willingly break out for publicity shots. He took the Cougars to their first Rose Bowl, but his WSU years ended in bizarre fashion when a Spokane grand jury indicted him for false draft registration as a Native American during World War I. Dietz was acquitted.

QUOTE "There are four important stages in your life. You're born, you play the Huskies, you get married and you die."—WSU guard Dan Lynch, 1984, on the rivalry with Washington

WASHINGTON STATE ANNUAL STATISTICAL LEADERS

YR	RUSHING	YDS	ATT	AVG	PASSING	ATT	CMP	PCT	YDS	RECEIVING	REC	YDS	AVG
1950	Blackie Bower	483	109	4.4	Bob Gambold	96	49	.51	705	Ed Barker	25	331	13.2
1951	Byron Bailey	695	149	4.7	Bob Burkhart	145	70	.48	1,153	Ed Barker	46	864	18.8
1952	Al Charlton	396	115	3.4	Bob Burkhart	93	42	.45	732	Ed Barker	37	504	13.6
1953	Wayne Berry	388	92	4.2	Wayne Berry	51	25	.49	389	Russ Quackenbush	12	137	11.4
1954	Duke Washington	616	105	5.9	Bob Iverson	98	45	.46	496	Russ Quackenbush	19	270	14.2
1955	Reynaldo Alvarado	286	72	4.0	Bob Iverson	95	49	.52	568	Arnie Pelluer	17	215	12.6
1956	Chuck Morrell	528	121	4.4	Bob Newman	170	91	.54	1,240	Bill Steiger	39	607	15.6
1957	Carl Ketchie	419	84	5.0	Bob Newman	188	104	.55	1,391	Don Ellingson	45	559	12.4
1958	Chuck Morrell	571	133	4.3	Bob Newman	79	51	.65	541	Gail Cogdill	21	479	22.8
1959	Keith Lincoln	670	124	5.4	Mel Melin	98	41	.42	526	Gail Cogdill	28	531	19.0
1960	Keith Lincoln	543	121	4.5	Mel Melin	221	119	.54	1,638	Hugh Campbell	66	881	13.4
1961	George Reed	489	131	3.7	Mel Melin	134	66	.49	814	Hugh Campbell	53	723	13.6
1962	George Reed	503	132	3.8	Dave Mathieson	198	104	.53	1,492	Hugh Campbell	57	848	14.9
1963	Clancy Williams	523	105	5.0	Dave Mathieson	175	85	.49	859	R. Gerald Shaw	32	309	9.6
1964	Clancy Williams	783	147	5.3	Dave Peterson	77	36	.47	478	Clancy Williams	17	210	12.4
1965	Larry Eilmes	818	180	4.5	Tom Roth	190	98	.52	1,257	Doug Flansburg	46	578	12.6
1966	Ammon McWashington	298	94	3.2	Jerry Henderson	174	95	.55	989	Doug Flansburg	54	613	11.3
1967	Mark Williams	415	114	3.6	Jerry Henderson	144	67	.47	836	Doug Flansburg	39	461	11.8
1968	Richard Smith	326	105	3.1	Jerry Henderson	246	137	.56	1,586	Ron Souza	33	343	10.3
1969	Richard Smith	485	134	3.6	Jack Wigmore	149	65	.44	876	Fred Moore	31	523	16.9
1970	Robert Ewen	667	142	4.7	Ty Paine	267	123	.46	1,581	Ed Armstrong	33	488	14.8
1971	Bernard Jackson	1,189	177	6.7	Ty Paine	217	91	.42	1,206	Ike Nelson	23	349	15.2
1972	Ken Grandberry	833	214	3.9	Ty Paine	241	111	.46	1,349	Ken Grandberry	28	273	9.7
1973	Andrew Jones	1,059	207	5.1	Chuck Peck	145	76	.52	1,023	Fritz Brayton	23	175	7.6
1974	Ron Cheatham	616	110	5.6	John Hopkins	82	45	.55	522	Carl Barschig	32	423	13.2
1975	Vaughn Williams	662	134	4.9	John Hopkins	146	81	.56	1,022	Brian Kelly	28	371	13.3
1976	Dan Doornink	422	129	3.3	Jack Thompson	355	208	.59	2,762	Mike Levenseller	67	1,124	16.8
1977	Dan Doornink	591	144	4.1	Jack Thompson	329	192	.58	2,372	Brian Kelly	44	675	15.3
1978	Tali Ena	728	132	5.5	Jack Thompson	348	175	.50	2,333	Tali Ena	42	409	9.7
1979	Tali Ena	844	158	5.3	Steve Grant	224	120	.54	1,565	Jim Whatley	31	513	16.5
1980	Tim Harris	801	167	4.8	Samoa Samoa	200	105	.53	1,668	Pat Beach	20	318	15.9
1981	Tim Harris	931	161	5.8	Clete Casper	156	84	.54	1,008	Jeff Keller	39	535	13.7
1982	Tim Harris	684	147	4.7	Clete Casper	184	91	.50	1,072	Mike Peterson	26	440	16.9
1983	Kerry Porter	1,000	195	5.1	Ricky Turner	172	100	.58	1,351	John Marshall	21	328	15.6
1984	Rueben Mayes	1,632	258	6.3	Mark Rypien	271	134	.49	1,927	John Marshall	34	534	15.7
1985	Rueben Mayes	1,236	228	5.4	Mark Rypien	273	159	.58	2,174	Rick Chase	37	411	11.1
1986	Kerry Porter	921	205	4.5	Ed Blount	227	117	.52	1,882	Michael James	33	481	14.6
1987	Richard Calvin	822	180	4.6	Timm Rosenbach	390	222	.57	2,446	Steve Broussard	59	701	11.9
1988	Steve Broussard	1,280	222	5.8	Timm Rosenbach	338	218	.65	3,097	Tim Stallworth	63	1,151	18.3
1989	Steve Broussard	1,237	260	4.8	Brad Gossen	137	88	.64	1,372	Steve Broussard	39	326	8.4
1990	Shaumbe Wright Fair	739	162	4.6	Drew Bledsoe	189	92	.49	1,368	Phillip Bobo	51	758	14.9
1991	Shaumbe Wright Fair	843	187	4.5	Drew Bledsoe	358	199	.56	2,741	Phillip Bobo	54	759	14.1
1992	Shaumbe Wright Fair	1,330	264	5.0	Drew Bledsoe	432	241	.56	3,246	C.J. Davis	63	1,024	16.3
1993	Kevin Hicks	497	128	3.9	Mike Pattinson	200	110	.55	1,430	Brett Carolan	49	591	12.1
1994	Frank Madu	494	143	3.5	Chad Davis	339	197	.58	2,299	Jay Dumas	41	402	9.8
1995	Frank Madu	870	173	5.0	Chad Davis	301	174	.58	1,868	Jay Dumas	50	463	9.3
1996	Michael Black	948	182	5.2	Ryan Leaf	373	194	.52	2,811	Chad Carpenter	47	623	13.3
1997	Michael Black	1,181	242	4.9	Ryan Leaf	410	227	.55	3,968	Kevin McKenzie	55	911	16.6
1998	Kevin Brown	1,046	215	4.9	Steve Birnbaum	235	114	.49	1,677	Leaford Hackett	54	680	12.6
1999	Deon Burnett	974	209	4.7	Steve Birnbaum	307	174	.57	2,022	Nian Taylor	51	627	12.3
2000	Dave Minnich	754	165	4.6	Jason Gesser	246	128	.52	1,967	Milton Wynn	52	964	18.5
2001	Dave Minnich	815	192	4.2	Jason Gesser	375	199	.53	3,010	Nakoa McElrath	72	1,163	16.2
2002	Jermaine Green	829	150	5.5	Jason Gesser	402	236	.59	3,408	Jerome Riley	57	929	16.5
2003	Jonathan Smith	961	224	4.3	Matt Kegel	394	218	.55	2,947	Devard Darling	50	830	16.6
2004	Jerome Harrison	900	174	5.2	Alex Brink	194	97	.50	1,305	Jason Hill	45	1,007	22.4

Receiving leaders by receptions
All statistics include postseason

WASHINGTON STATE ALL-TIME SCORES

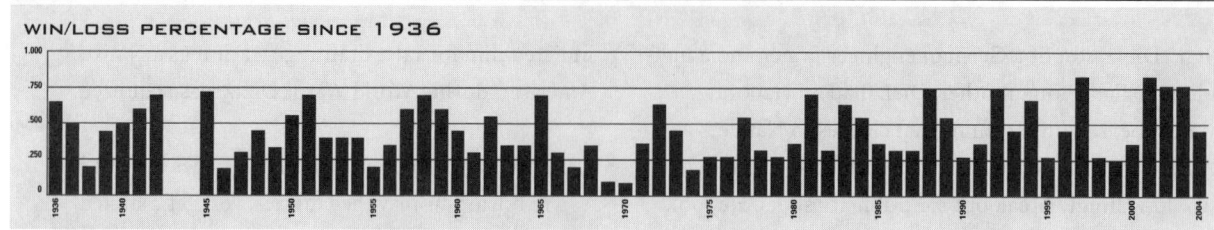

WIN/LOSS PERCENTAGE SINCE 1936

WILLIAM GOODYEAR
1894 (.500)   1-1

1894   1-1-0
N18 ● at Idaho   10   0
N29 ● at Spokane HS   0 18

FRED WAITE
1895 (1.000)   2-0

1895   2-0-0
N9   ● Idaho   10   4
N28 ● at Spokane AC   26   4

DAVID A. BRODIE
1896 (.833)   2-0-1

1896   2-0-1
N4   ● Lewiston AA   26   0
N26 ● Co. C NGW   22   0
D5   ● at Lewiston AA   6   6

ROBERT R. GAILEY
1897 (.000)   2-0

1897   2-0-0
N13 ● at Spokane AC   16   8
N25 ● at Whitman   16   4

FRANK SHIVELY
1898-99 (.500)   1-1-1

1898   0-0-1
N5   ● Whitman   0   0

1899   1-1-0
O28 ● Idaho   11   0
N10 ● at Whitman   10 11

WILLIAM ALLEN
1900, '02 (.650)   6-3-1

1900   4-0-1
O13 ● at Lewiston AA   2   0
O20 ● Spokane AC   6   0
N10 ● at Walla Walla AC 5   0
N24 ● at Spokane AC   21   0
N30 = at Washington   5   5

WILLIAM NAMACK
1901 (.800)   4-1

1901   4-1-0
O18 ● Lewiston-Clark State 16 0
O25 ● at Idaho   0   5
N1   ● Washington   10   0
N9   ● Oregon   16   0
N28 ● at Wittman   5   2

WILLIAM ALLEN

1902   2-3-0
O11 ● at Lewis-Clark State 0 12
O18 ● Pacific   5   6
O24 ● Idaho   17   0
N1   ● Whitman   6   5
N27 ● at Washington   0 16

JAMES N. ASHMORE
1903 (.500)   3-3-2

1903   3-3-2
O3   ● Spokane HS   40   0
O14 = Puget Sound   0   0
O23 ● at Idaho   0 32
O30 ● Washington   0 10
N7   ● at Oregon   0   0
N11 ● at Oregon State   0   6
N21 ● Montana   34   0
N26 ● at Whitman   18   6

EVERETT M. SWEELEY
1904-05 (.500)   6-6

1904   2-2-0
O21 ● Idaho   0   5
O29 ● at Washington   6 12
N16 ● at Montana   6   5
N24 ● at Whitman   34   4

1905   4-4-0
S30 ● Spokane HS   51   0
O7   ● Lewiston HS   52   0
O11 ● Montana State   32   0
O18 ● Willamette *SAL*   6 11
O21 ● at Oregon State   0 29
O28 ● Montana   28   6
N10 ● at Idaho   0   5
N30 ● at Whitman   6 10

JOHN R. BENDER
1906-07, '12-14 (.636)   21-12

1906   6-0-0
O13 ● Blair Bus. Coll. 11   0
O19 ● at Montana   5   0
N3   ● at Spokane AC   8   0
N9   ● Idaho   10   0
N17 ● at Spokane AC   8   0
N24 ● Whitman   6   0

1907   7-1-0
O5   ● Ea. Washington   46   0
O12 ● Blair Bus.Coll.   86   0
O18 ● Montana   38   0
O26 ● Spokane AC   70   0
N8   ● at Idaho   4   5
N21 ● at Washington   11   5
N28 ● Whitman   16   8
D25 ● St. Louis *Spo*   11   0

WALTER RHEINSCHILD
1908 (.833)   4-0-2

1908   4-0-2
O10 ● E. Washington   73   0
O17 ● Spokane YMCA   33   0
O30 ● Bremerton Navy   44   0
N7   ● at Washington   6   6
N14 = Idaho   4   4
N21 ● Whitman   4   0

W.S. KIENHOLZ
1909 (.800)   4-1

1909   4-1-0
O20 ● Puget Sound   74   0
N5   ● at Idaho   18   0
N16 ● Whitworth   38   0
N28 ● at Whitman   23   6
D4   ● Denver *Spo*   6 11

OSCAR P. OSTHOFF
1910-11 (.455)   5-6

1910   2-3-0
O21 ● Idaho   5   9
O29 ● Oregon State *Port* 3   9
N1   ● Multnomah AC *Port* 9   0
N12 ● Washington *Spo*   0 16
N24 ● at Whitman   8   0

1911   3-3-0
O7   ● Gonzaga   58   0
O20 ● at Idaho   17   0
O27 ● Oregon   0   6
N11 ● at Oregon State   0   6
N18 ● Whitman *Spo*   11   0
N30 ● at Washington   6 30

JOHN R. BENDER

1912   2-3-0
O18 ● Idaho   0   13
O26 ● at Oregon   7   0
N1   ● Oregon State   10   9
N9   ● Whitman *Spo*   0   30
N28 ● at Washington   0 19

1913   4-4-0
O4   ● Bremerton Navy   26 12
O11 ● Montana   34   9
O17 ● at Idaho   0   3
O25 ● at Multnomah AC   0   7
N1   ● Gonzaga   26   0
N8   ● Whitman   23   0
N15 ● at Oregon State   2 10
N27 ● at Washington   0 20

1914   2-4-0
O6   ● Montana   0 10
O17 ● Oregon *Port*   0   7
O24 ● Oregon State   0   7
N7   ● Idaho   3   0
N14 ● Whitman *Spo*   7   6
N26 ● at Washington   0 45

WILLIAM H. DIETZ
1915-17 (.875)   17-2-1

1915   7-0-0
O9   ● Oregon   28   3
O16 ● at Oregon State   29   0
O30 ● at Idaho   41   0
N6   ● Montana   27   7
N16 ● Whitman   17   0
N25 ● at Gonzaga   48   0

ROSE BOWL
J1   ● Brown   14   0

1916   4-2-0
O14 ● Oregon State   10 13
O28 ● at Montana   27   0
N4   ● Idaho   31   0
N11 ● Oregon *Port*   3 12 *
N25 ● at Gonzaga   18   0
N30 ● at Whitman   46   0

1917-1958
PACIFIC COAST

1917   6-0-1 (3-0-0)
O13 = 362nd Infantry *Tac* 0   0
O20 ● Oregon   26   3
O27 ● Whitman   19   0
N3   ● at Idaho   19   0
N10 ● at Oregon State   6   0
N17 ● Montana *Spo*   28   0
N29 ● at Washington   14   0

EMORY ALVORD
1918 (.500)   1-1

1918   1-1-0
N28 ● Gonzaga   20   6
D7   ● at Idaho   6   7

GUS WELCH
1919-22 (.611)   16-10-1

1919   5-2-0 (2-2-0)
O18 ● Multnomah AC *Spo* 49   0
O25 ● at California   14   0
N1   ● Idaho   37   0
N8   ● Oregon *Port*   7   0
N15 ● Washington   7 13
N22 ● Oregon State *Port* 0   6
N27 ● at Montana   42 14

1920   5-1-0 (1-1-0)
O9   ● at Gonzaga   35   0
O15 ● at Idaho   14   7
O30 ● Montana   31   0
N6   ● at California   0 49
N13 ● Oregon State   28   0
N25 ● at Nebraska   21 20

1921   4-2-1 (2-1-1)
O15 ● at Gonzaga   54   7
O21 ● Idaho   20   3
O29 ● California *Port* 0 14
N5   = Oregon   7   7
N12 ● at Oregon State   7   3
N24 ● at Washington   14   0
D3   ● Southern Cal *Pas* 7 28

1922   2-5-0 (1-5-0)
O14 ● at Gonzaga   10   7
O20 ● at Idaho   18   9
O28 ● Washington   13 16
N4   ● at California   0 61
N11 ● at Oregon   0 13
N25 ● Oregon State *Port* 0 16
N30 ● Southern Cal *Pas* 3 41

A.A. EXENDINE
1923-25 (.348)   6-13-4

1923   2-4-1 (1-3-1)
O6   ● Pacific   19   0
O13 ● at Gonzaga   14 27
O19 ● Idaho   0 14
O27 ● California *Port* 0   9
N3   ● Oregon   13   7
N17 ● Oregon State *Tac* 3   3
N24 ● at Washington   7 24

1924   1-5-2 (0-4-1)
O4   ● Pacific   65   0
O11 ● Gonzaga   12 14
O17 ● at Idaho   3 19
O25 ● at California   7 20
N8   ● Oregon State *Port* 13 14
N15 ● Oregon *Port*   7   7
N22 ● at Washington   0 14
N27 ● at Gonzaga   7   7

1925   3-4-1 (2-3-0)
O3   ● at Montana   9   0
O17 ● Idaho   6   7
O31 ● Washington   0 23
N7   ● at California   0 35
N21 ● at Gonzaga   0   0
N28 ● at Southern Cal   17 12
D25 ● at Hawaii All Stars 24   7
J1   ● at Hawaii   11 20

D.E. HOLLINGBERY
1926-42 (.625)   93-53-14

1926   6-1-0 (4-1-0)
O2   ● Albertson   35   0
O9   ● at Southern Cal   7 16
O16 ● Montana   14   6
O23 ● at Washington   9   6
N6   ● at Idaho   6   0
N13 ● Oregon   7   0
N25 ● at Gonzaga   7   0

1927   3-3-2 (1-3-1)
S24 ● Carroll   6   6
O1   ● Albertson   53   0
O8   ● Montana   35   0
O15 ● at Gonzaga   13   0
O22 ● at Washington   0 14
O29 ● at Oregon State   6 13
N11 ● Idaho   7   7
N19 ● at Southern Cal   0 27

THE SCHOOLS

1928 — 7-3-0 (4-3-0)
S22	●	Whitman	33 6
S29	●	at Gonzaga	3 0
O6	|	at Montana	26 6
O13	●	at California	3 13
O20	●	Oregon State	9 7
O27	●	Albertson	51 0
N3	●	at Idaho	26 0
N10	●	UCLA *Port*	38 0
N17	●	at Southern Cal	13 27
N29	●	at Washington	0 6

1929 — 10-2-0 (4-2-0)
S28	●	Albertson	48 0
O5	●	Carroll	38 0
O12	●	at California	0 14
O19	●	Washington	20 13
O26	●	Whitman	58 6
N2	●	Oregon State *Port*	9 0
N9	●	Idaho	41 7
N16	●	at Montana	13 0
N23	●	at Gonzaga	27 0
N30	●	at Southern Cal	7 27
D25	●	at Hawaii All Stars	12 0
J1	●	at Hawaii	28 7

1930 — 9-1-0 (6-0-0)
S27	●	Coll. of Idaho	47 12
O4	●	at California	16 0
O11	●	Southern Cal	7 6
O18	●	at Gonzaga	24 0
O25	●	Montana	61 0
N1	●	Oregon State *Port*	14 7
N8	●	at Idaho	33 7
N15	●	at Washington	3 0
N29	●	Villanova *Phil*	13 0
ROSE BOWL			
J1		Alabama	0 24

1931 — 6-4-0 (4-3-0)
S26	●	Albertson	41 0
O3	●	UCLA	13 0
O10	|	at Southern Cal	6 38
O17	|	California *Port*	7 13
O24	●	at Montana	13 0
O31	●	Oregon State *Port*	7 6
N7	●	Idaho	9 8
N14	●	at Washington	0 12
N21	●	at Gonzaga	13 6
D5	|	at Tulane	14 28

1932 — 7-1-1 (5-1-1)
S24	●	Albertson	40 0
O1	●	at Southern Cal	0 20
O8	●	Willamette	30 0
O15	●	at California	7 2
O22	●	at Oregon State	7 6
O29	●	Montana	31 0
N5	●	Idaho	12 0
N12	=	at Washington	0 0
N24	●	at UCLA	3 0

1933 — 5-3-1 (3-3-1)
S30	●	Puget Sound	56 0
O7	●	at Southern Cal	0 33
O14	●	at Montana	13 7
O21	=	California *Port*	6 6
O28	●	Oregon State *Port*	0 2
N4	●	Gonzaga	16 0
N11	●	at Idaho	14 6
N25	●	Washington	17 6
N30	|	at UCLA	0 7

1934 — 4-3-1 (4-0-1)
S29	●	Montana	27 0
O6	●	at Southern Cal	19 0
O13	●	at Gonzaga	6 13
O27	●	Oregon State	31 0
N2	●	Saint Mary's-Cal *SF*	6 9
N10	●	Idaho	19 0
N24	=	at Washington	0 0
D1	●	at Detroit	0 6

1935 — 5-3-1 (3-2-0)
S28	●	Puget Sound	46 6
O5	●	Willamette	30 0
O12	●	at Montana	13 7
O19	●	at Washington	0 21
O26	●	Oregon State *Port*	26 13
N2	●	Gonzaga	0 7
N9	●	at Idaho	6 0
N16	●	at Southern Cal	10 20
N30	=	Saint Mary's-Cal *SF*	7 7

1936 — 6-3-1 (6-2-1)
S26	●	Montana	19 0
O3	●	Stanford	14 13
O10	●	at Idaho	14 0
O17	=	at Southern Cal	0 0
O24	●	Oregon	3 0
O31	●	at California	14 13
N7	|	Oregon State	6 16
N14	●	at UCLA	32 7
N26	●	at Washington	0 40
D5	●	at Gonzaga	6 13

1937 — 3-3-3 (3-3-2)
S25	|	at Gonzaga	0 0
O2	●	Idaho	13 0
O9	●	at California	0 27
O16	=	Washington	7 7
O23	●	at UCLA	3 0
O30	|	Southern Cal	0 0
N6	●	Oregon *Port*	6 10
N13	●	at Stanford	0 23
N20	|	at Oregon State	7 0

1938 — 2-8-0 (1-7-0)
S24	|	Oregon	2 10
O1	|	California	3 27
O8	|	at Stanford	0 8
O15	|	at Southern Cal	6 19
O22	|	Oregon State *Port*	6 7
O29	●	at Gonzaga	15 13
N5	|	UCLA	0 21
N12	●	at Idaho	12 0
N26	●	at Washington	0 26
D3	|	at Oklahoma	0 28

1939 — 4-5-0 (3-5-0)
S23	●	Gonzaga	19 6
O7	|	at Southern Cal	0 27
O14	●	Washington	6 0
O21	●	at California	7 13
O28	●	at Oregon State	0 13
N4	●	at Oregon	0 38 *
N11	●	Idaho	21 13
N18	●	at Stanford	7 0
N30	●	at UCLA	7 24

1940 — 4-4-2 (3-4-2)
S28	=	at Southern Cal	14 14
O5	●	Montana	13 0
O12	●	at California	9 6
O19	●	Stanford	14 26
O26	●	Oregon	6 6
N2	●	Idaho *Boi*	26 0
N9	●	at Oregon State	0 21
N16	●	at UCLA	26 34
N23	●	at Gonzaga	14 7
N30	|	at Washington	9 33

1941 — 6-4-0 (5-3-0)
S26	●	at UCLA	6 7
O4	●	California	13 6
O11	|	Washington	13 23
O18	●	at Southern Cal	6 7
O25	●	Oregon State	7 0
N1	●	at Oregon	13 0
N8	●	Idaho	26 0
N15	●	at Stanford	14 13
N22	●	at Gonzaga	59 0
D6	|	Texas A&M *Tac*	0 7

1942 — 6-2-2 (5-1-1)
S26	●	at Stanford	6 0
O3	●	Oregon	7 0
O10	●	Montana	68 16
O17	●	at Southern Cal	12 26
O24	●	Oregon State *Port*	26 13
N7	●	Michigan State *Spo*	25 13
N14	●	at Idaho	0 0
N21	=	Second Air Force *Spo*	6 6
N28	●	at Washington	0 0
D5	|	Texas A&M *SA*	0 21

1943-1944
NO TEAM WWII

PHIL SARBOE
1945-49 (.402)   17-26-3

1945 — 6-2-1 (6-2-1)
S29	●	at Idaho	43 12
O6	●	Oregon State	33 0
O13	●	at Washington	0 6
O20	●	at Oregon	13 26
O27	●	at Idaho	21 0
N3	●	at California	7 7
N10	●	Oregon	20 13
N17	●	at Oregon State	13 6
N24	●	Washington	7 0

1946 — 1-6-1 (1-5-1)
S27	●	at Southern Cal	7 13
O5	●	Idaho	32 0
O12	●	Washington	7 21
O19	=	at Oregon	0 0
O26	●	Oregon State	12 13
N2	●	at California	14 47
N16	●	at Stanford	26 27
N30	●	at Michigan State	20 26

1947 — 3-7-0 (2-5-0)
S20	●	Penn State *Her*	6 27
S27	●	at Southern Cal	0 21
O4	●	at Idaho	7 0
O11	●	Michigan State	7 21
O18	●	at California	6 21
O25	●	Montana	12 13
O31	●	Portland	35 0
N8	●	Oregon	6 12
N15	●	at Oregon State	14 13
N22	●	at Washington	0 20

1948 — 4-5-1 (4-3-1)
S18	●	at UCLA	26 48
O2	●	Stanford	14 7
O9	●	at Montana	48 0
O16	●	Washington	10 0
O23	●	at Oregon	7 33
O30	●	Idaho	19 14
N6	=	Oregon State	26 26
N13	●	at California	14 44
N20	●	at Michigan State	0 40
N27	●	Penn State *Tac*	0 7

1949 — 3-6-0 (2-6-0)
S17	●	Utah State	33 0
S24	●	Montana	13 7
O1	●	at Southern Cal	7 35
O8	●	Oregon	0 21
O15	●	at Idaho	35 13
O22	●	UCLA	20 27
O29	●	at Oregon State	6 35
N5	●	at California	14 33
N19	●	at Washington	21 34

FOREST EVASHEVSKI
1950-51 (.632)   11-6-2

1950 — 4-3-2 (2-3-2)
S23	●	at Utah State	46 6
S30	●	at UCLA	0 42
O7	=	Southern Cal	20 20
O14	●	at Montana	14 7
O28	=	Idaho	7 7
N4	●	at Oregon	21 13 *
N11	●	at Stanford	17 26 *
N18	●	Oregon State	21 7
N25	●	Washington *Spo*	21 52

1951 — 7-3-0 (4-3-0)
S22	|	at Southern Cal	21 31
S29	●	Santa Clara *Spo*	34 20
O5	●	Oklahoma State *Spo*	27 13
O13	●	California	35 42
O20	●	at Oregon State	26 13
O27	●	Oregon	41 6
N3	●	at Stanford	13 21
N10	●	at Idaho	9 6
N17	●	Montana	47 10
N24	●	at Washington	27 25

AL KIRCHER
1952-55 (.350)   13-25-2

1952 — 4-6-0 (3-4-0)
S19	|	at Southern Cal	7 35
S27	|	Stanford	13 14
O4	●	at Baylor	7 31
O18	●	at Ohio State	7 35
O25	●	Oregon State	33 20
N1	●	Idaho	36 6
N8	●	at Oregon	19 6
N15	●	at California	13 28
N22	●	at Oklahoma State	9 7
N29	●	Washington *Spo*	27 33

1953 — 4-6-0 (3-4-0)
S19	|	Southern Cal	13 29
S26	●	at Pacific	26 20
O3	●	at Iowa	12 54
O10	●	Oregon	7 0
O17	●	at Idaho	30 13
O24	●	at UCLA	7 44
O31	●	at Stanford	19 48
N7	●	TCU *Spo*	7 21
N14	●	at Oregon State	0 7
N21	●	at Washington	25 20

1954 — 4-6-0 (3-4-0)
S17	●	at Southern Cal	0 39
S25	●	Pacific *Spo*	18 0
O2	●	at Texas	14 40
O9	●	Oregon State	34 6
O16	●	at California	7 17
O23	●	Idaho	0 10
O30	●	at Stanford	30 26
N6	●	at Michigan State	6 54
N13	●	at Oregon	14 26
N20	●	Washington	26 7

1955 — 1-7-2 (1-5-1)
S17	●	at Southern Cal	12 50
S24	●	at Kansas	0 13
O1	●	UCLA	0 55
O8	=	at California	20 20
O15	●	at Idaho	9 0
O22	●	at Oregon State	6 14
O29	●	at Pacific	0 30
N5	●	at Oregon	0 35
N12	=	San Jose State	13 13
N19	●	at Washington	7 27

JIM SUTHERLAND
1956-63 (.488)   37-39-4

1956 — 3-6-1 (2-5-1)
S22	●	Stanford *Spo*	26 40
S29	●	San Jose State	33 18
O6	●	at Idaho	33 19
O13	●	at UCLA	0 28
O20	●	Oregon State	0 21
O27	●	at Pacific	12 33
N3	●	Southern Cal	12 28
N10	=	at Oregon	7 7
N17	●	at California	14 13
N24	●	Washington *Spo*	26 40

1957 — 6-4-0 (5-3-0)
S21	●	at Nebraska	34 12
S28	●	California	13 7
O5	●	at Iowa	13 20
O12	●	at Stanford	21 18
O19	●	Oregon	13 14
O26	●	at Southern Cal	13 12
N2	●	at Oregon State	25 39
N9	●	UCLA *Spo*	13 19
N16	●	Idaho	21 13
N23	●	at Washington	27 7

1958 — 7-3-0 (6-2-0)
S20	●	Stanford	40 6
S27	●	at Northwestern	28 29
O4	●	at California	14 34
O11	●	at Idaho	8 0
O18	●	at Oregon	6 0
O25	●	Southern Cal *Spo*	6 14
N1	●	at UCLA	38 20
N8	●	Oregon State	7 0
N15	●	at Pacific	34 0
N22	●	Washington *Spo*	18 14

1959-1961 INDEPENDENT

1959 — 6-4-0
S19	●	California *Spo*	6 20
S25	●	at San Jose State	30 6
O3	●	at Oregon	6 14
O10	●	at Pacific	20 12
O17	●	at Stanford	36 19
O24	●	Idaho	27 5
O31	●	at Oregon State	14 0
N14	●	Oregon	6 7
N21	●	at Washington	0 20
N26	●	at Houston	32 18

1960 — 4-5-1
S17	●	Stanford *Spo*	15 14
S23	●	at Denver	26 28
O1	●	at Arizona State	21 24
O8	=	at California	21 21
O15	●	at Oregon	12 21
O22	●	Pacific	51 12
O29	●	at San Jose State	29 6
N5	●	Oregon State	10 20
N12	●	at Idaho	18 7
N19	●	Washington *Spo*	7 8

1961 — 3-7-0

Date	Result	Conf	Opponent	WSU	Opp
S23			at Missouri	6	28
S30			Utah State Spo	14	34
O7			at Texas	8	41
O14	●		Idaho	34	0
O21			at Indiana	7	33
O28			San Jose State Spo	19	21
N4			at Oregon State	6	14
N11	●		Oregon	22	21
N18	●		at Stanford	30	0
N25			at Washington	17	21

1962-1967 AAWU

1962 — 5-4-1 (1-1-0)

Date	Result	Conf	Opponent	WSU	Opp
S22	●		San Jose State	49	8
S29	●		at Wyoming	21	15
O6	=		at Arizona State	24	24
O13	●	|	Stanford Spo	21	6
O20	●		Indiana Spo	21	15
O27			at Pacific	12	13
N3			Oregon State	12	18
N10			at Oregon	10	28
N17	●		at Idaho	22	14
N24		|	Washington Spo	21	26

1963 — 3-6-1 (1-1-0)

Date	Result	Conf	Opponent	WSU	Opp
S21			at Texas Tech	7	16
S28	=		at Iowa	14	14
O5	●		Arizona Spo	7	2
O12			San Jose State	8	13
O19			at Oregon State	6	30
O26			at Army	0	23
N2	●		Idaho	14	10
N9			Oregon	7	21
N16	●	|	at Stanford	32	15
N23		|	at Washington	0	16

BERT CLARK
1964-67 (.388) 15-24-1

1964 — 3-6-1 (1-2-1)

Date	Result	Conf	Opponent	WSU	Opp
S19	●	|	Stanford Spo	29	23
S26			Wyoming	7	28
O3			at Arizona	12	28
O10	●		Pacific	50	0
O17	●		at San Jose State	16	14
O24			at Idaho	13	28
O31		|	Oregon State	7	24
N7	=	|	at Oregon	21	21
N14			at Texas Tech	10	28
N21		|	Washington Spo	0	14

1965 — 7-3-0 (2-1-0)

Date	Result	Conf	Opponent	WSU	Opp
S18	●		at Iowa	7	0
S25	●		at Minnesota	14	13
O2			Idaho	13	17
O9	●		Villanova Spo	24	14
O16	●		Arizona Spo	21	3
O23	●		at Indiana	8	7
O30	●	|	at Oregon State	10	8
N6	●	|	Oregon	27	7
N13			at Arizona State	6	7
N20		|	at Washington	9	27

1966 — 3-7-0 (1-3-0)

Date	Result	Conf	Opponent	WSU	Opp
S17		|	California Spo	6	21
S23			at Houston	7	21
O1			Baylor Spo	14	20
O9	●		Arizona State	24	15
O15			at Utah	15	26
O22	●		at Idaho	14	7
O29		|	Oregon State	13	41
N5	●	|	at Oregon	14	13
N12			at Arizona	18	28
N19		|	Washington Spo	7	19

1967 — 2-8-0 (1-5-0)

Date	Result	Conf	Opponent	WSU	Opp
S15		|	at Southern Cal	0	49
S23			at Oklahoma	0	21
S30		|	UCLA Spo	23	51
O7			at Baylor	7	10
O14		|	at Stanford	10	31
O21			Arizona State Spo	20	31
O28		|	at Oregon State	7	35
N4		|	Oregon	13	17
N11	●		Idaho	52	14
N18	●	|	at Washington	9	7

1968-Present Pac-10

JIM SWEENEY
1968-75 (.308) 26-59-1

1968 — 3-6-1 (1-3-1)

Date	Result	Conf	Opponent	WSU	Opp
S21	●		Idaho Spo	14	7
S28		|	at UCLA	21	31
O5			Utah	14	17
O12			at Arizona State	14	41
O19	=	|	Stanford Spo	21	21
O26		|	Oregon State	8	16
N2			at Arizona	14	28
N9		|	at Oregon	13	27
N16	●		at San Jose State	46	0
N23	●	|	Washington Spo	24	0

1969 — 1-9-0 (0-7-0)

Date	Result	Conf	Opponent	WSU	Opp
S20	●		at Illinois	19	18
S27			at Iowa	35	61
O4		|	Oregon	24	25
O11		|	UCLA Spo	14	46
O18		|	at Stanford	0	49
O25		|	California Spo	0	17
N1			Pacific	20	27
N8		|	at Southern Cal	7	28
N15		|	at Oregon State	3	38
N22		|	at Washington	21	30

1970 — 1-10-0 (0-7-0)

Date	Result	Conf	Opponent	WSU	Opp
S12			at Kansas	31	48
S19	●		Idaho Spo	44	16
S26			at Michigan State	14	28
O3		|	at Oregon	13	28
O10			at Arizona State	30	37
O17		|	Stanford Spo	16	63
O24		|	at California	0	45
O31		|	at UCLA	9	54
N7		|	Southern Cal Spo	33	70
N14		|	Oregon State Spo	16	28
N21		|	Washington Spo	25	43

1971 — 4-7-0 (2-5-0)

Date	Result	Conf	Opponent	WSU	Opp
S11			at Kansas	0	34
S18			Arizona Spo	28	39
S25	●		at Minnesota	31	20
O2	●		at Utah	34	12
O9		|	UCLA Spo	21	34
O16		|	California Spo	23	24
O23	●	|	at Stanford	24	23
O30	●	|	Oregon Spo	31	21
N6		|	at Southern Cal	20	30
N13		|	at Oregon State	14	21
N20		|	at Washington	20	28

1972 — 7-4-0 (4-3-0)

Date	Result	Conf	Opponent	WSU	Opp
S9	●		at Kansas	18	17
S16		|	at California	23	37
S23	●		at Arizona	28	6
S30			Utah	25	44
O7	●		Idaho	35	14
O14	●	|	at Oregon	31	14
O21	●	|	Oregon State	37	7
O28		|	at UCLA	20	35
N4		|	Southern Cal SEA	3	44
N11	●	|	Stanford	27	13
N18	●	|	Washington Spo	27	10

1973 — 5-6-0 (4-3-0)

Date	Result	Conf	Opponent	WSU	Opp
S15			at Kansas	8	29
S22			at Arizona State	9	20
S29	●		Idaho	51	24
O6			at Ohio State	3	27
O13		|	at Southern Cal	35	46
O20		|	UCLA Spo	13	24
O27		|	at Stanford	14	45
N3	●	|	Oregon	21	14
N10	●	|	at Oregon State	13	7
N17	●	|	California	31	28
N24	●	|	at Washington	52	26

1974 — 2-9-0 (1-6-0)

Date	Result	Conf	Opponent	WSU	Opp
S14			Kansas Spo	7	14
S21	●		Idaho	17	10
S28			at Illinois	19	21
O5			Ohio State SEA	7	42
O12		|	Southern Cal Spo	7	54
O19		|	at UCLA	13	17
O26		|	Stanford	18	20
N2	●	|	at Oregon	21	16
N9		|	Oregon State	3	17
N16		|	at California	33	37
N23		|	Washington Spo	17	24

1975 — 3-8-0 (0-7-0)

Date	Result	Conf	Opponent	WSU	Opp
S13	●		at Kansas	18	14
S20	●		at Utah	30	14
S27		|	California	21	33
O4			at Illinois	21	27
O11		|	at Southern Cal	10	28
O18		|	UCLA Spo	23	37
O25		|	at Stanford	14	54
N1		|	Oregon	14	26
N8		|	at Oregon State	0	7
N15	●		Idaho	84	27
N22		|	at Washington	27	28

JACKIE SHERRILL
1976 (.273) 3-8

1976 — 3-8-0 (2-5-0)

Date	Result	Conf	Opponent	WSU	Opp
S11			at Kansas	16	35
S18			at Minnesota	14	28
S25			at Wisconsin	26	35
O2	●		Idaho	45	6
O9		|	Southern Cal SEA	14	23
O16		|	at UCLA	3	62
O23		|	Stanford	16	22
O30	●	|	at Oregon	23	22
N6	●	|	Oregon State	29	24
N13		|	at California	22	23
N20		|	Washington Spo	32	51

WARREN POWERS
1977 (.545) 6-5

1977 — 6-5-0 (3-4-0)

Date	Result	Conf	Opponent	WSU	Opp
S10	●		at Nebraska	19	10
S17	●		at Michigan State	23	21
S24			at Kansas	12	14
S30		|	at Southern Cal	7	41
O8	●	|	California	17	10
O15		|	UCLA Spo	16	27 †
O22		|	at Stanford	29	31
O29	●	|	Oregon	56	20
N5	●	|	at Oregon State	24	10
N12	●		Idaho	45	17
N19		|	at Washington	15	35

JIM WALDEN
1978-86 (.430) 41-55-4

1978 — 3-7-1 (1-7-0)

Date	Result	Conf	Opponent	WSU	Opp
S9	●		Nevada-Las Vegas Spo	34	7
S16	●		Idaho	28	0
S23	●	|	Arizona State Spo	51	26
S30	=		at Army	21	21
O14		|	at UCLA	31	45
O21		|	Stanford	27	43
O28		|	at Oregon	7	31
N4		|	Oregon State	31	32
N11		|	at California	14	22
N18		|	at Arizona	24	31
N25		|	Washington Spo	8	38

1979 — 3-8-0 (2-6-0)

Date	Result	Conf	Opponent	WSU	Opp
S8		|	Arizona Spo	7	22
S15	●		Montana Spo	34	14
S22			at Ohio State	29	45
S29			Syracuse BUF	25	52
O6		|	at Southern Cal	21	50
O13	●	|	UCLA	17	14
O20		|	at Arizona State	17	28
O27		|	Oregon	26	37
N3	●	|	at Oregon State	45	42
N10		|	California	13	45
N17		|	at Washington	7	17

1980 — 4-7-0 (3-4-0)

Date	Result	Conf	Opponent	WSU	Opp
S13			San Jose State Spo	26	31
S20			at Tennessee	23	35
S27	●		Army	31	18
O4			Pacific	22	24
O11		|	at Arizona State	21	27
O18	●	|	at Arizona	38	14
O25		|	Stanford	34	48
N1		|	at Oregon	10	20
N8	●	|	Oregon State	28	7
N15	●	|	at California	31	17
N22		|	Washington Spo	23	30

1981 — 8-3-1 (5-2-1)

Date	Result	Conf	Opponent	WSU	Opp
S12	●		Montana State Spo	33	21
S19	●		at Colorado	14	10
S26	●	|	Arizona State	24	21
O3	●		Pacific	31	0
O10	●	|	at Oregon State	23	0
O17	=	|	UCLA	17	17
O24	●	|	at Arizona	34	19
O31		|	at Southern Cal	17	41
N7	●	|	Oregon	39	7
N14	●	|	California Spo	19	0
N21		|	at Washington	10	23
HOLIDAY BOWL					
D18			Brigham Young	36	38

1982 — 3-7-1 (2-4-1)

Date	Result	Conf	Opponent	WSU	Opp
S11	●		Idaho Spo	34	14
S18			Colorado Spo	0	12
S25			at Minnesota	11	41
O2			at Tennessee	3	10
O9	=	|	Oregon State	14	14
O16		|	at UCLA	17	42
O23		|	Stanford	26	31
O30		|	Arizona	17	34
N6	●	|	at Oregon	10	3
N13		|	at California	14	34
N20	●	|	Washington	24	20

1983 — 7-4-0 (5-3-0)

Date	Result	Conf	Opponent	WSU	Opp
S3	●		Montana State Spo	27	7
S10			at Michigan	17	20
S17		|	Arizona	6	45
S24	●		Nevada-Las Vegas Spo	41	28
O8		|	at Southern Cal	17	38
O15		|	UCLA	14	24
O22	●	|	at Arizona State	31	21
O29	●	|	Oregon	24	7
N5	●	|	at Oregon State	27	9
N12	●	|	California	16	6
N19	●	|	at Washington	17	6

1984 — 6-5-0 (4-3-0)

Date	Result	Conf	Opponent	WSU	Opp
S1			at Tennessee	27	34
S8	●		Utah	42	40
S15			at Ohio State	0	44
S22	●		Ball State	16	14
O6		|	Southern Cal	27	29
O13		|	at UCLA	24	27
O20	●	|	at Stanford	49	42
O27	●	|	at Oregon	50	41
N3	●	|	Oregon State	20	3
N10	●	|	at California	33	7
N17		|	Washington	29	38

1985 — 4-7-0 (3-5-0)

Date	Result	Conf	Opponent	WSU	Opp
A31		|	Oregon	39	42
S7	●	|	California	20	19
S14		|	at Arizona	7	12
S21			at Utah	37	44
S28			at Ohio State	32	48
O12	●	|	at Oregon State	34	0
O19		|	UCLA	30	31
O26		|	Arizona State	16	21
N2		|	at Southern Cal	13	31
N16	●		Montana State	64	14
N23	●	|	at Washington	21	20

1986 — 3-7-1 (2-6-1)

Date	Result	Conf	Opponent	WSU	Opp
S6	●		Nevada-Las Vegas	34	14
S13			San Jose State	13	20
S20		|	at California	21	31
S27	=	|	at Arizona State	21	21
O4	●	|	Oregon State	24	14
O11	●	|	Southern Cal	34	14
O25		|	at UCLA	16	54
N1		|	at Stanford	12	42
N8		|	Arizona	6	31
N15		|	at Oregon	17	27
N22		|	Washington	23	44

DENNIS ERICKSON
1987-88 (.543) 12-10-1

1987 — 3-7-1 (1-5-1)

Date	Result	Conf	Opponent	WSU	Opp
S5	●		Fresno State	41	24
S12	●		Wyoming	43	28
S19			at Michigan	18	44
S26			at Colorado	17	26
O10		|	Stanford	7	44
O17		|	at Arizona State	7	38
O24	●	|	Arizona	45	28
O31		|	at Southern Cal	7	42
N14		|	Oregon	17	31
N21		|	at Washington	19	34
N28	=	|	California TOK	17	17

1988 — 9-3-0 (5-3-0)

Date	Result	Conf	Opponent	WSU	Opp
S3	●		at Illinois	44	7
S10	●		at Minnesota	41	9
S17		|	Oregon	28	43
O1	●		at Tennessee	52	24
O8	●	|	California	44	13
O15		|	at Arizona	28	45
O22		|	Arizona State	28	31
O29	●	|	at UCLA	34	30
N5	●	|	at Stanford	24	21
N12	●	|	Oregon State	36	27
N19		|	Washington	32	31
ALOHA BOWL					
D25	●		Houston	24	22

MIKE PRICE
1989-2002 (.516)   83-78

1989   6-5-0 (3-5-0)

S2	●	Idaho	41	7
S7	●	at Brigham Young	46	41
S16	● |	Oregon State	41	3
S23	● |	at Wyoming	29	23
S30	|	Southern Cal	17	18
O7	● |	at Oregon	51	38
O14	|	Stanford	31	13
O21	|	Arizona	21	23
O28	|	at Arizona State	39	44
N11	|	at California	26	38
N18	|	at Washington	9	20

1990   3-8-0 (2-6-0)

S1	●	at TCU	21	3
S8		Wyoming	13	34
S15		at Brigham Young	36	50
S22	● |	California	41	31
S29	|	UCLA	20	30
O6	|	at Southern Cal	17	30
O20	● |	at Oregon State	55	24
O27	|	at Arizona	34	42
N3	|	at Stanford	13	31
N10	|	Arizona State	26	51
N17	|	Washington	10	55

1991   4-7-0 (3-5-0)

S7	|	at Oregon	14	40
S14		Fresno State	30	34
S21		at Ohio State	19	33
S28	●	at Nevada-Las Vegas	40	13
O5	|	Oregon State	55	7
O12	|	Southern Cal	27	34
O19	|	at Arizona State	17	3
N2	|	at UCLA	3	44
N9	|	Arizona	40	27
N16	|	Stanford	14	49
N23	|	at Washington	21	56

1992   9-3-0 (5-3-0)

S5	●	Montana	25	13
S12	|	at Arizona	23	20
S26	●	at Fresno State	39	37
O3	●	Temple	51	10
O10	● |	at Oregon State	35	10
O17	|	UCLA	30	17
O24	|	at Southern Cal	21	31
O31	|	Oregon	17	34
N7	|	Arizona State	20	18
N14	|	at Stanford	3	40
N21	● |	Washington	42	23
COPPER BOWL				
D29	●	Utah	31	28

1993   5-6-0 (3-5-0)

S4	|	at Michigan	14	41
S11	● |	Montana State	54	14
S18	|	Oregon State	51	6
S25	|	at Southern Cal	3	34
O2	● |	at Pacific	12	0
O9	● |	Arizona State	44	25
O16	● |	California	34	7
O23	|	at Arizona	6	9
O30	|	at Oregon	23	46
N6	|	UCLA	27	40
N20	|	at Washington	3	26

1994   8-4-0 (5-3-0)

S1	●	Illinois CHI	10	9
S10	●	Fresno State	24	3
S24	● |	at UCLA	21	0
O1		at Tennessee	9	10
O8	● |	Oregon	21	7
O15	|	Arizona	7	10
O22	● |	at Arizona State	28	21
O29	● |	at California	26	23
N5	|	Southern Cal	10	23
N12	|	at Oregon State	3	21
N19	● |	Washington	23	6
ALAMO BOWL				
D31	●	Baylor	10	3

1995   3-8-0 (2-6-0)

S2		at Pittsburgh	13	17
S9	●	Montana	38	21
S23	● |	UCLA	24	15
S30		at Nebraska	21	35
O7	● |	Oregon State	40	14
O14	|	at Southern Cal	14	26
O21	|	at Oregon	7	26
O28	|	Arizona	14	24
N4	|	at California	11	27
N11	|	Stanford	24	36
N18	|	at Washington	30	33

1996   5-6 (3-5)

A31		at Colorado	19	37
S7	●	at Temple	38	34
S21	● |	Oregon	55	44
S28	●	San Jose State	52	16
O5		at Arizona	26	34
O12	● |	at Oregon State	24	3
O19	● |	California	21	18
O26	|	Southern Cal	24	29
N9	|	at UCLA	14	38
N16	|	at Stanford	17	33
N23	|	Washington	24	31

1997   10-2 (7-1)

A30	● |	UCLA	37	34
S13	● |	at Southern Cal	28	21
S20	● |	at Illinois	35	22
S27	● |	Boise State	58	0
O4	|	at Oregon	24	13
O18	● |	California	63	37
O25	● |	Arizona	35	34
N1	|	at Arizona State	31	44
N8	● |	La. Lafayette	77	7
N15	● |	Stanford	38	28
N22	● |	at Washington	41	35
ROSE BOWL				
J1		Michigan	16	21

1998   3-8 (0-8)

S5	●	Illinois	20	13
S12	●	at Boise State	33	21
S19	●	Idaho	24	16
S26	|	at California	14	24
O3	|	at UCLA	17	49
O10	|	Oregon	29	51
O17	|	Southern Cal	14	42
O31	|	Arizona State	28	38
N7	|	at Arizona	7	41
N14	|	at Stanford	28	38
N21	|	Washington	9	16

1999   3-9 (1-7)

S4		Utah	7	27
S11	|	at Stanford	17	54
S18		Idaho PULL	17	28
S25	|	Arizona	24	30
O2	● |	California	31	7
O9	●	La. Lafayette	44	0
O23	|	at Arizona State	21	33
O30	|	Oregon State	13	27
N6	|	at Oregon	10	52
N13	|	Southern Cal	28	31
N20	|	at Washington	14	24
N27	●	at Hawaii	22	14

2000   4-7 (2-6)

S2	|	Stanford	10	24
S16	●	at Utah	38	21
S23		Idaho	34	38
S30	● |	at California	21	17
O7	●	Boise State	42	35
O14	|	at Arizona	47	53
O21	|	Arizona State	20	23
O28	|	at Oregon State	9	38
N4	|	Oregon	24	27
N11	|	at Southern Cal	33	27
N18	|	Washington	3	51

2001   10-2 (6-2)

A30	● |	Idaho	36	7
S8	● |	at Boise State	41	20
S22	● |	California	51	20
S29	● |	at Arizona	48	21
O6	● |	Oregon State	34	27
O13	● |	at Stanford	45	39
O18	● |	Montana State	53	28
O27	|	Oregon	17	24
N3	● |	UCLA	20	14
N10	● |	at Arizona State	28	16
N17	|	at Washington	14	26
SUN BOWL				
D31	●	Purdue	33	27

2002   10-3 (7-1)

A31	●	Nevada	31	7
S7	●	Idaho	49	14
S14		at Ohio State	7	25
S21	●	Montana State	45	28
S28	● |	at California	48	38
O5	● |	Southern Cal	30	27
O12	● |	at Stanford	36	11
O26	● |	at Arizona	21	13
N2	● |	Arizona State	44	22
N9	● |	Oregon	32	21
N23	|	Washington	26	29
D7	● |	at UCLA	48	27
ROSE BOWL				
J1		Oklahoma	14	34

BILL DOBA
2003-Present (.625)   15-9

2003   10-3 (6-2)

A30	●	Idaho	25	0
S6		at Notre Dame	26	29
S13	●	at Colorado	47	26
S20	●	New Mexico	23	13
S27	● |	at Oregon	55	16
O4	|	Arizona	30	7
O18	● |	at Stanford	24	14
O25	● |	Oregon State	36	30
N1	|	at Southern Cal	16	43
N8	● |	UCLA	31	13
N15	● |	Arizona State	34	19
N22	|	at Washington	19	27
HOLIDAY BOWL				
D30	●	Texas	28	20

2004   5-6 (3-5)

S3	●	at New Mexico	21	17
S11		Sea Colorado	12	20
S18	●	Idaho	49	8
S25	● |	at Arizona	20	19
O9		Oregon	38	41
O16	|	Stanford	17	23
O23	|	at Oregon State	19	38
O30	|	Southern Cal	12	42
N6	● |	at UCLA	31	29
N13	|	at Arizona State	28	45
N20	|	Washington	28	25

WEST VIRGINIA

BY MIKE VACCARO

LONG BEFORE MAJOR HARRIS AND Sam Huff, long before Don Nehlen and Bobby Bowden, West Virginia's football ties were rooted in a simple, humble history, not unlike West Virginia itself. In 1891, a band of West Virginia students became intrigued at the stories they'd heard of "foot-ball," the relatively new sport gaining popularity at universities all across the country. Quickly, they gathered equipment and uniforms (expensive, even by those primitive standards) and found an opponent, Washington & Jefferson College of nearby Washington, Pa., which was in its second year fielding a football team.

Robert Bivens, who had played at Princeton for a time before transferring to WVU, was named field captain. Frederick Emory, a professor who'd played at Yale, one of the original football superpowers, was appointed team adviser. Preparation was sketchy; the team practiced for two weeks on a cow pasture known as baseball grounds, and the results were predictably disastrous, a 72-0 loss in cold, blustery conditions on Thanksgiving Day on a level field in south Morgantown. But from that indignity has grown a program that has filled the small college town with life and energy almost every year since.

From its first postseason appearance in the 1922 East-West Bowl—when crowds gathered in Morgantown to receive telegraph reports about the game against Gonzaga, which was being played in San Diego—to the 1989 Fiesta Bowl, when West Virginia played Notre Dame in a winner-take-all showdown for the national title, Mountaineers football has seized the state, and Mountaineer Field has become one of the great game-day sites in all of college football.

TRADITION Game days in West Virginia have always been loud, colorful events, often highlighted by the regular reports of the mascot's musket. In the 1940s and 1950s, the most popular chant was "West By God Virginia!" Now, the team runs through a man-made tunnel of band members before games, a carryover from the original Mountaineer Field. The school's Mountaineer Marching Band is one of the nation's best, a 350-piece

PROFILE

West Virginia University
Morgantown, W.Va.
Founded: 1867
Enrollment: 17,517
Colors: Old Gold and Blue
Nickname: Mountaineers
Stadium: Mountaineer Field at Milan Puskar Stadium
    Opened in 1980
    AstroPlay; 63,500 capacity
First football game: 1891
All-time record: 631–437–45 (.587)
Bowl record: 9–15
Big East championships: 3 (1 outright)
First-round NFL draftees: 8
Website: www.msnsportsnet.com

THE BEST OF TIMES

West Virginia has finished in the top 10 of both major polls twice in its history, both under Don Nehlen. In 1988 and 1993, the Mountaineers went 11–0 before losing bowl games to finish fifth and seventh, respectively, in the AP poll.

THE WORST OF TIMES

Frank Cignetti had the great misfortune of bridging two legends, Bobby Bowden and Don Nehlen. His legacy was secured by four losing seasons in four years on the job from 1976 to 1979.

CONFERENCE

West Virginia was an independent from 1891 to 1924, 1928 to 1949 and 1968 to 1990. It also has been a part of three conferences: the West Virginia Intercollegiate Athletic Conference from 1925 to 1927, the Southern Conference from 1950 to 1967 and the Big East since 1991.

DISTINGUISHED ALUMNI

Jerry West; Don Knotts, actor; Emily Morey-Holton, president of NASA research center; David Selby, actor; Rod Thorn, NBA executive

FIGHT SONG

HAIL WEST VIRGINIA
Let's give a rah for West Virginia,
And let us pledge to her anew,
Others may like black or crimson,
But for us it's Gold and Blue.
Let all our troubles be forgotten,
Let college spirit rule,
We'll join and give our loyal efforts
For the good of our old school.
It's West Virginia, it's West Virginia,
The pride of every Mountaineer,
Come on you old grads, join with us young lads.
It's West Virginia now we cheer!
Now is the time boys to make a big noise
No matter what the people say,
For there is naught to fear, the gang's all here,
So hail West Virginia, hail.

While WVU served as Bobby Bowden's apprenticeship, Don Nehlen is the king of Mountaineers coaches.

group whose nickname is the Pride of West Virginia, and whose signature formation is an outline of the state's boundaries that provides a rousing finale to the "Hail West Virginia" song at every home game.

BEST PLAYER Although West Virginia has produced a wealth of well-known players through the years, from Sam Huff to Jeff Hostetler, Darryl Talley to Major Harris, there is only one name that still conjures magic, more than 80 years after he played his last down, nearly 40 years after drawing his last breath. Ira Errett "Rat" Rodgers is the preeminent athlete in West Virginia history, a fullback from 1915 to 1919 who was called "the finest all-around football player in the land" by columnist Grantland Rice. Rodgers came to national prominence after West Virginia's 25-0 victory over Princeton in 1919, passing for 162 yards and two touchdowns. During that season, he accounted for 147 points, still a school single-season record.

BEST COACH While Bobby Bowden coached the team for six years before heading off into legend at Florida State—he went 42–26 with two Peach Bowl appearances at WVU—it is Don Nehlen who is the undisputed king of Mountaineer coaches. In 1980, Nehlen inherited a team that had suffered through four straight losing seasons; his second year as coach was the first of three straight 9–3 seasons. By far, the highlight of Nehlen's tenure—and West Virginia's football history—was the 1988 team that won its first 11 games and faced Notre Dame in the Fiesta Bowl for the national championship. In 1993, he guided the Mountaineers to a second 11–0 start before losing to Florida in the Sugar Bowl. Nehlen was 149–93–4 in 21 seasons in Morgantown, and guided the Mountaineers to 13 bowls. "Don Nehlen is considered to be the E.F. Hutton of college coaching, because when he speaks, out of respect for his wisdom and experience, we all listen," Purdue coach Joe Tiller said the week

RECORDS

RUSHING YARDS

GAME	
337	Kay-Jay Harris vs. East Carolina, Sept. 4, 2004 (25 att.)
SEASON	
1,710	Avon Cobourne, 2002 (335 att.)
CAREER	
5,164	Avon Cobourne, 1999-2002 (1,050 att.)

PASSING YARDS

GAME	
429	Marc Bulger vs. Missouri, Dec. 26, 1998 (34 of 40)
SEASON	
3,607	Marc Bulger, 1998 (274 of 419)
CAREER	
8,153	Marc Bulger, 1996-99 (630 of 1,023)

RECEIVING YARDS

GAME	
209	Chris Henry vs. Syracuse, Nov. 22, 2003 (6 rec.)
SEASON	
1,043	David Saunders, 1996 (76 rec.)
CAREER	
2,608	David Saunders, 1995-98 (191 rec.)

POINTS

GAME	
37	Ira Errett Rodgers vs. Marietta, Sept. 27, 1919 (5 TDs, 7 PATs); Rodgers vs. Ohio Wesleyan, Nov. 22, 1919 (5 TDs, 7 PATs)
SEASON	
147	Ira Errett Rodgers, 1919 (19 TDs, 33 PATs)
CAREER	
323	Paul Woodside, 1981-84 (74 FGs, 101 PATs)

CONSENSUS ALL-AMERICANS

1919	Ira Rodgers,	B
1934	Tod Goodwin,	E
1955	Bruce Bosley,	T
1982	Darryl Talley,	LB
1985	Brian Jozwiak,	OL
1992	Mike Compton,	C
1994	Todd Sauerbrun,	P
1995	Aaron Beasley,	DB
1996	Canute Curtis,	LB
2003	Grant Wiley,	LB

Nehlen retired. "College football certainly will miss one of the icons of our profession."

BEST TEAM It wasn't just that the Mountaineers were winning; it was how much they were winning by. As the early weeks of the 1988 season progressed, that was the striking thing. They beat Bowling Green 62-14. Cal State Fullerton was crushed 45-10. Maryland was obliterated 55-24. Pitt was squashed in the Backyard Brawl, 31-10. On and on it went. Led by sophomore quarterback Major Harris, West Virginia's offense seemed unstoppable. Harris grew up in Pittsburgh and became one of that city's great high school athletes in the mid-1980s; still, most recruiters saw him as a defensive back. Don Nehlen saw something else when he spotted Harris at one of his high school camps. "We had probably 40 quarterbacks in camp," Nehlen said. "We'd teach them in the morning and afternoon, then at night they'd split up into six-man teams for touch games. So I watched Major one night, playing touch, and he was running all over the place. I said to myself, 'Man, if they can't touch him, they've got to have a tough time tackling him.'" Harris' powers were never more in evidence than during a three-week stretch when Boston College, Penn State and Cincinnati fell under the Mountaineers steamroller by scores of 59-19, 51-30 and 51-13. Despite the traditional cries levied against East Coast schools, there was little doubt who Notre Dame's opponent in the Fiesta Bowl would be. But it was at Tempe, Ariz., where the magic finally ran out for West Virginia. Harris was limited to 166 passing yards and one touchdown, Notre Dame dashed out to a 16-0 lead and the Fighting Irish wrapped up the 17th national title in school history, 34-21.

BIGGEST GAME Miami was 12–0 in its short history in the Big East; the Hurricanes had not lost a game of any kind in November in nine years, since a fellow named Flutie plunged a knife in their hearts. West Virginia had a better record (9–0 to 8–1) than the fourth-ranked Canes

> *Watching Major Harris play touch football, Nehlen thought, "Man, if they can't touch him, they've got to have a tough time tackling him."*

entering the game on Nov. 20, 1993. But it was still a defining moment in Mountaineers football. And when the 17-14 victory was complete, in front of 70,222 fans at Mountaineer Field, it not only proved the arrival of West Virginia as a national championship player, but also announced the Big East as more than Miami and a batch of patsies. There were five lead changes in the game; the winning touchdown turned out to be a 19-yard run by Robert Walker with 6:08 left in the fourth quarter. Then Miami's withering threats were turned back by a stubborn Mountaineers defense. "We needed the elements to all come together to win this game," West Virginia coach Don Nehlen said when it was over. "And that's exactly what happened."

BIGGEST UPSET Nobody knew what to expect from Jeff Hostetler when the Hollsopple, Pa., native transferred to Morgantown from Penn State. Hostetler had lost out to Todd Blackledge for the starting quarterback's job in State College, and arrived at West Virginia completely unproven. He wasted little time changing that—in his first game, Sept. 11, 1982, he threw for 321 yards and four touchdowns as the Mountaineers rocked ninth-ranked Oklahoma 41-27 in Norman. Hostetler completed 17 of 37 passes, and his last scoring toss, to Wayne Brown midway through the fourth quarter, snapped a 27-27 tie. Despite a 9–3 record and Peach Bowl victory the previous year, this game truly signaled the arrival of something new in West Virginia's football history, and not only because it handed Barry Switzer his first opening-day loss in 10 years as Sooners coach. Hostetler described his afternoon thusly: "I just threw 'em up and the good Lord collected 'em." Nehlen was a bit more effusive: "For a guy who had never taken a snap for West Virginia University, and then to come out and do what he did today, well, I just don't have the right words to describe it. Jeff just has to go down in history."

HEARTBREAKER On Oct. 26, 1996, West Virginia was 7–0 and grinding toward an eighth straight victory when it led Miami 7-3 late in a hard-fought game in Morgantown. But when Brian West tried to punt the ball from deep in

West Virginia territory, Miami safety Tremain Mack zoomed in around the left side and smothered the ball just as it left West's foot. Jack Hallmon recovered the ball and handed it off to fellow defensive back Nate Brooks to complete a staggering 20-yard touchdown play with 21 seconds left. Nehlen would describe this as "the toughest loss I've ever been associated with," and a stunned West, in the locker room afterward, called it "a nightmare. I've never seen anything like it before."

CONTROVERSY It was a galling way for the game to end and, in retrospect, a disheartening way for a season to turn. Marvin Graves' 17-yard touchdown pass to Chris Gedney in the game's final minute allowed Syracuse to beat the Mountaineers 20-17 on Oct. 17, 1992. But it's how the score came to pass that hurt. Earlier in the drive, Graves had been pushed hard out-of-bounds after picking up a first down. He then lost his temper and fired the ball at the tackler, WVU's Tommy Orr. That touched off an ugly bench-clearing brawl that ultimately resulted in three Mountaineers defensive regulars—Mike Collins, Tom Briggs and Leroy Axem—getting ejected. Only Ken Warren, an obscure sub lineman, was thrown out for Syracuse; inexplicably, Graves, who started the melee, was allowed to stay in. As a result, he not only threw the winning score, he did so at the expense of backup safety John Harper—in the game only because Collins was in the locker room. "I don't think I've ever had one taken from me like that," Nehlen said afterward. "It's a crime." Whatever it was called, it threw a wrench into West Virginia's season. The Mountaineers were 3–0–2 entering the game, but the loss to Syracuse started a three-game losing streak that ultimately kept WVU out of the bowl picture.

NICKNAME The Mountaineer, in addition to being emblematic of West Virginia's proud history as a haven for outdoorsmen, became the school nickname after the state motto was coined: "Mountaineers are always free." Prior to 1905, West Virginia football players were referred to as the Snakes.

MASCOT The Mountaineer is a member of the student body chosen for outstanding enthusiasm, character, community service and academics. Candidates write essays describing why they want to be the mascot, and finalists are then chosen following a "cheer-off" at the next-to-last home basketball game each season. The costume is tailored to fit each year's winner, and male Mountaineers customarily

grow beards during their tenure. The mascot's rifle is a genuine flintlock that requires the user to know the amount of gunpowder needed to fire off the traditional charge.

UNIFORMS West Virginia's official school colors of old gold and blue were adopted by the school's upperclassmen in 1890. The football uniform has been virtually unchanged since Nehlen became the coach in 1980, with the helmet featuring a blue background and the "Flying WV" logo in old gold. The Mountaineers traditionally wear gold pants and blue jerseys at home, with gold pants and white jerseys on the road. They will wear blue pants on occasion at home and on the road.

STADIUM Opened in 1980, Mountaineer Field has been twice expanded, from the original 50,000 seats to 63,500, all of them unobstructed. The seats are arrayed in an acoustically friendly bowl shape that holds noise very well. The new Mountaineer Field replaced a smaller one that opened in 1924 and grew along with the program until it could grow no longer.

In 2004, WVU added 18 stadium suites and club seating in the north end zone to the renamed Milan Puskar Stadium. Milan "Mike" Puskar is a local businessman who donated $20 million to the school in 2003.

RIVAL West Virginia and Pittsburgh have staged the Backyard Brawl since 1895, though Pitt's attention during much of that time was divided between the Mountaineers and Penn State. Once that longtime rivalry was discontinued by Penn State's entry into the Big Ten in 1993, the Brawl became the unquestioned grudge match for both teams. Although West Virginia won the first three games in the series, two of them via shutout, Pitt holds a decisive advantage, helped by a stretch from 1924 to 1951 when it won 23 of 25 meetings. Perhaps the most thrilling game in the series came in 1997, when Pitt won 41-38 in triple overtime.

LORE Art "Pappy" Lewis was the man who put West Virginia football on the map. Though the Mountaineers had already appeared in and won three bowl games (1922 East-West against Gonzaga, 1938 Sun against Texas Tech, 1949 Sun against Texas-El Paso), it was Lewis who engineered the program's first true golden age. From 1952 through 1957, the school went 44–13–1, won 30 consecutive games in the Southern Conference and made its first major bowl appearance in the 1954 Sugar Bowl (a 42-19 loss to Georgia Tech).

QUIRK Todd Sauerbrun may well have been the most accomplished punter in college football history. As a senior in 1994, he set an NCAA record with a 48.4-yard punting average, which helped boost his career record to an NCAA-best 46.3 yards. During an otherwise dismal 31-0 loss to Nebraska during the 1994 Kickoff Classic, Sauerbrun booted a rocket that traveled 90 yards, one of 32 that traveled farther than 50 yards that year.

QUOTE "This really is almost heaven."—John Denver, before singing "Take Me Home, Country Roads" at the opening of Mountaineer Field in 1980

WEST VIRGINIA ANNUAL STATISTICAL LEADERS

YR	RUSHING	YDS	ATT	AVG	PASSING	ATT	CMP	PCT	YDS	RECEIVING	REC	YDS	AVG
1940	Glenn Ellis	272	62	4.4	Dick McElwee	18	8	.44	139	Bob Mellace	8	163	20.4
1941	Dick McElwee	457	115	4.0	William Bell	52	19	.37	198	Dick McElwee	8	97	12.1
1942		NA	NA	NA		NA	NA	NA	NA		NA	NA	NA
1943		NA	NA	NA		NA	NA	NA	NA		NA	NA	NA
1944		NA	NA	NA		NA	NA	NA	NA		NA	NA	NA
1945		NA	NA	NA		NA	NA	NA	NA		NA	NA	NA
1946	Jim Devonshire	228	67	3.4	Russell Combs	40	17	.43	204	Chet Spelock	7	76	10.9
1947	Rex Bumgardner	351	65	5.4	Russell Combs	60	29	.48	481	Bernie Huntz	8	206	25.8
1948	Victor Bonfili	535	125	4.3	Jimmy Walthall	178	89	.50	1,222	Victor Bonfili	24	244	10.2
1949	Pete Ziniach	546	129	4.2	Jimmy Walthall	152	65	.43	741	Clarence Cox	23	345	15.0
1950	Bill Lohr	287	75	3.8	Kent Barges	99	40	.40	661	Paul Bischoff	35	581	16.6
1951	Dick Luciani	523	105	5.0	Gerald Fisher	99	39	.39	591	Paul Bischoff	30	366	12.2
1952	Jack Stone	379	64	5.9	Fred Wyant	128	55	.43	867	Paul Bischoff	31	402	13.0
1953	Tommy Allman	501	88	5.7	Fred Wyant	102	41	.40	642	Bill Marker	16	301	18.8
1954	Dick Nicholson	416	62	6.7	Fred Wyant	97	40	.41	563	Bill Hillen	9	98	10.9
1955	Bob Moss	807	98	8.2	Fred Wyant	74	38	.51	591	Joe Kopnisky	12	141	11.8
1956	Larry Krutko	584	124	4.7	Mickey Trimarki	98	33	.34	419	Joe Kopnisky	19	295	15.5
1957	Larry Krutko	403	100	4.0	Dick Longfellow	78	32	.41	405	Ralph Anastasio	7	108	15.4
1958	Ray Peterson	333	81	4.1	Dick Longfellow	156	79	.51	948	Mel Reight	31	329	10.6
1959	Ray Peterson	505	116	4.4	Danny Williams	99	28	.28	310	John Marra	16	177	11.1
1960	Bob Benke	187	50	3.7	Dale Evans	85	34	.40	466	Bob Timmerman	9	99	11.0
1961	Glen Holton	372	79	4.7	Fred Colvard	71	31	.44	482	Steve Berzansky	10	116	11.6
1962	Tom Woodeshick	433	89	4.9	Jerry Yost	152	75	.49	1,134	Gene Heeter	19	284	14.9
1963	Dick Leftridge	393	79	5.0	Jerry Yost	140	62	.44	685	Steve Berzansky	12	125	10.4
1964	Dick Leftridge	534	125	4.3	Allen McCune	127	73	.57	1,034	Milt Clegg	31	437	14.1
1965	Garrett Ford Sr.	894	140	6.4	Allen McCune	182	91	.50	1,274	Bob Dunlevy	29	480	16.6
1966	Garrett Ford Sr.	1,068	236	4.5	Tom Digon	54	28	.52	323	Larry Sine	9	99	11.0
1967	Ben Siegfried	334	93	3.6	Tom Digon	108	62	.57	684	Oscar Patrick	19	326	17.2
1968	Eddie Silverio	559	143	3.9	Mike Sherwood	264	151	.57	1,998	Oscar Patrick	50	770	15.4
1969	Bob Gresham	1,155	206	5.6	Mike Sherwood	116	61	.53	773	Bob Gresham	15	147	9.8
1970	Bob Gresham	866	140	6.2	Mike Sherwood	193	117	.61	1,550	Chris Potts	31	346	11.2
1971	Kerry Marbury	890	145	6.1	Bernie Galiffa	238	121	.51	1,543	Harry Blake	27	388	14.4
1972	Kerry Marbury	775	150	5.2	Bernie Galiffa	334	164	.49	2,496	Marshall Mills	39	659	16.9
1973	Dwayne Woods	818	186	4.4	Ade Dillon	97	46	.47	762	Dave Jagdmann	30	424	14.1
1974	Artie Owens	1,130	174	6.5	Chuck Fiorante	87	43	.49	592	Marshall Mills	36	445	12.4
1975	Artie Owens	1,055	159	6.6	Dan Kendra	189	98	.52	1,315	Steve Lewis	21	296	14.1
1976	Dwayne Woods	588	121	4.9	Dan Kendra	233	113	.48	1,476	Steve Lewis	48	737	15.4
1977	Dave Riley	616	125	4.9	Dan Kendra	226	121	.54	1,674	Cedric Thomas	37	699	18.9
1978	Dane Conwell	412	88	4.7	Dutch Hoffman	238	105	.44	1,475	Steve Lewis	38	629	16.6
1979	Robert Alexander	656	118	5.6	Oliver Luck	231	103	.45	1,292	Darrell Miller	33	507	15.4
1980	Robert Alexander	1,064	204	5.2	Oliver Luck	254	135	.53	1,874	Cedric Thomas	31	607	19.6
1981	Curlin Beck	497	123	4.0	Oliver Luck	394	216	.55	2,448	Mark Raugh	64	601	9.4
1982	Curlin Beck	350	76	4.6	Jeff Hostetler	292	137	.47	1,916	Mark Raugh	32	423	13.2
1983	Tom Gray	498	110	4.5	Jeff Hostetler	309	173	.56	2,345	Rich Hollins	50	781	15.6
1984	Ron Wolfley	475	127	3.7	Kevin White	232	128	.55	1,727	Willie Drewrey	36	594	16.5
1985	John Holifield	595	140	4.3	Mike Timko	84	44	.52	567	Tom Gray	26	233	9.0
1986	Undra Johnson	652	138	4.7	Mike Timko	189	90	.48	1,191	Harvey Smith	28	456	16.3
1987	Anthony Brown	975	199	4.9	Major Harris	155	79	.51	1,200	John Talley	25	307	12.3
1988	Anthony Brown	962	178	5.4	Major Harris	186	105	.56	1,915	Calvin Phillips	24	611	25.5
1989	Major Harris	936	155	6.0	Major Harris	245	142	.58	2,058	Reggie Rembert	47	850	18.1
1990	Michael Beasley	607	125	4.9	Greg Jones	247	121	.49	1,481	James Jett	31	652	21.0
1991	Adrian Murrell	904	201	4.5	Darren Studstill	168	85	.51	1,055	Alex Shook	23	246	10.7
1992	Adrian Murrell	1,145	222	5.2	Darren Studstill	159	89	.56	1,065	Ed Hill	43	540	12.6
1993	Robert Walker	1,250	214	5.8	Jake Kelchner	174	110	.63	1,688	Mike Baker	42	714	17.0
1994	Robert Walker	749	179	4.2	Chad Johnston	242	124	.51	1,863	Rahsaan Vanterpool	50	849	17.0
1995	Robert Walker	508	122	4.2	Chad Johnston	248	127	.51	2,019	David Saunders	38	682	17.9
1996	Amos Zereoue	1,035	222	4.7	Chad Johnston	334	167	.50	1,958	David Saunders	76	1,043	13.7
1997	Amos Zereoue	1,589	281	5.7	Marc Bulger	323	192	.59	2,465	Shawn Foreman	77	928	12.1
1998	Amos Zereoue	1,462	283	5.2	Marc Bulger	419	274	.65	3,607	David Saunders	77	883	11.5
1999	Avon Cobourne	1,139	224	5.1	Marc Bulger	239	145	.61	1,729	Khori Ivy	53	666	12.6
2000	Avon Cobourne	1,018	224	4.5	Brad Lewis	238	123	.52	1,819	Antonio Brown	51	877	17.2
2001	Avon Cobourne	1,298	267	4.9	Brad Lewis	237	135	.57	1,339	A.J. Nastasi	42	334	8.0
2002	Avon Cobourne	1,710	335	5.1	Rasheed Marshall	259	139	.54	1,616	Miquelle Henderson	40	496	12.4
2003	Quincy Wilson	1,380	282	4.9	Rasheed Marshall	215	109	.51	1,729	Chris Henry	41	1,006	24.5
2004	Kay-Jay Harris	959	165	5.8	Rasheed Marshall	242	144	.60	1,886	Chris Henry	52	872	16.8

Receiving leaders by receptions
All statistics include postseason

WEST VIRGINIA ALL-TIME SCORES

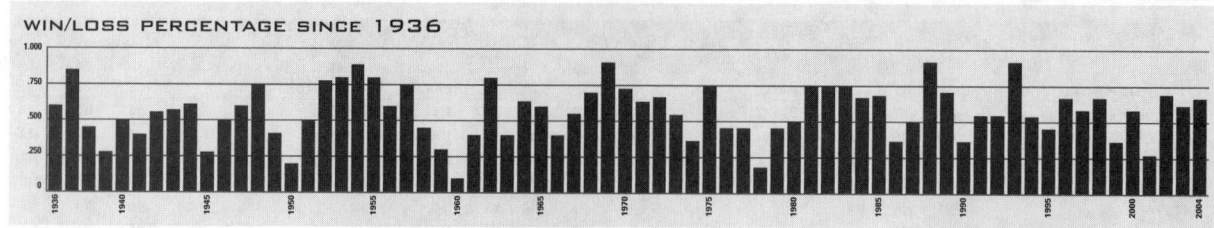

WIN/LOSS PERCENTAGE SINCE 1936

FREDERICK LINCOLN EMORY
1891 (.000)   0-1

1891
			0-1-0
N28		Wash. & Jeff.	0 72

1892
NO TEAM

F. WILLIAM "JOHN" RANE
1893-94 (.571)   4-3

1893
			2-1-0
O7	●	at Mt. Pleasant	12 0
N25	●	at Union Town	12 2
N30		at Wash. & Jeff.	0 58

1894
			2-2-0
O20	●	Mt Pleasant	16 0
O27		at Connelville	0 36
N10	●	Bethany	6 0
N17		at Marietta	6 16

HARRY McCRORY
1895 (.833)   5-1

1895
			5-1-0
O5	●	at Mt. Pleasant	6 0
O19	●	at Latrobe	10 0
O26	●	Pittsburgh	8 0
N9	●	at Marietta	6 0
N23	●	at Wash. & Jeff.	0 4
N27	●	at Wash. & Lee	28 6

THOMAS G. "DOGGY" TRENCHARD
1896 (.333)   3-7-2

1896
			3-7-2
S26	●	Grove City	6 0
O15		at Lafayette	0 18
O16		at Lafayette	0 6
O17		at Lafayette	0 34
O24	●	at Pittsburgh AC	4 0
N7	=	at Duquesne AC	0 0
N13		at Latrobe	0 5
N14	●	at Latrobe	4 0
N21		at Duquesne	0 6
N26	=	Pittsburgh AC AA	0 0
N26		at Mahoning CC	0 26
N30		at Centre	0 6

GEORGE R. KREBS
1897 (.550)   5-4-1

1897
			5-4-1
O6	●	at Marietta	6 0
O9		at Pittsbugh AC	0 5
O14	●	Westminster	18 0
O23		at Wash. & Jeff.	0 12
O30	=	at Pittsburg College	0 0
N4	●	at Wash. & Lee	14 0
N5		at Ohio U.	0 12
N6	●	at Ohio State	24 0 *
N17	●	at Bethany	30 0
N25		at Latrobe	0 16

HARRY ANDERSON
1898 (.857)   6-1

1898
			6-1-0
O7	●	Westminster	24 0
O15	●	at Marietta	6 5
O27		at Pittsburgh AC	0 18
O29	●	at Marietta	6 0
N4	●	at Pittsburgh	6 0 *
N14	●	at Virginia	6 0
N15	●	at Ohio U.	16 0

LOUIS YEAGER
1899, 1901-02 (.571)   12-9

1899
			2-3-0
O11	●	Grove City	6 0
O21		at Wash. & Jeff.	0 29
O23		at Marietta	5 23
N4	●	at Waynesburg	17 6
N30		at Waynesburg	0 20

JOHN E. HILL
1900 (.571)   4-3

1900
			4-3-0
O6	●	Pittsburgh	6 5
O20	●	Moneseen AC	24 6
O27	●	at Marietta	6 19
N3		at Ohio State	0 27
N5	●	at Ohio Wesleyan	6 5
N10	●	at California, Pa.	11 6
N17		at Wash. & Jeff.	0 36

LOUIS YEAGER

1901
			3-2-0
O5		Pittsburgh	0 12
O19	●	Grove City	37 0
N9	●	Westminster	31 0
N13		at Wash. & Jeff.	0 22
N24	●	Marietta	5 0

1902
			7-4-0
S27	●	Alumni	11 6
O4	●	Westminster	25 0
O11		at Ohio State	0 30
O18		Alumni	0 6
O22	●	at Pittsburgh	23 6
O24	●	at Marietta	12 6
N1		at Georgetown	0 5
N15	●	Grove City	53 0
N19		at Wash. & Jeff.	0 23
N22	●	at Wash. & Lee	17 5
N27	●	W. V. Wesleyan	78 0

H.E. TROUT
1903 (.875)   7-1

1903
			7-1-0
O3	●	Pittsburgh	24 6
O10	●	Grove City	21 0
O16	●	at Marietta	18 11
O19	●	at W.V. Weslayan	39 0
O24	●	Westminster	21 0
O31		at Ohio State	6 34
N14	●	at Bethany	11 5
N26	●	Wash. & Jeff.	6 0

ANTHONY CHEZ
1904 (.667)   6-3

1904
			6-3-0
S24	●	Westminster	15 0
O1	●	California, Pa.	16 0
O7	●	Ohio Wesleyan	19 11
O15		at Penn State	0 34
O22		at Michigan	0 130
N8		at Pittsburgh	0 53
N15	●	Alumni	18 0
N19	●	at Washington, Mo.	6 5
N24	●	at Marietta	25 0

CARL FORKUM
1905-06 (.684)   13-6

1905
			8-1-0
S30	●	Westminster	15 0
O7	●	Califonia, Pa.	12 0
O14	●	Ohio U.	28 0
O21	●	Bethany	46 0
N4	●	Kentucky	45 0
N11	●	at California, Pa.	17 10
N18	●	at Bethany	24 0
N25		at Penn State	0 6
N30	●	at Marietta	17 6

1906
			5-5-0
S29		Ohio U.	6 9
O6	●	Connelville	37 0
O13	●	California, Pa.	11 0
O20		at Marietta	2 4
O27	●	Grove City	25 0
N3	●	Carnigie Tech	51 0
N10		at Pittsburgh	0 17
N11	●	W. V. Wesleyan	54 4
N23		at Penn State	0 10 *
N29		at Wash. & Jeff.	6 29

CLARENCE RUSSELL
1907 (.600)   6-4

1907
			6-4-0
S28	●	Ohio U.	35 5
O2	●	Parkersburg YMCA	55 0
O5	●	Cal St. Pa.	36 0
O16	●	W. V. Wesleyan	65 0
O26		at Marietta	2 4
N2		at Navy	0 6
N9		at Pittsburgh	0 10
N16	●	Westminster	27 0
N28		at Wash. & Jeff.	5 13
N29	●	Alumni	11 0

C.A. LEUDER
1908-11 (.561)   17-13-3

1908
			5-3-0
S26		at Pennsylvania	0 6
O17	●	at Carnegie Tech	16 0
O24		at Penn State	0 12
O31	●	at Marietta	12 0
N7		at Pittsburgh	0 11
N14	●	Pitt. Lyceum	4 0
N21	●	Bethany	47 0
N28	●	Westminster	22 0

1909
			4-3-2
O2	●	Waynesburg	15 0
O9		at Pennsylvania	0 12
O16	●	Slippery Rock	40 5
O23	=	Bucknell	6 6
O30	●	Marietta PAR	3 0
N6	=	Pittsburgh	0 0
N13		at Penn State	0 40
N17	●	W.V. Wesleyan	49 0
N25	●	Wash. & Jeff.	5 18

1910
			2-4-1
O1	●	Westminster	6 0
O8		at Pennsylvania	0 38
O15	=	Bethany	0 0
O22		Bucknell	0 9
O29		at Marietta	5 10
N5		at Pittsburgh	0 38
N12	●	at Bethany	9 0

1911
			6-3-0
S30	●	Waynesburg	17 0
O14	●	Ohio U.	3 0
O21	●	Westminster	3 0
O28	●	Marshall	17 15
N4	●	Wash. & Jeff.	6 5
N11		at Navy	0 32
N18	●	Allegheny	6 10
N25	●	W.V. Wesleyan	36 0
N30		at Denison	3 5

W.P. EDMUNDS
1912 (.667)   6-3

1912
			6-3-0
O5	●	W. V. Wesleyan	14 19
O12	●	Westminster	7 0
O13	●	Geneva	20 13
O26	●	Ohio U.	6 0
N2	●	Allegheny	8 7
N9	●	at Marietta	22 6
N16		at Virginia Tech	0 41
N23	●	Waynesburg	48 0
N28		at Denison	6 17

E.R. SWEETLAND
1913 (.444)   3-4-2

1913
			3-4-2
S27	●	Davidson & Elkins	43 0
O4	●	Waynesburg	45 0
O11		at Pittsburgh	0 40
O18	●	W.V. Wesleyan FAI	0 21
O25	=	Morris-Harvey	0 0
N1	=	Marietta	14 14
N8		Wash. & Jeff.	0 34
N15		Wash. & Lee CHWV	0 28
N27	●	Villanova	70

SOL METZGER
1914-15 (.618)   10-6-1

1914
			5-4-0
O3	●	Marshall	20 0
O10	●	Bethany	13 0
O17	●	Dusquesne	37 0
O22		at North Carolina St.	13 26
O31		at Wash. & Jeff.	0 48
N7	●	Davis & Elkins	55 0
N14		Wash. & Lee CHWV	6 8
N21	●	Marietta CLK	6 0
N26		W.V. Wesleyan FAI	9 14

1915
			5-2-1
S25		at Pennsylvania	0 7
O2	=	Wash. & Jeff.	6 6
O16	●	Geneva	33 0
O23		Wash. & Lee	0 1 f
N6	●	at Marshall	92 6
N13	●	Virginia Tech	19 0
N19	●	Marietta PAR	28 0
N25	●	W. V. Wesleyan FAI	30 0

MONT McINTIRE
1916-20 (.667)   24-11-4

1916
			5-2-2
S30		at Pennsylvania	0 3
O14	●	Virginia Tech	20 0
O21		at Navy	7 12
O28	●	Davis & Elkins	58 0
N4	●	Gettysburg	12 6
N11	=	at Rutgers	0 0
N18	=	at Dartmouth	7 7
N25	●	Catholic	40 3
N30	●	W. V. Wesleyan FAI	54 7

1917
			6-3-1
S29		Pittsburgh	9 14
O6	●	at Navy	7 0
O13	●	Carlisle	21 0
O20		at Dartmouth	2 6
O27	●	Gettysburg	60 0
N3	=	at Rutgers	7 7
N10	●	Virginia Tech HUN	27 3
N17	●	Wash. & Jeff. FAI	7 0
N24		W.V. Wesleyan CLK	0 20
N29	●	North Carolina St.	21 0

1918
NO TEAM WWI

1919
			8-2-0
S27	●	Marietta	61 0
O4	●	Westminster	55 0
O11		at Pittsburgh	0 26
O18	●	at Maryland	27 0
O25	●	Bethany WHE	60 0
N1	●	at Princeton	25 0
N8		Centre CHWV	6 14
N15	●	at Rutgers	30 7
N22	●	Ohio Wesleyan	55 0
N25	●	Wash. & Jeff.	7 0

1920 — 5-4-1

S25	●	W.V. Wesleyan Fai	14	0
O2	=	Lehigh	7	7
O9		at Pittsburgh	13	34
O16	●	George Washington	81	0
O23		at Yale	0	24
O30		at Princeton	3	10
N6	●	Wash. & Lee ChWV	14	10
N13	●	Rutgers	17	0
N20	●	Bethany	20	0
N25		at Wash. & Jeff.	0	28

CLARENCE SPEARS
1921-24 (.808) 30-6-3

1921 — 5-4-1

S24	●	W. V. Wesleyan Fai	34	3
O1	●	Cincinnati	50	0
O8		at Pittsburgh	14	21 *
O15	●	Ohio U.	7	0
O22	=	Bucknell	0	0
O29		at Lehigh	12	21
N5	●	Wash. & Lee ChWV	28	7
N12	●	at Virginia	7	0
N19		at Rutgers	7	17
N24		Wash. & Jeff.	0	13

1922 — 10-0-1

S30	●	W. V. Wesleyan Fai	20	3
O7	●	Marietta	55	0
O14	●	at Pittsburgh	9	6
O21	=	Wash. & Lee ChWV	12	12
O28	●	Rutgers	28	0
N4	●	at Cincinnati	34	0
N11	●	at Indiana	33	0
N18	●	Virginia	13	0
N25	●	Ohio U.	28	0
N30	●	Wash. & Jeff.	14	0
		EAST-WEST BOWL		
D25	●	Gonzaga	21	13

1923 — 7-1-1

S24	●	W. V. Wesleyan Fai	21	7
O6	●	Allegheny	28	0
O13	●	at Pittsburgh	13	7
O20	●	Marshall	81	0
O27	=	Penn State Brnx	13	13
N6	●	Rutgers NYC	27	7
N10	●	Wash. & Lee ChWV	63	0
N17	●	St. Louis	49	0
N29		Wash. & Jeff.	2	7

1924 — 8-1-0

S27	●	W. V. Wesleyan	21	6
O4	●	Allegheny	35	6
O11		at Pittsburgh	7	14
O18	●	Geneva	55	0
O25	●	Centre NYC	13	6
N1	●	Bethany	71	6
N8	●	Colgate	34	2
N15	●	Wash. & Lee ChWV	6	0
N27	●	Wash. & Jeff.	40	7

IRA ERRETT RODGERS
1925-30, '43-45 (.578) 44-31-8

1925 — 8-1-0

S26	●	Allegheny Eri	18	0
O3	●	Davis & Elkins	6	0
O10		at Pittsburgh	7	15
O17	●	Grove City	54	3
O24	●	W.V. Wesleyan	16	0
O31	●	Wash. & Lee ChWV	21	0
N7	●	at Boston College	21	0
N14	●	Penn State	14	0
N26	●	Wash. & Jeff.	19	0

1926 — 6-4-0

S25	●	Davis & Elkins	18	6
O2	●	Wash. & Lee ChWV	18	0
O9	●	Allegheny	54	0
O16	●	at Georgetown	13	10
O23	●	W. V. Wesleyan	7	0
O30		Missouri	0	27
N6		at Pittsburgh	7	17
N13	●	Centre Par	21	0
N20		at Carnegie Tech	0	20
N25		Wash. & Jeff.	3	13

1927 — 2-4-3

S24	●	W. V. Wesleyan	27	7
O1	=	Wash. & Lee ChWV	6	6
O8		at Pittsburgh	0	40
O15	=	Lafayette	7	7
O22		at Georgetown	0	25
O29		Carnegie Tech	7	13
N5		at Missouri	0	13
N12	●	Davis & Elkins	15	12
N24	=	Wash. & Jeff.	6	6

1928 — 8-2-0

S22		Davis & Elkins	0	7
S29	●	W.V. Wesleyan	12	0
O6	●	Haskell Whe	28	7
O13	●	at Pittsburgh	9	6
O20	●	Wash. & Lee ChWV	22	0
O27	●	at Lafayette	17	0
N6	●	Fordham Brnx	18	0
N10	●	Oklahoma State	32	6
N17		at Georgetown	0	12
N29	●	Wash. & Jeff.	14	0

1929 — 4-3-3

S21	●	W. V. Wesleyan	16	0
S28		Davis & Elkins	6	13
O5	=	Duquesne	7	7
O12		at Pittsburgh	7	27
O19	●	Wash. & Lee ChWV	26	6
O26	●	at Oklahoma State	9	6
N5	=	Fordham NYC	0	0
N9		Detroit	0	36
N16	=	at Georgetown	0	0
N28	●	Wash. & Jeff.	6	0

1930 — 5-5-0

S19	●	at Duquesne	7	0
S27	●	W. V. Wesleyan	26	0
O4		Pittsburgh	0	16
O11	●	Wash. & Lee ChWV	33	13
O17		at Detroit	0	23
O24	●	at Georgetown	14	7
N1		Fordham NYC	2	18
N8	●	Kansas State	23	7
N22		Wash. & Jeff.	6	7
N27		Oregon State Chi	0	12

EARLE "GREASY" NEALE
1931-33 (.435) 12-16-3

1931 — 4-6-0

S26	●	Duquesne	14	6
O3		Fordham NYC	7	20
O10		at Pittsburgh	0	34
O17	●	Wash. & Lee ChWV	19	0
O23		at Detroit	7	9
O31		Kansas State	0	19
N7	●	W. V. Wesleyan	12	7
N14		at Georgetown	0	13
N21	●	Penn State	19	0
N28		Wash. & Jeff. Whe	13	14

1932 — 5-5-0

S23		at Duquesne	0	3
O1		Pittsburgh	0	40
O7		at Temple	13	14
O15	●	W. V. Wesleyan	14	0
O21		at Detroit	13	26
O29	●	at Marquette	34	7
N5	●	Georgetown	19	0
N12	●	Wash. & Lee ChWV	19	0
N19	●	Davis & Elkins	25	12
N26		Wash. & Jeff. Whe	0	13

1933 — 3-5-3

S23	=	Wash. & Lee ChWV	0	0
S29		at Duquesne	7	19
O7		at Pittsburgh	0	21
O14		Fordham NYC	0	20
O21		at Temple	7	13
O28	=	Davis & Elkins	7	7
N4	=	Marquette	13	13
N11		at Wisconsin	6	25
N18	●	W. V. Wesleyan	26	13
N25	●	at Georgetown	14	12
N30	●	Wash. & Jeff.	7	2

CHARLES C. "TRUSTY" TALLMAN
1934-36 (.552) 15-12-2

1934 — 6-4-0

S22	●	W. V. Wesleyan	19	0
S28	●	at Duquesne	7	0
O6		Pittsburgh	6	27
O13	●	Wash. & Lee ChWV	12	0
O19		at Temple	13	28
O27	●	Davis & Elkins	12	7
N3	●	Ohio U. Par	7	2
N10		Fordham NYC	20	27
N17		George Washington	7	10
N29	●	Wash. & Jeff. AtC	14	12

1935 — 3-4-2

S28	=	W. V. Wesleyan	0	0
O5	●	at Davis & Elkins	20	0
O12		at Pittsburgh	6	24
O18		at George Washington	7	15
O26		Temple	6	19
N2	●	Wash. & Lee ChWV	20	0
N16		Duquesne	0	19
N23	●	Wash. & Jeff.	51	0
N28	=	at Loyola-New Orleans	19	19

1936 — 6-4-0

S19	●	Waynesburg	7	0
S26	●	at Cincinnati	40	6
O3		at Pittsburgh	0	34
O10	●	Wash. & Lee ChWV	28	7
O17	●	W. V. Wesleyan	15	0
O24	●	Centre Lou	26	13
O31	●	Western Maryland	33	20
N7		Georgetown	0	28
N14		at Western Reserve	0	7
N26		at George Washington	2	7

MARSHALL "LITTLE SLEEPY" GLENN
1937-39 (.534) 14-12-3

1937 — 8-1-1

S25	●	at W. V. Wesleyan	14	0
O2		Pittsburgh	0	20
O9	●	Wash. & Lee ChWV	6	0
O16	●	at Xavier	13	7
O23	●	Waynesburg	13	0
O30	●	Western Maryland Balt	64	0
N6	=	at Georgetown	6	6
N13	●	Toledo	34	0
N25	●	George Washington	26	0
		SUN BOWL		
J1	●	Texas Tech	7	6

1938 — 4-5-1

S24		at Pittsburgh	0	19
O1	●	W. V. Wesleyan	38	6
O8	=	Wash. & Lee ChWV	6	6
O15		Michigan State	0	26
O22	●	at Creighton	20	13
O29	●	Youngstown St.	27	7
N5		at Western Reserve	0	7
N12		Georgetown	0	14
N19		Manhattan Brnx	0	13
N24	●	at George Washington	7	6

1939 — 2-6-1

S30	●	W. V. Wesleyan	44	0
O7		at Pittsburgh	0	20
O14	●	at Cincinnati	7	0
O21		Wash. & Lee ChWV	0	9
O27	=	South Carolina Ora	6	6
N4		at Georgetown	0	14
N11		Manhattan	7	19
N18		at Kentucky	6	13
D2		George Washington	0	13

WILLIAM F. "BILL" KERN
1940-42, '46-47 (.510) 24-23-1

1940 — 4-4-1

S28	●	Westminster	47	0
O5		Fordham NYC	7	20
O12		at Penn State	13	17
O19	●	W. V. Wesleyan	32	0
O25		at George Washington	0	19
N2	●	Wash. & Lee ChWV	12	7
N9	=	Cincinnati	7	7
N17	●	Kentucky	9	7
N23		at Michigan State	0	17

1941 — 4-6-0

S27	●	Waynesburg	13	7
O4		at Navy	0	40
O11	●	W. V. Wesleyan	20	0
O18		Fordham NYC	0	27
O25		at Kentucky	6	18
N1	●	Wash. & Lee ChWV	7	6
N8	●	Kansas	21	0
N15		at Penn State	0	7
N22		at Army	6	7
N29		Michigan State	12	14

1942 — 5-4-0

S26	●	Wash. & Lee ChWV	21	7
O3		at Boston College	0	33
O10	●	South Carolina	13	0
O17		Fordham NYC	14	23
O24	●	Waynesburg	27	0
O31	●	Penn State	24	0
N14	●	at Kentucky	7	0
N21		at Michigan State	0	7
N28		at Miami, Fla.	13	21

IRA ERRETT RODGERS

1943 — 4-3-0

O2		Virginia ChWV	0	6
O9		at Pittsburgh	0	20
O16	●	Maryland	6	2
O23	●	Carnegie Tech	32	0
O30		at Penn State	7	32
N6	●	at Lehigh	53	6
N13	●	Bethany	26	13

1944 — 5-3-1

S23		at Pittsburgh	13	26
S30	●	Case	32	7
O7		Virginia ChWV	6	24
O14	=	at Maryland	6	6
O21	●	Bethany	20	0
O28	●	at Penn State	28	27
N4	●	Temple	6	0
N11	●	Lehigh	71	0
N18		at Kentucky	9	40

1945 — 2-6-1

S22	●	Otterbien	42	7
S29		at Pittsburgh	0	20
O6	●	Drexel	42	0
O12		at Syracuse	0	12
O19		at Temple	12	28
O27	=	Maryland	13	13
N3		Virginia ChWV	7	13
N10		Kentucky	6	19
N17		Ohio U.	0	14

WILLIAM F. "BILL" KERN

1946 — 5-5-0

S21	●	Otterbien	13	7
S28		at Pittsburgh	7	33
O5	●	Waynesburg	42	0
O12	●	Wash. & Lee ChWV	6	0
O18		at Temple	0	6
O26	●	Syracuse	13	0
N2		at Army	0	19
N9	●	Fordham	39	0
N16		at Kentucky	0	13
N23		at Virginia	0	21

1947 — 6-4-0

S27	●	Otterbien	59	0
O4	●	Wash. & Lee ChWV	35	6
O11	●	Waynesburg	60	7
O18	●	at NYU	40	0
O25		at Penn State	14	21
N1		Maryland DC	0	27
N8		Kentucky	6	15
N15		Virginia	0	6
N22	●	Temple	21	0
N29	●	at Pittsburgh	17	2

DUDLEY S. DeGROOT
1948-49 (.587) 13-9-1

1948 — 9-3-0

S19	●	Waynesburg	29	16
S25	●	Wooster	34	6
O2	●	Temple Her	27	7
O9		at Pittsburgh	6	16
O16		at Penn State	7	37
O23	●	Wash. & Lee ChWV	14	7
O30	●	South Carolina	35	12
N6	●	Ohio U.	48	6
N13		at Virginia	0	7
N20	●	Western Reserve	20	0
N27	●	Maryland	16	14
		SUN BOWL		
J1	●	Texas El Paso	21	12

1949 — 4-6-1

S17	●	Waynesburg	42	7
S24		at Ohio U.	7	17
O1	●	Wash. & Lee ChWV	28	20
O8		Pittsburgh	7	20
O14		at Boston U.	20	52
O22	●	Quantico Marines	47	26
O29		at Virginia	14	19
N5		Penn State	14	34
N12	=	Texas El Paso	13	13
N19	●	at Western Reserve	28	20
N24		at Maryland	7	47

1950-1967
SOUTHERN

ART "PAPPY" LEWIS
1950-59 (.602) 58-38-2

1950 — 2-8-0 (1-3-0)

S23	●	Western Reserve	38	13
S30	|	Wash. & Lee Lyn	7	26
O6	|	at George Washington	14	21
O14	● |	Richmond	46	7
O21		Fordham	23	27
O28		Virginia	21	28
N4		at Pittsburgh	7	21
N11		at Penn State	0	27
N18	|	Maryland	0	41
N25		at Texas El Paso	7	48

1951 5-5-0 (2-3-0)

S22	●	Waynesburg	20	9
S28	● |	at Furman	18	7
O6	|	Wash. & Lee	0	34
O13	● |	Richmond	24	0
O20	●	Geneva	89	0
O27		at Penn State	7	13
N3	●	Western Reserve	35	7
N10	|	South Carolina	13	34
N17		at Pittsburgh	12	32
N24	|	at Maryland	7	54

1952 7-2-0 (5-1-0)

S27	|	Furman	14	22
O4	●	Waynesburg	49	12
O11		Penn State	21	35
O18	● |	Wash. & Leen CMB	31	13
O25	●	at Pittsburgh	16	0
N1	● |	George Washington	24	0
N8	● |	VMI ROA	39	21
N15	● |	Virginia Tech	27	7
N22	● |	at South Carolina	13	6

1953 8-2-0 (4-0-0)

S26	●	at Pittsburgh	17	7
O3	●	Waynesburg	47	19
O10	● |	Wash. & Lee	40	14
O16	● |	at George Washington	27	6
O24	● |	VMI	52	20
O31	●	at Penn State	20	19
N7	● |	Virginia Tech BLU	12	7
N14		South Carolina	14	20
N21	●	at North Carolina St.	61	0
		SUGAR BOWL		
J1		Georgia Tech	19	42

1954 8-1-0 (3-0-0)

O2	●	at South Carolina	26	6
O9	● |	George Washington	13	7
O16	●	at Penn State	19	14
O23	● |	VMI BLU	40	6
O30		Pittsburgh	10	13
N6	●	Fordham	39	9
N13	● |	at William & Mary	20	6
N20	●	North Carolina St.	28	3
N27	●	at Virginia	14	10

1955 8-2-0 (4-0-0)

S24	● |	Richmond	33	12
O1	●	Wake Forest	46	0
O8	● |	VMI BLU	47	12
O15	● |	William & Mary	39	13
O22	●	Penn State	21	7
O29	●	at Marquette	39	0
N4	● |	at George Washington	13	7
N12		at Pittsburgh	7	26
N19		Syracuse	13	20
N25	●	at North Carolina St.	27	7

1956 6-4-0 (5-0-0)

S22		Pittsburgh	13	14
S29	● |	Richmond	30	6
O6	●	at Texas	7	6
O13		at Syracuse	20	27
O20	● |	at William & Mary	20	13
O27		at Penn State	6	16
N3	● |	George Washington	14	0
N10	● |	VMI	13	6
N17	● |	Furman	7	0
N23		at Miami, Fla.	0	18

1957 7-2-1 (3-0-0)

S21	=	Virginia	6	6
S28	● |	Virginia Tech	14	0
O5		at Wisconsin	13	45
O12	●	at Boston U.	46	6
O18	● |	at George Washington	34	14
O26	● |	William & Mary	19	0
N2		at Penn State	6	27
N9	●	at Pittsburgh	7	6
N16	●	at Wake Forest	27	14
N23	●	Syracuse	7	0

1958 4-5-1 (4-0-0)

S20	● |	Richmond	66	22
S27		at Oklahoma	14	47
O4		at Indiana	12	13
O11		Boston U.	30	36
O18		at Pittsburgh	8	15
O25	● |	Virginia Tech RICH	21	20
N1	● |	George Washington	35	12
N8	=	Penn State	14	14
N15	● |	at William & Mary	56	6
N22		Syracuse	12	15

1959 3-7-0 (2-2-0)

S19		at Maryland	7	27
S26	● |	Richmond	10	7
O2	● |	at George Washington	10	8
O9		at Boston U.	0	7
O17	●	Pittsburgh	23	15
O24		at Syracuse	0	44
O31		Penn State	10	28
N7		at Southern Cal	0	36
N14	|	Virginia Tech	0	12
N21	|	Citadel	14	20

GENE CORUM
1960-65 (.492) 29-30-2

1960 0-8-2 (0-2-1)

S17		Maryland	8	31
S24	|	Virginia Tech RICH	0	15
O1		at Illinois	0	33
O8	= |	Richmond	6	6
O15		at Pittsburgh	0	42
O22		Syracuse	0	45
O29		at Penn State	13	34
N5	=	Boston U.	7	7
N12		Oregon PORT	6	20
N19	|	George Washington	0	26

1961 4-6-0 (2-1-0)

S16	|	Richmond	26	35
S23		at Vanderbilt	6	16
S30		at Syracuse	14	29
O7	● |	Virginia Tech	28	0
O14	●	at Pittsburgh	20	6
O21		at Boston U.	6	12
O28	●	at Army	7	3
N4	● |	at George Washington	12	7
N11		Penn State	6	20
N18		Indiana	9	17

1962 8-2-0 (4-0-0)

S22	●	Vanderbilt	26	0
S29	● |	Virginia Tech RICH	14	0
O6	●	Boston U.	7	0
O13	●	at Pittsburgh	15	8
O20	● |	George Washington	27	25
O27		Oregon State PORT	22	51
N3	● |	William & Mary	28	13
N10		at Penn State	6	34
N17	● |	Citadel	49	0
N24	●	at Syracuse	17	6

1963 4-6-0 (3-1-0)

S21		Navy	7	51
S28	●	Boston U.	34	0
O5		Oregon	0	35
O12	● |	William & Mary	20	16
O19		Pittsburgh	10	13
O26		Penn State	9	20
N2	● |	George Washington	20	16
N9		Syracuse	13	15
N16	|	Virginia Tech	3	28
N28	● |	Furman	38	7

1964 7-4-0 (5-0-0)

S19	● |	at Richmond	20	10
S26	● |	Citadel	7	3
O3		at Rice	0	24
O10		at Pittsburgh	0	14
O17	● |	at Virginia Tech	23	10
O24		Penn State	8	37
O31	●	Kentucky	26	21
N7	● |	at George Washington	20	19
N14	● |	William & Mary	24	14
N21	●	Syracuse	28	27
		LIBERTY BOWL		
D19		Utah	6	32

1965 6-4-0 (4-0-0)

S19	● |	Richmond	56	0
S25	● |	at William & Mary	34	14
O2	●	Pittsburgh	63	48
O9	● |	at Citadel	25	2
O16		Virginia RICH	0	41
O23		at Penn State	6	44
O30		at Kentucky	8	28
N6	●	Virginia Tech	31	22
N13		Syracuse	19	41
N20	● |	George Washington	37	24

JIM CARLEN
1966-69 (.646) 25-13-3

1966 3-5-2 (3-0-0)

S17		at Duke	15	34
S24	● |	William & Mary	24	13
O1	=	at Virginia Tech	13	13
O8		at Pittsburgh	14	17
O15		at Maryland	9	28
O22		Penn State	6	38
O29	=	Kentucky	14	14
N5	● |	Citadel	35	0
N12	● |	at George Washington	21	6
N19		Syracuse	7	34

1967 5-4-1 (3-0-1)

S9	●	Villanova	40	0
S16	● |	at Richmond	27	6
S23	● |	VMI	21	9
S30		at Syracuse	6	23
O7	●	Pittsburgh	15	0
O21		at Penn State	14	21
O28		Virginia Tech	7	20
N4		at Kentucky	7	22
N11	= |	at William & Mary	16	16
N18	● |	Davidson	35	0

1968-1990
INDEPENDENT

1968 7-3-0

S21	●	Richmond	17	0
S28	●	at Pittsburgh	38	15
O5		Penn State	20	31
O11	●	VMI ROA	14	7
O19	●	William & Mary RICH	20	0
O26		at Virginia Tech	12	27
N2		Kentucky	16	35
N9	●	at Citadel	17	0
N16	●	Villanova	30	20
N23	●	Syracuse	23	6

1969 10-1-0

S13	●	Cincinnati	57	11
S20	●	Maryland	31	7
S27	●	at Tulane	35	17
O4	●	VMI	32	0
O11		at Penn State	0	20
O25	●	Pittsburgh	49	18
N1	●	at Kentucky	7	6
N8	●	at William & Mary	31	0
N15	●	Richmond	33	21
N22	●	at Syracuse	13	10
		PEACH BOWL		
D30	●	South Carolina	14	3

BOBBY BOWDEN
1970-75 (.618) 42-26

1970 8-3-0

S12	●	William & Mary	43	7
S19	●	Richmond	49	10
S26	●	VMI	47	10
O3	●	at Indiana	16	10
O10		Duke	13	21
O17		at Pittsburgh	35	36
O24	●	Colorado St	24	21
O31		at Penn State	8	42
N7	●	at East Carolina	28	14
N14	●	Syracuse	28	19
N28	●	at Maryland	20	10

1971 7-4-0

S11	●	Boston College	45	14
S18		at California	10	20
S25	●	at Richmond	16	3
O2	●	Pittsburgh	20	9
O9	●	at William & Mary	28	23
O16	●	East Carolina	44	21
O23	●	Temple	43	33
O30		Penn State	7	35
N6		at Duke	15	31
N13	●	VMI	28	3
N20		at Syracuse	24	28

1972 8-4-0

S9	●	Villanova	25	6
S16	●	Richmond	28	7
S23	●	at Virginia	48	10
S30		at Stanford	35	41
O7	●	William & Mary	49	34
O14		at Temple	36	39
O21	●	Tulane	31	19
O28		Penn State	19	28
N4	●	at Pittsburgh	38	20
N11	●	VMI	50	24
N18	●	Syracuse	43	12
		PEACH BOWL		
D29		North Carolina St.	13	49

1973 6-5-0

S15	●	at Maryland	20	13
S22	●	Virginia Tech	24	10
S29	●	at Illinois	17	10
O6		Indiana	14	28
O13		Pittsburgh	7	35
O20		at Richmond	17	38
O27		at Penn State	14	62
N2	●	at Miami, Fla.	20	14
N10		Boston College	13	25
N17	●	Virginia	42	17
N24	●	at Syracuse	24	14

1974 4-7-0

S14		Richmond	25	29
S21	●	Kentucky	16	3
S28		at Tulane	14	17
O5	●	at Indiana	24	0
O12		at Pittsburgh	14	31
O19		Miami, Fla.	20	21
O26		Penn State	12	21
N2		at Boston College	3	35
N9	●	Syracuse	39	11
N16		Temple	21	35
N23	●	at Virginia Tech	22	21

1975 9-3-0

S13	●	Temple	50	7
S20	●	at California	28	10
S27	●	Boston College	35	18
O4	●	at SMU	28	22
O11		at Penn State	0	39
O18		Tulane	14	16
O24	●	Virginia Tech	10	7
N1	●	Kent	38	13
N8	●	Pittsburgh	17	14
N15	●	at Richmond	31	13
N22		at Syracuse	19	20
		PEACH BOWL		
D31	●	North Carolina St.	13	10

FRANK CIGNETTI
1976-79 (.386) 17-27

1976 5-6-0

S11	●	Villanova	28	7
S18		Maryland	3	24
S25		at Kentucky	10	14
O2	●	Richmond	9	6
O9	●	at Temple	42	0
O16		at Boston College	3	14
O23		Penn State	0	33
O30		at Virginia Tech	7	24
N6	●	at Tulane	32	28
N13		at Pittsburgh	16	24
N20	●	Syracuse	34	28

1977 5-6-0

S10	●	Richmond	36	0
S17	●	at Maryland	24	16
S24		at Kentucky	13	28
O1	●	at Virginia	13	0
O8	●	Temple	38	16
O15		Boston College	24	28
O22		at Penn State	28	49
O29		Villanova	36	41
N5		Pittsburgh	3	44
N12	●	Virginia Tech	20	14
N19		at Syracuse	9	28

1978 2-9-0

S9	●	Richmond	14	12
S16		at Oklahoma	10	52
S23		at North Carolina St.	15	29
S30		California	21	28
O7		Syracuse	15	31
O14		at Virginia Tech	3	16
O21		at Temple	27	28
O28		Penn State	21	49
N4	●	Virginia	20	17
N11		at Pittsburgh	7	52
N18		at Colorado State	14	50

1979 5-6-0

S8		Temple	16	38
S15		Syracuse ERUT	14	24
S22		North Carolina St.	14	38
S29	●	at Richmond	20	18
O6	●	Kentucky	10	6
O13	●	at Boston College	20	18
O20	●	Tulane	27	17
O27		at Penn State	6	31
N3	●	Virginia Tech	34	23
N10		Pittsburgh	17	24
N17		at Arizona State	7	42

DON NEHLEN
1980-2000 (.614) 149-93-4

1980 6-6-0

S6 ●	Cincinnati	41	27
S13 ●	at Colorado State	52	24
S20	Maryland	11	14
S27 ●	Richmond	31	28
O4 ●	Virginia	45	21
O11	at Hawaii	13	16
O18	at Pittsburgh	14	42
O25	Penn State	15	20
N1	at Virginia Tech	11	34
N8 ●	at Temple	41	28
N15 ●	at Rutgers	24	15
N22	Syracuse	7	20

1981 9-3-0

S12 ●	at Virginia	32	18
S19 ●	at Maryland	17	13
S26 ●	Colorado State	49	3
O3 ●	at Boston College	38	10
O10	Pittsburgh	0	17
O17 ●	Virginia Tech	27	6
O24	at Penn State	7	30
O31 ●	East Carolina	20	3
N7 ●	Temple	24	19
N14 ●	Rutgers	20	3
N21	at Syracuse	24	27
	PEACH BOWL		
D31 ●	Florida	26	6

1982 9-3-0

S11 ●	at Oklahoma	41	27
S18 ●	Maryland	19	18
S25 ●	Richmond	43	10
O2	at Pittsburgh	13	16
O9 ●	Boston College	20	13
O16 ●	at Virginia Tech	16	6
O23	Penn State	0	24
O30 ●	East Carolina	30	3
N6 ●	at Temple	20	17
N11 ●	Rutgers *ERut*	44	17
N20 ●	Syracuse	26	0
	GATOR BOWL		
D30	Florida State	12	31

1983 9-3-0

S3 ●	Ohio U.	55	3
S10 ●	Pacific	48	7
S17 ●	at Maryland	31	21
S24 ●	at Boston College	27	17
O1 ●	Pittsburgh	24	21
O15 ●	Virginia Tech	13	0
O22	at Penn State	23	41
O29	at Miami, Fla.	3	20
N5 ●	Temple	27	9
N12 ●	Rutgers	35	7
N19	at Syracuse	16	27
	HALL OF FAME CLASSIC		
D22 ●	Kentucky	20	16

1984 8-4-0

S1 ●	Ohio U.	38	0
S8 ●	Louisville	30	6
S15 ●	at Virginia Tech	14	7
S22	Maryland	17	20
S29 ●	at Pittsburgh	28	10
O13 ●	Syracuse	20	10
O20 ●	Boston College	21	20
O27 ●	Penn State	17	14
N3	Virginia	7	27
N10	Rutgers *ERut*	19	23
N17	at Temple	17	19
	BLUEBONNET BOWL		
D31 ●	TCU	31	14

1985 7-3-1

S7 ●	Louisville	52	13
S14 ●	Duke	20	18
S21	at Maryland	0	28
S28 =	Pittsburgh	10	10
O5 ●	Virginia Tech	24	9
O19 ●	at Boston College	13	6
O26	at Penn State	0	27
N2	at Virginia	7	27
N9 ●	Rutgers	27	0
N16 ●	Temple	23	10
N30 ●	at Syracuse	13	10

1986 4-7-0

S6 ●	Northern Illinois	47	14
S13 ●	at East Carolina	24	21
S20	Maryland	3	24
S27	at Pittsburgh	16	48
O4	at Virginia Tech	7	13
O11	Miami, Fla.	14	58
O25	Boston College	10	19
N1	Penn State	0	19
N8 ●	Rutgers *ERut*	24	17
N15 ●	at Louisville	42	19
N22	Syracuse	23	34

1987 6-6-0

S5 ●	Ohio U.	23	3
S12	at Ohio State	3	24
S19	at Maryland	20	25
S26	Pittsburgh	3	6
O3 ●	East Carolina	49	0
O17 ●	Cincinnati	45	17
O24 ●	at Boston College	37	16
O31	at Penn State	21	25
N7 ●	Virginia Tech	28	16
N14 ●	Rutgers	37	13
N21	at Syracuse	31	32
	SUN BOWL		
D25	Oklahoma State	33	35

1988 11-1-0

S3 ●	Bowling Green	62	14
S10 ●	Fullerton St.	45	10
S17 ●	Maryland	55	24
S24 ●	at Pittsburgh	31	10
O1 ●	at Virginia Tech	22	10
O8 ●	at East Carolina	30	10
O22 ●	Boston College	59	19
O29 ●	Penn State	51	30
N5 ●	at Cincinnati	51	13
N12 ●	Rutgers *ERut*	35	25
N19 ●	Syracuse	31	9
	FIESTA BOWL		
J2	Notre Dame	21	34

1989 8-3-1

S2 ●	Ball State	35	10
S9 ●	at Maryland	14	10
S16 ●	South Carolina	45	21
S23 ●	at Louisville	30	21
S30 =	Pittsburgh	31	31
O7	Virginia Tech	10	12
O21 ●	Cincinnati	69	3
O28 ●	at Boston College	44	30
N4	at Penn State	9	19
N11 ●	Rutgers	21	20
N23 ●	at Syracuse	24	17
	GATOR BOWL		
D30	Clemson	7	27

1990 4-7-0

S1 ●	Kent	35	24
S8	Maryland	10	14
S22	Louisville	7	9
S29 ●	at Pittsburgh	38	24
O6	at Virginia Tech	21	26
O13 ●	Cincinnati	28	20
O27	Boston College	14	27
N3	Penn State	19	31
N10 ●	Rutgers *ERut*	28	3
N17	Syracuse	7	31
N22	at South Carolina	10	29

1991-PRESENT
Big East

1991 6-5-0 (3-4-0)

A31 |	Pittsburgh	3	34
S7 ●	Bowling Green	24	17
S14 ●	South Carolina	21	16
S21 ●	at Maryland	37	7
O5 |	Virginia Tech	14	20
O12 ● |	Temple	10	9
O19 ● |	at Boston College	31	24
O26	at Penn State	6	51
N2 ● |	Rutgers	28	3
N9 |	at Miami, Fla.	3	27
N23 |	at Syracuse	10	16

1992 5-4-2 (2-3-1)

S5 =	Miami, Ohio	29	29
S12 ● |	at Pittsburgh	44	6
S19 ●	Maryland	34	33
S26 ● |	at Virginia Tech	16	7
O3 = |	Boston College	24	24
O17 |	Syracuse	17	20
O24	Penn State	26	40
O31 |	at Miami, Fla.	23	35
N7 ●	East Carolina	41	28
N14 |	at Rutgers	9	13
N21 ●	Louisiana Tech	23	3

1993 11-1-0 (7-0-0)

S4 ●	Eastern Michigan	48	6
S18 ●	at Maryland	42	37
S25 ●	Missouri	35	3
O2 ● |	Virginia Tech	14	13
O9 ●	Louisville	36	34
O23 ● |	Pittsburgh	42	21
O30 ● |	at Syracuse	43	0
N6 ● |	Rutgers	58	22
N13 ● |	at Temple	49	7
N20 ● |	Miami, Fla.	17	14
N27 ● |	at Boston College	17	14
	SUGAR BOWL		
J1	Florida	7	41

1994 7-6-0 (4-3-0)

A28	Nebraska *ERut*	0	31
S3 ●	Ball State	16	14
S10 |	at Rutgers	12	17
S17	Maryland	13	24
S22 |	at Virginia Tech	6	34
O1 ●	at Missouri	34	10
O15 ● |	at Pittsburgh	47	41
O22 |	Miami, Fla.	6	38
O29 ●	Louisiana Tech	52	16
N12 ● |	at Temple	55	17
N19 ● |	Boston College	21	20
N24 ● |	Syracuse	13	0
	CARQUEST BOWL		
J2	South Carolina	21	24

1995 5-6-0 (4-3-0)

S2	Purdue	24	26
S9 ● |	Temple	24	3
S16	at Maryland	17	31
S23 ●	Kent	45	6
S30	at East Carolina	20	23
O14 ● |	at Boston College	31	19
O21 |	at Syracuse	0	22
O28 |	Virginia Tech	0	27
N4 ● |	Rutgers	59	26
N18 |	at Miami, Fla.	12	17
N24 ● |	Pittsburgh	21	0

1996 8-4 (4-3)

A31 ● |	at Pittsburgh	34	0
S7 ●	Western Michigan	34	9
S14 ●	East Carolina	10	9
S21 ●	at Purdue	20	6
S28 ●	Maryland	13	0
O5 ● |	Boston College	34	17
O19 ● |	at Temple	30	10
O26 |	Miami, Fla.	7	10
N2 |	Syracuse	7	30
N9 ● |	at Rutgers	55	14
N23 |	at Virginia Tech	14	31
	GATOR BOWL		
J1	North Carolina	13	20

1997 7-5 (4-3)

A30 ●	Marshall	42	31
S6 ●	East Carolina	24	17
S13 |	at Boston College	24	31
S27 ● |	at Miami, Fla.	28	17
O4 ● |	Rutgers	48	0
O11 ●	at Maryland	31	14
O25 ● |	Virginia Tech	30	17
N1 |	at Syracuse	10	40
N15 ● |	Temple	41	21
N22	at Notre Dame	14	21
N28 |	Pittsburgh	38	41
	CARQUEST BOWL		
D29	Georgia Tech	30	35

1998 8-4 (5-2)

S5	Ohio State	17	34
S19 ●	Maryland	42	20
S26 ●	Tulsa	44	21
O3 ●	at Navy	45	24
O10 ● |	at Temple	37	7
O24 |	Miami, Fla.	31	34
O31 |	at Virginia Tech	13	27
N7 ● |	Syracuse	35	28
N14 ● |	at Rutgers	28	14
N21 ● |	Boston College	35	10
N27 ● |	at Pittsburgh	52	14
	INSIGHT.COM BOWL		
D26	Missouri	31	34

1999 4-7 (3-4)

S4	East Carolina *CHAR*	23	30
S11 ●	Miami, Ohio	43	27
S18	at Maryland	0	33
S25 |	at Syracuse	7	30
O2	Navy	28	31
O16 ● |	Rutgers	62	16
O23 ● |	Temple	20	17
O30 |	at Miami, Fla.	20	28
N6 |	Virginia Tech	20	22
N13 |	at Boston College	17	34
N27 ● |	at Pittsburgh	52	21

2000 7-5 3-4

S2 ● |	Boston College	34	14
S16 ●	Maryland	30	17
S23 |	Miami, Fla.	10	47
S328 ● |	at Temple	29	24
O7 ●	Idaho	28	16
O12 |	at Virginia Tech	20	48
O21	Notre Dame	28	42
N4 |	Syracuse	27	31
N11 ● |	at Rutgers	31	24
N18 ●	East Carolina	42	24
N24 |	at Pittsburgh	28	38
	MUSIC CITY BOWL		
D28 ●	Mississippi	49	38

RICH RODRIGUEZ
2001-PRESENT (.571) 28-21

2001 3-8 (1-6)

S1 |	at Boston College	10	34
S8 ●	Ohio U.	20	3
S22 ●	Kent	34	14
S29	at Maryland	20	32
O6 |	Virginia Tech	0	35
O13	at Notre Dame	24	34
O27 |	at Miami, Fla.	3	45
N3 ● |	Rutgers	80	7
N10 |	at Syracuse	13	24
N17 |	Temple	14	17
N24 |	Pittsburgh	17	23

2002 9-4 (6-1)

A31 ●	U.T. Chattanooga	56	7
S7	at Wisconsin	17	34
S14 ●	at Cincinnati	35	32
S28 ●	East Carolina	37	17
O5	Maryland	17	48
O12 ● |	at Rutgers	40	0
O19 ● |	Syracuse	34	7
O26 |	Miami, Fla.	23	40
N2 ● |	at Temple	46	20
N9 ● |	Boston College	24	14
N20 ● |	at Virginia Tech	21	18
N30 ● |	at Pittsburgh	24	17
	CONTINENTAL TIRE BOWL		
D28	Virginia	22	48

2003 8-5 (6-1)

A30	Wisconsin	17	24
S6 ●	at East Carolina	48	7
S13	Cincinnati	13	15
S20	at Maryland	7	34
O2 |	at Miami, Fla.	20	22
O11 ● |	Rutgers	34	19
O22 ● |	Virginia Tech	28	7
N1 ●	Central Florida	36	18
N8 ● |	at Boston College	35	28
N15 ● |	Pittsburgh	52	31
N22 ● |	at Syracuse	34	23
N29 ● |	Temple	45	28
	GATOR BOWL		
J1	Maryland	7	41

2004 8-4 (4-2)

S4 ●	East Carolina	56	23
S11 ●	at Central Florida	45	20
S18 ●	Maryland	19	16
S25 ●	James Madison	45	10
O2	at Virginia Tech	13	19
O14 ● |	at Connecticut	31	19
O21 ● |	Syracuse	27	6
O30 ● |	at Rutgers	35	30
N6 ● |	Temple	42	21
N13 |	Boston College	17	36
N25 |	at Pittsburgh	13	16
	GATOR BOWL		
J1	Florida State	18	30

Neutral Site key: *AtC* Atlantic City, NJ / *Balt* Baltimore, MD / *Blu* Bluefield, WV / *Brnx* Bronx, NY / *ChWV* Charleston, WV / *Char* Charlotte, NC / *Chi* Chicago, IL / *Clk* Clarksburg, WV / *Cmb* Cumberland, MD / *ERut* East Rutherford, NJ / *Eri* Erie, PA / *Fai* Fairmount, WV / *Her* Hershey, PA / *Hun* Huntington, WV / *Lou* Louisville, KY / *Lyn* Lynchburg, VA / *NYC* New York, NY / *Ora* Orangeburg, SC / *Par* Parkersburg, WV / *Port* Portland, OR / *Rich* Richmond, VA / *Roa* Roanoke, VA / *DC* Washington, DC / *Whe* Wheeling, WV

f Forfeit † Game Later Forfieted # Disputed Victor * Disputed Score || Designated Conference Game |2 Counted Twice in Conference Standings

WESTERN MICHIGAN

BY ED KRZEMIENSKI

WHEN THE STATE OF MICHIGAN decided in 1903 that it needed a third school for training teachers, it chose Kalamazoo as the site and named the school Western State Normal College. Thus, Western Michigan University was born. In recent years, with strong support from the Kalamazoo community, WMU has spread its recruiting net beyond the Midwest. Although still heavily dependent on the talent pools of Michigan and Illinois, WMU has brought in players from Florida, California and even Hawaii and American Samoa. It paid off initially, as Western Michigan won or shared the MAC West title in two of coach Gary Darnell's first four years. What goes up must come down, though, and in 2004, Darnell's squad lost 10 straight games to end the season at 1–10. The school named Darnell's former offensive coordinator, Bill Cubit, as its new coach following that disappointing season.

TRADITION Before home games, the team touches a sign above the exit door to the field that reads, "Our House." During home games, the PA announcer at Waldo Stadium announces, to the delight of the crowd, "Here comes Amtrak!" when a train passes by.

BEST PLAYER At the end of his career as a Broncos running back in 1978, Jerome Persell held the gold, silver and bronze medals of seasonal rushing records at Western. Although those and his career mark of 4,190 yards have since been surpassed, Persell still ranks as the greatest Bronco of all time. In 1976 he placed second nationally with an average of 150.5 yards rushing per game; the following year he ranked fourth in the nation in rushing and ninth in scoring. For his efforts, Persell was first-team All-MAC and was named the MAC Offensive Player of the Year and team MVP in each of his three varsity seasons. Persell never played professionally.

BEST COACH Al Molde did not take long to turn around the Western Michigan football program. Inheriting a team that won only three games the previous season, Molde won five games in his first season in 1987 and won the MAC outright in 1988. The latter year, Molde took the Broncos to the California Bowl (along with the 1961 Aviation Bowl, the second postseason appearance Western Michigan had ever made) and won MAC Coach of the Year honors. From 1987 to 1996, Molde went 62–47–2, tying him with William Spaulding for the most victories in school history.

BEST TEAM The 1988 Broncos began their season with five straight wins, including a season-opening upset of Wisconsin. Led by six first-team All-MAC players, including

PROFILE
Western Michigan University
Kalamazoo, Mich.
Founded: 1903
Enrollment: 23,309
Colors: Brown and Gold
Nickname: Broncos
Stadium: Waldo Stadium
    Opened in 1939
    NeXturf; 30,200 capacity
First football game: 1906
All-time record: 475–372–24 (.559)
Bowl record: 0–2
Mid-American Conference championships:
2 (1 outright)
First-round NFL draftees: 1
Website: www.wmubroncos.com

THE BEST OF TIMES
From 1988 to 1995, Western Michigan had seven winning seasons, including a MAC championship in 1988.

THE WORST OF TIMES
From 1951 to 1960, Western Michigan did not experience a single winning season.

CONFERENCE
Except for a brief stint in the Michigan Collegiate Conference (from 1927-30), Western Michigan was an independent through the early decades of its program. The Broncos joined the Mid-American Conference in 1948, and have remained there since.

DISTINGUISHED ALUMNI
Tim Allen, comedian; Dennis Archer, Detroit mayor; Jim Bouton, baseball pitcher and best-selling author; Neil Smith, New York Rangers general manager; Luther Vandross, singer

FIGHT SONG
WMU FIGHT
Fight on, fight on for Western,
Take the ball, make a score, win the game,
Onward for the brown and gold,
Push 'em back, push 'em back,
Bring us fame!

Fight on, fight on for Western,
Over one, over all we will reign,
Fight, Broncos, fight,
Fight with all your might,
Western win this game!
B-R-O-N-C-O, B-R-O-N-C-O, GOOO
BRONCOS! W-M-U!

Buster Bronco belongs to the giant-fluffy-goofy phylum of the college mascot kingdom.

MAC offensive Player of the Year Tony Kimbrough at quarterback, Western ended its regular season at 9–2 overall and 7–1 in the MAC. With its first and only outright conference championship (Western shared a title with Miami in 1966), the Broncos traveled to Fresno for the California Bowl. Before a hostile crowd of 31,272, they rolled up 503 total yards, including 366 in the air by Kimbrough, and 30 points, but fell to Fresno State 35-30. Molde's team sent five players to the pros, including Kimbrough, who played in the Canadian Football League, and defensive end Joel Smeenge, who went on to a successful career with the New Orleans Saints and Jacksonville Jaguars of the NFL.

BIGGEST GAME Needing a victory to secure a MAC title in 1988, the Broncos traveled to Muncie, Ind., to take on the Cardinals of Ball State. Cold, wet and windy, the day saw the Cardinals take an early lead before WMU quarterback Kimbrough tied the score on a pass to Bruce Boyko. Kicker John Creek emerged as the Broncos' hero, though, as he connected on three short field goals to give Western a 16-7 lead. Ball State added a late touchdown to close the final gap to 16-13, but the game and the conference title went to the Broncos.

BIGGEST UPSET In 1988, Western set the tone for two teams when it defeated Wisconsin 24-14 to open the season. For the Broncos, it marked the school's first victory over a Big Ten team in the modern era. For the Badgers, it began a three-year nightmare that resulted in four total victories.

HEARTBREAKER Losing to rival Central Michigan is never easy, but doing so after entering the game as 20-point favorites is even more painful. Yet that's exactly what Western Michigan did when it traveled to Mount Pleasant to face the woeful Chippewas in 2000. The Broncos entered the game with an 8–1 record, while the Chippewas, at 1–8, were in the midst of the mirror-image season. Nevertheless, behind a stifling defense, the Chippewas upset the Broncos 21-17. Western Michigan is 1–11–1 at Mount Pleasant since 1977.

STADIUM Built for an original outlay of $250,000 in 1939, Waldo Stadium was constructed as part of an athletic complex and named for the school's first president, Dwight B. Waldo. From 1973 to 1991, the stadium had artificial turf, then Prescription Athletic Turf, before returning to the fake stuff (NeXturf) in 2001. Although Waldo Stadium seats a maximum of 30,200 fans, the school set the MAC

RECORDS

RUSHING YARDS

	GAME
279	Lovell Coleman vs. Central Michigan, Sept. 20, 1958
	SEASON
1,668	Shawn Faulkner, 1983 (394 att.)
	CAREER
4,219	Robert Sanford, 1997-2000 (838 att.)

PASSING YARDS

	GAME
450	Chad Munson vs. William & Mary, Sept. 6, 2003 (24 of 35)
	SEASON
3,639	Tim Lester, 1999 (282 of 470)
	CAREER
11,299	Tim Lester, 1996–99 (875 of 1,507)

RECEIVING YARDS

	GAME
263	Corey Alston vs. Eastern Michigan, Nov. 1, 1997 (9 rec.)
	SEASON
1,121	Steve Neal, 1998 (63 rec.)
	CAREER
3,599	Steve Neal, 1997-2000 (235 rec.)

POINTS

	GAME
52	Walt Olsen vs. Grand Rapids Veterinary, 1916 (8 TDs, 4 PATs)
	SEASON
138	Walt Olsen, 1916 (17 TDs, 36 PATs)
	CAREER
307	Brad Selent, 1997-2000 (50 FGs, 157 PATs)

CONSENSUS ALL-AMERICANS

1982	Matt Meares, OL

home attendance mark in 2000 with 36,361. In fact, Western Michigan has broken the MAC single-game home attendance record four times and has enjoyed that advantage, going 21–4 at home from 1997 to 2001.

RIVAL Western Michigan considers Central Michigan its prime rival, and the feeling is mutual. The teams first met in 1907, but did not begin a fairly consistent annual rivalry until 1943. When Central joined Western in the MAC in 1975, meetings between the two were guaranteed. Despite being only a short bus ride away, the trip to Mount Pleasant has been a painfully long journey for the Broncos. Since the teams began play in the MAC together, the Broncos have just one win at Central Michigan's Kelly/Shorts Stadium.

NICKNAME Located on Prospect Hill, later known as Normal Hill, Western Michigan first took Hilltoppers for its nickname. As the campus began to spread beyond the hill—and in an effort to distinguish itself from Western Kentucky, which also used the moniker—the school held a contest in 1939 to come up with a new name. Assistant coach John Gill suggested Broncos. In support of the decision, the W club's semi-annual publication *The Hilltopper* was renamed *The Bronco*.

MASCOT Buster Bronco, a cheerleader in horse's clothing, debuted in 1988 and has appeared at all Western Michigan games ever since. Buster is a dark-brown horse clad in basketball high-tops and a WMU shirt. With bipedal ability and a Bullwinkle-esque face, Buster belongs to the giant-fluffy-goofy phylum of the college mascot kingdom.

UNIFORMS Legend has it that Waldo chose the school's colors in 1906 at the behest of his only assistant, Josephine Wing. Pointing to a batch of brown-eyed Susan flowers outside the window, Wing suggested their gold-and-brown scheme for the school. That much has remained unchanged. Helmets, on the other hand, have undergone several incarnations. For a while, a brown bucking bronco appeared on a white shell; at other times helmets have been plain white or yellow. Currently, the helmets are gold with the profile of a bronco applied. The team wears brown home and white away jerseys, both with gold numbers and gold pants. In 1998, black was added as an accent color.

NUMBERS Western Michigan opened its 1916 season with a 93-0 win over the Grand Rapids Veterinary school. Too bad the team was not yet known as the Broncos; the irony might have been complete.

LORE In 1916, Western Michigan lost to the Notre Dame JV 10-6. It was during this game that George Gipp dropkicked his record-breaking 62-yard field goal. Contrary to legend, it was not a spontaneous decision by Gipp; he had announced his intent to kick in advance. Maybe he felt the wind pick up.

QUIRK From the don't-try-this-with-your-dog file comes Jason Babin, a Western Michigan defensive end with a strange pregame ritual. On Friday nights before games, Babin ate an entire bucket of fried chicken—bones and all—to psych himself up. It worked: Babin won MAC defensive Player of the Year honors following his junior and senior seasons in 2002 and 2003, respectively.

QUOTE "It was time for us to win one of those games or quit opening our mouths."—Gary Darnell, after Western Michigan upset Iowa in the second game of the 2000 season. Darnell had earlier stated that it was his intention to compete with Big Ten teams

WESTERN MICHIGAN ANNUAL STATISTICAL LEADERS

YR	RUSHING	YDS	ATT	AVG	PASSING	ATT	CMP	PCT	YDS	RECEIVING	REC	YDS	AVG
1947	Arthur Gillespie	436	129	3.4	Nick Milosevich	105	49	.47	580	Carl Schiller	47	327	7.0
1948	Harry Hildreth	396	77	5.1	Hilton Foster	58	28	.48	436	George Mesko	15	305	20.3
1949	Arnold Thompson	243	56	4.3	Robert White	146	54	.37	870	Pat Clysdale	19	291	15.3
1950	Bob Morse	369	60	6.2	Norm Harris	135	40	.30	684	Chas Atkcounis	7	201	28.7
1951	Earl Montross	556	105	5.3	Owen Bennett	102	38	.37	661	Len Johnston	21	405	19.3
1952	Bill Brown	364	85	4.3	Charles Higgins	142	57	.40	868	John Smith	17	336	19.8
1953	John Kelder	220	66	3.3	Louis Fierens	31	9	.29	116	Bernard Porter	9	190	21.1
1954	Charles Nidiffer	271	85	3.2	Jerry Ganzel	115	41	.36	624	John Berryman	11	208	18.9
1955	Charles Nidiffer	478	107	4.5	Robert Mason	74	23	.31	254	John Berryman	13	185	14.2
1956	Buryl Breed	493	119	4.1	Robert Mason	74	28	.38	427	Joe Grigg	7	153	21.9
1957	Lovell Coleman	384	80	4.8	Jim Kolk	45	25	.56	473	Jesse Madden	7	228	32.6
1958	Lovell Coleman	1,068	174	6.1	Jim Kolk	28	12	.43	158	Jesse Madden	7	101	14.4
1959	Lovell Coleman	466	126	3.7	Ed Chlebek	67	32	.48	555	Jesse Madden	12	297	24.8
1960	Lloyd Swelnis	479	79	6.1	Ed Chlebek	72	51	.71	626	Dennis Holland	10	149	14.9
1961	Bob White	278	70	4.0	Ed Chlebek	79	45	.57	577	Dennis Holland	10	96	9.6
1962	Bill Schlee	599	120	5.0	Roger Theder	124	58	.47	824	Jim Bedner	12	255	21.3
1963	George Archer	397	90	4.4	Ken Barnhill	93	36	.39	668	Tom Patterson	15	269	17.9
1964	Troy Allen	195	67	2.9	Bob Radlinski	93	38	.41	469	Stan Williams	7	77	11.0
1965	Steve Terlep	361	105	3.4	Ron Seifert	116	55	.47	660	Dave Mollard	25	269	10.8
1966	Tim Majerle	731	204	3.6	Jim Boreland	118	47	.40	756	Dave Mollard	27	361	13.4
1967	Jack Foster	377	90	4.2	Jim Boreland	90	42	.47	620	Marty Barski	28	392	14.0
1968	Kenneth Woodside	474	134	3.5	Mark Bordeax	171	83	.49	1,143	Alan Bellile	30	394	13.1
1969	Paul Schneider	554	112	4.9	Ted Grignon	109	47	.43	549	Greg Flaska	37	433	11.7
1970	Roger Lawson	1,205	168	7.2	Ted Grignon	123	62	.50	1,001	Greg Flaska	17	372	21.9
1971	Larry Cates	819	162	5.1	Ted Grignon	129	68	.53	912	Dave Hallabrin	22	294	13.4
1972	Larry Cates	660	122	5.4	Steve Doolittle	101	40	.40	518	Bob Gavinski	17	290	17.1
1973	Paul Jorgensen	482	111	4.3	Paul Jorgensen	106	41	.39	664	Frank Mumford	13	225	17.3
1974	Dan Matthews	769	142	5.4	Paul Jorgensen	119	53	.45	701	Greg Cowser	32	403	12.6
1975	Dan Matthews	873	181	4.8	Sollie Boone	77	23	.30	318	Ted Forrest	21	286	13.6
1976	Jerome Persell	1,505	269	5.6	Pepper Powers	103	46	.45	571	Tom Henry	17	225	13.2
1977	Jerome Persell	1,339	264	5.1	Albert Little	121	50	.41	802	Tim Clysdale	19	228	12.0
1978	Jerome Persell	1,346	309	4.4	Albert Little	138	61	.44	828	Tim Clysdale	18	213	11.8
1979	Larry Caper	844	168	5.0	Albert Little	67	32	.48	342	Tim Clysdale	16	207	12.9
1980	Craig Morrow	778	150	5.2	Tom George	124	59	.48	644	Reggie Hinton	29	429	14.8
1981	Shawn Faulkner	701	155	4.5	Tom George	207	104	.50	1,419	Bob Phillips	53	809	15.3
1982	Shawn Faulkner	910	206	4.4	Chris Conklin	137	76	.55	853	Bob Phillips	39	577	14.8
1983	Shawn Faulkner	1,668	394	4.2	Steve Hoffman	213	125	.59	1,407	Kelly Spielmaker	48	653	13.6
1984	Otis Cheathem	778	190	4.1	Steve Hoffman	265	151	.57	1,732	Cliff Read	47	591	12.6
1985	Lewis Howard	819	177	4.6	Chris Conklin	244	133	.55	1,574	Paul Sorce	47	567	12.1
1986	Joe Glenn	602	152	4.0	Chris Conklin	261	127	.49	1,668	Kelly Spielmaker	43	575	13.4
1987	Robert Davis	477	115	4.1	Dave Kruse	278	125	.45	1,592	Jamie Hence	50	858	17.2
1988	Robert Davis	1,054	226	4.7	Tony Kimbrough	324	186	.57	2,465	Bruce Boyko	44	583	13.3
1989	Dan Boggan	744	208	3.6	Brad Tayles	321	147	.46	1,909	Ulric King	32	435	13.6
1990	Corey Sylve	840	147	5.7	Brad Tayles	345	171	.50	2,397	Paul Agema	57	785	13.8
1991	Corey Sylve	711	176	4.0	Brad Tayles	328	162	.49	1,949	John Morton	39	588	15.1
1992	Jim Vackaro	893	183	4.9	Brad Tayles	376	183	.49	2,462	Ulric King	48	732	15.3
1993	Dave Madsen	571	140	4.1	Jay McDonagh	283	174	.61	1,974	Andre Wallace	55	599	10.9
1994	Jim Vackaro	910	187	4.9	Jay McDonagh	293	172	.59	2,136	Andre Wallace	68	758	11.1
1995	Jim Vackaro	702	128	5.5	Jay McDonagh	316	183	.58	2,038	Tony Knox	43	430	10.0
1996	Bruno Heppell	700	160	4.4	Tim Lester	363	203	.56	2,189	Tony Knox	71	754	10.6
1997	Robert Sanford	1,033	216	4.8	Tim Lester	268	154	.57	2,160	Jake Moreland	36	406	11.3
1998	Darnell Fields	1,016	189	5.4	Tim Lester	406	236	.58	3,311	Steve Neal	63	1,121	17.8
1999	Robert Sanford	1,092	221	4.9	Tim Lester	470	282	.60	3,639	Steve Neal	74	1,113	15.0
2000	Robert Sanford	1,571	293	5.4	Jeff Welsh	354	207	.58	2,537	Steve Neal	67	848	12.7
2001	Philip Reed	539	122	4.4	Jeff Welsh	213	134	.63	1,702	Josh Bush	48	617	12.9
2002	Philip Reed	1,053	221	4.8	Chad Munson	309	162	.52	2,160	Antonio Thomas	45	439	9.8
2003	Philip Reed	744	189	3.9	Chad Munson	266	150	.56	2,123	Kendrick Mosley	77	1,019	13.2
2004	Trovon Riley	691	172	4.0	Ryan Cubit	290	170	.59	1,887	Greg Jennings	74	1,092	14.8

Receiving leaders by receptions
All statistics include postseason

THE SCHOOLS

WESTERN MICHIGAN ALL-TIME SCORES

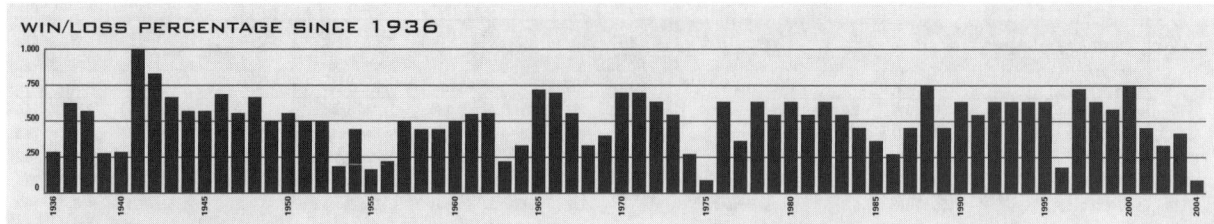

WIN/LOSS PERCENTAGE SINCE 1936

MELVIN "TUBBY" MYERS
1906 (.333)   1-2

1906   1-2-0
N17		Eastern Michigan	5	14
U		Kalamazoo *Unk*	0	14
U	●	Wayland HS *Unk*	21	0

WILLIAM SPAULDING
1907-21 (.706)   62-25-3

1907   3-2-1
U	●	Grand Rapids HS *Unk*	9	0
U		Albion *Unk*	0	5
U		Olivet *Unk*	0	3
U	=	Central Michigan *Unk*	27	0 *
N9	●	Eastern Michigan	6	0
U	=	Ferris St. *Unk*	0	0

1908   3-3-0
U	●	Mc Fadden's PC *Unk*	20	0
O10		Michigan State	0	35
U		Olivet *Unk*	0	34
U		Albion *Unk*	0	24
U	●	Central Michigan *Unk*	11	5
U	●	Kalamazoo *Unk*	2	0

1909   7-0-0
U	●	Otsego Indy's *Unk*	61	0
U	●	Albion *Unk*	6	0
U	●	Battle Creek HS *Unk*	15	0
U	●	Dowagiac HS *Unk*	47	0
U	●	Benton Harbor Coll. *Unk*	28	3
U	●	Kalamazoo *Unk*	26	5
U	●	Central Michigan *Unk*	11	0

1910   4-1-1
U	=	Hillsdale *Unk*	3	3
U		Albion *Unk*	0	6
U	●	Culver Military Acad. *Unk*	22	5
U	●	Central Michigan *Unk*	16	6
U	●	Hope *Unk*	6	0
U	●	Kalamazoo *Unk*	28	0

1911   2-3-0
U		Hillsdale *Unk*	6	14
U		Albion *Unk*	5	12
U		Culver Military Acad. *Unk*	3	27
U	●	Battle Creek TS *Unk*	62	6
U	●	Hope *Unk*	34	0

1912   3-2-1
U	●	Culver Military Acad. *Unk*	19	13
U	●	Albion *Unk*	6	3
U		Michigan State JV *Unk*	0	20
U	●	Hope *Unk*	54	0
U	=	Hillsdale *Unk*	7	7
N15		at Eastern Michigan	0	7 *

1913   4-0-0
U	●	Albion *Unk*	20	3
U	●	Culver Military Acad. *Unk*	13	6
U	●	Hope *Unk*	14	0
N1	●	Eastern Michigan	12	6

1914   6-0-0
U	●	Battle Creek TS *Unk*	28	0
U	●	Olivet *Unk*	3	0
U	●	Albion *Unk*	43	0
U	●	Ferris St. *Unk*	68	0
U	●	Hillsdale *Unk*	28	7
N14	●	at Eastern Michigan	10	0

1915   5-1-0
U		Hillsdale *Unk*	16	20
U	●	Albion *Unk*	54	7
U	●	Alma *Unk*	79	0
U	●	Olivet *Unk*	40	0
N6	●	Eastern Michigan	19	0
U	●	Culver Military Acad. *Unk*	83	16

1916   5-1-0
U	●	Grand Rapids Veterinary *Unk*	93	0
U	●	Albion *Unk*	37	0
U	●	Indiana, Pa. *Unk*	94	6
U	●	Michigan State JV *Unk*	77	3
U		Notre Dame JV *Unk*	6	10
U	●	Ohio Northern *Unk*	82	19

1917   4-3-0
U	●	Albion *Unk*	26	6
O10		Michigan	13	17
U	●	Notre Dame JV *Unk*	83	0
N3	●	Michigan State	14	0
U	●	Camp Custer *Unk*	61	7
U		Detroit *Unk*	6	35
U		Indiana, Pa. *Unk*	0	40

1918   3-2-0
U		Albion *Unk*	12	14
N2		Michigan State	7	16
U	●	Hillsdale *Unk*	103	0
U	●	Hop *Unk*	62	0
U	●	Notre Dame JV *Unk*	39	0

1919   4-1-0
U	●	Wayne St. *Unk*	88	0
O11	●	Michigan State	21	18
U	●	Wabash *Unk*	27	13
O25		Notre Dame *Unk*	0	53
U	●	Albion *Unk*	20	7

1920   3-4-0
U	●	Olivet *Unk*	47	7
O9		at Notre Dame	0	42 *
U		Chicago YMCA *Unk*	6	10
U		Marquette *Unk*	7	46
U	●	Jope *Unk*	46	0
U	●	Earlham *Unk*	6	0
U		Wabash *Unk*	7	27

1921   6-2-0
U	●	Ferris St.	49	0
U		at Albion	20	9
U	●	Notre Dame JV	7	0
U		Chicago YMCA	3	7
O22		at Michigan State	14	17
U	●	Earlham	42	7
U	●	Hope	65	0
U	●	Milwaukee Engineers	62	0

MILTON OLANDER
1922-23 (.893)   12-1-1

1922   6-0-0
U	●	Defiance	19	0
U	●	at Valparaiso	7	0
U	●	Albion	10	0
U	●	Chicago YMCA	13	0
U	●	Notre Dame JV	44	0
U	●	at Earlham	67	0

1923   6-1-1
S29	●	Notre Dame JV	15	0
O6	●	Valparaiso	7	0
O13	●	Alma	21	7
O20	=	at St. Viator	7	7
O29	●	Western Kentucky	26	0
N10	●	Earlham	46	0
N17	●	Chicago YMCA	32	0
N29		at Albion	6	7

EARL MARTINEAU
1924-28 (.711)   26-10-2

1924   5-1-1
U	●	Alma	7	0
O4		Notre Dame JV	7	15
O11	●	St. Viator	6	0
O25	●	at Western Kentucky	14	0
N1	●	Wisconsin-Oshkosh	23	7
U	=	Chicago YMCA	18	18
N27	●	Albion	26	6

1925   6-2-1
S26	●	Western Kentucky *Unk*	20	0
O3		Bradley *Unk*	2	6
O10		St. Thomas *Unk*	13	27
O17	●	Valparaiso *Unk*	45	0
U	●	Notre Dame JV *Unk*	21	0
U	●	Wisconsin-Oshkosh *Unk*	7	6
U	=	Central Michigan	0	0
U	●	Chicago YMCA *Unk*	14	6
N26	●	Albion *Unk*	3	2

1926   7-1-0
S25	●	Olivet	25	0
O2		Bradley	0	12
O9	●	Albion	28	0
O16	●	at Western Kentucky	3	2
O23	●	Chicago YMCA	7	0
O30	●	Valparaiso	37	0
N13	●	Notre Dame JV	12	6
N20	●	Wisconsin-Oshkosh	20	0

1927   3-4-0
O8		at Lombard	6	18
O15		Notre Dame JV	0	18
O22		at Central Michigan	12	18
O29	●	Wayne St.	44	0
N5	●	at Wisconsin-Oshkosh	19	6
N12		Eastern Michigan	0	6
N26	●	Albion	19	6

1928   5-2-0
U	●	Chicago YMCA *Unk*	26	0
O6	●	Ferris St. *Unk*	14	0
O13		Lombard *Unk*	0	14
O27	●	Wayne St. *Unk*	45	0
U	●	Michigan JV *Unk*	6	0
N10		at Eastern Michigan	9	18
U	●	Central Michigan	19	0

MITCHELL "MIKE" GARY
1929-41 (.628)   59-34-5

1929   5-2-1
U	●	Ferris St. *Unk*	41	0
U	●	Illinois JV *Unk*	20	0
U		Notre Dame JV *Unk*	7	13
U	●	Lombard *Unk*	14	6
O26	●	Wayne St. *Unk*	40	0
N2	=	Eastern Michigan	7	7
N9	●	at Central Michigan	25	6
U		Michigan JV *Unk*	7	12

1930   5-1-1
U	●	Ferris St.	46	0
U	●	Central Michigan	54	0
O18		at Eastern Michigan	0	19
U	●	at Wayne St.	52	0
U	●	Michigan JV	14	6
N8	●	at No. Iowa	26	0
N27	=	Western Kentucky	0	0

1931   5-2-0
S26	●	Ferris St.	25	0
O2		at Detroit	0	20
U		at Michigan JV	0	19
U	●	Notre Dame JV	27	6
N7	●	at No. Iowa	14	0
N14	●	Western Kentucky	13	0
N21	●	at Central Michigan	7	6

1932   6-0-1
S24	●	Hope	31	6
O1	●	at North Central	27	0
O8	=	DePaul	0	0
O15	●	at St. Viator	7	0
O29	●	No. Iowa	26	0
N5	●	Central Michigan	7	0
N12	●	Adrian	76	0

1933   3-3-1
S30		North Central	0	7
O6		at Detroit	0	26
O14	●	at No. Iowa	8	6
O21	=	Carroll	0	0
O28		DePaul	6	25
N4	●	at Central Michigan	13	0 *
N11	●	St. Viator	33	0

1934   7-1-0
O5		at Detroit	7	25
O13	●	at Carroll	25	7
O20	●	No. Iowa	7	0
O27	●	DePaul	13	0
N3	●	Central Michigan	13	0
N9	●	at St. Viator	19	7
N24	●	West Chester St.	13	7
N29	●	at Western Kentucky	7	6

1935   5-3-0
S28	●	Illinois Coll. *Unk*	13	0
O5	●	Western Kentucky *Unk*	6	0
O12		Chicago *Unk*	6	31
O19		No. Iowa *Unk*	14	21
O26		DePaul *Unk*	0	26
N9	●	Central Michigan	13	0
N16	●	Butler *Unk*	19	7
N23	●	West Chester St. *Unk*	7	6

1936   2-5-0
S25		at Detroit	0	40
O10		Miami, Ohio	0	6 *
O17	●	Valparaiso	7	0
O24		No. Iowa	6	12
O31		at DePaul	7	19
N7	●	Central Michigan	33	0
N14		at Butler	7	13

1937   5-3-0
O1		at Detroit	7	20
O9	●	Illinois Coll.	37	0
O16		at No. Iowa	7	0
O23		St. Viator	7	13
O30	●	Western Kentucky	13	7
N6	●	at Central Michigan	7	0
N13	●	at Butler	14	13
N20		DePaul	0	12

1938   4-3-0
S24	●	Illinois Coll.	28	0
S30		at Detroit	0	7
O8	●	No. Iowa	20	0
O15		at Akron	0	6
O29		Western Kentucky	6	13
N5	●	at Butler	13	0
N12	●	Central Michigan	35	0

1939   2-6-1
S29		at Detroit	0	14
O7	●	Miami, Ohio	6	0
O14	●	Akron	6	0
O21	=	at No. Iowa	13	13
O28		at Toledo	0	6
N4		Western Kentucky	14	20
N11		Butler	0	12
N18		Ohio U.	6	13
U		at Wayne St.	6	7

1940   2-5-0
O5		Wayne St.	6	13
O12		at Ohio U.	7	20
O19		No. Iowa	19	20
O26		Toledo	0	12
N2		at Western Kentucky	6	25
N9	●	at Miami, Ohio	20	13
N16	●	Manchester	19	14

1941 — 8-0-0

S27	●	at Western Reserve	7	0
O3	●	Butler	14	6
O18	●	at No. Iowa	28	7
O25	●	Toledo	34	0
N1	●	Western Kentucky	21	7
N8	●	Manchester	12	0
N15	●	at Wayne St.	34	0
N20	●	Ripon	35	7

JOHN GILL
1942-52 (.594) 50-34-1

1942 — 5-1-0

S26		at Dayton	0	21
O10	●	Toledo	13	0
O17	●	No. Iowa	14	7
O24	●	Butler	13	7
U	●	Grosse Isle Navy	13	2
N14	●	Wayne St.	13	0

1943 — 4-2-0

U	●	at Central Michigan	19	0
S25		at Michigan	6	57
U	●	Alma	54	0
U	●	Xavier	60	0
O16	●	Miami, Ohio	6	0
N6		Great Lakes NAS	6	32

1944 — 4-3-0

U	●	Fort Sheridan	67	0
U	●	Wabash	20	0
U		Bunker Hill Navy	7	33
S30		at Miami, Ohio	6	32
O7	●	Central Michigan	35	14
O14		at Great Lakes NAS	0	38
U	●	at Wooster	27	0

1945 — 4-3-0

S22	●	Alma	21	13
S29		at Central Michigan	0	6
O6	●	at Ohio U.	21	20
O13		Miami, Ohio	13	21
O27		Great Lakes NAS	0	39
N3	●	at Valparaiso	26	6
N10	●	Wooster	66	0

1946 — 5-2-1

S28	●	Ripon	47	0
O5		Ohio U.	7	25
O12	●	Butler	19	0
O19	=	at No. Iowa	0	0
O26	●	at Western Kentucky	32	21
N2	●	Central Michigan	27	21
N9	●	Valparaiso	26	13
N16		at Miami, Ohio	0	20

1947 — 5-4-0

S26		at Xavier	0	19
O4	●	Washington, Mo.	14	0
O11	●	at Central Michigan	20	12
O18	●	No. Iowa	14	0
O25		at Butler	20	21
N1	●	Western Kentucky	38	0
N8		at Illinois	14	60
N27		at Oklahoma City	7	35
U	●	Beloit	12	0

1948-PRESENT
MAC

1948 — 6-3-0 (3-1-0)

S25	● |	Western Reserve	26	0
O2	●	at Beloit	33	0
O9	●	Central Michigan	7	0
O16		at No. Iowa	6	13
O23		Xavier	20	39
O30	|	at Miami, Ohio	28	34
N6	● |	Butler	20	7
N13	●	at Washington, Mo.	19	6
N20	● |	at Ohio U.	40	7

1949 — 4-4-0 (2-3-0)

S24	●	No. Iowa	20	6
O1	|	Ohio U.	6	16
O8	|	at Cincinnati	6	27
O15		Washington, Mo.	0	12
O22	●	at Central Michigan	35	8
O29	|	Miami, Ohio	20	34
N5	● |	at Butler	40	6
N12	● |	at Western Reserve	21	14

1950 — 5-4-0 (1-3-0)

S23	●	Northern Illinois	40	13
S30	●	Central Michigan	21	13
O7	●	Toledo	54	19
O14	|	at Miami, Ohio	0	35
O21	●	at Washington, Mo.	26	7
O28	|	Cincinnati	6	27
N4	●	Butler	34	13
N11	|	Western Reserve	0	26
N18	|	at Ohio U.	7	10

1951 — 4-4-0 (0-4-0)

S22	|	Kent State	19	48
S29	●	at Toledo	14	6
O6	|	Ohio U.	0	13
O13	|	Miami, Ohio	27	34
O20	●	Washington, Mo.	12	7
N3	●	at Butler	20	0
N10	|	at Western Reserve	26	27
N17	●	Central Michigan	46	25

1952 — 4-4-0 (1-4-0)

S20	|	at Kent State	13	20
S27	●	Illinois Wesleyan	44	6
O4	●	at Central Michigan	18	0
O11	|	at Miami, Ohio	6	55
O18	● |	Toledo	19	14
O25	●	at Washington, Mo.	28	20
N1	|	Ohio U.	13	28
N8	|	Western Reserve	13	16

JACK PETOSKEY
1953-56 (.257) 8-25-2

1953 — 1-6-1 (0-4-1)

S26		at Central Michigan	0	21
O3	●	at Illinois Wesleyan	20	7
O10	|	Miami, Ohio	6	52
O17	|	at Toledo	7	19
O24		Washington, Mo.	7	18
O31	|	Ohio U.	12	67
N7	= |	at Western Reserve	14	14
N14	|	Kent State	0	40

1954 — 4-5-0 (3-4-0)

S25		Central Michigan	19	25
O2	|	at Marshall	13	47
O9	● |	Bowling Green	20	15
O16	|	Toledo	7	19
O23	●	at Washington, Mo.	7	6
O31	|	at Miami, Ohio	0	48
N6	● |	Ohio U.	19	6
N13	● |	Western Reserve	38	0
N20	|	at Kent State	13	20

1955 — 1-7-1 (0-5-0)

S17	=	Great Lakes NAS	13	13
S24		at Central Michigan	12	27
O1	|	Bowling Green	0	35
O8	|	Marshall	0	28
O15	|	at Toledo	0	6
O22		Washington, Mo.	14	26
N5	|	at Ohio U.	14	40
N12	●	Western Reserve	13	0
N19	|	Kent State	14	25

1956 — 2-7-0 (1-4-0)

S22		Central Michigan	7	14
S29	|	Bowling Green	13	27
O6	|	at Marshall	0	13
O13	● |	Toledo	26	15
O20		at Washington, Mo.	7	13
O27		at Great Lakes NAS	6	13
N3	|	Ohio U.	0	27
N10	●	at Western Reserve	42	19
N17	|	Kent State	13	27

MERLE SCHLOSSER
1957-63 (.461) 28-33-3

1957 — 4-4-1 (1-4-1)

S21	●	at Central Michigan	33	0
S28	|	Miami, Ohio	0	20
O5	|	Marshall	7	12
O12	= |	at Bowling Green	14	14
O19	●	Youngstown St.	25	14
O26	|	at Toledo	16	27 *
N2	|	at Ohio U.	7	20
N9	●	Western Reserve	20	0
N16	● |	Kent State	28	20

1958 — 4-5-0 (2-4-0)

S20		Central Michigan	32	33
S27	|	at Miami, Ohio	20	34
O4	● |	at Marshall	30	24
O11	|	Bowling Green	6	40
O18	●	at Washington, Mo.	34	2
O25	|	Toledo	6	21
N1	● |	Ohio U.	21	14
N8	●	Western Reserve	33	0
N15	|	at Kent State	6	32

1959 — 4-5-0 (3-3-0)

S19		at Central Michigan	15	21
S26	|	Miami, Ohio	0	21
O3	● |	Marshall	51	0
O10	|	at Bowling Green	0	34
O17	●	Washington, Mo.	78	0
O24	● |	at Toledo	24	14
O31	|	at Ohio U.	9	12
N7	● |	Kent State	7	0
N14		Detroit	0	14

1960 — 4-4-1 (2-4-0)

S17	●	Central Michigan	31	0
S24	|	at Miami, Ohio	14	15
O1	=	Baldwin-Wallace	28	28
O8	|	Bowling Green	13	14
O15	●	at Washington, Mo.	43	0
O22	● |	Toledo	7	3
O29	|	Ohio U.	0	24
N5	|	at Kent State	3	10
N12	● |	Marshall	34	12

1961 — 5-4-1 (4-1-1)

S16	●	at Central Michigan	27	21
S23		at Detroit	14	21
S30	● |	Miami, Ohio	6	3
O7	|	at Bowling Green	0	21
O21	● |	at Toledo	7	0
O28	● |	Marshall	20	0
N4	● |	Kent State	14	0
N11		Utah State	22	65
N18	= |	at Ohio U.	20	20
		AVIATION BOWL		
D9		New Mexico	12	28

1962 — 5-4-0 (3-3-0)

S15	●	Central Michigan	28	0
S22		at Louisville	21	27
S29	|	at Miami, Ohio	7	17
O6	|	Bowling Green	6	10
O20	● |	Toledo	21	0
O27	● |	at Marshall	12	0
N3	● |	at Kent State	19	6
N10	●	Brigham Young	28	20
N17	|	Ohio U.	16	32

1963 — 2-7-0 (2-4-0)

S21		at Wisconsin	0	41
S28		at Central Michigan	14	30
O5	|	Miami, Ohio	19	27
O12	|	at Bowling Green	7	16
O19	● |	Kent State	26	12
O26	● |	at Toledo	18	7
N2	|	Marshall	7	20
N9	|	at Ohio U.	13	27
N16		Louisville	7	21

BILL DOOLITTLE
1964-74 (.541) 53-49-2

1964 — 3-6-0 (2-4-0)

S19	●	at Louisville	10	7
S26		Central Michigan	6	18
O3	|	at Miami, Ohio	0	35
O10	|	Bowling Green	8	28
O17	● |	at Kent State	12	9
O24	|	Toledo	13	21
O31	|	at Marshall	7	16
N7	● |	Ohio U.	13	8
N14		at Brigham Young	8	43

1965 — 6-2-1 (3-2-1)

S18	●	Louisville	17	13
S25	●	at Central Michigan	21	13
O2	|	Miami, Ohio	9	36
O9	|	at Bowling Green	17	21
O16	= |	Kent State	10	10
O23	● |	at Toledo	3	0
O30	● |	Marshall	17	14
N6	● |	at Ohio U.	17	6
N13	●	Montana	17	14

1966 — 7-3-0 (5-1-0)

S17	●	Lamar Tech	16	14
S24	●	Central Michigan	31	14
O1	|	at Miami, Ohio	9	26
O8	● |	Bowling Green	16	14
O15	● |	at Kent State	23	20
O22	● |	Toledo	14	13
O29	● |	at Marshall	35	29
N5	● |	Ohio U.	20	13
N12		at Xavier	6	21
N19		at West Texas St.	7	30

1967 — 5-4-0 (4-2-0)

S16	● |	Miami, Ohio	24	14
S23		Arkansas State	8	21
S29		at Brigham Young	19	44
O7	● |	at Bowling Green	10	6
O14	● |	Kent State	16	7
O21	|	at Toledo	9	35
O28	● |	Marshall	42	10
N4	|	at Ohio U.	10	20
N11	●	Xavier	18	7

1968 — 3-6-0 (2-4-0)

S14	●	Arkansas State	20	0
S21		Brigham Young	7	17
S28	|	at Miami, Ohio	0	28
O5	|	Bowling Green	10	17
O12	● |	at Kent State	14	0
O19	|	Toledo	6	30
O26	● |	at Marshall	40	12
N2	|	Ohio U.	27	34
N9		at West Texas St.	36	53

1969 — 4-6-0 (1-4-0)

S13	●	Central Michigan	24	0
S20		at Pacific	0	21
S27	|	Miami, Ohio	20	24
O4	|	at Bowling Green	10	21
O11	● |	Kent State	33	13
O18	|	at Toledo	13	38
O25	●	Marshall	48	14
N1	|	at Ohio U.	17	22
N8		West Texas St.	20	28
N15	●	at Northern Illinois	31	22

1970 — 7-3-0 (2-3-0)

S12	●	at Central Michigan	41	0
S19	●	Brigham Young	35	17
S26	|	at Miami, Ohio	12	23
O3	● |	Bowling Green	23	3
O10	|	at Kent State	22	25
O17	|	Toledo	0	20
O24	●	at Marshall	34	3
O31	● |	Ohio U.	52	23
N7	●	at West Texas St.	20	0
N14	●	Northern Illinois	38	18

1971 — 7-3-0 (2-3-0)

S11	●	Illinois St.	35	7
S18	●	at Ball State	9	0
S25	●	Northern Illinois	27	17
O2	|	at Bowling Green	6	23
O9	● |	Kent State	31	0
O16	|	at Toledo	24	35
O23	●	Marshall	37	0
O30	● |	at Ohio U.	28	14
N6	|	Miami, Ohio	6	7
N13	●	Pacific	25	21

1972 — 7-3-1 (2-2-1)

S9	●	Long Beach St.	28	20
S16		at Fresno State	14	41
S23	●	at Northern Illinois	14	10
S30	= |	Bowling Green	13	13
O7	● |	at Kent State	13	12
O14	|	Toledo	13	20
O21	●	at Marshall	34	0
O28	● |	Ohio U.	34	17
N4	|	at Miami, Ohio	8	38
N11	●	Ball State	31	14
N18	●	Idaho	27	16

1973 — 6-5-0 (1-4-0)

S8	●	at Central Michigan	18	13
S15	●	Long Beach St.	13	8
S22	●	Northern Illinois	28	14
S29	|	at Bowling Green	20	31
O6	|	Kent State	15	39
O13	● |	at Toledo	24	22
O20	●	Marshall	21	7
O27	|	at Ohio U.	0	16
N3	|	Miami, Ohio	9	24
N10	●	Ball State	30	13
N17		at Texas-Arlington	12	31

1974 — 3-8-0 (0-5-0)

S7	●	Texas-Arlington	33	6
S14		at Eastern Michigan	19	20
S21	●	at Northern Illinois	30	13
S28	│	Bowling Green	13	21
O5	│	at Kent State	6	28
O12	│	Toledo	24	31
O19	●	at Marshall	20	17
O26	│	Ohio U.	3	26
N2	│	at Miami, Ohio	0	31
N9		Central Michigan	6	42
N16		at Long Beach St.	33	34

ELLIOT UZELAC 1975-81 (.494) 38-39

1975 — 1-10-0 (0-7-0)

S6	│	at Central Michigan	0	34
S13		Akron	21	27
S20		at Minnesota	0	38
S27	│	Northern Illinois	0	20
O4	│	at Bowling Green	0	28
O11	│	Kent State	17	22
O18	│	Toledo Clev	7	25
O25		at Marshall	19	21
N1	│	at Ohio U.	10	24
N8	│	Miami, Ohio	21	44
N15	●	Eastern Michigan	24	14

1976 — 7-4-0 (6-3-0)

S11	● │	Eastern Michigan	31	13
S18	● │	at Northern Illinois	37	6
S25		at Minnesota	10	21
O2	│	Bowling Green	28	31
O9	│	at Kent State	12	24
O16	● │	Toledo	34	21
O23	●	Marshall	31	21
O30	● │	Ohio U.	21	10
N6	│	at Miami, Ohio	0	31
N13	● │	at Ball State	24	10
N20	● │	Central Michigan	42	14

1977 — 4-7-0 (3-5-0)

S10		at Minnesota	7	10
S17		Texas-Arlington	10	17
S24	● │	Northern Illinois	49	21
O1	│	at Bowling Green	14	34
O8	│	Kent State	16	20
O15	● │	at Toledo	28	7
O22	●	Marshall	53	29
O29	● │	at Ohio U.	28	22
N5	│	Miami, Ohio	8	14
N12	│	Ball State	25	29
N19	│	at Central Michigan	23	28

1978 — 7-4-0 (5-4-0)

S9	●	Illinois St.	27	17
S16	● │	at Northern Illinois	44	30
S23	│	at Miami, Ohio	3	7
S30	● │	Bowling Green	24	20
O7	● │	at Kent State	14	0
O14	● │	Toledo	17	7
O21	● │	Eastern Michigan	32	0
O28	│	Ohio U.	7	10
N4	●	at Marshall	24	6
N11	│	at Ball State	14	20
N18	│	Central Michigan	14	35

1979 — 6-5-0 (5-4-0)

S8	│	at Central Michigan	0	10
S15		at South Carolina	7	24
S22	● │	Northern Illinois	45	17
S29	│	Bowling Green	3	15
O6	│	Kent State	13	18
O13	│	at Toledo	0	17
O20	●	Grand Valley St.	37	0
O27	● │	at Ohio U.	20	6
N3	● │	Miami, Ohio	24	3
N10	● │	Ball State	20	10
N17	● │	at Eastern Michigan	17	7

1980 — 7-4-0 (6-3-0)

S6	● │	Eastern Michigan	37	0
S13	●	at Illinois St.	31	17
S20	● │	at Northern Illinois	35	6
S27		at Michigan State	7	33
O4	│	Bowling Green	14	17
O11	● │	at Kent State	28	21
O18	● │	Toledo	17	7
O25	● │	at Ball State	17	15
N1	● │	Ohio U.	13	7
N8	│	at Miami, Ohio	24	34
N15	│	Central Michigan	10	22

1981 — 6-5-0 (5-4-0)

S12	● │	at Kent State	20	17
S19	●	Marshall	14	3
S26		at Wisconsin	10	21
O3	● │	at Bowling Green	21	7
O10	│	Central Michigan	13	15
O17	│	at Miami, Ohio	19	20
O24	● │	Ball State	14	3
O31	● │	at Northern Illinois	23	12
N7	│	Toledo	14	28
N14	│	at Ohio U.	20	37
N21	● │	Eastern Michigan	38	7

JACK HARBAUGH 1982-86 (.482) 25-27-3

1982 — 7-2-2 (5-2-2)

S4	●	Grand Valley St.	28	3
S11	●	at Marshall	34	0
S25	● │	Kent State	24	14
O2	│	at Bowling Green	3	7
O9	= │	at Central Michigan	18	18
O16	● │	Miami, Ohio	10	0
O23	│	at Ball State	6	13
O30	● │	Northern Illinois	27	3
N6	● │	at Toledo	17	10
N13	● │	Ohio U.	16	7
N20	= │	at Eastern Michigan	3	3

1983 — 6-5-0 (4-5-0)

S10	●	at Texas-Arlington	21	14
S17	●	at Illinois St.	14	13
S24	│	Central Michigan	14	32
O1	● │	at Miami, Ohio	20	18
O8	│	at Northern Illinois	3	27
O15	│	Bowling Green	20	23
O22	│	Ball State	20	24
O29	● │	at Ohio U.	16	14
N5	│	Toledo	16	20
N12	● │	at Kent State	21	13
N19	● │	Eastern Michigan	14	10

1984 — 5-6-0 (3-6-0)

S8	● │	Miami, Ohio	17	13
S15	●	Illinois St.	41	14
S22	│	at Central Michigan	19	38
S29	●	Marshall	42	7
O6	│	Northern Illinois	15	20
O13	│	at Bowling Green	7	34
O20	│	at Ball State	20	23
O27	● │	Ohio U.	33	14
N3	│	at Toledo	13	17
N10	● │	Kent State	13	9
N17	│	at Eastern Michigan	14	24

1985 — 4-6-1 (4-4-1)

S7	│	at Northern Illinois	0	17
S14		at Army	6	48
S28		at Michigan State	3	7
O5	│	Bowling Green	7	48
O12	│	Central Michigan	17	24
O19	= │	at Miami, Ohio	10	10
O26	● │	Ball State	34	0
N2	● │	Toledo	18	13
N9	│	at Ohio U.	15	21
N16	● │	at Kent State	34	3
N23	● │	Eastern Michigan	38	21

1986 — 3-8-0 (3-5-0)

S6	│	at Eastern Michigan	14	21
S13		Temple	17	49 †
S20		Long Beach St.	13	14
S27		at Michigan State	10	45
O4	│	at Bowling Green	3	17
O11	│	Central Michigan	10	18
O18	● │	Miami, Ohio	27	17
O25	│	at Ball State	10	24
N1	│	at Toledo	7	28
N8	● │	Ohio U.	45	17
N15	● │	Kent State	27	7

AL MOLDE 1987-96 (.568) 62-47-2

1987 — 5-6-0 (4-4-0)

S5	●	Akron	24	19
S12		at Illinois St.	6	20
S19		Northern Illinois	14	34
S26	● │	at Bowling Green	34	27
O3	● │	Toledo	21	14
O10	│	Miami, Ohio	0	17
O17	│	at Kent State	13	27
O24	│	Eastern Michigan	17	23
O31	│	at Central Michigan	27	30
N7	● │	Ball State	31	16
N21	● │	at Ohio U.	31	13

1988 — 9-3-0 (7-1-0)

S3	●	at Wisconsin	24	14
S10	● │	at Toledo	31	9
S17	●	Illinois St.	44	14
O1	● │	Bowling Green	37	10
O8	● │	at Miami, Ohio	41	18
O15	│	Kent State	28	45
O22	● │	at Eastern Michigan	31	24
O29	● │	Central Michigan	42	24
N5	● │	at Ball State	16	13
N12		at Northern Illinois	7	15
N19	● │	Ohio U.	23	16
		CALIFORNIA BOWL		
D10		Fresno State	30	35

1989 — 5-6-0 (3-5-0)

S2	●	Temple	31	24
S9	●	Louisiana Tech	24	20
S16		at Maryland	0	23
S23	● │	at Kent State	26	4
S30	│	Eastern Michigan	20	21
O14	│	Central Michigan	6	34
O21	│	at Ball State	13	14
O28	● │	Ohio U.	28	13
N4	│	at Toledo	18	19
N11	│	Bowling Green	30	31
N18	● │	at Miami, Ohio	14	7

1990 — 7-4-0 (5-3-0)

S8	│	at Eastern Michigan	24	27
S15	●	Louisiana Tech	27	21
S22	● │	Kent State	37	10
S29		at Iowa State	20	34
O6	●	at Akron	24	20
O13	│	at Central Michigan	13	20
O20	● │	Ball State	14	13
O27	● │	at Ohio U.	31	23
N3	│	Toledo	9	37
N10	● │	at Bowling Green	19	13
N17	● │	Miami, Ohio	31	17

1991 — 6-5-0 (4-4-0)

A31	● │	Kent State	13	10
S7	●	Akron	35	12
S14		at Florida State	0	58
S21	│	Toledo	13	23
S28	● │	Ohio U.	35	9
O5	● │	at Ball State	25	16
O12	●	at Northern Illinois	22	10
O19	│	at Eastern Michigan	24	42
O26	│	Bowling Green	10	23
N9	● │	Miami, Ohio	24	23
N16	│	at Central Michigan	17	27

1992 — 7-3-1 (6-3-0)

S3	│	at Bowling Green	19	29
S12	=	at TCU	17	17
S19	●	Akron	24	20
S26	● │	at Ohio U.	19	3
O3	● │	Ball State	21	14
O10	│	at Toledo	12	21
O17	● │	Eastern Michigan	20	19
O24	● │	at Kent State	26	13
O31	●	Northern Illinois	13	7
N7	│	at Miami, Ohio	7	20
N14	● │	Central Michigan	19	14

1993 — 7-3-1 (6-1-1)

S2		Youngstown St.	13	17
S11		at Purdue	13	28
S18	● │	Akron	20	3
S25	● │	Miami, Ohio	17	0
O2	● │	at Kent State	27	21
O9	│	Central Michigan	18	23
O23	● │	at Eastern Michigan	21	20
O30	●	at Army	20	7
N6	● │	at Ohio U.	34	28
N13	● │	Toledo	39	26
N20	= │	at Bowling Green	14	14

1994 — 7-4-0 (5-3-0)

S3	● │	at Miami, Ohio	28	25
S8	●	Western Illinois	43	7
S17	●	at Iowa State	23	19
S24	● │	Akron	19	6
O1	● │	Kent State	24	10
O8	│	at Central Michigan	28	35
O15	│	at Ball State	13	16
O22	● │	Eastern Michigan	33	14
N5	● │	Ohio U.	15	3
N12	│	at Toledo	34	37
N19		at La. Lafayette	14	17

1995 — 7-4-0 (6-2-0)

A31	●	Weber St.	28	21
S9		at Indiana	10	24
S14	│	Toledo	21	31
S23	│	at Ball State	0	10
S30	● │	at Kent State	52	6
O7	● │	Akron	7	3
O14	● │	at Ohio U.	34	17
O21		at Auburn	13	34
O28	● │	Bowling Green	17	0
N11	● │	at Eastern Michigan	23	13
N18	● │	Central Michigan	48	31

1996 — 2-9 (2-6)

A29		Eastern Illinois	20	28
S7		at West Virginia	9	34
S14	│	Eastern Michigan	12	19
S21	│	at Central Michigan	28	38
S28	│	at Akron	7	27
O5	│	Ball State	5	28
O12		at Wyoming	28	42
O26	│	at Toledo	7	10
N2	│	Ohio U.	0	38
N9	● │	at Bowling Green	16	13
N16	● │	Kent State	76	27

GARY DARNELL 1997-2004 (.500) 46-46

1997 — 8-3 (6-2)

A28	●	Temple	34	14
S6		at Michigan State	10	42
S13	● │	at Northern Illinois	21	13
S20	│	Toledo	13	23
S27	│	at Ohio U.	7	31
O4	● │	Ball State	21	13
O11	● │	at Bowling Green	34	21
O18	● │	Kent State	50	27
N1	● │	at Eastern Michigan	41	38
N8	● │	Central Michigan	38	24
N15	●	at La. Monroe	32	19

1998 — 7-4 (5-3)

S3	● │	Northern Illinois	37	23
S12		at Indiana	30	45
S19	│	at Toledo	7	35
S26	│	Ohio U.	35	37
O3	●	La. Monroe	27	14
O10	●	at Vanderbilt	27	24
O17	● │	Eastern Michigan	45	35
O24	│	at Central Michigan	24	26
O31	● │	at Kent State	48	23
N7	● │	at Ball State	24	23
N14	● │	Bowling Green	56	27

1999 — 7-5 (6-2)

S4		at Florida	26	55
S11	●	Youngstown St.	46	28
S18		at Missouri	34	48
S25	● │	at Northern Illinois	24	21
O2	● │	Central Michigan	38	16
O9	● │	at Eastern Michigan	40	37
O16	● │	Buffalo	45	17
O23	● │	Ball State	28	0
O30	● │	at Akron	24	10
N13	│	Marshall	17	31
N20	│	at Toledo	21	45
		MAC CHAMPIONSHIP GAME		
D3		Marshall *HUN*	30	34

2000 — 9-3 (7-1)

A31		at Wisconsin	7	19
S9	●	at Iowa	27	21
S16	●	Indiana St.	56	0
S23	● │	Toledo	21	14
S30	● │	Ohio U.	23	10
O5	● │	at Marshall	30	10
O21	● │	Northern Illinois	52	22
O28	● │	at Kent State	42	0
N4	● │	at Ball State	42	3
N11	│	at Central Michigan	17	21
N18	● │	Eastern Michigan	28	0
		MAC CHAMPIONSHIP GAME		
D2		Marshall *HUN*	14	19

2001 — 5-6 (4-4)

A30	●	Illinois St.	48	7
S8		at Virginia Tech	0	31
S22		at Michigan	21	38
S29	● │	at Eastern Michigan	31	10
O6	● │	Akron	31	14
O13	● │	Bowling Green	37	28
O20	│	at Northern Illinois	12	20
O27	│	at Miami, Ohio	11	25
N6	│	at Toledo	35	41
N17	● │	Central Michigan	20	17
N24	│	Ball State	31	35

2002   4-8   (3-5)

A29	●	Indiana St.	48	17
S7		at Michigan	12	35
S14		at Purdue	24	28
S28		Virginia Tech	0	30
O5	●	at Buffalo	31	17
O12		Central Florida	27	31
O19		at Bowling Green	45	48
O26		Northern Illinois	20	24
N2		at Ball State	7	17
N9	●	Eastern Michigan	33	31
N16		Toledo	21	42
N23	●	at Central Michigan	35	10

2003   5-7   (4-4)

A30		at Michigan State	21	26
S6	●	William & Mary	56	24
S13		Virginia	16	59
S27	●	at Ohio U.	39	32
O4	●	at Eastern Michigan	31	3
O11		Bowling Green	21	32
O18		at Northern Illinois	10	37
O25		Marshall	21	41
N1		at Connecticut	27	41
N8	●	Ball State	28	20
N15	●	Central Michigan	44	21
N22		at Toledo	17	34

2004   1-10   (0-8)

S2	●	Tenn-Martin	42	0
S11		at Virginia Tech	0	63
S18		at Illinois	27	30
S25		at Ball State	14	41
O9		Toledo	33	59
O16		Eastern Michigan	31	35
O23		Northern Illinois	38	59
O30		at Central Michigan	21	24
N6		at Bowling Green	0	52
N13		Miami, Ohio	21	42
N20		at Marshall	21	31

THE SCHOOLS

WISCONSIN

BY TODD JONES

WISCONSIN FOOTBALL IS AS SUBTLE as cannon fire at dawn. The Badgers play a tough, physical game with few gimmicks and many bruises. Heisman Trophy winners Alan Ameche and Ron Dayne are exemplars of smash-mouth Badgers football. Four decades apart, the two running backs hammered opponents with a power that resonated throughout the football-mad state. The head-banging style of play has linked Wisconsin fans through good times and bad. They know their Badgers will provide a consistent blue-collar effort when they gather on fall afternoons in the eclectic state capital of Madison.

TRADITION Music has long been part of the Wisconsin football experience. William Purdy composed "On, Wisconsin" in 1909 and alumnus Carl Beck wrote the lyrics. About 2,500 high schools and colleges use its melody as their fight song. Wisconsin has appropriated the Budweiser commercial jingle and made it its own with 79,500 fans singing, "When you say Wisconsin, you've said it all." They lock arms, dance and wave their arms when "Varsity" is played. The press box actually sways at the end of the third quarter when thousands of fans jump up and down to House of Pain's rap anthem "Jump Around." Music defines pregame and postgame festivities, too. The Wisconsin marching band plays at Union South before kickoff and then takes part in the "run-on" into the stadium along with the Bucky Wagon, a restored fire engine carrying cheerleaders and the Bucky Badger mascot. A postgame celebration called the fifth quarter is held win or lose. The band marches in formation onto the field and then breaks into various songs with fans and, sometimes, players singing and dancing along.

BEST PLAYER The names and jersey numerals of Ameche (35) and Dayne (33) are immortalized on the facade of Camp Randall Stadium's second deck. Each running back led Wisconsin to the Rose Bowl and each won the Heisman Trophy. Ameche won his Heisman in 1954 after The Horse from Kenosha, Wis., ended his career with a then-NCAA-record 3,345 rushing yards. Although he also played linebacker, the bruising Ameche relinquished the title of the school's greatest player to Dayne four decades later. There was nothing fancy about Dayne. The tailback with 254 pounds of muscle packed onto a 5'10" frame took the ball, scattered defenders like

PROFILE

University of Wisconsin, Madison
Madison, Wis.
Founded: 1848
Enrollment: 28,585
Colors: Cardinal and White
Nickname: Badgers
Stadium: Camp Randall Stadium
    Opened in 1917
    FieldTurf; 80,000 capacity
First football game: 1889
All-time record: 564–449–53 (.554)
Bowl record: 8–8
Big Ten Conference championships: 11
(6 outright)
Heisman Trophy: Alan Ameche, 1954; Ron Dayne, 1999
First-round NFL draftees: 23
Website: www.uwbadgers.com

THE BEST OF TIMES

From 1896 to 1901, the Badgers went 51–6–1, including 9–0 in 1901. They outscored opponents 1,622-110 during those six seasons and posted 44 shutouts. Three Rose Bowl victories—1994, 1999 and 2000—and six other bowl trips (three of them wins) since 1995 have made modern-day heroes of coach Barry Alvarez and Heisman winner Ron Dayne.

THE WORST OF TIMES

The Badgers suffered through 10 consecutive losing seasons from 1964 to 1973, including 18 defeats in a row and a span of 1–27–2. They went 0–9–1 in 1967 and 0–10 in 1968.

CONFERENCE

Wisconsin was a charter member of the Western Conference in 1896, and has remained in the league since. The league was popularly known as the Big Ten since 1917, but didn't officially change its name to the Big Ten Conference until 1987.

DISTINGUISHED ALUMNI

Charles Lindbergh; Bud Selig; Frank Lloyd Wright; Stephen E. Ambrose, historian; Jim Lovell, astronaut; D. Wayne Lukas, thoroughbred trainer; John Muir, naturalist; Arthur Nielsen Sr., creator of Nielsen ratings; Dick Cheney

FIGHT SONG

ON, WISCONSIN
On Wisconsin, On Wisconsin
Plunge right through that line,
Run the ball clear down the field, boys
Touchdown sure this time
On Wisconsin, On Wisconsin
Fight on for her fame,
Fight, Fellows, Fight, Fight, Fight
We'll win this game!

The head-banging style of play has linked Wisconsin fans through good times and bad.

bowling pins, got up and did it again. His quiet, no-nonsense style matched his personality. Dayne arrived at Wisconsin as a shy kid from New Jersey hoping to start a new life after divorce and drugs had ravaged his family. He left Madison four years later still a man of few words, but with rushing records that screamed for attention. Dayne won the 1999 Heisman Trophy as a senior after rushing for 2,034 yards and 20 touchdowns. That year he became the first player to lead the Big Ten in rushing, scoring and all-purpose yards. Dayne finished as college football's career rushing leader with 6,397 yards, not counting bowl games. He was one of four players to run for 1,000 yards in each of four seasons and outrushed opposing teams 29 times in 43 career starts.

BEST COACH Nothing came easy to Barry Alvarez. He grew up in a blue-collar neighborhood in the western Pennsylvania mining town of Burgettstown and later played linebacker at Nebraska, although he described himself as "short, slow and fat." His belief in toughness, discipline and hard work was sorely needed at Wisconsin. The Badgers had endured five straight losing seasons, and had gone 6–27 in the previous three years, before

Alvarez took over in 1990. He came to an athletic department that had a $2.1 million deficit and inherited a football program that had averaged 41,734 fans—the school's lowest mark in 44 years—the previous season. His first Wisconsin team went 1–10, but Alvarez kept working. Three years later, the Badgers went 10–1–1 and won the Rose Bowl. Alvarez learned how to maintain success as an assistant under Iowa coach Hayden Fry and Notre Dame coach Lou Holtz. His work ethic, and ability to recruit New York and New Jersey, ensured Wisconsin remained a Big Ten force and perennial bowl game victor. Alvarez is the only Big Ten coach to win consecutive Rose Bowls. In April 2004, he also became Wisconsin's athletic director.

BEST TEAM The 1998 Badgers epitomized the power football Alvarez loves. Wisconsin went 11–1 for its best winning percentage (.916) in the modern era and won its third Rose Bowl in seven years. Dayne rumbled for 1,525 yards and 15 TDs behind a line anchored by behemoth tackle Aaron Gibson (6'6", 370 pounds). While the Badgers averaged 31.8 points per game, their defense allowed only 10.2, lowest in the nation. Tom Burke led

RECORDS

RUSHING YARDS

	GAME
339	Ron Dayne vs. Hawaii, Nov. 30, 1996 (36 att.)
	SEASON
2,109	Ron Dayne, 1996 (325 att.)
	CAREER
7,125	Ron Dayne, 1996-99 (1,220 att.)

PASSING YARDS

	GAME
423	Darrell Bevell, vs. Minnesota, Oct. 23, 1993 (31 of 48)
	SEASON
2,390	Darrell Bevell, 1993 (187 of 276)
	CAREER
7,686	Darrell Bevell, 1992-95 (646 of 1,052)

RECEIVING YARDS

	GAME
258	Lee Evans vs. Michigan State, Nov. 15, 2003 (10 rec.)
	SEASON
1,545	Lee Evans, 2001 (75 rec.)
	CAREER
3,468	Lee Evans, 1999-2003 (175 rec.)

POINTS

	GAME
30	Anthony Davis vs. Minnesota, Nov. 23, 2002 (5 TDs); Billy Marek vs. Minnesota, Nov. 23, 1974 (5 TDs)
	SEASON
126	Ron Dayne, 1996 (21 TDs)
	CAREER
426	Ron Dayne, 1996-99 (71 TDs)

CONSENSUS ALL-AMERICANS

1912	Robert Butler, T
1913	Ray Keeler, G
1915	Howard Buck, T
1919	Charles Carpenter, C
1920	Ralph Scott, T
1923	Marty Below, T
1930	Milo Lubratovich, T
1942	Dave Schreiner, E
1954	Alan Ameche, B
1959	Dan Lanphear, T
1962	Pat Richter, E
1975	Dennis Lick, T
1981	Tim Krumrie, DL
1994	Cory Raymer, C
1998	Aaron Gibson, OL
1998	Tom Burke, DL
1999	Ron Dayne, RB
1999	Chris McIntosh, OL
2000	Jamar Fletcher, DB
2004	Erasmus James, DL

the nation with 22 sacks and Jamar Fletcher had an NCAA-high six interceptions. Wisconsin allowed a school-record-low five rushing TDs. The Badgers won their first nine games and were ranked No. 8 before losing 27-10 at Michigan in mid-November. Lingering distaste from that defeat was washed away by a Rose Bowl win over No. 6 UCLA. Dayne ran for 246 yards and four touchdowns in the 38-31 victory. The Badgers ended the season ranked No. 6.

BIGGEST GAME UCLA was in its hometown but didn't have the crowd at the 1994 Rose Bowl. Over 70,000 Wisconsin fans crammed into the stadium to see a Badgers team that had won the school's first Big Ten title in 31 years. "I've never been on a team where everybody was so focused on one goal— winning—not just for the team, but for an entire state," said freshman linebacker Tarek Saleh. Wisconsin won 21-16 for the school's first New Year's Day bowl victory. Badgers tailback Brent Moss was named the game's MVP after running for 158 yards and two touchdowns on 36 carries. Clinging to a 14-10 lead in the fourth quarter, quarterback Darrell Bevell scored on a 79-yard keeper that Wisconsin fans call The Run. UCLA answered with a touchdown, then drove on the game's final possession to the Badgers' 18-yard line before time ran out. Wisconsin's first bowl game in 10 years, and first bowl win in 12, legitimized the program's turnaround under Alvarez.

BIGGEST UPSET Paul Brown brought the second, and best, of his three Ohio State teams to Madison in 1942. The Buckeyes were 5–0 and ranked No. 1 when they met the 5–0–1 and No. 6-ranked Badgers. Nearly 45,000 attended the homecoming game. Over 200 radio stations broadcast the action to U.S. servicemen in Alaska, Hawaii, Canada and South America. The British Broadcasting Company carried the game to England, Ireland, Australia, Africa and India. Wisconsin led 10-0 at halftime after a second quarter in which fullback Pat Harder ran for an eight-yard TD and kicked a 37-yard field goal. The Buckeyes drew within 10-7 early in the fourth quarter on a TD run by Paul Sarringhaus, but Elroy "Crazy Legs" Hirsch tossed a 14-yard TD pass to ensure the Badgers' 17-7 victory. Ohio

State fans called the defeat "the bad water game" because half the OSU team got dysentery before the game from drinking rusty water on the train ride from Columbus. The Buckeyes rebounded to finish 9–1.

ALL-TIME TEAM	

In conjunction with the centennial celebration of college football in 1969, Wisconsin fans selected the school's all-time team. The 11-man unit features 1954 Heisman Trophy winner Alan Ameche, who was voted All-Time Greatest Player. The vote was conducted 30 years before running back Ron Dayne won the Heisman Trophy for the Badgers.

1951-54	Alan Ameche, HB
1961-63	Ken Bowman, OL
1913-15	Howard Buck, OL
1941-42	Pat Harder, HB
1942	Elroy "Crazy Legs" Hirsch, WR
1957-59	Dan Lanphear, OL
1914	Arlie Mucks, Sr., OL
1960-62	Pat Richter, WR
1940-42	Dave Schreiner, E
1962	Ron Vander Kelen, QB
1946-49	Robert "Red" Wilson, OL

HEARTBREAKER One of the most beloved Wisconsin teams was the "Hard Rocks" of 1951. Those Badgers led the nation in defense, allowing only 154.8 yards per game. The defense actually outscored opponents 58-53. Defensive stars Pat O'Donahue, Hal Faverty and Ed Withers helped produce six straight victories to end the season, but a trip to Illinois in the season's second game cost Wisconsin a Rose Bowl berth. The Badgers led 10-7 at halftime, and on their first possession of the second half they drove 10 minutes to the Illini 1-yard line. Wisconsin failed to score on four plays. Rollie Strehlow lost three yards on a first-down run. The Badgers were penalized five yards for illegal motion on second down. John Coatta gained five on a run, but the freshman Ameche was stopped for no gain on third down. Ameche was stopped for no gain again on fourth down from the 4. Illinois then drove 96 yards for a touchdown. Wisconsin lost 14-10 despite having more first downs (20-8) and more total yards (274-142). The Badgers finished the season 7–1–1, including a 6-6 tie with Ohio State.

WILDEST FINISH The Badgers trailed Iowa 17-0 in the fourth quarter on Oct. 11, 1969. They were already 0–3 in John Coatta's third and final season. Wisconsin had gone 0–10 the previous season, and 0–9–1 in 1967. The Badgers faced Iowa in the throes of an 18-game losing streak, dating to a 21-21 tie against Iowa on Oct. 21, 1967. They had not won since beating Minnesota 7-6 in the final game of the 1966 season. So another defeat seemed imminent even when Alan Thompson scored for Wisconsin on a two-yard run. He added a six-yard TD run to cut the deficit to 17-14. Badgers quarterback Neil Graff then threw a 17-yard TD pass to Randall Marks for a 21-17 lead with 2:08 remaining. Iowa's Dennis Green then fumbled the kickoff out of the end zone while trying to make a return. The safety closed the scoring on Wisconsin's 23-17 win. Hundreds of fans from the Camp

Randall Stadium crowd of 53,1714 stormed the field with 1:10 remaining, which delayed the game's finish. The Badgers ended the season 3–7.

STADIUM It now hosts a classic horseshoe football structure, but previously the site of Camp Randall Stadium served as a military training center. Wisconsin's famous Iron Brigade drilled on the 53 acres of Camp Randall, and 1,400 Confederate prisoners were held there during the Civil War. Before and after that war, the site was home to Wisconsin's state fair. In 1893, the state legislature fulfilled the desires of Civil War veterans and purchased the land and gave it to the school to serve as a memorial park for athletics. The football team began playing games at Camp Randall in 1913, but two years later, temporary wooden bleachers collapsed. The state legislature responded by appropriating $15,000 to build concrete stands on the field's western side. The field was dedicated in 1917 and the stadium grew in size over subsequent decades. A $109.3 million renovation was scheduled to increase capacity to 80,000 for the 2005 season.

RIVAL The most-played rivalry in Division I-A history took on special meaning long before the Paul Bunyan's Axe trophy was created. Minnesota became an immediate villain in 1890 by beating the Badgers 63-0 in the series' first game. Wisconsin was outscored 161-16 while losing the first four games before beating the Golden Gophers 6-0 in 1894 when Ikey Karel scored on a 40-yard touchdown run. The *Milwaukee Journal* wrote: "When little Karel had done it, he sat down and wept. The excitement was too much for him." Wisconsin students celebrated with a campus bonfire that night and serenaded university president Charles Kendall Adams at his home. Such emotion still defines the annual game between schools from bordering states. Since 1948, the victors have gained possession of Paul Bunyan's Axe, created that year by the Wisconsin letterwinners' group, the National W Club. Wisconsin fans still take delight in the 23-21 upset of No. 3 Minnesota in 1961 that cost the Golden Gophers a share of the Big Ten title.

NICKNAME In the 1820s, lead miners in Wisconsin burrowed tunnels into hillsides during the winter because they had no shelter. People said they "lived like badgers," and soon Wisconsin became known as the Badger State. The school adopted the name Badgers from those miners.

MASCOT Wisconsin used to use a real badger on a leash at games but stopped in 1940 when the animal proved too vicious; it was donated to the Madison zoo. Arthur Lentz, a PR man in the athletic department, came up with the idea of a cartoon badger and hired illustrator Art Evans, who drew one in a cardinal-and-white sweater. In 1949, art department student Connie Conrad was commissioned to mold a papier-mâché head of a badger. Bill Sagal, a cheerleader and gymnast, wore the outfit at that year's homecoming game. A school committee named the mascot Bucky Badger after deciding that Buckingham U. Badger, a name apparently from the lyrics of a song, encouraged the football team to buck through the line.

UNIFORMS The Badgers have always worn cardinal red uniforms with the exception of one game in 1923. For an unknown reason, they wore all black that day against Indiana. Wisconsin won 52-0, but then went back to its traditional red-and-white uniforms. A "W" has usually been on the Badgers' helmets, with the current design dating to 1991.

NUMBERS The Badgers were ranked No. 1 for the only time after a 20-6 win over Illinois on Oct. 4, 1952. They lost to Ohio State 23-14 the next week … Wisconsin upset No. 4 Nebraska 21-20 at Camp Randall in 1974 when Gregg Bohlig completed a 77-yard TD pass to Jeff Mack with 3:29 remaining … Billy Marek ran for 3,709 yards and 44 TDs from 1972 to 1975. He averaged 5.2 yards per carry in his career. In 1974 he ran for 304 yards and 5 TDs against Minnesota … Four Badgers have their numbers retired: Elroy "Crazy Legs" Hirsch (40), Alan Ameche (35), Dave Schreiner (80) and Allan Shafer (83). Shafer died from head injuries suffered in a 1944 home game against Iowa … Wisconsin upset No. 1-ranked Northwestern 37-6 in a homecoming game at Camp Randall on Nov. 10, 1962 … The 1901 Badgers went 9–0 with eight shutouts and outscored opponents 317-5.

LORE Pat O'Dea came to Wisconsin from Melbourne, Australia, in 1896 as a rugby player and left two years later with the nickname the Kangaroo Kicker. He had a 110-yard punt (fields were that long then), drop-kicked field goals of 65 and 55 yards and also place-kicked a 57-yard field goal while totaling 32 career field goals. Walter Camp wrote that O'Dea "put the foot in football as no man ever has or as no man probably ever will again." Many believed O'Dea died while serving Australia in World War I, but he actually had disappeared into anonymity. He took a new name, Charles J. Mitchell, to avoid the attention he had

gained as a football player. In 1934, a San Francisco newspaper made national news by revealing Mitchell's true identity when he was working at a California lumber company. That year, as Pat O'Dea once again, he was guest of honor at Wisconsin's homecoming game against Illinois … The four-season coaching era of Dr. Clarence Spears ended in chaos. He was fired after a 1–7 record in 1935, but he didn't go down alone with the ship. Team captain John Golemgeske told a university athletic council that Dr. Walter Meanwell, the AD and basketball coach, had instructed him at a season-ending party to circulate a petition calling for Spears' firing. Team trainer Bill Fallon and his assistant, Red Smith, told the council that Spears had ordered whiskey to be put in the coffee served to players at halftime of the Minnesota game. Smith also alleged the coach had given whiskey to two players after the Northwestern game. Spears denied the whiskey charges when the board of regents ordered an investigation. The regents fired Spears anyway, but also fired Fallon and Meanwell, despite his successful 20 seasons as the school's basketball coach. Six members of the athletic council resigned.

QUOTE "Why not Wisconsin? Someone has to win the Big Ten Conference title. It might as well be us." — Joe Panos, starting right offensive tackle and co-captain of the 1993 co-Big Ten champions

WISCONSIN ANNUAL STATISTICAL LEADERS

YR	RUSHING	YDS	ATT	AVG	PASSING	ATT	CMP	PCT	YDS	RECEIVING	REC	YDS	AVG
1946	Earl Maves	538	92	5.8	Lisle Blackbourne	26	10	.38	175	Tom Bennett	6	124	20.7
1947	Clarence Self	526	75	7.0	Earl Girard	55	25	.45	322	Tom Bennett	7	95	13.6
1948	Ben Bendrick	327	64	5.1	Bob Petruska	26	11	.42	125	Jim Embach	5	92	18.4
1949	Bob Teague	521	96	5.4	Bob Petruska	106	45	.42	620	Hal Haberman	17	194	11.4
1950	Rollie Strehlow	398	101	3.9	John Coatta	108	65	.60	727	Gene Felker	23	266	11.6
1951	Alan Ameche	824	157	5.2	John Coatta	185	91	.49	1,154	Jerry Witt	17	371	21.8
1952	Alan Ameche	1,079	233	4.6	Jim Haluska	225	123	.55	1,552	Jerry Witt	27	387	14.3
1953	Alan Ameche	801	165	4.9	Jim Miller	69	36	.52	683	Norbert Esser	19	238	12.5
1954	Alan Ameche	641	146	4.4	Jim Miller	88	46	.52	608	Ron Locklin	22	218	9.9
1955	Charles Thomas	477	98	4.9	Jim Haluska	132	71	.54	1,036	Dave Howard	15	273	18.2
1956	Danny Lewis	554	100	5.5	Sid Williams	19	10	.53	216	Dave Howard	16	247	15.4
1957	Danny Lewis	611	95	6.4	Sid Williams	54	25	.46	451	Earl Hill	11	197	17.9
1958	John Hobbs	401	117	3.4	Dale Hackbart	99	46	.46	641	Ron Steiner	11	171	15.5
1959	Dale Hackbart	387	103	3.8	Dale Hackbart	108	51	.47	734	Alan Schoonover	10	290	29.0
1960	Tom Wiesner	374	87	4.3	Ron Miller	188	97	.52	1,351	Pat Richter	25	362	14.5
1961	Jim Nettles	213	39	5.5	Ron Miller	198	104	.53	1,487	Pat Richter	47	817	17.4
1962	Ralph Kurek	367	67	5.5	Ron Vander Kelen	216	124	.57	1,582	Pat Richter	49	694	14.2
1963	Louis Holland	511	88	5.8	Harold Brandt	181	86	.48	1,006	Rick Reichardt	26	383	14.7
1964	Ronald Smith	438	101	4.3	Harold Brandt	176	85	.48	1,059	Jimmy Jones	34	529	15.6
1965	Tom Jankowski	271	86	3.2	Chuck Burt	235	121	.51	1,143	Dennis Lager	39	396	10.2
1966	Wayne Todd	480	128	3.8	John Boyajian	129	64	.50	863	Tom McCauley	46	689	15.0
1967	John Smith	362	96	3.8	John Boyajian	152	79	.52	966	Tom McCauley	37	525	14.2
1968	Wayne Todd	364	100	3.6	John Ryan	202	84	.42	855	Mel Reddick	34	375	11.0
1969	Alan Thompson	907	214	4.2	Neil Graff	191	93	.49	1,086	Stu Voigt	39	439	11.3
1970	Rufus Ferguson	588	130	4.5	Neil Graff	174	83	.48	1,313	Larry Mialik	33	702	21.3
1971	Rufus Ferguson	1,222	249	4.9	Neil Graff	186	97	.52	1,300	Albert Hannah	39	608	15.6
1972	Rufus Ferguson	1,004	215	4.7	Rudy Steiner	150	62	.41	1,080	Jeff Mack	27	528	19.6
1973	Billy Marek	1,207	241	5.0	Gregg Bohlig	172	78	.45	1,211	Jack Novak	13	282	21.7
1974	Billy Marek	1,215	205	5.9	Gregg Bohlig	143	79	.55	1,212	Jeff Mack	16	353	22.1
1975	Billy Marek	1,281	272	4.7	Mike Carroll	123	58	.47	708	Ray Bailey	18	223	12.4
1976	Larry Canada	993	221	4.5	Mike Carroll	262	132	.50	1,627	David Charles	34	449	13.2
1977	Mike Morgan	478	124	3.9	Anthony Dudley	127	64	.50	877	David Charles	29	437	15.1
1978	Ira Matthews	654	130	5.0	Mike Kalasmiki	231	107	.46	1,378	David Charles	38	573	15.1
1979	Dave Mohapp	603	117	5.2	Mike Kalasmiki	137	72	.53	1,082	Tom Stauss	38	660	17.4
1980	John Williams	526	119	4.4	John Josten	138	53	.38	622	Tim Stracka	28	462	16.5
1981	John Williams	634	116	5.5	Jess Cole	215	90	.42	1,269	Michael Jones	24	421	17.5
1982	Troy King	715	106	6.7	Randy Wright	330	174	.53	2,292	Tim Stracka	35	614	17.5
1983	Gary Ellerson	777	161	4.8	Randy Wright	323	173	.54	2,329	Al Toon	45	881	19.6
1984	Marck Harrison	848	179	4.7	Mike Howard	314	182	.58	2,127	Al Toon	54	750	13.9
1985	Larry Emery	1,113	224	5.0	Bud Keyes	147	60	.41	829	Tim Fullington	21	403	19.2
1986	Larry Emery	855	193	4.4	Bud Keyes	174	93	.53	1,002	Reggie Tompkins	32	443	13.8
1987	Marvin Artley	955	148	6.5	Tony Lowery	89	42	.47	572	Scott Bestor	18	257	14.3
1988	Marvin Artley	516	132	3.9	Tony Lowery	121	67	.55	712	Scott Bestor	26	327	12.6
1989	Jimmy Henderson	426	102	4.2	Sean Wilson	129	66	.51	667	Craig Hudson	24	206	8.6
1990	Robert Williams	541	139	3.9	Tony Lowery	280	159	.57	1,757	Tim Ware	24	473	19.7
1991	Terrell Fletcher	446	109	4.1	Tony Lowery	158	87	.55	965	Lee DeRamus	23	374	16.3
1992	Brent Moss	739	165	4.5	Darrell Bevell	245	125	.51	1,479	Lee DeRamus	42	680	16.2
1993	Brent Moss	1,637	312	5.2	Darrell Bevell	276	187	.68	2,390	Lee DeRamus	54	920	17.0
1994	Terrell Fletcher	1,476	244	6.0	Darrell Bevell	231	139	.60	1,544	Tony Simmons	22	588	26.7
1995	Carl McCullough	1,038	236	4.4	Darrell Bevell	300	195	.65	2,273	Michael London	41	587	14.3
1996	Ron Dayne	2,109	325	6.5	Mike Samuel	254	148	.58	1,752	Donald Hayes	44	629	14.3
1997	Ron Dayne	1,457	263	5.5	Mike Samuel	254	141	.56	1,896	Donald Hayes	45	618	13.7
1998	Ron Dayne	1,525	295	5.2	Mike Samuel	172	90	.52	1,175	Chris Chambers	28	563	20.1
1999	Ron Dayne	2,034	337	6.0	Brooks Bollinger	140	82	.59	1,133	Chris Chambers	41	578	14.1
2000	Michael Bennett	1,681	310	5.4	Brooks Bollinger	209	110	.53	1,479	Chris Chambers	52	813	15.6
2001	Anthony Davis	1,466	291	5.0	Brooks Bollinger	177	91	.51	1,257	Lee Evans	75	1,545	20.6
2002	Anthony Davis	1,555	300	5.2	Brooks Bollinger	245	131	.53	1,758	Brandon Williams	52	663	12.8
2003	Dwayne Smith	857	165	5.2	Jim Sorgi	248	140	.56	2,251	Lee Evans	64	1,213	19.0
2004	Anthony Davis	973	201	4.8	John Stocco	321	169	.53	1,999	Brandon Williams	42	517	12.3

Receiving leaders by receptions
All statistics include postseason

WISCONSIN ALL-TIME SCORES

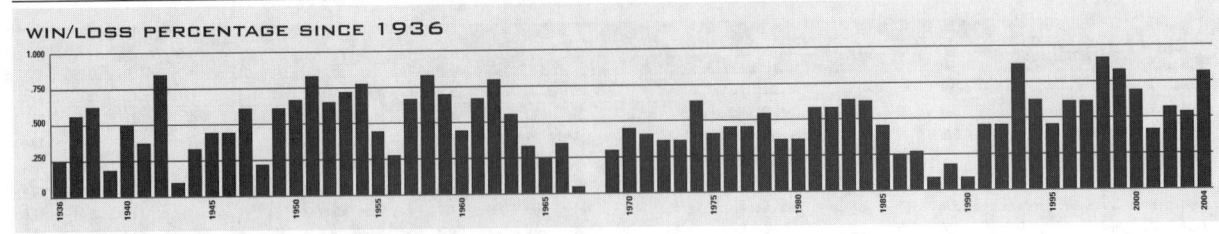

WIN/LOSS PERCENTAGE SINCE 1936

ALVIN KLETSCH		
1889 (.000)		0-2

1889   0-2-0
N23	Calumet Club	0	27
D14	at Beloit	0	4

TED MESTRE		
1890 (.250)		1-3

1890   1-3-0
N1 ●	U.W. Whitewater	106	0
N15	at Minnesota	0	63
N22	Lake Forest	6	16
N26	Northwestern	10	22

HERB ALWARD		
1891 (.700)		3-1-1

1891   3-1-1
O17 ●	at Beloit	40	4
O24	at Minnesota	12	26
O31 =	Northwestern	0	0
N14 ●	Lake Forest	6	4
N29 ●	Northwestern	40	0

FRANK CRAWFORD		
1892 (.571)		4-3

1892   4-3-0
O1 ●	Beloit	32	4
O15	Michigan	6	10
O19	at Purdue	4	32 *
O22 ●	Lake Forest *MIL*	10	6
O29 ●	Minnesota	4	32
N19 ●	at Northwestern	26	6
N24 ●	Northwestern *MIL*	20	6

PARKE DAVIS		
1893 (.667)		4-2

1893   4-2-0
O14 ●	Chicago *MIL*	0	22
O21 ●	Lake Forest	24	0
O28 ●	Beloit	18	0
N4 ●	at Michigan	34	18
N11 ●	at Minnesota	0	40
N18 ●	Purdue	36	30

H.O. STICKNEY		
1894-95 (.700)		10-4-1

1894   5-2-0
O6 ●	Chicago AC	22	4
O15 ●	Purdue	0	1 *f*
O20 ●	at Chicago	30	0
O27 ●	at Chicago AC	4	16
O29 ●	Iowa	44	0
N3 ●	at Beloit	46	0
N17 ●	Minnesota	6	0

1895   5-2-1
S21 ●	Northwestern *MIL*	12	6
S30 ●	Iowa State	28	6 *
O5 ●	Armour	32	4
O12 ●	Lake Forest	26	5
O19 ●	Grinnell	14	4
O26 =	Illinois	10	10
N2 ●	at Chicago	12	22
N16 ●	at Minnesota	10	14

1896-PRESENT		
BIG 10		
PHIL KING		
1896-1902, '05 (.851) 65-11-1		

1896   7-1-1 (2-0-1)
O10 ●	Lake Forest	34	0
O14 ●	Madison HS	18	0
O17 ●	Rush Medical	50	0
O24 ●	Grinnell	54	6
O31 ●	at Beloit	6	0
N7 ●	Chicago	24	0
N21 ●	Minnesota	6	0
N26 =	at Northwestern	6	6
D19	Carlisle Indians *CHI*	8	18

1897   9-1-0 (3-0-0)
O2 ●	Lake Forest	30	0
O6 ●	Madison HS	8	0
O9 ●	Rush Medical	28	0
O16 ●	U.W. Platteville	20	0
O23 ●	Madison HS	29	0
O30 ●	at Minnesota	39	0
N6 ●	Beloit	11	0
N13 ●	at Chicago	25	8
N20 ●	U.W. Alumni	0	6
N25 ●	at Northwestern	22	0

1898   9-1-0 (2-1-0)
O1 ●	Ripon	52	0
O5 ●	Madison HS	21	0
O8 ●	Dixon	76	0
O15 ●	Rush Medical	42	0
O22 ●	Beloit *MIL*	17	0
O29 ●	Minnesota	28	0 *
N5 ●	U.W. Alumni	12	11
N12	at Chicago	0	6
N19 ●	U.W. WhiteWater	22	0
N24 ●	at Northwestern	47	0

1899   9-2-0 (4-1-0)
S30 ●	Lake Forest	45	0
O6 ●	Beloit *MIL*	36	0
O14 ●	Northwestern	38	0
O21	at Yale	0	6
O28 ●	Rush Medical	17	0
N4 ●	U.W. Alumni	17	5
N11 ●	Illinois *MIL*	23	0
N18 ●	at Minnesota	19	0
N25 ●	Lawrence	58	0
N30 ●	Michigan *CHI*	17	5
D9	Chicago	0	17

1900   8-1-0 (2-1-0)
S29 ●	Ripon	50	0
O6 ●	Chicago P&S	5	0
O13 ●	Beloit *MIL*	11	0
O20 ●	Upper Iowa	64	0
O27 ●	Grinnell	45	0
N3	at Minnesota	5	6
N10 ●	Notre Dame	54	0
N17 ●	at Chicago	39	5
N24 ●	Illinois	27	0

1901   9-0-0 (2-0-0)
S28 ●	Milwaukee Medical	26	0
O5 ●	Hyde Park HS	62	0
O12 ●	Beloit *MIL*	40	0
O19 ●	Knox	23	5
O26 ●	Kansas	50	0
N2 ●	Nebraska *MIL*	18	0
N9 ●	Iowa State	45	0
N16 ●	at Minnesota	18	0
N28 ●	at Chicago	35	0

1902   6-3-0 (1-3-0)
S27 ●	Lawrence	11	0
O4 ●	Hyde Park HS	24	5
O11 ●	Lawrence	52	0
O18 ●	Beloit *MIL*	52	6
O25 ●	Kansas	38	0
N1	Michigan *CHI*	0	6
N8 ●	at Northwestern	51	0
N15	at Minnesota	0	11
N27	at Chicago	0	11

ART CURTIS		
1903-04 (.639)		11-6-1

1903   6-3-1 (0-3-1)
O3 ●	North Central	28	0
O10 ●	Lawrence	40	7
O17 ●	Beloit	87	0
O21 ●	Osteopaths	32	0
O24 ●	Knox	54	6
O31 ●	Chicago	6	15
N7 ●	U.W. Oshkosh	52	0
N14	at Michigan	0	16
N21 =	Northwestern *CHI*	6	6
N26	at Minnesota	0	17

1904   5-3-0 (0-3-0)
O1 ●	Ft. Sheridan	45	0
O8 ●	Marquette	33	0
O15 ●	Notre Dame *MIL*	58	0
O22 ●	Drake	82	0
O29	Michigan	0	28
N5 ●	Beloit	36	0
N12	at Minnesota	0	28
N24	at Chicago	11	18

PHIL KING		

1905   8-2-0 (1-2-0)
S23 ●	at Company I.	16	0
S30 ●	North Central	49	0
O4 ●	Marquette	29	0
O7 ●	Lawrence	34	0
O14 ●	Notre Dame *MIL*	21	0
O21	Chicago	0	4
O28 ●	U.W. Alumni	17	0
N4	at Minnesota	16	12
N11 ●	Beloit	44	0
N18	at Michigan	0	12

CHARLES HUTCHINS		
1906-07 (.850)		8-1-1

1906   5-0-0 (3-0-0)
O13 ●	Lawrence	5	0
O20 ●	North Dakota	10	0
N3 ●	Iowa	18	4
N10 ●	at Illinois	16	6
N17 ●	Purdue	29	5

1907   3-1-1 (3-1-1)
O26 ●	Illinois	4	15
N2 ●	at Iowa	6	5
N9 ●	Indiana	11	8
N16 ●	at Purdue	12	6
N23 =	Minnesota	17	17

J.A. BARRY		
1908-10 (.656)		9-4-3

1908   5-1-0 (2-1-0)
O10 ●	Lawrence	35	0
O17 ●	at Indiana	16	0
O24 ●	U.W. JV	24	15
O31 ●	Marquette	9	6
N7 ●	at Minnesota	5	0
N21	Chicago	12	18

1909   3-1-1 (2-1-1)
O9 ●	Lawrence	22	0
O23 ●	Indiana	6	3
O30 ●	at Northwestern	21	11
N13	Minnesota	6	34
N20 =	at Chicago	6	6

1910   1-2-2 (1-2-1)
O8 ●	Lawrence	6	6
O22 ●	Indiana *IND*	3	12
O29 =	Northwestern	0	0
N12 ●	at Minnesota	0	28
N19 ●	Chicago	10	0

J.R. RICHARDS		
1911, '17, '19-22 (.738)		29-9-4

1911   5-1-1 (2-1-1)
O7 ●	Lawrence	15	0
O14 ●	Ripon	24	0
O21 ●	Colorado College	26	0
O28 ●	at Northwestern	28	3
N4 ●	Iowa	12	0
N18 =	Minnesota	6	6
N25	at Chicago	0	5

WILLIAM JUNEAU		
1912-15 (.679)		18-8-2

1912   7-0-0 (5-0-0)
O5 ●	Lawrence	13	0
O12	Northwestern	56	0
O19	Purdue	41	0
N2	Chicago	30	12
N9	Arkansas	64	7
N16	at Minnesota	14	0
N23	at Iowa	28	10

1913   3-3-1 (1-2-1)
O4 ●	Lawrence	58	7
O11 ●	Marquette	13	0
O18	at Purdue	7	7
O25	Michigan State	7	12
N1	Minnesota	3	21
N8	Ohio State	12	0
N22	at Chicago	0	19

1914   4-2-1 (2-2-1)
O3 ●	Lawrence	21	0
O10 ●	Marquette	48	0
O17 ●	Purdue	14	7
O24	at Ohio State	7	6
O31 =	Chicago	0	0
N14	at Minnesota	3	14
N21	Illinois	9	24

1915   4-3-0 (2-3-0)
O2 ●	Lawrence	82	0
O8 ●	Marquette	85	0
O16 ●	at Purdue	28	3
O23 ●	Ohio State	21	0
O30 ●	at Chicago	13	14
N13	at Illinois	3	17
N20	Minnesota	3	20

PAUL WITHINGTON		
1916 (.643)		4-2-1

1916   4-2-1 (1-2-1)
O7 ●	Lawrence	20	0
O14 ●	South Dakota St.	28	3
O21 ●	Haskell Indians	13	0
O28 ●	Chicago	30	7
N4	at Ohio State	13	14
N18	at Minnesota	0	54
N25 =	Illinois	0	0

THE SCHOOLS

J.R. RICHARDS

1917 4-2-1 (3-2-0)
O6	•	Beloit	34	0
O13	=	Notre Dame	0	0
O20		at Illinois	0	7
O27	•	Iowa	20	0
N3	•	Minnesota	10	7
N10		Ohio State	3	16
N24		at Chicago	18	0

GUY LOWMAN 1918 (.500)   3-3

1918 3-3-0 (1-2-0)
O26		Camp Grant	0	7
N2	•	Beloit	21	0
N9		Illinois	0	22
N16		at Minnesota	0	6
N23	•	at Ohio State	14	3
N28	•	Michigan State	7	6

J.R. RICHARDS

1919 5-2-0 (3-2-0)
O4	•	Ripon	37	0
O11	•	Marquette	13	0
O18	•	at Northwestern	10	6
O25	•	at Illinois	14	10
N1		Minnesota	7	19
N15		Ohio State	0	3
N22	•	at Chicago	10	3

1920 6-1-0 (4-1-0)
O2	•	Lawrence	60	0
O9	•	Michigan State	27	0
O16	•	Northwestern	27	7
O23		at Ohio State	7	13
N6	•	at Minnesota	3	0
N13	•	Illinois	14	9
N20	•	at Chicago	3	0

1921 5-1-1 (3-1-1)
O1	•	Lawrence	28	0
O8	•	South Dakota St.	24	3
O15	•	at Northwestern	27	0
O22	•	at Illinois	20	0
O29	•	Minnesota	35	0
N12	=	Michigan	7	7
N19		at Chicago	0	3

1922 4-2-1 (2-2-1)
O7	•	Carleton	41	0
O14	•	South Dakota St.	20	6
O21	•	Indiana	20	0
N4	•	at Minnesota	14	0
N11		Illinois	0	3
N18		at Michigan	6	13
N25	=	at Chicago	0	0

JACK RYAN 1923-24 (.467)   5-6-4

1923 3-3-1 (1-3-1)
O6	•	Coe	7	3
O13	•	Michigan State	21	0
O20		at Indiana	52	0
O27	=	Minnesota	0	0
N10		at Illinois	0	10
N17		Michigan	3	6
N24		at Chicago	6	13

1924 2-3-3 (0-2-2)
S27	•	North Dakota St.	25	0
O4	•	Iowa State	17	0
O11	=	Coe	7	7
O18	=	Minnesota	7	7
O25		at Michigan	0	21
N8		Notre Dame	3	38
N15		Iowa	7	21
N22	•	at Chicago	0	0

GEORGE LITTLE 1925-26 (.750)   11-3-2

1925 6-1-1 (3-1-1)
O3	•	Iowa State	30	0
O10	•	Franklin	35	0
O17		Michigan	0	21
O24	•	Purdue	7	0
O31	=	at Minnesota	12	12
N7	•	at Iowa	6	0
N14	•	Michigan State	21	10
N21	•	at Chicago	20	7

1926 5-2-1 (3-2-1)
O2		Cornell Coll.	38	0
O9	•	Kansas	13	0
O16	=	at Purdue	0	0
O23	•	Indiana	27	2
O30		Minnesota	10	16
N6		at Michigan	0	37
N13	•	Iowa	20	10
N20	•	at Chicago	14	7

GLENN THISTLETHWAITE 1927-31 (.611)   26-16-3

1927 4-4-0 (1-4-0)
O1	•	Cornell Coll.	31	6
O8	•	at Kansas	26	6
O15		Michigan	0	14
O22	•	Purdue	12	6
O29	•	at Minnesota	7	13
N5	•	Grinnell	20	2
N12		Iowa	0	16
N19		at Chicago	0	6

1928 7-1-1 (3-1-1)
O6	•	Notre Dame	22	6
O13	•	Cornell Coll.	49	0
O13	•	North Dakota St.	13	7
O20	=	at Purdue	19	19
O27	•	at Michigan	7	0
N3	•	Alabama	15	0
N10	•	Chicago	25	0
N17	•	at Iowa	13	0
N24		Minnesota	0	6

1929 4-5-0 (1-4-0)
S28	•	Ripon	22	0
S28	•	South Dakota St.	21	0
O5	•	Colgate	13	6
O12		Northwestern	0	7
O19		Notre Dame Chi	0	19
O26		Iowa	0	14
N2		Purdue	0	13
N9	•	at Chicago	20	6
N23		at Minnesota	12	13

1930 6-2-1 (2-2-1)
O4	•	Lawrence	53	6
O4	•	Carleton	28	0
O11	•	Chicago	34	0
O18	•	Pennsylvania	27	0
O25		at Purdue	6	7
N1	=	at Ohio State	0	0
N8	•	South Dakota St.	58	7
N15		at Northwestern	7	20
N22	•	Minnesota	14	0

1931 5-4-1 (3-3-0)
O3	•	Bradley	33	6
O3	•	North Dakota St.	12	7
O10	•	Auburn	7	7
O17	•	Purdue	21	14
O24		at Pennsylvania	13	27
O31		at Minnesota	0	14
N7	•	at Illinois	7	6
N14		Ohio State	0	6
N21	•	at Chicago	12	7
N28		at Michigan	0	16

CLARENCE SPEARS 1932-35 (.438)   13-17-2

1932 6-1-1 (4-1-1)
O1	•	Marquette	7	2
O8	•	Iowa	34	0
O15		at Purdue	6	7
O22	•	Coe	39	0
O29	=	at Ohio State	7	7
N5	•	Illinois	20	12
N12	•	Minnesota	20	13
N19	•	at Chicago	18	7

1933 2-5-1 (0-5-1)
O7	•	Marquette	19	0
O14		at Illinois	0	21
O21		at Iowa	7	26
O28		Purdue	0	14
N4	=	at Chicago	0	0
N11	•	West Virginia	25	6
N18	•	Ohio State	0	6
N25		at Minnesota	3	6

1934 4-4-0 (2-3-0)
O6	•	Marquette	3	0
O13	•	South Dakota St.	28	7
O20		at Purdue	0	14
O27		at Notre Dame	0	19
N3		at Northwestern	0	7
N10	•	at Michigan	10	0
N17	•	Illinois	7	3
N24		Minnesota	0	34

1935 1-7-0 (1-4-0)
S28		South Dakota St.	6	13
O5		Marquette	0	33
O12		Notre Dame	0	27
O19		Michigan	12	20
O26		at Chicago	7	13
N9	•	Purdue	8	0
N16		at Northwestern	13	32
N23		at Minnesota	7	33

HARRY STUHLDREHER 1936-48 (.425)   45-62-6

1936 2-6-0 (0-4-0)
S26	•	South Dakota St.	24	7
O3		Marquette	6	12
O10		at Purdue	14	35
O17		at Notre Dame	0	27
O31		Chicago	6	7
N7		at Northwestern	18	26
N14	•	Cincinnati	27	6
N21		Minnesota	0	24

1937 4-3-1 (2-2-1)
S25	•	South Dakota St.	32	0
O2	•	Marquette	12	0
O9	•	at Chicago	27	0
O16		Iowa	13	6
O23		at Pittsburgh	0	21
O30		Northwestern	6	14
N13	=	Purdue	7	7
N20		at Minnesota	6	13

1938 5-3-0 (3-2-0)
O1	•	Marquette	27	0
O8	•	at Iowa	31	13
O15		Pittsburgh	6	26
O22		at Purdue	7	13
O29	•	Indiana	6	0
N5	•	at Northwestern	20	13
N12		at UCLA	14	7
N19		Minnesota	0	21

1939 1-6-1 (0-5-1)
S30	•	Marquette	14	13
O7		Texas	7	17
O14		Indiana	0	14
O21		at Northwestern	7	13
O28		Iowa	13	19
N11		at Illinois	0	7
N18	=	Purdue	7	7
N25		at Minnesota	6	23

1940 4-4-0 (3-3-0)
O5		Marquette	33	19
O12		at Iowa	12	30
O19		Northwestern	7	27
O26	•	at Purdue	14	13
N2	•	Illinois	13	6
N9		at Columbia	6	7
N16	•	Indiana	27	10
N23		Minnesota	13	22

1941 3-5-0 (3-3-0)
O4		Marquette	7	28
O11	•	at Northwestern	14	41
O18	•	Iowa	23	0
O25	•	Indiana	27	25
N1		Syracuse	20	27
N8		at Ohio State	34	46
N15	•	Purdue	13	0
N22		at Minnesota	6	41

1942 8-1-1 (4-1-0)
S19		Camp Grant	7	0
S26	=	Notre Dame	7	7
O3	•	Marquette	35	7
O10	•	Missouri	17	9
O17	•	Great Lakes NAS Chi	13	7
O24	•	at Purdue	13	0
O31	•	Ohio State	17	7
N7		at Iowa	0	6
N14	•	at Northwestern	20	19
N21	•	Minnesota	20	6

1943 1-9-0 (1-6-0)
S18		Marquette	7	33
S25		at Camp Grant	7	10
O2	•	at Iowa	7	5
O9		Illinois	7	25
O16		Notre Dame	0	50
O23		at Indiana	0	34
O30		Purdue	0	32
N6		Northwestern	0	41
N13		at Michigan	0	27
N20		at Minnesota	13	25

1944 3-6-0 (2-4-0)
S30	•	at Northwestern	7	6
O7	•	Marquette	21	2
O14		Ohio State	7	20
O21		at Notre Dame	13	28
O28		Great Lakes NAS	12	40
N4		at Purdue	0	35
N11	•	Iowa	26	7
N18		at Michigan	0	14
N25		Minnesota	26	28

1945 3-4-2 (2-3-1)
S22	=	at Great Lakes NAS	0	0
S29	•	Marquette	40	13
O6		Purdue	7	13
O13		at Ohio State	0	12
O20	•	Illinois	7	7
N3	•	at Iowa	27	7
N10		Northwestern	14	28
N17		Navy Balt	7	36
N24	•	at Minnesota	26	12

1946 4-5-0 (2-5-0)
S21	•	Marquette	34	0
S28	•	at California	28	7
O5		at Northwestern	0	28
O12	•	Ohio State	20	7
O19		at Illinois	21	27
N2	•	at Purdue	24	20
N9		Iowa	7	21
N16		at Michigan	6	28
N23		Minnesota	0	6

1947 5-3-1 (3-2-1)
S27		Purdue	32	14
O4	=	at Indiana	7	7
O11		California	7	48
O18	•	at Yale	9	0
O25	•	Marquette	35	12
N1	•	at Northwestern	29	0
N8	•	Iowa	46	14
N15		Michigan	6	40
N22		at Minnesota	0	21

1948 2-7-0 (1-5-0)
S25		Indiana	7	35
O2	•	Illinois	20	16
O9		at California	14	40
O16		Yale	7	17
O23		at Ohio State	32	34
O30		at Iowa	13	19
N6		Northwestern	7	16
N13	•	Marquette	26	0
N20		Minnesota	0	16

IVY WILLIAMSON 1949-55 (.672)   41-19-4

1949 5-3-1 (3-2-1)
S24	•	Marquette	41	0
O1	=	at Illinois	13	13
O8		California	20	35
O15	•	Navy	48	13
O22		Ohio State	0	21
O29	•	at Indiana	30	14
N5	•	at Northwestern	14	6
N12	•	Iowa	35	13
N19		at Minnesota	6	14

1950 6-3-0 (5-2-0)
S30	•	Marquette	28	6
O7	•	at Illinois	7	6
O14	•	at Iowa	14	0
O21	•	at Michigan	13	26
O28	•	Northwestern	14	13
N4	•	Purdue	33	7
N11	•	at Ohio State	14	19
N18	•	at Pennsylvania	0	20
N25	•	Minnesota	14	0

1951 7-1-1 (5-1-1)
S29	•	Marquette	22	6
O6	•	at Illinois	10	14
O13	=	Ohio State	6	6
O20	•	at Purdue	31	7
O27	•	at Northwestern	41	0
N3	•	Indiana	6	0
N10	•	Pennsylvania	16	7
N17	•	Iowa	34	7
N24	•	at Minnesota	30	6

1952 6-3-1 (4-1-1)
S27	•	Marquette	42	19
O4	•	Illinois	20	6
O11		at Ohio State	14	23
O18	•	at Iowa	42	13
O25		UCLA	7	20
N1	•	at Rice	21	7
N8	•	Northwestern	24	20
N15	•	at Indiana	37	14
N22	=	Minnesota	21	21
		ROSE BOWL		
J1		Southern Cal	0	7

THE SCHOOLS

1953   6-2-1 (4-1-1)
S26 ●	Penn State	20	0
03 ●	Marquette	13	11
09	at UCLA	0	13
O17 ●	at Purdue	28	19
O24	Ohio State	19	20
O31 ●	Iowa	10	6
N7 ●	at Northwestern	34	13
N14 ●	Illinois	34	7
N21 =	at Minnesota	21	21

1954   7-2-0 (5-2-0)
S25 ●	Marquette	52	14
02 ●	at Michigan State	6	0
09 ●	Rice	13	7
O16 ●	Purdue	20	6
O23 ●	at Ohio State	14	31
O30 ●	at Iowa	7	13
N6 ●	Northwestern	34	13
N13 ●	at Illinois	27	14
N20 ●	Minnesota	27	0

1955   4-5-0 (3-4-0)
S24 ●	Marquette	28	14
01 ●	Iowa	37	14
08 ●	at Purdue	9	0
O14 ●	at Southern Cal	21	33
O22 ●	Ohio State	16	26
O29 ●	Michigan State	0	27
N5 ●	at Northwestern	41	14
N12 ●	Illinois	14	17
N19 ●	at Minnesota	6	21

MILT BRUHN
1956-66 (.534)   52-45-6

1956   1-5-3 (0-4-3)
S29 ●	Marquette	41	0
06 ●	Southern Cal	6	13
O13	at Iowa	7	13
O20 =	Purdue	6	6
O27	at Ohio State	0	21
N3	at Michigan State	0	33
N10 ●	Northwestern	7	17
N17 =	at Illinois	13	13
N24 =	Minnesota	13	13

1957   6-3-0 (4-3-0)
S28 ●	Marquette	60	6
05 ●	West Virginia	45	13
O12 ●	at Purdue	23	14
O19	at Iowa	7	21
O26 ●	Ohio State	13	16
N2 ●	Michigan State	7	21
N9 ●	at Northwestern	41	12
N16 ●	Illinois	24	13
N23 ●	at Minnesota	14	6

1958   7-1-1 (5-1-1)
S26 ●	at Miami, Fla.	20	0
04 ●	Marquette	50	0
O11 ●	Purdue	31	6
O18 ●	Iowa	9	20
O25 =	at Ohio State	7	7
N1 ●	at Michigan State	9	7
N8 ●	Northwestern	17	13
N15 ●	at Illinois	31	12
N22 ●	Minnesota	27	12

1959   7-3-0 (5-2-0)
S26 ●	Stanford	16	14
03 ●	Marquette	44	6
O10 ●	at Purdue	0	21
O17 ●	Iowa	25	16
O24 ●	Ohio State	12	3
O31 ●	at Michigan	19	10
N7 ●	at Northwestern	24	19
N14 ●	Illinois	6	9
N21 ●	at Minnesota	11	7
ROSE BOWL			
J1	Washington	8	44

1960   4-5-0 (2-5-0)
S24 ●	at Stanford	24	7
01 ●	Marquette	35	6
08 ●	Purdue	24	13
O15	at Iowa	21	28
O22	at Ohio State	7	34
O29 ●	Michigan	16	13
N5	Northwestern	0	21
N12	at Illinois	14	35
N19	Minnesota	7	26

1961   6-3-0 (4-3-0)
S23 ●	Utah	7	0
S30 ●	Michigan State	0	20
07	at Indiana	6	3
O14 ●	Oregon State	23	20
O21	at Iowa	15	47
O28	Ohio State	21	30
N11 ●	at Northwestern	29	10
N18 ●	Illinois	55	7
N25 ●	at Minnesota	23	21

1962   8-2-0 (6-1-0)
S29 ●	New Mexico St.	69	13
06 ●	Indiana	30	6
O13 ●	Notre Dame	17	8
O20 ●	Iowa	42	14
O27	at Ohio State	7	14
N3 ●	at Michigan	34	12
N10 ●	Northwestern	37	6
N17 ●	at Illinois	35	6
N24 ●	Minnesota	14	9
ROSE BOWL			
J1	Southern Cal	37	42

1963   5-4-0 (3-4-0)
S21 ●	Western Michigan	41	0
S28 ●	at Notre Dame	14	9
O12 ●	Purdue	38	20
O19 ●	at Iowa	10	7
O26 ●	Ohio State	10	13
N2 ●	at Michigan State	13	30
N9 ●	Northwestern	17	14
N16 ●	Illinois	7	17
N28 ●	at Minnesota	0	14

1964   3-6-0 (2-5-0)
S19 ●	Kansas State	17	7
S26 ●	Notre Dame	7	31
O10	at Purdue	7	28
O17 ●	Iowa	31	21
O24	at Ohio State	3	28
O31	Michigan State	6	22
N7 ●	at Northwestern	13	17
N14 ●	at Illinois	0	29
N21 ●	Minnesota	14	7

1965   2-7-1 (2-5-0)
S18 =	Colorado	0	0
S25 ●	Southern Cal	6	26
02 ●	Iowa	16	13
09	at Nebraska	0	37
O16 ●	at Northwestern	21	7
O23	Ohio State	10	20
O30	at Michigan	14	50
N6	at Purdue	7	45
N13	Illinois	0	51
N20	at Minnesota	7	42

1966   3-6-1 (2-4-1)
S17 ●	Iowa State	20	10
S24 ●	at Southern Cal	3	38
01 ●	at Iowa	7	0
08	Nebraska	3	31
O15 =	Northwestern	3	3
O22 ●	at Ohio State	13	24
O29 ●	Michigan	17	28
N5 ●	Purdue	0	23
N12 ●	at Illinois	14	49
N19 ●	Minnesota	7	6

JOHN COATTA
1967-69 (.117)   3-26-1

1967   0-9-1 (0-6-1)
S23	at Washington	0	17
S30	Arizona State	16	42
07	at Michigan State	7	35
O14	Pittsburgh	11	13
O21 =	Iowa	21	21
O28	Northwestern	13	17
N4	at Indiana	9	14
N11	at Ohio State	15	17
N18	Michigan	14	27
N25	at Minnesota	14	21

1968   0-10-0 (0-7-0)
S21	at Arizona State	7	55
S28	Washington	17	21
05	Michigan State	0	39
O12	Utah State	0	20
O19	at Iowa	0	41
O26	at Northwestern	10	13
N2	Indiana	20	21
N9	Ohio State	8	43
N16	at Michigan	9	34
N23	Minnesota	15	23

1969   3-7-0 (3-4-0)
S20	Oklahoma	21	48
S27	UCLA	23	34
04	Syracuse	7	43
O11 ●	Iowa	23	17
O18 ●	at Northwestern	7	27
O25 ●	Indiana	36	34
N1 ●	at Michigan	7	35
N8	Ohio State	7	62
N15 ●	Illinois	55	14
N22	at Minnesota	10	35

JOHN JARDINE
1970-77 (.443)   37-47-3

1970   4-5-1 (3-4-0)
S19	at Oklahoma	7	21
S26 =	TCU	14	14
03 ●	Penn State	29	16
O10	at Iowa	14	24
O17	Northwestern	14	24
O24 ●	at Indiana	30	12
O31	Michigan	15	29
N7	Ohio State	7	24
N14	at Illinois	29	17
N21 ●	Minnesota	39	14

1971   4-6-1 (3-5-0)
S11 ●	Northern Illinois	31	0
S18 =	at Syracuse	20	20
S25	LSU	28	38
02	at Northwestern	11	24
09 ●	Indiana	35	29
O16 ●	Michigan State	31	28
O23	at Ohio State	6	31
O30	at Iowa	16	20
N6 ●	Purdue	14	10
N13	Illinois	27	35
N20	at Minnesota	21	23

1972   4-7-0 (2-6-0)
S16 ●	Northern Illinois	31	7
S23 ●	Syracuse	31	7
S30	at LSU	7	27
07 ●	Northwestern	21	14
O14	at Indiana	7	33
O21	at Michigan State	0	31
O28	Ohio State	20	28
N4 ●	Iowa	16	14
N11	at Purdue	6	27
N18	at Illinois	7	27
N25	Minnesota	6	14

1973   4-7-0 (3-5-0)
S15 ●	Purdue	13	14
S22	Colorado	25	28
S29	at Nebraska	16	20
06 ●	Wyoming	37	28
O13	Ohio State	0	24
O20	at Michigan	6	35
O27 ●	Indiana	31	7
N3	at Michigan State	0	21
N10 ●	Iowa	35	7
N17	Northwestern	36	34
N24	at Minnesota	17	19

1974   7-4-0 (5-3-0)
S14 ●	at Purdue	28	14
S21 ●	Nebraska	21	20
S28	at Colorado	21	24
05 ●	Missouri	59	20
O12	at Ohio State	7	52
O19 ●	Michigan	20	24
O26 ●	at Indiana	35	25
N2 ●	Michigan State	21	28
N9 ●	at Iowa	28	15
N16 ●	at Northwestern	52	7
N23 ●	Minnesota	49	14

1975   4-6-1 (3-4-1)
S13 ●	Michigan	6	23
S20 ●	South Dakota	48	7
S27	at Missouri	21	27
04 ●	Kansas	7	41
O11 ●	at Purdue	17	14
O18	at Ohio State	0	56
O25 ●	Northwestern	17	14
N1 ●	Illinois	18	9
N8 ●	at Iowa	28	45
N15 =	Indiana	9	9
N22	at Minnesota	3	24

1976   5-6-0 (3-5-0)
S11 ●	at Michigan	27	40
S18 ●	North Dakota	45	9
S25 ●	Washington State	35	26
02	at Kansas	24	34
09 ●	Purdue	16	18
O16 ●	Ohio State	20	30
O23 ●	at Northwestern	28	25
O30 ●	Illinois	25	31
N6 ●	Iowa	38	21
N13 ●	at Indiana	14	15
N20 ●	Minnesota	26	17

1977   5-6-0 (3-6-0)
S10 ●	at Indiana	30	14
S17 ●	Northern Illinois	14	3
S24 ●	at Oregon	22	10
01 ●	Northwestern	19	7
08 ●	Illinois	26	0
O15 ●	at Michigan	0	56
O22 ●	Michigan State	7	9
O29 ●	at Ohio State	0	42
N5 ●	Purdue	0	22
N12 ●	Iowa	8	24
N19 ●	at Minnesota	7	13

DAVE McCLAIN
1978-85 (.522)   46-42-3

1978   5-4-2 (3-4-2)
S16 ●	Richmond	7	6
S23 ●	at Northwestern	28	7
S30 ●	Oregon	22	19
07 ●	Indiana	34	7
O14 =	at Illinois	20	20
O21 ●	Michigan	0	42
O28 ●	at Michigan State	2	55
N4 ●	Ohio State	14	49
N11 ●	Purdue	24	24
N18 ●	at Iowa	24	38
N25 ●	Minnesota	48	10

1979   4-7-0 (3-5-0)
S8 ●	at Purdue	20	41
S15 ●	Air Force	38	0
S22 ●	UCLA	12	37
S29 ●	at San Diego State	17	24
06 ●	Indiana	0	3
O13 ●	Michigan State	38	29
O20 ●	at Ohio State	0	59
O27 ●	Iowa	13	24
N3 ●	at Michigan	0	54
N10 ●	Northwestern	28	3
N17 ●	at Minnesota	42	37

1980   4-7-0 (3-5-0)
S13	Purdue	6	12
S20	Brigham Young	3	28
S27	at UCLA	0	35
04 ●	San Diego State	35	12
O11	at Indiana	0	24
O18 ●	at Michigan State	17	7
O25	Ohio State	0	21
N1	at Iowa	13	22
N8	Michigan	0	24
N15 ●	at Northwestern	39	19
N22 ●	Minnesota	25	7

1981   7-5-0 (6-3-0)
S12	Michigan	21	14
S19	UCLA	13	31
S26 ●	Western Michigan	21	10
03 ●	Purdue	20	14
O10	Ohio State	24	21
O17	at Michigan State	14	33
O24	at Illinois	21	23
O31 ●	Northwestern	52	0
N7 ●	at Indiana	28	7
N14	Iowa	7	17
N21 ●	at Minnesota	26	21
GARDEN STATE BOWL			
D13	Tennessee	21	28

1982   7-5-0 (5-4-0)
S11	at Michigan	9	20
S18	UCLA	26	51
S25 ●	Toledo	36	27
02 ●	at Purdue	35	31
09 ●	at Ohio State	6	0
O16 ●	Michigan State	24	23
O23	Illinois	28	29
O30 ●	Northwestern	54	20
N6	Indiana	17	20
N13 ●	at Iowa	14	28
N20 ●	Minnesota	24	0
INDEPENDENCE BOWL			
D11 ●	Kansas State	14	3

THE SCHOOLS

1983 — 7-4-0 (5-4-0)

S10	●	Northern Illinois	37 9
S17	●	Missouri	21 20
S24		Michigan	21 38
O1	●	at Northwestern	49 0
O8		Illinois	15 27
O15	●	at Minnesota	56 17
O22	●	Indiana	45 14
O29		at Ohio State	27 45
N5		Iowa	14 34
N12	●	at Purdue	42 38
N19	●	Michigan State	32 0

1984 — 7-4-1 (5-3-1)

S8	●	Northern Illinois	27 14
S15	●	at Missouri	35 34
S22		at Michigan	14 20
S29	●	Northwestern	31 16
O6		at Illinois	6 22
O13		Minnesota	14 17
O20	●	at Indiana	20 16
O27		Ohio State	16 14
N3	=	at Iowa	10 10
N10	●	Purdue	30 13
N17	●	at Michigan State	20 10
HALL OF FAME CLASSIC			
D29		Kentucky	19 20

1985 — 5-6-0 (2-6-0)

S14	●	Northern Illinois	38 11
S21	●	Nevada-Las Vegas	26 23
S28	●	at Wyoming	41 17
O5		at Michigan	6 33
O12		Iowa	13 23
O19		Northwestern	14 17
O26		at Illinois	25 38
N2	●	Indiana	31 20
N9		at Minnesota	18 27
N16	●	at Ohio State	12 7
N23		Michigan State	7 41

JIM HILLES
1986 (.250) — 3-9

1986 — 3-9-0 (2-6-0)

S6		at Hawaii	17 20
S13	●	Northern Illinois	35 20
S20	●	at Nevada-Las Vegas	7 17
S27		Wyoming	12 21
O4		Michigan	17 34
O11		at Iowa	6 17
O18	●	at Northwestern	35 27
O25	●	Illinois	15 9
N1		at Indiana	7 21
N8		Minnesota	20 27
N15		Ohio State	17 30
N22		at Michigan State	13 23

DON MORTON
1987-89 (.182) — 6-27

1987 — 3-8-0 (1-7-0)

S12	●	Hawaii	28 7
S19		Utah	28 31
S26	●	Ball State	30 13
O3		at Michigan	0 49
O10		Iowa	10 31
O17		at Illinois	14 16
O24		Northwestern	24 27
O31		at Purdue	14 49
N7	●	Ohio State	26 24
N14		at Minnesota	19 22
N21		Michigan State	9 30

1988 — 1-10-0 (1-7-0)

S3		Western Michigan	14 24
S17		Northern Illinois	17 19
S24		at Miami, Fla.	3 23
O1		Michigan	14 62
O8		at Iowa	6 31
O15		Illinois	6 34
O22		at Northwestern	14 35
O29		Purdue	6 9
N5		at Ohio State	12 34
N12	●	Minnesota	14 7
N19		at Michigan State	0 36

1989 — 2-9-0 (1-7-0)

S9		Miami, Fla.	3 51
S16	●	Toledo	23 10
S23		at California	14 20
O7		at Michigan	0 24
O14		Iowa	24 31
O21	●	Northwestern	35 31
O28		at Illinois	9 32
N4		at Minnesota	22 24
N11		Indiana	17 45
N18		at Ohio State	22 42
N25		Michigan State	3 31

BARRY ALVAREZ
1990-Present (.599) 107-71-4

1990 — 1-10-0 (0-8-0)

S8		California	12 28
S15	●	Ball State	24 7
S22	●	Temple	18 24
O6		Michigan	3 41
O13		at Iowa	10 30
O20		at Northwestern	34 44
O27		Illinois	3 21
N3		Minnesota	3 21
N10		at Indiana	7 20
N17		Ohio State	10 35
N24		at Michigan State	9 14

1991 — 5-6-0 (2-6-0)

S14	●	W. Illinois	31 13
S21	●	Iowa State	7 6
S28	●	Eastern Michigan	21 6
O5		at Ohio State	16 31
O12		Iowa	6 10
O19		at Purdue	7 28
O26		Indiana	20 28
N2		at Illinois	6 22
N9		Michigan State	7 20
N16	●	at Minnesota	19 16
N23		Northwestern	32 14

1992 — 5-6-0 (3-5-0)

S12		at Washington	10 27
S19		Bowling Green	39 18
S26	●	Northern Illinois	18 17
O3		Ohio State	20 16
O10		at Iowa	22 23
O17		Purdue	19 16
O24		at Indiana	3 10
O31		Illinois	12 13
N7		at Michigan State	10 26
N14	●	Minnesota	34 6
N21		at Northwestern	25 27

1993 — 10-1-1 (6-1-1)

S4	●	Nevada	35 17
S11	●	at SMU	24 16
S18	●	Iowa State	28 7
S25	●	at Indiana	27 15
O9	●	Northwestern	53 14
O16	●	at Purdue	42 28
O23		at Minnesota	21 28
O30		Michigan	13 10
N6	=	Ohio State	14 14
N20	●	at Illinois	35 10
D5	●	Michigan State [Tok]	41 20
ROSE BOWL			
J1	●	UCLA	21 16

1994 — 7-4-1 (4-3-1)

S10	●	Eastern Michigan	56 0
S17		at Colorado	17 55
S24		Indiana	62 13
O1		at Michigan State	10 29 †
O8		at Northwestern	46 14
O15	=	Purdue	27 27
O22		Minnesota	14 17
O29	●	at Michigan	31 19
N5		at Ohio State	3 24
N12	●	Cincinnati	38 7
N19	●	Illinois	19 13
HALL OF FAME BOWL			
J2	●	Duke	34 20

1995 — 4-5-2 (3-4-1)

S2		Colorado	7 43
S16	=	at Stanford	24 24
S23	●	SMU	42 0
S30	●	at Penn State	17 9
O14		Ohio State	16 27
O21		at Northwestern	0 35
O28	●	Michigan State	45 14
N4		at Purdue	27 38
N11	●	at Minnesota	34 27
N18		Iowa	20 33
N25	=	Illinois	3 3

1996 — 8-5 (3-5)

S7	●	Eastern Michigan	24 3
S14	●	at Nevada-Las Vegas	52 17
S21	●	Stanford	14 0
S28	●	Penn State	20 23
O12	●	at Ohio State	14 17
O19		Northwestern	30 34
O26		at Michigan State	13 30
N2	●	Purdue	33 25
N9	●	Minnesota	45 28
N16		Iowa	0 31
N23	●	at Illinois	35 15
N30	●	at Hawaii	59 10
COPPER BOWL			
D27	●	Utah	38 10

1997 — 8-5 (5-3)

A24		Syracuse [ERut]	0 34
S6	●	Boise State	28 24
S13		at San Jose State	56 10
S20		San Diego State	36 10
S27	●	Indiana	27 26
O4	●	at Northwestern	26 25
O11	●	Illinois	31 7
O18		at Purdue	20 45
O25	●	at Minnesota	22 21
N8	●	Iowa	13 10
N15		Michigan	16 26
N22		at Penn State	10 35
OUTBACK BOWL			
J1		Georgia	6 33

1998 — 11-1 (7-1)

S5	●	at San Diego State	26 14
S12	●	Ohio U.	45 0
S19	●	Nevada-Las Vegas	52 7
S26	●	Northwestern	38 7
O3		at Indiana	24 20
O10	●	Purdue	31 24
O17	●	at Illinois	37 3
O24	●	at Iowa	31 0
N7	●	Minnesota	26 7
N14		at Michigan	10 27
N21	●	Penn State	24 3
ROSE BOWL			
J1	●	UCLA	38 31

1999 — 10-2 (7-1)

S4	●	Murray St.	49 10
S11	●	Ball State	50 10
S18		at Cincinnati	12 17
S25		Michigan	16 21
O2	●	at Ohio State	42 17
O9		at Minnesota	20 17
O16	●	Indiana	59 0
O23	●	Michigan State	40 10
O30	●	at Northwestern	35 19
N6	●	at Purdue	28 21
N13	●	Iowa	41 3
ROSE BOWL			
J1	●	Stanford	17 9

2000 — 9-4 (4-4)

A31	●	Western Michigan	19 7
S9	●	Oregon	27 23
S16	●	Cincinnati	28 25
S23		Northwestern	44 47
S30		at Michigan	10 13
O7		Ohio State	7 23
O14	●	at Michigan State	17 10
O21		Purdue	24 30
O28	●	at Iowa	13 7
N4		Minnesota	41 20
N11	●	at Indiana	43 20
N25	●	at Hawaii	34 18
SUN BOWL			
D29		UCLA	21 20

2001 — 5-7 (3-5)

A25	●	Virginia	26 17
S1		at Oregon	28 31
S8		Fresno St.	20 32
S22	●	at Penn State	18 6
S29	●	Western Ky.	24 6
O6		Indiana	32 63
O13	●	at Ohio State	20 17
O20		at Illinois	35 42
O27		Michigan State	28 42
N3	●	Iowa	34 28
N17		Michigan	17 20
N24		at Minnesota	31 42

2002 — 8-6 (2-6)

A23	●	Fresno State	23 21
A31	●	at Nevada-Las Vegas	27 7
S7	●	West Virginia	34 17
S14	●	Northern Illinois	24 21
S21	●	Arizona	31 10
O5		Penn State	31 34
O12		at Indiana	29 32
O19		Ohio State	14 19
O26	●	at Michigan State	42 24
N2		at Iowa	3 20
N9		Illinois	20 37
N16		at Michigan	14 21
N23	●	Minnesota	49 31
ALAMO BOWL			
D28	●	Colorado	31 28

2003 — 7-6 (4-4)

A30	●	at West Virginia	24 17
S6	●	Akron	48 31
S13		Nevada-Las Vegas	5 23
S20	●	North Carolina	38 27
S27		at Illinois	38 20
O4	●	at Penn State	30 23
O11	●	Ohio State	17 10
O18		Purdue	23 26
O25	●	at Northwestern	7 16
N8	●	at Minnesota	34 37
N15	●	Michigan State	56 21
N22		Iowa	21 27
MUSIC CITY BOWL			
D31	●	Auburn	14 28

2004 — 9-3 (6-2)

S4	●	Central Florida	34 6
S11	●	Nevada-Las Vegas	18 3
S18	●	at Arizona	9 7
S25	●	Penn State	16 3
O2	●	Illinois	24 7
O9	●	at Ohio State	24 13
O16	●	at Purdue	20 17
O23	●	Northwestern	24 12
N6	●	Minnesota	38 14
N13		at Michigan State	14 49
N20		at Iowa	7 30
OUTBACK BOWL			
J1		Georgia	21 24

Neutral Site key: *Ind* Indianapolis, Ind. / *Mil* Milwaukee, Wisc. / *Chi* Chicago, Ill. / *Balt* Baltimore, Md. / *ERut* East Rutherford, N.J. / *Tok* Tokyo, Japan
f Forfeit † Game Later Forfeited # Disputed Victor * Disputed Score ‖ Designated Conference Game |2 Counted Twice in Conference Standings

WYOMING

BY DERRICK GOOLD

Forget being the only game in town; University of Wyoming football is the only game in a vast, sparsely populated state, at its only four-year school. On game days, War Memorial Stadium becomes the third-largest city in the state—a concentration of 7% of its population. The school's dorms are the most densely populated area of the state. There is no collegiate or big league professional competition for the Cowboys within state borders. Pro baseball, in the form of a Class-A team, returned in 2001 for the first time in 60 years. From Jackson Hole to Chugwater to Thermopolis, the Pokes rule the range. And they take the wide-open nature of the state to heart in the trademark of the football team. Self-proclaimed as Receiver U, Wyoming has produced two of the NCAA's top career wideouts—Marcus Harris and Ryan Yarborough—and All-America tight end/decathlete Jay Novacek. Fanned by coach Joe Glenn (hired in December 2002) and the Cowboys' upsets of Colorado State and BYU in 2003, Wyoming was considered the Mountain West Conference 2004 Team on the Rise in a vote conducted by the *Las Vegas Review-Journal*. The Cowboys received 53.3% of the media vote, more than twice the percentage of the next program. The University of Wyoming sits at the highest altitude of any Division I-A school in the country—7,200 feet above sea level—and aspirations are also on the rise after years of, as one sportswriter jotted, "cheering for one-win seasons."

TRADITION The true coup of Cowboys football is Tailgate Park. Less than two decades ago, Wyoming copied Southern college football tailgating to spur fan interest. The school brought in live music and food vendors. Hay bales were tugged in and arranged for folks to sit on. The tailgating became instant tradition. In 2003, Pepsi swooped in as a sponsor for Cowboy Tailgate, providing an inflatable football-tossing game called Quarterback Challenge for the festivities. Also added through the years: Wyoming athletics trivia contests and face-painting. Players sing the school fight song, "Ragtime Cowboy Joe," after each victory.

BEST PLAYER Eddie "Boom Boom" Talboom played his freshman season at Notre Dame in 1941, but after serving four years in the Army, and a few more years working odd jobs, he attempted a return to college football. He wanted to leave South Bend for Tennessee, but Tennessee had too many tailbacks. It was suggested he go elsewhere to play—

PROFILE

University of Wyoming
Laramie, Wyo.
Founded: 1886
Enrollment: 9,352
Colors: Brown and Wyoming Prairie Gold
Nickname: Cowboys
Stadium: War Memorial Stadium
  Built in 1950
  Grass; 33,500 capacity
First football game: 1893
All-time record: 458–477–28 (.490)
Bowl record: 5–6
First-round NFL draftees: 3
Website: www.wyomingathletics.com

THE BEST OF TIMES

Lloyd Eaton guided Wyoming to back-to-back 10–1 seasons in 1966 and 1967. The Cowboys' lone defeats: a 12-10 loss at archrival Colorado State in 1966 and 20-13 loss to LSU in the Sugar Bowl on New Year's Day 1968.

THE WORST OF TIMES

From 2000 to 2002, Wyoming staggered to a 5–29 record under Vic Koenning, including a mind-numbing 1–16 mark on the road. The Pokes' only Mountain West Conference win in that period was a 2002 upset of Air Force.

CONFERENCE

After spending nearly four decades (1962-98) as a member of the Western Athletic Conference, Wyoming was one of eight WAC schools that jumped to form the Mountain West Conference in 1999.

DISTINGUISHED ALUMNI

Dick Cheney; Curt Gowdy; Dr. Jerry Buss, owner, Los Angeles Lakers; Alan Simpson, U.S. senator; Gerry Spence, lawyer and author

FIGHT SONG

RAGTIME COWBOY JOE
He always sings
Raggy music to the cattle
as he swings
back and forward in the saddle
on a horse—a pretty good horse!
He's got syncopated guitar,
and you ought to hear the meter
to the roar of his repeater;
how they run—YES RUN!
when they hear him 'a-comin',
cause the western folks all know,
he's a high-falootin', rootin', tootin',
son of a gun from ol' Wyoming,
Ragtime Cowboy.
Talk about your Cowboy,
Ragtime Cowboy Joe!

THE SCHOOLS

so he went way elsewhere. When he arrived in Laramie, Talboom was 28 and the perfect fit for coach Bowden Wyatt's single-wing offense. Talboom became the school's first All-America selection and the first three-time all-conference pick. Boom Boom scored 303 points total in three seasons and set 13 school scoring records. Talboom, who died in 1998, posthumously became the first Wyoming player inducted into the College Football Hall of Fame in 2000—in his hometown of South Bend, Ind.—and Oct. 14, 2000, was declared Eddie Talboom Day in Wyoming.

BEST COACH Although his tenure ended with the Black-14 controversy—which involved the expulsion of 14 black athletes for a political protest in 1969—and a 1–9 season, Lloyd Eaton led Wyoming to a 57–33–2 record in his nine seasons on the high prairie. He won 16 consecutive conference games and lost to rival Colorado State just once in nine games. With Eaton, the Cowboys went to consecutive bowls in 1966 and 1967—defeating Florida State in the Sun Bowl and losing to LSU in the Sugar Bowl.

> *At 7,200 feet above sea level, War Memorial Stadium has the highest altitude of any Division I-A football field.*

BEST TEAM Coming off a 10–3 season in which they won nine straight games to close the regular season, the Cowboys won 10 games to start the 1988 campaign. The Pokes scored more than 40 points in seven of those victories and won the WAC title. Like the other great Wyoming teams, however, the 1988 group also lost its bowl game—62-14 to Heisman winner Barry Sanders' Oklahoma State team in the Holiday Bowl. Piloting the nation's third-highest scoring offense (41.4 points per game), quarterback Randy Welniak won the WAC Offensive Player of the Year award with 2,791 passing yards and 3,206 total yards.

BIGGEST GAME Capping a 10–0 season in 1950, the Cowboys defeated Washington & Lee 20-7 in the 1951 Gator Bowl, the first bowl game for both schools and the only bowl appearance by Washington & Lee. Talboom, who scored a total of 130 points that season (still the school record), handled the offense—passing for 141 yards, rushing for 31 and accounting for two touchdowns. It was the final game of Talboom's career, and he won the bowl's MVP

RECORDS

RUSHING YARS

	GAME
302	Kevin Lowe vs. South Dakota, Sept. 1, 1984 (10 att.)
	SEASON
1,455	Ryan Christopherson, 1994 (300 att.)
	CAREER
2,906	Ryan Christopherson, 1991-94 (585 att.)

PASSING YARDS

	GAME
485	Josh Wallwork vs. Idaho, Aug. 31, 1996 (29 of 53)
	SEASON
4,090	Josh Wallwork, 1996 (286 of 458)
	CAREER
7,945	Tom Corontzos, 1988-91 (579 of 1,066)

RECEIVING YARDS

	GAME
260	Marcus Harris vs. Fresno State, Oct. 15, 1994 (10 rec.)
	SEASON
1,650	Marcus Harris, 1996 (109 rec.)
	CAREER
4,518	Marcus Harris, 1993-96 (259 rec.)

POINTS

	GAME
29	Eddie Talboom vs. Colorado State, Oct. 1, 1949 (4 TDs, 5 PATs)
	SEASON
130	Eddie Talboom, 1950 (15 TDs, 40 PATs)
	CAREER
324	Sean Fleming, 1988-91 (153 PATs, 57 FGs)

CONSENSUS ALL-AMERICANS

1983	Jack Weil, P
1984	Jay Novacek, TE
1996	Marcus Harris, WR
1997	Brian Lee, DB

award. He did not attend the awards ceremony because he left for the Senior Bowl immediately after the game.

BIGGEST UPSET The Cowboys had lost 21 of their previous 28 games coming into their game with 11th-ranked Arizona State on Sept. 30, 1972. Wyoming had been outscored 97-28 in its previous two outings. ASU had won 30 of its past 31 games, but came ill-prepared for the option attack. The Cowboys led 23-7 at halftime. Wyoming had three 100-yard rushers and 472 total rushing yards en route to a 45-43 stunner. Quarterback Steve Cockreham, of Lusk, Wyo., earned national attention and player of the week awards for his performance: rushing for 177 yards and three touchdowns and throwing for 103 yards and another touchdown.

HEARTBREAKER Besides boasting the only undefeated, untied record in the country in 1967, the Cowboys, who finished the season ranked sixth in the AP poll (still the highest ever for the school), took a 4–0 bowl record into the Sugar Bowl. Their opponent, LSU, had won its four previous bowl games. Many bowl organizers were hesitant to woo Wyoming, thinking the Pokes had an easy schedule. Wyoming held a 13-0 lead at halftime, outgaining LSU 215 yards to 38. LSU took its first lead with 4:22 remaining in the game. With 39 seconds left, the Cowboys regained possession and quarterback Paul Toscano drove the team 77 yards. But on the final play of the game, receiver Gene Huey was wrangled down five yards shy of the game-winning score. The Bayou Bengals won 20-13.

STADIUM War Memorial Stadium (capacity 33,500) opened in 1950 to replace Corbett Field. The War is the highest Division I-A football stadium in the country at 7,200 feet above sea level. Boosted by the altitude, the Cowboys won 69 percent of their home games in the first decade of War Memorial, going 30–9–4.

RIVAL There's been a trophy for the winner only since 1968, but the Cowboys' skirmish with nearby Colorado State dates back to 1899. The rivalry is still considered one of the oldest interstate rivalries west of the Mississippi River. In 2004, the schools played for the 59th consecutive year. The winner receives the Bronze Boot. Mounted on a base, it is a military boot that was originally worn by a CSU graduate in Vietnam.

CONTROVERSY Eventually they would come to be

known as the Black-14 and would be cited years later as a reason why Wyoming struggled to attract African-American athletes, but in 1969 they were just angry football players. Fourteen members of the football team approached coach Lloyd Eaton about wearing black armbands during a home game against BYU. The players wanted to protest discrimination by the Mormon church. (Until 1978, black men could not become Mormon priests.) The Cowboys were 4–0 at the time, ranked 16th in the AP Poll. Eaton, obligated to follow a school rule prohibiting demonstration by team members, kicked the 14 players off the team. His decision was announced at 3:15 a.m. the day of the game, which Wyoming went on to win 40-7. The university's Board of Trustees concurred with Eaton's decision—which he clearly wrestled with. Eaton then lobbied for the rule to change with an eye on reinstating the players, who left the school anyway. Though he planned on retiring, in part because of the Black-14 decision, Eaton returned for one more season, and the Cowboys went 1–9. National coverage of the Black-14 spread around the country, and the university subsequently had difficulty recruiting black athletes. Wyoming had nine losing seasons in the next 11 years.

NICKNAME Predating the football program, a 220-pound "ex-Harvard cowpuncher" named Fred Bush was convinced to enroll in a few classes and play for the school's pickup football team. In 1891, Bush arrived for a game decked out in a checkered shirt and a Stetson. "Hey, look at the cowboy!" someone yelled. And, as many of the players were actually former cowboys, the name stuck.

MASCOT In 1950, the Farthing Family and Cheyenne Quarterback Club donated a brown-and-white Shetland pony to serve as the Cowboys' mascot. The pony was dubbed Cowboy Joe. Currently Cowboy Joe IV circles the field whenever Wyoming scores.

UNIFORMS A "W" was Wyoming's first helmet emblem, but in the 1920s, equipment manager Deane Hunton found a photo of rodeo cowboy Guy Holt and his ride, Steamboat, the winner of the Worst Horse award at Frontier Park in Cheyenne in 1909. Hunton traced the image's profile and a logo was made for the school's sports teams. Wyoming license plates feature a similar picture—but it is actually a profile of a different rider and horse. The colors brown and Wyoming Prairie gold were borrowed from the indigenous brown-eyed

Susans, which were used to decorate the first alumni banquet in 1895.

NUMBERS On Nov. 5, 1949, Wyoming pummeled what is now Northern Colorado 103-0 to set the Division I-A single-game scoring record. It was a game the Cowboys didn't want to play for a reason: they had hoped to find a more competitive opponent. Leading 42-0 at halftime, coach Bowden Wyatt said if anyone else scored, "they would have to walk home." The team scored 61 points despite the risk of hiking.

No word if he followed through on the threat. The Cowboys scored 15 touchdowns that day and totaled 812 yards.

QUOTE "I could use all of my 1,000 words on that lovable, lamented sacred place known as Corbett Field, which spawned numerous loyal fans and moral victories, [and] where sometimes nearly 4,000 folks would gather for the fall Saturday rituals cheering for a one-win season."
—Journalist Larry Birleffi, who covered Wyoming football for 53 years

WYOMING ANNUAL STATISTICAL LEADERS

YR	RUSHING	YDS	ATT	AVG	PASSING	ATT	CMP	PCT	YDS	RECEIVING	REC	YDS	AVG
1951	Harry Geldien	502	158	3.2	Harry Geldien	74	41	.55	491	Dewey McConnell	47	775	16.5
1952	Chuck Spaulding	512	167	3.1	Chuck Spaulding	135	53	.39	703	Harry Geldien	11	216	19.6
1953	Joe Mastrogiavanni	624	144	4.3	Joe Mastrovgiavanni	129	60	.47	890	Chick Magagna	8	177	22.1
1954	Jerry Jester	750	122	6.1	Joe Mastrovgiavanni	113	50	.44	798	John Watts	10	291	29.1
1955	Jerry Jester	696	140	5.0	Joe Mastrovgiavanni	54	20	.37	329	Bob Marshall	4	95	23.8
1956	Jim Crawford	1,104	200	5.5	Larry Zowada	96	41	.43	878	John Watts	10	287	28.7
1957	Greg Maushart	516	111	4.6	Larry Zowada	123	63	.51	862	Russ Mather	12	319	26.6
1958	Dick Hamilton	381	62	6.1	Jim Walden	50	21	.42	491	Bob Sawyer	7	215	30.7
1959	Jerry Hill	579	97	6.0	Jim Walden	101	45	.45	882	Dick Hamilton	9	245	27.2
1960	Jerry Hill	636	144	4.4	Chuck Lamson	42	20	.48	243	Mark Smolinski	8	88	11.0
1961	Chuck Lamson	451	93	4.8	Andy Melosky	72	33	.46	464	Mike Walker	9	118	13.1
1962	Rick Desmarais	301	77	3.9	Jeff Hartmap	42	25	.60	287	Tom Delaney	13	146	11.2
1963	Wayne Linton	317	82	3.9	Tom Wilkinson	137	64	.47	902	Tom Delaney	19	301	15.8
1964	Jeff Hartman	301	77	3.9	Tom Wilkinson	115	60	.52	1,021	Darryl Alleman	32	519	16.2
1965	Jim Klick	534	131	4.1	Tom Wilkinson	154	84	.55	1,313	Bill Prout	28	325	11.6
1966	Jim Klick	597	145	4.1	Rick Egloff	188	83	.44	1,181	Jerry Marion	33	612	18.5
1967	Jim Klick	583	155	3.8	Paul Toscano	241	134	.56	1,191	Gene Huey	53	868	16.4
1968	Dave Hampton	749	137	5.5	Skip Jacobson	151	81	.54	1,008	Gene Huey	43	626	14.6
1969	Forrest Franklin	541	151	3.6	Ed Synakowski	200	94	.47	1,053	Bill Kyranris	35	571	16.3
1970	Forrest Franklin	542	149	3.6	Scott Freeman	164	67	.41	605	Ken Hustad	25	238	9.5
1971	Forrest Franklin	534	196	2.7	Gary Fox	328	171	.52	2,336	Scott Freeman	44	803	18.3
1972	Charles Shaw	797	158	5.0	Steve Cockreham	137	61	.45	1,010	Scott Freeman	26	429	16.5
1973	Andy Dixon	487	90	5.4	Steve Cockreham	209	89	.43	1,639	Archie Gray	40	988	24.7
1974	Robbie Wright	604	140	4.3	Rick Costello	249	118	.47	1,639	Archie Gray	27	394	14.6
1975	Lawrence Gaines	894	161	5.6	Steve Trusso	48	24	.50	381	John Arnold	23	376	16.3
1976	Robbie Wright	718	135	5.3	Don Clayton	65	21	.32	409	Walter Howard	16	305	19.1
1977	Myron Hardeman	1,165	186	6.3	Don Clayton	92	35	.38	530	Walter Howard	24	491	20.5
1978	Myron Hardeman	658	119	5.5	Marc Cousins	138	52	.38	928	Dan Pittman	15	367	24.5
1979	Phil Davis	629	240	2.6	Phil Davis	241	113	.47	1,687	Dan Pittman	41	733	17.9
1980	Mandel Robinson	873	152	5.7	Phil Davis	147	63	.43	1,143	Steve Martinez	27	513	19.0
1981	Phil Davis	575	142	4.0	Phil Davis	145	75	.52	1,173	Steve Martinez	37	629	17.0
1982	Walter Goffigan	586	121	4.8	Craig Johnson	175	79	.45	1,130	Steve Martinez	35	546	15.6
1983	Walter Goffigan	827	161	5.1	Brad Baumberger	189	112	.59	1,551	Chris Kolodzieski	43	576	13.4
1984	Dave Evans	979	183	5.3	Scott Runyan	148	68	.46	1,353	Allyn Griffin	38	835	22.0
1985	Toriane Taylor	692	136	5.1	Scott Runyan	153	62	.41	919	Allyn Griffin	43	668	15.5
1986	Gerald Abraham	668	139	4.8	Scott Runyan	271	138	.51	1,651	James Loving	54	673	12.5
1987	Gerald Abraham	1,305	238	5.5	Craig Burnett	467	258	.55	3,131	Anthony Sargent	68	929	13.7
1988	Dabby Dawson	1,119	151	7.4	Randy Welniak	354	199	.56	2,791	Ted Gilmore	40	594	14.9
1989	Dabby Dawson	1,005	182	5.5	Tom Corontzos	280	153	.55	2,005	Gordy Wood	60	632	10.5
1990	Dwight Driver	684	154	4.4	Tom Corontzos	399	211	.53	2,956	Shawn Wiggins	58	1,018	17.6
1991	Terrance Hendricks	815	164	5.0	Tom Corontzos	363	203	.56	2,686	Ryan Yarborough	53	1,081	20.4
1992	Dwight Driver	1,027	229	4.5	Joe Hughes	373	216	.58	2,706	Ryan Yarborough	86	1,351	15.7
1993	Ryan Christopherson	1,042	222	4.7	Joe Hughes	414	236	.57	3,372	Ryan Yarborough	75	1,584	21.1
1994	Ryan Christopherson	1,455	300	4.9	John Gustin	306	181	.59	2,757	Marcus Harris	71	1,431	20.2
1995	Len Sexton	810	129	6.3	Josh Wallwork	271	163	.60	2,363	Marcus Harris	78	1,423	18.2
1996	Len Sexton	826	164	5.0	Josh Wallwork	458	286	.62	4,090	Marcus Harris	109	1,650	15.1
1997	Marques Brigham	696	153	4.5	Jay Stoner	299	149	.50	1,890	Wendell Montgomery	58	905	15.6
1998	Marques Brigham	1,114	259	4.3	Jay Stoner	316	183	.58	2,373	Wendell Montgomery	57	789	13.8
1999	Cliff Brye	451	76	5.9	Jay Stoner	222	135	.61	1,859	Wendell Montgomery	41	733	17.9
2000	Nate Scott	645	110	5.9	Jay Stoner	275	171	.62	1,552	Ryan McGuffey	63	696	11.0
2001	Nate Scott	550	111	5.0	Casey Bramlet	432	225	.52	3,069	Ryan McGuffey	65	751	11.6
2002	Derek Armah	596	124	4.8	Casey Bramlet	464	277	.60	3,290	Jovon Bouknight	63	689	10.9
2003	Derek Armah	683	177	3.9	Casey Bramlet	425	241	.57	3,037	Ryan McGuffey	68	815	12.0
2004	Ivan Harrison	587	159	3.7	Corey Bramlet	334	195	.58	2,409	Jovon Bouknight	63	1,075	17.1

All statistics include postseason

WYOMING ALL-TIME SCORES

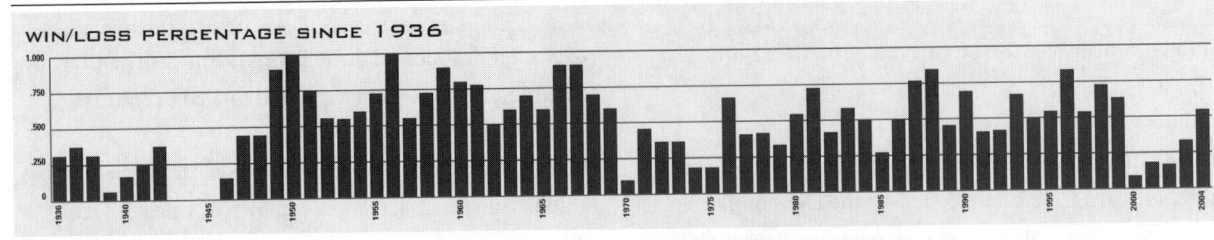

WIN/LOSS PERCENTAGE SINCE 1936

FRED HESS
1893, '98 (.200)   1-4

1893   1-0-0
F22 ● Cheyenne HS   14   0

FRED HESS / J.F. SOULE
1894 (1.000)   3-0

1894   3-0-0
O13 ● Laramie Town Team   14   0
N29 ● Wilson Beauties   16   0
D25 ● #5 Hose Co.   16   6

J.F. SOULE
1895-97 '99 (.786)   5-1-1

1895   1-0-0
N29 ● No. Colorado   34   0

1896   2-0-0
O31 ● at No. Colorado   10   6
N7   ● Denver Manual HS   18   14

1897   2-0-0
N25 ● Alumni   4   0
D16 ● Cheyenne   16   0

FRED HESS

1898   0-4-0
O15   Colorado Mines   0   29
N5   at Colorado Mines   0   50
N24   Denver   0   5
N29   Laramie HS   8   11

J.F. SOULE

1899   0-1-0
N30   at Colorado State   0   12
D16 = No. Colorado   5   5

WILLIAM McMURRAY
1900-06 (.589)   16-11-1

1900   3-3-0
O27 ● Laramie Town Team   27   0
N3   at Denver AC   0   33
N5   ● at Colorado   6   10
N17 ● Utah YMCA   16   0
N24 ● at Colorado State   0   16
N29 ● No. Colorado   56   0

1901   1-0-0
N28 ● Laramie AC   38   0

1902   1-0-0
D13 ● Cheyenne HS   18   0

1903   3-2-0
O16 ● Laramie HS   15   0
O24 ● Laramie AC   6   0
N14 ● at Colorado State   0   17
N21 ● at Utah State   0   46
N26 ● Laramie AC   11   0

1904   4-1-1
O15 ● Cheyenne HS   56   0
O31 ● Utah   0   23
N8   ● at Cheyenne HS   12   6
N12 ● Faculty   11   0
N19 ● at Fort Warren   12   0
N24 = Colorado State   6   6

1905-1937
ROCKY MOUNTAIN

1905   3-4-0 (0-4-0)
O7   at Utah   0   31
O15   at Colorado Mines   0   28
O21   at Colorado   0   69
N5   ● No. Colorado   22   0
N18   at Cheyenne HS   10   0
N25   at Colorado State   5   34
N30   Fort Warren   26   0

1906   1-1-0 (0-1-0)
O15   Colorado Mines   0   35
O29   Laramie HS   12   0

ROBERT EHLMAN
1907-08 (.500)   3-3

1907   2-1-0 (0-1-0)
O12   Fort Warren   12   2
O19   at Colorado Mines   0   77
N29 ● at Fort Russell   56   0

1908   1-2-0 (0-2-0)
O27 ● Fort Warren   66   0
N7   at Utah   0   75
N14   at Colorado State   0   20

HAROLD I. DEAN
1909-11 (.479)   11-12-1

1909   3-5-0 (0-4-0)
O2   ● at Cheyenne HS   30   0
O9   at Denver   0   56
O12 ● Laramie HS   25   0
O16   at Colorado State   3   32
O30   Colorado College   5   44
N6   at Fort Russell   6   15
N13   Fort Russell   18   0
N20   Colorado Mines   6   23

1910   4-4-0 (1-4-0)
O1   ● at Cheyenne HS   61   12
O8   ● at Denver   3   17
O15   at Colorado College   0   23
O22   at Colorado   3   14 *
N8   ● All Star Team   17   0
N12   at Colorado Mines   8   9
N19 ● Nebraska Wesleyan   5   0
N24 ● Colorado State   10   0

1911   4-3-1 (2-3-0)
S30 ● Laramie HS   74   0
O7   at Colorado College   9   29
O14 = at So. Dakota Mines   0   0
O21 ● Colorado Mines   5   0
O28   at Colorado   3   18
N13 ● Nebraska Wesleyan   21   0
N18   Denver   0   6
N30 ● at Colorado State   27   0

LEON C. EXCELBY
1912 (.222)   2-7

1912   2-7-0 (0-6-0)
O5   at Utah   0   9
O12   at Colorado College   0   35
O19   at Colorado Mines   0   42
O26   at Colorado   0   75
N2   at Utah State   0   53
N9   ● So. Dakota Mines   14   3
N16   Chadron St.   25   0
N23   Kearney St.   25   41
N28   Colorado State   0   33

RALPH W. THACKER
1913-14 (.091)   1-10

1913   0-5-0 (0-5-0)
O4   Colorado   0   7
O11   at Colorado College   0   49
O18   Colorado Mines   0   40
N8   Denver   0   26
N27   at Colorado State   0   61

1914   1-5-0 (0-5-0)
S30 ● Cheyenne HS   18   10
O10   at Utah   0   20
O17   Colorado Mines   0   25
O24   at Colorado State   10   48
N7   at Utah State   3   24
N21   Denver   0   31

JOHN CORBETT
1915-23 (.266)   15-44-3

1915   2-6-0 (1-5-0)
S25 ● Laramie HS   19   0
O2   at Colorado   0   30
O9   at Utah   7   70
O16   at Colorado Mines   0   19
O23   Denver   7   19
O27 ● Utah State   13   7
N6   Colorado State   0   47 *
N19   at Nebraska Wesleyan   9   20

1916   1-4-0 (1-4-0)
S30 ● at Colorado State   0   40
O7   Colorado   10   16
O14   Denver   10   19
O21 ● at Utah State   23   10
O28   Colorado Mines   7   30

1917   3-4-0 (1-4-0)
O6   ● Colorado State   6   0
O13   Colorado Mines   3   51
O20   at Utah   0   14
O24   at Utah State   0   57
N3   Denver   0   18
N10 ● No. Colorado   7   0
N29 ● at No. Colorado   8   0

1918
NO TEAM-FLU EPIDEMIC

1919   3-5-0 (3-3-0)
S27   Colorado State   0   28
O4   at Colorado State   0   14
O11 ● Montana St.   6   0
O18 ● Colorado Mines   16   6
O25 ● at Denver   36   6
N8   Nebraska Wesleyan   10   14
N15   at Creighton   0   41
N20   Utah State   0   6

1920   4-5-1 (2-5-1)
O2   Colorado State   0   13
O9   ● at Denver   10   7
O16   at Colorado State   0   42
O23   Colorado   0   7
O30 ● at Colorado Mines   14   7
N2   ● at Nebraska Wesleyan   14   7
N7   at Colorado College   17   20
N13   Denver   0   3
N20 = at Utah   0   0
N25 ● at Ogden AC   3   0

1921   1-4-2 (1-3-2)
O1   = at Colorado State   7   7
O8   Colorado College   0   10
O11 ● at Utah State   3   14 *
O15   at Utah   3   14
O22 = Colorado Mines   14   7
O29 = at Denver   9   9
N11   at Idaho   3   31

1922   1-8-0 (1-7-0)
S30   at Colorado College   0   20
O7   at Colorado Mines   0   32
O14   Colorado State   0   60
O25   Utah   0   27
N4   at Denver   0   7
N11   at Utah State   0   25 *
N14   at Brigham Young   0   7
N21   at Gonzaga   0   77
N30 ● Brigham Young   13   0

1923   0-8-0 (0-7-0)
S29   at Colorado State   0   33
O6   Colorado College   7   34
O13   at Utah   0   79
O20   Faculty   0   14
O27   Colorado Mines   0   20
N3   at Denver   0   45
N16   Utah State   6   20
N24   at Colorado   3   20

"LONE STAR" DIETZ
1924-26 (.440)   10-13-2

1924   2-6-0 (2-6-0)
O11   at Denver   0   7
O18 ● No. Colorado   33   6
O25   Colorado   0   21
N1   at Colorado Mines   3   6
N5   ● Montana St.   18   17
N15   at Utah   0   28
N19   at Utah State   2   25
N22   at Colorado College   3   28

1925   6-3-0 (4-3-0)
O3   ● Kearney St.   34   0
O10 ● at Western St.   7   0
O17 ● Colorado Mines   43   0
O24 ● Regis   24   0
O30 ● at Montana St.   7   0
N5   ● at Utah State   13   26
N11 ● No. Colorado   13   10
N18 ● Utah   6   7
N26 ● at Colorado State   0   40

1926   2-4-2 (1-2-2)
O6   Nebraska Wesleyan   7   14
O9   ● Kearney St.   48   0
O16 = at Colorado   13   13
O23 | Utah State   6   6
N6   ● at Colorado College   0   25
N13 | Montana St. CAS   0   10
N20   at Regis   7   22
N25 | Western St.   71   0

GEORGE McLAREN
1927-29 (.269)   7-19

1927   4-5-0 (1-4-0)
S24 ● Black Hills St.   31   6
O1   at Creighton   0   13
O8   at Denver   0   7
O15 ● Chadron St.   30   13
O22   at Utah State   0   42
O29 ● Colorado College   8   12
N11   Montana St. SHE   0   6
N19 ● Montezuma Coll.   26   0
N24 ● at No. Colorado   27   6

1928   2-7-0 (0-5-0)
S22 ● Black Hills St.   31   6
S29 ● Kearney St.   19   6
O6   at Chicago   0   47
O19 ● Utah State   6   24
O27 ● No. Colorado   0   28
N3   at Denver   7   26
N10 ● at Montana St.   7   14
N17 ● at Chadron St.   0   31
N24 | at Colorado College   25   48

1929 — 1-7-0 (0-7-0)

S27	●	Black Hills St.	13	6
O4		at Colorado State	7	20
O12		at Denver	6	19
O26		Utah State	7	12
N2		at No. Colorado	0	6
N11		Montana St.	0	13
N16		Utah	0	44
N23		at Brigham Young	0	40

JOHN RHODES
1930-32 (.407)   10-15-2

1930 — 2-5-1 (1-5-1)

S27		at Brigham Young	12	19
O4		at Utah	0	72
O11		Montana St.	13	20
O25		at Utah State	8	13
N1	=	No. Colorado	6	6
N8	●	at Colorado State	21	6
N15		at Denver	7	19
N29		at New Mexico	19	6

1931 — 6-4-0 (3-2-0)

S19	●	at Fort Warren	59	0
S26	●	at Chadron St.	35	0
O3		at Creighton	0	3
O10	●	at No. Colorado	13	6
O17	●	at Montana St.	32	13
O24		Utah State	0	12
N7		Colorado State	6	26
N13	●	at Brigham Young	13	7
N21		Santa Clara	0	6
N26	●	at New Mexico	12	2

1932 — 2-6-1 (1-4-1)

O1	●	Chadron St.	28	6
O7		at St. Louis	6	20
O15	●	Montana St.	13	7
O22		Colorado College *CHE*	6	15
O29		Brigham Young	0	25
N5		Denver	0	7
N11	=	No. Colorado	0	0
N19		at Creighton	0	34
N24		at Colorado State	0	23

WILLARD WITTE
1933-38 (.357)   16-30-3

1933 — 2-6-1 (1-6-1)

S23	●	at Fort Warren	33	0
S30		Colorado State	0	7
O7	=	at Colorado College	0	0
O14		Montana St.	0	7
O21		at No. Colorado	0	27
O28		at Colorado	12	40
N4		at Utah State	0	27
N25	●	Western St.	6	0
N30		at Brigham Young	0	3 *

1934 — 3-5-0 (2-4-0)

S22	●	at Fort Warren	40	0
S29		at Nebraska	0	50
O6	●	Brigham Young	6	0 *
O13		at Montana St.	25	6
O20		Utah State	0	19
O27		at Denver	0	9
N3		at Colorado State	0	16
N17		No. Colorado	6	9

1935 — 4-4-0 (3-4-0)

S22	●	at Fort Warren	15	0
S28		Colorado State	3	12
O5	●	Colorado Mines	40	0
O11		at Denver	0	14
O26		Brigham Young	6	13
N2	●	at Montana St.	6	2
N9	●	at Utah State	0	16 *
N23	●	at Colorado	6	0

1936 — 2-5-1 (2-4-1)

O2		at No. Colorado	7	13
O10		Utah State	0	25
O17	=	at Colorado State	0	0
O24		at Denver	14	25
O31	●	Colorado Mines	27	0
N7	●	Montana St.	19	6
N21		at Brigham Young	7	32
N28		Arizona *PHO*	0	58

1937 — 3-5-0 (2-4-0)

S25	●	at Fort Warren	20	0
O2		at Nevada	7	9
O9		at Colorado College	6	9
O16	●	at Colorado State	7	0
O23		at Utah State	7	34
N6		Brigham Young	0	19
N13		at Denver	6	21
N25	●	No. Colorado	33	0

1938-1947
MOUNTAIN STATES

1938 — 2-5-1 (1-4-1)

S17	●	at Fort Warren	20	7
S24		at Texas Tech	0	35 *
O1	=	Colorado State	0	0
O8		at Brigham Young	13	22 *
O22		Denver	0	6
O29		at Colorado	6	20
N12	●	at Utah State	27	13 *
N19		Utah	0	39

JOEL HUNT
1939 (.063)   0-7-1

1939 — 0-7-1 (0-5-1)

S29		at New Mexico	7	34
O7		at Utah	0	60
O13		at Denver	7	32
O28		Colorado	7	27
N4		at Colorado State	0	22
N10		at St. Louis	6	39
N18		Utah State	13	20
N25	=	Brigham Young	7	7

OKIE BLANCHARD
1940 (.167)   1-7-1

1940 — 1-7-1 (0-5-1)

S28	●	New Mexico	7	3
O5	=	Colorado State	0	0
O11		Brigham Young	0	20
O19		at Denver	9	41
O26		at Colorado	0	62
N2		Chadron St.	9	12
N9		Utah	7	34
N16		at Wichita St.	0	2
N23		at Utah State	0	16

"BUNNY" OAKES
1941-46 (.250)   6-20-2

1941 — 2-7-1 (1-5-0)

S26	●	at No. Colorado	19	6
O4		at Colorado State	0	27
O11		at Utah	6	60
O18		Denver	0	40
O25		at Colorado	0	27
N1		at Colorado College	0	16
N8		Brigham Young	7	23
N15	●	Utah State	12	6
N20	=	Colorado Mines	0	0
N29		at New Mexico	0	28

1942 — 3-5-0 (1-5-0)

S26		Colorado State	0	10
O2	●	at Brigham Young	13	6
O10	●	No. Colorado	33	0
O17		at Denver	14	17
O24	●	at Colorado Mines	26	6
O31		at Colorado	7	28
N14		Utah	7	34
N21		at Utah State	6	14

1943-1945
NO TEAM WWII

1946 — 1-8-1 (0-6-0)

S21	●	No. Colorado	7	0
S28	●	Colorado Mines	7	7
O5		Colorado State	0	7
O12		Colorado	0	20
O19		at Minnesota	0	46
O26		at Utah	7	27
N2		at Brigham Young	3	6
N9		Denver	6	19
N16		at Utah State	7	21
N24		at San Francisco	7	39

BOWDEN WYATT
1947-52 (.693)   39-17-1

1947 — 4-5-0 (2-4-0)

S27		at Arizona	7	27
O4	●	Brigham Young	12	7
O11	●	Colorado Mines	53	6
O18	●	Utah State	33	19
O25		Utah	7	26
N1	●	at No. Colorado	44	14
N8		at Denver	7	27
N15		at Colorado	6	21
N22		at Colorado State	6	21

1948-1961
SKYLINE

1948 — 4-5-0 (0-5-0)

S25		Colorado College	61	7
O2	●	No. Colorado	48	0
O9	●	Idaho St.	40	13
O16		Colorado State	20	21
O23		at Utah	7	19
O30		at Utah State	34	45
N13		Montana St. *BILL*	46	12
N20		at Brigham Young	14	15
N27		at Denver	0	13

1949 — 9-1-0 (5-0-0)

S17	●	at Idaho St.	58	13
S24	●	at New Mexico	41	14
O1	●	at Colorado State	8	0
O8	●	Montana St. *BILL*	48	0
O15	●	Utah State	27	0
O22	●	Utah	13	0
O29	●	Brigham Young	45	0
N5	●	at No. Colorado	103	0
N12		at Baylor	13	32 *
N24	●	at Denver	25	6

1950 — 10-0-0 (5-0-0)

S16	●	Montana St.	61	13
S23	●	Baylor	7	0
O7	●	Colorado State	34	0
O14	●	at Utah State	40	7
O21	●	at Utah	53	13
O28	●	New Mexico	44	0
N4	●	at Idaho	14	7
N11	●	at Brigham Young	48	0
N23	●	at Denver	42	12
GATOR BOWL				
J1	●	Wash. & Lee	20	7

1951 — 7-2-1 (4-1-1)

S15	●	Florida *JACF*	0	13
S22	●	Idaho	28	0
S29	●	Denver	20	14
O6	●	Utah State	37	0
O13		at Colorado State	7	14
O20	=	Brigham Young	20	20
O27	●	at Utah	13	0
N3		at Montana	34	7
N10	●	at New Mexico	41	7
N24	●	at Arizona State	20	7

1952 — 5-4-0 (4-3-0)

S27	●	Montana	14	0
O4	●	at Utah State	14	0
O11		Colorado State	0	14
O18	●	New Mexico	0	7
O25		Utah	21	27
N1	●	at Brigham Young	24	13
N8	●	at Kansas State	20	7
N27	●	at Denver	21	14
D6		at Houston	0	20

PHIL DICKENS
1953-56 (.720)   29-11-1

1953 — 5-4-1 (3-2-1)

S19	●	New Mexico State	47	0
S26	●	at Montana	27	7
O3	●	Utah State	20	13
O10	●	Colorado State	21	14
O17		at Iowa	7	21
O24		at Utah	12	13
O31	●	at Brigham Young	27	0
N7		at Oklahoma State	14	20
N14		at New Mexico	7	9
N26	=	at Denver	13	13

1954 — 6-4-0 (5-1-0)

S18		Oklahoma State	6	14
S25		Kansas State	13	21
O2	●	Denver	23	21
O9		at Colorado State	34	0
O16	●	New Mexico	9	7
O23		Utah	7	14
N6		at Utah State	21	12
N13		at Brigham Young	34	13
N20	●	at Tulsa	28	27
N27		at Arizona	40	42

1955 — 8-3-0 (5-2-0)

S17	●	at Kansas State	38	20
S24	●	Montana *BILL*	35	6
O1	●	Utah State	21	13
O8		Colorado State	13	14
O15	●	Tulsa	23	19
O22	●	at Utah	23	13
O29	●	Brigham Young	14	6
N12	●	at New Mexico	20	0
N24		Denver	3	6
D3		at Houston	14	26
SUN BOWL				
J2	●	Texas Tech	21	14

1956 — 10-0-0 (7-0-0)

S15	●	Western St.	40	13
S22	●	at Arizona	26	20
S29	●	Denver	27	0
O6	●	at Colorado State	20	12
O13	●	New Mexico	20	13
O20	●	Utah	30	20
O27	●	Kansas State	27	15
N3	●	at Utah State	21	0
N10	●	Montana *BILL*	34	13
N17	●	at Brigham Young	7	6

BOB DEVANEY
1957-61 (.750)   35-10-5

1957 — 4-3-3 (3-2-2)

S21	●	Kansas State	12	7
S28	●	Montana *BILL*	20	0
O5	=	Utah State	19	19
O12	●	Colorado State	27	13
O19	=	Brigham Young	0	0
O26		at Utah	15	23
N2		Air Force	7	7
N9		at Oklahoma State	6	39
N16	●	at New Mexico	20	13
N28		at Denver	13	14

1958 — 8-3-0 (6-1-0)

S20		at Kansas State	14	17
S27	●	Montana *BILL*	21	14
O4	●	Denver	15	12
O11	●	Oregon State	28	0
O18	●	at Colorado State	7	6
O25	●	New Mexico	12	13
N1	●	Utah	25	20
N8	●	at Utah State	41	13
N15		at Air Force	6	21
N22	●	at Brigham Young	22	14
SUN BOWL				
D31	●	Hardin Simmons	14	6

1959 — 9-1-0 (7-0-0)

S19	●	Montana *BILL*	58	0
S26		Air Force	7	20
O3	●	Utah State	27	2
O10	●	Colorado State	29	0
O17	●	Brigham Young	21	6
O24	●	at Utah	21	7
O31	●	at North Carolina St.	26	0
N7	●	at San Jose State	28	7
N14	●	at New Mexico	25	20
N21	●	at Denver	45	0

1960 — 8-2-0 (6-1-0)

S17	●	Montana *BILL*	14	0
S24	●	New Mexico	13	3
O1		at Arizona	19	21
O8	●	Denver	41	2
O15	●	at Colorado State	40	8
O22	●	Air Force	15	0
O29	●	Utah	17	7
N5	●	at Utah State	13	17
N12	●	at Texas Tech	10	7
N19	●	at Brigham Young	30	6

1961　　6-1-2 (5-0-1)

S16	●	at Montana	29	0
S23	●	North Carolina St.	15	14
S30	=	at Kansas	6	6
O7	=	Utah State	6	6
O14	●	Colorado State	18	7
O21	●	Brigham Young	36	8
O28	●	at Utah	13	6
N4		at Arizona	15	20
N11	●	at New Mexico	33	7

1962-1998
WAC

LLOYD EATON
1962-70 (.630)　　57-33-2

1962　　5-5-0 (2-2-0)

S15	●	at Montana	13	0
S22		New Mexico	21	25
S29		Washington State	15	21
O6	●	Utah	16	7
O13	●	at Texas-El Paso	14	6
O20	●	Arizona	31	8
O27	●	at Colorado State	28	7
N3		at Air Force	14	35
N10		Utah State	6	20
N17		at Brigham Young	7	14

1963　　6-4-0 (2-3-0)

S21	●	at Montana	35	0
S28	●	Utah State	21	14
O5		Kansas	21	25
O12		Colorado State	21	3
O19	●	Brigham Young	41	14
O26	●	at Utah	26	23
N2		at Arizona	7	15
N9		at New Mexico	6	17
N16		at Arizona State	6	35
D7	●	at Texas-El Paso	7	6

1964　　6-2-2 (2-2-0)

S19	●	Colorado State	31	7
S26	●	at Washington State	28	7
O3	●	at Kansas	17	14
O10	●	Utah	14	13
O17		Texas-El Paso	20	6
O23		at Arizona	7	15
O31		New Mexico	6	17
N7	=	at Utah State	20	20
N14	=	at Air Force	7	7
N21		at Brigham Young	31	11

1965　　6-4-0 (3-2-0)

S18	●	Air Force	31	14
S25	●	at Colorado State	33	14
O2		Arizona	19	0
O9		at Utah	3	42
O16	●	Texas-El Paso	38	14
O23	●	Brigham Young	34	6
N6	●	at New Mexico	27	9
N13		at Army	0	13
N20		at Arizona State	10	14
N27		at Southern Cal	6	56

1966　　10-1-0 (5-0-0)

S17	●	at Air Force	13	0
S24	●	Arizona State	23	6
O1	●	Arizona	36	6
O8	●	Utah	40	7
O15	●	New Mexico	37	7
O22	●	Utah State	35	10
O29		at Colorado State	10	12
N5	●	at Wichita St.	55	0
N12	●	at Texas-El Paso	31	7
N19	●	at Brigham Young	47	14
		SUN BOWL		
D24	●	Florida State	28	20

1967　　10-1-0 (5-0-0)

S16	●	at Arizona	36	17
S23	●	Air Force	37	10
S30	●	Colorado State	13	10
O7	●	Brigham Young	26	10
O14	●	at Utah	28	0
O21	●	Wichita St.	30	7
O28	●	at Arizona State	15	13
N4	●	at San Jose State	28	7
N11	●	at New Mexico	42	6
N18	●	at Texas-El Paso	21	19
		SUGAR BOWL		
J1		LSU	13	20

1968　　7-3-0 (6-1-0)

S14		at Nebraska	10	13
S21	●	Utah State	48	3
S28		at Air Force	3	10
O5	●	Arizona State	27	13
O12	●	at Brigham Young	20	17
O19	●	Utah	20	9
O26	●	New Mexico	35	6
N2	●	at Colorado State	46	14
N16	●	at Texas-El Paso	26	19
N23		at Arizona	7	14

1969　　6-4-0 (4-3-0)

S20	●	Arizona	23	7
S27	●	at Air Force	27	25
O4	●	Colorado State	39	3
O11	●	Texas-El Paso	37	9
O18	●	Brigham Young	40	7
O25	●	San Jose State	16	7
N1		at Arizona State	14	30
N8		at Utah	10	34
N15		at New Mexico	12	24
N22		at Houston	14	41

1970　　1-9-0 (1-6-0)

S19	●	Air Force	17	41
S26		Utah State	29	42
O3		Arizona State	3	52
O10	●	at Colorado State	16	6
O17		Utah	16	20
O24		New Mexico	7	17
O31		at Brigham Young	3	23
N7		at Texas-El Paso	7	47
N14		at Houston	0	28
N21		at Arizona	12	38

FRITZ SHURMUR
1971-74 (.341)　　15-29

1971　　5-6-0 (3-4-0)

S11	●	South Dakota	42	28
S18	●	at Colorado	13	56
S25		at Air Force	19	23
O2	●	Colorado State	17	6
O9	●	Arizona	14	3
O16		Brigham Young	17	35
O23		Texas-El Paso	7	12
O30	●	at Utah	29	16
N6	●	at Utah State	31	29
N13		at Arizona State	19	52
N20		at New Mexico	14	49

1972　　4-7-0 (3-4-0)

S9	●	Idaho St.	30	14
S16		at Air Force	14	45
S23		at Kansas	14	52
S30	●	Arizona State	45	43
O7		New Mexico	14	17
O14	●	at Colorado State	28	9
O21		Utah	6	27
O28		Utah State	23	35
N4		at Brigham Young	14	33
N11		at Texas-El Paso	13	20
N18	●	at Arizona	22	14

1973　　4-7-0 (3-4-0)

S15	●	Arizona	7	21
S22	●	Pacific	49	14
S29	●	Texas-El Paso	31	8
O6		at Wisconsin	28	37
O13		at Utah	16	50
O20		Colorado State	35	3
O27		Brigham Young	41	21
N3		at Utah State	20	31
N10		at Arizona State	0	47
N17		at New Mexico	21	23
N24		at Houston	0	35

1974　　2-9-0 (1-6-0)

S14		Utah State	7	17
S21		at Texas	7	34
S28	●	Air Force	20	16
O5		Arizona State	10	16
O12		at Brigham Young	7	38
O19		New Mexico	21	32
O26	●	Utah	31	13
N2		at Colorado State	6	11
N9		at Texas-El Paso	13	35
N16		Pacific	14	50
N23		at Arizona	14	21

FRED AKERS
1975-76 (.435)　　10-13

1975　　2-9-0 (1-6-0)

S13		Idaho St.	3	16
S20		at Colorado	10	27
S27		Arizona	0	14
O4		Colorado State	0	3
O11		at Utah	13	16
O18	●	Texas-El Paso	31	14
O25		Brigham Young	20	33
N1		at Utah State	21	27
N8		at Arizona State	20	21
N15		at New Mexico	32	38
N22	●	at Air Force	24	10

1976　　8-4-0 (6-1-0)

S11	●	South Dakota	48	7
S18	●	at Michigan State	10	21
S25	●	Utah State	20	3
O2	●	Arizona State	13	10
O9	●	at Brigham Young	34	29
O16	●	New Mexico	24	23
O23	●	Utah	45	22
O30		at Colorado State	16	19
N6	●	at Arizona	26	24
N13	●	at Texas-El Paso	14	10
N20		at Air Force	21	41
		FIESTA BOWL		
D25		Oklahoma	7	41

BILL LEWIS
1977-79 (.386)　　13-21-1

1977　　4-6-1 (4-3-0)

S10	=	Air Force	0	0
S17	●	Texas-El Paso	27	17
S24		at Michigan State	16	34
O1	●	Arizona	13	12
O8		at Utah	13	23
O22		Brigham Young	7	10
O29	●	Colorado State	29	13
N5		at Arizona State	0	45
N12		at Utah State	31	32
N19	●	at New Mexico	23	21
N26		at LSU	7	66

1978　　5-7-0 (4-2-0)

S16	●	South Dakota	30	11
S23		at Texas	3	17
S30		Utah State	13	20
O7		New Mexico	15	19
O14	●	San Diego State	31	22
O21	●	Utah	34	21
O28	●	at Colorado State	13	3
N4		at Brigham Young	14	48
N11		at Nevada-Las Vegas	10	12
N18		at Hawaii	22	27
N25	●	at Texas-El Paso	51	21
D2		at LSU	17	24

1979　　4-8-0 (2-5-0)

S8		at Washington	2	38
S15		at Northwestern	22	27
S22	●	Richmond	9	7
S29		Colorado State	16	20
O6	●	Texas-El Paso	23	3
O13		at Utah	14	24
O20		Brigham Young	14	54
O27		Nevada-Las Vegas	24	28
N3		at San Diego State	21	31
N10	●	Arkansas State	17	14
N17		at Hawaii	21	13
N24		at New Mexico	3	17

PAT DYE
1980 (.545)　　6-5

1980　　6-5-0 (4-4-0)

S13	●	Oregon State	30	10
S20	●	Richmond	35	14
S27	●	Hawaii	45	20
O4		New Mexico	21	24
O11		at Brigham Young	17	52
O18	●	Utah	24	21
O25	●	San Diego State	34	9
N1		at Colorado State	25	28
N8		at Nevada-Las Vegas	26	33
N15		at Air Force	7	25
N22	●	at Texas-El Paso	52	7

AL KINCAID
1981-85 (.500)　　29-29

1981　　8-3-0 (6-2-0)

S5	●	Fullerton St.	38	13
S12		at Oklahoma	20	37
S19	●	at Air Force	17	10
O3	●	Nevada-Las Vegas	45	21
O10		Hawaii	9	14
O17	●	Texas-El Paso	63	12
O24	●	Brigham Young	33	20
O31	●	Colorado State	55	21
N7	●	at San Diego State	24	13
N14		at Utah	27	30
N21	●	at New Mexico	13	12

1982　　5-7-0 (2-6-0)

S4		New Mexico	20	41
S11		at Colorado State	3	9
S18	●	Long Beach St.	36	27
S25	●	at Colorado	24	10
O2		at Hawaii	28	10
O9		San Diego State	21	24
O16		Fullerton St.	16	20
O23	●	Utah	16	13
O30		at Air Force	34	44
N6		at Brigham Young	13	23
N13	●	Wichita St.	24	20
N20		at Texas-El Paso	32	39

1983　　7-5-0 (5-3-0)

S3	●	South Dakota	34	13
S10		at Nebraska	20	56
S17	●	Air Force	14	7
S24		at Kansas State	25	27
O1	●	Texas-El Paso	49	17
O8		Brigham Young	10	41
O15		at Utah	14	69
O22	●	Colgate	49	29
N5		at New Mexico	10	17
N12	●	at San Diego State	33	21
N19	●	Colorado State	42	17
N26	●	at Hawaii	31	13

1984　　6-6-0 (4-4-0)

S1	●	South Dakota	31	13
S8		at Nebraska	7	42
S15	●	Air Force	26	20
S22		at Oregon State	14	41
S29	●	Utah	21	14
O6		San Diego State	0	21
O13		at Brigham Young	38	41
O20	●	New Mexico	59	21
O27	●	at Colorado State	43	34
N3		at Hawaii	28	31
N10	●	South Dakota St.	45	29
N17		at Texas-El Paso	22	35

1985　　3-8-0 (2-6-0)

S7		at Baylor	18	39
S14		Air Force	7	49
S21	●	Fullerton St.	31	8
S28	●	Wisconsin	17	41
O4		at Utah	20	37
O12		Hawaii	18	26
O26		Colorado State	19	30
N2		at Brigham Young	0	59
N9	●	San Diego State	41	20
N16	●	at New Mexico	16	41
D6	●	Texas-El Paso MEL	24	21

DENNIS ERICKSON
1986 (.500)　　6-6

1986　　6-6-0 (4-4-0)

S6		Baylor	28	31
S13	●	Pacific	23	20
S20	●	at Air Force	23	17
S27		at Wisconsin	21	12
O4		at Iowa State	10	21
O11	●	Utah	38	14
O18		Brigham Young	22	34
O25		at Colorado State	15	20
N1	●	New Mexico	35	25
N8	●	Texas-El Paso	41	12
N15	●	at San Diego State	24	31
N29		at Hawaii	19	35

PAUL ROACH
1987-90 (.700)   35-15

1987   10-3-0 (8-0-0)

S5	● Air Force	27	13
S12	at Washington State	28	43
S19	Oklahoma State	29	35
S26	● Iowa State	34	17
O3	● San Diego State	52	10
O10	● at Brigham Young	29	27
O17	● Houston	37	35
O31	● Colorado State	20	15
N7	● at New Mexico	59	16
N14	● at Utah	31	7
N21	● at Texas-El Paso	37	13
N28	● at Hawaii	24	20
HOLIDAY BOWL			
D30	Iowa	19	20

1988   11-2-0 (8-0-0)

S1	● Brigham Young	24	14
S8	● at Louisville	44	9
S17	● Louisiana Tech	38	6
S24	● at Air Force	48	45
O1	● Fullerton St.	35	16
O8	● at San Diego State	55	27
O15	● New Mexico	55	7
O22	● Utah	61	18
O29	● at Colorado State	48	14
N5	● Texas-El Paso	51	6
N12	at Houston	10	34
N19	● at Hawaii	28	22
HOLIDAY BOWL			
D30	Oklahoma State	14	62

1989   5-6-0 (5-3-0)

S2	Louisville	21	28
S9	at Air Force	7	45
S16	● Hawaii	20	15
S23	● Washington State	23	29
S30	at Oklahoma State	7	27
O7	at Brigham Young	20	36
O14	● Utah	45	24
O28	● at New Mexico	24	23
N4	● Colorado State	56	35
N11	● at San Diego State	17	27
N18	● Texas-El Paso	41	10

1990   9-4-0 (5-3-0)

S1	● Temple	38	23
S8	● at Washington State	34	13
S15	● Arkansas State	34	27
S22	● Air Force	24	12
S29	● at Utah	28	10
O6	● San Diego State	52	51
O13	● New Mexico	25	22
O20	● Weber St.	21	12
O27	● at Texas-El Paso	17	10
N3	at Colorado State	8	17
N10	Brigham Young	14	45
N17	at Hawaii	17	38
COPPER BOWL			
D31	California	15	17

JOE TILLER
1991-96 (.564)   39-30-1

1991   4-6-1 (2-5-1)

A31	Hawaii	17	32
S7	at Colorado	13	30
S14	● La. Lafayette	28	15
S21	● Texas Tech	22	17
S28	= Texas-El Paso	28	28
O5	at Air Force	28	51
O12	Utah	42	57
O19	● at New Mexico	39	19
O26	● Colorado State	35	28
N2	at San Diego State	22	24
N9	at Brigham Young	31	56

1992   5-7-0 (3-5-0)

S5	● Nevada	25	6
S12	at Texas Tech	32	49
S19	Air Force	28	42
S26	at Louisville	26	24
O3	San Jose State	24	26
O10	● New Mexico	35	21
O17	Brigham Young	28	31
O24	● at Colorado State	31	14
O31	at Fresno State	31	42
N7	San Diego State	17	6
N14	at Utah	7	38
N21	at Hawaii	18	42

1993   8-4-0 (6-2-0)

S4	Oregon State	16	27
S11	● No. Iowa	45	42
S18	● at San Jose State	36	25
S25	● Utah	28	12
O2	● at Air Force	31	18
O9	● at Texas-El Paso	33	26
O23	● Hawaii	48	10
O30	● Fresno State	32	28
N13	at New Mexico	7	10
N20	Colorado State	21	41
N27	● at San Diego State	43	38
COPPER BOWL			
D29	Kansas State	17	52

1994   6-6-0 (4-4-0)

S3	● Texas-El Paso	36	13
S10	at Oregon State	31	44
S17	● Tulsa	17	7
S24	at Utah	7	41
O1	at Nebraska	32	42
O8	● La. Monroe	28	14
O15	at Fresno State	24	38
O22	● San Diego State	52	35
O29	Air Force	17	34
N5	at Colorado State	24	35
N12	● New Mexico	38	28
N19	● at Hawaii	13	10

1995   6-5-0 (4-4-0)

S9	at Air Force	10	34
S16	● Hawaii	52	6
S23	● Oklahoma State	45	25
O7	at Tulsa	6	35
O14	● Louisville	27	20
O21	at Brigham Young	20	23
O28	● Colorado State	24	31
N4	Utah	24	30
N11	● at San Diego State	34	31
N18	● Fresno State	38	10
N25	● at Texas-El Paso	42	19

1996   10-2 (7-1)

A31	● Idaho	40	38
S7	● at Iowa State	41	38
S14	● Hawaii	66	0
S21	● Air Force	22	19
S28	● at Nevada-Las Vegas	33	21
O5	● at San Jose State	45	22
O12	● Western Michigan	42	28
O19	● Fresno State	42	21
N2	● SMU	59	17
N7	at San Diego State	24	28
N16	● at Colorado State	25	24
WAC CHAMPIONSHIP			
D7	Brigham Young *LV*	25	28

DANA DIMEL
1997-99 (.629)   22-13

1997   7-6 (4-4)

A28	at Ohio State	10	24
S6	● Iowa State	56	10
S13	● at Hawaii	35	6
S20	● San Jose State	30	10
S27	at Colorado	19	20
O4	● Montana	28	13
O11	at Nevada	34	30
O18	● Colorado State	7	14
O25	at SMU	17	22
N1	● San Diego State	41	17
N8	● Nevada-Las Vegas	35	23
N15	● at Air Force	3	14
N22	● at Fresno State	7	24

1998   8-3 (6-2)

S12	● Montana St.	17	9
S19	at Georgia	9	16
S26	● Louisiana Tech	31	19
O3	● Utah	27	24
O10	● SMU	12	7
O17	● at Nevada-Las Vegas	28	25
O24	● Rice	34	24
O31	● at TCU	34	27
N7	● at Colorado State	27	19
N14	● Air Force	3	10
N21	● at Tulsa	0	35

1999-PRESENT
MOUNTAIN WEST

1999   7-4 (4-3)

S4	at Tennessee	17	42
S11	● Weber St.	41	16
S25	● at Air Force	10	7
O2	● Idaho	28	13
O9	Nevada-Las Vegas	32	35
O16	● at La. Monroe	38	20
O23	Colorado State	13	24
N6	● at Utah	43	29
N13	● Brigham Young	31	17
N20	● New Mexico	42	28
N27	at San Diego State	7	39

VIC KOENNING
2000-02 (.147)   5-29

2000   1-10 (0-7)

A31	at Auburn	21	35
S9	at Texas A&M	3	51
S16	● Central Michigan	31	10
S23	Nevada	28	35
S30	at New Mexico	10	45
O7	San Diego State	0	34
O14	Air Force	26	51
O21	at Nevada-Las Vegas	23	42
O26	at Brigham Young	7	19
N11	Utah	0	34
N16	at Colorado State	13	37

2001   2-9 (0-7)

S1	● Furman	20	14
S6	Texas A&M	20	28
S22	● at Utah State	43	42
S29	Colorado State	14	42
O6	New Mexico	29	30
O13	at Air Force	13	24
O20	at Utah	0	35
O27	Nevada-Las Vegas	26	47
N10	Brigham Young	34	41
N17	at San Diego State	16	38
N24	at Kansas	14	27

2002   2-10 (1-6)

A31	Tennessee *NASH*	7	47
S7	at Central Michigan	20	32
S14	Boise State	13	35
S21	at Washington	7	38
O5	● Citadel	34	10
O12	at Colorado State	36	44
O19	San Diego State	20	24
O26	● Air Force	34	26
N2	at Nevada-Las Vegas	48	49
N9	at Brigham Young	31	35
N16	Utah	18	23
N30	at New Mexico	20	49

JOE GLENN
2003-PRESENT (.458)   11-13

2003   4-8 (2-5)

A30	● Montana St.	21	10
S6	at Oklahoma State	24	48
S13	Kansas	35	42
S20	at Air Force	29	35
S27	at Boise State	17	33
O11	● at Utah State	48	21
O18	Brigham Young	13	10
O25	at San Diego State	20	25
N1	● Colorado State	35	28
N15	at Utah	17	47
N22	New Mexico	3	26
N29	Nevada-Las Vegas	24	35

2004   7-5 (3-4)

S4	● Appalachian St.	53	7
S11	at Texas A&M	0	31
S25	● Mississippi	37	32
O2	● La. Monroe	31	10
O9	● San Diego State	20	10
O16	at Brigham Young	13	24
O22	at Colorado State	7	30
O30	● Air Force	43	26
N6	● at Nevada-Las Vegas	53	45
N13	Utah	28	45
N20	at New Mexico	9	16
LAS VEGAS BOWL			
D23	● UCLA	24	21

THE SCHOOLS

The Roots of the Game

*The Resilient Glory
of Ivy League Football*

BY BRUCE WOOD

AFTER PRACTICALLY INVENTING THE GAME LATE IN the 19th century and helping define it over the first half of the 20th, the Ivy League slid steadily off the national college football map in the second half of the 20th century.

So why should we care about it in the early years of the 21st? Why should we pay attention to a Division I-AA conference that the major networks and national newspapers now largely ignore, that hasn't had a team finish in the major college Top 20 since 1970 and won't ever again? Why should we care about a league that hasn't produced a Heisman Trophy winner since 1951, more than half a century ago?

Because, explains Jeff Orleans, the Ivy League's executive director, in addition to being there at the beginning, "We also invented everything that is wrong with college football. From people playing in their seventh year to people being paid under the table, to disputes about the role of television.

"At one time or another, because we've played football for so long, we've seen everything that can go wrong. So we've got a lot of experience trying to fix it. If we can stay true to trying to do it right, then we should matter to college football and people should continue to care about us."

***

College football got its start on Nov. 6, 1869, in New Brunswick, N.J., when Princeton defeated Rutgers, 6-4, in a rough-and-tumble game more akin to soccer than football. By 1922, the Tigers had won 15 national football championships of one variety or another, a number surpassed to this day only by the 18 Yale has claimed, the last in 1927.

The history of the early days of college football was virtually written at the eight institutions that would later become the Ivy League. Walter Camp played seven years at Yale and is considered the father of American football. As an influential member of the Rules Committee from 1879

to 1925, he was instrumental in introducing plays from scrimmage, the use of a quarterback, set plays, and first downs. Even today's point values can be traced back to Camp, who coached Yale to a 67–2 record from 1888 to 1892.

Amos Alonzo Stagg lettered five years at Yale. Pop Warner coached at Cornell. John Heisman played club football at Brown and then on the varsity team at Pennsylvania, where he later coached briefly.

The Ivy League started the game and then helped to change it by opening the door to African-Americans. In January 1916, Brown's Fritz Pollard was the first African-American to play in the Rose Bowl. The following season, he became the first black All-America selection. In 1921, he became the first black coach in NFL history with the Akron Pros. Harvard tackle Chester "Chet" Pierce was the first African-American player to play against a white college in the South, when the Crimson traveled to Virginia in 1947, the same year Jackie Robinson broke the color barrier in major league baseball. When Dennis Coleman called signals for Brown and Marty Vaughn was under center for Penn at Franklin Field on Oct. 6, 1973, it marked the first time in more than 100 years of major college football that both starting quarterbacks were black.

***

Although *New York Herald Tribune* sportswriter Caswell Adams is generally credited with the first reference to the "Ivy" league in 1937, Brown, Columbia, Cornell, Dartmouth, Harvard, Pennsylvania, Princeton and Yale were not part of a conference and were only loosely affiliated at the time.

Surprisingly, formal roots of what is often referred to as the "Ancient Eight" date only to November 1945, when the Ivy Group Agreement was signed in response to growing concerns among the eight Eastern schools about the proper place of football in an academic setting. Among the conditions of the agreement that would be the philosophical bedrock of the future Ivy League: there would be no football scholarships, and players would be representative of the student body as a whole.

In February 1952, the presidents of the schools that would become the Ivy League took another step toward formalizing the conference when they agreed to a ban on spring practice and postseason games, and agreed to play one another at least once every five years. When the Ivy

"We also invented everything that is wrong with college football."

Group Agreement was reissued in February 1954, it was with the understanding that the schools would begin annual round-robin play in 1956. That decision, and the folding of all other sports into the same philosophical tent in the landmark 1954 agreement, essentially signaled the birth of the Ivy League as it is known today. Although alumni and critics who fondly remembered national championships and Rose Bowl appearances of the halcyon days rued what they termed the "de-emphasis of football," the conference would be a national player for a few more years. In 1960, Yale went undefeated and finished No. 14 in the final Associated Press poll. It was the first Ivy team to be ranked at season's end since Princeton in 1952.

In 1970, unbeaten Dartmouth, which recorded six shutouts and led the nation in scoring defense, finished No. 14 in the polls while beating out Penn State for the Lambert Trophy, emblematic of Eastern supremacy.

But that would be the final time any Ivy League team ended a season ranked in the major college Top 20. Any chance it would happen again disappeared in January 1978 when, unhappy about sharing the growing pot of TV revenues with schools they argued weren't pulling their weight, the nation's new high-profile football powers forced legislation through the NCAA creating Division I-AA.

Largely because they couldn't claim average paid attendance of 17,000 per game, seven of the eight Ivy League schools were automatically consigned to the lower division. Yale, which met the attendance criteria, voluntarily moved down with its brethren.

No longer would players from Harvard, Princeton, Yale and the rest of the Ivies vie with those from USC, Texas and Alabama for All-America honors. An Ivy League team could go through the season unscored upon and still wouldn't rub elbows in the Associated Press poll with Oklahoma, Nebraska or Ohio State.

***

So, again, let's pose the question, why should we continue to care?

Not because of what Ivy football isn't anymore, say those around the league. We should care because of what the Ivy League is: a conference populated by true student-athletes who play a surprisingly good brand of football.

"The perception is definitely below the actual level of play," says Jay Fiedler, the former Dartmouth quarterback who replaced Dan Marino with the Miami Dolphins. "The biggest difference from Division I-A is the depth. You aren't going to find 40 or 50 guys on an Ivy League team that are top caliber, but there are some very good players in the Ivy League. Just look at the number of guys who have gone on to the NFL." In fact, in the fall of 2003, all eight Ivy League schools had players on NFL rosters. It marked the first time the conference could claim that distinction since 1928.

Penn coach Al Bagnoli watched the overall level of Ivy play improve while leading the Quakers to six titles in his first 12 years in Philadelphia. Part of the improvement can be traced back to the decision to eliminate freshman football teams in 1993 and let freshmen compete on the varsity for the first time. Part can be tracked back to the start of limited spring practice in 1994—the first time more than one day of spring practice was allowed in the Ivy League since 1952—and part to the result of restraints being placed on I-A schools.

"I think I-AA football in general is a much higher level and much higher quality than most people would realize," says Bagnoli. "At I-A scholarship schools, scholarships have been repeatedly cut. When I first started it was 140 scholarships, then it went to 120, then 110, then 95, and now it's at 85. Obviously, you have a lot more kids available that maybe at one time would be at Notre Dame if they had 40 scholarships in a given year. Or would be at Stanford, or Cal-Berkeley, or whatever school that has pretty good academics."

As expensive as they are selective, the Ivy League schools draw from a player pool too shallow to ever be competitive on the football field with a Stanford, a Cal or even a Duke. But while the admissions floor for athletes is substantially higher than it is at all but a few other schools nationally, each institution does have spots in the lower academic "bands" of each recruiting class for elite athletes. And while there are no scholarships per se, large endowments allow the Ivy League schools to offer generous financial-aid packages to all qualified students—including those who block and tackle.

As a result, the eight schools are filled with bright student-athletes eager and able to process everything their

coaches can throw at them. The innovative product on the field—the Ivy League has become one of the most pass-happy leagues in the nation in recent years—reflects that.

"One of the exciting things about being a coach in this league is, it's hard to overload your kids," says Bagnoli. "The concern is not like, 'Oh jeez, if we have 20 different formations, can our kids remember them all?' So if you have a creative coaching staff, you can remain pretty much at the cutting edge and your kids can absorb it. You don't have to worry about information overload. Consequently, you get a much more wide-open style of play."

According to Orleans, the league's coaches are unanimous in their belief that the level of play in the Ivy League is better now than it was a decade ago.

"The number of guys we've had drafted by the NFL and signed as free agents, and the number who stick, which is kind of a funny index, is up," Orleans says. "We've played some very good football against teams that have had a fair amount of success in the I-AA playoffs. Our league from top to bottom is stronger and much more competitive internally than it was 10 years ago."

But improvement on the gridiron has not come at the expense of other athletic programs, which Orleans believes is another reason why the Ivy League model matters.

"Without denying that football includes the most people, the most money and is the most visible on campus, we've tried to promote the interest in excellence of all our other men's and women's sports, so that all our sports, including football, feel they are a part of a single athletic program," says Orleans. "While some sports may be more visible than others, they are all important."

"There are no soft majors in our league," says Bagnoli. "Everybody has to take a real major. They have to do what every other student does. Their extracurricular happens to be a very visible one in terms of football, but it's no different than the kid on the debate team. They have to take the exact same courses as someone in the engineering club or someone who is president of their fraternity. They are not sheltered by any stretch in terms of their academic selections."

With no scholarships hanging over their heads, Ivy League football players are under no obligation to keep playing. Those who do choose to do so for the pure love of the game.

"No doubt about it," says Fiedler, "there are a lot of guys who don't play a full four years, where at scholarship schools you are going to stick it out. But the guys who do stick it out and stay involved have a passion for the game

that compares to, or is superior to, anyone out there."

Like all his peers, Bagnoli has had his share of players quit to take advantage of the myriad opportunities available to students at Ivy League schools. Those who do make it four years, he says, make the conference special.

"We really have a good story to tell as a league," he says. "We may be the last bastion of kids playing at this level because they love the game, they like the challenge both in the classroom and on the football field. I think they are playing for all the right reasons. And we are also playing within the philosophical context of our institutions. The institution is governing the program instead of the other way around."

Ultimately, Orleans, like Bagnoli and Fiedler, would say that the true measure of the Ivy League really isn't how many of its graduates are playing on Sunday. Or how league teams fare against relatively like-minded schools such as Colgate and Lehigh, which have enjoyed great success in recent years in the I-AA playoffs. The true measure of the Ivy League, they'll say, is the people it turns out, be they musicians, politicians or record-setting tight ends. People like Kurt Schmoke, a letterman on Yale's unbeaten 1968 team, a Rhodes Scholar and later the first black mayor of Baltimore. Like former Pennsylvania star Gavin O'Connor, director of *Miracle*, the hit movie about the 1980 U.S. Olympic ice hockey team. Like Reggie Williams, the former Dartmouth and Cincinnati Bengals standout who now heads up Disney Sports Attractions.

Scan the press guide of any Ivy League football team and the list of well-known graduates who have made and continue to make their mark after football will make your head spin.

"What that doesn't talk about is the other 99 percent of our football alumni who are professionals of one sort or another, teachers or lawyers or business folks active in their communities," Orleans says. "We think the qualities you see in [former Dartmouth linebacker and Olympic shot-putter] Adam Nelson, [San Francisco 49ers tight end] Eric Johnson or George Wood [a former Cornell standout killed in Iraq in 2003], you see in all their lesser-known teammates.

"I think part of the reason why we matter," he continues, "is when people look at us they see something they think is true, and hope is true, in a lot of other teams and conferences. We've become kind of a symbol of it."

While he believes wholeheartedly in the Ivy League way, Orleans is guarded about suggesting it is the only way or that the Ivies have a monopoly on doing things correctly.

"I'd like to paraphrase something [former Yale President]

Bart Giamatti said in an interview with a student radio station probably 18 years ago," Orleans says. "He said our job is to do what we do as well as we can do it. And lead by example. Because it's hard enough to get your own stuff right without trying to tell other people what to do. We have some circumstances that other people don't, so our model isn't necessarily going to translate. But what we can do is demonstrate that whatever model you pick, if it's an honest model and you do it honestly, people will care about you."

Orleans points to the Southern Conference as a league that has worked hard to do things the right way, but also its own way. "There's a set of schools in the Southern that are private, selective institutions that are increasingly good institutions academically," he says. "They are not in a situation where they can afford to give up grants in aid. They are in a conference with enough range in academic profile that they probably couldn't use the same kind of academic regulation that we use.

"But they have a clear set of standards for what they think is right and wrong. In between the ACC and SEC, they've been able to find a continuing niche where people respect them and care about them because their fans see they have a clear sense of what they are doing." Orleans believes the Ivy League does as well.

"In some ways, when we are at our best, we really do symbolize something that is unique," he says. "That is really focusing on academic standards, making clear the students are playing because they want to—because they don't have athletic scholarships—and emphasizing the games against each other, whether there is a playoff or not, whether there is a bowl or not.

"In the end, I think we matter because we represent an attempt to play really good collegiate football with real college students. And that, however exciting BCS football is, fans of BCS football, many of them, wonder whether those are really still college games played by college students."

BROWN

BY BRUCE WOOD

IT WAS WHERE JOHN HEISMAN FIRST played college football. It's the school that produced Joe Paterno, co-captain of the 1949 squad. It was an assistant coaching stop for Weeb Ewbank, who went on to lead the New York Jets to one of the greatest upsets in sports history in Super Bowl III. It was home to Frederick Douglass "Fritz" Pollard, the first African-American coach in pro football. Brown may no longer play at the college game's highest level, but its impact on football has resonated through the ages.

TRADITION The Brown band plays "Ever True to Brown" after every touchdown. The music continues quietly, with the band turning the volume back up after a successful extra point or two-point conversion. After Brown victories, players gather in the locker room and sing "The Mighty Bears."

BEST PLAYER No less than Walter Camp called Fritz Pollard "one of the greatest runners these eyes have ever seen." The first black player to make Camp's All-America first team, Pollard was just 5'8" and weighed 160 pounds, but he made up for his lack of size with rocket speed.

(Away from the football field, he won the intercollegiate hurdles championship two years in a row.) After helping Brown to a berth in the 1916 Rose Bowl, Pollard led the team to an 8–1 record the following season, gaining 243 all-purpose yards against Harvard and 294 yards against Yale. After graduation, he played professionally and later became the first African-American coach in pro football history, leading the Akron Indians and the Hammond Pros.

BEST COACH From 1959 to 1972, Brown averaged less than one Ivy League win per year, going a sickly 12–83–3 in the conference. Then John Anderson, fresh off an 8–0 season as head coach at Middlebury, took over in 1973. In his first season, Anderson led the Bears to a 4–3 Ivy League record, only their second winning mark in the conference since it was formed in 1956. Anderson went on to post a winning record in each of his first eight years, guiding Brown to a share of the 1976 Ivy League title, the Bears' first conference championship. Known for his innovative offensive plays, Anderson finished with a 60–39–3 record over 11 seasons.

BEST TEAM They were called the Iron Men. Against Yale and Dartmouth on consecutive Saturdays in 1926, the same 11 men played every minute for Brown,

PROFILE
Brown University
Providence, R.I.
Founded: 1764
Enrollment: 5,701
Colors: Seal Brown, Cardinal Red and White
Nickname: Bears
Stadium: Brown Stadium
    Opened in 1925
    Grass; 20,000 capacity
First football game: 1878
All-time record: 540–519–40 (.510)
Bowl record: 0–1
Ivy League championships: 2 (shared)
Website: www.brownbears.com

THE BEST OF TIMES
The 1932 Cinderella team beat seven consecutive undefeated opponents before losing its finale to undefeated, untied, unscored-upon Colgate before a record crowd of 33,000 in Providence.

THE WORST OF TIMES
Brown had one winning season (5–4 in 1964) and a combined 26–95–4 record from 1959 to 1972.

CONFERENCE
Brown was an original member of the Ivy League when the conference began formal play in 1956.

DISTINGUISHED ALUMNI
Joe Paterno; Ted Turner; Mary Chapin Carpenter, singer; Laura Linney, actress; Bill Wirtz, president of the Chicago Blackhawks

FIGHT SONG
EVER TRUE TO BROWN
We are ever true to Brown,
For we love our college dear,
And wherever we may go,
We are ready with a cheer.
And the people always say (What do they say?)
That you can't outshine Brown men (or women!)
With their Rah! Rah! Rah! and their Ki! Yi! Yi!
And their B-R-O-W-N

Bruno III had a short mascot career after climbing a tree to avoid the crowd at a game.

winning the first game 7-0 and the second 10-0. After starting his second-string team in an easy win over Norwich, coach Tuss McLaughry went back to the Iron Men the next week against Harvard. A crowd of 53,896 watched Brown go without subs until less than two minutes remained in another shutout, 21-0. Brown's sole blemish that fall would be a season-ending 10-10 tie with Colgate. The 9–0–1 team remains the only undefeated squad in school history.

BIGGEST GAME Seven weeks in a row, the 1932 Cinderella Bears played an undefeated team; each time, they emerged victorious. The eighth and final week of the season brought yet another undefeated opponent. But Colgate wasn't just unbeaten—no team had even scored on the Red Raiders, who had won their eight games by a collective margin of 243-0. With a possible Rose Bowl berth on the line, the Bears instead saw their dreams vanish, suffering a 21-0 loss before 33,000, the largest home crowd in school history.

BIGGEST UPSET The Bears brought a 3–2–1 record into their Nov. 5, 1910, game at Yale. The 5–1–1 Bulldogs

had been national champions in 1909, and they also had history on their side: Yale had not lost any of the previous 13 games in the series, shutting out the Bears eight times. But Brown had other plans. Consensus All-America Bill Sprackling threw for a touchdown and kicked three field goals as the Bears shocked Yale 21-0.

WILDEST FINISH Still angry over a disputed Hail Mary touchdown pass on the final play of the 1998 Yale game that cost them a share of the Ivy League championship, the Bears were looking for payback against the Bulldogs in 1999. Brown quickly fell behind by 14 points, but rallied back, and after James Perry's pass to tight end David Brookman with 14 seconds left, the Bears were just one point behind, 24-23. Brown lined up for the extra point and a tie, but Yale's Ben Blake broke through the line and blocked Sean Jensen's kick. Somehow, Brown's Michael Powell recovered the ball and pitched it to Rob School, who ran it in for a two-point conversion and an improbable win. It was Yale's only loss of the year. "I've been in this for 24 years and I've never seen that one," Bulldogs coach Jack Siedlecki said

RECORDS

RUSHING YARDS

	GAME
267	Michael Malan vs. Fordham, Oct. 6, 2001 (32 att.)
	SEASON
1,498	Nick Hartigan, 2003 (275 att.)
	CAREER
3,266	Michael Malan, 1999-2001 (602 att.)

PASSING YARDS

	GAME
494	Kyle Slager vs. Rhode Island, Oct. 5, 2002 (44 of 58)
	SEASON
3,255	James Perry, 1999 (309 of 467)
	CAREER
9,294	James Perry, 1997-99 (789 of 1,309)

RECEIVING YARDS

	GAME
269	Chas Gessner vs. Rhode Island, Sept. 29, 2001 (19 rec.)
	SEASON
1,434	Sean Morey, 1997 (74 rec.)
	CAREER
3,850	Sean Morey, 1995-98 (251 rec.)

POINTS

	GAME
30	Michael Malan vs. Fordham, Oct. 6, 2001 (5 TDs); Gus Russ vs. Vermont, Nov. 18, 1905 (5 TDs)
	SEASON
102	Nick Hartigan, 2004 (17 TDs)
	CAREER
252	Michael Malan, 1999-2001 (42 TDs)

CONSENSUS ALL-AMERICANS

1902	Thomas Barry	B
1906	John Mayhew	B
1909	Adrian Regnier	E
1910	Bill Sprackling	B
1912	George Crowther	B
1916	Fritz Pollard	B
1996	Paul Choquette	TE
1997	Sean Morey	WR
1997	Roderic Parson	DB
1998	Zach Burns	TE
2000	Stephen Campbell	WR
2001	Chas Gessner	WR

afterward. "We made the play to win the game and it actually cost us the game instead."

STADIUM Brown Stadium was built in 1925 on a piece of land originally referred to as both Cat Swamp and Fifteen-Acre Plot. The project was paid for with a $500,000 subscription campaign that asked, "How many seats will you build in the Brown Amphitheatre?" Each seat went for $25. While the unique trapezoid-shape facility was a source of great pride, the first season hardly went as planned. Despite playing nine of its 10 games at home, Brown went a mediocre 5–4–1. After a 3-0 loss to Harvard on Nov. 14, 1925, Crimson fans made off with the stadium's new goalposts.

RIVAL Harvard slapped a 58-0 hurt on Brown when the teams first met in 1893, and the Bears have been looking for revenge ever since. It hasn't helped that three times—in 1975, 1983 and 1987—Brown has lost to Harvard to cost the Bears a share of the Ivy League crown.

NICKNAME In 1904, Brown graduate and future U.S. senator Theodore Francis Green suggested that the school use Bears as a nickname. Explained Green, "While somewhat unsociable, he is good-natured and clean. While courageous and ready to fight, he does not look for trouble for its own sake, nor is he bloodthirsty. He is not one of a herd but acts independently. He is intelligent and capable of being educated."

MASCOT The first live bear to represent Brown on the sideline, curiously named Helen, was greeted by a standing ovation at

the 1905 Dartmouth game. Bruno came on the scene in 1921, but he died after eating chemicals in the biology building. In 1936, Bruno III arrived, but he too had a short career; the meek bear was farmed out to a zoo after climbing a tree to escape the crowd at a game. Finally, a costumed bear took over as mascot in 1963.

UNIFORMS The name of the school aside, Brown's first uniforms in 1878 were all white with dark socks. By the 1916 Rose Bowl, the team was wearing dark-brown jerseys with numbers and lighter-brown pants. Players on the 1955 team were early converts to plastic helmets and face masks; the helmet was white with a brown stripe down the middle. Since then, Brown's helmets have gone through numerous variations, at different times featuring the word Bruins to a large B to a stylized paw print.

LORE On Nov. 6, 1915, Brown was deadlocked in a scoreless tie in New Haven, facing fourth down deep in Yale territory. Team captain Harold P. "Buzz" Andrews had made a couple of kicks in practice but had never tried a field goal in a game, much less made one. Andrews lined up and launched a dropkick from 22 yards out. His kick sailed straight between the goalposts, giving Brown the only points scored by either team that day as well as a berth in the Rose Bowl. The kick wasn't just the biggest of Andrews' career—it was the only kick of his career.

QUOTE "They're not 'iron men.' They are just 11 college boys having a good time playing football."

—Tuss McLaughry, on his famed 1926 team

ALL-TIME TEAM

For the 125th anniversary of Brown football in 2003, more than 1,500 alumni and fans selected the all-time team via Internet and mail-in ballots.

OFFENSE

1924-26	Orland Smith,	OL
1926-28	Louis Farber,	OL
1929-31	Paul Mackesey,	OL
1931-32	Thomas Gilbane,	OL
1946-47	Lou Regine,	OL
1953-55	Jim McGuinness,	OL
1956, 1958	Don Warburton,	OL
1977-79	John Sinnott,	OL
1981-83	Bob Mangiacotti,	OL
1998-2000	Drew Inzer,	OL
1979-81	Steve Jordan,	TE
1993-96	Paul Choquette,	TE
1974-76	Robert Farnham,	WR
1995-98	Sean Morey,	WR
1997-2000	Stephen Campbell,	WR
1999-2002	Chas Gessner,	WR
1915-16	Fritz Pollard,	B
1924-25	Jackson Keefer,	B
1957-59	Paul Choquette Jr.,	RB
1999-2001	Michael Malan,	RB
1963-65	Robert Hall,	QB
1996-99	James Perry,	QB
1973-75	Jose Violante,	PK
1992-94	Bob Warden,	PK
1965-67	Dave Jollin,	KR
1977-79	Joe Jamiel,	KR

DEFENSE

1947-49	Don Colo,	DL
1955-57	Gil Robertshaw,	DL
1975-77	Kevin Rooney,	DL
1976-78	Mike Lancaster,	DL
1981-83	John Daniel,	DL
1983-85	Ted Moskala,	DL
1985-86	Bill Perry,	DL
1993-96	Brendan Finneran,	DL
1946-49	Milton Hodosh,	LB
1974-76	Scott Nelson,	LB
1975-77	Lou Cole,	LB
1978-80	John Prassas,	LB
1978-80	John Woodring,	LB
1994-97	Joe Karcutskie,	LB
1925-27	Roy "Red" Randall,	DB
1937-39	John McLaughry,	DB
1947-49	Joe Paterno,	DB
1953-54	David Zucconi,	DB
1976-78	Ron Brown,	DB
1985-87	Walt Cataldo,	DB
1993-96	Greg Parker,	DB
1994-97	Roderic Parson,	DB
1964-66	Joe Randall,	P
1985-87	Alex Kos,	P

BROWN ANNUAL STATISTICAL LEADERS

YR	RUSHING	YDS	ATT	AVG	PASSING	ATT	CMP	PCT	YDS	RECEIVING	REC	YDS	AVG
1956	John McTigue	329	86	3.8	Frank Finney	107	51	.48	617	Richard Bence	13	144	11.1
1957	Paul Choquette	362	90	4.0	Frank Finney	101	48	.48	632	Jon Jensen	14	210	15.0
1958	Paul Choquette	576	123	4.7	Frank Finney	142	71	.50	982	Bill Traub	19	253	13.3
1959	Paul Choquette	617	179	3.4	Nicholas Pannes	102	28	.27	275	Charles Olobri	18	214	11.9
1960	Raymond Barry	464	133	3.5	Nelson Rohrbach	156	76	.49	858	Roger Cirone	17	289	17.0
1961	Raymond Barry	334	90	3.7	Nelson Rohrbach	111	44	.40	411	David Nelson	9	106	11.8
1962	John Kelly	311	70	4.4	James Dunda	139	65	.47	928	John Parry	27	385	14.3
1963	Jan Moyer	289	60	4.8	James Dunda	89	44	.49	588	John Parry	39	457	11.7
1964	Robert Hall	399	97	4.1	James Dunda	115	50	.43	621	John Parry	30	348	11.6
1965	Robert Hall	557	158	3.5	Robert Hall	254	135	.53	1,340	John Hutchinson	41	356	8.7
1966	Neal Weinstock	360	91	4.0	John McMahon	86	35	.41	420	John Olson	15	200	13.3
1967	Stephen Wormith	356	105	3.4	Harold Phillips	152	58	.38	714	Gregory Kontos	36	638	17.7
1968	Thomas Lemire	699	172	4.1	Bryan Marini	107	46	.43	394	Gregory Kontos	31	312	10.1
1969	Gerald Hart	370	76	4.9	Bryan Marini	72	27	.38	284	Gregory Brown	15	193	12.9
1970	Gary Bonner	674	135	5.0	Robert Flanders	83	27	.33	375	Kurt Franke	11	172	15.6
1971	Gary Bonner	621	163	3.8	Bob Zink	111	51	.46	633	Louis Regine	31	452	14.6
1972	Leonard Cherry	442	122	3.6	Pete Beatrice	201	86	.43	1,131	Louis Regine	51	681	13.4
1973	Mike Sokolowski	426	110	3.9	Pete Beatrice	111	65	.59	894	Jeff Smith	10	200	20.0
1974	Kevin Slattery	533	105	5.1	Pete Beatrice	140	75	.54	990	Ken O'Keefe	9	236	26.2
1975	Kevin Slattery	705	174	4.1	Bob Bateman	206	112	.54	1,428	Bob Farnham	56	701	12.5
1976	Wally Shields	521	103	5.1	Paul Michalko	187	89	.48	1,113	Bob Farnham	41	507	12.4
1977	Seth Morris	656	134	4.9	Mark Whipple	143	77	.54	989	Mark Farnham	25	384	15.4
1978	Rick Villella	735	150	4.9	Mark Whipple	197	98	.50	1,376	Mark Farnham	36	550	15.3
1979	Rick Villella	481	109	4.4	Larry Carbone	165	87	.53	1,178	Paul Farnham	31	400	12.9
1980	Steve Curtin	665	132	5.0	Larry Carbone	217	117	.54	1,587	Mitch Metz	40	501	12.5
1981	Rod Jones	482	98	4.9	Hank Landers	301	131	.44	1,913	Steve Jordan	38	693	18.2
1982	Joe Potter	607	121	5.0	Joe Potter	219	111	.51	1,516	Paul Farnham	34	550	16.2
1983	Steve Heffernan	676	156	4.3	Joe Potter	244	121	.50	1,438	Brad McCaulley	33	439	13.3
1984	Jamie Potkul	525	128	4.1	Steve Kettleberger	183	92	.50	1,191	Brad McCaulley	34	500	14.7
1985	Jamie Potkul	1,015	239	4.2	Steve Kettleberger	183	95	.52	1,108	Brian Heffernan	22	240	10.9
1986	Lane Wood	419	95	4.4	Mark Donovan	239	120	.50	1,777	Dave Fielding	37	721	19.5
1987	Kirk Little	893	190	4.7	Mark Donovan	143	61	.43	747	Jamie Simone	22	291	13.2
1988	Lane Wood	506	135	3.7	Danny Clark	143	61	.43	726	Matt Merrick	25	290	11.6
1989	Nick Badalato	527	112	4.7	Danny Clark	197	115	.58	1,172	Mike Geroux	23	376	16.3
1990	Rodney Vincent	397	99	4.0	Mike Lenkaitis	217	120	.55	1,222	Rodd Torbert	67	908	13.6
1991	Joel Brown	821	199	4.1	Jeff Barrett	186	107	.58	1,276	Rodd Torbert	36	543	15.1
1992	Joel Brown	740	164	4.5	Bill Pienjas	213	116	.54	1,194	Nate Taylor	51	647	12.7
1993	Marquis Jessie	823	179	4.6	Trevor Yankoff	131	61	.47	833	Charlie Buckley	31	535	17.3
1994	Paul Fichiera	861	164	5.3	Jason McCullough	260	126	.48	1,724	Charlie Buckley	32	455	14.2
1995	Marquis Jessie	728	141	5.2	Jason McCullough	351	190	.54	2,402	Jason Dummert	40	525	13.1
1996	Marquis Jessie	910	210	4.3	Jason McCullough	393	204	.52	2,609	Sean Morey	60	939	15.7
1997	Azibo Smith	564	117	4.8	James Perry	396	206	.52	2,874	Sean Morey	74	1,434	19.4
1998	Kevin Coyne	514	124	4.1	James Perry	444	274	.62	3,165	Sean Morey	83	1,023	12.3
1999	Michael Malan	994	187	5.6	James Perry	467	309	.66	3,255	Steve Campbell	89	1,107	12.4
2000	Michael Malan	1,213	245	5.3	Eric Webber	431	289	.67	3,175	Steve Campbell	120	1,332	11.1
2001	Michael Malan	1,059	170	6.2	Kyle Rowley	307	191	.62	2,386	Chas Gessner	83	1,182	14.2
2002	Joe Rackley	572	150	3.8	Kyle Slager	340	230	.68	2,609	Chas Gessner	114	1,166	10.2
2003	Nick Hartigan	1,498	275	5.4	Kyle Slager	359	219	.61	2,398	Lonnie Hill	76	869	11.4
2004	Nick Hartigan	1,263	323	3.9	Joe DiGiacomo	216	112	.52	1,514	Jarrett Schreck	62	1,035	16.7

THE SCHOOLS

BROWN ALL-TIME SCORES

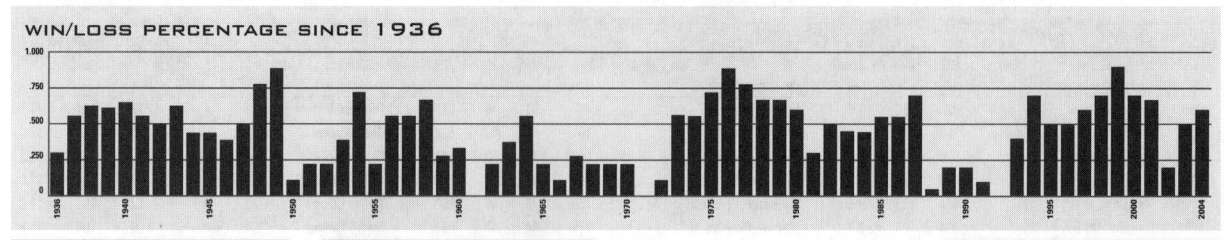

WIN/LOSS PERCENTAGE SINCE 1936

THE SCHOOLS

NO HEAD COACH

1878 0-1-0
O26	Amherst	0	1

1879
NO TEAM

1880 0-1-0
N13	at Yale	0	8

1881-1885
NO TEAM

1886 1-1-0
U	●	Providence HS *U*	70	0
U	●	Boston U. *U*	6	10

1887-1888
NO TEAM

1889 2-2-0
U	●	Pawtucket CC *U*	14	0
O19		MIT	0	48
U	●	Tufts *U*	16	0
U	●	Boston AC *U*	0	16

1890 2-4-1
U	=	MIT *U*	8	8
U	●	Fall River *U*	0	8
U	●	Tufts *U*	14	0
U	●	Boston AC *U*	12	26
N8		Trinity	16	20
U	●	Harvard JV *U*	22	8
N22		Wesleyan	6	34

1891 4-6-1
S30	●	at MIT	6	4
O3		Trinity	0	8
O10	●	at Fall River	18	4
O17		at Andover	0	26
O24		at Bowdoin	18	22
O31		MIT	6	14
N7	●	Bowdoin	18	0
N14		at Williams	0	58
N21	●	at WPI	32	6
N23		Detroit AC		
N26		Tufts	12	34

M. HOWLAND
1892 (.450) 4-5-1

1892 4-5-1
O1	●	WPI	8	4
O81	●	at Fall River	24	0
O12	●	at Andover	6	4
O15		MIT	6	30
O22		Tufts	4	24
N2		MIT	6	12
N5	=	Trinity	0	0
N12		Bowdoin	0	8
N16		at WPI	0	4
N19	●	Wesleyan	6	0

WILLIAM ODLIN
1893 (.667) 6-3

1893 6-3-0
O4		at Yale	0	18
O7	●	at WPI	30	0
O14	●	Boston AC	0	6
O18	●	Trinity	34	0
O21	●	at Andover	10	0
O25		at Harvard	0	58
N4	●	MIT	36	0
N11	●	at MIT	28	6
N18	●	Tufts	30	6

W.G. NORTON
1894 (.667) 10-5

1894 10-5-0
S29	●	Fort Adams	56	0
O3		at Yale	0	28
O6	●	at Boston AC	28	0
O10		at Harvard	4	18
O13	●	at Army	10	8
O20	●	at Andover	14	0
O24	●	Wesleyan	26	0
O27		at MIT	4	8
O31	●	Tufts	30	0
N3		Yale	0	12
N7	●	at Orange AA	12	10
N17		at Harvard	0	18
N21	●	Bowdoin	42	0
N24	●	at Dartmouth	20	4
N29	●	MIT	16	4

WALLACE MOYLE
1895-97 (.543) 18-15-2

1895 7-6-1
S28	●	Newton AA	22	0
O2		at Yale	0	4
O12	●	Tufts	28	0
O19		at Harvard	6	26
O23	●	at MIT	14	0
O26	●	Lehigh	22	4
O30		at Pennsylvania	0	12
N2	●	Wesleyan	10	5
N5		at Crescent AC	0	16
N9	=	Yale	6	6
N13	●	MIT	28	0
N16		at Cornell	4	6
N23		Army *Nwa*	0	26
N28	●	Dartmouth	10	4

1896 4-5-1
S26	●	WPI	20	0
O7		at Yale	0	18
O10	●	Amherst	44	6
O17		at Harvard	0	12
O24	●	Lehigh	16	0
O28		at Pennsylvania	0	16
O31	=	Dartmouth	10	10
N7		Yale	6	18
N21		at Army	6	8
N26	●	at Carlisle	24	12

1897 7-4-0
S25	●	Tufts	24	0
O6	●	Wesleyan	24	12
O9	●	Boston U.	44	0
O16	●	at Andover	20	4
O20		at Yale	14	18
O23		at Harvard	0	18
O30		Pennsylvania	0	40
N6	●	at Newton	24	0
N13	●	Carlisle	18	14
N20		at Army	0	42
N27	●	Wesleyan	12	4

E.N. ROBINSON
1898-1901, '04-07, '10-25
140-82-12 (.624)

1898 6-4-0
O1	●	Holy Cross	19	0
O5	●	Tufts	29	6
O8		at Pennsylvania	0	18
O12	●	Colby	41	5
O19		at Yale	6	22
O26	●	Boston College	6	0
O29		at Princeton	0	23
N5	●	Newton AC	16	5
N12		at Harvard	6	17
N19	●	Dartmouth	12	0

1899 7-3-1
S30	●	at Holy Cross	19	0
O4	●	Tufts	6	0
O7	=	Pennsylvania	6	6
O14	●	Campello	25	0
O21		at Harvard	0	11
O28	●	Newton AC	35	0
N4		at Princeton	6	18
N11	●	MIT	38	0
N18	●	Boston College	18	0
N25	●	Dartmouth	16	5
N30		at Chicago	6	17

1900 7-3-1
S29	●	Colby	27	0
O3	●	Holy Cross	18	0
O6	●	MIT	22	0
O13		at Pennsylvania	0	12
O20	●	at Chicago	11	6
O27		Princeton	5	17
N3	●	Needhamon	12	5
N10	●	Tufts	26	5
N17		at Harvard	6	11
N24	=	Syracuse	6	6
N29	●	Dartmouth	12	5

1901 4-7-1
S28	●	Boston College	12	0
O2	●	Colby	16	0
O5		Syracuse	0	20
O9	●	Manhattan AC	6	5
O12		at Pennsylvania	0	26
O19		at Princeton	0	35
O26	=	Holy Cross	6	6
N2		at Harvard	0	48
N6		at Homestead AC	0	34
N9		Lafayette	6	11
N16	●	Union	24	5
N27		Dartmouth	0	22

J.A. GAMMONS
1902, '08-09 (.621) 17-10-2

1902 5-4-1
O1	=	Vermont	0	0
O4	●	Wesleyan	5	0
O11		Yale	0	10
O18	●	at Pennsylvania	15	6
O25		at Harvard	0	6
N1	●	at Lafayette	5	6
N5	●	Tufts	45	12
N8	●	at Columbia	28	0
N15	●	Springfield	11	0
N23	●	Dartmouth	6	12

D.S. FULTZ
1903 (.550) 5-4-1

1903 5-4-1
S26	●	Colby	23	0
O3	●	Wesleyan	11	0
O10	●	Princeton	0	29
O17		at Pennsylvania	0	30
O24		at Harvard	0	29
O31	●	Williams	22	0
N7	●	Vermont	24	0
N14		at Syracuse	12	5
N21	=	Springfield	6	6
N26		Dartmouth	0	62

E.N. ROBINSON

1904 6-5-0
O1		Maine	0	6
O8	●	Massachusetts	27	0
O12	●	Wesleyan	12	0
O15		at Pennsylvania	0	6
O19		Amherst	0	5
O22	●	Bowdoin	22	0
O29	●	Vermont	33	0
N2	●	Tufts	41	0
N5		at Yale	0	22
N12	●	Colby	41	0
N19		Dartmouth	5	12

1905 7-4-0
S23	●	New Hampshire	16	5
S27	●	Massachusetts	24	0
S30	●	WPI	42	0
O7	●	Colby	70	0
O14	●	Maine	34	0
O21		at Pennsylvania	6	8
O28		at Harvard	0	10
N4	●	Syracuse	27	0
N11		at Yale	0	11
N18	●	Vermont	56	0
N25		Dartmouth	6	24

1906 6-3-0
S29	●	New Hampshire	12	0
O6	●	Wesleyan	17	0
O10	●	Massachusetts	17	0
O20		at Pennsylvania	0	14
O27	●	Norwich	26	4
N3		at Harvard	5	9
N10		at Yale	0	5
N17	●	Vermont	12	0
N24	●	Dartmouth	23	0

1907 7-3-0
S21	●	New Hampshire	16	0
S28	●	Massachusetts	5	0
O5	●	Norwich	24	0
O12	●	Maine	40	0
O19		at Pennsylvania	0	11
O26	●	Williams	24	11
N2		at Harvard	5	6
N9		at Yale	0	22
N16	●	Vermont	36	0
N23	●	Amherst	18	0

J.A. GAMMONS

1908 5-3-1
S19	●	New Hampshire	34	0
S26	●	Bates	35	4
O3	●	Colgate	6	0
O10	●	Bowdoin	12	0
O17		at Pennsylvania	0	12
O24		Lafayette	6	8
O31	●	at Harvard	2	6
N7	=	at Yale	10	10
N14	●	Vermont	12	0

1909 7-3-0
S29	●	Rhode Island	6	0
O2	●	Colgate	14	0
O6	●	Bates	17	0
O9	●	Amherst	10	0
O16		at Pennsylvania	5	13
O23		at Harvard	0	11
O30	●	Massachusetts	12	3
N6		at Yale	0	23
N13	●	Vermont	17	0
N20	●	Carlisle *NYC*	21	8

THE SCHOOLS

E.N. ROBINSON

1910 — 7-2-1
S24	●	Norwich	31	0
O1	●	Rhode Island	5	0
O8	=	Colgate	0	0
O15		Pennsylvania	0	20
O22		at Harvard	0	12
O29	●	Tufts	27	9
N5	●	at Yale	21	0
N12	●	Vermont	50	0
N19	●	Massachusetts	49	0
N24	●	Carlisle	15	6

1911 — 7-3-1
S23	●	New Hampshire	56	0
S30	●	Rhode Island	12	0
O7	●	Massachusetts	26	0
O14	●	Bowdoin	33	0
O21	●	at Pennsylvania	6	0
O28		at Harvard	6	20
N4	●	Tufts	30	0
N11		at Yale	0	15
N18	●	Vermont	6	0
N25	=	Trinity	6	6
N30		Carlisle	6	12

1912 — 6-4-0
S28	●	Colby	3	0
O5	●	Rhode Island	14	0
O12		Wesleyan	6	7
O19	●	Pennsylvania	30	7
O26		at Harvard	10	30
N2	●	Vermont	12	7
N9		at Yale	0	10
N16	●	Lafayette	21	7
N23	●	Norwich	21	7
N28		Carlisle	0	32

1913 — 4-5-0
S27		Colby	0	10
O4	●	Rhode Island	19	0
O11	●	Ursinus	6	0
O18		at Pennsylvania	0	23
O25	●	Springfield	26	6
N1	●	Vermont	19	0
N8		at Yale	0	17
N15		at Harvard	0	37
N27		Carlisle	0	13

1914 — 5-2-2
S26	●	Norwich	24	0
O3	●	Rhode Island	20	0
O10	=	Amherst	0	0
O17	●	Wesleyan	16	0
O24		Cornell NYC	7	28
O31	●	Vermont	12	9
N7		at Yale	6	14
N14	=	at Harvard	0	0
N26	●	Carlisle	20	14

1915 — 5-4-1
S25	●	Rhode Island	38	0
O2	=	Trinity	0	0
O9		Amherst	0	7
O16	●	Williams	33	0
O23		Syracuse	0	6
O30	●	Vermont	46	0
N6	●	Yale	3	0
N13		Harvard	7	16
N27	●	Carlisle	39	3

ROSE BOWL
J1		Washington State	0	14

1916 — 8-1-0
S30	●	Rhode Island	18	0
O7	●	Trinity	42	0
O14	●	Amherst	69	0
O21	●	at Williams	20	0
O28	●	Rutgers	21	3
N4	●	Vermont	42	0
N11		at Yale	21	6
N18	●	at Harvard	21	0
N25		Colgate	0	28

1917 — 8-2-0
S29	●	Rhode Island	27	0
O6	●	Johns Hopkins	20	0
O13	●	at Holy Cross	27	6
O20	●	Boston College	7	2
O27	●	Colgate	7	6
N3		Syracuse	0	6
N10		at USN Reserve	0	35
N17	●	Camp Devens	40	0
N24	●	Colby	19	7
N29	●	Dartmouth U	13	0

1918 — 2-3-0
N3		Camp Devens	7	19
N10		at Syracuse	0	53
N17		at League Island Navy	7	23
N24	●	Dartmouth U	28	0
N28		at Harvard	6	3

1919 — 5-4-1
S27	●	Rhode Island	27	0
O4	●	Bowdoin	7	0
O11		at Colgate	0	14
O18		at Harvard	0	7
O25	●	Norwich	20	0
N1		Syracuse	0	13
N8		at Yale	0	14
N15	●	Dartmouth U	7	6
N22	●	New Hampshire	6	0
N27	=	at Columbia	7	7

1920 — 6-3-0
S25	●	Rhode Island	25	0
O2	●	Amherst	13	0
O9	●	Maine	32	6
O16	●	Colgate	14	0
O23	●	Springfield	14	0
O30	●	Vermont	35	0
N6	●	at Yale	10	14
N13		at Harvard	0	27
N20		Dartmouth U	6	14

1921 — 5-3-1
S24	●	Rhode Island	6	0
O1	●	Colby	12	7
O8	●	NYU	13	0
O15		at Syracuse	0	28
O22	=	Springfield	0	0
O29		at Yale	7	45
N5	●	St. Bonaventure	55	0
N12		at Harvard	7	9
N19	●	Colgate	7	0

1922 — 6-2-1
S30	●	Rhode Island	27	0
O7	●	Colby	13	0
O14	=	Syracuse	0	0
O21	●	at Lehigh	6	2
O28	●	Boston U.	16	6
N4		at Yale	0	20
N11	●	Bates	27	12
N18	●	at Harvard	3	0
N25		Dartmouth U	0	7

1923 — 6-4-0
S29	●	Haverford	34	0
O6	●	Colby	33	0
O13		at Wash. & Jeff.	7	12
O20	●	Boston U.	20	3
O27		at Yale	0	21
N3	●	St. Bonaventure	19	0
N10		Dartmouth U	14	16
N17	●	at Harvard	20	7
N24	●	New Hampshire	6	0
D1		Lehigh	6	12

1924 — 5-4-0
O4	●	Colby	45	0
O11		at Chicago	7	19
O18	●	Boston U.	35	0
O25		at Yale	3	13
N1		at Dartmouth	3	10
N8		Haskell	13	17
N15	●	at Harvard	7	0
N22	●	New Hampshire	21	0
N29	●	Colgate	20	6

1925 — 5-4-1
S26	●	Rhode Island	33	0
O3	●	Colby	33	0
O10		Pennsylvania	0	9
O17	●	Bates	48	0
O24		Yale	7	20
O31		Dartmouth	0	14
N7	●	Boston U.	42	6
N14		at Harvard	0	3
N21	●	New Hampshire	38	14
N28	=	Colgate	14	14

D.O. McLAUGHRY
1926-40 (.565)   76-58-5

1926 — 9-0-1
S25	●	Rhode Island	14	0
O2	●	Colby	35	0
O9	●	Lehigh	32	0
O16	●	Bates	27	14
O23	●	at Yale	7	0
O30	●	at Dartmouth	10	0
N6	●	Norwich	27	0
N13	●	at Harvard	21	0
N20	●	New Hampshire	40	12
N27	=	Colgate	10	10

1927 — 3-6-1
S24	●	Rhode Island	27	0
O1	●	Albright	20	0
O8		at Pennsylvania	6	14
O15		at Yale	0	19
O22		Lebanon Valley	12	13
O29		Temple	0	7
N5		Dartmouth	7	19
N12		at Harvard	6	18
N19	●	New Hampshire	31	13
N26	=	Colgate	0	0

1928 — 8-1-0
O6	●	WPI	32	0
O13	●	Dayton	13	7
O20		at Yale	14	32
O27	●	Tufts	19	13
N3	●	Holy Cross	6	0
N10	●	at Dartmouth	14	0
N17	●	New Hampshire	20	0
N24	●	Rhode Island	33	7
N29	●	Colgate	16	13

1929 — 5-5-0
S28		at Springfield	6	14
O5	●	Rhode Island	14	6
O12	●	at Princeton	13	12
O19		at Yale	6	14
O26		Syracuse	0	6
N2	●	at Holy Cross	15	14
N9		Dartmouth	6	13
N16	●	Norwich	66	6
N23	●	New Hampshire	14	7
N30		Colgate	0	32

1930 — 6-3-1
S27	●	Rhode Island	7	0
O4	●	WPI	54	0
O11	●	at Princeton	7	0
O18		at Yale	0	21
O25	●	Holy Cross	13	0
N1	=	at Syracuse	16	16
N8	●	Tufts	32	7
N15	●	Columbia	6	0
N22		New Hampshire	0	7
N29		Colgate	0	27

1931 — 7-3-0
S26	●	Colby	22	0
O3	●	Rhode Island	18	0
O10	●	at Princeton	19	7
O17	●	Tufts	33	12
O24	●	Lehigh	33	0
O31		at Holy Cross	0	33
N7	●	Ohio Wesleyan	26	13
N14		Columbia	7	9
N21	●	New Hampshire	19	13
N28		Colgate	7	13

1932 — 7-1-0
O1	●	Rhode Island	19	0
O8	●	Springfield	13	6
O15	●	at Yale	7	2
O22	●	Tufts	11	0
O29	●	at Harvard	14	0
N5	●	Holy Cross	10	7
N12		at Columbia	7	6
N19		Colgate	0	21

1933 — 3-5-0
O7	●	Rhode Island	26	0
O14	●	Springfield	13	6
O21		at Yale	6	14
O28		at Holy Cross	7	19
N4		Princeton	0	33
N11	●	at Syracuse	10	7
N18		at Harvard	6	12
N25		Colgate	0	25

1934 — 3-6-0
S29	●	Boston U.	18	0
O6	●	Rhode Island	13	0
O13		at Harvard	0	13
O20		at Yale	0	37
O27		Syracuse	0	33
N3	●	Springfield	13	7
N10		at Columbia	0	39
N17	●	Holy Cross	7	20
D1		Colgate	13	20

1935 — 1-8-0
O5		Rhode Island	7	13
O12		Springfield	0	20
O19		Dartmouth	0	41
O26		at Syracuse	0	19
N2		at Harvard	0	33
N9		at Yale	0	20
N16	●	Boston U.	14	0
N23		at Columbia	0	18
N30		Colgate	0	33

1936 — 3-7-0
S26		Connecticut	0	27
O3	●	Rhode Island	7	6
O10		at Harvard	0	28
O17		at Dartmouth	0	34
O24		at Pennsylvania	6	48
O31	●	Tufts	38	7
N7	●	at Yale	6	14
N14		Holy Cross	0	32
N21	●	Colby	19	6
N28		Colgate	0	32

1937 — 5-4-0
S25	●	Connecticut	20	0
O2	●	Rhode Island	13	6
O9		at Harvard	7	34
O16		Dartmouth	0	41
O23		at Columbia	7	6
O30	●	Tufts	19	0
N6		at Yale	0	19
N13		Holy Cross	0	7
N25	●	at Rutgers	7	6

1938 — 5-3-0
O1	●	at Harvard	20	13
O8	●	Lafayette	20	0
O15	●	at Dartmouth	13	34
O22	●	Rhode Island	40	21
O29	●	Tufts	48	0
N5		at Yale	14	20
N12		at Holy Cross	12	14
N26		Columbia	36	27

1939 — 5-3-1
S30	●	Rhode Island	34	0
O7	●	Amherst	20	14
O14		at Colgate	0	10
O21	●	Holy Cross	0	20
O28	●	at Princeton	12	26
N4	●	Tufts	54	7
N11	=	at Yale	14	14
N18	●	Connecticut	41	0
N30	●	Rutgers	13	0

1940 — 6-3-1
S28	●	at Wesleyan	41	0
O5	●	Rhode Island	20	17
O12	●	Colgate	3	20
O19	●	Tufts	26	6
O26	●	Holy Cross	9	6
N2	●	at Yale	6	2
N9	●	at Army	13	9
N16		at Harvard	0	14
N23		Dartmouth	6	20
N30	=	Columbia	0	0

J.N. STAHLEY
1941-43 (.560)   14-11

1941 — 5-4-0
S27	●	Wesleyan	20	6
O4		at Columbia	6	13
O11	●	Rhode Island	14	7
O18	●	Tufts	28	6
O25	●	at Lafayette	13	0
N1	●	at Yale	7	0
N8		Holy Cross	0	13
N15		at Harvard	7	23
N22		Rutgers	7	13

1942 — 4-4-0

O3		Rhode Island	28	0
O10		at Columbia	28	21
O17		Lafayette	7	0
O24		at Princeton	13	32
O31		at Yale	0	27
N7		Holy Cross	20	14
N14		at Harvard	0	7
N21		Colgate	0	13

1943 — 5-3-0

S25	•	Tufts	35	6
O2		at Holy Cross	0	20
O9	•	Camp Kilmer	62	3
O16	•	at Princeton	28	20
O30	•	Coast Guard	34	31
N6		at Yale	21	20
N20		at Army	0	59
N27		Colgate	14	21

C.A. ENGLE — 1944-49 (.577) — 28-20-4

1944 — 3-4-1

S30	•	Tufts	44	0
O7		at Army	7	59
O14	=	at Holy Cross	24	24
O28		Dartmouth	13	14
N4		Coast Guard	0	20
N11		at Yale	0	13
N18		at Columbia	12	0
N25		Colgate	32	20

1945 — 3-4-1

S29		at Pennsylvania	0	50
O6	•	Boston College	51	6
O20		Holy Cross	0	25
O27		at Columbia	6	27
N3	•	Coast Guard	33	6
N10		at Yale	20	7
N17		at Harvard	7	14
N24	=	Colgate	6	6

1946 — 3-5-1

S28	•	Canisius	14	6
O5		at Princeton	12	33
O12		Rhode Island	29	0
O19		Dartmouth	20	13
O26		Boston U.	14	14
N2		at Holy Cross	19	21
N9		at Yale	0	49
N16		at Harvard	0	28
N23		Colgate	14	20

1947 — 4-4-1

S27	•	Connecticut	33	13
O4		at Princeton	7	21
O11		Rhode Island	55	6
O18		at Dartmouth	10	13
O25	=	at Colgate	13	13
N1		Holy Cross	20	19
N8		at Yale	20	14
N15		at Harvard	7	13
N22		Rutgers	20	27

1948 — 7-2-0

S25		at Yale	13	28
O2	•	at Princeton	23	20
O9	•	Rhode Island	33	0
O16	•	at Holy Cross	14	6
O23	•	Connecticut	49	6
O30	•	at Rutgers	20	6
N6	•	Western Reserve	36	0
N13		at Harvard	19	30
N20	•	Colgate	35	7

1949 — 8-1-0

O1	•	Holy Cross	28	6
O8	•	Rhode Island	46	0
O15	•	at Princeton	14	27
O22	•	Lehigh	48	0
O29	•	at Western Reserve	28	14
N5	•	at Yale	14	0
N12	•	at Harvard	28	14
N19	•	at Columbia	16	7
N26	•	Colgate	41	26

G.G. ZITRIDES — 1950 (.111) — 1-8

1950 — 1-8-0

S30		at Yale	12	36
O7		at Holy Cross	21	41
O14	•	Rhode Island	55	13
O21		Princeton	0	34
O28		Colgate	34	35
N4		at Rutgers	12	15
N11		at Pennsylvania	0	50
N18		at Harvard	13	14
N25		Columbia	0	33

A.E. KELLEY — 1951-58 (.444) — 31-39-2

1951 — 2-7-0

S29		Temple	14	20
O6		at Yale	14	13
O13		Rhode Island	20	13
O20		Colgate	14	32
O27		Holy Cross	6	41
N3		at Princeton	0	12
N10		Rutgers	21	28
N17		at Harvard	21	34
N24		at Columbia	14	29

1952 — 2-7-0

O4		at Yale	0	28
O11		Rhode Island	6	7
O18		at Holy Cross	0	46
O25		Rutgers	7	19
N1		at Princeton	0	39
N8	•	Connecticut	21	13
N15		Harvard	28	21
N22		at Columbia	0	14
N29		Colgate	27	33

1953 — 3-5-1

S26		Amherst	6	7
O3		at Yale	0	13
O10		Rhode Island	13	19
O17		at Rutgers	27	20
O24	•	Holy Cross	6	0
O31		at Princeton	13	27
N7	•	Connecticut	42	7
N14		at Harvard	20	27
N21	=	Colgate	7	7

1954 — 6-2-1

S25	•	Columbia	18	7
O2		at Yale	24	26
O9	•	Rhode Island	35	0
O16	•	Princeton	21	20
O23		Temple	14	19
O30	•	at Lehigh	34	6
N6	•	Springfield	40	7
N13	=	at Harvard	21	21
N25	•	Colgate	18	14

1955 — 2-7-0

S24		at Columbia	12	14
O1		at Yale	20	27
O8	•	Dartmouth	7	0
O15		Rutgers	12	14
O22		Rhode Island	7	19
O29		at Princeton	7	14
N5		Cornell	7	20
N12		at Harvard	14	6
N24		Colgate	0	25

1956-PRESENT IVY LEAGUE

1956 — 5-4-0 (3-4-0)

S29	•	at Columbia	20	0
O6	•	at Yale	2	20
O13		Dartmouth	7	14
O20		at Pennsylvania	7	14
O27	•	Rhode Island	27	7
N3		at Princeton	7	21
N10	•	Cornell	13	6
N17	•	at Harvard	21	12
N24	•	Colgate	20	0

1957 — 5-4-0 (3-4-0)

S28		Columbia	20	23
O5	•	at Yale	21	20
O12		at Dartmouth	0	35
O19		Pennsylvania	20	7
O26	•	Rhode Island	21	7
N2		Princeton	0	7
N9		at Cornell	6	13
N16	•	at Harvard	33	6
N23	•	Colgate	33	7

1958 — 6-3-0 (4-3-0)

S27	•	at Columbia	22	0
O4		Yale	35	29
O11		Dartmouth	0	20
O18		at Pennsylvania	20	21
O25	•	Rhode Island	47	6
N1		at Princeton	18	28
N8	•	Cornell	12	8
N15	•	at Harvard	29	22
N22	•	Colgate	28	6

JOHN McLAUGHRY — 1959-66 (.261) — 17-51-3

1959 — 2-6-1 (1-5-1)

S26		Columbia	6	21
O3		at Yale	0	17
O10	=	at Dartmouth	0	0
O17		at Pennsylvania	9	36
O24	•	Rhode Island	6	0
O31		at Princeton	0	7
N7		at Cornell	0	19
N14	•	Harvard	16	6
N21		Colgate	14	33

1960 — 3-6-0 (1-6-0)

S24		Columbia	0	37
O1		at Yale	0	9
O8		Dartmouth	0	20
O15		at Pennsylvania	7	36
O22	•	Rhode Island	36	14
O29		at Princeton	21	54
N5		Cornell	7	6
N12		at Harvard	8	22
N19	•	Colgate	21	14

1961 — 0-9-0 (0-7-0)

S30		Columbia	0	50
O7		at Yale	3	14
O14		at Dartmouth	0	34
O21		at Pennsylvania	0	7
O28		Rhode Island	9	12
N4		Princeton	0	52
N11		at Cornell	0	25
N18		at Harvard	6	21
N25		Colgate	6	30

1962 — 1-6-2 (0-6-1)

S22	•	at Colgate	6	2
S29		at Columbia	20	22
O6	=	Yale	6	6
O13		Dartmouth	0	41
O20		at Pennsylvania	15	18
O27	=	Rhode Island	12	12
N3		at Princeton	12	28
N10		Cornell	26	28
N17		at Harvard	19	31

1963 — 3-5-0 (2-5-0)

S28		Columbia	14	41
O5	•	Yale	12	7
O12		at Dartmouth	7	14
O19	•	Pennsylvania	41	13
O26	•	Rhode Island	33	7
N2		at Princeton	13	34
N9		at Cornell	25	28
N16		Harvard	12	24

1964 — 5-4-0 (3-4-0)

S26		Lafayette	20	3
O3	•	Pennsylvania	3	0
O10		at Yale	7	15
O17		at Dartmouth	14	24
O24	•	Rhode Island	30	14
O31		Princeton	0	14
N7	•	Cornell	31	28
N14		at Harvard	7	19
N21	•	Columbia	7	0

1965 — 2-7-0 (1-6-0)

S25		Rhode Island	6	14
O2		at Pennsylvania	0	7
O9		Yale	0	3
O16		Dartmouth	9	35
O23	•	Colgate	6	0
O30		at Princeton	27	45
N6		at Cornell	21	41
N13		Harvard	8	17
N20	•	at Columbia	51	7

1966 — 1-8-0 (0-7-0)

S24	•	Rhode Island	40	14
O1		Pennsylvania	0	20
O8		at Yale	0	24
O15		at Dartmouth	14	49
O22		Colgate	7	48
O29		Princeton	7	24
N5		Cornell	14	23
N12		at Harvard	7	24
N19		at Columbia	38	40

LEN JARDINE — 1967-72 (.176) — 9-44-1

1967 — 2-6-1 (1-5-1)

S30		Rhode Island	8	12
O7		at Pennsylvania	7	28
O14		Yale	0	35
O21		Dartmouth	6	41
O28	•	Colgate	7	0
N4		at Princeton	14	48
N11	=	at Cornell	14	14
N18		Harvard	6	21
N25	•	Columbia	14	7

1968 — 2-7-0 (0-7-0)

S28	•	Rhode Island	10	9
O5		Pennsylvania	13	17
O12		at Yale	13	35
O19		at Dartmouth	0	48
O26	•	Colgate	27	19
N2		Princeton	7	50
N9		Cornell	0	31
N16		at Harvard	7	31
N23		at Columbia	20	46

1969 — 2-7-0 (1-6-0)

S27	•	Rhode Island	21	0
O4		at Pennsylvania	2	23
O11		Yale	13	27
O18		Dartmouth	13	38
O25		Colgate	6	20
N1		at Princeton	6	33
N8		at Cornell	7	14
N15	•	Harvard	24	17
N22		Columbia	3	18

1970 — 2-7-0 (1-6-0)

S26	•	Rhode Island	21	14
O3		Pennsylvania	9	17
O10		at Yale	0	28
O17		at Dartmouth	14	42
O24		Colgate	6	10
O31		Princeton	14	42
N7		Cornell	21	35
N14		at Harvard	10	17
N21	•	at Columbia	17	12

1971 — 0-9-0 (0-7-0)

S25		Rhode Island	21	34
O2		at Pennsylvania	16	17
O9		Yale	10	17
O16		Dartmouth	7	10
O23		at Colgate	32	42
O30		at Princeton	21	49
N6		at Cornell	7	21
N13		Harvard	19	24
N20		Columbia	6	24

1972 — 1-8-0 (1-6-0)

S23		Holy Cross	24	30
S30		Rhode Island	17	21
O7	•	Pennsylvania	28	20
O14		at Yale	19	53
O21		at Dartmouth	20	49
N4		Princeton	10	31
N11		Cornell	28	48
N18		at Harvard	14	21
N25		at Columbia	12	28

JOHN ANDERSON — 1973-83 (.603) — 60-39-3

1973 — 4-3-1 (4-3-0)

S29	=	Rhode Island	20	20
O6		at Pennsylvania	20	28
O13	•	Yale	34	25
O20		Dartmouth	16	28
N3	•	at Princeton	7	6
N10	•	at Cornell	17	7
N17		Harvard	32	35
N24	•	Columbia	37	14

1974 — 5-4-0 (4-3-0)

S21		at Holy Cross	10	45
S28	•	Rhode Island	45	15
O5		Pennsylvania	9	14
O12		at Yale	0	24
O19		Dartmouth	6	7
N2	•	Princeton	17	13
N9		Cornell	16	8
N16	•	at Harvard	10	7
N23	•	at Columbia	28	19

1975 6-2-1 (5-1-1)

S27	●		Rhode Island	41	20
O4	●	|	at Pennsylvania	17	8
O11	●	|	Yale	27	12
O18	=	|	at Dartmouth	10	10
O25			at Holy Cross	20	21
N1	●	|	at Princeton	24	16
N8	●	|	at Cornell	45	23
N15		|	Harvard	26	45
N22	●	|	Columbia	48	13

1976 8-1-0 (6-1-0)

S18	●	|	Yale	14	6
S25	●		Rhode Island	3	0
O2	●	|	at Princeton	13	7
O9		|	Pennsylvania	6	7
O16	●	|	at Cornell	28	12
O23	●		Holy Cross	28	18
O30	●	|	at Harvard	16	14
N6	●	|	Dartmouth	35	21
N13	●	|	at Columbia	28	17

1977 7-2-0 (5-2-0)

S17		|	at Yale	9	10
S24	●		Rhode Island	28	10
O1	●	|	Princeton	10	7
O8		|	at Pennsylvania	7	14
O15	●	|	Cornell	21	3
O22	●		at Holy Cross	44	13
O29	●	|	Harvard	20	15
N5	●	|	at Dartmouth	13	10
N12	●	|	Columbia	21	14

1978 6-3-0 (5-2-0)

S23		|	Yale	0	21
S30			Rhode Island	3	17
O7	●	|	at Princeton	44	16
O14	●	|	Pennsylvania	14	0
O21	●	|	at Cornell	21	13
O28	●		Holy Cross	31	25
N4	●	|	at Harvard	31	30
N11		|	Dartmouth	21	31
N18	●	|	at Columbia	24	12

1979 6-3-0 (5-2-0)

S22		|	at Yale	12	13
S29	●		Rhode Island	31	13
O6	●	|	Princeton	31	12
O13	●	|	at Pennsylvania	24	18
O20	●	|	Cornell	28	7
O27			at Holy Cross	7	14
N3	●	|	Harvard	23	14
N10		|	at Dartmouth	10	24
N17	●	|	Columbia	31	14

1980 6-4-0 (4-3-0)

S20		|	Yale	17	45
S27			Bucknell	20	28
O4	●	|	at Princeton	28	11
O11	●	|	Pennsylvania	42	22
O18	●	|	at Cornell	32	25
O25	●		Holy Cross	21	3
N1		|	at Harvard	16	17
N15		|	Dartmouth	24	28
N22	●	|	at Columbia	31	13
N29	●		Rhode Island	9	3

1981 3-7-0 (2-5-0)

S19		|	at Yale	7	28
S26			at Army	17	23
O3		|	Princeton	17	20
O10	●	|	at Pennsylvania	26	24
O17		|	Cornell	9	14
O24			at Holy Cross	24	34
O31		|	Harvard	7	41
N7	●		Rhode Island	10	8
N14		|	at Dartmouth	13	38
N21	●	|	Columbia	23	20

1982 5-5-0 (3-4-0)

S18	●	|	Yale	28	21
S25	●		Rhode Island	24	20
O2		|	at Princeton	23	28
O9		|	Pennsylvania	21	24
O16	●	|	at Cornell	38	19
O23			Holy Cross	6	17
O30		|	at Harvard	0	34
N6	●		at William & Mary	23	22
N13		|	Dartmouth	16	22
N20	●	|	at Columbia	35	21

1983 4-5-1 (4-2-1)

S17	●	|	at Yale	26	24
S24			Rhode Island	16	30
O1		|	Princeton	16	27
O8	=	|	at Pennsylvania	24	24
O15	●	|	Cornell	14	3
O22			at Holy Cross	10	31
O29		|	Harvard	10	17
N5			at Penn State	21	38
N12	●	|	at Dartmouth	25	7
N19	●	|	Columbia	42	36

JOHN ROSENBERG
1984-89 (.415) 23-33-3

1984 4-5-0 (4-3-0)

S22	●	|	Yale	27	14
S29			Rhode Island	13	34
O6	●	|	at Princeton	32	30
O13		|	Pennsylvania	14	41
O20	●	|	at Cornell	13	9
O27			Holy Cross	17	38
N3		|	at Harvard	10	24
N10		|	Dartmouth	11	27
N17	●	|	at Columbia	28	14

1985 5-4-1 (4-3-0)

S21		|	Yale	9	10
S28	●		Rhode Island	32	27
O5	●	|	Princeton	17	0
O12		|	Pennsylvania	14	17
O19	●	|	Cornell	22	0
O26	=		Holy Cross	20	20
N2		|	Harvard	17	25
N9			Richmond	13	29
N16	●	|	Dartmouth	22	0
N23	●	|	Columbia	34	0

1986 5-4-1 (4-2-1)

S20	●	|	Yale	21	7
S27	●		at Rhode Island	27	7
O4	●	|	at Princeton	24	10
O11		|	Pennsylvania	0	34
O18		|	at Cornell	9	27
O25			Holy Cross	7	22
N1	●	|	at Harvard	31	19
N8			Colgate	3	27
N15	=	|	Dartmouth	21	21
N22	●	|	at Columbia	45	7

1987 7-3-0 (5-2-0)

S19	●	|	at Yale	17	7
S26	●		Rhode Island	17	15
O3	●	|	Princeton	13	7
O10		|	at Pennsylvania	17	38
O17	●	|	Cornell	23	15
O24			at Holy Cross	0	41
O31		|	Harvard	9	14
N7	●		at Lehigh	10	7
N14	●	|	at Dartmouth	19	0
N21	●	|	Columbia	19	16

1988 0-9-1 (0-6-1)

S17	=	|	Yale	24	24
S24			at Rhode Island	10	17
O1		|	at Princeton	27	31
O8		|	Pennsylvania	0	10
O15		|	at Cornell	0	35
O22			Holy Cross	14	35
O29		|	at Harvard	3	28
N5			Maine	10	37
N12		|	Dartmouth	24	37
N19		|	at Columbia	13	31

1989 2-8-0 (2-5-0)

S16		|	at Yale	3	12
S23			at Colgate	7	42
S30			Rhode Island	13	18
O7		|	Princeton	15	38
O14		|	at Pennsylvania	30	32
O21	●	|	Cornell	28	7
O28			at Holy Cross	13	49
N4		|	Harvard	14	27
N11		|	at Dartmouth	6	12
N18	●	|	Columbia	41	28

MICKEY KWIATKOWSKI
1990-93 (.175) 7-33

1990 2-8-0 (2-5-0)

S15		|	Yale	21	27
S22			at Rhode Island	3	23
S29			Fordham	28	35
O6		|	at Princeton	23	27
O13			Holy Cross	0	55
O20	●	|	Pennsylvania	24	17
O27		|	at Cornell	7	34
N3		|	at Harvard	37	52
N10		|	Dartmouth	0	29
N17	●	|	at Columbia	17	0

1991 1-9-0 (1-6-0)

S21		|	at Yale	20	36
S28			at Marshall	0	46
O5			Rhode Island	36	38
O12		|	Princeton	37	59
O19			at Holy Cross	28	42
O26		|	at Pennsylvania	19	28
N2		|	Cornell	17	20
N9		|	Harvard	29	35
N16		|	at Dartmouth	13	45
N23	●	|	Columbia	28	23

1992 0-10-0 (0-7-0)

S19		|	Yale	17	22
S26			at Bucknell	14	33
O3			at William & mary	6	51
O10		|	at Princeton	14	28
O17			Lehigh	24	31
O24		|	Pennsylvania	0	38
O31		|	at Cornell	6	16
N7		|	at Harvard	19	29
N14		|	Dartmouth	28	51
N21		|	at Columbia	28	34

1993 4-6-0 (3-4-0)

S18	●	|	at Yale	12	3
S25			at Lehigh	35	42
O2			Rhode Island	7	30
O9		|	Princeton	16	34
O16	●		Bucknell	21	12
O23		|	at Pennsylvania	9	34
O30		|	Cornell	3	21
N6	●	|	Harvard	43	29
N13		|	at Dartmouth	16	39
N20	●	|	Columbia	28	23

MARK WHIPPLE
1994-97 (.575) 23-17

1994 7-3-0 (4-3-0)

S17		|	at Yale	16	27
S24	●		at Rhode Island	32	29
O1	●		Colgate	26	7
O8		|	at Princeton	10	31
O15	●		Holy Cross	20	18
O22		|	Pennsylvania	0	24
O29	●	|	at Cornell	16	3
N5	●	|	at Harvard	23	17
N12	●	|	Dartmouth	27	14
N19	●	|	at Columbia	59	27

1995 5-5-0 (2-5-0)

S16		|	at Yale	38	42
S23	●		Rhode Island	31	28
S30	●		at Holy Cross	37	14
O7		|	Princeton	19	21
O14	●		Colgate	21	6
O21		|	at Pennsylvania	21	58
O28		|	Cornell	28	38
N4	●	|	Harvard	47	8
N11		|	at Dartmouth	7	10
N18	●	|	Columbia	33	14

1996 5-5 (4-3)

S21		|	Yale	0	30
S28			at Rhode Island	13	28
O5			at Colgate	27	44
O12	●	|	at Princeton	27	23
O19	●		Fordham	27	14
O26	●	|	Pennsylvania	27	21
N2	●	|	at Cornell	35	21
N9	●	|	at Harvard	31	7
N16		|	Dartmouth	24	27
N23		|	at Columbia	27	31

1997 6-4 (3-4)

S20	●	|	at Yale	52	14
S27	●		Lafayette	35	27
O4	●		at Fordham	45	14
O11		|	Princeton	13	30
O18	●		Rhode Island	23	15
O25		|	at Pennsylvania	10	31 †
N1	●	|	Cornell	37	12
N8		|	Harvard	10	27
N15		|	at Dartmouth	7	13
N22	●	|	Columbia	42	11

PHIL ESTES
1998-Present (.609) 42-27

1998 7-3 (5-2)

S19		|	Yale	28	30
S26	●		at Lafayette	23	21
O3			at Rhode Island	16	44
O10		|	at Princeton	17	31
O17	●		Fordham	38	27
O24	●	|	Pennsylvania	58	51
O31	●	|	at Cornell	20	7
N7	●	|	at Harvard	27	6
N14	●	|	Dartmouth	28	21
N21	●	|	at Columbia	10	3

1999 9-1 (6-1)

S18	●	|	at Yale	25	24
S25	●		Lafayette	35	28
O2		|	Cornell	28	33
O9	●	|	Princeton	53	30
O16	●		Rhode Island	27	25
O23	●	|	at Pennsylvania	44	37
O30	●		at Fordham	37	18
N6	●	|	Harvard	17	10
N13	●	|	at Dartmouth	35	28
N20	●	|	Columbia	23	6

2000 7-3 (4-3)

S16	●		San Diego	36	20
S23		|	Harvard	37	42
S30	●		Rhode Island	29	19
O7	●		at Fordham	44	17
O14		|	at Princeton	28	55
O21	●	|	Cornell	56	40
O28		|	at Pennsylvania	38	41
N4	●	|	Yale	28	14
N11	●	|	at Dartmouth	34	26
N18	●	|	Columbia	45	27

2001 6-3 (5-2)

S22		|	at Harvard	20	27
S29			Rhode Island	38	42
O6	●		Fordham	40	23
O13	●	|	Princeton	35	24
O20	●	|	at Cornell	49	21
O27		|	Pennsylvania	14	27
N3	●	|	at Yale	37	34
N10	●	|	Dartmouth	41	16
N17	●	|	at Columbia	45	21

2002 2-8 (2-5)

S21			at Towson	42	56
S28		|	Harvard	24	26
O5			at Rhode Island	28	38
O12			at Fordham	17	24
O19		|	at Princeton	14	16
O26		|	Cornell	7	10
N2		|	at Pennsylvania	7	31
N9		|	Yale	27	31
N16	●	|	at Dartmouth	21	18
N23	●	|	Columbia	35	28

2003 5-5 (4-3)

S20	●		at SUNY-Albany	21	3
S27		|	at Harvard	14	52
O4			Rhode Island	9	27
O11			Fordham	21	24
O18		|	Princeton	14	34
O25	●	|	at Cornell	21	7
N1		|	Pennsylvania	21	24
N8	●	|	at Yale	55	44
N15	●	|	Dartmouth	26	21
N22	●	|	at Columbia	42	10

2004 6-4 (3-4)

S18	●		Albany	35	7
S25		|	Harvard	34	35
O2	●		at Rhode Island	20	13
O9	●		at Fordham	27	20
O16		|	at Princeton	10	24
O23		|	at Pennsylvania	16	20
O30	●	|	Cornell	21	17
N6	●	|	Yale	24	17
N13		|	at Dartmouth	7	20
N20	●	|	Columbia	33	21

Neutral Site Key: ***Nwb*** Newburgh, NY / ***NYC*** New York, NY / ***U*** Unknown, Unknown

f **Forfeit** † **Game Later Forfieted** # **Disputed Victor** * **Disputed Score** || **Designated Conference Game** |2 **Counted Twice in Conference Standings**

COLUMBIA

BY BRUCE WOOD

LEGENDARY COLUMBIA COACH KNUTE Rockne? It almost happened. After finishing the 1925 season with a 6–3–1 record, Columbia set its sights even higher by offering Rockne a contract that would make him the highest-paid coach in the country. But when sportswriter Grantland Rice broke the story before Rockne could finalize his release, the legendary coach had no choice but to stay in South Bend. Under Rockne's leadership, Notre Dame would become a college football dynasty. Columbia enjoyed its fair share of winning seasons, but that would all become a distant memory by the second half of the 20th century, when the Lions set records for futility that stand to this day. With just one winning season from 1972 to 2004, Columbia hasn't turned the corner yet.

TRADITION In 1961, Columbia wrapped up a 6–1 conference slate with a 37-6 victory over Penn to clinch a share of the school's only Ivy League title. Each year, the 1961 team hosts a party for all returning players during homecoming weekend.

BEST PLAYER After a fine career at Brooklyn's Erasmus Hall High School, Sid Luckman stayed in New York to play for Lions coach Lou Little. Luckman earned All-America honors at quarterback in 1938, leading Columbia to a 27-14 victory over Yale and a 20-18 upset of Army. He was featured on the cover of *Life* magazine on Oct. 24, 1938, under the headline "Best Passer." Luckman, who went on to a distinguished NFL career, is the only Columbia player enshrined in both the College and Pro Football halls of fame.

BEST COACH Spirited away from Georgetown, Lou Little went 43–15–3 in his first seven seasons at Columbia, leading the Lions to a stunning Rose Bowl victory in 1934. Before the 1948 season, Little was almost lured away by Yale; one of Columbia president-elect Dwight Eisenhower's first executive tasks was to keep Little coaching the Lions. Little, heralded as the best-dressed coach in the game, remained in Morningside Heights until 1956; with a 110–116–10 record over 27 years, he has more victories than the next three coaches on Columbia's wins list combined.

BEST TEAM Other Columbia squads have won more games, and the 1934 Rose Bowl victory garnered more attention. But

PROFILE

Columbia University
New York, N.Y.
Founded: 1754
Enrollment: 7,248
Colors: Columbia Blue and White
Nickname: Lions
Stadium: Lawrence A. Wien Stadium at Baker Field
   Opened in 1984
   Astroturf XL; 17,000 capacity
First football game: 1870
All-time record: 355–573–44 (.388)
Bowl record: 1–0
Ivy League championships: 1 (shared)
First-round NFL draftees: 3
Website: www.gocolumbialions.com

THE BEST OF TIMES

On Oct. 8, 1988, the Lions ended the then-longest Division I-AA losing streak (since surpassed by Prairie View A&M) at 44 games when a 48-yard Princeton field goal fell short on the final play of the game to give Columbia a 16-13 win.

THE WORST OF TIMES

The Columbia Class of 1988 graduated without seeing the Lions win. They were 0–39 during that time and in the midst of a 44-game winless streak.

CONFERENCE

Columbia was an original member of the Ivy League when the conference began formal play in 1956.

DISTINGUISHED ALUMNI

Art Garfunkel; Ruth Bader Ginsberg; George Stephanopoulos; David Stern; Allen Ginsberg; Jack Kerouacs

FIGHT SONG

ROAR LION
When the bold teams of old wore the blue and white,
Deeds of fame made their name here at old Columbia,
Nowadays, we can praise fighting teams again,
Hear the Lion roar his pride,
While the men of Morningside,
Follow the blue and white to victory!
Roar, Lion, Roar
And wake the echoes of the Hudson Valley
Fight on to victory evermore
While the sons of Knickerbocker
Rally 'round Columbia, Columbia!
Shouting her name forever
Roar, Lion, Roar
For Alma Mater on the Hudson shore!

coach Buff Donelli's 1961 Lions stand out as the school's only Ivy League championship team. Led by quarterback Tom Vassell, Columbia opened with a 50-0 thrashing of Brown and ran a 6–1 record against Ivy League teams for a share of the conference title with Harvard. The Lions scored a league-leading 30.6 points per game in conference play.

BIGGEST GAME Thinking it was a joke, Little hung up the phone when Stanford's athletic director called to invite his team to play in the 1934 Rose Bowl. At 7–1, Columbia was a good team, but its ledger was marred by a 20-0 loss to Princeton. Although Little soon realized the invitation was sincere, few gave the Lions much of a chance against a mighty Stanford team that was ranked No. 2 in the nation at the time. Still, Columbia made the trip out West. Aided by a wet field and Little's sound defensive schemes, the Lions shocked Stanford 7-0 behind a 17-yard touchdown run by fullback Al Barabas.

BIGGEST UPSET Forty-four consecutive losses. By 1988,

The night before homecoming each year, the 1961 Ivy title team hosts a party for returning players.

Division I-AA Columbia had surpassed Northwestern's Division I-A losing streak and was staring down the barrel at Macalester's all-divisions mark of 50 straight defeats. On Oct. 8, Princeton brought its 2–1 record to Wien Stadium and was favored to win by three touchdowns. Columbia hung in through three quarters and erased a 13-9 Princeton lead on Solomon Johnson's two-yard TD run with 5:13 remaining. The Tigers got the ball back and drove down the field. On the game's final play, Princeton's 48-yard field goal attempt fell short, and the exuberant Columbia fans tore down the goalposts, carrying them back to the school's Morningside Heights campus.

WILDEST FINISH With Columbia leading NYU 6-0 late in a 1922 game, the Lions faced fourth down deep in their own territory and set up to punt. The snap went over the punter's head and an NYU player retrieved the ball in the end zone, but not before it bounced into the grandstand and back onto the field. The referee ruled it a touchdown for NYU, giving the Purple Violets a 7-6 victory. (After

RECORDS

RUSHING YARDS

	GAME
236	Johnathan Reese vs. Dartmouth, Oct. 21, 2000 (25 att.)
	SEASON
1,330	Johnathan Reese, 2000 (263 att.)
	CAREER
3,321	Johnathan Reese, 1998-2001 (739 att.)

PASSING YARDS

	GAME
466	John Witkowski vs. Dartmouth, Nov. 6, 1982 (39 of 64)
	SEASON
3,152	John Witkowski, 1983 (234 of 429)
	CAREER
7,849	John Witkowski, 1981-83 (613 of 1,176)

RECEIVING YARDS

	GAME
214	Bill Wazevich vs. Princeton, Oct. 7, 1967 (12 rec.)
	SEASON
1,000	Don Lewis, 1982 (84 rec.)
	CAREER
2,384	Bill Reggio, 1981-83 (170 rec.)

POINTS

	GAME
30	Eugene Rossides vs. Cornell, Nov. 3, 1945 (5 TDs)
	SEASON
114	Johnathan Reese, 2000 (19 TDs)
	CAREER
270	Lou Kusserow, 1945-48 (45 TDs)

CONSENSUS ALL-AMERICANS

1900-01	Bill Morley, B
1901	Harold Weekes, B
1903	Richard Smith, B
1942	Paul Governali, B
1947	Bill Swiacki, E
2004	Wade Fletcher, TE

the game, the ref needed a police escort to the subway.) He later checked the rule book, realized he had made a mistake and called both schools on Monday to change the touchdown to a safety, granting Columbia a 6-2 win. The Purple Violets, however, weren't buying it; the disputed touchdown gave them the lead, NYU officials argued, and therefore they had sat on the ball. Had it been ruled a safety, they would have played for a win. Convinced he was right, the referee refused to award NYU the victory. Although Columbia lists the game as a 6-2 win, to this day NYU considers the same game a 7-6 victory for the Purple Violets.

STADIUM After playing for years on a two-acre lot between Low Library and Butler Hall, the Lions moved to a 15,000-seat stadium at the northern tip of Manhattan in 1923. Lawrence A. Wien Stadium, which seats 17,000, was built in 1984. With panoramic views of the New Jersey Palisades and the confluence of the Harlem and Hudson rivers, Wien Stadium is considered one of the most beautiful places in the country to watch a college football game.

RIVAL Any win during Columbia's record-setting losing streak in the 1980s would have been welcome. Ending the historic slide against Princeton in 1988 only made it sweeter; the Tigers were led by brothers Jason and Judd Garrett, who had started their college careers with the Lions. Still, Princeton keeps finding ways to get Columbia's goat. In 1995, the Lions jumped out to a 3–0 Ivy record but were then pummeled by Princeton 44-14. Columbia failed to win another game the rest of the year.

ALL-CENTURY TEAM	
Chosen in 2000 by a committee of sports historians and journalists.	
1899-1901	William Morley, DB
1899-1901	Harold Weekes, RB
1922-24	Walter Koppisch, RB
1931-33	Cliff Montgomery, QB
1936-38	Sid Luckman, QB/DB/P/K
1940-42	Paul Governali, QB/P
1945-48	Lou Kusserow, RB
1945-48	Gene Rossides, QB
1946-47	Bill Swiacki, E
1954-56	Claude Benham, QB
1959, 1961	Russ Warren, RB/P
1962-64	Archie Roberts, QB
1966-68	Marty Domres, QB
1969-70	George Starke, TE
1970-72	Paul Kaliades, LB
1971-73	Ted Gregory, DB
1973-75	Doug Jackson, RB
1974-76	Ed Backus, DB
1981-83	Don Lewis, WR
1981-83	Bill Reggio, WR
1981-83	John Witkowski, QB
1990-92	Des Werthman, LB/RB/K
1993-96	Marcellus Wiley, DE/RB
1993-96	Rory Wilfork, LB

NICKNAME The nickname Lions was officially adopted by the school in 1910. Later, Columbia grad Howard Dietz, Metro Goldwyn Mayer's vice president for advertising and public relations, based MGM's famous lion, Leo, on his alma mater's mascot.

MASCOT Stirring up crowds at Wien Stadium on Saturdays is a student dressed in a furry brown lion suit, complete with oversize feet, a mane and a toothy grin that closely resembles the school's stylized logo.

UNIFORMS Drawn from the school's Philolexian and Peithologian societies, Columbia's blue-and-white color scheme first appeared in 1852. Over the years, the Lions' uniform has included different amounts of dark blue, but the signature color has always been a sky-colored shade that is widely referred to as Columbia blue. The team's helmets have gone through a number of variations, including one that featured a leaping lion not unlike the one used by the Detroit Lions.

QUOTE "I did not come to Columbia to fail." —Lou Little in 1930, after being named head coach

THE SCHOOLS

COLUMBIA ANNUAL STATISTICAL LEADERS

YR	RUSHING	YDS	ATT	AVG	PASSING	ATT	CMP	PCT	YDS	RECEIVING	REC	YDS	AVG
1956		NA	NA	NA	Claude Benham	86	45	.52	709	Ron Szcypkowski	14	170	12.1
1957	Brad Howard	397	93	4.3	Richard Donelli	96	52	.54	589	Ron Szcypkowski	12	120	10.0
1958	Harvey Brookins	292	94	3.1	Richard Donelli	88	41	.47	390	Bob Federspiel	15	147	9.8
1959	Harvey Brookins	303	63	4.7	Tom Vasell	143	56	.39	739	Bob Federspiel	20	312	15.6
1960	Tom Haggerty	345	81	4.3	Tom Vasell	122	57	.47	850	Bob Federspiel	20	306	15.3
1961	Tom Haggerty	647	131	4.9	Tom Vasell	101	52	.51	639	Dick Hassan	14	208	14.9
1962	Tom O'Connor	250	83	3.0	Archie Roberts	170	102	.60	1,076	Al Butts	18	235	13.1
1963	Archie Roberts	341	121	2.8	Archie Roberts	164	101	.62	1,184	Bob Donohue	26	328	12.6
1964	Archie Roberts	169	145	1.2	Archie Roberts	196	110	.56	1,444	Roger Dennis	33	524	15.9
1965	Roger Dennis	209	72	2.9	Rick Ballantine	108	54	.50	617	Roger Dennis	18	282	15.7
1966	John O'Connor	526	128	4.1	Marty Dormes	129	64	.50	908	Garry Zawadzkas	20	272	13.6
1967	Jim O'Connor	399	103	3.9	Marty Dormes	229	121	.53	1,378	Bill Wazevich	45	593	13.2
1968	Marty Dormes	198	153	1.3	Marty Dormes	344	183	.53	2,206	Bill Wazevich	47	618	13.1
1969	John Sefcik	535	148	3.6	Jim Romanosky	81	36	.44	394	George Starke	24	293	12.2
1970	Tom Hurley	375	98	3.8	Don Jackson	195	89	.46	1,156	Mike Jones	36	362	10.1
1971	Steve Howland	360	128	2.8	Don Jackson	158	77	.49	1,155	Jesse Parks	30	558	18.6
1972	George Georges	540	127	4.3	Don Jackson	189	89	.47	1,136	Jesse Parks	33	441	13.4
1973	George Georges	363	117	3.1	Geoff Cummings	117	56	.48	617	Mike Telep	43	572	13.3
1974	Glen Smith	323	79	4.1	Mike Delaney	136	63	.46	813	Dexter Brown	26	374	14.4
1975	Doug Jackson	914	174	5.3	Mike Delaney	124	54	.44	580	Dexter Brown	18	185	10.3
1976	Paul McCormick	444	87	5.1	Kevin Burns	80	30	.38	374	Artie Pulsinelli	12	183	15.3
1977	Gerry Fitzpatrick	473	91	5.2	Kevin Burns	143	60	.42	770	Artie Pulsinelli	22	320	14.5
1978	Pat Britt	545	134	4.1	Larry Biondi	74	34	.46	490	Artie Pulsinelli	21	306	14.6
1979	Joe Cabrera	278	56	5.0	Bob Conroy	165	70	.42	920	Eric Blattman	18	213	11.8
1980	Joe Cabrera	597	148	4.0	Greg Gennaro	96	42	.44	620	Bill Donley	19	288	15.2
1981	Jim McHale	475	108	4.4	John Witkowski	294	129	.44	1,647	Bill Reggio	29	439	15.1
1982	Jim McHale	472	133	3.5	John Witkowski	453	250	.55	3,050	Don Lewis	84	1,000	11.9
1983	Mike Goldman	726	173	4.2	John Witkowski	429	234	.55	3,152	Bill Reggio	71	958	13.5
1984	Jimmy Henderson	444	56	7.9	Henry Santos	174	88	.51	1,074	Dan Upperco	38	489	12.9
1985	John Chirico	518	133	3.9	Henry Santos	337	179	.53	1,608	Mark Milam	35	323	9.2
1986	John Chirico	319	71	4.5	David Putelo	182	89	.49	894	Dan Botich	23	234	10.2
1987	Chris Konovalchik	418	111	3.8	David Putelo	197	85	.43	859	Ron Kalyan	17	220	12.9
1988	Greg Abbruzzese	723	137	5.3	Chris Della Pietra	64	25	.39	427	Matt Less	14	158	11.3
1989	J.R. Clearfield	175	37	4.7	Bruce Mayhew	225	140	.62	1,526	Matt Less	61	707	11.6
1990	Greg Abbruzzese	380	105	3.6	Bruce Mayhew	346	193	.56	2,234	Gary Comstock	68	816	12.0
1991	Solomon Johnson	522	104	5.0	John Tribolet	250	120	.48	1,448	Mike Sardo	42	512	12.2
1992	John Klosek	274	57	4.8	Chad Andrzejewski	346	186	.54	1,997	Mike Sardo	60	571	9.5
1993	Marcellus Wiley	421	126	3.3	Jamie Schwalbe	189	101	.53	1,140	Brian Bassett	34	398	11.7
1994	Mike Cavanaugh	622	108	5.8	Jamie Schwalbe	300	165	.55	2,119	Brian Bassett	62	793	12.8
1995	John Harper	526	141	3.7	Mike Cavanaugh	138	71	.51	996	David Ramirez	46	708	15.4
1996	Jason Bivens	649	239	2.7	Bobby Thomason	256	123	.48	1,264	Bert Bondi	48	483	10.1
1997	Norman Hayes	456	130	3.5	Bobby Thomason	232	96	.41	1,135	Bert Bondi	39	516	13.2
1998	Norman Hayes	514	152	3.4	Paris Childress	163	88	.54	974	Mark Cannan	30	388	12.9
1999	Johnathan Reese	607	159	3.8	Jeff McCall	141	78	.55	817	Armand Dawkins	44	503	11.4
2000	Johnathan Reese	1,330	263	5.1	Jeff McCall	227	131	.58	1,614	Doug Peck	39	560	14.4
2001	Johnathan Reese	967	218	4.4	Jeff McCall	280	166	.59	1,819	Doug Peck	57	822	14.4
2002	Rashad Biggers	442	110	4.0	Steve Hunsberger	370	212	.57	2,023	Zach Van Zant	51	592	11.6
2003	Ayo Oluwole	215	903	4.2	Jeff Otis	372	217	.58	2,552	Wade Fletcher	59	874	14.8
2004	Rashad Biggers	197	770	3.9	Jeff Otis	330	189	.57	1,870	Wade Fletcher	52	575	11.1

Receiving leaders by receptions

COLUMBIA ALL-TIME SCORES

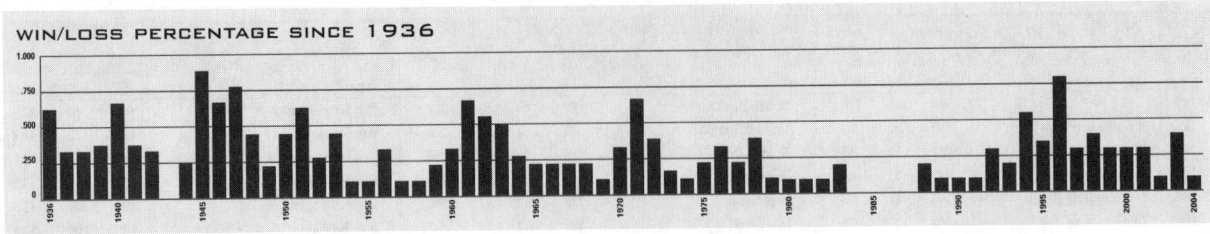

WIN/LOSS PERCENTAGE SINCE 1936

NO HEAD COACH

1870　　　　0-1-0
| N5 | at Rutgers | 3 | 6 |

1872　　　　1-2-1
N2	= Rutgers	0	0
N9	at Rutgers	5	7
N16	at Yale	0	3
N23	● Stevens	6	0

1873　　　　2-1-0
O25	● at Stevens	2	1
N1	at Rutgers	4	5
N8	● Rutgers	4	3

1874　　　　1-5-0
O24	at Rutgers	1	6
O31	at Stevens	2	4
N7	at Princeton	0	6
N14	● Rutgers	4	1
N21	at Yale	1	5
D5	at Yale	1	6

1875　　　　4-1-1
N2	= at Rutgers	1	1
N4	● at Stevens	2	1
N6	● at CCNY	5	0
N13	at Princeton	2	6
N20	● CCNY	6	0
D4	● at Yale	3	2

1876　　　　1-3-0
N4	at Stevens	3	5
N11	Princeton	0	3
N18	● Stevens	4	0
D9	Yale *Hob*	0	2

1877　　　　2-2-0
O27	Harvard	0	6
N6	● Rutgers	6	0
N13	● at Stevens	1	0
N24	at Princeton	0	4

1878　　　　0-0-2
| N5 | = Stevens | 0 | 0 |
| N16 | = at Pennsylvania | 0 | 0 |

1879　　　　0-3-2
O25	= at Stevens	0	0
N1	at Princeton	0	2
N8	at Pennsylvania	0	1
N20	= Rutgers	0	0
N22	Yale *Hob*	0	2

1880　　　　1-2-0
N6	Harvard	0	3
N10	at Yale	0	13
N13	● Rutgers	3	0

1881　　　　3-3-1
O31	● at Stevens	3	1
N5	at Harvard	0	1
N8	= at Rutgers	0	0
N12	at Princeton	0	1
N16	Yale *NYC*	0	1
N23	● Rutgers	1	0
N26	● at Pennsylvania	2	0

1882　　　　0-5-0
N7	Princeton *NYC*	0	8
N9	at Rutgers	1	2
N11	at Harvard	0	3
N18	at Yale	0	11
N25	at Princeton	0	3

1883　　　　1-3-0
O20	● CCNY	12	0
O27	at Stevens	0	19
N14	at Pennsylvania	1	35
N17		Yale *NYC*	0	93

1884　　　　1-1-0
| O15 | at Rutgers | 5 | 35 |
| U | ● CCNY *U* | 16 | 0 |

1885-1888
NO TEAM

1889　　　　2-7-2
O5	Crescent AC *Sta*	0	30
O9	= Lafayette	10	10
O12	at Trinity	4	24
O26	Yale	0	62
N2	at Lehigh	6	51
N6	Princeton	0	71
N9	Pennsylvania	0	24
N14	● at Stevens	12	6
N20	● Manhattan AC	22	0
N23	= at Amherst	0	0
N26	Cornell	0	20

1890　　　　1-6-1
O4	at Orange AC	0	21
O18	Wesleyan *NYC*	0	4
O22	Pennsylvania *NYC*	0	18
O30	● Fordham *NYC*	40	0
N1	Crescent AC *Bkln*	0	29
N4	Princeton *NYC*	0	85
N15	= Rutgers *NYC*	6	6
N22	at Cornell	0	36

1891　　　　1-5-0
O10	● Berkeley AC	32	0
O14	Manhattan AC	0	28
O17	Crescent AC *Bkln*	0	42
O21	at Stevens	0	52
O24	Trinity	0	54
O28	at Rutgers	0	44

1892-1898
NO TEAM

GEORGE F. SANFORD
1899-1901 (.681)　　　24-11-1

1899　　　　9-3-0
S23	● Walton	30	6
S30	● at Rutgers	26	0
O7	● at Union	21	0
O14	Princeton	0	11
O18	● NYU	40	0
O21	● Amherst	18	0
O28	● Yale	5	0
N1	● at Stevens	46	0
N7	Cornell	0	29
N11	● at Army	16	0
N18	● Dartmouth	22	0
N30	Carlisle	0	45

1900　　　　7-3-1
O3	● at Rutgers	11	0
O6	● Wesleyan	12	0
O10	= Williams	0	0
O13	at Harvard	0	24
O17	● Stevens	45	0
O20	at Pennsylvania	0	30
O27	Yale	5	12
N6	● Princeton	6	5
N10	● at Buffalo	17	0
N17	● at Navy	11	0
N29	● Carlisle	17	6

1901　　　　8-5-0
S28	at Buffalo	0	5
O2	● at Rutgers	27	0
O5	● Williams	5	0
O12	at Harvard	0	18
O19	● Hamilton	12	0
O26	at Yale	5	10
O30	● Haverford	29	6
N2	● Pennsylvania	10	0
N5	● Georgetown	18	0
N9	● Syracuse	5	11
N16	● Cornell	0	24
N22	● at Navy	6	5
N28	● Carlisle	40	12

WILLIAM F. MORLEY
1902-05 (.688)　　　26-11-3

1902　　　　6-4-1
O4	● at Rutgers	43	0
O8	● Fordham	45	0
O11	● Buffalo	5	0
O15	● Swarthmore	24	0
O18	● Hamilton	35	0
O25	at Princeton	0	21
N1	at Pennsylvania	0	17
N8	● Brown	0	28
N15	Amherst	0	29
N19	● at Navy	5	0
N27	= Syracuse	6	6

1903　　　　9-1-0
S26	● Wesleyan	10	0
S30	● Alumni	16	0
O3	● Union	36	0
O7	● Hamilton	29	0
O10	● Williams	5	0
O14	● Swarthmore	5	0
O17	● Amherst	12	0
O22	● Pennsylvania	18	6
O31	at Yale	0	25
N14	at Cornell	17	12

1904　　　　7-3-0
S24	● Union	10	0
S28	● Franklin & Marshall	28	0
O1	● Wesleyan	16	0
O4	● Tufts	31	0
O8	● Williams	11	0
O12	● Swarthmore	12	0
O15	Amherst	0	12
O21	at Pennsylvania	0	16
O29	Yale	0	34
N12	● Cornell	12	6

1905　　　　4-3-2
S30	● Union	23	0
O4	● Seton Hall	21	0
O7	= Wesleyan	0	0
O14	● Williams	11	5
O21	● Amherst	10	10
O28	● Princeton	0	12
N4	Yale	0	53
N18	● at Cornell	12	6
N25	● Pennsylvania	0	23

1906-1914
NO TEAM

T. NELSON METCALF
1915-17 (.474)　　　8-9-2

1915　　　　5-0-0
U	● St. Lawrence *U*	57	0
U	● Stevens *U*	15	6
U	● Connecticut *U*	17	6
U	● NYU *U*	19	16
U	● Wesleyan *U*	18	0

1916　　　　1-5-2
U	Hamilton *U*	7	14
U	● Vermont *U*	6	0
U	Union	0	3
U	= Williams *U*	0	0
U	= Stevens *U*	0	0
U	Swarthmore	0	18
U	Wesleyan *U*	0	40
U	NYU *U*	0	6

1917　　　　2-4-0
U	● Union *U*	21	0
U	● Williams *U*	6	9
U	Amherst *U*	6	14
U	● Hobart *U*	70	0
U	Wesleyan *U*	0	6
U	NYU *U*	7	9

FRED DAWSON
1918-19 (.567)　　　7-5-3

1918　　　　5-1-0
U	● Merritt *U*	7	0
U	● Amherst *U*	21	7
U	● Union	33	0
U	● Wesleyan *U*	14	0
U	● NYU	12	0
N28	at Syracuse	0	20

1919　　　　2-4-3
U	= USS Arizona *U*	0	0
U	● Vermont *U*	7	0
U	Williams *U*	0	25
U	● Amherst *U*	9	7
U	NYU *U*	12	27
U	= Union *U*	0	0
U	Stevens *U*	0	13
U	Wesleyan *U*	13	28
N27	= Brown	7	7

FRANK O'NEILL
1920-22 (.440)　　　11-14

1920　　　　4-4-0
U	● Trinity *U*	21	0
U	● NYU *U*	14	7
U	● Amherst *U*	20	7
U	Wesleyan *U*	0	10
U	● Williams *U*	20	14
U	Swarthmore	7	21
N13	at Cornell	7	34
N20	Pennsylvania	7	27

1921　　　　2-6-0
O1	Amherst	7	9
O8	● Wesleyan	14	3
O15	● NYU	19	0
O22	at Dartmouth	7	31
O29	Williams	0	20
N5	Cornell *NYC*	7	41
N12	● Ohio U.	21	23
N24	Colgate	14	21

1922　　　　5-4-0
S30	● Ursinus	48	7
O7	● Amherst	43	6
O14	● Wesleyan	10	6
O21	● NYU	6	2
O28	● Williams	10	13
N4	at Cornell	0	56
N11	● Middlebury	17	6
N18	Dartmouth *NYC*	7	28
N30	Colgate	6	59

PERCY D. HAUGHTON
1923-24 (.607) 8-5-1

1923 4-4-1

S29	●	Ursinus	13	0
O6	=	Amherst	0	0
O13	●	Wesleyan	12	6
O20		at Pennsylvania	7	19
O27		Williams	0	10
N3	●	Middlebury	9	6
N10		Cornell NYC	0	35
N17	●	NYU	21	0
N29		Dartmouth NYC	6	31

PAUL WITHINGTON
1924 (.375) 1-2-1

1924 5-3-1

S27	●	Haverford	29	3
O4	●	St. Lawrence	52	0
O11	●	Wesleyan	35	0
O18		at Pennsylvania	7	10
O25	●	Williams	27	3
N1		at Cornell	0	14
N8	●	NYU	40	0
N15	=	at Army	14	14
N27		Syracuse NYC	6	9

CHARLES F. CROWLEY
1925-29 (.609) 26-16-4

1925 6-3-1

S26	●	Haverford	59	0
O3	●	Johns Hopkins	47	0
O10		at Ohio State	0	9
O17	●	Wesleyan	64	0
O24	●	Williams	26	0
O31		Cornell NYC	14	17
N7	=	NYU	6	6
N14	●	Army NYC	21	7
N21	●	Alfred	46	0
N26		Syracuse NYC	5	16

1926 6-3-0

S25	●	Vermont	14	0
O2	●	Union	26	0
O9	●	Wesleyan	41	0
O16		Ohio State NYC	7	32
O23	●	Duke	24	0
O30	●	Cornell NYC	17	9
N6	●	William & Mary	13	10
N13		at Pennsylvania	0	3
N25		Syracuse NYC	2	19

1927 5-2-2

S24	●	Vermont	32	0
O1	●	Union	28	0
O8	●	Wesleyan	28	0
O15		Colgate	7	13
O22	●	Williams	19	0
O29	=	at Cornell	0	0
N5	=	Johns Hopkins	7	7
N12		at Pennsylvania	0	27
N24	●	Syracuse NYC	14	7

1928 5-3-1

S29	●	Vermont	20	0
O6	●	Union	27	0
O13	●	Wesleyan	31	7
O20		at Dartmouth	7	21
O27	●	Williams	20	6
N3	=	Cornell	0	0
N10	●	Johns Hopkins	14	13
N17		at Pennsylvania	7	34
N29		Syracuse	6	14

1929 4-5-0

S28	●	Middlebury	38	6
O5	●	Union	31	0
O12	●	Wesleyan	52	0
O19		Dartmouth	0	34
O26	●	Williams	33	0
N2		at Cornell	6	12
N9		Colgate	0	33
N16		Pennsylvania	0	20
N28		Syracuse	0	6

LOU LITTLE
1930-56 (.487) 110-116-10

1930 5-4-0

S27	●	Middlebury	48	0
O4	●	Union	25	0
O11	●	Wesleyan	48	0
O18		at Dartmouth	0	52
O25	●	Williams	3	0
N1	●	Cornell	10	7
N8		Colgate	0	54
N15		at Brown	0	6
N27		Syracuse	7	19

1931 7-1-1

S26	●	Middlebury	61	0
O3	●	Union	51	0
O10	●	at Wesleyan	37	0
O17	●	Dartmouth	19	6
O24	●	Williams	19	0
O31		at Cornell	0	13
N7	●	Virginia	27	0
N14	●	at Brown	9	7
N21	=	Syracuse	0	0

1932 7-1-1

S24	●	Middlebury	51	0
O1	●	Lehigh	41	6
O8	●	Princeton	20	7
O15	●	Virginia	22	6
O22	●	Williams	46	0
O29	●	Cornell	6	0
N5	●	at Navy	7	6
N12		Brown	6	7
N19	=	Syracuse	0	0

1933 8-1-0

O7	●	Lehigh	39	0
O14	●	Virginia	15	6
O21		at Princeton	0	20
O28	●	Penn State	33	0
N4	●	at Cornell	9	6
N11	●	Navy	14	7
N18	●	Lafayette	46	6
N25	●	Syracuse	16	0
		ROSE BOWL		
J1	●	Stanford	7	0

1934 7-1-0

O6	●	at Yale	12	6
O13	●	VMI	29	6
O20		Navy	7	18
O27	●	Penn State	14	7
N3	●	Cornell	14	0
N10	●	Brown	39	0
N17	●	at Pennsylvania	13	12
N25	●	Syracuse	12	0

1935 4-4-1

O5	●	VMI	12	0
O12	●	Rutgers	20	6
O19		at Pennsylvania	0	34
O26		Michigan	7	19
N2	=	at Cornell	7	7
N9		Syracuse	2	14
N16		at Navy	7	28
N23	●	Brown	18	0
N30	●	Dartmouth	13	7

1936 5-3-0

O3	●	Maine	34	0
O10		Army BRNX	16	27
O17	●	VMI	38	0
O24		at Michigan	0	1
O31	●	Cornell	20	1
N7		at Dartmouth	13	2
N14	●	Syracuse	17	0
N28	●	Stanford NYC	7	0

1937 2-5-2

O2	●	Williams	40	6
O9		at Army	18	21
O16	●	Pennsylvania	26	6
O23		Brown	6	7
O30		at Cornell	0	14
N6		at Navy	6	13
N13	=	Syracuse	6	6
N20		Dartmouth	0	27
N27	=	Stanford	0	0

1938 3-6-0

O1	●	at Yale	27	14
O8	●	at Army	20	18
O15		Colgate	0	12
O22		at Pennsylvania	13	14
O29		Cornell	7	23
N5	●	Virginia	39	0
N12		Navy	9	14
N19		Syracuse	12	13
N26		at Brown	27	36

1939 2-4-2

O7		at Yale	7	10
O14	=	Army	6	6
O21		Princeton	7	14
O28	●	VMI	26	7
N4		at Cornell	7	13
N11	●	at Navy	19	13
N18		Tulane	0	25
N25	=	Colgate	0	0

1940 5-2-2

O5	●	Maine	15	0
O12	●	at Dartmouth	20	6
O19	●	Georgia	19	13
O26		Syracuse	0	3
N2		at Cornell	0	27
N9	●	Wisconsin	7	6
N16	=	Navy	0	0
N23	●	Colgate	20	17
N30	=	at Brown	0	0

1941 3-5-0

O4	●	Brown	13	6
O11	●	at Princeton	21	0
O18		Georgia	3	7
O25		at Army	0	13
N1	●	Cornell	7	0
N8		at Pennsylvania	16	19
N15		Michigan	0	28
N22		Colgate	21	30

1942 3-6-0

S26	●	Fort Monmouth	39	0
O3	●	Maine	34	2
O10		Brown	21	28
O17		Army	6	34
O24		at Pennsylvania	12	42
O31	●	Cornell	14	13
N7		Colgate	26	35
N14		Navy BALT	9	13
N21		Dartmouth	13	26

1943 0-8-0

O2		Princeton	7	26
O9		Yale	7	20
O16		Army	0	52
O23		Pennsylvania	0	33
O30		at Cornell	6	3
N6		at Dartmouth	13	47
N13		Navy	0	61
N20		Colgate	0	41

1944 2-6-0

S30	●	Union	21	0
O7	●	Syracuse	26	2
O14		at Yale	10	27
O28		Colgate	0	6
N4		Cornell	7	25
N11		at Pennsylvania	7	35
N18		Brown	0	12
N25		Dartmouth	0	18

1945 8-1-0

S29	●	Lafayette	40	14
O6	●	Syracuse	32	0
O13	●	Yale	27	13
O20	●	Colgate	31	7
O27	●	Brown	27	6
N3	●	Cornell	34	26
N10		at Pennsylvania	7	32
N17	●	at Princeton	32	7
N24	●	Dartmouth	21	0

1946 6-3-0

S28	●	Rutgers	13	7
O5	●	Navy	23	14
O12	●	at Yale	28	20
O19		at Army	14	48
O26	●	at Dartmouth	33	13
N2		Cornell	0	12
N9		Pennsylvania	6	41
N16	●	Lafayette	46	0
N23	●	Syracuse	59	21

1947 7-2-0

S27	●	Rutgers	40	28
O4	●	at Navy	13	6
O11		Yale	7	17
O18		at Pennsylvania	14	34
O25	●	Army	21	20
N1	●	at Cornell	22	0
N8	●	Dartmouth	15	0
N15	●	Holy Cross	10	0
N22	●	Syracuse	28	8

1948 4-5-0

S25	●	Rutgers	27	6
O2		at Harvard	24	33
O9	●	at Yale	34	28
O16		Pennsylvania	14	20
O23		Princeton	14	16
O30		Cornell	13	20
N6		at Dartmouth	21	26
N13	●	Navy	13	0
N20	●	Syracuse	34	28

1949 2-7-0

S24	●	Amherst	27	7
O1	●	Harvard	14	7
O8		Yale	7	33
O15		at Pennsylvania	7	27
O22		at Army	6	63
O29		at Cornell	0	54
N5		Dartmouth	14	35
N12		at Navy	0	34
N19		Brown	7	16

1950 4-5-0

S30	●	Hobart	42	12
O7	●	at Harvard	28	7
O14		at Yale	14	20
O21		Pennsylvania	0	34
O28		Army	0	34
N4	●	Cornell	20	19
N11		at Dartmouth	7	14
N18		Navy	7	29
N25	●	at Brown	33	0

1951 5-3-0

O6	●	Harvard	35	0
O13	●	Yale	14	0
O20		at Pennsylvania	13	28
O27		at Army	9	14
N3	●	at Cornell	21	20
N10	●	Dartmouth	21	6
N17		Navy	7	21
N24	●	Brown	29	14

1952 2-6-1

S27		Princeton	0	14
O4	●	at Harvard	16	7
O11		at Yale	28	35
O18		Pennsylvania	17	27
O25	=	Army	14	14
N1		Cornell	14	21
N8		at Dartmouth	14	38
N15		at Navy	0	28
N22	●	Brown	14	0

1953 4-5-0

S26	●	Lehigh	14	7
O3		at Princeton	19	20
O10		at Yale	7	13
O17	●	Harvard	6	0
O24		at Army	7	40
O31		at Cornell	13	27
N7	●	Dartmouth	25	19
N14		Navy	6	14
N21	●	Rutgers	27	13

1954 1-8-0

S25		Brown	7	18
O2		Princeton	20	54
O9		Yale	7	13
O16	●	at Harvard	7	6
O23		Army	12	67
O30		Cornell	0	26
N6		at Dartmouth	0	26
N13		at Navy	6	51
N20		Rutgers	12	45

1955 1-8-0

S24	●	Brown	14	12
O1		at Princeton	7	20
O8		at Yale	14	46
O15		Harvard	7	21
O22		at Army	0	45
O29		at Cornell	19	34
N5		Dartmouth	7	14
N12		Navy	0	47
N19		Rutgers	6	12

1956-PRESENT
IVY LEAGUE

1956 3-6-0 (2-5-0)

S29		ǀ	Brown	0	20
O6		ǀ	at Princeton	0	39
O13		ǀ	Yale	19	33
O20	●	ǀ	Harvard	26	20
O27			Army	0	60
N3	●	ǀ	Cornell	25	19
N10		ǀ	at Dartmouth	0	14
N17		ǀ	at Pennsylvania	6	20
N24	●		at Rutgers	18	12

THE SCHOOLS

THE SCHOOLS

ALDO T. DONELLI 1957-67 (.313) 30-67-2

1957 — 1-8-0 (1-6-0)
S28	•	at Brown	23	20
O5		Princeton	6	47
O12		at Yale	0	19
O19		at Harvard	6	19
O26		Lehigh	6	40
N2		at Cornell	0	8
N9		Dartmouth	0	7
N16		Pennsylvania	6	28
N23		Rutgers	7	26

1958 — 1-8-0 (1-6-0)
S27		Brown	0	22
O4		at Princeton	8	43
O11	•	Yale	13	0
O18		Harvard	0	26
O25		at Buffalo	14	34
N1		Cornell	0	25
N8		at Dartmouth	0	38
N15		at Pennsylvania	0	42
N22		at Rutgers	0	61

1959 — 2-7-0 (1-6-0)
S26	•	at Brown	21	6
O3		Princeton	0	22
O10		at Yale	0	14
O17		at Harvard	22	38
O24		Holy Cross	0	34
O31		at Cornell	7	13
N7		Dartmouth	0	22
N14		Pennsylvania	6	24
N21		Rutgers	26	16

1960 — 3-6-0 (3-4-0)
S24	•	Brown	37	0
O1		at Princeton	0	49
O8		at Yale	8	30
O15		Harvard	7	8
O22		Holy Cross	6	27
O29	•	Cornell	44	6
N5		at Dartmouth	6	22
N12	•	at Pennsylvania	16	6
N19		Rutgers	2	43

1961 — 6-3-0 (6-1-0)
S30	•	at Brown	50	0
O7		Princeton	20	30
O14	•	at Yale	11	0
O21		at Harvard	26	14
O28		Lehigh	7	14
N4	•	at Cornell	35	7
N11		Dartmouth	35	14
N18	•	Pennsylvania	37	6
N25		at Rutgers	19	32

1962 — 5-4-0 (4-3-0)
S29	•	Brown	22	20
O6		at Princeton	0	33
O13	•	Yale	14	10
O20		Harvard	14	36
O27	•	Lehigh	22	15
N3	•	Cornell	25	21
N10		at Dartmouth	0	42
N17	•	at Pennsylvania	21	7
N24		Rutgers	6	22

1963 — 4-4-1 (2-4-1)
S28	•	at Brown	41	14
O5		Princeton	6	7
O12		at Yale	7	19
O19	=	at Harvard	3	3
O26	•	Lehigh	42	21
N2		at Cornell	17	18
N9		Dartmouth	6	47
N16	•	Pennsylvania	33	8
N23		at Rutgers	35	28

1964 — 2-6-1 (1-5-1)
S26	•	Colgate	21	14
O3		at Princeton	13	23
O10		Harvard	0	3
O17	=	at Yale	9	9
O24		Rutgers	35	38
O31		Cornell	20	57
N7		at Dartmouth	14	31
N14	•	Pennsylvania	33	12
N21		at Brown	0	7

1965 — 2-7-0 (1-6-0)
S25		Lafayette	10	14
O2		Princeton	0	31
O9		at Harvard	6	21
O16	•	Yale	21	7
O23	•	at Rutgers	12	7
O30		at Cornell	6	20
N6		Dartmouth	0	47
N13		at Pennsylvania	21	31
N20		Brown	7	51

1966 — 2-7-0 (2-5-0)
S24		Colgate	0	38
O1		at Princeton	12	14
O8		Harvard	7	34
O15		at Yale	21	44
O22		at Rutgers	34	37
O29		Cornell	6	31
N5		at Dartmouth	14	56
N12	•	Pennsylvania	22	14
N19	•	Brown	40	38

1967 — 2-7-0 (0-7-0)
S30	•	Colgate	17	14
O7		Princeton	14	28
O14		at Harvard	13	49
O21		Yale	7	21
O28	•	Rutgers	24	13
N4		at Cornell	14	27
N11		Dartmouth	7	13
N18		at Pennsylvania	6	26
N25		at Brown	7	14

FRANK NAVARRO 1968-73 (.315) 16-36-2

1968 — 2-7-0 (2-5-0)
S28		Lafayette	14	36
O5		at Princeton	16	44
O12		Harvard	14	21
O19		at Yale	7	29
O26		Rutgers	17	28
N2	•	Cornell	34	25
N9		at Dartmouth	19	31
N16		at Pennsylvania	7	13
N23	•	Brown	46	20

1969 — 1-8-0 (1-6-0)
S27		Lafayette	22	36
O4		Princeton	7	21
O11		at Harvard	0	51
O18		Yale	6	41
O25		at Rutgers	14	21
N1		at Cornell	3	10
N8		Dartmouth	7	37
N15		Pennsylvania	7	17
N22	•	at Brown	18	3

1970 — 3-6-0 (1-6-0)
S26	•	Lafayette	23	9
O3		at Princeton	22	24
O10	•	Harvard	28	21
O17		at Yale	15	32
O24	•	Rutgers	30	14
O31		Cornell	20	31
N7		at Dartmouth	0	55
N14		at Pennsylvania	14	21
N21		Brown	12	17

1971 — 6-3-0 (5-2-0)
S25		at Lafayette	0	3
O2	•	Princeton	22	20
O9		at Harvard	19	21
O16	•	Yale	15	14
O23	•	at Rutgers	17	16
O30		at Cornell	21	24
N6	•	Dartmouth	31	29
N13	•	Pennsylvania	17	3
N20	•	at Brown	24	6

1972 — 3-5-1 (2-4-1)
S30	•	at Fordham	44	0
O7	=	at Princeton	0	0
O14		Harvard	18	20
O21		at Yale	14	28
O28		Rutgers	3	6
N4	•	Cornell	14	0
N11		at Dartmouth	8	38
N18		at Pennsylvania	14	20
N25	•	Brown	28	12

1973 — 1-7-1 (1-6-0)
S29	=	Bucknell	0	0
O6		Princeton	14	13
O13		at Harvard	0	57
O20		Yale	0	29
O27		at Rutgers	2	28
N3		at Cornell	14	44
N10		Dartmouth	6	24
N17		Pennsylvania	8	42
N24		at Brown	14	37

WILLIAM V. CAMPBELL 1974-79 (.231) 12-41-1

1974 — 1-8-0 (0-7-0)
S28		Lafayette	0	15
O5		at Princeton	13	40
O12		Harvard	6	34
O19		at Yale	2	42
O26	•	Bucknell	38	33
N2		Cornell	0	24
N9		at Dartmouth	0	21
N16		at Pennsylvania	3	21
N23		Brown	19	28

1975 — 2-7-0 (2-5-0)
S27		at Lafayette	7	10
O4		Princeton	7	27
O11		at Harvard	30	35
O18		Yale	7	34
O25		at Rutgers	0	41
N1	•	at Cornell	42	19
N8		Dartmouth	17	22
N15	•	Pennsylvania	28	25
N22		at Brown	13	48

1976 — 3-6-0 (2-5-0)
S18		at Harvard	10	34
S25	•	Lafayette	38	31
O2	•	at Pennsylvania	14	10
O9		Princeton	6	9
O16		at Yale	6	37
O23		Rutgers ERut	0	47
O30		at Dartmouth	14	34
N6	•	Cornell	35	17
N13		Brown	17	28

1977 — 2-7-0 (1-6-0)
S17		Harvard	7	21
S24	•	Lafayette	21	10
O1	•	Pennsylvania	30	18
O8		at Princeton	7	28
O15		Yale	20	42
O22		Colgate	36	48
O29		Dartmouth	7	14
N5		at Cornell	7	20
N12		at Brown	14	21

1978 — 3-5-1 (2-4-1)
S23	•	at Harvard	21	19
S30	•	Lafayette	21	0
O7		at Pennsylvania	19	31
O14		at Princeton	14	10
O21	=	at Yale	3	3
O28		Rutgers ERut	0	69
N4		at Dartmouth	7	37
N11		Cornell	14	35
N18		Brown	12	24

1979 — 1-8-0 (1-6-0)
S22		Harvard	7	26
S29		at Lafayette	7	14
O6	•	Pennsylvania	12	7
O13		at Princeton	7	35
O20		Yale	7	37
O27		Colgate	14	24
N3		Dartmouth	0	17
N10		at Cornell	7	24
N17		at Brown	14	31

ROBERT J. NASO 1980-84 (.102) 4-43-2

1980 — 1-9-0 (0-7-0)
S20		at Harvard	6	26
S27	•	Lafayette	6	0
O4		at Pennsylvania	13	24
O11		Princeton	19	31
O18		at Yale	10	30
O25		at Colgate	22	35
N1		Holy Cross	0	26
N8		at Dartmouth	0	48
N15		Cornell	0	24
N22		Brown	13	31

1981 — 1-9-0 (1-6-0)
S19		Harvard	6	23
S26		Lafayette	13	28
O3	•	Pennsylvania	20	9
O10		at Princeton	14	21
O17		Yale	17	48
O24		Colgate	3	41
O31		at Holy Cross	7	14
N7		Dartmouth	7	21
N14		at Cornell	9	15
N21		at Brown	20	23

1982 — 1-9-0 (1-6-0)
S18		Harvard	16	27
S25		Lafayette	23	53
O2		Pennsylvania	31	51
O9	•	Princeton	35	14
O16		Yale	10	36
O23		Bucknell	25	42
O30		Army	8	41
N6		Dartmouth	41	56
N13		Cornell	26	35
N20		Brown	21	35

1983 — 1-7-2 (1-5-1)
S17		Harvard	14	43
S24		Lafayette	29	34
O1		Pennsylvania	10	35
O8		Princeton	26	35
O15	•	Yale	21	18
O22	=	Bucknell	31	31
O29		Holy Cross	28	77
N5	=	Dartmouth	17	17
N12		Cornell	6	31
N19		Brown	36	42

1984 — 0-9-0 (0-7-0)
S22		Harvard	21	35
S29		Lafayette	14	23
O6		Pennsylvania	7	35
O13		Princeton	8	38
O20		Yale	21	28
O27		Colgate	16	35
N3		Dartmouth	9	41
N10		Cornell	7	19
N17		Brown	14	28

JAMES W. GARRETT 1985 (.000) 0-10

1985 — 0-10-0 (0-7-0)
S21		Harvard	17	49
S28		Lafayette	0	20
O5		Pennsylvania	14	46
O12		Princeton	0	31
O19		Yale	12	28
O26		Bucknell	10	13
N2		Colgate	11	55
N9		Dartmouth	3	34
N16		Cornell	8	21
N23		Brown	0	34

LARRY McELREAVY 1986-88 (.067) 2-28

1986 — 0-10-0 (0-7-0)
S20		Harvard	0	34
S27		Lafayette	21	26
O4		Pennsylvania	7	42
O1		Princeton	14	20
O18		Yale	0	47
O25		Colgate	8	54
N1		Villanova	34	42
N8		Dartmouth	0	41
N15		Cornell	0	28
N22		Brown	7	45

1987 — 0-10-0 (0-7-0)
S19		Harvard	0	35
S26		Lafayette	7	38
O3		Pennsylvania	0	23
O10		Princeton	8	38
O17		Yale	13	27
O24		Bucknell	20	62
O31		Lehigh	10	26
N7		Dartmouth	10	12
N14		Cornell	20	31
N21		Brown	16	19

1988 — 2-8-0 (2-5-0)
S17		Harvard	7	41
S24		Lafayette	3	49
O1		Pennsylvania	10	24
O8	•	Princeton	16	13
O15		Yale	10	24
O22		Bucknell	7	21
O29		Lehigh	27	56
N5		Dartmouth	10	20
N12		Cornell	19	42
N19	•	Brown	31	13

RAY TELLIER		
1989-2002 (.307)		41-97-2

1989
1-9-0 (1-6-0)

S16		Harvard	10	26
S23		at Villanova	0	38
S30		at Lafayette	14	52
O7		Pennsylvania	21	24
O14		at Princeton	8	24
O21		Yale	0	23
O28		Bucknell	12	27
N4		Dartmouth	12	13
N11	●	at Cornell	25	19
N18		at Brown	28	41

1990
1-9-0 (1-6-0)

S15		Harvard	6	9
S22		at Bucknell	16	41
S29		at Lehigh	9	42
O6		Lafayette	34	41
O13		at Pennsylvania	6	21
O20		at Yale	7	31
O27	●	Princeton	7	15
N3		at Dartmouth	20	34
N10		Cornell	0	41
N17		Brown	0	17

1991
1-9-0 (1-6-0)

S21		at Harvard	16	21
S28		Lehigh	9	22
O5		Fordham	16	20
O12	●	Pennsylvania	20	14
O19		at Lafayette	15	30
O26		Yale	9	36
N2		at Princeton	6	22
N9		Dartmouth	19	28
N16		at Cornell	21	28
N23		at Brown	23	28

1992
3-7-0 (2-5-0)

S19		Harvard	20	27
S26	●	at Fordham	18	9
O3		Colgate	29	34
O10		Bucknell	22	29
O17		at Pennsylvania	21	34
O24		at Yale	0	23
O31		Princeton	7	34
N7		at Dartmouth	19	38
N14	●	Cornell	35	30
N21	●	Brown	34	28

1993
2-8-0 (1-6-0)

S18		at Harvard	3	30
S25	●	Fordham	7	0
O2		at Colgate	24	27
O9		Lafayette	6	58
O16		Pennsylvania	7	36
O23		Yale	28	35
O30		at Princeton	3	14
N6		Dartmouth	25	42
N13	●	at Cornell	29	24
N20		at Brown	23	28

1994
5-4-1 (3-4-0)

S17		Harvard	32	39
S24	=	at Lehigh	28	28
O1	●	Lafayette	28	13
O8	●	at Fordham	24	13
O15		at Pennsylvania	3	12
O22	●	at Yale	30	9
O29	●	Princeton	17	10
N5		at Dartmouth	13	14
N12	●	Cornell	38	33
N19		Brown	27	59

1995
3-6-1 (3-4-0)

S16	●	at Harvard	28	24
S23		St. Mary's-Cal	14	34
S30	=	at Lafayette	10	10
O7	●	Pennsylvania	24	14
O14		Lehigh	35	37
O21	●	Yale	21	7
O28		at Princeton	14	44
N4		Dartmouth	27	43
N11		at Cornell	14	35
N18		at Brown	14	33

1996
8-2 (5-2)

S21	●	Harvard	20	13
S28	●	at Fordham	17	10
O5	●	at Holy Cross	42	16
O12	●	at Pennsylvania	20	19
O19	●	Lafayette	3	0
O26	●	at Yale	13	10
N2		Princeton	11	14
N9		at Dartmouth	0	40
N16	●	Cornell	24	10
N23	●	Brown	31	27

1997
3-7 (2-5)

S20		at Harvard	7	45
S27	●	Towson	16	6
O4		at Lafayette	3	31
O11		Holy Cross	16	45
O18		Pennsylvania	7	24	†
O25	●	Yale	21	10
N1	●	Princeton	17	0
N8		Dartmouth	21	23
N15		at Cornell	22	33
N22		at Brown	11	42

1998
4-6 (3-4)

S19	●	Harvard	24	0
S26		at Bucknell	20	27
O3	●	at St. Mary's-Cal	20	17
O10		Lehigh	19	20
O17		at Pennsylvania	0	20
O24		at Yale	14	37
O31		Princeton	0	20
N7	●	at Dartmouth	24	14
N14	●	Cornell	22	10
N21		Brown	3	10

1999
3-7 (1-6)

S18		at Harvard	7	24
S25	●	Towson	28	13
O2		at Lehigh	13	63
O9	●	Bucknell	10	7
O16		Pennsylvania	17	41
O23		Yale	29	41
O30		at Princeton	15	44
N6	●	Dartmouth	21	14
N13		at Cornell	29	31
N20		at Brown	6	23

2000
3-7 (1-6)

S16	●	Fordham	43	26
S23		at Bucknell	10	12
S30		Princeton	24	27
O7	●	Lafayette	47	22
O14		at Pennsylvania	25	43
O21	●	Dartmouth	49	21
O28		at Yale	0	41
N4		at Harvard	0	34
N11		Cornell	31	35
N18		at Brown	27	45

2001
3-7 (3-4)

S22		Bucknell	20	23
S29		at Princeton	11	44
O6		at Lafayette	14	31
O13		Pennsylvania	7	35
O20	●	at Dartmouth	27	20
O27	●	Yale	28	14
N3		at Harvard	33	45
N10	●	at Cornell	35	28
N17		Brown	21	45
N24		at Fordham	10	41

2002
1-9 (0-7)

S21	●	Fordham	13	11
S28		at Colgate	6	38
O5		Princeton	32	35
O12		Lafayette	21	28
O19		at Pennsylvania	10	44
O26		Dartmouth	23	24
N2		at Yale	7	35
N9		at Harvard	7	28
N16		Cornell	14	17
N23		at Brown	28	35

BOB SHOOP		
2003-Present (.250)		5-15

2003
4-6 (3-4)

S20		Fordham	30	37
S27	●	Bucknell	19	16
O4	●	at Princeton	33	27
O11		at Lafayette	27	41
O18		Pennsylvania	7	31
O25		at Dartmouth	21	26
N1		Yale	14	29
N8	●	Harvard	16	13
N15	●	at Cornell	34	21
N22		Brown	10	42

2004
1-9 (1-6)

S18		Fordham	14	17
S25		at Bucknell	13	42
O2		Princeton	26	27
O9		Lafayette	14	35
O16		at Pennsylvania	3	14
O23	●	Dartmouth	9	6
O30		at Yale	14	21
N6		at Harvard	0	38
N13		Cornell	26	32
N20		at Brown	21	33

CORNELL

BY BRUCE WOOD

To BE IN ITHACA, N.Y., ON GAME DAY is to be taken to another era. The Cornell football players finish their pregame meal and meet up with the Big Red marching band for a traditional musical escort to Schoellkopf Field. Fans break from their tailgating and assemble along the route. As the sea of red nears the stadium, the band strikes up "Give My Regards to Davy" in mock honor of David Fletcher Hoy, the school's disciplinarian during the early 1900s, the scourge of every undergrad looking for good fun. And now it is time to play. The days when Ivy League football commanded the nation's center stage may be long gone, but on these Saturday afternoons in the air far above Cayuga's waters, the echoes of its great past—in custom, in song and in spirit—most definitely live on.

TRADITION Immediately after the last play of Cornell's home opener, the entire freshman class takes to the field to join the team on the gridiron. Three years later, the same students, now seniors, reunite on Schoellkopf Field after the final home game, celebrating their memories of Ithaca with the football team.

BEST PLAYER The 1971 Heisman Trophy narrowly eluded running back Ed Marinaro, who found fame as the leading rusher in college football history well before TV audiences came to know him as Officer Joe Coffey on *Hill Street Blues*. With his relentless running style, Marinaro won the triple crown in his senior year, leading the nation in rushing, all-purpose yards and scoring.

BEST COACH Glenn Scobey "Pop" Warner, a Cornell alum, had a solid 36–13–3 record in his two short stints on the Cornell sideline. But the winningest coach in school history? "Gloomy" Gil Dobie. A Scotsman who had not lost a single game in nine seasons with the Washington Huskies (58–0–3), Dobie came to Cornell with college football's first long-term contract and produced three undefeated teams and two unofficial national championships. Between 1920 and 1935, Dobie's teams went 82–36 with seven ties. As the school's admissions requirements became more ambitious in 1934, Dobie suffered his first losing season. The following year, his team went without a win. Dobie, who once barked, "You can't win games with Phi Beta Kappas," left.

BEST TEAM What could have been. Under the leadership of Carl "The Gray Fox" Snavely, Cornell went 8–0 in 1939,

---

beating Ohio State, Syracuse and Penn State to win the Lambert Trophy as the best team in the East. They were ranked fourth in the nation and were poised for a Rose Bowl berth against Southern California. After clobbering Penn 26-0, the Big Red looked unstoppable. Sadly, they were stopped; Cornell's president, Edmund Ezra Day, felt it was time for the players to concentrate on their studies, and the team never made the trip out West.

> *The 1971 Heisman Trophy narrowly eluded Ed Marinaro, who graduated as the leading rusher in college history.*

BIGGEST GAME Cornell and Harvard squared off in a 1915 showdown of two undefeated teams. What's more, Harvard was riding a 33-game winning streak. But Cornell's defense met their task, shutting down the Crimson offense as senior Charley Barrett scored the day's only touchdown to lead Cornell to a stunning 10-0 victory. The Big Red finished the year with a 9–0 record and a national championship.

BIGGEST UPSET Nationally ranked Ohio State took the opening kickoff in a 1939 game in Columbus and cut the Cornell defense into stripes with an 86-yard touchdown drive that consisted of 19 straight rushing plays. The Buckeyes held the Big Red with ease and then marched 72 yards down the field on their next possession for another TD: 14-0. Then, somehow, Cornell's Walt "Pop" Scholl burst off tackle for a 79-yard touchdown run; next, it was Scholl hitting "Swifty" Bohrman downfield for another touchdown. Cornell's defense dug in. Hal McCullough added a third score, and Nick Drahos tacked on a 28-yard field goal for good measure as the Big Red miraculously came from behind to post a 23-14 victory over the previously unbeaten Buckeyes.

WILDEST FINISH On Nov. 16, 1940, second-ranked Cornell's 18-game unbeaten streak appeared to be over when, on fourth down, Dartmouth batted away a last-chance pass into the end zone with only seconds left to play. Referee Red Friesell spotted the ball and indicated that the incomplete pass had actually occurred on third down. Despite protests from the Dartmouth bench, Friesell stuck to his guns and granted the Big Red one

RECORDS

RUSHING YARDS

	GAME	
288	Scott Oliaro vs. Yale, Nov. 3, 1990 (35 att.)	
	SEASON	
1,881	Ed Marinaro, 1971 (356 att.)	
	CAREER	
4,715	Ed Marinaro, 1969-71 (918 att.)	

PASSING YARDS

	GAME	
446	Ricky Rahne vs. Brown, Oct. 21, 2000 (29 of 62)	
	SEASON	
2,944	Ricky Rahne, 2000 (252 of 479)	
	CAREER	
7,710	Ricky Rahne, 1998-2001 (678 of 1,226)	

RECEIVING YARDS

	GAME	
204	Joe Splendorio vs. Brown, Oct. 2, 1999 (11 rec.)	
	SEASON	
1,042	Eric Krawczyk, 1997 (89 rec.)	
	CAREER	
2,569	Keith Ferguson, 1999-2002 (202 rec.)	

POINTS

	GAME	
32	Ed Marinaro vs. Pennsylvania, Nov. 20, 1971 (5 TDs, 1 two-pt. conv.)	
	SEASON	
148	Ed Marinaro, 1971 (24 TDs, 2 two-pt. conv.)	
	CAREER	
318	Ed Marinaro, 1969-71 (52 TDs, 3 two-pt. conv.)	

CONSENSUS ALL-AMERICANS

1895	Clinton Wyckoff, B
1900	Raymond Starbuck, B
1901-02	William Warner, G
1901	Sanford Hunt, G
1906	Elmer Thompson, G
1906	William Newman, C
1908	Bernard O'Rourke, G
1914	John O'Hearn, E
1914-15	Charles Barrett, B
1915	Murray Shelton, E
1921-22	Edgar Kaw, B
1923	George Pfann, B
1938	Brud Holland, E
1939-40	Nick Drahos, T
1971	Ed Marinaro, RB
1982	Dan Suren, TE
1986	Tom McHale, DE
1993	Chris Zingo, LB
1996	Chad Levitt, RB

final snap. This time, Walter Scholl connected with Bill Murphy for a touchdown and an apparent 7-3 Cornell win. Two days later, Dartmouth captain Lou Young received a telegram from Friesell: "I want to be the first to admit my very grave error on the extra down." After reviewing the game film, Cornell officials wired Hanover to concede defeat, 3-0, in what will forever be known in Ithaca as the Fifth Down Game.

STADIUM Financed largely by the family of a former Cornell player and coach, Schoellkopf Field opened in 1915 and is set on the highest tract of land on campus. The stands to the east were replaced by the famous crescent-shaped structure in 1924, expanding seating from 9,000 to 21,500. Permanent steel stands were erected on the west side in 1947, and artificial turf was installed in 1971. A state-of-the-art press box, complete with an elevator, was built in 1986. In 2004, Cornell began work on an $8 million project to construct a Hall of Fame room and a Traditions room in a building next to the stadium.

RIVAL From 1895 to 1963, Cornell closed every season with a game against Penn, always in Philadelphia and often on Thanksgiving. Although the Big Red faced the Quakers in the final game in roughly half the following 23 seasons, the Cornell-Penn finale wasn't restored as a tradition until the Ivy League reworked the schedule for 1988. That year, an already heated rivalry only intensified when previously unbeaten Penn ceded a share of the Ivy crown to Cornell with a 19-6 loss in a game that featured nine personal fouls.

ALL-TIME TEAM

Chosen in 2003 by representatives of the Cornell Football Association.

OFFENSE

1938-40	Nick Drahos	OT
1946	Frank Wydo	OT
1899-1902	William Warner	OG
1936-38	Sid Roth	OG
1989-90	Chris Field	OG
1992-95	Greg Bloedorn	OC
1936-38	Brud Holland	TE
1995-97	Eric Krawczyk	WR
1998-2000	Joe Splendorio	WR
1961-63	Gary Wood	QB
1969-71	Ed Marinaro	RB
1981-83	Derrick Harmon	RB
1993-96	Chad Levitt	RB
1948-50	Jeff Fleischmann	FB
1986-88	Scott Malaga	FB
1961-63	Pete Gogolak	PK
1955-57	Bo Roberson	RET
1964-66	Pete Larson	RET

DEFENSE

1912-14	John O'Hearn	DE
1986	Tom McHale	DE
1994-96	Seth Payne	DE
1963-65	Phil Ratner	DL
1966-68	John Sponheimer	DL
1971-73	Mike Phillips	DL
1938-40	Walt Matuszczak	LB
1971-73	Bob Lally	LB
1987-89	Mitch Lee	LB
1991-93	Chris Zingo	LB
1920-22	Eddie Kaw	DB
1921-23	George Pfann	DB
1945-49	Hillary Chollet	DB
1985-87	Mike Raich	DB
1946-48	Bob Dean	P
1984-86	Erik Bernstein	P

NICKNAME Working up some lyrics for a new football song in 1905, Cornell alum Romeyn Berry found himself at a loss—the team had no nickname. Berry simply glossed in a reference to the Big Red Team, and with that the nickname was born.

MASCOT Touchdown, a Maine-bred bear, once had to be coaxed down from the goalposts. And then things got worse; in Detroit for a game against Michigan, Touchdown got loose and ran rampant through the Tuller Hotel. Cornell would go through three other live bears before the school finally settled on a student in costume.

UNIFORMS Cornell's uniforms have ranged from maroon to scarlet to the current bright red. Why the changes? In 1869, a student publication suggested the official color should be "the bright red of the carnelian," and the school agreed. It might not have been a problem had the students realized that carnelian, a semiprecious stone, varies from bright orange to dark reddish-brown.

LORE Herberton L. Williams, comptroller and general manager of the Campbell Soup Company, attended an 1898 game and was so impressed by Cornell's distinctive uniforms that he insisted the company use the same color scheme on its cans. The following year, Campbell's came out with its red-and-white labels, which it has used ever since.

QUOTE "I refuse to allow 40 men to go 400 miles merely to agitate a bag of wind."—Cornell president Andrew Dickson White, nixing an 1873 trip to Cleveland to play the University of Michigan

CORNELL ANNUAL STATISTICAL LEADERS

YR	RUSHING	YDS	ATT	AVG	PASSING	ATT	CMP	PCT	YDS	RECEIVING	REC	YDS	AVG
1946	Walt Kretz	594	88	6.8	John Burns	99	48	.48	593	Hillary Chollet	12	305	25.4
1947	Norm Dawson	293	66	4.4	Pete Dorset	77	39	.51	568	Bernie Babula	12	301	25.1
1948	Frank Miller	598	98	6.1	Pete Dorset	74	28	.38	437	Hillary Chollet	8	106	13.3
1949	Jeff Fleischmann	579	106	5.5	Pete Dorset	111	55	.50	845	Walt Bruska	14	289	20.6
1950	Jeff Fleischmann	538	146	3.7	Rocco Calvo	94	51	.54	730	Vic Pujo	24	420	17.5
1951	Stu Metz	431	77	5.6	Rocco Calvo	77	38	.49	675	Dick Cliggott	14	291	20.8
1952	Bob Engel	364	106	3.4	John Jaeckel	96	33	.34	453	Dick Cliggott	25	372	14.9
1953	Guy Bedrossian	336	111	3.0	Bill DeGraaf	85	28	.33	351	Bruce Brenner	14	226	16.1
1954	Dick Jackson	445	76	5.9	Bill DeGraaf	94	31	.33	433	Dick Jackson	17	196	11.5
1955	Irv Roberson	503	83	6.1	Bill DeGraaf	97	44	.45	629	Stan Intihar	12	145	12.1
1956	Irv Roberson	480	106	4.5	Art Boland	107	43	.40	572	Bob McAniff	15	206	13.7
1957	Bob McAniff	700	140	5.0	Tom Brogan	50	23	.46	387	John Webster	12	180	15.0
1958	Terry Wilson	521	121	4.3	Tom Skypock	121	55	.45	784	Nick Iuvonen	16	301	18.8
1959	Dan Bidwell	474	109	4.3	Dave McKelvey	67	23	.34	245	John Sandusky	8	116	14.5
1960	Pat Pennucci	285	77	3.7	Scott Brown	85	34	.40	519	Pat Pennucci	16	222	13.9
1961	Gary Wood	449	94	4.8	Gary Wood	75	28	.37	456	Ken Hoffman	10	159	15.9
1962	Gary Wood	889	173	5.1	Gary Wood	117	60	.51	890	Ed Burnap	17	260	15.3
1963	Gary Wood	818	166	4.9	Gary Wood	119	48	.40	545	Bill Ponzer	13	162	12.5
1964	Bill Wilson	659	189	3.5	Marty Sponaugle	55	23	.42	319	Pete Larson	13	191	14.7
1965	Bill Wilson	848	181	4.7	Marty Sponaugle	115	45	.39	582	Ron Gervase	19	248	13.1
1966	Pete Larson	979	206	4.8	Bill Abel	138	64	.46	953	Ron Gervase	36	559	15.5
1967	Bill Huling	369	88	4.2	Bill Robertson	175	94	.54	1,347	Bill Murphy	50	853	17.1
1968	Chris Ritter	341	87	3.9	Bill Robertson	197	81	.41	1,156	Chris Ritter	30	507	16.9
1969	Ed Marinaro	1,409	277	5.1	Rick Furbush	37	23	.62	294	Erv Bratcher	8	113	14.1
1970	Ed Marinaro	1,425	285	5.0	Rick Furbush	104	57	.55	876	Tom Albright	21	300	14.3
1971	Ed Marinaro	1,881	356	5.3	Mark Allen	90	39	.43	496	Tom Albright	21	274	13.0
1972	Dan Malone	913	196	4.7	Mark Allen	181	91	.50	1,235	George Milosevic	37	564	15.2
1973	Don Fanelli	403	99	4.1	Mark Allen	272	119	.44	1,590	Bruce Starks	31	483	15.6
1974	Dan Malone	532	139	3.8	Kevin Sigler	248	143	.58	1,648	Bruce Starks	47	619	13.2
1975	Tim LaBeau	482	106	4.5	Garland Burns	81	21	.26	285	Bruce Starks	14	185	13.2
1976	Neal Hall	330	91	3.6	Jim Hofher	139	63	.45	740	Eamon McEneaney	35	383	10.9
1977	Craig Jaeger	440	103	4.3	Jim Hofher	118	60	.51	745	Dave Rupert	26	423	16.3
1978	Joe Holland	1,396	273	5.1	Jim Hofher	85	44	.52	487	Brad Decker	17	200	11.8
1979	Tom Weidenkopf	571	118	4.8	Mike Tanner	73	41	.56	595	Mark Turley	26	381	14.7
1980	Steve Vago	513	114	4.5	Mike Ryan	109	53	.49	786	Alva Taylor	13	199	15.3
1981	Derrick Harmon	893	173	5.2	Chris Metz	77	33	.43	507	Derrick Harmon	21	285	13.6
1982	Derrick Harmon	905	157	5.8	Jeff Hammond	176	89	.51	1,064	Dan Suren	26	287	11.0
1983	Derrick Harmon	1,276	216	5.9	Shawn Maguire	205	110	.54	1,009	Derrick Harmon	36	270	7.5
1984	Tony Baker	847	165	5.1	Shawn Maguire	221	119	.54	1,112	John Tagliaferri	30	266	8.9
1985	John Tagliaferri	583	153	3.8	Marty Stallone	138	76	.55	817	John Tagliaferri	61	358	5.9
1986	Jeff Johnson	902	191	4.7	Marty Stallone	226	110	.49	1,446	Jeff Johnson	29	246	8.5
1987	Scott Magala	647	168	3.9	Dave Dase	198	100	.51	1,302	Sam Brickley	56	518	9.3
1988	Scott Magala	1,097	256	4.3	Aaron Sumida	141	69	.49	1,132	Sam Brickley	29	533	18.4
1989	John McNiff	753	160	4.7	Chris Cochrane	236	115	.49	1,322	Scott Oliaro	30	230	7.7
1990	John McNiff	998	176	5.7	Chris Cochrane	175	107	.61	1,266	Scott Oliaro	25	347	13.9
1991	John McNiff	806	203	4.0	Bill Lazor	217	129	.59	1,461	Mike Jamin	35	486	13.9
1992	Scott Oliaro	834	181	4.6	Bill Lazor	328	169	.52	2,206	Mike Jamin	49	794	16.2
1993	Pete Fitzpatrick	789	179	4.4	Bill Lazor	328	172	.52	2,030	Ned Burke	40	328	8.2
1994	Chad Levitt	1,319	275	4.8	Per Larson	154	76	.49	1,092	Aaron Berryman	36	565	15.7
1995	Chad Levitt	1,428	292	4.9	Steve Joyce	274	156	.57	2,255	Ron Mateo	47	695	14.8
1996	Chad Levitt	1,435	267	5.4	Scott Carroll	262	125	.48	1,583	Steve Busch	57	720	12.6
1997	Brad Kiesendahl	513	102	5.0	Scott Carroll	239	131	.55	1,378	Eric Krawczyk	89	1,042	11.7
1998	Deon Harris	757	221	3.4	Mike Hood	294	173	.59	1,910	Joe Splendorio	46	677	14.7
1999	Deon Harris	605	149	4.1	Ricky Rahne	388	225	.58	2,762	Joe Splendorio	65	944	14.5
2000	Evan Simmons	649	145	4.5	Ricky Rahne	479	252	.53	2,944	Joe Splendorio	46	630	13.7
2001	Evan Simmons	598	123	4.9	Ricky Rahne	355	199	.56	1,984	Keith Ferguson	50	507	10.1
2002	Marcus Blanks	598	129	4.6	Mick Razzano	276	137	.50	1,556	Keith Ferguson	70	852	12.2
2003	Joshua Johnston	446	103	4.3	D.J. Busch	227	118	.52	1,320	John Kellner	49	582	11.9
2004	Joshua Johnston	475	156	3.0	D.J. Busch	234	121	.52	1,534	Brian Romney	60	766	12.8

Receiving leaders by receptions

THE SCHOOLS

CORNELL ALL-TIME SCORES

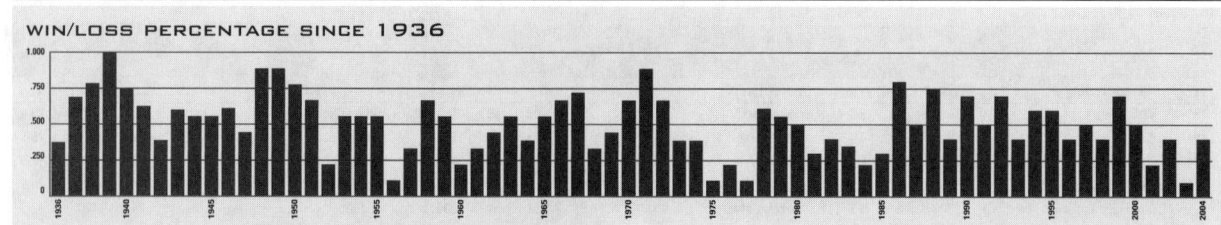

WIN/LOSS PERCENTAGE SINCE 1936

NO HEAD COACH

1887   0-2-0
U	Union *U*	10	24
N26	Lehigh	10	38

1888   4-2-0
O20 ●	Palmyra	26	0
O27 ●	Williams	20	0
N3 ●	Union	30	0
N10 ●	Lafayette	0	16
N17 ●	Bucknell	20	0
D1	at Lehigh	0	4

1889   7-2-0
O5 ●	Bucknell	66	0
O12 ●	Lafayette	10	0
O15	at Yale	6	60
O19 ●	Rochester	124	0
N2 ●	Stevens	38	4
N9 ●	Yale	0	70
N23 ●	Michigan *BUF*	66	0
N26 ●	at Columbia	20	0
N28 ●	Lafayette *SYR*	24	0

1890   8-4-0
O1 ●	Rochester	98	0
O4 ●	at Union	32	0
O8 ●	at Williams	8	18
O18 ●	at Trinity	26	0
O29 ●	at Amherst	0	18
N1 ●	at Harvard	0	77
N5 ●	at Wesleyan	2	4
N8 ●	Bucknell	26	0
N15 ●	at Michigan	20	5
N22 ●	Columbia	36	0
N27 ●	at Chicago AC	12	8
D6 ●	Fordham	82	4

1891   7-3-0
O3 ●	Syracuse	68	0
O10 ●	Bucknell	0	4
O17 ●	Stevens	72	0
O24 ●	Lafayette	30	0
N7 ●	Lehigh	24	0
N14 ●	at Princeton	0	6
N21 ●	Michigan *DET*	58	12
N23 ●	at Detroit AC	32	0
N25 ●	at Chicago AC	4	12
N28 ●	Michigan *CHI*	10	0

1892   10-1-0
S28 ●	at Syracuse AC	16	0
O1 ●	Syracuse	58	0
O8 ●	Bucknell	54	0
O15 ●	Dickinson	58	0
O22 ●	at Lehigh	76	0
O29 ●	at Williams	24	12
N5 ●	Harvard *U*	14	20
N8 ●	Michigan	44	0
N12 ●	MIT	44	12
N18 ●	at Manhattan AC	16	0
N22 ●	at Michigan	30	10

1893   3-6-1
S30 ●	Syracuse	50	0
O7 ●	Gettysburg	16	0
O14 ●	Union	18	6
O21 ●	Princeton	0	46
O24 ●	Tufts	0	6
O28 =	Williams	10	10
N4 ●	Harvard	0	34
N8 ●	Tufts	0	6
N11 ●	Lehigh	0	14
N18 ●	Pennsylvania *MAN*	0	50

MARSHALL NEWELL
1894-95 (.526)   9-8-2

1894   6-4-1
S26 ●	Syracuse	39	0
O6 ●	Union	37	0
O13 ●	Lafayette	24	0
O20 ●	Princeton *NYC*	4	12
O27 ●	Harvard *U*	12	22
N3 ●	Michigan	22	0
N9 ●	at Crescent AC	22	0
N14 =	at Williams	0	0
N17 ●	at Pennsylvania	0	6
N24 ●	at Michigan	4	12
N29 ●	Lehigh	10	6

1895   3-4-1
S26 ●	Syracuse	8	0
O5 =	Penn State	0	0
O12 ●	Western Reserve	12	4
O19 ●	Lafayette	0	6
O26 ●	at Harvard	0	25
N9 ●	Princeton *NYC*	0	6
N16 ●	Brown	6	4
N28 ●	at Pennsylvania	2	46

JOSEPH BEACHAM
1896 (.611)   5-3-1

1896   5-3-1
S26 ●	Colgate	6	0
O3 ●	Syracuse	22	0
O10 ●	Western Reserve	48	0
O17 ●	Tufts	18	0
O24 ●	Harvard	4	13
O31 ●	at Princeton	0	7
N7 ●	Bucknell	54	0
N14 =	at Williams	0	0
N26 ●	at Pennsylvania	10	32

GLENN "POP" WARNER
1897-98, '04-06 (.721)   36-13-3

1897   5-3-1
S25 ●	Colgate	6	0
O3 ●	Syracuse	16	0
O9 ●	Tufts	15	0
O16 ●	at Lafayette	4	4
O23 ●	Princeton	0	10
O27 ●	at Harvard	5	24
O30 ●	Penn State	45	0
N6 ●	at Williams	42	0
N25 ●	at Pennsylvania	0	4

1898   10-2-0
S21 ●	Syracuse	28	0
S24 ●	Colgate	29	5
S28 ●	Hamilton	41	0
O1 ●	Trinity	47	0
O5 ●	at Syracuse	30	0
O12 ●	Carlisle	23	6
O19 ●	Buffalo	27	0
O22 ●	at Princeton	0	6
O29 ●	Oberlin	6	0
N5 ●	at Williams	12	0
N12 ●	Lafayette	47	0
N24 ●	at Pennsylvania	6	12

PERCY HAUGHTON
1899-1900 (.773)   17-5

1899   7-3-0
S23 ●	Colgate *RSP*	42	0
S27 ●	Syracuse	17	0
S30 ●	Hamilton	12	0
O7 ●	Williams	12	0
O14 ●	at Chicago	6	17
O21 ●	Lehigh	6	0
N1 ●	Princeton	5	0
N7 ●	at Columbia	29	0
N11 ●	Lafayette	5	6
N30 ●	at Pennsylvania	0	29

1900   10-2-0
S22 ●	Colgate	16	0
S29 ●	Syracuse	6	0
O3 ●	Rochester	6	0
O6 ●	Bucknell	6	0
O13 ●	Wash. & Jeff.	16	5
O20 ●	Union	11	0
O27 ●	Dartmouth	23	6
N3 ●	at Princeton	12	0
N10 ●	Oberlin	29	0
N17 ●	at Lafayette	0	17
N24 ●	Vermont	42	0
N29 ●	at Pennsylvania	0	27

RAYMOND STARBUCK
1901-02 (.826)   19-4

1901   11-1-0
S28 ●	Colgate	17	0
O2 ●	Rochester	50	0
O5 ●	Bucknell	6	0
O9 ●	Hamilton	39	0
O12 ●	Union	24	0
O19 ●	Carlisle *BUF*	17	0
O26 ●	Oberlin	29	0
N2 ●	Princeton	6	8
N9 ●	Lehigh	30	0
N16 ●	at Columbia	24	0
N23 ●	Vermont	68	0
N28 ●	at Pennsylvania	23	6

1902   8-3-0
S27 ●	Colgate	5	0
O1 ●	Rochester	31	0
O4 ●	Union	42	0
O8 ●	Hobart	57	0
O11 ●	Williams	37	6
O18 ●	Carlisle	6	10
O25 ●	Oberlin	57	0
N1 ●	at Princeton	0	10
N8 ●	Wash. & Jeff.	50	0
N15 ●	Lafayette	28	0
N27 ●	at Pennsylvania	11	12

WILLIAM WARNER
1903 (.650)   6-3-1

1903   6-3-1
S26 ●	Hobart	12	0
S30 ●	Alfred	26	0
O3 ●	Rochester	11	0
O10 ●	Colgate	12	0
O17 ●	Bucknell	6	0
O24 ●	Western Reserve	41	0
O31 ●	at Princeton	0	44
N7 =	Lehigh	0	0
N14 ●	Columbia	12	17
N26 ●	at Pennsylvania	0	42

GLENN "POP" WARNER

1904   7-3-0
S28 ●	Colgate	17	0
O1 ●	Rochester	29	6
O5 ●	Hobart	24	0
O8 ●	Hamilton	34	0
O15 ●	Bucknell	24	12
O22 ●	Franklin & Marshall	36	5
O29 ●	Princeton	6	18
N5 ●	Lehigh	50	5
N12 ●	at Columbia	6	12
N24 ●	at Pennsylvania	0	34

1905   6-4-0
S27 ●	Hamilton	5	0
S30 ●	Colgate	12	11
O4 ●	Hobart	28	0
O7 ●	Bucknell	24	0
O21 ●	Pittsburgh	30	0
O28 ●	Haverford	57	0
N4 ●	Swarthmore	0	14
N11 ●	at Princeton	6	16
N18 ●	Columbia	6	12
N30 ●	at Pennsylvania	5	6

1906   8-1-2
S29 =	Colgate	0	0
O3 ●	Hamilton	21	0
O6 ●	Oberlin	25	5
O10 ●	Niagara	23	6
O13 ●	Bucknell	24	6
O20 ●	Bowdoin	72	0
O27 ●	Princeton *NYC*	5	14
N3 ●	Pittsburgh	23	0
N10 ●	Holy Cross	16	6
N17 ●	Swarthmore	28	0
N29 =	at Pennsylvania	0	0

HENRY SCHOELLKOPF
1907-08 (.816)   15-3-1

1907   8-2-0
S28 ●	Hamilton	23	0
O2 ●	Oberlin	22	5
O5 ●	Niagara	47	0
O12 ●	Colgate	18	0
O19 ●	Penn State	6	8
O26 ●	Princeton	6	5
N2 ●	Pittsburgh	18	5
N9 ●	at Army	14	10
N16 ●	Swarthmore	18	0
N28 ●	at Pennsylvania	4	12

1908   7-1-1
O3 ●	Hamilton	11	0
O10 ●	Oberlin	23	10
O17 ●	Colgate	9	0
O24 ●	Vermont	9	0
O31 ●	Penn State	10	4
N7 ●	Amherst	6	0
N14 =	at Chicago	6	6
N21 ●	Trinity	18	6
N26 ●	at Pennsylvania	4	17

GEORGE WALDER
1909 (.438)   3-4-1

1909   3-4-1
O2 ●	Rensselaer	16	3
O9 ●	Oberlin	16	6
O16 ●	Fordham	6	12
O23 ●	Vermont	16	0
O30 ●	Williams	0	3
N6 ●	at Harvard	0	18
N13 =	Chicago	6	6
N25 ●	at Pennsylvania	6	17

DANIEL REED
1910-11 (.694)   12-5-1

1910   5-2-1
O1 ●	Hobart	50	0
O8 ●	Rensselaer	24	0
O15 ●	Oberlin	0	0
O22 ●	St. Bonaventure	47	0
O29 ●	Vermont	15	5
N5 ●	at Harvard	5	27
N12 ●	Chicago	18	0
N24 ●	at Pennsylvania	6	12

1911   7-3-0

S23	•	Allegheny	35	0
S30	•	Colgate	6	0
O7	•	Oberlin	15	3
O14		Penn State	0	5
O21	•	Wash. & Jeff.	6	0
O28	•	Pittsburgh	9	3
N4	•	Williams	15	14
N11	•	Michigan	6	0
N18		at Chicago	0	6
N30		at Pennsylvania	9	21

AL SHARPE
1912-17 (.616)   34-21-1

1912   3-7-0

S21	•	Wash. & Jeff.	3	0
S28	•	Colgate	7	13
O5	•	Oberlin	0	13
O12	•	NYU	14	6
O19	•	Penn State	6	29
O26	•	Bucknell	14	0
N2	•	Williams	10	24
N9	•	Dartmouth	0	24
N16		at Michigan	7	20
N28		at Pennsylvania	2	7

1913   5-4-1

S27	•	Ursinus	41	0
O1	=	Colgate	0	0
O4	•	Oberlin	37	12
O11	•	Carlisle	0	7
O18	•	Bucknell	10	7
O25	•	Pittsburgh	7	20
N1		at Harvard	6	23
N8	•	Michigan	0	17
N15	•	Lafayette	10	3
N27		at Pennsylvania	21	0

1914   8-2-0

S26	•	Ursinus	28	0
S30	•	Pittsburgh	3	9
O3	•	Colgate	3	7
O10	•	Carlisle	21	0
O17	•	Bucknell	48	0
O24	•	Brown NYC	28	7
O31	•	Holy Cross	48	3
N7	•	Franklin & Marshall	26	3
N14		at Michigan	28	13
N26		at Pennsylvania	24	12

1915   9-0-0

S25	•	Gettysburg	13	0
O2	•	Oberlin	34	7
O9	•	Williams	46	6
O16	•	Bucknell	41	0
O23		at Harvard	10	0
O30	•	Virginia Tech	45	0
N6		at Michigan	34	7
N13	•	Wash. & Lee	40	21
N25		at Pennsylvania	24	9

1916   6-2-0

O7	•	Gettysburg	26	0
O14	•	Williams	42	0
O21	•	Bucknell	19	0
O28		at Harvard	0	23
N4	•	Carnegie Tech	15	7
N11	•	Michigan	23	20
N18	•	Massachusetts	37	0
N30		at Pennsylvania	3	23

1917   3-6-0

S29	•	Oberlin	22	0
O6	•	Williams	10	14
O13	•	47th Infantry	0	6
O20	•	Colgate	0	20
O27	•	Bucknell	20	0
N3	•	Carnegie Tech	20	0
N10		at Michigan	0	42
N17	•	Fordham	6	27
N29		at Pennsylvania	0	37

1918
NO TEAM WWI

JOHN RUSH
1919 (.492)   3-5

1919   3-5-0

O4	•	Oberlin	9	0
O11	•	Williams	3	0
O18	•	Colgate	0	21
O25	•	Dartmouth NYC	0	9
N1	•	Lafayette	2	21
N8	•	Carnegie Tech	20	0
N15	•	Penn State	0	20
N27		at Pennsylvania	0	24

GIL DOBIE
1920-35 (.684)   82-36-7

1920   6-2-0

O2	•	Rochester	13	6
O9	•	St. Bonaventure	55	7
O16	•	Union	60	0
O23	•	Colgate	42	6
O30	•	Rutgers	24	0
N6	•	Dartmouth NYC	3	14
N13	•	Columbia	34	7
N25		at Pennsylvania	0	28

1921   8-0-0

O1	•	St. Bonaventure	41	0
O8	•	Rochester	55	0
O15	•	Western Reserve	110	0
O22	•	Colgate	31	7
O29	•	Dartmouth	59	7
N5	•	Columbia NYC	41	7
N12	•	Springfield	14	0
N24		at Pennsylvania	41	0

1922   8-0-0

S30	•	St. Bonaventure	55	6
O7	•	Niagara	66	0
O14	•	New Hampshire	68	7
O21	•	Colgate	14	0
N4	•	Columbia	56	0
N11	•	Dartmouth NYC	23	0
N18	•	Albright	48	14
N30		at Pennsylvania	9	0

1923   8-0-0

S29	•	St. Bonaventure	41	6
O6	•	Susquehanna	84	0
O13	•	Williams	28	6
O20	•	Colgate	34	7
N3		at Dartmouth	32	7
N10	•	Columbia NYC	35	0
N17	•	Johns Hopkins	52	0
N29		at Pennsylvania	14	7

1924   4-4-0

S27	•	St. Bonaventure	56	0
O4	•	Niagara	27	0
O11	•	Williams	7	14
O18	•	Rutgers	0	10
N1	•	Columbia	14	0
N8	•	Susquehanna	91	0
N15	•	Dartmouth NYC	14	27
N27		at Pennsylvania	0	20

1925   6-2-0

S26	•	Susquehanna	80	0
O3	•	Niagara	26	0
O10	•	Williams	48	0
O17	•	Rutgers	41	0
O31	•	Columbia NYC	17	14
N7		at Dartmouth	13	62
N14	•	Canisius	33	0
N26		at Pennsylvania	0	7

1926   6-1-1

S25	•	Geneva	6	0
O2	•	Niagara	28	0
O9	•	Williams	49	0
O16	•	Michigan State	24	14
O30	•	Columbia NYC	9	17
N6	•	St. Bonaventure	41	0
N13	•	Dartmouth	24	23
N25	=	at Pennsylvania	10	10

1927   3-3-2

S25	•	Clarkson	41	0
O1	•	Niagara	19	6
O9	•	Richmond	53	0
O22	•	Princeton	10	21
O29	=	Columbia	0	0
N5	•	St. Bonaventure	6	6
N12		at Dartmouth	7	53
N24		at Pennsylvania	0	35

1928   3-3-2

O6	•	Clarkson	20	0
O13	•	Niagara	34	0
O20	•	Hampden Sydney	18	6
O27		at Princeton	0	3
N3		at Columbia	0	0
N10	•	St. Bonaventure	0	0
N17	•	Dartmouth	0	28
N29		at Pennsylvania	0	49

1929   6-2-0

S28	•	Clarkson	60	0
O5	•	Niagara	22	6
O12	•	Hampden Sydney	40	6
O19	•	Princeton	13	7
N2	•	Columbia	12	6
N16	•	Western Reserve	36	0
N23		at Dartmouth	14	18
N28		at Pennsylvania	7	17

1930   6-2-0

S27	•	Clarkson	66	0
O4	•	Niagara	61	14
O11	•	Hampden Sydney	47	6
O18		at Princeton	12	7
N1		at Columbia	7	10
N8	•	Hobart	54	0
N15	•	Dartmouth	13	19
N27		at Pennsylvania	13	7

1931   7-1-0

S26	•	Clarkson	68	0
O3	•	Niagara	37	6
O10	•	Richmond	27	0
O17	•	Princeton	33	0
O31	•	Columbia	13	0
N7	•	Alfred	54	0
N14		at Dartmouth	0	14
N26		at Pennsylvania	7	0

1932   5-2-1

S24	•	Buffalo	72	0
O1	•	Niagara	7	0
O8	•	Richmond	27	0
O15	=	at Princeton	0	0
O29		at Columbia	0	6
N5	•	Albright	40	14
N12	•	Dartmouth	21	6
N24		at Pennsylvania	7	13

1933   4-3-0

S30	•	St. Lawrence	48	7
O7	•	Richmond	28	7
O14		at Michigan	0	40
O21	•	Syracuse	7	14
N4	•	Columbia	6	9
N18		at Dartmouth	7	0
N30		at Pennsylvania	20	12

1934   2-5-0

S29	•	St. Lawrence	14	0
O6	•	Richmond	0	6
O13	•	Syracuse	7	20
O27		at Princeton	0	45
N3		at Columbia	0	14
N17	•	Dartmouth	21	6
N29		at Pennsylvania	13	23

1935   0-6-1

S28	•	St. Lawrence	6	12
O12		at Syracuse	14	21
O19	•	Western Reserve	19	33
O26	•	Princeton	0	54
N2	=	Columbia	7	7
N16		at Dartmouth	6	41
N28		at Pennsylvania	7	33

CARL SNAVELY
1936-44 (.633)   46-26-3

1936   3-5-0

S26	•	Alfred	74	0
O3		at Yale	0	23
O17	•	Syracuse	20	7
O24	•	Penn State	13	7
O31		at Columbia	13	20
N7		at Princeton	13	41
N14	•	Dartmouth	6	20
N26		at Pennsylvania	6	14

1937   5-2-1

S25	•	Penn State	26	19
O2	•	Colgate	40	7
O9		at Princeton	20	7
O16	•	Syracuse	6	14
O23		at Yale	0	9
O30	•	Columbia	14	0
N13	=	at Dartmouth	6	6
N25		at Pennsylvania	34	20

1938   5-1-1

O1	•	Colgate	15	6
O8		at Harvard	20	0
O15		at Syracuse	17	19
O22	•	Penn State	21	6
O29		at Columbia	23	7
N12	•	Dartmouth	14	7
N24	=	at Pennsylvania	0	0

1939   8-0-0

O7	•	Syracuse	19	6
O14		at Princeton	20	7
O21	•	Penn State	47	0
O28		at Ohio State	23	14
N4	•	Columbia	13	7
N11	•	Colgate	14	12
N18		at Dartmouth	35	6
N25		at Pennsylvania	26	0

1940   6-2-0

O5	•	Colgate	34	0
O12		at Army	45	0
O19	•	Syracuse	33	6
O26	•	Ohio State	21	7
N2	•	Columbia	27	0
N9		at Yale	21	0
N16		at Dartmouth	0	3
N23		at Pennsylvania	20	22

1941   5-3-0

O4	•	Syracuse	6	0
O11		at Harvard	7	0
O18	•	Navy BALT	0	14
O25	•	Colgate	21	2
N1		at Columbia	0	7
N8	•	Yale	21	7
N15	•	Dartmouth	33	19
N22		at Pennsylvania	0	16

1942   3-5-1

S26	•	Lafayette	20	16
O3	•	Colgate	6	18
O10		at Army	8	28
O17	=	Penn State	0	0
O24		at Syracuse	7	12
O31		at Columbia	13	14
N7		at Yale	13	7
N14	•	Dartmouth NYC	21	19
N21		at Pennsylvania	7	34

1943   6-4-0

S18	•	Bucknell	7	6
S25	•	Sampson NTS	27	13
O2	•	Navy BALT	7	46
O9		at Princeton	30	0
O16	•	Holy Cross	20	7
O23	•	Colgate SYR	7	20
O30	•	Columbia	33	6
N6	•	Penn State	13	0
N13	•	Dartmouth BOS	0	20
N20		at Pennsylvania	14	20

1944   5-4-0

S23	•	at Syracuse	39	6
S30	•	Bucknell	26	0
O7		at Yale	7	16
O14	•	Colgate	7	14
O28	•	Sampson NTS	13	6
N4	•	Columbia	25	7
N11	•	Navy BALT	0	48
N18	•	Dartmouth	14	13
N25		at Pennsylvania	0	20

ED McKEEVER
1945-46 (.583)   10-7-1

1945   5-4-0

S22	•	at Syracuse	26	14
S29	•	Bucknell	19	8
O6	•	U.S. Sub Base	39	0
O13	•	Princeton	6	14
O27		at Yale	7	18
N3		at Columbia	26	34
N10	•	Colgate	20	6
N17		at Dartmouth	20	13
N24		at Pennsylvania	6	59

1946   5-3-1

S28	•	Bucknell	21	0
O5		at Army	21	46
O12	•	Colgate	13	9
O19	=	Yale	6	6
O26		at Princeton	14	7
N2		at Columbia	12	0
N9	•	Syracuse	7	14
N16	•	Dartmouth	21	7
N30		at Pennsylvania	20	26

GEORGE "LEFTY" JAMES 1947-60 (.532)		66-58-2

1947   4-5-0

S27	●	Lehigh	27 0
O4	●	at Yale	0 14
O11	●	at Colgate	27 18
O18	●	Navy	19 38
O25	●	at Princeton	28 21
N1		Columbia	0 22
N8	●	Syracuse	12 6
N15	●	at Dartmouth	13 21
N29	●	at Pennsylvania	0 21

1948   8-1-0

S25	●	NYU	47 6
O2	●	Navy BALT	13 7
O9	●	Harvard	40 6
O16	●	at Syracuse	34 7
O23		Army	6 27
O30	●	at Columbia	20 13
N6	●	Colgate	14 6
N13	●	Dartmouth	27 26
N27	●	at Pennsylvania	23 14

1949   8-1-0

S24	●	Niagara	27 0
O1	●	Colgate	39 27
O8	●	at Harvard	33 14
O15	●	at Yale	48 14
O22	●	Princeton	14 12
O29	●	Columbia	54 0
N5	●	Syracuse	33 7
N12	●	at Dartmouth	7 16
N26	●	at Pennsylvania	9 21

1950   7-2-0

S30	●	Lafayette	27 0
O7	●	at Syracuse	26 7
O14	●	at Harvard	28 7
O21	●	Yale	7 0
O28	●	at Princeton	0 27
N4	●	at Columbia	19 20
N11	●	Colgate	26 18
N18	●	Dartmouth	24 0
N25	●	at Pennsylvania	13 6

1951   6-3-0

S29	●	Syracuse	21 14
O6	●	at Colgate	41 18
O13	●	Harvard	42 6
O20	●	at Yale	27 0
O27	●	at Princeton	15 53
N3		Columbia	20 21
N10	●	Michigan	20 7
N17	●	at Dartmouth	21 13
N24	●	at Pennsylvania	0 7

1952   2-7-0

S27		Colgate	7 14
O4		Navy	7 31
O11	●	at Syracuse	6 26
O18	●	at Yale	0 13
O25		Princeton	0 27
N1	●	at Columbia	21 14
N8	●	at Michigan	7 49
N15	●	Dartmouth	13 7
N27	●	at Pennsylvania	7 14

1953   4-3-2

S26	●	Colgate	27 7
O3		Rice	7 28
O10		Navy	6 26
O17	=	Yale	0 0
O24	●	at Princeton	26 19
O31	●	Columbia	27 13
N7		Syracuse	0 26
N14	●	at Dartmouth	28 26
N26	=	at Pennsylvania	7 7

1954   5-4-0

S25		Colgate	14 19
O2	●	at Rice	20 41
O9		Harvard	12 13
O16		at Yale	21 47
O23	●	at Princeton	27 0
O30	●	at Columbia	26 0
N6	●	Syracuse	14 6
N13	●	Dartmouth	40 21
N25	●	at Pennsylvania	20 6

1955   5-4-0

S24		Lehigh	14 6
O1		Colgate	6 21
O8	●	at Harvard	20 7
O15		at Yale	6 34
O22		Princeton	20 26
O29	●	Columbia	34 19
N5	●	at Brown	20 7
N12		at Dartmouth	0 7
N24	●	at Pennsylvania	39 7

1956-PRESENT IVY LEAGUE

1956   1-8-0 (1-6-0)

S29		at Colgate	6 34
O6		Navy	0 14
O13		Harvard	7 32
O20		at Yale	7 25
O27		Princeton	21 32
N3		at Columbia	19 25
N10		at Brown	6 13
N17		Dartmouth	14 27
N22	●	at Pennsylvania	20 7

1957   3-6-0 (3-4-0)

S28		Colgate	13 14
O5	●	at Harvard	20 6
O12		Syracuse	0 34
O19		Yale	7 18
O26	●	at Princeton	14 47
N2	●	Columbia	8 0
N9	●	Brown	13 6
N16		at Dartmouth	19 20
N28		at Pennsylvania	6 14

1958   6-3-0 (5-2-0)

S27	●	Colgate	13 0
O4	●	Harvard	21 14
O11		at Syracuse	0 55
O18	●	at Yale	12 7
O25	●	Princeton	34 8
N1	●	at Columbia	25 0
N8		at Brown	8 12
N15		Dartmouth	15 32
N27	●	at Pennsylvania	19 7

1959   5-4-0 (3-4-0)

S26	●	at Colgate	20 15
O3	●	Lehigh	13 6
O10	●	at Harvard	20 16
O17		Yale	0 23
O24		at Princeton	0 20
O31	●	Columbia	13 7
N7	●	Brown	19 0
N14		at Dartmouth	12 21
N26		at Pennsylvania	13 28

1960   2-7-0 (1-6-0)

S24		Colgate	8 28
O1	●	Bucknell	15 7
O8		Harvard	12 0
O15		at Yale	6 22
O22		Princeton	18 21
O29		at Columbia	6 44
N5		at Brown	6 7
N12		Dartmouth	0 20
N24		at Pennsylvania	7 18

TOM HARP 1961-65 (.456)		19-23-3

1961   3-6-0 (2-5-0)

S30	●	Colgate	34 0
O7		at Harvard	0 14
O14		Navy	7 31
O21		Yale	0 12
O28		at Princeton	25 30
N4		Columbia	7 35
N11	●	Brown	25 0
N18		at Dartmouth	14 15
N25	●	at Pennsylvania	31 0

1962   4-5-0 (4-3-0)

S29		Colgate	12 23
O6	●	Harvard	14 12
O13		at Navy	0 41
O20		at Yale	8 26
O27	●	Princeton	35 34
N3		at Columbia	21 25
N10	●	at Brown	28 26
N17		Dartmouth	21 28
N24	●	at Pennsylvania	29 22

1963   5-4-0 (4-3-0)

S28	●	Colgate	17 21
O5	●	Lehigh	24 0
O12		Harvard	14 21
O19	●	Yale	13 10
O26		Princeton	14 51
N2	●	Columbia	18 17
N9	●	Brown	28 25
N16		Dartmouth	7 12
N28	●	Pennsylvania	17 8

1964   3-5-1 (3-4-0)

S26		Buffalo	9 9
O3		at Colgate	3 8
O10	●	Pennsylvania	33 0
O17		at Harvard	0 16
O24		Yale	21 23
O31	●	at Columbia	57 20
N7		at Brown	28 31
N14		Dartmouth	33 15
N21		at Princeton	12 17

1965   4-3-2 (3-3-1)

S25	=	Colgate	0 0
O2	●	at Lehigh	49 13
O9		Princeton	27 36
O16	=	Harvard	3 3
O23		at Yale	14 24
O30	●	Columbia	20 6
N6	●	Brown	41 21
N13		at Dartmouth	0 20
N25	●	at Pennsylvania	38 14

JACK MUSICK 1966-74 (.574)		45-33-3

1966   6-3-0 (4-3-0)

S24		at Buffalo	28 21
O1	●	Colgate	15 14
O8	●	Pennsylvania	45 28
O15		at Harvard	0 21
O22	●	Yale	16 14
O29		at Columbia	31 6
N5	●	at Brown	23 14
N12		Dartmouth	23 32
N19		at Princeton	0 7

1967   6-2-1 (4-2-0)

S30	●	Bucknell	23 7
O7	●	at Colgate	23 7
O14	●	Princeton	47 13
O21		Harvard	12 14
O28		at Yale	7 41
N4	●	Columbia	27 14
N11	=	Brown	14 14
N18	●	at Dartmouth	24 21
N25	●	at Pennsylvania	33 14

1968   3-6-0 (1-6-0)

S28	●	Colgate	17 0
O5	●	Rutgers	17 16
O12		Pennsylvania	8 10
O19		at Harvard	0 10
O26		Yale	13 25
N2		at Columbia	25 34
N9	●	at Brown	31 0
N16		Dartmouth	6 27
N23		at Princeton	13 41

1969   4-5-0 (4-3-0)

S27	●	Colgate	24 28
O4		at Rutgers	7 21
O11		Princeton	17 24
O18	●	Harvard	41 24
O25		at Yale	0 17
N1	●	Columbia	10 3
N8	●	Brown	14 7
N15		at Dartmouth	7 24
N22	●	at Pennsylvania	28 14

1970   6-3-0 (4-3-0)

S26	●	at Colgate	17 7
O3	●	Lehigh	41 14
O10	●	Pennsylvania	32 31
O17		at Harvard	24 27
O24		Yale	7 38
O31	●	at Columbia	31 20
N7	●	at Brown	35 21
N14		Dartmouth	0 24
N21	●	at Princeton	6 3

1971   8-1-0 (6-1-0)

S25	●	Colgate	38 20
O2	●	at Rutgers	31 17
O9		Princeton	19 8
O16		Harvard	21 16
O23	●	at Yale	31 10
O30		Columbia	24 23
N6	●	Brown	21 7
N13		at Dartmouth	14 24
N20	●	at Pennsylvania	41 13

1972   6-3-0 (4-3-0)

S30	●	Colgate	37 7
O7	●	Rutgers	36 22
O14	●	Pennsylvania	24 20
O21		at Harvard	15 33
O28	●	Yale	24 13
N4		at Columbia	0 14
N11	●	at Brown	48 28
N18		Dartmouth	22 31
N25	●	at Princeton	22 15

1973   3-5-1 (2-5-0)

S29	●	at Colgate	35 21
O6	=	Lehigh	7 7
O13	●	Princeton	37 6
O20		Harvard	15 21
O27		at Yale	3 20
N3	●	Columbia	44 14
N10		Brown	7 17
N17		at Dartmouth	0 17
N24		at Pennsylvania	22 31

1974   3-5-1 (1-5-1)

S28	●	Colgate	40 21
O5	●	Bucknell	24 0
O12	=	Pennsylvania	28 28
O19	●	at Harvard	27 39
O26		Yale	3 27
N2	●	at Columbia	24 0
N9	●	at Brown	8 16
N16		Dartmouth	9 21
N23	●	at Princeton	20 41

GEORGE SEIFERT 1975-76 (.167)		3-15

1975   1-8-0 (0-7-0)

S27		Colgate	22 24
O4	●	at Bucknell	21 6
O11		Princeton	8 16
O18		Harvard	13 34
O25		at Yale	14 20
N1		Columbia	19 42
N8		Brown	23 45
N15		at Dartmouth	10 33
N22		at Pennsylvania	21 27

1976   2-7-0 (2-5-0)

S18		Princeton	0 3
S25		Colgate	20 25
O2		at Rutgers	14 21
O9	●	at Harvard	9 3
O16		Brown	12 8
O23		Dartmouth	0 35
O30		at Yale	6 14
N6		at Columbia	17 35
N13	●	Pennsylvania	31 13

BOB BLACKMAN 1977-82 (.412)		23-33-1

1977   1-8-0 (1-6-0)

S17		at Pennsylvania	7 17
S24		Colgate	22 28
O1		Rutgers	14 30
O8		Harvard	7 17
O15		at Brown	3 21
O22		at Dartmouth	13 17
O29		Yale	0 28
N5	●	Columbia	20 7
N12		at Princeton	0 34

1978   5-3-1 (3-3-1)

S23	=	Princeton	14 14
S30	●	at Colgate	21 12
O7	●	Bucknell	24 0
O14	●	at Harvard	25 20
O21	●	Brown	13 21
O28	●	Dartmouth	7 14
N4		at Yale	14 42
N11	●	at Columbia	35 14
N18	●	Pennsylvania	35 17

THE SCHOOLS

1979 — 5-4-0 (4-3-0)

Date		Opponent		
S22	•	at Pennsylvania	52	13
S29	•	Colgate	36	21
O6		Bucknell	0	10
O13	•	Harvard	41	14
O20		at Brown	7	28
O27		at Dartmouth	21	10
N3		Yale	20	23
N10	•	Columbia	24	7
N17		at Princeton	14	26

1980 — 5-5-0 (5-2-0)

Date		Opponent		
S20	•	Princeton	17	7
S27		at Colgate	20	38
O4		Rutgers	3	44
O11		at Harvard	12	20
O18		Brown	25	32
O25	•	Dartmouth	7	3
N1		at Bucknell	16	33
N8	•	at Yale	24	6
N15		at Columbia	24	0
N22	•	Pennsylvania	31	9

1981 — 3-7-0 (2-5-0)

Date		Opponent		
S19		at Pennsylvania	22	29
S26		Colgate	10	34
O3		at Rutgers	17	31
O10		Harvard	10	27
O17	•	at Brown	14	9
O24		at Dartmouth	7	42
O31	•	Bucknell	22	15
N7		Yale	17	23
N14	•	Columbia	15	9
N21		at Princeton	14	37

1982 — 4-6-0 (3-4-0)

Date		Opponent		
S18		Princeton	36	41
S25		Colgate	6	21
O2		Boston U.	6	17
O9		at Harvard	13	25
O16		Brown	19	38
O23		Dartmouth	13	14
O30		Merchant Marines	34	0
N6		at Yale	26	20
N13		at Columbia	35	26
N20		Pennsylvania	23	0

MAXIE BAUGHAN
1983-88 (.492) — 28-29-2

1983 — 3-6-1 (3-3-1)

Date		Opponent		
S17		at Pennsylvania	7	28
S24		Colgate	7	60
O16		at Cincinnati	20	48
O8	=	Harvard	3	3
O15		at Brown	3	14
O22		at Dartmouth	17	31
O29		at Boston U.	0	41
N5	•	Yale	41	7
N12	•	Columbia	31	6
N19		at Princeton	32	30

1984 — 2-7-0 (2-5-0)

Date		Opponent		
S22		Princeton	9	17
S29		Colgate	7	35
O6		at Bucknell	7	10
O13		at Harvard	18	24
O20		Brown	9	13
O27	•	Dartmouth	13	10
N3		at Yale	14	21
N10		at Columbia	19	7
N17		Pennsylvania	0	24

1985 — 3-7-0 (2-5-0)

Date		Opponent		
S21		at Pennsylvania	6	10
S28		Colgate	20	21
O5		Lafayette	3	17
O12		Harvard	17	20
O19		at Brown	0	22
O26		Dartmouth	17	20
N2	•	at Bucknell	26	13
N9	•	at Yale	20	1
N16	•	Columbia	21	8
N23		at Princeton	27	33

1986 — 8-2-0 (6-1-0)

Date		Opponent		
S20	•	Princeton	39	8
S27		at Colgate	21	12
O4		at Lafayette	22	33
O11	•	at Harvard	3	0
O18	•	Brown	27	9
O25	•	at Dartmouth	10	7
N1		Bucknell	16	3
N8	•	Yale	15	0
N15	•	at Columbia	28	0
N22		Pennsylvania	21	31

1987 — 5-5-0 (4-3-0)

Date		Opponent		
S19	•	at Pennsylvania	17	13
S26		Colgate	3	27
O3		Lafayette	17	12
O10	•	Harvard	29	17
O17		at Brown	15	23
O24	•	Dartmouth	21	14
O31		Bucknell	6	20
N7		at Yale	9	28
N14	•	Columbia	31	20
N21		at Princeton	6	23

1988 — 7-2-1 (6-1-0)

Date		Opponent		
S17		Princeton	17	26
S24	•	Colgate	17	14
O1		at Lehigh	14	27
O8	•	at Harvard	19	17
O15	•	Brown	35	0
O22	•	at Dartmouth	24	7
O29	=	at Lafayette	21	21
N5	•	Yale	26	0
N12	•	at Columbia	42	19
N19	•	Pennsylvania	19	6

JACK FOUTS
1989 (.400) — 4-6

1989 — 4-6-0 (2-5-0)

Date		Opponent		
S16	•	at Bucknell	20	9
S23		Northeastern	0	20
O7	•	Lafayette	24	23
O14	•	Harvard	28	0
O21		at Brown	7	28
O28		Dartmouth	14	28
N4		at Yale	19	34
N11		Columbia	19	25
N18		at Princeton	7	21
N23	•	at Pennsylvania	20	6

JIM HOFHER
1990-97 (.550) — 44-36

1990 — 7-3-0 (6-1-0)

Date		Opponent		
S15	•	Princeton	17	14
S22		at Colgate	24	59
S29		Bucknell	21	42
O6	•	at Harvard	20	17
O13	•	at Lafayette	38	6
O20		Dartmouth	6	11
O27	•	Brown	34	7
N3	•	at Yale	41	31
N10	•	at Columbia	41	0
N17	•	Pennsylvania	21	15

1991 — 5-5-0 (4-3-0)

Date		Opponent		
S21		at Princeton	0	18
S28		Colgate	13	31
O5	•	at Bucknell	23	7
O12		at Stanford	6	56
O19	•	Harvard	22	17
O26		at Dartmouth	25	31
N2	•	at Brown	20	17
N9	•	Yale	31	6
N16	•	Columbia	28	21
N23		at Pennsylvania	13	14

1992 — 7-3-0 (4-3-0)

Date		Opponent		
S19		Princeton	20	22
S26	•	Lehigh	29	23
O3	•	Lafayette	44	33
O10	•	at Harvard	31	13
O17	•	at Colgate	25	7
O24	•	Dartmouth	26	16
O31	•	Brown	16	6
N7	•	at Yale	35	14
N14	•	at Columbia	30	35
N21		Pennsylvania	7	14

1993 — 4-6-0 (3-4-0)

Date		Opponent		
S18		at Princeton	12	18
S25		Colgate	6	22
O2		at Lehigh	13	35
O9	•	Harvard	27	0
O16	•	Fordham	48	6
O23		at Dartmouth	27	28
O30	•	at Brown	21	3
N6	•	Yale	21	0
N13		Columbia	24	29
N20		at Pennsylvania	14	17

1994 — 6-4-0 (3-4-0)

Date		Opponent		
S17		Princeton	31	16
S24	•	at Fordham	13	6
O1	•	Lehigh	21	17
O8	•	at Harvard	18	13
O15	•	at Bucknell	29	28
O22	•	Dartmouth	17	14
O29		Brown	3	16
N5		at Yale	14	24
N12		at Columbia	33	38
N19		Pennsylvania	14	18

1995 — 6-4-0 (5-2-0)

Date		Opponent		
S16		at Princeton	22	24
S23	•	Holy Cross	28	19
S30	•	at Dartmouth	24	19
O7		Harvard	28	27
O14		Bucknell	7	10
O21		at Lehigh	23	34
O28	•	at Brown	38	28
N4	•	Yale	38	10
N11	•	Columbia	35	14
N18	•	at Pennsylvania	18	37

1996 — 4-6 (4-3)

Date		Opponent		
S21	•	Princeton	33	27
S28		at Lafayette	19	30
O5		at Buffalo	24	41
O12	•	at Harvard	20	13
O19		Colgate	21	31
O26		Dartmouth	21	38
N2		Brown	21	35
N9	•	at Yale	28	20
N16		at Columbia	10	24
N23	•	Pennsylvania	24	21

1997 — 5-5 (3-4)

Date		Opponent		
S21	•	Princeton	14	10
S28		Colgate	38	44
O4		at Dartmouth	20	24
O11		Harvard	9	34
O18	•	Lafayette	41	34
O25		at Fordham	45	13
N1		at Brown	12	37
N8	•	Yale	37	10
N15	•	Columbia	33	22
N22		at Pennsylvania	20	33 †

PETE MANGURIAN
1998-2000 (.533) — 16-14

1998 — 4-6 (1-6)

Date		Opponent		
S19		at Princeton	0	6
S26	•	at Holy Cross	17	9
O3		Buffalo	34	31
O10		at Harvard	12	19
O17	•	Bucknell	23	19
O24		Dartmouth	14	11
O31		Brown	7	20
N7		at Yale	21	28
N14		at Columbia	10	22
N21		Pennsylvania	21	35

1999 — 7-3 (5-2)

Date		Opponent		
S18	•	at Princeton	20	3
S25	•	Fordham	42	14
O2	•	at Brown	33	28
O9	•	Harvard	24	23
O16		at Colgate	16	55
O23		at Dartmouth	17	20
O30	•	Wagner	31	14
N6		Yale	20	37
N13	•	Columbia	31	29
N20	•	at Pennsylvania	20	12

2000 — 5-5 (5-2)

Date		Opponent		
S16		at Bucknell	15	38
S23		Yale	24	23
S30		at Lehigh	16	35
O7	•	at Harvard	29	28
O14		Colgate	16	23
O21		at Brown	40	56
O28	•	Princeton	25	24
N4	•	Dartmouth	49	31
N11	•	at Columbia	35	31
N18		Pennsylvania	15	45

TIM PENDERGAST
2001-03 (.241) — 7-22

2001 — 2-7 (2-5)

Date		Opponent		
S22		at Yale	13	40
S29		at Colgate	32	35
O6		Lehigh	35	38
O13		Harvard	6	26
O20		Brown	21	49
O27	•	at Princeton	10	7
N3	•	at Dartmouth	28	24
N10		Columbia	28	35
N17		at Pennsylvania	14	38

2002 — 4-6 (3-4)

Date		Opponent		
S21		at Bucknell	3	14
S28		Yale	23	50
O5		Towson	35	31
O12		at Harvard	23	52
O19		Colgate	13	42
O26	•	at Brown	10	7
N2		Princeton	25	32
N9	•	Dartmouth	21	19
N16	•	at Columbia	17	14
N21		Pennsylvania	0	31

2003 — 1-9 (0-7)

Date		Opponent		
S20	•	Bucknell	21	19
S27		at Yale	7	21
O4		Colgate	24	27
O11		Harvard	0	27
O18		Georgetown	20	42
O25		Brown	7	21
N1		at Princeton	6	28
N8		at Dartmouth	17	26
N15		Columbia	21	34
N22		at Pennsylvania	7	59

JIM KNOWLES
2004-Present (.400) — 4-6

2004 — 4-6 (4-3)

Date		Opponent		
S18		at Bucknell	9	15
S25	•	Yale	19	7
O2		at Towson	11	21
O9		at Harvard	24	34
O16		Colgate	6	10
O23		at Brown	17	21
O30	•	Princeton	21	20
N6	•	Dartmouth	14	7
N13	•	at Columbia	32	26
N20		Pennsylvania	14	20

Neutral Site key: *U* Unknown, Unknown / *Balt* Baltimore, MD / *Bos* Boston, MA / *Buf* Buffalo, NY / *Syr* Syracuse, NY / *Chi* Chicago, IL / *Det* Detroit, MI / *RSp* Richfield Springs, NY / *NYC* New York, NY / *Man* Manheim, PA
ƒ Forfeit † Game Later Forfeited ● Disputed Victor * Disputed Score || Designated Conference Game |2 Counted Twice in Conference Standings

DARTMOUTH

BY BRUCE WOOD

THERE IS PRIDE, AND THEN THERE is Dartmouth football pride. In 1970, an undefeated Dartmouth team did not allow a single point in the season's final four games on the way to a perfect 9–0 record and an undisputed Ivy League crown. The Big Green were also awarded the Lambert Trophy as best team in the East, which prompted Joe Paterno to suggest a matchup between Dartmouth and his 7–3 Penn State Nittany Lions. Ivy League schools, however, were barred from postseason play, a fact that didn't stop Big Green coach Bob Blackman from proudly countering, "I'd prefer to play a team with a better record."

TRADITION For many years, Dartmouth's old guard steadfastly refused to call the alumni weekend "homecoming" and bristled when anyone else did. Homecoming was for schools that welcomed their alumni back one weekend a year, and at Dartmouth the feeling was alumni were always welcomed back. Whatever the weekend is called, it's kicked off with Friday's Dartmouth Night, which centers on a huge

bonfire on the Green, followed by a Saturday afternoon football game, usually against Harvard or Yale. On Dartmouth Night, a parade of students and returning alumni make their way down Hanover's Main Street to the campus, where they gather for speeches by the football coach and team captains. The bonfire (built by the freshman class) is lit, and everyone joins in the singing of old school songs. When players cross the Green on their way to Memorial Field the next morning, the ground is still steaming, and the smell of wood smoke hangs in the air.

BEST PLAYER At halfback, Bob MacLeod was one of the country's top players from 1936 to 1938, averaging almost six yards a carry during his storied career. But it was his play on the other side of the ball that led the famed sportswriter Grantland Rice to call him "the best defensive back of the year" for 1938. MacLeod was a consensus All-American that year and the only unanimous pick by NFL coaches for the All-America team.

BEST COACH It's a well-known story that during his 16-year career, Dartmouth coach Bob Blackman wanted the best quarterback in the Ivy League under center and the Ivy's next-best quarterback on his bench so he

couldn't play for Harvard, Yale or Princeton. An aggressive recruiter and innovative strategist, Blackman compiled a 104–37–3 overall record and a 79–24–2 Ivy League mark between 1956 and 1970. During his tenure, the Big Green won seven Ivy titles as well as two Lambert Trophies as the top team in the East.

BEST TEAM In 1970, Bob Blackman's final team was not only his best, it was arguably the finest in Dartmouth history. The Big Green finished the season unbeaten and were ranked No. 14 in the nation—the last time an Ivy League school finished in the Top 20. Led by hard-hitting defensive back Murry Bowden, Dartmouth allowed only 42 points all year, the fewest surrendered by any team in the country.

BIGGEST GAME In 1965, the final game of the season pitted Dartmouth against Princeton. Both teams had matching 8–0 records, and the winner would walk away as

> *"Dartmouth has never had any great love for Harvard, and Harvard has never wasted any affection on the Hanover college."*
> *—The Boston Globe (1903)*

Ivy champ. With 45,725 in attendance, Dartmouth's Mickey Beard piled up 229 yards and three touchdowns—one passing and two rushing—in a stunning 28-14 Big Green victory. The bells of Dartmouth's Rollins Chapel rang through the night and into the next day in honor of the championship win.

BIGGEST UPSET Unbeaten Harvard came into the fifth game of the 1973 season having outscored its opponents 118-22. Visiting Dartmouth was 1–3 and a bleak 13-point underdog. Aided by a series of inspired goal-line stands, the Big Green shocked the Crimson, 24-18. Dartmouth went on to close out its season without another loss, earning its fifth consecutive Ivy League crown.

WILDEST FINISH It was late in the 1993 Dartmouth-Princeton game and payback time for the Tigers; for two years in a row, the Big Green had beaten Princeton in the final game of the year. This time, the Tigers were in

RECORDS

RUSHING YARDS

	GAME	
229	Al Rosier vs. Brown, Nov. 16, 1991 (25 att.)	
	SEASON	
1,432	Al Rosier, 1991 (258 att.)	
	CAREER	
2,252	Al Rosier, 1989-91 (448 att.)	

PASSING YARDS

	GAME	
419	Jay Fiedler vs. Yale, Oct. 17, 1992 (20 of 31)	
	SEASON	
2,913	Brian Mann, 2002 (253 of 423)	
	CAREER	
6,684	Jay Fiedler, 1991-93 (456 of 813)	

RECEIVING YARDS

	GAME	
219	Jack Daly vs. Colgate, Oct. 2, 1982 (9 rec.)	
	SEASON	
1,076	John Hyland, 1993 (62 rec.)	
	CAREER	
2,605	Craig Morton, 1986-88 (138 rec.)	

POINTS

	GAME	
44	Fred Jennings vs. Amherst, Oct. 22, 1898 (7 TDs, 9 PATs)	
	SEASON	
125	Myles Lane, 1927 (18 TDs, 17 PATs)	
	CAREER	
307	Myles Lane, 1925-27 (48 TDs, 19 PATs)	

CONSENSUS ALL-AMERICANS

1903	Henry Hooper, C
1903	Myron Witham, B
1904	Joseph Gilman, G
1905	Ralph Glaze, E
1908	George Schildmiller, E
1908	Clark Tobin, G
1912	Wesley Englehorn, T
1913	Robert Hogsett, E
1914-15	Clarence Spears, G
1917	Eugene Neely, G
1919	Adolph Youngstrom, G
1924-25	Carl Diehl, G
1925	George Tully, E
1925	Andy Oberlander, B
1938	Bob MacLeod, B
1991	Al Rosier, RB
1992	Dennis Durkin, PK
1996	Brian Larsen, OL
1997	Zach Walz, LB
2002	Casey Cramer, TE

complete control, leading 22-8 in the fourth quarter. But then Dartmouth's Jay Fiedler came alive. First, he passed for a touchdown. Then he ran one in, following it with a throw on the two-point conversion to tie the game at 22-22. With snow swirling around Memorial Field, Fiedler capped the dramatic comeback by hitting John Hyland from 38 yards out with 1:12 left on the clock for yet another TD and a stirring 28-22 Dartmouth win.

STADIUM The 1923 Dartmouth powerhouse lost just one game all season. Unfortunately for the Big Green, the 32-7 defeat at the hands of Cornell came on the day the college dedicated Memorial Field before a crowd of 14,000. The stadium is named in honor of Dartmouth's World War I veterans; 112 alumni died in the war, and 3,407 served. In 1968, construction of the east grandstand and the addition of temporary bleachers behind the end zones expanded capacity to 20,416.

RIVAL For the Harvard game, Dartmouth players do just about everything short of foaming at the mouth. It's been that way for as long as anyone can remember. When the Big Green beat the Crimson for their first win in the series, the *Boston Globe* captured the heated rivalry: "Dartmouth has never had any great love for Harvard, and Harvard has never wasted any affection on the Hanover college." The year was 1903.

NICKNAME Dartmouth was founded in 1769 in part to educate Native Americans, and its teams were called the Indians by sportswriters well before the 1920s. Although an

Indian caricature with war paint came to symbolize the team, the nickname was never formally adopted by the college. Recommitting the school to its founding mission in 1972, president John Kemeny officially dropped the nickname that Dartmouth never had actually adopted in the first place. The college's teams have since been referred to by their other longstanding nickname, the Big Green.

MASCOT Looking for a suitable replacement for the Indian mascot, Dartmouth has seen several variations of an antlered "DartMoose" since 1990. The last one, a tall inflatable moose, was banished after numerous complaints from alumni.

UNIFORMS The Dartmouth helmet is among the most distinctive ones in the college game, with a block D in the front and pairs of parallel stripes that separate over the top.

LORE One of the first great passers in college football, All-American Andrew "Swede" Oberlander was known for getting the ball to receivers at exactly the right time. Asked how he did it, Oberlander said that as soon as the ball was snapped he'd recite the following: *Ten thousand Swedes jumped out of the weeds at the Battle of Copenhagen.* "After reciting the jingle to myself," he added, "I'd let the ball go, confident my ends would be downfield by then."

QUOTE "… Dartmouth, football champion of the East, is also champion of the world." —Damon Runyon in 1925, after the Big Green capped an undefeated season as national champions

---

ALL-TIME TEAM

Former Dartmouth sports information director Jack DeGange selected this team in 2004.

OFFENSE

1914-15	Clarence Spears,	OG
1997-2000	Caleb Moore	OG
1965-67	Hank Paulson,	OT
1994-95	Brian Larsen,	OT
1903	Henry Hooper,	C
2000-03	Casey Cramer,	TE
1986-88	Craig Morton,	WR
1991-93	Jay Fiedler,	QB
1925-27	Myles Lane,	RB
1936-38	Bob MacLeod,	RB
1989-91	Al Rosier,	RB
1990-92	Dennis Durkin,	K

DEFENSE

1946-48	Dale Armstrong,	DE
1968-70	Barry Brink,	DT
1975-77	Gregg Robinson,	DT
1978-80	Jerry Pierce,	MG
1960-62	Don McKinnon,	LB
1968-70	Murry Bowden,	LB
1976	Reggie Williams,	LB
1994-97	Zach Walz,	LB
1946-48	Joe Sullivan,	DB
1968-70	Willie Bogan,	DB
1994-97	Lloyd Lee,	DB
1996-99	Wayne Schlobohm,	P

DARTMOUTH ANNUAL STATISTICAL LEADERS

YR	RUSHING	YDS	ATT	AVG	PASSING	ATT	CMP	PCT	YDS	RECEIVING	REC	YDS	AVG
1950	Bill Roberts	527	110	4.8	John Clayton	116	55	.47	673	John McDonald	17	220	12.9
1951	Rick Jennison	255	69	3.7	Gene Howard	75	28	.37	453	John McDonald	14	189	13.5
1952	Rick Collins	368	76	4.8	Jim Miller	148	69	.47	895	Dave Thielscher	30	425	14.2
1953	Lou Turner	400	83	4.8	Leo McKenna	79	41	.52	649	Dave McLaughlin	41	592	14.4
1954	Lou Turner	356	89	4.0	Bill Beagle	145	76	.52	867	Monte Pascoe	24	335	14.0
1955	Lou Rovero	421	91	4.6	Bill Beagle	155	75	.48	812	Monte Pascoe	24	331	13.8
1956	Lou Rovero	508	109	4.7	Mike Brown	78	34	.44	530	Ron Fraser	13	158	12.2
1957	Jake Crouthamel	462	105	4.4	Dave Bradley	77	34	.44	587	Dave Moss	12	368	30.7
1958	Jake Crouthamel	722	123	5.9	Bill Gundy	87	40	.46	572	Jim Burke	12	219	18.3
1959	Jake Crouthamel	579	159	3.6	Bill Gundy	87	48	.55	566	Al Rozycki	25	242	9.7
1960	Al Rozycki	725	169	4.3	Jack Kinderdine	172	81	.47	985	Al Rozycki	25	242	9.7
1961	John Krumme	416	99	4.2	Bill King	98	49	.50	711	John Krumme	17	192	11.3
1962	Tom Spangenberg	675	123	5.5	Bill King	117	67	.57	1,043	Tom Spangenberg	23	353	15.3
1963	Tom Spangenberg	463	117	4.0	Dana Kelly	148	88	.59	1,062	Scott Creelman	24	435	18.1
1964	Bob O'Brien	308	68	4.5	Mickey Beard	84	45	.54	627	Bob MacLeod	27	412	15.3
1965	Pete Walton	641	124	5.2	Mickey Beard	116	60	.52	959	Bill Calhoun	16	345	21.6
1966	Pete Walton	585	102	5.7	Mickey Beard	137	75	.55	1,079	Bill Calhoun	21	388	18.5
1967	Steve Luxford	371	86	4.3	Bill Koenig	102	35	.34	623	Bob Mlakar	25	367	14.7
1968	Clark Beier	481	97	5.0	Bill Koenig	98	36	.37	689	Randy Wallick	19	419	22.1
1969	John Short	707	116	6.1	Jim Chasey	111	62	.56	892	Bob Mlakar	17	187	11.0
1970	John Short	787	165	4.8	Jim Chasey	146	86	.59	1,058	Bob Brown	27	323	12.0
1971	Rick Klupchak	638	106	6.0	Bill Pollock	70	33	.47	520	Tyrone Byrd	19	339	17.8
1972	Rick Klupchak	750	113	6.6	Steve Stetson	139	72	.52	1,159	Tyrone Byrd	19	339	17.8
1973	Ellis Rowe	445	102	4.4	Tom Snickenberger	97	48	.49	481	Tom Fleming	12	233	19.4
1974	John Souba	340	81	4.2	Tom Snickenberger	99	56	.57	615	Alex Kandabarrow	20	293	14.7
1975	Curt Oberg	500	126	4.0	Mike Bralt	169	92	.54	1,155	Tom Fleming	24	523	21.8
1976	Sam Coffey	764	154	5.0	Kevin Case	146	88	.60	1,073	Harry Wilson	40	646	16.2
1977	Curt Oberg	620	138	4.5	Steve Ferraris	122	68	.56	756	Jeff Nadherny	26	317	12.2
1978	Jeff Dufresne	730	190	3.8	Buddy Teevens	194	117	.60	1,396	Dave Shula	49	646	13.2
1979	Jeff Dufresne	449	117	3.8	Jeff Kemp	182	81	.45	915	Dave Shula	32	408	12.8
1980	Jeff Dufresne	488	143	3.4	Jeff Kemp	216	117	.54	1,470	Dave Shula	52	758	14.6
1981	Sean Maher	707	145	4.9	Frank Polsinello	112	63	.56	766	Shaun Teevens	37	520	14.1
1982	Richard Weissman	605	124	4.9	Mike Caraviello	105	60	.57	833	Jack Daly	55	1,034	18.8
1983	Richard Weissman	584	178	3.3	Frank Polsinello	229	141	.62	1,952	Jack Daly	56	889	15.9
1984	Lorenzo Chambers	632	136	4.6	Mike Caraviello	249	132	.53	1,706	Scott Truitt	37	558	15.1
1985	Ernie Torain	432	116	3.7	David Gabianelli	175	87	.50	1,150	Scott Truitt	32	522	16.3
1986	Ernie Torain	640	192	3.3	David Gabianelli	259	141	.54	2,264	Craig Morton	44	1,063	24.2
1987	Chris Pollard	364	97	3.8	Chris Rorke	219	101	.46	1,222	Craig Morton	41	651	15.9
1988	David Clark	669	123	5.4	Mark Johnson	350	196	.56	2,262	Craig Morton	53	891	16.8
1989	David Clark	1,063	219	4.9	Mark Johnson	298	151	.51	1,681	Tom Parker	51	587	11.5
1990	Shon Page	1,087	217	5.0	Matt Brzica	136	64	.47	705	Mike Bobo	23	300	13.0
1991	Al Rosier	1,432	258	5.6	Jay Fiedler	219	121	.55	1,394	Mike Bobo	55	725	13.2
1992	Greg Hoffmeister	650	121	5.4	Jay Fiedler	273	175	.64	2,748	Matt Brzica	53	965	18.2
1993	Pete Oberle	660	164	4.0	Jay Fiedler	321	160	.50	2,542	John Hyland	62	1,076	17.4
1994	Pete Oberle	625	154	4.1	Jerry Singleton	87	50	.57	620	David Shearer	37	589	15.9
1995	Greg Smith	826	178	4.6	Jon Aljiancic	122	49	.40	693	Eric Morton	17	281	16.5
1996	Greg Smith	885	224	4.0	Jon Aljiancic	230	139	.60	1,856	Zach Ellis	32	623	19.5
1997	Dylan Karczewski	541	158	3.4	Peter Sellers	278	139	.50	1,634	Zach Ellis	37	537	14.5
1998	Reggie Belhomme	366	128	2.9	Mike Coffey	265	144	.54	1,543	Adam Young	39	433	11.1
1999	Reggie Belhomme	532	159	3.3	Brian Mann	313	188	.60	1,848	Reggie Belhomme	34	222	6.5
2000	Reggie Belhomme	513	120	4.3	Greg Smith	222	133	.60	1,423	Damien Roomets	43	483	11.2
2001	Michael Gratch	916	194	4.7	Greg Smith	190	117	.62	1,289	Casey Cramer	37	525	14.2
2002	Mike Giles	585	151	3.9	Brian Mann	423	253	.60	2,913	Jay Barnard	83	899	10.8
2003	Chris Little	538	150	3.6	Charlie Rittgers	312	177	.57	2,138	Jay Barnard	70	861	12.3
2004	Chad Gaudet	389	99	3.9	Charlie Rittgers	320	170	.53	1,866	Bob Murphy	49	560	11.4

DARTMOUTH ALL-TIME SCORES

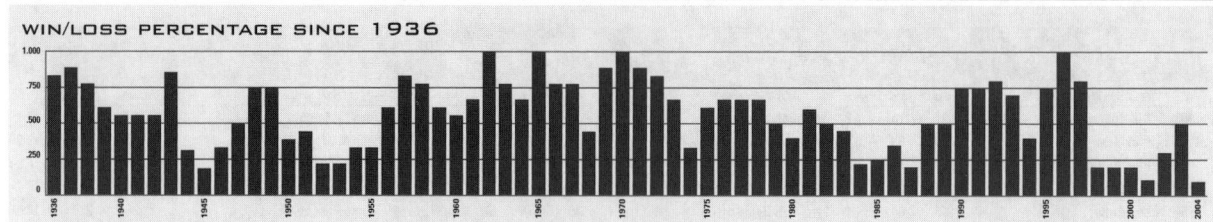

WIN/LOSS PERCENTAGE SINCE 1936

NO HEAD COACH

1881   1-0-1
N12	●	at Amherst	1	0
N19	=	at Amherst	0	0

1882   1-1-0
O28	●	McGill	5	0
N4		at Harvard	0	8

1883   0-1-0
O27		at Amherst	3	5

1884   1-2-1
O25	●	Yale	0	113
N12		Harvard	0	29
U	=	Tufts	10	10
U	●	at Tufts	20	0

1885
NO TEAM

1886   2-2-0
O16		at Andover	11	18
O23	●	MIT	11	6
O27	●	at Vermont	91	0
O30		Harvard *U*	0	70

1887   3-1-1
O15	●	at Tufts	52	0
O22	=	at Stevens	4	4
O26	●	Amherst	52	0
N5	●	at MIT	15	24
N19	●	at Trinity	66	0

1888   3-4-0
O27		at Harvard	0	74
O31	●	at Exeter	10	12
N3	●	at Andover	4	14
N10	●	MIT	30	0
N17	●	Williams	36	6
N19	●	at Stevens	0	30
N29	●	at Amherst	40	0

1889   7-1-0
O9		at Harvard	0	38
O12	●	at Andover	45	4
O19	●	at Exeter	34	0
O26	●	at Andover	20	4
N2	●	Amherst	60	6
N9	●	at Williams	20	9
N16	●	MIT	42	6
N28	●	at Stevens	18	5

1890   4-4-0
O4	●	Andover	10	5
O8		at Harvard	0	43
O11	●	Vermont	71	0
O18		at Harvard	0	64
O25	●	at Andover	10	0
N1	●	Bowdoin	42	0
N8		at Amherst	0	4
N15		at Williams	0	6

1891   2-2-1
O3		at Harvard	0	16
O14	=	Amherst	14	14
O24		at Williams	6	14
N4	●	at Stevens	32	12
N14	●	at MIT		86

1892   5-3-0
O1		at Harvard	0	48
O8	●	Springfield	10	8
O15	●	at Andover	26	0
O22		at Boston AA	8	30
O26	●	at Wesleyan	20	8
N5		Tufts	12	10
N19	●	Williams	24	12
N24		at Amherst	2	30

WALLACE MOYLE
1893-94 (.563)   9-7

1893   4-3-0
S30		at Harvard	0	16
O4	●	at Trinity	16	6
O14		at Yale	0	28
O18		at Harvard	0	36
N1	●	at Williams	20	0
N11	●	Tufts	14	4
N18	●	Amherst	34	0

1894   5-4-0
S29		at Harvard	0	22
O17		Yale *SPR*	0	34
O20	●	at Tufts	12	0
O27	●	Bowdoin	42	0
N3	●	at Bowdoin	14	0
N10	●	Williams	10	0
N17	●	Amherst	30	0
N24	●	Brown	4	20
N29		at Chicago AC	0	4

WILLIAM WURTENBERG
1895-99 (.500)   23-23-2

1895   7-5-1
S28	●	Exeter	50	0
O2		at Harvard	0	4
O5	●	at So. Berwick	10	6
O9	=	at Bowdoin	10	10
O12	●	Bates	38	0
O16		at Yale	0	26
O19	●	MIT	30	0
O23	●	Boston U.	12	0
O26		at Army	0	6
O30		at Yale	0	32
N9	●	Amherst	20	0
N16	●	at Williams	10	5
N28		at Brown	4	10

1896   5-2-1
O3	●	at Worcester AC	30	0
O10		at Pennsylvania	0	16
O17		Yale *PROV*	0	42
O24	●	Bowdoin	28	10
O31	=	at Brown	10	10
N14	●	at Amherst	32	0
N21	●	Williams	10	0
N26	●	Newton AC	12	6

1897   4-3-0
S25	●	Exeter	34	0
O2		at Harvard	0	13
O16		at Pennsylvania	0	14
O30		at Princeton	0	30
N3	●	Amherst	54	0
N13	●	at Williams	52	0
N20	●	at Newton AC	24	0

1898   5-6-0
S24	●	Exeter	23	5
O1		at Harvard	0	21
O8	●	Bowdoin	35	6
O15	●	Vermont	45	6
O22	●	at Amherst	64	6
O29	●	at Williams	10	6
N5		Wesleyan	5	23
N12	●	at Chicago AC	5	17
N19		at Brown	0	12
N24		at Cincinnati	12	17
D3		at Carlisle	6	17

1899   2-7-0
S30	●	Exeter	16	5
O7	●	Bowdoin	37	0
O14		Yale *NTH*	0	12
O21		Williams	10	12
O28		at Army	2	6
N4		at Wesleyan	0	11
N11		at Harvard	0	11
N18		at Columbia	0	22
N25		at Brown	5	16

FREDERICK JENNINGS
1900 (.375)   2-4-2

1900   2-4-2
O6	●	Exeter	10	0
O13		Yale *NTH*	0	17
O20	●	Tufts	12	0
O27		at Cornell	6	23
N3		at Wesleyan	5	16
N10	=	Union	0	0
N17	=	at Vermont	0	0
N29		at Brown	5	12

WALTER McCORNACK
1901-02 (.825)   16-3-1

1901   10-1-0
O2	●	New Hampshire	51	0
O5	●	Trinity	23	0
O9	●	Boston College	45	0
O12	●	Tufts	22	0
O19	●	at Williams	6	2
O26	●	at Bowdoin	35	12
N2	●	Wesleyan	29	12
N9	●	Vermont	22	0
N16		at Harvard	12	27
N23	●	St. Paul's	24	0
N27	●	at Brown	22	0

1902   6-2-1
O4	●	Vermont	11	0
O8	=	Massachusetts	0	0
O11	●	Tufts	29	0
O18	●	at Williams	18	0
O25	●	Amherst	6	12
N1	●	at Wesleyan	12	5
N8	●	Springfield	11	0
N15		at Harvard	6	16
N23	●	Brown *U*	12	6

FRED FOLSOM
1903-06 (.816)   29-5-4

1903   9-1-0
S26	●	Massachusetts	12	0
O3	●	Holy Cross	18	0
O7	●	at Vermont	36	0
O14	●	Union	34	0
O17	●	at Williams	17	0
O24		at Princeton	0	17
O31	●	Wesleyan	34	6
N7	●	at Amherst	18	0
N14	●	at Harvard	11	0
N26	●	Brown *U*	62	0

1904   7-0-1
S28	●	Massachusetts	17	0
O8	●	Vermont	37	0
O15	●	at Williams	11	0
O22	●	at Holy Cross	18	4
O29	●	at Wesleyan	33	0
N5	=	at Harvard	0	0
N12	●	Amherst	15	4
N19	●	Brown *U*	12	5

1905   7-1-2
S16	●	Norwich	34	0
S23	●	Massachsetts	18	0
O4	●	Vermont	12	0
O7	●	Holy Cross	16	6
O21	●	Colgate	10	16
O28	●	Williams	24	0
N4		at Princeton	6	0
N11	=	at Amherst	0	0
N18	●	at Harvard	6	6
N25	●	at Brown	24	6

1906   6-3-1
S22	●	Norwich	5	0
S29	●	Vermont	8	0
O6	●	Holy Cross	16	0
O13	●	Maine	4	0
O20	●	Massachusetts	26	0
O27	=	at Williams	0	0
N3		at Princeton	0	42
N10	●	at Amherst	4	0
N17	●	at Harvard	9	22
N24		Brown *U*	0	23

JOHN O'CONNOR
1907-08 (.882)   14-1-2

1907   8-0-1
S28	●	Norwich	12	0
O5	=	Vermont	0	0
O9	●	New Hampshire St.	10	0
O12	●	Massachusetts	6	0
O19	●	at Maine	27	0
O26	●	at Amherst	15	10
U	●	Tufts	6	0
N9	●	Holy Cross	52	0
N16	●	at Harvard	22	0

1908   6-1-1
S30	●	Vermont	11	0
O3	●	Massachusetts	23	0
O10	●	Tufts	18	0
O17	=	at Williams	0	0
O24	●	at Holy Cross	18	5
O31	●	Amherst	17	0
N7		Princeton	10	6
N14	●	at Harvard	0	6

WALTER LILLARD
1909 (.750)   5-1-2

1909   5-1-2
S29	●	Massachusetts	23	0
O2	=	Vermont	0	0
O9	●	Bowdoin	15	0
O16	●	Williams	18	0
O23	●	at Amherst	12	0
O30	●	Holy Cross	12	0
N6	=	at Princeton	6	6
N13		at Harvard	3	12

WILLIAM RANDALL
1910 (.714)   5-2

1910   5-2-0
O1	●	Massachusetts	6	0
U	●	Colby	18	0
U	●	Vermont	33	0
U	●	at Williams	39	0
O29		Princeton *UNK*	0	6
U	●	at Amherst	15	3
N12		at Harvard	0	18

FRANK CAVANAUGH
1911-16 (.806) 42-9-3

1911 8-2-0
S27	•	Norwich	18	3
S30	•	MAC	22	0
O4	•	Bowdoin	23	0
O7	•	Colby	12	0
O14	•	Holy Cross	6	0
O21	•	Williams	23	5
O28	•	Vermont	12	0
N4	•	at Amherst	18	6
N11		at Princeton	0	3
N18		at Harvard	3	5

1912 7-2-0
S21	•	Bates	26	0
S28	•	Norwich	41	9
O5	•	MAC	47	0
O12	•	Vermont	55	0
O19	•	at Williams	21	0
O26		at Princeton	7	22
N2	•	Amherst	60	0
N9	•	at Cornell	24	0
N16		at Harvard	0	3

1913 7-1-0
S27	•	MAC	13	3
O4	•	Colby	53	0
O11	•	Vermont	33	7
O18	•	Williams	48	6
O25	•	at Princeton	6	0
N1	•	at Amherst	21	7
N8	•	at Pennsylvania	34	21
N15		Carlisle NYC	10	35

1914 8-1-0
S26	•	MAC	29	6
O3	•	Norwich	74	0
O10	•	at Williams	21	3
O17	•	at Vermont	42	0
O24		at Princeton	12	16
O31	•	Amherst	32	0
N7	•	Tufts	68	0
N14	•	at Pennsylvania	41	0
N21	•	Syracuse	40	0

1915 7-1-1
S25	•	MAC	13	0
O2	•	Maine	32	0
O9	•	Tufts	20	7
O16	•	Vermont	60	0
O23		at Princeton	7	30
O30	•	at Amherst	26	0
N6	•	Pennsylvania Bos	7	3
N13	•	Bates	29	0
N20	=	at Syracuse	0	0

1916 5-2-2
S23	•	New Hampshire St.	33	0
S30	•	Boston College	32	6
O7	•	Lebanon Valley	47	0
O14	•	MAC	62	0
O21		at Georgetown	0	10
O28		at Princeton	3	7
N4	•	Syracuse Spr	15	10
N11	=	at Pennsylvania	7	7
N18	=	West Virginia	7	7

CLARENCE SPEARS
1917-20 (.694) 21-9-1

1917 5-3-0
O6	•	Springfield	14	0
O13	•	Middlebury	32	6
O20	•	West Virginia	6	2
O27	•	New Hampshire St.	21	6
N3	•	Penn State	10	7
N10		Pennsylvania Bos	0	7
N17		at Tufts	0	27
N29		Brown U	0	13

1918 3-3-0
O26	•	Norwich	20	0
N3		Syracuse	6	34
N10	•	US Marines	26	0
N17	•	Middlebury	26	0
N24		Brown U	0	28
N28		at Pennsylvania	0	21

1919 6-1-1
S27	•	Springfield	40	0
O4	•	Norwich	13	0
O11	•	MAC	27	7
O18	•	Penn State	19	13
O25	•	Cornell NYC	9	0
N1	=	Colgate	7	7
N8	•	Pennsylvania NYC	20	19
N15		Brown U	6	7

1920 7-2-0
O2	•	Norwich	31	0
O9		at Penn State	7	14
O16	•	Holy Cross	27	14
O23		Syracuse	0	10
O30	•	Tufts	34	7
N6	•	Cornell NYC	14	3
N13	•	at Pennsylvania	44	7
N20	•	Brown U	14	6
N27	•	at Washington	28	7 *

JACKSON CANNELL
1921-22, '29-33 (.661) 39-19-4

1921 6-2-1
S24	•	Norwich	34	3
O1	•	Middlebury	28	3
O8	•	New Hampshire	24	0
O15	•	Tennessee	14	3
O22	•	Columbia	31	7
O29		at Cornell	7	59
N12	=	Pennsylvania NYC	14	14
N19		Syracuse NYC	7	14
N27	•	Georgia Atl	7	0

1922 6-3-0
S30	•	Norwich	20	0
O7	•	Maine	19	0
O14	•	Middlebury	21	0
O21		Vermont	3	6
O28		at Harvard	3	12
N4	•	Boston U.	10	7
N11		Cornell NYC	0	23
N18	•	Columbia NYC	28	7
N25	•	Brown U	7	0

JESSE HAWLEY
1923-28 (.790) 39-10-1

1923 8-1-0
S29	•	Norwich	13	0
O6	•	Maine	6	0
O13	•	Boston U.	24	0
O20	•	at Vermont	27	2
O27	•	at Harvard	16	0
N3		Cornell	7	32
N10	•	Brown U	16	14
N17	•	Colby	62	0
N29	•	Columbia NYC	31	6

1924 7-0-1
S27	•	Norwich	40	0
O4	•	McGill	52	0
O11	•	Vermont	38	0
O18	=	at Yale	14	14
O25	•	at Harvard	6	0
N1	•	Brown	10	3
N8	•	Boston U.	38	0
N15	•	Cornell NYC	27	14

1925 8-0-0
S26	•	Norwich	59	0
O3	•	Hobart	34	0
O10	•	Vermont	50	0
O17	•	Maine	56	0
O24	•	at Harvard	32	9
O31	•	at Brown	14	0
N7	•	Cornell	62	13
N14	•	at Chicago	33	7

1926 4-4-0
S25	•	Norwich	59	0
O2	•	Hobart	50	0
O9	•	Virginia Tech	21	0
O16		Yale	7	14
O23		Harvard	12	16
O30		Brown	0	10
N6	•	Boston U.	32	0
N13		at Cornell	23	24

1927 7-1-0
S24	•	Norwich	47	0
O1	•	Hobart	46	0
O8	•	Allegheny	38	7
O15	•	Temple	47	7
O22	•	at Harvard	30	6
O29		at Yale	0	19
N5	•	at Brown	19	7
N12	•	Cornell	53	7

1928 5-4-0
S29	•	Norwich	39	6
O6	•	Hobart	44	0
O13	•	Allegheny	37	12
O20	•	Columbia	21	7
O27		at Harvard	7	19
N3		at Yale	0	18
N10		Brown	0	14
N17	•	at Cornell	28	0
N24		at Northwestern	6	27

JACKSON CANNELL

1929 7-2-0
S28	•	Norwich	67	0
O5	•	Hobart	68	0
O12	•	Allegheny	53	0
O19	•	at Columbia	34	0
O26	•	at Harvard	34	7
N2		at Yale	12	16
N9	•	at Brown	13	6
N23	•	Cornell	18	14
N30		Navy Phil	6	13

1930 7-1-1
S27	•	Norwich	79	0
O4	•	Bates	20	0
O11	•	Boston U.	74	0
O18	•	Columbia	52	0
O25	•	at Harvard	7	2
N1	=	at Yale	0	0
N8	•	Allegheny	43	14
N15	•	at Cornell	19	13
N29		at Stanford	7	14

1931 5-3-1
S26	•	Norwich	56	6
O3	•	Buffalo	61	0
O10	•	Holy Cross	14	7
O17		at Columbia	6	19
O24	•	Lebanon Valley	20	6
O31	=	at Yale	33	33
N7		at Harvard	6	7
N14	•	Cornell	14	0
N28		Stanford Bos	6	32

1932 4-4-0
S24	•	Norwich	73	0
O1	•	Vermont	32	0
O8	•	Lafayette	6	0
O15		at Pennsylvania	7	14
O22		at Harvard	7	10
O26		at Yale	0	6
N5	•	New Hampshire	25	0
N12		at Cornell	6	21

1933 4-4-1
S30	•	Norwich	41	0
O7	•	Vermont	39	6
O14	•	Bates	14	0
O21	•	at Pennsylvania	14	7
O28	=	at Harvard	7	7
N4		at Yale	13	1
N11		at Princeton	0	7
N18		Cornell	0	7
N25		at Chicago	0	39

EARL BLAIK
1934-40 (.734) 45-15-4

1934 6-3-0
S29	•	Norwich	39	0
O6	•	Vermont	32	0
O13	•	Maine	27	0
O20	•	Virginia	27	0
O27	•	at Harvard	10	0
N3		at Yale	2	7
N10	•	New Hampshire	21	7
N17		at Cornell	6	21
N24		at Princeton	13	38

1935 8-2-0
S28	•	Norwich	39	0
O5	•	Vermont	47	0
O12	•	Bates	59	0
O19	•	at Brown	41	0
O26	•	at Harvard	14	6
N2	•	at Yale	14	6
N9	•	William & Mary	34	0
N16	•	Cornell	41	6
N23		at Princeton	6	26
N30		at Columbia	7	13

1936 7-1-1
S26	•	Norwich	58	0
O3	•	Vermont	56	0
O10		Holy Cross	0	7
O17	•	Brown	34	0
O24	•	at Harvard	26	7
O31	•	at Yale	11	7
N7	•	Columbia	20	13
N14	•	at Cornell	20	6
N21	=	at Princeton	13	13

1937 7-0-2
S25	•	Bates	39	0
O2	•	Amherst	31	7
O9	•	Springfield	42	0
O16	•	at Brown	41	0
O23	•	at Harvard	20	2
O30	=	at Yale	9	9
N6	•	at Princeton	33	9
N13	=	Cornell	6	6
N20	•	at Columbia	27	0

1938 7-2-0
S24	•	Bates	46	0
O1	•	St. Lawrence	51	0
O8	•	at Princeton	22	0
O15	•	Brown	34	13
O22	•	at Harvard	13	7
O29	•	at Yale	24	6
N5	•	Dickinson	44	6
N12		at Cornell	7	14
N26		at Stanford	13	23

1939 5-3-1
S30	•	St. Lawrence	41	9
O7	•	Hampden Sydney	34	6
O14	=	Navy Balt	0	0
O21	•	Lafayette	14	0
O28	•	at Harvard	16	0
N4	•	at Yale	33	0
N11		at Princeton	7	9
N18		Cornell	6	35
D2		Stanford NYC	3	14

1940 5-4-0
S28	•	St. Lawrence	36	0
O5		Franklin & Marshall	21	23
O12		Columbia	6	20
O19		at Yale	7	13
O26	•	at Harvard	7	6
N2	•	Sewanee	26	0
N9		at Princeton	9	14
N16	•	Cornell	3	0
N23	•	at Brown	20	6

DeORMOND McLAUGHRY
1941-42, '45-54 (.433) 44-58-3

1941 5-4-0
S27	•	Norwich	35	0
O4	•	Amherst	47	7
O11	•	Colgate	18	6
O18		at Harvard	0	7
O25	•	at Yale	7	0
N1		William & Mary	0	3
N8	•	at Princeton	20	13
N15		at Cornell	19	33
N22		at Georgia	0	35

1942 5-4-0
S26	•	at Holy Cross	17	6
O3	•	Miami, Ohio	58	7
O10		Colgate	19	27
O17	•	at Harvard	14	2
O24		at Yale	7	17
O31		William & Mary	14	35
N7	•	at Princeton	19	7
N14		Cornell NYC	19	21
N21	•	at Columbia	26	13

EARL BROWN
1943-44 (.567) 8-6-1

1943 6-1-0
S25	•	at Holy Cross	3	0
O2	•	Coast Guard	47	0
O9		at Pennsylvania	6	7
O30	•	at Yale	20	6
N6	•	Columbia	47	13
N13	•	Cornell Bos	20	0
N20	•	at Princeton	42	13

1944 2-5-1
S30	=	Holy Cross	6	6
O7		at Pennsylvania	6	20
O14		Notre Dame	0	64
O28	•	at Brown	14	13
N4		at Yale	0	6
N11		Coast Guard	0	19
N18		at Cornell	13	14
N25	•	at Columbia	18	0

DeORMOND McLAUGHRY

1945 1-6-1
S29		Holy Cross	6	13
O6		at Pennsylvania	0	12
O13		at Notre Dame	0	34
O27	•	at Syracuse	8	0
N3		at Yale	0	6
N10	=	at Princeton	13	13
N17		Cornell	13	20
N24		at Columbia	0	21

1946 — 3-6-0

S28 •	at Holy Cross	3	0
O5 •	Syracuse	20	14
O12	at Pennsylvania	6	39
O19	at Brown	13	20
O26	Columbia	13	33
N2	at Yale	2	33
N9	Harvard	7	21
N16	at Cornell	7	21
N23 •	at Princeton	20	13

1947 — 4-4-1

S27 =	at Holy Cross	0	0
O4 •	at Syracuse	28	7
O11	Pennsylvania	0	32
O18 •	Brown	13	10
O25	at Harvard	14	13
N1	at Yale	14	23
N8	Columbia	0	15
N15 •	Cornell	21	13
N22	at Princeton	12	14

1948 — 6-2-0

O2	at Pennsylvania	13	26
O9 •	Holy Cross	19	6
O16 •	Colgate	41	16
O23 •	at Harvard	14	7
O30 •	at Yale	41	14
N6 •	Columbia	26	21
N13 •	at Cornell	26	27
N20 •	at Princeton	33	13

1949 — 6-2-0

O1 •	at Pennsylvania	0	21
O8 •	Holy Cross	31	7
O15 •	Colgate	27	13
O22 •	at Harvard	27	13
O29 •	at Yale	34	13
N5 •	at Columbia	35	14
N12 •	Cornell	16	7
N19 •	at Princeton	13	19

1950 — 3-5-1

S30 =	Holy Cross	21	21
O7	at Michigan	7	27
O14	at Pennsylvania	26	42
O21	Lehigh	14	16
O28 •	at Harvard	27	7
N4 •	at Yale	7	0
N11 •	Columbia	14	7
N18 •	at Cornell	0	24
N25 •	at Princeton	7	13

1951 — 4-5-0

S29 •	Fordham	6	14
O6 •	at Pennsylvania	14	39
O13 •	at Army	28	14
O20 •	Syracuse	14	0
O27 •	at Harvard	26	20
N3 •	at Yale	14	10
N10 •	at Columbia	6	21
N17 •	Cornell	13	21
N24 •	at Princeton	0	13

1952 — 2-7-0

S27 •	Holy Cross	9	27
O4 •	at Pennsylvania	0	7
O11 •	at Army	7	37
O18 •	Rutgers	29	20
O25 •	at Harvard	19	26
N1 •	at Yale	7	21
N8 •	Columbia	38	14
N15 •	at Cornell	7	13
N22 •	at Princeton	0	33

1953 — 2-7-0

S26 •	Holy Cross	6	28
O3 •	at Navy	7	55
O10 •	at Army	0	27
O17 •	Colgate	14	24
O24 •	at Harvard	14	20
O31 •	at Yale	32	0
N7 •	at Columbia	19	25
N14 •	Cornell	26	28
N21 •	at Princeton	34	12

1954 — 3-6-0

S25 •	Holy Cross	27	26
O2 •	Navy	7	42
O9 •	at Army	6	60
O16 •	Colgate	7	13
O23 •	at Harvard	13	7
O30 •	at Yale	7	13
N6 •	Columbia	26	0
N13 •	at Cornell	21	40
N20 •	at Princeton	7	49

1955 — 3-6-0

S24	at Colgate	20	21
O1	Holy Cross	21	29
O8	at Brown	0	7
O15	Lafayette	13	21
O22 •	Harvard	14	9
O29	at Yale	0	20
N5 •	at Columbia	14	7
N12 •	Cornell	7	0
N19	at Princeton	3	6

1956-PRESENT
IVY LEAGUE

1956 — 5-3-1 (4-3-0)

S29 •	New Hampshire	13	0
O6 •	at Pennsylvania	7	14
O13 •	at Brown	14	7
O20 =	Holy Cross	7	7
O27 •	at Harvard	21	28
N3 •	at Yale	0	19
N10 •	Columbia	14	0
N17 •	at Cornell	27	14
N24 •	at Princeton	19	0

1957 — 7-1-1 (5-1-1)

S28 •	New Hampshire	27	0
O5 •	at Pennsylvania	6	3
O12 •	Brown	35	0
O19 •	at Holy Cross	14	7
O26 •	at Harvard	26	0
N2 =	at Yale	14	14
N9 •	at Columbia	7	0
N16 •	Cornell	20	19
N23 •	at Princeton	14	34

1958 — 7-2-0 (6-1-0)

S27 •	Lafayette	20	0
O4 •	Pennsylvania	13	12
O11 •	at Brown	20	0
O18 •	Holy Cross	8	14
O25 •	at Harvard	8	16
N1 •	at Yale	22	14
N8 •	Columbia	38	0
N15 •	at Cornell	32	15
N22 •	at Princeton	21	12

1959 — 5-3-1 (5-1-1)

S26 •	Holy Cross	8	31
O3 •	at Pennsylvania	0	13
O10 =	Brown	0	0
O17 •	at Boston College	12	35
O24 •	at Harvard	9	0
O31 •	at Yale	12	8
N7 •	at Columbia	22	0
N14 •	Cornell	21	12
N21 •	at Princeton	12	7

1960 — 5-4-0 (4-3-0)

S24 •	New Hampshire	7	6
O1 •	Pennsylvania	15	0
O8 •	at Brown	20	0
O15 •	Holy Cross	8	9
O22 •	at Harvard	6	9
O29 •	at Yale	0	29
N5 •	Columbia	22	6
N12 •	at Cornell	20	0
N19 •	at Princeton	0	7

1961 — 6-3-0 (5-2-0)

S30 •	New Hampshire	28	3
O7 •	at Pennsylvania	30	0
O14 •	Brown	34	0
O21 •	at Holy Cross	13	17
O28 •	at Harvard	15	21
N4 •	at Yale	24	8
N11 •	at Columbia	14	35
N18 •	Cornell	15	14
N25 •	at Princeton	24	6

1962 — 9-0-0 (7-0-0)

S29 •	Massachusetts	22	3
O6 •	Pennsylvania	17	0
O13 •	at Brown	41	0
O20 •	Holy Cross	10	0
O27 •	at Harvard	24	6
N3 •	at Yale	9	0
N10 •	Columbia	42	0
N17 •	at Cornell	28	21
N24 •	at Princeton	38	27

1963 — 7-2-0 (5-2-0)

S28 •	Bucknell	20	18
O5 •	at Pennsylvania	28	0
O12 •	Brown	14	7
O19 •	Holy Cross	13	8
O26 •	at Harvard	13	17
N2 •	at Yale	6	10
N9 •	at Columbia	47	6
N16 •	Cornell	12	7
N30 •	at Princeton	22	21

1964 — 6-3-0 (4-3-0)

S26 •	at New Hampshire	40	0
O3 •	Boston U.	28	6
O10	Princeton	7	37
O17 •	Brown	24	14
O24 •	at Harvard	48	0
O31 •	at Yale	15	24
N7 •	Columbia	31	14
N14 •	at Cornell	15	33
N21 •	at Pennsylvania	27	7

1965 — 9-0-0 (7-0-0)

S25 •	New Hampshire	56	6
O2 •	at Holy Cross	27	6
O9 •	Pennsylvania	24	19
O16 •	at Brown	35	9
O23 •	at Harvard	14	0
O30 •	at Yale	20	17
N6 •	at Columbia	47	0
N13 •	Cornell	20	0
N20 •	at Princeton	28	14

1966 — 7-2-0 (6-1-0)

S24 •	Massachusetts	17	7
O1 •	at Holy Cross	6	7
O8 •	Princeton	31	13
O15 •	Brown	49	14
O22 •	at Harvard	14	19
O29 •	at Yale	28	13
N5 •	Columbia	56	14
N12 •	at Cornell	32	23
N19 •	at Pennsylvania	40	21

1967 — 7-2-0 (5-2-0)

S30 •	at Massachusetts	28	10
O7 •	Holy Cross	24	8
O14 •	Pennsylvania	23	0
O21 •	at Brown	41	6
O28 •	at Harvard	23	21
N4 •	at Yale	15	56
N11 •	at Columbia	13	7
N18 •	Cornell	21	24
N25 •	at Princeton	17	14

1968 — 4-5-0 (3-4-0)

S28 •	New Hampshire	21	0
O5 •	at Holy Cross	17	29
O12 •	Princeton	7	34
O19 •	Brown	48	0
O26 •	at Harvard	7	22
N2 •	at Yale	27	47
N9 •	Columbia	31	19
N16 •	at Cornell	27	6
N23 •	at Pennsylvania	21	26

1969 — 8-1-0 (6-1-0)

S27 •	at New Hampshire	31	0
O4 •	Holy Cross	38	6
O11 •	Pennsylvania	41	0
O18 •	at Brown	38	13
O25 •	at Harvard	24	10
N1 •	at Yale	42	21
N8 •	at Columbia	37	7
N15 •	Cornell	24	7
N22 •	at Princeton	7	35

1970 — 9-0-0 (7-0-0)

S26 •	Massachusetts	27	0
O3 •	at Holy Cross	50	14
O10 •	Princeton	38	0
O17 •	Brown	42	14
O24 •	at Harvard	37	14
O31 •	at Yale	10	0
N7 •	Columbia	55	0
N14 •	at Cornell	24	0
N21 •	at Pennsylvania	28	0

1971 — 8-1-0 (6-1-0)

S25 •	at Massachusetts	31	7
O2 •	Holy Cross	28	9
O9 •	Pennsylvania	19	3
O16 •	at Brown	10	7
O23 •	at Harvard	16	13
O30 •	Yale	17	15
N6 •	at Columbia	29	31
N13 •	Cornell	24	14
N20 •	at Princeton	33	7

1972 — 7-1-1 (5-1-1)

S30 •	New Hampshire	24	14
O7 •	at Holy Cross	17	7
O14 •	Princeton	35	14
O21 •	Brown	49	20
O28 =	at Harvard	21	21
N4 •	at Yale	14	45
N11 •	Columbia	38	8
N18 •	at Cornell	31	22
N25 •	at Pennsylvania	31	17

1973 — 6-3-0 (6-1-0)

S29 •	at New Hampshire	9	10
O6 •	Holy Cross	0	10
O13 •	Pennsylvania	16	22
O20 •	at Brown	28	16
O27 •	at Harvard	24	18
N3 •	Yale	24	13
N10 •	at Columbia	24	6
N17 •	Cornell	17	0
N24 •	at Princeton	42	24

1974 — 3-6-0 (3-4-0)

S28 •	Massachusetts	0	14
O5 •	at Holy Cross	3	14
O12 •	Princeton	7	14
O19 •	at Brown	7	6
O26 •	Harvard	15	17
N2 •	at Yale	9	14
N9 •	Columbia	21	0
N16 •	at Cornell	21	9
N23 •	at Pennsylvania	20	27

1975 — 5-3-1 (4-2-1)

S27 •	at Massachusetts	3	7
O4 •	Holy Cross	28	7
O11 •	Pennsylvania	19	14
O18 =	Brown	10	10
O25 •	at Harvard	10	24
N1 •	at Yale	14	16
N8 •	at Columbia	22	17
N15 •	Cornell	33	10
N22 •	at Princeton	21	16

1976 — 6-3-0 (4-3-0)

S18 •	Pennsylvania	20	0
S25 •	New Hampshire	24	13
O2 •	at Holy Cross	45	7
O9 •	at Yale	14	18
O16 •	Harvard	10	17
O23 •	at Cornell	35	0
O30 •	Columbia	34	14
N6 •	at Brown	21	35
N13 •	at Princeton	33	7

1977 — 6-3-0 (4-3-0)

S17 •	Princeton	14	11
S24 •	Holy Cross	17	14
O1 •	at Boston U.	38	0
O8 •	at Yale	3	0
O15 •	at Harvard	25	31
O22 •	Cornell	17	13
O29 •	at Columbia	14	7
N5 •	Brown	10	13
N12 •	at Pennsylvania	3	7

1978 — 6-3-0 (6-1-0)

S23 •	Pennsylvania	31	21
S30 •	at Holy Cross	0	35
O7 •	Boston U.	17	20
O14 •	Yale	10	3
O21 •	at Harvard	19	24
O28 •	at Cornell	14	7
N4 •	Columbia	37	7
N11 •	at Brown	31	21
N18 •	at Princeton	28	21

1979 4-4-1 (4-3-0)

S22		Princeton	0	16
S29	=	New Hampshire	10	10
O6		Holy Cross	7	13
O13		Yale	0	3
O20	●	Harvard	10	7
O27		Cornell	10	21
N3	●	Columbia	17	0
N10	●	Brown	24	10
N17	●	Pennsylvania	20	6

1980 4-6-0 (4-3-0)

S20	●	Pennsylvania	40	7
S27		New Hampshire	7	24
O4		at Holy Cross	6	17
O11		at William & Mary	14	17
O18	●	Harvard	30	12
O25		at Cornell	3	7
N1		Yale	7	35
N8	●	Columbia	48	0
N15	●	at Brown	28	24
N22		at Princeton	24	27

1981 6-4-0 (6-1-0)

S19	●	Princeton	32	13
S26		at Massachusetts	8	10
O3		Holy Cross	0	28
O10		William & Mary	7	12
O17	●	at Harvard	24	10
O24		Cornell	42	7
O31		at Yale	3	24
N7	●	at Columbia	21	7
N14	●	Brown	38	13
N21	●	at Pennsylvania	33	13

1982 5-5-0 (5-2-0)

S18		Pennsylvania	0	21
S25		at Holy Cross	12	28
O2		Colgate	21	38
O9		at William & Mary	16	24
O16	●	Harvard	14	12
O23	●	at Cornell	14	13
O30		Yale	21	22
N6	●	Columbia	56	41
N13	●	at Brown	22	16
N20	●	at Princeton	43	20

1983 4-5-1 (4-2-1)

S17	●	Princeton	21	3
S24		at Army	12	13
O1		Holy Cross	14	41
O8		William & Mary	17	21
O15	●	at Harvard	28	12
O22	●	Cornell	31	17
O29	●	at Yale	24	21
N5	=	at Columbia	17	17
N12		Brown	7	25
N19		at Pennsylvania	14	38

1984 2-7-0 (2-5-0)

S22		Pennsylvania	24	55
S29		New Hampshire	10	38
O6		at Holy Cross	20	30
O13		at Yale	18	28
O20		Harvard	7	21
O27		at Cornell	10	13
N3	●	Columbia	41	9
N10	●	at Brown	27	11
N17		at Princeton	17	21

1985 2-7-1 (2-4-1)

S21		Princeton	3	10
S28		at New Hampshire	7	23
O5		Holy Cross	14	17
O12		Colgate	28	54
O19		at Harvard	7	17
O26	●	at Cornell	20	17
N2	=	Yale	17	17
N9	●	at Columbia	34	3
N16		Brown	0	22
N23		at Pennsylvania	14	19

1986 3-6-1 (3-3-1)

S20		Pennsylvania	7	21
S27		New Hampshire	12	66
O4		at Navy	0	45
O11		at Holy Cross	7	48
O18		Harvard	26	42
O25		Cornell	7	10
N1	●	at Yale	39	13
N8	●	Columbia	41	0
N15	=	at Brown	21	21
N22	●	at Princeton	28	6

1987 2-8-0 (1-6-0)

S19		Princeton	3	34
S26		at New Hampshire	3	41
O3	●	Davidson	38	7
O10		Holy Cross	23	62
O17		at Harvard	3	42
O24		at Cornell	14	21
O31		Yale	7	17
N7	●	at Columbia	12	10
N14		Brown	0	19
N21		at Pennsylvania	7	49

1988 5-5-0 (4-3-0)

S17		Pennsylvania	27	33
S24		Lehigh	16	41
O1		at Davidson	24	3
O8		at Holy Cross	3	17
O15	●	Harvard	38	7
O22		Cornell	7	24
O29		at Yale	13	22
N5	●	Columbia	20	10
N12	●	at Brown	37	24
N19	●	at Princeton	24	17

1989 5-5-0 (4-3-0)

S16		Princeton	14	20
S23	●	Boston U.	28	27
S30		at Bucknell	20	36
O7		Holy Cross	7	33
O14		Yale	19	24
O21		at Harvard	5	6
O28	●	at Cornell	28	14
N4	●	at Columbia	13	12
N11	●	Brown	12	6
N18	●	at Pennsylvania	24	0

1990 7-2-1 (6-1-0)

S15		Pennsylvania	6	16
S22	●	Lehigh	33	14
S29	=	at New Hampshire	21	21
O6		at Holy Cross	10	21
O13	●	Yale	27	17
O20	●	at Cornell	11	6
O27	●	Harvard	17	0
N3	●	Columbia	34	20
N10	●	at Brown	29	0
N17	●	at Princeton	23	6

1991 7-2-1 (6-0-1)

S21	●	at Pennsylvania	21	15
S28	●	Bucknell	34	16
O5		at Lehigh	28	30
O12		Holy Cross	6	23
O19	●	at Yale	28	24
O26	●	Cornell	31	25
N2	=	at Harvard	31	31
N9	●	at Columbia	28	19
N16	●	Brown	45	13
N23	●	Princeton	31	13

1992 8-2-0 (6-1-0)

S19	●	Pennsylvania	36	17
S26	●	at New Hampshire	27	45
O3	●	Bucknell	44	14
O10	●	at Holy Cross	48	0
O17	●	Yale	39	27
O24		at Cornell	16	26
O31	●	at Harvard	31	7
N7	●	Columbia	38	19
N14	●	at Brown	51	28
N21	●	at Princeton	34	20

1993 7-3-0 (6-1-0)

S18		at Pennsylvania	6	10
S25		Holy Cross	7	13
O2	●	at Bucknell	31	13
O9		New Hampshire	7	14
O16	●	at Yale	31	14
O23	●	Cornell	28	27
O30	●	Harvard	39	34
N6	●	at Columbia	42	25
N13	●	Brown	39	16
N20	●	Princeton	28	22

1994 4-6-0 (2-5-0)

S17		at Colgate	16	20
S24		Pennsylvania	11	13
O1	●	Fordham	31	14
O8		at Lafayette	27	15
O15	●	Yale	14	13
O22		at Cornell	14	17
O29		Harvard	12	35
N5	●	Columbia	14	13
N12		at Brown	14	27
N19		at Princeton	13	20

1995 7-2-1 (4-2-1)

S16		at Pennsylvania	12	20
S23	●	at Fordham	34	14
S30		Cornell	19	24
O7	●	Lafayette	14	7
O14	●	at Yale	22	7
O21	●	Colgate	35	14
O28	●	at Harvard	23	7
N4	●	at Columbia	43	27
N11	●	Brown	10	7
N18	=	Princeton	10	10

1996 10-0 (7-0)

S21	●	Pennsylvania	24	22
S28	●	at Fordham	21	14
O5	●	Fordham	20	7
O12	●	Holy Cross	35	7
O19	●	Yale	40	6
O26	●	at Cornell	38	21
N2	●	at Harvard	6	3
N9	●	Columbia	40	0
N16	●	at Brown	27	24
N23	●	at Princeton	24	0

1997 8-2 (6-1)

S20	●	at Pennsylvania	23	15
S27	●	at Holy Cross	35	6
O4	●	Cornell	24	20
O11	●	at Fordham	31	10
O18	●	at Yale	21	7
O25		Lehigh	26	46
N1		Harvard	0	24
N8	●	at Columbia	23	21
N15	●	Brown	13	7
N22	●	Princeton	12	9

1998 2-8 (1-6)

S19		Pennsylvania	14	17
S26		at Maine	3	14
O3	●	Lafayette	13	10
O10		at Colgate	24	45
O17	●	Yale	22	19
O24		at Cornell	11	14
O31		Harvard	7	20
N7		Columbia	14	24
N14		at Brown	21	28
N21		at Princeton	13	35

1999 2-8 (2-5)

S18		at Pennsylvania	6	17
S25		Colgate	3	35
O2		at Lafayette	10	20
O9		Lehigh	14	30
O16		at Yale	3	44
O23	●	Cornell	20	17
O30		at Harvard	21	63
N6		at Columbia	14	21
N13		Brown	28	35
N20	●	Princeton	19	18

2000 2-8 (1-6)

S16		Colgate	24	42
S23		at New Hampshire	21	42
S30		at Pennsylvania	14	48
O7		Yale	14	24
O14	●	Holy Cross	31	14
O21		at Columbia	21	49
O28		Harvard	7	49
N4		at Cornell	31	49
N11		Brown	26	34
N18	●	at Princeton	42	37

2001 1-8 (1-6)

S22		New Hampshire	38	42
S29		Pennsylvania	20	21
O7	●	at Yale	32	27
O13		at Holy Cross	17	49
O20		Columbia	20	27
O27		at Harvard	21	31
N3		Cornell	24	28
N10		at Brown	16	41
N17		Princeton	14	35

2002 3-7 (2-5)

S21		at Colgate	26	30
S28		New Hampshire	26	29
O5		at Pennsylvania	14	49
O12	●	Yale	20	17
O19		Holy Cross	44	36
O26	●	at Columbia	24	23
N2		Harvard	26	31
N9		at Cornell	19	21
N16		Brown	18	21
N23		at Princeton	30	38

2003 5-5 (4-3)

S20		Colgate	9	31
S27		at New Hampshire	17	42
O4		Pennsylvania	20	33
O11		at Yale	17	40
O18	●	at Holy Cross	24	20
O25	●	Columbia	26	21
N1	●	at Harvard	30	16
N8	●	Cornell	26	17
N15		at Brown	21	26
N22	●	Princeton	21	15

2004 1-9 (1-6)

S18		at Colgate	15	17
S25		New Hampshire	24	45
O2		at Pennsylvania	0	35
O9		Yale	14	24
O16		Holy Cross	0	24
O23		at Columbia	6	9
O30		Harvard	12	13
N6		at Cornell	7	14
N13	●	Brown	20	7
N20		at Princeton	10	17

HARVARD

BY BRUCE WOOD

ALARMED BY THE INCREASING brutality in football, president Theodore Roosevelt, a Harvard alum, called for a meeting at the White House in 1906 with representatives of Harvard, Yale and Princeton. Walter Camp, the Father of American Football and a rules committee member, suggested widening the field by 40 feet. But Harvard balked at the idea—the school had just built a new football stadium, and the structure wouldn't allow for changes in the field's parameters. Because of Harvard's insistence, the group came up with another idea: the forward pass. The rest is football history.

TRADITION Every time the Crimson score against Yale, the Little Red Flag—a silk banner adorned with an H and mounted on a walking stick—is waved in celebration. The pennant is carried by Harvard's Most Loyal Fan, traditionally acknowledged as the person who has seen the most games of the historic series.

BEST PLAYER A consensus All-America in 1912 and 1913, Charles Brickley is considered the finest dropkicker of all time; he still holds Harvard's single-season and career scoring records. After graduating, Brickley played pro football and went on to form Brickley's New York Giants, an early forerunner to the present-day NFL team.

BEST COACH Percy Haughton, a former Crimson punter, led Harvard to a blistering 71–7–5 record in his nine seasons as head coach. In addition to winning three unofficial national championships, Haughton's teams won 22 games in a row between 1912 and 1914.

BEST TEAM Outscoring its opponents by 229-19, the 1919 Crimson team won the last of Harvard's national championships and capped the season with a 7-6 Rose Bowl victory over Oregon. The only blemish to its undefeated season was a 10-10 tie with a good but not great 4–2–1 Princeton team.

BIGGEST GAME Part social gathering, part football contest, the 100th edition of The Game—the annual showdown between Harvard and Yale—saw the Crimson

PROFILE
Harvard University
Cambridge, Mass.
Founded: 1636
Enrollment: 6,562
Colors: Crimson, Black and White
Nickname: Crimson
Stadium: Harvard Stadium
    Opened in 1903
    Grass; 30,323 capacity
First football game: 1874
All-time record: 767–365–50 (.670)
Bowl record: 1–0
Ivy League championships: 11 (5 outright)
Website: www.gocrimson.com

THE BEST OF TIMES
The Crimson posted a winning record in 42 straight seasons from 1881 to 1923.

THE WORST OF TIMES
Six consecutive losing seasons from 1991 to 1996, including a 12-game home winless streak between 1994 and 1996.

CONFERENCE
Harvard was an original member of the Ivy League when the conference began formal play in 1956.

DISTINGUISHED ALUMNI
John F. Kennedy; Bill Gates; Al Gore; Al Franken; Tommy Lee Jones; John Updike; Michael Crichton, novelist; Yo-Yo Ma, cellist; Conan O'Brien, talk-show host

FIGHT SONG
TEN THOUSAND MEN OF HARVARD
Ten Thousand Men of Harvard want
victory today
For they know that o'er old Eli
Fair Harvard holds sway.
So then we'll conquer all old Eli's men,
And when the game ends we'll sing again:
Ten thousand men of Harvard gained
vict'ry today

Harvard Stadium was the first permanent structure in the world to be built of reinforced concrete.

prevail 16-7 at the Yale Bowl on Nov. 19, 1983. A crowd of more than 70,000, many of them luminaries, looked on as every living captain from both teams met at midfield for the coin toss. Hamilton Fish Jr., former congressman and the 1909 Harvard captain, was there, as was Henry Ketcham, captain of the 1913 Yale team. Beyond bragging rights, the victory gave the Crimson a share of the 1983 Ivy League championship.

BIGGEST UPSET All that stood between the powerhouse 1979 Yale team and a perfect season was the sweetest win of all—a victory at home over Harvard. With six losses and only two wins (over hapless Columbia and winless Penn), the Crimson weren't expected to put up much of a fight. But Harvard's defense forced six fumbles and picked off three passes as the Crimson stunned the Yale Bowl crowd of 72,000 with a shocking 22-7 win over the heavily favored Bulldogs.

WILDEST FINISH At the 1968 Harvard-Yale game, the Crimson quickly fell behind 22-0. Trailing 29-13 in the closing moments, Harvard's Bruce Freeman, a backup receiver, caught a touchdown pass with 42 seconds left; a successful two-point conversion closed the gap to 29-21. The Crimson then tried an onside kick, recovered by Harvard sophomore Bill Kelly. On the final play from scrimmage, backup quarterback Frank Champi avoided the Bulldogs' rush and found captain Vic Gatto alone in the end zone to make it 29-27. With time expired, Champi hit an open Pete Varney for the two-point conversion. The headline in the next day's *Harvard Crimson* famously offered the stunning news: "Harvard Beats Yale, 29-29."

STADIUM Harvard Stadium celebrated its centennial in 2003, no mean feat for a facility that many considered a great folly; back in 1903, no one knew for sure whether

RECORDS

RUSHING YARDS

GAME
323 — Matt Johnson vs. Brown, Nov. 9, 1991 (30 att.)

SEASON
1,302 — Clifton Dawson, 2004 (248 att.)

CAREER
3,330 — Chris Menick, 1996-99 (726 att.)

PASSING YARDS

GAME
443 — Neil Rose vs. Dartmouth, Nov. 2, 2002 (36 of 50)

SEASON
2,655 — Neil Rose, 2000 (203 of 339)

CAREER
5,949 — Neil Rose, 1999-2002 (455 of 729)

RECEIVING YARDS

GAME
257 — Carl Morris vs. Dartmouth, Nov. 2, 2002 (21 rec.)

SEASON
1,288 — Carl Morris, 2002 (90 rec.)

CAREER
3,488 — Carl Morris, 1999-2002 (245 rec.)

POINTS

GAME
30 — Tom Ossman vs. Brown, Nov. 17, 1951 (5 TDs)

SEASON
108 — Clifton Dawson, 2004 (18 TDs)

CAREER
215 — Charles Brickley, 1911-14 (23 TDs, 25 FGs, 2 PATs)

CONSENSUS ALL-AMERICANS

1889	Arthur Cumnock, E
1889	James Lee, B
1889-90	John Cranston, G/C
1890	Dudley Dean, B
1890	John Corbett, B
1890, 1892	Frank Hallowell, E
1890-93	Marshall Newell, T
1891	Everett Lake, B
1892-93	William Lewis, C
1892, 1894	Bertram Waters, G/T
1892-93, 1895	Charles Brewer, B
1895-96	Norman Cabot, E
1896	Edgar Wrightington, B
1897	Alan Doucette, C
1897-98	Benjamin Dibblee, B
1898	Walter Boal, G
1898-1900	Charles Daly, B
1898, 1900	John Hallowell, E
1899-1901	David Campbell, E
1901	Oliver Cutts, T
1901	Crawford Blagden, T
1901	William Lee, G
1901	Charles Barnard, G
1901	Robert Kernan, B
1901-02	Thomas Graydon, B
1901-02	Edward Bowditch, E
1903	Daniel Knowlton, T
1903	Andrew Marshall, G
1904-05	Daniel Hurley, B
1905	Beaton Squires, T
1905	Karl Brill, T
1905-06	Francis Burr, G
1906	Charles Osborne, T
1907	Patrick Grant, C
1907	John Wendell, B
1908	Charles Nourse, C
1908	Hamilton Corbett, B
1908-09	Hamilton Fish, T
1909	Wayland Minot, B
1910	Robert McKay, T
1910-11	Percy Wendell, B
1910-11	Robert Fisher, G
1912	Samuel Felton, E
1912-13	Charles Brickley, B

(Continued on next page)

the game of football was just another fad. Given to the school as a gift from the Class of 1879, the stadium was the first permanent structure in the world to be built of reinforced concrete. Upon its completion in a quick 4½ months, it was considered an engineering masterpiece.

RIVAL It all started on Aug. 3, 1852, on the waters of New Hampshire's Lake Winnipesaukee. Crews from Harvard and Yale competed in a two-mile race, which the Crimson handily won by two lengths. Whatever the venue or sport, it's been Harvard vs. Yale ever since. The football series kicked off in New Haven in 1875, when nearly 2,000 fans paid 50 cents apiece to witness a Harvard victory, 4 goals to 0. By 1891, the matchup was so eagerly anticipated that scalpers were busted for selling counterfeit tickets. Things got just as heated on the field; played before 25,000 in Springfield, Mass., the 1894 game was so hard-fought that seven players had to be carted off the field in what was described as "dying" condition.

NICKNAME Harvard Magenta doesn't have the same ring as Harvard Crimson, but it was the school's nickname until May 1875, when a student-wide election gave the nod to Crimson. The first connection between Harvard and crimson can be traced to 1858, when rowers Charles Eliot and Benjamin

CONSENSUS ALL-AMERICANS (CONT.)

1912-14	Stanley Pennock,	G
1913	Harvey Hitchcock,	T
1913-15	Edward Mahan,	B
1914	Huntington Hardwick,	E
1914	Walter Trumbull,	T
1915	Joseph Gilman,	T
1915	Richard King,	B
1916	Harrie Dadmun,	G
1919	Edward Casey,	B
1920	Tom Woods,	G
1921	John Brown,	G
1922-23	Charles Hubbard,	G
1929-30	Ben Ticknor,	C
1931	Barry Wood,	B
1941	Endicott Peabody,	G
1982	Mike Corbat,	OL
1984	Roger Caron,	OL
1999	Isaiah Kacyvenski,	LB
2000	Mike Clare,	OL
2002	Carl Morris,	WR
2003	Dante Balestracci,	LB
2004	Clifton Dawson,	RB

ALL-TIME TEAM

As chosen by Bernie Corbett, the Voice of Harvard Football and co-author of The Only Game That Matters: The Harvard/Yale Rivalry.

OFFENSE

1973-75	Danny Jiggetts,	T
1982-84	Roger Caron,	T
1995-97	Matt Birk,	T
1932-34	Herman Gundlach Jr.,	G
1967-68	Tommy Lee Jones,	G
1928-30	Ben Ticknor,	C
1995, 1997-99	Chris Eitzmann,	TE
1965-67	Carter Lord,	WR
1972-74	Pat McInally,	WR
1999-2002	Carl Morris,	WR
1929-31	Barry Wood,	QB
2001-04	Ryan Fitzpatrick,	QB
1951-53	Dick Clasby,	RB
1996-99	Chris Menick,	RB
1913-15	Eddie Mahan,	FB
1916, 1919	Edward Casey,	FB
1912-14	Charlie Brickley,	PK

DEFENSE

1912-14	Stanley Pennock,	DE
1994-97	Tim Fleiszer,	DE
1994-97	Chris Smith,	DE
1890-93	Marshall Newell,	DT
1907-09	Hamilton Fish,	DT
1909-11	Bob Fisher,	DT
1939-41	Endicott Peabody,	DT
1965-67	Donald Chiofaro,	LB
1981-83	Joe Azelby,	LB
1996-99	Isaiah Kacyvenski,	LB
2000-03	Dante Balestracci,	LB
1920-22	George Owen,	DB
1946-48	Kenny O'Donnell,	DB
1963-65	John Dockery,	DB
1964, 1968	Pat Conway,	DB
1984-85	Cecil Cox,	DB
1981-83	Jim Villanueva,	PK

Crowninshield gave their teammates crimson scarves in order to help spectators identify the Harvard crew. Eliot went on to become Harvard's president in 1869.

UNIFORMS From the second half of the 20th century, Harvard uniforms have stayed pretty much the same. But there was nothing subtle about the changes Arthur Valpey made when he took over the program in 1948. A former Michigan assistant coach, Valpey brought with him a variation of the Wolverines' distinctive winged-helmet design, as well as new uniforms featuring black nylon pants and crimson socks. After his second season ended with a 1–8 record and no Ivy wins, Valpey and his uniforms were canned.

LORE When Harvard squared off against the Carlisle Indian School in 1903, Carlisle coach Pop Warner brought out the old hidden-ball trick on a kickoff for a TD. In 1908, Harvard coach Percy Haughton decided to fight fire with fire. He had three footballs dyed to match his team's crimson jerseys. The oddly colored footballs never made it onto the field, but Harvard nonetheless handed Warner's team its only loss of the year, 17-0.

QUOTE "Gentlemen, you are now going out to play football against Harvard. Never again in your whole life will you do anything so important."—Yale coach Thomas A.D. Jones, before The Game in 1923

HARVARD ALL-TIME SCORES

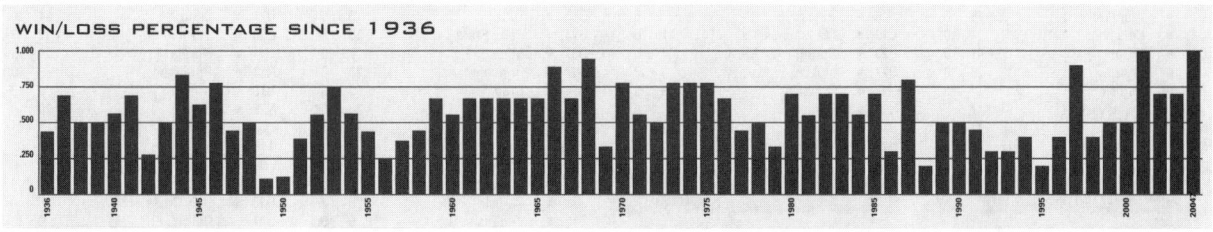

WIN/LOSS PERCENTAGE SINCE 1936

NO HEAD COACH

1874 — 2-1-1
Y14	● McGill	3	0
Y15	= McGill	0	0
O23	● at McGill	3	0
E4	Tufts	0	1

1875 — 4-0-0
O30	● at Canada All-Stars	1	0
O27	● at Tufts	1	0
N13	● at Yale	4	0
Y8	● at Canada All-Stars	1	0

1876 — 3-1-0
O28	● at Canada All-Stars	2	0
O30	● at McGill	1	0
N18	● at Yale	0	1
P28	Princeton	1	0

1877 — 3-1-0
O23	● at Tufts	3	0
O26	● at McGill	1	0
N3	● at Princeton	0	1
N5	● at Columbia	6	0

1878 — 1-2-0
N9	● at Amherst	3	0
N16	● Princeton *U*	0	1
N23	Yale *Bos*	0	1

1879 — 2-1-2
O25	● at Britannia	2	0
N1	● at Britannia	1	0
N3	= at McGill	0	0
N8	= at Yale	0	0
N15	Princeton *U*	0	1

1880 — 2-2-2
O23	= at Britannia	0	0
N1	● at Ottawa	2	1
N2	= at Montreal	0	0
N6	● at Columbia	3	0
N13	● Princeton *U*	1	2
N20	Yale *Bos*	0	1

LUCIUS N. LITTAUER
1881 (.813) — 6-1-1
1881 — 6-1-1
O20	● at Montreal	2	0
O22	● at Ottawa	9	1
O29	● at Britannia	2	0
O31	● Michigan *Bos*	4	0
N2	● Pennsylvania *NYC*	2	0
N5	● Columbia	1	0
N12	● at Yale	0	1
N19	= Princeton *U*	0	0

NO HEAD COACH

1882 — 7-1-0
O7	● MIT	1	0
O14	● MIT	3	0
O21	● McGill	2	0
O28	● at Amherst	1	0
N4	● Dartmouth	8	0
N11	● Columbia	3	0
N18	● Princeton	2	1
N25	Yale	0	1

1883 — 8-2-0
O6	● Wesleyan	23	1
O13	● Pennsylvania	4	0
O20	● Stevens	14	4
O27	● at MIT	14	1
N3	● at Wesleyan	18	6
N6	● Stevens	11	2
N10	● Williams	39	0
N17	● at Princeton	7	26
N22	● Michigan	3	0
N29	Yale *NYC*	2	23

1884 — 7-4-0
O18	● MIT	43	5
O22	Pennsylvania	0	4
O25	● at MIT	42	0
O29	● Trinity	67	0
N1	● at Wesleyan	0	16
N5	● Williams	23	0
N8	● at Ottawa	20	6
N12	● at Dartmouth	29	0
N15	● Tufts	51	0
N19	● Princeton	6	36
N22	at Yale	0	52

1885
NO TEAM

FRANK A. MASON
1886 (.857) — 12-2
1886 — 12-2-0
O2	● at Tufts	82	0
O6	● at MIT	54	0
O9	● Tufts	46	0
O16	● Stevens	44	0
O20	● MIT	59	0
O23	● at Andover	86	0
O30	● Dartmouth *U*	70	0
N3	● at Exeter	158	0
N6	● Wesleyan	34	0
N10	● Graduates	38	0
N13	at Princeton	0	12
N17	● at MIT	62	0
N20	● Yale	4	29
N25	● at Pennsylvania	28	0

NO HEAD COACH

1887 — 10-1-0
O1	● at Tufts	86	0
O5	● at Exeter	68	0
O8	● MIT	62	0
O15	● Williams	52	6
O22	● Amherst	98	0
O29	● Tufts	68	0
N2	● Exeter	54	0
N5	● Wesleyan	110	0
N12	● Princeton	12	0
N19	● Pennsylvania	42	0
N24	Yale *NYC*	8	17

1888 — 12-1-0
O3	● at Worcester	70	0
O6	● MIT	18	0
O10	● at Exeter	30	6
O13	● at Wesleyan	34	0
O17	● at Williams	14	6
O20	● Andover	68	0
O24	● Worcester	68	0
O27	● Dartmouth	74	0
O31	● MIT	42	0
N3	● Amherst	102	0
N10	● Wesleyan	50	2
N17	at Princeton	6	18
N19	● at Pennsylvania	50	0

1889 — 9-2-0
O2	● Exeter	28	0
O5	● Stevens	28	4
O9	● Dartmouth	38	0
O12	● MIT	62	0
O16	● Williams	41	0
O19	● Andover	41	0
O26	● Wesleyan	64	0
N2	● Pennsylvania	35	0
N9	● at Wesleyan	67	2
N16	● Princeton	15	41
N23	Yale *SPR*	0	6

GEORGE STEWART / GEORGE ADAMS
1890-92 (.944) — 34-2
1890 — 11-0-0
O4	● Exeter	41	0
O8	● Dartmouth	43	0
O11	● Amherst	74	6
O13	● Williams	38	0
O18	● Dartmouth	64	0
O22	● Bowdoin	54	0
O25	● Wesleyan	55	0
N1	● Cornell	77	0
N8	● Orange AC	33	0
N15	● at Amherst	64	0
N22	● Yale *SPR*	12	6

1891 — 13-1-0
O3	● Dartmouth	16	0
O7	● Exeter	17	0
O10	● Amherst	18	0
O14	● at MIT	26	0
O17	● Williams	26	0
O21	● at Andover	76	0
O24	● Amherst	39	0
O28	● Bowdoin	79	0
O31	● Springfield	34	0
N4	● at Wesleyan	124	0
N7	● Springfield	44	4
N11	● at Trinity	38	0
N14	● Boston AC	51	12
N21	● Yale *SPR*	0	10

1892 — 10-1-0
O1	● Dartmouth	48	0
O5	● Exeter	62	0
O8	● Amherst	26	0
O15	● Williams	55	0
O19	● Boston AA	40	0
O22	● Chicago AC	32	0
O29	● MIT	34	0
N2	● Amherst	32	10
N5	● Cornell *U*	20	14
N12	● Boston AA	16	12
N19	● Yale *SPR*	0	6

GEORGE STEWART / EVERETT LAKE
1893 (.923) — 12-1
1893 — 12-1-0
S30	● Dartmouth	16	0
O4	● Exeter	54	0
O7	● Amherst	32	0
O11	● MIT	34	0
O14	● Williams	52	0
O18	● Dartmouth	36	0
O21	● Graduates	6	0
O25	● Brown	58	0
O28	● at Andover	60	5
N4	● Cornell *NYC*	34	0
N11	● Boston AA	10	0
N25	Yale *SPR*	0	6
N30	● Pennsylvania	26	4

WILLIAM A. BROOKS
1894 (.846) — 11-2
1894 — 11-2-0
S29	● Dartmouth	22	0
O3	● Exeter	48	0
O6	● Andover	46	0
O10	● Brown	18	4
O17	● Orange AC	14	0
O20	● Amherst	30	0
O24	● Williams	32	0
O27	● Cornell *U*	22	12
N3	● Boston AA	40	0
N10	● Chicago AC	36	0
N17	● Brown	18	0
N24	Yale	4	12
N29	at Pennsylvania	4	18

ROBERT W. EMMONS
1895 (.773) — 8-2-1
1895 — 8-2-1
O2	● Dartmouth	4	0
O5	● Amherst	24	0
O9	● Exeter	42	0
O12	● at Army	4	0
O16	● Williams	32	0
O19	● Brown	26	6
O26	● Cornell	25	0
N2	at Princeton	4	12
N9	● Michigan	4	0
N16	= Boston AA	0	0
N23	Pennsylvania	14	17

BERTRAM G. WATERS
1896 (.636) — 7-4
1896 — 7-4-0
S26	● Williams	6	0
O3	● Trinity	34	0
O7	● Newton AA	18	0
O10	● Wesleyan	28	0
O17	● Brown	12	0
O24	● at Cornell	13	4
O28	● Graduates	5	8
O31	● Carlisle	4	0
N7	● Princeton	0	12
N14	● Boston AA	6	8
N21	● at Pennsylvania	6	8

W. CAMERON FORBES
1897-98 (.935) — 21-1-1
1897 — 10-1-1
S25	● Williams	20	0
S29	● Bowdoin	24	0
O2	● Dartmouth	13	0
O9	● Amherst	38	0
O16	● Army	10	0
O20	● Newton AA	24	0
O23	● Brown	18	0
O25	● Newtowne AC	22	0
O27	● Cornell	24	5
N6	● Wesleyan	34	0
N13	= Yale	0	0
N20	at Pennsylvania	6	15

1898 — 11-0-0
S24	● Williams	11	0
S28	● Bowdoin	28	6
O1	● Dartmouth	21	0
O8	● Amherst	53	2
O15	● at Army	28	0
O19	● Newtowne AC	22	0
O22	● Chicago AC	39	0
O29	● Carlisle	11	5
N5	● Pennsylvania	10	0
N12	● Brown	17	6
N19	● at Yale	17	0

BENJAMIN H. DIBBLEE
1899-1900 (.932) — 20-1-1
1899 — 10-0-1
S30	● Williams	29	0
O4	● Bowdoin	13	0
O7	● Wesleyan	20	0
O11	● Amherst	41	0
O14	● at Army	18	0
O18	● Bates	29	0
O21	● Brown	11	0
O28	● Carlisle	22	10
N4	● at Pennsylvania	16	0
N11	● Dartmouth	11	0
N18	= Yale	0	0

1900   10-1-0

S29	●	Wesleyan	24	0
O3	●	Williams	12	0
O6	●	Bowdoin	12	0
O10	●	Amherst	18	0
O13	●	Columbia	24	0
O17	●	Bates	41	0
O20	●	at Army	29	0
O27	●	Carlisle	17	5
N3	●	Pennsylvania	17	5
N17	●	Brown	11	6
N24	●	at Yale	0	28

WILLIAM T. REID
1901,'05-06 (.897)   30-3-1

1901   12-0-0

S28	●	Williams	16	0
O2	●	Bowdoin	12	0
O5	●	Bates	16	6
O9	●	Amherst	11	0
O12	●	Columbia	18	0
O16	●	Wesleyan	16	0
O19	●	at Army	6	0
O26	●	Carlisle	29	0
N2	●	Brown	48	0
N9	●	at Pennsylvania	33	6
N16	●	Dartmouth	27	12
N23	●	Yale	22	0

JOHN W. FARLEY
1902 (.917)   11-1

1902   11-1-0

S27	●	Williams	11	0
O1	●	Bowdoin	17	6
O4	●	Bates	23	0
O8	●	Amherst	6	0
O11	●	Maine	22	0
O15	●	Wesleyan	35	5
O18	●	at Army	14	6
O25	●	Brown	6	0
N1	●	Carlisle	23	0
N8	●	Pennsylvania	11	0
N15	●	Dartmouth	16	6
N22	●	at Yale	0	23

JOHN S. CRANSTON
1903 (.750)   9-3

1903   9-3-0

S23	●	Williams	17	0
S26	●	Bowdoin	24	0
O3	●	Maine	6	0
O7	●	Bates	23	0
O10	●	Amherst	0	5
O14	●	Wesleyan	17	6
O17	●	at Army	5	0
O24	●	Brown	29	0
O31	●	Carlisle	12	11
N7	●	at Pennsylvania	17	10
N14	●	Dartmouth	0	11
N21	●	Yale	0	16

EDGAR N. WRIGHTINGTON
1904 (.750)   7-2-1

1904   7-2-1

S28	●	Williams	24	0
O5	●	Bowdoin	17	0
O8	●	Maine	23	0
O12	●	Bates	11	0
O15	●	at Army	4	0
O22	●	Carlisle	12	0
O29	●	Pennsylvania	0	11
N5	=	Dartmouth	0	0
N12	●	Holy Cross	28	5
N19	●	at Yale	0	12

WILLIAM T. REID

1905   8-2-1

S30	●	Williams	12	0
O3	●	Bowdoin	16	0
O7	●	Maine	22	0
O10	●	Bates	34	6
O14	●	Springfield YMCA	12	0
O21	●	at Army	6	0
O28	●	Brown	10	0
N4	●	Carlisle	23	11
N11	●	at Pennsylvania	6	12
N18	=	Dartmouth	6	6
N25	●	Yale	0	6

1906   10-1-0

S22	●	Williams	7	0
S26	●	Bowdoin	10	0
S29	●	Maine	17	0
O6	●	Bates	27	6
O13	●	Massachusetts	21	0
O20	●	Springfield YMCA	44	0
O27	●	at Army	5	0
N3	●	Brown	9	5
N10	●	Carlisle	5	0
N17	●	Dartmouth	22	9
N24	●	at Yale	0	6

JOSHUA CRANE
1907 (.700)   7-3

1907   7-3-0

S28	●	Bowdoin	5	0
O2	●	Maine	30	0
O5	●	Bates	33	4
O12	●	Williams	18	0
O19	●	at Navy	6	0
O26	●	Springfield YMCA	9	5
N2	●	Brown	6	5
N9	●	Carlisle	15	23
N16	●	Dartmouth	0	22
N23	●	Yale	0	12

PERCY D. HAUGHTON
1908-16 (.886)   71-7-5

1908   9-0-1

S19	●	Bowdoin	5	0
S26	●	Maine	16	0
O3	●	Bates	18	0
O10	●	Williams	10	0
O17	●	Springfield YMCA	44	0
O24	=	at Navy	6	6
O31	●	Brown	6	2
N7	●	Carlisle	17	0
N14	●	Dartmouth	6	0
N21	●	at Yale	4	0

1909   8-1-0

S25	●	Bates	11	0
O2	●	Bowdoin	17	0
O9	●	Williams	8	6
O16	●	Maine	17	0
O23	●	Brown	11	0
O30	●	at Army	9	0
N6	●	Cornell	18	0
N13	●	Dartmouth	12	3
N20	●	Yale	0	8

1910   8-0-1

S24	●	Bates	22	0
O1	●	Bowdoin	32	0
O8	●	Williams	21	0
O15	●	Amherst	17	0
O22	●	Brown	12	0
O29	●	at Army	6	0
N5	●	Cornell	27	5
N12	●	Dartmouth	18	0
N19	=	at Yale	0	0

1911   6-2-1

S30	●	Bates	15	0
O7	●	Holy Cross	8	0
O14	●	Williams	18	0
O21	●	Amherst	11	0
O28	●	Brown	20	6
N4	●	at Princeton	6	8
N11	●	Carlisle	15	18
N18	●	Dartmouth	5	3
N25	=	Yale	0	0

1912   9-0-0

S28	●	Maine	7	0
O5	●	Holy Cross	19	0
O12	●	Williams	26	3
O19	●	Amherst	46	0
O26	●	Brown	30	10
N2	●	Princeton	16	6
N9	●	Vanderbilt	9	3
N16	●	Dartmouth	3	0
N23	●	at Yale	20	0

1913   9-0-0

S27	●	Maine	34	0
O4	●	Bates	14	0
O11	●	Williams	23	3
O18	●	Holy Cross	47	7
O25	●	Penn State	29	0
N1	●	Cornell	23	6
N8	●	at Princeton	3	0
N15	●	Brown	37	0
N22	●	Yale	15	5

1914   7-0-2

S26	●	Bates	44	0
O3	●	Springfield	44	0
O10	●	Wash. & Jeff.	10	9
O17	●	Tufts	13	6
O24	=	Penn State	13	13
O31	●	Michigan	7	0
N7	●	Princeton	20	0
N14	=		0	0
N21	●	at Yale	36	0

1915   8-1-0

S25	●	Colby	39	6
O2	●	Massachusetts	7	0
O9	●	Carlisle	29	7
O16	●	Virginia	9	0
O23	●	Cornell	0	10
O30	●	Penn State	13	0
N6	●	at Princeton	10	6
N13	●	Brown	16	7
N20	●	Yale	41	0

1916   7-3-0

S23	●	Colby	10	0
S30	●	Bates	26	0
O7	●	Tufts	3	7
O14	●	North Carolina	21	0
O21	●	Massachusetts	47	0
O28	●	Cornell	23	0
N4	●	Virginia	51	0
N11	●	Princeton	3	0
N18	●	Brown	0	21
N25	●	at Yale	3	6

WINGATE ROLLINS
1917 (.643)   3-1-3

1917   3-1-3

U	●	Dean Acad. *U*	27	0
U	●	Bump Island NR *U*	35	0
U	●	1st Maine Hvy. Aty. *U*	13	0
U	=	Depot Brigade *U*	0	0
U	=	Portland NR *U*	0	0
U	=	Camp Devens *U*	0	0
U		New Port NR *U*	0	14

POOCH DONOVAN
1918 (.667)   2-1

1918   2-1-0

N9	●	Tufts	7	0
N23	●	Boston College	14	6
N28	●	Brown	3	6

ROBERT T. FISHER
1919-25 (.734)   43-14-5

1919   9-0-1

S27	●	Bates	53	0
O4	●	Boston College	17	0
O11	●	Colby	35	0
O18	●	Brown	7	0
O25	●	Virginia	47	0
N1	●	Springfield	20	0
N8	=	at Princeton	10	10
N15	●	Tufts	23	0
N22	●	Yale	10	3

ROSE BOWL

J1	●	Oregon	7	6

1920   8-0-1

S25	●	Holy Cross	3	0
O2	●	Maine	41	0
O9	●	Valparasio	21	0
O16	●	Williams	38	0
O23	●	Centre	31	14
O30	●	Virginia	24	0
N6	=	Princeton	14	14
N13	●	Brown	27	0
N20	●	at Yale	9	0

1921   7-2-1

S17	●	Boston U.	10	0
S24	●	Middlebury	16	0
O1	●	Holy Cross	3	0
O8	●	Indiana	19	0
O15	●	Georgia	10	7
O22	=	Penn State	21	21
O29	●	Centre	0	6
N5	●	at Princeton	3	10
N12	●	Brown	9	7
N19	●	Yale	10	3

1922   7-2-0

S30	●	Middlebury	20	0
O7	●	Holy Cross	20	0
O14	●	Bowdoin	15	0
O21	●	Centre	24	10
O28	●	Dartmouth	12	3
N4	●	Florida	24	0
N11	●	Princeton	3	10
N18	●	Brown	0	3
N25	●	at Yale	10	3

1923   4-3-1

O6	●	Rhode Island	35	0
O13	=	Middlebury	6	6
O20	●	Holy Cross	6	0
O27	●	Dartmouth	0	16
N3	●	Tufts	16	0
N10	●	at Princeton	5	0
N17	●	Brown	7	20
N24	●	Yale	0	13

1924   4-4-0

O4	●	Virginia	14	0
O11	●	Middlebury	16	6
O18	●	Holy Cross	12	6
O25	●	Dartmouth	0	6
N1	●	Boston U.	13	0
N8	●	Princeton	0	34
N15	●	Brown	0	7
N22	●	at Yale	6	19

1925   4-3-1

O3	●	Rensselaer	18	6
O10	●	Middlebury	68	0
O17	●	Holy Cross	6	7
O24	●	Dartmouth	9	32
O31	●	William & Mary	14	7
N7	●	at Princeton	0	36
N14	●	Brown	3	0
N21	=	Yale	0	0

ARNOLD HORWEEN
1926-30 (.549)   21-17-3

1926   3-5-0

O2	●	Genoa	7	16
O9	●	Holy Cross	14	19
O16	●	William & Mary	27	7
O23	●	Dartmouth	16	12
O30	●	Tufts	69	6
N6	●	Princeton	0	12
N13	●	Brown	0	21
N20	●	at Yale	7	12

1927   4-4-0

O1	●	Vermont	21	3
O8	●	Purdue	0	19
O15	●	Holy Cross	14	6
O22	●	Dartmouth	6	30
O29	●	Indiana	26	6
N5	●	at Pennsylvania	0	24
N12	●	Brown	18	6
N19	●	Yale	0	14

1928   5-2-1

O6	●	Springfield	30	0
O13	●	North Carolina	20	0
O20	●	Army	0	15
O27	●	Dartmouth	19	7
N3	●	Lehigh	39	0
N10	●	Pennsylvania	0	7
N17	=	Holy Cross	0	0
N24	●	at Yale	17	0

1929   5-2-1

O5	●	Bates	48	0
O12	●	New Hampshire	35	0
O19	=	Army	20	20
O26	●	Dartmouth	7	34
N2	●	Florida	14	0
N9		at Michigan	12	14
N16	●	Holy Cross	12	6
N23	●	Yale	10	6

1930   4-4-1

S27	●	Coast Guard	33	0
O4	●	Vermont	35	0
O11	●	Springfield	27	0
O18	●	Army	0	6
O25	●	Dartmouth	2	7
N1	=	William & Mary	13	13
N8	●	Michigan	3	6
N15	●	Holy Cross	0	27
N22	●	at Yale	3	0

EDWARD L. CASEY
1931-34 (.641)   20-11-1

1931   7-1-0
O3	●	Bates	28	0
O10	●	New Hampshire	39	0
O17	●	at Army	14	13
O24	●	Texas	35	7
O31	●	Virginia	19	0
N7	●	Dartmouth	7	6
N14	●	Holy Cross	7	0
N21		Yale	0	3

1932   5-3-0
O1	●	Buffalo	66	0
O8	●	New Hampshire	40	0
O15	●	Penn State	46	13
O22	●	Dartmouth	10	7
O29		Brown	0	14
N5		Army	0	46
N12	●	Holy Cross	7	0
N19		at Yale	1	6

1933   5-2-1
O7	●	Bates	33	0
O14	●	New Hampshire	34	0
O21	●	Holy Cross	7	10
O28	=	Dartmouth	7	7
N4	●	Lehigh	27	0
N11		Army	0	27
N18	●	Brown	12	6
N25	●	Yale	19	6

1934   3-5-0
O6	●	Bates	12	0
O13	●	Brown	13	0
O20		Holy Cross	6	26
O27		Dartmouth	0	10
N3		Princeton	0	19
N10		Army	6	27
N17	●	New Hampshire	47	3
N24		at Yale	0	14

RICHARD C. HARLOW
1935-42, '45-47 (.533) 45-39-7

1935   3-5-0
O5	●	Springfield	20	0
O12		Holy Cross	0	13
O19		at Army	0	13
O26		Dartmouth	6	14
N2	●	Brown	33	0
N9		at Princeton	0	35
N16	●	New Hampshire	41	0
N23		Yale	7	14

1936   3-4-1
O3	●	Amherst	38	6
O10	●	Brown	28	0
O17		Army	0	32
O24		Dartmouth	7	26
O31	=	Princeton	14	14
N7	●	Virginia	65	0
N14		Navy	13	20
N21		at Yale	13	14

1937   5-2-1
O2	●	Springfield	54	0
O9	●	Brown	34	7
O16	=	Navy *BALT*	0	0
O23		Dartmouth	2	20
O30	●	at Princeton	34	6
N6		Army	6	7
N13	●	Davidson	15	0
N20	●	Yale	13	6

1938   4-4-0
O1		Brown	13	20
O8		Cornell	0	20
O15		Army	17	20
O22		Dartmouth	7	13
O29	●	Princeton	26	7
N5	●	Chicago	47	13
N12	●	Virginia	40	13
N19		at Yale	7	0

1939   4-4-0
O7	●	Bates	20	0
O14	●	at Chicago	61	0
O21		Pennsylvania	7	22
O28		Dartmouth	0	16
N4		at Princeton	6	9
N11	●	Army	15	0
N18	●	New Hampshire	46	0
N25		Yale	7	20

1940   3-2-3
O5	●	Amherst	13	0
O12		Michigan	0	26
O19	=	Army	6	6
O26		Dartmouth	6	7
N2	=	Princeton	0	0
N9	=	at Pennsylvania	10	10
N16	●	Brown	14	0
N23	●	at Yale	28	0

1941   5-2-1
O4		at Pennsylvania	0	19
O11		Cornell	0	7
O18	●	Dartmouth	7	0
O25	=	Navy	0	0
N1	●	at Princeton	6	4
N8	●	Army	20	6
N15	●	Brown	23	7
N22	●	Yale	14	0

1942   2-6-1
S26		N.C. Pre-Flight	0	13
O3		Pennsylvania	7	19
O10	=	William & Mary	7	7
O17		Dartmouth	2	14
O24		Army	0	14
O31	●	Princeton	19	14
N7		at Michigan	7	35
N14	●	Brown	7	0
N21		at Yale	3	7

HENRY N. LAMAR
1943-44 (.682)   7-3-1

1943   2-2-1
O16	●	Camp Edwards	7	0
O23		WORC Poly	0	13
O30	●	at Camp Edwards	14	7
N6		Tufts	7	13
N13	=	Boston College	6	6

1944   5-1-0
S16	●	Tufts	19	12
S23	●	Bates	43	6
S30	●	WORC Poly	13	0
O7	●	Boston College	13	0
O14		Melville PT Boat	0	13
O28	●	at Tufts	12	6

RICHARD C. HARLOW

1945   5-3-0
S29		Tufts	6	7
O6	●	Rochester	21	13
O13		New London Sub Base	7	18
O27	●	Coast Guard	25	0
N10	●	Kings Point	28	7
N17	●	Brown	14	7
N24	●	Boston U.	60	0
D1		at Yale	0	28

1946   7-2-0
S28	●	Connecticut	7	0
O5	●	Tufts	49	0
O12	●	at Princeton	13	12
O19	●	Coast Guard	69	0
O26	●	Holy Cross	13	6
N2		Rutgers	0	13
N9	●	at Dartmouth	21	7
N16	●	Brown	28	0
N23		Yale	14	27

1947   4-5-0
S27	●	Western Maryland	52	0
O4	●	Boston U.	19	14
O11		at Virginia	0	47
O18	●	Holy Cross	7	0
O25		Dartmouth	13	14
N1		Rutgers	7	31
N8		Princeton	7	33
N15	●	Brown	13	7
N22		at Yale	21	31

ARTHUR VALPEY
1948-49 (.294)   5-12

1948   4-4-0
O2	●	Columbia	33	24
O9		at Cornell	6	40
O16		at Army	7	20
O23		Dartmouth	7	14
O30	●	Holy Cross	20	13
N6		at Princeton	7	47
N13	●	Brown	30	19
N20	●	Yale	20	7

1949   1-8-0
S24		at Stanford	0	44
O1		at Columbia	7	14
O8		Cornell	14	33
O15		Army	14	54
O22		Dartmouth	13	27
O29	●	Holy Cross	22	14
N5		Princeton	13	33
N12	●	Brown	14	28
N19		at Yale	6	29

LLOYD P. JORDAN
1950-56 (.440)   24-31-3

1950   1-7-0
O7		Columbia	7	28
O14		Cornell	7	28
O21		Army	0	49
O28		Dartmouth	7	27
N4		Holy Cross	7	26
N11		at Princeton	26	63
N18	●	Brown	14	13
N25		Yale	6	14

1951   3-5-1
S22	●	Springfield	21	13
S29	●	Holy Cross	6	33
O6		at Columbia	0	35
O13		at Cornell	6	42
O20	●	Army	22	21
O27		Dartmouth	20	26
N10		Princeton	13	54
N17	●	Brown	34	21
N24	=	at Yale	21	21

1952   5-4-0
S27	●	Springfield	27	7
O4		Columbia	7	16
O11	●	Washington, Mo.	42	0
O18	●	Colgate	21	20
O25	●	Dartmouth	26	19
N1		Davidson	35	26
N8		at Princeton	21	41
N15		at Brown	21	28
N22		Yale	14	41

1953   6-2-0
O3	●	Ohio U.	16	0
O10		Colgate	28	26
O17		at Columbia	0	6
O24	●	Dartmouth	20	14
O31	●	Davidson	42	6
N7		Princeton	0	6
N14	●	Brown	27	20
N21	●	at Yale	13	0

1954   4-3-1
O2		Massachusetts	7	13
O9	●	at Cornell	13	12
O16		Columbia	6	7
O23		Dartmouth	7	13
O30	●	Ohio U.	27	13
N6	●	at Princeton	14	9
N13	=	Brown	21	21
N20	●	Yale	13	9

1955   3-4-1
O1	●	Massachusetts	60	6
O8		Cornell	7	20
O15	●	at Columbia	21	7
O22		at Dartmouth	9	14
O29	●	Bucknell	26	26
N5	●	Princeton	7	6
N12		Brown	6	14
N19		at Yale	7	21

1956-Present
Ivy League

1956   2-6-0 (2-5-0)
O6		Tufts	13	19
O13	●	at Cornell	32	7
O20		at Columbia	20	26
O27	●	Dartmouth	28	21
N3		Pennsylvania	14	28
N10		at Princeton	20	35
N17		Brown	12	21
N24		Yale	14	42

JOHN M. YOVICSIN
1957-70 (.644)   78-42-5

1957   3-5-0 (2-5-0)
O5		Cornell	6	20
O12	●	Ohio U.	14	7
O19	●	Columbia	19	6
O26		Dartmouth	0	26
N2	●	at Pennsylvania	13	6
N9		Princeton	20	28
N16		Brown	6	33
N23		at Yale	0	54

1958   4-5-0 (3-4-0)
S27		Buffalo	3	6
O4		at Cornell	14	21
O11	●	Lehigh	20	0
O18	●	at Columbia	26	0
O25	●	Dartmouth	16	8
N1		Pennsylvania	6	19
N8		at Princeton	14	16
N15		Brown	22	29
N22	●	Yale	28	0

1959   6-3-0 (4-3-0)
S26	●	Massachusetts	36	22
O3	●	Bucknell	20	6
O10		Cornell	16	20
O17	●	Columbia	38	22
O24		Dartmouth	0	9
O31	●	at Pennsylvania	12	0
N7	●	Princeton	14	0
N14		at Brown	6	16
N21	●	at Yale	35	6

1960   5-4-0 (4-3-0)
S24	●	Holy Cross	13	6
O1		Massachsetts	12	27
O8		at Cornell	0	12
O15	●	at Columbia	8	7
O22	●	Dartmouth	9	6
O29	●	Pennsylvania	8	0
N5		at Princeton	12	14
N12	●	Brown	22	8
N19		Yale	6	39

1961   6-3-0 (6-1-0)
S30		Lehigh	17	22
O7		Cornell	14	0
O14		Colgate	0	15
O21		Columbia	14	26
O28	●	Dartmouth	21	15
N4	●	at Pennsylvania	37	6
N11	●	Princeton	9	7
N18	●	Brown	21	6
N25	●	at Yale	27	0

1962   6-3-0 (5-2-0)
S29	●	Lehigh	27	7
O6		at Cornell	12	14
O13		Holy Cross	20	34
O20	●	at Columbia	36	14
O27		Dartmouth	6	24
N3	●	Pennsylvania	36	0
N10		at Princeton	20	0
N17	●	Brown	31	19
N24	●	Yale	14	6

1963   5-2-2 (4-2-1)
S28	=	Massachsetts	0	0
O5	●	Rutgers	28	0
O12	●	Cornell	21	14
O19	=	Columbia	3	3
O26	●	Dartmouth	17	13
N2		at Pennsylvania	2	7
N9	●	Princeton	21	7
N16	●	at Brown	24	12
N30		at Yale	6	20

1964   6-3-0 (5-2-0)
S26	●	Massachusetts	20	14
O3	●	Bucknell	21	24
O10	●	at Columbia	3	0
O17	●	Cornell	16	0
O24		Dartmouth	0	48
O31	●	Pennsylvania	34	0
N7		at Princeton	0	16
N14	●	Brown	19	7
N21	●	Yale	18	14

1074 HARVARD

THE SCHOOLS

1965 5-2-2 (3-2-2)

S25 ●	Holy Cross	17	7
O2 ●	Tufts	33	0
O9 ●	Columbia	21	6
O16 =	at Cornell	3	3
O23	Dartmouth	0	14
O30 =	at Pennsylvania	10	10
N6	Princeton	6	14
N13 ●	at Brown	17	8
N20 ●	at Yale	13	0

1966 8-1-0 (6-1-0)

S24 ●	Lafayette	30	7
O1 ●	Tufts	45	0
O8 ●	at Columbia	34	7
O15 ●	Cornell	21	0
O22 ●	Dartmouth	19	14
O29 ●	Pennsylvania	27	7
N5	at Princeton	14	18
N12 ●	Brown	24	7
N19 ●	Yale	17	0

1967 6-3-0 (4-3-0)

S30 ●	Lafayette	51	0
O7 ●	Boston U.	29	14
O14 ●	Columbia	49	13
O21 ●	at Cornell	14	12
O28	Dartmouth	21	23
N4 ●	at Pennsylvania	45	7
N11	Princeton	6	45
N18 ●	at Brown	21	6
N25	at Yale	20	24

1968 8-0-1 (6-0-1)

S28 ●	Holy Cross	27	20
O5 ●	Bucknell	59	0
O12 ●	at Columbia	21	14
O19 ●	Cornell	10	0
O26 ●	Dartmouth	22	7
N2 ●	Pennsylvania	28	6
N9 ●	at Princeton	9	7
N16 ●	Brown	31	7
N23 =	Yale	29	29

1969 3-6-0 (2-5-0)

S27 ●	Holy Cross	13	0
O4	Boston U.	10	13
O11 ●	Columbia	51	0
O18	at Cornell	24	41
O25	Dartmouth	10	24
N1 ●	at Pennsylvania	20	6
N8	Princeton	20	51
N15	at Brown	17	24
N22	at Yale	0	7

1970 7-2-0 (5-2-0)

S26 ●	Northeastern	28	7
O3 ●	Rutgers	39	9
O10	at Columbia	21	28
O17 ●	Cornell	27	24
O24	Dartmouth	14	37
O31 ●	Pennsylvania	38	23
N7 ●	at Princeton	29	7
N14 ●	Brown	17	10
N21 ●	Yale	14	12

JOSEPH RESTIC
1971-93 (.545) 117-97-6

1971 5-4-0 (4-3-0)

S25	Holy Cross	16	21
O2 ●	Northeastern	17	7
O9 ●	Columbia	21	19
O16	at Cornell	16	21
O23	Dartmouth	13	16
O30 ●	at Pennsylvania	28	27
N6	Princeton	10	21
N13 ●	at Brown	24	19
N20 ●	at Yale	35	16

1972 4-4-1 (3-3-1)

S30	Massachusetts	19	28
O7 ●	Boston U.	33	14
O14 ●	at Columbia	20	18
O21 ●	Cornell	33	15
O28 =	Dartmouth	21	21
N4	Pennsylvania	27	38
N11	at Princeton	7	10
N18 ●	Brown	21	14
N25	Yale	17	28

1973 7-2-0 (5-2-0)

S29 ●	Massachusetts	24	7
O6 ●	Boston U.	16	0
O13 ●	Columbia	57	0
O20 ●	at Cornell	21	15
O27	Dartmouth	18	24
N3 ●	at Pennsylvania	34	30
N10 ●	Princeton	19	14
N17 ●	at Brown	35	32
N24	at Yale	0	35

1974 7-2-0 (6-1-0)

S28 ●	Holy Cross	24	14
O5	Rutgers	21	24
O12 ●	at Columbia	34	6
O19 ●	Cornell	39	27
O26 ●	at Dartmouth	17	15
N2 ●	Pennsylvania	39	0
N9 ●	at Princeton	34	17
N16	Brown	7	10
N23 ●	Yale	21	16

1975 7-2-0 (6-1-0)

S27 ●	Holy Cross	18	7
O4	Boston U.	9	13
O11 ●	Columbia	35	30
O18 ●	at Cornell	34	13
O25 ●	Dartmouth	24	10
N1 ●	at Pennsylvania	21	3
N8	Princeton	20	24
N15 ●	at Brown	45	26
N22 ●	Yale	10	7

1976 6-3-0 (4-3-0)

S18 ●	Columbia	34	10
S25 ●	Massachusetts	24	13
O2 ●	Boston U.	37	14
O9	Cornell	3	9
O16 ●	at Dartmouth	17	10
O23 ●	at Princeton	20	14
O30	Brown	14	16
N6 ●	at Pennsylvania	20	8
N13	Yale	7	21

1977 4-5-0 (4-3-0)

S17 ●	at Columbia	21	7
S24	Massachusetts	0	17
O1	Colgate	21	38
O8 ●	at Cornell	17	7
O15 ●	Dartmouth	31	25
O22	Princeton	7	20
O29	at Brown	15	20
N5 ●	Pennsylvania	34	15
N12	at Yale	7	24

1978 4-4-1 (2-4-1)

S23	Columbia	19	21
S30 ●	Massachusetts	10	0
O7 ●	Colgate	24	21
O14	Cornell	20	25
O21 ●	Dartmouth	24	19
O28 =	at Princeton	24	24
N4	Brown	30	31
N11 ●	at Pennsylvania	17	13
N18	Yale	28	35

1979 3-6-0 (3-4-0)

S22 ●	at Columbia	26	7
S29	Massachusetts	7	20
O6	Boston U.	10	14
O13	at Cornell	14	41
O20	Dartmouth	7	10
O27	Princeton	7	9
N3	at Brown	14	23
N10 ●	Pennsylvania	41	26
N17 ●	at Yale	22	7

1980 7-3-0 (4-3-0)

S20 ●	Columbia	26	6
S27 ●	Holy Cross	14	13
O4 ●	at Army	15	10
O11 ●	Cornell	20	12
O18	at Dartmouth	12	30
O25	at Princeton	3	7
N1 ●	Brown	17	16
N8 ●	William & Mary	24	13
N15 ●	at Pennsylvania	28	17
N22	Yale	0	14

1981 5-4-1 (4-2-1)

S19 ●	at Columbia	23	6
S26	Holy Cross	19	33
O3	Army	13	27
O10 ●	at Cornell	27	10
O17	Dartmouth	10	24
O24 =	Princeton	17	17
O31 ●	at Brown	41	7
N7 ●	at William & Mary	23	14
N14 ●	Pennsylvania	45	7
N21	at Yale	0	28

1982 7-3-0 (5-2-0)

S18 ●	Columbia	27	16
S25 ●	Massachusetts	31	14
O2	at Army	13	17
O9 ●	Cornell	25	13
O16	at Dartmouth	12	14
O23 ●	at Princeton	27	15
O30 ●	Brown	34	0
N6 ●	at Holy Cross	24	17
N13	at Pennsylvania	21	23
N20 ●	Yale	45	7

1983 6-2-2 (5-1-1)

S17 ●	at Columbia	43	14
S24	Massachusetts	7	21
O1 ●	Army	24	21
O8 =	at Cornell	3	3
O15	Dartmouth	12	28
O22 ●	Princeton	28	26
O29 ●	at Brown	17	10
N5 =	Holy Cross	10	10
N12 ●	Pennsylvania	28	0
N19 ●	at Yale	16	7

1984 5-4-0 (5-2-0)

S22 ●	at Columbia	35	21
S29	Holy Cross	14	24
O6	at Army	11	33
O13 ●	Cornell	24	18
O20 ●	at Dartmouth	21	7
O27 ●	at Princeton	17	15
N3 ●	Brown	24	10
N10	at Pennsylvania	7	38
N17	Yale	27	30

1985 7-3-0 (5-2-0)

S21 ●	at Columbia	49	17
S28 ●	Massachusetts	10	3
O5	William & Mary	14	21
O12 ●	at Cornell	20	17
O19 ●	Dartmouth	17	7
O26	Princeton	6	11
N2 ●	at Brown	25	17
N9 ●	at Holy Cross	28	20
N16 ●	Pennsylvania	17	6
N23	at Yale	6	17

1986 3-7-0 (3-4-0)

S20 ●	Columbia	34	0
S27	Holy Cross	0	41
O4	William & Mary	0	24
O11	Cornell	0	3
O18 ●	at Dartmouth	42	26
O25	at Princeton	3	14
N1	Brown	19	31
N8	Massachusetts	7	17
N15	at Pennsylvania	10	17
N22 ●	Yale	24	17

1987 8-2-0 (6-1-0)

S19 ●	at Columbia	35	0
S26 ●	Northeastern	27	24
O3 ●	Bucknell	33	14
O10	at Cornell	17	29
O17 ●	Dartmouth	42	3
O24 ●	Princeton	24	19
O31 ●	at Brown	14	9
N7	at Holy Cross	6	41
N14 ●	Pennsylvania	31	14
N21 ●	at Yale	14	10

1988 2-8-0 (2-5-0)

S17 ●	Columbia	41	7
S24	Massachusetts	28	45
O1	at Holy Cross	20	35
O8	Cornell	17	19
O15	at Dartmouth	7	38
O22	at Princeton	8	23
O29 ●	Brown	28	3
N5	Boston U.	23	24
N12	at Pennsylvania	13	52
N19	Yale	17	26

1989 5-5-0 (5-2-0)

S16 ●	at Columbia	26	10
S23	Holy Cross	17	31
S30	at Army	28	56
O7	Lehigh	28	50
O14	at Cornell	0	28
O21 ●	Dartmouth	6	5
O28	Princeton	14	28
N4 ●	at Brown	27	14
N11 ●	Pennsylvania	24	15
N18 ●	at Yale	37	20

1990 5-5-0 (3-4-0)

S15 ●	at Columbia	9	6
S22 ●	Northeastern	26	0
S29	at Holy Cross	14	35
O6	Cornell	17	20
O13 ●	Fordham	19	13
O20 ●	at Princeton	23	20
O27	at Dartmouth	0	17
N3 ●	Brown	52	37
N10	at Pennsylvania	20	24
N17	Yale	19	34

1991 4-5-1 (4-2-1)

S21 ●	Columbia	21	16
S28	at Army	20	21
O5	Holy Cross	13	28
O12	at Fordham	7	14
O19	at Cornell	17	22
O26 ●	Princeton	24	21
N2 =	Dartmouth	31	31
N9 ●	at Brown	35	29
N16 ●	Pennsylvania	22	18
N23	at Yale	13	23

1992 3-7-0 (3-4-0)

S19 ●	at Columbia	27	20
S26	William & Mary	16	36
O3	at Holy Cross	7	30
O10	Cornell	13	31
O17	at Lafayette	29	31
O24	at Princeton	6	21
O31	Dartmouth	7	31
N7 ●	Brown	29	19
N14	at Pennsylvania	19	21
N21 ●	Yale	14	0

1993 3-7-0 (1-6-0)

S18 ●	Columbia	30	3
S25	at William & Mary	17	45
O2 ●	Lafayette	21	16
O9	at Cornell	0	27
O16 ●	Holy Cross	41	25
O23	Princeton	10	21
O30	at Dartmouth	34	39
N6	at Brown	29	43
N13	Pennsylvania	20	27
N20	at Yale	31	33

TIMOTHY L. MURPHY
1994-Present (.606) 66-43

1994 4-6-0 (2-5-0)

S17 ●	at Columbia	39	32
S24	Bucknell	23	42
O1 ●	at Holy Cross	27	17
O8	Cornell	13	18
O15 ●	Colgate	35	27
O22	at Princeton	7	18
O29 ●	at Dartmouth	35	12
N5	Brown	17	23
N12	at Pennsylvania	0	33
N19	Yale	13	32

1995 2-8-0 (1-6-0)

S16	Columbia	24	28
S23 ●	at Colgate	28	8
S30	Fordham	21	24
O7	at Cornell	27	28
O14	Holy Cross	22	27
O21	Princeton	3	14
O28	Dartmouth	7	23
N4	at Brown	8	47
N11	Pennsylvania	21	38
N18 ●	at Yale	22	21

1996 4-6 (2-5)

S21	at Columbia	13	20
S28 ●	at Bucknell	30	7
O5	Lafayette	7	17
O12	Cornell	13	20
O19 ●	at Holy Cross	28	25
O26 ●	at Princeton	24	0
N2	Dartmouth	3	6
N9	Brown	7	31
N16	at Pennsylvania	12	17
N23 ●	Yale	26	21

1997   9-1   (7-0)
S20 ●	Columbia	45	7
S27 ●	at Lehigh	35	30
O4	Bucknell	20	24
O11 ●	at Cornell	34	9
O18 ●	Holy Cross	52	24
O25 ●	Princeton	14	12
N1 ●	at Dartmouth	24	0
N8 ●	at Brown	27	10
N15 ●	Pennsylvania	33	0
N22 ●	at Yale	17	7

1998   4-6   (3-4)
S19 ●	at Columbia	0	24
S26 ●	at Colgate	14	34
O3	Lehigh	17	21
O10 ●	Cornell	19	12
O17 ●	Holy Cross	20	14
O24 ●	at Princeton	23	22
O31 ●	at Dartmouth	20	7
N7 ●	Brown	6	27
N14 ●	at Pennsylvania	10	41
N21 ●	Yale	7	9

1999   5-5   (3-4)
S18 ●	Columbia	24	7
S25 ●	at Holy Cross	25	17
O2	Colgate	21	24
O9	at Cornell	23	24
O16 ●	at Fordham	37	30
O23 ●	Princeton	13	6
O30 ●	Dartmouth	63	21
N6	at Brown	10	17
N13 ●	Pennsylvania	17	21
N20	at Yale	21	24

2000   5-5   (4-3)
S16 ●	Holy Cross	25	27
S23 ●	at Brown	42	37
S30 ●	at Lafayette	42	19
O7	Cornell	28	29
O14	Lehigh	13	45
O21 ●	at Princeton	35	21
O28 ●	at Dartmouth	49	7
N4 ●	Columbia	34	0
N11 ●	at Pennsylvania	35	36
N18	Yale	24	34

2001   9-0   (7-0)
S22 ●	Brown	27	20
S29 ●	Lafayette	38	14
O6 ●	Northeastern	35	20
O13 ●	at Cornell	26	6
O20 ●	Princeton	28	26
O27 ●	Dartmouth	31	21
N3 ●	at Columbia	45	33
N10 ●	Pennsylvania	28	21
N17 ●	at Yale	35	23

2002   7-3   (6-1)
S21 ●	Holy Cross	28	23
S28 ●	at Brown	26	24
O5 ●	at Lehigh	35	36
O12 ●	Cornell	52	23
O19 ●	Northeastern	14	17
O26 ●	at Princeton	24	17
N2 ●	at Dartmouth	31	26
N9 ●	Columbia	28	7
N16 ●	at Pennsylvania	9	44
N23 ●	Yale	20	13

2003   7-3   (4-3)
S20 ●	at Holy Cross	43	23
S27 ●	Brown	52	14
O4 ●	Northeastern	28	20
O11 ●	at Cornell	27	0
O18 ●	Lafayette	34	27
O25 ●	Princeton	43	40
N1 ●	Dartmouth	16	30
N8 ●	at Columbia	13	16
N15 ●	Pennsylvania	24	32
N22 ●	at Yale	37	19

2004   10-0   (7-0)
S18 ●	Holy Cross	35	0
S25 ●	at Brown	35	34
O2 ●	at Lafayette	38	23
O9 ●	Cornell	34	24
O16 ●	Northeastern	41	14
O23 ●	at Princeton	39	14
O30 ●	at Dartmouth	13	12
N6 ●	Columbia	38	0
N13 ●	at Pennsylvania	31	10
N20 ●	Yale	35	3

Neutral Site key: U Unknown, Unknown / Spr Springfield, MA / Bos Boston, MA / Balt Baltimore, MD / NYC New York, NY

Months: Y May / E June / P April

ƒ Forfeit   † Game Later Forfeited   # Disputed Victor   * Disputed Score || Designated Conference Game   2 Counted Twice in Conference Standings

HARVARD ANNUAL STATISTICAL LEADERS

YR	RUSHING	YDS	ATT	AVG	PASSING	ATT	CMP	PCT	YDS	RECEIVING	REC	YDS	AVG
1954	Matthew Botsford	456	108	4.2	Matthew Botsford	47	19	.40	250	Robert Cochran	13	210	16.2
1955	Matthew Botsford	323	86	3.8	Matthew Botsford	49	21	.43	316	Robert Morrison	8	120	15.0
1956	Anthony Gianelly	316	80	4.0	John Simourian	66	30	.45	329	Phil Haughey	11	141	12.8
1957	Chet Boulris	393	85	4.6	Richard McLaughlin	55	28	.51	282	Thomas Hooper	16	171	10.7
1958	Chet Boulris	493	124	4.0	Charlie Frank	82	31	.38	258	Stuart Hershon	8	99	12.4
1959	Chet Boulris	628	125	5.0	Charlie Ravenell	87	34	.39	460	Chet Boulris	9	70	7.8
1960	Hobart Armstrong	339	79	4.3	Terry Bartolet	53	23	.43	393	Robert Messenbaugh	11	166	15.1
1961	William Grana	431	94	4.6	William Humenuk	31	13	.42	195	William Taylor	7	58	8.3
1962	William Taylor	450	71	6.3	Michael Bassett	50	25	.50	451	William Taylor	12	315	26.3
1963	Walter Grant	332	73	4.5	Michael Bassett	79	39	.49	559	L. Scott Harshbarger	14	194	13.9
1964	Walter Grant	278	93	3.0	Thomas Bilodeau	61	38	.62	379	Walter Grant	20	175	8.8
1965	Walter Grant	559	118	4.7	John McClusky	85	31	.36	293	Robert Leo	9	126	14.0
1966	Robert Leo	827	130	6.4	Richard Zimmerman	103	51	.50	639	Carter Lord	19	248	13.1
1967	Victor Gatto	752	184	4.1	Richard Zimmerman	139	62	.45	1,143	Carter Lord	39	774	19.8
1968	Victor Gatto	678	149	4.6	George Lalich	110	55	.50	628	Richard Varney	20	306	15.3
1969	Ralph Hornblower	620	136	4.6	David Smith	59	22	.37	284	Richard Varney	20	265	13.3
1970	Theodore DeMars	512	96	5.3	Eric Crone	71	35	.49	531	William Craven	18	293	16.3
1971	Theodore DeMars	704	135	5.2	James Stoeckel	79	39	.49	487	Richard Gatto	25	251	10.0
1972	Theodore DeMars	673	140	4.8	Eric Crone	115	45	.39	588	John Hagerty	19	332	17.5
1973	Neal Miller	661	130	5.1	James Stoeckel	208	112	.54	1,391	Patrick McInally	56	752	13.4
1974	Thomas Winn	433	98	4.4	Milton Holt	204	108	.53	1,456	Patrick McInally	46	655	14.2
1975	Thomas Winn	630	137	4.6	James Kubacki	137	77	.56	1,273	James Curry	32	641	20.0
1976	Thomas Winn	656	139	4.7	James Kubacki	145	66	.46	945	Thomas Winn	19	265	13.9
1977	Christopher Doherty	308	64	4.8	Larry Brown	139	79	.57	1,186	James Curry	28	440	15.7
1978	Ralph Polillio	585	130	4.5	Larry Brown	178	101	.57	1,575	Ralph Polillio	25	403	16.1
1979	Jon Hollingworth	315	106	3.0	Burke St. John	150	68	.45	1,010	Rich Horner	40	712	17.8
1980	Jim Callinan	455	104	4.4	Brian Buckley	167	89	.53	1,123	Tom Beatrice	23	245	10.7
1981	Jim Callinan	1,054	209	5.0	Ron Cuccia	116	50	.43	687	Jim Callinan	18	204	11.3
1982	Mike Granger	442	109	4.1	Don Allard	204	109	.53	1,560	John O'Brien	26	253	9.7
1983	Steve Ernst	761	138	5.5	Greg Guzzi	107	60	.56	729	John O'Brien	47	519	11.0
1984	Robert Santiago	822	138	6.0	Brian White	113	66	.58	934	Robert Santiago	24	296	12.3
1985	Robert Santiago	793	174	4.6	Brian White	184	84	.46	1,273	Robert Santiago	27	279	10.3
1986	Brian O'Neil	425	98	4.3	Tom Yohe	102	45	.44	596	Joe Connelly	18	246	13.7
1987	Tony Hinz	789	139	5.7	Tom Yohe	321	158	.49	2,134	Brian Barringer	49	537	11.0
1988	Tony Hinz	686	148	4.6	Tom Yohe	225	117	.52	1,677	Don Gajewski	40	533	13.3
1989	Jim Reidy	477	99	4.8	Tom Perry	268	121	.45	1,513	Mark Bianchi	28	397	14.2
1990	Matt Johnson	535	99	5.4	Adam Lazarre-White	98	48	.49	616	Andy Lombara	21	299	14.2
1991	Matt Johnson	744	121	6.1	Mike Giardi	161	79	.49	1,193	Robb Hirsch	32	438	13.7
1992	Mike Hill	391	89	4.4	Mike Giardi	172	90	.52	1,271	Robb Hirsch	17	126	7.4
1993	Mark Cote	569	116	4.9	Mike Giardi	244	114	.47	1,734	Mark Begert	31	522	16.8
1994	Eion Hu	1,038	234	4.4	Vin Ferrara	211	124	.59	1,500	Mike Halligan	26	376	14.5
1995	Eion Hu	1,175	230	5.1	Vin Ferrara	281	146	.52	1,522	Colby Skelton	35	496	14.2
1996	Eion Hu	961	250	3.8	Rich Linden	145	85	.59	899	Colby Skelton	49	691	14.1
1997	Chris Menick	1,267	247	5.1	Rich Linden	286	164	.57	2,099	Terence Patterson	45	459	10.2
1998	Chris Menick	768	186	4.1	Rich Linden	228	117	.51	1,201	Terence Patterson	40	385	9.6
1999	Chris Menick	969	194	5.0	Brad Wilford	296	162	.55	1,866	Terence Patterson	54	537	9.9
2000	Nick Palazzo	740	130	5.7	Neil Rose	339	203	.60	2,655	Carl Morris	60	920	15.3
2001	Nick Palazzo	556	108	5.1	Neil Rose	198	127	.64	1,830	Carl Morris	71	943	13.3
2002	Ryan Fitzpatrick	523	115	4.5	Neil Rose	186	123	.66	1,438	Carl Morris	90	1,288	14.3
2003	Clifton Dawson	1,187	215	5.5	Ryan Fitzpatrick	178	107	.60	1,770	Brian Edwards	47	864	18.4
2004	Clifton Dawson	1,302	248	5.3	Ryan Fitzpatrick	276	158	.57	1,986	Corey Mazza	51	773	15.2

Receiving leaders by receptions

PENNSYLVANIA

BY BRUCE WOOD

ONE OF THE WORST RUNS IN IVY League play has been followed by one of the best. From 1978 to 1981, the once-proud Quakers, whose history includes a berth in the 1917 Rose Bowl, averaged less than one win per year. Things got so bad that before the 1982 season, one poll ranked Penn the third-worst team in the country. Undaunted, the Quakers shocked Dartmouth 21-0 in their opener and went on to earn a share of their first Ivy title in 23 years. Since 1982, the Quakers have been the dominant team in Ivy League play, amassing 12 championships in 23 years.

TRADITION After the third quarter, the marching band breaks into "Drink a Highball," and for decades the Penn faithful joined in the drinking as well as the singing. When alcohol was banned from the school's stadium in the 1970s, students found new meaning in the song's final words, "Here's a toast to dear old Penn." Inspired by the cult movie *The Rocky Horror Picture Show*, the home crowd now marks the start of the fourth quarter by raining down thousands of slices of toast toward the field. The tradition is so ingrained that two Penn engineering students designed the Toast Zamboni, a modified street sweeper that can vacuum up the pieces of toast that make it onto the field.

BEST PLAYER The son of a Bethlehem, Pa., steelworker, Chuck Bednarik served as a waist gunner on a B-24 over Germany in World War II before coming home to play center and linebacker for the Quakers. Once on the field, Bednarik wouldn't leave. Through four years, he played every down, 60 minutes a game, earning first-team All-America honors as a junior and senior. In his final year, he became the first offensive lineman to win the Maxwell Award as the nation's outstanding player. Bednarik went on to a standout 14-year career with the Philadelphia Eagles, and he was inducted into both the College and Pro Football halls of fame.

BEST COACH In his first 13 years as head coach, Al Bagnoli has guided Penn to an impressive 99–29 record and six Ivy League championships. The foundation for Penn's modern success was laid by Jerry Berndt, who guided the Quakers to four Ivy titles from 1982 to 1985. But Bagnoli still has a way to go to match the standard set by George Munger. A Penn alum, Munger was teaching math and sacred studies at Philadelphia's Episcopal Academy when he decided to give college coaching a try. He was tapped to lead the Quakers in 1938 at the age of 28. In 16 seasons, he crafted an 82–42–10 record, winning or sharing the unofficial Ivy crown nine times.

PROFILE

University of Pennsylvania
Philadelphia, Pa.
Founded: 1740
Enrollment: 10,047
Colors: Red and Blue
Nickname: Quakers
Stadium: Franklin Field
  Opened in 1895
  Sprinturf; 52,593 capacity
First football game: 1876
All-time record: 777–435–42 (.636)
Bowl record: 0–1
Ivy League championships: 13 (10 outright)
First-round NFL draftees: 2
Website: www.pennathletics.com

THE BEST OF TIMES

After winning just three Ivy League games from 1978 to 1981, the Quakers exploded on the conference to capture five consecutive titles from 1982 to 1986.

THE WORST OF TIMES

The 1960s were unkind to the Quakers, who went 18–51–1 in Ivy League play during the decade and were outscored by Princeton 305-57 while losing nine of 10 games to their rival.

CONFERENCE

Pennsylvania was an original member of the Ivy League when the conference began formal play in 1956.

DISTINGUISHED ALUMNI

Donald Trump; Walter Annenberg; Charles Addams, creator of *The Addams Family*; Candice Bergen, actress; Maury Povich, talk-show host; Harold Prince, Broadway producer; Ed Rendell, Pennsylvania governor; Arlen Specter, U.S. senator

FIGHT SONG

FIGHT ON PENNSYLVANIA
Fight on, Pennsylvania, put the ball across that line.
Fight, you Pennsylvanians, there it goes across this time.
Red and blue we're with you
And we're cheering for your men.
So it's fight, fight, fight, Pennsylvan-i-a,
Fight on for Penn!

BEST TEAM From 1894 to 1898, the Quakers pounded nearly everyone they met, winning 67 games against only two losses. But the 1897 squad, led by former Yale guard George Woodruff, was something special, posting an undefeated season and a school-record 15 wins. Four team members were honored as All-Americas: tackle John Outland (the namesake of the Outland Trophy), guard Truxtun Hare, end Sam Boyle and back John Minds.

Inspired by The Rocky Horror Picture Show, students mark the end of the "Drink a Highball" singing by sailing slices of toast onto the field.

BIGGEST GAME On Nov. 13, 1982, the 6–2 Quakers were poised to clinch a share of the Ivy League title; only Harvard stood in their way. With 34,746 fans looking on, Penn took a comfortable 20-0 lead into the fourth quarter, only to watch helplessly as the Crimson roared back with three quick touchdowns to take a 21-20 lead. With 1:24 left, the Quakers took possession and marched down to the Harvard 21. Dave Shulman lined up for a potential 38-yard game-winning field goal with three seconds left, but his kick sailed wide left. It wasn't over, though: Harvard was flagged for roughing the kicker on the play. Shulman then calmly kicked a 27-yarder to give the Quakers their first title since 1959. Fans immediately

swarmed the field and tore down the goalposts, lugging them out of the stadium and into the nearby Schuylkill River.

BIGGEST UPSET Penn was a serious underdog coming into the 1902 Thanksgiving Day contest against Cornell. The Quakers had lost four of their previous six games, and their anemic offense had been held scoreless in their past two contests. Cornell, on the other hand, had won three of four games by a combined 135-10. What's more, the Big Red were confident they could repeat the pounding they dished out on Penn the previous year. Leading 11-0 at halftime, the Big Red offered to shorten the rest of the game to keep the score from getting out of hand and to save Penn the agony of a humiliating defeat. The Quakers rebuffed them and returned to the field. Penn went on to rally for two touchdowns and left Ithaca with a shocking 12-11 victory.

WILDEST FINISH On Oct. 28, 2000, the Quakers trailed Brown 38-20 with less than five minutes to play, and any hopes of an Ivy League championship were slipping away. Penn

RECORDS

RUSHING YARDS

GAME	
272	Terrance Stokes vs. Princeton, Nov. 6, 1993 (42 att.)
SEASON	
1,450	Jim Finn, 1998 (323 att.)
CAREER	
3,181	Kris Ryan, 1998-2001 (611 att.)

PASSING YARDS

GAME	
476	Gavin Hoffman vs. Brown, Oct. 28, 2000 (38 of 52)
SEASON	
3,214	Gavin Hoffman, 2000 (272 of 386)
CAREER	
7,542	Gavin Hoffman, 1999-2001 (651 of 1,004)

RECEIVING YARDS

GAME	
284	Don Clune vs. Harvard, Oct. 30, 1971 (8 rec.)
SEASON	
1,112	Rob Milanese, 2002 (85 rec.)
CAREER	
3,409	Rob Milanese, 1999-2002 (259 rec.)

POINTS

GAME	
36	Jim Finn vs. Brown, Oct. 24, 1998 (6 TDs)
SEASON	
109	Howard Berry, 1917 (10 TDs, 8 FGs, 25 PATs)
CAREER	
218	Jason Feinberg, 1998-2000 (41 FGs, 95 PATs)

CONSENSUS ALL-AMERICANS

1891	John Adams, C
1892	Harry Thayer, B
1894	Arthur Knipe, B
1894-95	George Brooke, B
1894-96	Charles Gelbert, E
1895-96	Charles Wharton, G
1895	Alfred Bull, C
1896	Wylie Woodruff, G
1897	John Minds, B
1897-98	John Outland, T/B
1897-1900	T. Truxton Hare, G
1898-99	Pete Overfield, C
1899	Josiah McCracken, B
1904	Frank Piekarski, G
1904	Vincent Stevenson, B
1904	Andrew Smith, B
1905	Otis Lamson, T
1905	Robert Torrey, C

(Continued on next page)

quarterback Gavin Hoffman led his team to three touchdowns in the final 4:37, finishing the furious rally with a seven-yard TD pass to Rob Milanese with 28 seconds left to pull out a 41-38 victory. Penn, which had lost to Yale the previous week, went on to sweep its remaining three games to claim the Ivy crown with a 6–1 record.

STADIUM Franklin Field, the oldest college football stadium in the nation, has roots dating to 1895, when a 10,000-seat facility was built for the first running of the Penn Relays track meet. The home of the Penn football team and site of the first stadium scoreboard soon proved inadequate to handle big crowds. In 1903, the wooden stands were demolished in favor of a 20,000-seat brick horseshoe, the first of its kind. In 1925, Franklin Field became the first two-tier football stadium in the country; by then, its seating capacity topped 78,205. From 1958 to 1970, the Philadelphia Eagles played their home games at Franklin Field. In 2004, the stadium and field underwent a number of improvements, including a new high-tech scoreboard and Sprinturf playing surface.

RIVAL Since the start of formal Ivy League competition in 1956, only nine times have teams with unbeaten conference records met on the final day of the season. Twice those games pitted Penn against Cornell, whom the Quakers used to play annually on Thanksgiving. In 1986, the Quakers' Rich Comizio and Chris Flynn combined for 251 rushing yards against a Cornell defense that had been allowing a league-low 52 yards rushing per game. Penn won the game and the championship on the road, 31-21. Again in 2000, the outright Ivy title was at stake in Ithaca, and again the Quakers prevailed in the battle of conference unbeatens, 45-15. In recent years, Penn has tended to view Princeton as its chief rival, but the Tigers look to Yale as theirs.

NICKNAME There was a time when Philadelphia sports-writers referred to all the college teams they covered as Quakers, invoking the city's historic ties to William Penn and the Society of Friends. St. Joseph's eventually became the Hawks, Temple the Owls and LaSalle the Explorers. Only with Penn did the Quakers moniker stick.

UNIFORMS Penn's red-and-blue color scheme can be traced back at least as far as the letters on the lid of the school's 1871 College Hall cornerstone. They were made official in a resolution adopted by the university on May 17, 1910, that read, "The colors shall be red and blue. The colors shall conform to the present standards used by the United States government in its flags." The school has since moved to a burgundy red and darker blue.

QUOTE "We played the game because we love it. We loved the game beyond the prize."—Four-time All-America Truxtun Hare in 1900, ruing the increasing professionalism in college football

CONSENSUS ALL-AMERICANS (CONT.)	
1906-07	August Ziegler, G
1906, 1908	William Hollenback, B
1907	Dexter Draper, T
1908	Hunter Scarlett, E
1910	Ernest Cozens, C
1910, 1912	E. LeRoy Mercer, B
1917, 1919	Henry Miller, E
1922	John Thurman, T
1924	Ed McGinley, T
1927	Ed Hake, T
1928	Paul Scull, B
1943	Bob Odell, B
1945	George Savitsky, T
1947-48	Chuck Bednarik, C
1986	Marty Peterson, OL
1988	John Zinser, OL
1990	Joe Valerio, OL
1993, 1995	Miles Macik, WR
1994	Pat Goodwillie, LB
1995	Tom McGarrity, DL
1996	Mitch Marrow, DL
2001	Jeff Hatch, OL
2003	Chris Clark, OL

PENNSYLVANIA ALL-TIME SCORES

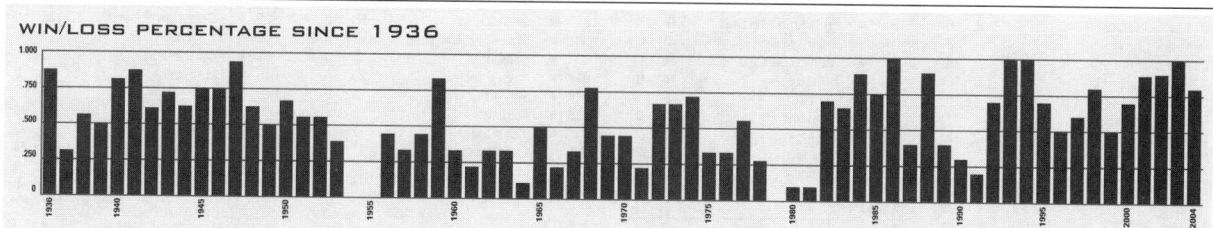

WIN/LOSS PERCENTAGE SINCE 1936

NO HEAD COACH

1876   1-2-0
N1		Princeton	0	6
N17	●	All Philadelphia	4	0
N25		at Princeton	0	6

1877
NO TEAM

1878   1-2-1
O19		at Princeton	0	2
N2	●	Swarthmore	9	0
N9		Princeton	1	2
N16	=	Columbia	0	0

1879   2-2-0
O18		at Princeton	0	6
N1		Yale *Hob*	0	3
N8		Columbia	1	0
N15		Widener	7	0

1880   3-2-0
O23	●	Crescent AC	5	0
O30		at Princeton	0	1
N6	●	Stevens	3	0
N13		at Stevens	5	0
N17		Yale *NYC*	0	8

1881   0-5-0
O29		Princeton	0	7
N2		Harvard *NYC*	0	2
N5		at Princeton	0	4
N19		Rutgers	1	2
N26		Columbia	0	2

1882   2-4-0
O14	●	Crescent AC	5	0
O28		at Princeton	0	8
N4		Rutgers	1	3
N11		Princeton	0	10
N18		at Rutgers	0	1
N25	●	Lafayette	1	0

1883   6-2-1
O13		at Harvard	0	4
O20	●	Johns Hopkins	26	6
O27	●	Lafayette	44	4
N3		at Princeton	6	39
N10	●	Johns Hopkins	30	0
N14	●	Columbia	35	1
N17	●	Rutgers	18	0
N24	●	Graduates	38	7
N29	●	Stevens	6	6

1884   5-1-1
O22	●	at Harvard	4	0
O25		Princeton	0	31
N1	●	Lafayette	21	0
N8	●	Stevens	30	0
N15	●	Johns Hopkins	33	0
N20	=	Graduates	16	16
N27	●	Wesleyan *NYC*	14	12

FRANK DOLE
1885-87 (.547)   23-19-1

1885   8-5-0
O7	●	Graduates	42	0
O10	●	Lehigh	54	0
O14	●	Swarthmore	68	6
O17	●	Graduates	6	5
O24		Princeton	0	57
O28	●	Lafayette	54	10
O31		at Princeton	10	80
N4		at Lafayette	30	22
N7	●	Wesleyan *NYC*	18	25
N14		Yale	5	53
N18	●	Lehigh	35	0
N21		at Stevens	23	9
N26		Princeton	10	76

1886   9-7-1
S30	●	Schuylkill	64	0
O2	●	Tioga	18	0
O9	●	Lehigh	26	4
O13	●	Graduates	4	0
O16		Princeton	0	30
O18	=	Graduates	6	6
O20		at Lafayette	0	12
O23		at Princeton	9	55
O27	●	Wesleyan *NYC*	14	0
O30	●	Lafayette	20	10
N3	●	Haverford	16	4
N6		Princeton	6	28
N10	●	Rutgers	65	0
N13		at Yale	0	75
N15	●	Vineland	96	6
N18		at Lehigh	0	28
N25		Harvard	0	28

1887   6-7-0
O8	●	Graduates	14	6
O12	●	Tioga	46	0
O15	●	Graduates	18	0
O19		Princeton	0	57
O22		Princeton	0	42
O29		Yale	0	50
N2	●	Rutgers	13	10
N5		Princeton	0	95
N9	●	Haverford	36	0
N12	●	Lehigh	6	4
N16		Lafayette	0	20
N19		Harvard	0	42
N24	●	Wesleyan *NYC*	4	10

E.O. WAGENHURST
1888-91 (.679)   38-18

1888   9-7-0
O3	●	Graduates	20	6
O6	●	Stevens	48	0
O10		at Princeton	0	63
O13		Yale	0	34
O17	●	at Swarthmore	44	6
O20		at Princeton	0	38
O24	●	Tioga	12	4
O27	●	at Lehigh	36	0
N3		at Yale	0	58
N7		Lafayette	6	12
N10		Princeton	0	4
N19		Harvard	0	50
N21	●	at Lafayette	50	0
N27	●	Wesleyan *NYC*	18	6
N30	●	at Johns Hopkins	24	10
D1	●	at Navy	20	9

1889   7-6-0
O3	●	Philly All Stars	30	6
O5	●	Swarthmore	82	0
O12	●	at Rutgers	4	0
O19	●	Lehigh	6	4
O26		Princeton	4	72
O30		Yale	10	20
N2		at Harvard	0	35
N6	●	at Lafayette	8	10
N9	●	at Columbia	24	0
N16	●	Rutgers	14	0
N20		at Lehigh	0	8
N23	●	Lafayette	14	0
N28		Wesleyan *NYC*	2	10

1890   11-3-0
O1	●	at Swarthmore	10	0
O4	●	Rutgers	16	4
O10	●	Penn State	20	0
O15		at Princeton	0	18
O18	●	Lehigh	8	0
O22	●	Columbia *NYC*	18	0
O25	●	Franklin & Marshall	28	0
O31	●	Virginia *DC*	72	0
N5	●	Schuylkill	34	10
N8		at Princeton	0	6
N15		at Yale	0	60
N22	●	at Lehigh	17	14
N26	●	Wesleyan *NYC*	16	10
D13	●	Rutgers *NYC*	13	10

1891   11-2-0
O3	●	All Philadelphia	4	0
O8	●	Schuylkill	24	0
O10	●	Haverford	34	0
O17	●	at Orange AC	26	0
O21	●	Rutgers	32	6
O24	●	at Lehigh	42	0
O28	●	Lafayette	15	6
O31	●	Trinity	28	5
N7		Princeton	0	24
N14		Yale	0	48
N18	●	at Lafayette	12	10
N21	●	Lehigh	32	0
N25	●	Wesleyan	18	10

GEORGE WOODRUFF
1892-1901 (.887)   124-15-2

1892   15-1-0
S28	●	at Swarthmore	22	0
O1	●	Penn State	20	0
O5	●	Haverford	56	0
O11	●	at Virginia	32	0
O12	●	at Navy	16	0
O15	●	Crescent AC *BKLN*	23	0
O19	●	Dickinson	78	0
O21	●	Williams	50	0
O22	●	Franklin & Marshall	34	0
O26		at Lafayette	8	6
O29	●	Chicago AC	12	10
N5	●	Princeton *MAN*	6	4
N8	●	Lehigh	4	0
N12		Yale *NYC*	0	28
N16	●	Lafayette	10	4
N25	●	Wesleyan *MAN*	34	0

1893   12-3-0
S30	●	Franklin & Marshall	48	0
O4	●	Gettysburg	74	0
O7	●	Columbia AC	30	0
O9	●	at Columbia AC	20	6
O10	●	at Georgetown	12	0
O11	●	at Navy	34	0
O14	●	Volunteer AC	34	0
O18	●	at Lehigh	32	6
O21	●	at Crescent AC	40	0
O25	●	Penn State	18	6
O28	●	Lafayette	82	0
N4		Princeton *MAN*	0	4
N11		Yale *NYC*	6	14
N18	●	Cornell *MAN*	50	0
N30		at Harvard	4	26

1894   12-0-0
O3	●	at Franklin & Marshall	34	0
O6	●	Swarthmore	66	0
O10	●	Crescent AC	22	0
O13	●	Georgetown	46	0
O17	●	Lehigh	30	0
O20	●	at Crescent AC	80	0
O26	●	Virginia *DC*	14	6
O27	●	at Navy	12	0
O31	●	Lafayette	26	0
N10	●	Princeton *THE*	12	0
N17	●	Cornell	6	0
N29	●	Harvard	18	4

1895   14-0-0
O1	●	Swarthmore	40	0
O2	●	Bucknell	40	0
O5	●	Franklin & Marshall	42	0
O9	●	at Crescent AC	32	0
O14	●	Lehigh	54	0
O16	●	Carlisle	36	0
O19	●	Virginia	54	0
O23	●	at Duquesne AC	30	0
O26	●	Lafayette	30	0
O30	●	Brown	12	0
N1	●	Chicago AC	12	4
N9	●	Penn State	35	4
N23	●	at Harvard	17	14
N28	●	Cornell	46	2

1896   14-1-0
S26	●	Franklin & Marshall	24	0
S30	●	Gettysburg	32	0
O3	●	Bucknell	40	0
O7	●	at Navy	8	0
O10	●	Dartmouth	16	0
O14	●	Virginia	20	0
O17	●	Lehigh	34	0
O21	●	Amherst	14	0
O24		Lafayette	4	6
O28	●	Brown	16	0
N3	●	Dickinson	30	2
N7	●	Carlisle	21	0
N14	●	Penn State	27	0
N21	●	Harvard	8	6
N26	●	Cornell	32	10

1897   15-0-0
S22	●	at Bucknell	17	0
S25	●	Franklin & Marshall	33	0
S29	●	Wash. & Jeff.	18	4
O2	●	Bucknell	33	0
O6	●	Gettysburg	57	0
O9	●	Lehigh	58	0
O13	●	Virginia	42	0
O16	●	Dartmouth	14	0
O20	●	Penn State	24	0
O23	●	Lafayette	46	0
O30	●	at Brown	40	0
N6	●	Carlisle	20	10
N13	●	Wesleyan	22	0
N20	●	Harvard	15	6
N25	●	Cornell	4	0

1898   12-1-0
S24	●	Franklin & Marshall	41	0
S28	●	Gettysburg	50	0
O1	●	Penn State	40	0
O5	●	Mansfield	50	0
O8	●	Brown	18	0
O12	●	Virginia	34	0 *
O15	●	Lehigh	40	0
O19	●	Wesleyan	17	0
O22	●	Lafayette	32	0
O29	●	Chicago	23	11
N5		at Harvard	0	10
N12	●	Carlisle	35	5
N24	●	Cornell	12	6

1899   8-3-2
S27	●	Franklin & Marshall	48	0
S30	●	Lehigh	20	0
O4	●	Bucknell	47	10
O7	=	at Brown	6	6
O11	●	Virginia	33	6
O14	●	Carlisle	5	16
O18	●	Wesleyan	17	6
O21		Lafayette	0	6
O28	=	at Chicago	5	5
N4		Harvard	0	16
N11	●	Michigan	11	10
N17	●	Penn State	47	0
N30	●	Cornell	29	0

1900			12-1-0	
S29	●	Lehigh	27	6
O3	●	Franklin & Marshall	47	0
O6	●	Haverford	38	0
O10	●	Dickinson	35	0
O13	●	Brown	12	0
O17	●	Penn State	17	6 *
O20	●	Columbia	30	0
O27	●	Chicago	41	0
N3		at Harvard	5	17
N10	●	Lafayette	12	5
N17	●	Carlisle	16	6
N21	●	at Navy	28	6
N29	●	Cornell	27	0

1901			10-5-0	
S28	●	Lehigh	28	0
O2	●	Franklin & Marshall	6	0
O5	●	Penn State	23	6
O9	●	Swarthmore	28	0
O12	●	Brown	26	0
O16	●	Virginia	20	5
O19	●	Bucknell	6	0
O21		at Navy	5	6
O23	●	Gettysburg	22	0
O26	●	at Chicago	11	0
N2		at Columbia	0	10
N9		Harvard	6	33
N16	●	Carlisle	16	14
N23		at Army	0	24
N28		Cornell	6	23

CARL WILLIAMS
1902-07 (.838) 60-10-4

1902			9-4-0	
S27	●	Lehigh	12	0
O1	●	Franklin & Marshall	16	0
O4	●	Penn State	17	0
O8	●	Haverford	18	5
O11	●	Swarthmore	11	6
O15	●	Gettysburg	36	0
O18		Brown	6	15
O22		at Navy	6	10
O25	●	Bucknell	6	5
N1	●	Columbia	17	0
N8		at Harvard	0	11
N15		Carlisle	0	5
N27	●	Cornell	12	11

1903			9-3-0	
S26	●	Dickinson	27	0
S30	●	Franklin & Marshall	17	0
O3	●	Lehigh	16	0
O7	●	Haverford	58	0
O10	●	Penn State	39	0
O14	●	Gettysburg	72	0
O17	●	Brown	30	0
O22		at Columbia	6	18
O31	●	Bucknell	47	6
N7		Harvard	10	17
N14		Carlisle	6	16
N26	●	Cornell	42	0

1904			12-0-0	
S24	●	Penn State	6	0
S28	●	Swarthmore	6	4
O1	●	Virginia	24	0
O5	●	Franklin & Marshall	34	0
O8	●	Lehigh	24	0
O12	●	Gettysburg	21	0
O15	●	Brown	6	0
O21	●	Columbia	16	0
O29	●	at Harvard	11	0
N5	●	Lafayette	22	0
N12	●	Carlisle	18	0
N24	●	Cornell	34	0

1905			12-0-1	
S30	●	Lehigh	35	0
O4	●	Gettysburg	16	6
O7	●	Swarthmore	11	4
O11	●	Franklin & Marshall	38	0
O14	●	North Carolina	17	0
O18	●	Ursinus	39	0
O21	●	Brown	8	6
)28	●	Carlisle	6	0
N4	=	Lafayette	6	6
N11	●	Harvard	12	6
N18	●	Villanova	42	0
N25	●	at Columbia	23	0
N30	●	Cornell	6	5

1906			7-2-3	
S29	●	Lehigh	32	6
O3	=	Gettysburg	6	6
O6	●	North Carolina	11	0
O10	●	Franklin & Marshall	47	6
O13		Swarthmore	0	4
O17	●	Medico Chicago	31	0
O20	●	Brown	14	0
O27		Carlisle	6	24
N10	=	Lafayette	0	0
N17	●	Michigan	17	0
N24	●	Villanova	22	12
N29	=	Cornell	0	0

1907			11-1-0	
S28	●	North Carolina	37	0
O2	●	Villanova	16	0
O5	●	Bucknell	29	2
O9	●	Franklin & Marshall	57	0
O12	●	Swarthmore	16	8
O16	●	Gettysburg	23	0
O19	●	Brown	11	0
O26		Carlisle	6	26
N2	●	Lafayette	15	0
N9	●	Penn State	28	0
N16	●	at Michigan	6	0
N28	●	Cornell	12	4

SOL METZGER
1908 (.958) 11-0-1

1908			11-0-1	
S26	●	West Virginia	6	0
S30	●	Ursinus	30	0
O3	●	Bucknell	16	0
O7	●	Villanova	11	0
O10	●	Penn State	6	0
O14	●	Gettysburg	23	4
O17	●	Brown	12	0
O24	=	Carlisle	6	6
O31	●	at Carnegie Tech	25	10
N7	●	Lafayette	34	4
N14	●	at Michigan	29	0
N26	●	Cornell	17	4

ANDREW SMITH
1909-12 (.733) 30-10-3

1909			7-1-2	
S25	●	Gettysburg	20	0
S29	●	Ursinus	22	0
O2	●	Dickinson	18	0
O9	●	West Virginia	12	0
O16	●	Brown	13	5
O23	=	Penn State	3	3
O30	●	Carlisle	29	6
N6	=	Lafayette	6	6
N13		Michigan	6	12
N25	●	Cornell	17	6

1910			9-1-1	
S24		Ursinus	5	8
S28	●	Dickinson	18	0
O1	●	Gettysburg	29	0
O5	●	Franklin & Marshall	17	0
O8	●	West Virginia	38	0
O15	●	at Brown	20	0
O22	●	Penn State	10	0
O29	●	Carlisle	17	5
N5	●	Lafayette	18	0
N12	=	Michigan	0	0
N24	●	Cornell	12	6

1911			7-4-0	
S30	●	Gettysburg	5	3
O4	●	Franklin & Marshall	14	0
O7	●	Ursinus	9	0
O11	●	Dickinson	22	10
O14	●	Villanova	22	0
O21		Brown	0	6
O28		Penn State	6	22
N4		Carlisle	0	16
N11	●	Lafayette	23	6
N18		at Michigan	9	11
N30	●	Cornell	21	9

1912			7-4-0	
S28	●	Gettysburg	25	0
O2	●	Franklin & Marshall	35	0
O5	●	Dickinson	16	0
O9	●	Ursinus	34	0
O12		Swarthmore	3	6
O19		at Brown	7	30
O26		Lafayette	3	7
N2		Penn State	0	14
N9	●	Michigan	27	21
N16	●	Carlisle	34	26
N28	●	Cornell	7	2

GEORGE BROOKE
1913-15 (.517) 13-12-4

1913			6-3-1	
S27	●	Gettysburg	53	0
O1	●	Franklin & Marshall	13	6
O4	●	Lafayette	10	0
O11	●	Swarthmore	20	0
O18	●	Brown	23	0
O25	=	Carlisle	7	7
N1	●	Penn State	17	0
N8		Dartmouth	21	34
N15		at Michigan	0	13
N27		Cornell	0	21

1914			4-4-1	
S26	●	Gettysburg	14	0
O3		Franklin & Marshall	0	10
O10	=	Lafayette	0	0
O17	●	Navy	13	6
O24	●	Carlisle	7	0
O31	●	Swarthmore	40	6
N7		at Michigan	3	34
N14		Dartmouth	0	41
N26		Cornell	12	24

1915			3-5-2	
S25	●	West Virginia	7	0
S29	●	Albright	63	0
O2	●	Franklin & Marshall	10	6
O9		Penn State	3	13
O16	=	at Navy	7	7
O23		Pittsburgh	7	14
O30		Lafayette	0	17
N6		Dartmouth *Bos*	3	7
N13	=	Michigan	0	0
N25		Cornell	9	24

BOB FOLWELL
1916-19 (.718) 27-10-2

1916			7-3-1	
S30	●	West Virginia	3	0
O7	●	Franklin & Marshall	27	0
O14		Swarthmore	0	6
O21	●	Penn State	15	0
O28		Pittsburgh	0	20
N4	●	Lafayette	19	0
N11	=	Dartmouth	7	7
N18	●	Michigan	10	7
N25	●	W.V. Wesleyan	16	0
N30	●	Cornell	23	3
		ROSE BOWL		
J1		Oregon	0	14

1917			9-2-0	
O3	●	Albright	73	10
O6		at Georgia Tech	0	41
O13	●	Swarthmore	10	0
O20	●	Bucknell	20	6
O27		Pittsburgh	6	14
N3	●	Lafayette	27	0
N6	●	Widener	23	0
N10	●	Dartmouth *Bos*	7	0
N17	●	Michigan	16	0
N24	●	Carlisle	26	0
N29	●	Cornell	37	0

1918			5-3-0	
O19	●	USS Minnesota	27	0
O26		Naval Yard	0	7
N3		Swarthmore	12	20
N7	●	St. Joseph's	12	0
N10	●	Lafayette	34	0
N16		at Pittsburgh	0	37
N24	●	Swarthmore	13	7
N28	●	Dartmouth	21	0

1919			6-2-1	
S27	●	Bucknell	16	0
O4	●	Widener	54	0
O11	●	Delaware	89	0
O18	●	Swarthmore	55	7
O25	●	Lafayette	23	0
N1		Penn State	0	10
N8		Dartmouth *NYC*	19	20
N15	=	Pittsburgh	3	3
N27	●	Cornell	24	0

JOHN HEISMAN
1920-22 (.607) 16-10-2

1920			6-4-0	
S25	●	Delaware	35	0
O2	●	Bucknell	7	0
O9	●	Swarthmore	21	0
O16	●	Lafayette	7	0
O23		VMI	7	27
O30		Penn State	7	28
N6		Pittsburgh	21	27
N13		Dartmouth	7	44
N20	●	Columbia *NYC*	27	7
N25	●	Cornell	28	0

1921			4-3-2	
S24	●	Delaware	89	0
O1	●	Franklin & Marshall	20	0
O8	●	Gettysburg	7	0
O15	=	Swarthmore	7	7
O22	●	VMI	21	7
O29		Pittsburgh	0	28
N5		Lafayette	6	38
N12	=	Dartmouth *NYC*	14	14
N24		Cornell	0	41

1922			6-3-0	
S30	●	Franklin & Marshall	14	0
O7	●	Sewanee	27	0
O14	●	Maryland	12	0
O21	●	Swarthmore	14	6
O28	●	Navy	13	7
N4		Alabama	7	9
N11		Pittsburgh	6	7
N18	●	Penn State	7	6
N30		Cornell	0	9

LOUIS YOUNG
1923-29 (.758) 49-15-2

1923			5-4-0	
S29	●	Franklin & Marshall	20	0
O6		Maryland	0	3
O13	●	Swarthmore	13	10
O20	●	Columbia	19	7
O27	●	Centre	24	0
N3	●	Pittsburgh	6	0
N10		Lafayette	6	8
N17		Penn State	0	21
N29		Cornell	7	14

1924			9-1-1	
S27	●	Ursinus	34	0
O1	●	Drexel	52	0
O4	●	Franklin & Marshall	26	0
O11	●	Swarthmore	25	7
O18	●	Columbia	10	7
O25	●	Virginia	27	0
N1	●	Lafayette	6	3
N8	●	Georgetown	3	0
N15	=	Penn State	0	0
N27	●	Cornell	20	0
J1		at California	0	14

1925			7-2-0	
S26	●	Ursinus	32	0
O3	●	Swarthmore	26	13
O10	●	at Brown	9	0
O17	●	at Yale	16	13
O24	●	Chicago	7	0
O31		Illinois	2	24
N7	●	Haverford	66	0
N14		Pittsburgh	0	14
N26	●	Cornell	7	0

1926			7-1-1	
S25	●	Franklin & Marshall	41	0
O2	●	Johns Hopkins	40	7
O9	●	Swarthmore	44	0
O16	●	Chicago	27	0
O23	●	Williams	36	0
O30		at Illinois	0	3
N6	●	Penn State	3	0
N13	●	Columbia	3	0
N25	=	Cornell	10	10

1927			6-4-0	
S24	●	Franklin & Marshall	8	0
O1	●	Swarthmore	33	0
O8	●	Brown	14	6
O15		Penn State	0	20
O22		Chicago	7	13
O29		Navy	6	12
N5	●	Harvard	24	0
N12	●	Columbia	27	0
N24	●	Cornell	35	0
D31		at California	13	27

1928		8-1-0	
S29	•	Ursinus	34 0
O6	•	Franklin & Marshall	46 0
O13	•	Swarthmore	67 0
O20	•	Penn State	14 0
O27	•	Navy	0 6
N3	•	at Chicago	20 13
N10	•	at Harvard	7 0
N17	•	Columbia	34 7
N29	•	Cornell	49 0

1929		7-2-0	
S28	•	Franklin & Marshall	14 7
O5	•	Swarthmore	20 6
O12	•	Virginia Tech	14 8
O19	•	California	7 12
O26	•	Lehigh	10 7
N2	•	Navy	7 2
N9	•	Penn State	7 19
N16	•	at Columbia	20 0
N28	•	Cornell	17 7

LUDLOW WRAY
1930 (.556)   5-4

1930		5-4-0	
O4	•	Swarthmore	63 0
O11	•	Virginia	40 6
O18	•	at Wisconsin	0 27
O25	•	Lehigh	40 0
N1	•	Kansas	21 6
N8	•	Notre Dame	20 60
N15	•	Georgia Tech	34 7
N27	•	Cornell	7 13
D6	•	Navy	0 26

HARVEY HARMAN
1931-37 (.571)   31-23-2

1931		6-3-0	
O3	•	Swarthmore	32 7
O10	•	Franklin & Marshall	14 0
O17	•	Lehigh	32 0
O24	•	Wisconsin	27 13
O31	•	Lafayette	3 0
N7	•	at Notre Dame	0 49
N14	•	Georgia Tech	13 12
N26	•	Cornell	0 7
D5	•	Navy	0 6

1932		6-2-0	
O1	•	Franklin & Marshall	38 0
O8	•	Swarthmore	54 0
O15	•	Dartmouth	14 7
O22	•	Lehigh	33 6
O29	•	Navy	14 0
N5	•	Pittsburgh	12 19
N12	•	at Ohio State	0 19
N24	•	Cornell	13 7

1933		2-4-1	
O14	•	Franklin & Marshall	9 0
O21	•	Dartmouth	7 14
O28	•	Navy	0 13
N4	•	Lafayette	16 7
N11	•	Ohio State	7 20
N18	=	Penn State	6 6
N30	•	Cornell	12 20

1934		4-4-0	
O6	•	Ursinus	6 7
O13	•	at Yale	6 14
O20	•	Rutgers	27 19
O27	•	Navy	0 17
N3	•	Lafayette	41 0
N10	•	Penn State	3 0
N17	•	Columbia	12 13
N29	•	Cornell	23 13

1935		4-4-0	
O5	•	at Princeton	6 7
O12	•	Yale	20 31
O19	•	Columbia	34 0
O26	•	Lafayette	67 0
N2	•	at Michigan	6 16
N9	•	Navy	0 13
N16	•	Penn State	33 6
N28	•	Cornell	33 7

1936		7-1-0	
O3	•	Lafayette	35 0
O10	•	at Yale	0 7
O17	•	Princeton	7 0
O24	•	Brown	48 6
O31	•	Navy	16 6
N7	•	Michigan	27 7
N14	•	Penn State	19 12
N26	•	Cornell	14 6

1937		2-5-1	
O2	•	Maryland	28 21
O9	•	at Yale	7 27
O16	•	at Columbia	6 26
O23	=	Georgetown	0 0
O30	•	Navy	14 7
N6	•	Penn State	0 7
N13	•	Michigan	0 7
N25	•	Cornell	20 34

GEORGE MUNGER
1938-53 (.649)   82-42-10

1938		3-2-3	
O1	•	Lafayette	34 6
O8	•	Yale	21 0
O15	•	at Princeton	0 13
O22	•	Columbia	14 13
O29	=	Navy	0 0
N5	•	at Michigan	13 19
N12	•	Penn State	7 7
N24	•	Cornell	0 0

1939		4-4-0	
O7	•	Lafayette	6 0
O14	•	at Yale	6 0
O21	•	at Harvard	22 7
O28	•	North Carolina	6 30
N4	•	Navy	13 6
N11	•	Penn State	0 10
N18	•	Michigan	17 19
N25	•	Cornell	0 26

1940		6-1-1	
O5	•	Maryland	51 0
O12	•	Yale	50 7
O19	•	Princeton	46 28
O26	•	at Michigan	0 14
N2	•	Navy	20 0
N9	=	Harvard	10 10
N16	•	Army	48 0
N23	•	Cornell	22 20

1941		7-1-0	
O4	•	Harvard	19 0
O11	•	at Yale	28 13
O18	•	at Princeton	23 0
O25	•	Maryland	55 6 *
N1	•	Navy	6 13
N8	•	Columbia	19 16
N15	•	Army	14 7
N22	•	Cornell	16 0

1942		5-3-1	
S26	•	Georgia Pre-Flight	6 14
O3	•	at Harvard	19 7
O10	•	at Yale	35 6
O17	•	Princeton	6 6
O24	•	Columbia	42 12
O31	•	Army	19 0
N7	•	Navy	0 7
N14	•	Penn State	7 13
N21	•	Cornell	34 7

1943		6-2-1	
S25	•	Princeton	47 9
O2	•	Yale	41 7
O9	•	Dartmouth	7 6
O16	•	Lakehurst NAS	74 6
O23	•	at Columbia	33 0
O30	=	Army	13 13
N6	•	Navy	7 24
N13	•	North Carolina	6 9
N20	•	Cornell	20 14

1944		5-3-0	
S30	•	Duke	18 7
O7	•	Dartmouth	20 6
O14	•	William & Mary	46 0
O28	•	Navy	0 26
N4	•	Michigan	19 41
N11	•	Columbia	35 7
N18	•	Army	7 62
N25	•	Cornell	20 0

1945		6-2-0	
S29	•	Brown	50 0
O6	•	Dartmouth	12 0
O13	•	North Carolina	49 0
O27	•	Navy	7 14
N3	•	Princeton	28 0
N10	•	Columbia	32 7
N17	•	Army	0 61
N24	•	Cornell	59 6

1946		6-2-0	
O5	•	Lafayette	66 0
O12	•	Dartmouth	39 6
O19	•	Virginia	40 0
O26	•	Navy	32 19
N2	•	Princeton	14 17
N9	•	at Columbia	41 6
N16	•	Army	7 34
N30	•	Cornell	26 20

1947		7-0-1	
O4	•	Lafayette	59 0
O11	•	at Dartmouth	32 0
O18	•	Columbia	34 14
O25	•	Navy	21 0
N1	•	at Princeton	26 7
N8	•	Virginia	19 7
N15	=	Army	7 7
N29	•	Cornell	21 0

1948		5-3-0	
O2	•	Dartmouth	26 13
O9	•	Princeton	29 7
O16	•	at Columbia	20 14
O23	•	Navy	20 14
O30	•	Wash. & Lee	40 7
N6	•	Penn State	0 13
N13	•	Army	20 26
N27	•	Cornell	14 23

1949		4-4-0	
O1	•	Dartmouth	21 0
O8	•	at Princeton	14 13
O15	•	Columbia	27 7
O22	•	Navy	28 7
O29	•	Pittsburgh	21 22
N5	•	Virginia	14 26
N12	•	Army	13 14
N26	•	Cornell	21 29

1950		6-3-0	
S30	•	Virginia	21 7
O7	•	at California	7 14
O14	•	Dartmouth	42 26
O21	•	at Columbia	34 0
O28	•	Navy	30 7
N4	•	Army	13 28
N11	•	Brown	50 0
N18	•	Wisconsin	20 0
N25	•	Cornell	6 13

1951		5-4-0	
S29		California	0 35
O6	•	Dartmouth	39 14
O13		Princeton	7 13
O20		Columbia	28 13
O27	•	Navy	14 0
N3		William & Mary	12 20
N10		at Wisconsin	7 16
N17		Army	7 6
N24	•	Cornell	7 0

1952		4-3-2	
S27	=	Notre Dame	7 7
O4	•	Dartmouth	7 0
O11	•	at Princeton	13 7
O18	•	at Columbia	27 17
O25	•	Navy	7 7
N1	•	Penn State	7 14
N8	•	Georgia	27 34
N15	•	Army	13 14
N27	•	Cornell	14 7

1953		3-5-1	
S26	•	Vanderbilt	13 7
O3	•	Penn State	13 7
O10	•	California	0 40
O17	•	Ohio State	6 12
O24	•	Navy	9 6
O31	•	at Michigan	14 24
N7	•	Notre Dame	20 28
N14	•	Army	14 21
N26	=	Cornell	7 7

STEVE SEBO
1954-59 (.343)   18-35-1

1954		0-9-0	
S25		Duke	0 52
O2		William & Mary	7 27
O9		at Princeton	7 13
O16		George Washington	27 32
O23		Navy	6 52
O30		Penn State	13 35
N6		Notre Dame	7 42
N13		Army	0 35
N25		Cornell	6 20

1955		0-9-0	
S24		Virginia Tech	0 33
O1		at California	7 27
O8		Princeton	0 7
O15		George Washington	6 25
O22		Navy	0 33
O29		Penn State	0 20
N5		Notre Dame	14 46
N12		Army	0 40
N24		Cornell	7 39

1956-PRESENT
IVY LEAGUE

1956		4-5-0 (4-3-0)	
S29	•	Penn State	0 34
O6	|	Dartmouth	14 7
O13	•	Princeton	0 34
O20	•	Brown	14 7
O27	•	Navy	6 54
N3	•	at Harvard	28 14
N10	•	at Yale	7 40
N17	|	Columbia	20 6
N22	|	Cornell	7 20

1957		3-6-0 (3-4-0)	
S28	•	Penn State	14 19
O5	|	Dartmouth	3 6
O12	|	at Princeton	9 13
O19	•	at Brown	7 20
O26	•	Navy	7 35
N2	|	Harvard	6 13
N9	|	Yale	33 20
N16	•	at Columbia	28 6
N28	•	Cornell	14 6

1958		4-5-0 (4-3-0)	
S27	•	Penn State	0 43
O4	|	at Dartmouth	12 13
O11	|	Princeton	14 20
O18	|	Brown	21 20
O25	•	Navy	8 50
N1	|	at Harvard	19 6
N8	|	at Yale	30 6
N15	|	Columbia	42 0
N27	|	Cornell	7 19

1959		7-1-1 (6-1-0)	
S26	•	Lafayette	26 0
O3	|	Dartmouth	13 0
O10	|	at Princeton	18 0
O17	|	Brown	36 9
O24	=	Navy	22 22
O31	|	Harvard	0 12
N7	|	Yale	28 12
N14	|	at Columbia	24 6
N26	|	Cornell	28 13

JOHN STIEGMAN
1960-64 (.267)   12-33

1960		3-6-0 (2-5-0)	
S24	•	Lafayette	35 14
O1	|	at Dartmouth	0 15
O8	|	Princeton	0 21
O15	|	Brown	36 7
O22	•	Navy	0 27
O29	|	at Harvard	0 8
N5	|	at Yale	9 34
N12	|	Columbia	6 16
N24	•	Cornell	18 7

1961		2-7-0 (1-6-0)	
S30	•	Lafayette	14 7
O7	|	Dartmouth	0 30
O14	|	at Princeton	3 9
O21	|	Brown	7 0
O28	|	Rutgers	6 20
N4	|	Harvard	6 37
N11	|	Yale	0 23
N18	|	at Columbia	6 37
N25	|	Cornell	0 31

1962		3-6-0 (2-5-0)	
S29	•	Lafayette	13 11
O6	|	at Dartmouth	0 17
O13	|	Princeton	8 21
O20	|	Brown	18 15
O27	|	Rutgers	7 12
N3	|	at Harvard	0 36
N10	|	at Yale	15 12
N17	|	Columbia	7 21
N24	|	Cornell	22 29

THE SCHOOLS

1963 3-6-0 (1-6-0)

S28	●	Lafayette	47	0
O5		Dartmouth	0	28
O12		at Princeton	0	34
O19		at Brown	13	41
O26	●	Rutgers	7	6
N2	●	Harvard	7	2
N9		Yale	7	28
N16		at Columbia	8	33
N28		Cornell	8	17

1964 1-8-0 (0-7-0)

S26	●	Lehigh	13	6
O3		at Brown	0	3
O10		at Cornell	0	33
O17		Rutgers	7	10
O24		Princeton	0	55
O31		at Harvard	0	34
N7		Yale	9	21
N14		at Columbia	12	33
N21		Dartmouth	7	27

BOB ODELL 1965-70 (.454) 24-29-1

1965 4-4-1 (2-4-1)

S25	●	Lehigh	20	14
O2	●	Brown	7	0
O9		at Dartmouth	19	24
O16	●	Bucknell	16	13
O23		at Princeton	0	51
O30	=	Harvard	10	10
N6		at Yale	19	21
N13	●	Columbia	31	21
N25		Cornell	14	38

1966 2-7-0 (1-6-0)

S24	●	Lehigh	38	28
O1	●	at Brown	20	0
O8		at Cornell	28	45
O15		Bucknell	21	28
O22		Princeton	13	30
O29		at Harvard	7	27
N5		Yale	14	17
N12	●	at Columbia	14	22
N19		Dartmouth	21	40

1967 3-6-0 (2-5-0)

S30	●	Lehigh	35	23
O7	●	Brown	28	7
O14		at Dartmouth	0	23
O21	●	Bucknell	27	28
O28		at Princeton	14	28
N4		Harvard	7	45
N11		at Yale	22	44
N18	●	Columbia	26	6
N25		Cornell	14	33

1968 7-2-0 (5-2-0)

S28	●	Bucknell	27	10
O5	●	at Brown	17	13
O12	●	at Cornell	10	8
O19	●	Lehigh	34	0
O26	●	Princeton	19	14
N2		at Harvard	6	28
N9		Yale	13	30
N16	●	Columbia	13	7
N23	●	Dartmouth	26	21

1969 4-5-0 (2-5-0)

S27	●	Bucknell	28	17
O4	●	Brown	23	2
O11		at Dartmouth	0	41
O18	●	Lehigh	13	7
O25		at Princeton	0	42
N1		Harvard	6	20
N8		at Yale	3	21
N15	●	at Columbia	17	7
N22		Cornell	14	28

1970 4-5-0 (2-5-0)

S26	●	Lehigh	24	0
O3	●	at Brown	17	9
O10		at Cornell	31	32
O17	●	Lafayette	31	20
O24		Princeton	16	22
O31		at Harvard	23	38
N7		Yale	22	32
N14	●	Columbia	21	14
N21		Dartmouth	0	28

HARRY GAMBLE 1971-80 (.385) 34-55-2

1971 2-7-0 (1-6-0)

S25	●	Lehigh	28	14
O2	●	Brown	17	16
O9		at Dartmouth	3	19
O16		Lafayette	15	17
O23		at Princeton	0	31
O30		Harvard	27	28
N6		at Yale	14	24
N13		at Columbia	3	17
N20		Cornell	13	41

1972 6-3-0 (4-3-0)

S29	●	Lafayette	55	12
O7		at Brown	20	28
O14		at Cornell	20	24
O21	●	at Lehigh	30	27
O28	●	Princeton	15	10
N4	●	at Harvard	38	27
N11	●	Yale	48	30
N18	●	Columbia	20	14
N25		Dartmouth	17	31

1973 6-3-0 (5-2-0)

S29		at Lafayette	14	16
O6	●	Brown	28	20
O13	●	at Dartmouth	22	16
O20	●	Lehigh	27	20
O27	●	at Princeton	24	0
N3		Harvard	30	34
N10	●	at Yale	21	24
N17	●	at Columbia	42	8
N24	●	Cornell	31	22

1974 6-2-1 (4-2-1)

S27	●	Lehigh	28	18
O5	●	at Brown	14	9
O12	=	at Cornell	28	28
O19	●	at Lafayette	37	7
O26	●	Princeton	20	18
N2		at Harvard	0	39
N9		Yale	12	37
N16	●	Columbia	21	3
N23		Dartmouth	27	20

1975 3-6-0 (2-5-0)

S27		at Lehigh	23	34
O4		Brown	8	17
O11		at Dartmouth	14	19
O18	●	Lafayette	13	0
O25	●	at Princeton	24	20
N1		Harvard	3	21
N8		at Yale	14	24
N15	●	at Columbia	25	28
N22	●	Cornell	27	21

1976 3-6-0 (2-5-0)

S18		at Dartmouth	0	20
S24		Lehigh	20	24
O2		Columbia	10	14
O9	●	at Brown	7	6
O16	●	at Lafayette	15	14
O23		Yale	7	21
O30	●	at Princeton	10	9
N6		Harvard	8	20
N13		at Cornell	13	31

1977 5-4-0 (4-3-0)

S17	●	Cornell	17	7
S24	●	at Lehigh	7	19
O1		at Columbia	18	30
O8	●	Brown	14	7
O15	●	Lafayette	42	7
O22		at Yale	21	27
O29	●	Princeton	21	10
N5	●	at Harvard	15	34
N12		Dartmouth	7	3

1978 2-6-1 (1-5-1)

S23		at Dartmouth	21	31
S29	●	Lehigh	21	13
O7	●	Columbia	31	19
O14		at Brown	0	14
O21		at Lafayette	19	20
O28	=	Yale	17	17
N4		at Princeton	0	21
N11		Harvard	13	17
N18		at Cornell	17	35

1979 0-9-0 (0-7-0)

S22		Cornell	13	52
S29		at Lehigh	7	31
O6		at Columbia	7	12
O13		Brown	18	24
O19		Lafayette	7	9
O27		at Yale	6	24
N3		Princeton	10	38
N10		at Harvard	26	41
N17		Dartmouth	6	20

1980 1-9-0 (1-6-0)

S20		at Dartmouth	7	40
S26		Lehigh	6	35
O4	●	Columbia	24	13
O11		at Brown	22	42
O18		at Lafayette	0	3
O25		Yale	0	8
N1		at Princeton	21	28
N8		Villanova	3	34
N15		Harvard	17	28
N22		at Cornell	9	31

JERRY BERNDT 1981-85 (.612) 29-18-2

1981 1-9-0 (1-6-0)

S19	●	Cornell	29	22
S26		at Lehigh	0	58
O3		at Columbia	9	20
O10		Brown	24	26
O24		at Yale	3	24
O31		Princeton	30	38
N7		Delaware	6	40
N14		at Harvard	7	45
N21		Dartmouth	13	33
N26		at Richmond	12	18

1982 7-3-0 (5-2-0)

S18	●	at Dartmouth	21	0
S25	●	Lehigh	20	17
O2	●	Columbia	51	31
O9	●	at Brown	24	21
O16		at Lafayette	20	35
O23	●	Yale	27	14
O30		at Princeton	14	17
N6	●	Colgate	21	13
N13	●	Harvard	23	21
N20		at Cornell	0	23

1983 6-3-1 (5-1-1)

S17	●	Cornell	28	7
S24		at Delaware	7	40
S30	●	Columbia	35	10
O8	=	Brown	24	24
O15	●	Lafayette	28	20
O22	●	at Yale	17	0
O29	●	Princeton	28	27
N5		Colgate	20	34
N12	●	at Harvard	0	28
N19	●	Dartmouth	38	14

1984 8-1-0 (7-0-0)

S22	●	at Dartmouth	55	24
S29	●	Davidson	19	14
O6		Columbia	35	7
O13	●	at Brown	41	14
O20	●	at Army	13	48
O27	●	Yale	34	21
N3	●	at Princeton	27	17
N10	●	Harvard	38	7
N17	●	at Cornell	24	0

1985 7-2-1 (6-1-0)

S21	●	at Cornell	10	6
S28		Army	3	41
O5	●	at Columbia	46	14
O12	●	Brown	17	14
O19	●	at Davidson	15	0
O26	●	Yale	23	7
N2	●	Princeton	31	21
N9	=	at Colgate	27	27
N16		at Harvard	6	17
N23	●	Dartmouth	19	14

ED ZUBROW 1986-88 (.767) 23-7

1986 10-0-0 (7-0-0)

S20		at Dartmouth	21	7
S27	●	Bucknell	10	7
O4	●	Columbia	42	7
O11	●	at Brown	34	0
O18	●	at Navy	30	26
O25	●	Yale	24	6
N1	●	at Princeton	23	10
N8	●	Lafayette	42	14
N15	●	Harvard	17	10
N22	●	at Cornell	31	21

1987 4-6-0 (3-4-0)

S19		Cornell	13	17
S26		at Bucknell	24	32
O3	●	at Columbia	23	0
O10	●	Brown	38	17
O17		Navy	28	38
O24		at Yale	22	28
O31		Princeton	7	17
N7	●	at Lafayette	23	14
N14		at Harvard	14	31
N21	●	Dartmouth	49	17

1988 9-1-0 (6-1-0)

S17	●	at Dartmouth	33	27
S24	●	Bucknell	38	35
O1	●	Columbia	24	10
O8	●	at Brown	10	0
O15	●	Colgate	33	22
O22	●	Yale	10	3
O29	●	at Princeton	31	23
N5	●	at Lafayette	31	17
N12	●	at Harvard	52	13
N19		Dartmouth	6	19

GARY STEELE 1989-91 (.300) 9-21

1989 4-6-0 (2-5-0)

S16		at Colgate	14	21
S23		Lafayette	25	12
O7		at Columbia	24	21
O14	●	Brown	32	30
O21	●	Bucknell	25	24
O28		at Yale	22	23
N4		Princeton	8	30
N11		at Harvard	15	24
N18		Dartmouth	0	24
N23		Cornell	6	20

1990 3-7-0 (3-4-0)

S15	●	at Dartmouth	16	6
S22		Holy Cross	3	17
S29		at Lafayette	13	20
O6		Lehigh	16	22
O13	●	Columbia	21	6
O20		at Brown	17	24
O27		Yale	10	27
N3		at Princeton	20	34
N10		Harvard	24	20
N17		at Cornell	15	21

1991 2-8-0 (2-5-0)

S21		Dartmouth	15	21
S28		at Holy Cross	0	45
O5		Lafayette	12	20
O12		at Columbia	14	20
O19		at Lehigh	17	28
O26	●	Brown	28	19
N2		at Yale	12	31
N9		Princeton	12	17
N16		at Harvard	18	22
N23	●	Cornell	14	13

AL BAGNOLI 1992-Present (.773) 99-29

1992 7-3-0 (5-2-0)

S19		at Dartmouth	17	36
S26	●	Colgate	24	0
O3	●	at Fordham	13	10
O10		William & Mary	19	21
O17	●	Columbia	34	21
O24	●	at Brown	38	0
O31	●	Yale	13	10
N7		at Princeton	14	20
N14	●	Harvard	21	19
N21	●	at Cornell	14	7

1993 10-0-0 (7-0-0)

S18	●	Dartmouth	10	6
S25	●	at Bucknell	42	19
O2	●	Fordham	34	30
O9	●	at Colgate	30	12
O16	●	at Columbia	36	7
O23	●	Brown	34	9
O30	●	at Yale	48	7
N6	●	Princeton	30	14
N13	●	at Harvard	27	20
N20	●	Cornell	17	14

1994 9-0-0 (7-0-0)

S17	●	Lafayette	27	7
S24	●	at Dartmouth	13	11
O8	●	Holy Cross	59	8
O15	●	Columbia	12	3
O22	●	at Brown	24	0
O29	●	Yale	14	6
N5	●	at Princeton	33	19
N12	●	Harvard	33	0
N19		at Cornell	18	14

1995 — 7-3-0 (5-2-0)

Date		Opponent		
S16	●	Dartmouth	20	12
S23	●	at Lafayette	28	8
S30	●	Bucknell	20	19
O7		at Columbia	14	24
O14		at William & Mary	34	48
O21	●	Brown	58	21
O28	●	at Yale	16	6
N4		Princeton	9	22
N11	●	at Harvard	38	21
N18	●	Cornell	37	18

1996 — 5-5 (3-4)

Date		Opponent		
S21		at Dartmouth	22	24
S28	●	Colgate	38	7
O5	●	at Bucknell	30	21
O12		Columbia	19	20
O19		Lehigh	24	28
O26		at Brown	21	27
N2	●	Yale	20	3
N9		at Princeton	10	6
N16	●	Harvard	17	12
N23		at Cornell	21	24

1997 — 6-4 (5-2)

Date		Opponent		
S20		Dartmouth	15	23
S27		at Bucknell	16	20
O4	●	Towson	26	14
O11		at Lehigh	7	24
O18	●	at Columbia	24	7 †
O25	●	Brown	31	10 †
N1	●	at Yale	26	7 †
N8	●	Princeton	20	17 †
N15		at Harvard	0	33
N22	●	Cornell	33	20 †

1998 — 8-2 (6-1)

Date		Opponent		
S19	●	at Dartmouth	17	14
S26		Richmond	18	34
O3	●	Bucknell	20	10
O10	●	at Fordham	34	31
O17	●	Columbia	20	0
O24		at Brown	51	58
O31	●	Yale	34	21
N7	●	at Princeton	27	14
N14	●	Harvard	41	10
N21	●	at Cornell	35	21

1999 — 5-5 (4-3)

Date		Opponent		
S18	●	Dartmouth	17	6
S25		Villanova	6	34
O2		Bucknell	16	23
O9	●	Fordham	35	18
O16	●	at Columbia	41	17
O23		Brown	37	44
O30		at Yale	19	23
N6	●	Princeton	41	13
N13	●	at Harvard	21	17
N20		Cornell	12	20

2000 — 7-3 (6-1)

Date		Opponent		
S16		at Lehigh	10	17
S23	●	Lafayette	45	28
S30	●	Dartmouth	48	14
O7		at Holy Cross	17	34
O14	●	Columbia	43	25
O21		at Yale	24	27
O28	●	Brown	41	38
N4	●	at Princeton	40	24
N11	●	Harvard	36	35
N18	●	at Cornell	45	15

2001 — 8-1 (6-1)

Date		Opponent		
S22	●	at Lafayette	37	0
S29	●	at Dartmouth	21	20
O6	●	Holy Cross	43	7
O13	●	at Columbia	35	7
O20	●	Yale	21	3
O27	●	at Brown	27	14
N3	●	Princeton	21	10
N10	●	at Harvard	21	28
N17	●	Cornell	38	14

2002 — 9-1 7-0

Date		Opponent		
S21	●	at Lafayette	52	21
S28	●	Lehigh	24	21
O5	●	Dartmouth	49	14
O10		at Villanova	3	17
O19	●	Columbia	44	10
O26	●	at Yale	41	20
N2	●	Brown	31	7
N9	●	at Princeton	44	13
N16	●	Harvard	44	9
N23	●	at Cornell	31	0

2003 — 10-0 (7-0)

Date		Opponent		
S20	●	Duquesne	51	10
S27	●	at Lehigh	31	24
O4	●	at Dartmouth	33	20
O11	●	Bucknell	14	13
O18	●	at Columbia	31	7
O25	●	Yale	34	31
N1	●	at Brown	24	21
N8	●	Princeton	37	7
N15	●	at Harvard	32	24
N22	●	Cornell	59	7

2004 — 8-2 (6-1)

Date		Opponent		
S18	●	at San Diego	61	18
S25	●	Villanova	13	16
O2	●	Dartmouth	35	0
O9	●	at Bucknell	32	25
O16		Columbia	14	3
O23	●	at Yale	17	7
O30	●	Brown	20	16
N6	●	at Princeton	16	15
N13		Harvard	10	31
N20	●	at Cornell	20	14

Neutral Site key: U Unknown, Unknown / DC Washington, DC / Hob Hoboken, NJ / NYC New York, NY / Bkln Brooklyn, NY / Man Manheim, PA / Tre Trenton, NJ / Bos Boston, MA
ƒ Forfeit † Game Later Forfieted # Disputed Victor * Disputed Score || Designated Conference Game 2 Counted Twice in Conference Standings

PENNSYLVANIA ANNUAL STATISTICAL LEADERS

YR	RUSHING	YDS	ATT	AVG	PASSING	ATT	CMP	PCT	YDS	RECEIVING	REC	YDS	AVG
1961	John Owens	294	96	3.1	Luther Gray	46	16	.35	150	Ron Allshouse	12	125	10.4
1962	John Owens	407	114	3.6	John Owens	50	22	.44	265	Ron Allshouse	18	318	17.7
1963	Bruce Molloy	455	144	3.2	Donald Challis	64	28	.44	318	Ed Miller	11	131	11.9
1964	Bruce Molloy	407	147	2.8	Tom Kennedy	71	26	.37	283	Harrison Clement	14	161	11.5
1965	Bruce Molloy	393	85	4.6	Bill Creeden	95	45	.47	501	Rick Owens	43	451	10.5
1966	Cabot Knowlton	531	109	4.9	Bill Creeden	265	121	.46	1,842	Rick Owens	28	439	15.7
1967	Cabot Knowlton	830	186	4.5	Bill Creeden	164	70	.43	870	Rick Owens	24	266	11.1
1968	Gerry Santini	880	241	3.7	Bernie Zbrzeznj	188	101	.54	1,278	Pete Blumenthal	39	506	13.0
1969	Bob Sudhaus	394	118	3.3	John Brown	91	44	.48	493	Pete Blumenthal	25	277	11.1
1970	Bob Hoffman	428	103	4.2	Pancho Micir	214	104	.49	1,292	Bruce Batch	27	338	12.5
1971	Ron Dawson	432	115	3.8	Gary Shue	135	65	.48	1,016	Don Clune	40	891	22.3
1972	Adolph Bellizeare	849	168	5.1	Tom Pinto	74	34	.46	694	Don Clune	28	646	23.1
1973	Adolph Bellizeare	746	159	4.7	Marty Vaughn	206	114	.55	1,926	Don Clune	53	882	16.6
1974	Jack Wixted	790	141	5.6	Marty Vaughn	213	112	.53	1,503	Bob Bucola	39	593	15.2
1975	Jack Wixted	556	120	4.6	Bob Graustein	183	107	.58	1,197	Ron Kellogg	32	432	13.5
1976	Denis Grosvener	257	64	4.0	Bob Graustein	230	127	.55	1,429	Tim Kelly	22	344	15.6
1977	Denis Grosvener	743	185	4.0	Tom Roland	49	16	.33	189	Nelson Johnson	8	111	13.9
1978	Denis Grosvener	805	190	4.2	Tom Roland	47	22	.47	300	Steve Routh	10	171	17.1
1979	Rick Beauvis	352	76	4.6	Doug Marzonie	136	59	.43	944	Nelson Johnson	22	444	20.2
1980	Rick Beauvis	550	133	4.1	Gary Vura	63	22	.35	284	Jerry Smith	16	285	17.8
1981	Steve Rubin	271	81	3.3	Doug Marzonie	199	85	.43	893	Karl Hall	38	615	16.2
1982	Steve Flacco	466	82	5.7	Gary Vura	275	148	.54	1,771	Jeff Schulte	25	267	10.7
1983	Chuck Nolan	556	128	4.3	John McGeehan	169	79	.47	1,266	Rich Syrek	19	432	22.7
1984	Rich Comizio	596	112	5.3	John McGeehan	169	95	.56	1,493	Warren Buehler	23	509	22.1
1985	Rich Comizio	779	171	4.6	Jim Crocicchia	208	113	.54	1,250	Brian Moyer	27	335	12.4
1986	Rich Comizio	1,104	201	5.5	Jim Crocicchia	176	90	.51	1,200	Brent Novoselsky	18	337	18.7
1987	Chris Flynn	751	150	5.0	John Keller	81	51	.63	580	Brent Novoselsky	15	174	11.6
1988	Bryan Keys	1,165	248	4.7	Malcolm Glover	190	103	.54	1,498	Scott Sandler	33	534	16.2
1989	Bryan Keys	1,302	254	5.1	Malcolm Glover	273	147	.54	1,733	Dave Whaley	47	622	13.2
1990	Steve Hooper	607	114	5.3	Doug Hensch	197	91	.46	1,088	Mohamed Ali	21	378	18.0
1991	Sundiata Rush	787	188	4.2	Jimmy McGeehan	179	74	.41	848	Mike Baker	28	256	9.1
1992	Sundiata Rush	960	190	5.1	Jimmy McGeehan	160	86	.54	909	Cache Miller	36	375	10.4
1993	Terrance Stokes	1,211	256	4.7	Jimmy McGeehan	318	183	.58	2,197	Miles Macik	72	840	11.7
1994	Terrance Stokes	1,052	243	4.3	Mark DeRosa	244	152	.62	1,832	Miles Macik	60	708	11.8
1995	Aman Abye	695	145	4.8	Mark DeRosa	292	157	.54	2,053	Miles Macik	68	817	12.0
1996	Jasen Scott	1,193	290	4.1	Tom MacLeod	150	75	.50	720	Mark Fabish	29	302	10.4
1997	Jim Finn	801	155	5.2	Matt Rader	289	164	.57	1,832	Doug O'Neill	32	430	13.4
1998	Jim Finn	1,450	323	4.5	Matt Rader	279	172	.62	2,026	Doug O'Neill	42	506	12.0
1999	Kris Ryan	1,197	214	5.6	Gavin Hoffman	336	200	.60	2,328	Rob Milanese	41	702	17.1
2000	Kris Ryan	683	129	5.3	Gavin Hoffman	386	272	.70	3,214	Rob Milanese	76	936	13.1
2001	Kris Ryan	1,304	267	4.9	Gavin Hoffman	282	179	.63	2,000	Rob Milanese	57	659	11.6
2002	Stephen Faulk	467	128	3.6	Mike Mitchell	371	241	.65	2,803	Rob Milanese	85	1,112	13.1
2003	Sam Mathews	1,266	276	4.6	Mike Mitchell	319	200	.63	2,470	Dan Castles	71	1,067	15.0
2004	Sam Mathews	716	178	4.0	Patrick McDermott	295	159	.54	1,995	Dan Castles	70	966	13.8

Receiving leaders by receptions

PRINCETON

BY BRUCE WOOD

THE HISTORY OF COLLEGE FOOTBALL begins with a baseball game. On May 2, 1866, Princeton—then known as the College of New Jersey—humiliated nearby Rutgers on the diamond 40-2. Seeking payback, Rutgers student William Leggett sent a missive to Princeton, challenging the school to a three-match series in a whole new ball game. According to Leggett's rules, there would be 25 men to a side, a round ball and two goalposts set 100 yards apart. Players could kick or hit the ball, but no one would be allowed to pick it up and run with it, and certainly there would be no passing. The first team to score six goals would win.

Princeton accepted the challenge and Rutgers found its sweet revenge, winning the inaugural game of what would become collegiate football, 6 goals to 4, on Nov. 6, 1869.

TRADITION Long after other schools had abandoned it, Princeton continued to have success with its trademark single-wing offense. On Nov. 23, 1996, in a final salute to venerable Palmer Stadium, which was playing host to its last game before meeting with the wrecking ball, Tigers coach Steve Tosches dusted off the single wing. Before the surprised Dartmouth defense could catch on, Tosches switched back to his regular offense. Despite the emotional start, the Tigers dropped their Palmer finale, 24-0.

One of the oldest series in college football (beginning in 1897) has one of the newest traditions. In 2004, Princeton began playing Dartmouth for the "Sawhorse Dollar." The framed 1917 bill, one-third larger than today's currency and featuring a painting of the Pilgrims landing at Plymouth Rock next to George Washington's portrait, gets its name from the crisscrossing of the words "United States" and "of America" on the back.

BEST PLAYER Because he weighed just 155 pounds as a high school senior in Maumee, Ohio, there were concerns about how good a match Dick Kazmaier and football would be. There was no reason to worry. Even though most Division I schools had abandoned single-wing formations by the late 1940s, Princeton still used them exclusively, and they perfectly suited Kazmaier's blazing speed, quick moves and deadly arm. Kazmaier led Princeton to perfect seasons

PROFILE

Princeton University
Princeton, N.J.
Founded: 1746
Enrollment: 4,600
Colors: Orange and Black
Nickname: Tigers
Stadium: Princeton Stadium
　Opened in 1998
　Grass; 27,800 capacity
First football game: 1869
All-time record: 757–347–49 (.678)
Ivy League championships: 8 (3 outright)
Heisman Trophy: Dick Kazmaier, 1951
First-round NFL draftees: 1
Website: www.goprincetontigers.com

THE BEST OF TIMES

From 1933 to 1935, Princeton went 25–1 with two undefeated national championship teams.

THE WORST OF TIMES

Great seasons had bitter endings in 1951, when Dartmouth beat Princeton in a winner-take-all finale for the Ivy League title, and again in 1952, when the Big Green won a season-ending showdown to share the title with the Tigers.

CONFERENCE HISTORY

Princeton was an original member of the Ivy League when it began formal play in 1956.

DISTINGUISHED ALUMNI

Woodrow Wilson; Bill Bradley; Toni Morrison; Donald Rumsfeld; Ralph Nader; Brooke Shields; Steve Forbes, publisher; John Nash, Nobel Prize winner

FIGHT SONG

THE CANNON SONG
In Princeton town we've got a team
that knows the way to play.
With Princeton spirit back of them,
they're sure to win the day.
With cheers and song we'll rally 'round
the cannon as of yore,
And Nassau's walls will echo with
the Princeton Tiger's roar:
(And then we'll) crash through that line of
blue, and send the back on 'round the end!
Fight, fight for ev'ry yard,
Princeton's honor to defend.
Rah! Rah! Rah!
Rah! Tiger sis boom bah!
And locomotives by the score!
For we'll fight with a vim
that is dead sure to win,
for Old Nassau

All the Team of Destiny did in 1922 was win.

in 1950 and 1951, guiding his team to victory in his last 22 games. In what is still discussed as one of the greatest athletic displays in college football history, Kazmaier led Princeton to a crushing 53-15 win over 12th-ranked Cornell in his senior year, completing 15 of 17 passes for 236 yards and three touchdowns, rushing for 124 and two more touchdowns and scoring a safety on defense. Kazmaier finished his career with 35 TD passes, 20 rushing TDs and 4,354 all-purpose yards. He was awarded the Heisman Trophy in 1951 and, as a national sensation, even graced the cover of *Time* magazine.

BEST COACH Charlie Caldwell had a tough act to follow—his own. As a Princeton undergrad, he played wingback on the undefeated 1922 "Team of Destiny" that brought Princeton a national championship. He returned as head coach in 1945 and helped the Tigers win 24 consecutive games—and 33 of 34—from 1949 to 1952. Under his direction, Princeton won the Lambert Trophy as the best college football team in the East two years in a row. Caldwell's focus on success wasn't limited to athletics; he once said that "if a college coach doesn't understand how the curriculum operates, what

challenges his boys face in other phases of university life, he is in for trouble." Tragically, Caldwell was diagnosed with cancer early in the 1957 season and died within weeks at age 56.

BEST TEAM In terms of raw talent and offensive stats, the Tigers definitely had better squads than the one they fielded in 1922. But all the Team of Destiny did was win. With only three returning starters, Princeton used daring offensive plays and pure guts to keep other teams guessing; they finished their eight-game season without a loss. Although they would score only 127 points all year, they held their opponents to a mere 34, including five shutouts.

BIGGEST GAME The 1922 Tigers were picked to finish behind both Yale and Harvard, but with four wins in a row—all shutouts—Princeton was on a roll. One problem: it had to travel to the University of Chicago to play the toughest game on its schedule. The Tigers trailed Amos Alonzo Stagg's heavily favored Maroons 18-7 with less than six minutes to play, when Princeton's Howdy Gray recovered a fumble in

RECORDS

RUSHING YARDS
GAME
299 Keith Elias vs. Lafayette, Sept. 26, 1992 (25 att.)
SEASON
1,731 Keith Elias, 1993 (305 att.)
CAREER
4,208 Keith Elias, 1991-93 (736 att.)

PASSING YARDS
GAME
501 Bob Holly vs. Yale, Nov. 14, 1981 (36 of 55)
SEASON
3,175 Doug Butler, 1983 (224 of 398)
CAREER
7,291 Doug Butler, 1983-85 (542 of 988)

RECEIVING YARDS
GAME
370 Michael Lerch vs. Brown, Oct. 12, 1991 (9 rec.)
SEASON
1,321 Derek Graham, 1983 (84 rec.)
CAREER
2,798 Derek Graham, 1981, 1983-84 (172 rec.)

POINTS
GAME
30 Ellis Moore vs. Harvard, Nov. 11, 1967 (5 TDs)
SEASON
130 Keith Elias, 1993 (21 TDs, 2 two-pt. conv.)
CAREER
320 Keith Elias, 1991-93 (52 TDs, 6 two-pt. conv.)

CONSENSUS ALL-AMERICANS

1889	Hector Cowan, T
1889	William George, C
1889	Edgar Allan Poe, B
1889	Roscoe Channing, B
1889	Knowlton Ames, B
1890	Ralph Warren, E
1890-91	Sheppard Homans, B
1890-91	Jesse Riggs, G
1891-93	Philip King, B
1892-94	Arthur Wheeler, G
1893	Thomas Trenchard, E
1893	Franklin Morse, B
1893-95	Langdon Lea, G
1895	Dudley Riggs, G
1896	William Church, T
1896	Robert Gailey, C
1896	John Baird, B
1896-97	Addison Kelly, B
1897	Garrett Cochran, E
1898	Lew Palmer, E
1898-99	Arthur Hillebrand, T
1899	Arthur Poe, E
1899	Howard Reiter, B
1901	Ralph Davis, E

(Continued on next page)

midair and ran 40 yards for a touchdown, closing the gap to 18-14. On Princeton's next possession, Harry Crum squeaked in from one yard out on fourth down to give the Tigers a 21-18 lead. But there was enough time left on the clock, and Princeton could not stop Chicago as it drove down the field in the final minute. Only a spirited Princeton goal-line stand preserved the 21-18 win, the centerpiece of the Tigers' 8–0 national championship season.

BIGGEST UPSET Unbeaten Yale was 8–0 and looking for its 15th consecutive win over Princeton on Nov. 14, 1981. Trailing 21-0 in the second quarter, the Tigers looked even worse than their 3–4–1 record would indicate. But behind quarterback Bob Holly's three touchdown passes, they fought back to take a 22-21 lead. Yale answered by scoring 10 points, a challenge Princeton met with a lone field goal. Bulldogs 31, Tigers 25. With 1:39 left, Princeton took over on its own 24. Holly drove the Tigers to the Yale 20-yard line and, with time running out, desperately threw into the end zone. The Bulldogs, however, were called for pass interference, and on the next play Holly took the snap and scrambled into the end zone for a 35-31 Princeton victory. Holly's stats for the day: four touchdown passes and an Ivy-record 501 passing yards.

WILDEST FINISH In a 1974 home game against the Tigers' oldest rivals, Walt Snickenberger's one-yard run lifted Princeton into a 6-6 tie against Rutgers with 22 seconds left to play. All the Tigers had to do was kick the extra point for the victory. There was one problem, though: after the touchdown, fans had torn down the goalposts. Coach Bob Casciola asked for time to put up another set, but the referees ruled that it had been Princeton's responsibility to control the home crowd and denied his request. Forced to go for a two-point conversion, the Tigers' pass into the end zone sailed incomplete, sealing a bizarre tie.

STADIUM The challenge was daunting: to replace the crumbling Palmer Stadium while keeping alive the storied

CONSENSUS ALL-AMERICANS (CONT.)	
1902-03	John DeWitt, G
1903	Howard Henry, E
1903	J. Dana Kafer, B
1904, 1906	James Cooney, T
1905, 1907	James McCormick, B
1906	Edward Dillon, B
1906-07	L. Casper Wister, E
1907	Edwin Harlan, B
1908	Frederick Tibbott, B
1910	Talbot Pendleton, B
1911	Sanford White, E
1911	Edward Hart, T
1911	Joseph Duff, G
1912	John Logan, G
1913-14	Harold Ballin, T
1916	Frank Hogg, G
1918	Frank Murrey, B
1920	Donold Lourie, B
1920-21	Stan Keck, G
1922	C. Herbert Treat, T
1925	Ed McMillan, C
1935	John Weller, G
1951	Dick Kazmaier, TB
1952	Frank McPhee, E
1965	Stas Maliszewski, G
1987	Dean Cain, DB
1989	Judd Garrett, RB
1992-93	Keith Elias, TB
2001	Taylor Northrop, PK

legacy of one of the great structures in college football. Princeton's solution was novel. Opened in 1998, the school's two-tiered stadium is tucked into a horseshoe-shaped, walled building erected on the footprint of old Palmer Stadium, which served the school proudly for 83 years. Palmer was completed in 1914, in just over four months, at a cost of $300,000. Construction of Princeton Stadium, which required the Tigers to play the entire 1997 season on the road, took more than a year. Cost: $45 million.

RIVAL Geography may be destiny, and it certainly makes Penn a natural rival, but nothing gets Princeton pulses racing quite like the Yale game. The Tigers have played the Bulldogs more times than any other opponent; they have also lost more games to the Bulldogs than to any other team. The series, which began with a 3-0 Princeton win in 1873, is the second oldest in college football. (Much to the chagrin of the other five schools in the Ivy League conference, Princeton and Yale join Harvard in what the trio call HYP, or the Big Three.)

NICKNAME Woodrow Wilson's class gave Princeton a pair of lion sculptures to guard the main entrance to Nassau Hall in 1879, but for some reason the school settled on the name Tigers. It might have stemmed from the football team's orange-and-black-striped jerseys. Or it might have come from sportswriters, who compared the players to fighting cats. It might even date to the Civil War, when New York's Seventh Regiment passed through Princeton and answered the students' applause with a tiger roar. Whatever its origins, credit Princeton students with flexibility: in 1911, they replaced the lions with a pair of bronze tigers.

MASCOT Bulldogs are one thing; a live tiger is something else entirely. In 1923, the father of junior Albert Howard shipped a tiger he had captured in India to the campus. Princeton had its first mascot, but not for long; concerns about public safety quickly led the school to donate the wild cat to the zoo.

UNIFORMS The helmet design immortalized by the Michigan Wolverines actually got its start at Princeton. Coach Fritz Crisler created a design that (sort of) resembled a tiger with its ears pinned back in a series of orange stripes running from front to back. The pattern, Crisler reasoned, could even yield results on the field, as it might help quarterbacks spot their receivers more easily. Of course, when Michigan hired Crisler away, he took the distinctive pattern with him. Eventually, Princeton would abandon the Crisler helmet, but with the opening of the new Princeton Stadium in 1998, the Tigers returned to the gridiron wearing their throwback lids.

LORE The character Allenby in F. Scott Fitzgerald's novel *This Side of Paradise* was based on Hobey Baker, a Princeton football and ice hockey legend who was a senior at the school in 1914 when Fitzgerald was a freshman. Baker, whose 92 points in 1912 stood as a Princeton football record until 1974, is the only athlete enshrined in both the College Football Hall of Fame and the Hockey Hall of Fame. The dashing quarterback and dropkicker, who refused to cover his wavy blond hair with a helmet in either of his sports, twice made All-America in football and ice hockey. After graduation he took flying lessons and buzzed the 1916 Princeton-Yale football game. He went on to fly with Eddie Rickenbacker in World War I, shooting down three German planes in dogfights, only to die in a plane crash shortly after the armistice at age 26. The Hobey Baker Memorial Award, the Heisman Trophy of ice hockey, is awarded annually in his honor.

QUIRK On Nov. 23, 1935, Princeton faced Dartmouth in a battle of two unbeaten teams. A sellout crowd of 56,000 sat through a massive snowstorm to witness one of the strangest moments in Princeton football history. With the Tigers threatening on the Dartmouth 2-yard line, a lone figure jumped out of the stands and lined up with the Dartmouth defense. The mysterious 12th man lasted for just a play, but he made the most of it: the Big Green stuffed the Tigers short of the goal line. One play, however, did not make the game as Princeton won handily, 26-6.

QUOTE "I thought it was nice, and then I went back to class." —Dick Kazmaier, upon learning he had won the 1951 Heisman

ALL-CENTURY TEAM

A 10-person committee from the Princeton Football Association selected the squad in 1999.

1919-30	Bill Roper, coach

OFFENSE

1904-06	Jim Cooney, T
1912-14	Harold Ballin, T
1919-21	Stan Keck, G
1931-33	Charles Ceppi, OL
1933-35	John Weller, G
1950-52	Frank McPhee, E
1983-84	Derek Graham, WR
1983-85	Doug Butler, QB
1948-50	George Chandler, B
1962-64	Cosmo Iacavazzi, B
1949-51	Dick Kazmaier, TB
1991-93	Keith Elias, TB
1963-65	Charlie Gogolak, PK

DEFENSE

1905-07	Lou Wister, E
1901-03	John DeWitt, G
1909-11	Ed Hart, T
1948-50	Hollie Donan, DL
1904-07	James McCormick, B
1948-50	Reddy Finney, LB
1963-65	Stas Maliszewski, G
1918-20	Frank Murrey, B
1919-21	Donold Lourie, B
1939-41	Bob Peters, B
1947-49	George Sella, B
1995-98	Matt Evans, P
1911-13	Hobey Baker, KR

PRINCETON ALL-TIME SCORES

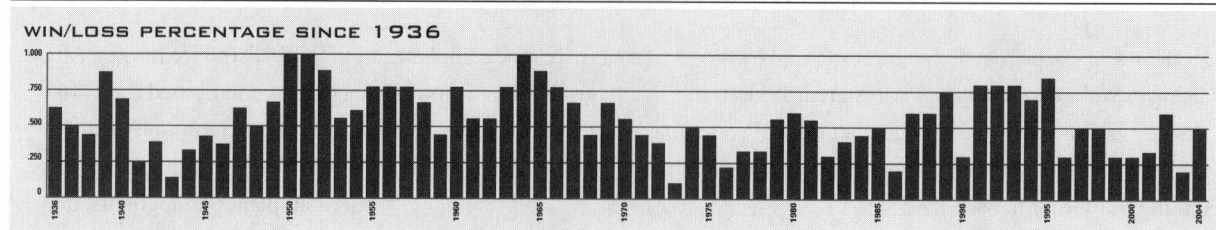

WIN/LOSS PERCENTAGE SINCE 1936

THE SCHOOLS

NO HEAD COACH

1869   1-1-0
N6	●	at Rutgers	4 6
N13	●	Rutgers	8 0

1870   1-0-0
N12	●	Rutgers	6 2

1872   1-0-0
N16	●	Rutgers	4 1

1873   1-0-0
N15	●	at Yale	3 0

1874   2-0-0
N7	●	Columbia	6 0
N18	●	Rutgers	6 0

1875   2-0-0
N13	|	Columbia	6 2
N20	●	Stevens	6 0

1876   3-2-0
N1	●	Pennsylvania	6 0
N11	●	Columbia	3 0
N25	●	Pennsylvania	6 0
N30	●	Yale *HOE*	0 2
P28	●	at Harvard	0 1

1877   2-0-1
N17	●	Harvard	1 0
N24	●	Columbia	4 0
D8	●	Yale *HOE*	0 0

1878   6-0-0
O19	●	Pennsylvania	2 0
O26	●	Stevens	4 0
N2	●	Rutgers	5 0
N9	●	at Pennsylvania	2 1
N16	●	Harvard *U*	1 0
N28	●	Yale *HOB*	1 0

1879   4-0-1
O18	●	Pennsylvania	6 0
N1	●	Columbia	2 0
N8	●	Stevens	7 0
N15	●	Harvard *U*	1 0
N27	=	Yale *HOB*	0 0

1880   4-0-1
O23	●	Stevens	6 0
O30	●	Pennsylvania	1 0
N2	●	Rutgers	8 0
N13	●	Harvard *U*	2 1
N25	=	Yale *NYC*	0 0

1881   7-0-2
O15	●	Rutgers	3 0
O22	●	Stevens	7 0
O29	●	at Pennsylvania	7 0
N4	●	Michigan	1 0
N5	●	Pennsylvania	4 0
N10	●	at Rutgers	1 0
N12	●	Columbia	1 0
N19	=	Harvard *U*	0 0
N24	=	Yale *NYC*	0 0

1882   7-2-0
O11	●	Graduates	5 0
O14	●	Rutgers	5 0
O28	●	Pennsylvania	8 0
N7	●	Columbia	8 0
N11	●	at Pennsylvania	10 0
N14	●	at Rutgers	3 0
N18	●	at Harvard	1 2
N25	●	Columbia	3 0
D1	●	Yale *NYC*	1 2

1883   7-1-0
O17	●	at Rutgers	20 0
O22	●	Lafayette	54 7
O24	●	at Stevens	15 5
O27	●	Rutgers	61 0
N3	●	Pennsylvania	39 6
N6	●	Wesleyan *NYC*	24 0
N17	●	Harvard	26 7
N24	●	Yale *NYC*	0 6

1884   9-0-1
O10	●	Rutgers	23 5
O13	●	at Stevens	4 0
O15	●	at Wesleyan	22 2
O18	●	Rutgers	35 0
O25	●	at Pennsylvania	31 0
O29	●	Lafayette	140 0
N1	●	Stevens	56 0
N8	●	Johns Hopkins	57 0
N19	●	at Harvard	36 6
N27	=	Yale *NYC*	0 0

1885   9-0-0
O3	●	at Stevens	94 0
O14	●	Stevens	76 0
O24	●	at Pennsylvania	57 0
O31	●	Pennsylvania	80 10
N7	●	at Columbia Law	64 0
N11	●	Johns Hopkins	10 0
N14	●	Wesleyan	76 0
N21	●	at Yale	6 5
N26	●	at Pennsylvania	76 10

1886   7-0-1
O9	●	Stevens	58 0
O13	●	at Stevens	61 6
O16	●	at Pennsylvania	30 0
O23	●	Pennsylvania	55 9
N6	●	at Pennsylvania	28 6
N13	●	Harvard	12 0
N20	●	at Wesleyan	76 6
N25	=	Yale	0 0

1887   7-2-0
O8	●	Lafayette	47 0
O12	●	at Rutgers	30 0
O15	●	Lehigh	80 0
O19	●	Pennsylvania	57 0
O22	●	at Pennsylvania	42 0
O29	●	Wesleyan	69 0
N5	●	at Pennsylvania	95 0
N12	●	at Harvard	0 12
N19	●	Yale *NYC*	0 12

1888   11-1-0
O3	●	Lehigh	65 0
O6	●	Crescent AC *NYC*	31 0
O10	●	Pennsylvania	63 0
O13	●	Stevens	80 0
O20	●	Pennsylvania	38 0
O24	●	at Rutgers	80 0
O27	●	Rutgers	82 0
O31	●	Johns Hopkins	104 0
N6	●	Wesleyan *NYC*	44 0
N10	●	at Pennsylvania	4 0
N17	●	Harvard	18 6
N24	●	Yale *NYC*	0 10

1889   10-0-0
O5	●	Lehigh	16 0
O12	●	at Lehigh	16 4
O19	●	Stevens	49 0
O26	●	at Pennsylvania	72 4
N2	●	at Wesleyan	98 0
N6	●	at Columbia	71 0
N16	●	at Harvard	41 15
N23	●	Orange AC	54 6
N28	●	Yale *NYC*	10 0
N30	●	at Washington AC	57 0

1890   11-1-1
O1	●	Franklin & Marshall	33 16
O8	●	Rutgers	27 0
O11	=	Orange AC	0 0
O15	●	Pennsylvania	18 0
O18	●	Crescent AC *BKLN*	12 0
O22	●	Lafayette	26 6
O25	●	Lehigh	50 0
O29	●	at Columbia AC	60 0
N1	●	Virginia *BALT*	115 0
N4	●	Columbia *NYC*	85 0
N8	●	Pennsylvania	6 0
N15	●	Wesleyan *BKLN*	46 4
N27	●	Yale *BKLN*	0 32

1891   12-1-0
O3	●	Rutgers	12 0
O7	●	at Lehigh	18 0
O10	●	Crescent AC *BKLN*	28 0
O14	●	Lehigh	30 0
O17	●	at Franklin & Marshall	44 0
O20	●	at Lafayette	24 0
O24	●	New York AC	28 0
O28	●	Manhattan AC	78 0
O31	●	Wesleyan	73 0
N4	●	at Orange AC	26 0
N7	●	Pennsylvania *MAN*	24 0
N14	●	Cornell	6 0
N26	●	Yale *NYC*	0 19

1892   13-2-0
O1	●	Rutgers	30 0
O5	●	at Lehigh	16 0
O8	●	Lafayette	40 0
O12	●	at Columbia AC	42 0
O15	●	at Navy	28 0
O19	●	Lehigh	50 0
O21	●	New York AC *NYC*	40 0
O22	●	Crescent AC *NYC*	42 0
O27	●	Manhattan AC	46 0
O29	●	Wesleyan *NYC*	60 0
N2	●	Chicago AC	12 0
N5	●	Pennsylvania *MAN*	4 6
N19	●	at Orange AC	23 0
N24	●	Yale *NYC*	0 12
N26	●	Manhattan AC *NYC*	40 0

1893   11-0-0
S30	●	Lafayette	20 0
O7	●	at Lehigh	12 0
O14	●	Crescent AC *BKLN*	26 0
O18	●	Lawrenceville	8 4
O21	●	Cornell *NYC*	46 0
O25	●	Lehigh	28 6
O28	●	Wesleyan *NYC*	76 0
N4	●	Pennsylvania *MAN*	4 0
N11	●	at Orange AC	8 0
N18	●	at Army	36 4
N30	●	Yale *NYC*	6 0

1894   8-2-0
S29	●	Lafayette	40 0
O3	●	at Lehigh	8 0
O10	●	Rutgers	48 0
O13	●	Virginia *BALT*	12 0
N20	●	Cornell *NYC*	12 4
O27	●	Lehigh	32 0
N3	●	Volunteers	40 0
N10	●	Pennsylvania	0 12
N17	●	at Orange AC	16 4
D1	●	Yale *NYC*	0 24

1895   10-1-1
O2	●	at Elizabeth AC	38 0
O5	●	Rutgers	22 0
O9	●	Virginia *BALT*	36 0
O12	●	Lafayette	14 0
O16	●	at Lawrenceville	38 0
O19	●	Seminary	10 4
O23	●	at Lehigh	16 0
O26	●	Union	22 0
O30	=	at Orange AC	0 0
N2	●	Harvard	12 4
N9	●	Cornell *NYC*	6 0
N23	●	Yale *NYC*	10 20

1896   10-0-1
O3	●	Rutgers	44 0
O7	=	at Lafayette	0 0
O10	●	Lehigh	16 0
O14	●	Carlisle	22 6
O17	●	at Army	11 0
O21	●	Virginia	48 0
O24	●	Penn State	39 0
O28	●	at Lawrenceville	46 0
O31	●	Cornell	37 0
N7	●	at Harvard	12 0
N21	●	Yale *NYC*	24 6

1897   10-1-0
O2	●	Lehigh	43 0
O6	●	Rutgers	53 0
O9	●	at Navy	28 0
O13	●	Penn State	34 0
O16	●	Carlisle	18 0
O20	●	Franklin & Marshall	54 0
O23	●	at Cornell	10 0
O27	●	Elizabeth AC	12 0
O30	●	Dartmouth	30 0
N6	●	Lafayette	57 0
N20	●	at Yale	0 6

1898   11-0-1
S24	●	Lehigh	21 0
O1	●	Stevens	42 0
O8	●	Franklin & Marshall	58 0
O12	●	Lafayette	34 0
O14	●	at Maryland AC	24 0
O15	●	at Navy	30 0
O22	●	Cornell	6 0
O26	●	Penn State	5 0
O29	●	Brown	23 0
N2	●	Virginia	12 0
N5	=	at Army	5 5
N12	●	Yale	6 0

1899   12-1-0
S30	●	at Maryland AC	28 0
O7	●	at Navy	5 0
O11	●	Lafayette	12 0
O14	●	at Columbia	11 0
O18	●	Penn State	12 0
O21	●	at Army	23 0
O28	●	Lehigh	17 0
N1	●	at Cornell	0 5
N4	●	Brown	18 6
N8	●	North Carolina	30 0
N11	●	at Carlisle	12 0
N18	●	Wash. & Jeff.	6 0
N25	●	at Yale	11 10

1900   8-3-0
S29	●	Stevens	40 0
O6	●	Lehigh	12 5
O10	●	Penn State	26 0
O12	●	at Johns Hopkins	11 0
O13	●	at Navy	5 0
O17	●	Syracuse	43 0
O20	●	at Lafayette	5 0
O27	●	at Brown	17 5
N3	●	Cornell	0 12
N6	●	at Columbia	5 6
N17	●	Yale	5 29

LANGDON LEA
1901 (.864) — 9-1-1

1901 — 9-1-1

S28	• Villanova	35	0
O2	• Haverford	47	0
O5	• NYU	23	0
O9	• Lehigh	35	0
O16	• Dickinson	23	0
O19	• Brown	35	0
O23	• Orange AC	29	0
O26	• Lafayette	6	0
N2	• at Cornell	8	6
N9	= at Army	6	6
N16	• at Yale	0	12

GARRETT COCHRAN
1902 (.889) — 8-1

1902 — 8-1-0

S27	• Swarthmore	18	0
O1	• Lehigh	23	0
O4	• at Navy	11	0
O11	• Haverford	30	0
O18	• Wash. & Jeff.	23	5
O22	• Dickinson	23	0
O25	• Columbia	21	0
N1	• Cornell	10	0
N15	• Yale	5	12

A.R.T. HILLENBRAND
1903-05 (.871) — 27-4

1903 — 11-0-0

S26	• Swarthmore	34	0
O3	• Georgetown	5	0
O7	• Gettysburg	68	0
O10	• at Brown	29	0
O14	• Lehigh	12	0
O17	• Carlisle	11	0
O21	• Bucknell	17	0
O24	• Dartmouth	17	0
O31	• Cornell	44	0
N7	• Lafayette	11	0
N14	• at Yale	11	6

1904 — 8-2-0

S28	• Dickinson	12	0
O1	• Georgetown	10	0
O5	• Wesleyan	39	0
O8	• Wash. & Jeff.	16	0
O12	• Lafayette	5	0
O15	• at Navy	9	10
O26	• Lehigh	60	0
O29	• at Cornell	18	6
N5	• at Army	12	6
N12	• Yale	0	12

1905 — 8-2-0

S23	• Villanova	41	0
S30	• Wash. & Jeff.	23	0
O7	• Georgetown	34	0
O11	• Lehigh	29	6
O14	• Bucknell	48	0
O21	• Lafayette	22	4
O28	• at Columbia	12	0
N4	• Dartmouth	0	6
N11	• Cornell	16	6
N18	• at Yale	4	23

BILL ROPER
1906-08, '10-11, '19-30 (.729) — 89-28-16

1906 — 9-0-1

S29	• Villanova	24	0
O3	• Stevens	22	0
O6	• Wash. & Jeff.	6	0
O10	• Lehigh	52	0
O13	• at Navy	5	0
O20	• Bucknell	32	4
O27	• Cornell NYC	14	5
N3	• Dartmouth	42	0
N10	• at Army	8	0
N17	= Yale	0	0

1907 — 7-2-0

S28	• Stevens	47	0
O5	• Wesleyan	53	0
O9	• Bucknell	52	0
O12	• Villanova	45	5
O19	• Wash. & Jeff.	40	0
O26	• at Cornell	5	6
N2	• Carlisle NYC	16	0
N9	• Amherst	14	0
N16	• at Yale	10	12

1908 — 5-2-3

S26	• Springfield	18	0
O3	• Stevens	21	0
O10	= Lafayette	0	0
O14	• Villanova	6	0
O17	• Virginia Tech	10	4
O21	• Fordham	17	0
O25	= Syracuse	0	0
O31	= at Army	0	0
N7	• Dartmouth U	6	10
N14	• Yale	6	11

JAMES McCORMICK
1909 (.722) — 6-2-1

1909 — 6-2-1

S29	• Stevens	47	12
O2	• Villanova	12	0
O9	• Fordham	3	0
O13	• Virginia Tech	8	6
O16	• Sewanee	20	0
O23	• Lafayette	0	6
O30	• at Navy	5	3
N6	• Dartmouth U	6	6
N13	• Yale	0	17

BILL ROPER

1910 — 7-1-0

S24	• Stevens	18	0
O1	• Villanova	36	0
O8	• NYU	12	0
O15	• at Lafayette	3	0
O22	• Carlisle	6	0
O29	• Dartmouth U	6	0
N5	• Holy Cross	17	0
N12	• Yale	3	5

1911 — 8-0-2

S30	• Stevens	37	0
O3	• Rutgers	37	0
O7	• Villanova	31	0
O11	= Lehigh	6	6
O14	• Colgate	31	0
O21	= at Navy	0	0
O28	• Holy Cross	20	0
N4	• Harvard	8	6
N11	• Dartmouth	3	0
N18	• at Yale	6	3

LOGAN CUNNINGHAM
1912 (.833) — 7-1-1

1912 — 7-1-1

S28	• Stevens	65	0
O2	• Rutgers	41	6
O5	• Lehigh	35	0
O12	• Virginia Tech	31	0
O19	• Syracuse	62	0
O26	• Dartmouth	22	7
N2	• at Harvard	6	16
N9	• NYU	54	0
N16	= Yale	6	6

W.G. ANDREWS
1913 (.688) — 5-2-1

1913 — 5-2-1

S27	• Rutgers	14	3
O4	• Fordham	69	0
O11	• Bucknell	28	6
O18	• Syracuse	13	0
O25	• Dartmouth	0	6
N1	• Holy Cross	54	0
N8	• Harvard	0	3
N15	= at Yale	3	3

WILDER PENFIELD
1914 (.688) — 5-2-1

1914 — 5-2-1

S26	• Rutgers	12	0
O3	• Bucknell	10	0
O10	• Syracuse	12	9 *
O17	• Lafayette	16	0
O24	• Dartmouth	16	12
O31	• Williams	7	7
N7	• at Harvard	0	20
N14	• Yale	14	19

JOHN RUSH
1915-16 (.750) — 12-4

1915 — 6-2-0

S25	• Georgetown	13	0
O2	• Rutgers	10	0
O9	• Syracuse	3	0
O16	• Lafayette	40	3
O23	• Dartmouth	30	7
O30	• Williams	27	0
N6	• Harvard	6	10
N13	• at Yale	7	13

1916 — 6-2-0

S30	• at Holy Cross	21	0
O7	• North Carolina	29	0
O14	• Tufts	3	0
O21	• Lafayette	33	0
O28	• Dartmouth	7	3
N4	• Bucknell	42	0
N11	• at Harvard	0	3
N18	• Yale	0	10

NO HEAD COACH

1917 — 2-0-0

U	• 37th Fort Dixon U	7	0
U	• Wissahickon Barracks U	43	0

1918 — 3-0-0

U	• Navy Pay Sch. U	26	0
U	• Gov. Areo U	7	0
U	• Camp Upton U	28	7

BILL ROPER

1919 — 4-2-1

O4	• Trinity	28	0
O11	• Lafayette	9	6
O18	• Rochester	34	0
O25	• Colgate	0	7
N1	• West Virginia	0	25
N8	= Harvard	10	10
N15	• at Yale	13	6

1920 — 6-0-1

O2	• Swarthmore	17	6
O9	• Maryland	35	0
O16	• Wash. & Lee	34	0
O23	• Navy	14	0
O30	• West Virginia	10	3
N6	= at Harvard	14	14
N13	• Yale	20	0

1921 — 4-3-0

O1	• Swarthmore	21	7
O8	• Colgate	19	0
O15	• at Navy	0	13
O22	• Chicago	0	9
O29	• Virginia	34	0
N5	• Harvard	10	3
N12	• at Yale	7	13

1922 — 8-0-0

S30	• Johns Hopkins	30	0
O7	• Virginia	5	0
O14	• Colgate	10	0
O21	• Maryland	26	0
O28	• at Chicago	21	18
N4	• Swarthmore	22	13
N11	• at Harvard	10	3
N18	• Yale	3	0

1923 — 3-3-1

O6	• Johns Hopkins	16	7
O13	• Georgetown	17	0
O20	• Notre Dame	2	25
O27	= Navy BALT	3	3
N3	• Swarthmore	35	6
N10	• Harvard	0	5
N17	• at Yale	0	27

1924 — 4-2-1

O4	• Amherst	40	6
O11	= Lehigh	0	0
O18	• Navy	17	14
O25	• Notre Dame	0	12
N1	• Swarthmore	21	6
N8	• at Harvard	34	0
N15	• Yale	0	10

1925 — 5-1-1

O3	• Amherst	20	0
O10	• Wash. & Lee	15	6
O17	= Navy BALT	10	10
O24	• Colgate	0	9
O31	• Swarthmore	19	7
N7	• Harvard	36	0
N14	• at Yale	25	12

1926 — 5-1-1

O2	• Amherst	14	7
O9	= Wash. & Lee	7	7
O16	• Navy	13	27
O23	• Lehigh	7	6
O30	• Swarthmore	27	0
N6	• at Harvard	12	0
N13	• Yale	10	7

1927 — 6-1-0

O1	• Amherst	14	0
O8	• Lehigh	42	0
O15	• Wash. & Lee	13	0
O22	• at Cornell	21	10
O29	• William & Mary	35	7
N5	• Ohio State	20	0
N12	• at Yale	6	14

1928 — 5-1-2

O6	• Vermont	50	0
O13	= Virginia	0	0
O20	• Lehigh	47	0
O27	• Cornell	3	0
N3	= at Ohio State	6	6
N10	• Wash. & Lee	25	12
N17	• Yale	12	2
N24	• Navy PHIL	0	9

1929 — 2-4-1

O5	• Amherst	7	0
O12	• Brown	12	13
O19	• at Cornell	7	13
O26	= Navy	13	13
N2	• Chicago	7	15
N9	• Lehigh	20	0
N16	• at Yale	0	13

1930 — 1-5-1

O4	• Amherst	23	0
O11	• Brown	0	7
O18	• Cornell	7	12
O25	• Navy	0	31
N1	= at Chicago	0	0
N8	• Lehigh	9	13
N15	• Yale	7	10

AL WITTMER
1931 (.125) — 1-7

1931 — 1-7-0

O3	• Amherst	27	0
O10	• Brown	7	19
O17	• at Cornell	0	33
O24	• Navy	0	15
O31	• Michigan	0	21
N7	• Lehigh	7	19
N14	• Wash. & Lee	0	6
N28	• at Yale	14	51

FRITZ CRISLER
1932-37 (.765) — 35-9-5

1932 — 2-2-3

O1	• Amherst	22	0
O8	• at Columbia	7	20
O15	= Cornell	0	0
O22	• Navy	0	0
O29	• at Michigan	7	14
N5	= Lehigh	53	0
N12	• Yale	7	7

1933 — 9-0-0

O7	• Amherst	40	0
O14	• Williams	45	0
O21	• Columbia	20	0
O28	• Wash. & Lee	6	0
N4	• at Brown	33	0
N11	• Dartmouth	7	0
N18	• Navy	13	0
N25	• Rutgers	26	6
D2	• at Yale	27	2

1934 — 7-1-0

O6	• Amherst	75	0
O13	• Williams	35	6
O20	• Wash. & Lee	14	12
O27	• Cornell	45	0
N3	• at Harvard	19	0
N10	• Lehigh	54	0
N17	• Yale	0	7
N24	• Dartmouth	38	13

THE SCHOOLS

1935 — 9-0-0

Date		Opponent		
O5	●	Pennsylvania	7	6
O12	●	Williams	14	7
O19	●	Rutgers	29	6
O26	●	at Cornell	54	0
N2	●	Navy	26	0
N9	●	Harvard	35	0
N16	●	Lehigh	27	0
N23	●	Dartmouth	26	6
N30	●	at Yale	38	7

1936 — 4-2-2

O3	●	Williams	27	7
O10	●	Rutgers	20	0
O17		at Pennsylvania	0	7
O24	●	Navy	7	0
O31	=	at Harvard	14	14
N7	●	Cornell	41	13
N14		Yale	23	26
N21	=	Dartmouth	13	13

1937 — 4-4-0

O2	●	Virginia	26	0
O9		Cornell	7	20
O16		at Chicago	16	7
O23	●	Rutgers	6	0
O30		Harvard	6	34
N6		Dartmouth	9	33
N13		at Yale	0	26
N20	●	Navy	26	6

TAD WIEMAN
1938-42 (.524)   20-18-3

1938 — 3-4-1

O1	●	Williams	39	0
O8		Dartmouth	0	22
O15	●	Pennsylvania	13	0
O22	=	Navy BALT	13	13
O29		at Harvard	7	26
N5		at Rutgers	18	20
N12	●	Yale	20	7
N19		Army	7	19

1939 — 7-1-0

O7	●	Williams	26	6
O14		Cornell	7	20
O21	●	at Columbia	14	7
O28	●	Brown	26	12
N4	●	Harvard	9	6
N11	●	Dartmouth	9	7
N18	●	at Yale	13	7
N25	●	Navy	28	0

1940 — 5-2-1

O5	●	Vanderbilt	7	6
O12	●	Navy	6	12
O19		at Pennsylvania	28	46
O26	●	Rutgers	28	13
N2	=	at Harvard	0	0
N9	●	Dartmouth	14	9
N16	●	Yale	10	7
N23	●	Army	26	19

1941 — 2-6-0

O4	●	Williams	20	7
O11		Columbia	0	21
O18		Pennsylvania	0	23
O25		at Vanderbilt	7	46
N1		Harvard	4	6
N8		Dartmouth	13	20
N15	●	at Yale	20	6
N22		Navy	0	23

1942 — 3-5-1

S26	●	Lakehurst NAS	20	6
O3		Williams	7	19
O10	●	Navy NYC	10	0
O17	=	at Pennsylvania	6	6
O24	●	Brown	32	13
O31		at Harvard	14	19
N7		Dartmouth	7	19
N14		Yale NYC	6	13
N21		Army BRNX	7	40

HARRY MAHNKEN
1943-44 (.200)   2-8

1943 — 1-6-0

S25	●	at Pennsylvania	9	47
O2	●	at Columbia	26	7
O9		Cornell	0	30
O16		Brown	20	28
O23		Villanova	22	45
N13		at Yale	6	27
N20		Dartmouth	13	42

1944 — 1-2-0

N11	●	Muhlenberg	16	6
N18	●	Swarthmore	0	3
N25		Atlantic City NAS	6	31

CHARLIE CALDWELL
1945-56 (.694)   70-30-3

1945 — 2-3-2

O6	=	Lafayette	7	7
O13	●	at Cornell	14	6
O27	●	Rutgers	14	6
N3		at Pennsylvania	0	28
N10	=	Dartmouth	13	13
N17		Columbia	7	32
N24		Yale	14	20

1946 — 3-5-0

O5	●	Brown	33	12
O12		Harvard	12	13
O19	●	Rutgers	14	7
O26		Cornell	7	14
N2	●	at Pennsylvania	17	14
N9	●	Virginia	6	20
N16	●	at Yale	2	30
N23		Dartmouth	13	20

1947 — 5-3-0

O4	●	Brown	21	7
O11	●	at Rutgers	7	13
O18	●	Colgate	20	7
O25	●	Cornell	21	28
N1	●	Pennsylvania	7	26
N8	●	at Harvard	33	7
N15	●	Yale	17	0
N22	●	Dartmouth	14	12

1948 — 4-4-0

O2	●	Brown	20	23
O9	●	at Pennsylvania	7	29
O16	●	Rutgers	6	22
O23	●	at Columbia	16	14
O30	●	Virginia	55	14
N6	●	Harvard	47	7
N13	●	at Yale	20	14
N20	●	Dartmouth	13	33

1949 — 6-3-0

S24	●	Lafayette	26	14
O1		Navy BALT	7	28
O8		Pennsylvania	13	14
O15	●	Brown	27	14
O22	●	at Cornell	12	14
O29	●	Rutgers	34	14
N5	●	at Harvard	33	13
N12	●	Yale	21	13
N19	●	Dartmouth	19	13

1950 — 9-0-0

S30	●	Williams	66	0
O7	●	Rutgers	34	28
O14	●	Navy	20	14
O21	●	at Brown	34	0
O28	●	Cornell	27	0
N4	●	Colgate	45	7
N11	●	Harvard	63	26
N18	●	at Yale	47	12
N25	●	Dartmouth	13	7

1951 — 9-0-0

S29	●	NYU	54	20
O6	●	at Navy	24	20
O13	●	at Pennsylvania	13	7
O20	●	Lafayette	60	7
O27	●	Cornell	53	15
N3	●	Brown	12	0
N10	●	at Harvard	54	13
N17	●	Yale	27	0
N24	●	Dartmouth	13	0

1952 — 8-1-0

S27	●	at Columbia	14	0
O4	●	Rutgers	61	19
O11	●	Pennsylvania	7	13
O18	●	Lafayette	48	0
O25	●	at Cornell	27	0
N1	●	Brown	39	0
N8	●	Harvard	41	21
N15	●	at Yale	27	21
N22	●	Dartmouth	33	0

1953 — 5-4-0

S26	●	Lafayette	20	14
O3	●	Columbia	20	19
O10	●	Rutgers	9	7
O17		Navy	7	65
O24		Cornell	19	26
O31		Brown	27	13
N7		at Harvard	6	0
N14		Yale	24	26
N21		Dartmouth	12	34

1954 — 5-3-1

S25	●	Rutgers	10	8
O2	●	at Columbia	54	20
O9	●	Pennsylvania	13	7
O16	●	at Brown	20	21
O23	●	Cornell	0	27
O30	=	Colgate	6	6
N6		Harvard	9	14
N13	●	at Yale	21	14
N20	●	Dartmouth	49	7

1955 — 7-2-0

S24	●	Rutgers	41	7
O1	●	Columbia	20	7
O8	●	at Pennsylvania	7	0
O15	●	Colgate	6	15
O22	●	at Cornell	26	20
O29	●	Brown	14	7
N5		at Harvard	6	7
N12	●	Yale	13	0
N19	●	Dartmouth	6	3

1956-Present
IVY LEAGUE

1956 — 7-2-0 (5-2-0)

S29	●	Rutgers	28	6
O6	●	Columbia	39	0
O13	●	at Pennsylvania	34	0
O20	●	Colgate	28	20
O27	●	Cornell	32	21
N3	●	Brown	21	7
N10	●	Harvard	35	20
N17		at Yale	20	42
N24		Dartmouth	0	19

DICK COLMAN
1957-68 (.694)   75-33

1957 — 7-2-0 (6-1-0)

S28	●	Rutgers	7	0
O5	●	at Columbia	47	6
O12	●	Pennsylvania	13	9
O19	●	Colgate	10	12
O26	●	Cornell	47	14
N2	●	at Brown	7	0
N9	●	at Harvard	28	20
N16		Yale	13	20
N23	●	Dartmouth	34	14

1958 — 6-3-0 (5-2-0)

S27	●	Rutgers	0	28
O4	●	Columbia	43	8
O11	●	at Pennsylvania	20	14
O18	●	Colgate	40	13
O25	●	at Cornell	8	34
N1	●	Brown	28	18
N8	●	Harvard	16	14
N15	●	at Yale	50	14
N22	●	Dartmouth	12	21

1959 — 4-5-0 (3-4-0)

S26	●	Rutgers	6	8
O3	●	at Columbia	22	0
O10	●	Pennsylvania	0	18
O17	●	Colgate	42	7
O24	●	Cornell	20	0
O31	●	Brown	7	0
N7		at Harvard	0	14
N14		Yale	20	38
N21	●	Dartmouth	7	12

1960 — 7-2-0 (6-1-0)

S24	●	Rutgers	8	13
O1	●	Columbia	49	0
O8	●	at Pennsylvania	21	0
O15	●	Colgate	36	26
O22	●	at Cornell	21	18
O29	●	Brown	54	21
N5	●	Harvard	14	12
N12		at Yale	22	43
N19	●	Dartmouth	7	0

1961 — 5-4-0 (5-2-0)

S30	●	Rutgers	13	16
O7	●	at Columbia	30	20
O14	●	Pennsylvania	9	3
O21	●	Colgate	0	15
O28	●	Cornell	30	25
N4	●	at Brown	52	0
N11	●	at Harvard	7	9
N18	●	Yale	26	16
N25	●	Dartmouth	6	24

1962 — 5-4-0 (4-3-0)

S29	●	Rutgers	15	7
O6	●	Columbia	33	0
O13	●	at Pennsylvania	21	8
O20	●	Colgate	15	16
O27	●	at Cornell	34	35
N3	●	Brown	28	12
N10	●	Harvard	0	20
N17	●	at Yale	14	10
N24	●	Dartmouth	27	38

1963 — 7-2-0 (5-2-0)

S28	●	Rutgers	24	0
O5	●	at Columbia	7	6
O12	●	Pennsylvania	34	0
O19	●	Colgate	42	0
O26	●	Cornell	51	14
N2	●	Brown	34	13
N9	●	at Harvard	7	21
N16	●	Yale	27	7
N30	●	Dartmouth	21	22

1964 — 9-0-0 (7-0-0)

S26	●	Rutgers	10	7
O3	●	Columbia	23	13
O10	●	at Dartmouth	37	7
O17	●	Colgate	9	0
O24	●	at Pennsylvania	55	0
O31	●	at Brown	14	0
N7	●	Harvard	16	0
N14	●	at Yale	35	14
N21	●	Cornell	17	12

1965 — 8-1-0 (6-1-0)

S25	●	Rutgers	32	6
O2	●	at Columbia	31	0
O9	●	at Cornell	36	27
O16	●	Colgate	27	0
O23	●	Pennsylvania	51	0
O30	●	Brown	45	27
N6	●	at Harvard	14	6
N13	●	Yale	31	6
N20	●	Dartmouth	14	28

1966 — 7-2-0 (6-1-0)

S24	●	Rutgers	16	12
O1	●	Columbia	14	12
O8	●	at Dartmouth	13	31
O15		Colgate	0	7
O22	●	at Pennsylvania	30	13
O29	●	at Brown	24	7
N5	●	Harvard	18	14
N12	●	at Yale	13	7
N19	●	Cornell	7	0

1967 — 6-3-0 (4-3-0)

S30	●	Rutgers	22	21
O7	●	at Columbia	28	14
O14		at Cornell	13	47
O21	●	Colgate	28	0
O28	●	Pennsylvania	28	14
N4	●	Brown	48	14
N11	●	at Harvard	45	6
N18		Yale	7	29
N25	●	Dartmouth	14	17

1968 — 4-5-0 (4-3-0)

S28	●	Rutgers	14	20
O5	●	Columbia	44	16
O12	●	at Dartmouth	34	7
O19	●	Colgate	7	14
O26	●	at Pennsylvania	14	19
N2	●	at Brown	50	7
N9	●	Harvard	7	9
N16	●	at Yale	17	42
N23	●	Cornell	41	13

JACK McCANDLESS
1969-72 (.514)   18-17-1

1969 — 6-3-0 (6-1-0)

S27		at Rutgers	0	29
O4	●	at Columbia	21	7
O11	●	at Cornell	24	17
O18	●	Colgate	28	35
O25	●	Pennsylvania	42	0
N1	●	Brown	33	6
N8	●	at Harvard	51	20
N15		Yale	14	17
N22	●	Dartmouth	35	7

1970 — 5-4-0 (3-4-0)

S26	●	Rutgers	41 14
O3	●	Columbia	24 22
O10		at Dartmouth	0 38
O17	●	Colgate	34 14
O24	●	at Pennsylvania	22 16
O31	●	at Brown	42 14
N7		Harvard	7 29
N14		at Yale	22 27
N21		Cornell	3 6

1971 — 4-5-0 (3-4-0)

S25		Rutgers	18 33
O2		at Columbia	20 22
O9		at Cornell	8 19
O16	●	Colgate	35 12
O23	●	Pennsylvania	31 0
O30	●	Brown	49 21
N6	●	at Harvard	21 10
N13		Yale	6 10
N20		Dartmouth	7 33

1972 — 3-5-1 (2-4-1)

S30	●	Rutgers	7 6
O7	=	Columbia	0 0
O14		at Dartmouth	14 35
O21		Colgate	26 35
O28		at Pennsylvania	10 15
N4	●	at Brown	31 10
N11	●	Harvard	10 7
N18		at Yale	7 31
N25		Cornell	15 22

BOB CASCIOLA — 1973-77 (.322) — 14-30-1

1973 — 1-8-0 (0-7-0)

S29		Rutgers	14 39
O6		at Columbia	13 14
O13		at Cornell	6 37
O20	●	Colgate	37 21
O27		Pennsylvania	0 24
N3		Brown	6 7
N10		at Harvard	14 19
N17		Yale	13 30
N24		Dartmouth	24 42

1974 — 4-4-1 (3-4-0)

S28	=	Rutgers	6 6
O5	●	Columbia	40 13
O12	●	at Dartmouth	14 7
O19	●	Colgate	33 24
O26	●	at Pennsylvania	18 20
N2	●	at Brown	13 17
N9		Harvard	17 34
N16	●	at Yale	6 19
N23	●	Cornell	41 20

1975 — 4-5-0 (3-4-0)

S27	●	Rutgers	10 7
O4	●	at Columbia	27 7
O11	●	at Cornell	16 8
O18		Colgate	21 22
O25		Pennsylvania	20 24
N1		Brown	16 24
N8	●	at Harvard	24 20
N15		Yale	13 24
N22		Dartmouth	16 21

1976 — 2-7-0 (2-5-0)

S18	●	at Cornell	3 0
S25		Rutgers	0 17
O2		Brown	7 13
O9	●	at Columbia	9 6
O16		Colgate	7 17
O23		Harvard	14 20
O30		Pennsylvania	9 10
N6		at Yale	7 39
N13		Dartmouth	7 33

1977 — 3-6-0 (3-4-0)

S17		at Dartmouth	11 14
S24		Rutgers	6 10
O1		at Brown	7 10
O8	●	Columbia	28 7
O15		Colgate	13 31
O22	●	at Harvard	20 7
O29		at Pennsylvania	10 21
N5		Yale	8 44
N12	●	Cornell	34 0

FRANK NAVARRO — 1978-84 (.455) — 29-35-3

1978 — 2-5-2 (1-4-2)

S23	=	at Cornell	14 14
S30		Rutgers ERUT	0 24
O7		Brown	16 44
O14		at Columbia	10 14
O21	●	Colgate	13 12
O28	=	Harvard	24 24
N4	●	Pennsylvania	21 0
N11		at Yale	7 23
N18		Dartmouth	21 28

1979 — 5-4-0 (5-2-0)

S22	●	at Dartmouth	16 0
S29		Rutgers	14 38
O6		at Brown	12 31
O13	●	Columbia	35 7
O20		Colgate	6 17
O27	●	at Harvard	9 7
N3	●	at Pennsylvania	38 10
N10		Yale	10 35
N17	●	Cornell	26 14

1980 — 6-4-0 (4-3-0)

S20	●	at Cornell	7 17
S27		at Rutgers	13 44
O4		Brown	11 28
O11	●	at Columbia	31 19
O18	●	Colgate	14 10
O25	●	Harvard	7 3
N1	●	Pennsylvania	28 21
N8	●	Maine	24 7
N15	●	at Yale	13 25
N22	●	Dartmouth	27 24

1981 — 5-4-1 (5-1-1)

S19	●	at Dartmouth	13 32
S26		Delaware	8 61
O3	●	at Brown	20 17
O10	●	Columbia	21 14
O17		at Army	0 34
O24	=	at Harvard	17 17
O31	●	at Pennsylvania	38 30
N7		Maine	44 55
N14	●	Yale	35 31
N21	●	Cornell	37 14

1982 — 3-7-0 (3-4-0)

S18	●	at Cornell	41 36
S25		at Delaware	17 35
O2	●	Brown	28 23
O9		at Columbia	14 35
O16		Army	14 20
O23		Harvard	15 27
O30	●	Pennsylvania	17 14
N6		Lafayette	37 47
N13		at Yale	19 37
N20		Dartmouth	20 43

1983 — 4-6-0 (2-5-0)

S17		at Dartmouth	3 21
S24	●	Bucknell	46 28
O1	●	at Brown	27 16
O8	●	Columbia	35 26
O15		Navy	29 37
O22		at Harvard	26 28
O29		at Pennsylvania	27 28
N5	●	Lafayette	41 33
N12	●	Yale	21 28
N19	●	Cornell	30 32

1984 — 4-5-0 (3-4-0)

S22	●	at Cornell	17 9
S29	●	Bucknell	20 14
O6	●	Brown	30 32
O13	●	at Columbia	38 8
O20		at Navy	3 41
O27		Harvard	15 17
N3		Pennsylvania	17 27
N10		at Yale	24 27
N17	●	Dartmouth	21 17

RON ROGERSON — 1985-86 (.350) — 7-13

1985 — 5-5-0 (5-2-0)

S21	●	at Dartmouth	10 3
S28		Lehigh	13 34
O5		at Brown	0 17
O12	●	Columbia	31 0
O19		Colgate	44 49
O26	●	at Harvard	11 6
N2		at Pennsylvania	21 31
N9		William & Mary	28 33
N16	●	Yale	21 12
N23	●	Cornell	33 27

1986 — 2-8-0 (2-5-0)

S20		at Cornell	8 39
S27		Northwestern	0 37
O4		Brown	10 24
O11		at Columbia	20 14
O18		at Lehigh	28 48
O25		Harvard	14 3
N1		Pennsylvania	10 23
N8		at William & Mary	14 32
N15		at Yale	13 14
N22		Dartmouth	6 28

STEVE TOSCHES — 1987-99 (.600) — 77-51-2

1987 — 6-4-0 (4-3-0)

S19	●	at Dartmouth	34 3
S26	●	at Davidson	42 6
O3		at Brown	7 13
O10	●	Columbia	38 8
O17	●	Lehigh	16 15
O24		at Harvard	19 24
O31	●	at Pennsylvania	17 7
N7		Colgate	15 39
N14		Yale	19 34
N21	●	Cornell	23 6

1988 — 6-4-0 (4-3-0)

S17	●	at Cornell	26 17
S24		Holy Cross	26 30
O1	●	Brown	31 27
O8		at Columbia	13 16
O15	●	at Bucknell	41 35
O22	●	Harvard	23 8
O29		Pennsylvania	23 31
N5	●	Colgate	45 13
N12	●	at Yale	24 7
N19		Dartmouth	17 24

1989 — 7-2-1 (6-1-0)

S16	●	at Dartmouth	20 14
S23	=	William & Mary	31 31
S30		at Holy Cross	0 46
O7	●	at Brown	38 15
O14	●	Columbia	24 8
O21	●	Fordham	38 20
O28	●	at Harvard	28 14
N4	●	at Pennsylvania	30 8
N11		Yale	7 14
N18	●	Cornell	21 7

1990 — 3-7-0 (2-5-0)

S15		at Cornell	14 17
S22	●	Fordham	23 14
S29		at Colgate	13 39
O6	●	Brown	27 23
O13		at Bucknell	9 14
O20		Harvard	20 23
O27		at Columbia	15 17
N3	●	Pennsylvania	34 20
N10		at Yale	7 34
N17		Dartmouth	6 23

1991 — 8-2-0 (5-2-0)

S21	●	Cornell	18 0
S28	●	at Fordham	20 17
O5	●	Colgate	30 21
O12	●	at Brown	59 37
O19	●	Bucknell	31 7
O26	●	at Harvard	21 24
N2	●	Columbia	22 6
N9	●	at Pennsylvania	17 12
N16	●	Yale	22 16
N23	●	at Dartmouth	13 31

1992 — 8-2-0 (6-1-0)

S19	●	at Cornell	22 20
S26	●	Lafayette	38 35
O3	●	at Lehigh	38 28
O10	●	Brown	28 14
O17		at Holy Cross	7 10
O24	●	at Harvard	21 6
O31	●	at Columbia	34 7
N7	●	Pennsylvania	20 14
N14	●	at Yale	36 7
N21		Dartmouth	20 34

1993 — 8-2-0 (5-2-0)

S18	●	Cornell	18 12
S25	●	at Lafayette	21 7
O2	●	Holy Cross	38 0
O9	●	at Brown	34 16
O16	●	Lehigh	31 23
O23	●	at Harvard	21 10
O30	●	Columbia	14 3
N6	●	at Pennsylvania	14 30
N13	●	Yale	28 7
N20		at Dartmouth	22 28

1994 — 7-3-0 (4-3-0)

S17		at Cornell	16 31
S24	●	Colgate	29 3
O1	●	Bucknell	12 7
O8	●	Brown	31 10
O15	●	at Fordham	27 20
O22	●	Harvard	18 7
O29		at Columbia	10 17
N5		Pennsylvania	19 33
N12	●	at Yale	19 6
N19	●	Dartmouth	20 13

1995 — 8-1-1 (5-1-1)

S16	●	Cornell	24 22
S23	●	Bucknell	20 3
S30	●	at Colgate	34 23
O7	●	at Brown	21 19
O14	●	Lafayette	41 0
O21	●	at Harvard	13 3
O28	●	Columbia	44 14
N4	●	at Pennsylvania	22 9
N11	●	Yale	13 21
N18	=	at Dartmouth	10 10

1996 — 3-7 (2-5)

S21		at Cornell	27 33
S28	●	Holy Cross	37 30
O5		at Lehigh	14 20
O12		Brown	23 27
O19		at Bucknell	6 10
O26		Harvard	0 24
N2	●	at Columbia	14 11
N9		Pennsylvania	6 10
N16	●	at Yale	17 13
N23		Dartmouth	0 24

1997 — 5-5 (5-2)

S21		at Cornell	10 14
S28	●	Fordham EWI	9 7
O4	●	at Holy Cross	21 7
O11	●	at Brown	30 13
O18	●	at Colgate	31 28
O25		Harvard	12 14
N1		at Columbia	0 17
N8	●	at Pennsylvania	17 20 †
N15	=	Yale ERUT	9 9
N22		at Dartmouth	9 12

1998 — 5-5 (4-3)

S19	●	Cornell	6 0
S26		at Lehigh	24 31
O3		at Fordham	17 20
O10	●	Brown	31 17
O17	●	at Lafayette	20 0
O24		Harvard	22 23
O31	●	at Columbia	20 0
N7		Pennsylvania	14 27
N14	●	at Yale	28 31
N21	●	Dartmouth	35 13

1999 — 3-7 (1-6)

S18		Cornell	3 20
S25		Lehigh	0 31
O2	●	Fordham	27 0
O9		at Brown	30 53
O16	●	Lafayette	22 10
O23		at Harvard	6 13
O30	●	Columbia	44 15
N6		at Pennsylvania	13 41
N13		Yale	21 23
N20		at Dartmouth	18 19

ROGER HUGHES — 2000-Present (.388) — 19-30

2000 — 3-7 (3-4)

S16		at Lafayette	17 24
S23		Lehigh	18 20
S30	●	at Columbia	27 24
O7		at Colgate	6 34
O14	●	Brown	55 28
O21		Harvard	21 35
O28		at Cornell	24 25
N4		Pennsylvania	24 40
N11	●	at Yale	19 14
N18		Dartmouth	37 42

2001   3-6   (3-4)

S22		Lehigh	10	34
S29	●	Columbia	44	11
O6		Colgate	10	35
O13		Brown	24	35
O20		Harvard	26	28
O27		Cornell	7	10
N3		Pennsylvania	10	21
N10	●	Yale	34	14
N17	●	Dartmouth	35	14

2002   6-4   (4-3)

S21		at Lehigh	24	31
S28	●	Lafayette	34	19
O5	●	at Columbia	35	32
O12	●	Colgate	14	10
O19	●	Brown	16	14
O26		Harvard	17	24
N2	●	at Cornell	32	25
N9		Pennsylvania	13	44
N16	●	at Yale	3	7
N23	●	Dartmouth	38	30

2003   2-8   (2-5)

S20		Lehigh	13	28
S27		at Lafayette	13	28
O4		Columbia	27	33
O11		Colgate	3	30
O18	●	Brown	34	14
O25		at Harvard	40	43
N1	●	Cornell	28	6
N8		at Pennsylvania	7	37
N15		Yale	24	27
N22		at Dartmouth	15	21

2004   5-5   (3-4)

S18	●	Lafayette	35	18
S25	●	at San Diego	24	17
O2	●	at Columbia	27	26
O9		at Colgate	26	29
O16	●	Brown	24	10
O23		Harvard	14	39
O30		at Cornell	20	21
N6		Pennsylvania	15	16
N13		at Yale	9	21
N20	●	Dartmouth	17	10

PRINCETON ANNUAL STATISTICAL LEADERS

YR	RUSHING	YDS	ATT	AVG	PASSING	ATT	CMP	PCT	YDS	RECEIVING	REC	YDS	AVG
1954	Royce Flippen	494	94	5.3	Royce Flippen	38	17	.45	193	Frank Agnew	14	196	14.0
1955	Dick Martin	546	126	4.3	Sid Pinch	43	19	.44	220	Frank Agnew	10	142	14.2
1956	Tom Morris	546	95	5.7	Jim Mottley	42	26	.62	481	Jack Sapoch	10	102	10.2
1957	Fred Tiley	592	127	4.7	Tom Morris	47	24	.51	213	Jack Sapoch	11	99	9.0
1958	Hugh Scott	429	99	4.3	Hugh Scott	24	12	.50	132	Jim Blair	5	186	37.2
1959	Dan Sachs	450	114	3.9	Mike Ippolito	41	20	.49	285	Jim Blair	22	238	10.8
1960	Hugh Scott	760	140	5.4	Hugh Scott	47	24	.51	367	Jim Blair	11	176	16.0
1961	Greg Riley	459	90	5.1	Pete Porietis	44	25	.57	304	Barry Schuman	15	178	11.9
1962	Greg Riley	492	109	4.5	Greg Riley	50	26	.52	291	John Henrich	15	133	8.9
1963	Cosmo Iacavazzi	675	164	4.1	Don McKay	29	16	.55	253	Jack Singer	5	54	10.8
1964	Cosmo Iacavazzi	909	172	5.3	Don McKay	75	33	.44	419	Doug Tufts	15	215	14.3
1965	Ron Landeck	850	188	4.5	Ron Landeck	144	75	.52	1,099	Lauson Cashdollar	30	373	12.4
1966	Dick Bracken	436	135	3.2	Dick Bracken	73	29	.40	370	Steve Pierce	17	225	13.2
1967	Ellis Moore	484	122	4.0	Bob Weber	46	20	.43	368	Mike Garton	21	225	10.7
1968	Brian McCullough	778	163	4.8	Scott MacBean	43	27	.63	286	Mark Biros	12	157	13.1
1969	Brian McCullough	481	127	3.8	Scott MacBean	192	107	.56	1,383	Rod Bordley	30	351	11.7
1970	Hank Bjorklund	1,081	179	6.0	Rod Plummer	134	64	.48	888	Pete Hauck	22	370	16.8
1971	Hank Bjorklund	944	194	4.9	Rod Plummer	88	45	.51	682	Doug Blake and Bill Skinner	21	267	12.7
1972	Jud Wagenseller	353	102	3.5	Fred Dalzell	136	65	.48	649	Kerry Brown	31	436	14.1
1973	Walt Snickenberger	935	176	5.3	Ron Beible	161	79	.49	1,023	Bill Skinner	27	299	11.1
1974	Walt Snickenberger	1,041	214	4.9	Ron Beible	187	91	.49	1,136	Kevin Gropp	23	243	10.6
1975	Bob Reid	340	87	3.9	Ron Beible	244	123	.50	1,503	Neil Chamberlin	44	519	11.8
1976	Bobby Isom	439	118	3.7	Kirby Lockhart	98	50	.51	500	Dan Fournier	27	342	12.7
1977	Bobby Isom	918	220	4.2	Kirby Lockhart	89	49	.55	546	Rich Keefe	17	205	12.1
1978	William Crissy	649	159	4.1	Ken Barrett	107	52	.49	574	William Crissy	24	294	12.3
1979	William Crissy	622	153	4.1	Steve Reynolds	97	51	.53	574	Lew Leone	20	267	13.4
1980	Larry Van Pelt	550	121	4.5	Mark Lockenmeyer	185	110	.59	1,284	William Crissy	55	653	11.9
1981	Larry Van Pelt	528	107	4.9	Bob Holly	338	206	.61	2,622	Scott Oostdyk	37	403	10.9
1982	Brent Woods	411	142	2.9	Brent Woods	435	220	.51	2,668	Kevin Guthrie	75	1,003	13.4
1983	Ralph Ferraro	1,012	254	4.0	Doug Butler	398	224	.56	3,175	Kevin Guthrie	88	1,260	14.3
1984	Dan Pelligrino	410	109	3.8	Doug Butler	309	164	.53	2,179	Derek Graham	62	959	15.5
1985	Butch Climmons	449	118	3.8	Doug Butler	281	154	.55	1,937	Butch Climmons	28	301	10.8
1986	Jerry Santillo	437	104	4.2	Brad Hammond	91	44	.48	593	Jeff Baker	24	315	13.1
1987	Judd Garrett	822	190	4.3	Jason Garrett	251	162	.65	2,057	John Garrett	45	617	13.7
1988	Judd Garrett	940	190	4.9	Jason Garrett	299	204	.68	2,217	Judd Garrett	66	634	9.6
1989	Judd Garrett	1,347	307	4.4	Joel Sharp	181	103	.57	1,378	Judd Garrett	34	351	10.3
1990	Erick Hamilton	699	138	5.1	Joel Sharp	219	102	.47	1,339	Mark Rodgers	19	368	19.4
1991	Keith Elias	902	186	4.8	Chad Roghair	239	147	.62	1,886	Michael Lerch	47	886	18.9
1992	Keith Elias	1,575	245	6.4	Joel Foote	131	74	.56	918	Michael Lerch	30	579	19.3
1993	Keith Elias	1,731	305	5.7	Joel Foote	191	113	.59	1,632	Marc Ross	29	586	20.2
1994	Bill Jordan	880	204	4.3	Harry Nakielny	115	56	.49	720	Dave Scoggin	30	405	13.5
1995	Marc Washington	937	230	4.1	Brock Harvey	127	65	.51	835	Kevin Duffy	41	583	14.2
1996	Marc Washington	611	154	4.0	Brett Budzinski	224	110	.49	1,160	Kevin Duffy	35	507	14.5
1997	Gerry Giurato	509	147	3.5	Harry Nakielny	275	117	.43	1,236	Ray Canole	34	363	10.7
1998	Derek Theisen	487	114	4.3	John Burnham	255	143	.56	1,905	Ryan Crowley	43	494	11.5
1999	Kyle Brandt	466	87	5.4	Tommy Crenshaw	281	157	.56	1,662	Phil Wendler	74	822	11.1
2000	Cameron Atkinson	413	94	4.4	Jon Blevins	105	62	.59	840	Chisom Opara	51	689	13.5
2001	Cameron Atkinson	660	114	5.8	David Splithoff	231	137	.59	1,690	Chisom Opara	36	581	16.1
2002	Cameron Atkinson	1,122	187	6.0	David Splithoff	142	85	.60	1,223	Chisom Opara	57	772	13.5
2003	Jon Veach	642	141	4.6	Matt Verbit	327	174	.53	2,499	Blair Morrison	50	734	14.7
2004	Jon Veach	625	152	4.1	Matt Verbit	291	167	.57	1,768	Greg Fields	49	511	10.4

Receiving leaders by receptions

YALE

BY BRUCE WOOD

WHEN NOTRE DAME BEGAN USING a shift in its backfield, legendary coach Knute Rockne was asked how he had come up with the maneuver. Rockne reportedly said, "Where everything else in football came from—Yale." Rockne may not have used those exact words, but there is no doubt about Yale's place in football history. Walter Camp, a Yale player and coach and a member of every football rules committee from 1879 to 1925, is credited with introducing many of the game's most fundamental concepts, from first downs and the use of a quarterback to plays from scrimmage and the game's first scoring system.

TRADITION After every victory, the Yale players gather on the field, take off their helmets and pump them in the air while singing a rendition of the fight song "Bulldog."

BEST PLAYER Even before Garry Trudeau immortalized him as the character B.D. in "Doonesbury," quarterback Brian Dowling was a campus legend. In 1965, he arrived at Yale having not lost a game since junior high and promptly led the freshman squad to a 6–0 record. He helped the varsity team win its opener in 1966, but the following week he was sidelined for the rest of the season. After sitting out the only loss of the 1967 season with a wrist injury, he guided Yale to an 8–0–1 mark in his senior year. Dowling's record in games he started and finished from seventh grade through college was 65–0–1.

BEST COACH Carm Cozza's career at Yale started with a dubious distinction. In the 1965 season opener, Cozza lost to Connecticut, the first time the Elis had stumbled against an in-state rival in 90 years. Despite the initial embarrassment, Cozza went on to lead the Bulldogs to a 179–119–5 record during his 32-year career at Yale, including 10 Ivy League championships.

BEST TEAM Yale's 1909 national championship team finished 10–0. The Bulldogs weren't only undefeated—they did not give up a single point all year. Their closest game was an 8-0 win at Harvard. The 1909 Bulldogs had no fewer than six All-Americas: captain Ted Coy, Carroll Cooney, Hamlin Andrus, Henry Hobbs, John Kilpatrick and Stephen Philbin.

BIGGEST GAME The annual matchup against Harvard is known as The Game. In 1968, it was THE GAME, as both

PROFILE

Yale University
New Haven, Conn.
Founded: 1701
Enrollment: 5,242
Colors: Yale Blue and White
Nickname: Bulldogs
Stadium: Yale Bowl
    Opened in 1914
    Grass; 64,269 capacity
First football game: 1872
All-time record: 828–320–55 (.711)
Ivy League championships: 13 (6 outright)
Heisman Trophy: Larry Kelley, 1936; Clint Frank, 1937
First-round NFL draftees: 2
Website: www.yale.edu/athletics

THE BEST OF TIMES

The 13–0 national champions of 1888 outscored their opponents 698-0, one of 11 unscored-upon seasons in school history.

THE WORST OF TIMES

Yale lost eight of nine games against Harvard between 1912 and 1922, by a combined score of 154-20.

CONFERENCE

Yale was an original member of the Ivy League when it began formal play in 1956.

DISTINGUISHED ALUMNI

Cole Porter; George H.W. Bush; George W. Bush; John Kerry; Jodie Foster; Oliver Stone; Angela Bassett, actress; Joseph F. Cullman III, CEO of Philip Morris and sponsor of original women's pro tennis tour; Bart Giamatti, baseball commissioner

FIGHT SONG

DOWN THE FIELD
March, march on down the field,
Fighting for Eli.
Break through that crimson line,
Their strength to defy.
We'll give a long cheer for Eli's men.
We're here to win again.
Harvard's team may fight to the end,
But Yale will win!

BULLDOG
Bulldog, bulldog, bow-wow-wow, Eli Yale!
Bulldog, bulldog, bow-wow-wow, our team can never fail!
When the sons of Eli break through the line,
That is the sign we hail.
Bulldog, bulldog, bow-wow-wow, Eli Yale!

teams entered the contest undefeated for the first time since 1909. A sellout crowd of 40,280 at Harvard Stadium watched the Bulldogs vault to a 22-0 lead in the first half. After Dowling's TD run gave Yale a 29-13 lead in the fourth quarter, the Bulldogs looked to be on their way to a sure and easy victory. But with 3:34 remaining, Yale fumbled deep in Harvard territory, and the Crimson rallied for two touchdowns in the final minute for an improbable 29-29 tie.

The Game pits Harvard and Yale in the last—and most important—contest of the year. During the Depression, scalpers commanded $50 a seat.

credited with the wisecrack, and a nickname was born.

WILDEST FINISH After losing every game against Ivy League opponents in 1997, Yale opened the 1998 season against conference favorite Brown. The Bulldogs stayed close, but with 59 seconds left, Brown scored a touchdown to go up 28-24. Scrappy Yale quarterback Joe Walland engineered a last-minute 79-yard drive, capped by a 27-yard Hail Mary pass to Jake Borden in a crowded end zone, for a dramatic 30-28 Bulldogs victory.

BIGGEST UPSET On Nov. 17, 1934, Yale squared off against Princeton, which entered the game with 15 straight wins, having outscored its opponents 459-29 during the run. "Laughing" Larry Kelley pulled down a 43-yard TD catch on a fake punt for the day's only score as Yale shocked the Tigers 7-0. All 11 Bulldogs played every down. When a Princeton substitute ran onto the field but was not sure whom to replace on offense, a Yale player yelled out to one of the officials, "Maybe that sub is in for me, sir. I've been playing in Princeton's backfield all afternoon." Kelley was mistakenly

STADIUM On Nov. 21, 1914, the Yale Bowl was packed with more than 75,000 fans for the stadium's opening, but Harvard spoiled the day with a 36-0 victory over the Bulldogs. A registered national historic landmark, the Bowl was referred to as the Coliseum in its original 1912 plans and later served as the inspiration for the Rose Bowl's design. Legendary Yale coach Carm Cozza has spearheaded a $27 million fund-raising campaign for a new scoreboard, an upgrade of the skyboxes and

RECORDS

RUSHING YARDS
	GAME
235	Robert Carr vs. Cornell, Sept. 28, 2002 (28 att.)
	SEASON
1,442	Rich Diana, 1981 (293 att.)
	CAREER
3,393	Robert Carr, 2001-04 (738 att.)

PASSING YARDS
	GAME
438	Alvin Cowan vs. Harvard, Nov. 22, 2003 (34 of 64)
	SEASON
2,994	Alvin Cowan, 2003 (227 of 381)
	CAREER
5,481	Alvin Cowan, 2001-04 (428 of 733)

RECEIVING YARDS
	GAME
258	Ralph Plumb vs. Brown, Nov. 6, 2004 (18 rec.)
	SEASON
1,007	Eric Johnson, 2000 (86 rec.)
	CAREER
2,396	Ralph Plumb, 2001-04 (195 rec.)

POINTS
	GAME
30	Joe Crowley vs. St. John's, Nov. 7, 1931 (5 TDs)
	SEASON
96	John Pagliaro, 1976 (16 TDs)
	CAREER
205	Mike Murawczyk, 1997-2000 (36 FGs, 97 PATs)

CONSENSUS ALL-AMERICANS

1889	Amos Alonzo Stagg, E
1889	Charles Gill, T
1889-91	Pudge Heffelfinger, G
1890	William Rhodes, T
1890-91	Thomas McClung, B
1891-94	Frank Hinkey, E
1891	John Hartwell, E
1891	Wallace Winter, T
1892	A. Hamilton Wallis, T
1892	Vance McCormick, B
1893-94	William Hickok, G
1893-94	Frank Butterworth, B
1894	Philip Stillman, C
1894	George Adee, B
1895	Samuel Thorne, B
1895-96	Fred Murphy, T
1896	Clarence Fincke, B
1897	John Hall, E
1897	Charles DeSaulles, B
1897-98	Burr Chamberlin, T
1897-1900	Gordon Brown, G

(Continued on next page)

construction of Bulldog Plaza, which will feature the name of every football player in the school's history.

RIVAL Started in 1875 when Yale guaranteed Harvard $75 to play a rugby-style match at Hamilton Park in New Haven, The Game annually pits Harvard and Yale in the last—and most important—contest of the season for both teams. Tickets to the first match went for 50 cents; by 1937, scalpers were demanding as much as $50 a ticket. Even today, Harvard vs. Yale at the Bowl easily surpasses 50,000 in attendance.

NICKNAME The Elis trace their roots to Elihu Yale, whose gift of books and other valuables in 1718 gave the Collegiate School not only a new name but also the nickname Old Eli. The nickname Bulldogs came about after rower Andrew Graves bought a dog named Handsome Dan from a New Haven blacksmith in 1889.

MASCOT In 1889, bulldog Handsome Dan became the first college mascot in the country; press reports at the time described him as "a cross between an alligator and a horned frog." In all, there have been 15 Handsome Dans, including Dan IV, whose caretaker was future secretary of state Cyrus Vance, and Dan XII, the only female bulldog, chosen in recognition of the university's admitting women for the first time in 1969.

CONSENSUS ALL-AMERICANS (CONT.)	
1898-99	Malcolm McBride, B
1899	Albert Sharpe, B
1899-1900	George Stillman, T
1900	Herman Olcott, C
1900	Perry Hale, B
1900	William Fincke, B
1900, 1902	George Chadwick, B
1900, 1903	James Bloomer, T/G
1901-02	Henry Holt, C
1902	Edgar Glass, C
1902-04	James Hogan, T
1902, 1904	Ralph Kinney, T/G
1902, 1904-05	Thomas Shevlin, E
1903	Charles Rafferty, E
1903	W. Ledyard Mitchell, B
1905	Roswell Tripp, G
1905	Howard Roome, B
1905	Guy Hutchinson, B
1906	Robert Forbes, E
1906	Hugh Knox, B
1906	Paul Veeder, B
1906-07	L. Horatio Biglow, T
1907	Clarence Alcott, E
1907	Thomas A.D. Jones, B
1907-09	Edward Coy, B
1908	William Goebel, G
1908-09	Hamlin Andrus, G
1909	Henry Hobbs, T
1909	Carroll Cooney, C
1909	Stephen Philbin, B
1909-10	John Kilpatrick, E
1911-12	Douglass Bomeisler, E
1911	Arthur Howe, B
1911-12	Henry Ketcham, C
1913	Nelson Talbott, T
1914	Harry LeGore, B
1916	Clinton Black, G
1920	Tim Callahan, G
1921	Malcolm Aldrich, B
1923	Century Milstead, T
1923	William Mallory, B
1924	Dick Luman, E
1927	Bill Webster, G
1927	John Charlesworth, C
1936	Larry Kelley, E
1937	Clint Frank, B
1944	Paul Walker, E
1984	John Zanieski, DL
2003	Nate Lawrie, TE
2004	Rory Hennessey, OL

UNIFORMS Yale's early uniforms were light blue and white until improvements in dyes brought the current dark blue. Numbers were added in 1927. Helmets have evolved over the years from brown leather to white, to white with blue trim, to plain white again, to white with a bulldog logo. The logo was replaced in the 1960s with players' numbers and, several years later, with the Y that currently adorns the helmets.

LORE From 1896 to 1916, fictional Yale football hero Frank Merriwell was the star of Street & Smith's wildly popular *Tip Top Weekly* dime novel series. Merriwell, described by one reviewer as having a "body like Tarzan's and a head like Einstein's," also starred in his own NBC radio show on Saturday mornings from 1947 to 1949.

QUOTE "Yale was the first to have the true feeling of the game, a game which means spirit, body contact and team play, all the finest elements of competition."—Michigan coach Fielding H. Yost

YALE ALL-TIME SCORES

WIN/LOSS PERCENTAGE SINCE 1936

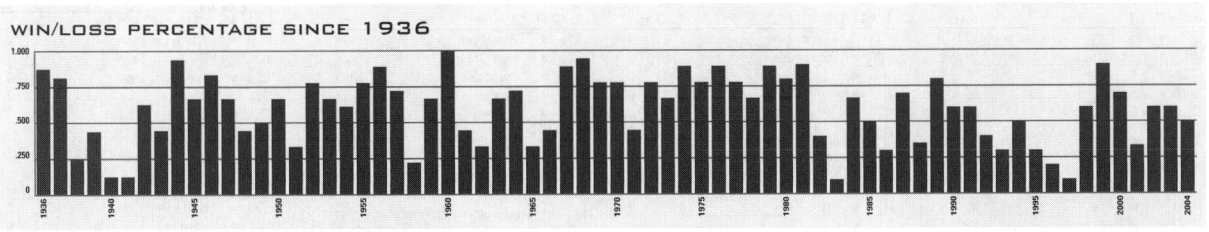

NO HEAD COACH

1872 1-0-0

N16	•	Columbia	3	0

1873 2-1-0

O25	•	Rutgers	3	1
N15	•	Princeton	0	3
D6	•	Eton	2	1

1874 3-0-0

N18	•	Stevens	6	0
N21	•	Columbia	5	1
D5	•	Columbia	6	1

1875 2-2-0

N6	•	Rutgers	4	1
N13	•	Harvard	0	4
N20	•	Wesleyan	6	0
D4	•	Columbia	2	3

1876 3-0-0

N18	•	Harvard	1	0
N30	•	Princeton Hob	2	0
D9	•	Columbia Hob	2	0

1877 3-0-1

N3	•	Tufts	1	0
N21	•	Trinity	7	0
N24	•	Stevens Hob	13	0
D8	=	Princeton Hob	0	0

1878 4-1-1

N2	•	Amherst	2	0
N9	•	Trinity U	2	0
N13	•	Trinity U	3	0
N16	•	Amherst U	0	0
N23	•	Harvard Bos	1	0
N28	•	Princeton Hob	0	1

1879 3-0-2

N1	•	Pennsylvania Hob	3	0
N8	•	Harvard	0	0
N15	•	Rutgers	5	0
N22	•	Columbia Hob	2	0
N27	=	Princeton Hob	0	0

1880 4-0-1

N10	•	Columbia	13	0
N13	•	Brown	8	0
N17	•	Pennsylvania NYC	8	0
N20	•	Harvard Bos	1	0
N25	•	Princeton NYC	0	0

1881 5-0-1

O29	•	at Amherst	2	0
N2	•	Michigan	2	0
N5	•	Amherst	4	0
N12	•	Harvard	1	0
N16	•	Columbia NYC	1	0
N24	=	Princeton NYC	0	0

1882 8-0-0

O7	•	Wesleyan	9	0
O21	•	Rutgers	9	0
O28	•	at Rutgers	5	0
N4	•	MIT	6	0
N8	•	at Amherst	9	0
N18	•	Columbia	11	0
N25	•	at Harvard	1	0
D1	•	Princeton NYC	2	1

1883 9-0-0

S26	•	Wesleyan	60	0
S29	•	at Wesleyan	94	0
O6	•	Stevens	48	0
N6	•	Rutgers Bkln	97	0
N14	•	Brooklyn Tech Bkln	49	0
N17	•	Columbia NYC	93	0
N21	•	Michigan	64	0
N24	•	Princeton NYC	6	0
N29	•	Harvard NYC	23	2

1884 8-0-1

O1	•	Wesleyan	31	0
O11	•	Stevens	96	0
O18	•	Wesleyan U	63	0
O22	•	at Rutgers	76	10
O25	•	at Dartmouth	113	0
N5	•	Wesleyan	46	0
N19	•	Graduates	18	0
N22	•	Harvard	52	0
N27	=	Princeton	0	0

1885 7-1-0

O10	•	at Stevens	55	0
O14	•	Wesleyan Hart	18	0
O28	•	Wesleyan	71	0
O31	•	MIT Bos	51	0
N3	•	Crescent AC	52	0
N14	•	at Pennsylvania	53	5
N21	•	Princeton	5	6
N26	•	Wesleyan NYC	61	0

1886 9-0-1

O6	•	Wesleyan	75	0
O9	•	at Wesleyan	62	0
O16	•	MIT	96	0
O20	•	at Stevens	54	0
O23	•	at Williams	76	0
O30	•	Wesleyan	136	0
N2	•	Crescent AC NYC	84	0
N13	•	Pennsylvania	75	0
N20	•	at Harvard	29	4
N25	=	at Princeton	0	0

1887 9-0-0

O5	•	Wesleyan	38	0
O15	•	at Wesleyan	106	0
O22	•	at Williams	74	0
O29	•	at Pennsylvania	50	0
N5	•	Rutgers	74	0
N8	•	Crescent AC NYC	68	0
N12	•	Wesleyan	76	4
N19	•	Princeton NYC	12	0
N24	•	Harvard NYC	17	8

WALTER CAMP
1888-92 (.971) 68-2

1888 13-0-0

S29	•	Wesleyan	76	0
O6	•	Rutgers	65	0
O13	•	at Pennsylvania	34	0
O16	•	at Wesleyan	46	0
O19	•	at Amherst	39	0
O20	•	at Williams	30	0
O24	•	MIT Hart	68	0
O27	•	Stevens	69	0
N3	•	Pennsylvania	58	0
N6	•	Crescent AC Bkln	28	0
N10	•	Amherst	70	0
N17	•	Wesleyan	105	0
N24	•	Princeton NYC	10	0

1889 16-1-0

S28	•	Wesleyan	38	0
O2	•	Williams	36	0
O9	•	at Wesleyan	63	5
O15	•	Cornell	60	6
O19	•	Amherst	42	0
O24	•	at Trinity	64	0
O26	•	at Columbia	62	0
O30	•	at Pennsylvania	20	10
O31	•	Stevens Brnx	30	0
N5	•	Crescent AC Bkln	5	0
N9	•	at Cornell	70	0
N12	•	at Amherst	32	0
N13	•	at Williams	70	0
N16	•	Wesleyan NYC	52	0
N20	•	at Crescent AC	18	0
N23	•	Harvard Spr	6	0
N28	•	Princeton NYC	0	10

1890 13-1-0

O1	•	Wesleyan	8	0
O4	•	Crescent AC Bkln	18	6
O8	•	at Wesleyan	34	0
O11	•	Lehigh	26	0
O15	•	Trinity	40	0
O18	•	Orange AC U	16	0
O22	•	Williams	36	0
O25	•	at Amherst	12	0
N1	•	Wesleyan	76	0
N4	•	Crescent AC Bkln	52	0
N8	•	Rutgers	70	0
N15	•	Pennsylvania	60	0
N22	•	Harvard Spr	6	12
N27	•	Princeton Bkln	32	0

1891 13-0-0

S30	•	Wesleyan	28	0
O3	•	Crescent AC Bkln	26	0
O7	•	at Trinity	36	0
O10	•	Williams U	46	0
O14	•	Springfield YMCA	28	0
O24	•	Orange AC U	36	0
O31	•	Lehigh	38	0
N3	•	Crescent AC Bkln	70	0
N7	•	Wesleyan	76	0
N11	•	Amherst	27	0
N14	•	Pennsylvania NYC	48	0
N21	•	Harvard Spr	10	0
N26	•	Princeton NYC	19	0

1892 13-0-0

O5	•	Wesleyan	6	0
O8	•	Crescent AC Bkln	28	0
O12	•	Williams	32	0
O15	•	Manhattan AC NYC	22	0
O19	•	Amherst	29	0
O22	•	Orange AC U	58	0
O26	•	at Springfield YMCA	50	0
O29	•	Tufts	44	0
N5	•	Wesleyan	72	0
N8	•	New York AC NYC	48	0
N12	•	Pennsylvania NYC	28	0
N19	•	Harvard Spr	6	0
N24	•	Princeton NYC	12	0

WILLIAM RHODES
1893-94 (.963) 26-1

1893 10-1-0

O4	•	Brown	18	0
O7	•	Crescent AC Bkln	16	0
O14	•	Dartmouth	28	0
O18	•	Amherst	46	0
O21	•	Orange AC U	50	0
O25	•	Williams	82	0
O28	•	at Army	28	0
N7	•	New York AC NYC	42	0
N11	•	Pennsylvania NYC	14	6
N25	•	Harvard Spr	6	0
N30	•	Princeton NYC	0	6

1894 16-0-0

S29	•	at Trinity	42	0
O3	•	Brown	28	0
O6	•	Crescent AC	10	0
O10	•	Williams	23	4
O13	•	Lehigh NYC	34	0
O17	•	Dartmouth Spr	34	0
O20	•	Orange AC U	24	0
O24	•	Boston AA	23	0
O27	•	at Army	12	5
O31	•	Volunteer AC	42	0
N3	•	at Brown	12	0
N7	•	Tufts	67	0
N10	•	Lehigh NYC	50	0
N14	•	Chicago AC	48	0
N24	•	Harvard Spr	12	4
D1	•	Princeton NYC	24	0

JOHN HARTWELL
1895 (.933) 13-0-2

1895 13-0-2

S28	•	at Trinity	8	0
O2	•	Brown	4	0
O5	•	at Union	26	0
O9	•	Amherst	36	0
O12	•	Crescent AC	8	2
O16	•	Dartmouth	26	0
O19	•	Orange AC U	24	12
O23	•	Williams	54	0
O26	=	Boston AC	0	0
O30	•	Dartmouth	32	0
N2	•	at Army	28	8
N6	•	Carlisle	18	0
N9	=	at Brown	6	6
N16	•	Orange AC U	26	0
N23	•	Princeton NYC	20	10

SAMUEL B. THORNE
1896 (.864) 13-1

1896 13-1-0

S26	•	at Trinity	6	0
S30	•	Amherst	12	0
O7	•	Brown	18	0
O10	•	Orange AC U	12	0
O14	•	Willliams	22	0
O17	•	Dartmouth Prov	42	0
O21	•	Wesleyan	16	0
O24	•	Carlisle U	12	6
O28	•	Elizabeth AC	12	6
O31	•	at Army	16	2
N3	•	Boston AA	10	0
N7	•	at Brown	18	6
N14	•	New Jersey AC	16	0
N21	•	Princeton NYC	6	24

F. BUTTERWORTH
1897-98 (.864) 18-2-2

1897 9-0-2

S29	•	at Trinity	10	0
O2	•	Wesleyan	30	0
O6	•	Amherst	18	0
O9	•	Williams	32	0
O16	•	at Newton AA	10	0
O20	•	Brown	18	14
O23	•	Carlisle NYC	24	9
O30	=	Army	6	6
N6	•	Chicago AC	16	6
N13	=	at Harvard	0	0
N20	•	Princeton	6	0

1898 9-2-0

S24	•	at Trinity	18	0
O1	•	Wesleyan	5	0
O5	•	Amherst	34	0
O8	•	Williams	23	0
O15	•	at Newton AA	6	0
O19	•	Brown	22	6
O22	•	Carlisle	18	5
O29	•	at Army	10	0
N5	•	Chicago AC	10	0
N12	•	at Princeton	0	6
N19	•	Harvard	0	17

JAMES O. RODGERS
1899 (.750) 7-2-1

1899 7-2-1

S30	•	Amherst	23	0
O4	•	Trinity	46	0
O7	•	Bates	28	0
O14	•	Dartmouth Ntn	12	0
O21	•	Wisconsin	6	0
O28	•	at Columbia	0	5
N4	•	Army	24	0
N11	•	Penn State	42	0
N18	=	at Harvard	0	0
N25	•	Princeton	10	11

THE SCHOOLS

MALCOLM McBRIDE
1900 (1.000) — 12-0

1900 — 12-0-0

Date		Opponent		
S29	•	Trinity	22	0
O3	•	Amherst	27	0
O6	•	Tufts	30	0
O10	•	Bates	50	0
O13	•	Dartmouth NTN	17	0
O17	•	Bowdoin	30	0
O20	•	Wesleyan	38	0
O27	•	at Columbia	12	5
N3	•	at Army	18	0
N10	•	Carlisle	35	0
N17	•	at Princeton	29	5
N24	•	Harvard	28	0

GEORGE STILLMAN
1901 (.885) — 11-1-1

1901 — 11-1-1

Date		Opponent		
S28	•	Trinity	23	0
O2	•	Amherst	6	0
O5	•	Tufts	29	5
O9	•	Wesleyan	24	0
O12	•	at Navy	24	0
O16	•	Bowdoin	45	0
O19	•	Penn State	22	0
O22	•	Bates	21	0
O26	•	Columbia	10	5
N2	=	at Army	5	5
N9	•	Orange AC	30	0
N16	•	Princeton	12	0
N23	•	at Harvard	0	22

JOSEPH SWAN
1902 (.958) — 11-0-1

1902 — 11-0-1

Date		Opponent		
S27	•	Trinity	40	0
O1	•	Tufts	34	6
O4	•	Amherst	23	0
O8	•	Wesleyan	35	0
O11	•	at Brown	10	0
O15	•	Vermont	32	0
O18	•	Penn State	11	0
O25	•	Syracuse	24	0
N1	=	at Army	6	6
N8	•	Bucknell	36	5
N15	•	at Princeton	12	5
N22	•	Harvard	23	0

G.B. CHADWICK
1903 (.917) — 11-1

1903 — 11-1-0

Date		Opponent		
S26	•	Trinity	35	0
S30	•	Tufts	19	0
O3	•	Vermont	46	0
O7	•	Wesleyan	33	0
O10	•	Springfield	22	0
O14	•	Holy Cross	36	10
O17	•	Penn State	27	0
O24	•	at Army	17	5
O31	•	Columbia	25	0
N7	•	Syracuse	30	0
N14	•	Princeton	6	11
N21	•	at Harvard	16	0

C.D. RAFFERTY
1904 (.909) — 10-1

1904 — 10-1-0

Date		Opponent		
S28	•	Wesleyan	22	0
O1	•	Trinity	42	0
O5	•	Holy Cross	23	0
O8	•	Penn State	24	0
O12	•	Springfield	6	0
O15	•	Syracuse	17	9
O22	•	at Army	6	11
O29	•	at Columbia	34	0
N5	•	Brown	22	0
N12	•	at Princeton	12	0
N19	•	Harvard	12	0

J.E. OWSLEY
1905 (1.000) — 10-0

1905 — 10-0-0

Date		Opponent		
O4	•	Wesleyan	27	0
O7	•	Syracuse	16	0
O11	•	Springfield	29	0
O14	•	Holy Cross	30	0
O21	•	Penn State	12	0
O28	•	Army	20	0
N4	•	at Columbia	53	0
N11	•	Brown	11	0
N18	•	Princeton	23	4
N25	•	at Harvard	6	0

FOSTER ROCKWELL
1906 (.950) — 9-0-1

1906 — 9-0-1

Date		Opponent		
O3	•	Wesleyan	21	0
O6	•	Syracuse	51	0
O10	•	Springfield	12	0
O13	•	Holy Cross	17	0
O20	•	Penn State	10	0
O27	•	Amherst	12	0
N3	•	at Army	10	6
N10	•	Brown	5	0
N17	=	at Princeton	0	0
N24	•	Harvard	6	0

WILLIAM KNOX
1907 (.950) — 9-0-1

1907 — 9-0-1

Date		Opponent		
O2	•	Wesleyan	25	0
O5	•	Syracuse	11	0
O9	•	Springfield	18	0
O12	•	Holy Cross	52	0
O19	•	at Army	0	0
O26	•	Villanova	45	0
N2	•	Wash. & Jeff.	11	0
N9	•	Brown	22	0
N16	•	Princeton	12	10
N23	•	at Harvard	12	0

L.H. BIGLOW
1908 (.883) — 7-1-1

1908 — 7-1-1

Date		Opponent		
S30	•	Wesleyan	16	0
O3	•	Syracuse	5	0
O10	•	Holy Cross	18	0
O17	•	at Army	6	0
O24	•	Wash. & Jeff.	38	0
O31	•	Massachusetts	49	0
N7	=	Brown	10	10
N14	•	at Princeton	11	6
N21	•	Harvard	0	4

HOWARD JONES
1909, '13 (.825) — 15-2-3

1909 — 10-0-0

Date		Opponent		
S29	•	Wesleyan	11	0
O2	•	Syracuse	15	0
O6	•	Holy Cross	12	0
O9	•	Springfield	36	0
O16	•	at Army	17	0
O23	•	Colgate	36	0
O30	•	Amherst	34	0
N6	•	Brown	23	0
N13	•	Princeton	17	0
N20	•	at Harvard	8	0

EDWARD COY
1910 (.700) — 6-2-2

1910 — 6-2-2

Date		Opponent		
S28	•	Wesleyan	22	0
O1	•	Syracuse	12	6
O5	•	Tufts	17	0
O8	•	Holy Cross	12	0
O15	•	at Army	3	9
O22	=	Vanderbilt	0	0
O29	•	Colgate	19	0
N5	•	Brown	0	21
N12	•	at Princeton	5	3
N19	=	Harvard	0	0

JOHN FIELD
1911 (.750) — 7-2-1

1911 — 7-2-1

Date		Opponent		
S27	•	Wesleyan	21	0
S30	•	Holy Cross	26	0
O7	•	Syracuse	12	0
O14	•	Virginia Tech	33	0
O21	•	at Army	0	6
O28	•	Colgate	23	0
N4	•	NYU	28	3
N11	•	Brown	15	0
N18	•	Princeton	3	6
N25	=	at Harvard	0	0

ARTHUR HOWE
1912 (.833) — 7-1-1

1912 — 7-1-1

Date		Opponent		
S25	•	Wesleyan	10	3
S28	•	Holy Cross	7	0
O5	•	Syracuse	21	0
O12	•	Lafayette	16	0
O19	•	at Army	6	0
O26	•	Wash. & Jeff.	13	3
N9	•	Brown	0	0
N16	=	at Princeton	6	6
N23	•	Harvard	0	20

HOWARD JONES

1913 — 5-2-3

Date		Opponent		
S24	•	Wesleyan	21	0
S27	•	Holy Cross	10	0
O4	=	Maine	0	0
O11	•	Lafayette	27	0
O18	•	Lehigh	37	0
O25	•	Wash. & Jeff.	0	0
N1	•	Colgate	6	16
N8	•	Brown	17	0
N15	•	Princeton	3	3
N22	•	at Harvard	5	15

FRANK HINKEY
1914-15 (.611) — 11-7

1914 — 7-2-0

Date		Opponent		
S26	•	Maine	20	0
O3	•	Virginia	21	0
O10	•	Lehigh	20	3
O17	•	Notre Dame	28	0
O24	•	Wash. & Jeff.	7	13
O31	•	Colgate	49	7
N7	•	Brown	14	6
N14	•	at Princeton	19	14
N21	•	Harvard	0	36

1915 — 4-5-0

Date		Opponent		
S25	•	Maine	37	0
O2		Virginia	0	10
O9		Lehigh	7	6
O16	•	Springfield	19	0
O23		Wash. & Jeff.	7	16
O30		Colgate	0	15
N6		Brown	0	3
N13	•	Princeton	13	7
N20	•	at Harvard	0	41

THOMAS A.D. JONES
1916-17, '20-27 (.759) — 60-15-4

1916 — 8-1-0

Date		Opponent		
S30	•	Carnegie Tech	25	0
O7	•	Virginia	61	3
O14	•	Lehigh	12	0
O20	•	Virginia Tech	19	0
O28	•	Wash. & Jeff.	36	14
N4	•	Colgate	7	3
N11	•	Brown	6	21
N18	•	at Princeton	10	0
N25	•	Harvard	6	3

1917 — 3-0-0

Date		Opponent		
O27	•	at Loomis Inst	7	0
N10	•	N.H. Naval Base	33	0
N17	•	Trinity	7	0

1918

NO TEAM WWI

ALBERT SHARPE
1919 (.625) — 5-3

1919 — 5-3-0

Date		Opponent		
O4	•	Springfield	20	0
O11	•	North Carolina	34	7
O18	•	Boston College	3	5
O25	•	Tufts	37	0
N1	•	Maryland	31	0
N8	•	Brown	14	0
N15	•	Princeton	6	13
N22	•	at Harvard	3	10

THOMAS A.D. JONES

1920 — 5-3-0

Date		Opponent		
O2	•	Carnegie Tech	44	0
O9	•	North Carolina	21	0
O16	•	Boston College	13	21
O23	•	West Virginia	24	0
O30	•	Colgate	21	7
N6	•	Brown	14	10
N13	•	at Princeton	0	20
N20	•	Harvard	0	9

1921 — 8-1-0

Date		Opponent		
S24	•	Bates	28	0
O1	•	Vermont	14	0
O8	•	North Carolina	34	0
O15	•	Williams	23	0
O22	•	Army	14	7
O29	•	Brown	45	7
N5	•	Maryland	28	0
N12	•	Princeton	13	7
N19	•	at Harvard	3	10

1922 — 6-3-1

Date		Opponent		
S23	•	Bates	48	0
S30	•	Carnegie Tech	13	0
O7	•	North Carolina	18	0
O14	•	Iowa	0	6
O21	•	Williams	38	0
O28	=	Army	7	7
N4	•	Brown	20	0
N11	•	Maryland	45	3
N18	•	at Princeton	0	3
N25	•	Harvard	3	10

1923 — 8-0-0

Date		Opponent		
O6	•	North Carolina	53	0
O13	•	Georgia	40	0
O20	•	Bucknell	29	14
O27	•	Brown	21	0
N3	•	Army	31	10
N10	•	Maryland	16	14
N17	•	Princeton	27	0
N24	•	at Harvard	13	0

1924 — 6-0-2

Date		Opponent		
O4	•	North Carolina	27	0
O11	•	Georgia	7	6
O18	=	Dartmouth	14	14
O25	•	Brown	13	3
N1	=	Army	7	7
N8	•	Maryland	47	0
N15	•	at Princeton	10	0
N22	•	Harvard	19	6

1925 — 5-2-1

Date		Opponent		
O3	•	Middlebury	53	0
O10	•	Georgia	35	7
O17	•	Pennsylvania	13	16
O24	•	at Brown	20	7
O31	•	Army	28	7
N7	•	Maryland	43	14
N14	•	Princeton	12	25
N21	=	at Harvard	0	0

1926 — 4-4-0

Date		Opponent		
O2	•	Boston U.	51	0
O9	•	Georgia	10	0
O16	•	Dartmouth	14	7
O23	•	Brown	0	7
O30	•	Army	0	33
N6	•	Maryland	0	15
N13	•	at Princeton	7	10
N20	•	Harvard	12	7

1927 — 7-1-0

Date		Opponent		
O1	•	Bowdoin	41	0
O8	•	Georgia	10	14
O15	•	Brown	19	0
O22	•	Army	10	6
O29	•	Dartmouth	19	0
N5	•	Maryland	30	6
N12	•	Princeton	14	6
N19	•	at Harvard	14	0

MARVIN STEVENS
1928-32 (.625) — 21-11-8

1928 — 4-4-0

Date		Opponent		
O6	•	Maine	27	0
O13	•	Georgia	21	6
O20	•	Brown	32	14
O27	•	Army	6	18
N3	•	Dartmouth	18	0
N10	•	Maryland	0	6
N17	•	at Princeton	2	12
N24	•	Harvard	0	17

THE SCHOOLS

1929 — 5-2-1

Date		Opponent		
O5	•	Vermont	89	0
O12		at Georgia	0	15
O19	•	Brown	14	6
O26	•	Army	21	13
N2	•	Dartmouth	16	12
N9	=	Maryland	13	13
N16	•	Princeton	13	0
N23		at Harvard	6	10

1930 — 5-2-2

Date		Opponent		
S27	•	Maine	38	0
O4	•	Maryland	40	13
O11		Georgia	14	18
O18	•	Brown	21	0
O25	=	Army	7	7
N1	=	Dartmouth	0	0
N8	•	Alfred	66	0
N15		at Princeton	10	7
N22		Harvard	0	13

1931 — 5-1-2

Date		Opponent		
O3	•	Maine	19	0
O10		Georgia	7	26
O17		at Chicago	27	0
O24	=	Army	6	6
O31	•	Dartmouth	33	33
N7	•	St. John's	52	0
N21		at Harvard	3	0
N28	•	Princeton	51	14

1932 — 2-2-3

Date		Opponent		
O1	=	Bates	0	0
O8	=	Chicago	7	7
O15		Brown	2	7
O22		Army	0	20
O26	•	Dartmouth	6	0
N12	=	at Princeton	7	7
N19	•	Harvard	19	0

REGINALD ROOT — 1933 (.500) — 4-4

1933 — 4-4-0

Date		Opponent		
O7	•	Maine	14	7
O14	•	Wash. & Lee	14	0
O21	•	Brown	14	6
O28	•	Army	0	21
N4	•	Dartmouth	14	13
N11		Georgia	0	7
N25		at Harvard	6	19
D2		Princeton	2	27

RAYMOND POND — 1934-40 (.544) — 30-25-2

1934 — 5-3-0

Date		Opponent		
O6		Columbia	6	12
O13	•	Pennsylvania	14	6
O20	•	Brown	37	0
O27		Army	12	20
N3	•	Dartmouth	7	2
N10		Georgia	7	14
N17		at Princeton	7	0
N24	•	Harvard	14	0

1935 — 6-3-0

Date		Opponent		
O5	•	New Hampshire	34	0
O12		at Pennsylvania	31	20
O19	•	Navy	7	6
O26		Army	8	14
N2		Dartmouth	6	14
N9	•	Brown	20	0
N16	•	Lafayette	55	0
N23		at Harvard	14	7
N30		Princeton	7	38

1936 — 7-1-0

Date		Opponent		
O3	•	Cornell	23	0
O10	•	Pennsylvania	7	0
O17	•	Navy BALT	12	7
O24	•	Rutgers	28	0
O31		Dartmouth	7	11
N7	•	Brown	14	6
N14		at Princeton	26	23
N21	•	Harvard	14	13

1937 — 6-1-1

Date		Opponent		
O2	•	Maine	26	0
O9	•	Pennsylvania	27	7
O16	•	Army	15	7
O23	•	Cornell	9	0
O30	=	Dartmouth	9	9
N6	•	Brown	19	0
N13	•	Princeton	26	0
N20		at Harvard	6	13

1938 — 2-6-0

Date		Opponent		
O1		Columbia	14	27
O8		at Pennsylvania	0	21
O15	•	Navy	9	7
O22		Michigan	13	15
O29		Dartmouth	6	24
N5	•	Brown	20	14
N12		at Princeton	7	20
N19		Harvard	0	7

1939 — 3-4-1

Date		Opponent		
O7	•	Columbia	10	7
O14		Pennsylvania	0	6
O21	•	Army	20	15
O28		at Michigan	7	27
N4		Dartmouth	0	33
N11	=	Brown	14	14
N18		Princeton	7	13
N25	•	at Harvard	20	7

1940 — 1-7-0

Date		Opponent		
O5		Virginia	14	19
O12		at Pennsylvania	7	50
O19	•	Dartmouth	13	7
O26		Navy	0	21
N2		Brown	2	6
N9		Cornell	0	21
N16		at Princeton	7	10
N23		Harvard	0	28

EMERSON NELSON — 1941 (.125) — 1-7

1941 — 1-7-0

Date		Opponent		
O4	•	Virginia	21	19
O11		Pennsylvania	13	28
O18		Army	7	20
O25		Dartmouth	0	7
N1		Brown	0	7
N8		at Cornell	7	21
N15		Princeton	6	20
N22		at Harvard	0	14

HOWARD ODELL — 1942-47 (.692) — 35-15-2

1942 — 5-3-0

Date		Opponent		
O3	•	Lehigh	33	6
O10		Pennsylvania	6	35
O17		Navy BALT	6	13
O24	•	Dartmouth	17	7
O31	•	Brown	27	0
N7		Cornell	7	13
N14	•	Princeton NYC	13	6
N21	•	Harvard	7	3

1943 — 4-5-0

Date		Opponent		
S11	•	Muhlenberg	13	6
S18		Rochester	12	14
S25	•	Coast Guard	20	12
O2		at Pennsylvania	7	41
O9	•	at Columbia	20	7
O23		Army	7	39
O30		Dartmouth	6	20
N6		Brown	20	21
N13	•	Princeton	27	6

1944 — 7-0-1

Date		Opponent		
S30	•	Coast Guard	7	3
O7	•	Cornell	16	7
O14	•	Columbia	27	10
O28	•	Rochester	32	0
N4	•	Dartmouth	6	0
N11	•	Brown	13	0
N18	•	North Carolina	13	6
N25	=	Virginia	6	6

1945 — 6-3-0

Date		Opponent		
S29	•	Tufts	27	7
O6		Holy Cross	0	21
O13		at Columbia	13	27
O27	•	Cornell	18	7
N3	•	Dartmouth	6	0
N10		Brown	7	20
N17	•	Coast Guard	41	6
N24	•	at Princeton	20	14
D1	•	Harvard	28	0

1946 — 7-1-1

Date		Opponent		
S28	•	Kings Point	33	0
O5	•	Colgate	27	6
O12	•	Columbia	20	28
O19	=	at Cornell	6	6
O26	•	Coast Guard	47	14
N2	•	Dartmouth	33	2
N9	•	Brown	49	0
N16	•	Princeton	30	2
N23	•	at Harvard	27	14

1947 — 6-3-0

Date		Opponent		
S27	•	Kings Point	34	13
O4	•	Cornell	14	0
O11	•	at Columbia	17	7
O18	•	Wisconsin	0	9
O25	•	Springfield	49	0
N1	•	Dartmouth	23	14
N8	•	Brown	14	20
N15	•	at Princeton	0	17
N22	•	Harvard	31	21

HERMAN HICKMAN — 1948-51 (.486) — 16-17-2

1948 — 4-5-0

Date		Opponent		
S25	•	Brown	28	13
O2	•	Connecticut	7	0
O9		Columbia	28	34
O16	•	at Wisconsin	17	7
O23		Vanderbilt	0	35
O30		Dartmouth	14	41
N6	•	Kings Point	52	0
N13		Princeton	14	20
N20		at Harvard	7	20

1949 — 4-4-0

Date		Opponent		
S24	•	Connecticut	26	0
O8	•	at Columbia	33	7
O15		Cornell	14	48
O22	•	Holy Cross	14	7
O29		Dartmouth	13	34
N5		Brown	0	14
N12	•	at Princeton	13	21
N19	•	Harvard	29	6

1950 — 6-3-0

Date		Opponent		
S23	•	Connecticut	25	0
S30	•	Brown	36	12
O7	•	Fordham	21	14
O14	•	Columbia	20	14
O21		at Cornell	0	7
O28	•	Holy Cross	14	13
N4		Dartmouth	0	7
N18		Princeton	12	47
N25	•	at Harvard	14	6

1951 — 2-5-2

Date		Opponent		
S22	•	Bates	48	0
S29	=	Navy	7	7
O6		Brown	13	14
O13		at Columbia	0	14
O20		Cornell	0	27
O27	•	Colgate	27	7
N3		Dartmouth	10	14
N17		at Princeton	0	27
N24	•	Harvard	21	21

JORDAN OLIVAR — 1952-62 (.646) — 61-32-6

1952 — 7-2-0

Date		Opponent		
S20	•	Connecticut	34	13
S27		Navy BALT	0	31
O4	•	Brown	28	0
O11	•	Columbia	35	28
O18	•	Cornell	13	0
O25	•	Lafayette	47	0
N1	•	Dartmouth	21	7
N15		Princeton	21	27
N22	•	at Harvard	41	14

1953 — 5-2-2

Date		Opponent		
S26	•	Connecticut	32	0
O3	•	Brown	13	0
O10	•	Columbia	13	7
O17	=	at Cornell	0	0
O24	=	Colgate	7	7
O31		Dartmouth	0	32
N7	•	Temple	32	6
N14	•	at Princeton	26	24
N21		Harvard	0	13

1954 — 5-3-1

Date		Opponent		
S25	•	Connecticut	27	0
O2	•	Brown	26	24
O9		at Columbia	13	7
O16	•	Cornell	47	21
O23	=	Colgate	13	13
O30	•	Dartmouth	13	7
N6		Army	7	48
N13	•	Princeton	14	21
N20		at Harvard	9	13

1955 — 7-2-0

Date		Opponent		
S24	•	Connecticut	14	0
O1	•	Brown	27	20
O8	•	Columbia	46	14
O15	•	Cornell	34	6
O22		Colgate	0	7
O29	•	Dartmouth	20	0
N5	•	Army	14	12
N12		at Princeton	0	13
N19	•	Harvard	21	7

1956-PRESENT — IVY LEAGUE

1956 — 8-1-0 (7-0-0)

Date		Opponent		
S29	•	Connecticut	19	14
O6	•	Brown	20	2
O13	•	at Columbia	33	19
O20	•	Cornell	25	7
O27		Colgate	6	14
N3	•	Dartmouth	19	0
N10	•	Pennsylvania	40	7
N17	•	Princeton	42	20
N24	•	at Harvard	42	14

1957 — 6-2-1 (4-2-1)

Date		Opponent		
S28	•	Connecticut	27	0
O5		Brown	20	21
O12		Columbia	19	0
O19		at Cornell	18	7
O26	•	Colgate	20	0
N2	=	Dartmouth	14	14
N9		at Pennsylvania	20	33
N16	•	at Princeton	20	13
N23	•	Harvard	54	0

1958 — 2-7-0 (0-7-0)

Date		Opponent		
S27	•	Connecticut	8	6
O4		at Brown	29	35
O11		at Columbia	0	13
O18		Cornell	7	12
O25	•	Colgate	14	7
N1		Dartmouth	14	22
N8		Pennsylvania	6	30
N15		Princeton	14	50
N22		at Harvard	0	28

1959 — 6-3-0 (4-3-0)

Date		Opponent		
S26	•	Connecticut	20	0
O3	•	Brown	17	0
O10		Columbia	14	0
O17	•	at Cornell	23	0
O24		Colgate	21	0
O31		Dartmouth	8	12
N7		at Pennsylvania	12	28
N14		at Princeton	38	20
N21		Harvard	6	35

1960 — 9-0-0 (7-0-0)

Date		Opponent		
S24	•	Connecticut	11	8
O1		Brown	9	0
O8	•	Columbia	30	8
O15	•	Cornell	22	6
O22	•	Colgate	36	14
O29	•	Dartmouth	29	0
N5	•	Pennsylvania	34	9
N12	•	Princeton	43	22
N19	•	at Harvard	39	6

1961 — 4-5-0 (3-4-0)

Date		Opponent		
S30	•	Connecticut	18	0
O7	•	Brown	14	3
O14		Columbia	0	11
O21	•	at Cornell	12	0
O28		Colgate	8	14
N4		Dartmouth	8	24
N11	•	at Pennsylvania	23	0
N18	•	at Princeton	16	26
N25		Harvard	0	27

THE SCHOOLS

1962   2-5-2 (1-5-1)
S29	●	Connecticut	18	14
O6	=	at Brown	6	6
O13		at Columbia	10	14
O20	●	Cornell	26	8
O27	●	Colgate	14	14
N3		Dartmouth	0	9
N10		Pennsylvania	12	15
N17	●	Princeton	10	14
N24		at Harvard	6	14

JOHN PONT
1963-64 (.694)   12-5-1

1963   6-3-0 (4-3-0)
S28	●	Connecticut	3	0
O5		Brown	7	12
O12	●	Columbia	19	7
O19		at Cornell	10	13
O26	●	Colgate	31	0
N2	●	Dartmouth	10	6
N9	●	at Pennsylvania	28	7
N16	●	at Princeton	7	27
N30	●	Harvard	20	6

1964   6-2-1 (4-2-1)
S26	●	Connecticut	21	6
O3	●	Lehigh	54	0
O10	●	Brown	15	7
O17	=	Columbia	9	9
O24	●	at Cornell	23	21
O31	●	Dartmouth	24	15
N7	●	at Pennsylvania	21	9
N14		Princeton	14	35
N21		at Harvard	14	18

CARMEN COZZA
1965-96 (.599)   179-119-5

1965   3-6-0 (3-4-0)
S25		Connecticut	6	13
O2		Colgate	0	7
O9	●	at Brown	3	0
O16		at Columbia	7	21
O23	●	Cornell	24	14
O30		Dartmouth	17	20
N6	●	Pennsylvania	21	19
N13		at Princeton	6	31
N20		Harvard	0	13

1966   4-5-0 (3-4-0)
S24	●	Connecticut	16	0
O1		Rutgers	14	17
O8	●	Brown	24	0
O15	●	Columbia	44	21
O22		at Cornell	14	16
O29		Dartmouth	13	28
N5	●	at Pennsylvania	17	14
N12		Princeton	7	13
N19		at Harvard	0	17

1967   8-1-0 (7-0-0)
S30		Holy Cross	14	26
O7	●	Connecticut	14	6
O14	●	at Brown	35	0
O21	●	at Columbia	21	7
O28	●	Cornell	41	7
N4	●	Dartmouth	56	15
N11	●	Pennsylvania	44	22
N18	●	at Princeton	29	7
N25	●	Harvard	24	20

1968   8-0-1 (6-0-1)
S28	●	Connecticut	31	14
O5	●	Colgate	49	14
O12	●	Brown	35	13
O19	●	Columbia	29	7
O26	●	at Cornell	25	13
N2	●	Dartmouth	47	27
N9	●	at Pennsylvania	30	13
N16	●	Princeton	42	17
N23	=	at Harvard	29	29

1969   7-2-0 (6-1-0)
S27		Connecticut	15	19
O4	●	Colgate	40	21
O11	●	at Brown	27	13
O18	●	at Columbia	41	6
O25	●	Cornell	17	0
N1		Dartmouth	21	42
N8	●	Pennsylvania	21	3
N15	●	at Princeton	17	14
N22	●	Harvard	7	0

1970   7-2-0 (5-2-0)
S26	●	Connecticut	10	0
O3		Colgate	39	7
O10		Brown	28	0
O17		Columbia	32	15
O24	●	at Cornell	38	7
O31		Dartmouth	0	10
N7	●	at Pennsylvania	32	22
N14	●	Princeton	27	22
N21		at Harvard	12	14

1971   4-5-0 (3-4-0)
S25	●	Connecticut	23	0
O2		Colgate	21	28
O9	●	at Brown	17	10
O16		at Columbia	14	15
O23		Cornell	10	31
O30		at Dartmouth	15	17
N6	●	Pennsylvania	24	14
N13	●	at Princeton	10	6
N20		Harvard	16	35

1972   7-2-0 (5-2-0)
S30	●	Connecticut	28	7
O7		Colgate	27	7
O14	●	Brown	53	19
O21	●	Columbia	28	14
O28		at Cornell	13	24
N4	●	Dartmouth	45	14
N11	●	at Pennsylvania	30	48
N18	●	Princeton	31	7
N25	●	at Harvard	28	17

1973   6-3-0 (5-2-0)
S29		Connecticut	13	27
O6	●	Colgate	24	18
O13		at Brown	25	34
O20	●	at Columbia	29	0
O27	●	Cornell	20	3
N3		at Dartmouth	13	24
N10	●	Pennsylvania	24	21
N17	●	at Princeton	30	13
N24	●	Harvard	35	0

1974   8-1-0 (6-1-0)
S28	●	Connecticut	20	7
O5	●	Colgate	30	7
O12	●	Brown	24	0
O19	●	Columbia	42	2
O26	●	at Cornell	27	3
N2	●	Dartmouth	14	9
N9	●	at Pennsylvania	37	12
N16	●	Princeton	19	6
N23		at Harvard	16	21

1975   7-2-0 (5-2-0)
S27	●	Connecticut	35	14
O4	●	Colgate	24	10
O11		at Brown	12	27
O18	●	at Columbia	34	7
O25	●	Cornell	20	14
N1	●	Dartmouth	16	14
N8	●	Pennsylvania	24	14
N15	●	at Princeton	24	13
N22		Harvard	7	10

1976   8-1-0 (6-1-0)
S18		at Brown	6	14
S25	●	Connecticut	21	10
O2	●	Lehigh	21	6
O9	●	Dartmouth	18	14
O16	●	Columbia	37	6
O23	●	at Pennsylvania	21	7
O30		Cornell	14	6
N6	●	Princeton	39	7
N13	●	at Harvard	21	7

1977   7-2-0 (6-1-0)
S17	●	Brown	10	9
S24	●	Connecticut	23	12
O1		Miami, Ohio	14	28
O8		Dartmouth	0	3
O15	●	at Columbia	42	20
O22	●	Pennsylvania	27	21
O29	●	at Cornell	28	0
N5	●	at Princeton	44	8
N12	●	Harvard	24	7

1978   5-2-2 (4-1-2)
S23	●	at Brown	21	0
S30	●	Connecticut	21	7
O7		Rutgers	27	28
O14		at Dartmouth	3	10
O21	=	Columbia	3	3
O28	=	at Pennsylvania	17	17
N4	●	Cornell	42	14
N11	●	Princeton	23	7
N18	●	at Harvard	35	28

1979   8-1-0 (6-1-0)
S22	●	Brown	13	12
S29	●	Connecticut	24	17
O6	●	Colgate	27	0
O13		Dartmouth	3	0
O20	●	at Columbia	37	7
O27	●	Pennsylvania	24	6
N3	●	at Cornell	23	20
N10	●	at Princeton	35	10
N17		Harvard	7	22

1980   8-2-0 (6-1-0)
S20	●	at Brown	45	17
S27	●	Connecticut	20	10
O4	●	Air Force	17	16
O11		at Boston College	9	27
O18	●	Columbia	30	10
O25	●	at Pennsylvania	8	0
N1	●	at Dartmouth	35	7
N8		Cornell	6	24
N15	●	Princeton	25	13
N22	●	at Harvard	14	0

1981   9-1-0 (6-1-0)
S19	●	Brown	28	7
S26	●	Connecticut	27	18
O3	●	Navy	23	19
O10	●	at Holy Cross	29	28
O17	●	at Columbia	48	17
O24	●	Pennsylvania	24	3
O31	●	Dartmouth	24	3
N7	●	at Cornell	23	17
N14	●	at Princeton	31	35
N21	●	Harvard	28	0

1982   4-6-0 (3-4-0)
S18	●	at Brown	21	28
S25	●	Connecticut	7	17
O2		Holy Cross	6	10
O9	●	Boston U.	27	24
O16	●	Columbia	36	10
O23	●	at Pennsylvania	14	27
O30	●	at Dartmouth	22	21
N6		Cornell	20	26
N13	●	Princeton	37	19
N20		at Harvard	7	45

1983   1-9-0 (1-6-0)
S17		Brown	24	26
S24		Connecticut	12	38
O1		William & Mary *Non*	14	26
O8		Boston College	7	42
O15		Columbia	18	21
O22		Pennsylvania	0	17
O29		Dartmouth	21	24
N5		at Cornell	7	41
N12		at Princeton	28	21
N19		Harvard	7	16

1984   6-3-0 (5-2-0)
S22		at Brown	14	27
S29		Connecticut	0	20
O6	●	Morgan St.	41	0
O13	●	Dartmouth	28	18
O20	●	Columbia	28	21
O27	●	at Pennsylvania	21	34
N3	●	Cornell	21	14
N10	●	Princeton	27	24
N17	●	at Harvard	30	27

1985   4-4-1 (3-3-1)
S21	●	Brown	10	9
O5		at Army	16	59
O12	●	Holy Cross	19	15
O19	●	at Columbia	28	12
O26	●	Pennsylvania	7	23
N2	=	at Dartmouth	17	17
N9		Cornell	14	20
N16	●	at Princeton	12	21
N23	●	Harvard	17	6

1986   3-7-0 (2-5-0)
S20		at Brown	7	21
S27	●	Connecticut	12	17
O4		Army	24	41
O11	●	Colgate	28	23
O18	●	Columbia	47	0
O25		at Pennsylvania	6	24
N1	●	Dartmouth	13	39
N8		at Cornell	0	15
N15	●	Princeton	14	13
N22		at Harvard	17	24

1987   7-3-0 (5-2-0)
S19		Brown	7	17
S26	●	Connecticut	30	27
O3		at Hawaii	10	62
O10	●	William & Mary	40	34
O17	●	at Columbia	27	13
O24	●	Pennsylvania	28	22
O31	●	at Dartmouth	17	7
N7	●	Cornell	28	9
N14	●	at Princeton	34	19
N21		Harvard	10	14

1988   3-6-1 (3-4-0)
S17	=	at Brown	24	24
S24	●	Connecticut	0	41
O1		at Navy	7	41
O8		Army	18	33
O15	●	Columbia	24	10
O22		at Pennsylvania	3	10
O29	●	Dartmouth	22	13
N5		Cornell	0	26
N12		Princeton	7	24
N19	●	at Harvard	26	17

1989   8-2-0 (6-1-0)
S16	●	Brown	12	3
S23	●	Lehigh	33	17
S30	●	Connecticut	20	31
O7	●	Colgate	36	15
O14	●	at Dartmouth	24	19
O21	●	at Columbia	23	0
O28	●	Pennsylvania	23	22
N4	●	Cornell	34	19
N11	●	at Princeton	14	7
N18	●	Harvard	20	37

1990   6-4-0 (5-2-0)
S15	●	at Brown	27	21
S22	●	Lafayette	18	17
S29	●	Connecticut	7	44
O6	●	Colgate	7	30
O13		at Dartmouth	17	27
O20	●	Columbia	31	7
O27	●	at Pennsylvania	27	10
N3	●	Cornell	31	41
N10	●	Princeton	34	7
N17	●	at Harvard	34	19

1991   6-4-0 (4-3-0)
S21	●	Brown	36	20
S28	●	at Lafayette	24	14
O5		Connecticut	20	34
O12	●	at Colgate	25	7
O19		Dartmouth	24	28
O26	●	at Columbia	36	9
N2	●	Pennsylvania	31	12
N9		at Cornell	6	31
N16	●	at Princeton	16	22
N23	●	Harvard	23	13

1992   4-6-0 (2-5-0)
S19	●	at Brown	22	17
S28	●	Holy Cross	7	3
O3		at Connecticut	20	40
O10	●	Fordham	31	12
O17		at Dartmouth	27	39
O24	●	Columbia	23	0
O31	●	at Pennsylvania	10	13
N7		Cornell	14	35
N14		Princeton	7	36
N21		at Harvard	0	14

1993   3-7-0 (2-5-0)
S18		Brown	3	12
S25	●	Connecticut	14	25
O2		at Central Florida	28	42
O9	●	at Holy Cross	31	27
O16		Dartmouth	14	31
O23	●	at Columbia	35	28
O30		Pennsylvania	7	48
N6		at Cornell	0	21
N13		at Princeton	7	28
N20	●	Harvard	33	31

1994   5-5-0 (3-4-0)
S17	●	at Brown	27	16
S24	●	Holy Cross	47	22
O1	●	Connecticut	28	17
O8		Lehigh	32	36
O15		at Dartmouth	13	14
O22		Columbia	9	30
O29	●	at Pennsylvania	6	14
N5	●	Cornell	24	14
N12		Princeton	6	19
N19	●	at Harvard	32	13

1995		3-7-0 (2-5-0)	
S16 •	Brown	42	38
S23	at Lehigh	10	21
S30	Connecticut	20	39
O7 •	at Holy Cross	28	17
O14	Dartmouth	7	22
O21	at Columbia	7	21
O28	Pennsylvania	6	16
N4	at Cornell	10	38
N11 •	at Princeton	21	13
N18	Harvard	21	22

1996		2-8 (1-6)	
S21 •	at Brown	30	0
S28	Connecticut	6	42
O5	at Army	13	39
O12 •	Bucknell	23	21
O19	at Dartmouth	6	40
O26	Columbia	10	13
N2	at Pennsylvania	3	20
N9	Cornell	20	28
N16	Princeton	13	17
N23	at Harvard	21	26

JACK SIEDLECKI
1997-Present (.544)   43-36

1997		1-9 (0-7)	
S20	Brown	14	52
S27	Connecticut	0	28
O3 •	Valparaiso CHI	34	14
O11	Bucknell	24	25
O18	Dartmouth	7	21
O25	at Columbia	10	21
N1	Pennsylvania	7	26 †
N8	at Cornell	10	37
N15	Princeton ERut	0	9
N22	Harvard	7	17

1998		6-4 (5-2)	
S19	at Brown	30	28
S26	Connecticut	21	63
O3	Colgate	17	35
O10 •	Holy Cross	15	7
O17	at Dartmouth	19	22
O24	Columbia	37	14
O31	at Pennsylvania	21	34
N7 •	Cornell	28	21
N14 •	Princeton	31	28
N21	at Harvard	9	7

1999		9-1 (6-1)	
S18	Brown	24	25
S25 •	Valparaiso	48	2
O2 •	at San Diego	17	6
O9 •	at Holy Cross	34	14
O16 •	Dartmouth	44	3
O23	at Columbia	41	29
O30 •	Pennsylvania	23	19
N6 •	at Cornell	37	20
N13 •	at Princeton	23	21
N20 •	Harvard	24	21

2000		7-3 (4-3)	
S16 •	Dayton	42	6
S23	at Cornell	23	24
S30 •	Holy Cross	33	27
O7 •	at Dartmouth	24	14
O14 •	at Fordham	24	17
O21 •	Pennsylvania	27	24
O28 •	Columbia	41	0
N4	at Brown	14	28
N11	Princeton	14	19
N18 •	at Harvard	34	24

2001		3-6 (1-6)	
S22 •	Cornell	40	13
S29 •	at Holy Cross	23	22
O7	Dartmouth	27	32
O13 •	Fordham	36	27
O20	at Pennsylvania	3	21
O27	at Columbia	14	28
N3	Brown	34	37
N10	at Princeton	14	34
N17	Harvard	23	35

2002		6-4 (4-3)	
S21 •	San Diego	49	14
S28 •	at Cornell	50	23
O5 •	Holy Cross	28	19
O12	at Dartmouth	17	20
O19	at Lehigh	7	14
O26	Pennsylvania	20	41
N2 •	Columbia	35	7
N9 •	at Brown	31	27
N16 •	Princeton	7	3
N23	at Harvard	13	20

2003		6-4 (4-3)	
S20 •	Towson	62	28
S27 •	Cornell	21	7
O4	at Holy Cross	41	16
O11 •	Dartmouth	40	17
O18	at Colgate	40	52
O25	at Pennsylvania	31	34
N1 •	at Columbia	29	14
N8	Brown	44	55
N15 •	at Princeton	27	24
N22	Harvard	19	37

2004		5-5 (3-4)	
S18	at Dayton	24	17
S25	at Cornell	7	19
O2	Colgate	31	28
O9 •	at Dartmouth	24	14
O16	Lehigh	24	30
O23	Pennsylvania	7	17
O30 •	Columbia	21	1
N6	at Brown	17	24
N13	Princeton	21	9
N20	at Harvard	3	35

THE SCHOOLS

Neutral Site key: *U* Unknown, Unknown / *SPR* Springfield, MA / *PROV* Providence, RI / *NTN* Newton, MA / *BALT* Baltimore, MD / *HOB* Hoboken, NJ / *ERUT* East Rutherford, NJ / *NYC* New York, NY / *BKLN* Brooklyn, NY / *BOS* Boston, MA / *BRNX* Bronx, NY / *NOR* Norfolk, VA / *CHI* Chicago, IL / *HART* Hartford, CT

ƒ Forfeit † Game Later Forfieted # Disputed Victor * Disputed Score || Designated Conference Game 2 Counted Twice in Conference Standings

YALE ANNUAL STATISTICAL LEADERS

YR	RUSHING	YDS	ATT	AVG	PASSING	ATT	CMP	PCT	YDS	RECEIVING	REC	YDS	AVG
1963	Chuck Mercein	422	88	4.8	Brian Rapp	83	36	.43	477	Steve Lawrence	10	109	10.9
1964	Chuck Mercein	755	141	5.4	Ed McCarthy	132	61	.46	908	Bob Kenney	19	275	14.5
1965	Don Barrows	330	106	3.1	Watts Humphrey	118	49	.42	576	Jim Groninger	23	235	10.2
1966	Don Barrows	394	110	3.6	Pete Doherty	192	90	.47	978	Bob Kenney	37	414	11.2
1967	Calvin Hill	463	102	4.5	Brian Dowling	98	44	.45	684	Bruce Weinstein	16	318	19.9
1968	Calvin Hill	680	138	4.9	Brian Dowling	160	92	.58	1,554	Del Marting	28	428	15.3
1969	Don Martin	518	148	3.5	Joe Massey	195	99	.51	1,280	Rich Maher	30	363	12.1
1970	Dick Jauron	962	182	5.3	Joe Massey	120	61	.51	889	Rich Maher	16	247	15.4
1971	Dick Jauron	930	173	5.4	Roly Purrington	76	32	.42	353	Rich Maher	19	304	16.0
1972	Dick Jauron	1,055	160	6.6	Roly Purrington	78	36	.46	439	Paul Sortal	15	198	13.2
1973	Rudy Green	793	161	4.9	Tom Doyle	84	38	.45	449	Bob Fernandez	23	261	11.3
1974	Rudy Green	759	142	5.3	Tom Doyle	97	46	.47	712	Gary Fencik	32	491	15.3
1975	Don Gesicki	873	190	4.6	Stone Phillips	129	59	.46	969	Gary Fencik	42	729	17.4
1976	John Pagliaro	1,023	179	5.7	Stone Phillips	63	31	.49	531	John Spagnola	12	238	19.8
1977	John Pagliaro	1,159	239	4.8	Bob Rizzo	113	61	.54	979	John Spagnola	35	593	16.9
1978	Ken Hill	910	183	5.0	Pat O'Brien	153	75	.49	1,242	John Spagnola	41	723	17.6
1979	Ken Hill	669	167	4.0	John Rogan	96	40	.42	686	Dan Stratton	32	629	19.7
1980	Rich Diana	1,074	229	4.7	John Rogan	117	55	.47	891	Curt Grieve	32	580	18.1
1981	Rich Diana	1,442	293	4.9	John Rogan	192	95	.49	1,267	Curt Grieve	51	791	15.5
1982	Paul Andrie	976	231	4.2	Joe Dufek	215	112	.52	1,284	Rick Crews	36	401	11.1
1983	Paul Andrie	717	174	4.1	Mike Curtin	136	65	.48	837	Kevin Moriarty	27	478	17.7
1984	Ted Macauley	454	105	4.3	Mike Curtin	121	60	.50	718	Mike Luzzi	19	244	12.8
1985	Ted Macauley	550	157	3.5	Mike Curtin	169	82	.49	1,160	Dean Athanasia	31	355	11.5
1986	Kevin Brice	529	103	5.1	Kelly Ryan	286	138	.48	1,739	Dean Athanasia	40	434	10.9
1987	Mike Stewart	954	210	4.5	Kelly Ryan	282	170	.60	2,110	Tom Szuba	44	582	13.2
1988	Buddy Zachery	820	148	5.5	Mark Brubaker	111	51	.46	564	Kevin Callahan	16	165	10.3
1989	Darin Kehler	903	210	4.3	Darin Kehler	118	59	.50	870	Chris Kouri	19	157	8.3
1990	Kevin Callahan	546	122	4.5	Darin Kehler	111	55	.50	764	Kevin Callahan	17	183	10.8
1991	Chris Kouri	1,101	209	5.3	Nick Crawford	84	34	.40	672	Ya-Sin Shabazz	10	175	17.5
1992	Keith Price	1,141	245	4.7	Steve Mills	118	61	.52	863	Keith Price	16	151	9.4
1993	Bob Nelson	544	162	3.4	Steve Mills	237	132	.56	1,894	Dave Iwan	46	873	19.0
1994	Bob Nelson	717	138	5.2	Chris Hetherington	167	86	.51	1,119	Dan Iwan	28	452	16.1
1995	Kena Heffernan	652	161	4.0	Chris Hetherington	178	94	.53	1,169	Jon Aram	40	590	14.8
1996	Jabbar Craigwell	456	130	3.5	Blake Kendall	148	58	.39	766	Clint Rodriguez	34	707	20.8
1997	Jake Fuller	484	125	3.9	Joe Walland	167	70	.42	767	Jake Borden	25	379	15.2
1998	Rashad Bartholomew	941	213	4.4	Joe Walland	318	179	.56	1,858	Ken Marschner	36	389	10.8
1999	Rashad Bartholomew	841	214	3.9	Joe Walland	302	181	.60	2,207	Eric Johnson	67	858	12.8
2000	Rashad Bartholomew	1,232	216	5.7	Peter Lee	310	192	.62	2,207	Eric Johnson	86	1,007	11.7
2001	T.J. Hyland	433	86	5.0	Peter Lee	236	123	.52	1,357	Billy Brown	71	946	13.3
2002	Robert Carr	1,083	236	4.6	Jeff Mroz	244	135	.55	1,731	Ralph Plumb	55	592	10.8
2003	Robert Carr	800	170	4.7	Alvin Cowan	381	227	.60	2,994	Nate Lawrie	72	810	11.2
2004	Robert Carr	1,185	252	4.7	Alvin Cowan	325	181	.56	2,140	Ralph Plumb	79	939	11.9

Receiving leaders by receptions

The Pride and the Passion

The Long, Hard Evolution of Black College Football

BY MICHAEL HURD

O N A SUNNY TALLAHASSEE AFTERNOON IN THE EARLY 1960s, before his Florida A&M Rattlers took the practice field, Jake Gaither called his coaching staff over to the blocking sled he was standing on to share his vision of what integration would mean for black colleges. A former preacher's son, Gaither gave what amounted to a sermon that day, though his tone was closer to a eulogy.

Coach Gaither, who was born in Dayton, Tenn., site of the famous Scopes monkey trial, explained to his assistants that the evolution of American society was about to steamroll black college football as they knew it. "He said, 'You know, integration is going to be a good thing,' " one of his assistants, Robert Mungen, recalled, " 'but the ones that are going to be hurt are the black schools.' I couldn't understand what he was talking about. I thought he was just being old and fogyish. But it became a reality. Coach had been right, but he was that kind of way; he could foresee things, like Nostradamus. Most of our players came from black high schools in the state. We had a lot of players from Miami, but all that ceased with integration. As soon as integration came in, the [white] schools saw the contributions that black athletes could make at their schools."

Many white Southern coaches, of course, had known for years what black athletes could do for their programs, but there was no way before the '60s that a black man would suit up for Louisiana State, Ole Miss, Georgia or Florida State. And despite rumblings for most of the decade, it really wasn't until 1970, after Sam Cunningham, a black tailback for USC, rushed for 135 yards and scored two touchdowns in the Trojans' 41-21 win over Alabama in Birmingham, that the most tangible changes began to take effect. Bear Bryant had already signed running back Wilbur Jackson as the school's first black football scholarship player the previous spring. Southern Cal's rout of Alabama ensured that Jackson would be the first of many.

Once the floodgates opened, recruiters were flowing into black neighborhoods with scholarship papers in hand and grand promises of stardom. Inevitably, white and black coaches crossed each other's paths and the recruiting games were on. Gaither often told a story about pulling up to a player's home

just as Bryant was walking out. The two old friends greeted each other and talked for a bit, then Gaither went into the house and introduced himself. "I'm Jake Gaither," he announced. The player's mother looked at him and said, bewildered, "You can't be Jake Gaither. Jake Gaither just left!"

Soon enough, black coaches and colleges had trouble getting access to blue-chip recruits who only had eyes for the white schools and their national television exposure, huge stadiums, state-of-the-art athletic facilities, multimillion-dollar budgets and wealthy alumni. Black college programs would never be able to compete with any of that.

"They used to say I had a farm system, and I told them they were right," Gaither would recount years later. "My boys did come off the farm. Right here under their noses was the greatest talent in the world, and they didn't want it. But, now you can't turn around without a scout from every white school down here beating the bushes for black [high school] players."

Gaither, Eddie Robinson at Grambling, John Merritt at Tennessee State, Billy Nicks at Prairie View, Earl Banks at Morgan State and their peers had built reputations on the talents of homegrown kids fed to them by their former players, many of whom were now high school coaches themselves. These were solid-gold pipelines that produced some of the best talent in college football history. All told, they produced 17 College Football Hall of Fame members and 17 Pro Football Hall of Fame members, including Walter Payton (Jackson State), the NFL's former career rushing leader; Jerry Rice (Mississippi Valley State), the NFL's all-time leading receiver; and the league's first modern-day black head coach, Art Shell (Maryland Eastern Shore). But soon that kind of talent stopped coming around. Robinson continued to charm some of the top black players in Louisiana into coming to Grambling well into the late '70s, but eventually even he couldn't recruit successfully against Louisiana State and the other Southeastern and Southwest Conference schools.

***

In many ways, the decline of black college football programs mirrored their awkward beginnings. During the close of the 19th century, which saw the advent of college football itself, many black college presidents were reluctant to organize teams at all. What little money the schools had would be better spent, they reasoned, on infrastructure, books, lab equipment, teacher salaries. Why budget for games? Some of the schools did have intramural teams, but it was not until the Christmas season of 1892 that black colleges finally began intercollegiate play. On a

snowy afternoon in Salisbury, N.C., Livingstone hosted Biddle University from nearby Charlotte. The crowd that watched Biddle win that day 4-0 was mostly made up of Livingstone students who could not afford to go home for Christmas break, and they were likely unaware of the historical significance of what they were witnessing.

It was not until after the turn of the century, as the number of black colleges soared, that more schools began to field teams of "volunteer" students, coached by men who had learned the game while attending Eastern schools. Collectively, the men who ran these early programs— "missionary" coaches—were one or two generations removed from slavery and were primarily classroom teachers; they coached as an unpaid side job. Samuel Howard Archer, for example, had played at Colgate, graduating in 1902, then went to Morehouse College in Atlanta, where he guided undefeated teams from 1905 through 1908. Illustrating the importance of teaching duties, Archer did not coach for another seven years because of his academic responsibilities.

Most of the schools held to their conflicted attitude about playing football, though Howard, Tuskegee, Lincoln (Pa.), and Morgan State were already building strong programs. By the 1920s, Cleve Abbott's Tuskegee teams dominated black college football, raising the level of play along the way. Abbott had been a center on the Dakota State College (S.D.) football team and the first black to captain a team at a white institution. At Tuskegee, he became the first black coach to win 200 games (202–95–27), building a dynasty around All-America running back Ben Stevenson, one of the most versatile players in college football history. Stevenson was hailed by many as the first black college superstar and at least the equal in talent to Illinois great Red Grange.

The '20s also brought a legitimacy to black college football, as sportswriters for the *Pittsburgh Courier*, a nationally distributed publication for the black community, collaborated with black college coaches—and later, black NFL scouts—to begin selecting annual black college All-America teams, as well as an annual black college national champion. The first black college national champions were named in 1920, when Howard (7–0) shared the honor with Talladega (Ala.) College (5–0–1).

The '20s belonged to Abbott, Stevenson and the rest of the

Long before Bill Walsh was anointed a genius, Jake Gaither was considered the finest offensive mind in college football.

Tuskegee Tigers, who won or shared six of the first 11 national titles. Their record in those years—1924-27, 1929 and 1930—was a phenomenal 56–0–4, but only in 1929 and 1930 did they win the crown outright.

The next decade would see an influx of great coaches, starting with Eddie Hurt at Morgan State. During one stretch of Hurt's 31-year tenure, his teams had six consecutive undefeated seasons. A former All-America receiver at Howard, Hurt was the first coach to use a four-man defensive front, devising the scheme in 1937. His career record was 175–52–18, including a 1943 team that was undefeated, untied and unscored upon.

Earl "Papa Bear" Banks, who followed, revered Hurt and thought the great coach's stellar record could never be topped. He was wrong. When Banks was inducted into the College Football Hall of Fame in 1992, it was the reward for a career at Morgan State where he never had a losing season from1960 to 1973.

Morgan State was the only school to win more than one national title from 1930-39, as more black schools jumped into the intercollegiate football fray and talent began to disperse. Among the schools earning their first title: Wilberforce of Ohio (which later became Central State), Kentucky State, Texas College, Virginia State, West Virginia State, Florida A&M and Langston. Texas College was guided by a young Arnett "Ace" Mumford, a future College Football Hall of Fame coach who left Texas College in 1936 for Southern University, where he won five more black college championships. FAMU was coached by William "Big Bill" Bell, an Army veteran, who hired Jake Gaither after his success at the prep level.

Long before Bill Walsh was anointed an offensive genius, Gaither was considered the finest offensive mind in college football. Walsh would have his West Coast offense, but Gaither created the split-line T and tutored his peers, black and white, on how to effectively incorporate speed into their offensive systems. Of course, that was a lot easier said than done, unless your players were track stars in football togs—which a lot of Gaither's were, including "The World's Fastest Human," Bob Hayes. Georgia Tech's legendary Bobby Dodd said that Gaither's split-line T (with its wide splits between linemen) was "one of the finest offensive ideas to come along in years." The split-line T was the first system to pressure defenses to adjust their alignments to an offense, reversing what was then the trend.

"We used to be jealous of Jake because they had all the speed," Florida State coach Bobby Bowden once recalled. "In [the '60s], I'd go over and watch his practices and he'd have those big ol' lineman splits, and if you moved [your defense] outside they'd look at the hole inside. All he wanted was a lane."

That's where the speed came in, and Gaither's teams had plenty of it. One season he had nine Olympic-caliber sprinters, including Hayes, in the lineup. Gaither was the first to coach "speed," and often described the perfect football player as "mo-bile, a-gile and hos-tile." The Rattlers lit up the scoreboard like a pinball machine. Two of Gaither's teams scored over 500 points in a season, and the coach finished his career with an astonishing 203–36–4 record. When he retired in 1969, his .844 winning percentage was the highest among all NCAA coaches with more than 200 wins.

Meanwhile, two years after Jackie Robinson broke the color line in Major League Baseball, Eddie Robinson was about to send the first of hundreds of black players to professional football. Paul Younger was a big, bruising runner whose style reminded sports information director Collie Nicholson, a former Marine war correspondent, of a tank. A star—and a nickname—was born. Younger signed a $6,000 free agent contract with the Los Angeles Rams in 1949 and became the first player from a historically black college or university to make an NFL roster.

After Younger, Robinson would send to the pros the first black college player drafted as a No. 1 overall pick—defensive lineman Buck Buchanan, to the Kansas City Chiefs in 1963; the first regular starting black quarterback—James "Shack" Harris, who was drafted by Buffalo in 1969 and became a starter with the Los Angeles Rams in 1974; and the first black quarterback to lead a team to the Super Bowl—Doug Williams, who was also the game's MVP in Washington's 42-10 win over Denver in Super Bowl XXII.

Robinson built the program with invaluable aid and support from school president Ralph Waldo Emerson Jones ("Prez"), and Nicholson, the innovative publicist who set up the first NCAA football game played outside of the U.S.: Grambling's 1976 contest against Morgan State in Tokyo, where the No. 1 sports show was *Grambling Football Highlights*. It was Nicholson who also thought it would be a great idea for archrivals Grambling and Southern to play their annual game in New Orleans. That's how the Bayou Classic came about, the only black college game with a national television contract (NBC) and one of the largest black entertainment events in the country.

The football team from the tiny school in rural Louisiana became the best-known black college team in the country and, arguably, the world. Even the Grambling band got a taste of fame as part of the pregame entertainment for the first Super Bowl.

If Robinson and Gaither were the most famous black college football coaches of their day, many prominent men were in their shadow. John Merritt of Tennessee State had plenty of success against Robinson, and so did Southern's Ace Mumford. "He beat me so much," Robinson once joked, "I thought I had stolen something." At Tennessee State, the flamboyant, cigar-chomping Merritt—who was inducted into the College Football Hall of Fame in 1994—built his teams on pass-happy offenses. "I just love to see it in the air," he'd say, and he groomed several quarterbacks who regularly made him downright giddy, including Eldridge "The Lord's Prayer" Dickey, Joe "747" Adams and, the best of the bunch, a star-crossed talent named "Jefferson Street" Joe Gilliam.

From that group of great coaches, Robinson would be the last man standing and, when he finally left the sideline in 1997, the G-Men were no longer the most feared team in the SWAC. It was difficult to fathom Grambling on the losing end more often than not, but by that time so was the rest of black college football. In 1978, for instance, Florida A&M won the first 1-AA championship game, beating Massachusetts, 35-28. No black college team has advanced that far since. In fact, black college teams have won only 8 of their 44 1-AA playoff games, and only three teams have advanced as far as the semifinals since FAMU got there.

***

To be sure, the football played now at the traditional black colleges and universities is not what it used to be. But today's games are still fun and exciting, and the teams all cling to proud legacies. There is simply a dearth of talent.

Black college players don't show up much on NFL draft lists anymore. Only two black college players were drafted in 2004 (Southern cornerback Lenny Williams and Hampton defensive end Isaac Hilton), both in the seventh round. Compare that to 11 Jackson State players taken in 1968, a record for Mississippi schools. The last two black college players taken in the first round were also from Jackson State: wide receiver Sylvester Morris (Kansas City) and cornerback Rashard Anderson (Carolina) in 2000.

And while the football programs may be hurting, the schools continue to give minorities opportunities to be, in some cases, the first in their families to attend college. The facilities continue to improve, with high-tech buildings wired for the computer age, but the mission is the same: nurturing and turning out educated and productive citizens.

So ol' Coach Gaither, who passed away in 1994, was right. He did, in fact, see the future for black colleges back in the 1960s, but even he and Eddie Robinson, and the legions of coaches and players who passed through black college football programs, would likely admit that the sport's loss was the nation's gain.

GRAMBLING

BY MICHAEL HURD

IT'S NOT TRUE THAT EDDIE ROBINSON invented black college football, but if he had ever applied for a patent it would have been expeditiously approved. Working from his tiny backwoods football lab in Northern Louisiana, Robinson assembled a program that still carries the banner for black college football. He sent Tank Younger to the Los Angeles Rams in 1949 as the first black college player to make it in the National Football League. He sent James Harris to the Buffalo Bills in 1969 as the NFL's first legitimate black quarterback, and later Doug Williams became the first black quarterback to lead a team into, and win, the Super Bowl.

Grambling is black college football, and the play of Robinson's teams made it so—with a lot of help from sports information director Collie Nicholson. As Robinson was revered as a coach, so was Nicholson as a publicist, getting the Grambling name out largely through the black press and making Robinson and his team household names among black fans across the country. It was also Nicholson who took a crash course in Japanese in order to negotiate sponsor contracts for the G-Men to play Morgan State in Tokyo in 1976, the first time a regular-season college football game had been played on foreign soil. Nicholson conceived of the idea for the Bayou Classic, the annual catfight between

Grambling and archrival Southern played in New Orleans' Superdome, and the only black college game carried nationally on network TV. The game and its surrounding events over the Thanksgiving weekend are the most popular holiday sports event for many African-Americans.

TRADITION According to the folks at Grambling, their biggest tradition is "producing superstars." Sounds a bit arrogant, but it actually makes sense for a program that was once known as The Cradle of the Pros. The team's best days are history, but at its peak, the Tigers had some big-time stars who went on to shine: seven first-round draft picks, four players in the Pro Football Hall of Fame, four players and Robinson in the College Football Hall of Fame.

STADIUM Eddie G. Robinson Stadium opened in 1983 and seats 19,600. Before that, home games were played on campus in an antiquated facility (Grambling Stadium) with wooden bleachers that may have seated 5,000. But Grambling was America's Team long before the Dallas Cowboys. There have been seasons when the team played only two or three home games, with the rest on the road, where the team headlined various "classic" games in major markets such as New York, Los Angeles and Dallas. But the team has also played "home" games in Shreveport, 65 miles west of Grambling, at Independence Stadium (site of the Independence Bowl).

PROFILE

Grambling State University
Grambling, La.
Founded: 1901
Enrollment: 4,300
Colors: Black and Gold
Nickname: Tigers
Stadium: Eddie G. Robinson Stadium
   Opened in 1983
   Grass; 19,600 capacity
First football game: 1926
All-time record: 466–188–15 (.708)
Bowl record: 7–6
SWAC championships: 22 (10 outright)
First-round NFL draftees: 5
Website:
www.gram.edu/sports/football/index.htm

THE BEST OF TIMES

From 1971 to 1980, Grambling won or shared eight SWAC championships and was named black college national champion five times.

THE WORST OF TIMES

In Eddie Robinson's waning years, the Tigers suffered three consecutive losing seasons (1995-97), including back-to-back 3–8 finishes. Grambling hadn't had consecutive losing seasons in almost 50 years.

CONFERENCE

Grambling has been a member of the Southwestern Athletic Conference since 1958.

DISTINGUISHED ALUMNI

Tommie Agee, baseball player; Willis Reed, NBA player

FIGHT SONG

FIGHT FOR DEAR OLD GRAMBLING!
Fight, for dear old Grambling,
Fight, we're going to win.
Light, the torch of victory,
We will win this game.

Rah! Rah! Rah!

Fight for dear old Grambling,
Fight, we're going to win.
There's no doubt that we are
The pride of the USA.

BEST PLAYER Good grief! Well, there's Tank Younger, Buck Buchanan (the first black college player taken as a No. 1 overall draft pick), James Harris and Doug Williams. Each had a historic career (first black this or that), but Williams still holds most of Grambling's passing records and was a serious Heisman candidate. The nod goes to him.

BEST COACH Robinson was hired in 1941 to coach football and basketball and teach physical education. In his first season, he had no assistants and no budget for replacing equipment. He handled virtually everything himself, from mowing the field to taping players' ankles to writing accounts of the games for the local newspaper. In his first season, the team went 3–5. But the next season he led them to a perfect 9–0 record. In 56 years with the Tigers, he won 408 games (losing 165, with 15 ties), took the Southwestern Athletic Conference title 17 times, was named black college national champion nine times and had a streak of 27 consecutive winning seasons (1960-86). He is still the only black college coach to grace the cover of *Sports Illustrated*. Respect? Even in Baton Rouge—home of Grambling's main rival, Southern— there's a street named after after him. The College

> *Even in Baton Rouge, home of Grambling's main rival, Southern, there's a street named after Eddie Robinson.*

Football Hall of Fame waived the requirement that a coach be retired for three years before consideration for the Hall. Robinson retired following the 1997 season and was inducted in 1999.

BEST TEAM The 1942 team has been called the "un" team, as in undefeated, untied and unscored on. The ragtag squad was only Robinson's second but finished 9–0. No NCAA team since then has matched the "un" team's accomplishment. At the time, Grambling had only 67 men enrolled in school and 33 were on the football team, including Fred Hobdy, who later would coach basketball at Grambling for 28 years (1959-1986) and become the most successful coach in Louisiana history, winning 572 (against 288 losses). Hobdy's 1961 team, led by future NBA star Willis Reed, won the National Athletic Intercollegiate Association (NAIA) championship. After the "un" team's big season, Grambling did not field a team for the next two years as many of the school's male students went off to fight in World War II.

BIGGEST GAME In 1968, Grambling lost to Morgan State 9-7 before a near sellout crowd of 64,204 fans in Yankee Stadium in the first of the big showcase ("classic") games for black college teams. ABC televised the game. The previous week, Grambling had lost to Alcorn State 28-13 before

RECORDS

RUSHING YARDS

	GAME	
	NA	
	SEASON	
1,417	Eric Gant, 1992 (229 att.)	
	CAREER	
3,795	Eric Gant, 1990-93 (634 att.)	

PASSING YARDS

	GAME	
532	Bruce Eugene, Texas Southern, Nov. 2, 2002 (24 of 54)	
	SEASON	
3,286	Doug Williams, 1977 (181 of 352)	
	CAREER	
8,411	Doug Williams, 1974-77 (484 of 1,009)	

RECEIVING YARDS

	GAME	
330	Nate Singleton, vs. Virginia Union, Sept. 14, 1991 (16 rec.)	
	SEASON	
1,162	Scotty Anderson, 1999 (65 rec.)	
	CAREER	
2,718	Trumaine Johnson, 1979-82 (135 rec.)	

POINTS

	GAME	
	NA	
	SEASON	
150	John Christophe, 1948 (25 TDs)	
	CAREER	
369	Tank Younger, 1945-48 (60 TDs, 9 PATs)	

FIRST-TEAM ALL-AMERICANS

1962	Junious "Buck" Buchanan, T
1964	Alphonse Dotson, OT
1965	Willie Young, OG
1965	Frank Cornish, DT
1969	Billy Manning, C
1970	Richard Harris, DE
1970	Charles Roundtree, DT
1971	Solomon Freelon, OG
1971	John Mendenhall, DE
1972	Steve Dennis, DB
1972-74	Gary Johnson, DT
1973	Willie Bryant, DB
1975	Sammie White, WR
1975	James Hunter, DB
1979	Joe Gordon, DT
1979	Aldrich Allen, LB
1979	Robert Salters, DB

(Continued on next page)

60,294 fans at the Los Angeles Coliseum and that game also drew a huge crowd. Combined attendance for the two games marked the first time that a black college led the nation in attendance for the first two weeks of a season.

BIGGEST UPSET In 1955, Grambling handed Jake Gaither and his Florida A&M crew their only defeat in a 7–1–1 season in the Orange Blossom Classic. The game, played in the Orange Bowl, was for the black college national championship. Grambling, with defensive end Willie Davis, beat FAMU and running back Willie Galimore 28-21, leading to Grambling's first black college title. The Tigers were 10–0 for the season and FAMU's 21 points marked the only game that year in which Grambling gave up more than one touchdown. Played before a large group of NFL scouts, the game is also credited as the beginning of national focus on Robinson and his program.

RIVAL Southern, and it's as edgy as a holiday family dinner because, like any down-and-dirty rivalry, the Tigers from Grambling and the Jaguars from Southern—180 miles south in Baton Rouge—would just as soon scratch each other's eyes out. It's as good a college football rivalry as there is and the series has been played practically even. Families, churches, friends and neighbors separate for the days leading up to the game, which for the past 31 years has been played in New Orleans as the Bayou Classic. "For three days, it's the place to be for Grambling and Southern fans," said Marino Casem, former athletic director and head football coach at Southern. "A fan who doesn't show up is probably sick or out of the country. But, wherever he is, he's probably got two tickets in his pocket."

NICKNAME Grambling formed its first football team in

FIRST-TEAM ALL-AMERICANS (CONT.)		
1980, 1982	Trumaine Johnson, WR	
1980	Mike Barker, DT	
1981	Andre Robinson, LB	
1983	Robert Smith, DL	
1985	James Harris, LB	
1990	Walter Dean, RB	
1990	Jake Reed, WR	
1994	Curtis Ceaser, WR	
2001	Robert Taylor, LB	
2002	Tramon Douglas, WR	
2002	Terry Riley, OL	
2002-03	Bruce Eugene, QB	

ALL-TIME TEAM

Michael Hurd, author of Black College Football, 1892-1992, *compiled the team in 2004 for this encyclopedia. Players were chosen weighted by their play at Grambling, not in pro football. Also considered were All-America honors and national and school records held.*

OFFENSE
1959-63	Lane Howell, OL
1962-65	Alphonse Dotson, OL
1962-65	Willie Young, OL
1964-67	Woody Peoples, OL
1975-78	Bruce Radford, OL
1966-69	Charlie Joiner, WR
1972-76	Sammy White, WR
2000-03	Tramon Douglas, WR
1974-78	Doug Williams, QB
1945-48	Paul "Tank" Younger, RB
1990-93	Eric Gant, RB

DEFENSE
1952-55	Willie Davis, DL
1958-61	Ernie Ladd, DL
1959-62	Junious "Buck" Buchanan, DL
1971-74	Gary "Big Hands" Johnson, DL
1958-61	Garland Boyette, LB
1968-71	John Mendenhall, LB
1972-75	Robert Pennywell, LB
1958-62	Willie Brown, DB
1972-75	James Hunter, DB
1977-80	Everson Walls, DB
1979-82	Albert Lewis, DB

1926 and the head coach was a math teacher, Ralph Waldo Emerson Jones, who was also the school's baseball coach. Jones didn't have much of a team and in part because of that he wanted a nickname that would indicate the team's ferocity. Hence Tigers. Affectionately nicknamed Prez, Jones was Grambling's president (1936-1977), guiding force and football marketing visionary.

UNIFORMS Under Eddie Robinson, Grambling's use of black, bright gold and red uniforms, in an almost infinite variety of combinations, made Grambling one of the most distinctive-looking schools in the country. But with the 2005 season, the Tigers announced they'd unveil a new helmet logo, replacing the stylized oval G that was similar to that worn by the Green Bay Packers and Georgia Bulldogs. The move was prompted by the discovery that the school had let its copyright on the use of the logo (on a black helmet, with a yellow oval) expire.

LORE Ernie Ladd was one of the first of the behemoth Grambling defensive linemen to terrorize American and National Football League offenses. Getting around or fighting off Ladd—who was 6'9", 310 pounds—was a futile all-day project, and off the field he gravitated toward the dinner table as voraciously as he did opposing backfields. Thus, his recruiting trip to Grambling in 1957 is legend. Eddie Robinson had sent Dr. Charles Henry to Orange, Texas, to retrieve Ladd, who proceeded to literally eat his way to Grambling. During the five-hour drive, Henry was forced to stop and call Robinson, advising him: "Hold the dining hall open, I don't know if I have enough money to feed him!" Ladd had already eaten breakfast (twice) and downed a huge lunch. That evening, when he got to the Grambling dining hall,

Ladd loaded his tray and announced to Robinson: "I like the way you feed here."

QUOTE "When our student body begins to appeal, 'Hold that line, Louisiana Negro Normal and Industrial Institute, hold that line!' before they can get that cheer out of their mouths, gentlemen, the other team has already scored."—Grambling president Ralph Waldo Emerson "Prez" Jones, in 1946, explaining to the Louisiana state legislature why the school's name should be shortened to Grambling, from Louisiana Negro Normal and Industrial Institute

THE SCHOOLS

A PROUD LEGACY

BY MICHAEL HURD

Among the nation's historically black colleges and universities, Grambling has by far the best-known football program, but it's hardly the only one. Here are capsule histories of 18 other schools in the Southwestern Athletic Conference and the Mid-Eastern Athletic Conference.

ALABAMA A&M UNIVERSITY
Normal, Ala.

Alabama A&M is located in the northern Alabama community of Normal, just outside of Huntsville, where Civil War history meets Star Wars future. During the war, Huntsville was home to the Confederate Army's Camp Bradford. Today, the area is a hotbed of space technology, which includes NASA's nearby Marshall Space Flight Center. Among the space agency's contractors is the Alabama A&M physics department. The Bulldogs football program, however, has been pretty down-to-earth through the years. As a member of the Southern Intercollegiate Athletic Conference for 51 years (1947-97), A&M won just six outright conference championships. The Bulldogs joined the SWAC in 1999.

GLORY DAYS From 1960 to 1964, the Bulldogs were 37–5–1, including an undefeated season (8–0) in 1963, the only one in school history, and a SIAC co-championship in 1962.

BEST PLAYER Wide receiver John Stallworth grew up in Tuscaloosa, in the shadows of Alabama Crimson Tide football, but in an era when Bear Bryant was only just beginning to recruit black players. So Stallworth was an All-SIAC receiver for the Bulldogs in 1972 and 1973, and a black college All-America in 1973. A fourth-round NFL pick, Stallworth played all 14 of his pro seasons with the Pittsburgh Steelers. He caught 537 passes for 8,723 yards and 63 touchdowns, all team records; was an All-Pro (1979); and played on all four Steelers Super Bowl champions. Stallworth, who scored the winning touchdown on a 73-yard, over-the-shoulder catch and run in Super Bowl XIV against the Los Angeles Rams, holds Super Bowl records for career average per catch (24.4 yards) and single-game average (40.33 yards

in Super Bowl XIV). He was inducted into the Division II football National Hall of Fame in 2000 and to the Pro Football Hall of Fame in 2002.

BEST COACH Lewis "Sugar Bear" Crews starred at A&M as a running back and quarterback before World War II (1936-41) and returned in 1960 to begin a 16-year run as head coach. He turned around a program with only one winning season (5–2–1, 1955) in the previous 10 years. In his first seven seasons with the Bulldogs, Crews, built a 50–10–1 record that included four one-loss seasons and the undefeated season in 1963. His career record was 93–53–3, the most wins in school history. "Sugar Bear was a one-man coaching staff," Joe Kent, a quarterback on Crews' first Bulldogs squad, once said. "It was amazing to me how he did it. We won all those games with no staff at all."

BEST TEAM The 1989 Bulldogs went to the Division II playoffs, losing in the first round to Jacksonville State 33-9 and finishing the year with an 8–4 record. That year, wide receiver Barry Wagner set a school record with 106 catches for 1,812 yards, which made him second only to Jerry Rice among black college players for single-season catches and yards. Under head coach Anthony Jones, the 2003 Bulldogs cracked the national rankings for the first time in school history when they were briefly ranked 24th in the ESPN/*USA Today* Division I-AA poll late in their 8–4 season.

ALABAMA STATE UNIVERSITY
Montgomery, Ala.

Montgomery, Ala., where Alabama State University was founded in 1867, served briefly as the capital of the Confederacy in 1861. Nearly a century later, in 1956, Alabama State students and faculty were on the front lines of the year-long Montgomery bus boycott led by Dr. Martin Luther King Jr., which ignited the civil rights movement. Not surprisingly, given Montgomery's status as the Cradle of the Confederacy, the school was punished severely for its activism. First Alabama State lost state funding, then its accreditation. But the school quickly recovered from both setbacks, and as the civil rights movement picked up steam in the 1960s, Alabama State's football program thrived as well.

GLORY DAYS Since the Hornets first started playing intercollegiate football in 1901, Alabama State has had only 14 seasons in which they won seven or more games—and

four of those came in succession (1966-69), the first three under Whitney Van Cleve, the last with Henry Holbert at the helm. In those four years, the Hornets had a combined record of 32–7–1.

BEST PLAYER Eddie Robinson Jr. is no relation to the famous Grambling coach, but the Hornets linebacker also left his mark on SWAC football. The hard-hitting defender, who was inducted into the SWAC Hall of Fame in 1998 (the youngest ever, at age 28), went to Alabama State on an academic scholarship, majoring in chemistry. Switching from lineman to linebacker in his sophomore season, he piled up 233 tackles and 11 sacks, twice winning SWAC Defensive Player of the Year. He was also a two-time Division I-AA and Sheridan Black College All-America. As a senior, Robinson was a SWAC All-Academic choice with a 3.53 GPA and was awarded an NCAA Postgraduate Scholarship. His success in the Blue-Gray all-star game, where he made 16 tackles and forced a fumble, helped Robinson to become a second-round draft pick of the Houston Oilers in 1992. Robinson started as a rookie and played in the NFL for 11 years, finishing his career in 2002 with a one-year stint with the Buffalo Bills.

BEST COACH Houston "The Quiet Storm" Markam guided Alabama State from 1987 to 1997, the longest tenure of any Hornets football coach. In his 11 seasons, Markam compiled a 69–47–4 record, including only the second undefeated season in school history, an 11–0–1 mark in 1991. (The other was 5–0 in 1909.) Markam was named Black College Coach of the Year in 1991.

BEST TEAM The 1991 squad, without question. Led by Robinson, Alabama State went 11–0–1, setting a school mark for most wins in a season. The Hornets earned their lone SWAC championship and played in the inaugural Heritage Bowl, which matched the SWAC and MEAC champions, defeating North Carolina A&T in Miami 36-13. Other standouts on the team that year were offensive linemen Jackie Rowan and Patrick Johnson, both black college All-Americas.

ALCORN STATE UNIVERSITY
Alcorn State, Miss.

After World War II, a quiet, studious Army veteran from Mississippi returned to his home state and enrolled at Alcorn State University, founded in 1871 and located in

Alcorn, 80 miles southwest of Jackson. Medgar Evers not only met his wife, Myrlie, at Alcorn State, but he was also active in various campus activities, including playing a little football for the Braves. His destiny, of course, was not to achieve football fame, but to become a powerful civil rights leader and eventually a national martyr to the cause.

GLORY DAYS The 1968 and 1969 teams, coached by Marino Casem, had a combined 17–1–1 record and were both named black college national champs. The teams featured several black college All-Americas: Willie Alexander, a cornerback who would play nine years in the NFL with the Houston Oilers; offensive linemen Willie Peake and Willie Young; quarterback Marvin Weeks; linebacker Rayford Jenkins; and two other defensive backs, David Hadley, who played two years with the Kansas City Chiefs, and Cleophus Johnson. The Braves shared the 1968 SWAC title with Grambling and Texas Southern, but won the championship outright in 1969 and 1970.

BEST PLAYER When Steve McNair came out of high school in Mt. Olive, Miss., Alcorn State was the only program that recruited him to play quarterback. In high school, he had played both quarterback and defensive back, and the bigger schools thought the athletically gifted McNair—one opponent described him as a "big ol' strong country boy"—would be much better as a defensive back. He might have been, but it's hard today to imagine McNair being better at defending passes than throwing them. He set the NCAA single-season passing record, averaging 527.18 yards per game, and he holds the completion percentage record for a season (73.6%). As a senior in 1994, McNair finished third in the Heisman Trophy voting behind Colorado's Rashaan Salaam and Penn State's Ki-Jana Carter, and he was a first-round pick of the Houston Oilers. McNair was the first player in collegiate history to accumulate 16,000 yards (16,823) of total offense. In the process, he also set five NCAA records and an additional 31 Division I-AA records. The Oilers were relocated to Tennessee in 1998 and rechristened the Titans in 1999. In 2000, McNair led his team to a berth in Super Bowl XXXIV, where the Titans' thrilling fourth-quarter rally fell a yard short in a 23-16 loss to the St. Louis Rams.

BEST COACH That naturally raspy voice, not to mention the respect he earned over two decades as The Man at Alcorn State, made the nickname almost automatic: Marino Casem, a.k.a. The Godfather, coached the Braves to a 132–65–8 record from 1964 to 1985, during which period Alcorn State captured seven SWAC championships

and four black college national championships. The Godfather was named both the National Black College and SWAC Coach of the Year a total of seven times. As athletic director, he was responsible for the construction of Alcorn State's athletics complex, and he was instrumental in the designing and planning of Jack Spinks Stadium, which opened in 1992. In 1986, Casem became athletic director at rival Southern University and quickly converted Southern's program into the top overall outfit in the SWAC. Between 1986 and his retirement in 1999 Casem guided Southern to seven SWAC Commissioner Cups, six SWAC men's all-sport trophies and nine SWAC women's all-sport trophies. Always affable, personable and quotable, Casem was inducted into the College Football Hall of Fame in 2003.

BEST TEAM In 1984, Casem guided the Braves to an undefeated and untied regular season—their first since 1931. The 9–0 record also made his team only the second in black college history to finish the regular season ranked No. 1 in the Division I-AA poll (Grambling was the other, in 1979). However, the Braves lost in the D1-AA quarterfinals to Louisiana Tech, 44-21. The team featured cornerback Issiac Holt (a second-round pick of the Minnesota Vikings in the 1985 draft) and won Alcorn's most recent black college national championship.

ARKANSAS-PINE BLUFF
Pine Bluff, Ark.

Located 42 miles southeast of Little Rock, the school was founded as Branch Normal College in 1873 and was renamed the University of Arkansas at Pine Bluff when it became a part of the state university system in 1972. The Golden Lions have been playing football since 1928 but have never been nationally ranked or earned a conference title, winning as many as nine games in a season only twice (1990, 1994). The wins in the 1990 campaign were later forfeited when the National Association of Intercollegiate Athletics uncovered 140 allegations of improprieties in the program, all of which led to the Lions receiving a two-year ban from competition. The program restarted in 1993 as a member of the NCAA and the SWAC.

GLORY DAYS After his pass-happy offense gained notoriety at Mississippi Valley, Archie Cooley took the head-coaching job at UAPB in 1987. In three of his four star-crossed years there, Cooley had winning seasons, including a combined 16–3 record in 1989 and 1990 seasons. The latter season produced a 9–1 finish, the best in school history. However, all of that was washed away after an NAIA probe that resulted in the forfeit of

22 wins from 1987 to 1990, Cooley's resignation and the NAIA's ban.

BEST PLAYER Most of the college scholarship offers that L.C. Greenwood got in 1964 as a senior at Canton (Miss.) High School were academic. The oldest of nine siblings, Greenwood was contemplating medical school. He chose the Golden Lions, in part, because of the school's strong chemistry and biology departments. Also, Greenwood said, "the only schools I knew about to attend were black colleges." With the Lions, Greenwood played both defensive end and tackle, and was named to the *Ebony* magazine All-America squad as a senior (1969). A 10th-round pick by the Pittsburgh Steelers, the 6'6", 260-pound Greenwood, wearing his signature gold-colored shoes, was a member of the famed Steel Curtain defense. He began wearing gold-painted cleats in 1974 to establish his identity. "I'd be running all over the field making tackles on the other sideline," Greenwood said. "Then I'd hear the public address announcer say, 'Joe Greene on the tackle.' I'd get up and look around, and Joe was nowhere around." Greenwood led the Steelers in sacks six times in a 13-year career in which he totaled 73.5 sacks and 14 fumble recoveries.

BEST COACH Golden Lions alum Lee Hardman was chosen in 1993 to rebuild the program after its forced hiatus. His first team finished 5–6, but for the next seven seasons, the Lions had .500 or better records. Twice Hardman led teams to the NAIA playoffs, in 1994 advancing to the Division I title game (a 13-12 loss to Northeastern Oklahoma State) and in 1995 losing in the semifinals (17-14 to Northeastern Oklahoma State). Then, after three consecutive losing seasons, Hardman was forced to resign in 2003. With a record of 64–57, he left as UAPB's all-time winningest coach.

BEST TEAM The ill-fated 1990 team featured running back Ivory Lee Brown, who would be a seventh-round pick by the Arizona Cardinals. Brown was part of Cooley's high-powered run-and-shoot offense that put up 407 points for the season, while a potent defense allowed only 50. The defense posted four shutouts and allowed only two opponents to score in double digits.

BETHUNE-COOKMAN COLLEGE
Daytona Beach, Fla.

In 1904, Mary McLeod Bethune, the great educator and civil rights activist, founded the school that today bears her name. The school was initially named the Daytona Educational and Industrial Training School for Negro Girls. It became coed in 1923 when it merged with Cookman

Institute, but didn't pick up its present name until 1931, after evolving into a junior college. Bethune's energy and enthusiasm for helping black communities spilled over to the Wildcats football program, which began in 1925, where she could often be found leading cheers on the sideline during games. A couple of times a week after practice, the team would walk to her house and serenade her with "Let Me Call You Sweetheart."

GLORY DAYS From 1945 to 1953, the Wildcats played in eight black college bowl games. Rudolph "Bunky" Matthews was head coach for all but one of those seasons, and his 1947 team finished 10–2. Bethune-Cookman also won two SIAC titles during that span (1949, 1952), but wouldn't win another until 1973. Among Matthews' stars were two black college All-Americas: receiver Jack "Cy" McClairen and quarterback Raymon Thornton. McClairen went on to play six years in the NFL with the Pittsburgh Steelers.

BEST PLAYER Offensive lineman Larry Little was All-SIAC for three consecutive years (1964-66), then signed as a free agent with the San Diego Chargers. Two years later he was traded to the Miami Dolphins, where he would earn a reputation as the prototypical NFL pulling guard—even though he maintained that pass-blocking was his real strength. Whatever, he was arguably the best ever to play his position in the NFL, leading the powerful Dolphins sweeps that featured running backs Larry Csonka, Mercury Morris and Jim Kiick and took Miami to Super Bowl victories in 1972 and 1973. Little was the first player to be named the NFL Players Association AFC Lineman of the Year for three consecutive seasons (1970-72). In 1993, Little was inducted into the Pro Football Hall of Fame and named to Sheridan's All-Time Black College Football Team.

BEST COACH At the helm from 1946 to 1959, Matthews led the Wildcats to an 80–42–6 record, the best in school history. Matthews, who had an English literature degree from Morehouse, brought an intensely personal passion to the game. "He coached by himself. He knew the game and he showed us how to do it," recalled Rufus "Buddy" Young, a fullback and linebacker for Matthews (1946-50). "And if we didn't do it right, he'd yell, 'Do it this way! I want it done right!' And we would do it his way."

BEST TEAM Led by junior quarterback Allen Suber and senior defensive back Rashean Mathis, the MEAC Offensive and Defensive players of the year, the 2002 Wildcats finished with an overall 11–2 record and won the MEAC championship. Operating out of coach Alvin Wyatt's "Wyattbone" option offense, Suber rushed 158 times for 1,035 yards and 15 touchdowns and threw 164 times for 1,307 yards 8 TDs. Mathis, a three-time Division I-AA All-America, was the first defensive back to win the Buck

Buchanan Award, presented to the top D1-AA defender. He set several D1-AA marks, including passes intercepted in a season (14) and career (31). Mathis was a second-round pick of the Jacksonville Jaguars in 2003 and started all 16 games as a rookie.

DELAWARE STATE UNIVERSITY
Dover, Del.

The Hornets didn't have much of a sting in the first half-century after the program's beginning in 1924, when they played only one game—and lost. Things didn't get much better for Delaware State until the 1980s, when the program began to thrive and become a force in the MEAC. Still, just two of the school's 15 coaches have had winning records.

GLORY DAYS The Hornets enjoyed 12 winning seasons from 1983 to 1995, recording a combined record of 91–45–1 and winning five MEAC titles (1985, 1987-89, 1991). Among the standouts from that era: wide receiver John Taylor (1982-85), who would later become an NFL All-Pro wideout; running back Gene Lake (1982-84), whose 1,722 yards in 1984 is still a school record; and defensive back Joe Burton (1983-86). Both Lake and Burton were D1-AA All-America selections, as was offensive lineman Rod Milstead (1988-91), who later played five years in the NFL. Milstead, a 1991 Walter Camp All-America as well as a Sheridan Black College All-America, anchored a 1991 team that pulled off a huge upset over heavily favored Youngstown State in the second game of the season. Youngstown would go on to win the D1-AA national championship that year, but on Sept. 29 at Alumni Stadium in Dover, the Hornets beat Jim Tressel's Penguins 33-29, putting together four defensive stops down the fourth-quarter stretch to clinch the win. The 1991 Hornets finished 9–2 overall and had a 5–1 MEAC record, tying North Carolina A&T for the conference title.

BEST PLAYER Taylor, because of his career in the NFL, is the best-known, but quarterback Rahsaan Matthews was the program's most productive player. Matthews, who owns all of the school's passing records, was named a Sheridan Black College All-America in 2000, a season in which the Hornets offense averaged 35 points per game, good enough to rank No. 19 among Division I-AA teams.

BEST COACH Bill Collick guided the Hornets from 1985 to 1996 and is one of only two coaches in school history with more than 50 wins (81–48); Ed Jackson (54–23–3; 1933-45, 1953-56) is the other. Collick was MEAC Coach of the Year in 1985 and is the winningest coach in Delaware State history. He coached 63 All-MEAC selections, six All-Americas and at least 20 players who went on to sign

professional contracts. Collick also achieved success as DSU's head wrestling coach, leading the Hornets to their lone MEAC wrestling title in 1984. Collick was inducted into the Delaware Sports Hall of Fame in 1998.

BEST TEAM The 1934 Hornets finished 8–0, the only undefeated season in school history when more than one game was played. Seven of their eight wins were shutouts; the only score by opponents came on a safety. Best among modern teams was the 1985 squad, led by Taylor and Burton, which went 9–2 overall and 5–0 in conference play, winning the school's first MEAC championship. The 1985 Hornets earned their first-ever Top 20 national ranking— No. 12 in the Division I-AA poll.

FLORIDA A&M UNIVERSITY
Tallahassee, Fla.

Here's the Cliffs Notes version of Florida A&M University Football 101: Jake Gaither. Two words, one man. At one time, Gaither enjoyed a virtual monopoly on black football players in Florida. The key to his recruiting success? The fact that nearly 90% of the state's black high school coaches were Gaither's former players, who collectively formed a human pipeline pumping talent to Tallahassee. And the key to their loyalty? Respect bordering on awe for Gaither. Their crosstown neighbors at Florida State University eventually overshadowed Florida A&M's success, but even the Seminoles' longtime mentor, Bobby Bowden, was in awe of Gaither, a man Bowden has said was like a father figure to him.

GLORY DAYS Gaither coached the Rattlers from 1945 to 1969 and put FAMU football on the map. His teams won six black college national titles and 22 SIAC championships, and he produced 36 black college All-Americas.

BEST PLAYER Willie "Gallopin' Gal" Galimore, later a great running back for the Chicago Bears, still holds FAMU records for rushing yards in a season (3,592), rushing yards in a game (295), longest run from scrimmage (98 yards), touchdowns in a game (four, a mark he shares with two other Rattlers) and touchdowns in a season (16). A three-time black college All-America (1954-56) and a first-team NAIA All-America in 1954, Galimore led FAMU to four SIAC titles (1953-56). Some historians credit Galimore with being the first player to spike the ball after scoring a touchdown. Sadly, he and teammate John Farrington were killed in an auto accident in 1964 as they drove back to Bears training camp. In 1999, Galimore was inducted into the College Football Hall of Fame.

BEST COACH One of the greatest, most revered coaches in all of football history, Gaither once famously described his ideal football player as "mo-bile, a-gile and hos-tile." In 25 years, Gaither never had a losing season, in great measure because he was a master motivator. When sprinter Bob Hayes returned from the 1964 Tokyo Olympics with the label World's Fastest Human, his fame didn't sit well with some of his teammates. So at a team meeting, Gaither stepped in: "I said, 'Tell you how you can get just as much publicity as he gets.' They said, 'How, Coach?' I said, 'Outrun him.'" The first black coach inducted into the College Football Hall of Fame (1975), Gaither was a low-key but strict disciplinarian, and an innovative genius whose split-line-T offense emphasized speed, speed and more speed, something his teams always had plenty of. Florida A&M football will forever be coiled in the shadow of the Papa Rattler.

BEST TEAM William "Big Bill" Bell's 1938 squad did not give up a point through its first seven games before squeezing out a 9-7 win over Kentucky State in the season finale in the Orange Blossom Classic, finishing 8–0 and earning the school's first black college national title. The game's winning points came after Kentucky State was backed up against its own goal line with the score tied in the third quarter, and a Kentucky State lateral sailed out of the back of the end zone for a safety.

HAMPTON UNIVERSITY
Hampton, Va.

Having a gospel group that doubles as a football team, or vice versa, is a pretty righteous notion. When Joe Taylor became head coach at Hampton in 1992, among the character-building programs he instituted was the formation of a gospel choir comprising players and coaches. It was a tip of the hat to the world-renowned Jubilee Singers at Fisk University, some of whom were members of that school's football team in the early 1900s. And it helped turn Hampton around. In the six decades before Taylor arrived on the scene, football rarely offered much to sing about at Hampton. The school had dominated the Central Intercollegiate Athletic Association from 1913 to 1931, winning eight conference championships outright and one co-championship (1914), and a black college championship in 1922 under Gideon Smith. But after winning the title in 1931, the Pirates wouldn't claim another for 54 years, when Fred Freeman's 1985 squad finished 10–2.

GLORY DAYS From 1992 to 1999, the Pirates claimed three CIAA championships, two MEAC titles and two black college national championships. Hampton also defeated

Southern 24-3 in the 1999 Heritage Bowl and made four trips to the postseason.

BEST PLAYER. Defensive end Reggie Doss was a seventh-round pick of the Los Angeles Rams in 1978 after a stellar career at Hampton, where his school record for most tackles in a season (156 in 1977) stood for nearly two decades. Doss' 15 assisted tackles against Virginia Union in 1977 remains a school single-game record, as does his 75 assists for that season. A versatile athlete, Doss also played tight end and linebacker, and was twice named All-CIAA. Doss spent his entire 10-year NFL career as a defensive end for the Rams, retiring in 1987.

BEST COACH Smith (1921-40) had 97 career wins, and his teams won five CIAA titles and a black college national championship (1922). But Taylor, a tough disciplinarian, overtook Smith as the school's career leader in wins (109) when the Pirates finished 7–4 in 2003. In 2000, the All-America Football Foundation honored Taylor with the Johnny Vaught Lifetime Achievement Award. Before the Pirates joined the MEAC in 1995, Taylor had led them to three consecutive CIAA titles and two consecutive Division II playoff appearances. In 1993, he led the Pirates to an undefeated regular season and the quarterfinal round of the Division II playoffs, with Hampton becoming the first CIAA team in history to win 12 games in a season, posting an overall mark of 12–1.

BEST TEAM In their last season of Division II competition, the 1994 Pirates finished 10–1 and were awarded the Sheridan Broadcasting Network's (SBN) Jake Gaither Trophy, which annually recognizes the black college national champion. The team was led on the field by quarterback Matt Montgomery, Hampton's all-time leader in career passing (7,839 yards) and total offense (8,311 yards). The Pirates broke the CIAA total offense record that year with 5,575 yards, becoming the first CIAA team to finish the season averaging more than 500 yards of total offense per game. Hampton dominated its final seven opponents, averaging 54.2 points per game while limiting teams to 14.2 points per contest, to extend its CIAA winning streak to 23 games.

HOWARD UNIVERSITY
Washington, D.C.

Howard is an urban school just southeast of downtown Washington, D.C., that has produced numerous social and political leaders, both in the U.S. and abroad, including Andrew Young (Class of 1951), former U.S. ambassador to the United Nations and former mayor of Atlanta. The football program, however, which first fielded an intercollegiate team in 1894, has not enjoyed as much renown. Even so, from 1919 to 1929, Howard's Thanksgiving Day game against Lincoln (Pa.) University was always a huge social event in Washington, and was the inspiration for Florida A&M to start its Orange Blossom Classic.

GLORY DAYS You have to go back to the Roaring '20s to find Howard's era of football dominance. The Bison shared black college national championships three times in the decade (1920, 1925-26), led by Ed Morrison and Louis Watson, the latter coach winning the second and third titles.

BEST PLAYER Running back Harvey Reed (1984-87) still holds five Bison career records, including rushing yards (4,142), rushing touchdowns (47) and points scored (294). An eighth-round pick of the Chicago Bears in 1988, Reed was a black college All-America as well as the Sheridan Broadcasting Network Black College Player of the Year. Former Bison star Steve Wilson (1975-78) played 10 years in the NFL—three with the Dallas Cowboys, seven with the Denver Broncos—as both a defensive back and a wide receiver before returning in 1989 as Howard's head coach. In 13 seasons, Wilson produced the most wins in school history, 77, while losing 67 games. His 1993 squad, led by quarterback Jay "Sky" Walker, posted an 11–0 regular-season record, Howard's first undefeated season in 67 years.

BEST COACH Hard-driving taskmaster Morrison was hired in 1920 to give the Bison an edge over then-archrival Lincoln, which had won two of the last three games against Howard and tied the third 0-0. Morrison installed his "straight backs" offense, a scheme that was a forerunner to the I-formation. Using that innovative system, Morrison's charges beat the Lions 42-0 to close the coach's first season with a 7–0 record and a tie with Talledega (Ala.) College for the first-ever black college national championship. Morrison won 25 of 35 games (with five ties) from 1920 to 1928. In the 1920 and 1921 seasons, his teams had a string of 13 consecutive shutouts, a remarkable run that ended with a 13-7 loss to Lincoln. The Lions beat Howard again in 1922, 13-12, and that led to Watson taking over for Morrison in 1923. Watson's challenge to his teams: "I don't want any opponent to earn a first down!" The Bison defense didn't accomplish that, but in sharing two championships (tying Tuskegee in 1925 and 1926), the Bison shut out 13 of their 15 opponents. Watson was 23–3–5 in his four seasons at the helm.

BEST TEAM Morrison's 1920 team, the Thundering Herd, was unscored on (132-0) in winning all seven of its games and earning a share of the first-ever black college

national title. The team featured black college All-America receiver Eddie Hurt, who would go on to become a legend himself as head coach at Morgan State.

JACKSON STATE UNIVERSITY
Jackson, Miss.

After a low-key start in 1910 with "volunteer" students and a suspension of all athletics during World War II, the modern Jackson State program began in 1946. The Tigers won three black college national championships (1962, 1985, 1996) as well as 15 (outright and shared) SWAC titles. And yet the Jackson State football legacy is one of the most underrated in black college football history, probably because the school is surrounded by perennial black college powers: Grambling to the west, Florida A&M to the east, Tennessee State to the north and in-state Mississippi rival Alcorn State to the south. Beginning in 1971, Jackson State had only three losing seasons (1984, 2003-04) over the next three-plus decades.

GLORY DAYS From 1980 to 1996, the Tigers were SWAC champs or co-champs 10 times. They were co-champs with Grambling in 1985 and then won the title outright for the next three years, compiling a SWAC-record 28 consecutive conference wins from 1985 to 1989. During that span, Jackson State made eight D1-AA playoff appearances. Of course, the 1970s hadn't been too shabby either. From 1970 to 1976, the Tigers produced four first-round NFL draft picks—tight end Jerome Barkum (1972), defensive end Don Reese (1974), running back Walter Payton (1975) and linebacker Robert Brazile (1975).

BEST PLAYER Receiver Willie Richardson (1959-62) was a four-time black college All-America. Defensive back Lem Barney (1967-77), with his signature backpedal style, revolutionized the way cornerbacks cover receivers as a seven-time Pro-Bowler with the Detroit Lions. Offensive tackle Jackie Slater (1976-95) spent 20 seasons with the Los Angeles Rams, playing the most games (259) as an offensive lineman in NFL history. But when it comes to great players in Jackson State football lore, one towers above the rest—and he almost didn't go there. Walter Payton, recruited by Kansas State in 1971 out of newly integrated Columbia (Miss.) High School, was on his way to Manhattan when he stopped in at Jackson State to visit his brother Eddie. Goodbye, K-State. Payton canceled his trip and in the next four years became one of the greatest players in college football history. At J-State, Payton set nine school records, including career touchdowns (66) and rushing yards (3,563). In 1973, he led the nation in scoring with 160 points, and his 464 career points was an NCAA record. Payton joined the Chicago

Bears as the fourth overall pick of the 1975 draft. As a Bear, Payton continued to set records in a Hall of Fame pro career in which he rushed for 16,726 yards. Payton died of bile duct cancer in 1999. The Walter Payton Award is given to the outstanding player in Division I-AA.

BEST COACH W.C. Gorden, Tigers head coach from 1976 to 1991, led his teams to eight SWAC titles and nine of Jackson State's 12 NCAA playoff appearances. Gorden, whose career mark at J-State was 119–48–5, won 76 of his 93 conference games and was named SWAC Coach of the Year six times. In 1997, he was named to the Mississippi Sports Hall of Fame.

BEST TEAM The most talented may well have been the 1968 squad, coached by Rod Paige, who would go on to become U.S. secretary of education. That team sent 11 players to the pros despite a 3–6 finish. But John Merritt's 1962 Tigers get the nod as the best team in J-State history. The team rolled up a 10–1 record, marking the first time the Tigers had won 10 games in a season, a feat they've repeated only twice since, in 1978 and 1996. The 1962 outfit featured wide receiver Willie Richardson (43 receptions, 896 yards, 11 touchdowns), quarterback Roy Curry (1,862 yards passing, 15 TDs) and linemen Ben McGee and Verlon Biggs. Oh, yes, and a freshman punter named Lem Barney.

MISSISSIPPI VALLEY STATE
Itta Bena, Miss.

Itta Bena is a tiny town smack in the heart of the Mississippi Delta, but it can legitimately claim two bona fide American icons: B.B. King and Jerry Rice. The King of the Blues was born in Itta Bena (pop. 2,208), and Rice began his meteoric rise to football megastardom in the hometown of the Mississippi Valley State University Delta Devils. Rice went on to become the king of wide receivers, but the Mississippi Valley State program has mostly sung the blues. In 37 years as a member of the SWAC, Mississippi Valley State has never won a league title and has had only 14 winning seasons since beginning play in 1953.

GLORY DAYS For two seasons, 1983 and 1984, the Devils were college football's greatest show on turf. In head coach Archie Cooley's version of the run-and-shoot offense, quarterback Willie "Satellite" Totten threw, threw and, if that failed, threw some more—as in 75 times against Louisiana Tech in 1984. Totten set 50 NCAA passing records, but you'd throw it a lot too if Jerry Rice were your main receiver.

BEST PLAYER For some reason, NFL scouts doubted Rice would adjust to the pro game, and there were questions about his speed. Yeah, right. At Valley, Rice set NCAA receiving records and followed that by breaking all of the NFL's major pass-catching marks. Rice totaled a Division I-AA-record 4,693 yards from 1981 to 1984 and set 18 D1-AA marks during his four-year career with the Devils, including most TD catches in a season (27 in 1984). A consensus All-America that year, Rice had more than 100 receptions in both his junior and senior seasons. He picked up 1,682 yards in 1984, topping 1,000 yards receiving for the third consecutive year. "A lot of scouts thought we just lined up and ran deep," said Cooley. "What it all meant was that Jerry hadn't had a white coach, so there were doubts." They didn't last long.

BEST COACH It's Cooley, if for no other reason than his colorful nature. The man they called Gunslinger—he wore a cowboy hat on the sideline—devised a version of the run-and-shoot offense that was much more shoot than run. Cooley's seven years (1980-86) were the most productive in school history. Though he compiled a modest 40–24–3 record, it was good enough to earn the top spot among all MVSU coaches for most wins.

BEST TEAM The 1984 Delta Devils finished 9–2 and tied for No. 6 nationally in the D1-AA poll. In the process, Valley put up 628 points, averaging 60.9 points per game, still a record for both D1-A and D1-AA teams. Totten threw 56 touchdown passes, also the record for both divisions, and set a D1-AA mark with 455.7 yards passing per game (518 attempts, 324 completions, 22 interceptions, 4,557 yards). The Devils set the tone by opening the year with an 86-0 trouncing of Kentucky State. Valley scored 49 points or more in nine games, 65 or more in six games and more than 80 points twice. Moving up in competition, the Delta Devils got their comeuppance in their final game of the season, losing to Louisiana Tech 66–19 in the first round of the 1984 D1-AA playoffs.

MORGAN STATE UNIVERSITY
Baltimore, Md.

The Baltimore Conference of the Methodist Episcopal Church founded Morgan State in 1867 as the Centenary Biblical Institute. The school's mission was to train young men in ministry. By that measure, it was a resounding success, but in the next century the school would produce two coaches—Eddie Hurt and Earl Banks—who could preach the gospel of football like few others. Over the years, Morgan State produced four Pro Football Hall of Famers: Willie Lanier, Leroy Kelley, Len Ford and Roosevelt Brown. However, another player would also achieve legendary status, but not in football. Clarence Gaines, a little-known lineman on the Bears' black college national championship teams of 1943 and 1944, would become one of the most successful coaches in college basketball history, compiling an 828–447 record in 47 years as head coach at Winston-Salem State, and earning the nickname Big House.

GLORY DAYS In a remarkable 57-game span from 1931 to 1938, Morgan State went undefeated, going 54–0–3. The streak, orchestrated by Hurt, is the third-longest in NCAA football history. The 1933 and 1937 teams (9–0 and 7–0, respectively) won the school's first two black college national championships. The Bears claimed four more championships in the 1940s—two outright (1943-44) and two shared (with Tennessee State in 1946, with Southern in 1949).

BEST PLAYER When Lanier walked-on in 1963, Banks had never even heard of him. But by the time Lanier graduated from Morgan State four seasons later, just about everybody in football had heard of the cerebral but hard-hitting, undersized linebacker known as Contact. Lanier was a Small College All-America his junior and senior seasons, and was a black college All-America as a junior. Named to the SBN All-Time Black College Team in 1992, Lanier appeared much smaller than his listed height of 6'1", but he was a 245-pound knockout punch looking for a place to land. The Kansas City Chiefs drafted Lanier in the second round of the 1967 draft, and made him the first black middle linebacker in pro football. He intercepted 27 passes for 440 yards in his 11-year NFL career and was named to six Pro Bowls. Lanier was inducted into the Pro Football Hall of Fame in 1986 and the College Football Hall of Fame in 2000.

BEST COACH "Papa Bear" Banks is in the College Football Hall of Fame, but even he admitted that "the greatest coach at Morgan State was Eddie Hurt. You could never do better than him." Hurt coached football, basketball and track and field at Morgan State for 40 years, beginning in 1929, and won multiple CIAA titles in each sport. An All-America receiver at Howard, Hurt coached Morgan State to 13 CIAA championships and six black college national titles. Banks succeeded Hurt in 1960 and over 14 seasons posted a fantastic .756 winning percentage, including a 31-game winning streak from 1965 to 1968 (the seventh-longest winning streak in college football history), three undefeated regular seasons (1965-67) and five CIAA titles. In 1967, Banks won his only black college national championship, sharing the title with Grambling. He was CIAA Coach of the Year three times (1962, 1965-66) and was inducted into the College Football Hall of Fame in 1992.

BEST TEAM In 1966, Morgan State went undefeated (8–0) and beat West Chester (Pa.) 14-6 in the Tangerine Bowl, marking the only appearance by a black college team in the bowl game's history. Lanier was the game's MVP.

NORFOLK STATE UNIVERSITY
Norfolk, Va.

The Spartans have carved a nice little niche in the football-rich Hampton Roads area, where three other black colleges—Hampton, Virginia State, Virginia Union—are within 100 miles of each other. Norfolk State (enrollment 6,186) is Virginia's largest public historically black university and one of the largest HBCUs in the nation. After several decades as a member of the NCAA Division II CIAA, the Spartans moved up to Division I-AA and joined the MEAC in 1997.

GLORY DAYS From 1974 to 1976, NSU won three straight CIAA championships, posting a 23–11 record in the first three seasons of William "Dick" Price's tenure. Leaders on those teams were defensive tackle Moses Trotter (1974) and defensive back James Flowers (1976), both *Pittsburgh Courier* All-Americas. Flowers was also named to the Associated Press D1-AA All-America team in 1976.

BEST PLAYER The aerial combination of quarterback Aaron Sparrow and wide receiver James Roe locked up every Spartans major career passing and receiving record from 1992 to 1995. Sparrow is NSU's leader in career passing yards (8,743 yards, 79 TDs, 38 INTs). Roe caught 239 passes for 4,468 yards, averaged 18.7 yards per catch, scored 46 TDs and had 291 career points. Both Sparrow and Roe were All-Americas in 1994 and 1995.

BEST COACH Price coached the Spartans from 1974 to 1983, compiling a record of 61–42–4. He also won two NCAA Division II track titles during his tenure, and later became the school's athletic director. In 1997, NSU named its new football stadium (which at 30,000 capacity is the largest in the MEAC) after Price. Norfolk State joined the CIAA in 1963, but didn't win a league title until Price's first season as head coach in 1974, when he guided the team to a 7–1 MEAC record and a 7–4 mark overall.

BEST TEAM The 1984 Spartans, under coach Willard Bailey, went 10–2, setting school records for most wins in a season and longest winning streak (eight games). Bailey's group, led by quarterback Willie Gillus, won the CIAA championship and advanced to the NCAA Division II playoffs for the first and only time in school history. The team lost to Towson State in the first round 31–21.

NORTH CAROLINA A&T UNIVERSITY
Greensboro, N.C.

Many of the central figures in the Greensboro, N.C., lunch-counter sit-ins that galvanized the civil rights movement throughout the segregated South in the 1960s were students from North Carolina A&T—among them a gregarious Aggies quarterback and future preacher named Jesse Jackson. The Aggies had been members of the CIAA for 46 years (1924-70), scattering a mere four conference championships during that span. However, the 1968 team, coached by Hornsby Howell, finished 8–1 and earned the Aggies' first-ever black college national championship. North Carolina A&T joined the MEAC in 1971.

GLORY DAYS The 1990s were pretty exciting for the Aggies. Bill Hayes took over as coach for Mo Forte in 1988, and within three seasons, the Aggies had only their second MEAC championship (their first was in 1986). They followed that with another conference title in 1992, and from 1990 to 1993 A&T was 35–11. The 1992 and 1999 teams also appeared in the D1-AA playoffs. The 1999 team was 11–2 and was named black college national champion.

BEST PLAYER Defensive end Elvin Bethea was a two-time black college All-America lineman for the Aggies and was a third-round draft pick of the Houston Oilers in 1968. The durable Bethea retired in 1983 holding several Oilers records: most seasons (16), most career regular-season games played (210), most consecutive regular-season games played (135), most career sacks (105) and most sacks in a season (16 in 1973). Bethea was a Pro Bowler eight times, was All-Pro four times and was All-AFC six times. He was inducted into the Pro Football Hall of Fame in 2003.

BEST COACH Hayes is by far the most successful coach in the program's history, posting a 106–64 record in 15 years with the Aggies. His total wins are almost double those for his closest competitors, Bert Piggott (56), Hornsby Howell (55) and Big Bill Bell (55). In 1991, Hayes was named Sheridan Broadcasting Network Coach of the Year, after a 9–2 finish and an appearance in the inaugural Heritage Bowl, a 36-13 loss to Alabama State. Hayes received the SBN coaching honor again in 1999.

BEST TEAM Hayes' 1999 conference champions, led by black college All-America defensive back Darryl Klugh, is considered the finest team in school history. The team went 11–2—the first time the Aggies had won more than nine games in a season—was named black college national champion and was slotted No. 10 nationally by the Sports Network. The 1999 Aggies were 8–0 in the MEAC and earned the school's only D1-AA playoff win, a 24–10 first-round victory over No. 1-seeded Tennessee State.

PRAIRIE VIEW A&M UNIVERSITY
Prairie View, Texas

Founded in 1878 in Prairie View, a town on the site of a former cotton plantation 40 miles west of Houston, the school has always been a keystone—academically, athletically, socially, culturally—of African-American life in Texas. From 1940 to 1969, the Prairie View Interscholastic League was the governing body for all black high school athletic programs in the state, and Prairie View was a magnet in the 1950s and 1960s for talented black high school athletes. But in the integration era, the football program found it increasingly difficult to recruit blue-chip talent and the team nosedived. The result? A nine-year, 80-game losing streak that began on Oct. 28, 1989, and ended Sept. 26, 1998—the longest losing streak in NCAA history. Ouch.

GLORY DAYS During the 1950s and 1960s, Prairie View peaked as a dominant force in black college football, earning a reputation as the "Black Notre Dame." In one 12-season span (1953-64), the Panthers were named black college national champions five times (1953-54, 1958, 1963-64).

BEST PLAYER Ken Houston started his career at Prairie View (1963-67) as a linebacker but would become one of the best strong safeties ever to play the game. A two-time black college All-America, Houston had a 14-year NFL career (six seasons with the Houston Oilers, eight with the Washington Redskins). He returned nine interceptions for touchdowns during his career, an NFL record until 2001. In 1986, he was inducted into the Pro Football Hall of Fame.

BEST COACH Billy Nicks arrived at Prairie View in 1945 after a successful coaching start at his alma mater, Morris Brown, where he produced a black college national championship (1941). Nicks' first tour of duty at Prairie View lasted all of three mediocre seasons, with a 15–9–3 record earning him a demotion to assistant coach. Nicks took charge of the program again in 1952 and, over the next 14 years, never had a losing season and won eight conference titles in the ultracompetitive SWAC. In 1963, he became the first black college coach to be named NAIA Division I Coach of the Year. Nicks is a member of the NAIA Coaches Hall of Fame and in 1999 was inducted into the College Football Hall of Fame. "He was a classic coach," said Houston. "He looked the part and he got his players to play. He didn't play favorites. If we were going on a trip and there were star players missing when we got ready to leave, he'd say, 'We got 11? Roll this bus.'"

BEST TEAM Black college football was reaching its zenith in the 1960s, when SWAC teams won or shared seven black college national titles, with the Panthers winning it all twice, in 1963 (10–1) and 1964 (9–0). Though both squads were coached by Nicks, the former group was Prairie View's all-time best, possessing a wealth of future NFL and AFL talent, including wide receiver Otis Taylor, defensive back Jim Kearney and tight end Alvin Reed. The only blemish on the 1963 team was a 33-27 loss to St. John's (Minn.) in the NAIA Division I national championship game, the first time ever a black college team had played for that title.

SOUTH CAROLINA STATE UNIVERSITY
Orangeburg, S.C.

Located in Orangeburg, S.C., South Carolina State is rightfully proud of an Army ROTC program that produces more African-American military officers than any other college or university in the country. In football, South Carolina State gave starts to two of the game's most revered players: Marion Motley and David "Deacon" Jones. Motley, who played most of his career in the AAFC and is a Hall of Famer, played for S.C. State in his freshman season (1939) before transferring cross-country to the University of Nevada, Reno. Jones, a civil rights militant, played his freshman season in Orangeburg but then sat out a year to regroup from his social activism. "I was tired," he said. "You got spit on and all that, and I wondered, 'What am I living for?'" Jones, one of the greatest defensive ends in NFL history, completed his college football career at Mississippi Vocational College (now Mississippi Valley State University) before embarking on his illustrious Hall of Fame career in the NFL.

GLORY DAYS During Willie Jeffries' first stint as head coach at South Carolina State, the Bulldogs won five consecutive MEAC championships (1974-78) and compiled a 50–13–4 record. The 1975 team allowed just 29 points in 10 games.

BEST PLAYER As a standout linebacker for the New York Giants, Harry Carson surprised head coach Bill Parcells with a Gatorade shower near the end of one of the resurgent Giants' wins, and so started a trend that swept the sport. At S.C. State, Carson played linebacker and defensive end and was a two-time black college All-America. A first-team All-America selection in 1975, Carson set school and conference records with 17 sacks and 112 tackles as anchor of the record-setting 1975 defense. A two-time all-conference choice, Carson became the first player in MEAC history to win back-to-back Defensive Player of the Year honors, in 1974 and

1975. Rated the No. 1 inside linebacker in NFL history by *Pro Football Weekly*, Carson was named to the All-Rookie team after his first NFL season. He was named to the All-NFL team seven times and to the All-NFC team eight times.

BEST COACH Willie Jeffries, best known as the first African-American to lead a Division I-A team (Wichita State, 1979-83), coached at S.C. State in two different stints (1973-78, 1989-2001), compiling a 128–77–4 record. His teams were MEAC champs six times, and he won two black college national championships (1976-77). In 2002, Jeffries received the Lifetime Achievement Award from the Black Coaches Association.

BEST TEAM Good as the 8–2–1 Carson-led 1975 outfit was, the 1976 team gets the edge for giving up only 34 points, finishing with a 10–1 record and being named black college national champion.

SOUTHERN UNIVERSITY
Baton Rouge, La.

Bad enough that Southern has always languished in arch-rival Grambling's shadow, but just down the street in Baton Rouge is LSU, for Billy Cannon's sake! Yet, in football-mad Louisiana, the Jaguars have always rallied a faithful, rabid following with an intimidating chant: "Who dat talkin' 'bout beatin' them Jags?" Not many teams could do it, let alone talk about it, especially from the 1940s through the 1960s, when the Jags took a backseat to no one—including Grambling.

GLORY DAYS In one magical five-season stretch just after World War II, Southern went 47–4–3 from 1946 to 1950 and won the school's first three black college national championships (1948-50) under legendary coach Arnett "Ace" Mumford. For the three national championship seasons, the Jags' combined record was 32–0–2. Odie Posey, the greatest running back in Southern University history, led those teams. In 1949, Posey rushed for 1,399 yards, still a school record.

BEST PLAYER Coming out of high school in New Orleans, defensive back Aeneas Williams received an offer for an academic scholarship from Dartmouth, but decided to stay closer to home and play at Southern—as a walk-on. Williams became a two-time black college All-America (1989-90) and had 11 interceptions his senior year. A third-round pick of the Phoenix Cardinals, Williams was named the NFC's Defensive Rookie of the Year in 1991 and is an eight-time Pro Bowler.

BEST COACH Grambling coach Eddie Robinson on Ace Mumford: "He beat me so often, I thought I had stolen something." Mumford and Robinson went head-to-head only six times, mainly because Grambling didn't join the SWAC until 1958 and Mumford retired at the end of the 1961 season. The record? Mumford 5, Robinson 1. Mumford's career began in 1924 at Jarvis Christian College in Hawkins, Texas. He also coached at Bishop College and Texas College before taking over at Southern in 1936. Mumford won six black college national championships (including one at Texas College in 1935) and had a 38-game unbeaten streak from 1948 to 1951. In 36 years as a head coach, he compiled a 233–85–23 record. Mumford was inducted into the College Football Hall of Fame in 2001.

BEST TEAM Quarterback Warren Braden, a two-time black college All-America (1948-49), and Posey, a shifty breakaway back, starred on the 1948 team that put together the only perfect season in Southern history. The team, coached by Mumford, scored 395 points and gave up only 33, shutting out eight opponents.

TEXAS SOUTHERN
Houston, Texas

Founded in 1947, Texas Southern is one of the youngest schools among historically black colleges. TSU has produced major players in Texas politics, sending Barbara Jordan and Mickey Leland to the U.S. Congress and producing U.S. secretary of education Rod Paige, who from 1971 to 1975 coached the football team, winning 26 of 51 games. Located just east of downtown Houston, TSU was at the center of local civil rights activism in the 1960s; Muhammad Ali made a celebrated visit there before refusing induction into the military in April 1967. Quite a few individual stars have come out of the TSU football program: defensive end Michael Strahan, wide receivers Homer Jones, Warren Wells and Kenny Burrough, running back Willie Ellison and offensive lineman Winston Hill. Even so, the Tigers have been consistent only in their mediocrity since the early 1960s.

GLORY DAYS TSU had at least seven wins in nine of the 13 seasons covering 1951-63. Quarterback Audrey Ford, a two-time black college All-America, led the team in the early 1950s. Later in the decade, William "Rock" Glosson, a two-time black college All-America wide receiver, was the marquee player for the Tigers.

BEST PLAYER Strahan was such a dominant defensive end, opposing players could only double-team and hold him. These tactics so rarely drew a penalty flag that

outraged TSU coaches began referring to "the Strahan rules." Despite playing only one year of high school football, in his senior college season (1992), Strahan was named first-team Associated Press D1-AA All-America, Sheridan Network's Black College Player of the Year, D1-AA and Black College Defensive Player of the Year and SWAC Player of the Year (for the second consecutive season). A second-round draft pick by the New York Giants, Strahan became the NFL's single-season sacks leader in 2001 with 22.5. Strahan still holds Texas Southern records for most sacks in a season (19 in 1992) and career (41.5).

BEST COACH Alexander Durley, a former math teacher and librarian, took the reins in 1949 as the second head coach in TSU history. Over the next 15 years, he built a solid program, going 101–54–7, with just three losing seasons. Despite his success, Durley's only SWAC title was shared with Wiley in 1956. His teams finished second five times in nine SWAC seasons.

BEST TEAM The 1952 Tigers were 10–0–1 and named co-black college national champions, the only time Texas Southern has ever received such consideration. The Tigers shared the title with three other teams, including 8–0–1 Lincoln (Mo.). Lincoln and TSU, the only undefeated black college teams that year, played to an early-season 13-13 tie. Florida A&M (8–2) and Virginia State (8–1) also claimed shares in the championship. The Tigers outscored their 1952 opponents 429-100.

THE ANNUAL REVIEW

What follows is a year-by-year rundown of 136 seasons of college football, incorporating poll rankings, All-America teams, Heisman Trophy balloting, award winners, conference standings, bowl game results and the NCAA's team and individual statistical leaders.

Poll Progression Charts. From 1936 on, each season begins with a chart, listing the nation's top teams from one week to the next along with the results for all the games involving ranked teams, so that you can monitor the precise fluctuations in the race for the national title. (You can see, for instance, that the last time a No. 1 team won and dropped in the polls was on Nov. 2, 2002, when Miami was pressured by Rutgers before prevailing 42-17, while No. 2 Oklahoma beat No. 3 Colorado. The Sooners claimed the top spot in the next day's poll.) The offerings include the writers poll published by the Associated Press (AP) since 1936; the coaches poll sponsored by United Press International (UP in our shorthand), then CNN from 1993-96 and finally ESPN and USA Today; and, at season's end, Richard Billingsley's final computer rankings (RB).

Consensus All-Americans. Beginning with Caspar Whitney's first All-America team of 1889, we've listed consensus All-Americans and all of the first-team All-Americans chosen by selectors recognized by the NCAA. The selectors are abbreviated as follows: AA-All-America Board; AP-Associated Press; WC-Walter Camp; CN-Cable News Network/Sports Illustrated.com; CM-Collier's Magazine; CP-Central Press; FM-Football World Magazine; FC-American Football Coaches Association; FN-Football News; FW-Football Writers Association of America; IN-International News Service; LK-Look Magazine; LM-Liberty Magazine; FM-Frank Menke Syndicate; NW-Newsweek; NA-North American Newspaper Alliance; NE-

Newspaper Enterprise Association; SN-Sporting News; UP-United Press; PI-United Press International; CW-Caspar Whitney; and CF-Walter Camp Foundation.

Conference Standings. The last year of pure parity in college football was 1869, when both teams finished 1-1. Since then, ranking teams has been slightly more complicated. This section contains a review of major-college records assembled through Richard Billingsley's all-time scores database and NCAA sources. The teams are ranked based on their winning percentages, using an NCAA formula that counts ties as half a win and half a loss. We have tried to use the contemporaneous names for each conference with one exception: the Big Ten, which was called the Western Conference well into the 1970s.

NCAA Statistical Leaders. The numbers simply don't exist to reliably determine the statistical leaders in college football's first 60 seasons. It wasn't until 1937 when Homer Cooke, founder of what would become the NCAA Statistics Service, began contacting every school in the country to request figures that the NCAA tabulated national rankings. In Cooke's early years, the standings were often tabulated without reports from one or more games. Those discrepancies, coupled with missing data from the 1950s, make most recordkeeping unreliable. That is until 1970 when the NCAA dispensed with accumulated totals and determined the champions of most categories on a per-game basis.

Point of Departure. Unlike the NCAA, we have decided to include military teams like Great Lakes Naval Academy and Randolph Field in the annual leaders categories because they competed against college teams and were football powers during the first and second World Wars. As the statistics reflect, acknowledging those service teams provides a more accurate snapshot of the sport during that era.

Poll Positions

It's Writers vs. Coaches in Football's Ballot Bowl

BY JOE POSNANSKI

OLD JOKE: EVERY MORNING, TWO GUYS STAND IN FRONT of the same store and watch the same beautiful woman walk by. After she passes, they argue about what perfume she's wearing. The woman walks around the corner and the men go back and forth, one shouting, "Chanel No. 5," the other screaming, "White Diamonds."

Then they go to work.

This happens every day.

"Look," the store owner finally says. "Every day you two guys stand here. You never buy anything. All you ever do is argue about this girl's perfume, and you've never even met her. Why don't you just ask her what perfume she wears?"

The two guys look at him like he's crazy.

"What fun would that be?" they ask.

That, as Woody Allen might say, is the key joke when it comes to the two major polls—the writers poll and the coaches poll—that for more than half a century have picked college football's national champion.

The poll system is absurd, even laughable if you want to spend any time thinking about it. Imagine any other sports league finishing its season and then going to a group of sportswriters and coaches and saying, "Okay, you saw the teams play, tell us which one is the best."

Every year, people shout, "This is no way to pick a champion? What do sportswriters know? And as for the coaches, they don't even see the other teams. Why don't you simply match up the best teams? Why don't you have a playoff, like every other college sport?"

And every year the college football people look at the critics like they're crazy.

"What fun would that be?" they ask.

***

The first Associated Press college football poll was in 1936. It was the brainchild of a fairly extraordinary and forgotten man, Alan J. Gould, the sports editor of the AP. Gould lived something of a Forrest Gump life: Somehow he managed to be everywhere. He was there when Gene Tunney beat Jack

Dempsey. He was there when Gene Sarazen hit the double eagle at the Masters. He was there when Jesse Owens won four gold medals in Berlin. Later, when Gould was the AP's executive editor, he was the one who made the right presidential call in 1948: "Truman," he told his reporters, "seems to be winning."

His passion was for college sports. In 1935 he started devising his own list of Top 10 college football teams in his column. That first year it was entirely his opinion. In the end, Gould named Minnesota, Princeton and Southern Methodist as tri-champions.

This created quite a fuss: who was this Alan J. Gould fellow to decide the college football national championship? When he made the mistake of not putting Minnesota alone at No. 1, his likeness was hanged in effigy in a small Minnesota town. "It created a storm," is how Gould explained it in an interview a few years before his death in 1993. And Gould loved the storm—what, after all, are sports all about? Gould decided he was on to something, and he began to poll other sportswriters regarding who they thought was the best college football team in all the land. And then he tabulated and released their Top 10 picks.

"Newspapers wanted material to fill space between games," Gould would later say. "That's all I had in mind, something to keep the pot boiling. Sports then was living off controversy, opinion, whatever. This was just another exercise in hoopla."

The first full AP poll, in 1936, was as baffling as any that would follow. Nobody seems to know for sure how voters were chosen, but we know that 44 sportswriters voted that first year, and that they voted for Minnesota (7–1) as No. 1. The team that beat Minnesota—Northwestern—was also 7–1, but was ranked seventh in the poll. Louisiana State (9–0–1)—the national champion choice of the Williamson Poll, a power rating invented by geologist (and Sugar Bowl committee member) Paul Williamson—was ranked No. 2 in the AP poll.

And so began seven decades (and counting) of puzzling picks, kicked off by Gould's little exercise in hoopla.

***

Eventually, United Press, the AP's direct competitor, decided it needed its own college football poll. There's no surviving story about the birth of the coaches poll, but it's easy to imagine a meeting in the UP executive offices:

Editor 1: We need our own college football poll.

Editor 2: How about we poll the sportswriters?

The coaches and sportswriters almost always agreed. All was right with the world. And then came 1990.

Editor 1: AP's already got the sportswriters. We need our own thing. How about we set up a playoff system, where the best teams in America would play each other in a sort of tournament, and the winner of that would be the national champion?

(Editor 1 and Editor 2 look at each other and shake their heads. "What fun would that be?" they ask.)

Editor 1: I've got it! We'll poll the coaches.

And so it came to pass. In 1950, for the first time, there were two major polls, AP's poll of 44 sportswriters and UP's poll of 35 coaches. The numbers would change (now 65 writers and broadcasters and 61 coaches vote), but the systems would more or less remain the same. That first year, the coaches and sportswriters agreed: Oklahoma was the best team in the country. The Sooners were 10–0 in 1950, and even though they lost to Kentucky in the Sugar Bowl, the voting was done before the bowl games. (That would change in time, but that story comes later.)

While there were occasional disagreements—the writers going with Ohio State, the coaches with UCLA in 1954; the writers picking Auburn, the coaches Ohio State in 1957—the two polls were mostly in agreement well into the 1980s. In 1958, United Press merged with International News Service and became UPI. From that year (when both the writers and coaches voted Louisiana State No. 1) until 1989 (when both polls picked Miami), the coaches and writers agreed 27 out of 32 years. That means 84% of the time, there was a clear-cut national champion.

There was peace in college football.

In the 1965 season, AP, for the first time, had its final poll after the bowl games. Up to this point, the bowls had been seen as nothing but exhibitions—"They are a reward for the players," Woody Hayes had said—and they were supposed to be off-limits when it came to voting the national champion.

But in 1964, this line of thinking had produced an unsatisfying result. There had been two undefeated teams going into the bowls, Alabama and Arkansas. The writers and coaches both picked Alabama. But then Arkansas proceeded to beat Nebraska in the Cotton Bowl while Alabama lost to Texas in the Orange Bowl. So there was Arkansas, unbeaten, and without its deserved national championship.

So the next year the AP pushed its voting back until after the bowl games. The move turned out to be perfectly timed. There were three undefeated teams going into the bowls: Michigan State, Arkansas and Nebraska. The coaches refused to wait for the bowls ("You can't judge a team by a bowl game," one coach reportedly grumbled to UPI. "Those kids have a month to do whatever they want before that game"). They chose Michigan State.

The writers waited. And everything changed. Michigan State lost to UCLA in the Rose Bowl. Arkansas lost to Louisiana State in the Cotton Bowl. And then, in the big game, Alabama beat Nebraska 39-28 in the Orange Bowl. All three undefeated teams had lost. And the writers chose ... Alabama.

A new era in college football was ushered in.

Well, not immediately. There was uproar about the sportswriters placing such an emphasis on bowl games, and it was so intense that the AP went back to voting before the bowl games for the next two years. But by 1968, the system looked so silly that the AP permanently went back to the postbowl vote. There was no holding back. The polls mattered. And the bowls mattered.

In 1970, the coaches still refused to wait until after the bowls. They picked Texas, which ended up losing to Notre Dame by 13 in the Cotton Bowl. Meanwhile, the writers waited and chose undefeated Nebraska, which won the Orange Bowl.

Three years later, with the coaches still refusing to wait until after the bowl games, they chose Alabama, which was undefeated as it went to the Sugar Bowl to face Notre Dame. Notre Dame was also undefeated, and the Fighting Irish won the game 24-23. The writers voted for Notre Dame, and Alabama was left waving a fairly humorous "UPI National Champion" banner. After that embarrassment, the coaches decided in 1974 to vote after the bowls.

There were two other split titles. In 1974, the writers named Oklahoma No. 1, but the coaches kept them out of the poll entirely because the Sooners were still on probation and chose Southern Cal. And in 1978, when the writers (suckers for the story angle) went for aging coach Bear Bryant and his Alabama team. The coaches, noting that Southern Cal had actually beaten Alabama during the regular season, voted for the Trojans.

Other than those exceptions, for 32 blissful years the coaches and writers agreed every single year. Sure, there was

always talk about the need for a playoff, and there were always newspaper columns mocking the system. But there wasn't much strife. The coaches and sportswriters almost always agreed. All was right in the world.

And then came 1990.

***

I was a copy editor at *The Charlotte Observer* in North Carolina when news came in that Colorado had been voted the national champion by the Associated Press. This was a huge story in ACC country, where most people felt Georgia Tech deserved the top spot. After all, the Yellow Jackets had gone unbeaten, 11–0–1, the only blotch a tie with North Carolina. And Georgia Tech had thumped Nebraska in the Citrus Bowl.

And Colorado? Well, the Buffaloes had lost a game and tied a game, and they needed two miracles to have a record that good. In their final drive at Missouri, the Buffaloes had inexplicably been given five downs, an astonishing gaffe that allowed Colorado to score a last-minute touchdown and win. Then, in the Orange Bowl against Notre Dame, a debatable clipping call nullified a spectacular Rocket Ismail punt return for a touchdown. Colorado won 10-9.

Appalled at the writers' ignorance, and because I never did have a copy editor's sense of balance, my headline was "Georgia Tech Robbed of National Championship." Then, because we had the holiday skeleton crew in—that was the only reason I was writing a headline on something that important to begin with—the headline actually appeared in the newspaper. I assumed everyone would share my fury.

The reaction was very different from the one I expected. People were mad, all right. But as it turned out, they were mad at me. Why? Because in the headline (and, for that matter in the story I put together), I had all but ignored the fact that the coaches had selected Georgia Tech as national champions. It had been so long since we'd had a split national champion—12 years, in fact—that the concept simply slipped past me. By throwing all my rage at the writers, I had, in fact, rejected the coaches poll (which, a year later, became known as the *USA Today*/CNN poll, and in 1995, ESPN replaced CNN in the title).

The letters received by the paper went something like this:
Dear [Moron, Loser, etc.],

I have been a subscriber for 10 years [a million years, two weeks, etc.] and I have never been so insulted [enraged, humiliated, etc.] as I was by the headline that said Georgia Tech did not win the national championship. In fact, if you knew anything at all [had any brains in your head, etc.], you would know that Georgia Tech did win the national championship, as voted by the coaches, who are the only people qualified to vote for the national championship [10,000 times smarter than sportswriters, the greatest people on planet earth, etc.].
Cancel my subscription.

That year was a turning point, all right. For the first time in the 40-year coexistence of the two polls, there was a violent dispute over which team was the best. All the other split national champions had been simple differences of opinion. But here, everybody disagreed with everybody. The coaches picked Georgia Tech by just one point, 847-846. And the writers went against their usual philosophy and bypassed the undefeated team. Many argued that Colorado wasn't worthy because of the nature of their tainted win over Missouri. Everybody argued about whether sportswriters or coaches were more qualified to vote. It was mayhem.

And when the writers and coaches disagreed again the next year—this time the writers went with undefeated Miami while the coaches went with undefeated Washington—the outcry was deafening. The system had to be changed.

Starting in 1992, college football had something called the Bowl Coalition, which led to something called the Bowl Alliance, which led to the Bowl Championship Series—which isn't a series at all—which was designed to match up big conferences in the bowl games and end the confusion.

Which, of course, it did not.

In 2004, after the BCS system had been overhauled for about the 28th time, the regular season ended with five undefeated teams, three of them—Auburn, Oklahoma, Southern California—from BCS powerhouse conferences. The BCS bumped Auburn out of the national championship game, leading at least one Alabama sportswriter to receive very angry hate mail. After the season ended, the Associated Press demanded that its poll no longer be used in the Bowl Championship Series.

And yet the polls go on. As do the arguments.

***

A few years ago, a coach I like very much asked me how it was possible for a sportswriter to rate college football teams. "What do sportswriters know about football?" he asked. "Have you ever played? Have you ever coached? All you guys do is sit up in the press box, eat your free lunches, look at the statistics and watch a few highlights. How could you possibly vote for the national champion?"

"Well," I said, "how can coaches vote? You guys obviously

don't know anything about other teams from other conferences. You can't even tell us about your next opponent until Tuesday when you've had a chance to study them. You have personal biases about certain coaches. There are always stories that many coaches don't even vote themselves; they have their sports information directors vote. At Maryland, Jerry Claiborne said his wife did the voting."

"His wife probably knows more about football than any sportswriter," the coach said. "I mean, give me a small break. We had a punt blocked once, and I had a sportswriter ask:

'Coach, why didn't you just block that guy?' You get that? Why didn't we just block him?"

"If coaches are so smart about football," I said, "they might be able to tell us something after the game instead of saying, 'I need to look at the film.'"

This went on for a while, until the secretary came in and said, "Why don't you just both admit that neither coaches nor sportswriters should be voting for the national championship?"

We both looked at her like she was mad.

"What fun would that be?" we asked.

Between the Numbers

Mathematical Rankings in College Football

BY RICHARD BILLINGSLEY

"THE RECOGNITION OF THE STATISTICAL ANALYSIS OF a season is important to incorporate now that we are moving into the 21st century." That's how Bowl Championship Series chairman Roy Kramer explained, in 1998, the addition of computer rankings to the BCS formula that would be used to match the No. 1 and No. 2 teams in college football. Few people, perhaps not even Kramer himself, recognized that in addition to building a bridge to a new century, the new BCS formula was actually tapping into one of the richest traditions in the history of the sport, that of mathematical rankings.

America's long fascination with ranking college teams can be traced to 1926, when a professor of economics at the University of Illinois, Frank Dickinson, released the first mathematical ranking, one that attempted to come up with a scientific answer to the perennial question, "Who's No. 1?" This was 10 years before the first Associated Press poll and 24 years before the first coaches poll (then for United Press) in 1950. The development of mathematical systems, and later polls, provided clear signs of the expanding universe of college football.

In the earliest years of the game, of course, there was no need for a ranking system. The "best team" in college football always came from a handful of Eastern schools that would later become known as the Ivy League: Princeton, Yale, Harvard and Pennsylvania dominated football from its inception as a college sport in 1869 through the late 1800s. By the turn of the century, though, the spread of college football across the country was producing a wave of challengers. Fielding Yost's great Michigan squads of 1901-04, which compiled an astounding record of 43–0–1, were the first teams outside the East to challenge the Ivy League for national supremacy. The 11–0–0 Wolverines of 1901 defeated Stanford 49-0 in the first Rose Bowl and steamrolled their way to a second consecutive 11–0–0 season a year later. They would remain undefeated until the final game of the 1905 season.

But soon it became difficult to determine "Who's No. 1?" It was impossible for the great Michigan and Minnesota teams of the early 1900s—or the exemplary Notre Dame and Pittsburgh clubs in the following decade—to tour the country playing head-to-head against the other contenders, from Vanderbilt in the South to Stanford and California on the West Coast. A few select intersectional games did occur during that period, but they were a rarity and took place only after days of travel by train.

By the mid-1920s, Professor Dickinson began tinkering with a mathematical means of settling disputes taking place between East Coast and West Coast teams, and everyone in between, with different schools proclaiming themselves unofficial "national champions."

Dickinson's timing was perfect: the 1920s and 1930s were the Golden Age for the college game. Great rivalries were being born: Southern California-Notre Dame, Texas-Oklahoma, Alabama-Tennessee, Michigan-Ohio State. Great traditions were being established: Bevo first roamed the sideline at Austin in 1916; the 12th man first warmed the hearts of the Texas A&M faithful in 1922; the Hedges were one foot tall at Georgia's Sanford Stadium in 1929. The "i" was first dotted in Script Ohio in 1936, one year after the Downtown Athletic Club started awarding a trophy to college football's outstanding player.

Bowl games became a favorite part of America's sports landscape, as the Orange and Sugar bowls joined the Rose in 1935 and the Cotton kicked off in 1937. Crowds flocked to stadiums in astounding numbers. On Nov. 26, 1927, an estimated 120,000 gathered at Soldier Field in Chicago to witness Notre Dame defeat Southern California 7-6. The massive stadiums we all know today as the Big House (Michigan), the Horse Shoe (Ohio State), The Swamp (Florida) and Death Valley (LSU) were all constructed from 1924 to 1929.

Mathematical rankings (defined as any system that rates teams using a mathematical formula based on tangible factors such as wins, losses and scores) flourished during the same period, and to some degree, their success—like so much else in the sport—can partially be credited to Notre Dame. Dickinson's math rankings caught the eye of Irish coach Knute Rockne, who asked the professor to backdate two seasons of his system. The results? The Irish were named Dickinson's national champion for 1924, thus giving Notre Dame the distinction of becoming the first "scientific"

champion in college football. Dickinson's system, like virtually every one since, was based on a private formula, which gave different weights to a team's wins based on the score and the quality of each opponent.

Rockne wasn't the only one fascinated by Dickinson's mathematical approach to naming national champions. From 1926 to 1935 a number of mathematical systems were born, some of which have survived the test of time, with their "No. 1" teams still recorded in the *NCAA Records Book* as "unofficial College Football Champions."

Among the early selectors, six systems gained considerable acclaim. They would be joined in succeeding decades by two other notable systems. All had a major impact on the sport:

Dickinson System (1926). Dickinson's rankings were arguably the best known of the early systems, widely reported in newspapers and accompanied at season's end by a trophy presentation.

Houlgate System (1927). Deke Houlgate of Los Angeles was syndicated in newspapers as well as the annual *Football Thesaurus* from 1946 to 1958.

Dunkel Index (1929). Created by Dick Dunkel Sr., it is still one of the most respected mathematical ranking systems in the world, its formula unchanged since its inception more than 75 years ago. The Index is now in the hands of a third-generation Dunkel.

Boand System (1930). Also known as the Azzi Ratem System. Developed by William Boand, it appeared in many newspapers over the next three decades, as well as the *Illustrated Football Annual* (1932-42), and weekly in the *Football News* from 1942 to 1944 and again from 1951 to 1960.

Williamson System (1932). Geologist Paul Williamson of New Orleans was a Sugar Bowl committeeman, and was syndicated throughout the South.

Poling System (1935). The ratings of Richard Poling, a former player for Ohio Wesleyan, appeared in several newspapers and were published annually in the *Football Review Supplement.*

DeVold System (1945). Harry DeVold, a former player for Cornell, first appeared in the *Football News* in 1962 and continues today.

Herman Matthews Grid Ratings (1966). Gained

> ## *Professor Dickinson's system caught the eye of Knute Rockne, who asked him to backdate it to 1924.*

considerable acclaim with national distribution by Scripps-Howard News Services.

Each system had its followers, and each had a slightly different formula. The Dunkel Index was among the first systems that didn't merely rank teams but also created numerical "power ratings," which attempted to identify the expected scoring differential of any upcoming game.

While interest in mathematical rankings rose in the early '30s, the Associated Press turned up the volume on the "Who's No. 1?" debate in 1936 when it began to publish a weekly poll of sportswriters ranking the top teams in the country. The very first AP poll (Oct. 19, 1936), tabulating the votes of 35 nationwide sportswriters, found Minnesota (3–0) to be the nation's most respected team with 32 No. 1 votes, solidly ahead of No. 2 Duke (5–0). In the 69 years since, human voters and the mathematicians have battled for the right to declare their choice as a "true" national champion. In 1950, United Press joined the race and began publishing a poll based on the votes of a board of coaches.

Perceived flaws in each approach sparked an unending debate. Early mathematical formulas relied heavily on margin of victory, often without collapsing runaway scores. Sportswriters and coaches often ignored the strength of a team's schedule, relying more heavily on wins and losses regardless of the quality of the opposition. Even more alarming was the personal bias factor: sportswriters favoring teams from their geographical regions, coaches voting for teams in their own conferences.

To some degree, this bias was a natural consequence of the lack of sufficient information. Without television coverage and only limited radio broadcasts, human nature dictated that voters would favor teams they knew more about. Even now, in the age of *SportsCenter*, those regional biases remain.

From the late 1930s through the mid-1960s, the main discussion centered on whether the bowl games should be included in the final rankings. Mathematicians insisted that all games be counted; otherwise, a true champion could not be declared. Sportswriters, bowing to pressure from the NCAA, which deemed bowl games "postseason" play, refused to recognize bowls as part of the championship process.

The debate took off in 1938 after the sportswriters in the AP poll picked TCU as No. 1 while four of the six math-based systems favored Tennessee, which played a superior schedule. But that was nothing compared to three post-WWII donnybrooks:

1947. Michigan and Notre Dame, both unbeaten, battled back and forth between No. 1 and No. 2 in the regular season. The Irish claimed the top spot in the final AP poll after a season-ending 38-7 win over No. 3 USC, but five of the six mathematicians picked Michigan after the Wolverines shut out the Trojans 49-0 in the Rose Bowl. (Only the pre-bowl Williamson System stuck it out with the Irish.) The two teams played comparable schedules. Notre Dame's dominance of the game from 1940 to 1946 heavily influenced the human voters; Michigan's dominant margins of victory (they outscored opponents 394-53, with five shutouts) heavily influenced the mathematicians.

1953. The tables were turned six years later: Notre Dame became the mathematicians' unanimous pick after AP and UP champion Maryland lost to Oklahoma 7-0 in the Orange Bowl. Clearly, naming a national champion before the bowl games was risky business. In fact, three AP-UP champs went on to lose bowl games in one four-year stretch: Oklahoma was beaten 13-7 by Bear Bryant's great Kentucky team in the 1950 Sugar Bowl; General Bob Neyland's undefeated Tennessee squad of 1951 lost to Maryland 28-13 in the 1951 Sugar Bowl; and Maryland in 1953. (Michigan State, AP-UP champ in 1952, didn't play in a bowl that season.)

1954. This was the year the pigskin hit the fan. For four years the AP and UP had agreed on their choice for a national champion, and as long as the humans agreed, a majority of the public seemed satisfied. But in 1954 the AP favored Ohio State and UP voted for UCLA. Both were undefeated, as was Oklahoma, voted No. 3 by both services. Of the three, only Ohio State played in a bowl, beating Southern California 20-7 in the Rose. The public waited anxiously for the math polls to break the tie, and they did, falling solidly behind the Buckeyes.

Only twice in the next 14 years (1957, 1965) did the humans disagree on a choice for national champion. But the mathematicians' continued preference for waiting until after the bowls, and the public's increasingly vocal preference for that method, eventually forced the wire service polls to give in. Beginning in 1969 (after a one-year special vote in 1965), the Associated Press moved to a postbowl final vote. The UPI, after three split national championships and near-constant controversy over the next five years, followed suit in 1974.

Ironically, the very moment when mathematical rankings seemed to be least relevant—in the mid-1970s, after the coaches began voting after bowl games—coincided with an explosion of computing technology that enabled the mathematical rankings to become more sophisticated, easier to compute—and more numerous.

An unlikely source helped bring mathematical ratings back into circulation. In 1979, after several years of postbowl game controversies, the sports department of *The New York Times* commissioned its own mathematical system, one that explicitly factored in both strength of schedule and strength of opponents' schedules; gave greater weight to late-season games; and collapsed runaway scores. Other systems had been doing this before, but the *Times'* system made these innovations explicit and deepened the understanding of these factors for a general audience.

If college football had developed a playoff system to determine a national champion, the significance of any rankings (either voter-based or mathematically based) would have greatly diminished or simply been assimilated into a larger framework of factors used to select and seed the playoff field. (See the NCAA and March Madness.) Instead, college football's postseason steered clear of a playoff system, and by the end of the 1990s the mathematicians returned to a prominent—and controversial—role in the national championship debate.

Criticism of the current computer rankings' complexity notwithstanding, their usefulness is more manifest now than ever before. In the absence of a playoff, with nearly 120 schools in Division I-A and relatively few intersectional games, the need for a rational, scientific approach to rating schools is self-evident. If anything, the gap among the top 10 teams in the land in any year has narrowed, making it all the more difficult to judge, at the end of a season, who deserves to be No. 1.

Compare the present environment to, say, 1950, when there were no scholarship limitations and the powerful schools hoarded the great players and stuffed rosters with qualified backups. Injuries didn't have the same impact on a team as they do today. Innovative coaching minds, ever-more-complicated schemes and scholarship limits created what we know today as "parity," and it's the presence of parity—and the ongoing absence of a national championship tournament—that makes mathematical rankings more necessary than ever.

Mathematical rankings have been a part of college football for more than 75 years—and they're sharper, smarter, more scientifically based today than ever before. Computer

analysts for college football don't know anywhere near as much about X's and O's as coaches do, and their algorithms aren't as easily understood as the colorful words of sportswriters, but they have a deep respect and appreciation for the game of college football. Agree with the specific results of computer analyses or not, but to ignore their value reflects a disregard for objectivity in the decisionmaking process.

Does that mean computers are infallible and better than human beings with regard to ranking teams? No. Computers are programmed by human beings and are as susceptible to flawed logic in their conception as any other system.

There are also areas about which reasonable people can differ, and it's in these particulars that the individual BCS computer rankings differ. For instance, although the strength of a team's schedule is always a primary factor in any good system, how is that strength of schedule calculated—strictly by wins and losses, by strength of conference or by rank of opponent? What is the starting position for the teams each season; should everyone start equal or should there be a preseason ranking? Should each win or loss in the season count equally or should the most recent performances carry more weight? Should margin of victory be used? If so, should it be capped at a particular level? Should that level be 21 points, 28 points or more? Should the site of a game factor into the equation? All of these perspectives had to be dealt with, and the only way to do so was to bring together a cross-section of proven, respected computer formulas, because no single formula could accomplish all of the above criteria. And this is what the BCS did.

The BCS determined that no single program should be the sole factor in seeding teams to play for a championship. By using a select group of respected, time-tested computer programs, in conjunction with a human element (i.e., polls), the BCS sought to provide a more reliable blend of judgments. Computers serve as a great resource tool, reflecting strength of opponent and conference in comparison to wins and losses. Human input can weigh in on injuries, weather conditions, impact of rivalries and other factors that even a good computer formula simply cannot analyze.

Together they represent the best college football can achieve without a playoff. Until it's settled on the field in a national championship tournament of some type, even if it's two teams selected to play in a "College Bowl" after the four major bowls, the job of determining a national champion—as well as the most worthy opponents for a game to be designated as a national championship game—will be, at best, an imprecise blend of art and science.

As it was in Professor Dickinson's day, college football leaves us with no definitive answer to the eternal question, "Who's No. 1?" Consequently it's important that we use all the tools at our disposal. Thankfully, that array is vastly more sophisticated and accessible than it was 80 years ago.

Getting There From Here

A Practical Guide to a College Playoff

By Michael MacCambridge

F AR FROM THE GOLDEN DOME, THE BIG HOUSE AND THE Swamp, across the Atlantic Ocean and several time zones removed from the pageantry of college football, there is another sports organization that doesn't bother with a playoff at the end of its season.

It's the English Premiership soccer league, the dominant sports entity in England and among the most celebrated in the world. As in many other top-class soccer leagues around the globe, there is no postseason for the league championship because there's no need for one. In the Premiership, 20 teams begin each season in August, playing a double round-robin schedule of home-and-away dates against every other team in the league. At the end of the 38-game regular season in May, everyone has had one home and one road game against everyone else, and whoever tops the table is the clear and undisputed champion.

Contrast the Premiership setup with the sport closer to home that doesn't bother with a playoff: big-time college football. There are nearly six times as many teams playing major college football (117 teams played football in Division I-A in 2004), and they play just 11 or 12 games per season, most against regional and conference opponents. For this reason—so many teams, so few games—it's probably more difficult to identify the best two teams at the end of the regular season in college football than in any other sport.

And yet, this is our sport with no tournament.

While many of the details about how college football crowns its mythical national champions have changed in the past 70 years, the central fact—the mythical part—remains stubbornly unmoved. The bowls-and-polls structure of college football is big-time sports' greatest anomaly, an institution suffused with opinion and arbitrary judgments in a universe whose very foundation is the idea of meritocracy and tangible results.

Yes, Southern California's win over Oklahoma in the 2005 Orange Bowl was convincing, but both Auburn and Utah finished undefeated as well—yet those schools had no

suitable forum in which to prove themselves. As long as instances like that exist—and in the absence of a championship playoff, they must continue to exist—the criticism of the BCS won't abate.

The public knows this, and among the hottest topics in American sports, none is so clearly one-sided. Recent surveys showed that sports fans favor a playoff by a 9-1 margin.

Besides the present system being arbitrary and wildly unpopular, it lacks drama. "It won't work," said the savvy Texas athletic director DeLoss Dodds in 1998. "We've got four major bowls now, but we've got only one that people care about. The other bowls are hurt. People aren't going to travel to them, and people aren't going to watch them on TV, because those games are not a progression into something, and people don't care about the end of anything but 1 vs. 2. The way to do it is to go with a progression toward 1 vs. 2, and that's a playoff. The bowls know this."

Which is perhaps one reason why so many in the BCS resist even discussing the merits of a playoff, insisting that any talk is foolish because a playoff flatly won't happen. Many insiders flatly disagree. "What we're experiencing now," said Dodds, "is the transition from what was to what's gonna be— and what's gonna be is a playoff."

Of course, saying that a college playoff won't happen is far different than saying one shouldn't happen. So let's skip the Machiavellian rhetoric of the BCS and move on to the logistics of the more interesting question:

How would a playoff happen?

In general, there are two different paths to a playoff: a revolutionary method, in which the NCAA regains effective control of the sport from the BCS and tears down many of the conventions established in the past decade; or an evolutionary one, in which the BCS solidifies its control over the game for the foreseeable future by delivering—at long last—what the public wants.

The two plans would eventually lead to a similar outcome. But for either plan to have a chance, there are a few conditions that must be met, at least according to the college administrators, university athletic directors and television networks that have studied the problem over the past 20 years.

THE PREREQUISITES

Any playoff plan that ultimately comes into being will include the following elements. (These stipulations have been

dictated by the market; their integration increases the likelihood of earning NCAA approval; each answers a criticism of playoff opponents; and, not incidentally, they make sense.)

Eight Teams. "The magic number is eight," says former CBS Sports president Neal Pilson. "I've always felt that was the best combination in terms of extending the season, in terms of the number of teams that should be involved. Sixteen is too cumbersome, and four involves too many arbitrary choices."

In most years, there are at least four—and often more—teams with a plausible claim on a national title. Eight would bring the ideal balance, giving all truly worthy contenders a shot without unduly watering down the regular season.

January Playoff. Around 95% of NCAA schools have final exams in December, not January, which is why a playoff in January makes both economic and academic sense. Though Divisions I-AA, II and III all hold 16- to 28-team playoffs in November and December, there is virtually no support in Division I-A for a December tournament. And the bowls have been trending later, with 25 of the 2004 season's 28 bowl games played on or after Dec. 23, when schools are on their winter break.

An eight-team playoff means that just four teams would have longer seasons than they do currently. Many seniors from the best schools in the country already play during those weekends, in senior all-star games. Playing the tournament into mid-January would still cause football players in Division I-A to miss less class time than do Division I-A basketball players, whose nonconference tournaments and midweek games exact a greater toll. And under either of the following plans, Division I-A football players would actually continue to miss less class time than football players in the NCAA's other divisions.

Survival of the Bowls. When Florida State coach Bobby Bowden says, "I'm not one for eliminating the bowls, because they're so much a part of the American tradition," he echoes the opinion of most coaches.

Among the canards of playoff opponents is the idea that a playoff would kill the tradition of the bowls. This is patently false. With the four major bowls hosting the four quarterfinal games on or around New Year's Day, interest in all four games would be heightened. And, as explained below, a playoff plan

> *Among the canards of playoff opponents is that a playoff would kill the tradition of the bowls.*

would offer something extra for the major bowls.

An eight-team playoff would also have no effect on the minor bowls. The Sun Bowl and Peach Bowl wouldn't be part of determining a national champion, but those bowls have never figured into the national title chase. Minor bowls would survive a football playoff, just as the NIT survived the expansion of the Big Dance in basketball. Besides, ESPN needs programming in late December.

Lid on Regular-Season Schedule. The people who've opposed the playoff idea on the grounds that it would be too much of a burden for student-athletes are, curiously, the same people who added conference championship games in the 1990s and who were pushing for a 12th regular-season game (possibly coming as soon as 2006). If a playoff system were realized, it likely would accompany a return to an 11-game regular season, and a complete prohibition on preseason games like the ousted Kickoff and Pigskin classics and the current BCA Classic.

"To justify ourselves going into January, I think we'd have to do something on the front end," says former Brigham Young coach LaVell Edwards, whose BYU team labored through a 15-game season beginning with the Pigskin Classic in 1996. For teams playing in a preseason game, notes Edwards, "you're bringing your guys in the first of August, and if a team goes all the way through, you're looking at six months of college football— while a guy's in school. And to me, that's brutal."

So accompanying any playoff plan would likely be a rule limiting regular-season play to 11 games, played on or around the 13 Saturdays that fall every year in the months of September, October and November. With those variables set, college football could have an eight-team playoff with the first round to be held on New Year's Eve and New Year's Day in the major bowl games currently aligned with the BCS.

There are two ways to arrive at that end.

COME THE REVOLUTION

In 1992, the SEC played its first conference title game, which was created in the belief that a supersize conference (12 or more teams) needed a championship game lest it occasionally end a season with two undefeated teams that had never played each other.

The hypothesis has been tested and found wanting. Since 1992, the NCAA has seen 33 conference championship games (13 in the SEC, nine in the Big 12, eight in the MAC, three in the WAC), and there's yet to be a conference championship matchup between two undefeated teams. Take it a step further: there's yet to be a conference championship game between two teams that were undefeated in their own conference.

In a sport in which games are scarce, conference title games waste a valuable resource. They've proved to be little more than a moneymaking contrivance for the conferences. Too often, the game forces a national championship contender to defeat again a team it's already vanquished, and in past years the BCS formula actually penalized those contenders for doing so.

Twice in the history of the Big 12 (whose coaches voted 12-0 against a title game when it was proposed), the conference title game has cost the conference a spot in the national title game.

So if the groundswell of public opinion and collegiate sentiment brought down the BCS and the NCAA regained control of the sport, the extraneous conference championship games could well be the first thing to go.

What would survive in the aftermath is a system in which the bowls remain in place, while merging with a tournament not that different from NCAA basketball.

Five Automatic Bids for Major Conferences. The five major conferences in the sport—Big 12, Big Ten, SEC, ACC, Pac-Ten—would each be guaranteed a spot in the eight-team field. (The decimated Big East would no longer, on merit, deserve inclusion among the top-tier conferences.)

Sixth Automatic Bid to Highest-Rated Remaining Conference Champion. Call it Cinderella's ticket to the ball. This provision, by dictating that the sixth automatic bid would come from among the champions of Division I-A's other conferences—Big East, Mountain West, Conference USA, MAC, WAC, Sun Belt—would allow upstart teams from upstart conferences to get a shot. It would offer Cinderella teams like Tulane in 1998, Marshall in 1999 and Utah in 2004 a real opportunity to prove themselves. Or be exposed.

Two At-Large Bids From 11 Other Contenders. After those six spots are taken, an NCAA selection committee would examine 11 other teams (armed with polls and every one of the BCS computer rankings, of course). Those teams would be the second-rated schools in the five major conferences, the other five conference champions whose champions hadn't yet earned a bid, and the nation's top independent.

Selection Weekend. The eight-team bracket would be announced on the first Sunday in December, a weekend that would celebrate college football, with the Heisman Trophy and other awards presented on Saturday night and the eight-team championship bracket and other bowl bids announced Sunday evening. The eight teams would be bracketed into four major bowl games—one on New Year's Eve, the other three on New Year's Day. (The lineup for the 2004-05 bowl season might have been: Sugar: Auburn-California; Fiesta: Texas-Utah; Rose: USC-Michigan; Orange: Oklahoma-Virginia Tech.) The four winners of those bowl games would advance to the national semifinals (about which more later).

One of the great appeals of the revolutionary method is that it would create an instant national classic, pretty much turning January into National Football Month in America, with both college and pro playoffs building to championship games. But it would also perform the neatest trick in modern sports: create an NCAA-sanctioned playoff that would increase revenue while reducing commercialism.

Not only would the bowls still survive, they'd be able to retain their original identity. Since NCAA rules stipulate that all of its championship tournaments must be played at "clean" venues, free of commercial markings, the title sponsors would be out the window. The Fiesta Bowl would no longer need to resemble a four-hour corn chip commercial. And don't cry for the men in the loud blazers: the extra money generated by TV revenue for a playoff tournament would more than make up for the relatively small amount of lost revenue in title sponsorships.

Everything in this plan makes sense—and, of course, that's just the problem. It is in many ways too clean, too precise, too sensible.

Let's now consider the more realistic possibility.

EVOLUTIONARY THEORY

The very reason that college football doesn't have a playoff, of course, is the alliance of powers against it.

The NCAA began to lose control of the sport with the landmark 1984 Supreme Court decision that deregulated college football broadcasts. And while the organization has done a remarkable job with the NCAA men's basketball tournament, that has not made it welcome in football circles.

"Nobody wants to share the money with the NCAA, like the basketball tournament is shared," said one conference commissioner at the dawn of the BCS. "If you earn it, you ought to be able to keep it. With the basketball tournament money, they form a committee to divide up where the money goes—everybody gets this, everybody gets that. And with

football, you can bet that by the time the legislation got done it would be a Christmas tree, and every special cause would be hung on it in terms of the money. Because, of course, the money would be huge."

Actually, this concern is no more substantial than the supposed concern about class time or the demise of the bowls. In 1997, the NCAA reorganized to a more federated form of government, with each subdivision in football gaining greater control over its affairs. Part of the change was a special provision explicitly stating that if a Division I-A football playoff came about, Division I-A would control the purse strings.

But, as has become clear with the extreme financial inequality in bowl revenues (the six BCS conferences comprise less than 55% of Division I-A membership, but keep more than 92% of BCS bowl-game revenue), the BCS conferences have no interest in sharing with the rest of Division I-A.

Sooner or later, the BCS seems likely to act in its own self-interest to forestall someone else pushing through a playoff plan. The most likely short-term method is the "plus-one" concept, which would simply take the two worthiest teams for a championship following the BCS bowls. If such a plan were enacted, it seems it would inevitably be a stopgap for the more logical 8-4-2 progression of a three-round tournament. And as the 2004 season illustrated, the "plus-one" system is also no guarantee of a clean finish: three Division I-A schools finished the bowls unbeaten.

If the BCS is here to stay, then it's also obvious that the conference championships are here to stay. In the event of an eight-team playoff, the conference championship games would take on another aspect entirely, becoming the de facto first round of a larger tournament.

How large would that tournament be? With the ACC adding a title game in 2005, three of the five dominant conferences in the sport will have conference title games. Because the revenue generated by the conference championships is already on the table, it's unlikely that it would be taken off. More likely would be an increase in the number of large conferences and, in the meantime, an increased number of "play-in" games featuring champions of different conferences playing each other the same weekend as the conference championship games. So imagine the first weekend of December with eight first-round playoff games. The 16 qualifying teams: Big 12 North champion, Big 12 South champion, ACC Atlantic champion, ACC Coastal champion, SEC West champion, SEC East champion, Pac-10 champion, Big Ten champion,

Big East champion, Conference USA champion, Mountain West champion, WAC champion, MAC champion and three at-large bids. (At some point, the Sun Belt might prove itself worthy of a spot in the final 16, but the fledgling conference has yet to see one of its teams even finish in the Top 25, so it wouldn't merit an automatic bid in a 16-team field.) The 2004 qualifiers would have been Colorado, Oklahoma, Virginia Tech, Miami, Auburn, Tennessee, USC, Michigan, Pittsburgh, Louisville, Utah, Boise State, Toledo, Texas, California and Georgia.

If this did happen, the logical next step would be to seed at least the top eight teams rather than dictating the same matchups each season. The 2004 field might have been seeded as follows:

No. 1 USC vs. Toledo

No. 8 Georgia vs. Boise State

No. 5 California vs. Louisville

No. 4 Texas vs. Pittsburgh

No. 6 Utah vs. Michigan

No. 3 Auburn vs. Tennessee (SEC championship)

No. 7 Virginia Tech vs. Miami, Fla. (hypothetical ACC championship)

No. 2 Oklahoma vs. Colorado (Big 12 championship)

Here, of course, is where it gets messy.

What do you do when two teams from different divisions of the same conference finish in the Top 5? Are you better off seeding all 16 teams, regardless of conference affiliation (meaning, for instance, that No. 3 Auburn might draw Pittsburgh rather than higher-ranked Tennessee for its game)?

And what about large conferences that don't have the stature to have both divisional winners included? Would the MAC need to play its conference championship the final weekend in November (thus creating the prospect of a grueling 16-game season for any MAC upstart that advanced to the finals)?

The main problem with a 16-team playoff is something playoff opponents and proponents have agreed on for a long time: it unduly dilutes the significance of the regular season, which remains one of college football's most enduring strengths. A 16-team playoff would turn late-season poll-bowl showdowns into simple warmups for the Big Gridiron Dance.

And yet, to look at that slate of eight games and compare it to the confusion and anticlimactic air of the current setup, it's still a clear improvement. The eight winners could be reseeded for the New Year's Day bowl games. The eight losers would all get invites to minor bowls.

ANNUAL REVIEW

And then the two divergent methods—Revolution vs. Evolution—would begin to come together.

THE ENDGAME

Both scenarios result in a New Year's Eve/New Year's Day bonanza of four quarterfinal bowl games, beginning with a prime-time New Year's Eve clash in the Sugar Bowl, followed by a New Year's Day tripleheader in the Fiesta Bowl, Rose Bowl and Orange Bowl.

Now we set out to crown college football's first true national champion, with one more crucial wrinkle. The four winners of the New Year's Day games would advance to college football's Final Four. And just as with the basketball tournament, all three games—both semifinals and the championship—would be played at a single location. Tradition and politics dictate that the location would rotate among the four major bowls, and would constitute a magnificent payoff for them.

By having all three games played at the same place, each of the four major bowls would host the national title game every fourth year (just as they do now), but they would be guaranteed three extra sellouts over that span, as well as a quadrennial experience of being in the national spotlight for a week in mid-January.

A portion of tickets would be reserved for the schools that qualify in each successive round, but most could be sold through a lottery system—similar to basketball's Final Four—to fans around the country who want to be a part of the spectacle.

And any team that made it to the Final Four would have just three postseason road trips: the first weekend in December, the New Year's Day bowls, then the Final Four. That's the same number of trips made by basketball teams that reach the Final Four. The week of class time missed by the two championship-game participants—who would stay in the city for an extra week awaiting the title game—would occur early in the semester, and would still result in less class time missed than in several other NCAA sports.

Finally, and best of all, college football would end with a bang and not a ballot. A true champion. More revenue and less commercialism. A unifying spectacle for all of college football.

"This is a plan that could work," says a member of the NCAA committee that studied it in 1994. "You've got it sized up right, you've got the plan and you've got the politics. I'm going to tell you exactly how it works: it works when the public clamor is combined with college presidents—on campuses where there is a pressing need for money—realizing the dollar value. Then it will happen."

The inherent flaws of any BCS setup have already prompted public clamor. It will now be up to playoff advocates—and collegiate athletic pragmatists—to mount another charge. The stakes are high, but the reward is a grand one. Once the playoff question is resolved, the rest of college football's arguments can be settled on the field.

And the word "mythical" can finally be retired.

1869

CONFERENCE STANDINGS

Independents	Overall W	L	T
Princeton	1	1	0
Rutgers	1	1	0

1870

CONFERENCE STANDINGS

Independents	Overall W	L	T
Princeton	1	0	0
Rutgers	1	1	0
Columbia	0	1	0

1871

No Football

1872

CONFERENCE STANDINGS

Independents	Overall W	L	T
Yale	1	0	0
Princeton	1	0	0
Rutgers	1	1	1
Columbia	1	2	1

1873

CONFERENCE STANDINGS

Independents	Overall W	L	T
Princeton	1	0	0
Columbia	2	1	0
Yale	2	1	0
Rutgers	1	2	0

1874

CONFERENCE STANDINGS

Independents	Overall W	L	T
Yale	3	0	0
Princeton	2	0	0
Harvard	2	1	1
Rutgers	2	2	0
Columbia	1	5	0

1875

CONFERENCE STANDINGS

Independents	Overall W	L	T
Harvard	4	0	0
Princeton	2	0	0
Columbia	4	1	1
Yale	2	2	0
Rutgers	1	1	1

1876

CONFERENCE STANDINGS

Independents	Overall W	L	T
Yale	3	0	0
Rutgers	1	0	0
Harvard	3	1	0
Princeton	3	2	0
Pennsylvania	1	2	0
Columbia	1	3	0
Northwestern	0	1	0

1877

CONFERENCE STANDINGS

Independents	Overall W	L	T
Yale	3	0	1
Princeton	2	0	1
Harvard	4	1	0
Columbia	2	2	0
Rutgers	0	3	0

1878

CONFERENCE STANDINGS

Independents	Overall W	L	T
Princeton	6	0	0
Yale	4	1	1
Columbia	0	0	2
Pennsylvania	1	2	1
Rutgers	1	2	1
Harvard	1	2	0
Brown	0	1	0

1879

CONFERENCE STANDINGS

Independents	Overall W	L	T
Princeton	4	0	1
Yale	3	0	2
Michigan	1	0	1
Harvard	2	1	2
Pennsylvania	2	2	0
Navy	0	0	1
Rutgers	1	2	3
Columbia	0	3	2

1880

CONFERENCE STANDINGS

Independents	Overall W	L	T
Michigan	1	0	0
Yale	4	0	1
Princeton	4	0	1
Harvard	2	2	2
Rutgers	2	2	0
Pennsylvania	2	2	0
Columbia	1	2	0
Brown	0	1	0

1881

CONFERENCE STANDINGS

Independents	Overall W	L	T
Yale	5	0	1
Princeton	7	0	2
Harvard	6	1	1
Dartmouth	1	0	1
Columbia	3	3	1
Rutgers	2	4	1
Kentucky	1	2	0
Michigan	0	3	0
Pennsylvania	0	5	0

1882

CONFERENCE STANDINGS

Independents	Overall W	L	T
Yale	8	0	0
Navy	1	0	0
Harvard	7	1	0
Princeton	7	2	0
Rutgers	6	4	0
Minnesota	1	1	0
Dartmouth	1	1	0
Northwestern	1	1	0
Pennsylvania	2	4	0
Columbia	0	5	0

1883

CONFERENCE STANDINGS

Independents	Overall W	L	T
Yale	8	0	0
Princeton	7	1	0
Harvard	8	2	0
Pennsylvania	6	2	1
California	2	1	1
Minnesota	1	2	0
Columbia	1	3	0
Michigan	1	4	0
Rutgers	1	6	0
Navy	0	1	0
Dartmouth	0	1	0

1884

CONFERENCE STANDINGS

Independents	Overall W	L	T
California	2	0	0
Michigan	2	0	0
Navy	1	0	0
Princeton	9	0	1
Yale	8	0	1
Pennsylvania	5	1	1
Harvard	7	4	0
Columbia	1	1	0
Rutgers	3	4	0
Dartmouth	1	2	1

1885

CONFERENCE STANDINGS

Independents	Overall W	L	T
Princeton	9	0	0
Michigan	3	0	0
California	4	0	1
Yale	7	1	0
Pennsylvania	8	5	0
Navy	1	2	0
Rutgers	0	1	0

1886

CONFERENCE STANDINGS

Independents	Overall W	L	T
Michigan	2	0	0
Yale	9	0	1
Princeton	7	0	1
Harvard	12	2	0
California	6	2	1
Pennsylvania	9	7	1
Navy	3	3	0
Dartmouth	2	2	0
Brown	1	1	0
Rutgers	1	3	0
Northwestern	0	1	0
Minnesota	0	2	0

1887

CONFERENCE STANDINGS

Independents	Overall W	L	T
Yale	9	0	0
California	4	0	0
Michigan	3	0	0
Penn State	2	0	0
Minnesota	2	0	0
Harvard	10	1	0
Princeton	7	2	0
Navy	3	1	0
Dartmouth	3	1	1
Pennsylvania	6	7	0
Rutgers	2	6	0
Cornell	0	2	0
Purdue	0	1	0
Notre Dame	0	1	0
Indiana	0	1	0
Cornell	0	2	0

1888

CONFERENCE STANDINGS

Independents	Overall W	L	T
Yale	13	0	0
Southern Cal	2	0	0
Duke	1	0	0
Wake Forest	1	0	0
Harvard	12	1	0
Princeton	11	1	0
California	6	1	0
Michigan	4	1	0
Cornell	4	2	0
Virginia	2	1	0
Northwestern	2	1	0
Pennsylvania	9	7	0
Minnesota	1	1	0
Indiana	0	0	1
Dartmouth	3	4	0
Notre Dame	1	2	0
Navy	1	3	0
Rutgers	1	6	1
Penn State	0	2	1
North Carolina	0	2	0

1889

CONSENSUS ALL-AMERICANS

POS	Name	SCHOOL	CW
B	Edgar Allan Poe	Princeton	•
B	James Lee	Harvard	•
B	Roscoe Channing	Princeton	•
B	Knowlton Ames	Princeton	•
E	Arthur Cumnock	Harvard	•
E	Amos Alonzo Stagg	Yale	•
T	Hector Cowan	Princeton	•
T	Charles Gill	Yale	•
G	John Cranston	Harvard	•
G	Pudge Heffelfinger	Yale	•
C	William George	Princeton	•

CONFERENCE STANDINGS

Independents	Overall W	L	T
Princeton	10	0	0
Southern Cal	2	0	0
Notre Dame	1	0	0
Yale	16	1	0
Dartmouth	7	1	0
Harvard	9	2	0
Cornell	7	2	0
Navy	4	1	1
Minnesota	3	1	0
Northwestern	4	1	1
Virginia	4	2	0
Purdue	2	1	0
Duke	2	1	0
Pennsylvania	7	6	0
Wake Forest	3	3	0
Penn State	2	2	0
Brown	2	2	0
North Carolina	1	2	0
Michigan	1	2	0
Columbia	2	7	2
Rutgers	1	4	0
Wisconsin	0	2	0
Iowa	0	1	0
Indiana	0	1	0
Syracuse	0	1	0
Washington	0	1	0
Wisconsin	0	2	0

1890

CONSENSUS ALL-AMERICANS

POS	Name	SCHOOL	CW
B	Dudley Dean	Harvard	•
B	John Corbett	Harvard	•
B	Thomas McClung	Yale	•
B	Sheppard Homans	Princeton	•
E	Frank Hallowell	Harvard	•
E	Ralph Warren	Princeton	•
T	Marshall Newell	Harvard	•
T	William Rhodes	Yale	•
G	Jesse Riggs	Princeton	•
G	Pudge Heffelfinger	Yale	•
C	John Cranston	Harvard	•

CONFERENCE STANDINGS

Independents	Overall W	L	T
Harvard	11	0	0
California	4	0	0
Nebraska	2	0	0
Vanderbilt	1	0	0
Yale	13	1	0
Princeton	11	1	1
Michigan	4	1	0
Pennsylvania	11	3	0
Navy	5	1	1
Minnesota	5	1	1
Northwestern	4	1	1
Virginia	5	2	0
Cornell	8	4	0
Missouri	2	1	0
Syracuse	7	4	0
Rutgers	5	5	1
Dartmouth	4	4	0
Purdue	3	3	0
Penn State	2	2	0
Iowa	1	1	0
Washington	0	0	1
Brown	2	4	1
Kansas	1	2	0
Illinois	1	2	0
Pittsburgh	1	2	0
Ohio State	1	3	0
Wisconsin	1	3	0
Columbia	1	6	1
Army	0	1	0
Duke	0	1	0
Colorado	0	4	0

1891
Consensus All-Americans

POS	Name	School	CW
B	Philip King	Princeton	•
B	Everett Lake	Harvard	•
B	Thomas McClung	Yale	•
B	Sheppard Homans	Princeton	•
E	Frank Hinkey	Yale	•
E	John Hartwell	Yale	•
T	Wallace Winter	Yale	•
T	Marshall Newell	Harvard	•
G	Jesse Riggs	Princeton	•
G	Pudge Heffelfinger	Yale	•
C	John Adams	Pennsylvania	•

Conference standings

Independents	Overall W	L	T
Yale	13	0	0
Purdue	4	0	0
Duke	3	0	0
Wake Forest	1	0	0
Kansas	7	0	1
Harvard	13	1	0
Princeton	12	1	0
Pennsylvania	11	2	0
Illinois	5	1	0
Penn State	6	2	0
Army	4	1	1
Vanderbilt	3	1	0
Missouri	3	1	0
Stanford	3	1	0
Navy	5	2	0
Cornell	7	3	0
Wisconsin	3	1	1
Minnesota	3	1	1
Virginia	2	1	2
Rutgers	8	6	0
California	4	3	0
Nebraska	2	2	0
Dartmouth	2	2	1
Ohio State	2	2	0
Northwestern	2	2	3
Kentucky	1	1	0
Michigan	4	5	0
Brown	4	6	0
Iowa	2	3	0
Syracuse	4	7	0
Southern Cal	1	2	0
Pittsburgh	2	5	0
Colorado	1	4	0
Indiana	1	5	0
Columbia	1	5	0
Tennessee	0	1	0
West Virginia	0	1	0
North Carolina	0	2	0

1892
Consensus All-Americans

POS	Name	School	CW
B	Vance McCormick	Yale	•
B	Charles Brewer	Harvard	•
B	Philip King	Princeton	•
B	Harry Thayer	Pennsylvania	•
E	Frank Hinkey	Yale	•
E	Frank Hallowell	Harvard	•
T	A. Hamilton Wallis	Yale	•
T	Marshall Newell	Harvard	•
G	Bertram Waters	Harvard	•
G	Arthur Wheeler	Princeton	•
C	William Lewis	Harvard	•

Conference standings

Independents	Overall W	L	T
Yale	13	0	0
Purdue	8	0	0
Minnesota	5	0	0
North Carolina St.	1	0	0
Utah State	1	0	0
Pennsylvania	15	1	0
Harvard	10	1	0
Cornell	10	1	0
Wake Forest	4	0	1
Kansas	7	1	0
Princeton	13	2	0
North Carolina	5	1	0
Penn State	5	1	0
Iowa State	1	0	1
Notre Dame	1	0	1
Navy	5	2	0
Army	3	1	1
Pittsburgh	4	2	0
Stanford	1	0	2
Illinois	7	4	1
Dartmouth	5	3	0
Ohio State	5	3	0
Northwestern	5	3	2
California	2	1	1
Auburn	3	2	0
Michigan	7	5	0
Virginia	3	2	1
Iowa	3	2	1
Wisconsin	4	3	0
Vanderbilt	4	4	0
Nebraska	2	2	1
Alabama	2	2	0
Colorado	2	2	0
Indiana	2	2	0
Washington	1	1	0
Virginia Tech	1	1	0
Georgia	1	1	0
Brown	4	5	1
Rutgers	3	5	1
Kentucky	2	4	1
Missouri	1	2	0
Tennessee	2	5	0
Duke	1	3	0
South Carolina	0	1	0
Utah	0	1	0
New Mexico	0	2	0
Georgia Tech	0	3	0
Maryland	0	3	0
Syracuse	0	8	1

1893
Consensus All-Americans

POS	Name	School	CW
B	Philip King	Princeton	•
B	Charles Brewer	Harvard	•
B	Franklin Morse	Princeton	•
B	Frank Butterworth	Yale	•
E	Frank Hinkey	Yale	•
E	Thomas Trenchard	Princeton	•
T	Langdon Lea	Princeton	•
T	Marshall Newell	Harvard	•
G	Arthur Wheeler	Princeton	•
G	William Hickok	Yale	•
C	William Lewis	Harvard	•

Conference standings

Independents	Overall W	L	T
Princeton	11	0	0
Maryland	6	0	0
Minnesota	6	0	0
Texas	4	0	0
North Carolina St.	2	0	0
Wyoming	1	0	0
Stanford	8	0	1
Harvard	12	1	0
Yale	10	1	0
Vanderbilt	6	1	0
Pennsylvania	12	3	0
Oregon State	4	1	0
Penn State	4	1	0
Mississippi	4	1	0
Notre Dame	4	1	0
California	5	1	1
Duke	3	1	0
Southern Cal	3	1	0
New Mexico	3	1	0
Auburn	2	0	2
Virginia	8	3	0
Michigan	7	3	0
Purdue	5	2	1
Kentucky	5	2	1
Brown	6	3	0
Wisconsin	4	2	0
West Virginia	2	1	0
Navy	5	3	0
Georgia Tech	2	1	1
Nebraska	3	2	1
Missouri	4	3	0
Dartmouth	4	3	0
Illinois	3	2	3
Colorado	3	3	0
Boston College	3	3	0
Georgia	2	2	1
Ohio State	4	5	0
Army	4	5	0
North Carolina	3	4	0
Iowa	3	4	0
Cornell	3	6	1
Northwestern	2	5	3
Colorado State	2	4	0
Tennessee	2	4	0
Tulane	1	2	0
Wake Forest	1	2	0
Syracuse	4	9	1
Washington	1	3	1
Kansas	2	5	0
Indiana	1	4	1
Pittsburgh	1	4	0
LSU	0	1	0
New Mexico State	0	1	0
Virginia Tech	0	2	0
Iowa State	0	3	0
Alabama	0	4	0
Rutgers	0	4	0

1894

CONSENSUS ALL-AMERICANS

POS	Name	School	CW
B	George Adee	Yale	•
B	Arthur Knipe	Pennsylvania	•
B	George Brooke	Pennsylvania	•
B	Frank Butterworth	Yale	•
E	Frank Hinkey	Yale	•
E	Charles Gelbert	Pennsylvania	•
T	Bertram Waters	Harvard	•
T	Langdon Lea	Princeton	•
G	Arthur Wheeler	Princeton	•
G	William Hickok	Yale	•
C	Philip Stillman	Yale	•

CONFERENCE STANDINGS

Independents

	Overall W L T		
Yale	16	0	0
Pennsylvania	12	0	0
Wyoming	3	0	0
Southern Cal	1	0	0
Penn State	6	0	1
Purdue	9	1	0
Colorado	8	1	0
Vanderbilt	7	1	0
Michigan	9	1	1
Mississippi	6	1	0
Texas	6	1	0
Harvard	11	2	0
Georgia	5	1	0
Iowa State	5	1	0
Princeton	8	2	0
Virginia	8	2	0
Virginia Tech	4	1	0
Nebraska	6	2	0
Alabama	3	1	0
Minnesota	3	1	0
Wisconsin	5	2	0
Kentucky	5	2	0
Navy	4	1	2
Notre Dame	3	1	1
Brown	10	5	0
North Carolina	6	3	0
Stanford	6	3	0
LSU	2	1	0
Arkansas	2	1	0
Oregon State	2	1	0
Illinois	4	3	0
Army	3	2	0
Cornell	6	4	1
Missouri	4	3	0
Dartmouth	5	4	0
Ohio State	6	5	0
Syracuse	6	5	0
Iowa	4	4	1
Maryland	4	3	0
West Virginia	2	2	0
Washington State	1	1	0
Texas A&M	1	1	0
Pittsburgh	1	1	0
New Mexico	1	1	1
Washington	1	1	1
Northwestern	4	5	0
Kansas	2	3	1
Rutgers	4	6	0
Oregon	1	2	1
Utah	1	2	0
California	0	1	2
Auburn	1	3	0
Boston College	1	6	0
Indiana	0	4	0
Duke	0	1	0
Colorado State	0	1	0
South Carolina	0	2	0
Georgia Tech	0	3	0
North Carolina St.	0	2	0
Tulane	0	4	0

1895

CONSENSUS ALL-AMERICANS

POS	Name	School	CW
B	Clinton Wyckoff	Cornell	•
B	Samuel Thorne	Yale	•
B	Charles Brewer	Harvard	•
B	George Brooke	Pennsylvania	•
E	Norman Cabot	Harvard	•
E	Charles Gelbert	Pennsylvania	•
T	Langdon Lea	Princeton	•
T	Fred Murphy	Yale	•
G	Charles Wharton	Pennsylvania	•
G	Dudley Riggs	Princeton	•
C	Alfred Bull	Pennsylvania	•

CONFERENCE STANDINGS

Independents

	Overall W L T		
Pennsylvania	14	0	0
Texas	5	0	0
Oregon	4	0	0
LSU	3	0	0
New Mexico State	2	0	0
Washington State	2	0	0
Wyoming	1	0	0
Arkansas	1	0	0
Yale	13	0	2
Washington	4	0	1
Stanford	4	0	1
Michigan	8	1	0
Princeton	10	1	1
Missouri	7	1	0
Kansas	6	1	0
North Carolina	7	1	1
Colorado	5	1	0
West Virginia	5	1	0
Virginia	9	2	0
Harvard	8	2	1
Notre Dame	3	1	0
Navy	5	2	0
Army	5	2	0
Minnesota	7	3	0
Syracuse	6	2	2
California	3	1	1
Wisconsin	5	2	1
Nebraska	6	3	0
Virginia Tech	4	2	0
Auburn	2	1	0
South Carolina	2	1	0
Mississippi	2	1	0
Illinois	4	2	1
Vanderbilt	5	3	1
Tulane	3	2	0
Northwestern	6	5	0
Dartmouth	7	5	1
Indiana	4	3	1
Brown	7	6	1
Ohio State	4	4	2
Iowa State	3	3	0
Purdue	3	3	0
Penn State	2	2	3
Wake Forest	0	0	1
Kentucky	4	5	0
Cornell	3	4	1
Rutgers	3	4	0
Georgia	3	4	0
Boston College	2	4	2
North Carolina St.	1	2	1
Iowa	2	5	0
Southern Cal	0	1	1
Oregon State	0	2	1
Pittsburgh	1	6	0
Mississippi State	0	2	0
Oklahoma	0	1	0
Utah	0	1	0
Alabama	0	4	0

1896

CONSENSUS ALL-AMERICANS

POS	Name	School	CW
B	Clarence Fincke	Yale	•
B	Edgar Wrightington	Harvard	•
B	Addison Kelly	Princeton	•
B	John Baird	Princeton	•
E	Norman Cabot	Harvard	•
E	Charles Gelbert	Pennsylvania	•
T	William Church	Princeton	•
T	Fred Murphy	Yale	•
G	Charles Wharton	Pennsylvania	•
G	Wylie Woodruff	Pennsylvania	•
C	Robert Gailey	Princeton	•

CONFERENCE STANDINGS

Big 10	Conf. W	L	T	Overall W	L	T
Wisconsin	2	0	1	7	1	1
Michigan	2	1	0	9	1	0
Northwestern	2	1	1	6	1	2
Chicago	3	2	0	11	2	1
Minnesota	1	2	0	8	2	0
Illinois	0	2	1	4	2	1
Purdue	0	2	1	4	2	1

Independents	Overall W	L	T
LSU	6	0	0
Colorado	5	0	0
Tennessee	4	0	0
Georgia	4	0	0
Wyoming	2	0	0
Oklahoma	2	0	0
North Carolina St.	1	0	0
Lafayette	11	0	1
Princeton	10	0	1
Pennsylvania	14	1	0
Yale	13	1	0
Iowa	7	1	1
Texas A&M	2	0	1
Washington State	2	0	1
Iowa State	8	2	0
Indiana	6	2	0
Auburn	3	1	0
Virginia	7	2	2
Boston College	5	2	0
Kansas	7	3	0
Maryland	6	2	2
California	6	2	2
Virginia Tech	5	2	1
Dartmouth	5	2	1
Alabama	2	1	0
Clemson	2	1	0
Arkansas	2	1	0
Oregon	2	1	0
Nebraska	6	3	1
Texas	4	2	1
Harvard	7	4	0
Navy	5	3	0
Stanford	2	1	1
Cornell	5	3	1
Syracuse	5	3	2
Utah	3	2	0
Tulane	3	2	0
Missouri	7	5	0
Army	3	2	1
Notre Dame	4	3	0
Vanderbilt	3	2	2
Ohio State	5	5	1
TCU	1	1	1
Georgia Tech	1	1	1
Rutgers	6	6	0
Brown	4	5	1
North Carolina	3	4	1
Penn State	3	4	0
Washington	2	3	0
Michigan State	1	2	1
West Virginia	3	7	2
Pittsburgh	3	6	0
Kentucky	3	6	0
Mississippi	1	2	0
Oregon State	1	2	0
South Carolina	1	3	0
Kansas State	0	1	1
Utah State	0	1	0
Tulsa	0	1	0
New Mexico State	0	2	0
Southern Cal	0	3	0
Mississippi State	0	4	0

1897

CONSENSUS ALL-AMERICANS

POS	Name	School	CW
B	Charles DeSaulles	Yale	•
B	Benjamin Dibblee	Harvard	•
B	Addison Kelly	Princeton	•
B	John Minds	Pennsylvania	•
E	Garrett Cochran	Princeton	•
E	John Hall	Yale	•
T	Burr Chamberlain	Yale	•
T	John Outland	Pennsylvania	•
G	T. Truxton Hare	Pennsylvania	•
G	Gordon Brown	Yale	•
C	Alan Doucette	Harvard	•

CONFERENCE STANDINGS

Big 10	Conf. W	L	T	Overall W	L	T
Wisconsin	3	0	0	9	1	0
Chicago	3	1	0	8	1	0
Michigan	2	1	0	6	1	1
Illinois	1	1	0	6	2	0
Purdue	1	2	0	5	3	1
Northwestern	0	3	0	5	3	0
Minnesota	0	3	0	4	4	0

Independents	Overall W	L	T
Pennsylvania	15	0	0
Oklahoma	2	0	0
Wyoming	2	0	0
Oregon State	2	0	0
Washington State	2	0	0
Alabama	1	0	0
Vanderbilt	6	0	1
Princeton	10	1	0
Yale	9	0	2
Navy	8	1	0
Harvard	10	1	1
Colorado	7	1	0
Southern Cal	5	1	0
Nebraska	5	1	0
Arkansas	2	0	1
Auburn	2	0	1
Army	6	1	1
Indiana	6	1	1
Kansas	8	2	0
Stanford	4	1	0
Tennessee	4	1	0
Texas	6	2	0
Notre Dame	4	1	1
Iowa State	3	1	0
TCU	3	1	0
New Mexico State	1	0	1
Virginia	6	2	1
Virginia Tech	5	2	0
North Carolina	7	3	0
Georgia	2	1	0
Michigan State	4	2	1
Brown	7	4	0
Syracuse	5	3	1
Cornell	5	3	1
Boston College	4	3	0
Dartmouth	4	3	0
West Virginia	5	4	1
Iowa	4	4	0
Clemson	2	2	0
Oregon	1	1	0
LSU	1	1	0
Missouri	5	6	0
Kansas State	1	2	1
Penn State	3	6	0
Kentucky	2	4	0
Maryland	2	4	0
Texas A&M	1	2	0
Washington	1	2	0
North Carolina St.	1	2	0
Rutgers	2	6	0
Pittsburgh	1	3	0
California	0	3	2
Utah	1	5	0
Ohio State	1	7	1
Arizona State	0	1	0
Georgia Tech	0	1	0
South Carolina	0	3	0

1898
CONSENSUS ALL-AMERICANS

POS	Name	School	CW	WC
B	Charles Daly	Harvard	•	•
B	John Outland	Pennsylvania		•
B	Benjamin Dibblee	Harvard	•	•
B	Malcolm McBride	Yale	•	
B	Charles Romeyn	Army	•	
B	Clarence Herschberger	Chicago		•
E	Lew Palmer	Princeton	•	•
E	John Hallowell	Harvard	•	•
T	Arthur Hillebrand	Princeton	•	•
T	Burr Chamberlain	Yale	•	•
G	T. Truxton Hare	Pennsylvania	•	•
G	Gordon Brown	Yale		•
G	Walter Boal	Harvard	•	
C	Pete Overfield	Pennsylvania		•
C	William Cunningham	Michigan	•	

CONFERENCE STANDINGS

Big 10	CONF. W L T	OVERALL W L T
Michigan	3 0 0	10 0 0
Chicago	3 1 0	9 2 0
Wisconsin	2 1 0	9 1 0
Illinois	1 1 0	4 5 0
Minnesota	1 2 0	4 5 0
Northwestern	0 4 0	9 4 1
Purdue	0 1 0	3 3 0

Independents	OVERALL W L T
Harvard	11 0 0
North Carolina	9 0 0
Kentucky	7 0 0
Oklahoma	2 0 0
LSU	1 0 0
Princeton	11 0 1
Pennsylvania	12 1 0
California	8 0 2
Kansas	7 1 0
Navy	7 1 0
West Virginia	6 1 0
Cornell	10 2 0
Texas	5 1 0
Yale	9 2 0
Southern Cal	5 1 1
Syracuse	8 2 1
Clemson	3 1 0
Oregon	3 1 0
Nebraska	8 3 0
Indiana	4 1 2
Pittsburgh	5 2 1
Notre Dame	4 2 0

Texas A&M	4 2 0
Georgia	4 2 0
Utah	2 1 0
New Mexico State	2 1 0
Auburn	2 1 0
Arkansas	2 1 0
Stanford	5 3 1
Brown	6 4 0
Penn State	6 4 0
Virginia Tech	3 2 0
Iowa State	3 2 0
Army	3 2 1
Michigan State	4 3 0
Virginia	6 5 0
Colorado	4 4 0
Kansas State	1 1 2
Washington	1 1 0
Tulane	1 1 0
Mississippi	1 1 0
Washington State	0 0 1
Dartmouth	5 6 0
Iowa	3 4 2
Ohio State	3 5 0
Oregon State	1 2 1
South Carolina	1 2 0
Boston College	2 5 1
TCU	1 3 1
Maryland	2 5 1
Missouri	1 4 1
Rutgers	1 6 1
Vanderbilt	1 5 0
Wyoming	0 4 0
Georgia Tech	0 3 0
North Carolina St.	0 1 0
Utah State	0 1 0

1899
CONSENSUS ALL-AMERICANS

POS	Name	School	CW	WC
B	Charles Daly	Harvard	•	•
B	Isaac Seneca	Carlisle	*	•
B	Josiah McCracken	Pennsylvania	*	•
B	Malcolm McBride	Yale	•	•
B	Howard Reiter	Princeton	•	
B	Albert Sharpe	Yale	•	
E	David Campbell	Harvard	•	•
E	Arthur Poe	Princeton	•	•
T	Arthur Hillebrand	Princeton	•	•
T	George Stillman	Yale	•	•
G	T. Truxton Hare	Pennsylvania	•	•
G	Gordon Brown	Yale		•
C	Pete Overfield	Pennsylvania	•	•

CONFERENCE STANDINGS

Big 10	CONF. W L T	OVERALL W L T
Chicago	4 0 0	12 0 2
Wisconsin	4 1 0	9 2 0
Northwestern	2 2 0	7 6 0
Michigan	1 1 0	8 2 0
Purdue	1 2 0	4 4 1
Minnesota	0 3 0	6 3 2
Illinois	0 3 0	3 5 1

Independents	OVERALL W L T
Kansas	10 0 0
Arizona State	3 0 0
New Mexico State	1 0 0
Utah State	1 0 0
Harvard	10 0 1
Ohio State	9 0 1
Iowa	8 0 1
Princeton	12 1 0
Boston College	8 1 1
California	7 1 1
Missouri	9 2 0
Virginia Tech	4 1 0
Colorado	7 2 0
Vanderbilt	7 2 0
Columbia	9 3 0
Yale	7 2 1
Texas	6 2 0
Indiana	6 2 0
Washington	4 1 1
Alabama	3 1 0
Tennessee	5 2 0
Cornell	7 3 0
Auburn	3 1 1
Arkansas	3 1 1
Pittsburgh	3 1 1
Pennsylvania	8 3 2
Brown	7 3 1

North Carolina	7 3 1
Kentucky	5 2 2
Clemson	4 2 0
Texas A&M	4 2 0
Utah	2 1 0
Oklahoma	2 1 0
Notre Dame	6 3 1
Navy	5 3 0
Baylor	2 1 1
Oregon State	3 2 0
Oregon	3 2 1
Virginia	4 3 2
Iowa State	5 4 1
Syracuse	4 4 0
Washington State	1 1 0
New Mexico	1 1 0
Arizona	1 1 1
TCU	0 0 1
Army	4 5 0
Mississippi	3 4 0
Southern Cal	2 3 1
Georgia	2 3 1
Penn State	4 6 1
West Virginia	2 3 0
South Carolina	2 3 0
Kansas State	2 3 0
North Carolina St.	1 2 2
Colorado State	1 2 1
Michigan State	2 4 1
Stanford	2 5 2
Tulsa	0 1 1
Wyoming	0 1 1
Dartmouth	2 7 0
LSU	1 4 0
Maryland	1 4 0
Rutgers	2 9 0
Nebraska	1 7 1
Tulane	0 6 1
Georgia Tech	0 5 0

1900
CONSENSUS ALL-AMERICANS

POS	Name	School	CW	WC
B	Bill Morley	Columbia	•	•
B	George Chadwick	Yale	•	•
B	Perry Hale	Yale	*	•
B	William Fincke	Yale		•
B	Charles Daly	Harvard	•	
B	Raymond Starbuck	Cornell	•	
E	John Hallowell	Harvard	•	•
E	David Campbell	Harvard	•	
E	William Smith	Army	•	
T	George Stillman	Yale	•	
T	James Bloomer	Yale	•	
G	T. Truxton Hare	Pennsylvania	•	•
G	Gordon Brown	Yale	•	•
C	Herman Olcott	Yale	•	
C	Walter Bachman	Lafayette	•	

CONFERENCE STANDINGS

Big 10	Conf. W	L	T	Overall W	L	T
Minnesota	3	0	1	10	0	2
Iowa	2	0	1	7	0	1
Wisconsin	2	1	0	8	1	0
Michigan	3	2	0	7	2	1
Northwestern	2	1	2	7	2	3
Chicago	2	3	1	7	5	1
Indiana	1	2	1	4	2	2
Illinois	1	3	2	7	3	2
Purdue	0	4	0	4	4	0

Rocky Mountain	Conf. W	L	T	Overall W	L	T
Colorado Coll.	4	0	0	6	2	0
Colorado Mines	3	1	0	4	2	0
Colorado	2	2	0	6	4	0
Colorado State	0	2	0	1	2	0
No. Colorado	0	3	0	0	4	0

Independents	Overall W	L	T
Yale	12	0	0
Clemson	6	0	0
Texas	6	0	0
Tulane	5	0	0
Auburn	4	0	0
Baylor	3	0	0
Pennsylvania	12	1	0
Harvard	10	1	0
Washington State	4	0	1
Ohio State	8	1	1
Cornell	10	2	0
Nebraska	6	1	1
Syracuse	7	2	1
Stanford	7	2	1
Virginia	7	2	1
Arizona	3	1	0
Princeton	8	3	0
Oklahoma	3	1	1
North Carolina	4	1	3
Brown	7	3	1
Columbia	7	3	1
Army	7	3	1
Navy	6	3	0
Tulsa	2	1	0
Notre Dame	6	3	1
California	4	2	1
Arkansas	2	1	1
Tennessee	3	2	1
West Virginia	4	3	0
South Carolina	4	3	0
Pittsburgh	5	4	0
Missouri	4	4	1
Vanderbilt	4	4	1
Rutgers	4	4	0
New Mexico State	3	3	1
Wyoming	3	3	0
Virginia Tech	3	3	1
Oregon	3	3	1
Texas A&M	2	2	1
Utah	2	2	0
LSU	2	2	0
Southern Cal	1	1	1
Arizona State	1	1	0
Maryland	3	4	1
Penn State	4	6	1
Kentucky	4	6	0
Alabama	2	3	0
Washington	1	2	2
Dartmouth	2	4	2
Kansas	2	5	2
Kansas State	2	4	0
Georgia	2	4	0
Iowa State	2	5	1
Michigan State	1	3	0
Utah State	0	1	0
Mississippi	0	3	0
Georgia Tech	0	4	0
North Carolina St.	0	4	0

1901
CONSENSUS ALL-AMERICANS

POS	Name	School	CW	WC
B	Robert Kernan	Harvard	•	•
B	Charles Daly	Army	•	•
B	Thomas Graydon	Harvard	•	•
B	Harold Weekes	Columbia		•
B	Bill Morley	Columbia		•
E	David Campbell	Harvard		•
E	Ralph Davis	Princeton		•
E	Edward Bowditch	Harvard		•
E	Neil Snow	Michigan		•
T	Oliver Cutts	Harvard		•
T	Paul Bunker	Army		•
T	Crawford Blagden	Harvard		•
G	William Warner	Cornell		•
G	William Lee	Harvard	•	
G	Charles Barnard	Harvard	•	
G	Sanford Hunt	Cornell	•	
C	Henry Holt	Yale		•
C	Walter Bachman	Lafayette	•	

CONFERENCE STANDINGS

Big 10	Conf. W	L	T	Overall W	L	T
Michigan	4	0	0	11	0	0
Wisconsin	2	0	0	9	0	0
Minnesota	3	1	0	9	1	1
Illinois	4	2	0	8	2	0
Northwestern	3	2	0	8	2	1
Indiana	1	2	0	6	3	0
Chicago	0	5	2	5	5	2
Purdue	0	3	1	4	4	1
Iowa	0	3	0	6	3	0

Rocky Mountain	Conf. W	L	T	Overall W	L	T
Colorado	2	0	0	5	1	1
Colorado Coll.	2	1	0	5	1	0
Colorado Mines	1	2	0	1	3	0
Colorado State	0	2	0	1	2	0

Independents	Overall W	L	T
Harvard	12	0	0
Wyoming	1	0	0
California	9	0	1
Cornell	11	1	0
Dartmouth	10	1	0
Georgia Tech	4	0	1
Yale	11	1	1
Syracuse	7	1	0
Princeton	9	1	1
Virginia Tech	6	1	0
Notre Dame	8	1	1
LSU	5	1	0
Vanderbilt	6	1	1
Virginia	8	2	0
Washington State	4	1	0
Arizona	4	1	0
North Carolina	7	2	0
Texas	8	2	1
Pittsburgh	7	2	1
Nebraska	6	2	0
Army	5	1	2
Utah	3	1	0
Clemson	3	1	1
Pennsylvania	10	5	0
Tulane	4	2	0
New Mexico State	2	1	0
Penn State	5	3	0
Baylor	5	3	0
Columbia	8	5	0
Ohio State	5	3	1
Oklahoma	3	2	0
West Virginia	3	2	0
Alabama	2	1	2
Navy	6	4	1
Stanford	3	2	2
Tennessee	3	3	2
Washington	3	3	0
Mississippi State	2	2	1
Utah State	2	2	1
Oregon	3	4	1
Kansas State	3	4	1
Michigan State	3	4	1
South Carolina	3	4	0
Auburn	2	3	1
Kansas	3	5	2
Oklahoma State	2	3	0
Brown	4	7	1
Arkansas	3	5	0
TCU	1	2	1
Mississippi	2	4	0
North Carolina St.	1	2	0
Iowa State	2	6	2
Missouri	2	6	1
Kentucky	2	6	1
Georgia	1	5	2
Boston College	2	7	0
Texas A&M	1	4	0
Maryland	1	7	0
New Mexico	0	3	1
Rutgers	0	7	0
Tulsa	0	1	0
Southern Cal	0	1	0

BOWL GAMES

DATE	GAME	SCORE
J1	Rose	Michigan 49, Stanford 0

1902
CONSENSUS ALL-AMERICANS

POS	Name	School	CW	WC
B	Foster Rockwell	Yale	•	•
B	George Chadwick	Yale	•	•
B	Thomas Graydon	Harvard	•	•
B	Thomas Barry	Brown	•	
E	Thomas Shevlin	Yale	•	•
E	Edward Bowditch	Harvard	•	•
T	Ralph Kinney	Yale	•	•
T	James Hogan	Yale	•	•
T	Paul Bunker	Army	•	*
G	Edgar Glass	Yale	•	•
G	John DeWitt	Princeton		•
G	William Warner	Cornell	•	
C	Henry Holt	Yale		•
C	Robert Boyers	Army	•	

CONFERENCE STANDINGS

Big 10	Conf. W	L	T	Overall W	L	T
Michigan	5	0	0	11	0	0
Chicago	5	1	0	11	1	0
Minnesota	3	1	0	9	2	1
Illinois	4	2	0	10	2	1
Purdue	2	2	0	7	2	1
Wisconsin	1	3	0	6	3	0
Iowa	0	3	0	5	4	0
Northwestern	0	4	0	6	6	0
Indiana	0	4	0	3	5	1

Rocky Mountain	Conf. W	L	T	Overall W	L	T
Colorado	4	0	0	5	1	0
Utah	1	0	1	5	2	1
Colorado Mines	2	1	1	4	1	2
Colorado College	2	2	0	3	4	0
Colorado State	1	3	2	1	3	2
Denver	1	3	0	3	4	1
Utah State	0	2	0	0	4	0

Independents	Overall W	L	T
Nebraska	9	0	0
California	8	0	0
Arizona	5	0	0
Wyoming	1	0	0
Yale	11	0	1
Harvard	11	1	0
Vanderbilt	8	1	0
Princeton	8	1	0
Texas A&M	7	0	2
Clemson	6	1	0
LSU	6	1	0
South Carolina	6	1	0
Stanford	6	1	0
Virginia	8	1	1
Washington	5	1	0
Army	6	1	1
Tennessee	6	2	0
Oregon State	4	1	1
Cornell	8	3	0
Syracuse	6	2	1
Dartmouth	6	2	1
Notre Dame	6	2	1
North Carolina	5	1	3
Penn State	7	3	0
Ohio State	6	2	2
Pennsylvania	9	4	0
Oklahoma	6	3	0
Arkansas	6	3	0
Arizona State	2	1	0
Iowa State	6	3	1
Texas	6	3	1
Georgia	4	2	1
Oregon	3	1	3
West Virginia	7	4	0
Missouri	5	3	0
Kansas	6	4	0
Columbia	6	4	1
Virginia Tech	3	2	1
Mississippi	4	3	0
Brown	5	4	1
Alabama	4	4	0
Pittsburgh	5	6	1
Michigan State	4	5	0
Baylor	3	4	2
North Carolina St.	3	4	2
Maryland	3	5	2
Washington State	2	3	0
Southern Cal	2	3	0
Kentucky	3	5	1
Auburn	2	4	1
New Mexico State	0	1	2
Rutgers	3	7	0
Tulane	1	4	2
Navy	2	7	1
Kansas State	2	6	0
Mississippi State	1	4	1
Georgia Tech	0	6	2
TCU	0	5	1
Tulsa	0	1	0
Boston College	0	9	0

1903
CONSENSUS ALL-AMERICANS

POS	Name	School	CW	WC
B	Willie Heston	Michigan	•	•
B	J. Dana Kafer	Princeton	•	•
B	James Johnson	Carlisle		•
B	Richard Smith	Columbia		•
B	Myron Witham	Dartmouth	•	
B	W. Ledyard Mitchell	Yale	•	
E	Howard Henry	Princeton	•	•
E	Charles Rafferty	Yale	•	•
T	Daniel Knowlton	Harvard	•	•
T	James Hogan	Yale	•	•
T	Fred Schacht	Minnesota	•	
G	John DeWitt	Princeton	•	•
G	Andrew Marshall	Harvard	•	
G	James Bloomer	Yale	•	
C	Henry Hooper	Dartmouth	•	•

CONFERENCE STANDINGS

Big 10	Conf. W	L	T	Overall W	L	T
Minnesota	3	0	1	14	0	1
Michigan	3	0	1	11	0	1
Chicago	4	1	1	10	2	1
Northwestern	1	0	2	10	1	3
Iowa	1	1	0	9	2	0
Indiana	1	2	0	4	4	0
Illinois	1	5	0	8	6	0
Wisconsin	0	3	1	6	3	1
Purdue	0	2	0	4	2	0

Rocky Mountain	Conf. W	L	T	Overall W	L	T
Colorado	6	0	0	8	2	0
Utah State	1	0	0	3	0	0
Colorado State	5	1	0	6	1	0
Colorado Mines	2	3	0	3	3	0
Colorado College	1	3	0	4	5	0
Denver	1	5	0	6	7	0
Utah	0	4	0	3	5	0

Independents	Overall W	L	T
Princeton	11	0	0
Nebraska	10	0	0
Arizona State	2	0	0
Arizona	2	0	0
Notre Dame	8	0	1
Yale	11	1	0
Columbia	9	1	0
Dartmouth	9	1	0
Iowa State	8	1	0
West Virginia	7	1	0
Kentucky	7	1	0
New Mexico	3	0	1
Stanford	8	0	3
Washington	6	1	0
Virginia Tech	5	1	0
New Mexico State	2	0	1
Vanderbilt	6	1	1
Michigan State	6	1	1
South Carolina	8	2	0
Mississippi State	3	0	2
California	6	1	2
Harvard	9	3	0
Pennsylvania	9	3	0
Virginia	7	2	1
Texas	5	1	2
Clemson	4	1	1
Ohio State	8	3	0
Army	6	2	1
Texas A&M	7	3	1
Kansas	6	3	0
North Carolina	6	3	0
Southern Cal	4	2	0
Cornell	6	3	1
Oregon	4	2	1
Maryland	7	4	0
Penn State	5	3	0
Mississippi	2	1	1
Wyoming	3	2	0
Auburn	4	3	0
Baylor	4	3	1
Syracuse	5	4	0
Brown	5	4	1
Oklahoma	5	4	3
North Carolina St.	4	4	0
Rutgers	4	4	0
Washington State	3	3	2
Tulane	2	2	1
Tennessee	4	5	0
LSU	4	5	0
Kansas State	3	4	1
Arkansas	3	4	0
Georgia	3	4	0
Alabama	3	4	0
Navy	4	7	1
Oregon State	2	4	1
Georgia Tech	2	5	0
Oklahoma State	0	2	2
Missouri	1	7	1
Pittsburgh	0	8	1
TCU	0	7	0

1904
CONSENSUS ALL-AMERICANS

POS	Name	School	CW	WC
B	Daniel Hurley	Harvard	•	•
B	Walter Eckersall	Chicago	•	*
B	Vincent Stevenson	Pennsylvania		•
B	Willie Heston	Michigan		•
B	Andrew Smith	Pennsylvania		•
B	Foster Rockwell	Yale	•	
B	Henry Torney	Army	•	
E	Thomas Shevlin	Yale	•	
E	Fred Speik	Chicago	•	
T	James Hogan	Yale	•	
T	James Cooney	Princeton	•	•
G	Frank Piekarski	Pennsylvania	•	•
G	Joseph Gilman	Dartmouth	•	
G	Ralph Kinney	Yale		
C	Arthur Tipton	Army	•	•

1905
CONSENSUS ALL-AMERICANS

POS	Name	School	CW	WC
B	Walter Eckersall	Chicago	•	•
B	Howard Roome	Yale		•
B	John Hubbard	Amherst		•
B	James McCormick	Princeton		•
B	Guy Hutchinson	Yale	•	
B	Daniel Hurley	Harvard	•	
B	Henry Torney	Army	•	
E	Thomas Shevlin	Yale	•	•
E	Ralph Glaze	Dartmouth		•
E	Mark Catlin	Chicago	•	
T	Otis Lamson	Pennsylvania	•	•
T	Beaton Squires	Harvard	•	
T	Karl Brill	Harvard	•	
G	Roswell Tripp	Yale	•	•
G	Francis Burr	Harvard	•	•
C	Robert Torrey	Pennsylvania	•	•

CONFERENCE STANDINGS (1904)

Big 10	CONF. W	L	T	OVERALL W	L	T
Minnesota	3	0	0	13	0	0
Michigan	2	0	0	10	0	0
Chicago	5	1	1	8	1	1
Illinois	3	1	1	9	2	1
Northwestern	1	2	0	8	2	0
Purdue	1	2	0	9	3	0
Iowa	0	3	0	7	4	0
Wisconsin	0	3	0	5	3	0
Indiana	0	3	0	6	4	0

Rocky Mountain	CONF. W	L	T	OVERALL W	L	T
Colorado Mines	4	0	1	4	0	1
Colorado	4	1	0	6	2	1
Utah	3	1	0	7	1	0
Colorado College	3	3	1	6	3	1
Denver	2	5	0	2	5	0
Colorado State	0	4	0	0	4	1
Utah State	0	1	0	4	8	0

Independents	OVERALL W	L	T
Pennsylvania	12	0	0
Pittsburgh	10	0	0
Vanderbilt	9	0	0
Auburn	5	0	0
Arizona State	4	0	0
New Mexico	1	0	0
Dartmouth	7	0	1
Yale	10	1	0
Kentucky	9	1	0
Michigan State	8	1	0
Southern Cal	6	1	0
Georgia Tech	8	1	1
Kansas	8	1	1
California	6	1	1
Princeton	8	2	0
Army	7	2	0
Iowa State	7	2	0
Navy	7	2	1
Stanford	7	2	1
Harvard	7	2	1
Texas	6	2	0
Wyoming	4	1	1
Tulane	5	2	0
Alabama	7	3	0
Columbia	7	3	0
Nebraska	7	3	0
Cornell	7	3	0
West Virginia	6	3	0
Virginia	6	3	0
Syracuse	6	3	0
North Carolina	5	2	2
Texas A&M	4	2	0
Oregon State	4	2	0
North Carolina St.	3	1	2
Arizona	3	1	2
Washington	4	2	1
Virginia Tech	5	3	0
Notre Dame	5	3	0
Oregon	5	3	0
Penn State	6	4	0
Mississippi	4	3	0
Arkansas	4	3	0
Oklahoma	4	3	1
South Carolina	4	3	1
Ohio State	6	5	0
Brown	6	5	0
Clemson	3	3	1
Washington State	2	2	0
LSU	3	4	0
Tennessee	3	5	1
Maryland	2	4	2
New Mexico State	1	2	1
Missouri	3	6	0
Baylor	2	5	1
Mississippi State	2	5	0
TCU	1	4	1
Rutgers	1	6	2
Georgia	1	5	0
Kansas State	1	6	0
Oklahoma State	0	4	1

CONFERENCE STANDINGS (1905)

Big 10	CONF. W	L	T	OVERALL W	L	T
Chicago	7	0	0	10	0	0
Michigan	2	1	0	12	1	0
Minnesota	2	1	0	10	1	0
Purdue	1	1	1	6	1	1
Wisconsin	1	2	0	8	2	0
Indiana	0	1	1	8	1	1
Iowa	0	2	0	8	2	0
Northwestern	0	2	0	8	2	1
Illinois	0	3	0	5	4	0

Rocky Mountain	CONF. W	L	T	OVERALL W	L	T
Colorado	2	0	0	8	1	0
Colorado Mines	4	0	1	5	0	1
Colorado College	2	0	2	5	1	2
Utah	4	2	0	6	2	0
Colorado State	2	4	0	3	4	0
Denver	1	4	1	3	5	2
Wyoming	0	4	0	3	4	0
Utah State	0	1	0	2	2	1

Independents	OVERALL W	L	T
Yale	10	0	0
Stanford	8	0	0
LSU	3	0	0
New Mexico State	3	0	0
Pennsylvania	12	0	1
Georgia Tech	6	0	1
Kansas	10	1	0
Virginia Tech	9	1	0
West Virginia	8	1	0
Navy	10	1	1
Vanderbilt	7	1	0
Pittsburgh	10	2	0
Michigan State	9	2	0
Nebraska	8	2	0
Princeton	8	2	0
Dartmouth	7	1	2
New Mexico	5	1	1
Texas A&M	7	2	0
Oklahoma	7	2	0
Harvard	8	2	1
Ohio State	8	2	2
Kansas State	6	2	0
North Carolina St.	4	1	1
Syracuse	8	3	0
Penn State	8	3	0
California	4	1	2
Iowa State	6	3	0
Oregon State	6	3	0
Arizona	4	2	0
Southern Cal	6	3	1
Kentucky	6	3	1
South Carolina	4	2	1
Brown	7	4	0
Oregon	4	2	2
Washington	4	2	2
Cornell	6	4	0
Maryland	6	4	0
Alabama	6	4	0
Clemson	3	2	1
North Carolina	4	3	1
Texas	5	4	0
Missouri	5	4	0
Virginia	5	4	0
Notre Dame	5	4	0
Columbia	4	3	2
Army	4	4	1
Washington State	4	4	0
TCU	4	4	0
Mississippi State	3	4	0
Tennessee	3	5	1
Rutgers	3	6	0
Auburn	2	4	0
Tulsa	1	2	0
Oklahoma State	1	3	2
Arkansas	2	6	0
Georgia	1	5	0
Baylor	1	6	0
Tulane	0	1	0
Mississippi	0	2	0
Arizona State	0	3	0

1906
CONSENSUS ALL-AMERICANS

POS	Name	School	CW	WC
B	Walter Eckersall	Chicago	•	•
B	Hugh Knox	Yale	•	•
B	Edward Dillon	Princeton	•	
B	John Mayhew	Brown		•
B	William Hollenback	Pennsylvania	•	
B	Paul Veeder	Yale		•
E	Robert Forbes	Yale	•	•
E	L. Casper Wister	Princeton	•	•
T	L. Horatio Biglow	Yale	•	•
T	James Cooney	Princeton	•	
T	Charles Osborne	Harvard		•
G	Francis Burr	Harvard	•	•
G	Elmer Thompson	Cornell		•
G	August Ziegler	Pennsylvania	•	
C	William Dunn	Penn State		•
C	William Newman	Cornell	•	

1907
CONSENSUS ALL-AMERICANS

POS	Name	School	CW	WC
B	John Wendell	Harvard	•	•
B	Thomas A. D. Jones	Yale	•	•
B	Edwin Harlan	Princeton		•
B	James McCormick	Princeton		•
B	Edward Coy	Yale	•	
B	Peter Hauser	Carlisle	•	
E	Bill Dague	Navy		•
E	Clarence Alcott	Yale		•
E	Albert Exendine	Carlisle	•	
E	L. Casper Wister	Princeton	•	
T	Dexter Draper	Pennsylvania	•	•
T	L. Horatio Biglow	Yale	•	•
G	August Ziegler	Pennsylvania	•	•
G	William Erwin	Army		•
C	Adolph Schulz	Michigan		•
C	Patrick Grant	Harvard	•	

CONFERENCE STANDINGS (1906)

Big 10	CONF. W	L	T	OVERALL W	L	T
Wisconsin	3	0	0	5	0	0
Minnesota	2	0	0	4	1	0
Michigan	1	0	0	4	1	0
Chicago	3	1	0	4	1	0
Illinois	1	3	0	1	3	1
Indiana	0	2	0	4	2	0
Iowa	0	1	0	2	3	0
Purdue	0	3	0	0	5	0
Northwestern	0	0	0	0	0	0

Rocky Mountain	CONF. W	L	T	OVERALL W	L	T
Colorado Mines	3	0	2	3	0	2
Utah	3	1	0	4	1	0
Colorado College	2	2	1	3	2	2
Denver	2	3	0	2	3	0
Colorado	1	2	2	2	3	4
Colorado State	1	2	1	1	2	1
Utah State	0	1	0	3	1	0
Wyoming	0	1	0	1	1	0

Independents	OVERALL W	L	T
Washington State	6	0	0
New Mexico State	4	0	0
Princeton	9	0	1
Yale	9	0	1
Oregon	5	0	1
Harvard	10	1	0
Texas	9	1	0
Iowa State	9	1	0
Vanderbilt	8	1	0
Ohio State	8	1	0
Notre Dame	6	1	0
Texas A&M	6	1	0
Penn State	8	1	1
Alabama	5	1	0
Cornell	8	1	2
Clemson	4	0	3
Navy	8	2	2
New Mexico	3	1	0
Southern Cal	2	0	2
Virginia	7	2	2
Michigan State	7	2	2
Kansas	7	2	2
Kansas State	5	2	0
Oregon State	4	1	2
Pennsylvania	7	2	3
Missouri	5	2	1
Syracuse	6	3	0
Brown	6	3	0
Virginia Tech	5	2	2
Oklahoma	5	2	2
Rutgers	5	2	2
Mississippi	4	2	0
Washington	4	1	4
Dartmouth	6	3	1
Florida	5	3	0
Maryland	5	3	0
North Carolina St.	3	1	4
Georgia Tech	5	3	1
Nebraska	6	4	0
Pittsburgh	6	4	0
Kentucky	4	3	0
West Virginia	5	5	0
LSU	2	2	2
Mississippi State	2	2	1
Army	3	5	1
Arkansas	2	4	2
Georgia	2	4	1
TCU	2	5	0
Oklahoma State	1	4	2
North Carolina	1	4	2
Tennessee	1	6	2
Auburn	1	5	1
Tulane	0	4	1
Arizona State	0	2	0

CONFERENCE STANDINGS (1907)

Big 10	CONF. W	L	T	OVERALL W	L	T
Chicago	4	0	0	4	1	0
Wisconsin	3	1	1	3	1	1
Illinois	3	2	0	3	2	0
Iowa	1	1	0	3	2	0
Minnesota	0	1	1	2	2	1
Indiana	0	3	0	2	3	1
Purdue	0	3	0	0	5	0
Northwestern	0	0	0	0	0	0

Missouri Valley	CONF. W	L	T	OVERALL W	L	T
Nebraska	1	0	0	8	2	0
Iowa*	1	0	0	3	2	0
Kansas	1	1	0	5	3	0
Missouri	1	2	0	7	2	0
Washington, Mo.	0	1	0	1	5	0

* Footnote- Iowa held dual Membership in Big 10

Rocky Mountain	CONF. W	L	T	OVERALL W	L	T
Utah State	1	0	0	6	0	0
Colorado Mines	5	1	0	5	1	0
Utah	4	1	0	6	3	0
Colorado College	3	2	0	5	2	0
Colorado	3	2	0	5	3	0
Denver	1	4	0	2	6	0
Wyoming	0	1	0	2	1	0
Colorado State	0	4	0	0	4	0

Independents	OVERALL W	L	T
Oregon State	6	0	0
New Mexico State	3	0	0
South Carolina	3	0	0
New Mexico	1	0	0
Yale	9	0	1
Dartmouth	8	0	1
North Carolina St.	6	0	1
Notre Dame	6	0	1
Pennsylvania	11	1	0
Washington State	7	1	0
Kentucky	9	1	1
Michigan	5	1	0
Oregon	5	1	0
Southern Cal	5	1	0
Texas	6	1	1
Texas A&M	6	1	1
Pittsburgh	8	2	0
Cornell	8	2	0
Navy	9	2	1
Vanderbilt	5	1	1
Virginia Tech	7	2	0
Princeton	7	2	0
Ohio State	7	2	1
Tennessee	7	2	1
Iowa State	6	2	0
Alabama	5	1	2
Florida	4	1	1
Auburn	6	2	1
Army	6	2	1
Harvard	7	3	0
Brown	7	3	0
LSU	7	3	0
Mississippi State	6	3	0
Virginia	6	3	1
Michigan State	4	2	1
Kansas State	5	3	0
TCU	4	2	2
Syracuse	5	3	1
Penn State	6	4	0
West Virginia	6	4	0
Tulane	3	2	0
Georgia	4	3	1
Baylor	4	3	1
Georgia Tech	4	4	0
Clemson	4	4	0
Oklahoma	4	4	0
North Carolina	4	4	1
Arkansas	3	4	1
Washington	4	4	2
Rutgers	3	5	1
Maryland	3	6	0
Oklahoma State	1	3	1
Mississippi	0	6	0

ANNUAL REVIEW

1908

CONSENSUS ALL-AMERICANS

POS	Name	School	WC
B	Edward Coy	Yale	•
B	Frederick Tibbott	Princeton	•
B	William Hollenback	Pennsylvania	•
B	Walter Steffen	Chicago	•
B	Ed Lange	Navy	
B	Hamilton Corbett	Harvard	
E	Hunter Scarlett	Pennsylvania	•
E	George Schildmiller	Dartmouth	•
T	Hamilton Fish	Harvard	•
T	Frank Horr	Syracuse	
T	Percy Northcroft	Navy	
G	Clark Tobin	Dartmouth	•
G	William Goebel	Yale	
G	Hamlin Andrus	Yale	
G	Bernard O'Rourke	Cornell	
C	Charles Nourse	Harvard	•

CONFERENCE STANDINGS

Big 10	Conf.			Overall		
	W	L	T	W	L	T
Chicago	5	0	0	5	0	1
Illinois	4	1	0	5	1	1
Wisconsin	2	1	0	5	1	0
Purdue	1	3	0	4	3	0
Indiana	1	3	0	3	4	0
Minnesota	0	2	0	3	2	1
Northwestern	0	2	0	2	2	0
Iowa	0	1	0	2	5	0

Missouri Valley	Conf.			Overall		
	W	L	T	W	L	T
Kansas	4	0	0	9	0	0
Nebraska	2	1	0	7	2	1
Iowa State	2	1	0	6	3	0
Missouri	3	2	0	6	2	0
Drake	1	2	0	5	2	0
Washington, Mo.	0	2	0	4	4	1
Iowa*	0	4	0	2	5	0

* Footnote- Iowa held Membership in Big 10

Rocky Mountain	Conf.			Overall		
	W	L	T	W	L	T
Denver	5	0	0	7	1	0
Colorado	3	2	0	5	2	0
Colorado College	2	2	0	5	2	0
Utah	2	2	0	3	2	1
Colorado State	1	2	0	1	3	0
Colorado Mines	1	3	0	2	3	0
Utah State	0	1	0	4	2	0
Wyoming	0	2	0	1	2	0

Independents	Overall		
	W	L	T
LSU	10	0	0
Arizona	5	0	0
Pennsylvania	11	0	1
Harvard	9	0	1
Virginia	7	0	1
Washington	6	0	1
Notre Dame	8	1	0
Tulane	7	1	0
Michigan State	6	0	2
North Carolina St.	6	1	0
Auburn	6	1	0

	W	L	T
Oklahoma	8	1	1
Cornell	7	1	1
Yale	7	1	1
New Mexico	5	1	0
Washington State	4	0	2
Dartmouth	6	1	1
Alabama	6	1	1
Navy	9	2	1
Tennessee	7	2	0
Army	6	1	2
Vanderbilt	7	2	1
Kansas State	6	2	0
Pittsburgh	8	3	0
Oregon	5	2	0
Southern Cal	3	1	1
Florida	5	2	1
Georgia	5	2	1
Michigan	5	2	1
Georgia Tech	6	3	0
TCU	6	3	0
New Mexico State	4	2	0
Syracuse	6	3	1
Princeton	5	2	3
West Virginia	5	3	0
Brown	5	3	1
Ohio State	6	4	0
Oklahoma State	4	3	0
Kentucky	4	3	0
Oregon State	4	3	1
Arkansas	5	4	0
Virginia Tech	5	4	0
Texas	5	4	0
Penn State	5	5	0
North Carolina	3	3	3
Mississippi State	3	4	0
Tulsa	2	3	0
Rutgers	3	5	1
South Carolina	3	5	1
Texas A&M	3	5	0
Baylor	3	5	0
Mississippi	3	5	0
Boston College	2	4	2
Maryland	4	7	0
Wake Forest	1	5	0
Clemson	1	6	0

1909

CONSENSUS ALL-AMERICANS

POS	Name	School	WC
B	John McGovern	Minnesota	•
B	Stephen Philbin	Yale	•
B	Wayland Minot	Harvard	•
B	Edward Coy	Yale	•
E	Adrien Regnier	Brown	•
E	John Kilpatrick	Yale	•
T	Hamilton Fish	Harvard	•
T	Henry Hobbs	Yale	•
G	Albert Benbrook	Michigan	•
G	Hamlin Andrus	Yale	•
C	Carroll Cooney	Yale	•

CONFERENCE STANDINGS

Big 10	Conf.			Overall		
	W	L	T	W	L	T
Minnesota	3	0	0	6	1	0
Chicago	4	1	1	4	1	2
Illinois	3	1	0	5	2	0
Wisconsin	2	1	1	3	1	1
Indiana	1	3	0	4	3	0
Northwestern	1	3	0	1	3	1
Iowa	0	1	0	2	4	1
Purdue	0	4	0	2	5	0

Missouri Valley	Conf.			Overall		
	W	L	T	W	L	T
Missouri	4	0	1	7	0	1
Kansas	3	1	0	8	1	0
Drake	2	1	0	6	1	0
Iowa*	1	3	1	2	4	1
Nebraska	0	1	1	3	3	2
Iowa State	0	2	1	4	3	1
Washington, Mo.	0	2	0	3	4	0

* Footnote- Iowa held Membership in Big 10

Rocky Mountain	Conf.			Overall		
	W	L	T	W	L	T
Colorado	3	0	0	6	0	0
Denver	3	0	0	7	2	0
Utah	2	1	0	4	1	0
Colorado College	3	2	0	5	2	0
Colorado Mines	2	3	0	3	3	0
Colorado State	1	2	0	1	2	0
Utah State	0	2	0	2	2	1
Wyoming	0	4	0	3	5	0

Independents	Overall		
	W	L	T
Yale	10	0	0
Arkansas	7	0	0
Washington	7	0	0
Texas A&M	7	0	1
Notre Dame	7	0	1
Kentucky	9	1	0
Harvard	8	1	0
Michigan State	8	1	0
Virginia	7	1	0
Michigan	6	1	0
North Carolina St.	6	1	0

	W	L	T
Virginia Tech	6	1	0
Penn State	5	0	2
Florida	6	1	1
Pennsylvania	7	1	2
Washington State	4	1	0
Georgia Tech	7	2	0
Kansas State	7	2	0
LSU	6	2	0
Dartmouth	5	1	2
Alabama	5	1	2
Arizona	3	1	0
Princeton	6	2	1
Pittsburgh	6	2	1
North Carolina	5	2	0
Auburn	5	2	0
Vanderbilt	7	3	0
Ohio State	7	3	0
Brown	7	3	0
TCU	5	2	1
Clemson	6	3	0
New Mexico	4	2	0
Southern Cal	3	1	2
Tulsa	2	1	0
Oregon State	4	2	1
Oklahoma State	5	3	0
Baylor	5	3	0
Oklahoma	6	4	0
Army	3	2	0
Oregon	3	2	0
Navy	4	3	1
Texas	4	3	1
Mississippi State	5	4	0
Tulane	4	3	2
Mississippi	4	3	2
West Virginia	4	3	2
Syracuse	4	5	1
Boston College	3	4	1
Cornell	3	4	1
Rutgers	3	5	1
Wake Forest	2	4	0
New Mexico State	1	3	1
Maryland	2	5	0
Georgia	1	4	2
South Carolina	2	6	0
Tennessee	1	6	2

1910
CONSENSUS ALL-AMERICANS

POS	Name	School	WC
B	Earl Sprackling	Brown	•
B	Percy Wendell	Harvard	•
B	Talbot Pendleton	Princeton	•
B	E. LeRoy Mercer	Pennsylvania	•
E	John Kilpatrick	Yale	•
E	Stanfield Wells	Michigan	•
T	Robert McKay	Harvard	•
T	James Walker	Minnesota	•
G	Robert Fisher	Harvard	•
G	Albert Benbrook	Michigan	•
C	Ernest Cozens	Pennsylvania	•

CONFERENCE STANDINGS

Big 10	CONF. W L T			OVERALL W L T		
Illinois	4	0	0	7	0	0
Minnesota	2	0	0	6	1	0
Indiana	3	1	0	6	1	0
Iowa	1	1	0	5	2	0
Wisconsin	1	2	1	1	2	2
Northwestern	1	2	1	1	3	1
Chicago	2	4	0	2	5	0
Purdue	0	4	0	1	5	0

Missouri Valley	CONF. W L T			OVERALL W L T		
Nebraska	2	0	0	7	1	0
Iowa*	3	1	0	5	2	0
Missouri	2	1	1	4	2	2
Iowa State	2	2	0	4	4	0
Kansas	1	1	1	6	1	1
Washington, Mo.	0	2	0	3	4	0
Drake	0	3	0	2	5	0

* Footnote- Iowa held Membership in Big 10

Rocky Mountain	CONF. W L T			OVERALL W L T		
Colorado College	5	0	0	7	0	0
Colorado	4	0	0	6	0	0
Utah	4	2	0	4	2	0
Denver	3	2	0	4	3	1
Colorado Mines	2	4	0	2	4	0
Wyoming	1	4	0	4	4	0
Utah State	0	2	0	5	2	0
Colorado State	0	5	0	0	5	0

Independents	OVERALL W L T		
Pittsburgh	9	0	0
Washington	6	0	0
Arizona	5	0	0
Vanderbilt	8	0	1
Navy	8	0	1
Harvard	8	0	1
Southern Cal	7	0	1
Kansas State	10	1	0
Texas A&M	8	1	0
Princeton	7	1	0
Mississippi	7	1	0

	W	L	T
Arkansas	7	1	0
Pennsylvania	9	1	1
Michigan State	6	1	0
Auburn	6	1	0
Florida	6	1	0
North Carolina St.	4	0	2
Baylor	6	1	1
Oregon	4	1	0
Kentucky	7	2	0
Mississippi State	7	2	0
Brown	7	2	1
Virginia Tech	6	2	0
Virginia	6	2	0
Texas	6	2	0
Army	6	2	0
Ohio State	6	1	3
Notre Dame	4	1	1
Michigan	3	0	3
Georgia	6	2	1
Dartmouth	5	2	0
Yale	6	2	2
Penn State	5	2	1
Cornell	5	2	1
Oklahoma	4	2	1
Georgia Tech	5	3	0
New Mexico State	3	2	0
Oregon State	3	2	1
Maryland	4	3	1
Clemson	4	3	1
Rutgers	3	2	3
Syracuse	5	4	1
Alabama	4	4	0
South Carolina	4	4	0
Tulsa	1	1	0
Oklahoma State	3	4	0
Washington State	2	3	0
Tennessee	3	5	1
West Virginia	2	4	1
North Carolina	3	6	0
TCU	2	6	1
Wake Forest	2	7	0
LSU	1	5	0
Boston College	0	4	2
New Mexico	0	3	0
Tulane	0	7	0

1911
CONSENSUS ALL-AMERICANS

POS	Name	School	WC
B	Arthur Howe	Yale	•
B	Percy Wendell	Harvard	•
B	Jim Thorpe	Carlisle	•
B	Jack Dalton	Navy	•
E	Douglass Bomeisler	Yale	•
E	Sanford White	Princeton	•
T	Edward Hart	Princeton	•
T	Leland Devore	Army	•
G	Robert Fisher	Harvard	•
G	Joseph Duff	Princeton	•
C	Henry Ketcham	Yale	•

CONFERENCE STANDINGS

Big 10	CONF. W L T			OVERALL W L T		
Minnesota	3	0	1	6	0	1
Chicago	5	1	0	6	1	0
Wisconsin	2	1	1	5	1	1
Illinois	2	2	1	4	2	1
Iowa	2	2	0	3	4	0
Purdue	1	3	0	3	4	0
Northwestern	1	4	0	3	4	0
Indiana	0	3	1	3	3	1

Missouri Valley	CONF. W L T			OVERALL W L T		
Iowa State	2	0	1	6	1	1
Nebraska	2	0	1	5	1	2
Kansas	1	1	1	4	2	2
Washington, Mo.	0	0	2	4	2	2
Missouri	0	2	2	2	4	2
Drake	0	2	1	5	2	1

Rocky Mountain	CONF. W L T			OVERALL W L T		
Colorado	5	0	0	6	0	0
Utah State	1	0	0	5	0	0
Utah	3	1	1	5	1	1
Denver	3	1	1	5	2	1
Colorado College	3	2	0	4	3	0
Wyoming	2	3	0	4	3	1
Colorado Mines	1	5	0	2	5	0
Colorado State	0	6	0	0	6	0

Independents	OVERALL W L T		
Oklahoma	8	0	0
Washington	7	0	0
New Mexico State	7	0	0
Penn State	8	0	1
Florida	5	0	1
Princeton	8	0	2
Vanderbilt	8	1	0
Notre Dame	6	0	2
Texas A&M	6	1	0
Georgia	7	1	1
Navy	6	0	3
Michigan State	5	1	0
North Carolina	6	1	1

	W	L	T
Army	6	1	1
Dartmouth	8	2	0
Virginia	8	2	0
Virginia Tech	6	1	2
Yale	7	2	1
Mississippi State	7	2	1
Michigan	5	1	2
Harvard	6	2	1
Georgia Tech	6	2	1
Arkansas	6	2	1
Oregon State	5	2	0
Oklahoma State	5	2	0
Texas	5	2	0
Cornell	7	3	0
Kentucky	7	3	0
Arizona	3	1	1
Brown	7	3	1
West Virginia	6	3	0
Mississippi	6	3	0
LSU	6	3	0
Alabama	5	2	2
Auburn	4	2	1
Pennsylvania	7	4	0
North Carolina St.	5	3	0
Tulane	5	3	1
Syracuse	5	3	2
Ohio State	5	3	2
Oregon	3	2	0
Pittsburgh	4	3	1
Kansas State	5	4	1
Rutgers	4	4	1
Washington State	3	3	0
Maryland	4	4	2
TCU	4	5	0
Tennessee	3	4	2
Baylor	3	4	2
Clemson	3	5	0
Wake Forest	3	5	0
New Mexico	1	3	1
South Carolina	1	4	2
Boston College	0	7	0

1912
CONSENSUS ALL-AMERICANS

POS	Name	School	WC
B	George Crowther	Brown	•
B	Charles Brickley	Harvard	•
B	Jim Thorpe	Carlisle	•
B	E. LeRoy Mercer	Pennsylvania	•
E	Samuel Felton	Harvard	•
E	Douglass Bomeisler	Yale	•
T	Wesley Englehorn	Dartmouth	•
T	Robert Butler	Wisconsin	•
G	Stanley Pennock	Harvard	•
G	John Logan	Princeton	•
C	Henry Ketcham	Yale	•

1913
CONSENSUS ALL-AMERICANS

POS	Name	School	IN	WC
B	Charles Brickley	Harvard	•	•
B	Edward Mahan	Harvard	•	•
B	Jim Craig	Michigan	•	
B	Ellery Huntington	Colgate		•
B	Gus Dorais	Notre Dame	•	•
E	Robert Hogsett	Dartmouth	•	•
E	Louis Merrillat	Army	•	•
T	Harold Ballin	Princeton	•	•
T	Nelson Talbott	Yale		•
T	Miller Pontius	Michigan	•	
T	Harvey Hitchcock	Harvard	•	
G	John Brown	Navy	•	•
G	Stanley Pennock	Harvard		•
G	Ray Keeler	Wisconsin	•	•
C	Paul Des Jardien	Chicago	•	•

CONFERENCE STANDINGS

Big 10

	CONF. W L T			OVERALL W L T		
Wisconsin	5	0	0	7	0	0
Chicago	6	1	0	6	1	0
Purdue	2	2	1	4	2	1
Minnesota	2	2	0	4	3	0
Northwestern	2	3	0	2	3	1
Illinois	1	3	1	3	3	1
Iowa	1	3	0	4	3	0
Indiana	0	5	0	2	5	0

Missouri Valley

	CONF. W L T			OVERALL W L T		
Nebraska	2	0	0	7	1	0
Iowa State	2	0	0	6	2	0
Drake	2	2	0	4	3	0
Missouri	2	3	0	5	3	0
Kansas	1	2	0	4	4	0
Washington, Mo.	0	2	0	4	4	0

Rocky Mountain

	CONF. W L T			OVERALL W L T		
Colorado Mines	6	1	0	9	1	0
Utah	4	1	1	5	1	1
Colorado	4	2	0	6	3	0
Colorado State	3	2	0	3	2	0
Utah State	1	2	1	4	2	1
Colorado College	2	4	0	5	4	0
Denver	1	3	0	2	6	1
Wyoming	0	6	0	2	7	0

Independents

	OVERALL W L T		
Harvard	9	0	0
Penn State	8	0	0
Notre Dame	7	0	0
Washington	6	0	0
TCU	8	1	0
Texas A&M	8	1	0
Michigan State	7	1	0
Texas	7	1	0
Vanderbilt	8	1	1
Princeton	7	1	1
Yale	7	1	1

New Mexico State	5	1	0
Auburn	6	1	1
Georgia	6	1	1
Maryland	6	1	1
Kansas State	8	2	0
Kentucky	7	2	0
Dartmouth	7	2	0
Oklahoma State	6	2	0
Michigan	5	2	0
South Carolina	5	2	1
Florida	5	2	1
Ohio State	6	3	0
West Virginia	6	3	0
Virginia	6	3	0
Navy	6	3	0
Arizona	2	1	0
Pennsylvania	7	4	0
Mississippi	5	3	0
Army	5	3	0
Tulane	5	3	0
Georgia Tech	5	3	1
Alabama	5	3	1
Brown	6	4	0
Rice	3	2	0
North Carolina St.	4	3	0
LSU	4	3	0
Mississippi State	4	3	0
Oklahoma	5	4	0
Rutgers	5	4	0
Virginia Tech	5	4	0
Tennessee	4	4	0
Clemson	4	4	0
Syracuse	4	5	0
North Carolina	3	4	1
Oregon State	3	4	0
Oregon	3	4	0
Arkansas	4	6	0
Washington State	2	3	0
Baylor	3	5	0
Memphis	1	2	1
Boston College	2	4	1
Pittsburgh	3	6	0
Cornell	3	7	0
Wake Forest	2	6	0
Tulsa	1	3	0
New Mexico	0	4	0

CONFERENCE STANDINGS

Big 10

	CONF. W L T			OVERALL W L T		
Chicago	7	0	0	7	0	0
Minnesota	2	1	0	5	2	0
Iowa	2	1	0	5	2	0
Purdue	2	1	2	4	1	2
Illinois	2	2	1	4	2	1
Wisconsin	1	2	1	3	3	1
Indiana	2	4	0	3	4	0
Ohio State	1	2	0	4	2	1
Northwestern	0	6	0	1	6	0

Missouri Valley

	CONF. W L T			OVERALL W L T		
Missouri	4	0	0	7	1	0
Nebraska	3	0	0	8	0	0
Kansas	3	2	0	5	3	0
Iowa State	2	2	0	4	4	0
Drake	1	3	0	4	3	1
Kansas State	0	2	0	3	4	1
Washington, Mo.	0	4	0	1	5	0

Rocky Mountain

	CONF. W L T			OVERALL W L T		
Colorado	4	0	1	5	1	1
Colorado Mines	5	1	0	5	1	0
Colorado State	3	2	0	3	2	0
Colorado College	2	2	1	5	2	1
Utah State	1	1	0	3	3	0
Utah	1	3	0	2	4	1
Denver	1	3	0	2	5	0
Wyoming	0	5	0	0	5	0

Independents

	OVERALL W L T		
Harvard	9	0	0
Auburn	8	0	0
Washington	7	0	0
Notre Dame	7	0	0
Michigan State	7	0	0
Rice	4	0	0
New Mexico State	7	0	1
Army	8	1	0
Virginia	7	1	0

Texas	7	1	0
Dartmouth	7	1	0
Michigan	6	1	0
North Carolina St.	6	1	0
Virginia Tech	7	1	1
Navy	7	1	1
Mississippi State	6	1	1
Arkansas	7	2	0
Georgia Tech	7	2	0
LSU	6	1	2
Georgia	6	2	0
Kentucky	6	2	0
Oklahoma	6	2	0
Pittsburgh	6	2	1
Tulsa	5	2	0
Princeton	5	2	1
Maryland	6	3	0
Tennessee	6	3	0
Rutgers	6	3	0
Alabama	6	3	0
TCU	3	1	2
Pennsylvania	6	3	1
Mississippi	6	3	1
Yale	5	2	3
Vanderbilt	5	3	0
Syracuse	6	4	0
New Mexico	3	2	0
Florida	4	3	0
South Carolina	4	3	0
Oklahoma State	4	3	0
Boston College	4	3	1
Oregon State	3	2	3
North Carolina	5	4	0
Cornell	5	4	1
Washington State	4	4	0
Baylor	4	4	2
Clemson	4	4	0
Oregon	3	3	1
Arizona	2	2	0
Brown	4	5	0
Texas A&M	3	4	2
West Virginia	3	4	2
Tulane	3	5	0
Penn State	2	6	0
Memphis	1	3	0
North Texas	0	1	0
Wake Forest	0	8	0

1914
CONSENSUS ALL-AMERICANS

POS	Name	School	MS	WC
B	John Maulbetsch	Michigan	•	•
B	Edward Mahan	Harvard		•
B	Charles Barrett	Cornell	•	
B	John Spiegel	Wash. & Jeff.	•	
B	Harry LeGore	Yale	•	
E	Huntington Hardwick	Harvard	•	•
E	John O'Hearn	Cornell		•
E	Perry Graves	Illinois	•	
T	Harold Ballin	Princeton		•
T	Walter Trumbull	Harvard		•
G	Stanley Pennock	Harvard	•	•
G	Ralph Chapman	Illinois		•
G	Clarence Spears	Dartmouth	•	
C	John McEwan	Army		•

OTHERS RECEIVING FIRST-TEAM HONORS

POS	Name	School	MS	WC
B	Milt Ghee	Dartmouth		•
B	Frederick Bradlee	Harvard		•
T	Vic Halligan	Nebraska	•	
G	Arlie Mucks	Wisconsin	•	
C	Robert Peck	Pittsburgh	•	

1915
CONSENSUS ALL-AMERICANS

POS	Name	School	MS	WC
B	Charles Barrett	Cornell	•	•
B	Edward Mahan	Harvard	•	•
B	Richard King	Harvard		•
B	Bart Macomber	Illinois		•
B	Eugene Mayer	Virginia	•	
B	Neno Jerry DaPrato	Michigan State	•	
E	Murray Shelton	Cornell		•
E	Guy Chamberlin	Nebraska	•	
T	Joseph Gilman	Harvard	•	
T	Howard Buck	Wisconsin	•	
G	Clarence Spears	Dartmouth	•	•
G	Harold White	Syracuse	•	
C	Robert Peck	Pittsburgh	•	•

OTHERS RECEIVING FIRST-TEAM HONORS

POS	Name	School	MS	WC
E	Bob Higgins	Penn State	•	
E	Bert Baston	Minnesota		•
T	M.M. Witherspoon	Wash. & Jeff.	•	
T	Earl Abell	Colgate		•
G	Christopher Schlachter	Syracuse		•

CONFERENCE STANDINGS

Big 10

	Conf. W L T			Overall W L T		
Illinois	6	0	0	7	0	0
Minnesota	3	1	0	6	1	0
Chicago	4	2	1	4	2	1
Purdue	2	2	0	5	2	0
Ohio State	2	2	0	5	2	0
Wisconsin	2	2	1	4	2	1
Iowa	1	2	0	4	3	0
Indiana	1	4	0	3	4	0
Northwestern	0	6	0	1	6	0

Missouri Valley

	Conf. W L T			Overall W L T		
Nebraska	3	0	0	7	0	1
Missouri	4	1	0	5	3	0
Iowa State	2	1	0	4	3	0
Kansas	2	2	0	5	2	1
Drake	0	3	1	4	3	1
Washington, Mo.	0	3	1	3	3	1
Kansas State	0	3	0	1	5	1

Rocky Mountain

	Conf. W L T			Overall W L T		
Colorado Mines	5	0	1	5	0	1
Colorado	4	1	0	5	1	0
Colorado College	3	1	1	4	1	1
Colorado State	3	3	0	3	4	0
Utah	2	3	0	3	3	0
Utah State	1	2	0	2	5	0
Denver	1	4	0	5	4	0
Wyoming	0	5	0	1	5	0

Independents

	Overall W L T		
Tennessee	9	0	0
Army	9	0	0
Texas	8	0	0
Auburn	8	0	1
Washington	6	0	1
North Carolina	10	1	0
Dartmouth	8	1	0
Pittsburgh	8	1	0
Virginia	8	1	0
Oregon State	7	0	2
Harvard	7	0	2

Oklahoma	9	1	1
Texas A&M	6	1	1
Cornell	8	2	0
Arizona	4	1	0
Yale	7	2	0
Notre Dame	6	2	0
Mississippi State	6	2	0
Tulsa	6	2	0
Georgia Tech	6	2	0
Virginia Tech	6	2	1
Oklahoma State	6	2	1
Michigan State	5	2	0
Florida	5	2	0
New Mexico	3	1	1
Princeton	5	2	1
Michigan	6	3	0
Navy	6	3	0
Brown	5	2	2
New Mexico State	4	2	1
Oregon	4	2	1
Kentucky	5	3	0
Maryland	5	3	0
Clemson	5	3	1
Penn State	5	3	1
Rutgers	5	3	1
Syracuse	5	3	2
Arizona State	4	3	0
Southern Cal	4	3	0
Rice	3	2	3
Alabama	5	4	0
Boston College	5	4	0
West Virginia	5	4	0
Mississippi	5	4	1
South Carolina	5	5	1
TCU	4	4	2
LSU	4	4	1
Pennsylvania	4	4	1
North Texas	3	3	0
Tulane	3	3	1
North Carolina St.	2	3	1
Baylor	3	5	2
Texas-El Paso	2	3	0
Georgia	3	5	1
Memphis	3	5	0
Arkansas	3	6	0
Wake Forest	3	6	0
Washington State	2	4	0
Vanderbilt	2	6	0

CONFERENCE STANDINGS

Big 10

	Conf. W L T			Overall W L T		
Minnesota	3	0	1	6	0	1
Illinois	3	0	2	5	0	2
Chicago	4	2	0	5	2	0
Ohio State	2	1	1	5	1	1
Purdue	2	2	0	3	3	1
Wisconsin	2	3	0	4	3	0
Iowa	1	2	0	3	4	0
Indiana	1	3	0	3	3	1
Northwestern	0	5	0	2	5	0

Missouri Valley

	Conf. W L T			Overall W L T		
Nebraska	4	0	0	8	0	0
Kansas	3	1	0	6	2	0
Iowa State	2	1	0	6	2	0
Washington, Mo.	1	1	0	3	2	0
Missouri	1	3	1	2	5	1
Drake	1	4	0	2	6	0
Kansas State	0	2	1	3	4	1

Rocky Mountain

	Conf. W L T			Overall W L T		
Colorado State	7	0	0	7	0	0
Utah	4	2	0	5	2	0
Colorado Mines	4	2	0	4	2	0
Colorado College	3	2	0	6	2	0
Denver	2	3	0	4	3	0
Wyoming	1	5	0	2	6	0
Colorado	1	5	0	1	6	0
Utah State	0	3	0	3	4	0

SWC

	Conf. W L T			Overall W L T		
Oklahoma	3	0	0	10	0	0
Baylor	3	0	0	7	1	0
Texas	2	2	0	6	3	0
Texas A&M	1	1	0	6	2	0
Arkansas	1	1	0	4	2	1
Rice	1	2	0	5	3	0
Oklahoma State	0	3	0	4	5	1

Independents

	Overall W L T		
Cornell	9	0	0
Pittsburgh	8	0	0
Washington State	7	0	0
Washington	7	0	0

Columbia	5	0	0
Georgia Tech	7	0	1
Vanderbilt	9	1	0
Virginia	8	1	0
Harvard	8	1	0
Rutgers	7	1	0
Notre Dame	7	1	0
Syracuse	9	1	2
Dartmouth	7	1	1
Michigan State	5	1	0
Kentucky	6	1	1
Tulsa	6	1	1
North Texas	4	1	0
Oregon	7	2	0
Penn State	7	2	0
Auburn	6	2	0
Princeton	6	2	0
LSU	6	2	0
Alabama	6	2	0
New Mexico State	3	1	0
New Mexico	3	1	0
Mississippi State	5	2	1
West Virginia	5	2	1
Maryland	6	3	0
Georgia	5	2	2
Arizona	5	3	0
Oregon State	5	3	0
California	8	5	0
Army	5	3	1
South Carolina	5	3	1
Arizona State	3	2	0
Texas-El Paso	3	2	0
Florida	4	3	0
Memphis	4	3	0
Michigan	4	3	1
North Carolina	4	3	1
Brown	5	4	1
Virginia Tech	4	4	0
Tulane	4	4	0
Tennessee	4	4	0
North Carolina St.	3	3	1
Yale	4	5	0
TCU	4	5	0
Southern Cal	3	4	0
Wake Forest	3	4	0
Boston College	3	4	0
Pennsylvania	3	5	2
Navy	3	5	1
Clemson	2	4	2
SMU	2	5	0
Mississippi	2	6	0

BOWL GAMES

DATE	GAME	SCORE
J1	Rose	Washington State 14, Brown 0

ANNUAL REVIEW

1916
CONSENSUS ALL-AMERICANS

POS	Name	School	IN	MS	WC
B	Elmer Oliphant	Army	•	•	•
B	Oscar Anderson	Colgate	•		•
B	Fritz Pollard	Brown		•	•
B	Charles Harley	Ohio State	•		•
E	Bert Baston	Minnesota	•	•	•
E	James Herron	Pittsburgh			•
T	Clarence Horning	Colgate			•
T	D. Belford West	Colgate	•	•	•
G	Clinton Black	Yale		•	
G	Harrie Dadmun	Harvard			•
G	Frank Hogg	Princeton		•	•
C	Robert Peck	Pittsburgh	•	•	•

OTHERS RECEIVING FIRST-TEAM HONORS

B	Stan Cofall	Notre Dame		•	
B	Claire Long	Minnesota		•	
B	Andy Hastings	Pittsburgh	•		
E	Charlie Comerford	Yale		•	
E	George Moseley	Yale			•
T	Bob Karch	Ohio State			•
T	George Hauser	Minnesota	•		
G	Claude Thornhill	Pittsburgh	•		

CONFERENCE STANDINGS

Big 10	Conf. W L T			Overall W L T		
Ohio State	4	0	0	7	0	0
Northwestern	4	1	0	6	1	0
Minnesota	3	1	0	6	1	0
Illinois	2	2	1	3	3	1
Wisconsin	1	2	1	4	2	1
Iowa	1	2	0	4	3	0
Indiana	0	3	1	2	4	1
Purdue	0	4	1	2	4	1

Missouri Valley	Conf. W L T			Overall W L T		
Nebraska	3	1	0	6	2	0
Missouri	3	1	1	6	1	1
Iowa State	2	1	1	5	2	1
Kansas State	1	1	1	6	1	1
Kansas	1	2	1	4	3	1
Drake	1	3	0	3	5	0
Washington, Mo.	0	2	0	3	3	1

Pacific Coast	Conf. W L T			Overall W L T		
Washington	3	0	1	6	0	1
Oregon	2	0	1	7	0	1
California	0	3	0	6	4	1
Oregon State	0	2	0	4	5	0

Rocky Mountain	Conf. W L T			Overall W L T		
Colorado State	6	0	1	6	0	1
Colorado College	4	1	0	6	1	0
Denver	3	2	0	4	2	1
Utah	2	2	0	3	2	0
Colorado Mines	2	2	1	3	2	1
Wyoming	1	4	0	1	4	0
Colorado	1	5	0	1	5	1
Utah State	0	3	0	1	5	1

SWC	Conf. W L T			Overall W L T		
Texas	6	1	0	7	2	0
Baylor	3	1	0	9	1	0
Rice	2	1	0	6	1	2
Oklahoma	2	1	0	6	5	0
Texas A&M	2	2	0	6	3	0
Arkansas	0	2	0	4	4	0
Oklahoma State	0	3	0	4	4	0

Independents	Overall W L T		
Tulsa	10	0	0
Army	9	0	0
Pittsburgh	8	0	0
Georgia Tech	8	0	1
Tennessee	8	0	1
Yale	8	1	0
Brown	8	1	0
Notre Dame	8	1	0
Vanderbilt	7	1	1
Penn State	8	2	0
LSU	7	1	2
Michigan	7	2	0
Virginia Tech	7	2	0
Cornell	6	2	0
Auburn	6	2	0
Princeton	6	2	0
Boston College	6	2	0
Maryland	6	2	0
TCU	6	2	1
Kentucky	4	1	2
Harvard	7	3	0
Pennsylvania	7	3	1
Alabama	6	3	0
Georgia	6	3	0
Dartmouth	5	2	2
West Virginia	5	2	2
Washington State	4	2	0
Navy	6	3	1
Michigan State	4	2	1
Southern Cal	5	3	0
Arizona	5	3	0
New Mexico	3	2	0
Rutgers	3	2	2
North Texas	4	3	1
Tulane	4	3	1
North Carolina	5	4	0
Syracuse	5	4	0
Mississippi State	4	4	1
Wake Forest	3	3	0
Virginia	4	5	0
Memphis	2	3	1
Clemson	3	6	0
Mississippi	3	6	0
North Carolina St.	2	5	0
Columbia	1	5	2
South Carolina	2	7	0
Texas-El Paso	2	3	0
SMU	0	8	2
Arizona State	0	3	0
New Mexico State	0	4	0
Florida	0	5	0

BOWL GAMES

DATE	GAME	SCORE
J1	Rose	Oregon 14, Pennsylvania 0

1917
CONSENSUS ALL-AMERICANS

POS	Name	School	IN	MS	NE
B	Elmer Oliphant	Army	•	•	•
B	Ben Boynton	Williams	•		•
B	Everett Strupper	Georgia Tech		•	•
B	Charles Harley	Ohio State	•		•
E	Charles Bolen	Ohio State	•		•
E	Paul Robeson	Rutgers		•	
E	Henry Miller	Pennsylvania	•		
T	Alfred Cobb	Syracuse	•		
T	George Hauser	Minnesota	•		
G	Dale Seis	Pittsburgh	•		
G	John Sutherland	Pittsburgh	•		
G	Eugene Neely	Dartmouth	•		
C	Frank Rydzewski	Notre Dame	•		•

OTHERS RECEIVING FIRST-TEAM HONORS

B	George McLaren	Pittsburgh	•		•
B	J. Howard Berry	Pennsylvania	•		
E	Clifford Carlson	Pittsburgh	•		
E	Ernest Von Heimburg	Navy	•		
T	Walker Carpenter	Georgia Tech			•
T	Wilbur Henry	Wash. & Jeff.	•		
G	C.G. Higgins	Chicago	•		
G	Frank Culver	Michigan	•		
C	Russell Bailey	West Virginia	•		

CONFERENCE STANDINGS

Big 10	Conf. W L T			Overall W L T		
Ohio State	4	0	0	8	0	1
Minnesota	3	1	0	4	1	0
Northwestern	3	2	0	5	2	0
Wisconsin	3	2	0	4	2	1
Illinois	2	2	1	5	2	1
Chicago	2	2	1	3	2	1
Indiana	1	2	0	5	2	0
Michigan	0	1	0	8	2	0
Purdue	0	4	0	3	4	0
Iowa	0	2	0	3	5	0

Missouri Valley	Conf. W L T			Overall W L T		
Nebraska	2	0	0	5	2	0
Kansas	3	1	0	6	2	0
Iowa State	3	1	0	5	2	0
Kansas State	2	2	0	6	2	0
Missouri	2	4	0	3	5	0
Washington, Mo.	1	2	0	4	3	0
Drake	0	3	0	0	5	2

Pacific Coast	Conf. W L T			Overall W L T		
Washington State	3	0	0	6	0	1
California	2	1	0	5	5	1
Oregon State	1	2	1	4	2	1
Oregon	1	2	0	4	3	0
Washington	0	2	1	1	2	1

Rocky Mountain	Conf. W L T			Overall W L T		
Denver	5	0	0	9	0	0
Utah State	4	0	1	7	0	1
Colorado	4	2	0	6	2	0
Colorado Mines	3	2	0	5	3	0
Colorado College	2	3	0	3	3	0
Utah	2	3	0	2	4	0
Wyoming	1	4	0	3	4	0
Colorado State	0	7	1	0	7	1

SWC	Conf. W L T			Overall W L T		
Texas A&M	3	0	0	8	0	0
Baylor	2	1	0	6	2	1
Rice	1	1	0	7	1	0
Oklahoma	1	1	1	6	4	1
Texas	2	4	0	4	4	0
Oklahoma State	1	2	0	4	5	0
Arkansas	0	1	1	5	1	1

Independents	Overall W L T		
Pittsburgh	10	0	0
Georgia Tech	9	0	0
Columbia	5	0	0
Yale	3	0	0
Princeton	2	0	0
Navy	7	1	0
Army	7	1	0
North Texas	6	1	0
Mississippi State	6	1	0
Syracuse	8	1	1
Rutgers	7	1	1
Pennsylvania	9	2	0
Notre Dame	6	1	1
TCU	8	2	0
Brown	8	2	0
Clemson	6	2	0
Boston College	6	2	0
Auburn	6	2	1
North Carolina St.	6	2	1
Virginia Tech	6	2	1
Alabama	5	2	1
New Mexico State	4	2	0
West Virginia	6	3	1
Southern Cal	4	2	1
Harvard	3	1	3
Tulane	5	3	0
Vanderbilt	5	3	0
Dartmouth	5	3	0
Memphis	3	2	0
Arizona	3	2	0
Maryland	4	3	1
SMU	3	2	3
Penn State	5	4	0
Texas-El Paso	0	0	1
Kentucky	3	5	1
South Carolina	3	5	0
LSU	3	5	0
Cornell	3	6	0
Florida	2	4	0
New Mexico	1	2	0
Mississippi	1	4	1
Wake Forest	1	6	1
Tulsa	0	8	1
Michigan State	0	9	0

BOWL GAMES

DATE	GAME	SCORE
J1	Rose	Mare Island Marines 19, Camp Lewis 7

1918
CONSENSUS ALL-AMERICANS

POS	Name	School	MS	WC
B	Frank Murrey	Princeton	•	•
B	Tom Davies	Pittsburgh	•	•
B	Wolcott Roberts	Navy	•	•
B	George McLaren	Pittsburgh	•	
E	Paul Robeson	Rutgers	•	•
E	Bill Fincher	Georgia Tech	•	
T	Wilbur Henry	Wash. & Jeff.	•	
T	Leonard Hilty	Pittsburgh		•
T	Lou Usher	Syracuse	•	
T	Joe Guyon	Georgia Tech	•	
G	Joe Alexander	Syracuse	•	•
G	Lyman Perry	Navy	•	
C	Ashel Day	Georgia Tech	•	
C	John Depler	Illinois	•	

	Others receiving first-team honors			
B	Frank Steketee	Michigan		•
E	Robert Hopper	Pennsylvania		•

CONFERENCE STANDINGS
CONFERENCES PLAYED AN ABBREVIATED SCHEDULE DUE TO WORLD WAR 1

Big 10

	CONF.			OVERALL		
	W	L	T	W	L	T
Illinois	4	0	0	5	2	0
Michigan	2	0	0	5	0	0
Purdue	1	0	0	3	3	0
Iowa	2	1	0	6	2	1
Minnesota	2	1	0	5	2	1
Northwestern	1	1	0	2	2	1
Wisconsin	1	2	0	3	3	0
Ohio State	0	3	0	3	3	0
Chicago	0	5	0	0	5	0
Indiana	0	0	0	2	2	0

Missouri Valley

	CONF.			OVERALL		
	W	L	T	W	L	T
Washington, Mo.	2	0	0	6	0	0
Nebraska	2	0	0	2	3	1
Kansas State	1	1	0	4	1	0
Kansas	1	1	0	2	2	0
Drake	0	1	0	3	2	0
Iowa State	0	1	0	0	3	0

Pacific Coast

	CONF.			OVERALL		
	W	L	T	W	L	T
California	2	0	0	7	2	0
Oregon	2	1	0	4	2	0
Washington	1	1	0	1	1	0
Oregon State	0	2	0	2	4	0
Stanford	0	1	0	0	4	0
Washington State	0	0	0	1	1	0

Rocky Mountain

	CONF.			OVERALL		
	W	L	T	W	L	T
Colorado Mines	2	0	0	4	0	0
Denver	3	1	0	3	2	0
Colorado College	1	2	0	1	2	0
Colorado State	0	2	0	0	2	0
Colorado	0	3	0	2	3	0

SWC

	CONF.			OVERALL		
	W	L	T	W	L	T
Texas	4	0	0	9	0	0
Oklahoma	2	0	0	6	0	0
Texas A&M	1	1	0	6	1	0
Rice	1	1	0	1	5	1
SMU	1	2	0	4	2	0
Oklahoma State	0	2	0	4	2	0
Arkansas	0	1	0	3	2	0
Baylor	0	2	0	0	6	0

Independents

	OVERALL		
	W	L	T
Virginia Tech	7	0	0
Princeton	3	0	0
Army	1	0	0
Georgia Tech	6	1	0
Syracuse	5	1	0
Columbia	5	1	0
Navy	4	1	0
Pittsburgh	4	1	0
Maryland	4	1	1
Tulane	4	1	1
Rutgers	5	2	0
Boston College	5	2	0
Clemson	5	2	0
Vanderbilt	4	2	0
Notre Dame	3	1	2
Kentucky	2	1	0
Harvard	2	1	0
Pennsylvania	5	3	0
South Carolina	2	1	1
Mississippi State	3	2	0
TCU	4	3	0
Michigan State	4	3	0
Dartmouth	3	3	0
Southern Cal	2	2	2
Brown	2	3	0
Penn State	1	2	1
North Texas	1	2	1
Wake Forest	1	2	0
Tulsa	1	2	0
Auburn	2	5	0
Mississippi	1	3	0
North Carolina St.	1	3	0
Memphis	1	4	0
Florida	0	1	0

BOWL GAMES

DATE	GAME	SCORE
J1	Rose	Great Lakes NAS 17, Mare Island Marines 0

1919
CONSENSUS ALL-AMERICANS

POS	Name	School	MS	WC
B	Charles Harley	Ohio State	•	•
B	Ira Rodgers	West Virginia	•	•
B	Edward Casey	Harvard	•	•
B	Bo McMillin	Centre	•	
B	Ben Boynton	Williams	•	
E	Bob Higgins	Penn State	•	
E	Henry Miller	Pennsylvania	•	
E	Lester Belding	Iowa	•	
T	Wilbur Henry	Wash. & Jeff.	•	•
T	D. Belford West	Colgate	•	•
G	Joe Alexander	Syracuse	•	•
G	Adolph Youngstrom	Dartmouth	•	•
C	James Weaver	Centre	•	
C	Charles Carpenter	Wisconsin	•	

CONFERENCE STANDINGS

Big 10

	CONF.			OVERALL		
	W	L	T	W	L	T
Illinois	6	1	0	6	1	0
Ohio State	3	1	0	6	1	0
Chicago	4	2	0	5	2	0
Wisconsin	3	2	0	5	2	0
Minnesota	3	2	0	4	2	1
Iowa	2	2	0	5	2	0
Michigan	1	4	0	3	4	0
Northwestern	1	4	0	2	5	0
Indiana	0	2	0	3	4	0
Purdue	0	3	0	2	4	1

Missouri Valley

	CONF.			OVERALL		
	W	L	T	W	L	T
Missouri	4	0	1	5	1	2
Iowa State	3	1	1	5	2	1
Washington, Mo.	2	2	0	5	2	0
Drake	2	2	0	4	3	0
Kansas	1	1	1	3	2	3
Kansas State	0	3	1	3	5	1
Grinnell	0	3	0	1	4	1

Pacific Coast

	CONF.			OVERALL		
	W	L	T	W	L	T
Washington	2	1	0	5	1	0
Oregon	2	1	0	5	2	0
California	2	2	0	6	2	1
Washington State	2	2	0	5	2	0
Stanford	1	1	0	4	3	0
Oregon State	1	3	0	4	4	1

Rocky Mountain

	CONF.			OVERALL		
	W	L	T	W	L	T
Colorado State	7	1	0	7	1	0
Utah	4	1	0	5	2	0
Colorado College	3	1	1	4	2	1
Utah State	3	2	0	5	2	0
Wyoming	3	3	0	3	5	0
Colorado	2	3	1	2	3	1
Denver	0	4	1	1	5	1
Colorado Mines	0	4	1	0	4	2

SWC

	CONF.			OVERALL		
	W	L	T	W	L	T
Texas A&M	4	0	0	10	0	0
Rice	3	1	0	8	1	0
Oklahoma	2	1	0	5	2	3
Texas	3	2	0	6	3	0
Arkansas	1	2	0	3	4	0
SMU	0	2	1	5	4	1
Baylor	0	3	1	5	3	1
Oklahoma State	0	2	0	3	3	2

Independents

	OVERALL		
	W	L	T
Notre Dame	9	0	0
Harvard	9	0	1
Tulsa	8	0	1
Alabama	8	1	0
Auburn	8	1	0
Penn State	7	1	0
Arizona	7	1	0
Navy	6	1	0
Dartmouth	6	1	1
West Virginia	8	2	0
Southern Cal	4	1	0
New Mexico	3	0	2
North Carolina St.	7	2	0
LSU	6	2	0
Mississippi State	6	2	0
Vanderbilt	5	1	2
Syracuse	8	3	0
Pittsburgh	6	2	1
Tulane	6	2	1
Pennsylvania	6	2	1
Georgia Tech	7	3	0
Clemson	6	2	2
Army	6	3	0
Princeton	4	2	1
Boston College	5	3	0
Rutgers	5	3	0
Florida	5	3	0
Yale	5	3	0
Georgia	4	2	3
North Carolina	4	3	1
Maryland	5	4	0
Virginia Tech	5	4	0
Brown	5	4	1
Mississippi	4	4	0
North Texas	4	4	0
Michigan State	4	4	1
Tennessee	3	3	3
Nebraska	3	3	2
Kentucky	3	4	1
Memphis	3	4	0
New Mexico State	2	3	1
Texas-El Paso	2	4	0
Columbia	2	4	3
Cornell	3	5	0
Virginia	2	5	2
Wake Forest	2	6	0
UCLA	2	6	0
TCU	2	6	0
South Carolina	1	7	1
Arizona State	0	2	0

BOWL GAMES

DATE	GAME	SCORE
J1	Rose	Harvard 7, Oregon 6

ANNUAL REVIEW

1920
CONSENSUS ALL-AMERICANS

POS	Name	School	FM	IN	MS	WC
B	George Gipp	Notre Dame	•	•	•	•
B	Donald Lourie	Princeton		•		•
B	Gaylord Stinchcomb	Ohio State		•	•	•
B	Charles Way	Penn State	•		•	
E	Luke Urban	Boston College	•		•	
E	Charles Carney	Illinois				•
E	Bill Fincher	Georgia Tech		•		•
T	Stan Keck	Princeton	•	•	•	•
T	Ralph Scott	Wisconsin				•
G	Tim Callahan	Yale		•		•
G	Tom Woods	Harvard	•			•
G	Iolas Huffman	Ohio State			•	
C	Herb Stein	Pittsburgh		•		•

OTHERS RECEIVING FIRST-TEAM HONORS

B	Bo McMillin	Centre		•		
B	Tom Davies	Pittsburgh		•		•
B	Walter French	Army		•		
B	Arnold Horween	Harvard				•
B	Ben Boynton	Williams			•	
E	Armant Legendre	Princeton		•		•
E	Roger Kiley	Notre Dame		•		
E	Frank Weston	Wisconsin				•
T	Bob Sedgwick	Harvard		•		
T	Bertrand Gulick	Syracuse				•
T	Charles McGuire	Chicago				•
G	Paul Griffiths	Penn State		•		•
G	James Tolbert	Harvard				•
C	Joe Alexander	Syracuse		•		•

CONFERENCE STANDINGS

Big 10	CONF. W L T			OVERALL W L T		
Ohio State	5	0	0	7	1	0
Wisconsin	4	1	0	6	1	0
Indiana	3	1	0	5	2	0
Illinois	4	2	0	5	2	0
Iowa	3	2	0	5	2	0
Michigan	2	2	0	5	2	0
Northwestern	2	3	0	3	4	0
Chicago	2	4	0	3	4	0
Purdue	0	4	0	2	5	0
Minnesota	0	6	0	1	6	0

Missouri Valley	CONF. W L T			OVERALL W L T		
Oklahoma	4	0	1	6	0	1
Missouri	5	1	0	7	1	0
Kansas	3	2	0	5	2	1
Iowa State	3	2	0	4	4	0
Drake	1	3	1	4	5	1
Washington, Mo.	1	4	0	4	4	0
Grinnell	0	2	1	3	3	1
Kansas State	0	3	1	3	3	3

Pacific Coast	CONF. W L T			OVERALL W L T		
California	3	0	0	9	0	0
Stanford	2	1	0	4	3	0
Washington State	1	1	0	5	1	0
Oregon	1	1	1	3	2	1
Oregon State	1	2	1	2	2	2
Washington	0	3	0	1	5	0

Rocky Mountain	CONF. W L T			OVERALL W L T		
Colorado State	6	0	1	6	1	1
Colorado College	4	1	1	5	1	1
Colorado	3	1	2	4	1	2
Utah State	2	1	1	4	2	1
Utah	1	2	1	1	5	1
Denver	2	4	0	3	4	0
Wyoming	2	5	1	4	5	1
Colorado Mines	0	6	0	0	6	0

SWC	CONF. W L T			OVERALL W L T		
Texas	5	0	0	9	0	0
Texas A&M	5	1	0	6	1	1
Arkansas	2	0	1	3	2	2
Rice	2	2	1	4	2	2
Baylor	1	2	1	4	4	1
SMU	0	4	1	3	5	2
Oklahoma State	0	3	0	0	7	1

Independents	OVERALL W L T		
Notre Dame	9	0	0
Boston College	8	0	0
Southern Cal	6	0	0
Tulsa	10	0	1
Harvard	8	0	1
Georgia	8	0	1
Princeton	6	0	1
Alabama	10	1	0
TCU	9	1	0
Duke	4	0	1
Georgia Tech	8	1	0
Penn State	7	0	2
North Texas	7	1	0
Pittsburgh	6	0	2
Arizona	6	1	0
New Mexico State	5	1	1
Tennessee	7	2	0
Army	7	2	0
Maryland	7	2	0
Dartmouth	7	2	0
Auburn	7	2	0
Cornell	6	2	0
Navy	6	2	0
Syracuse	6	2	1
Tulane	6	2	1
North Carolina St.	7	3	0
Brown	6	3	0
Florida	6	3	0
Virginia	5	2	2
Yale	5	3	0
Mississippi State	5	3	0
Nebraska	5	3	1
Vanderbilt	5	3	1
LSU	5	3	1
Pennsylvania	6	4	0
Mississippi	4	3	0
South Carolina	5	4	0
West Virginia	5	4	1
Columbia	4	4	0
New Mexico	3	3	0
Kentucky	3	4	1
Clemson	4	6	1
Michigan State	4	6	0
Virginia Tech	4	6	0
Texas-El Paso	2	4	0
North Carolina	2	6	0
Wake Forest	2	7	0
Rutgers	2	7	0
Memphis	0	5	0
UCLA	0	5	0

BOWL GAMES

DATE	GAME	SCORE
J1	Rose	California 28, Ohio State 0
J1	Fort Worth Classic	Centre 63, TCU 7

1921
CONSENSUS ALL-AMERICANS

POS	Name	School	WC
B	Aubrey Devine	Iowa	•
B	Glenn Killinger	Penn State	•
B	Bo McMillin	Centre	
B	Malcolm Aldrich	Yale	
B	Edgar Kaw	Cornell	•
E	Brick Muller	California	•
E	Eddie Anderson	Notre Dame	
T	Dan McMillan	California	
T	Iolas Huffman	Ohio State	•
G	Frank Schwab	Lafayette	
G	John Brown	Harvard	
G	Stan Keck	Princeton	
C	Herb Stein	Pittsburgh	

OTHERS RECEIVING FIRST-TEAM HONORS

POS	Name	School	WC
E	James Roberts	Centre	•
T	Russell Stein	Wash. & Jeff.	•
T	Charles McGuire	Chicago	•
C	Henry Vick	Michigan	

CONFERENCE STANDINGS

Big 10	CONF. W L T			OVERALL W L T		
Iowa	5	0	0	7	0	0
Chicago	4	1	0	6	1	0
Ohio State	4	1	0	5	2	0
Wisconsin	3	1	1	5	1	1
Michigan	2	1	1	5	1	1
Minnesota	2	4	0	3	4	0
Indiana	1	2	0	3	4	0
Illinois	1	4	0	3	4	0
Purdue	1	4	0	1	6	0
Northwestern	0	5	0	1	6	0

Missouri Valley	CONF. W L T			OVERALL W L T		
Nebraska	3	0	0	7	1	0
Missouri	4	2	0	6	2	0
Kansas State	4	2	0	5	3	0
Kansas	3	3	0	4	3	0
Drake	2	2	0	5	2	0
Iowa State	3	4	0	4	4	0
Oklahoma	2	3	0	5	3	0
Washington, Mo.	2	3	0	4	3	1
Grinnell	0	4	0	2	5	0

Pacific Coast	CONF. W L T			OVERALL W L T		
California	4	0	0	9	0	1
Washington State	2	1	1	4	2	1
Stanford	1	1	1	4	2	2
Oregon State	1	2	1	4	3	2
Oregon	0	1	2	5	1	3
Washington	0	3	1	3	4	1

Rocky Mountain	CONF. W L T			OVERALL W L T		
Utah State	4	0	0	7	1	0
Colorado	4	0	1	4	1	1
Utah	2	1	1	3	2	1
Denver	2	2	1	4	2	1
Colorado State	2	2	1	2	3	1
Colorado College	2	4	0	4	4	0
Wyoming	1	3	2	1	4	2
Colorado Mines	1	5	0	1	5	0

SWC	CONF. W L T			OVERALL W L T		
Texas A&M	3	0	2	6	1	2
Texas	1	0	1	6	1	1
Arkansas	2	1	0	5	3	1
Baylor	2	2	0	8	3	0
Oklahoma State	1	1	0	5	4	1
Rice	1	2	1	4	4	1
SMU	0	4	0	1	6	1

Independents	OVERALL W L T		
Lafayette	9	0	0
Cornell	7	0	0
Wash. & Jeff.	10	0	1
Vanderbilt	7	0	1
Notre Dame	10	1	0
Southern Cal	10	1	0
Penn State	8	0	2
Yale	8	1	0
Navy	6	1	0
LSU	6	1	1
Syracuse	7	2	0
Arizona	7	2	0
Duke	6	1	2
Harvard	7	2	1
South Carolina	5	1	2
Dartmouth	6	2	1
Tulsa	6	3	0
TCU	6	3	1
Florida	6	3	2
Pittsburgh	5	3	1
Brown	5	3	1
Army	6	4	0
Princeton	4	3	0
Boston College	4	3	1
Pennsylvania	4	3	2
West Virginia	5	4	1
North Texas	3	3	0
New Mexico	2	2	0
New Mexico State	2	2	0
Memphis	4	5	1
Rutgers	4	5	0
Tulane	4	6	0
Michigan State	3	5	0
Mississippi	3	6	0
Columbia	2	6	0
Wake Forest	2	8	0
UCLA	0	5	0
Texas-El Paso	0	5	0

BOWL GAMES

DATE	GAME	SCORE
D26	San Diego East-West Christmas Classic	Centre 38, Arizona 0
J2	Rose	California 0, Wash. & Jeff. 0
J2	Dixie Classic	Texas A&M 22, Centre 14

1922
CONSENSUS ALL-AMERICANS

POS	Name	School	WC
B	Harry Kipke	Michigan	•
B	Gordon Locke	Iowa	•
B	John Thomas	Chicago	•
B	Edgar Kaw	Cornell	•
E	Brick Muller	California	•
E	Wendell Taylor	Navy	•
T	C. Herbert Treat	Princeton	•
T	John Thurman	Pennsylvania	•
G	Frank Schwab	Lafayette	•
G	Charles Hubbard	Harvard	•
C	Ed Garbisch	Army	•

CONFERENCE STANDINGS

Big 10	Conf. W L T	Overall W L T
Iowa	5 0 0	7 0 0
Michigan	4 0 0	6 0 1
Chicago	4 0 1	5 1 1
Wisconsin	2 2 1	4 2 1
Minnesota	2 3 1	3 3 1
Illinois	2 4 0	2 5 0
Northwestern	1 3 1	3 3 1
Ohio State	1 4 0	3 4 0
Indiana	0 2 1	1 4 2
Purdue	0 3 1	1 5 1

Missouri Valley	Conf. W L T	Overall W L T
Nebraska	5 0 0	7 1 0
Drake	4 0 0	7 0 0
Kansas State	3 1 2	5 1 2
Missouri	4 3 0	5 3 0
Oklahoma	1 2 2	2 3 3
Iowa State	2 4 0	2 6 0
Kansas	1 3 1	3 4 1
Grinnell	1 3 0	3 4 1
Washington, Mo.	0 5 1	1 5 1

Pacific Coast	Conf. W L T	Overall W L T
California	4 0 0	9 0 0
Oregon	3 0 1	6 1 1
Washington	4 1 1	6 1 1
Southern Cal	3 1 0	10 1 0
Stanford	1 3 0	4 5 0
Oregon State	1 3 0	3 4 0
Washington State	1 5 0	2 5 0
Idaho	0 4 0	3 5 0

Rocky Mountain	Conf. W L T	Overall W L T
Utah	5 0 0	7 1 0
Colorado State	5 1 1	5 2 1
Denver	3 1 1	6 1 1
Colorado Mines	4 2 1	4 2 1
Utah State	3 3 0	5 4 0
Colorado College	2 3 1	3 3 1
Colorado	2 3 0	4 4 0
Brigham Young	1 5 0	1 5 0
Wyoming	1 7 0	1 8 0

Southern	Conf. W L T	Overall W L T
Florida State	7 1 0	10 2 0
North Carolina	5 0 0	9 1 0
Vanderbilt	4 0 0	8 0 1
Georgia Tech	4 0 0	7 2 0
Virginia Tech	3 0 0	8 1 1
Florida	2 0 0	7 2 0
Tennessee	4 2 0	8 2 0
Auburn	2 1 0	8 2 0

	Conf.	Overall
Alabama	3 2 1	6 3 1
Kentucky	2 2 0	6 3 0
Virginia	1 1 1	4 4 1
Mississippi State	2 3 0	3 4 2
Wash. & Jeff.	1 2 0	5 3 1
Clemson	1 2 0	5 4 0
Maryland	1 2 0	4 5 1
LSU	1 2 0	3 7 0
Georgia	1 3 1	5 4 1
Tulane	1 4 0	4 4 0
South Carolina	0 3 0	5 4 0
Mississippi	0 2 0	4 5 1
North Carolina St.	0 5 0	4 6 0
Sewanee	1 3 1	3 4 1

SWC	Conf. W L T	Overall W L T
Baylor	5 0 0	8 3 0
Texas	2 1 0	7 2 0
SMU	2 2 0	6 3 1
Texas A&M	2 2 0	5 4 0
Oklahoma State	2 3 0	4 4 1
Arkansas	1 3 0	4 5 0
Rice	1 4 0	4 4 0

Independents	Overall W L T
Princeton	8 0 0
Tulsa	8 0 0
Cornell	8 0 0
West Virginia	10 0 1
Army	8 0 2
Notre Dame	8 1 1
Pittsburgh	8 2 0
Harvard	7 2 0
Syracuse	6 1 2
Duke	7 2 1
Brown	6 2 1
Boston College	6 2 1
New Mexico State	5 2 0
Navy	5 2 0
North Texas	5 2 1
Arizona	6 3 0
Pennsylvania	6 3 0
Dartmouth	6 3 0
Memphis	5 2 2
Yale	6 3 1
Penn State	6 4 1
Rutgers	5 4 0
Columbia	5 4 0
Texas-El Paso	5 4 0
New Mexico	3 4 0
UCLA	2 3 1
Wake Forest	3 5 2
Michigan State	3 5 2
TCU	2 5 3
Arizona State	0 3 1

BOWL GAMES

DATE	GAME	SCORE
D25	San Diego East-West Christmas Classic	West Virginia 21, Gonzaga 13
J1	Rose	Southern Cal 14, Penn State 3

1923
CONSENSUS ALL-AMERICANS

POS	Name	School	FW	WC
B	George Pfann	Cornell		•
B	Red Grange	Illinois	•	•
B	William Mallory	Yale	•	•
B	Harry Wilson	Penn State	•	
E	Pete McRae	Syracuse	•	
E	Ray Ecklund	Minnesota		•
E	Lynn Bomar	Vanderbilt	•	
T	Century Milstead	Yale	•	•
T	Marty Below	Wisconsin	•	•
G	Charles Hubbard	Harvard		•
G	James McMillen	Illinois	•	
C	Jack Blott	Michigan	•	

OTHERS RECEIVING FIRST-TEAM HONORS

POS	Name	School	FW	WC
B	John Levi	Haskell		•
B	Earl Martineau	Minnesota		•
E	Homer Hazel	Rutgers		•
T	Frank Sundstrom	Cornell	•	
G	Joe Bedenk	Penn State		•

CONFERENCE STANDINGS

Big 10	Conf. W L T	Overall W L T
Illinois	5 0 0	8 0 0
Michigan	4 0 0	8 0 0
Chicago	5 1 0	7 1 0
Minnesota	2 1 1	5 1 1
Iowa	3 3 0	5 3 0
Indiana	2 2 0	3 4 0
Wisconsin	1 3 1	3 3 1
Ohio State	1 4 0	3 4 1
Purdue	1 4 0	2 5 1
Northwestern	0 6 0	2 6 0

Missouri Valley	Conf. W L T	Overall W L T
Nebraska	3 0 2	4 2 2
Kansas	3 0 3	5 0 3
Drake	3 1 0	5 2 0
Iowa State	3 2 1	4 3 1
Kansas State	2 2 2	4 2 2
Oklahoma	2 4 0	3 5 0
Missouri	1 3 2	2 3 3
Grinnell	1 3 0	2 6 0
Washington, Mo.	1 4 0	3 5 0

Pacific Coast	Conf. W L T	Overall W L T
California	5 0 0	9 0 1
Washington	4 1 0	10 1 1
Stanford	2 2 0	7 2 0
Southern Cal	2 2 0	6 2 0
Idaho	2 2 1	5 2 1
Oregon State	1 3 1	4 5 2
Washington State	1 3 1	2 4 1
Oregon	0 4 1	3 4 1

Rocky Mountain	Conf. W L T	Overall W L T
Colorado	8 0 0	9 0 0
Colorado College	5 1 1	6 1 1
Colorado State	5 1 1	5 2 1
Utah State	4 2 0	5 2 0
Denver	4 3 0	6 3 0
Utah	2 3 0	4 3 0
Montana St.	1 2 0	5 4 0
Brigham Young	1 5 0	2 5 0
Colorado Mines	1 5 0	2 5 0
No. Colorado	0 2 0	2 3 1
Wyoming	0 7 0	0 8 0

Southern	Conf. W L T	Overall W L T
Vanderbilt	4 0 1	5 2 1
Wash. & Lee	4 0 1	6 3 1
VMI	5 1 0	9 1 0

	Conf.	Overall
Virginia Tech	4 1 0	6 3 0
Alabama	5 1 1	7 2 1
Tennessee	4 2 0	5 4 1
Maryland	2 1 0	7 2 1
Florida	1 0 2	6 1 2
North Carolina	2 1 1	5 3 1
Georgia	3 2 0	5 3 1
Mississippi State	2 1 2	5 2 2
Tulane	2 2 1	6 3 1
Clemson	1 1 1	5 2 1
Georgia Tech	0 0 4	3 2 4
Auburn	0 1 3	3 3 3
Kentucky	0 2 2	4 3 2
North Carolina St.	1 4 0	3 7 0
Virginia	0 3 1	3 5 1
Sewanee	0 2 0	5 4 1
Mississippi	0 4 0	4 6 0
South Carolina	0 4 0	4 6 0
LSU	0 3 0	3 5 1

SWC	Conf. W L T	Overall W L T
SMU	5 0 0	9 0 0
Texas	2 0 1	8 0 1
TCU	2 1 0	4 5 0
Arkansas	2 2 0	6 2 1
Baylor	1 1 2	5 1 2
Oklahoma State	1 3 0	2 8 0
Rice	1 4 0	3 5 0

Independents	Overall W L T
Yale	8 0 0
New Mexico State	8 0 0
Cornell	8 0 0
Notre Dame	9 1 0
Syracuse	8 1 0
Dartmouth	8 1 0
West Virginia	7 1 1
Boston College	7 1 1
Rutgers	7 1 1
Army	6 2 1
Penn State	6 2 1
Navy	5 1 3
Wake Forest	6 3 0
Memphis	6 3 0
Arizona State	4 2 0
Arizona	5 3 0
Brown	6 4 0
Harvard	4 3 1
Duke	5 4 0
Pittsburgh	5 4 0
Pennsylvania	5 4 0
Columbia	4 4 1
Princeton	3 3 1
Texas-El Paso	3 4 0
New Mexico	3 5 0
North Texas	3 5 0
Michigan State	3 5 0
Tulsa	2 5 1
UCLA	2 5 0

BOWL GAMES

DATE	GAME	SCORE
J1	Rose	Navy 14, Washington 14

1924

Consensus All-Americans

POS	Name	HT	WT	School	AA	FM	IN	LM	NE	WC
B	Red Grange	5-10	170	Illinois	•	•	•	•	•	•
B	Harry Stuhldreher	5-7	151	Notre Dame	•	•	•	•		•
B	Jimmy Crowley	5-11	162	Notre Dame	•	•	•			•
B	Elmer Layden	6-0	162	Notre Dame	•	•		•		
E	Jim Lawson	5-11	190	Stanford	•	•		•		
E	Dick Luman	6-1	176	Yale	•	•	•			
E	Henry Wakefield	5-10	160	Vanderbilt		•		•		
T	Ed McGinley	5-11	185	Pennsylvania	•	•	•		•	•
T	Ed Weir	6-1	194	Nebraska	•	•	•		•	
G	Joe Pondelik	5-11	215	Chicago	•	•		•		
G	Carl Diehl	6-1	205	Dartmouth			•	•	•	
C	Edwin Horrell	5-11	185	California		•	•	•	*	

Others Receiving First-Team Honors

POS	Name	School					
B	Homer Hazel	Rutgers			•		•
B	Eddie Dooley	Dartmouth		•			
B	Charles Darling	Boston College				•	
B	Raymond Pond	Yale					•
B	Walter Koppisch	Columbia				•	
E	Edmond Stout	Princeton					•
E	Henry Bjorkman	Dartmouth				•	
E	Hilary Mahaney	Holy Cross				•	
E	Charley Berry	Lafayette					•
T	Frank Gowdy	Chicago		•			
T	Bob Beattie	Princeton					•
G	Gus Farwick	Army	•		•		
G	Alton Papworth	Pennsylvania	•				
G	Edgar Garbisch	Army		•		*	
G	Edliff Slaughter	Michigan				•	
C	Winslow Lovejoy	Yale	•	•			

Conference Standings

Big 10

	Conf. W L T			Overall W L T		
Chicago	3	0	3	4	1	3
Iowa	3	1	1	6	1	1
Illinois	3	1	1	6	1	1
Michigan	4	2	0	6	2	0
Purdue	2	2	0	5	2	0
Minnesota	1	2	1	3	3	2
Ohio State	1	3	2	2	3	3
Northwestern	1	3	0	4	4	0
Indiana	1	3	0	4	4	0
Wisconsin	0	2	2	2	3	3

Missouri Valley

	Conf. W L T			Overall W L T		
Missouri	5	1	0	7	2	0
Nebraska	3	1	0	5	3	0
Drake	3	1	1	5	2	1
Grinnell	2	1	0	3	3	0
Iowa State	3	2	0	4	3	1
Oklahoma	2	3	1	2	5	1
Kansas	2	4	1	2	5	1
Kansas State	1	4	1	3	4	1
Washington, Mo.	0	4	0	4	4	0

Pacific Coast

	Conf. W L T			Overall W L T		
Stanford	3	0	1	7	1	1
California	2	0	2	8	0	2
Washington	3	1	1	8	1	1
Idaho	4	2	0	5	2	0
Southern Cal	2	1	0	9	2	0
Oregon	2	2	1	4	3	2
Oregon State	1	4	0	3	5	0
Washington State	0	4	1	1	5	2
Montana	0	3	0	4	4	0

Rocky Mountain

	Conf. W L T			Overall W L T		
Colorado	5	0	1	8	1	1
Colorado State	4	2	0	4	2	0
Montana St.	2	1	1	5	1	1
Utah State	3	2	1	4	2	1
Colorado College	4	3	0	5	3	0
Denver	3	2	2	4	2	2
Utah	2	2	1	3	4	1
Colorado Mines	3	4	1	4	4	1
Wyoming	2	6	0	2	6	0
Brigham Young	0	3	1	2	3	1
No. Colorado	0	4	0	2	5	0

Southern

	Conf. W L T			Overall W L T		
Alabama	5	0	0	8	1	0
Georgia	5	1	0	7	3	0
Florida	2	0	1	6	2	2
Tulane	4	1	0	8	1	0
Wash. & Lee	4	1	1	6	3	1
South Carolina	3	2	0	7	3	0
Sewanee	3	2	0	6	4	0
Virginia	3	2	0	5	4	0
Mississippi State	3	2	0	5	4	0
Georgia Tech	3	2	1	5	3	1
Vanderbilt	3	3	0	6	3	1
Virginia Tech	2	2	3	4	2	3
VMI	2	3	1	6	3	1
Kentucky	2	3	0	4	5	0
North Carolina	2	3	0	4	5	0
Maryland	1	2	1	3	3	3
Auburn	2	4	1	4	4	1
North Carolina St.	1	4	1	2	6	2
LSU	0	3	0	5	4	0
Mississippi	0	3	0	4	5	0
Tennessee	0	4	0	3	5	0
Clemson	0	3	0	2	6	0

SWC

	Conf. W L T			Overall W L T		
Baylor	5	0	0	8	3	0
Texas	2	1	0	7	2	0
SMU	2	2	0	6	3	1
Texas A&M	2	2	0	5	4	0
Oklahoma State	2	3	0	4	4	1
Arkansas	1	3	0	4	5	0

Independents

	Overall W L T		
Notre Dame	10	0	0
Dartmouth	7	0	1
West Virginia	8	1	0
Yale	6	0	2
Pennsylvania	9	1	1
Rutgers	7	1	1
New Mexico	5	1	0
Arizona State	6	1	1
Wake Forest	7	2	0
Syracuse	8	2	1
Army	5	1	2
New Mexico State	7	3	0
Boston College	6	3	0
Penn State	6	3	1
Princeton	4	2	1
Michigan State	5	3	0
Pittsburgh	5	3	1
North Texas	5	3	1
Columbia	5	3	1
Texas-El Paso	3	2	1
Brown	5	4	0
Harvard	4	4	0
Cornell	4	4	0
Duke	4	5	0
Arizona	2	4	0
Navy	2	6	0
Tulsa	1	6	1
UCLA	0	5	3
Memphis	1	7	0

Bowl Games

DATE	GAME	SCORE
D25	Los Angeles Christmas Festival	Southern Cal 20, Missouri 7
J1	Rose	Notre Dame 27, Stanford 10
J1	Dixie Classic	West Virginia Wesleyan 9, SMU 7

1925

Consensus All-Americans

POS	Name	HT	WT	School	AA	AP	CM	FW	IN	LM	NE	UP
B	**Andy Oberlander**	6-0	197	Dartmouth	•	•	•	•	•	•		
B	**Red Grange**	5-10	170	Illinois		•	•	•	•	•	•	•
B	**Ernie Nevers**	6-0	200	Stanford	•	•	•			•	•	
B	**Benny Friedman**	5-8	170	Michigan	•				•		•	
B	**George Wilson**	5-11	190	Washington	•	•	•	•	•			
E	**Bennie Oosterbaan**	6-0	180	Michigan	•		•			•	•	
E	**George Tully**	5-10	175	Dartmouth		•					•	
T	**Ed Weir**	6-1	194	Nebraska	•	•	•	•	•	•	•	
T	**Ralph Chase**	6-3	202	Pittsburgh	•	•	•	•				
G	**Carl Diehl**	6-1	205	Dartmouth			•		•	•	•	
G	**Ed Hess**	6-1	190	Ohio State			•			•	•	•
C	**Ed McMillan**	6-0	208	Princeton	•	•	•			*	•	

	Others receiving first-team honors											
B	J. Edward Tryon			Colgate			•					
B	Charles Flourney			Tulane						•		
B	Jacob Slagle			Princeton						•		
E	Charles Born			Army		•						
E	George Thayer			Pennsylvania			•					
E	Ted Sloan			Drake			•					
E	Dick Romney			Iowa					•			
T	Edgar Lindenmeyer			Missouri					•	•		
T	John Joss			Yale					•			
T	Nate Parker			Dartmouth					•			
G	Herbert Sturhahn			Yale	•	•						
G	Harry Hawkins			Michigan		•						
G	Brice Taylor			Southern Cal		•						
G	Dana Carey			California			•					
C	Tim Lowry			Northwestern		•						
C	Robert Brown			Michigan						•	•	•

Conference Standings

Big 10

	CONF. W L T			OVERALL W L T		
Michigan	5	1	0	7	1	0
Northwestern	3	1	0	5	3	0
Wisconsin	3	1	1	6	1	1
Iowa	2	2	0	5	3	0
Illinois	2	2	0	5	3	0
Chicago	2	2	0	3	5	1
Minnesota	1	1	1	5	2	1
Ohio State	1	3	1	4	3	1
Purdue	0	3	1	3	4	1
Indiana	0	3	1	3	4	1

Missouri Valley

	CONF. W L T			OVERALL W L T		
Missouri	5	1	0	6	1	1
Drake	5	2	0	5	3	0
Kansas State	3	2	1	5	2	1
Iowa State	3	2	1	4	3	1
Oklahoma	3	3	1	4	3	1
Nebraska	2	2	1	4	2	2
Grinnell	2	2	1	3	3	2
Kansas	2	5	1	2	5	1
Oklahoma State	0	3	1	2	5	1
Washington, Mo.	1	4	1	2	5	1

Pacific Coast

	CONF. W L T			OVERALL W L T		
Washington	5	0	0	10	1	1
Stanford	4	1	0	7	2	0
Southern Cal	3	2	0	11	2	0
Oregon State	3	2	0	7	2	0
California	2	2	0	6	3	0
Washington State	2	3	0	3	4	1
Idaho	2	3	0	3	5	0
Montana	1	4	0	3	4	1
Oregon	0	5	0	1	5	1

Rocky Mountain

	CONF. W L T			OVERALL W L T		
Colorado State	8	0	0	9	1	0
Utah State	5	1	0	6	1	0
Utah	5	1	0	6	2	0
Colorado	5	2	0	6	3	0
Wyoming	4	3	0	6	3	0
Colorado College	4	4	0	5	4	1
Brigham Young	3	3	0	3	3	0
Western St.	2	4	0	3	4	0
Colorado Mines	2	6	0	2	7	0
Montana St.	1	4	0	6	5	0
Denver	1	6	0	1	6	0
No. Colorado	0	6	0	2	6	1

Southern

	CONF. W L T			OVERALL W L T		
Alabama	7	0	0	10	0	0
Tulane	5	0	0	9	0	1
North Carolina	4	0	1	7	1	1
Washington & Lee	5	1	0	5	5	0
Virginia	4	1	1	7	1	1
Georgia Tech	4	1	1	6	2	1
Kentucky	4	2	0	6	3	0
Florida	3	2	0	8	2	0
Auburn	3	2	1	5	3	1
Vanderbilt	3	3	0	6	3	0
Virginia Tech	3	3	1	5	3	2
South Carolina	2	2	0	7	3	0
Tennessee	2	2	1	5	2	1
VMI	2	4	0	6	4	0
Georgia	2	4	0	4	5	0
Sewanee	1	4	0	4	4	1
Mississippi State	1	4	0	3	4	1
LSU	0	2	1	5	3	1
North Carolina St.	0	4	1	3	5	1
Mississippi	0	4	0	5	5	0
Maryland	0	4	0	2	5	1
Clemson	0	4	0	1	7	0

SWC

	CONF. W L T			OVERALL W L T		
TCU	2	0	1	7	1	1
Texas A&M	4	1	0	7	1	1
Texas	2	1	1	6	2	1
Arkansas	2	2	1	4	4	1
SMU	1	1	2	5	2	2
Rice	1	2	1	4	4	1

Independents

	OVERALL W L T		
Dartmouth	8	0	0
West Virginia	8	1	0
Pittsburgh	8	1	0
Syracuse	8	1	1
Texas-El Paso	5	1	1
Princeton	5	1	1
Pennsylvania	7	2	0
Army	7	2	0
Texas Tech	6	1	2
Notre Dame	7	2	1
Cornell	6	2	0
Tulsa	6	2	0
Boston College	6	2	0
Arizona State	6	2	0
Wake Forest	6	2	1
Yale	5	2	1
Navy	5	2	1
Columbia	6	3	1
New Mexico State	5	3	1
UCLA	5	3	1
North Texas	6	4	0
Harvard	4	3	1
Brown	5	4	1
Penn State	4	4	1
Arizona	3	3	1
Duke	4	5	0
Michigan State	3	5	0
New Mexico	2	4	1
Rutgers	2	7	0
Memphis	0	7	1

Bowl Games

DATE	GAME	SCORE
J1	**Rose**	Alabama 20, Washington 19

1926

CONSENSUS ALL-AMERICANS

POS	Name	HT	WT	School	AA	AP	CM	IN	NE	UP
B	Benny Friedman	5-8	172	Michigan		•	•	•	•	•
B	Mort Kaer	5-11	167	Southern Cal	•	•	•	•	•	
B	Ralph Baker	5-10	172	Northwestern	•			•		
B	Herb Joesting	6-1	192	Minnesota	•	•	•	•		•
E	Bennie Oosterbaan	6-0	186	Michigan	•	•	•	•	•	•
E	Vic Hanson	5-10	174	Syracuse	•	•	•	•		•
T	Frank Wickhorst	6-0	218	Navy	•	•	•	•	•	•
T	Bud Sprague	6-2	210	Army				•		
G	Harry Connaughton	6-2	275	Georgetown		•	•		•	•
G	Bernie Shively	6-4	208	Illinois	•	•	•	•	•	•
C	Bud Boeringer	6-1	186	Notre Dame	•	•	•	•	•	•

OTHERS RECEIVING FIRST-TEAM HONORS

B	Roy Randall	Brown
B	George Wilson	Army
B	George Wilson	Lafayette
B	Tom Hamilton	Navy
B	Charles Rogers	Pennsylvania
B	Marty Karow	Ohio State
E	Ted Shipkey	Stanford
E	Hoyt Winslett	Alabama
E	Hal Broda	Brown
T	Lloyd Yoder	Carnegie Tech
T	Orland Smith	Brown
T	Lonnie Stiner	Nebraska
T	Bob Johnson	Northwestern
T	Al Lassman	NYU
G	Herbert Sturhahn	Yale
G	Edwin Hayes	Ohio State
C	John Butler	Pennsylvania

CONFERENCE STANDINGS

Big 10

	CONF. W L T	OVERALL W L T
Northwestern	5 0 0	7 1 0
Michigan	5 0 0	7 1 0
Ohio State	3 1 0	7 1 0
Purdue	2 1 1	5 2 1
Wisconsin	3 2 1	5 2 1
Illinois	2 2 0	6 2 0
Minnesota	2 2 0	5 3 0
Indiana	0 4 0	3 5 0
Iowa	0 5 0	3 5 0
Chicago	0 5 0	2 6 0

Missouri Valley

	CONF. W L T	OVERALL W L T
Oklahoma State	3 0 1	3 4 1
Nebraska	5 1 0	6 2 0
Missouri	4 1 0	5 1 2
Grinnell	3 1 1	6 1 1
Oklahoma	3 2 1	5 2 1
Iowa State	3 3 1	4 3 1
Kansas State	2 2 0	5 3 0
Drake	1 4 0	2 6 0
Kansas	1 5 0	2 6 0
Washington, Mo.	0 6 0	1 7 0

Pacific Coast

	CONF. W L T	OVERALL W L T
Stanford	4 0 0	10 0 1
Southern Cal	5 1 0	8 2 0
Oregon State	4 1 0	7 1 0
Washington State	4 1 0	6 1 0
Washington	3 2 0	8 2 0
Idaho	1 4 0	3 4 1
Oregon	1 4 0	2 4 1
Montana	0 4 0	3 5 0
California	0 5 0	3 6 0

Rocky Mountain

	CONF. W L T	OVERALL W L T
Utah	5 0 0	7 0 0
Montana St.	4 0 0	4 2 1
Colorado State	5 2 0	6 2 1
Colorado College	5 2 0	5 2 0
Utah State	4 1 2	5 1 2
Denver	4 4 0	4 4 0
No. Colorado	3 3 0	6 4 0
Wyoming	1 2 2	2 4 2
Colorado	2 5 1	3 5 1
Brigham Young	1 4 1	1 5 1
Colorado Mines	1 5 0	1 6 0
Western St.	0 7 0	0 8 0

Southern

	CONF. W L T	OVERALL W L T
Alabama	8 0 0	9 0 1
Tennessee	5 1 0	8 1 0
Vanderbilt	4 1 0	8 1 0
South Carolina	4 2 0	6 4 0
Georgia	4 2 0	5 4 0
Virginia	4 2 1	6 2 2
Virginia Tech	3 2 1	5 3 1
Wash. & Lee	3 2 1	4 3 2
Georgia Tech	4 3 0	4 5 0
LSU	3 3 0	6 3 0
Auburn	3 3 0	5 4 0
North Carolina	3 3 0	4 5 0
Mississippi	2 2 0	5 4 0
Mississippi State	2 3 0	5 4 0
VMI	2 4 0	5 5 0
Tulane	2 4 0	3 5 1
Maryland	1 3 1	5 4 1
Florida	1 4 1	2 6 2
Kentucky	1 4 1	2 6 1
Clemson	1 3 0	2 7 0
North Carolina St.	0 4 0	4 6 0
Sewanee	0 5 0	2 6 0

SWC

	CONF. W L T	OVERALL W L T
SMU	5 0 0	8 0 1
Baylor	3 1 1	6 3 1
Texas	2 2 0	5 4 0
Arkansas	2 2 0	5 5 0
TCU	1 1 2	6 1 2
Texas A&M	1 3 1	5 3 1
Rice	0 4 0	4 4 1

Independents

	OVERALL W L T
Miami, Fla.	8 0 0
Navy	9 0 1
Brown	9 0 1
Notre Dame	9 1 0
Boston College	6 0 2
Army	7 1 1
Pennsylvania	7 1 1
Cornell	6 1 1
Arizona	5 1 1
Princeton	5 1 1
Tulsa	7 2 0
Syracuse	7 2 1
Texas Tech	6 1 3
Arizona State	4 1 1
Columbia	6 3 0
Pittsburgh	5 2 2
New Mexico	4 2 1
UCLA	5 3 0
North Texas	5 3 1
New Mexico State	5 3 1
West Virginia	6 4 0
Penn State	5 4 0
Wake Forest	5 4 1
Yale	4 4 0
Dartmouth	4 4 0
Michigan State	3 4 1
Texas-El Paso	3 4 0
Harvard	3 5 0
Duke	3 6 0
Rutgers	3 6 0
Memphis	1 8 0

BOWL GAMES

DATE	GAME	SCORE
J1	Rose	Alabama 7, Stanford 7

1927
CONSENSUS ALL-AMERICANS

POS	Name	HT	WT	School	AA	AP	CM	IN	NA	NE	UP
B	Gibby Welch	5-11	170	Pittsburgh	•	•	•	•	•	•	•
B	Morley Drury	6-0	185	Southern Cal	•	•	•	•	•		•
B	Red Cagle	5-9	167	Army	•		•	•	•		•
B	Herb Joesting	6-1	192	Minnesota	•	•	•	•	•		•
E	Bennie Oosterbaan	6-0	186	Michigan	•	•	•	•	•		•
E	Tom Nash	6-3	200	Georgia	•		•	•	•		•
T	Jesse Hibbs	5-11	185	Southern Cal	•		•	•			•
T	Ed Hake	6-0	190	Pennsylvania	•			•	•		•
G	Bill Webster	6-0	200	Yale	•	•	•		•		•
G	John P. Smith	5-9	164	Notre Dame	•	•	•	•	•		•
C	Larry Bettencourt	5-10	187	Saint Mary's-Cal	•	•					
C	John Charlesworth	5-11	198	Yale			•		•		•

	OTHERS RECEIVING FIRST-TEAM HONORS										
B	Bill Spears			Vanderbilt		•		•			
B	Mike Miles			Princeton				•			
B	Christy Flanagan			Notre Dame					•		•
E	Ivey Shiver			Georgia		•		•			
T	Sidney Quarrier			Yale		•					
T	Bud Sprague			Army		•		*			
T	Leo Raskowski			Ohio State			•		•		
T	John H. Smith			Pennsylvania			•				
T	Bill Kern			Pittsburgh					•		
G	Russ Crane			Illinois			•				
G	Harold Hanson			Minnesota					•		•
C	Bill Reitsch			Illinois			•				

CONFERENCE STANDINGS

Big 10

	Conf. W L T			Overall W L T		
Illinois	5	0	0	7	0	1
Minnesota	3	0	1	6	0	2
Michigan	3	2	0	6	2	0
Chicago	3	3	0	4	5	0
Purdue	2	2	0	6	2	0
Ohio State	2	3	0	4	4	0
Northwestern	2	3	0	4	4	0
Indiana	1	2	1	3	4	1
Wisconsin	1	4	0	4	4	0
Iowa	1	4	0	4	4	0

Missouri Valley

	Conf. W L T			Overall W L T		
Missouri	5	1	0	7	2	0
Nebraska	4	1	0	6	2	0
Oklahoma State	2	1	0	4	4	0
Iowa State	3	2	0	4	3	1
Kansas	3	3	1	3	4	1
Washington, Mo.	2	2	1	5	2	2
Oklahoma	2	3	0	3	3	2
Kansas State	2	4	0	3	5	0
Drake	1	2	0	3	6	0
Grinnell	0	5	0	0	7	1

Pacific Coast

	Conf. W L T			Overall W L T		
Southern Cal	4	0	1	8	1	1
Stanford	4	0	1	8	2	1
Idaho	2	0	2	4	1	3
Washington	4	2	0	9	2	0
California	2	3	0	7	3	0
Oregon State	2	3	0	3	3	1
Washington State	1	3	1	3	3	2
Oregon	0	4	1	2	4	1
Montana	0	4	0	3	4	1

Rocky Mountain

	Conf. W L T			Overall W L T		
Colorado State	7	1	0	7	1	0
Denver	5	1	0	5	2	0
Montana St.	3	1	0	4	4	0
Colorado College	5	2	0	6	2	0
Utah	3	1	1	3	3	1
Colorado	4	4	0	4	5	0
Utah State	3	3	1	3	4	1
Brigham Young	2	4	0	2	4	1
Colorado Mines	2	5	0	2	5	0
Wyoming	1	4	0	4	5	0
Western St.	1	5	0	1	6	0
No. Colorado	1	6	0	2	7	0

Southern

	Conf. W L T			Overall W L T		
North Carolina St.	4	0	0	9	1	0
Georgia Tech	7	0	1	8	1	1
Tennessee	5	0	1	8	0	1
Georgia	6	1	0	9	1	0
Vanderbilt	5	0	2	8	1	2
Florida	5	2	0	7	3	0
Mississippi	3	2	0	5	3	1
Virginia	4	4	0	5	4	0
Clemson	2	2	0	5	3	1
Alabama	3	4	1	5	4	1
LSU	2	3	1	4	4	1
Mississippi State	2	3	0	5	3	0
Virginia Tech	2	3	0	5	4	0
Wash. & Lee	2	3	0	4	4	1
Maryland	3	5	0	4	7	0
VMI	2	4	0	6	4	0
South Carolina	2	4	0	4	5	0
Tulane	2	5	1	2	5	1
North Carolina	2	5	0	4	6	0
Sewanee	1	4	0	2	6	0
Kentucky	1	5	0	3	6	1
Auburn	0	6	1	0	7	2

SWC

	Conf. W L T			Overall W L T		
Texas A&M	4	0	1	8	0	1
SMU	4	1	0	7	2	0
Arkansas	3	1	0	8	1	0
Texas	2	2	1	6	2	1
TCU	1	2	2	4	3	2
Rice	1	3	0	2	6	1
Baylor	0	5	0	2	7	0

Independents

	Overall W L T		
New Mexico	8	0	1
Army	9	1	0
Tulsa	8	1	0
Dartmouth	7	1	0
Yale	7	1	0
Princeton	6	1	0
Pittsburgh	8	1	1
Notre Dame	7	1	1
UCLA	6	2	1
Penn State	6	2	1
Navy	6	3	0
Columbia	5	2	2
Arizona	4	2	1
Memphis	5	3	1
Pennsylvania	6	4	0
Syracuse	5	3	2
Texas Tech	5	4	0
Rutgers	4	4	0
Harvard	4	4	0
Boston College	4	4	0
Cornell	3	3	2
Texas-El Paso	2	2	2
Michigan State	4	5	0
Duke	4	5	0
Arizona State	2	3	1
West Virginia	2	4	3
New Mexico State	3	5	0
Miami, Fla.	3	6	1
Brown	3	6	1
Wake Forest	2	6	2
North Texas	1	6	2

BOWL GAMES

DATE	GAME	SCORE
J2	Rose	Stanford 7, Pittsburgh 6

1928

Consensus All-Americans

POS	Name	HT	WT	School	AA	AP	CM	IN	NA	NE	UP
B	Red Cagle	5-9	167	Army	•	•	•	•	•	•	•
B	Paul Scull	5-8	187	Pennsylvania	•		•	•	•	•	
B	Ken Strong	6-0	201	NYU	•		•	•		•	•
B	Howard Harpster	6-1	160	Carnegie Mellon	•		•	•			•
B	Charles Carroll	6-0	190	Washington	•	•		•			
E	Irv Phillips	6-1	188	California	•		•	•		•	•
E	Wes Fesler	6-0	173	Ohio State	•	•	•			•	•
T	Otto Pommerening	6-0	178	Michigan	•		•	•		•	
T	Mike Getto	6-2	198	Pittsburgh	•		•	•			•
G	Seraphim Post	6-0	190	Stanford	•	•	•	•		•	•
G	Don Robesky	5-11	198	Stanford	•		•	•			
G	Edward Burke	6-0	180	Navy	•		•				•
C	Pete Pund	6-0	195	Georgia Tech	•		•	•		•	

Others Receiving First-Team Honors

B	Earl Clark	Colorado College	•
B	Warner Mizell	Georgia Tech	• •
B	Don Williams	Southern Cal	•
B	Lloyd Brazil	Detroit	•
E	Ike Frankian	Saint Mary's-Cal	•
E	Dale Van Sickel	Florida	• • •
E	Kenneth Haycraft	Minnesota	•
E	Theodore Rosenzweig	Carnegie Mellon	•
T	Albert Nowack	Illinois	• •
T	Frank Speer	Georgia Tech	•
T	Fred Miller	Notre Dame	•
T	Jesse Hibbs	Southern Cal	•
T	Forrest Douds	Wash. & Jeff.	• •
G	George Gibson	Minnesota	• •
G	Dan McMullen	Nebraska	•
G	Leroy Wietz	Illinois	•
G	Peter Westra	Iowa	•
C	Charles Howe	Princeton	• •

Conference Standings

Big 10

	Conf. W L T			Overall W L T		
Illinois	4	1	0	7	1	0
Wisconsin	3	1	1	7	1	1
Minnesota	4	2	0	6	2	0
Iowa	3	2	0	6	2	0
Ohio State	3	2	0	5	2	1
Purdue	2	2	1	5	2	1
Northwestern	2	3	0	5	3	0
Michigan	2	3	0	3	4	1
Indiana	2	4	0	4	4	0
Chicago	0	5	0	2	7	0

Big 6

	Conf. W L T			Overall W L T		
Nebraska	5	0	0	7	1	1
Oklahoma	3	2	0	5	3	0
Missouri	3	2	0	4	4	0
Iowa State	2	2	1	2	5	1
Kansas	1	3	1	2	4	2
Kansas State	0	5	0	3	5	0

Pacific Coast

	Conf. W L T			Overall W L T		
Southern Cal	4	0	1	9	0	1
California	3	0	2	6	2	2
Stanford	4	1	1	8	3	1
Oregon	4	2	0	9	2	0
Washington State	4	3	0	7	3	0
Oregon State	2	3	0	6	3	0
Idaho	2	3	0	3	4	1
Washington	2	4	0	7	4	0
UCLA	0	4	0	4	4	1
Montana	0	5	0	4	5	1

Rocky Mountain

	Conf. W L T			Overall W L T		
Utah	4	0	1	5	0	2
Colorado	5	1	0	5	1	0
Colorado State	6	2	0	6	2	0
Utah State	4	2	1	5	3	1
Colorado College	5	3	0	5	3	0
Montana St.	3	2	0	4	4	1
Denver	3	4	1	4	4	1
No. Colorado	3	4	0	4	4	0
Brigham Young	1	3	1	3	3	1
Colorado Mines	2	5	0	2	5	0
Wyoming	0	5	0	2	7	0
Western St.	0	6	0	0	7	0

Southern

	Conf. W L T			Overall W L T		
Georgia Tech	7	0	0	10	0	0
Tennessee	6	0	1	9	0	1
Florida	6	1	0	8	1	0
Virginia Tech	4	1	0	7	2	0
Alabama	6	2	0	6	3	0
LSU	3	1	1	6	2	1
Vanderbilt	4	2	0	8	2	0
Clemson	4	2	0	8	3	0
Tulane	3	3	1	6	3	1
Mississippi	3	3	0	5	4	0
South Carolina	2	2	1	6	2	2
North Carolina	2	2	2	5	3	2
Kentucky	2	2	1	4	3	1
Maryland	2	3	1	6	3	1
VMI	2	3	1	5	3	2
Georgia	2	4	0	4	5	0
North Carolina St.	1	3	1	4	5	1
Mississippi State	1	4	0	2	4	2
Virginia	1	6	0	2	6	1
Wash. & Lee	1	6	0	2	8	0
Sewanee	0	5	0	2	7	0
Auburn	0	7	0	1	8	0

SWC

	Conf. W L T			Overall W L T		
Texas	5	1	0	7	2	0
Arkansas	3	1	0	7	2	0
Baylor	3	2	0	8	2	0
TCU	3	2	0	8	2	0
SMU	2	2	1	6	3	1
Texas A&M	1	3	1	5	4	1
Rice	0	5	0	2	7	0

Independents

	Overall W L T		
Boston College	9	0	0
Detroit	9	0	0
Brown	8	1	0
Pennsylvania	8	1	0
West Virginia	8	2	0
Army	8	2	0
Tulsa	7	2	1
Arizona	5	1	2
Princeton	5	1	2
Pittsburgh	6	2	1
Harvard	5	2	1
New Mexico	5	2	1
Rutgers	6	3	0
Navy	5	3	1
Columbia	5	3	1
Memphis	5	3	2
Arizona State	3	2	1
Notre Dame	5	4	0
Dartmouth	5	4	0
Duke	5	5	0
Texas Tech	4	4	1
Syracuse	4	4	1
Miami, Fla.	4	4	1
Yale	4	4	0
Cornell	3	3	2
North Texas	4	5	0
New Mexico State	4	5	0
Michigan State	3	4	1
Texas-El Paso	3	4	1
Penn State	3	5	1
Wake Forest	2	6	2

Bowl Games

DATE	GAME	SCORE
J1	Rose	Georgia Tech 8, California 7

1929

CONSENSUS ALL-AMERICANS

POS	Name	HT	WT	School	AA	AP	CM	IN	NA	NE	UP
B	Frank Carideo	5-7	175	Notre Dame	•	•	•	•	•	•	•
B	Ralph Welch	6-1	189	Purdue	•	•	•		•	•	•
B	Red Cagle	5-9	167	Army	•	•	•	•			
B	Gene McEver	5-10	185	Tennessee					•	•	•
E	Joe Donchess	6-0	175	Pittsburgh	•	•	•	•	•	•	•
E	Wes Fesler	6-0	183	Ohio State		•					
T	Bronko Nagurski	6-2	217	Minnesota		•	•	•	•	•	
T	Elmer Sleight	6-2	193	Purdue	•	•		•		•	•
G	Jack Cannon	5-11	193	Notre Dame	•	•	•	•	•	•	•
G	Ray Montgomery	6-1	188	Pittsburgh	•		•	•	•		•
C	Ben Ticknor	6-2	193	Harvard	•	•	•	•	•		•

	OTHERS RECEIVING FIRST-TEAM HONORS		
B	Bill Banker	Tulane	•
B	Toby Uansa	Pittsburgh	•
B	Tony Holm	Alabama	•
B	Willis Glassgow	Iowa	• •
B	Earl Pomeroy	Utah	•
B	Alton Marsters	Dartmouth	•
B	Merle Hufford	Washington	•
E	Francis Tappaan	Southern Cal	• • •
E	Wear Schoonover	Arkansas	•
E	Robert Tanner	Minnesota	•
T	George Ackerman	Saint Mary's-Cal	•
T	Lou Gordon	Illinois	•
T	Ray Richards	Nebraska	•
T	Marion Hammon	SMU	•
G	Bert Schwarz	California	•
G	Harry Anderson	Northwestern	•
G	John Brown	Vanderbilt	•
C	Roy Riegels	California	•

CONFERENCE STANDINGS

Big 10

	CONF. W L T			OVERALL W L T		
Purdue	5	0	0	8	0	0
Illinois	3	1	1	6	1	1
Minnesota	3	2	0	6	2	0
Northwestern	3	2	0	6	3	0
Iowa	2	2	2	4	2	2
Ohio State	2	2	1	4	3	1
Michigan	1	3	1	5	3	1
Indiana	1	3	1	2	6	1
Chicago	1	3	0	7	3	0
Wisconsin	1	4	0	4	5	0

Big 6

	CONF. W L T			OVERALL W L T		
Nebraska	3	0	2	4	1	3
Missouri	3	1	1	5	2	1
Kansas State	3	2	0	3	5	0
Oklahoma	2	2	1	3	3	2
Kansas	2	3	0	4	4	0
Iowa State	0	5	0	1	7	0

Pacific Coast

	CONF. W L T			OVERALL W L T		
Southern Cal	6	1	0	10	2	0
Stanford	5	1	0	9	2	0
California	4	1	0	7	1	1
Oregon	4	1	0	7	3	0
Washington State	4	2	0	10	2	0
UCLA	1	3	0	4	4	0
Oregon State	1	4	0	5	4	0
Idaho	1	4	0	4	5	0
Montana	0	4	1	3	5	1
Washington	0	5	1	2	6	1

Rocky Mountain

	CONF. W L T			OVERALL W L T		
Utah	6	0	0	7	0	0
Colorado	4	1	1	5	1	1
Denver	4	1	1	5	1	1
Brigham Young	4	2	0	5	3	0
Montana St.	2	1	0	6	2	0
No. Colorado	3	2	0	4	3	0
Colorado College	4	3	0	4	3	0
Colorado State	4	4	0	5	4	0
Utah State	3	4	0	3	4	0
Colorado Mines	1	5	0	2	5	0
Western St.	0	5	0	2	5	0
Wyoming	0	7	0	1	7	0

Southern

	CONF. W L T			OVERALL W L T		
Tulane	6	0	0	9	0	0
Tennessee	6	0	1	9	0	1
North Carolina	7	1	0	9	1	0
Florida	6	1	0	8	2	0
Vanderbilt	5	1	0	7	2	0
Kentucky	3	1	1	6	1	1
VMI	4	2	0	8	2	0
Georgia	4	2	0	6	4	0
Duke	2	1	0	4	6	0
LSU	3	2	0	6	3	0
Alabama	4	3	0	6	3	0
Clemson	3	3	0	8	3	0
Virginia Tech	2	3	0	5	4	0
Georgia Tech	3	5	0	3	6	0
Virginia	1	3	2	4	3	2
Maryland	1	3	1	4	4	2
South Carolina	2	5	0	6	5	0
Wash. & Lee	1	4	1	3	5	1
Mississippi	0	4	2	1	6	2
Mississippi State	0	3	1	1	5	2
Sewanee	0	4	1	2	5	2
Auburn	0	7	0	2	7	0
North Carolina St.	0	5	0	1	8	0

SWC

	CONF. W L T			OVERALL W L T		
Northwestern	5	0	0	7	1	0
TCU	4	0	1	9	0	1
SMU	3	0	2	6	0	4
Arkansas	3	2	0	7	2	0
Baylor	2	2	1	7	3	1
Texas	2	2	2	5	2	2
Texas A&M	2	3	0	5	4	0
Rice	0	5	0	2	7	0

Independents

	OVERALL W L T		
Notre Dame	9	0	0
Pittsburgh	9	1	0
Memphis	8	0	2
Arizona	7	1	0
Dartmouth	7	2	0
Pennsylvania	7	2	0
Texas-El Paso	6	1	2
Boston College	7	2	1
Cornell	6	2	0
Navy	6	2	2
Harvard	5	2	1
Yale	5	2	1
Penn State	6	3	0
Syracuse	6	3	0
Tulsa	6	3	1
Michigan State	5	3	0
Miami, Fla.	3	2	0
Army	6	4	1
New Mexico State	3	2	3
Rutgers	5	4	0
North Texas	4	3	2
West Virginia	4	3	3
Wake Forest	6	5	1
Brown	5	5	0
Columbia	3	5	0
New Mexico	2	4	2
Princeton	2	4	1
Texas Tech	1	7	2
Arizona State	0	6	0

BOWL GAMES

DATE	GAME	SCORE
J1	Rose	Southern Cal 47, Pittsburgh 14

1930

CONSENSUS ALL-AMERICANS

POS	Name	HT	WT	School	AA	AP	CM	IN	NA	NE	UP
B	Frank Carideo	5-7	175	Notre Dame	•	•	•	•	•	•	•
B	Marchy Schwartz	5-11	172	Notre Dame		•	•	•	•	•	•
B	Erny Pinckert	6-0	189	Southern Cal	•	•			•	•	
B	Leonard Macaluso	6-2	210	Colgate		•	•	•	•		•
E	Wes Fesler	6-0	185	Ohio State	•	•	•	•	•	•	•
E	Frank Baker	6-2	175	Northwestern	•	•		•	•	•	•
T	Fred Sington	6-2	215	Alabama	•	•	•	•	•	•	•
T	Milo Lubratovich	6-2	216	Wisconsin						•	•
G	Ted Beckett	6-1	190	California	•		•		•		
G	Barton Koch	5-10	195	Baylor		•		•	•	•	
C	Ben Ticknor	6-2	193	Harvard	•	•	•	•	•	•	•

OTHERS RECEIVING FIRST-TEAM HONORS

B	Marty Brill	Notre Dame	•
B	Fayette Russell	Northwestern	•
B	Bobby Dodd	Tennessee	• •
B	Orv Mohler	Southern Cal	*
B	Jim Murphy	Fordham	•
B	Phil Moffatt	Stanford	•
E	Jerry Dalrymple	Tulane	• • •
E	Garrett Arbelbide	Southern Cal	•
T	Mel Hein	Washington State	• •
T	Glen Edwards	Washington State	• •
T	Hugh Rhea	Nebraska	•
T	Jack Price	Army	•
G	Frederick Linehan	Yale	•
G	Bert Metzger	Notre Dame	• •
G	Wade Woodworth	Northwestern	• •
G	Ralph Maddox	Georgia	•
G	Henry Wisniewski	Fordham	•

CONFERENCE STANDINGS

Big 10

	Conf. W	L	T	Overall W	L	T
Michigan	5	0	0	8	0	1
Northwestern	5	0	0	7	1	0
Purdue	4	2	0	6	2	0
Wisconsin	2	2	1	6	2	1
Ohio State	2	2	1	5	2	1
Minnesota	1	3	0	3	4	1
Indiana	1	3	0	2	5	1
Illinois	1	4	0	3	5	0
Iowa	0	1	0	4	4	0
Chicago	0	4	0	2	5	2

Big 6

	Conf. W	L	T	Overall W	L	T
Kansas	4	1	0	6	2	0
Oklahoma	3	1	1	4	3	1
Kansas State	3	2	0	5	3	0
Nebraska	2	2	1	4	3	2
Missouri	1	2	2	2	5	2
Iowa State	0	5	0	0	9	0

Pacific Coast

	Conf. W	L	T	Overall W	L	T
Washington State	6	0	0	9	1	0
Southern Cal	5	1	0	8	2	0
Stanford	4	1	0	9	1	1
Oregon	3	1	0	7	2	0
Washington	3	4	0	5	4	0
Oregon State	2	3	0	7	3	0
Montana	1	3	0	5	3	0
California	1	4	0	4	5	0
UCLA	1	4	0	3	5	0
Idaho	0	5	0	4	7	0

Rocky Mountain

	Conf. W	L	T	Overall W	L	T
Utah	7	0	0	8	0	0
Colorado	5	1	1	6	1	1
Brigham Young	4	1	1	5	2	4
Denver	4	3	0	5	4	0
Colorado State	3	3	1	3	5	1
No. Colorado	2	2	3	2	2	3
Montana St.	1	1	0	6	3	0
Utah State	3	4	1	3	5	1
Colorado College	2	4	2	2	4	2
Wyoming	1	5	1	2	5	1
Colorado Mines	1	4	0	1	5	0
Western St.	0	5	0	0	6	0

Southern

	Conf. W	L	T	Overall W	L	T
Alabama	8	0	0	10	0	0
Tulane	5	0	0	8	1	0
Tennessee	6	1	0	9	1	0
Duke	4	1	1	8	1	2
Vanderbilt	5	2	0	8	2	0
Maryland	4	2	0	7	5	0
Florida	4	2	1	6	3	1
North Carolina	4	2	2	5	3	2
Clemson	3	2	0	8	2	0
Georgia	3	2	1	7	2	1
Kentucky	4	3	0	5	3	0
South Carolina	4	3	0	6	4	0
Virginia Tech	2	3	1	5	3	1
Mississippi State	2	3	0	2	7	0
Georgia Tech	2	4	1	2	6	1
LSU	2	4	0	6	4	0
Virginia	2	5	0	4	6	0
Sewanee	1	4	0	3	6	1
Mississippi	1	5	0	3	5	1
North Carolina St.	1	5	0	2	8	0
Auburn	1	6	0	3	7	0
Wash. & Lee	0	4	1	3	6	1
VMI	0	5	0	3	6	0

SWC

	Conf. W	L	T	Overall W	L	T
Texas	4	1	0	8	1	1
Baylor	3	1	1	6	3	1
TCU	4	2	0	9	2	1
SMU	2	2	1	6	3	1
Arkansas	2	2	0	3	6	0
Rice	2	4	0	8	4	0
Texas A&M	0	5	0	2	7	0

Independents

	Overall W	L	T
Notre Dame	10	0	0
Army	9	1	1
Texas-El Paso	7	1	1
Dartmouth	7	1	1
Arizona	6	1	1
Tulsa	7	2	0
Cornell	6	2	0
Michigan State	5	1	2
Pittsburgh	6	2	1
Syracuse	5	2	2
Yale	5	2	2
Memphis	6	3	1
Brown	6	3	1
New Mexico State	5	3	0
Wake Forest	5	3	1
Columbia	5	4	0
Pennsylvania	5	4	0
North Texas	5	4	1
Navy	6	5	0
Boston College	5	5	0
West Virginia	5	5	0
Harvard	4	4	1
Rutgers	4	5	0
New Mexico	4	5	0
Penn State	3	4	2
Miami, Fla.	3	4	1
Arizona State	3	5	1
Texas Tech	3	6	0
Princeton	1	5	1

BOWL GAMES

DATE	GAME	SCORE
J1	Rose	Alabama 24, Washington State 0

1931

Consensus All-Americans

POS	Name	HT	WT	School	AA	AP	CM	IN	LM	NE	UP
B	Gus Shaver	5-11	185	Southern Cal	•		•	•		•	•
B	Marchy Schwartz	5-11	178	Notre Dame	•	•	•	•	•	•	•
B	Pug Rentner	6-1	185	Northwestern	•	•	•	•	•	•	•
B	Barry Wood	6-1	173	Harvard		•	•	•		•	
E	Jerry Dalrymple	5-10	175	Tulane	•	•	•	•	•	•	•
E	Vernon Smith	6-2	190	Georgia	•	•	•				
T	Jesse Quatse	5-8	198	Pittsburgh	•			•			
T	Jack Riley	6-2	218	Northwestern	•			•		•	•
T	Dallas Marvil	6-3	227	Northwestern		•	•			•	
G	Biggie Munn	5-10	217	Minnesota	•	•	•	•		•	•
G	John Baker	5-10	185	Southern Cal	•			•		•	•
C	Tommy Yarr	5-11	197	Notre Dame	•	•	•				

Others Receiving First-Team Honors

POS	Name	School	AA	AP	CM	IN	LM	NE	UP
B	Johnny Cain	Alabama	•					•	
B	Erny Pinckert	Southern Cal		•		•			
B	Don Zimmerman	Tulane				•			
B	Rusty Gill	California				•			
E	John Orsi	Colgate	•			•			
E	Paul Moss	Purdue				•			
E	Henry Cronkite	Kansas State						•	•
T	Paul Schwegler	Washington		•	•				
T	Jack Price	Army				•			
T	Joe Kurth	Notre Dame					•	•	
G	Nordy Hoffman	Notre Dame		•	•				
G	Herman Hickman	Tennessee				•			
C	Maynard Morrison	Michigan		•		•			
C	Stan Williamson	Southern Cal				•			
C	Charles Miller	Purdue							•

Conference Standings

Big 10

	Conf. W L T			Overall W L T		
Purdue	5	1	0	9	1	0
Michigan	5	1	0	8	1	1
Northwestern	5	1	0	7	1	1
Ohio State	4	2	0	6	3	0
Minnesota	3	2	0	7	3	0
Wisconsin	3	3	0	5	4	1
Indiana	1	4	2	2	5	2
Chicago	1	4	0	2	6	1
Iowa	0	3	1	1	6	1
Illinois	0	6	1	2	6	1

Big 6

	Conf. W L T			Overall W L T		
Nebraska	5	0	0	8	2	0
Iowa State	3	1	0	5	3	0
Kansas State	3	2	0	8	2	0
Kansas	1	3	0	5	5	0
Oklahoma	1	4	0	4	7	1
Missouri	1	4	0	2	8	0

Border

	Conf. W L T			Overall W L T		
Arizona State	3	1	0	6	2	0
New Mexico	1	1	1	3	3	1
Arizona	1	1	1	3	5	1
No. Arizona	2	3	0	3	5	0
New Mexico State	1	2	0	6	4	0

Pacific Coast

	Conf. W L T			Overall W L T		
Southern Cal	7	0	0	10	1	0
California	4	1	0	8	2	0
Oregon	3	1	1	6	2	2
Washington State	4	3	0	6	4	0
Washington	3	3	1	5	3	1
Stanford	2	2	1	7	2	2
Oregon State	1	3	1	6	3	1
Idaho	1	4	0	3	4	0
UCLA	0	3	0	3	4	1
Montana	0	5	0	1	6	0

Rocky Mountain

	Conf. W L T			Overall W L T		
Utah	6	0	0	7	2	0
Utah State	5	2	0	6	2	0
Colorado State	5	2	0	5	4	0
Colorado	3	2	0	5	3	0
Wyoming	3	2	0	6	4	0
Colorado College	4	3	0	4	4	0
Brigham Young	2	3	0	4	4	0
Denver	3	5	0	4	6	0
No. Colorado	2	4	1	2	4	1
Western St.	1	5	0	1	6	0
Colorado Mines	0	4	1	1	5	1
Montana St.	0	2	0	1	5	1

Southern

	Conf. W L T			Overall W L T		
Tulane	8	0	0	11	1	0
Tennessee	6	0	1	9	0	1
Alabama	7	1	0	9	1	0
Georgia	6	1	0	8	2	0
Maryland	4	1	1	8	1	1
Kentucky	4	2	2	5	2	2
LSU	3	2	0	5	4	0
Sewanee	3	3	0	6	3	1
Auburn	3	3	0	5	3	1
Duke	3	3	1	5	3	2
South Carolina	3	3	1	5	4	1
North Carolina	2	3	3	4	3	3
Vanderbilt	3	4	0	5	4	0
Wash. & Lee	2	3	0	4	5	1
Florida	2	4	2	2	6	2
Georgia Tech	2	4	1	2	7	1
VMI	2	4	0	3	6	1
North Carolina St.	2	4	0	3	6	0
Virginia Tech	1	4	1	3	4	2
Clemson	1	4	0	1	6	2
Mississippi	1	5	0	2	6	1
Virginia	0	5	1	1	7	2
Mississippi State	0	5	0	2	6	0

SWC

	Conf. W L T			Overall W L T		
Texas	5	1	0	7	2	0
SMU	5	0	1	9	1	1
TCU	4	1	1	9	2	1
Texas A&M	3	2	0	7	3	0
Rice	3	3	0	6	4	0
Texas	2	3	0	6	4	0
Baylor	1	5	0	3	6	0
Arkansas	0	4	0	3	5	1

Independents

	Overall W L T		
Pittsburgh	8	1	0
Harvard	7	1	0
Cornell	7	1	0
Texas-El Paso	7	1	0
Columbia	7	1	1
Syracuse	7	1	1
Army	8	2	1
Yale	5	1	2
North Texas	8	3	0
Tulsa	8	3	0
Notre Dame	6	2	1
Brown	7	3	0
Texas Tech	6	3	0
Pennsylvania	6	3	0
Dartmouth	5	3	1
Michigan State	5	3	1
Boston College	6	4	0
Rutgers	4	3	1
Navy	5	5	1
Wake Forest	4	4	0
West Virginia	4	6	0
Miami, Fla.	4	8	0
Memphis	2	5	2
Penn State	2	8	0
Princeton	1	7	0

Bowl Games

DATE	GAME	SCORE
J1	Rose	Southern Cal 21, Tulane 12

1932

CONSENSUS ALL-AMERICANS

POS	Name	HT	WT	School	AA	AP	CM	FW	IN	LM	NE	UP
B	Harry Newman	5-7	175	Michigan	•	•	•	•	•	•	•	•
B	Warren Heller	6-0	170	Pittsburgh	•	•	•	•	•	•	•	
B	Don Zimmerman	5-10	190	Tulane		•	•		•	•	•	
B	Jimmy Hitchcock	5-11	172	Auburn	•	•	•	•		•	•	
E	Paul Moss	6-2	185	Purdue	•	•	•	•		•	•	
E	Joe Skladany	5-10	185	Pittsburgh		•		•	•	•	•	
T	Joe Kurth	6-2	204	Notre Dame	•	•	•	•	•	•	•	
T	Ernie Smith	6-2	215	Southern Cal	•	•	•	•	•		•	
G	Milt Summerfelt	6-0	181	Army		•	•	•	•		•	
G	Bill Corbus	5-11	188	Stanford	•					•	•	
C	Pete Gracey	6-0	188	Vanderbilt					•	•	•	

	OTHERS RECEIVING FIRST-TEAM HONORS											
B	Roy Horstmann			Purdue		•						
B	Angel Brovelli			Saint Mary's-Cal			•					
B	Frank Christensen			Utah				•				
B	George Melinkovich			Notre Dame					•			
E	Ted Petoskey			Michigan		•						
E	Jose Martinez-Zorrilla			Cornell		•						
E	Dave Nisbet			Washington		•			•			
G	Robert Smith			Colgate		•		•				
G	John Vaught			TCU		•						
G	Aaron Rosenberg			Southern Cal			•					
G	Joe Gailus			Ohio State					•			
C	Art Krueger			Marquette		•						
C	Lawrence Ely			Nebraska		•	•					
C	Chuck Bernard			Michigan				•		•		

CONFERENCE STANDINGS

Big 10

	CONF. W L T			OVERALL W L T		
Michigan	6	0	0	8	0	0
Purdue	5	0	1	7	0	1
Wisconsin	4	1	1	6	1	1
Ohio State	2	1	2	4	1	3
Northwestern	2	3	1	3	4	1
Minnesota	2	3	0	5	3	0
Illinois	2	4	0	5	4	0
Indiana	1	4	1	3	4	1
Chicago	1	4	0	3	4	1
Iowa	0	5	0	1	7	0

Big 6

	CONF. W L T			OVERALL W L T		
Nebraska	5	0	0	7	1	1
Kansas	3	2	0	5	3	0
Oklahoma	3	2	0	4	4	1
Kansas State	2	3	0	4	4	0
Missouri	1	3	1	1	7	1
Iowa State	0	4	1	3	4	1

Border

	CONF. W L T			OVERALL W L T		
Texas Tech	2	0	0	10	2	0
Arizona	3	2	0	4	5	0
Northern Arizona	2	2	1	3	2	2
Arizona State	2	2	1	3	3	1
New Mexico State	1	2	1	4	5	1
New Mexico	1	3	1	1	6	11

Pacific Coast

	CONF. W L T			OVERALL W L T		
Southern Cal	6	0	0	10	0	0
Washington State	5	1	1	7	1	1
UCLA	4	2	0	6	4	0
Washington	3	2	2	6	2	2
California	2	2	1	7	3	2
Oregon	2	2	1	6	3	1
Stanford	1	3	1	6	4	1
Oregon State	1	4	0	4	6	0
Idaho	1	4	0	3	5	0
Montana	0	5	0	2	7	0

Rocky Mountain

	CONF. W L T			OVERALL W L T		
Utah	6	0	0	6	1	1
Brigham Young	5	1	0	8	1	0
Denver	4	1	1	4	3	1
Colorado College	5	2	0	5	2	0
Colorado State	4	3	1	4	3	1
Utah State	3	3	0	4	4	0
No. Colorado	2	2	1	4	2	1
Colorado	2	4	0	2	4	0
Wyoming	1	4	1	2	6	1
Colorado Mines	1	5	0	1	7	0
Montana St.	0	3	0	3	3	1
Western St.	0	5	0	1	5	0

Southern

	CONF. W L T			OVERALL W L T		
LSU	4	0	0	6	3	1
Tennessee	7	0	1	9	0	1
Auburn	6	0	1	9	0	1
Virginia Tech	6	1	0	8	1	0
Alabama	5	2	0	8	2	0
Vanderbilt	4	1	2	6	1	2
North Carolina St.	3	1	1	6	1	2
Tulane	5	2	1	6	2	1
Duke	5	3	0	7	3	0
Georgia Tech	4	4	1	4	5	1
South Carolina	2	2	2	5	4	2
Kentucky	4	5	0	4	5	0
Virginia	2	3	0	5	4	0
Mississippi	2	3	0	5	6	0
Georgia	2	4	2	2	5	2
Maryland	2	4	0	5	6	0
North Carolina	2	5	1	3	5	2
VMI	1	4	0	2	8	0
Wash. & Lee	1	4	0	1	9	0
Florida	1	6	0	3	6	0
Clemson	0	4	0	3	5	1
Mississippi State	0	4	0	3	5	0
Sewanee	0	6	0	2	7	1

SWC

	CONF. W L T			OVERALL W L T		
TCU	6	0	0	10	0	1
Texas	5	1	0	8	2	0
Rice	3	3	0	7	3	0
Texas A&M	1	2	2	4	4	2
Baylor	1	4	1	3	5	1
SMU	1	4	1	3	7	2

Independents

	OVERALL W L T		
Colgate	9	0	0
Brown	7	1	0
Michigan State	7	1	0
North Texas	8	1	1
Columbia	7	1	1
Tulsa	7	1	1
Pittsburgh	8	1	2
Army	8	2	0
Notre Dame	7	2	0
Pennsylvania	6	2	0
Rutgers	6	3	1
Texas-El Paso	7	3	0
Cornell	5	2	1
Harvard	5	3	0
Boston College	4	2	2
Miami, Fla.	4	3	1
West Virginia	5	5	0
Dartmouth	4	4	0
Syracuse	4	4	1
Wake Forest	3	3	2
Princeton	2	2	3
Yale	2	2	3
Memphis	4	5	0
Penn State	2	5	0
Navy	2	6	1

BOWL GAMES

DATE	GAME	SCORE
J2	Rose	Southern Cal 35, Pittsburgh 0

1933

CONSENSUS ALL-AMERICANS

POS	Name	HT	WT	School	AA	AP	CM	FW	IN	LM	NE	UP
B	Cotton Warburton	5-7	147	Southern Cal	•	•	•	•	•	•	•	•
B	George Sauer	6-2	195	Nebraska	•	•	•	•	•	•		•
B	Beattie Feathers	5-10	180	Tennessee	•	•	•	•	•	•		
B	Duane Purvis	6-1	190	Purdue	•	•		•		•	•	
E	Joe Skladany	5-10	190	Pittsburgh	•	•	•	•	•	•		•
E	Paul Geisler	6-2	189	Centenary	•	•		•			•	
T	Fred Crawford	6-2	195	Duke	•	•		•	•	•		•
T	Francis Wistert	6-3	212	Michigan	•	•		•	•		•	
G	Bill Corbus	5-11	195	Stanford	•	•	•	•	•	•		
G	Aaron Rosenberg	6-0	210	Southern Cal	•		•	•		•		•
C	Chuck Bernard	6-2	215	Michigan	•	•	•	•	•	•		•

OTHERS RECEIVING FIRST-TEAM HONORS

POS	Name	School								
B	Pug Lund	Minnesota		•						
B	Jack Buckler	Army		•						
B	Norman Franklin	Oregon State								•
E	Bill Smith	Washington	•							
E	Frank Larson	Minnesota				•				
E	Tony Matal	Columbia			•					
E	Edgar Manske	Northwestern							•	
T	Charles Ceppi	Princeton	•			•		•		
T	Ade Schwammel	Oregon State	•							
T	John Dempsey	Bucknell								
T	John Yezerski	Saint Mary's-Cal								
G	Francis Schammel	Iowa	•			•		•	•	
G	Larry Stevens	Southern Cal			•					

CONFERENCE STANDINGS

Big 10	CONF.			OVERALL		
	W	L	T	W	L	T
Michigan	5	0	1	7	0	1
Ohio State	4	1	0	7	1	0
Purdue	3	1	1	6	1	1
Minnesota	2	0	4	4	0	4
Illinois	3	2	0	5	3	0
Iowa	3	2	0	5	3	0
Northwestern	1	4	1	1	5	2
Chicago	0	3	2	3	3	2
Indiana	0	3	2	1	5	2
Wisconsin	0	5	1	2	5	1

Big 6	CONF.			OVERALL		
	W	L	T	W	L	T
Nebraska	5	0	0	8	1	0
Kansas State	4	1	0	6	2	1
Oklahoma	3	2	0	4	4	1
Kansas	2	3	0	5	4	1
Iowa State	1	4	0	3	5	1
Missouri	0	5	0	1	8	0

Border	CONF.			OVERALL		
	W	L	T	W	L	T
Texas Tech	1	0	0	8	1	0
Northern Arizona	4	1	0	5	1	0
Arizona	3	2	0	5	3	0
New Mexico	2	2	0	3	4	1
Arizona State	2	3	0	3	5	0
New Mexico State	0	4	0	2	6	0

Pacific Coast	CONF.			OVERALL		
	W	L	T	W	L	T
Oregon	4	1	0	9	1	0
Stanford	4	1	0	8	2	1
Southern Cal	4	1	1	10	1	1
Oregon State	2	1	1	6	2	2
Washington State	3	3	1	5	3	1
California	2	2	2	6	3	2
Washington	3	4	0	5	4	0
UCLA	1	3	1	6	4	1
Idaho	1	4	0	4	4	0
Montana	0	4	0	3	4	0

Rocky Mountain	CONF.			OVERALL		
	W	L	T	W	L	T
Utah	5	1	0	5	3	0
Colorado State	5	1	1	5	1	1
Denver	5	1	1	5	3	1
Colorado	5	2	0	7	2	0
Brigham Young	5	3	0	5	4	0
Utah State	4	3	0	4	4	0
No. Colorado	3	3	0	4	3	0
Colorado College	2	4	1	2	5	1
Montana St.	1	3	0	2	5	0
Wyoming	1	6	1	2	6	1
Colorado Mines	1	5	0	1	5	0
Western St.	0	5	0	0	5	0

SEC	CONF.			OVERALL		
	W	L	T	W	L	T
Alabama	5	0	1	7	1	1
LSU	3	0	2	7	0	3
Georgia	3	1	0	8	2	0
Tennessee	5	2	0	7	3	0
Tulane	4	2	1	6	3	1
Mississippi	2	2	1	6	3	2
Vanderbilt	2	2	2	4	3	3
Auburn	2	2	0	5	5	0
Florida	2	3	0	5	3	1
Kentucky	2	3	0	5	5	0
Georgia Tech	2	5	0	5	5	0
Mississippi State	1	5	1	3	6	1
Sewanee	0	6	0	3	6	0

Southern	CONF.			OVERALL		
	W	L	T	W	L	T
Duke	4	0	0	9	1	0
South Carolina	3	0	0	6	3	1
North Carolina	2	1	0	4	5	0
VMI	2	1	1	2	7	1
Virginia Tech	1	1	3	4	3	3
Wash. & Lee	1	1	1	4	4	2
Clemson	1	1	0	3	6	2
Virginia	1	3	1	2	6	2
Maryland	1	4	0	3	7	0
North Carolina St.	0	4	0	1	5	3

SWC	CONF.			OVERALL		
	W	L	T	W	L	T
Arkansas	4	1	0	7	3	1
TCU	4	2	0	9	2	1
Baylor	4	2	0	6	4	0
Texas A&M	2	2	1	6	3	1
Texas	2	3	1	4	5	2
SMU	2	4	0	4	7	1
Rice	1	5	0	3	8	0

Independents	OVERALL		
	W	L	T
Princeton	9	0	0
Army	9	1	0
Boston College	8	1	0
Columbia	8	1	0
Pittsburgh	8	1	0
Tulsa	6	1	0
Memphis	7	1	1
Miami, Fla.	5	1	2
Harvard	5	2	1
Rutgers	6	3	1
Michigan State	4	2	2
Cornell	4	3	0
Navy	5	4	0
Dartmouth	4	4	1
Syracuse	4	4	0
Yale	4	4	0
Penn State	3	3	1
North Texas	3	4	2
West Virginia	3	5	3
Notre Dame	3	5	1
Brown	3	5	0
Pennsylvania	2	4	1
Texas-El Paso	3	6	0
Wake Forest	0	5	1

BOWL GAMES

DATE	GAME	SCORE
J1	Dixie Classic	Arkansas 7, Centenary 7
J1	Rose	Columbia 7, Stanford 0

ANNUAL REVIEW

1934

Consensus All-Americans

POS	Name	HT	WT	School	AA	AP	CM	IN	LM	NA	NE	SN	UP
B	Bobby Grayson	5-11	186	Stanford	•	•	•	•	•	•	•	•	•
B	Pug Lund	5-11	185	Minnesota	•	•	•	•	•	•	•	•	•
B	Dixie Howell	5-10	164	Alabama	•		•	•	•	•	•	•	
B	Fred Borries	6-0	175	Navy		•	•					•	•
E	Don Hutson	6-1	185	Alabama	•	•	•	•	•		•	•	•
E	Frank Larson	6-3	190	Minnesota	•	•	•	•		•	•	•	•
T	Bill Lee	6-2	225	Alabama	•	•	•	•	•		•	•	•
T	Bob Reynolds	6-4	220	Stanford	•	•	•	•	•		•		
G	Chuck Hartwig	6-0	190	Pittsburgh	•	•	•	•			•	•	
G	Bill Bevan	5-11	194	Minnesota		•		•	•		•	•	•
C	Darrell Lester	6-4	218	TCU	•	•	•				•		
C	George Shotwell	NA	NA	Pittsburgh		•	•						
C	Jack Robinson	6-3	195	Notre Dame	•								

Others Receiving First-Team Honors

B	Jay Berwanger	Chicago	•
B	Bill Wallace	Rice	• •
B	Arleigh Williams	California	•
B	Ed Goddard	Washington State	•
B	Bones Hamilton	Stanford	•
B	Isadore Weinstock	Pittsburgh	•
B	Bobby Wilson	SMU	•
B	Duane Purvis	Purdue	•
E	Monk Moscrip	Stanford	•
E	Merle Wendt	Ohio State	•
E	Joe Bogdanski	Colgate	•
T	George Maddox	Kansas State	•
T	Ed Widseth	Minnesota	•
T	James Steen	Syracuse	•
T	Slade Cutter	Navy	• •
T	Cash Gentry	Oklahoma	•
T	Clyde Carter	SMU	•
G	George Barclay	North Carolina	• • •
G	Regis Monahan	Ohio State	•
G	Ken Ormiston	Pittsburgh	•
C	Ellmore Patterson	Chicago	•
C	Elmer Ward	Utah State	•
C	Elwood Kalbaugh	Princeton	•

Conference Standings

Big 10

	Conf. W L T			Overall W L T		
Minnesota	5	0	0	8	0	0
Ohio State	5	1	0	7	1	0
Illinois	4	1	0	7	1	0
Purdue	3	1	0	5	3	0
Wisconsin	2	3	0	4	4	0
Northwestern	2	3	0	3	5	0
Chicago	2	4	0	4	4	0
Indiana	1	3	1	3	3	2
Iowa	1	3	1	2	5	1
Michigan	0	6	0	1	7	0

Big 6

	Conf. W L T			Overall W L T		
Kansas State	5	0	0	7	2	1
Nebraska	4	1	0	6	3	0
Oklahoma	2	2	1	3	4	2
Kansas	1	2	2	3	4	3
Iowa State	1	3	1	5	3	1
Missouri	0	5	0	0	8	1

Border

	Conf. W L T			Overall W L T		
Texas Tech	1	0	0	7	2	1
New Mexico	3	1	0	8	1	0
Arizona	2	1	1	7	2	1
Arizona State	2	2	1	4	3	1
New Mexico State	0	1	3	4	1	3
Northern Arizona	0	3	1	1	5	1

Pacific Coast

	Conf. W L T			Overall W L T		
Stanford	5	0	0	9	1	1
Washington State	4	0	1	4	3	1
Washington	5	1	1	6	1	1
Oregon	4	2	0	6	4	0
California	3	2	0	6	6	0
UCLA	2	3	0	7	3	0
Southern Cal	1	4	1	4	6	1
Idaho	1	4	0	3	5	0
Oregon State	0	5	2	3	6	2
Montana	0	4	1	2	5	1

Rocky Mountain

	Conf. W L T			Overall W L T		
No. Colorado	6	1	0	6	1	0
Colorado	6	1	0	6	1	2
Colorado State	6	1	1	6	2	1
Utah State	4	1	1	5	1	1
Utah	4	2	0	5	3	0
Denver	4	4	0	5	5	1
Brigham Young	3	5	0	4	5	0
Wyoming	2	4	0	3	5	0
Colorado Mines	1	6	0	1	6	0
Colorado College	1	6	0	1	7	0
Montana St.	0	4	0	2	5	0
Western St.	0	3	0	2	5	0

SEC

	Conf. W L T			Overall W L T		
Tulane	8	0	0	10	1	0
Alabama	7	0	0	10	0	0
Tennessee	5	1	0	8	2	0
LSU	4	2	0	7	2	2
Georgia	3	2	0	7	3	0
Vanderbilt	4	3	0	6	3	0
Florida	2	2	1	6	3	1
Mississippi	2	3	1	4	5	1
Kentucky	1	3	0	5	5	0
Auburn	1	6	0	2	8	0
Mississippi State	0	5	0	4	6	0
Sewanee	0	4	0	2	7	0
Georgia Tech	0	6	0	1	9	0

Southern

	Conf. W L T			Overall W L T		
Wash. & Lee	4	0	0	7	3	0
North Carolina	2	0	1	7	1	1
Duke	3	1	0	7	2	0
Maryland	3	1	0	7	3	0
Clemson	2	1	0	5	4	0
Virginia Tech	3	3	0	5	5	0
South Carolina	2	3	0	5	4	0
North Carolina St.	1	3	1	2	6	1
Virginia	1	4	0	3	6	0
VMI	0	5	0	1	8	0

SWC

	Conf. W L T			Overall W L T		
Rice	5	1	0	9	1	1
Texas	4	1	1	7	2	1
SMU	3	2	1	8	2	2
TCU	3	3	0	8	4	0
Arkansas	2	3	1	4	4	2
Texas A&M	1	4	1	2	7	2
Baylor	1	5	0	3	7	0

Independents

	Overall W L T		
Pittsburgh	8	1	0
Navy	8	1	0
Michigan State	8	1	0
Princeton	7	1	0
Columbia	7	1	0
Temple	7	1	2
Syracuse	6	2	0
Bucknell	7	2	2
Army	7	3	0
Tulsa	5	2	1
Dartmouth	6	3	0
Notre Dame	6	3	0
Yale	5	3	0
Miami, Fla.	5	3	1
Rutgers	5	3	1
West Virginia	6	4	0
North Texas	5	4	0
Boston College	5	4	0
Penn State	4	4	0
Texas-El Paso	4	4	0
Pennsylvania	4	4	0
Memphis	3	3	2
Harvard	3	5	0
Brown	3	6	0
Wake Forest	3	7	0
Cornell	2	5	0

Bowl Games

DATE	GAME	SCORE
J1	Rose	Alabama 29, Stanford 13
J1	Sugar	Tulane 20, Temple 14
J1	Orange	Bucknell 26, Miami, Fla. 0

1935

Consensus All-Americans

POS	Name	HT	WT	School	AA	AP	CM	IN	LM	NA	NE	SN	UP
B	Jay Berwanger	6-0	195	Chicago	•	•	•	•	•	•	•	•	•
B	Bobby Grayson	5-11	190	Stanford	•	•	•	•	•	•	•	•	•
B	Bobby Wilson	5-10	147	SMU	•	•	•	•	•		•	•	•
B	Riley Smith	6-1	195	Alabama	•	•	•	•			•		
E	Wayne Millner	6-0	184	Notre Dame	•					•		•	•
E	James Moscrip	6-0	186	Stanford	•	•	•		•		•	•	•
E	Gaynell Tinsley	6-0	188	LSU	•	•	•	•		•	•	•	
T	Ed Widseth	6-2	220	Minnesota	•			•		•	•	•	•
T	Larry Lutz	6-0	201	California	•	•				•		•	•
G	John Weller	6-0	195	Princeton	•	•	•	•	•	•	•		•
G	Sidney Wagner	5-11	186	Michigan State	•					•		•	
G	J.C. Wetsel	5-10	185	SMU	•								
C	Gomer Jones	5-8	210	Ohio State	•					•		•	•
C	Darrell Lester	6-4	218	TCU	*	•	•	•				•	•

	Others receiving first-team honors												
B	Bill Shakespeare			Notre Dame	•								
B	Ed Goddard			Washington State					•				
B	Sheldon Beise			Minnesota					•				
B	Ozzie Simmons			Iowa							•		
B	Sammy Baugh			TCU							•		
E	Bill Shuler			Army			•						
E	Merle Wendt			Ohio State						•		•	
T	Dick Smith			Minnesota	•	•	•	•			•	•	
T	Truman Spain			SMU					•				
T	Charles Wasicek			Colgate					•				
T	Art Detzel			Pittsburgh						•			
G	Paul Tangora			Northwestern	•						•		
G	Inwood Smith			Ohio State			•						
G	Ed Michaels			Villanova					•				
G	Dub Wheeler			Oklahoma						•			

Heisman Trophy Voting

	PLAYER	POS	SCHOOL	TOTAL
1	Jay Berwanger	RB	Chicago	84
2	Monk Meyer	HB	Army	29
3	Bill Shakespeare	HB	Notre Dame	23
4	Pepper Constable	FB	Princeton	20

Conference Standings

Big 10

	CONF. W L T			OVERALL W L T		
Minnesota	5	0	0	8	0	0
Ohio State	5	0	0	7	1	0
Purdue	3	3	0	4	4	0
Indiana	2	2	1	4	3	1
Northwestern	2	3	1	4	3	1
Michigan	2	3	0	4	4	0
Chicago	2	3	0	4	4	0
Iowa	1	2	2	4	2	2
Illinois	1	4	0	3	5	0
Wisconsin	1	4	0	1	7	0

Big 6

	CONF. W L T			OVERALL W L T		
Nebraska	4	0	1	6	2	1
Oklahoma	3	2	0	6	3	0
Kansas	2	2	1	4	4	1
Kansas State	1	2	2	2	4	3
Iowa State	1	3	1	2	4	3
Missouri	0	2	3	3	3	3

Border

	CONF. W L T			OVERALL W L T		
Arizona	4	0	0	7	2	0
New Mexico State	4	1	0	7	1	2
New Mexico	3	2	0	6	4	0
Arizona State	2	3	1	2	5	1
Northern Arizona	0	3	1	3	3	3
Texas Tech	0	1	0	5	3	2
Texas-El Paso	0	3	0	1	8	0

Pacific Coast

	CONF. W L T			OVERALL W L T		
California	4	1	0	9	1	0
Stanford	4	1	0	8	1	0
UCLA	4	1	0	8	2	0
Oregon	3	2	0	6	3	0
Washington State	3	2	0	5	3	1
Washington	4	3	0	5	3	0
Oregon State	2	3	1	6	4	1
Southern Cal	2	4	0	5	7	0
Idaho	1	5	0	2	7	0
Montana	0	5	1	1	5	2

Rocky Mountain

	CONF. W L T			OVERALL W L T		
Colorado	5	1	0	5	4	0
Utah State	5	1	1	5	2	1
Utah	4	1	1	4	3	1
Denver	5	2	0	6	3	0
No. Colorado	2	1	0	4	3	0
Colorado College	4	2	1	4	3	1
Brigham Young	3	4	0	4	4	0
Wyoming	3	4	0	4	4	0
Colorado State	2	4	1	3	4	1
Montana St.	1	5	0	2	6	1
Colorado Mines	1	6	0	1	6	0
Western St.	0	4	0	1	6	0

SEC

	CONF. W L T			OVERALL W L T		
LSU	5	0	0	9	2	0
Vanderbilt	5	1	0	7	3	0
Mississippi	3	1	0	9	3	0
Auburn	5	2	0	8	2	0
Alabama	4	2	0	6	2	1
Tulane	3	3	0	6	4	0
Kentucky	3	3	0	5	4	0
Georgia Tech	3	4	0	5	5	0
Mississippi State	2	3	0	8	3	0
Tennessee	2	3	0	4	5	0
Georgia	2	4	0	6	4	0
Florida	1	6	0	3	7	0
Sewanee	0	6	0	2	7	0

Southern

	CONF. W L T			OVERALL W L T		
Duke	5	0	0	8	2	0
North Carolina	4	1	0	8	1	0
Maryland	3	1	1	7	2	2
Clemson	2	1	0	6	3	0
Virginia Tech	3	3	1	4	3	2
North Carolina St.	2	2	0	6	4	0
Wash. & Lee	1	3	1	3	4	1
South Carolina	1	4	0	3	7	0
Virginia	0	3	2	1	5	4
VMI	0	3	1	2	7	1

SWC

	CONF. W L T			OVERALL W L T		
Michigan	6	0	0	8	0	0
SMU	6	0	0	12	1	0
TCU	5	1	0	12	1	0
Rice	3	3	0	8	3	0
Baylor	3	3	0	8	3	0
Arkansas	2	4	0	5	5	0
Texas	1	5	0	4	6	0
Texas A&M	1	5	0	3	7	0

Independents

	OVERALL W L T		
Princeton	9	0	0
Notre Dame	7	1	1
Syracuse	6	1	1
Dartmouth	8	2	0
Pittsburgh	7	1	2
Michigan State	6	2	0
Army	6	2	1
Boston College	6	3	0
Yale	6	3	0
Miami, Fla.	5	3	0
North Texas	5	3	1
Navy	5	4	0
Pennsylvania	4	4	0
Penn State	4	4	0
Columbia	4	4	1
Rutgers	4	5	0
West Virginia	3	4	2
Harvard	3	5	0
Wake Forest	2	7	0
Memphis	1	6	1
Brown	1	8	0
Cornell	0	6	1

Bowl Games

DATE	GAME	SCORE
J1	Rose	Stanford 7, SMU 0
J1	Sugar	TCU 3, LSU 2
J1	Orange	Catholic 20, Mississippi 19
J1	Sun	Hardin-Simmons 14, New Mexico St. 14

ANNUAL REVIEW

1936 POLL PROGRESSION

AP	OCTOBER 19 POLL		OCT. 24 GAMES
1	Minnesota	3-0-0	beat # 5 Purdue 33-0
2	Duke	5-0-0	lost to Tennessee 13-15
3	Army	3-0-0	beat Springfield 33-0
4	Northwestern	3-0-0	beat Illinois 13-2
5	Purdue	3-0-0	lost to # 1 Minnesota 0-33
6	Southern Cal	3-0-1	beat Stanford 14-7
7	Notre Dame	3-0-0	lost to # 9 Pittsburgh 0-26
8	Washington	3-1-0	beat California 13-0
9	Pittsburgh	3-1-0	beat # 7 Notre Dame 26-0
10	Yale	3-0-0	beat Rutgers 28-0
11	Duquesne	4-0-0	lost to W. V. Wesleyan 0-2
12	Saint Mary's-Cal	3-0-1	lost to # 16 Fordham 6-7
13	LSU	3-0-1	beat Arkansas 19-7
14	Texas A&M	4-0-0	tied Baylor 0-0
15	Nebraska	2-1-0	beat Oklahoma 14-0
16	Fordham	3-0-0	beat # 12 Saint Mary's-Cal 7-6
17	Holy Cross	4-0-0	beat Carnegie Tech 7-0
18	Tulane	3-0-1	beat North Carolina 21-7
19	SMU	3-1-0	bye week
20	Marquette	3-0-0	beat Michigan State 13-7

AP	OCTOBER 26 POLL		OCT. 31 GAMES
1	Minnesota	4-0-0	lost to # 3 Northwestern 0-6
2	Pittsburgh	4-1-0	tied # 5 Fordham 0-0
3	Northwestern	4-0-0	beat # 1 Minnesota 6-0
4	Washington	4-1-0	beat Oregon 7-0
5	Fordham	4-0-0	tied # 2 Pittsburgh 0-0
6	Army	4-0-0	lost to Colgate 7-14
7	Southern Cal	4-0-1	bye week
8	LSU	4-0-1	beat Vanderbilt 19-0
9	Tulane	4-0-1	beat Louisiana Tech 22-13
10	Marquette	4-0-0	beat # 20 Saint Mary's-Cal 20-6
11	Nebraska	3-1-0	beat Missouri 20-0
12	Yale	4-0-0	lost to Dartmouth 7-11
13	Duke	5-1-0	beat Wash & Lee 51-0
14	Holy Cross	5-0-0	lost to Temple 0-3
15	SMU	3-1-0	beat Texas 14-7
16	Auburn	4-0-1	lost to # 19 Santa Clara 0-12
17	Princeton	3-1-0	tied Harvard 14-14
18	Purdue	3-1-0	beat Carnegie Tech 7-6
19	Santa Clara	4-0-0	beat # 16 Auburn 12-0
20	Pennsylvania	3-1-0	beat Navy 16-6
20	Saint Mary's-Cal	3-1-1	lost to # 10 Marquette 6-20

AP	NOVEMBER 2 POLL		NOV. 7 GAMES
1	Northwestern	5-0-0	beat Wisconsin 26-18
2	Minnesota	4-1-0	beat Iowa 52-0
3	Fordham	4-0-1	beat Purdue 15-0
4	Marquette	5-0-0	beat Creighton 7-6
5	Pittsburgh	4-1-1	beat Penn State 24-7
6	Washington	5-1-0	tied Stanford 14-14
7	LSU	5-0-1	beat Mississippi State 12-0
8	Nebraska	4-1-0	beat Kansas 26-0
9	Santa Clara	5-0-0	beat Portland 26-0
10	Tulane	5-0-1	lost to Alabama 7-34
11	Southern Cal	4-0-1	lost to California 7-13
12	SMU	4-1-0	lost to Texas A&M 6-22
13	Notre Dame	4-1-0	lost to Navy 0-3
14	Alabama	5-0-1	beat Tulane 34-7
15	Duke	6-1-0	beat Wake Forest 20-0
16	Pennsylvania	4-1-0	beat Michigan 27-7
17	Washington State	5-0-1	lost to Oregon State 6-16
18	Dartmouth	5-1-0	beat Columbia 20-13
19	Tennessee	3-2-1	beat Maryville 34-0
20	Auburn	4-1-1	beat Georgia Tech 13-12

AP	NOVEMBER 9 POLL		NOV. 14 GAMES
1	Northwestern	6-0-0	beat Michigan 9-0
2	Minnesota	5-1-0	beat Texas 47-19
3	Fordham	5-0-1	bye week
4	Alabama	6-0-1	beat Georgia Tech 20-16
5	Pittsburgh	5-1-1	beat # 6 Nebraska 19-6
6	Nebraska	5-1-0	lost to # 5 Pittsburgh 6-19
7	LSU	6-0-1	beat Auburn 19-6
8	Marquette	6-0-0	beat Mississippi 33-0
9	Santa Clara	6-0-0	bye week
10	Washington	5-1-1	beat # 15 Southern Cal 12-0
11	Pennsylvania	5-1-0	beat Penn State 19-12
12	Dartmouth	6-1-0	beat Cornell 20-6
13	Duke	7-1-0	beat North Carolina 27-7
14	Washington State	5-1-1	beat UCLA 32-7
15	Southern Cal	4-1-1	lost to # 10 Washington 0-12
15	Texas A&M	6-1-1	beat Utah 20-7
17	Holy Cross	6-1-0	beat Brown 32-0
18	TCU	5-2-1	beat Centenary 26-0
19	SMU	4-2-0	lost to Arkansas 0-17
19	Temple	5-1-1	beat Villanova 6-0

AP	NOVEMBER 16 POLL		NOV. 21 GAMES
1	Northwestern	7-0-0	lost to # 11 Notre Dame 6-26
2	Minnesota	6-1-0	beat Wisconsin 24-0
3	Fordham	5-0-1	tied Georgia 7-7
4	Pittsburgh	6-1-1	bye week
5	LSU	7-0-1	beat La. Lafayette 93-0
6	Washington	6-1-1	bye week
7	Marquette	7-0-0	lost to # 20 Duquesne 0-13
8	Alabama	7-0-1	bye week
9	Santa Clara	6-0-0	beat Saint Mary's-Cal 19-0
10	Pennsylvania	6-1-0	bye week
11	Notre Dame	5-2-0	beat # 1 Northwestern 26-6
12	Dartmouth	7-1-0	tied Princeton 13-13
13	Nebraska	5-2-0	beat Kansas State 40-0
14	Texas A&M	6-1-1	lost to Centenary 0-3
15	Washington State	6-1-1	bye week
16	Duke	8-1-0	bye week
17	Holy Cross	7-1-0	tied St. Anselm 0-0
18	Ohio State	4-3-0	beat Michigan 21-0
19	Tennessee	5-2-1	bye week
20	Duquesne	6-2-0	beat # 7 Marquette 13-0
20	Temple	6-1-1	lost to Iowa 0-25

AP	NOVEMBER 23 POLL		NOV. 28 GAMES
1	Minnesota	7-1-0	regular season complete
2	LSU	8-0-1	beat # 19 Tulane 33-0
3	Alabama	7-0-1	beat Vanderbilt 14-6
4	Pittsburgh	6-1-1	beat Carnegie Tech 31-14
5	Santa Clara	7-0-0	bye week
6	Washington	6-1-1	beat # 20 Wash. State 40-0
7	Northwestern	7-1-0	regular season complete
8	Fordham	5-0-2	lost to NYU 6-7
9	Notre Dame	6-2-0	bye week
10	Nebraska	6-2-0	beat Oregon State 32-14
11	Duke	8-1-0	beat North Carolina St. 13-0
12	Duquesne	7-2-0	regular season complete
13	Pennsylvania	6-1-0	beat Cornell 14-6
14	Dartmouth	7-1-1	regular season complete
15	Marquette	7-1-0	regular season complete
16	Yale	7-1-0	regular season complete
17	Tennessee	5-2-1	beat Kentucky 7-6
18	TCU	7-2-1	tied SMU 0-0
19	Tulane	6-2-1	lost to # 2 LSU 0-33
20	Washington State	6-1-1	lost to # 6 Washington 0-40

AP	NOVEMBER 30 FINAL POLL	RECORD	BOWL BID	DATE	BOWL RESULT	RB	RECORD
1	Minnesota	7-1-0				1	7-1-0
2	LSU	9-0-1	Sugar Bowl	J1	lost to # 6 Santa Clara 14-21	5	9-1-1
3	Pittsburgh	7-1-1	Rose Bowl	J1	beat # 5 Washington 21-0	2	8-1-1
4	Alabama	8-0-1				6	8-0-1
5	Washington	7-1-1	Rose Bowl	J1	lost to # 3 Pittsburgh 0-21	8	7-2-1
6	Santa Clara	7-0-0	Sugar Bowl	J1	beat # 2 LSU 21-14	3	8-1-0
7	Northwestern	7-1-0				4	7-1-0
8	Notre Dame	6-2-0				12	6-2-1
9	Nebraska	7-2-0				10	7-2-0
10	Pennsylvania	7-1-0				23	7-1-0
11	Duke	9-1-0				9	9-1-0
12	Yale	7-1-0				15	7-1-0
13	Dartmouth	7-1-1				13	7-1-1
14	Duquesne	7-2-0	Orange Bowl	J1	beat Mississippi State 13-12	24	8-2-0
15	Fordham	5-1-2				17	5-1-2
16	TCU	7-2-2	Cotton Bowl	J1	beat #20 Marquette 16-6	7	9-2-2
17	Tennessee	6-2-1				45	6-2-2
18	Arkansas	6-3-0				18	7-3-0
19	Navy	6-3-0				11	6-3-0
20	Marquette	7-1-0	Cotton Bowl	J1	lost to #16 TCU 6-16	14	7-2-0

1936

Consensus All-Americans

POS	Name	HT	WT	School	AA	AP	CM	IN	LM	NA	NE	SN	UP
B	Sammy Baugh	6-2	180	TCU			•	•		•	•	•	•
B	Ace Parker	5-11	175	Duke	•	•	•	•	•	•	•		•
B	Ray Buivid	6-1	193	Marquette	•	•	•	•	•		•	•	
B	Sam Francis	6-1	207	Nebraska	•	•	•	•	•		•	•	•
E	Larry Kelley	6-1	190	Yale	•	•	•	•	•	•	•	•	•
E	Gaynell Tinsley	6-0	196	LSU	•	•	•	•	•	•	•	•	•
T	Ed Widseth	6-2	220	Minnesota	•	•	•	•	•	•	•	•	•
T	Averell Daniell	6-3	200	Pittsburgh	•	•	•				•		•
G	Steve Reid	5-9	192	Northwestern	•	•		•			•		•
G	Max Starcevich	5-10	198	Washington	•	•	•	•			•		
C	Alex Wojciechowicz	6-0	192	Fordham	•			•			•		
C	Mike Basrak	6-1	210	Duquesne	•	•		•	•				

	Others Receiving First-Team Honors												
B	Nello Falaschi			Santa Clara	•			•					
B	Kent Ryan			Utah State	•								
B	Clint Frank			Yale	•		•						
B	Jim Cain			Washington					•				
B	Ed Goddard			Washington State							•		
B	Andy Uram			Minnesota							•		
T	Frank Kinard			Mississippi	•			•					
T	Marcel Chesbro			Colgate							•		
T	Ed Franco			Fordham					•				
G	Joe Routt			Texas A&M	•			•					
G	Bill Glassford			Pittsburgh					•		•		
G	Alex Drobnitch			Denver					•				
G	Arthur White			Alabama							•		
G	John Lautar			Notre Dame							•		
C	Bob Herwig			California						•		•	

Heisman Trophy Voting

	PLAYER	POS	SCHOOL	TOTAL
1	Larry Kelley	E	Yale	213
2	Sam Francis	FB	Nebraska	47
3	Ray Buivid	HB	Marquette	46
4	Sammy Baugh	QB	TCU	40
5	Clint Frank	QB	Yale	33
6	Ace Parker	HB	Duke	28
7	Ed Widseth	T	Minnesota	25

Conference Standings

Big 10

	CONF. W L T			OVERALL W L T		
Northwestern	6	0	0	7	1	0
Minnesota	4	1	0	7	1	0
Ohio State	4	1	0	5	3	0
Indiana	3	1	1	5	2	1
Purdue	3	1	1	5	2	1
Illinois	2	2	1	4	3	1
Chicago	1	4	0	2	5	1
Iowa	0	4	1	3	4	1
Wisconsin	0	4	0	2	6	0
Michigan	0	5	0	1	7	0

Big 6

	CONF. W L T			OVERALL W L T		
Nebraska	5	0	0	7	2	0
Missouri	3	1	1	6	2	1
Kansas State	2	1	2	4	3	2
Oklahoma	1	2	2	3	3	3
Iowa State	1	3	1	3	3	2
Kansas	0	5	0	1	6	1

Border

	CONF. W L T			OVERALL W L T		
Arizona	3	0	1	5	2	3
Texas-El Paso	2	1	1	5	3	1
New Mexico State	3	2	0	6	4	1
Northern Arizona	2	2	1	3	4	1
Texas Tech	0	0	1	5	4	1
Arizona State	2	4	0	4	5	0
New Mexico	1	4	0	2	7	0

Pacific Coast

	CONF. W L T			OVERALL W L T		
Washington	7	0	1	7	2	1
Washington State	6	2	1	6	3	1
California	4	3	0	6	5	0
Southern Cal	3	2	2	4	2	3
UCLA	4	3	1	6	3	1
Stanford	2	3	2	2	5	2
Oregon State	3	5	0	4	6	0
Montana	1	3	0	6	3	0
Oregon	1	6	1	2	6	1
Idaho	0	4	0	3	7	0

Rocky Mountain

	CONF. W L T			OVERALL W L T		
Utah State	6	0	1	7	0	1
Denver	6	1	1	7	1	1
Utah	5	2	0	6	3	0
Colorado	4	2	0	4	3	0
No. Colorado	4	3	0	5	4	0
Brigham Young	4	4	0	4	5	0
Colorado State	3	4	1	4	4	1
Colorado College	3	4	0	3	4	1
Wyoming	2	4	1	2	5	1
Montana St.	1	4	0	3	5	0
Western St.	1	5	0	1	6	0
Colorado Mines	0	6	0	2	6	0

SEC

	CONF. W L T			OVERALL W L T		
LSU	6	0	0	9	1	1
Alabama	5	0	1	8	0	1
Auburn	4	1	1	7	2	2
Tennessee	3	1	2	6	2	2
Mississippi State	3	2	0	7	3	1
Georgia	3	3	0	5	4	1
Georgia Tech	3	3	1	5	5	1
Tulane	2	3	1	6	3	1
Vanderbilt	1	3	1	3	5	1
Kentucky	1	3	0	6	4	0
Florida	1	5	0	4	6	0
Mississippi	0	3	1	5	5	2
Sewanee	0	5	0	0	6	1

Southern

	CONF. W L T			OVERALL W L T		
Duke	7	0	0	9	1	0
North Carolina	5	1	0	8	2	0
Furman	4	1	0	7	2	0
VMI	4	2	0	6	4	0
Maryland	3	2	0	6	5	0
Clemson	3	2	0	5	5	0
Davidson	4	3	0	5	4	0
Wash. & Lee	2	2	0	4	5	0
Wake Forest	2	3	0	5	4	0
Virginia Tech	3	5	0	5	5	0
North Carolina St.	2	4	0	3	7	0
South Carolina	2	5	0	5	7	0
Richmond	1	3	0	4	4	2
Citadel	0	4	0	4	6	0
William & Mary	0	4	0	1	8	0

SWC

	CONF. W L T			OVERALL W L T		
Arkansas	5	1	0	7	3	0
TCU	4	1	1	9	2	2
Texas A&M	3	2	1	8	3	1
Baylor	3	2	1	6	3	1
SMU	2	3	1	5	4	1
Rice	1	5	0	5	5	0
Texas	1	5	0	2	6	1

Independents

	OVERALL W L T		
Santa Clara	8	1	0
Yale	7	1	0
Pennsylvania	7	1	0
Pittsburgh	8	1	1
Dartmouth	7	1	1
Duquesne	8	2	0
Marquette	7	2	0
Michigan State	6	1	2
Boston College	6	1	2
Villanova	7	2	1
Holy Cross	7	2	1
Fordham	5	1	2
North Texas	6	2	1
Notre Dame	6	2	1
Miami, Fla.	6	2	2
Army	6	3	0
Navy	6	3	0
Saint Mary's-Cal	6	3	1
Temple	6	3	2
Columbia	5	3	0
Princeton	4	2	2
West Virginia	6	4	0
Harvard	3	4	1
Cornell	3	5	0
Penn State	3	5	0
Brown	3	7	0
Virginia	2	7	0
Rutgers	1	6	1
Syracuse	1	7	0
Memphis	0	9	0

Bowl Games

DATE	GAME	SCORE
J1	Bacardi	Auburn 7, Villanova 7
J1	Rose	Pittsburgh 21, Washington 0
J1	Sugar	Santa Clara 21, LSU 14
J1	Cotton	TCU 16, Marquette 6
J1	Orange	Duquesne 13, Mississippi State 12
J1	Sun	Hardin-Simmons 34, Texas-El Paso 6

1937 POLL PROGRESSION

AP OCTOBER 18 POLL — Oct. 23 Games

#	Team	Record	Result
1	California	5-0-0	beat # 11 Southern Cal 20-6
2	Alabama	4-0-0	beat George Wash. 19-0
3	Pittsburgh	3-0-1	beat # 16 Wisconsin 21-0
4	Minnesota	3-1-0	bye week
5	Yale	3-0-0	beat # 19 Cornell 9-0
6	LSU	4-0-0	lost to # 20 Vanderbilt 6-7
7	Northwestern	3-0-0	lost to # 12 Ohio State 0-7
8	Nebraska	2-0-1	beat Missouri 7-0
9	Fordham	2-0-1	beat TCU 7-6
10	Duke	3-0-1	beat Colgate 13-0
11	Southern Cal	3-1-0	lost to # 1 California 6-20
12	Ohio State	2-1-0	beat # 7 Northwestern 7-0
13	Texas A&M	2-1-0	lost to # 15 Baylor 0-13
14	Santa Clara	3-0-0	bye week
15	Baylor	4-0-0	beat # 13 Texas A&M 13-0
16	Wisconsin	4-0-0	lost to # 3 Pittsburgh 0-21
17	Syracuse	3-0-0	lost to Maryland 0-13
18	Dartmouth	4-0-0	beat Harvard 20-2
19	Cornell	3-1-0	lost to # 5 Yale 0-9
20	Auburn	2-0-2	beat Georgia Tech 21-0
20	Holy Cross	4-0-0	beat W. Maryland 6-0
20	Vanderbilt	4-0-0	beat # 6 LSU 7-6

AP OCTOBER 25 POLL — Oct. 30 Games

#	Team	Record	Result
1	California	6-0-0	beat UCLA 27-14
2	Pittsburgh	4-0-1	beat Carnegie Tech 25-14
3	Alabama	5-0-0	beat Kentucky 41-0
4	Minnesota	3-1-0	lost to Notre Dame 6-7
5	Yale	4-0-0	tied # 9 Dartmouth 9-9
6	Baylor	5-0-0	beat TCU 6-0
7	Vanderbilt	5-0-0	lost to Georgia Tech 0-14
8	Ohio State	3-1-0	beat Chicago 39-0
9	Dartmouth	5-0-0	tied # 5 Yale 9-9
10	Fordham	3-0-1	beat # 15 North Carolina 14-0
11	Nebraska	3-0-1	beat Indiana 7-0
12	Auburn	3-0-2	lost to Rice 7-13
13	Duke	4-0-1	beat Wash. & Lee 43-0
14	Santa Clara	4-0-0	beat Marquette 38-0
15	North Carolina	4-0-1	lost to # 10 Fordham 0-14
16	LSU	4-1-0	beat Loyola, New Orleans 52-6
17	Villanova	3-0-1	beat # 18 Detroit 7-0
18	Detroit	5-0-0	lost to # 17 Villanova 0-7
19	Holy Cross	5-0-0	tied Temple 0-0
20	Arkansas	3-1-1	beat Texas A&M 26-13

AP NOVEMBER 1 POLL — Nov. 6 Games

#	Team	Record	Result
1	California	7-0-0	tied Washington 0-0
2	Alabama	6-0-0	beat # 19 Tulane 9-6
3	Pittsburgh	5-0-1	beat # 12 Notre Dame 21-6
4	Baylor	6-0-0	lost to Texas 6-9
5	Fordham	4-0-1	beat Purdue 21-3
6	Nebraska	4-0-1	tied Kansas 13-13
7	Yale	4-0-1	beat Brown 19-0
8	Ohio State	4-1-0	lost to Indiana 0-10
9	Dartmouth	5-0-1	beat Princeton 33-9
10	Santa Clara	5-0-0	beat Portland 27-0
11	Duke	5-0-1	beat Wake Forest 67-0
12	Notre Dame	3-1-1	lost to # 3 Pittsburgh 6-21
13	Villanova	4-0-1	beat Marquette 25-7
14	Minnesota	3-2-0	beat Iowa 35-10
15	Tennessee	4-1-1	lost to Auburn 7-20
16	Arkansas	4-1-1	lost to Rice 20-26
17	Duquesne	4-1-0	lost to Carnegie Tech 0-6
18	LSU	5-1-0	beat Miss. State 41-0
19	Northwestern	4-1-0	lost to Illinois 0-6
19	Tulane	4-1-1	lost to # 2 Alabama 6-9

AP NOVEMBER 8 POLL — Nov. 13 Games

#	Team	Record	Result
1	Pittsburgh	6-0-1	beat # 11 Nebraska 13-7
2	California	7-0-1	beat Oregon 26-0
3	Alabama	7-0-0	beat Georgia Tech 7-0
4	Fordham	5-0-1	bye week
5	Dartmouth	6-0-1	tied Cornell 6-6
6	Yale	5-0-1	beat Princeton 26-0
7	Santa Clara	6-0-0	beat Gonzaga 27-0
8	Duke	6-0-1	lost to North Carolina 6-14
9	Villanova	5-0-1	beat Boston U. 12-0
10	Minnesota	4-2-0	beat Northwestern 7-0
11	Nebraska	4-0-2	lost to # 1 Pittsburgh 7-13
12	LSU	6-1-0	beat # 14 Auburn 9-7
13	Baylor	6-1-0	lost to SMU 7-13
14	Auburn	4-1-2	lost to # 12 LSU 7-9
15	Rice	3-2-1	tied Texas A&M 6-6
16	Colorado	6-0-0	beat Colo. Coll. 35-6
17	Indiana	4-2-0	beat Iowa 3-0
18	Notre Dame	3-2-1	beat Army 7-0
19	Holy Cross	6-0-1	beat Brown 7-0
20	Arkansas	4-2-1	beat Mississippi 32-6

AP NOVEMBER 15 POLL — Nov. 20 Games

#	Team	Record	Result
1	Pittsburgh	7-0-1	beat Penn State 28-7
2	California	8-0-1	beat #13 Stanford 13-0
3	Alabama	8-0-0	bye week
4	Fordham	5-0-1	beat Saint Mary's-Cal 6-0
5	Yale	6-0-1	lost to Harvard 6-13
6	Santa Clara	7-0-0	bye week
7	Minnesota	5-2-0	beat Wisconsin 13-6
8	LSU	7-1-0	beat Northwestern St. 52-0
9	Dartmouth	6-0-2	beat Columbia 27-0
10	Villanova	6-0-1	beat Temple 33-0
11	Nebraska	4-1-2	beat Iowa 28-0
12	Notre Dame	4-2-1	beat Northwestern 7-0
13	Stanford	4-2-1	lost to #2 California 0-13
14	Holy Cross	7-0-1	tied Carnegie Tech 0-0
15	Rice	3-2-2	lost to TCU 2-7
16	Colorado	7-0-0	bye week
17	North Carolina	6-1-1	bye week
18	Vanderbilt	7-1-0	bye week
19	Ohio State	5-2-0	beat Michigan 21-0
20	Indiana	5-2-0	lost to Purdue 7-13

AP NOVEMBER 22 POLL — Nov. 27 Games

#	Team	Record	Result
1	Pittsburgh	8-0-1	beat # 18 Duke 10-0
2	California	9-0-1	regular season complete
3	Fordham	6-0-1	beat NYU 20-7
4	Alabama	8-0-0	beat # 12 Vanderbilt 9-7
5	Minnesota	6-2-0	regular season complete
6	Dartmouth	7-0-2	regular season complete
7	Villanova	7-0-1	beat Loyola, Marymount 25-0
8	Santa Clara	7-0-0	bye week
9	Notre Dame	5-2-1	beat Southern Cal 13-6
10	LSU	8-1-0	beat Tulane 20-7
11	Nebraska	5-1-2	beat Kansas State 3-0
12	Vanderbilt	7-1-0	lost to # 4 Alabama 7-9
13	Washington	5-2-2	bye week
14	TCU	3-4-2	beat SMU 3-0
15	Yale	6-1-1	regular season complete
16	Colorado	7-0-0	beat Denver 34-7
17	Holy Cross	7-0-2	beat Boston College 20-0
18	Duke	7-1-1	lost to # 1 Pittsburgh 0-10
19	North Carolina	6-1-1	beat Virginia 40-0
20	Tulsa	6-1-1	lost to Arkansas 7-20

AP NOVEMBER 29 FINAL POLL

#	Team	Record	Bowl Bid	Date	Bowl Result	RB	Record
1	Pittsburgh	9-0-1				1	9-0-1
2	California	9-0-1	Rose Bowl	J1	beat # 4 Alabama 13-0	2	10-0-1
3	Fordham	7-0-1				5	7-0-1
4	Alabama	9-0-0	Rose Bowl	J1	lost to # 2 California 0-13	3	9-1-0
5	Minnesota	6-2-0				12	6-2-0
6	Villanova	8-0-1				18	8-0-1
7	Dartmouth	7-0-2				7	7-0-2
8	LSU	9-1-0	Sugar Bowl	J1	lost to # 9 Santa Clara 0-6	6	9-2-0
9	Notre Dame	6-2-1				8	6-2-1
9	Santa Clara	7-0-0	Sugar Bowl	J1	beat # 8 LSU 6-0	4	9-0-0
11	Nebraska	6-1-2				11	6-1-2
12	Yale	6-1-1				9	6-1-1
13	Ohio State	6-2-0				10	6-2-0
14	Arkansas	6-2-2				30	6-2-2
14	Holy Cross	8-0-2				26	8-0-2
15	TCU	4-4-2				25	4-4-2
17	Colorado	8-0-0	Cotton Bowl	J1	lost to # 18 Rice 14-28	24	8-1-0
18	Rice	4-3-2	Cotton Bowl	J1	beat # 17 Colorado 28-14	22	6-3-2
19	North Carolina	7-1-1				13	7-1-1
20	Duke	7-2-1				16	7-2-1

1937

CONSENSUS ALL-AMERICANS

POS	Name	HT	WT	School	AA	AP	CM	IN	LM	NA	NE	NW	SN	UP
B	Clint Frank	5-10	190	Yale	•	•	•	•	•	•	•	•	•	•
B	Marshall Goldberg	5-11	185	Pittsburgh	•	•	•	•	•	•		•	•	•
B	Byron "Whizzer" White	6-1	185	Colorado	•	•	•	•	•			•		•
B	Sam Chapman	6-0	190	California	•	•	•		•			•		
E	Chuck Sweeney	6-0	190	Notre Dame	•									
E	Andy Bershak	6-0	190	North Carolina		•			•			•	•	
T	Ed Franco	5-8	196	Fordham	•	•								•
T	Tony Matisi	6-0	224	Pittsburgh	•	•								
G	Joe Routt	6-0	193	Texas A&M	•	•		•		•		•		•
G	Leroy Monsky	6-0	198	Alabama	•	•	•	•						•
C	Alex Wojciechowicz	6-0	196	Fordham	•	•				•				•

OTHERS RECEIVING FIRST-TEAM HONORS

POS	Name	School	AA	AP	CM	IN	LM	NA	NE	NW	SN	UP
B	Corby Davis	Indiana	•				•	•		•		
B	Joe Kilgrow	Alabama				•				•		
B	George Karamatic	Gonzaga				•		•		•		
E	Perry Schwartz	California	•									
E	Ray King	Minnesota	•			•				•		
E	Brud Holland	Cornell		•	•							
E	John Wysocki	Villanova					•	•		•		
E	Frank Souchak	Pittsburgh					•					
E	Jim Benton	Arkansas								•		
E	Bill Daddio	Pittsburgh								•		
T	Ed Beinor	Notre Dame	•				•					
T	Vic Markov	Washington				•	•	•				
T	Frank Kinard	Mississippi					•			•		
T	J.B. Hale	TCU					•					
T	Al Babartsky	Fordham						•				
T	Fred Shirey	Nebraska								•		
G	Gus Zarnas	Ohio State	•							•		
G	Phil Dougherty	Santa Clara				•						
G	Vard Stockton	California				•	•	•		•		
C	Carl Hinkle	Vanderbilt		•	•		•					
C	Charles Brock	Nebraska								•		
C	Bob Herwig	California					•					

HEISMAN TROPHY VOTING

	PLAYER	POS	SCHOOL	TOTAL
1	Clint Frank	QB	Yale	524
2	Byron "Whizzer" White	HB	Colorado	264
3	Marshall Goldberg	RB	Pittsburgh	211
4	Alex Wojciechowicz	C/LB	Fordham	85

AWARD WINNERS

PLAYER	POS	SCHOOL	AWARD NAME
Clint Frank	HB	Yale	Maxwell

CONFERENCE STANDINGS

Big 10

	Conf. W	L	T	Overall W	L	T
Minnesota	5	0	0	6	2	0
Ohio State	5	1	0	6	2	0
Indiana	3	2	0	5	3	0
Northwestern	3	3	0	4	4	0
Michigan	3	3	0	4	4	0
Wisconsin	2	2	1	4	3	1
Purdue	2	2	1	4	3	1
Illinois	2	3	0	3	3	2
Chicago	0	4	0	1	6	0
Iowa	0	5	0	1	7	0

Big 6

	Conf. W	L	T	Overall W	L	T
Nebraska	3	0	2	6	1	2
Oklahoma	3	1	1	5	2	2
Kansas	2	1	2	3	4	2
Missouri	2	2	1	3	6	1
Kansas State	1	4	0	4	5	0
Iowa State	1	4	0	3	6	0

Border

	Conf. W	L	T	Overall W	L	T
Texas Tech	3	0	0	8	4	0
New Mexico State	4	1	0	7	2	0
Arizona	3	1	0	8	2	0
Texas-El Paso	2	1	1	7	1	2
New Mexico	2	3	1	4	4	1
Northern Arizona	1	4	0	5	5	0
Arizona State	0	5	0	0	8	1

Pacific Coast

	Conf. W	L	T	Overall W	L	T
California	6	0	1	10	0	1
Stanford	4	2	1	4	3	2
Washington	4	2	2	7	2	2
Washington State	3	3	2	3	3	3
Idaho	2	2	0	4	3	1
Oregon State	2	3	3	3	3	3
Southern Cal	2	3	2	4	4	2
Oregon	2	5	0	4	6	0
UCLA	1	5	1	2	6	1
Montana	0	1	0	7	1	0

Rocky Mountain

	Conf. W	L	T	Overall W	L	T
Colorado	7	0	0	8	1	0
Brigham Young	5	2	0	6	3	0
Denver	5	2	0	6	3	0
Utah	5	2	0	5	3	0
Colorado College	3	3	0	5	4	0
Utah State	2	4	1	2	4	2
Wyoming	2	4	0	3	5	0
No. Colorado	2	4	0	2	6	0
Western St.	2	6	0	5	3	0
Colorado Mines	1	5	0	2	5	0
Colorado State	1	6	0	1	7	0
Montana St.	0	3	1	3	4	1

SEC

	Conf. W	L	T	Overall W	L	T
Alabama	6	0	0	9	1	0
LSU	5	1	0	9	2	0
Auburn	4	1	2	6	2	3
Vanderbilt	4	2	0	7	2	0
Mississippi State	3	2	0	5	4	1
Georgia Tech	3	2	1	6	3	1
Tennessee	4	3	0	6	3	1
Florida	3	4	0	4	7	0
Tulane	2	3	1	5	4	1
Georgia	1	2	2	6	3	2
Mississippi	0	4	0	4	5	1
Kentucky	0	5	0	4	6	0
Sewanee	0	6	0	2	7	0

Southern

	Conf. W	L	T	Overall W	L	T
Maryland	2	0	0	8	2	0
North Carolina	4	0	1	7	1	1
Duke	5	1	0	7	2	1
Clemson	2	0	1	4	4	1
VMI	4	2	0	5	5	0
North Carolina St.	4	2	1	5	3	1
South Carolina	2	2	1	5	6	1
Citadel	2	3	0	7	4	0
Richmond	2	3	0	5	4	1
Wash. & Lee	2	3	0	4	5	0
Furman	1	2	2	4	3	2
Virginia Tech	2	4	0	5	5	0
William & Mary	1	3	0	4	5	0
Wake Forest	1	4	0	3	6	0
Davidson	1	6	0	2	8	0

SWC

	Conf. W	L	T	Overall W	L	T
Rice	4	1	1	6	3	2
TCU	3	1	2	4	4	2
Arkansas	3	2	1	6	2	2
Baylor	3	3	0	7	3	0
Texas A&M	2	2	2	5	2	2
SMU	2	4	0	5	6	0
Texas	1	5	0	2	6	1

Independents

	Overall W	L	T
Santa Clara	9	0	0
Pittsburgh	9	0	1
Villanova	8	0	1
Fordham	7	0	1
Holy Cross	8	0	2
Dartmouth	7	0	2
West Virginia	8	1	1
Yale	6	1	1
Michigan State	8	2	0
Army	7	2	0
Notre Dame	6	2	1
Detroit	7	3	0
Harvard	5	2	1
Syracuse	5	2	1
Cornell	5	2	1
Penn State	5	3	0
Duquesne	6	4	0
Brown	5	4	0
Rutgers	5	4	0
Princeton	4	4	0
Boston College	4	4	1
Miami, Fla.	4	4	1
Navy	4	4	1
North Texas	4	4	2
Memphis	3	6	0
Columbia	2	5	2
Pennsylvania	2	5	1
Virginia	2	7	0

BOWL GAMES

DATE	GAME	SCORE
J1	Orange	Auburn 6, Michigan State 0
J1	Rose	California 13, Alabama 0
J1	Cotton	Rice 28, Colorado 14
J1	Sugar	Santa Clara 6, LSU 0
J1	Sun	West Virginia 7, Texas Tech 6

1937 NCAA MAJOR COLLEGE STATISTICAL LEADERS

INDIVIDUAL LEADERS

PASSING/COMPLETIONS	G	ATT	COM	PCT	INT	I%	YDS	YDA	COM.PG
1 Davey O'Brien, TCU	10	234	94	40.2	18	7.7	969	4.1	9.4
2 Dwight Sloan, Arkansas	9	164	78	47.6	9	5.5	1074	6.5	8.7
3 Billy Patterson, Baylor	9	196	72	36.7	15	7.7	1109	5.7	8.0
4 Tommy Thompson, Tulsa	10	128	53	41.4	5	3.9	956	7.5	5.3
5 Jack Robbins, Arkansas	8	113	49	43.3	13	11.5	780	6.9	6.1
6 Joseph Gray, Oregon State	7	109	48	44.0	13	11.9	477	4.4	6.9
7 Edward Boell, NYU	8	81	47	58.0	9	11.1	507	6.3	5.9
7 Gene Barnett, Texas Tech	11	120	47	39.2	4	3.3	510	4.3	4.3
9 Frank Filchock, Indiana	8	92	45	48.9	10	10.9	585	6.4	5.6
10 Kenny Washington, UCLA	9	85	41	48.2	6	7.1	390	4.6	4.6

ALL-PURPOSE YARDS	G	RUSH	REC	INT	PR	KR	YDS	TPG
1 Byron "Whizzer" White, Colorado	8	1121	0	103	587	159	1970	246.3

RUSHING/YARDS	G	ATT	YDS	AVG	YPG
1 Byron "Whizzer" White, Colorado	8	181	1121	6.2	140.1
2 Walter Mayberry, Florida	11	164	818	5.0	74.4
3 Bob Holmes, Texas Tech	11	142	760	5.4	69.1
4 Elmer Tarbox, Texas Tech	11	126	737	5.8	67.0
5 Marshall Goldberg, Pittsburgh	10	115	701	6.1	70.1
6 Clint Frank, Yale	8	157	667	4.2	83.4
7 Dick Cassiano, Pittsburgh	10	69	620	9.0	62.0
8 Charlie Holm, Alabama	9	117	607	5.2	67.4
9 Ambrose Schindler, Southern Cal	10	134	599	4.5	59.9
10 Eric Tipton, Duke	10	125	594	4.8	59.4
10 Joe Kilgrow, Alabama	9	128	594	4.6	66.0

RUSHING/YARDS PER CARRY	G	ATT	YDS	YPC
1 Dick Cassiano, Pittsburgh	10	69	620	9.0
2 George Cafego, Tennessee	10	72	501	7.0
3 Byron "Whizzer" White, Colorado	8	181	1121	6.2
4 Marshall Goldberg, Pittsburgh	10	115	701	6.1
5 Harold Van Every, Minnesota	8	88	526	6.0
6 Elmer Tarbox, Texas Tech	11	126	737	5.8
7 Elmore Hackney, Duke	10	85	490	5.8
8 Bob Holmes, Texas Tech	11	142	760	5.4
9 Charlie Holm, Alabama	9	117	607	5.2
10 Johnny Pingel, Michigan State	9	116	590	5.1

*-Based on top 30 rushers

RECEIVING/RECEPTIONS	G	REC	YDS	YPR	YPG	RPG
1 Jim Benton, Arkansas	10	48	814	17.0	81.4	4.8
2 Ray Hamilton, Arkansas	10	29	306	10.6	30.6	2.9
3 Herschel Ramsey, Texas Tech	11	27	337	12.5	30.6	2.5
4 Sam Boyd, Baylor	9	23	365	15.9	40.6	2.6
5 Harry Shorten, NYU	9	23	323	14.0	35.9	2.6
6 Johnny Hall, TCU	9	21	203	9.7	22.6	2.3
7 Jack Robbins, Arkansas	8	20	361	18.1	45.1	2.5
7 Walter Nelson, Michigan State	9	18	388	21.6	43.1	2.0
7 Frank Steen, Rice	10	18	263	14.6	26.3	1.8
8 Don Looney, TCU	10	18	181	10.1	18.1	1.8

PUNTING	PUNT	YDS	AVG
1 Johnny Pingel, Michigan State	49	2101	42.9
2 Byron "Whizzer" White, Colorado	63	2679	42.5
3 Jerry Dowd, Saint Mary's-Cal	91	3851	42.3
4 Joe Woitkowski, Fordham	36	1521	42.3
5 Ray King, Minnesota	21	883	42.1
6 George Cafego, Tennessee	59	2480	42.0
7 Eric Tipton, Duke	90	3656	40.6
8 Larry Atwell, Brown	30	1213	40.4
9 Bob Bailey, Clemson	53	2120	40.0
10 James Fenton, Auburn	60	2400	40.0

SCORING	TDS	XPT	FG	PTS
1 Byron "Whizzer" White, Colorado	16	23	1	122
2 Andy Farkas, Detroit	19	0	1	117
3 William Tranavitch, Rutgers	13	12	0	90
4 Victor Bottari, California	12	0	0	72
5 Clint Frank, Yale	11	0	0	66
6 Paul Shu, VMI	9	11	0	65
7 Elmore Hackney, Duke	9	10	0	64
8 Walter Nielsen, Arizona	8	9	2	63
9 Harry Clark, West Virginia	10	0	0	60
9 William Osmanski, Holy Cross	10	0	0	60

TEAM LEADERS

RUSHING OFFENSE	G	YDS	YPG
1 Colorado	8	2480	310.0
2 North Carolina	9	2285	253.9
3 Pittsburgh	10	2530	253.0
4 Tulane	10	2401	240.1
5 Minnesota	8	1887	235.9
5 Harvard	8	1887	235.9
7 Texas Tech	11	2538	230.7
8 Alabama	9	1992	221.3
9 California	10	2210	221.0
10 Navy	9	1973	219.2

PASSING OFFENSE	G	ATT	COM	INT	PCT	YDS	YPA	YPG	I%	YPC
1 Arkansas	10	310	136	30	43.9	1850	6.0	185.0	9.7	13.6
2 TCU	10	244	99	20	40.6	1005	4.1	100.5	8.2	10.2
3 NYU	9	171	85	18	49.7	1097	6.4	121.9	10.5	12.9
4 Columbia	9	181	83	14	45.9	1070	5.9	118.9	7.7	12.9
5 Baylor	9	201	79	20	39.3	1223	6.1	135.9	10.0	15.5
6 SMU	11	203	74	30	36.9	1053	5.2	95.7	14.8	14.2
7 Southern Cal	10	143	64	14	44.8	751	5.3	75.1	9.8	11.7
7 Tulsa	10	163	63	14	38.7	1149	7.0	114.9	8.6	18.2
9 Oklahoma	9	125	61	10	48.8	528	4.2	58.7	8.0	8.7
9 Texas Tech	11	170	61	14	35.9	643	3.8	58.5	8.2	10.5

Ranking based on number of completions

TOTAL OFFENSE	G	YDS	YPG
1 Colorado	8	3003	375.4
2 North Carolina	9	2933	325.9
3 Minnesota	8	2428	303.5
4 Harvard	8	2427	303.4
5 NYU	9	2699	299.9
6 Fordham	8	2355	294.4
7 Navy	9	2642	293.6
8 Texas Tech	11	3181	289.2
9 Pittsburgh	10	2864	286.4
10 Arkansas	10	2823	282.3

RUSHING DEFENSE	G	YDS	YPG
1 Santa Clara	8	202	25.3
2 Pittsburgh	10	405	40.5
3 Washington	9	445	49.4
4 Oklahoma	9	536	59.6
5 Dartmouth	6	367	61.2
6 Illinois	8	520	65.0
6 Ohio State	8	520	65.0
8 Michigan State	9	588	65.3
9 Alabama	9	589	65.4
10 Tulane	10	667	66.7

PASSING DEFENSE	G	ATT	COM	PCT	YPC	INT	I%	YDS	YPA	YPG
1 Harvard	8	81	16	19.8	15.5	11	13.6	248	3.1	31.0
2 Chicago	5	49	13	26.5	13.2	11	22.4	171	3.5	34.2
3 Michigan State	9	85	24	28.2	12.9	13	15.3	310	3.6	34.4
4 Iowa State	5	57	12	21.1	15.8	14	24.6	190	3.3	38.0
5 Oklahoma	9	95	31	32.6	11.3	15	15.8	349	3.7	38.8
6 Clemson	9	83	27	32.5	13.2	13	15.7	356	4.3	39.6
7 Princeton	8	94	26	27.7	12.2	13	13.8	318	3.4	39.8
8 California	10	134	39	29.1	10.5	24	17.9	410	3.1	41.0
9 Florida	11	124	39	31.5	12.1	16	12.9	472	3.8	42.9
10 Marquette	9	94	27	28.7	14.7	15	16.0	396	4.2	44.0

Based on 37 teams whose opponents had the lowest pass completion percentage.

TOTAL DEFENSE	G	YDS	YPG
1 Santa Clara	8	559	69.9
2 Pittsburgh	10	928	92.8
3 Oklahoma	9	885	98.3
4 Michigan State	9	898	99.8
5 Washington	9	947	105.2
6 Dartmouth	6	672	112.0
7 California	10	1126	112.6
8 Ohio State	8	924	115.5
9 Alabama	9	1042	115.8
10 Tulane	10	1167	116.7

SCORING OFFENSE	G	PTS	AVG
1 Colorado	8	248	31.0

SCORING DEFENSE	G	PTS	AVG
1 Santa Clara	8	9	1.1

1938 POLL PROGRESSION

AP October 17 Poll | Oct. 22 Games

#	Team	Record	Result
1	Pittsburgh	4-0-0	beat SMU 34-7
2	Minnesota	4-0-0	bye week
3	California	5-0-0	beat Washington 14-7
4	Dartmouth	4-0-0	beat Harvard 13-7
5	Notre Dame	3-0-0	beat #14 Carnegie Tech 7-0
6	Santa Clara	3-0-0	beat Arkansas 21-6
7	TCU	4-0-0	beat #18 Marquette 21-0
8	Tennessee	4-0-0	beat Citadel 44-0
9	Duke	4-0-0	beat Wake Forest 7-0
10	Syracuse	3-0-0	lost to Michigan State 12-19
11	Fordham	2-0-1	beat Oregon 26-0
12	Michigan	2-1-0	beat Yale 15-13
13	Carnegie Tech	3-0-0	lost to #6 Notre Dame 0-7
14	Oklahoma	3-0-0	beat Nebraska 14-0
15	Alabama	3-1-0	beat Sewanee 32-0
16	Vanderbilt	4-0-0	lost to LSU 0-7
17	Baylor	4-0-0	tied Texas A&M 6-6
18	Northwestern	2-0-1	beat Illinois 13-0
19	North Carolina	3-1-0	beat Davidson 34-0
20	Villanova	3-0-0	beat Detroit 13-6

AP October 24 Poll | Oct. 29 Games

#	Team	Record	Result
1	Pittsburgh	5-0-0	beat #9 Fordham 24-13
2	Minnesota	4-0-0	lost to #12 Northwestern 3-6
3	California	6-0-0	beat Oregon State 13-7
4	TCU	5-0-0	beat Baylor 39-7
5	Santa Clara	4-0-0	beat Michigan State 7-6
6	Dartmouth	5-0-0	beat Yale 24-6
7	Notre Dame	4-0-0	beat Army 19-7
8	Tennessee	5-0-0	beat LSU 14-6
9	Fordham	3-0-1	lost to #1 Pittsburgh 13-24
10	Oklahoma	4-0-0	beat Tulsa 28-6
11	Duke	5-0-0	beat North Carolina 14-0
12	Northwestern	3-0-1	beat #2 Minnesota 6-3
13	Michigan	3-1-0	beat Illinois 14-0
14	Holy Cross	4-1-0	beat Colgate 21-0
15	Villanova	4-0-0	tied South Carolina 6-6
16	Carnegie Tech	3-1-0	beat Akron 27-13
17	Cornell	3-1-0	beat Columbia 23-7
18	Alabama	4-1-0	beat Kentucky 26-6
19	Southern Cal	4-1-0	beat Oregon 31-7
20	Ohio State	2-1-1	beat NYU 32-0

AP October 31 Poll | Nov. 5 Games

#	Team	Record	Result
1	Pittsburgh	6-0-0	lost to #19 Carnegie Tech 10-20
2	TCU	6-0-0	beat Tulsa 21-0
3	California	7-0-0	lost to #13 Southern Cal 7-13
4	Notre Dame	5-0-0	beat Navy 15-0
5	Dartmouth	6-0-0	beat Dickinson 44-6
6	Tennessee	6-0-0	beat U. T. Chattanooga 45-0
7	Northwestern	4-0-1	lost to Wisconsin 13-20
8	Santa Clara	5-0-0	bye week
9	Duke	6-0-0	bye week
10	Fordham	3-1-1	beat Saint Mary's-Cal 3-0
11	Oklahoma	5-0-0	beat Kansas State 26-0
12	Minnesota	4-1-0	beat Iowa 28-0
13	Holy Cross	5-1-0	beat Temple 33-0
14	Southern Cal	5-1-0	beat #3 California 13-7
15	Alabama	5-1-0	beat Tulane 3-0
16	Cornell	4-1-0	bye week
16	Michigan	4-1-0	beat Penn 19-13
18	Iowa State	6-0-0	beat Drake 14-0
19	Carnegie Tech	4-1-0	beat #1 Pittsburgh 20-10
19	Texas A&M	3-2-1	lost to SMU 7-10

AP November 7 Poll | Nov. 12 Games

#	Team	Record	Result
1	TCU	7-0-0	beat Texas 28-6
2	Notre Dame	6-0-0	beat #12 Minnesota 19-0
3	Pittsburgh	6-1-0	beat Nebraska 19-0
4	Tennessee	7-0-0	beat Vanderbilt 14-0
5	Dartmouth	7-0-0	lost to #20 Cornell 7-14
6	Carnegie Tech	5-1-0	beat Duquesne 21-0
7	Duke	6-0-0	beat Syracuse 21-0
8	Santa Clara	5-0-0	lost to Saint Mary's-Cal 0-7
9	Southern Cal	6-1-0	lost to Washington 6-7
10	Oklahoma	6-0-0	beat Missouri 21-0
11	Holy Cross	6-1-0	beat Brown 14-12
12	Minnesota	5-1-0	lost to Notre Dame 0-19
13	Fordham	4-1-1	tied North Carolina 0-0
14	California	7-1-0	beat Oregon 20-0
15	Wisconsin	4-2-0	beat UCLA 14-7
16	Alabama	6-1-0	tied Georgia Tech 14-14
17	Northwestern	4-1-1	tied #17 Michigan 0-0
18	Michigan	5-1-0	tied #18 Northwestern 0-0
19	Villanova	5-0-1	beat Temple 20-0
20	Cornell	4-1-0	beat #5 Dartmouth 14-7

AP November 14 Poll | Nov. 19 Games

#	Team	Record	Result
1	Notre Dame	7-0-0	beat #16 Northwestern 9-7
2	TCU	8-0-0	beat Rice 29-7
3	Tennessee	8-0-0	bye week
4	Duke	7-0-0	beat North Carolina St. 7-0
5	Pittsburgh	7-1-0	beat Penn State 26-0
6	Carnegie Tech	6-1-0	bye week
7	Oklahoma	7-0-0	beat Iowa State 10-0
8	Cornell	5-1-0	bye week
9	California	8-1-0	beat Stanford 6-0
10	Holy Cross	7-1-0	bye week
11	Santa Clara	6-1-0	beat San Francisco 7-0
12	Wisconsin	5-2-0	lost to Minnesota 0-21
13	Southern Cal	6-2-0	bye week
14	Dartmouth	7-1-0	bye week
15	Villanova	6-0-1	beat Boston U. 39-6
16	Northwestern	4-1-2	lost to #1 Notre Dame 7-9
17	Michigan	6-1-0	beat Ohio State 18-0
18	Fordham	4-1-2	beat South Carolina 13-0
19	Texas Tech	8-0-0	beat New Mexico 17-7
20	Alabama	6-1-1	beat Vanderbilt 7-0

AP November 21 Poll | Nov. 26 Games

#	Team	Record	Result
1	Notre Dame	8-0-0	bye week
2	TCU	9-0-0	beat SMU 20-7
3	Duke	8-0-0	beat #4 Pittsburgh 7-0
4	Pittsburgh	8-1-0	lost to #3 Duke 0-7
4	Tennessee	8-0-0	beat Kentucky 46-0
6	Oklahoma	8-0-0	beat Oklahoma State 19-0
7	Carnegie Tech	6-1-0	beat North Carolina St. 14-0
8	Minnesota	6-2-0	regular season complete
9	California	9-1-0	bye week
10	Cornell	5-1-0	tied Pennsylvania 0-0
11	Holy Cross	7-1-0	beat Boston College 29-7
12	Michigan	6-1-1	regular season complete
13	Dartmouth	7-1-0	lost to Stanford 13-23
14	Southern Cal	6-2-0	beat UCLA 42-7
15	Northwestern	4-2-2	regular season complete
16	Villanova	7-0-1	beat Manhattan 20-0
17	Texas Tech	9-0-0	beat Marquette 21-2
18	Fordham	5-1-2	beat NYU 25-0
19	Santa Clara	6-1-0	lost to Detroit 6-7
20	Georgetown	8-0-0	regular season complete

AP November 28 Poll | Dec. 3 Games

#	Team	Record	Result
1	Notre Dame	8-0-0	lost to #8 Southern Cal 0-13
2	TCU	10-0-0	regular season complete
3	Duke	9-0-0	regular season complete
4	Tennessee	9-0-0	beat Mississippi 47-0
5	Oklahoma	9-0-0	beat Washington State 28-0
6	Carnegie Tech	7-1-0	regular season complete
7	Pittsburgh	8-2-0	regular season complete
8	Southern Cal	7-2-0	beat #1 Notre Dame 13-0
9	Holy Cross	8-1-0	regular season complete
10	Minnesota	6-2-0	
11	Cornell	5-1-1	regular season complete
12	California	9-1-0	bye week
13	Fordham	6-1-2	regular season complete
14	Texas Tech	10-0-0	regular season complete
15	Villanova	8-0-1	regular season complete
16	Michigan	6-1-1	
17	Alabama	7-1-1	regular season complete
18	Tulane	7-2-1	regular season complete
19	Northwestern	4-2-2	
20	Dartmouth	7-2-0	regular season complete

AP December 5 Final Poll

#	Team	RECORD	BOWL BID	DATE	BOWL RESULT	RB	RECORD
1	TCU	10-0-0	Sugar Bowl	J2	beat #6 Carnegie Tech 15-7	2	11-0-0
2	Tennessee	10-0-0	Orange Bowl	J2	beat #4 Oklahoma 17-0	1	11-0-0
3	Duke	9-0-0	Rose Bowl	J2	lost to #7 Southern Cal 3-7	6	9-1-0
4	Oklahoma	10-0-0	Orange Bowl	J2	lost to #2 Tennessee 0-17	9	10-1-0
5	Notre Dame	8-1-0				3	8-1-0
6	Carnegie Tech	7-1-0	Sugar Bowl	J2	lost to #1 TCU 7-15	15	7-2-0
7	Southern Cal	8-2-0	Rose Bowl	J2	beat #3 Duke 7-3	5	9-2-0
8	Pittsburgh	8-2-0				7	8-2-0
9	Holy Cross	8-1-0				22	8-1-0
10	Minnesota	6-2-0				8	6-2-0
11	Texas Tech	10-0-0	Cotton Bowl	J2	lost to Saint Mary's-Cal 13-20	19	10-1-0
12	Cornell	5-1-1				25	5-1-1
13	Alabama	7-1-1				10	7-1-1
14	California	10-1-0				4	10-1-0
15	Fordham	6-1-2				11	6-1-2
16	Michigan	6-1-1				16	6-1-1
17	Northwestern	4-2-2				12	4-2-2
18	Villanova	8-0-1				23	8-0-1
19	Tulane	7-2-1				27	7-2-1
20	Dartmouth	7-2-0				17	7-2-0

1938

CONSENSUS ALL-AMERICANS

POS	Name	HT	WT	School	AA	AP	CM	IN	LM	NE	NW	SN	UP
B	Davey O'Brien	5-7	150	TCU	•	•	•	•	•	•	•	•	•
B	Marshall Goldberg	6-0	190	Pittsburgh	•	•	•	•	•	•	•	•	•
B	Bob MacLeod	6-0	190	Dartmouth	•	•	•	•	•	•	•	•	
B	Vic Bottari	5-9	182	California	•				•	•	•		
E	Waddy Young	6-2	203	Oklahoma	•	•	•	•	•	•			
E	Brud Holland	6-1	205	Cornell	•	•	•			•	•		
E	Bowden Wyatt	6-1	190	Tennessee	•	•	•		•				
T	Ed Beinor	6-2	207	Notre Dame	•	•	•	•	•	•	•		
T	Alvord Wolff	6-2	220	Santa Clara	•	•	•		•	•	•		
G	Ralph Heikkinen	5-10	185	Michigan	•	•	•	•	•	•	•		
G	Ed Bock	6-0	202	Iowa State	•	•				•			
C	Ki Aldrich	5-11	195	TCU	•	•				•	•	•	

OTHERS RECEIVING FIRST-TEAM HONORS

POS			AA	AP	CM	IN	LM	NE	NW	SN	UP
B	Parker Hall	Mississippi	•								•
B	Johnny Pingel	Michigan State	•			•					
B	Howard Weiss	Wisconsin					•				
B	George Cafego	Tennessee						•	•		
B	Sid Luckman	Columbia									•
B	Eric Tipton	Duke									•
E	Earl Brown	Notre Dame	•						•		
E	John Wysocki	Villanova									•
E	Bill Daddio	Pittsburgh					•				
T	Bob Voigts	Northwestern	•								
T	Bill McKeever	Cornell				•					
T	I.B. Hale	TCU									•
G	Harry Smith	Southern Cal	•				•				
G	Sid Roth	Cornell				•					
G	Francis Twedell	Minnesota					•				
G	Bob Suffridge	Tennessee									•
C	Dan Hill	Duke	•				•	•	•		

HEISMAN TROPHY VOTING

	PLAYER	POS	SCHOOL	TOTAL
1	Davey O'Brien	QB	TCU	519
2	Marshall Goldberg	RB	Pittsburgh	294
3	Sid Luckman	QB	Columbia	154
4	Bob MacLeod	HB	Dartmouth	78
5	Vic Bottari	RB	California	67
6	Howard Weiss	FB	Wisconsin	60
7	George Cafego	TB	Tennessee	55
8	Ki Aldrich	C	TCU	48
9	Whitey Beinor	TB	Notre Dame	47
10	Dan Hill	C	Duke	38

AWARD WINNERS

PLAYER	POS	SCHOOL	AWARD NAME
Davey O'Brien	QB	TCU	Maxwell

CONFERENCE STANDINGS

Big 10

	Conf. W L T			Overall W L T		
Minnesota	4	1	0	6	2	0
Michigan	3	1	1	6	1	1
Purdue	3	1	1	5	1	2
Wisconsin	3	2	0	5	3	0
Northwestern	2	1	2	4	2	2
Ohio State	3	2	1	4	3	1
Illinois	2	3	0	3	5	0
Iowa	1	3	1	1	6	1
Indiana	1	4	0	1	6	1
Chicago	0	4	0	1	6	1

Big 6

	Conf. W L T			Overall W L T		
Oklahoma	5	0	0	10	1	0
Iowa State	3	1	1	7	1	1
Missouri	2	3	0	6	3	0
Nebraska	2	3	0	3	5	1
Kansas State	1	3	1	4	4	1
Kansas	1	4	0	3	6	0

Border

	Conf. W L T			Overall W L T		
Texas Tech	2	0	0	10	1	0
New Mexico State	4	1	0	7	2	0
New Mexico	4	2	0	8	3	0
Texas-El Paso	3	2	0	6	3	0
Northern Arizona	1	2	0	2	6	1
Arizona State	0	4	0	3	6	0
Arizona	0	3	0	3	6	0

Mountain States

	Conf. W L T			Overall W L T		
Utah	4	0	2	7	1	2
Brigham Young	3	2	1	4	3	1
Denver	3	2	1	4	4	1
Colorado	3	2	1	3	4	1
Utah State	3	3	0	4	4	0
Wyoming	1	4	1	2	5	1
Colorado State	0	4	2	1	5	2

Pacific Coast

	Conf. W L T			Overall W L T		
California	6	1	0	10	1	0
Southern Cal	6	1	0	9	2	0
UCLA	4	3	1	7	4	1
Oregon State	4	3	1	5	3	1
Oregon	4	4	0	4	5	0
Washington	3	4	1	3	5	1
Idaho	2	3	1	6	3	1
Stanford	2	5	0	3	6	0
Washington State	1	7	0	2	8	0
Montana	0	1	0	5	3	1

SEC

	Conf. W L T			Overall W L T		
Tennessee	7	0	0	11	0	0
Alabama	4	1	1	7	1	1
Tulane	4	1	1	7	2	1
Mississippi	3	2	0	9	2	0
Georgia Tech	2	1	3	3	4	3
Vanderbilt	4	3	0	6	3	0
Auburn	3	3	1	4	5	1
Florida	2	2	1	4	6	1
Georgia	1	2	1	5	4	1
LSU	2	4	0	6	4	0
Mississippi State	1	4	0	4	6	0
Kentucky	0	4	0	2	7	0
Sewanee	0	6	0	1	8	0

Southern

	Conf. W L T			Overall W L T		
Duke	5	0	0	9	1	0
Clemson	3	0	1	7	1	1
North Carolina	4	1	0	6	2	1
VMI	4	0	3	6	1	4
Richmond	3	2	1	6	3	1
North Carolina St.	3	3	1	3	7	1
South Carolina	2	2	0	6	4	1
Washington & Lee	2	2	0	4	4	1
Wake Forest	3	4	1	4	5	1
Virginia Tech	2	3	2	3	5	2
Citadel	2	3	0	6	5	0
Maryland	1	2	0	2	7	0
Davidson	2	6	0	4	6	0
Furman	0	4	1	2	7	1
William & Mary	0	4	0	3	7	0

SWC

	Conf. W L T			Overall W L T		
TCU	6	0	0	11	0	0
SMU	4	2	0	6	4	0
Baylor	3	2	1	7	2	1
Rice	3	3	0	4	6	0
Texas A&M	2	3	1	4	4	1
Arkansas	1	5	0	2	7	1
Texas	1	5	0	1	8	0

Independents

	Overall W L T		
Memphis	10	0	0
Georgetown	8	0	0
Villanova	8	0	1
Holy Cross	8	1	0
Notre Dame	8	1	0
Rutgers	7	1	0
Miami, Fla.	8	2	0
Pittsburgh	8	2	0
Army	8	2	0
Cornell	5	1	1
Carnegie Tech	7	2	0
Dartmouth	7	2	0
Boston College	6	1	2
Fordham	6	1	2
Santa Clara	6	2	0
Michigan State	6	3	0
North Texas	7	4	0
Brown	5	3	0
Syracuse	5	3	0
Pennsylvania	3	2	3
Navy	4	3	2
Virginia	4	4	1
Harvard	4	4	0
West Virginia	4	5	1
Penn State	3	4	1
Princeton	3	4	1
Columbia	3	6	0
Yale	2	6	0

BOWL GAMES

DATE	GAME	SCORE
J2	Rose	Southern Cal 7, Duke 3
J2	Orange	Tennessee 17, Oklahoma 0
J2	Sugar	TCU 15, Carnegie Mellon 7
J2	Sun	Utah 26, New Mexico 0
J2	Cotton	Saint Mary's-Cal 20, Texas Tech 13

1938 NCAA MAJOR COLLEGE STATISTICAL LEADERS

INDIVIDUAL LEADERS

PASSING/COMPLETIONS

		G	ATT	COM	PCT	INT	I%	YDS	YDA	COM.PG
1	Davey O'Brien, TCU	10	167	93	55.7	4	2.4	1457	8.7	9.3
2	Billy Patterson, Baylor	10	206	84	40.8	17	8.3	1334	6.5	8.4
3	Hugh McCullough, Oklahoma	10	111	70	63.1	6	5.4	647	5.8	7.0
4	Sid Luckman, Columbia	9	132	66	50.0	8	6.1	856	6.5	7.3
5	Lemuel Cooke, Navy	9	122	63	51.6	7	5.7	815	6.7	7.0
5	Paul Christman, Missouri	9	145	63	43.4	19	13.1	1087	7.5	7.0
7	Johnny Pingel, Michigan State	9	101	54	53.5	NA	NA	571	5.7	6.0
7	Everett Kischer, Iowa State	9	107	54	50.5	8	7.5	653	6.1	6.0
9	Parker Hall, Mississippi	11	99	51	51.5	6	6.1	860	8.7	4.6
10	Gilbert Humphrey, Yale	8	104	49	47.1	8	7.7	603	5.8	6.1

ALL-PURPOSE YARDS

		G	RUSH	REC	INT	PR	KR	YDS	YPG
1	Parker Hall, Mississippi	11	698	0	128	0	594	1420	129.1

RUSHING/YARDS

		G	ATT	YDS	AVG	YPG
1	Len Eshmont, Fordham	9	132	831	6.3	92.3
2	Dick Cassiano, Pittsburgh	10	141	742	5.3	74.2
3	Parker Hall, Mississippi	11	108	698	6.5	63.5
4	Dominic Principe, Fordham	9	121	692	5.7	76.9
5	Bob O'Mara, Duke	9	156	685	4.4	76.1
6	Warren Brunner, Tulane	10	136	662	4.9	66.2
7	Elmer Tarbox, Texas Tech	10	127	637	5.0	63.7
8	Harold Stebbins, Pittsburgh	10	136	616	4.5	61.6
9	Victor Bottari, California	11	159	578	3.6	52.5
10	Kenny Washington, UCLA	10	147	573	3.9	57.3

RUSHING/YARDS PER CARRY

		G	ATT	YDS	YPC
1	Parker Hall, Mississippi	11	108	698	6.5
2	George Muha, Carnegie Tech	7	81	514	6.3
3	Len Eshmont, Fordham	9	132	831	6.3
4	Dominic Principe, Fordham	9	121	692	5.7
5	Dick Cassiano, Pittsburgh	10	141	742	5.3
6	Henry Wilder, Iowa State	9	105	545	5.2
7	Johnny Pingel, Michigan State	9	110	556	5.0
8	Elmer Tarbox, Texas Tech	10	127	637	5.0
9	Dick Todd, Texas A&M	9	99	493	5.0
10	Warren Brunner, Tulane	10	136	662	4.9

*-Based on top 20 rushers

RECEIVING/RECEPTIONS

		G	REC	YDS	YPR	YPG	RPG
1	Sam Boyd, Baylor	10	32	537	16.8	53.7	3.2
2	Charles Heileman, Iowa State	9	29	320	11.0	35.6	3.2
3	Bill Dewell, SMU	10	26	437	16.8	43.7	2.6
4	James Starmer, Missouri	9	25	437	17.5	48.6	2.8
5	Michael Lukac, Temple	10	23	350	15.2	35.0	2.3
5	Bill Jennings, Oklahoma	10	23	217	9.4	21.7	2.3
7	Earle Clark, TCU	10	22	411	18.7	41.1	2.2
8	Eugene Corrotto, Oklahoma	10	21	188	9.0	18.8	2.1
9	Bud Orf, Missouri	9	18	218	12.1	24.2	2.0
10	Elmer Tarbox, Texas Tech*	10	17	364	21.4	36.4	1.7

* Six players tied for number of receptions, but Tarbox had the most yardage.

PUNTING

		PUNT	YDS	AVG
1	Jerry Dowd, Saint Mary's-Cal	62	2711	43.7
2	Johnny Pingel, Michigan State	99	4138	41.8
3	Neil Cavette, Georgia Tech	46	1909	41.5
4	Nile Kinnick, Iowa	41	1686	41.1
5	Kay Eakin, Arkansas	41	1683	41.1
6	George Stirnweiss, North Carolina	60	2455	40.9
7	Carl Nery, Duquesne	49	1985	40.5
8	Eric Tipton, Duke	59	2378	40.3
9	Michael Kabealo, Ohio State	42	1692	40.3
10	Dick McGowen, Auburn	55	2214	40.3

PUNT AND KICKOFF RETURNS/YARDS

		RET	YDS	AVG
1	Parker Hall, Mississippi	32	594	18.6
2	Spec Kelly, Auburn	31	559	18.0
3	Dick Todd, Texas A&M	32	506	15.8
4	Billy Patterson, Baylor	37	488	13.2
5	Shad Bryant, Clemson	27	487	18.0
6	Davey O'Brien, TCU	37	458	12.4
7	Grenny Lansdell, Southern Cal	27	438	16.2
8	Tony Canadeo, Gonzaga	25	432	17.3
9	Warren Brunner, Tulane	28	416	14.9
10	Mike Klotovich, Saint Mary's-Cal	28	393	14.0

SCORING

		TDS	XPT	FG	PTS
1	Parker Hall, Mississippi	11	7	0	73
2	Irving Hall, Brown	10	9	0	69
3	Dick Cassiano, Pittsburgh	11	0	0	66
4	Victor Bottari, California	8	13	0	61
5	William Osmanski, Holy Cross	10	0	0	60
5	Connie Sparks, TCU	10	0	0	60
5	Elmer Tarbox, Texas Tech	10	0	0	60
8	Bill Hutchinson, Dartmouth	7	12	1	57
9	Charles Long, Army	6	14	0	50
10	Seven tied	–	–	–	48

INTERCEPTIONS

		INT	YDS
1	Elmer Tarbox, Texas Tech	11	89
2	Parker Hall, Mississippi	7	128
3	Russell Busk, Iowa	6	98
3	Davey O'Brien, TCU	6	86
3	Otis Rogers, Oklahoma	6	47
3	Nile Kinnick, Iowa	6	39
3	George Watson, North Carolina	6	36
8	Dudley Akins, Texas Tech*	5	117
8	Bill Schneller, Mississippi*	5	110
8	Val Boehm, Xavier*	5	67

* Six tied with 5; these three players had the most yards.

TEAM LEADERS

RUSHING OFFENSE

		G	ATT	YDS	AVG	YPG
1	Fordham	9	567	2674	4.7	297.1
2	Tulane	10	547	2541	4.6	254.1
3	Penn State	8	397	2012	5.1	251.5
4	Carnegie Tech	7	341	1751	5.1	250.1
5	Texas Tech	10	470	2501	5.3	250.1
6	Dartmouth	7	323	1663	5.1	237.6
7	Pittsburgh	10	543	2280	4.2	228.0
8	Army	10	422	2196	5.2	219.6
9	Minnesota	8	452	1717	3.8	214.6
10	Brown	8	383	1705	4.5	213.1

PASSING OFFENSE/YPG

		G	ATT	COM	INT	PCT	YDS	YPA	YPG	I%	YPC
1	TCU	10	201	108	7	53.7	1641	8.2	164.1	3.5	15.2
2	Yale	8	196	92	15	46.9	1080	5.5	135.0	7.7	11.7
2	Missouri	9	172	79	23	45.9	1215	7.1	135.0	13.4	15.4
4	Baylor	10	216	86	18	39.8	1349	6.2	134.9	8.3	15.7
5	Arkansas	9	250	78	34	31.2	1169	4.7	129.9	13.6	15.0
6	SMU	10	203	75	21	36.9	1282	6.3	128.2	10.3	17.1
7	Navy	9	202	87	16	43.1	1132	5.6	125.8	7.9	13.0
8	Chicago	7	161	60	17	37.3	841	5.2	120.1	10.6	14.0
9	NYU	8	183	78	17	42.6	921	5.0	115.1	9.3	11.8
10	Oklahoma	10	213	108	16	50.7	1082	5.1	108.2	7.5	10.0

TOTAL OFFENSE

		G	P	YDS	AVG	YPG
1	Fordham	9	649	3074	4.7	341.6
2	TCU	10	677	3332	4.9	333.2
3	Texas Tech	10	570	3266	5.7	326.6
4	Army	10	579	3243	5.6	324.3
5	Dartmouth	7	405	2133	5.3	304.7
6	Missouri	9	563	2716	4.8	301.8
7	NYU	8	515	2404	4.7	300.5
8	Navy	9	599	2635	4.4	292.8
9	Carnegie Tech	7	384	2046	5.3	292.3
10	Tulane	10	606	2898	4.8	289.8

RUSHING DEFENSE

		G	ATT	YDS	AVG	YPG
1	Oklahoma	10	285	433	1.5	43.3
2	Alabama	7	219	319	1.5	45.6
3	Duke	9	253	508	2.0	56.4
4	Georgetown	6	234	353	1.5	58.8
5	Santa Clara	8	272	485	1.8	60.6
6	Southern Cal	10	340	640	1.9	64.0
7	Fordham	9	303	597	2.0	66.3
8	Carnegie Tech	6	208	485	2.3	80.8
9	Cornell	7	241	586	2.4	83.7
10	Xavier	8	281	678	2.4	84.8

PASSING DEFENSE

		G	ATT	COM	PCT	YPC	INT	I%	YDS	YPA	YPG
1	Penn State	8	59	10	16.9	10.5	14	23.7	105	1.8	13.1
2	Colgate	7	62	14	22.6	13.1	4	6.5	184	3.0	26.3
3	Lafayette	8	67	24	35.8	9.8	14	20.9	236	3.5	29.5
4	Alabama	7	61	18	29.5	12.6	13	21.3	226	3.7	32.3
5	Georgia Tech	6	51	16	31.4	13.3	5	9.8	212	4.2	35.3
6	Fordham	9	120	31	25.8	11.2	17	14.2	348	2.9	38.7
7	Idaho	6	69	13	18.8	18.8	13	18.8	244	3.5	40.7
8	Bucknell	8	68	25	36.8	13.4	9	13.2	334	4.9	41.8
9	Carnegie Tech	6	53	15	28.3	17.3	14	26.4	260	4.9	43.3
10	Vanderbilt	9	77	32	41.6	12.3	7	9.1	395	5.1	43.9

TOTAL DEFENSE

		G	P	YDS	AVG	YPG
1	Alabama	7	280	545	1.9	77.9
2	Oklahoma	10	457	966	2.1	96.6
3	Fordham	9	423	945	2.2	105.0
4	Duke	9	336	961	2.9	106.8
5	Georgetown	6	321	652	2.0	108.7
6	Southern Cal	10	481	1113	2.3	111.3
7	Santa Clara	8	412	962	2.3	120.3
8	Carnegie Tech	6	261	745	2.9	124.2
9	Xavier	8	388	1129	2.9	141.1
10	Lafayette	8	373	1130	3.0	141.3

SCORING OFFENSE

		G	PTS	AVG
1	Dartmouth	9	254	28.2
2	Tennessee	10	276	27.6
3	Texas Tech	10	274	27.4

Based on top 15 teams in winning percentage.

SCORING DEFENSE

		G	PTS	AVG
1	Duke	9	0	0.0
2	Oklahoma	10	12	1.2
3	Tennessee	10	16	1.6

Based on top 15 teams in winning percentage.

1939 POLL PROGRESSION

AP October 16 Poll — Oct. 21 Games

1	Pittsburgh	3-0-0	lost to Duquesne 13-21
2	Notre Dame	3-0-0	beat Navy 14-7
3	Oklahoma	2-0-1	beat Kansas 27-7
4	Tulane	3-0-0	tied # 14 North Carolina 14-14
5	Tennessee	3-0-0	beat # 8 Alabama 21-0
6	Michigan	2-0-0	beat Chicago 85-0
7	Southern Cal	2-0-1	bye week
8	Alabama	3-0-0	lost to # 5 Tennessee 0-21
9	Texas A&M	4-0-0	beat TCU 20-6
10	Ohio State	2-0-0	beat Minnesota 23-20
11	Oregon	2-0-1	lost to Gonzaga 7-12
12	Cornell	2-0-0	beat Penn State 47-0
13	Duke	2-1-0	beat Syracuse 33-6
14	North Carolina	4-0-0	tied # 4 Tulane 14-14
15	Carnegie Tech	3-0-0	lost to NYU 0-6
16	Nebraska	2-0-1	beat # 19 Baylor 20-0
17	Mississippi	4-0-0	beat St. Louis 42-0
18	SMU	1-1-1	beat Marquette 16-0
19	Baylor	3-0-0	lost to # 16 Nebraska 0-20
20	Saint Mary's-Cal	2-0-0	bye week

AP October 23 Poll — Oct. 28 Games

1	Tennessee	4-0-0	beat Mercer 17-0
2	Notre Dame	4-0-0	beat Carnegie Tech 7-6
3	Michigan	3-0-0	beat Yale 27-7
4	Ohio State	3-0-0	lost to # 7 Cornell 14-23
5	Texas A&M	5-0-0	beat Baylor 20-0
6	Oklahoma	3-0-1	beat Oklahoma State 41-0
7	Cornell	3-0-0	beat # 4 Ohio State 23-14
8	Southern Cal	2-0-1	beat California 26-0
9	Tulane	3-0-1	beat # 14 Mississippi 18-6
10	Nebraska	3-0-1	beat Kansas State 25-9
11	Duquesne	4-0-0	beat Texas Tech 13-0
12	Duke	3-1-0	beat Wake Forest 6-0
13	North Carolina	4-0-1	beat # 16 Pennsylvania 30-6
14	Mississippi	4-0-0	lost to # 9 Tulane 6-18
15	Oregon State	4-0-0	beat Washington State 13-0
16	Pennsylvania	3-0-0	lost to # 13 North Carolina 6-30
17	SMU	2-1-1	bye week
18	Pittsburgh	3-1-0	lost to Fordham 13-27
19	NYU	3-1-0	beat Georgia 14-13
20	Alabama	3-1-0	beat Mississippi State 7-0

AP October 30 Poll — Nov. 4 Games

1	Tennessee	5-0-0	beat # 18 LSU 20-0
2	Michigan	4-0-0	lost to Illinois 7-16
3	Cornell	4-0-0	beat Columbia 13-7
4	Notre Dame	5-0-0	beat Army 14-0
5	Texas A&M	6-0-0	beat Arkansas 27-0
6	Oklahoma	4-0-1	beat Iowa State 38-6
7	Southern Cal	3-0-1	beat # 11 Oregon State 19-7
8	Tulane	4-0-1	bye week
9	North Carolina	5-0-1	beat North Carolina St. 17-0
10	Nebraska	4-0-1	lost to Missouri 13-27
11	Oregon State	5-0-0	lost to # 7 Southern Cal 7-19
12	Duke	4-1-0	beat Georgia Tech 7-6
13	Duquesne	5-0-0	beat Marquette 21-13
14	Ohio State	3-1-0	beat Indiana 24-0
15	Kentucky	5-0-0	tied # 19 Alabama 7-7
16	SMU	2-1-1	beat Texas 10-0
17	NYU	4-1-0	beat Lafayette 14-0
18	LSU	4-1-0	lost to # 1 Tennessee 0-20
19	Alabama	4-1-0	tied # 15 Kentucky 7-7
20	UCLA	4-0-1	beat California 20-7

AP November 6 Poll — Nov. 11 Games

1	Tennessee	6-0-0	beat Citadel 34-0
2	Texas A&M	7-0-0	beat # 13 SMU 6-2
3	Notre Dame	6-0-0	lost to Iowa 6-7
4	Southern Cal	4-0-1	beat Stanford 33-0
5	Cornell	5-0-0	beat Colgate 14-12
6	Oklahoma	5-0-1	beat Kansas State 13-10
7	Tulane	4-0-1	beat # 20 Alabama 13-0
8	North Carolina	6-0-1	beat Davidson 32-0
9	Ohio State	4-1-0	beat Chicago 61-0
10	Michigan	4-1-0	lost to Minnesota 7-20
11	UCLA	5-0-1	bye week
12	Duquesne	6-0-0	beat North Carolina St. 7-0
13	SMU	3-1-1	lost to # 2 Texas A&M 2-6
14	Dartmouth	5-0-1	lost to Princeton 7-9
15	Duke	5-1-0	beat VMI 20-7
16	Santa Clara	3-1-2	beat Michigan State 6-0
17	NYU	5-1-0	lost to Missouri 7-20
18	Kentucky	5-0-1	lost to Georgia Tech 6-13
19	Mississippi	5-1-0	beat Southern Miss 27-7
20	Alabama	4-1-1	lost to # 7 Tulane 0-13

AP November 13 Poll — Nov. 18 Games

1	Tennessee	7-0-0	beat Vanderbilt 13-0
2	Texas A&M	8-0-0	beat Rice 19-0
3	Southern Cal	5-0-1	bye week
4	Cornell	6-0-0	beat # 20 Dartmouth 35-6
5	Oklahoma	6-0-1	lost to # 12 Missouri 6-7
6	Tulane	5-0-1	beat Columbia 25-0
7	North Carolina	7-0-1	lost to # 13 Duke 3-13
8	Ohio State	5-1-0	beat Illinois 21-0
9	Notre Dame	6-1-0	beat Northwestern 7-0
10	Duquesne	7-0-0	bye week
11	UCLA	5-0-1	tied # 14 Santa Clara 0-0
12	Missouri	6-1-0	beat # 5 Oklahoma 7-6
13	Duke	6-1-0	beat # 7 North Carolina 13-3
14	Santa Clara	4-1-2	tied # 11 UCLA 0-0
15	Iowa	5-1-0	beat # 20 Minnesota 13-9
16	Clemson	6-1-0	beat Southwestern 21-6
17	SMU	3-2-1	lost to Arkansas 0-14
18	Holy Cross	6-1-0	beat Carnegie Tech 21-0
19	Oregon State	6-1-0	beat California 21-0
20	Dartmouth	5-1-1	lost to # 4 Cornell 6-35
20	Minnesota	2-3-1	lost to # 15 Iowa 9-13

AP November 20 Poll — Nov. 25 Games

1	Texas A&M	9-0-0	bye week
2	Tennessee	8-0-0	bye week
3	Cornell	7-0-0	beat Pennsylvania 26-0
4	Southern Cal	5-0-1	beat # 7 Notre Dame 20-12
5	Tulane	6-0-1	beat Sewanee 52-0
6	Ohio State	6-1-0	lost to Michigan 14-21
7	Notre Dame	7-1-0	lost to # 4 Southern Cal 12-20
8	Duke	7-1-0	beat North Carolina St. 28-0
9	Iowa	6-1-0	tied Northwestern 7-7
10	Missouri	7-1-0	beat Kansas 20-0
11	Holy Cross	7-1-0	bye week
12	Duquesne	7-0-0	beat Carnegie Tech 22-7
13	UCLA	5-0-2	tied Oregon State 13-13
14	Oklahoma	6-1-1	lost to Nebraska 7-13
15	Clemson	7-1-0	beat Furman 14-3
16	Georgetown	7-0-0	regular season complete
17	North Carolina	7-1-1	bye week
17	Santa Clara	4-1-3	beat Saint Mary's-Cal 7-0
19	Georgia Tech	5-2-0	beat Florida 21-7
19	Princeton	6-1-0	beat Navy 28-0

AP November 27 Poll — Dec. 2 Games

1	Texas A&M	9-0-0	beat Texas 20-0
1	Southern Cal	6-0-1	beat Washington 9-7
3	Cornell	8-0-0	regular season complete
4	Tennessee	8-0-0	beat Kentucky 19-0
5	Tulane	7-0-1	beat LSU 33-20
6	Duquesne	8-0-0	tied Detroit 10-10
7	Duke	8-1-0	regular season complete
8	Missouri	8-1-0	regular season complete
9	Iowa	6-1-1	regular season complete
10	Holy Cross	7-1-0	lost to Boston College 0-14
11	Notre Dame	7-2-0	regular season complete
12	Ohio State	6-2-0	regular season complete
13	UCLA	5-0-3	beat Washington State 24-7
14	Clemson	8-1-0	regular season complete
15	Michigan	6-2-0	regular season complete
16	North Carolina	8-1-1	beat Virginia 19-0
17	Georgetown	7-0-1	
18	Nebraska	7-1-1	regular season complete
19	San Jose State	12-0-0	beat Drake 12-0
20	Santa Clara	5-1-3	regular season complete

AP December 4 Poll — Dec. 9 Games

1	Texas A&M	10-0-0	regular season complete
2	Tennessee	9-0-0	beat Auburn 7-0
3	Southern Cal	7-0-1	tied # 9 UCLA 0-0
4	Cornell	8-0-0	
5	Tulane	8-0-1	regular season complete
6	Duke	8-1-0	
7	Missouri	8-1-0	
8	Iowa	6-1-1	
9	UCLA	6-0-3	tied # 3 Southern Cal 0-0
10	Duquesne	8-0-1	regular season complete
11	Notre Dame	7-2-0	
12	Ohio State	6-2-0	
13	Georgia Tech	7-2-0	regular season complete
14	Boston College	9-1-0	regular season complete
15	Clemson	8-1-0	
16	Santa Clara	5-1-3	
17	Nebraska	7-1-1	
18	Fordham	6-2-0	regular season complete
18	San Jose State	13-0-0	regular season complete
20	Georgetown	7-0-1	

AP	DECEMBER 11 FINAL POLL	RECORD	BOWL BID	DATE	BOWL RESULT	RB	RECORD
1	Texas A&M	10-0-0	Sugar Bowl	J1	beat # 5 Tulane 14-13	1	11-0-0
2	Tennessee	10-0-0	Rose Bowl	J1	lost to # 3 Southern Cal 0-14	3	10-1-0
3	Southern Cal	7-0-2	Rose Bowl	J1	beat # 2 Tennessee 14-0	2	8-0-2
4	Cornell	8-0-0				4	8-0-0
5	Tulane	8-0-1	Sugar Bowl	J1	lost to # 1 Texas A&M 13-14	5	8-1-1
6	Missouri	8-1-0	Orange Bowl	J1	lost to # 16 Georgia Tech 7-21	11	8-2-0
7	UCLA	6-0-4				18	6-0-4
8	Duke	8-1-0				7	8-1-0
9	Iowa	6-1-1				16	6-1-1
10	Duquesne	8-0-1				8	8-0-1
11	Boston College	9-1-0	Cotton Bowl	J1	lost to # 12 Clemson 3-6	30	9-2-0
12	Clemson	8-1-0	Cotton Bowl	J1	beat # 11 Boston College 6-3	20	9-1-0
13	Notre Dame	7-2-0				6	7-2-0
14	Santa Clara	5-1-3				14	5-1-3
15	Ohio State	6-2-0				21	6-2-0
16	Georgia Tech	7-2-0	Orange Bowl	J1	beat # 6 Missouri 21-7	10	8-2-0
17	Fordham	6-2-0				9	6-2-0
18	Nebraska	7-1-1				13	7-1-1
19	Oklahoma	6-2-1				15	6-2-1
20	Michigan	6-2-0				17	6-2-0

1939

Consenus All-Americans

POS	NAME	HT	WT	SCHOOL	AA	AP	CM	IN	LM	NE	NW	SN	UP
B	Nile Kinnick	5-8	167	Iowa	•	•	•	•	•	•	•	•	•
B	Tom Harmon	6-0	195	Michigan	•	•		•	•	•	•	•	•
B	John Kimbrough	6-2	210	Texas A&M	•	•		•	•	•	•	•	•
B	George Cafego	6-0	174	Tennessee				•		•	•	•	•
E	Esco Sarkkinen	6-0	192	Ohio State	•		•		•	•		•	•
E	Ken Kavanaugh	6-3	203	LSU				•	•	•	•	•	•
T	Nick Drahos	6-3	200	Cornell				•	•	•	•	•	•
T	Harley McCollum	6-4	235	Tulane	•	•			•	•	•	•	•
G	Harry Smith	5-11	218	Southern Cal	•	•	•	•	•	•	•	•	•
G	Ed Molinski	5-10	190	Tennessee	•	•		•	•	•	•	•	•
C	John Schiechl	6-2	220	Santa Clara	•	•		•					

	OTHERS RECEIVING FIRST-TEAM HONORS												
B	Paul Christman			Missouri		•	•		•				
B	Banks McFadden			Clemson		•	•		•				
B	Donald Scott			Ohio State					•				
B	Kenny Washington			UCLA					•				
E	Bud Kerr			Notre Dame	•				•				
E	Paul Severin			North Carolina					•				
E	Frank Ivy			Oklahoma					•				
E	Harlan Gustafson			Pennsylvania					•				
E	Dave Rankin			Purdue					•				
T	Jim Reeder			Illinois				•					
T	Joe Boyd			Texas A&M			•		•				
T	Harry Stella			Army				•		•	•	•	
G	Bob Suffridge			Tennessee				•		•		•	•
C	John Haman			Northwestern				•		•		•	•
C	Carey Cox			Alabama					•				

Heisman Trophy Voting

	PLAYER	POS	SCHOOL	TOTAL
1	Nile Kinnick	HB	Iowa	651
2	Tom Harmon	HB	Michigan	405
3	Paul Christman	QB	Missouri	391
4	George Cafego	TB	Tennessee	296

Award Winners

PLAYER	POS	SCHOOL	AWARD NAME
Nile Kinnick	HB	Iowa	Maxwell

Conference Standings

Big 10

	CONF. W L T			OVERALL W L T		
Ohio State	5	1	0	6	2	0
Iowa	4	1	1	6	1	1
Michigan	3	2	0	6	2	0
Purdue	2	1	2	3	3	2
Northwestern	3	2	1	3	4	1
Illinois	3	3	0	3	4	1
Minnesota	2	3	1	3	4	1
Indiana	2	3	0	2	4	2
Wisconsin	0	5	1	1	6	1
Chicago	0	3	0	2	6	0

Big 6

	CONF. W L T			OVERALL W L T		
Missouri	5	0	0	8	2	0
Nebraska	4	1	0	7	1	1
Oklahoma	3	2	0	6	2	1
Kansas State	1	4	0	4	5	0
Kansas	1	4	0	2	6	0
Iowa State	1	4	0	2	7	0

Border

	CONF. W L T			OVERALL W L T		
Arizona State	4	0	0	8	2	1
New Mexico	4	2	0	8	2	0
Texas-El Paso	3	2	0	5	4	0
Texas Tech	1	1	0	5	5	1
Arizona	1	2	0	6	4	0
New Mexico State	1	4	0	3	6	0
Northern Arizona	0	4	0	1	6	1

Mountain States

	CONF. W L T			OVERALL W L T		
Colorado	5	1	0	5	3	0
Utah	4	1	1	6	1	2
Denver	3	2	1	5	3	1
Brigham Young	2	2	2	5	2	2
Utah State	2	3	1	3	4	1
Colorado State	2	4	0	2	7	0
Wyoming	0	5	1	0	7	1

Pacific Coast

	CONF. W L T			OVERALL W L T		
Southern Cal	5	0	2	8	0	2
Oregon State	6	1	1	9	1	1
UCLA	5	0	3	6	0	4
Washington	4	4	0	4	5	0
Oregon	3	3	1	3	4	1
Washington State	3	5	0	4	5	0
Montana	1	2	0	3	6	0
California	2	5	0	3	7	0
Stanford	0	6	1	1	7	1
Idaho	0	3	0	2	6	0

SEC

	CONF. W L T			OVERALL W L T		
Tennessee	6	0	0	10	1	0
Georgia Tech	6	0	0	8	2	0
Tulane	5	0	0	8	1	1
Mississippi State	3	2	0	8	2	0
Auburn	3	3	1	5	5	1
Mississippi	2	2	0	7	2	0
Kentucky	2	2	1	6	2	1
Alabama	2	3	1	5	3	1
Georgia	1	3	0	5	6	0
LSU	1	5	0	4	5	0
Vanderbilt	1	6	0	2	7	1
Florida	0	3	1	5	5	1
Sewanee	0	3	0	3	5	0

Southern

	CONF. W L T			OVERALL W L T		
Duke	5	0	0	8	1	0
Clemson	4	0	0	9	1	0
North Carolina	5	1	0	8	1	1
Richmond	3	1	1	7	1	2
VMI	3	1	1	6	3	1
Wake Forest	3	3	0	7	3	0
Furman	3	3	0	5	4	0
William & Mary	1	1	1	6	2	1
North Carolina St.	2	4	0	2	8	0
Wash. & Lee	1	2	0	3	4	1
Virginia Tech	1	4	1	4	5	1
South Carolina	1	3	0	3	6	1
Davidson	1	7	0	2	7	0
Citadel	0	4	0	3	8	0
Maryland	0	1	0	2	7	0

SWC

	CONF. W L T			OVERALL W L T		
Texas A&M	6	0	0	11	0	0
Baylor	4	2	0	7	3	0
SMU	4	2	0	6	3	1
Texas	3	3	0	5	4	0
Arkansas	2	3	1	4	5	1
TCU	1	5	0	3	7	0
Rice	0	5	1	1	9	1

Independents

	OVERALL W L T		
San Jose State	13	0	0
Cornell	8	0	0
Duquesne	8	0	1
Georgetown	7	0	1
Princeton	7	1	0
North Texas	6	1	0
Rutgers	7	1	1
Boston College	9	2	0
Holy Cross	7	2	0
Notre Dame	7	2	0
Fordham	6	2	0
Penn State	5	1	2
Santa Clara	5	1	3
Brown	5	3	1
Dartmouth	5	3	1
NYU	5	4	0
Pittsburgh	5	4	0
Virginia	5	4	0
Miami, Fla.	5	5	0
Michigan State	4	4	1
Pennsylvania	4	4	0
Harvard	4	4	0
Syracuse	3	3	2
Army	3	4	2
Yale	3	4	1
Saint Mary's-Cal	3	4	1
Navy	3	5	1
Carnegie Tech	3	5	0
Columbia	2	4	2
Memphis	3	7	0
West Virginia	2	6	1

Bowl Games

DATE	GAME	SCORE
J1	Sun	Arizona State 0, Catholic 0
J1	Cotton	Clemson 6, Boston College 3
J1	Orange	Georgia Tech 21, Missouri 7
J1	Rose	Southern Cal 14, Tennessee 0
J1	Sugar	Texas A&M 14, Tulane 13

1939 NCAA Major College Statistical Leaders

Individual Leaders

PASSING/COMPLETIONS	G	ATT	COM	PCT	INT	I%	YDS	YPA	COM.PG
1 Kay Eakin, Arkansas	10	193	78	40.4	18	9.3	962	5.0	7.8
2 Paul Christman, Missouri	9	136	63	46.3	12	8.8	677	5.0	7.0
3 Doc Plunkett, Vanderbilt	10	163	61	37.4	19	11.7	867	5.3	6.1
4 Harold Hursh, Indiana	8	125	59	47.2	11	8.8	913	7.3	7.4
5 Charles Edwards, Citadel	11	108	53	49.1	10	9.3	602	5.6	4.8
6 Glenn Cowart, TCU	10	110	51	46.4	5	4.6	639	5.8	5.1
7 Jim Lalanne, North Carolina	10	96	50	52.1	11	11.5	602	6.3	5.0
7 Ernie Lain, Rice	11	122	50	41.0	8	6.6	580	4.8	4.5
9 Edward Boell, NYU	8	87	45	51.7	12	13.8	431	5.0	5.6
10 Marion Pugh, Texas A&M	10	84	43	51.2	10	11.9	458	5.5	4.3

ALL-PURPOSE YARDS	G	RUSH	REC	INT	PR	KR	YDS	YPG
1 Tom Harmon, Michigan	8	868	110	98	0	132	1208	151.0

RUSHING/YARDS	G	ATT	YDS	AVG	YPG
1 John Polanski, Wake Forest	10	137	882	6.4	88.2
2 Tom Harmon, Michigan	8	129	868	6.7	108.5
3 Kenny Washington, UCLA	10	168	811	4.8	81.1
4 Red Mayberry, Wake Forest	10	148	784	5.3	78.4
5 Johnny Knolla, Creighton	9	106	720	6.8	80.0
6 Harold Van Every, Minnesota	8	132	676	5.1	84.5
7 Grenny Lansdell, Southern Cal	9	136	675	5.0	75.0
8 John Black, Arizona	10	173	630	3.6	63.0
8 Tony Gallovich, Wake Forest	10	100	622	6.2	62.2
10 Jack Crain, Texas	9	92	610	6.6	67.8

RUSHING/YARDS PER CARRY	G	ATT	YDS	YPC
1 Jackie Robinson, UCLA	10	42	514	12.2
2 Jim Strausbaugh, Ohio State	8	71	526	7.4
3 Harvey Johnson, Mississippi State	10	87	592	6.8
4 Johnny Knolla, Creighton	9	106	720	6.8
5 Tom Harmon, Michigan	8	129	868	6.7
6 Jack Crain, Texas	9	92	610	6.6
7 John Polanski, Wake Forest	10	137	882	6.4
8 Tony Gallovich, Wake Forest	10	100	622	6.2
9 George McAfee, Duke	9	96	596	6.2
10 Red Mayberry, Wake Forest	10	148	784	5.3

*-Based on top 20 rushers

RECEIVING/RECEPTIONS	G	REC	YDS	YPR	YPG	RPG
1 Ken Kavanaugh, LSU	9	30	467	15.6	51.9	3.3
2 Don Looney, TCU	10	29	405	14.0	40.5	2.9
3 Robert David, Citadel	11	28	360	12.9	32.7	2.5
4 George Radman, North Carolina	10	25	247	9.9	24.7	2.5
5 Joe Anderson, Vanderbilt	10	23	181	7.9	18.1	2.3
6 Bill Jennings, Oklahoma	9	21	244	11.6	27.1	2.3
7 Earle Clark, TCU	10	19	328	17.3	32.8	1.9
7 Ed Hiestand, Vanderbilt	10	19	289	15.2	28.9	1.9
7 Durwood Horner, TCU	10	19	224	11.8	22.4	1.9
10 Ralph Atwood, Arkansas	10	18	183	10.2	18.3	1.8

PUNTING	PUNT	YDS	AVG
1 Harry Dunkle, North Carolina	37	1725	46.6
2 Stanley Nyhan, Tulane	38	1692	44.5
3 Charley Boswell, Alabama	38	1643	43.2
4 Neil Cavette, Georgia Tech	31	1336	43.1
5 Dick McGowen, Auburn	92	3959	43.0
6 Banks McFadden, Clemson	56	2393	42.7
7 Bill Sewell, Washington State	38	1620	42.6
8 Nelson Catlett, VMI	47	1992	42.4
9 Herschel Mosley, Alabama	51	2143	42.0
10 Charles O'Rourke, Boston College	47	1950	41.5

PUNT RETURNS/YARDS	PR	YDS	AVG
1 Bosh Pritchard, VMI	42	583	13.9
2 Derace Moser, Texas A&M	24	404	16.8
3 Dick McGowen, Auburn	37	379	10.2
4 George McAfee, Duke	37	365	9.9
5 Olie Cordill, Rice	26	351	13.5
6 William Conatser, Texas A&M	24	339	14.1
7 George Kiick, Bucknell	36	334	9.3
8 Ernie Steele, Washington	26	318	12.2
9 Jack Crain, Texas	17	317	18.6
10 Red Mayberry, Wake Forest	34	300	8.8

KICKOFF RETURNS/YARDS	KR	YDS	AVG
1 Nile Kinnick, Iowa	15	377	25.1
2 Red Mayberry, Wake Forest	8	328	41.0
3 Winfred Bynum, Centenary	9	287	31.9
4 George Clay, Tulane	6	229	38.2
5 Johnny Knolla, Creighton	10	216	21.6
6 R. H. Miller, Chicago	12	212	17.7
7 Melvin Seelye, Kansas State	10	210	21.0
8 Harold Van Every, Minnesota	8	198	24.8
9 Bob Olson, Oregon State	5	186	37.2
10 Jim Groves, Stanford	7	181	25.9

SCORING	TDS	XPT	FG	PTS
1 Tom Harmon, Michigan	14	15	1	102
2 John Polanski, Wake Forest	13	6	0	84
3 Vito Ananis, Boston College	12	1	0	73
4 Harvey Johnson, Mississippi State	10	2	0	62
5 John Kimbrough, Texas A&M	10	0	0	60
6 Jack Crain, Texas	8	8	0	56
7 Bobby Kellogg, Tulane	8	7	0	55
8 Ray Hare, Gonzaga	8	6	0	54
8 Ken Kavanaugh, LSU	9	0	0	54
8 Grenny Lansdell, Southern Cal	9	0	0	54
8 Red Mayberry, Wake Forest	9	0	0	54

INTERCEPTIONS	INT	YDS
1 Harold Van Every, Minnesota	8	59
1 Nile Kinnick, Iowa	8	52
3 Bosh Pritchard, VMI	7	199
3 John Black, Arizona	7	69
5 Dick McGowen, Auburn	6	134
5 Thomas Harrison, Florida	6	68
5 Pete Cignetti, Boston College	6	41
5 Kay Eakin, Arkansas	6	40
5 Hal McCullough, Cornell	6	3
10 Ray Portillo, Oklahoma State*	5	114

* Nine tied with 5; Portillo had the most yards.

Team Leaders

RUSHING OFFENSE	G	ATT	YDS	AVG	YPG
1 Wake Forest	10	516	2903	5.6	290.3
2 Tulane	9	573	2348	4.1	260.9
3 Tennessee	10	510	2553	5.0	255.3
4 Minnesota	8	470	1891	4.0	236.4
5 Boston College	10	460	2236	4.9	223.6
6 Clemson	9	436	1972	4.5	219.1
7 Cornell	8	391	1726	4.4	215.8
8 Ohio State	8	380	1711	4.5	213.9
9 Mississippi	9	399	1890	4.7	210.0
10 Brown	9	414	1861	4.5	206.8

PASSING OFFENSE/YPG	G	ATT	COM	INT	PCT	YDS	YPA	YPG	I%	YPC
1 TCU	10	245	120	16	49.0	1485	6.1	148.5	6.5	12.4
2 Princeton	8	153	67	12	43.8	1055	6.9	131.9	7.8	15.7
3 Indiana	8	142	69	14	48.6	1032	7.3	129.0	9.9	15.0
4 Vanderbilt	10	214	84	22	39.3	1146	5.4	114.6	10.3	13.6
5 Southern Cal	9	183	84	12	45.9	1008	5.5	112.0	6.6	12.0
6 Lehigh	9	176	65	17	36.9	989	5.6	109.9	9.7	15.2
7 Arkansas	10	242	91	25	37.6	1091	4.5	109.1	10.3	12.0
8 Oregon	8	137	58	11	42.3	866	6.3	108.3	8.0	14.9
9 LSU	9	159	67	16	42.1	918	5.8	102.0	10.1	13.7
10 Kansas	7	121	51	12	42.1	708	5.9	101.1	9.9	13.9

TOTAL OFFENSE	G	P	YDS	AVG	YPG
1 Ohio State	8	514	2474	4.8	309.3
2 Tennessee	10	590	3083	5.2	308.3
3 Mississippi	9	519	2770	5.3	307.8
4 Southern Cal	9	606	2763	4.6	307.0
5 Wake Forest	10	563	3062	5.4	306.2
6 Creighton	9	583	2692	4.6	299.1
7 Boston College	10	565	2990	5.3	299.0
8 Brown	9	549	2663	4.9	295.9
9 Cornell	8	481	2354	4.9	294.3
10 Minnesota	8	544	2296	4.2	287.0

RUSHING DEFENSE	G	ATT	YDS	AVG	YPG
1 San Jose State	13	387	444	1.2	34.2
2 Texas A&M	10	272	415	1.5	41.5
3 Boston College	10	294	583	2.0	58.3
4 Tulane	9	287	547	1.9	60.8
5 Tennessee	10	331	631	1.9	63.1
6 Georgetown	5	190	327	1.7	65.4
7 Southern Cal	9	291	649	2.2	72.1
8 Mississippi	9	302	675	2.2	75.0
9 Santa Clara	9	328	703	2.1	78.1
10 Baylor	10	306	804	2.6	80.4

PASSING DEFENSE	G	ATT	COM	PCT	YPC	INT	I%	YDS	YPA	YPG
1 Kansas	7	77	25	32.5	9.6	6	7.8	239	3.1	34.1
2 Texas A&M	10	175	48	27.4	7.3	28	16.0	348	2.0	34.8
3 Xavier	9	83	19	22.9	16.5	12	14.5	314	3.8	34.9
4 Clemson	9	86	28	32.6	11.9	15	15.1	333	3.9	37.0
5 San Jose State	13	195	45	23.1	10.7	29	14.9	483	2.5	37.2
6 Tennessee	10	128	49	38.3	8.0	22	17.2	392	3.1	39.2
7 VMI	10	143	42	29.4	9.6	16	11.2	402	2.8	40.2
8 Pittsburgh	9	96	31	32.3	12.2	15	15.6	379	3.9	42.1
9 Princeton	8	86	28	32.6	12.3	13	15.1	345	4.0	43.1
10 Georgia	7	68	24	35.3	12.7	10	14.7	304	4.5	43.4

TOTAL DEFENSE	G	P	YDS	AVG	YPG
1 San Jose State	13	582	927	1.6	71.3
2 Texas A&M	10	447	763	1.7	76.3
3 Tennessee	10	459	1023	2.2	102.3
4 Boston College	10	454	1029	2.3	102.9
5 Georgetown	5	258	591	2.3	118.2
6 Arizona	10	537	1333	2.5	133.3
7 Southern Cal	9	439	1228	2.8	136.4
8 Florida	11	529	1505	2.8	136.8
9 Xavier	9	419	1245	3.0	138.3
10 Manhattan	5	262	698	2.7	139.6

SCORING OFFENSE	G	PTS	AVG
1 Utah	9	256	28.4

SCORING DEFENSE	G	PTS	AVG
1 Tennessee	10	0	0.0

1940 POLL PROGRESSION

AP October 14 Poll — Oct. 19 Games

#	Team	Record	Result
1	Cornell	2-0-0	beat Syracuse 33-6
2	Texas A&M	3-0-0	beat TCU 21-7
3	Michigan	3-0-0	beat Illinois 28-0
4	Northwestern	2-0-0	beat Wisconsin 27-7
5	Tennessee	3-0-0	beat Alabama 27-12
6	Notre Dame	2-0-0	beat Carnegie Tech 61-0
7	Minnesota	2-0-0	beat # 15 Ohio State 13-7
8	Boston College	3-0-0	beat Idaho 60-0
9	Pennsylvania	2-0-0	beat Princeton 46-28
10	Stanford	3-0-0	beat # 19 Washington State 26-14
11	Fordham	2-0-0	beat Pittsburgh 24-12
12	Clemson	4-0-0	bye week
13	Mississippi	4-0-0	beat Duquesne 14-6
14	Texas	3-0-0	beat Arkansas 21-0
15	Ohio State	2-1-0	lost to # 7 Minnesota 7-13
16	Washington	2-1-0	beat # 18 Oregon State 19-0
17	Southern Cal	1-0-2	beat Oregon 13-0
18	Oregon State	2-0-1	lost to # 16 Washington 0-19
19	Washington State	2-0-1	lost to # 10 Stanford 14-26
20	Iowa	2-0-0	lost to Indiana 6-10

AP October 21 Poll — Oct. 26 Games

#	Team	Record	Result
1	Cornell	3-0-0	beat Ohio State 21-7
2	Notre Dame	3-0-0	beat Illinois 26-0
3	Michigan	4-0-0	beat # 8 Pennsylvania 14-0
4	Texas A&M	4-0-0	beat Baylor 14-7
5	Tennessee	4-0-0	beat Florida 14-0
6	Minnesota	3-0-0	beat Iowa 34-6
7	Northwestern	3-0-0	beat Indiana 20-7
8	Pennsylvania	3-0-0	lost to # 3 Michigan 0-14
9	Stanford	4-0-0	beat # 17 Southern Cal 21-7
10	Boston College	4-0-0	beat St. Anselm 55-0
11	Fordham	3-0-0	lost to Saint Mary's-Cal 6-9
12	Texas	4-0-0	lost to Rice 0-13
13	Clemson	4-0-0	beat South Carolina 21-13
14	Mississippi	5-0-0	lost to Arkansas 20-21
15	Georgetown	4-0-0	beat NYU 26-0
16	Washington	3-1-0	beat California 7-6
17	Southern Cal	2-0-2	lost to # 9 Stanford 7-21
18	Nebraska	2-1-0	beat Missouri 20-7
19	SMU	3-0-1	bye week
20	Columbia	3-0-0	lost to Syracuse 0-3

AP October 28 Poll — Nov. 2 Games

#	Team	Record	Result
1	Cornell	4-0-0	beat Columbia 27-0
2	Notre Dame	4-0-0	beat Army 7-0
3	Michigan	5-0-0	bye week
4	Minnesota	4-0-0	beat # 8 Northwestern 13-12
5	Texas A&M	5-0-0	beat Arkansas 17-0
6	Stanford	5-0-0	beat UCLA 20-14
7	Tennessee	5-0-0	beat LSU 28-0
8	Northwestern	4-0-0	lost to # 4 Minnesota 12-13
9	Boston College	5-0-0	beat Manhattan 25-0
10	Clemson	5-0-0	lost to Tulane 0-13
11	Georgetown	5-0-0	beat Syracuse 28-6
12	Nebraska	3-1-0	beat Oklahoma 13-0
13	Washington	4-1-0	bye week
14	Navy	5-0-0	lost to # 15 Pennsylvania 0-20
15	Pennsylvania	3-1-0	beat # 14 Navy 20-0
16	SMU	3-0-1	beat Texas 21-13
17	Detroit	5-0-0	lost to Tulsa 0-7
18	Duke	3-1-0	beat Georgia Tech 41-7
18	Penn State	4-0-0	beat South Carolina 12-0
20	Mississippi State	4-0-1	beat Southwestern 13-0
20	Santa Clara	2-1-1	beat San Francisco 27-0

AP November 4 Poll — Nov. 9 Games

#	Team	Record	Result
1	Cornell	5-0-0	beat Yale 21-0
2	Minnesota	5-0-0	beat # 3 Michigan 7-6
3	Michigan	5-0-0	lost to # 2 Minnesota 6-7
4	Texas A&M	6-0-0	beat # 14 SMU 19-7
5	Tennessee	6-0-0	beat Southwestern 41-0
6	Stanford	6-0-0	beat # 11 Washington 20-10
7	Notre Dame	5-0-0	beat Navy 13-7
8	Boston College	6-0-0	beat Boston U. 21-0
9	Georgetown	6-0-0	beat Maryland 41-0
10	Northwestern	4-1-0	beat Illinois 32-14
11	Washington	4-1-0	lost to # 6 Stanford 10-20
12	Duke	4-1-0	beat Davidson 46-13
12	Nebraska	4-1-0	beat Iowa 14-6
14	SMU	4-0-1	lost to # 4 Texas A&M 7-19
15	Pennsylvania	4-1-0	tied Harvard 10-10
16	Penn State	5-0-0	tied Syracuse 13-13
17	Fordham	4-1-0	beat Purdue 13-7
18	Lafayette	5-0-0	beat Wash. & Jeff 25-0
19	Mississippi State	5-0-1	beat LSU 22-7
19	Santa Clara	3-1-1	bye week

AP November 11 Poll — Nov. 16 Games

#	Team	Record	Result
1	Minnesota	6-0-0	beat Purdue 33-6
2	Cornell	6-0-0	lost to Dartmouth 0-3
3	Texas A&M	7-0-0	beat Rice 25-0
4	Stanford	7-0-0	beat # 19 Oregon State 28-14
5	Tennessee	7-0-0	beat Virginia 41-14
6	Michigan	5-1-0	beat # 10 Northwestern 20-13
7	Notre Dame	6-0-0	lost to Iowa 0-7
8	Boston College	7-0-0	beat Georgetown 19-18
9	Georgetown	7-0-0	lost to Boston College 18-19
10	Northwestern	5-1-0	lost to # 6 Michigan 13-20
11	Nebraska	5-1-0	beat Pittsburgh 9-7
12	Duke	5-1-0	lost to North Carolina 3-6
13	Fordham	5-1-0	bye week
14	Alabama	5-1-0	beat Georgia Tech 14-13
15	Mississippi State	6-0-1	beat Milsaps 46-13
16	Santa Clara	3-1-1	beat Loyola, Marymount 27-0
17	Mississippi	7-1-0	beat Memphis 38-7
17	Washington	4-2-0	beat Southern Cal 14-0
18	Oregon State	5-1-1	lost to # 4 Stanford 14-28
20	Penn State	5-0-1	beat NYU 25-0
20	SMU	4-1-1	beat Arkansas 28-0

AP November 18 Poll — Nov. 23 Games

#	Team	Record	Result
1	Minnesota	7-0-0	beat Wisconsin 22-13
2	Texas A&M	8-0-0	bye week
3	Stanford	8-0-0	bye week
4	Boston College	8-0-0	beat Auburn 33-7
5	Cornell	6-1-0	lost to # 12 Pennsylvania 20-22
6	Tennessee	8-0-0	beat Kentucky 33-0
7	Michigan	6-1-0	beat Ohio State 40-0
8	Nebraska	6-1-0	beat Iowa State 21-12
9	Georgetown	7-1-0	beat George Washington 8-0
10	Northwestern	5-2-0	beat Notre Dame 20-0
11	Mississippi	8-1-0	lost to # 16 Mississippi State 0-19
12	Pennsylvania	5-1-1	beat # 5 Cornell 22-20
13	Washington	5-2-0	beat UCLA 41-0
14	Notre Dame	6-1-0	lost to Northwestern 0-20
15	Fordham	5-1-0	beat Arkansas 27-7
16	Mississippi State	7-0-1	beat # 11 Mississippi 19-0
17	Alabama	6-1-0	beat Vanderbilt 25-21
18	SMU	5-1-1	beat Baylor 7-4
19	Santa Clara	4-1-1	beat Saint Mary's-Cal 19-7
20	Penn State	6-0-1	lost to Pittsburgh 7-20
20	Texas Tech	7-0-1	beat St. Louis 7-6

AP November 25 Poll — Nov. 30 Games

#	Team	Record	Result
1	Minnesota	8-0-0	regular season complete
2	Texas A&M	8-0-0	lost to Texas 0-7
3	Stanford	8-0-0	beat California 13-7
4	Boston College	9-0-0	beat Holy Cross 7-0
5	Michigan	7-1-0	regular season complete
6	Tennessee	9-0-0	beat Vanderbilt 20-0
7	Northwestern	6-2-0	regular season complete
8	Nebraska	7-1-0	beat Kansas State 20-0
9	Georgetown	8-1-0	regular season complete
10	Pennsylvania	6-1-1	regular season complete
11	Mississippi State	8-0-1	beat # 17 Alabama 13-0
12	Washington	6-2-0	beat Washington State 33-9
13	Cornell	6-2-0	regular season complete
14	Fordham	6-1-0	beat NYU 26-0
15	Santa Clara	5-1-1	beat Oklahoma 33-13
16	SMU	6-1-1	beat TCU 16-0
17	Alabama	7-1-0	lost to # 11 Mississippi State 0-13
18	Lafayette	8-0-0	beat Lehigh 13-0
18	Texas Tech	8-0-1	lost to New Mexico 14-19
20	Duke	6-2-0	beat Pittsburgh 12-7
20	Hardin-Simmons	8-0-0	beat Loyola, Marymount 40-6

AP December 2 Final Poll

#	Team	Record	Bowl Bid	Date	Bowl Result	RB	Record
1	Minnesota	8-0-0				3	8-0-0
2	Stanford	9-0-0	Rose Bowl	J1	beat # 7 Nebraska 21-13	1	10-0-0
3	Michigan	7-1-0				6	7-1-0
4	Tennessee	10-0-0	Sugar Bowl	J1	lost to # 5 Boston College 13-19	5	10-1-0
5	Boston College	10-0-0	Sugar Bowl	J1	beat # 4 Tennessee 19-13	4	11-0-0
6	Texas A&M	8-1-0	Cotton Bowl	J1	beat # 12 Fordham 13-12	2	9-1-0
7	Nebraska	8-1-0	Rose Bowl	J1	lost to # 2 Stanford 13-21	11	8-2-0
8	Northwestern	6-2-0				12	6-2-0
9	Mississippi State	8-0-1	Orange Bowl	J1	beat # 13 Georgetown 14-7	7	10-0-1
10	Washington	7-2-0				19	7-2-0
11	Santa Clara	6-1-1				20	6-1-1
12	Fordham	7-1-0	Cotton Bowl	J1	lost to # 6 Texas A&M 12-13	13	7-2-0
13	Georgetown	8-1-0	Orange Bowl	J1	lost to # 9 Mississippi State 7-14	21	8-2-0
14	Pennsylvania	6-1-1				14	6-1-1
15	Cornell	6-2-0				17	6-2-0
16	SMU	7-1-1				8	8-1-1
17	Hardin-Simmons	9-0-0				22	9-0-0
18	Duke	7-2-0				16	7-2-0
19	Lafayette	9-0-0				15	9-0-0

1940

Consensus All-Americans

POS	Name	HT	WT	School	AA	AP	CM	IN	LM	NE	NW	SN	UP
B	Tom Harmon	6-0	195	Michigan	•	•	•	•	•	•	•	•	•
B	John Kimbrough	6-2	221	Texas A&M	•	•	•	•	•	•	•	•	•
B	Frank Albert	5-9	170	Stanford	•	•	•	•	•		•	•	•
B	George Franck	6-0	175	Minnesota	•	•	•	•			•	•	•
E	Gene Goodreault	5-10	184	Boston College	•		•	•				•	•
E	Dave Rankin	6-1	190	Purdue	•			•			•	•	•
T	Nick Drahos	6-3	212	Cornell	•	•	•	•		•	•	•	•
T	Alf Bauman	6-1	210	Northwestern	•	•			•				
T	Urban Odson	6-3	247	Minnesota					•	•	•		•
G	Bob Suffridge	6-0	190	Tennessee	•	•	•	•	•	•	•	•	•
G	Marshall Robnett	6-1	205	Texas A&M	•					•		•	•
C	Rudy Mucha	6-2	210	Washington	•	•		•			•	•	•

	Others receiving first-team honors		
B	Francis Reagan	Pennsylvania	
B	Charles O'Rourke	Boston College	
B	Hugh Gallarneau	Stanford	
E	Paul Severin	North Carolina	
E	Buddy Elrod	Mississippi State	
E	Ed Frutig	Michigan	
E	Jay MacDowell	Washington	
T	Bob Reinhard	California	
T	Forrest Behm	Nebraska	
T	Mike Enich	Iowa	
G	Warren Alfson	Nebraska	
G	Augie Lio	Georgetown	
G	Ray Frankowski	Washington	
G	Helge Pukema	Minnesota	
G	Ed Molinski	Tennessee	
C	Chet Gladchuk	Boston College	
C	Ray Frick	Pennsylvania	
C	Leon Gajecki	Penn State	

Heisman Trophy Voting

	PLAYER	POS	SCHOOL	TOTAL
1	Tom Harmon	HB	Michigan	1303
2	John Kimbrough	RB	Texas A&M	841
3	George Franck	HB	Minnesota	102
4	Frankie Albert	QB	Stanford	90
5	Paul Christman	QB	Missouri	66

Award Winners

PLAYER	POS	SCHOOL	AWARD NAME
Tom Harmon	HB	Michigan	Maxwell

Conference Standings

Big 10

	CONF. W L T			OVERALL W L T		
Minnesota	6	0	0	8	0	0
Michigan	3	1	0	7	1	0
Northwestern	4	2	0	6	2	0
Wisconsin	3	3	0	4	4	0
Ohio State	3	3	0	4	4	0
Iowa	2	3	0	4	4	0
Indiana	2	3	0	3	5	0
Purdue	1	4	0	2	6	0
Illinois	0	5	0	1	7	0

Big 6

	CONF. W L T			OVERALL W L T		
Nebraska	5	0	0	8	2	0
Oklahoma	4	1	0	6	3	0
Missouri	3	2	0	6	3	0
Iowa State	2	3	0	4	5	0
Kansas State	1	4	0	2	7	0
Kansas	0	5	0	2	7	0

Border

	CONF. W L T			OVERALL W L T		
Arizona State	3	0	1	7	2	2
Arizona	3	1	0	7	2	0
Texas-El Paso	3	1	1	4	4	1
New Mexico	4	2	0	5	4	0
New Mexico State	1	4	0	3	6	0
Texas Tech	0	1	0	9	1	1
Northern Arizona	0	5	0	2	6	0

Mountain States

	CONF. W L T			OVERALL W L T		
Utah	5	1	0	7	2	0
Denver	4	1	1	6	2	1
Colorado	4	1	1	5	3	1
Brigham Young	2	3	1	2	4	2
Utah State	2	4	0	2	5	1
Colorado State	1	3	2	3	5	2
Wyoming	0	5	1	1	7	1

Pacific Coast

	CONF. W L T			OVERALL W L T		
Stanford	7	0	0	10	0	0
Washington	7	1	0	7	2	0
Oregon State	4	3	1	5	3	1
Washington State	3	4	2	4	4	2
Oregon	3	4	1	4	4	1
California	3	4	0	4	6	0
Southern Cal	2	3	2	3	4	2
Montana	1	2	0	4	4	1
UCLA	1	6	0	1	9	0
Idaho	0	4	0	1	7	1

SEC

	CONF. W L T			OVER. W L T		
Tennessee	5	0	0	10	1	0
Mississippi State	4	0	1	10	0	1
Mississippi	3	1	0	9	2	0
Alabama	4	2	0	7	2	0
Auburn	3	2	1	6	4	1
LSU	3	3	0	6	4	0
Georgia	2	3	1	5	4	1
Florida	2	3	0	5	5	0
Kentucky	1	2	2	5	3	2
Tulane	1	3	0	5	5	0
Georgia Tech	1	5	0	3	7	0
Vanderbilt	0	5	1	3	6	1
Sewanee	0	1	0	3	5	0

Southern

	CONF. W L T			OVERALL W L T		
Clemson	4	0	0	6	2	1
Duke	4	1	0	7	2	0
Wake Forest	4	2	0	7	3	0
William & Mary	2	1	1	6	2	1
Richmond	3	2	0	7	3	0
North Carolina	3	2	0	6	4	0
Virginia Tech	2	3	0	5	5	0
North Carolina St.	3	5	0	3	6	0
South Carolina	1	3	0	3	6	0
Maryland	0	1	1	2	6	1
Davidson	1	5	0	5	5	0
Citadel	0	4	0	5	4	0

SWC

	CONF. W L T			OVERALL W L T		
Texas A&M	5	1	0	9	1	0
SMU	5	1	0	8	1	1
Texas	4	2	0	8	2	0
Rice	4	2	0	7	3	0
TCU	2	4	0	3	7	0
Arkansas	1	5	0	4	6	0
Baylor	0	6	0	4	6	0

Independents

	OVERALL W L T		
Boston College	11	0	0
Lafayette	9	0	0
Hardin-Simmons	9	0	0
Santa Clara	6	1	1
Penn State	6	1	1
Pennsylvania	6	1	1
Georgetown	8	2	0
Notre Dame	7	2	0
Detroit	7	2	0
Fordham	7	2	0
Cornell	6	2	0
Navy	6	2	1
Princeton	5	2	1
North Texas	6	3	0
Columbia	5	2	2
Brown	6	3	1
Rutgers	5	3	0
Harvard	3	2	3
Dartmouth	5	4	0
Memphis	5	5	0
West Virginia	4	4	1
Virginia	4	5	0
Pittsburgh	3	4	1
Syracuse	3	4	1
Michigan State	3	4	1
Miami, Fla.	3	7	0
Army	1	7	1
Yale	1	7	0

Bowl Games

DATE	GAME	SCORE
J1	Orange	Mississippi State 14, Georgetown 7
J1	Rose	Stanford 21, Nebraska 13
J1	Sugar	Boston College 19, Tennessee 13
J1	Cotton	Texas A&M 13, Fordham 12
J1	Sun	Case Western Reserve 26, Arizona State 13

1940 NCAA MAJOR COLLEGE STATISTICAL LEADERS

INDIVIDUAL LEADERS

PASSING/COMPLETIONS

		G	ATT	COM	PCT	INT	I%	YDS	YPA	COM.PG
1	Billy Sewell, Washington State	10	174	86	49.4	17	9.8	1023	5.9	8.6
2	David Allerdice, Princeton	8	144	76	52.8	17	11.8	989	6.9	9.5
2	Johnny Supulski, Manhattan	9	148	76	51.4	17	11.5	1190	8.0	8.4
4	Paul Christman, Missouri	9	154	69	44.8	14	9.1	1131	7.3	7.7
5	Bill Dudley, Virginia	9	140	67	47.9	9	6.4	722	5.2	7.4
6	Andy Tomasic, Temple	9	115	56	48.7	11	9.6	646	5.6	6.2
7	Ray Mallouf, SMU	10	107	54	50.5	9	8.4	692	6.5	5.4
8	Harold Hursh, Indiana	8	111	53	47.7	10	9.0	699	6.3	6.6
9	Jack Jacobs, Oklahoma	9	99	49	49.5	12	12.1	584	5.9	5.4
10	Marion Pugh, Texas A&M	9	86	48	55.8	5	5.8	653	7.6	5.3

ALL-PURPOSE YARDS

		G	RUSH	REC	INT	PR	KR	YDS	YPG
1	Tom Harmon, Michigan	8	844	0	20	244	204	1312	164.0

RUSHING/YARDS

		G	ATT	YDS	AVG	YPG
1	Al Ghesquiere, Detroit	9	146	957	6.6	106.3
2	Tom Harmon, Michigan	8	186	844	4.5	105.5
3	Johnny Knolla, Creighton	10	181	813	4.5	81.3
4	Merle Hapes, Mississippi	11	120	807	6.7	73.4
5	Bob Westfall, Michigan	8	190	807	4.2	100.9
6	Harvey Johnson, Mississippi State	10	117	721	6.2	72.1
7	Tony Gallovich, Wake Forest	10	124	709	5.7	70.9
8	Bobby Robertson, Southern Cal	9	147	694	4.7	77.1
9	Jim Reynolds, Oklahoma State	10	202	685	3.4	68.5
10	John Polanski, Wake Forest	10	147	655	4.5	65.5

RUSHING/YARDS PER CARRY

		G	ATT	YDS	YPC
1	James Farrell, Lafayette	9	81	585	7.2
2	Merle Hapes, Mississippi	11	120	807	6.7
3	Al Ghesquiere, Detroit	9	146	957	6.6
4	Bud Nygren, San Jose State	12	100	624	6.2
5	Harvey Johnson, Mississippi State	10	117	721	6.2
6	Walter Zirinski, Lafayette	9	108	638	5.9
7	Tony Gallovich, Wake Forest	10	124	709	5.7
8	Hugh Gallarneau, Stanford	9	106	597	5.6
9	Francis Reagan, Pennsylvania	8	124	652	5.3
10	Len Eshmont, Fordham	8	118	620	5.3

*-Based on top 20 rushers

RECEIVING/RECEPTIONS

		G	REC	YDS	YPR	YPG	RPG
1	Eddie Bryant, Virginia	9	30	222	7.4	24.7	3.3
2	Steve Lach, Duke	9	26	333	12.8	37.0	2.9
3	Bill Jennings, Oklahoma	9	26	292	11.2	32.4	2.9
4	Lenny Krouse, Penn State	8	25	420	16.8	52.5	3.1
4	Dick Humbert, Richmond	9	25	390	15.6	43.3	2.8
6	Don Vosberg, Marquette	9	24	526	21.9	58.4	2.7
7	Johnny Allen, San Jose State	12	21	373	17.8	31.1	1.8
7	Nick Gianakos, Virginia	9	21	296	14.1	32.9	2.3
7	Felix Fletcher, Washington State	10	20	274	13.7	27.4	2.0
7	Don Greeley, Washington State	10	20	188	9.4	18.8	2.0
9	Phil Roach, TCU	10	20	179	9.0	17.9	2.0

PUNTING

		PUNT	YDS	AVG
1	Owen Price, Texas-El Paso	30	1440	48.0
2	Jack Jacobs, Oklahoma	33	1483	44.9
3	Dick McGowen, Auburn	43	1879	43.7
4	Sherwood Fries, Colorado State	60	2553	42.6
5	Paul McClung, Colorado	41	1722	42.0
6	Norm Standlee, Stanford	28	1171	41.8
7	Don Scott, Ohio State	39	1630	41.8
8	Art Jones, Richmond	65	2713	41.7
9	Steve Lach, Duke	31	1280	41.3
10	Leonard Isberg, Oregon	36	1484	41.2

PUNT RETURNS/YARDS

		PR	YDS	AVG
1	Junie Hovious, Mississippi	33	498	15.1
2	Art Jones, Richmond	33	481	14.6
3	Tony Gallovich, Wake Forest	35	429	12.3
4	Ernie Steele, Washington	30	425	14.2
5	Eddie Bryant, Virginia	28	421	15.0
6	Marvin Bell, Utah State	35	408	11.7
7	Jackie Robinson, UCLA	19	399	21.0
8	Bill Geyer, Colgate	34	392	11.5
9	George Moyer, Lafayette	28	388	13.9
10	Johnny Knolla, Creighton	36	378	10.5

KICKOFF RETURNS/YARDS

		KR	YDS	AVG
1	Jack Emigh, Montana	18	395	21.9
2	Noah Mullins, Kentucky	11	394	35.8
3	Bill Dudley, Virginia	14	356	25.4
4	Bill Geyer, Colgate	13	351	27.0
5	George Franck, Minnesota	6	305	50.8
6	George Nixon, Idaho	11	286	26.0
7	Leo Stasica, Colorado	8	269	33.6
8	Chuck Peters, Penn State	5	261	52.2
9	Johnny Knolla, Creighton	11	257	23.4
10	Leland Morris, Syracuse	6	246	41.0

SCORING

		TDS	XPT	FG	PTS
1	Tom Harmon, Michigan	16	18	1	117
2	Francis Reagan, Pennsylvania	17	1	0	103
3	Walter Zirinski, Lafayette	10	14	3	83
4	Frank Maznicki, Boston College	10	19	0	79
5	Merle Hapes, Mississippi	12	0	0	72
6	Mike Holovak, Boston College	11	1	0	67
7	Junie Hovious, Mississippi	9	11	0	65
8	Tony Gallovich, Wake Forest	9	9	0	63
9	John Martin, Oklahoma	10	0	0	60
9	Owen Price, Texas-El Paso	10	0	0	60

INTERCEPTIONS

		INT	YDS
1	Dick Morgan, Tulsa	7	210
1	Jack Crain, Texas	7	160
1	Junie Hovious, Mississippi	7	146
1	Joe Muha, VMI	7	108
1	John Hanna, Santa Clara	7	92
1	Walter Williams, Boston U.	7	72
1	Noble Doss, Texas	7	33
8	E.H. Wheeler, Virginia Tech*	6	84
8	Bill Dudley, Virginia*	6	83
8	T.A. Weems, Rice*	6	79

* Eight tied with 6; these three players had the most yards.

TEAM LEADERS

RUSHING OFFENSE

		G	ATT	YDS	AVG	YPG
1	Lafayette	9	492	2758	5.6	306.4
2	Texas Tech	10	580	2637	4.5	263.7
3	Detroit	9	495	2183	4.4	242.6
4	Michigan	8	471	1921	4.1	240.1
5	Tennessee	10	476	2394	5.0	239.4
6	Navy	9	525	2019	3.8	224.3
7	Penn State	8	423	1785	4.2	223.1
8	Minnesota	8	407	1782	4.4	222.8
9	Boston College	10	489	2227	4.6	222.7
10	Colgate	8	425	1767	4.2	220.9

PASSING OFFENSE/YPG

		G	ATT	COM	INT	PCT	YDS	YPA	YPG	I%	YPC
1	Cornell	8	152	83	14	54.6	1490	9.8	186.3	9.2	18.0
2	Georgia	8	175	74	17	42.3	1164	6.7	145.5	9.7	15.7
3	Manhattan	9	179	87	20	48.6	1292	7.2	143.6	11.2	14.9
4	Texas-El Paso	9	201	89	15	44.3	1280	6.4	142.2	7.5	14.4
5	Missouri	9	174	75	15	43.1	1248	7.2	138.7	8.6	16.6
6	Marquette	9	185	72	21	38.9	1227	6.6	136.3	11.4	17.0
7	Princeton	8	169	80	20	47.3	1066	6.3	133.3	11.8	13.3
8	Georgia Tech	7	164	67	15	40.9	905	5.5	129.3	9.2	13.5
9	Washington, Mo.	9	168	77	15	45.8	1144	6.8	127.1	8.9	14.9
10	Washington State	10	210	99	22	47.1	1206	5.7	120.6	10.5	12.2

TOTAL OFFENSE

		G	P	YDS	AVG	YPG
1	Lafayette	9	577	3314	5.7	368.
2	Cornell	8	496	2945	5.9	368.
3	Texas Tech	10	701	3376	4.8	337.
4	Detroit	9	661	2901	4.4	322.
5	Boston College	10	623	3177	5.1	317.
6	Navy	9	690	2850	4.1	316.
7	Missouri	9	550	2799	5.1	311.
8	Texas-El Paso	9	614	2790	4.5	310.
9	Mississippi	11	611	3406	5.6	309.
10	Duke	9	518	2783	5.4	309.

RUSHING DEFENSE

		G	ATT	YDS	AVG	YPG
1	Texas A&M	9	305	399	1.3	44.3
2	Navy	9	249	443	1.8	49.2
3	Mississippi State	10	350	505	1.4	50.5
4	Santa Clara	8	241	429	1.8	53.6
5	Arizona	9	320	488	1.5	54.2
6	Boston College	10	334	600	1.8	60.0
7	Detroit	9	300	572	1.9	63.6
8	San Jose State	12	383	834	2.2	69.5
9	Lafayette	9	307	634	2.1	70.4
10	Duquesne	7	218	498	2.3	71.1

PASSING DEFENSE

		G	ATT	COM	PCT	YPC	INT	I%	YDS	YPA	YPG
1	Harvard	8	101	27	26.7	9.9	20	19.8	266	2.6	33.3
2	Utah State	7	71	24	33.8	11.3	6	8.5	272	3.8	38.9
3	Indiana	8	67	22	32.8	15.8	11	16.4	347	5.2	43.4
4	West Virginia	9	81	34	42.0	11.9	10	12.4	403	5.0	44.8
5	Montana	7	62	22	35.5	14.4	12	19.4	316	5.1	45.1
6	Richmond	8	108	38	35.2	9.6	12	11.1	363	3.4	45.4
7	Michigan	8	86	24	27.9	15.6	16	18.6	374	4.3	46.8
8	Navy	9	94	35	37.2	12.0	13	13.8	421	4.5	46.8
9	Wake Forest	10	111	34	30.6	13.9	11	9.9	471	4.2	47.1
10	Cornell	8	113	42	37.2	9.0	24	21.2	380	3.4	47.5

TOTAL DEFENSE

		G	P	YDS	AVG	YPG
1	Navy	9	343	864	2.5	96.
2	Santa Clara	8	360	876	2.4	109.
3	Boston College	10	468	1117	2.4	111.
4	San Jose State	12	546	1517	2.8	126.
5	Mississippi State	10	533	1270	2.4	127.
6	Penn State	8	324	1073	3.3	134.
7	Tennessee	10	499	1365	2.7	136.
8	Alabama	9	454	1246	2.7	138.
9	Detroit	9	436	1260	2.9	140.
10	Nebraska	9	409	1299	3.2	144.

SCORING OFFENSE

		G	PTS	AVG
1	Boston College	10	320	32.0
2	Tennessee	10	318	31.8
3	Georgetown	9	273	30.3
4	Lafayette	9	238	26.4
5	Michigan	8	196	24.5

*Based on top 15 teams in winning percentage.

SCORING DEFENSE

		G	PTS	AVG
1	Tennessee	10	26	2.6
2	Lafayette	9	33	3.7
3	Texas A&M	9	34	3.8
4	Georgetown	9	37	4.1
5	Michigan	8	34	4.3

*Based on top 15 teams in winning percentage.

1941 POLL PROGRESSION

AP October 13 Poll / Oct. 18 Games

	Team	Record	Oct. 18 Games
1	Minnesota	2-0-0	beat Pittsburgh 39-0
2	Texas	3-0-0	beat Arkansas 48-14
3	Duke	3-0-0	beat Colgate 27-14
4	Fordham	2-0-0	beat West Virginia 27-0
5	Northwestern	2-0-0	lost to #6 Michigan 7-14
6	Michigan	3-0-0	beat #5 Northwestern 14-7
7	Navy	3-0-0	beat Cornell 14-0
8	Notre Dame	3-0-0	beat Carnegie Tech 16-0
9	Santa Clara	3-0-0	beat Michigan State 7-0
10	Ohio State	2-0-0	beat Purdue 16-14
11	Pennsylvania	2-0-0	beat Princeton 23-0
12	Rice	2-0-0	lost to LSU 0-27
13	Clemson	4-0-0	bye week
14	Texas A&M	3-0-0	beat TCU 14-0
15	Nebraska	2-0-0	lost to Indiana 13-21
16	Oregon State	2-1-0	bye week
17	Tulane	2-1-0	beat North Carolina 52-6
18	Vanderbilt	3-0-0	beat Georgia Tech 14-7
19	Mississippi State	2-0-1	beat Union 56-7
20	Columbia	2-0-0	lost to Georgia 3-7

AP October 20 Poll / Oct. 25 Games

	Team	Record	Oct. 25 Games
1	Minnesota	3-0-0	beat #3 Michigan 7-0
2	Texas	4-0-0	beat Rice 40-0
3	Michigan	4-0-0	lost to #1 Minnesota 0-7
4	Duke	4-0-0	beat Pittsburgh 27-7
5	Navy	4-0-0	tied Harvard 0-0
6	Fordham	3-0-0	beat TCU 28-14
7	Notre Dame	4-0-0	beat Illinois 49-14
8	Santa Clara	4-0-0	lost to Oklahoma 6-16
9	Texas A&M	4-0-0	beat Baylor 48-0
10	Tulane	3-1-0	lost to Mississippi 13-20
11	Ohio State	3-0-0	lost to #13 Northwestern 7-14
12	Pennsylvania	3-0-0	beat Maryland 55-6
13	Northwestern	2-1-0	beat #11 Ohio State 14-7
14	Clemson	4-0-0	lost to South Carolina 14-18
15	Vanderbilt	4-0-0	beat Princeton 46-7
16	Oregon	3-1-0	lost to UCLA 7-14
17	Temple	4-0-0	beat Bucknell 41-14
18	Oregon State	2-1-0	lost to Washington State 0-7
19	Stanford	3-1-0	beat Washington 13-7
19	Villanova	3-0-0	lost to Manhattan 6-9

AP October 27 Poll / Nov. 1 Games

	Team	Record	Nov. 1 Games
1	Minnesota	4-0-0	beat #9 Northwestern 8-7
1	Texas	5-0-0	beat #20 SMU 34-0
3	Fordham	4-0-0	beat Purdue 17-0
4	Duke	5-0-0	beat Georgia Tech 14-0
5	Texas A&M	5-0-0	beat Arkansas 7-0
6	Notre Dame	5-0-0	tied #14 Army 0-0
7	Michigan	4-1-0	beat Illinois 20-0
8	Pennsylvania	4-0-0	lost to #11 Navy 6-13
9	Northwestern	3-1-0	lost to #1 Minnesota 7-8
10	Vanderbilt	5-0-0	lost to Tulane 14-34
11	Navy	4-0-1	beat #8 Pennsylvania 13-6
12	Stanford	4-1-0	beat Santa Clara 27-7
13	Temple	5-0-0	lost to Boston College 0-31
14	Army	4-0-0	tied #6 Notre Dame 0-0
15	Alabama	4-1-0	Beat Kentucky 30-0
16	Duquesne	5-0-0	beat Villanova 7-0
17	Mississippi	3-1-1	beat Marquette 12-6
17	Mississippi State	3-0-1	beat Southwestern 20-6
19	Missouri	4-1-0	beat Michigan State 19-0
20	SMU	3-1-0	lost to #2 Texas 0-34

AP November 3 Poll / Nov. 8 Games

	Team	Record	Nov. 8 Games
1	Texas	6-0-0	tied Baylor 7-7
2	Minnesota	5-0-0	beat Nebraska 9-0
3	Fordham	5-0-0	lost to Pittsburgh 0-13
4	Duke	6-0-0	beat Davidson 56-0
5	Texas A&M	6-0-0	beat SMU 21-10
6	Navy	5-0-1	lost to #7 Notre Dame 13-20
7	Notre Dame	5-0-1	beat #6 Navy 20-13
8	Michigan	5-1-0	bye week
9	Stanford	5-1-0	beat Southern Cal 13-0
10	Northwestern	3-2-0	beat Indiana 20-14
11	Army	4-0-1	lost to Harvard 6-20
12	Duquesne	6-0-0	beat Saint Mary's-Cal 9-0
13	Alabama	5-1-0	beat #14 Tulane 19-14
14	Tulane	4-2-0	lost to #13 Alabama 14-19
15	Mississippi State	4-0-1	beat Auburn 14-7
16	Mississippi	4-1-1	beat LSU 13-12
17	Missouri	5-1-0	beat NYU 26-0
18	Syracuse	5-1-0	lost to Penn State 19-34
19	Pennsylvania	4-1-0	beat Columbia 19-16
20	Ohio State	4-1-0	beat Wisconsin 46-34

AP November 10 Poll / Nov. 15 Games

	Team	Record	Nov. 15 Games
1	Minnesota	6-0-0	beat Iowa 34-13
2	Texas	6-0-1	lost to TCU 7-14
3	Duke	7-0-0	beat North Carolina 20-0
4	Texas A&M	7-0-0	beat Rice 19-6
5	Notre Dame	6-0-1	beat #8 Northwestern 7-6
6	Stanford	6-1-0	lost to Washington State 13-14
7	Michigan	5-1-0	beat Columbia 28-0
8	Northwestern	4-2-0	lost to #5 Notre Dame 6-7
9	Alabama	6-1-0	beat Georgia Tech 20-0
10	Duquesne	7-0-0	beat #13 Mississippi State 16-0
11	Fordham	5-1-0	bye week
12	Navy	5-1-0	bye week
13	Mississippi State	5-0-1	lost to #10 Duquesne 0-16
14	Pennsylvania	5-1-0	beat #19 Army 14-7
15	Mississippi	5-1-0	bye week
16	Missouri	6-1-0	beat Oklahoma 28-0
17	Harvard	3-2-1	beat Brown 23-7
18	Boston College	5-2-0	lost to Tennessee 7-14
19	Army	4-1-1	lost to #14 Pennsylvania 7-14
20	Ohio State	5-1-0	beat Illinois 12-7

AP November 17 Poll / Nov. 22 Games

	Team	Record	Nov. 22 Games
1	Minnesota	7-0-0	beat Wisconsin 41-6
2	Texas A&M	8-0-0	bye week
3	Duke	8-0-0	beat North Carolina St. 55-6
4	Notre Dame	7-0-1	beat Southern Cal 20-18
5	Michigan	6-1-0	tied #14 Ohio State 20-20
6	Duquesne	8-0-0	regular season complete
7	Alabama	7-1-0	lost to Vanderbilt 0-7
8	Missouri	7-1-0	beat Kansas 45-6
9	Texas	6-1-1	bye week
10	Northwestern	4-3-0	beat Illinois 27-0
11	Navy	5-1-1	beat Princeton 23-0
12	Pennsylvania	6-1-0	beat Cornell 16-0
14	Ohio State	6-1-0	tied #5 Michigan 20-20
15	Mississippi	5-1-1	beat Arkansas 18-0
16	Oregon State	6-2-0	beat Montana 27-0
17	Stanford	6-2-0	bye week
18	Clemson	6-1-0	beat Furman 34-6
19	TCU	6-2-0	tied Rice 0-0
20	Georgia	6-1-1	beat Dartmouth 35-0
20	Washington	4-3-0	lost to Oregon 16-19

AP November 24 Poll / Nov. 29 Games

	Team	Record	Nov. 29 Games
1	Minnesota	8-0-0	regular season complete
2	Texas A&M	8-0-0	lost to #10 Texas 0-23
3	Duke	9-0-0	regular season complete
4	Notre Dame	8-0-1	regular season complete
5	Duquesne	8-0-0	
6	Michigan	6-1-1	regular season complete
7	Missouri	8-1-0	regular season complete
8	Fordham	6-1-0	beat NYU 30-9
9	Northwestern	5-3-0	regular season complete
10	Texas	6-1-1	beat #2 Texas A&M 23-0
11	Navy	6-1-1	beat Army 14-6
12	Vanderbilt	8-1-0	lost to Tennessee 7-26
13	Pennsylvania	7-1-0	regular season complete
14	Mississippi	6-1-1	lost to Miss. St. 0-6
15	Ohio State	6-1-1	regular season complete
16	Clemson	7-1-0	lost to Auburn 7-28
17	Oregon State	6-2-0	beat Oregon 12-7
18	Alabama	7-2-0	beat Miami, Fla. 21-7
19	Harvard	5-2-1	regular season complete
20	Georgia	7-1-1	beat Georgia Tech 21-0

AP December 1 Final Poll

	Team	Record	Bowl Bid	Date	Bowl Result	RB	Record
1	Minnesota	8-0-0				1	8-0-0
2	Duke	9-0-0	Rose Bowl	J1	lost to #12 Oregon State 16-20	8	9-1-0
3	Notre Dame	8-0-1				5	8-0-1
4	Texas	7-1-1				2	8-1-1
5	Michigan	6-1-1				6	6-1-1
6	Fordham	7-1-0	Sugar Bowl	J1	beat #7 Missouri 2-0	10	8-1-0
7	Missouri	8-1-0	Sugar Bowl	J1	lost to #6 Fordham 0-2	21	8-2-0
8	Duquesne	8-0-0				12	8-0-0
9	Texas A&M	8-1-0	Cotton Bowl	J1	lost to #20 Alabama 21-29	4	9-2-0
10	Navy	7-1-1				14	7-1-1
11	Northwestern	5-3-0				20	5-3-0
12	Oregon State	7-2-0	Rose Bowl	J1	beat #2 Duke 20-16	7	8-2-0
13	Ohio State	6-1-1				15	6-1-1
14	Georgia	8-1-1	Orange Bowl	J1	beat TCU 40-26	18	9-1-1
15	Pennsylvania	7-1-0				11	7-1-0
16	Mississippi State	7-1-1				9	8-1-1
17	Mississippi	6-2-1				22	6-2-1
18	Tennessee	8-2-0				13	8-2-0
19	Washington State	6-3-0				16	6-4-0
20	Alabama	8-2-0	Cotton Bowl	J1	beat #9 Texas A&M 29-21	3	9-2-0

1941

CONSENSUS ALL-AMERICANS

POS	Name	HT	WT	School	AA	AP	CM	IN	LM	NE	NW	SN	UP
B	Bob Westfall	5-8	190	Michigan	•		•	•	•	•	•	•	•
B	Bruce Smith	6-0	193	Minnesota	•	•	•	•	•	•	•		•
B	Frank Albert	5-9	173	Stanford	•	•	•	•		•	•	•	•
B	Bill Dudley	5-10	175	Virginia		•	•		•	•	•		•
B	Frank Sinkwich	5-8	180	Georgia	•	•				•			•
E	Holt Rast	6-1	185	Alabama	•		•	•	•	•	•		•
E	Bob Dove	6-2	195	Notre Dame	•		•			•		•	•
T	Dick Wildung	6-0	210	Minnesota	•	•	•	•	•	•	•	•	•
T	Ernie Blandin	6-3	245	Tulane			•		•	•	•	•	•
G	Endicott Peabody	6-0	181	Harvard	•	•	•	•	•	•	•		•
G	Ray Frankowski	5-10	210	Washington	•					•	•		•
C	Darold Jenkins	6-0	195	Missouri	•	•				•	•		•

	OTHERS RECEIVING FIRST-TEAM HONORS		
B	Steve Lach	Duke	• • •
B	Derace Moser	Texas A&M	•
E	Dave Schreiner	Wisconsin	•
E	Malcolm Kutner	Texas	• •
E	John Rokisky	Duquesne	• • •
E	Jim Lansing	Fordham	•
E	Joe Blalock	Clemson	•
T	Alf Bauman	Northwestern	• •
T	Bob Reinhard	California	• • •
G	Ralph Fife	Pittsburgh	•
G	Bernie Crimmins	Notre Dame	• • •
G	Chal Daniel	Texas	• • •
C	Vince Banonis	Detroit	• • •

HEISMAN TROPHY VOTING

	PLAYER	POS	SCHOOL	TOTAL
1	Bruce Smith	HB	Minnesota	554
2	Angelo Bertelli	QB	Notre Dame	345
3	Frank Albert	QB	Stanford	336
4	Frank Sinkwich	HB	Georgia	249
5	Bill Dudley	HB	Virginia	237
6	Endicott Peabody	G	Harvard	153
7	Edgar Jones	RB	Pittsburgh	151
8	Bob Westfall	FB	Michigan	147
9	Steve Lach	HB	Duke	126
10	Jack Crain	RB	Texas	102

AWARD WINNERS

PLAYER	POS	SCHOOL	AWARD NAME
Bill Dudley	HB	Virginia	Maxwell

CONFERENCE STANDINGS

Big 10

	CONF. W	L	T	OVERALL W	L	T
Minnesota	5	0	0	8	0	0
Ohio State	3	1	1	6	1	1
Michigan	3	1	1	6	1	1
Northwestern	4	2	0	5	3	0
Wisconsin	3	3	0	3	5	0
Iowa	2	4	0	3	5	0
Purdue	1	3	0	2	5	1
Indiana	1	3	0	2	6	0
Illinois	0	5	0	2	6	0

Big 6

	CONF. W	L	T	OVERALL W	L	T
Missouri	5	0	0	8	2	0
Oklahoma	3	2	0	6	3	0
Nebraska	3	2	0	4	5	0
Kansas	2	3	0	3	6	0
Kansas State	1	3	1	2	5	2
Iowa State	0	4	1	2	6	1

Border

	CONF. W	L	T	OVERALL W	L	T
Arizona	5	0	0	7	3	0
Texas Tech	2	0	0	9	2	0
West Texas State	4	1	0	8	2	0
Hardin-Simmons	3	1	0	7	3	1
New Mexico	3	2	1	5	4	1
Texas-El Paso	3	4	0	4	5	1
Arizona State	2	4	1	5	5	1
Northern Arizona	1	5	0	3	5	0
New Mexico State	0	6	0	2	7	0

Mountain States

	CONF. W	L	T	OVERALL W	L	T
Utah	4	0	2	6	0	2
Brigham Young	3	1	2	4	3	2
Denver	3	1	2	4	3	2
Colorado State	3	2	1	4	2	1
Colorado	3	2	1	3	4	1
Wyoming	1	5	0	2	7	1
Utah State	0	6	0	0	8	0

Pacific Coast

	CONF. W	L	T	OVERALL W	L	T
Oregon State	7	2	0	8	2	0
Washington State	5	3	0	6	4	0
Washington	5	3	0	5	4	0
Stanford	4	3	0	6	3	0
Oregon	4	4	0	5	5	0
UCLA	3	4	1	5	5	1
California	3	4	0	4	5	0
Southern Cal	2	4	1	2	6	1
Montana	1	3	0	6	3	0
Idaho	0	4	0	4	5	0

SEC

	CONF. W	L	T	OVERALL W	L	T
Mississippi State	4	0	1	8	1	1
Tennessee	3	1	0	8	2	0
Alabama	5	2	0	9	2	0
Georgia	3	1	1	9	1	1
Mississippi	2	1	1	6	2	1
Vanderbilt	3	2	0	8	2	0
LSU	2	2	2	4	4	2
Tulane	2	3	0	5	4	0
Georgia Tech	2	4	0	3	6	0
Florida	1	3	0	4	6	0
Auburn	0	4	1	4	5	1
Kentucky	0	4	0	5	4	0

Southern

	CONF. W	L	T	OVERALL W	L	T
Duke	5	0	0	9	1	0
South Carolina	4	0	1	4	4	1
Clemson	5	1	0	7	2	0
William & Mary	4	1	0	8	2	0
Virginia Tech	4	2	0	6	4	0
VMI	4	2	0	4	6	0
Wake Forest	4	2	1	5	5	1
North Carolina St.	3	4	2	4	5	2
Furman	2	3	2	3	4	2
Wash. & Lee	1	2	2	1	6	2
North Carolina	2	4	0	3	7	0
Maryland	1	2	0	3	5	1
Davidson	1	5	1	1	6	3
Citadel	0	2	1	4	3	1
George Washington	0	4	1	1	7	1
Richmond	0	6	0	2	7	0

SWC

	CONF. W	L	T	OVERALL W	L	T
Texas A&M	5	1	0	9	2	0
Texas	4	1	1	8	1	1
TCU	4	1	1	7	3	1
Rice	3	2	1	6	3	1
SMU	2	4	0	5	5	0
Baylor	1	4	1	3	6	1
Arkansas	0	6	0	3	7	0

Independents

	OVERALL W	L	T
Duquesne	8	0	0
Notre Dame	8	0	1
Virginia	8	1	0
Fordham	8	1	0
North Texas	7	1	0
Pennsylvania	7	1	0
Navy	7	1	1
Miami, Fla.	8	2	0
Penn State	7	2	0
Rutgers	7	2	0
Temple	7	2	0
Boston College	7	3	0
Syracuse	5	2	1
Harvard	5	2	1
Memphis	6	3	0
Cornell	5	3	0
Michigan State	5	3	1
Army	5	3	1
Dartmouth	5	4	0
Brown	5	4	0
Villanova	4	4	0
West Virginia	4	6	0
Columbia	3	5	0
Pittsburgh	3	6	0
Princeton	2	6	0
Yale	1	7	0

BOWL GAMES

DATE	GAME	SCORE
J1	Cotton	Alabama 29, Texas A&M 21
J1	Orange	Georgia 40, TCU 26
J1	Rose	Oregon Sate 20, Duke 16
J1	Sugar	Fordham 2, Missouri 0
J1	Sun	Tulsa 6, Texas Tech 0

1941 NCAA Major College Statistical Leaders

Individual Leaders

PASSING/COMPLETIONS	G	ATT	COM	PCT	INT	I%	YDS	YPA	COM.PG
1 Bud Schwenk, Washington, Mo.	9	234	114	48.7	19	8.1	1457	6.2	12.7
2 Owen Price, Texas-El Paso	9	208	94	45.2	19	9.1	997	4.8	10.4
3 Angelo Bertelli, Notre Dame	9	124	70	56.5	11	8.9	1037	8.4	7.8
3 Paul Governali, Columbia	8	167	70	41.9	10	6.0	810	4.9	8.8
5 Derace Moser, Texas A&M	10	166	67	40.4	19	11.5	912	5.5	6.7
6 Elmer Madarik, Detroit	9	128	64	50.0	7	5.5	874	6.8	7.1
7 Johnny Podesto, Saint Mary's-Cal	9	142	61	43.0	20	14.1	1000	7.0	6.8
8 John Cochran, Wake Forest	10	139	59	42.4	20	14.4	1125	8.1	5.9
9 Jimmy Richardson, Marquette	9	91	58	63.7	7	7.7	536	5.9	6.4
10 Bill Dudley, Virginia	9	107	57	53.3	8	7.5	856	8.0	6.3

ALL-PURPOSE YARDS	G	RUSH	REC	INT	PR	KR	YDS	YPG
1 Bill Dudley, Virginia	9	968	60	76	481	89	1674	186.0

RUSHING/YARDS	G	ATT	YDS	AVG	YPG
1 Frank Sinkwich, Georgia	10	209	1103	5.3	110.3
2 Bill Dudley, Virginia	9	155	968	6.2	107.6
3 Bob Steuber, Missouri	9	113	855	7.6	95.0
4 John Grigas, Holy Cross	10	179	826	4.6	82.6
5 Pat Harder, Wisconsin	8	142	731	5.1	91.4
6 Bob Westfall, Michigan	8	156	688	4.4	86.0
7 Bill Daley, Minnesota	8	158	685	4.3	85.6
8 Maurice Wade, Missouri	9	105	681	6.5	75.7
9 Andy Tomasic, Temple	9	173	677	3.9	75.2
10 Dick Fisher, Ohio State	8	134	674	5.0	84.3

RUSHING/YARDS PER CARRY	G	ATT	YDS	YPC
1 Bob Steuber, Missouri	9	113	855	7.6
2 Isadore Spector, Utah	8	78	559	7.2
3 Maurice Wade, Missouri	9	105	681	6.5
4 Bill Dudley, Virginia	9	155	968	6.2
5 Harry Ice, Missouri	9	98	603	6.2
6 Frank Sinkwich, Georgia	10	209	1103	5.3
7 George Sutch, Temple	9	107	561	5.2
8 Pat Harder, Wisconsin	8	142	731	5.1
9 Dick Fisher, Ohio State	8	134	674	5.0
10 Bill Busik, Navy	9	124	609	4.9

*-Based on top 20 rushers

RECEIVING/RECEPTIONS	G	REC	YDS	YPR	YPG	RPG
1 Hank Stanton, Arizona	10	50	820	16.4	82.0	5.0
2 Allen Lindow, Washington, Mo.	9	39	472	12.1	52.4	4.3
3 Lenny Krouse, Penn State	9	32	536	16.8	59.6	3.6
4 Bill Pufalt, Washington, Mo.	9	29	405	14.0	45.0	3.2
5 Walter McDonald, Tulane	9	27	437	16.2	48.6	3.0
6 Milton Crain, Baylor	10	26	152	5.8	15.2	2.6
7 Marshall Spivey, Texas A&M	10	25	363	14.5	36.3	2.5
7 Clarence Turley, Washington, Mo.	9	25	262	10.5	29.1	2.8
7 Robert Henderson, Texas A&M	10	25	229	9.2	22.9	2.5
10 Howard Keating, Detroit	9	24	277	11.5	30.8	2.7

PUNTING	PUNT	YDS	AVG
1 Owen Price, Texas-El Paso	40	1813	45.3
2 Merle Hapes, Mississippi	32	1425	44.5
3 Bill Busik, Navy	41	1797	43.8
4 Preston Johnston, SMU	67	2857	42.6
5 Robert Riddell, Denver	35	1465	41.9
6 Booty Payne, Clemson	47	1960	41.7
7 Harry Dunkle, North Carolina	71	2954	41.6
8 Jim Blumenstock, Fordham	62	2571	41.5
9 J.E. Dickson, Rice	63	2603	41.3
10 Emil Banjavcic, Arizona	41	1662	40.5

PUNT RETURNS/YARDS	PR	YDS	AVG
1 Bill Geyer, Colgate	33	616	18.7
2 Bob Margarita, Brown	40	549	13.7
3 Bill Hillenbrand, Indiana	41	524	12.8
4 Bill Dudley, Virginia	28	481	17.2
5 Van Davis, Georgia	36	464	12.9
6 Junie Hovious, Mississippi	36	457	12.7
7 Thomas Roblin, Oregon	30	428	14.3
8 Andy Tomasic, Temple	31	420	13.5
9 Don Austin, Texas Tech	29	397	13.7
10 Henry Mazur, Army	36	387	10.8

KICKOFF RETURNS/YARDS	KR	YDS	AVG
1 Earl Ray, Wyoming	23	496	21.6
2 Bill Geyer, Colgate	15	350	23.3
3 Owen Price, Texas-El Paso	10	282	28.2
4 Monk Gafford, Auburn	13	271	20.8
5 Royal Lohry, Iowa State	9	270	30.0
6 Vern Lockard, Colorado	11	268	24.4
7 Charles McNulty, Manhattan	10	261	26.1
8 John Polanski, Wake Forest	8	257	32.1
9 Harold Stockbridge, Rice	10	253	25.3
9 Stanley Szymakowski, Lehigh	10	245	24.5

SCORING	TDS	XPT	FG	PTS
1 Bill Dudley, Virginia	18	23	1	134
2 Jack Crain, Texas	11	23	1	92
3 Jack Jenkins, Vanderbilt	12	15	1	90
4 Winston Siegfried, Duke	13	2	0	80
5 Charlie Timmons, Clemson	9	23	0	77
6 Van Davis, Georgia	12	1	0	73
7 Pat Harder, Wisconsin	10	9	1	72
7 John Petrella, Penn State	12	0	0	72
9 Bob Steuber, Missouri	9	14	0	68
10 Fred Evans, Notre Dame	11	1	0	67

INTERCEPTIONS	INT	YDS
1 Bobby Robertson, Southern Cal	9	126
1 Bill Sibley, Texas A&M	9	57
3 Clyde Ehrhardt, Georgia	8	162
3 Owen Price, Texas-El Paso	8	124
3 Dale Bradley, Nebraska	8	115
6 Edgar Jones, Pittsburgh*	6	215
6 Bob Dethman, Oregon State*	6	119
6 Andy Tomasic, Temple*	6	83
6 Noble Doss, Texas*	6	82
6 Jack Jacobs, Oklahoma*	6	77

* Eight players tied with 6; these had the most yards.

Team Leaders

RUSHING OFFENSE	G	ATT	YDS	AVG	YPG
1 Missouri	9	488	2769	5.7	307.7
2 Duke	9	498	2392	4.8	265.8
3 Minnesota	8	476	2062	4.3	257.8
4 Utah	8	398	2054	5.2	256.8
5 Syracuse	8	395	2007	5.1	250.9
6 Navy	9	494	2249	4.6	249.9
7 Georgia	10	511	2397	4.7	239.7
8 Texas	10	460	2372	5.2	237.2
9 Clemson	9	437	2132	4.9	236.9
10 Michigan	8	420	1871	4.5	233.9

PASSING OFFENSE/YPG	G	ATT	COM	INT	PCT	YDS	YPA	YPG	I%	YPC
1 Arizona	10	231	106	18	45.9	1777	7.7	177.7	7.8	16.8
2 Texas A&M	10	294	126	30	42.9	1657	5.6	165.7	10.2	13.2
3 Washington, Mo.	9	238	116	20	48.7	1472	6.2	163.6	8.4	12.7
4 Detroit	9	185	94	11	50.8	1307	7.1	145.2	6.0	13.9
5 Notre Dame	9	148	81	14	54.7	1223	8.3	135.9	9.5	15.1
6 Texas-El Paso	9	261	112	27	42.9	1219	4.7	135.4	10.3	10.9
7 Wake Forest	10	197	88	24	44.7	1335	6.8	133.5	12.2	15.2
8 San Francisco	6	102	41	10	40.2	756	7.4	126.0	9.8	18.4
9 Saint Mary's-Cal	9	165	69	23	41.8	1116	6.8	124.0	13.9	16.2
10 SMU	10	200	68	17	34.0	1201	6.0	120.1	8.5	17.7

TOTAL OFFENSE	G	P	YDS	AVG	YPG
1 Duke	9	619	3350	5.4	372.2
2 Arizona	10	668	3573	5.3	357.3
3 Georgia	10	695	3504	5.0	350.4
4 Utah	8	496	2803	5.7	350.4
5 Texas	10	621	3500	5.6	350.0
6 Missouri	9	557	3102	5.6	344.7
7 Tulane	9	640	2951	4.6	327.9
8 Fordham	8	515	2616	5.1	327.0
9 Detroit	9	631	2881	4.6	320.1
10 Clemson	9	559	2879	5.2	319.9

RUSHING DEFENSE	G	ATT	YDS	AVG	YPG
1 Duquesne	8	235	448	1.9	56.0
2 Georgia	10	323	596	1.8	59.6
3 Texas Tech	10	328	617	1.9	61.7
4 Navy	9	311	560	1.8	62.2
5 Texas	10	323	659	2.0	65.9
6 Tulane	9	311	597	1.9	66.3
7 Santa Clara	9	302	598	2.0	66.4
8 Notre Dame	9	340	611	1.8	67.9
9 Utah	8	268	602	2.2	75.3
10 Rice	10	357	812	2.3	81.2

PASSING DEFENSE	G	ATT	COM	PCT	YPC	INT	I%	YDS	YPA	YPG
1 Purdue	8	74	21	28.4	10.3	11	14.9	217	2.9	27.1
2 Boston U.	8	85	23	27.1	12.2	15	17.7	280	3.3	35.0
3 Denver	9	98	34	34.7	10.5	17	17.4	357	3.6	39.7
4 Idaho	9	105	30	28.6	12.4	17	16.2	371	3.5	41.2
5 Lafayette	9	105	39	37.1	10.7	24	22.9	418	4.0	46.4
6 Harvard	8	97	27	27.8	13.9	9	9.3	376	3.9	47.0
7 Florida	8	98	23	23.5	16.6	16	16.3	381	3.9	47.6
8 Mississippi State	7	95	28	29.5	12.0	16	16.8	336	3.5	48.0
9 San Jose State	10	122	40	32.8	12.3	20	16.4	490	4.0	49.0
9 Villanova	7	89	30	33.7	11.4	15	16.9	343	3.9	49.0

TOTAL DEFENSE	G	P	YDS	AVG	YPG
1 Duquesne	8	363	885	2.4	110.6
2 Navy	9	449	1258	2.8	139.8
3 Detroit	9	453	1282	2.8	142.4
4 Notre Dame	9	481	1283	2.7	142.6
5 Georgia	10	499	1429	2.9	142.9
6 Texas Tech	10	512	1432	2.8	143.2
7 Duke	9	433	1311	3.0	145.7
8 San Jose State	10	467	1465	3.1	146.5
9 Virginia	9	496	1362	2.7	151.3
10 Rutgers	8	390	1211	3.1	151.4

SCORING OFFENSE	G	PTS	AVG
1 Duke	9	311	34.6
2 Texas	10	338	33.8
3 Virginia	9	279	31.0
4 Georgia	10	279	27.9
5 Texas A&M	10	266	26.6
6 Utah	8	209	26.1
7 Vanderbilt	10	260	26.0
8 Clemson	9	233	25.9
9 Arizona	10	253	25.3
9 William & Mary	10	253	25.3

SCORING DEFENSE	G	PTS	AVG
1 Duquesne	8	23	2.9
2 Texas Tech	10	30	3.0
3 Oregon State	9	33	3.7
4 Navy	9	34	3.8
5 Missouri	9	37	4.1
6 Duke	9	41	4.6
7 Texas A&M	10	46	4.6
8 Virginia	9	42	4.7
9 Minnesota	8	38	4.8
10 Detroit	9	43	4.8

ANNUAL REVIEW

1942 POLL PROGRESSION

AP October 12 Poll / Oct. 17 Games

#	Team	Record	Result
1	Ohio State	3-0-0	beat Purdue 26-0
2	Georgia	4-0-0	beat Tulane 40-0
3	Michigan	2-1-0	beat Northwestern 34-16
4	Alabama	3-0-0	beat #15 Tennessee 8-0
5	Illinois	3-0-0	beat #19 Iowa 12-7
6	Georgia Tech	3-0-0	beat Davidson 33-0
7	Wisconsin	3-0-1	beat Great Lakes NAS 13-7
8	Pennsylvania	2-1-0	tied Princeton 6-6
9	Colgate	4-0-0	lost to Duke 0-34
10	Washington State	3-0-0	lost to Southern Cal 12-26
11	Boston College	2-0-0	beat N.C. Pre-Flight 7-6
12	Vanderbilt	3-0-0	lost to Mississippi State 0-33
13	Duquesne	3-0-0	lost to North Carolina 6-13
14	Minnesota	1-2-0	beat Nebraska 15-2
15	Santa Clara	3-0-0	beat Oregon State 7-0
16	Tennessee	2-0-1	lost to #4 Alabama 0-8
17	TCU	3-0-0	beat Texas A&M 7-2
18	Army	2-0-0	beat Columbia 34-6
19	Iowa	3-1-0	lost to #5 Illinois 7-12
20	Texas	3-1-0	beat Arkansas 47-6

AP October 19 Poll / Oct. 24 Games

#	Team	Record	Result
1	Ohio State	4-0-0	beat Northwestern 20-6
2	Georgia	5-0-0	beat Cincinnati 35-13
3	Alabama	4-0-0	beat Kentucky 14-0
4	Michigan	3-1-0	lost to #13 Minnesota 14-16
5	Illinois	4-0-0	lost to #8 Notre Dame 14-21
6	Georgia Tech	4-0-0	beat Navy 21-0
7	Wisconsin	4-0-1	beat Purdue 13-0
8	Notre Dame	2-1-1	beat #5 Illinois 21-14
9	Santa Clara	4-0-0	lost to #14 UCLA 6-14
10	Boston College	3-0-0	beat Wake Forest 27-0
11	Army	3-0-0	beat Harvard 14-0
12	TCU	4-0-0	beat Pensacola NAS 21-0
13	Minnesota	2-2-0	beat #4 Michigan 16-14
14	UCLA	2-2-0	beat #9 Santa Clara 14-6
15	Texas	4-1-0	beat Rice 12-7
16	Mississippi State	2-2-0	beat Florida 26-12
17	Pennsylvania	2-1-1	beat Columbia 42-12
17	Tennessee	2-1-1	beat Furman 52-7
19	North Carolina	3-0-1	lost to Tulane 14-29
20	Syracuse	4-0-0	beat Cornell 12-7

AP October 26 Poll / Oct. 31 Games

#	Team	Record	Result
1	Ohio State	5-0-0	lost to Wisconsin 7-17
2	Georgia	6-0-0	beat #3 Alabama 21-10
3	Alabama	5-0-0	lost to #2 Georgia 10-21
4	Notre Dame	3-1-1	beat Navy 9-0
5	Georgia Tech	5-0-0	beat Duke 26-7
6	Wisconsin	5-0-1	beat Ohio State 17-7
7	Boston College	4-0-0	beat Georgetown 47-0
8	Army	4-0-0	lost to #14 Pennsylvania 0-19
9	TCU	5-0-0	lost to Baylor 7-10
10	Minnesota	3-2-0	beat Northwestern 19-7
11	UCLA	3-2-0	beat Stanford 20-7
11	Illinois	4-1-0	lost to #13 Michigan 14-28
13	Michigan	3-2-0	beat #12 Illinois 28-14
14	Pennsylvania	3-1-1	beat #8 Army 19-0
15	Syracuse	5-0-0	lost to N.C. Pre-Flight 0-9
15	Tulsa	5-0-0	beat Drake 40-0
17	Texas	5-1-0	beat SMU 21-7
17	William & Mary	4-0-1	beat Dartmouth 35-14
19	LSU	5-1-0	beat #20 Tennessee 0-26
20	Tennessee	3-1-1	beat #19 LSU 26-0

AP November 2 Poll / Nov. 7 Games

#	Team	Record	Result
1	Georgia	7-0-0	beat Florida 75-0
2	Wisconsin	6-0-1	lost to Iowa 0-6
3	Georgia Tech	6-0-0	beat Kentucky 47-7
4	Notre Dame	4-1-1	beat #19 Army 13-0
5	Boston College	5-0-0	beat Temple 28-0
6	Ohio State	5-1-0	beat Pittsburgh 59-19
7	Minnesota	4-2-0	lost to Indiana 0-7
8	Alabama	5-1-0	beat South Carolina 29-0
9	Pennsylvania	4-1-1	lost to Navy 0-7
10	UCLA	4-2-0	lost to Oregon 7-14
11	Michigan	4-2-0	beat Harvard 35-7
12	Tulsa	6-0-0	beat Oklahoma State 34-6
13	Tennessee	4-1-1	beat Cincinnati 34-12
14	Texas	6-1-0	beat #16 Baylor 20-0
15	Santa Clara	5-1-0	beat Saint Mary's-Cal 20-7
16	Baylor	6-1-0	lost to #14 Texas 0-20
17	William & Mary	5-0-1	beat Randolph Macon 40-0
18	Fresno State	7-0-0	lost to San Francisco 13-33
19	Army	4-1-0	lost to #4 Notre Dame 0-13
20	Illinois	4-2-0	beat Northwestern 14-7

AP November 9 Poll / Nov. 14 Games

#	Team	Record	Result
1	Georgia	8-0-0	beat U.T. Chattanooga 40-0
2	Georgia Tech	7-0-0	beat #5 Alabama 7-0
3	Boston College	6-0-0	beat Fordham 56-6
4	Notre Dame	5-1-1	lost to #6 Michigan 20-32
5	Alabama	6-1-0	lost to #2 Georgia Tech 0-7
6	Michigan	5-2-0	beat #4 Notre Dame 32-20
7	Wisconsin	6-1-1	beat Northwestern 20-19
8	Texas	7-1-0	lost to TCU 7-13
9	Tulsa	7-0-0	beat Baylor 24-0
10	Ohio State	6-1-0	beat #13 Illinois 44-20
11	Tennessee	5-1-1	beat Mississippi 14-0
12	Iowa	6-2-0	lost to Minnesota 7-27
13	Illinois	5-2-0	lost to #10 Ohio State 20-44
14	Washington State	5-1-0	beat Idaho 7-0
15	William & Mary	6-0-1	beat VMI 27-6
16	Minnesota	4-3-0	beat Iowa 27-7
17	Pennsylvania	4-2-1	lost to Penn State 7-13
18	UCLA	4-3-0	bye week
19	Hardin-Simmons	8-0-0	beat Arizona 34-26
20	Williams	7-0-0	lost to Amherst 6-12

AP November 16 Poll / Nov. 21 Games

#	Team	Record	Result
1	Georgia	9-0-0	lost to Auburn 13-27
2	Georgia Tech	8-0-0	beat Florida 20-7
3	Boston College	7-0-0	beat Boston U. 37-0
4	Michigan	6-2-0	beat #5 Ohio State 7-21
5	Ohio State	7-1-0	beat #4 Michigan 21-7
6	Tulsa	8-0-0	beat Creighton 33-19
7	Wisconsin	7-1-1	beat #10 Minnesota 20-6
8	Notre Dame	5-2-1	beat Northwestern 27-20
9	Alabama	6-2-0	beat Vanderbilt 27-7
10	Minnesota	5-3-0	lost to #7 Wisconsin 6-20
11	Tennessee	6-1-1	beat Kentucky 26-0
12	Washington State	6-1-0	tied 2nd Air Force 6-6
13	William & Mary	7-0-1	lost to N.C. Pre-Flight 0-14
14	Santa Clara	6-1-0	lost to St. Mary's Pre-Flight 6-13
15	Texas	7-2-0	bye week
15	Southern Cal	3-3-1	bye week
17	Hardin-Simmons	7-0-0	tied Texas Tech 0-0
18	Indiana	5-3-0	beat Purdue 20-0
18	TCU	6-2-0	lost to Rice 0-21
18	UCLA	4-3-0	beat Washington 14-10

AP November 23 Poll / Nov. 28 Games

#	Team	Record	Result
1	Boston College	8-0-0	lost to Holy Cross 12-55
2	Georgia Tech	9-0-0	lost to #5 Georgia 0-34
3	Ohio State	8-1-0	beat Iowa Pre-Flight 41-12
4	Wisconsin	8-1-1	regular season complete
5	Georgia	9-1-0	beat #2 Georgia Tech 34-0
6	Tulsa	9-0-0	beat Arkansas 40-7
7	Alabama	7-2-0	lost to Georgia Pre-Flight 19-35
8	Notre Dame	6-2-1	beat #14 Southern Cal 13-0
9	Michigan	6-3-0	beat Iowa 28-14
10	Tennessee	7-1-1	beat Vanderbilt 19-7
11	UCLA	5-3-0	bye week
12	Santa Clara	6-2-0	beat Loyola, Marymount 21-0
12	Stanford	5-4-0	beat St. Mary's Pre-Flight 28-13
14	Southern Cal	3-3-1	lost to #8 Notre Dame 0-13
15	Washington State	6-1-1	tied Washington 0-0
16	Auburn	5-4-1	beat Clemson 41-13
16	Mississippi State	7-2-0	beat San Francisco 19-7
18	Texas	7-2-0	beat Texas A&M 12-6
19	William & Mary	7-1-1	beat Richmond 10-0 & beat Oklahoma 14-7
20	Minnesota	5-4-0	regular season complete

AP November 30 Final Poll

#	Team	Record	Bowl Bid	Date	Bowl Result	RB	Record
1	Ohio State	9-1-0				2	9-1-0
2	Georgia	10-1-0	Rose Bowl	J1	beat #13 UCLA 9-0	1	11-1-0
3	Wisconsin	8-1-1				11	8-1-1
4	Tulsa	10-0-0	Sugar Bowl	J1	lost to #7 Tennessee 7-14	12	10-1-0
5	Georgia Tech	9-1-0	Cotton Bowl	J1	lost to #11 Texas 7-14	10	9-2-0
6	Notre Dame	7-2-1				13	7-2-2
7	Tennessee	8-1-1	Sugar Bowl	J1	beat #4 Tulsa 14-7	3	9-1-1
8	Boston College	8-1-0	Orange Bowl	J1	lost to #10 Alabama 21 37	24	8-2-0
9	Michigan	7-3-0				9	7-3-0
10	Alabama	7-3-0	Orange Bowl	J1	beat #8 Boston College 37-21	7	8-3-0
11	Texas	8-2-0	Cotton Bowl	J1	beat #5 Georgia Tech 14-7	4	9-2-0
12	Stanford	6-4-0				19	6-4-0
13	UCLA	5-3-0	Rose Bowl	J1	lost to #2 Georgia 0-9	39	7-4-0
14	William & Mary	9-1-1				18	9-1-1
15	Santa Clara	7-2-0				23	7-2-0
16	Auburn	6-4-1				43	6-4-1
17	Washington State	6-1-2				33	6-2-2
18	Mississippi State	7-2-0				5	8-2-0
19	Holy Cross	5-4-1				48	5-4-1
19	Minnesota	5-4-0				21	5-4-0
19	Penn State	6-1-1				17	6-1-1

1942

Consensus All-Americans

POS	Name	HT	WT	School	AA	AP	CM	IN	LM	NE	NW	SN	UP
B	Frank Sinkwich	5-8	185	Georgia	•	•	•	•	•	•	•	•	•
B	Paul Governali	5-11	186	Columbia	•	•	•				•	•	•
B	Mike Holovak	6-2	214	Boston College	•	•		•		•	•		•
B	Billy Hillenbrand	6-0	195	Indiana	•	•		•					•
E	Dave Schreiner	6-2	198	Wisconsin	•	•	•	•	•	•	•	•	•
E	Bob Dove	6-2	195	Notre Dame	•				•	•		•	•
T	Dick Wildung	6-0	215	Minnesota	•	•	•		•	•	•	•	•
T	Albert Wistert	6-2	205	Michigan	•		•			•		•	•
G	Chuck Taylor	5-11	200	Stanford	•	•			•	•	•		•
G	Harvey Hardy	5-10	185	Georgia Tech					•	•	•		•
G	Julie Franks	6-0	187	Michigan					•	•	•		
C	Joe Domnanovich	6-1	200	Alabama	•	•	•		•		•	•	•

Others receiving first-team honors

B	Pat Harder			Wisconsin	•
B	Glenn Dobbs			Tulsa	• • •
B	Roy Gafford			Auburn	•
B	Bob Kennedy			Washington State	•
B	Angelo Bertelli			Notre Dame	•
B	Jackie Fellows			Fresno State	•
B	Bob Steuber			Missouri	•
E	Bob Shaw			Ohio State	•
E	Don Currivan			Boston College	• •
E	Bernard Kuczynski			Pennsylvania	•
T	Clyde Johnson			Kentucky	•
T	Robin Olds			Army	•
T	Charles Csuri			Ohio State	•
T	Derrell Palmer			TCU	•
T	Don Whitmire			Alabama	•
T	Gil Bouley			Boston College	•
G	Lindell Houston			Ohio State	• •
G	Garrard Ramsey			William and Mary	•
G	Alex Agase			Illinois	• •
G	Merv Pregulman			Michigan	•
C	Fred Naumetz			Boston College	•
C	Spencer Moseley			Yale	•

Heisman Trophy Voting

	PLAYER	POS	SCHOOL	TOTAL
1	Frank Sinkwich	HB	Georgia	1059
2	Paul Governali	QB	Columbia	218
3	Clint Castleberry	RB	Georgia Tech	99
4	Mike Holovak	RB	Boston College	90
5	Bill Hillenbrand	HB	Indiana	86
6	Angelo Bertelli	QB	Notre Dame	75
7	Dick Wildung	T	Minnesota	71
8	Gene Fekete	FB	Ohio State	65
9	Glenn Dobbs	RB	Tulsa	63
10	Dave Schreiner	E	Wisconsin	60

Award Winners

PLAYER	POS	SCHOOL	AWARD NAME
Paul Governali	QB	Columbia	Maxwell

Conference Standings

Big 10

	CONF. W L T	OVERALL W L T
Ohio State	5 1 0	9 1 0
Wisconsin	4 1 0	8 1 1
Michigan	3 2 0	7 3 0
Illinois	3 2 0	6 4 0
Iowa	3 3 0	6 4 0
Minnesota	3 3 0	5 4 0
Indiana	2 2 0	7 3 0
Purdue	1 4 0	1 8 0
Northwestern	0 6 0	1 9 0

Big 6

	CONF. CW GL CT	OVER. W L T
Missouri	4 0 1	8 3 1
Oklahoma	3 1 1	3 5 2
Nebraska	3 2 0	3 7 0
Kansas State	2 3 0	3 8 0
Iowa State	1 4 0	3 6 0
Kansas	1 4 0	2 8 0

Border

	CONF. W L T	OVERALL W L T
Hardin-Simmons	4 0 1	9 1 1
Texas Tech	3 0 1	4 5 1
West Texas State	5 2 0	7 2 0
Arizona	4 2 0	6 4 0
Texas-El Paso	4 3 0	5 4 0
New Mexico	3 4 0	4 5 2
Arizona State	2 5 0	2 8 0
Northern Arizona	1 4 0	1 5 0
New Mexico State	0 6 0	1 8 0

Mountain States

	CONF. W L T	OVERALL W L T
Colorado	5 1 0	7 2 0
Utah	5 1 0	6 3 0
Denver	3 2 1	6 3 1
Utah State	2 3 1	6 3 1
Colorado State	2 3 0	4 3 0
Brigham Young	1 4 0	2 5 0
Wyoming	1 5 0	3 5 0

Pacific Coast

	CONF. W L T	OVERALL W L T
UCLA	6 1 0	7 4 0
Washington State	5 1 1	6 2 2
Stanford	5 2 0	6 4 0
Southern Cal	4 2 1	5 5 1
Oregon State	4 4 0	4 5 1
Washington	3 3 2	4 3 3
California	3 4 0	5 5 0
Oregon	2 5 0	2 6 0
Idaho	1 5 0	3 7 0
Montana	0 6 0	0 8 0

SEC

	CONF. W L T	OVERALL W L T
Georgia	6 1 0	11 1 0
Tennessee	4 1 0	9 1 1
Georgia Tech	4 1 0	9 2 0
Mississippi State	5 2 0	8 2 0
Alabama	4 2 0	8 3 0
LSU	3 2 0	7 3 0
Auburn	3 3 0	6 4 1
Vanderbilt	2 4 0	6 4 0
Florida	1 3 0	3 7 0
Tulane	1 4 0	4 5 0
Kentucky	0 5 0	3 6 1
Mississippi	0 5 0	2 7 0

Southern

	CONF. W L T	OVERALL W L T
William & Mary	4 0 0	9 1 1
Virginia Tech	5 1 0	7 2 1
Wake Forest	6 1 1	6 2 1
North Carolina	3 1 1	5 2 2
Duke	3 1 1	5 4 1
North Carolina St.	3 1 2	4 4 2
Furman	3 3 0	3 6 0
Citadel	2 2 0	5 2 0
Clemson	2 3 1	3 6 1
VMI	2 4 1	3 5 1
Davidson	2 4 1	2 6 1
George Washington	2 4 0	3 6 0
Maryland	1 2 0	7 2 0
South Carolina	1 4 0	1 7 1
Richmond	1 5 0	3 6 1
Wash. & Lee	0 4 0	1 8 0

SWC

	CONF. W L T	OVERALL W L T
Texas	5 1 0	9 2 0
Rice	4 1 1	7 2 1
TCU	4 2 0	7 3 0
Baylor	3 2 1	6 4 1
Texas A&M	2 3 1	4 5 1
SMU	1 4 1	3 6 2
Arkansas	0 6 0	3 7 0

Independents

	OVERALL W L T
Georgia Pre-Flight	7 1 1
Penn State	6 1 1
Boston College	8 2 0
Miami, Fla.	7 2 0
Santa Clara	7 2 0
N.C. Pre-Flight	8 2 1
Jacksonville NAS	9 3 0
Notre Dame	7 2 2
Colgate	6 2 1
Great Lakes NAS	8 3 1
Iowa Pre-Flight	7 3 0
St. Mary's Pre-Flight	7 3 1
Syracuse	6 3 0
Army	6 3 0
Duquesne	6 3 1
Yale	5 3 0
Pennsylvania	5 3 1
West Virginia	5 4 0
Dartmouth	5 4 0
Navy	5 4 0
Michigan State	4 3 2
Holy Cross	5 4 1
Brown	4 4 0
Rutgers	3 4 1
Princeton	3 5 1
Cornell	3 5 1
North Texas	3 5 0
Pittsburgh	3 6 0
Columbia	3 6 0
Virginia	2 6 1
Harvard	2 6 1
Memphis	2 7 0

Bowl Games

DATE	GAME	SCORE
J1	Orange	Alabama 37, Boston College 21
J1	Rose	Georgia 9, UCLA 0
J1	Sugar	Tennessee 14, Tulsa 7
J1	Cotton	Texas 14, Georgia Tech 7
J1	Sun	Second Air Force 13, Hardin-Simmons 7

1942 NCAA MAJOR COLLEGE STATISTICAL LEADERS

INDIVIDUAL LEADERS

PASSING/COMPLETIONS		G	ATT	COM	PCT	INT	I%	YDS	YPA	COM.PG
1	Ray Evans, Kansas	10	200	101	50.5	9	4.5	1117	5.6	10.1
2	Otto Graham, Northwestern	10	182	89	48.9	18	9.9	1092	6.0	8.9
3	Paul Governali, Columbia	9	165	87	52.7	18	10.9	1442	8.7	9.7
4	Frank Sinkwich, Georgia	11	166	84	50.6	7	4.2	1392	8.4	7.6
5	Tabb Gillette, Virginia	9	144	82	56.9	14	9.7	920	6.4	9.1
6	Angelo Bertelli, Notre Dame	11	162	72	44.4	16	9.9	1039	6.4	6.5
7	Vic Clark, Texas-El Paso	9	136	71	52.2	12	8.8	846	6.2	7.9
8	Glenn Dobbs, Tulsa	10	107	67	62.6	4	3.7	1066	10.0	6.7
9	Tom Mont, Maryland	9	127	66	52.0	12	9.5	1076	8.5	7.3
9	Emery Nix, TCU	10	154	66	42.9	9	5.8	672	4.4	6.6

ALL-PURPOSE YARDS	G	RUSH	REC	INT	PR	KR	YDS	YPG
NA								

RUSHING/YARDS		G	ATT	YDS	AVG	YPG
1	Rudy Mobley, Hardin-Simmons	9	187	1281	6.9	142.3
2	Bob Steuber, Missouri	12	149	1098	7.4	91.5
3	Camp Wilson, Hardin-Simmons	9	196	981	5.0	109.0
4	Mike Holovak, Boston College	9	174	965	5.5	107.2
5	Gene Fekete, Ohio State	10	185	910	4.9	91.0
6	Bruce Smith, Great Lakes NAS	12	144	849	5.9	70.8
7	Bob Kennedy, Washington State	10	226	813	3.6	81.3
8	Frank Sinkwich, Georgia	11	175	795	4.5	72.3
9	Elroy Hirsch, Wisconsin	10	141	767	5.4	76.7
10	Roy Dale McKay, Texas	10	132	701	5.3	70.1

RUSHING/YARDS PER CARRY		G	ATT	YDS	YPC
1	Bob Steuber, Missouri	12	149	1098	7.4
2	Charlie Trippi, Georgia	11	98	673	6.9
3	Rudy Mobley, Hardin-Simmons	9	187	1281	6.9
4	Bruce Smith, Great Lakes NAS	12	144	849	5.9
5	Mike Holovak, Boston College	9	174	965	5.5
6	Elroy Hirsch, Wisconsin	10	141	767	5.4
7	Roy Dale McKay, Texas	10	132	701	5.3
8	Jackie Field, Texas	10	122	646	5.3
9	Joe Day, Oregon State	10	123	630	5.1
10	Camp Wilson, Hardin-Simmons	9	196	981	5.0

*-Based on top 15 rushers

RECEIVING/RECEPTIONS		G	REC	YDS	YPR	YPG	RPG
1	Bill Rogers, Texas A&M	10	39	432	11.1	43.2	3.9
2	Albert Salem, Texas-El Paso	9	36	401	11.1	44.6	4.0
3	Sax Judd, Tulsa	10	35	509	14.5	50.9	3.5
4	Van Davis, Georgia	11	33	455	13.8	41.4	3.0
5	Harding Miller, SMU	11	32	531	16.6	48.3	2.9
6	Van Hall, TCU	10	27	231	8.6	23.1	2.7
7	John Ferguson, California	10	26	338	13.0	33.8	2.6
8	Otto Schnellbacher, Kansas	10	25	366	14.6	36.6	2.5
9	George Poschner, Georgia*	10	24	493	20.5	49.3	2.4
9	John Kelleher, Columbia*	9	24	412	17.2	45.8	2.7

*Six players tied with 24; these had the most yards.

PUNTING		PUNT	YDS	AVG
1	Bobby Cifers, Tennessee	37	1586	42.9
2	Art Faircloth, North Carolina St.	54	2279	42.2
3	John Strzykalski, Marquette	42	1760	41.9
4	Tom Douglas, Dartmouth	60	2485	41.4
5	Mike Cooke, North Carolina	45	1860	41.3
6	Barney Welch, Texas A&M	39	1609	41.3
7	Joe Muha, VMI	44	1804	41.0
8	Jerry Moore, Vanderbilt	40	1608	40.2
9	Joe Colone, Penn State	46	1845	40.1
10	Earl Dolaway, Indiana	30	1202	40.1

PUNT RETURNS/YARDS		PR	YDS	AVG
1	Bill Hillenbrand, Indiana	23	481	20.9

KICKOFF RETURNS/YARDS		KR	YDS	AVG
1	Frank Porto, California	17	483	28.4

SCORING		TDS	XPT	FG	PTS
1	Bob Steuber, Missouri	18	13	0	121
2	Frank Sinkwich, Georgia	16	0	0	96
2	Rudy Mobley, Hardin-Simmons	16	0	0	96
4	Gene Fekete, Ohio State	10	29	1	92
5	Paul Sarringhaus, Ohio State	13	0	0	78
6	Ralph Tate, Oklahoma State	10	12	0	72
7	Robert Kennedy, Washington State	11	3	0	69
8	John Bezemes, Holy Cross	11	0	0	66

INTERCEPTIONS		INT	YDS
1	Ray Evans, Kansas	10	76

TEAM LEADERS

RUSHING OFFENSE		G	ATT	YDS	AVG	YPG
1	Hardin-Simmons	9	508	2767	5.4	307.4
2	Boston College	9	538	2635	4.9	292.8
3	Ohio State	10	571	2833	5.0	283.3
4	Missouri	12	597	3230	5.4	269.2
5	Texas	10	532	2496	4.7	249.6
6	Iowa Pre-Flight	10	515	2493	4.8	249.3
7	Auburn	9	500	2223	4.4	247.0
8	Great Lakes NAS	12	619	2906	4.7	242.2
9	Pennsylvania	9	518	2162	4.2	240.2
10	Georgia	11	491	2624	5.3	238.5

PASSING OFFENSE/YPG		G	ATT	COM	INT	PCT	YDS	YPA	YPG	I%	YPC
1	Tulsa	10	245	138	9	56.3	2339	9.5	233.9	3.7	16.9
2	Georgia	11	245	122	18	49.8	2101	8.6	191.0	7.4	17.2
3	Columbia	9	199	96	21	48.2	1661	8.3	184.6	10.6	17.3
4	Creighton	9	157	78	13	49.7	1393	8.9	154.8	8.3	17.9
5	Maryland	9	170	90	15	52.9	1364	8.0	151.6	8.8	15.2
6	Virginia	9	222	110	22	49.5	1307	5.9	145.2	9.9	11.9
7	SMU	11	271	111	30	41.0	1535	5.7	139.5	11.1	13.8
8	Texas-El Paso	9	199	89	19	44.7	1195	6.0	132.8	9.6	13.4
9	Saint Mary's-Cal	10	184	79	16	42.9	1246	6.8	124.6	8.7	15.8
10	Georgia Tech	10	178	68	18	38.2	1208	6.8	120.8	10.1	17.8

TOTAL OFFENSE		G	P	YDS	AVG	YPG
1	Georgia	11	736	4725	6.4	429.
2	Tulsa	10	627	4261	6.8	426
3	Boston College	9	672	3697	5.5	410.
4	Ohio State	10	680	3975	5.8	397
5	Missouri	12	NA	4272	NA	356.
6	Hardin-Simmons	9	574	3130	5.5	347
7	Iowa Pre-Flight	10	NA	3356	NA	335.
8	Georgia Tech	10	NA	3304	NA	330
9	Indiana	10	620	3301	5.3	330
10	Texas	10	679	3205	4.7	320.

RUSHING DEFENSE		G	ATT	YDS	AVG	YPG
1	Boston College	9	294	440	1.5	48.9
2	Texas	10	306	575	1.9	57.5
3	William & Mary	11	329	734	2.2	66.7
4	Alabama	10	329	743	2.3	74.3
5	Tennessee	10	347	760	2.2	76.0
6	Miami, Fla.	9	341	717	2.1	79.7
7	Tulsa	10	345	839	2.4	83.9
8	North Carolina Navy	10	358	842	2.4	84.2
9	Minnesota	9	320	762	2.4	84.7
10	Saint Mary's-Cal	10	337	852	2.5	85.2

PASSING DEFENSE		G	ATT	COM	PCT	YPC	INT	I%	YDS	YPA	YPG
1	Harvard	9	81	29	35.8	14.1	6	7.4	409	5.0	45.4
2	Texas-El Paso	8	105	40	38.1	9.1	5	4.8	363	3.5	45.4
3	Miami, Fla.	9	115	46	40.0	9.5	19	16.5	437	3.8	48.6
4	Penn State	8	93	32	34.4	12.2	11	11.8	389	4.2	48.6
5	South Carolina	9	99	32	32.3	14.2	15	15.2	453	4.6	50.3
6	Lafayette	9	105	35	33.3	13.0	17	16.2	455	4.3	50.6
7	Manhattan	8	75	32	42.7	13.0	8	10.7	415	5.5	51.9
8	Richmond	10	130	33	25.4	15.8	14	10.8	520	4.0	52.0
9	Washington	10	129	41	31.8	13.6	22	10.1	556	4.3	55.6
10	Detroit	9	156	42	26.9	11.9	18	11.5	501	3.2	55.7

TOTAL DEFENSE		G	P	YDS	AVG	YPG
1	Texas	10	483	1173	2.4	117.
2	Miami, Fla.	9	456	1154	2.5	128.
3	Boston College	9	501	1186	2.4	131
4	William & Mary	11	NA	1516	NA	137.
5	North Carolina Navy	10	NA	1428	NA	142.
6	Tennessee	10	484	1435	3.0	143.
7	Minnesota	9	437	1314	3.0	146.
8	Tulsa	10	489	1487	3.0	148.
9	Holy Cross	10	483	1494	3.1	149.
10	Great Lakes NAS	12	NA	1917	NA	159.

SCORING OFFENSE		G	PTS	AVG
1	Tulsa	10	427	42.7

SCORING DEFENSE		G	PTS	AVG
1	Tulsa	10	32	3.2

1943 POLL PROGRESSION

AP October 4 Poll — Oct. 9 Games

	Team	Record	Result
1	Notre Dame	2-0-0	beat # 2 Michigan 35-12
2	Michigan	3-0-0	lost to # 1 Notre Dame 12-35
3	Army	2-0-0	beat Temple 51-0
4	Navy	2-0-0	beat # 5 Duke 14-13
5	Duke	3-0-0	lost to # 4 Navy 13-14
6	Pennsylvania	2-0-0	beat # 14 Dartmouth 7-6
7	Purdue	3-0-0	beat Camp Grant 19-0
8	Iowa Pre-Flight	3-0-0	beat Iowa 25-0
9	Minnesota	2-0-0	bye week
10	Southern Cal	2-0-0	beat St. Mary's Pre-Flight 13-0
11	Southwestern Texas	3-0-0	N/A
12	Great Lakes NAS	3-1-0	beat # 18 Ohio State 13-6
13	Memphis Naval	3-0-0	N/A
14	Dartmouth	2-0-0	lost to # 6 Pennsylvania 6-7
15	Del Monte Pre-Flight	2-0-0	beat Pleasonton Navy 34-6
16	March Field	2-0-0	beat UCLA 47-7
17	LSU	2-0-0	lost to Texas A&M 13-28
18	Ohio State	1-1-0	lost to # 12 Great Lakes NAS 6-13
19	Northwestern	1-1-0	bye week
20	College of Pacific	3-0-0	beat California 12-6

AP October 11 Poll — Oct. 16 Games

	Team	Record	Result
1	Notre Dame	3-0-0	beat Wisconsin 50-0
2	Army	3-0-0	beat Columbia 52-0
3	Navy	3-0-0	beat Penn State 14-6
4	Pennsylvania	3-0-0	beat Lakehurst NAS 74-6
5	Purdue	4-0-0	beat Ohio State 30-7
6	Duke	3-1-0	beat North Carolina 14-7
7	Iowa Pre-Flight	4-0-0	beat Missouri 21-6
8	Southern Cal	3-0-0	beat San Francisco 34-0
9	Michigan	3-1-0	bye week
10	College of Pacific	4-0-0	beat# 11 Del Monte Pre-Flight 16-7
11	Del Monte Pre-Flight	3-0-0	lost to # 10 Pacific 7-16
12	March Field	3-0-0	beat San Diego Naval 7-0
13	Minnesota	2-0-0	beat Camp Grant 13-7
14	Great Lakes	4-1-0	lost to # 7 Navy 7-24
15	Memphis Naval	3-0-0	N/A
16	Dartmouth	2-1-0	bye week
17	Southwestern Texas	4-0-0	N/A
18	Texas A&M	3-0-0	beat TCU 13-0
19	Washington	2-0-0	bye week
20	Georgia	3-1-0	lost to Daniel Field 7-18

AP October 18 Poll — Oct. 23 Games

	Team	Record	Result
1	Notre Dame	4-0-0	beat Illinois 47-0
2	Army	5-0-0	beat Yale 39-7
3	Navy	4-0-0	beat Georgia Tech 28-14
4	Purdue	5-0-0	beat Iowa 28-7
5	Pennsylvania	4-0-0	beat Columbia 33-0
6	College of Pacific	5-0-0	lost to # 7 Southern Cal 0-6
7	Southern Cal	4-0-0	beat # 6 Pacific 6-0
8	Iowa Pre-Flight	5-0-0	beat Fort Riley 19-2
9	Duke	4-1-0	bye week
10	Michigan	3-1-0	beat Minnesota 49-6
11	Minnesota	3-0-0	lost to Michigan 6-49
12	Southwestern Texas	5-0-0	N/A
13	Texas A&M	4-0-0	tied North Texas AC 0-0
14	March Field	4-0-0	lost to Washington 7-27
15	Del Monte Pre-Flight	3-1-0	beat San Francisco 34-0
16	Texas	3-1-0	beat Rice 58-0
17	Northwestern	2-1-0	beat Ohio State 13-0
18	Colorado College	4-0-0	beat Colorado 16-6
19	Memphis Naval	3-0-0	N/A
20	Camp Grant	2-3-1	tied Fort Riley 13-13

AP October 25 Poll — Oct. 30 Games

	Team	Record	Result
1	Notre Dame	5-0-0	beat # 3 Navy 33-6
2	Army	5-0-0	tied # 6 Pennsylvania 13-13
3	Navy	5-0-0	lost to # 1 Notre Dame 6-33
4	Purdue	6-0-0	beat Wisconsin 32-0
5	Southern Cal	5-0-0	beat # 20 California 13-0
6	Pennsylvania	5-0-0	tied # 2 Army 13-13
7	Michigan	4-1-0	beat Illinois 42-6
8	Duke	4-1-0	beat Georgia Tech 14-7
9	Iowa Pre-Flight	6-0-0	beat Marquette 46-19
10	College of Pacific	5-1-0	bye week
11	Washington	4-0-0	regular season complete
12	Texas	4-1-0	beat SMU 20-0
13	Tulsa	4-0-0	tied Southwestern Texas 6-6
14	Louisiana-Lafayette	1-0-0	beat UCLA 26-7
15	Northwestern	3-1-0	beat Minnesota 42-6
16	Colorado College	5-0-0	bye week
17	Del Monte Pre-Flight	3-1-0	bye week
18	Great Lakes NAS	5-2-0	beat Western Michigan 32-6
19	Texas A&M	4-0-1	beat Arkansas 13-0
20	California	2-3-0	lost to # 5 Southern Cal 0-13

AP November 1 Poll — Nov. 6 Games

	Team	Record	Result
1	Notre Dame	6-0-0	beat #3 Army 26-0
2	Purdue	7-0-0	beat Minnesota 14-7
3	Army	5-0-1	lost to # 1 Notre Dame 0-26
4	Southern Cal	6-0-0	lost to San Diego Naval 7-10
5	Pennsylvania	5-0-1	lost to # 7 Navy 7-24
6	Michigan	5-1-0	beat Indiana 23-6
7	Navy	5-1-0	beat # 5 Pennsylvania 24-7
8	Iowa Pre-Flight	7-0-0	bye week
9	Duke	5-1-0	beat North Carolina St. 75-0
10	College of Pacific	5-1-0	beat Saint Mary's-Cal 19-7
11	Washington	4-0-0	
12	Northwestern	4-1-0	beat Wisconsin 41-0
13	Texas	5-1-0	bye week
14	Del Monte Pre-Flight	4-1-0	beat UCLA 26-7
15	Louisiana-Lafayette	2-0-0	tied Arkansas A&M 20-20
16	Texas A&M	5-0-1	beat SMU 22-0
17	Arkansas-Monticello	0-0-0	N/A
18	Colorado College	5-0-0	bye week
19	Tulsa	4-0-1	beat Oklahoma State 55-6
20	LSU	5-1-0	lost to Georgia Tech 7-42

AP November 8 Poll — Nov. 13 Games

	Team	Record	Result
1	Notre Dame	7-0-0	beat # 8 Northwestern 25-6
2	Purdue	8-0-0	bye week
3	Navy	6-1-0	beat Columbia 61-0
4	Michigan	6-1-0	beat Wisconsin 27-0
5	Iowa Pre-Flight	7-0-0	beat Camp Grant 28-13
6	Army	5-1-1	beat Sampson USN 16-7
7	Duke	6-1-0	beat Virginia 49-0
8	Northwestern	5-1-0	lost to # 1 Notre Dame 6-25
9	Southern Cal	6-1-0	lost to # 15 March Field 0-35
10	Pennsylvania	5-1-1	lost to North Carolina 6-9
11	College of Pacific	6-1-0	beat Yuma Field 43-0
12	Washington	4-0-0	
13	Del Monte Pre-Flight	5-1-0	bye week
14	Texas A&M	6-0-1	beat Rice 20-0
15	March Field	6-1-0	beat # 9 Southern Cal 35-0
16	Texas	5-1-0	beat TCU 46-7
17	Tulsa	5-0-1	bye week
18	Dartmouth	4-1-0	beat Cornell 20-0
19	Georgia Tech	4-3-0	beat Tulane 33-0
20	San Diego Naval	6-1-0	beat San Pedro NAS

AP November 15 Poll — Nov. 20 Games

	Team	Record	Result
1	Notre Dame	8-0-0	beat # 2 Iowa Pre-Flight 14-13
2	Iowa Pre-Flight	8-0-0	lost to # 1 Notre Dame 13-14
3	Purdue	8-0-0	beat Indiana 7-0
4	Michigan	7-1-0	beat Ohio State 45-7
5	Navy	7-1-0	bye week
6	Duke	7-1-0	beat North Carolina 27-6
7	Army	6-1-1	beat Brown 59-0
8	March Field	7-1-0	bye week
9	Northwestern	5-2-0	beat Illinois 53-6
10	Texas	6-1-0	bye week
11	Washington	4-0-0	
12	Texas A&M	7-0-1	bye week
13	College of Pacific	7-1-0	bye week
14	Del Monte Pre-Flight	5-1-0	beat St. Mary's Pre-Flight 37-14
15	Georgia Tech	5-3-0	beat Clemson 41-6
16	Tulsa	5-0-1	bye week
17	Bainbridge NTS	7-0-0	regular season complete
18	San Diego Naval	7-1-0	regular season complete
19	Pennsylvania	5-2-1	beat Cornell 20-14
20	Dartmouth	5-1-0	beat Princeton 42-13

AP November 22 Poll — Nov. 27 Games

	Team	Record	Result
1	Notre Dame	9-0-0	lost to Great Lakes NAS 14-19
2	Iowa Pre-Flight	8-1-0	beat Minnesota 32-0
3	Michigan	8-1-0	regular season complete
4	Purdue	9-0-0	regular season complete
5	Duke	8-1-0	regular season complete
6	Navy	7-1-0	beat # 7 Army 13-0
7	Army	7-1-1	lost to # 6 Navy 0-13
8	Northwestern	6-2-0	regular season complete
9	March Field	7-1-0	beat San Diego Naval 13-2
10	Del Monte Pre-Flight	6-1-0	beat California 47-0
11	Washington	4-0-0	
12	Texas	6-1-0	beat # 16 Texas A&M 27-13
13	Dartmouth	6-1-0	regular season complete
14	Georgia Tech	6-3-0	beat Georgia 48-0
15	Bainbridge NTS	7-0-0	
16	Texas A&M	7-0-1	lost to # 12 Texas 13-27
17	Colorado College	5-0-0	regular season complete
18	Pennsylvania	6-2-1	regular season complete
19	Randolph Field	9-0-0	lost to La. Lafayette 0-6
20	Tulsa	5-0-1	beat Arkansas 61-0

AP	NOVEMBER 29 FINAL POLL	RECORD	BOWL BID	DATE	BOWL RESULT	RB	RECORD
1	Notre Dame	9-1-0				1	9-1-0
2	Iowa Pre-Flight	9-1-0				2	9-1-0
3	Michigan	8-1-0				3	8-1-0
4	Navy	8-1-0				5	8-1-0
5	Purdue	9-0-0				4	9-0-0
6	Great Lakes NAS	10-2-0				8	10-2-0
7	Duke	8-1-0				11	8-1-0
8	Del Monte Pre-Flight	7-1-0				21	7-1-0
9	Northwestern	6-2-0				9	6-2-0
10	March Field	8-1-0				10	9-1-0
11	Army	7-2-1				18	7-2-1
12	Washington	4-0-0	Rose Bowl	J1	lost to Southern Cal 0-29	27	4-1-0
13	Georgia Tech	7-3-0	Sugar Bowl	J1	beat # 15 Tulsa 20-18	6	8-3-0
14	Texas	7-1-0	Cotton Bowl	J1	tied Randolph Field 7-7	7	7-1-1
15	Tulsa	6-0-1	Sugar Bowl	J1	lost to # 13 Georgia Tech 18-20	15	6-1-1
16	Dartmouth	6-1-0				32	6-1-0
17	Bainbridge NTS	7-0-0				20	7-0-0
18	Colorado College	7-0-0				16	7-0-0
19	College of Pacific	7-1-0				28	7-2-0
20	Pennsylvania	6-2-1				22	6-2-1

1943

CONSENSUS ALL-AMERICANS

POS	Name	HT	WT	School	AA	AP	CM	FN	IN	LK	SN	UP
B	Angelo Bertelli	6-1	173	Notre Dame	•		•	•	•	•		•
B	Creighton Miller	6-0	185	Notre Dame	•	•	•	•	•	•	•	•
B	Bill Daley	6-2	206	Michigan	•	•	•	•	•	•		•
B	Bob Odell	5-11	182	Pennsylvania		•	•	•		•		•
E	Ralph Heywood	6-2	195	Southern Cal	•	•	•	•	•			•
E	John Yonakor	6-4	220	Notre Dame	•	•	•		•	•	•	•
T	Jim White	6-2	210	Notre Dame	•	•	•	•		•	•	•
T	Don Whitmire	5-11	215	Navy	•	•			•	•	•	•
G	Alex Agase	5-10	190	Purdue	•			•	•	•	•	•
G	Pat Filley	5-8	175	Notre Dame	•	•		•	•	•		•
C	Casimir Myslinski	5-11	186	Army	•	•	•	•	•	•	•	•

	OTHERS RECEIVING FIRST-TEAM HONORS											
B	Otto Graham			Northwestern	•	•		•				
B	John Podesto			Pacific								•
B	Tony Butkovich			Purdue						•		
E	Pete Pihos			Indiana	•	•		•				
E	Joe Parker			Texas				•				
E	Herb Hein			Northwestern				•				
E	Albert Channell			Navy					•			
E	Bob Gantt			Duke						•		
T	Pat Preston			Duke			•					
T	Art McCaffray			Pacific				•				
T	Frank Merritt			Army				•				
T	Merv Pregulman			Michigan			*		•	•	•	
G	John Steber			Georgia Tech	•	•		•				
G	George Brown			Navy				•				
G	Harold Fisher			Southwestern						•		

HEISMAN TROPHY VOTING

	PLAYER	POS	SCHOOL	TOTAL
1	Angelo Bertelli	QB	Notre Dame	648
2	Bob Odell	HB	Pennsylvania	177
3	Otto Graham	QB	Northwestern	140
4	Creighton Miller	HB	Notre Dame	134
5	Eddie Prokop	RB	Georgia Tech	85
6	Hal Hamburg	HB	Navy	73
7	Bill Dailey	FB	Michigan	71
8	Tony Butkovich	FB	Purdue	65
9	Jim White	T	Notre Dame	52

AWARD WINNERS

PLAYER	POS	SCHOOL	AWARD NAME
Bob Odell	HB	Pennsylvania	Maxwell

CONFERENCE STANDINGS

CONFERENCES PLAYED AN ABBREVIATED SCHEDULE DUE TO WORLD WAR II

Big 10

	CONF. W L T			OVERALL W L T		
Purdue	6	0	0	9	0	0
Michigan	6	0	0	8	1	0
Northwestern	5	1	0	6	2	0
Indiana	2	3	1	4	4	2
Minnesota	2	3	0	5	4	0
Illinois	2	4	0	3	7	0
Ohio State	1	4	0	3	6	0
Wisconsin	1	6	0	1	9	0
Iowa	0	4	1	1	6	1

Big 6

	CONF. W L T			OVERALL W L T		
Oklahoma	5	0	0	7	2	0
Iowa State	3	2	0	4	4	0
Missouri	3	2	0	3	5	0
Kansas	2	3	0	4	5	1
Nebraska	2	3	0	2	6	0
Kansas State	0	5	0	1	7	0

Border

	CONF. W L T			OVERALL W L T		
New Mexico	1	0	0	3	2	0
Northern Arizona	0	1	0	1	1	0
New Mexico State	0	0	0	4	0	0
Texas Tech	0	0	0	4	6	0

Mountain States

	CONF. W L T			OVERALL W L T		
Colorado	2	0	0	5	2	0
Utah	0	2	0	0	7	0
Denver	0	0	0	2	5	0

Pacific Coast

	CONF. W L T			OVERALL W L T		
Southern Cal	4	0	0	8	2	0
California	2	2	0	4	6	0
Washington	0	1	0	4	1	0
UCLA	0	4	0	1	8	0

SEC

	CONF. W L T			OVERALL W L T		
Georgia Tech	3	0	0	8	3	0
LSU	2	2	0	6	3	0
Tulane	1	1	0	3	3	0
Georgia	0	3	0	6	4	0

Southern

	CONF. W L T			OVERALL W L T		
Duke	4	0	0	8	1	0
Maryland	2	0	0	4	5	0
South Carolina	2	1	0	5	2	0
Wake Forest	3	2	0	4	5	0
North Carolina	2	2	0	6	3	0
Richmond	1	1	0	6	1	0
VMI	2	3	0	2	6	0
Clemson	2	3	0	2	6	0
North Carolina St.	1	4	0	3	6	0
Davidson	0	3	0	0	5	0

SWC

	CONF. W L T			OVERALL W L T		
Texas	5	0	0	7	1	1
Texas A&M	4	1	0	7	2	1
Rice	2	3	0	3	7	0
SMU	2	3	0	2	7	0
TCU	1	4	0	2	6	0
Arkansas	1	4	0	2	7	0

Independents

	OVERALL W L T		
Colorado College	7	0	0
Bainbridge NTS	7	0	0
Notre Dame	9	1	0
Iowa Pre-Flight	9	1	0
March Field	9	1	0
Boston College	4	0	1
Navy	8	1	0
Del Monte Pre-Flight	7	1	0
Randolph Field	9	1	1
Dartmouth	6	1	0
Great Lakes NAS	10	2	0
Miami, Fla.	5	1	0
Georgia Pre-Flight	5	1	0
Pacific	7	2	0
San Diego Naval	7	2	0
Army	7	2	1
Pennsylvania	6	2	1
Brown	5	3	0
Penn State	5	3	1
Cornell	6	4	0
Rutgers	3	2	0
West Virginia	4	3	0
Harvard	2	2	1
Yale	4	5	0
Virginia	3	4	1
Pittsburgh	3	5	0
Camp Grant	2	6	2
Princeton	1	6	0
Columbia	0	8	0

BOWL GAMES

DATE	GAME	SCORE
J1	Orange	LSU 19, Texas A&M 14
J1	Sugar	Georgia Tech 20, Tulsa 18
J1	Rose	Southern Cal 29, Washington 0
J1	Cotton	Randolph Field 7, Texas 7
J1	Sun	Southwestern Texas 7, New Mexico 0

1943 NCAA MAJOR COLLEGE STATISTICAL LEADERS

INDIVIDUAL LEADERS

PASSING/COMPLETIONS	G	ATT	COM	PCT	INT	I%	YDS	YPA	COM.PG
1 Johnny Cook, Georgia	10	157	73	46.5	20	12.7	1007	6.4	7.3
2 Bob Hoernschemeyer, Indiana	10	154	69	44.8	15	9.7	1133	7.4	6.9
3 Eddie Prokop, Georgia Tech	10	133	66	49.6	17	12.8	806	6.1	6.6
4 Tony Hubka, Temple	8	109	59	54.1	10	9.2	549	5.0	7.4
5 Howard Tippee, Iowa State	8	122	56	45.9	13	10.7	637	5.2	7.0
6 David Marshall, Princeton	7	120	52	43.3	17	14.2	588	4.9	7.4
7 James Hallmark, Texas A&M	9	120	48	40.0	14	11.7	719	6.0	5.3
8 Don Kasprzak, Dartmouth	7	92	46	50.0	8	8.7	644	7.0	6.6
8 Jim Lucas, TCU	8	132	46	34.8	15	11.4	622	4.7	5.8
10 Clyde LeForce, Tulsa	7	90	43	47.8	5	5.6	557	6.2	6.1

ALL-PURPOSE YARDS	G	RUSH	REC	INT	PR	KR	YDS	YPG
1 Stan Koslowski, Holy Cross	8	784	63	50	438	76	1411	176.4

RUSHING/YARDS	G	ATT	YDS	AVG	YPG
1 Creighton Miller, Notre Dame	10	151	911	6.0	91.1
2 Steve Van Buren, LSU	8	150	847	5.6	105.9
3 Tony Butkovich, Purdue	9	142	833	5.9	92.6
4 Bill Daley, Michigan	9	120	817	6.8	90.8
5 Stan Koslowski, Holy Cross	8	161	784	4.9	98.0
6 Eddie Bray, Illinois	10	117	739	6.3	73.9
7 Jim Mello, Notre Dame	10	137	704	5.1	70.4
8 Ernie Parks, Ohio State	9	161	693	4.3	77.0
9 Dean Sensanbaugher, Ohio State	9	150	677	4.5	75.2
10 Joseph Kane, Pennsylvania	9	104	671	6.5	74.6

RUSHING/YARDS PER CARRY	G	ATT	YDS	YPC
1 Bill Daley, Michigan	9	120	817	6.8
2 Joseph Kane, Pennsylvania	9	104	671	6.5
3 Eddie Bray, Illinois	10	117	739	6.3
4 Creighton Miller, Notre Dame	10	151	911	6.0
5 Tony Butkovich, Purdue	9	142	833	5.9
6 Steve Van Buren, LSU	8	150	847	5.6
7 Jim Mello, Notre Dame	10	137	704	5.1
8 Stan Koslowski, Holy Cross	8	161	784	4.9
9 Dean Sensanbaugher, Ohio State	9	150	677	4.5
10 Ernie Parks, Ohio State	9	161	693	4.3

*-Based on top 10 rushers

RECEIVING/RECEPTIONS	G	REC	YDS	YPR	YPG	RPG
1 Neill Armstrong, Oklahoma State	7	39	317	8.1	45.3	5.6
2 Marion Flanagan, Texas A&M	9	23	403	17.5	44.8	2.6
3 James Dorough, Georgia Tech	10	20	290	14.5	29.0	2.0
3 Pete Pihos, Indiana	10	20	241	12.1	24.1	2.0
5 Billy Collins, VMI	8	19	333	17.5	41.6	2.4
5 Ben Jones, Arkansas	9	19	279	14.7	31.0	2.1
5 Tom Rock, Columbia	8	19	250	13.2	31.3	2.4

PUNTING	PUNT	YDS	AVG
1 Harold Cox, Arkansas	37	1518	41.0
2 Frank Meuhlheuser, Colgate	32	1258	39.3
3 Stan Koslowski, Holy Cross	40	1570	39.3
4 John Monahan, Dartmouth	37	1448	39.1
5 Stanley Turner, Texas A&M	72	2742	38.1
6 George Maxon, Army	35	1321	37.7

PUNT RETURNS/YARDS	PR	YDS	AVG
1 Marion Flanagan, Texas A&M	49	475	9.7

KICKOFF RETURNS/YARDS	KR	YDS	AVG
1 Paul Copoulos, Marquette	11	384	34.9

SCORING	TDS	XPT	FG	PTS
1 Steve Van Buren, LSU	14	14	0	98
2 Tony Butkovich, Purdue	16	0	0	96
3 Bob Brumley, Oklahoma	10	16	1	79
4 Johnny Cook, Georgia	13	0	0	78
4 Creighton Miller, Notre Dame	13	0	0	78
6 Stan Koslowski, Holy Cross	11	9	0	75
7 Charles Avery, Minnesota	12	0	0	72
7 Howard Blose, Cornell	12	0	0	72
9 Elroy Hirsch, Michigan	11	2	0	68
10 Eddie Prokop, Georgia Tech	7	24	0	66

INTERCEPTIONS	INT	YDS
1 Jay Stoves, Washington	7	139

TEAM LEADERS

RUSHING OFFENSE	G	ATT	YDS	AVG	YPG
1 Iowa Pre-Flight	10	481	3244	6.7	324.4
2 Notre Dame	10	625	3137	5.0	313.7
3 Duke	9	487	2660	5.5	295.6
4 Michigan	9	508	2648	5.2	294.2
5 Washington	4	197	1170	5.9	292.5
6 Army	10	499	2568	5.1	256.8
7 Texas	8	362	2016	5.6	252.0
8 Minnesota	9	410	2202	5.4	244.7
9 Navy	9	444	2165	4.9	240.6
10 Holy Cross	8	449	1876	4.2	234.5

PASSING OFFENSE/YPG	G	ATT	COM	INT	PCT	YDS	YPA	YPG	I%	YPC
1 Brown	8	142	67	13	47.2	1065	7.5	133.1	9.2	15.9
2 Tulsa	7	141	69	7	48.9	931	6.6	133.0	5.0	13.5
3 Texas A&M	9	197	78	24	39.6	1186	6.0	131.8	12.2	15.2
4 Georgia	9	164	75	21	45.7	1146	7.0	127.3	12.8	15.3
5 Arkansas	8	212	80	28	37.7	1015	4.8	126.9	13.2	12.7
6 Indiana	10	168	76	16	45.2	1241	7.4	124.1	9.5	16.3
7 Dartmouth	7	123	62	13	50.4	849	6.9	121.3	10.6	13.7
8 Georgia Tech	9	159	79	20	49.7	1011	6.4	112.3	12.6	12.8
9 Notre Dame	10	106	60	12	56.6	1043	9.8	104.3	11.3	17.4
10 Princeton	7	144	62	18	43.1	721	5.0	103.0	12.5	11.6

TOTAL OFFENSE	G	P	YDS	AVG	YPG
1 Notre Dame	10	734	4180	5.7	418.0
2 Iowa Pre-Flight	10	583	3929	6.7	392.9
3 Washington	4	250	1499	6.0	374.8
4 Duke	9	566	3299	5.8	366.6
5 Michigan	9	582	3269	5.6	363.2
6 Army	10	639	3545	5.5	354.5
7 Texas	8	498	2814	5.7	351.8
8 Tulsa	7	425	2379	5.6	339.9
9 Georgia	9	593	2969	5.0	329.9
10 Holy Cross	8	587	2628	4.5	328.5

RUSHING DEFENSE	G	ATT	YDS	AVG	YPG
1 Duke	9	235	355	1.5	39.4
2 Tulsa	7	229	327	1.4	46.7
3 Penn State	9	312	505	1.6	56.1
4 Washington	4	112	245	2.2	61.3
5 Holy Cross	8	254	517	2.0	64.6
6 Texas	8	223	556	2.5	69.5
7 Navy	9	347	667	1.9	74.1
8 Army	10	347	765	2.2	76.5
9 Texas A&M	9	361	773	2.1	85.9
10 Southern Cal	8	311	715	2.3	89.4

PASSING DEFENSE	G	ATT	COM	PCT	YPC	YDS	YPA	YPG
1 North Carolina	8	92	29	31.5	10.1	292	3.2	36.5
2 Texas A&M	9	138	33	23.9	12.3	407	2.9	45.2
3 Iowa State	8	86	29	33.7	13.8	400	4.7	50.0
4 Columbia	8	78	33	42.3	12.3	406	5.2	50.8
5 Northwestern	8	67	28	41.8	14.8	415	6.2	51.9
6 Indiana	10	103	39	37.9	14.2	555	5.4	55.5
7 Purdue	9	113	38	33.6	13.5	514	4.5	57.1
8 Wisconsin	9	72	29	40.3	18.0	523	7.3	58.1

TOTAL DEFENSE	G	P	YDS	AVG	YPG
1 Duke	9	405	1095	2.7	121.7
2 Tulsa	7	383	881	2.3	125.9
3 Penn State	9	439	1176	2.7	130.7
4 Texas A&M	9	488	1178	2.4	130.9
5 Holy Cross	8	371	1104	3.0	138.0
6 Texas	8	357	1110	3.1	138.8
7 Army	10	521	1525	2.9	152.5
8 Navy	9	499	1451	2.9	161.2
9 Southern Cal	8	413	1299	3.1	162.4
10 Michigan	8	460	1313	2.9	164.1

SCORING OFFENSE	G	PTS	AVG
1 Duke	9	335	37.2

SCORING DEFENSE	G	PTS	AVG
1 Duke	9	34	3.8

1944 POLL PROGRESSION

AP	OCTOBER 9 POLL		OCT. 14 GAMES
1	Notre Dame	2-0-0	beat Dartmouth 64-0
2	North Carolina Pre-Flight	3-0-0	N/A
3	Army	3-0-0	beat Pittsburgh 69-7
4	Randolph Field	3-0-0	beat SMU 41-0
5	Great Lakes NAS	3-0-1	beat Western Michigan 38-0
6	Navy	1-1-0	beat Duke 7-0
7	Purdue	2-1-0	lost to # 11 Iowa Pre-Flight 6-13
8	Ohio State	2-0-0	beat # 19 Wisconsin 20-7
9	Pennsylvania	2-0-0	beat William & Mary 46-0
10	Georgia Tech	2-0-0	beat Auburn 27-0
11	Iowa Pre-Flight	3-1-0	beat # 7 Purdue 13-6
12	Michigan	3-1-0	beat Northwestern 27-0
13	Tulsa	2-0-0	beat Texas Tech 34-7
14	Illinois	2-1-1	beat Iowa 40-6
15	2nd Air Force	4-1-0	beat New Mexico 89-6
16	Tennessee	2-0-0	beat Florida 40-0
17	Wake Forest	3-0-0	beat VMI 38-7
18	Bainbridge NTS	4-0-0	beat Camden Pros 47-7
19	Indiana	2-1-0	beat Nebraska 54-0
19	Wisconsin	2-0-0	lost to # 8 Ohio State 7-20

AP	OCTOBER 16 POLL		OCT. 21 GAMES
1	Notre Dame	3-0-0	beat Wisconsin 28-13
2	Army	3-0-0	beat Coast Guard 76-0
3	Randolph Field	4-0-0	beat Camp Polk 67-0
4	Ohio State	3-0-0	beat # 6 Great Lakes NAS 26-6
5	Iowa Pre-Flight	4-1-0	beat Fort Warren 30-0
6	Great Lakes NAS	4-0-1	lost to # 4 Ohio State 6-26
7	Pennsylvania	3-0-0	bye week
8	Georgia Tech	3-0-0	beat # 9 Navy 17-15
9	Navy	2-1-0	lost to # 8 Georgia Tech 15-17
10	North Carolina Pre-Flight	3-0-1	N/A
11	Purdue	2-2-0	beat Iowa 26-7
12	California	3-0-1	lost to Fleet City 2-19
13	Tulsa	3-0-0	beat Mississippi 47-0
14	March Field	2-1-1	beat El Toro Marines 20-14
15	Michigan	4-1-0	bye week
16	Southern Cal	2-0-2	beat Washington 38-7
17	Tennessee	3-0-0	tied Alabama 0-0
18	Bainbridge NTS	3-0-0	bye week
19	2nd Air Force	5-1-0	beat U.T. Arlington 68-0
20	Indiana	3-1-0	beat Northwestern 14-7

AP	OCTOBER 23 POLL		OCT. 28 GAMES
1	Notre Dame	4-0-0	beat # 14 Illinois 13-7
2	Army	4-0-0	beat Duke 27-7
3	Randolph Field	5-0-0	beat Morris Field 19-0
4	Ohio State	4-0-0	beat Minnesota 34-14
5	Georgia Tech	4-0-0	beat Georgia Pre-Flight 13-7
6	Iowa Pre-Flight	5-1-0	beat Marquette 26-0
7	Pennsylvania	3-0-0	lost to # 12 Navy 0-26
8	Tulsa	4-0-0	lost to Oklahoma State 40-46
9	North Carolina Pre-Flight	4-0-1	N/A
10	Purdue	3-2-0	lost to Michigan 14-40
11	4th Air Force	3-0-1	N/A
12	Navy	2-2-0	beat # 7 Pennsylvania 26-0
13	Bainbridge NTS	3-0-0	beat Maxwell Field 15-7
14	Illinois	4-1-1	lost to # 1 Notre Dame 7-13
15	2nd Air Force	4-1-0	lost to Norman NAS 6-13
16	Great Lakes NAS	4-1-1	beat Wisconsin 40-12
17	Indiana	4-1-0	beat Iowa 32-0
18	Wake Forest	5-0-0	beat Miami, Fla. 27-0
19	3rd Air Force	4-0-0	N/A
20	Mississippi State	4-0-0	bye week
20	Tennessee	3-0-1	beat Clemson 26-7

AP	OCTOBER 30 POLL		NOV. 4 GAMES
1	Army	5-0-0	beat Villanova 83-0
2	Notre Dame	5-0-0	lost to # 6 Navy 13-32
3	Ohio State	5-0-0	beat Indiana 21-7
4	Randolph Field	6-0-0	beat U.T. Arlington 68-0
5	Georgia Tech	5-0-0	lost to Duke 13-19
6	Navy	3-2-0	beat # 2 Notre Dame 32-13
7	Iowa Pre-Flight	6-1-0	beat Tulsa 47-27
8	North Carolina Pre-Flight	5-0-1	lost to # 12 Bainbridge NTS 20-49
9	Illinois	4-2-1	bye week
10	Michigan	5-1-0	beat Pennsylvania 41-19
11	4th Air Force	4-0-1	N/A
12	Bainbridge NTS	4-0-0	beat # 8 North Carolina Pre-Flight 49-20
13	Southern Cal	4-0-2	beat San Diego Navy 28-21
14	Great Lakes NAS	5-1-1	beat Marquette 45-7
15	Indiana	5-1-0	lost to Ohio State 7-21
16	Tennessee	4-0-1	beat LSU 13-0
17	Wake Forest	6-0-0	beat Clemson 13-7
18	Mississippi State	4-0-0	beat Kentucky 26-0
19	Alabama	3-0-2	lost to Georgia 7-14
19	Oklahoma State	5-0-0	lost to Norman NAS 0-15

AP	NOVEMBER 6 POLL		NOV. 11 GAMES
1	Army	6-0-0	beat # 5 Notre Dame 59-0
2	Ohio State	6-0-0	beat Pittsburgh 54-19
3	Navy	4-2-0	beat Cornell 48-0
4	Randolph Field	7-0-0	beat Maxwell Field 25-0
5	Notre Dame	5-1-0	lost to # 1 Army 0-59
6	Bainbridge NAS	5-0-0	beat Cherry Point 50-7
7	Iowa Pre-Flight	7-1-0	beat Bunker Hill 33-7
8	Michigan	6-1-0	beat # 10 Illinois 14-0
9	4th Air Force	5-0-1	N/A
10	Illinois	4-2-1	lost to # 8 Michigan 0-14
11	Southern Cal	5-0-2	bye week
12	Wake Forest	7-0-0	lost to # 20 Duke 0-34
13	Georgia Tech	5-1-0	beat Tulane 34-7
14	Great Lakes NAS	6-1-0	beat Morris Field 12-10
15	Norman NAS	5-0-0	beat Lubbock Field 42-0
16	North Carolina Pre-Flight	5-1-1	N/A
17	El Toro, CA Marines	4-1-0	N/A
18	Tennessee	5-0-1	bye week
19	Mississippi State	5-0-0	beat Auburn 26-21
20	Duke	2-4-0	beat # 12 Wake Forest 34-0

AP	NOVEMBER 13 POLL		NOV. 18 GAMES
1	Army	7-0-0	beat Pennsylvania 62-7
2	Randolph Field	8-0-0	beat Southwestern, Texas 54-0
3	Navy	5-2-0	beat # 14 Purdue 32-0
4	Ohio State	7-0-0	beat Illinois 26-12
5	Michigan	7-1-0	beat Wisconsin 14-0
6	Bainbridge NTS	6-0-0	beat Camp Lejeune 33-6
7	Iowa Pre-Flight	8-1-0	beat Missouri 51-7
8	4th Air Force	6-0-1	N/A
9	Georgia Tech	6-1-0	beat LSU 14-6
10	Duke	3-4-0	beat South Carolina 34-7
11	Notre Dame	5-2-0	beat Northwestern 21-0
12	Southern Cal	5-0-2	beat California 32-0
13	Great Lakes NAS	7-1-1	beat Marquette 32-0
14	Purdue	5-3-0	lost to # 3 Navy 0-32
15	El Toro, CA Marines	5-1-0	N/A
16	Mississippi State	6-0-0	lost to Alabama 0-19
17	Tennessee	5-0-1	beat Temple 27-14
18	Norman NAS	6-0-0	regular season complete
19	North Carolina Pre-Flight	6-1-1	N/A
20	Yale	6-0-0	beat North Carolina 13-6

AP	NOVEMBER 20 POLL		NOV. 25 GAMES
1	Army	8-0-0	bye week
2	Navy	6-2-0	bye week
3	Ohio State	8-0-0	beat # 6 Michigan 18-14
4	Randolph Field	9-0-0	beat Amarillo Field 33-0
5	Bainbridge NTS	7-0-0	beat # 14 Camp Peary 21-13
6	Michigan	8-1-0	lost to # 3 Ohio State 14-18
7	Iowa Pre-Flight	9-1-0	beat Iowa 30-6
8	Southern Cal	6-0-2	beat UCLA 40-13
9	4th Air Force	7-0-1	N/A
10	Georgia Tech	7-1-0	lost to # 18 Notre Dame 0-21
11	Duke	4-4-0	beat North Carolina 33-0
12	Great Lakes NAS	8-1-2	beat Fort Warren 28-7
13	Alabama	4-1-2	beat Mississippi State 19-0
14	Camp Peary	4-0-0	lost to # 5 Bainbridge NTS 13-21
15	Tennessee	6-0-1	beat Kentucky 21-7
16	El Toro, CA Marines	6-1-0	N/A
17	Norman NAS	6-0-0	
18	Notre Dame	6-2-0	beat # 10 Georgia Tech 21-0
19	2nd Air Force	9-2-0	tied March Field 0-0
20	North Carolina Pre-Flight	6-2-1	N/A

AP	NOVEMBER 27 POLL		DEC. 2 GAMES
1	Army	8-0-0	beat # 2 Navy 23-7
2	Navy	6-2-0	lost to # 1 Army 7-23
3	Ohio State	9-0-0	regular season complete
4	Randolph Field	10-0-0	bye week
5	Bainbridge NTS	8-0-0	bye week
6	Iowa Pre-Flight	10-1-0	regular season complete
7	Southern Cal	7-0-2	regular season complete
8	Michigan	8-2-0	regular season complete
9	Notre Dame	7-2-0	beat # 12 Great Lakes NAS 28-7
10	Tennessee	7-0-1	regular season complete
11	Duke	5-4-0	regular season complete
12	Great Lakes NAS	9-1-1	lost to # 9 Notre Dame 7-28
13	Norman NAS	6-0-0	
14	4th Air Force	7-0-2	N/A
15	Oklahoma State	7-1-0	regular season complete
16	Alabama	5-1-2	regular season complete
17	Camp Peary	6-2-0	regular season complete
18	El Toro, CA Marines	7-1-0	N/A
19	Yale	7-0-1	regular season complete
20	2nd Air Force	9-2-1	beat Peru St. 38-0

AP	DECEMBER 4 FINAL POLL	RECORD	BOWL BID	DATE	BOWL RESULT	RB	RECORD
1	Army	9-0-0				1	9-0-0
2	Ohio State	9-0-0				2	9-0-0
3	Randolph Field	10-0-0	Treasury Bowl	D16	beat # 20 2nd Air Force 13-6	5	12-0-0
4	Navy	6-3-0				9	6-3-0
5	Bainbridge NTS	8-0-0				13	9-0-0
6	Iowa Pre-Flight	10-1-0				6	10-1-0
7	Southern Cal	7-0-2	Rose Bowl	J1	beat # 12 Tennessee 25-0	16	8-0-2
8	Michigan	8-2-0				4	8-2-0
9	Notre Dame	8-2-0				3	8-2-0
10	4th Air Force	7-0-2				NR	7-0-2
11	Duke	5-4-0	Sugar Bowl	J1	beat Alabama 29-26	21	6-4-0
12	Tennessee	7-0-1	Rose Bowl	J1	lost to # 7 Southern Cal 0-25	31	7-1-1
13	Georgia Tech	8-2-0	Orange Bowl	J1	lost to Tulsa 12-26	11	8-3-0
14	Norman NAS	6-0-0				8	6-0-0
15	Illinois	5-4-1				33	5-4-1
16	El Toro, CA Marines	7-1-0				NR	7-1-0
17	Great Lakes NAS	9-2-1				12	9-2-1
18	Fort Pierce	7-0-0				22	9-0-0
19	St. Mary's Pre-Flight	4-4-0				58	4-4-0
20	2nd Air Force	10-2-1	Treasury Bowl	D16	lost to # 3 Randolph Field 6-13	41	10-4-1

1944

CONSENSUS ALL-AMERICANS

POS	Name	HT	WT	School	AA	AP	CM	FN	FW	IN	LK	NE	SN	UP
B	Les Horvath	5-10	167	Ohio State	•	•	•	•	•	•	•	•	•	•
B	Glenn Davis	5-9	170	Army	•	•		•		•	•	•	•	•
B	Doc Blanchard	6-0	205	Army	•	•	•		•	•	•		•	•
B	Bob Jenkins	6-1	195	Navy	•		•					•	•	•
E	Phil Tinsley	6-1	188	Georgia Tech	•	•	•	•		•	•	•	•	•
E	Paul Walker	6-3	203	Yale		•	•	•	•				•	•
E	Jack Dugger	6-3	210	Ohio State	•			•		•			•	•
T	Don Whitmire	5-11	215	Navy	•	•	•	•	•	•	•		•	•
T	John Ferraro	6-3	235	Southern Cal	•		•	•	•	•	•		*	•
G	Bill Hackett	5-9	191	Ohio State	•		•		•	•			•	•
G	Ben Chase	6-1	195	Navy	•			•		•			•	•
C	John Tavener	6-0	220	Indiana				•	•		•		•	•

	OTHERS RECEIVING FIRST-TEAM HONORS													
B	Bob Fenimore			Oklahoma State	•	•	•	•		•				
B	Doug Kenna			Army		•								
B	Boris Dimancheff			Purdue				•						
B	Buddy Young			Illinois						•				
B	Earl Girard			Wisconsin						•				
E	Hubert Bechtol			Texas		•								
E	Barney Poole			Army						•				
T	Bill Willis			Ohio State						•		•	•	
T	George Savitsky			Pennsylvania						•				
G	Hamilton Nichols			Rice						•				
G	John Green			Army		•								
G	Joe Stanowicz			Army				•		•			•	
G	Bill Hachten			California				•						
G	Ellis Jones			Tulsa						•				
G	Clyde Flowers			TCU						•				
G	Ralph Serpico			Illinois						•				
C	Tex Warrington			Auburn	•	•	•			•				
C	Felto Prewitt			Tulsa				•						

HEISMAN TROPHY VOTING

	PLAYER	POS	SCHOOL	TOTAL
1	Les Horvath	QB	Ohio State	412
2	Glenn Davis	HB	Army	287
3	Doc Blanchard	FB	Army	237
4	Don Whitmire	T	Navy	115
5	Buddy Young	HB	Illinois	105
6	Bob Kelly	HB	Notre Dame	76
7	Bob Jenkins	HB	Navy	60
8	Doug Kenna	QB	Army	56
9	Bob Fenimore	HB	Oklahoma State	54
10	Thomas McWilliams	TB	Mississippi State	37

AWARD WINNERS

PLAYER	POS	SCHOOL	AWARD NAME
Glenn Davis	HB	Army	Maxwell

CONFERENCE STANDINGS

CONFERENCES PLAYED AN ABBREVIATED SCHEDULE DUE TO WORLD WAR II

Big 10

	Conf. W L T			Overall W L T		
Ohio State	6	0	0	9	0	0
Michigan	5	2	0	8	2	0
Purdue	4	2	0	5	5	0
Minnesota	3	2	1	5	3	1
Indiana	4	3	0	7	3	0
Illinois	3	3	0	5	4	1
Wisconsin	2	4	0	3	6	0
Northwestern	0	5	1	1	7	1
Iowa	0	6	0	1	7	0

Big 6

	Conf. W L T			Overall W L T		
Oklahoma	4	0	1	6	3	1
Iowa State	3	1	1	6	1	1
Missouri	2	1	2	3	5	2
Nebraska	2	3	0	2	6	0
Kansas	1	4	0	3	6	1
Kansas State	1	4	0	2	5	2

Border

	Conf. W L T			Overall W L T		
Texas Tech	2	0	0	4	7	0
West Texas State	1	1	0	4	3	0
New Mexico	1	2	0	1	7	0
Northern Arizona	0	1	0	2	2	0

Mountain States

	Conf. W L T			Overall W L T		
Colorado	2	0	0	6	2	0
Denver	2	1	1	4	3	2
Utah	1	2	1	5	2	1
Utah State	0	2	0	3	3	0

Pacific Coast

	Conf. W L T			Overall W L T		
Southern Cal	3	0	2	8	0	2
Washington	1	1	0	5	3	0
UCLA	1	2	1	4	5	1
California	1	3	1	3	6	1

SEC

	Conf. W L T			Over. W L T		
Vanderbilt	0	0	0	3	0	1
Georgia Tech	4	0	0	8	3	0
Tennessee	5	0	1	7	1	1
Georgia	4	2	0	7	3	0
Alabama	3	1	2	5	2	2
Mississippi State	3	2	0	6	2	0
LSU	2	3	1	2	5	1
Mississippi	2	3	0	2	6	0
Tulane	1	2	0	4	3	0
Kentucky	1	5	0	3	6	0
Florida	0	3	0	4	3	0
Auburn	0	4	0	4	4	0

Southern

	Conf. W L T			Overall W L T		
Duke	4	0	0	6	4	0
Wake Forest	6	1	0	8	1	0
Clemson	3	1	0	4	5	0
William & Mary	2	1	1	5	2	1
North Carolina St.	3	2	0	7	2	0
Maryland	1	1	0	1	7	1
South Carolina	1	3	0	3	4	2
VMI	1	5	0	1	8	0
North Carolina	0	3	1	1	7	1
Richmond	0	4	0	2	6	0

SWC

	Conf. W L T			Overall W L T		
Baylor	0	0	0	0	0	0
TCU	3	1	1	7	3	1
Texas	3	2	0	5	4	0
Arkansas	2	2	1	5	5	1
Texas A&M	2	3	0	7	4	0
SMU	2	3	0	5	5	0
Rice	2	3	0	5	6	0

Independents

	Overall W L T		
Randolph Field	12	0	0
Army	9	0	0
Fort Pierce	9	0	0
Bainbridge NTS	9	0	0
Norman NAS	6	0	0
Yale	7	0	1
Iowa Pre-Flight	10	1	0
Michigan State	6	1	0
Harvard	5	1	0
Notre Dame	8	2	0
Camp Peary	4	1	0
Great Lakes NAS	9	2	1
Virginia	6	1	2
March Field	7	2	2
Second Air Force	10	4	1
Penn State	6	3	0
Navy	6	3	0
Pennsylvania	5	3	0
West Virginia	5	3	1
Rutgers	3	2	0
Boston College	4	3	0
Cornell	5	4	0
St. Mary's Pre-Flight	4	4	0
Pittsburgh	4	5	0
Brown	3	4	1
Syracuse	2	4	1
Princeton	1	2	0
Dartmouth	2	5	1
Columbia	2	6	0
Miami, Fla.	1	7	1

BOWL GAMES

DATE	GAME	SCORE
J1	Cotton	Oklahoma State 34, TCU 0
J1	Sugar	Duke 29, Alabama 26
J1	Rose	Southern Cal 25, Tennessee 0
J1	Orange	Tulsa 26, Georgia Tech 12
J1	Sun	Southwestern 35, U. of Mexico 0

1944 NCAA MAJOR COLLEGE STATISTICAL LEADERS

Individual Leaders

PASSING/COMPLETIONS

		G	ATT	COM	PCT	INT	I%	YDS	YPA	COM.PG
1	Paul Rickards, Pittsburgh	9	178	84	47.2	20	11.2	997	5.6	9.3
2	Frank Dancewicz, Notre Dame	10	153	68	44.4	12	7.8	989	6.5	6.8
3	James Cashion, Texas A&M	11	113	59	52.2	12	10.6	852	7.5	5.4
4	Bob Waterfield, UCLA	10	136	55	40.4	19	14.0	901	6.6	5.5
5	Allan Dekdebrun, Cornell	9	121	53	43.8	13	10.7	648	5.4	5.9
6	Gordon Long, Arkansas	11	155	51	32.9	19	12.3	823	5.3	4.6
7	Bobby Layne, Texas	9	91	50	54.9	5	5.5	662	7.3	5.6
8	Bob Fenimore, Oklahoma State	8	79	49	62.0	5	6.3	861	10.9	6.1
9	John Yungwirth, Northwestern	9	99	48	48.5	11	11.1	613	6.2	5.3
9	James Youel, Great Lakes NAS	12	113	48	42.5	6	5.3	818	7.2	4.0

ALL-PURPOSE YARDS

		G	RUSH	REC	INT	PR	KR	YDS	YPG
1	Wayne "Red" Williams, Minnesota	9	911	0	0	242	314	1467	163.0

RUSHING/YARDS

		G	ATT	YDS	AVG	YPG
1	Wayne "Red" Williams, Minnesota	9	136	911	6.7	101.2
2	Les Horvath, Ohio State	9	163	905	5.6	100.6
3	Bob Fenimore, Oklahoma State	8	162	897	5.5	112.1
4	Curtis Kuykendall, Auburn	8	127	841	6.6	105.1
5	Buddy Young, Illinois	10	94	840	8.9	84.0
6	Boris Dimancheff, Purdue	10	175	830	4.7	83.0
7	Paul Patterson, Illinois	10	131	790	6.0	79.0
8	John Duda, Virginia	9	125	716	5.7	79.6
9	Dub Jones, Tulane	7	140	700	5.0	100.0
10	Bob Kelly, Notre Dame	10	136	681	5.0	68.1

RUSHING/YARDS PER CARRY

		G	ATT	YDS	YPC
1	Glenn Davis, Army	9	58	667	11.5
2	Buddy Young, Illinois	10	94	840	8.9
3	Anthony Minisi, Pennsylvania	8	78	551	7.1
4	Wayne "Red" Williams, Minnesota	9	136	911	6.7
5	Curtis Kuykendall, Auburn	8	127	841	6.6
6	Buster Stephens, Tennessee	8	101	631	6.2
7	Paul Patterson	10	131	790	6.0
8	Billy Rutland, Georgia	9	100	599	6.0
9	Camp Wilson, Tulsa	9	98	573	5.8
10	John Duda, Virginia	9	125	716	5.7

*-Based on top 20 rushers

RECEIVING/RECEPTIONS

		G	REC	YDS	YPR	YPG	RPG
1	Reid Moseley, Georgia	9	32	506	15.8	56.2	3.6
2	Neill Armstrong, Oklahoma State	8	27	325	12.0	40.6	3.4
3	Barney White, Tulsa	9	25	450	18.0	50.0	2.8
4	John Howell, Texas A&M	11	24	394	16.4	35.8	2.2
5	Robert Folsom, SMU	10	21	246	11.7	24.6	2.1
6	Abe Addams, Indiana	9	21	332	15.8	36.9	2.3
7	Pat Thrash, South Carolina	9	20	298	14.9	33.1	2.2
7	Lamar Dingler, Arkansas	11	20	291	14.6	26.5	1.8
7	George Gilbert, Columbia	8	20	218	10.9	27.3	2.5
10	Cecil Hankins, Oklahoma State	8	19	474	24.9	59.3	2.4
10	Merle Gibson, TCU	10	19	371	19.5	37.1	1.9

PUNTING

		PUNT	YDS	AVG
1	Bob Waterfield, UCLA	60	2575	42.9
2	Bob Wiese, Michigan	24	988	41.2
3	Jack Breslin, Michigan State	20	816	40.8
4	Walter Sheridan, Holy Cross	37	1503	40.6
5	Bobby Goff, Texas A&M	50	2014	40.3
6	Sid Tinsley, Clemson	52	2066	39.7
7	Louis Yacopec, Pittsburgh	24	951	39.6
8	Tom Davis, Duke	32	1226	38.3
9	Wayne Morgan, Columbia	24	915	38.1
10	Bob Kelly, Notre Dame	26	983	37.8

PUNT RETURNS/YARDS

		PR	YDS	AVG
1	Joe Stuart, California	39	372	9.5
2	Elwood Petchel, Penn State	22	328	14.9
3	Glenn Davis, Army	16	294	18.4

KICKOFF RETURNS/YARDS

		KR	YDS	AVG
1	Paul Copoulos, Marquette	14	337	24.1
2	Joe Stuart, California	15	317	21.1

SCORING

		TDS	XPT	FG	PTS
1	Glenn Davis, Army	20	0	0	120
2	Bob Kelley, Notre Dame	13	6	0	84
2	Tom McWilliams, Mississippi State	14	0	0	84
4	Richard Brinkley, Wake Forest	13	0	0	78
4	Buddy Young, Illinois	13	0	0	78
6	Bob Fenimore, Oklahoma State	12	5	0	77
7	Keith DeCourcey, Washington	12	0	0	72
7	Boris Dimancheff, Purdue	12	0	0	72
7	Les Horvath, Ohio State	12	0	0	72
7	Fred Robbins, Lafayette	12	0	0	72

INTERCEPTIONS

		INT	YDS
1	Jim Hardy, Southern Cal	8	73
2	Joe Stuart, California	7	NA

Team Leaders

RUSHING OFFENSE

		G	ATT	YDS	AVG	YPG
1	Army	9	381	2687	7.1	298.6
2	Tulane	7	385	2074	5.4	296.3
3	Illinois	10	449	2940	6.5	294.0
4	Auburn	6	319	1752	5.5	292.0
5	Ohio State	9	542	2506	4.6	278.4
6	Virginia	9	481	2468	5.1	274.2
7	Minnesota	9	452	2381	5.3	264.6
8	Randolph Field	10	424	2574	6.1	257.4
9	Michigan	10	528	2541	4.8	254.1
10	Navy	9	470	2166	4.6	240.7

PASSING OFFENSE

		G	ATT	COM	INT	PCT	YDS	YPA	YPG	I%	YPC
1	Tulsa	9	178	102	11	57.3	1857	10.4	206.3	6.2	18.2
2	Georgia Tech	6	125	53	10	42.4	852	6.8	142.0	8.0	16.1
3	Georgia	9	153	73	13	47.7	1244	8.1	138.2	8.5	17.0
4	Army	9	120	64	8	53.3	1190	9.9	132.2	6.7	18.6
5	Oklahoma State	8	110	63	8	57.3	1008	9.2	126.0	7.3	16.0
6	Pittsburgh	9	212	97	28	45.8	1117	5.3	124.1	13.2	11.5
7	Notre Dame	10	181	81	16	44.8	1229	6.8	122.9	8.8	15.2
8	Texas	9	166	88	12	53.0	1092	6.6	121.3	7.2	12.4
9	Randolph Field	10	160	66	12	41.3	1196	7.5	119.6	7.5	18.1
10	Texas A&M	11	177	88	18	49.7	1300	7.3	118.2	10.2	14.8

TOTAL OFFENSE

		G	P	YDS	AVG	YPG
1	Tulsa	9	576	3912	6.8	434.7
2	Army	9	501	3877	7.7	430.8
3	Randolph Field	10	584	3770	6.5	377.0
4	Auburn	6	399	2191	5.5	365.2
5	Ohio State	9	635	3264	5.1	362.7
6	Illinois	10	521	3559	6.8	355.9
7	Notre Dame	10	690	3552	5.1	355.2
8	Georgia	9	680	3193	4.7	354.8
9	Navy	9	620	3159	5.1	351.0
10	Tulane	7	463	2381	5.1	340.1

RUSHING DEFENSE

		G	ATT	YDS	AVG	YPG
1	Randolph Field	10	289	296	1.0	29.6
2	Navy	9	282	484	1.7	53.8
3	Virginia	9	276	499	1.8	55.4
4	Army	9	298	518	1.7	57.6
5	Texas A&M	11	390	845	2.2	76.8
6	Wake Forest	7	207	573	2.8	81.9
7	Tulsa	9	249	737	3.0	81.9
8	Yale	5	181	414	2.3	82.8
9	Southern Cal	9	277	759	2.7	84.3
10	Michigan State	6	220	532	2.4	88.7

PASSING DEFENSE

		G	ATT	COM	PCT	YPC	INT	I%	YDS	YPA	YPG
1	Michigan State	6	66	14	21.2	11.4	12	18.2	160	2.4	26.7
2	Colgate	6	66	15	22.7	15.9	10	15.2	238	3.6	39.7
3	Virginia	9	120	33	27.5	11.3	17	14.2	373	3.1	41.4
4	Alabama	7	97	30	30.9	10.7	14	14.4	320	3.3	45.7
5	Wake Forest	7	96	28	29.2	11.9	12	12.5	334	3.5	47.7
6	Northwestern	9	90	32	35.6	14.4	9	10.0	462	5.1	51.3
7	South Carolina	9	108	36	33.3	13.4	17	15.7	483	4.5	53.7
8	Great Lakes NAS	12	197	65	33.0	10.0	24	12.2	648	3.3	54.0
9	Florida	7	83	25	30.1	15.6	14	16.9	389	4.7	55.6
10	TCU	10	128	48	37.5	11.8	16	12.5	567	4.4	56.7

TOTAL DEFENSE

		G	P	YDS	AVG	YPG
1	Virginia	9	394	872	2.2	96.9
2	Randolph Field	10	516	1108	2.1	110.8
3	Michigan State	6	286	692	2.4	115.3
4	Army	9	499	1162	2.3	129.1
5	Wake Forest	7	303	907	3.0	129.6
6	Navy	9	447	1227	2.7	136.3
7	Yale	5	260	707	2.7	141.4
8	Alabama	7	365	1008	2.8	144.0
9	Southern Cal	9	434	1385	3.2	153.9
10	Texas A&M	11	607	1754	2.9	159.5

SCORING OFFENSE

		G	PTS	AVG
1	Army	9	504	56.0

SCORING DEFENSE

		G	PTS	AVG
1	Army	9	35	3.9

ANNUAL REVIEW

1945 POLL PROGRESSION

AP OCTOBER 8 POLL — OCT. 13 GAMES

#	Team	Record	Result
1	Army	2-0-0	beat # 9 Michigan 28-7
2	Navy	2-0-0	beat Penn State 28-0
3	Notre Dame	2-0-0	beat Dartmouth 34-0
4	Ohio State	2-0-0	beat Wisconsin 12-0
5	Minnesota	2-0-0	beat Fort Warren 14-0
6	Southern Cal	3-0-0	lost to San Diego Navy 6-33
7	Alabama	2-0-0	beat South Carolina 55-0
8	Indiana	2-0-1	beat Nebraska 54-14
9	Michigan	3-1-0	lost to # 1 Army 7-28
10	Texas	3-0-0	beat Oklahoma 12-7
11	Pennsylvania	2-0-0	beat North Carolina 49-0
12	Holy Cross	2-0-0	beat Villanova 26-7
13	Duke	2-1-0	beat Wake Forest 26-19
14	Oklahoma State	2-0-0	beat SMU 26-12
15	Purdue	3-0-0	beat Iowa 40-0
16	Tulsa	3-0-0	beat Texas Tech 18-7
17	Texas A&M	3-0-0	lost to LSU 12-31
18	Tennessee	2-0-0	beat U.T. Chattanooga 30-0
19	Saint Mary's-Cal	2-0-0	beat Pacific 61-0
20	Mississippi State	2-0-0	beat Detroit 41-6
20	Virginia	2-0-0	bye week

AP OCTOBER 15 POLL — OCT. 20 GAMES

#	Team	Record	Result
1	Army	3-0-0	beat Melville, R.I. 55-13
2	Navy	3-0-0	beat Georgia Tech 20-6
3	Notre Dame	3-0-0	beat Pittsburgh 39-9
4	Ohio State	3-0-0	lost to # 9 Purdue 13-35
5	Minnesota	3-0-0	beat Northwestern 30-7
6	Alabama	3-0-0	beat Tennessee 25-7
7	Pennsylvania	3-0-0	bye week
8	Indiana	3-0-1	beat Iowa 52-20
9	Purdue	4-0-0	beat # 4 Ohio State 35-13
10	Texas	4-0-0	beat Arkansas 34-7
11	Saint Mary's-Cal	3-0-0	beat Mc Clellan Field 58-0
12	Georgia	4-0-0	lost to LSU 0-32
13	Michigan	3-2-0	bye week
14	Southern Cal	3-1-0	beat Pacific 52-0
15	Oklahoma State	3-0-0	beat Utah 46-6
16	Duke	3-1-0	bye week
17	Columbia	3-0-0	beat Colgate 31-7
18	Tulsa	4-0-0	beat Nevada 40-0
19	Holy Cross	3-0-0	beat Brown 25-0
20	Mississippi State	3-0-0	beat Maxwell 16-6

AP OCTOBER 22 POLL — OCT. 27 GAMES

#	Team	Record	Result
1	Army	4-0-0	beat # 19 Duke 48-13
2	Notre Dame	4-0-0	beat Iowa 56-0
3	Navy	4-0-0	beat # 7 Pennsylvania 14-7
4	Purdue	5-0-0	lost to Northwestern 14-26
5	Minnesota	4-0-0	lost to # 12 Ohio State 7-20
6	Alabama	4-0-0	beat Georgia 28-14
7	Pennsylvania	3-0-0	lost to # 3 Navy 7-14
8	Indiana	4-0-1	beat # 14 Tulsa 7-2
9	Texas	5-0-0	lost to Rice 6-7
10	Saint Mary's-Cal	4-0-0	bye week
11	Columbia	4-0-0	beat Brown 27-6
12	Ohio State	3-1-0	beat # 5 Minnesota 20-7
13	LSU	3-1-0	beat Vanderbilt 39-7
14	Tulsa	5-0-0	lost to # 8 Indiana 2-7
15	Holy Cross	4-0-0	beat Colgate 21-0
16	Michigan	3-2-0	beat Illinois 19-0
17	Oklahoma State	4-0-0	beat TCU 25-12
18	Mississippi State	4-0-0	bye week
19	Duke	3-1-0	lost to # 1 Army 13-48
20	Southern Cal	4-1-0	lost to Washington 7-13

AP OCTOBER 29 POLL — NOV. 3 GAMES

#	Team	Record	Result
1	Army	5-0-0	beat Villanova 54-0
2	Notre Dame	5-0-0	tied # 3 Navy 6-6
3	Navy	5-0-0	tied # 2 Notre Dame 6-6
4	Alabama	5-0-0	beat Kentucky 60-19
5	Indiana	5-0-1	beat Cornell Coll. 46-6
6	Ohio State	4-1-0	beat # 20 Northwestern 16-14
7	Pennsylvania	3-1-0	beat Princeton 28-0
8	Saint Mary's-Cal	4-0-0	beat Southern Cal 26-0
9	Oklahoma State	5-0-0	bye week
10	Michigan	4-2-0	beat # 16 Minnesota 26-0
11	Holy Cross	5-0-0	beat New London Sub Base 20-6
12	Columbia	5-0-0	beat Cornell 34-26
13	Purdue	5-1-0	beat Pittsburgh 28-0
14	Oklahoma	4-2-0	lost to TCU 7-13
15	Mississippi State	4-0-0	lost to Tulane 13-14
16	Minnesota	4-1-0	lost to # 10 Michigan 0-26
17	LSU	4-1-0	beat Mississippi 32-13
18	Duke	3-2-0	beat Georgia Tech 14-6
19	Washington	4-1-0	beat Oregon 7-0
20	Northwestern	2-2-1	lost to # 6 Ohio State 14-16

AP NOVEMBER 5 POLL — NOV. 10 GAMES

#	Team	Record	Result
1	Army	6-0-0	beat # 2 Notre Dame 48-0
2	Notre Dame	5-0-1	lost to # 1 Army 0-48
3	Alabama	6-0-0	bye week
4	Navy	5-0-1	beat # 7 Michigan 33-7
5	Saint Mary's-Cal	5-0-0	beat Fresno State 32-6
6	Indiana	6-0-1	beat # 20 Minnesota 49-0
7	Michigan	5-2-0	lost to # 4 Navy 7-33
8	Ohio State	5-1-0	beat Pittsburgh 14-0
9	Pennsylvania	4-1-0	beat # 10 Columbia 32-7
10	Columbia	6-0-0	lost to # 9 Pennsylvania 7-32
11	Oklahoma State	5-0-0	beat # 19 Tulsa 12-6
12	Purdue	6-1-0	beat Miami, Ohio 21-7
13	Holy Cross	6-0-0	beat Coast Guard 39-6
14	LSU	5-1-0	lost to Mississippi State 20-27
15	Virginia	5-0-0	beat Richmond 45-0 N11
16	Duke	4-2-0	beat North Carolina St. 26-13
17	Texas	6-1-0	beat Baylor 21-14
18	Washington	5-1-0	lost to Oregon State 6-7
19	Tulsa	5-1-0	lost to #11 Oklahoma State 6-12
20	Minnesota	4-2-0	lost to # 6 Indiana 0-49

AP NOVEMBER 12 POLL — NOV. 17 GAMES

#	Team	Record	Result
1	Army	7-0-0	beat # 6 Pennsylvania 61-0
2	Navy	6-0-1	beat Wisconsin 36-7
3	Alabama	6-0-0	beat Vanderbilt 71-0
4	Indiana	7-0-1	beat Pittsburgh 19-0
5	Saint Mary's-Cal	6-0-0	lost to UCLA 7-13
6	Pennsylvania	5-1-0	lost to # 1 Army 0-61
7	Notre Dame	5-1-1	beat Northwestern 34-7
8	Oklahoma State	6-0-0	beat Texas Tech 46-6
9	Ohio State	6-1-0	beat Illinois 27-2
10	Holy Cross	7-0-0	lost to Temple 6-14
11	Purdue	7-1-0	lost to # 14 Michigan 13-27
12	Penn State	5-1-0	lost to Michigan State 0-33
13	Virginia	6-0-0	beat Oceana 40-0
14	Michigan	5-3-0	beat # 11 Purdue 27-13
15	Oklahoma	5-3-0	lost to Missouri 6-14
16	Mississippi State	5-1-0	beat Northwestern St. 54-0
17	Texas	7-1-0	beat TCU 20-0
18	Tennessee	6-1-0	bye week
19	Tulsa	5-2-0	beat Baylor 26-7
20	Duke	5-2-0	bye week

AP	NOVEMBER 19 POLL		NOV. 24 GAMES
1	Army	8-0-0	bye week
2	Navy	7-0-1	bye week
3	Alabama	7-0-0	beat Pensacola NAS 55-6
4	Indiana	8-0-1	beat # 18 Purdue 26-0
5	Notre Dame	6-1-1	beat Tulane 32-6
6	Oklahoma State	7-0-0	beat Oklahoma 47-0
7	Ohio State	7-1-0	lost to # 8 Michigan 3-7
8	Michigan	6-3-0	beat #7 Ohio State 7-3
9	Saint Mary's-Cal	6-1-0	regular season complete
10	Texas	8-1-0	bye week
11	Pennsylvania	5-2-0	beat Cornell 59-6
12	UCLA	5-2-0	lost to California 0-6
13	Virginia	7-0-0	lost to Maryland 13-19
14	Tennessee	6-1-0	beat Kentucky 14-0
15	Duke	5-2-0	beat North Carolina 14-7
16	Missouri	5-3-0	beat Kansas 33-12
17	Tulsa	6-2-0	beat Arkansas 45-13 (N23)
18	Purdue	7-2-0	lost to # 4 Indiana 0-26
19	LSU	6-2-0	bye week
20	Mississippi State	6-1-0	lost to Mississippi 6-7

AP	NOVEMBER 26 POLL		DEC. 1 GAMES
1	Army	8-0-0	beat # 2 Navy 32-13
2	Navy	7-0-1	lost to # 1 Army 13-32
3	Alabama	8-0-0	beat Mississippi State 55-13
4	Indiana	9-0-1	regular season complete
5	Notre Dame	7-1-1	lost to Great Lakes NAS 7-39
6	Oklahoma State	8-0-0	regular season complete
7	Michigan	7-3-0	regular season complete
8	Pennsylvania	6-2-0	regular season complete
9	Saint Mary's-Cal	6-1-0	
10	Texas	8-1-0	beat Texas A&M 20-10
11	Duke	6-2-0	regular season complete
12	Ohio State	7-2-0	regular season complete
13	Holy Cross	8-1-0	regular season complete
14	Missouri	6-3-0	regular season complete
15	Tulsa	7-2-0	beat Hondo AAF 20-18
16	Southern Cal	6-3-0	beat UCLA 26-15
17	Tennessee	7-1-0	beat Vanderbilt 45-0
18	Clemson	6-2-1	lost to Wake Forerst 6-13
19	Columbia	8-1-0	regular season complete
20	Virginia	7-1-0	lost to North Carolina 18-27

AP	DECEMBER 3 FINAL POLL	RECORD	BOWL BID	DATE	BOWL RESULT	RB	RECORD
1	Army	9-0-0				1	9-0-0
2	Navy	7-1-1				3	7-1-1
3	Alabama	9-0-0	Rose Bowl	J1	beat #11 Southern Cal 34-14	5	10-0-0
4	Indiana	9-0-1				4	9-0-1
5	Oklahoma State	8-0-0	Sugar Bowl	J1	beat # 7 Saint Mary's-Cal 33-13	2	9-0-0
6	Michigan	7-3-0				7	7-3-0
7	Saint Mary's-Cal	6-1-0	Sugar Bowl	J1	lost to # 5 Oklahoma State 13-33	21	6-2-0
8	Pennsylvania	6-2-0				10	6-2-0
9	Notre Dame	7-2-1				6	7-2-1
10	Texas	9-1-0	Cotton Bowl	J1	beat Missouri 40-27	10	10-1-0
11	Southern Cal	7-3-0	Rose Bowl	J1	lost to # 3 Alabama 14-34	32	7-4-0
12	Ohio State	7-2-0				8	7-2-0
13	Duke	6-2-0				12	6-2-0
14	Tennessee	8-1-0				13	8-1-0
15	LSU	7-2-0				11	7-2-0
16	Holy Cross	8-1-0	Orange Bowl	J1	lost to Miami, Fla. 6-13	23	8-2-0
17	Tulsa	8-2-0	Oil Bowl	J1	lost to # 18 Georgia 6-20	16	8-3-0
18	Georgia	8-2-0	Oil Bowl	J1	beat # 17 Tulsa 20-6	15	9-2-0
19	Wake Forest	4-3-1	Gator Bowl	J1	beat South Carolina 26-14	25	5-3-1
20	Columbia	8-1-0				19	8-1-0

1945

CONSENSUS ALL-AMERICANS

POS	Name	HT	WT	School	AA	AP	CM	FC	FW	IN	LK	NE	SN	UP
B	Glenn Davis	5-9	170	Army	•	•	•	•	•	•	•	•	•	•
B	Doc Blanchard	6-0	205	Army	•	•	•	•	•	•	•	•	•	•
B	Herman Wedemeyer	5-10	173	Saint Mary's-Cal	•	•	•	•	•	•	•		•	•
B	Bob Fenimore	6-2	188	Oklahoma State	•	•		•		•		•	•	•
E	Dick Duden	6-2	203	Navy	•	•	•	•	•			•	•	•
E	Hubert Bechtol	6-2	190	Texas	•	•				•	•		•	•
E	Bob Ravensberg	6-1	180	Indiana		•			•		•	•	•	•
E	Max Morris	6-2	195	Northwestern	•			•		•		•	•	•
T	Tex Coulter	6-3	220	Army	•	•	•	•	•	•	•	•	•	•
T	George Savitsky	6-3	250	Pennsylvania	•	•	•	•	•		•	•	•	•
G	Warren Amling	6-0	197	Ohio State	•	•	•	•	•		•	•	•	•
G	John Green	5-11	190	Army	•	•	•	•	•	•	•		•	•
C	Vaughn Mancha	6-0	235	Alabama		•	•	•	•		•		•	•

	OTHERS RECEIVING FIRST-TEAM HONORS				AA	AP	CM	FC	FW	IN	LK	NE	SN	UP
B	Harry Gilmer			Alabama			•			•			•	
B	Arnold Tucker			Army								•		
B	Tom McWilliams			Army								•		
E	Hank Foldberg			Army					•	•				
E	Dick Pitzer			Army						•				
T	Albert Nemetz			Army			•							
T	Mike Castronis			Georgia							•			
T	Tom Hughes			Purdue							•			
G	John Mastrangelo			Notre Dame						•				
G	Al Sparlis			UCLA							•			
G	Art Gerometta			Army			•		•					
C	Dick Scott			Navy							•			
C	Herschel Fuson			Army							•			

HEISMAN TROPHY VOTING

	PLAYER	POS	SCHOOL	TOTAL
1	Doc Blanchard	FB	Army	860
2	Glenn Davis	HB	Army	638
3	Bob Fenimore	HB	Oklahoma State	187
4	Herman Wedemeyer	HB	Saint Mary's-Cal	152
5	Harry Gilmer	HB	Alabama	132
6	Frank Dancewicz	QB	Notre Dame	56
7	Warren Amling	G	Ohio State	42
8	Pete Pihos	FB	Indiana	38

AWARD WINNERS

PLAYER	POS	SCHOOL	AWARD NAME
Doc Blanchard	FB	Army	Maxwell

CONFERENCE STANDINGS

CONFERENCES PLAYED AN ABBREVIATED SCHEDULE DUE TO WORLD WAR II

Big 10

	CONF.			OVERALL		
	W	L	T	W	L	T
Indiana	5	0	1	9	0	1
Michigan	5	1	0	7	3	0
Ohio State	5	2	0	7	2	0
Purdue	3	3	0	7	3	0
Northwestern	3	3	1	4	4	1
Wisconsin	2	3	1	3	4	2
Illinois	1	4	1	2	6	1
Minnesota	1	5	0	4	5	0
Iowa	1	5	0	2	7	0

Big 6

	CONF.			OVERALL		
	W	L	T	W	L	T
Missouri	5	0	0	6	4	0
Oklahoma	4	1	0	5	5	0
Iowa State	2	2	1	4	3	1
Nebraska	2	3	0	4	5	0
Kansas	1	3	1	4	5	1
Kansas State	0	5	0	1	7	0

Border

	CONF.			OVERALL		
	W	L	T	W	L	T
Arizona	1	0	0	5	0	0
New Mexico	1	0	1	6	1	1
Texas Tech	1	0	1	3	5	2
Northern Arizona	0	1	0	2	3	0
West Texas State	0	2	0	2	6	0

Mountain States

	CONF.			OVERALL		
	W	L	T	W	L	T
Denver	4	1	0	4	5	1
Colorado	3	1	0	5	3	0
Utah	3	2	0	4	4	0
Utah State	1	3	0	4	3	0
Colorado State	0	4	0	2	5	1

Pacific Coast

	CONF.			OVERALL		
	W	L	T	W	L	T
Southern Cal	5	1	0	7	4	0
Washington State	6	2	1	6	2	1
Washington	6	3	0	6	3	0
Oregon State	4	4	0	4	4	1
UCLA	2	3	0	5	4	0
California	2	4	1	4	5	1
Oregon	3	6	0	3	6	0
Idaho	1	5	0	1	7	0
Montana	0	1	0	1	4	0

SEC

	CONF.			OVERALL		
	W	L	T	W	L	T
Alabama	6	0	0	10	0	0
Tennessee	3	1	0	8	1	0
LSU	5	2	0	7	2	0
Georgia	4	2	0	9	2	0
Mississippi	3	3	0	4	5	0
Georgia Tech	2	2	0	4	6	0
Mississippi State	2	3	0	6	3	0
Auburn	2	3	0	5	5	0
Vanderbilt	2	4	0	3	6	0
Florida	1	3	1	4	5	1
Tulane	1	3	1	2	6	1
Kentucky	0	5	0	2	8	0

Southern

	CONF.			OVERALL		
	W	L	T	W	L	T
Duke	4	0	0	6	2	0
Wake Forest	3	1	1	5	3	1
William & Mary	4	2	0	6	3	0
Clemson	2	1	1	6	3	1
Maryland	3	2	0	6	2	1
VMI	3	2	0	5	4	0
North Carolina	2	2	0	5	5	0
North Carolina St.	2	4	0	3	6	0
Virginia Tech	2	5	0	2	6	0
South Carolina	0	2	2	2	4	3
Richmond	0	4	0	2	6	0

SWC

	CONF.			OVERALL		
	W	L	T	W	L	T
Texas	5	1	0	10	1	0
SMU	4	2	0	5	6	0
Texas A&M	3	3	0	6	4	0
TCU	3	3	0	5	5	0
Rice	3	3	0	5	6	0
Baylor	2	4	0	5	5	1
Arkansas	1	5	0	3	7	0

Independents

	OVERALL		
	W	L	T
Army	9	0	0
Columbia	8	1	0
Miami, Fla.	9	1	1
Navy	7	1	1
Holy Cross	8	2	0
Virginia	7	2	0
Notre Dame	7	2	1
Pennsylvania	6	2	0
Saint Mary's-Cal	6	2	0
Rutgers	5	2	0
Yale	6	3	0
Great Lakes NAS	6	3	1
Harvard	5	3	0
Penn State	5	3	0
Michigan State	5	3	1
Cornell	5	4	0
Brown	3	4	1
Boston College	3	4	0
Princeton	2	3	2
Pittsburgh	3	7	0
West Virginia	2	6	1
Dartmouth	1	6	1
Syracuse	1	6	0

BOWL GAMES

DATE	GAME	SCORE
J1	Rose	Alabama 34, Southern Cal 14
J1	Oil	Georgia 20, Tulsa 6
J1	Orange	Miami, Fla. 13, Holy Cross 6
J1	Sun	New Mexico 34, Denver 24
J1	Sugar	Oklahoma State 33, Saint Mary's-Cal 13
J1	Cotton	Texas 40, Missouri 27
J1	Gator	Wake Forest 26, South Carolina 14
J1	Raisin	Drake 13, Fresno State 12

1945 NCAA MAJOR COLLEGE STATISTICAL LEADERS

INDIVIDUAL LEADERS

PASSING/COMPLETIONS

		G	ATT	COM	PCT	INT	I%	YDS	YPA	COM.PG
1	Al Dekdebrun, Cornell	9	194	90	46.4	15	7.7	1227	6.3	10.0
2	Leon Joslin, TCU	10	142	69	48.6	11	7.7	955	6.7	6.9
3	Jerry Niles, Iowa	9	179	63	35.2	15	8.4	872	4.9	7.0
4	Herman Wedemeyer, Saint Mary's-Cal	8	103	59	57.3	5	4.9	1040	10.1	7.4
4	Jack Price, Baylor	11	125	59	47.2	16	12.8	708	5.7	5.4
6	Harry Gilmer, Alabama	9	88	57	64.8	3	3.4	905	10.3	6.3
7	Art Dakos, Yale	9	109	56	51.4	10	9.2	723	6.6	6.2
8	Bob DeMoss, Purdue	10	117	55	47.0	12	10.3	742	6.3	5.5
9	Russell Reader, Michigan State	9	90	53	58.9	5	5.6	613	6.8	5.9
10	Ed Holtsinger, Georgia Tech	9	116	49	42.4	9	7.8	682	5.9	5.4

ALL-PURPOSE YARDS

		G	RUSH	REC	INT	PR	KR	YDS	YPG
1	Bob Fenimore, Oklahoma State	8	1048	12	129	157	231	1577	197.1

RUSHING/YARDS

		G	ATT	YDS	AVG	YPG
1	Bob Fenimore, Oklahoma State	8	142	1048	7.4	131.0
2	Glenn Davis, Army	9	82	944	11.5	104.9
3	Ollie Cline, Ohio State	9	171	931	5.4	103.4
4	Walter Schlinkman, Texas Tech	10	145	871	6.0	87.1
5	Ed Cody, Purdue	10	157	847	5.4	84.7
6	Stan Koslowski, Holy Cross	9	186	841	4.5	93.4
7	George Taliaferro, Indiana	10	156	728	4.7	72.8
8	Doc Blanchard, Army	9	101	718	7.1	79.8
9	Lowell Tew, Alabama	9	88	715	8.1	79.4
10	Linwood Sexton, Wichita State	8	120	707	5.9	88.4

RUSHING/YARDS PER CARRY

		G	ATT	YDS	YPC
1	Glenn Davis, Army	9	82	944	11.5
2	Lowell Tew, Alabama	9	88	715	8.1
3	Gene Knight, LSU	9	85	679	8.0
4	Guy Brown, Detroit	9	82	610	7.4
5	Bob Fenimore, Oklahoma State	8	142	1048	7.4
6	Cal Rossi, UCLA	6	95	679	7.1
7	Doc Blanchard, Army	9	101	718	7.1
8	Walter Schlinkman, Texas Tech	10	145	871	6.0
9	Linwood Sexton, Wichita State	8	120	707	5.9
10	Dick Conners, Northwestern	9	116	671	5.8

*-Based on top 20 rushers

RECEIVING/RECEPTIONS

		G	REC	YDS	YPR	YPG	RPG
1	Reid Moseley, Georgia	10	31	662	21.4	66.2	3.1
1	Gene Wilson, SMU	11	31	311	10.0	28.3	2.8
1	Steve Contos, Michigan State	9	31	285	9.2	31.7	3.4
4	Hub Bechtol, Texas	10	25	389	15.6	38.9	2.5
5	Denny O'Connor, Saint Mary's-Cal	8	23	373	16.2	46.6	2.9
5	Bill Canfield, Purdue	10	23	314	13.7	31.4	2.3
7	Joe Joiner, Baylor	11	21	319	15.2	29.0	1.9
7	Paul Walker, Yale	9	21	277	13.2	30.8	2.3
7	Wallace Jones, Kentucky	6	19	369	19.4	61.5	3.2
9	Jesse Mason, TCU	10	19	218	11.5	21.8	1.9

PUNTING

		PUNT	YDS	AVG
1	Howard Maley, SMU	59	2458	41.7
2	Harry Ghaul, Miami, Fla.	63	2584	41.0
3	Floyd Lang, Penn State	22	893	40.6
4	Herman Wedemeyer, Saint Mary's-Cal	24	963	40.1
5	Stan Koslowski, Holy Cross	37	1471	39.8
6	Robert Evans, Pennsylvania	40	1570	39.3
7	Bob Fenimore, Oklahoma State	23	897	39.0
8	Hardy Brown, Tulsa	40	1552	38.8
9	Jimmy Plyler, Texas	49	1897	38.7
10	George Blanda, Kentucky	32	1232	38.5

PUNT RETURNS/YARDS

		PR	YDS	AVG
1	Jake Leicht, Oregon	28	395	14.1
2	Jimmy Jo Robinson, Pittsburgh	17	307	18.1
3	Jack Burns, Temple	NA	301	NA

KICKOFF RETURNS/YARDS

		KR	YDS	AVG
1	Allen Dekdebrun, Cornell	14	321	22.9

SCORING

		TDS	XPT	FG	PTS
1	Doc Blanchard, Army	19	1	0	115
2	Glenn Davis, Army	18	0	0	108
3	Harry Ghaul, Miami, Fla.	13	22	0	100
4	Lou Kusserow, Columbia	15	0	0	90
5	Stan Koslowski, Holy Cross	12	15	0	87
6	Bob Fenimore, Oklahoma State	12	0	0	72
6	Ed Cody, Purdue	12	0	0	72
8	Herman Wedemeyer, Saint Mary's-Cal	9	17	0	71
8	William Cromer, Colorado State	10	11	0	71
10	Five tied	11	0	0	66

INTERCEPTIONS

		INT	YDS
1	Jake Leicht, Oregon	9	195
1	Herman Wedemeyer, Saint Mary's-Cal	9	120

TEAM LEADERS

RUSHING OFFENSE

		G	ATT	YDS	AVG	YPG
1	Army	9	424	3238	7.6	359.8
2	LSU	9	443	2705	6.1	300.6
3	Alabama	9	440	2679	6.1	297.7
4	Oklahoma State	9	383	2293	6.0	286.6
5	Notre Dame	9	451	2395	5.3	266.1
6	Maryland	7	345	1846	5.4	263.7
7	Mississippi State	8	443	2028	4.6	253.5
8	Ohio State	9	505	2133	4.2	237.0
9	Colorado College	8	366	1882	5.1	235.3
10	Indiana	10	484	2331	4.8	233.1

PASSING OFFENSE/YPG

		G	ATT	COM	INT	PCT	YDS	YPA	YPG	I%	YPC
1	Saint Mary's-Cal	8	150	74	16	49.3	1290	8.6	161.3	10.7	17.4
2	Cornell	9	207	95	17	45.9	1351	6.5	150.1	8.2	14.2
3	Georgia	9	159	71	17	44.7	1335	8.4	148.3	10.7	18.8
4	Oklahoma State	8	113	54	11	47.8	1070	9.5	133.8	9.7	19.8
5	Wake Forest	5	93	44	8	47.3	634	6.8	126.8	8.6	14.4
6	Alabama	9	117	71	4	60.7	1116	9.5	124.0	3.4	15.7
7	SMU	11	263	123	26	46.8	1310	5.0	119.1	9.9	10.7
8	TCU	10	190	87	19	45.8	1183	6.2	118.3	10.0	13.6
9	Colgate	6	94	46	8	48.9	694	7.4	115.7	8.5	15.1
10	South Carolina	7	103	44	14	42.7	808	7.8	115.4	13.6	18.4

TOTAL OFFENSE

		G	P	YDS	AVG	YPG
1	Army	9	526	4164	7.9	462.7
2	Alabama	9	557	3795	6.8	421.7
3	Oklahoma State	8	496	3363	6.8	420.4
4	Saint Mary's-Cal	8	502	2995	6.0	374.4
5	Georgia	9	575	3291	5.7	365.7
6	LSU	9	539	3269	6.1	363.2
7	Notre Dame	9	626	3180	5.1	353.3
8	Maryland	7	427	2433	5.7	347.6
9	Indiana	10	619	3254	5.3	325.4
10	Yale	9	648	2911	4.5	323.4

RUSHING DEFENSE

		G	ATT	YDS	AVG	YPG
1	Alabama	9	320	305	1.0	33.9
2	Tennessee	7	231	385	1.7	55.0
3	Temple	8	296	520	1.8	65.0
4	Saint Mary's-Cal	8	240	591	2.5	73.9
5	Penn State	8	295	634	2.1	79.3
6	Yale	9	300	721	2.4	80.1
7	Army	9	357	728	2.0	80.9
8	Texas	10	353	813	2.3	81.3
9	Mississippi State	8	256	670	2.6	83.8
10	Tulsa	10	353	850	2.4	85.0

PASSING DEFENSE

		G	ATT	COM	PCT	YPC	YDS	YPA	YPG
1	Holy Cross	8	104	27	26.0	11.1	301	2.9	37.6
2	Virginia	6	63	18	28.6	14.8	267	4.2	44.5
3	Texas A&M	10	119	37	31.1	12.1	446	3.7	44.6
4	Iowa	9	83	32	38.6	13.5	433	5.2	48.1
5	Georgia	6	72	25	34.7	11.6	289	4.0	48.2
6	Pittsburgh	10	103	39	37.9	12.8	501	4.9	50.1
7	Michigan State	9	99	34	34.3	14.6	497	5.0	55.2
8	Virginia Tech	6	85	27	31.8	12.4	334	3.9	55.7
9	Illinois	9	118	34	28.8	15.2	518	4.4	57.6
10	Florida	9	104	40	38.5	13.4	536	5.2	59.6

TOTAL DEFENSE

		G	P	YDS	AVG	YPG
1	Alabama	9	452	989	2.2	109.9
2	Temple	8	403	1005	2.5	125.6
3	Holy Cross	8	371	1131	3.0	141.4
4	Mississippi State	8	365	1191	3.3	148.9
5	Saint Mary's-Cal	8	397	1236	3.1	154.5
6	Tulsa	10	491	1550	3.2	155.0
7	Yale	9	427	1441	3.4	160.1
8	Tennessee	7	368	1142	3.1	163.1
9	Indiana	10	536	1641	3.1	164.1
10	Army	9	515	1528	3.0	169.8

SCORING OFFENSE

		G	PTS	AVG
1	Army	9	412	45.8

SCORING DEFENSE

		G	PTS	AVG
1	Saint Mary's-Cal	8	32	4.0

ANNUAL REVIEW

1946 POLL PROGRESSION

AP	October 7 Poll		Oct. 12 Games
1	Texas	3-0-0	beat Oklahoma 20-13
2	Army	3-0-0	beat # 4 Michigan 20-13
3	Notre Dame	2-0-0	beat Purdue 49-6
4	Michigan	2-0-0	lost to # 2 Army 13-20
5	UCLA	2-0-0	beat # 17 Stanford 26-6
6	Alabama	3-0-0	beat La. Lafayette 54-0
7	Pennsylvania	1-0-0	beat Dartmouth 39-6
8	Georgia	2-0-0	beat # 19 Kentucky 28-13
9	Tennessee	2-0-0	beat U.T. Chattanooga 47-7
10	Northwestern	2-0-0	beat Minnesota 14-7
11	Columbia	2-0-0	beat # 15 Yale 28-20
12	Illinois	2-1-0	lost to Indiana 7-14
13	LSU	2-0-0	beat Texas A&M 33-9
14	Ohio State	1-0-1	lost to Wisconsin 7-20
15	Yale	2-0-0	lost to # 11 Columbia 20-28
16	Saint Mary's-Cal	2-0-0	lost to California 13-20
17	Stanford	2-0-0	lost to # 5 UCLA 6-26
18	Arkansas	2-0-1	beat Baylor 13-0
19	Kentucky	3-0-0	lost to # 8 Georgia 13-28
19	North Carolina St.	2-0-0	beat Davidson 25-0

AP	October 14 Poll		Oct. 19 Games
1	Army	4-0-0	beat # 11 Columbia 48-14
2	Notre Dame	3-0-0	bye week
3	Texas	4-0-0	beat # 14 Arkansas 20-0
4	UCLA	3-0-0	beat California 13-6
5	Michigan	2-1-0	tied # 10 Northwestern 14-14
6	Pennsylvania	2-0-0	beat Virginia 40-0
7	Alabama	4-0-0	lost to # 9 Tennessee 0-12
8	Georgia	3-0-0	beat Oklahoma State 33-13
9	Tennessee	3-0-0	beat # 7 Alabama 12-0
10	Northwestern	3-0-0	tied # 5 Michigan 14-14
11	Columbia	3-0-0	lost to # 1 Army 14-48
12	LSU	3-0-0	lost to Georgia Tech 7-26
13	Oklahoma	1-2-0	beat Kansas State 28-7
14	Arkansas	3-0-1	lost to # 3 Texas 0-20
15	North Carolina	2-0-1	beat Navy 21-14
16	Rice	2-1-0	beat SMU 21-7
17	Duke	1-2-0	beat Richmond 41-0
18	Indiana	2-2-0	lost to Iowa 0-13
19	William & Mary	3-1-0	beat Wash. & Lee 34-18
20	Tulsa	4-0-0	lost to Detroit 14-20
20	Wisconsin	3-1-0	lost to Illinois 21-27

AP	October 21 Poll		Oct. 26 Games
1	Army	5-0-0	beat # 13 Duke 19-0
2	Notre Dame	3-0-0	beat # 17 Iowa 41-6
3	Texas	5-0-0	lost to # 16 Rice 13-18
4	Tennessee	4-0-0	lost to Wake Forest 6-19
5	UCLA	4-0-0	beat Santa Clara 33-7
6	Pennsylvania	3-0-0	beat Navy 32-19
7	Georgia	4-0-0	beat Furman 70-7
8	Michigan	2-1-1	lost to Illinois 9-13
9	Northwestern	3-0-1	beat Pacific 26-13
10	North Carolina	3-0-1	beat Florida 40-19
11	Alabama	4-1-0	beat Kentucky 21-7
12	North Carolina St.	4-0-0	lost to Virginia Tech 6-14
13	Duke	2-2-0	lost to # 1 Army 0-19
14	Oklahoma	2-2-0	beat Iowa State 63-0
15	Georgia Tech	3-1-0	beat Auburn 27-6
16	Rice	3-1-0	beat # 3 Texas 18-13
17	Iowa	3-1-0	lost to # 2 Notre Dame 6-41
18	William & Mary	4-1-0	beat VMI 41-0
19	Oregon	3-0-1	beat Idaho 26-13
20	Harvard	4-0-0	beat Holy Cross 13-6

AP	October 28 Poll		Nov. 2 Games
1	Army	6-0-0	beat West Virginia 19-0
2	Notre Dame	4-0-0	beat Navy 28-0
3	Pennsylvania	4-0-0	lost to Princeton 14-17
4	UCLA	5-0-0	beat Saint Mary's-Cal 46-20
5	Georgia	5-0-0	beat # 15 Alabama 14-0
6	Northwestern	4-0-1	lost to Ohio State 27-39
7	Texas	5-1-0	beat SMU 19-3
8	Rice	4-1-0	beat Texas Tech 41-6
9	North Carolina	4-0-1	lost to # 10 Tennessee 14-20
10	Tennessee	4-1-0	beat # 9 North Carolina 20-14
11	Illinois	4-2-0	beat Iowa 7-0
12	Wake Forest	4-1-0	beat U.T. Chattanooga 32-14
13	Michigan	2-2-1	beat Minnesota 21-0
14	Oklahoma	3-2-0	beat TCU 14-12
15	Alabama	5-1-0	lost to # 5 Georgia 0-14
16	Georgia Tech	4-1-0	beat # 19 Duke 14-0
17	Harvard	5-0-0	lost to Rutgers 0-13
18	Wisconsin	3-2-0	bye week
19	Duke	2-3-0	lost to # 16 Georgia Tech 0-14
20	Indiana	3-3-0	beat Pittsburgh 20-6

AP	November 4 Poll		Nov. 9 Games
1	Army	7-0-0	tied # 2 Notre Dame 0-0
2	Notre Dame	5-0-0	tied # 1 Army 0-0
3	Georgia	6-0-0	beat Florida 33-14
4	UCLA	6-0-0	beat Oregon 14-0
5	Rice	5-1-0	lost to Arkansas 0-7
6	Texas	6-1-0	beat Baylor 22-7
7	Tennessee	5-1-0	beat Mississippi 18-14
8	Georgia Tech	5-1-0	beat Navy 28-20
9	Pennsylvania	4-1-0	beat Columbia 41-16
10	Illinois	5-2-0	bye week
11	Michigan	3-2-1	beat Michigan State 55-7
12	Ohio State	3-1-2	beat Pittsburgh 20-13
13	Wake Forest	5-1-0	lost to Duke 0-13
14	Southern Cal	4-2-0	beat California 14-0
15	Wisconsin	4-2-0	lost to Iowa 7-21
16	Oklahoma	4-2-0	lost to Kansas 13-16
17	North Carolina	4-1-1	beat William & Mary 21-7
18	Northwestern	4-1-1	lost to Indiana 6-7
19	LSU	5-1-0	beat Alabama 31-21
20	North Carolina St.	5-1-0	lost to Vanderbilt 0-7

AP	November 11 Poll		Nov. 16 Games
1	Army	7-0-1	beat # 5 Pennsylvania 34-7
2	Notre Dame	5-0-1	beat Northwestern 27-0
3	Georgia	7-0-0	beat Auburn 41-0
4	UCLA	7-0-0	beat Montana 61-7
5	Pennsylvania	5-1-0	lost to # 1 Army 7-34
6	Texas	7-1-0	lost to TCU 0-14
7	Georgia Tech	6-1-0	beat Tulane 35-7
8	Tennessee	6-1-0	beat Boston College 33-13
9	Illinois	5-2-0	beat # 13 Ohio State 16-7
10	Michigan	4-2-1	beat Wisconsin 28-6
11	LSU	6-1-0	beat Miami, Fla. 20-7
12	Southern Cal	5-2-0	bye week
13	Ohio State	4-1-2	lost to # 9 Illinois 7-16
14	Rice	5-2-0	beat Texas A&M 27-10
15	North Carolina	5-1-1	beat Wake Forest 26-14
16	Iowa	5-3-0	lost to Minnesota 6-16
17	Arkansas	5-2-1	beat SMU 13-0
18	Yale	5-1-1	beat Princeton 30-2
19	Holy Cross	3-4-0	bye week
20	Duke	3-4-0	beat South Carolina 39-0

AP	November 18 Poll		Nov. 23 Games
1	Army	8-0-1	bye week
2	Notre Dame	6-0-1	beat Tulane 41-0
3	Georgia	8-0-0	beat U.T. Chattanooga 48-27
4	UCLA	8-0-0	beat # 10 Southern Cal 13-6
5	Illinois	6-2-0	beat Northwestern 20-0
6	Georgia Tech	7-1-0	beat Furman 41-7
7	Tennessee	7-1-0	beat Kentucky 7-0
8	Michigan	5-2-1	beat Ohio State 58-6
9	LSU	7-1-0	beat Fordham 40-0
10	Southern Cal	5-2-0	lost to # 4 UCLA 6-13
11	Arkansas	6-2-1	bye week
12	Rice	6-2-0	beat TCU 13-0
13	Pennsylvania	5-2-0	bye week
14	North Carolina	6-1-1	beat Duke 22-7
15	Yale	6-1-1	beat Harvard 27-14
16	Delaware	8-0-0	beat # 19 Muhlenberg 20-12
17	Texas	7-2-0	bye week
18	Oklahoma	5-3-0	beat Nebraska 27-6
19	Muhlenberg	8-0-0	lost to # 16 Delaware 12-20
19	Tulsa	8-1-0	bye week

AP	November 25 Poll		Nov. 30 Games
1	Army	8-0-1	beat Navy 21-18
2	Notre Dame	7-0-1	beat # 16 Southern Cal 26-6
3	Georgia	9-0-0	beat # 7 Georgia Tech 35-7
4	UCLA	9-0-0	beat Nebraska 18-0
5	Illinois	7-2-0	regular season complete
6	Michigan	6-2-1	regular season complete
7	Georgia Tech	8-1-0	lost to # 3 Georgia 7-35
8	Tennessee	8-1-0	beat Vanderbilt 7-6
9	LSU	8-1-0	beat Tulane 41-27
10	Arkansas	6-2-1	lost to Tulsa 13-14
11	North Carolina	7-1-1	beat Virginia 49-14
12	Yale	7-1-1	regular season complete
13	Rice	7-2-0	beat Baylor 38-6
14	Pennsylvania	5-2-0	beat Cornell 26-20
15	Delaware	9-0-0	regular season complete
16	Southern Cal	5-3-0	lost to # 2 Notre Dame 6-26
17	Boston College	6-2-0	lost to Holy Cross 6-13
17	Oklahoma	6-3-0	beat Oklahoma State 73-12
19	Mississippi State	8-1-0	lost to Alabama 7-24
20	Texas	7-2-0	beat Texas A&M 24-7

AP	December 2 Final Poll	Record	Bowl Bid	Date	Bowl Result	RB	Record
1	Notre Dame	8-0-1				2	8-0-1
2	Army	9-0-1				1	9-0-1
3	Georgia	10-0-0	Sugar Bowl	J1	beat # 9 North Carolina 20-10	3	11-0-0
4	UCLA	10-0-0	Rose Bowl	J1	lost to # 5 Illinois 14-45	11	10-1-0
5	Illinois	7-2-0	Rose Bowl	J1	beat # 4 UCLA 45-14	4	8-2-0
6	Michigan	6-2-1				9	6-2-1
7	Tennessee	9-1-0	Orange Bowl	J1	lost to # 10 Rice 0-8	7	9-2-0
8	LSU	9-1-0	Cotton Bowl	J1	tied # 16 Arkansas 0-0	8	9-1-1
9	North Carolina	8-1-1	Sugar Bowl	J1	lost to # 3 Georgia 10-20	15	8-2-1
10	Rice	8-2-0	Orange Bowl	J1	beat # 7 Tennessee 8-0	6	9-2-0
11	Georgia Tech	8-2-0	Oil Bowl	J1	beat Saint Mary's-Cal 41-19	10	9-2-0
12	Yale	7-1-1				20	7-1-1
13	Pennsylvania	6-2-0				13	6-2-0
14	Oklahoma	7-3-0	Gator Bowl	J1	beat # 18 North Carolina St. 34-13	29	8-3-0
15	Texas	8-2-0				5	8-2-0
16	Arkansas	6-3-1	Cotton Bowl	J1	tied # 8 LSU 0-0	31	6-3-2
17	Tulsa	9-1-0				14	9-1-0
18	North Carolina St.	8-2-0	Gator Bowl	J1	lost to # 14 Oklahoma 13-34	41	8-3-0
19	Delaware	9-0-0	Cigar Bowl	J1	beat Rollins 21-7	26	10-0-0
20	Indiana	6-3-0				12	6-3-0

1946

CONSENSUS ALL-AMERICANS

POS	Name	HT	WT	School	AA	AP	CM	FC	FW	IN	NE	SN	UP
B	John Lujack	6-0	180	Notre Dame	•	•	•	•	•	•	•	•	•
B	Charley Trippi	5-11	185	Georgia	•	•	•	•	•	•	•	•	•
B	Glenn Davis	5-9	170	Army	•	•	•	•	•	•	•	•	•
B	Doc Blanchard	6-0	205	Army	•	•	•	•	•	•	•	•	•
E	Burr Baldwin	6-1	196	UCLA	•	•	•	•		•	•		•
E	Hubert Bechtol	6-2	201	Texas	•	•	•	•	•	•	•	•	•
E	Hank Foldberg	6-1	200	Army	•		•	•		•	•		•
T	George Connor	6-3	225	Notre Dame	•	•	•	•	•	•	•	•	•
T	Warren Amling	6-0	197	Ohio State	•	•	•	•	*	•	•	•	•
T	Dick Huffman	6-2	230	Tennessee	•	•	•	•	•		•		
G	Alex Agase	5-10	191	Illinois	•	•	•	•		•	•	•	•
G	Weldon Humble	6-1	214	Rice	•	•	•		•		•		•
C	Paul Duke	6-1	210	Georgia Tech	•	•	•	•		•		•	

OTHERS RECEIVING FIRST-TEAM HONORS

E	Elmer Madar	Michigan	•								
T	George Savitsky	Pennsylvania				•					
G	John Mastrangelo	Notre Dame		•		•			•		
C	George Strohmeyer	Notre Dame				•		•	•		

* FW named Amling as a G

HEISMAN TROPHY VOTING

	PLAYER	POS	SCHOOL	TOTAL
1	Glenn Davis	HB	Army	792
2	Charley Trippi	HB	Georgia	435
3	John Lujack	QB	Notre Dame	379
4	Doc Blanchard	FB	Army	267
5	Arnie Tucker	QB	Army	257
6	Herman Wedemeyer	HB	Saint Mary's-Cal	101
7	Burr Baldwin	E	UCLA	49
8	Bobby Layne	QB	Texas	45

AWARD WINNERS

PLAYER	POS	SCHOOL	AWARD NAME
Charley Trippi	HB	Georgia	Maxwell
George Connor	T	Notre Dame	Outland

CONFERENCE STANDINGS

Big 10

	CONF. W L T			OVERALL W L T		
Illinois	6	1	0	8	2	0
Michigan	5	1	1	6	2	1
Indiana	4	2	0	6	3	0
Iowa	3	3	0	5	4	0
Minnesota	3	4	0	5	4	0
Ohio State	2	3	1	4	3	2
Northwestern	2	3	1	4	4	1
Wisconsin	2	5	0	4	5	0
Purdue	0	5	1	2	6	1

Big 6

	CONF. W L T			OVERALL W L T		
Kansas	4	1	0	7	2	1
Oklahoma	4	1	0	8	3	0
Missouri	3	2	0	5	4	1
Nebraska	3	2	0	3	6	0
Iowa State	1	4	0	2	6	1
Kansas State	0	5	0	0	9	0

Border

	CONF. W L T			OVERALL W L T		
Hardin-Simmons	6	0	0	11	0	0
Texas Tech	3	1	0	8	3	0
New Mexico	4	2	1	5	5	2
Arizona	2	2	1	4	4	2
West Texas State	3	4	0	5	5	0
Northern Arizona	1	2	1	5	2	2
Texas-El Paso	2	4	0	3	6	0
Arizona State	1	4	1	2	7	2
New Mexico State	1	4	0	4	5	0

Mountain States

	CONF. W L T			OVERALL W L T		
Utah State	4	1	1	7	2	1
Denver	4	1	1	5	5	1
Utah	4	2	0	8	3	0
Brigham Young	3	2	1	5	4	1
Colorado	3	2	1	5	4	1
Colorado State	1	5	0	2	7	0
Wyoming	0	6	0	1	8	1

Pacific Coast

	CONF. W L T			OVERALL W L T		
UCLA	7	0	0	10	1	0
Oregon State	6	1	1	7	1	1
Southern Cal	5	2	0	5	4	0
Washington	5	3	0	5	4	0
Stanford	3	3	1	5	3	1
Oregon	3	4	1	4	4	1
Montana	1	3	0	4	4	0
Washington State	1	5	1	1	6	1
California	1	6	0	2	7	0
Idaho	0	5	0	1	8	0

SEC

	CONF. W L T			OVERALL W L T		
Georgia	5	0	0	11	0	0
Tennessee	5	0	0	9	2	0
LSU	5	1	0	9	1	1
Georgia Tech	4	2	0	9	2	0
Mississippi State	3	2	0	8	2	0
Alabama	4	3	0	7	4	0
Vanderbilt	3	4	0	5	4	0
Kentucky	2	3	0	7	3	0
Tulane	2	4	0	3	6	0
Auburn	1	5	0	4	6	0
Mississippi	1	6	0	2	7	0
Florida	0	5	0	0	9	0

Southern

	CONF. W L T			OVERALL W L T		
North Carolina	4	0	1	8	2	1
William & Mary	7	1	0	8	2	0
North Carolina St.	6	1	0	8	3	0
South Carolina	4	2	0	5	3	0
Duke	3	2	0	4	5	0
Richmond	3	2	2	6	2	2
Virginia Tech	3	3	3	3	4	3
George Washington	1	1	0	4	3	0
VMI	2	3	1	4	5	1
Wake Forest	2	3	0	6	3	0
Clemson	2	3	0	4	5	0
Maryland	2	5	0	3	6	0
Wash. & Lee	1	4	0	2	6	0
Furman	1	4	0	2	8	0
Davidson	1	5	0	4	5	0
Citadel	1	5	0	3	5	0

SWC

	CONF. W L T			OVERALL W L T		
Purdue	6	0	0	9	0	0
Rice	5	1	0	9	2	0
Arkansas	5	1	0	6	3	2
Texas	4	2	0	8	2	0
Texas A&M	3	3	0	4	6	0
SMU	2	4	0	4	5	1
TCU	2	4	0	2	7	1
Baylor	0	6	0	1	8	0

Independents

	OVERALL W L T		
Delaware	10	0	0
Army	9	0	1
Notre Dame	8	0	1
Yale	7	1	1
Miami, Fla.	8	2	0
Rutgers	7	2	0
Harvard	7	2	0
Penn State	6	2	0
Pennsylvania	6	2	0
North Texas	7	3	1
Columbia	6	3	0
Saint Mary's-Cal	6	3	0
Boston College	6	3	0
Cornell	5	3	1
Montana St.	5	3	2
Holy Cross	5	4	0
West Virginia	5	5	0
Michigan State	5	5	0
Virginia	4	4	1
Syracuse	4	5	0
Houston	4	6	0
Brown	3	5	1
Pittsburgh	3	5	1
Princeton	3	5	0
Dartmouth	3	6	0
Navy	1	8	0

BOWL GAMES

DATE	GAME	SCORE
J1	Tangerine	Catawba 31, Maryville 6
J1	Cotton	Arkansas 0, LSU 0
J1	Sun	Cincinnati 18, Virginia Tech 6
J1	Oil	Georgia Tech 41, Saint Mary's-Cal 19
J1	Rose	Illinois 45, UCLA 14
J1	Gator	Oklahoma 34, North Carolina St. 13
J1	Sugar	Georgia 20, North Carolina 10
J1	Orange	Rice 8, Tennessee 0
J1	Raisin	San Jose State 20, Utah State 0
J1	Harbor	Montana State 13, New Mexico 13
J4	Alamo	Hardin-Simmons 20, Denver 0

1946 NCAA Major College Statistical Leaders

Individual Leaders

PASSING/COMPLETIONS		G	ATT	COM	PCT	INT	I%	YDS	YPA	TD	TD%	COM.PG
1	Travis Tidwell, Auburn	10	158	79	50.0	10	6.3	943	6.0	5	3.2	7.9
2	Bobby Layne, Texas	10	140	77	55.0	14	10.0	1122	8.0	6	4.3	7.7
3	Ben Raimondi, Indiana	9	138	74	53.6	8	5.8	956	6.9	7	5.1	8.2
4	Harry Gilmer, Alabama	11	160	69	43.1	10	6.3	930	5.8	5	3.1	6.3
5	Bob Thomason, VMI	10	126	66	52.4	4	3.2	833	6.6	10	7.9	6.6
6	Charlie Conerly, Mississippi	9	124	64	51.6	13	10.5	641	5.2	3	2.4	7.1
7	Vic Clark, Texas-El Paso	8	107	61	57.0	8	7.5	604	5.6	6	5.6	7.6
7	Clyde LeForce, Tulsa	10	125	61	48.8	7	5.6	807	6.5	7	5.6	6.1
9	Bob DeMoss, Purdue	8	122	59	48.4	9	7.4	814	6.7	6	4.9	7.4
10	Dick Working, Washington & Lee	7	108	56	51.9	14	13.0	741	6.9	8	7.4	8.0
10	Bill Mackrides, Nevada	8	115	56	48.7	7	6.1	1254	10.9	17	14.8	7.0

ALL-PURPOSE YARDS		G	RUSH	REC	INT	PR	KR	YDS	YPG
1	Rudy Mobley, Hardin-Simmons	10	1262	13	79	273	138	1765	176.5

RUSHING/YARDS		G	ATT	YDS	AVG	YPG
1	Rudy Mobley, Hardin-Simmons	10	227	1262	5.6	126.2
2	Gene Roberts, U.T. Chattanooga	10	167	1113	6.7	111.3
3	Charlie Justice, North Carolina	10	131	943	7.2	94.3
4	Joe Golding, Oklahoma	10	126	902	7.2	90.2
5	Levi Jackson, Yale	9	134	806	6.0	89.6
6	Roger Stephens, Cincinnati	10	101	774	7.7	77.4
7	Travis Tidwell, Auburn	10	181	772	4.3	77.2
8	Charley Trippi, Georgia	10	115	744	6.5	74.4
9	Art Hodges, Wichita State	10	152	733	4.8	73.3
10	Glenn Davis, Army	10	123	712	5.8	71.2

RUSHING/YARDS PER CARRY		G	ATT	YDS	YPC
1	Roger Stephens, Cincinnati	10	101	774	7.7
2	Charlie Justice, North Carolina	10	131	943	7.2
3	Joe Golding, Oklahoma	10	126	902	7.2
4	George Guerre, Michigan State	10	90	633	7.0
5	Joseph Rogers, Villanova	10	90	620	6.9
6	Wally Kretz, Cornell	9	89	602	6.8
7	Gene Roberts, U.T. Chattanooga	10	167	1113	6.7
8	Forrest Hall, San Francisco	9	89	579	6.5
9	Charley Trippi, Georgia	10	115	744	6.5
10	Levi Jackson, Yale	9	134	806	6.0

*-Based on top 20 rushers

RECEIVING/RECEPTIONS		G	REC	YDS	YPR	YPG	RPG
1	Neill Armstrong, Oklahoma State	10	32	479	15.0	47.9	3.2
2	James Montgomery, Arizona State	11	32	399	12.5	36.3	2.9
3	Broughton Williams, Florida	8	29	490	16.9	61.3	3.6
3	Red O'Quinn, Wake Forest	9	29	441	15.2	49.0	3.2
5	Barney Poole, Mississippi	9	28	277	9.9	30.8	3.1
6	John Roderick, Yale	9	27	403	14.9	44.8	3.0
7	George Blomquist, North Carolina St.	10	26	403	15.5	40.3	2.6
8	Sam Marusich, Texas-El Paso	9	26	382	14.7	42.4	2.9
9	Lou Mihajlovich, Indiana	9	25	300	12.0	33.3	2.8
10	Ted Cook, Alabama	11	24	377	15.7	34.3	2.2

PUNTING		PUNT	YDS	AVG
1	John Galvin, Purdue	30	1286	42.9
2	Fred Wendt, Texas-El Paso	46	1969	42.8
3	Charley Loiacano, Lafayette	43	1832	42.6
4	Leslie Palmer, North Carolina St.	31	1296	41.8
5	Harry Ghaul, Miami, Fla.	59	2449	41.5
6	Jerry Moore, Vanderbilt	53	2178	41.1
7	Charlie Conerly, Mississippi	57	2331	40.9
8	Don Rezzer, Denver	30	1221	40.7
9	Bill Long, Oklahoma State	38	1543	40.6
10	Billy Richards, SMU	63	2552	40.5

PUNT RETURNS/YARDS		PR	YDS	AVG
1	Harry Gilmer, Alabama	37	436	11.8
2	Herman Wedemeyer, Saint Mary's-Cal	26	397	15.3
3	Clyde LeForce, Tulsa	25	382	15.3
4	Walt Slater, Tennessee	26	347	13.3
5	George Clark, Duke	21	344	16.4
6	Travis Tidwell, Auburn	29	341	11.8
7	Lindy Berry, TCU	23	315	13.7
8	Shorty McWilliams, Mississippi State	19	306	16.1
9	Joe Wright, Detroit	19	305	16.1
10	Harold Griffin, Florida	15	302	20.1

KICKOFF RETURNS/YARDS		KR	YDS	AVG
1	Forrest Hall, San Francisco	15	573	38.2
2	Bob Longacre, William & Mary	9	375	41.7
3	Charlie Justice, North Carolina	10	344	34.4
4	Louie Viau, Kings Point	10	343	34.3
5	Harold Griffin, Florida	13	311	23.9
6	Art Hodges, Wichita State	14	296	21.1
7	Howard Turner, North Carolina St.	7	275	39.3
8	Wally Kretz, Cornell	11	273	24.8
9	Don Phelps, Kentucky	6	270	45.0
10	Charley Loiacano, Lafayette	15	265	17.7

SCORING		TDS	XPT	FG	PTS
1	Gene Roberts, U.T. Chattanooga	18	9	0	117
2	Rudy Mobley, Hardin-Simmons	16	0	0	96
3	Forrest Hall, San Francisco	13	9	0	87
4	Charley Trippi, Georgia	14	0	0	84
5	Herman Hering, Rutgers	12	8	0	80
6	Glenn Davis, Army	13	0	0	78
7	Charlie Justice, North Carolina	12	0	0	72
8	Clyde LeForce, Tulsa	5	34	1	67
9	Jack Cloud, William & Mary	11	0	0	66
10	Doc Blanchard, Army	10	2	0	62

INTERCEPTIONS		INT	YDS
1	Larry Hatch, Washington	8	114
1	Harry Gilmer, Alabama	8	79
1	Arnold Tucker, Army	8	57
4	Phil O'Donnell, Harvard	7	176

Team Leaders

RUSHING OFFENSE		G	ATT	YDS	AVG	YPG
1	Notre Dame	9	567	3061	5.4	340.1
2	Hardin-Simmons	10	540	2906	5.4	290.6
3	Utah	8	418	2108	5.0	263.5
4	Detroit	10	510	2632	5.2	263.2
5	UCLA	10	508	2598	5.1	259.8
6	Oklahoma	10	499	2354	4.7	235.4
7	North Carolina	10	452	2341	5.2	234.1
8	Yale	9	452	2100	4.6	233.3
9	Pennsylvania	8	378	1865	4.9	233.1
10	Army	10	454	2242	4.9	224.2

PASSING OFFENSE/YPG		G	ATT	COM	INT	PCT	YDS	YPA	TD	YPG	I%	YPC
1	Nevada	8	156	68	14	43.6	1569	10.1	20	198.1	9.0	23.1
2	Georgia	10	206	112	9	54.4	1737	8.4	23	173.7	4.4	15.5
3	Texas	10	186	99	19	53.2	1569	8.4	12	156.9	10.2	15.8
4	Oklahoma State	11	252	107	25	42.5	1652	6.6	13	150.2	9.9	15.4
5	Michigan	9	162	73	22	45.1	1322	8.2	10	146.9	13.6	18.1
6	Boston College	9	175	82	14	46.9	1266	7.2	14	140.7	8.0	15.4
7	Indiana	9	185	95	15	51.4	1264	6.8	8	140.4	8.1	13.3
8	Marquette	9	189	90	19	47.6	1243	6.6	13	138.1	10.1	13.8
9	Princeton	8	167	68	14	40.7	1096	6.6	4	137.0	8.4	16.1
10	Washington & Lee	8	165	87	20	52.7	1085	6.6	12	135.6	12.1	12.5

TOTAL OFFENSE		G	P	YDS	AVG	YPG
1	Notre Dame	9	690	3972	5.8	441.3
2	Georgia	10	622	3946	6.3	394.6
3	Nevada	8	484	3114	6.4	389.3
4	UCLA	10	646	3779	5.8	377.9
5	Hardin-Simmons	10	642	3594	5.6	359.4
6	Michigan	9	579	3166	5.5	351.8
7	Boston College	9	598	3159	5.3	351.0
8	Yale	9	598	3095	5.2	343.9
9	Utah	8	531	2747	5.2	343.4
10	Pennsylvania	8	503	2720	5.4	340.0

RUSHING DEFENSE		G	ATT	YDS	AVG	YPG
1	Oklahoma	10	359	580	1.6	58.0
2	Mississippi State	10	334	664	2.0	66.4
3	Harvard	9	330	679	2.1	75.4
4	South Carolina	8	292	637	2.2	79.6
5	Notre Dame	9	321	753	2.3	83.7
6	North Carolina St.	10	360	850	2.4	85.0
7	Yale	9	310	769	2.5	85.4
8	William & Mary	10	349	895	2.6	89.5
9	Tulsa	10	360	930	2.6	93.0
10	Texas	10	374	934	2.5	93.4

PASSING DEFENSE		G	ATT	COM	PCT	YPC	YDS	YPA	YPG
1	Holy Cross	9	107	35	32.7	13.8	483	4.5	53.7
2	West Texas St.	10	124	43	34.7	13.3	570	4.6	57.0
3	Notre Dame	9	144	54	37.5	9.7	522	3.6	58.0
4	Indiana	9	127	39	30.7	13.8	538	4.2	59.8
5	Florida	9	84	39	46.4	14.3	557	6.6	61.9
6	Rice	10	168	62	36.9	10.2	630	3.8	63.0
7	Detroit	10	160	55	34.4	11.5	634	4.0	63.4
8	Penn State	8	133	46	34.6	11.1	509	3.8	63.6
9	West Virginia	10	131	47	35.9	13.7	642	4.9	64.2
10	Navy	9	115	43	37.4	13.4	578	5.0	64.2

TOTAL DEFENSE		G	P	YDS	AVG	YPG
1	Notre Dame	9	465	1275	2.7	141.7
2	Oklahoma	10	539	1550	2.9	155.0
3	Penn State	8	454	1271	2.8	158.9
4	North Carolina St.	10	501	1621	3.2	162.1
5	Rice	10	547	1663	3.0	166.3
6	Davidson	9	432	1498	3.5	166.4
7	Hardin-Simmons	10	537	1673	3.1	167.3
8	Mississippi State	10	502	1695	3.4	169.5
9	Harvard	9	501	1536	3.1	170.7
10	Texas	10	562	1760	3.1	176.0

SCORING OFFENSE	G	PTS	AVG
1	Georgia	10	372	37.2

SCORING DEFENSE	G	PTS	AVG
1	Notre Dame	9	24	2.7

1947 POLL PROGRESSION

AP October 6 Poll — Oct. 11 Games

1	Notre Dame	1-0-0	beat Purdue 22-7
2	Michigan	2-0-0	beat Pittsburgh 69-0
3	Texas	3-0-0	beat # 15 Oklahoma 34-14
4	Georgia Tech	2-0-0	beat VMI 20-0
5	Army	2-0-0	tied Illinois 0-0
6	Illinois	2-0-0	tied Army 0-0
7	Pennsylvania	1-0-0	beat Dartmouth 32-0
8	California	3-0-0	beat Wisconsin 48-7
9	Georgia	2-1-0	lost to Kentucky 0-26
10	Vanderbilt	2-0-0	beat # 18 Mississippi 10-6
11	Columbia	2-0-0	lost to # 14 Yale 7-17
12	Penn State	2-0-0	beat Fordham 75-0
13	Duke	2-0-0	tied Navy 14-14
14	Yale	2-0-0	beat # 11 Columbia 17-7
15	Oklahoma	2-0-0	lost to # 3 Texas 14-34
16	Rice	0-1-1	beat Tulane 33-0
17	Minnesota	2-0-0	beat Northwestern 37-21
18	Mississippi	3-0-0	lost to # 10 Vanderbilt 6-10
19	North Carolina	1-1-0	lost to Wake Forest 7-19
20	Southern Cal	1-0-1	beat Ohio State 32-0

AP October 13 Poll — Oct. 18 Games

1	Michigan	3-0-0	beat Northwestern 49-21
2	Notre Dame	2-0-0	beat Nebraska 31-0
3	Texas	4-0-0	beat Arkansas 21-6
4	California	4-0-0	beat Washington State 21-6
5	Georgia Tech	3-0-0	beat Auburn 27-7
6	Illinois	2-0-1	beat # 13 Minnesota 40-13
7	Army	2-0-1	beat Virginia Tech 40-0
8	Pennsylvania	2-0-0	beat Columbia 34-14
9	Penn State	3-0-0	beat Syracuse 40-0
10	Vanderbilt	3-0-0	lost to # 20 Kentucky 0-14
11	Southern Cal	2-0-1	beat Oregon State 48-6
12	Yale	3-0-0	lost to Wisconsin 0-9
13	Minnesota	3-0-0	lost to # 6 Illinois 13-40
14	Wake Forest	3-0-0	beat Geo. Washington 39-7
15	Rice	1-1-1	lost to SMU 0-14
16	Virginia	3-0-0	beat Wash. & Lee 32-7
17	Duke	2-0-1	beat Maryland 19-7
18	North Carolina St.	2-1-0	lost to Florida 6-7
19	UCLA	2-1-0	beat Stanford 39-6
20	Kentucky	3-1-0	beat # 10 Vanderbilt 14-0

AP October 20 Poll — Oct. 25 Games

1	Michigan	4-0-0	beat Minnesota 13-6
2	Notre Dame	3-0-0	beat Iowa 21-0
3	Texas	5-0-0	beat Rice 12-0
4	California	5-0-0	lost to # 10 Southern Cal 14-39
5	Illinois	3-0-1	lost to Purdue 7-14
6	Army	3-0-1	lost to Columbia 20-21
7	Georgia Tech	4-0-0	beat Citadel 38-0
8	Pennsylvania	3-0-0	beat Navy 21-0
9	Penn State	4-0-0	beat West Virginia 21-14
10	Southern Cal	3-0-1	beat # 4 California 39-14
11	Wake Forest	4-0-0	lost to # 15 Duke 6-13
12	SMU	4-0-0	beat # 16 UCLA 7-0
13	Virginia	4-0-0	beat VMI 35-6
14	Kentucky	4-1-0	beat Michigan State 7-6
15	Duke	3-0-1	beat # 11 Wake Forest 13-6
16	UCLA	3-1-0	lost to # 12 SMU 0-7
17	Baylor	4-0-0	lost to Texas A&M 0-24
18	LSU	3-1-0	beat # 19 Vanderbilt 19-13
19	Vanderbilt	3-1-0	lost to # 18 LSU 13-19
20	San Fransisco	4-1-0	lost to Oregon 7-34

AP October 27 Poll — Nov. 1 Games

1	Notre Dame	4-0-0	beat Navy 27-0
2	Michigan	5-0-0	beat # 11 Illinois 14-7
3	Texas	6-0-0	lost to # 8 SMU 13-14
4	Pennsylvania	4-0-0	beat Princeton 26-7
5	Southern Cal	4-0-1	beat Washington 19-0
6	Georgia Tech	5-0-0	beat # 9 Duke 7-0
7	Penn State	5-0-0	beat Colgate 46-0
8	SMU	5-0-0	beat # 3 Texas 14-13
9	Duke	4-0-1	lost to # 6 Georgia Tech 0-7
10	Army	3-1-1	beat Wash. & Lee 65-13
11	Illinois	3-1-1	lost to # 2 Michigan 7-14
12	Virginia	5-0-0	beat Richmond 34-0
13	Kentucky	5-1-0	lost to # 18 Alabama 0-13
14	California	5-1-0	beat # 19 UCLA 6-0
15	Wake Forest	4-1-0	lost to William & Mary 0-21
16	Purdue	3-2-0	beat Iowa 21-0
17	LSU	4-1-0	lost to Mississippi 18-20
18	Alabama	4-2-0	beat # 13 Kentucky 13-0
19	UCLA	3-2-0	lost to # 14 California 0-6
20	Columbia	3-2-0	beat Cornell 22-0

AP November 3 Poll — Nov. 8 Games

1	Notre Dame	5-0-0	beat # 9 Army 27-7
2	Michigan	6-0-0	beat Indiana 35-0
3	SMU	6-0-0	beat Texas A&M 13-0
4	Pennsylvania	5-0-0	beat # 10 Virginia 19-7
5	Southern Cal	5-0-1	beat Stanford 14-0
6	Georgia Tech	6-0-0	beat Navy 16-14
7	Penn State	6-0-0	beat Temple 7-0
8	Texas	6-1-0	beat Baylor 28-7
9	Army	4-1-1	lost to # 1 Notre Dame 7-27
10	Virginia	6-0-0	lost to # 4 Pennsylvania 7-19
11	Illinois	3-2-1	beat Western Michigan 60-14
12	California	6-1-0	beat Washington 13-7
13	Duke	4-1-1	lost to Missouri 7-28
14	Purdue	4-2-0	lost to Minnesota 21-26
15	William & Mary	5-1-0	beat VMI 28-20
16	Alabama	5-2-0	bye week
17	Columbia	4-2-0	beat Dartmouth 15-0
18	North Carolina	4-2-0	beat North Carolina St. 41-6
19	Wisconsin	4-1-1	beat Iowa 46-14
20	Yale	5-1-0	lost to Brown 14-20

AP November 10 Poll — Nov. 15 Games

1	Notre Dame	6-0-0	beat Northwestern 26-19
2	Michigan	7-0-0	beat # 9 Wisconsin 40-6
3	Pennsylvania	6-0-0	tied # 13 Army 7-7
4	SMU	7-0-0	beat Arkansas 14-6
5	Southern Cal	6-0-1	bye week
6	Georgia Tech	7-0-0	lost to # 14 Alabama 7-14
7	Texas	7-1-0	beat TCU 20-0
8	Penn State	7-0-0	beat Navy 20-7
9	Wisconsin	5-1-1	lost to # 2 Michigan 6-40
10	California	7-1-0	beat Montana 60-14
11	Illinois	4-2-1	beat Ohio State 28-7
12	William & Mary	6-1-0	beat Wash. & Lee 45-6
13	Army	4-2-1	tied # 3 Pennsylvania 7-7
14	Alabama	5-2-0	beat # 6 Georgia Tech 14-7
15	Mississippi	6-2-0	beat U.T. Chattanooga 52-0
16	Virginia	6-1-0	beat West Virginia 6-0
17	Missouri	6-2-0	lost to Oklahoma 12-21
18	Utah	7-0-0	lost to Idaho 6-7
19	North Carolina	5-2-0	beat Maryland 19-0
20	Minnesota	5-2-0	lost to Iowa 7-13

AP	NOVEMBER 17 POLL		NOV. 22 GAMES
1	Michigan	8-0-0	beat Ohio State 21-0
2	Notre Dame	7-0-0	beat Tulane 59-6
3	SMU	8-0-0	beat Baylor 10-0
4	Southern Cal	6-0-1	beat # 18 UCLA 6-0
5	Penn State	8-0-0	beat Pittsburgh 29-0
6	Pennsylvania	6-0-1	bye week
7	Texas	8-1-0	bye week
8	Alabama	6-2-0	beat LSU 41-12
9	California	8-1-0	beat Stanford 21-18
10	Georgia Tech	7-1-0	beat Furman 51-0
11	Army	4-2-2	bye week
12	Illinois	5-2-1	lost to Northwestern 13-28
13	North Carolina	6-2-0	beat Duke 21-0
14	William & Mary	7-1-0	beat Bowling Green 20-0
15	Mississippi	7-2-0	bye week
16	Virginia	7-1-0	lost to North Carolina St. 2-7
17	Kansas	6-0-2	beat Missouri 20-14
18	UCLA	5-3-0	lost to # 4 Southern Cal 0-6
19	Columbia	6-2-0	beat Syracuse 28-8
20	Rice	4-3-1	beat TCU 7-0

AP	NOVEMBER 24 POLL		NOV. 29 GAMES
1	Notre Dame	8-0-0	bye week
2	Michigan	9-0-0	regular season complete
3	SMU	9-0-0	tied TCU 19-19
4	Southern Cal	7-0-1	bye week
5	Penn State	9-0-0	regular season complete
6	Alabama	7-2-0	beat Miami, Fla. 21-6
7	Texas	8-1-0	beat Texas A&M 32-13
8	Pennsylvania	6-0-1	beat Cornell 21-0
9	Georgia Tech	8-1-0	beat Georgia 7-0
10	North Carolina	7-2-0	beat Virginia 40-7
11	California	9-1-0	regular season complete
12	Army	4-2-2	beat Navy 21-0
13	Kansas	7-0-2	beat Arizona 54-28
14	William & Mary	8-1-0	beat Richmond 35-0
15	Mississippi	7-2-0	beat Mississippi State 33-14
16	Columbia	7-2-0	regular season complete
17	UCLA	5-4-0	regular season complete
18	Rice	5-3-1	beat Baylor 34-6
19	Minnesota	6-3-0	regular season complete
20	Oklahoma	6-2-1	beat Oklahoma State 21-13

AP	DECEMBER 1 POLL		DEC. 6 GAMES
1	Notre Dame	8-0-0	beat # 3 Southern Cal 38-7
2	Michigan	9-0-0	
3	Southern Cal	7-0-1	lost to # 1 Notre Dame 7-38
4	SMU	9-0-1	regular season complete
5	Penn State	9-0-0	
6	Texas	9-1-0	regular season complete
7	Alabama	8-2-0	regular season complete
8	Pennsylvania	7-0-1	regular season complete
9	Georgia Tech	9-1-0	regular season complete
10	North Carolina	8-2-0	regular season complete
11	Army	5-2-2	regular season complete
12	Mississippi	8-2-0	regular season complete
13	Kansas	8-0-2	regular season complete
14	William & Mary	9-1-0	regular season complete
15	California	9-1-0	
16	North Carolina St.	5-3-1	regular season complete
17	Rice	6-3-1	regular season complete
18	Oklahoma	7-2-1	regular season complete
19	UCLA	5-4-0	
20	Catawba	9-1-0	N/A

AP	DECEMBER 8 FINAL POLL	RECORD	BOWL BID	DATE	BOWL RESULT	RB	RECORD
1	Notre Dame	9-0-0				2	9-0-0
2	Michigan	9-0-0	Rose Bowl	J1	beat # 8 Southern Cal 49-0	1	10-0-0
3	SMU	9-0-1	Cotton Bowl	J1	tied # 4 Penn State 13-13	4	9-0-2
4	Penn State	9-0-0	Cotton Bowl	J1	tied # 3 SMU 13-13	9	9-0-1
5	Texas	9-1-0	Sugar Bowl	J1	beat # 6 Alabama 27-7	3	10-1-0
6	Alabama	8-2-0	Sugar Bowl	J1	lost to # 5 Texas 7-27	10	8-3-0
7	Pennsylvania	7-0-1				6	7-0-1
8	Southern Cal	7-1-1	Rose Bowl	J1	lost to # 2 Michigan 0-49	11	7-2-1
9	North Carolina	8-2-0				7	8-2-0
10	Georgia Tech	9-1-0	Orange Bowl	J1	beat # 12 Kansas 20-14	5	10-1-0
11	Army	5-2-2				8	5-2-2
12	Kansas	8-0-2	Orange Bowl	J1	lost to # 10 Georgia Tech 14-20	14	8-1-2
13	Mississippi	8-2-0	Delta Bowl	J1	beat TCU 13-9	15	9-2-0
14	William & Mary	9-1-0	Dixie Bowl	J1	lost to Arkansas 19-21	26	9-2-0
15	California	9-1-0				16	9-1-0
16	Oklahoma	7-2-1				21	7-2-1
17	North Carolina St.	5-3-1				20	5-3-1
18	Rice	6-3-1				13	6-3-1
19	Duke	4-3-2				44	4-3-2
20	Columbia	7-2-0				12	7-2-0

1947

CONSENSUS ALL-AMERICANS

POS	Name	HT	WT	School	AP	CM	FC	FW	IN	NE	SN	UP
B	John Lujack	6-0	180	Notre Dame	•	•	•	•	•	•	•	•
B	Bob Chappuis	6-0	180	Michigan	•	•	•	•	•	•	•	•
B	Doak Walker	5-11	170	SMU	•	•		•	•		•	•
B	Charley Conerly	6-0	184	Mississippi			•	•	•			
B	Bobby Layne	6-0	191	Texas			•			•	•	
E	Paul Cleary	6-1	195	Southern Cal	•		•	•	•	•	•	•
E	Bill Swiacki	6-2	198	Columbia	•	•	•		•	•	•	
T	Bob Davis	6-4	220	Georgia Tech	•	•	•	•	•		•	•
T	George Connor	6-3	225	Notre Dame	•	•		•	•	•	•	•
G	Joe Steffy	5-11	190	Army		•	•	•	•	•	•	•
G	Bill Fischer	6-2	230	Notre Dame	•		•		•	•	•	
C	Chuck Bednarik	6-3	220	Pennsylvania	•	•	•	•	•	•	•	•

OTHERS RECEIVING FIRST-TEAM HONORS

POS		School	
B	Bump Elliott	Michigan	•
B	Ray Evans	Kansas	• •
B	Tony Minisi	Pennsylvania	•
E	Leon Hart	Notre Dame	•
E	Barney Poole	Mississippi	• • •
T	George Savitsky	Pennsylvania	•
T	John Ferraro	Southern Cal	•
T	Dick Harris	Texas	•
T	Ziggy Czarobski	Notre Dame	• •
G	Rod Franz	California	•
G	Steve Suhey	Penn State	• • •
C	Dick Scott	Navy	• • • •

HEISMAN TROPHY VOTING

	PLAYER	POS	SCHOOL	TOTAL
1	John Lujack	QB	Notre Dame	742
2	Bob Chappuis	HB	Michigan	555
3	Doak Walker	RB	SMU	196
4	Charley Conerly	HB	Mississippi	186
5	Harry Gilmer	HB	Alabama	115
6	Bobby Layne	QB	Texas	75
7	Chuck Bednarik	C	Pennsylvania	65
8	Bill Swiacki	E	Columbia	61

AWARD WINNERS

PLAYER	POS	SCHOOL	AWARD NAME
Doak Walker	HB	SMU	Maxwell
Joe Steffy	G	Army	Outland

CONFERENCE STANDINGS

Big 10

	CONF. W L T			OVERALL W L T		
Michigan	6	0	0	10	0	0
Wisconsin	3	2	1	5	3	1
Minnesota	3	3	0	6	3	0
Illinois	3	3	0	5	3	1
Purdue	3	3	0	5	4	0
Indiana	2	3	1	5	3	1
Iowa	2	3	1	3	5	1
Northwestern	2	4	0	3	6	0
Ohio State	1	4	1	2	6	1

Big 6

	CONF. W L T			OVERALL W L T		
Kansas	4	0	1	8	1	2
Oklahoma	4	0	1	7	2	1
Missouri	3	2	0	6	4	0
Nebraska	2	3	0	2	7	0
Iowa State	1	4	0	3	6	0
Kansas State	0	5	0	0	10	0

Border

	CONF. W L T			OVERALL W L T		
Texas Tech	4	0	0	6	5	0
Hardin-Simmons	5	1	0	8	3	0
West Texas State	5	2	0	7	4	0
Arizona	3	2	0	5	4	1
Texas-El Paso	3	3	1	5	3	1
Arizona State	3	4	0	4	7	0
New Mexico	1	5	1	4	5	1
New Mexico State	1	4	0	3	6	0
Northern Arizona	0	4	0	1	7	0

MAC

	CONF. W L T			OVERALL W L T		
Cincinnati	3	1	0	7	3	0
Case Western Reserve	2	1	0	4	5	0
Butler	1	3	0	0	0	0
Ohio U	1	3	0	3	5	1

Mountain States

	CONF. W L T			OVERALL W L T		
Utah	6	0	0	8	1	1
Denver	3	2	1	5	4	1
Utah State	3	3	0	6	5	0
Colorado	3	3	0	4	5	0
Colorado State	2	3	1	5	4	1
Wyoming	2	4	0	4	5	0
Brigham Young	1	5	0	3	7	0

Pacific Coast

	CONF. W L T			OVERALL W L T		
Southern Cal	6	0	0	7	2	1
California	5	1	0	9	1	0
Oregon	5	1	0	7	3	0
UCLA	4	2	0	5	4	0
Montana	2	1	0	7	4	0
Oregon State	3	4	0	5	5	0
Washington	2	5	0	3	6	0
Washington State	2	5	0	3	7	0
Idaho	1	4	0	4	4	0
Stanford	0	7	0	0	9	0

SEC

	CONF. W L T			OVERALL W L T		
Mississippi	6	1	0	9	2	0
Georgia Tech	4	1	0	10	1	0
Alabama	5	2	0	8	3	0
Georgia	3	3	0	7	4	1
Vanderbilt	3	3	0	6	4	0
Mississippi State	2	2	0	7	3	0
Tulane	2	3	2	2	5	2
LSU	2	3	1	5	3	1
Kentucky	2	3	0	8	3	0
Tennessee	2	3	0	5	5	0
Auburn	1	5	0	2	7	0
Florida	0	3	1	4	5	1

Southern

	CONF. W L T			OVERALL W L T		
William & Mary	6	1	0	9	2	0
North Carolina	4	1	0	8	2	0
South Carolina	4	1	1	6	2	1
Duke	3	1	1	4	3	2
Wash. & Lee	3	2	0	5	5	0
Maryland	3	2	1	7	2	2
North Carolina St.	3	2	1	5	3	1
Virginia Tech	4	3	0	4	5	0
Davidson	3	3	1	6	3	1
Wake Forest	3	4	0	6	4	0
VMI	2	3	1	3	5	1
Clemson	1	3	0	4	5	0
Citadel	1	4	0	3	5	0
Furman	1	4	0	2	7	0
Richmond	1	5	0	3	7	0
George Washington	0	4	0	1	7	1

SWC

	CONF. W L T			OVERALL W L T		
SMU	5	0	1	9	0	2
Texas	5	1	0	10	1	0
Rice	4	2	0	6	3	1
TCU	2	3	1	4	5	2
Arkansas	1	4	1	6	4	1
Texas A&M	1	4	1	3	6	1
Baylor	1	5	0	5	5	0

Independents

	OVERALL W L T		
Notre Dame	9	0	0
Penn State	9	0	1
Pennsylvania	7	0	1
Rutgers	8	1	0
North Texas	10	2	0
Nevada	9	2	0
Michigan State	7	2	0
Columbia	7	2	0
Memphis	6	2	1
San Francisco	7	3	0
Virginia	7	3	0
Yale	6	3	0
Army	5	2	2
Villanova	6	3	1
Princeton	5	3	0
West Virginia	6	4	0
Boston College	5	4	0
Brown	4	4	1
Dartmouth	4	4	1
Harvard	4	5	0
Cornell	4	5	0
Syracuse	3	6	0
Houston	3	8	0
Miami, Fla.	2	7	1
Navy	1	7	1
Pittsburgh	1	8	0
Florida State	0	5	0

BOWL GAMES

DATE	GAME	SCORE
D6	Great Lakes	Kentucky 24, Villanova 14
J1	Tangerine	Catawba 7, Marshall 0
J1	Dixie	Arkansas 21, William & Mary 19
J1	Gator	Georgia 20, Maryland 20
J1	Orange	Georgia Tech 20, Kansas 14
J1	Sun	Miami, Ohio 13, Texas Tech 12
J1	Rose	Michigan 49, Southern Cal 0
J1	Delta	Mississippi 13, TCU 9
J1	Salad	Nevada 13, North Texas 6
J1	Sugar	Texas 27, Alabama 7
J1	Cotton	Penn State 13, SMU 13
J1	Raisin	Pacific 26, Wichita State 14
J1	Harbor	Hardin-Simmons 53, San Diego State 0

1947 NCAA MAJOR COLLEGE STATISTICAL LEADERS

INDIVIDUAL LEADERS

PASSING/COMPLETIONS	G	ATT	COM	PCT	INT	I%	YDS	YPA	TD	TD%	COM.PG
1 Charlie Conerly, Mississippi	10	233	133	57.1	7	3.0	1367	5.9	18	7.7	13.3
2 Johnny Rauch, Georgia	11	181	98	54.1	10	5.5	1352	7.5	10	5.5	8.9
3 Fred Enke Jr., Arizona	10	184	88	47.8	10	5.4	1406	7.6	11	6.0	8.8
4 Rex Olsen, Brigham Young	10	158	79	50.0	13	8.2	982	6.2	7	4.4	7.9
5 Dick Working, Washington & Lee	10	143	78	54.5	9	6.3	895	6.3	6	4.2	7.8
6 Norm Van Brocklin, Oregon	10	168	76	45.2	12	7.1	939	5.6	9	5.4	7.6
7 Perry Moss, Illinois	9	127	71	59.9	7	5.5	719	5.7	5	3.9	7.9
8 Frank Downing, Lafayette	9	126	67	53.2	11	8.7	731	5.8	4	3.2	7.4
9 Bobby Layne, Texas	10	115	63	54.9	7	6.1	965	8.4	9	7.8	6.3
10 Tex Furse, Yale *	9	99	61	61.6	5	5.1	722	7.3	1	1.0	6.8

* Two others tied with 61 completions, but they had a lower completion percentage.

ALL-PURPOSE YARDS	G	RUSH	REC	INT	PR	KR	YDS	YPG
1 Wilton Davis, Hardin-Simmons	10	1173	79	0	295	251	1798	179.8

RUSHING/YARDS	G	ATT	YDS	AVG	YPG
1 Wilton Davis, Hardin-Simmons	10	193	1173	6.1	117.3
2 Lou Gambino, Maryland	10	125	904	7.2	90.4
3 Frank Neilson, Utah	10	152	885	5.8	88.5
4 Harry Szulborski, Purdue	9	136	851	6.3	94.6
5 Bobby Forbes, Florida	10	118	766	6.5	76.6
6 Elwyn Rowan, Army	9	123	750	6.1	83.3
7 Ed Smith, Texas-El Paso	9	135	742	5.5	82.4
8 Charles Hall, Arizona	10	124	686	5.5	68.6
9 Linwood Sexton, Wichita State	10	92	685	7.4	68.5
10 Mike Kaysserian, Detroit	10	87	684	7.9	68.4

RUSHING/YARDS PER CARRY	G	ATT	YDS	YPC
1 Jack Kurkowski, Detroit	10	61	614	10.1
2 Mike Kaysserian, Detroit	10	87	684	7.9
3 Linwood Sexton, Wichita State	10	92	685	7.4
4 Lou Gambino, Maryland	10	125	904	7.2
5 Jack Weisenburger, Michigan	9	101	682	6.8
6 Bobby Forbes, Florida	10	118	766	6.5
7 Harry Szulborski, Purdue	9	136	851	6.3
8 Elwyn Rowan, Army	9	123	750	6.1
9 Wilton Davis, Hardin-Simmons	10	193	1173	6.1
10 Art Hodges, Wichita State	10	108	630	5.8

*-Based on top 20 rushers

RECEIVING/RECEPTIONS	G	REC	YDS	TD	YPR	YPG	RPG
1 Barney Poole, Mississippi	10	52	513	8	9.9	51.3	5.2
2 Dan Edwards, Georgia	11	38	540	4	14.2	49.1	3.5
3 Vince Cisterna, Northern Arizona	9	33	441	2	13.4	49.0	3.7
4 John Smith, Arizona	10	31	568	6	18.3	56.8	3.1
4 Bill Swiacki, Columbia	9	31	517	4	16.7	57.4	3.4
4 George Brodnax, Georgia Tech	10	31	400	5	12.9	40.0	3.1
7 Tom Bienemann, Drake	9	30	345	4	11.5	38.3	3.3
8 John Setear, Yale	9	28	290	1	10.4	32.2	3.1
9 Jim Powell, Tennessee	10	27	407	3	15.1	40.7	2.7
10 Lou Mihajlovich, Indiana	9	26	349	2	13.4	38.8	2.9

PUNTING	PUNT	YDS	AVG
1 Leslie Palmer, North Carolina St.	65	2816	43.3
2 Forrest Bast, Lehigh	56	2419	43.2
3 Fred Folger, Duke	68	2910	42.8
4 Jack Pesek, Nebraska	42	1793	42.7
5 Charlie Justice, North Carolina	61	2538	41.6
6 George Grimes, Virginia	50	2040	40.8
7 Zack Clinard, Vanderbilt	50	2030	40.6
8 Harry Ghaul, Miami, Fla.	63	2539	40.3
9 Bob Dean, Cornell	41	1648	40.2
10 Norm Van Brocklin, Oregon	66	2647	40.1

PUNT RETURNS/YARDS	PR	YDS	AVG
1 Lindy Berry, TCU	42	493	11.7
2 Jake Leicht, Oregon	35	480	13.7

KICKOFF RETURNS/YARDS	KR	YDS	AVG
1 Doak Walker, SMU	10	387	38.7
2 Garner Barnett, Arizona State	15	373	24.9
3 Herman Wedemeyer, Saint Mary's-Cal	20	361	18.1

SCORING	TDS	XPT	FG	PTS
1 Lou Gambino, Maryland	16	0	0	96
2 Jack Cloud, William & Mary	15	0	0	90
2 Wilton Davis, Hardin-Simmons	15	0	0	90
4 Doak Walker, SMU	11	18	1	87
5 Terry Brennan, Notre Dame	11	0	0	66
5 Mike Kaysserian, Detroit	11	0	0	66
7 J.R. Boone, Tulsa	10	1	0	61
8 Elwyn Rowan, Army *	10	0	0	60

* Tied with seven others.

INTERCEPTIONS	INT	YDS
1 John Bruce, William & Mary	9	78
2 George Sims, Baylor	8	208
2 Phil O'Donnell, Harvard	8	171
2 Ed Stec, Bucknell	8	NA
5 Jackie Jensen, California	7	114
5 Allen Davis, Utah	7	NA
5 Van Heuitt, Saint Mary's-Cal	7	NA
5 Billy Vigh, Rutgers	7	NA
5 Darrell Royal, Oklahoma	7	38
5 Paul Page, SMU	7	37

TEAM LEADERS

RUSHING OFFENSE	G	ATT	YDS	AVG	YPG
1 Detroit	10	504	3197	6.3	319.7
2 Penn State	9	527	2713	5.1	301.4
3 Wichita State	10	457	2904	6.4	290.4
4 Notre Dame	9	514	2464	4.8	273.8
5 Hardin-Simmons	10	511	2693	5.3	269.3
6 Missouri	10	566	2581	4.6	258.1
7 Oklahoma	10	535	2484	4.6	248.4
8 California	10	463	2470	5.3	247.0
8 Army	9	443	2223	5.0	247.0
10 Michigan	9	429	2149	5.0	238.8

PASSING OFFENSE/YPG	G	ATT	COM	INT	PCT	YDS	YPA	TD	YPG	I%	YPC
1 Michigan	9	153	77	16	50.3	1565	10.2	15	173.9	10.5	20.3
2 Arizona	10	226	107	14	47.3	1680	7.4	13	168.0	6.2	15.7
3 Indiana	9	164	83	17	50.6	1393	8.5	10	154.8	10.4	16.8
4 Mississippi	10	256	147	8	57.4	1496	5.8	19	149.6	3.1	10.2
5 Clemson	9	153	67	19	43.8	1331	8.7	12	147.9	12.4	19.9
6 Brigham Young	10	215	100	18	46.5	1433	6.7	11	143.3	8.4	14.3
7 San Francisco	10	175	79	11	45.1	1407	8.0	8	140.7	6.3	17.8
8 Texas A&M	10	251	117	28	46.6	1389	5.5	10	138.9	11.2	11.9
9 Notre Dame	9	154	86	9	55.8	1213	7.9	12	134.8	5.8	14.1
10 Wake Forest	10	207	86	19	41.5	1327	6.4	9	132.7	9.2	15.4

TOTAL OFFENSE	G	P	YDS	AVG	YPG
1 Michigan	9	582	3714	6.4	412.7
2 Notre Dame	9	668	3677	5.5	408.6
3 Detroit	10	652	4002	6.1	400.2
4 Penn State	9	606	3275	5.4	363.9
5 California	10	627	3625	5.8	362.5
6 Hardin-Simmons	10	634	3573	5.6	357.3
7 Wichita State	10	550	3478	6.3	347.8
8 Missouri	10	707	3428	4.8	342.8
9 San Francisco	10	617	3385	5.5	338.5
9 Nevada	10	684	3385	4.9	338.5

RUSHING DEFENSE	G	ATT	YDS	AVG	YPG
1 Penn State	9	240	153	0.6	17.0
2 William & Mary	10	307	615	2.0	61.5
3 Georgia Tech	10	380	743	2.0	74.3
4 North Carolina	10	347	881	2.5	88.1
5 Boston College	9	295	805	2.7	89.4
6 Holy Cross	10	371	899	2.4	89.9
7 South Carolina	9	329	820	2.5	91.1
8 Alabama	10	342	912	2.7	91.2
9 Utah	9	319	831	2.6	92.3
10 UCLA	9	338	838	2.5	93.1

PASSING DEFENSE	G	ATT	COM	PCT	YPC	INT	I%	YDS	YPA	TD	YPG
1 North Carolina St.	9	86	31	36.0	11.4	15	17.4	354	4.1	1	39.3
2 Colorado College	9	85	24	28.2	15.9	9	10.6	382	4.5	5	42.4
3 Maryland	10	132	40	30.3	11.2	20	15.2	446	3.4	3	44.6
4 Davidson	10	130	40	30.8	12.2	13	10.0	486	3.7	2	48.6
5 Iowa State	9	91	33	36.3	14.7	11	12.1	486	5.3	5	54.0
6 Notre Dame	9	155	53	34.2	9.5	11	7.1	504	3.3	2	56.0
7 Penn State	9	147	40	27.2	13.5	22	15.0	538	3.7	2	59.8
8 Lehigh	9	128	41	32.0	13.1	19	14.8	539	4.2	4	59.9
9 Georgia	11	116	45	38.8	15.1	16	13.8	678	5.8	6	61.6
10 San Francisco	10	148	45	30.4	13.8	17	11.5	620	4.2	4	62.0

TOTAL DEFENSE	G	P	YDS	AVG	YPG
1 Penn State	9	387	691	1.8	76.8
2 William & Mary	10	466	1345	2.9	134.5
3 Georgia Tech	10	535	1418	2.7	141.8
4 Davidson	10	502	1487	3.0	148.7
5 Georgia	11	531	1763	3.3	160.3
6 Holy Cross	10	528	1658	3.1	165.8
7 South Carolina	9	469	1509	3.2	167.7
8 Notre Dame	9	535	1514	2.8	168.2
9 North Carolina St.	9	413	1518	3.7	168.7
10 Pennsylvania	8	417	1401	3.4	175.1

SCORING OFFENSE	G	PTS	AVG
1 Michigan	9	345	38.3
2 Penn State	9	319	35.4
3 Notre Dame	9	291	32.3
4 Nevada	10	308	30.8
5 William & Mary	10	301	30.1
6 Rutgers	9	262	29.1
7 Kansas	10	290	29.0
8 Detroit	10	276	27.6
9 California	10	275	27.5
10 Pennsylvania	8	219	27.4

SCORING DEFENSE	G	PTS	AVG
1 Penn State	9	27	3.0
2 Georgia Tech	10	35	3.5
3 Pennsylvania	8	35	4.4
4 Notre Dame	9	52	5.8
5 Michigan	9	53	5.9
6 Kentucky	10	59	5.9
7 North Carolina St.	9	57	6.3
8 William & Mary	10	66	6.6
9 Texas	10	67	6.7
10 Southern Cal	9	65	7.2

ANNUAL REVIEW

1948 POLL PROGRESSION

October 4 Poll — Oct. 9 Games

AP	Team	Record	Result
1	Notre Dame	2-0-0	beat Michigan State 26-7
2	North Carolina	2-0-0	beat Wake Forest 28-6
3	Northwestern	2-0-0	beat # 8 Minnesota 19-16
4	SMU	2-0-0	lost to Missouri 14-20
5	Army	2-0-0	beat Illinois 26-21
6	Georgia Tech	2-0-0	beat Wash. & Lee 27-0
7	Michigan	2-0-0	beat # 15 Purdue 40-0
8	Minnesota	2-0-0	lost to # 3 Northwestern 16-19
9	California	3-0-0	beat Wisconsin 40-14
10	Penn State	1-0-0	beat Syracuse 34-14
11	Ohio State	2-0-0	lost to Iowa 7-14
12	Pennsylvania	1-0-0	beat Princeton 29-17
13	Arkansas	3-0-0	lost to Baylor 7-23
14	Mississippi	2-0-0	beat Vanderbilt 20-7
15	Purdue	0-2-0	lost to # 7 Michigan 0-40
16	Texas	2-1-0	lost to Oklahoma 14-20
17	Indiana	2-0-0	lost to TCU 6-7
18	Harvard	1-0-0	lost to Cornell 6-40
19	Nevada	2-0-0	beat North Texas 48-7
20	Tennessee	0-1-1	beat U.T. Chattanooga 26-0

October 11 Poll — Oct. 16 Games

AP	Team	Record	Result
1	North Carolina	3-0-0	beat North Carolina St. 14-0
2	Notre Dame	3-0-0	beat Nebraska 44-13
3	Northwestern	3-0-0	lost to # 4 Michigan 0-28
4	Michigan	3-0-0	beat # 3 Northwestern 28-0
5	Army	3-0-0	beat Harvard 20-7
6	California	4-0-0	beat Oregon State 42-0
7	Georgia Tech	3-0-0	beat Auburn 27-0
8	Pennsylvania	2-0-0	beat Columbia 20-14
9	Penn State	2-0-0	beat West Virginia 37-7
10	Mississippi	3-0-0	lost to Tulane 7-20
11	Minnesota	2-1-0	beat Illinois 6-0
12	Missouri	2-1-0	beat Navy 35-14
13	Cornell	3-0-0	beat Syracuse 34-7
14	SMU	2-1-0	beat Rice 33-7
15	Clemson	3-0-0	bye week
16	Georgia	2-1-0	beat LSU 22-0
17	Nevada	3-0-0	beat Saint Mary's-Cal 48-20
18	Duke	1-0-2	beat Maryland 13-12
19	Baylor	2-0-1	beat Texas Tech 13-0
20	Oklahoma	2-1-0	beat Kansas State 42-0

October 18 Poll — Oct. 23 Games

AP	Team	Record	Result
1	Michigan	4-0-0	beat # 13 Minnesota 27-14
2	Notre Dame	4-0-0	beat Iowa 27-12
3	North Carolina	4-0-0	beat LSU 34-7
4	California	5-0-0	beat Washington 21-0
5	Army	4-0-0	beat # 12 Cornell 27-6
6	Georgia Tech	4-0-0	beat Florida 42-7
7	Pennsylvania	3-0-0	beat Navy 20-14
8	Penn State	3-0-0	tied # 19 Michigan State 14-14
9	Missouri	3-1-0	beat Iowa State 49-7
10	Northwestern	3-1-0	beat Syracuse 48-0
11	SMU	3-1-0	beat Santa Clara 33-0
12	Cornell	4-0-0	lost to # 5 Army 6-27
13	Minnesota	3-1-0	lost to # 1 Michigan 14-27
14	Clemson	3-0-0	beat South Carolina 13-7
15	Duke	2-0-2	beat Virginia Tech 7-0
16	Nevada	4-0-0	beat Tulsa 65-14
17	Tulane	3-1-0	beat Auburn 21-6
18	Oklahoma	3-1-0	beat TCU 21-18
19	Michigan State	2-2-0	tied # 8 Penn State 14-14
20	Mississippi	3-1-0	beat Boston College 32-13

October 25 Poll — Oct. 30 Games

AP	Team	Record	Result
1	Michigan	5-0-0	beat Illinois 28-20
2	Notre Dame	5-0-0	beat Navy 41-7
3	North Carolina	5-0-0	beat Tennessee 14-7
4	California	6-0-0	beat Southern Cal 13-7
5	Army	5-0-0	beat Virginia Tech 49-7
6	Georgia Tech	5-0-0	beat Duke 19-7
7	Pennsylvania	4-0-0	beat Wash. & Lee 40-7
8	Missouri	4-1-0	beat Kansas State 49-7
9	Northwestern	4-1-0	beat Ohio State 21-7
10	Nevada	5-0-0	beat Oklahoma City 79-13
11	SMU	4-1-0	beat Texas 21-6
12	Penn State	3-0-1	beat Colgate 32-13
13	Clemson	4-0-0	beat Boston College 26-19
14	Oregon	5-1-0	beat Saint Mary's-Cal 14-13
15	Minnesota	3-2-0	beat Indiana 30-7
16	Oklahoma	4-1-0	beat Iowa State 33-6
17	Michigan State	2-2-1	beat Oregon State 46-21
18	Georgia	4-1-0	beat Alabama 35-0
19	Tulane	4-1-0	beat Mississippi State 9-0
20	Baylor	4-0-1	beat TCU 6-3

November 1 Poll — Nov. 6 Games

AP	Team	Record	Result
1	Notre Dame	6-0-0	beat Indiana 42-6
2	Michigan	6-0-0	beat Navy 35-0
3	North Carolina	6-0-0	tied William & Mary 7-7
4	Army	6-0-0	beat Stanford 43-0
5	California	7-0-0	beat UCLA 28-13
6	Georgia Tech	6-0-0	lost to Tennessee 6-13
7	Pennsylvania	5-0-0	lost to # 14 Penn State 0-13
8	SMU	5-1-0	beat Texas A&M 20-14
9	Missouri	5-1-0	lost to # 15 Oklahoma 7-41
10	Northwestern	5-1-0	beat Wisconsin 16-7
11	Nevada	6-0-0	lost to Santa Clara 0-14
12	Clemson	5-0-0	beat Furman 41-0
13	Georgia	5-1-0	beat Florida 20-12
14	Penn State	4-0-1	beat # 7 Pennsylvania 13-0
15	Oklahoma	5-1-0	beat # 9 Missouri 41-7
16	Oregon	6-1-0	beat Washington 13-7
17	Michigan State	3-2-1	beat Marquette 47-0
18	Wake Forest	4-2-0	beat Duke 27-20
19	Minnesota	4-2-0	beat Purdue 34-7
20	Tulane	5-1-0	beat VMI 28-7

November 8 Poll — Nov. 13 Games

AP	Team	Record	Result
1	Michigan	7-0-0	beat Indiana 54-0
2	Notre Dame	7-0-0	beat # 8 Northwestern 12-7
3	Army	7-0-0	beat # 17 Pennsylvania 26-20
4	California	8-0-0	beat Washington State 44-14
5	Penn State	5-0-1	beat Temple 47-0
6	North Carolina	6-0-1	beat Maryland 49-20
7	SMU	6-1-0	beat Arkansas 14-12
8	Northwestern	6-1-0	lost to # 2 Notre Dame 7-12
9	Oklahoma	6-1-0	beat Nebraska 41-14
10	Clemson	6-0-0	beat # 19 Wake Forest 21-14
11	Georgia Tech	6-1-0	lost to Alabama 12-14
12	Michigan State	4-2-1	beat Iowa State 48-7
13	Georgia	6-1-0	beat Auburn 42-14
14	Minnesota	5-2-0	beat Iowa 28-21
15	Oregon	7-1-0	beat UCLA 26-7
16	Nevada	6-1-0	beat Fresno State 53-7
17	Pennsylvania	5-1-0	lost to # 3 Army 20-26
18	Tennessee	4-2-1	lost to Mississippi 13-16
19	Wake Forest	5-2-0	lost to # 10 Clemson 14-21
20	Missouri	5-2-0	beat Colorado 27-13

AP	NOVEMBER 15 POLL		NOV. 20 GAMES
1	Michigan	8-0-0	beat # 18 Ohio State 13-3
2	Notre Dame	8-0-0	bye week
3	Army	8-0-0	bye week
4	California	9-0-0	beat Stanford 7-6
5	North Carolina	7-0-1	beat Duke 20-0
6	Penn State	6-0-1	lost to Pittsburgh 0-7
7	Northwestern	6-2-0	beat Illinois 20-7
8	Oklahoma	7-1-0	beat Kansas 60-7
9	Clemson	7-0-0	beat Citadel 20-0
10	SMU	7-1-0	beat Baylor 13-6
11	Georgia	7-1-0	beat Furman 33-0
12	Michigan State	5-2-1	beat Washington State 40-0
13	Oregon	8-1-0	beat Oregon State 10-0
14	Tulane	7-1-0	beat Cincinnati 6-0
15	Minnesota	6-2-0	beat Wisconsin 16-0
16	Pennsylvania	5-2-0	bye week
17	Mississippi	7-1-0	bye week
18	Ohio State	6-2-0	lost to # 1 Michigan 3-13
19	Cornell	7-1-0	bye week
20	Georgia Tech	6-2-0	beat Citadel 54-0

AP	NOVEMBER 22 POLL		NOV. 27 GAMES
1	Michigan	9-0-0	regular season complete
2	Notre Dame	8-0-0	beat Washington 46-0
3	Army	8-0-0	tied Navy 21-21
4	North Carolina	8-0-1	beat Virginia 34-12
5	California	10-0-0	regular season complete
6	Oklahoma	8-1-0	beat Oklahoma St. 19-15
7	Northwestern	7-2-0	regular season complete
8	SMU	8-1-0	tied TCU 7-7
9	Clemson	8-0-0	beat Auburn 7-6
10	Oregon	9-1-0	regular season complete
11	Michigan State	6-2-1	tied Santa Clara 21-21
12	Georgia	8-1-0	beat Georgia Tech 21-13
13	Minnesota	7-2-0	regular season complete
14	Tulane	8-1-0	beat LSU 46-0
15	Vanderbilt	6-2-1	beat Tennessee 28-6
16	Mississippi	7-1-0	beat Mississippi State 34-7
17	Ohio State	6-3-0	regular season complete
18	Penn State	6-1-1	beat Washington State 7-0
19	Pennsylvania	5-2-0	lost to Cornell 14-23
20	William & Mary	5-2-2	beat Arkansas 9-0

AP	NOVEMBER 29 FINAL POLL	RECORD	BOWL BID	DATE	BOWL RESULT	RB	RECORD
1	Michigan	9-0-0				1	9-0-0
2	Notre Dame	9-0-0				4	9-0-1
3	North Carolina	9-0-1	Sugar Bowl	J1	lost to # 5 Oklahoma 6-14	3	9-1-1
4	California	10-0-0	Rose Bowl	J1	lost to # 7 Northwestern 14-20	8	10-1-0
5	Oklahoma	9-1-0	Sugar Bowl	J1	beat # 3 North Carolina 14-6	2	10-1-0
6	Army	8-0-1				5	8-0-1
7	Northwestern	7-2-0	Rose Bowl	J1	beat # 4 California 20-14	6	8-2-0
8	Georgia	9-1-0	Orange Bowl	J1	lost to Texas 28-41	19	9-2-0
9	Oregon	9-1-0	Cotton Bowl	J1	lost to # 10 SMU 13-21	14	9-2-0
10	SMU	8-1-1	Cotton Bowl	J1	beat # 9 Oregon 21-13	7	9-1-1
11	Clemson	9-0-0	Gator Bowl	J1	beat Missouri 24-23	9	11-0-0
12	Vanderbilt	7-2-1				21	8-2-1
13	Tulane	9-1-0				12	9-1-0
14	Michigan State	6-2-2				29	6-2-2
15	Mississippi	8-1-0				10	8-1-0
16	Minnesota	7-2-0				16	7-2-0
17	William & Mary	6-2-2	Delta Bowl	J1	beat Oklahoma State 20-0	28	7-2-2
18	Penn State	7-1-1				11	7-1-1
19	Cornell	8-1-0				13	8-1-0
20	Wake Forest	6-3-0	Dixie Bowl	J1	lost to Baylor 7-20	40	6-4-0

1948

CONSENSUS ALL-AMERICANS

POS	Name	HT	WT	School	AA	AP	FC	FW	IN	NE	SN	UP
B	Doak Walker	5-11	168	SMU	•	•	•	•	•	•	•	•
B	Charlie Justice	5-10	165	North Carolina	•	•	•		•	•	•	•
B	Jackie Jensen	5-11	195	California	•	•	•	•	•	•	•	•
B	Emil Sitko	5-8	180	Notre Dame			•			•		
B	Clyde Scott	6-0	175	Arkansas		•		•				
E	Dick Rifenburg	6-3	197	Michigan	•	•	•		•	•	•	•
E	Leon Hart	6-4	225	Notre Dame	•		•	•	•	•	•	•
T	Leo Nomellini	6-2	248	Minnesota	•	•	•	•		•	•	•
T	Alvin Wistert	6-3	218	Michigan	•	•	•	•	•	•	•	•
G	Buddy Burris	5-11	214	Oklahoma	•	•	•		•		•	•
G	Bill Fischer	6-2	233	Notre Dame	•		•	•	•	•	•	•
C	Chuck Bednarik	6-3	220	Pennsylvania	•	•	•	•	•	•	•	•

OTHERS RECEIVING FIRST-TEAM HONORS

POS	Name	School								
B	John Rauch	Georgia		•			•	•		
B	Stan Heath	Nevada								•
B	Bobby Stuart	Army		•						
B	Art Murakowski	Northwestern		•						
B	Bobby Gage	Clemson							•	
B	Pete Elliott	Michigan							•	
B	George Taliaferro	Indiana							•	
B	Jack Cloud	William & Mary					•			
E	Art Weiner	North Carolina				•				
E	George Brodnax	Georgia Tech			•					
E	Sam Tamburo	Penn State			•		•			
E	Barney Poole	Mississippi		•			•			
E	Dale Armstrong	Dartmouth							•	
T	Laurie Niemi	Washington State							•	
T	Paul Lea	Tulane							•	
T	Jim Turner	California							•	
G	William Healy	Georgia Tech					•	•	•	•
G	Joe Henry	Army					•	•		
G	Marty Wendell	Notre Dame			•					
G	Rod Franz	California			•					
C	Alex Sarkisian	Northwestern			•					

FW named Hart as a T; AP named Bill Fischer as a T; IN named Nomellini as a G; NE named Healy as a T

HEISMAN TROPHY VOTING

	PLAYER	POS	SCHOOL	TOTAL
1	Doak Walker	RB	SMU	778
2	Charlie Justice	RB	North Carolina	443
3	Chuck Bednarik	C	Pennsylvania	336
4	Jackie Jensen	RB	California	143
5	Stan Heath	QB	Nevada	113
6	Norm Van Brocklin	QB	Oregon	83
7	Emil Sitko	HB	Notre Dame	73
8	Jack Mitchell	QB	Oklahoma	68

AWARD WINNERS

PLAYER	POS	SCHOOL	AWARD NAME
Chuck Bednarik	C	Pennsylvania	Maxwell
Bill Fischer	G	Notre Dame	Outland

CONFERENCE STANDINGS

Big 10

	CONF. W L T			OVERALL W L T		
Michigan	6	0	0	9	0	0
Northwestern	5	1	0	8	2	0
Minnesota	5	2	0	7	2	0
Ohio State	3	3	0	6	3	0
Iowa	2	4	0	4	5	0
Purdue	2	4	0	3	6	0
Indiana	2	4	0	2	7	0
Illinois	2	5	0	3	6	0
Wisconsin	1	5	0	2	7	0

Big 7

	CONF. W L T			OVERALL W L T		
Oklahoma	5	0	0	10	1	0
Missouri	5	1	0	8	3	0
Kansas	4	2	0	7	3	0
Colorado	2	3	0	3	6	0
Iowa State	2	4	0	4	6	0
Nebraska	2	4	0	2	8	0
Kansas State	0	6	0	1	9	0

Border

	CONF. W L T			OVERALL W L T		
Texas Tech	5	0	0	7	3	0
Texas-El Paso	4	1	1	8	2	1
Arizona	3	2	0	6	5	0
Arizona State	3	2	0	5	5	0
Hardin-Simmons	3	2	1	6	2	3
West Texas St.	2	3	0	6	5	0
Northern Arizona	1	2	0	4	5	0
New Mexico	1	6	0	2	9	0
New Mexico State	0	4	0	3	7	0

MAC

	CONF. W L T			OVERALL W L T		
Miami, Ohio	4	0	0	3	6	0
Western Michigan	3	1	0	6	3	0
Cincinnati	3	1	0	3	6	1
Ohio U	2	3	0	3	6	0
Western Reserve	1	4	0	1	8	1
Butler	0	4	0	0	0	0

Pacific Coast

	CONF. W L T			OVERALL W L T		
Oregon	7	0	0	9	2	0
California	6	0	0	10	1	0
Southern Cal	4	2	0	6	3	1
Washington State	4	3	1	4	5	1
Stanford	3	4	0	4	6	0
Oregon State	2	3	2	5	4	3
Washington	2	5	1	2	7	1
UCLA	2	6	0	3	7	0
Idaho	1	5	0	3	6	0
Montana	0	3	0	3	7	0

SEC

	CONF. W L T			OVERALL W L T		
Georgia	6	0	0	9	2	0
Mississippi	6	1	0	8	1	0
Tulane	5	1	0	9	1	0
Vanderbilt	4	2	1	8	2	1
Georgia Tech	4	3	0	7	3	0
Alabama	4	4	1	6	4	1
Mississippi State	3	3	0	4	4	1
Tennessee	2	3	1	4	4	2
Kentucky	1	3	1	5	3	2
Florida	1	5	0	5	5	0
LSU	1	5	0	3	7	0
Auburn	0	7	0	1	8	1

Skyline

	CONF. W L T			OVERALL W L T		
Utah	5	0	0	8	1	1
Colorado State	4	1	0	8	3	0
Denver	2	2	0	4	5	1
Utah State	2	3	0	5	6	0
Brigham Young	1	3	0	5	6	0
Wyoming	0	5	0	4	5	0

Southern

	CONF. W L T			OVERALL W L T		
Clemson	5	0	0	11	0	0
North Carolina	4	0	1	9	1	1
VMI	5	1	0	6	3	0
William & Mary	5	1	1	7	2	2
Wake Forest	5	2	0	6	4	0
Virginia	4	2	0	5	3	1
Maryland	4	2	0	6	4	0
Duke	3	2	1	4	3	2
Richmond	3	3	1	5	3	2
Wash. & Lee	2	2	0	4	6	0
George Washington	2	4	0	4	6	0
Furman	2	4	0	2	6	1
Davidson	2	5	0	3	5	1
South Carolina	1	3	0	3	5	0
North Carolina St.	1	4	1	3	6	1
Virginia Tech	0	6	1	0	8	1
Citadel	0	5	0	2	7	0

SWC

	CONF. W L T			OVERALL W L T		
SMU	5	0	1	9	1	1
Texas	4	1	1	7	3	1
Baylor	3	2	1	6	3	2
Rice	3	2	1	5	4	1
Arkansas	2	4	0	5	5	0
TCU	1	4	1	4	5	1
Texas A&M	0	5	1	0	9	1

Independents

	OVERALL W L T		
Notre Dame	9	0	0
Penn State	9	0	1
Pennsylvania	7	0	1
Rutgers	8	1	0
North Texas	10	2	0
Nevada	9	2	0
Michigan State	7	2	0
Columbia	7	2	0
Memphis	6	2	1
San Francisco	7	3	0
Virginia	7	3	0
Yale	6	3	0
Army	5	2	2
Villanova	6	3	1
Princeton	5	3	0
West Virginia	6	4	0
Boston College	5	4	0
Brown	4	4	1
Dartmouth	4	4	1
Harvard	4	5	0
Cornell	4	5	0
Syracuse	3	6	0
Houston	3	8	0
Miami, Fla.	2	7	1
Navy	1	7	1
Pittsburgh	1	8	0
Florida State	0	5	0

BOWL GAMES

DATE	GAME	SCORE
D18	Shrine	Hardin-Simmons 40, Ouachita 12
D30	Camellia	Hardin-Simmons 49, Wichita State 12
J1	Tangerine	Murray St. 21, Sul Ross St. 21
J1	Dixie	Baylor 20, Wake Forest 7
J1	Gator	Clemson 24, Missouri 23
J1	Rose	Northwestern 20, California 14
J1	Sugar	Oklahoma 14, North Carolina 6
J1	Cotton	SMU 21, Oregon 13
J1	Orange	Texas 41, Georgia 28
J1	Harbor	Villanova 27, Nevada 7
J1	Sun	West Virginia 21, Texas-El Paso 12
J1	Delta	William & Mary 20, Oklahoma State 0
J1	Salad	Drake 14, Arizona 13
J1	Raisin	Occidental 21, Colorado State 20

1948 NCAA MAJOR COLLEGE STATISTICAL LEADERS

INDIVIDUAL LEADERS

PASSING/COMPLETIONS	G	ATT	COM	PCT	INT	I%	YDS	YPA	TD	TD%	COM.PG
1 Stan Heath, Nevada	9	222	126	56.8	9	4.1	2005	9.0	22	9.9	14.0
2 Jim Finks, Tulsa	10	214	115	53.7	16	7.5	1376	6.4	7	3.3	11.5
3 Bobby Thomason, VMI	9	177	95	53.7	NA	NA	1252	7.1	14	7.9	10.6
4 Jimmy Walthall, West Virginia	11	164	83	50.6	16	9.8	1136	6.9	12	7.3	7.5
4 Eddie Songin, Boston College	9	169	83	49.1	15	8.9	1172	6.9	13	7.7	9.2
6 Gil Johnson, SMU	10	125	76	60.8	13	10.4	1022	8.2	9	7.2	7.6
7 Michael Boyda, Washington & Lee	10	157	75	47.8	14	8.9	1000	6.4	5	3.2	7.5
8 John Ford, Hardin-Simmons	8	121	72	59.5	NA	NA	1114	9.2	9	7.4	9.0
9 Jimmy Southard, Georgia Tech	10	121	71	58.7	NA	NA	1130	9.3	7	5.8	7.1
9 Johnny Rauch, Georgia	10	141	71	50.4	13	9.2	1307	9.3	5	3.6	7.1*

ALL-PURPOSE YARDS	G	RUSH	REC	INT	PR	KR	YDS	YPG
1 Lou Kusserow, Columbia	9	766	463	19	130	359	1737	193.0

RUSHING/YARDS	G	ATT	YDS	AVG	YPG
1 Fred Wendt, Texas-El Paso	10	184	1570	8.5	157.0
2 Ed Price, Tulane	10	188	1178	6.3	117.8
3 Jackie Jensen, California	10	137	1010	7.4	101.0
4 Harry Szulborski, Purdue	9	183	989	5.4	109.9
5 Wilton Davis, Hardin-Simmons	8	135	889	6.6	111.1
6 Gil Stephenson, Army	9	153	887	5.8	98.6
7 Johnny Papit, Virginia	9	135	884	6.5	98.2
8 Charles Hunsinger, Florida	10	116	842	7.3	84.2
9 George Thomas, Oklahoma	10	126	835	6.6	83.5
10 Jay Van Noy, Utah State	10	145	825	5.7	82.5

RUSHING/YARDS PER CARRY	G	ATT	YDS	YPC
1 Fred Wendt, Texas-El Paso	10	184	1570	8.5
2 John Panelli, Notre Dame	10	92	692	7.5
3 Pug Gabrel, Texas-El Paso	10	110	820	7.5
4 Jackie Jensen, California	10	137	1010	7.4
5 Charles Hunsinger, Florida	10	116	842	7.3
6 Bob Stuart, Army	9	114	801	7.0
7 George Thomas, Oklahoma	10	126	835	6.6
7 Wilton Davis, Hardin-Simmons	8	135	889	6.6
9 Johnny Papit, Virginia	9	135	884	6.5
10 Ray Borneman, Texas	10	110	700	6.4

*-Based on top 22 rushers

RECEIVING/RECEPTIONS	G	REC	YDS	TD	YPR	YPG	RPG
1 Johnny "Red" O'Quinn, Wake Forest	9	39	605	7	15.5	67.2	4.3
2 Jim Powell, Tennessee	10	36	462	2	12.8	46.2	3.6
2 Bob McChesney, Hardin-Simmons	8	36	445	5	12.4	55.6	4.5
4 Robert Larsen, Arizona	10	35	408	0	11.7	40.8	3.5
4 Jimmy Ford, Tulsa	10	35	403	2	11.5	40.3	3.5
6 James Lukens, Washington & Lee	10	33	439	1	13.3	43.9	3.3
7 Art Weiner, North Carolina	10	31	481	6	15.5	48.1	3.1
7 Morris Bailey, TCU	10	29	346	1	11.9	34.6	2.9
9 Dick Wilkins, Oregon	10	27	520	5	19.3	52.0	2.7
9 Brian Bell, Washington & Lee	10	27	409	4	15.1	40.9	2.7

PUNTING		PUNT	YDS	AVG
1 Charlie Justice, North Carolina		62	2728	44.0
2 Hall Haynes, Santa Clara		47	2045	43.5
3 Dike Eddleman, Illinois		59	2531	42.9
4 Paul Stombaugh, Furman		72	3031	42.1
5 Doak Walker, SMU		35	1474	42.1
6 Albin Collins, LSU		65	2691	41.4
7 George Taliaferro, Indiana		55	2233	40.6
8 Levi Jackson, Yale		49	1989	40.6
9 Michael Boyda, Washington & Lee		47	1908	40.6
10 Harry Ghaul, Miami, Fla.		69	2781	40.3

PUNT RETURNS/YARDS		PR	YDS	AVG
1 Lee Nalley, Vanderbilt		43	791	18.4
2 Jack Mitchell, Oklahoma		22	515	23.4
3 Hal Littleford, Tennessee		36	448	12.4
4 Henry Pryor, Rutgers		24	444	18.5
5 George Sims, Baylor		15	375	25.0
6 William Doherty, Villanova		25	365	14.6
7 Wilford White, Arizona State		16	354	22.1
8 Charlie Justice, North Carolina		19	332	17.5
9 Bud French, Kansas		25	302	12.1
10 Bobby Vinson, Army		25	295	11.8

KICKOFF RETURNS/YARDS		KR	YDS	AVG
1 Billy Gregus, Wake Forest		19	503	26.5
1 John Freeman, Portland		21	503	24.0
3 Jerry Williams, Washington State		16	478	29.9
4 Jerry Hiller, Marquette		20	462	23.1
5 Bob Goode, Texas A&M		16	407	25.4
6 Ray Malcolm, Montana		17	406	23.9
7 Brooks Biddle, Washington		18	385	21.4
8 Andy Davis, George Washington		19	382	20.1
9 Leonard Corbin, Case Western Reserve		15	378	25.2
10 Lou Kusserow, Columbia		13	359	27.6

SCORING		TDS	XPT	FG	PTS
1 Fred Wendt, Texas-El Paso		20	32	0	152
2 Lou Kusserow, Columbia		18	0	0	108
3 Wilford White, Arizona State		11	20	3	95
4 Dick Talboom, Wyoming		11	28	0	94
5 Joe Geri, Georgia		9	36	0	90
6 Doak Walker, SMU		11	22	0	88
7 Ray Mathews, Clemson		13	0	0	78
8 Jay Van Noy, Utah State		11	7	0	73
9 Six tied		12	0	0	72

INTERCEPTIONS		INT	YDS
1 Jay Van Noy, Utah State		8	228
1 Eli Maricich, Georgia		8	189
1 Bill Olson, Columbia		8	124

TEAM LEADERS

RUSHING OFFENSE	G	ATT	YDS	AVG	YPG
1 Texas-El Paso	10	614	3783	6.2	378.3
2 Army	9	509	2955	5.8	328.3
3 Notre Dame	10	600	3194	5.3	319.4
4 Michigan State	10	498	3041	6.1	304.1
5 Oklahoma	10	555	2964	5.3	296.4
6 California	10	536	2788	5.2	278.8
7 Missouri	10	512	2665	5.2	266.5
8 Detroit	9	431	2285	5.3	253.9
9 Cornell	9	497	2283	4.6	253.7
10 Hardin-Simmons	8	377	2025	5.4	253.1

PASSING OFFENSE	G	ATT	COM	YPC	PCT	YDS	YPA	TD	YPG
1 Nevada	9	245	140	16.4	57.1	2295	9.4	27	255.0
2 Georgia Tech	10	206	112	15.6	54.4	1746	8.5	14	174.6
3 Tulsa	10	265	130	12.1	49.1	1576	5.9	7	157.6
4 San Francisco	9	216	95	14.4	44.0	1364	6.3	11	151.6
5 Georgia	10	162	83	18.1	51.2	1506	9.3	7	150.6
6 Michigan	9	168	77	17.6	45.8	1355	8.1	16	150.6
7 SMU	10	183	109	13.5	59.6	1471	8.0	17	147.1
8 Boston College	9	202	97	13.6	48.0	1318	6.5	14	146.4
9 Minnesota	9	168	79	16.2	47.0	1283	7.6	9	142.6
10 VMI	9	192	98	13.1	51.0	1281	6.7	15	142.3

TOTAL OFFENSE	G	P	YDS	AVG	YPG
1 Nevada	9	630	4383	7.0	487.0
2 Texas-El Paso	10	664	4249	6.4	424.9
3 Army	9	622	3711	6.0	412.3
4 Michigan State	10	627	4027	6.4	402.7
5 Notre Dame	10	708	3964	5.6	396.4
6 Hardin-Simmons	8	498	3139	6.3	392.4
7 Oklahoma	10	654	3802	5.8	380.2
8 Miami, Ohio	9	546	3412	6.2	379.1
9 California	10	692	3726	5.4	372.6
10 Missouri	10	679	3695	5.4	369.5

RUSHING DEFENSE	G	ATT	YDS	AVG	YPG
1 Georgia Tech	10	374	749	2.0	74.9
2 Penn State	9	311	750	2.4	83.3
3 Minnesota	9	312	786	2.5	87.3
4 Michigan	9	373	789	2.1	87.7
5 North Carolina	10	363	885	2.4	88.5
6 Pennsylvania	8	299	714	2.4	89.3
7 Vanderbilt	11	428	993	2.3	90.3
8 Georgia	10	371	946	2.5	94.6
9 California	10	379	957	2.5	95.7
10 Clemson	10	376	1001	2.7	100.1

PASSING DEFENSE	G	ATT	COM	PCT	YPC	YDS	YPA	TD	YPG
1 Northwestern	9	129	42	32.6	11.6	487	3.8	2	54.1
2 Brigham Young	11	144	55	38.2	10.9	599	4.2	1	54.5
3 Maryland	10	130	45	34.6	12.2	550	4.2	5	55.0
4 Brown	9	128	43	33.6	11.7	504	3.9	6	56.0
5 Richmond	10	151	50	33.1	11.8	590	3.9	5	59.0
6 Rice	10	134	54	40.3	11.9	645	4.8	6	64.5
7 Utah	10	152	52	34.2	12.6	655	4.3	3	65.5
8 Montana St.	9	93	41	44.1	14.8	608	6.5	7	67.6
9 Hardin-Simmons	8	89	44	49.4	12.3	542	6.1	2	67.8
10 South Carolina	8	125	47	37.6	11.8	555	4.4	7	69.4

TOTAL DEFENSE	G	P	YDS	AVG	YPG
1 Georgia Tech	10	524	1513	2.9	151.3
2 Penn State	9	454	1424	3.1	158.2
3 Clemson	10	529	1760	3.3	176.0
4 North Carolina	10	558	1767	3.2	176.7
5 Villanova	10	544	1840	3.4	184.0
6 Vanderbilt	11	634	2044	3.2	185.8
7 Minnesota	9	481	1674	3.5	186.0
8 Maryland	10	550	1862	3.4	186.2
9 Army	9	583	1676	2.9	186.2
10 Tennessee	10	590	1875	3.2	187.5

SCORING OFFENSE	G	PTS	AVG
1 Nevada	9	400	44.4
2 Michigan State	10	359	35.9
3 Texas-El Paso	10	349	34.9
4 Lafayette	8	277	34.6
5 Oklahoma	10	336	33.6
6 Army	9	294	32.7
7 Notre Dame	10	320	32.0
8 Missouri	10	308	30.8
9 Vanderbilt	11	328	29.8
10 Arizona State	9	264	29.3

SCORING DEFENSE	G	PTS	AVG
1 Michigan	9	44	4.9
2 Clemson	10	53	5.3
3 Tulane	10	60	6.0
4 Penn State	9	55	6.1
5 Vanderbilt	11	73	6.6
6 William & Mary	10	67	6.7
7 Georgia Tech	10	69	6.9
8 California	10	80	8.0
8 North Carolina	10	80	8.0
10 Oregon	10	82	8.2

1949 POLL PROGRESSION

October 3 Poll — Oct. 8 Games

AP	Team	Rec	Result
1	Michigan	2-0-0	lost to #7 Army 7-21
2	Notre Dame	2-0-0	beat Purdue 35-12
3	Oklahoma	2-0-0	beat #12 Texas 20-14
4	Tulane	2-0-0	beat S.E. Louisiana 40-0
5	Minnesota	2-0-0	beat #20 Northwestern 21-7
6	North Carolina	2-0-0	beat South Carolina 28-13
7	Army	2-0-0	beat #1 Michigan 21-7
8	Southern Cal	2-0-0	tied #11 Ohio State 13-13
9	SMU	2-0-0	bye week
10	California	3-0-0	beat Wisconsin 35-20
11	Ohio State	2-0-0	tied #8 Southern Cal 13-13
12	Texas	3-0-0	lost to #3 Oklahoma 14-20
13	Michigan State	1-1-0	beat Maryland 14-7
14	Duke	2-0-0	lost to Navy 14-28
15	Kentucky	3-0-0	beat Georgia 25-0
16	Villanova	3-0-0	beat Saint Mary's-Cal 28-20
17	Cornell	2-0-0	beat Harvard 33-14
18	UCLA	3-0-0	beat Stanford 14-7
19	Pittsburgh	2-0-0	beat West Virginia 20-7
20	Missouri	0-2-0	beat Oklahoma State 21-7
20	Pennsylvania	2-0-0	beat Columbia 27-7

October 10 Poll — Oct. 15 Games

AP	Team	Rec	Result
1	Notre Dame	3-0-0	beat #4 Tulane 46-7
2	Army	3-0-0	beat Harvard 54-14
3	Oklahoma	3-0-0	beat Kansas 48-26
4	Tulane	3-0-0	lost to #1 Notre Dame 7-46
5	Minnesota	3-0-0	beat #11 Ohio State 27-0
6	North Carolina	3-0-0	beat Wake Forest 28-14
7	Michigan	2-1-0	lost to Northwestern 20-21
8	Kentucky	4-0-0	beat Citadel 44-0
9	California	4-0-0	beat #12 Southern Cal 16-10
10	SMU	2-0-0	lost to Rice 27-41
11	Ohio State	2-0-1	lost to #5 Minnesota 0-27
12	Southern Cal	2-0-1	lost to #9 California 10-16
13	UCLA	4-0-0	lost to Santa Clara 0-14
14	Cornell	3-0-0	beat Yale 48-14
15	Pittsburgh	3-0-0	beat Miami, Ohio 35-26
16	Texas	3-1-0	beat Arkansas 27-14
17	Villanova	4-0-0	lost to Tulsa 19-21
18	Navy	2-1-0	lost to Wisconsin 13-48
19	Michigan State	2-1-0	beat William & Mary 42-13
20	Baylor	3-0-0	beat Texas Tech 28-7

October 17 Poll — Oct. 22 Games

AP	Team	Rec	Result
1	Notre Dame	4-0-0	bye week
2	Army	4-0-0	beat Columbia 63-6
3	Minnesota	4-0-0	lost to #12 Michigan 7-14
4	Oklahoma	4-0-0	beat Nebraska 48-0
5	California	5-0-0	beat Washington 21-7
6	North Carolina	4-0-0	lost to LSU 7-13
7	Kentucky	5-0-0	lost to #17 SMU 7-20
8	Cornell	4-0-0	beat Princeton 14-12
9	Rice	3-1-0	beat #10 Texas 17-15
10	Texas	4-1-0	lost to #9 Rice 15-17
11	Baylor	4-0-0	beat Texas A&M 21-0
12	Michigan	2-2-0	beat #3 Minnesota 14-7
13	Northwestern	2-2-0	lost to Iowa 21-28
14	Pennsylvania	3-0-0	beat Navy 28-7
15	Michigan State	3-1-0	beat Penn State 24-0
16	Pittsburgh	4-0-0	lost to Indiana 14-48
17	SMU	2-1-0	beat #7 Kentucky 20-7
18	Missouri	2-2-0	beat Iowa State 32-0
19	Southern Cal	2-1-1	beat Oregon 40-13
20	Tulane	3-1-0	beat Auburn 14-6

October 24 Poll — Oct. 29 Games

AP	Team	Rec	Result
1	Notre Dame	4-0-0	beat Navy 40-0
2	Army	5-0-0	beat VMI 40-14
3	Oklahoma	5-0-0	beat Iowa State 34-7
4	California	6-0-0	beat #20 UCLA 35-21
5	Rice	4-1-0	beat Texas Tech 28-0
6	Michigan	3-2-0	beat Illinois 13-0
7	Minnesota	4-1-0	lost to Purdue 7-13
8	Cornell	5-0-0	beat Columbia 54-0
9	Pennsylvania	4-0-0	lost to Pittsburgh 21-22
10	Baylor	5-0-0	beat TCU 40-14
11	SMU	3-1-0	beat #19 Texas 7-6
12	Michigan State	4-1-0	beat Temple 62-14
13	North Carolina	4-1-0	lost to Tennessee 6-35
14	Kentucky	5-1-0	beat Cincinnati 14-7
15	Southern Cal	3-1-1	beat Washington 40-28
16	Missouri	3-2-0	beat Nebraska 21-20
17	LSU	3-2-0	beat Mississippi 34-7
18	Ohio State	3-1-1	beat Northwestern 24-7
19	Texas	4-2-0	lost to #11 SMU 6-7
20	UCLA	5-1-0	lost to #4 California 21-35

October 31 Poll — Nov. 5 Games

AP	Team	Rec	Result
1	Notre Dame	5-0-0	beat #10 Michigan State 34-21
2	Army	6-0-0	beat Fordham 35-0
3	Oklahoma	6-0-0	beat Kansas State 39-0
4	California	7-0-0	beat Washington State 33-14
5	Michigan	4-2-0	beat Purdue 20-12
6	Baylor	6-0-0	lost to Texas 0-20
7	Cornell	6-0-0	beat Syracuse 33-7
8	Rice	5-1-0	beat Arkansas 14-0
9	SMU	4-1-0	tied Texas A&M 27-27
10	Michigan State	5-1-0	lost to #1 Notre Dame 21-34
11	Ohio State	4-1-1	beat Pittsburgh 14-10
12	Southern Cal	4-1-1	lost to Stanford 13-34
13	Kentucky	6-1-0	beat Xavier 21-7
14	Tennessee	4-1-1	lost to Georgia Tech 13-30
15	Iowa	4-2-0	lost to Minnesota 7-55
16	Duke	5-1-0	lost to Wake Forest 7-27
17	LSU	4-2-0	beat Vanderbilt 33-13
18	Boston	5-0-0	beat Temple 28-7
19	Virginia	6-0-0	beat #20 Pennsylvania 26-14
20	Fordham	4-0-0	lost to Army 0-35
20	Pennsylvania	4-1-0	lost to #19 Virginia 14-26

November 7 Poll — Nov. 12 Games

AP	Team	Rec	Result
1	Notre Dame	6-0-0	beat North Carolina 42-6
2	Army	7-0-0	beat Pennsylvania 14-13
3	Oklahoma	7-0-0	beat Missouri 27-7
4	California	8-0-0	beat Oregon 41-14
5	Michigan	5-2-0	beat Indiana 20-7
6	Cornell	7-0-0	lost to Dartmouth 7-16
7	Rice	6-1-0	beat Texas A&M 13-0
8	Michigan State	5-2-0	lost to Oregon State 20-25
9	Minnesota	5-2-0	beat Pittsburgh 24-7
10	Virginia	7-0-0	bye week
11	Ohio State	5-1-1	beat Illinois 30-17
12	SMU	4-1-1	beat Arkansas 34-6
13	Texas	5-3-0	lost to TCU 13-14
14	Kentucky	7-1-0	beat Florida 35-0
15	Boston	6-0-0	lost to Maryland 13-14
16	LSU	5-2-0	beat Mississippi State 34-7
17	Stanford	5-2-1	beat Idaho 63-0
18	Wake Forest	4-4-0	lost to North Carolina St. 14-27
19	College of Pacific	7-0-0	N/A
20	Santa Clara	6-1-1	beat Saint Mary's-Cal 19-6

AP	NOVEMBER 14 POLL		NOV. 19 GAMES
1	Notre Dame	7-0-0	beat Iowa 28-7
2	Oklahoma	8-0-0	beat # 19 Santa Clara 28-21
3	California	9-0-0	beat # 12 Stanford 33-14
4	Army	8-0-0	bye week
5	Michigan	6-2-0	tied # 7 Ohio State 7-7
6	Rice	7-1-0	beat TCU 20-14
7	Ohio State	6-1-1	tied # 5 Michigan 7-7
8	Minnesota	6-2-0	beat Wisconsin 14-6
9	Virginia	7-0-0	lost to # 19 Tulane 14-28
10	SMU	5-1-1	lost to # 15 Baylor 26-35
11	Kentucky	8-1-0	lost to Tennessee 0-6
12	Stanford	6-2-1	lost to # 3 California 14-33
13	LSU	6-2-0	beat S.E. Louisiana 48-7
14	Dartmouth	6-1-0	lost to Princeton 13-19
15	Baylor	7-1-0	beat # 10 SMU 35-26
16	Maryland	6-1-0	bye week
17	Cornell	7-1-0	bye week
18	Michigan State	5-3-0	beat Arizona 75-0
19	Santa Clara	7-1-1	lost to # 2 Oklahoma 21-28
19	Tulane	6-1-1	beat # 9 Virginia 28-14

AP	NOVEMBER 21 POLL		NOV. 26 GAMES
1	Notre Dame	8-0-0	beat # 17 Southern Cal 32-0
2	California	10-0-0	regular season complete
3	Oklahoma	9-0-0	beat Oklahoma State 41-0
4	Army	8-0-0	beat Navy 38-0
5	Ohio State	6-1-2	regular season complete
6	Michigan	6-2-1	regular season complete
7	Rice	8-1-0	beat # 9 Baylor 21-7
8	Minnesota	7-2-0	regular season complete
9	Baylor	8-1-0	lost to # 7 Rice 7-21
10	Tulane	7-1-1	lost to # 13 LSU 0-21
11	College of Pacific	9-0-0	N/A
12	Stanford	6-3-1	regular season complete
13	LSU	7-2-0	beat # 10 Tulane 21-0
14	Santa Clara	7-2-1	regular season complete
15	Maryland	6-1-0	beat West Virginia 47-7
16	Villanova	8-1-0	regular season complete
17	Southern Cal	5-2-1	lost to # 1 Notre Dame 0-32
18	Tennessee	6-2-1	beat Vanderbilt 26-20
19	North Carolina	6-3-0	beat Virginia 14-7
20	Cornell	7-1-0	beat Pennsylvania 29-21
20	Kentucky	8-2-0	beat Miami, Fla. 21-6

AP	NOVEMBER 28 FINAL POLL	RECORD	BOWL BID	DATE	BOWL RESULT	RB	RECORD
1	Notre Dame	9-0-0				1	10-0-0
2	Oklahoma	10-0-0	Sugar Bowl	J2	beat # 9 LSU 35-0	2	11-0-0
3	California	10-0-0	Rose Bowl	J2	lost to # 6 Ohio State 14-17	5	10-1-0
4	Army	9-0-0				3	9-0-0
5	Rice	9-1-0	Cotton Bowl	J2	beat # 16 North Carolina 27-13	6	10-1-0
6	Ohio State	6-1-2	Rose Bowl	J2	beat # 3 California 17-14	4	7-1-2
7	Michigan	6-2-1				7	6-2-1
8	Minnesota	7-2-0				10	7-2-0
9	LSU	8-2-0	Sugar Bowl	J2	lost to # 2 Oklahoma 0-35	13	8-3-0
10	College of Pacific	10-0-0				NR	10-0-0
11	Kentucky	9-2-0	Orange Bowl	J2	lost to Santa Clara 13-21	19	9-3-0
12	Cornell	8-1-0				8	8-1-0
13	Villanova	8-1-0				20	8-1-0
14	Maryland	7-1-0	Gator Bowl	J2	beat # 20 Missouri 20-7	15	9-1-0
15	Santa Clara	7-2-1	Orange Bowl	J2	beat # 11 Kentucky 21-13	18	8-2-1
16	North Carolina	7-3-0	Cotton Bowl	J2	lost to # 5 Rice 13-27	23	7-4-0
17	Tennessee	7-2-1				12	7-2-1
18	Princeton	6-3-0				44	6-3-0
19	Michigan State	6-3-0				40	6-3-0
20	Baylor	8-2-0				9	8-2-0
20	Missouri	7-3-0	Gator Bowl	J2	lost to # 14 Maryland 7-20	38	7-4-0

1949

CONSENSUS ALL-AMERICANS

POS	Name	HT	WT	School	AA	AP	FC	FW	IN	NE	SN	UP
B	Emil Sitko	5-8	180	Notre Dame	•	•	•	•	•	•	•	•
B	Doak Walker	5-11	170	SMU	•	•		•	•	•	•	•
B	Arnold Galiffa	6-2	190	Army		•	•	•		•	•	•
B	Bob Williams	6-1	180	Notre Dame	•		•		•		•	
E	Leon Hart	6-5	260	Notre Dame	•	•	•	•	•	•	•	•
E	James Williams	6-0	197	Rice		•	•	•		•		
T	Leo Nomellini	6-2	255	Minnesota	•	•		•		•	•	•
T	Alvin Wistert	6-3	223	Michigan	•			•		•	•	•
G	Rod Franz	6-1	198	California	•	•	•	•		•	•	•
G	Ed Bagdon	5-10	200	Michigan State			•	•		•	•	•
C	Clayton Tonnemaker	6-3	240	Minnesota		•	•	•		•	•	•

OTHERS RECEIVING FIRST-TEAM HONORS

B	Lynn Chandnois			Michigan State			•		•			
B	Charlie Justice			North Carolina	•	•	•					
B	Eddie Price			Tulane					•			
B	Darrell Royal			Oklahoma					•			
B	Eddie LeBaron			Pacific			•		•			
B	John Papit			Virginia					•			
B	George Thomas			Oklahoma					•			
B	Randall Clay			Texas					•			
B	George Sella			Princeton					•			
E	Art Weiner			North Carolina					•		•	•
E	Jim Owens			Oklahoma					•			
E	Dan Foldberg			Army					•			
E	Ken Rose			Stanford					•			
E	Ken Powell			North Carolina					•			
T	Allen Wahl			Michigan				•	•			
T	Wade Walker			Oklahoma		•	•	•	•			
T	Jim Martin			Notre Dame		•		•				
T	Jim Turner			California					•			
T	Thurman McGraw			Colorado State					•			
G	John Schweder			Pennsylvania		•			•			
G	Stan West			Oklahoma	•				•			
G	Bernie Barkouskie			Pittsburgh			•		•		•	
G	Bud McFadin			Texas					•			
G	Bob Gain			Kentucky					•			
G	Forrest Klein			California					•			
C	Tom Novak			Nebraska					•			
C	Joe Watson			Rice					•		•	

FC named Franz as a T; FC named Walker as a G; NE named Nomellini as a G; FC selected Barkouskie as a T

HEISMAN TROPHY VOTING

	PLAYER	POS	SCHOOL	TOTAL
1	Leon Hart	E	Notre Dame	995
2	Charlie Justice	RB	North Carolina	272
3	Doak Walker	RB	SMU	229
4	Arnold Galiffa	QB	Army	196
5	Bob Williams	QB	Notre Dame	189
6	Eddie LeBaron	QB	Pacific	122
7	Clayton Tonnemaker	C	Minnesota	81
8	Emil Sitko	HB	Notre Dame	79

AWARD WINNERS

PLAYER	POS	SCHOOL	AWARD NAME
Leon Hart	E	Notre Dame	Maxwell
Ed Bagdon	G	Michigan State	Outland

CONFERENCE STANDINGS

Big 10

	CONF.			OVERALL		
	W	L	T	W	L	T
Ohio State	4	1	1	7	1	2
Michigan	4	1	1	6	2	1
Minnesota	4	2	0	7	2	0
Wisconsin	3	2	1	5	3	1
Illinois	3	3	1	3	4	2
Iowa	3	3	0	4	5	0
Northwestern	3	4	0	4	5	0
Purdue	2	4	0	4	5	0
Indiana	0	6	0	1	8	0

Big 7

	CONF.			OVERALL		
	W	L	T	W	L	T
Oklahoma	5	0	0	11	0	0
Missouri	5	1	0	7	4	0
Iowa State	3	3	0	5	3	1
Nebraska	3	3	0	4	5	0
Kansas	2	4	0	5	5	0
Colorado	1	4	0	3	7	0
Kansas State	1	5	0	2	8	0

Border

	CONF.			OVERALL		
	W	L	T	W	L	T
Texas Tech	5	0	0	7	5	0
Arizona State	4	1	0	7	3	0
Texas-El Paso	4	2	0	8	2	1
Hardin-Simmons	4	2	0	6	4	1
West Texas State	3	2	0	5	4	0
Arizona	2	4	0	2	7	1
New Mexico State	1	4	0	4	6	0
New Mexico	1	6	0	2	8	0
Northern Arizona	0	3	0	1	6	1

MAC

	CONF.			OVERALL		
	W	L	T	W	L	T
Cincinnati	4	0	0	7	4	0
Miami, Ohio	3	1	0	5	4	0
Ohio U	2	2	1	4	4	1
Western Michigan	2	3	0	4	4	0
Case Western Reserve	1	3	0	4	5	1
Butler	0	3	0	0	0	0

Pacific Coast

	CONF.			OVERALL		
	W	L	T	W	L	T
California	7	0	0	10	1	0
UCLA	5	2	0	6	3	0
Stanford	4	2	0	7	3	1
Southern Cal	4	2	0	5	3	1
Oregon State	5	3	0	7	3	0
Oregon	2	5	0	4	6	0
Washington	2	5	0	3	7	0
Washington State	2	6	0	3	6	0
Idaho	1	4	0	3	5	0
Montana	0	3	0	5	4	0

SEC

	CONF.			OVERALL		
	W	L	T	W	L	T
Tulane	5	1	0	7	2	1
Kentucky	4	1	0	9	3	0
Tennessee	4	1	1	7	2	1
Georgia Tech	5	2	0	7	3	0
LSU	4	2	0	8	3	0
Alabama	4	3	1	6	3	1
Vanderbilt	4	4	0	5	5	0
Auburn	2	4	2	2	4	3
Mississippi	2	4	0	4	5	1
Florida	1	4	1	4	5	1
Georgia	1	4	1	4	6	1
Mississippi State	0	6	0	0	8	1

Skyline

	CONF.			OVERALL		
	W	L	T	W	L	T
Wyoming	5	0	0	9	1	0
Colorado State	4	1	0	9	1	0
Denver	2	2	0	4	6	0
Utah	2	3	0	2	7	1
Utah State	1	3	0	3	7	0
Brigham Young	0	5	0	0	11	0

Southern

	CONF.			OVERALL		
	W	L	T	W	L	T
North Carolina	5	0	0	7	4	0
Maryland	4	0	0	9	1	0
Wash. & Lee	3	1	1	3	5	1
Duke	4	2	0	6	3	0
William & Mary	4	2	0	6	4	0
VMI	3	2	1	3	5	1
South Carolina	3	3	0	4	6	0
Wake Forest	3	3	0	4	6	0
Furman	3	3	0	3	6	0
Clemson	2	2	0	4	4	2
Citadel	2	2	0	4	5	0
George Washington	2	3	0	4	5	0
North Carolina St.	3	6	0	3	7	0
Richmond	2	6	0	3	7	0
Virginia Tech	1	5	2	1	7	2
Davidson	1	5	0	2	8	0

SWC

	CONF.			OVERALL		
	W	L	T	W	L	T
Rice	6	0	0	10	1	0
Baylor	4	2	0	8	2	0
TCU	3	3	0	6	3	1
Texas	3	3	0	6	4	0
SMU	2	3	1	5	4	1
Arkansas	2	4	0	5	5	0
Texas A&M	0	5	1	1	8	1

Independents

	OVERALL		
	W	L	T
Notre Dame	10	0	0
Army	9	0	0
Memphis	9	1	0
Florida State	9	1	0
Brown	8	1	0
Cornell	8	1	0
Villanova	8	1	0
Virginia	7	2	0
Santa Clara	8	2	1
Boston U.	6	2	0
Dartmouth	6	2	0
North Texas	8	4	0
Miami, Fla.	6	3	0
Michigan State	6	3	0
Rutgers	6	3	0
Princeton	6	3	0
Pittsburgh	6	3	0
Fordham	5	3	0
Penn State	5	4	0
Houston	5	4	1
Pennsylvania	4	4	0
Yale	4	4	0
Boston College	4	4	1
Syracuse	4	5	0
West Virginia	4	6	1
Navy	3	5	1
Columbia	2	7	0
Harvard	1	8	0

BOWL GAMES

DATE	GAME	SCORE
D31	Raisin	San Jose State 20, Texas Tech 13
J1	Salad	Xavier 33, Arizona State 21
J2	Tangerine	St. Vincent 7, Emory & Henry 6
J2	Gator	Maryland 20, Missouri 7
J2	Rose	Ohio State 17, California 14
J2	Sugar	Oklahoma 35, LSU 0
J2	Cotton	Rice 27, North Carolina 13
J2	Sun	Texas-El Paso 33, Georgetown 20
J2	Orange	Santa Clara 21, Kentucky 13

1949 NCAA Major College Statistical Leaders

Individual Leaders

PASSING/COMPLETIONS	G	ATT	COM	PCT	INT	I%	YDS	YPA	TD	TD%	COM.PG
1 Adrian Burk, Baylor	10	191	110	57.6	6	3.1	1428	7.5	14	7.3	11.0
2 Tom O'Malley, Cincinnati	10	225	108	48.0	15	6.7	1617	7.2	16	7.1	10.8
3 Eddie Songin, Boston College	9	210	106	50.5	15	7.1	1318	6.3	8	3.8	11.8
3 Lindy Berry, TCU	10	220	106	48.2	23	10.5	1445	6.6	11	5.0	10.6
5 Paul Campbell, Texas	10	182	91	50.0	12	6.6	1312	7.5	7	3.9	9.1
6 Buddy Lex, William & Mary	10	168	90	53.6	13	7.7	1325	7.9	18	10.7	9.0
7 Ed Jesse, Nevada	9	185	89	48.1	13	7.0	1159	6.3	5	2.7	9.9
8 Eddie Kriwiel, Wichita State	10	184	88	47.8	22	12.0	1253	6.8	10	5.4	8.8
9 Dick Doheny, Fordham	8	140	87	62.1	5	3.6	1127	8.1	13	9.3	10.9
9 Jim Powers, Southern Cal	9	148	87	58.8	11	7.4	1215	8.2	12	8.1	9.7

ALL-PURPOSE YARDS	G	RUSH	REC	INT	PR	KR	YPG
1 Johnny Papit, Virginia	9	1214	0	0	0	397	179.0

RUSHING/YARDS	G	ATT	YDS	AVG	YPG
1 John Dottley, Mississippi	10	208	1312	6.3	131.2
2 Johnny Papit, Virginia	9	197	1214	6.2	134.9
3 Ed Price, Tulane	10	171	1137	6.6	113.7
4 John Pont, Miami, Ohio	9	128	977	7.6	108.6
5 Johnny Bright, Drake	9	170	975	5.7	108.3
6 Al Egler, Colgate	9	142	933	6.6	103.7
7 Lynn Chandnois, Michigan State	9	129	885	6.9	98.3
8 Pug Gabrel, Texas El-Paso	10	145	881	6.1	88.1
9 George Thomas, Oklahoma	10	133	859	6.5	85.9
10 Ollie Matson, San Francisco	10	156	853	5.5	85.3

RUSHING/YARDS PER CARRY	G	ATT	YDS	YPC
1 John Pont, Miami, Ohio	9	128	977	7.6
2 Lynn Chandnois, Michigan State	9	129	885	6.9
3 Ed Price, Tulane	10	171	1137	6.6
4 Al Egler, Colgate	9	142	933	6.6
5 Walker Jones, Wyoming	10	119	777	6.5
6 John Karras, Illinois	9	127	826	6.5
7 George Thomas, Oklahoma	10	133	859	6.5
8 Charles Hunsinger, Florida	10	122	774	6.3
9 Lindell Pearson, Oklahoma	10	119	753	6.3
10 John Dottley, Mississippi	10	208	1312	6.3

*-Based on top 20 rushers

RECEIVING/RECEPTIONS	G	REC	YDS	TD	YPR	RPG	YPG
1 Art Weiner, North Carolina	10	52	762	7	14.7	5.2	76.2
2 Alex Loyd, Oklahoma State	10	47	669	2	14.2	4.7	66.9
3 Vito Ragazzo, William & Mary	10	44	793	15	18.0	4.4	79.3
4 Ben Procter, Texas	10	43	724	5	16.8	4.3	72.4
5 Pete Brown, Davidson	10	43	509	2	11.8	4.3	50.9
6 Jim Kelly, Cincinnati	10	42	478	2	11.4	4.2	47.8
6 J.D. Ison, Baylor	10	42	457	6	10.9	4.2	45.7
9 Gene Ackerman, Missouri	10	40	576	2	14.4	4.0	57.6
9 Al Pfeifer, Fordham	8	38	477	8	12.6	4.8	59.6
10 Mott Price, Davidson	10	37	538	1	14.5	3.7	53.8
10 Morris Bailey, TCU	10	37	501	3	13.5	3.7	50.1

PUNTING	PUNT	YDS	AVG
1 Paul Stombaugh, Furman	57	2550	44.7
2 Charlie Justice, North Carolina	63	2777	44.1
3 Hal Haynes, Santa Clara	58	2558	44.1
4 Ed Brown, San Francisco	51	2178	42.7
5 John Caputo, Utah State	65	2730	42.0
6 Harold Chaffee, Colorado State	33	1386	42.0
7 Jackie Calvert, Clemson	25	1045	41.8
8 Bob Manire, Colorado	35	1463	41.8
9 Fred Montsdeoca, Florida	62	2579	41.6
10 William Hardisty, Pittsburgh	39	1607	41.2

PUNT RETURNS/YARDS	PR	YDS	AVG
1 Lee Nalley, Vanderbilt	35	498	14.2
2 Gene Gibson, Cincinnati	21	438	20.9
3 Jimmy Nutter, Wichita State	23	426	18.5
4 Selmer Pederson, Wyoming	24	386	16.1
5 Frank Neilson, Utah	27	356	13.2
6 Lindy Berry, TCU	18	334	18.6
7 Mitford Johnson, Baylor	21	334	15.9
8 Jimmy Jordan, Georgia Tech	20	306	15.3
9 Jack Christiansen, Colorado State	20	301	15.1
10 Ollie Matson, San Francisco	17	298	17.5

KICKOFF RETURNS/YARDS	KR	YDS	AVG
1 Johnny Subda, Nevada	18	444	24.7
2 Jay Van Noy, Utah State	19	441	23.2
3 Bennie Aldridge, Oklahoma State	19	404	21.3
4 Vernon Wynott, Columbia	18	399	22.2
5 Johnny Papit, Virginia	17	397	23.4
6 Woodley Lewis, Oregon	9	387	43.0
7 John Pont, Miami, Ohio	13	385	29.6
8 Hi Faubion, Kansas State	17	383	22.5
8 Ernie Johnson, UCLA	17	383	22.5
10 Jack O'Loughlin, Montana	16	368	23.0

SCORING	TDS	XPT	FG	PTS
1 George Thomas, Oklahoma	19	3	0	117
2 Vito Ragazzo, William & Mary	15	0	0	90
3 John Dottley, Mississippi	14	0	0	84
4 Doak Walker, SMU	11	17	0	83
5 Eddie Talboom, Wyoming	8	31	0	79
6 James Cain, Army	13	0	0	78
6 James Monachino, California	13	0	0	78
6 Gil Stephenson, Army	13	0	0	78
9 Randy Clay, Texas	8	28	0	76
9 John Glorioso, Missouri	8	28	0	76

INTERCEPTIONS	INT	YDS
1 Bobby Wilson, Mississippi	10	70
2 Jimmy Glisson, Tulane	9	141
2 Bill Sheffold, Oregon State	9	138
2 Jim Rinehart, Arkansas	9	NA
2 Charles Lentz, Michigan	9	NA
2 George Skipworth, Duke	9	88
2 J.W. Sherrill, Tennessee	9	NA

Team Leaders

RUSHING OFFENSE	G	ATT	YDS	AVG	YPG
1 Texas El-Paso	10	626	3332	5.3	333.2
2 Oklahoma	10	564	3203	5.7	320.3
3 Villanova	9	461	2642	5.7	293.6
4 Notre Dame	10	568	2914	5.1	291.4
5 Wyoming	10	501	2841	5.7	284.1
6 Army	9	523	2485	4.8	276.1
7 Illinois	9	484	2460	5.1	273.3
8 Boston U.	8	423	2162	5.1	270.3
9 Cornell	9	471	2420	5.1	268.9
10 Idaho	8	379	2042	5.4	255.3

PASSING OFFENSE/YPG	G	ATT	COM	INT	PCT	YDS	YPA	TD	YPG	I%	YPC
1 Fordham	8	185	108	12	58.4	1467	7.9	16	183.4	6.5	13.6
2 Southern Cal	9	225	128	12	56.9	1582	7.0	14	175.8	5.3	12.4
3 Oklahoma State	10	254	114	18	44.9	1755	6.9	13	175.5	7.1	15.4
4 William & Mary	10	218	112	16	51.4	1730	7.9	23	173.0	7.3	15.4
5 TCU	10	264	121	28	45.8	1693	6.4	15	169.3	10.6	14.0
6 Cincinnati	10	234	111	18	47.4	1664	7.1	16	166.4	7.7	15.0
7 Texas	10	209	105	13	50.2	1659	7.9	10	165.9	6.2	15.8
8 SMU	10	195	99	11	50.8	1621	8.3	11	162.1	9.7	16.4
9 Denver	10	208	99	25	47.6	1612	7.8	9	161.2	12.0	16.3
10 Davidson	10	267	127	24	47.6	1578	5.9	7	157.8	9.0	12.4

TOTAL OFFENSE	G	P	YDS	AVG	YPG
1 Notre Dame	10	722	4348	6.0	434.8
2 Villanova	9	624	3896	6.2	432.9
3 Oklahoma	10	676	4093	6.1	409.3
4 Texas El-Paso	10	715	3997	5.6	399.7
5 Army	9	650	3542	5.4	393.6
6 Boston U.	8	555	3094	5.6	386.8
7 Mississippi	10	680	3864	5.7	386.4
8 Missouri	10	746	3859	5.2	385.9
9 Cornell	9	601	3429	5.7	381.0
10 Miami, Ohio	9	592	3421	5.8	380.1

RUSHING DEFENSE	G	ATT	YDS	AVG	YPG
1 Oklahoma	10	343	556	1.6	55.6
2 Kentucky	11	455	788	1.7	71.6
3 Minnesota	9	349	742	2.1	82.4
4 Notre Dame	10	417	864	2.1	86.4
5 Maryland	9	356	844	2.4	93.8
6 Army	9	393	906	2.3	100.7
7 Villanova	9	362	924	2.6	102.7
8 Virginia	9	373	931	2.5	103.4
9 LSU	10	447	1074	2.4	107.4
10 Duke	9	355	980	2.8	108.9

PASSING DEFENSE	G	ATT	COM	PCT	YPC	INT	I%	YDS	YPA	TD	YPG
1 Miami, Fla.	9	122	40	32.8	12.3	10	8.2	492	4.0	4	54.7
2 Miami, Ohio	9	127	39	30.7	12.7	20	15.8	495	3.9	5	55.0
3 Wyoming	10	161	48	29.8	12.0	18	11.2	576	3.6	1	57.6
4 Purdue	10	106	41	38.7	13.5	5	4.7	553	5.2	7	61.4
5 Iowa State	9	112	39	34.8	15.2	15	13.4	593	5.3	0	65.9
6 Nebraska	9	125	52	41.6	11.4	18	14.4	595	4.8	6	66.1
7 Texas	10	194	71	36.6	9.9	13	6.7	706	3.6	4	70.6
8 Wichita State	10	130	50	38.5	14.2	16	12.3	708	5.4	7	70.8
9 Tennessee	10	161	64	39.8	11.8	26	16.2	752	4.7	4	75.2
10 Alabama	10	172	61	35.5	12.5	15	8.7	761	4.4	1	76.1

TOTAL DEFENSE	G	P	YDS	AVG	YPG
1 Kentucky	11	653	1692	2.6	153.8
2 Army	9	594	1670	2.8	185.6
3 Maryland	9	549	1686	3.1	187.3
4 Wyoming	10	604	1895	3.1	189.5
5 Villanova	9	526	1815	3.5	201.7
6 Oklahoma	10	633	2027	3.2	202.7
7 Texas	10	627	2060	3.3	206.0
8 Minnesota	9	570	1940	3.4	215.6
9 LSU	10	620	2158	3.5	215.8
10 Drake	9	574	1952	3.4	216.9

SCORING OFFENSE	G	PTS	AVG
1 Army	9	354	39.3
2 Wyoming	10	375	37.5
3 Oklahoma	10	364	36.4
4 Notre Dame	10	360	36.0
5 Arizona State	9	321	35.7
6 Michigan State	9	309	34.3
7 Cornell	9	284	31.6
8 California	10	305	30.5
9 Rutgers	9	266	29.6
10 Villanova	9	265	29.4

SCORING DEFENSE	G	PTS	AVG
1 Kentucky	11	53	4.8
2 Wyoming	10	65	6.5
3 LSU	10	74	7.4
4 Army	9	68	7.6
5 Maryland	9	75	8.3
6 Rice	10	84	8.4
7 Colorado State	10	86	8.6
7 Notre Dame	10	86	8.6
9 Oklahoma	10	88	8.8
10 Minnesota	9	80	8.9

1950 POLL PROGRESSION

Pre-Season 1950 / Sept 30 Games

AP	Team	Record	Result
1	Notre Dame	0-0-0	beat # 20 North Carolina 14-7
2	Army	0-0-0	beat Colgate 28-0
3	Michigan	0-0-0	lost to # 19 Michigan State 7-14
4	Tennessee	0-0-0	lost to Mississippi State 0-7
5	Texas	0-0-0	beat Purdue 34-26
6	Oklahoma	0-0-0	beat Boston College 28-0
7	Stanford	0-0-0	beat San Francisco 55-7
8	Illinois	0-0-0	beat Ohio U 28-2
9	Cornell	0-0-0	beat Lafayette 27-0
10	SMU	0-0-0	beat # 11 Ohio State 32-27
11	Ohio State	0-0-0	lost to # 10 SMU 27-32
12	Southern Cal	0-0-0	lost to Iowa 14-20
13	Kentucky	0-0-0	beat Mississippi 27-0
14	California	0-0-0	beat Oregon 28-7
15	Maryland	0-0-0	beat Navy 35-21
16	Duke	0-0-0	beat Pittsburgh 28-14
17	Missouri	0-0-0	lost to Clemson 0-34
18	Minnesota	0-0-0	lost to Washington 13-28
19	Michigan State	0-0-0	beat # 3 Michigan 14-7
20	North Carolina	0-0-0	lost to # 1 Notre Dame 7-14

October 2 Poll / Oct 7 Games

UP	AP	Team	Record	Result
1	1	Notre Dame	1-0-0	lost to Purdue 14-28
3	2	Michigan State	2-0-0	lost to Maryland 7-34
4	3	SMU	2-0-0	beat Missouri 21-0
2	4	Army	1-0-0	beat Penn State 41-7
5	5	Oklahoma	1-0-0	beat Texas A&M 34-28
8	6	Kentucky	3-0-0	beat Dayton 40-0
6	7	Texas	2-0-0	bye week
9	8	Stanford	2-0-0	beat Oregon State 21-7
7	9	California	2-0-0	beat # 20 Pennsylvania 14-7
18	10	Washington	2-0-0	beat # 13 UCLA 21-20
16	11	North Carolina	1-1-0	tied Georgia 0-0
14	12	Alabama	2-0-0	lost to Vanderbilt 22-27
10	13	UCLA	2-0-0	lost to # 10 Washington 20-21
13	14	Duke	2-0-0	lost to Tennessee 7-28
17	15	Illinois	1-0-0	lost to Wisconsin 6-7
11	16	Cornell	1-0-0	beat Syracuse 26-7
15	17	Iowa	1-0-0	lost to Indiana 7-20
	18	Clemson	2-0-0	beat North Carolina St. 27-0
12	19	Michigan	0-1-0	beat Dartmouth 27-7
	20	Pennsylvania	1-0-0	lost to # 9 California 7-14
19		Princeton	1-0-0	beat Rutgers 34-28
20		Tennessee	1-1-0	beat # 14 Duke 28-7

October 9 Poll / Oct 14 Games

UP	AP	Team	Record	Result
1	1	Army	2-0-0	beat # 18 Michigan 27-6
2	2	SMU	3-0-0	beat Oklahoma State 56-0
3	3	Oklahoma	2-0-0	beat # 4 Texas 14-13
4	4	Texas	2-0-0	lost to # 3 Oklahoma 13-14
7	5	Kentucky	4-0-0	beat Cincinnati 41-7
5	6	Stanford	3-0-0	beat Santa Clara 23-13
6	7	California	3-0-0	beat Southern Cal 13-7
8	8	Maryland	2-1-0	beat Georgetown 25-14
10	9	Purdue	1-1-0	lost to Miami, Fla. 14-20
9	10	Notre Dame	1-1-0	beat Tulane 13-9
11	11	Washington	3-0-0	beat Oregon State 35-6
12	12	Ohio State	1-1-0	beat Indiana 26-14
16	13	Clemson	3-0-0	bye week
14	14	Tennessee	2-1-0	beat U.T. Chattanooga 41-0
15	15	Rice	2-0-0	beat Pittsburgh 14-7
17	16	Wisconsin	2-0-0	beat Iowa 14-0
13	17	Cornell	2-0-0	beat Harvard 28-7
18	18	Michigan	1-1-0	lost to # 1 Army 6-27
20	19	Vanderbilt	3-0-0	beat Mississippi 20-14
19	20	Michigan State	2-1-0	beat William & Mary 33-14

October 16 Poll / Oct 21 Games

UP	AP	Team	Record	Result
1	1	Army	3-0-0	beat Harvard 49-0
2	2	Oklahoma	3-0-0	beat Kansas State 58-0
3	3	SMU	4-0-0	beat # 15 Rice 42-21
5	4	Kentucky	5-0-0	beat Villanova 34-7
4	5	California	4-0-0	beat Oregon State 27-0
6	6	Stanford	4-0-0	lost to UCLA 7-21
7	7	Texas	2-1-0	beat Arkansas 19-14
11	8	Maryland	3-1-0	lost to North Carolina St. 13-16
8	9	Ohio State	2-1-0	beat Minnesota 48-0
9	10	Washington	4-0-0	lost to Illinois 13-20
10	11	Notre Dame	2-1-0	lost to Indiana 7-20
14	12	Clemson	3-0-0	tied South Carolina 14-14
17	13	Vanderbilt	4-0-0	lost to Florida 27-31
19	14	Miami, Fla.	3-0-0	beat Boston U. 34-7
16	15	Rice	3-0-0	lost to # 3 SMU 21-42
15	16	Wisconsin	3-0-0	lost to Michigan 13-26
13	17	Cornell	3-0-0	beat Yale 7-0
12	18	Tennessee	3-1-0	beat Alabama 14-9
	18	Wake Forest	3-0-1	beat George Washington 13-7
	20	Northwestern	3-0-0	beat Pittsburgh 28-23
18		Georgia	2-0-2	tied LSU 13-13
19		Texas A&M	3-1-0	beat TCU 42-23
19		Wyoming	4-0-0	beat Utah 53-13

October 23 Poll / Oct 28 Games

UP	AP	Team	Record	Result
2	1	SMU	5-0-0	bye week
1	2	Army	4-0-0	beat Columbia 34-0
3	3	Oklahoma	4-0-0	beat Iowa State 20-7
6	4	Kentucky	6-0-0	beat Georgia Tech 28-14
4	5	California	5-0-0	beat Saint Mary's-Cal 40-25
5	6	Ohio State	3-1-0	beat Iowa 83-21
7	7	Texas	3-1-0	beat Rice 35-7
8	8	Tennessee	4-1-0	beat Wash. & Lee 27-20
14	9	Northwestern	4-0-0	lost to Wisconsin 13-14
10	10	Cornell	4-0-0	lost to Princeton 0-27
	11	Miami, Fla.	4-0-0	beat Pittsburgh 28-0
9	12	Illinois	3-1-0	beat # 19 Indiana 20-0
11	13	Texas A&M	4-1-0	lost to Baylor 20-27
12	14	Michigan	2-2-0	tied Minnesota 7-7
16	15	Michigan State	4-1-0	beat Notre Dame 36-33
	16	Clemson	3-0-1	beat Wake Forest 13-12
	17	Wake Forest	4-0-1	lost to Clemson 12-13
19	18	UCLA	3-2-0	beat Purdue 20-6
16	19	Indiana	2-1-1	lost to # 12 Illinois 0-20
	20	Florida	4-1-0	beat Furman 19-7
12		Pennsylvania	3-1-0	beat Navy 30-7
17		Princeton	4-0-0	beat # 10 Cornell 27-0
18		Wyoming	5-0-0	beat New Mexico 44-0
20		Washington	4-1-0	beat Stanford 21-7

October 30 Poll / Nov 4 Games

UP	AP	Team	Record	Result
1	1	SMU	5-0-0	lost to # 7 Texas 20-23
2	2	Army	5-0-0	beat # 15 Pennsylvania 28-13
3	3	Oklahoma	5-0-0	beat Colorado 27-18
3	4	Ohio State	4-1-0	beat Northwestern 32-0
6	5	Kentucky	7-0-0	beat # 17 Florida 40-6
5	6	California	6-0-0	beat # 12 Washington 14-7
7	7	Texas	4-1-0	beat # 1 SMU 23-20
13	8	Miami, Fla.	5-0-0	beat Georgetown 42-7
9	9	Princeton	5-0-0	beat Colgate 45-7
8	10	Illinois	4-1-0	beat Michigan 7-0
11	11	Tennessee	5-1-0	beat North Carolina 16-0
10	12	Washington	5-1-0	lost to # 6 California 7-14
12	13	Michigan State	5-1-0	beat Indiana 35-0
18	14	Clemson	4-0-1	beat Duquesne 53-20
14	15	Pennsylvania	4-1-0	lost to # 2 Army 13-28
15	16	Maryland	4-2-0	beat George Washington 23-7
	17	Florida	5-1-0	lost to # 5 Kentucky 6-40
17	18	Wyoming	6-0-0	beat Idaho 14-7
16	19	UCLA	4-2-0	beat Oregon State 20-13
20	20	Wisconsin	4-1-0	beat Purdue 33-7
19		Georgia	3-0-3	lost to Alabama 7-14

November 6 Poll — Nov 11 Games

AP	Team	Record	Game
1	Army	6-0-0	beat New Mexico 51-0
2	Ohio State	5-1-0	beat # 15 Wisconsin 19-14
3	Oklahoma	6-0-0	beat # 19 Kansas 33-13
4	Kentucky	8-0-0	beat Mississippi State 48-21
5	Texas	5-1-0	beat Baylor 27-20
6	California	7-0-0	beat # 19 UCLA 35-0
7	SMU	5-1-0	lost to Texas A&M 20-25
8	Princeton	6-0-0	beat Harvard 63-26
9	Miami, Fla.	6-0-0	tied Louisville 13-13
10	Illinois	5-1-0	beat Iowa 21-7
11	Tennessee	6-1-0	beat Tenn. Tech 48-14
12	Michigan State	6-1-0	beat Minnesota 27-0
13	Clemson	5-0-1	beat Boston College 35-14
14	Wyoming	7-0-0	beat Brigham Young 48-0
15	Wisconsin	5-1-0	lost to # 2 Ohio State 14-19
16	Nebraska	4-1-1	beat Kansas State 49-21
17	Washington	5-2-0	beat Oregon 27-13
18	Maryland	5-2-0	tied North Carolina 7-7
19	Kansas	5-2-0	lost to # 3 Oklahoma 13-33
19	Lehigh	7-0-0	N/A
19	UCLA	5-2-0	lost to # 6 California 0-35

November 13 Poll — Nov 18 Games

UP	AP	Team	Record	Game
3	1	Ohio State	6-1-0	lost to # 8 Illinois 7-14
2	2	Oklahoma	7-0-0	beat Missouri 41-7
1	3	Army	7-0-0	beat Stanford 7-0
4	4	California	8-0-0	beat San Francisco 13-7
5	5	Kentucky	9-0-0	beat North Dakota 83-0
6	6	Texas	6-1-0	beat TCU 21-7
7	7	Princeton	7-0-0	beat Yale 47-12
8	8	Illinois	6-1-0	beat # 1 Ohio State 14-7
9	9	Tennessee	7-1-0	beat Mississippi 35-0
10	10	Michigan State	7-1-0	beat Pittsburgh 19-0
13	11	Clemson	6-0-1	beat Furman 57-2
11	12	Texas A&M	6-2-0	lost to Rice 13-21
14	13	Wyoming	8-0-0	bye week
12	14	SMU	5-2-0	beat Arkansas 14-7
14	15	Wisconsin	5-2-0	lost to # 20 Pennsylvania 0-20
	16	Wake Forest	5-1-1	tied North Carolina St. 6-6
	17	Miami, Fla.	6-0-1	beat Florida 20-14
18	18	Nebraska	5-1-1	beat Iowa State 20-13
17	19	Washington	6-2-0	beat Southern Cal 28-13
16	20	Pennsylvania	5-2-0	beat # 15 Wisconsin 20-0
	18	Michigan	3-3-1	beat Northwestern 34-23
	19	Georgia	4-1-3	beat Auburn 12-10
	19	Maryland	5-2-1	beat West Virginia 41-0
	19	Notre Dame	4-3-0	tied Iowa 14-14

November 20 Poll — Nov 25 Games

UP	AP	Team	Record	Game
1	1	Oklahoma	8-0-0	beat # 16 Nebraska 49-35
2	2	Army	8-0-0	bye week
3	3	Kentucky	10-0-0	lost to # 9 Tennessee 0-7
4	4	California	9-0-0	tied Stanford 7-7
5	5	Texas	7-1-0	bye week
6	6	Illinois	7-1-0	lost to Northwestern 7-14
7	7	Princeton	8-0-0	beat Dartmouth 13-7
8	8	Ohio State	6-2-0	lost to Michigan 3-9
8	9	Tennessee	8-1-0	beat # 3 Kentucky 7-0
10	10	Michigan State	8-1-0	regular season complete
12	11	Clemson	7-0-1	beat Auburn 41-0
15	12	Wyoming	8-0-0	beat Denver 42-12
11	13	Pennsylvania	6-2-0	lost to Cornell 6-13
16	14	Miami, Fla.	7-0-1	beat Iowa 14-6
13	15	SMU	6-2-0	lost to Baylor 0-3
17	16	Nebraska	6-1-1	lost to # 1 Oklahoma 35-49
	17	Alabama	7-2-0	beat Florida 41-13
14	18	Washington	7-2-0	beat Washington State 52-21
	19	Washington & Lee	7-2-0	beat Richmond 67-7
	20	Loyola, Marymount	7-0-0	lost to Santa Clara 26-28
17		Stanford	5-3-1	tied California 7-7
19		Maryland	6-2-1	bye week
20		Vanderbilt	7-2-0	lost to Tulane 6-35

November 27 Final Poll

UP	AP	Team	Record	Bowl Bid	Date	Bowl Result	RB	Record
1	1	Oklahoma	9-0-0	Sugar Bowl	J1	lost to # 7 Kentucky 7-13	3	10-1-0
2	2	Army	8-0-0				5	8-1-0
4	3	Texas	7-1-0	Cotton Bowl	J1	lost to # 4 Tennessee 14-20	4	9-2-0
5	4	Tennessee	9-1-0	Cotton Bowl	J1	beat # 3 Texas 20-14	1	11-1-0
3	5	California	9-0-1	Rose Bowl	J1	lost to # 9 Michigan 6-14	6	9-1-1
6	6	Princeton	9-0-0				7	9-0-0
7	7	Kentucky	10-1-0	Sugar Bowl	J1	beat # 1 Oklahoma 13-7	2	11-1-0
8	8	Michigan State	8-1-0				11	8-1-0
9	9	Michigan	5-3-1	Rose Bowl	J1	beat # 5 California 14-6	9	6-3-1
10	10	Clemson	8-0-1	Orange Bowl	J1	beat # 15 Miami, Fla. 15-14	16	9-0-1
13	11	Washington	8-2-0				20	8-2-0
14	12	Wyoming	9-0-0	Gator Bowl	J1	beat # 18 Wash. & Lee 20-7	8	10-0-0
12	13	Illinois	7-2-0				12	7-2-0
11	14	Ohio State	6-3-0				13	6-3-0
16	15	Miami, Fla.	8-0-1	Orange Bowl	J1	lost to # 10 Clemson 14-15	22	9-1-1
16	16	Alabama	8-2-0				17	9-2-0
18	17	Nebraska	6-2-1				28	6-2-1
	18	Tulsa	8-1-1				30	9-1-1
	18	Washington & Lee	8-2-0	Gator Bowl	J1	lost to # 12 Wyoming 7-20	36	8-3-0
20	20	Tulane	6-2-0				21	6-2-1
15		SMU	6-2-0				18	6-4-0
19		Stanford	5-3-2				44	5-3-2

1950

Consensus All-Americans

POS	Name	HT	WT	School	AA	AP	FC	FW	IN	NE	SN	UP
B	Vic Janowicz	5-9	189	Ohio State	•	•	•	•	•	•	•	•
B	Kyle Rote	6-0	190	SMU	•	•	•	•	•	•	•	•
B	Babe Parilli	6-1	183	Kentucky	•		•	•		•	•	
B	Leon Heath	6-1	195	Oklahoma	•		•	•		•	•	
E	Dan Foldberg	6-1	185	Army	•	•	•	•	•	•	•	•
E	Bill McColl	6-4	225	Stanford	•	•	•	•	•	•	•	•
T	Bob Gain	6-3	230	Kentucky	•	•	•	•	•	•	•	•
T	Jim Weatherall	6-4	220	Oklahoma	•	•	•	•	•	•	•	•
G	Bud McFadin	6-3	225	Texas	•	•	•	•	•	•	•	•
G	Les Richter	6-2	220	California	•	•						
C	Jerry Groom	6-3	215	Notre Dame					•	•	•	•

Others Receiving First-Team Honors

POS	Player	School							
B	Bob Williams	Notre Dame							
B	Bob Reynolds	Nebraska		•		•	•		
B	Don Heinrich	Washington		•					
B	Everett Grandelius	Michigan State			•	•			
B	Dick Kazmaier	Princeton		•					
B	Eddie Talboom	Wyoming					•		
B	Johnny Bright	Drake					•		
B	Ed Withers	Wisconsin					•		
B	Francis Bagnell	Pennsylvania					•		
B	Bob Smith	Texas A&M					•		
B	Jackie Calvert	Clemson					•		
E	Bucky Curtis	Vanderbilt			•	•			
E	Don Stonesifer	Northwestern		•					
E	Jim Doran	Iowa State				•		•	
T	Holland Donan	Princeton			•			•	
T	Allen Wahl	Michigan	•			•			
T	Charles Shira	Army					•		
T	J.D. Kimmel	Army					•		
G	Bob Ward	Maryland	•		•			•	
G	Ted Daffer	Tennessee			•	•			
G	Bill Ciarvino	Lehigh					•		
G	Bernard Lemonick	Pennsylvania					•		
G	Jerome Helluin	Tulane					•		
C	Redmond Finney	Princeton				•	•	•	
C	Bob McCullough	Ohio State		•					
C	Bill Vohaska	Illinois		•					
C	Irvin Holdash	North Carolina	•						
C	Donn Moomaw	UCLA					•		

Janowicz and Richter were selected to the AP's first-ever All-American defensive team, but not on offense.

Heisman Trophy Voting

	PLAYER	POS	SCHOOL	TOTAL
1	Vic Janowicz	HB	Ohio State	633
2	Kyle Rote	HB	SMU	280
3	Francis Bagnell	B	Pennsylvania	231
4	Babe Parilli	QB	Kentucky	214
5	Bob Reynolds	HB	Nebraska	174
6	Bob Williams	QB	Notre Dame	159
7	Leon Heath	FB	Oklahoma	125
8	Dan Foldberg	E	Army	103

Award Winners

PLAYER	POS	SCHOOL	AWARD NAME
Francis Bagnell	HB	Pennsylvania	Maxwell
Bob Gain	T	Kentucky	Outland

Conference Standings

Big 10	Conf. W	L	T	Overall W	L	T
Michigan	4	1	1	6	3	1
Ohio State	5	2	0	6	3	0
Wisconsin	5	2	0	6	3	0
Illinois	4	2	0	7	2	0
Northwestern	3	3	0	6	3	0
Iowa	2	4	0	3	5	1
Minnesota	1	4	1	1	7	1
Indiana	1	4	0	3	5	1
Purdue	1	4	0	2	7	0

Big 7	Conf. W	L	T	Overall W	L	T
Oklahoma	6	0	0	10	1	0
Nebraska	4	2	0	6	2	1
Missouri	3	2	1	4	5	1
Kansas	3	3	0	6	4	0
Iowa State	2	3	1	3	6	1
Colorado	2	4	0	5	4	1
Kansas State	0	6	0	1	9	1

Border	Conf. W	L	T	Overall W	L	T
Texas Tech	5	0	0	7	5	0
Arizona State	4	1	0	7	3	0
Texas-El Paso	4	2	0	8	2	1
Hardin-Simmons	4	2	0	6	4	1
West Texas State	3	2	0	5	4	0
Arizona	2	4	0	2	7	1
New Mexico State	1	4	0	4	6	0
New Mexico	1	6	0	2	8	0
Northern Arizona	0	3	0	1	6	1

MAC	Conf. W	L	T	Overall W	L	T
Miami, Ohio	4	0	0	9	1	0
Cincinnati	3	1	0	8	4	0
Ohio U	2	2	0	6	4	0
Western Michigan	1	3	0	5	4	0
Case Western Reserve	1	3	0	2	8	0

Pacific Coast	Conf. W	L	T	Overall W	L	T
California	5	0	1	9	1	1
Washington	6	1	0	8	2	0
UCLA	5	2	0	6	3	0
Stanford	2	2	2	5	3	2
Idaho	1	1	1	3	5	1
Washington State	2	3	2	4	3	2
Southern Cal	1	3	2	2	5	2
Oregon State	2	5	0	3	6	0
Oregon	0	7	0	1	9	0

SEC	Conf. W	L	T	Overall W	L	T
Kentucky	5	1	0	11	1	0
Tennessee	4	1	0	11	1	0
Alabama	6	2	0	9	2	0
Tulane	3	1	1	6	2	1
Georgia Tech	4	2	0	5	6	0
Georgia	3	2	1	6	3	3
Vanderbilt	3	4	0	7	4	0
Mississippi State	3	4	0	4	5	0
LSU	2	3	2	4	5	2
Florida	2	4	0	5	5	0
Mississippi	1	5	0	5	5	0
Auburn	0	7	0	0	10	0

Skyline	Conf. W	L	T	Overall W	L	T
Wyoming	5	0	0	10	0	0
Colorado State	4	1	0	6	3	0
Denver	2	2	1	3	8	1
Utah	1	2	2	3	4	3
Brigham Young	1	3	1	4	5	1
Utah State	0	5	0	2	9	0

Southern	Conf. W	L	T	Overall W	L	T
Clemson	3	0	1	9	0	1
Washington & Lee	6	1	0	8	3	0
VMI	5	1	0	6	4	0
Wake Forest	6	1	1	6	1	2
Maryland	4	1	1	7	2	1
Duke	5	2	0	7	3	0
George Washington	4	3	0	5	4	0
North Carolina St.	4	4	1	5	4	1
North Carolina	3	3	1	3	5	2
William & Mary	3	3	0	4	7	0
Citadel	2	3	0	4	6	0
South Carolina	2	4	1	3	4	2
Furman	2	4	0	2	9	1
West Virginia	1	4	0	2	8	0
Davidson	1	5	0	3	6	0
Richmond	1	8	0	2	8	0
Virginia Tech	0	9	0	0	10	0

SWC	Conf. W	L	T	Overall W	L	T
Texas	6	0	0	9	2	0
Baylor	4	2	0	7	3	0
Texas A&M	3	3	0	7	4	0
TCU	3	3	0	5	5	0
Rice	2	4	0	6	4	0
SMU	2	4	0	6	4	0
Arkansas	1	5	0	2	8	0

Independent	Overall W	L	T
Princeton	9	0	0
Florida State	8	0	0
Michigan State	8	1	0
Army	8	1	0
Miami, Fla.	9	1	1
Memphis	9	2	0
Virginia	8	2	0
North Texas	8	2	0
Cornell	7	2	0
Pennsylvania	6	3	0
Yale	6	3	0
Penn State	5	3	1
Syracuse	5	5	0
Rutgers	4	4	0
Notre Dame	4	4	1
Columbia	4	5	0
Houston	4	6	0
Dartmouth	3	5	1
Navy	3	6	0
Harvard	1	7	0
Brown	1	8	0
Pittsburgh	1	8	0
Boston College	0	9	1

Bowl Games

DATE	GAME	SCORE
D9	Presidential Cup	Texas A&M 40, Georgia 20
J1	Tangerine	Morris Harvey 35, Emory & Henry 6
J1	Orange	Clemson 15, Miami, Fla. 14
J1	Salad	Miami, Ohio 34, Arizona State 21
J1	Rose	Michigan 14, California 6
J1	Sugar	Kentucky 13, Oklahoma 7
J1	Cotton	Tennessee 20, Texas 14
J1	Gator	Wyoming 20, Wash. & Lee 7
J1	Sun	West Texas State 14, Cincinnati 13

1950 NCAA MAJOR COLLEGE STATISTICAL LEADERS

Individual Leaders

PASSING/COMPLETIONS	G	ATT	COM	PCT	INT	I%	YDS	YPA	TD	TD%	COM.PG
1 Don Heinrich, Washington	10	221	134	60.6	9	4.1	1846	8.4	14	6.3	13.4
2 Dave Cunningham, Utah	9	217	119	54.8	12	5.5	1146	5.3	13	6.0	13.2
3 Bill Weeks, Iowa State	10	220	116	52.7	16	7.3	1552	7.1	9	4.1	11.6
4 Babe Parilli, Kentucky	11	203	114	56.2	12	5.9	1627	8.0	23	11.3	10.4
5 Don Klosterman, Loyola-Marymount	9	207	113	54.6	11	5.3	1582	7.6	19	9.2	12.6
6 Ed Ford, Hardin-Simmons	10	199	111	55.8	7	3.5	1777	8.9	12	6.0	11.1
7 Fred Benners, SMU	10	192	109	56.8	12	6.3	1361	7.1	9	4.7	10.9
8 Billy Cox, Duke	10	206	108	52.4	15	7.3	1428	6.9	8	3.9	10.8
9 Chuck Maloy, Holy Cross	10	242	104	43.0	19	7.9	1572	6.5	14	5.8	10.4
10 Bob Williams, Notre Dame	9	210	99	47.1	15	7.1	1035	4.9	10	4.8	11.0

ALL-PURPOSE YARDS	G	RUSH	REC	INT	PR	KR	YDS	YPG
1 Wilford White, Arizona State	10	1502	225	0	64	274	2065	206.5

RUSHING/YARDS	G	ATT	YDS	AVG	YPG
1 Wilford White, Arizona State	10	199	1502	7.5	150.2
2 Bobby Reynolds, Nebraska	9	193	1342	7.0	149.1
3 Bob Smith, Texas A&M	10	199	1302	6.5	130.2
4 Johnny Bright, Drake	9	183	1232	6.7	136.9
5 Wade Stinson, Kansas	10	167	1129	6.8	112.9
6 Hugh McElhenny, Washington	10	179	1107	6.2	110.7
7 Everett Grandelius, Michigan State	9	163	1023	6.3	113.7
8 John Dottley, Mississippi	10	191	1007	5.3	100.7
9 Steve Wadiak, South Carolina	10	162	998	6.2	99.8
10 Jake Roberts, Tulsa	11	138	954	6.9	86.7

RUSHING/YARDS PER CARRY	G	ATT	YDS	YPC
1 Wilford White, Arizona State	10	199	1502	7.5
2 Bobby Marlow, Alabama	11	118	882	7.5
3 Bobby Reynolds, Nebraska	9	193	1342	7.0
4 Jake Roberts, Tulsa	11	138	954	6.9
5 Wade Stinson, Kansas	10	167	1129	6.8
6 Johnny Bright, Drake	9	183	1232	6.7
7 Max Clark, Houston	10	129	860	6.7
8 Bob Smith, Texas A&M	10	199	1302	6.5
9 Billy Vessels, Oklahoma	10	135	870	6.4
10 John Olszewski, California	10	151	950	6.3

*-Based on top 20 rushers

RECEIVING/RECEPTIONS	G	REC	YDS	TD	YPR	YPG	RPG
1 Gordon Cooper, Denver	10	46	569	8	12.4	56.9	4.6
2 Tom Bienemann, Drake	9	45	615	2	13.7	68.3	5.0
3 Jim Doran, Iowa State	10	42	652	6	15.5	65.2	4.2
3 Don Stonesifer, Northwestern	9	42	560	5	13.3	62.2	4.7
5 Ceep Youmans, Duke	10	40	446	1	11.2	44.6	4.0
6 Bill McColl, Stanford	10	39	671	4	17.2	67.1	3.9
7 Sy Wilhelmi, Iowa State	10	38	442	2	11.6	44.2	3.8
7 Herman Fisher, Nevada	9	38	434	1	11.4	48.2	4.2
9 Fred Snyder, Loyola-Marymount	9	36	596	9	16.6	66.2	4.0
9 John Thomas, Oregon State	9	36	350	1	9.7	38.9	4.0

PUNTING	PUNT	YDS	AVG
1 Zack Jordan, Colorado	38	1830	48.2
2 Pat Brady, Nevada	35	1642	46.9
3 Milt Smith, Utah	47	2030	43.2
4 Bud Wallace, North Carolina	27	1150	42.6
5 Rex Berry, Brigham Young	28	1187	42.4
6 James Hammond, Wisconsin	26	1079	41.5
7 Dolph Simons, Kansas	32	1318	41.2
8 Larry Isbell, Baylor	56	2307	41.2
9 Bob Moore, UCLA	63	2583	41.0
10 Glenn Drahn, Iowa	56	2296	41.0

PUNT RETURNS/YARDS	PR	YDS	AVG
1 Dave Waters, Washington & Lee	30	445	14.8
2 Jesse Thomas, Michigan State	18	358	19.9
3 Bert Rechichar, Tennessee	20	349	17.5
4 Bobby Dan Dillon, Texas	15	334	22.3
5 Bob Shemonski, Maryland	28	334	11.9
6 Duane Rice, Colorado State	16	328	20.5
7 Gene Gibson, Cincinnati	16	322	20.1
8 Johnny Cole, Arkansas	16	293	18.3
9 George Kinek, Tulane	20	277	13.9
10 Alex Webster, North Carolina St.	14	276	19.7

KICKOFF RETURNS/YARDS	KR	YDS	AVG
1 Chuck Hill, New Mexico	27	729	27.0
2 Sterling Wingo, Virginia Tech	20	462	23.1
3 John Henry Johnson, Saint Mary's-Cal	16	423	26.4
4 Ralph Longmore, Duquesne	19	402	21.2
5 Sammy Hurt, U.T. Chattanooga	22	368	16.7
6 George Bean, Utah	21	366	17.4
7 William Lohr, West Virginia	19	362	19.1
8 William Farris, Richmond	18	355	19.7
9 Ted Narleski, UCLA	14	348	24.9
10 Norm Rohter, Marquette	15	342	22.8

SCORING	TDS	XPT	FG	PTS
1 Bobby Reynolds, Nebraska	22	25	0	157
2 Wilford White, Arizona State	22	1	1	136
3 Eddie Talboom, Wyoming	15	40	0	130
4 Johnny Bright, Drake	18	0	0	108
5 Johnny Turco, Holy Cross	17	0	0	102
6 Bob Shemonski, Maryland	16	1	0	97
7 Max Clark, Houston	11	24	0	90
7 Merwin Hodel, Colorado	15	0	0	90
7 Billy Vessels, Oklahoma	15	0	0	90
10 Fred Cone, Clemson	14	2	0	86

INTERCEPTIONS	INT	YDS
1 Hank Rich, Arizona State	12	135
2 Al Brosky, Illinois	11	96
3 Tom Hardiman, Georgetown	9	155

Team Leaders

RUSHING OFFENSE	G	ATT	YDS	AVG	YPG
1 Arizona State	10	620	3470	5.6	347.0
2 Princeton	9	503	2929	5.8	325.4
3 Nebraska	9	510	2894	5.7	321.6
4 Kansas	10	524	3116	5.9	311.6
5 Tulsa	11	619	3384	5.5	307.6
6 Washington & Lee	10	578	2995	5.2	299.5
7 Pacific	11	619	3278	5.3	298.0
8 Clemson	9	504	2648	5.3	294.2
9 Oklahoma	10	562	2931	5.2	293.1
10 Army	9	477	2568	5.4	285.3

PASSING OFFENSE/YPG	G	ATT	COM	INT	PCT	YDS	YPA	TD	YPG	I%	YPC
1 SMU	10	296	156	24	52.7	2146	7.3	14	214.6	8.1	13.8
2 Hardin-Simmons	10	228	130	8	57.0	2061	9.0	15	206.1	3.5	15.9
3 Washington	10	260	149	12	57.3	2041	7.9	14	204.1	4.6	13.7
4 Loyola-Marymount	9	228	122	12	53.5	1674	7.3	20	186.0	5.3	13.7
5 Duke	10	236	121	21	51.3	1639	6.9	10	163.9	8.9	13.5
6 George Washington	9	228	113	17	49.6	1475	6.5	7	163.9	7.5	13.0
7 Holy Cross	10	247	105	20	42.5	1585	6.4	14	158.5	8.1	15.1
8 Drake	9	182	101	11	55.5	1420	7.8	12	157.8	6.0	14.1
9 Iowa State	10	226	117	18	51.8	1574	7.0	9	157.4	8.0	13.5
10 Kentucky	11	230	125	14	54.3	1714	7.5	27	155.8	6.1	13.7

TOTAL OFFENSE	G	P	YDS	AVG	YPG
1 Arizona State	10	792	4704	5.9	470.4
2 Princeton	9	617	3903	6.3	433.7
3 Tulsa	11	783	4747	6.1	431.5
4 Clemson	9	630	3881	6.2	431.2
5 Loyola-Marymount	9	775	3781	4.9	420.1
6 Alabama	11	773	4576	5.9	416.0
7 Oklahoma	10	706	4154	5.9	415.4
8 Washington	10	694	4116	5.9	411.6
9 Nebraska	9	618	3666	5.9	407.3
10 Pacific	11	800	4399	5.5	399.9

RUSHING DEFENSE	G	ATT	YDS	AVG	YPG
1 Ohio State	9	341	576	1.7	64.0
2 Princeton	9	326	611	1.9	67.9
3 Wake Forest	9	330	626	1.9	69.6
4 San Francisco	11	435	820	1.9	74.5
5 Wyoming	9	343	788	2.3	87.6
6 Tulane	9	373	824	2.2	91.6
7 Kentucky	11	482	1021	2.1	92.8
8 Michigan State	9	344	874	2.5	97.1
9 Maryland	10	421	1016	2.4	101.6
10 Loyola-Marymount	9	348	960	2.8	106.7

PASSING DEFENSE	G	ATT	COM	PCT	YPC	INT	I%	YDS	YPA	TD	YPG
1 Tennessee	11	149	65	43.6	11.4	23	15.4	743	5.0	2	67.5
2 Indiana	9	127	51	40.2	12.3	12	9.5	629	5.0	3	69.9
3 Tulsa	11	181	59	32.6	13.1	12	6.6	770	4.3	3	70.0
4 Duke	10	147	67	45.6	10.6	17	11.6	707	4.8	3	70.7
5 Montana	9	127	48	37.8	13.8	19	15.0	661	5.2	4	73.4
6 Iowa State	10	113	42	37.2	17.6	9	8.0	741	6.6	4	74.1
7 Penn State	9	141	52	36.9	12.9	18	12.8	671	4.8	8	74.6
8 Harvard	8	101	35	34.7	17.1	2	2.0	599	5.9	6	74.9
9 Army	9	155	59	38.1	11.5	18	11.6	679	4.4	1	75.4
10 Mississippi State	9	102	49	48.0	14.3	7	6.9	703	6.9	7	78.1

TOTAL DEFENSE	G	P	YDS	AVG	YPG
1 Wake Forest	9	491	1469	3.0	163.2
2 Kentucky	11	671	1895	2.8	172.3
3 Wyoming	9	493	1559	3.2	173.2
4 Army	9	637	1705	2.7	189.4
5 Miami, Fla.	10	653	1968	3.0	196.8
6 Cornell	9	547	1788	3.3	198.7
7 Tennessee	11	673	2208	3.3	200.7
8 Tulane	9	557	1807	3.2	200.8
9 Mississippi State	9	470	1828	3.9	203.1
10 San Francisco	11	693	2240	3.2	203.6

SCORING OFFENSE	G	PTS	AVG
1 Princeton	9	349	38.8

SCORING DEFENSE	G	PTS	AVG
1 Army	9	40	4.4

1951 POLL PROGRESSION

Pre-Season 1951 | Sept 29 Games

AP	Team	Record	Result
1	Tennessee	0-0-0	beat Mississippi State 14-0
2	Michigan State	0-0-0	beat #17 Michigan 25-0
3	Ohio State	0-0-0	beat SMU 7-0
4	Oklahoma	0-0-0	beat William & Mary 49-7
5	California	0-0-0	beat #19 Pennsylvania 35-0
6	Kentucky	0-0-0	lost to Mississippi 17-21
6	Texas A&M	0-0-0	beat Texas Tech 20-7
8	Washington	0-0-0	beat Minnesota 25-20
9	Alabama	0-0-0	lost to LSU 7-13
10	Illinois	0-0-0	beat UCLA 27-13
11	Texas	0-0-0	beat Purdue 14-0
12	Nebraska	0-0-0	lost to TCU 7-28
13	Baylor	0-0-0	bye week
14	Notre Dame	0-0-0	beat Indiana 48-6
15	Wisconsin	0-0-0	beat Marquette 22-6
16	Maryland	0-0-0	beat Washington & Lee 54-14
17	Michigan	0-0-0	lost to #2 Michigan State 0-25
18	Princeton	0-0-0	beat NYU 54-20
19	Pennsylvania	0-0-0	lost to #5 California 0-35
20	Cornell	0-0-0	beat Syracuse 21-14

October 1 Poll | Oct 6 Games

UP	AP	Team	Record	Result
2	1	Michigan State	2-0-0	beat #7 Ohio State 24-20
1	2	California	2-0-0	beat Minnesota 55-14
3	3	Tennessee	1-0-0	beat #16 Duke 26-0
5	4	Oklahoma	1-0-0	lost to #10 Texas A&M 7-14
4	5	Notre Dame	1-0-0	beat Detroit 40-6
	6	Texas	2-0-0	beat North Carolina 45-20
8	7	Ohio State	1-0-0	lost to #1 Michigan State 20-24
7	8	Illinois	1-0-0	beat Wisconsin 14-10
12	9	Maryland	1-0-0	beat George Washington 33-6
10	10	Texas A&M	2-0-0	beat #4 Oklahoma 14-7
13	11	Georgia Tech	2-0-0	beat #17 Kentucky 13-7
9	12	Washington	2-0-0	lost to Southern Cal 13-20
11	13	Georgia	2-0-0	lost to Mississippi State 0-6
15	14	Princeton	2-0-0	beat Navy 24-20
	15	Oregon State	1-1-0	beat Idaho 34-6
19	16	Duke	2-0-0	lost to #3 Tennessee 0-26
	17	Kentucky	1-2-0	lost to #11 Georgia Tech 7-13
	18	Clemson	2-0-0	beat North Carolina St. 6-0
17	19	Baylor	1-0-0	beat Tulane 27-14
	20	Kansas	2-0-0	lost to Colorado 27-35
14		Tulane	1-0-0	lost to #19 Baylor 14-27
16		Southern Cal	2-0-0	beat #12 Washington 20-13
18		Wisconsin	1-0-0	lost to #8 Illinois 10-14
19		Cornell	1-0-0	beat Colgate 41-18

October 8 Poll | Oct 13 Games

UP	AP	Team	Record	Result
2	1	Michigan State	3-0-0	beat Marquette 20-14
1	2	California	3-0-0	beat Washington State 42-35
3	3	Tennessee	2-0-0	beat U.T. Chattanooga 42-13
5	4	Texas A&M	3-0-0	beat Trinity 53-14
6	5	Notre Dame	2-0-0	lost to SMU 20-27
4	6	Texas	3-0-0	beat #11 Oklahoma 9-7
7	7	Illinois	2-0-0	beat Syracuse 41-20
8	8	Georgia Tech	3-0-0	beat LSU 25-7
11	9	Ohio State	1-1-0	tied Wisconsin 6-6
9	10	Maryland	2-0-0	beat Georgia 43-7
14	11	Oklahoma	1-1-0	lost to #6 Texas 7-9
10	12	Baylor	2-0-0	beat Arkansas 9-7
13	13	Princeton	2-0-0	beat Pennsylvania 13-7
12	14	Southern Cal	3-0-0	beat #18 Oregon State 16-14
15	15	Holy Cross	2-0-0	lost to Tulane 14-20
24	16	Clemson	3-0-0	lost to #20 Pacific 7-21
	17	Cornell	2-0-0	beat Harvard 42-6
19	18	Oregon State	2-1-0	lost to #14 Southern Cal 14-16
22	19	Stanford	3-0-0	beat UCLA 21-7
	20	Pacific	3-0-0	beat #16 Clemson 21-7
17		Mississippi	3-0-0	lost to Vanderbilt 20-34
20		Washington	2-1-0	beat Oregon 63-6

October 15 Poll | Oct 20 Games

UP	AP	Team	Record	Result
1	1	California	4-0-0	lost to #11 Southern Cal 14-21
2	2	Tennessee	3-0-0	beat Alabama 27-13
3	3	Michigan State	4-0-0	beat Penn State 32-21
4	4	Texas	4-0-0	lost to Arkansas 14-16
6	5	Georgia Tech	4-0-0	beat Auburn 27-7
5	6	Texas A&M	4-0-0	lost to TCU 14-20
8	7	Maryland	3-0-0	beat North Carolina 14-7
7	8	Illinois	3-0-0	beat #20 Washington 27-20
10	9	Princeton	3-0-0	beat Lafayette 60-7
9	10	Baylor	3-0-0	beat Texas Tech 40-20
11	11	Southern Cal	4-0-0	beat #1 California 21-14
15	12	Villanova	3-0-0	lost to Kentucky 13-35
12	13	Stanford	4-0-0	beat Santa Clara 21-14
16	14	Cornell	3-0-0	beat Yale 27-0
13	15	SMU	2-2-0	lost to Rice 7-28
22	16	Pacific	4-0-0	lost to Boston U. 12-27
14	17	Ohio State	1-1-1	lost to Indiana 10-32
17	18	Northwestern	3-0-0	beat Navy 16-7
20	19	Oklahoma	1-2-0	beat Kansas 33-21
19	20	Washington	3-1-0	lost to #8 Illinois 20-27

October 22 Poll | Oct 27 Games

UP	AP	Team	Record	Result
1	1	Tennessee	4-0-0	beat Tenn. Tech 68-0
2	2	Michigan State	5-0-0	beat Pittsburgh 53-26
4	3	Georgia Tech	5-0-0	beat Vanderbilt 8-7
3	4	Illinois	4-0-0	beat Indiana 21-0
6	5	Maryland	4-0-0	beat LSU 27-0
5	6	Southern Cal	5-0-0	beat TCU 28-26
7	7	Baylor	4-0-0	tied Texas A&M 21-21
9	8	Princeton	4-0-0	beat #12 Cornell 53-15
8	9	California	4-1-0	beat Oregon State 35-14
10	10	Texas	4-1-0	beat Rice 14-6
16	11	Stanford	5-0-0	beat Washington 14-7
11	12	Cornell	4-0-0	lost to #8 Princeton 15-53
17	13	Northwestern	4-0-0	lost to #14 Wisconsin 0-41
14	14	Wisconsin	2-1-1	beat #13 Northwestern 41-0
12	15	Notre Dame	3-1-0	beat Purdue 30-9
13	16	Texas A&M	4-1-0	tied Baylor 21-21
17	17	Kentucky	3-3-0	beat Florida 14-6
19	18	Washington State	3-2-0	beat Oregon 41-6
19	19	Arkansas	3-2-0	lost to Santa Clara 12-21
	20	San Francisco	5-0-0	bye week
19		Oklahoma	2-2-0	beat Colorado 55-14

October 29 Poll | Nov. 3 Games

UP	AP	Team	Record	Result
1	1	Tennessee	5-0-0	beat North Carolina 27-0
3	2	Michigan State	6-0-0	bye week
2	3	Illinois	5-0-0	beat #15 Michigan 7-0
6	4	Maryland	5-0-0	beat Missouri 35-0
5	5	Georgia Tech	6-0-0	tied Duke 14-14
8	6	Princeton	5-0-0	beat Brown 12-0
4	7	Southern Cal	6-0-0	beat Army 28-6
10	8	Baylor	4-0-1	lost to TCU 7-20
7	9	California	5-1-0	lost to UCLA 7-21
9	10	Wisconsin	3-1-1	beat Indiana 6-0
11	11	Stanford	6-0-0	beat #16 Washington State 21-13
12	12	Texas	5-1-0	beat SMU 20-13
13	13	Notre Dame	4-1-0	beat Navy 19-0
17	14	Kentucky	4-3-0	beat #19 Miami, Fla. 32-0
19	15	Michigan	3-2-0	lost to #3 Illinois 0-7
16	16	Washington State	4-2-0	lost to #11 Stanford 13-21
15	17	Oklahoma	3-2-0	beat Kansas State 33-0
14	18	Texas A&M	4-1-1	lost to Arkansas 21-33
19	19	Miami, Fla.	4-1-0	lost to #14 Kentucky 0-32
	20	San Francisco	5-0-0	beat Santa Clara 26-7
17		TCU	3-3-0	beat #8 Baylor 20-7

NOVEMBER 5 POLL — NOV 10 GAMES

UP	AP	Team		
1	1	Tennessee	6-0-0	beat Washington & Lee 60-14
2	2	Illinois	6-0-0	beat Iowa 40-13
5	3	Maryland	6-0-0	beat Navy 40-21
6	4	Princeton	6-0-0	beat Harvard 54-13
3	5	Michigan State	6-0-0	beat # 11 Notre Dame 35-0
4	6	Southern Cal	7-0-0	lost to # 7 Stanford 20-27
9	7	Stanford	7-0-0	beat # 6 Southern Cal 27-20
7	8	Georgia Tech	6-0-1	beat VMI 34-7
8	9	Wisconsin	4-1-1	beat Pennsylvania 16-7
10	10	Texas	6-1-0	lost to # 16 Baylor 6-18
11	11	Notre Dame	5-1-0	lost to #5 Michigan State 0-35
13	12	Kentucky	5-3-0	beat Tulane 37-0
12	13	TCU	4-3-0	bye week
14	14	Oklahoma	4-2-0	beat Missouri 34-20
	15	San Francisco	6-0-0	beat San Diego Navy 26-7
16	16	Baylor	4-1-1	beat # 10 Texas 18-6
20	17	California	5-2-0	beat Washington 37-28
	17	Washington State	4-3-0	beat Idaho 9-6
	19	Pacific	6-1-0	lost to Denver 33-35
18	18	Arkansas	4-3-0	lost to Rice 0-6
23	20	Ohio State	3-2-1	beat Pittsburgh 16-14
15		UCLA	3-3-0	beat Oregon State 7-0
17		Michigan	3-3-0	lost to Cornell 7-20
17		Kansas	5-2-0	beat Loyola Marymount 34-26

NOVEMBER 12 POLL — NOV 17 GAMES

UP	AP	Team		
1	1	Michigan State	7-0-0	beat Indiana 30-36
2	2	Tennessee	7-0-0	beat Mississippi 46-21
3	3	Illinois	7-0-0	tied Ohio State 0-0
4	4	Stanford	8-0-0	beat Oregon State 35-14
5	5	Maryland	7-0-0	beat North Carolina St. 53-0
6	6	Princeton	7-0-0	beat Yale 27-0
7	7	Georgia Tech	7-0-1	beat Alabama 27-7
8	8	Wisconsin	5-1-1	beat Iowa 34-7
11	9	Kentucky	6-3-0	beat George Washington 47-13
10	10	Baylor	5-1-1	beat Wake Forest 42-0
9	11	Southern Cal	7-1-0	bye week
13	12	Oklahoma	5-2-0	beat Iowa State 35-6
12	13	TCU	4-3-0	lost to # 15 Texas 21-32
14	14	San Francisco	7-0-0	beat Pacific 47-14
16	15	Texas	6-2-0	beat # 13 TCU 32-21
14	16	California	5-3-0	beat Oregon 28-26
	17	Washington State	5-3-0	beat Montana 47-10
15	18	UCLA	4-3-0	tied Washington 20-20
	19	Rice	4-3-0	beat Texas A&M 28-13
	20	Cincinnati	9-0-0	lost to Xavier 0-26
17		Holy Cross	6-1-0	beat Quantico Marines 39-14
17		Cornell	5-2-0	beat Dartmouth 21-13
19		San Francisco	7-0-0	beat Pacific 47-14

NOVEMBER 19 POLL — NOV 24 GAMES

UP	AP	Team		
1	1	Tennessee	8-0-0	beat # 9 Kentucky 28-0
2	2	Michigan State	8-0-0	beat Colorado 45-7
3	3	Stanford	9-0-0	lost to California 7-20
4	4	Maryland	8-0-0	beat West Virginia 54-7
6	5	Princeton	8-0-0	beat Dartmouth 13-0
5	6	Illinois	7-0-1	beat Northwestern 3-0
7	7	Georgia Tech	8-0-1	beat Davidson 34-7
8	8	Wisconsin	6-1-1	beat Minnesota 30-6
11	9	Kentucky	7-3-0	lost to # 1 Tennessee 0-28
9	10	Baylor	6-1-1	beat SMU 14-13
10	11	Southern Cal	7-1-0	lost to UCLA 7-21
12	12	Oklahoma	6-2-0	beat Nebraska 27-0
15	13	San Francisco	8-0-0	beat Loyola Marymount 20-2
13	14	Texas	7-2-0	bye week
	15	Virginia	7-1-0	beat William & Mary 46-0
16	16	Holy Cross	7-1-0	beat Temple 41-7
19	17	Washington State	6-3-0	beat Washington 27-25
16	18	Rice	5-3-0	lost to TCU 6-22
18	19	California	7-2-0	beat Stanford 20-7
	20	Bucknell	9-0-0	regular season complete
14		Ohio State	4-2-2	lost to Michigan 0-7
20		UCLA	4-3-1	beat # 11 Southern Cal 21-7
20		Notre Dame	6-2-0	tied Iowa 20-20
20		Cornell	4-4-0	beat Indiana 21-13
20		Purdue	6-2-0	lost to Pennsylvania 0-7
20		Pacific	6-3-0	lost to San Jose State (N23)

NOVEMBER 26 POLL — DEC 1 GAMES

UP	AP	Team		
1	1	Tennessee	9-0-0	beat Vanderbilt 35-27
2	2	Michigan State	9-0-0	regular season complete
3	3	Maryland	9-0-0	regular season complete
4	4	Illinois	8-0-1	regular season complete
5	5	Princeton	9-0-0	regular season complete
6	6	Georgia Tech	9-0-1	beat Georgia 48-6
7	7	Wisconsin	7-1-1	regular season complete
8	8	Stanford	9-1-0	regular season complete
9	9	Baylor	7-1-1	beat Rice 34-13
11	10	Oklahoma	7-2-0	beat Oklahoma State 41-6
10	11	TCU	5-4-0	beat SMU 13-2
12	12	California	8-2-0	regular season complete
17	13	Virginia	8-1-0	regular season complete
16	14	San Francisco	9-0-0	regular season complete
15	15	UCLA	5-3-1	regular season complete
13	16	Texas	7-2-0	lost to Texas A&M 21-22
20	17	Kentucky	7-4-0	regular season complete
	18	Washington State	7-3-0	regular season complete
14	19	Holy Cross	8-1-0	lost to Boston College 14-19
20	20	Southern Cal	7-2-0	lost to Notre Dame 12-19
17		Michigan	4-5-0	regular season complete
17		Purdue	5-4-0	regular season complete

DECEMBER 3 FINAL POLL

UP	AP	Team	RECORD	BOWL BID	DATE	BOWL RESULT	RB	RECORD
1	1	Tennessee	10-0-0	Sugar Bowl	J1	lost to # 3 Maryland 13-28	4	10-1-0
2	2	Michigan State	9-0-0				1	9-0-0
3	3	Maryland	9-0-0	Sugar Bowl	J1	beat # 1 Tennessee 28-13	3	10-0-0
4	4	Illinois	8-0-1	Rose Bowl	J1	beat # 7 Stanford 40-7	2	9-0-1
5	5	Georgia Tech	10-0-1	Orange Bowl	J1	beat # 9 Baylor 17-14	6	11-0-1
6	6	Princeton	9-0-0				5	9-0-0
7	7	Stanford	9-1-0	Rose Bowl	J1	lost to # 4 Illinois 7-40	8	9-2-0
8	8	Wisconsin	7-1-1				11	7-1-1
9	9	Baylor	8-1-1	Orange Bowl	J1	lost to # 5 Georgia Tech 14-17	7	8-2-1
11	10	Oklahoma	8-2-0				12	8-2-0
10	11	TCU	6-4-0	Cotton Bowl	J1	lost to # 15 Kentucky 7-20	31	6-5-0
12	12	California	8-2-0				10	8-2-0
	13	Virginia	8-1-0				18	8-1-0
14	14	San Francisco	9-0-0				14	9-0-0
17	15	Kentucky	7-4-0	Cotton Bowl	J1	beat # 11 TCU 20-7	15	8-4-0
	16	Boston U.	6-4-0				61	6-4-0
17	17	UCLA	5-3-1				27	5-3-1
14	18	Washington State	7-3-0				54	7-3-0
	19	Clemson	7-2-0	Gator Bowl	J1	lost to Miami, Fla. 0-14	23	7-3-0
17	19	Holy Cross	8-2-0				41	8-2-0
13		Notre Dame	7-2-1				13	7-2-1
14		Purdue	5-4-0				28	5-4-0
20		Kansas	8-2-0				26	8-2-0

ANNUAL REVIEW

1951

Consensus All-Americans

POS	Name	HT	WT	School	AA	AP	FC	FW	IN	NE	SN	UP
B	Dick Kazmaier	5-11	171	Princeton	•	•	•	•	•	•	•	•
B	Hank Lauricella	5-10	169	Tennessee	•	•	•	•	•	•	•	•
B	Babe Parilli	6-1	188	Kentucky	•			•	•	•	•	•
B	Johnny Karras	5-11	171	Illinois	•		•		•	•		•
E	Bill McColl	6-4	225	Stanford	•		•	•	•	•	•	•
E	Bob Carey	6-5	215	Michigan State	•	•			•	•		•
T	Don Coleman	5-10	185	Michigan State	•	•	•	•	•	•	•	•
T	Jim Weatherall	6-4	230	Oklahoma	•	*	•		•	•	•	•
G	Bob Ward	5-10	185	Maryland	•		•	•	•	•	•	•
G	Les Richter	6-2	230	California	•		•		•	•	•	•
C	Dick Hightower	6-1	215	SMU	•		•		•	•		•

	Others receiving first-team honors											
B	Larry Isbell			Baylor			•	•	•			
B	Frank Gifford			Southern Cal				•				
B	Ollie Matson			San Francisco			•			•	•	
B	Gary Kerkorian			Stanford				•				
B	Ed Modzelewski			Maryland				•				
B	Al Dorow			Michigan State				•				
B	Hugh McElhenny			Washington				•				
B	Bobby Dillon			Texas						•		
B	Harry Agganis			Boston U.						•		
E	Stan Williams			Baylor				•				
E	Bill Howton			Rice				•				
E	Hal Faverty			Wisconsin						•		
E	Ed Bell			Pennsylvania						•		
E	Frank McPhee			Princeton						•		
E	Pat O'Donahue			Wisconsin						•		
E	Dewey McConnell			Wyoming						•		
T	Jack Little			Texas A&M				•				
T	Bob Toneff			Notre Dame			•					
T	Charles Ulrich			Illinois						•		
T	Lamar Wheat			Georgia Tech				•				
T	Bill Pearman			Tennessee						•		
T	Doug Conway			TCU						•		
G	Ray Beck			Georgia Tech	•	•	•	•				
G	Nick Liotta			Villanova				•				
G	Marv Matuszak			Tulsa			•					
G	Ted Daffer			Tennessee						•	•	
G	George Mrkonic			Kansas						•		
G	Joe Palumbo			Virginia						•		
C	Doug Moseley			Kentucky			•	•				
C	Pat Cannamela			Southern Cal						•	•	
C	George Tarasovic			LSU						•		
C	Charles Boerio			Illinois						•		

AP named Weatherall, Richter and Beck to its first-team All-American defense, but not on offense.

Heisman Trophy Voting

	PLAYER	POS	SCHOOL	1ST	2ND	3RD	TOTAL
1	Dick Kazmaier	HB	Princeton	506	107	45	1777
2	Hank Lauricella	RB	Tennessee	45	108	73	424
3	Babe Parilli	QB	Kentucky	32	79	90	344
4	Bill McColl	E	Stanford	42	56	75	313
5	John Bright	RB	Drake	31	49	39	230
6	John Karras	HB	Illinois	15	60	58	223
7	Larry Isbell	QB	Baylor	29	24	28	163
8	Hugh McElhenny	FB	Washington	18	17	15	103
9	Ollie Matson	FB	San Francisco	6	28	21	95
10	Don Coleman	T	Michigan State	6	23	29	93

Award Winners

PLAYER	POS	SCHOOL	TOTAL
Dick Kazmaier	HB	Princeton	Maxwell
Jim Weatherall	T	Oklahoma	Outland

Conference Standings

Big 10	CONF. W	L	T	OVERALL W	L	T
Illinois	5	0	1	9	0	1
Purdue	4	1	0	5	4	0
Wisconsin	5	1	1	7	1	1
Michigan	4	2	0	4	5	0
Ohio State	2	2	2	4	3	2
Northwestern	2	4	0	5	4	0
Minnesota	1	4	1	2	6	1
Indiana	1	5	0	2	7	0
Iowa	0	5	1	2	5	2

Big 7	CONF. W	L	T	OVERALL W	L	T
Oklahoma	6	0	0	8	2	0
Colorado	5	1	0	7	3	0
Kansas	4	2	0	8	2	0
Iowa State	2	4	0	4	4	1
Kansas State*	1	4	1	1	7	1
Nebraska	1	4	1	1	8	1
Missouri	1	5	0	2	8	0

* Later Forfeited to 0-6-0

Border	CONF. W	L	T	OVERALL W	L	T
Texas Tech	5	0	0	7	4	0
Arizona State	4	1	0	6	3	1
Hardin-Simmons	4	1	0	6	6	0
Arizona	4	2	0	6	5	0
Texas-El Paso	3	4	0	3	7	0
New Mexico	2	3	0	4	7	0
West Texas State	1	5	0	2	7	0
New Mexico State	1	5	0	1	9	0
Northern Arizona	0	2	0	1	7	0

MAC	CONF. W	L	T	OVERALL W	L	T
Cincinnati	3	0	0	10	1	0
Miami, Ohio	3	1	0	7	3	0
Kent State	2	1	0	4	3	2
Ohio U	2	2	0	5	4	1
Case Western Reserve	1	3	0	2	6	1
Western Michigan	0	4	0	4	4	0

Pacific Coast	CONF. W	L	T	OVERALL W	L	T
Stanford	6	1	0	9	2	0
UCLA	4	1	1	5	3	1
California	5	2	0	8	2	0
Southern Cal	4	2	0	7	3	0
Washington State	4	3	0	7	3	0
Oregon State	3	5	0	4	6	0
Washington	1	5	1	3	6	1
Oregon	1	6	0	2	8	0
Idaho	0	3	0	2	7	0

SEC	CONF. W	L	T	OVERALL W	L	T
Georgia Tech	7	0	0	11	0	1
Tennessee	5	0	0	10	1	0
LSU	4	2	1	7	3	1
Mississippi	4	2	1	6	3	1
Kentucky	3	3	0	8	4	0
Auburn	3	4	0	5	5	0
Vanderbilt	3	5	0	6	5	0
Alabama	3	5	0	5	6	0
Florida	2	4	0	5	5	0
Georgia	2	4	0	5	5	0
Mississippi State	2	5	0	4	5	0
Tulane	1	5	0	4	6	0

Skyline	CONF. W	L	T	OVERALL W	L	T
Utah	4	1	0	7	4	0
Wyoming	4	1	1	7	2	1
Denver	4	3	0	6	4	0
Brigham Young	2	2	1	6	3	1
Colorado State	2	3	1	5	4	1
Utah State	2	3	1	3	5	1
Montana	1	4	0	2	7	0

Southern	CONF. W	L	T	OVERALL W	L	T
Maryland	5	0	0	10	0	0
VMI	5	0	0	7	3	0
William & Mary	5	1	0	7	3	0
Wash. & Lee	5	1	0	6	4	0
Clemson	3	1	0	7	3	0
Duke	4	2	0	5	4	1
Wake Forest	5	3	0	6	4	0
South Carolina	5	3	0	5	4	0
George Washington	2	3	1	2	6	1
West Virginia	2	3	0	5	5	0
North Carolina	2	3	0	2	8	0
North Carolina St.	2	6	0	3	7	0
Richmond	2	6	0	3	8	0
Citadel	1	3	0	4	6	0
Furman	1	4	1	3	6	1
Davidson	1	5	0	1	8	0
Virginia Tech	1	7	0	2	8	0

SWC	CONF. W	L	T	OVERALL W	L	T
TCU	5	1	0	6	5	0
Baylor	4	1	1	8	2	1
Texas	3	3	0	7	3	0
Rice	3	3	0	5	5	0
Arkansas	2	4	0	5	5	0
Texas A&M	1	3	2	5	3	2
SMU	1	4	1	3	6	1

Independents	OVERALL W	L	T
Princeton	9	0	0
Michigan State	9	0	0
San Francisco	9	0	0
Virginia	8	1	0
Holy Cross	8	2	0
Notre Dame	7	2	1
Florida State	6	2	0
Miami, Fla.	8	3	0
North Texas	8	4	0
Cornell	6	3	0
Memphis	5	3	0
Columbia	5	3	0
Boston U.	6	4	0
Pennsylvania	5	4	0
Penn State	5	4	0
Syracuse	5	4	0
Pacific	6	5	0
Rutgers	4	4	0
Dartmouth	4	5	0
Harvard	3	5	1
Boston College	3	6	0
Yale	2	5	2
Pittsburgh	3	7	0
Navy	2	6	1
Army	2	7	0
Brown	2	7	0

Bowl Games

DATE	GAME	SCORE
J1	Tangerine	Stetson 35, Arkansas State 20
J1	Orange	Georgia Tech 17, Baylor 14
J1	Salad	Houston 26, Dayton 21
J1	Rose	Illinois 40, Stanford 7
J1	Cotton	Kentucky 20, TCU 7
J1	Gator	Miami, Fla. 14, Clemson 0
J1	Sugar	Maryland 28, Tennessee 13
J1	Sun	Texas Tech 25, Pacific 14

1951 NCAA MAJOR COLLEGE STATISTICAL LEADERS

INDIVIDUAL LEADERS

PASSING/COMPLETIONS	G	ATT	COM	PCT	INT	I%	YDS	YPA	TD	TD%	COM.PG
1 Don Klosterman, Loyola-Marymount	9	315	159	50.5	21	6.7	1843	5.9	9	2.9	17.7
2 Babe Parilli, Kentucky	11	239	136	56.9	12	5.0	1643	6.9	19	8.0	12.4
3 Don Leahy, Marquette	11	232	127	54.7	15	6.5	1543	6.7	12	5.2	11.5
4 Tom Dublinski, Utah	11	239	124	51.9	11	4.6	1418	5.9	14	5.9	11.3
5 Don Babers, Oklahoma State	10	247	121	49.0	13	5.3	1352	5.5	10	4.1	12.1
6 Bob Hart, Hardin-Simmons	12	229	117	51.1	14	6.1	1380	6.0	8	3.5	9.8
7 Zeke Bratkowski, Georgia	10	248	116	46.8	29	11.7	1578	6.4	6	2.4	11.6
8 Bill Wade, Vanderbilt	11	223	111	49.8	10	4.5	1609	7.2	13	5.8	10.1
9 Fred Benners, SMU	10	204	108	52.9	12	5.9	1306	6.4	9	4.4	10.8
10 Larry Isbell, Baylor	10	214	105	49.1	18	8.4	1430	6.7	10	4.7	10.5

ALL-PURPOSE YARDS	G	RUSH	REC	INT	PR	KR	YDS	YPG
1 Ollie Matson, San Francisco	9	1566	58	18	115	280	2037	226.3

RUSHING/YARDS	G	ATT	YDS	AVG	YPG
1 Ollie Matson, San Francisco	9	245	1566	6.4	174.0
2 Frank Goode, Hardin-Simmons	12	270	1399	5.2	116.6
3 Howard Waugh, Tulsa	11	165	1118	6.8	101.6
4 Gene Shannon, Houston	10	144	1059	7.4	105.9
5 Tommy McCormick, Pacific	10	191	1001	5.2	100.1
6 Hugh McElhenny, Washington	10	169	936	5.5	93.6
7 Johnny Bright, Drake	9	160	927	5.8	103.0
8 John Kastan, Boston U.	10	133	886	6.7	88.6
9 Hank Lauricella, Tennessee	10	111	881	7.9	88.1
10 Buck McPhail, Oklahoma	10	101	865	8.6	86.5

RUSHING/YARDS PER CARRY	G	ATT	YDS	YPC
1 Buck McPhail, Oklahoma	10	101	865	8.6
2 Hank Lauricella, Tennessee	10	111	881	7.9
3 Dick Modzelewski, Maryland	9	113	834	7.4
4 Gene Shannon, Houston	10	144	1059	7.4
5 Glenn Lippman, Texas A&M	10	118	801	6.8
6 Howard Waugh, Tulsa	11	165	1118	6.8
7 John Kastan, Boston U.	10	133	886	6.7
8 Ollie Matson, San Francisco	9	245	1566	6.4
9 Ray Oliverson, Brigham Young	10	129	822	6.4
10 Jack Crocker, Tulsa	11	133	817	6.1
*-Based on top 20 rushers				

RECEIVING/RECEPTIONS	G	REC	YDS	TD	YPR	YPG	RPG
1 Dewey McConnell, Wyoming	10	47	725	8	15.4	72.5	4.7
2 Ed Barker, Washington State	10	46	864	9	18.8	86.4	4.6
3 Jim David, Colorado State	10	46	551	5	12.0	55.1	4.6
4 Karl Kluckhohn, Colgate	9	45	616	5	13.7	68.4	5.0
4 Fred Snyder, Loyola-Marymount	9	45	539	2	12.0	59.9	5.0
6 Bill McColl, Stanford	10	42	607	7	14.5	60.7	4.2
6 Harry Babcock, Georgia	10	41	666	2	16.2	66.6	4.1
8 Ben Roderick, Vanderbilt	11	40	627	5	15.7	57.0	3.6
8 George Wooden, Oklahoma State	10	40	502	2	12.6	50.2	4.0
8 Wesley Bomm, Columbia	8	40	444	1	11.1	55.5	5.0
8 Jimmy Walker, Texas El-Paso	10	40	440	3	11.0	44.0	4.0

PUNTING	PUNT	YDS	AVG
1 Chuck Spaulding, Wyoming	37	1610	43.5
2 Des Koch, Southern Cal	33	1429	43.3
3 Bobby Wilson, Alabama	65	2724	41.9
4 Jerry Norton, SMU	32	1338	41.8
5 Joe Bevere, Drake	47	1941	41.3
6 Red Smith, Duke	47	1913	40.7
7 Dave Mann, Oregon State	45	1827	40.6
8 Bob Moore, UCLA	52	2096	40.3
9 Bud Wallace, North Carolina	65	2613	40.2
10 Avatus Stone, Syracuse	52	2090	40.2

PUNT RETURNS/YARDS	PR	YDS	AVG
1 Tom Murphy, Holy Cross	25	533	21.3
2 Johnny Williams, Southern Cal	39	438	11.2
3 Selmer Pederson, Wyoming	39	420	10.8
4 Robert Lary, Texas A&M	24	388	16.2
5 James Lesane, Virginia	35	387	11.1
6 John Hall, Florida	24	369	15.4
7 Billy Stephens, South Carolina	19	355	18.7
8 Bud Carson, North Carolina	25	318	12.7
9 Bill Blackstock, Tennessee	12	311	25.9
10 Lindy Hanson, Boston U.	21	306	14.6

KICKOFF RETURNS/YARDS	KR	YDS	AVG
1 Chuck Hill, New Mexico	17	504	29.6
2 Robert Byrne, Montana	21	446	21.2
3 Johnny Williams, Southern Cal	15	408	27.2
3 Alex Webster, North Carolina St.	15	408	27.2
5 Robert Mischak, Army	12	376	31.3
6 Larry Parker, North Carolina	17	372	21.9
7 Harry Jones, Kentucky	15	371	24.7
8 Steve Wadiak, South Carolina	13	350	26.9
9 Gilbert Gonzales, Arizona	13	348	26.8
10 Bino Barreira, George Washington	19	341	17.9

SCORING	TDS	XPT	FG	PTS
1 Ollie Matson, San Francisco	21	0	0	126
2 Hugh McElhenny, Washington	17	23	0	125
3 Bill Parsons, Tulsa	16	0	0	96
4 Ray Oliverson, Brigham Young	15	0	0	90
4 John Kastan, Boston U.	15	0	0	90
6 Frank Goode, Hardin-Simmons	14	0	0	84
6 Harold Payne, Tennessee	14	0	0	84
6 Johnny Bright, Drake	14	0	0	84
6 Eddie Macon, Pacific	14	0	0	84
10 Four tied	—	—	—	78

INTERCEPTIONS	INT	YDS
1 George Shaw, Oregon	13	136
2 Bill Albrecht, Washington	12	140
3 Alfred Brosky, Illinois	10	183
3 Robert Reid, Baylor	10	130
5 Eddie Macon, Pacific	9	245
6 Pete Konek, Kansas	8	180
6 Lester Kennedy, Tulane	8	103
6 Chester Lyssy, Hardin-Simmons	8	96
6 John Thompson, Texas Tech	8	74
6 Mike Zinkiewicz, Holy Cross	8	72

TEAM LEADERS

RUSHING OFFENSE	G	ATT	YDS	AVG	YPG
1 Arizona State	10	559	3348	6.0	334.8
2 Tulsa	11	647	3622	5.6	329.3
3 Maryland	9	496	2906	5.9	322.9
4 Oklahoma	10	589	3160	5.4	316.0
5 Pacific	10	678	3153	4.7	315.3
6 Tennessee	10	532	3068	5.8	306.8
7 California	10	551	3044	5.5	304.4
8 Michigan State	9	530	2630	5.0	292.2
9 Princeton	9	522	2604	5.0	289.3
10 San Francisco	9	520	2544	4.9	282.7

PASSING OFFENSE/YPG	G	ATT	COM	INT	PCT	YDS	YPA	TD	YPG	I%	YPC
1 Loyola-Marymount	9	324	164	22	50.6	1895	5.8	10	210.6	6.8	11.6
2 Missouri	10	284	124	30	43.7	1762	6.2	12	176.2	10.6	14.2
3 SMU	10	286	144	23	50.4	1734	6.1	11	173.4	8.0	12.0
4 Colgate	9	235	110	20	46.8	1560	6.6	13	173.3	8.5	14.2
5 Boston U.	10	212	117	17	55.2	1680	7.9	16	168.0	8.0	14.4
6 Washington	10	257	123	21	47.9	1622	6.3	12	162.2	8.2	13.2
7 Oregon	10	314	134	26	42.7	1620	5.2	24	162.0	8.3	12.1
8 Georgia	10	263	121	32	46.0	1618	6.2	7	161.8	12.2	13.4
9 Oklahoma State	10	291	143	19	49.1	1603	5.5	11	160.3	6.5	11.2
10 Iowa State	9	218	109	18	50.0	1425	6.5	16	158.3	8.3	13.1

TOTAL OFFENSE	G	P	YDS	AVG	YPG
1 Tulsa	11	836	5282	6.3	480.2
2 Maryland	9	616	3810	6.2	423.3
3 Princeton	9	671	3753	5.6	417.0
4 Arizona State	10	689	4162	6.0	416.2
5 Cincinnati	11	796	4491	5.6	408.3
6 Oklahoma	10	693	4062	5.9	406.2
7 Holy Cross	10	810	4055	5.0	405.5
8 Michigan State	9	667	3627	5.4	403.0
9 Pacific	10	844	4016	4.8	401.6
10 California	10	685	3980	5.8	398.0

RUSHING DEFENSE	G	ATT	YDS	AVG	YPG
1 San Francisco	9	288	464	1.6	51.6
2 Wisconsin	9	344	599	1.7	66.6
3 Princeton	9	359	669	1.9	74.3
4 Maryland	9	321	680	2.1	75.6
5 Holy Cross	10	415	973	2.3	97.3
6 Oklahoma	10	418	1049	2.5	104.9
7 Georgia Tech	11	477	1164	2.4	105.8
8 Tennessee	10	460	1071	2.3	107.1
9 Southern Cal	11	466	1179	2.5	107.2
10 Illinois	9	422	1020	2.4	113.3

PASSING DEFENSE	G	ATT	COM	PCT	YPC	INT	I%	YDS	YPA	TD	YPG
1 Washington & Lee	10	151	53	35.1	12.8	24	15.9	679	4.5	5	67.9
2 Miami, Fla.	10	174	65	37.4	10.8	11	6.3	700	4.0	6	70.0
3 Columbia	8	141	50	35.5	12.5	7	5.0	624	4.4	2	78.0
3 Indiana	9	128	53	41.4	13.2	14	10.9	702	5.5	8	78.0
5 Vanderbilt	11	125	53	42.4	16.2	18	14.4	861	6.9	3	78.3
6 Purdue	9	128	48	37.5	15.4	10	7.8	737	5.8	8	81.9
7 Colorado State	10	167	71	42.5	11.8	10	6.0	838	5.0	7	83.8
8 Furman	10	151	68	45.0	12.4	14	9.3	841	5.6	7	84.1
9 Boston U.	10	178	60	33.7	14.2	18	10.1	853	4.8	5	85.3
10 Denver	10	165	70	42.4	12.3	21	12.7	863	5.2	4	86.3

TOTAL DEFENSE	G	P	YDS	AVG	YPG
1 Wisconsin	9	539	1393	2.6	154.8
2 Princeton	9	513	1592	3.1	176.9
3 Georgia Tech	11	708	2190	3.1	199.1
4 Kentucky	11	630	2265	3.6	205.9
5 San Francisco	9	561	1885	3.4	209.4
6 Illinois	9	552	1954	3.5	217.1
7 Holy Cross	10	647	2212	3.4	221.2
8 Oklahoma	10	655	2215	3.4	221.5
9 Virginia	9	553	1995	3.6	221.7
10 Denver	10	617	2230	3.6	223.0

SCORING OFFENSE	G	PTS	AVG
1 Maryland	9	353	39.2

SCORING DEFENSE	G	PTS	AVG
1 Wisconsin	9	53	5.9

1952 POLL PROGRESSION

Pre-Season 1952 — Sept 27 Games

UP	AP	Team	Record	Result
1	1	Michigan State	0-0-0	beat Michigan 27-13
2	2	Maryland	0-0-0	beat Auburn 13-7
3	3	Georgia Tech	0-0-0	beat Florida 17-14
4	4	Oklahoma	0-0-0	tied Colorado 21-21
6	5	Illinois	0-0-0	beat Iowa State 33-7
8	6	Tennessee	0-0-0	beat Mississippi State 14-7
7	7	Wisconsin	0-0-0	beat Marquette 42-19
5	8	California	0-0-0	beat Missouri 28-14
11	9	TCU	0-0-0	lost to # 18 UCLA 0-14
9	10	Notre Dame	0-0-0	tied # 11 Pennsylvania 7-7
10	11	Texas	0-0-0	beat North Carolina 28-7
13	11	Pennsylvania	0-0-0	tied # 10 Notre Dame 7-7
	13	Stanford	0-0-0	beat # 15 Washington State 14-13
18	14	Princeton	0-0-0	beat Columbia 14-0
17	15	Washington State	0-0-0	lost to # 13 Stanford 13-14
13	16	Southern Cal	0-0-0	beat Northwestern 31-0
12	17	Kansas	0-0-0	beat Santa Clara 21-9
15	18	UCLA	0-0-0	beat # 9 TCU 14-0
19	19	Duke	0-0-0	beat SMU 14-7
	20	Ohio State	0-0-0	beat Indiana 33-13
16		Purdue	0-0-0	tied Penn State 20-20
20		Syracuse	0-0-0	beat Boston U. 34-21
20		Virginia	0-0-0	beat Vanderbilt 27-0

September 29 Poll — Oct 4 Games

UP	AP	Team	Record	Result
1	1	Michigan State	1-0-0	beat Oregon State 17-14
4	2	Illinois	1-0-0	lost to # 8 Wisconsin 6-20
5	3	Maryland	2-0-0	beat Clemson 28-0
2	4	California	2-0-0	beat Minnesota 49-13
3	5	Texas	2-0-0	lost to # 19 Notre Dame 3-14
7	6	Georgia Tech	2-0-0	beat SMU 20-7
6	7	Southern Cal	2-0-0	beat Army 22-0
8	8	Wisconsin	1-0-0	lost to # 2 Illinois 20-6
9	9	Kansas	2-0-0	beat Colorado 21-12
12	10	Duke	2-0-0	beat # 11 Tennessee 7-0
11	11	Tennessee	1-0-0	lost to # 10 Duke 0-7
15	12	Villanova	2-0-0	beat Detroit 21-7
13	13	Princeton	1-0-0	beat Rutgers 61-19
16	14	UCLA	2-0-0	beat Washington 32-7
13	15	Ohio State	1-0-0	lost to Purdue 14-21
19	16	Virginia	1-0-0	beat Virginia Tech 42-0
	17	Rice		
	18	Mississippi	1-0-1	beat Auburn 20-7
18	19	Notre Dame	0-0-1	beat # 5 Texas 14-3
10	20	Oklahoma	0-0-1	beat Pittsburgh 49-20
17		Pennsylvania	0-0-1	beat Dartmouth 7-0
20		Georgia	2-0-0	beat North Carolina 49-0

October 6 Poll — Oct 11 Games

UP	AP	Team	Record	Result
3	1	Wisconsin	2-0-0	lost to Ohio State 14-23
1	2	Michigan State	2-0-0	beat Texas A&M 48-6
2	3	California	3-0-0	beat Oregon 41-7
4	4	Maryland	3-0-0	beat # 19 Georgia 37-0
5	5	Georgia Tech	3-0-0	beat Tulane 14-0
8	6	Duke	3-0-0	beat South Carolina 33-7
6	7	Southern Cal	3-0-0	beat San Diego Navy 20-6
9	8	Notre Dame	1-0-1	lost to Pittsburgh 19-22
10	9	Kansas	3-0-0	beat Iowa State 43-0
12	10	Princeton	2-0-0	lost to Pennsylvania 7-13
11	11	UCLA	3-0-0	beat Rice 20-0
7	12	Oklahoma	1-0-1	beat Texas 49-20
18	13	Illinois	1-1-0	beat Washington 48-14
	14	Villanova	3-0-0	beat Wake Forest 20-0
19	15	Virginia	2-0-0	beat George Washington
16	16	Purdue	1-0-1	beat Iowa 41-14
	17	Navy	2-0-0	beat William & Mary 14-0
17	18	Alabama	3-0-0	beat Virginia Tech 33-0
13	19	Georgia	3-0-0	lost to # 4 Maryland 0-37
	20	Penn State	2-0-1	beat West Virginia 35-21
14		Texas	2-1-0	lost to # 12 Oklahoma 20-49
15		Pennsylvania	1-0-1	beat # 10 Princeton 13-7
19		Baylor	2-0-0	lost to Arkansas 17-20

October 13 Poll — Oct 18 Games

UP	AP	Team	Record	Result
1	1	Michigan State	3-0-0	beat Syracuse 48-7
3	2	Maryland	4-0-0	beat # 20 Navy 38-7
2	3	California	4-0-0	beat Santa Clara 27-7
4	4	Georgia Tech	4-0-0	beat Auburn 33-0
8	5	Duke	4-0-0	beat North Carolina St. 57-0
5	6	Oklahoma	2-0-1	beat # 8 Kansas 42-20
7	7	Southern Cal	4-0-0	beat Oregon State 28-6
6	8	Kansas	4-0-0	lost to # 6 Oklahoma 20-42
9	9	Purdue	2-0-1	lost to Notre Dame 14-26
10	10	UCLA	4-0-0	beat # 13 Stanford 24-14
17	11	Virginia	3-0-0	beat VMI 33-14
14	12	Wisconsin	2-1-0	beat Iowa 42-13
18	13	Stanford	4-0-0	lost to # 10 UCLA 14-24
11	14	Pennsylvania	2-0-1	beat Columbia 27-17
15	15	Villanova	4-0-0	beat Boston College 28-7
12	16	Ohio State	2-1-0	beat Washington State 35-7
13	17	Illinois	2-1-0	lost to Minnesota 7-13
19	18	Alabama	4-0-0	lost to Tennessee 0-20
	19	Penn State	3-0-1	beat Nebraska 10-0
15	20	Navy	3-0-0	lost to # 2 Maryland 7-38
20		Pittsburgh	2-1-0	beat Army 22-14

October 20 Poll — Oct 25 Games

UP	AP	Team	Record	Result
1	1	Michigan State	4-0-0	beat # 17 Penn State 34-7
2	2	Maryland	5-0-0	beat LSU 34-6
4	3	Oklahoma	3-0-1	beat Kansas State 49-6
3	4	California	5-0-0	lost to # 7 Southern Cal 0-10
7	5	Georgia Tech	5-0-0	beat Vanderbilt 30-0
6	6	Duke	5-0-0	beat # 9 Virginia 21-7
8	7	Southern Cal	5-0-0	beat # 4 California 10-0
15	8	UCLA	5-0-0	beat# 10 Wisconsin 20-7
9	9	Virginia	4-0-0	lost to # 6 Duke 7-21
12	10	Wisconsin	3-1-0	lost to # 8 UCLA 7-20
13	11	Pennsylvania	3-0-1	tied Navy 7-7
16	12	Villanova	5-0-0	beat Xavier 34-20
10	13	Tennessee	3-1-0	beat Wofford 50-0
16	14	Ohio State	3-1-0	lost to Iowa 0-8
11	15	Kansas	4-1-0	beat SMU 26-0
19	16	Notre Dame	2-1-1	beat North Carolina 34-14
18	17	Penn State	4-0-1	lost to# 1 Michigan State 7-34
	18	Pittsburgh	3-1-0	lost to West Virginia 0-16
14	19	Michigan	2-0-0	beat Minnesota 21-0
	20	Texas	3-2-0	beat Rice 20-7
20		Minnesota	2-2-0	lost to # 19 Michigan 0-21
20		Illinois	2-2-0	lost to Purdue 12-40

October 27 Poll — Nov. 1 Games

UP	AP	Team	Record	Result
1	1	Michigan State	5-0-0	beat # 8 Purdue 14-7
2	2	Maryland	6-0-0	beat Boston U. 34-7
4	3	Oklahoma	4-0-1	beat Iowa State 41-0
5	4	Georgia Tech	6-0-0	beat # 6 Duke 28-7
3	5	Southern Cal	6-0-0	bye week
7	6	Duke	6-0-0	lost to# 4 Georgia Tech 7-28
6	7	UCLA	6-0-0	beat # 11 California 28-7
8	8	Purdue	3-1-1	lost to # 1 Michigan State 7-14
10	9	Kansas	5-1-0	beat Kansas State 26-6
13	10	Villanova	6-0-0	tied Parris Isl. Marines 20-20
9	11	California	5-1-0	lost to # 7 UCLA 7-28
15	12	Tennessee	4-1-0	beat North Carolina 41-14
11	13	Notre Dame	3-1-1	beat Navy 17-6
16	14	Texas	4-2-0	beat SMU 31-14
14	15	Michigan	3-2-0	lost to Illinois 13-22
	16	Virginia	4-1-0	lost to South Carolina 14-21
12	17	Pennsylvania	3-0-2	lost to Penn State 7-14
17	18	Wisconsin	3-2-0	beat Rice 21-7
	19	Alabama	5-1-0	beat Georgia 34-19
	20	Florida	4-2-0	beat Auburn 31-21
17		Princeton	4-1-0	beat Brown 39-0
19		Baylor	4-1-0	tied TCU 20-20
20		Illinois	2-3-0	beat # 15 Michigan 22-13
20		Pittsburgh	3-2-0	beat Indiana 28-7
20		Washington	4-2-0	beat Oregon State 38-13

UP	AP	NOVEMBER 3 POLL		NOV. 8 GAMES
1	1	Michigan State	6-0-0	beat Indiana 41-14
2	2	Maryland	7-0-0	bye week
4	3	Georgia Tech	7-0-0	beat Army 45-6
5	4	Oklahoma	5-0-1	lost to # 10 Notre Dame 21-27
3	5	UCLA	7-0-0	beat Oregon State 57-0
6	6	Southern Cal	6-0-0	beat Stanford 54-7
7	7	Kansas	6-1-0	lost to Nebraska 13-14
10	8	Tennessee	5-1-0	beat LSU 22-3
9	9	Purdue	3-2-1	tied Minnesota 14-14
8	10	Notre Dame	4-1-1	beat # 4 Oklahoma 27-21
13	11	Villanova	6-0-1	lost to Tulsa 6-42
11	12	Duke	6-1-0	lost to Navy 6-16
12	13	Texas	5-2-0	beat Baylor 35-33
18	14	Mississippi	5-0-2	beat Houston 6-0
14	15	Penn State	5-1-1	lost to Syracuse 7-25
	16	Alabama	6-1-0	beat U.T. Chattanooga 42-28
	17	Florida	5-2-0	bye week
16	18	Wisconsin	4-2-0	beat Northwestern 24-20
15	19	Princeton	5-1-0	beat Harvard 41-21
	20	Holy Cross	5-1-0	beat Colgate 13-7
16		California	5-2-0	lost to Washington 7-22
19		Arkansas	2-5-0	lost to Rice 33-35
19		Illinois	3-3-0	beat Iowa 33-13

UP	AP	NOVEMBER 10 POLL		NOV. 15 GAMES
1	1	Michigan State	7-0-0	beat # 6 Notre Dame 21-3
2	2	Georgia Tech	8-0-0	beat # 12 Alabama 7-3
3	3	Maryland	7-0-0	lost to # 11 Mississippi 14-21
4	4	UCLA	8-0-0	bye week
5	5	Southern Cal	7-0-0	beat # 17 Washington 33-0
6	6	Notre Dame	5-1-1	lost to # 1 Michigan State 3-21
8	7	Tennessee	6-1-0	beat # 18 Florida 26-12
7	8	Oklahoma	5-1-1	beat Missouri 47-7
10	9	Texas	6-2-0	beat TCU 14-7
9	10	Purdue	3-2-2	lost to # 20 Michigan 10-21
12	11	Mississippi	6-0-2	beat # 3 Maryland 21-14
13	12	Alabama	7-1-0	lost to # 2 Georgia Tech 3-7
	13	Syracuse	5-2-0	beat Colgate 20-14
13	14	Pittsburgh	5-2-0	beat North Carolina St. 48-6
11	15	Wisconsin	5-2-0	beat Indiana 37-14
15	16	Princeton	6-1-0	beat Yale 27-21
	17	Washington	6-2-0	lost to # 5 Southern Cal 0-33
	18	Florida	5-2-0	lost to # 7 Tennessee 12-26
17	19	Kansas	6-2-0	beat Oklahoma State 12-7
	20	Michigan	4-3-0	beat # 10 Purdue 21-10
16		Duke	6-2-0	beat Wake Forest 14-7
18		Villanova	6-1-1	bye week
19		Illinois	4-3-0	lost to Ohio State 7-27
19		Navy	4-2-1	beat Columbia 28-0

UP	AP	NOVEMBER 17 POLL		NOV. 22 GAMES
1	1	Michigan State	8-0-0	beat Marquette 62-13
4	2	Georgia Tech	9-0-0	beat Florida State 30-0
3	3	UCLA	8-0-0	lost to # 4 Southern Cal 12-14
2	4	Southern Cal	8-0-0	beat # 3 UCLA 14-12
5	5	Oklahoma	6-1-1	beat Nebraska 34-13
8	6	Mississippi	7-0-2	bye week
6	7	Tennessee	7-1-0	tied Kentucky 14-14
6	8	Maryland	7-1-0	lost to # 14 Alabama 7-27
10	9	Notre Dame	5-2-1	beat Iowa 27-0
9	10	Texas	7-2-0	bye week
	11	Tulsa	6-1-1	beat Arkansas 44-34
13	12	Michigan	5-3-0	lost to Ohio State 7-27
11	13	Wisconsin	6-2-0	tied Minnesota 21-21
14	14	Alabama	7-2-0	beat # 8 Maryland 27-7
	15	Syracuse	6-2-0	beat Fordham 26-13
12	16	Pittsburgh	6-2-0	lost to Penn State 0-17
14	17	Princeton	7-1-0	beat Dartmouth 33-0
	18	Kansas	7-2-0	lost to Missouri 19-20
19	19	Houston	6-2-0	bye week
20	20	Duke	7-2-0	beat North Carolina 34-0
16		Purdue	3-3-2	beat Indiana 21-16
16		Army	4-3-1	bye week
18		Navy	5-2-1	bye week
20		Kentucky	5-3-1	tied # 7 Tennessee 14-14

UP	AP	NOVEMBER 24 POLL		NOV. 29 GAMES
1	1	Michigan State	9-0-0	regular season complete
2	2	Southern Cal	9-0-0	lost to # 7 Notre Dame 0-9
3	3	Georgia Tech	10-0-0	beat Georgia 23-9
5	4	Oklahoma	7-1-1	beat Oklahoma State 54-7
4	5	UCLA	8-1-0	regular season complete
7	6	Mississippi	7-0-2	beat Mississippi State 20-14
6	7	Notre Dame	6-2-1	beat # 2 Southern Cal 9-0
9	8	Alabama	8-2-0	beat Auburn 21-0
8	9	Tennessee	7-1-1	beat Vanderbilt 46-0
10	10	Texas	7-2-0	beat Texas A&M 32-12
	11	Tulsa	7-1-1	bye week
11	12	Wisconsin	6-2-1	regular season complete
14	13	Duke	8-2-0	regular season complete
13	14	Purdue	4-3-2	regular season complete
12	15	Maryland	7-2-0	regular season complete
	16	Syracuse	7-2-0	regular season complete
17	17	Florida	6-3-0	bye week
16	18	Princeton	8-1-0	regular season complete
	19	Kentucky	5-3-2	bye week
	20	Virginia	7-2-0	beat William & Mary 20-13
14		tie- Ohio State	6-3-0	regular season complete
18		Pittsburgh	6-3-0	regular season complete
19		Navy	5-2-1	beat Army 7-0
19		Houston	6-2-0	beat Detroit 33-19

UP	AP	DECEMBER 1 FINAL POLL	RECORD	BOWL BID	DATE	BOWL RESULT	RB	RECORD
1	1	Michigan State	9-0-0				2	9-0-0
2	2	Georgia Tech	11-0-0	Sugar Bowl	J1	beat # 7 Mississippi 24-7	1	12-0-0
3	3	Notre Dame	7-2-1				7	7-2-1
4	4	Oklahoma	8-1-1				9	8-1-1
5	5	Southern Cal	9-1-0	Rose Bowl	J1	beat # 11 Wisconsin 7-0	3	10-1-0
6	6	UCLA	8-1-0				4	8-1-0
7	7	Mississippi	8-0-2	Sugar Bowl	J1	lost to # 2 Georgia Tech 7-24	5	8-1-2
8	8	Tennessee	8-1-1	Cotton Bowl	J1	lost to # 10 Texas 0-16	12	8-2-1
9	9	Alabama	9-2-0	Orange Bowl	J1	beat Syracuse 61-6	6	10-2-0
11	10	Texas	8-2-0	Cotton Bowl	J1	beat # 8 Tennessee 16-0	8	9-2-0
10	11	Wisconsin	6-2-1	Rose Bowl	J1	lost to # 5 Southern Cal 0-7	19	6-3-1
	12	Tulsa	7-1-1	Gator Bowl	J1	lost to # 15 Florida 13-14	26	8-2-1
13	11	Maryland	7-2-0				10	7-2-0
	14	Syracuse	7-2-0	Orange Bowl	J1	lost to Alabama 6-61	25	7-3-0
	15	Florida	6-3-0	Gator Bowl	J1	beat # 12 Tulsa 14-13	16	8-3-0
18	16	Duke	8-2-0				13	8-2-0
15	17	Ohio State	6-3-0				23	6-3-0
12	18	Purdue	4-3-2				34	4-3-2
14	19	Princeton	8-1-0				11	8-1-0
19	20	Kentucky	5-3-2				31	5-4-2
15		Pittsburgh	6-3-0				35	6-3-0
17		Navy	6-2-1				14	6-2-1
19		Houston	8-2-0				17	8-2-0

ANNUAL REVIEW

1952

CONSENSUS ALL-AMERICANS

POS	Name	HT	WT	School	AA	AP	FC	FW	IN	NE	SN	UP
B	Jack Scarbath	6-1	190	Maryland	•	•	•	•	•	•	•	•
B	Johnny Lattner	6-1	190	Notre Dame	•	•	•	•	•	•	•	•
B	Billy Vessels	6-0	185	Oklahoma	•	•	•	•	•	•	•	•
B	Jim Sears	5-9	167	Southern Cal	•		•			•	•	
E	Frank McPhee	6-3	203	Princeton	•	•	•	•	•	•	•	•
E	Bernie Flowers	6-1	189	Purdue	•	•			•	•	•	•
T	Dick Modzelewski	6-0	235	Maryland	•	•		•		•	•	•
T	Hal Miller	6-4	235	Georgia Tech	•		•		•	•	•	•
G	John Michels	5-10	195	Tennessee	•	•	•	•	•	•	•	•
G	Elmer Willhoite	6-2	216	Southern Cal	•	•	•	•	•	•		•
C	Donn Moomaw	6-4	220	UCLA	•	•		•	•	•		•

OTHERS RECEIVING FIRST-TEAM HONORS

B	Gene Filipski			Villanova				•				
B	Paul Giel			Minnesota		•	•					
B	Don McAuliffe			Michigan State		•			•			
B	Buck McPhail			Oklahoma		•						
B	Don Heinrich			Washington						•	•	
B	Leon Hardeman			Georgia Tech	•				•	•		
B	Bobby Moorhead			Georgia Tech					•			
B	John Olszewski			California					•	•		
B	Paul Cameron			UCLA					•			
B	Lowell Perry			Michigan					•			
E	Tom Stolhandske			Texas		•	•		•			
E	Ed Bell			Pennsylvania		•	•		•			
E	Buck Martin			Georgia Tech		•						
E	Joe Collier			Northwestern					•			
E	Steve Meilinger			Kentucky					•			
E	Tom Scott			Virginia					•			
T	Kline Gilbert			Mississippi		•		•				
T	Ed Meadows			Duke		•						
T	David Suminski			Wisconsin					•			
T	Doug Atkins			Tennessee	•				•			
T	Harvey Achziger			Colorado State					•			
T	Bob Fleck			Syracuse					•			
T	Jerry Minnick			Nebraska					•			
T	Oliver Spencer			Kansas					•			
G	Harley Sewell			Texas		•	•		•			
G	Marv Matuszak			Tulsa		•						
G	Steve Eisenhauer			Navy					•	•	•	
G	Mike Takacs			Ohio State					•			
C	Tom Catlin			Oklahoma	•		•	•	•	•		
C	Pete Brown			Georgia Tech	•							
C	Dick Tamburo			Michigan State		•			•			
C	Joe Schmidt			Pittsburgh					•			
C	George Morris			Georgia Tech					•			

*   AP named Weatherall, Richter and Beck to its first-team All-American defense, but not on offense.

HEISMAN TROPHY VOTING

	PLAYER	POS	SCHOOL	1ST	2ND	3RD	TOTAL
1	Billy Vessels	HB	Oklahoma	98	91	49	525
2	Jack Scarbath	QB	Maryland	70	57	43	367
3	Paul Giel	TB	Minnesota	76	38	25	329
4	Donn Moomaw	LB	UCLA	54	32	31	257
5	Johnny Lattner	HB	Notre Dame	35	45	58	253
6	Paul Cameron	HB	UCLA	40	35	28	218
7	Jim Sears	HB	Southern Cal	38	21	17	173
8	Don McAuliffe	HB	Michigan State	26	29	28	164
9	Don Heinrich	QB	Washington	19	28	40	153
10	Tom Catlin	C	Oklahoma	25	26	23	150

AWARD WINNERS

PLAYER	POS	SCHOOL	AWARD NAME
Johnny Lattner	HB	Notre Dame	Maxwell
Dick Modzelewski	T	Maryland	Outland

CONFERENCE STANDINGS

Big 10

	CONF. W	L	T	OVERALL W	L	T
Wisconsin	4	1	1	6	3	1
Purdue	4	1	1	4	3	2
Ohio State	5	2	0	6	3	0
Michigan	4	2	0	5	4	0
Minnesota	3	1	2	4	3	2
Illinois	2	5	0	4	5	0
Northwestern	2	5	0	2	6	1
Iowa	2	5	0	2	7	0
Indiana	1	5	0	2	7	0

Big 7

	CONF. W	L	T	OVERALL W	L	T
Oklahoma	5	0	1	8	1	1
Missouri	5	1	0	5	5	0
Nebraska	3	2	1	5	4	1
Kansas	3	3	0	7	3	0
Colorado	2	2	2	6	2	2
Colorado	2	2	2	6	2	2
Kansas State	0	6	0	1	9	0

Border

	CONF. W	L	T	OVERALL W	L	T
Arizona State	4	0	0	6	3	0
Texas Tech	2	1	1	3	7	1
Arizona	3	2	0	6	4	0
Hardin-Simmons	2	2	1	5	3	2
Texas-El Paso	2	3	1	5	5	1
New Mexico State	1	2	1	2	6	1
West Texas State	1	4	0	3	6	0
Northern Arizona	0	1	0	3	4	0
Kansas State	0	6	0	1	9	0

MAC

	CONF. W	L	T	OVERALL W	L	T
Cincinnati	3	0	0	8	1	1
Miami, Ohio	4	1	0	8	1	0
Ohio U	5	2	0	6	2	1
Bowling Green	2	2	0	7	2	0
Kent State	2	2	0	5	4	0
Case Western Reserve	1	4	0	5	4	0
Western Michigan	1	4	0	4	4	0
Toledo	1	4	0	4	5	0

Pacific Coast

	CONF. W	L	T	OVERALL W	L	T
Southern Cal	6	0	0	10	1	0
UCLA	5	1	0	8	1	0
Washington	6	2	0	7	3	0
California	3	3	0	7	3	0
Washington State	3	4	0	4	6	0
Stanford	2	5	0	5	5	0
Oregon	2	5	0	2	7	1
Idaho	1	3	0	4	4	1
Oregon State	1	6	0	2	7	0

SEC

	CONF. W	L	T	OVERALL W	L	T
Georgia Tech	6	0	0	12	0	0
Tennessee	5	0	1	8	2	1
Mississippi	4	0	2	8	1	2
Alabama	4	2	0	10	2	0
Georgia	4	3	0	7	4	0
Florida	3	3	0	8	3	0
Mississippi State	3	4	0	5	4	0
Tulane	3	5	0	5	5	0
Kentucky	1	3	2	5	4	2
LSU	2	5	0	3	7	0
Vanderbilt	1	4	1	3	5	2
Auburn	0	7	0	2	8	0

Skyline

	CONF. W	L	T	OVERALL W	L	T
Utah	5	0	0	6	3	1
New Mexico	5	1	0	7	2	0
Colorado State	5	2	0	6	4	0
Wyoming	4	3	0	5	4	0
Brigham Young	3	4	0	4	6	0
Utah State	3	4	0	3	7	1
Montana	1	5	0	2	7	1
Denver	0	7	0	3	7	0

Southern

	CONF. W	L	T	OVERALL W	L	T
Duke	5	0	0	8	2	0
Maryland	1	0	0	7	2	0
West Virginia	5	1	0	7	2	0
Wake Forest	5	1	0	5	4	1
William & Mary	4	1	0	4	5	0
George Washington	4	2	1	5	3	1
Virginia Tech	4	4	0	5	6	0
Furman	2	2	1	6	3	1
South Carolina	3	4	0	5	5	0
Wash. & Lee	3	4	0	3	7	0
VMI	2	3	1	3	6	1
North Carolina St.	2	4	0	3	7	0
North Carolina	1	2	0	2	6	0
Citadel	1	3	1	3	5	1
Davidson	1	6	0	2	7	0
Clemson	0	2	0	2	6	1
Richmond	0	6	0	1	9	0

SWC

	CONF. W	L	T	OVERALL W	L	T
Texas	6	0	0	9	2	0
Rice	4	2	0	5	5	0
SMU	3	2	1	4	5	1
TCU	2	2	2	4	4	2
Baylor	1	3	2	4	4	2
Texas A&M	1	4	1	3	6	1
Arkansas	1	5	0	2	8	0

Independents

	OVERALL W	L	T
Michigan State	9	0	0
Princeton	8	1	0
Virginia	8	2	0
Yale	7	2	0
Notre Dame	7	2	1
Penn State	7	2	1
Navy	6	2	1
North Texas	7	3	0
Syracuse	7	3	0
Pittsburgh	6	3	0
Harvard	5	4	0
Pennsylvania	4	3	2
Rutgers	4	4	1
Army	4	4	1
Boston College	4	4	1
Miami, Fla.	4	7	0
Columbia	2	6	1
Cornell	2	7	0
Memphis	2	7	0
Dartmouth	2	7	0
Brown	2	7	0
Florida State	1	8	1

BOWL GAMES

DATE	GAME	SCORE
J1	Tangerine	Texas A&M-Commerce 33, Tennessee Tech 0
J1	Orange	Alabama 61, Syracuse 6
J1	Gator	Florida 14, Tulsa 13
J1	Sugar	Georgia Tech 24, Mississippi 7
J1	Rose	Southern Cal 7, Wisconsin 0
J1	Cotton	Texas 16, Tennessee 0
J1	Sun	Pacific 26, Southern Miss 7

1952 NCAA Major College Statistical Leaders

Individual Leaders

PASSING/COMPLETIONS

		G	ATT	COM	PCT	INT	I%	YDS	YPA	TD	TD%	COM.PG
1	Don Heinrich, Washington	10	270	137	50.7	17	6.3	1647	6.1	13	4.8	13.7
2	Tommy O'Connell, Illinois	9	224	133	59.4	17	7.6	1761	7.9	12	5.4	14.8
3	Zeke Bratkowski, Georgia	11	262	131	50.0	16	6.1	1824	7.0	12	4.6	11.9
4	Chuck Maloy, Holy Cross	10	288	126	43.8	16	5.6	1514	5.3	13	4.5	12.6
5	Johnny Borton, Ohio State	9	196	115	58.7	6	3.1	1555	7.9	15	7.7	12.8
6	Jim Haluska, Wisconsin	9	199	112	56.3	18	9.0	1410	7.1	12	6.0	12.4
7	Roger Franz, Fordham	8	216	105	48.6	12	5.6	1392	6.4	4	2.8	13.1
8	Dale Samuels, Purdue	9	185	104	56.2	6	3.2	1131	6.1	10	5.4	11.6
9	Ted Marchibroda, Detroit	9	240	103	42.9	13	5.4	1637	6.8	9	3.8	11.4
10	Dick Shinaut, Texas-El Paso	11	208	102	49.0	15	7.2	1520	7.3	13	6.3	9.3

ALL-PURPOSE YARDS

		G	RUSH	REC	INT	PR	KR	YDS	YPG
1	Billy Vessels, Oklahoma	10	1072	165	10	120	145	1512	151.2

RUSHING/YARDS

		G	ATT	YDS	AVG	YPG
1	Howie Waugh, Tulsa	10	164	1372	8.4	137.2
2	Billy Vessels, Oklahoma	10	161	1072	6.7	107.2
3	Buck McPhail, Oklahoma	10	161	1018	6.3	101.8
4	Bobby Marlow, Alabama	11	176	950	5.4	86.4
4	Dick Clasby, Harvard	9	205	950	4.6	105.6
6	Alan Ameche, Wisconsin	9	205	946	4.6	105.1
7	Rod Williams, Hardin-Simmons	10	180	898	5.0	89.8
8	Gene Filipski, Villanova	9	138	889	6.4	98.8
9	Dick Curran, Arizona State	9	114	870	7.6	96.7
10	John Olszewski, California	10	160	845	5.3	84.5

RUSHING/YARDS PER CARRY

		G	ATT	YDS	YPC
1	Howie Waugh, Tulsa	10	164	1372	8.4
2	Dick Curran, Arizona State	9	114	870	7.6
3	Dick Stults, San Jose State	9	118	801	6.8
4	Billy Vessels, Oklahoma	10	161	1072	6.7
5	Gene Filipski, Villanova	9	138	889	6.4
6	Buck McPhail, Oklahoma	10	161	1018	6.3
7	Homer Smith, Princeton	9	133	821	6.2
8	Joe Fortunato, Mississippi State	9	128	779	6.1
9	Tom McCormick, Pacific	9	142	782	5.5
10	Billy Reynolds, Pittsburgh	9	135	748	5.5

*-Based on top 20 rushers

RECEIVING/RECEPTIONS

		G	REC	YDS	TD	YPR	YPG	RPG
1	Ed Brown, Fordham	8	57	774	6	13.6	96.8	7.1
2	Joe McClaran, Drake	9	47	666	6	14.2	74.0	5.2
3	John Carroll, Holy Cross	10	46	609	4	13.2	60.9	4.6
4	Rocky Ryan, Illinois	9	45	714	5	15.9	79.3	5.0
4	Rex Smith, Illinois	9	45	642	4	14.3	71.3	5.0
6	Al Ward, Columbia	9	43	615	3	14.3	68.3	4.8
6	Bernie Flowers, Purdue	9	43	603	7	14.0	67.0	4.8
6	George Black, Washington	10	42	637	7	15.2	63.7	4.2
9	Monte Brethauer, Oregon	10	41	486	2	11.9	48.6	4.1
9	Jimmy Byron, VMI*	10	40	755	8	18.9	75.5	4.0

*Four tied with 40; Byron had the most yards.

PUNTING

		PUNT	YDS	AVG
1	Des Koch, Southern Cal	47	2043	43.5
2	Zack Koch, Southern Cal	57	2474	43.4
3	Paul Chapman, Citadel	61	2519	41.3
4	Jerry Norton, SMU	44	1813	41.2
5	Bud Wallace, North Carolina	70	2877	41.1
6	Jerry Jeffries, Hardin-Simmons	46	1877	40.8
7	Roger Franz, Fordham	36	1469	40.8
8	Jack Williams, Virginia Tech	66	2686	40.7
9	Buddy Bellis, Montana	61	2483	40.7
10	Udell Westover, Brigham Young	40	1620	40.5

PUNT RETURNS/YARDS

		PR	YDS	AVG
1	Horton Nesrsta, Rice	44	536	12.2
2	Jim Sears, Southern Cal	30	478	15.9
3	Eddie Knowles, Virginia	32	365	11.4
4	Billy Anderson, Virginia Tech	20	334	16.7
5	Cecil Ingram, Alabama	30	329	11.0
6	Gil Reich, Kansas	19	327	17.2
7	Harold Farmer, Wyoming	24	264	11.0
8	Paul Larson, California	24	261	10.9
9	Billy Polson, Houston	22	260	11.8
10	John Zibnack, Denver	18	258	14.3

KICKOFF RETURNS/YARDS

		KR	YDS	AVG
1	Curly Powell, VMI	27	517	19.1
2	Larry Spencer, Wake Forest	11	464	42.2
3	Fob James, Auburn	17	414	24.4
4	Don Ellis, Texas A&M	17	413	24.3
4	Don Booth, Virginia Tech	18	413	22.9
6	Jerry Blitz, Harvard	13	392	30.2
7	Carroll Hardy, Colorado	12	386	32.2
8	Ken Kessaris, Brown	13	379	29.2
9	Richard Towers, Kansas State	18	378	21.0
10	Robert Mercier, Columbia	16	361	22.6

SCORING

		TDS	XPT	FG	PTS
1	Jackie Parker, Mississippi State	16	24	0	120
2	Billy Vessels, Oklahoma	18	0	0	108
3	Robert Haner, Villanova	13	21	0	99
4	Buford Long, Florida	14	0	0	84
5	Billy Quinn, Texas	13	0	0	78
5	Tom McCormick, Pacific	13	0	0	78
7	Tom Miner, Tulsa	5	41	1	74
8	Five tied	—	—	—	72

INTERCEPTIONS

		INT	YDS
1	Cecil Ingram, Alabama	10	163
2	Bobby Renn, Davidson	9	121
2	Jim Psaltis, Southern Cal	9	113
4	Bill Stits, UCLA	8	235
4	Joe McNicholas, Villanova	8	102
4	Jack Sherry, Penn State	8	101
4	Al Brosky, Illinois	8	77
4	Don Eyer, Penn State	8	67
4	Joe Boring, Texas A&M	8	67
4	Ron Fraley, TCU	8	36

Team Leaders

RUSHING OFFENSE

		G	ATT	YDS	AVG	YPG
1	Tulsa	10	540	3215	6.0	321.5
2	Oklahoma	10	609	3036	5.0	303.6
3	California	10	553	2814	5.1	281.4
4	San Jose State	9	439	2478	5.6	275.3
5	Michigan State	9	508	2452	4.8	272.4
6	Texas	10	610	2695	4.4	269.5
7	Princeton	9	474	2410	5.1	267.8
8	West Virginia	9	487	2375	4.9	263.9
9	Arizona	10	479	2548	5.3	254.8
10	Virginia	10	559	2525	4.5	252.5

PASSING OFFENSE/YPG

		G	ATT	COM	INT	PCT	YDS	YPA	TD	YPG	I%	YPC
1	Fordham	8	277	136	15	49.1	1806	6.5	13	225.8	5.4	13.3
2	Illinois	9	245	141	20	57.6	1929	7.9	13	214.3	8.2	13.7
3	Detroit	9	264	112	18	42.4	1769	6.7	11	196.6	6.8	15.8
4	Ohio State	9	217	124	9	57.1	1709	7.9	16	189.9	4.1	13.8
5	Cincinnati	10	194	116	9	59.8	1864	9.6	15	186.4	4.6	16.1
6	Oregon	10	285	126	32	44.2	1720	6.0	9	172.0	11.2	13.7
7	Pennsylvania	9	192	98	13	51.0	1547	8.1	10	171.9	6.8	15.8
8	Washington	10	285	142	21	49.8	1708	6.0	13	170.8	7.4	12.0
9	Georgia	11	266	134	16	50.4	1878	7.1	13	170.7	6.0	14.0
10	Wisconsin	9	211	117	19	55.5	1476	7.0	13	164.0	9.0	12.6

TOTAL OFFENSE

		G	P	YDS	AVG	YPG
1	Tulsa	10	685	4666	6.8	466.6
2	San Jose State	9	612	3871	6.3	430.1
3	Michigan State	9	667	3858	5.8	428.7
4	Princeton	9	643	3852	6.0	428.0
5	Oklahoma	10	721	4255	5.9	425.5
6	Wisconsin	9	603	3497	5.2	388.6
7	Cincinnati	10	658	3882	5.9	388.2
8	Texas	10	767	3865	5.0	386.5
9	Mississippi	10	749	3831	5.1	383.1
10	West Virginia	9	633	3395	5.4	377.2
10	Maryland	9	648	3395	5.2	377.2

RUSHING DEFENSE

		G	ATT	YDS	AVG	YPG
1	Michigan State	9	342	755	2.2	83.9
2	Navy	9	421	843	2.0	93.7
3	UCLA	9	360	847	2.4	94.1
4	Princeton	9	373	865	2.3	96.1
5	Wake Forest	10	418	997	2.4	99.7
6	Holy Cross	10	449	1039	2.3	103.9
7	Yale	9	378	950	2.5	105.6
8	Georgia Tech	11	473	1175	2.5	106.8
9	Syracuse	9	357	964	2.7	107.1
10	Fordham	8	357	885	2.5	110.6

PASSING DEFENSE

		G	ATT	COM	PCT	YPC	INT	I%	YDS	YPA	TD	YPG
1	Virginia	10	161	50	31.1	10.1	16	10.0	503	3.1	3	50.3
2	Duke	10	125	44	35.2	11.7	14	11.2	516	4.1	1	51.6
3	Tennessee	10	116	44	37.9	12.1	10	8.6	531	4.6	3	53.1
4	Brigham Young	10	105	43	41.0	14.1	13	12.4	605	5.8	5	60.5
5	Georgia Tech	11	191	71	37.2	10.3	NA	NA	730	3.8	0	66.4
6	Southern Cal	10	184	62	33.7	10.8	31	16.8	668	3.6	1	66.8
7	Alabama	11	160	68	42.5	11.1	24	15.0	755	4.7	6	68.6
8	Vanderbilt	10	152	58	38.2	12.1	20	13.2	703	4.6	4	70.3
9	Mississippi State	9	133	50	37.6	12.7	9	6.8	636	4.8	4	70.7
10	Colgate	9	187	61	32.6	10.7	20	10.7	652	3.5	7	72.4

TOTAL DEFENSE

		G	P	YDS	AVG	YPG
1	Tennessee	10	578	1667	2.9	166.7
2	Georgia Tech	11	664	1905	2.9	173.2
3	Southern Cal	10	642	1775	2.8	177.5
4	Virginia	10	657	1963	3.0	196.3
5	Maryland	9	516	1808	3.5	200.9
6	Navy	9	604	1884	3.1	209.3
7	West Virginia	9	612	1901	3.1	211.2
8	Duke	10	623	2121	3.4	212.1
9	Wake Forest	10	586	2142	3.7	214.2
10	Houston	10	637	2150	3.4	215.0

SCORING OFFENSE

		G	PTS	AVG
1	Oklahoma	10	407	40.7

SCORING DEFENSE

		G	PTS	AVG
1	Southern Cal	10	47	4.7

ANNUAL REVIEW

1953 POLL PROGRESSION

Pre-Season 1953 | Sept. 26 Games

AP	Team	Record	Result
1	Notre Dame	0-0-0	beat # 6 Oklahoma 28-21
2	Michigan State	0-0-0	beat Iowa 21-7
3	Georgia Tech	0-0-0	tied # 15 Florida 0-0
4	UCLA	0-0-0	beat Kansas 19-7
5	Alabama	0-0-0	tied LSU 7-7
6	Oklahoma	0-0-0	lost to # 1 Notre Dame 21-28
7	Ohio State	0-0-0	beat Indiana 36-12
8	Southern Cal	0-0-0	beat Minnesota 17-7
9	Maryland	0-0-0	beat Wash. & Lee 52-0
10	Duke	0-0-0	beat Wake Forest 19-0
11	Texas	0-0-0	beat Villanova 41-12
12	Rice	0-0-0	bye week
13	Navy	0-0-0	tied William & Mary 6-6
14	California	0-0-0	beat Oregon State 26-0
15	Florida	0-0-0	tied # 3 Georgia Tech 0-0
16	West Virginia	0-0-0	beat # 17 Pittsburgh 17-7
17	Pittsburgh	0-0-0	lost to # 16 West Virginia 7-17
18	Tennessee	0-0-0	lost to Mississippi State 0-26
19	Princeton	0-0-0	beat Lafayette 20-14
20	Baylor	0-0-0	bye week

September 28 Poll | Oct. 3 Games

AP	Team	Record	Result
1	Notre Dame	1-0-0	beat Purdue 37-7
2	Michigan State	1-0-0	beat Minnesota 21-0
3	Maryland	2-0-0	beat Clemson 20-0
4	Michigan	1-0-0	beat Tulane 26-7
5	UCLA	2-0-0	beat Oregon 12-0
6	Ohio State	1-0-0	beat California 33-19
7	Southern Cal	2-0-0	beat Indiana 27-14
8	Oklahoma	0-1-0	tied Pittsburgh 7-7
9	Georgia Tech	1-0-1	beat SMU 6-4
10	Baylor	1-0-0	beat Miami, Fla. 21-13
11	Mississippi State	2-0-0	beat North Texas 21-6
12	Duke	1-0-0	beat Tennessee 21-7
13	West Virginia	1-0-0	beat Waynesburg 47-19
14	Rice	1-0-0	beat Cornell 28-7
15	Mississippi	2-0-0	lost to Auburn 0-13
16	Wisconsin	1-0-0	beat Marquette 13-11
17	Texas	1-1-0	beat Houston 28-7
18	Georgia	2-0-0	lost to Texas A&M 12-14
19	LSU	1-0-1	beat Boston College 42-6
20	Holy Cross	1-0-0	beat Colgate 19-6

October 5 Poll | Oct. 10 Games

UP	AP	Team	Record	Result
1	1	Notre Dame	2-0-0	bye week
2	2	Michigan State	2-0-0	beat TCU 26-19
4	3	Ohio State	2-0-0	lost to Illinois 20-41
5	4	Maryland	3-0-0	beat Georgia 40-13
7	5	Michigan	2-0-0	beat Iowa 14-13
3	6	UCLA	3-0-0	beat Wisconsin 13-0
6	7	Southern Cal	3-0-0	tied Washington 13-13
10	8	Duke	3-0-0	beat Purdue 20-14
8	9	Baylor	2-0-0	beat Arkansas 14-7
9	10	Georgia Tech	2-0-1	beat Tulane 27-13
11	11	Rice	2-0-0	beat Hardin Simmons 40-0
16	12	West Virginia	2-0-0	beat Wash. & Lee 40-14
13	13	Mississippi State	3-0-0	tied Auburn 21-21
12	14	LSU	2-0-1	tied Kentucky 6-6
14	15	Texas	2-1-0	lost to # 16 Oklahoma 14-19
15	16	Oklahoma	0-1-1	beat # 15 Texas 19-14
	17	Pittsburgh	0-1-1	beat Nebraska 14-6
	18	Northwestern	2-0-0	lost to Minnesota 13-30
20	19	Holy Cross	2-0-0	beat Bucknell 40-0
18	20	Pennsylvania	2-0-0	lost to California 0-40
	20	Southern Mississippi	3-0-0	beat La. Lafayette 41-14
17		Navy	1-0-1	beat Cornell 20-6
19		Wisconsin	2-0-0	lost to # 6 UCLA 0-13 (09)

October 12 Poll | Oct. 17 Games

UP	AP	Team	Record	Result
1	1	Notre Dame	2-0-0	beat # 15 Pittsburgh 23-14
2	2	Michigan State	3-0-0	beat Indiana 47-18
4	3	Maryland	4-0-0	beat North Carolina 26-0
3	4	UCLA	4-0-0	lost to Stanford 20-21
6	5	Michigan	3-0-0	beat Northwestern 20-12
5	6	Georgia Tech	3-0-1	beat # 19 Auburn 36-6
8	7	Duke	4-0-0	lost to Army 13-14
7	8	Baylor	3-0-0	beat Vanderbilt 47-6
11	9	Illinois	2-0-1	beat Minnesota 27-7
13	10	West Virginia	3-0-0	beat George Washington 27-6
12	11	Rice	3-0-0	lost to SMU 7-12
9	12	Oklahoma	1-1-1	beat Kansas 45-0
10	13	Southern Cal	3-0-1	beat Oregon State 37-0
15	14	Navy	2-0-1	beat Princeton 65-7
16	15	Pittsburgh	1-1-1	lost to # 1 Notre Dame 14-23
16	16	California	2-2-0	beat San Jose State 34-14
19	17	Ohio State	2-1-0	beat Pennsylvania 12-6
	18	Southern Mississippi	4-0-0	beat S.E. Louisiana 7-0
	19	Auburn	2-0-1	lost to # 6 Georgia Tech 6-36
14	20	Mississippi State	3-0-1	lost to Kentucky 13-32
16		SMU	1-1-0	beat # 11 Rice 12-7
	19	Utah	4-0-0	beat Denver 40-6

October 19 Poll | Oct. 24 Games

UP	AP	Team	Record	Result
1	1	Notre Dame	3-0-0	beat # 4 Georgia Tech 27-14
2	2	Michigan State	4-0-0	lost to Purdue 0-6
3	3	Maryland	5-0-0	beat Miami, Fla. 30-0
4	4	Georgia Tech	4-0-1	lost to # 1 Notre Dame 14-27
5	5	Michigan	4-0-0	lost to Minnesota 0-22
6	6	Baylor	4-0-0	beat Texas A&M 14-13
7	7	Illinois	3-0-1	beat Syracuse 20-13
12	8	West Virginia	4-0-0	beat VMI 52-20
8	9	Oklahoma	2-1-1	beat Colorado 27-20
11	10	Navy	3-0-1	lost to Pennsylvania 6-9
9	11	Southern Cal	4-0-1	beat California 32-20
10	12	UCLA	4-1-0	beat Washington State 44-7
14	13	SMU	2-1-0	beat Kansas 14-6
14	14	LSU	3-0-2	tied Florida 21-21
17	15	Texas A&M	4-0-1	lost to Baylor 13-14
15	16	Duke	4-1-0	beat North Carolina St. 31-0
	17	Kentucky	2-2-1	beat Villanova 19-0
	18	Pittsburgh	1-2-1	lost to Northwestern 21-27
	19	Southern Mississippi	5-0-0	lost to Memphis 13-27
	20	Stanford	3-2-0	beat Washington 13-7
15		California	3-2-0	lost to # 11 Southern Cal 20-32
17		Iowa	2-2-0	beat Indiana 19-13
17		Mississippi	4-1-0	beat Arkansas 28-0
20		Ohio State	3-1-0	beat Wisconsin 20-19

October 26 Poll | Oct. 31 Games

UP	AP	Team	Record	Result
1	1	Notre Dame	4-0-0	beat # 20 Navy 38-7
2	2	Maryland	6-0-0	beat South Carolina 24-6
3	3	Baylor	5-0-0	beat TCU 25-7
5	4	Illinois	4-0-1	beat Purdue 21-0
10	5	West Virginia	5-0-0	beat Penn State 20-19
6	6	Michigan State	4-1-0	beat Oregon State 34-6
4	7	Southern Cal	5-0-1	lost to Oregon 7-13
9	8	Georgia Tech	4-1-1	beat Vanderbilt 43-0
7	9	Oklahoma	3-1-1	beat Kansas State 34-0
8	10	UCLA	5-1-0	beat California 20-7
12	11	SMU	3-1-0	lost to Texas 7-16
11	12	Rice	4-1-0	lost to # 19 Kentucky 13-19
16	13	Duke	5-1-0	beat Virginia 48-6
13	14	Minnesota	2-3-0	beat Pittsburgh 35-14
15	15	Army	4-1-0	tied Tulane 0-0
13	16	Michigan	4-1-0	beat Pennsylvania 24-14
18	17	Stanford	4-2-0	beat Washington State 48-19
	18	Mississippi	5-1-0	beat LSU 27-16
	19	Kentucky	3-2-1	beat # 12 Rice 19-13
	20	Navy	3-1-1	lost to # 1 Notre Dame 7-38
17		Purdue	1-4-0	lost to# 4 Illinois 0-21
18		tie-Stanford	4-2-0	beat Washington State 48-19
18		Kansas State	5-1-0	lost to # 9 Oklahoma 0-34
18		Ohio State	4-1-0	beat Northwestern 27-13

November 2 Poll / Nov. 7 Games

UP	AP	Team	Record	Nov. 7 Games
1	1	Notre Dame	5-0-0	beat Pennsylvania 28-20
2	2	Maryland	7-0-0	beat George Washington 27-6
3	3	Baylor	6-0-0	lost to # 19 Texas 20-21
4	4	Illinois	5-0-1	beat # 17 Michigan 19-3
5	5	Michigan State	5-1-0	beat # 16 Ohio State 28-13
7	6	Georgia Tech	5-1-1	beat Clemson 20-7
9	7	West Virginia	6-0-0	beat Virginia Tech 12-7
6	8	Oklahoma	4-1-1	beat Missouri 14-7
8	9	UCLA	6-1-0	bye week
17	10	Duke	6-1-0	tied Navy 0-0
13	11	Stanford	5-2-0	lost to # 17 Southern Cal 20-23
14	12	Mississippi	6-1-0	beat North Texas 40-7
14	13	Minnesota	3-3-0	beat Indiana 28-20
	14	Kentucky	4-2-1	beat Vanderbilt 40-14
	15	Auburn	4-1-1	beat Miami, Fla. 29-20
12	16	Ohio State	5-1-0	lost to # 5 Michigan State 13-28
	17	Michigan	5-1-0	lost to # 4 Illinois 3-19
11	18	Southern Cal	5-1-1	beat # 11 Stanford 23-20
16	19	Texas	4-3-0	beat # 3 Baylor 21-20
18	20	Alabama	3-1-3	beat U. T. Chattanooga 21-14
19		LSU	3-1-3	lost to Tennessee 14-32
20		Wisconsin	4-2-0	beat Northwestern 34-13
20		SMU	3-2-0	beat Texas A&M 23-0

November 9 Poll / Nov. 14 Games

UP	AP	Team	Record	Nov. 14 Games
1	1	Notre Dame	6-0-0	beat North Carolina 34-14
2	2	Maryland	8-0-0	beat # 11 Mississippi 38-0
3	3	Illinois	6-0-1	lost to Wisconsin 7-34
4	4	Michigan State	6-1-0	beat Michigan 14-6
7	5	Georgia Tech	6-1-1	lost to Alabama 6-13
6	6	Oklahoma	5-1-1	beat Iowa State 47-0
5	7	UCLA	6-1-0	beat Washington 22-6
9	8	West Virginia	7-0-0	lost to South Carolina 14-20
8	9	Baylor	6-1-0	lost to Houston 7-37
11	10	Texas	5-3-0	beat TCU 13-3
12	11	Mississippi	7-1-0	lost to # 2 Maryland 0-38
10	12	Southern Cal	6-1-1	bye week
20	13	Kentucky	5-2-1	beat Memphis 20-7
17	14	Duke	6-1-1	bye week
16	15	Minnesota	4-3-0	lost to Iowa 0-27
13	16	Rice	5-2-0	beat Texas A&M 34-7
14	17	Stanford	5-3-0	beat San Jose State 54-0
	18	Tennessee	4-2-1	beat Florida 9-7
	19	Texas Tech	7-1-0	beat Tulsa 49-7
20	20	Auburn	5-1-1	beat Georgia 39-18
14		Michigan	5-2-0	lost to # 4 Michigan State 6-14
17		Wisconsin	5-2-0	beat # 3 Illinois 34-7
17		Pennsylvania	3-4-0	lost to Army 14-21

November 16 Poll / Nov. 21 Games

UP	AP	Team	Record	Nov. 21 Games
1	1	Notre Dame	7-0-0	tied # 20 Iowa 14-14
2	2	Maryland	9-0-0	beat # 11 Alabama 21-0
3	3	Michigan State	7-1-0	beat Marquette 21-15
5	4	Oklahoma	6-1-1	beat Nebraska 30-7
4	5	UCLA	7-1-0	beat # 9 Southern Cal 13-0
6	6	Texas	6-3-0	bye week
10	7	Illinois	6-1-1	beat Northwestern 39-14
7	8	Wisconsin	6-2-0	tied Minnesota 21-21
8	9	Southern Cal	6-1-1	lost to # 5 UCLA 0-13
11	10	Rice	6-2-0	beat TCU 19-6
12	11	Alabama	5-1-3	lost to # 2 Maryland 0-21
9	12	Georgia Tech	6-2-1	beat # 15 Duke 13-10
15	13	Kentucky	6-2-1	beat Tennessee 27-21
14	14	Auburn	6-1-1	beat Clemson 45-19
17	15	Duke	6-1-1	lost to # 12 Georgia Tech 10-13
13	16	Stanford	6-3-0	tied California 21-21
	17	Texas Tech	8-1-0	beat Houston 41-21
	18	South Carolina	6-2-0	beat Wofford 49-0
	19	West Virginia	7-1-0	beat North Carolina St. 61-0
19	20	Iowa	5-3-0	tied # 1 Notre Dame 14-14
15		Army	6-1-1	bye week
17		Ohio State	6-2-0	lost to Michigan 0-20
20		Michigan	5-3-0	beat Ohio State 20-0
20		SMU	5-2-0	lost to Baylor 21-27

November 23 Poll / Nov. 28 Games

UP	AP	Team	Record	Nov. 28 Games
1	1	Maryland	10-0-0	regular season complete
2	2	Notre Dame	7-0-1	beat # 20 Southern Cal 48-14
4	3	Michigan State	8-1-0	regular season complete
5	4	Oklahoma	7-1-1	beat Oklahoma State 42-7
3	5	UCLA	8-1-0	regular season complete
6	6	Illinois	7-1-1	regular season complete
8	7	Texas	6-3-0	beat Texas A&M 21-12
7	8	Rice	7-2-0	beat # 17 Baylor 41-19
10	9	Iowa	5-3-1	regular season complete
9	10	Georgia Tech	7-2-1	beat Georgia 28-12
15	11	West Virginia	8-1-0	regular season complete
14	12	Wisconsin	6-2-1	regular season complete
11	13	Kentucky	7-2-1	regular season complete
11	14	Texas Tech	9-1-0	beat Hardin Simmons 46-12
	15	South Carolina	7-2-0	lost to Wake Forest 13-19
17	16	Auburn	7-1-1	lost to Alabama 7-10
13	17	Baylor	7-2-0	lost to # 8 Rice 19-41
19	18	Army	6-1-1	beat Navy 20-7
16	19	Stanford	6-3-1	regular season complete
18	20	Southern Cal	6-2-1	lost to # 2 Notre Dame 14-48
20		Oklahoma State	7-2-0	lost to # 4 Oklahoma 7-42

November 30 Final Poll

UP	AP	Team	Record	Bowl Bid	Date	Bowl Result	RB	Record
1	1	Maryland	10-0-0	Orange Bowl	J1	lost to # 4 Oklahoma 0-7	3	10-1-0
2	2	Notre Dame	8-0-1				1	9-0-1
3	3	Michigan State	8-1-0	Rose Bowl	J1	beat # 5 UCLA 28-20	4	9-1-0
5	4	Oklahoma	8-1-1	Orange Bowl	J1	beat # 1 Maryland 7-0	2	9-1-1
4	5	UCLA	8-1-0	Rose Bowl	J1	lost to # 3 Michigan State 20-28	5	8-2-0
6	6	Rice	8-2-0	Cotton Bowl	J1	beat # 13 Alabama 28-6	9	9-2-0
7	7	Illinois	7-1-1				10	7-1-1
9	8	Georgia Tech	7-2-1	Sugar Bowl	J1	beat# 10 West Virginia 42-19	6	9-2-1
10	9	Iowa	5-3-1				19	5-3-1
13	10	West Virginia	8-1-0	Sugar Bowl	J1	lost to # 8 Georgia Tech 19-42	23	8-2-0
8	11	Texas	7-3-0				16	7-3-0
12	12	Texas Tech	10-1-0	Gator Bowl	J1	beat # 17 Auburn 35-13	7	11-1-0
11	13	Alabama	6-2-3	Cotton Bowl	J1	lost to # 6 Rice 6-28	11	6-3-3
16	14	Army	7-1-1				18	7-1-1
14	15	Wisconsin	6-2-1				14	6-2-1
15	16	Kentucky	7-2-1				8	7-2-1
	17	Auburn	7-2-1	Gator Bowl	J1	lost to # 12 Texas Tech 13-35	17	7-3-1
18	18	Duke	7-2-1				12	7-2-1
17	19	Stanford	6-3-1				37	6-3-1
19	20	Michigan	6-3-0				20	6-3-0
20		Ohio State	6-3-0				25	6-3-0

1953

CONSENSUS ALL-AMERICANS

POS	Name	HT	WT	School	AA	AP	FC	FW	IN	NE	SN	UP
B	Johnny Lattner	6-1	190	Notre Dame	•	•	•	•	•	•	•	•
B	Paul Giel	5-11	185	Minnesota	•	•	•	•	•	•	•	•
B	Paul Cameron	6-0	185	UCLA	•	•	•	•	•		•	•
B	J.C. Caroline	6-0	184	Illinois		•	•			•	•	•
E	Don Dohoney	6-1	193	Michigan State	•	•	•		•	•	•	•
E	Carlton Massey	6-4	210	Texas	•					•		
T	Stan Jones	6-0	235	Maryland	•	•	•	•	•	•	•	•
T	Art Hunter	6-2	226	Notre Dame	•			•	•		•	•
G	J.D. Roberts	5-10	210	Oklahoma	•	•	•	•	•	•		•
G	Crawford Mims	5-10	200	Mississippi		•	•	•		•		•
C	Larry Morris	6-0	205	Georgia Tech	•	•					•	•

OTHERS RECEIVING FIRST-TEAM HONORS

POS	Name	School			FC		IN	NE	SN	
B	Alan Ameche	Wisconsin						•	•	
B	Bob Garrett	Stanford						•		
B	Kosse Johnson	Rice			•			•		
B	Jackie Parker	Mississippi State			•					
B	Bernie Faloney	Maryland			•		•			
E	Ken Buck	Pacific			•					
E	John Carson	Georgia			•					
E	Steve Meilinger	Kentucky		•		•		•		
E	Sam Morley	Stanford			•					
E	Joe Collier	Northwestern					•			
T	Ed Meadows	Duke			•					
T	Jack Shanafelt	Pennsylvania		•		•				
T	Jim Ray Smith	Baylor			•					
T	John Hudson	Rice					•			
G	Milt Bohart	Washington			•					
G	Ray Correll	Kentucky			•					
G	Bob Fleck	Syracuse			•	•				
G	Steve Eisenhauer	Navy		•						
C	Matt Hazeltine	California			•	•				
C	Jerry Hilgenberg	Iowa								
C	Bob Orders	West Virginia					•			

AP named Weatherall, Richter and Beck to its first-team All-American defense, but not on offense.

HEISMAN TROPHY VOTING

	PLAYER	POS	SCHOOL	1ST	2ND	3RD	TOTAL
1	Johnny Lattner	HB	Notre Dame	384	283	132	1850
2	Paul Giel	TB	Minnesota	366	295	106	1794
3	Paul Cameron	HB	UCLA	44	89	134	444
4	Bernie Faloney	QB	Maryland	46	34	52	258
5	Bob Garrett	QB	Stanford	32	43	49	231
6	Alan Ameche	FB	Wisconsin	25	38	60	211
7	J.C. Caroline	HB	Illinois	15	37	74	193
8	J.D. Roberts	G	Oklahoma	6	21	48	108
9	Lamar McHan	QB	Arkansas	15	12	9	78
10	Steve Meilinger	E	Kentucky	12	10	9	65

AWARD WINNERS

PLAYER	POS	SCHOOL	AWARD NAME
Johnny Lattner	HB	Notre Dame	Maxwell
J.D. Roberts	G	Oklahoma	Outland

CONFERENCE STANDINGS

ACC

	Conf.			Overall		
	W	L	T	W	L	T
Duke	4	0	0	7	2	1
Maryland	3	0	0	10	1	0
South Carolina	2	3	0	7	3	0
North Carolina	2	3	0	4	6	0
Wake Forest	2	3	0	3	6	1
Clemson	1	2	0	3	5	1
North Carolina St.	0	3	0	1	9	0

Big 10

	Conf.			Overall		
	W	L	T	W	L	T
Michigan State	5	1	0	9	1	0
Illinois	5	1	0	7	1	1
Wisconsin	4	1	1	6	2	1
Ohio State	4	3	0	6	3	0
Michigan	3	3	0	6	3	0
Iowa	3	3	0	5	3	1
Minnesota	3	3	1	4	4	1
Purdue	2	4	0	2	7	0
Indiana	1	5	0	2	7	0
Northwestern	0	6	0	3	6	0

Big 7

	Conf.			Overall		
	W	L	T	W	L	T
Oklahoma	6	0	0	9	1	1
Kansas State	4	2	0	6	3	1
Missouri	4	2	0	6	4	0
Colorado	2	4	0	6	4	0
Nebraska	2	4	0	3	6	1
Kansas	2	4	0	2	8	0
Iowa State	1	5	0	2	7	0

Border

	Conf.			Overall		
	W	L	T	W	L	T
Texas Tech	5	0	0	11	1	0
Hardin-Simmons	4	1	0	6	5	0
Texas-El Paso	4	2	0	8	2	0
Arizona	3	2	0	4	5	1
Arizona State	1	3	0	4	5	1
New Mexico State	1	4	0	2	7	0
West Texas State	0	6	0	1	8	1

MAC

	Conf.			Overall		
	W	L	T	W	L	T
Ohio U	5	0	1	6	2	1
Miami, Ohio	3	0	1	7	1	1
Kent State	3	1	0	7	2	0
Toledo	2	3	0	3	6	0
Case Western Reserve	1	2	1	5	3	1
Western Michigan	0	4	1	1	6	1
Bowling Green	0	4	0	1	8	0

Pacific Coast

	Conf.			Overall		
	W	L	T	W	L	T
UCLA	6	1	0	8	2	0
Stanford	5	1	1	6	3	1
Southern Cal	4	2	1	6	3	1
California	2	2	2	4	4	2
Washington State	3	4	0	4	6	0
Oregon State	3	5	0	3	6	0
Washington	2	4	1	3	6	1
Oregon	2	5	1	4	5	1
Idaho	0	3	0	1	8	0

SEC

	Conf.			Overall		
	W	L	T	W	L	T
Alabama	4	0	3	6	3	3
Georgia Tech	4	1	1	9	2	1
Kentucky	4	1	1	7	2	1
Mississippi	4	1	1	7	2	1
Auburn	4	2	1	7	3	1
Mississippi State	3	1	3	5	2	3
Tennessee	3	2	1	6	4	1
LSU	2	3	3	5	3	3
Florida	1	3	2	3	5	2
Vanderbilt	1	5	0	3	7	0
Georgia	1	5	0	3	8	0
Tulane	0	7	0	1	8	1

Skyline

	Conf.			Overall		
	W	L	T	W	L	T
Utah	5	0	0	8	2	0
Utah State	5	2	0	8	3	0
Wyoming	4	2	1	5	4	1
New Mexico	3	2	1	5	3	1
Colorado State	3	4	0	4	5	0
Montana	2	4	0	3	5	0
Denver	1	5	1	3	5	2
Brigham Young	1	5	1	2	7	1

SWC

	Conf.			Overall		
	W	L	T	W	L	T
Rice	5	1	0	9	2	0
Texas	5	1	0	7	3	0
Baylor	4	2	0	7	3	0
SMU	3	3	0	5	5	0
Arkansas	2	4	0	3	7	0
Texas A&M	1	5	0	4	5	1
TCU	1	5	0	3	7	0

Independents

	Overall		
	W	L	T
Notre Dame	9	0	1
Army	7	1	1
Harvard	6	2	0
Penn State	6	3	0
Yale	5	2	2
Syracuse	5	3	1
Boston College	5	3	1
Memphis	6	4	0
Princeton	5	4	0
Cornell	4	3	2
Navy	4	3	2
Florida State	5	5	0
Miami, Fla.	4	5	0
Columbia	4	5	0
Brown	3	5	1
Pennsylvania	3	5	1
Pittsburgh	3	5	1
North Texas	3	6	1
Rutgers	2	6	0
Dartmouth	2	7	0
Virginia	1	8	0

BOWL GAMES

DATE	GAME	SCORE
J1	Tangerine	Arkansas State 7, Texas A&M-Commerce 7
J1	Rose	Michigan State 28, UCLA 20
J1	Sugar	Georgia Tech 42, West Virginia 19
J1	Orange	Oklahoma 7, Maryland 0
J1	Cotton	Rice 28, Alabama 6
J1	Gator	Texas Tech 35, Auburn 13
J1	Sun	Texas-El Paso 37, Southern Miss 14

1953 NCAA MAJOR COLLEGE STATISTICAL LEADERS

INDIVIDUAL LEADERS

PASSING/COMPLETIONS	G	ATT	COM	PCT	INT	I%	YDS	YPA	TD	TD%	COM.PG
1 Bob Garrett, Stanford	10	205	118	57.6	10	4.9	1637	8.0	17	8.3	11.8
2 Zeke Bratkowski, Georgia	11	224	113	50.4	23	10.3	1461	6.5	6	2.7	10.3
3 Sandy Lederman, Washington	10	189	92	48.7	14	7.4	1157	6.1	8	4.2	9.2
4 Paul Larson, California	10	171	85	49.7	16	9.4	1431	8.4	6	3.5	8.5
5 Tony Rados, Penn State	9	171	81	47.4	12	7.0	1025	6.0	8	4.7	9.0
6 Don Rydalch, Utah	10	128	78	60.9	8	6.3	980	7.7	7	5.5	7.8
6 Lamar McHan, Arkansas	10	150	78	52.0	11	7.3	1107	7.4	8	5.3	7.8
8 Richard Carr, Columbia	9	191	77	40.3	18	9.4	1367	7.2	13	6.8	8.6
9 Don Ellis, Texas A&M	10	171	76	44.4	14	8.2	950	5.6	4	2.3	7.6
10 Dick Thomas, Northwestern	9	145	74	51.0	7	4.8	933	6.4	5	3.5	8.2
10 Cotton Davidson, Baylor	10	156	74	47.4	16	10.3	1092	7.0	9	5.8	7.4

ALL-PURPOSE YARDS	G	RUSH	REC	INT	PR	KR	YDS	YPG
1 J.C. Caroline, Illinois	9	1256	52	0	129	33	1470	163.3

RUSHING/YARDS	G	ATT	YDS	AVG	YPG
1 J.C. Caroline, Illinois	9	194	1256	6.5	139.6
2 Kosse Johnson, Rice	10	187	944	5.0	94.4
3 Ken Cardella, Arizona	10	148	915	6.2	91.5
4 Bob Watkins, Ohio State	9	153	875	5.7	97.2
5 Neil Worden, Notre Dame	10	145	859	5.9	85.9
6 Dicky Maegle, Rice	10	114	833	7.3	83.3
7 Alan Ameche, Wisconsin	9	165	801	4.9	89.0
8 Larry Grigg, Oklahoma	10	130	792	6.1	79.2
9 Bobby Cavazos, Texas Tech	11	97	757	7.8	68.8
10 Chet Hanulak, Maryland	10	77	753	9.8	75.3

RUSHING/YARDS PER CARRY	G	ATT	YDS	YPC
1 Chet Hanulak, Maryland	10	77	753	9.8
2 Dick Imer, Montana	8	86	703	8.2
3 Bobby Cavazos, Texas Tech	11	97	757	7.8
4 Dicky Maegle, Rice	10	114	833	7.3
5 J.C. Caroline, Illinois	9	194	1256	6.5
6 Ken Cardella, Arizona	10	148	915	6.2
7 Larry Grigg, Oklahoma	10	130	792	6.1
8 Neil Worden, Notre Dame	10	145	859	5.9
9 Bob Watkins, Ohio State	9	153	875	5.7
10 Bill Bowman, William & Mary	10	132	722	5.5

*-Based on top 20 rushers

RECEIVING/RECEPTIONS	G	REC	YDS	TD	YPR	YPG	RPG
1 John Carson, Georgia	11	45	663	4	14.7	60.3	4.1
1 Ken Buck, Pacific	10	45	660	5	14.7	66.0	4.5
1 Sam Morley, Stanford	10	45	594	6	13.2	59.4	4.5
4 John Steinberg, Stanford	10	32	425	3	13.3	42.5	3.2
5 Dave McLaughlin, Dartmouth	9	31	592	6	19.1	65.8	3.4
6 Floyd Sagely, Arkansas	10	30	542	3	18.1	54.2	3.0
6 John Allen, Arizona State	10	30	505	8	16.8	50.5	3.0
6 Chester Lyssy, Hardin-Simmons	11	30	389	5	13.0	35.4	2.7
6 Jim Garrity, Penn State	9	30	349	3	11.6	38.8	3.3
10 Dale Hopp, Columbia	9	29	437	4	15.1	48.6	3.2
10 Andy Nacrelli, Fordham	9	29	428	3	14.8	47.6	3.2

PUNTING	PUNT	YDS	AVG
1 Zeke Bratkowski, Georgia	50	2130	42.6
2 Bart Starr, Alabama	30	1242	41.4
3 Paul Cameron, UCLA	31	1280	41.3
4 Dick Clasby, Harvard	30	1230	41.0
5 Jack Williams, Virginia Tech	30	1227	40.9
6 Lamar McHan, Arkansas	46	1849	40.2
7 Homer Smith, Princeton	30	1200	40.0
8 Tom Yewcic, Michigan State	31	1234	39.8
9 Walt Hynoski, Pennsylvania	37	1469	39.7
10 George Broeder, Iowa	34	1350	39.7

PUNT RETURNS/YARDS	PR	YDS	AVG
1 Paul Giel, Minnesota	17	288	16.9
2 Paul Cameron, UCLA	21	284	13.5
3 Bobby Lee, New Mexico	13	252	19.4
4 Eddie West, North Carolina St.	23	239	10.4
5 Jimmy Wade, Tennessee	18	235	13.1
6 Jack Stone, West Virginia	13	233	17.9
7 Lamar McHan, Arkansas	21	233	11.1
8 Ron Drzewiecki, Marquette	10	232	23.2
9 Lenny Moore, Penn State	13	228	17.5
10 Merrill Green, Oklahoma	5	225	45.0

KICKOFF RETURNS/YARDS	KR	YDS	AVG
1 Max McGee, Tulane	17	371	21.8
2 Howard Cassady, Ohio State	15	343	22.9
3 L.G. Dupre, Baylor	14	340	24.3
4 Johnny Lattner, Notre Dame	8	331	41.4
5 Carl Bolt, Washington & Lee	12	325	27.1
6 Jim Thacker, Davidson	12	311	25.9
7 Ken Keller, North Carolina	13	299	23.0
8 Bill Teer, North Carolina St.	12	289	24.1
9 Charles Horton, Vanderbilt	15	284	18.9
10 Jim Bradley, New Mexico State	15	281	18.7

SCORING	TDS	XPT	FG	PTS
1 Earl Lindley, Utah State	13	3	0	81
2 Bobby Cavazos, Texas Tech	13	2	0	80
3 Larry Grigg, Oklahoma	13	0	0	78
3 Fred Mahaffey, Denver	13	0	0	78
3 Johnny Mapp, VMI	13	0	0	78
6 Robert Burgmeier, Detroit	12	0	0	72
6 Paul Cameron, UCLA	12	0	0	72
6 Jimmy Wade, Tennessee	12	0	0	72
9 Don Lewis, Texas Tech	11	1	0	67
9 Joe Mastrogiovanni, Wyoming	9	13	0	67

INTERCEPTIONS	INT	YDS
1 Bob Garrett, Stanford	9	80
2 Bobby Luna, Alabama	6	158
2 Paul Larson, California	6	102
2 Ralph Carr, Oregon State	6	86
2 Levi Johns, LSU	6	80
2 Charlie Sumner, William & Mary	6	70
2 Jerry Barger, Duke	6	55

TEAM LEADERS

RUSHING OFFENSE	G	ATT	YDS	AVG	YPG
1 Oklahoma	10	591	3069	5.2	306.9
2 Cincinnati	10	463	2947	6.4	294.7
3 Texas Tech	11	567	3172	5.6	288.4
4 Notre Dame	10	616	2881	4.7	288.1
5 West Virginia	9	477	2536	5.3	281.8
6 Illinois	9	478	2481	5.2	275.7
7 Rice	10	547	2735	5.0	273.5
8 Arizona	10	505	2689	5.3	268.9
9 Maryland	10	483	2578	5.3	257.8
10 Furman	9	459	2242	4.9	249.1

PASSING OFFENSE/YPG	G	ATT	COM	INT	PCT	YDS	YPA	TD	YPG	I%	YPC
1 Stanford	10	230	130	13	56.5	1795	7.8	19	179.5	5.7	13.8
2 Pacific	10	235	113	16	48.1	1716	7.3	15	171.6	6.8	15.2
3 Dartmouth	9	177	90	18	50.9	1493	8.4	15	165.9	10.2	16.6
4 California	10	195	94	19	48.2	1612	8.3	7	161.2	9.7	17.1
5 Columbia	9	192	77	18	40.1	1367	7.1	13	151.9	9.4	17.8
6 Syracuse	9	175	92	11	52.6	1320	7.5	11	146.7	6.3	14.3
7 Georgia	11	247	118	25	47.8	1575	6.4	8	143.2	10.1	13.3
8 Mississippi	10	169	75	17	44.4	1411	8.3	6	141.1	10.1	18.8
9 Baylor	10	199	98	18	49.3	1394	7.0	10	139.4	9.1	14.2
10 Washington	10	224	106	19	47.3	1369	6.1	8	136.9	8.5	12.9

TOTAL OFFENSE	G	P	YDS	AVG	YPG
1 Cincinnati	10	577	4095	7.1	409.5
2 Notre Dame	10	753	3839	5.1	383.9
3 West Virginia	9	593	3398	5.7	377.6
4 Texas Tech	11	694	4141	6.0	376.5
5 Utah	10	722	3751	5.2	375.1
6 Maryland	10	593	3595	6.1	359.5
7 Rice	10	682	3586	5.3	358.6
8 Illinois	9	575	3205	5.6	356.1
9 Oklahoma	10	652	3521	5.4	352.1
10 Army	9	622	3136	5.0	348.4

RUSHING DEFENSE	G	ATT	YDS	AVG	YPG
1 Maryland	10	362	839	2.3	83.9
2 Syracuse	9	328	920	2.8	102.2
3 Holy Cross	10	403	1069	2.7	106.9
4 West Virginia	9	351	975	2.8	108.3
5 UCLA	9	375	1021	2.7	113.4
6 Army	9	392	1031	2.6	114.6
7 Iowa	9	367	1051	2.9	116.8
8 Navy	9	412	1084	2.6	120.4
9 Notre Dame	10	394	1207	3.1	120.7
10 Texas-El Paso	9	384	1107	2.9	123.0

PASSING DEFENSE	G	ATT	COM	PCT	YPC	INT	I%	YDS	YPA	TD	YPG
1 Richmond	9	104	34	32.7	10.7	14	13.5	363	3.5	0	40.3
2 Cincinnati	10	135	43	31.9	9.7	13	9.6	417	3.1	2	41.7
3 Marquette	10	115	41	35.7	10.9	13	11.3	448	3.9	2	44.8
4 Tennessee	11	148	59	39.9	10.1	16	10.8	594	4.0	2	54.0
5 Brown	9	112	43	38.4	11.9	11	9.8	512	4.6	4	56.9
6 Oregon	10	104	41	39.4	14.1	8	7.7	578	5.6	2	57.8
7 Kansas State	10	111	52	46.8	11.5	14	12.6	597	5.4	2	59.7
8 Kansas	10	105	44	41.9	13.9	14	13.3	610	5.8	3	61.0
9 Arizona State	10	138	52	37.7	11.8	8	5.8	613	4.4	5	61.3
10 Mississippi State	10	119	50	42.0	12.8	8	6.7	639	5.4	2	63.9

TOTAL DEFENSE	G	P	YDS	AVG	YPG
1 Cincinnati	10	527	1843	3.5	184.3
2 UCLA	9	520	1696	3.3	188.4
3 Maryland	10	577	1932	3.3	193.2
4 Yale	9	494	1754	3.6	194.9
5 Syracuse	9	489	1769	3.6	196.6
6 Oklahoma	10	583	1969	3.4	196.9
7 Texas -El Paso	9	515	1787	3.5	198.6
8 Wichita State	9	490	1789	3.7	198.8
9 Detroit	10	586	1996	3.4	199.6
10 West Virginia	9	516	1835	3.6	203.9

SCORING OFFENSE	G	PTS	AVG
1 Texas Tech	11	428	38.9

SCORING DEFENSE	G	PTS	AVG
1 Maryland	10	31	3.1

1954 POLL PROGRESSION

AP Pre-Season 1954 — Sept. 18 Games

AP	Team	Record	Result
1	Notre Dame	0-0-0	bye week
2	Oklahoma	0-0-0	beat # 12 California 27-13
3	Maryland	0-0-0	beat Kentucky 20-0
4	Texas	0-0-0	beat LSU 20-6
5	Illinois	0-0-0	bye week
6	Michigan State	0-0-0	bye week
7	Georgia Tech	0-0-0	beat Tulane 28-0
8	UCLA	0-0-0	beat San Diego NTC 67-0
9	Wisconsin	0-0-0	bye week
10	Mississippi	0-0-0	beat North Texas 35-12
11	Iowa	0-0-0	bye week
12	California	0-0-0	lost to # 2 Oklahoma 13-27
13	Army	0-0-0	bye week
14	Alabama	0-0-0	lost to Southern Miss 2-7
15	Duke	0-0-0	beat Idaho 41-0
16	Rice	0-0-0	beat Florida 34-14
17	Southern Cal	0-0-0	beat Washington State 39-0
18	Oregon	0-0-0	beat Idaho 41-0
19	Texas Tech	0-0-0	beat Texas A&M 41-9
20	Ohio State	0-0-0	bye week

AP September 20 Poll — Sept. 25 Games

AP	Team	Record	Result
1	Oklahoma	1-0-0	beat # 20 TCU 21-16
2	Notre Dame	0-0-0	beat #4 Texas 21-0
3	Maryland	1-0-0	bye week
4	Texas	1-0-0	lost to # 2 Notre Dame 0-21
5	Georgia Tech	1-0-0	lost to Florida 12-13
6	Illinois	0-0-0	lost to Penn State 12-14
7	Michigan State	0-0-0	lost to # 12 Iowa 10-14
8	UCLA	1-0-0	beat Kansas 32-7
9	Mississippi	1-0-0	beat Kentucky 28-9
10	Baylor	1-0-0	beat Vanderbilt 25-19
11	Wisconsin	0-0-0	beat Marquette 52-14
12	Iowa	0-0-0	beat # 7 Michigan State 14-10
13	Rice	1-0-0	bye week
14	Texas Tech	1-0-0	beat West Texas State 33-7
15	Southern Cal	1-0-0	beat Pittsburgh 27-7
16	Oregon	1-0-0	lost to Stanford 13-18
17	California	0-1-0	beat San Jose State 45-0
18	Army	0-0-0	lost to South Carolina 20-34
19	Duke	0-0-0	beat Pennsylvania 52-0
20	TCU	1-0-0	lost to # 1 Oklahoma 16-21

AP September 27 Poll — Oct. 2 Games

UP	AP	Team	Record	Result
1	1	Notre Dame	1-0-0	lost to # 19 Purdue 14-27
2	2	Oklahoma	2-0-0	bye week
3	3	Iowa	1-0-0	beat Montana 48-6
4	4	UCLA	2-0-0	beat # 6 Maryland 12-7
5	5	Wisconsin	1-0-0	beat # 13 Michigan State 6-0
6	6	Maryland	1-0-0	lost to # 4 UCLA 7-12
7	7	Duke	1-0-0	beat Tennessee 7-6
10	8	Mississippi	2-0-0	beat Villanova 52-0
8	9	Southern Cal	2-0-0	beat Northwestern 12-7
9	10	Penn State	1-0-0	beat Syracuse 13-0
13	11	Baylor	2-0-0	lost to Miami, Fla. 13-19
16	12	Texas	1-1-0	beat Washington St. 40-14
	13	Michigan State	0-1-0	lost to # 5 Wisconsin 0-6
11	14	Ohio State	1-0-0	beat # 18 California 21-13
15	15	South Carolina	1-0-0	lost to West Virginia 6-26
17	16	Rice	1-0-0	beat Cornell 41-20
12	17	Texas Tech	2-0-0	tied Oklahoma State 13-13
19	18	California	1-1-0	lost to # 14 Ohio State 13-21
14	19	Purdue	1-0-0	beat # 1 Notre Dame 27-14
17	20	Florida	1-1-0	beat Auburn 19-13
	20	TCU	1-1-0	lost to Arkansas 13-20

October 4 Poll — Oct. 9 Games

UP	AP	Team	Record	Result
1	1	Oklahoma	2-0-0	beat # 15 Texas 14-7
2	2	UCLA	3-0-0	beat Washington 21-20
4	3	Wisconsin	2-0-0	beat # 11 Rice 13-7
5	4	Iowa	2-0-0	lost to Michigan 13-14
3	5	Purdue	2-0-0	tied # 6 Duke 13-13
6	6	Duke	2-0-0	tied # 5 Purdue 13-13
7	7	Mississippi	3-0-0	beat Vanderbilt 22-7
9	8	Notre Dame	1-1-0	beat Pittsburgh 33-0
8	9	Southern Cal	3-0-0	beat TCU 7-20
10	10	Ohio State	2-0-0	beat Illinois 40-7
11	11	Rice	2-0-0	lost to # 3 Wisconsin 7-13
12	12	Penn State	2-0-0	beat Virginia 34-7
15	13	Maryland	1-1-0	tied Wake Forest 13-13
17	14	Florida	2-1-0	lost to Clemson 7-14
14	15	Texas	2-1-0	lost to # 1 Oklahoma 7-14
20	16	West Virginia	1-0-0	beat George Washington 13-7
13	17	Stanford	3-0-0	lost to # 19 Navy 0-25
16	18	Minnesota	2-0-0	beat Northwestern 26-7
20	19	Navy	2-0-0	beat # 17 Stanford 25-0
	19	Virginia Tech	3-0-0	bye week
18		Michigan State	0-2-0	beat Indiana 21-14
18		Texas Tech	2-0-1	beat Texas-El Paso 55-28

October 11 Poll — Oct. 16 Games

UP	AP	Team	Record	Result
1	1	Oklahoma	3-0-0	beat Kansas 65-0
2	2	Wisconsin	3-0-0	beat # 5 Purdue 20-6
3	3	UCLA	4-0-0	beat Stanford 72-0
4	4	Ohio State	3-0-0	beat # 13 Iowa 20-14
5	5	Purdue	2-0-1	lost to # 2 Wisconsin 6-20
6	6	Duke	2-0-1	lost to # 18 Army 14-28
8	7	Mississippi	4-0-0	beat Tulane 34-7
7	8	Notre Dame	2-1-0	beat Michigan State 20-19
11	9	Navy	3-0-0	lost to Pittsburgh 19-21
10	9	Penn State	3-0-0	lost to West Virginia 14-19
9	11	Minnesota	3-0-0	beat Illinois 19-6
16	12	Arkansas	3-0-0	beat Texas 20-7
14	13	Iowa	2-1-0	lost to # 4 Ohio State 14-20
	14	West Virginia	2-0-0	beat Penn State 19-14
15	15	Rice	2-1-0	lost to SMU 6-20
	16	Virginia Tech	3-0-0	beat Richmond 19-12
13	17	Colorado	3-0-0	beat Iowa State 20-0
12	18	Army	2-1-0	beat # 6 Duke 28-14
17	19	Georgia Tech	3-1-0	beat Auburn 14-7
	20	Texas Tech	3-0-1	lost to LSU 13-20
18		Texas	2-2-0	lost to # 12 Arkansas 7-20
18		Michigan State	1-2-0	lost to # 8 Notre Dame 19-20
20		Southern Cal	3-1-0	beat Oregon 24-14

October 18 Poll — Oct. 23 Games

UP	AP	Team	Record	Result
1	1	Oklahoma	4-0-0	beat Kansas State 21-0
2	2	Wisconsin	4-0-0	lost to # 4 Ohio State 14-31
3	3	UCLA	5-0-0	beat Oregon State 61-0
4	4	Ohio State	4-0-0	beat # 2 Wisconsin 31-14
5	5	Mississippi	5-0-0	lost to # 7 Arkansas 0-6
6	6	Notre Dame	3-1-0	bye week
8	7	Arkansas	4-0-0	beat # 5 Mississippi 6-0
6	8	Minnesota	4-0-0	lost to Michigan 0-34
9	9	Army	3-1-0	beat Columbia 67-12
12	10	West Virginia	3-0-0	beat VMI 40-6
10	11	Colorado	5-0-0	lost to Nebraska 6-20
15	12	Alabama	4-1-0	lost to Mississippi State 7-12
11	13	Purdue	2-1-1	beat Michigan State 27-13
	14	Virginia Tech	4-0-0	beat Virginia 6-0
	15	Georgia Tech	4-1-0	lost to Kentucky 6-13
	16	Miami, Fla.	4-0-0	beat Maryland 9-7
13	17	Southern Cal	4-1-0	beat California 29-27
	18	Florida	3-2-0	lost to LSU 7-20
18	19	Duke	2-1-1	beat North Carolina St. 21-7
18	20	TCU	3-2-0	beat Penn State 20-7
14		SMU	2-1-0	beat Kansas 36-18
16		Iowa	2-2-0	beat Indiana 27-14
17		Penn State	3-1-0	lost to # 20 TCU 7-20
19		Yale	4-0-0	tied Colgate 13-13

October 25 Poll — Oct. 30 Games

UP	AP	Team	Record	Result
2	1	Ohio State	5-0-0	beat Northwestern 14-7
2	2	Oklahoma	5-0-0	beat Colorado 13-6
1	3	UCLA	6-0-0	beat California 27-6
4	4	Arkansas	5-0-0	beat Texas A&M 14-7
5	5	Army	4-1-0	beat Virginia 21-20
6	6	Notre Dame	3-1-0	beat # 15 Navy 6-0
10	7	West Virginia	4-0-0	lost to Pittsburgh 10-13
7	8	Wisconsin	4-1-0	lost to Iowa 7-13
8	9	Purdue	3-1-1	beat Illinois 28-14
15	10	Miami, Fla.	5-0-0	beat Fordham 75-7
11	11	Michigan	4-1-0	lost to Indiana 9-13
14	12	Mississippi	5-1-0	beat LSU 21-6
9	13	Southern Cal	5-1-0	beat Oregon State 30-0
	14	Virginia Tech	5-0-0	tied William & Mary 7-7
17	15	Navy	4-1-0	lost to # 6 Notre Dame 0-6
18	16	Duke	3-1-1	beat Georgia Tech 21-20
16	17	TCU	4-2-0	beat Baylor 7-12
12	18	SMU	3-1-0	tied Texas 13-13
13	19	Rice	3-2-0	beat Vanderbilt 34-13
19	20	Cincinnati	6-0-0	beat Pacific 13-7
20		Alabama	4-2-0	tied Georgia 0-0

November 1 Poll — Nov. 6 Games

UP	AP	Team	Record	Result
1	1	UCLA	7-0-0	beat Oregon 41-0
2	2	Ohio State	6-0-0	beat Pittsburgh 26-0
3	3	Oklahoma	6-0-0	beat Iowa State 40-0
4	4	Arkansas	6-0-0	beat # 15 Rice 28-15
5	5	Notre Dame	4-1-0	beat Pennsylvania 42-7
10	6	Miami, Fla.	6-0-0	lost to Auburn 13-14
6	7	Army	5-1-0	beat Yale 48-7
7	8	Purdue	4-1-1	lost to # 12 Iowa 14-25
9	9	Mississippi	6-1-0	beat Memphis 51-0
8	10	Southern Cal	6-1-0	beat Stanford 21-7
11	11	Duke	4-1-1	lost to # 19 Navy 7-40
12	12	Iowa	4-2-0	beat # 8 Purdue 25-14
17	13	Cincinnati	7-0-0	beat Arizona State 34-7
14	14	Minnesota	5-1-0	beat Oregon State 44-6
13	15	Rice	4-2-0	lost to # 4 Arkansas 15-28
15	16	Wisconsin	4-2-0	beat Northwestern 34-13
18	17	West Virginia	4-1-0	beat Fordham 39-9
	17	Virginia Tech	5-0-1	beat George Washington 20-13
18	19	Navy	4-2-0	beat # 11 Duke 40-7
	19	Baylor	5-2-0	beat Texas 13-7
	10	Nebraska	4-2-0	beat Kansas 41-20
	10	Pittsburgh	3-3-0	lost to Ohio State 0-26
15		SMU	3-1-1	beat Texas A&M 6-3
18		Penn State	4-2-0	beat Holy Cross 39-7

November 8 Poll — Nov. 13 Games

UP	AP	Team	Record	Result
1	1	UCLA	8-0-0	bye week
2	2	Ohio State	7-0-0	beat Purdue 28-6
3	3	Oklahoma	7-0-0	beat Missouri 34-13
4	4	Arkansas	7-0-0	lost to # 19 SMU 14-21
5	5	Notre Dame	5-1-0	beat North Carolina 42-13
6	6	Army	6-1-0	beat Pennsylvania 35-0
8	7	Mississippi	7-1-0	beat Houston 26-0
7	8	Southern Cal	7-1-0	beat Washington 41-0
9	9	Iowa	5-2-0	lost to # 13 Minnesota 20-22
10	10	Navy	5-2-0	beat Columbia 51-6
14	11	Miami, Fla.	6-1-0	bye week
17	12	Cincinnati	8-0-0	lost to Wichita 0-13
12	13	Minnesota	6-1-0	beat # 9 Iowa 22-20
11	14	Wisconsin	5-2-0	beat Illinois 27-14
	15	Virginia Tech	6-0-1	beat Waynesburg 20-6
19	16	West Virginia	5-1-0	beat William & Mary 20-6
	17	Maryland	4-2-1	beat Clemson 16-0
13	18	Baylor	6-2-0	bye week
15	19	SMU	4-1-1	beat # 4 Arkansas 21-14
	20	Georgia	6-1-1	lost to Auburn 0-35
15		tie-Purdue	4-2-1	lost to # 2 Ohio State 6-28
18		Miami, Ohio	7-0-0	lost to Dayton 12-20
20		tie-Michigan	5-2-0	beat Michigan State 33-7
20		Penn State	5-2-0	beat Rutgers 37-14

UP	AP	November 15 Poll		Nov. 20 Games
2	1	Ohio State	8-0-0	beat # 12 Michigan 21-7
1	2	UCLA	8-0-0	beat # 7 Southern Cal 34-0
3	3	Oklahoma	8-0-0	beat Nebraska 55-7
4	4	Notre Dame	6-1-0	beat # 19 Iowa 34-18
5	5	Army	7-1-0	bye week
8	6	Mississippi	8-1-0	bye week
7	7	Navy	6-2-0	bye week
6	7	Southern Cal	8-1-0	lost to # 2 UCLA 0-34
10	9	Arkansas	7-1-0	lost to LSU 6-7
12	10	Minnesota	7-1-0	lost to # 17 Wisconsin 0-27
9	11	SMU	5-1-1	lost to # 20 Baylor 21-33
11	12	Michigan	6-2-0	lost to # 1 Ohio State 7-21
17	13	Maryland	5-2-1	beat George Washington 48-6
	14	West Virginia	6-1-0	beat North Carolina St. 28-3
	15	Virginia Tech	7-0-1	bye week
15	16	Miami, Fla.	6-1-0	beat Alabama 23-7
13	17	Wisconsin	6-2-0	beat # 10 Minnesota 27-0
18	18	Auburn	5-3-0	beat Clemson 27-6
16	19	Iowa	5-3-0	lost to # 4 Notre Dame 18-34
18	20	Baylor	6-2-0	beat # 11 SMU 33-21
14		Georgia Tech	6-3-0	bye week
17		Wichita State	7-1-0	beat Detroit 20-0

UP	AP	November 22 Poll		Nov. 27 Games
2	1	Ohio State	9-0-0	regular season complete
1	2	UCLA	9-0-0	regular season complete
3	3	Oklahoma	9-0-0	beat Oklahoma State 14-0
4	4	Notre Dame	7-1-0	beat # 17 Southern Cal 23-17
5	5	Army	7-1-0	lost to # 6 Navy 20-27
6	6	Navy	6-2-0	beat # 5 Army 27-20
7	7	Mississippi	8-1-0	beat Mississippi State 14-0
8	8	Wisconsin	7-2-0	regular season complete
11	9	Baylor	7-2-0	lost to Rice 14-20
14	10	Maryland	6-2-1	beat Missouri 74-14
10	11	Miami, Fla.	7-1-0	beat Florida 14-0
18	12	West Virginia	7-1-0	beat Virginia 14-10
9	13	Arkansas	7-2-0	beat Houston 19-0
12	14	Michigan	6-3-0	regular season complete
	15	Auburn	6-3-0	beat Alabama 28-0
	16	Virginia Tech	7-0-1	beat VMI 46-9
13	17	Southern Cal	8-2-0	lost to # 4 Notre Dame 17-23
	18	Kentucky	7-3-0	regular season complete
15	19	Penn State	7-2-0	regular season complete
16	20	Duke	6-2-1	beat North Carolina 47-12
	20	Minnesota	7-2-0	regular season complete
17		SMU	5-2-1	beat TCU 21-6
18		Rice	6-3-0	beat # 9 Baylor 20-14
20		Georgia Tech	6-3-0	beat Georgia 7-3
20		Wichita State	8-1-0	beat Tulsa 33-19 (N25)

UP	AP	November 29 Final Poll	RECORD	BOWL BID	DATE	BOWL RESULT	RB	RECORD
2	1	Ohio State	9-0-0	Rose Bowl	J1	beat # 17 Southern Cal 20-7	1	10-0-0
1	2	UCLA	9-0-0				3	9-0-0
3	3	Oklahoma	10-0-0				2	10-0-0
4	4	Notre Dame	8-1-0				4	9-1-0
5	5	Navy	7-2-0	Sugar Bowl	J1	beat # 6 Mississippi 21-0	5	8-2-0
6	6	Mississippi	9-1-0	Sugar Bowl	J1	lost to # 5 Navy 0-21	7	9-2-0
7	7	Army	7-2-0				8	7-2-0
12	8	Maryland	7-2-1				11	7-2-1
10	9	Wisconsin	7-2-0				6	7-2-0
8	10	Arkansas	8-2-0	Cotton Bowl	J1	lost to Georgia Tech 6-14	20	8-3-0
9	11	Miami, Fla.	8-1-0				10	8-1-0
	12	West Virginia	8-1-0				18	8-1-0
	13	Auburn	7-3-0	Gator Bowl	D31	beat # 18 Baylor 33-13	21	8-3-0
14	14	Duke	7-2-1	Orange Bowl	J1	beat Nebraska 34-7	9	8-2-1
15	15	Michigan	6-3-0				23	6-3-0
	16	Virginia Tech	8-0-1				27	8-0-1
11	17	Southern Cal	8-3-0	Rose Bowl	J1	lost to # 1 Ohio State 7-20	22	8-4-0
	18	Baylor	7-3-0	Gator Bowl	D31	lost to # 13 Auburn 13-33	25	7-4-0
18	19	Rice	7-3-0				17	7-3-0
15	20	Penn State	7-2-0				24	7-2-0
13		Georgia Tech	7-3-0	Cotton Bowl	J1	beat #10 Arkansas 14-6	14	8-3-0
17		SMU	6-3-1				19	6-3-1
18		Denver	9-1-0				NR	9-1-0
20		Minnesota	7-2-0				12	7-2-0

1954

Consensus All-Americans

POS	Name	HT	WT	School	AA	AP	FC	FW	IN	NE	SN	UP
B	Ralph Guglielmi	6-0	185	Notre Dame	•	•	•	•	•	•	•	•
B	Howard Cassady	5-10	177	Ohio State	•	•	•	•	•	•	•	•
B	Alan Ameche	6-0	215	Wisconsin	•	•	•	•	•	•	•	•
B	Dicky Maegle	6-0	175	Rice	•	•	•	•	•	•		•
E	Max Boydston	6-2	207	Oklahoma	•	•		•	•	•	•	•
E	Ron Beagle	6-0	185	Navy	•	•		•			•	
T	Jack Ellena	6-3	214	UCLA	•	•	•		•	•	•	•
T	Sid Fournet	5-11	225	LSU		•	•	•	•	•		•
G	Bud Brooks	5-11	200	Arkansas	•	•	•	•	•	•		•
G	Calvin Jones	6-0	200	Iowa	•			•			•	•
C	Kurt Burris	6-1	209	Oklahoma		•	•	•	•		•	•

Others receiving first-team honors

B	Tommy Bell	Army				•	•				
B	Bob Davenport	UCLA				•					
B	Paul Larson	California				•					
B	Bob McNamara	Minnesota				•					
E	Dean Dugger	Ohio State				•					
E	Frank McDonald	Miami			•		•				
E	Don Holleder	Army			•		•				
T	Darris McCord	Tennessee				•					
T	Art Walker	Michigan			•		•				
T	Rex Boggan	Mississippi				•					
T	Frank Varrichione	Notre Dame						•			
G	Tom Bettis	Purdue				•	•				
G	Frank Mincevich	South Carolina					•				
G	Jim Salsbury	UCLA			•		•				
G	Ralph Chesnauskas	Army			•						
C	Hal Easterwood	Mississippi State				•					
C	Matt Hazeltine	California				•					

FW named Brooks as a T

Heisman Trophy Voting

	PLAYER	POS	SCHOOL	1ST	2ND	3RD	TOTAL
1	Alan Ameche	FB	Wisconsin	214	157	112	1068
2	Kurt Burris	LB	Oklahoma	180	111	76	838
3	Howard Cassady	HB	Ohio State	137	139	121	810
4	Ralph Guglielmi	QB	Notre Dame	112	128	99	691
5	Paul Larson	QB	California	50	42	37	271
6	Dicky Maegle	RB	Rice	36	53	44	258
7	Jack Ellena	T	UCLA	23	40	44	193
8	George Shaw	QB	Oregon	32	33	20	182
9	Pete Vann	QB	Army	20	22	30	134
10	Bob McNamara	FB	Minnesota	16	15	26	104

Award Winners

PLAYER	POS	SCHOOL	AWARD NAME
Ron Beagle	E	Navy	Maxwell
Bill Brooks	G	Arkansas	Outland

Conference Standings

ACC

	Conf. W L T			Overall W L T		
Duke	4	0	0	8	2	1
Maryland	4	0	1	7	2	1
North Carolina	4	2	0	4	5	1
South Carolina	3	3	0	6	4	0
Clemson	1	2	0	5	5	0
Wake Forest	1	4	1	2	7	1
Virginia	0	2	0	3	6	0
North Carolina St.	0	4	0	2	8	0

Big 10

	Conf. W L T			Overall W L T		
Ohio State	7	0	0	10	0	0
Wisconsin	5	2	0	7	2	0
Michigan	5	2	0	6	3	0
Minnesota	4	2	0	7	2	0
Iowa	4	3	0	5	4	0
Purdue	3	3	0	5	3	1
Indiana	2	4	0	3	6	0
Michigan State	1	5	0	3	6	0
Northwestern	1	5	0	2	7	0
Illinois	0	6	0	1	8	0

Big 7

	Conf. W L T			Overall W L T		
Oklahoma	6	0	0	10	0	0
Nebraska	4	2	0	6	5	0
Colorado	3	2	1	7	2	1
Missouri	3	2	1	4	5	1
Kansas State	3	3	0	7	3	0
Iowa State	1	5	0	3	6	0
Kansas	0	6	0	0	10	0

Border

	Conf. W L T			Overall W L T		
Texas Tech	4	0	0	7	2	1
Arizona State	3	1	0	5	5	0
Texas-El Paso	4	2	0	8	3	0
Arizona	3	2	0	7	3	0
Hardin-Simmons	2	3	0	4	6	0
West Texas State	1	5	0	1	8	0
New Mexico State	0	4	0	0	9	0

MAC

	Conf. W L T			Overall W L T		
Miami, Ohio	4	0	0	8	1	0
Kent State	4	1	0	8	2	0
Ohio U	5	2	0	6	3	0
Toledo	3	2	0	6	2	1
Western Michigan	3	4	0	4	5	0
Case Western Reserve	2	3	0	3	4	1
Marshall	2	5	0	4	5	0
Bowling Green	0	6	0	2	7	0

Pacific Coast

	Conf. W L T			Overall W L T		
UCLA	6	0	0	9	0	0
Southern Cal	6	1	0	8	4	0
Oregon	5	3	0	6	4	0
California	4	3	0	5	5	0
Washington State	3	4	0	4	6	0
Stanford	2	4	0	4	6	0
Idaho	1	2	0	4	5	0
Washington	1	6	0	2	8	0
Oregon State	1	6	0	1	8	0

SEC

	Conf. W L T			Overall W L T		
Mississippi	6	0	0	9	2	0
Georgia Tech	6	2	0	8	3	0
Kentucky	5	2	0	7	3	0
Florida	5	2	0	5	5	0
Georgia	3	2	1	6	3	1
Auburn	3	3	0	8	3	0
Mississippi State	3	3	0	6	4	0
Alabama	3	3	2	4	5	2
LSU	2	5	0	5	6	0
Tulane	1	6	1	1	6	3
Tennessee	1	5	0	4	6	0
Vanderbilt	1	5	0	2	7	0

Skyline

	Conf. W L T			Overall W L T		
Denver	6	1	0	9	1	0
Wyoming	5	1	0	6	4	0
Utah State	4	3	0	4	6	0
New Mexico	3	3	0	5	5	0
Utah	3	3	0	4	7	0
Colorado State	3	4	0	3	7	0
Montana	1	5	0	3	6	0
Brigham Young	1	6	0	1	8	0

SWC

	Conf. W L T			Overall W L T		
Arkansas	5	1	0	8	3	0
SMU	4	1	1	6	3	1
Rice	4	2	0	7	3	0
Baylor	4	2	0	7	4	0
Texas	2	3	1	4	5	1
TCU	1	5	0	4	6	0
Texas A&M	0	6	0	1	9	0

Independents

	Overall W L T		
Notre Dame	9	1	0
Boston College	8	1	0
Miami, Fla.	8	1	0
Navy	8	2	0
Army	7	2	0
Penn State	7	2	0
Brown	6	2	1
Florida State	8	4	0
Princeton	5	3	1
Yale	5	3	1
Harvard	4	3	1
Cornell	5	4	0
Syracuse	4	4	0
Memphis	3	4	3
Pittsburgh	4	5	0
North Texas	4	6	0
Rutgers	3	6	0
Dartmouth	3	6	0
Columbia	1	8	0
Virginia	1	8	0
Pennsylvania	0	9	0

Bowl Games

DATE	GAME	SCORE
D 31	Gator	Auburn 33, Baylor 13
J 1	Tangerine	Nebraska-Omaha 7, Eastern Kentucky 6
J 1	Orange	Duke 34, Nebraska 7
J 1	Cotton	Georgia Tech 14, Arkansas 6
J 1	Sugar	Navy 21, Mississippi 0
J 1	Rose	Ohio State 20, Southern Cal 7
J 1	Sun	Texas-El Paso 47, Florida State 20

1954 NCAA MAJOR COLLEGE STATISTICAL LEADERS

INDIVIDUAL LEADERS

PASSING/COMPLETIONS		G	ATT	COM	PCT	INT	I%	YDS	YPA	TD	TD%	COM.PG
1	Paul Larson, California	10	195	125	64.1	8	4.1	1537	7.9	10	5.1	12.5
2	George Shaw, Oregon	10	196	91	46.4	11	5.6	1358	6.9	10	5.1	9.1
3	Len Dawson, Purdue	9	167	87	52.1	8	4.8	1464	8.8	15	9.0	9.7
4	John Brodie, Stanford	10	163	81	49.7	16	9.8	937	5.7	2	1.2	8.1
5	Ken Ford, Hardin-Simmons	10	146	78	53.4	9	6.2	948	6.5	7	4.8	7.8
6	Bill Beagle, Dartmouth	9	145	76	52.4	10	6.9	867	6.0	5	3.5	8.4
7	Dave Dungan, Utah	11	128	74	57.8	4	3.1	862	6.7	5	3.9	6.7
8	John Stephans, Holy Cross	10	149	73	49.0	11	7.4	800	5.4	8	5.4	7.3
9	Mackie Prickett, South Carolina	10	116	68	58.6	9	7.8	682	5.9	1	0.9	6.8
9	Ralph Guglielmi, Notre Dame	10	127	68	53.4	7	5.5	1162	9.1	6	4.7	6.8

ALL-PURPOSE YARDS		G	RUSH	REC	INT	PR	KR	YDS	YPG
1	Art Luppino, Arizona	10	1359	50	84	68	632	2193	219.3

RUSHING/YARDS		G	ATT	YDS	AVG	YPG
1	Art Luppino, Arizona	10	179	1359	7.6	135.9
2	Lenny Moore, Penn State	9	136	1082	8.0	120.2
3	Tommy Bell, Army	9	96	1020	10.6	113.3
4	Sam Pino, Boston U.	9	154	933	6.1	103.7
5	Dicky Maegle, Rice	10	144	905	6.3	90.5
6	Dick Imer, Montana	9	111	889	8.0	98.8
7	Joe Childress, Auburn	10	148	836	5.7	83.6
8	John Bayuk, Colorado	10	145	824	5.7	82.4
9	Fred Mahaffey, Denver	10	143	813	5.7	81.3
10	Tom Tracy, Tennessee	10	116	794	6.8	79.4

RUSHING/YARDS PER CARRY		G	ATT	YDS	YPC
1	Tommy Bell, Army	9	96	1020	10.6
2	Dick Imer, Montana	9	111	889	8.0
3	Lenny Moore, Penn State	9	136	1082	8.0
4	Art Luppino, Arizona	10	179	1359	7.6
5	Tom Tracy, Tennessee	10	116	794	6.8
6	Dicky Maegle, Rice	10	144	905	6.3
7	Sam Pino, Boston U.	9	154	933	6.1
8	Fred Mahaffey, Denver	10	143	813	5.7
9	John Bayuk, Colorado	10	145	824	5.7
10	Joe Childress, Auburn	10	148	836	5.7

*-Based on top 10 rushers

RECEIVING/RECEPTIONS		G	REC	YDS	TD	YPR	YPG	RPG
1	Jim Hanifan, California	10	44	569	7	12.9	56.9	4.4
2	John Stewart, Stanford	10	36	577	2	16.0	57.7	3.6
3	Jim Carmichael, California	10	33	420	2	12.7	42.0	3.3
4	Carl Brazell, South Carolina	10	29	241	1	8.3	24.1	2.9
5	Jerry Mertens, Drake	9	28	495	4	17.7	55.0	3.1
5	Jim Pyburn, Auburn	10	28	460	4	16.4	46.0	2.8
7	Andrew Nacrelli, Fordham	9	25	493	2	19.7	54.8	2.8
7	Max Pierce, Utah	11	25	457	3	18.3	41.5	2.3
7	Larry Ross, Denver	10	25	378	4	15.1	37.8	2.5
7	Robert Dee, Holy Cross	10	25	236	2	9.4	23.6	2.5

PUNTING		PUNT	YDS	AVG
1	A.L. Terpening, New Mexico	41	1869	45.6
2	Ted Rohde, Kansas	29	1270	43.8
3	Bobby Brengle, Tennessee	30	1275	42.5
4	Ray Taylor, TCU	44	1844	41.9
5	Carroll Hardy, Colorado	26	1082	41.6
6	Walt Hynoski, Pennsylvania	47	1941	41.3
7	James Withrow, Oregon State	30	1215	40.5
8	Bobby Collins, Mississippi State	33	1330	40.3
8	John Caruso, Tulane	33	1330	40.3
10	Bob Heydenfeldt, UCLA	26	1037	39.9

PUNT RETURNS/YARDS		PR	YDS	AVG
1	Dicky Maegle, Rice	15	293	19.5
2	Jack Yohe, William & Mary	13	277	21.3
3	Earl Smith, Iowa	15	267	17.8
4	Sam Brown, UCLA	10	262	26.2
5	Bob McNamara, Minnesota	14	252	18.0
6	Lee Riley, Detroit	13	240	18.5
7	Fred Tesone, Denver	13	230	17.7
8	Gordon Malloy, Miami, Fla.	9	223	24.8
9	Ron Waller, Maryland	13	199	15.3
10	Ron Younker, Penn State	12	193	16.1

KICKOFF RETURNS/YARDS		KR	YDS	AVG
1	Art Luppino, Arizona	20	632	31.6
2	George Marinkov, North Carolina St.	13	465	35.8
3	Lon Turner, Dartmouth	17	407	23.9
4	Jackie Simpson, Florida	13	324	24.9
5	Dick Mackey, Arizona State	17	323	19.0
6	Gene Hendrix, Drake	17	317	18.6
7	Ron Drzewiecki, Marquette	12	315	26.3
8	Frank Eidom, SMU	13	292	22.5
9	Paul Larson, California	10	285	28.5
9	Dick Imer, Montana	11	285	25.9

SCORING		TDS	XPT	FG	PTS
1	Art Luppino, Arizona	24	22	0	166
2	Buddy Leake, Oklahoma	9	25	0	79
3	Tommy Bell, Army	13	0	0	78
3	Lenny Moore, Penn State	13	0	0	78
5	Fred Mahaffey, Denver	12	1	0	73
6	Dicky Maegle, Rice	12	0	0	72
7	Rusty Fairly, Denver	9	16	0	70
8	Carroll Hardy, Colorado	9	14	0	68
9	Six tied	—	—	—	66

INTERCEPTIONS		INT	YDS
1	Gary Glick, Colorado State	8	168
2	Rusty Fairly, Denver	7	62
2	Jerry Barger, Duke	7	50
2	Whitey Rouviere, Miami, Fla.	7	18
2	Dick Jackson, Cornell	7	NA
6	James Miller, Wisconsin	6	117
6	Pat Oleksiak, Tennessee	6	99
6	Lenny Moore, Penn State	6	96
6	George Walker, Arkansas	6	90
6	Dick Mackey, Arizona State	6	83
6	Mackie Prickett, South Carolina	6	63

TEAM LEADERS

RUSHING OFFENSE		G	ATT	YDS	AVG	YPG
1	Army	9	468	2898	6.2	322.0
2	Texas Tech	10	562	3164	5.6	316.4
3	Colorado	10	492	3160	6.4	316.0
4	Oklahoma	10	591	2962	5.0	296.2
5	UCLA	9	454	2578	5.7	286.4
6	Miami, Fla.	9	497	2558	5.1	284.2
7	Arizona	10	502	2765	5.5	276.5
8	Penn State	9	421	2415	5.7	268.3
9	Navy	10	507	2677	5.3	267.2
10	Nebraska	10	467	2657	5.7	265.7

PASSING OFFENSE/YPG		G	ATT	COM	INT	PCT	YDS	YPA	TD	YPG	I%	YPC
1	Purdue	9	195	99	11	50.8	1596	8.2	15	177.3	5.6	16.1
2	California	10	228	139	13	61.0	1724	7.6	11	172.4	5.7	12.4
3	Oregon	10	229	107	13	46.7	1601	7.0	13	160.1	5.7	15.0
4	Mississippi	10	175	81	9	46.3	1554	8.9	10	155.4	5.1	19.2
5	Notre Dame	10	178	89	9	50.0	1460	8.2	11	146.0	5.1	16.4
6	Dartmouth	9	220	112	20	51.0	1301	5.9	8	144.6	9.1	11.6
7	Missouri	10	188	92	11	49.0	1399	7.4	14	139.9	5.9	15.2
8	Holy Cross	10	247	118	20	47.8	1391	5.6	15	139.1	8.1	11.8
9	Washington	10	237	109	16	46.0	1360	5.7	6	136.0	6.8	12.5
10	Hardin-Simmons	10	228	111	17	48.7	1352	5.9	11	135.2	7.5	12.2

TOTAL OFFENSE		G	P	YDS	AVG	YPG
1	Army	9	575	4038	7.0	448.7
2	Texas Tech	10	677	4223	6.2	422.3
3	Arizona	10	643	4020	6.3	402.0
4	Navy	9	620	3544	5.7	393.8
5	Mississippi	10	663	3868	5.8	386.8
6	Notre Dame	10	729	3853	5.3	385.3
7	Oklahoma	10	679	3827	5.6	382.7
8	Denver	10	637	3718	5.8	371.8
9	Boston U.	9	557	3304	5.9	367.1
10	UCLA	9	561	3299	5.9	366.6

RUSHING DEFENSE		G	ATT	YDS	AVG	YPG
1	UCLA	9	314	659	2.1	73.2
2	Oklahoma	10	378	870	2.3	87.0
3	Mississippi	10	375	901	2.4	90.1
4	Clemson	10	388	969	2.5	96.9
5	Navy	9	353	923	2.6	102.6
6	Notre Dame	10	354	1094	3.1	109.4
7	West Virginia	9	361	990	2.7	110.0
8	Wisconsin	9	359	1045	2.9	116.1
9	Wichita State	10	393	1170	3.0	117.0
10	Cincinnati	10	368	1184	3.2	118.4

PASSING DEFENSE		G	ATT	COM	PCT	YPC	INT	I%	YDS	YPA	TD	YPG
1	Alabama	11	122	43	35.2	11.7	10	8.2	504	4.1	0	45.8
2	Richmond	9	97	33	34.0	12.8	12	12.4	424	4.4	1	47.1
3	Detroit	9	98	39	39.8	11.1	11	11.2	432	4.4	2	48.0
4	Kansas State	10	111	45	40.5	11.4	6	5.4	515	4.6	6	51.5
5	Arkansas	10	122	48	39.3	11.2	17	13.9	538	4.4	1	53.8
6	Boston College	9	130	42	32.3	12.5	11	8.5	524	4.0	3	58.2
7	Georgia Tech	10	118	51	43.2	11.5	15	12.7	587	5.0	3	58.7
8	Auburn	10	105	44	41.9	13.7	12	11.4	601	5.7	5	60.1
9	Florida	10	104	47	45.2	13.2	7	6.7	619	6.0	0	61.9
9	Texas A&M	10	98	45	45.9	13.8	8	8.2	619	6.3	11	61.9

TOTAL DEFENSE		G	P	YDS	AVG	YPG
1	Mississippi	10	537	1723	3.2	172.3
2	Richmond	9	505	1570	3.1	174.4
3	Clemson	10	528	1761	3.3	176.1
4	Boston College	9	511	1661	3.3	184.6
5	Oklahoma	10	561	1863	3.3	186.3
6	West Virginia	9	521	1680	3.2	186.7
7	Denver	10	559	1886	3.4	188.6
8	UCLA	9	530	1708	3.2	189.8
9	Navy	9	495	1714	3.5	190.4
10	Cincinnati	10	521	1984	3.8	198.4

SCORING OFFENSE		G	PTS	AVG
1	UCLA	9	367	40.8

SCORING DEFENSE		G	PTS	AVG
1	UCLA	9	40	4.4

1955 POLL PROGRESSION

AP Pre-Season 1955 — Sept. 17 Games

Rank	Team	Record	Result
1	UCLA	0-0-0	beat Texas A&M 21-0
2	Oklahoma	0-0-0	bye week
3	Michigan	0-0-0	bye week
4	Ohio State	0-0-0	bye week
5	Maryland	0-0-0	beat Missouri 13-12
6	Notre Dame	0-0-0	bye week
7	Army	0-0-0	bye week
8	Navy	0-0-0	bye week
9	Miami, Fla.	0-0-0	lost to #10 Georgia Tech 6-14
10	Georgia Tech	0-0-0	beat #9 Miami, Fla. 14-6
11	Rice	0-0-0	bye week
12	Iowa	0-0-0	bye week
13	Southern Cal	0-0-0	beat Washington St. 50-12
14	Wisconsin	0-0-0	bye week
15	Mississippi	0-0-0	beat Georgia 26-13
16	SMU	0-0-0	bye week
17	Auburn	0-0-0	bye week
18	Duke	0-0-0	bye week
19	West Virginia	0-0-0	bye week
20	Purdue	0-0-0	bye week

AP September 19 Poll — Sept. 24 Games

Rank	Team	Record	Result
1	UCLA	1-0-0	lost to #5 Maryland 0-7
2	Georgia Tech	1-0-0	beat #19 Florida 14-7
3	Oklahoma	0-0-0	beat North Carolina 13-6
4	Michigan	0-0-0	beat Missouri 42-7
5	Maryland	1-0-0	beat #1 UCLA 7-0
6	Ohio State	0-0-0	beat Nebraska 28-20
7	Pittsburgh	1-0-0	beat Syracuse 22-12
8	Mississippi	1-0-0	lost to Kentucky 14-21
9	Navy	0-0-0	beat William & Mary 7-0
10	Southern Cal	1-0-0	beat Oregon 42-15
11	Notre Dame	0-0-0	beat SMU 17-0
12	Texas Tech	1-0-0	lost to TCU 0-32
13	Rice	0-0-0	beat Alabama 20-0
14	Army	0-0-0	beat Furman 81-0
15	Miami, Fla.	0-1-0	bye week
16	LSU	1-0-0	lost to Texas A&M 0-28
17	Arkansas	1-0-0	beat Oklahoma State 21-0
18	Baylor	1-0-0	beat Villanova 19-2
19	Florida	1-0-0	lost to #2 Georgia Tech 7-14
19	Purdue	0-0-0	beat Pacific 14-7

UP AP September 26 Poll — Oct. 1 Games

UP	AP	Team	Record	Result
1	1	Maryland	2-0-0	beat #20 Baylor 20-6
2	2	Michigan	1-0-0	beat Michigan State 14-7
3	3	Georgia Tech	2-0-0	beat SMU 20-7
5	4	Notre Dame	1-0-0	beat Indiana 19-0
4	5	Oklahoma	1-0-0	beat #12 Pittsburgh 26-14
7	6	Army	1-0-0	beat #18 Penn State 35-6
6	7	UCLA	1-1-0	beat Washington St. 55-0
10	8	Ohio State	1-0-0	lost to Stanford 0-6
8	9	Southern Cal	2-0-0	beat Texas 19-7
9	10	TCU	2-0-0	beat Arkansas 26-0
11	11	Rice	1-0-0	tied LSU 20-20
12	12	Pittsburgh	2-0-0	lost to #5 Oklahoma 14-26
	13	West Virginia	1-0-0	beat Wake Forest 46-0
13	14	Iowa	1-0-0	lost to #17 Wisconsin 14-37
15	15	Navy	1-0-0	beat South Carolina 26-0
16	16	Duke	1-0-0	beat Tennessee 21-0
14	17	Wisconsin	1-0-0	beat #14 Iowa 37-14
	18	Penn State	1-0-0	lost to #6 Army 6-35
	19	Washington	2-0-0	beat Oregon 19-7
	20	Baylor	2-0-0	lost to #1 Maryland 6-20
17		Mississippi	1-1-0	beat North Texas 33-0
18		SMU	0-1-0	lost to #3 Georgia Tech 7-20
19		Colorado	1-0-0	beat Kansas 12-0
20		Michigan State	1-0-0	lost to #2 Michigan 7-14
20		Miami, Fla.	0-1-0	beat Florida State 34-0 (S30)

UP AP October 3 Poll — Oct. 8 Games

UP	AP	Team	Record	Result
1	1	Maryland	3-0-0	beat Wake Forest 28-7
2	2	Michigan	2-0-0	beat #6 Army 26-2
3	3	Oklahoma	2-0-0	beat Texas 20-0
4	4	Georgia Tech	3-0-0	beat LSU 7-0
5	5	Notre Dame	2-0-0	beat #15 Miami, Fla. 14-0
6	6	Army	2-0-0	lost to #2 Michigan 2-26
8	7	UCLA	2-1-0	beat Oregon State 38-0
7	8	TCU	3-0-0	beat Alabama 21-0
9	9	Wisconsin	2-0-0	beat Purdue 9-0
10	10	Southern Cal	3-0-0	lost to Washington 0-7
14	11	West Virginia	2-0-0	beat VMI 47-12
12	12	Navy	2-0-0	beat Pittsburgh 21-0
11	13	Duke	2-0-0	beat William & Mary 47-7
19	14	Auburn	2-1-0	beat #19 Kentucky 14-14
13	15	Miami, Fla.	1-1-0	lost to #5 Notre Dame 0-14
	16	Clemson	3-0-0	lost to Rice 7-21
18	17	Purdue	2-0-0	lost to Wisconsin 0-9
	18	Washington	3-0-0	beat Southern Cal 7-0
	19	Kentucky	2-1-0	tied #14 Auburn 14-14
14	20	Stanford	2-1-0	lost to Michigan State 14-38
14		tie-Michigan State	1-1-0	beat #20 Stanford 38-14
17		Ohio State	1-1-0	beat Illinois 27-12
19		tie-Colorado	2-0-0	beat Oregon 13-6

UP AP October 10 Poll — Oct. 15 Games

UP	AP	Team	Record	Result
1	1	Michigan	3-0-0	beat Northwestern 14-2
2	2	Maryland	4-0-0	beat North Carolina 25-7
3	3	Oklahoma	3-0-0	beat Kansas 44-6
4	4	Notre Dame	3-0-0	lost to #13 Michigan State 7-21
5	5	Georgia Tech	4-0-0	lost to #17 Auburn 12-14
8	6	Wisconsin	3-0-0	lost to #16 Southern Cal 21-33
6	7	TCU	4-0-0	lost to #19 Texas A&M 16-19
9	8	Navy	3-0-0	beat Penn State 34-14
7	9	UCLA	3-1-0	beat Stanford 21-13
15	10	West Virginia	3-0-0	beat William & Mary 39-13
	11	Duke	3-0-0	beat #14 Ohio State 20-14
12	12	Washington	4-0-0	lost to Baylor 7-13
11	13	Michigan State	3-1-0	beat #4 Notre Dame 21-7
17	14	Ohio State	2-1-0	lost to #11 Duke 14-20
14	15	Rice	2-0-1	lost to SMU 0-20
16	16	Southern Cal	3-1-0	beat #6 Wisconsin 33-21
17	17	Auburn	2-0-1	beat #5 Georgia Tech 14-12
13	18	Army	2-1-0	lost to Syracuse 0-13
	19	Texas A&M	3-1-0	beat #7 TCU 19-16
19	20	Colorado	3-0-0	beat Kansas State 34-13
20		Kentucky	2-1-1	lost to Mississippi State 14-20
15		Purdue	2-1-0	tied Iowa 20-20
19		Mississippi	3-1-0	beat Tulane 27-13
19		Miami, Fla.	1-2-0	bye week

UP AP October 17 Poll — Oct. 22 Games

UP	AP	Team	Record	Result
1	1	Michigan	4-0-0	beat Minnesota 14-13
2	2	Maryland	5-0-0	beat Syracuse 34-13
3	3	Oklahoma	4-0-0	beat #14 Colorado 56-21
4	4	Navy	4-0-0	beat Pennsylvania 33-0
7	5	Duke	4-0-0	lost to Pittsburgh 7-26
6	6	Michigan State	3-1-0	beat Illinois 21-7
5	7	UCLA	4-1-0	beat Iowa 33-13
11	8	West Virginia	4-0-0	beat Penn State 21-7
8	9	Auburn	3-0-1	beat Furman 52-0
9	10	Southern Cal	4-1-0	beat California 33-6
10	11	Notre Dame	3-1-0	beat Purdue 22-7
13	12	Texas A&M	4-1-0	beat #16 Baylor 19-7
12	13	Georgia Tech	4-1-0	beat Florida State 34-0
17	14	Colorado	4-0-0	lost to #3 Oklahoma 21-56
15	15	Wisconsin	3-1-0	lost to Ohio State 16-26
19	16	Baylor	4-1-0	lost to #12 Texas A&M 7-19
	17	Boston College	3-0-0	tied Marquette 13-13
14	18	TCU	4-1-0	beat Miami, Fla. 21-19
	19	Yale	4-0-0	lost to Colgate 0-7
	20	Holy Cross	4-0-0	beat Boston U. 20-12
16		Purdue	2-1-1	lost to #11 Notre Dame 7-22
17		tie-Iowa	2-1-1	lost to #7 UCLA 13-33 (O21)
20		tie-SMU	2-2-0	beat Kansas 33-14
20		tie-Washington	4-1-0	tied Stanford 7-7

UP AP October 24 Poll — Oct. 29 Games

UP	AP	Team	Record	Result
2	1	Maryland	6-0-0	beat South Carolina 27-0
3	2	Oklahoma	5-0-0	beat Kansas State 40-7
1	3	Michigan	5-0-0	beat Iowa 33-21
4	4	Navy	5-0-0	lost to #9 Notre Dame 7-21
6	5	Michigan State	4-1-0	beat Wisconsin 27-0
5	6	UCLA	5-1-0	beat California 47-0
11	7	West Virginia	6-0-0	beat Marquette 39-0
8	8	Auburn	4-0-1	lost to Tulane 13-27
7	9	Notre Dame	4-1-0	beat #4 Navy 21-7
9	10	Southern Cal	5-1-0	lost to Minnesota 19-25
10	11	Texas A&M	5-1-0	tied Arkansas 7-7
12	12	Georgia Tech	5-1-0	beat #17 Duke 27-0
16	13	Holy Cross	4-1-0	lost to Syracuse 9-49
13	14	TCU	5-1-0	beat Baylor 28-6
15	15	Ohio State	3-2-0	beat Northwestern 49-0
16	16	Pittsburgh	4-2-0	lost to Miami, Fla. 7-21
14	17	Duke	4-1-0	lost to #12 Georgia Tech 0-27
	18	Miami, Ohio	5-0-0	beat Kent State 19-7
16	19	Washington	4-1-1	tied Stanford 7-7
	20	Mississippi	5-1-0	beat LSU 29-26

UP AP October 31 Poll — Nov. 5 Games

UP	AP	Team	Record	Result
3	1	Maryland	7-0-0	beat LSU 13-0
2	2	Oklahoma	6-0-0	beat Missouri 20-0
1	3	Michigan	6-0-0	lost to Illinois 6-25
5	4	Michigan State	5-1-0	beat Purdue 27-0
4	5	UCLA	6-1-0	beat Pacific 34-0
6	6	Notre Dame	5-1-0	beat Pennsylvania 46-14
8	7	West Virginia	6-0-0	beat George Washington 13-7
7	8	Georgia Tech	6-1-0	tied Tennessee 7-7
10	9	Navy	5-1-0	tied Duke 7-7
9	10	TCU	6-1-0	bye week
11	11	Ohio State	4-2-0	beat Indiana 20-13
12	12	Texas A&M	5-1-1	beat SMU 13-2
	13	Miami, Ohio	6-0-0	beat Bowling Green 7-0
13	14	Auburn	4-1-1	beat #20 Mississippi State 27-26
17	15	Mississippi	6-1-0	beat Memphis 39-6
15	16	Southern Cal	6-1-0	lost to Stanford 20-28
	17	Kentucky	4-2-1	lost to Vanderbilt 0-34
	18	Syracuse	3-2-0	lost to Penn State 20-21
19	19	Army	5-1-0	lost to Yale 12-14
20		Mississippi State	6-1-0	lost to #14 Auburn 26-27
14		Purdue	3-2-1	lost to #4 Michigan State 0-27
15		Duke	4-2-0	tied #9 Navy 7-7
18		Miami, Fla.	2-3-0	beat Boston College 14-7 (N4)

UP AP November 7 Poll — Nov. 12 Games

UP	AP	Team	Record	Result
1	1	Oklahoma	7-0-0	beat Iowa State 52-0
2	2	Maryland	8-0-0	beat Clemson 25-12
3	3	Michigan State	6-1-0	beat Minnesota 42-14
4	4	UCLA	7-1-0	beat Washington 19-17
5	5	Notre Dame	6-1-0	beat North Carolina 27-7
10	6	West Virginia	7-0-0	lost to Pittsburgh 7-26
6	7	Michigan	6-1-0	beat Indiana 30-0
7	8	TCU	6-1-0	beat Texas 47-0
9	9	Texas A&M	6-1-1	beat Rice 20-12
10	10	Ohio State	5-2-0	beat #20 Iowa 20-10
8	11	Georgia Tech	6-1-1	beat Alabama 26-2
13	12	Auburn	5-1-1	beat Georgia 16-13
12	13	Navy	5-1-1	beat Columbia 14-7
14	14	Mississippi	7-1-0	beat Houston 27-11
	15	Miami, Ohio	7-0-0	beat Dayton 7-0
15	16	Illinois	4-3-0	beat Wisconsin 17-14
	17	Pittsburgh	5-3-0	beat West Virginia 26-7
17	18	Duke	4-2-1	beat South Carolina 41-7
18	19	Mississippi State	6-2-0	lost to LSU 7-34
	20	Iowa	3-3-1	lost to #10 Ohio State 10-20
	20	Miami, Fla.	3-3-0	beat Bucknell 46-0
16		Stanford	4-3-1	beat Oregon 44-7
18		Yale	6-1-0	lost to Princeton 0-13

UP	AP	November 14 Poll		Nov. 19 Games
1	1	Oklahoma	8-0-0	beat Nebraska 41-0
3	2	Maryland	9-0-0	beat George Washington 19-0
2	3	Michigan State	7-1-0	beat Marquette 33-0
4	4	Notre Dame	7-1-0	beat Iowa 17-14
5	5	UCLA	8-1-0	beat Southern Cal 17-7
6	6	Michigan	7-1-0	lost to #9 Ohio State 0-17
7	7	TCU	7-1-0	beat Rice 35-0
9	8	Texas A&M	7-1-1	bye week
8	9	Ohio State	6-2-0	beat #6 Michigan 17-0
10	10	Georgia Tech	7-1-1	bye week
11	11	Navy	6-1-1	bye week
12	12	Auburn	6-1-1	beat Clemson 21-0
15	13	West Virginia	7-1-0	lost to Syracuse 13-20
13	14	Mississippi	8-1-0	bye week
15	15	Pittsburgh	6-3-0	beat Penn State 20-0
	16	Miami, Ohio	8-0-0	bye week
	17	Tennessee	5-2-1	lost to Kentucky 0-23
17	18	Stanford	5-3-1	beat California 19-0
	19	Oregon State	6-2-0	lost to Oregon 0-28
14	20	Duke	5-2-1	beat Wake Forest 14-0
18		Iowa	3-4-1	lost to #4 Notre Dame 14-17
18		Miami, Fla.	4-3-0	beat Alabama 34-12 (N18)

UP	AP	November 21 Poll		Nov. 26 Games
1	1	Oklahoma	9-0-0	beat Oklahoma State 53-0
2	2	Michigan State	8-1-0	regular season complete
3	3	Maryland	10-0-0	regular season complete
4	4	UCLA	9-1-0	regular season complete
5	5	Notre Dame	8-1-0	lost to Southern Cal 20-42
6	6	Ohio State	7-2-0	regular season complete
7	7	TCU	8-1-0	beat SMU 20-13
8	8	Texas A&M	7-1-1	lost to Texas 6-21
9	9	Georgia Tech	7-1-1	beat Georgia 21-3
11	10	Auburn	7-1-1	beat Alabama 26-0
10	11	Navy	6-1-1	lost to Army 6-14
12	12	Michigan	7-2-0	regular season complete
13	13	Pittsburgh	7-3-0	regular season complete
	14	Miami, Fla.	5-3-0	beat Florida 7-6
15	15	Mississippi	8-1-0	beat Mississippi State 26-0
	16	Miami, Ohio	8-0-0	beat Cincinnati 14-0
14	17	Stanford	6-3-1	regular season complete
17	18	Duke	6-2-1	beat North Carolina 6-0
	19	Vanderbilt	7-2-0	lost to Tennessee 14-20
	20	Syracuse	5-3-0	
15		West Virginia	7-2-0	beat North Carolina St. 27-7
17		Washington	5-4-1	regular season complete
19		Southern Cal	5-4-0	beat #5 Notre Dame 42-20
19		Iowa	3-5-1	regular season complete

UP	AP	November 28 Final Poll	Record	Bowl Bid	Date	Bowl Result	RB	Record
1	1	Oklahoma	10-0-0	Orange Bowl	J2	beat #3 Maryland 20-6	1	11-0-0
2	2	Michigan State	8-1-0	Rose Bowl	J2	beat #4 UCLA 17-14	5	9-1-0
3	3	Maryland	10-0-0	Orange Bowl	J2	lost to #1 Oklahoma 6-20	2	10-1-0
4	4	UCLA	9-1-0	Rose Bowl	J2	lost to #2 Michigan State 14-17	8	9-2-0
6	5	Ohio State	7-2-0				7	7-2-0
5	6	TCU	9-1-0	Cotton Bowl	J2	lost to #10 Mississippi 13-14	9	9-2-0
7	7	Georgia Tech	8-1-1	Sugar Bowl	J2	beat #11 Pittsburgh 7-0	4	9-1-1
10	8	Auburn	8-1-1	Gator Bowl	D31	lost to Vanderbilt 13-25	14	8-2-0
8	9	Notre Dame	8-2-0				6	8-2-0
9	10	Mississippi	9-1-0	Cotton Bowl	J2	beat #6 TCU 14-13	3	10-1-0
11	11	Pittsburgh	7-3-0	Sugar Bowl	J2	lost to #7 Georgia Tech 0-7	29	7-4-0
13	12	Michigan	7-2-0				12	7-2-0
12	13	Southern Cal	6-4-0				20	6-4-0
18	14	Miami, Fla.	6-3-0				18	6-3-0
20	15	Miami, Ohio	9-0-0				NR	9-0-0
20	16	Stanford	6-3-1				19	6-3-1
14	17	Texas A&M	7-2-1				16	7-2-1
20	18	Navy	6-2-1				15	6-2-1
17	19	West Virginia	8-2-0				25	8-2-0
15	20	Army	6-3-0				10	6-3-0
15		Duke	7-2-1				13	7-2-1
19		Iowa	3-5-1				32	3-5-1

1955

CONSENSUS ALL-AMERICANS

POS	Name	HT	WT	School	AA	AP	FC	FW	IN	NE	SN	UP
B	Howard Cassady	5-10	172	Ohio State	•	•	•	•	•	•	•	•
B	Jim Swink	6-1	180	TCU	•	•	•	•	•	•	•	•
B	Earl Morrall	6-1	180	Michigan State	•	•	•	•	•		•	
B	Paul Hornung	6-2	205	Notre Dame	•		•		•	•	•	•
E	Ron Beagle	6-0	186	Navy	•	•	•	•	•	•	•	•
E	Ron Kramer	6-3	218	Michigan	•	•	•	•	•	•	•	•
T	Norman Masters	6-2	225	Michigan State				•	•	•		•
T	Bruce Bosley	6-2	225	West Virginia	•	•		•		•	•	
G	Bo Bolinger	5-10	206	Oklahoma	•	•	•	•	•	•		•
G	Calvin Jones	6-0	220	Iowa	•				•			
G	Hardiman Cureton	6-0	213	UCLA	•	•	•	•		•	•	•
C	Bob Pellegrini	6-2	225	Maryland	•	•	•	•	•	•	•	•

OTHERS RECEIVING FIRST-TEAM HONORS

B	Jon Arnett	Southern Cal	• •
B	Joe Childress	Auburn	•
B	Art Davis	Mississippi State	•
B	Don Schaefer	Notre Dame	• • •
B	Tommy McDonald	Oklahoma	•
B	Bob Davenport	UCLA	•
E	Harold Burnine	Missouri	•
E	Rommie Loudd	UCLA	•
E	Howard Schnellenberger	Kentucky	•
T	Herb Gray	Texas	•
T	Sam Huff	West Virginia	• •
T	Frank D'Agostino	Auburn	• •
T	Paul Wiggin	Stanford	•
T	John Witte	Oregon State	•
T	Mike Sandusky	Maryland	•
G	Jim Parker	Ohio State	•
G	Tony Sardisco	Tulane	•
G	James D. Brown	UCLA	•
G	Pat Bisceglia	Notre Dame	•
G	Scott Suber	Mississippi State	•
C	Hugh Pitts	TCU	•

HEISMAN TROPHY VOTING

	PLAYER	POS	SCHOOL	1ST	2ND	3RD	TOTAL
1	Howard Cassady	HB	Ohio State	594	179	79	2219
2	Jim Swink	RB	TCU	128	120	118	742
3	George Welsh	QB	Navy	56	70	75	383
4	Earl Morrall	QB	Michigan State	23	97	60	323
5	Paul Hornung	QB	Notre Dame	33	72	78	321
6	Bob Pellegrini	C	Maryland	38	64	52	294
7	Ron Beagle	E	Navy	21	44	61	212
8	Ron Kramer	E	Michigan	12	50	56	192
9	Bo Bolinger	G	Oklahoma	14	32	42	148
10	Calvin Jones	G	Iowa	14	40	16	138

AWARD WINNERS

PLAYER	POS	SCHOOL	AWARD NAME
Howard Cassady	HB	Ohio State	Maxwell
Calvin Jones	G	Iowa	Outland

CONFERENCE STANDINGS

ACC

	CONF. W L T			OVERALL W L T		
Maryland	4	0	0	10	1	0
Duke	4	0	0	7	2	1
Clemson	3	1	0	7	3	0
Wake Forest	3	3	1	5	4	1
North Carolina	3	3	0	3	7	0
South Carolina	1	5	0	3	6	0
North Carolina St.	0	2	1	4	5	1
Virginia	0	4	0	1	9	0

Big 10

	CONF. W L T			OVERALL W L T		
Ohio State	6	0	0	7	2	0
Michigan State	5	1	0	9	1	0
Michigan	5	2	0	7	2	0
Purdue	4	2	1	5	3	1
Illinois	3	3	1	5	3	1
Wisconsin	3	4	0	4	5	0
Iowa	2	3	1	3	5	1
Minnesota	2	5	0	3	6	0
Indiana	1	5	0	3	6	0
Northwestern	0	6	1	0	8	1

Big 7

	CONF. W L T			OVERALL W L T		
Oklahoma	6	0	0	11	0	0
Nebraska	5	1	0	5	5	0
Colorado	3	3	0	6	4	0
Kansas State	3	3	0	4	6	0
Kansas	1	4	1	3	6	1
Iowa State	1	4	1	1	7	1
Missouri	1	5	0	1	9	0

Border

	CONF. W L T			OVERALL W L T		
Texas Tech	3	0	1	7	3	1
Arizona State	4	1	0	8	2	1
Hardin-Simmons	3	2	0	5	5	0
Texas-El Paso	3	2	1	6	2	2
Arizona	1	2	1	5	4	1
West Texas State	1	4	1	4	4	1
New Mexico State	0	4	0	3	7	0

MAC

	CONF. W L T			OVERALL W L T		
Miami, Ohio	5	0	0	8	1	0
Bowling Green	4	1	1	7	1	1
Kent State	4	1	1	6	2	1
Ohio U	3	3	0	5	4	0
Toledo	2	4	0	3	5	1
Marshall	1	5	0	3	6	0
Western Michigan	0	5	0	1	7	1

Pacific Coast

	CONF. W L T			OVERALL W L T		
UCLA	6	0	0	9	2	0
Oregon State	5	2	0	6	3	0
Stanford	3	2	1	6	3	1
Oregon	4	3	0	6	4	0
Washington	4	3	1	5	4	1
Southern Cal	3	3	0	6	4	0
California	1	5	1	2	7	1
Washington State	1	5	1	1	7	2
Idaho	0	4	0	2	7	0

SEC

	CONF. W L T			OVERALL W L T		
Mississippi	5	1	0	10	1	0
Auburn	5	1	1	8	2	1
Georgia Tech	4	1	1	9	1	1
Tennessee	3	2	1	6	3	1
Vanderbilt	4	3	0	8	3	0
Mississippi State	4	4	0	6	4	0
Kentucky	3	3	1	6	3	1
Tulane	3	3	1	5	4	1
LSU	2	3	1	3	5	2
Florida	3	5	0	4	6	0
Georgia	2	5	0	4	6	0
Alabama	0	7	0	0	10	0

Skyline

	CONF. W L T			OVERALL W L T		
Colorado State	6	1	0	8	2	0
Utah	4	1	0	6	3	0
Denver	5	2	0	8	2	0
Wyoming	5	2	0	8	3	0
Utah State	3	4	0	4	6	0
Montana	2	4	0	3	7	0
New Mexico	1	5	0	2	8	0
Brigham Young	0	7	0	1	9	0

SWC

	CONF. W L T			OVERALL W L T		
TCU	5	1	0	9	2	0
Texas A&M	4	1	1	7	2	1
Texas	4	2	0	5	5	0
Arkansas	3	2	1	5	4	1
Baylor	2	4	0	5	5	0
SMU	2	4	0	4	6	0
Rice	0	6	0	2	7	1

Independents

	OVERALL W L T		
Notre Dame	8	2	0
Princeton	7	2	0
Yale	7	2	0
Navy	6	2	1
Boston College	5	2	1
Army	6	3	0
Miami, Fla.	6	3	0
Pittsburgh	7	4	0
Syracuse	5	3	0
Penn State	5	4	0
Cornell	5	4	0
North Texas	5	4	1
Florida State	5	5	0
Air Force	4	4	0
Harvard	3	4	1
Rutgers	3	5	0
Dartmouth	3	6	0
Memphis	2	7	0
Brown	2	7	0
Columbia	1	8	0
Pennsylvania	0	9	0

BOWL GAMES

DATE	GAME	SCORE
D31	Gator	Vanderbilt 25, Auburn 13
J2	Tangerine	Juniata 6, Missouri Valley 6
J2	Rose	Michigan State 17, UCLA 14
J2	Cotton	Mississippi 14, TCU 13
J2	Sugar	Georgia Tech 7, Pittsburgh 0
J2	Orange	Oklahoma 20, Maryland 6
J2	Sun	Wyoming 21, Texas Tech 14

1955 NCAA Major College Statistical Leaders

Individual Leaders

Passing/Completions

		G	ATT	COM	PCT	INT	I%	YDS	YPA	TD	TD%	COM.PG
1	George Welsh, Navy	9	150	94	62.7	6	4.0	1319	8.8	8	5.3	10.4
2	Claude Benham, Columbia	9	188	89	47.3	15	8.0	999	5.3	7	3.7	9.9
3	Len Dawson, Purdue	9	155	87	56.1	14	9.0	1005	6.5	7	4.5	9.7
4	John Brodie, Stanford	10	133	76	57.1	7	5.3	1024	7.7	5	3.8	7.6
5	Bill Beagle, Dartmouth	9	155	75	48.4	12	7.7	812	5.2	6	3.9	8.3
6	Ken Ford, Hardin-Simmons	10	135	73	54.1	10	7.4	854	6.3	8	5.9	7.3
7	James Haluska, Wisconsin	9	132	71	53.8	10	7.6	1036	7.8	6	4.6	7.9
8	Nick Consoles, Wake Forest	10	123	66	53.7	8	6.5	787	6.4	6	4.9	6.6
9	Joe Clements, Texas	10	128	65	50.8	13	10.2	818	6.4	6	4.7	6.5
10	John Roach, SMU	10	141	64	45.4	14	9.9	907	6.4	6	4.3	6.4

All-Purpose Yards

		G	RUSH	REC	INT	PR	KR	YDS	YPG
1	Jim Swink, TCU	10	1283	111	46	64	198	1702	170.2

Rushing/Yards

		G	ATT	YDS	AVG	YPG
1	Art Luppino, Arizona	10	209	1313	6.3	131.3
2	Jim Swink, TCU	10	157	1283	8.2	128.3
3	Howard Cassady, Ohio State	9	161	958	6.0	106.4
4	Fob James, Auburn	10	123	879	7.1	87.9
5	Sam Brown, UCLA	10	130	829	6.4	82.9
6	Bob Moss, West Virginia	10	98	807	8.2	80.7
7	Joel Wells, Clemson	10	135	782	5.8	78.2
8	Bob Pascal, Duke	10	156	750	4.8	75.0
9	James Bakhtiar, Virginia	10	158	733	4.6	73.3
10	Jim Shanley, Oregon	10	100	711	7.1	71.1

Rushing/Yards Per Carry

		G	ATT	YDS	YPC
1	Bob Moss, West Virginia	10	98	807	8.2
2	Jim Swink, TCU	10	157	1283	8.2
3	Fob James, Auburn	10	123	879	7.1
4	Jim Shanley, Oregon	10	100	711	7.1
5	Tommy McDonald, Oklahoma	10	103	702	6.8
6	Sam Brown, UCLA	10	130	829	6.4
7	Art Luppino, Arizona	10	209	1313	6.3
8	Credell Green, Washington	10	108	652	6.0
9	Howard Cassady, Ohio State	9	161	958	6.0
10	Joel Wells, Clemson	10	135	782	5.8

*-Based on top 20 rushers

Receiving/Receptions

		G	REC	YDS	TD	YPR	YPG	RPG
1	Harold Burnine, Missouri	10	44	594	2	13.5	59.4	4.4
2	John Bredice, Boston U.	8	35	468	4	13.4	58.5	4.4
3	Bill Barnes, Wake Forest	10	31	349	0	11.3	34.9	3.1
4	Ron Beagle, Navy	9	30	451	4	15.0	50.1	3.3
5	Terry Hurley, Montana	10	25	431	2	17.2	43.1	2.5
6	Jim Orr, Georgia	10	24	443	3	18.5	44.3	2.4
6	Gary Sanders, Colorado State	10	24	351	3	14.6	35.1	2.4
6	Monte Pascoe, Dartmouth	9	24	331	3	13.8	36.8	2.7
6	Charles Massegee, Hardin-Simmons	10	24	321	4	13.4	32.1	2.4
6	George Seitz, Columbia	9	24	286	1	11.9	31.8	2.7

Punting

		PUNT	YDS	AVG
1	Don Chandler, Florida	22	975	44.3
2	Earl Morrall, Michigan State	22	944	42.9
3	Ted Rohde, Kansas	20	846	42.3
4	William Schmitt, Pittsburgh	22	931	42.3
5	Kelvin Kleber, Minnesota	32	1347	42.1
6	Ray Westfall, Oregon State	30	1254	41.8
7	Homer Jenkins, Colorado	32	1306	40.8
8	Clarence McCluskey, Arizona	33	1340	40.6
9	Lou Mele, Utah	31	1259	40.6
10	Bobby Wolfenden, Virginia Tech	29	1157	39.9

Punt Returns/Yards

		PR	YDS	AVG
1	Mike Sommer, George Washington	24	330	13.8
2	Jon Arnett, Southern Cal	16	282	17.6
3	Jackie Simpson, Florida	17	267	15.7
4	Ron Lind, Drake	12	253	21.1
5	John Majors, Tennessee	21	234	11.1
6	Terry Barr, Michigan	15	222	14.8
7	Charles Horton, Vanderbilt	21	220	10.5
8	Dewey Tompkins, Pacific	14	210	15.0
9	Howard Cassady, Ohio State	17	205	12.1
10	Tommy McDonald, Oklahoma	10	199	19.9

Kickoff Returns/Yards

		KR	YDS	AVG
1	Sam Woolwine, VMI	22	471	21.4
2	Jon Arnett, Southern Cal	15	417	27.8
3	Ron Lind, Drake	19	392	20.6
4	Carl Brazell, South Carolina	12	378	31.5
5	Lee Hermsen, Marquette	16	372	23.3
6	Billy Odom, Florida State	13	358	27.5
7	Walter Fondren, Texas	15	341	22.7
8	Jim Brown, Syracuse	10	320	32.0
9	Rex Fischer, Nebraska	16	316	19.8
10	Howard Cassady, Ohio State	10	313	31.3

Scoring

		TDS	XPT	FG	PTS
1	Jim Swink, TCU	20	5	0	125
2	Jon Arnett, Southern Cal	15	18	0	108
3	Tommy McDonald, Oklahoma	16	0	0	96
3	Ed Vereb, Maryland	16	0	0	96
3	Art Luppino, Arizona	13	18	0	96
6	Howard Cassady, Ohio State	15	0	0	90
7	Paige Cothren, Mississippi	6	20	6	74
8	Charles Horton, Vanderbilt	12	1	0	73
9	Sam Brown, UCLA	9	15	0	69
10	Jack Morris, Oregon	8	19	0	67

Interceptions

		INT	YDS
1	Sam Wesley, Oregon State	7	61
2	Milton Campbell, Indiana	6	111
2	Dale Boyd, Duke	6	88
2	Dick James, Oregon	6	68
5	Tony Teresa, San Jose State	5	112
5	Bill Barnes, Wake Forest	5	99
5	Lou Mele, Utah	5	95
5	Claude Benham, Columbia	5	71
5	Paul Hornung, Notre Dame	5	59
5	Jerry Curtright, Missouri	5	47

Team Leaders

Rushing Offense

		G	ATT	YDS	AVG	YPG
1	Oklahoma	10	661	3289	5.0	328.9
2	TCU	10	555	2857	5.1	285.7
3	Army	9	461	2555	5.5	283.9
4	Ohio State	9	508	2504	4.9	278.2
5	Notre Dame	10	601	2727	4.5	272.7
6	West Virginia	10	489	2639	5.4	263.9
7	Oregon	10	513	2527	4.9	252.7
8	Wichita State	10	505	2484	4.9	248.4
9	Miami, Fla.	9	467	2201	4.7	244.6
10	Auburn	10	468	2413	5.2	241.3

Passing Offense/YPG

		G	ATT	COM	INT	PCT	YDS	YPA	TD	YPG	I%	YPC
1	Navy	9	195	116	8	59.5	1666	8.5	13	185.1	4.1	14.4
2	Stanford	10	244	130	15	53.3	1605	6.6	11	160.5	6.1	12.3
3	Hardin-Simmons	10	244	132	15	54.1	1517	6.2	15	151.7	6.1	11.5
4	Denver	10	160	80	11	50.0	1465	9.2	19	146.5	6.9	18.3
5	Wisconsin	9	171	84	13	49.1	1309	7.7	11	145.4	7.6	15.6
6	Drake	8	135	68	9	50.4	1093	8.1	11	136.6	6.7	16.1
7	Purdue	9	191	104	18	54.5	1213	6.4	8	134.8	9.4	11.7
8	Texas	10	209	96	20	45.9	1291	6.2	11	129.1	9.6	13.4
9	Wake Forest	10	180	92	15	51.1	1291	7.2	9	129.1	8.3	14.0
10	Michigan State	9	98	52	9	53.1	1124	11.5	7	124.9	9.2	21.6

Total Offense

		G	P	YDS	AVG	YPG
1	Oklahoma	10	756	4107	5.4	410.7
2	West Virginia	10	642	3845	6.0	384.5
3	Denver	10	606	3689	6.1	368.9
4	Michigan State	9	521	3280	6.3	364.4
5	Navy	9	625	3227	5.2	358.6
6	Notre Dame	10	722	3573	4.9	357.3
7	Stanford	10	737	3551	4.8	355.1
8	TCU	10	637	3531	5.5	353.1
9	Miami, Fla.	9	562	3104	5.5	344.9
10	Mississippi	10	609	3396	5.6	339.6

Rushing Defense

		G	ATT	YDS	AVG	YPG
1	Maryland	10	342	759	2.2	75.9
2	Army	9	340	732	2.2	81.3
3	Holy Cross	10	374	951	2.5	95.1
4	Auburn	10	405	1078	2.7	107.8
5	Wichita State	10	428	1131	2.6	113.1
6	Oklahoma	10	426	1136	2.7	113.6
7	Boston College	8	268	940	3.5	117.5
8	West Virginia	10	406	1267	3.1	126.7
9	Colgate	9	358	1154	3.2	128.2
10	Vanderbilt	10	466	1298	2.8	129.8

Passing Defense

		G	ATT	COM	PCT	YPC	INT	I%	YDS	YPA	TD	YPG
1	Florida	10	92	37	40.2	11.4	3	3.3	420	4.6	2	42.0
2	Navy	9	101	36	35.6	10.8	8	7.9	387	3.8	0	43.0
3	Michigan	9	86	28	32.6	14.4	10	11.6	402	4.7	4	44.7
4	Nebraska	10	103	28	27.2	16.0	10	9.7	449	4.4	3	44.9
5	George Washington	9	107	36	33.6	11.6	18	16.8	417	3.9	2	46.3
6	Kentucky	10	96	36	37.5	13.3	13	13.5	479	5.0	4	47.9
7	Detroit	9	93	34	36.6	13.9	5	5.4	474	5.1	3	52.7
8	Harvard	8	89	37	41.6	12.4	6	6.7	460	5.2	4	57.5
9	Indiana	9	93	37	39.8	14.4	13	14.0	533	5.7	6	59.2
10	Washington	10	119	55	46.2	10.9	14	11.8	600	5.0	3	60.0

Total Defense

		G	P	YDS	AVG	YPG
1	Army	9	499	1446	2.9	160.7
2	Maryland	10	537	1691	3.1	169.1
3	Navy	9	481	1635	3.4	181.7
4	Auburn	10	531	1832	3.5	183.2
5	Holy Cross	10	539	1835	3.4	183.5
6	Oklahoma	10	578	1864	3.2	186.4
7	Detroit	9	484	1747	3.6	194.1
8	West Virginia	10	560	1948	3.5	194.8
9	George Washington	9	527	1779	3.4	197.7
10	Georgia Tech	10	516	1999	3.9	199.9

Scoring Offense

		G	PTS	AVG
1	Oklahoma	10	365	36.5

Scoring Defense

		G	PTS	AVG
1	Georgia Tech	10	46	4.6
2	Oklahoma	10	54	5.4

1956 POLL PROGRESSION

Pre-Season 1956 — Sept. 22 Games

AP	Team	Record	Result
1	Oklahoma	0-0-0	bye week
2	Michigan State	0-0-0	bye week
3	Notre Dame	0-0-0	lost to SMU 13-19
4	Georgia Tech	0-0-0	beat Kentucky 14-6
5	Ohio State	0-0-0	bye week
6	Maryland	0-0-0	lost to Syracuse 12-26
7	TCU	0-0-0	beat Kansas 32-0
8	Michigan	0-0-0	bye week
9	Texas A&M	0-0-0	beat Villanova 19-0
10	Pittsburgh	0-0-0	beat West Virginia 14-13
11	Army	0-0-0	bye week
12	Tennessee	0-0-0	bye week
13	Mississippi	0-0-0	beat North Texas 45-0
14	Stanford	0-0-0	beat Washington State 40-26
15	Southern Cal	0-0-0	beat Texas 44-20
16	Duke	0-0-0	lost to South Carolina 0-7
17	UCLA	0-0-0	beat Utah 13-7
18	Miami, Fla.	0-0-0	bye week
19	Yale	0-0-0	bye week
20	Illinois	0-0-0	bye week

September 24 Poll — Sept. 29 Games

AP	Team	Record	Result
1	Oklahoma	0-0-0	beat North Carolina 36-0
2	Georgia Tech	1-0-0	beat #5 SMU 9-7
3	Michigan State	0-0-0	beat #12 Stanford 21-7
4	TCU	1-0-0	bye week
5	SMU	1-0-0	lost to #2 Georgia Tech 7-9
6	Southern Cal	1-0-0	beat Oregon State 21-13
7	Syracuse	1-0-0	lost to #10 Pittsburgh 7-14
8	Ohio State	0-0-0	beat Nebraska 34-7
9	Mississippi	1-0-0	beat Kentucky 37-7
10	Pittsburgh	0-0-0	beat #7 Syracuse 14-7
11	Texas A&M	1-0-0	beat LSU 9-6
12	Stanford	1-0-0	lost to #3 Michigan State 7-21
13	Michigan	0-0-0	beat UCLA 42-13
14	Notre Dame	0-1-0	bye week
15	Vanderbilt	1-0-0	beat U.T. Chattanooga 46-7
16	Army	0-0-0	beat VMI 32-12
17	South Carolina	2-0-0	lost to Miami, Fla. 6-14
18	Oregon	1-0-0	beat Idaho 21-14
19	Florida	1-0-0	tied Clemson 20-20
20	North Carolina St.	1-0-0	lost to Virginia Tech 6-35

October 1 Poll — Oct. 6 Games

UP	AP	Team	Record	Result
1	1	Oklahoma	1-0-0	beat Kansas State 66-0
2	2	Michigan State	1-0-0	beat #5 Michigan 9-0
3	3	Georgia Tech	2-0-0	bye week
5	4	Ohio State	1-0-0	beat Stanford 32-20
4	5	Michigan	1-0-0	lost to #2 Michigan State 0-9
8	6	Mississippi	2-0-0	beat Houston 14-0
7	7	Pittsburgh	2-0-0	lost to California 0-14
6	8	TCU	1-0-0	beat Arkansas 41-6
10	9	Tennessee	1-0-0	beat Duke 33-20
9	10	Southern Cal	2-0-0	beat Wisconsin 13-6
12	11	Texas A&M	2-0-0	beat Texas Tech 40-7
13	12	SMU	1-1-0	beat Missouri 33-27
17	13	Illinois	1-0-0	lost to Washington 13-28
18	14	Miami, Fla.	1-0-0	beat Boston College 27-6
11	15	Army	1-0-0	beat Penn State 14-7
16	16	Baylor	2-0-0	beat Maryland 14-0
17		Syracuse	1-1-0	bye week
	18	Vanderbilt	2-0-0	beat Alabama 32-7
18	20	Iowa	1-0-0	beat Oregon State 14-13
14		Navy	1-0-0	beat Cornell 14-0
15		Minnesota	1-0-0	beat Purdue 21-14
	18	Notre Dame	0-1-0	beat Indiana 20-6

October 8 Poll — Oct. 13 Games

UP	AP	Team	Record	Result
1	1	Oklahoma	2-0-0	beat Texas 45-0
2	2	Michigan State	2-0-0	beat Indiana 53-6
5	3	Georgia Tech	2-0-0	beat LSU 39-7
3	4	TCU	2-0-0	beat Alabama 23-6
4	5	Ohio State	2-0-0	beat Illinois 26-6
6	6	Tennessee	2-0-0	beat U.T. Chattanooga 42-20
8	7	Mississippi	3-0-0	beat #13 Vanderbilt 16-0
7	8	Southern Cal	3-0-0	bye week
9	9	Texas A&M	3-0-0	tied Houston 14-14
12	10	Baylor	3-0-0	beat Arkansas 14-7
16	11	Miami, Fla.	2-0-0	beat Maryland 13-6
10	12	Michigan	1-1-0	beat #15 Army 48-14
	13	Vanderbilt	3-0-0	lost to #7 Mississippi 0-16
16	14	Navy	2-0-0	lost to Tulane 6-21
11	15	Army	2-0-0	lost to #12 Michigan 14-48
16		George Washington	3-0-0	tied Boston U. 20-20
13	17	Minnesota	2-0-0	tied Northwestern 0-0
15	18	Notre Dame	1-1-0	lost to Purdue 14-28
14	19	SMU	2-1-0	lost to Duke 6-14
	20	South Carolina	3-1-0	beat Virginia 27-13
20		West Virginia	2-1-0	lost to Syracuse 20-27
18		Iowa	2-0-0	beat Wisconsin 13-7
19		Stanford	1-2-0	beat San Jose State 40-20
20		Pittsburgh	2-1-0	bye week

October 15 Poll — Oct. 20 Games

UP	AP	Team	Record	Result
1	1	Oklahoma	3-0-0	beat Kansas 34-12
2	2	Michigan State	3-0-0	beat Notre Dame 47-14
3	3	Georgia Tech	3-0-0	beat Auburn 28-7
5	4	TCU	3-0-0	lost to #14 Texas A&M 6-7
4	5	Ohio State	3-0-0	lost to Penn State 6-7
8	6	Mississippi	4-0-0	lost to #19 Tulane 3-10
6	7	Tennessee	3-0-0	beat Alabama 24-0
7	8	Michigan	2-1-0	beat Northwestern 34-20
9	9	Southern Cal	3-0-0	beat Washington 35-7
10	10	Baylor	4-0-0	bye week
11	11	Miami, Fla.	3-0-0	tied Georgia 7-7
15	12	Iowa	3-0-0	beat Hawaii 34-0
14	13	Syracuse	2-1-0	beat Army 7-0
14	14	Texas A&M	3-0-1	beat #4 TCU 7-6
18	15	Clemson	3-0-1	bye week
16	16	Pittsburgh	2-1-0	beat Duke 27-14
17	17	Purdue	2-1-0	tied Wisconsin 6-6
	18	Virginia Tech	4-1-0	beat Richmond 46-14
	19	Tulane	3-1-0	beat #6 Mississippi 10-3
	20	South Carolina	4-1-0	bye week
17		Stanford	2-2-0	beat Oregon 21-7
18		Clemson	3-0-1	bye week
18		Washington	3-1-0	lost to #9 Southern Cal 7-35

October 22 Poll — Oct. 27 Games

UP	AP	Team	Record	Result
1	1	Michigan State	4-0-0	lost to Illinois 13-20
2	2	Oklahoma	4-0-0	beat Notre Dame 40-0
3	3	Georgia Tech	4-0-0	beat #15 Tulane 40-0
4	4	Tennessee	4-0-0	beat Maryland 34-7
5	5	Michigan	3-1-0	lost to Minnesota 0-7
6	6	Southern Cal	4-0-0	lost to Stanford 19-27
7	7	Texas A&M	4-0-1	beat #8 Baylor 19-13
9	8	Baylor	4-0-0	lost to #7 Texas A&M 13-19
8	9	Ohio State	3-1-0	beat Wisconsin 21-0
16	10	Mississippi	4-1-0	lost to Arkansas 0-14
9	11	TCU	3-1-0	lost to #19 Miami, Fla. 0-14
15	12	Iowa	4-0-0	beat Purdue 21-20
11	13	Pittsburgh	3-1-0	beat Oregon 14-7
12	14	Syracuse	3-1-0	beat Boston U. 21-7
13	15	Tulane	4-1-0	lost to #3 Georgia Tech 0-40
	16	Virginia Tech	5-1-0	beat Virginia 14-7
	17	George Washington	4-0-1	beat William & Mary 16-14
17	18	Penn State	3-1-0	beat West Virginia 16-6
19	19	Miami, Fla.	3-0-1	beat #11 TCU 14-0
20	20	Clemson	3-0-1	beat South Carolina 7-0
14		Minnesota	3-0-1	beat #5 Michigan 20-7
18		Stanford	3-2-0	beat #6 Southern Cal 27-19

October 29 Poll — Nov. 3 Games

UP	AP	Team	Record	Result
1	1	Oklahoma	5-0-0	beat Colorado 27-19
2	2	Georgia Tech	5-0-0	beat Duke 7-0
3	3	Tennessee	5-0-0	beat North Carolina 20-0
4	4	Michigan State	4-1-0	beat Wisconsin 33-0
5	5	Texas A&M	5-0-1	beat Arkansas 27-0
6	6	Ohio State	4-1-0	beat Northwestern 6-2
8	7	Iowa	5-0-0	lost to #17 Michigan 14-17
7	8	Minnesota	4-0-1	beat #11 Pittsburgh 9-6
12	9	Miami, Fla.	4-0-1	beat Florida State 20-7
9	10	Stanford	4-2-0	lost to UCLA 13-14
10	11	Pittsburgh	4-1-0	lost to #8 Minnesota 6-9
11	12	Penn State	4-1-0	lost to #17 Syracuse 9-13
17	13	Clemson	4-0-1	beat #16 Virginia Tech 21-6
	14	George Washington	5-0-1	lost to West Virginia 0-14
16	15	Baylor	4-1-0	lost to TCU 6-7
	16	Virginia Tech	6-1-0	lost to #13 Clemson 6-21
13	17	Michigan	3-2-0	beat #7 Iowa 17-14
17	18	Oregon State	4-2-0	beat Washington 28-20
15	19	Syracuse	4-1-0	beat #12 Penn State 13-9
14	20	Southern Cal	5-0-1	beat Washington State 28-12
19		Princeton	5-0-0	beat Brown 21-7
20		Colorado	5-1-0	lost to #1 Oklahoma 19-27

November 5 Poll — Nov. 10 Games

UP	AP	Team	Record	Result
1	1	Oklahoma	6-0-0	beat Iowa State 44-0
2	2	Georgia Tech	6-0-0	lost to #3 Tennessee 0-6
3	3	Tennessee	6-0-0	beat #2 Georgia Tech 6-0
4	4	Michigan State	5-1-0	beat Purdue 12-9
5	5	Texas A&M	6-0-1	beat SMU 33-7
6	6	Minnesota	5-0-1	lost to #15 Iowa 0-7
7	7	Ohio State	5-1-0	beat Indiana 35-14
8	8	Miami, Fla.	5-1-0	bye week
11	9	Syracuse	5-1-0	beat Holy Cross 41-20
9	10	Michigan	4-2-0	beat Illinois 17-7
15	11	Purdue	5-0-1	tied Maryland 6-6
12	12	Navy	5-1-0	tied Duke 7-7
18	13	Florida	5-1-1	beat Georgia 28-0
14	14	Oregon State	5-2-0	beat Stanford 20-19
10	15	Iowa	5-1-0	beat #6 Minnesota 7-0
15	16	Southern Cal	5-1-0	beat California 20-7
17	17	TCU	4-2-0	lost to Texas Tech 7-21
	18	Colorado	5-2-0	tied Missouri 14-14
	19	UCLA	5-2-0	beat Washington 13-9
15	20	Pittsburgh	4-2-0	beat Notre Dame 26-13
	20	Stanford	4-3-0	lost to Oregon State 19-20
19		Army	4-2-0	beat William & Mary 34-6
19		Mississippi	5-2-0	beat Memphis 26-0

November 12 Poll — Nov. 17 Games

UP	AP	Team	Record	Result
2	1	Tennessee	7-0-0	beat #19 Mississippi 27-7
1	2	Oklahoma	7-0-0	beat Missouri 67-14
4	3	Michigan State	6-1-0	lost to #17 Minnesota 13-14
5	4	Georgia Tech	6-1-0	beat Alabama 27-0
3	5	Texas A&M	7-0-1	beat Rice 21-7
6	6	Ohio State	6-1-0	beat #7 Iowa 0-6
7	7	Iowa	6-1-0	beat #6 Ohio State 6-0
10	8	Miami, Fla.	5-0-1	beat #13 Clemson 21-0
11	9	Syracuse	6-1-0	beat Colgate 61-7
9	10	Michigan	5-2-0	beat Indiana 49-26
8	11	Oregon State	6-2-0	beat Idaho 14-10
14	12	Florida	6-1-1	bye week
	13	Clemson	5-0-2	lost to #8 Miami, Fla. 0-21
12	14	Southern Cal	6-1-0	lost to Oregon 0-7
13	15	Navy	5-1-1	beat Virginia 34-0
16	16	Pittsburgh	5-2-0	beat Army 20-7
15	17	Minnesota	5-2-0	beat #3 Michigan State 14-13
	18	George Washington	6-1-1	beat Citadel 20-0
	19	Mississippi	6-2-0	lost to #1 Tennessee 7-27
17	20	Princeton	7-0-0	lost to Yale 20-42
18		Yale	6-1-0	beat #20 Princeton 42-20
19		West Virginia	5-3-0	beat Furman 7-0
19		Army	5-2-0	lost to #16 Pittsburgh 7-20

UP	AP	NOVEMBER 19 POLL		NOV. 24 GAMES
1	1	Oklahoma	8-0-0	beat Nebraska 54-6
2	2	Tennessee	8-0-0	beat Kentucky 20-7
4	3	Iowa	7-1-0	beat Notre Dame 48-0
3	4	Texas A&M	8-0-1	bye week
5	5	Georgia Tech	7-1-0	beat # 13 Florida 28-0
6	6	Miami, Fla.	6-0-1	beat West Virginia 18-0
7	7	Minnesota	6-1-1	tied Wisconsin 13-13
10	8	Syracuse	7-1-0	regular season complete
10	9	Michigan	6-2-0	beat # 12 Ohio State 19-0
8	10	Michigan State	6-2-0	beat Kansas State 38-17
9	11	Oregon State	7-2-0	tied Oregon 14-14
13	12	Ohio State	6-2-0	lost to # 9 Michigan 0-19
15	13	Florida	6-1-1	lost to # 5 Georgia Tech 0-28
12	14	Pittsburgh	6-2-0	tied Penn State 7-7
14	15	Navy	6-1-1	bye week
19	16	Baylor	6-2-0	beat SMU 26-0
	17	George Washington	7-1-1	regular season complete
17	18	TCU	5-3-0	beat Rice 20-17
18	19	Wyoming	10-0-0	regular season complete
	20	Colorado	6-2-1	beat Arizona 38-7
16		Yale	7-1-0	beat Harvard 42-14
19		Southern Cal	6-2-0	beat UCLA 10-7
19		Purdue	2-4-2	beat Indiana 39-20
19		Penn State	6-2-0	tied #14 Pittsburgh 7-7

UP	AP	NOVEMBER 26 POLL		DEC 1 GAMES
1	1	Oklahoma	9-0-0	beat Oklahoma State 53-0
2	2	Tennessee	9-0-0	beat Vanderbilt 27-7
3	3	Iowa	8-1-0	regular season complete
5	4	Georgia Tech	8-1-0	beat Georgia 35-0
4	5	Texas A&M	8-0-1	beat Texas 34-21
6	6	Miami, Fla.	7-0-1	beat # 18 Florida 20-7
7	7	Michigan	7-2-0	regular season complete
9	8	Syracuse	7-1-0	
8	9	Michigan State	7-2-0	regular season complete
10	10	Minnesota	6-1-2	regular season complete
11	11	Oregon State	7-2-1	regular season complete
12	12	Pittsburgh	6-2-1	regular season complete
16	13	Navy	6-1-1	tied Army 7-7
14	14	TCU	6-3-0	beat SMU 21-6
12	15	Baylor	7-2-0	beat Rice 46-13
	16	George Washington	7-1-1	
15	17	Southern Cal	7-2-0	beat Notre Dame 28-20
	18	Florida	6-2-1	lost to # 6 Miami, Fla. 7-20
	19	Colorado	7-2-1	regular season complete
	20	Ohio State	6-3-0	regular season complete
17		Yale	8-1-0	regular season complete
18		Wyoming	10-0-0	regular season complete
19		Duke	5-4-1	regular season complete
19		Texas-El Paso	9-1-0	regular season complete

UP	AP	DECEMBER 3 FINAL POLL	RECORD	BOWL BID	DATE	BOWL RESULT	RB	RECORD
1	1	Oklahoma	10-0-0				1	10-0-0
2	2	Tennessee	10-0-0	Sugar Bowl	J1	lost to # 11 Baylor 7-13	2	10-1-0
3	3	Iowa	8-1-0	Rose Bowl	J1	beat # 10 Oregon State 35-19	5	9-1-0
4	4	Georgia Tech	9-1-0	Gator Bowl	D29	beat # 13 Pittsburgh 21-14	3	10-1-0
5	5	Texas A&M	9-0-1				4	9-0-1
6	6	Miami, Fla.	8-0-1				6	8-1-1
7	7	Michigan	7-2-0				8	7-2-0
8	8	Syracuse	7-1-0	Cotton Bowl	J1	lost to # 14 TCU 27-28	13	7-2-0
10	9	Michigan State	7-2-0				7	7-2-0
13	10	Oregon State	7-2-1	Rose Bowl	J1	lost to # 3 Iowa 19-35	39	7-3-1
11	11	Baylor	8-2-0	Sugar Bowl	J1	beat # 2 Tennessee 13-7	9	9-2-0
9	12	Minnesota	6-1-2				10	6-1-2
12	13	Pittsburgh	6-2-1	Gator Bowl	D29	lost to # 4 Georgia Tech 14-21	18	7-3-1
14	14	TCU	7-3-0	Cotton Bowl	J1	beat # 8 Syracuse 28-27	12	8-3-0
	15	Ohio State	6-3-0				16	6-3-0
19	16	Navy	6-1-2				19	6-1-2
	17	George Washington	7-1-1	Sun Bowl	J1	beat Texas El-Paso 13-0	26	8-1-1
15	18	Southern Cal	8-2-0				11	8-2-0
	19	Clemson	7-1-2	Orange Bowl	J1	lost to # 20 Colorado 21-27	30	7-2-2
18	20	Colorado	7-2-1	Orange Bowl	J1	beat # 19 Clemson 27-21	29	8-2-1
16		Wyoming	10-0-0				15	10-0-0
17		Yale	8-1-0				23	8-1-0
20		Duke	5-4-1				33	5-4-1

1956

Consensus All-Americans

POS	Name	HT	WT	School	AA	AP	FC	FW	IN	NE	SN
B	Jim Brown	6-2	212	Syracuse	•	•	•	•	•	•	•
B	John Majors	5-10	162	Tennessee	•	•	•	•		•	•
B	Tommy McDonald	5-9	169	Oklahoma	•	•	•	•	•	•	•
B	John Brodie	6-1	190	Stanford		•	•	•	•	•	
E	Joe Walton	5-11	205	Pittsburgh	•	•	•	•	•	•	•
E	Ron Kramer	6-3	220	Michigan	•	•	•	•	•	•	•
T	John Witte	6-2	232	Oregon State	•	•	•	•	•	•	
T	Lou Michaels	6-2	229	Kentucky		•	•		•		•
G	Jim Parker	6-2	251	Ohio State	•	•	•	•	•	•	•
G	Bill Glass	6-4	220	Baylor	•	•	•	•		•	•
C	Jerry Tubbs	6-2	205	Oklahoma	•	•	•	•	•	•	•

	Others receiving first-team honors							
B	Bill Barnes	Wake Forest				•		
B	Jim Crawford	Wyoming				•		
B	Paul Hornung	Notre Dame				•		
B	Jack Pardee	Texas A&M				•		
B	Don Bosseler	Miami, Fla.		•				
E	Buddy Cruze	Tennessee				•		
E	Bill Steiger	Washington State				•		
T	Norman Hamilton	TCU				•		
T	Bob Hobert	Minnesota				•		
T	Alex Karras	Iowa		•		•		
T	Charles Krueger	Texas A&M			•			
T	Paul Wiggin	Stanford					•	
T	Ed Gray	Oklahoma					•	
G	John Barrow	Florida				•		
G	Sam Valentine	Penn State				•		
C	Don Stephenson	Georgia Tech				•		

Heisman Trophy Voting

	PLAYER	POS	SCHOOL	1ST	2ND	3RD	TOTAL
1	Paul Hornung	QB	Notre Dame	197	162	151	1066
2	John Majors	RB	Tennessee	172	171	136	994
3	Tommy McDonald	HB	Oklahoma	205	122	114	973
4	Jerry Tubbs	C	Oklahoma	121	137	87	724
5	Jim Brown	HB	Syracuse	118	68	71	561
6	Ron Kramer	E	Michigan	70	104	100	518
7	John Brodie	QB	Stanford	39	52	60	281
8	Jim Parker	G	Ohio State	34	51	44	248
9	Kenny Ploen	QB	Iowa	36	10	22	150
10	Jim Arnett	HB	Southern Cal	20	25	18	128

Award Winners

PLAYER	POS	SCHOOL	AWARD NAME
Tommy McDonald	HB	Oklahoma	Maxwell
Jim Parker	G	Ohio State	Outland

Conference Standings

ACC

	Conf. W L T			Overall W L T		
Clemson	4	0	1	7	2	2
Duke	4	1	0	5	4	1
South Carolina	5	2	0	7	3	0
Maryland	2	2	1	2	7	1
North Carolina	2	3	1	2	7	1
North Carolina St.	2	4	0	3	7	0
Wake Forest	1	5	1	2	5	3
Virginia	1	4	0	3	7	0

Big 10

	Conf. W L T			Overall W L T		
Iowa	5	1	0	9	1	0
Michigan	5	2	0	7	2	0
Minnesota	4	1	2	6	1	2
Michigan State	4	2	0	7	2	0
Ohio State	4	2	0	6	3	0
Northwestern	3	3	1	4	4	1
Purdue	1	4	2	3	4	2
Illinois	1	4	2	2	5	2
Wisconsin	0	4	3	1	5	3
Indiana	1	5	0	3	6	0

Big 7

	Conf. W L T			Overall W L T		
Oklahoma	6	0	0	10	0	0
Colorado	4	1	1	8	2	1
Missouri	3	2	1	4	5	1
Nebraska	3	3	0	4	6	0
Kansas	2	4	0	3	6	1
Kansas State	2	4	0	3	7	0
Iowa State	0	6	0	2	8	0

Border

	Conf. W L T			Overall W L T		
Texas-El Paso	5	0	0	9	2	0
Arizona State	3	1	0	9	1	0
West Texas State	2	2	0	8	2	0
Arizona	1	2	0	4	6	0
Hardin-Simmons	1	3	0	4	6	0
New Mexico State	0	4	0	1	9	0

Ivy League

	Conf. W L T			Overall W L T		
Yale	7	0	0	8	1	0
Princeton	5	2	0	7	2	0
Dartmouth	4	3	0	5	3	1
Pennsylvania	4	3	0	4	5	0
Brown	3	4	0	5	4	0
Columbia	2	5	0	3	6	0
Harvard	2	5	0	2	6	0
Cornell	1	6	0	1	8	0

MAC

	Conf. W L T			Overall W L T		
Bowling Green	5	0	1	8	0	1
Miami, Ohio	4	0	1	7	1	1
Kent State	4	2	0	7	2	0
Marshall	2	4	0	3	6	0
Ohio U	2	4	0	2	7	0
Western Michigan	1	4	0	2	7	0
Toledo	1	5	0	1	7	1

Pacific Coast

	Conf. W L T			Overall W L T		
Oregon State	6	1	1	7	3	1
Southern Cal	5	2	0	8	2	0
UCLA	5	2	0	7	3	0
Washington	4	4	0	5	5	0
Oregon	3	3	2	4	4	2
Stanford	3	4	0	4	6	0
Washington State	2	5	1	3	6	1
California	2	5	0	3	7	0
Idaho	0	4	0	2	7	0

SEC

	Conf. W L T			Overall W L T		
Tennessee	6	0	0	10	1	0
Georgia Tech	7	1	0	10	1	0
Florida	5	2	0	6	3	1
Mississippi	4	2	0	7	3	0
Auburn	4	3	0	7	3	0
Kentucky	4	4	0	6	4	0
Tulane	3	3	0	6	4	0
Vanderbilt	2	5	0	5	5	0
Mississippi State	2	5	0	4	6	0
Alabama	2	5	0	2	7	1
LSU	1	5	0	3	7	0
Georgia	1	6	0	3	6	1

Skyline

	Conf. W L T			Overall W L T		
Wyoming	7	0	0	10	0	0
Utah	5	1	0	5	5	0
Utah State	4	3	0	6	4	0
Denver	4	3	0	6	4	0
Colorado State	2	4	1	2	7	1
New Mexico	2	4	0	4	6	0
Brigham Young	1	5	1	2	7	1
Montana	1	6	0	1	9	0

SWC

	Conf. W L T			Overall W L T		
Texas A&M	6	0	0	9	0	1
TCU	5	1	0	8	3	0
Baylor	4	2	0	9	2	0
Arkansas	3	3	0	6	4	0
SMU	2	4	0	4	6	0
Rice	1	5	0	4	6	0
Texas	0	6	0	1	9	0

Independents

	Overall W L T		
Miami, Fla.	8	1	1
Syracuse	7	2	0
Navy	6	1	2
North Texas	7	2	1
Air Force	6	2	1
Penn State	6	2	1
Pittsburgh	7	3	1
Army	5	3	1
Boston College	5	4	0
Memphis	5	4	1
Florida State	5	4	1
Rutgers	3	7	0
Texas Tech	2	7	1
Notre Dame	2	8	0

Bowl Games

DATE	GAME	SCORE
D29	Gator	Georgia Tech 21, Pittsburgh 14
J1	Tangerine	West Texas State 20, Southern Miss 13
J1	Orange	Colorado 27, Clemson 21
J1	Rose	Iowa 35, Oregon State 19
J1	Sugar	Baylor 13, Tennessee 7
J1	Cotton	TCU 28, Syracuse 27
J1	Sun	George Washington 13, Texas-El Paso 0

1956 NCAA Major College Statistical Leaders

Individual Leaders

PASSING/COMPLETIONS	G	ATT	COM	PCT	INT	I%	YDS	YPA	TD	TD%	COM.PG
1 John Brodie, Stanford	10	240	139	57.9	14	5.8	1633	6.8	12	5.0	13.9
2 Bob Newman, Washington State	10	170	91	53.5	8	4.7	1240	7.3	8	4.7	9.1
3 Bob Reinhart, San Jose State	10	172	90	52.3	5	2.9	1138	6.6	10	5.8	9.0
4 Guy Martin, Colgate	9	170	88	51.8	15	8.8	1100	6.5	9	5.3	9.8
5 Gene Saur, Hardin-Simmons	10	133	78	58.6	10	7.5	968	7.3	8	6.0	7.8
6 Ralph Hunsaker, Arizona	10	148	75	50.7	12	8.1	823	5.6	4	2.7	7.5
7 Joe Clements, Texas	10	151	74	49.0	16	10.6	793	5.3	7	4.6	7.4
8 Tom Flores, Pacific	10	127	73	57.5	8	6.3	1119	8.8	11	8.7	7.3
9 Charlie Arnold, SMU	10	157	71	45.2	14	8.9	964	6.1	8	5.1	7.1
9 Carroll Johnston, Brigham Young	10	167	71	42.5	15	9.0	945	5.7	8	4.8	7.1

ALL-PURPOSE YARDS	G	RUSH	REC	INT	PR	KR	YDS	YPG
1 Jack Hill, Utah State	10	920	215	132	21	403	1691	169.1

RUSHING/YARDS	G	ATT	YDS	AVG	YPG
1 Jim Crawford, Wyoming	10	200	1104	5.5	110.4
2 Bill Barnes, Wake Forest	10	168	1010	6.0	101.0
3 Jim Brown, Syracuse	8	158	986	6.2	123.3
4 Jack Hill, Utah State	10	140	920	6.6	92.0
5 Jim Bakhtiar, Virginia	10	203	879	4.3	87.9
6 Mel Dillard, Purdue	9	193	873	4.5	97.0
7 Tommy McDonald, Oklahoma	10	119	853	7.2	85.3
8 Clendon Thomas, Oklahoma	10	104	817	7.9	81.7
9 Don Clark, Ohio State	9	139	797	5.7	88.6
10 C.R. Roberts, Southern Cal	10	120	775	6.5	77.5

RUSHING/YARDS PER CARRY	G	ATT	YDS	YPC
1 Tommy Lorino, Auburn	10	82	692	8.4
2 Clendon Thomas, Oklahoma	10	104	817	7.9
3 Tommy McDonald, Oklahoma	10	119	853	7.2
4 Bob Mulgado, Arizona State	10	107	721	6.7
5 Jack Hill, Utah State	10	140	920	6.6
6 C.R. Roberts, Southern Cal	10	120	775	6.5
7 Jim Brown, Syracuse	8	158	986	6.2
8 Ed Sutton, North Carolina	10	120	748	6.2
9 Bill Barnes, Wake Forest	10	168	1010	6.0
10 Don Clark, Ohio State	9	139	797	5.7

*-Based on top 20 rushers

RECEIVING/RECEPTIONS	G	REC	YDS	TD	YPR	YPG	RPG
1 Art Powell, San Jose State	10	40	583	5	14.6	58.3	4.0
2 Bill Steiger, Washington State	10	39	607	5	15.6	60.7	3.9
3 Connie Baird, Hardin-Simmons	10	37	455	1	12.3	45.5	3.7
4 Brad Bomba, Indiana	9	31	407	1	13.1	45.2	3.4
5 Larry Aldrich, Idaho	9	30	409	1	13.6	45.4	3.3
5 Charles James, Missouri	10	30	362	3	12.1	36.2	3.0
7 Al Jamison, Colgate	9	29	289	6	10.0	32.1	3.2
8 Paul Camera, Stanford	10	28	350	2	12.5	35.0	2.8
9 Farrell Funston, Pacific	10	27	563	5	20.9	56.3	2.7
9 Don Ellingsen, Washington State	10	27	455	1	16.9	45.5	2.7
9 Johnny Wilson, Denver	10	27	383	4	14.2	38.3	2.7

PUNTING	PUNT	YDS	AVG
1 Kirk Wilson, UCLA	30	1479	49.3
2 Larry Barnes, Colorado State	27	1212	44.9
3 John Majors, Tennessee	26	1118	43.0
4 Boyd Dowler, Colorado	41	1726	42.1
5 Jim Wood, Oklahoma State	34	1421	41.8
6 Ted Rohde, Kansas	26	1082	41.6
7 Ernie Zampese, Southern Cal	27	1112	41.2
8 Jack Hill, Utah State	29	1195	41.2
9 Wally Vale, North Carolina	31	1274	41.1
10 Jerry Lott, New Mexico	33	1346	40.8

PUNT RETURNS/YARDS	PR	YDS	AVG
1 Billy Stacy, Mississippi State	24	290	12.1
2 Ron Lind, Drake	14	268	19.1
3 Phil King, Vanderbilt	20	247	12.4
4 Charlie Sidwell, William & Mary	8	205	25.6
5 Leroy Phelps, Oregon	12	204	17.0
6 Joe Morrison, Cincinnati	6	198	33.0
7 Luther Carr, Washington	12	179	14.9
8 Victor Rabbits, West Virginia	12	177	14.8
9 Jefferson Davis, Georgia	6	176	29.3
9 Jim Shanley, Oregon	10	176	17.6

KICKOFF RETURNS/YARDS	KR	YDS	AVG
1 Sam Woolwine, VMI	18	503	27.9
2 Paul Hornung, Notre Dame	16	496	31.0
3 Charlie Sidwell, William & Mary	20	467	23.4
4 Jack Hill, Utah State	14	403	28.8
5 Lynn White, New Mexico	14	368	26.3
6 Weldon Jackson, Brigham Young	15	358	23.9
7 Art Powell, San Jose State	15	352	23.5
8 Robert Fee, Indiana	15	326	21.7
8 Ron Lind, Drake	15	326	21.7
10 Walter Fondren, Texas	17	325	19.1

SCORING	TDS	XPT	FG	PTS
1 Clendon Thomas, Oklahoma	18	0	0	108
2 Jim Brown, Syracuse	14	22	0	106
3 Jack Hill, Utah State	15	15	0	105
4 Tommy McDonald, Oklahoma	17	0	0	102
5 Jim Crawford, Wyoming	14	12	0	96
6 Bob Kyasky, Army	14	1	0	85
7 John Bayuk, Colorado	11	0	0	66
7 John Call, Colgate	11	0	0	66
9 Dean Derby, Washington	7	18	1	63
10 Hewes Agnew, Princeton	10	1	0	61

INTERCEPTIONS	INT	YDS
1 Jack Hill, Utah State	7	132
1 Milt Plum, Penn State	7	72
3 John Bookman, Miami, Fla.	6	137
3 Tommy McDonald, Oklahoma	6	136
3 Ernie Zampese, Southern Cal	6	98
3 James Ridlon, Syracuse	6	70
7 Joe Brodsky, Florida	5	244
7 Darrell Roberts, California	5	81
7 Ronnie Morris, Tulsa	5	0

Team Leaders

RUSHING OFFENSE	G	ATT	YDS	AVG	YPG
1 Oklahoma	10	675	3910	5.8	391.0
2 Virginia Tech	10	621	2835	4.6	283.5
3 Auburn	10	515	2760	5.4	276.0
3 Army	9	481	2484	5.2	276.0
5 Ohio State	9	524	2468	4.7	274.2
6 Southern Cal	10	560	2695	4.8	269.5
7 Washington	10	583	2688	4.6	268.8
8 Yale	9	463	2385	5.2	265.0
9 Texas A&M	10	564	2638	4.7	263.8
10 Michigan State	9	486	2312	4.8	256.9

PASSING OFFENSE	G	ATT	COM	INT	PCT	YDS	YPA	TD	I%	YPC	YPG
1 Washington State	10	281	150	15	53.4	2068	7.4	13	5.3	13.8	206.8
2 Stanford	10	305	170	18	55.7	2044	6.7	16	5.9	12.0	204.4
3 Pacific	10	231	124	11	53.7	1889	8.2	13	4.8	15.2	188.9
4 San Jose State	10	294	147	15	50.0	1881	6.4	15	5.1	12.8	188.1
5 Hardin-Simmons	10	249	131	23	52.6	1569	6.3	9	9.2	12.0	156.9
6 Rice	10	194	107	15	55.2	1373	7.1	7	7.7	12.8	137.3
7 Navy	9	172	89	13	51.7	1197	7.0	10	7.6	13.4	133.0
8 Texas	10	228	108	22	47.4	1303	5.7	9	9.6	12.1	130.3
9 Colgate	9	184	92	16	50.0	1161	6.3	11	8.7	12.6	129.0
10 Brigham Young	10	264	105	23	39.8	1286	4.9	12	8.7	12.2	128.6

TOTAL OFFENSE	G	P	YDS	AVG	YPG
1 Oklahoma	10	775	4817	6.2	481.7
2 Hardin-Simmons	10	786	3912	5.0	391.2
3 Auburn	10	670	3749	5.6	374.9
4 Pacific	10	684	3645	5.3	364.5
5 Arizona State	10	625	3609	5.8	360.9
6 Michigan State	9	585	3231	5.5	359.0
7 TCU	10	718	3563	5.0	356.3
8 Virginia Tech	10	726	3559	4.9	355.9
9 Yale	9	574	3199	5.6	355.4
10 Denver	10	676	3505	5.2	350.5

RUSHING DEFENSE	G	ATT	YDS	AVG	YPG
1 Miami, Fla.	10	425	1069	2.5	106.9
2 Navy	9	400	1018	2.5	113.1
3 Holy Cross	9	372	1110	3.0	123.3
4 Georgia Tech	10	405	1284	3.2	128.4
5 Boston College	9	402	1171	2.9	130.1
6 Texas A&M	10	437	1302	3.0	130.2
7 West Virginia	10	467	1369	2.9	136.9
8 Oklahoma	10	487	1383	2.8	138.3
9 Iowa	9	430	1285	3.0	142.8
10 Mississippi	10	454	1449	3.2	144.9

PASSING DEFENSE	G	ATT	COM	PCT	YPC	INT	I%	YDS	YPA	TD	YPG
1 Villanova	9	113	35	31.0	11.3	10	8.9	394	3.5	4	43.8
2 Dartmouth	9	108	38	35.2	10.7	15	13.9	408	3.8	4	45.3
3 South Carolina	10	107	43	40.2	11.1	7	6.5	476	4.4	3	47.6
4 Penn State	9	121	30	24.8	14.5	18	14.9	434	3.6	2	48.2
5 TCU	10	114	34	29.8	14.6	19	16.7	497	4.4	4	49.7
5 Wake Forest	10	143	47	32.9	10.6	13	9.1	497	3.5	1	49.7
7 Mississippi	10	118	48	40.7	10.5	21	17.8	506	4.3	1	50.6
8 Clemson	10	128	50	39.1	10.5	12	9.4	526	4.1	0	52.6
8 Auburn	10	109	45	41.3	11.7	4	3.7	528	4.8	4	52.8
10 North Carolina St.	10	95	44	46.3	12.1	9	9.5	530	5.6	5	53.0

TOTAL DEFENSE	G	P	YDS	AVG	YPG
1 Miami, Fla.	10	590	1894	3.2	189.4
2 Oklahoma	10	634	1938	3.1	193.8
3 Mississippi	10	572	1955	3.4	195.5
4 South Carolina	10	558	1998	3.6	199.8
5 Georgia Tech	10	537	2003	3.7	200.3
6 Navy	9	543	1840	3.4	204.4
7 Auburn	10	540	2083	3.9	208.3
8 Texas A&M	10	601	2088	3.5	208.8
9 Penn State	9	534	1903	3.6	211.4
10 Pittsburgh	10	591	2154	3.6	215.4

SCORING OFFENSE	G	PTS	AVG
1 Oklahoma	10	466	46.6

SCORING DEFENSE	G	PTS	AVG
1 Georgia Tech	10	33	3.3

ANNUAL REVIEW

1957 POLL PROGRESSION

Pre-Season 1957 / Sept. 21 Games

AP	Team	Record	Result
1	Oklahoma	0-0-0	beat # 8 Pittsburgh 26-0
2	Texas A&M	0-0-0	beat Maryland 21-13
3	Michigan State	0-0-0	bye week
4	Minnesota	0-0-0	bye week
5	Tennessee	0-0-0	bye week
6	Michigan	0-0-0	bye week
7	Baylor	0-0-0	beat Villanova 7-0
8	Pittsburgh	0-0-0	lost to # 1 Oklahoma 0-26
9	Iowa	0-0-0	bye week
10	Duke	0-0-0	beat South Carolina 26-14
11	Georgia Tech	0-0-0	beat # 20 Kentucky 13-0
12	Navy	0-0-0	beat Boston College 46-6
13	Oregon State	0-0-0	beat # 19 Southern Cal 20-0
14	Miami, Fla.	0-0-0	lost to Houston 0-7
15	Auburn	0-0-0	bye week
16	Penn State	0-0-0	bye week
17	Ohio State	0-0-0	bye week
18	Notre Dame	0-0-0	bye week
19	Southern Cal	0-0-0	lost to # 13 Oregon State 0-20
20	Kentucky	0-0-0	lost to # 11 Georgia Tech 0-13

September 23 Poll / Sept. 28 Games

UP	AP	Team	Record	Result
1	1	Oklahoma	1-0-0	bye week
2	2	Texas A&M	1-0-0	beat Texas Tech 21-0
3	3	Georgia Tech	1-0-0	tied # 15 SMU 0-0
4	4	Michigan State	0-0-0	beat Indiana 54-0
7	5	Navy	1-0-0	beat William & Mary 33-6
5	6	Minnesota	0-0-0	beat Washington 46-7
9	7	Duke	1-0-0	beat Virginia 40-0
8	8	Tennessee	0-0-0	lost to Auburn 0-7
10	9	Oregon State	1-0-0	beat Kansas 34-6
6	10	Michigan	0-0-0	beat Southern Cal 16-6
11	11	Baylor	1-0-0	beat # 14 Houston 14-6
12	12	Iowa	0-0-0	beat Utah State 70-14
14	13	Texas	1-0-0	beat Tulane 20-6
	14	Houston	1-0-0	lost to # 11 Baylor 6-14
16	15	SMU	1-0-0	tied # 3 Georgia Tech 0-0
18	16	Pittsburgh	0-1-0	beat Oregon 6-3
16	16	Stanford	1-0-0	beat Northwestern 26-6
20	18	Rice	1-0-0	bye week
	19	Mississippi	1-0-0	beat Kentucky 15-0
18	19	Penn State	0-0-0	beat Pennsylvania 19-14
13		Ohio State	0-0-0	lost to TCU 14-18
15		UCLA	1-0-0	beat Illinois 16-6 (S27)

September 30 Poll / Oct. 5 Games

UP	AP	Team	Record	Result
1	1	Oklahoma	1-0-0	beat Iowa State 40-14
2	2	Michigan State	1-0-0	beat California 19-0
3	3	Minnesota	1-0-0	beat Purdue 21-17
9	4	Duke	2-0-0	beat Maryland 14-0
4	5	Texas A&M	2-0-0	beat Missouri 28-0
6	6	Navy	2-0-0	lost to North Carolina 7-13
10	7	Auburn	1-0-0	beat U.T. Chattanooga 40-7
7	8	Iowa	1-0-0	beat Washington State 20-13
5	9	Oregon State	2-0-0	beat Northwestern 22-13
8	10	Michigan	1-0-0	beat Georgia 26-0
11	11	Baylor	2-0-0	lost to Miami, Fla. 7-13
12	12	Army	1-0-0	beat Penn State 27-13
15	13	North Carolina St.	2-0-0	beat Clemson 13-7
	14	Georgia Tech	1-0-1	bye week
19	15	Mississippi	2-0-0	beat Hardin-Simmons 34-7
	16	Notre Dame	1-0-0	beat Indiana 26-0
18	17	Stanford	2-0-0	lost to Rice 7-34
13	17	TCU	1-0-1	lost to Arkansas 7-20
16	19	UCLA	2-0-0	lost to Oregon 0-21
17	20	Texas	2-0-0	lost to South Carolina 21-27
14		Georgia Tech	1-0-1	bye week
20		Penn State	1-0-0	lost to # 12 Army 13-27

October 7 Poll / Oct. 12 Games

UP	AP	Team	Record	Result
1	1	Oklahoma	2-0-0	beat Texas 21-7
2	2	Michigan State	2-0-0	beat # 6 Michigan 35-6
3	3	Texas A&M	3-0-0	beat Houston 28-6
4	4	Minnesota	2-0-0	beat Northwestern 41-6
7	5	Duke	3-0-0	beat # 15 Rice 7-6
5	6	Michigan	2-0-0	lost to # 2 Michigan State 6-35
6	7	Oregon State	3-0-0	beat Idaho 20-0
9	8	Iowa	2-0-0	beat Indiana 47-7
10	9	Auburn	2-0-0	beat Kentucky 6-0
8	10	Army	2-0-0	lost to # 12 Notre Dame 21-23
13	11	Arkansas	3-0-0	beat Baylor 20-17
11	12	Notre Dame	2-0-0	beat # 10 Army 23-21
14	13	North Carolina St.	3-0-0	beat Florida State 7-0
17	14	Mississippi	3-0-0	beat Vanderbilt 28-0
11	15	Rice	2-0-0	lost to # 5 Duke 6-7
	16	Wisconsin	2-0-0	beat Purdue 23-14
15	17	Georgia Tech	1-0-1	lost to LSU 13-20
16	18	North Carolina	2-1-0	beat Miami, Fla. 20-13
	19	Tennessee	1-1-0	beat U.T. Chattanooga 28-13
	20	Pittsburgh	2-1-0	beat Nebraska 34-0
17		Navy	2-1-0	beat California 21-6
19		Pittsburgh	2-1-0	beat Nebraska 34-0
20		TCU	1-1-1	beat Alabama 28-0

October 14 Poll / Oct. 19 Games

UP	AP	Team	Record	Result
1	1	Michigan State	3-0-0	lost to Purdue 13-20
2	2	Oklahoma	3-0-0	beat Kansas 47-0
4	3	Texas A&M	4-0-0	beat TCU 7-0
3	4	Minnesota	3-0-0	lost to Illinois 13-34
6	5	Duke	4-0-0	beat Wake Forest 34-7
5	6	Iowa	3-0-0	beat Wisconsin 21-7
7	7	Oregon State	4-0-0	lost to UCLA 7-26
8	8	Notre Dame	3-0-0	bye week
9	9	Auburn	3-0-0	beat Georgia Tech 3-0
11	10	Arkansas	4-0-0	lost to Texas 0-17
11	11	Mississippi	4-0-0	beat Tulane 50-0
12	12	North Carolina St.	4-0-0	tied Miami, Fla. 0-0
12	13	Wisconsin	3-0-0	lost to Iowa 7-21
	14	North Carolina	3-1-0	lost to Maryland 7-21
17	15	Navy	3-1-0	beat Georgia 27-14
13	16	Pittsburgh	3-1-0	lost to #19 Army 13-29
	17	LSU	3-1-0	beat Kentucky 21-0
	18	Michigan	2-1-0	beat Northwestern 34-13
16	19	Army	2-1-0	beat # 16 Pittsburgh 29-13
14	19	Rice	2-1-0	beat SMU 27-21
	19	Washington State	3-1-0	lost to Oregon 13-14
17		Ohio State	3-1-0	beat Indiana 56-0
19		UCLA	3-1-0	beat # 7 Oregon State 26-7
19		TCU	2-1-1	lost to # 3 Texas A&M 0-7

October 21 Poll / Oct. 26 Games

UP	AP	Team	Record	Result
1	1	Oklahoma	4-0-0	beat Colorado 14-13
3	2	Texas A&M	5-0-0	beat Baylor 14-0
2	3	Iowa	4-0-0	beat Northwestern 6-0
4	4	Duke	5-0-0	tied # 11 North Carolina St. 14-14
6	5	Auburn	4-0-0	beat Houston 48-7
9	6	Mississippi	5-0-0	lost to Arkansas 6-12
5	7	Notre Dame	3-0-0	beat Pittsburgh 13-7
7	8	Michigan State	3-1-0	beat # 16 Illinois 19-14
8	9	Army	3-1-0	beat Virginia 20-12
18	10	LSU	4-1-0	lost to Florida 14-22
14	11	North Carolina St.	4-0-1	tied # 4 Duke 14-14
10	12	Ohio State	3-1-0	beat Wisconsin 16-13
11	13	Rice	3-1-0	lost to Texas 14-19
12	14	Minnesota	3-1-0	lost to # 20 Michigan 7-24
12	15	UCLA	4-1-0	lost to Stanford 6-20
20	16	Illinois	2-2-0	lost to # 8 Michigan State 14-19
15	17	Navy	4-1-0	beat Pennsylvania 35-7
19	18	Oregon	4-1-0	beat California 24-6
17	19	Texas	3-2-0	beat Rice 19-14
16	20	Michigan	3-1-0	beat # 14 Minnesota 24-7
20		Oregon State	4-1-0	lost to Washington 6-19

October 28 Poll / Nov. 2 Games

UP	AP	Team	Record	Result
2	1	Texas A&M	6-0-0	beat # 11 Arkansas 7-6
1	2	Oklahoma	5-0-0	beat Kansas State 13-0
3	3	Iowa	5-0-0	tied # 12 Michigan 21-21
4	4	Auburn	5-0-0	beat # 19 Florida 13-0
5	5	Notre Dame	4-0-0	lost to # 16 Navy 6-20
6	6	Michigan State	4-1-0	beat Wisconsin 21-7
7	7	Duke	5-0-1	lost to Georgia Tech 0-13
9	8	Ohio State	4-1-0	beat Northwestern 47-6
8	9	Army	4-1-0	beat Colgate 53-7
10	10	North Carolina St.	4-0-2	beat Wake Forest 19-0
13	11	Arkansas	5-1-0	lost to # 1 Texas A&M 6-7
12	12	Michigan	4-1-0	tied # 3 Iowa 21-21
16	13	Texas	4-2-0	lost to SMU 12-19
16	14	Mississippi	5-1-0	beat Houston 20-7
11	15	Oregon	5-1-0	beat Stanford 27-26
13	16	Navy	5-1-0	beat # 5 Notre Dame 20-6
15	17	Tennessee	4-1-0	beat North Carolina 35-0
16	18	Colorado	3-2-1	lost to Missouri 6-9
	19	Florida	3-1-0	lost to # 4 Auburn 0-13
20	20	Dartmouth	5-0-0	tied Yale 14-14
19		Texas-El Paso	5-0-0	lost to Hardin-Simmons 20-33
20		Arizona State	5-0-0	beat New Mexico State 21-0

November 4 Poll / Nov. 9 Games

UP	AP	Team	Record	Result
1	1	Texas A&M	7-0-0	beat SMU 19-6
2	2	Oklahoma	6-0-0	beat # 19 Missouri 39-14
3	3	Auburn	6-0-0	beat # 17 Mississippi State 15-7
4	4	Michigan State	5-1-0	beat # 15 Notre Dame 34-6
5	5	Iowa	5-0-1	beat Minnesota 44-20
6	6	Ohio State	5-1-0	beat Purdue 20-7
8	7	Navy	6-1-0	beat # 16 Duke 6-6
7	8	Army	5-1-0	beat Utah 39-33
10	9	Tennessee	5-1-0	beat # 18 Georgia Tech 21-6
12	10	North Carolina St.	5-0-2	lost to William & Mary 6-7
9	11	Michigan	4-1-1	lost to Illinois 19-20
13	12	Arkansas	5-2-0	lost to Rice 7-13
10	13	Oregon	5-1-0	lost to Washington 6-13
15	14	Mississippi	6-1-0	beat LSU 14-12
13	15	Notre Dame	4-1-0	lost to # 4 Michigan State 6-34
16	16	Duke	5-1-1	tied # 7 Navy 6-6
	17	Mississippi State	5-1-0	lost to # 3 Auburn 7-15
17	18	Georgia Tech	3-2-1	lost to # 9 Tennessee 6-21
	19	Missouri	5-1-1	lost to # 2 Oklahoma 14-39
	20	VMI	6-0-1	beat Lehigh 12-7
17		TCU	4-2-1	bye week
17		Penn State	4-2-0	beat Marquette 20-7
17		Arizona State	6-0-0	beat Texas-El Paso 43-7

November 11 Poll / Nov. 16 Games

UP	AP	Team	Record	Result
1	1	Texas A&M	8-0-0	lost to # 20 Rice 6-7
2	2	Oklahoma	7-0-0	lost to Notre Dame 0-7
3	3	Auburn	7-0-0	beat Georgia 6-0
4	4	Michigan State	6-1-0	beat Minnesota 42-13
5	5	Iowa	6-0-1	lost to # 6 Ohio State 13-17
6	6	Ohio State	6-1-0	beat # 5 Iowa 17-13
7	7	Tennessee	6-1-0	beat # 8 Mississippi 7-14
11	8	Mississippi	7-1-0	beat # 7 Tennessee 14-7
8	9	Navy	6-1-1	beat George Washington 52-0
9	10	Army	6-1-0	beat Tulane 20-14
10	11	Duke	5-1-2	beat # 14 Clemson 7-6
	12	Mississippi State	5-2-0	beat LSU 14-6
	13	VMI	7-0-1	beat Citadel 33-7
14	14	Clemson	5-2-0	lost to # 11 Duke 6-7
	15	Illinois	3-4-0	lost to Wisconsin 13-24
15	16	Oregon	6-2-0	beat Southern Cal 16-7
	17	TCU	4-2-1	lost to Texas 2-14
	18	Michigan	4-2-1	beat Indiana 27-13
	19	North Carolina St.	5-1-2	beat Virginia Tech 12-0
15	20	Rice	4-3-0	beat # 1 Texas A&M 7-6
12		Arizona State	7-0-0	beat Montana St. 53-13
13		Wisconsin	4-3-0	beat Illinois 24-13
15		Dartmouth	6-0-1	beat Cornell 20-19
15		Stanford	5-3-0	lost to Oregon State 14-24
15		Arkansas	5-3-0	lost to SMU 22-27
20		Notre Dame	4-2-0	beat # 2 Oklahoma 7-0
20		Penn State	5-2-0	beat Holy Cross 14-10
20		UCLA	6-2-0	beat Pacific 21-0

UP	AP	NOVEMBER 18 POLL		NOV. 23 GAMES
1	1	Michigan State	7-1-0	beat Kansas State 27-9
3	2	Auburn	8-0-0	beat Florida State 29-7
2	3	Ohio State	7-1-0	beat #19 Michigan 31-14
4	4	Texas A&M	8-1-0	bye week
6	5	Mississippi	8-1-0	bye week
5	6	Oklahoma	7-1-0	beat Nebraska 32-7
7	7	Navy	7-1-1	bye week
8	8	Iowa	6-1-1	beat #9 Notre Dame 21-13
9	9	Notre Dame	5-2-0	lost to #8 Iowa 13-21
10	10	Army	7-1-0	bye week
11	11	Duke	6-1-2	lost to North Carolina 13-21
16	12	Tennessee	6-2-0	lost to Kentucky 6-20
13	13	Rice	5-3-0	beat TCU 20-0
	14	Mississippi State	6-2-0	bye week
12	15	Oregon	7-2-0	lost to Oregon State 7-10
	16	VMI	8-0-1	bye week
14	17	Arizona State	8-0-0	beat Pacific 41-0
14	18	Wisconsin	5-3-0	beat Minnesota 14-6
17	19	Michigan	5-2-1	lost to #3 Ohio State 14-31
18	20	North Carolina St.	6-1-2	beat South Carolina 29-26
19		Clemson	5-3-0	beat Wake Forest 13-6
19		Dartmouth	7-0-1	lost to Princeton 14-34
19		Penn State	6-2-0	lost to Pittsburgh 13-14
19		UCLA	7-2-0	beat Southern Cal 20-9

UP	AP	NOVEMBER 25 POLL		NOV. 30 GAMES
3	1	Auburn	9-0-0	beat Alabama 40-0
1	2	Ohio State	8-1-0	regular season complete
2	3	Michigan State	8-1-0	regular season complete
5	4	Texas A&M	8-1-0	lost to Texas 7-9
6	5	Oklahoma	8-1-0	beat Oklahoma State 53-6
4	6	Iowa	7-1-1	regular season complete
8	7	Mississippi	8-1-0	tied #13 Mississippi State 7-7
7	8	Navy	7-1-1	beat #10 Army 14-0
10	9	Rice	6-3-0	beat Baylor 20-0
9	10	Army	7-1-0	lost to #8 Navy 0-14
13	11	Arizona State	9-0-0	beat Arizona 47-7
11	12	Notre Dame	5-3-0	beat Southern Cal 40-12
19	13	Mississippi State	6-2-0	tied #7 Mississippi 7-7
12	14	Wisconsin	6-3-0	regular season complete
14	15	North Carolina St.	7-1-2	regular season complete
15	16	Duke	6-2-2	regular season complete
	17	VMI	8-0-1	beat Virginia Tech 14-6
	18	Tennessee	6-3-0	beat Vanderbilt 20-6
	19	Oregon State	8-2-0	regular season complete
	20	Florida	5-2-1	beat Miami, Fla. 14-0
15		Texas	5-3-1	beat #4 Texas A&M 9-7 (N28)
17		Oregon	7-3-0	regular season complete
17		UCLA	8-2-0	regular season complete
19		Clemson	6-3-0	beat Furman 45-6
19		Princeton	7-2-0	regular season complete
19		Illinois	4-5-0	regular season complete
19		North Carolina	6-3-0	lost to Virginia 13-20

UP	AP	DECEMBER 2 FINAL POLL	RECORD	BOWL BID	DATE	BOWL RESULT	RB	RECORD
2	1	Auburn	10-0-0				1	10-0-0
1	2	Ohio State	8-1-0	Rose Bowl	J1	beat Oregon 10-7	3	9-1-0
3	3	Michigan State	8-1-0				5	8-1-0
4	4	Oklahoma	9-1-0	Orange Bowl	J1	beat #16 Duke 48-21	2	10-1-0
6	5	Navy	8-1-1	Cotton Bowl	J1	beat #8 Rice 20-7	9	9-1-1
5	6	Iowa	7-1-1				4	7-1-1
8	7	Mississippi	8-1-1	Sugar Bowl	J1	beat #11 Texas 39-7	6	9-1-1
7	8	Rice	7-3-0	Cotton Bowl	J1	lost to #5 Navy 7-20	11	7-4-0
10	9	Texas A&M	8-2-0	Gator Bowl	D28	lost to #13 Tennessee 0-3	8	8-3-0
9	10	Notre Dame	6-3-0				10	7-3-0
11	11	Texas	6-3-1	Sugar Bowl	J1	lost to #7 Mississippi 7-39	18	6-4-1
12	12	Arizona State	10-0-0				13	10-0-0
16	13	Tennessee	7-3-0	Gator Bowl	D28	beat #9 Texas A&M 3-0	7	8-3-0
	14	Mississippi State	6-2-1				25	6-2-1
20	15	North Carolina St.	7-1-2				21	7-1-2
14	16	Duke	6-2-2	Orange Bowl	J1	lost to #4 Oklahoma 21-48	30	6-3-2
	17	Florida	6-2-1				15	6-2-1
13	18	Army	7-2-0				17	7-2-0
14	19	Wisconsin	6-3-0				23	6-3-0
	20	VMI	9-0-1				19	9-0-1
17		Oregon	7-3-0	Rose Bowl	J1	lost to #2 Ohio State 7-10	31	7-4-0
18		Clemson	7-3-0				39	7-3-0
18		UCLA	8-2-0				14	8-2-0

1957

CONSENSUS ALL-AMERICANS

POS	Name	HT	WT	School	AA	AP	FC	FW	IN	NE	SN	UP
B	John David Crow	6-2	214	Texas A&M	•	•	•	•	•	•	•	•
B	Walt Kowalczyk	6-0	205	Michigan State		•	•	•		•	•	•
B	Bob Anderson	6-2	200	Army			•	•	•	•	•	•
B	Clendon Thomas	6-2	188	Oklahoma		•				•	•	•
E	Jimmy Phillips	6-2	205	Auburn	•	•	•	•	•	•	•	•
E	Dick Wallen	6-0	185	UCLA	•	•	•	•	•			
T	Lou Michaels	6-2	235	Kentucky	•	•	•	•	•	•	•	•
T	Alex Karras	6-2	233	Iowa	•	•	•	•	•	•	•	•
G	Bill Krisher	6-1	213	Oklahoma	•	•	•	•	•	•	•	•
G	Al Ecuyer	5-10	190	Notre Dame			•		•		•	•
C	Dan Currie	6-3	225	Michigan State	•	•	•	•				

OTHERS RECEIVING FIRST-TEAM HONORS

B	Jim Bakhtiar			Virginia		•						
B	Lee Grosscup			Utah		•		•				
B	King Hill			Rice	•	•	•					
B	Bob Stransky			Colorado		•	•					
B	Jimmy Taylor			LSU		•						
B	Dick Christy			North Carolina St.	•							
B	Jim Pace			Michigan		•						
B	Tom Forrestal			Navy			•					
E	Fred Dugan			Dayton		•						
E	Jim Gibbons			Iowa		•			•	•	•	
T	Charlie Krueger			Texas A&M		•	•					
T	Tom Topping			Duke		•						
G	Bill Johnson			Tennessee		•		•				
G	Jack Simpson			Mississippi		•	•					
G	Aurelius Thomas			Ohio State		•	•					
C	Bob Reifsnyder			Navy		•	•		•			
C	Don Stephenson			Georgia Tech					•	•	•	

FC named Reifsnyder as a T

HEISMAN TROPHY VOTING

	PLAYER	POS	SCHOOL	1ST	2ND	3RD	TOTAL
1	John David Crow	RB	Texas A&M	241	176	108	1183
2	Alex Karras	DT	Iowa	128	109	91	693
3	Walt Kowalczyk	HB	Michigan State	116	93	96	630
4	Lou Michaels	T	Kentucky	60	57	36	330
5	Tom Forrestal	QB	Navy	34	42	46	232
6	Jim Phillips	E	Auburn	34	35	44	216
7	Bob Anderson	HB	Army	25	45	39	204
8	Dan Currie	C	Michigan State	49	16	18	197
9	Clendon Thomas	HB	Oklahoma	21	39	44	185
10	Lee Grosscup	QB	Utah	21	28	28	147

AWARD WINNERS

PLAYER	POS	SCHOOL	AWARD NAME
Bob Reifsnyder	T	Navy	Maxwell
Alex Karras	T	Iowa	Outland

CONFERENCE STANDINGS

ACC

	Conf. W L T			Overall W L T		
North Carolina St.	5	0	1	7	1	2
Duke	5	1	1	6	3	2
Clemson	4	3	0	7	3	0
North Carolina	4	3	0	6	4	0
Maryland	4	3	0	5	5	0
Virginia	2	4	0	3	6	1
South Carolina	2	5	0	5	5	0
Wake Forest	0	7	0	0	10	0

Big 10

	Conf. W L T			Overall W L T		
Ohio State	7	0	0	9	1	0
Michigan State	5	1	0	8	1	0
Iowa	4	1	1	7	1	1
Wisconsin	4	3	0	6	3	0
Purdue	4	3	0	5	4	0
Michigan	3	3	1	5	3	1
Illinois	3	4	0	4	5	0
Minnesota	3	5	0	4	5	0
Indiana	0	6	0	1	8	0
Northwestern	0	7	0	0	9	0

Big 7

	Conf. W L T			Overall W L T		
Oklahoma	6	0	0	10	1	0
Kansas	4	2	0	5	4	1
Colorado	3	3	0	6	3	1
Missouri	3	3	0	5	4	1
Iowa State	2	4	0	4	5	1
Kansas State	2	4	0	3	6	1
Nebraska	1	5	0	1	9	0

Border

	Conf. W L T			Overall W L T		
Arizona State	4	0	0	10	0	0
West Texas State	3	1	0	7	3	0
Texas-El Paso	3	2	0	6	3	0
Hardin-Simmons	3	2	0	5	5	0
New Mexico State	0	4	0	3	7	0
Arizona	0	4	0	1	8	1

Ivy League

	Conf. W L T			Overall W L T		
Princeton	6	1	0	7	2	0
Dartmouth	5	1	1	7	1	1
Yale	4	2	1	6	2	1
Brown	3	4	0	5	4	0
Pennsylvania	3	4	0	3	6	0
Cornell	3	4	0	3	6	0
Harvard	2	5	0	3	5	0
Columbia	1	6	0	1	8	0

MAC

	Conf. W L T			Overall W L T		
Miami, Ohio	5	0	0	6	3	0
Marshall	4	2	0	6	3	0
Bowling Green	3	1	2	6	1	2
Toledo	3	2	0	5	4	0
Western Michigan	1	4	1	4	4	1
Ohio U	1	4	1	2	6	1
Kent State	1	5	0	3	6	0

Pacific Coast

	Conf. W L T			Overall W L T		
Oregon State	6	2	0	8	2	0
Oregon	6	2	0	7	4	0
UCLA	5	2	0	8	2	0
Washington State	5	3	0	6	4	0
Stanford	4	3	0	6	4	0
Washington	3	4	0	3	6	1
California	1	6	0	1	9	0
Southern Cal	1	6	0	1	9	0
Idaho	0	3	0	4	4	1

SEC

	Conf. W L T			Overall W L T		
Auburn	7	0	0	10	0	0
Mississippi	5	0	1	9	1	1
Florida	4	2	1	6	2	1
Mississippi State	4	2	1	6	2	1
Tennessee	4	3	0	8	3	0
LSU	4	4	0	5	5	0
Vanderbilt	3	3	1	5	3	2
Georgia Tech	3	4	1	4	4	2
Georgia	3	4	0	3	7	0
Alabama	1	6	1	2	7	1
Tulane	1	5	0	2	8	0
Kentucky	1	7	0	3	7	0

Skyline

	Conf. W L T			Overall W L T		
Utah	5	1	0	6	4	0
Brigham Young	5	1	1	5	3	2
Denver	5	2	0	6	4	0
Wyoming	3	2	2	4	3	3
New Mexico	2	4	0	4	6	0
Colorado State	2	5	0	3	7	0
Montana	2	5	0	2	7	0
Utah State	1	5	1	2	7	1

SWC

	Conf. W L T			Overall W L T		
Minnesota	6	0	0	8	0	0
Rice	5	1	0	7	4	0
Texas	4	1	1	6	4	1
Texas A&M	4	2	0	8	3	0
SMU	3	3	0	4	5	1
Arkansas	2	4	0	6	4	0
TCU	2	4	0	5	4	1
Baylor	0	5	1	3	6	1

Independents

	Overall W L T		
Navy	9	1	1
Boston College	7	2	0
Army	7	2	0
Notre Dame	7	3	0
Penn State	6	3	0
Oklahoma State	6	3	1
Syracuse	5	3	1
Memphis	6	4	0
Rutgers	5	4	0
Miami, Fla.	5	4	1
Pittsburgh	4	6	0
Florida State	4	6	0
Air Force	3	6	1
Texas Tech	2	8	0

BOWL GAMES

DATE	GAME	SCORE
D28	Gator	Tennessee 3, Texas A&M 0
J1	Tangerine	Texas A&M-Commerce 10, Southern Miss 9
J1	Sun	Louisville 34, Drake 20
J1	Sugar	Mississippi 39, Texas 7
J1	Cotton	Navy 20, Rice 7
J1	Rose	Ohio State 10, Oregon 7
J1	Orange	Oklahoma 48, Duke 21

1957 NCAA Major College Statistical Leaders

Individual Leaders

PASSING/COMPLETIONS	G	ATT	COM	PCT	INT	I%	YDS	YPA	TD	TD%	COM.PG
1 Ken Ford, Hardin-Simmons	10	205	115	56.1	11	5.4	1254	6.1	14	6.8	11.5
2 Bob Newman, Washington State	10	188	104	55.3	13	6.9	1391	7.4	13	6.9	10.4
3 Lee Grosscup, Utah	10	137	94	68.6	2	1.5	1398	10.2	10	7.3	9.4
4 Bob Winters, Utah State	10	179	92	51.4	9	5.0	1139	6.4	7	3.9	9.2
5 Billy Baker, Furman	10	150	88	58.7	5	3.3	846	5.6	6	4.0	8.8
6 Tom Flores, Pacific	10	184	82	44.6	10	5.4	980	5.3	5	2.7	8.2
7 Tom Forrestal, Navy	10	159	80	50.3	17	10.7	1117	7.0	8	5.0	8.0
8 Jack Douglas, Stanford	10	146	78	53.4	6	4.1	957	6.6	10	6.9	7.8
9 Roger LaBrasca, Drake	8	145	74	51.0	10	6.9	1054	7.3	12	8.3	9.3
9 Tommy Greene, Holy Cross	9	159	74	46.5	12	7.6	1297	8.2	11	6.9	8.2

ALL-PURPOSE YARDS	G	RUSH	REC	INT	PR	KR	YDS	YPG
1 Overton Curtis, Utah State	10	616	193	60	44	695	1608	160.8

RUSHING/YARDS	G	ATT	YDS	AVG	YPG
1 Leon Burton, Arizona State	10	117	1126	9.6	112.6
2 Bob Stransky, Colorado	10	183	1097	6.0	109.7
3 Bob Anderson, Army	9	153	983	6.4	109.2
4 Bill Austin, Rutgers	9	193	946	4.9	105.1
5 Chuck Shea, Stanford	10	163	840	5.2	84.0
6 Jim Bakhtiar, Virginia	10	194	822	4.2	82.2
7 Clendon Thomas, Oklahoma	10	130	816	6.3	81.6
8 Jimmy Taylor, LSU	10	162	762	4.7	76.2
9 Nub Beamer, Oregon State	10	173	760	4.4	76.0
10 Wray Carlton, Duke	10	143	749	5.2	74.9

RUSHING/YARDS PER CARRY	G	ATT	YDS	YPC
1 Leon Burton, Arizona State	10	117	1126	9.6
2 Don Perkins, New Mexico	10	112	744	6.6
3 Bob Anderson, Army	9	153	983	6.4
4 Clendon Thomas, Oklahoma	10	130	816	6.3
5 Bob Stransky, Colorado	10	183	1097	6.0
6 Bobby Mulgado, Arizona State	10	121	681	5.6
7 Pete Hart, Hardin-Simmons	10	120	669	5.6
8 Jim Pace, Michigan	9	123	664	5.4
9 Pete Dawkins, Army	9	124	665	5.4
10 Wray Carlton, Duke	10	143	749	5.2

*-Based on top 20 rushers

RECEIVING/RECEPTIONS	G	REC	YDS	TD	YPR	YPG	RPG
1 Stuart Vaughan, Utah	10	53	756	5	14.3	75.6	5.3
2 Gary Kapp, Utah State	10	45	633	4	14.1	63.3	4.5
2 Don Ellingsen, Washington State	10	45	559	3	12.4	55.9	4.5
4 Fred Dugan, Dayton	10	37	546	3	14.8	54.6	3.7
5 Jim Gibbons, Iowa	9	36	587	4	16.3	65.2	4.0
6 Al Jamison, Colgate	9	33	420	6	12.7	46.7	3.7
7 Jerry Mertens, Drake	8	29	509	6	17.6	63.6	3.6
8 Gene Leek, Arizona	10	29	310	1	10.7	31.0	2.9
9 Chuck Chatfield, Pacific	10	28	404	1	14.4	40.4	2.8
9 Pete Jokanovich, Navy	10	28	339	0	12.1	33.9	2.8

PUNTING	PUNT	YDS	AVG
1 Dave Sherer, SMU	36	1620	45.0
2 Bobby Gordon, Tennessee	40	1708	42.7
3 Bobby Jordan, VMI	39	1642	42.1
4 Gerald Nesbit, Arkansas	32	1344	42.0
5 Kirk Wilson, UCLA	31	1302	42.0
6 Robert Haas, Missouri	27	1126	41.7
7 Bill Gundy, Dartmouth	23	934	40.6
8 Walter Fondren, Texas	37	1502	40.6
9 Larry DeVincentis, Cincinnati	39	1583	40.6
10 Lou Michaels, Kentucky	47	1908	40.6

PUNT RETURNS/YARDS	PR	YDS	AVG
1 Bobby Mulgado, Arizona State	14	267	19.1
2 Sterling Hammack, Oregon State	22	253	11.5
3 Jakie Sandefer, Oklahoma	17	249	14.6
4 Corbin Bailey, Virginia Tech	15	242	16.1
5 Bobby Gordon, Tennessee	22	231	10.5
6 Dave Parr, Villanova	9	208	23.1
7 Howard Cook, Colorado	14	186	13.3
8 Clendon Thomas, Oklahoma	7	178	25.4
9 Jim Shofner, TCU	11	168	15.3
10 John Maio, Boston U.	10	167	16.7

KICKOFF RETURNS/YARDS	KR	YDS	AVG
1 Overton Curtis, Utah State	23	695	30.2
2 Stan Dobosz, Florida State	19	390	20.5
3 Billy Cannon, LSU	11	343	31.2
4 Jim Jones, Washington	12	342	28.5
5 Dewey Bohling, Hardin-Simmons	18	337	18.7
6 Wilmer Fowler, Northwestern	14	336	24.0
7 Dick Haley, Pittsburgh	14	329	23.5
8 Dick Christy, North Carolina St.	7	318	45.4
9 Clarence Bruton, Marquette	12	310	25.8
9 Jim Shanley, Oregon	10	309	30.9

SCORING	TDS	XPT	FG	PTS
1 Leon Burton, Arizona State	16	0	0	96
2 Bobby Mulgado, Arizona State	9	36	1	93
3 Jimmy Taylor, LSU	12	14	0	86
4 Bob Anderson, Army	14	0	0	84
5 Dick Christy, North Carolina St.	13	2	1	83
6 William Atkins, Auburn	11	13	1	82
7 Joe Belland, Arizona State	13	0	0	78
8 Bob Stransky, Colorado	12	5	0	77
9 Bill Austin, Rutgers	12	2	0	74
10 Wray Carlton, Duke	10	11	0	71

INTERCEPTIONS	INT	YDS
1 Ray Toole, North Texas	7	133
2 Carroll Johnston, Brigham Young	7	89
3 Bobby Mulgado, Arizona State	6	113
3 James Dunn, Florida	6	71
5 Frank Finney, Brown	5	155
5 Bob Winters, Utah State	5	87
5 Reece Whitley, Virginia	5	81
5 John David Crow, Texas A&M	5	39
5 Barry Maroney, Cincinnati	5	27
5 Bobby Lackey, Texas	5	15

Team Leaders

RUSHING OFFENSE	G	ATT	YDS	AVG	YPG
1 Colorado	10	616	3224	5.2	322.4
2 Mississippi	10	582	3057	5.3	305.7
3 Ohio State	9	555	2681	4.8	297.9
4 Army	9	535	2674	5.0	297.1
5 Oklahoma	10	679	2970	4.4	297.0
6 Arizona State	10	520	2922	5.6	292.2
7 Wisconsin	9	503	2437	4.8	270.8
8 Michigan State	9	533	2367	4.4	263.0
9 Princeton	9	474	2323	4.9	258.1
10 Miami, Fla.	10	567	2540	4.5	254.0

PASSING OFFENSE	G	ATT	COM	INT	PCT	YDS	YPA	TD	I%	YPC	YPG
1 Utah	10	218	133	14	61.0	1952	9.0	5	6.4	14.7	195.2
2 Washington State	10	253	136	19	53.8	1808	7.1	17	7.5	13.3	180.8
3 Holy Cross	9	189	84	16	44.4	1508	8.0	12	8.5	18.0	167.6
4 Arizona	10	294	155	19	52.7	1540	5.2	4	6.5	9.9	154.0
5 Drake	8	174	86	12	49.4	1231	7.1	12	6.9	14.3	153.9
6 Arizona State	10	152	81	7	53.3	1527	10.0	19	4.6	18.9	152.7
7 Hardin-Simmons	10	242	135	13	55.8	1510	6.2	15	5.4	11.2	151.0
8 Navy	10	230	113	14	49.1	1469	6.4	15	6.1	13.0	146.9
9 Iowa	9	146	77	17	52.7	1289	8.8	11	11.6	16.7	143.2
10 Penn State	9	185	90	8	48.6	1187	6.4	11	4.3	13.2	131.9

TOTAL OFFENSE	G	P	YDS	AVG	YPG
1 Arizona State	10	672	4449	6.6	444.9
2 Colorado	10	743	4152	5.6	415.2
3 Navy	10	719	3844	5.3	384.4
4 Iowa	9	599	3459	5.8	384.3
5 Michigan State	9	669	3455	5.2	383.9
6 Army	9	648	3376	5.2	375.1
7 Oklahoma	10	776	3600	4.6	360.0
8 Mississippi	10	673	3556	5.3	355.6
9 Utah	10	628	3476	5.5	347.6
9 Rice	10	672	3476	5.2	347.6

RUSHING DEFENSE	G	ATT	YDS	AVG	YPG
1 Auburn	10	390	674	1.7	67.4
2 Miami, Fla.	10	418	998	2.4	99.8
3 Arizona State	10	381	1035	2.7	103.5
4 Princeton	9	338	974	2.9	108.2
5 Navy	10	427	1096	2.6	109.6
6 Iowa	9	372	1014	2.7	112.7
7 Boston College	9	381	1032	2.7	114.7
8 Michigan State	9	422	1055	2.5	117.2
9 Cincinnati	10	402	1220	3.0	122.0
10 Syracuse	9	368	1107	3.0	123.0

PASSING DEFENSE	G	ATT	COM	PCT	YPC	INT	I%	YDS	YPA	TD	YPG
1 Georgia Tech	10	73	31	42.5	10.8	7	9.6	334	4.6	1	33.4
2 Missouri	10	96	41	42.7	9.9	10	10.3	404	4.2	3	40.4
3 Tulane	10	94	33	35.1	12.5	10	10.6	413	4.4	5	41.3
4 Virginia Tech	10	108	38	35.2	12.8	9	8.3	485	4.5	3	48.5
5 Mississippi	10	133	45	33.8	11.1	19	14.3	500	3.8	1	50.0
6 Tennessee	10	109	49	45.0	10.2	6	5.5	501	4.6	3	50.1
7 Navy	10	127	39	30.7	13.6	20	15.8	530	4.2	1	53.0
7 Florida	9	107	39	36.4	12.2	15	14.0	477	4.5	1	53.0
9 Kentucky	10	115	37	32.2	14.4	12	10.4	531	4.6	1	53.1
10 Texas A&M	10	140	54	38.6	9.9	16	11.4	534	3.8	16	53.4

TOTAL DEFENSE	G	P	YDS	AVG	YPG
1 Auburn	10	529	1330	2.5	133.0
2 Navy	10	554	1626	2.9	162.6
3 Georgia Tech	10	546	1778	3.3	177.8
4 Tennessee	10	574	1847	3.2	184.7
5 Michigan State	9	556	1724	3.1	191.6
6 Miami, Fla.	10	579	2002	3.5	200.2
7 TCU	10	570	2022	3.5	202.2
8 Florida	9	494	1822	3.7	202.4
9 Cincinnati	10	556	2065	3.7	206.5
10 Mississippi	10	561	2074	3.7	207.4

SCORING OFFENSE	G	PTS	AVG
1 Arizona State	10	397	39.7

SCORING DEFENSE	G	PTS	AVG
1 Auburn	10	28	2.8

ANNUAL REVIEW

1958 Poll Progression

Pre-Season 1958 (AP) — Sept. 20 Games

AP	Team	Record	Result
1	Ohio State	0-0-0	bye week
2	Oklahoma	0-0-0	bye week
3	Notre Dame	0-0-0	bye week
4	Michigan State	0-0-0	bye week
5	Auburn	0-0-0	bye week
6	Mississippi	0-0-0	beat Memphis 17-0
7	Navy	0-0-0	bye week
8	TCU	0-0-0	beat Kansas 42-0
9	Army	0-0-0	bye week
10	North Carolina	0-0-0	lost to North Carolina St. 14-21
11	Texas	0-0-0	beat Georgia 13-8
12	Oregon State	0-0-0	lost to Southern Cal 0-21
13	Iowa	0-0-0	bye week
14	Wisconsin	0-0-0	bye week
15	Mississippi State	0-0-0	bye week
16	Miami, Fla.	0-0-0	bye week
17	SMU	0-0-0	bye week
18	Clemson	0-0-0	beat Virginia 20-15
19	Pittsburgh	0-0-0	beat UCLA 27-6
20	Texas A&M	0-0-0	lost to Texas Tech 14-15

September 22 Poll (UP AP) — Sept. 27 Games

UP	AP	Team	Record	Result
1	1	Ohio State	0-0-0	beat #20 SMU 23-20
2	2	Oklahoma	0-0-0	beat #13 West Virginia 47-14
6	3	Auburn	0-0-0	beat Tennessee 13-0
4	4	Michigan State	0-0-0	beat California 32-12
3	5	Notre Dame	0-0-0	beat Indiana 18-0
5	6	TCU	1-0-0	lost to Iowa 0-17
7	7	Pittsburgh	1-0-0	beat Holy Cross 17-0
11	8	Army	0-0-0	beat #18 South Carolina 45-8
10	9	Mississippi	1-0-0	beat #17 Kentucky 27-6
12	10	Washington State	1-0-0	lost to Northwestern 28-29
	11	Mississippi State	0-0-0	beat #18 Florida 14-7
8	12	Navy	0-0-0	beat William & Mary 14-0
	13	West Virginia	1-0-0	lost to #2 Oklahoma 14-47
9	14	Wisconsin	0-0-0	beat #15 Miami, Fla. 20-0
13	15	LSU	1-0-0	beat Alabama 13-3
	16	Miami, Fla.	0-0-0	lost to #14 Wisconsin 0-20
14	17	Kentucky	2-0-0	lost to #9 Mississippi 6-27
	18	Florida	1-0-0	lost to #11 Mississippi State 7-14
19	18	South Carolina	1-0-0	lost to #8 Army 8-45
	20	SMU	0-0-0	lost to #1 Ohio State 20-23
15		Southern Cal	1-0-0	lost to Michigan 19-20
16		Clemson	1-0-0	beat North Carolina 26-21
17		Purdue	0-0-0	beat Nebraska 28-0
18		Wake Forest	1-0-0	beat Virginia Tech 13-6
20		North Carolina St.	1-0-0	lost to Maryland 6-21

September 29 Poll (UP AP) — Oct. 4 Games

UP	AP	Team	Record	Result
1	1	Oklahoma	1-0-0	beat Oregon 6-0
4	2	Auburn	1-0-0	beat U.T. Chattanooga 30-8
3	3	Ohio State	1-0-0	beat Washington 12-7
2	4	Michigan State	1-0-0	tied #16 Michigan 12-12
5	5	Army	1-0-0	beat Penn State 26-0
10	6	Mississippi	2-0-0	beat Trinity 21-0
6	7	Notre Dame	1-0-0	beat #17 SMU 14-6
8	8	Iowa	1-0-0	tied Air Force 13-13
7	9	Wisconsin	1-0-0	beat Marquette 50-0
13	10	Clemson	2-0-0	beat Maryland 8-0
14	11	Mississippi State	1-0-0	lost to Tennessee 8-13
9	12	Pittsburgh	2-0-0	beat Minnesota 13-7
17	13	LSU	2-0-0	beat Hardin-Simmons 20-6
11	14	Purdue	1-0-0	beat Rice 24-0
12	15	Navy	1-0-0	beat Boston U. 28-14
15	16	Michigan	1-0-0	tied #4 Michigan State 12-12
17	17	SMU	0-1-0	lost to #7 Notre Dame 6-14
15	18	Texas	2-0-0	beat Texas Tech 12-7
	19	Houston	1-0-0	beat Cincinnati 34-13
	20	Vanderbilt	2-0-0	tied Alabama 0-0

October 6 Poll (UP AP) — Oct. 11 Games

UP	AP	Team	Record	Result
1	1	Auburn	2-0-0	beat Kentucky 8-0
2	2	Oklahoma	2-0-0	lost to #16 Texas 14-15
4	3	Army	2-0-0	beat #4 Notre Dame 14-2
3	4	Notre Dame	2-0-0	lost to #3 Army 2-14
5	5	Ohio State	2-0-0	beat Illinois 19-13
6	6	Wisconsin	2-0-0	beat #13 Purdue 31-6
9	7	Mississippi	3-0-0	beat Tulane 19-8
11	8	Clemson	3-0-0	beat Vanderbilt 12-7
7	9	Michigan State	1-0-1	lost to Pittsburgh 22-8
8	10	Pittsburgh	3-0-0	lost to #9 Michigan State 8-22
15	11	LSU	3-0-0	beat Miami, Fla. 41-0
13	12	Navy	2-0-0	beat #14 Michigan 20-14
10	13	Purdue	2-0-0	lost to #6 Wisconsin 6-31
12	14	Michigan	1-0-1	lost to #12 Navy 14-20
14	15	Oregon	1-1-0	beat Southern Cal 25-0
16	16	Texas	3-0-0	beat #2 Oklahoma 15-14
20	17	Iowa	1-0-1	beat Indiana 34-13
	18	SMU	0-2-0	beat Missouri 32-19
18	19	Colorado	2-0-0	beat Arizona 65-12
17	19	Houston	2-0-0	beat Wichita State 44-0
19		North Carolina St.	2-1-0	lost to Wake Forest 7-13
20		Pacific	2-0-0	beat Brigham Young 26-8

October 13 Poll (UP AP) — Oct. 18 Games

UP	AP	Team	Record	Result
1	1	Army	3-0-0	beat Virginia 35-6
2	2	Auburn	3-0-0	tied Georgia Tech 7-7
4	3	Ohio State	3-0-0	beat Indiana 49-8
3	4	Wisconsin	3-0-0	lost to #13 Iowa 9-20
5	5	Michigan State	2-0-1	lost to Purdue 6-14
6	6	Navy	3-0-0	lost to Tulane 6-14
7	7	Texas	4-0-0	beat Arkansas 24-6
8	8	Mississippi	4-0-0	beat Hardin-Simmons 24-0
9	9	LSU	4-0-0	beat Kentucky 32-7
12	10	Clemson	4-0-0	bye week
11	11	Oklahoma	3-0-0	beat Kansas 43-0
10	12	Notre Dame	2-1-0	beat Duke 9-7
13	13	Iowa	2-0-1	beat #4 Wisconsin 20-9
14	14	Oregon	2-1-0	lost to Washington State 0-6
	15	Houston	3-0-0	lost to Oklahoma State 0-7
	16	SMU	1-2-0	lost to Rice 7-13
19	17	Northwestern	3-0-0	beat #19 Michigan 55-24
	18	Florida	2-1-0	tied Vanderbilt 6-6
19	19	Michigan	1-1-1	lost to #17 Northwestern 24-55
	20	TCU	3-1-0	beat Texas A&M 24-0
15		Colorado	3-0-0	beat Iowa State 20-0
15		Purdue	2-1-0	beat #5 Michigan State 14-6
17		Pacific	3-0-0	lost to Cincinnati 6-12
18		Pittsburgh	3-1-0	beat West Virginia 15-8

October 20 Poll (UP AP) — Oct. 25 Games

UP	AP	Team	Record	Result
1	1	Army	4-0-0	tied Pittsburgh 14-14
2	2	Ohio State	4-0-0	tied #13 Wisconsin 7-7
5	3	LSU	5-0-0	beat Florida 10-7
4	4	Texas	5-0-0	lost to Rice 7-34
3	5	Auburn	3-0-1	beat Maryland 20-7
7	6	Mississippi	5-0-0	beat Arkansas 14-12
6	7	Iowa	3-0-1	beat #8 Northwestern 26-20
10	8	Northwestern	3-0-1	lost to #7 Iowa 20-26
8	9	Oklahoma	4-1-0	beat Kansas State 40-6
11	10	Clemson	4-0-0	lost to South Carolina 6-26
9	11	Notre Dame	3-1-0	lost to #15 Purdue 22-29
14	12	Colorado	4-0-0	beat Nebraska 27-16
12	13	Wisconsin	3-1-0	tied #2 Ohio State 7-7
17	14	Air Force	3-0-1	beat Utah 16-14
13	15	Purdue	3-1-0	beat #11 Notre Dame 29-22
16	16	TCU	4-1-0	bye week
	17	Georgia Tech	3-1-1	beat SMU 0-20
	18	Navy	3-1-0	beat Pennsylvania 50-8
	19	Mississippi State	3-1-0	lost to Alabama 7-9
15	20	Michigan State	2-1-1	lost to Illinois 0-16
18		Pittsburgh	4-1-0	tied #1 Army 14-14
		Oregon	2-2-0	lost to California 6-23
20		Pacific	3-1-0	lost to Marquette 18-28

October 27 Poll (UP AP) — Nov. 1 Games

UP	AP	Team	Record	Result
5	1	LSU	6-0-0	beat #6 Mississippi 14-0
1	2	Iowa	4-0-1	beat Michigan 37-14
2	3	Army	4-0-1	beat Colgate 68-6
4	4	Auburn	4-0-1	beat Florida 6-5
3	5	Ohio State	4-0-1	lost to #11 Northwestern 0-21
6	6	Mississippi	6-0-0	lost to #1 LSU 0-14
7	7	Oklahoma	5-1-0	beat #9 Colorado 23-7
9	8	Wisconsin	3-1-1	beat Michigan State 9-7
11	9	Colorado	5-0-0	lost to #7 Oklahoma 7-23
8	10	Purdue	4-1-0	beat Illinois 31-8
12	11	Northwestern	4-1-0	beat #5 Ohio State 21-0
10	12	Pittsburgh	4-1-1	lost to Syracuse 13-16
17	13	Air Force	4-0-1	beat Oklahoma State 33-29
13	14	Rice	4-2-0	bye week
14	15	Navy	4-1-0	lost to Notre Dame 20-40
16	16	Texas	5-1-0	lost to SMU 10-26
20	17	North Carolina	4-2-0	beat Tennessee 21-7
17	18	TCU	4-1-0	beat Baylor 22-0
	19	Clemson	4-1-0	beat Wake Forest 14-12
	20	Rutgers	5-0-0	beat Delaware 37-20
15		Notre Dame	3-2-0	beat #15 Navy 40-20
17		SMU	2-3-0	beat #16 Texas 26-10

November 3 Poll (UP AP) — Nov. 8 Games

UP	AP	Team	Record	Result
2	1	LSU	7-0-0	beat Duke 50-18
1	2	Iowa	5-0-1	beat Minnesota 28-6
3	3	Army	5-0-1	beat #13 Rice 14-7
6	4	Northwestern	5-1-0	lost to #7 Wisconsin 13-17
4	5	Auburn	5-0-1	beat Mississippi State 33-14
5	6	Oklahoma	5-1-0	beat Iowa State 20-0
7	7	Wisconsin	4-1-1	beat #4 Northwestern 17-13
8	8	Purdue	5-1-0	tied #6 Ohio State 14-14
11	9	Mississippi	6-1-0	beat Houston 56-7
14	10	Air Force	5-0-1	beat Denver 10-7
13	11	TCU	5-1-0	beat Marquette 36-0
12	12	Syracuse	5-1-0	beat Boston U. 42-0
14	13	Rice	4-2-0	lost to #3 Army 7-14
10	14	Notre Dame	4-2-0	lost to Pittsburgh 26-29
16	15	North Carolina	5-2-0	beat Virginia 42-0
9	16	Ohio State	4-1-1	tied #8 Purdue 14-14
17	17	Clemson	5-1-0	lost to Georgia Tech 0-13
	18	Rutgers	6-0-0	beat Lafayette 18-0
	19	Florida	2-3-1	beat Georgia 7-6
17	20	SMU	3-3-0	beat Texas A&M 33-0
19		Georgia Tech	4-2-1	beat #17 Clemson 13-0
20		Colorado	5-1-0	lost to Missouri 9-33
20		Texas A&M	3-4-0	lost to #20 SMU 0-33
20		Oregon State	5-2-0	lost to Washington State 0-7
20		Pittsburgh	4-2-1	beat #14 Notre Dame 29-26
20		VMI	6-0-1	tied Lehigh 7-7

November 10 Poll (UP AP) — Nov. 15 Games

UP	AP	Team	Record	Result
1	1	LSU	8-0-0	beat Mississippi State 7-6
2	2	Iowa	6-0-1	lost to #16 Ohio State 28-38
3	3	Army	6-0-1	beat Villanova 26-0
4	4	Auburn	6-0-1	beat Georgia 21-6
5	5	Wisconsin	5-1-1	beat Illinois 31-12
6	6	Oklahoma	6-1-0	beat Missouri 39-0
8	7	Mississippi	7-1-0	lost to Tennessee 16-18
7	8	Purdue	5-1-1	beat #13 Northwestern 23-6
14	9	TCU	6-1-0	beat Texas 22-8
12	10	Air Force	6-0-1	beat Wyoming 21-6
11	11	North Carolina	6-2-0	lost to Notre Dame 24-34
11	12	Syracuse	6-1-0	beat Colgate 47-0
9	13	Northwestern	5-2-0	lost to #8 Purdue 6-23
10	14	Pittsburgh	5-2-1	lost to Nebraska 6-14
17	15	SMU	4-3-0	lost to Arkansas 6-13
13	16	Ohio State	4-1-2	beat #2 Iowa 38-28
16	17	Rice	4-3-0	lost to Texas A&M 21-28
	18	Florida	3-3-1	beat Arkansas State 51-7
	19	Rutgers	7-0-0	lost to Quantico Marines 12-13
18	20	Georgia Tech	5-2-1	lost to Alabama 8-17
19		Navy	5-2-0	beat George Washington 28-8
20		Notre Dame	4-3-0	beat #11 North Carolina 34-24
20		California	5-3-0	beat Washington 12-7

UP	AP	November 17 Poll	RECORD	Nov. 22 Games
1	1	LSU	9-0-0	beat Tulane 62-0
3	2	Auburn	7-0-1	beat Wake Forest 21-7
2	3	Army	7-0-1	bye week
4	4	Oklahoma	7-1-0	beat Nebraska 40-7
5	5	Wisconsin	6-1-1	beat Minnesota 27-12
6	6	Iowa	6-1-1	beat # 15 Notre Dame 31-21
8	7	TCU	7-1-0	beat Rice 21-10
7	8	Purdue	6-1-1	tied Indiana 15-15
10	9	Air Force	7-0-1	beat New Mexico 45-7
11	10	Syracuse	7-1-0	beat West Virginia 15-12
9	11	Ohio State	5-1-2	beat Michigan 20-14
18	12	Florida	4-3-1	beat Florida State 21-7
14	13	Mississippi	7-2-0	bye week
	14	Vanderbilt	5-1-3	bye week
12	15	Notre Dame	5-3-0	lost to # 6 Iowa 21-31
17	16	Clemson	6-2-0	beat Boston College 34-12
	17	North Carolina	6-3-0	lost to Duke 6-7
18	18	Mississippi State	3-5-0	bye week
18	19	California	6-3-0	beat Stanford 16-15
13	20	Northwestern	5-3-0	lost to Illinois 20-27
15		Southern Cal	4-4-0	tied UCLA 15-15
16		Rice	4-4-0	lost to # 7 TCU 10-21
18		Oklahoma State	7-2-0	bye week
18		Pittsburgh	5-3-1	bye week

UP	AP	November 24 Poll	RECORD	Nov. 29 Games
1	1	LSU	10-0-0	regular season complete
4	2	Auburn	8-0-1	beat Alabama 14-8
5	3	Oklahoma	8-1-0	beat Oklahoma State 7-0
2	4	Iowa	7-1-1	regular season complete
2	5	Army	7-0-1	beat Navy 22-6
6	6	Wisconsin	7-1-1	regular season complete
7	7	TCU	8-1-0	lost to SMU 13-20
9	8	Air Force	8-0-1	beat Colorado 20-14
8	9	Ohio State	6-1-2	regular season complete
10	10	Syracuse	8-1-0	regular season complete
11	11	Purdue	6-1-2	regular season complete
12	12	Clemson	7-2-0	beat Furman 36-19
16	13	Mississippi	7-2-0	beat Mississippi State 21-0
15	14	Florida	5-3-1	beat Miami, Fla. 12-9
	15	Vanderbilt	5-1-3	lost to Tennessee 6-10
	16	South Carolina	6-3-0	beat Wake Forest 24-7
13	17	California	7-3-0	regular season complete
14	18	Notre Dame	5-4-0	beat Southern Cal 20-13
19	19	Pittsburgh	5-3-1	lost to Penn State 21-25
	20	Rutgers	8-1-0	regular season complete
17		Oklahoma State	7-2-0	lost to # 3 Oklahoma 0-7
18		Georgia Tech	5-3-1	lost to Georgia 3-16

UP	AP	December 1 Final Poll	RECORD	BOWL BID	DATE	BOWL RESULT	RB	RECORD
1	1	LSU	10-0-0	Sugar Bowl	J1	beat # 12 Clemson 7-0	1	11-0-0
2	2	Iowa	7-1-1	Rose Bowl	J1	beat # 16 California 38-12	4	8-1-1
3	3	Army	8-0-1				5	8-0-1
4	4	Auburn	9-0-1				2	9-0-1
5	5	Oklahoma	9-1-0	Orange Bowl	J1	beat # 9 Syracuse 21-6	3	10-1-0
8	6	Air Force	9-0-1	Cotton Bowl	J1	tied # 10 TCU 0-0	11	9-0-2
6	7	Wisconsin	7-1-1				7	7-1-1
7	8	Ohio State	6-1-2				6	6-1-2
10	9	Syracuse	8-1-0	Orange Bowl	J1	lost to # 5 Oklahoma 6-21	17	8-2-0
9	10	TCU	8-2-0	Cotton Bowl	J1	tied # 6 Air Force 0-0	10	8-2-1
12	11	Mississippi	8-2-0	Gator Bowl	D27	beat # 14 Florida 7-3	8	9-2-0
13	12	Clemson	8-2-0	Sugar Bowl	J1	lost to # 1 LSU 0-7	23	8-3-0
11	13	Purdue	6-1-2				9	6-1-2
15	14	Florida	6-3-1	Gator Bowl	D27	lost to # 11 Mississippi 3-7	21	6-4-1
	15	South Carolina	7-3-0				28	7-3-0
16	16	California	7-3-0	Rose Bowl	J1	lost to # 2 Iowa 12-38	40	7-4-0
14	17	Notre Dame	6-4-0				15	6-4-0
18	18	SMU	6-4-0				27	6-4-0
	19	Oklahoma State	7-3-0	Bluegrass Bowl	D13	beat Florida State 15-6	25	8-3-0
	20	Rutgers	8-1-0				39	8-1-0
17		Northwestern	5-4-0				14	5-4-0

ANNUAL REVIEW

1958

CONSENSUS ALL-AMERICANS

POS	Name	HT	WT	School	AP	FC	FW	NE	SN	UP
B	Randy Duncan	6-0	180	Iowa	•	•	•	•	•	•
B	Pete Dawkins	6-1	197	Army	•	•	•	•	•	•
B	Billy Cannon	6-1	200	LSU	•	•	•	•	•	•
B	Bob White	6-2	212	Ohio State			•	•	•	•
E	Buddy Dial	6-1	185	Rice	•		•	•	•	•
E	Sam Williams	6-5	225	Michigan State		•		•		
T	Ted Bates	6-2	215	Oregon State	•	•		•	•	•
T	Brock Strom	6-0	217	Air Force	•			•		•
G	John Guzik	6-3	223	Pittsburgh			•	•	•	•
G	Zeke Smith	6-2	210	Auburn	•	•		•		
G	George Deiderich	6-1	198	Vanderbilt	•	•	•			
C	Bob Harrison	6-2	206	Oklahoma	•		•	•	•	•

OTHERS RECEIVING FIRST-TEAM HONORS

POS	Name	School	
B	Bob Anderson	Army	•
B	Joe Kapp	California	•
B	Don Meredith	SMU	•
B	Nick Pietrosante	Notre Dame	• •
B	Billy Austin	Rutgers	•
E	Al Goldstein	North Carolina	• •
E	Jim Houston	Ohio State	• •
E	Curtis Merz	Iowa	•
E	Jim Wood	Oklahoma State	•
E	Monty Stickles	Notre Dame	•
T	Andrew Cvercko	Northwestern	•
T	Don Floyd	TCU	•
T	Vel Heckman	Florida	•
T	Gene Selawski	Purdue	•
T	Hogan Wharton	Houston	•
T	Ron Luciano	Syracuse	•
T	Jim Marshall	Ohio State	•
G	Bob Novogratz	Army	•
G	John Wooten	Colorado	•
G	Al Ecuyer	Notre Dame	• •
C	Max Fugler	LSU	•
C	Jackie Burkett	Auburn	•

HEISMAN TROPHY VOTING

	PLAYER	POS	SCHOOL	1ST	2ND	3RD	TOTAL
1	Pete Dawkins	HB	Army	296	195	116	1394
2	Randy Duncan	QB	Iowa	194	157	125	1021
3	Billy Cannon	HB	LSU	198	140	101	975
4	Bob White	RB	Ohio State	40	88	69	365
5	Joe Kapp	QB	California	47	27	32	227
6	Billy Austin	TB	Rutgers	26	41	37	197
7	Bob Harrison	C	Oklahoma	26	37	35	187
8	Dick Bass	RB	Pacific	14	17	20	96
9	Don Meredith	QB	SMU	10	12	21	75
10	Nick Pietrosante	FB	Notre Dame	8	14	18	70

AWARD WINNERS

PLAYER	POS	SCHOOL	AWARD NAME
Pete Dawkins	HB	Army	Maxwell
Zeke Smith	G	Auburn	Outland

CONFERENCE STANDINGS

ACC

	CONF. W L T	OVERALL W L T
Clemson	5 1 0	8 3 0
South Carolina	5 2 0	7 3 0
Duke	3 2 0	5 5 0
North Carolina	4 3 0	6 4 0
Maryland	3 3 0	4 6 0
Wake Forest	2 4 0	3 7 0
North Carolina St.	2 5 0	2 7 1
Virginia	1 5 0	1 9 0

Big 10

	CONF. W L T	OVERALL W L T
Iowa	5 1 0	8 1 1
Wisconsin	5 1 1	7 1 1
Ohio State	4 1 2	6 1 2
Purdue	3 1 2	6 1 2
Indiana	3 2 1	5 3 1
Illinois	4 3 0	4 5 0
Northwestern	3 4 0	5 4 0
Michigan	1 5 1	2 6 1
Minnesota	1 6 0	1 8 0
Michigan State	0 5 1	3 5 1

Big 7

	CONF. W L T	OVERALL W L T
Oklahoma	6 0 0	10 1 0
Missouri	4 1 1	5 4 1
Colorado	4 2 0	6 4 0
Kansas	3 2 1	4 5 1
Kansas State	2 4 0	3 7 0
Nebraska	1 5 0	3 7 0
Iowa State	0 6 0	4 6 0

Border

	CONF. W L T	OVERALL W L T
Hardin-Simmons	4 0 0	6 5 0
Arizona State	4 1 0	7 3 0
Arizona	2 1 0	3 7 0
New Mexico State	1 3 0	4 6 0
Texas-El Paso	1 4 0	2 7 0
West Texas State	1 4 0	1 9 0

Ivy

	CONF. W L T	OVERALL W L T
Dartmouth	6 1 0	7 2 0
Cornell	5 2 0	6 3 0
Princeton	5 2 0	6 3 0
Brown	4 3 0	6 3 0
Pennsylvania	4 3 0	4 5 0
Harvard	3 4 0	4 5 0
Columbia	1 6 0	1 8 0
Yale	0 7 0	2 7 0

MAC

	CONF. W L T	OVERALL W L T
Miami, Ohio	5 0 0	6 3 0
Kent State	5 1 0	7 2 0
Bowling Green	4 2 0	7 2 0
Ohio U	2 4 0	5 4 0
Western Michigan	2 4 0	4 5 0
Toledo	1 4 0	4 5 0
Marshall	1 5 0	3 6 0

Pacific Coast

	CONF. W L T	OVERALL W L T
California	6 1 0	7 4 0
Washington State	6 2 0	7 3 0
Southern Cal	4 2 1	4 5 1
Oregon State	5 3 0	6 4 0
Oregon	4 4 0	4 6 0
UCLA	2 4 1	3 6 1
Stanford	2 5 0	2 8 0
Washington	1 6 0	3 7 0
Idaho	0 3 0	4 5 0

SEC

	CONF. W L T	OVERALL W L T
LSU	6 0 0	11 0 0
Auburn	6 0 1	9 0 1
Mississippi	4 2 0	9 2 0
Vanderbilt	2 1 3	5 2 3
Tennessee	4 3 0	4 6 0
Kentucky	3 4 1	5 4 1
Alabama	3 4 1	5 4 1
Florida	2 3 1	6 4 1
Georgia Tech	2 3 1	5 4 1
Georgia	2 4 0	4 6 0
Tulane	1 5 0	3 7 0
Mississippi State	1 6 0	3 6 0

Skyline

	CONF. W L T	OVERALL W L T
Wyoming	6 1 0	8 3 0
New Mexico	5 1 0	7 3 0
Brigham Young	5 2 0	6 4 0
Colorado State	4 3 0	6 4 0
Utah	3 3 0	4 7 0
Utah State	2 5 0	3 7 0
Denver	2 5 0	2 8 0
Montana	0 7 0	0 10 0

SWC

	CONF. W L T	OVERALL W L T
TCU	5 1 0	8 2 1
SMU	4 2 0	6 4 0
Rice	4 2 0	5 5 0
Texas	3 3 0	7 3 0
Texas A&M	2 4 0	4 6 0
Arkansas	2 4 0	4 6 0
Baylor	1 5 0	3 7 0

Independents

	OVERALL W L T
Army	8 0 1
Air Force	9 0 2
Rutgers	8 1 0
Syracuse	8 2 0
Oklahoma State	8 3 0
Boston College	7 3 0
Navy	6 3 0
Penn State	6 3 1
Florida State	7 4 0
Notre Dame	6 4 0
Pittsburgh	5 4 1
Memphis	4 5 0
Texas Tech	3 7 0
Miami, Fla.	2 8 0

BOWL GAMES

DATE	GAME	SCORE
D13	Bluegrass	Oklahoma State 15, Florida State 6
D27	Gator	Mississippi 7, Florida 3
D27	Tangerine	Texas A&M-Commerce 26, Missouri Valley 7
D31	Sun	Wyoming 14, Hardin-Simmons 6
J1	Cotton	Air Force 0, TCU 0
J1	Rose	Iowa 38, California 12
J1	Sugar	LSU 7, Clemson 0
J1	Orange	Oklahoma 21, Syracuse 6

1958 NCAA MAJOR COLLEGE STATISTICAL LEADERS

INDIVIDUAL LEADERS

PASSING/COMPLETIONS	G	ATT	COM	PCT	INT	I%	YDS	YPA	TD	TD%	COM.PG
1 Buddy Humphrey, Baylor	10	195	112	57.4	8	4.1	1316	6.7	7	3.6	11.2
2 Ralph Hunsaker, Arizona	10	191	106	55.5	13	6.8	1129	5.9	5	2.6	10.6
3 Randy Duncan, Iowa	9	172	101	58.7	9	5.2	1347	7.8	11	6.4	11.2
4 Rich Mayo, Air Force	10	174	98	56.3	6	3.5	1019	5.9	11	6.3	9.8
5 Charles Milstead, Texas A&M	10	167	88	52.7	11	6.6	1135	6.8	5	3.0	8.8
6 Dick Longfellow, West Virginia	10	156	79	50.6	12	7.7	948	6.1	6	3.9	7.9
7 Bob Nicolet, Stanford	10	146	77	52.7	5	3.4	724	5.0	3	2.1	7.7
8 Dick Norman, Stanford	10	133	76	57.1	7	5.3	717	5.4	3	2.3	7.6
9 Arnold Dempsey, Virginia	10	152	74	48.7	11	7.2	697	4.6	2	1.3	7.4
10 Jack Lee, Cincinnati	10	130	71	54.6	11	8.5	951	7.3	5	3.9	7.1
10 Frank Finney, Brown	9	142	71	50.0	10	7.0	982	6.9	8	5.6	7.9

ALL-PURPOSE YARDS	G	RUSH	REC	INT	PR	KR	YDS	YPG
1 Dick Bass, Pacific	10	1361	121	5	164	227	1878	187.8

RUSHING/YARDS	G	ATT	YDS	AVG	YPG
1 Dick Bass, Pacific	10	205	1361	6.6	136.1
2 Bob White, Ohio State	9	218	859	3.9	95.4
3 Dwight Nichols, Iowa State	10	220	815	3.7	81.5
4 Pete Hart, Hardin-Simmons	10	163	785	4.8	78.5
5 Billy Austin, Rutgers	9	145	747	5.2	83.0
6 Jake Crouthamel, Dartmouth	9	123	722	5.9	80.2
7 Weldon Jackson, Brigham Young	10	101	698	6.9	69.8
8 Billy Cannon, LSU	10	115	686	6.0	68.6
9 Larry Hickman, Baylor	10	151	670	4.4	67.0
10 John Saunders, South Carolina	10	128	653	5.1	65.3

RUSHING/YARDS PER CARRY	G	ATT	YDS	YPC
1 Ray Jauch, Iowa	9	72	506	7.0
2 Weldon Jackson, Brigham Young	10	101	698	6.9
3 Wayne Schneider, Colorado State	10	84	580	6.9
4 Dick Bass, Pacific	10	205	1361	6.6
5 Sam Horner, VMI	10	102	612	6.0
6 Prentice Gautt, Oklahoma	10	105	627	6.0
7 Billy Cannon, LSU	10	115	686	6.0
8 Leon Burton, Arizona State	10	108	642	5.9
9 Duane Wood, Oklahoma State	10	83	492	5.9
10 Jake Crouthamel, Dartmouth	9	123	722	5.9

*-Based on top 60 rushers

RECEIVING/RECEPTIONS	G	REC	YDS	TD	YPR	YPG	RPG
1 Dave Hibbert, Arizona	10	61	606	4	9.9	60.6	6.1
2 Sonny Randle, Virginia	10	47	642	5	13.7	64.2	4.7
3 Chris Burford, Stanford	10	45	493	2	11.0	49.3	4.5
4 John Tracey, Texas A&M	10	37	466	2	12.6	46.6	3.7
5 Ray Siminski, Furman	9	35	568	5	16.2	63.1	3.9
6 Bob Simms, Rutgers	9	33	468	9	14.2	52.0	3.7
7 Irvin Nikolai, Stanford	10	32	343	0	10.7	34.3	3.2
8 Sonny Oates, Hardin-Simmons	10	31	402	0	13.0	40.2	3.1
8 Gerry Moore, Baylor	10	31	357	2	11.5	35.7	3.1
8 Mel Reight, West Virginia	10	31	329	2	10.6	32.9	3.1

PUNTING	PUNT	YDS	AVG
1 Bobby Walden, Georgia	44	1993	45.3
2 Boyd Dowler, Colorado	33	1429	43.3
3 Don Coker, North Carolina	31	1339	43.2
4 Tommy Davis, LSU	38	1623	42.7
5 Sam Horner, VMI	28	1193	42.6
5 Joe Delany, Georgia Tech	28	1193	42.6
7 Doug Hatcher, South Carolina	20	834	41.7
8 Dainard Paulson, Oregon State	35	1449	41.4
9 Brad Myers, Michigan	24	989	41.2
10 John Lands, Montana	23	943	41.0

PUNT RETURNS/YARDS	PR	YDS	AVG
1 Howard Cook, Colorado	24	242	10.1
2 John Horrillo, Oregon State	20	227	11.4
3 David Ray, Vanderbilt	10	199	19.9
4 Dwight Nichols, Iowa State	18	195	10.8
5 Dale Hackbart, Wisconsin	7	193	27.6
6 Jake Crouthamel, Dartmouth	11	188	17.1
7 Ronnie Morris, Tulsa	12	183	15.3
8 Dean Look, Michigan State	5	179	35.8
9 Jim Colclough, Boston College	19	177	9.3
10 Mike Quinlan, Air Force	11	172	15.6

KICKOFF RETURNS/YARDS	KR	YDS	AVG
1 Sonny Randle, Virginia	21	506	24.1
2 Wray Carlton, Duke	13	332	25.5
3 Billy Stacy, Mississippi State	12	309	25.8
4 Ronnie Morris, Tulsa	11	305	27.7
5 Warren Livingston, Arizona	12	302	25.2
6 Frank Reginelli, Marquette	14	301	21.5
7 Tom Newell, Drake	14	300	21.4
8 Jim Crotty, Notre Dame	12	297	24.8
9 Overton Curtis, Utah State	9	296	32.9
10 Claude King, Houston	10	291	29.1

SCORING	TDS	XPT	FG	PTS
1 Dick Bass, Pacific	18	8	0	116
2 Billy Austin, Rutgers	16	10	0	106
3 Ron Burton, Northwestern	12	4	0	76
4 Billy Cannon, LSU	11	8	0	74
4 Frank Finney, Brown	10	14	0	74
4 Pete Hart, Army	12	2	0	74
7 Bob White, Ohio State	12	0	0	72
8 Leon Burton, Arizona State	11	4	0	70
9 Calvin Bird, Kentucky	10	5	0	65
10 Bob Simms, Rutgers	9	10	0	64

KICK SCORING	XPA	XP	FG	PTS
1 Bobby Khayat, Mississippi	24	22	4	34
2 John Sheppard, Florida State	21	19	3	28
3 George Pupich, Air Force	16	12	5	27
4 Bill Bucek, Rice	14	12	4	24
5 Ben Grosse, Kansas State	8	8	5	23
6 Bob Prescott, Iowa	24	18	1	21
7 Tommy Wells, Georgia Tech	10	7	4	19
8 David Kilgore, Ohio State	17	15	1	18
8 Monty Stickles, Notre Dame	19	15	1	18
10 Charles Rash, Missouri	16	14	1	17

INTERCEPTIONS	INT	YDS
1 Jim Norton, Idaho	9	222
2 Dale Hackbart, Wisconsin	7	77
2 James Grazione, Villanova	7	76
4 Billy Austin, Rutgers	6	128
4 Dick Young, Wichita State	6	107
4 Ted Colna, George Washington	6	65
4 Ken Hohl, Holy Cross	6	22
8 Abner Haynes, North Texas	5	122
8 Jim Kerr, Penn State	5	122
8 Bill Bucek, Rice	5	84

TEAM LEADERS

RUSHING OFFENSE	G	ATT	YDS	AVG	YPG
1 Pacific	10	502	2596	5.2	259.6
2 Oklahoma	10	633	2574	4.1	257.4
3 Arizona State	10	548	2539	4.6	253.9
4 Brigham Young	10	538	2497	4.6	249.7
5 Colorado	10	523	2495	4.8	249.5
6 Penn State	10	597	2429	4.1	242.9
7 California	10	603	2380	3.9	238.0
8 Tulsa	10	582	2364	4.1	236.4
9 Iowa	9	444	2123	4.8	235.9
10 Purdue	9	550	2094	3.8	232.7

PASSING OFFENSE	G	ATT	COM	INT	PCT	YDS	YPA	TD	I%	YPC	YPG
1 Army	9	187	87	13	46.5	1550	8.3	13	7.0	17.8	172.2
2 Iowa	9	205	115	11	56.1	1530	7.5	11	5.4	13.3	170.0
3 San Jose State	9	253	131	6	51.8	1528	6.0	11	5.5	11.7	169.8
4 Baylor	10	253	140	11	55.3	1687	6.7	9	4.4	12.1	168.7
5 SMU	10	208	113	16	54.3	1661	8.0	15	7.7	14.7	166.1
6 Navy	9	194	106	14	54.6	1445	7.4	15	7.2	13.6	160.6
7 Stanford	10	305	164	14	53.8	1581	5.2	7	4.6	9.6	158.1
8 Notre Dame	10	198	94	22	47.5	1561	7.9	13	11.1	16.6	156.1
9 Texas A&M	10	233	119	16	51.1	1541	6.6	6	6.9	12.9	154.1
10 Washington State	10	188	115	10	61.2	1463	7.8	18	5.3	12.7	146.3

TOTAL OFFENSE	G	P	YDS	AVG	YPG
1 Iowa	9	649	3653	5.6	405.9
2 Pacific	10	657	3804	5.8	380.4
3 Arizona State	10	694	3795	5.5	379.5
4 Army	9	630	3380	5.4	375.6
5 Notre Dame	10	710	3697	5.2	369.7
6 Air Force	10	732	3605	4.9	360.5
7 Oklahoma	10	762	3517	4.6	351.7
8 Baylor	10	715	3356	4.7	335.6
9 Brown	9	622	3019	4.9	335.4
10 West Virginia	10	720	3319	4.6	331.9

RUSHING DEFENSE	G	ATT	YDS	AVG	YPG
1 Auburn	10	370	796	2.2	79.6
2 Tulsa	10	398	825	2.1	82.5
3 Pittsburgh	10	407	913	2.2	91.3
4 Army	9	346	837	2.4	93.0
5 Syracuse	9	382	849	2.2	94.3
6 Purdue	9	372	849	2.3	94.3
7 Florida	10	395	948	2.4	94.8
8 Boston College	10	404	1060	2.6	106.0
9 TCU	10	401	1104	2.8	110.4
10 LSU	10	461	1151	2.5	115.1

PASSING DEFENSE	G	ATT	COM	INT	PCT	YDS	YPA	TD	I%	YPC	YPG
1 Iowa State	10	109	41	15	37.6	390	3.6	2	13.8	9.5	39.0
2 Brown	9	108	36	NA	33.3	403	3.7	6	NA	11.2	44.8
3 Georgia Tech	10	129	55	12	42.6	571	4.4	3	9.3	10.4	57.1
4 Harvard	9	105	47	NA	44.8	526	5.0	2	NA	11.2	58.4
5 Colorado	10	129	50	9	38.8	590	4.6	6	7.0	11.8	59.0
6 Alabama	10	133	55	19	41.4	600	4.5	2	14.3	10.9	60.0
7 Washington State	10	140	55	NA	39.3	607	4.3	2	NA	11.0	60.7
8 Oregon	10	122	56	7	45.9	656	5.4	2	5.7	11.7	65.6
9 Georgia	10	141	58	NA	41.1	673	4.8	8	NA	11.6	67.3
10 Florida State	10	126	51	14	40.5	675	5.4	2	11.1	13.2	67.5

TOTAL DEFENSE	G	P	YDS	AVG	YPG
1 Auburn	10	521	1575	3.0	157.5
2 Purdue	9	485	1590	3.3	176.7
3 Army	9	561	1643	2.9	182.6
4 Harvard	9	512	1720	3.4	191.1
5 LSU	10	624	1934	3.1	193.4
6 Boston College	10	558	1942	3.5	194.2
7 Pittsburgh	10	569	1961	3.4	196.1
8 North Texas	10	542	2017	3.7	201.7
9 Georgia Tech	10	552	2018	3.7	201.8
10 Tulsa	10	595	2030	3.4	203.0

SCORING OFFENSE	G	PTS	AVG
1 Rutgers	9	301	33.4
2 Army	9	264	29.3
2 Syracuse	9	264	29.3
4 Oklahoma	10	279	27.9
5 LSU	10	275	27.5
6 Arizona State	10	271	27.1
7 West Virginia	10	268	26.8
8 Pacific	10	266	26.6
9 Iowa	9	234	26.0
10 Air Force	10	247	24.7

SCORING DEFENSE	G	PTS	AVG
1 Oklahoma	10	49	4.9
2 Oregon	10	50	5.0
3 LSU	10	53	5.3
4 Army	9	49	5.4
5 Auburn	10	62	6.2
6 Mississippi	10	65	6.5
7 Syracuse	9	59	6.6
8 Vanderbilt	10	71	7.1
9 Alabama	10	75	7.5
10 TCU	10	78	7.8

1959 POLL PROGRESSION

PRE-SEASON 1959 — SEPT. 19 GAMES

AP	Team	Record	Result
1	LSU	0-0-0	beat Rice 26-3
2	Oklahoma	0-0-0	bye week
3	Auburn	0-0-0	bye week
4	SMU	0-0-0	bye week
5	Army	0-0-0	bye week
6	Wisconsin	0-0-0	bye week
7	Ohio State	0-0-0	bye week
8	Mississippi	0-0-0	beat Houston 16-0
9	Iowa	0-0-0	bye week
10	Northwestern	0-0-0	bye week
11	Purdue	0-0-0	tied UCLA 0-0
12	North Carolina	0-0-0	lost to # 18 Clemson 18-20
13	TCU	0-0-0	beat Kansas 14-7
14	South Carolina	0-0-0	beat Duke 12-7
15	Air Force	0-0-0	bye week
16	Notre Dame	0-0-0	bye week
17	Texas	0-0-0	beat Nebraska 20-0
18	Clemson	0-0-0	beat # 12 North Carolina 20-18
19	Michigan State	0-0-0	bye week
20	Syracuse	0-0-0	bye week

SEPTEMBER 21 POLL — SEPT. 26 GAMES

UP	AP	Team	Record	Result
1	1	LSU	1-0-0	beat # 9 TCU 10-0
2	2	Oklahoma	0-0-0	lost to # 10 Northwestern 13-45
7	3	Auburn	0-0-0	lost to Tennessee 0-3
5	4	Mississippi	1-0-0	beat Kentucky 16-0
9	5	Clemson	1-0-0	beat Virginia 47-0
11	6	SMU	0-0-0	lost to # 16 Georgia Tech 12-16
6	7	Army	0-0-0	beat Boston College 44-8
3	8	Wisconsin	0-0-0	beat Stanford 16-14
15	9	TCU	0-0-0	lost to # 1 LSU 0-10
14	10	Northwestern	0-0-0	beat # 2 Oklahoma 45-13
12	11	Southern Cal	1-0-0	beat Pittsburgh 23-0
4	12	Ohio State	0-0-0	lost to Duke 14-13
10	13	Iowa	0-0-0	beat California 42-12
13	14	Navy	1-0-0	beat William & Mary 29-2
8	15	Texas	1-0-0	beat Maryland 26-0
20	16	Georgia Tech	1-0-0	beat # 6 SMU 16-12
18	17	Georgia	1-0-0	beat Vanderbilt 21-6
17	18	Penn State	1-0-0	beat VMI 21-0
	19	Florida	1-0-0	beat Mississippi State 14-13
	20	South Carolina	1-0-0	beat Furman 30-0
16		Purdue	0-0-1	bye week
19		Maryland	1-0-0	lost to # 15 Texas 0-26

SEPTEMBER 28 POLL — OCT. 3 GAMES

UP	AP	Team	Record	Result
1	1	LSU	2-0-0	beat Baylor 22-0
2	2	Northwestern	1-0-0	beat # 5 Iowa 14-10
5	3	Mississippi	2-0-0	beat Memphis 43-0
4	4	Army	1-0-0	lost to Illinois 14-20
3	5	Iowa	1-0-0	lost to # 2 Northwestern 10-14
7	6	Clemson	2-0-0	lost to # 7 Georgia Tech 6-16
12	7	Georgia Tech	2-0-0	beat # 6 Clemson 16-6
10	8	Notre Dame	1-0-0	lost to Purdue 7-28
13	9	Tennessee	1-0-0	beat Mississippi State 22-6
8	10	Texas	2-0-0	beat California 33-0
6	11	Southern Cal	2-0-0	beat # 14 Ohio State 17-0
9	12	Wisconsin	1-0-0	beat Marquette 44-6
16	13	Georgia	2-0-0	lost to # 16 South Carolina 14-30
10	14	Ohio State	1-0-0	lost to # 11 Southern Cal 0-17
15	15	Navy	1-0-0	lost to SMU 7-20
	16	South Carolina	2-0-0	beat # 13 Georgia 30-14
	17	Auburn	0-1-0	beat Hardin-Simmons 35-12
	18	Air Force	1-0-0	beat Trinity 52-0
	19	Florida	2-0-0	beat Virginia 55-10
14	20	Syracuse	1-0-0	beat Maryland 29-0
17		Indiana	1-0-0	lost to Minnesota 14-24
18		Oklahoma	0-1-0	beat Colorado 42-12
19		Purdue	0-0-1	beat # 8 Notre Dame 28-7
20		Penn State	2-0-0	beat Colgate 58-20

OCTOBER 5 POLL — OCT. 10 GAMES

UP	AP	Team	Record	Result
1	1	LSU	3-0-0	beat Miami, Fla. 27-3
2	2	Northwestern	2-0-0	beat Minnesota 6-0
5	3	Georgia Tech	3-0-0	beat # 8 Tennessee 14-7
4	4	Texas	3-0-0	beat # 13 Oklahoma 19-12
7	5	Mississippi	3-0-0	beat Vanderbilt 33-0
3	6	Southern Cal	3-0-0	bye week
8	7	Purdue	1-0-1	beat # 9 Wisconsin 21-0
6	8	Tennessee	2-0-0	lost to # 3 Georgia Tech 7-14
9	9	Wisconsin	2-0-0	lost to # 7 Purdue 0-21
10	10	Iowa	1-1-0	beat Michigan State 37-8
13	11	South Carolina	3-0-0	lost to North Carolina 6-19
11	12	Syracuse	2-0-0	beat Navy 32-6
14	13	Oklahoma	1-1-0	lost to # 4 Texas 12-19
15	14	Auburn	1-1-0	beat Kentucky 33-0
	15	SMU	1-1-0	beat Missouri 23-2
12	16	Penn State	3-0-0	beat Army 17-11
18	17	Florida	3-0-0	tied Rice 13-13
19	18	Air Force	2-0-0	beat Idaho 21-0
	19	Arkansas	3-0-0	beat Baylor 23-7
	20	Illinois	1-1-0	beat Ohio State 9-0
16		Michigan State	1-1-0	lost to # 10 Iowa 8-37
16		SMU	1-1-0	beat Missouri 23-2 (09)
20		Duke	1-2-0	lost to Pittsburgh 0-12
20		Oregon	3-0-0	beat San Jose State 35-12

OCTOBER 12 POLL — OCT. 17 GAMES

UP	AP	Team	Record	Result
1	1	LSU	4-0-0	beat Kentucky 9-0
2	2	Northwestern	3-0-0	beat Michigan 20-7
3	3	Texas	4-0-0	beat # 12 Arkansas 13-12
4	4	Georgia Tech	4-0-0	lost to # 11 Auburn 6-7
7	5	Mississippi	4-0-0	beat Tulane 53-7
5	6	Purdue	2-0-1	lost to Ohio State 0-15
6	7	Southern Cal	3-0-0	beat # 18 Washington 22-15
8	8	Syracuse	3-0-0	beat Holy Cross 42-6
9	9	Iowa	2-1-0	lost to Wisconsin 16-25
10	10	Penn State	4-0-0	beat Boston U. 21-12
11	11	Auburn	2-1-0	beat # 4 Georgia Tech 7-6
14	12	Arkansas	4-0-0	lost to # 3 Texas 12-13
	13	Illinois	2-1-0	beat Minnesota 14-6
16	14	Tennessee	2-1-0	tied Alabama 7-7
15	15	Clemson	3-1-0	bye week
19	16	SMU	2-1-0	tied Rice 13-13
12	17	Air Force	3-0-0	lost to Oregon 3-20
18	18	Washington	4-0-0	lost to # 7 Southern Cal 15-22
19	19	Florida	3-0-1	lost to Vanderbilt 6-13
	20	Pittsburgh	3-1-0	lost to West Virginia 15-23
14		Notre Dame	2-1-0	lost to Michigan State 0-19
17		Oklahoma	1-2-0	beat Missouri 23-0

OCTOBER 19 POLL — OCT. 24 GAMES

UP	AP	Team	Record	Result
1	1	LSU	5-0-0	beat Florida 9-0
2	2	Northwestern	4-0-0	beat Notre Dame 30-24
3	3	Texas	5-0-0	beat Rice 28-6
5	4	Mississippi	5-0-0	beat # 10 Arkansas 28-0
4	5	Southern Cal	4-0-0	beat Stanford 30-28
6	6	Syracuse	4-0-0	beat West Virginia 44-0
8	7	Auburn	3-1-0	beat Miami, Fla. 21-6
7	8	Penn State	5-0-0	beat # 13 Illinois 20-9
9	9	Georgia Tech	4-1-0	beat Tulane 21-13
13	10	Arkansas	4-1-0	lost to # 4 Mississippi 0-28
11	11	Oregon	5-0-0	lost to Washington 10-13
10	12	Wisconsin	3-1-0	beat # 20 Ohio State 12-3
12	13	Illinois	3-1-0	lost to # 8 Penn State 9-20
14	14	Purdue	2-1-1	beat Iowa 14-7
	15	Iowa	2-2-0	lost to Purdue 7-14
20	16	TCU	3-2-0	beat Pittsburgh 13-3
15	17	Clemson	3-1-0	beat South Carolina 27-0
18	18	Oklahoma	2-2-0	beat Kansas 7-6
	19	Yale	4-0-0	beat Colgate 21-0
17	20	Ohio State	2-2-0	lost to # 12 Wisconsin 3-12
17		UCLA	1-1-1	lost to Air Force 7-20 (O23)
20		Tennessee	2-1-1	beat U.T. Chattanooga 23-0
20		Washington	4-1-0	beat # 11 Oregon 13-12
20		Indiana	3-1-0	lost to Michigan State 6-14

OCTOBER 26 POLL — OCT. 31 GAMES

UP	AP	Team	Record	Result
1	1	LSU	6-0-0	beat # 3 Mississippi 7-3
2	2	Northwestern	5-0-0	beat Indiana 30-13
3	3	Mississippi	6-0-0	lost to # 1 LSU 3-7
4	4	Texas	6-0-0	beat SMU 21-0
5	5	Syracuse	5-0-0	beat Pittsburgh 35-0
6	6	Southern Cal	5-0-0	beat California 14-7
7	7	Penn State	6-0-0	beat West Virginia 28-10
8	8	Auburn	4-1-0	beat Florida 6-0
10	9	Georgia Tech	5-1-0	lost to Duke 7-10
9	10	Wisconsin	4-1-0	beat Michigan 19-10
11	11	Purdue	3-1-1	tied Illinois 7-7
12	12	Clemson	4-1-0	beat Rice 19-0
15	13	Yale	5-0-0	lost to Dartmouth 8-12
	14	Georgia	5-1-0	beat Florida State 42-0
19	15	TCU	4-2-0	beat Baylor 14-0
15	16	Oregon	5-1-0	beat Idaho 45-7
	17	Arkansas	4-2-0	beat Texas A&M 12-7
13	18	Washington	5-1-0	beat UCLA 23-7
15	19	Oklahoma	3-2-0	lost to Nebraska 21-25
14	20	Tennessee	3-1-1	beat North Carolina 29-7
15		Air Force	4-1-0	tied Army 13-13
19		Michigan State	3-2-0	lost to Ohio State 24-30

NOVEMBER 2 POLL — NOV. 7 GAMES

UP	AP	Team	Record	Result
1	1	LSU	7-0-0	lost to # 13 Tennessee 13-14
2	2	Northwestern	6-0-0	lost to # 9 Wisconsin 19-24
3	3	Texas	7-0-0	beat Baylor 13-12
3	4	Syracuse	6-0-0	beat # 7 Penn State 20-18
6	5	Mississippi	6-1-0	beat U.T. Chattanooga 58-0
5	6	Southern Cal	6-0-0	beat West Virginia 36-0
7	7	Penn State	7-0-0	lost to # 4 Syracuse 18-20
9	8	Auburn	5-1-0	beat Mississippi State 31-0
8	9	Wisconsin	5-1-0	beat # 2 Northwestern 24-19
11	10	Clemson	5-1-0	beat Duke 6-0
14	11	Georgia	6-1-0	beat Florida 21-10
10	12	Washington	6-1-0	beat Oregon State 13-6
16	13	Tennessee	4-1-1	beat # 1 LSU 14-13
13	14	Purdue	3-1-2	lost to Michigan State 0-15
15	15	Oregon	6-1-0	beat California 10-0
	16	Arkansas	5-2-0	beat Rice 14-10
18	17	TCU	5-2-0	bye week
20	18	Air Force	4-1-1	lost to Missouri 0-13
15	19	Georgia Tech	5-2-0	beat Notre Dame 14-10
	20	North Texas	7-0-0	beat Louisville 39-7
16		Illinois	3-2-1	lost to Michigan 15-20
18		Ohio State	3-3-0	tied Indiana 0-0

NOVEMBER 9 POLL — NOV. 14 GAMES

UP	AP	Team	Record	Result
1	1	Syracuse	7-0-0	beat Colgate 71-0
2	2	Texas	8-0-0	lost to # 18 TCU 9-14
4	3	LSU	7-1-0	beat Mississippi State 27-0
3	4	Southern Cal	7-0-0	beat Baylor 17-8
7	5	Mississippi	7-1-0	beat # 9 Tennessee 37-7
6	6	Northwestern	6-1-0	lost to # 19 Michigan State 10-15
5	7	Wisconsin	6-1-0	lost to Illinois 6-9
8	8	Auburn	6-1-0	lost to # 12 Georgia 13-14
10	9	Tennessee	5-1-1	lost to # 5 Mississippi 7-37
9	10	Penn State	7-1-0	beat Holy Cross 46-0
11	11	Clemson	6-1-0	lost to Maryland 25-28
12	12	Georgia	7-1-0	beat # 8 Auburn 14-13
13	13	Washington	7-1-0	beat California 20-0
15	14	Oregon	7-1-0	beat Washington State 7-6
14	15	Georgia Tech	6-2-0	lost to Alabama 7-9
16	16	Iowa	4-3-0	beat Ohio State 16-7
17	17	North Texas	8-0-0	lost to Tulsa 0-7
19	18	TCU	5-2-0	beat # 2 Texas 14-9
17	19	Michigan State	4-3-0	beat # 6 Northwestern 15-10
17	20	Arkansas	6-2-0	beat SMU 17-14

UP	AP	November 16 Poll		Nov. 21 Games
1	1	Syracuse	8-0-0	beat Boston U. 46-0
3	2	Mississippi	8-1-0	bye week
4	3	LSU	8-1-0	beat Tulane 14-6
2	4	Southern Cal	8-0-0	lost to UCLA 3-10
6	5	Texas	8-1-0	bye week
7	6	Georgia	8-1-0	bye week
5	7	Penn State	8-1-0	lost to Pittsburgh 7-22
9	8	Northwestern	6-2-0	lost to Illinois 0-28
9	9	Wisconsin	6-2-0	beat Minnesota 11-7
11	10	TCU	6-2-0	beat Rice 35-6
12	11	Michigan State	5-3-0	lost to Miami, Fla. 13-18
14	12	Auburn	6-2-0	beat Southern Miss 28-7
13	13	Arkansas	7-2-0	beat Texas Tech 27-0
8	14	Washington	8-1-0	beat Washington State 20-0
16	15	Oregon	8-1-0	lost to Oregon State 7-15
14	16	Iowa	5-3-0	lost to Notre Dame 19-20
18	17	Alabama	5-1-2	beat Memphis 14-7
	18	Miami, Fla.	5-3-0	beat Michigan State 18-13
	19	Clemson	6-2-0	beat Wake Forest 33-31
	20	Tennessee	5-2-1	lost to Kentucky 0-20
17		Illinois	4-3-1	beat # 8 Northwestern 28-0
18		Iowa State	7-2-0	lost to Oklahoma 12-35
18		Wyoming	8-1-0	beat Denver 45-0

UP	AP	November 23 Poll		Nov. 28 Games
1	1	Syracuse	9-0-0	bye week
2	2	Mississippi	8-1-0	beat Mississippi State 42-0
3	3	LSU	9-1-0	regular season complete
4	4	Texas	8-1-0	beat Texas A&M 20-17
5	5	Wisconsin	7-2-0	regular season complete
6	6	Georgia	8-1-0	beat Georgia Tech 21-14
7	7	Southern Cal	8-1-0	lost to Notre Dame 6-16
9	8	TCU	7-2-0	beat SMU 19-0
8	9	Washington	9-1-0	regular season complete
10	10	Arkansas	8-2-0	regular season complete
11	11	Auburn	7-2-0	lost to # 19 Alabama 0-10
16	12	Miami, Fla.	6-3-0	lost to Florida 14-23
12	13	Illinois	5-3-1	regular season complete
14	14	Clemson	7-2-0	beat Furman 56-3
13	15	Penn State	8-2-0	regular season complete
	16	Pittsburgh	6-4-0	regular season complete
20	17	Oklahoma	6-3-0	beat Oklahoma State 17-7
	18	Missouri	6-4-0	regular season complete
20	19	Alabama	6-1-2	beat # 11 Auburn 10-0
	20	UCLA	4-3-1	beat Utah 21-6
15		Michigan State	5-4-0	regular season complete
17		Oregon	8-2-0	regular season complete
18		Northwestern	6-3-0	regular season complete
19		Wyoming	9-1-0	regular season complete

UP	AP	November 30 Poll		Dec. 5 Games
1	1	Syracuse	9-0-0	beat # 17 UCLA 36-8
2	2	Mississippi	9-1-0	regular season complete
3	3	LSU	9-1-0	
4	4	Texas	9-1-0	regular season complete
5	5	Georgia	9-1-0	regular season complete
6	6	Wisconsin	7-2-0	
8	7	TCU	8-2-0	regular season complete
7	8	Washington	9-1-0	
9	9	Arkansas	8-2-0	
10	10	Clemson	8-2-0	regular season complete
13	11	Alabama	7-1-2	regular season complete
11	12	Illinois	5-3-1	
12	13	Southern Cal	8-2-0	regular season complete
14	14	Penn State	8-2-0	
15	15	Oklahoma	7-3-0	regular season complete
18	16	Wyoming	9-1-0	regular season complete
	17	UCLA	5-3-1	lost to # 1 Syracuse 8-36
	18	Florida	5-4-1	regular season complete
	19	Notre Dame	5-5-0	regular season complete
19	20	Missouri	6-4-0	
15		Northwestern	6-3-0	regular season complete
15		Michigan State	5-4-0	regular season complete
19		Auburn	7-3-0	regular season complete

UP	AP	December 7 Final Poll	RECORD	BOWL BID	DATE	BOWL RESULT	RB	RECORD
1	1	Syracuse	10-0-0	Cotton Bowl	J1	beat # 4 Texas 23-14	1	11-0-0
2	2	Mississippi	9-1-0	Sugar Bowl	J1	beat # 3 LSU 21-0	2	10-1-0
3	3	LSU	9-1-0	Sugar Bowl	J1	lost to # 2 Mississippi 0-21	3	9-2-0
4	4	Texas	9-1-0	Cotton Bowl	J1	lost to # 1 Syracuse 14-23	4	9-2-0
5	5	Georgia	9-1-0	Orange Bowl	J1	beat # 18 Missouri 14-0	5	10-1-0
6	6	Wisconsin	7-2-0	Rose Bowl	J1	lost to # 8 Washington 8-44	7	7-3-0
8	7	TCU	8-2-0	Bluebonnet Bowl	D19	lost to # 11 Clemson 7-23	12	8-3-0
7	8	Washington	9-1-0	Rose Bowl	J1	beat # 6 Wisconsin 44-8	6	10-1-0
9	9	Arkansas	8-2-0	Gator Bowl	J2	beat Georgia Tech 14-7	14	9-2-0
13	10	Alabama	7-1-2	Liberty Bowl	D19	lost to # 12 Penn State 0-7	18	7-2-2
11	11	Clemson	8-2-0	Bluebonnet Bowl	D19	beat # 7 TCU 23-7	11	9-2-0
10	12	Penn State	8-2-0	Liberty Bowl	D19	beat # 10 Alabama 7-0	17	9-2-0
12	13	Illinois	5-3-1				8	5-3-1
13	14	Southern Cal	8-2-0				19	8-2-0
17	15	Oklahoma	7-3-0				20	7-3-0
	16	Wyoming	9-1-0				22	9-1-0
18	17	Notre Dame	5-5-0				23	5-5-0
20	18	Missouri	6-4-0	Orange Bowl	J1	lost to # 5 Georgia 0-14	49	6-5-0
20	19	Florida	5-4-1				16	5-4-1
19	20	Pittsburgh	6-4-0				36	6-4-0
15		Auburn	7-3-0				15	7-3-0
16		Michigan State	5-4-0				10	5-4-0

1959

CONSENSUS ALL-AMERICANS

POS	Name	HT	WT	School	AP	FC	FW	NE	SN	PI
B	Richie Lucas	6-1	185	Penn State		•	•	•	•	•
B	Billy Cannon	6-1	208	LSU	•	•	•	•	•	•
B	Charlie Flowers	6-0	198	Mississippi	•	•	•	•	•	•
B	Ron Burton	5-9	185	Northwestern		•	•		•	•
E	Bill Carpenter	6-2	210	Army	•	•	•	•		•
E	Monty Stickles	6-4	225	Notre Dame					•	•
T	Dan Lanphear	6-2	214	Wisconsin	•	•	•	•	•	•
T	Don Floyd	6-3	215	TCU	•	•			•	•
G	Roger Davis	6-2	228	Syracuse	•	•	•	•	•	•
G	Bill Burrell	6-0	210	Illinois	•	•			•	•
C	Maxie Baughan	6-1	212	Georgia Tech	•	•				

	OTHERS RECEIVING FIRST-TEAM HONORS									
B	Dean Look			Michigan State		•				
B	Don Meredith			SMU		•				
B	Dwight Nichols			Iowa State		•				
B	Jack Spikes			TCU		•				
B	Bob Schloredt			Washington	•					
B	Jim Mooty			Arkansas	•					
E	Carroll Dale			Virginia Tech			•	•		
E	Marlin McKeever			Southern Cal	•		•			
E	Don Norton			Iowa		•				
E	Chris Burford			Stanford		•				
E	Fred Mautino			Syracuse	•					
T	Mike McGee			Duke		•				
T	Ken Rice			Auburn		•	•			
T	Robert Yates			Syracuse				•		
G	Maurice Doke			Texas		•				
G	Pat Dye			Georgia		•				
G	Marvin Terrell			Mississippi		•				
G	Zeke Smith			Auburn	•			•		
C	Jim Andreotti			Northwestern		•				
C	E.J. Holub			Texas Tech		•	•			

FW named Roger Davis as a T; NEA named McKeever as a G

HEISMAN TROPHY VOTING

	PLAYER	POS	SCHOOL	1ST	2ND	3RD	TOTAL
1	Billy Cannon	HB	LSU	519	147	78	1929
2	Richie Lucas	QB	Penn State	97	109	104	613
3	Don Meredith	QB	SMU	26	67	74	286
4	Bill Burrell	G	Illinois	23	47	33	196
5	Charlie Flowers	FB	Mississippi	11	58	44	193
6	Dean Look	HB	Michigan State	23	41	25	176
7	Dale Hackbart	QB	Wisconsin	19	21	35	134
8	Dwight Nichols	RB	Iowa State	21	25	13	126
9	Monty Stickles	E	Notre Dame	16	21	36	126
10	Ron Burton	RB	Northwestern	10	28	36	122

AWARD WINNERS

PLAYER	POS	SCHOOL	AWARD NAME
Richie Lucas	QB	Penn State	Maxwell
Mike McGee	T	Duke	Outland

CONFERENCE STANDINGS

ACC	Conf. W L T			Overall W L T		
Clemson	6	1	0	9	2	0
North Carolina	5	2	0	5	5	0
Maryland	4	2	0	5	5	0
South Carolina	4	3	0	6	4	0
Wake Forest	4	3	0	6	4	0
Duke	2	3	0	4	6	0
North Carolina St.	0	6	0	1	9	0
Virginia	0	5	0	0	10	0

Big 10	Conf. W L T			Overall W L T		
Wisconsin	5	2	0	7	3	0
Michigan State	4	2	0	5	4	0
Purdue	4	2	1	5	2	2
Illinois	4	2	1	5	3	1
Northwestern	4	3	0	6	3	0
Iowa	3	3	0	5	4	0
Michigan	3	4	0	4	5	0
Indiana	2	4	1	4	4	1
Ohio State	2	4	1	3	5	1
Minnesota	1	6	0	2	7	0

Big 7	Conf. W L T			Overall W L T		
Oklahoma	5	1	0	7	3	0
Missouri	4	2	0	6	5	0
Iowa State	3	3	0	7	3	0
Colorado	3	3	0	5	5	0
Kansas	3	3	0	5	5	0
Nebraska	2	4	0	4	6	0
Kansas State	1	5	0	2	8	0

Border	Conf. W L T			Overall W L T		
Arizona State	5	0	0	10	1	0
Arizona	2	1	0	4	6	0
New Mexico State	2	2	0	8	3	0
Hardin-Simmons	2	2	0	3	7	0
Texas-El Paso	2	3	0	3	7	0
West Texas State	0	5	0	1	9	0

Ivy	Conf. W L T			Overall W L T		
Pennsylvania	6	1	0	7	1	1
Dartmouth	5	1	1	5	3	1
Yale	4	3	0	6	3	0
Harvard	4	3	0	6	3	0
Cornell	3	4	0	5	4	0
Princeton	3	4	0	4	5	0
Brown	1	5	1	2	6	1
Columbia	1	6	0	2	7	0

MAC	Conf. W L T			Overall W L T		
Bowling Green	6	0	0	9	0	0
Ohio U	4	2	0	7	2	0
Miami, Ohio	3	2	0	5	4	0
Kent State	3	3	0	5	3	0
Western Michigan	3	3	0	4	5	0
Marshall	1	4	0	1	8	0
Toledo	0	6	0	2	6	1

AAWU	Conf. W L T			Overall W L T		
Washington	3	1	0	10	1	0
Southern Cal	3	1	0	8	2	0
UCLA	3	1	0	5	4	1
California	1	3	0	2	8	0
Stanford	0	4	0	3	7	0

SEC	Conf. W L T			Overall W L T		
Georgia	7	0	0	10	1	0
Mississippi	5	1	0	10	1	0
LSU	5	1	0	9	2	0
Alabama	4	1	2	7	2	2
Auburn	4	3	0	7	3	0
Vanderbilt	3	2	2	5	3	2
Georgia Tech	3	3	0	6	5	0
Tennessee	3	4	1	5	4	1
Florida	2	4	0	5	4	1
Kentucky	1	6	0	4	6	0
Tulane	0	5	1	3	6	1
Mississippi State	0	7	0	2	7	0

Skyline	Conf. W L T			Overall W L T		
Wyoming	7	0	0	9	1	0
Colorado State	5	2	0	6	4	0
New Mexico	4	2	0	7	3	0
Utah	3	2	0	5	5	0
Utah State	2	5	0	5	6	0
Brigham Young	2	5	0	3	7	0
Denver	2	5	0	2	8	0
Montana	1	5	0	1	8	0

SWC	Conf. W L T			Overall W L T		
Arkansas	5	1	0	9	2	0
Texas	5	1	0	9	2	0
TCU	5	1	0	8	3	0
SMU	2	3	1	5	4	1
Baylor	2	4	0	4	6	0
Rice	1	4	1	1	7	2
Texas A&M	0	6	0	3	7	0

Independents	Overall W L T		
Syracuse	11	0	0
Penn State	9	2	0
Oregon	8	2	0
Rutgers	6	3	0
Memphis	6	4	0
Oklahoma State	6	4	0
Pittsburgh	6	4	0
Washington State	6	4	0
Miami, Fla.	6	4	0
Boston College	5	4	0
Air Force	5	4	1
Navy	5	4	1
Notre Dame	5	5	0
Army	4	4	1
Florida State	4	6	0
Texas Tech	4	6	0
Oregon State	3	7	0

BOWL GAMES

DATE	GAME	SCORE
D19	Bluebonnet	Clemson 23, TCU 7
D19	Liberty	Penn State 7, Alabama 0
D 31	Sun	New Mexico State 28, North Texas 8
J1	Tangerine	Middle Tennessee 21, Presbyterian 12
J1	Orange	Georgia 14, Missouri 0
J1	Sugar	Mississippi 21, LSU 0
J1	Cotton	Syracuse 23, Texas 14
J1	Rose	Washington 44, Wisconsin 8
J2	Gator	Arkansas 14, Georgia Tech 7

1959 NCAA Major College Statistical Leaders

Individual Leaders

	PASSING/COMPLETIONS	G	ATT	COM	PCT	INT	I%	YDS	YPA	TD	TD%	COM.PG
1	Dick Norman, Stanford	10	263	152	57.8	12	4.6	1963	7.5	11	4.2	15.2
2	Jack Lee, Cincinnati	10	232	132	56.9	6	2.6	1535	6.6	7	3.0	13.2
3	Pete Hall, Marquette	10	237	120	50.6	14	5.9	1589	6.7	7	3.0	12.0
4	Rich Mayo, Air Force	10	211	110	52.1	10	4.7	1212	5.7	6	2.8	11.0
5	Don Meredith, SMU	10	181	105	58.0	10	5.5	1266	7.0	11	6.1	10.5
5	Joe Caldwell, Army	9	188	105	55.9	7	3.7	1343	7.1	9	4.8	11.7
5	Charley Johnson, New Mexico State	10	199	105	52.8	8	4.0	1449	7.3	18	9.1	10.5
8	Fran Curci, Miami, Fla.	10	195	100	51.3	14	7.2	1068	5.5	5	2.6	10.0
8	Gale Weidner, Colorado	10	207	100	48.3	13	6.3	1200	5.8	7	3.4	10.0
10	Dick Soergel, Oklahoma State	10	155	93	60.0	4	2.6	1102	7.1	8	5.2	9.3

	ALL-PURPOSE YARDS	G	RUSH	REC	INT	PR	KR	YDS	YPG
1	Pervis Atkins, New Mexico State	10	971	301	23	241	264	1800	180.0

	RUSHING/YARDS	G	ATT	YDS	AVG	YPG
1	Pervis Atkins, New Mexico State	10	130	971	7.5	97.1
2	Tom Watkins, Iowa State	10	158	843	5.3	84.3
3	Dwight Nichols, Iowa State	10	207	746	3.6	74.6
4	Dick Bass, Pacific	9	139	742	5.3	82.4
5	Billy Brown, New Mexico	10	95	740	7.8	74.0
6	Charlie Flowers, Mississippi	10	141	733	5.2	73.3
7	Abner Haynes, North Texas	10	116	730	6.3	73.0
8	Bob Crandall, New Mexico	10	116	729	6.3	72.9
9	Fred Doelling, Pennsylvania	9	133	707	5.3	78.6
10	Nolan Jones, Arizona State	11	143	689	4.8	62.6

	RUSHING/YARDS PER CARRY	G	ATT	YDS	YPC
1	Billy Brown, New Mexico	10	95	740	7.8
2	Pervis Atkins, New Mexico State	10	130	971	7.5
3	Charles Bowers, Hardin-Simmons	10	86	619	7.2
4	Ernie Davis, Syracuse	10	98	686	7.0
5	Ger Schwedes, Syracuse	10	90	567	6.3
6	Abner Haynes, North Texas.	10	116	730	6.3
7	Bob Crandall, New Mexico	10	116	729	6.3
8	Jerry Hill, Wyoming	10	97	579	6.0
9	Larry Wilson, Utah	10	98	559	5.7
10	Joe Bellino, Navy	10	99	564	5.7

*-Based on top 42 rushers

	RECEIVING/RECEPTIONS	G	REC	YDS	TD	YPR	YPG	RPG
1	Chris Burford, Stanford	10	61	756	6	12.4	75.6	6.1
2	Bill Carpenter, Army	9	43	591	3	13.7	65.7	4.8
3	Dick Evans, VMI	10	35	698	9	19.9	69.8	3.5
4	Ben Robinson, Stanford	10	34	595	2	17.5	59.5	3.4
5	Bill Miller, Miami, Fla.	10	33	395	1	12.0	39.5	3.3
6	Paul Maguire, Citadel	10	32	549	10	17.2	54.9	3.2
7	Ed Kovac, Cincinnati	10	31	332	5	10.7	33.2	3.1
7	Bud Whitehead, Florida State	10	31	320	2	10.3	32.0	3.1
9	Don Norton, Iowa	9	30	428	4	14.3	47.6	3.3
9	Glynn Gregory, SMU	10	30	369	2	12.3	36.9	3.0
9	Bill Voss, Hardin-Simmons	10	30	319	4	10.6	31.9	3.0

	PUNTING	PUNT	YDS	AVG
1	John Hadl, Kansas	43	1961	45.6
2	Dainard Paulson, Oregon State	32	1459	45.6
3	Bobby Joe Green, Florida	54	2425	44.9
4	Joe Zuger, Arizona State	42	1882	44.8
5	Gary Dunn, Brigham Young	39	1747	44.8
6	Lamont Miller, Utah State	26	1157	44.5
7	Willie Vasquez, Texas-El Paso	23	1021	44.4
8	Paul Gustafson, Montana	26	1131	43.5
9	Keith Lincoln, Washington State	41	1779	43.4
10	Paul Maguire, Citadel	32	1370	42.8

	PUNT RETURNS/YARDS	PR	YDS	AVG
1	Pervis Atkins, New Mexico State	16	241	15.1
2	George Fleming, Washington	23	231	10.0
3	Billy Cannon, LSU	15	221	14.7
4	Charley Britt, Georgia	18	213	11.8
5	Jacque MacKinnon, Colgate	12	210	17.5
6	Gerald Mauren, Iowa	10	181	18.1
7	George Usry, Clemson	16	175	10.9
7	John Majors, Tennessee	22	175	8.0
9	David Ames, Richmond	7	174	24.9
10	Gordon Speer, Rice	12	172	14.3

	KICKOFF RETURNS/YARDS	KR	YDS	AVG
1	Don Perkins, New Mexico	15	520	34.7
2	Ronald Miller, Oregon State	15	453	30.2
3	Calvin Bird, Kentucky	14	426	30.4
4	Paul Choquette, Brown	15	354	23.6
5	Tom Gravins, Virginia	17	346	20.4
6	Terry Terrebone, Tulane	13	335	25.8
7	Walter Mince, Arizona	14	329	23.5
8	Joe Allen, Hardin-Simmons	16	325	20.3
9	Alger Pugh, Virginia Tech	12	305	25.4
10	Sandy Stephens, Minnesota	11	299	27.2

	SCORING	TDS	XPT	FG	PTS
1	Pervis Atkins, New Mexico State	17	5	0	107
2	Skip Face, Stanford	11	25	3	100
2	Nolan Jones, Arizona State	11	25	3	100
2	Ger Schwedes, Syracuse	16	4	0	100
5	Abner Haynes, North Texas	14	6	0	90
5	Ed Kovac, Cincinnati	15	0	0	90
7	Larry Wilson, Utah	13	6	0	84
8	Bruce Maher, Detroit	11	8	0	74
8	Don Perkins, New Mexico	12	2	0	74
10	Bill Mathis, Clemson	11	4	0	70

	KICK SCORING	XPA	XP	FG	PTS
1	Bobby Khayat, Mississippi	29	25	5	40
2	Danny Villanueva, New Mexico State	35	28	3	37
3	Edgar Beach, New Mexico	32	28	2	34
4	Durward Pennington, Georgia	28	26	2	32
5	Karl Holzwarth, Wisconsin	10	10	7	31
6	Nolan Jones, Arizona State	25	21	3	30
7	Skip Face, Stanford	20	19	3	28
7	George Fleming, Washington	21	16	4	28
9	Sam Stellatella, Penn State	23	20	2	26
9	Ed Dyas, Auburn	17	14	4	26

	INTERCEPTIONS	INT	YDS
1	Bud Whitehead, Florida State	6	111
1	Bob Cyphers, Dayton	6	62
1	Bob Schloredt, Washington	6	53
1	George Fleming, Washington	6	27
1	Tony Banfield, Oklahoma State	6	12
6	Rich Lucas, Penn State	5	114
6	Alger Pugh, Virginia Tech	5	103
6	Willie Wood, Southern Cal	5	83
6	Terry Parks, North Texas	5	80
6	Don Johnston, Washington State	5	51
6	Russ Morris, Vanderbilt	5	40
6	Chuck Roberts, New Mexico	5	37
6	Nick Pannes, Brown	5	24
6	Ed Hino, George Washington	5	14

Team Leaders

	RUSHING OFFENSE	G	ATT	YDS	AVG	YPG
1	Syracuse	10	578	3136	5.4	313.6
2	North Texas	10	534	2908	5.4	290.8
3	New Mexico	10	535	2898	5.4	289.8
4	Oklahoma	10	620	2735	4.4	273.5
5	Utah	10	551	2570	4.7	257.0
6	Wyoming	10	550	2520	4.6	252.0
7	Southern Cal	10	583	2493	4.3	249.3
8	Mississippi	10	528	2391	4.5	239.1
9	Iowa	9	440	2151	4.9	239.0
10	Iowa State	10	502	2287	4.6	228.7

	PASSING OFFENSE/YPG	G	ATT	COM	INT	PCT	YPA	TD	YPG	I%	YPC	YDS
1	Stanford	10	307	176	18	57.3	7.4	11	227.8	5.9	12.9	2278
2	Marquette	10	281	139	18	49.5	6.7	10	187.0	6.4	13.5	1870
3	San Jose State	10	268	149	19	55.6	6.9	12	185.2	7.1	12.4	1852
4	Army	9	260	133	15	51.2	6.3	10	182.3	5.8	12.3	1641
5	Boston College	9	222	111	11	50.0	7.1	10	175.3	5.0	14.2	1578
6	Cincinnati	10	241	135	6	56.0	6.6	9	158.5	2.5	11.7	1585
7	New Mexico State	10	216	114	9	52.8	7.3	18	157.3	4.2	13.8	1573
8	Hardin-Simmons	10	275	134	23	48.7	5.6	8	154.2	8.4	11.5	1542
9	Pacific	9	196	88	10	44.9	7.0	5	152.3	5.1	15.6	1371
10	Wake Forest	10	218	90	18	41.3	6.9	13	149.8	8.3	16.6	1498

	TOTAL OFFENSE	G	P	YDS	AVG	YPG
1	Syracuse	10	738	4515	6.1	451.5
2	Iowa	9	632	3399	5.4	377.7
3	New Mexico State	10	618	3756	6.1	375.6
4	North Texas	10	655	3713	5.7	371.3
5	Mississippi	10	698	3686	5.3	368.6
6	Utah	10	712	3651	5.1	365.1
7	Wyoming	10	686	3577	5.2	357.7
8	New Mexico	10	639	3562	5.6	356.2
9	Stanford	10	665	3467	5.2	346.7
10	Oklahoma	10	731	3405	4.7	340.5

	RUSHING DEFENSE	G	ATT	YDS	AVG	YPG
1	Syracuse	10	302	193	0.6	19.3
2	LSU	10	390	908	2.3	90.8
3	Mississippi	10	384	939	2.4	93.9
4	Southern Cal	10	408	981	2.4	98.1
5	TCU	10	404	1017	2.5	101.7
6	Clemson	10	391	1085	2.8	108.5
7	Pennsylvania	9	401	988	2.5	109.8
8	Wyoming	10	433	1098	2.5	109.8
9	South Carolina	10	376	1115	3.0	111.5
10	Detroit	10	383	1129	2.9	112.9

	PASSING DEFENSE	G	ATT	COM	PCT	YPC	INT	I%	YDS	YPA	TD	YPG
1	Alabama	10	116	46	39.7	9.9	20	17.2	457	3.9	1	45.7
2	Montana	9	96	35	36.5	11.9	9	9.4	415	4.3	5	46.1
3	LSU	10	169	56	33.1	9.4	13	7.7	524	3.1	0	52.4
4	Mississippi	10	132	61	46.2	8.7	17	12.9	533	4.0	1	53.3
5	Iowa State	10	141	50	35.5	11.1	22	15.6	553	3.9	1	55.3
6	North Texas	10	138	49	35.5	11.9	18	13.0	581	4.2	0	58.1
7	Wake Forest	10	128	57	44.5	10.9	15	11.7	621	4.9	7	62.1
8	Kentucky	10	146	58	39.7	10.8	12	8.2	626	4.3	2	62.6
9	Auburn	10	173	62	35.8	10.3	14	8.1	636	3.7	3	63.6
10	Tennessee	10	133	62	46.6	10.8	13	9.8	668	5.0	4	66.8

	TOTAL DEFENSE	G	P	YDS	AVG	YPG
1	Syracuse	10	486	962	2.0	96.2
2	LSU	10	559	1432	2.6	143.2
3	Mississippi	10	516	1472	2.9	147.2
4	Alabama	10	549	1799	3.3	179.9
5	Wyoming	10	572	1805	3.2	180.5
6	Auburn	10	565	1825	3.2	182.5
7	Southern Cal	10	603	1844	3.1	184.4
8	Illinois	9	533	1713	3.2	190.3
9	TCU	10	578	1945	3.4	194.5
10	North Texas	10	553	1965	3.6	196.5

	SCORING OFFENSE	G	PTS	AVG
1	Syracuse	10	390	39.0
2	New Mexico State	10	332	33.2
3	Mississippi	10	329	32.9
4	North Texas	10	295	29.5
5	Wyoming	10	287	28.7
6	Clemson	10	262	26.2
7	New Mexico	10	260	26.0
8	Iowa	9	233	25.9
9	Penn State	10	255	25.5
10	Iowa State	10	248	24.8

	SCORING DEFENSE	G	PTS	AVG
1	Mississippi	10	21	2.1
2	LSU	10	29	2.9
3	Alabama	10	52	5.2
3	TCU	10	52	5.2
5	Auburn	10	58	5.8
6	Syracuse	10	59	5.9
7	Wyoming	10	62	6.2
8	Washington	10	65	6.5
9	Texas	10	73	7.3
10	North Texas	10	75	7.5

1960 POLL PROGRESSION

AP Pre-Season — Sept. 17 Games

Rank	Team	Record	Result
1	Syracuse	0-0-0	bye week
2	Mississippi	0-0-0	beat Houston 42-0
3	Washington	0-0-0	beat Pacific 55-6
4	Texas	0-0-0	lost to Nebraska 13-14
5	Illinois	0-0-0	bye week
6	Southern Cal	0-0-0	lost to Oregon State 0-14
7	Pittsburgh	0-0-0	lost to UCLA 7-8
8	Michigan State	0-0-0	bye week
9	Clemson	0-0-0	bye week
10	Oklahoma	0-0-0	bye week
11	TCU	0-0-0	lost to Kansas 7-21
12	Auburn	0-0-0	bye week
13	Georgia	0-0-0	lost to Alabama 6-21
14	Northwestern	0-0-0	bye week
15	Iowa	0-0-0	bye wee
16	Ohio State	0-0-0	bye week
17	Notre Dame	0-0-0	bye week
18	Tennessee	0-0-0	bye week
19	Arkansas	0-0-0	beat Oklahoma State 9-0
20	Penn State	0-0-0	beat Boston U. 20-0

AP September 19 Poll — Sept 24 Games

Rank	Team	Record	Result
1	Mississippi	1-0-0	beat Kentucky 21-6
2	Syracuse	0-0-0	beat Boston U. 35-7
3	Washington	1-0-0	beat Idaho 41-12
4	Illinois	0-0-0	beat Indiana 17-6
5	Alabama	0-0-0	tied Tulane 6-6
6	Michigan State	0-0-0	tied #17 Pittsburgh 7-7
7	Kansas	1-0-0	beat Kansas State 41-0
8	UCLA	1-0-0	tied Purdue 27-27
9	Clemson	0-0-0	beat Wake Forest 28-7
10	Oregon State	1-0-0	lost to #19 Iowa 12-22
11	Penn State	1-0-0	bye week
12	Nebraska	1-0-0	lost to Minnesota 14-26
13	Georgia Tech	1-0-0	beat Rice 16-13
14	Northwestern	0-0-0	beat Oklahoma 19-3
15	Texas	0-1-0	beat Maryland 34-0
16	Missouri	1-0-0	beat Oklahoma State 28-7
17	Pittsburgh	0-1-0	tied #6 Michigan State 7-7
18	LSU	1-0-0	bye week
19	Iowa	0-0-0	beat #10 Oregon State 22-12
20	Ohio State	0-0-0	beat SMU 24-0

UP AP September 26 Poll — Oct. 1 Games

UP	AP	Team	Record	Result
2	1	Mississippi	2-0-0	beat Memphis 31-20
1	2	Syracuse	1-0-0	beat #5 Kansas 14-7
3	3	Washington	2-0-0	lost to #17 Navy 14-15
4	4	Illinois	1-0-0	beat West Virginia 33-0
5	5	Kansas	2-0-0	lost to #2 Syracuse 7-14
6	6	Northwestern	1-0-0	lost to #8 Iowa 0-42
10	7	Clemson	1-0-0	beat Virginia Tech 13-7
8	8	Iowa	1-0-0	beat #6 Northwestern 42-0
7	9	Ohio State	1-0-0	beat Southern Cal 20-0
9	10	Georgia Tech	2-0-0	lost to Florida 17-18
11	11	Tennessee	1-0-0	tied Mississippi State 0-0
18	12	Notre Dame	1-0-0	lost to Purdue 19-51
15	13	Texas	1-1-0	beat Texas Tech 17-0
17	14	Arkansas	2-0-0	beat TCU 7-0
14	15	Alabama	1-0-1	beat Vanderbilt 21-0
15	16	UCLA	1-0-1	bye week
17	17	Navy	2-0-0	beat #3 Washington 15-14
12	18	Minnesota	1-0-0	beat Indiana 42-0
20	19	Missouri	2-0-0	beat #20 Penn State 21-8
	20	Penn State	1-0-0	lost to #19 Missouri 8-21
13		Michigan State	0-0-1	beat Michigan 24-17
20		Michigan	1-0-0	lost to Michigan State 17-24

UP AP October 3 Poll — Oct. 8 Games

UP	AP	Team	Record	Result
1	1	Syracuse	2-0-0	beat Holy Cross 15-6
2	2	Mississippi	3-0-0	beat Vanderbilt 26-0
3	3	Iowa	2-0-0	beat #13 Michigan State 27-15
4	4	Illinois	2-0-0	lost to #5 Ohio State 7-34
5	5	Ohio State	2-0-0	beat #4 Illinois 34-7
6	6	Navy	3-0-0	beat SMU 26-7
7	7	Purdue	1-0-1	lost to Wisconsin 13-24
11	8	Clemson	2-0-0	beat Virginia 21-7
10	9	Arkansas	3-0-0	lost to #20 Baylor 14-28
13	10	Kansas	2-1-0	beat Iowa State 28-14
8	11	Missouri	3-0-0	beat Air Force 34-8
15	12	Washington	2-1-0	beat Stanford 29-10
14	13	Michigan State	1-0-1	lost to #3 Iowa 15-27
9	14	Minnesota	2-0-0	beat Northwestern 7-0
	15	Texas	2-1-0	beat Oklahoma 24-0
19	16	UCLA	1-0-1	bye week
18	17	Alabama	2-0-1	bye week
16	18	Army	3-0-0	lost to Penn State 16-27
	19	Florida	3-0-0	lost to Rice 0-10
12	20	Baylor	2-0-0	beat #9 Arkansas 28-14
17		Air Force	2-0-0	lost to Missouri 8-34
20		Iowa State	3-0-0	lost to Kansas 14-28

UP AP October 10 Poll — Oct. 15 Games

UP	AP	Team	Record	Result
1	1	Mississippi	4-0-0	beat Tulane 26-13
3	2	Iowa	3-0-0	beat #12 Wisconsin 28-21
2	3	Ohio State	3-0-0	lost to Purdue 21-24
4	4	Syracuse	3-0-0	beat #20 Penn State 21-15
5	5	Navy	4-0-0	beat Air Force 35-3
6	6	Missouri	4-0-0	beat Kansas State 45-0
	7	Baylor	3-0-0	beat Texas Tech 14-7
11	8	Clemson	3-0-0	lost to Maryland 17-19
10	9	Kansas	3-1-0	tied Oklahoma 13-13
8	10	Minnesota	3-0-0	beat Illinois 21-10
9	11	Texas	3-1-0	lost to Arkansas 23-24
	12	Wisconsin	3-0-0	lost to #2 Iowa 21-28
13	13	Washington	3-1-0	beat #15 UCLA 10-8
14	14	Michigan State	1-1-1	beat Notre Dame 21-0
16	15	Alabama	2-0-1	lost to Tennessee 7-20
15		UCLA	1-0-1	lost to #13 Washington 8-10
	17	Oregon State	3-1-0	beat Idaho 28-0
	18	Arizona State	4-0-0	beat Brigham Young 31-0
	19	Georgia Tech	3-1-0	lost to Auburn 7-9
17	20	Penn State	2-1-0	lost to #4 Syracuse 15-21
17		North Carolina St.	4-0-0	lost to Duke 13-17
19		Michigan	2-1-0	beat Northwestern 14-7
19		New Mexico State	4-0-0	beat McMurry 47-17

UP AP October 17 Poll — Oct. 22 Games

UP	AP	Team	Record	Result
1	1	Iowa	4-0-0	beat #10 Purdue 21-14
2	2	Mississippi	5-0-0	beat #14 Arkansas 10-7
3	3	Syracuse	4-0-0	beat West Virginia 45-0
4	4	Navy	5-0-0	beat Pennsylvania 27-0
6	5	Missouri	5-0-0	beat Iowa State 34-8
5	6	Minnesota	4-0-0	beat Michigan 10-0
7	7	Baylor	4-0-0	beat Texas A&M 14-0
9	8	Washington	4-1-0	beat #18 Oregon State 30-29
10	9	Ohio State	3-1-0	beat #11 Wisconsin 34-7
8	10	Purdue	2-1-1	lost to #1 Iowa 14-21
12	11	Wisconsin	3-1-0	lost to #9 Ohio State 7-34
15	12	Tennessee	3-0-1	beat U.T. Chattanooga 35-0
13	13	Michigan State	2-1-1	beat Indiana 35-0
11	14	Arkansas	4-1-0	lost to #2 Mississippi 7-10
14	15	Kansas	3-1-1	beat Oklahoma State 14-7
	16	Texas	3-2-0	lost to #20 Rice 0-7
18	17	Auburn	3-1-0	beat Miami, Fla. 20-7
	18	Oregon State	4-1-0	lost to #8 Washington 29-30
	19	UCLA	1-1-1	beat Stanford 26-8
18	20	Rice	3-1-0	beat #16 Texas 7-0
16		Michigan	3-1-0	lost to #6 Minnesota 0-10
17		Clemson	3-1-0	lost to Duke 6-21
18		New Mexico State	5-0-0	beat Wichita State 40-8
18		Duke	3-1-0	beat Clemson 21-6

UP AP October 24 Poll — Oct. 29 Games

UP	AP	Team	Record	Result
1	1	Iowa	5-0-0	beat #19 Kansas 21-7
2	2	Mississippi	6-0-0	tied LSU 6-6
3	3	Syracuse	5-0-0	lost to Pittsburgh 0-10
5	4	Navy	6-0-0	beat Notre Dame 14-7
	5	Missouri	6-0-0	beat Nebraska 28-0
4	6	Minnesota	5-0-0	beat Kansas State 48-7
7	7	Baylor	5-0-0	lost to TCU 6-14
8	8	Ohio State	4-1-0	beat #10 Michigan State 21-10
9	9	Washington	5-1-0	beat Oregon 7-6
10	10	Michigan State	3-1-1	lost to #8 Ohio State 10-21
11	11	Tennessee	4-0-1	beat North Carolina 27-14
13	12	Arkansas	4-2-0	beat Texas A&M 7-3
12	13	Rice	4-1-0	beat Texas Tech 30-6
	14	Auburn	4-1-0	beat Florida 10-7
16	15	Duke	4-1-0	beat Georgia Tech 6-0
15		Oregon State	4-2-0	lost to California 6-14
14		Purdue	2-1-1	lost to Illinois 12-14
17	18	New Mexico State	6-0-0	beat Arizona State 27-24
15	19	Kansas	4-1-1	lost to #1 Iowa 7-21
18		Wyoming	5-1-0	beat Utah 17-7
18		Colorado	4-1-0	beat Oklahoma 7-0
20		UCLA	2-1-1	beat North Carolina St. 7-0

UP AP October 31 Poll — Nov. 5 Games

UP	AP	Team	Record	Result
1	1	Iowa	6-0-0	lost to #3 Minnesota 10-27
4	2	Missouri	7-0-0	beat #18 Colorado 16-6
2	3	Minnesota	6-0-0	beat #1 Iowa 27-10
3	4	Navy	7-0-0	lost to #13 Duke 10-19
5	5	Ohio State	5-1-0	beat Indiana 36-7
6	6	Mississippi	6-0-1	beat U.T. Chattanooga 45-0
7	7	Washington	6-1-0	beat Southern Cal 34-0
8	8	Tennessee	5-0-1	lost to Georgia Tech 7-14
9	9	Syracuse	5-1-0	lost to Army 6-9
10	10	Rice	5-1-0	lost to #16 Arkansas 0-3
11	11	Baylor	5-1-0	lost to Texas 7-12
	12	Auburn	5-1-0	beat Mississippi State 27-12
12	13	Duke	5-1-0	beat #4 Navy 19-10
20	14	Pittsburgh	3-2-2	beat Notre Dame 20-13
18	15	UCLA	3-1-1	beat California 28-0
13	16	Arkansas	5-2-0	beat #10 Rice 3-0
16	17	Michigan State	3-2-1	beat Purdue 17-13
16	18	Colorado	5-1-0	lost to #2 Missouri 6-16
	18	Utah State	7-0-0	beat Wyoming 17-13
18	20	New Mexico State	7-0-0	bye week
14		Wyoming	6-1-0	lost to #18 Utah State 13-17
14		Wisconsin	4-2-0	lost to Northwestern 0-21

UP AP November 7 Poll — Nov. 12 Games

UP	AP	Team	Record	Result
1	1	Minnesota	7-0-0	lost to Purdue 14-23
2	2	Missouri	8-0-0	beat Oklahoma 41-9
3	3	Ohio State	6-1-0	lost to #5 Iowa 12-35
4	4	Mississippi	7-0-1	beat #14 Tennessee 24-3
6	5	Iowa	6-1-0	beat #3 Ohio State 35-12
5	6	Washington	7-1-0	beat California 27-7
8	7	Duke	6-1-0	beat Wake Forest 34-7
9	8	Navy	7-1-0	beat Virginia 41-8
7	9	Arkansas	6-2-0	beat SMU 26-3
11	10	Auburn	6-1-0	beat Georgia 9-6
14	11	UCLA	4-1-1	beat Air Force 22-0
10	12	Pittsburgh	4-2-2	tied Army 7-7
11	13	Michigan State	4-2-1	beat Northwestern 21-18
14	14	Tennessee	5-1-1	lost to #4 Mississippi 3-24
16	15	New Mexico State	7-0-0	beat West Texas State 35-15
13	16	Rice	5-2-0	beat Texas A&M 21-14
18	17	Syracuse	5-2-0	beat Colgate 46-6
	17	Yale	7-0-0	beat Princeton 43-22
19	19	Utah State	8-0-0	beat Pacific 45-6
17		Florida	6-2-0	beat Tulane 21-6
	20	Baylor	5-2-0	beat Southern Cal 35-14

UP	AP	November 14 Poll		Nov. 19 Games
1	1	Missouri	9-0-0	lost to Kansas 7-23
3	2	Iowa	7-1-0	beat Notre Dame 28-0
2	3	Mississippi	8-0-1	bye week
4	4	Minnesota	7-1-0	beat Wisconsin 26-7
5	5	Washington	8-1-0	beat Washington State 8-7
6	6	Duke	7-1-0	lost to North Carolina 6-7
8	7	Arkansas	7-2-0	beat Texas Tech 34-6
7	8	Navy	8-1-0	bye week
10	9	Auburn	7-1-0	beat Florida State 57-21
9	10	Ohio State	6-2-0	beat Michigan 7-0
11	11	UCLA	5-1-1	lost to Southern Cal 6-17
12	12	Michigan State	5-2-1	beat Detroit 43-15
	13	Purdue	3-4-1	beat Indiana 35-6
20	14	New Mexico State	8-0-0	beat Hardin-Simmons 40-3
14	14	Rice	6-2-0	beat TCU 23-0
	14	Syracuse	6-2-0	beat Miami, Fla. 21-14
18	14	Yale	8-0-0	beat Harvard 39-6
16	18	Alabama	6-1-1	beat Tampa 34-6
18	19	Florida	7-2-0	bye week
	19	Oregon	7-2-0	tied Oregon State 14-14
13		Kansas	6-2-1	beat #1 Missouri 23-7
15		Baylor	6-2-0	beat SMU 20-7
16		Utah State	9-0-0	lost to Utah 0-6
20		Pittsburgh	4-2-3	lost to Penn State 3-14

UP	AP	November 21 Poll		Nov. 26 Games
1	1	Minnesota	8-1-0	regular season complete
2	2	Iowa	8-1-0	regular season complete
3	3	Mississippi	8-0-1	beat Mississippi State 35-9
4	4	Washington	9-1-0	regular season complete
5	5	Missouri	9-1-0	regular season complete
6	6	Arkansas	8-2-0	regular season complete
7	7	Navy	8-1-0	beat Army 17-12
9	8	Auburn	8-1-0	lost to #17 Alabama 0-3
8	9	Ohio State	7-2-0	regular season complete
10	10	Kansas	7-2-1	regular season complete
13	11	Duke	7-2-0	bye week
11	12	Rice	7-2-0	lost to #19 Baylor 7-12
16	13	Yale	9-0-0	regular season complete
12	14	Michigan State	6-2-1	regular season complete
18	15	New Mexico State	9-0-0	beat Texas-El Paso 27-15
	15	Penn State	6-3-0	regular season complete
19	17	Alabama	7-1-1	beat #8 Auburn 3-0
14	17	Syracuse	7-2-0	regular season complete
15	19	Baylor	7-2-0	beat #12 Rice 12-7
19	19	Florida	7-2-0	beat Miami, Fla. 18-0
17		Purdue	4-4-1	regular season complete

UP	AP	November 28 Final Poll	RECORD	BOWL BID	DATE	BOWL RESULT	RB	RECORD
1	1	Minnesota	8-1-0	Rose Bowl	J2	lost to #6 Washington 7-17	5	8-2-0
3	2	Mississippi	9-0-1	Sugar Bowl	J2	beat Rice 14-6	1	10-0-1
2	3	Iowa	8-1-0				2	8-1-0
6	4	Navy	8-1-0	Orange Bowl	J2	lost to #5 Missouri 14-21	10	9-2-0
4	5	Missouri	9-1-0	Orange Bowl	J2	beat #4 Navy 21-14	4	10-1-0
5	6	Washington	9-1-0	Rose Bowl	J2	beat #1 Minnesota 17-7	3	10-1-0
7	7	Arkansas	8-2-0	Cotton Bowl	J2	lost to #10 Duke 6-7	17	8-3-0
8	8	Ohio State	7-2-1				6	7-2-0
9	9	Alabama	8-1-1	Bluebonnet Bowl	D17	tied Texas 3-3	7	8-1-2
11	10	Duke	7-2-0	Cotton Bowl	J2	beat #7 Arkansas 7-6	15	8-3-0
9	11	Kansas	7-2-1				18	7-2-1
12	12	Baylor	8-2-0	Gator Bowl	D31	lost to #18 Florida 12-13	20	8-3-0
14	13	Auburn	8-2-0				13	8-2-0
18	14	Yale	9-0-0				9	9-0-0
13	15	Michigan State	6-2-1				8	6-2-1
	16	Penn State	6-3-0	Liberty Bowl	D17	beat Oregon 41-12	22	7-3-0
18	17	New Mexico State	10-0-0	Sun Bowl	D31	beat Utah State 20-13	14	11-0-0
16	18	Florida	8-2-0	Gator Bowl	D31	beat #12 Baylor 13-12	12	9-2-0
15	19	Purdue	4-4-1				19	4-4-1
	19	Syracuse	7-2-0				11	7-2-0
17		Texas	7-3-0	Bluebonnet Bowl	D17	tied #9 Alabama 3-3	16	7-3-1
18		Tennessee	6-2-2				27	6-2-2

ANNUAL REVIEW

1960

CONSENSUS ALL-AMERICANS

POS	Name	HT	WT	School	AP	FC	FW	NE	SN	PI
B	Jake Gibbs	6-0	185	Mississippi	•	•	•	•	•	•
B	Joe Bellino	5-9	181	Navy	•	•	•	•	•	•
B	Bob Ferguson	6-0	217	Ohio State	•	•	•	•	•	•
B	Ernie Davis	6-2	205	Syracuse			•		•	
E	Mike Ditka	6-3	215	Pittsburgh	•	•	•	•	•	•
E	Danny LaRose	6-4	220	Missouri	•	•		•	•	•
T	Bob Lilly	6-5	250	TCU	•	•	•	•	•	•
T	Ken Rice	6-3	250	Auburn	•	•	•	•	•	•
G	Tom Brown	6-0	225	Minnesota	•	•	•	•	•	•
G	Joe Romig	5-10	197	Colorado		•	•		•	
C	E.J. Holub	6-4	215	Texas Tech	•	•	•	•	•	•

OTHERS RECEIVING FIRST-TEAM HONORS

POS	Name	School						
B	Ed Dyas	Auburn			•			
B	Larry Ferguson	Iowa			•			
B	Roman Gabriel	North Carolina St.			•			
B	John Hadl	Kansas			•			
B	Bill Kilmer	UCLA			•	•		
B	Pervis Atkins	New Mexico State	•					
E	Bill Miller	Miami			•			
E	Claude Moorman	Duke			•			
T	Jerry Beabout	Purdue			•			
T	Merlin Olsen	Utah State			•	•		
G	Wayne Harris	Arkansas			•			
G	Mark Manders	Iowa			•		•	
G	Ben Balme	Yale	•					
C	Roy McKasson	Washington	•		•	•		

NE named Holub as a G

HEISMAN TROPHY VOTING

	PLAYER	POS	SCHOOL	1ST	2ND	3RD	TOTAL
1	Joe Bellino	HB	Navy	436	196	93	1303
2	Tom Brown	G	Minnesota	127	121	108	731
3	Jake Gibbs	QB	Mississippi	74	77	77	453
4	Ed Dyas	FB	Auburn	46	63	55	319
5	Bill Kilmer	HB	UCLA	55	42	31	280
6	Mike Ditka	E	Pittsburgh	17	52	68	223
7	Tom Matte	QB	Ohio State	17	42	30	165
8	Danny LaRose	E	Missouri	16	28	32	136
9	Pervis Atkins	HB	New Mexico State	25	18	13	124
10	E.J. Holub	C	Texas Tech	14	23	29	117

AWARD WINNERS

PLAYER	POS	SCHOOL	AWARD NAME
Joe Bellino	HB	Navy	Maxwell
Tom Brown	G	Minnesota	Outland

CONFERENCE STANDINGS

ACC

	Conf. W	L	T	Overall W	L	T
Duke	5	1	0	8	3	0
North Carolina St.	4	1	1	6	3	1
Maryland	5	2	0	6	4	0
Clemson	4	2	0	6	4	0
South Carolina	3	3	1	3	6	1
North Carolina	2	5	0	3	7	0
Wake Forest	2	5	0	2	8	0
Virginia	0	6	0	0	10	0

Big 10

	Conf. W	L	T	Overall W	L	T
Minnesota	6	1	0	8	2	0
Iowa	5	1	0	8	1	0
Ohio State	5	2	0	7	2	0
Michigan State	4	2	0	6	2	1
Michigan	3	4	0	5	4	0
Illinois	3	4	0	5	4	0
Northwestern	3	4	0	5	4	0
Purdue	3	4	0	4	4	1
Wisconsin	2	5	0	4	5	0
Indiana	0	7	0	1	8	0

Big 8

	Conf. W	L	T	Overall W	L	T
Kansas*	6	0	1	7	2	1
Missouri**	6	1	0	10	1	0
Colorado***	5	2	0	6	4	0
Iowa State	4	3	0	7	3	0
Oklahoma	2	4	1	3	6	1
Nebraska	2	5	0	4	6	0
Oklahoma State	2	5	0	3	7	0
Kansas State	0	7	0	1	9	0

*Later forfeited to 4-2-1
** 7-0-0
*** 6-1-0

Border

	Conf. W	L	T	Overall W	L	T
New Mexico State	4	0	0	11	0	0
Arizona	3	0	0	7	3	0
Arizona State	3	2	0	7	3	0
Texas-El Paso	2	3	0	4	5	1
West Texas State	1	4	0	3	7	0
Hardin-Simmons	0	4	0	0	10	0

Ivy

	Conf. W	L	T	Overall W	L	T
Yale	7	0	0	9	0	0
Princeton	6	1	0	7	2	0
Harvard	4	3	0	5	4	0
Dartmouth	4	3	0	5	4	0
Columbia	3	4	0	3	6	0
Pennsylvania	2	5	0	3	6	0
Brown	1	6	0	3	6	0
Cornell	1	6	0	2	7	0

MAC

	Conf. W	L	T	Overall W	L	T
Ohio U	6	0	0	10	0	0
Bowling Green	5	1	0	8	1	0
Kent State	4	2	0	6	3	0
Miami, Ohio	2	3	0	5	5	0
Western Michigan	2	4	0	4	4	1
Marshall	1	4	0	2	7	1
Toledo	0	6	0	2	7	0

AAWU

	Conf. W	L	T	Overall W	L	T
Washington	4	0	0	10	1	0
Southern Cal	3	1	0	4	6	0
UCLA	2	2	0	7	2	1
California	1	3	0	2	7	1
Stanford	0	4	0	0	10	0

SEC

	Conf. W	L	T	Overall W	L	T
Mississippi	5	0	1	10	0	1
Florida	5	1	0	9	2	0
Alabama	5	1	1	8	1	2
Auburn	5	2	0	8	2	0
Georgia	4	3	0	6	4	0
Tennessee	3	2	2	6	2	2
Georgia Tech	4	4	0	5	5	0
LSU	2	3	1	5	4	1
Kentucky	2	4	1	5	4	1
Tulane	1	4	1	3	6	1
Mississippi State	0	5	1	2	6	1
Vanderbilt	0	7	0	3	7	0

Skyline

	Conf. W	L	T	Overall W	L	T
Utah State	6	1	0	9	2	0
Wyoming	6	1	0	8	2	0
Utah	5	1	0	7	3	0
New Mexico	4	2	0	5	5	0
Montana	2	5	0	5	5	0
Brigham Young	2	5	0	3	8	0
Denver	1	6	0	3	7	0
Colorado State	1	6	0	2	8	0

SWC

	Conf. W	L	T	Overall W	L	T
Arkansas	6	1	0	8	3	0
Baylor	5	2	0	8	3	0
Texas	5	2	0	7	3	1
Rice	5	2	0	7	4	0
TCU	3	3	1	4	4	2
Texas Tech	1	5	1	3	6	1
Texas A&M	0	4	3	1	6	3
SMU	0	6	1	0	9	1

Independents

	Overall W	L	T
Rutgers	8	1	0
Navy	9	2	0
Memphis	8	2	0
Syracuse	7	2	0
Penn State	7	3	0
Oregon	7	3	1
Oregon State	6	3	1
Army	6	3	1
Miami, Fla.	6	4	0
Houston	6	4	0
Pittsburgh	4	3	3
Washington State	4	5	1
Air Force	4	6	0
Florida State	3	6	1
Boston College	3	6	1
Notre Dame	2	8	0

BOWL GAMES

DATE	GAME	SCORE
D17	Bluebonnet	Alabama 3, Texas 3
D17	Liberty	Penn State 41, Oregon 12
D30	Tangerine	Citadel 27, Tennessee Tech 0
D31	Gator	Florida 13, Baylor 12
D31	Sun	New Mexico State 20, Utah State 13
J2	Cotton	Duke 7, Arkansas 6
J2	Sugar	Mississippi 14, Rice 6
J2	Orange	Missouri 21, Navy 14
J2	Rose	Washington 17, Minnesota 7

1960 NCAA Major College Statistical Leaders

Individual Leaders

	PASSING/COMPLETIONS	G	ATT	COM	PCT	INT	I%	YDS	YPA	TD	TD%	COM.PG
1	Harold Stephens, Hardin-Simmons	10	256	145	56.6	14	5.5	1254	4.9	3	1.2	14.5
2	Norm Snead, Wake Forest	10	259	123	47.4	14	5.4	1676	6.5	10	3.9	12.3
3	Melvin Melin, Washington State	10	221	119	53.8	13	5.9	1638	7.4	11	5.0	11.9
4	Charley Johnson, New Mexico State	10	199	109	54.8	6	3.0	1511	7.6	13	6.5	10.9
5	Fran Tarkenton, Georgia	10	185	108	58.4	12	6.5	1189	6.4	7	3.8	10.8
5	Rich Mayo, Air Force	10	238	108	45.4	18	7.6	1168	4.9	7	2.9	10.8
7	Roman Gabriel, North Carolina St.	10	186	105	56.5	7	3.8	1176	6.3	8	4.3	10.5
8	Ron Miller, Wisconsin	9	188	97	51.6	16	8.5	1351	7.2	8	4.3	10.8
9	Dick Norman, Stanford	10	201	95	47.3	13	6.5	1057	5.3	4	2.0	9.5
10	John Furman, Texas-El Paso	10	192	94	49.0	7	3.7	1094	5.7	4	2.1	9.4

	ALL-PURPOSE YARDS	G	RUSH	REC	INT	PR	KR	YDS	YPG
1	Pervis Atkins, New Mexico State	10	611	468	23	218	293	1613	161.3

	RUSHING/YARDS	G	ATT	YDS	AVG	YPG
1	Bob Gaiters, New Mexico State	10	197	1338	6.8	133.8
2	Tom Larscheid, Utah State	10	124	1044	8.4	104.4
3	Ernie Davis, Syracuse	9	112	877	7.8	97.4
4	Bob Ferguson, Ohio State	9	160	853	5.3	94.8
5	Dave Hoppmann, Iowa State	10	161	844	5.2	84.4
6	Joe Bellino, Navy	10	168	834	5.0	83.4
7	Bill Kilmer, UCLA	10	163	803	4.9	80.3
8	Hugh Scott, Princeton	9	140	760	5.4	84.4
9	Robert Thompson, Arizona	10	92	732	8.0	73.2
10	Al Rozycki, Dartmouth	9	169	725	4.3	80.6

	RUSHING/YARDS PER CARRY	G	ATT	YDS	YPC
1	Pervis Atkins, New Mexico State	10	65	611	9.4
2	Tom Larscheid, Utah State	10	124	1044	8.4
3	Robert Thompson, Arizona	10	92	732	8.0
4	Ernie Davis, Syracuse	9	112	877	7.8
5	Larry Ferguson, Iowa	9	90	665	7.4
6	Ken Bolin, Houston	10	75	542	7.2
7	Norris Stevenson, Missouri	10	85	610	7.2
8	Bob Gaiters, New Mexico State	10	197	1338	6.8
9	Mike Quinlan, Air Force	10	93	585	6.3
10	Bobby Santiago, New Mexico	10	98	591	6.0

*-Based on top 40 rushers

	RECEIVING/RECEPTIONS	G	REC	YDS	TD	YPR	YPG	RPG
1	Hugh Campbell, Washington State	10	66	881	10	13.3	88.1	6.6
2	Claude Moorman, Duke	10	46	431	2	9.4	43.1	4.6
3	Del Williams, Texas-El-Paso	10	36	414	2	11.5	41.4	3.6
4	Bob Coolbaugh, Richmond	10	35	380	2	10.9	38.0	3.5
5	Joe Kehoe, Virginia	10	34	378	2	11.1	37.8	3.4
6	Reg Carolan, Idaho	10	33	498	3	15.1	49.8	3.3
7	Fred Brown, Georgia	10	31	275	3	8.9	27.5	3.1
8	Tom Hutchinson, Kentucky	10	30	455	4	15.2	45.5	3.0
8	E.A. Sims, New Mexico State	10	30	415	2	13.8	41.5	3.0
8	Bobby Crespino, Mississippi	10	30	408	4	13.6	40.8	3.0
8	Gary Collins, Maryland	10	30	404	4	13.5	40.4	3.0

	PUNTING	PUNT	YDS	AVG
1	Dick Fitzsimmons, Denver	25	1106	44.2
2	Bobby Walden, Georgia	38	1657	43.6
3	Kent Rockholt, San Jose State	33	1412	42.8
4	Willie Vasquez, Texas-El Paso	31	1318	42.5
5	Bill Kilmer, UCLA	35	1481	42.3
6	Jerry Stovall, LSU	64	2694	42.1
7	Jim Bakken, Wisconsin	36	1508	41.9
8	George Canale, Tennessee	26	1084	41.7
9	Tom Gilburg, Syracuse	28	1159	41.4
10	Laurien Stapp, Alabama	42	1726	41.1

	PUNT RETURNS/YARDS	PR	YDS	AVG
1	Lance Alworth, Arkansas	18	307	17.1
2	Pat Fischer, Nebraska	13	276	21.2
3	Glen Adams, Army	16	270	16.9
4	Arny Byrd, Rutgers	14	249	17.8
5	Donnie Smith, Missouri	10	230	23.0
6	Ossie McCarty, Arizona State	16	223	13.9
7	Earl Stoudt, Richmond	18	223	12.4
8	Bake Turner, Texas Tech	25	221	8.8
9	John Sullivan, Princeton	9	219	24.3
10	Pervis Atkins, New Mexico State	10	218	21.8

	KICKOFF RETURNS/YARDS	KR	YDS	AVG
1	Bruce Samples, Brigham Young	23	577	25.1
2	Tom Hennessey, Holy Cross	12	401	33.4
3	Herman Urenda, Pacific	15	389	25.9
4	Skip Face, Stanford	19	387	20.4
5	Dennis Condie, Maryland	10	352	35.2
6	Jack Richardson, Kansas State	12	345	28.8
7	Calvin Bird, Kentucky	14	344	24.6
8	Tom Watkins, Iowa State	14	332	23.7
9	Lance Alworth, Arkansas	14	328	23.4
9	Nicholas Russo, Villanova	15	328	21.9

	SCORING	TDS	XPT	FG	PTS
1	Bob Gaiters, New Mexico State	23	7	0	145
2	Joe Bellino, Navy	18	2	0	110
3	Nolan Jones, Arizona State	8	27	6	93
4	Tom Larscheid, Utah State	15	2	0	92
5	Pervis Atkins, New Mexico State	12	8	0	80
6	Bob Ferguson, Ohio State	13	0	0	78
6	Tommy Mason, Tulane	13	0	0	78
6	Donnie Smith, Missouri	13	0	0	78
9	Hugh Campbell, Washington State	11	10	0	76
9	Joe Hernandez, Arizona	12	4	0	76

	KICK SCORING	XPA	XP	FG	PTS
1	Ed Dyas, Auburn	13	12	13	51
2	Nolan Jones, Arizona State	25	25	6	43
3	Durward Pennington, Georgia	18	16	8	40
4	Edgar Beach, New Mexico	29	27	4	39
4	Bill Tobin, Missouri	33	30	3	39
6	John Suder, Kansas	30	27	3	36
7	George Fleming, Washington	25	23	4	35
7	Jack Carter, Memphis State	36	29	2	35
9	Tommy Wells, Georgia Tech	13	10	8	34
10	Lon Armstrong, Clemson	25	24	3	33

	INTERCEPTIONS	INT	YDS
1	Bob O'Billovich, Montana	7	71
1	Ray Timmons, Miami, Fla.	7	46
3	Bryant Harvard, Auburn	6	113
3	Thomas O'Rourke, Villanova	6	91
3	Mickey Bruce, Oregon	6	68
3	Grimm Mason, Oregon State	6	41
3	Del Williams, Texas-El Paso	6	39
3	Bobby Bethune, Mississippi State	6	30
9	Bill Munsey, Minnesota*	5	130
9	James Boylan, Washington State*	5	82

*-Six tied with five; these had the most yards.

Team Leaders

	RUSHING OFFENSE	G	ATT	YDS	AVG	YPG
1	Utah State	10	553	3120	5.6	312.0
2	Memphis	10	484	2782	5.7	278.2
3	New Mexico State	10	452	2639	5.8	263.9
4	Syracuse	9	451	2309	5.1	256.6
5	Wyoming	10	595	2553	4.3	255.3
6	Iowa	9	439	2284	5.2	253.8
7	Missouri	10	571	2500	4.4	250.0
8	Arizona State	10	548	2489	4.5	248.9
9	Southern Miss	10	532	2445	4.6	244.5
10	Princeton	9	464	2132	4.6	236.9

	PASSING OFFENSE	G	ATT	COM	INT	PCT	YDS	YPA	TD	I%	YPC	YPG
1	Washington State	10	247	132	16	53.4	1855	7.5	14	6.5	14.1	185.5
2	Wisconsin	9	229	113	17	49.3	1526	6.7	8	7.4	13.5	169.6
3	Wake Forest	10	265	125	15	47.2	1692	6.4	10	5.7	13.5	169.2
4	Kentucky	10	220	114	14	51.8	1633	7.4	13	6.4	14.3	163.3
5	Baylor	10	205	109	14	53.2	1618	7.9	9	6.8	14.8	161.8
6	New Mexico State	10	218	113	8	51.8	1557	7.1	14	3.7	13.8	155.7
7	Detroit	9	201	96	10	47.8	1386	6.9	11	5.0	14.4	154.0
8	San Jose State	9	213	105	7	49.3	1382	6.5	8	3.3	13.2	153.6
9	Denver	10	230	107	18	46.5	1489	6.5	9	7.8	13.9	148.9
10	VMI	10	214	103	14	48.1	1424	6.7	8	6.5	13.8	142.4

	TOTAL OFFENSE	G	P	YDS	AVG	YPG
1	New Mexico State	10	670	4196	6.3	419.6
2	Memphis	10	612	3744	6.1	374.4
2	Utah State	10	638	3744	5.9	374.4
4	Mississippi	10	646	3624	5.6	362.4
5	Southern Miss	10	670	3467	5.2	346.7
6	Wyoming	10	706	3333	4.7	333.3
7	Arizona State	10	683	3331	4.9	333.1
8	Oregon	10	650	3311	5.1	331.1
9	Oregon State	10	613	3306	5.4	330.6
10	Washington State	10	645	3295	5.1	329.5

	RUSHING DEFENSE	G	ATT	YDS	AVG	YPG
1	Wyoming	10	345	824	2.4	82.4
2	Utah State	10	369	847	2.3	84.7
3	Alabama	10	378	891	2.4	89.1
4	Mississippi	10	386	892	2.3	89.2
5	Yale	9	369	945	2.6	105.0
6	Memphis	10	386	1080	2.8	108.0
7	Southern Miss	10	373	1082	2.9	108.2
8	Missouri	10	377	1092	2.9	109.2
9	Florida	10	397	1105	2.8	110.5
10	Washington	10	363	1117	3.1	111.7

	PASSING DEFENSE	G	ATT	COM	PCT	YPC	INT	I%	YDS	YPA	TD	YPG
1	Iowa State	10	93	29	31.2	10.4	7	7.5	302	3.2	2	30.2
2	Dayton	10	96	32	33.3	14.2	10	10.4	454	4.7	4	45.4
3	Kansas	10	113	43	38.1	11.2	12	10.6	483	4.3	4	48.3
4	Kentucky	10	124	47	37.9	11.1	17	13.7	522	4.2	3	52.2
5	Tennessee	10	130	58	44.6	9.3	13	10.0	538	4.1	2	53.8
6	Colorado	10	119	46	38.7	12.1	11	9.2	557	4.7	1	55.7
7	Citadel	10	126	54	42.9	10.6	16	12.7	570	4.5	4	57.0
8	Syracuse	9	129	47	36.4	11.0	11	8.5	516	4.0	1	57.3
9	Auburn	10	132	46	34.8	12.8	21	15.9	590	4.5	3	59.0
10	Kansas State	10	105	53	50.5	11.7	7	6.7	619	5.9	1	61.9

	TOTAL DEFENSE	G	P	YDS	AVG	YPG
1	Wyoming	10	477	1496	3.1	149.6
2	Alabama	10	536	1576	2.9	157.6
3	Mississippi	10	542	1686	3.1	168.6
4	Syracuse	9	520	1559	3.0	173.2
5	Auburn	10	526	1741	3.3	174.1
6	Kentucky	10	545	1831	3.4	183.1
7	Kansas	10	555	1872	3.4	187.2
8	Army	10	530	1916	3.6	191.6
9	Missouri	10	563	1493	2.7	194.3
10	Utah State	10	566	1945	3.4	194.5

	SCORING OFFENSE	G	PTS	AVG
1	New Mexico State	10	374	37.4
2	Memphis	10	303	30.3
3	Yale	9	253	28.1
4	Missouri	10	274	27.4
5	Mississippi	10	266	26.6
6	Utah Sate	10	261	26.1
7	Iowa	9	234	26.0
8	Princeton	9	232	25.8
9	Washington	10	255	25.5
10	Rutgers	9	225	25.0

	SCORING DEFENSE	G	PTS	AVG
1	LSU	10	50	5.0
2	Alabama	10	53	5.3
3	Rice	10	58	5.8
4	Mississippi	10	64	6.4
5	Utah State	10	65	6.5
6	Wyoming	10	71	7.1
7	Dartmouth	9	66	7.3
8	Florida	10	74	7.4
9	Texas	10	75	7.5
10	Rutgers	9	69	7.7

1961 POLL PROGRESSION

AP PRE-SEASON — SEPT. 23 GAMES

AP		Record	Result
1	Iowa	0-0-0	bye week
2	Ohio State	0-0-0	bye week
3	Alabama	0-0-0	beat Georgia 32-6
4	Texas	0-0-0	beat California 28-3
5	LSU	0-0-0	lost to Rice 3-16
6	Michigan State	0-0-0	bye week
7	Penn State	0-0-0	beat Navy 20-10
8	Kansas	0-0-0	lost to TCU 16-17
9	Mississippi	0-0-0	beat Arkansas 16-0
10	Syracuse	0-0-0	beat Oregon State 19-8

AP SEPTEMBER 25 POLL — SEPT. 30 GAMES

AP		Record	Result
1	Iowa	0-0-0	beat California 28-7
2	Mississippi	1-0-0	beat Kentucky 20-6
3	Ohio State	0-0-0	tied TCU 7-7
4	Alabama	1-0-0	beat Tulane 9-0
5	Syracuse	1-0-0	beat West Virginia 29-14
6	Texas	1-0-0	beat Texas Tech 42-14
7	Rice	1-0-0	lost to Georgia Tech 0-24
8	Penn State	1-0-0	lost to Miami, Fla. 8-25
9	UCLA	1-0-0	lost to Michigan 6-29
10	Michigan State	0-0-0	beat Wisconsin 20-0

UP AP OCTOBER 2 POLL — OCT. 7 GAMES

UP	AP		Record	Result
1	1	Iowa	1-0-0	beat Southern Cal 35-34
2	2	Mississippi	2-0-0	beat Florida State 33-0
3	3	Georgia Tech	2-0-0	lost to LSU 0-10
7	4	Alabama	2-0-0	beat Vanderbilt 35-6
5	5	Texas	2-0-0	beat Washington State 41-0
4	6	Michigan State	1-0-0	beat Stanford 31-3
9	7	Syracuse	2-0-0	lost to Maryland 21-22
	8	Ohio State	0-0-1	beat UCLA 13-3
8	9	Michigan	1-0-0	beat Army 38-8
10	10	Baylor	2-0-0	bye week
6		Missouri	2-0-0	tied California 14-14

UP AP OCTOBER 9 POLL — OCT. 14 GAMES

UP	AP		Record	Result
1	1	Mississippi	3-0-0	beat Houston 47-7
5	2	Iowa	2-0-0	beat Indiana 27-8
4	3	Alabama	3-0-0	beat North Carolina St. 26-7
3	4	Texas	3-0-0	beat Oklahoma 28-7
6	5	Michigan State	2-0-0	beat #6 Michigan 28-0
2	6	Michigan	2-0-0	lost to #5 Michigan State 0-28
8	7	Ohio State	1-0-1	beat Illinois 44-0
7	8	Notre Dame	2-0-0	beat Southern Cal 30-0
9	9	Baylor	2-0-0	lost to Arkansas 13-23
10	10	Maryland	3-0-0	lost to North Carolina 8-14

UP AP OCTOBER 16 POLL — OCT. 21 GAMES

UP	AP		Record	Result
2	1	Michigan State	3-0-0	beat Notre Dame 17-7
1	2	Mississippi	4-0-0	beat Tulane 41-0
3	3	Texas	4-0-0	beat #10 Arkansas 33-7
6	4	Iowa	3-0-0	beat Wisconsin 47-15
4	5	Alabama	4-0-0	beat Tennessee 34-3
5	6	Notre Dame	3-0-0	lost to Michigan State 7-17
7	7	Ohio State	2-0-1	beat Northwestern 10-0
8	8	Georgia Tech	3-1-0	beat Auburn 7-6
9	9	Colorado	3-0-0	beat Kansas State 13-0
11	10	Arkansas	3-1-0	lost to #3 Texas 7-33
10	10	LSU	3-1-0	beat Kentucky 24-14

UP AP OCTOBER 23 POLL — OCT. 28 GAMES

UP	AP		Record	Result
1	1	Michigan State	4-0-0	beat Indiana 35-0
2	2	Mississippi	5-0-0	beat Vanderbilt 47-0
3	3	Texas	5-0-0	beat Rice 34-7
4	4	Alabama	5-0-0	beat Houston 17-0
5	5	Iowa	4-0-0	lost to Purdue 9-23
6	6	Ohio State	3-0-1	beat Wisconsin 30-21
8	7	LSU	4-1-0	beat Florida 23-0
9	8	Notre Dame	3-1-0	lost to Northwestern 10-12
7	9	Georgia Tech	4-1-0	beat Tulane 35-0
10	10	Colorado	4-0-0	beat Oklahoma 22-14

UP AP OCTOBER 30 POLL — NOV. 4 GAMES

UP	AP		Record	Result
1	1	Michigan State	5-0-0	lost to Minnesota 0-13
2	2	Mississippi	6-0-0	lost to #6 LSU 7-10
3	3	Texas	6-0-0	beat SMU 27-0
4	4	Alabama	6-0-0	beat Mississippi State 24-0
5	5	Ohio State	4-0-1	beat #9 Iowa 29-13
7	6	LSU	5-1-0	beat #2 Mississippi 10-7
6	7	Georgia Tech	5-1-0	beat Florida 20-0
8	8	Colorado	5-0-0	beat #10 Missouri 7-6
9	9	Iowa	4-1-0	lost to #5 Ohio State 13-29
11	10	Missouri	5-0-1	lost to #8 Colorado 6-7

UP AP NOVEMBER 6 POLL — NOV. 11 GAMES

UP	AP		Record	Result
1	1	Texas	7-0-0	beat Baylor 33-7
2	2	Alabama	7-0-0	beat Richmond 66-0
3	3	Ohio State	5-0-1	beat Indiana 16-7
4	4	LSU	6-1-0	beat North Carolina 30-0
5	5	Minnesota	5-1-0	beat Iowa 16-9
7	6	Michigan State	5-1-0	lost to Purdue 6-7
8	7	Mississippi	6-1-0	beat U.T. Chattanooga 54-0
9	8	Colorado	6-0-0	lost to Utah 12-21
6	9	Georgia Tech	6-1-0	lost to Tennessee 6-10
10	10	Missouri	5-1-1	lost to Oklahoma 0-7

UP AP NOVEMBER 13 POLL — NOV. 18 GAMES

UP	AP		Record	Result
1	1	Texas	8-0-0	lost to TCU 0-6
2	2	Alabama	8-0-0	beat Georgia Tech 10-0
3	3	Ohio State	6-0-1	beat Oregon 22-12
5	4	LSU	7-1-0	beat Mississippi State 14-6
4	5	Minnesota	6-1-0	beat #7 Purdue 10-7
6	6	Mississippi	7-1-0	beat Tennessee 24-10
7	7	Purdue	5-2-0	lost to #5 Minnesota 7-10
10	8	Colorado	6-1-0	beat Nebraska 7-0
8	9	Michigan State	5-2-0	beat Northwestern 21-13
13	10	Syracuse	6-2-0	lost to Notre Dame 15-17

UP AP NOVEMBER 20 POLL — NOV. 25 GAMES

UP	AP		Record	Result
1	1	Alabama	9-0-0	bye week
2	2	Ohio State	7-0-1	beat Michigan 50-20
3	3	Minnesota	7-1-0	lost to Wisconsin 21-23
4	4	LSU	8-1-0	beat Tulane 62-0
5	5	Texas	8-1-0	beat Texas A&M 25-0
6	6	Mississippi	8-1-0	bye week
8	7	Colorado	7-1-0	beat Iowa State 34-0
7	8	Michigan State	6-2-0	beat Illinois 34-7
10	9	Arkansas	7-2-0	beat Texas Tech 28-0
	10	Kansas	6-2-1	lost to Missouri 7-10
9		Michigan	6-2-0	lost to #2 Ohio State 20-50

UP AP NOVEMBER 27 POLL — DEC. 2 GAMES

UP	AP		Record	Result
2	1	Alabama	9-0-0	beat Auburn 34-0
1	2	Ohio State	8-0-1	regular season complete
3	3	LSU	9-1-0	regular season complete
4	4	Texas	9-1-0	regular season complete
5	5	Mississippi	8-1-0	beat Mississippi State 37-7
6	6	Colorado	8-1-0	beat Air Force 29-12
7	7	Minnesota	7-2-0	regular season complete
8	8	Michigan State	7-2-0	regular season complete
9	9	Arkansas	8-2-0	regular season complete
11	10	Missouri	7-2-1	regular season complete

DECEMBER 4 FINAL POLL

UP	AP		RECORD	BOWL BID	DATE	BOWL RESULTS	RB	RECORDS
1	1	Alabama	10-0-0	Sugar Bowl	J1	beat #9 Arkansas 10-3	1	11-0-0
2	2	Ohio State	8-0-1				2	8-0-1
4	3	Texas	9-1-0	Cotton Bowl	J1	beat #5 Mississippi 12-7	4	10-1-0
3	4	LSU	9-1-0	Orange Bowl	J1	beat #7 Colorado 25-7	6	10-1-0
5	5	Mississippi	9-1-0	Cotton Bowl	J1	lost to #3 Texas 7-12	5	9-2-0
6	6	Minnesota	7-2-0	Rose Bowl	J1	beat #16 UCLA 21-3	3	8-2-0
7	7	Colorado	9-1-0	Orange Bowl	J1	lost to #4 LSU 7-25	9	9-2-0
9	8	Michigan State	7-2-0				7	7-2-0
8	9	Arkansas	8-2-0	Sugar Bowl	J1	lost to #1 Alabama 3-10	12	8-3-0
10	10	Utah State	9-0-1	Gotham Bowl	J1	lost to Baylor 9-24	19	9-1-1
11	11	Missouri	7-2-1				11	7-2-1
11	12	Purdue	6-3-0				8	6-3-0
13	13	Georgia Tech	7-3-0	Gator Bowl	D30	lost to #17 Penn State 15-30	28	7-4-0
16	14	Syracuse	7-3-0	Liberty Bowl	D16	beat Miami, Fla. 15-14	24	8-3-0
	15	Rutgers	9-0-0				14	9-0-0
	16	UCLA	7-3-0	Rose Bowl	J1	lost to #6 Minnesota 3-21	31	7-4-0
	17	Arizona	8-1-1				16	8-1-1
19	17	Penn State	6-3-0	Gator Bowl	D30	beat #13 Georgia Tech 30-15	21	8-3-0
	17	Rice	7-3-0	Bluebonnet Bowl	D16	lost to Kansas 7-33	29	7-4-0
14	20	Duke	7-3-0				15	7-3-0
15		Kansas	6-3-1	Bluebonnet Bowl	D16	beat #17 Rice 33-7	23	7-3-1
17		Wyoming	6-1-2				20	6-1-2
18		Wisconsin	6-3-0				10	6-3-0
19		Penn State	7-3-0	Gator Bowl	D30	beat #13 Georgia Tech 30-15	21	8-3-0

1961

Consensus All-Americans

POS	Name	HT	WT	School	AP	FC	FW	NE	SN	PI
B	**Ernie Davis**	6-2	210	Syracuse	•	•	•	•	•	•
B	**Bob Ferguson**	6-0	217	Ohio State	•	•	•	•	•	•
B	**Jimmy Saxton**	5-11	160	Texas	•	•	•	•	•	•
B	**Sandy Stephens**	6-0	215	Minnesota	•		•	•	•	•
E	**Gary Collins**	6-3	205	Maryland		•	•	•	•	•
E	**Bill Miller**	6-0	188	Miami	•		•	•	•	•
T	**Billy Neighbors**	5-11	229	Alabama	•	•	*	•	•	•
T	**Merlin Olsen**	6-5	265	Utah State	•	•	•	•	•	•
G	**Roy Winston**	6-1	225	LSU	•	•	•	•	•	•
G	**Joe Romig**	5-10	199	Colorado	•	•	•	•	•	•
C	**Alex Kroll**	6-2	228	Rutgers	•	•	•	•	•	•

	OTHERS RECEIVING FIRST-TEAM HONORS		
B	Billy Ray Adams	Mississippi	•
B	Lance Alworth	Arkansas	•
B	Roman Gabriel	North Carolina St.	• •
B	John Hadl	Kansas	•
E	Jerry Hillebrand	Colorado	• •
E	Greg Mather	Navy	•
E	Bob Mitinger	Penn State	•
E	Pat Richter	Wisconsin	•
T	Bobby Bell	Minnesota	• • •
T	Ed Blaine	Missouri	•
T	Don Talbert	Texas	•
G	Dave Behrman	Michigan State	• •
C	Ron Hull	UCLA	•
C	Bill Van Buren	Iowa	•

FW named Neighbors as a G

Heisman Trophy Voting

	PLAYER	POS	SCHOOL	1ST	2ND	3RD	TOTAL
1	Ernie Davis	HB	Syracuse	179	103	81	824
2	Bob Ferguson	FB	Ohio State	122	156	93	771
3	Jimmy Saxton	RB	Texas	81	105	98	551
4	Sandy Stephens	QB	Minnesota	104	78	68	543
5	Pat Trammel	QB	Alabama	76	45	44	362
6	Joe Romig	G	Colorado	55	40	34	279
7	John Hadl	QB	Kansas	33	25	23	172
8	Gary Collins	TE	Maryland	28	31	21	167
9	Roman Gabriel	QB	North Carolina St.	23	27	32	155
10	Merlin Olsen	DT	Utah State	13	19	16	93

Award Winners

PLAYER	POS	SCHOOL	AWARD NAME
Bob Ferguson	FB	Ohio State	Maxwell
Merlin Olsen	T	Utah State	Outland

Conference Standings

ACC

	CONF. W L T	OVERALL W L T
Duke	5 1 0	7 3 0
North Carolina	4 3 0	5 5 0
Maryland	3 3 0	7 3 0
Clemson	3 3 0	5 5 0
South Carolina	3 4 0	4 6 0
Wake Forest	3 4 0	4 6 0
North Carolina St.	3 4 0	4 6 0
Virginia	2 4 0	4 6 0

Big 10

	CONF. W L T	OVERALL W L T
Ohio State	6 0 0	8 0 1
Minnesota	6 1 0	8 2 0
Michigan State	5 2 0	7 2 0
Purdue	4 2 0	6 3 0
Wisconsin	4 3 0	6 3 0
Michigan	3 3 0	6 3 0
Iowa	2 4 0	5 4 0
Northwestern	2 4 0	4 5 0
Indiana	0 6 0	2 7 0
Illinois	0 7 0	0 9 0

Big 8

	CONF. W L T	OVERALL W L T
Colorado	7 0 0	9 2 0
Missouri	5 2 0	7 2 1
Kansas	5 2 0	7 3 1
Oklahoma	4 3 0	5 5 0
Iowa State	3 4 0	5 5 0
Oklahoma State	2 5 0	4 6 0
Nebraska	2 5 0	3 6 1
Kansas State	0 7 0	2 8 0

Border

	CONF. W L T	OVERALL W L T
Arizona State	3 0 0	7 3 0
West Texas State	3 1 0	6 4 0
New Mexico State	2 1 0	5 4 1
Texas-El Paso	1 3 0	3 7 0
Hardin-Simmons	0 4 0	0 10 0

Ivy

	CONF. W L T	OVERALL W L T
Columbia	6 1 0	6 3 0
Harvard	6 1 0	6 3 0
Dartmouth	5 2 0	6 3 0
Princeton	5 2 0	5 4 0
Yale	3 4 0	4 5 0
Cornell	2 5 0	3 6 0
Pennsylvania	1 6 0	2 7 0
Brown	0 7 0	0 9 0

MAC

	CONF. W L T	OVERALL W L T
Bowling Green	5 1 0	8 1 0
Western Michigan	4 1 1	5 3 1
Miami, Ohio	3 2 0	6 4 0
Ohio U	3 2 1	5 3 1
Toledo	2 4 0	3 7 0
Marshall	1 4 0	2 7 1
Kent State	1 5 0	2 8 0

AAWU

	CONF. W L T	OVERALL W L T
UCLA	3 1 0	7 4 0
Washington	2 1 1	5 4 1
Southern Cal	2 1 1	4 5 1
Stanford	1 3 0	4 6 0
California	1 3 0	1 8 1

SEC

	CONF. W L T	OVERALL W L T
Alabama	7 0 0	11 0 0
LSU	6 0 0	10 1 0
Mississippi	5 1 0	9 2 0
Georgia Tech	4 3 0	7 4 0
Tennessee	4 3 0	6 4 0
Florida	3 3 0	4 5 1
Auburn	3 4 0	6 4 0
Kentucky	2 4 0	5 5 0
Georgia	2 5 0	3 7 0
Mississippi State	1 5 0	5 5 0
Tulane	1 5 0	2 8 0
Vanderbilt	1 6 0	2 8 0

Skyline

	CONF. W L T	OVERALL W L T
Utah State	5 0 1	9 1 1
Wyoming	5 0 1	6 1 2
New Mexico	3 3 0	7 4 0
Utah	3 3 0	6 4 0
Montana	2 4 0	2 6 0
Brigham Young	2 4 0	2 8 0
Colorado State	0 6 0	0 10 0

SWC

	CONF. W L T	OVERALL W L T
Texas	6 1 0	10 1 0
Arkansas	6 1 0	8 3 0
Rice	5 2 0	7 4 0
Texas A&M	3 4 0	4 5 1
TCU	2 4 1	3 5 2
Baylor	2 5 0	6 5 0
Texas Tech	2 5 0	4 6 0
SMU	1 5 1	2 7 1

Independents

	OVERALL W L T
Rutgers	9 0 0
Arizona	8 1 1
Memphis	8 2 0
Syracuse	8 3 0
Penn State	8 3 0
Navy	7 3 0
Miami, Fla.	7 4 0
Army	6 4 0
Houston	5 4 1
Oregon State	5 5 0
Notre Dame	5 5 0
Florida State	4 5 1
Oregon	4 6 0
Boston College	4 6 0
Washington State	3 7 0
Air Force	3 7 0
Pittsburgh	3 7 0

Bowl Games

DATE	GAME	SCORE
N23	**Mercy**	Fresno State 36, Bowling Green 6
D9	**Gotham**	Baylor 24, Utah State 9
D9	**Aviation**	New Mexico 28, Western Michigan 12
D16	**Bluebonnet**	Kansas 33, Rice 7
D16	**Liberty**	Syracuse 15, Miami, Fla. 14
D29	**Tangerine**	Lamar 21, Middle Tennessee 14
D30	**Gator**	Penn State 30, Georgia Tech 15
D30	**Sun**	Villanova 17, Wichita State 9
J1	**Orange**	LSU 25, Colorado 7
J1	**Sugar**	Alabama 10, Arkansas 3
J1	**Rose**	Minnesota 21, UCLA 3
J1	**Cotton**	Texas 12, Mississippi 7

1961 NCAA Major College Statistical Leaders

Individual Leaders

PASSING/COMPLETIONS	G	ATT	COM	PCT	INT	I%	YDS	YPA	TD	TD%	COM.PG
1 Chon Gallegos, San Jose State	10	197	117	59.4	13	6.6	1480	7.5	14	7.1	11.7
2 Ron Miller, Wisconsin	9	198	104	52.5	11	5.6	1487	7.5	11	5.6	11.6
3 Roman Gabriel, North Carolina St.	10	186	99	53.2	6	3.2	937	5.0	8	4.3	9.9
4 Ron Klemick, Navy	10	183	86	47.0	13	7.1	1045	5.7	6	3.3	8.6
5 Billy Canty, Furman	10	168	84	50.0	12	7.1	884	5.3	8	4.8	8.4
5 John Furman, Texas-El Paso	10	180	84	46.7	10	5.6	1026	5.7	10	5.6	8.4
7 Matthew Szykowny, Iowa	9	139	79	56.8	15	10.8	1078	7.8	7	5.0	8.8
7 Eddie Wilson, Arizona	10	154	79	51.3	7	4.6	1294	8.4	10	6.5	7.9
9 Pat McCarthy, Holy Cross	10	165	76	46.1	11	6.7	1081	6.6	11	6.7	7.6
10 Pat Trammell, Alabama	10	133	75	56.4	2	1.5	1035	7.8	8	6.0	7.5

ALL-PURPOSE YARDS	G	RUSH	REC	PR	KR	YDS	YPG
1 Jim Pilot, New Mexico State	10	1278	20	161	147	1606	160.6

RUSHING/YARDS	G	ATT	YDS	AVG	YPG
1 Jim Pilot, New Mexico State	10	191	1278	6.7	127.8
2 Pete Pedro, West Texas State	10	137	976	7.1	97.6
3 Bob Ferguson, Ohio State	9	202	938	4.6	104.2
4 Dave Hoppmann, Iowa State	10	229	920	4.0	92.0
5 James Saxton, Texas	10	107	846	7.9	84.6
6 Ernie Davis, Syracuse	10	150	823	5.5	82.3
7 Tom Larscheid, Utah State	10	121	773	6.4	77.3
8 Tom Campbell, Furman	10	157	767	4.9	76.7
9 Robert Thompson, Arizona	10	103	752	7.3	75.2
10 Earl Stoudt, Richmond	10	162	704	4.4	70.4

RUSHING/YARDS PER CARRY	G	ATT	YDS	YPC
1 James Saxton, Texas	10	107	846	7.9
2 Robert Thompson, Arizona	10	103	752	7.3
3 Pete Pedro, West Texas State	10	137	976	7.1
4 Angelo Dabiero, Notre Dame	10	92	637	6.9
5 Jim Pilot, New Mexico State	10	191	1278	6.7
6 Tom Larscheid, Utah State	10	121	773	6.4
7 Billy Ray Adams, Mississippi	10	91	574	6.3
8 Alan White, Wake Forest	10	93	586	6.3
9 Mike McClellan, Oklahoma	10	82	508	6.2
10 Mike Haffner, UCLA	10	117	696	5.9

*-Based on top 42 rushers

RECEIVING/RECEPTIONS	G	REC	YDS	TD	YPR	YPG
1 Hugh Campbell, Washington State	10	53	723	5	13.6	72.3
2 Pat Richter, Wisconsin	9	47	817	8	17.4	90.8
3 Bill Miller, Miami, Fla.	10	43	640	2	14.9	64.0
4 Al Snyder, Holy Cross	10	38	558	5	14.7	55.8
5 Oscar Donahue, San Jose State	10	35	527	5	15.1	52.7
6 Larry Vargo, Detroit	9	32	601	8	18.8	66.8
6 Tom Hutchinson, Kentucky	10	32	543	4	17.0	54.3
8 Buddy Iles, TCU	10	31	479	2	15.5	47.9
9 Gary Collins, Maryland	10	30	428	4	14.3	42.8
10 Royce Cassell, New Mexico State	10	29	519	7	17.9	51.9
10 Joe Borich, Utah	10	29	486	5	16.8	48.6

PUNTING	PUNT	YDS	AVG
1 Joe Zuger, Arizona State	31	1305	42.1
2 Henry Lesesne, Vanderbilt	41	1702	41.5
3 Russ Warren, Columbia	25	1028	41.1
4 Jim Bakken, Wisconsin	39	1583	40.6
5 Clyde Marsh, Citadel	46	1863	40.5
5 Bill Wright, Brigham Young	46	1863	40.5
7 Terry Isaacson, Air Force	39	1572	40.3
8 Dick Fitzsimmons, New Mexico	39	1568	40.2
9 Eddie Werntz, Clemson	56	2251	40.2
10 Bill Ruby, Wake Forest	55	2211	40.2

PUNT RETURNS/YARDS	PR	YDS	AVG
1 Lance Alworth, Arkansas	28	336	12.0
2 Jay Wilkinson, Duke	22	328	14.9
3 Tom Larscheid, Utah State	12	281	23.4
3 Darrell Cox, Kentucky	21	281	13.4
5 Fred Colvard, West Virginia	12	196	16.3
6 Tom Brown, Maryland	8	194	24.3
7 John Hadl, Kansas	17	191	11.2
7 W.E. Richardson, Alabama	21	191	9.1
9 Larry Cox, Xavier	13	183	14.1
10 Al Snyder, Holy Cross	10	182	18.2

KICKOFF RETURNS/YARDS	KR	YDS
1 Dick Mooney, Idaho	23	494
2 Paul Allen, Brigham Young	12	481
3 Ken Bolin, Houston	19	437
4 Terry Isaacson, Air Force	20	397
5 Jack Morris, South Carolina	13	375
6 Mack Burton, San Jose State	14	368
6 Jerry Logan, West Texas State	15	368
8 Paul Costa, Notre Dame	16	359
9 Rudy Carvajal, California	20	358
10 Larry McIntire, Tulane	15	348

SCORING	TDS	XPT	FG	PTS
1 Jim Pilot, New Mexico State	21	12	0	138
2 Pete Pedro, West Texas State	22	0	0	132
3 Tom Larscheid, Utah State	15	6	0	96
4 Ernie Davis, Syracuse	15	4	0	94
4 Wendell Harris, LSU	8	28	6	94
6 Bob Smith, UCLA	10	16	3	85
7 Robert Thompson, Arizona	13	4	0	82
8 Nolan Jones, Arizona State	8	20	3	77
9 Butch Blume, Rice	6	20	6	74
10 Sam Mudie, Rutgers	10	10	0	70

KICK SCORING	XPA	XP	FG	PTS
1 Greg Mather, Navy	23	22	11	55
2 Tim Davis, Alabama	27	22	9	49
3 Wendell Harris, LSU	29	26	6	44
4 Pete Smolanovich, New Mexico State	39	38	1	41
4 Jack Carter, Memphis	43	38	1	41
6 Carl Choate, Baylor	23	23	5	38
6 Dick Heydt, Army	28	26	4	38
6 Butch Blume, Rice	22	20	6	38
9 Jim Turner, Utah State	36	30	2	36
10 Dick Van Raaphorst, Ohio State	27	23	4	35
10 Don Jonas, Penn State	22	17	6	35

INTERCEPTIONS	INT
1 Joe Zuger, Arizona State	10
2 Tom Brown, Maryland	8
3 Junior Edge, North Carolina	7
4 Sam Mudie, Rutgers	6
4 John Maisel, Oklahoma State	6
4 Tony Carmignani, Furman	6
4 Bob McDonough, Air Force	6
8 Stinson Jones, VMI *	5
8 Jackie Farland, Boston U. *	5
8 Angelo Dabiero, Notre Dame *	5
8 John Snider, Syracuse *	5

*-Ten tied with five; these had the most yards.

Team Leaders

RUSHING OFFENSE	G	ATT	YDS	AVG	YPG
1 New Mexico State	10	489	2991	6.1	299.1
2 Texas	10	552	2858	5.2	285.8
3 Utah State	10	534	2818	5.3	281.8
4 Ohio State	9	522	2447	4.7	271.9
5 West Texas State	10	461	2475	5.4	247.5
6 Wyoming	9	535	2205	4.1	245.0
7 Michigan State	9	463	2135	4.6	237.2
8 Bowling Green	9	519	2132	4.1	236.9
9 Mississippi	10	472	2360	5.0	236.0
10 Memphis State	10	435	2341	5.4	234.1

PASSING OFFENSE	G	ATT	COM	INT	PCT	YDS	YPA	TD	I%	YPC	YPG
1 Wisconsin	9	226	117	12	51.8	1696	7.5	13	5.3	14.5	188.4
2 Mississippi	10	202	109	8	54.0	1827	9.0	19	4.0	16.8	182.7
3 Detroit	9	245	103	20	42.0	1639	6.7	13	8.2	15.9	182.1
4 Holy Cross	10	242	108	14	44.6	1625	6.7	13	5.8	15.0	162.5
5 Washington State	10	231	117	17	50.6	1561	6.8	10	7.4	13.3	156.1
5 San Jose State	10	223	127	15	57.0	1561	7.0	15	6.7	12.3	156.1
7 Navy	10	244	110	20	45.1	1545	6.3	8	8.2	14.0	154.5
8 Iowa	9	172	94	17	54.7	1319	7.7	9	9.9	14.0	146.6
9 Maryland	10	215	115	17	53.5	1464	6.8	12	7.9	12.7	146.4
10 Arizona	10	180	90	8	50.0	1456	8.1	12	4.4	16.2	145.6

TOTAL OFFENSE	G	P	YDS	AVG
1 Mississippi	10	674	4187	6.2
2 New Mexico State	10	631	4009	6.4
3 Utah State	10	669	3911	5.8
4 Texas	10	700	3831	5.5
5 Arizona	10	588	3782	6.4
6 Penn State	10	706	3691	5.2
7 Memphis	10	610	3690	6.0
8 Ohio State	9	612	3142	5.1
9 Arizona State	10	658	3353	5.1
10 West Texas State	10	575	3290	5.7

RUSHING DEFENSE	G	ATT	YDS	AVG	YPG
1 Utah State	10	325	508	1.6	50.8
2 Alabama	10	321	550	1.7	55.0
3 Villanova	9	290	640	2.2	71.1
4 LSU	10	386	794	2.1	79.4
5 Mississippi	10	378	804	2.1	80.4
6 Minnesota	9	364	759	2.1	84.3
7 Bowling Green	9	317	780	2.5	86.7
8 Wyoming	9	319	803	2.5	89.2
9 Texas	10	376	902	2.4	90.2
10 Georgia Tech	10	365	949	2.6	94.9

PASSING DEFENSE	G	ATT	COM	PCT	YPC	INT	I%	YDS	YPA	TD	YPG
1 Pennsylvania	9	124	44	35.5	11.6	14	11.3	512	4.1	4	56.9
2 Yale	9	111	48	43.2	10.9	11	9.9	523	4.7	5	58.1
3 Arkansas	10	121	57	47.1	11.0	10	8.3	629	5.2	5	62.9
4 Mississippi	10	149	58	38.9	11.2	13	8.7	649	4.4	1	64.9
5 Dartmouth	9	110	44	40.0	13.4	12	10.9	591	5.4	4	65.7
6 Columbia	9	124	42	33.9	14.1	14	11.3	592	4.8	6	65.8
7 Southern Cal	10	111	50	45.0	13.3	10	9.0	666	6.0	6	66.6
8 Brown	9	90	40	44.4	15.0	9	10.0	600	6.7	9	66.7
9 Oregon	10	112	50	44.6	13.4	8	7.1	672	6.0	1	67.2
10 Kansas State	10	109	42	38.5	16.4	10	9.2	687	6.3	6	68.7

TOTAL DEFENSE	G	P	YDS	AVG
1 Alabama	10	524	1326	2.5
2 Utah State	10	512	1393	2.7
3 Mississippi	10	527	1453	2.8
4 Bowling Green	9	460	1456	3.2
5 Wyoming	9	438	1511	3.4
6 LSU	10	564	1703	3.0
7 Villanova	9	470	1559	3.3
8 Texas	10	577	1761	3.1
9 Missouri	10	560	1769	3.2
10 Arkansas	10	548	1774	3.2

SCORING OFFENSE	G	PTS	AVG
1 Utah State	10	387	38.7
2 New Mexico State	10	341	34.1
3 Memphis	10	332	33.2
4 Mississippi	10	326	32.6
5 West Texas State	10	309	30.9
6 Texas	10	291	29.1
7 Arizona	10	288	28.8
8 Arizona State	10	287	28.7
8 Alabama	10	287	28.7
10 Rutgers	9	246	27.3

SCORING DEFENSE	G	PTS	AVG
1 Alabama	10	22	2.2
2 Mississippi	10	40	4.0
3 Bowling Green	9	42	4.7
4 LSU	10	50	5.0
4 Georgia Tech	10	50	5.0
6 Michigan State	9	50	5.6
7 Missouri	10	57	5.7
8 Texas	10	59	5.9
9 Miami, Fla.	10	70	7.0
10 Memphis	10	75	7.5

1962 POLL PROGRESSION

AP PRE-SEASON / SEPT. 22 GAMES

AP	Team	Record	Result
1	Ohio State	0-0-0	bye week
2	Texas	0-0-0	beat Oregon 25-13
3	Alabama	0-0-0	beat Georgia 35-0
4	Michigan State	0-0-0	bye week
5	LSU	0-0-0	beat Texas A&M 21-0
6	Mississippi	0-0-0	beat Memphis 21-7
7	Purdue	0-0-0	tied # 10 Washington 7-7
8	Duke	0-0-0	lost to Southern Cal 7-14
9	Penn State	0-0-0	beat Navy 41-7
10	Washington	0-0-0	tied # 7 Purdue 7-7

AP SEPTEMBER 24 POLL / SEPT. 29 GAMES

AP	Team	Record	Result
1	Alabama	1-0-0	beat Tulane 44-6
2	Ohio State	0-0-0	beat North Carolina 41-7
3	Texas	1-0-0	beat Texas Tech 34-0
4	Penn State	1-0-0	beat Air Force 20-6
5	LSU	1-0-0	tied Rice 6-6
6	Michigan State	0-0-0	lost to Stanford 13-16
7	Mississippi	1-0-0	beat Kentucky 14-0
8	Georgia Tech	1-0-0	beat Florida 17-0
9	Southern Cal	1-0-0	beat SMU 33-3
10	Missouri	1-0-0	tied Minnesota 0-0

UP AP OCTOBER 1 POLL / OCT. 6 GAMES

UP	AP	Team	Record	Result
1	1	Ohio State	1-0-0	lost to UCLA 7-9
2	2	Alabama	2-0-0	beat Vanderbilt 17-7
3	3	Texas	2-0-0	beat Tulane 35-0
4	4	Penn State	2-0-0	beat Rice 18-7
5	5	Georgia Tech	2-0-0	lost to LSU 7-10
6	6	Southern Cal	2-0-0	beat Iowa 7-0
7	7	Mississippi	2-0-0	beat Houston 40-7
8	8	Washington	1-0-1	beat Kansas State 41-0
10	9	Miami, Fla.	2-0-0	beat Florida State 7-6
9	10	Army	2-0-0	lost to Michigan 7-17

UP AP OCTOBER 8 POLL / OCT. 13 GAMES

UP	AP	Team	Record	Result
2	1	Alabama	3-0-0	beat Houston 14-3
1	2	Texas	3-0-0	beat Oklahoma 9-6
3	3	Penn State	3-0-0	lost to Army 6-9
4	4	Southern Cal	3-0-0	bye week
5	5	Mississippi	3-0-0	bye week
	6	LSU	2-0-1	beat Miami, Fla. 17-3
6	7	Washington	2-0-1	beat Oregon State 14-13
7	8	Arkansas	3-0-0	beat Baylor 28-21
9	9	Purdue	1-0-1	lost to Miami, Ohio 7-10
	10	Ohio State	1-1-0	beat Illinois 51-15
8		UCLA	1-0-0	beat Colorado State 35-7 (O12)
10		Northwestern	2-0-0	beat Minnesota 34-22

UP AP OCTOBER 15 POLL / OCT. 20 GAMES

UP	AP	Team	Record	Result
1	1	Texas	4-0-0	beat # 7 Arkansas 7-3
2	2	Alabama	4-0-0	beat Tennessee 27-7
5	3	Southern Cal	3-0-0	beat California 32-6
10	4	LSU	3-0-1	beat Kentucky 7-0
4	5	Mississippi	3-0-0	beat Tulane 21-0
7	6	Ohio State	2-1-0	lost to # 8 Northwestern 14-18
6	7	Arkansas	4-0-0	lost to # 1 Texas 3-7
3	8	Northwestern	3-0-0	beat # 6 Ohio State 18-14
9	9	Washington	3-0-1	beat Stanford 14-0
8	10	Wisconsin	3-0-0	beat Iowa 42-14

UP AP OCTOBER 22 POLL / OCT. 27 GAMES

UP	AP	Team	Record	Result
1	1	Texas	5-0-0	tied Rice 14-14
3	2	Alabama	5-0-0	beat Tulsa 35-6
2	3	Northwestern	4-0-0	beat Notre Dame 35-6
5	4	Southern Cal	4-0-0	beat Illinois 28-16
4	5	Wisconsin	4-0-0	lost to Ohio State 7-14
8	6	LSU	4-0-1	beat Florida 23-0
6	7	Mississippi	4-0-0	beat Vanderbilt 35-0
7	8	Washington	4-0-1	tied Oregon 21-21
	9	Arkansas	4-1-0	beat Hardin-Simmons 49-7
9	10	Michigan State	3-1-0	beat Indiana 26-8
10		Auburn	4-0-0	beat Clemson 17-14

UP AP OCTOBER 29 POLL / NOV. 3 GAMES

UP	AP	Team	Record	Result
1	1	Northwestern	5-0-0	beat Indiana 26-21
2	2	Alabama	6-0-0	beat Mississippi State 20-0
3	3	Southern Cal	5-0-0	beat # 9 Washington 14-0
6	4	LSU	5-0-1	lost to # 6 Mississippi 7-15
5	5	Texas	5-0-1	beat SMU 6-0
4	6	Mississippi	5-0-0	beat # 4 LSU 15-7
7	7	Michigan State	4-1-0	lost to Minnesota 7-28
9	8	Arkansas	5-1-0	beat Texas A&M 17-7
8	9	Washington	4-0-2	lost to # 3 Southern Cal 0-14
	20	Auburn	5-0-0	lost to Florida 3-22
16		Nebraska	6-0-0	lost to Missouri 7-16

UP AP NOVEMBER 5 POLL / NOV. 10 GAMES

UP	AP	Team	Record	Result
1	1	Northwestern	6-0-0	lost to # 8 Wisconsin 6-37
3	2	Southern Cal	6-0-0	beat Stanford 39-14
2	3	Alabama	7-0-0	beat Miami, Fla. 36-3
4	4	Mississippi	6-0-0	beat U.T. Chattanooga 52-7
5	5	Texas	6-0-1	beat Baylor 27-12
8	6	Arkansas	6-1-0	beat Rice 28-14
6	7	Missouri	6-0-1	beat Colorado 57-0
7	8	Wisconsin	5-1-0	beat # 1 Northwestern 37-6
10	9	LSU	5-1-1	beat TCU 5-0
9	10	Minnesota	4-1-1	beat Iowa 10-0

UP AP NOVEMBER 12 POLL / NOV. 17 GAMES

UP	AP	Team	Record	Result
2	1	Alabama	8-0-0	lost to Georgia Tech 6-7
1	2	Southern Cal	7-0-0	beat Navy 13-6
3	3	Mississippi	7-0-0	beat Tennessee 19-6
4	4	Wisconsin	6-1-0	beat Illinois 35-6
5	5	Texas	7-0-1	beat TCU 14-0
6	6	Missouri	7-0-1	lost to Oklahoma 0-13
9	7	Arkansas	7-1-0	beat SMU 9-7
7	8	Minnesota	5-1-1	beat Purdue 7-6
	9	Northwestern	6-1-0	lost to Michigan State 7-31
10	10	LSU	6-1-1	beat Mississippi State 28-0

UP AP NOVEMBER 19 POLL / NOV. 24 GAMES

UP	AP	Team	Record	Result
1	1	Southern Cal	8-0-0	beat UCLA 14-3
2	2	Mississippi	8-0-0	bye week
3	3	Wisconsin	7-1-0	beat # 5 Minnesota 14-9
4	4	Texas	8-0-1	beat Texas A&M 13-3
5	5	Minnesota	6-1-1	lost to # 3 Wisconsin 9-14
6	6	Alabama	8-1-0	bye week
7	7	Arkansas	8-1-0	beat Texas Tech 34-0
8	8	LSU	7-1-1	beat Tulane 38-3
9	9	Penn State	8-1-0	beat Pittsburgh 16-0
10	10	Oklahoma	6-2-0	beat Nebraska 34-6

UP AP NOVEMBER 26 POLL / DEC. 1 GAMES

UP	AP	Team	Record	Result
1	1	Southern Cal	9-0-0	beat Notre Dame 25-0
2	2	Wisconsin	8-1-0	regular season complete
3	3	Mississippi	8-0-0	beat Mississippi State 13-6
4	4	Texas	9-0-1	regular season complete
5	5	Alabama	8-1-0	beat Auburn 38-0
6	6	Arkansas	9-1-0	regular season complete
6	7	LSU	8-1-1	regular season complete
8	8	Oklahoma	7-2-0	beat Oklahoma State 37-6
9	9	Penn State	9-1-0	regular season complete
10	10	Minnesota	6-2-1	regular season complete

UP AP DECEMBER 3 FINAL POLL

UP	AP	Team	Record	Bowl Bid	Date	Bowl Result	RB	Record
1	1	Southern Cal	10-0-0	Rose Bowl	J1	beat # 2 Wisconsin 42-37	2	11-0-0
2	2	Wisconsin	8-1-0	Rose Bowl	J1	lost to # 1 Southern Cal 37-42	6	8-2-0
3	3	Mississippi	9-0-0	Sugar Bowl	J1	beat # 6 Arkansas 17-13	1	10-0-0
4	4	Texas	9-0-1	Cotton Bowl	J1	lost to # 7 LSU 13-0	5	9-1-1
5	5	Alabama	9-1-0	Orange Bowl	J1	beat # 8 Oklahoma 17-0	3	10-1-0
6	6	Arkansas	9-1-0	Sugar Bowl	J1	lost to # 3 Mississippi 13-17	10	9-2-0
8	7	LSU	8-1-1	Cotton Bowl	J1	beat # 4 Texas 13-0	4	9-1-1
7	8	Oklahoma	8-2-0	Orange Bowl	J1	lost to # 5 Alabama 0-17	14	8-3-0
9	9	Penn State	9-1-0	Gator Bowl	D29	lost to Florida 7-17	12	9-2-0
10	10	Minnesota	6-2-1				7	6-2-1

1962

CONSENSUS ALL-AMERICANS

POS	Name	HT	WT	School	AP	FC	FW	NE	SN	PI
B	Terry Baker	6-3	191	Oregon State	•	•	•	•	•	•
B	Jerry Stovall	6-2	195	LSU	•	•	•	•	•	•
B	Mel Renfro	5-11	190	Oregon				•	•	•
B	George Saimes	5-10	186	Michigan State	•	•	•	•		•
E	Hal Bedsole	6-5	225	Southern Cal		•	•	•	•	•
E	Pat Richter	6-5	229	Wisconsin	•	•	•		•	
T	Bobby Bell	6-4	214	Minnesota	•	•	•	•	•	•
T	Jim Dunaway	6-4	260	Mississippi				•	•	•
G	Johnny Treadwell	6-1	194	Texas	•	•	•	•		•
G	Jack Cvercko	6-0	230	Northwestern				•	•	•
C	Lee Roy Jordan	6-2	207	Alabama	•	•	•	•	•	•

OTHERS RECEIVING FIRST-TEAM HONORS

B	George Mira	Miami, Fla.	•		•			
B	Tom Myers	Northwestern			•			
B	Glynn Griffing	Mississippi			•			
B	Dave Hoppman	Iowa State			•			
B	Bill Moore	Arkansas				•	•	
B	Roger Kochman	Penn State		•				
B	Eldon Fortie	Brigham Young			•			
E	Conrad Hitchler	Missouri			•			
E	Dave Robinson	Penn State	•		•	•		
T	Steve Barnett	Oregon		•	•			
T	Don Brumm	Purdue		•	•			
T	Fred Miller	LSU			•			
G	Jean Berry	Duke			•			
G	Leon Cross	Oklahoma			•			
G	Rufus Guthrie	Georgia Tech	•	•	•			
G	Damon Bame	Southern Cal	•					
C	Donald McKinnon	Dartmouth			•	•		

Notes: NEA named McKinnon as a G

HEISMAN TROPHY VOTING

	PLAYER	POS	SCHOOL	1ST	2ND	3RD	TOTAL
1	Terry Baker	QB	Oregon State	172	74	43	707
2	Jerry Stovall	HB	LSU	112	100	82	618
3	Bobby Bell	T	Minnesota	56	95	71	429
4	Lee Roy Jordan	LB	Alabama	70	35	41	321
5	George Mira	QB	Miami, Fla.	41	53	55	284
6	Pat Richter	E	Wisconsin	55	40	31	276
7	George Saimes	HB	Michigan State	48	36	38	254
8	Billy Lothridge	QB	Georgia Tech	24	35	20	162
9	Ron Vander Kelen	QB	Wisconsin	23	22	26	139
10	Eldon Fortie	TB	Brigham Young	25	22	17	136

AWARD WINNERS

PLAYER	POS	SCHOOL	AWARD NAME
Terry Baker	QB	Oregon State	Maxwell
Bobby Bell	T	Minnesota	Outland

CONFERENCE STANDINGS

ACC

	Conf.			Overall		
	W	L	T	W	L	T
Duke	6	0	0	8	2	0
Clemson	5	1	0	6	4	0
Maryland	5	2	0	6	4	0
South Carolina	3	4	0	4	5	1
North Carolina St.	3	4	0	3	6	1
North Carolina	3	4	0	3	7	0
Virginia	1	4	0	5	5	0
Wake Forest	0	7	0	0	10	0

Big 10

	Conf.			Overall		
	W	L	T	W	L	T
Wisconsin	6	1	0	8	2	0
Minnesota	5	2	0	6	2	1
Northwestern	4	2	0	7	2	0
Ohio State	4	2	0	6	3	0
Michigan State	3	3	0	5	4	0
Purdue	3	3	0	4	4	1
Iowa	3	3	0	4	5	0
Illinois	2	5	0	2	7	0
Indiana	1	5	0	3	6	0
Michigan	1	6	0	2	7	0

Big 8

	Conf.			Overall		
	W	L	T	W	L	T
Oklahoma	7	0	0	8	3	0
Missouri	5	1	1	8	1	2
Nebraska	5	2	0	9	2	0
Kansas	4	2	1	6	3	1
Iowa State	3	4	0	5	5	0
Oklahoma State	2	5	0	4	6	0
Colorado	1	6	0	2	8	0
Kansas State	0	7	0	0	10	0

Ivy

	Conf.			Overall		
	W	L	T	W	L	T
Dartmouth	7	0	0	9	0	0
Harvard	5	2	0	6	3	0
Princeton	4	3	0	5	4	0
Columbia	4	3	0	5	4	0
Cornell	4	3	0	4	5	0
Pennsylvania	2	5	0	3	6	0
Yale	1	5	1	2	5	2
Brown	0	6	1	1	6	2

MAC

	Conf.			Overall		
	W	L	T	W	L	T
Bowling Green	5	0	1	7	1	1
Ohio U	5	1	0	8	2	0
Miami, Ohio	3	1	1	8	1	1
Western Michigan	3	3	0	5	4	0
Kent State	2	4	0	3	6	0
Toledo	1	5	0	3	6	0
Marshall	0	5	0	4	6	0

AAWU

	Conf.			Overall		
	W	L	T	W	L	T
Southern Cal	4	0	0	11	0	0
Washington	4	1	0	7	1	2
Washington State	1	1	0	5	4	1
Stanford	2	3	0	5	5	0
UCLA	1	3	0	4	6	0
California	0	4	0	1	9	0

SEC

	Conf.			Overall		
	W	L	T	W	L	T
Mississippi	6	0	0	10	0	0
Alabama	6	1	0	10	1	0
LSU	5	1	0	9	1	1
Georgia Tech	5	2	0	7	3	1
Florida	4	2	0	7	4	0
Auburn	4	3	0	6	3	1
Georgia	2	3	1	3	4	3
Kentucky	2	3	1	3	5	2
Mississippi State	2	5	0	3	6	0
Tennessee	2	6	0	4	6	0
Vanderbilt	1	6	0	1	9	0
Tulane	0	7	0	0	10	0

SWC

	Conf.			Overall		
	W	L	T	W	L	T
Texas	6	0	1	9	1	1
Arkansas	6	1	0	9	2	0
TCU	5	2	0	6	4	0
Baylor	3	4	0	4	6	0
Texas A&M	3	4	0	3	7	0
Rice	2	4	1	2	6	2
SMU	2	5	0	2	8	0
Texas Tech	0	7	0	1	9	0

WAC

	Conf.			Overall		
	W	L	T	W	L	T
Wyoming	2	2	0	5	5	0
Arizona	2	2	0	5	5	0
Brigham Young	2	2	0	4	6	0
Arizona State	1	1	0	7	2	1
Utah	1	2	1	4	5	1

Independents

	Overall		
	W	L	T
Memphis	8	1	0
Penn State	9	2	0
Oregon State	9	2	0
Utah State	8	2	0
Boston College	8	2	0
Villanova	7	3	0
Oregon	6	3	1
Houston	7	4	0
Miami, Fla.	7	4	0
Army	6	4	0
Florida State	4	3	3
Navy	5	5	0
Pittsburgh	5	5	0
Notre Dame	5	5	0
Syracuse	5	5	0
Air Force	5	5	0
Rutgers	5	5	0
Texas-El Paso	4	5	0
New Mexico State	4	6	0
Colorado State	0	10	0

BOWL GAMES

DATE	GAME	SCORE
D15	Gotham	Nebraska 36, Miami, Fla. 34
D15	Liberty	Oregon State 6, Villanova 0
D22	Bluebonnet	Missouri 14, Georgia Tech 10
D22	Tangerine	Houston 49, Miami, Ohio 21
D29	Gator	Florida 17, Penn State 7
D31	Sun	West Texas State 15, Ohio U 14
J1	Orange	Alabama 17, Oklahoma 0
J1	Cotton	LSU 13, Texas 0
J1	Sugar	Mississippi 17, Arkansas 13
J1	Rose	Southern Cal 42, Wisconsin 37

1962 NCAA MAJOR COLLEGE STATISTICAL LEADERS

INDIVIDUAL LEADERS

PASSING/COMPLETIONS	G	ATT	COM	PCT	INT	I%	YDS	YPA	TD	TD%	COM.PG
1 Don Trull, Baylor	10	229	125	54.6	12	5.2	1627	7.1	11	4.8	12.5
2 George Mira, Miami, Fla.	10	260	122	46.9	16	6.2	1572	6.0	10	3.9	12.2
3 Dick Shiner, Maryland	10	203	121	59.6	16	7.9	1324	6.5	4	2.0	12.1
4 Tom Myers, Northwestern	9	195	116	59.5	14	7.2	1537	7.9	13	6.7	12.9
5 Terry Baker, Oregon State	10	203	112	55.2	5	2.5	1738	8.6	15	7.4	11.2
6 Jerry Gross, Detroit	9	212	105	49.5	13	6.1	1317	6.2	6	2.8	11.7
7 Dave Mathieson, Washington State	10	198	104	52.5	8	4.0	1472	7.4	12	6.1	10.4
8 Junior Edge, North Carolina	10	185	103	55.7	12	6.5	1234	6.7	7	3.8	10.3
9 Archie Roberts, Columbia	9	170	102	60.0	6	3.5	1076	6.3	6	3.5	11.3
10 Gary Cuozzo, Virginia	10	181	98	54.1	9	5.0	1136	6.3	6	3.3	9.8

ALL-PURPOSE YARDS	G	RUSH	REC	PR	KR	YDS	YPG
1 Gary Wood, Cornell	9	889	7	69	430	1395	155.0

RUSHING/Yards	G	ATT	YDS	AVG	YPG
1 Jim Pilot, New Mexico State	10	208	1247	6.0	124.7
2 Eldon Fortie, Brigham Young	10	199	1149	5.8	114.9
3 Gale Sayers, Kansas	10	158	1125	7.1	112.5
4 Gary Wood, Cornell	9	173	889	5.1	98.8
5 Joe Don Looney, Oklahoma	10	137	852	6.2	85.2
6 Pete Pedro, West Texas State	10	134	831	6.2	83.1
7 Johnny Roland, Missouri	10	159	830	5.2	83.0
8 Dave Casinelli, Memphis	9	173	826	4.8	91.8
9 Bobby Santiago, New Mexico	10	151	806	5.3	80.6
10 Dave Hoppmann, Iowa State	10	198	798	4.0	79.8

RUSHING/Yards Per Carry	G	ATT	YDS	YPC
1 Gale Sayers, Kansas	10	158	1125	7.1
2 Willie Brown, Southern Cal	10	80	555	6.9
3 Tony Lorick, Arizona State	10	105	704	6.7
4 John Cook, Furman	10	99	655	6.6
5 Joe Don Looney, Oklahoma	10	137	852	6.2
6 Pete Pedro, West Texas State	10	134	831	6.2
7 Sherman Lewis, Michigan State	9	98	590	6.0
8 Jim Pilot, New Mexico State	10	208	1247	6.0
9 Mel Renfro, Oregon	10	126	753	6.0
10 Junior Coffey, Washington	10	98	581	5.9

*-Based on top 42 rushers

RECEIVING/Receptions	G	REC	YDS	TD	YPR	YPG	RPG
1 Vern Burke, Oregon State	10	69	1007	10	14.6	100.7	6.9
2 John Simmons, Tulsa	10	65	860	9	13.2	86.0	6.5
3 Hugh Campbell, Washington State	10	57	849	7	14.9	84.9	5.7
4 Tom Brown, Maryland	10	47	557	4	11.9	55.7	4.7
5 James Cure, Marshall	10	46	667	3	14.5	66.7	4.6
6 Paul Flatley, Northwestern	9	45	632	5	14.0	70.2	5.0
6 Bob Lacey, North Carolina	10	44	668	5	15.2	66.8	4.4
7 Bill Turner, California	10	44	537	6	12.2	53.7	4.4
6 Art Graham, Boston College	10	41	823	7	20.1	82.3	4.1
6 Al Snyder, Holy Cross	10	41	703	6	17.1	70.3	4.1
9 Jim Kelly, Notre Dame	10	41	523	4	12.8	52.3	4.1

PUNTING	PUNT	YDS	AVG
1 Joe Don Looney, Oklahoma	34	1474	43.4
2 Dave Marion, Wyoming	36	1544	42.9
3 Cotton Clark, Alabama	21	893	42.5
4 George Canale, Tennessee	53	2221	41.9
5 Bob Paterson, San Jose State	37	1524	41.2
6 Chuck Raisig, Penn State	35	1439	41.1
7 Hagood Clarke, Florida	46	1886	41.0
8 Dick Fitzsimmons, New Mexico	41	1681	41.0
9 Jon Kilgore, Auburn	57	2320	40.7
10 Danny Thomas, SMU	69	2808	40.7

PUNT RETURNS/Yards	PR	YDS	AVG
1 Darrell Roberts, Utah State	16	333	20.8
2 Ken Hatfield, Arkansas	18	267	14.8
3 Woody Houston, New Mexico State	22	266	12.1
4 Jay Wilkinson, Duke	28	259	9.3
5 Paul Lea, Oklahoma	17	254	14.9
6 Dave Marion, Wyoming	9	244	27.1
7 Cotton Clark, Alabama	16	243	15.2
8 Ken Waldrop, Army	18	235	13.1
9 Russell Vollmer, Memphis	11	224	20.4
10 Nat Whitmyer, Washington	17	220	12.9

KICKOFF RETURNS/Yards	KR	YDS	AVG
1 Donnie Frederick, Wake Forest	29	660	22.8
2 Jerry Graves, Tulane	21	513	24.4
3 Jim Blakeney, California	18	456	25.3
4 Gary Wood, Cornell	20	430	21.5
5 Billy Gambrell, South Carolina	17	422	24.8
6 Marvin Woodson, Indiana	16	418	26.1
7 Ronnie Graham, Rice	20	418	20.9
8 Larry Coyer, Marshall	13	393	30.2
9 Ronnie Jackson, North Carolina	17	386	22.7
10 Eddie Taylor, Citadel	18	377	20.9

SCORING	TDS	XPT	FG	PTS
1 Jerry Logan, West Texas State	13	32	0	110
2 Cotton Clark, Alabama	15	2	0	92
2 Jim Pilot, New Mexico State	15	2	0	92
4 Billy Lothridge, Georgia Tech	9	20	5	89
5 Eldon Fortie, Brigham Young	14	2	0	86
5 Bill King, Dartmouth	14	2	0	86
7 Billy Moore, Arkansas	14	0	0	84
7 Bob Jencks, Miami, Ohio	6	24	8	84
9 Johnny Roland, Missouri	13	0	0	78
9 Mel Renfro, Oregon	13	0	0	78
9 Pat McCarthy, Holy Cross	12	6	0	78

KICK SCORING	XPA	XP	FG	PTS
1 Bob Jencks, Miami, Ohio	26	24	8	48
1 Bill Wellstead, Dartmouth	30	27	7	48
3 John Seedborg, Arizona State	39	37	3	46
4 Tom McKnelly, Arkansas	37	33	3	42
5 Al Woodall, Auburn	20	17	8	41
6 John Gavin, Air Force	21	18	7	39
6 Billy Reynolds, Duke	23	18	7	39
8 Jim McKee, Ohio U	31	25	4	37
9 Gary Kroner, Wisconsin	27	27	3	36
10 Buck Corey, Oregon	31	29	2	35
10 Billy Lothridge, Georgia Tech	24	20	5	35

INTERCEPTIONS	INT	YDS
1 Byron Beaver, Houston	10	56
2 Gene Frantz, Brigham Young	9	133
2 Tom MacDonald, Notre Dame	9	81
2 Dan Espalin, Oregon State	9	67
5 Jerry Richardson, West Texas State	8	100
6 Jim McGowan, Boston College	7	182
6 Billy Ryan, North Texas	7	174
6 David Gibson, West Texas State	7	129
9 Jerry Logan, West Texas State *	6	168
9 Tom Brown, Maryland *	6	122
9 Steve Shafer, Utah State *	6	82

*-Five tied with six; these had the most yards.

TEAM LEADERS

RUSHING OFFENSE	G	ATT	YDS	AVG	YPG
1 Ohio State	9	528	2510	4.8	278.9
2 Oklahoma	10	561	2659	4.7	265.9
3 Michigan State	9	498	2383	4.8	264.8
4 Kansas	10	520	2610	5.0	261.0
5 West Texas State	10	506	2555	5.0	255.5
6 Missouri	10	585	2549	4.4	254.9
7 Washington	10	597	2514	4.2	251.4
8 Utah State	10	538	2464	4.6	246.4
9 Nebraska	10	541	2455	4.5	245.5
10 New Mexico	10	527	2428	4.6	242.8

PASSING OFFENSE	G	ATT	COM	INT	PCT	YDS	YPA	TD	I%	YPC	YPG
1 Tulsa	10	295	154	17	52.2	1993	6.8	18	5.8	12.9	199.3
2 Northwestern	9	225	130	15	57.8	1758	7.8	13	6.7	13.5	195.3
3 Oregon State	10	234	124	7	53.0	1951	8.3	19	3.0	15.7	195.1
4 California	10	272	146	20	53.7	1795	6.6	15	7.4	12.3	179.5
5 Baylor	10	254	133	14	52.4	1714	6.7	12	5.5	12.9	171.4
6 Washington State	10	234	118	11	50.4	1644	7.0	13	4.7	13.9	164.4
7 Wisconsin	9	216	112	9	51.9	1444	6.7	14	4.2	12.9	160.4
8 Florida State	10	223	118	8	52.9	1596	7.2	12	3.6	13.5	159.6
9 Miami, Fla.	10	260	122	16	46.9	1572	6.0	10	6.2	12.9	157.2
10 Auburn	10	258	122	15	47.3	1512	5.9	6	5.8	12.4	151.2

TOTAL OFFENSE	G	P	YDS	AVG	YPG
1 Arizona State	10	629	3844	6.1	384.4
2 Oregon State	10	675	3752	5.6	375.2
3 Oklahoma	10	677	3693	5.5	369.3
4 Mississippi	9	627	3276	5.2	364.0
5 Dartmouth	9	598	3275	5.5	363.9
6 Northwestern	9	674	3267	4.8	363.0
7 Arkansas	10	717	3570	5.0	357.0
8 Utah State	10	701	3535	5.0	353.5
9 Oregon	10	654	3530	5.4	353.0
10 Wisconsin	9	600	3142	5.2	349.1

RUSHING DEFENSE	G	ATT	YDS	AVG	YPG
1 Minnesota	9	362	470	1.3	52.2
2 Alabama	10	321	601	1.9	60.1
3 Mississippi	9	300	610	2.0	67.8
4 LSU	10	349	832	2.4	83.2
5 Memphis	9	321	758	2.4	84.2
6 Bowling Green	9	316	788	2.5	87.6
7 Arkansas	10	381	907	2.4	90.7
8 Auburn	10	411	930	2.3	93.0
9 Michigan State	9	368	851	2.3	94.6
10 Villanova	9	359	857	2.4	95.2

PASSING DEFENSE	G	ATT	COM	PCT	YPC	INT	I%	YDS	YPA	TD	YPG
1 New Mexico	10	117	46	39.3	12.3	15	12.8	568	4.9	3	56.8
2 Boston U.	9	94	36	38.3	15.5	8	8.5	558	5.9	6	62.0
3 Memphis	9	115	49	42.6	11.6	18	15.7	566	4.9	1	62.9
4 Missouri	10	150	59	39.3	11.6	17	11.3	686	4.6	3	68.6
5 Yale	9	110	54	49.1	11.5	8	7.3	621	5.6	5	69.0
6 Florida State	10	148	67	45.3	10.3	13	8.8	693	4.7	3	69.3
7 Oklahoma	10	162	59	36.4	12.2	16	9.9	718	4.4	3	71.8
8 Kansas State	10	115	51	44.3	14.3	9	7.8	727	6.3	7	72.7
9 Texas-El Paso	9	121	44	36.4	15.2	11	9.1	669	5.5	7	74.3
10 Mississippi	9	146	60	41.1	11.2	7	4.8	670	4.6	2	74.4

TOTAL DEFENSE	G	P	YDS	AVG	YPG
1 Mississippi	9	446	1280	2.9	142.2
2 Memphis	9	436	1324	3.0	147.1
3 Alabama	10	542	1598	2.9	159.8
4 Minnesota	9	568	1505	2.6	167.2
5 Missouri	10	532	1811	3.4	181.1
6 Dartmouth	9	470	1664	3.5	184.9
6 Bowling Green	9	467	1664	3.6	184.9
8 Villanova	9	504	1701	3.4	189.0
9 Michigan State	9	553	1753	3.2	194.8
10 Auburn	10	599	1973	3.3	197.3

SCORING OFFENSE	G	PTS	AVG
1 Wisconsin	9	285	31.7
2 Arizona State	10	304	30.4
3 West Texas State	10	297	29.7
4 Memphis	9	261	29.0
5 Arkansas	10	286	28.6
6 Oregon State	10	273	27.3
7 Utah State	10	273	27.3
8 Alabama	10	272	27.2
9 Oklahoma	10	267	26.7
10 Northwestern	9	237	26.3

SCORING DEFENSE	G	PTS	AVG
1 LSU	10	34	3.4
2 Alabama	10	39	3.9
3 Oklahoma	10	44	4.4
4 Mississippi	9	40	4.4
5 Missouri	10	52	5.2
6 Southern Cal	10	55	5.5
7 Texas	10	59	5.9
8 Dartmouth	9	57	6.3
9 Minnesota	9	61	6.8
10 Florida State	10	69	6.9

1963 POLL PROGRESSION

AP	PRE-SEASON		SEPT. 21 GAMES
1	Southern Cal	0-0-0	beat Colorado 14-0
2	Mississippi	0-0-0	tied Memphis 0-0
3	Alabama	0-0-0	beat Georgia 32-7
4	Oklahoma	0-0-0	beat Clemson 31-14
5	Texas	0-0-0	beat Tulane 21-0
6	Northwestern	0-0-0	beat Missouri 23-12
7	Wisconsin	0-0-0	beat Western Michigan 41-0
8	Arkansas	0-0-0	beat Oklahoma State 21-0
9	Navy	0-0-0	beat West Virginia 51-7
10	Ohio State	0-0-0	bye week
10	Washington	0-0-0	lost to Air Force 7-10

AP	SEPTEMBER 23 POLL		SEPT. 28 GAMES
1	Southern Cal	1-0-0	lost to # 3 Oklahoma 12-17
2	Alabama	1-0-0	beat Tulane 28-0
3	Oklahoma	1-0-0	beat # 1 Southern Cal 17-12
4	Texas	1-0-0	beat Texas Tech 49-7
5	Navy	1-0-0	beat William & Mary 28-0
6	Wisconsin	1-0-0	beat Notre Dame 14-9
7	Northwestern	1-0-0	beat Indiana 34-21
8	Arkansas	1-0-0	lost to Missouri 6-7
9	Georgia Tech	1-0-0	beat Clemson 27-0
10	Pittsburgh	1-0-0	beat Washington 13-6

UP	AP	SEPTEMBER 30 POLL		OCT. 5 GAMES
1	1	Oklahoma	2-0-0	bye week
2	2	Alabama	2-0-0	beat Vanderbilt 21-6
3	3	Texas	2-0-0	beat Oklahoma State 34-7
4	4	Northwestern	2-0-0	lost to Illinois 9-10
5	4	Wisconsin	2-0-0	bye week
7	6	Navy	2-0-0	beat Michigan 26-13
6	7	Georgia Tech	2-0-0	lost to LSU 6-7
9	8	Southern Cal	1-1-0	beat Michigan State 13-10
8	9	Pittsburgh	2-0-0	beat California 35-15
	10	Mississippi	1-0-1	beat Houston 20-6
10		Ohio State	1-0-0	beat Indiana 21-0
10		Nebraska	2-0-0	beat Iowa State 21-7

UP	AP	OCTOBER 7 POLL		OCT. 12 GAMES
1	1	Oklahoma	2-0-0	lost to # 2 Texas 7-28
2	2	Texas	3-0-0	beat # 1 Oklahoma 28-7
3	3	Alabama	3-0-0	lost to Florida 6-10
6	4	Navy	3-0-0	lost to SMU 28-32
5	5	Wisconsin	2-0-1	beat Purdue 0-0
4	6	Pittsburgh	3-0-0	bye week
9	7	Southern Cal	2-1-0	lost to Notre Dame 14-17
7	8	Ohio State	2-0-1	tied Illinois 20-20
8	9	Penn State	3-0-0	lost to Army 7-10
	10	Mississippi	2-0-1	bye week
10		Nebraska	3-0-0	lost to Air Force 13-17

UP	AP	OCTOBER 14 POLL		OCT. 19 GAMES
1	1	Texas	4-0-0	beat Arkansas 17-13
2	2	Wisconsin	3-0-0	beat Iowa 10-7
3	3	Pittsburgh	3-0-0	beat West Virginia 13-10
4	4	Ohio State	2-0-1	lost to Southern Cal 3-32
7	5	Mississippi	2-0-1	beat Tulane 21-0
5	6	Oklahoma	2-1-0	beat Kansas 21-18
8	7	Illinois	2-0-1	beat Minnesota 16-6
6	8	Georgia Tech	3-1-0	lost to Auburn 21-29
8	9	Alabama	3-1-0	beat Tennessee 35-0
	10	Navy	3-1-0	beat VMI 21-12
10	10	Northwestern	3-1-0	beat Miami, Ohio 37-6

UP	AP	OCTOBER 21 POLL		OCT. 26 GAMES
1	1	Texas	5-0-0	beat Rice 10-6
2	2	Wisconsin	4-0-0	lost to Ohio State 10-13
3	3	Pittsburgh	4-0-0	lost to # 10 Navy 12-24
4	4	Illinois	3-0-1	beat UCLA 18-12
6	5	Mississippi	3-0-1	beat Vanderbilt 27-7
5	6	Alabama	4-1-0	beat Houston 21-13
7	7	Oklahoma	3-1-0	beat Kansas State 34-9
8	8	Auburn	5-0-0	bye week
9	9	Northwestern	4-1-0	lost to Michigan State 7-15
10	10	Navy	4-1-0	beat # 3 Pittsburgh 24-12
10		Southern Cal	3-2-0	beat California 36-6

UP	AP	OCTOBER 28 POLL		NOV. 2 GAMES
1	1	Texas	6-0-0	beat SMU 17-12
2	2	Illinois	4-0-1	beat Purdue 41-21
3	3	Mississippi	4-0-1	beat LSU 37-3
5	4	Navy	5-1-0	beat Notre Dame 35-14
7	5	Auburn	5-0-0	beat Florida 19-0
8	6	Oklahoma	4-1-0	beat Colorado 35-0
4	7	Alabama	5-1-0	beat Mississippi State 20-19
6	8	Wisconsin	4-1-0	lost to Michigan State 13-30
	9	Ohio State	3-1-1	beat Iowa 7-3
	10	Pittsburgh	4-1-0	beat Syracuse 35-27
9		Southern Cal	4-2-0	lost to Washington 7-22
10		Syracuse	5-1-0	lost to # 10 Pittsburgh 27-35

UP	AP	NOVEMBER 4 POLL		NOV. 9 GAMES
1	1	Texas	7-0-0	beat Baylor 7-0
2	2	Illinois	5-0-1	lost to Michigan 8-14
3	3	Mississippi	5-0-1	beat Tampa 41-0
4	4	Navy	6-1-0	beat Maryland 42-7
5	5	Auburn	6-0-0	lost to Mississippi State 10-13
6	6	Oklahoma	5-1-0	beat Iowa State 24-14
7	7	Alabama	6-1-0	bye week
9	8	Pittsburgh	5-1-0	beat Notre Dame 27-7
8	9	Michigan State	4-1-1	beat Purdue 23-0
	10	Ohio State	4-1-1	lost to Penn State 7-10
10		Nebraska	6-1-0	beat Kansas 23-9

UP	AP	NOVEMBER 11 POLL		NOV. 16 GAMES
1	1	Texas	8-0-0	beat TCU 17-0
2	2	Navy	7-1-0	beat Duke 38-25
3	3	Mississippi	6-0-1	beat Tennessee 20-0
4	4	Michigan State	5-1-1	beat Notre Dame 12-7
5	5	Oklahoma	6-1-0	beat Missouri 13-3
6	6	Pittsburgh	6-1-0	beat Army 28-0
7	7	Alabama	6-1-0	beat Georgia Tech 27-11
8	8	Illinois	5-1-1	beat Wisconsin 17-7
10	9	Auburn	6-1-0	beat Georgia 14-0
9	10	Nebraska	7-1-0	beat Oklahoma State 20-16

UP	AP	NOVEMBER 18 POLL		NOV. 23 GAMES
1	1	Texas	9-0-0	bye week
2	2	Navy	8-1-0	bye week
3	3	Mississippi	6-0-1	bye week
5	4	Michigan State	6-1-1	game postponed to N28
4	5	Pittsburgh	7-1-0	game postponed to D7
6	6	Oklahoma	7-1-0	lost to # 10 Nebraska 20-29
7	7	Alabama	7-1-0	bye week
8	8	Illinois	6-1-1	game postponed to N28
10	9	Auburn	7-1-0	beat Florida State 21-15
9	10	Nebraska	8-1-0	beat # 6 Oklahoma 29-20

UP	AP	NOVEMBER 25 POLL		NOV. 30 GAMES
1	1	Texas	9-0-0	beat Texas A&M 15-13
2	2	Navy	8-1-0	bye week
4	3	Mississippi	7-0-1	tied Mississippi State 10-10
3	4	Michigan State	6-1-1	lost to # 8 Illinois 0-13
5	5	Pittsburgh	7-1-0	beat Miami, Fla. 31-20
7	6	Alabama	7-1-0	lost to # 9 Auburn 8-10
6	7	Nebraska	9-1-0	regular season complete
8	8	Illinois	6-1-1	beat # 4 Michigan State 13-0
9	9	Auburn	8-1-0	beat # 6 Alabama 10-8
10	10	Oklahoma	7-2-0	beat Oklahoma State 34-10

UP	AP	DECEMBER 2 POLL		DEC. 7 GAMES
1	1	Texas	10-0-0	regular season complete
2	2	Navy	8-1-0	beat Army 21-15
4	3	Illinois	7-1-1	regular season complete
3	4	Pittsburgh	8-1-0	beat Penn State 22-21
6	5	Auburn	9-1-0	regular season complete
5	6	Nebraska	9-1-0	
7	7	Mississippi	7-0-2	regular season complete
8	8	Oklahoma	8-2-0	regular season complete
9	9	Alabama	7-2-0	beat Miami, Fla. 17-12
10	10	Michigan State	6-2-1	regular season complete

UP	AP	DECEMBER 9 FINAL POLL	RECORD	BOWL BID	DATE	BOWL RESULT	RB	RECORD
1	1	Texas	10-0-0	Cotton Bowl	J1	beat # 2 Navy 28-6	1	11-0-0
2	2	Navy	9-1-0	Cotton Bowl	J1	lost to # 1 Texas 6-28	11	9-2-0
4	3	Illinois	7-1-1	Rose Bowl	J1	beat Washington 17-7	2	8-1-1
3	4	Pittsburgh	9-1-0				4	9-1-0
6	5	Auburn	9-1-0	Orange Bowl	J1	lost to # 6 Nebraska 7-13	8	9-2-0
5	6	Nebraska	9-1-0	Orange Bowl	J1	beat # 5 Auburn 13-7	3	10-1-0
7	7	Mississippi	7-0-2	Sugar Bowl	J1	lost to # 8 Alabama 7-12	6	7-1-2
9	8	Alabama	8-2-0	Sugar Bowl	J1	beat # 7 Mississippi 12-7	5	9-2-0
10	9	Michigan State	6-2-1				9	6-2-1
8	10	Oklahoma	8-2-0				7	8-2-0

1963

CONSENSUS ALL-AMERICANS

POS	Name	HT	WT	School	AP	FC	FW	NE	SN	PI
B	Roger Staubach	6-2	190	Navy	•	•	•	•	•	•
B	Sherman Lewis	5-8	154	Michigan State	•	•	•	•	•	
B	Jim Grisham	6-2	205	Oklahoma		•		•	•	•
B	Gale Sayers	6-0	196	Kansas		•		•	•	
B	Paul Martha	6-1	180	Pittsburgh		•				•
E	Vern Burke	6-4	195	Oregon State	•	•	•	•		•
E	Lawrence Elkins	6-1	187	Baylor		•		•	•	
T	Scott Appleton	6-3	235	Texas	•	•	•	•	•	•
T	Carl Eller	6-6	241	Minnesota	•	•	•	•	•	
G	Bob Brown	6-5	259	Nebraska	•	•	•	•	•	
G	Rick Redman	5-11	210	Washington	•	•		•	•	•
C	Dick Butkus	6-3	234	Illinois	•	•	•	•	•	•

OTHERS RECEIVING FIRST-TEAM HONORS

B	Tommy Ford			Texas				•		
B	Billy Lothridge			Georgia Tech	•			•		
B	Jimmy Sidle			Auburn	•			•		
B	Don Trull			Baylor				•		
B	Tom Vaughn			Iowa State				•		
B	Tommy Crutcher			TCU			•			
B	Jay Wilkinson			Duke			•	•		•
E	Bob Lacey			North Carolina	•			•		
E	Jim Kelly			Notre Dame			•			•
E	David Parks			Texas Tech	•					
E	Billy Martin			Georgia Tech			•			
T	Ernie Borghetti			Pittsburgh			•			
T	Ken Kortas			Louisville			•			
T	Harry Schuh			Memphis			•			
G	Steve DeLong			Tennessee			•			
G	Mike Reilly			Iowa		•				
G	Damon Bame			Southern Cal	•					
C	Kenny Dill			Mississippi		•				

FW named Wilkinson as an E

HEISMAN TROPHY VOTING

	PLAYER	POS	SCHOOL	1ST	2ND	3RD	TOTAL
1	Roger Staubach	QB	Navy	517	132	45	1860
2	Billy Lothridge	QB	Georgia Tech	65	119	71	504
3	Sherman Lewis	RB	Michigan State	53	80	50	369
4	Don Trull	QB	Baylor	20	68	57	253
5	Scott Appleton	T	Texas	27	33	47	194
6	Dick Butkus	C	Illinois	10	49	44	172
7	Jimmy Sidle	QB	Auburn	11	28	34	123
8	Terry Isaacson	RB	Air Force	17	20	13	104
9	Jay Wilkinson	RB	Duke	3	20	35	84
10	George Mira	QB	Miami, Fla.	6	16	30	80

AWARD WINNERS

PLAYER	POS	SCHOOL	AWARD NAME
Roger Staubach	QB	Navy	Maxwell
Scott Appleton	T	Texas	Outland

CONFERENCE STANDINGS

ACC

	CONF. W L T			OVERALL W L T		
North Carolina	6	1	0	9	2	0
North Carolina St.	6	1	0	8	3	0
Duke	5	2	0	5	4	1
Clemson	5	2	0	5	4	1
Maryland	2	5	0	3	7	0
South Carolina	1	5	1	1	8	1
Wake Forest	1	5	0	1	9	0
Virginia	0	5	1	2	7	1

Big 10

	CONF. W L T			OVERALL W L T		
Illinois	5	1	1	8	1	1
Michigan State	4	1	1	6	2	1
Ohio State	4	1	1	5	3	1
Purdue	4	3	0	5	4	0
Wisconsin	3	4	0	5	4	0
Northwestern	3	4	0	5	4	0
Michigan	2	3	2	3	4	2
Iowa	2	3	1	3	3	2
Minnesota	2	5	0	3	6	0
Indiana	1	5	0	3	6	0

Big 8

	CONF. W L T			OVERALL W L T		
Nebraska	7	0	0	10	1	0
Oklahoma	6	1	0	8	2	0
Missouri	5	2	0	7	3	0
Kansas	3	4	0	5	5	0
Iowa State	3	4	0	4	5	0
Colorado	2	5	0	2	8	0
Kansas State	1	5	0	2	7	0
Oklahoma State	0	6	0	1	8	0

Ivy

	CONF. W L T			OVERALL W L T		
Dartmouth	5	2	0	7	2	0
Princeton	5	2	0	7	2	0
Harvard	4	2	1	5	2	2
Yale	4	3	0	6	3	0
Cornell	4	3	0	5	4	0
Columbia	2	4	1	4	4	1
Brown	2	5	0	3	5	0
Pennsylvania	1	6	0	3	6	0

MAC

	CONF. W L T			OVERALL W L T		
Ohio U	5	1	0	6	4	0
Miami, Ohio	4	1	1	5	3	2
Bowling Green	4	2	0	8	2	0
Marshall	3	2	1	5	4	1
Western Michigan	2	4	0	2	7	0
Kent State	1	5	0	3	5	1
Toledo	1	5	0	2	7	0

AAWU

	CONF. W L T			OVERALL W L T		
Washington	4	1	0	6	5	0
Southern Cal	3	1	0	7	3	0
UCLA	2	2	0	2	8	0
Washington State	1	1	0	3	6	1
California	1	3	0	4	5	1
Stanford	1	4	0	3	7	0

SEC

	CONF. W L T			OVERALL W L T		
Mississippi	5	0	1	7	1	2
Auburn	6	1	0	9	2	0
Alabama	6	2	0	9	2	0
Mississippi State	4	1	2	7	2	2
LSU	4	2	0	7	4	0
Georgia Tech	4	3	0	7	3	0
Florida	3	3	1	6	3	1
Tennessee	3	5	0	5	5	0
Georgia	2	4	0	4	5	1
Vanderbilt	0	5	2	1	7	2
Kentucky	0	5	1	3	6	1
Tulane	0	6	1	1	8	1

SWC

	CONF. W L T			OVERALL W L T		
Texas	7	0	0	11	0	0
Baylor	6	1	0	8	3	0
Rice	4	3	0	6	4	0
Arkansas	3	4	0	5	5	0
TCU	2	4	1	4	5	1
Texas Tech	2	5	0	5	5	0
SMU	2	5	0	4	7	0
Texas A&M	1	5	1	2	7	1

WAC

	CONF. W L T			OVERALL W L T		
Arizona State	3	0	0	8	1	0
New Mexico	3	1	0	6	4	0
Arizona	2	2	0	5	5	0
Utah	2	2	0	4	6	0
Wyoming	2	3	0	6	4	0
Brigham Young	0	4	0	2	8	0

Independents

	OVERALL W L T		
Memphis	9	0	1
Pittsburgh	9	1	0
Navy	9	2	0
Syracuse	8	2	0
Utah State	8	2	0
Oregon	8	3	0
Army	7	3	0
Penn State	7	3	0
Boston College	6	3	0
Air Force	7	4	0
Oregon State	5	5	0
Florida State	4	5	1
New Mexico State	3	6	1
Rutgers	3	6	0
Texas-El Paso	3	7	0
Colorado State	3	7	0
Miami, Fla.	3	7	0
Notre Dame	2	7	0
Houston	2	8	0

BOWL GAMES

DATE	GAME	SCORE
D21	Bluebonnet	Baylor 14, LSU 7
D21	Liberty	Mississippi State 16, North Carolina St. 12
D28	Gator	North Carolina 35, Air Force 0
D28	Tangerine	Western Kentucky 27, Coast Guard 0
D31	Sun	Oregon 21, SMU 14
J1	Rose	Illinois 17, Washington 7
J1	Sugar	Alabama 12, Mississippi 7
J1	Orange	Nebraska 13, Auburn 7
J1	Cotton	Texas 28, Navy 6

ANNUAL REVIEW

1963 NCAA MAJOR COLLEGE STATISTICAL LEADERS

INDIVIDUAL LEADERS

PASSING/COMPLETIONS	G	ATT	COM	PCT	INT	I%	YDS	YPA	TD	TD%	COM.PG
1 Don Trull, Baylor	10	308	174	56.5	12	3.9	2157	7.0	12	3.9	17.4
2 George Mira, Miami, Fla.	10	335	172	51.3	14	4.2	2155	6.4	10	3.0	17.2
3 Jerry Rhome, Tulsa	10	258	150	58.1	13	5.0	1909	7.4	10	3.9	15.0
4 Bill Munson, Utah State	10	201	120	59.7	3	1.5	1699	8.5	12	6.0	12.0
5 Dick Shiner, Maryland	10	222	108	48.6	8	3.6	1165	5.2	10	4.5	10.8
6 Roger Staubach, Navy	10	161	107	66.5	6	3.7	1474	9.2	7	4.4	10.7
7 Tom LaFramboise, Louisville	10	204	104	51.0	12	5.9	1205	5.9	9	4.4	10.4
8 Larry Rakestraw, Georgia	10	209	103	49.3	14	6.7	1297	6.2	7	3.4	10.3
9 Archie Roberts, Columbia	9	164	101	61.6	10	6.1	1184	7.2	11	6.7	11.2
9 Bob Berry, Oregon	10	171	101	59.1	7	4.1	1675	9.8	16	9.4	10.1
9 Scotty Glacken, Duke	10	200	101	50.5	8	4.0	1265	6.3	12	6.0	10.1
9 Craig Morton, California	10	207	101	48.8	12	5.8	1475	7.1	14	6.8	10.1
9 Merv Holland, George Washington	9	215	101	47.0	11	5.1	1312	6.1	8	3.7	11.2

ALL-PURPOSE YARDS	G	RUSH	REC	PR	KR	YDS	YPG
1 Gary Wood, Cornell	9	818	15	57	618	1508	167.6

RUSHING/YARDS	G	ATT	YDS	AVG	YPG
1 Dave Casinelli, Memphis	10	219	1016	4.6	101.6
2 Jimmy Sidle, Auburn	10	185	1006	5.4	100.6
3 Gale Sayers, Kansas	10	132	917	6.9	91.7
4 Jack Mahone, Marshall	10	163	884	5.4	88.4
5 Jim Grisham, Oklahoma	10	153	861	5.6	86.1
6 Bob Schweickert, Virginia Tech	10	155	839	5.4	83.9
7 Mike Garrett, Southern Cal	10	128	833	6.5	83.3
8 Gary Wood, Cornell	9	166	818	4.9	90.9
9 Tony Lorick, Arizona State	9	105	805	7.7	89.4
10 Terry Isaacson, Air Force	10	162	801	4.9	80.1

RUSHING/YARDS PER CARRY	G	ATT	YDS	YPC
1 Tony Lorick, Arizona State	9	105	805	7.7
2 Larry Campbell, Utah State	10	82	585	7.1
3 Gale Sayers, Kansas	10	132	917	6.9
4 Charley Taylor, Arizona State	9	88	595	6.8
5 Mike Garrett, Southern Cal	10	128	833	6.5
6 Sherman Lewis, Michigan State	9	90	577	6.4
7 Benny Nelson, Alabama	10	97	613	6.3
8 Rudy Johnson, Nebraska	10	91	573	6.3
9 Walt Mainer, Xavier	10	120	744	6.2
10 Pat Donnelly, Navy	10	99	603	6.1

*-Based on top 42 rushers

RECEIVING/RECEPTIONS	G	REC	YDS	TD	YPR	YPG	P
1 Lawrence Elkins, Baylor	10	70	873	8	12.5	87.3	
2 Vern Burke, Oregon State	10	48	794	9	16.5	79.4	
3 Stan Crisson, Duke	10	48	559	7	11.6	55.9	
2 Bob Lacey, North Carolina	10	48	533	1	11.1	53.3	
5 Darryl Hill, Maryland	10	43	516	7	12.0	51.6	
6 Bob Long, Wichita State	9	42	653	9	15.5	72.6	
7 Nick Spinelli, Miami, Fla.	10	41	501	4	12.2	50.1	
8 James Ingram, Baylor	10	40	537	4	13.4	53.7	
2 James Cure, Marshall	10	40	534	2	13.4	53.4	
10 Jim Curry, Cincinnati	9	39	621	3	15.9	69.0	
10 John Simmons, Tulsa	10	39	543	3	13.9	54.3	
10 John Parry, Brown	8	39	457	4	11.7	57.1	

PUNTING		PUNT	YDS	AVG
1 Danny Thomas, SMU		48	2110	44.0
2 Len Frketich, Oregon State		24	1013	42.2
3 Kroghie Andresen, Citadel		38	1581	41.6
4 James Keller, Texas A&M		66	2739	41.5
5 Merlin Norenberg, Northwestern		32	1325	41.4
6 Norm Limpert, Bowling Green		42	1735	41.3
7 Olie Cordill, Memphis		22	909	41.3
8 Frank Lambert, Mississippi		37	1524	41.2
9 Jon Kilgore, Auburn		51	2101	41.2
10 Billy Lothridge, Georgia Tech		46	1886	41.0

PUNT RETURNS/YARDS		PR	YDS	AVG
1 Ken Hatfield, Arkansas		21	350	16.7
2 Larry Elliott, Oklahoma State		11	225	20.5
3 Gene Fleming, Rice		22	224	10.2
4 Junior Powell, Penn State		18	221	12.3
5 Joe Labruzzo, LSU		9	215	23.9
6 Jim Gray, Toledo		13	212	16.3
7 Rickie Harris, Arizona		12	209	17.4
8 George Rose, Auburn		23	205	8.9
9 Tom Vaughn, Iowa State		13	204	15.7
9 Jimmy Heidel, Mississippi		18	200	11.1

KICKOFF RETURNS/YARDS		KR	YDS	A
1 Gary Wood, Cornell		19	618	3
2 Steve Bramwell, Washington		18	565	3
3 Tom Blanchfield, California		16	470	2
4 Donny Anderson, Texas Tech		18	448	2
5 Larry Elliott, Oklahoma State		20	437	2
6 Joe Lopasky, Houston		16	423	2
7 Floyd Hudlow, Arizona		13	422	3
8 Robert Dunn, Villanova		14	416	2
9 Dick Drummond, George Washington		16	403	2
10 Jim Blakeney, California		14	397	2

SCORING		TDS	XPT	FG	PTS
1 Cosmo Iacavazzi, Princeton		14	0	0	84
1 Dave Casinelli, Memphis		14	0	0	84
3 Terry Isaacson, Air Force		13	2	0	80
4 Jay Wilkinson, Duke		12	0	0	72
4 Rick Leeson, Pittsburgh		7	15	5	72
6 Billy Lothridge, Georgia Tech		3	15	12	69
7 Henry Schichtle, Wichita State		7	17	3	68
8 Benny Nelson, Alabama		10	2	0	62
9 Nine tied		–	–	–	60

KICK SCORING		XPA	XP	FG	PTS
1 Fred Marlin, Navy		41	37	5	52
2 Hugh Crosby, Texas		24	24	9	51
2 Billy Lothridge, Georgia Tech		19	15	12	51
4 Alva Holaday, Air Force		25	23	7	44
5 Woody Woodall, Auburn		23	23	6	41
6 H.L. Daniels, Texas Tech		18	15	8	39
7 George Jarman, Oklahoma		32	29	3	38
8 Charles Gogolak, Princeton		35	31	2	37
9 Pete Gogolak, Cornell		18	18	6	36
9 Braden Beck, Stanford		12	12	8	36
9 Justin Canale, Mississippi State		20	15	7	36

INTERCEPTIONS		INT	
1 Dick Kern, William & Mary		8	1
2 Bruce Bennett, Florida		6	
2 Mike Dundy, Illinois		6	
2 Larry Shields, Oklahoma		6	
2 Ollie Ross, West Texas State		6	
6 Walter Roberts, San Jose State		5	
6 Sonny Fisher, Mississippi State		5	
6 Tom MacDonald, Notre Dame		5	
6 James Hudson, Texas		5	
6 Dick McCauley, Northwestern		5	
6 Jimmy Heidel, Mississippi		5	

TEAM LEADERS

RUSHING OFFENSE	G	ATT	YDS	AVG	YPG
1 Nebraska	10	561	2626	4.7	262.6
2 Princeton	9	509	2246	4.4	249.6
3 Army	10	564	2479	4.4	247.9
4 Oklahoma	10	562	2469	4.4	246.9
5 Kansas	10	512	2431	4.7	243.1
6 Cincinnati	10	462	2320	5.0	232.0
7 Texas	10	590	2316	3.9	231.6
8 Pittsburgh	10	501	2302	4.6	230.2
9 Air Force	10	496	2297	4.6	229.7
10 Memphis	10	509	2292	4.5	229.2

PASSING OFFENSE	G	ATT	COM	INT	PCT	YDS	YPA	TD	I%	YPC	YPG
1 Tulsa	10	352	199	22	56.5	2448	7.0	14	6.3	12.3	244.8
2 Miami, Fla.	10	338	173	14	51.2	2183	6.5	10	4.1	12.6	218.3
3 Baylor	10	320	177	13	55.3	2159	6.7	12	4.1	12.2	215.9
4 Utah State	10	241	133	7	55.2	1852	7.7	14	2.9	13.9	185.2
5 Oregon	10	212	118	10	55.7	1851	8.7	17	4.7	15.7	185.1
6 San Jose State	10	248	136	17	54.8	1834	7.4	14	6.9	13.5	183.4
7 Wichita	9	172	97	6	56.4	1571	9.1	13	3.5	16.2	174.6
8 Navy	10	186	121	8	65.1	1690	9.1	8	4.3	14.0	169.0
9 Mississippi	9	191	104	12	54.5	1500	7.9	17	6.3	14.4	166.7
10 Northwestern	9	192	98	16	51.0	1473	7.7	7	8.3	15.0	163.7

TOTAL OFFENSE	G	P	YDS	AVG	Y
1 Utah State	10	669	3953	5.9	3
2 Wichita State	9	564	3496	6.2	3
3 Pittsburgh	10	706	3772	5.3	3
4 Oregon	10	635	3607	5.7	3
5 Arizona State	9	563	3235	5.7	3
6 Navy	10	656	3512	5.4	3
7 Cincinnati	10	616	3494	5.7	3
8 Nebraska	10	685	3476	5.1	3
9 Tulsa	10	652	3415	5.2	3
10 North Carolina	10	730	3414	4.7	3

RUSHING DEFENSE	G	ATT	YDS	AVG	YPG
1 Mississippi	9	315	696	2.2	77.3
2 Texas	10	319	802	2.5	80.2
3 Southern Miss	9	304	724	2.4	80.4
4 Michigan State	9	343	738	2.2	82.0
5 Memphis	10	342	833	2.4	83.3
6 Clemson	10	344	931	2.7	93.1
7 Utah State	10	403	932	2.3	93.2
8 Syracuse	10	358	938	2.6	93.8
9 Pittsburgh	10	352	970	2.8	97.0
10 Wichita State	9	295	876	3.0	97.3

PASSING DEFENSE	G	ATT	COM	PCT	YPC	INT	I%	YDS	YPA	TD	YPG
1 Texas-El Paso	10	104	35	33.7	12.5	7	6.7	438	4.2	5	43.8
2 Southern Miss	9	115	49	42.6	9.3	14	12.2	457	4.0	3	50.8
3 Mississippi	9	123	47	38.2	11.1	13	10.6	522	4.2	3	58.0
4 Ohio U	10	125	49	39.2	12.7	6	4.8	621	5.0	5	62.1
5 Toledo	10	101	38	37.6	15.0	6	5.9	569	5.6	5	63.2
6 Boston U.	8	108	46	42.6	11.0	6	5.6	507	4.7	1	63.4
7 Harvard	9	127	50	39.4	12.7	11	8.7	634	5.0	3	70.4
8 Princeton	9	162	68	42.0	9.8	13	8.0	667	4.1	2	74.1
9 Georgia Tech	10	152	60	39.5	12.4	9	5.9	743	4.9	2	74.3
9 VMI	10	143	64	44.8	11.6	8	5.6	743	5.2	5	74.3

TOTAL DEFENSE	G	P	YDS	AVG	Y
1 Southern Miss	9	419	1181	2.8	1
2 Mississippi	9	438	1218	2.8	1
3 Memphis	10	500	1637	3.3	1
4 Michigan State	9	516	1567	3.0	1
5 Clemson	10	544	1847	3.4	1
6 Princeton	9	519	1715	3.3	1
7 Auburn	10	584	1910	3.3	1
8 Utah State	10	599	1925	3.2	1
9 Florida	10	555	1942	3.5	1
9 Texas	10	530	1942	3.7	1

SCORING OFFENSE	G	PTS	AVG
1 Utah State	10	317	31.7
2 Navy	10	314	31.4
3 Arizona State	9	249	27.7
4 Princeton	9	247	27.4
5 Nebraska	10	260	26.0
6 Wichita State	9	233	25.9
7 Syracuse	10	255	25.5
8 Oregon	10	253	25.3
9 Air Force	10	249	24.9
10 Cincinnati	10	238	23.8

SCORING DEFENSE	G	PTS	AVG
1 Mississippi	9	33	3.7
2 Memphis	10	52	5.2
3 Texas	10	65	6.5
4 Michigan State	9	63	7.0
5 Southern Miss	9	64	7.1
6 Mississippi State	10	82	8.2
7 Harvard	9	76	8.4
8 Missouri	10	86	8.6
9 Yale	9	78	8.7
10 Alabama	10	88	8.8

1964 POLL PROGRESSION

AP PRE-SEASON / SEPT. 26 GAMES

AP		Team	Record	Sept. 26 Games
1		Mississippi	0-0-0	lost to Kentucky 21-27
2		Oklahoma	0-0-0	lost to Southern Cal 14-40
3		Illinois	0-0-0	beat California 20-14
4		Texas	0-0-0	beat Texas Tech 23-0
5		Ohio State	0-0-0	beat SMU 27-8
6		Alabama	0-0-0	beat Tulane 36-6
7		Washington	0-0-0	beat Baylor 35-14
8		Auburn	0-0-0	beat Tennessee 3-0
9		Syracuse	0-0-0	beat Kansas 38-6
10		Navy	0-0-0	beat William & Mary 35-6

UP AP SEPTEMBER 28 POLL / OCT. 3 GAMES

UP	AP	Team	Record	Oct. 3 Games
1	1	Texas	2-0-0	beat Army 17-6
2	2	Southern Cal	2-0-0	lost to Michigan State 7-17
4	3	Illinois	1-0-0	beat Northwestern 17-6
3	4	Alabama	2-0-0	beat Vanderbilt 24-0
6	5	Ohio State	1-0-0	beat Indiana 17-9
5		Navy	2-0-0	lost to # 8 Michigan 0-21
8	7	Auburn	2-0-0	lost to Kentucky 0-20
9	8	Michigan	1-0-0	beat # 6 Navy 21-0
7		Notre Dame	1-0-0	beat Purdue 34-15
	10	Washington	1-1-0	lost to Iowa 18-28
10		Army	2-0-0	lost to # 1 Texas 6-17

UP AP OCTOBER 5 POLL / OCT. 10 GAMES

UP	AP	Team	Record	Oct. 10 Games
1	1	Texas	3-0-0	beat Oklahoma 28-7
2	2	Illinois	2-0-0	lost to # 4 Ohio State 0-26
3	3	Alabama	3-0-0	beat North Carolina St. 21-0
6	4	Ohio State	2-0-0	beat # 2 Illinois 26-0
7	5	Kentucky	3-0-0	lost to Florida State 6-48
5	6	Notre Dame	2-0-0	beat Air Force 34-7
4	7	Michigan	2-0-0	beat # 10 Michigan State 17-10
8	8	Nebraska	3-0-0	beat South Carolina 28-6
	9	Arkansas	3-0-0	beat Baylor 17-6
	9	Michigan State	1-1-0	lost to # 7 Michigan 10-17
9		UCLA	3-0-0	lost to Syracuse 0-39
10		Syracuse	2-1-0	beat UCLA 39-0

UP AP OCTOBER 12 POLL / OCT. 17 GAMES

UP	AP	Team	Record	Oct. 17 Games
1	1	Texas	4-0-0	lost to # 8 Arkansas 13-14
2	2	Ohio State	3-0-0	beat Southern Cal 17-0
3	3	Alabama	4-0-0	beat Tennessee 19-8
4	4	Notre Dame	3-0-0	beat UCLA 24-0
5	5	Michigan	3-0-0	lost to Purdue 20-21
6	6	Nebraska	4-0-0	beat Kansas State 47-0
7	7	Syracuse	3-1-0	beat Penn State 21-14
10	8	Arkansas	4-0-0	beat # 1 Texas 14-13
	9	LSU	3-0-0	beat Kentucky 27-7
	10	Florida State	4-0-0	beat Georgia 17-14
8		Georgia Tech	4-0-0	beat Auburn 7-3
9		Florida	3-0-0	beat South Carolina 37-0

UP AP OCTOBER 19 POLL / OCT. 24 GAMES

UP	AP	Team	Record	Oct. 24 Games
1	1	Ohio State	4-0-0	beat Wisconsin 28-3
3	2	Notre Dame	4-0-0	beat Stanford 28-6
2	3	Alabama	5-0-0	beat # 9 Florida 17-14
4	4	Arkansas	5-0-0	beat Wichita State 17-0
5	5	Nebraska	5-0-0	beat Colorado 21-3
6	6	Texas	4-1-0	beat Rice 6-3
7	7	LSU	4-0-0	tied Tennessee 3-3
8	8	Syracuse	4-1-0	lost to Oregon State 13-31
10	9	Florida	4-0-0	lost to # 3 Alabama 14-17
	10	Florida State	5-0-0	lost to Virginia Tech 11-20
9		Georgia Tech	5-0-0	beat Tulane 7-6

UP AP OCTOBER 26 POLL / OCT. 31 GAMES

UP	AP	Team	Record	Oct. 31 Games
1	1	Ohio State	5-0-0	beat Iowa 21-19
2	2	Notre Dame	5-0-0	beat Navy 40-0
3	3	Alabama	6-0-0	beat Mississippi State 23-6
5	4	Arkansas	6-0-0	beat Texas A&M 17-0
4	5	Nebraska	6-0-0	beat Missouri 9-0
6	6	Texas	5-1-0	beat SMU 7-0
10	7	Oregon	6-0-0	lost to Stanford 8-10
7	8	Georgia Tech	6-0-0	beat Duke 21-8
	9	LSU	4-0-1	beat Mississippi 11-10
	10	Florida	4-1-0	beat Auburn 14-0
8		Michigan	4-1-0	beat Northwestern 35-0
9		Illinois	4-1-0	lost to Purdue 14-26

UP AP NOVEMBER 2 POLL / NOV. 7 GAMES

UP	AP	Team	Record	Nov. 7 Games
1	1	Notre Dame	6-0-0	beat Pittsburgh 17-15
2	2	Ohio State	6-0-0	beat Penn State 0-27
3	3	Alabama	7-0-0	beat # 8 LSU 17-9
4	4	Arkansas	7-0-0	beat Rice 21-0
5	5	Nebraska	7-0-0	beat Kansas 14-7
7	6	Texas	6-1-0	beat Baylor 20-14
6	7	Georgia Tech	7-0-0	lost to Tennessee 14-22
9	8	LSU	5-0-1	lost to # 3 Alabama 9-17
10	9	Florida	5-1-0	lost to Georgia 7-14
10	10	Purdue	5-1-0	lost to Michigan State 7-21
8		Michigan	5-1-0	beat Illinois 21-6

UP AP NOVEMBER 9 POLL / NOV. 14 GAMES

UP	AP	Team	Record	Nov. 14 Games
1	1	Notre Dame	7-0-0	beat Michigan State 34-7
2	2	Alabama	8-0-0	beat # 10 Georgia Tech 24-7
3	3	Arkansas	8-0-0	beat SMU 44-0
4	4	Nebraska	8-0-0	beat Oklahoma State 27-14
5	5	Texas	7-1-0	beat TCU 28-13
6	6	Michigan	6-1-0	beat Iowa 34-20
7	7	Ohio State	6-1-0	beat Northwestern 10-0
8	8	Oregon State	7-1-0	lost to Stanford 7-16
10	9	LSU	5-1-1	beat Mississippi State 14-10
9	10	Georgia Tech	7-1-0	lost to # 2 Alabama 7-24

UP AP NOVEMBER 16 POLL / NOV. 21 GAMES

UP	AP	Team	Record	Nov. 21 Games
1	1	Notre Dame	8-0-0	beat Iowa 28-0
2	2	Alabama	9-0-0	bye week
3	3	Arkansas	9-0-0	beat Texas Tech 17-0
4	4	Nebraska	9-0-0	lost to Oklahoma 7-17
5	5	Texas	8-1-0	bye week
6	6	Michigan	7-1-0	beat # 7 Ohio State 10-0
7	7	Ohio State	7-1-0	lost to # 6 Michigan 0-10
8	8	LSU	6-1-1	beat Tulane 13-3
9	9	Syracuse	7-2-0	lost to West Virginia 27-28
10	10	Oregon	7-1-1	lost to Oregon State 6-7

UP AP NOVEMBER 23 POLL / NOV. 28 GAMES

UP	AP	Team	Record	Nov. 28 Games
1	1	Notre Dame	9-0-0	lost to Southern Cal 17-20
2	2	Alabama	9-0-0	beat Auburn 21-14
3	3	Arkansas	10-0-0	regular season complete
4	4	Michigan	8-1-0	regular season complete
5	5	Texas	8-1-0	beat Texas A&M 26-7
7	6	LSU	7-1-1	bye week
6	7	Nebraska	9-1-0	regular season complete
9	8	Oregon State	8-2-0	regular season complete
8	9	Ohio State	7-2-0	regular season complete
10	10	Florida State	8-1-1	regular season complete

UP AP NOVEMBER 30 FINAL POLL

UP	AP	Team	Record	Bowl Bid	Date	Bowl Result	RB	Record
1	1	Alabama	10-0-0	Orange Bowl	J1	lost to # 5 Texas 17-21	3	10-1-0
2	2	Arkansas	10-0-0	Cotton Bowl	J1	beat # 6 Nebraska 10-7	1	11-0-0
3	3	Notre Dame	9-1-0				6	9-1-0
4	4	Michigan	8-1-0	Rose Bowl	J1	beat # 8 Oregon State 34-7	4	9-1-0
5	5	Texas	9-1-0	Orange Bowl	J1	beat # 1 Alabama 21-17	2	10-1-0
6	6	Nebraska	9-1-0	Cotton Bowl	J1	lost to # 2 Arkansas 7-10	7	9-2-0
7	7	LSU	7-1-1	Sugar Bowl	J1	beat Syracuse 13-10	9	8-2-1
8	8	Oregon State	8-2-0	Rose Bowl	J1	lost to # 4 Michigan 7-34	21	8-3-0
9	9	Ohio State	7-2-0				5	7-2-0
10	10	Southern Cal	7-3-0				15	7-3-0

1964

CONSENSUS ALL-AMERICANS

POS	Name	HT	WT	School	AP	CP	FC	FW	NE	PI
B	John Huarte	6-0	180	Notre Dame	•			•		•
B	Gale Sayers	6-0	194	Kansas	•	•	•	•	•	•
B	Lawrence Elkins	6-1	187	Baylor	•		•	•		•
B	Tucker Frederickson	6-2	210	Auburn	•	•	•	•		•
E	Jack Snow	6-2	210	Notre Dame	•	•	•		•	•
E	Fred Biletnikoff	6-1	186	Florida State	•	•	•	•		•
T	Larry Kramer	6-2	240	Nebraska	•	•	•	•		•
T	Ralph Neely	6-5	243	Oklahoma	•			•		•
G	Rick Redman	5-11	215	Washington	•		•	•		•
G	Glenn Ressler	6-2	230	Penn State	•		•		•	•
C	Dick Butkus	6-3	237	Illinois	•	•	•	•	•	•

OTHERS RECEIVING FIRST-TEAM HONORS

B	Floyd Little	Syracuse			•	•		•	
B	Craig Morton	California			•	•		•	
B	Jerry Rhome	Tulsa			•			•	
B	Bob Schweickert	Virginia Tech				•		•	
B	Bob Timberlake	Michigan	•			•		•	
B	Clarence Williams	Washington State	•			•			
B	Bob Berry	Oregon			•				
B	Larry Dupree	Florida			•				
B	Tom Nowatzke	Indiana			•				
B	Cosmo Iacavazzi	Princeton			•				
B	Jim Grabowski	Illinois			•				
B	Mike Garrett	Southern Cal			•				
B	Ken Willard	North Carolina			•				
B	Arnold Chonko	Ohio State						•	
B	Brian Piccolo	Wake Forest			•				
E	Donny Anderson	Texas Tech	•					•	
E	Karl Noonan	Iowa						•	
E	Alphonse Dotson	Grambling						•	
T	Steve DeLong	Tennessee	•			•	•	•	
T	Stas Maliszewski	Princeton				•			
T	Jim Wilson	Georgia	•	•		•		•	
T	Bill Yearby	Michigan			•			•	
T	Remi Prudhomme	LSU				•			
T	Harry Schuh	Memphis						•	
G	Ronnie Caveness	Arkansas	•	•		•		•	
G	Tommy Nobis	Texas	•			•		•	
G	Bill Fisk	Southern Cal	•						
G	Al Atkinson	Villanova		•		•			
G	Wayne Freeman	Alabama				•			
G	Jack O'Billovich	Oregon State				•			
C	Dwight Kelley	Ohio State				•			
C	Pat Killorin	Syracuse	•						
LB	Jim Carroll	Notre Dame			•				
LB	Carl McAdams	Oklahoma						•	

HEISMAN TROPHY VOTING

	PLAYER	POS	SCHOOL	TOTAL
1	John Huarte	QB	Notre Dame	1026
2	Jerry Rhome	QB	Tulsa	952
3	Dick Butkus	LB	Illinois	505
4	Bob Timberlake	QB	Michigan	361
5	Jack Snow	E	Notre Dame	187
6	Tucker Frederickson	FB	Auburn	184
7	Craig Morton	QB	California	181
8	Steve DeLong	MG	Tennessee	176
9	Cosmo Iacavazzi	RB	Princeton	165
10	Brian Piccolo	RB	Wake Forest	124

AWARD WINNERS

PLAYER	POS	SCHOOL	AWARD NAME
Glenn Ressler	C-G	Penn State	Maxwell
Steve DeLong	T	Tennessee	Outland

CONFERENCE STANDINGS

ACC

	CONF. W L T			OVERALL W L T		
North Carolina St.	5	2	0	5	5	0
Duke	3	2	1	4	5	1
North Carolina	4	3	0	5	5	0
Wake Forest	4	3	0	5	5	0
Maryland	4	3	0	5	5	0
South Carolina	2	3	1	3	5	2
Clemson	2	4	0	3	7	0
Virginia	1	5	0	5	5	0

Big 10

	CONF. W L T			OVERALL W L T		
Michigan	6	1	0	9	1	0
Ohio State	5	1	0	7	2	0
Purdue	5	2	0	6	3	0
Illinois	4	3	0	6	3	0
Minnesota	4	3	0	5	4	0
Michigan State	3	3	0	4	5	0
Wisconsin	2	5	0	3	6	0
Northwestern	2	5	0	3	6	0
Iowa	1	5	0	3	6	0
Indiana	1	5	0	2	7	0

Big 8

	CONF. W L T			OVERALL W L T		
Nebraska	6	1	0	9	2	0
Oklahoma	5	1	1	6	4	1
Kansas	5	2	0	6	4	0
Missouri	4	2	1	6	3	1
Oklahoma State	3	4	0	4	6	0
Kansas State	3	4	0	3	7	0
Colorado	1	6	0	2	8	0
Iowa State	0	7	0	1	8	1

Ivy

	CONF. W L T			OVERALL W L T		
Princeton	7	0	0	9	0	0
Harvard	5	2	0	6	3	0
Yale	4	2	1	6	2	1
Dartmouth	4	3	0	6	3	0
Brown	3	4	0	5	4	0
Cornell	3	4	0	3	5	1
Columbia	1	5	1	2	6	1
Pennsylvania	0	7	0	1	8	0

MAC

	CONF. W L T			OVERALL W L T		
Bowling Green	5	1	0	9	1	0
Marshall	4	2	0	7	3	0
Miami, Ohio	4	2	0	6	3	1
Ohio U	3	2	1	5	4	1
Western Michigan	2	4	0	3	6	0
Kent State	1	4	1	3	5	1
Toledo	1	5	0	2	8	0

AAWU

	CONF. W L T			OVERALL W L T		
Oregon State	3	1	0	8	3	0
Southern Cal	3	1	0	7	3	0
Washington	5	2	0	6	4	0
UCLA	2	2	0	4	6	0
Stanford	3	4	0	5	5	0
Oregon	1	2	1	7	2	1
Washington State	1	2	1	3	6	1
California	0	4	0	3	7	0

SEC

	CONF. W L T			OVERALL W L T		
Alabama	8	0	0	10	1	0
Florida	4	2	0	7	3	0
Kentucky	4	2	0	5	5	0
LSU	4	2	1	8	2	1
Georgia	3	2	0	7	3	1
Auburn	3	3	0	6	4	0
Mississippi	2	4	1	5	5	1
Mississippi State	2	5	0	4	6	0
Vanderbilt	1	4	1	3	6	1
Tennessee	1	5	1	4	5	1
Tulane	1	5	0	3	7	0

SWC

	CONF. W L T			OVERALL W L T		
Arkansas	7	0	0	11	0	0
Texas	6	1	0	10	1	0
Baylor	4	3	0	5	5	0
Texas Tech	3	3	1	6	4	1
Rice	3	3	1	4	5	1
TCU	3	4	0	4	6	0
Texas A&M	1	6	0	1	9	0
SMU	0	7	0	1	9	0

WAC

	CONF. W L T			OVERALL W L T		
Utah	3	1	0	9	2	0
New Mexico	3	1	0	9	2	0
Arizona	3	1	0	6	3	1
Wyoming	2	2	0	6	2	2
Arizona State	0	2	0	8	2	0
Brigham Young	0	4	0	3	6	1

Independents

	OVERALL W L T		
Notre Dame	9	1	0
Florida State	9	1	1
Georgia Tech	7	3	0
Rutgers	6	3	0
Boston College	6	3	0
Syracuse	7	4	0
Penn State	6	4	0
New Mexico State	6	4	0
Memphis	5	4	0
Utah State	5	4	1
Colorado State	5	6	0
Miami, Fla.	4	5	1
Air Force	4	5	1
Army	4	6	0
Pittsburgh	3	5	2
Navy	3	6	1
Houston	2	6	1
Texas-El Paso	0	8	2

BOWL GAMES

DATE	GAME	SCORE
D12	Tangerine	East Carolina 14, Massachusetts 13
D19	Bluebonnet	Tulsa 14, Mississippi 7
D19	Liberty	Utah 32, West Virginia 6
D26	Sun	Georgia 7, Texas Tech 0
J1	Cotton	Arkansas 10, Nebraska 7
J1	Sugar	LSU 13, Syracuse 10
J1	Rose	Michigan 34, Oregon State 7
J1	Orange	Texas 21, Alabama 17
J2	Gator	Florida State 36, Oklahoma 19

1964 NCAA Major College Statistical Leaders

Individual Leaders

PASSING/COMPLETIONS	G	ATT	COM	PCT	INT	I%	YDS	YPA	TD	TD%	COM.PG
1 Jerry Rhome, Tulsa	10	326	224	68.7	4	1.2	2870	8.8	32	9.8	22.4
2 Craig Morton, California	10	308	185	60.1	9	2.9	2121	6.9	13	4.2	18.5
3 Gary Snook, Iowa	9	311	151	48.6	14	4.5	2062	6.6	11	3.5	16.8
4 John Torok, Arizona State	10	251	139	55.4	14	5.6	2356	9.4	20	8.0	13.9
5 Tom LaFramboise, Louisville	10	242	122	50.4	18	7.4	1380	5.7	4	1.7	12.2
6 Steve Tensi, Florida State	10	204	121	59.3	10	4.9	1681	8.2	14	6.9	12.1
6 Richie Badar, Indiana	9	245	121	49.4	15	6.1	1571	6.4	9	3.7	13.4
8 Roger Staubach, Navy	10	204	119	58.3	10	4.9	1131	5.5	4	2.0	11.9
9 Terry Southall, Baylor	10	225	118	52.4	20	8.9	1623	7.2	10	4.4	11.8
10 Dan Simrell, Toledo	10	215	115	53.5	13	6.1	1239	5.8	4	1.9	11.5

ALL-PURPOSE YARDS	G	RUSH	REC	PR	KR	YDS	YPG
1 Donny Anderson, Texas Tech	10	966	396	28	320	1710	171.0

RUSHING/YARDS	G	ATT	YDS	AVG	YPG
1 Brian Piccolo, Wake Forest	10	252	1044	4.1	104.4
2 Jim Grabowski, Illinois	9	186	1004	5.4	111.6
3 Al Nelson, Cincinnati	10	201	973	4.8	97.3
4 Donny Anderson, Texas Tech	10	211	966	4.6	96.6
5 Jim Nance, Syracuse	10	190	951	5.0	95.1
6 Mike Garrett, Southern Cal	10	217	948	4.4	94.8
7 Ray Handley, Stanford	10	197	936	4.8	93.6
8 Cosmo Iacavazzi, Princeton	9	172	909	5.3	101.0
9 Bo Hickey, Maryland	10	182	894	4.9	89.4
10 Jack Mahone, Marshall	10	190	878	4.6	87.8

RUSHING/YARDS PER CARRY	G	ATT	YDS	YPC
1 Dick Gordon, Michigan State	9	123	741	6.0
2 Stew Williams, Bowling Green	10	109	609	5.6
3 Floyd Little, Syracuse	10	149	828	5.6
4 Ron Coleman, Utah	10	108	596	5.5
5 Jack Lentz, Holy Cross	10	148	800	5.4
6 Jim Grabowski, Illinois	9	186	1004	5.4
7 Clarence Williams, Washington State	10	147	783	5.3
8 Cosmo Iacavazzi, Princeton	9	172	909	5.3
9 Chuck Mercein, Yale	9	141	737	5.2
10 Gale Sayers, Kansas	10	122	633	5.2

*-Based on top 42 rushers

RECEIVING/RECEPTIONS	G	REC	YDS	TD	YPR	YPG	RPG
1 Howard Twilley, Tulsa	10	95	1178	13	12.4	117.8	9.5
2 Jack Snow, Notre Dame	10	60	1114	9	18.6	111.4	6.0
3 Karl Noonan, Iowa	9	59	933	4	15.8	103.7	6.6
4 Fred Biletnikoff, Florida State	10	57	987	11	17.3	98.7	5.7
5 Jack Schraub, California	10	52	633	2	12.2	63.3	5.2
6 Lawrence Elkins, Baylor	10	50	851	7	17.0	85.1	5.0
7 Bob Daugherty, Tulsa	10	48	498	4	10.4	49.8	4.8
8 Charles Casey, Florida	10	47	673	4	14.3	67.3	4.7
8 Henry Burch, Toledo	9	47	420	1	8.9	46.7	5.2
10 Bill Malinchak, Indiana	9	46	634	5	13.8	70.4	5.1

PUNTING	PUNT	YDS	AVG
1 Frank Lambert, Mississippi	50	2205	44.1
2 David Lewis, Stanford	34	1486	43.7
3 Doug Dusenbury, Kansas State	61	2647	43.4
4 Buddy French, Alabama	42	1802	42.9
5 Danny Thomas, SMU	58	2488	42.9
6 Larry Seiple, Kentucky	35	1474	42.1
7 Norm Limpert, Bowling Green	31	1305	42.1
8 Lou Bobich, Michigan State	37	1536	41.5
9 Mickey Rice, Idaho	55	2283	41.5
10 Ron Widby, Tennessee	74	3041	41.1

PUNT RETURNS/YARDS	PR	YDS	AVG
1 Ken Hatfield, Arkansas	31	729	44.1
2 David Ferguson, Rice	34	381	11.2
3 Wayne Swinford, Georgia	34	343	10.1
4 Steve Bramwell, Washington	29	314	10.8
5 Jeff Jordan, Tulsa	21	285	13.6
6 Kent Oborn, Brigham Young	22	278	12.6
7 Floyd Little, Syracuse	11	270	24.5
8 Curley Waters, West Texas State	18	265	14.7
9 Floyd Hudlow, Arizona	8	251	31.4
10 Joe Vargo, Penn State	19	233	12.3

KICKOFF RETURNS/YARDS	KR	YDS	AVG
1 Don Bland, Mississippi State	20	558	27.9
2 Larry Elliott, Oklahoma State	20	508	25.4
3 Ron Smith, Wisconsin	19	481	25.3
4 Roger Davis, Virginia	21	461	22.0
5 John Gutekunst, Duke	21	458	21.8
6 Chuck Hughes, Texas-El Paso	17	446	26.2
7 Barry Ellman, Pennsylvania	15	421	28.1
8 Tom Vaughn, Iowa State	17	402	23.6
9 Willie Loper, Toledo	16	399	24.9
10 Bob Hall, Brown	19	395	20.8

SCORING	TDS	XPT	FG	PTS
1 Brian Piccolo, Wake Forest	17	9	0	111
2 Howard Twilley, Tulsa	13	32	0	110
3 Al Nelson, Cincinnati	13	4	0	82
4 Bob Timberlake, Michigan	8	20	4	80
5 Jim Nance, Syracuse	13	0	0	78
6 Kent McCloughan, Nebraska	12	2	0	74
7 Tom Nowatzke, Indiana	10	10	1	73
7 Doug Moreau, LSU	4	10	13	73
9 Floyd Little, Syracuse	12	0	0	72
10 David Ray, Alabama	2	23	12	71

KICK SCORING	XPA	XP	FGA	FG	PTS
1 David Ray, Alabama	25	23	17	12	59
2 Charles Gogolak, Princeton	26	25	16	9	52
3 Les Murdock, Florida State	26	22	14	9	49
4 David Conway, Texas	24	24	12	7	45
5 Tom McKnelly, Arkansas	28	27	11	6	45
6 Doug Moreau, LSU	9	6	20	13	45
7 Bernardo Bramson, Maryland	18	17	17	9	44
8 Braden Beck, Stanford	16	15	16	9	42
8 Billy Carl Irwin, Mississippi	23	21	11	7	42
10 George Squires, Wyoming	21	20	12	7	41

INTERCEPTIONS	INT	YDS
1 Tony Carey, Notre Dame	8	121
2 George Donnelly, Illinois	8	54
3 Jeff Jordan, Tulsa	7	124
3 C.D. Lowery, Utah	7	92
3 Arnie Chonko, Ohio State	7	72
3 Jim Hunt, California	7	65
3 Teddy Roberts, Texas Tech	7	62
8 Ken Boston, Missouri *	6	166
8 Les Palm, Oregon *	6	73
8 Winfred Bailey, Florida State *	6	69

*-Six tied with six; these had the most yards.

Team Leaders

RUSHING OFFENSE	G	ATT	YDS	AVG	YPG
1 Syracuse	10	544	2510	4.6	251.0
2 Bowling Green	10	491	2393	4.9	239.3
3 Cincinnati	10	493	2383	4.8	238.3
4 Michigan	9	516	2141	4.1	237.9
5 Oklahoma	10	502	2276	4.1	227.6
6 Nebraska	10	538	2265	4.2	226.5
7 Princeton	9	432	1968	4.6	218.7
8 Dartmouth	9	394	1958	5.0	217.6
9 Villanova	8	411	1715	4.2	214.4
10 New Mexico	11	550	2331	4.2	211.9

PASSING OFFENSE	G	ATT	COM	INT	PCT	YDS	YPA	TD	I%	YPC	YPG
1 Tulsa	10	377	244	12	64.7	3179	8.4	34	3.2	13.0	317.9
2 Arizona State	10	281	151	19	53.7	2559	9.1	23	6.8	16.9	255.9
3 Iowa	9	321	154	14	48.0	2125	6.6	11	4.4	13.8	236.1
4 California	10	316	192	9	60.8	2187	6.9	14	2.9	11.4	218.7
5 Notre Dame	10	222	120	13	54.1	2105	9.5	16	5.9	17.5	210.5
6 Florida State	10	249	147	10	59.0	2027	8.1	15	4.0	13.8	202.7
7 Baylor	10	282	141	21	50.0	2023	7.2	13	7.5	14.3	202.3
8 Oregon	10	259	132	13	51.0	1793	6.9	17	5.0	13.6	179.3
9 Indiana	9	250	123	15	49.2	1597	6.4	9	6.0	13.0	177.4
10 Southern Cal	10	221	112	11	50.7	1704	7.7	11	5.0	15.2	170.4

TOTAL OFFENSE	G	P	YDS	AVG	YPG
1 Tulsa	10	729	4618	6.3	461.8
2 Notre Dame	10	694	4014	5.8	401.4
3 Arizona State	10	646	3762	5.8	376.2
4 Dartmouth	9	573	3284	5.7	364.9
5 Southern Cal	10	659	3526	5.4	352.6
6 Nebraska	10	696	3485	5.0	348.5
7 Utah State	10	616	3484	5.7	348.4
8 Michigan	9	659	3074	4.7	341.6
9 Florida State	10	658	3410	5.2	341.0
10 Bowling Green	10	637	3343	5.2	334.3

RUSHING DEFENSE	G	ATT	YDS	AVG	YPG
1 Washington	10	346	613	1.8	61.3
2 Notre Dame	10	351	687	2.0	68.7
3 Florida State	10	355	750	2.1	75.0
4 Auburn	10	376	819	2.2	81.9
5 Rutgers	9	324	757	2.3	84.1
6 Texas	10	390	844	2.2	84.4
7 Villanova	8	323	683	2.1	85.4
8 Syracuse	10	368	861	2.3	86.1
9 Michigan	9	326	781	2.4	86.8
10 Illinois	9	323	786	2.4	87.3

PASSING DEFENSE	G	ATT	COM	PCT	YPC	INT	I%	YDS	YPA	TD	YPG
1 Kent State	9	118	41	34.7	11.8	7	5.9	482	4.1	4	53.6
2 Florida	10	150	57	38.0	11.2	16	10.7	640	4.3	3	64.0
3 Nebraska	10	135	60	44.4	11.1	7	5.2	665	4.9	1	66.5
4 LSU	10	142	61	43.0	11.3	9	6.3	689	4.9	2	68.9
5 Boston College	9	112	45	40.2	14.5	7	6.3	652	5.8	4	72.4
6 Xavier	10	136	61	44.9	12.3	8	5.9	750	5.5	4	75.0
7 Citadel	10	162	59	36.4	12.8	6	3.7	755	4.7	6	75.5
8 Ohio U	10	155	64	41.3	12.3	7	4.5	789	5.1	4	78.9
9 VMI	10	132	63	47.7	12.6	4	3.0	796	6.0	8	79.6
10 SMU	10	128	61	47.7	13.1	9	7.0	797	6.2	8	79.7

TOTAL DEFENSE	G	P	YDS	AVG	YPG
1 Auburn	10	495	1647	3.3	164.7
2 Nebraska	10	517	1670	3.2	167.0
3 LSU	10	529	1757	3.3	175.7
4 Arkansas	10	567	1805	3.2	180.5
5 Florida State	10	550	1811	3.3	181.1
6 Syracuse	10	525	1859	3.5	185.9
7 Bowling Green	10	527	1883	3.6	188.3
8 Alabama	10	560	1912	3.4	191.2
9 Villanova	8	488	1555	3.2	194.4
10 Florida	10	535	1944	3.6	194.4

SCORING OFFENSE	G	PTS	AVG
1 Tulsa	10	384	38.4
2 Utah State	10	294	29.4
3 Notre Dame	10	287	28.7
4 Bowling Green	10	275	27.5
5 Dartmouth	9	235	26.1
6 Syracuse	10	254	25.4
7 Nebraska	10	249	24.9
8 Villanova	8	193	24.1
9 Princeton	9	216	24.0
10 Alabama	10	233	23.3

SCORING DEFENSE	G	PTS	AVG
1 Arkansas	10	57	5.7
2 Colgate	9	52	5.8
3 Villanova	8	47	5.9
4 Princeton	9	53	5.9
5 Utah	10	62	6.2
6 Texas	10	64	6.4
7 Florida State	10	66	6.6
8 Alabama	10	67	6.7
9 Nebraska	10	75	7.5
10 Arizona	10	76	7.6

1965 POLL PROGRESSION

Pre-Season 1965 — Sept. 18 Games

AP	Team	Record	Result
1	Nebraska	0-0-0	beat TCU 34-14
2	Texas	0-0-0	beat Tulane 31-0
3	Notre Dame	0-0-0	beat California 48-6
4	Michigan	0-0-0	beat North Carolina 31-24
5	Alabama	0-0-0	lost to Georgia 17-18
6	Arkansas	0-0-0	beat Oklahoma State 28-14
7	Southern Cal	0-0-0	tied Minnesota 20-20
8	LSU	0-0-0	beat Texas A&M 10-0
9	Purdue	0-0-0	beat Miami, Ohio 38-0
10	Ohio State	0-0-0	bye week

September 20 Poll — Sept. 25 Games

AP	Team	Record	Result
1	Notre Dame	1-0-0	lost to # 6 Purdue 21-25
2	Nebraska	1-0-0	beat Air Force 27-17
3	Texas	1-0-0	beat Texas Tech 33-7
4	Michigan	1-0-0	beat California 10-7
5	Arkansas	1-0-0	beat Tulsa 20-12
6	Purdue	1-0-0	beat # 1 Notre Dame 25-21
7	LSU	1-0-0	beat Rice 42-14
8	Florida	1-0-0	lost to Mississippi State 13-18
9	Syracuse	1-0-0	lost to Miami, Fla. 0-24
10	Kentucky	1-0-0	beat Mississippi 16-7

September 27 Poll — Oct. 2 Games

UP	AP	Team	Record	Result
1	1	Texas	2-0-0	beat Indiana 27-12
2	2	Purdue	2-0-0	tied SMU 14-14
3	3	Nebraska	2-0-0	beat Iowa St. 44-0
4	4	Arkansas	2-0-0	beat TCU 28-0
6	5	LSU	2-0-0	lost to Florida 7-14
8	6	Kentucky	2-0-0	lost to Auburn 18-23
5	7	Michigan	2-0-0	lost to # 10 Georgia 7-15
9	8	Notre Dame	1-1-0	beat Northwestern 38-7
7	9	Michigan State	2-0-0	beat Illinois 22-12
	10	Georgia	2-0-0	beat # 7 Michigan 15-7
10		Southern Cal	1-0-1	beat Oregon State 26-12 (O1)

October 4 Poll — Oct. 9 Games

UP	AP	Team	Record	Result
2	1	Texas	3-0-0	beat Oklahoma 19-0
1	2	Nebraska	3-0-0	beat Wisconsin 37-0
3	3	Arkansas	3-0-0	beat Baylor 38-7
5	4	Georgia	3-0-0	beat Clemson 23-9
4	5	Michigan State	3-0-0	beat Michigan 24-7
7	6	Purdue	2-0-1	beat Iowa 17-14
6	7	Notre Dame	2-1-0	beat Army 17-0
8	8	Southern Cal	2-0-1	beat Washington 34-0
10	9	Mississippi State	3-0-0	beat Southern Miss
	10	Florida	2-1-0	beat Mississippi 17-0
10		Oregon	3-0-0	lost to Stanford 14-17

October 11 Poll — Oct. 16 Games

UP	AP	Team	Record	Result
2	1	Texas	4-0-0	lost to # 3 Arkansas 24-27
1	2	Nebraska	4-0-0	beat Kansas State 41-0
3	3	Arkansas	4-0-0	beat # 1 Texas 27-24
4	4	Michigan State	4-0-0	beat Ohio State 32-7
5	5	Georgia	4-0-0	lost to Florida State 3-10
7	6	Southern Cal	3-0-1	beat Stanford 14-0
6	7	Purdue	3-0-1	beat Michigan 17-15
8	8	Notre Dame	3-1-0	bye week
9	9	Florida	3-1-0	beat North Carolina St. 28-6
	10	Mississippi State	4-0-0	lost to Memphis 13-33

October 18 Poll — Oct. 23 Games

UP	AP	Team	Record	Result
2	1	Arkansas	5-0-0	beat North Texas 55-20
3	2	Michigan State	5-0-0	beat # 6 Purdue 14-10
1	3	Nebraska	5-0-0	beat Colorado 38-13
4	4	Southern Cal	4-0-1	lost to # 7 Notre Dame 7-28
6	5	Texas	4-1-0	lost to Rice 17-20
5	6	Purdue	4-0-1	lost to # 2 Michigan State 10-14
7	7	Notre Dame	3-1-0	beat # 4 Southern Cal 28-7
8	8	Florida	4-1-0	bye week
9	9	LSU	4-1-0	beat South Carolina 21-7
10	10	Georgia	4-1-0	lost to Kentucky 10-28

October 25 Poll — Oct. 30 Games

UP	AP	Team	Record	Result
1	1	Michigan State	6-0-0	beat Northwestern 49-7
3	2	Arkansas	6-0-0	beat Texas A&M 31-0
2	3	Nebraska	6-0-0	beat Missouri 16-14
4	4	Notre Dame	4-1-0	beat Navy 29-3
6	5	LSU	5-1-0	lost to Mississippi 0-23
7	6	Purdue	4-1-0	lost to Illinois 0-21
5	7	Florida	4-1-0	lost to Auburn 17-28
9	8	Southern Cal	4-1-1	bye week
	9	Texas	4-2-0	lost to SMU 14-31
	10	Alabama	4-1-1	beat Mississippi State 10-7
8		Missouri	4-1-1	lost to # 3 Nebraska 14-16
10		UCLA	3-1-1	beat Air Force 10-0

November 1 Poll — Nov. 6 Games

UP	AP	Team	Record	Result
1	1	Michigan State	7-0-0	beat Iowa 35-0
3	2	Arkansas	7-0-0	beat Rice 31-0
2	3	Nebraska	7-0-0	beat Kansas 42-6
4	4	Notre Dame	5-1-0	beat Pittsburgh 69-13
7	5	Alabama	5-1-0	beat LSU 31-7
5	6	Southern Cal	4-1-1	beat California 35-0
8	7	Georgia Tech	5-1-1	lost to Tennessee 7-21
6	8	UCLA	4-1-1	beat Washington 28-24
	9	Missouri	4-2-1	beat Colorado 20-7
10	10	Kentucky	5-2-0	beat Vanderbilt 34-0
9		Texas Tech	6-1-0	beat New Mexico State 48-9

November 8 Poll — Nov. 13 Games

UP	AP	Team	Record	Result
1	1	Michigan State	8-0-0	beat Indiana 27-13
3	2	Arkansas	8-0-0	beat SMU 24-3
2	3	Nebraska	8-0-0	beat Oklahoma State 21-17
4	4	Notre Dame	6-1-0	beat North Carolina 17-0
6	5	Alabama	6-1-0	beat South Carolina 35-14
5	6	Southern Cal	5-1-1	beat Pittsburgh 28-0
7	7	UCLA	5-1-1	beat Stanford 30-13
9	8	Tennessee	4-0-2	lost to Mississippi 13-14
8	9	Missouri	5-2-1	beat Oklahoma 30-0
10	10	Kentucky	6-2-0	lost to Houston 21-38

November 15 Poll — Nov. 20 Games

UP	AP	Team	Record	Result
1	1	Michigan State	9-0-0	beat # 4 Notre Dame 12-3
2	2	Arkansas	9-0-0	beat # 9 Texas Tech 42-24
3	3	Nebraska	9-0-0	bye week
4	4	Notre Dame	7-1-0	lost to # 1 Michigan State 3-12
6	5	Alabama	7-1-1	bye week
5	6	Southern Cal	6-1-1	lost to # 7 UCLA 16-20
7	7	UCLA	6-1-1	beat # 6 Southern Cal 20-16
8	8	Missouri	6-2-1	beat Kansas 44-20
9	9	Texas Tech	8-1-0	lost to # 2 Arkansas 24-42
	10	Florida	6-2-0	lost to Miami, Fla. 13-16
10		Purdue	6-2-1	beat Indiana 26-21

November 22 Poll — Nov. 27 Games

UP	AP	Team	Record	Result
1	1	Michigan State	10-0-0	regular season complete
2	2	Arkansas	10-0-0	regular season complete
3	3	Nebraska	9-0-0	beat Oklahoma 21-9
4	4	UCLA	7-1-1	bye week
5	5	Alabama	7-1-1	beat Auburn 30-3
7	6	Notre Dame	7-2-0	tied Miami, Fla. 0-0
6	7	Missouri	7-2-1	regular season complete
10	8	Southern Cal	6-2-1	beat Wyoming 56-6
8	9	Tennessee	5-1-2	beat Vanderbilt 21-3
9	10	Texas Tech	8-2-0	regular season complete

November 29 Poll / January 3 Final Poll

UP	AP	Team	Record	Bowl Bid	Date	Bowl Result	RB	AP	January 3 Final Poll	Record
1	1	Michigan State	10-0-0	Rose Bowl	J1	lost to # 5 UCLA 12-14	3	1	Alabama	9-1-1
2	2	Arkansas	10-0-0	Cotton Bowl	J1	lost to LSU 7-14	1	2	Michigan State	10-1-0
3	3	Nebraska	10-0-0	Orange Bowl	J1	lost to # 4 Alabama 28-39	2	3	Arkansas	10-1-0
4	4	Alabama	8-1-1	Orange Bowl	J1	beat # 3 Nebraska 39-28	5	4	UCLA	8-2-1
5	5	UCLA	7-1-1	Rose Bowl	J1	beat # 1 Michigan State 14-12	4	5	Nebraska	10-1-0
6	6	Missouri	7-2-1	Sugar Bowl	J1	beat Florida 20-18	16	6	Missouri	8-2-1
7	7	Tennessee	6-1-2	Bluebonnet Bowl	D18	beat Tulsa 27-6	10	7	Tennessee	8-1-2
9	8	Southern Cal	7-2-1				13	8	LSU	8-3-0
8	9	Notre Dame	7-2-1				7	9	Notre Dame	7-2-1
10	10	Texas Tech	8-2-0	Gator Bowl	D31	lost to Georgia Tech 21-31	9	10	Southern Cal	7-2-1

1965

CONSENSUS ALL-AMERICANS

POS	Offense	HT	WT	School	AP	CP	FC	FW	NE	PI
B	Mike Garrett	5-9	185	Southern Cal	•	•	•	•	•	•
B	Jim Grabowski	6-2	211	Illinois	•	•	•	•	•	•
B	Bob Griese	6-1	185	Purdue			•	•		•
B	Donny Anderson	6-3	210	Texas Tech	•	•	•	•	•	•
E	Howard Twilley	5-10	180	Tulsa	•	•	•	•		•
E	Freeman White	6-5	220	Nebraska			•	•	•	•
T	Sam Ball	6-4	241	Kentucky			•	•	•	•
T	Glen Ray Hines	6-5	235	Arkansas	•		•	•	•	•
G	Dick Arrington	5-11	232	Notre Dame	•	•		•	•	•
G	Stas Maliszewski	6-1	215	Princeton		•			•	
C	Paul Crane	6-2	188	Alabama	•		•	•		•

	OTHERS RECEIVING FIRST-TEAM HONORS									
B	Clint Jones			Michigan State				•		
B	Floyd Little			Syracuse			•		•	
B	Steve Spurrier			Florida					•	
B	Steve Juday			Michigan State	•					
E	Bobby Crockett			Arkansas				•		
E	Chuck Casey			Florida					•	
E	Gene Washington			Michigan State	•					
T	Wayne Foster			Washington State				•		
T	Ron Goovert			Michigan State				•		
T	George Patton			Georgia	•			•		
T	Karl Singer			Purdue	•					
T	Francis Peay			Missouri				•		
G	Doug Van Horn			Ohio State	•	•		•		
G	Harold Lucas			Michigan State	•			•	•	
K	Charlie Gogolak			Princeton		•				

AP named Patton as an MG; CP and NE named Lucas as an MG; CP named Van Horn as a T

POS	Defense	HT	WT	School	AP	CP	FC	FW	NE	PI
E	Aaron Brown	6-4	230	Minnesota	•	•		•	•	•
E	Bubba Smith	6-7	268	Michigan State			•	•		•
T	Walt Barnes	6-3	235	Nebraska	•	•	•	•	•	•
T	Loyd Phillips	6-3	221	Arkansas	•		•	•	•	•
T	Bill Yearby	6-3	222	Michigan	•		•	•		•
LB	Carl McAdams	6-3	215	Oklahoma	•	•	•	•	•	•
LB	Tommy Nobis	6-2	230	Texas	•	•	•	•	•	•
LB	Frank Emanuel	6-3	228	Tennessee	•	•	•	•	•	•
B	George Webster	6-4	204	Michigan State	•	•	•	•	•	•
B	Johnny Roland	6-2	198	Missouri	•	•	•	•	•	•
B	Nick Rassas	6-0	185	Notre Dame	•	•	•	•	•	•

	OTHERS RECEIVING FIRST-TEAM HONORS									
DL	Tony Jeter			Nebraska		•				
DL	Jerry Shay			Purdue		•				
DL	Ed Weisacosky			Miami, Fla.	•					
DL	Joe Fratangelo			North Carolina	•					
DL	Jack Thornton			Auburn				•		
DL	Lynn Matthews			Florida				•		
LB	Dwight Kelley			Ohio State	•					
DB	Bruce Bennett			Florida				•		

FW picked one team and did not distinguish between offense and defense; AP named Nobis as an offensive G

HEISMAN TROPHY VOTING

	PLAYER	POS	SCHOOL	1ST	2ND	3RD	TOTAL
1	Mike Garrett	TB	Southern Cal	179	143	103	926
2	Howard Twilley	E	Tulsa	101	78	69	528
3	Jim Grabowski	FB	Illinois	97	72	46	481
4	Donny Anderson	RB	Texas Tech	78	57	60	408
5	Floyd Little	HB	Syracuse	51	42	50	287
6	Steve Juday	QB	Michigan State	53	40	42	281
7	Tommy Nobis	LB	Texas	27	37	50	205
8	Bob Griese	QB	Purdue	32	36	25	193
9	Steve Spurrier	QB	Florida	17	14	14	93
10	Steve Sloan	QB	Alabama	18	15	8	92

AWARD WINNERS

PLAYER	POS	SCHOOL	AWARD NAME
Tommy Nobis	LB	Texas	Maxwell
Tommy Nobis	LB	Texas	Outland

CONFERENCE STANDINGS

ACC

	CONF. W L T			OVERALL W L T		
Duke	4	2	0	6	4	0
South Carolina	4	2	0	5	5	0
North Carolina St.	4	3	0	6	4	0
Clemson	4	3	0	5	5	0
Maryland	3	3	0	4	6	0
North Carolina	3	3	0	4	6	0
Virginia	2	4	0	4	6	0
Wake Forest	1	5	0	3	7	0

Big 10

	CONF. W L T			OVERALL W L T		
Michigan State	7	0	0	10	1	0
Ohio State	6	1	0	7	2	0
Purdue	5	2	0	7	2	1
Minnesota	5	2	0	5	4	1
Illinois	4	3	0	6	4	0
Northwestern	3	4	0	4	6	0
Michigan	2	5	0	4	6	0
Wisconsin	2	5	0	2	7	1
Indiana	1	6	0	2	8	0
Iowa	0	7	0	1	9	0

Big 8

	CONF. W L T			OVERALL W L T		
Nebraska	7	0	0	10	1	0
Missouri	6	1	0	8	2	1
Colorado	4	2	1	6	2	2
Iowa State	3	3	1	5	4	1
Oklahoma	3	4	0	3	7	0
Oklahoma State	2	5	0	3	7	0
Kansas	2	5	0	2	8	0
Kansas State	0	7	0	0	10	0

Ivy

	CONF. W L T			OVERALL W L T		
Dartmouth	7	0	0	9	0	0
Princeton	6	1	0	8	1	0
Harvard	3	2	2	5	2	2
Cornell	3	3	1	4	3	2
Yale	3	4	0	3	6	0
Pennsylvania	2	4	1	4	4	1
Brown	1	6	0	2	7	0
Columbia	1	6	0	2	7	0

MAC

	CONF. W L T			OVERALL W L T		
Bowling Green	5	1	0	7	2	0
Miami, Ohio	5	1	0	7	3	0
Western Michigan	3	2	1	6	2	1
Kent State	3	2	1	5	4	1
Marshall	2	4	0	5	5	0
Toledo	2	4	0	5	5	0
Ohio U	0	6	0	0	10	0

AAWU

	CONF. W L T			OVERALL W L T		
UCLA	4	0	0	8	2	1
Southern Cal	4	1	0	7	2	1
Washington State	2	1	0	7	3	0
Washington	4	3	0	5	5	0
Stanford	2	3	0	6	3	1
California	2	3	0	5	5	0
Oregon State	1	3	0	5	5	0
Oregon	0	5	0	4	5	1

SEC

	CONF. W L T			OVERALL W L T		
Alabama	6	1	1	9	1	1
Auburn	4	1	1	5	5	1
Florida	4	2	0	7	4	0
Tennessee	3	1	2	8	1	2
Mississippi	5	3	0	7	4	0
LSU	3	3	0	8	3	0
Kentucky	3	3	0	6	4	0
Georgia	3	3	0	6	4	0
Mississippi State	1	5	0	4	6	0
Vanderbilt	1	5	0	2	7	1
Tulane	1	5	0	2	8	0

SWC

	CONF. W L T			OVERALL W L T		
Arkansas	7	0	0	10	1	0
Texas Tech	5	2	0	8	3	0
TCU	5	2	0	6	5	0
Texas	3	4	0	6	4	0
Baylor	3	4	0	5	5	0
SMU	3	4	0	4	5	1
Texas A&M	1	6	0	3	7	0
Rice	1	6	0	2	8	0

WAC

	CONF. W L T			OVERALL W L T		
Brigham Young	4	1	0	6	4	0
Arizona State	3	1	0	6	4	0
Wyoming	3	2	0	6	4	0
New Mexico	2	3	0	3	7	0
Utah	1	3	0	3	7	0
Arizona	1	4	0	3	7	0

Independents

	OVERALL W L T		
New Mexico State	8	2	0
Utah State	8	2	0
Notre Dame	7	2	1
Texas-El Paso	8	3	0
Virginia Tech	7	3	0
Syracuse	7	3	0
Georgia Tech	7	3	1
Boston College	6	4	0
Miami, Fla.	5	4	1
Memphis	5	5	0
Penn State	5	5	0
Navy	4	4	2
Army	4	5	1
Florida State	4	5	1
Houston	4	5	1
Colorado State	4	6	0
Air Force	3	6	1
Rutgers	3	6	0
Pittsburgh	3	7	0

BOWL GAMES

DATE	GAME	SCORE
D11	Tangerine	East Carolina 31, Maine 0
D18	Liberty	Mississippi 13, Auburn 7
D18	Bluebonnet	Tennessee 27, Tulsa 6
D31	Gator	Georgia Tech 31, Texas Tech 21
D31	Sun	Texas-El Paso 13, TCU 12
J1	Orange	Alabama 39, Nebraska 28
J1	Sugar	Missouri 20, Florida 18
J1	Cotton	LSU 14, Arkansas 7
J1	Rose	UCLA 14, Michigan State 12

1965 NCAA Major College Statistical Leaders

Individual Leaders

PASSING/COMPLETIONS	G	ATT	COM	PCT	INT	I%	YDS	YPA	TD	TD%	COM.PG
1 Bill Anderson, Tulsa	10	509	296	58.2	14	2.8	3464	6.8	30	5.9	29.6
2 Billy Stevens, Texas El-Paso	10	432	196	45.4	29	6.7	3042	7.0	21	4.9	19.6
3 Tom Wilson, Texas Tech	10	283	172	60.8	16	5.7	2119	7.5	18	6.4	17.2
4 Vidal Carlin, North Texas	10	341	159	46.6	18	5.3	1723	5.1	12	3.5	15.9
5 Steve Spurrier, Florida	10	287	148	51.6	13	4.5	1893	6.6	14	4.9	14.8
6 Ken Lucas, Pittsburgh	10	268	144	53.7	15	5.6	1921	7.2	10	3.7	14.4
7 Bob Griese, Purdue	10	238	142	59.7	8	3.4	1719	7.2	11	4.6	14.2
8 Bob Hall, Brown	9	254	135	53.1	17	6.7	1340	5.3	8	3.2	15.0
9 Carroll Williams, Xavier	10	262	128	48.9	14	5.3	1847	7.0	20	7.6	12.8
10 Chuck Burt, Wisconsin	10	235	121	51.5	22	9.4	1143	4.9	5	2.1	12.1

ALL-PURPOSE YARDS	G	RUSH	REC	PR	KR	YDS	YPG
1 Floyd Little, Syracuse	10	1065	248	423	254	1990	199

RUSHING/YARDS	G	ATT	YDS	AVG	YPG
1 Mike Garrett, Southern Cal	10	267	1440	5.4	144.0
2 Jim Grabowski, Illinois	10	252	1258	5.0	125.8
3 Jim Bohl, New Mexico State	10	182	1187	6.5	118.7
4 Roy Shivers, Utah State	10	189	1138	6.0	113.8
5 Pete Pifer, Oregon State	10	234	1095	4.7	109.5
6 Floyd Little, Syracuse	10	193	1065	5.5	106.5
7 Ray McDonald, Idaho	10	213	1000	4.7	100.0
8 Bill Asbury, Kent State	10	238	998	4.2	99.8
9 Bobby Burnett, Arkansas	10	232	947	4.1	94.7
10 Charlie Brown, Missouri	10	174	937	5.4	93.7

RUSHING/YARDS PER CARRY	G	ATT	YDS	YPC
1 Mel Farr, UCLA	10	112	785	7.0
2 Jim Bohl, New Mexico State	10	182	1187	6.5
3 Garrett Ford, West Virginia	10	140	894	6.4
4 Roy Shivers, Utah State	10	189	1138	6.0
5 Larry Csonka, Syracuse	10	136	795	5.9
6 Harry Wilson, Nebraska	10	120	672	5.6
7 Floyd Little, Syracuse	10	193	1065	5.5
8 Bob Apisa, Michigan State	10	121	666	5.5
9 Mike Garrett, Southern Cal	10	267	1440	5.4
10 Charlie Brown, Missouri	10	174	937	5.4

*-Based on top 40 rushers

RECEIVING/RECEPTIONS	G	REC	YDS	TD	YPR	YPG	RPG
1 Howard Twilley, Tulsa	10	134	1779	16	13.3	177.9	13.
2 Chuck Hughes, Texas El-Paso	10	80	1519	12	19.0	151.9	8.
3 Neal Sweeney, Tulsa	10	78	883	8	11.3	88.3	7.
4 John Love, North Texas	10	76	994	7	13.1	99.4	7.
5 George Pearce, William & Mary	10	61	796	6	13.0	79.6	6.
6 Ken McLean, Texas A&M	10	60	835	3	13.9	83.5	6.
6 Donny Anderson, Texas Tech	10	60	797	7	13.3	79.7	6.
8 Charles Casey, Florida	10	58	809	8	13.9	80.9	5.
9 Harlan Lane, Baylor	10	56	643	3	11.5	64.3	5.
10 Jack Clancy, Michigan	10	52	762	5	14.7	76.2	5.

PUNTING	PUNT	YDS	AVG
1 Dave Lewis, Stanford	29	1302	44.9
2 Joe Payton, Arizona	56	2498	44.6
3 Chuck Kolb, Arizona State	65	2860	44.0
4 Phil Scoggins, Texas A&M	88	3837	43.6
5 David Conway, Texas	52	2252	43.3
6 Jerry DePoyster, Wyoming	36	1559	43.3
7 Rodney Stewart, Duke	41	1755	42.8
8 Joe Rodriguez, Idaho	36	1516	42.1
9 Dick McGraw, Mississippi State	48	2021	42.1
10 Mike Bragg, Richmond	67	2794	41.7

PUNT RETURNS/YARDS	PR	YDS	AVG
1 Nick Rassas, Notre Dame	24	459	19.1
2 Larry Wachholtz, Nebraska	31	452	14.6
3 Charlie Greer, Colorado	26	431	16.6
4 Johnny Roland, Missouri	32	430	13.4
5 Floyd Little, Syracuse	18	423	23.5
6 Marcus Rhoden, Mississippi State	19	413	21.7
7 Doug Cunningham, Mississippi	33	405	12.3
8 Mike Carroll, New Mexico State	28	384	13.7
9 Joe Souliere, Bowling Green	18	372	20.7
10 Eddie Willis, VMI	24	349	14.5

KICKOFF RETURNS/YARDS	KR	YDS	AV
1 Eric Crabtree, Pittsburgh	24	636	26
2 Steve Bramwell, Washington	22	573	26
3 Donny Anderson, Texas Tech	22	541	24
4 Bob Grim, Oregon State	23	524	22
5 Dan Bland, Mississippi State	20	499	25
6 Donald Dennis, West Texas State	17	482	28
7 Tom Barrington, Ohio State	14	480	34
8 Mike Junker, Xavier	22	479	2
9 Preston Ridlehuber, Georgia	20	468	23
10 Benny Galloway, South Carolina	19	463	24

SCORING	TDS	XPT	FG	PTS
1 Howard Twilley, Tulsa	16	31	0	127
2 Floyd Little, Syracuse	19	0	0	114
3 Donny Anderson, Texas Tech	17	0	0	102
4 Mike Garrett, Southern Cal	16	0	0	96
4 Roy Shivers, Utah State	16	0	0	96
4 Mickey Jackson, Marshall	16	0	0	96
4 Bobby Burnett, Arkansas	16	0	0	96
8 Ray McDonald, Idaho	15	0	0	90
9 Charley Harraway, San Jose State	14	0	0	84
10 Charley Gogolak, Princeton	0	33	16	81

KICK SCORING	XPA	XP	FGA	FG	PTS
1 Charles Gogolak, Princeton	33	33	23	16	81
2 Ronny South, Arkansas	44	42	11	6	60
3 Frank Rogers, Colorado	18	16	17	13	55
4 Dick Kenney, Michigan State	23	20	18	11	53
5 Joe Cook, Texas El-Paso	41	37	10	5	52
5 Bob Wolfe, Colorado State	33	28	15	8	52
7 Ken Ivan, Notre Dame	31	27	11	7	48
8 Bob Etter, Georgia	18	16	13	10	46
9 Dave Conway, Texas	24	21	16	8	45
9 Jerry DePoyster, Wyoming	26	21	18	8	45
9 Larry Wachholtz, Nebraska	39	36	6	3	45

INTERCEPTIONS	INT	Y
1 Bob Sullivan, Maryland	10	
2 Jim Miller, New Mexico State	8	1
2 Billy Devrow, Southern Miss	8	
4 Henry King, Utah State	7	1
4 Ron Bostwick, Texas El-Paso	7	1
4 Tony Golmont, North Carolina St.	7	
4 Dick Gingrich, Penn State	7	
8 Nick Rassas, Notre Dame	6	1
8 David Fronek, Wisconsin	6	1

Team Leaders

RUSHING OFFENSE	G	ATT	YDS	AVG	YPG
1 Nebraska	10	573	2900	5.1	290.0
2 Southern Cal	10	527	2562	4.9	256.2
3 Missouri	10	566	2473	4.4	247.3
4 Syracuse	10	536	2390	4.5	239.0
5 Cornell	9	476	2143	4.5	238.1
6 Michigan State	10	547	2375	4.3	237.5
7 Dartmouth	9	462	2107	4.6	234.1
8 Arkansas	10	516	2261	4.4	226.1
9 Penn State	10	525	2247	4.3	224.7
10 Princeton	9	461	1991	4.3	221.2

PASSING OFFENSE	G	ATT	COM	INT	PCT	YDS	YPA	TD	I%	YPC	YPG
1 Tulsa	10	510	296	14	58.0	3464	6.8	30	2.8	11.7	346.4
2 Texas El-Paso	10	446	202	30	45.3	3211	7.2	23	6.7	15.9	321.1
3 North Texas State	10	420	194	23	46.2	2172	5.2	14	5.5	11.2	217.2
4 Louisville	10	297	134	20	45.1	2149	7.2	13	6.7	16.0	214.9
5 Texas Tech	10	291	173	16	59.5	2126	7.3	18	5.5	12.3	212.6
6 Pittsburgh	10	289	155	16	53.6	2065	7.1	12	5.5	13.3	206.5
7 Florida	10	309	158	13	51.1	2033	6.6	16	4.2	12.9	203.3
8 Oregon	10	301	139	20	46.2	2022	6.7	16	6.6	14.5	202.2
9 Brigham Young	10	264	128	15	48.5	1920	7.3	21	5.7	15.0	192.0
10 Kentucky	10	236	124	19	52.5	1902	8.1	11	8.1	15.3	190.2

TOTAL OFFENSE	G	P	YDS	AVG	
1 Tulsa	10	780	4278	5.5	4
2 Nebraska	10	760	4040	5.3	4
3 Southern Cal	10	682	3748	5.5	3
4 Brigham Young	10	695	3691	5.3	3
5 Texas El-Paso	10	707	3653	5.2	3
6 Princeton	9	646	3277	5.1	3
7 Arkansas	10	692	3602	5.2	3
8 Dartmouth	9	608	3239	5.3	3
9 Utah State	10	693	3563	5.1	3
10 Michigan State	10	717	3561	5.0	3

RUSHING DEFENSE	G	ATT	YDS	AVG	YPG
1 Michigan State	10	338	456	1.3	45.6
2 Buffalo	10	421	737	1.8	73.7
3 Southern Miss	9	335	673	2.0	74.8
4 Arkansas	10	355	749	2.1	74.9
5 Notre Dame	10	389	754	1.9	75.4
6 Utah State	10	372	839	2.3	83.9
7 Cincinnati	10	367	841	2.3	84.1
8 Florida	10	408	884	2.2	88.4
9 Dartmouth	9	339	801	2.4	89.0
10 Miami, Ohio	10	373	898	2.4	89.8

PASSING DEFENSE	G	ATT	COM	PCT	YPC	INT	I%	YDS	YPA	TD	YPG
1 Toledo	10	146	57	39.0	12.2	13	8.9	698	4.8	2	69.8
2 Columbia	9	140	53	37.9	13.2	12	8.6	700	5.0	4	77.8
3 Colgate	10	189	71	37.6	11.0	21	11.1	778	4.1	6	77.8
4 Bowling Green	9	144	65	45.1	11.2	8	5.6	730	5.1	4	81.1
5 Citadel	10	132	66	50.0	12.3	9	6.8	812	6.2	7	81.2
6 Iowa State	10	150	61	40.7	13.5	8	5.3	821	5.5	4	82.1
7 Holy Cross	10	136	61	44.9	13.7	10	7.4	833	6.1	4	83.3
8 Vanderbilt	10	151	77	51.0	11.0	14	9.3	847	5.6	4	84.7
9 Southern Miss	9	189	67	35.4	11.6	20	10.6	777	4.1	2	86.3
10 Yale	9	166	77	46.4	10.2	14	8.4	783	4.7	4	87.0

TOTAL DEFENSE	G	P	YDS	AVG
1 Southern Miss	9	524	1450	2.8
2 Michigan State	10	572	1699	3.0
3 Toledo	10	593	1820	3.1
4 Buffalo	10	621	1831	2.9
5 Bowling Green	9	499	1680	3.4
6 Notre Dame	10	598	1944	3.3
7 Florida	10	617	2017	3.3
8 Nebraska	10	607	2028	3.3
9 Miami (Ohio)	10	544	2088	3.8
10 Harvard	9	557	1887	3.4

SCORING OFFENSE	G	PTS	AVG
1 Arkansas	10	324	32.4
2 Nebraska	10	321	32.1
3 Tulsa	10	315	31.5
4 Princeton	9	281	31.2
5 Texas El-Paso	10	304	30.4
6 Dartmouth	9	271	30.1
7 West Virginia	10	279	27.9
8 Utah State	10	271	27.1
9 Notre Dame	10	270	27.0
10 Colorado State	10	264	26.4

SCORING DEFENSE	G	PTS	AVG
1 Michigan State	10	62	6.2
2 Southern Miss	9	60	6.7
3 Harvard	9	62	6.9
4 Notre Dame	10	73	7.3
5 Buffalo	10	78	7.8
6 Dartmouth	9	71	7.9
7 Alabama	10	79	7.9
8 Missouri	10	83	8.3
9 Nebraska	10	90	9.0

1966 POLL PROGRESSION

AP PRE-SEASON — SEPT. 17 GAMES

AP	Team	Record	Result
1	Alabama	0-0-0	bye week
2	Michigan State	0-0-0	beat North Carolina St. 28-10
3	Nebraska	0-0-0	beat TCU 14-10
4	UCLA	0-0-0	beat Pittsburgh 57-14
5	Arkansas	0-0-0	beat Oklahoma State 14-10
6	Notre Dame	0-0-0	bye week
7	Syracuse	0-0-0	bye week
8	Purdue	0-0-0	beat Ohio U. 42-3
9	Southern Cal	0-0-0	beat Texas 10-6
10	Tennessee	0-0-0	bye week

UP AP SEPTEMBER 19 POLL — SEPT. 24 GAMES

UP	AP	Team	Record	Result
1	1	Michigan State	1-0-0	beat Penn State 42-8
2	2	UCLA	1-0-0	beat Syracuse 31-12
4	3	Alabama	0-0-0	beat Louisiana Tech 34-0
5	4	Nebraska	1-0-0	beat Utah State 28-7
3	5	Southern Cal	1-0-0	beat Wisconsin 38-3
9	6	Arkansas	1-0-0	beat Tulsa 27-8
7	7	Purdue	1-0-0	lost to # 8 Notre Dame 14-26
	8	Notre Dame	0-0-0	beat # 7 Purdue 26-14
6	9	Michigan	1-0-0	beat California 17-7
	10	Baylor	1-0-0	lost to Colorado 7-13
8		Florida	1-0-0	beat Mississippi State 28-7
10		Missouri	1-0-0	beat Illinois 21-14

UP AP SEPTEMBER 26 POLL — OCT. 1 GAMES

UP	AP	Team	Record	Result
1	1	Michigan State	2-0-0	beat Illinois 26-10
2	2	UCLA	2-0-0	beat Missouri 24-15
4	3	Alabama	1-0-0	beat Mississippi 17-7
3	4	Notre Dame	1-0-0	beat Northwestern 35-7
5	5	Southern Cal	2-0-0	beat Oregon State 21-0
6	6	Nebraska	2-0-0	beat Iowa State 12-6
9	7	Arkansas	2-0-0	beat TCU 21-0
7	8	Michigan	2-0-0	lost to North Carolina 7-21
10	9	Georgia Tech	2-0-0	beat Clemson 13-12
	10	Tennessee	1-0-0	beat Rice 23-3
8		Florida	2-0-0	beat Vanderbilt 13-0

UP AP OCTOBER 3 POLL — OCT. 8 GAMES

UP	AP	Team	Record	Result
1	1	Michigan State	3-0-0	beat Michigan 20-7
2	2	UCLA	3-0-0	beat Rice 27-24
3	3	Notre Dame	2-0-0	beat Army 35-0
4	4	Alabama	2-0-0	beat Clemson 26-0
6	5	Arkansas	3-0-0	lost to Baylor 0-7
5	6	Southern Cal	3-0-0	beat Washington 17-14
8	7	Nebraska	3-0-0	beat Wisconsin 31-3
7	8	Tennessee	2-0-0	lost to # 9 Georgia Tech 3-6
10	9	Georgia Tech	3-0-0	beat # 8 Tennessee 6-3
9	10	Florida	3-0-0	beat Florida State 22-19

UP AP OCTOBER 10 POLL — OCT. 15 GAMES

UP	AP	Team	Record	Result
1	1	Michigan State	4-0-0	beat Ohio State 11-8
2	2	Notre Dame	3-0-0	beat North Carolina 32-0
3	3	Alabama	3-0-0	beat Tennessee 11-10
4	4	UCLA	4-0-0	beat Penn State 49-11
5	5	Southern Cal	4-0-0	beat Stanford 21-7
6	6	Nebraska	4-0-0	beat Kansas State 21-10
7	7	Georgia Tech	4-0-0	beat Auburn 17-3
8	8	Florida	4-0-0	beat North Carolina St. 17-10
9	9	Purdue	3-1-0	beat Michigan 22-21
	10	Baylor	3-1-0	bye week
10		Oklahoma	3-0-0	beat Kansas 35-0

UP AP OCTOBER 17 POLL — OCT. 22 GAMES

UP	AP	Team	Record	Result
1	1	Notre Dame	4-0-0	beat # 10 Oklahoma 38-0
2	2	Michigan State	5-0-0	beat # 9 Purdue 41-20
3	3	UCLA	5-0-0	beat California 28-15
4	4	Alabama	4-0-0	beat Vanderbilt 42-6
5	5	Southern Cal	5-0-0	beat Clemson 30-0
6	6	Georgia Tech	5-0-0	beat Tulane 35-17
7	7	Nebraska	5-0-0	beat Colorado 21-19
8	8	Florida	5-0-0	beat LSU 28-7
9	9	Purdue	4-1-0	lost to # 2 Michigan State 20-41
10	10	Oklahoma	4-0-0	lost to # 1 Notre Dame 0-38

UP AP OCTOBER 24 POLL — OCT. 29 GAMES

UP	AP	Team	Record	Result
1	1	Notre Dame	5-0-0	beat Navy 31-7
2	2	Michigan State	6-0-0	beat Northwestern 22-0
3	3	UCLA	6-0-0	beat Air Force 38-13
4	4	Alabama	5-0-0	beat Mississippi State 27-14
5	5	Southern Cal	6-0-0	lost to Miami, Fla. 7-10
6	6	Georgia Tech	6-0-0	beat Duke 48-7
7	7	Florida	6-0-0	beat Auburn 30-27
8	8	Nebraska	6-0-0	beat Missouri 35-0
9	9	Arkansas	5-1-0	beat Texas A&M 34-0
10	10	Wyoming	6-0-0	lost to Colorado State 10-12

UP AP OCTOBER 31 POLL — NOV. 5 GAMES

UP	AP	Team	Record	Result
1	1	Notre Dame	6-0-0	beat Pittsburgh 40-0
2	2	Michigan State	7-0-0	beat Iowa 56-7
3	3	UCLA	7-0-0	lost to Washington 3-16
4	4	Alabama	6-0-0	beat LSU 21-0
5	5	Georgia Tech	7-0-0	beat Virginia 14-13
6	6	Nebraska	7-0-0	beat Kansas 24-13
7	7	Florida	7-0-0	lost to Georgia 10-27
8	8	Arkansas	6-1-0	beat Rice 31-20
9	9	Southern Cal	6-1-0	beat California 35-9
10	10	Tennessee	4-2-0	beat U.T. Chattanooga 28-10

UP AP NOVEMBER 7 POLL — NOV. 12 GAMES

UP	AP	Team	Record	Result
1	1	Notre Dame	7-0-0	beat Duke 64-0
2	2	Michigan State	8-0-0	beat Indiana 37-19
3	3	Alabama	7-0-0	beat South Carolina 24-0
4	4	Nebraska	8-0-0	beat Oklahoma State 21-6
5	5	Georgia Tech	8-0-0	beat Penn State 21-0
6	6	Arkansas	7-1-0	beat SMU 22-0
7	7	Southern Cal	7-1-0	bye week
8	8	UCLA	7-1-0	beat Stanford 10-0
9	9	Georgia	7-1-0	beat Auburn 21-13
	10	Tennessee	5-2-0	lost to Mississippi 7-14
10		Florida	7-1-0	beat Tulane 31-10

UP AP NOVEMBER 14 POLL — NOV. 19 GAMES

UP	AP	Team	Record	Result
1	1	Notre Dame	8-0-0	tied # 2 Michigan State 10-10
2	2	Michigan State	9-0-0	tied # 1 Notre Dame 10-10
3	3	Alabama	8-0-0	bye week
4	4	Nebraska	9-0-0	bye week
5	5	Georgia Tech	9-0-0	bye week
6	6	Arkansas	8-1-0	lost to Texas Tech 16-21
7	7	Southern Cal	7-1-0	lost to # 8 UCLA 7-14
8	8	UCLA	8-1-0	beat # 7 Southern Cal 14-7
9	9	Georgia	8-1-0	bye week
	10	Purdue	7-2-0	beat Indiana 51-6
10		Florida	8-1-0	bye week

UP AP NOVEMBER 21 POLL — NOV. 26 GAMES

UP	AP	Team	Record	Result
2	1	Notre Dame	8-0-1	beat # 10 Southern Cal 51-0
1	2	Michigan State	9-0-1	regular season complete
3	3	Alabama	8-0-0	beat Southern Miss 34-0
4	4	Nebraska	9-0-0	lost to Oklahoma 9-10
5	5	Georgia Tech	9-0-0	lost to # 7 Georgia 14-23
6	6	UCLA	9-1-0	regular season complete
7	7	Georgia	8-1-0	beat # 5 Georgia Tech 23-14
8	8	Purdue	8-2-0	regular season complete
9	9	Florida	8-1-0	lost to Miami, Fla. 16-21
10	10	Southern Cal	7-2-0	lost to # 1 Notre Dame 0-51

UP AP NOVEMBER 28 POLL — DEC. 3 GAMES

UP	AP	Team	Record	Result
1	1	Notre Dame	9-0-1	regular season complete
2	2	Michigan State	9-0-1	
3	3	Alabama	9-0-0	beat Auburn 31-0
4	4	Georgia	9-1-0	regular season complete
5	5	UCLA	9-1-0	
7	6	Nebraska	9-1-0	regular season complete
6	7	Purdue	8-2-0	
8	8	Georgia Tech	9-1-0	regular season complete
10	9	Miami, Fla.	7-2-1	regular season complete
9	10	SMU	8-2-0	regular season complete

AP DECEMBER 5 FINAL POLL

AP	Team	Record	Bowl Bid	Date	Bowl Results	RB	Records
1	Notre Dame	9-0-1				1	9-0-1
2	Michigan State	9-0-1				3	9-0-1
3	Alabama	10-0-0	Sugar Bowl	J2	beat # 6 Nebraska 34-7	2	11-0-0
4	Georgia	9-1-0	Cotton Bowl	D31	beat # 10 SMU 24-9	5	10-1-0
5	UCLA	9-1-0				4	9-1-0
6	Nebraska	9-1-0	Sugar Bowl	J2	lost to # 3 Alabama 7-34	8	9-2-0
7	Purdue	8-2-0	Rose Bowl	J2	beat Southern Cal 14-13	9	9-2-0
8	Georgia Tech	9-1-0	Orange Bowl	J2	lost to Florida 12-27	7	9-2-0
9	Miami, Fla.	7-2-1	Liberty Bowl	D10	beat Virginia Tech 14-7	18	8-2-1
10	SMU	8-2-0	Cotton Bowl	D31	lost to # 4 Georgia 9-24	19	8-3-0

1966

CONSENSUS ALL-AMERICANS

POS	Offense	HT	WT	School	AP	CP	FC	FW	NE	PI
B	Steve Spurrier	6-2	203	Florida	•	•	•	•	•	•
B	Nick Eddy	6-0	195	Notre Dame	•	•	•	•	•	•
B	Mel Farr	6-2	208	UCLA	•	•		•	•	•
B	Clint Jones	6-0	206	Michigan State	•	•		•		•
E	Jack Clancy	6-1	192	Michigan	•	•	•	•		•
E	Ray Perkins	6-0	184	Alabama	•	•	•	•		•
T	Cecil Dowdy	6-0	206	Alabama	•	•	•	•	•	•
T	Ron Yary	6-6	265	Southern Cal	•	•	•	•		•
G	Tom Regner	6-1	245	Notre Dame	•	•	•	•	•	•
G	LaVerne Allers	6-0	209	Nebraska	•	•		•		•
C	Jim Breland	6-2	223	Georgia Tech	•	•	•	•		•

OTHERS RECEIVING FIRST-TEAM HONORS

B	Lenny Snow			Georgia Tech				•		
B	Bob Griese			Purdue				•		
B	Floyd Little			Syracuse				•		•
B	Larry Csonka			Syracuse			•			
E	Gene Washington			Michigan State				•		•
E	Jim Bierne			Purdue			•			
E	Austin Denney			Tennessee				•		
T	Maurice Moorman			Texas A&M				•		
T	Wayne Mass			Clemson			•			
T	Jerry West			Michigan State				•		
G	Gary Bugenhagen			Syracuse	•			•		
G	Ed Chandler			Georgia				•		
C	Ray Pryor			Ohio State			•			

FW named Yary as a G; FC named Dowdy as a G; AP named Bugenhagen as a T

POS	Defense	HT	WT	School	AP	CP	FC	FW	NE	PI
E	Bubba Smith	6-7	283	Michigan State	•	•	•	•	•	•
E	Alan Page	6-5	238	Notre Dame	•	•		•	•	•
T	Loyd Phillips	6-3	230	Arkansas	•	•	•	•	•	•
T	Tom Greenlee	6-0	195	Washington	•		•			•
MG	Wayne Meylan	6-0	239	Nebraska	•		•	•		•
MG	John LaGrone	5-10	232	SMU	•	•		•		•
LB	Jim Lynch	6-1	225	Notre Dame	•	•	•	•	•	•
LB	Paul Naumoff	6-1	209	Tennessee	•	•		•	•	•
B	George Webster	6-4	218	Michigan State	•	•	•	•	•	•
B	Tom Beier	5-11	197	Miami (Fla.)	•		•		•	•
B	Nate Shaw	6-2	205	Southern Cal	•		•	•		•

OTHERS RECEIVING FIRST-TEAM HONORS

T	Dennis Byrd			North Carolina St.					•	•
T	Pete Duranko			Notre Dame				•		•
T	George Patton			Georgia	•	•				
MG	John Richardson			UCLA				•		
LB	Bob Matheson			Duke	•					
LB	Townsend Clarke			Army			•			
B	Frank Loria			Virginia Tech	•		•			
B	Larry Wachholtz			Michigan State				•		
B	Bobby Johns			Alabama			•			
B	E. Winters Mabry			Dartmouth			•			
B	Ray Perkins			Alabama				•		

AP and FC named Greenlee as an E

HEISMAN TROPHY VOTING

	PLAYER	POS	SCHOOL	1ST	2ND	3RD	TOTAL
1	Steve Spurrier	QB	Florida	433	150	80	1659
2	Bob Griese	QB	Purdue	184	95	74	816
3	Nick Eddy	HB	Notre Dame	39	120	99	456
4	Gary Beban	QB	UCLA	23	76	97	318
5	Floyd Little	HB	Syracuse	25	70	81	296
6	Clint Jones	RB	Michigan State	22	43	52	204
7	Mel Farr	HB	UCLA	10	29	27	115
8	Terry Hanratty	QB	Notre Dame	12	23	16	98
9	Loyd Phillips	T	Arkansas	13	10	8	67
10	George Patton	DT	Georgia	1	23	17	62

AWARD WINNERS

PLAYER	POS	SCHOOL	AWARD NAME
Jim Lynch	LB	Notre Dame	Maxwell
Loyd Phillips	T	Arkansas	Outland

CONFERENCE STANDINGS

ACC

	CONF. W L T			OVERALL W L T		
Clemson	6	1	0	6	4	0
North Carolina St.	5	2	0	5	5	0
Maryland	3	3	0	4	6	0
Virginia	3	3	0	4	6	0
Duke	2	3	0	5	5	0
Wake Forest	2	4	0	3	7	0
South Carolina	1	3	0	1	9	0
North Carolina	1	4	0	2	8	0

Big 10

	CONF. W L T			OVERALL W L T		
Michigan State	7	0	0	9	0	1
Purdue	6	1	0	9	2	0
Michigan	4	3	0	6	4	0
Illinois	4	3	0	4	6	0
Minnesota	3	3	1	4	5	1
Ohio State	3	4	0	4	5	0
Northwestern	2	4	1	3	6	1
Wisconsin	2	4	1	3	6	1
Indiana	1	5	1	1	8	1
Iowa	1	6	0	2	8	0

Big 8

	CONF. W L T			OVERALL W L T		
Nebraska	6	1	0	9	2	0
Colorado	5	2	0	7	3	0
Missouri	4	2	1	6	3	1
Oklahoma State	4	2	1	4	5	1
Oklahoma	4	3	0	6	4	0
Iowa State	2	3	2	2	6	2
Kansas	0	6	1	2	7	1
Kansas State	0	6	1	0	9	1

Ivy

	CONF. W L T			OVERALL W L T		
Harvard	6	1	0	8	1	0
Dartmouth	6	1	0	7	2	0
Princeton	6	1	0	7	2	0
Cornell	4	3	0	6	3	0
Yale	3	4	0	4	5	0
Columbia	2	5	0	2	7	0
Pennsylvania	1	6	0	2	7	0
Brown	0	7	0	1	8	0

MAC

	CONF. W L T			OVERALL W L T		
Miami, Ohio	5	1	0	9	1	0
Western Michigan	5	1	0	7	3	0
Bowling Green	4	2	0	6	3	0
Ohio U.	3	3	0	5	5	0
Kent State	2	4	0	4	6	0
Toledo	1	5	0	2	7	1
Marshall	1	5	0	2	8	0

AAWU

	CONF. W L T			OVERALL W L T		
Southern Cal	4	1	0	7	4	0
UCLA	3	1	0	9	1	0
Oregon State	3	1	0	7	3	0
Washington	4	3	0	6	4	0
California	2	3	0	3	7	0
Washington State	1	3	0	3	7	0
Oregon	1	3	0	3	7	0
Stanford	1	4	0	5	5	0

SEC

	CONF. W L T			OVERALL W L T		
Alabama	6	0	0	11	0	0
Georgia	6	0	0	10	1	0
Florida	5	1	0	9	2	0
Mississippi	5	2	0	8	3	0
Tennessee	4	2	0	8	3	0
LSU	3	3	0	5	4	1
Kentucky	2	4	0	3	6	1
Auburn	1	5	0	4	6	0
Mississippi State	0	6	0	2	8	0
Vanderbilt	0	6	0	1	9	0

SWC

	CONF. W L T			OVERALL W L T		
SMU	6	1	0	8	3	0
Arkansas	5	2	0	8	2	0
Texas	5	2	0	7	4	0
Texas A&M	4	3	0	4	5	1
Baylor	3	4	0	5	5	0
Texas Tech	2	5	0	4	6	0
TCU	2	5	0	2	8	0
Rice	1	6	0	2	8	0

WAC

	CONF. W L T			OVERALL W L T		
Wyoming	5	0	0	10	1	0
Brigham Young	3	2	0	8	2	0
Utah	3	2	0	5	5	0
Arizona State	3	2	0	5	5	0
Arizona	1	4	0	3	7	0
New Mexico	0	5	0	2	8	0

Independents

	OVERALL W L T		
Notre Dame	9	0	1
Georgia Tech	9	2	0
Houston	8	2	0
Army	8	2	0
Memphis	7	2	0
Virginia Tech	8	2	1
Miami, Fla.	8	2	1
Syracuse	8	3	0
New Mexico State	7	3	0
Colorado State	7	3	0
Texas-El Paso	6	4	0
Rutgers	5	4	0
Tulane	5	4	1
Florida State	6	5	0
Penn State	5	5	0
Air Force	4	6	0
Boston College	4	6	0
Navy	4	6	0
Utah State	4	6	0
Pittsburgh	1	9	0

BOWL GAMES

DATE	GAME	SCORE
D10	Liberty	Miami, Fla. 14, Virginia Tech 7
D10	Tangerine	Morgan St. 14, West Chester 6
D17	Bluebonnet	Texas 19, Mississippi 0
D24	Sun	Wyoming 28, Florida State 20
D31	Cotton	Georgia 24, SMU 9
D31	Gator	Tennessee 18, Syracuse 12
J2	Orange	Florida 27, Georgia Tech 12
J2	Sugar	Alabama 34, Nebraska 7
J2	Rose	Purdue 14, Southern Cal 13

1966 ANNUAL REVIEW 1279

1966 NCAA Major College Statistical Leaders

Individual Leaders

Passing/Completions	G	ATT	COM	PCT	INT	I%	YDS	YPA	TD	TD%	COM.PG
1 John Eckman, Wichita State	10	458	195	42.6	34	7.4	2339	5.1	7	1.5	19.5
2 Mark Reed, Arizona	10	365	193	52.9	16	4.4	2368	6.5	20	5.5	19.3
3 Steve Spurrier, Florida	10	291	179	61.5	8	2.8	2012	6.9	16	5.5	17.9
4 Terry Southall, Baylor	10	337	173	51.3	23	6.8	1986	5.9	16	4.8	17.3
5 Hank Washington, West Texas State	10	281	163	58.0	16	5.7	2107	7.5	17	6.1	16.3
6 Danny Holman, San Jose State	10	260	160	61.5	12	4.6	1925	7.4	12	4.6	16.0
7 Benny Russell, Louisville	10	310	142	45.8	12	3.9	2016	6.5	14	4.5	14.2
8 Virgil Carter, Brigham Young	10	293	141	48.1	16	5.5	2182	7.4	21	7.2	14.1
9 Billy Stevens, Texas-El Paso	10	305	140	45.9	17	5.6	2088	6.8	19	6.2	14.0
10 Dewey Warren, Tennessee	10	229	136	59.4	7	3.1	1716	7.5	18	7.9	13.6

All-Purpose Yards	G	RUSH	REC	PR	KR	YDS	YPG
1 Frank Quayle, Virginia	10	727	420	30	439	1616	161.6

Rushing/Yards	G	ATT	YDS	TD	AVG	YPG
1 Ray McDonald, Idaho	10	259	1329	14	5.1	132.9
2 Don Fitzgerald, Kent State	10	296	1245	12	4.2	124.5
3 Jim Bohl, New Mexico State	10	218	1148	13	5.3	114.8
4 Pete Pifer, Oregon State	10	230	1088	12	4.7	108.8
5 Chris Gilbert, Texas	10	206	1080	6	5.2	108.0
6 Garrett Ford, West Virginia	10	236	1068	7	4.5	106.8
7 Dick Post, Houston	10	185	1061	5	5.7	106.1
8 Cornelius Davis, Kansas State	10	210	1028	6	4.9	102.8
9 Larry Csonka, Syracuse	10	197	1012	7	5.1	101.2
10 Pete Larson, Cornell	9	206	979	9	4.8	108.8

Rushing/Yards Per Carry	G	ATT	YDS	YPC
1 Bobby Leo, Harvard	9	130	827	6.4
2 Mel Farr, UCLA	10	138	809	5.9
3 Vic Gatto, Harvard	9	121	700	5.8
4 Dick Post, Houston	10	185	1061	5.7
5 Jack Layland, Pacific	11	145	830	5.7
6 Clem Turner, Cincinnati	10	153	840	5.5
7 Jim Bohl, New Mexico State	10	218	1148	5.3
8 Chris Gilbert, Texas	10	206	1080	5.2
9 Larry Csonka, Syracuse	10	197	1012	5.1
10 Ray McDonald, Idaho	10	259	1329	5.1

*-Based on top 34 rushers

Receiving/Receptions	G	REC	YDS	TD	YPR	YPG	RPG
1 Glenn Meltzer, Wichita State	10	91	1115	4	12.3	111.5	9.1
2 Jack Clancy, Michigan	10	76	1079	4	14.2	107.9	7.6
2 Jim Greth, Arizona	10	76	1003	8	13.2	100.3	7.6
4 John Love, North Texas	10	68	1130	10	16.6	113.0	6.8
5 Chuck Albertson, William & Mary	10	67	792	4	11.8	79.2	6.7
6 Jim Beirne, Purdue	10	64	768	8	12.0	76.8	6.4
7 Dick Trapp, Florida	10	63	872	7	13.8	87.2	6.3
8 John Wright, Illinois	10	60	831	4	13.9	83.1	6.0
9 Jim Zamberlan, Louisville	10	59	747	4	12.7	74.7	5.9
10 Phil Odle, Brigham Young	10	58	920	5	15.9	92.0	5.8
10 Dave Szymakowski, West Texas State	10	58	842	6	14.5	84.2	5.8

Punting	PUNT	YDS	AVG
1 Ron Widby, Tennessee	48	2104	43.8
2 Gary Houser, Oregon State	45	1971	43.8
3 Donnie Gibbs, TCU	61	2611	42.8
4 Mike Bragg, Richmond	58	2482	42.8
5 Joe Randall, Brown	61	2605	42.7
6 Bill Bradley, Texas	45	1913	42.5
7 Dave Morgan, Kansas	46	1950	42.4
8 Steve O'Neal, Texas A&M	67	2834	42.3
9 Randy Cardin, San Jose State	66	2785	42.2
10 Bob Coble, Kansas State	70	2919	41.7
10 Brant Conley, Tulsa	68	2836	41.7
10 Dan Darragh, William & Mary	45	1877	41.7

Punt Returns/Yards	PR	YDS	TD	AVG
1 Vic Washington, Wyoming	34	443	2	13.0
2 Dicky Lyons, Kentucky	25	419	2	16.8
3 Kent Oborn, Brigham Young	31	393	1	12.7
4 Don Bean, Houston	19	384	3	20.2
5 Martine Bercher, Arkansas	24	375	3	15.6
6 Doug Cunningham, Mississippi	33	369	2	11.2
7 Reg Matthews, Texas-El Paso	19	367	2	19.3
8 Doug James, Princeton	23	365	1	15.9
9 Billy Woods, North Texas	20	351	3	17.6
10 Sammy Grezaffi, LSU	25	309	1	12.4

Kickoff Returns/Yards	KR	YDS	TD	AVG
1 Marcus Rhoden, Mississippi State	26	572	1	22.0
2 John Ginter, Indiana	26	532	0	20.5
3 Tom Schinke, Wisconsin	21	527	0	25.1
4 Gary Rowe, North Carolina St.	20	505	0	25.3
5 Jim Baker, Rutgers	22	495	1	22.5
6 Tom Busch, Iowa State	18	484	0	26.9
7 Dave Riggs, North Carolina	23	480	0	20.9
8 Bob Baxter, Memphis	19	449	0	23.6
9 Andy Beath, Duke	25	447	0	17.9
10 Frank Quayle, Virginia	18	439	0	24.4

Scoring	TDS	XPT	FG	PTS
1 Ken Hebert, Houston	11	41	2	113
2 Jim Bohl, New Mexico State	15	8	0	98
3 Leeland Jones, Buffalo	16	0	0	96
4 Floyd Little, Syracuse	15	2	0	92
5 Ray McDonald, Idaho	15	0	0	90
6 Marvin Hubbard, Colgate	13	7	1	88
6 John Love, North Texas	10	26	0	88
8 Tom Francisco, Virginia Tech	14	0	0	84
9 Bob Griese, Purdue	6	33	4	81
10 Four tied	–	–	–	72

Kick Scoring	XPA	XP	FGA	FG	PTS
1 Jerry DePoyster, Wyoming	39	32	38	13	71
2 Bob Etter, Georgia	22	21	15	12	57
3 Steve Davis, Alabama	28	25	18	10	55
4 Tom Fambrough, West Texas State	35	33	10	6	51
4 Kurt Zimmerman, UCLA	33	33	11	6	51
6 Jimmy Keyes, Mississippi	20	20	17	10	50
7 Harold Deters, North Carolina St.	19	19	22	10	49
8 Al Lavan, Colorado State	30	27	10	7	48
9 Bunky Henry, Georgia Tech	32	32	10	5	47
9 Joe Azzaro, Notre Dame	38	35	5	4	47
9 Ken Hebert, Houston	46	41	7	2	47

Interceptions	INT	YDS	TD
1 Henry King, Utah State	11	180	2
1 Charlie West, Texas-El Paso	11	105	1
3 Tom Wilson, Colgate	8	125	0
3 Abelardo Alba, New Mexico State	8	112	1
3 Don Peterson, San Jose State	8	110	0
3 Gerald Warfield, Mississippi	8	77	0
7 Tom Schoen, Notre Dame*	7	112	2
7 Gus Holloman, Houston*	7	105	0
7 Gary Adams, Arkansas*	7	93	0
7 Bobby Roberts, Brigham Young*	7	87	1

*-Eleven tied with 7; these had the most yards

Team Leaders

Rushing Offense	G	ATT	YDS	AVG	TD	YPG
1 Harvard	9	514	2421	4.7	24	269.0
2 Dartmouth	9	453	2298	5.1	23	255.3
3 Idaho	10	539	2435	4.5	20	243.5
4 Houston	10	439	2420	5.5	21	242.0
5 Colgate	10	532	2367	4.4	28	236.7
6 UCLA	10	503	2338	4.6	28	233.8
7 Oregon State	10	530	2335	4.4	19	233.5
8 Michigan State	10	523	2305	4.4	29	230.5
9 Tulane	10	513	2297	4.5	14	229.7
10 Colorado	10	523	2224	4.3	21	222.4

Passing Offense	G	ATT	COM	INT	PCT	YDS	YPA	TD	I%	YPC	YPG
1 Tulsa	10	387	205	19	53.0	2720	7.0	22	4.9	13.3	272.0
2 North Texas	10	415	184	31	44.3	2595	6.3	25	7.5	14.1	259.5
3 Arizona	10	407	210	19	51.6	2551	6.3	20	4.7	12.1	255.1
4 Florida State	10	351	187	14	53.3	2467	7.0	13	4.0	13.2	246.7
5 Brigham Young	10	329	161	21	48.9	2416	7.3	22	6.4	15.0	241.6
6 Texas-El Paso	10	360	165	19	45.8	2410	6.7	24	5.3	14.6	241.0
7 Wichita State	10	460	196	34	42.6	2347	5.1	7	7.4	12.0	234.7
8 West Texas State	10	309	174	19	56.3	2313	7.5	17	6.2	13.3	231.3
9 Florida	10	328	199	11	60.7	2242	6.8	17	3.4	11.3	224.2
10 Louisville	10	322	149	14	46.3	2157	6.7	14	4.4	14.5	215.7

Total Offense	G	P	YDS	AVG	TD	YPG
1 Houston	10	678	4372	6.4	44	437.2
2 Brigham Young	10	748	4006	5.4	36	400.6
3 Notre Dame	10	703	3915	5.6	44	391.5
4 West Texas State	10	672	3898	5.8	36	389.8
5 Dartmouth	9	610	3499	5.7	37	388.8
6 Florida State	10	735	3746	5.1	34	374.6
7 UCLA	10	682	3735	5.5	35	373.5
8 Tulsa	10	704	3618	5.1	28	361.8
9 Florida	10	714	3611	5.1	30	361.1
10 Idaho	10	746	3590	4.8	23	359.0

Rushing Defense	G	ATT	YDS	AVG	TD	YPG
1 Wyoming	10	357	385	1.1	2	38.5
2 North Texas	10	408	513	1.3	5	51.3
3 Michigan State	10	336	514	1.5	6	51.4
4 Southern Miss	10	376	600	1.6	6	60.0
5 Virginia Tech	10	363	723	2.0	4	72.3
6 Texas-El Paso	10	374	728	1.9	10	72.8
7 Syracuse	10	341	738	2.2	5	73.8
8 Mississippi	10	410	741	1.8	3	74.1
9 Notre Dame	10	384	793	2.1	2	79.3
10 Alabama	10	336	797	2.4	2	79.7

Passing Defense	G	ATT	COM	PCT	YPC	INT	I%	YDS	YPA	TD	YPG
1 Toledo	10	142	56	39.4	12.6	9	6.3	704	5.0	8	70.4
2 Oklahoma	10	171	75	43.9	11.6	15	8.8	873	5.1	1	87.3
3 Xavier	10	169	74	43.8	12.4	6	3.6	915	5.4	4	91.5
4 Missouri	10	159	68	42.8	13.6	14	8.8	922	5.8	1	92.2
5 Alabama	10	208	86	41.3	11.0	24	11.5	944	4.5	3	94.4
6 Tennessee	10	187	76	40.6	12.4	16	8.6	946	5.1	3	94.6
7 Michigan	10	196	82	41.8	11.6	9	4.6	953	4.9	6	95.3
8 Harvard	9	176	70	39.8	12.3	14	8.0	863	4.9	1	95.9
9 Colgate	10	217	88	40.6	11.0	28	12.9	966	4.5	4	96.6
10 South Carolina	10	154	72	46.8	13.4	13	8.4	968	6.3	8	96.8

Total Defense	G	P	YDS	AVG	TD	YPG
1 Southern Miss	10	602	1637	2.7	12	163.7
2 Alabama	10	544	1741	3.2	5	174.1
3 Mississippi	10	621	1751	2.8	6	175.1
4 Notre Dame	10	633	1876	3.0	3	187.6
5 Wyoming	10	668	1883	2.8	9	188.3
6 Georgia Tech	10	602	2066	3.4	8	206.6
7 Miami, Fla.	10	646	2068	3.2	9	206.8
8 Michigan State	10	596	2093	3.5	13	209.3
9 Toledo	10	607	2097	3.5	21	209.7
10 Tennessee	10	628	2099	3.3	8	209.9

Scoring Offense	G	PTS	AVG
1 Notre Dame	10	362	36.2
2 Houston	10	335	33.5
3 Wyoming	10	327	32.7
4 New Mexico State	10	321	32.1
5 Dartmouth	9	273	30.3
6 North Texas	10	298	29.8
7 Michigan State	10	293	29.3
7 Texas-El Paso	10	293	29.3
9 Purdue	10	283	28.3
10 UCLA	10	281	28.1

Scoring Defense	G	PTS	AVG
1 Alabama	10	37	3.7
2 Notre Dame	10	38	3.8
3 Mississippi	10	46	4.6
4 Colgate	10	67	6.7
5 Harvard	9	60	6.7
6 Wyoming	10	69	6.9
7 Arkansas	10	73	7.3
8 Miami, Ohio	10	76	7.6
9 Georgia Tech	10	81	8.1

ANNUAL REVIEW

1967 POLL PROGRESSION

AP	PRE-SEASON		SEPT. 16 GAMES
1	Notre Dame	0-0-0	bye week
2	Alabama	0-0-0	bye week
3	Michigan State	0-0-0	bye week
4	Texas	0-0-0	bye week
5	Miami, Fla.	0-0-0	bye week
6	Georgia	0-0-0	bye week
7	Southern Cal	0-0-0	beat Washington State 49-0
8	UCLA	0-0-0	beat #9 Tennessee 20-16
9	Tennessee	0-0-0	lost to #8 UCLA 16-20
10	Colorado	0-0-0	beat Baylor 27-7

AP	SEPTEMBER 18 POLL		SEPT. 23 GAMES
1	Notre Dame	0-0-0	beat California 41-0
2	Alabama	0-0-0	tied Florida State 37-37
3	Michigan State	0-0-0	lost to Houston 7-37
4	Southern Cal	1-0-0	beat #5 Texas 17-13
5	Texas	0-0-0	lost to #4 Southern Cal 13-17
6	UCLA	1-0-0	beat Pittsburgh 40-8
7	Georgia	0-0-0	beat Mississippi State 30-0
8	Miami, Fla.	0-0-0	lost to Northwestern 7-12
9	Colorado	1-0-0	beat Oregon 17-13
10	Nebraska	1-0-0	bye week

UP	AP	SEPTEMBER 25 POLL		SEPT. 30 GAMES
1	1	Notre Dame	1-0-0	lost to #10 Purdue 21-28
3	2	Southern Cal	2-0-0	beat Michigan State 21-17
4	3	Houston	2-0-0	beat Wake Forest 50-6
2	4	UCLA	2-0-0	beat Washington State 51-23
5	5	Georgia	1-0-0	beat Clemson 24-17
7	6	Colorado	2-0-0	bye week
6	7	Nebraska	1-0-0	beat Minnesota 7-0
	8	Texas	0-1-0	lost to Texas Tech 13-19
9	9	Alabama	0-0-1	beat Southern Miss 25-3
8	10	Purdue	1-0-0	beat #1 Notre Dame 28-21
10		Missouri	2-0-0	beat Northwestern 13-6

UP	AP	OCTOBER 2 POLL		OCT. 7 GAMES
1	1	Southern Cal	3-0-0	beat Stanford 30-0
3	2	Houston	3-0-0	lost to North Carolina St. 6-16
2	3	UCLA	3-0-0	beat Penn State 17-15
4	4	Purdue	2-0-0	beat Northwestern 25-16
5	5	Georgia	2-0-0	beat South Carolina 21-0
7	6	Notre Dame	1-1-0	beat Iowa 56-6
6	7	Nebraska	2-0-0	beat Kansas State 16-14
9	8	Colorado	2-0-0	beat Iowa State 34-0
10	9	Alabama	1-0-1	beat Mississippi State 13-0
	10	Texas Tech	2-0-0	lost to Mississippi State 3-7
8		Missouri	2-0-0	beat Arizona 17-3

UP	AP	OCTOBER 9 POLL		OCT. 14 GAMES
1	1	Southern Cal	4-0-0	beat #5 Notre Dame 24-7
2	2	Purdue	3-0-0	beat Ohio State 41-6
4	3	Georgia	3-0-0	lost to Mississippi 20-29
3	4	UCLA	4-0-0	beat California 37-14
5	5	Notre Dame	2-1-0	lost to #1 Southern Cal 7-24
7	6	Colorado	3-0-0	beat Missouri 23-9
6	7	Alabama	2-0-1	beat Vanderbilt 35-21
9	8	Nebraska	3-0-0	lost to Kansas 0-10
	9	North Carolina St.	4-0-0	beat Maryland 31-9
	10	Houston	3-1-0	bye week
8		Missouri	3-0-0	lost to #6 Colorado 9-23
9		LSU	3-0-0	lost to Miami, Fla. 15-17

UP	AP	OCTOBER 16 POLL		OCT. 21 GAMES
1	1	Southern Cal	5-0-0	beat Washington 23-6
2	2	Purdue	4-0-0	lost to Oregon State 14-22
3	3	UCLA	5-0-0	beat Stanford 21-16
4	4	Colorado	4-0-0	beat Nebraska 21-16
6	5	North Carolina St.	5-0-0	beat Wake Forest 24-7
5	6	Alabama	3-0-1	lost to #6 Tennessee 13-24
7	7	Tennessee	2-1-0	beat #7 Alabama 24-13
8	8	Georgia	3-1-0	beat VMI 56-6
10	9	Houston	3-1-0	beat Mississippi State 43-6
9	10	Wyoming	5-0-0	beat Wichita State 30-7

UP	AP	OCTOBER 23 POLL		OCT. 28 GAMES
1	1	Southern Cal	6-0-0	beat Oregon 28-6
2	2	UCLA	6-0-0	bye week
3	3	Colorado	5-0-0	lost to Oklahoma State 7-10
4	4	Tennessee	3-1-0	beat LSU 17-14
5	5	North Carolina St.	6-0-0	beat Duke 28-7
6	6	Georgia	4-1-0	beat Kentucky 31-7
7	7	Purdue	4-1-0	beat Iowa 41-22
8	8	Wyoming	6-0-0	beat Arizona State 15-13
9	9	Houston	4-1-0	lost to Mississippi 13-14
	10	Indiana	5-0-0	beat Arizona 42-7
10		Notre Dame	3-2-0	beat Michigan State 24-12

UP	AP	OCTOBER 30 POLL		NOV. 4 GAMES
1	1	Southern Cal	7-0-0	beat California 31-12
2	2	UCLA	6-0-0	tied Oregon State 16-16
3	3	Tennessee	4-1-0	beat Tampa 38-0
4	4	North Carolina St.	7-0-0	beat Virginia 30-8
5	5	Georgia	5-1-0	lost to Houston 14-15
6	6	Purdue	5-1-0	beat Illinois 42-9
8	7	Indiana	6-0-0	beat Wisconsin 14-9
7	8	Wyoming	7-0-0	beat San Jose State 28-7
9	9	Colorado	5-1-0	lost to Oklahoma 0-23
10	10	Notre Dame	4-2-0	beat Navy 43-14

UP	AP	NOVEMBER 6 POLL		NOV. 11 GAMES
1	1	Southern Cal	8-0-0	lost to Oregon State 0-3
2	2	Tennessee	5-1-0	beat Tulane 35-14
3	3	North Carolina St.	8-0-0	lost to Penn State 8-13
3	4	UCLA	6-0-1	beat Washington 48-0
5	5	Purdue	6-1-0	beat Minnesota 41-12
6	6	Indiana	7-0-0	beat Michigan State 14-13
7	7	Wyoming	8-0-0	beat New Mexico 42-6
9	8	Oklahoma	5-1-0	beat Iowa State 52-14
8	9	Notre Dame	5-2-0	beat Pittsburgh 38-0
	10	Houston	5-2-0	beat Memphis 35-18
10		Alabama	5-1-1	beat LSU 7-6
10		Minnesota	6-1-0	lost to #5 Purdue 12-41

UP	AP	NOVEMBER 13 POLL		NOV. 18 GAMES
1	1	UCLA	7-0-1	lost to #4 Southern Cal 20-21
2	2	Tennessee	6-1-0	beat Mississippi 20-7
4	3	Purdue	7-1-0	beat Michigan State 21-7
3	4	Southern Cal	8-1-0	beat #1 UCLA 21-20
5	5	Indiana	8-0-0	lost to Minnesota 7-33
6	6	Wyoming	9-0-0	beat Texas-El Paso 21-19
7	7	Oklahoma	6-1-0	beat Kansas 14-10
8	8	Oregon State	6-2-1	beat Oregon 14-10
9	9	Notre Dame	6-2-0	beat Georgia Tech 36-6
10	10	North Carolina St.	8-1-0	lost to Clemson 6-14

UP	AP	NOVEMBER 20 POLL		NOV. 25 GAMES
1	1	Southern Cal	9-1-0	regular season complete
2	2	Tennessee	7-1-0	beat Kentucky 17-7
3	3	Purdue	8-1-0	lost to Indiana 14-19
4	4	UCLA	7-1-1	lost to Syracuse 14-32
5	5	Oklahoma	7-1-0	beat Nebraska 21-14
6	6	Notre Dame	7-2-0	beat Miami, Fla. 24-22
7	7	Wyoming	10-0-0	regular season complete
8	8	Oregon State	7-2-1	regular season complete
9	9	Alabama	7-1-1	regular season complete
	10	Houston	7-2-0	lost to Tulsa 13-22
10		Miami, Fla.	6-2-0	lost to #6 Notre Dame 22-24

UP	AP	NOVEMBER 27 FINAL POLL	RECORD	BOWL BID	DATE	BOWL RESULT	RB	RECORD
1	1	Southern Cal	9-1-0	Rose Bowl	J1	beat #4 Indiana 14-3	1	10-1-0
2	2	Tennessee	8-1-0	Orange Bowl	J1	lost to #3 Oklahoma 24-26	3	9-2-0
3	3	Oklahoma	8-1-0	Orange Bowl	J1	beat #2 Tennessee 26-24	2	10-1-0
6	4	Indiana	9-1-0	Rose Bowl	J1	lost to #1 Southern Cal 3-14	12	9-2-0
4	5	Notre Dame	8-2-0				4	8-2-0
5	6	Wyoming	10-0-0	Sugar Bowl	J1	lost to LSU 13-20	7	10-1-0
8	7	Oregon State	7-2-1				8	7-2-1
7	8	Alabama	7-1-1	Cotton Bowl	J1	lost to Texas A&M 16-20	13	8-2-1
9	9	Purdue	8-2-0				6	8-2-0
	10	Penn State	8-2-0	Gator Bowl	D30	tied Florida State 17-17	11	8-2-1
10		UCLA	7-2-1				5	7-2-1

1967

CONSENSUS ALL-AMERICANS

POS	Offense	HT	WT	School	AP	CP	FC	FW	NE	PI
B	Gary Beban	6-0	191	UCLA	•	•	•	•	•	•
B	Leroy Keyes	6-3	199	Purdue	•	•	•	•	•	•
B	O.J. Simpson	6-2	205	Southern Cal	•	•	•	•	•	•
B	Larry Csonka	6-3	230	Syracuse	•	•	•	•	•	•
E	Dennis Homan	6-0	182	Alabama	•	•	•	•	•	•
E	Ron Sellers	6-4	187	Florida State	•	•	•		•	
T	Ron Yary	6-6	245	Southern Cal	•	•	•	•	•	•
T	Ed Chandler	6-2	222	Georgia	•		•	•	•	•
G	Harry Olszewski	5-11	237	Clemson	•		•	•	•	•
G	Rich Stotter	5-11	225	Houston	•		•	•	•	•
C	Bob Johnson	6-4	232	Tennessee	•	•	•	•	•	•

OTHERS RECEIVING FIRST-TEAM HONORS

E	Ken Hebert			Houston		•				
E	Ted Kwalick			Penn State			•		•	
E	Jim Seymour			Notre Dame			•			•
T	Larry Slagle			UCLA					•	
G	Garry Cassells			Indiana		•		•		
G	Bob Kalsu			Oklahoma			•			
G	Phil Tucker			Texas Tech					•	
PK	Jerry DePoyster			Wyoming		•				

POS	Defense	HT	WT	School	AP	CP	FC	FW	NE	PI
E	Ted Hendricks	6-8	222	Miami, Fla.	•	•	•	•	•	•
E	Tim Rossovich	6-5	235	Southern Cal	•		•	•		•
T	Dennis Byrd	6-4	250	NC State	•	•	•	•	•	•
MG	Granville Liggins	5-11	216	Oklahoma	•	•	•	•	•	•
MG	Wayne Meylan	6-0	231	Nebraska	•	•	•	•	•	•
LB	Adrian Young	6-1	210	Southern Cal	•	•	•	•		•
LB	Don Manning	6-2	204	UCLA	•				•	•
B	Tom Schoen	5-11	178	Notre Dame	•	•	•	•	•	•
B	Frank Loria	5-9	174	Virginia Tech	•	•	•			•
B	Bobby Johns	6-1	180	Alabama			•		•	•
B	Dick Anderson	6-2	204	Colorado					•	•

OTHERS RECEIVING FIRST-TEAM HONORS

E	Bob Stein			Minnesota				•	•	
E	John Garlington			LSU						•
E	Kevin Hardy			Notre Dame		•				•
E	Bill Staley			Utah State			•			
T	Mike Dirks			Wyoming					•	
T	Greg Pipes			Baylor		•		•		
T	Jess Lewis			Oregon State		•				
MG	Jon Sandstrom			Oregon State				•		
LB	Corby Robertson			Texas				•		
LB	Bill Hobbs			Texas A&M		•				
LB	Tom Beutler			Toledo			•			
LB	D.D. Lewis			Mississippi State					•	
LB	Fred Carr			UTEP					•	
B	Fred Combs			North Carolina St.				•		
B	Harry Cheatwood			Oklahoma State			•			
B	Jim Smith			Oregon						
B	Al Dorsey			Tennessee						•

AP named Liggins as a LB

HEISMAN TROPHY VOTING

	PLAYER	POS	SCHOOL	1ST	2ND	3RD	TOTAL
1	Gary Beban	QB	UCLA	369	332	197	1968
2	O.J. Simpson	TB	Southern Cal	261	359	221	1722
3	Leroy Keyes	HB	Purdue	278	142	248	1366
4	Larry Csonka	FB	Syracuse	22	20	30	136
5	Kim Hammond	QB	Florida State	17	15	9	90
6	Bob Johnson	C	Tennessee	13	10	17	76
7	Granville Liggins	NG	Oklahoma	2	11	33	61
8	Dewey Warren	QB	Tennessee	4	13	18	56
9	Wayne Meylan	MG	Nebraska	11	5	12	55
10	Terry Hanratty	QB	Notre Dame	1	12	27	54

AWARD WINNERS

PLAYER	POS	SCHOOL	AWARD NAME
Gary Beban	QB	UCLA	Maxwell
Ron Yary	T	Southern Cal	Outland
O.J. Simpson	RB	Southern Cal	Camp

CONFERENCE STANDINGS

ACC

	CONF. W L T			OVERALL W L T		
Clemson	6	0	0	6	4	0
North Carolina St.	5	1	0	9	2	0
South Carolina	4	2	0	5	5	0
Virginia	3	3	0	5	5	0
Wake Forest	3	4	0	4	6	0
Duke	2	4	0	4	6	0
North Carolina	2	5	0	2	8	0
Maryland	0	6	0	0	9	0

Big 10

	CONF. W L T			OVERALL W L T		
Indiana	6	1	0	9	2	0
Minnesota	6	1	0	8	2	0
Purdue	6	1	0	8	2	0
Ohio State	5	2	0	6	3	0
Illinois	3	4	0	4	6	0
Michigan	3	4	0	4	6	0
Michigan State	3	4	0	3	7	0
Northwestern	2	5	0	3	7	0
Iowa	0	6	1	1	8	1
Wisconsin	0	6	1	0	9	1

Big 8

	CONF. W L T			OVERALL W L T		
Oklahoma	7	0	0	10	1	0
Colorado	5	2	0	9	2	0
Kansas	5	2	0	5	5	0
Missouri	4	3	0	7	3	0
Nebraska	3	4	0	6	4	0
Oklahoma State	3	4	0	4	5	1
Iowa State	1	6	0	2	8	0
Kansas State	0	7	0	1	9	0

Ivy

	CONF. W L T			OVERALL W L T		
Yale	7	0	0	8	1	0
Dartmouth	5	2	0	7	2	0
Cornell	4	2	1	6	2	1
Harvard	4	3	0	6	3	0
Princeton	4	3	0	6	3	0
Pennsylvania	2	5	0	3	6	0
Brown	1	5	1	2	6	1
Columbia	0	7	0	2	7	0

MAC

	CONF. W L T			OVERALL W L T		
Toledo	5	1	0	9	1	0
Miami, Ohio	4	2	0	6	4	0
Western Michigan	4	2	0	5	4	0
Ohio U.	4	2	0	5	5	0
Bowling Green	2	4	0	6	4	0
Kent State	2	4	0	5	5	0
Marshall	0	6	0	0	10	0

AAWU

	CONF. W L T			OVERALL W L T		
Southern Cal	6	1	0	10	1	0
UCLA	4	1	1	7	2	1
Oregon State	4	1	1	7	2	1
Stanford	3	4	0	5	5	0
Washington	3	4	0	5	5	0
California	2	3	0	5	5	0
Oregon	1	5	0	2	8	0
Washington State	1	5	0	2	8	0

SEC

	CONF. W L T			OVERALL W L T		
Tennessee	6	0	0	9	2	0
Alabama	5	1	0	8	2	1
Georgia	4	2	0	7	4	0
Florida	4	2	0	6	4	0
Mississippi	4	2	1	6	4	1
LSU	3	2	1	7	3	1
Auburn	3	3	0	6	4	0
Kentucky	1	6	0	2	8	0
Vanderbilt	0	6	0	2	7	1
Mississippi State	0	6	0	1	9	0

SWC

	CONF. W L T			OVERALL W L T		
Texas A&M	6	1	0	7	4	0
Texas Tech	5	2	0	6	4	0
Texas	4	3	0	6	4	0
TCU	4	3	0	4	6	0
Arkansas	3	3	1	4	5	1
SMU	3	4	0	3	7	0
Baylor	1	5	1	1	8	1
Rice	1	6	0	4	6	0

WAC

	CONF. W L T			OVERALL W L T		
Wyoming	5	0	0	10	1	0
Arizona State	4	1	0	8	2	0
Brigham Young	3	2	0	6	4	0
Utah	2	3	0	4	7	0
Arizona	1	4	0	3	6	1
New Mexico	0	5	0	1	9	0

Independents

	OVERALL W L T		
Syracuse	8	2	0
Notre Dame	8	2	0
Army	8	2	0
Penn State	8	2	1
Utah State	7	2	1
New Mexico State	7	2	1
Texas-El Paso	7	2	1
Florida State	7	2	2
Houston	7	3	0
Virginia Tech	7	3	0
Memphis	6	3	0
Miami, Fla.	7	4	0
Navy	5	4	1
Colorado State	4	5	1
Rutgers	4	5	0
Boston College	4	6	0
Georgia Tech	4	6	0
Tulane	3	7	0
Air Force	2	6	2
Pittsburgh	1	9	0

BOWL GAMES

DATE	GAME	SCORE
D2	Pasadena	West Texas State 35, Cal St. Northridge 13
D16	Liberty	North Carolina St. 14, Georgia 7
D16	Tangerine	Tennessee-Martin 25, West Chester 8
D23	Bluebonnet	Colorado 31, Miami, Fla. 21
D30	Gator	Florida State 17, Penn State 17
D30	Sun	Texas-El Paso 14, Mississippi 7
J1	Sugar	LSU 20, Wyoming 13
J1	Orange	Oklahoma 26, Tennessee 24
J1	Rose	Southern Cal 14, Indiana 3
J1	Cotton	Texas A&M 20, Alabama 16

1967 NCAA Major College Statistical Leaders

Individual Leaders

PASSING/COMPLETIONS	G	ATT	COM	PCT	INT	I%	YDS	YPA	TD	TD%	COM.PG
1 Terry Stone, New Mexico	10	336	160	47.6	19	5.7	1946	5.8	9	2.7	16.0
2 Jimmy Poole, Davidson	9	264	157	59.5	12	4.6	1611	6.1	9	3.4	17.4
3 Sal Olivas, New Mexico State	10	321	156	48.6	16	5.0	2225	6.9	18	5.6	15.6
4 Mike Livingston, SMU	10	250	152	60.8	14	5.6	1750	7.0	10	4.0	15.2
5 Kim Hammond, Florida State	10	241	140	58.1	10	4.2	1991	8.3	15	6.2	14.0
6 Paul Toscano, Wyoming	10	241	134	55.6	10	4.2	1791	7.4	18	7.5	13.4
7 John Cartwright, Navy	10	241	129	53.5	9	3.7	1537	6.4	9	3.7	12.9
8 John Schneider, Toledo	10	245	127	51.8	11	4.5	1650	6.7	10	4.1	12.7
9 Marty Domres, Columbia	9	229	121	52.8	12	5.2	1378	6.0	6	2.6	13.4
10 Steve Ramsey, North Texas	9	269	119	44.2	19	7.1	1732	6.4	21	7.8	13.2

ALL-PURPOSE YARDS	G	RUSH	REC	PR	KR	YDS	YPG
1 O.J. Simpson, Southern Cal	9	1415	109	0	176	1700	188.

RUSHING/YARDS	G	ATT	YDS	TD	AVG	YPG
1 O.J. Simpson, Southern Cal	9	266	1415	11	5.3	157.2
2 Eugene Morris, West Texas State	10	191	1274	11	6.7	127.4
3 Max Anderson, Arizona State	10	191	1188	10	6.2	118.8
4 Butch Colson, East Carolina	10	252	1135	14	4.5	113.5
5 Larry Csonka, Syracuse	10	261	1127	8	4.3	112.7
6 Doug Dalton, New Mexico State	10	177	1123	10	6.3	112.3
7 Paul Gipson, Houston	10	187	1100	11	5.9	110.0
8 Buddy Gore, Clemson	10	230	1045	8	4.5	104.5
9 Chris Gilbert, Texas	10	205	1019	9	5.0	101.9
10 Ron Johnson, Michigan	10	220	1005	7	4.6	100.5

RUSHING/YARDS PER CARRY	G	ATT	YDS	YPC
1 Eugene Morris, West Texas State	10	191	1274	6.7
2 Leroy Keyes, Purdue	10	149	986	6.6
3 Doug Dalton, New Mexico State	10	177	1123	6.3
4 Max Anderson, Arizona State	10	191	1188	6.2
5 Bill Mayo, Dayton	10	128	771	6.0
6 Paul Gipson, Houston	10	187	1100	5.9
7 Charles Jarvis, Army	10	144	774	5.4
8 O.J. Simpson, Southern Cal	9	266	1415	5.3
9 Al Moore, Miami, Ohio	10	135	717	5.3
10 Chris Gilbert, Texas	10	205	1019	5.0

*-Based on top 34 rushers

RECEIVING/RECEPTIONS	G	REC	YDS	TD	YPR	YPG	RPG
1 Bob Goodridge, Vanderbilt	10	79	1114	6	14.1	111.4	7.9
2 Rick Eber, Tulsa	10	78	1168	12	15.0	116.8	7.8
3 Phil Odle, Brigham Young	10	77	971	9	12.6	97.1	7.
4 Ron Sellers, Florida State	10	70	1228	8	17.5	122.8	7.0
5 Ace Hendricks, New Mexico	10	67	1094	6	16.3	109.4	6.7
6 Rob Taylor, Navy	10	61	818	6	13.4	81.8	6.1
7 Richard Trapp, Florida	10	58	708	1	12.2	70.8	5.8
7 Emilio Vallez, New Mexico	10	58	650	4	11.2	65.0	5.8
9 Jerry Levias, SMU	10	57	724	7	12.7	72.4	5.7
10 Allan Bream, Iowa	10	55	703	5	12.8	70.3	5.5

PUNTING	PUNT	YDS	AVG
1 Zenon Andrusyshyn, UCLA	34	1503	44.2
2 Ken Hebert, Houston	42	1831	43.6
3 Gary Houser, Oregon State	40	1736	43.4
4 Dale Livingston, Western Michigan	49	2122	43.3
5 Eddie Ray, LSU	52	2226	42.8
6 Tom Galloway, Texas-El Paso	62	2647	42.7
7 Bob Coble, Kansas State	61	2605	42.7
8 Steve O'Neal, Texas A&M	81	3402	42.0
9 Dickie Dunaway, Southern Miss	58	2430	41.9
10 Bill Bradley, Texas	65	2717	41.8

PUNT RETURNS/YARDS	PR	YDS	TD	AVG
1 Mike Battle, Southern Cal	47	570	2	12.1
2 Vic Washington, Wyoming	53	565	1	10.7
3 Don Bean, Houston	45	522	2	11.6
4 Jimmy Carter, Auburn	38	473	2	12.4
5 John Mallory, West Virginia	36	453	2	12.6
6 Tom Schoen, Notre Dame	42	447	1	10.6
7 Benny Goodwin, Oklahoma State	35	422	1	12.1
8 Frank Loria, Virginia Tech	30	420	1	14.0
9 Fred Combs, North Carolina St.	22	417	2	19.0
10 Charles Greer, Colorado	28	408	1	14.6

KICKOFF RETURNS/YARDS	KR	YDS	TD	AVG
1 Joe Casas, New Mexico	23	602	1	26
2 Dave Strong, Vanderbilt	28	577	0	20
3 Charlie Smith, Utah	20	544	1	27
4 Nick Pappas, Memphis	17	527	1	3
5 Ron Johnson, Michigan	26	498	0	19
6 Jim Kirkpatrick, Purdue	20	487	0	24
7 Altie Taylor, Utah State	15	478	1	3
8 Dicky Lyons, Kentucky	18	474	1	26
9 Curley Watters, West Texas State	20	460	1	23
10 Kenny Dutton, Maryland	24	454	0	18

SCORING	TDS	XPT	FG	PTS
1 Leroy Keyes, Purdue	19	0	0	114
2 Roland Moss, Toledo	16	0	0	96
2 David Dickey, Arkansas	16	0	0	96
4 Butch Colson, East Carolina	15	2	0	92
5 Don Abbey, Penn State	9	25	3	88
6 Ken Hebert, Houston	7	38	2	86
7 Doug Dalton, New Mexico State	14	0	0	84
8 Rick Eber, Tulsa	13	2	0	80
9 Ron Shanklin, North Texas	13	0	0	78
10 Dicky Lyons, Kentucky	11	4	1	73

KICK SCORING	XPA	XP	FGA	FG	PTS
1 Gerald Warren, North Carolina St.	19	19	22	17	70
2 Jerry DePoyster, Wyoming	31	21	37	15	66
3 Zenon Andrusyshyn, UCLA	35	31	27	11	64
4 Dennis Patera, Brigham Young	35	29	22	11	62
5 Joe Azzaro, Notre Dame	40	37	10	8	61
6 Karl Kremser, Tennessee	32	30	15	10	60
7 Jerry Waddles, Texas-El Paso	38	30	18	9	57
8 Ken Juskowich, West Virginia	22	20	23	12	56
9 Al Gonzales, New Mexico State	42	37	8	6	55
10 Grant Guthrie, Florida State	27	26	14	9	53

INTERCEPTIONS	INT	YDS
1 Steve Haterius, West Texas State	11	90
2 Ron Davidson, Virginia Tech	9	149
3 Wes Plummer, Arizona State	8	161
3 Jim Bevans, Army	8	124
3 Steve Bailey, Xavier	8	42
6 Bill Hobbs, Texas A&M *	7	162
6 Kerr Kump, VMI *	7	160
6 Mike Jones, Tennessee *	7	150
6 Dick Stiverson, Wichita State *	7	111
6 Bobby Roberts, Brigham Young *	7	96

*-Twelve tied with seven; these had the most yards.

Team Leaders

RUSHING OFFENSE	G	ATT	YDS	AVG	TD	YPG
1 Houston	10	553	2709	4.9	29	270.9
2 West Texas State	10	449	2497	5.6	22	249.7
3 Texas Tech	10	558	2444	4.4	19	244.4
4 Oregon State	10	582	2389	4.1	21	238.9
5 LSU	10	554	2361	4.3	27	236.1
6 East Carolina	10	569	2316	4.1	22	231.6
7 Syracuse	10	561	2298	4.1	16	229.8
8 Southern Cal	10	568	2285	4.0	19	228.5
9 Colorado State	10	571	2282	4.0	20	228.2
10 Yale	9	504	2053	4.1	24	228.1

PASSING OFFENSE	G	ATT	COM	INT	PCT	YDS	YPA	TD	I%	YPC	YPG
1 Texas-El Paso	9	367	164	26	44.7	2710	7.4	28	7.1	16.5	301.1
2 Tulsa	10	389	207	24	53.2	2639	6.8	26	6.2	12.7	263.9
3 Florida State	10	352	190	21	54.0	2584	7.3	18	6.0	13.6	258.4
4 New Mexico	10	416	193	27	46.4	2491	6.0	13	6.5	12.9	249.1
5 New Mexico State	10	333	163	16	48.9	2359	7.1	18	4.8	14.5	235.9
6 Davidson	9	323	192	14	59.4	2080	6.4	14	4.3	10.8	231.1
7 Brigham Young	10	370	177	17	47.8	2264	6.1	20	4.6	12.8	226.4
8 North Texas	9	334	145	22	43.4	2012	6.0	25	6.6	13.9	223.6
9 SMU	10	330	189	23	57.3	2207	6.7	13	7.0	11.7	220.7
10 Wyoming	10	278	156	11	56.1	2077	7.5	20	4.0	13.3	207.7

TOTAL OFFENSE	G	P	YDS	AVG	TD	YPG
1 Houston	10	738	4279	5.8	41	42
2 Purdue	10	778	4236	5.4	41	42
3 New Mexico State	10	734	4181	5.7	41	4
4 Arizona State	10	756	4148	5.5	44	41
5 West Texas State	10	681	4066	6.0	32	4
6 Brigham Young	10	816	3962	4.9	33	3
7 Notre Dame	10	788	3911	5.0	42	3
8 Texas-El Paso	9	679	3476	5.1	39	3
9 Tulsa	10	787	3818	4.9	40	3
10 Florida State	10	723	3786	5.2	29	3

RUSHING DEFENSE	G	ATT	YDS	AVG	TD	YPG
1 Wyoming	10	376	423	1.1	6	42.3
2 Syracuse	10	354	548	1.5	9	54.8
3 Southern Miss	9	350	541	1.5	5	60.1
4 Nebraska	10	420	675	1.6	7	67.5
5 Virginia Tech	10	365	724	2.0	3	72.4
6 Missouri	10	438	739	1.7	3	73.9
7 Arizona State	10	401	789	2.0	13	78.9
8 North Texas	9	376	712	1.9	10	79.1
9 Utah State	10	373	808	2.2	8	80.8
10 West Virginia	10	425	821	1.9	8	82.1

PASSING DEFENSE	G	ATT	COM	PCT	YPC	INT	I%	YDS	YPA	TD	YPG
1 Nebraska	10	207	78	37.7	11.6	11	5.3	901	4.4	1	90.1
2 Virginia	10	170	76	44.7	12.1	13	7.7	918	5.4	2	91.8
2 Oregon	10	143	65	45.5	14.1	7	4.9	918	6.4	6	91.8
4 Oklahoma State	10	175	71	40.6	13.3	11	6.3	945	5.4	4	94.5
5 Georgia	10	214	77	36.0	12.3	18	8.4	947	4.4	5	94.7
6 Kent State	10	229	92	40.2	10.7	15	6.6	986	4.3	5	98.6
7 Dayton	10	199	89	44.7	11.1	11	5.5	990	5.0	1	99.0
8 Columbia	9	119	47	39.5	19.2	10	8.4	901	7.6	9	100.1
9 Missouri	10	188	88	46.8	11.5	11	5.9	1013	5.4	5	101.3
10 Toledo	10	206	84	40.8	12.1	16	7.8	1014	4.9	4	101.4

TOTAL DEFENSE	G	P	YDS	AVG	TD	YPG
1 Nebraska	10	627	1576	2.5	8	1
2 Missouri	10	626	1752	2.8	8	1
3 Wyoming	10	652	1852	2.8	13	1
4 Syracuse	10	588	1921	3.3	15	1
5 Toledo	10	618	1984	3.2	9	1
6 Southern Miss	9	567	1794	3.2	13	1
7 North Texas	9	632	1821	2.9	16	2
8 Southern Cal	10	634	2031	3.2	9	2
9 West Virginia	10	654	2036	3.1	13	2
10 Houston	10	677	2076	3.1	17	2

SCORING OFFENSE	G	PTS	AVG
1 Texas-El Paso	9	323	35.9
2 Arizona State	10	350	35.0
3 New Mexico State	10	346	34.6
4 Notre Dame	10	337	33.7
5 Houston	10	322	32.2
6 Yale	9	278	30.9
6 North Texas	9	278	30.9
8 Tulsa	10	304	30.4
9 Purdue	10	291	29.1
10 Harvard	9	256	28.4

SCORING DEFENSE	G	PTS	AVG
1 Oklahoma	10	68	6.8
2 Missouri	10	76	7.6
3 Toledo	10	83	8.3
3 Nebraska	10	83	8.3
5 Southern Cal	10	84	8.4
6 North Carolina St.	10	87	8.7
7 Colorado	10	92	9.2
8 Army	10	94	9.4
9 Wyoming	10	99	9.9

ANNUAL REVIEW

1968 POLL PROGRESSION

AP Pre-Season / Sept. 14 Games

AP	Team	Record	Sept. 14 Games
1	Purdue	0-0-0	bye week
2	Southern Cal	0-0-0	bye week
3	Notre Dame	0-0-0	bye week
4	Oklahoma	0-0-0	bye week
5	Texas	0-0-0	bye week
6	Oregon State	0-0-0	bye week
7	Florida	0-0-0	bye week
8	Penn State	0-0-0	bye week
9	Tennessee	0-0-0	tied Georgia 17-17
10	Alabama	0-0-0	bye week
11	Ohio State	0-0-0	bye week
12	Texas A&M	0-0-0	bye week
13	Indiana	0-0-0	bye week
14	Nebraska	0-0-0	beat Wyoming 13-10
15	Minnesota	0-0-0	bye week
16	UCLA	0-0-0	bye week
17	Arizona State	0-0-0	bye week
18	LSU	0-0-0	bye week
19	Syracuse	0-0-0	bye week

AP September 16 Poll / Sept. 21 Games

AP	Team	Record	Sept. 21 Games
1	Purdue	0-0-0	beat Virginia 44-6
2	Southern Cal	0-0-0	beat Minnesota 29-20
3	Notre Dame	0-0-0	beat # 5 Oklahoma 45-21
4	Texas	0-0-0	tied # 11 Houston 20-20
5	Oklahoma	0-0-0	lost to # 3 Notre Dame 21-45
6	Florida	0-0-0	beat Air Force 23-20
7	Alabama	0-0-0	beat Virginia Tech 14-7
8	Oregon State	0-0-0	lost to Iowa 20-21
9	Ohio State	0-0-0	bye week
10	Penn State	0-0-0	beat Navy 31-6
11	Houston	0-0-0	tied # 4 Texas 20-20
12	Tennessee	0-0-1	bye week
13	Texas A&M	0-0-0	lost to # 20 LSU 12-13
14	Nebraska	1-0-0	beat Utah 31-0
15	Indiana	0-0-0	beat Baylor 40-36
16	Minnesota	0-0-0	lost to Southern Cal 20-29
17	UCLA	0-0-0	beat Pittsburgh 63-7
18	Georgia	0-0-1	bye week
19	Miami, Fla.	0-0-0	beat Northwestern 28-7
20	LSU	0-0-0	beat # 13 Texas A&M 13-12

UP AP September 23 Poll / Sept. 28 Games

UP	AP	Team	Record	Sept. 28 Games
2	1	Purdue	1-0-0	beat # 2 Notre Dame 37-22
1	2	Notre Dame	1-0-0	lost to # 1 Purdue 22-37
3	3	Southern Cal	1-0-0	beat Northwestern 24-7
4	4	Penn State	1-0-0	beat Kansas State 25-9
14	5	Florida	1-0-0	beat Florida State 9-3
13	6	Texas	0-0-1	lost to Texas Tech 22-31
7	7	Alabama	1-0-0	beat Southern Miss 17-14
5	8	UCLA	1-0-0	beat Washington State 31-21
8	9	Nebraska	2-0-0	beat # 17 Minnesota 17-14
11	10	Houston	1-0-1	bye week
15	11	Ohio State	0-0-0	beat SMU 35-14
6	12	Kansas	1-0-0	beat # 13 Indiana 38-20
12	13	Indiana	1-0-0	lost to # 12 Kansas 20-38
9	14	LSU	1-0-0	beat Rice 21-7
10	15	Miami, Fla.	1-0-0	beat Georgia Tech 10-7
19	16	Tennessee	0-0-1	beat Memphis 24-17
	17	Minnesota	0-1-0	lost to # 9 Nebraska 14-17
	18	Oregon State	0-1-0	beat Utah 24-21
18	19	Arizona State	1-0-0	beat Texas-El Paso 31-19
	20	Wyoming	1-1-0	lost to Air Force 3-10
16		North Carolina St.	2-0-0	lost to Oklahoma 14-28
17		Michigan State	1-0-0	beat Baylor 28-10
20		Florida State	1-0-0	lost to # 5 Florida 3-9

UP AP September 30 Poll / Oct. 5 Games

UP	AP	Team	Record	Oct. 5 Games
1	1	Purdue	2-0-0	beat Northwestern 43-6
2	2	Southern Cal	2-0-0	beat # 13 Miami, Fla. 28-3
3	3	Penn State	2-0-0	beat West Virginia 31-20
10	4	Florida	2-0-0	beat Mississippi State 31-14
8	5	Notre Dame	1-1-0	beat Iowa 51-28
7	6	Ohio State	1-0-0	beat Oregon 21-6
6	7	Nebraska	3-0-0	bye week
5	8	Kansas	2-0-0	beat New Mexico 68-7
4	9	UCLA	2-0-0	lost to Syracuse 7-20
9	10	LSU	2-0-0	beat Baylor 48-16
11	11	Alabama	2-0-0	lost to Mississippi 8-10
15	12	Houston	1-0-1	beat Cincinnati 71-33
12	13	Miami, Fla.	2-0-0	lost to # 2 Southern Cal 3-28
16	14	Arizona State	2-0-0	lost to Wyoming 13-27
19	15	Tennessee	1-0-1	beat Rice 52-0
13	16	Georgia	1-0-1	beat South Carolina 21-20
	17	Texas A&M	1-1-0	lost to Florida State 14-20
17	18	California	2-0-0	beat San Jose State 46-0
18	19	Michigan State	2-0-0	beat Wisconsin 39-0
14	20	Arkansas	2-0-0	beat TCU 17-7
20		Mississippi	2-0-0	beat # 11 Alabama 10-8

AP October 7 Poll / Oct. 12 Games

AP	Team	Record	Oct. 12 Games
1	Purdue	3-0-0	lost to # 4 Ohio State 0-13
2	Southern Cal	3-0-0	beat # 18 Stanford 27-24
3	Penn State	3-0-0	beat UCLA 21-6
4	Ohio State	2-0-0	beat # 1 Purdue 13-0
5	Notre Dame	2-1-0	beat Northwestern 27-7
6	Kansas	3-0-0	beat # 9 Nebraska 23-13
7	Florida	3-0-0	beat Tulane 24-3
8	LSU	3-0-0	lost to Miami, Fla. 0-30
9	Nebraska	3-0-0	lost to # 6 Kansas 13-23
10	Tennessee	2-0-1	beat Georgia Tech 24-7
11	Houston	2-0-1	lost to Oklahoma State 17-21
12	Michigan State	3-0-0	lost to Michigan 14-28
13	Mississippi	3-0-0	lost to # 17 Georgia 7-21
14	Arkansas	3-0-0	beat Baylor 35-19
15	Syracuse	2-1-0	beat Pittsburgh 50-17
16	California	3-0-0	lost to Army 7-10
17	Georgia	2-0-1	beat # 13 Mississippi 21-7
18	Stanford	3-0-0	lost to # 2 Southern Cal 24-27
19	Florida State	2-1-0	bye week
20	Oregon State	2-1-0	lost to Kentucky 34-35
	Wyoming	2-2-0	beat Brigham Young 20-17

UP AP October 14 Poll / Oct. 19 Games

UP	AP	Team	Record	Oct. 19 Games
1	1	Southern Cal	4-0-0	beat Washington 14-7
2	2	Ohio State	3-0-0	beat Northwestern 45-21
3	3	Penn State	4-0-0	bye week
4	4	Kansas	4-0-0	beat Oklahoma State 49-14
5	5	Purdue	3-1-0	beat Wake Forest 28-27
6	6	Notre Dame	3-1-0	beat Illinois 58-8
7	7	Florida	4-0-0	lost to North Carolina 7-22
8	8	Tennessee	3-0-1	beat Alabama 10-9
10	9	Arkansas	4-0-0	lost to # 17 Texas 29-39
9	10	Georgia	3-0-1	beat Vanderbilt 32-6
13	11	Syracuse	3-1-0	bye week
11	12	Miami, Fla.	3-1-0	beat Virginia Tech 13-0
14	13	Nebraska	3-1-0	lost to # 20 Missouri 14-16
12	14	Stanford	3-1-0	tied Washington St. 21-21
15	15	Texas Tech	3-0-1	tied Mississippi State 28-28
	16	Mississippi	3-1-0	beat Southern Miss 21-13
	17	Texas	2-1-1	beat # 9 Arkansas 39-29
18	18	Michigan	3-1-0	beat # 19 Indiana 27-22
	19	Indiana	3-1-0	lost to # 18 Michigan 22-27
	20	LSU	3-1-0	beat Kentucky 13-3
17	20	Missouri	3-1-0	beat # 13 Nebraska 16-14
16		Houston	2-1-1	bye week
19		California	3-1-0	beat UCLA 39-15
20		Michigan State	3-1-0	lost to Minnesota 13-14
		Minnesota	2-2-0	beat Michigan State 14-13

UP AP October 21 Poll / Oct. 26 Games

UP	AP	Team	Record	Oct. 26 Games
1	1	Southern Cal	5-0-0	bye week
2	2	Ohio State	4-0-0	beat Illinois 31-24
3	3	Kansas	5-0-0	beat Iowa State 46-25
4	4	Penn State	4-0-0	beat Boston College 29-0
5	5	Notre Dame	4-1-0	lost to Michigan State 17-21
6	6	Tennessee	4-0-1	bye week
7	7	Purdue	4-1-0	beat Iowa 44-14
8	8	Georgia	4-0-1	beat Kentucky 35-14
9	9	Miami, Fla.	4-1-0	lost to Auburn 6-31
10	10	Syracuse	3-1-0	lost to California 0-43
13	11	California	4-1-0	beat Syracuse 43-0
14	12	Michigan	4-1-0	beat Minnesota 33-20
12	13	Texas	3-1-1	beat Rice 38-14
11	14	Missouri	4-1-0	beat Kansas State 56-20
19	15	Florida	4-1-0	tied Vanderbilt 14-14
14	16	Arkansas	4-1-0	beat North Texas 17-15
19	17	Mississippi	4-1-0	lost to Houston 7-29
16	18	LSU	4-1-0	beat TCU 10-7
19	19	Texas Tech	3-0-2	lost to SMU 18-39
	20	Florida State	3-1-0	beat South Carolina 35-28
17		Houston	2-1-1	beat # 17 Mississippi 29-7
17		SMU	4-1-0	beat # 19 Texas Tech 39-18
19		Oregon State	3-2-0	beat Washington State 16-8

UP AP October 28 Poll / Nov. 2 Games

UP	AP	Team	Record	Nov. 2 Games
1	1	Southern Cal	5-0-0	beat Oregon 20-13
2	2	Ohio State	5-0-0	beat # 16 Michigan State 25-20
3	3	Kansas	6-0-0	beat Colorado 27-14
4	4	Penn State	5-0-0	beat Army 28-24
5	5	Tennessee	4-0-1	beat UCLA 42-18
6	6	Purdue	5-1-0	beat Illinois 35-17
7	7	Georgia	5-0-1	tied # 15 Houston 10-10
8	8	California	5-1-0	tied Washington 7-7
10	9	Michigan	5-1-0	beat Northwestern 35-0
9	10	Missouri	5-1-0	beat Oklahoma State 42-7
11	11	Texas	4-1-1	beat # 13 SMU 38-7
15	12	Notre Dame	4-2-0	beat Navy 45-14
14	13	SMU	5-1-0	lost to # 11 Texas 7-38
12	14	LSU	5-1-0	lost to Mississippi 24-27
13	15	Houston	3-1-1	tied # 7 Georgia 10-10
19	16	Michigan State	4-2-0	lost to # 2 Ohio State 20-25
17	17	Arkansas	5-1-0	beat Texas A&M 25-22
16	18	Florida State	4-1-0	lost to Virginia Tech 22-40
	19	Ohio U.	6-0-0	beat Western Michigan 34-27
19	20	Florida	4-1-1	lost to Auburn 13-24
18		Alabama	4-2-0	beat Mississippi State 20-13
19		Oregon State	4-2-0	beat Stanford 29-7

UP AP November 4 Poll / Nov. 9 Games

UP	AP	Team	Record	Nov. 9 Games
1	1	Southern Cal	6-0-0	beat # 11 California 35-17
2	2	Ohio State	6-0-0	beat Wisconsin 43-0
3	3	Kansas	7-0-0	lost to Oklahoma 23-27
4	4	Penn State	6-0-0	beat Miami, Fla. 22-7
5	5	Tennessee	5-0-1	lost to # 18 Auburn 14-28
6	6	Purdue	6-1-0	lost to Minnesota 13-27
7	7	Michigan	6-1-0	beat Illinois 36-0
8	8	Missouri	6-1-0	beat Iowa State 42-7
10	9	Georgia	5-0-2	beat Florida 51-0
9	10	Texas	5-1-1	beat Baylor 47-26
11	11	California	5-1-1	lost to # 1 Southern Cal 17-35
12	12	Notre Dame	5-2-0	beat Pittsburgh 56-7
13	13	Houston	3-1-2	beat Memphis 27-7
15	14	Arkansas	6-1-0	beat Rice 46-21
14	15	Oregon State	5-2-0	beat UCLA 45-21
18	16	Ohio U.	7-0-0	beat Bowling Green 28-27
18	17	Michigan State	4-3-0	lost to Indiana 22-24
	18	Auburn	5-2-0	beat # 5 Tennessee 28-14
	19	Wyoming	6-2-0	bye week
	20	LSU	5-2-0	lost to Alabama 7-16
16		Yale	6-0-0	beat Pennsylvania 30-13
17		Miami, Fla.	5-2-0	lost to # 4 Penn State 7-22
18		Alabama	5-2-0	beat # 20 LSU 16-7

UP	AP	NOVEMBER 11 POLL		NOV. 16 GAMES
1	1	Southern Cal	7-0-0	beat # 13 Oregon State 17-13
2	2	Ohio State	7-0-0	beat Iowa 33-27
3	3	Penn State	7-0-0	beat Maryland 57-13
4	4	Michigan	7-1-0	beat Wisconsin 34-9
5	5	Georgia	6-0-2	beat # 12 Auburn 17-3
6	6	Missouri	7-1-0	lost to Oklahoma 14-28
7	7	Kansas	7-1-0	beat Kansas State 38-29
8	8	Texas	6-1-1	beat TCU 47-21
11	9	Notre Dame	6-2-0	beat Georgia Tech 34-6
13	10	Arkansas	7-1-0	beat SMU 35-29
10	11	Tennessee	5-1-1	beat Mississippi 31-0
9	12	Auburn	6-2-0	lost to # 5 Georgia 3-17
14	13	Oregon State	6-2-0	lost to # 1 Southern Cal 13-17
12	14	Houston	4-1-2	beat Idaho 77-3
15	15	Purdue	6-2-0	beat Michigan State 9-0
16	16	Alabama	6-2-0	beat Miami, Fla. 14-6
17	17	Ohio U.	8-0-0	beat Cincinnati 60-48
	18	California	5-2-1	beat Oregon 36-8
	19	Indiana	6-2-0	lost to Minnesota 6-20
	20	Wyoming	6-2-0	beat Texas-El Paso
18		Yale	7-0-0	beat Princeton 42-17
18		Texas Tech	5-1-2	lost to Baylor 28-42

UP	AP	NOVEMBER 18 POLL		NOV. 23 GAMES
1	1	Southern Cal	8-0-0	beat UCLA 28-16
2	2	Ohio State	8-0-0	beat # 4 Michigan 50-14
3	3	Penn State	8-0-0	beat Pittsburgh 65-9
4	4	Michigan	8-1-0	lost to # 2 Ohio State 14-50
5	5	Georgia	7-0-2	bye week
7	6	Texas	7-1-1	bye week
6	7	Kansas	8-1-0	beat # 13 Missouri 21-19
8	8	Tennessee	6-1-1	beat Kentucky 24-7
9	9	Arkansas	8-1-0	beat Texas Tech 42-7
10	10	Notre Dame	7-2-0	bye week
11	11	Houston	5-1-2	beat Tulsa 100-6
16	12	Purdue	7-2-0	beat Indiana 38-35
13	13	Missouri	7-2-0	lost to # 7 Kansas 19-21
14	14	Oklahoma	5-3-0	beat Nebraska 47-0
15	15	Alabama	7-2-0	bye week
12	16	Oregon State	6-3-0	beat Oregon 41-19
17	17	Ohio U.	9-0-0	beat No. Illinois 28-12
	18	California	6-2-1	lost to Stanford 0-20
	19	Auburn	6-3-0	bye week
	20	Wyoming	7-2-0	lost to Arizona 7-14
18		Yale	8-0-0	tied Harvard 29-29
19		SMU	6-3-0	beat Baylor 33-17
19		Minnesota	5-4-0	beat Wisconsin 23-15

UP	AP	NOVEMBER 25 POLL		NOV. 30 GAMES
2	1	Ohio State	9-0-0	regular season complete
1	2	Southern Cal	9-0-0	tied # 9 Notre Dame 21-21
3	3	Penn State	9-0-0	bye week
4	4	Georgia	7-0-2	beat Georgia Tech 47-8
5	5	Kansas	9-1-0	regular season complete
6	6	Texas	7-1-1	beat Texas A&M 35-14
7	7	Tennessee	7-1-1	beat Vanderbilt 10-7
8	8	Arkansas	9-1-0	regular season complete
9	9	Notre Dame	7-2-0	tied # 2 Southern Cal 21-21
11	10	Houston	6-1-2	lost to Florida State 20-40
10	11	Oklahoma	6-3-0	beat Oklahoma State 41-7
12	12	Purdue	8-2-0	regular season complete
13	13	Michigan	8-2-0	regular season complete
14	14	Oregon State	7-3-0	regular season complete
15	15	Alabama	7-2-0	beat Auburn 24-16
16	16	Missouri	7-3-0	regular season complete
17	17	Ohio U.	10-0-0	regular season complete
	18	Auburn	6-3-0	lost to Alabama 16-24
	19	Arizona	8-1-0	lost to # 20 Arizona State 7-30
	20	Arizona State	7-2-0	beat # 19 Arizona 30-7
18		Florida State	7-2-0	beat # 10 Houston 40-20 (N29)
19		SMU	7-3-0	regular season complete
19		Minnesota		regular season complete
19		Stanford		regular season complete

UP	AP	DECEMBER 2 POLL	RECORD	BOWL BID	DATE	BOWL RESULT
1	1	Ohio State	9-0-0	Rose Bowl	J1	beat # 2 Southern Cal 27-16
2	2	Southern Cal	9-1-0	Rose Bowl	J1	lost to # 1 Ohio State 16-27
3	3	Penn State	9-0-0	Orange Bowl	J1	beat # 6 Kansas 15-14
4	4	Georgia	8-0-2	Sugar Bowl	J1	lost to # 9 Arkansas 2-16
5	5	Texas	8-1-1	Cotton Bowl	J1	beat # 8 Tennessee 36-13
6	6	Kansas	9-1-0	Orange Bowl	J1	lost to # 3 Penn State 14-15
8	7	Notre Dame	7-2-1			
7	8	Tennessee	8-1-1	Cotton Bowl	J1	lost to #5 Texas 13-36
9	9	Arkansas	9-1-0	Sugar Bowl	J1	beat # 4 Georgia 16-2
10	10	Oklahoma	7-3-0	Bluebonnet Bowl	D31	lost to # 20 SMU 27-28
11	11	Purdue	8-2-0			
12	12	Alabama	8-2-0	Gator Bowl	D28	lost to # 16 Missouri 10-35
15	13	Michigan	8-2-0			
13	14	Oregon State	7-3-0			
18	15	Ohio U.	10-0-0	Tangerine Bowl	D27	lost to Richmond 42-49
17	16	Missouri	7-3-0	Gator Bowl	D28	beat # 12 Alabama 35-10
	17	Arizona State	8-2-0			
20	18	Houston	6-2-2			
14	19	Florida State	8-2-0			
16	20	SMU	7-3-0	Bluebonnet Bowl	D31	beat # 10 Oklahoma 28-27
18		Minnesota	6-4-0			
20		Stanford	6-3-1			

RB	AP	JANUARY 3 FINAL POLL	RECORD
1	1	Ohio State	10-0-0
2	2	Penn State	11-0-0
5	3	Texas	9-1-1
3	4	Southern Cal	9-1-1
10	5	Notre Dame	7-2-1
9	6	Arkansas	10-1-0
7	7	Kansas	9-2-0
12	8	Georgia	8-1-2
14	9	Missouri	8-3-0
11	10	Purdue	8-2-0
18	11	Oklahoma	7-4-0
16	12	Michigan	8-2-0
6	13	Tennessee	8-2-1
17	14	SMU	8-3-0
27	15	Oregon State	7-3-0
13	16	Auburn	7-4-0
15	17	Alabama	8-3-0
21	18	Houston	6-2-2
19	19	LSU	8-3-0
40	20	Ohio U.	10-1-0

1968

CONSENSUS ALL-AMERICANS

POS	OFFENSE	HT	WT	School	AP	CP	FC	FW	NE	PI
B	O.J. Simpson	6-2	205	Southern Cal	•	•	•	•	•	•
B	Leroy Keyes	6-3	205	Purdue	•	•	•	•	•	•
B	Terry Hanratty	6-1	200	Notre Dame	•	•	•		•	•
B	Chris Gilbert	5-11	176	Texas	•		•	•		•
E	Ted Kwalick	6-4	230	Penn State	•	•	•	•	•	•
E	Jerry LeVias	5-10	170	SMU		•	•	•	•	•
T	Dave Foley	6-5	246	Ohio State	•	•	•	•	•	•
T	George Kunz	6-5	240	Notre Dame	•	•	•	•	•	•
G	Charles Rosenfelder	6-1	220	Tennessee	•	•	•	•	•	•
G	Jim Barnes	6-4	227	Arkansas	•	•	•			
G	Mike Montler	6-4	235	Colorado	•	•		•		
C	John Didion	6-4	242	Oregon State	•	•	•	•	•	•

OTHERS RECEIVING FIRST-TEAM HONORS

B	Ron Johnson	Michigan	•
B	Bobby Douglass	Kansas	• •
B	Paul Gipson	Houston	• •
B	Bill Enyart	Oregon State	• •
E	Ron Sellers	Florida State	• •
E	Jim Seymour	Notre Dame	• •
T	John Shinners	Xavier	•
G	Joe Armstrong	Nebraska	•
G	Guy Dennis	Florida	•

AP named Montler as a T; NE named Keyes as a DB

POS	DEFENSE	HT	WT	School	AP	CP	FC	FW	NE	PI
E	Ted Hendricks	6-8	222	Miami, Fla.	•	•	•	•	•	•
E	John Zook	6-4	230	Kansas	•	•	•	•	•	
T	Bill Stanfill	6-5	245	Georgia	•	•	•	•	•	•
T	Joe Greene	6-4	274	North Texas	•	•	•	•	•	
MG	Ed White	6-3	245	California	•	•	•	•	•	•
MG	Chuck Kyle	6-1	225	Purdue	•	•	•	•	•	
LB	Steve Kiner	6-1	205	Tennessee	•	•	•	•		
LB	Dennis Onkotz	6-2	205	Penn State	•	•	•			
B	Jake Scott	6-1	188	Georgia	•	•	•	•	•	•
B	Roger Wehrli	6-0	184	Missouri	•	•	•	•	•	•
B	Al Worley	6-0	175	Washington	•	•	•	•		

OTHERS RECEIVING FIRST-TEAM HONORS

E	Ron Carpenter	North Carolina St.	•
T	Loyd Wainscott	Texas	• •
T	David Campbell	Auburn	•
LB	Bob Babich	Miami, Ohio	•
LB	Ken Johnson	Army	•
LB	Mike Widger	Virginia Tech	•
LB	Mike Hall	Alabama	•
LB	Chip Healy	Vanderbilt	•
LB	Ron Pritchard	Arizona State	•
LB	Dale McCullers	Florida State	•
LB	Bill Hobbs	Texas A&M	•
B	Mike Battle	Southern Cal	• •
B	Al Brenner	Michigan State	• •
B	Jim Weatherford	Tennessee	•

FC named White as a T

HEISMAN TROPHY VOTING

	PLAYER	POS	SCHOOL	1ST	2ND	3RD	TOTAL
1	O.J. Simpson	TB	Southern Cal	855	128	82	2853
2	Leroy Keyes	HB	Purdue	49	358	240	1103
3	Terry Hanratty	QB	Notre Dame	22	86	149	387
4	Ted Kwalick	TE	Penn State	14	69	74	254
5	Ted Hendricks	DE	Miami, Fla.	7	52	49	174
6	Ron Johnson	HB	Michigan	12	36	50	158
7	Bob Douglass	QB	Kansas	9	33	39	132
8	Chris Gilbert	RB	Texas	12	34	20	124
9	Brian Dowling	QB	Yale	15	25	24	119
10	Ron Sellers	WR	Florida State	7	25	20	91

AWARD WINNERS

PLAYER	POS	SCHOOL	AWARD NAME
O.J. Simpson	RB	Southern Cal	Maxwell
Bill Stanfill	T	Georgia	Outland
O.J. Simpson	RB	Southern Cal	Camp

CONFERENCE STANDINGS

ACC

	CONF. W L T	OVERALL W L T
North Carolina St.	6 1 0	6 4 0
Clemson	4 1 1	4 5 1
Virginia	3 2 0	7 3 0
South Carolina	4 3 0	4 6 0
Duke	3 4 0	4 6 0
Wake Forest	2 3 1	2 7 1
Maryland	2 5 0	2 8 0
North Carolina	1 6 0	3 7 0

Big 10

	CONF. W L T	OVERALL W L T
Ohio State	7 0 0	10 0 0
Michigan	6 1 0	8 2 0
Purdue	5 2 0	8 2 0
Minnesota	5 2 0	6 4 0
Indiana	4 3 0	6 4 0
Iowa	4 3 0	5 5 0
Michigan State	2 5 0	5 5 0
Illinois	1 6 0	1 9 0
Northwestern	1 6 0	1 9 0
Wisconsin	0 7 0	0 10 0

Big 8

	CONF. W L T	OVERALL W L T
Kansas	6 1 0	9 2 0
Oklahoma	6 1 0	7 4 0
Missouri	5 2 0	8 3 0
Nebraska	3 4 0	6 4 0
Colorado	3 4 0	4 6 0
Kansas State	2 5 0	4 6 0
Oklahoma State	2 5 0	3 7 0
Iowa State	1 6 0	3 7 0

Ivy

	CONF. W L T	OVERALL W L T
Yale	6 0 1	8 0 1
Harvard	6 0 1	8 0 1
Pennsylvania	5 2 0	7 2 0
Princeton	4 3 0	4 5 0
Dartmouth	3 4 0	4 5 0
Columbia	2 5 0	2 7 0
Cornell	1 6 0	3 6 0
Brown	0 7 0	2 7 0

MAC

	CONF. W L T	OVERALL W L T
Ohio U.	6 0 0	10 1 0
Miami, Ohio	5 1 0	7 3 0
Bowling Green	3 2 1	6 3 1
Toledo	3 2 1	5 4 1
Western Michigan	2 4 0	3 6 0
Kent State	1 5 0	1 9 0
Marshall	0 6 0	0 9 1

Pac 8

	CONF. W L T	OVERALL W L T
Southern Cal	6 0 0	9 1 1
Oregon State	5 1 0	7 3 0
Stanford	3 3 1	6 3 1
California	2 2 1	7 3 1
Oregon	2 4 0	4 6 0
UCLA	2 4 0	3 7 0
Washington State	1 3 1	3 6 1
Washington	1 5 1	3 5 2

SEC

	CONF. W L T	OVERALL W L T
Georgia	5 0 1	8 1 2
Tennessee	4 1 1	8 2 1
Alabama	4 2 0	8 3 0
LSU	4 2 0	8 3 0
Auburn	4 2 0	7 4 0
Mississippi	3 2 1	7 3 1
Florida	3 2 1	6 3 1
Vanderbilt	2 3 1	5 4 1
Mississippi State	1 4 1	0 8 2
Kentucky	0 7 0	3 7 0

SWC

	CONF. W L T	OVERALL W L T
Arkansas	6 1 0	10 1 0
Texas	6 1 0	9 1 1
SMU	5 2 0	8 3 0
Texas Tech	4 3 0	5 3 2
Baylor	3 4 0	3 7 0
Texas A&M	2 5 0	3 7 0
TCU	2 5 0	3 7 0
Rice	0 7 0	0 9 1

WAC

	CONF. W L T	OVERALL W L T
Wyoming	6 1 0	7 3 0
Arizona State	5 1 0	8 2 0
Arizona	5 1 0	8 3 0
Texas-El Paso	3 3 0	4 5 1
Utah	2 3 0	3 7 0
Colorado State	1 4 0	2 8 0
Brigham Young	1 5 0	2 8 0
New Mexico	0 7 0	0 10 0

Independents

	OVERALL W L T
Penn State	11 0 0
Rutgers	8 2 0
Notre Dame	7 2 1
Florida State	8 3 0
Utah State	7 3 0
Air Force	7 3 0
Army	7 3 0
Houston	6 2 2
Boston College	6 3 0
Virginia Tech	7 4 0
Syracuse	6 4 0
New Mexico State	5 5 0
Miami, Fla.	5 5 0
Georgia Tech	4 6 0
Navy	2 8 0
Tulane	2 8 0
Pittsburgh	1 9 0

BOWL GAMES

DATE	GAME	SCORE
D7	Pasadena	Grambling 34, Cal St. Sacramento 7
D14	Liberty	Mississippi 34, Virginia Tech 17
D27	Tangerine	Richmond 49, Ohio 42
D28	Sun	Auburn 34, Arizona 10
D28	Gator	Missouri 35, Alabama 10
D30	Peach	LSU 31, Florida State 27
D31	Bluebonnet	SMU 28, Oklahoma 27
J1	Sugar	Arkansas 16, Georgia 2
J1	Rose	Ohio State 27, Southern Cal 16
J1	Orange	Penn State 15, Kansas 14
J1	Cotton	Texas 36, Tennessee 13

1968 ANNUAL REVIEW 1287

1968 NCAA Major College Statistical Leaders

Individual Leaders

PASSING/COMPLETIONS	G	ATT	COM	PCT	INT	I%	YDS	YPA	TD	TD%	COM.PG
1 Chuck Hixson, SMU	10	468	265	56.6	23	4.9	3103	6.6	21	4.5	26.5
2 Greg Cook, Cincinnati	10	411	219	53.3	17	4.1	3272	8.0	25	6.1	21.9
3 Gordon Slade, Davidson	9	322	190	59.0	13	4.0	2109	6.5	14	4.4	21.1
4 Marty Domres, Columbia	9	344	183	53.2	15	4.4	2206	6.4	11	3.2	20.3
5 Steve Ramsey, North Texas	10	332	177	53.3	17	5.1	2516	7.6	24	7.2	17.7
6 Tommy Pharr, Mississippi State	10	319	173	54.2	18	5.6	1838	5.8	9	2.8	17.3
7 Edd Hargett, Texas A&M	10	348	169	48.6	14	4.0	2321	6.7	16	4.6	16.9
8 Mike Stripling, Tulsa	10	347	164	47.3	15	4.3	1968	5.7	8	2.3	16.4
9 Bill Cappleman, Florida State	10	287	162	56.4	11	3.8	2410	8.4	25	8.7	16.2
9 Leo Hart, Duke	10	301	162	53.8	11	3.7	2238	7.4	11	3.7	16.2

ALL-PURPOSE YARDS	G	RUSH	REC	PR	KR	YDS	YPG
1 O.J. Simpson, Southern Cal	10	1709	126	0	131	1966	196.6

RUSHING/YARDS	G	ATT	YDS	TD	AVG	YPG
1 O.J. Simpson, Southern Cal	10	355	1709	22	4.8	170.9
2 Eugene Morris, West Texas State	10	262	1571	17	6.0	157.1
3 Paul Gipson, Houston	10	242	1550	13	6.4	155.0
4 Steve Owens, Oklahoma	10	357	1536	21	4.3	153.6
5 Art Malone, Arizona State	10	235	1431	15	6.1	143.1
6 Ron Johnson, Michigan	10	255	1391	19	5.5	139.1
7 Bill Enyart, Oregon State	10	293	1304	17	4.5	130.4
8 Ron Poe James, New Mexico State	10	225	1291	12	5.7	129.1
9 Frank Quayle, Virginia	10	175	1213	12	6.9	121.3
10 Bryant Mitchell, Rutgers	10	238	1204	9	5.1	120.4

RUSHING/YARDS PER CARRY	G	ATT	YDS	YPC
1 Frank Quayle, Virginia	10	175	1213	6.9
2 Paul Gipson, Houston	10	242	1550	6.4
3 John Riggins, Kansas	10	140	866	6.2
4 Chris Gilbert, Texas	10	184	1132	6.2
5 Art Malone, Arizona State	10	235	1431	6.1
6 Ed Podolak, Iowa	10	154	937	6.1
7 Eugene Morris, West Texas State	10	262	1571	6.0
8 Ron Poe James, New Mexico State	10	225	1291	5.7
9 Ron Johnson, Michigan	10	255	1391	5.5
10 Charley Jarvis, Army	10	208	1110	5.3

*-Based on top 32 rushers

RECEIVING/RECEPTIONS	G	REC	YDS	TD	YPR	YPG	RPG
1 Ron Sellers, Florida State	10	86	1496	12	17.4	149.6	8.6
2 Jerry Levias, SMU	10	80	1131	8	14.1	113.1	8.0
2 Tom Rossley, Cincinnati	10	80	1072	4	13.4	107.2	8.0
4 Gene Washington, Stanford	10	71	1117	8	15.7	111.7	7.1
5 Barry Moore, North Texas	10	69	1053	7	15.3	105.3	6.9
6 Harry Wood, Tulsa	10	65	988	5	15.2	98.8	6.5
6 Henley Carter, Duke	10	65	892	2	13.7	89.2	6.5
8 Sammy Milner, Mississippi State	10	64	909	5	14.2	90.9	6.4
9 Mike Kelly, Davidson	9	63	936	11	14.9	104.0	7.0
10 John Sias, Georgia Tech	10	61	902	4	14.8	90.2	6.1

PUNTING	PUNT	YDS	AVG
1 Danny Pitcock, Wichita State	71	3067	43.2
2 Benny Rhoads, Cincinnati	45	1913	42.5
3 Bob Coble, Kansas State	77	3249	42.2
4 Zenon Andrusyshyn, UCLA	55	2316	42.1
5 Bob Jacobs, Wyoming	72	3031	42.1
6 Ken Sanders, Tulane	63	2640	41.9
7 Bill Bell, Kansas	41	1714	41.8
8 Roy Gerela, New Mexico State	57	2371	41.6
9 Julian Fagan, Mississippi	75	3120	41.6
10 Mike Hall, TCU	51	2117	41.5

PUNT RETURNS/YARDS	PR	YDS	TD	AVG
1 Roger Wehrli, Missouri	41	478	0	11.7
2 Jake Scott, Georgia	35	440	1	12.6
2 Lenny Randle, Arizona State	37	440	2	11.9
4 George Burrell, Pennsylvania	33	436	1	13.2
5 Larry Alford, Texas Tech	38	430	1	11.3
6 Curley Watters, West Texas State	21	368	2	17.5
7 Doug Mathews, Vanderbilt	30	354	2	11.8
8 Mark Williams, Washington State	20	333	3	16.7
9 Bob Zimpfer, Bowling Green	24	332	1	13.8
10 Kerr Kump, VMI	32	327	1	10.2

KICKOFF RETURNS/YARDS	KR	YDS	TD	AVG
1 Mike Adamle, Northwestern	34	732	0	21.5
2 Bobby Hall, North Carolina St.	29	721	0	24.9
3 J.D. Lewis, Pittsburgh	31	650	0	21.0
4 Jeff Allen, Iowa State	23	599	0	26.0
5 David Smith, Mississippi State	27	590	0	21.9
6 Mack Herron, Kansas State	21	583	2	27.8
7 Frank Slaton, San Jose State	24	578	0	24.1
8 Ed Hicklin, Duke	27	555	0	20.6
9 Don McCauley, North Carolina	25	553	0	22.1
10 Bill Carey, Columbia	27	528	0	19.6

SCORING	TDS	XPT	FG	PTS
1 Jim O'Brien, Cincinnati	12	31	13	142
2 O.J. Simpson, Southern Cal	22	0	0	132
3 Steve Owens, Oklahoma	21	0	0	126
4 Ron Johnson, Michigan	19	2	0	116
5 Bob Houmard, Ohio U.	19	0	0	114
5 Eugene Morris, West Texas State	19	0	0	114
7 Bill Enyart, Oregon State	17	0	0	102
8 Dave Bennett, Boston College	16	0	0	96
8 James Otis, Ohio State	16	0	0	96
8 Bill Burnett, Arkansas	16	0	0	96
8 Art Malone, Arizona State	16	0	0	96

KICK SCORING	XPA	XP	FGA	FG	PTS
1 Paul Ray Powell, Arizona State	55	47	15	10	77
2 Jim O'Brien, Cincinnati	34	31	25	13	70
3 Bob Jacobs, Wyoming	29	26	28	14	68
4 Clarence Redic, West Texas State	35	34	28	11	67
5 Ardie Jensen, Army	32	31	18	11	64
6 John Riley, Auburn	26	25	26	12	61
6 Terry Leiweke, Houston	57	52	11	3	61
8 Scott Hempel, Notre Dame	51	45	9	5	60
8 Bill Bell, Kansas	53	45	9	5	60
10 Kenneth Crots, Toledo	29	29	17	9	56

INTERCEPTIONS	INT	YDS	TD
1 Al Worley, Washington	14	130	1
2 Jerry Todd, Memphis	11	79	0
3 Tom Curtis, Michigan	10	182	0
3 Jake Scott, Georgia	10	175	2
3 Paul Shires, Houston	10	45	0
6 John Pollock, Rutgers	9	180	1
6 Bill Young, Tennessee	9	53	0
8 Jim McCall, Army	8	137	1
8 Rick Reed, Washington State	8	137	0
8 Jimmy Livingston, SMU	8	104	0
8 John Salmon, Boston College	8	83	0
8 Rich Moriarty, Arizona	8	75	0
8 Neal Smith, Penn State	8	74	0

Team Leaders

RUSHING OFFENSE	G	ATT	YDS	AVG	TD	YPG
1 Houston	10	633	3617	5.7	36	361.7
2 Texas	10	642	3315	5.2	37	331.5
3 Ohio State	9	589	2758	4.7	33	306.4
4 Notre Dame	10	657	3059	4.7	38	305.9
5 Kansas	10	594	2999	5.0	33	299.9
6 Princeton	9	580	2653	4.6	26	294.8
7 Arizona State	10	625	2903	4.6	37	290.3
8 West Texas State	10	570	2878	5.0	26	287.8
9 Virginia	10	573	2800	4.9	27	280.0
10 Penn State	10	614	2739	4.5	33	273.9

PASSING OFFENSE	G	ATT	COM	INT	PCT	YDS	YPA	TD	I%	YPC	YPG
1 Cincinnati	10	433	226	22	52.2	3358	7.8	25	5.1	14.9	335.8
2 SMU	10	485	270	24	55.7	3130	6.5	21	5.0	11.6	313.0
3 Texas-El Paso	10	455	199	21	43.7	2884	6.3	20	4.6	14.5	288.4
4 Florida State	10	356	195	13	54.8	2844	8.0	29	3.7	14.6	284.4
5 Duke	10	346	186	14	53.8	2653	7.7	11	4.1	14.3	265.3
6 North Texas	10	357	180	19	50.4	2546	7.1	25	5.3	14.1	254.6
7 Stanford	10	297	157	18	52.9	2516	8.5	18	6.1	16.0	251.6
8 Tulsa	10	435	213	19	49.0	2515	5.8	12	4.4	11.8	251.5
9 Columbia	9	351	186	15	53.0	2246	6.4	12	4.3	12.1	249.6
10 Davidson	9	327	192	14	58.7	2139	6.5	14	4.3	11.1	237.7

TOTAL OFFENSE	G	P	YDS	AVG	TD	YPG
1 Houston	10	846	5620	6.6	55	562.0
2 Notre Dame	10	909	5044	5.5	51	504.4
3 Boston College	9	739	4161	5.6	34	462.3
4 Yale	9	756	4107	5.4	45	456.3
5 Ohio State	9	762	4041	5.3	41	449.0
6 Texas	10	796	4476	5.6	43	447.6
7 Arizona State	10	848	4473	5.3	50	447.3
8 Cincinnati	10	801	4421	5.5	37	442.1
9 Kansas	10	777	4420	5.7	47	442.0
10 Iowa	10	759	4404	5.8	45	440.4

RUSHING DEFENSE	G	ATT	YDS	AVG	TD	YPG
1 Arizona State	10	403	570	1.4	10	57.0
2 Miami, Ohio	10	359	775	2.2	5	77.5
3 Wyoming	10	458	782	1.7	6	78.2
4 Notre Dame	10	358	793	2.2	11	79.3
5 Southern Miss	10	347	815	2.3	12	81.5
6 Penn State	10	404	831	2.1	6	83.1
7 Alabama	10	401	849	2.1	7	84.9
8 Auburn	10	410	878	2.1	9	87.8
9 Tennessee	10	371	933	2.5	6	93.3
10 Houston	10	413	947	2.3	13	94.7

PASSING DEFENSE	G	ATT	COM	PCT	YPC	INT	I%	YDS	YPA	TD	YPG
1 Kent State	10	183	75	41.0	14.3	10	5.5	1076	5.9	9	107.6
2 Toledo	10	249	106	42.6	10.8	17	6.8	1141	4.6	8	114.1
3 Western Michigan	9	200	80	40.0	12.9	20	10.0	1034	5.2	3	114.9
4 Davidson	9	137	71	51.8	14.7	10	7.3	1045	7.6	8	116.1
5 Missouri	10	185	74	40.0	15.8	17	9.2	1169	6.3	7	116.9
6 Harvard	9	196	96	49.0	11.1	17	8.7	1064	5.4	4	118.2
7 West Virginia	10	203	91	44.8	13.4	14	6.9	1215	6.0	4	121.5
8 Nebraska	10	251	107	42.6	11.5	8	3.2	1230	4.9	2	123.0
9 Bowling Green	10	239	110	46.0	11.4	20	8.4	1250	5.2	7	125.0
10 Xavier	10	225	102	45.3	12.4	16	7.1	1269	5.6	9	126.9

TOTAL DEFENSE	G	P	YDS	AVG	TD	YPG
1 Wyoming	10	732	2068	2.8	14	206.8
2 Miami, Ohio	10	632	2324	3.7	13	232.4
3 Georgia	10	650	2351	3.6	9	235.1
4 Syracuse	10	705	2354	3.3	18	235.4
5 Alabama	10	682	2387	3.5	13	238.7
6 Arizona State	10	734	2396	3.3	21	239.6
7 Arizona	10	749	2406	3.2	14	240.6
8 Missouri	10	683	2411	3.5	16	241.1
9 Bowling Green	10	675	2452	3.6	19	245.2
10 Notre Dame	10	644	2490	3.9	23	249.0

SCORING OFFENSE	G	PTS	AVG
1 Houston	10	425	42.5
2 Arizona State	10	414	41.4
3 Kansas	10	380	38.0
4 Notre Dame	10	376	37.6
4 Ohio U.	10	376	37.6
6 Yale	9	317	35.2
7 Texas	10	343	34.3
8 Penn State	10	339	33.9
9 Arkansas	10	334	33.4
10 Ohio State	9	296	32.9

SCORING DEFENSE	G	PTS	AVG
1 Georgia	10	98	9.8
2 Miami (Ohio)	10	99	9.9
3 Harvard	9	90	10.0
4 California	11	114	10.4
5 Alabama	10	104	10.4
6 Penn State	10	106	10.6
7 Tennessee	10	110	11.0
8 Arizona	10	115	11.5
9 Wyoming	10	118	11.8
10 Missouri	10	126	12.6

ANNUAL REVIEW

1969 POLL PROGRESSION

PRE-SEASON — SEPT. 20 GAMES

AP	Team	Record	Result
1	Ohio State	0-0-0	bye week
2	Arkansas	0-0-0	beat Oklahoma State 39-0
3	Penn State	0-0-0	beat Navy 45-22
4	Texas	0-0-0	beat California 17-0
5	Southern Cal	0-0-0	beat Nebraska 31-21
6	Oklahoma	0-0-0	beat Wisconsin 48-21
7	Houston	0-0-0	lost to Florida 34-59
8	Georgia	0-0-0	beat Tulane 35-0
9	Mississippi	0-0-0	beat Memphis 28-3
10	Missouri	0-0-0	beat Air Force 19-17
11	Notre Dame	0-0-0	beat Northwestern 35-10
12	Michigan State	0-0-0	beat Washington 27-11
13	Alabama	0-0-0	beat Virginia Tech 17-13
14	Indiana	0-0-0	beat Kentucky 58-30
15	Tennessee	0-0-0	beat U.T. Chattanooga 31-0
16	Stanford	0-0-0	beat San Jose State 63-21
17	UCLA	0-0-0	beat Pittsburgh 42-8
18	Purdue	0-0-0	beat TCU 42-35
19	Minnesota	0-0-0	lost to Arizona State 26-48
20	Auburn	0-0-0	beat Wake Forest 57-0

SEPTEMBER 22 POLL — SEPT. 27 GAMES

UP	AP	Team	Record	Result
1	1	Ohio State	0-0-0	beat TCU 62-0
2	2	Penn State	1-0-0	beat Colorado 27-3
4	3	Arkansas	1-0-0	beat Tulsa 55-0
3	4	Texas	1-0-0	beat Texas Tech 49-7
5	5	Southern Cal	1-0-0	beat Northwestern 48-6
6	6	Oklahoma	1-0-0	beat Pittsburgh 37-8
7	7	Georgia	1-0-0	beat Clemson 30-0
13	8	Mississippi	1-0-0	lost to Kentucky 9-10
8	9	Notre Dame	1-0-0	lost to # 16 Purdue 14-28
11	10	Indiana	1-0-0	lost to California 14-17
12	11	Missouri	1-0-0	beat Illinois 37-6
10	12	Florida	1-0-0	beat Mississippi State 47-35
15	13	Michigan State	1-0-0	beat SMU 23-15
9	14	UCLA	2-0-0	beat Wisconsin 34-23
	15	Alabama	1-0-0	beat Southern Miss 63-14
14	16	Purdue	1-0-0	beat # 9 Notre Dame 28-14
17	17	Auburn	1-0-0	lost to # 19 Tennessee 19-45
18	18	Arizona State	1-0-0	lost to Oregon State 7-30
19		Tennessee	1-0-0	beat # 17 Auburn 45-19
20		Michigan	1-0-0	beat Washington 45-7
16		Stanford		beat Oregon 28-0
19		LSU	1-0-0	beat Rice 42-0
20		Wyoming	1-0-0	beat Air Force 27-25

SEPTEMBER 29 POLL — OCT. 4 GAMES

UP	AP	Team	Record	Result
1	1	Ohio State	1-0-0	beat Washington 41-14
2	2	Penn State	2-0-0	beat Kansas State 17-14
3	3	Arkansas	2-0-0	beat TCU 24-6
4	4	Texas	2-0-0	beat Navy 56-17
5	5	Southern Cal	2-0-0	beat Oregon State 31-7
6	6	Oklahoma	2-0-0	bye week
7	7	Georgia	2-0-0	beat South Carolina 41-16
8	8	Purdue	2-0-0	beat # 17 Stanford 36-35
9	9	Missouri	2-0-0	beat # 13 Michigan 40-17
12	10	Tennessee	2-0-0	beat Memphis 55-16
10	11	UCLA	3-0-0	beat Northwestern 36-0
14	12	Florida	2-0-0	beat Florida State 21-6
11	13	Michigan	2-0-0	lost to # 9 Missouri 17-40
13	14	Michigan State	2-0-0	lost to Notre Dame 28-42
17	15	Alabama	2-0-0	beat # 20 Mississippi 33-32
15	16	LSU	2-0-0	beat Baylor 63-8
16	17	Stanford	2-0-0	lost to # 8 Purdue 35-36
	18	West Virginia	3-0-0	beat VMI 32-0
18	19	Wyoming	2-0-0	beat Colorado State 39-3
	20	Mississippi	1-1-0	lost to # 15 Alabama 32-33
19		Kansas State	2-0-0	lost to # 2 Penn State 14-17
20		Florida State	2-0-0	lost to # 12 Florida 6-21

OCTOBER 6 POLL — OCT. 11 GAMES

UP	AP	Team	Record	Result
1	1	Ohio State	2-0-0	beat # 19 Michigan State 54-21
2	2	Texas	3-0-0	beat # 8 Oklahoma 27-17
5	3	Arkansas	3-0-0	beat Baylor 21-7
3	4	Southern Cal	3-0-0	beat # 16 Stanford 26-24
4	5	Penn State	3-0-0	beat # 17 West Virginia 20-0
7	6	Georgia	3-0-0	lost to Mississippi 17-25
6	7	Missouri	3-0-0	beat # 20 Nebraska 17-7
8	8	Oklahoma	2-0-0	lost to # 2 Texas 17-27
9	9	Purdue	3-0-0	lost to Michigan 20-31
11	10	Tennessee	3-0-0	beat Georgia Tech 26-8
10	11	UCLA	4-0-0	beat Washington State 46-14
12	12	Florida	3-0-0	beat Tulane 18-17
15	13	Alabama	3-0-0	lost to Vanderbilt 10-14
13	14	LSU	3-0-0	beat Miami, Fla. 20-0
14	15	Notre Dame	2-1-0	beat Army 45-0
	16	Stanford	2-1-0	lost to # 4 Southern Cal 24-26
	17	West Virginia	4-0-0	lost to # 5 Penn State 0-20
16	18	Wyoming	3-0-0	beat Texas-El Paso 37-9
	19	Michigan State	2-1-0	lost to # 1 Ohio State 21-54
	20	Auburn	2-1-0	beat Clemson 51-0
20		Nebraska	2-1-0	lost to # 7 Missouri 7-17

OCTOBER 13 POLL — OCT. 18 GAMES

UP	AP	Team	Record	Result
1	1	Ohio State	3-0-0	beat Minnesota 34-7
2	2	Texas	4-0-0	bye week
3	3	Southern Cal	4-0-0	tied # 11 Notre Dame 14-14
6	4	Arkansas	4-0-0	bye week
4	5	Penn State	4-0-0	beat Syracuse 15-14
5	6	Missouri	4-0-0	beat Oklahoma State 31-21
7	7	Tennessee	4-0-0	beat # 20 Alabama 41-14
8	8	UCLA	5-0-0	beat California 32-0
9	9	LSU	4-0-0	beat Kentucky 37-10
13	10	Florida	4-0-0	beat North Carolina 52-2
10	11	Notre Dame	3-1-0	tied # 3 Southern Cal 14-14
11	12	Oklahoma	2-1-0	beat Colorado 42-30
14	13	Michigan	3-1-0	lost to Michigan State 12-23
14	14	Georgia	3-1-0	beat Vanderbilt 40-8
15	15	Auburn	3-1-0	beat Georgia Tech 17-14
12	16	Wyoming	4-0-0	beat Brigham Young 40-7
19	17	Purdue	3-1-0	beat Iowa 35-31
18	18	Stanford	2-2-0	beat Washington State 49-0
19	19	Mississippi	2-2-0	beat Southern Miss 69-7
	20	Alabama	3-1-0	lost to # 7 Tennessee 14-41
16		Kansas State	3-1-0	beat Iowa State 34-7
17		California	3-1-0	lost to # 8 UCLA 0-32
19		Colorado	3-1-0	lost to # 12 Oklahoma 30-42

OCTOBER 20 POLL — OCT. 25 GAMES

UP	AP	Team	Record	Result
1	1	Ohio State	4-0-0	beat Illinois 41-0
2	2	Texas	4-0-0	beat Rice 31-0
3	3	Tennessee	5-0-0	bye week
4	4	Arkansas	4-0-0	beat Wichita State 52-14
7	5	Missouri	5-0-0	lost to Colorado 24-31
5	6	UCLA	6-0-0	tied # 19 Stanford 20-20
8	7	Southern Cal	4-0-1	beat Georgia Tech 29-18
6	8	Penn State	5-0-0	beat Ohio U. 42-3
8	9	LSU	5-0-0	beat # 14 Auburn 21-20
10	10	Florida	5-0-0	beat Vanderbilt 41-20
11	11	Oklahoma	3-1-0	lost to Kansas State 21-59
12	12	Notre Dame	3-1-1	beat Tulane 37-0
16	13	Georgia	4-1-0	beat Kentucky 30-0
18	14	Auburn	4-1-0	lost to # 9 LSU 20-21
15	15	Purdue	4-1-0	beat Northwestern 45-20
12	16	Wyoming	5-0-0	beat San Jose State 16-7
	17	Mississippi	3-2-0	lost to Houston 11-25
17	18	Kansas State	4-1-0	beat Oklahoma 59-21
14	19	Stanford	3-2-0	tied # 6 UCLA 20-20
	20	Air Force	3-2-0	beat Colorado State 28-7

OCTOBER 27 POLL — NOV. 1 GAMES

UP	AP	Team	Record	Result
1	1	Ohio State	5-0-0	beat Northwestern 35-6
2	2	Texas	5-0-0	beat SMU 45-14
3	3	Tennessee	5-0-0	beat # 11 Georgia 17-3
4	4	Arkansas	5-0-0	beat Texas A&M 35-13
5	5	Penn State	6-0-0	beat Boston College 38-16
7	6	Southern Cal	5-0-1	beat California 14-9
9	7	Florida	6-0-0	lost to # 17 Auburn 12-38
6	8	LSU	6-0-0	lost to Mississippi 23-26
8	9	UCLA	6-0-1	beat Washington 57-14
12	10	Notre Dame	4-1-1	beat Navy 47-0
11	11	Georgia	5-1-0	lost to # 3 Tennessee 3-17
10	12	Kansas State	5-1-0	lost to # 14 Missouri 38-41
15	13	Purdue	5-1-0	beat Illinois 49-22
14	14	Missouri	5-1-0	beat # 12 Kansas State 41-38
13	15	Wyoming	6-0-0	lost to Arizona State 14-30
16	16	Stanford	3-2-1	beat Oregon State 33-0
	17	Auburn	4-2-0	beat # 7 Florida 38-12
17	18	Colorado	4-2-0	lost to Nebraska 7-20
	19	Air Force	4-2-0	beat Navy 13-6
	20	Michigan	4-2-0	beat Wisconsin 35-7
17		Oklahoma	3-2-0	beat Iowa State 37-14

NOVEMBER 3 POLL — NOV. 8 GAMES

UP	AP	Team	Record	Result
1	1	Ohio State	6-0-0	beat Wisconsin 62-7
2	2	Texas	6-0-0	beat Baylor 56-14
3	3	Tennessee	6-0-0	beat South Carolina 29-14
6	4	Arkansas	6-0-0	beat Rice 30-6
4	5	Penn State	7-0-0	bye week
5	6	Southern Cal	6-0-1	beat Washington State 28-7
7	7	UCLA	7-0-1	bye week
10	8	Notre Dame	5-1-1	beat Pittsburgh 49-7
8	9	Missouri	6-1-0	beat # 20 Oklahoma 44-10
9	10	Purdue	6-1-0	beat Michigan State 41-13
18	11	Auburn	5-2-0	beat Mississippi State 52-13
11	12	LSU	6-1-0	beat Alabama 20-15
	13	Florida	6-1-0	tied # 16 Georgia 13-13
12	14	Stanford	4-2-1	beat Washington 21-7
	15	Kansas State	5-2-0	lost to Oklahoma State 19-28
15	16	Georgia	5-2-0	tied # 13 Florida 13-13
16	17	Mississippi	4-3-0	beat U.T. Chattanooga 21-0
13	18	Michigan	5-2-0	beat Illinois 57-0
	19	Air Force	5-2-0	beat Utah State 38-13
	20	Nebraska	5-2-0	beat Iowa State 17-3
	20	Arizona State	4-2-0	lost to # 9 Missouri 10-44
14		Houston	4-2-0	beat Tulsa 47-14
16		Wyoming	6-1-0	lost to Utah 10-34
18		Utah	6-1-0	beat Wyoming 34-10

NOVEMBER 10 POLL — NOV. 15 GAMES

UP	AP	Team	Record	Result
1	1	Ohio State	7-0-0	beat # 10 Purdue 42-14
2	2	Texas	7-0-0	beat TCU 69-7
3	3	Tennessee	7-0-0	lost to # 18 Mississippi 0-38
5	4	Arkansas	7-0-0	beat SMU 28-15
4	5	Penn State	7-0-0	beat Maryland 48-0
6	6	Southern Cal	7-0-1	beat Washington 16-7
7	7	UCLA	7-0-1	beat Oregon 13-10
8	8	Missouri	7-1-0	beat Iowa State 40-13
11	9	Notre Dame	6-1-1	beat Georgia Tech 38-20
9	10	Purdue	7-1-0	lost to # 1 Ohio State 14-42
13	11	Auburn	6-2-0	beat # 16 Georgia 16-3
10	12	LSU	7-1-0	beat Mississippi State 61-6
12	13	Stanford	5-2-1	beat # 20 Air Force 47-34
15	14	Michigan	6-2-0	beat Iowa 51-6
	15	Florida	6-1-1	beat Kentucky 31-6
	16	Georgia	5-2-1	lost to # 11 Auburn 3-16
	17	Nebraska	6-2-0	beat Kansas State 10-7
13	18	Houston	6-2-0	beat Wyoming 41-14
	18	Mississippi	5-3-0	beat # 3 Tennessee 38-0
	20	Air Force	6-2-0	lost to # 13 Stanford 34-47
16		Utah	7-1-0	lost to Arizona 16-17

UP	AP	NOVEMBER 17 POLL		NOV. 22 GAMES
1	1	Ohio State	8-0-0	lost to # 12 Michigan 12-24
2	2	Texas	8-0-0	bye week
4	3	Arkansas	8-0-0	bye week
3	4	Penn State	8-0-0	beat Pittsburgh 27-7
5	5	Southern Cal	8-0-1	beat # 6 UCLA 14-12
7	6	UCLA	8-0-1	lost to # 5 Southern Cal 12-14
6	7	Missouri	8-1-0	beat Kansas 69-21
9	8	Notre Dame	7-1-1	beat Air Force 13-6
10	9	Tennessee	7-1-0	beat Kentucky 31-26
8	10	LSU	8-1-0	beat Tulane 27-0
11	11	Auburn	7-2-0	bye week
12	12	Michigan	7-2-0	beat # 1 Ohio State 24-12
13	13	Mississippi	6-3-0	bye week
14	14	Stanford	6-2-1	beat California 29-28
16	15	Florida	7-1-1	bye week
19	16	Nebraska	7-2-0	beat Oklahoma 44-14
16	17	Purdue	7-2-0	beat Indiana 44-21
	18	West Virginia	8-1-0	beat Syracuse 13-10
15	19	Houston	7-2-0	beat Florida State 41-13
	20	Toledo	9-0	beat Xavier 35-0
18		Georgia	5-3-1	bye week

UP	AP	NOVEMBER 24 POLL		NOV. 29 GAMES
1	1	Texas	8-0-0	beat Texas A&M 49-12
3	2	Arkansas	8-0-0	beat Texas Tech 33-0
2	3	Penn State	9-0-0	beat North Carolina St. 33-8
6	4	Ohio State	8-1-0	regular season complete
4	5	Southern Cal	9-0-1	regular season complete
5	6	Missouri	9-1-0	regular season complete
8	7	Michigan	8-2-0	regular season complete
9	8	Notre Dame	8-1-1	regular season complete
7	9	LSU	9-1-0	regular season complete
11	10	Tennessee	8-1-0	beat Vanderbilt 40-27
10	11	UCLA	8-1-1	regular season complete
15	12	Auburn	7-2-0	beat Alabama 49-26
12	13	Nebraska	8-2-0	regular season complete
14	14	Mississippi	6-3-0	beat Mississippi State 48-22
13	15	Stanford	7-2-1	regular season complete
18	16	Purdue	8-2-0	regular season complete
	17	Florida	7-1-1	beat Miami, Fla. 35-16
16	18	Houston	8-2-0	regular season complete
17	19	West Virginia	9-1-0	regular season complete
	20	Toledo	10-0	regular season complete
18		Arizona State	7-2-0	beat Arizona 38-24
18		San Diego State	9-0-0	beat Long Beach State 36-32

UP	AP	DECEMBER 1 POLL		DEC. 6 GAMES
1	1	Texas	9-0-0	beat # 2 Arkansas 15-14
3	2	Arkansas	9-0-0	lost to # 1 Texas 14-15
2	3	Penn State	10-0-0	regular season complete
5	4	Ohio State	8-1-0	
4	5	Southern Cal	9-0-1	
6	6	Missouri	9-1-0	
8	7	Michigan	8-2-0	
7	8	LSU	9-1-0	
9	9	Notre Dame	8-1-1	
10	10	UCLA	8-1-1	
12	11	Auburn	8-2-0	regular season complete
11	12	Tennessee	9-1-0	regular season complete
12	13	Nebraska	8-2-0	
15	14	Mississippi	7-3-0	regular season complete
19	15	Purdue	8-2-0	
18	16	West Virginia	9-1-0	
14	17	Stanford	7-2-1	
17	18	Florida	8-1-1	regular season complete
16	19	Houston	8-2-0	
	20	Toledo	10-0	
19		San Diego State	10-0-0	See Bowl Games

UP	AP	DECEMBER 8 POLL	RECORD	BOWL BID	DATE	BOWL RESULT	RB	UP	AP	JANUARY 2 FINAL POLL	RECORD
1	1	Texas	10-0-0	Cotton Bowl	J1	beat # 9 Notre Dame 21-17	1	1	1	Texas	11-0-0
2	2	Penn State	10-0-0	Orange Bowl	J1	beat # 6 Missouri 10-3	2	2	2	Penn State	11-0-0
3	3	Arkansas	9-1-0	Sugar Bowl	J1	lost to # 13 Mississippi 22-27	3	4	3	Southern Cal	10-0-1
5	4	Ohio State	8-1-0				4	5	4	Ohio State	8-1-0
4	5	Southern Cal	9-0-1	Rose Bowl	J1	beat # 7 Michigan 10-3	10	9	5	Notre Dame	8-2-1
6	6	Missouri	9-1-0	Orange Bowl	J1	lost to # 2 Penn State 3-10	7	6	6	Missouri	9-2-0
8	7	Michigan	8-2-0	Rose Bowl	J1	lost to # 5 Southern Cal 3-10	12	3	7	Arkansas	9-2-0
7	8	LSU	9-1-0				11	13	8	Mississippi	8-3-0
9	9	Notre Dame	8-1-1	Cotton Bowl	J1	lost to # 1 Texas 17-21	13	8	9	Michigan	8-3-0
10	10	UCLA	8-1-1				8	7	10	LSU	9-1-0
11	11	Tennessee	9-1-0	Gator Bowl	D27	lost to # 15 Florida 13-14	15	12	11	Nebraska	9-2-0
15	12	Auburn	8-2-0	Bluebonnet Bowl	D31	lost to # 17 Houston 7-36	14	16	12	Houston	9-2-0
13	13	Mississippi	7-3-0	Sugar Bowl	J1	beat # 3 Arkansas 27-22	20	10	13	UCLA	8-1-1
12	14	Nebraska	8-2-0	Sun Bowl	D20	beat Georgia 45-6	5	17	14	Florida	9-1-1
17	15	Florida	8-1-1	Gator Bowl	D27	beat # 11 Tennessee 14-13	6	11	15	Tennessee	9-2-0
14	16	Stanford	7-2-1				23		16	Colorado	8-3-0
16	17	Houston	8-2-0	Bluebonnet Bowl	D31	beat # 12 Auburn 36-7	18	18	17	West Virginia	10-1-0
18	18	Purdue	8-2-0				9	18	18	Purdue	8-2-0
18	19	West Virginia	9-1-0	Peach Bowl	D30	beat South Carolina 14-3	22	14	19	Stanford	7-2-1
	20	Toledo	10-0-0	Tangerine Bowl	D26	beat Davidson 56-33	16	15	20	Auburn	8-3-0
18		San Diego State	11-0-0	Pasadena Bowl	D6	beat Boston U. 28-7	NR	18		San Diego State	11-0-0

1969

CONSENSUS ALL-AMERICANS

POS	OFFENSE	HT	WT	School	AP	CP	FC	FW	NE	PI
B	Mike Phipps	6-3	206	Purdue	•	•	•	•	•	•
B	Steve Owens	6-2	215	Oklahoma	•	•	•	•	•	•
B	Jim Otis	6-0	214	Ohio State	•	•		•	•	•
B	Bob Anderson	6-0	208	Colorado	•			•	•	•
E	Jim Mandich	6-3	222	Michigan	•	•	•	•	•	•
E	Walker Gillette	6-5	200	Richmond	•			•	•	•
E	Carlos Alvarez	5-11	180	Florida			•	•	•	•
T	Bob McKay	6-6	245	Texas	•	•	•	•	•	•
T	John Ward	6-5	248	Oklahoma State	•	•		•	•	•
G	Chip Kell	6-0	255	Tennessee	•	•	•	•		•
G	Bill Bridges	6-2	230	Houston	•	•	•	•		
C	Rodney Brand	6-2	218	Arkansas	•	•	•	•	•	•

	OTHERS RECEIVING FIRST-TEAM HONORS									
B	Steve Worster			Texas				•		
B	Warren Muir			South Carolina			•			
B	Charlie Pittman			Penn State			•			
B	Rex Kern			Ohio State			•			
E	Chuck Dicus			Arkansas			•			
E	Charles Speyrer			Texas			•			
T	Jim Reilly			Notre Dame			•			
T	Bob Asher			Vanderbilt			•		•	
T	Sid Smith			Southern Cal			•			•
G	Bobby Wuensch			Texas			•			
G	Ron Saul			Michigan State			•		•	
G	Mike Carroll			Missouri					•	
G	Larry DiNardo			Notre Dame						•

FC named Kell as a C

POS	DEFENSE	HT	WT	School	AP	CP	FC	FW	NE	PI
E	Jim Gunn	6-1	210	Southern Cal	•	•	•	•		•
E	Phil Olsen	6-5	255	Utah State	•			•	•	
T	Mike Reid	6-3	240	Penn State	•	•	•	•	•	•
T	Mike McCoy	6-5	274	Notre Dame	•	•	•	•	•	•
MG	Jim Stillwagon	6-0	216	Ohio State	•	•	•	•	•	•
LB	Steve Kiner	6-1	215	Tennessee	•	•	•	•	•	•
LB	Dennis Onkotz	6-2	212	Penn State	•	•	•	•	•	•
LB	Mike Ballou	6-3	230	UCLA	•	•		•		
B	Jack Tatum	6-0	204	Ohio State	•	•	•	•	•	•
B	Buddy McClinton	5-11	190	Auburn	•	•	•	•	•	
B	Tom Curtis	6-1	190	Michigan	•	•		•		•

	OTHERS RECEIVING FIRST-TEAM HONORS									
E	Bill Brundige			Colorado				•		
E	Floyd Reese			UCLA			•			
E	Rick Campbell			Texas Tech			•			
T	Al Cowlings			Southern Cal			•			
LB	George bevan			LSU				•	•	
LB	Cliff Powell			Arkansas			•			
LB	Don Parish			Stanford		•				
LB	Glen Halsell			Texas			•			
LB	John Small			Citadel					•	
LB	Jim Corigall			Kent State				•		
B	Denton Fox			Texas Tech			•			
B	Glenn Cannon			Mississippi				•		
B	Curtis Johnson			Toledo					•	
B	Neal Smith			Penn State					•	•
K	Bob Jacobs			Wyoming				•		

HEISMAN TROPHY VOTING

	PLAYER	POS	SCHOOL	1ST	2ND	3RD	TOTAL
1	Steve Owens	FB	Oklahoma	294	218	170	1488
2	Mike Phipps	QB	Purdue	226	230	196	1334
3	Rex Kern	QB	Ohio State	154	134	126	856
4	Archie Manning	QB	Mississippi	120	76	70	582
5	Mike Reid	DT	Penn State	61	39	36	297
6	Mike McCoy	DT	Notre Dame	31	65	67	290
7	Jim Otis	FB	Ohio State	12	27	31	121
8	Jim Plunkett	QB	Stanford	21	16	25	120
9	Steve Kiner	LB	Tennessee	14	20	27	109
10	Jack Tatum	DB	Ohio State	13	22	22	105

AWARD WINNERS

PLAYER	POS	SCHOOL	AWARD NAME
Mike Reid	DT	Penn State	Maxwell
Mike Reid	DT	Penn State	Outland
Steve Owens	RB	Oklahoma	Camp

CONFERENCE STANDINGS

ACC	Conf. W L T	Overall W L T
South Carolina	6 0 0	7 4 0
North Carolina St.	3 2 1	3 6 1
North Carolina	3 3 0	5 5 0
Clemson	3 3 0	4 6 0
Duke	3 3 1	3 6 1
Maryland	3 3 0	3 7 0
Wake Forest	2 5 0	3 7 0
Virginia	1 5 0	3 7 0

Big 10	Conf. W L T	Overall W L T
Ohio State	6 1 0	8 1 0
Michigan	6 1 0	8 3 0
Purdue	5 2 0	8 2 0
Minnesota	4 3 0	4 5 1
Iowa	3 4 0	5 5 0
Indiana	3 4 0	4 6 0
Wisconsin	3 4 0	3 7 0
Northwestern	3 4 0	3 7 0
Michigan State	2 5 0	4 6 0
Illinois	0 7 0	0 10 0

Big 8	Conf. W L T	Overall W L T
Nebraska	6 1 0	9 2 0
Missouri	6 1 0	9 2 0
Colorado	5 2 0	8 3 0
Oklahoma	4 3 0	6 4 0
Oklahoma State	3 4 0	5 5 0
Kansas State	3 4 0	5 5 0
Iowa State	1 6 0	3 7 0
Kansas	0 7 0	1 9 0

Big West	Conf. W L T	Overall W L T
San Diego State	6 0 0	10 0 0
Long Beach State	3 2 1	8 3 0
Pacific	2 2 0	7 3 0
San Jose State	1 1 0	2 8 0
Fresno State	1 3 0	6 4 0
UC-Santa Barbara	1 3 0	6 4 0
Los Angeles State	0 4 0	0 9 0

Ivy	Conf. W L T	Overall W L T
Dartmouth	6 1 0	8 1 0
Yale	6 1 0	7 2 0
Princeton	6 1 0	6 3 0
Cornell	4 3 0	4 5 0
Pennsylvania	2 5 0	4 5 0
Harvard	2 5 0	3 6 0
Brown	1 6 0	2 7 0
Columbia	1 6 0	1 8 0

MAC	Conf. W L T	Overall W L T
Toledo	5 0 0	10 0 0
Bowling Green	4 1 0	6 4 0
Miami, Ohio	2 3 0	7 3 0
Ohio U	2 3 0	5 4 1
Kent State	1 4 0	5 5 0
Western Michigan	1 4 0	4 6 0

Pac 8	Conf. W L T	Overall W L T
Southern Cal	6 0 0	10 0 1
UCLA	5 1 1	8 1 1
Stanford	5 1 1	7 2 1
Oregon State	4 3 0	6 4 0
Oregon	2 3 0	5 5 1
California	2 4 0	5 5 0
Washington	1 6 0	1 9 0
Washington State	0 7 0	1 9 0

SEC	Conf. W L T	Overall W L T
Tennessee	5 1 0	9 2 0
LSU	4 1 0	9 1 0
Auburn	5 2 0	8 3 0
Florida	3 1 1	9 1 1
Mississippi	4 2 0	8 3 0
Georgia	2 3 1	5 5 1
Vanderbilt	2 3 0	4 6 0
Alabama	2 4 0	6 5 0
Kentucky	1 6 0	2 8 0
Mississippi State	0 5 0	3 7 0

SWC	Conf. W L T	Overall W L T
Texas	7 0 0	11 0 0
Arkansas	6 1 0	9 2 0
Texas Tech	4 3 0	5 5 0
TCU	4 3 0	4 6 0
SMU	3 4 0	3 7 0
Rice	2 5 0	3 7 0
Texas A&M	2 5 0	3 7 0
Baylor	0 7 0	0 10 0

WAC	Conf. W L T	Overall W L T
Arizona State	6 1 0	8 2 0
Utah	5 1 0	8 2 0
Wyoming	4 3 0	6 4 0
Brigham Young	4 3 0	6 4 0
Arizona	3 3 0	3 7 0
Texas-El Paso	2 5 0	4 6 0
New Mexico	1 5 0	4 6 0
Colorado State	0 4 0	4 6 0

Independents	Overall W L T
Penn State	11 0 0
West Virginia	10 1 0
Houston	9 2 0
Notre Dame	8 2 1
Rutgers	6 3 0
Florida State	6 3 1
Air Force	6 4 0
Boston College	5 4 0
Syracuse	5 5 0
New Mexico State	5 5 0
Virginia Tech	4 5 1
Army	4 5 1
Miami, Fla.	4 6 0
Pittsburgh	4 6 0
Georgia Tech	4 6 0
Utah State	3 7 0
Tulane	3 7 0
Navy	1 9 0

BOWL GAMES

DATE	GAME	SCORE
D6	Pasadena	San Diego State 28, Boston U. 7
D13	Liberty	Colorado 47, Alabama 33
D20	Sun	Nebraska 45, Georgia 6
D26	Tangerine	Toledo 56, Davidson 33
D27	Gator	Florida 14, Tennessee 13
D30	Peach	West Virginia 14, South Carolina 3
D31	Bluebonnet	Houston 36, Auburn 7
J1	Sugar	Mississippi 27, Arkansas 22
J1	Orange	Penn State 10, Missouri 3
J1	Rose	Southern Cal 10, Michigan 3
J1	Cotton	Texas 21, Notre Dame 17

1969 NCAA Major College Statistical Leaders

Individual Leaders

PASSING/COMPLETIONS	G	ATT	COM	PCT	INT	I%	YDS	YPA	TD	TD%	COM.PG
1 John Reaves, Florida	10	396	222	56.1	19	4.8	2896	7.3	24	6.1	22.2
2 Chuck Hixson, SMU	10	362	217	59.9	15	4.1	2313	6.4	9	2.5	21.7
3 Dennis Shaw, San Diego State	10	335	199	59.4	26	7.8	3185	9.5	39	11.6	19.9
4 Gordon Slade, Davidson	10	321	198	61.7	12	3.7	2177	6.8	21	6.5	19.8
5 Jim Plunkett, Stanford	10	336	197	58.6	15	4.5	2673	8.0	20	6.0	19.7
6 Lynn Dickey, Kansas State	10	372	196	52.7	19	5.1	2476	6.7	14	3.8	19.6
7 Steve Ramsey, North Texas	10	414	195	47.1	31	7.5	2828	6.8	24	5.8	19.5
8 Bill Cappleman, Florida State	10	344	183	53.2	18	5.2	2467	7.2	14	4.1	18.3
9 Charlie Richards, Richmond	10	356	175	49.2	15	4.2	2556	7.2	21	5.9	17.5
10 Mike Phipps, Purdue	10	321	169	52.6	18	5.6	2527	7.9	23	7.2	16.9

ALL-PURPOSE YARDS	G	RUSH	REC	PR	KR	YDS	YPG
1 Lynn Moore, Army	10	983	44	223	545	1795	179.5

RUSHING/YARDS	G	ATT	YDS	TD	AVG	YPG
1 Steve Owens, Oklahoma	10	358	1523	23	4.3	152.3
2 Ed Marinaro, Cornell	9	277	1409	14	5.1	156.6
3 Joe Moore, Missouri	10	260	1312	5	5.0	131.2
4 Jim Strong, Houston	10	190	1293	11	6.8	129.3
5 Clarence Davis, Southern Cal	10	282	1275	9	4.5	127.5
6 John Isenbarger, Indiana	10	233	1217	5	5.2	121.7
7 Ron Poe James, New Mexico State	10	258	1181	8	4.6	118.1
8 Don McCauley, North Carolina	10	204	1092	8	5.4	109.2
9 Duane Thomas, West Texas State	10	199	1072	10	5.4	107.2
10 Lee Bouggess, Louisville	10	267	1064	6	4.0	106.4

RUSHING/YARDS PER CARRY	G	ATT	YDS	YPC
1 Bob Duncan, Citadel	10	136	936	6.9
2 Jim Strong, Houston	10	190	1293	6.8
3 Bill Taylor, Michigan	10	123	808	6.6
4 Dave Buchanan, Arizona State	10	143	908	6.3
5 Tony Harris, Toledo	10	146	849	5.8
6 Bob Gresham, West Virginia	10	190	1057	5.6
7 Ted Heiskell, Houston	10	158	870	5.5
8 Duane Thomas, West Texas State	10	199	1072	5.4
9 Don McCauley, North Carolina	10	204	1092	5.4
10 John Isenbarger, Indiana	10	233	1217	5.2

*-Based on top 32 rushers

RECEIVING/RECEPTIONS	G	REC	YDS	TD	YPR	YPG	RPG
1 Jerry Hendren, Idaho	10	95	1452	12	15.3	145.2	9.5
2 Carlos Alvarez, Florida	10	88	1329	12	15.1	132.9	8.8
3 Tim Delaney, San Diego Sate	10	85	1259	14	14.8	125.9	8.5
4 Barry Moore, North Texas	10	71	1130	5	15.9	113.0	7.1
5 Mike Kelly, Davidson	10	70	891	6	12.7	89.1	7.0
6 Sammy Milner, Mississippi State	10	64	745	6	11.6	74.5	6.4
7 Elmo Wright, Houston	10	63	1275	14	20.2	127.5	6.3
8 Todd Snyder, Ohio U	10	62	835	8	13.5	83.5	6.2
9 George Hannen, Davidson	10	58	709	8	12.2	70.9	5.8
10 Walker Gillette, Richmond	10	57	1090	11	19.1	109.0	5.7
10 Fred Mathews, Bowling Green	10	57	528	6	9.3	52.8	5.7

PUNTING	PUNT	YDS	AVG
1 Ed Marsh, Baylor	68	2965	43.6
2 Spike Jones, Georgia	71	3089	43.5
3 Ken Sanders, Tulane	66	2858	43.3
4 Mike Nehl, Oregon State	56	2414	43.1
5 Pat Barrett, Miami, Fla.	45	1940	43.1
6 Ken Duncan, Tulsa	34	1452	42.7
7 Bob Jacobs, Wyoming	79	3358	42.5
8 Stefan Schroeder, Pacific	53	2237	42.2
9 Zenon Andrusyshyn, UCLA	47	1979	42.1
10 Jess Garcia, Utah State	87	3645	41.9

PUNT RETURNS/YARDS	PR	YDS	TD	AVG
1 Chris Farasopoulos, Brigham Young	35	527	1	15.1
2 George Hannen, Davidson	21	471	3	22.4
3 Bobby Majors, Tennessee	37	457	2	12.4
4 Larry Zelina, Ohio State	23	431	2	18.7
5 Bill Cornman, Pacific	34	430	1	12.6
6 Billy Watson, Citadel	27	397	2	14.7
7 Joe Bullard, Tulane	19	395	1	20.8
8 Bernie Barbour, North Texas	36	371	0	10.3
9 Tom Deckert, San Diego State	26	346	0	13.3
10 Lenny Randle, Arizona State	22	343	3	15.6

KICKOFF RETURNS/YARDS	KR	YDS	TD	AVG
1 Stan Brown, Purdue	26	698	2	26.8
2 Gordon Utgard, Baylor	37	669	0	18.1
3 Dave Garnett, Pittsburgh	25	653	0	26.1
4 Gary Hammond, SMU	27	617	0	22.9
5 Doug Mathews, Vanderbilt	26	607	0	23.3
6 Bob Warren, Brown	26	599	0	23.0
7 Eric Allen, Michigan State	29	598	0	20.6
8 Arnold Thomas, Southern Miss	31	585	0	18.9
9 Bob Darby, California	23	556	0	24.2
10 Chris Farasopul, Brigham Young	17	548	1	32.2

SCORING	TDS	XPT	FG	PTS
1 Steve Owens, Oklahoma	23	0	0	138
2 Mack Herron, Kansas State	21	0	0	126
3 Bill Burnett, Arkansas	20	0	0	120
4 Bob Anderson, Colorado	19	0	0	114
5 Tommy Durrance, Florida	18	2	0	110
6 Stan Brown, Purdue	18	0	0	108
6 Tom Reynolds, San Diego State	18	0	0	108
8 Jim Braxton, West Virginia	12	24	3	105
9 Jim Otis, Ohio State	16	0	0	96
10 Bob Moore, Oregon	15	2	0	92

KICK SCORING	XPA	XP	FGA	FG	PTS
1 Bob Jacobs, Wyoming	23	22	27	18	76
2 Dennis Leuthauser, Air Force	32	27	25	16	75
3 Henry Brown, Missouri	39	35	20	12	71
3 Steve Horowitz, Stanford	44	41	18	10	71
3 Ed Gallardo, Arizona State	48	41	16	10	71
6 John Riley, Auburn	46	39	21	10	69
7 George Hunt, Tennessee	38	35	13	10	65
8 Mark Lumpkin, LSU	44	38	13	8	62
8 Al Limahelu, San Diego State	60	59	8	1	62
10 Bill McClard, Arkansas	44	40	9	7	61
10 Happy Feller, Texas	45	43	8	6	61

INTERCEPTIONS	INT	YDS	TD
1 Seth Miller, Arizona State	11	63	0
2 Neal Smith, Penn State	10	78	1
3 Jeff Ford, Georgia Tech	9	257	3
3 Jay Morrison, New Mexico	9	144	0
3 Mike Sensibaugh, Ohio State	9	125	0
3 Buddy McClinton, Auburn	9	92	0
7 Tom Curtis, Michigan *	8	165	0
7 David Berrong, Memphis *	8	136	0
7 John Gates, Oklahoma State *	8	113	0
7 L.D. Rowden, Houston *	8	113	1
7 Bob Wroe, Columbia *	8	92	0

*-Ten tied with eight; these players had the most yards.

Team Leaders

RUSHING OFFENSE	G	ATT	YDS	AVG	TD	YPG
1 Texas	10	684	3630	5.3	51	363.0
2 Houston	10	583	3170	5.4	32	317.0
3 Ohio State	9	599	2774	4.6	36	308.2
4 Dartmouth	9	537	2654	4.9	22	294.9
5 West Virginia	10	625	2925	4.7	30	292.5
6 Notre Dame	10	663	2905	4.4	31	290.5
7 Michigan	10	625	2776	4.4	37	277.6
8 Oklahoma	10	639	2664	4.2	31	266.4
9 North Carolina	10	630	2615	4.2	16	261.5
10 Arizona State	10	553	2513	4.5	32	251.3

PASSING OFFENSE	G	ATT	COM	INT	PCT	YDS	YPA	TD	I%	YPC	YPG
1 San Diego State	10	417	244	28	58.5	3742	9.0	43	6.7	15.3	374.2
2 Florida	10	413	233	20	56.4	3016	7.3	24	4.8	12.9	301.6
3 Stanford	10	382	217	17	56.8	2985	7.8	26	4.5	13.8	298.5
4 North Texas	10	447	206	36	46.1	2944	6.6	25	8.1	14.3	294.4
5 Idaho	10	469	223	33	47.5	2741	5.8	16	7.0	12.3	274.1
6 Alabama	10	328	195	11	59.5	2707	8.3	14	3.4	13.9	270.7
7 Purdue	10	333	176	20	52.9	2679	8.0	23	6.0	15.2	267.9
8 Richmond	10	373	185	16	49.6	2651	7.1	23	4.3	14.3	265.1
9 Florida State	10	356	191	19	53.7	2550	7.2	16	5.3	13.4	255.0
10 Kansas State	10	379	197	19	52.0	2501	6.6	14	5.0	12.7	250.1

TOTAL OFFENSE	G	P	YDS	AVG	TD	YPG
1 San Diego State	10	840	5322	6.3	61	532.2
2 Houston	10	835	5138	6.2	53	513.8
3 Stanford	10	840	4944	5.9	43	494.4
4 Ohio State	9	829	4439	5.4	53	493.2
5 Texas	10	817	4721	5.8	56	472.1
6 Missouri	10	859	4507	5.2	44	450.7
7 Notre Dame	10	868	4489	5.2	44	448.9
8 Florida	10	826	4348	5.3	43	434.8
9 Purdue	10	794	4325	5.4	47	432.5
10 UCLA	10	762	4304	5.6	43	430.4

RUSHING DEFENSE	G	ATT	YDS	AVG	TD	YPG
1 LSU	10	353	389	1.1	5	38.9
2 Wyoming	10	395	663	1.7	10	66.3
3 Auburn	10	392	796	2.0	6	79.6
4 Pacific	10	400	834	2.1	3	83.4
5 Toledo	10	453	838	1.8	7	83.8
6 Notre Dame	10	374	851	2.3	8	85.1
7 Miami, Ohio	10	410	858	2.1	11	85.8
8 Texas	10	420	900	2.1	6	90.0
9 Yale	9	442	819	1.9	12	91.0
10 Houston	10	406	944	2.3	10	94.4

PASSING DEFENSE	G	ATT	COM	PCT	YPC	INT	I%	YDS	YPA	TD	YPG
1 Dayton	10	156	68	43.6	13.2	11	7.1	900	5.8	5	90.0
2 Dartmouth	9	192	80	41.7	10.3	19	9.9	821	4.3	4	91.2
3 Pennsylvania	9	166	72	43.4	11.5	18	10.8	826	5.0	6	91.8
4 Penn State	10	221	86	38.9	11.3	24	10.9	972	4.4	3	97.2
5 Xavier	10	169	80	47.3	12.4	10	5.9	992	5.9	9	99.2
6 Buffalo	9	157	71	45.2	12.8	6	3.8	911	5.8	4	101.2
7 Virginia	10	173	72	41.6	14.9	11	6.4	1073	6.2	10	107.3
8 Syracuse	10	232	106	45.7	10.2	13	5.6	1082	4.7	9	108.2
9 Duke	10	159	71	44.7	15.7	10	6.3	1112	7.0	11	111.2
10 Wake Forest	10	171	93	54.4	12.5	13	7.6	1161	6.8	11	116.1

TOTAL DEFENSE	G	P	YDS	AVG	TD	YPG
1 Toledo	10	703	2091	3.0	18	209.1
2 Yale	9	646	1932	3.0	16	214.7
3 Penn State	10	681	2181	3.2	10	218.1
4 Notre Dame	10	664	2187	3.3	14	218.7
5 Syracuse	10	659	2236	3.4	16	223.6
6 Texas	10	707	2260	3.2	11	226.0
7 LSU	10	714	2285	3.2	13	228.5
8 Buffalo	9	565	2065	3.7	11	229.4
9 Dartmouth	9	611	2077	3.4	12	230.8
10 Virginia	10	643	2358	3.7	21	235.8

SCORING OFFENSE	G	PTS	AVG
1 San Diego State	10	464	46.4
2 Ohio State	9	383	42.6
3 Texas	10	414	41.4
4 Houston	10	386	38.6
5 Arizona State	10	383	38.3
6 Auburn	10	363	36.3
7 Missouri	10	362	36.2
8 Purdue	10	354	35.4
9 LSU	10	349	34.9
9 Michigan	10	349	34.9
9 Stanford	10	349	34.9

SCORING DEFENSE	G	PTS	AVG
1 Arkansas	10	76	7.6
2 Penn State	10	87	8.7
3 LSU	10	91	9.1
4 Buffalo	9	89	9.9
5 Georgia	10	101	10.1
6 Texas	10	102	10.2
7 UCLA	10	103	10.3
8 Ohio State	9	93	10.3
9 Utah	10	107	10.7

1970 POLL PROGRESSION

AP	PRE-SEASON		SEPT. 12 GAMES
1	Ohio State	0-0-0	bye week
2	Texas	0-0-0	bye week
3	Southern Cal	0-0-0	beat # 16 Alabama 42-21
4	Arkansas	0-0-0	lost to # 10 Stanford 28-34
5	Mississippi	0-0-0	bye week
6	Notre Dame	0-0-0	bye week
7	Penn State	0-0-0	bye week
8	Michigan	0-0-0	bye week
9	Nebraska	0-0-0	beat Wake Forest 36-12
10	Stanford	0-0-0	beat # 4 Arkansas 34-28
11	Missouri	0-0-0	beat Baylor 38-0
12	LSU	0-0-0	bye week
13	Houston	0-0-0	bye week
14	Kansas State	0-0-0	beat Utah State 37-0
15	Florida	0-0-0	beat Duke 21-19
16	Alabama	0-0-0	lost to # 3 Southern Cal 21-42
17	South Carolina	0-0-0	lost to Georgia Tech 20-23
18	UCLA	0-0-0	beat Oregon State 14-9
19	Arizona State	0-0-0	bye week
20	Auburn	0-0-0	bye week
20	Oklahoma	0-0-0	Beat SMU 28-11
20	West Virginia	0-0-0	beat William & Mary 43-7

AP	SEPTEMBER 14 POLL		SEPT. 19 GAMES
1	Ohio State	0-0-0	bye week
2	Texas	0-0-0	beat California 56-15
3	Southern Cal	1-0-0	tied # 9 Nebraska 21-21
4	Stanford	1-0-0	beat San Jose State 34-3
5	Mississippi	0-0-0	beat Memphis 47-13
6	Notre Dame	0-0-0	beat Northwestern 35-14
7	Penn State	0-0-0	beat Navy 55-7
8	Michigan	0-0-0	beat Arizona 20-9
9	Nebraska	1-0-0	tied # 3 Southern Cal 21-21
10	Missouri	1-0-0	beat Minnesota 34-12
11	Arkansas	0-1-0	beat Oklahoma State 23-7
12	LSU	0-0-0	lost to Texas A&M 18-20
13	Kansas State	1-0-0	lost to Kentucky 3-16
14	Florida	1-0-0	beat Mississippi State 34-13
15	Houston	0-0-0	beat Syracuse 42-15
16	UCLA	1-0-0	beat Pittsburgh 24-15
17	West Virginia	1-0-0	beat Richmond 49-10
18	Oklahoma	1-0-0	beat Wisconsin 21-7
19	Georgia	0-0-0	lost to Tulane 14-17
20	Arizona State	0-0-0	beat Colorado State 38-9

UP	AP	SEPTEMBER 21 POLL		SEPT. 26 GAMES
2	1	Ohio State	0-0-0	beat Texas A&M 56-13
1	2	Texas	1-0-0	beat Texas Tech 35-13
4	3	Stanford	2-0-0	beat Oregon 33-10
3	4	Penn State	1-0-0	lost to # 18 Colorado 13-41
7	5	Mississippi	1-0-0	beat Kentucky 20-17
9	6	Notre Dame	1-0-0	beat Purdue 48-0
5	7	Southern Cal	1-0-1	beat Iowa 48-0
8	8	Nebraska	1-0-1	beat Army 28-0
6	9	Missouri	2-0-0	lost to # 20 Air Force 14-37
10	10	Michigan	1-0-0	beat Washington 17-3
11	11	Houston	1-0-0	lost to Oklahoma State 17-26
18	12	Arkansas	1-1-0	beat Tulsa 49-7
15	13	Florida	2-0-0	lost to Alabama 15-46
13	14	Oklahoma	2-0-0	lost to Oregon State 14-23
12	15	UCLA	2-0-0	beat Northwestern 12-7
19	16	West Virginia	2-0-0	beat VMI 47-10
14	17	Tennessee	1-0-0	lost to Auburn 23-36
16	18	Colorado	1-0-0	beat # 4 Penn State 41-13
	29	Georgia Tech	2-0-0	beat Miami, Fla. 31-21
	20	Air Force	2-0-0	beat # 9 Missouri 37-14
16		Purdue	1-0-0	lost to # 6 Notre Dame 0-48
19		Auburn	1-0-0	beat # 17 Tennessee 36-23
19		Washington	1-0-0	lost to # 10 Michigan 3-17

UP	AP	SEPTEMBER 28 POLL		OCT. 3 GAMES
1	1	Ohio State	1-0-0	beat Duke 34-10
2	2	Texas	2-0-0	beat # 13 UCLA 20-17
5	3	Stanford	3-0-0	lost to Purdue 14-26
3	4	Notre Dame	2-0-0	beat Michigan State 29-0
4	5	Southern Cal	2-0-1	beat Oregon State 45-13
6	6	Nebraska	2-0-1	beat Minnesota 35-10
8	7	Mississippi	2-0-0	beat # 17 Alabama 48-23
7	8	Colorado	2-0-0	lost to Kansas State 20-21
9	9	Michigan	2-0-0	beat Texas A&M 14-10
10	10	Air Force	3-0-0	beat Colorado State 37-22
12	11	Arkansas	2-1-0	beat TCU 49-14
11	12	Auburn	2-0-0	beat Kentucky 33-15
13	13	UCLA	3-0-0	lost to # 2 Texas 17-20
17	14	West Virginia	3-0-0	beat Indiana 16-10
16	15	Georgia Tech	3-0-0	beat Clemson 28-7
17	16	Penn State	1-1-0	lost to Wisconsin 16-29
19	17	Alabama	2-1-0	lost to # 7 Mississippi 23-48
15	18	Arizona State	3-0-0	beat Wyoming 52-3
	19	North Carolina	3-0-0	beat Vanderbilt 10-7
	20	Missouri	2-1-0	beat Oklahoma State 40-20
13		Oklahoma	2-1-0	bye week
20		San Diego State	3-0-0	beat Brigham Young 31-11

UP	AP	OCTOBER 5 POLL		OCT. 10 GAMES
1	1	Ohio State	2-0-0	beat Michigan State 29-0
2	2	Texas	3-0-0	beat Oklahoma 41-9
3	3	Notre Dame	3-0-0	beat Army 51-10
4	4	Southern Cal	3-0-1	lost to # 12 Stanford 14-24
6	5	Mississippi	3-0-0	beat Georgia 31-21
5	6	Nebraska	3-0-1	beat # 16 Missouri 21-7
8	7	Michigan	3-0-0	beat Purdue 29-0
7	8	Air Force	4-0-0	beat Tulane 24-3
9	9	Auburn	3-0-0	beat Clemson 44-0
10	10	Arkansas	3-1-0	beat Baylor 41-7
16	11	West Virginia	4-0-0	lost to Duke 13-21
12	12	Stanford	3-1-0	beat # 4 Southern Cal 24-14
15	13	Georgia Tech	4-0-0	lost to # 20 Tennessee 6-17
11	14	Arizona State	3-0-0	beat Washington State 37-30
13	15	UCLA	3-1-0	lost to Oregon 40-41
13	16	Missouri	3-1-0	lost to # 6 Nebraska 7-21
18	17	Colorado	3-1-0	beat Iowa State 61-10
	18	North Carolina	4-0-0	lost to South Carolina 21-35
	19	LSU	2-1-0	beat Pacific 34-0
17	20	Tennessee	2-1-0	beat # 13 Georgia Tech 17-6
19		Oklahoma	2-1-0	lost to # 2 Texas 9-41
20		San Diego State	4-0-0	beat Southern Miss 41-14

UP	AP	OCTOBER 12 POLL		OCT. 17 GAMES
1	1	Ohio State	3-0-0	beat Minnesota 28-8
2	2	Texas	4-0-0	bye week
3	3	Notre Dame	4-0-0	beat # 18 Missouri 24-7
5	4	Mississippi	4-0-0	lost to Southern Miss 14-30
4	5	Nebraska	4-0-1	beat Kansas 41-20
7	6	Michigan	4-0-0	beat Michigan State 34-20
6	7	Air Force	5-0-0	beat Navy 26-3
8	8	Auburn	4-0-0	beat # 16 Georgia Tech 31-7
9	9	Stanford	4-1-0	beat Washington State 63-16
10	10	Arkansas	4-1-0	bye week
12	11	Southern Cal	3-1-1	beat Washington 28-25
11	12	Arizona State	4-0-0	beat Brigham Young 27-3
13	13	Colorado	3-1-0	lost to Oklahoma 15-23
14	14	Tennessee	3-1-0	beat Alabama 24-0
	15	LSU	3-1-0	beat Kentucky 14-7
15	16	Georgia Tech	4-1-0	lost to # 8 Auburn 7-31
	17	Texas Tech	4-1-0	lost to Mississippi State 16-20
	18	Missouri	3-2-0	lost to # 3 Notre Dame 7-24
15	19	Houston	2-1-0	beat Oregon State 19-16
15	19	UCLA	3-2-0	beat California 24-21
14		South Carolina	3-1-1	lost to Maryland 15-21
19		San Diego State	5-0-0	beat San Jose State 32-6
19		West Virginia	4-1-0	lost to Pittsburgh 35-36

UP	AP	OCTOBER 19 POLL		OCT. 24 GAMES
1	1	Ohio State	4-0-0	beat Illinois 48-29
2	2	Texas	4-0-0	beat Rice 45-21
3	3	Notre Dame	5-0-0	bye week
4	4	Nebraska	5-0-1	beat Oklahoma State 65-31
7	5	Michigan	5-0-0	beat Minnesota 39-13
5	6	Auburn	5-0-0	lost to # 14 LSU 9-17
6	7	Air Force	6-0-0	beat Boston College 35-10
8	8	Stanford	5-1-0	beat # 16 UCLA 9-7
9	9	Arkansas	5-1-0	beat Wichita State 62-0
11	10	Southern Cal	4-1-1	lost to Oregon 7-10
12	11	Tennessee	4-1-0	beat Florida 38-7
10	12	Arizona State	5-0-0	beat Texas-El Paso 42-13
13	13	Mississippi	4-1-0	beat Vanderbilt 26-16
17	14	LSU	4-1-0	beat # 6 Auburn 17-9
14	15	Houston	3-1-0	lost to Alabama 21-30
16	16	UCLA	4-2-0	lost to # 8 Stanford 7-9
15	17	San Diego State	6-0-0	bye week
	18	Pittsburgh		beat Miami, Fla. 28-17
	19	Colorado	3-2-0	lost to Missouri 16-30
17	19	Toledo	6-0-0	beat Kent State 34-17

UP	AP	OCTOBER 26 POLL		OCT. 31 GAMES
2	1	Texas	5-0-0	beat SMU 42-15
1	2	Ohio State	5-0-0	beat # 20 Northwestern 24-10
3	3	Notre Dame	5-0-0	beat Navy 56-7
4	4	Nebraska	6-0-1	beat Colorado 29-13
5	5	Michigan	6-0-0	beat Wisconsin 29-15
6	6	Stanford	6-1-0	beat Oregon State 48-10
7	7	Air Force	7-0-0	beat Arizona 23-20
8	8	Arkansas	6-1-0	beat Texas A&M 45-6
9	9	Tennessee	5-1-0	beat Wake Forest 41-7
11	10	LSU	5-1-0	bye week
10	11	Arizona State	6-0-0	bye week
12	12	Auburn	5-1-0	beat Florida 63-14
13	13	Mississippi	5-1-0	bye week
14	14	San Diego State	6-0-0	beat Fresno State 56-14
18	15	Pittsburgh	5-1-0	lost to Syracuse 13-43
15	16	Oregon	5-2-0	lost to Washington 23-25
	17	Missouri	4-2-0	lost to Kansas State 13-17
	18	Southern Cal	4-2-1	lost to California 10-13
16	19	UCLA	4-3-0	beat Washington State 54-9
	20	Northwestern	3-3-0	lost to # 2 Ohio State 10-24
16		Yale	5-0-0	lost to Dartmouth 0-10
18		Dartmouth	5-0-0	beat Yale 10-0
18		Toledo	7-0-0	beat Miami, Ohio 14-13

UP	AP	NOVEMBER 2 POLL		NOV. 7 GAMES
1	1	Texas	6-0-0	beat Baylor 21-14
2	2	Notre Dame	6-0-0	beat Pittsburgh 46-14
3	3	Ohio State	6-0-0	beat Wisconsin 24-7
4	4	Nebraska	7-0-1	beat Iowa State 54-29
6	5	Michigan	7-0-0	beat Illinois 42-0
5	6	Stanford	7-1-0	beat Washington 29-22
8	7	Arkansas	6-1-0	beat Rice 38-14
10	8	Tennessee	6-1-0	beat South Carolina 20-18
7	9	Air Force	8-0-0	lost to Oregon 35-46
9	10	Auburn	6-1-0	beat Mississippi State 56-0
12	11	LSU	5-1-0	beat # 19 Alabama 14-9
11	12	Arizona State	6-0-0	beat San Jose State 46-10
13	13	Mississippi	5-1-0	beat # 18 Houston 24-13
14	14	San Diego State	7-0-0	beat Pacific 14-13
17	15	Toledo	8-0-0	beat No. Illinois 45-7
16	16	UCLA	5-3-0	bye week
15	17	Dartmouth	6-0-0	beat Columbia 55-0
	17	Houston	3-2-0	lost to # 13 Mississippi 13-24
17	19	Alabama	5-3-0	lost to # 11 LSU 9-14
	20	Syracuse	4-3-0	beat Army 31-29

November 9 Poll — Nov. 14 Games

UP	AP	Team	Record	Result
1	1	Notre Dame	7-0-0	beat Georgia Tech 10-7
1	2	Texas	7-0-0	beat TCU 58-0
3	3	Ohio State	7-0-0	beat Purdue 10-7
4	4	Nebraska	8-0-1	beat # 20 Kansas State 51-13
5	5	Michigan	8-0-0	beat Iowa 55-0
6	6	Stanford	8-1-0	lost to # 13 Air Force 14-31
8	7	Arkansas	7-1-0	beat SMU 36-3
7	8	Auburn	7-1-0	lost to Georgia 17-31
9	9	LSU	6-1-0	beat Mississippi State 38-7
10	10	Tennessee	7-1-0	bye week
11	11	Arizona State	7-0-0	beat Utah 37-14
13	12	Mississippi	6-1-0	beat U. T. Chattanooga 44-7
12	13	Air Force	8-1-0	beat # 6 Stanford 31-14
17	14	San Diego State	8-0-0	beat U.C.-Santa Barbara 64-7
14	15	Dartmouth	7-0-0	beat Cornell 24-0
19	16	Toledo	9-0-0	beat Dayton 31-7
17	17	UCLA	5-3-0	lost to Washington 20-61
15	18	Southern Cal	5-3-1	bye week
	19	Oregon	6-3-0	tied Army 22-22
	20	Kansas State	6-3-0	lost to # 4 Nebraska 13-51
15		Alabama	5-4-0	beat Miami, Fla. 32-8

November 16 Poll — Nov. 21 Games

UP	AP	Team	Record	Result
1	1	Texas	8-0-0	bye week
2	2	Notre Dame	8-0-0	beat # 7 LSU 3-0
3	3	Nebraska	9-0-1	beat Oklahoma 28-21
5	4	Michigan	9-0-0	lost to # 5 Ohio State 9-20
4	5	Ohio State	8-0-0	beat # 4 Michigan 20-9
6	6	Arkansas	8-1-0	beat # 19 Texas Tech 24-10
7	7	LSU	7-1-0	lost to # 2 Notre Dame 0-3
9	8	Tennessee	7-1-0	beat Kentucky 45-0
10	9	Arizona State	8-0-0	beat New Mexico 33-21
8	10	Air Force	9-1-0	lost to Colorado 19-49
11	11	Stanford	8-2-0	lost to California 14-22
12	12	Mississippi	7-1-0	bye week
13	13	Auburn	7-2-0	bye week
14	14	San Diego State	9-0-0	lost to Long Beach State 11-27
18	15	Toledo	10-0-0	beat Colorado State 24-14
14	16	Dartmouth	8-0-0	beat Pennsylvania 28-0
	17	Georgia Tech	7-3-0	bye week
	18	Northwestern	5-4-0	beat Michigan State 23-20
	19	Texas Tech	8-2-0	lost to # 6 Arkansas 10-24
	20	Penn State	6-3-0	beat Pittsburgh 35-15
14		San Diego State	9-0-0	lost to Long Beach State 11-27 (N20)
16		Alabama	6-4-0	bye week
16		Southern Cal	5-3-1	lost to UCLA 20-45

November 23 Poll — Nov. 28 Games

UP	AP	Team	Record	Result
1	1	Texas	8-0-0	beat Texas A&M 52-14
2	2	Ohio State	9-0-0	regular season complete
4	3	Nebraska	10-0-1	regular season complete
3	4	Notre Dame	9-0-0	lost to Southern Cal 28-38
6	5	Arkansas	9-1-0	bye week
8	6	LSU	7-2-0	beat Tulane 26-14
5	7	Tennessee	8-1-0	beat Vanderbilt 24-6
7	8	Michigan	9-1-0	regular season complete
9	9	Arizona State	9-0-0	bye week
10	10	Mississippi	7-1-0	lost to Mississippi State 14-19
11	11	Auburn	7-2-0	beat Alabama 33-28
16	12	Air Force	9-2-0	regular season complete
12	13	Stanford	8-3-0	
13	14	Dartmouth	9-0-0	regular season complete
16	15	Toledo	11-0-0	regular season complete
	16	Georgia Tech	7-3-0	beat Georgia 17-7
	17	Penn State	7-3-0	regular season complete
	18	Northwestern	6-4-0	regular season complete
	19	Colorado	6-4-0	regular season complete
	20	Washington	6-4-0	regular season complete
14		UCLA	6-4-0	bye week
15		Alabama	6-4-0	lost to # 11 Auburn 28-33
16		Houston	6-3-0	beat Florida State 53-21 (N26)
19		San Diego State	9-1-0	lost to Iowa State 22-28
19		Florida State	7-3-0	lost to Houston 21-53 (N26)

November 30 Poll — Dec. 5 Games

UP	AP	Team	Record	Result
1	1	Texas	9-0-0	beat # 4 Arkansas 42-7
2	2	Ohio State	9-0-0	
3	3	Nebraska	10-0-1	
5	4	Arkansas	9-1-0	lost to # 1 Texas 7-42
4	5	Tennessee	9-1-0	beat UCLA 28-17
6	6	Notre Dame	9-1-0	regular season complete
7	7	Michigan	9-1-0	
8	8	LSU	8-2-0	beat # 16 Mississippi 61-17
9	9	Arizona State	9-0-0	beat Arizona 10-6
10	10	Auburn	8-2-0	
	11	Air Force	9-2-0	
11	12	Stanford	8-3-0	
20	13	Georgia Tech	8-3-0	
16	14	Toledo	11-0-0	
12	15	Dartmouth	9-0-0	
15	16	Mississippi	7-2-0	lost to # 8 LSU 17-61
	17	Southern Cal	6-4-1	regular season complete
	18	Penn State	7-3-0	
	19	Northwestern	6-4-0	
16	20	Oklahoma	7-4-0	regular season complete
14		Houston	7-3-0	beat Miami, Fla. 36-3
16		Colorado	6-4-0	regular season complete
16		UCLA	6-4-0	lost to Tennessee 17-28

December 7 Poll / January 5 Final Poll

UP	AP	Team	Record	Bowl Bid	Date	Bowl Result	RB	AP	Team	Record
1	1	Texas	10-0-0	Cotton Bowl	J1	lost to # 6 Notre Dame 11-24	1	1	Nebraska	11-0-1
2	2	Ohio State	9-0-0	Rose Bowl	J1	lost to # 12 Stanford 17-27	2	2	Notre Dame	10-1-0
3	3	Nebraska	10-0-1	Orange Bowl	J1	beat # 5 LSU 17-12	3	3	Texas	10-1-0
4	4	Tennessee	10-1-0	Sugar Bowl	J1	beat # 11 Air Force 34-13	5	4	Tennessee	11-1-0
6	5	LSU	9-2-0	Orange Bowl	J1	lost to # 3 Nebraska 12-17	4	5	Ohio State	9-1-0
5	6	Notre Dame	9-1-0	Cotton Bowl	J1	beat # 1 Texas 24-11	7	6	Arizona State	11-0-0
7	7	Michigan	9-1-0				11	7	LSU	9-3-0
8	8	Arizona State	10-0-0	Peach Bowl	D30	beat North Carolina 48-26	10	8	Stanford	9-3-0
12	9	Arkansas	9-2-0				6	9	Michigan	9-1-0
9	10	Auburn	8-2-0	Gator Bowl	J2	beat Mississippi 35-28	9	10	Auburn	9-2-0
11	11	Air Force	9-2-0	Sugar Bowl	J1	lost to # 4 Tennessee 13-34	12	11	Arkansas	9-2-0
10	12	Stanford	8-3-0	Rose Bowl	J1	beat # 2 Ohio State 27-17	NR	12	Toledo	12-0-0
17	13	Georgia Tech	8-3-0	Sun Bowl	D19	beat # 19 Texas Tech 17-9	15	13	Georgia Tech	9-3-0
14	14	Dartmouth	9-0-0				8	14	Dartmouth	9-0-0
17	15	Toledo	11-0-0	Tangerine Bowl	D28	beat William & Mary 40-12	18	15	Southern Cal	6-4-1
19	16	Southern Cal	6-4-1				13	16	Air Force	9-3-0
13	17	Houston	8-3-0				23	17	Tulane	8-4-0
19	18	Penn State	7-3-0				20	18	Penn State	7-3-0
	19	Texas Tech	8-3-0	Sun Bowl	D19	lost to # 13 Georgia Tech 9-17	17	19	Houston	8-3-0
15	20	Oklahoma	7-4-0	Bluebonnet Bowl	D31	tied Alabama 24-24	19	20	Mississippi	7-4-0
16		Colorado	6-4-0	Liberty Bowl	D12	lost to Tulane 3-17	25	20	Oklahoma	7-4-1

1970

CONSENSUS ALL-AMERICANS

POS	Offense	HT	WT	School	AP	CP	FC	FW	NE	PI
QB	Jim Plunkett	6-3	204	Stanford		•	•	•	•	•
RB	Steve Worster	6-0	210	Texas	•	•	•	•	•	•
RB	Don McCauley	6-0	211	North Carolina	•	•	•	•	•	•
E	Tom Gatewood	6-2	208	Notre Dame		•	•	•	•	•
E	Ernie Jennings	6-0	172	Air Force	•	•	•		•	
E	Elmo Wright	6-0	195	Houston	•	•	•	•	•	
T	Dan Dierdorf	6-4	250	Michigan	•	•	•		•	
T	Bobby Wuensch	6-3	230	Texas	•	•		•	•	
T	Bob Newton	6-4	248	Nebraska	•	•	•	•	•	
G	Chip Kell	6-0	240	Tennessee	•	•	•		•	•
G	Larry DiNardo	6-1	235	Notre Dame	•	•	•		•	•
C	Don Popplewell	6-2	240	Colorado	•	•	•	•	•	•

OTHERS RECEIVING FIRST-TEAM HONORS

				School						
QB	Joe Theisman			Notre Dame	•					
RB	John Brockington			Ohio State		•				
RB	Ed Marinaro			Cornell		•				
RB	Leon Burns			Long Beach State				•		
E	Chuck Dicus			Arkansas		•				
E	Jim Braxton			West Virginia	•					
E	Jan White			Ohio State				•		
G	Henry Allison			San Diego State						•
K	Marv Bateman			Utah						•
K	Bill McClard			Arkansas		•				

FC named Newton as a G; FC named Kell as a C

POS	Defense	HT	WT	School	AP	CP	FC	FW	NE	PI
E	Bill Atessis	6-3	255	Texas	•	•	•	•	•	
E	Charlie Weaver	6-2	214	Southern Cal	•	•	•	•	•	
T	Rock Perdoni	5-11	236	Georgia Tech	•	•	•	•	•	
T	Dick Bumpas	6-1	225	Arkansas	•	•			•	
MG	Jim Stillwagon	6-0	220	Ohio State	•	•	•	•	•	•
LB	Jack Ham	6-3	212	Penn State	•	•	•	•	•	•
LB	Mike Anderson	6-3	225	LSU	•	•	•	•	•	•
B	Jack Tatum	6-0	208	Ohio State	•	•	•	•	•	•
B	Larry Willingham	6-1	185	Auburn			•	•	•	•
B	Dave Elmendorf	6-1	190	Texas A&M	•	•			•	
B	Tommy Casanova	6-1	191	LSU	•	•		•		

OTHERS RECEIVING FIRST-TEAM HONORS

				School						
E	Jack Youngblood			Florida		•		•		
T	Bruce James			Arkansas				•		
T	Marty Huff			Michigan				•		
T	Jimmy Poston			South Carolina		•				
T	Mel Long			Toledo					•	
T	Win Headley			Wake Forest				•		
T	Joe Ehrmann			Syracuse				•		
MG	Henry Hill			Michigan		•				
LB	Jerry Murtaugh			Nebraska				•		
LB	Jackie Walker			Tennessee					•	
B	Clarence Scott			Kansas State				•		
B	Murry Bowden			Dartmouth			•			
B	Dick Harris			South Carolina			•			
B	Mike Sensibaugh			Ohio State		•			•	
B	Clarence Ellis			Notre Dame				•		

FC named White as a T

HEISMAN TROPHY VOTING

	PLAYER	POS	SCHOOL	1ST	2ND	3RD	TOTAL
1	Jim Plunkett	QB	Stanford	510	285	129	2229
2	Joe Theismann	QB	Notre Dame	242	255	174	1410
3	Archie Manning	QB	Mississippi	138	133	169	849
4	Steve Worster	FB	Texas	47	81	95	398
5	Rex Kern	QB	Ohio State	17	39	59	188
6	Pat Sullivan	QB	Auburn	24	37	34	180
7	Jack Tatum	DB	Ohio State	8	48	53	173
8	Ernie Jennings	WR	Air Force	18	20	24	118
9	Don McCauley	RB	North Carolina	6	10	19	57
10	Lynn Dickey	QB	Kansas State	6	6	19	49

AWARD WINNERS

PLAYER	POS	SCHOOL	AWARD NAME
Jim Plunkett	QB	Stanford	Maxwell
Jim Stillwagon	MG	Ohio State	Outland
Jim Plunkett	QB	Stanford	Camp
Jim Stillwagon	MG	Ohio State	Lombardi

CONFERENCE STANDINGS

ACC

	Conf. W L T			Overall W L T		
Wake Forest	5	1	0	6	5	0
North Carolina	5	2	0	8	4	0
Duke	5	2	0	6	5	0
South Carolina	3	2	1	4	6	1
North Carolina St.	2	3	1	3	7	1
Clemson	2	4	0	3	8	0
Maryland	2	4	0	2	9	0
Virginia	0	6	0	5	6	0

Big 10

	Conf. W L T			Overall W L T		
Ohio State	7	0	0	9	1	0
Michigan	6	1	0	9	1	0
Northwestern	6	1	0	6	4	0
Iowa	3	3	1	3	6	1
Wisconsin	3	4	0	4	5	1
Michigan State	3	4	0	4	6	0
Minnesota	2	4	1	3	6	1
Purdue	2	5	0	4	6	0
Illinois	1	6	0	3	7	0
Indiana	1	6	0	1	9	0

Big 8

	Conf. W L T			Overall W L T		
Nebraska	7	0	0	11	0	1
Oklahoma	5	2	0	7	4	1
Kansas State	5	2	0	6	5	0
Colorado	3	4	0	6	5	0
Missouri	3	4	0	5	6	0
Kansas	2	5	0	5	6	0
Oklahoma State	2	5	0	4	7	0
Iowa State	1	6	0	5	6	0

Big West

	Conf. W L T			Overall W L T		
Long Beach State	5	1	0	9	2	0
San Diego State	5	1	0	9	2	0
Fresno State	4	2	0	8	4	0
Pacific	2	3	0	5	6	0
San Jose State	2	3	0	2	9	0
UC-Santa Barbara	1	5	0	2	9	0
Los Angeles State	0	4	0	1	9	0

Ivy

	Conf. W L T			Overall W L T		
Dartmouth	7	0	0	9	0	0
Yale	5	2	0	7	2	0
Harvard	5	2	0	7	2	0
Cornell	4	3	0	6	3	0
Princeton	3	4	0	5	4	0
Pennsylvania	2	5	0	4	5	0
Columbia	1	6	0	3	6	0
Brown	1	6	0	2	7	0

MAC

	Conf. W L T			Overall W L T		
Toledo	5	0	0	11	0	0
Miami, Ohio	3	2	0	7	3	0
Ohio U	3	2	0	4	5	0
Western Michigan	2	3	0	7	3	0
Kent State	1	4	0	3	7	0
Bowling Green	1	4	0	2	6	1

Pac 8

	Conf. W L T			Overall W L T		
Stanford	6	1	0	9	3	0
Washington	4	3	0	6	4	0
Oregon	4	3	0	6	4	1
UCLA	4	3	0	6	5	0
California	4	3	0	6	5	0
Southern Cal	3	4	0	6	4	1
Oregon State	3	4	0	6	5	0
Washington State	0	7	0	1	10	0

SEC

	Conf. W L T			Overall W L T		
LSU	5	0	0	9	3	0
Tennessee	4	1	0	11	1	0
Auburn	5	2	0	9	2	0
Mississippi	4	2	0	7	4	0
Florida	3	3	0	7	4	0
Georgia	3	3	0	5	5	0
Mississippi State	3	4	0	6	5	0
Alabama	3	4	0	6	5	1
Vanderbilt	1	5	0	4	7	0
Kentucky	0	7	0	2	9	0

SWC

	Conf. W L T			Overall W L T		
Texas	7	0	0	10	1	0
Arkansas	6	1	0	9	2	0
Texas Tech	5	2	0	8	4	0
Rice	3	4	0	5	5	0
SMU	3	4	0	5	6	0
TCU	3	4	0	4	6	1
Baylor	1	6	0	2	9	0
Texas A&M	0	7	0	2	9	0

WAC

	Conf. W L T			Overall W L T		
Arizona State	7	0	0	11	0	0
New Mexico	5	1	0	7	3	0
Utah	4	2	0	6	4	0
Texas-El Paso	4	3	0	6	4	0
Arizona	2	4	0	4	6	0
Colorado State	1	3	0	4	7	0
Brigham Young	1	6	0	3	8	0
Wyoming	1	6	0	1	9	0

Independents

	Overall W L T		
Notre Dame	10	1	0
Boston College	8	2	0
Georgia Tech	9	3	0
Air Force	9	3	0
Houston	8	3	0
West Virginia	8	3	0
Penn State	7	3	0
Tulane	8	4	0
Florida State	7	4	0
Syracuse	6	4	0
Rutgers	5	5	0
Utah State	5	5	0
Pittsburgh	5	5	0
Virginia Tech	5	6	0
New Mexico State	4	6	0
Miami, Fla.	3	8	0
Navy	2	9	0
Army	1	9	1

BOWL GAMES

DATE	GAME	SCORE
D12	Liberty	Tulane 17, Colorado 3
D19	Sun	Georgia Tech 17, Texas Tech 9
D19	Pasadena	Long Beach State 24, Louisville 24
D28	Tangerine	Toledo 40, William & Mary 12
D30	Peach	Arizona State 48, North Carolina 26
D31	Bluebonnet	Alabama 24, Oklahoma 24
J1	Sugar	Tennessee 34, Air Force 13
J1	Orange	Nebraska 17, LSU 12
J1	Cotton	Notre Dame 24, Texas 11
J1	Rose	Stanford 27, Ohio State 17
J2	Gator	Auburn 35, Mississippi 28

1970 NCAA Major College Statistical Leaders

Individual Leaders

PASSING	G	ATT	COM	PCT	INT	I%	YDS	YPA	TD	TD%	COM.PG
1 Sonny Sixkiller, Washington	10	362	186	51.4	22	6.1	2303	6.4	15	4.1	18.6
2 Bob Parker, Air Force	11	402	199	49.5	15	3.7	2789	6.9	21	5.2	18.1
3 Mark Thompson, Davidson	10	352	179	50.9	18	5.1	2202	6.3	14	4.0	17.9
4 Chuck Hixson, SMU	9	285	160	56.1	18	6.3	1763	6.2	10	3.5	17.8
5 Brian Sipe, San Diego State	11	337	195	57.9	20	5.9	2618	7.8	23	6.8	17.7
6 Jim Plunkett, Stanford	11	358	191	53.4	18	5.0	2715	7.6	18	5.0	17.4
7 Dan Fouts, Oregon	11	361	188	52.1	24	6.7	2390	6.6	16	4.4	17.1
7 John Reaves, Florida	11	376	188	50.0	19	5.1	2549	6.8	13	3.5	17.1
9 Pat Sullivan, Auburn	10	281	167	59.4	12	4.3	2586	9.2	17	6.1	16.7
10 John Read, Pacific	9	309	149	48.2	19	6.2	1697	5.5	13	4.2	16.6

ALL-PURPOSE	G	RUSH	REC	RET	YDS	YPG
1 Don McCauley, North Carolina	11	1720	235	66	2021	183.7
2 Ed Marinaro, Cornell	9	1425	129	0	1554	172.7
3 Phil Mosser, William & Mary	11	1286	139	447	1872	170.2
4 Larry McCutcheon, Colorado State	11	1008	486	316	1810	164.5
5 Brian Bream, Air Force	10	1276	237	0	1513	151.3
6 Eric Allen, Michigan State	10	811	125	575	1511	151.1
7 Henry Hawthorne, Kansas State	11	399	501	748	1648	149.8
8 Clarence Davis, Southern Cal	11	972	203	444	1619	147.2
9 Gary Hammond, SMU	11	891	489	224	1604	145.8
10 Jake Green, Colorado State	11	468	459	679	1601	145.5

RUSHING/Yards Per Game	G	ATT	YDS	TD	AVG	YPG
1 Ed Marinaro, Cornell	9	285	1425	12	5.0	158.3
2 Don McCauley, North Carolina	11	324	1720	19	5.3	156.4
3 Hank Bjorklund, Princeton	8	179	1081	7	6.0	135.1
4 Gary Kosins, Dayton	9	344	1172	18	3.4	130.2
5 Brian Bream, Air Force	10	294	1276	19	4.3	127.6
6 Mike Adamle, Northwestern	10	304	1255	8	4.1	125.5
7 Roger Lawson, Western Michigan	10	168	1205	13	7.2	120.5
8 Bill Gary, Ohio U.	9	265	1064	11	4.0	118.2
9 Phil Mosser, William & Mary	11	212	1286	9	6.1	116.9
10 John Brockington, Ohio State	9	240	1041	15	4.3	115.7

RUSHING/Yards Per Carry	G	ATT	YDS	YPC
1 Roger Lawson, Western Michigan	10	168	1205	7.2
2 Bob Duncan, Citadel	9	139	881	6.3
3 Phil Mosser, William & Mary	11	212	1286	6.1
4 Hank Bjorklund, Princeton	8	179	1081	6.0
5 John Riggins, Kansas	11	209	1131	5.4
6 Don McCauley, North Carolina	11	324	1720	5.3
7 Dick Jauron, Yale	9	182	962	5.3
8 Monroe Eley, Arizona State	8	141	739	5.2
9 Sam Scarber, New Mexico	10	184	961	5.2
10 Johnny Musso, Alabama	11	226	1137	5.0

*-Based on top 24 rushers

RECEIVING	G	REC	YDS	TD	YPR	YPG	RPG
1 Mike Mikolayunas, Davidson	10	87	1128	8	13.0	112.8	8.7
2 Tom Gatewood, Notre Dame	10	77	1123	7	14.6	112.3	7.7
3 Don Fair, Toledo	11	76	893	4	11.8	81.2	6.9
4 Mike Siani, Villanova	11	74	1358	12	18.4	123.5	6.7
4 Ernie Jennings, Air Force	11	74	1289	17	17.4	117.2	6.7
4 Wes Chesson, Duke	11	74	1080	3	14.6	98.2	6.7
4 David Smith, Mississippi State	11	74	987	6	13.3	89.7	6.7
8 Tim Delaney, San Diego State	10	62	794	6	12.8	79.4	6.2
9 Bob Newland, Oregon	11	67	1123	7	16.8	102.1	6.1
10 J.D. Hill, Arizona State	10	58	908	10	15.7	90.8	5.8

PUNTING	PUNT	YDS	AVG
1 Marv Bateman, Utah	65	2971	45.7
2 Ray Guy, Southern Miss	69	3126	45.3
3 Jim McCann, Arizona State	48	2026	42.2
4 Mike Parrott, Houston	64	2656	41.5
5 Paul Staroba, Michigan	54	2241	41.5
6 Ron Davis, Idaho	88	3643	41.4
7 Scott Hamm, Air Force	53	2184	41.2
8 Bob Jacobs, Wyoming	84	3444	41.0
9 Ken Duncan, Tulsa	67	2747	41.0
10 Jack Anderson, Clemson	35	1435	41.0

PUNT RETURNS	PR	YDS	TD	AVG
1 Steve Holden, Arizona State	17	327	2	19.2
2 Bob Wicks, Utah State	16	279	2	17.4
3 Ralph McGill, Tulsa	27	460	2	17.0
4 Greg Campbell, Louisville	16	267	2	16.7
5 Raymond Brown, West Texas State	15	250	0	16.7
6 Don Kelley, Clemson	24	389	2	16.2
7 Craig Burns, LSU	21	339	2	16.1
8 Tom Myers, Syracuse	29	436	0	15.0
9 Mike Reynolds, Texas-El Paso	25	375	2	15.0
10 Gary Windy, Illinois	17	252	1	14.8

KICKOFF RETURNS	KR	YDS	TD	AVG
1 Stan Brown, Purdue	19	638	3	33.6
2 Macon Hughes, Rice	15	459	2	30.6
3 Jim Krieg, Washington	19	576	2	30.3
4 Dick Harris, South Carolina	30	880	1	29.3
5 Rod Foster, Harvard	11	307	0	27.9
6 Jon Robertson, San Diego State	20	557	1	27.9
7 Henry Hawthorne, Kansas State	23	632	0	27.5
8 Ron Po James, New Mexico State	25	680	0	27.2
9 Cliff Branch, Colorado	21	564	2	26.9
10 Dick Graham, Oklahoma State	17	449	2	26.4

SCORING	TDS	XPT	FG	PTS	PTPG
1 Brian Bream, Air Force	20	0	0	120	12.0
1 Gary Kosins, Dayton	18	0	0	108	12.0
3 Don McCauley, North Carolina	21	0	0	126	11.5
4 Fred Willis, Boston College	16	0	0	96	10.7
5 Ernie Jennings, Air Force	19	0	0	114	10.4
6 John Short, Dartmouth	15	0	0	90	10.0
6 John Brockington, Ohio State	15	0	0	90	10.0
8 Ed Marinaro, Cornell	14	2	0	86	9.6
9 Steve Worster, Texas	14	0	0	84	8.4
9 J.D. Hill, Arizona State	14	0	0	84	8.4

KICK SCORING	XPA	XP	FGA	FG	PTS	PTPG
1 Bill McClard, Arkansas	51	50	15	10	80	7.3
2 Gardner Jett, Auburn	44	41	12	10	71	7.1
3 Happy Feller, Texas	57	55	14	5	70	7.0
3 Dave Haney, Colorado	36	34	18	12	70	7.0
5 George Hunt, Tennessee	43	42	21	10	72	6.5
5 Tom Duncan, Toledo	44	36	21	12	72	6.5
7 Don Ekstrand, Arizona State	47	38	12	9	65	6.5
8 Paul Rogers, Nebraska	52	48	12	7	69	6.3
9 Matias Garza, West Texas State	32	29	21	11	62	6.2
10 Kim Braswell, Georgia	24	22	17	13	61	6.1

INTERCEPTIONS	INT	YDS	TD	INT/GM
1 Mike Sensibaugh, Ohio State	8	40	0	1.00
2 Bobby Majors, Tennessee	10	177	0	0.91
3 Neovia Greyer, Wisconsin	9	116	0	0.90
4 Jeff Varnadoe, Citadel	9	251	3	0.82
4 Tim Priest, Tennessee	9	174	0	0.82
4 Paul Ellis, Tulane	9	109	0	0.82
7 Raymond Brown, West Texas State	8	162	1	0.80
7 Tom Elias, Western Michigan	8	136	1	0.80
9 Joe Bullard, Tulane	8	167	1	0.73
9 Craig Burns, LSU	8	117	0	0.73
9 Ron Ayala, Southern Cal	8	113	0	0.73
9 Dan Hansen, Brigham Young	8	108	0	0.73
9 Bo Davies, South Carolina	8	41	0	0.73

Team Leaders

RUSHING OFFENSE	G	ATT	YDS	AVG	TD	YPG
1 Texas	10	715	3745	5.2	51	374.5
2 New Mexico	10	637	3501	5.5	33	350.1
3 Ohio State	9	564	2761	4.9	32	306.8
4 Colorado	10	625	2998	4.8	29	299.8
5 Arizona State	10	595	2982	5.0	22	298.2
6 North Carolina	11	732	3137	4.3	31	285.2
7 Penn State	10	617	2768	4.5	31	276.8
8 Cincinnati	11	639	3011	4.7	27	273.7
9 Dartmouth	9	510	2368	4.6	30	263.1
10 Western Michigan	10	558	2631	4.7	22	263.1

PASSING OFFENSE	G	ATT	COM	INT	PCT	YDS	YPA	TD	I%	YPC	YPG
1 Auburn	10	311	181	12	58.2	2885	9.3	17	3.9	15.9	288.5
2 Oregon	11	441	230	28	52.2	3100	7.0	22	6.4	13.5	281.8
3 San Diego State	11	390	215	24	55.1	3029	7.8	28	6.2	14.1	275.4
4 Washington	10	415	213	26	51.3	2723	6.6	22	6.3	12.8	272.3
5 Stanford	11	391	206	21	52.7	2950	7.5	18	5.4	14.3	268.2
6 Florida State	11	345	175	16	50.7	2837	8.2	17	4.6	16.2	257.9
7 Air Force	11	404	200	15	49.5	2801	6.9	21	3.7	14.0	254.6
8 Notre Dame	10	283	162	15	57.2	2527	8.9	16	5.3	15.6	252.7
9 Villanova	11	385	193	18	50.1	2709	7.0	23	4.7	14.0	246.3
10 Florida	11	396	195	21	49.2	2622	6.6	15	5.3	13.4	238.4

TOTAL OFFENSE	G	P	YDS	AVG	TD	YPG
1 Arizona State	10	870	5145	5.9	42	514.5
2 Notre Dame	10	924	5105	5.5	45	510.5
3 Auburn	10	684	4850	7.1	43	485.0
4 Texas	10	840	4681	5.6	56	468.1
5 Southern Cal	11	869	4956	5.7	44	450.5
6 Dartmouth	9	713	3892	5.5	39	432.4
7 Stanford	11	866	4687	5.4	39	426.1
8 West Virginia	11	823	4677	5.7	42	425.2
9 Air Force	11	902	4660	5.2	46	423.6
10 Colorado	10	840	4229	5.0	35	422.9

RUSHING DEFENSE	G	ATT	YDS	AVG	TD	YPG
1 LSU	11	356	574	1.6	2	52.2
2 Tennessee	11	428	972	2.3	6	88.4
3 Dartmouth	9	384	820	2.1	4	91.1
4 North Carolina	11	405	1048	2.6	12	95.3
5 Notre Dame	10	376	962	2.6	6	96.2
6 Penn State	10	442	1008	2.3	12	100.8
7 Miami, Ohio	10	504	1050	2.1	8	105.0
8 Michigan	10	416	1051	2.5	5	105.1
9 Yale	9	407	958	2.4	6	106.4
10 Ohio State	9	391	965	2.5	4	107.2

PASSING DEFENSE	G	ATT	COM	PCT	YPC	INT	I%	YDS	YPA	TD	YPG
1 Toledo	11	251	88	35.1	9.7	24	9.6	856	3.4	1	77.8
2 Northwestern	10	191	61	31.9	13.0	18	9.4	793	4.2	4	79.3
3 Miami, Ohio	10	191	84	44.0	10.5	14	7.3	881	4.6	6	88.1
4 Dayton	10	221	74	33.5	12.5	15	6.8	928	4.2	3	92.8
5 Dartmouth	9	188	76	40.4	11.3	18	9.6	857	4.6	2	95.2
6 San Diego State	11	230	85	37.0	12.5	12	5.2	1062	4.6	6	96.5
7 Bowling Green	9	164	77	47.0	12.1	12	7.3	935	5.7	5	103.9
8 Tulane	11	247	106	42.9	11.2	28	11.3	1184	4.8	1	107.6
9 Rice	10	191	86	45.0	12.6	19	10.0	1087	5.7	5	108.7
10 Harvard	9	195	82	42.1	11.9	16	8.2	979	5.0	7	108.8

TOTAL DEFENSE	G	P	YDS	AVG	TD	YPG
1 Toledo	11	727	2044	2.8	8	185.8
2 Dartmouth	9	572	1677	2.9	6	186.3
3 Miami, Ohio	10	695	1931	2.8	14	193.1
4 San Diego State	11	742	2263	3.0	16	205.7
5 Notre Dame	10	658	2207	3.4	10	220.7
6 Tulane	11	801	2497	3.1	15	227.0
7 Arizona State	10	729	2378	3.3	15	237.8
8 Dayton	10	703	2423	3.4	18	242.3
9 LSU	11	746	2689	3.6	10	244.5
10 Ohio State	9	628	2224	3.5	11	247.1

SCORING OFFENSE	G	PTS	AVG
1 Texas	10	412	41.2
2 Nebraska	11	409	37.2
3 Arkansas	11	402	36.5
4 Arizona State	10	357	35.7
5 Auburn	10	355	35.5
6 Dartmouth	9	311	34.6
7 Washington	10	334	33.4
8 San Diego State	11	364	33.1
9 Notre Dame	10	330	33.0
10 Air Force	11	353	32.1

SCORING DEFENSE	G	PTS	AVG
1 Dartmouth	9	42	4.7
2 Toledo	11	76	6.9
3 LSU	11	96	8.7
4 Michigan	10	90	9.0
5 Tennessee	11	103	9.4
6 Notre Dame	10	97	9.7
7 Cincinnati	11	108	9.8
8 Ohio State	9	93	10.3
9 Yale	9	97	10.8
10 San Diego State	11	123	11.2

1971 POLL PROGRESSION

AP	PRE-SEASON		SEPT. 11 GAMES
1	Notre Dame	0-0-0	bye week
2	Nebraska	0-0-0	beat Oregon 34-7
3	Texas	0-0-0	bye week
4	Michigan	0-0-0	beat # 20 Northwestern 21-6
5	Southern Cal	0-0-0	lost to # 16 Alabama 10-17
6	Auburn	0-0-0	bye week
7	Arkansas	0-0-0	beat California 51-20
8	Tennessee	0-0-0	bye week
9	LSU	0-0-0	lost to Colorado 21-31
10	Oklahoma	0-0-0	bye week
11	Ohio State	0-0-0	beat Iowa 52-21
12	Penn State	0-0-0	bye week
13	Syracuse	0-0-0	bye week
14	Arizona State	0-0-0	bye week
15	UCLA	0-0-0	lost to Pittsburgh 25-29
16	Alabama	0-0-0	beat # 5 Southern Cal 17-10
17	Georgia Tech	0-0-0	lost to South Carolina 7-24
18	Georgia	0-0-0	beat Oregon State 56-25
19	Stanford	0-0-0	beat Missouri 19-0
20	Northwestern	0-0-0	lost to # 4 Michigan 6-21

UP	AP	SEPTEMBER 13 POLL		SEPT. 18 GAMES
1	1	Nebraska	1-0-0	beat Minnesota 35-7
2	2	Notre Dame	0-0-0	beat Northwestern 50-7
3	3	Texas	0-0-0	beat UCLA 28-10
5	4	Michigan	1-0-0	beat Virginia 56-0
4	5	Ohio State	1-0-0	bye week
9	6	Arkansas	1-0-0	beat Oklahoma State 31-10
10	7	Auburn	1-0-0	beat U.T. Chattanooga 60-7
7	8	Tennessee	0-0-0	beat Santa Barbara 48-6
6	9	Alabama	1-0-0	beat Southern Miss 42-6
12	10	Oklahoma	0-0-0	beat SMU 30-0
13	11	Georgia	1-0-0	beat Tulane 17-7
8	12	Colorado	1-0-0	beat Wyoming 56-13
11	13	Stanford	1-0-0	beat Army 38-3
16	14	Penn State	0-0-0	beat Navy 56-3
19	15	Syracuse	0-0-0	tied Wisconsin 20-20
15	16	Arizona State	0-0-0	beat # 20 Houston 18-17
17	17	Southern Cal	0-1-0	beat Rice 24-0
	18	Michigan State	1-0-0	lost to Georgia Tech 0-10
	19	South Carolina	1-0-0	lost to Duke 12-28
20	20	Houston	1-0-0	lost to # 16 Arizona State 17-18
14		Washington	1-0-0	beat Purdue 38-35
18		LSU	0-1-0	beat Texas A&M 37-0

UP	AP	SEPTEMBER 20 POLL		SEPT. 25 GAMES
1	1	Nebraska	2-0-0	beat Texas A&M 34-7
2	2	Notre Dame	1-0-0	beat Purdue 8-7
3	3	Texas	1-0-0	beat Texas Tech 28-0
4	4	Michigan	2-0-0	beat UCLA 38-0
7	5	Auburn	2-0-0	beat # 9 Tennessee 10-9
5	6	Ohio State	1-0-0	lost to # 10 Colorado 14-20
9	7	Arkansas	2-0-0	lost to Tulsa 20-21
6	8	Alabama	2-0-0	beat Florida 38-0
8	9	Tennessee	1-0-0	lost to # 5 Auburn 9-10
10	10	Colorado	2-0-0	beat # 6 Ohio State 20-14
11	11	Oklahoma	1-0-0	beat Pittsburgh 55-29
	12	Penn State	1-0-0	beat Iowa 44-14
12	13	Stanford	2-0-0	beat Oregon 38-17
13	14	Georgia	2-0-0	beat Clemson 28-0
16	15	Arizona State	1-0-0	beat Utah 41-21
17	16	Southern Cal	1-1-0	beat Illinois 28-0
14	17	Washington	2-0-0	beat TCU 44-26
18	18	LSU	1-1-0	beat Wisconsin 38-28
	19	Toledo	2-0-0	beat Texas-Arlington 23-0
	20	Duke	2-0-0	beat Virginia 28-0
19		North Carolina	2-0-0	beat Maryland 35-14
19		Georgia Tech	1-1-0	lost to Army 13-16

UP	AP	SEPTEMBER 27 POLL		OCT. 2 GAMES
1	1	Nebraska	3-0-0	beat Utah State 42-6
2	2	Michigan	3-0-0	beat Navy 46-0
3	3	Texas	2-0-0	beat Oregon 35-7
4	4	Notre Dame	2-0-0	beat Michigan State 14-2
7	5	Auburn	2-0-0	beat Kentucky 38-6
6	6	Colorado	3-0-0	beat Kansas State 31-21
5	7	Alabama	3-0-0	beat Mississippi 40-6
8	8	Oklahoma	2-0-0	beat # 17 Southern Cal 33-20
11	9	Penn State	2-0-0	beat Air Force 16-14
9	10	Stanford	3-0-0	lost to # 19 Duke 3-9
13	11	Georgia	3-0-0	beat Mississippi State 35-7
15	12	Tennessee	1-1-0	beat Florida 20-13
12	13	Arizona State	2-0-0	beat Texas-El Paso 24-7
17	14	Ohio State	1-1-0	beat California 35-3
10	15	Washington	3-0-0	beat Illinois 52-14
16	16	LSU	2-1-0	beat Rice 38-3
14	17	Southern Cal	2-1-0	lost to # 8 Oklahoma 20-33
	18	Arkansas	2-1-0	beat TCU 49-15
	19	Duke	3-0-0	beat # 10 Stanford 9-3
18	20	North Carolina	3-0-0	beat North Carolina State 27-7

UP	AP	OCTOBER 4 POLL		OCT. 9 GAMES
1	1	Nebraska	4-0-0	beat Missouri 36-0
2	2	Michigan	4-0-0	beat Michigan State 24-13
3	3	Texas	3-0-0	lost to # 8 Oklahoma 27-48
6	4	Auburn	3-0-0	beat Southern Miss 27-14
7	5	Colorado	4-0-0	beat Iowa State 24-14
4	6	Alabama	4-0-0	beat Vanderbilt 42-0
5	7	Notre Dame	3-0-0	beat Miami, Fla. 17-0
8	8	Oklahoma	3-0-0	beat # 3 Texas 48-27
11	9	Penn State	3-0-0	beat Army 42-0
10	10	Georgia	4-0-0	beat Mississippi 38-7
9	11	Washington	4-0-0	lost to # 19 Stanford 6-17
14	12	Arizona State	3-0-0	beat Colorado State 42-0
11	13	Tennessee	2-1-0	beat Georgia Tech 10-6
15	14	Duke	4-0-0	lost to Clemson 0-3
13	15	Ohio State	2-1-0	beat Illinois 24-10
16	16	LSU	3-1-0	beat Florida 48-7
18	17	Arkansas	3-1-0	beat Baylor 35-7
17	18	North Carolina	4-0-0	lost to Tulane 29-37
	19	Stanford	3-1-0	beat # 11 Washington 17-6
	20	Toledo	4-0-0	beat Bowling Green 24-7

UP	AP	OCTOBER 11 POLL		OCT. 16 GAMES
1	1	Nebraska	5-0-0	beat Kansas 55-0
2	2	Oklahoma	4-0-0	beat # 6 Colorado 45-17
3	3	Michigan	5-0-0	beat Illinois 35-6
4	4	Alabama	5-0-0	beat # 14 Tennessee 32-15
7	5	Auburn	4-0-0	beat Georgia Tech 31-14
5	6	Colorado	5-0-0	lost to # 2 Oklahoma 17-45
6	7	Notre Dame	4-0-0	beat North Carolina 16-0
8	8	Georgia	5-0-0	beat Vanderbilt 24-0
9	9	Penn State	4-0-0	beat Syracuse 31-0
10	10	Texas	3-1-0	lost to # 16 Arkansas 7-31
11	11	Arizona State	4-0-0	lost to Oregon State 18-24
12	12	LSU	4-1-0	beat Kentucky 17-13
15	13	Ohio State	3-1-0	beat Indiana 27-7
14	14	Tennessee	3-1-0	lost to # 4 Alabama 15-32
13	15	Stanford	4-1-0	beat Southern Cal 33-18
17	16	Arkansas	4-1-0	beat # 10 Texas 31-7
	17	Toledo	5-0-0	beat Western Michigan 35-24
18	18	Washington	4-1-0	lost to Oregon 21-23
16	19	Florida State	5-0-0	lost to Florida 15-17
	20	Purdue	2-2-0	beat Northwestern 21-20

UP	AP	OCTOBER 18 POLL		OCT. 23 GAMES
1	1	Nebraska	6-0-0	beat Oklahoma State 41-13
2	2	Oklahoma	5-0-0	beat Kansas State 75-28
3	3	Michigan	6-0-0	beat Minnesota 35-7
4	4	Alabama	6-0-0	beat Houston 34-20
5	5	Auburn	5-0-0	beat Clemson 35-13
6	6	Notre Dame	5-0-0	lost to Southern Cal 14-28
8	7	Penn State	5-0-0	beat TCU 66-14
7	8	Georgia	6-0-0	beat Kentucky 34-0
9	9	Arkansas	5-1-0	beat North Texas 60-21
10	10	Stanford	5-1-0	lost to Washington State 23-24
12	11	Colorado	5-1-0	beat Missouri 27-7
11	12	Ohio State	4-1-0	beat Wisconsin 31-6
13	13	LSU	5-1-0	bye week
14	14	Arizona State	4-1-0	beat New Mexico 60-28
	15	Toledo	6-0-0	beat Dayton 35-7
	16	Texas	3-2-0	beat Rice 39-10
16	17	Purdue	3-2-0	lost to Illinois 7-21
16	18	Tennessee	3-2-0	beat Mississippi State 10-7
	19	Duke	5-1-0	lost to Navy 14-15
	20	Air Force	4-1-0	beat Colorado State 17-12
15		Houston	4-1-0	lost to # 4 Alabama 20-34

UP	AP	OCTOBER 25 POLL		OCT. 30 GAMES
1	1	Nebraska	7-0-0	beat # 9 Colorado 31-7
2	2	Oklahoma	6-0-0	beat Iowa State 43-12
3	3	Michigan	7-0-0	beat Indiana 61-7
4	4	Alabama	7-0-0	beat Mississippi State 41-10
5	5	Auburn	6-0-0	beat Florida 40-7
7	6	Penn State	6-0-0	beat West Virginia 35-7
6	7	Georgia	7-0-0	beat South Carolina 24-0
8	8	Arkansas	6-1-0	lost to Texas A&M 9-17
9	9	Colorado	6-1-0	lost to # 1 Nebraska 7-31
10	10	Ohio State	5-1-0	beat Minnesota 14-12
12	11	LSU	5-1-0	lost to Mississippi 22-24
11	12	Notre Dame	5-1-0	beat Navy 21-0
15	13	Arizona State	5-1-0	beat Air Force 44-28
17	14	Texas	4-2-0	beat SMU 22-18
13	15	Toledo	7-0-0	beat Miami, Ohio 45-6
14	16	Tennessee	4-2-0	beat Tulsa 38-3
	17	Stanford	5-2-0	beat Oregon State 31-24
18	18	Air Force	5-1-0	lost to Arizona State 28-44
16	19	Florida State	6-1-0	lost to Houston 7-14
	20	Southern Cal	3-4-0	beat California 28-0

UP	AP	NOVEMBER 1 POLL		NOV. 6 GAMES
1	1	Nebraska	8-0-0	beat Iowa State 37-0
2	2	Oklahoma	7-0-0	beat Missouri 20-3
3	3	Michigan	8-0-0	beat Iowa 63-7
4	4	Alabama	8-0-0	beat # 18 LSU 14-7
5	5	Auburn	7-0-0	beat Mississippi State 30-21
7	6	Penn State	7-0-0	beat Maryland 63-27
6	7	Georgia	8-0-0	beat Florida 49-7
9	8	Notre Dame	6-1-0	beat Pittsburgh 56-7
8	9	Ohio State	6-1-0	lost to Michigan State 10-17
10	10	Arizona State	6-1-0	beat Brigham Young 38-13
15	11	Tennessee	5-2-0	beat South Carolina 35-6
12	12	Stanford	6-2-0	beat UCLA 20-9
11	13	Colorado	6-2-0	beat Kansas 35-14
14	14	Toledo	8-0-0	beat No. Illinois 23-8
17	15	Texas	5-2-0	beat Baylor 24-0
12	16	Arkansas	6-2-0	tied Rice 24-24
20	17	Southern Cal	4-4-0	beat Washington State 30-20
18	18	LSU	5-2-0	lost to # 4 Alabama 7-14
16	19	Houston	5-2-0	beat Memphis 35-7
	20	Washington	6-2-0	beat California 30-7
19		North Carolina	6-2-0	beat Clemson 26-13

November 8 Poll — Nov. 13 Games

UP	AP	Team	Record	Result
1	1	Nebraska	9-0-0	beat Kansas State 44-17
2	2	Oklahoma	8-0-0	beat Kansas 56-10
3	3	Michigan	9-0-0	beat Purdue 20-17
4	4	Alabama	9-0-0	beat Miami, Fla. 31-3
7	5	Penn State	8-0-0	beat North Carolina St. 35-3
5	6	Auburn	8-0-0	beat # 7 Georgia 35-20
6	7	Georgia	9-0-0	lost to # 6 Auburn 20-35
8	8	Notre Dame	7-1-0	beat Tulane 21-7
9	9	Arizona State	7-1-0	beat Wyoming 52-19
10	10	Stanford	7-2-0	lost to San Jose State 12-13
12	11	Tennessee	6-2-0	bye week
11	12	Colorado	7-2-0	beat Oklahoma State 40-6
15	13	Texas	6-2-0	beat TCU 31-0
13	14	Toledo	9-0-0	beat Marshall 43-0
15	15	Southern Cal	5-4-0	beat # 19 Washington 13-12
19	16	Ohio State	6-2-0	lost to Northwestern 10-14
	17	Arkansas	6-2-1	beat SMU 18-13
14	18	Houston	6-2-0	beat Virginia Tech 56-29
	19	Washington	7-2-0	lost to # 15 Southern Cal 12-13
	20	LSU	5-3-0	beat Mississippi State 28-3
15		North Carolina	7-2-0	beat Virginia 32-20
15		Michigan State	5-4-0	beat Minnesota 40-25
19		Florida State	6-2-0	lost to Georgia Tech 6-12

November 15 Poll — Nov. 20 Games

UP	AP	Team	Record	Result
1	1	Nebraska	10-0-0	bye week
2	2	Oklahoma	9-0-0	bye week
3	3	Michigan	10-0-0	beat Ohio State 10-7
4	4	Alabama	10-0-0	bye week
5	5	Auburn	9-0-0	bye week
6	6	Penn State	9-0-0	beat Pittsburgh 55-18
7	7	Notre Dame	8-1-0	lost to # 14 LSU 8-28
9	8	Georgia	9-1-0	bye week
8	9	Arizona State	8-1-0	beat San Jose State 49-6
10	10	Colorado	8-2-0	beat Air Force 53-17
11	11	Tennessee	6-2-0	beat Kentucky 21-7
14	12	Texas	7-2-0	bye week
12	13	Toledo	10-0-0	beat Kent State 41-6
18	14	LSU	6-3-0	beat # 7 Notre Dame 28-8
16	15	Southern Cal	6-4-0	tied UCLA 7-7
13	16	Houston	7-2-0	beat Miami, Fla. 27-6
19	17	Arkansas	7-2-1	beat Texas Tech 15-0
20	18	Stanford	7-3-0	beat California 14-0
	19	Michigan State	6-4-0	lost to Northwestern 7-28
	20	Mississippi	8-2-0	bye week
17		North Carolina	8-2-0	beat Duke 38-0

November 22 Poll — Nov. 27 Games

UP	AP	Team	Record	Result
1	1	Nebraska	10-0-0	beat # 2 Oklahoma 35-31
2	2	Oklahoma	9-0-0	lost to # 1 Nebraska 31-35
3	3	Alabama	10-0-0	beat # 5 Auburn 31-7
5	4	Michigan	11-0-0	regular season complete
4	5	Auburn	9-0-0	lost to # 3 Alabama 7-31
6	6	Penn State	10-0-0	bye week
7	7	Georgia	9-1-0	beat Georgia Tech 28-24
8	8	Colorado	9-2-0	regular season complete
9	9	Arizona State	9-1-0	beat Arizona 31-0
10	10	LSU	7-3-0	beat Tulane 36-7
11	11	Tennessee	7-2-0	beat Vanderbilt 19-7
18	12	Texas	7-2-0	beat Texas A&M 34-14
14	13	Notre Dame	8-2-0	regular season complete
12	14	Toledo	11-0-0	regular season complete
13	15	Houston	8-2-0	beat Utah 42-16
16	16	Stanford	8-3-0	regular season complete
18	17	Arkansas	8-2-1	regular season complete
	18	Mississippi	8-2-0	beat Mississippi State 48-0
15	19	North Carolina	9-2-0	regular season complete
	20	Washington	8-3-0	beat Washington State 28-20
17		Iowa State	7-3-0	beat San Diego State 48-31
20		Florida State	7-3-0	beat Pittsburgh 31-13

November 29 Poll — Dec. 4 Games

UP	AP	Team	Record	Result
1	1	Nebraska	11-0-0	beat Hawaii 45-3
2	2	Alabama	11-0-0	regular season complete
3	3	Oklahoma	9-1-0	beat Oklahoma State 58-14
4	4	Michigan	11-0-0	
5	5	Penn State	10-0-0	lost to # 12 Tennessee 11-31
6	6	Auburn	9-1-0	regular season complete
8	7	Georgia	10-1-0	regular season complete
7	8	Colorado	9-2-0	
9	9	Arizona State	10-1-0	regular season complete
10	10	LSU	8-3-0	regular season complete
11	11	Texas	8-2-0	regular season complete
12	12	Tennessee	8-2-0	beat # 5 Penn State 31-11
13	13	Toledo	11-0-0	
	14	Notre Dame	8-2-0	
14	15	Houston	9-2-0	regular season complete
16	16	Arkansas	8-2-1	
15	16	Stanford	8-3-0	
	18	Mississippi	9-2-0	regular season complete
17	18	North Carolina	9-2-0	
20	20	Washington	8-3-0	regular season complete
18		Iowa State	8-3-0	regular season complete
19		Florida State	8-3-0	regular season complete

December 6 Poll / January 3 Final Poll

UP	AP	Team	Record	Bowl Bid	Date	Bowl Result	RB	AP	January 3 Final Poll	Record
1	1	Nebraska	12-0-0	Orange Bowl	J1	beat # 2 Alabama 38-6	1	1	Nebraska	13-0-0
2	2	Alabama	11-0-0	Orange Bowl	J1	lost to # 1 Nebraska 6-38	2	2	Oklahoma	11-1-0
3	3	Oklahoma	10-1-0	Sugar Bowl	J1	beat # 5 Auburn 40-22	9	3	Colorado	10-2-0
4	4	Michigan	11-0-0	Rose Bowl	J1	lost to # 16 Stanford 12-13	3	4	Alabama	11-1-0
5	5	Auburn	9-1-0	Sugar Bowl	J1	lost to # 3 Oklahoma 22-40	5	5	Penn State	11-1-0
8	6	Georgia	10-1-0	Gator Bowl	D31	beat North Carolina 7-3	7	6	Michigan	11-1-0
7	7	Colorado	9-2-0	Bluebonnet Bowl	D31	beat # 15 Houston 29-17	6	7	Georgia	11-1-0
6	8	Arizona State	10-1-0	Fiesta Bowl	D27	beat Florida State 45-38	8	8	Arizona State	11-1-0
9	9	Tennessee	9-2-0	Liberty Bowl	D20	beat # 18 Arkansas 14-13	4	9	Tennessee	10-2-0
11	10	Penn State	10-1-0	Cotton Bowl	J1	beat # 12 Texas 30-6	16	10	Stanford	9-3-0
10	11	LSU	8-3-0	Sun Bowl	D18	beat Iowa State 33-15	11	11	LSU	9-3-0
12	12	Texas	8-2-0	Cotton Bowl	J1	lost to # 10 Penn State 6-30	10	12	Auburn	9-2-0
15	13	Notre Dame	8-2-0				13		Notre Dame	8-2-0
13	14	Toledo	11-0-0	Tangerine Bowl	D28	beat Richmond 28-3	NR	14	Toledo	12-0-0
14	15	Houston	9-2-0	Bluebonnet Bowl	D31	lost to # 7 Colorado 17-29	14	15	Mississippi	10-2-0
16	16	Stanford	8-3-0	Rose Bowl	J1	beat # 4 Michigan 13-12	20	16	Arkansas	8-3-1
20	17	Mississippi	9-2-0	Peach Bowl	D30	beat Georgia Tech 41-18	18	17	Houston	9-3-0
20	18	Arkansas	8-2-1	Liberty Bowl	D20	lost to # 9 Tennessee 13-14	15	18	Texas	8-3-0
	19	Northwestern	7-4-0				19	19	Washington	8-3-0
	20	Washington	8-3-0				30	20	Southern Cal	6-4-1
17		Iowa State	8-3-0	Sun Bowl	D18	lost to # 11 LSU 15-33				
18		North Carolina	9-2-0	Gator Bowl	D31	lost to # 6 Georgia 3-7				
19		Florida State	8-3-0	Fiesta Bowl	D27	lost to # 8 Arizona State 38-45				

1971

CONSENSUS ALL-AMERICANS

POS	Offense	HT	WT	School	AP	FC	FW	NE	PI
QB	Pat Sullivan	6-0	191	Auburn	•	•	•	•	•
RB	Ed Marinaro	6-3	210	Cornell	•	•	•	•	•
RB	Greg Pruitt	5-9	176	Oklahoma	•	•	•	•	•
RB	Johnny Musso	5-11	194	Alabama	•	•	•	•	•
E	Terry Beasley	5-11	184	Auburn	•	•	•	•	•
E	Johnny Rodgers	5-10	171	Nebraska	•	•	•	•	•
T	Jerry Sisemore	6-4	255	Texas	•	•	•	•	•
T	Dave Joyner	6-0	235	Penn State	•	•	•		•
G	Royce Smith	6-3	240	Georgia	•	•	•	•	•
G	Reggie McKenzie	6-4	232	Michigan	•	•	•	•	
C	Tom Brahaney	6-2	231	Oklahoma	•	•	•	•	•

	OTHERS RECEIVING FIRST-TEAM HONORS								
RB	Eric Allen			Michigan State		•			
RB	Lydell Mitchell			Penn State	•				
RB	Bobby Moore			Oregon				•	
E	Doug Kingsriter			Minnesota	•				
T	John Hannah			Alabama		•			
T	John Vella			Southern Cal	•			•	
C	Tom DeLeone			Ohio State	•				

FC named Joyner as a G

POS	Defense	HT	WT	School	AP	FC	FW	NE	PI
E	Walt Patulski	6-5	235	Notre Dame	•	•	•	•	•
E	Willie Harper	6-3	207	Nebraska	•	•	•	•	•
T	Larry Jacobson	6-6	250	Nebraska	•	•	•	•	
T	Mel Long	6-1	230	Toledo	•		•	•	•
T	Sherman White	6-5	250	California	•	•	•	•	
LB	Mike Taylor	6-2	224	Michigan	•	•	•	•	•
LB	Jeff Siemon	6-2	225	Stanford	•	•	•	•	•
B	Bobby Majors	6-1	197	Tennessee	•	•	•	•	•
B	Clarence Ellis	6-0	178	Notre Dame	•	•	•	•	
B	Ernie Jackson	5-10	170	Duke	•	•			
B	Tommy Casanova	6-2	195	LSU	•	•			

	OTHERS RECEIVING FIRST-TEAM HONORS								
E	Herb Orvis			Colorado		•			
E	Smylie Gebhart			Georgia Tech	•				
T	Ron Curl			Michigan State		•			
T	Ronnie Estay			LSU		•			
T	Rich Glover			Nebraska	•				
LB	Jackie Walker			Tennessee			•		
LB	Dave Chaney			San Jose State	•		•		
LB	Charlie Zapiec			Penn State	•				
B	Eric Hutchinson			Northwestern			•		
B	Tom Darden			Michigan	•				
B	Tom Myers			Syracuse	•				
B	Craig Clemons			Iowa				•	
K	Bill McClard			Arkansas			•		

HEISMAN TROPHY VOTING

	PLAYER	POS	SCHOOL	TOTAL
1	Pat Sullivan	QB	Auburn	1597
2	Ed Marinaro	RB	Cornell	1445
3	Greg Pruitt	RB	Oklahoma	586
4	Johnny Musso	RB	Alabama	365
5	Lydell Mitchell	RB	Penn State	251
6	Jack Mildren	QB	Oklahoma	208
7	Jerry Tagge	QB	Nebraska	168
8	Chuck Ealy	QB	Toledo	137
9	Walt Patulski	DE	Notre Dame	121
10	Eric Allen	RB	Michigan State	109

AWARD WINNERS

PLAYER	POS	SCHOOL	AWARD NAME
Ed Marinaro	RB	Cornell	Maxwell
Larry Jacobson	DT	Nebraska	Outland
Pat Sullivan	QB	Auburn	Camp
Walt Patulski	DE	Notre Dame	Lombardi

CONFERENCE STANDINGS

ACC	CONF. W L T			OVERALL W L T		
North Carolina	6	0	0	9	3	0
Clemson	5	2	0	5	6	0
South Carolina	4	2	0	6	5	0
Duke	3	3	0	6	5	0
Wake Forest	2	4	0	6	5	0
Virginia	2	4	0	3	8	0
North Carolina St.	2	5	0	3	8	0
Maryland	1	5	0	2	9	0

Big 10	CONF. W L T			OVERALL W L T		
Michigan	8	0	0	11	1	0
Northwestern	6	3	0	7	4	0
Ohio State	5	3	0	6	4	0
Michigan State	5	3	0	6	5	0
Illinois	5	3	0	5	6	0
Wisconsin	3	5	0	4	6	1
Minnesota	3	5	0	4	7	0
Purdue	3	5	0	3	7	0
Indiana	2	6	0	3	8	0
Iowa	1	8	0	1	10	0

Big 8	CONF. W L T			OVERALL W L T		
Nebraska	7	0	0	13	0	0
Oklahoma	6	1	0	11	1	0
Colorado	5	2	0	10	2	0
Iowa State	4	3	0	8	4	0
Kansas State	2	5	0	5	6	0
Oklahoma State	2	5	0	4	6	1
Kansas	2	5	0	4	7	0
Missouri	0	7	0	1	10	0

Big West	CONF. W L T			OVERALL W L T		
Long Beach State	5	1	0	8	4	0
San Jose State	4	1	0	5	5	1
Fresno State	3	2	0	6	4	0
San Diego State	2	3	0	6	5	0
UC-Santa Barbara	2	3	0	3	8	0
Pacific	1	4	0	3	8	0
Los Angeles State	0	3	0	2	8	0

Ivy	CONF. W L T			OVERALL W L T		
Dartmouth	6	1	0	8	1	0
Cornell	6	1	0	8	1	0
Columbia	5	2	0	6	3	0
Harvard	4	3	0	5	4	0
Yale	3	4	0	4	5	0
Princeton	3	4	0	4	5	0
Pennsylvania	1	6	0	2	7	0
Brown	0	7	0	0	9	0

MAC	CONF. W L T			OVERALL W L T		
Toledo	5	0	0	11	0	0
Bowling Green	4	1	0	6	4	0
Western Michigan	2	3	0	7	3	0
Miami, Ohio	2	3	0	7	3	0
Ohio U	2	3	0	5	5	0
Kent State	0	5	0	3	8	0

Pac 8	CONF. W L T			OVERALL W L T		
Stanford	6	1	0	9	3	0
Southern Cal	3	2	1	6	4	1
Washington	4	3	0	8	3	0
California	4	3	0	6	5	0
Oregon State	3	3	0	5	6	0
Oregon	2	4	0	5	6	0
Washington State	2	5	0	4	7	0
UCLA	1	4	1	2	7	1

SEC	CONF. W L T			OVERALL W L T		
Alabama	7	0	0	11	1	0
Georgia	5	1	0	11	1	0
Auburn	5	1	0	9	2	0
Tennessee	4	2	0	10	2	0
Mississippi	4	2	0	10	2	0
LSU	3	2	0	9	3	0
Vanderbilt	1	5	0	4	6	1
Florida	1	6	0	4	7	0
Kentucky	1	6	0	3	8	0
Mississippi State	1	7	0	2	9	0

SWC	CONF. W L T			OVERALL W L T		
Texas	6	1	0	8	3	0
Arkansas	5	1	1	8	3	1
TCU	5	2	0	6	4	1
Texas A&M	4	3	0	5	6	0
SMU	3	4	0	4	7	0
Rice	2	4	1	3	7	1
Texas Tech	2	5	0	4	7	0
Baylor	0	7	0	1	9	0

WAC	CONF. W L T			OVERALL W L T		
Arizona State	7	0	0	11	1	0
New Mexico	5	1	0	6	3	2
Arizona	3	3	0	5	6	0
Wyoming	3	4	0	5	6	0
Brigham Young	3	4	0	5	6	0
Utah	3	4	0	3	8	0
Colorado State	1	4	0	3	8	0
Texas-El Paso	1	6	0	5	6	0

Independents	OVERALL W L T		
Penn State	11	1	0
Boston College	9	2	0
Notre Dame	8	2	0
Houston	9	3	0
Utah State	8	3	0
Florida State	8	4	0
West Virginia	7	4	0
Air Force	6	4	0
Army	6	4	0
Georgia Tech	6	6	0
Syracuse	5	5	1
New Mexico State	5	5	1
Miami, Fla.	4	7	0
Virginia Tech	4	7	0
Rutgers	4	7	0
Navy	3	8	0
Tulane	3	8	0
Pittsburgh	3	8	0

BOWL GAMES

DATE	GAME	SCORE
D18	Sun	LSU 33, Iowa State 15
D18	Pasadena	Memphis 28, San Jose State 9
D20	Liberty	Tennessee 14, Arkansas 13
D27	Fiesta	Arizona State 45, Florida State 38
D28	Tangerine	Toledo 28, Richmond 3
D30	Peach	Mississippi 41, Georgia Tech 18
D31	Bluebonnet	Colorado 29, Houston 17
D31	Gator	Georgia 7, North Carolina 3
J1	Sugar	Oklahoma 40, Auburn 22
J1	Orange	Nebraska 38, Alabama 6
J1	Cotton	Penn State 30, Texas 6
J1	Rose	Stanford 13, Michigan 12

1971 NCAA Major College Statistical Leaders

Individual Leaders

PASSING	G	ATT	COM	PCT	INT	I%	YDS	YPA	TD	TD%	COM.PG
1 Brian Sipe, San Diego State	11	369	196	53.1	21	5.7	2532	6.9	17	4.6	17.8
2 Don Strock, Virginia Tech	11	356	195	54.8	19	5.3	2577	7.2	12	3.4	17.7
3 John Reaves, Florida	11	356	193	54.2	21	5.9	2104	5.9	17	4.8	17.5
4 Gary Huff, Florida State	11	327	184	56.3	18	5.5	2736	8.4	23	7.0	16.7
5 Pat Sullivan, Auburn	10	281	162	57.7	11	3.9	2012	7.2	20	7.1	16.2
6 Gary Fox, Wyoming	11	328	171	52.1	20	6.1	2336	7.1	14	4.3	15.5
7 Don Bunce, Stanford	11	297	162	54.5	16	5.4	2265	7.6	13	4.4	14.7
8 Joe Ferguson, Arkansas	11	271	160	59.0	12	4.4	2203	8.1	11	4.1	14.5
9 Dennis Morrison, Kansas State	11	333	157	47.1	14	4.2	1800	5.4	8	2.4	14.3
10 Carlos Brown, Pacific	11	320	154	48.1	22	6.9	1607	5.0	5	1.6	14.0

ALL-PURPOSE	G	RUSH	REC	PR	KR	YDS	YPG
1 Ed Marinaro, Cornell	9	1881	51	0	0	1932	214.7
2 Bernard Jackson, Washington State	11	1189	185	0	744	2118	192.5
3 Robert Newhouse, Houston	11	1757	35	0	196	1988	180.7
4 Eric Allen, Michigan State	11	1494	275	0	193	1962	178.4
5 Greg Pruitt, Oklahoma	11	1665	108	1	172	1946	176.9
6 Howard Stevens, Louisville	10	1429	168	24	120	1741	174.1
7 Phil Mosser, William & Mary	10	885	212	0	617	1714	171.4
8 Johnny Rodgers, Nebraska	12	259	872	548	304	1983	165.3
9 Paul Loughran, Temple	9	468	198	291	502	1459	162.1
10 Woodrow Green, Arizona State	10	1209	94	165	152	1620	162.0

RUSHING/Yards Per Game	G	ATT	YDS	TD	AVG	YPG
1 Ed Marinaro, Cornell	9	356	1881	24	5.3	209.0
2 Robert Newhouse, Houston	11	277	1757	12	6.3	159.7
3 Greg Pruitt, Oklahoma	11	178	1665	17	9.4	151.4
4 Howard Stevens, Louisville	10	250	1429	12	5.7	142.9
5 Lydell Mitchell, Penn State	11	254	1567	26	6.2	142.5
6 Eric Allen, Michigan State	11	259	1494	18	5.8	135.8
7 Charlie Davis, Colorado	11	219	1386	10	6.3	126.0
8 Bobby Moore, Oregon	10	249	1211	7	4.9	121.1
9 Woodrow Green, Arizona State	10	208	1209	9	5.8	120.9
10 Paul Miles, Bowling Green	10	274	1185	7	4.3	118.5

RUSHING/Yards Per Carry	G	ATT	YDS	YPC
1 Greg Pruitt, Oklahoma	11	178	1665	9.4
2 Jon Hall, Citadel	11	169	1230	7.3
3 Bernard Jackson, Washington State	11	177	1189	6.7
4 Fred Henry, New Mexico	10	176	1129	6.4
5 Robert Newhouse, Houston	11	277	1757	6.3
6 Charlie Davis, Colorado	11	219	1386	6.3
7 Lydell Mitchell, Penn State	11	254	1567	6.2
8 Jack Mildren, Oklahoma	11	193	1140	5.9
9 Woodrow Green, Arizona State	10	208	1209	5.8
10 Eric Allen, Michigan State	11	259	1494	5.8

*-Based on top 24 rushers

RECEIVING	G	REC	YDS	TD	YPR	YPG	RPG
1 Tom Reynolds, San Diego State	10	67	1070	7	16.0	107.0	6.7
2 Brian Baima, Citadel	11	64	1237	13	19.3	112.5	5.8
3 Rhett Dawson, Florida State	11	62	817	7	13.2	74.3	5.6
4 Mike Reppond, Arkansas	10	56	986	3	17.6	98.6	5.6
5 Terry Beasley, Auburn	10	55	846	12	15.4	84.6	5.5
6 Bob Wicks, Utah State	11	58	862	5	14.9	78.4	5.3
7 Leland Glass, Oregon	9	46	584	6	12.7	64.9	5.1
8 Willie Hatter, Northern Illinois	10	50	615	1	12.3	61.5	5.0
9 Geoff DeLapp, California	10	48	464	1	9.7	46.4	4.8
10 Jim Butler, Tulsa	11	50	486	0	9.7	44.2	4.5

PUNTING	PUNT	YDS	AVG
1 Marv Bateman, Utah	68	3271	48.1
2 Jim Benien, Oklahoma State	77	3504	45.5
3 Lowell Ramsey, Wake Forest	46	2001	43.5
4 Dave Green, Ohio U	33	1416	42.9
5 Ray Guy, Southern Miss	73	3132	42.9
6 Russell Brown, William & Mary	51	2183	42.8
7 Nick Vidnovic, North Carolina	60	2568	42.8
8 Darryl Haas, Air Force	67	2814	42.0
8 Tom Moore, Navy	67	2814	42.0
10 Steve Hunter, Idaho	73	3059	41.9

PUNT RETURNS	PR	YDS	TD	AVG
1 Golden Richards, Brigham Young	33	624	4	18.9
2 Ed Rideout, Boston College	15	271	1	18.1
3 Johnny Rodgers, Nebraska	33	548	3	16.6
4 Dean Campbell, Texas	14	232	0	16.6
5 Steven Solow, Pennsylvania	17	279	0	16.4
6 Cliff Branch, Colorado	31	505	4	16.3
7 Bill Cahill, Washington	26	421	1	16.2
8 John Sefcik, Columbia	22	310	0	14.1
9 Jeff Varnadoe, Citadel	33	455	2	13.8
10 Bobby McKinney, Alabama	25	326	1	13.0

KICKOFF RETURNS	KR	YDS	TD	AVG
1 Paul Loughran, Temple	15	502	1	33.5
2 Bob Allen, Ohio U	14	421	0	30.1
3 Greg Johnson, Wisconsin	19	540	0	28.4
4 Ray Taroli, Oregon State	32	908	1	28.4
5 Mike Fink, Missouri	21	594	2	28.3
6 John Chatman, Pittsburgh	16	447	0	27.9
7 Bruce Miller, Rutgers	19	524	1	27.6
8 Bernard Jackson, Washington State	27	744	2	27.6
9 Eddie Woodard, Kent State	23	632	1	27.5
10 Don Gilley, Wichita State	17	454	1	26.7
10 Benny Reed, Texas-El Paso	17	454	0	26.7

SCORING	TDS	XPT	FG	PTS	PTPG
1 Ed Marinaro, Cornell	24	4	0	148	16.4
2 Lydell Mitchell, Penn State	29	0	0	174	15.8
3 Eric Allen, Michigan State	18	2	0	110	10.0
3 Johnny Musso, Alabama	16	4	0	100	10.0
5 Joe Schwartz, Toledo	18	0	0	108	9.8
6 Jack Mildren, Oklahoma	17	4	0	106	9.6
7 Greg Pruitt, Oklahoma	17	0	0	102	9.3
8 Bill Butler, Kansas State	16	0	0	96	8.7
9 Larry Russell, Wake Forest	15	4	0	94	8.5
10 Johnny Rodgers, Nebraska	17	0	0	102	8.5
10 Hank Bjorklund, Princeton	11	2	0	68	8.5

KICK SCORING	XPA	XP	FGA	FG	PTS	PTPG
1 John Carroll, Oklahoma	62	53	12	9	80	7.3
2 Nick Mike-Mayer, Temple	28	26	17	12	62	6.9
3 Don Ekstrand, Arizona State	53	48	10	9	75	6.8
3 Dana Coin, Michigan	54	54	12	7	75	6.8
3 Bill Davis, Alabama	40	36	16	13	75	6.8
6 Albert Vitiello, Penn State	62	59	13	5	74	6.7
7 Bill McClard, Arkansas	38	35	22	12	71	6.5
8 Frank Fontes, Florida State	31	30	24	13	69	6.3
9 Rich Sanger, Nebraska	64	60	9	5	75	6.3
10 Rodrigo Garcia, Stanford	27	24	27	14	66	6.0
10 George Hunt, Tennessee	30	30	15	12	66	6.0

INTERCEPTIONS	INT	YDS	TD	INT/GM
1 Frank Polito, Villanova	12	261	2	1.20
2 Jackie Wallace, Arizona	11	135	1	1.00
3 Tom Myers, Syracuse	8	57	0	0.89
4 Dave Atkinson, Brigham Young	9	120	0	0.82
5 Pete Carroll, Pacific	8	131	0	0.73
6 Larry Marshall, Maryland	6	131	0	0.67
6 Nick Holm, Houston	6	45	0	0.67
8 Dan Hansen, Brigham Young *	7	233	2	0.64
8 Dave Chaney, San Jose State *	7	136	2	0.64
8 Willie Osley, Illinois *	7	127	1	0.64

*-Six tied with seven; these had the most yards.

Team Leaders

RUSHING OFFENSE	G	ATT	YDS	AVG	TD	YPG
1 Oklahoma	11	761	5196	6.8	56	472.4
2 New Mexico	11	747	4229	5.7	43	384.5
3 Michigan	11	768	3714	4.8	46	337.6
4 Alabama	11	705	3565	5.1	34	324.1
5 Cornell	9	578	2884	5.0	28	320.4
6 Penn State	11	619	3347	5.4	42	304.3
7 Wake Forest	11	744	3344	4.5	26	304.0
8 Georgia	11	691	3337	4.8	39	303.4
9 Colgate	10	672	3008	4.5	33	300.8
10 Arizona State	11	615	3278	5.3	29	298.0

PASSING OFFENSE	G	ATT	COM	INT	PCT	YDS	YPA	TD	I%	YPC	YPG
1 San Diego State	11	409	211	27	51.6	2765	6.8	18	6.6	13.1	251.4
2 Florida State	11	338	186	20	55.0	2750	8.1	23	5.9	14.8	250.0
3 Virginia Tech	11	368	202	20	54.9	2695	7.3	12	5.4	13.3	245.0
4 Washington	11	354	152	24	42.9	2606	7.4	18	6.8	17.1	236.9
5 Auburn	10	316	180	13	57.0	2277	7.2	24	4.1	12.7	227.7
6 Wyoming	11	346	176	22	50.9	2416	7.0	16	6.4	13.7	219.6
7 Stanford	11	328	176	16	53.7	2414	7.4	13	4.9	13.7	219.5
8 Arkansas	11	293	170	16	58.0	2327	7.9	11	5.5	13.7	211.5
9 Florida	11	381	205	23	53.8	2233	5.9	19	6.0	10.9	203.0
10 Utah State	11	300	150	11	50.0	2185	7.3	15	3.7	14.6	198.6

TOTAL OFFENSE	G	P	YDS	AVG	TD	YPG
1 Oklahoma	11	839	6232	7.4	66	566.5
2 New Mexico	11	862	5149	6.0	48	468.1
3 Arizona State	11	844	5121	6.1	52	465.5
4 Citadel	11	777	5030	6.5	46	457.3
5 Penn State	11	798	4995	6.3	60	454.1
6 Houston	11	836	4993	6.0	42	453.9
7 Arkansas	11	875	4898	5.6	43	445.3
8 Nebraska	12	976	5252	5.4	56	437.7
9 Colorado	11	820	4538	5.5	43	412.5
10 Michigan	11	882	4397	5.0	51	399.7

RUSHING DEFENSE	G	ATT	YDS	AVG	TD	YPG
1 Michigan	11	418	696	1.7	3	63.3
2 Nebraska	12	500	1031	2.1	7	85.9
3 Notre Dame	10	383	864	2.3	3	86.4
4 Western Michigan	10	407	932	2.3	7	93.2
5 Miami, Ohio	10	408	953	2.3	4	95.3
6 Georgia	11	424	1076	2.5	6	97.8
7 Toledo	11	539	1199	2.2	11	109.0
8 Alabama	11	423	1281	3.0	4	116.5
9 Stanford	11	519	1282	2.5	10	116.5
10 Penn State	11	483	1292	2.7	3	117.5

PASSING DEFENSE	G	ATT	COM	PCT	YPC	INT	I%	YDS	YPA	TD	YPG
1 Texas Tech	11	147	55	37.4	12.0	14	9.5	661	4.5	2	60.1
2 Cincinnati	11	164	66	40.2	11.3	18	11.0	748	4.6	5	68.0
3 Toledo	11	195	68	34.9	11.4	18	9.2	776	4.0	2	70.5
4 New Mexico State	11	176	63	35.8	13.7	12	6.8	865	4.9	3	78.6
5 Louisville	10	193	69	35.8	12.3	20	10.4	846	4.4	3	84.6
6 Miami, Ohio	10	211	92	43.6	10.2	14	6.6	940	4.5	4	94.0
7 Vanderbilt	11	196	89	45.4	11.6	13	6.6	1035	5.3	7	94.1
8 Kent State	11	177	82	46.3	12.9	11	6.2	1054	6.0	5	95.8
9 LSU	11	223	101	45.3	11.0	17	7.6	1108	5.0	4	100.7
10 Texas Arlington	11	194	85	43.8	13.3	13	7.0	1132	5.8	7	102.9

TOTAL DEFENSE	G	P	YDS	AVG	TD	YPG
1 Toledo	11	734	1975	2.7	13	179.5
2 Michigan	11	632	1977	3.1	9	179.7
3 Miami, Ohio	10	619	1893	3.1	8	189.3
4 Notre Dame	10	598	1981	3.3	11	198.1
5 Nebraska	12	769	2435	3.2	12	202.9
6 Louisville	10	666	2082	3.1	11	208.2
7 Alabama	11	663	2417	3.6	10	219.7
8 Stanford	11	761	2424	3.2	14	220.4
9 Georgia	11	690	2575	3.7	16	234.1
10 Boston College	11	732	2654	3.6	14	241.3

SCORING OFFENSE	G	PTS	AVG
1 Oklahoma	11	494	44.9
2 Penn State	11	454	41.3
3 Nebraska	12	469	39.1
4 Arizona State	11	417	37.9
5 Michigan	11	409	37.2
6 Citadel	11	366	33.3
7 Alabama	11	362	32.9
8 Washington	11	357	32.5
9 Toledo	11	355	32.3
10 Georgia	11	353	32.1

SCORING DEFENSE	G	PTS	AVG
1 Michigan	11	70	6.4
2 Alabama	11	84	7.6
3 Nebraska	12	98	8.2
4 Toledo	11	91	8.3
5 Notre Dame	10	86	8.6
6 Tennessee	11	108	9.8
7 Georgia	11	112	10.2
8 Boston College	11	117	10.6
9 Louisville	10	111	11.1
10 Stanford	11	123	11.2

1972 POLL PROGRESSION

Pre-Season | Sept. 9 Games

AP	Team	Record	Result
1	Nebraska	0-0-0	lost to UCLA 17-20
2	Colorado	0-0-0	beat California 20-10
3	Ohio State	0-0-0	bye week
4	Arkansas	0-0-0	lost to #8 Southern Cal 10-31
5	Penn State	0-0-0	bye week
6	Oklahoma	0-0-0	bye week
7	Alabama	0-0-0	beat Duke 35-12
8	Southern Cal	0-0-0	beat #4 Arkansas 31-10
9	Washington	0-0-0	beat Pacific 13-6
10	Michigan	0-0-0	bye week
11	LSU	0-0-0	bye week
12	Arizona State	0-0-0	bye week
13	Notre Dame	0-0-0	bye week
14	Texas	0-0-0	bye week
15	Tennessee	0-0-0	beat Georgia Tech 34-3
16	Mississippi	0-0-0	bye week
17	Georgia	0-0-0	bye week
18	Purdue	0-0-0	bye week
19	Florida State	0-0-0	beat Pittsburgh 19-7
20	Stanford	0-0-0	bye week

September 11 Poll | Sept. 16 Games

UP	AP	Team	Record	Result
2	1	Southern Cal	1-0-0	beat Oregon State 51-6
3	2	Colorado	1-0-0	beat Cincinnati 56-14
4	3	Ohio State	0-0-0	beat Iowa 21-0
1	4	Oklahoma	0-0-0	beat Utah State 49-0
5	5	Alabama	1-0-0	bye week
7	6	Penn State	0-0-0	lost to #7 Tennessee 21-28
6	7	Tennessee	1-0-0	beat #6 Penn State 28-21
11	8	UCLA	1-0-0	beat Pittsburgh 38-28
8	9	LSU	0-0-0	beat Pacific 31-13
9	10	Nebraska	0-1-0	beat Texas A&M 37-7
10	11	Michigan	0-0-0	beat Northwestern 7-0
15	12	Washington	1-0-0	beat Duke 14-6
12	13	Arizona State	1-0-0	beat Houston 33-28
14	14	Notre Dame	0-0-0	bye week
13	15	Texas	0-0-0	bye week
17	16	Georgia	0-0-0	beat Baylor 24-14
	17	Arkansas	0-1-0	bye week
19	18	Purdue	0-0-0	lost to Bowling Green 14-17
	19	Mississippi	0-0-0	beat Memphis 34-29
16	20	Florida State	1-0-0	beat Miami, Fla. 37-14
17		Iowa State	0-0-0	beat Colorado State 41-0
20		Auburn	1-0-0	bye week

September 18 Poll | Sept. 23 Games

UP	AP	Team	Record	Result
1	1	Southern Cal	2-0-0	beat Illinois 55-20
2	2	Oklahoma	1-0-0	beat Oregon 68-3
3	3	Colorado	2-0-0	beat Minnesota 38-6
5	4	Ohio State	1-0-0	bye week
4	5	Tennessee	2-0-0	beat Wake Forest 45-6
7	6	UCLA	2-0-0	lost to #12 Michigan 9-26
6	7	Alabama	1-0-0	beat Kentucky 35-0
9	8	LSU	1-0-0	beat Texas A&M 42-17
8	9	Nebraska	1-1-0	beat Army 77-7
10	10	Arizona State	2-0-0	beat Kansas State 56-14
13	11	Penn State	0-1-0	beat Navy 21-10
11	12	Michigan	1-0-0	beat #6 UCLA 26-9
13	13	Notre Dame	0-0-0	beat Northwestern 37-0
15	14	Texas	0-0-0	beat Miami, Fla. 23-10
17	15	Washington	2-0-0	beat Purdue 22-21
19	16	Georgia	1-0-0	lost to Tulane 13-24
16	17	Florida State	2-0-0	beat Virginia Tech 27-15
12	18	Michigan State	1-0-0	lost to Georgia Tech 16-21
	19	Stanford	1-0-0	beat Duke 10-6
	20	Mississippi	1-0-0	beat South Carolina 21-0
18		Iowa State	1-0-0	beat Utah 44-22
20		Arkansas	0-1-0	beat Oklahoma State 24-23

September 25 Poll | Sept. 30 Games

UP	AP	Team	Record	Result
1	1	Southern Cal	3-0-0	beat Michigan State 51-6
2	2	Oklahoma	2-0-0	beat Clemson 52-3
3	3	Colorado	3-0-0	lost to Oklahoma State 6-31
4	4	Tennessee	3-0-0	lost to Auburn 6-10
6	5	Ohio State	1-0-0	beat North Carolina 29-14
5	6	Alabama	2-0-0	beat Vanderbilt 48-21
7	7	Nebraska	2-1-0	beat Minnesota 49-0
8	8	Michigan	2-0-0	beat #18 Tulane 41-7
9	9	LSU	2-0-0	beat Wisconsin 27-7
10	10	Notre Dame	1-0-0	beat Purdue 35-14
11	11	Arizona State	3-0-0	lost to Wyoming 43-45
14	12	Texas	1-0-0	beat Texas Tech 25-20
16	13	Penn State	1-1-0	beat Iowa 14-10
12	14	Washington	3-0-0	beat Illinois 31-11
19	15	UCLA	2-0-0	beat Oregon 65-20
13	16	Florida State	3-0-0	beat Kansas 44-22
20	17	Mississippi	2-0-0	beat Southern Miss 13-9
	18	Tulane	2-0-0	lost to #8 Michigan 7-41
	19	Stanford	2-0-0	beat West Virginia 41-35
17	20	West Virginia	3-0-0	lost to Stanford 35-41
15		Iowa State	2-0-0	beat New Mexico 31-0
17		Air Force	2-0-0	beat Davidson 68-6

October 2 Poll | Oct. 7 Games

UP	AP	Team	Record	Result
1	1	Southern Cal	4-0-0	beat #15 Stanford 30-21
2	2	Oklahoma	3-0-0	bye week
4	3	Ohio State	2-0-0	beat California 35-18
3	4	Alabama	3-0-0	beat Georgia 25-7
6	5	Michigan	3-0-0	beat Navy 35-7
5	6	Nebraska	3-1-0	bye week
8	7	Notre Dame	2-0-0	beat Michigan State 16-0
7	8	LSU	3-0-0	beat Rice 12-6
10	9	Texas	2-0-0	beat Utah State 27-12
12	10	Tennessee	3-1-0	beat Memphis 38-7
9	11	Washington	4-0-0	beat Oregon 23-17
16	12	Colorado	3-1-0	beat Kansas State 38-17
11	13	Florida State	4-0-0	lost to Florida 13-42
13	14	UCLA	3-1-0	beat Arizona 42-31
18	15	Stanford	3-0-0	lost to #1 Southern Cal 21-30
19	16	Penn State	2-1-0	beat Illinois 35-17
14	17	Auburn	3-0-0	beat #18 Mississippi 19-13
	18	Mississippi	3-0-0	lost to #17 Auburn 13-19
15	19	Air Force	3-0-0	beat Colorado State 52-13
17	20	Iowa State	3-0-0	bye week
20		Arizona State	2-1-0	beat Oregon State 38-7

October 9 Poll | Oct. 14 Games

UP	AP	Team	Record	Result
1	1	Southern Cal	5-0-0	beat California 42-14
2	2	Oklahoma	3-0-0	beat #10 Texas 27-0
3	3	Alabama	4-0-0	beat Florida 24-7
4	4	Ohio State	3-0-0	beat Illinois 26-7
6	5	Michigan	4-0-0	beat Michigan State 10-0
5	6	Nebraska	4-0-0	beat Missouri 62-0
7	7	Notre Dame	3-0-0	beat Pittsburgh 42-16
8	8	LSU	4-0-0	beat #9 Auburn 35-7
9	9	Auburn	4-1-0	lost to #8 LSU 7-35
11	10	Texas	3-0-0	lost to #2 Oklahoma 0-27
12	11	Tennessee	4-1-0	bye week
10	12	Washington	5-0-0	lost to #17 Stanford 0-24
16	13	Colorado	4-1-0	beat #18 Iowa State 34-22
13	14	UCLA	4-1-0	beat Oregon State 37-7
15	15	Penn State	3-1-0	beat Army 45-0
15	16	Air Force	4-0-0	beat Boston College 13-9
20	17	Stanford	3-1-0	beat #12 Washington 24-0
14	18	Iowa State	4-1-0	lost to #13 Colorado 22-34
19	19	Oklahoma State	3-1-0	lost to Virginia Tech 32-34
	20	Arkansas	3-1-0	beat Baylor 31-20
18		Arizona State	3-1-0	beat Utah 59-48

October 16 Poll | Oct. 21 Games

UP	AP	Team	Record	Result
1	1	Southern Cal	6-0-0	beat #18 Washington 34-7
2	2	Oklahoma	4-0-0	lost to #9 Colorado 14-20
3	3	Alabama	5-0-0	beat #10 Tennessee 17-10
5	4	Ohio State	4-0-0	beat Indiana 44-7
4	5	Nebraska	4-1-0	beat Kansas 56-0
6	6	Michigan	5-0-0	beat Illinois 31-7
7	7	LSU	5-0-0	beat Kentucky 10-0
8	8	Notre Dame	4-0-0	lost to Missouri 26-30
10	9	Colorado	5-1-0	beat #2 Oklahoma 20-14
11	10	Tennessee	4-1-0	lost to #3 Alabama 10-17
9	11	UCLA	5-1-0	beat California 49-13
13	12	Penn State	4-1-0	beat Syracuse 17-0
12	13	Stanford	4-1-0	lost to Oregon 13-15
15	14	Auburn	4-1-0	beat Georgia Tech 24-14
	15	Texas	3-1-0	beat #17 Arkansas 35-15
14	16	Air Force	5-0-0	lost to Navy 17-21
	17	Arkansas	4-1-0	lost to #15 Texas 15-35
	18	Washington	5-1-0	lost to #1 Southern Cal 7-34
16	19	Arizona State	4-1-0	beat Brigham Young 49-17
	20	Iowa State	3-1-0	beat Kansas State 55-22

October 23 Poll | Oct. 28 Games

UP	AP	Team	Record	Result
1	1	Southern Cal	7-0-0	beat Oregon 18-0
2	2	Alabama	6-0-0	beat Southern Miss 48-11
4	3	Nebraska	5-1-0	beat Oklahoma State 34-0
3	4	Ohio State	5-0-0	beat Wisconsin 28-20
5	5	Michigan	6-0-0	beat Minnesota 42-0
6	6	LSU	6-0-0	bye week
7	7	Colorado	6-1-0	lost to Missouri 17-20
8	8	Oklahoma	4-1-0	beat Kansas State 52-0
9	9	UCLA	6-1-0	beat Washington State 35-20
11	10	Texas	4-1-0	beat Rice 45-9
10	11	Penn State	5-1-0	beat #18 West Virginia 28-19
12	12	Auburn	5-1-0	beat #17 Florida State 27-14
15	13	Notre Dame	4-1-0	beat TCU 21-0
16	14	Tennessee	4-2-0	beat Hawaii 34-2
14	15	Iowa State	4-1-0	beat Kansas 34-8
13	16	Arizona State	5-1-0	lost to Air Force 31-39
18	17	Florida State	6-1-0	lost to #12 Auburn 14-27
	18	Arkansas	4-2-0	beat North Texas 42-16
17	18	SMU	4-1-0	lost to Texas Tech 3-17
	18	West Virginia	5-2-0	lost to #11 Penn State 19-28

October 30 Poll | Nov. 4 Games

UP	AP	Team	Record	Result
1	1	Southern Cal	8-0-0	beat Washington State 44-3
2	2	Alabama	7-0-0	beat Mississippi State 58-14
3	3	Nebraska	6-1-0	beat #15 Colorado 33-10
5	4	Michigan	7-0-0	beat Indiana 21-7
4	5	Ohio State	6-0-0	beat Minnesota 27-19
7	6	LSU	7-0-0	beat Mississippi 17-16
6	7	Oklahoma	5-1-0	beat #14 Iowa State 20-6
8	8	UCLA	7-1-0	beat Stanford 28-23
9	9	Texas	5-1-0	beat SMU 17-9
11	10	Penn State	6-1-0	beat Maryland 46-16
10	11	Auburn	6-1-0	beat Florida 26-20
12	12	Notre Dame	5-1-0	beat Navy 42-23
16	13	Tennessee	4-2-0	beat Georgia 14-0
13	14	Iowa State	5-1-0	lost to #7 Oklahoma 6-20
15	15	Colorado	6-2-0	lost to #3 Nebraska 10-33
	16	Missouri	4-3-0	beat Kansas State 31-14
	17	Louisville	6-0-0	lost to Tulsa 26-28
16	18	Texas Tech	5-1-0	beat Rice 10-6
15	19	Air Force	6-1-0	lost to Army 14-17
	20	Arkansas	5-2-0	lost to Texas A&M 7-10
18		Stanford	5-2-0	lost to #8 UCLA 23-28

UP	AP	NOVEMBER 6 POLL		Nov. 11 Games
1	1	Southern Cal	9-0-0	bye week
3	2	Alabama	8-0-0	beat # 6 LSU 35-21
2	3	Nebraska	7-1-0	tied # 17 Iowa State 23-23
5	4	Michigan	8-0-0	beat Iowa 31-0
4	5	Ohio State	7-0-0	lost to Michigan State 12-19
6	6	LSU	7-0-0	lost to # 2 Alabama 21-35
7	7	Oklahoma	6-1-0	beat # 14 Missouri 17-6
8	8	UCLA	8-1-0	lost to Washington 21-30
9	9	Texas	6-1-0	beat Baylor 17-3
11	10	Penn State	7-1-0	beat North Carolina St. 37-22
10	11	Auburn	7-1-0	bye week
12	12	Notre Dame	6-1-0	beat Air Force 21-7
13	13	Tennessee	5-2-0	bye week
	14	Missouri	5-3-0	lost to # 7 Oklahoma 6-17
15	15	Texas Tech	7-3-0	lost to TCU 7-31
16	16	Colorado	6-3-0	beat Kansas 33-8
14	17	Iowa State	5-2-0	tied # 3 Nebraska 23-23
16	18	North Carolina	6-1-0	beat Virginia 23-3
	19	Arizona State	6-2-0	beat New Mexico 60-7
20	20	Stanford	5-3-0	lost to Washington State 13-27
20		Yale	5-1-0	lost to Pennsylvania 30-48

UP	AP	NOVEMBER 13 POLL		Nov. 18 Games
1	1	Southern Cal	9-0-0	beat # 14 UCLA 24-7
2	2	Alabama	9-0-0	beat Virginia Tech 52-13
3	3	Michigan	9-0-0	beat Purdue 9-6
4	4	Oklahoma	7-1-0	beat Kansas 31-7
5	5	Nebraska	7-1-1	beat Kansas State 59-7
8	6	Penn State	8-1-0	beat Boston College 45-26
6	7	Texas	7-1-0	beat TCU 27-0
7	8	LSU	7-1-0	beat Mississippi State 28-14
9	9	Ohio State	7-1-0	beat Northwestern 27-14
11	10	Notre Dame	7-1-0	beat Miami, Fla. 20-17
10	11	Auburn	7-1-0	beat Georgia 27-10
12	12	Iowa State	5-2-1	lost to # 19 Missouri 5-6
13	13	Tennessee	6-2-0	beat Mississippi 17-0
14	14	UCLA	8-2-0	lost to # 1 Southern Cal 7-24
15	15	Colorado	7-3-0	beat Air Force 38-7
17	16	North Carolina	7-1-0	beat Duke 14-0
16	17	Washington	8-2-0	lost to # 20 Washington St. 10-27
18	18	Arizona State	7-2-0	beat San Jose State 51-21
	19	Missouri	5-4-0	beat # 12 Iowa State 6-5
	20	Washington State	6-4-0	beat # 17 Washington 27-10
19		Utah State	6-3-0	beat Southern Miss 27-21

UP	AP	NOVEMBER 20 POLL		Nov. 25 Games
1	1	Southern Cal	10-0-0	bye week
2	2	Alabama	10-0-0	bye week
3	3	Michigan	10-0-0	lost to # 9 Ohio State 11-14
4	4	Oklahoma	8-1-0	beat # 5 Nebraska 17-14
5	5	Nebraska	8-1-1	lost to # 4 Oklahoma 14-17
7	6	Penn State	9-1-0	beat Pittsburgh 49-27
6	7	Texas	8-1-0	beat Texas A&M 38-3
9	8	LSU	8-1-0	tied Florida 3-3
8	9	Ohio State	8-1-0	beat # 3 Michigan 14-11
10	10	Auburn	8-1-0	bye week
11	11	Notre Dame	8-1-0	bye week
12	12	Tennessee	7-2-0	beat Kentucky 17-7
13	13	Colorado	8-3-0	regular season complete
	14	UCLA	8-3-0	regular season complete
16	15	North Carolina	8-1-0	beat East Carolina 42-19
16	16	Missouri	6-4-0	lost to Kansas 17-28
18	17	Iowa State	5-3-1	lost to Oklahoma State 14-45
14	18	Arizona State	8-2-0	beat Arizona 38-21
	19	Washington State	7-4-0	regular season complete
	20	Texas Tech	8-2-0	lost to Arkansas 14-24
15		Utah State	7-3-0	beat Weber St. 20-16

UP	AP	NOVEMBER 27 POLL		Dec. 2 Games
1	1	Southern Cal	10-0-0	beat # 10 Notre Dame 45-23
2	2	Alabama	10-0-0	lost to # 9 Auburn 16-17
3	3	Oklahoma	9-1-0	beat # 20 Oklahoma State 38-15
4	4	Ohio State	9-1-0	regular season complete
7	5	Penn State	10-1-0	regular season complete
5	6	Texas	9-1-0	regular season complete
6	7	Michigan	10-1-0	regular season complete
8	8	Nebraska	8-2-1	regular season complete
9	9	Auburn	8-1-0	beat # 2 Alabama 17-16
10	10	Notre Dame	8-1-0	lost to # 1 Southern Cal 23-45
12	11	LSU	8-1-1	beat Tulane 9-3
11	12	Tennessee	8-2-0	beat Vanderbilt 30-10
13	13	Colorado	8-3-0	
16	14	North Carolina	9-1-0	regular season complete
16	15	UCLA	8-3-0	
14	16	Arizona State	9-2-0	regular season complete
	17	Louisville	9-1-0	regular season complete
	18	West Virginia	8-3-0	regular season complete
15	19	Washington State	7-4-0	
	20	Oklahoma State	6-4-0	lost to # 3 Oklahoma 15-38
15		Utah State	8-3-0	regular season complete
17		Missouri	6-5-0	regular season complete

UP	AP	DECEMBER 4 POLL	RECORD	BOWL BID	DATE	BOWL RESULT	RB	AP	JANUARY 3 FINAL POLL	RECORD
1	1	Southern Cal	11-0-0	Rose Bowl	J1	beat # 3 Ohio State 42-17	1	1	Southern Cal	12-0-0
2	2	Oklahoma	10-1-0	Sugar Bowl	D31	beat # 5 Penn State 14-0	3	2	Oklahoma	11-1-0
3	3	Ohio State	9-1-0	Rose Bowl	J1	lost to # 1 Southern Cal 17-42	5	3	Texas	10-1-0
4	4	Alabama	10-1-0	Cotton Bowl	J1	lost to # 7 Texas 13-17	13	4	Nebraska	9-2-1
8	5	Penn State	10-1-0	Sugar Bowl	D31	lost to # 2 Oklahoma 0-14	2	5	Auburn	10-1-0
7	6	Auburn	9-1-0	Gator Bowl	D30	beat # 13 Colorado 24-3	4	6	Michigan	10-1-0
5	7	Texas	9-1-0	Cotton Bowl	J1	beat # 4 Alabama 17-13	6	7	Alabama	10-2-0
6	8	Michigan	10-1-0				7	8	Tennessee	10-2-0
9	9	Nebraska	8-2-1				9	9	Ohio State	9-2-0
10	10	LSU	9-1-1	Bluebonnet Bowl	D30	lost to # 11 Tennessee 17-24	10	10	Penn State	10-2-0
11	11	Tennessee	9-2-0	Bluebonnet Bowl	D30	beat # 10 LSU 24-17	8	11	LSU	9-2-1
12	12	Notre Dame	8-2-0	Orange Bowl	J1	lost to # 9 Nebraska 6-40	12	12	North Carolina	11-1-0
14	13	Colorado	8-3-0	Gator Bowl	D30	lost to # 6 Auburn 3-24	14	13	Arizona State	10-2-0
17	14	UCLA	8-3-0				15	14	Notre Dame	8-3-0
13	15	Arizona State	9-2-0	Fiesta Bowl	D23	beat Missouri 49-35	20	15	UCLA	8-3-0
14	16	North Carolina	9-1-0	Sun Bowl	D30	beat Texas Tech 32-28	17	16	Colorado	8-4-0
16	17	Louisville	9-1-0				34	17	North Carolina St.	8-3-1
	18	West Virginia	8-3-0				NR	18	Louisville	9-1-0
17	19	Washington State	7-4-0				16	19	Washington State	7-4-0
	20	Purdue	6-5-0				25	20	Georgia Tech	7-4-1
17		Utah State	8-3-0							
20		San Diego State	10-1-0							

1972

CONSENSUS ALL-AMERICANS

POS	Offense	HT	WT	School	AP	CF	FC	FW	NE	PI
QB	Bert Jones	6-3	205	LSU			•	•	•	•
RB	Greg Pruitt	5-9	177	Oklahoma	•	•		•	•	•
RB	Otis Armstrong	5-11	197	Purdue	•	•	•		•	•
RB	Woody Green	6-1	190	Arizona State	•			•	•	
WR	Johnny Rodgers	5-9	173	Nebraska	•	•	•	•	•	•
TE	Charles Young	6-4	228	Southern Cal	•	•	•	•	•	•
T	Jerry Sisemore	6-4	260	Texas	•	•	•	•	•	•
T	Paul Seymour	6-5	250	Michigan	•			•	•	•
G	John Hannah	6-3	282	Alabama	•	•	•	•	•	•
G	Ron Rusnak	6-1	223	North Carolina	•	•	•	•	•	
C	Tom Brahaney	6-2	227	Oklahoma	•	•	•	•	•	•

OTHERS RECEIVING FIRST-TEAM HONORS

POS		School	AP	CF	FC	FW	NE	PI
QB	John Hufnagel	Penn State	•			•		
QB	Gary Huff	Florida State					•	
RB	Sam Cunningham	Southern Cal			•	•		
RB	Dick Jauron	Yale			•	•		
WR	Steve Holden	Arizona State					•	
WR	Barry Smith	Florida State			•			
T	Daryl White	Nebraska					•	
T	John Hicks	Ohio State	•	•				
T	Pete Adams	Southern Cal				•		
G	Bill Singletary	Temple			•			
G	Jim Krapf	Alabama			•			
K	Ricky Townsend	Tennessee				•		

FC named Johnny Rodgers as a B

POS	Defense	HT	WT	School	AP	CF	FC	FW	NE	PI
E	Willie Harper	6-2	207	Nebraska	•	•	•	•	•	•
E	Bruce Bannon	6-3	224	Penn State	•	•	•	•	•	•
T	Greg Marx	6-5	265	Notre Dame	•	•	•	•	•	•
T	Dave Butz	6-7	279	Purdue	•	•	•	•	•	•
MG	Rich Glover	6-1	234	Nebraska	•	•	•	•	•	•
LB	Randy Gradishar	6-3	232	Ohio State	•	•	•	•	•	•
LB	John Skorupan	6-2	208	Penn State	•	•	•		•	•
B	Brad VanPelt	6-5	221	Michigan State	•	•	•	•	•	•
B	Cullen Bryant	6-2	215	Colorado	•	•	•	•	•	•
B	Robert Popelka	6-1	190	SMU	•	•			•	•
B	Randy Logan	6-2	192	Michigan	•	•	•	•	•	•

OTHERS RECEIVING FIRST-TEAM HONORS

POS		School	AP	CF	FC	FW	NE	PI
DL	Roger Goree	Baylor	•			•		
DL	John Grant	Southern Cal	•			•		
DL	Bud Magrum	Colorado			•			
DL	John LeHeup	South Carolina			•			
DL	Derland Moore	Oklahoma	•					
LB	Steve Brown	Oregon State		•	•			
LB	Tom Jackson	Louisville		•				
LB	Warren Capone	LSU				•		
LB	Jamie Rotella	Tennessee				•		
LB	John Mitchell	Alabama			•			
LB	Richard Wood	Southern Cal	•					
LB	Jim Youngblood	Tennessee Tech				•		
DB	Ray Guy	Southern Miss	•	•				
DB	Randy Rhino	Georgia Tech			•			
DB	Calvin Jones	Washington	•					
DB	Drane Scrivener	Tulsa						•
DB	Conrad Graham	Tennessee						•

FW named Ray Guy as a P.

HEISMAN TROPHY VOTING

	PLAYER	POS	SCHOOL	1ST	2ND	3RD	TOTAL
1	Johnny Rodgers	WR	Nebraska	301	151	105	1310
2	Greg Pruitt	HB	Oklahoma	117	223	169	966
3	Rich Glover	MG	Nebraska	99	125	105	652
4	Bert Jones	QB	LSU	61	61	46	351
5	Terry Davis	QB	Alabama	62	50	52	338
6	John Hufnagel	QB	Penn State	62	28	50	292
7	George Amundsen	QB	Iowa State	41	31	34	219
8	Otis Armstrong	HB	Purdue	44	24	28	208
9	Don Strock	QB	Virginia Tech	12	33	42	144
10	Gary Huff	QB	Florida State	20	24	30	138

AWARD WINNERS

PLAYER	POS	SCHOOL	AWARD NAME
Brad VanPelt	DB	Michigan State	Maxwell
Rich Glover	MG	Nebraska	Outland
Johnny Rodgers	WR	Nebraska	Camp
Rich Glover	MG	Nebraska	Lombardi

CONFERENCE STANDINGS

ACC

	CONF. W L T			OVERALL W L T		
North Carolina	6	0	0	11	1	0
North Carolina St.	4	1	1	8	3	1
Maryland	3	2	1	5	5	1
Duke	3	3	0	5	6	0
Clemson	2	4	0	4	7	0
Virginia	1	5	0	4	7	0
Wake Forest	1	5	0	2	9	0

Big 10

	CONF. W L T			OVERALL W L T		
Michigan	7	1	0	10	1	0
Ohio State	7	1	0	9	2	0
Purdue	6	2	0	6	5	0
Michigan State	5	2	1	5	5	1
Minnesota	4	4	0	4	7	0
Indiana	3	5	0	5	6	0
Illinois	3	5	0	3	8	0
Iowa	2	6	1	3	7	1
Wisconsin	2	6	0	4	7	0
Northwestern	1	8	0	2	9	0

Big 8

	CONF. W L T			OVERALL W L T		
Oklahoma	6	1	0	11	1	0
Nebraska	5	1	1	9	2	1
Colorado	4	3	0	8	4	0
Oklahoma State	4	3	0	6	5	0
Missouri	3	4	0	6	6	0
Iowa State	2	4	1	5	6	1
Kansas	2	5	0	4	7	0
Kansas State	1	6	0	3	8	0

Big West

	CONF. W L T			OVERALL W L T		
San Diego State	4	0	0	10	1	0
Pacific	3	1	0	8	3	0
Fresno State	1	3	0	6	4	1
Long Beach State	1	3	0	5	6	0
San Jose State	1	3	0	4	7	0

Ivy

	CONF. W L T			OVERALL W L T		
Dartmouth	5	1	1	7	1	1
Yale	5	2	0	7	2	0
Pennsylvania	4	3	0	6	3	0
Cornell	4	3	0	6	3	0
Harvard	3	3	1	4	4	1
Princeton	2	4	1	3	5	1
Columbia	2	4	1	3	5	1
Brown	1	6	0	1	8	0

MAC

	CONF. W L T			OVERALL W L T		
Kent State	4	1	0	6	4	1
Bowling Green	3	1	1	6	3	1
Western Michigan	2	2	1	7	3	1
Miami, Ohio	2	3	0	7	3	0
Toledo	2	3	0	6	5	0
Ohio U	1	4	0	3	8	0

Pac 8

	CONF. W L T			OVERALL W L T		
Southern Cal	7	0	0	12	0	0
UCLA	5	2	0	8	3	0
Washington	4	3	0	8	3	0
Washington State	4	3	0	7	4	0
California	3	4	0	3	8	0
Stanford	2	5	0	6	5	0
Oregon	2	5	0	4	7	0
Oregon State	1	6	0	2	9	0

SEC

	CONF. W L T			OVERALL W L T		
Alabama	7	1	0	10	2	0
Auburn	6	1	0	10	1	0
LSU	4	1	1	9	2	1
Tennessee	4	2	0	10	2	0
Georgia	4	3	0	7	4	0
Florida	3	3	1	5	5	1
Mississippi	2	5	0	5	5	0
Kentucky	2	5	0	3	8	0
Mississippi State	1	6	0	4	7	0
Vanderbilt	0	6	0	3	8	0

SWC

	CONF. W L T			OVERALL W L T		
Texas	7	0	0	10	1	0
Texas Tech	4	3	0	8	4	0
SMU	4	3	0	7	4	0
Arkansas	3	4	0	6	5	0
Rice	3	4	0	5	5	1
Baylor	3	4	0	5	6	0
TCU	2	5	0	5	6	0
Texas A&M	2	5	0	3	8	0

WAC

	CONF. W L T			OVERALL W L T		
Arizona State	5	1	0	10	2	0
Brigham Young	5	2	0	7	4	0
Utah	5	2	0	6	5	0
Arizona	4	3	0	4	7	0
Wyoming	3	4	0	4	7	0
New Mexico	2	4	0	3	8	0
Colorado State	1	4	0	1	10	0
Texas-El Paso	1	6	0	2	8	0

Independents

	OVERALL W L T		
Penn State	10	2	0
Notre Dame	8	3	0
Utah State	8	3	0
West Virginia	8	4	0
Florida State	7	4	0
Rutgers	7	4	0
Georgia Tech	7	4	1
Air Force	6	4	0
Army	6	4	0
Virginia Tech	6	4	1
Houston	6	4	1
Tulane	6	5	0
Syracuse	5	6	0
Miami, Fla.	5	6	0
Navy	4	7	0
Boston College	4	7	0
South Carolina	4	7	0
Pittsburgh	1	10	0

BOWL GAMES

DATE	GAME	SCORE
D18	Liberty	Georgia Tech 31, Iowa State 30
D23	Fiesta	Arizona State 49, Missouri 35
D29	Peach	North Carolina St. 49, West Virginia 13
D29	Tangerine	Tampa 21, Kent 18
D30	Gator	Auburn 24, Colorado 3
D30	Sun	North Carolina 32, Texas Tech 28
D30	Bluebonnet	Tennessee 24, LSU 17
D31	Sugar	Oklahoma 14, Penn State 0
J1	Orange	Nebraska 40, Notre Dame 6
J1	Rose	Southern Cal 42, Ohio State 17
J1	Cotton	Texas 17, Alabama 13

1972 NCAA Major College Statistical Leaders

Individual Leaders

PASSING	G	ATT	COM	PCT	INT	I%	YDS	YPA	TD	TD%	COM.PG
1 Don Strock, Virginia Tech	11	427	228	53.4	27	6.3	3243	7.6	16	3.8	20.7
2 Gary Huff, Florida State	11	385	206	53.5	23	6.0	2893	7.5	25	6.5	18.7
3 Tony Adams, Utah State	11	351	204	58.1	9	2.6	2797	8.0	22	6.3	18.5
4 Mike Boryla, Stanford	11	350	183	52.3	20	5.7	2284	6.5	14	4.0	16.6
5 Joe Pisarcik, New Mexico State	11	382	182	47.6	15	3.9	2179	5.7	8	2.1	16.5
6 Gary Keithley, Texas-El Paso	9	252	144	57.1	10	4.0	1870	7.4	7	2.8	16.0
7 Dan Fouts, Oregon	11	348	171	49.1	19	5.5	2041	5.9	12	3.5	15.5
8 Bruce Gadd, Rice	11	322	170	52.8	22	6.8	2064	6.4	11	3.4	15.5
9 Scotty Shipp, Davidson	10	286	149	52.1	22	7.7	1845	6.5	9	3.2	14.9
10 Buddy Palazzo, Southern Miss	11	289	160	55.4	16	5.5	1888	6.5	8	2.8	14.5
10 Tim Dydo, Xavier	11	327	160	48.9	18	5.5	1568	4.8	5	1.5	14.5

ALL-PURPOSE	G	RUSH	REC	PR	KR	YDS	YPG
1 Howard Stevens, Louisville	10	1294	221	377	240	2132	213.2
2 Pete Van Valkenburg, Brigham Young	10	1386	98	26	328	1838	183.8
3 Johnny Rodgers, Nebraska	11	267	942	618	184	2011	182.8
4 Steve Odom, Utah	11	59	663	244	984	1950	177.3
5 Otis Armstrong, Purdue	11	1361	55	0	452	1868	169.8
6 Woody Green, Arizona State	10	1363	115	12	117	1607	160.7
7 Adolph Bellizeare, Pennsylvania	9	849	149	129	263	1390	154.4
8 Dick Jauron, Yale	9	1055	75	41	207	1378	153.1
9 Paul Loughran, Temple	9	593	196	146	438	1373	152.6
10 Anthony Davis, Southern Cal	11	1034	115	44	468	1661	151.0

RUSHING/YARDS PER GAME	G	ATT	YDS	TD	AVG	YPG
1 Pete Van Valkenburg, Brigham Young	10	232	1386	12	6.0	138.6
2 Bob Hitchens, Miami, Ohio	10	326	1370	15	4.2	137.0
3 Woody Green, Arizona State	10	209	1363	15	6.5	136.3
4 Howard Stevens, Louisville	10	259	1294	13	5.0	129.4
5 Otis Armstrong, Purdue	11	243	1361	9	5.6	123.7
6 Mark Kellar, No. Illinois	11	285	1314	9	4.6	119.5
7 Carl Crumpler, East Carolina	11	340	1309	17	3.9	119.0
8 Dick Jauron, Yale	9	160	1055	12	6.6	117.2
9 Jim Jennings, Rutgers	11	287	1262	9	4.4	114.7
10 Mike Strachan, Iowa State	11	267	1260	8	4.7	114.5

RUSHING/YARDS PER CARRY	G	ATT	YDS	YPC
1 Dick Jauron, Yale	9	160	1055	6.6
2 Woody Green, Arizona State	10	209	1363	6.5
3 Pete Van Valkenburg, Brigham Young	10	232	1386	6.0
4 Mitchell True, Pacific	11	206	1164	5.7
5 Anthony Davis, Southern Cal	11	184	1034	5.6
6 Otis Armstrong, Purdue	11	243	1361	5.6
7 Puddin Jones, Houston	11	222	1216	5.5
8 Cleveland Cooper, Navy	11	192	1046	5.4
9 Adolph Bellizeare, Pennsylvania	9	168	849	5.1
10 Bob McCall, Arizona	11	228	1148	5.0

*-Based on top 26 rushers

RECEIVING	G	REC	YDS	TD	YPR	YPG	RPG
1 Tom Forzani, Utah State	11	85	1169	8	13.8	106.3	7.7
2 Clinton Graves, Temple	9	63	707	3	11.2	78.6	7.0
3 Barry Smith, Florida State	10	69	1243	13	18.0	124.3	6.9
4 Chip Regine, Brown	9	51	681	6	13.4	75.7	5.7
5 Walt Walker, Davidson	11	62	1031	8	16.6	93.7	5.6
5 Jeff Calabrese, Toledo	11	62	886	2	14.3	80.5	5.6
7 Bert Calland, Navy	11	61	650	2	10.7	59.1	5.5
8 Greg Taylor, Texas-El Paso	10	53	878	4	16.6	87.8	5.3
9 Ken Matthews, Long Beach State	11	58	938	2	16.2	85.3	5.3
10 Gary Barnes, Louisville	10	52	655	4	12.6	65.5	5.2

PUNTING	PUNT	YDS	AVG
1 Ray Guy, Southern Miss	58	2680	46.2
2 Bruce Barnes, UCLA	48	2078	43.3
3 Chuck Ramsey, Wake Forest	72	3110	43.2
4 Dan Marrelli, Utah	57	2462	43.2
5 Danny White, Arizona State	51	2193	43.0
6 Randy Lee, Tulane	70	2996	42.8
7 Greg Gantt, Alabama	44	1874	42.6
8 Gary Keithley, Texas-El Paso	47	2002	42.6
9 Marty Shuford, Arizona	77	3273	42.5
10 Bill Armstrong, California	64	2675	41.8

PUNT RETURNS	PR	YDS	TD	AVG
1 Randy Rhino, Georgia Tech	25	441	1	17.6
2 George Ewing, Tulane	16	264	3	16.5
3 Johnny Rodgers, Nebraska	39	618	2	15.8
4 Carl Roaches, Texas A&M	19	287	2	15.1
5 Gerald Tinker, Kent State	19	268	1	14.1
6 Lynn Swann, Southern Cal	18	253	1	14.1
7 Kris Silverthorn, SMU	32	443	2	13.8
8 Bill Simpson, Michigan State	21	286	2	13.6
9 Steve Haggerty, Colorado	26	352	1	13.5
10 Robert Smith, Maryland	23	308	1	13.4

KICKOFF RETURNS	KR	YDS	TD	AVG
1 Larry Williams, Texas Tech	16	493	0	30.8
2 Byron Florence, Northern Illinois	16	456	1	28.5
3 Fran Meagher, Holy Cross	16	451	1	28.2
4 Kerry Marbury, West Virginia	20	554	1	27.7
5 Theopolis Bell, Arizona	18	449	0	24.9
6 Doug Nettles, Vanderbilt	23	566	0	24.6
7 Earl Douthitt, Iowa	22	541	0	24.6
8 Eddie Woodard, Kent State	21	516	1	24.6
9 Steve Odom, Utah	41	984	0	24.0
10 Dornell Harris, Memphis	19	453	0	23.8

SCORING	TDS	XPT	FG	PTS	PTPG
1 Harold Henson, Ohio State	20	0	0	120	12.0
2 Kerry Marbury, West Virginia	18	0	0	108	10.8
3 Howard Stevens, Louisville	17	0	0	102	10.2
4 Anthony Davis, Southern Cal	18	0	0	108	9.8
5 Terry Metcalf, Long Beach State	16	2	0	98	9.8
6 Stan Fritts, North Carolina St.	17	4	0	106	9.6
7 Johnny Rodgers, Nebraska	17	0	0	102	9.3
7 Carl Crumpler, East Carolina	17	0	0	102	9.3
9 Bob Hitchens, Miami, Ohio	15	0	0	90	9.0
9 Woody Green, Arizona State	15	0	0	90	9.0

KICK SCORING	XPA	XP	FGA	FG	PTS	PTPG
1 Fred Lima, Colorado	36	35	34	15	80	7.3
2 Rich Sanger, Nebraska	62	58	14	6	76	6.9
3 Frank Nester, West Virginia	50	47	14	9	74	6.7
4 Dave Strock, Virginia Tech	30	28	29	15	73	6.6
5 Juan Cruz, Arizona State	62	53	12	6	71	6.5
6 Mike Rae, Southern Cal	52	43	10	8	67	6.1
6 Ricky Townsend, Tennessee	31	31	19	12	67	6.1
8 Don Grimes, Texas Tech	30	30	18	12	66	6.0
8 Ted Perry, Dartmouth	32	30	13	8	54	6.0
10 Rick Fulcher, Oklahoma	40	38	15	9	65	5.9

INTERCEPTIONS	INT	YDS	TD	INT/GM
1 Mike Townsend, Notre Dame	10	39	0	1.00
2 John Provost, Holy Cross	9	175	1	0.90
2 Harry Harrison, Mississippi	9	129	0	0.90
4 David Langner, Auburn	8	156	0	0.80
5 Peter Knight, Cornell	7	96	0	0.78
5 Denny Costello, Miami, Ohio	7	52	0	0.78
7 Ron Karlis, Western Michigan	8	247	2	0.73
7 Randy Rhino, Georgia Tech	8	171	1	0.73
7 Ray Guy, Southern Miss	8	137	0	0.73
7 Alvin Brown, Oklahoma State	8	117	0	0.73
7 Jackie Wallace, Arizona	8	115	1	0.73
7 Dave Atkinson, Brigham Young	8	88	1	0.73

Team Leaders

RUSHING OFFENSE	G	ATT	YDS	AVG	TD	YPG
1 Oklahoma	11	803	4057	5.1	39	368.8
2 UCLA	11	673	3810	5.7	38	346.4
3 Arizona State	11	619	3681	5.9	46	334.6
4 Oklahoma State	11	707	3497	4.9	24	317.9
5 Notre Dame	10	594	3043	5.1	28	304.3
6 Alabama	11	704	3332	4.7	42	302.9
7 Yale	9	538	2636	4.9	32	292.9
8 Miami, Ohio	10	683	2806	4.1	25	280.6
9 New Mexico	11	686	3085	4.5	25	280.5
10 Texas	10	598	2760	4.6	29	276.0

PASSING OFFENSE/YPG	G	ATT	COM	INT	PCT	YDS	YPA	TD	YPG	I%	YPC
1 Virginia Tech	11	440	233	28	53.0	3348	7.6	18	304.4	6.4	14.4
2 Utah State	11	392	222	13	56.6	3164	8.1	24	287.6	3.3	14.3
3 Florida State	11	389	209	23	53.7	2974	7.6	28	270.4	5.9	14.2
4 San Diego State	11	327	184	25	56.3	2525	7.7	18	229.5	7.7	13.7
5 Stanford	11	386	203	23	52.6	2509	6.5	16	228.1	6.0	12.4
6 West Virginia	11	334	161	18	48.2	2506	7.5	17	227.8	5.4	15.6
7 California	11	361	182	32	50.4	2444	6.8	20	222.2	8.9	13.4
8 Nebraska	11	306	161	20	52.6	2431	7.9	23	221.0	6.5	15.1
9 New Mexico State	11	412	195	16	47.3	2428	5.9	10	220.7	3.9	12.5
10 Texas-El Paso	10	323	169	12	52.3	2164	6.7	10	216.4	3.7	12.8

TOTAL OFFENSE	G	P	YDS	AVG	TD	YPG
1 Arizona State	11	856	5681	6.6	67	516.5
2 Oklahoma	11	953	5255	5.5	48	477.7
3 Nebraska	11	928	4843	5.2	60	440.3
4 Utah State	11	804	4783	5.9	40	434.8
5 North Carolina St.	11	846	4758	5.6	49	432.5
6 Southern Cal	11	830	4731	5.7	53	430.1
7 Notre Dame	10	766	4238	5.5	36	423.8
8 West Virginia	11	796	4531	5.7	51	411.9
9 Virginia Tech	11	857	4527	5.3	38	411.5
10 Alabama	11	832	4501	5.4	53	409.2

RUSHING DEFENSE	G	ATT	YDS	AVG	TD	YPG
1 Louisville	10	430	821	1.9	7	82.1
2 Western Michigan	11	454	980	2.2	14	89.1
3 Southern Cal	11	488	1036	2.1	9	94.2
4 Miami, Ohio	10	365	961	2.6	8	96.1
5 Pacific	11	428	1112	2.6	10	101.1
6 Oklahoma	11	409	1124	2.7	6	102.2
7 East Carolina	11	443	1200	2.7	15	109.1
8 Nebraska	11	516	1240	2.4	5	112.7
9 Bowling Green	10	458	1134	2.5	8	113.4
10 Alabama	11	459	1263	2.8	8	114.8

PASSING DEFENSE	G	ATT	COM	PCT	YPC	INT	I%	YDS	YPA	TD	YPG
1 Vanderbilt	11	164	61	37.2	14.5	11	6.7	883	5.4	5	80.3
2 Northwestern	11	129	57	44.2	15.6	7	5.4	889	6.9	8	80.8
3 Tennessee	11	213	85	39.9	10.6	20	9.4	904	4.2	4	82.2
4 Michigan	11	200	82	41.0	11.4	17	8.5	932	4.7	1	84.7
5 Toledo	11	177	70	39.5	13.5	13	7.3	947	5.4	8	86.1
6 Iowa	11	172	78	45.3	12.7	11	6.4	989	5.8	6	89.9
7 Baylor	11	199	72	36.2	13.8	18	9.1	995	5.0	4	90.5
8 Wichita State	11	209	76	36.4	13.5	27	12.9	1029	4.9	8	93.5
9 Marshall	10	154	66	42.9	14.4	8	5.2	951	6.2	2	95.1
10 Alabama	11	215	105	48.8	10.2	20	9.3	1071	5.0	7	97.4

TOTAL DEFENSE	G	P	YDS	AVG	TD	YPG
1 Louisville	10	689	2025	2.9	8	202.5
2 Alabama	11	674	2334	3.5	15	212.2
3 Michigan	11	680	2372	3.5	7	215.6
4 Nebraska	11	764	2411	3.2	11	219.2
5 Oklahoma	11	691	2494	3.6	8	226.7
6 Miami, Ohio	10	596	2276	3.8	15	227.6
7 Southern Cal	11	772	2534	3.3	14	230.4
8 Tennessee	11	738	2539	3.4	10	230.8
9 Tampa	11	730	2600	3.6	12	236.4
10 Bowling Green	10	661	2437	3.7	17	243.7

SCORING OFFENSE	G	PTS	AVG
1 Arizona State	11	513	46.6
2 Nebraska	11	461	41.9
3 Southern Cal	11	425	38.6
4 West Virginia	11	402	36.5
5 Alabama	11	393	35.7
6 Oklahoma	11	385	35.0
7 North Carolina St.	11	360	32.7
8 Penn State	11	358	32.5
9 Utah	11	354	32.2
10 UCLA	11	351	31.9

SCORING DEFENSE	G	PTS	AVG
1 Michigan	11	57	5.2
2 Oklahoma	11	74	6.7
3 Tennessee	11	83	7.5
4 Nebraska	11	91	8.3
5 Louisville	10	91	9.1
6 Tampa	11	114	10.4
7 Southern Cal	11	117	10.6
8 Texas	10	108	10.8
9 LSU	11	121	11.0
10 Miami, Ohio	10	116	11.6

1973 POLL PROGRESSION

PRE-SEASON / Sept. 8 Games

AP	Team	Record	Result
1	Southern Cal	0-0-0	bye week
2	Ohio State	0-0-0	bye week
3	Texas	0-0-0	bye week
4	Nebraska	0-0-0	beat #10 UCLA 40-13
5	Michigan	0-0-0	bye week
6	Alabama	0-0-0	bye week
7	Penn State	0-0-0	bye week
8	Notre Dame	0-0-0	bye week
9	Tennessee	0-0-0	bye week
10	UCLA	0-0-0	lost to #4 Nebraska 13-40
11	Colorado	0-0-0	bye week
12	Oklahoma	0-0-0	bye week
13	Auburn	0-0-0	bye week
14	Arizona State	0-0-0	bye week
15	Florida	0-0-0	bye week
16	LSU	0-0-0	bye week
17	North Carolina St.	0-0-0	beat East Carolina 57-8
18	Houston	0-0-0	bye week
19	North Carolina	0-0-0	bye week
20	Texas Tech	0-0-0	bye week

SEPTEMBER 10 POLL / Sept. 15 Games

AP	Team	Record	Result
1	Southern Cal	0-0-0	beat Arkansas 17-0
2	Nebraska	1-0-0	bye week
3	Ohio State	0-0-0	beat Minnesota 56-7
4	Texas	0-0-0	bye week
5	Michigan	0-0-0	beat Iowa 31-7
6	Alabama	0-0-0	beat California 66-0
7	Penn State	0-0-0	beat Stanford 20-6
8	Notre Dame	0-0-0	bye week
9	Tennessee	0-0-0	beat Duke 21-17
10	Colorado	0-0-0	lost to #15 LSU 6-17
11	Oklahoma	0-0-0	beat Baylor 42-14
12	Auburn	0-0-0	beat Oregon State 18-9
13	Arizona State	0-0-0	beat Oregon 26-20
14	Florida	0-0-0	beat Kansas State 21-10
15	LSU	0-0-0	beat #10 Colorado 17-6
16	UCLA	0-1-0	bye week
17	North Carolina St.	2-0-0	beat Virginia 43-23
18	Houston	0-0-0	beat Rice 24-6
19	North Carolina	0-0-0	beat William & Mary 34-27
20	Texas Tech	0-0-0	beat Utah 29-22

SEPTEMBER 17 POLL / Sept. 22 Games

UP	AP	Team	Record	Result
1	1	Southern Cal	1-0-0	beat Georgia Tech 23-6
2	2	Nebraska	1-0-0	beat #14 North Carolina St. 31-14
3	3	Ohio State	1-0-0	bye week
4	4	Alabama	1-0-0	beat Kentucky 28-14
6	5	Michigan	1-0-0	beat Stanford 47-10
5	6	Texas	0-0-0	lost to Miami, Fla. 15-20
7	7	Penn State	1-0-0	beat Navy 39-0
11	8	Notre Dame	1-0-0	beat Northwestern 44-0
8	9	Oklahoma	1-0-0	bye week
10	10	Tennessee	1-0-0	beat Army 37-18
9	11	LSU	1-0-0	beat Texas A&M 28-23
12	12	Auburn	1-0-0	beat U.T. Chatanooga 31-0
13	13	Arizona State	1-0-0	beat Washington State 20-9
16	14	North Carolina St.	2-0-0	lost to #2 Nebraska 14-31
14	15	Florida	1-0-0	beat Southern Miss 14-13
16	16	Houston	1-0-0	beat South Carolina 27-19
15	17	Oklahoma State	1-0-0	beat Arkansas 38-6
	18	UCLA	0-1-0	beat Iowa 55-18
	19	Colorado	0-1-0	beat Wisconsin 28-25
	20	Bowling Green	1-0-0	beat Dayton 31-16
18	20	Missouri	1-0-0	beat Virginia 31-7
19		Tulane	0-0-0	beat Boston College 21-16
19		North Carolina	1-0-0	lost to Maryland 3-23

SEPTEMBER 24 POLL / Sept. 29 Games

UP	AP	Team	Record	Result
1	1	Southern Cal	2-0-0	tied #8 Oklahoma 7-7
2	2	Nebraska	2-0-0	beat Wisconsin 20-16
3	3	Ohio State	1-0-0	beat TCU 37-3
4	4	Michigan	2-0-0	beat Navy 14-0
5	5	Alabama	2-0-0	beat Vanderbilt 44-0
6	6	Penn State	2-0-0	beat Iowa 27-8
7	7	Notre Dame	1-0-0	beat Purdue 20-7
8	8	Oklahoma	1-0-0	tied #1 Southern Cal 7-7
9	9	Tennessee	2-0-0	beat #11 Auburn 21-0
10	10	LSU	2-0-0	beat Rice 24-9
13	11	Auburn	2-0-0	lost to #9 Tennessee 0-21
11	12	Oklahoma State	2-0-0	beat So. Illinois 70-7
14	13	Arizona State	2-0-0	beat Colorado State 67-14
	14	Texas	0-1-0	beat Texas Tech 28-12
12		Houston	2-0-0	beat Memphis 35-21
15	16	Florida	2-0-0	lost to Mississippi State 12-33
		UCLA	1-1-0	beat Michigan State 34-21
18	18	Miami, Fla.	1-0-0	beat Florida State 14-10
	19	North Carolina St.	2-1-0	lost to Georgia 12-31
15	20	Missouri	2-0-0	beat North Carolina 27-14
15		SMU	2-0-0	beat Virginia Tech 37-6
18		Tulane	1-0-0	beat VMI 42-0

OCTOBER 1 POLL / Oct. 6 Games

UP	AP	Team	Record	Result
1	1	Ohio State	2-0-0	beat Washington St. 27-3
2	2	Nebraska	3-0-0	beat Minnesota 48-7
4	3	Alabama	3-0-0	beat Georgia 28-14
3	4	Southern Cal	2-0-1	beat Oregon State 21-7
5	5	Michigan	3-0-0	beat Oregon 24-0
6	6	Oklahoma	1-0-1	beat #17 Miami, Fla. 24-20
7	7	Penn State	3-0-0	beat Air Force 19-9
8	8	Notre Dame	2-0-0	beat Michigan State 14-10
9	9	Tennessee	3-0-0	beat Kansas 28-27
10	10	LSU	3-0-0	beat Florida 24-3
11	11	Oklahoma State	3-0-0	lost to Texas Tech 7-20
12	12	Arizona State	3-0-0	beat New Mexico 67-24
19	13	Texas	1-1-0	beat Wake Forest 41-0
13	14	Houston	3-0-0	beat San Diego State 14-9
15	15	Missouri	3-0-0	beat #19 SMU 17-7
	16	UCLA	2-1-0	beat Utah 66-16
17	17	Miami, Fla.	2-0-0	lost to #6 Oklahoma 20-24
	18	Colorado	2-1-0	beat Iowa State 23-16
14	19	SMU	3-0-0	lost to #15 Missouri 7-17
16	20	West Virginia	3-0-0	lost to Indiana 14-28
16		Tulane	2-0-0	beat Pittsburgh 24-6

OCTOBER 8 POLL / Oct. 13 Games

UP	AP	Team	Record	Result
1	1	Ohio State	3-0-0	beat Wisconsin 24-0
2	2	Nebraska	3-0-0	lost to #12 Missouri 12-13
3	3	Alabama	4-0-0	beat Florida 35-14
5	4	Southern Cal	3-0-1	beat Washington State 46-35
4	5	Michigan	4-0-0	beat Michigan State 31-0
6	6	Oklahoma	2-0-1	beat #13 Texas 52-13
7	7	Penn State	4-0-0	beat Army 54-3
8	8	Tennessee	4-0-0	beat Georgia Tech 20-14
9	9	Notre Dame	3-0-0	beat Rice 28-0
10	10	LSU	4-0-0	beat Auburn 20-6
12	11	Arizona State	4-0-0	beat San Jose State 28-3
14	12	Missouri	4-0-0	beat #2 Nebraska 13-12
16	13	Texas	2-1-0	lost to #6 Oklahoma 13-52
13	14	Houston	4-0-0	beat Virginia Tech 54-27
11	15	UCLA	3-1-0	beat Stanford 59-13
	16	Miami, Fla.	2-1-0	beat Boston College 15-10
17	17	Colorado	3-1-0	beat Air Force 38-17
15	18	Tulane	3-0-0	beat Duke 24-17
	19	Kansas	3-1-0	beat Kansas State 25-18
	20	Miami, Ohio	4-0-0	beat Ohio U. 10-6

OCTOBER 15 POLL / Oct. 20 Games

UP	AP	Team	Record	Result
1	1	Ohio State	4-0-0	beat Indiana 37-7
2	2	Alabama	5-0-0	beat #10 Tennessee 42-21
3	3	Oklahoma	3-0-1	beat #16 Colorado 34-7
4	4	Michigan	4-0-0	beat Wisconsin 35-6
6	5	Penn State	5-0-0	beat Syracuse 49-6
5	6	Southern Cal	4-0-1	beat Oregon 31-10
10	7	Missouri	5-0-0	beat Oklahoma State 13-9
8	8	Notre Dame	4-0-0	beat Army 62-3
7	9	LSU	5-0-0	beat Kentucky 28-21
9	10	Tennessee	5-0-0	lost to #2 Alabama 21-42
11	11	Nebraska	4-1-0	beat #18 Kansas 10-9
14	12	Arizona State	5-0-0	beat Brigham Young 52-12
12	13	UCLA	4-1-0	beat Washington State 24-13
13	14	Houston	5-0-0	beat #15 Miami, Fla. 30-7
16	15	Miami, Fla.	3-1-0	lost to #14 Houston 7-30
18	16	Colorado	4-1-0	lost to #3 Oklahoma 7-34
15	17	Tulane	4-0-0	beat North Carolina 16-0
18	18	Kansas	4-1-0	lost to #11 Nebraska 9-10
17	19	Arizona	5-0-0	lost to Texas Tech 17-31
18	20	Miami, Ohio	5-0-0	beat Bowling Green 31-8

OCTOBER 22 POLL / Oct. 27 Games

UP	AP	Team	Record	Result
1	1	Ohio State	5-0-0	beat Northwestern 60-0
2	2	Alabama	6-0-0	beat Virginia Tech 77-6
3	3	Oklahoma	4-0-1	beat Kansas State 56-14
4	4	Michigan	6-0-0	beat Minnesota 34-7
5	5	Penn State	6-0-0	beat West Virginia 62-14
6	6	Southern Cal	5-0-1	lost to #8 Notre Dame 14-23
9	7	Missouri	6-0-0	lost to Colorado 13-17
7	8	Notre Dame	5-0-0	beat #6 Southern Cal 23-14
8	9	LSU	6-0-0	beat South Carolina 33-29
12	10	Nebraska	5-1-0	tied Oklahoma State 17-17
10	11	Arizona State	6-0-0	beat Oregon State 44-14
10	12	Houston	6-0-0	lost to Auburn 0-7
13	13	UCLA	5-1-0	beat California 61-21
14	14	Tennessee	5-1-0	beat TCU 39-7
14	15	Tulane	5-0-0	beat Georgia Tech 23-14
17	16	Miami, Ohio	6-0-0	beat Toledo 16-0
	17	Kansas	4-2-0	beat Iowa State 22-20
16	18	Texas Tech	5-1-0	beat SMU 31-14
	19	Texas	3-2-0	beat Rice 55-13
	20	Richmond	6-0-0	lost to La. Monroe 8-14
17		SMU	4-1-0	lost to #18 Texas Tech 14-31

OCTOBER 29 POLL / Nov. 3 Games

UP	AP	Team	Record	Result
1	1	Ohio State	6-0-0	beat Illinois 30-0
2	2	Alabama	7-0-0	beat Mississippi State 35-0
3	3	Oklahoma	5-0-1	beat Iowa State 34-17
4	4	Michigan	7-0-0	beat Indiana 49-13
5	5	Notre Dame	6-0-0	beat Navy 44-7
6	6	Penn State	7-0-0	beat Maryland 42-22
7	7	LSU	7-0-0	beat Mississippi 51-14
8	8	Arizona State	7-0-0	lost to Utah 31-36
10	9	Southern Cal	5-1-1	beat California 50-14
9	10	UCLA	6-1-0	beat Washington 62-13
11	11	Tennessee	6-1-0	lost to Georgia 31-35
12	12	Missouri	6-1-0	beat Kansas State 31-7
15	13	Nebraska	5-1-1	beat #17 Colorado 28-16
13	14	Tulane	6-0-0	lost to Kentucky 7-34
17	15	Texas Tech	6-1-0	beat Rice 19-6
19	16	Miami, Ohio	7-0-0	beat Western Michigan 24-9
17	17	Colorado	5-2-0	lost to #13 Nebraska 16-28
16	18	Houston	6-1-0	beat Florida State 34-3
19	19	Auburn	5-2-0	lost to Florida 8-12
14	20	Texas	4-2-0	beat SMU 42-14

November 5 Poll — Nov. 10 Games

UP	AP	Team	Record	Result
1	1	Ohio State	7-0-0	beat Michigan State 35-0
2	2	Alabama	8-0-0	bye week
3	3	Oklahoma	6-0-1	beat #10 Missouri 31-3
4	4	Michigan	8-0-0	beat Illinois 21-6
5	5	Notre Dame	7-0-0	beat #20 Pittsburgh 31-10
6	6	Penn State	8-0-0	beat North Carolina St. 35-29
7	7	LSU	8-0-0	bye week
9	8	Southern Cal	6-1-1	beat Stanford 27-26
8	9	UCLA	7-1-0	beat Oregon 27-7
10	10	Missouri	7-1-0	lost to #3 Oklahoma 3-31
11	11	Nebraska	6-1-1	beat Iowa State 31-7
14	12	Texas Tech	7-1-0	beat TCU 24-10
12	13	Texas	5-2-0	beat Baylor 42-6
15	14	Arizona State	7-1-0	beat Wyoming 47-0
13	15	Houston	7-1-0	beat Colorado State 28-20
	16	Tennessee	6-2-0	bye week
15	17	Miami, Ohio	8-0-0	beat Kent State 20-10
	18	Kansas	5-2-1	beat Colorado 17-15
	19	Kent State	7-1-0	lost to Miami, Ohio 10-20
	20	Pittsburgh	5-2-1	lost to #5 Notre Dame 10-31
17		Tulane	6-1-0	beat Navy 17-15

November 12 Poll — Nov. 17 Games

UP	AP	Team	Record	Result
1	1	Ohio State	8-0-0	beat Iowa 55-13
2	2	Alabama	8-0-0	beat Miami, Fla. 43-13
3	3	Oklahoma	7-0-1	beat #18 Kansas 48-20
4	4	Michigan	9-0-0	beat Purdue 34-9
5	5	Notre Dame	8-0-0	bye week
6	6	Penn State	9-0-0	beat Ohio U. 49-10
7	7	LSU	8-0-0	beat Mississippi State 26-7
8	8	UCLA	8-0-0	beat Oregon State 56-14
9	9	Southern Cal	7-1-1	beat Washington 42-19
10	10	Nebraska	7-1-1	beat Kansas State 50-21
11	11	Texas	6-2-0	beat TCU 52-7
12	12	Texas Tech	8-1-0	beat Baylor 55-24
13	13	Arizona State	8-1-0	beat Texas-El Paso 54-13
15	14	Missouri	7-2-0	lost to Iowa State 7-17
14	15	Houston	8-1-0	bye week
19	16	Tennessee	6-2-0	lost to Mississippi 18-28
16	17	Miami, Ohio	9-0-0	beat Cincinnati 6-0
17	18	Kansas	6-2-1	lost to #3 Oklahoma 20-48
	19	Arizona	8-1-0	lost to Air Force 26-27
	20	North Carolina St.	6-3-0	beat Duke 21-3
19		Tulane	7-1-0	beat Vanderbilt 24-3

November 19 Poll — Nov. 24 Games

UP	AP	Team	Record	Result
1	1	Ohio State	9-0-0	tied #4 Michigan 10-10
2	2	Alabama	9-0-0	beat #7 LSU 21-7
3	3	Oklahoma	8-0-1	beat #10 Nebraska 27-0
4	4	Michigan	10-0-0	tied #1 Ohio State 10-10
5	5	Notre Dame	8-0-0	beat Air Force 48-15
6	6	Penn State	10-0-0	beat #20 Pittsburgh 35-13
7	7	LSU	9-0-0	lost to #2 Alabama 7-21
8	8	UCLA	9-1-0	lost to #9 Southern Cal 13-23
9	9	Southern Cal	8-1-1	beat #8 UCLA 23-13
10	10	Nebraska	8-1-1	lost to #3 Oklahoma 0-27
11	11	Texas	7-2-0	beat Texas A&M 42-13
13	12	Texas Tech	9-1-0	beat Arkansas 24-17
12	13	Arizona State	9-1-0	beat Arizona 55-19
14	14	Houston	8-1-0	beat Wyoming 35-0
15	15	Miami, Ohio	10-0-0	regular season complete
	16	North Carolina St.	7-3-0	beat Wake Forest 52-13
16	17	Tulane	8-1-0	lost to Maryland 9-42
	18	Oklahoma State	5-2-2	lost to Iowa State 12-28
	19	Missouri	7-3-0	lost to #20 Kansas 13-14
16	20	Kansas	6-3-1	beat #19 Missouri 14-13
		Pittsburgh	6-3-1	lost to #6 Penn State 13-35

November 26 Poll — Dec. 1 Games

UP	AP	Team	Record	Result
1	1	Alabama	10-0-0	beat Auburn 35-0
2	2	Oklahoma	9-0-1	beat Oklahoma State 45-18
3	3	Ohio State	9-0-1	regular season complete
5	4	Michigan	10-0-1	regular season complete
4	5	Notre Dame	9-0-0	beat Miami, Fla. 44-0
6	6	Penn State	11-0-0	regular season complete
7	7	Southern Cal	9-1-1	regular season complete
8	8	LSU	9-1-0	lost to Tulane 0-14
9	9	Texas	8-2-0	regular season complete
10	10	UCLA	9-2-0	regular season complete
11	11	Arizona State	10-1-0	regular season complete
13	12	Texas Tech	10-1-0	regular season complete
12	13	Nebraska	8-2-1	regular season complete
14	14	Houston	9-1-0	beat Tulsa 35-16
16	15	Miami, Ohio	10-0-0	
	16	North Carolina St.	8-3-0	regular season complete
15	17	Kansas	7-3-1	regular season complete
17	18	Maryland	8-3-0	regular season complete
	19	Tennessee	7-3-0	beat Vanderbilt 20-17
	20	Missouri	7-4-0	regular season complete

December 3 Poll

UP	AP	Team	Record	Bowl Bid	Date	Bowl Result
1	1	Alabama	11-0-0	Sugar Bowl	D31	lost to #3 Notre Dame 23-24
2	2	Oklahoma	10-0-1			
4	3	Notre Dame	10-0-0	Sugar Bowl	D31	beat #1 Alabama 24-23
3	4	Ohio State	9-0-1	Rose Bowl	J1	beat #7 Southern Cal 42-21
6	5	Michigan	10-0-1			
5	6	Penn State	11-0-0	Orange Bowl	J1	beat #13 LSU 16-9
7	7	Southern Cal	9-1-1	Rose Bowl	J1	lost to #4 Ohio State 21-42
8	8	Texas	8-2-0	Cotton Bowl	J1	lost to #12 Nebraska 3-19
9	9	UCLA	9-2-0			
10	10	Arizona State	10-1-0	Fiesta Bowl	D21	beat Pittsburgh 28-7
11	11	Texas Tech	10-1-0	Gator Bowl	D29	beat #20 Tennessee 28-19
11	12	Nebraska	8-2-1	Cotton Bowl	J1	beat #6 Texas 19-3
14	13	LSU	9-2-0	Orange Bowl	J1	lost to #6 Penn State 9-16
13	14	Houston	10-1-0	Bluebonnet Bowl	D29	beat #17 Tulane 47-7
17	15	Miami, Ohio	10-0-0	Tangerine Bowl	D22	beat Florida 16-7
	16	North Carolina St.	8-3-0	Liberty Bowl	D17	beat #19 Kansas 31-18
15	17	Tulane	9-2-0	Bluebonnet Bowl	D29	lost to #14 Houston 7-47
18	18	Maryland	8-3-0	Peach Bowl	D28	lost to Georgia 16-17
15	19	Kansas	7-3-1	Liberty Bowl	D17	lost to #16 North Carolina St. 18-31
	20	Tennessee	8-3-0	Gator Bowl	D29	lost to #11 Texas Tech 19-28
18		San Diego State	9-1-1			
18		Florida	7-4-0	Tangerine Bowl	D22	lost to #15 Miami, Ohio 7-16

January 3 Final Poll

RB	AP	Team	Record
1	1	Notre Dame	11-0-0
5	2	Ohio State	10-0-1
2	3	Oklahoma	10-0-1
4	4	Alabama	11-1-0
3	5	Penn State	12-0-0
6	6	Michigan	10-0-1
9	7	Nebraska	9-2-1
7	8	Southern Cal	9-2-1
12	9	Arizona State	11-1-0
10	10	Houston	11-1-0
11	11	Texas Tech	11-1-0
13	12	UCLA	9-2-0
8	13	LSU	9-3-0
17	14	Texas	8-3-0
NR	15	Miami, Ohio	11-0-0
18	16	North Carolina St.	9-3-0
16	17	Missouri	8-4-0
19	18	Kansas	7-4-1
14	19	Tennessee	8-4-0
23	20	Maryland	8-4-0
21	20	Tulane	9-3-0

ANNUAL REVIEW

1973

CONSENSUS ALL-AMERICANS

POS	Offense	HT	WT	School	AP	CP	FC	FW	NE	PI
QB	Dave Jaynes	6-2	212	Kansas	•	•	•		•	
RB	John Cappelletti	6-1	206	Penn State	•	•	•	•	•	•
RB	Roosevelt Leaks	5-11	209	Texas	•	•	•	•	•	•
RB	Woody Green	6-1	202	Arizona State		•	•		•	
RB	Kermit Johnson	6-0	185	UCLA			•	•		
WR	Lynn Swann	6-0	180	Southern Cal	•		•	•	•	•
TE	Dave Casper	6-3	252	Notre Dame	•	•	•	•	•	•
T	John Hicks	6-3	258	Ohio State	•	•	•	•	•	•
T	Booker Brown	6-3	270	Southern Cal			•	•		
G	Buddy Brown	6-2	242	Alabama	•	•	•	•	•	
G	Bill Yoest	6-0	235	North Carolina St.	•	•	•	•	•	
C	Bill Wyman	6-2	235	Texas	•	•	•	•	•	•

	OTHERS RECEIVING FIRST-TEAM HONORS									
QB	Danny White			Arizona State	•			•	•	
RB	Tony Dorsett			Pittsburgh	•				•	
RB	Archie Griffin			Ohio State					•	
WR	Wayne Wheeler			Alabama		•				
WR	Danny Buggs			West Virginia			•			
TE	Andre Tillman			Texas Tech		•				
T	Eddie Foster			Oklahoma					•	
T	Daryl White			Nebraska				•		•
T	Al Oliver			UCLA					•	
G	Tyler Lafauci			LSU	•	•			•	
K	Ricky Townsend			Tennessee				•		
KR	Steve Odom			Utah				•		

FC named Booker Brown as a G; AP named Buddy brown as a T

POS	Defense	HT	WT	School	AP	CP	FC	FW	NE	PI
L	John Dutton	6-7	248	Nebraska	•	•	•	•	•	•
L	Dave Gallagher	6-4	245	Michigan	•	•	•	•	•	•
L	Lucious Selmon	5-11	236	Oklahoma	•	•	•	•	•	•
L	Tony Cristiani	5-10	215	Miami, Fla.	•	•		•		
LB	Randy Gradishar	6-3	236	Ohio State	•	•	•	•	•	•
LB	Rod Shoate	6-1	214	Oklahoma	•	•		•	•	
LB	Richard Wood	6-2	217	Southern Cal	•	•	•	•	•	
B	Mike Townsend	6-3	183	Notre Dame	•	•	•	•	•	
B	Artimus Parker	6-3	215	Southern Cal	•	•		•		
B	Dave Brown	6-1	188	Michigan		•		•	•	•
B	Randy Rhino	5-10	179	Georgia Tech	•		•		•	

	OTHERS RECEIVING FIRST-TEAM HONORS									
L	Charlie Hall			Tulane			•			
L	Paul Vellano			Maryland		•				
L	Pat Donovan			Stanford	•					
L	Randy White			Maryland		•				
L	Bill Kollar			Montana State					•	
L	Ed Jones			Tennessee State					•	
L	Randy Crowder			Penn State					•	
L	Van DeCree			Ohio State				•		
L	Roger Stillwell			Stanford	•					
LB	Ed O'Neill			Penn State	•			•		
LB	Warren Capone			LSU		•			•	•
LB	Woodrow Lowe			Alabama		•			•	•
LB	Cleveland Vann			Oklahoma State			•			
B	John Moseley			Missouri			•			
B	Matt Blair			Iowa State				•		
B	Jimmy Allen			UCLA	•	•				
B	Harry Harrison			Mississippi					•	
P	Chuck Ramsey			Wake Forest	•					

FC named Shoate as a L

HEISMAN TROPHY VOTING

	PLAYER	POS	SCHOOL	1ST	2ND	3RD	TOTAL
1	John Cappelletti	HB	Penn State	229	142	86	1057
2	John Hicks	OT	Ohio State	114	64	54	524
3	Roosevelt Leaks	RB	Texas	74	80	100	482
4	David Jaynes	QB	Kansas	65	68	63	394
5	Archie Griffin	TB	Ohio State	45	63	65	326
6	Randy Gradishar	LB	Ohio State	47	53	35	282
7	Lucious Selmon	NG	Oklahoma	39	52	29	250
8	Woody Green	HB	Arizona State	31	55	44	247
9	Danny White	QB	Arizona State	32	22	26	166
10	Kermit Johnson	RB	UCLA	24	15	20	122

AWARD WINNERS

PLAYER	POS	SCHOOL	AWARD NAME
John Cappelletti	RB	Penn State	Maxwell
John Hicks	OT	Ohio State	Outland
John Cappelletti	RB	Penn State	Camp
John Hicks	OT	Ohio State	Lombardi

CONFERENCE STANDINGS

ACC

	CONF. W L T			OVERALL W L T		
North Carolina St.	6	0	0	9	3	0
Maryland	5	1	0	8	4	0
Clemson	4	2	0	5	6	0
Virginia	3	3	0	4	7	0
Duke	1	4	1	2	8	1
North Carolina	1	5	0	4	7	0
Wake Forest	0	5	1	1	9	1

Big 10

	CONF. W L T			OVERALL W L T		
Michigan	7	0	1	10	0	1
Ohio State	7	0	1	10	0	1
Minnesota	6	2	0	7	4	0
Illinois	4	4	0	5	6	0
Purdue	4	4	0	5	6	0
Michigan State	4	4	0	5	6	0
Northwestern	4	4	0	4	7	0
Wisconsin	3	5	0	4	7	0
Indiana	0	8	0	2	9	0
Iowa	0	8	0	0	11	0

Big 8

	CONF. W L T			OVERALL W L T		
Oklahoma	7	0	0	10	0	1
Nebraska	4	2	1	9	2	1
Kansas	4	2	1	7	4	1
Missouri	3	4	0	8	4	0
Oklahoma State	2	3	2	5	4	2
Kansas State	2	5	0	5	6	0
Colorado	2	5	0	5	6	0
Iowa State	2	5	0	4	7	0

Big West

	CONF. W L T			OVERALL W L T		
San Diego State	3	0	1	9	1	1
San Jose State	2	0	2	5	4	2
Pacific	2	1	1	7	2	1
Fresno State	1	3	0	2	9	0
Long Beach State	0	4	0	1	9	1

Ivy

	CONF. W L T			OVERALL W L T		
Dartmouth	6	1	0	6	3	0
Harvard	5	2	0	7	2	0
Pennsylvania	5	2	0	6	3	0
Yale	5	2	0	6	3	0
Brown	4	3	0	4	3	1
Cornell	2	5	0	3	5	1
Columbia	1	6	0	1	7	1
Princeton	0	7	0	1	8	0

MAC

	CONF. W L T			OVERALL W L T		
Miami, Ohio	5	0	0	10	0	0
Kent State	4	1	0	9	2	0
Bowling Green	2	3	0	7	3	0
Ohio U.	2	3	0	5	5	0
Western Michigan	1	4	0	6	5	0
Toledo	1	4	0	3	8	0

Pac 8

	CONF. W L T			OVERALL W L T		
Southern Cal	7	0	0	9	2	1
UCLA	6	1	0	9	2	0
Stanford	5	2	0	7	4	0
Washington State	4	3	0	5	6	0
California	2	5	0	4	7	0
Oregon State	2	5	0	2	9	0
Oregon	2	5	0	2	9	0
Washington	0	7	0	2	9	0

SEC

	CONF. W L T			OVERALL W L T		
Alabama	8	0	0	11	1	0
LSU	5	1	0	9	3	0
Mississippi	4	3	0	6	5	0
Tennessee	3	3	0	8	4	0
Georgia	3	4	0	7	4	1
Florida	3	4	0	7	5	0
Kentucky	3	4	0	5	6	0
Auburn	2	5	0	6	6	0
Mississippi State	2	5	0	4	5	2
Vanderbilt	1	5	0	5	6	0

SWC

	CONF. W L T			OVERALL W L T		
Texas	7	0	0	8	3	0
Texas Tech	6	1	0	11	1	0
Rice	4	3	0	5	6	0
SMU	3	3	1	6	4	1
Arkansas	3	3	1	5	5	1
Texas A&M	3	4	0	5	6	0
TCU	1	6	0	3	8	0
Baylor	0	7	0	2	9	0

WAC

	CONF. W L T			OVERALL W L T		
Arizona State	6	1	0	11	1	0
Arizona	6	1	0	8	3	0
Utah	4	2	0	7	5	0
Brigham Young	3	4	0	5	6	0
Wyoming	3	4	0	4	7	0
New Mexico	3	4	0	4	7	0
Colorado State	2	4	0	5	6	0
Texas-El Paso	0	7	0	0	11	0

Independents

	OVERALL W L T		
Penn State	12	0	0
Notre Dame	11	0	0
Houston	11	1	0
Tulane	9	3	0
Memphis	8	3	0
South Carolina	7	4	0
Utah State	7	4	0
Boston College	7	4	0
Air Force	6	4	0
Rutgers	6	5	0
West Virginia	6	5	0
Pittsburgh	6	5	1
Miami, Fla.	5	6	0
Georgia Tech	5	6	0
Navy	4	7	0
Virginia Tech	2	9	0
Syracuse	2	9	0
Army	0	10	0
Florida State	0	11	0

BOWL GAMES

DATE	GAME	SCORE
D17	Liberty	North Carolina St. 31, Kansas 18
D21	Fiesta	Arizona State 28, Pittsburgh 7
D22	Tangerine	Miami, Ohio 16, Florida 7
D28	Peach	Georgia 17, Maryland 16
D29	Bluebonnet	Houston 47, Tulane 7
D29	Sun	Missouri 34, Auburn 17
D29	Gator	Texas Tech 28, Tennessee 19
D31	Sugar	Notre Dame 24, Alabama 23
J1	Cotton	Nebraska 19, Texas 3
J1	Rose	Ohio State 42, Southern Cal 21
J1	Orange	Penn State 16, LSU 9

1973 NCAA Major College Statistical Leaders

Individual Leaders

PASSING	G	ATT	COM	PCT	INT	I%	YDS	YPA	TD	TD%	COM.PG
1 Jesse Freitas, San Diego State	11	347	227	65.4	17	4.9	2993	8.6	21	6.1	20.6
2 Gary Sheide, Brigham Young	10	294	177	60.2	12	4.1	2350	8.0	22	7.5	17.7
3 David Harper, Davidson	10	329	175	53.2	19	5.8	1885	5.7	11	3.3	17.5
4 Dave Jaynes, Kansas	11	330	172	52.1	9	2.7	2131	6.5	13	3.9	15.6
4 Bill Hatty, Villanova	11	341	172	50.4	19	5.6	1947	5.7	10	2.9	15.6
6 Gene Swick, Toledo	11	301	165	54.8	17	5.7	2234	7.4	15	5.0	15.0
6 Craig Kimball, San Jose State	11	305	165	54.1	14	4.6	1940	6.4	14	4.6	15.0
8 Danny White, Arizona State	11	265	146	55.1	12	4.5	2609	9.8	23	8.7	13.3
8 Jan Stuebbe, Colorado State	11	310	146	47.1	15	4.8	1938	6.3	11	3.6	13.3
10 Mark Allen, Cornell	9	272	119	43.8	11	4.0	1590	5.8	10	3.7	13.2

ALL-PURPOSE	G	RUSH	REC	PR	KR	YDS	YPG
1 Willard Harrell, Pacific	10	1319	18	88	352	1777	177.7
2 Walt Peacock, Louisville	11	1291	139	0	467	1897	172.5
3 Adolph Bellizeare, Pennsylvania	8	746	192	173	222	1333	166.6
4 Archie Griffin, Ohio State	10	1428	32	0	182	1642	164.2
5 Woody Green, Arizona State	10	1182	328	25	54	1589	158.9
6 Mark Van Eeghen, Colgate	10	1089	177	0	322	1588	158.8
7 Joe Washington, Oklahoma	11	1173	89	260	222	1744	158.5
8 Mike Esposito, Boston College	11	1293	126	0	318	1737	157.9
9 Mark Kellar, Northern Illinois	11	1719	17	0	0	1736	157.8
10 Tony Dorsett, Pittsburgh	11	1586	84	0	22	1692	153.8

RUSHING/Yards Per Game	G	ATT	YDS	TD	AVG	YPG
1 Mark Kellar, Northern Illinois	11	291	1719	16	5.9	156.3
2 Tony Dorsett, Pittsburgh	11	288	1586	12	5.5	144.2
3 Archie Griffin, Ohio State	10	225	1428	6	6.3	142.8
4 Roosevelt Leaks, Texas	10	229	1415	14	6.2	141.5
5 John Cappelletti, Penn State	11	286	1522	17	5.3	138.4
6 Willard Harrell, Pacific	10	209	1319	14	6.3	131.9
7 Jim Jennings, Rutgers	11	303	1353	21	4.5	123.0
8 Woody Green, Arizona State	10	184	1182	9	6.4	118.2
9 Dickey Morton, Arkansas	11	226	1298	5	5.7	118.0
10 Mike Esposito, Boston College	11	254	1293	15	5.1	117.5

RUSHING/Yards Per Carry	G	ATT	YDS	YPC
1 Kermit Johnson, UCLA	11	150	1129	7.5
2 Joe Washington, Oklahoma	11	176	1173	6.7
3 Woody Green, Arizona State	10	184	1182	6.4
4 Ben Malone, Arizona State	11	176	1129	6.4
5 Archie Griffin, Ohio State	10	225	1428	6.3
6 Willard Harrell, Pacific	10	209	1319	6.3
7 Roosevelt Leaks, Texas	10	229	1415	6.2
8 Tom Sloan, Temple	10	173	1036	6.0
9 Phil Rogers, Virginia Tech	10	175	1036	5.9
10 Mark Kellar, Northern Illinois	11	291	1719	5.9

*-Based on top 25 rushers

RECEIVING	G	REC	YDS	TD	YPR	YPG	RPG
1 Jay Miller, Brigham Young	11	100	1181	8	11.8	107.4	9.1
2 Pat McInally, Harvard	9	56	752	7	13.4	93.6	6.2
3 Hank Cook, New Mexico State	11	65	1111	8	17.1	101.0	5.9
4 Don Clune, Pennsylvania	9	53	882	7	16.6	98.0	5.9
5 Darold Nogle, San Diego State	11	59	945	6	16.0	85.9	5.4
6 Walt Walker, Davidson	10	52	606	2	11.7	60.6	5.2
7 Greg Hudson, Arizona State	11	54	788	7	14.6	71.6	4.9
8 Charles Dancer, Baylor	11	53	927	7	17.5	84.3	4.8
8 Willie Miller, Colorado State	11	53	793	6	15.0	72.1	4.8
10 Mike Telep, Columbia	9	43	572	1	13.3	63.6	4.8

PUNTING	PUNT	YDS	AVG
1 Chuck Ramsey, Wake Forest	87	3898	44.8
2 Mike Patrick, Mississippi State	60	2670	44.5
3 Steve Bauer, New Mexico	61	2696	44.2
4 Neil Clabo, Tennessee	56	2442	43.6
5 Skip Boyd, Washington	68	2917	42.9
6 Brian Doherty, Notre Dame	39	1665	42.7
7 Bob McKenzie, Oregon State	51	2173	42.6
8 Joe Marion, Wyoming	70	2982	42.6
9 Rod Blackford, Colorado State	68	2890	42.5
10 Jeff West, Cincinnati	55	2337	42.5

PUNT RETURNS	PR	YDS	TD	AVG
1 Gary Hayman, Penn State	23	442	1	19.2
2 Mike Fuller, Auburn	20	381	0	19.1
3 Rick Kimbrough, Mississippi	20	368	0	18.4
4 Tom Fleming, Dartmouth	14	258	1	18.4
5 Neal Colzie, Ohio State	38	639	2	16.8
6 John Moseley, Missouri	19	314	2	16.5
7 Danny Colbert, Tulsa	19	292	1	15.4
8 John Betham, Brigham Young	39	553	1	14.2
9 Craig Zaltosky, Stanford	21	299	1	14.2
10 Frank Polito, Villanova	20	280	2	14.0

KICKOFF RETURNS	KR	YDS	TD	AVG
1 Steve Odom, Utah	21	618	1	29.4
2 James Sykes, Rice	21	601	1	28.6
3 W.C. Paige, Texas-El Paso	17	451	0	26.5
4 Raymond Rhodes, Tulsa	19	501	0	26.4
5 Mike Fuller, Auburn	16	420	1	26.3
6 Larry Williams, Texas Tech	19	491	1	25.8
7 Douglas Jackson, Columbia	18	463	0	25.7
8 George Heath, Virginia Tech	16	411	0	25.7
9 John Moseley, Missouri	17	434	0	25.5
10 Burrell Duvauchelle, Harvard	15	381	0	25.4

SCORING	TDS	XPT	FG	PTS	PTPG
1 Jim Jennings, Rutgers	21	2	0	128	11.6
2 Larry Poole, Kent State	18	0	0	108	9.8
2 Steve Davis, Oklahoma	18	0	0	108	9.8
4 John Cappelletti, Penn State	17	0	0	102	9.3
4 Mike Esposito, Boston College	17	0	0	102	9.3
6 Willard Harrell, Pacific	15	2	0	92	9.2
7 Mark Van Eeghen, Colgate	15	0	0	90	9.0
8 Mark Kellar, Northern Illinois	16	2	0	98	8.9
9 Kermit Johnson, UCLA	16	0	0	96	8.7
10 Roosevelt Leaks, Texas	14	0	0	84	8.4
10 Woody Green, Arizona State	14	0	0	84	8.4
10 Barty Smith, Richmond	14	0	0	84	8.4

KICK SCORING	XPA	XP	FGA	FG	PTS	PTPG
1 Efren Herrera, UCLA	64	60	11	8	84	7.6
2 Danny Kush, Arizona State	58	49	7	6	67	7.4
3 Chris Bahr, Penn State	42	37	19	11	70	7.0
3 Bob Thomas, Notre Dame	45	43	18	9	70	7.0
5 Rod Garcia, Stanford	25	22	29	18	76	6.9
6 Bill Davis, Alabama	53	51	14	8	75	6.8
7 Tom Goedjen, Iowa State	25	25	24	15	70	6.4
8 Steve Mike-Mayer, Maryland	38	33	24	12	69	6.3
9 Dave Draudt, Miami, Ohio	21	20	27	14	62	6.2
10 Rick Fulcher, Oklahoma	53	49	11	6	67	6.1

INTERCEPTIONS	INT	YDS	TD	INT/GM
1 Mike Gow, Illinois	10	142	1	0.91
2 Tony Pawlik, Rutgers	8	137	0	0.80
3 John Provost, Holy Cross	8	138	0	0.73
3 Artimus Parker, Southern Cal	8	100	0	0.73
3 Barry Hill, Iowa State	8	99	0	0.73
3 Scott Wingfield, Vanderbilt	8	63	0	0.73
7 Jim Bolding, East Carolina	7	84	0	0.70
7 Joe Spicer, Miami, Ohio	7	64	0	0.70
9 Bob Fuhriman, Utah State	7	115	1	0.64
9 Bill Howe, Xavier	7	104	0	0.64
9 Danny Reece, Southern Cal	7	86	1	0.64
9 Dennis Downey, Oregon State	7	83	1	0.64

Team Leaders

RUSHING OFFENSE	G	ATT	YDS	AVG	TD	YPG
1 UCLA	11	690	4403	6.4	56	400.3
2 Alabama	11	664	4027	6.1	38	366.1
3 Oklahoma	11	755	3975	5.3	36	361.4
4 Ohio State	10	669	3588	5.4	41	358.8
5 Texas	10	638	3502	5.5	43	350.2
5 Notre Dame	10	673	3502	5.2	35	350.2
7 Houston	11	720	3798	5.3	29	345.3
8 Northern Illinois	11	664	3465	5.2	39	315.0
9 Arizona State	11	586	3412	5.8	41	310.2
10 SMU	11	659	3395	5.2	23	308.6

PASSING OFFENSE	G	ATT	COM	INT	PCT	YDS	YPA	TD	I%	YPC	YPG
1 San Diego State	11	385	247	24	64.2	3355	8.7	24	6.2	13.6	305.0
2 Brigham Young	11	410	235	19	57.3	2930	7.1	24	4.6	12.5	266.4
3 Arizona State	11	298	158	13	53.0	2808	9.4	25	4.4	17.8	255.3
4 Pennsylvania	9	246	133	11	54.1	2182	8.9	17	4.5	16.4	242.4
5 Tulsa	11	356	204	22	57.3	2601	7.3	21	6.2	12.8	236.5
6 Toledo	11	303	163	17	53.8	2234	7.4	15	5.6	13.7	203.1
7 Colorado State	11	371	169	19	45.6	2200	5.9	11	5.1	13.0	200.0
8 Washington	11	320	128	31	40.0	2154	6.7	18	9.7	16.8	195.8
9 Davidson	10	343	180	21	52.5	1952	5.7	11	6.1	10.8	195.2
10 Kansas	11	337	174	11	51.6	2139	6.3	13	3.3	12.3	194.5

TOTAL OFFENSE	G	P	YDS	AVG	TD	YPG
1 Arizona State	11	884	6220	7.0	66	565.5
2 Alabama	11	758	5288	7.0	55	480.7
3 UCLA	11	783	5177	6.6	62	470.6
4 Houston	11	901	5093	5.7	42	463.0
5 Notre Dame	10	815	4614	5.7	46	461.4
6 Temple	10	786	4555	5.8	46	455.5
7 Oklahoma	11	857	4986	5.8	51	453.3
8 Brigham Young	11	932	4811	5.2	42	437.4
9 San Diego State	11	819	4777	5.8	42	434.3
10 Texas	10	741	4218	5.7	47	421.8

RUSHING DEFENSE	G	ATT	YDS	AVG	TD	YPG
1 Miami, Ohio	10	424	770	1.8	2	77.0
2 Penn State	11	427	848	2.0	6	77.1
3 Notre Dame	10	390	824	2.1	3	82.4
4 Michigan	11	444	1075	2.4	2	97.7
5 Houston	11	431	1090	2.5	10	99.1
6 Cincinnati	11	491	1147	2.3	6	104.3
7 Oklahoma	11	475	1166	2.5	8	106.0
8 Maryland	11	467	1233	2.6	4	112.1
9 Pacific	10	407	1142	2.8	7	114.2
10 Long Beach State	11	499	1282	2.6	8	116.5

PASSING DEFENSE	G	ATT	COM	PCT	YPC	INT	I%	YDS	YPA	TD	YPG
1 Nebraska	11	142	40	28.2	11.0	15	10.6	439	3.1	1	39.9
2 Michigan State	11	139	54	38.8	11.4	14	10.1	613	4.4	4	55.7
3 Iowa	11	107	48	44.9	14.9	11	10.3	716	6.7	7	65.1
4 Ohio State	10	170	73	42.9	10.5	11	6.5	765	4.5	2	76.5
5 Texas A&M	11	146	59	40.4	14.3	7	4.8	844	5.8	11	76.7
6 Indiana	11	142	67	47.2	13.5	9	6.3	905	6.4	2	82.3
7 Illinois	11	187	71	38.0	12.8	23	12.3	912	4.9	2	82.9
8 Furman	11	184	83	45.1	11.3	17	9.2	935	5.1	4	85.0
9 Florida	11	165	72	43.6	13.0	10	6.1	938	5.7	7	85.3
10 Kansas	11	165	73	44.2	13.6	25	15.2	994	6.0	3	90.4

TOTAL DEFENSE	G	P	YDS	AVG	TD	YPG
1 Miami, Ohio	10	645	1774	2.8	6	177.4
2 Notre Dame	10	615	2012	3.3	7	201.2
3 Penn State	11	689	2253	3.3	13	204.8
4 Ohio State	10	613	2056	3.4	5	205.6
5 Michigan	11	661	2396	3.6	7	217.8
6 Oklahoma	11	712	2492	3.5	15	226.5
7 Dartmouth	9	621	2172	3.5	13	241.3
8 Florida	11	743	2656	3.6	18	241.5
9 Cincinnati	11	760	2665	3.5	12	242.3
10 Houston	11	714	2690	3.8	15	244.5

SCORING OFFENSE	G	PTS	AVG
1 Arizona State	11	491	44.6
2 UCLA	11	470	42.7
3 Alabama	11	454	41.3
4 Penn State	11	431	39.2
5 Ohio State	10	371	37.1
6 Texas	10	364	36.4
7 Oklahoma	11	400	36.4
8 Notre Dame	10	358	35.8
9 Temple	10	353	35.3
10 North Carolina St.	11	365	33.2

SCORING DEFENSE	G	PTS	AVG
1 Ohio State	10	43	4.3
2 Michigan	11	68	6.2
3 Notre Dame	10	66	6.6
4 Miami, Ohio	10	69	6.9
5 Alabama	11	89	8.1
6 Cincinnati	11	109	9.9
7 Pacific	10	109	10.9
8 Penn State	11	120	10.9
9 Richmond	10	112	11.2
10 Maryland	11	124	11.3

1974 POLL PROGRESSION

PRE-SEASON / SEPT. 7 GAMES

AP	Team	Record	Sept. 7 Games
1	Oklahoma	0-0-0	bye week
2	Ohio State	0-0-0	bye week
3	Notre Dame	0-0-0	beat Georgia Tech 31-7
4	Alabama	0-0-0	bye week
5	Southern Cal	0-0-0	bye week
6	Michigan	0-0-0	bye week
7	Nebraska	0-0-0	bye week
8	Penn State	0-0-0	bye week
9	LSU	0-0-0	bye week
10	Texas	0-0-0	bye week
11	Houston	0-0-0	lost to # 15 Arizona State 9-30
12	UCLA	0-0-0	tied Tennessee 17-17
13	Pittsburgh	0-0-0	bye week
14	Maryland	0-0-0	bye week
15	Arizona State	0-0-0	beat # 11 Houston 30-9
16	Tennessee	0-0-0	tied UCLA 17-17
17	Arizona	0-0-0	bye week
18	North Carolina St.	0-0-0	beat Wake Forest 33-15
19	Arkansas	0-0-0	bye week
20	Texas A&M	0-0-0	bye week

SEPTEMBER 9 POLL / SEPT. 14 GAMES

AP	Team	Record	Sept. 14 Games
1	Oklahoma	0-0-0	beat Baylor 28-11
2	Notre Dame	1-0-0	bye week
3	Alabama	0-0-0	beat # 14 Maryland 21-16
4	Ohio State	0-0-0	beat Minnesota 34-19
5	Southern Cal	0-0-0	lost to # 20 Arkansas 7-22
6	Michigan	0-0-0	beat Iowa 24-7
7	Nebraska	0-0-0	beat Oregon 61-7
8	Penn State	0-0-0	beat # 20 Stanford 24-20
9	LSU	0-0-0	beat Colorado 42-14
10	Texas	0-0-0	beat Boston College 42-19
11	Arizona State	1-0-0	bye week
12	UCLA	0-0-1	bye week
13	Pittsburgh	0-0-0	beat Florida State 9-6
14	Maryland	0-0-0	lost to # 3 Alabama 16-21
15	Tennessee	0-0-1	bye week
16	North Carolina St.	1-0-0	beat Duke 35-21
17	Arizona	0-0-0	beat San Diego State 17-10
18	Missouri	0-0-0	lost to Mississippi 0-10
19	Houston	0-1-0	beat Rice 21-0
20	Arkansas	0-0-0	beat # 5 Southern Cal 22-7
20	Stanford	0-0-0	lost to # 8 Penn State 20-24

SEPTEMBER 16 POLL / SEPT 21 GAMES

UP	AP	Team	Record	Sept 21 Games
2	1	Notre Dame	1-0-0	beat Northwestern 49-3
1	2	Ohio State	1-0-0	beat Oregon State 51-10
PB	3	Oklahoma	1-0-0	bye week
4	4	Nebraska	1-0-0	lost to Wisconsin 20-21
3	5	Alabama	1-0-0	beat Southern Miss 52-0
5	6	Michigan	1-0-0	beat Colorado 31-0
6	7	LSU	1-0-0	lost to Texas A&M 14-21
7	8	Penn State	1-0-0	lost to Navy 6-7
8	9	Texas	1-0-0	beat Wyoming 34-7
9	10	Arkansas	1-0-0	lost to Oklahoma State 7-26
10	11	Arizona State	1-0-0	beat TCU 37-7
11	12	UCLA	0-0-1	lost to Iowa 10-21
16	13	Southern Cal	0-1-0	bye week
14	14	Maryland	0-1-0	lost to Florida 10-17
18	15	North Carolina St.	2-0-0	beat Clemson 31-10
16	16	Pittsburgh	1-0-0	beat Georgia Tech 27-17
	17	Arizona	1-0-0	beat Indiana 35-20
12	17	Tennessee	0-0-1	beat Kansas 17-3
18	19	Houston	1-1-0	lost to Miami, Fla. 3-20
	19	Stanford	0-1-0	lost to Illinois 7-41
12		Texas A&M	1-0-0	beat # 7 LSU 21-14
14		Florida	1-0-0	beat # 14 Maryland 17-10
18		Georgia	1-0-0	lost to Mississippi State 14-38

SEPTEMBER 23 POLL / SEPT. 28 GAMES

UP	AP	Team	Record	Sept. 28 Games
1	1	Ohio State	2-0-0	beat SMU 28-9
2	2	Notre Dame	2-0-0	lost to Purdue 20-31
PB	3	Oklahoma	1-0-0	beat Utah State 72-3
3	4	Alabama	2-0-0	beat Vanderbilt 23-10
4	5	Michigan	2-0-0	beat Navy 52-0
5	6	Texas	2-0-0	lost to Texas Tech 3-26
6	7	Arizona State	2-0-0	lost to Missouri 0-9
14	8	Pittsburgh	2-0-0	lost to # 18 Southern Cal 7-16
7	9	Texas A&M	2-0-0	beat Washington 28-15
9	10	Nebraska	1-1-0	beat Northwestern 49-7
10	11	Wisconsin	2-0-0	lost to Colorado 21-24
8	12	Oklahoma State	2-0-0	lost to Baylor 14-31
13	13	North Carolina St.	3-0-0	beat Syracuse 28-22
11	14	Tennessee	1-0-1	lost to Auburn 0-21
18	15	Arizona	2-0-0	beat New Mexico 15-10
19	16	Illinois	2-0-0	beat Washington State 21-19
16	17	LSU	1-1-0	tied Rice 10-10
17	18	Southern Cal	0-1-0	beat # 8 Pittsburgh 16-7
20	19	Penn State	1-1-0	beat Iowa 27-0
12	20	Miami, Fla.	1-0-0	beat Tampa 28-26
14		Florida	2-0-0	beat Mississippi State 29-13

SEPTEMBER 30 POLL / OCT. 5 GAMES

UP	AP	Team	Record	Oct. 5 Games
1	1	Ohio State	3-0-0	beat Washington State 42-7
PB	2	Oklahoma	2-0-0	beat Wake Forest 63-0
2	3	Alabama	3-0-0	beat Mississippi 35-21
3	4	Michigan	3-0-0	beat Stanford 27-16
4	5	Texas A&M	3-0-0	lost to Kansas 10-28
5	6	Nebraska	2-1-0	beat Minnesota 54-0
6	7	Notre Dame	2-1-0	beat Michigan State 19-14
11	8	North Carolina St.	4-0-0	beat East Carolina 24-20
10	9	Southern Cal	1-1-0	beat Iowa 41-3
7	10	Texas Tech	2-0-1	beat Oklahoma State 14-13
9	11	Auburn	3-0-0	beat # 16 Miami, Fla. 3-0
15	12	Arizona	3-0-0	beat Texas-El Paso 42-13
8	13	Florida	3-0-0	beat LSU 24-14
14	14	Illinois	3-0-0	lost to California 14-31
12	15	Penn State	2-1-0	beat Army 21-14
12	16	Miami, Fla.	2-0-0	lost to # 11 Auburn 0-3
	17	Pittsburgh		lost to North Carolina 29-45
	18	Arizona State	2-1-0	beat Wyoming 16-10
16	19	Texas	2-1-0	beat Washington 35-21
	20	Arkansas	2-1-0	beat TCU 49-0
16		UCLA	1-1-1	beat Utah 27-14
16		Missouri	2-1-0	lost to Wisconsin 20-59
19		Oklahoma State	2-1-0	lost to Texas Tech 13-14
19		Mississippi	2-1-0	lost to # 3 Alabama 21-35

OCTOBER 7 POLL / OCT. 12 GAMES

UP	AP	Team	Record	Oct. 12 Games
1	1	Ohio State	4-0-0	beat # 13 Wisconsin 52-7
PB	2	Oklahoma	3-0-0	beat # 17 Texas 16-13
2	3	Alabama	4-0-0	beat Florida State 8-7
3	4	Michigan	4-0-0	beat Michigan State 21-7
4	5	Nebraska	3-1-0	lost to Missouri 10-21
8	6	Notre Dame	3-1-0	beat Rice 10-3
9	7	Southern Cal	2-1-0	beat Washington State 54-7
5	8	Florida	4-0-0	lost to Vanderbilt 10-24
7	9	Texas Tech	3-0-1	lost to # 16 Texas A&M 7-28
6	10	Auburn	4-0-0	beat Kentucky 31-13
11	11	North Carolina St.	5-0-0	beat Virginia 22-21
12	12	Arizona	4-0-0	beat Utah 41-8
11	13	Wisconsin	3-1-0	lost to # 1 Ohio State 7-52
15	14	Arkansas	3-1-0	lost to Baylor 17-21
13	15	Penn State	3-1-0	beat Wake Forest 55-0
16	16	Texas A&M	3-1-0	beat # 9 Texas Tech 28-7
16	17	Texas	3-1-0	lost to # 2 Oklahoma 13-16
19	18	Arizona State	3-1-0	bye week
14	19	Kansas	3-1-0	beat Kansas State 20-13
	20	Miami, Ohio	3-0-1	beat Ohio U. 31-3
16		UCLA	2-1-1	tied Stanford 13-13
20		Baylor	2-2-0	beat # 14 Arkansas 21-17
20		Tulane	3-0-0	beat Air Force 10-3

OCTOBER 14 POLL / OCT. 19 GAMES

UP	AP	Team	Record	Oct. 19 Games
1	1	Ohio State	5-0-0	beat Indiana 49-9
PB	2	Oklahoma	4-0-0	beat Colorado 49-14
2	3	Michigan	5-0-0	beat Wisconsin 24-20
3	4	Alabama	5-0-0	beat Tennessee 28-6
4	5	Auburn	5-0-0	beat Georgia Tech 31-22
5	6	Southern Cal	3-1-0	beat Oregon 16-7
7	7	Notre Dame	4-1-0	beat Army 48-0
6	8	Texas A&M	4-1-0	beat TCU 17-0
10	9	Arizona	5-0-0	lost to # 17 Texas Tech 8-17
8	10	North Carolina St.	6-0-0	lost to North Carolina 14-33
9	11	Penn State	4-1-0	beat Syracuse 30-14
14	12	Nebraska	3-2-0	beat # 13 Kansas 56-0
11	13	Kansas	4-1-0	lost to # 12 Nebraska 0-56
12	14	Florida	4-1-0	beat Florida State 24-14
17	15	Arizona State	3-1-0	beat Utah 32-0
20	16	Texas	3-2-0	beat Arkansas 38-7
	17	Texas Tech	3-1-1	beat # 9 Arizona 17-8
13	18	Maryland	3-2-0	beat Wake Forest 47-0
17	19	Miami, Ohio	4-0-1	beat Bowling Green 34-10
20	20	Tulane	4-0-0	beat Citadel 30-3
14		Vanderbilt	3-1-0	lost to Georgia 31-38
16		Miami, Fla.	3-1-0	beat West Virginia 21-20
17		Illinois	4-1-0	tied Michigan State 21-21

OCTOBER 21 POLL / OCT. 26 GAMES

UP	AP	Team	Record	Oct. 26 Games
1	1	Ohio State	6-0-0	beat Northwestern 55-7
PB	2	Oklahoma	5-0-0	beat Kansas State 63-0
2	3	Michigan	6-0-0	beat Minnesota 49-0
3	4	Alabama	6-0-0	beat TCU 41-3
4	5	Auburn	6-0-0	beat Florida State 38-6
5	6	Southern Cal	4-1-0	beat Oregon State 31-10
7	7	Notre Dame	5-1-0	beat Miami, Fla. 38-7
8	8	Texas A&M	5-1-0	beat Baylor 20-0
9	9	Nebraska	4-2-0	beat Oklahoma State 7-3
8	10	Penn State	5-1-0	beat West Virginia 21-12
15	11	Texas Tech	4-1-1	beat SMU 24-7
11	12	Florida	5-1-0	beat Duke 30-13
10	13	Texas	4-2-0	beat Rice 27-6
17	14	Arizona State	5-1-0	beat New Mexico 41-7
12	15	Maryland	4-2-0	beat # 17 North Carolina St. 20-10
14	16	Arizona	5-1-0	lost to Brigham Young 13-37
	17	North Carolina St.	6-1-0	lost to # 15 Maryland 10-20
18	18	Tulane	5-0-0	lost to Georgia Tech 7-27
16	19	Miami, Ohio	5-0-1	beat Toledo 38-22
		California	5-1-0	lost to UCLA 3-28
13		Miami, Fla.	4-1-0	lost to # 7 Notre Dame 7-38
18		Oklahoma State	3-2-0	lost to # 9 Nebraska 3-7
18		Mississippi State	5-1-0	beat Louisville 56-7
18		San Diego State	4-1-0	beat Long Beach State 27-17

OCTOBER 28 POLL / NOV. 2 GAMES

UP	AP	Team	Record	Nov. 2 Games
1	1	Ohio State	7-0-0	beat Illinois 49-7
PB	2	Oklahoma	6-0-0	beat Iowa State 28-10
2	3	Michigan	7-0-0	beat Indiana 21-7
3	4	Alabama	7-0-0	beat # 17 Mississippi State 35-0
4	5	Auburn	7-0-0	lost to # 11 Florida 14-25
6	6	Southern Cal	5-1-0	tied California 15-15
5	7	Notre Dame	6-1-0	beat Navy 14-6
7	8	Texas A&M	6-1-0	beat Arkansas 20-10
9	9	Nebraska	5-2-0	beat Colorado 31-15
8	10	Penn State	6-1-0	beat # 15 Maryland 24-17
10	11	Florida	6-1-0	beat # 5 Auburn 25-14
11	12	Texas	5-2-0	beat SMU 35-15
13	13	Texas Tech	5-1-1	lost to Rice 7-21
15	14	Arizona State	5-1-0	lost to Texas-El Paso 27-31
12	15	Maryland	5-2-0	lost to # 10 Penn State 17-24
14	16	Miami, Ohio	6-0-1	beat Western Michigan 31-0
15		Mississippi State	6-1-0	lost to # 4 Alabama 0-35
19	18	UCLA	4-1-2	lost to Washington 9-31
	19	Temple		lost to Cincinnati 20-22
	20	San Diego State	5-1-0	lost to North Texas State 9-14
	20	Wisconsin	4-3-0	lost to Michigan State 21-28
17		Oklahoma State	3-3-0	beat Kansas 24-13
17		Houston	5-2-0	beat Georgia 31-24

November 4 Poll — Nov. 9 Games

UP	AP	Team	Record	Nov. 9 Games
1	1	Ohio State	8-0-0	lost to Michigan State 13-16
PB	2	Oklahoma	7-0-0	beat Missouri 37-0
2	3	Alabama	8-0-0	beat LSU 30-0
2	4	Michigan	8-0-0	beat Illinois 14-6
4	5	Texas A&M	7-1-0	lost to SMU 14-18
7	6	Florida	7-1-0	lost to Georgia 16-17
6	7	Penn State	7-1-0	lost to North Carolina St. 7-12
5	8	Notre Dame	7-1-0	bye week
8	9	Nebraska	6-2-0	beat Iowa State 23-13
9	10	Auburn	7-1-0	beat Mississippi State 24-20
11	11	Southern Cal	5-1-1	beat Stanford 34-10
10	12	Texas	6-2-0	lost to Baylor 24-34
12	13	Miami, Ohio	7-0-1	beat Kent State 19-17
15	14	Maryland	5-3-0	beat Villanova 41-0
13	15	Houston	6-2-0	bye week
	16	Arizona State	5-2-0	lost to Brigham Young 18-21
	17	Oklahoma State	4-3-0	beat Kansas State 29-5
	18	California	5-2-1	beat Washington 52-26
14	19	Pittsburgh	6-2-0	beat Temple 35-24
	19	Texas Tech	5-2-1	beat TCU 28-0

November 11 Poll — Nov. 16 Games

UP	AP	Team	Record	Nov. 16 Games
PB	1	Oklahoma	8-0-0	beat Kansas 45-14
1	2	Alabama	9-0-0	beat Miami, Fla. 28-7
2	3	Michigan	9-0-0	beat Purdue 51-0
3	4	Ohio State	8-1-0	beat Iowa 35-10
4	5	Notre Dame	7-1-0	beat #17 Pittsburgh 14-10
6	6	Nebraska	7-2-0	beat Kansas State 35-7
5	7	Auburn	8-1-0	beat Georgia 17-13
7	8	Southern Cal	6-1-1	beat Washington 42-11
8	9	Florida	7-2-0	lost to Kentucky 24-41
9	10	Texas A&M	7-2-0	beat Rice 37-7
10	11	Penn State	7-2-0	beat Ohio U. 35-16
12	12	Miami, Ohio	8-0-1	beat Cincinnati 27-7
15	13	Maryland	6-3-0	beat Duke 56-13
14	14	Houston	6-2-0	beat Memphis 13-10
13	15	Michigan State	5-3-1	beat Indiana 19-10
11	16	North Carolina St.	8-2-0	beat Arizona State 35-14
16	17	Pittsburgh	7-2-0	lost to #5 Notre Dame 10-14
17	18	Oklahoma State	5-3-0	lost to Colorado 20-37
	19	California	6-2-1	beat Washington State 37-33
18	20	Texas Tech	6-2-1	lost to Baylor 10-17
19		Baylor	5-3-0	beat Texas Tech 17-10
19		Tulsa	6-3-0	beat Drake 52-14

November 18 Poll — Nov. 23 Games

UP	AP	Team	Record	Nov. 23 Games
PB	1	Oklahoma	9-0-0	beat #6 Nebraska 28-14
1	2	Alabama	10-0-0	bye week
2	3	Michigan	10-0-0	lost to #4 Ohio State 10-12
3	4	Ohio State	9-1-0	beat #3 Michigan 12-10
4	5	Notre Dame	8-1-0	beat Air Force 38-0
5	6	Nebraska	8-2-0	lost to #1 Oklahoma 14-28
6	7	Auburn	9-1-0	bye week
7	8	Southern Cal	7-1-1	beat UCLA 34-9
8	9	Texas A&M	8-2-0	bye week
9	10	Penn State	8-2-0	bye week
11	11	Maryland	7-3-0	beat Virginia 10-0
12	12	Miami, Ohio	9-0-1	regular season complete
10	13	North Carolina St.	9-2-0	regular season complete
17	14	Michigan State	6-3-1	beat Iowa 60-21
13	15	Houston	7-2-0	beat Florida State 23-8
16	16	Baylor	6-3-0	beat SMU 31-14
14	17	Texas	7-3-0	bye week
15	18	Pittsburgh	7-3-0	bye week
	19	California	7-2-1	lost to Stanford 20-22
	20	Florida	7-3-0	bye week
17		UCLA	6-2-2	lost to #8 Southern Cal 9-34
17		Tulsa	7-3-0	bye week
20		San Diego State	7-2-0	tied Bowling Green 21-21

November 25 Poll — Nov. 30 Games

UP	AP	Team	Record	Nov. 30 Games
PB	1	Oklahoma	10-0-0	beat Oklahoma State 44-13
1	2	Alabama	10-0-0	beat #7 Auburn 17-13
2	3	Ohio State	10-1-0	regular season complete
3	4	Michigan	10-1-0	regular season complete
5	5	Notre Dame	9-1-0	lost to #6 Southern Cal 24-55
4	6	Southern Cal	8-1-1	beat #5 Notre Dame 55-24
6	7	Auburn	9-1-0	lost to #1 Alabama 13-17
7	8	Texas A&M	8-2-0	lost to #17 Texas 3-32
8	9	Nebraska	8-3-0	regular season complete
9	10	Penn State	8-2-0	beat #18 Pittsburgh 31-10
11	11	Maryland	8-3-0	regular season complete
12	12	Miami, Ohio	9-0-1	
10	13	North Carolina St.	9-2-0	regular season complete
14	14	Michigan State	7-3-1	regular season complete
15	15	Houston	8-2-0	lost to Tulsa 14-30
13	16	Baylor	7-3-0	beat Rice 24-3
18	17	Texas	7-3-0	beat #8 Texas A&M 32-3
16	18	Pittsburgh	7-3-0	lost to #10 Penn State 10-31
	19	Wisconsin	7-4-0	regular season complete
18	20	Brigham Young	7-3-1	
16		Arizona	8-2-0	beat Arizona State 10-0
20		Florida	7-3-0	beat Miami, Fla. 31-7

December 2 Poll

UP	AP	Team	Record	Bowl Bid	Date	Bowl Result
PB	1	Oklahoma	11-0-0			
1	2	Alabama	11-0-0	Orange Bowl	J1	lost to #9 Notre Dame 11-13
2	3	Ohio State	10-1-0	Rose Bowl	J1	lost to #5 Southern Cal 17-18
3	4	Michigan	10-1-0			
4	5	Southern Cal	9-1-1	Rose Bowl	J1	beat #3 Ohio State 18-17
5	6	Auburn	9-2-0	Gator Bowl	D30	beat #11 Texas 27-3
6	7	Penn State	9-2-0	Cotton Bowl	J1	beat #12 Baylor 41-20
7	8	Nebraska	8-3-0	Sugar Bowl	D31	beat #18 Florida 13-10
8	9	Notre Dame	9-2-0	Orange Bowl	J1	beat #2 Alabama 13-11
11	10	Maryland	8-3-0	Liberty Bowl	D16	lost to Tennessee 3-7
10	11	Texas	8-3-0	Gator Bowl	D30	lost to #6 Auburn 3-27
12	12	Baylor	8-3-0	Cotton Bowl	J1	lost to #7 Penn State 20-41
9	13	North Carolina St.	9-2-0	Bluebonnet Bowl	D23	tied Houston 31-31
	14	Michigan State	7-3-1			
13	15	Miami, Ohio	9-0-1	Tangerine Bowl	D21	beat Georgia 21-10
16	16	Texas A&M	8-3-0			
15	17	Brigham Young	7-3-1			
14	18	Florida	8-3-0	Sugar Bowl	D31	lost to #8 Nebraska 10-13
18	19	Arizona	9-2-0			
	20	Pittsburgh	7-4-0			
	20	Wisconsin	7-4-0			
20		Tulsa	8-3-0			

January 3 Final Poll

RB	UP	AP	Team	Record
1	PB	1	Oklahoma	11-0-0
5	1	2	Southern Cal	10-1-1
4	5	3	Michigan	10-1-0
6	3	4	Ohio State	10-2-0
3	2	5	Alabama	11-1-0
2	4	6	Notre Dame	10-2-0
8	7	7	Penn State	10-2-0
7	6	8	Auburn	10-2-0
9	8	9	Nebraska	9-3-0
NR	10	10	Miami, Ohio	10-0-1
10	9	11	North Carolina St.	9-2-1
12	18	12	Michigan State	7-3-1
31	13	13	Maryland	8-4-0
13	14	14	Baylor	8-4-0
21	12	15	Florida	8-4-0
14	15	16	Texas A&M	8-3-0
20	17	17	Mississippi State	9-3-0
18		18	Texas	8-4-0
26	11	19	Houston	8-3-1
23	15	20	Tennessee	7-3-2
17	19		Tulsa	8-3-0

1974

CONSENSUS ALL-AMERICANS

POS	Offense	HT	WT	School	AP	CF	FC	FW	PI
QB	Steve Bartkowski	6-4	215	California	•				
RB	Archie Griffin	5-9	184	Ohio State	•	•	•	•	•
RB	Joe Washington	5-10	178	Oklahoma	•	•	•	•	•
RB	Anthony Davis	5-9	183	Southern Cal	•	•	•	•	•
WR	Pete Demmerle	6-1	190	Notre Dame	•	•	•		•
TE	Bennie Cunningham	6-5	252	Clemson	•		•		
T	Kurt Schumacher	6-4	250	Ohio State	•	•	•	•	•
T	Marvin Crenshaw	6-6	240	Nebraska			•	•	•
G	Ken Huff	6-4	261	North Carolina	•	•	•		
G	John Roush	6-0	252	Oklahoma			•		•
G	Gerry DiNardo	6-1	237	Notre Dame			•		•
C	Steve Myers	6-2	244	Ohio State	•				

OTHERS RECEIVING FIRST-TEAM HONORS

QB	Steve Joachim	Temple	•
QB	Tom Clements	Notre Dame	•
QB	David Humm	Nebraska	•
WR	Pat McInally	Harvard	• • •
WR	Larry Burton	Purdue	•
T	Bob Simmons	Texas	•
T	Chris Mackie	California	•
T	Craig Hertwig	Georgia	•
T	Al Krevis	Boston College	•
G	John Nessel	Penn State	•
C	Geoff Reece	Washington State	•
C	Aubrey Schulz	Baylor	•
C	Sylvester Croom	Alabama	•
C	Rik Bonness	Nebraska	•
K	Dave Lawson	Air Force	•

FC named McInally as a B; AP named Myers as a G

POS	Defense	HT	WT	School	AP	CF	FC	FW	PI
L	Randy White	6-4	238	Maryland	•	•	•	•	•
L	Mike Hartenstine	6-4	233	Penn State	•			•	•
L	Pat Donovan	6-5	240	Stanford			•	•	•
L	Jimmy Webb	6-5	245	Mississippi State		•	•		
L	Leroy Cook	6-4	205	Alabama	•	•			
MG	Louie Kelcher	6-5	275	SMU	•	•			
MG	Rubin Carter	6-3	260	Miami, Fla.			•		•
LB	Rod Shoate	6-1	213	Oklahoma	•	•	•	•	•
LB	Richard Wood	6-2	213	Southern Cal	•	•			•
LB	Ken Bernich	6-2	240	Auburn	•		•	•	•
LB	Woodrow Lowe	6-0	211	Alabama	•	•			•
B	Dave Brown	6-1	188	Michigan	•	•	•	•	•
B	Pat Thomas	5-9	180	Texas A&M	•		•		•
B	John Provost	5-10	180	Holy Cross	•	•			

OTHERS RECEIVING FIRST-TEAM HONORS

DL	Mack Mitchell	Houston	•
DL	Michael Fanning	Notre Dame	•
DL	Doug English	Texas	•
DL	Van DeCree	Ohio State	•
LB	Greg Collins	Notre Dame	•
LB	Brad Cousino	Miami, Ohio	•
LB	Bob Breunig	Arizona State	•
MG	Gary Burley	Pittsburgh	•
B	Randy Rhino	Georgia Tech	•
B	Charles Phillips	Southern Cal	•
B	Robert Giblin	Houston	•
B	Mike Williams	LSU	•
B	Neal Colzie	Ohio State	•
B	Randy Hughes	Oklahoma	•
P	Tom Skladany	Ohio State	•

FC named Carter as a DL

HEISMAN TROPHY VOTING

	PLAYER	POS	SCHOOL	1ST	2ND	3RD	TOTAL
1	Archie Griffin	TB	Ohio State	483	198	75	1920
2	Anthony Davis	TB	Southern Cal	120	148	163	819
3	Joe Washington	HB	Oklahoma	87	146	108	661
4	Tom Clements	QB	Notre Dame	26	49	68	244
5	David Humm	QB	Nebraska	23	46	49	210
6	Dennis Franklin	DE	Michigan	6	30	22	100
7	Rod Shoate	LB	Oklahoma	12	16	29	97
8	Gary Scheide	QB	Brigham Young	12	19	16	90
9	Randy White	DT	Maryland	9	20	18	85
10	Steve Bartkowski	QB	California	6	13	30	74

AWARD WINNERS

PLAYER	POS	SCHOOL	AWARD NAME
Steve Joachim	QB	Temple	Maxwell
Randy White	DT	Maryland	Outland
Archie Griffin	RB	Ohio State	Camp
Randy White	DT	Maryland	Lombardi

CONFERENCE STANDINGS

ACC	CONF. W L T			OVERALL W L T		
Maryland	6	0	0	8	4	0
North Carolina St.	4	2	0	9	2	1
Clemson	4	2	0	7	4	0
North Carolina	4	2	0	7	5	0
Duke	2	4	0	6	5	0
Virginia	1	5	0	4	7	0
Wake Forest	0	6	0	1	10	0

Big 10	CONF. W L T			OVERALL W L T		
Michigan	7	0	1	10	0	1
Ohio State	7	0	1	10	0	1
Minnesota	6	2	0	7	4	0
Illinois	4	4	0	5	6	0
Purdue	4	4	0	5	6	0
Michigan State	4	4	0	5	6	0
Northwestern	4	4	0	4	7	0
Wisconsin	3	5	0	4	7	0
Indiana	0	8	0	2	9	0
Iowa	0	8	0	0	11	0

Big 8	CONF. W L T			OVERALL W L T		
Oklahoma	7	0	0	10	0	1
Nebraska	4	2	1	9	2	1
Kansas	4	2	1	7	4	1
Missouri	3	4	0	8	4	0
Oklahoma State	2	3	2	5	4	2
Kansas State	2	5	0	5	6	0
Colorado	2	5	0	5	6	0
Iowa State	2	5	0	4	7	0

Big West	CONF. W L T			OVERALL W L T		
San Diego State	3	0	1	9	1	1
San Jose State	2	0	2	5	4	2
Pacific	2	1	1	7	2	1
Fresno State	1	3	0	2	9	0
Long Beach State	0	4	0	1	9	1

Ivy	CONF. W L T			OVERALL W L T		
Dartmouth	6	1	0	6	3	0
Harvard	5	2	0	7	2	0
Pennsylvania	5	2	0	6	3	0
Yale	5	2	0	6	3	0
Brown	4	3	0	4	3	1
Cornell	2	5	0	3	5	1
Columbia	1	6	0	1	7	1
Princeton	0	7	0	1	8	0

MAC	CONF. W L T			OVERALL W L T		
Miami, Ohio	5	0	0	10	0	0
Kent State	4	1	0	9	2	0
Bowling Green	2	3	0	7	3	0
Ohio U	2	3	0	5	5	0
Western Michigan	1	4	0	6	5	0
Toledo	1	4	0	3	8	0

PAC 8	CONF. W L T			OVERALL W L T		
Southern Cal	7	0	0	9	2	1
UCLA	6	1	0	9	2	0
Stanford	5	2	0	7	4	0
Washington State	4	3	0	5	6	0
California	2	5	0	4	7	0
Oregon State	2	5	0	2	9	0
Oregon	2	5	0	2	9	0
Washington	0	7	0	2	9	0

SEC	CONF. W L T			OVERALL W L T		
Alabama	8	0	0	11	1	0
LSU	5	1	0	9	3	0
Mississippi	4	3	0	6	5	0
Tennessee	3	3	0	8	4	0
Georgia	3	4	0	7	4	1
Florida	3	4	0	7	5	0
Kentucky	3	4	0	5	6	0
Auburn	2	5	0	6	6	0
Mississippi State	2	5	0	4	5	2
Vanderbilt	1	5	0	5	6	0

SWC	CONF. W L T			OVERALL W L T		
Texas	7	0	0	8	3	0
Texas Tech	6	1	0	11	1	0
Rice	4	3	0	5	6	0
SMU	3	3	1	6	4	1
Arkansas	3	3	1	5	5	1
Texas A&M	3	4	0	5	6	0
TCU	1	6	0	3	8	0
Baylor	0	7	0	2	9	0

WAC	CONF. W L T			OVERALL W L T		
Arizona State	6	1	0	11	1	0
Arizona	6	1	0	8	3	0
Utah	4	2	0	7	5	0
Brigham Young	3	4	0	5	6	0
Wyoming	3	4	0	4	7	0
New Mexico	3	4	0	4	7	0
Colorado State	2	4	0	5	6	0
Texas-El Paso	0	7	0	0	11	0

Independents	OVERALL W L T		
Penn State	12	0	0
Notre Dame	11	0	0
Houston	11	1	0
Tulane	9	3	0
Memphis	8	3	0
South Carolina	7	4	0
Utah State	7	4	0
Boston College	7	4	0
Air Force	6	4	0
Rutgers	6	5	0
West Virginia	6	5	0
Pittsburgh	6	5	1
Miami, Fla.	5	6	0
Georgia Tech	5	6	0
Navy	4	7	0
Virginia Tech	2	9	0
Syracuse	2	9	0
Army	0	10	0
Florida State	0	11	0

BOWL GAMES

DATE	GAME	SCORE
D16	Liberty	Tennessee 7, Maryland 3
D21	Tangerine	Miami, Ohio 21, Georgia 10
D23	Bluebonnet	Houston 31, North Carolina St. 31
D28	Sun	Mississippi State 26, North Carolina 24
D28	Fiesta	Oklahoma State 16, Brigham Young 6
D28	Peach	Texas Tech 6, Vanderbilt 6
D30	Gator	Auburn 27, Texas 3
D31	Sugar	Nebraska 13, Florida 10
J1	Orange	Notre Dame 13, Alabama 11
J1	Cotton	Penn State 41, Baylor 20
J1	Rose	Southern Cal 18, Ohio State 17

1974 ANNUAL REVIEW 1311

1974 NCAA Major College Statistical Leaders

Individual Leaders

PASSING

		G	ATT	COM	PCT	INT	I%	YDS	YPA	TD	TD%	COM.PG
1	Steve Bartkowski, California	11	325	182	56.0	7	2.2	2580	7.9	12	3.7	16.5
2	Gary Sheide, Brigham Young	11	300	181	60.3	19	6.3	2174	7.2	23	7.7	16.5
3	Gene Swick, Toledo	11	287	178	62.0	14	4.9	2235	7.8	13	4.5	16.2
4	Kevin Sigler, Cornell	9	248	143	57.7	14	5.6	1648	6.6	8	3.2	15.9
5	Craig Kimball, San Jose State	12	356	175	49.2	19	5.3	2401	6.7	23	6.5	14.6
6	Mark Driscoll, Colorado State	9	246	122	49.6	14	5.7	2016	8.2	19	7.7	13.6
7	Craig Penrose, San Diego State	10	235	132	56.2	9	3.8	1683	7.2	10	4.3	13.2
8	Jeb Blount, Tulsa	11	261	143	54.8	13	5.0	1860	7.1	15	5.7	13.0
9	Tom Vosberg, Dayton	11	305	141	46.2	18	5.9	1914	6.3	12	3.9	12.8
10	Steve Joachim, Temple	10	221	128	57.9	13	5.9	1950	8.8	20	9.0	12.8
10	Mike Cordova, Stanford	10	295	128	43.4	13	4.4	1569	5.3	10	3.4	12.8

ALL-PURPOSE

		G	RUSH	REC	PR	KR	YDS	YPG
1	Louie Giammona, Utah State	10	1534	79	16	355	1984	198.4
2	Willard Harrell, Pacific	10	1308	133	65	262	1768	176.8
3	Anthony Davis, Southern Cal	11	1354	87	0	467	1908	173.5
4	Joe Washington, Oklahoma	11	1321	71	332	180	1904	173.1
5	Jim Pooler, Northwestern	11	949	25	21	807	1802	163.8
6	Archie Griffin, Ohio State	11	1620	52	0	71	1743	158.5
7	Rick Upchurch, Minnesota	11	942	209	125	440	1716	156.0
8	James Betterson, North Carolina	11	1082	53	0	512	1647	149.7
9	Stanley Morgan, Tennessee	11	723	234	375	255	1587	144.3
10	Bill Marek, Wisconsin	9	1215	76	0	0	1291	143.4

RUSHING/YARDS PER GAME

		G	ATT	YDS	TD	AVG	YPG
1	Louie Giammona, Utah State	10	329	1534	8	4.7	153.4
2	Archie Griffin, Ohio State	11	236	1620	12	6.9	147.3
3	Bill Marek, Wisconsin	9	205	1215	18	5.9	135.0
4	Willard Harrell, Pacific	10	224	1308	12	5.8	130.8
5	Dave Preston, Bowling Green	11	324	1414	19	4.4	128.5
6	Andrew Johnson, Citadel	11	248	1373	7	5.5	124.8
7	Anthony Davis, Southern Cal	11	288	1354	13	4.7	123.1
8	Joe Washington, Oklahoma	11	194	1321	12	6.8	120.1
9	Fred Solomon, Tampa	11	193	1300	19	6.7	118.2
10	Walter Snickenberger, Princeton	9	214	1043	16	4.9	115.9

RUSHING/YARDS PER CARRY

		G	ATT	YDS	YPC
1	Archie Griffin, Ohio State	11	236	1620	6.9
2	Joe Washington, Oklahoma	11	194	1321	6.8
3	Fred Solomon, Tampa	11	193	1300	6.7
4	Laverne Smith, Kansas	11	176	1181	6.7
5	Artie Owens, West Virginia	11	174	1130	6.5
6	Gordon Bell, Michigan	11	174	1048	6.0
7	Bill Marek, Wisconsin	9	205	1215	5.9
8	Willard Harrell, Pacific	10	224	1308	5.8
9	Andrew Johnson, Citadel	11	248	1373	5.5
10	Sonny Collins, Kentucky	9	177	970	5.5

*-Based on top 25 rushers

RECEIVING

		G	REC	YDS	TD	YPR	YPG	RPG
1	Dwight McDonald, San Diego State	11	86	1157	7	13.5	105.2	7.8
2	John Ross, Toledo	11	77	866	2	11.2	78.7	7.0
3	Gary Pomeroy, Davidson	9	51	744	4	14.6	82.7	5.7
4	Dave Quehl, Holy Cross	11	62	801	6	12.9	72.8	5.6
5	Bruce Starks, Cornell	9	47	624	2	13.3	69.3	5.2
6	Pat McInally, Harvard	9	46	655	8	14.2	72.8	5.1
7	Steve Rivera, California	11	56	938	4	16.8	85.3	5.1
8	Willie Miller, Colorado State	11	53	1193	9	22.5	108.5	4.8
8	Theopolis Bell, Arizona	11	53	700	11	13.2	63.6	4.8
10	Steve Largent, Tulsa	11	52	844	14	16.2	76.7	4.7

PUNTING

		PUNT	YDS	AVG
1	Joe Parker, Appalachian State	63	2791	44.3
2	Johnny Evans, North Carolina St.	38	1653	43.5
3	Neil Clabo, Tennessee	64	2758	43.1
4	Joe Marion, Wyoming	56	2380	42.5
5	Skip Boyd, Washington	57	2405	42.2
6	Phil Waganheim, Maryland	52	2194	42.2
7	Dan Vess, Wichita State	73	3073	42.1
8	Mark Stanley, Texas A&M	59	2478	42.0
9	Bernie Ruoff, Syracuse	57	2388	41.9
10	Mitch Hoopes, Arizona	55	2299	41.8

PUNT RETURNS

		PR	YDS	TD	AVG
1	John Provost, Holy Cross	13	238	2	18.3
2	Adolph Bellizeare, Pennsylvania	14	255	2	18.2
3	Keith Wright, Memphis	13	218	1	16.8
4	Mike Fuller, Auburn	30	502	3	16.7
5	Devon Ford, Appalachian State	35	568	1	16.2
6	Martin Mitchell, Tulane	15	231	2	15.4
7	Joe Washington, Oklahoma	24	332	1	13.8
8	Wes Hankins, Oklahoma State	23	309	1	13.4
9	Tony Gillick, Missouri	12	160	1	13.3
10	Greg Johnson, Marshall	14	186	0	13.3

KICKOFF RETURNS

		KR	YDS	TD	AVG
1	Anthony Davis, Southern Cal	11	467	3	42.5
2	Luther Blue, Iowa State	12	393	1	32.8
3	Mike Carter, Princeton	14	402	0	28.7
4	Len Willis, Ohio State	14	401	2	28.6
5	James Betterson, North Carolina	18	512	0	28.4
6	Dick Pawlewicz, William & Mary	15	426	1	28.4
7	Mike Harris, Tampa	15	420	1	28.0
8	Tom Marvaso, Cincinnati	15	416	1	27.7
9	Bobby Ward, Memphis	16	438	0	27.4
10	Robert Dow, LSU	15	403	1	26.9

SCORING

		TDS	XPT	FG	PTS	PTPG
1	Bill Marek, Wisconsin	19	0	0	114	12.7
2	Keith Barnette, Boston College	22	2	0	134	12.2
3	Fred Solomon, Tampa	19	6	0	120	10.9
4	Walter Snickenberger, Princeton	16	0	0	96	10.7
5	Dave Preston, Bowling Green	19	0	0	114	10.4
6	Anthony Davis, Southern Cal	18	2	0	110	10.0
7	Steve Beaird, Baylor	16	0	0	96	8.7
8	Jim Germany, New Mexico State	14	2	0	86	8.6
9	Donald Fanelli, Cornell	10	0	0	60	8.6
10	Larry Poole, Kent State	15	0	0	90	8.2

KICK SCORING

		XPA	XP	FGA	FG	PTS	PTPG
1	Steve Mike-Mayer, Maryland	36	34	25	15	79	7.2
2	Don Bitterlich, Temple	44	44	15	9	71	7.1
3	Tom Klaban, Ohio State	51	50	10	8	74	6.7
4	Fred Steinfort, Boston College	46	44	15	9	71	6.5
5	Dave Lawson, Air Force	15	13	31	19	70	6.4
6	Clark Kemble, Colorado State	33	30	28	13	69	6.3
7	Bob Berg, New Mexico	17	14	24	18	68	6.2
8	Mark Adams, Vanderbilt	35	34	13	11	67	6.1
8	Al Knapp, Utah State	19	19	25	16	67	6.1
10	Ron Ploger, San Jose State	38	35	21	12	71	5.9

INTERCEPTIONS

		INT	YDS	TD	INT/GM
1	Mike Haynes, Arizona State	11	115	1	0.92
2	John Provost, Holy Cross	10	157	1	0.91
3	Barry Hill, Iowa State	9	90	0	0.82
4	A.J. Jacobs, Louisville	8	211	2	0.73
5	Dennis Anderson, Arizona	7	72	0	0.70
6	Tim Paul, Hawaii	6	60	0	0.67
7	Charles Phillips, Southern Cal	7	302	3	0.64
7	Ed Jones, Rutgers	7	94	0	0.64
7	Ken Shibata, Hawaii	7	49	0	0.64

Team Leaders

RUSHING OFFENSE

		G	ATT	YDS	AVG	TD	YPG
1	Oklahoma	11	813	4827	5.9	47	438.8
2	Ohio State	11	685	4006	5.8	46	364.2
3	Texas	11	674	3487	5.2	40	317.0
4	Houston	11	720	3448	4.8	27	313.5
5	Michigan	11	686	3372	4.9	31	306.5
6	Alabama	11	686	3288	4.8	32	298.9
7	Tampa	11	553	3182	5.8	30	289.3
8	Wisconsin	11	612	3162	5.2	38	287.5
8	Georgia Tech	11	650	3162	4.9	27	287.5
10	Kentucky	11	632	3124	4.9	24	284.0

PASSING OFFENSE

		G	ATT	COM	INT	PCT	YDS	YPA	TD	I%	YPC	YPG
1	Colorado State	11	367	171	24	46.6	2880	7.8	23	6.5	16.8	261.8
2	California	11	331	184	8	55.6	2599	7.9	14	2.4	14.1	236.3
3	San Diego State	11	358	174	18	48.6	2496	7.0	15	5.0	14.3	226.9
4	Tulsa	11	342	182	20	53.2	2417	7.1	20	5.8	13.3	219.7
5	San Jose State	12	394	188	22	47.7	2574	6.5	25	5.6	13.7	214.5
6	Toledo	11	309	187	14	60.5	2335	7.6	13	4.5	12.5	212.3
7	Brigham Young	11	321	192	22	59.8	2314	7.2	25	6.9	12.1	210.4
8	Temple	10	233	134	16	57.5	2027	8.7	20	6.9	15.1	202.7
9	Stanford	11	383	180	17	47.0	2195	5.7	15	4.4	12.2	199.5
10	Cornell	9	255	146	14	57.3	1735	6.8	9	5.5	11.9	192.8

TOTAL OFFENSE

		G	P	YDS	AVG	TD	YPG
1	Oklahoma	11	896	5585	6.2	60	507.7
2	Ohio State	11	783	4966	6.3	55	451.5
3	Temple	10	738	4473	6.1	44	447.3
4	Notre Dame	11	919	4779	5.2	39	434.5
5	North Carolina	11	810	4691	5.8	47	426.5
6	Vanderbilt	11	825	4570	5.5	37	415.5
7	Nebraska	11	815	4532	5.6	48	412.0
8	San Diego State	11	847	4521	5.3	37	411.0
9	Maryland	11	824	4484	5.4	37	407.6
10	Colorado State	11	803	4476	5.6	36	406.9

RUSHING DEFENSE

		G	ATT	YDS	AVG	TD	YPG
1	Notre Dame	11	488	1131	2.3	7	102.8
2	Michigan	11	438	1163	2.7	3	105.7
3	Brown	9	369	972	2.6	10	108.0
4	Brigham Young	11	473	1226	2.6	5	111.5
5	Miami, Ohio	10	454	1153	2.5	6	115.3
6	San Jose State	12	527	1394	2.6	15	116.2
7	Penn State	11	499	1322	2.6	8	120.2
8	Arizona State	12	588	1522	2.6	11	126.8
9	Yale	9	395	1149	2.9	3	127.7
10	Rutgers	11	530	1434	2.7	11	130.4

PASSING DEFENSE

		G	ATT	COM	PCT	YPC	INT	I%	YDS	YPA	TD	YPG
1	Iowa	11	130	50	38.5	14.5	6	4.6	723	5.6	7	65.7
2	Texas A&M	11	166	64	38.6	11.7	16	9.6	751	4.5	4	68.3
3	Furman	11	143	62	43.4	12.4	11	7.7	769	5.4	3	69.9
4	Texas Tech	11	174	63	36.2	12.6	16	9.2	796	4.6	6	72.4
5	Alabama	11	201	82	40.8	10.0	15	7.5	822	4.1	1	74.7
6	South Carolina	11	118	57	48.3	14.5	8	6.8	827	7.0	1	75.2
7	Tulane	11	142	62	43.7	14.5	13	9.2	902	6.4	4	82.0
8	Rice	11	154	67	43.5	13.7	11	7.1	919	6.0	3	83.5
9	Appalachian State	11	158	67	42.4	13.8	10	6.3	927	5.9	5	84.3
10	Georgia Tech	11	147	69	46.9	13.7	10	6.8	944	6.4	6	85.8

TOTAL DEFENSE

		G	P	YDS	AVG	TD	YPG
1	Notre Dame	11	693	2147	3.1	14	195.2
2	Texas A&M	11	688	2272	3.3	16	206.5
3	Michigan	11	659	2353	3.6	7	213.9
4	Miami, Ohio	10	640	2190	3.4	9	219.0
5	Alabama	11	679	2421	3.6	9	220.1
6	Oklahoma	11	745	2547	3.4	9	231.5
7	Rutgers	11	781	2643	3.4	19	240.3
8	Brown	9	576	2268	3.9	17	252.0
9	Houston	11	714	2779	3.9	17	252.6
10	Oklahoma State	11	736	2780	3.8	20	252.7

SCORING OFFENSE

		G	PTS	AVG
1	Oklahoma	11	473	43.0
2	Ohio State	11	420	38.2
3	Boston College	11	375	34.1
4	Temple	10	335	33.5
5	Texas	11	364	33.1
6	Nebraska	11	360	32.7
7	Southern Cal	11	345	31.4
8	Wisconsin	11	341	31.0
9	North Carolina	11	340	30.9
10	Michigan	11	324	29.5

SCORING DEFENSE

		G	PTS	AVG
1	Michigan	11	75	6.8
2	Yale	9	67	7.4
3	Alabama	11	83	7.5
4	Miami, Ohio	10	76	7.6
5	Oklahoma	11	92	8.4
6	Maryland	11	97	8.8
7	Ohio State	11	111	10.1
8	Penn State	11	122	11.1
8	Nebraska	11	122	11.1
10	Southern Cal	11	125	11.4

ANNUAL REVIEW

1975 POLL PROGRESSION

Pre-Season / Sept. 6 Games

AP			
1	Oklahoma	0-0-0	bye week
2	Alabama	0-0-0	lost to Missouri 7-20
3	Michigan	0-0-0	bye week
4	Ohio State	0-0-0	bye week
5	Southern Cal	0-0-0	bye week
6	Penn State	0-0-0	beat Temple 26-25
7	Nebraska	0-0-0	bye week
8	Auburn	0-0-0	bye week
9	Texas A&M	0-0-0	bye week
10	Notre Dame	0-0-0	bye week
11	Texas	0-0-0	bye week
12	Michigan State	0-0-0	bye week
13	North Carolina St.	0-0-0	beat East Carolina 26-3
14	UCLA	0-0-0	bye week
15	Florida	0-0-0	bye week
16	Arizona	0-0-0	bye week
17	Maryland	0-0-0	beat Villanova 41-0
18	Tennessee	0-0-0	bye week
19	Arkansas	0-0-0	bye week
20	Stanford	0-0-0	bye week

September 8 Poll / Sept. 13 Games

AP			
1	Oklahoma	0-0-0	beat Oregon 62-7
2	Michigan	0-0-0	beat Wisconsin 23-6
3	Ohio State	0-0-0	beat # 11 Michigan State 21-0
4	Southern Cal	0-0-0	beat Duke 35-7
5	Missouri	1-0-0	bye week
6	Nebraska	0-0-0	beat LSU 10-7
7	Auburn	0-0	lost to Memphis 20-31
8	Texas A&M	0-0-0	beat Mississippi 7-0
9	Notre Dame	0-0-0	beat Boston College 17-3
10	Penn State	1-0-0	beat Stanford 34-14
11	Michigan State	0-0-0	lost to # 3 Ohio State 0-21
12	Texas	0-0-0	beat Colorado State 46-0
13	Alabama	0-1-0	bye week
14	Maryland	1-0	lost to Tennessee 8-26
15	North Carolina St.	1-0-0	lost to Wake Forest 22-30
16	UCLA	0-0-0	beat Iowa State 37-21
17	Arizona	0-0-0	bye week
18	Pittsburgh	0-0-0	beat Georgia 19-3
19	Florida	0-0-0	beat SMU 40-14
20	Tennessee	0-0-0	beat Maryland 26-8

September 15 Poll / Sept. 20 Games

UP	AP			
1	1	Oklahoma	1-0-0	beat # 15 Pittsburgh 46-10
3	2	Michigan	1-0-0	tied Stanford 19-19
2	3	Ohio State	1-0-0	beat # 7 Penn State 17-9
4	4	Southern Cal	1-0-0	beat Oregon State 24-7
5	5	Missouri	1-0-0	beat Illinois 30-20
6	6	Nebraska	1-0-0	beat Indiana 45-0
8	7	Penn State	2-0-0	lost to # 3 Ohio State 9-17
7	8	Texas	1-0-0	beat Washington 28-10
9	9	Notre Dame	1-0-0	beat Purdue 17-0
10	10	Tennessee	1-0-0	lost to # 12 UCLA 28-34
11	11	Texas A&M	1-0-0	beat LSU 39-8
13	12	UCLA	1-0-0	beat # 10 Tennessee 34-28
12	13	Florida	1-0-0	lost to North Carolina St. 7-8
15	14	Alabama	0-1-0	beat Clemson 56-0
14	15	Pittsburgh	1-0-0	lost to # 1 Oklahoma 10-46
	16	Arkansas	1-0-0	lost to Oklahoma State 13-20
	17	Arizona	0-0-0	beat Pacific 16-0
16	18	Arizona State	1-0-0	beat TCU 33-10
17	19	Miami, Ohio	1-0-0	lost to Michigan State 13-14
19	20	West Virginia	1-0-0	beat California 28-10
20		San Diego State	2-0-0	beat North Texas 30-12

September 22 Poll / Sept. 27 Games

UP	AP			
1	1	Oklahoma	2-0-0	beat Miami, Fla. 20-17
2	2	Ohio State	2-0-0	beat North Carolina 32-7
3	3	Southern Cal	2-0-0	beat Purdue 19-6
4	4	Nebraska	2-0-0	beat TCU 56-14
5	5	Missouri	2-0-0	beat Wisconsin 27-21
6	6	Texas	2-0-0	beat Texas Tech 42-18
8	7	Notre Dame	2-0-0	beat Northwestern 31-7
7	8	Texas A&M	2-0-0	beat Illinois 43-13
10	9	Michigan	1-0-1	tied Baylor 14-14
9	10	UCLA	2-0-0	tied Air Force 20-20
11	11	Alabama	1-1-0	beat Vanderbilt 40-7
12	12	Penn State	2-1-0	beat Iowa 30-10
14	13	Arizona State	2-0-0	beat Brigham Young 20-0
14	14	West Virginia	2-0-0	beat Boston College 35-18
	15	Arizona	1-0-0	beat Wyoming 14-0
	16	Tennessee	1-1-0	beat Auburn 21-17
13	17	Oklahoma State	2-0-0	beat North Texas 61-7
	18	Stanford	0-1-1	lost to San Jose State 34-36
	19	Florida	1-1-0	beat Mississippi State 27-10
	20	Maryland	2-1	tied Kentucky 10-10
16		San Diego State	3-0-0	beat Utah State 19-10
17		Colorado	2-0-0	beat Wichita St. 52-0
19		Auburn	0-1-1	lost to # 16 Tennessee 17-21
20		Navy	2-0-0	lost to Washington 13-14
20		South Carolina	2-0-0	lost to Georgia 20-28

September 29 Poll / Oct. 4 Games

UP	AP			
2	1	Oklahoma	3-0-0	beat # 19 Colorado 21-20
1	2	Ohio State	3-0-0	beat # 13 UCLA 41-20
3	3	Southern Cal	3-0-0	beat Iowa 27-16
4	4	Nebraska	3-0-0	beat Miami, Fla. 31-16
5	5	Missouri	3-0-0	lost to # 12 Michigan 7-31
6	6	Texas A&M	3-0-0	beat Kansas State 10-0
7	7	Texas	3-0-0	beat Utah State 61-7
8	8	Notre Dame	3-0-0	lost to Michigan State 3-10
9	9	Alabama	2-1-0	beat Mississippi 32-6
10	10	Penn State	3-1-0	beat Kentucky 10-3
12	11	West Virginia	3-0-0	beat SMU 28-22
14	12	Michigan	1-0-2	beat # 5 Missouri 31-7
19	13	UCLA	2-0-1	lost to # 2 Ohio State 20-41
13	14	Arizona State	3-0-0	beat Idaho 29-3
11	15	Oklahoma State	3-0-0	beat Texas Tech 17-16
20	16	Tennessee	2-1-0	bye week
17	17	Arizona	3-0-0	beat Northwestern 41-6
15	18	Baylor	1-0-2	lost to South Carolina 13-24
16	19	Colorado	3-0-0	lost to # 1 Oklahoma 20-21
	20	Florida	2-1-0	beat LSU 34-6
18		San Diego State	4-0-0	beat Cal-St. Fullerton 59-14

October 6 Poll / Oct. 11 Games

UP	AP			
1	1	Ohio State	4-0-0	beat Iowa 49-0
2	2	Oklahoma	4-0-0	beat # 5 Texas 24-17
3	3	Southern Cal	4-0-0	beat Washington State 28-10
4	4	Nebraska	4-0-0	beat Kansas 16-0
5	5	Texas	4-0-0	lost to # 2 Oklahoma 17-24
6	6	Texas A&M	4-0-0	beat Texas Tech 38-9
7	7	Alabama	3-1-0	beat Washington 52-0
8	8	Michigan	2-0-2	beat Michigan State 16-6
9	9	Penn State	4-1-0	beat # 10 West Virginia 39-0
11	10	West Virginia	4-0-0	lost to # 9 Penn State 0-39
13	11	Arizona State	4-0-0	beat New Mexico 16-10
18	12	Missouri	3-1-0	beat # 14 Oklahoma State 41-14
12	13	Colorado	3-1-0	beat Miami, Fla. 23-10
10	14	Oklahoma State	4-0-0	lost to # 12 Missouri 14-41
16	15	Michigan State	3-1-0	lost to Michigan 6-16
15	15	Notre Dame	3-1-0	beat North Carolina 21-14
14	17	Arizona	4-0-0	beat Texas-El Paso 36-0
17	18	Florida	3-1-0	beat Vanderbilt 35-0
	19	Tennessee	2-1-0	beat LSU 24-10
	20	Miami, Ohio	3-1-0	beat Dayton 10-0
19		San Diego State	5-0-0	beat Fresno State 29-0
20		Kansas	2-1-0	beat Wisconsin 41-7

October 13 Poll / Oct. 18 Games

UP	AP			
1	1	Ohio State	5-0-0	beat Wisconsin 56-0
2	2	Oklahoma	5-0-0	beat Kansas State 25-3
3	3	Southern Cal	5-0-0	beat Oregon 17-3
4	4	Nebraska	5-0-0	beat Oklahoma State 28-20
5	5	Texas A&M	5-0-0	beat TCU 14-6
6	6	Alabama	4-1-0	beat # 16 Tennessee 30-7
7	7	Michigan	3-0-2	beat Northwestern 69-0
9	8	Texas	4-1-0	beat Arkansas 24-18
8	9	Penn State	5-1-0	beat Syracuse 19-7
10	10	Missouri	4-1-0	lost to # 12 Colorado 20-31
13	11	Arizona State	5-0-0	beat Colorado State 33-3
11	12	Colorado	4-1-0	beat # 10 Missouri 31-20
14	13	Arizona	4-0-0	beat Texas Tech 32-28
12	14	Florida	4-1-0	beat Florida State 34-8
15	15	Notre Dame	4-1-0	beat Air Force 31-30
16	16	Tennessee	3-1-0	lost to # 6 Alabama 7-30
	17	Michigan State	3-2-0	beat Minnesota 38-15
	18	UCLA	3-1-1	beat Washington State 37-23
	19	Maryland	4-1-1	beat Wake Forest 27-0
	20	Arkansas	4-1-0	lost to Texas 18-24
17		Pittsburgh	4-1-0	beat Army 52-20
18		San Diego State	6-0-0	beat New Mexico State 48-3
19		Miami, Ohio	4-1-0	beat Ohio U. 17-9

October 20 Poll / Oct. 25 Games

UP	AP			
1	1	Ohio State	6-0-0	beat Purdue 35-6
2	2	Oklahoma	6-0-0	beat Iowa State 39-7
3	3	Southern Cal	6-0-0	beat # 14 Notre Dame 24-17
4	4	Nebraska	6-0-0	beat # 10 Colorado 63-21
5	5	Texas A&M	6-0-0	beat Baylor 19-10
6	6	Alabama	5-1-0	beat TCU 45-0
7	7	Michigan	4-0-2	beat Indiana 55-7
8	8	Texas	5-1-0	beat Rice 41-9
9	9	Penn State	6-1-0	beat Army 31-0
10	10	Colorado	5-1-0	lost to # 4 Nebraska 21-63
11	11	Arizona State	6-0-0	beat Texas -El Paso 24-6
12	12	Florida	5-1-0	beat Duke 24-16
13	13	Arizona	5-0-0	lost to New Mexico 34-44
14	14	Notre Dame	5-1-0	lost to # 3 Southern Cal 17-24
15	15	Missouri	4-2-0	beat Kansas State 35-3
	16	Michigan State	4-2-0	lost to Illinois 19-21
16	17	Pittsburgh	5-1-0	lost to Navy 0-17
19	18	Maryland	5-1-1	bye week
18	19	UCLA	4-1-1	beat California 28-14
	20	South Carolina	5-1-0	lost to LSU 6-24
17		San Diego State	7-0-0	beat Pacific 31-13
19		Miami, Ohio	5-1-0	beat Bowling Green 20-17

October 27 Poll / Nov. 1 Games

UP	AP			
1	1	Ohio State	7-0-0	beat Indiana 24-14
2	2	Oklahoma	7-0-0	beat # 19 Oklahoma State 27-7
3	3	Nebraska	7-0-0	beat # 12 Missouri 30-7
4	4	Southern Cal	7-0-0	lost to California 14-28
5	5	Texas A&M	7-0-0	bye week
6	6	Alabama	6-1-0	beat Mississippi State 21-10
7	7	Michigan	5-0-2	beat Minnesota 28-21
8	8	Texas	6-1-0	beat SMU 30-22
9	9	Penn State	7-1-0	beat # 14 Maryland 15-13
11	10	Arizona State	7-0-0	beat Utah 40-14
10	11	Florida	6-1-0	beat Auburn 31-14
12	12	Missouri	5-2-0	lost to # 3 Nebraska 7-30
13	13	UCLA	5-1-1	lost to Washington 13-17
14	14	Maryland	5-1-1	lost to # 9 Penn State 13-15
18	15	Notre Dame	5-2-0	beat Navy 31-10
	16	Colorado	5-2-0	beat Iowa State 28-27
	17	Arizona	5-1-0	beat Brigham Young 36-20
14	18	San Diego State	7-0-0	beat Pacific 31-13
15	19	Miami, Ohio	6-1-0	beat Toledo 35-21
15	19	Oklahoma State	5-2-0	lost to # 2 Oklahoma 7-27

November 3 Poll — Nov. 8 Games

UP	AP	Team		Result
1	1	Ohio State	8-0-0	beat Illinois 40-3
2	2	Oklahoma	8-0-0	lost to Kansas 3-23
3	3	Nebraska	8-0-0	beat Kansas State 12-0
4	4	Texas A&M	7-0-0	beat SMU 36-3
5	5	Alabama	7-1-0	beat LSU 23-10
6	6	Michigan	6-0-2	beat Purdue 28-0
7	7	Texas	7-1-0	beat Baylor 37-21
8	8	Penn State	8-1-0	lost to North Carolina St. 14-15
9	9	Southern Cal	7-1-0	lost to Stanford 10-13
11	10	Arizona State	8-0-0	beat Wyoming 21-20
10	11	Florida	7-1-0	lost to Georgia 7-10
13	12	Notre Dame	6-2-0	beat Georgia Tech 24-3
12	13	San Diego State	8-0-0	lost to # 15 Arizona 24-31
	14	Colorado	6-2-0	beat Oklahoma State 17-7
15	15	Arizona	6-1-0	beat # 13 San Diego State 31-24
16	16	Maryland	5-2-1	beat Cincinnati 21-19
	17	Miami, Ohio	7-1-0	beat Western Michigan 44-21
15	18	California	5-3-0	beat Washington 27-24
	19	Missouri	5-3-0	beat Iowa State 44-14
14	20	Pittsburgh	6-2-0	lost to West Virginia 14-17

November 10 Poll — Nov. 15 Games

UP	AP	Team		Result
1	1	Ohio State	9-0-0	beat Minnesota 38-6
2	2	Nebraska	9-0-0	beat Iowa State 52-0
3	3	Texas A&M	8-0-0	beat Rice 33-14
4	4	Michigan	7-0-2	beat Illinois 21-15
5	5	Alabama	8-1-0	beat Southern Miss 27-6
7	6	Oklahoma	8-1-0	beat # 18 Missouri 28-27
6	7	Texas	8-1-0	beat TCU 27-11
8	8	Arizona State	9-0-0	beat Pacific 55-14
9	9	Notre Dame	7-2-0	lost to Pittsburgh 20-34
12	10	Colorado	7-2-0	beat # 17 Kansas 24-21
10	11	Penn State	8-2-0	bye week
11	12	Arizona	7-1-0	beat Colorado State 31-9
17	13	Southern Cal	7-2-0	lost to Washington 7-8
15	14	Florida	7-2-0	beat Kentucky 48-7
13	15	California	6-3-0	beat Air Force 31-14
	16	Miami, Ohio	8-1-0	beat Kent State 27-8
19	17	Kansas	6-3-0	lost to # 10 Colorado 21-24
16	18	Missouri	6-3-0	lost to # 6 Oklahoma 27-28
14	19	UCLA	6-2-1	beat Oregon State 31-9
19	20	Georgia	7-2-0	beat Auburn 28-13
17		Arkansas	6-2-0	beat SMU 35-7

November 17 Poll — Nov. 22 Games

UP	AP	Team		Result
1	1	Ohio State	10-0-0	beat # 4 Michigan 21-14
2	2	Nebraska	10-0-0	lost to # 7 Oklahoma 10-35
3	3	Texas A&M	9-0-0	bye week
5	4	Michigan	8-0-2	lost to # 1 Ohio State 14-21
4	5	Alabama	9-1-0	bye week
7	6	Texas	9-1-0	bye week
6	7	Oklahoma	9-1-0	beat # 2 Nebraska 35-10
8	8	Arizona State	10-0-0	bye week
9	9	Colorado	8-2-0	beat Kansas State 33-7
10	10	Penn State	8-2-0	beat # 17 Pittsburgh 7-6
11	11	Arizona	8-1-0	beat Utah 38-14
12	12	Florida	8-2-0	bye week
14	13	California	7-3-0	beat Stanford 48-15
15	14	UCLA	7-2-1	bye week
13	15	Georgia	8-2-0	bye week
	16	Miami, Ohio	9-1-0	beat Cincinnati 21-13
17	17	Pittsburgh	7-3-0	lost to # 10 Penn State 6-7
	18	Missouri	6-4-0	lost to Kansas 24-42
17	19	Arkansas	7-2-0	beat Texas Tech 31-14
	20	Maryland	7-2-1	beat Virginia 62-24
15		San Jose State	9-1-0	
19		West Virginia	8-2-0	lost to Syracuse 19-20
19		Tulsa	7-3-0	bye week

November 24 Poll — Nov. 29 Games

UP	AP	Team		Result
1	1	Ohio State	11-0-0	regular season complete
2	2	Texas A&M	9-0-0	beat # 5 Texas 20-10
3	3	Oklahoma	10-1-0	regular season complete
4	4	Alabama	9-1-0	beat Auburn 28-0
5	5	Texas	9-1-0	lost to # 2 Texas A&M 10-20
7	6	Michigan	8-1-2	regular season complete
6	7	Nebraska	10-1-0	regular season complete
8	8	Arizona State	10-0-0	beat # 12 Arizona 24-21
10	9	Colorado	9-2-0	regular season complete
9	10	Penn State	9-2-0	regular season complete
12	11	California	8-3-0	regular season complete
11	12	Arizona	9-1-0	lost to # 8 Arizona State 21-24
13	13	Florida	8-2-0	beat Miami, Fla. 15-11
16	14	UCLA	7-2-1	beat Southern Cal 25-22
14	15	Georgia	8-2-0	beat Georgia Tech 42-26
	16	Miami, Ohio	10-1-0	regular season complete
	17	Maryland	8-2-1	regular season complete
20	18	Kansas	7-4	regular season complete
17	19	Arkansas	8-2-0	bye week
15	20	San Jose State	9-1-0	lost to Hawaii 20-30
18		Tulsa	7-3-0	lost to Houston 30-42
19		Notre Dame	8-3-0	regular season complete

December 1 Poll / Bowl Bids / January 3 Final Poll

UP	AP	December 1 Poll	Record	Bowl Bid	Date	Bowl Result	RB	UP	AP	January 3 Final Poll	Record
1	1	Ohio State	11-0-0	Rose Bowl	J1	lost to # 11 UCLA 10-23	1	1	1	Oklahoma	11-1-0
2	2	Texas A&M	10-0-0	Liberty Bowl	D22	lost to Southern Cal 0-20	4	2	2	Arizona State	12-0-0
3	3	Oklahoma	10-1-0	Orange Bowl	J1	beat # 5 Michigan 14-6	3	3	3	Alabama	11-1-0
4	4	Alabama	10-1-0	Sugar Bowl	D31	beat # 8 Penn State 13-6	2	4	4	Ohio State	11-1-0
5	5	Michigan	8-1-2	Orange Bowl	J1	lost to # 3 Oklahoma 6-14	15	5	5	UCLA	9-2-1
6	6	Nebraska	10-1-0	Fiesta Bowl	D26	lost to # 7 Arizona State 14-17	8	7	6	Texas	10-2-0
7	7	Arizona State	11-0-0	Fiesta Bowl	D26	beat # 6 Nebraska 17-14	9	6	7	Arkansas	10-2-0
8	8	Penn State	9-2-0	Sugar Bowl	D31	lost to # 4 Alabama 6-13	7	8	8	Michigan	8-2-2
9	9	Texas	9-2-0	Bluebonnet Bowl	D27	beat # 10 Colorado 38-21	5	9	9	Nebraska	10-2-0
10	10	Colorado	9-3-0	Bluebonnet Bowl	D27	lost to # 9 Texas 21-38	11	10	10	Penn State	9-3-0
12	11	UCLA	8-2-1	Rose Bowl	J1	beat # 1 Ohio State 23-10	1	1	11	Texas A&M	10-2-0
11	12	Georgia	9-2-0	Cotton Bowl	J1	lost to # 18 Arkansas 10-31	16	16	12	Miami, Ohio	11-1-0
13	13	Florida	9-2-0	Gator Bowl	D29	lost to # 17 Maryland 0-13	16	11	13	Maryland	9-2-1
14	14	California	8-3-0				28	15	14	California	8-3-0
15	15	Arizona	9-2-0				14	13	15	Pittsburgh	8-4-0
20	16	Miami, Ohio	10-1-0	Tangerine Bowl	D20	beat South Carolina 20-7	10		16	Colorado	9-3-0
20	17	Maryland	8-2-1	Gator Bowl	D29	beat # 13 Florida 13-0	20	19	17	Southern Cal	8-4-0
15	18	Arkansas	8-2-0	Cotton Bowl	J1	beat # 12 Georgia 31-10	24	13	18	Arizona	9-2-0
18	19	Kansas	7-4	Sun Bowl	D26	lost to # 20 Pittsburgh 19-33	13	19	19	Georgia	9-3-0
	20	Pittsburgh	7-4-0	Sun Bowl	D26	beat # 19 Kansas 33-19	26	17	20	West Virginia	9-3-0
17		Notre Dame	8-3-0				12	17		Notre Dame	8-3-0
20		Tulsa	7-4-0								

1975

CONSENSUS ALL-AMERICANS

POS	Offense	HT	WT	School		AP	FC	FW	PI
QB	John Sciarra	5-10	178	UCLA		•	•		
RB	Archie Griffin	5-9	182	Ohio State		•	•	•	•
RB	Ricky Bell	6-2	215	Southern Cal		•	•	•	•
RB	Chuck Muncie	6-3	220	California		•	•	•	
E	Steve Rivera	6-0	185	California		•	•	•	
E	Larry Seivers	6-4	198	Tennessee		•		•	•
T	Bob Simmons	6-5	245	Texas		•	•	•	
T	Dennis Lick	6-3	262	Wisconsin		•		•	•
G	Randy Johnson	6-2	250	Georgia		•	•	•	
G	Ted Smith	6-1	242	Ohio State		•	•		
C	Rik Bonness	6-4	223	Nebraska		•	•	•	•

OTHERS RECEIVING FIRST-TEAM HONORS

QB	Marty Akins	Texas		•
QB	Gene Swick	Toledo		•
RB	Tony Dorsett	Pittsburgh	•	•
RB	Earl Campbell	Texas	•	
E	Don Buckey	North Carolina St.		•
E	Henry Marshall	Missouri	•	
E	Mike Barber	Louisiana Tech	•	
E	Ken MacAfee	Notre Dame		•
OL	Randy Cross	UCLA		•
OL	Ken Jones	Arkansas State		•
OL	Tom Rafferty	Penn State		•
OL	Marvin Powell	Southern Cal	•	
OL	Mark Koncar	Colorado	•	
OL	Terry Webb	Oklahoma		•
K	Bob Berg	New Mexico		•
KR	Joe Washington	Oklahoma		•

FC picked Bob Simmons as a G

POS	Defense	HT	WT	School		AP	FC	FW	PI
E	Leroy Cook	6-4	205	Alabama		•	•	•	•
E	Jimbo Elrod	6-0	210	Oklahoma		•	•	•	
T	Lee Roy Selmon	6-2	256	Oklahoma		•	•	•	•
T	Steve Niehaus	6-5	260	Notre Dame		•	•	•	•
MG	Dewey Selmon	6-1	257	Oklahoma		•	•	•	
LB	Ed Simonini	6-0	215	Texas A&M		•	•	•	•
LB	Greg Buttle	6-3	220	Penn State		•	•	•	•
LB	Sammy Green	6-2	228	Florida		•		•	
B	Chet Moeller	6-0	189	Navy		•	•	•	•
B	Tim Fox	6-0	186	Ohio State		•	•		
B	Pat Thomas	5-10	180	Texas A&M		•	•		

OTHERS RECEIVING FIRST-TEAM HONORS

DL	Ken Novak	Purdue		•
LB	Ray Preston	Syracuse	•	
LB	Reggie Williams	Dartmouth	•	
LB	Woodrow Lowe	Alabama		•
B	Don Dufek	Michigan	•	•
B	Wonder Monds	Nebraska		•
B	Mike Haynes	Arizona State	•	•
P	Tom Skladany	Ohio State		•

FC named Dewey Selmon as a DL

HEISMAN TROPHY VOTING

	PLAYER	POS	SCHOOL	1ST	2ND	3RD	TOTAL
1	Archie Griffin	TB	Ohio State	454	167	104	1800
2	Chuck Muncie	RB	California	145	104	87	730
3	Ricky Bell	TB	Southern Cal	70	169	160	708
4	Tony Dorsett	RB	Pittsburgh	66	149	120	616
5	Joe Washington	HB	Oklahoma	29	47	69	250
6	Jimmy DuBose	RB	Florida	19	13	29	112
7	John Sciarra	QB	UCLA	12	15	20	86
8	Gordon Bell	TB	Michigan	2	27	24	84
9	Lee Roy Selmon	DT	Oklahoma	7	22	14	79
10	Gene Swick	QB	Toledo	5	19	20	73

AWARD WINNERS

PLAYER	POS	SCHOOL	AWARD NAME
Archie Griffin	RB	Ohio State	Maxwell
Lee Roy Selmon	DT	Oklahoma	Outland
Archie Griffin	RB	Ohio State	Camp
Lee Roy Selmon	DT	Oklahoma	Lombardi

CONFERENCE STANDINGS

ACC

	CONF. W L T			OVERALL W L T		
Maryland	5	0	0	9	2	1
Duke	3	0	2	4	5	2
Wake Forest	3	3	0	3	8	0
North Carolina St.	2	2	1	7	4	1
Clemson	2	3	0	2	9	0
North Carolina	1	4	1	3	7	1
Virginia	0	4	0	1	10	0

Big 10

	CONF. W L T			OVERALL W L T		
Ohio State	8	0	0	11	1	0
Michigan	7	1	0	8	2	2
Michigan State	4	4	0	7	4	0
Illinois	4	4	0	5	6	0
Purdue	4	4	0	4	7	0
Wisconsin	3	4	1	4	6	1
Minnesota	3	5	0	6	5	0
Iowa	3	5	0	3	8	0
Northwestern	2	6	0	3	8	0
Indiana	1	6	1	2	8	1

Big 8

	CONF. W L T			OVERALL W L T		
Oklahoma	6	1	0	11	1	0
Nebraska	6	1	0	10	2	0
Colorado	5	2	0	9	3	0
Kansas	4	3	0	7	5	0
Oklahoma State	3	4	0	7	4	0
Missouri	3	4	0	6	5	0
Iowa State	1	6	0	4	7	0
Kansas State	0	7	0	3	8	0

Big West

	CONF. W L T			OVERALL W L T		
San Diego State	5	0	0	9	2	0
Long Beach Sate	4	1	0	9	2	0
San Diego State	3	2	0	8	3	0
Pacific	2	3	0	5	6	1
Fresno State	1	4	0	3	8	0
Cal-St. Fullerton	0	5	0	2	9	0

Ivy

	CONF. W L T			OVERALL W L T		
Harvard	6	1	0	7	2	0
Brown	5	1	1	6	2	1
Yale	5	2	0	7	2	0
Dartmouth	4	2	1	5	3	1
Princeton	3	4	0	4	5	0
Pennsylvania	2	5	0	3	6	0
Columbia	2	5	0	2	7	0
Cornell	0	7	0	1	8	0

MAC

	CONF. W L T			OVERALL W L T		
Miami, Ohio	6	0	0	10	1	0
Central Michigan	4	1	1	8	2	1
Ball State	4	2	0	9	2	0
Bowling Green	4	2	0	8	3	0
Toledo	4	4	0	5	6	0
Ohio U.	3	3	1	5	5	1
Northern Illinois	2	3	0	3	8	0
Kent State	1	6	0	4	7	0
Western Michigan	0	7	0	4	6	0

PAC 8

	CONF. W L T			OVERALL W L T		
UCLA	6	1	0	9	2	1
California	6	1	0	8	3	0
Stanford	5	2	0	6	4	1
Washington	5	2	0	6	5	0
Southern Cal	3	4	0	8	4	0
Oregon	2	5	0	3	8	0
Oregon State	1	6	0	1	10	0
Washington State	0	7	0	3	8	0

SEC

	CONF. W L T			OVERALL W L T		
Alabama	6	0	0	11	1	0
Florida	5	1	0	9	3	0
Georgia	5	1	0	9	3	0
Mississippi	5	1	0	6	5	0
Tennessee	3	3	0	7	5	0
Vanderbilt	2	4	0	7	4	0
Mississippi State*	1	4	1	6	4	1
Auburn	1	4	1	3	6	2
LSU	1	5	0	4	7	0
Kentucky	0	6	0	2	8	1

Later Forfeited to 0-6-0

SWC

	CONF. W L T			OVERALL W L T		
Arkansas	6	1	0	10	2	0
Texas	6	1	0	10	2	0
Texas A&M	6	1	0	10	2	0
Texas Tech	4	3	0	6	5	0
Baylor	2	5	0	3	6	2
SMU	2	5	0	4	7	0
Rice	1	6	0	2	9	0
TCU	1	6	0	1	10	0

WAC

	CONF. W L T			OVERALL W L T		
Arizona State	7	0	0	12	0	0
Arizona	5	2	0	9	2	0
Colorado State	4	2	0	6	5	0
New Mexico	4	3	0	6	5	0
Brigham Young	4	3	0	6	5	0
Utah	1	4	0	1	10	0
Wyoming	1	6	0	2	9	0
Texas-El Paso	0	6	0	1	10	0

Independents

	OVERALL W L T		
Rutgers	9	2	0
West Virginia	9	3	0
Penn State	9	3	0
Notre Dame	8	3	0
Virginia Tech	8	3	0
Pittsburgh	8	4	0
North Texas	7	4	0
Georgia Tech	7	4	0
Memphis	7	4	0
Boston College	7	4	0
Navy	7	4	0
South Carolina	7	5	0
Utah State	6	5	0
Syracuse	6	5	0
Tulane	4	7	0
Florida State	3	8	0
Air Force	2	8	1
Miami, Fla.	2	8	0
Houston	2	8	0
Army	2	9	0

BOWL GAMES

DATE	GAME	SCORE
D20	Tangerine	Miami, Ohio 20, South Carolina 7
D22	Liberty	Southern Cal 20, Texas A&M 0
D26	Fiesta	Arizona State 17, Nebraska 14
D26	Sun	Pittsburgh 33, Kansas 19
D27	Bluebonnet	Texas 38, Colorado 21
D29	Gator	Maryland 13, Florida 0
D31	Sugar	Alabama 13, Penn State 6
D31	Peach	West Virginia 13, North Carolina St. 10
J1	Cotton	Arkansas 31, Georgia 10
J1	Orange	Oklahoma 14, Michigan 6
J1	Rose	UCLA 23, Ohio State 10

1975 NCAA Major College Statistical Leaders

Individual Leaders

PASSING	G	ATT	COM	PCT	INT	I%	YDS	YPA	TD	TD%	COM.PG
1 Craig Penrose, San Diego State	11	349	198	56.7	24	6.9	2660	7.6	15	4.3	18.0
2 Gene Swick, Toledo	11	308	190	61.7	12	3.9	2487	8.1	15	4.9	17.3
2 Steve Myer, New Mexico	11	353	190	53.8	14	4.0	2501	7.1	21	5.9	17.3
4 Joe Bruner, La. Monroe	11	312	160	51.3	15	4.8	2025	6.5	7	2.2	14.5
5 Jack Henderson, Oregon	11	321	151	47.0	16	5.0	1492	4.6	6	1.9	13.7
6 Ron Beible, Princeton	9	244	123	50.4	10	4.1	1503	6.2	7	2.9	13.7
7 Pat Degnan, Utah	11	289	140	48.4	21	7.3	1621	5.6	7	2.4	12.7
8 Joe Roth, California	10	225	126	56.0	7	3.1	1880	8.4	14	6.2	12.6
9 Bob Bateman, Brown	9	206	112	54.4	7	3.4	1428	6.9	8	3.9	12.4
10 Gifford Nielsen, Brigham Young	9	180	110	61.1	7	3.9	1474	8.2	10	5.6	12.2

ALL-PURPOSE	G	RUSH	REC	PR	KR	YDS	YPG
1 Louie Giammona, Utah State	11	1454	33	124	434	2045	185.9
2 Ricky Bell, Southern Cal	11	1875	24	0	0	1899	172.6
3 Chuck Muncie, California	11	1460	392	0	19	1871	170.1
4 Tony Dorsett, Pittsburgh	11	1544	191	0	105	1840	167.3
5 John Zeglinski, Wake Forest	11	591	354	243	542	1730	157.3
6 Dan Watkins, Kent State	10	916	59	47	508	1530	153.0
7 Walter Peacock, Louisville	11	1013	0	43	612	1668	151.6
8 Herb Lusk, Long Beach State	11	1596	62	0	0	1658	150.7
9 Gordon Bell, Michigan	11	1335	67	18	207	1627	147.9
10 Archie Griffin, Ohio State	11	1357	158	0	91	1606	146.0

RUSHING/Yards Per Game	G	ATT	YDS	TD	AVG	YPG
1 Ricky Bell, Southern Cal	11	357	1875	13	5.3	170.5
2 Herb Lusk, Long Beach State	11	310	1596	13	5.1	145.1
3 Tony Dorsett, Pittsburgh	11	228	1544	11	6.8	140.4
4 Chuck Muncie, California	11	228	1460	13	6.4	132.7
5 Louie Giammona, Utah State	11	303	1454	11	4.8	132.2
6 Mike Voight, North Carolina	10	259	1250	11	4.8	125.0
7 Archie Griffin, Ohio State	11	245	1357	4	5.5	123.4
8 Gordon Bell, Michigan	11	255	1335	12	5.2	121.4
9 Fred Williams, Arizona State	11	248	1316	9	5.3	119.6
10 Jimmy DuBose, Florida	11	191	1307	6	6.8	118.8

RUSHING/Yards Per Carry	G	ATT	YDS	YPC
1 Jimmy DuBose, Florida	11	191	1307	6.8
2 Tony Dorsett, Pittsburgh	11	228	1544	6.8
3 Wendell Tyler, UCLA	11	187	1216	6.5
4 Chuck Muncie, California	11	228	1460	6.4
5 Dennis Bolden, Arkansas State	11	186	1191	6.4
6 Kevin Long, South Carolina	11	179	1114	6.2
7 Dan Saleet, Bowling Green	10	194	1114	5.7
8 Earl Campbell, Texas	11	198	1118	5.6
9 Cleveland Franklin, Baylor	11	200	1112	5.6
10 Archie Griffin, Ohio State	11	245	1357	5.5

*-Based on top 27 rushers

RECEIVING	G	REC	YDS	TD	YPR	YPG	RPG
1 Bob Farnham, Brown	9	56	701	2	12.5	77.9	6.2
2 Dave Quehl, Holy Cross	11	63	959	5	15.2	87.2	5.7
3 Steve Rivera, California	10	57	790	4	13.9	79.0	5.7
4 Preston Dennard, New Mexico	11	59	962	6	16.3	87.5	5.4
5 Pat Tilley, Louisiana Tech	10	53	926	6	17.5	92.6	5.3
6 Duke Fergerson, San Diego State	11	57	886	4	15.5	80.5	5.2
7 Tony Hill, Stanford	11	55	916	7	16.7	93.3	5.0
8 John Filliez, Marshall	11	54	657	7	12.2	59.7	4.9
9 Neil Chamberlin, Princeton	9	44	519	0	11.8	57.7	4.9
10 Greg Bauer, Oregon	11	52	616	4	11.8	56.0	4.7

PUNTING	PUNT	YDS	AVG
1 Tom Skladany, Ohio State	36	1681	46.7
2 Rick Engles, Tulsa	36	1678	46.6
3 Cliff Parsley, Oklahoma State	58	2598	44.8
4 Gavin Hedrick, Washington State	50	2235	44.7
5 Johnny Evans, North Carolina St.	42	1873	44.6
6 Jim Walton, Boston College	49	2171	44.3
7 Dennis Anderson, Arizona	53	2300	43.4
8 Bob Grupp, Duke	40	1720	43.0
9 Tommy Cheyne, Arkansas	37	1591	43.0
10 Don Fechtman, North Texas	66	2825	42.8

PUNT RETURNS	PR	YDS	TD	AVG
1 Donnie Ross, New Mexico State	21	338	1	16.1
2 Danny Reece, Southern Cal	26	409	1	15.7
3 Vernie Kelley, Pacific	19	294	0	15.5
4 Stanley Morgan, Tennessee	20	284	2	14.2
5 Henry Jenkins, Rutgers	20	277	1	13.8
6 Gordon Jones, Pittsburgh	28	373	0	13.3
7 Randy Rich, New Mexico	25	325	1	13.0
8 Devon Ford, Appalachian State	21	260	0	12.4
9 Ronnie Barber, LSU	14	173	0	12.4
10 Troy Slade, Duke	23	283	0	12.3

KICKOFF RETURNS	KR	YDS	TD	AVG
1 John Schultz, Maryland	13	403	1	31.0
2 Keith Jenkins, Cincinnati	15	437	1	29.1
3 Theopolis Bell, Arizona	16	453	0	28.3
4 Rick Neel, Auburn	17	474	1	27.9
5 Tim Morgan, Miami, Fla.	14	385	1	27.5
6 Mike Tsoutsouvas, Fresno State	13	354	0	27.2
7 Terry Eurick, Notre Dame	13	347	0	26.7
8 Robert Dow, LSU	23	598	0	26.0
9 Henry White, Colgate	13	335	0	25.8
10 Dave Schick, Iowa	24	610	1	25.4

SCORING	TDS	XPT	FG	PTS	PTPG
1 Pete Johnson, Ohio State	25	0	0	150	13.6
2 Dave Preston, Bowling Green	14	0	0	84	9.3
3 David Hines, Arkansas State	17	0	0	102	9.3
4 Herb Lusk, Long Beach State	16	0	0	96	8.7
5 Don Bitterlich, Temple	0	32	21	95	8.6
6 Ted Brown, North Carolina St.	13	6	0	84	8.4
7 Chuck Muncie, California	15	0	0	90	8.2
8 Walt Hodges, Central Michigan	12	0	0	72	8.0
9 Tony Dorsett, Pittsburgh	14	0	0	84	7.6
9 Steve Largent, Tulsa	14	0	0	84	7.6
9 John Sciarra, UCLA	14	0	0	84	7.6

FIELD GOALS	FGA	FGM	PCT	FGG
1 Don Bitterlich, Temple	31	21	0.68	1.91
2 Bob Berg, New Mexico	26	18	0.69	1.64
2 Chris Bahr, Penn State	33	18	0.55	1.64
4 Lou Rodriguez, San Jose State	32	16	0.50	1.45
5 David Jacobs, Syracuse	30	14	0.47	1.40
6 Lee Pistor, Arizona	19	15	0.79	1.36
6 Gary Davis, Appalachian State	20	15	0.75	1.36
6 Dan Shepherd, Cincinnati	22	15	0.68	1.36
9 Jose Violante, Brown	19	12	0.63	1.33
10 Chris Dennis, Miami, Fla.	21	13	0.62	1.30

INTERCEPTIONS	INT	YDS	TD	INT/GM
1 Jim Bolding, East Carolina	10	51	0	1.00
2 Cedric Brown, Kent State	8	107	1	0.89
3 Craig Cassady, Ohio State	8	78	0	0.73
4 Vernie Kelley, Pacific	8	51	0	0.67
5 Ed Oaks, Vanderbilt	7	117	0	0.64
5 Gerald Small, San Jose State	7	104	2	0.64
5 Billy Hardee, Virginia Tech	7	83	0	0.64
5 Preston Lanier, McNeese St.	7	80	0	0.64
5 Mike Lecklider, Ball State	7	61	0	0.64
5 Roy Gordon, Dayton	7	48	0	0.64
5 Mike Martinez, Arizona State	7	32	0	0.64

Team Leaders

RUSHING OFFENSE	G	ATT	YDS	AVG	TD	YPG
1 Arkansas State	11	746	3745	5.0	42	340.5
2 Michigan	11	686	3679	5.4	34	334.5
3 Georgia Tech	11	692	3627	5.2	32	329.7
4 UCLA	11	699	3619	5.2	40	329.0
5 Central Michigan	11	740	3613	4.9	32	328.5
6 Arkansas	11	659	3523	5.3	33	320.3
7 Kansas	11	670	3488	5.2	27	317.1
8 Ohio State	11	678	3480	5.1	43	316.4
9 Appalachian State	11	693	3438	5.0	32	312.5
10 Texas	11	656	3413	5.2	43	310.3

PASSING OFFENSE	G	ATT	COM	INT	PCT	YDS	YPA	TD	I%	YPC	YPG
1 San Diego State	11	411	238	27	57.9	3204	7.8	17	6.6	13.5	291.3
2 New Mexico	11	354	191	14	54.0	2529	7.1	22	4.0	13.2	229.9
3 California	11	307	170	9	55.4	2522	8.2	17	2.9	14.8	229.3
4 Toledo	11	312	190	12	60.9	2487	8.0	15	3.8	13.1	226.1
5 Louisiana Tech	10	265	143	12	54.0	2226	8.4	17	4.5	15.6	222.6
6 Stanford	11	374	189	20	50.5	2432	6.5	21	5.3	12.9	221.1
7 Tulsa	11	309	164	17	53.1	2417	7.8	19	5.5	14.7	219.7
8 Fresno State	11	330	168	30	50.9	2149	6.5	10	9.1	12.8	195.4
9 Brown	9	250	134	15	53.6	1726	6.9	9	6.0	12.9	191.8
10 La. Monroe	11	316	161	15	50.9	2030	6.4	7	4.7	12.6	184.5

TOTAL OFFENSE	G	P	YDS	AVG	TD	YPG
1 California	11	834	5044	6.0	43	458.5
2 Tulsa	11	800	4937	6.2	45	448.8
3 UCLA	11	828	4753	5.7	46	432.1
4 South Carolina	11	781	4746	6.1	41	431.5
5 Arizona	11	832	4666	5.6	40	424.2
6 Arizona State	11	861	4634	5.4	36	421.3
7 Appalachian State	11	861	4605	5.3	42	418.6
8 San Diego State	11	806	4520	5.6	35	410.9
9 Long Beach State	11	815	4509	5.5	35	409.9
10 Ohio State	11	785	4477	5.7	49	407.0

RUSHING DEFENSE	G	ATT	YDS	AVG	TD	YPG
1 Texas A&M	11	448	883	2.0	4	80.3
2 Miami, Ohio	11	462	947	2.0	8	86.1
3 Central Michigan	11	435	993	2.3	4	90.3
4 Alabama	11	460	1037	2.3	5	94.3
5 Arkansas State	11	475	1115	2.3	7	101.4
6 San Jose State	11	470	1133	2.4	7	103.0
7 Boston College	11	450	1269	2.8	11	115.4
8 Rutgers	11	465	1293	2.8	5	117.5
9 Michigan	11	484	1323	2.7	7	120.3
10 Navy	11	486	1341	2.8	7	121.9

PASSING DEFENSE	G	ATT	COM	PCT	YPC	INT	I%	YDS	YPA	TD	YPG
1 VMI	11	113	40	35.4	14.1	12	10.6	562	5.0	6	51.1
2 Florida State	11	116	53	45.7	13.2	11	9.5	698	6.0	4	63.5
3 Wisconsin	11	129	51	39.5	14.1	22	17.1	717	5.6	8	65.2
4 North Carolina St.	11	144	64	44.4	12.1	6	4.2	775	5.4	5	70.5
5 Navy	11	187	74	39.6	11.8	15	8.0	871	4.7	4	79.2
6 Baylor	11	154	69	44.8	13.0	12	7.8	896	5.8	5	81.5
7 Memphis	11	193	85	44.0	10.6	13	6.7	903	4.7	5	82.1
8 Bowling Green	11	196	78	39.8	11.7	17	8.7	914	4.7	5	83.1
9 Rutgers	11	212	88	41.5	10.7	19	9.0	940	4.4	2	85.5

TOTAL DEFENSE	G	P	YDS	AVG	TD	YPG
1 Texas A&M	11	645	2022	3.1	10	183.8
2 Alabama	11	677	2046	3.0	7	186.0
3 Navy	11	673	2212	3.3	11	201.1
4 Rutgers	11	677	2233	3.3	7	203.0
5 Central Michigan	11	625	2268	3.6	12	206.2
6 Miami, Ohio	11	679	2353	3.5	18	213.9
7 Arkansas State	11	711	2372	3.3	9	215.6
8 Nebraska	11	678	2465	3.6	15	224.1
9 Boston College	11	650	2563	3.9	15	233.0
10 Southern Miss	11	616	2572	4.2	16	233.8

SCORING OFFENSE	G	PTS	AVG
1 Ohio State	11	374	34.0
2 Tulsa	11	368	33.5
3 Texas	11	363	33.0
4 Alabama	11	361	32.8
5 Arkansas State	11	355	32.3
6 Nebraska	11	353	32.1
7 Rutgers	11	347	31.5
8 Appalachian State	11	337	30.6
9 Oklahoma	11	330	30.0
9 California	11	330	30.0
9 Arizona	11	330	30.0
9 Arizona State	11	330	30.0

SCORING DEFENSE	G	PTS	AVG
1 Alabama	11	66	6.0
2 Ohio State	11	79	7.2
3 Arkansas State	11	81	7.4
4 Rutgers	11	91	8.3
5 Citadel	11	97	8.8
6 Central Michigan	11	102	9.3
7 Florida	11	104	9.5
7 Texas A&M	11	104	9.5
9 Penn State	11	110	10.0

1976 POLL PROGRESSION

PRE-SEASON — Sept. 11 Games

AP	Team	Record	Result
1	Nebraska	0-0-0	tied LSU 6-6
2	Michigan	0-0-0	beat Wisconsin 40-27
3	Arizona State	0-0-0	lost to # 17 UCLA 10-28 S9
4	Ohio State	0-0-0	beat Michigan State 49-21
5	Oklahoma	0-0-0	beat Vanderbilt 24-3
6	Alabama	0-0-0	lost to Mississippi 7-10
7	Texas	0-0-0	lost to Boston College 13-14
8	Southern Cal	0-0-0	lost to Missouri 25-46
9	Pittsburgh	0-0-0	beat # 11 Notre Dame 31-10
10	Penn State	0-0-0	beat Stanford 15-12
11	Notre Dame	0-0-0	lost to # 9 Pittsburgh 10-31
12	Maryland	0-0-0	beat Richmond 31-7
13	Arkansas	0-0-0	beat Utah State 33-16
14	Texas A&M	0-0-0	beat Virginia Tech 19-0
15	California	0-0-0	lost to # 16 Georgia 24-36
16	Georgia	0-0-0	beat # 15 California 36-24
17	UCLA	0-0-0	beat # 3 Arizona State 28-10 S9
18	Florida	0-0-0	lost to North Carolina 21-24
19	Kansas	0-0-0	beat Washington State 35-16
20	Miami, Ohio	0-0-0	lost to Marshall 16-21

SEPTEMBER 13 POLL — Sept. 18 Games

UP	AP	Team	Record	Result
2	1	Michigan	1-0-0	beat Stanford 51-0
1	2	Ohio State	1-0-0	beat # 7 Penn State 12-7
4	3	Pittsburgh	1-0-0	beat Georgia Tech 42-14
5	4	Oklahoma	1-0-0	beat California 28-17
3	5	UCLA	1-0-0	beat Arizona 37-9
6	6	Missouri	1-0-0	lost to Illinois 6-31
7	7	Penn State	1-0-0	lost to # 2 Ohio State 7-12
8	8	Nebraska	0-0-1	beat Indiana 45-13
9	9	Georgia	1-0-0	beat Clemson 41-0
11	10	Maryland	1-0-0	beat West Virginia 24-3
10	11	Texas A&M	1-0-0	beat Kansas State 34-14
12	12	Arkansas	1-0-0	beat Oklahoma State 16-10
16	13	Kansas	2-0-0	beat Kentucky 37-16
13	14	Alabama	0-1-0	beat SMU 56-3
15	15	Boston College	1-0-0	bye week
14	16	LSU	0-0-1	beat Oregon State 28-11
17	17	North Carolina	2-0-0	beat Northwestern 12-0
	18	Arizona State	0-1-0	bye week
	19	Texas	0-1-0	beat North Texas 17-14
	20	Mississippi	1-1-0	beat Tulane 34-7
16		Texas Tech	1-0-0	bye week
16		North Carolina	2-0-0	beat Northwestern 12-0
19		Southern Cal	0-1-0	beat Oregon 53-0
20		Oklahoma State	1-0-0	lost to # 12 Arkansas 10-16

SEPTEMBER 20 POLL — Sept. 27 Games

UP	AP	Team	Record	Result
1	1	Michigan	2-0-0	beat Navy 70-14
2	2	Ohio State	2-0-0	lost to Missouri 21-22
3	3	Pittsburgh	2-0-0	beat Temple 21-7
5	4	Oklahoma	2-0-0	beat Florida State 24-9
4	5	UCLA	2-0-0	beat Air Force 40-7
6	6	Nebraska	1-0-1	beat TCU 64-10
7	7	Georgia	2-0-0	beat South Carolina 20-12
8	8	Maryland	2-0-0	beat Syracuse 42-28
9	9	Texas A&M	2-0-0	lost to Houston 10-21
12	10	Kansas	3-0-0	bye week
10	11	Penn State	1-1-0	lost to Iowa 6-7
11	12	Arkansas	2-0-0	lost to Tulsa 3-9
13	13	Alabama	1-1-0	beat Vanderbilt 42-14
14	14	Illinois	2-0-0	lost to Baylor 19-34
15	15	LSU	1-0-1	beat Rice 31-0
18	16	North Carolina	3-0-0	beat Army 34-32
	17	Mississippi	2-1-0	beat Southern Miss 28-0
17	18	Boston College	1-0-0	beat Tulane 27-3
	19	Southern Cal	1-1-0	beat Purdue 31-13
19	20	Texas Tech	1-0-0	beat New Mexico 20-16
19		Florida	1-1-0	beat Mississippi State 34-30

SEPTEMBER 29 POLL — Oct. 2 Games

UP	AP	Team	Record	Result
1	1	Michigan	3-0-0	beat Wake Forest 31-0
3	2	Pittsburgh	3-0-0	beat Duke 44-31
4	3	Oklahoma	3-0-0	beat Iowa State 24-10
2	4	UCLA	3-0-0	tied # 8 Ohio State 10-10
5	5	Nebraska	2-0-1	beat Miami, Fla. 17-9
6	6	Georgia	3-0-0	beat # 10 Alabama 21-0
7	7	Maryland	3-0-0	beat Villanova 20-9
8	8	Ohio State	2-1-0	tied # 4 UCLA 10-10
11	9	Kansas	3-0-0	beat Wisconsin 34-24
9	10	Alabama	2-1-0	lost to # 6 Georgia 0-21
13	11	LSU	2-0-1	lost to # 19 Florida 23-28
10	12	Missouri	2-1-0	beat # 14 North Carolina 24-3
12	13	Southern Cal	2-1-0	beat Iowa 55-0
14	14	North Carolina	4-0-0	lost to # 12 Missouri 3-24
16	15	Boston College	2-0-0	beat Navy 17-13
	16	Mississippi	3-1-0	lost to Auburn 0-10
	17	Texas Tech	2-0-0	bye week
15	18	Notre Dame	2-1-0	beat Michigan State 24-6
17	19	Florida	2-1-0	beat # 11 LSU 28-23
	20	Penn State	1-2-0	lost to Kentucky 6-22
		Houston	2-1-0	bye week
19		Tulsa	3-1-0	beat New Mexico State 32-7
20		Texas	1-1-0	beat Rice 42-15

OCTOBER 4 POLL — Oct. 9 Games

UP	AP	Team	Record	Result
1	1	Michigan	4-0-0	beat Michigan State 42-10
2	2	Pittsburgh	4-0-0	beat Louisville 27-6
3	3	Oklahoma	4-0-0	tied # 16 Texas 6-6
4	4	Georgia	4-0-0	lost to Mississippi 17-21
5	5	UCLA	3-0-1	beat Stanford 38-20
6	6	Nebraska	3-0-1	beat Colorado 24-12
7	7	Maryland	4-0-0	beat North Carolina St. 16-6
8	8	Kansas	4-0-0	lost to Oklahoma State 14-21
9	9	Missouri	3-1-0	beat Kansas State 28-21
11	10	Ohio State	2-1-1	beat Iowa 34-14
10	11	Southern Cal	3-1-0	beat Washington St. 23-14
13	12	Florida	3-1-0	bye week
17	13	Boston College	3-0-0	lost to Florida State 9-28
12	14	Notre Dame	3-1-0	bye week
18	15	Texas Tech	2-0-0	beat # 17 Texas A&M 27-16
14	16	Texas	2-1-0	tied # 3 Oklahoma 6-6
16	17	Texas A&M	3-1-0	lost to # 15 Texas Tech 16-27
15	18	Arkansas	3-1-0	bye week
	19	North Carolina	4-1-0	bye week
	20	LSU	2-1-1	beat Vanderbilt 33-20
19		Houston	2-1-0	beat West Texas St. 50-7
20		Tulsa	4-1-0	bye week

OCTOBER 11 POLL — Oct. 16 Games

UP	AP	Team	Record	Result
1	1	Michigan	5-0-0	beat Northwestern 38-7
2	2	Pittsburgh	5-0-0	beat Miami, Fla. 36-19
3	3	Nebraska	4-0-1	beat Kansas State 51-0
4	4	UCLA	4-0-1	beat Washington St. 62-3
6	5	Maryland	5-0-0	beat Wake Forest 17-15
5	6	Oklahoma	4-0-1	beat # 15 Kansas 28-10
7	7	Missouri	4-1-0	lost to Iowa State 17-21
8	8	Southern Cal	4-1-0	bye week
9	9	Ohio State	3-1-1	beat Wisconsin 30-20
10	10	Texas Tech	3-0-0	beat Rice 37-13
11	11	Georgia	4-1-0	beat Vanderbilt 45-0
12	12	Florida	3-1-0	beat Florida State 33-26
13	13	Texas	2-1-1	bye week
14	14	Notre Dame	3-1-0	beat Oregon 41-0
18	15	Kansas	4-1-0	lost to # 6 Oklahoma 10-28
	16	LSU	3-1-1	lost to Kentucky 7-21
20	17	Mississippi	4-2-0	lost to South Carolina 7-10
16	18	Arkansas	3-1-0	bye week
19	19	Houston	3-1-0	beat SMU 29-6
	20	Alabama	3-2-0	beat Tennessee 20-13
17		Tulsa	4-1-0	lost to Cincinnati 7-16
19		Oklahoma State	3-1-0	lost to Colorado 10-20

OCTOBER 18 POLL — Oct. 23 Games

UP	AP	Team	Record	Result
1	1	Michigan	6-0-0	beat Indiana 35-0
2	2	Pittsburgh	6-0-0	beat Navy 45-0
3	3	Nebraska	5-0-1	lost to # 17 Missouri 24-34
4	4	UCLA	5-0-1	beat California 35-19
5	5	Oklahoma	5-0-1	lost to Oklahoma State 24-31
7	6	Maryland	6-0-0	beat Duke 30-3
6	7	Southern Cal	4-1-0	beat Oregon State 56-0
9	8	Texas Tech	4-0-0	beat Arizona 52-27
8	9	Ohio State	4-1-0	beat Purdue 24-3
10	10	Georgia	5-1-0	beat Kentucky 31-7
11	11	Florida	4-1-0	beat Tennessee 20-18
12	12	Notre Dame	4-1-0	beat # 19 South Carolina 13-6
13	13	Texas	2-1-1	beat SMU 13-12
14	14	Houston	4-1-0	lost to # 15 Arkansas 7-14
15	15	Arkansas	3-1-0	beat # 14 Houston 14-7
18	16	Iowa State	5-1-0	lost to Colorado 14-33
16	17	Missouri	4-2-0	beat # 3 Nebraska 34-24
20	18	Alabama	4-2-0	beat Louisville 24-3
	19	South Carolina	5-2-0	lost to # 12 Notre Dame 6-13
	20	East Carolina	6-0-0	lost to North Carolina 10-12
	20	Mississippi State	5-1-0	beat Southern Miss 14-6
17		Cincinnati	6-1-0	bye week
19		Colorado	4-2-0	beat Iowa State 33-14

OCTOBER 25 POLL — Oct. 30 Games

UP	AP	Team	Record	Result
1	1	Michigan	7-0-0	beat Minnesota 45-0
2	2	Pittsburgh	7-0-0	beat Syracuse 23-13
3	3	UCLA	6-0-1	beat Washington 30-21
4	4	Southern Cal	5-1-0	beat California 20-6
5	5	Maryland	7-0-0	beat Kentucky 24-14
6	6	Texas Tech	5-0-0	beat # 15 Texas 31-28
7	7	Georgia	6-1-0	beat # 20 Cincinnati 31-17
8	8	Ohio State	5-1-1	beat Indiana 47-7
9	9	Nebraska	5-1-1	beat Kansas 31-3
10	10	Missouri	5-2-0	lost to # 16 Oklahoma State 19-20
11	11	Notre Dame	5-1-0	beat Navy 27-21
12	12	Florida	5-1-0	beat Auburn 24-19
13	13	Oklahoma	5-1-1	lost to # 19 Colorado 31-42
14	14	Arkansas	4-1-0	beat Rice 41-16
17	15	Texas	3-1-1	lost to # 6 Texas Tech 28-31
15	16	Oklahoma State	4-2-0	beat # 10 Missouri 20-19
18	17	Alabama	5-2-0	beat # 18 Mississippi State 34-17
	18	Mississippi State	6-1-0	lost to # 17 Alabama 17-34
16	19	Colorado	5-2-0	beat # 13 Oklahoma 42-31
18	20	Cincinnati	5-1-0	lost to # 7 Georgia 17-31
		Boston College	5-1-0	lost to Villanova 3-22

NOVEMBER 1 POLL — Nov. 6 Games

UP	AP	Team	Record	Result
1	1	Michigan	8-0-0	lost to Purdue 14-16
2	2	Pittsburgh	8-0-0	beat Army 37-7
3	3	UCLA	7-0-1	beat Oregon 46-0
4	4	Southern Cal	6-1-0	beat Stanford 48-24
5	5	Texas Tech	6-0-0	beat TCU 14-10
6	6	Maryland	8-0-0	beat Cincinnati 21-0
8	7	Georgia	7-1-0	beat # 10 Florida 41-27
7	8	Ohio State	6-1-1	beat Illinois 42-10
9	9	Nebraska	6-1-1	beat # 13 Oklahoma State 14-10
10	10	Florida	6-1-0	lost to # 7 Georgia 27-41
11	11	Notre Dame	6-1-0	lost to Georgia Tech 14-23
14	12	Arkansas	5-1-0	tied Baylor 7-7
12	13	Oklahoma State	5-2-0	lost to # 9 Nebraska 10-14
13	14	Colorado	6-2-0	lost to # 16 Missouri 7-16
15	15	Alabama	6-2-0	beat LSU 28-17
	16	Missouri	5-3-0	beat # 14 Colorado 16-7
	17	Oklahoma	5-2-1	beat Kansas State 49-20
	18	Texas A&M	6-2-0	bye week
17	19	Houston	5-2-0	beat # 20 Texas 30-0
	20	Texas	3-2-1	lost to # 19 Houston 0-30
16		Tulsa	5-2-0	beat Virginia Tech 35-31

November 8 Poll — Nov. 13 Games

UP	AP	Team	Record	Nov. 13 Games
1	1	Pittsburgh	9-0-0	beat West Virginia 24-16
2	2	UCLA	8-0-1	beat Oregon State 45-14
3	3	Southern Cal	7-1-0	beat Washington 20-3
4	4	Michigan	8-1-0	beat Illinois 38-7
5	5	Texas Tech	7-0-0	beat SMU 34-7
7	6	Maryland	9-0-0	beat Clemson 20-0
6	7	Georgia	8-1-0	beat Auburn 28-0
8	8	Ohio State	7-1-1	beat Minnesota 9-3
9	9	Nebraska	7-1-1	lost to Iowa State 28-37
12	10	Alabama	7-2-0	lost to # 18 Notre Dame 18-21
10	11	Missouri	6-3-0	lost to # 14 Oklahoma 20-27
11	12	Houston	6-2-0	bye week
16	13	Arkansas	5-1-1	lost to # 16 Texas A&M 10-31
14	14	Oklahoma	6-2-1	beat # 11 Missouri 27-20
15	15	Florida	6-2-0	lost to Kentucky 9-28
	16	Texas A&M	6-2-0	beat # 13 Arkansas 31-10
	17	Oklahoma State	5-3-0	beat Kansas State 45-21
19	18	Notre Dame	6-2-0	beat # 10 Alabama 21-18
	19	Colorado	6-3-0	beat Kansas 40-17
	20	South Carolina	6-3-0	lost to Wake Forest 7-10
13		Tulsa	6-2-0	beat Drake 45-20
16		Iowa State	7-2-0	beat # 9 Nebraska 37-28
18		Baylor	4-2-1	beat Rice 38-6
19		Brigham Young	7-2-0	beat New Mexico 21-8
19		Wyoming	7-2-0	beat Texas-El Paso 14-10

November 15 Poll — Nov. 20 Games

UP	AP	Team	Record	Nov. 20 Games
1	1	Pittsburgh	10-0-0	bye week
2	2	UCLA	9-0-1	lost to # 3 Southern Cal 14-24
3	3	Southern Cal	8-1-0	beat # 2 UCLA 24-14
4	4	Michigan	9-1-0	beat # 8 Ohio State 22-0
5	5	Texas Tech	8-0-0	lost to # 9 Houston 19-27
6	6	Georgia	9-1-0	bye week
7	7	Maryland	10-0-0	beat Virginia 28-0
8	8	Ohio State	8-1-1	lost to # 4 Michigan 0-22
13	9	Houston	6-2-0	beat # 5 Texas Tech 27-19
9	10	Oklahoma	7-2-1	bye week
12	11	Texas A&M	7-2-0	beat TCU 59-10
11	12	Nebraska	7-2-1	bye week
14	13	Notre Dame	7-2-0	beat Miami, Fla. 40-27
10	14	Iowa State	8-2-0	lost to # 16 Oklahoma State 21-42
16	15	Colorado	7-3-0	beat Kansas State 35-28
17	16	Oklahoma State	6-3-0	beat # 14 Iowa State 42-21
	17	Penn State	7-3-0	
	18	Alabama	7-3-0	bye week
	19	Missouri	6-4-0	lost to Kansas 14-41
18	19	Rutgers	10-0-0	beat Colgate 17-9 N18
15		Tulsa	7-2-0	lost to Wichita St. 13-30
19		Brigham Young	8-2-0	beat Utah 34-12
19		Wyoming	8-2-0	lost to Air Force 21-41

November 22 Poll — Nov. 27 Games

UP	AP	Team	Record	Nov. 27 Games
1	1	Pittsburgh	10-0-0	beat # 16 Penn State 24-7 (N26)
3	2	Michigan	10-1-0	regular season complete
2	3	Southern Cal	9-1-0	beat # 13 Notre Dame 17-13
4	4	Georgia	9-1-0	beat Georgia Tech 13-10
5	5	Maryland	11-0-0	regular season complete
6	6	UCLA	9-1-1	regular season complete
7	7	Houston	7-2-0	beat Rice 42-20
13	8	Oklahoma	7-2-1	beat # 10 Nebraska 20-17 (N26)
10	9	Texas Tech	8-1-0	beat Arkansas 30-7
8	10	Nebraska	7-2-1	lost to # 8 Oklahoma 17-20 (N26)
12	11	Texas A&M	8-2-0	beat Texas 27-3 (N25)
9	12	Ohio State	8-2-1	regular season complete
11	13	Notre Dame	8-2-0	lost to # 3 Southern Cal 13-17
15	14	Oklahoma State	7-3-0	beat Texas-El Paso 42-13
20	16	Penn State	7-3-0	lost to # 1 Pittsburgh 7-24 (N26)
16	17	Rutgers	11-0-0	regular season complete
	18	Alabama	7-3-0	beat Auburn 38-7
	19	Mississippi State	9-2-0	regular season complete
	19	North Carolina	9-2-0	regular season complete
17		Brigham Young	9-2-0	regular season complete
18		Baylor	6-2-1	beat TCU 24-19
19		Florida	7-3-0	beat Miami, Fla. 19-10

November 29 Poll / Bowls

UP	AP	Team	Record	Bowl Bid	Date	Bowl Result
1	1	Pittsburgh	11-0-0	Sugar Bowl	J1	beat # 5 Georgia 27-3
2	2	Michigan	10-1-0	Rose Bowl	J1	lost to # 3 Southern Cal 6-14
3	3	Southern Cal	10-1-0	Rose Bowl	J1	beat # 2 Michigan 14-6
5	4	Maryland	11-0-0	Cotton Bowl	J1	lost to # 6 Houston 21-30
4	5	Georgia	10-1-0	Sugar Bowl	J1	lost to # 1 Pittsburgh 3-27
7	6	Houston	8-2-0	Cotton Bowl	J1	beat # 4 Maryland 30-21
6	7	UCLA	9-1-1	Liberty Bowl	D20	lost to # 16 Alabama 6-36
9	8	Oklahoma	8-2-1	Fiesta Bowl	D25	beat Wyoming 41-7
8	9	Texas Tech	9-1-0	Bluebonnet Bowl	D31	lost to # 13 Nebraska 24-27
10	10	Texas A&M	9-2-0	Sun Bowl	J2	beat Florida 37-14
10	11	Ohio State	8-2-1	Orange Bowl	J1	beat # 12 Colorado 27-10
12	12	Colorado	8-3-0	Orange Bowl	J1	lost to # 11 Ohio State 10-27
19	13	Nebraska	7-3-1	Bluebonnet Bowl	D31	beat # 9 Texas Tech 27-24
14	14	Oklahoma State	8-3-0	Tangerine Bowl	D18	beat Brigham Young 49-21
13	15	Notre Dame	8-3-0	Gator Bowl	D27	beat # 20 Penn State 20-9
15	16	Alabama	8-3-0	Liberty Bowl	D20	beat # 7 UCLA 36-6
15	17	Rutgers	11-0-0			
17	18	Baylor	7-2-1			
	19	North Carolina	9-2-0	Peach Bowl	D31	lost to Kentucky 0-21
	20	Mississippi State	9-2-0			
	20	Penn State	7-4-0	Gator Bowl	D27	lost to # 15 Notre Dame 9-20
17		Brigham Young	9-2-0	Tangerine Bowl	D18	lost to # 14 Oklahoma State 21-49
20		Florida	8-3-0	Sun Bowl	J2	lost to # 10 Texas A&M 14-37

January 4 Final Poll

RB	UP	AP	Team	Record
1	1	1	Pittsburgh	12-0-0
2	2	2	Southern Cal	11-1-0
4	3	3	Michigan	10-2-0
7	4	4	Houston	10-2-0
6	6	5	Oklahoma	9-2-1
3	5	6	Ohio State	9-2-1
9	8	7	Texas A&M	10-2-0
8	11	8	Maryland	11-1-0
12	7	9	Nebraska	9-3-1
5	10	10	Georgia	10-2-0
10	9	11	Alabama	9-3-0
16	12	12	Notre Dame	9-3-0
13	13	13	Texas Tech	10-2-0
14	14	14	Oklahoma State	9-3-0
11	15	15	UCLA	9-2-1
19	16	16	Colorado	8-4-0
17	17	17	Rutgers	11-0-0
20	19	18	Kentucky	8-4-0
22	18	19	Iowa State	8-3-0
21		20	Mississippi State	9-2-0
25	19		Baylor	7-3-1

1976

CONSENSUS ALL-AMERICANS

POS	Offense	HT	WT	School	AP	FC	FW	PI
QB	**Tommy Kramer**	6-2	190	Rice	•	•		•
RB	**Tony Dorsett**	5-11	192	Pittsburgh	•	•	•	•
RB	**Ricky Bell**	6-2	218	Southern Cal	•	•	•	•
RB	**Rob Lytle**	6-1	195	Michigan	•	•		•
SE	**Larry Seivers**	6-4	200	Tennessee	•	•	•	•
TE	**Ken MacAfee**	6-4	251	Notre Dame	•			•
T	**Mike Vaughan**	6-5	275	Oklahoma	•	•	•	•
T	**Chris Ward**	6-4	274	Ohio State		•		
G	**Joel Parrish**	6-3	232	Georgia	•	•		•
G	**Mark Donahue**	6-3	245	Michigan	•			•
C	**Derrel Gofourth**	6-2	250	Oklahoma State		•		•
PK	**Tony Franklin**	5-10	170	Texas A&M				•

OTHERS RECEIVING FIRST-TEAM HONORS

POS		School	AP	FC	FW	PI
QB	Gifford Nielsen	Brigham Young			•	
RB	Terry Miller	Oklahoma State				•
SE	Luther Blue	Iowa State			•	
T	Steve Schindler	Boston College			•	
T	Warren Bryant	Kentucky		•		
T	Mike Wilson	Georgia	•			
T	Ted Albrecht	California	•			
T	Marvin Powell	Southern Cal	•			
G	T.J. Humphreys	Arkansas State	•			
C	Billy Bryan	Duke				•
C	John Yarno	Idaho	•			
K	Steve Little	Arkansas				•
KR	Jim Smith	Michigan	•		•	

FC named Ward as a T; AP named Smith as a SE

POS	Defense	HT	WT	School	AP	FC	FW	PI
E	**Ross Browner**	6-3	248	Notre Dame	•	•	•	•
E	**Bob Brudzinski**	6-4	228	Ohio State	•			•
T	**Wilson Whitley**	6-3	268	Houston	•	•	•	•
T	**Gary Jeter**	6-5	255	Southern Cal	•			•
T	**Joe Campbell**	6-6	255	Maryland				•
MG	**Al Romano**	6-3	230	Pittsburgh	•	•		•
LB	**Robert Jackson**	6-2	228	Texas A&M	•	•		•
LB	**Jerry Robinson**	6-3	208	UCLA	•			•
B	**Bill Armstrong**	6-4	205	Wake Forest	•	•		•
B	**Gary Green**	5-11	182	Baylor	•	•		•
B	**Dennis Thurman**	5-11	170	Southern Cal	•	•		•
B	**Dave Butterfield**	5-10	182	Nebraska		•		•

OTHERS RECEIVING FIRST-TEAM HONORS

POS		School	AP	FC	FW	PI
DL	Eddie Edwards	Miami	•			
DL	Mike Fultz	Nebraska				•
DL	Duncan McColl	Stanford				•
LB	Thomas Howard	Texas Tech				•
LB	Brian Ruff	Citadel	•			
LB	Calvin O'Neal	Michigan				•
LB	Kurt Allerman	Penn State				•
B	Eric Harris	Memphis			•	
B	Oscar Edwards	UCLA	•			
P	Russell Erxleben	Texas			•	

HEISMAN TROPHY VOTING

	PLAYER	POS	SCHOOL	1ST	2ND	3RD	TOTAL
1	**Tony Dorsett**	RB	Pittsburgh	701	112	30	2357
2	**Ricky Bell**	TB	Southern Cal	73	485	157	1346
3	**Rob Lytle**	RB	Michigan	35	85	138	413
4	**Terry Miller**	RB	Oklahoma State	18	43	57	197
5	**Tommy Kramer**	QB	Rice	6	7	31	63
6	**Gifford Nielson**	QB	Brigham Young	1	7	28	45
7	**Ray Goff**	QB	Georgia	2	12	14	44
8	**Mike Voight**	RB	North Carolina	1	7	24	41
9	**Joe Roth**	QB	California	0	6	20	32
10	**Jeff Dankworth**	QB	UCLA	2	6	13	31

AWARD WINNERS

PLAYER	POS	SCHOOL	AWARD NAME
Tony Dorsett	RB	Pittsburgh	Maxwell
Ross Browner	DE	Notre Dame	Outland
Tony Dorsett	RB	Pittsburgh	Camp
Wilson Whitley	DT	Houston	Lombardi

CONFERENCE STANDINGS

ACC

	CONF. W L T			OVERALL W L T		
Maryland	5	0	0	11	1	0
North Carolina	4	1	0	9	3	0
Wake Forest	3	3	0	5	6	0
Duke	2	3	1	5	5	1
North Carolina St.	2	3	0	3	7	1
Virginia	1	3	0	2	9	0
Clemson	0	4	1	3	6	2

Big 10

	CONF. W L T			OVERALL W L T		
Michigan	7	1	0	10	2	0
Ohio State	7	1	0	9	2	1
Minnesota	4	4	0	6	5	0
Indiana	4	4	0	5	6	0
Illinois	4	4	0	5	6	0
Purdue	4	4	0	5	6	0
Wisconsin	3	5	0	5	6	0
Iowa	3	5	0	5	6	0
Michigan State	3	5	0	4	6	1
Northwestern	1	7	0	1	10	0

Big 8

	CONF. W L T			OVERALL W L T		
Oklahoma	5	2	0	9	2	1
Oklahoma State	5	2	0	9	3	0
Colorado	5	2	0	8	4	0
Nebraska	4	3	0	9	3	1
Iowa State	4	3	0	8	3	0
Missouri	3	4	0	6	5	0
Kansas	2	5	0	6	5	0
Kansas State	0	7	0	1	10	0

Big West

	CONF. W L T			OVERALL W L T		
San Jose State	4	0	0	7	4	0
Fresno State	3	1	0	5	6	0
Long Beach State	2	2	0	8	3	0
Cal-St. Fullerton	1	3	0	3	7	1
Pacific	0	4	0	2	9	0

Ivy

	CONF. W L T			OVERALL W L T		
Brown	6	1	0	8	1	0
Yale	6	1	0	8	1	0
Harvard	4	3	0	6	3	0
Dartmouth	4	3	0	6	3	0
Pennsylvania	2	5	0	3	6	0
Columbia	2	5	0	3	6	0
Cornell	2	5	0	2	7	0
Princeton	2	5	0	2	7	0

MAC

	CONF. W L T			OVERALL W L T		
Ball State	4	1	0	8	3	0
Kent State	6	2	0	8	4	0
Ohio U	6	2	0	7	4	0
Western Michigan	6	3	0	7	4	0
Central Michigan	4	3	0	7	4	0
Bowling Green	4	3	0	6	5	0
Miami, Ohio	2	4	0	3	8	0
Toledo	2	6	0	3	8	0
Eastern Michigan	1	5	0	2	9	0
Northern Illinois	0	6	0	1	10	0

PAC 8

	CONF. W L T			OVERALL W L T		
Southern Cal	7	0	0	11	1	0
UCLA	6	1	0	9	2	1
Stanford	5	2	0	6	5	0
California	3	4	0	5	6	0
Washington	3	4	0	5	6	0
Washington State	2	5	0	3	8	0
Oregon	1	6	0	4	7	0
Oregon State	1	6	0	2	10	0

SEC

	CONF. W L T			OVERALL W L T		
Georgia	5	1	0	10	2	0
Alabama	5	2	0	9	3	0
Mississippi State*	4	2	0	9	2	0
Florida	4	2	0	8	4	0
Kentucky	4	2	0	8	4	0
Mississippi	3	4	0	5	6	0
LSU	2	4	0	6	4	1
Tennessee	2	4	0	6	5	0
Auburn	2	4	0	3	8	0
Vanderbilt	0	6	0	2	9	0

*Later Forfeited to 0-6-0

SWC

	CONF. W L T			OVERALL W L T		
Houston	7	1	0	10	2	0
Texas Tech	7	1	0	10	2	0
Texas A&M	6	2	0	10	2	0
Baylor	4	3	1	7	3	1
Texas	4	4	0	5	5	1
Arkansas	3	4	1	5	5	1
SMU	2	6	0	3	8	0
Rice	2	6	0	3	8	0

WAC

	CONF. W L T			OVERALL W L T		
Arizona State	7	0	0	12	0	0
Arizona	5	2	0	9	2	0
Colorado State	4	2	0	6	5	0
New Mexico	4	3	0	6	5	0
Brigham Young	4	3	0	6	5	0
Utah	1	4	0	1	10	0
Wyoming	1	6	0	2	9	0
Texas-El Paso	0	6	0	1	10	0

Independents

	OVERALL W L T		
Pittsburgh	12	0	0
Rutgers	11	0	0
Notre Dame	9	3	0
Boston College	8	3	0
Memphis	7	4	0
Penn State	7	5	0
South Carolina	6	5	0
North Texas	6	5	0
Virginia Tech	6	5	0
West Virginia	5	6	0
Army	5	6	0
Florida State	5	6	0
Georgia Tech	4	6	1
Air Force	4	7	0
Navy	4	7	0
Syracuse	3	8	0
Utah State	3	8	0
Miami, Fla.	3	8	0
Tulane	2	9	0

BOWL GAMES

DATE	GAME	SCORE
D13	**Independence**	McNeese St. 20, Tulsa 16
D18	**Tangerine**	Oklahoma State 49, Brigham Young 21
D20	**Liberty**	Alabama 36, UCLA 6
D25	**Fiesta**	Oklahoma 41, Wyoming 7
D27	**Gator**	Notre Dame 20, Penn State 9
D31	**Peach**	Kentucky 21, North Carolina 0
D31	**Bluebonnet**	Nebraska 27, Texas Tech 24
J1	**Sugar**	Pittsburgh 27, Georgia 3
J1	**Cotton**	Houston 30, Maryland 21
J1	**Orange**	Ohio State 27, Colorado 10
J1	**Rose**	Southern Cal 14, Michigan 6
J2	**Sun**	Texas A&M 37, Florida 14

1976 NCAA Major College Statistical Leaders

Individual Leaders

PASSING	G	ATT	COM	PCT	INT	I%	YDS	YPA	TD	TD%	COM.PG
1 Tommy Kramer, Rice	11	501	269	53.7	19	3.8	3317	6.6	21	4.2	24.5
2 Jack Thompson, Washington State	11	355	208	58.6	14	3.9	2762	7.8	20	5.6	18.9
3 Guy Benjamin, Stanford	9	295	170	57.6	17	5.8	1982	6.7	12	4.1	18.9
4 Gifford Nielsen, Brigham Young	11	372	207	55.6	19	5.1	3192	8.6	29	7.8	18.8
5 Joe Roth, California	10	295	154	52.2	18	6.1	1789	6.1	7	2.4	15.4
6 Leamon Hall, Army	11	344	162	47.1	27	7.8	2174	6.3	15	4.4	14.7
7 Jack Henderson, Oregon	11	298	157	52.7	16	5.4	1582	5.3	6	2.0	14.3
8 Bob Graustein, Pennsylvania	9	230	127	55.2	16	7.0	1429	6.2	2	0.9	14.1
9 Ed Smith, Michigan State	10	257	132	51.4	10	3.9	1749	6.8	13	5.1	13.2
10 Dan Hagemann, Utah	9	222	117	52.7	14	6.3	1585	7.1	10	4.5	13.0

ALL-PURPOSE	G	RUSH	REC	PR	KR	YDS	YPG
1 Tony Dorsett, Pittsburgh	11	1948	73	0	0	2021	183.7
2 Arthur Whittington, SMU	11	789	145	209	700	1843	167.5
3 Jerome Persell, Western Michigan	10	1505	38	0	18	1561	156.1
4 Ricky Bell, Southern Cal	10	1417	85	0	0	1502	150.2
5 Terry Miller, Oklahoma State	11	1541	0	0	92	1633	148.5
6 Andre Herrera, Southern Illinois	11	1588	26	-6	0	1608	146.2
7 James Sykes, Rice	11	435	653	0	464	1552	141.1
8 Rob Lytle, Michigan	11	1402	81	0	26	1509	137.2
9 Al Hunter, Notre Dame	11	1058	189	1	241	1489	135.4
10 Anthony Anderson, Temple	10	803	174	0	367	1344	134.4

RUSHING/YARDS PER GAME	G	ATT	YDS	TD	AVG	YPG
1 Tony Dorsett, Pittsburgh	11	338	1948	21	5.8	177.1
2 Jerome Persell, Western Michigan	10	269	1505	19	5.6	150.5
3 Andre Herrera, Southern Ilinois	11	287	1588	16	5.5	144.4
4 Ricky Bell, Southern Cal	10	276	1417	14	5.1	141.7
5 Terry Miller, Oklahoma State	11	268	1541	19	5.8	140.1
6 Mike Voight, North Carolina	11	315	1407	18	4.5	127.9
7 Rob Lytle, Michigan	11	203	1402	13	6.9	127.5
8 Derrick Jensen, Texas-Arlington	11	233	1266	7	5.4	115.1
9 John Pagliaro, Yale	9	179	1023	16	5.7	113.7
10 Mike Williams, New Mexico	11	258	1240	9	4.8	112.7

RUSHING/YARDS PER CARRY	G	ATT	YDS	YPC
1 Leroy Harris, Arkansas State	11	150	1046	7.0
2 Rob Lytle, Michigan	11	203	1402	6.9
3 Laverne Smith, Kansas	11	148	978	6.6
4 Ben Cowins, Arkansas	11	183	1162	6.3
5 Tony Dorsett, Pittsburgh	11	338	1948	5.8
6 Terry Miller, Oklahoma State	11	268	1541	5.8
7 Jeff Logan, Ohio State	11	204	1169	5.7
8 John Pagliaro, Yale	9	179	1023	5.7
9 Jerome Persell, Western Michigan	10	269	1505	5.6
10 Andre Herrera, Southern Illinois	11	287	1588	5.5

*-Based on top 38 rushers

RECEIVING	G	REC	YDS	TD	YPR	YPG	RPG
1 Billy Ryckman, Louisiana Tech	11	77	1382	10	17.9	125.6	7.0
2 James Sykes, Rice	11	76	653	2	8.6	59.4	6.9
3 Mike Levenseller, Washington State	11	67	1124	8	16.8	102.2	6.1
4 Doug Cunningham, Rice	10	57	770	3	13.5	77.0	5.7
5 David Oliver, La. Lafayette	11	59	876	10	14.8	79.6	5.4
6 Keith Hartwig, Arizona	11	54	1134	10	21.0	103.1	4.9
7 Tony Hill, Stanford	9	44	696	8	15.8	77.3	4.9
8 Greg Bauer, Oregon	11	53	632	2	11.9	57.5	4.8
8 Dan Doornink, Washington State	11	53	469	3	8.8	42.6	4.8
10 Jeff Gowan, Illinois State	10	48	696	1	14.5	69.6	4.8

PUNTING	PUNT	YDS	AVG
1 Russell Erxleben, Texas	61	2842	46.6
2 Johnny Evans, North Carolina St.	47	2168	46.1
3 Mike Deutsch, Colorado State	68	3134	46.1
4 Russ Henderson, Virginia	69	3168	45.9
5 Larry Swider, Pittsburgh	58	2600	44.8
6 Frank Corrall, UCLA	42	1874	44.6
7 Steve Little, Arkansas	63	2797	44.4
8 Joe Parker, Appalachian State	50	2210	44.2
9 Don Fechtman, North Texas	54	2381	44.1
10 Cliff Parsley, Oklahoma State	61	2666	43.7

PUNT RETURNS	PUNT	YDS	TD	AVG
1 Henry Jenkins, Rutgers	30	449	0	15.0
2 Keith Wright, Memphis	16	228	2	14.2
3 Will Mosley, Northwestern State	14	196	1	14.0
4 Preston Brown, Vanderbilt	16	213	1	13.3
5 Michael Coulter, UCLA	14	179	0	12.8
6 John Harris, Arizona State	15	188	1	12.5
7 Jim Smith, Michigan	15	313	0	12.5
8 Rick Morrison, Ball State	19	234	0	12.3
9 Stan Black, Mississippi State	16	196	0	12.2
10 Rich Mauti, Penn State	17	208	0	12.2

KICKOFF RETURNS	KR	YDS	TD	AVG
1 Ira Matthews, Wisconsin	14	415	2	29.6
2 Drew Hill, Georgia Tech	20	546	0	27.3
3 James Sykes, Rice	18	464	1	25.8
4 Billy Waddy, Colorado	22	566	1	25.7
5 Bruce Montagner, Indiana State	17	437	1	25.7
6 Steve Kuehl, Bowling Green	14	359	0	25.6
7 Art Gore, Duke	22	563	0	25.6
8 Robert Taylor, Idaho	16	401	1	25.1
9 Robert Dow, LSU	20	499	0	24.9
10 Luther Blue, Iowa State	14	349	1	24.9

SCORING	TDS	XPT	FG	PTS	PTPG
1 Tony Dorsett, Pittsburgh	22	2	0	134	12.2
2 Jerome Persell, Western Michigan	19	4	0	118	11.8
3 John Pagliaro, Yale	16	0	0	96	10.7
4 Terry Miller, Oklahoma State	19	0	0	114	10.4
5 Mike Voight, North Carolina	18	2	0	110	10.0
6 Pete Johnson, Ohio State	18	0	0	108	9.8
7 Arry Moody, Louisiana Tech	17	4	0	106	9.6
8 George Woodard, Texas A&M	17	0	0	102	9.3
9 Andre Herrera, Southern Illinois	16	2	0	98	8.9
10 Ricky Bell, Southern Cal	14	2	0	86	8.6

FIELD GOALS	FGA	FGM	PCT	FGG
1 Tony Franklin, Texas A&M	26	17	0.65	1.55
2 Craig Jones, VMI	18	15	0.83	1.50
3 Carson Long, Pittsburgh	23	16	0.70	1.45
3 Jim Breech, California	24	16	0.67	1.45
5 Brian Hall, Texas Tech	20	15	0.75	1.36
5 Dave Taylor, Brigham Young	29	15	0.52	1.36
7 Paul Marchese, Kent State	25	16	0.64	1.33
8 Pete Conaty, East Carolina	23	14	0.61	1.27
8 Rade Savich, Central Michigan	24	14	0.58	1.27
8 Tom Drake, Colorado State	27	14	0.52	1.27

INTERCEPTIONS	INT	YDS	TD	INT/GM
1 Anthony Francis, Houston	10	118	0	0.91
2 Bob Jury, Pittsburgh	9	105	0	0.82
3 Dennis Thurman, Southern Cal	8	170	1	0.73
3 Jeff Nixon, Richmond	8	132	0	0.73
3 Lester Hayes, Texas A&M	8	87	0	0.73
3 Ron Irving, La. Lafayette	8	26	1	0.73
7 Scott Erdmann, Wisconsin	7	143	1	0.64
7 John Harris, Arizona State	7	130	1	0.64
7 Mark Wood, Drake	7	98	0	0.64
7 Mike Galpin, Navy	7	87	0	0.64

Team Leaders

RUSHING OFFENSE	G	ATT	YDS	AVG	TD	YPG
1 Michigan	11	661	3989	6.0	42	362.6
2 UCLA	11	691	3755	5.4	41	341.4
3 Oklahoma	11	657	3540	5.4	33	321.8
4 Kansas	11	701	3271	4.7	29	297.4
5 East Carolina	11	734	3263	4.4	28	296.6
6 Yale	9	564	2658	4.7	24	295.3
7 Pittsburgh	11	671	3198	4.8	32	290.7
8 Texas Arlington	11	636	3153	5.0	26	286.6
9 Western Michigan	11	677	3136	4.6	32	285.1
10 Oklahoma State	11	672	3085	4.6	31	280.5

PASSING OFFENSE	G	ATT	COM	INT	PCT	YDS	YPA	TD	I%	YPC	YPG
1 Brigham Young	11	403	223	19	55.3	3386	8.4	31	4.7	15.2	307.8
2 Rice	11	504	270	19	53.6	3337	6.6	21	3.8	12.4	303.4
3 Washington State	11	442	250	22	56.6	3265	7.4	21	5.0	13.1	296.8
4 Louisiana Tech	11	307	159	19	51.8	2697	8.8	22	6.2	17.0	245.2
5 Stanford	11	408	223	23	54.7	2669	6.5	16	5.6	12.0	242.6
6 Utah	11	368	187	21	50.8	2603	7.1	14	5.7	13.9	236.6
7 San Jose State	11	323	178	11	55.1	2579	8.0	23	3.4	14.5	234.5
8 California	11	385	205	21	53.2	2365	6.1	10	5.5	11.5	215.0
9 Michigan State	11	337	171	13	50.7	2322	6.9	17	3.9	13.6	211.1
10 Arizona State	11	326	153	18	46.9	2304	7.1	16	5.5	15.1	209.5

TOTAL OFFENSE	G	P	YDS	AVG	TD	YPG
1 Michigan	11	760	4929	6.5	55	448.1
2 Iowa State	11	889	4836	5.4	47	439.6
3 Southern Cal	11	802	4757	5.9	49	432.5
4 UCLA	11	836	4690	5.6	48	426.4
5 San Jose State	11	781	4682	6.0	46	425.6
6 Brigham Young	11	857	4668	5.4	44	424.4
7 Louisiana Tech	11	818	4560	5.6	46	414.5
8 Houston	11	853	4555	5.3	41	414.1
9 Nebraska	12	913	4894	5.4	50	407.8
10 Bowling Green	11	890	4425	5.0	38	402.3

RUSHING DEFENSE	G	ATT	YDS	AVG	TD	YPG
1 Rutgers	11	407	923	2.3	4	83.9
2 Texas A&M	11	457	1064	2.3	7	96.7
3 Yale	9	362	966	2.7	6	107.3
4 Pittsburgh	11	495	1243	2.5	7	113.0
5 Michigan	11	457	1254	2.7	6	114.0
6 Maryland	11	466	1284	2.8	7	116.7
7 Notre Dame	11	483	1324	2.7	10	120.4
8 East Carolina	11	493	1353	2.7	10	123.0
9 Cincinnati	11	510	1367	2.7	10	124.3
10 Dartmouth	9	406	1138	2.8	7	126.4

PASSING DEFENSE	G	ATT	COM	PCT	YPC	INT	I%	YDS	YPA	TD	YPG
1 Western Michigan	11	175	74	42.3	11.7	10	5.7	863	4.9	6	78.5
2 Lamar	11	151	65	43.0	13.3	12	7.9	866	5.7	7	78.7
3 Vanderbilt	11	155	72	46.5	12.4	9	5.8	892	5.8	6	81.1
4 VMI	10	151	70	46.4	11.9	9	6.0	835	5.5	3	83.5
5 Ohio U	11	196	70	35.7	13.2	15	7.7	921	4.7	9	83.7
6 William & Mary	11	177	75	42.4	12.5	14	7.9	936	5.3	5	85.1
7 Florida State	11	135	68	50.4	14.0	5	3.7	949	7.0	7	86.3
8 Furman	11	174	68	39.1	14.2	10	5.7	965	5.5	8	87.7
9 Indiana State	10	129	65	50.4	13.5	8	6.2	880	6.8	5	88.0
10 Illinois State	11	173	71	41.0	13.7	9	5.2	970	5.6	6	88.2

TOTAL DEFENSE	G	P	YDS	AVG	TD	YPG
1 Rutgers	11	629	1971	3.1	9	179.2
2 Maryland	11	666	2321	3.5	11	211.0
3 East Carolina	11	712	2355	3.3	12	214.1
4 Texas A&M	11	722	2356	3.3	16	214.2
5 Yale	9	557	2034	3.7	9	226.0
6 Pittsburgh	11	726	2519	3.5	15	229.0
7 LSU	11	702	2564	3.7	19	233.1
8 Colgate	10	692	2407	3.5	17	240.7
9 Long Beach State	11	715	2649	3.7	14	240.8
10 Michigan	11	721	2666	3.7	10	242.4

SCORING OFFENSE	G	PTS	AVG
1 Michigan	11	426	38.7
2 UCLA	11	385	35.0
3 Southern Cal	11	372	33.8
4 Iowa State	11	369	33.5
5 Nebraska	12	389	32.4
6 Pittsburgh	11	354	32.2
6 San Jose State	11	354	32.2
8 Brigham Young	11	351	31.9
9 Louisiana Tech	11	336	30.5
10 Texas A&M	11	327	29.7

SCORING DEFENSE	G	PTS	AVG
1 Rutgers	11	81	7.4
1 Michigan	11	81	7.4
3 Maryland	11	85	7.7
4 Yale	9	77	8.6
5 Cincinnati	11	114	10.4
6 East Carolina	11	116	10.5
7 Georgia	11	118	10.7
8 Ball State	11	124	11.3
9 Brown	9	102	11.3
10 San Diego State	11	125	11.4

1977 POLL PROGRESSION

PRE-SEASON | SEPT. 10 GAMES

AP	Team	Record	SEPT. 10 GAMES
1	Oklahoma	0-0-0	beat Vanderbilt 25-23
2	Michigan	0-0-0	beat Illinois 37-9
3	Notre Dame	0-0-0	beat # 7 Pittsburgh 19-9
4	Southern Cal	0-0-0	beat Missouri 27-10
5	Ohio State	0-0-0	beat Miami, Fla. 10-0
6	Alabama	0-0-0	beat Mississippi 34-13
7	Pittsburgh	0-0-0	lost to # 3 Notre Dame 9-19
8	Texas Tech	0-0-0	beat Baylor 17-7
9	Texas A&M	0-0-0	beat Kansas 28-14
10	Maryland	0-0-0	beat Clemson 21-14
11	UCLA	0-0-0	lost to # 14 Houston 13-17
12	Colorado	0-0-0	beat Stanford 27-21
13	Penn State	0-0-0	bye week
14	Houston	0-0-0	beat # 11 UCLA 17-13
15	Nebraska	0-0-0	lost to Washington St. 10-19
16	Mississippi State	0-0-0	beat Washington 27-18
17	Arizona State	0-0-0	bye week
18	Florida	0-0-0	bye week
19	Georgia	0-0-0	beat Oregon 27-16
20	Oklahoma State	0-0-0	beat Tulsa 34-17

SEPTEMBER 12 POLL | SEPT. 17 GAMES

UP	AP	Team	Record	SEPT. 17 GAMES
1	1	Michigan	1-0-0	beat Duke 21-9
2	2	Southern Cal	1-0-0	beat Oregon State 17-10
4	3	Notre Dame	1-0-0	lost to Mississippi 13-20
3	4	Alabama	1-0-0	lost to Nebraska 24-31
6	5	Oklahoma	1-0-0	beat Utah 62-24
5	6	Ohio State	1-0-0	beat Minnesota 38-7
7	7	Texas A&M	1-0-0	beat Virginia Tech 27-6
8	8	Texas Tech	1-0-0	beat New Mexico 49-14
12	9	Houston	1-0-0	lost to # 10 Penn State 14-31
9	10	Penn State	1-0-0	beat # 9 Houston 31-14
10	11	Maryland	1-0-0	lost to West Virginia 16-24
11	12	Colorado	1-0-0	beat Kent State 42-0
	13	Mississippi State	2-0-0	bye week
13	14	UCLA	0-1-0	beat Kansas 17-7
19	15	Oklahoma State	1-0-0	lost to Arkansas 6-28
16	16	Pittsburgh	0-1-0	beat William & Mary 28-6
17	17	Georgia	1-0-0	lost to Clemson 6-7
13	18	Texas	1-0-0	beat Virginia 68-0
15	19	Florida	0-0-0	beat Rice 48-3
17	20	Brigham Young	1-0-0	bye week
18		South Carolina	2-0-0	beat Miami, Ohio 42-19
19		Iowa State	1-0-0	lost to Iowa 10-12

SEPTEMBER 19 POLL | SEPT. 24 GAMES

UP	AP	Team	Record	SEPT. 24 GAMES
1	1	Michigan	2-0-0	beat Navy 14-7
2	2	Southern Cal	2-0-0	beat TCU 51-0
4	3	Oklahoma	2-0-0	beat # 4 Ohio State 29-28
3	4	Ohio State	2-0-0	lost to # 3 Oklahoma 28-29
5	5	Penn State	2-0-0	beat Maryland 27-9
7	6	Texas A&M	2-0-0	beat # 7 Texas Tech 33-17
6	7	Texas Tech	2-0-0	lost to # 6 Texas A&M 17-33
8	8	Colorado	2-0-0	beat New Mexico 42-7
9	9	Texas	2-0-0	bye week
12	10	Alabama	1-1-0	beat Vanderbilt 24-12
14	11	Notre Dame	1-1-0	beat Purdue 31-24
16	12	Mississippi State	2-0-0	lost to Florida 22-24
10	13	Florida	1-0-0	beat Mississippi State 24-22
11	14	Nebraska	1-1-0	beat Baylor 31-10
13	15	Washington State	2-0-0	lost to Kansas 12-14
15	16	Arkansas	2-0-0	beat Tulsa 37-3
20	17	West Virginia	2-0-0	lost to Kentucky 13-28
	18	UCLA	1-1-0	lost to Minnesota 13-27
`	19	Houston	1-1-0	beat Utah 34-16
17	20	Brigham Young	1-0-0	beat Utah State 65-6
17		Pittsburgh	1-1-0	beat Temple 76-0
19		Oklahoma State	1-1-0	beat Texas-El Paso 54-0

SEPTEMBER 26 POLL | OCT 1 GAMES

UP	AP	Team	Record	OCT 1 GAMES
2	1	Oklahoma	3-0-0	beat Kansas 24-9
1	2	Southern Cal	3-0-0	beat Washington State 41-7 (S30)
3	3	Michigan	3-0-0	beat # 5 Texas A&M 41-3
4	4	Penn State	3-0-0	lost to Kentucky 20-24
5	5	Texas A&M	3-0-0	lost to # 3 Michigan 3-41
7	6	Ohio State	2-1-0	beat SMU 35-7
6	7	Colorado	3-0-0	beat Army 31-0
8	8	Texas	2-0-0	beat Rice 72-15
9	9	Florida	2-0-0	lost to LSU 14-36
12	10	Alabama	2-1-0	beat Georgia 18-10
10	11	Nebraska	2-1-0	beat Indiana 31-13
11	12	Arkansas	3-0-0	beat TCU 42-6
19	13	Texas Tech	2-1-0	beat North Carolina 10-7
15	14	Notre Dame	2-1-0	beat Michigan State 16-6
14	15	Brigham Young	2-0-0	beat New Mexico 54-19 (S30)
13	16	Pittsburgh	2-1-0	beat Boston College 45-7
16	17	California	2-1-0	beat San Jose State 52-3
	18	Mississippi State	2-1-0	beat Kansas State 24-21
17	19	Houston	2-1-0	beat Baylor 28-24
18	20	Arizona State	2-0-0	lost to Missouri 0-15
20		Wisconsin	3-0-0	beat Northwestern 19-7

OCTOBER 3 POLL | OCT. 8 GAMES

UP	AP	Team	Record	OCT. 8 GAMES
1	1	Southern Cal	4-0-0	lost to # 7 Alabama 20-21
3	2	Oklahoma	4-0-0	lost to # 5 Texas 6-13
2	3	Michigan	4-0-0	beat Michigan State 24-14
6	4	Ohio State	3-1-0	beat Purdue 46-0
4	5	Texas	3-0-0	beat # 2 Oklahoma 13-6
5	6	Colorado	4-0-0	beat Oklahoma State 29-13
8	7	Alabama	3-1-0	beat # 1 Southern Cal 21-20
9	7	Arkansas	4-0-0	bye week
7	9	Nebraska	3-1-0	beat Kansas State 26-9
11	10	Penn State	3-1-0	beat Utah State 16-7
13	11	Notre Dame	3-1-0	bye week
17	12	Texas A&M	3-1-0	bye week
12	13	Brigham Young	3-0-0	lost to Colorado State 19-24
14	14	California	4-0-0	lost to Washington State 10-17
14	15	Pittsburgh	3-1-0	tied # 20 Florida 17-17
PB	16	Kentucky	3-1-0	beat Mississippi State 23-7
16	17	Texas Tech	3-1-0	beat Arizona 32-26
19	18	LSU	2-1-0	beat Vanderbilt 28-15
20	19	Wisconsin	4-0-0	beat Illinois 26-0
18	20	Florida	2-1-0	tied # 15 Pittsburgh 17-17
15		Houston	3-1-0	bye week

OCTOBER 10 POLL | OCT. 15 GAMES

UP	AP	Team	Record	OCT. 15 GAMES
1	1	Michigan	5-0-0	beat # 14 Wisconsin 56-0
2	2	Texas	5-0-0	beat # 8 Arkansas 13-9
3	3	Colorado	5-0-0	tied Kansas 17-17
4	4	Alabama	4-1-0	beat Tennessee 24-10
5	5	Ohio State	4-1-0	beat Iowa 27-6
7	6	Southern Cal	4-1-0	beat Oregon 33-15
6	7	Oklahoma	4-1-0	beat Missouri 21-17
8	8	Arkansas	4-0-0	lost to # 2 Texas 9-13
9	9	Nebraska	4-1-0	lost to Iowa State 21-24
10	10	Penn State	4-1-0	beat Syracuse 31-24
12	11	Notre Dame	3-1-0	beat Army 24-0
PB	12	Kentucky	4-1-0	beat # 16 LSU 33-13
14	13	Texas A&M	3-1-0	beat Baylor 38-31
14	14	Wisconsin	5-0-0	lost to # 1 Michigan 0-56
15	15	Texas Tech	4-1-0	beat Rice 42-7
11	16	LSU	3-1-0	lost to # 12 Kentucky 13-33
12	17	Pittsburgh	3-1-1	beat Navy 34-17
	18	Florida	2-1-1	bye week
17	19	Houston	3-1-0	lost to SMU 23-37
20		California	4-1-0	beat Oregon State 41-17
18		North Texas	5-1-0	beat Texas-Arlington 15-6
18		Brigham Young	3-1-0	beat Colorado State 63-17
20		North Carolina St.	5-1-0	lost to North Carolina 14-27

OCTOBER 17 POLL | OCT. 22 GAMES

UP	AP	Team	Record	OCT. 22 GAMES
1	1	Michigan	6-0-0	lost to Minnesota 0-16
2	2	Texas	5-0-0	beat SMU 30-14
3	3	Alabama	5-1-0	beat Louisville 55-6
5	4	Ohio State	5-1-0	beat Northwestern 35-15
4	5	Southern Cal	5-1-0	lost to # 11 Notre Dame 19-49
6	6	Oklahoma	5-1-0	beat # 16 Iowa State 35-16
7	7	Colorado	5-0-1	lost to # 18 Nebraska 15-33
PB	8	Kentucky	5-1-0	beat Georgia 33-0
8	9	Arkansas	4-1-0	beat Houston 34-0
9	10	Penn State	5-1-0	beat West Virginia 49-28
10	11	Notre Dame	4-1-0	beat # 5 Southern Cal 49-19
11	12	Texas A&M	4-1-0	beat Rice 28-14
13	13	Texas Tech	5-1-0	bye week
12	14	Pittsburgh	4-1-1	beat Syracuse 28-21
14	15	California	5-1-0	lost to UCLA 19-21
18	16	Iowa State	5-1-0	lost to # 6 Oklahoma 16-35
15	17	Brigham Young	4-1-0	beat Wyoming 10-7
17	18	Nebraska	4-2-0	beat # 7 Colorado 33-15
	19	Florida	2-1-1	beat Tennessee 27-17
19	20	Clemson	5-1-0	beat North Carolina St. 7-3
16		North Texas	6-1-0	beat Memphis 20-19
20		Arizona State	4-1-0	beat Texas-El Paso 66-3

OCTOBER 24 POLL | OCT. 29 GAMES

UP	AP	Team	Record	OCT. 29 GAMES
1	1	Texas	6-0-0	beat # 14 Texas Tech 26-0
2	2	Alabama	6-1-0	beat Mississippi State 37-7
4	3	Ohio State	6-1-0	beat Wisconsin 42-0
3	4	Oklahoma	6-1-0	beat Kansas State 42-7
5	5	Notre Dame	5-1-0	beat Navy 43-10
6	6	Michigan	6-1-0	beat Iowa 23-6
PB	7	Kentucky	6-1-0	beat Virginia Tech 32-0
7	8	Arkansas	5-1-0	beat Rice 30-7
8	9	Penn State	6-1-0	beat Miami, Fla. 49-7
11	10	Southern Cal	5-2-0	lost to California 14-17
9	11	Texas A&M	5-1-0	beat SMU 38-21
10	12	Nebraska	5-2-0	beat Oklahoma State 31-14
12	13	Pittsburgh	5-1-1	beat Tulane 48-0
13	14	Texas Tech	5-1-0	lost to # 1 Texas 0-26
14	15	Colorado	5-1-1	lost to Missouri 14-24
16	16	Clemson	6-1-0	beat Wake Forest 26-0
15	17	Brigham Young	5-1-0	beat Arizona 34-14
	18	Florida	3-1-1	lost to Auburn 14-29
	19	Minnesota	5-2-0	lost to Indiana 22-34
	20	Florida State	5-1-0	beat North Texas 35-14
16		North Texas	7-1-0	lost to # 20 Florida State 14-35
18		Oklahoma State	4-3-0	lost to # 12 Nebraska 14-31
19		Iowa State	5-2-0	beat Kansas 41-3
20		Arizona State	5-1-0	beat Utah 47-19

OCTOBER 31 POLL | NOV. 5 GAMES

UP	AP	Team	Record	NOV. 5 GAMES
1	1	Texas	7-0-0	beat Houston 35-21
2	2	Alabama	7-1-0	beat # 18 LSU 24-3
3	3	Oklahoma	7-1-0	beat Oklahoma State 61-28
4	4	Ohio State	7-1-0	beat Illinois 35-0
5	5	Notre Dame	6-1-0	beat Georgia Tech 69-14
6	6	Michigan	7-1-0	beat Northwestern 63-20
PB	7	Kentucky	7-1-0	beat Vanderbilt 28-6
8	8	Arkansas	6-1-0	beat Baylor 35-9
7	9	Penn State	7-1-0	beat North Carolina St. 21-17
11	10	Texas A&M	6-1-0	bye week
10	11	Nebraska	6-2-0	beat Missouri 21-10
9	12	Pittsburgh	6-1-1	beat West Virginia 44-3
13	13	Clemson	7-1-0	tied North Carolina 13-13
12	14	Brigham Young	6-1-0	beat Utah 38-8
15	15	Florida State	6-1-0	beat Virginia Tech 23-21
	16	Southern Cal	5-3-0	beat Stanford 49-0
17	17	California	6-2-0	lost to Washington 31-50
	18	LSU	5-2-0	lost to # 2 Alabama 3-24
16	19	Arizona State	6-1-0	beat Wyoming 45-0
19		Iowa State	6-2-0	lost to Colorado 7-12
18		Stanford	6-2-0	lost to # 16 Southern Cal 0-49
19		North Carolina St.	6-3-0	lost to # 9 Penn State 17-21
20		North Texas	7-2-0	beat New Mexico State 45-17

November 7 Poll — Nov. 12 Games

UP	AP	Team	Record	Result
1	1	Texas	8-0-0	beat TCU 44-14
2	2	Alabama	8-1-0	beat Miami, Fla. 36-0
3	3	Oklahoma	8-1-0	beat Colorado 52-14
4	4	Ohio State	8-1-0	beat Indiana 35-7
5	5	Notre Dame	7-1-0	beat #15 Clemson 21-17
6	6	Michigan	8-1-0	beat Purdue 40-7
PB	7	Kentucky	8-1-0	beat Florida 14-7
7	8	Arkansas	7-1-0	beat #11 Texas A&M 26-20
8	9	Penn State	8-1-0	beat Temple 44-7
9	10	Pittsburgh	7-1-1	beat Army 52-26
11	11	Texas A&M	6-1-0	lost to #8 Arkansas 20-26
10	12	Nebraska	7-2-0	beat Kansas 52-7
12	13	Brigham Young	7-1-0	lost to Arizona State 13-24
14	14	Southern Cal	6-3-0	lost to Washington 10-28
16	15	Clemson	7-1-1	lost to #5 Notre Dame 17-21
16	16	Florida State	7-1-0	beat Memphis 30-9
13	17	Arizona State	7-1-0	beat Brigham Young 24-13
	18	Texas Tech	6-2-0	beat SMU 45-7
	19	North Carolina	6-2-1	beat Virginia 35-14
	20	Colgate	9-0-0	
15		Colorado	6-2-1	lost to #3 Oklahoma 14-52
18		North Texas	8-2-0	bye week

November 14 Poll — Nov. 19 Games

UP	AP	Team	Record	Result
1	1	Texas	9-0-0	beat Baylor 29-7
3	2	Alabama	9-1-0	bye week
2	3	Oklahoma	9-1-0	bye week
4	4	Ohio State	9-1-0	lost to #5 Michigan 6-14
5	5	Michigan	9-1-0	beat #4 Ohio State 14-6
6	6	Notre Dame	8-1-0	beat Air Force 49-0
PB	7	Kentucky	9-1-0	beat Tennessee 21-17
7	8	Arkansas	8-1-0	beat SMU 47-7
8	9	Penn State	9-1-0	beat #10 Pittsburgh 15-13
9	10	Pittsburgh	8-1-1	lost to #9 Penn State 13-15
10	11	Nebraska	8-2-0	bye week
11	12	Arizona State	8-1-0	lost to Colorado State 14-25
13	13	Florida State	8-1-0	lost to San Diego State 16-41
12	14	Texas A&M	6-2-0	beat TCU 52-23
15	15	Clemson	7-2-1	beat South Carolina 31-27
16	16	Texas Tech	7-2-0	lost to Houston 7-45
	17	Brigham Young	7-2-0	beat Long Beach State 30-27
16	18	North Carolina	7-2-1	beat Duke 16-3
	19	Washington	6-4-0	beat Washington St. 35-15
16	20	UCLA	7-3-0	bye week
14		North Texas	8-2-0	beat Louisiana Tech 41-14
19		Iowa State	7-3-0	beat Oklahoma State 21-13

November 21 Poll — Nov. 26 Games

UP	AP	Team	Record	Result
1	1	Texas	10-0-0	beat #12 Texas A&M 57-28
3	2	Alabama	9-1-0	beat Auburn 48-21
2	3	Oklahoma	9-1-0	beat #11 Nebraska 38-7 (N25)
4	4	Michigan	10-1-0	regular season complete
5	5	Notre Dame	9-1-0	bye week
6	6	Arkansas	9-1-0	beat Texas Tech 17-14
PB	7	Kentucky	10-1-0	regular season complete
7	8	Ohio State	9-2-0	regular season complete
8	9	Penn State	9-1-0	regular season complete
9	10	Pittsburgh	8-1-1	regular season complete
10	11	Nebraska	8-2-0	lost to #3 Oklahoma 7-38 (N25)
11	12	Texas A&M	7-2-0	lost to #1 Texas 28-57
14	13	Clemson	8-2-1	regular season complete
16	14	Washington	7-4-0	regular season complete
15	15	North Carolina	8-2-1	regular season complete
	16	San Diego State	9-1-0	beat San Jose State 37-34
17	17	UCLA	7-3-0	lost to Southern Cal 27-29 (N25)
18	18	Brigham Young	8-2-0	beat Texas-El Paso 68-19
	19	Arizona State	8-2-0	beat Arizona 23-7
	20	Florida State	8-2-0	bye week
12		Iowa State	8-3-0	regular season complete
13		North Texas	9-2-0	regular season complete
19		Colorado State	8-2-1	beat Utah State 13-10
20		Stanford	8-3-0	regular season complete

November 28 Poll

UP	AP	Team	Record	Bowl Bid	Date	Bowl Result
1	1	Texas	11-0-0	Cotton Bowl	J2	lost to #5 Notre Dame 10-38
2	2	Oklahoma	10-1-0	Orange Bowl	J2	lost to #6 Arkansas 6-31
3	3	Alabama	10-1-0	Sugar Bowl	J2	beat #9 Ohio State 35-6
4	4	Michigan	10-1-0	Rose Bowl	J2	lost to #13 Washington 20-27
5	5	Notre Dame	9-1-0	Cotton Bowl	J2	beat #1 Texas 38-10
6	6	Arkansas	10-1-0	Orange Bowl	J2	beat #2 Oklahoma 31-6
PB	7	Kentucky	10-1-0			
7	8	Penn State	10-1-0	Fiesta Bowl	D25	beat #15 Arizona State 42-30
8	9	Ohio State	9-2-0	Sugar Bowl	J2	lost to #3 Alabama 6-35
9	10	Pittsburgh	8-2-1	Gator Bowl	D30	beat #11 Clemson 34-3
10	11	Clemson	8-2-1	Gator Bowl	D30	lost to #10 Pittsburgh 3-34
13	12	Nebraska	8-3-0	Liberty Bowl	D19	beat #14 North Carolina 21-17
14	13	Washington	7-4-0	Rose Bowl	J2	beat #4 Michigan 27-20
11	14	North Carolina	8-2-1	Liberty Bowl	D19	lost to #12 Nebraska 17-21
12	15	Arizona State	9-2-0	Fiesta Bowl	D25	lost to #8 Penn State 30-42
18	16	San Diego State	10-1-0			
14	17	Brigham Young	9-2-0			
18	18	Texas A&M	7-3-0	Bluebonnet Bowl	D31	lost to #20 Southern Cal 28-47
	19	Florida State	8-2-0	Tangerine Bowl	D23	beat Texas Tech 40-17
20	20	Southern Cal	7-4-0	Bluebonnet Bowl	D31	beat #17 Texas A&M 47-28
14		Iowa State	8-3-0	Peach Bowl	D31	lost to North Carolina St.
17		North Texas	9-2-0			

January 3 Final Poll

RB	UP	AP	Team	Record
1	1	1	Notre Dame	11-1-0
3	2	2	Alabama	11-1-0
6	3	3	Arkansas	11-1-0
2	5	4	Texas	11-1-0
5	4	5	Penn State	11-1-0
4	PB	6	Kentucky	10-1-0
7	6	7	Oklahoma	10-2-0
10	7	8	Pittsburgh	9-2-1
8	8	9	Michigan	10-2-0
14	9	10	Washington	8-4-0
9	12	11	Ohio State	9-3-0
13	10	12	Nebraska	9-3-0
11	12	13	Southern Cal	8-4-0
16	11	14	Florida State	10-2-0
21	15	15	Stanford	9-3-0
NR	19	16	San Diego State	10-1-0
22	14	17	North Carolina	8-3-1
35	18	18	Arizona State	9-3-0
19		19	Clemson	8-3-1
28	16	20	Brigham Young	9-2-0
36	16		North Texas	9-2-0
30	19		North Carolina St.	8-4-0

1977

CONSENSUS ALL-AMERICANS

Offense

POS	Offense	HT	WT	School	AP	FC	FW	PI
QB	Guy Benjamin	6-4	202	Stanford			•	•
RB	Earl Campbell	6-1	220	Texas	•	•	•	•
RB	Terry Miller	6-0	196	Oklahoma State	•	•	•	•
RB	Charles Alexander	6-1	215	LSU		•	•	•
WR	John Jefferson	6-1	184	Arizona State	•		•	•
WR	Ozzie Newsome	6-4	210	Alabama	•	•	•	•
TE	Ken MacAfee	6-4	250	Notre Dame	•	•	•	•
T	Chris Ward	6-4	272	Ohio State	•	•	•	•
T	Dan Irons	6-7	260	Texas Tech	•	•	•	
G	Mark Donahue	6-3	245	Michigan	•	•	•	
G	Leotis Harris	6-1	254	Arkansas	•	•	•	
C	Tom Brzoza	6-3	240	Pittsburgh	•	•	•	
PK	Steve Little	6-0	179	Arkansas	•			

Others receiving first-team honors

POS		School				PI
QB	Matt Cavanaugh	Pittsburgh				•
QB	Doug Williams	Grambling				•
WR	Wes Chandler	Florida				•
T	Joe Bostic	Clemson			•	
T	Keith Dorney	Penn State			•	
T	Dennis Baker	Wyoming			•	
C	Tom Davis	Nebraska			•	
C	Walt Downing	Michigan			•	

FC named Jefferson as a RB

Defense

POS	Defense	HT	WT	School	AP	FC	FW	PI
L	Ross Browner	6-3	247	Notre Dame	•	•	•	•
L	Art Still	6-8	247	Kentucky	•	•	•	•
L	Brad Shearer	6-4	255	Texas	•	•	•	•
L	Randy Holloway	6-6	228	Pittsburgh	•	•	•	•
L	Dee Hardison	6-4	252	North Carolina	•		•	
LB	Jerry Robinson	6-3	208	UCLA	•	•	•	•
LB	Tom Cousineau	6-3	228	Ohio State	•		•	•
LB	Gary Spani	6-2	222	Kansas State	•		•	
B	Dennis Thurman	5-11	173	Southern Cal	•	•	•	•
B	Zac Henderson	6-1	184	Oklahoma	•	•	•	•
B	Luther Bradley	6-2	204	Notre Dame	•	•	•	
B	Bob Jury	6-0	190	Pittsburgh	•		•	

Others receiving first-team honors

POS		School				PI
MG	Aaron Brown	Ohio State				•
MG	Randy Sidler	Penn State				•
MG	Reggie Kinlaw	Oklahoma				•
LB	John Anderson	Michigan			•	
LB	Lucius Sanford	Georgia Tech			•	
LB	George Cumby	Oklahoma			•	
LB	Mike Woods	Cincinnati			•	
P	Russell Erxleben	Texas			•	

HEISMAN TROPHY VOTING

	PLAYER	POS	SCHOOL	1ST	2ND	3RD	TOTAL
1	Earl Campbell	RB	Texas	371	187	60	1547
2	Terry Miller	TB	Oklahoma State	125	159	119	812
3	Ken MacAfee	TE	Notre Dame	55	54	70	343
4	Doug Williams	QB	Grambling	36	52	54	266
5	Ross Browner	DE	Notre Dame	21	45	60	213
6	Guy Benjamin	QB	Stanford	14	17	35	111
7	Matt Cavanaugh	QB	Pittsburgh	6	17	34	86
8	Rick Leach	QB	Michigan	6	9	23	59
9	Charles Alexander	TB	LSU	2	13	22	54
10	Wes Chandler	WR	Florida	4	11	16	50

AWARD WINNERS

PLAYER	POS	SCHOOL	AWARD NAME
Tony Dorsett	RB	Pittsburgh	Maxwell
Ross Browner	DE	Notre Dame	Maxwell
Brad Shearer	DT	Texas	Outland
Ken MacAfee	TE	Notre Dame	Camp
Ross Browner	DE	Notre Dame	Lombardi

CONFERENCE STANDINGS

ACC

	Conf. W	L	T	Overall W	L	T
North Carolina	5	0	1	8	3	1
Clemson	4	1	1	8	3	1
North Carolina St.	4	2	0	8	4	0
Maryland	4	2	0	8	4	0
Duke	2	4	0	5	6	0
Virginia	1	5	0	1	9	1
Wake Forest	0	6	0	1	10	0

Big 10

	Conf. W	L	T	Overall W	L	T
Michigan	7	1	0	10	2	0
Ohio State	7	1	0	9	3	0
Michigan State	6	1	1	7	3	1
Indiana	4	3	1	5	5	1
Minnesota	4	4	0	7	5	0
Purdue	3	5	0	5	6	0
Iowa	3	5	0	4	7	0
Wisconsin	3	6	0	5	6	0
Illinois	2	6	0	3	8	0
Northwestern	1	8	0	1	10	0

Big 8

	Conf. W	L	T	Overall W	L	T
Oklahoma	7	0	0	10	2	0
Nebraska	5	2	0	9	3	0
Iowa State	5	2	0	8	4	0
Colorado	3	3	1	7	3	1
Missouri	3	4	0	4	7	0
Kansas	2	4	1	3	7	1
Oklahoma State	2	5	0	4	7	0
Kansas State	0	7	0	1	10	0

Big West

	Conf. W	L	T	Overall W	L	T
Fresno State	4	0	0	9	2	0
Pacific	3	1	0	6	5	0
San Jose State	2	2	0	4	7	0
Long Beach State	1	3	0	4	6	0
Cal-St. Fullerton	0	4	0	4	7	0

Ivy

	Conf. W	L	T	Overall W	L	T
Yale	6	1	0	7	2	0
Brown	5	2	0	7	2	0
Dartmouth	4	3	0	6	3	0
Pennsylvania	4	3	0	5	4	0
Harvard	4	3	0	4	5	0
Princeton	3	4	0	3	6	0
Columbia	1	6	0	2	7	0
Cornell	1	6	0	1	8	0

MAC

	Conf. W	L	T	Overall W	L	T
Miami, Ohio	5	0	0	10	1	0
Central Michigan	7	1	0	10	1	0
Ball State	5	1	0	9	2	0
Eastern Michigan	4	3	0	8	3	0
Bowling Green	4	3	0	5	7	0
Kent State	5	4	0	6	5	0
Western Michigan	3	5	0	4	7	0
Northern Illinois	2	5	0	3	8	0
Toledo	2	7	0	2	9	0
Ohio U	0	8	0	1	10	0

PAC 8

	Conf. W	L	T	Overall W	L	T
Washington	6	1	0	8	4	0
Stanford	5	2	0	9	3	0
Southern Cal	5	2	0	8	4	0
UCLA	5	2	0	7	4	0
California	3	4	0	7	4	0
Washington State	3	4	0	6	5	0
Oregon	1	6	0	2	9	0
Oregon State	0	7	0	2	9	0

SEC

	Conf. W	L	T	Overall W	L	T
Alabama	7	0	0	11	1	0
Kentucky	6	0	0	10	1	0
LSU	4	2	0	8	4	0
Auburn	4	2	0	5	6	0
Florida	3	3	0	6	4	1
Mississippi State*	2	4	0	5	6	0
Georgia	2	4	0	5	6	0
Mississippi	2	5	0	5	6	0
Tennessee	1	5	0	4	7	0
Vanderbilt	0	6	0	2	9	0

* Later Forfeited to 0-6-0

SWC

	Conf. W	L	T	Overall W	L	T
Texas	8	0	0	11	1	0
Arkansas	7	1	0	11	1	0
Texas A&M	6	2	0	8	4	0
Texas Tech	4	4	0	7	5	0
Houston	4	4	0	6	5	0
Baylor	3	5	0	5	6	0
SMU	3	5	0	4	7	0
TCU	1	7	0	2	9	0
Rice	0	8	0	1	10	0

WAC

	Conf. W	L	T	Overall W	L	T
Brigham Young	6	1	0	9	2	0
Arizona State	6	1	0	9	3	0
Colorado State	5	2	0	9	2	1
Wyoming	4	3	0	4	6	1
Arizona	3	4	0	5	7	0
New Mexico	2	5	0	5	7	0
Utah	2	5	0	3	8	0
Texas-El Paso	0	7	0	1	10	0

Independents

	Overall W	L	T
Penn State	11	1	0
Notre Dame	11	1	0
Florida State	10	2	0
North Texas	9	2	0
Pittsburgh	9	2	1
Rutgers	8	3	0
Army	7	4	0
Boston College	6	5	0
Memphis	6	5	0
Georgia Tech	6	5	0
Syracuse	6	5	0
Navy	5	6	0
West Virginia	5	6	0
South Carolina	5	7	0
Utah State	4	7	0
Virginia Tech	3	7	1
Tulane	3	8	0
Miami, Fla.	3	8	0
Air Force	2	8	1

BOWL GAMES

DATE	GAME	SCORE
D17	Independence	Louisiana Tech 24, Louisville 14
D19	Liberty	Nebraska 21, North Carolina 17
D22	All-American	Maryland 17, Minnesota 7
D23	Tangerine	Florida State 40, Texas Tech 17
D25	Fiesta	Penn State 42, Arizona State 30
D30	Gator	Pittsburgh 34, Clemson 3
D31	Peach	North Carolina St. 24, Iowa State 14
D31	Bluebonnet	Southern Cal 47, Texas A&M 28
D31	Sun	Stanford 24, LSU 14
J2	Orange	Arkansas 31, Oklahoma 6
J2	Sugar	Alabama 35, Ohio State 6
J2	Cotton	Notre Dame 38, Texas 10
J2	Rose	Washington 27, Michigan 20

1977 NCAA Major College Statistical Leaders

Individual Leaders

PASSING	G	ATT	COM	PCT	INT	I%	YDS	YPA	TD	TD%	COM.PG
1 Guy Benjamin, Stanford	10	330	208	63.0	15	4.5	2521	7.6	19	5.8	20.8
2 Jack Thompson, Washington State	11	329	192	58.4	13	4.0	2372	7.2	13	4.0	17.5
3 Ken Smith, Boston College	9	257	149	58.0	20	7.8	2073	8.1	17	6.6	16.6
4 Doug Williams, Grambling	11	352	181	51.4	18	5.1	3286	9.3	38	10.8	16.5
5 Mark Herrmann, Purdue	11	319	175	54.9	27	8.5	2453	7.7	18	5.6	15.9
6 Joe Davis, San Diego State	11	290	174	60.0	12	4.1	2360	8.1	24	8.3	15.8
7 Jim Freitas, Long Beach State	8	264	124	47.0	16	6.1	1358	5.1	15	5.7	15.5
8 Marc Wilson, Brigham Young	11	277	164	59.2	18	6.5	2418	8.7	24	8.7	14.9
9 Randy Hertel, Rice	11	356	156	43.8	24	6.7	1620	4.6	9	2.5	14.2
10 Randy Gomez, Utah	11	315	155	49.2	16	5.1	2126	6.7	12	3.8	14.1

ALL-PURPOSE	G	RUSH	REC	PR	KR	YDS	YPG
1 Earl Campbell, Texas	11	1744	111	0	0	1855	168.6
2 Henry White, Colgate	11	1032	306	67	448	1853	168.5
3 Larry Key, Florida State	11	1117	243	0	461	1821	165.5
4 Mose Rison, Central Michigan	10	1241	59	0	330	1630	163.0
5 Terry Miller, Oklahoma State	11	1680	2	0	104	1786	162.4
6 Charles Alexander, LSU	11	1686	80	0	0	1766	160.5
7 Joe Gattuso, Navy	11	1292	169	0	212	1673	152.1
8 Darrin Nelson, Stanford	11	1069	524	79	0	1672	152.0
9 David Turner, San Diego State	11	1252	417	0	0	1669	151.7
10 Robert Woods, Grambling	11	210	719	279	417	1625	147.7

RUSHING/ YARDS PER GAME	G	ATT	YDS	TD	AVG	YPG
1 Earl Campbell, Texas	11	267	1744	18	6.5	158.5
2 Charles Alexander, LSU	11	311	1686	17	5.4	153.3
3 Terry Miller, Oklahoma State	11	314	1680	14	5.4	152.7
4 Jerome Persell, Western Michigan	10	264	1339	14	5.1	133.9
5 John Pagliaro, Yale	9	239	1159	14	4.8	128.8
6 Bo Robinson, West Texas State	11	201	1399	12	7.0	127.2
7 Mose Rison, Central Michigan	10	238	1241	11	5.2	124.1
8 Amos Lawrence, North Carolina	10	193	1211	6	6.3	121.1
9 Bobby Windom, Eastern Michigan	11	246	1322	9	5.4	120.2
10 Darrell Lipford, Western Carolina	11	280	1318	16	4.7	119.8

RUSHING/YARDS PER CARRY	G	ATT	YDS	YPC
1 Henry White, Colgate	11	131	1032	7.9
2 Bo Robinson, West Texas State	11	201	1399	7.0
3 I.M. Hipp, Nebraska	11	197	1301	6.6
4 Earl Campbell, Texas	11	267	1744	6.5
5 Gwain Durden, U.T. Chattanooga	11	164	1049	6.4
6 Amos Lawrence, North Carolina	10	193	1211	6.3
7 Myron Hardeman, Wyoming	11	186	1165	6.3
8 Mike Smith, U.T. Chattanooga	11	172	1062	6.2
9 Darrin Nelson, Stanford	11	183	1069	5.8
10 Ron Springs, Ohio State	11	190	1092	5.7

RECEIVING	G	REC	YDS	TD	YPR	YPG	RPG
1 Wayne Tolleson, Western Carolina	11	73	1101	7	15.1	100.1	6.6
2 Emanuel Tolbert, SMU	11	64	996	6	15.6	90.5	5.8
3 Mike Moore, Grambling	11	60	1122	12	18.7	102.0	5.5
3 Paul Proffitt, Drake	11	60	778	5	13.0	70.7	5.5
5 Rod Foppe, Louisiana Tech	11	59	1274	5	21.6	115.8	5.4
5 Rick Morrison, Ball State	11	59	908	8	15.4	82.5	5.4
7 Dave Petzke, Northern Illinois	11	57	746	5	13.1	67.8	5.2
8 Steve Young, Wake Forest	10	51	483	3	9.5	48.3	5.1
9 Mike Riley, Citadel	11	56	724	2	12.9	65.8	5.1
10 David Houser, Rice	11	55	795	5	14.5	72.3	5.0
10 Todd Christensen, Brigham Young	10	50	603	5	12.1	60.3	5.0

PUNTING	PUNT	YDS	AVG
1 Jim Miller, Mississippi	66	3029	45.9
2 Craig Colquitt, Tennessee	66	2969	45.0
3 Gavin Hedrick, Washington State	53	2368	44.7
4 Steve Little, Arkansas	48	2127	44.3
5 Ken Rosenthal, SMU	62	2741	44.2
6 Rick Partridge, Utah	68	2980	43.8
7 Luke Prestridge, Baylor	63	2755	43.7
8 David Appleby, Texas A&M	57	2466	43.3
9 Mike Deutsch, Colorado State	71	3057	43.1
10 Mike Connell, Cincinnati	60	2568	42.8

PUNT RETURNS	PUNT	YDS	TD	AVG
1 Robert Woods, Grambling	11	279	3	25.4
2 Jimmy Cefalo, Penn State	18	247	2	13.7
3 Phil McConkey, Navy	19	257	1	13.5
4 Max Hudspeth, New Mexico	22	291	1	13.2
5 Jimmy Bryant, Utah State	18	226	0	12.6
6 Tony Nathan, Alabama	18	223	0	12.4
7 Johnnie Johnson, Texas	44	538	1	12.2
7 Vondell Robertson, Central Michigan	22	269	0	12.2
9 Freddie Nixon, Oklahoma	22	266	1	12.1
10 Gordon Jones, Pittsburgh	23	275	1	12.0

KICKOFF RETURNS	KR	YDS	TD	AVG
1 Tony Ball, U.T. Chattanooga	13	473	0	36.4
2 Larry Anderson, Louisiana Tech	14	435	2	31.1
3 James Otis Doss, Mississippi State	16	450	0	28.1
4 Steve Woods, Fresno State	16	447	1	27.9
5 Gary Moore, Tennessee	14	376	0	26.9
5 Tony Felder, Texas-Arlington	14	376	0	26.9
7 Joe Jamiel, Brown	11	293	0	26.6
8 Robert Woods, Grambling	16	417	2	26.1
9 Norman Warren, Kent State	22	569	1	25.9
10 Ralph Stringer, North Carolina St.	19	488	0	25.7

SCORING	TDS	XPT	FG	PTS	PTPG
1 Earl Campbell, Texas	19	0	0	114	10.4
2 Darrell Lipford, Western Carolina	18	0	0	108	9.8
3 Charles Alexander, LSU	17	2	0	104	9.5
4 John Pagliaro, Yale	14	0	0	84	9.3
5 Russell Erxleben, Texas	0	39	14	81	9.0
6 Mike Jones, North Texas	16	2	0	98	8.9
7 Joel Payton, Ohio State	13	2	0	80	8.9
8 Steve Little, Arkansas	0	37	19	94	8.5
9 Jerome Persell, Western Michigan	14	0	0	84	8.4
9 Ronnie Smith, San Diego State	14	0	0	84	8.4

FIELD GOALS	FGA	FGM	PCT	FGG
1 Paul Marchese, Kent State	27	18	0.67	1.80
2 Steve Little, Arkansas	30	19	0.63	1.73
3 Paul Rogind, Minnesota	26	18	0.69	1.64
4 John Roveta, La. Lafayette	25	19	0.76	1.58
5 Russell Erxleben, Texas	26	14	0.54	1.56
6 Hans Nielsen, Michigan State	28	17	0.61	1.55
7 Tom McNamara, Utah	23	16	0.70	1.45
7 Jim Breech, California	27	16	0.59	1.45
7 Tony Franklin, Texas A&M	28	16	0.57	1.45
7 Dave Jacobs, Syracuse	29	16	0.55	1.45

INTERCEPTIONS	INT	YDS	TD	INT/GM
1 Paul Lawler, Colgate	7	53	0	0.78
2 Leroy Paul, Texas Southern	8	113	0	0.73
2 John Sturges, Navy	8	88	0	0.73
4 Kevin White, Citadel	7	102	0	0.64
4 Zac Henderson, Oklahoma	7	89	0	0.64
4 Paul Murphy, Boston College	7	61	0	0.64
4 Bryan Ferguson, Miami, Fla.	7	50	0	0.64
4 Dave Abrams, Indiana	7	24	0	0.64
4 Charles Johnson, Grambling	7	14	0	0.64
10 Tom Pridemore, West Virginia	6	123	1	0.60
10 Sherman Taylor, Wichita State	6	41	0	0.60

Team Leaders

RUSHING OFFENSE	G	ATT	YDS	AVG	TD	YPG
1 Oklahoma	11	709	3618	5.1	40	328.9
2 Ohio State	11	731	3534	4.8	39	321.3
3 West Texas State	11	697	3503	5.0	32	318.5
4 Texas	11	646	3369	5.2	39	306.3
5 LSU	11	674	3352	5.0	35	304.7
6 U.T. Chattanooga	11	660	3332	5.0	26	302.9
7 Nebraska	11	655	3328	5.1	31	302.5
8 Texas A&M	11	709	3304	4.7	29	300.4
9 Alabama	11	697	3268	4.7	34	297.1
10 Central Michigan	11	741	3213	4.3	31	292.1

PASSING OFFENSE	G	ATT	COM	INT	PCT	YDS	YPA	TD	I%	YPC	YPG
1 Brigham Young	11	457	277	23	60.6	3758	8.2	41	5.0	13.6	341.6
2 Grambling	11	373	187	20	50.1	3360	9.0	38	5.4	18.0	305.5
3 Stanford	11	372	235	15	63.2	2856	7.7	20	4.0	12.2	259.6
4 California	11	391	214	16	54.7	2837	7.3	18	4.1	13.3	257.9
5 San Diego State	11	331	192	16	58.0	2685	8.1	26	4.8	14.0	244.1
6 Purdue	11	350	190	30	54.3	2631	7.5	18	8.6	13.8	239.2
7 Washington State	11	346	202	13	58.4	2581	7.5	14	3.8	12.8	234.6
8 Louisiana Tech	11	300	151	18	50.3	2552	8.5	9	6.0	16.9	232.0
9 Long Beach State	10	388	186	20	47.9	2249	5.8	19	5.2	12.1	224.9
10 Florida State	11	323	176	18	54.5	2466	7.6	18	5.6	14.0	224.2

TOTAL OFFENSE	G	P	YDS	AVG	TD	YPG
1 Colgate	11	794	5347	6.7	49	486.1
2 Grambling	11	805	5329	6.7	58	484.5
3 Brigham Young	11	881	5172	5.9	55	470.2
4 Southern Cal	11	839	4959	5.9	37	450.8
5 Notre Dame	11	918	4840	5.3	47	440.0
6 Texas	11	792	4805	6.1	53	436.8
7 Stanford	11	846	4750	5.6	32	431.8
8 Fresno State	11	873	4695	5.4	44	426.8
9 Penn State	11	865	4646	5.4	39	422.4
10 Arizona State	11	928	4643	5.0	45	422.1

RUSHING DEFENSE	G	ATT	YDS	AVG	TD	YPG
1 Jackson State	11	446	746	1.7	6	67.8
2 Cincinnati	11	478	871	1.8	8	79.2
3 Notre Dame	11	447	981	2.2	3	89.2
4 Texas	11	471	1002	2.1	5	91.1
5 Fresno State	11	494	1165	2.4	12	105.9
6 Louisiana Tech	11	481	1167	2.4	5	106.1
7 Central Michigan	11	475	1209	2.5	13	109.9
8 San Diego State	11	512	1243	2.4	12	113.0
9 Texas Southern	11	495	1249	2.5	16	113.5
10 Michigan	11	488	1287	2.6	6	117.0

PASSING DEFENSE	G	ATT	COM	PCT	YPC	INT	I%	YDS	YPA	TD	YPG
1 Tennessee State	9	156	52	33.3	11.8	10	6.4	611	3.9	4	67.9
2 Brown	9	158	75	47.5	10.3	9	5.7	776	4.9	3	86.2
3 Northern Illinois	11	165	74	44.8	13.2	9	5.5	974	5.9	8	88.5
4 Indiana	11	178	74	41.6	13.3	13	7.3	984	5.5	5	89.5
4 Arkansas	11	227	98	43.2	10.0	17	7.5	984	4.3	1	89.5
6 Wisconsin	11	149	58	38.9	17.3	7	4.7	1002	6.7	4	91.1
7 Nebraska	11	202	89	44.1	11.7	17	8.4	1037	5.1	6	94.3
8 Western Carolina	11	172	86	50.0	12.4	12	7.0	1066	6.2	3	96.9
9 Tennessee	11	179	78	43.6	13.7	10	5.6	1067	6.0	6	97.0
10 Northwestern State	11	188	73	38.8	14.7	12	6.4	1072	5.7	8	97.5

TOTAL DEFENSE	G	P	YDS	AVG	TD	YPG
1 Jackson State	11	688	2277	3.3	14	207.0
2 Tennessee State	9	609	1883	3.1	11	209.2
3 Louisiana Tech	11	708	2421	3.4	16	220.1
4 Central Michigan	11	671	2422	3.6	19	220.2
5 Texas	11	737	2461	3.3	13	223.7
6 Brown	9	573	2071	3.6	12	230.1
7 Ohio State	11	694	2539	3.7	10	230.8
8 Fresno State	11	750	2548	3.4	21	231.6
9 Kentucky	11	728	2590	3.6	12	235.5
10 Texas Southern	11	705	2606	3.7	25	236.9

SCORING OFFENSE	G	PTS	AVG
1 Grambling	11	462	42.0
2 Brigham Young	11	433	39.4
3 Texas	11	431	39.2
4 Oklahoma	11	395	35.9
5 Pittsburgh	11	394	35.8
6 Notre Dame	11	382	34.7
7 Colgate	11	380	34.5
8 Ball State	11	377	34.3
9 LSU	11	375	34.1
10 Arizona State	11	369	33.5

SCORING DEFENSE	G	PTS	AVG
1 North Carolina	11	81	7.4
2 Ohio State	11	85	7.7
3 Arkansas	11	95	8.6
4 Michigan	11	97	8.8
5 Kentucky	11	111	10.1
6 Tennessee State	9	91	10.1
7 Jackson State	11	112	10.2
8 Texas	11	114	10.4
9 Brown	9	96	10.7
9 Dartmouth	9	96	10.7

1978 POLL PROGRESSION

PRE-SEASON 1978 — Sept. 9 Games

AP	Team	Record	Result
1	Alabama	0-0-0	bye week
2	Arkansas	0-0-0	bye week
3	Penn State	0-0-0	beat Rutgers 26-10
4	Oklahoma	0-0-0	beat Stanford 35-29
5	Notre Dame	0-0-0	lost to Missouri 0-3
6	Michigan	0-0-0	bye week
7	Ohio State	0-0-0	bye week
8	Texas	0-0-0	bye week
9	Southern Cal	0-0-0	beat Texas Tech 17-9
10	Nebraska	0-0-0	beat California 36-26
11	Washington	0-0-0	lost to # 12 UCLA 7-10
12	UCLA	0-0-0	beat # 11 Washington 10-7
13	LSU	0-0-0	bye week
14	Pittsburgh	0-0-0	bye week
15	Kentucky	0-0-0	bye week
16	Texas A&M	0-0-0	beat Kansas 37-10
17	Florida State	0-0-0	beat Syracuse 28-0
18	Clemson	0-0-0	bye week
19	North Carolina	0-0-0	bye week
20	Iowa State	0-0-0	beat Rice 23-19

SEPTEMBER 11 POLL — Sept. 16 Games

UP	AP	Team	Record	Result
1	1	Alabama	1-0-0	beat # 11 Missouri 38-20
3	2	Arkansas	0-0-0	beat Vanderbilt 48-17
2	3	Oklahoma	1-0-0	beat West Virginia 52-10
4	4	Michigan	0-0-0	beat Illinois 31-0
8	5	Penn State	2-0-0	beat # 6 Ohio State 19-0
6	6	Ohio State	0-0-0	lost to # 5 Penn State 0-19
7	7	Texas	0-0-0	beat Rice 34-0
5	8	Alabama	1-0-0	beat Oregon 37-10
9	9	UCLA	1-0-0	beat Tennessee 13-0
11	10	Texas A&M	1-0-0	bye week
10	11	Missouri	1-0-0	lost to # 1 Alabama 20-38
14	12	Nebraska	1-1-0	beat Hawaii 56-10
13	13	LSU	0-0-0	beat Indiana 24-17
12	14	Pittsburgh	0-0-0	beat Tulane 24-6
16	15	Notre Dame	0-1-0	bye week
15	16	Florida State	1-0-0	beat Oklahoma State 38-20
17	17	Kentucky	0-0-0	tied South Carolina 14-14
19	18	Washington	0-1-0	beat Kansas 31-2
	19	Iowa State	1-0-0	beat San Diego State 14-13
17	20	Maryland	1-0-0	beat Louisville 24-17
20		Colorado	1-0-0	beat Miami, Fla. 17-7

SEPTEMBER 18 POLL — Sept. 23 Games

UP	AP	Team	Record	Result
1	1	Alabama	2-0-0	lost to # 7 Southern Cal 14-24
3	2	Arkansas	1-0-0	beat Oklahoma State 19-7
2	3	Oklahoma	2-0-0	beat Rice 66-7
4	4	Penn State	3-0-0	beat SMU 26-21
5	5	Michigan	1-0-0	beat # 14 Notre Dame 28-14
6	6	Texas	1-0-0	beat Wyoming 17-3
7	7	Southern Cal	2-0-0	beat # 1 Alabama 24-14
8	8	UCLA	2-0-0	lost to Kansas 24-28
10	9	Texas A&M	1-0-0	beat Boston College 37-2
11	10	LSU	1-0-0	beat Wake Forest 13-11
9	11	Pittsburgh	1-0-0	beat Temple 20-12
12	12	Nebraska	2-1-0	bye week
13	13	Florida State	2-0-0	beat Miami, Fla. 31-21
14	14	Notre Dame	0-1-0	lost to # 5 Michigan 14-28
17	15	Washington	1-1-0	lost to Indiana 7-14
19	16	Ohio State	0-1-0	beat Minnesota 27-10
	17	Missouri	1-1-0	beat Mississippi 45-14
16	18	Maryland	2-0-0	beat North Carolina 21-20
15	19	Colorado	2-0-0	beat San Jose State 22-7
20	20	Iowa State	2-0-0	beat Iowa 31-0
	18	Clemson	1-0-0	lost to Georgia 0-12
	20	Arizona State	2-0-0	lost to Washington State 26-51

SEPTEMBER 25 POLL — Sept. 30 Games

UP	AP	Team	Record	Result
1	1	Oklahoma	3-0-0	beat # 14 Missouri 45-23
4	2	Arkansas	2-0-0	beat Tulsa 21-13
2	3	Southern Cal	3-0-0	beat Michigan State 30-9 S29
3	4	Michigan	2-0-0	beat Duke 52-0
5	5	Penn State	4-0-0	beat TCU 58-0
6	6	Texas	2-0-0	beat Texas Tech 24-7
7	7	Alabama	2-1-0	beat Vanderbilt 51-28
8	8	Texas A&M	2-0-0	beat Memphis 58-0
10	9	Pittsburgh	2-0-0	beat North Carolina 20-16
9	10	Florida State	3-0-0	lost to Houston 21-27
11	11	LSU	2-0-0	beat Rice 37-7
12	12	Nebraska	2-1-0	beat Indiana 69-17
15	13	Ohio State	1-1-0	beat Baylor 34-28
17	14	Missouri	2-1-0	lost to # 1 Oklahoma 23-45
13	15	Maryland	3-0-0	beat Kentucky 20-3
14	16	Colorado	3-0-0	beat Northwestern 55-7
16	17	Iowa State	3-0-0	beat Drake 35-7
	18	UCLA	2-1-0	beat Minnesota 17-3
	19	Georgia	2-0-0	lost to South Carolina 10-27
19	20	Stanford	2-1-0	beat Tulane 17-14
18		Kentucky	1-0-1	lost to # 15 Maryland 3-20
20		Purdue	2-0-0	lost to Notre Dame 6-10

OCTOBER 2 POLL — Oct. 7 Games

UP	AP	Team	Record	Result
1	1	Oklahoma	4-0-0	beat # 6 Texas 31-10
2	2	Southern Cal	4-0-0	bye week
3	3	Michigan	3-0-0	beat Arizona 21-17
5	4	Arkansas	3-0-0	beat TCU 42-3
4	5	Penn State	5-0-0	beat Kentucky 30-0
6	6	Texas	3-0-0	lost to # 1 Oklahoma 10-31
7	7	Texas A&M	3-0-0	beat Texas Tech 38-9
8	8	Alabama	3-1-0	beat Washington 20-17
9	9	Pittsburgh	3-0-0	beat Boston College 32-15
10	10	Nebraska	3-1-0	beat # 15 Iowa State 23-0
11	11	LSU	3-0-0	beat Florida 34-21
13	12	Maryland	4-0-0	beat # 20 North Carolina St. 31-7
12	13	Colorado	4-0-0	beat Kansas 17-7
14	14	Ohio State	2-1-0	tied SMU 35-35
15	15	Iowa State	4-0-0	lost to # 10 Nebraska 0-23
16	16	UCLA	3-1-0	beat # 17 Stanford 27-26
17	17	Stanford	3-1-0	lost to # 16 UCLA 26-27
	18	Florida State	3-1-0	beat Cincinnati 26-21
20	19	Auburn	3-0-0	lost to Miami, Fla. 15-17
19	20	North Carolina St.	4-0-0	lost to # 12 Maryland 7-31
17		Houston	2-1-0	beat Baylor 20-18

OCTOBER 9 POLL — Oct. 14 Games

UP	AP	Team	Record	Result
1	1	Oklahoma	5-0-0	beat Kansas 17-16
2	2	Southern Cal	4-0-0	lost to Arizona State 7-20
5	3	Arkansas	4-0-0	bye week
3	3	Penn State	6-0-0	bye week
4	5	Michigan	4-0-0	lost to Michigan State 15-24
6	6	Texas A&M	4-0-0	lost to # 17 Houston 0-33
7	7	Alabama	4-1-0	beat Florida 23-12
8	8	Nebraska	4-1-0	beat Kansas State 48-14
9	9	Pittsburgh	4-0-0	lost to Notre Dame 17-26
11	10	Maryland	5-0-0	beat Syracuse 24-9
10	11	LSU	4-0-0	lost to Georgia 17-24
13	12	Texas	3-1-0	beat North Texas 26-16
12	13	Colorado	5-0-0	lost to Oklahoma State 20-24
14	14	UCLA	4-1-0	beat Washington St. 45-31
17	15	Florida State	4-1-0	lost to Mississippi State 27-55
	16	Ohio State	2-1-1	lost to Purdue 16-27
16	17	Houston	3-1-0	beat # 6 Texas A&M 33-0
20	18	Stanford	3-2-0	lost to Washington 31-34
15	19	Missouri	3-2-0	beat # 19 Iowa State 26-13
	20	Iowa State	4-1-0	lost to # 20 Missouri 13-26
18		Utah State	5-0-0	lost to Long Beach State 17-33
19		Navy	4-0-0	beat Duke 31-8

OCTOBER 16 POLL — Oct. 21 Games

UP	AP	Team	Record	Result
1	1	Oklahoma	6-0-0	beat Iowa State 34-6
2	2	Penn State	6-0-0	beat Syracuse 45-15
3	3	Arkansas	4-0-0	lost to # 8 Texas 21-28
4	4	Alabama	5-1-0	beat Tennessee 30-17
5	5	Nebraska	5-1-0	beat Colorado 52-14
6	6	Maryland	6-0-0	beat Wake Forest 39-0
7	7	Southern Cal	4-1-0	beat Oregon State 38-7
8	8	Texas	4-1-0	beat # 3 Arkansas 28-21
9	9	Michigan	4-1-0	beat Wisconsin 42-0
10	10	UCLA	5-1-0	beat California 45-0
11	11	Houston	4-1-0	beat SMU 42-28
14	12	Texas A&M	4-1-0	lost to Baylor 6-24
17	13	Missouri	4-2-0	beat Kansas State 56-14
12	14	Arizona State	5-1-0	bye week
15	15	Pittsburgh	4-1-0	beat Florida State 7-3
13	16	LSU	4-1-0	beat Kentucky 21-0
20	17	Navy	5-0-0	beat William & Mary 9-0
16	18	Georgia	4-1-0	beat Vanderbilt 31-10
19	19	Purdue	4-1-0	beat Illinois 13-0
18	20	Notre Dame	3-2-0	beat Air Force 38-15

OCTOBER 23 POLL — Oct. 28 Games

UP	AP	Team	Record	Result
1	1	Oklahoma	7-0-0	beat Kansas State 56-19
2	2	Penn State	7-0-0	beat West Virginia 49-21
3	3	Alabama	6-1-0	beat Virginia Tech 35-0
4	4	Nebraska	6-1-0	beat Oklahoma State 22-14
5	5	Maryland	7-0-0	beat Duke 27-0
6	6	Southern Cal	5-1-0	beat California 42-17
7	7	Texas	5-1-0	beat SMU 22-3
9	8	Michigan	5-1-0	beat Minnesota 42-10
11	9	Arkansas	4-1-0	lost to # 11 Houston 9-20
8	10	UCLA	6-1-0	beat Arizona 24-14 O27
10	11	Houston	5-1-0	beat # 9 Arkansas 20-9
12	12	Arizona State	5-1-0	lost to Washington 7-41
16	13	Missouri	5-2-0	lost to Colorado 27-28
14	14	LSU	5-1-0	bye week
15	15	Pittsburgh	5-1-0	lost to # 18 Navy 11-21
13	16	Georgia	5-1-0	beat Kentucky 17-16
17	17	Purdue	5-1-0	beat Iowa 34-7
18	18	Navy	6-0-0	beat # 15 Pittsburgh 21-11
19	19	Notre Dame	4-2-0	beat Miami, Fla. 20-0
20	20	Clemson	5-1-0	beat North Carolina St. 33-10

OCTOBER 30 POLL — Nov. 4 Games

UP	AP	Team	Record	Result
1	1	Oklahoma	8-0-0	beat Colorado 28-7
2	2	Penn State	8-0-0	beat # 5 Maryland 27-3
3	3	Alabama	7-1-0	beat Mississippi State 35-14
4	4	Nebraska	7-1-0	beat Kansas 63-21
5	5	Maryland	8-0-0	lost to # 2 Penn State 3-27
6	6	Southern Cal	6-1-0	beat Stanford 13-7
7	7	Texas	6-1-0	bye week
9	8	Michigan	6-1-0	beat Iowa 34-0
10	9	UCLA	7-1-0	beat Oregon 23-21
8	10	Houston	6-1-0	beat TCU 63-6
11	11	Navy	7-0-0	lost to # 15 Notre Dame 7-27
13	12	LSU	5-1-0	beat Mississippi 30-8
12	13	Georgia	6-1-0	beat VMI 41-3
14	14	Purdue	6-1-0	beat Northwestern 31-0
15	15	Notre Dame	5-2-0	beat # 11 Navy 27-7
16	16	Clemson	6-1-0	beat Wake Forest 51-6
17	17	Arkansas	4-2-0	beat Rice 37-7
PB	18	Michigan State	4-3-0	beat Illinois 59-19
	19	Pittsburgh	5-2-0	beat Syracuse 18-17
	20	Washington	5-3-0	beat Arizona 31-21
18		Colorado	6-2-0	lost to # 1 Oklahoma 7-28
19		Georgia Tech	6-2-0	bye week
20		Ohio State	4-2-1	beat Wisconsin 49-14

UP	AP	NOVEMBER 6 POLL		NOV. 11 GAMES
1	1	Oklahoma	9-0-0	lost to # 4 Nebraska 14-17
2	2	Penn State	9-0-0	beat North Carolina St. 19-10
3	3	Alabama	8-1-0	beat # 10 LSU 31-10
4	4	Nebraska	8-1-0	beat # 1 Oklahoma 17-14
5	5	Southern Cal	7-1-0	beat # 19 Washington 28-10
6	6	Texas	6-1-0	lost to # 8 Houston 7-10
7	7	Michigan	7-1-0	beat Northwestern 59-14
8	8	Houston	7-1-0	beat # 6 Texas 10-7
9	9	UCLA	8-1-0	lost to Oregon State 13-15
11	10	LSU	6-1-0	lost to # 3 Alabama 10-31
10	11	Georgia	7-1-0	beat Florida 24-22
12	12	Purdue	7-1-0	tied Wisconsin 24-24
14	13	Maryland	8-1-0	beat Virginia 17-7
13	14	Notre Dame	6-2-0	beat Tennessee 31-14
15	15	Clemson	7-1-0	beat North Carolina 13-9
16	16	Arkansas	5-2-0	beat Baylor 27-14
PB	17	Michigan State	5-3-0	beat Minnesota 33-9
18	18	Navy	7-1-0	lost to Syracuse 17-20
17	19	Washington	6-3-0	lost to # 5 Southern Cal 10-28
20	20	Pittsburgh	6-2-0	beat West Virginia 52-7
19		Georgia Tech	6-2-0	beat Air Force 42-21

UP	AP	NOVEMBER 13 POLL		NOV. 18 GAMES
1	1	Penn State	10-0-0	bye week
2	2	Nebraska	9-1-0	lost to Missouri 31-35
3	3	Alabama	9-1-0	bye week
4	4	Oklahoma	9-1-0	beat Oklahoma State 62-7
5	5	Southern Cal	8-1-0	beat # 14 UCLA 17-10
6	6	Houston	8-1-0	bye week
7	7	Michigan	8-1-0	beat # 15 Purdue 24-6
8	8	Georgia	8-1-0	tied Auburn 22-22
9	9	Texas	6-2-0	beat TCU 41-0
10	10	Notre Dame	7-2-0	beat # 20 Georgia Tech 38-21
11	11	Maryland	9-1-0	lost to # 12 Clemson 24-28
12	12	Clemson	8-1-0	beat # 11 Maryland 28-24
13	13	Arkansas	6-2-0	beat Texas A&M 26-7
15	14	UCLA	8-2-0	lost to # 5 Southern Cal 10-17
16	15	Purdue	7-1-1	lost to # 7 Michigan 6-24
PB	16	Michigan State	6-3-0	beat Northwestern 52-3
14	17	LSU	6-2-0	lost to Mississippi State 14-16
18	18	Pittsburgh	7-2-0	beat Army 35-17
17	19	Ohio State	6-2-1	beat Indiana 21-18
19	20	Georgia Tech	7-2-0	lost to # 10 Notre Dame 21-38
20		Stanford	6-4-0	beat California 30-10
20		Iowa State	7-3-0	beat Colorado 20-16

UP	AP	NOVEMBER 20 POLL		NOV. 25 GAMES
1	1	Penn State	10-0-0	beat # 15 Pittsburgh 17-10
2	2	Alabama	9-1-0	bye week
4	3	Southern Cal	9-1-0	beat # 8 Notre Dame 27-25
3	4	Oklahoma	10-1-0	regular season complete
5	5	Houston	8-1-0	lost to Texas Tech 21-22
6	6	Michigan	9-1-0	beat # 16 Ohio State 14-3
7	7	Nebraska	9-2-0	regular season complete
8	8	Notre Dame	8-2-0	lost to # 3 Southern Cal 25-27
9	9	Texas	7-2-0	lost to Baylor 14-38
10	10	Clemson	9-1-0	beat South Carolina 41-23
12	11	Arkansas	7-2-0	beat SMU 27-14
11	12	Georgia	8-1-1	bye week
16	13	Maryland	9-2-0	regular season complete
PB	14	Michigan State	7-3-0	beat Iowa 42-7
13	15	Pittsburgh	8-2-0	lost to # 1 Penn State 10-17
14	16	Ohio State	7-2-1	lost to # 6 Michigan 3-14
15	17	UCLA	8-3-0	regular season complete
19	18	Purdue	7-2-1	beat Indiana 20-7
17	19	Missouri	7-4-0	regular season complete
20	20	Iowa State	8-3-0	regular season complete
18		Stanford	7-4-0	regular season complete

UP	AP	NOVEMBER 27 POLL		DEC. 2 GAMES
1	1	Penn State	11-0-0	regular season complete
2	2	Alabama	9-1-0	beat Auburn 34-16
3	3	Southern Cal	10-1-0	beat Hawaii 21-5
4	4	Oklahoma	10-1-0	
5	5	Michigan	10-1-0	regular season complete
6	6	Nebraska	9-2-0	
7	7	Clemson	10-1-0	regular season complete
10	8	Arkansas	8-2-0	beat Texas Tech 49-7
11	9	Houston	8-2-0	beat Rice 49-25
9	10	Notre Dame	8-3-0	regular season complete
8	11	Georgia	8-1-1	beat Georgia Tech 29-28
PB	12	Michigan State	8-3-0	regular season complete
12	13	Maryland	9-2-0	
17	14	Texas	7-3-0	beat Texas A&M 22-7
15	15	UCLA	8-3-0	
13	16	Pittsburgh	8-3-0	regular season complete
14	17	Purdue	8-2-1	regular season complete
16	18	Missouri	7-4-0	
	19	Iowa State	8-3-0	
20	20	Ohio State	7-3-1	regular season complete
18		LSU	7-3-0	beat Wyoming 24-17
19		Stanford	7-4-0	

UP	AP	DECEMBER 4 POLL	RECORD	BOWL BID	DATE	BOWL RESULT	RB	UP	AP	JANUARY 3 FINAL POLL	RECORD
1	1	Penn State	11-0-0	Sugar Bowl	J1	lost to # 2 Alabama 7-14	2	2	1	Alabama	11-1-0
2	2	Alabama	10-1-0	Sugar Bowl	J1	beat # 1 Penn State 14-7	1	1	2	Southern Cal	12-1-0
3	3	Southern Cal	11-1-0	Rose Bowl	J1	beat # 5 Michigan 17-10	4	3	3	Oklahoma	11-1-0
4	4	Oklahoma	10-1-0	Orange Bowl	J1	beat # 6 Nebraska 31-24	3	4	4	Penn State	11-1-0
5	5	Michigan	10-1-0	Rose Bowl	J1	lost to # 3 Southern Cal 10-17	5	5	5	Michigan	10-2-0
6	6	Nebraska	9-2-0	Orange Bowl	J1	lost to # 4 Oklahoma 24-31	6	6	6	Clemson	11-1-0
8	7	Clemson	10-1-0	Gator Bowl	D29	beat # 20 Ohio State 17-15	7	6	7	Notre Dame	9-3-0
10	8	Arkansas	9-2-0	Fiesta Bowl	D25	tied # 15 UCLA 10-10	8	8	8	Nebraska	9-3-0
11	9	Houston	9-2-0	Cotton Bowl	J1	lost to # 10 Notre Dame 34-35	11	9	9	Texas	9-3-0
9	10	Notre Dame	8-3-0	Cotton Bowl	J1	beat # 9 Houston 35-34	9	11	10	Houston	9-3-0
7	11	Georgia	9-1-1	Bluebonnet Bowl	D31	lost to Stanford 22-25	10	10	11	Arkansas	9-2-1
PB	12	Michigan State	8-3-0				14	PB	12	Michigan State	8-3-0
12	13	Maryland	9-2-0	Sun Bowl	D23	lost to # 14 Texas 0-42	16	13	13	Purdue	9-2-1
14	14	Texas	8-3-0	Sun Bowl	D23	beat # 13 Maryland 42-0	23		14	UCLA	8-3-1
16	15	UCLA	8-3-0	Fiesta Bowl	D25	tied # 8 Arkansas 10-10	22	14	15	Missouri	8-4-0
13	16	Pittsburgh	8-3-0				15	15	16	Georgia	9-2-1
17	17	Purdue	8-2-1	Peach Bowl	D25	beat Georgia Tech 41-21	13	16	17	Stanford	8-4-0
15	18	Missouri	7-4-0	Liberty Bowl	D23	beat LSU 20-15	19	19	18	North Carolina St.	9-3-0
	19	Iowa State	8-3-0	Hall of Fame Classic	D20	lost to Texas A&M 12-28	20	18	19	Texas A&M	8-4-0
	20	Ohio State	7-3-1	Gator Bowl	D29	lost to # 7 Clemson 15-17	12		20	Maryland	9-3-0
18		LSU						27	17	Navy	9-3-0
19		Georgia Tech	7-4-0	Peach Bowl	D25	lost to # 17 Purdue 21-41	17	19		Arizona State	9-3-0
20		Stanford	7-4-0	Bluebonnet Bowl	D31	beat # 11 Georgia 25-22					

1978

CONSENSUS ALL-AMERICANS

POS	Offense	HT	WT	School	AP	FC	FW	PI
QB	Chuck Fusina	6-1	195	Penn State	•	•	•	•
RB	Billy Sims	6-0	205	Oklahoma	•	•	•	•
RB	Charles White	5-11	183	Southern Cal	•	•	•	•
RB	Ted Brown	5-10	195	North Carolina St.	•	•	•	•
RB	Charles Alexander	6-1	214	LSU	•	•		•
WR	Emanuel Tolbert	5-10	180	SMU	•		•	
TE	Kellen Winslow	6-6	235	Missouri	•	•		
T	Keith Dorney	6-5	257	Penn State	•	•	•	•
T	Kelvin Clark	6-4	275	Nebraska	•	•	•	•
G	Pat Howell	6-6	255	Southern Cal	•	•	•	•
G	Greg Roberts	6-3	238	Oklahoma	•	•	•	•
C	Dave Huffman	6-5	245	Notre Dame	•	•	•	•
C	Jim Ritcher	6-3	242	North Carolina St.	•	•	•	•

OTHERS RECEIVING FIRST-TEAM HONORS

RB	Rick Leach	Michigan	•
WR	Gordon Jones	Pittsburgh	•
WR	Jerry Butler	Clemson	•
WR	Kirk Gibson	Michigan State	•
TE	Mark Brammer	Michigan State	•
T	Matt Miller	Colorado	•
K	Tony Franklin	Texas A&M	•

POS	Defense	HT	WT	School	AP	FC	FW	PI
L	Al Harris	6-5	240	Arizona State	•	•	•	•
L	Bruce Clark	6-3	246	Penn State	•	•	•	•
L	Hugh Green	6-2	215	Pittsburgh	•	•	•	
L	Mike Bell	6-5	265	Colorado State	•	•	•	
L	Marty Lyons	6-6	250	Alabama	•	•	•	•
LB	Bob Golic	6-3	244	Notre Dame	•	•	•	•
LB	Jerry Robinson	6-3	209	UCLA	•	•	•	•
LB	Tom Cousineau	6-3	227	Ohio State	•	•	•	
B	Johnnie Johnson	6-2	183	Texas	•	•	•	
B	Kenny Easley	6-2	202	UCLA	•	•	•	•
B	Jeff Nixon	6-4	195	Richmond	•	•	•	

OTHERS RECEIVING FIRST-TEAM HONORS

DL	Jimmy Walker	Arkansas	•
DL	Dan Hampton	Arkansas	•
DL	Don Smith	Miami, Fla.	• •
DL	Reggie Kinlaw	Oklahoma	•
DL	Matt Millen	Penn State	•
LB	Ken Fantetti	Wyoming	•
LB	John Corker	Oklahoma State	•
B	Henry Williams	San Diego State	•
B	Pete Harris	Penn State	•
P	Russell Erxleben	Texas	•

HEISMAN TROPHY VOTING

	PLAYER	POS	SCHOOL	1ST	2ND	3RD	TOTAL
1	Billy Sims	HB	Oklahoma	151	152	70	827
2	Chuck Fusina	QB	Penn State	163	89	83	750
3	Rick Leach	QB	Michigan	89	58	52	435
4	Charles White	TB	Southern Cal	36	74	98	354
5	Charles Alexander	TB	LSU	42	51	54	282
6	Ted Brown	RB	North Carolina St.	5	19	29	82
	Steve Fuller	QB	Clemson	19	6	13	82
8	Eddie Lee Ivery	RB	Georgia Tech	11	19	10	81
9	Jack Thompson	QB	Washington State	13	11	11	72
10	Jerry Robinson	LB	UCLA	12	11	12	70

AWARD WINNERS

PLAYER	POS	SCHOOL	AWARD NAME
Chuck Fusina	QB	Penn State	Maxwell
Greg Roberts	G	Oklahoma	Outland
Billy Sims	RB	Oklahoma	Camp
Bruce Clark	D	Penn State	Lombardi

BOWL GAMES

DATE	GAME	SCORE
D16	Garden State	Arizona State 34, Rutgers 18
D16	Independence	East Carolina 35, Louisiana Tech 13
D20	All-American	Texas A&M 28, Iowa State 12
D22	Holiday	Navy 23, Brigham Young 16
D23	Liberty	Missouri 20, LSU 15
D23	Tangerine	North Carolina St. 30, Pittsburgh 17
D23	Sun	Texas 42, Maryland 0
D25	Fiesta	Arkansas 10, UCLA 10

DATE	GAME	SCORE
D25	Peach	Purdue 41, Georgia Tech 21
D29	Gator	Clemson 17, Ohio State 15
D31	Bluebonnet	Stanford 25, Georgia 22
J1	Sugar	Alabama 14, Penn State 7
J1	Cotton	Notre Dame 35, Houston 34
J1	Orange	Oklahoma 31, Nebraska 24
J1	Rose	Southern Cal 17, Michigan 10

CONFERENCE STANDINGS

ACC

	CONF. W L T	OVERALL W L T
Clemson	6 0 0	11 1 0
Maryland	5 1 0	9 3 0
North Carolina St.	4 2 0	9 3 0
North Carolina	3 3 0	5 6 0
Duke	2 4 0	4 7 0
Wake Forest	1 5 0	1 10 0
Virginia	0 6 0	2 9 0

Big 10

	CONF. W L T	OVERALL W L T
Michigan	7 1 0	10 2 0
Michigan State	7 1 0	8 3 0
Purdue	6 1 1	9 2 1
Ohio State	6 2 0	7 4 1
Minnesota	4 4 0	5 6 0
Wisconsin	3 4 2	5 4 2
Indiana	3 5 0	4 7 0
Iowa	2 6 0	2 9 0
Illinois	0 6 2	1 8 2
Northwestern	0 8 1	0 10 1

Big 8

	CONF. W L T	OVERALL W L T
Oklahoma	6 1 0	11 1 0
Nebraska	6 1 0	9 3 0
Iowa State	4 3 0	8 4 0
Missouri	4 3 0	8 4 0
Kansas State	3 4 0	4 7 0
Oklahoma State	3 4 0	3 8 0
Colorado	2 5 0	6 5 0
Kansas	0 7 0	1 10 0

Big West

	CONF. W L T	OVERALL W L T
Utah State	4 1 0	7 4 0
San Jose State	4 1 0	7 5 0
Pacific	3 2 0	4 8 0
Cal-St. Fullerton	2 3 0	5 7 0
Long Beach State	1 4 0	5 6 0
Fresno State	1 4 0	3 8 0

Ivy

	CONF. W L T	OVERALL W L T
Dartmouth	6 1 0	6 3 0
Brown	5 2 0	6 3 0
Yale	4 1 2	5 2 2
Cornell	3 3 1	5 3 1
Harvard	2 4 1	4 4 1
Columbia	2 4 1	3 5 1
Princeton	1 4 2	2 5 2
Pennsylvania	1 5 1	2 6 1

MAC

	CONF. W L T	OVERALL W L T
Ball State	8 0 0	10 1 0
Central Michigan	8 1 0	9 2 0
Miami, Ohio	5 2 0	8 2 1
Western Michigan	5 4 0	7 4 0
Bowling Green	3 5 0	4 7 0
Ohio U	3 5 0	3 8 0
Northern Illinois	2 4 0	5 6 0
Kent State	2 6 0	4 7 0
Toledo	2 7 0	2 9 0
Eastern Michigan	1 5 0	3 7 0

Pac 10

	CONF. W L T	OVERALL W L T
Southern Cal	6 1 0	12 1 0
UCLA	6 2 0	8 3 1
Washington	6 2 0	7 4 0
Arizona State	4 3 0	9 3 0
Stanford	4 3 0	8 4 0
California	3 4 0	6 5 0
Arizona	3 4 0	5 6 0
Oregon	2 5 0	2 9 0
Oregon State	2 6 0	3 7 1
Washington State	1 7 0	3 7 1

SEC

	CONF. W L T	OVERALL W L T
Alabama	6 0 0	11 1 0
Georgia	5 0 1	9 2 1
Auburn	3 2 1	6 4 1
LSU	3 3 0	8 4 0
Tennessee	3 3 0	5 5 1
Florida	3 3 0	4 7 0
Mississippi State	2 4 0	6 5 0
Mississippi	2 4 0	5 6 0
Kentucky	2 4 0	4 6 1
Vanderbilt	0 6 0	2 9 0

SWC

	CONF. W L T	OVERALL W L T
Houston	7 1 0	9 3 0
Arkansas	6 2 0	9 2 1
Texas	6 2 0	9 3 0
Texas Tech	5 3 0	7 4 0
Texas A&M	4 4 0	8 4 0
SMU	3 5 0	4 6 1
Baylor	3 5 0	3 8 0
Rice	2 6 0	2 9 0
TCU	0 8 0	2 9 0

WAC

	CONF. W L T	OVERALL W L T
Brigham Young	5 1 0	9 4 0
Utah	4 2 0	8 3 0
Wyoming	4 2 0	5 7 0
New Mexico	3 3 0	7 5 0
Colorado State	2 4 0	5 6 0
San Diego State	2 4 0	4 7 0
Texas-El Paso	1 5 0	1 11 0

Independents

	OVERALL W L T
Penn State	11 1 0
North Texas	9 2 0
Navy	9 3 0
East Carolina	9 3 0
Rutgers	9 3 0
Notre Dame	9 3 0
Florida State	8 3 0
Temple	7 3 1
Pittsburgh	8 4 0
Nevada-Las Vegas	7 4 0
Southern Miss	7 4 0
Louisville	7 4 0
Georgia Tech	7 5 0
Miami, Fla.	6 5 0
Hawaii	6 5 0
South Carolina	5 5 1
Cincinnati	5 6 0
Army	4 6 1
Memphis	4 7 0
Tulane	4 7 0
Virginia Tech	4 7 0
Air Force	3 8 0
Syracuse	3 8 0
West Virginia	2 9 0
Boston College	0 11 0

1978 NCAA Major College Statistical Leaders

Individual Leaders

Passing

		G	ATT	COM	PCT	INT	I%	YDS	YPA	TD	TD%	COM.PG
1	Steve Dils, Stanford	11	391	247	63.2	15	3.8	2943	7.5	22	5.6	22.5
2	Mike Ford, SMU	11	389	224	57.6	23	5.9	3007	7.7	17	4.4	20.4
3	Mark Halda, San Diego State	11	358	205	57.3	14	3.9	2262	6.3	14	3.9	18.6
4	Ed Luther, San Jose State	12	386	205	53.1	23	6.0	2275	5.9	13	3.4	17.1
5	Ed Smith, Michigan State	10	292	169	57.9	8	2.7	2226	7.6	20	6.8	16.9
6	Jack Thompson, Washington State	11	348	175	50.3	20	5.7	2333	6.7	17	4.9	15.9
7	Randy Hertel, Rice	10	279	156	55.9	11	3.9	1677	6.0	12	4.3	15.6
8	Mark Hutsell, East Tennessee State	11	294	171	58.2	15	5.1	2160	7.3	14	4.8	15.5
9	Paul McGaffigan, Long Beach State	11	302	170	56.3	13	4.3	2164	7.2	9	3.0	15.5
10	David Spriggs, New Mexico State	11	317	169	53.3	25	7.9	2558	8.1	17	5.4	15.4

All-Purpose

		G	RUSH	REC	PR	KR	YDS	YPG
1	Charles White, Southern Cal	12	1760	191	0	145	2096	174.7
2	Eddie Lee Ivery, Georgia Tech	11	1562	238	79	0	1879	170.8
3	Billy Sims, Oklahoma	11	1762	35	0	0	1797	163.4
4	Joe Holland, Cornell	9	1396	31	0	36	1463	162.6
5	Darrin Nelson, Stanford	11	1061	446	254	13	1774	161.3
6	Cormac Carney, Air Force	11	-9	870	67	807	1735	157.7
7	Obie Graves, Cal-St. Fullerton	12	1789	103	0	0	1892	157.7
8	Ottis Anderson, Miami, Fla.	11	1268	47	0	395	1710	155.5
9	Theotis Brown, UCLA	11	1199	74	0	434	1707	155.2
10	Bernard Jackson, North Texas	11	1453	76	0	75	1604	145.8

Rushing/Yards Per Game

		G	ATT	YDS	TD	AVG	YPG
1	Billy Sims, Oklahoma	11	231	1762	20	7.6	160.2
2	Joe Holland, Cornell	9	273	1396	16	5.1	155.1
3	Obie Graves, Cal-St. Fullerton	12	275	1789	9	6.5	149.1
4	Charles White, Southern Cal	12	342	1760	12	5.1	146.7
5	Eddie Lee Ivery, Georgia Tech	11	267	1562	9	5.9	142.0
6	Bernard Jackson, North Texas	11	269	1453	6	5.4	132.1
7	Nathan Poole, Louisville	11	212	1394	15	6.6	126.7
8	James Hadnot, Texas Tech	11	251	1369	5	5.5	124.5
9	Ted Brown, North Carolina St.	11	302	1350	11	4.5	122.7
10	Jerome Persell, Western Michigan	11	309	1346	6	4.4	122.4

Rushing/Yards Per Carry

		G	ATT	YDS	YPC
1	Billy Sims, Oklahoma	11	231	1762	7.6
2	Nathan Poole, Louisville	11	212	1394	6.6
3	Obie Graves, Cal-St. Fullerton	12	275	1789	6.5
4	Darrin Nelson, Stanford	11	167	1061	6.4
5	Bernell Quinn, Southern Illinois	9	152	939	6.2
6	Frank Mordica, Vanderbilt	11	173	1065	6.2
7	Theotis Brown, UCLA	11	200	1199	6.0
8	Emmett King, Houston	11	183	1095	6.0
9	Joe Morris, Syracuse	10	170	1001	5.9
10	Eddie Lee Ivery, Georgia Tech	11	267	1562	5.9

*-Based on top 38 rushers

Receiving

		G	REC	YDS	TD	YPR	YPG	RPG
1	Dave Petzke, Northern Illinois	11	91	1217	11	13.4	110.6	8.3
2	Gerald Harp, Western Carolina	11	62	1155	11	18.6	105.0	5.6
2	Emanuel Tolbert, SMU	11	62	1040	11	16.8	94.5	5.6
4	Vernon Henry, Long Beach State	11	60	985	6	16.4	89.5	5.5
4	Rick Beasley, Appalachian State	11	60	971	4	16.2	88.3	5.5
6	David Shula, Dartmouth	9	49	656	1	13.4	72.9	5.4
6	Phil Francis, Stanford	9	49	378	0	7.7	42.0	5.4
8	Cormac Carney, Air Force	11	57	870	8	15.3	79.1	5.2
9	Jeff Groth, Bowling Green	11	56	874	8	15.6	79.5	5.1
10	Jerry Butler, Clemson	11	54	864	3	16.0	78.5	4.9

Punting

		PUNT	YDS	AVG
1	Maury Buford, Texas Tech	71	3131	44.1
2	Tom Orosz, Ohio State	43	2464	43.9
3	Rick Partridge, Utah	56	1889	43.9
4	Russell Erxleben, Texas	72	3128	43.4
5	Scott Schafer, Air Force	62	2679	43.2
6	Jim Miller, Mississippi	76	3283	43.2
7	Eddie Hare, Tulsa	66	2846	43.1
8	Ray Stachowicz, Michigan State	39	1681	43.1
9	Guy McClure, Utah State	55	2367	43.0
10	Don Clayton, Wyoming	57	2446	42.9

Punt Returns

		PUNT	YDS	TD	AVG
1	Ira Matthews, Wisconsin	16	270	3	16.9
2	Richard Ellender, McNeese St.	22	349	3	15.9
3	Kenny Brown, Nebraska	19	278	1	14.6
4	Willie Jordan, Clemson	20	277	0	13.8
5	Gerald Hall, East Carolina	36	478	1	13.3
6	Darrin Nelson, Stanford	20	254	0	12.7
7	Larry Carter, Kentucky	29	354	2	12.2
8	Scott Woerner, Georgia	23	279	1	12.1
9	James Johnson, Eastern Michigan	24	287	2	12.0
10	Eddie Hood, Vanderbilt	14	166	0	11.9

Kickoff Returns

		KR	YDS	TD	AVG
1	Drew Hill, Georgia Tech	19	570	2	30.0
2	Howard Ballage, Colorado	18	530	1	29.4
3	Ken Hill, Yale	11	322	1	29.3
4	Jimmy Bryant, Utah State	20	551	1	27.5
5	Theotis Brown, UCLA	16	434	1	27.1
6	Sean McCall, Virginia	19	511	0	26.9
7	Jesse Williams, Richmond	17	455	1	26.8
8	Lindsay Scott, Georgia	20	529	1	26.4
9	Charles Fowler, Appalachian State	21	555	0	26.4
10	Ronnie Horton, East Tennessee State	17	447	1	26.3

Scoring

		TDS	XPT	FG	PTS	PTPG
1	Billy Sims, Oklahoma	20	0	0	120	10.9
2	Joe Holland, Cornell	16	0	0	96	10.7
3	Joe Cribbs, Auburn	16	2	0	98	9.8
4	Lester Brown, Clemson	17	0	0	102	9.3
5	Matt Bahr, Penn State	0	31	22	97	8.8
6	Charles Alexander, LSU	16	0	0	96	8.7
6	Nathan Poole, Louisville	16	0	0	96	8.7
8	Scott McConnell, Appalachian State	14	4	0	88	8.0
8	Willie Todd, Central Michigan	13	2	0	80	8.0
10	James Jones, Mississippi State	13	6	0	84	7.6

Field Goals

		FGA	FGM	PCT	FGG
1	Matt Bahr, Penn State	27	22	0.82	2.00
2	Steve Steinke, Utah State	24	18	0.75	1.64
3	Nathan Ritter, North Carolina St.	19	17	0.90	1.60
3	Doug Dobbs, Arkansas State	22	17	0.77	1.60
5	Berj Yepremian, Florida	20	16	0.80	1.50
5	Bill Adams, Texas Tech	20	16	0.80	1.50
5	Dave Jacobs, Syracuse	23	16	0.70	1.50
5	Ed Loncar, Maryland	26	16	0.62	1.50
5	Jim Sturch, Air Force	26	16	0.62	1.50
10	Rex Robinson, Georgia	17	15	0.88	1.40
10	Scott Sovereen, Purdue	21	15	0.71	1.40
10	Steven Duncan, San Diego State	23	15	0.65	1.40
10	Rade Savich, Central Michigan	24	15	0.63	1.40

Interceptions

		INT	YDS	TD	INT/GM
1	Pete Harris, Penn State	10	155	0	0.91
2	Chris Williams, LSU	8	72	0	0.73
3	Roland James, Tennessee	7	126	1	0.70
4	Arnie Pinkston, Yale	6	27	0	0.67
5	Jeff Nixon, Richmond	7	171	2	0.64
5	Glenn Verrette, Holy Cross	7	164	1	0.64
5	Marty Morrison, North Texas	7	111	1	0.64
5	Darrol Ray, Oklahoma	7	99	0	0.64
5	David Hill, SMU	7	88	2	0.64
5	Kim Anderson, Arizona State	7	44	0	0.64

Team Leaders

Rushing Offense

		G	ATT	YDS	AVG	TD	YPG
1	Oklahoma	11	721	4703	6.5	51	427.5
2	Nebraska	11	699	3715	5.3	40	337.7
3	Texas Arlington	11	664	3368	5.1	25	306.2
4	Cal-St. Fullerton	12	687	3632	5.3	28	302.7
5	Houston	11	663	3306	5.0	30	300.5
6	Clemson	11	681	3262	4.8	37	296.5
7	Ohio State	11	688	3160	4.6	35	287.3
8	Alabama	11	638	3158	4.9	31	287.1
9	Michigan	11	694	3152	4.5	31	286.5
10	Arkansas	11	677	3119	4.6	34	283.5

Passing Offense

		G	ATT	COM	INT	PCT	YDS	YPA	TD	I%	YPC	YPG
1	SMU	11	391	225	23	57.5	3038	7.8	18	5.9	13.5	276.2
2	Stanford	11	401	251	17	62.6	2947	7.3	24	4.2	11.7	267.9
3	Florida State	11	369	206	16	55.8	2749	7.4	23	4.3	13.3	249.9
4	California	11	345	189	24	54.8	2698	7.8	17	7.0	14.3	245.3
5	New Mexico State	11	341	180	29	52.8	2667	7.8	18	8.5	14.8	242.5
6	Mississippi State	11	311	177	18	56.9	2637	8.5	14	5.8	14.9	239.7
7	Michigan State	11	340	194	10	57.1	2631	7.7	22	2.9	13.7	239.2
8	Brigham Young	12	416	210	22	50.5	2858	6.9	14	5.3	13.6	238.2
9	Long Beach State	11	369	202	16	54.7	2521	6.8	9	4.3	12.5	229.2
10	Tennessee State	11	305	163	18	53.4	2455	8.0	15	5.9	15.1	223.2

Total Offense

		G	P	YDS	AVG	TD	YPG
1	Nebraska	11	897	5515	6.1	53	501.4
2	Oklahoma	11	816	5382	6.6	59	489.3
3	Michigan State	11	838	5294	6.3	54	481.3
4	Clemson	11	866	4804	5.5	44	436.7
5	Stanford	11	886	4791	5.4	38	435.5
6	Furman	11	817	4648	5.7	42	422.5
7	Cal-St. Fullerton	12	863	5053	5.9	36	421.1
8	Houston	11	852	4619	5.4	43	419.9
9	Arizona State	11	905	4566	5.0	41	415.1
10	Missouri	11	820	4557	5.6	45	414.3

Rushing Defense

		G	ATT	YDS	AVG	TD	YPG
1	Penn State	11	408	599	1.5	4	54.5
2	Southern Cal	12	471	1096	2.3	4	91.3
3	Arizona State	11	494	1074	2.2	13	97.6
4	U.T. Chattanooga	11	463	1098	2.4	11	99.8
5	Ball State	11	472	1124	2.4	4	102.2
6	Tennessee State	11	448	1193	2.7	8	108.5
7	Texas	11	535	1222	2.3	11	111.1
8	Michigan	11	426	1240	2.9	6	112.7
9	Pittsburgh	11	535	1243	2.3	10	113.0
10	Arkansas	11	468	1250	2.7	10	113.6

Passing Defense

		G	ATT	COM	PCT	YPC	INT	I%	YDS	YPA	TD	YPG
1	Boston College	11	155	73	47.1	9.8	10	6.5	716	4.6	3	65.1
2	East Carolina	11	180	70	38.9	12.0	19	10.6	837	4.7	3	76.1
3	Miami, Ohio	11	213	85	39.9	12.2	15	7.0	1039	4.9	5	94.5
4	Arkansas State	11	172	70	40.7	15.1	13	7.6	1054	6.1	3	95.8
4	Cincinnati	11	207	81	39.1	13.0	14	6.8	1054	5.1	11	95.8
4	William & Mary	11	181	88	48.6	12.0	7	3.9	1054	5.8	7	95.8
7	Northern Illinois	11	175	80	45.7	13.8	16	9.1	1100	6.3	2	100.0
8	Clemson	11	209	96	45.9	11.5	23	11.0	1103	5.3	4	100.3
9	Central Michigan	11	215	81	37.7	13.7	22	10.2	1111	5.2	6	101.0
10	Richmond	11	188	86	45.7	13.0	17	9.0	1114	5.9	10	101.3

Total Defense

		G	P	YDS	AVG	TD	YPG
1	Penn State	11	729	2243	3.1	10	203.9
2	East Carolina	11	720	2253	3.1	10	204.8
3	Ball State	11	719	2333	3.2	7	212.1
4	Michigan	11	665	2372	3.6	10	215.6
5	Tennessee State	11	689	2537	3.7	18	230.6
6	Texas A&M	11	716	2630	3.7	20	239.1
7	Central Michigan	11	738	2645	3.6	15	240.5
8	Texas	11	781	2646	3.4	17	240.5
9	Arkansas State	11	698	2668	3.8	15	242.5
10	Arkansas	11	706	2685	3.8	18	244.1

Scoring Offense

		G	PTS	AVG
1	Oklahoma	11	440	40.0
2	Nebraska	11	420	38.2
3	Michigan State	11	411	37.4
4	Michigan	11	362	32.9
5	Clemson	11	351	31.9
6	Missouri	11	348	31.6
7	Appalachian State	11	338	30.7
8	Alabama	11	331	30.1
8	Central Michigan	11	331	30.1
10	Houston	11	330	30.0

Scoring Defense

		G	PTS	AVG
1	Ball State	11	82	7.5
2	Michigan	11	88	8.0
3	Penn State	11	97	8.8
4	Purdue	11	109	9.9
5	Clemson	11	116	10.5
6	Central Michigan	11	119	10.8
7	Navy	11	120	10.9
8	East Carolina	11	123	11.2
9	Maryland	11	125	11.4
10	Rutgers	11	131	11.9

Turnover Margin

		G	FR	INT	TOT	FL	INTL	TOT	MAR
1	Penn State	11	14	28	42	6	14	20	2.0
2	North Texas	11	21	28	49	22	6	28	1.9
3	McNeese St.	11	20	24	44	14	11	25	1.7
4	Rutgers	11	16	23	39	11	10	21	1.6
4	Clemson	11	15	23	38	15	5	20	1.6

1979 POLL PROGRESSION

Pre-Season 1979 — Sept. 8 Games

AP	Team	Record	Result
1	Southern Cal	0-0-0	beat Texas Tech 21-7
2	Alabama	0-0-0	beat Georgia Tech 30-6
3	Oklahoma	0-0-0	bye week
4	Texas	0-0-0	bye week
5	Penn State	0-0-0	bye week
6	Purdue	0-0-0	beat Wisconsin 41-20
7	Michigan	0-0-0	beat Northwestern 49-7
8	Nebraska	0-0-0	bye week
9	Notre Dame	0-0-0	bye week
10	Michigan State	0-0-0	beat Illinois 33-16
11	Georgia	0-0-0	bye week
12	Missouri	0-0-0	beat San Diego State 45-15
13	Stanford	0-0-0	lost to Tulane 10-33
14	Texas A&M	0-0-0	lost to Brigham Young 17-18
15	Washington	0-0-0	beat Wyoming 38-2
16	Houston	0-0-0	beat UCLA 24-16
17	Pittsburgh	0-0-0	bye week
18	Arizona State	0-0-0	lost to California 9-17
19	Florida State	0-0-0	beat Southern Miss 17-14
20	Arkansas	0-0-0	bye week

September 10 Poll — Sept. 15 Games

UP	AP	Team	Record	Result
1	1	Southern Cal	1-0-0	beat Oregon State 42-5
2	2	Alabama	1-0-0	bye week
3	3	Oklahoma	0-0-0	beat Iowa 21-6
4	4	Texas	0-0-0	bye week
7	5	Purdue	1-0-0	lost to UCLA 21-31
5	6	Michigan	1-0-0	lost to # 9 Notre Dame 10-12
6	7	Penn State	0-0-0	beat Rutgers 45-10
8	8	Nebraska	0-0-0	beat Utah State 35-14
11	9	Notre Dame	0-0-0	beat # 6 Michigan 12-10
10	10	Michigan State	1-0-0	beat Oregon 41-17
12	11	Missouri	1-0-0	beat Illinois 14-6
14	12	Georgia	0-0-0	lost to Wake Forest 21-22
9	13	Houston	1-0-0	beat Florida 14-10
13	14	Washington	1-0-0	beat Utah 41-7
16	15	Ohio State	1-0-0	beat Minnesota 21-17
15	16	Pittsburgh	0-0-0	beat Kansas 24-0
17	17	Arkansas	0-0-0	beat Colorado State 36-3
18	18	Florida State	1-0-0	beat Arizona State 31-3
19	19	North Carolina St.	1-0-0	beat Virginia 31-27
	20	SMU	1-0-0	beat TCU 27-7
20		Brigham Young	1-0-0	beat Weber St. 48-3

September 17 Poll — Sept. 22 Games

UP	AP	Team	Record	Result
1	1	Southern Cal	2-0-0	beat Minnesota 48-14
2	2	Alabama	1-0-0	beat Baylor 45-0
3	3	Oklahoma	1-0-0	beat Tulsa 49-13
4	4	Texas	0-0-0	beat Iowa State 17-9
5	5	Notre Dame	1-0-0	lost to # 17 Purdue 22-28
6	6	Penn State	1-0-0	lost to Texas A&M 14-27
7	7	Nebraska	1-0-0	beat Iowa 24-21
8	8	Michigan State	2-0-0	beat Miami, Ohio 24-21
11	9	Missouri	2-0-0	beat Mississippi 33-7
9	10	Houston	2-0-0	bye week
12	11	Michigan	1-1-0	beat Kansas 28-7
10	12	Washington	2-0-0	beat Oregon 21-17
13	13	Pittsburgh	1-0-0	lost to North Carolina 7-17
14	14	Florida State	2-0-0	beat Miami, Fla. 40-23
16	15	Arkansas	1-0-0	beat Oklahoma State 27-7
15	16	Ohio State	2-0-0	beat Washington State 45-29
	17	Purdue	1-1-0	beat # 5 Notre Dame 28-22
	18	SMU	2-0-0	beat North Texas 20-9
20	19	North Carolina St.	2-0-0	beat West Virginia 38-14
18	20	UCLA	1-1-0	beat Wisconsin 37-12
17		LSU	1-0-0	beat Rice 47-3
19		Brigham Young	2-0-0	bye week

September 24 Poll — Sept. 29 Games

UP	AP	Team	Record	Result
1	1	Southern Cal	3-0-0	beat # 20 LSU 17-12
2	2	Alabama	2-0-0	beat Vanderbilt 66-3
3	3	Oklahoma	2-0-0	beat Rice 63-21
4	4	Texas	1-0-0	beat # 5 Missouri 21-0
7	5	Missouri	2-0-0	lost to # 4 Texas 0-21
5	6	Nebraska	2-0-0	beat # 18 Penn State 42-17
6	7	Michigan State	3-0-0	lost to # 15 Notre Dame 3-27
8	8	Houston	2-0-0	beat West Texas St. 49-10
9	9	Washington	3-0-0	beat Fresno State 49-14
12	10	Purdue	2-1-0	beat Oregon 13-7
13	11	Michigan	2-1-0	beat California 14-10
10	12	Florida State	3-0-0	beat Virginia Tech 17-10
14	13	Arkansas	2-0-0	beat Tulsa 33-8
11	14	Ohio State	3-0-0	beat # 17 UCLA 17-13
16	15	Notre Dame	1-1-0	beat # 7 Michigan State 27-3
19	16	North Carolina St.	3-0-0	beat Wake Forest 17-14
17	17	UCLA	2-1-0	lost to # 14 Ohio State 13-17
18	18	Penn State	1-1-0	lost to # 6 Nebraska 17-42
	19	SMU	3-0-0	lost to Tulane 17-24
15	20	LSU	2-0-0	lost to # 1 Southern Cal 12-17
20		North Carolina	2-0-0	beat Army 41-3

October 1 Poll — Oct. 6 Games

UP	AP	Team	Record	Result
1	1	Southern Cal	4-0-0	beat Washington State 50-21
2	2	Alabama	3-0-0	beat Wichita St. 38-0
3	3	Oklahoma	3-0-0	beat Colorado 49-24
4	4	Texas	2-0-0	beat Rice 26-9
5	5	Nebraska	3-0-0	beat New Mexico State 57-0
6	6	Houston	3-0-0	beat Baylor 13-10
7	7	Washington	4-0-0	beat Oregon State 41-0
8	8	Ohio State	4-0-0	beat Northwestern 16-7
10	9	Florida State	4-0-0	beat Louisville 27-0
9	10	Notre Dame	2-1-0	beat Georgia Tech 21-13
11	11	Michigan	3-1-0	beat # 16 Michigan State 21-7
13	12	Purdue	3-1-0	lost to Minnesota 14-31
12	13	Arkansas	3-0-0	beat TCU 16-13
15	14	North Carolina St.	4-0-0	lost to Auburn 31-44
17	15	Missouri	3-1-0	bye week
16	16	Michigan State	3-1-0	lost to # 11 Michigan 7-21
14	17	LSU	2-1-0	beat Florida 20-3
	16	North Carolina	3-0-0	beat Cincinnati 35-14
19	19	Tennessee	3-0-0	lost to Mississippi State 9-28
20	20	Brigham Young	3-0-0	beat Hawaii 38-15 OS

October 8 Poll — Oct. 13 Games

UP	AP	Team	Record	Result
1	1	Southern Cal	5-0-0	tied Stanford 21-21
2	2	Alabama	4-0-0	beat Florida 40-0
3	3	Oklahoma	4-0-0	lost to # 4 Texas 7-16
5	4	Texas	3-0-0	beat # 3 Oklahoma 16-7
4	5	Nebraska	4-0-0	beat Kansas 42-0
7	6	Washington	5-0-0	lost to Arizona State 7-12
6	7	Houston	4-0-0	beat Texas A&M 17-14
8	8	Ohio State	5-0-0	beat Indiana 47-6
10	9	Florida State	5-0-0	beat Mississippi State 17-6
9	10	Notre Dame	3-1-0	beat Air Force 38-13
11	11	Michigan	4-1-0	beat Minnesota 31-21
13	12	Arkansas	4-0-0	beat Texas Tech 20-6
12	13	LSU	3-1-0	lost to Georgia 14-21
14	14	North Carolina	4-0-0	lost to Wake Forest 19-24
15	15	Missouri	3-1-0	lost to Oklahoma State 13-14
16	16	Brigham Young	4-0-0	beat Utah State 48-24
19	17	North Carolina St.	4-1-0	beat Maryland 7-0
PB	18	Auburn	3-1-0	beat Vanderbilt 52-35
	19	Michigan State	3-2-0	lost to Wisconsin 29-38
	20	Purdue	3-2-0	beat Illinois 28-14
17		Pittsburgh	3-1-0	beat Cincinnati 35-0
18		Navy	4-0-0	beat William & Mary 24-7
20		Mississippi State	2-2-0	lost to # 9 Florida State 6-17

October 15 Poll — Oct. 20 Games

UP	AP	Team	Record	Result
1	1	Alabama	5-0-0	beat # 18 Tennessee 27-17
2	2	Texas	4-0-0	lost to # 10 Arkansas 14-17
3	3	Nebraska	5-0-0	beat Oklahoma State 36-0
4	4	Southern Cal	5-0-1	beat # 9 Notre Dame 42-23
5	5	Houston	5-0-0	beat SMU 37-10
6	6	Ohio State	6-0-0	beat Wisconsin 59-0
7	7	Florida State	6-0-0	bye week
8	8	Oklahoma	4-1-0	beat Kansas State 38-6
9	9	Notre Dame	4-1-0	lost to # 4 Southern Cal 23-42
10	10	Arkansas	5-0-0	beat # 2 Texas 17-14
11	11	Michigan	5-1-0	beat Illinois 27-7
12	12	Washington	5-1-0	lost to # 17 Pittsburgh 14-26
13	13	Brigham Young	5-0-0	beat Wyoming 54-14
PB	14	Auburn	4-1-0	beat Georgia Tech 38-14
17	15	North Carolina St.	5-1-0	lost to # 19 North Carolina 21-35
15	16	Purdue	4-2-0	beat Michigan State 14-7
14	17	Pittsburgh	4-1-0	beat # 12 Washington 26-14
19	18	Tennessee	4-1-0	lost to # 1 Alabama 17-27
18	19	North Carolina	4-1-0	beat # 15 North Carolina St. 35-21
16	20	Navy	5-0-0	beat Virginia 17-10
20		LSU	3-2-0	beat Kentucky 23-19

October 22 Poll — Oct. 27 Games

UP	AP	Team	Record	Result
1	1	Alabama	6-0-0	beat Virginia Tech 31-7
2	2	Nebraska	6-0-0	beat Colorado 38-10
3	3	Southern Cal	6-0-1	beat California 24-14
4	4	Arkansas	6-0-0	lost to # 6 Houston 10-13
5	4	Ohio State	7-0-0	beat Michigan State 42-0
4	6	Houston	6-0-0	beat # 4 Arkansas 13-10
7	7	Oklahoma	5-1-0	beat Iowa State 38-9
6	8	Florida State	7-0-0	beat LSU 24-19
9	9	Texas	4-1-0	beat SMU 30-6
10	10	Michigan	6-1-0	beat Indiana 27-21
11	11	Brigham Young	7-0-0	beat New Mexico 59-7
12	12	Pittsburgh	5-1-0	beat # 17 Navy 24-7
PB	13	Auburn	5-1-0	lost to # 18 Wake Forest 38-42
14	14	Notre Dame	4-2-0	beat South Carolina 18-17
13	15	North Carolina	5-1-0	tied East Carolina 24-24
16	16	Purdue	5-2-0	beat Northwestern 20-16
14	17	Navy	5-1-0	lost to # 12 Pittsburgh 7-24
18	18	Wake Forest	6-1-0	beat # 13 Auburn 42-38
	19	Tennessee	4-2-0	bye week
	20	Washington	5-2-0	beat UCLA 34-14
17		LSU	4-2-0	lost to # 8 Florida State 19-24
19		Penn State	4-2-0	beat West Virginia 31-6
20		Baylor	5-2-0	beat TCU 16-3

October 29 Poll — Nov. 3 Games

UP	AP	Team	Record	Result
1	1	Alabama	7-0-0	beat Mississippi State 24-7
2	2	Nebraska	7-0-0	beat Missouri 23-20
5	3	Southern Cal	7-0-1	beat Arizona 34-7
4	4	Houston	7-0-0	beat TCU 21-10
3	5	Ohio State	8-0-0	beat Illinois 44-7
6	6	Florida State	7-0-0	beat Cincinnati 26-21
7	7	Oklahoma	6-1-0	beat Oklahoma State 38-7
8	8	Texas	5-1-0	beat Texas Tech 14-6
9	9	Arkansas	6-1-0	beat Rice 34-7
10	10	Michigan	6-2-0	beat Wisconsin 54-0
11	11	Brigham Young	7-0-0	beat Colorado State 30-7
12	12	Pittsburgh	6-1-0	beat Syracuse 28-21
13	13	Notre Dame	5-2-0	beat Navy 14-0
14	14	Wake Forest	7-1-0	lost to Clemson 0-31
16	15	Purdue	6-2-0	beat Iowa 20-14
15	16	Washington	6-2-0	beat California 28-24
	17	Tennessee	4-2-0	lost to Rutgers 7-13
17	18	North Carolina	5-1-1	lost to Maryland 14-17
19	19	Penn State	5-2-0	lost to Miami, Fla. 10-26
PB	20	Auburn	5-2-0	beat Florida 19-13
18		Baylor	6-2-0	bye week
20		LSU		

November 5 Poll — Nov. 10 Games

UP	AP	Team	Record	Result
1	1	Alabama	8-0-0	beat LSU 3-0
2	2	Nebraska	8-0-0	beat Kansas State 21-12
5	3	Ohio State	9-0-0	beat Iowa 34-7
3	4	Southern Cal	8-0-1	beat #15 Washington 24-17
4	5	Houston	8-0-0	lost to #8 Texas 13-21
7	6	Oklahoma	7-1-0	beat Kansas 38-0
6	7	Florida State	8-0-0	beat #19 South Carolina 27-7
8	8	Texas	6-1-0	beat #5 Houston 21-13
9	9	Arkansas	7-1-0	beat #17 Baylor 29-20
10	10	Michigan	8-1-0	lost to #14 Purdue 21-24
11	11	Brigham Young	8-0-0	beat Long Beach State 31-17 N9
12	12	Pittsburgh	7-1-0	beat West Virginia 24-17
13	13	Notre Dame	6-2-0	lost to Tennessee 18-40
15	14	Purdue	7-2-0	beat #10 Michigan 24-21
14	15	Washington	7-2-0	lost to #4 Southern Cal 17-24
PB	16	Auburn	6-2-0	beat Mississippi State 14-3
16	17	Baylor	6-2-0	lost to #9 Arkansas 20-29
17	18	Clemson	6-2-0	beat North Carolina 19-10
	19	South Carolina	6-2-0	lost to #7 Florida State 7-27
19	20	Wake Forest	7-2-0	beat Duke 17-14
18		Temple	7-1-0	beat Akron 42-6
20		LSU	5-3-0	lost to #1 Alabama 0-3

November 12 Poll — Nov. 17 Games

UP	AP	Team	Record	Result
1	1	Alabama	9-0-0	beat Miami, Fla. 30-0
3	2	Ohio State	10-0-0	beat #13 Michigan 18-15
2	3	Nebraska	9-0-0	beat Iowa State 34-3
4	4	Southern Cal	9-0-1	bye week
5	5	Florida State	9-0-0	beat Memphis 66-17
6	6	Texas	7-1-0	beat TCU 35-10
7	7	Oklahoma	8-1-0	beat Missouri 24-22
9	8	Arkansas	8-1-0	beat Texas A&M 22-10
8	9	Houston	8-1-0	bye week
10	10	Brigham Young	9-0-0	beat Utah 27-0
11	11	Pittsburgh	8-1-0	beat Army 40-0
12	12	Purdue	8-2-0	beat Indiana 37-21
13	13	Michigan	8-2-0	lost to #2 Ohio State 15-18
14	14	Clemson	7-2-0	beat Notre Dame 16-10
PB	15	Auburn	7-2-0	beat Georgia 33-13
15	16	Washington	7-3-0	beat Washington St. 17-7
17	17	Wake Forest	8-2-0	lost to South Carolina 14-35
16	18	Temple	8-2-0	beat Villanova 42-10
18	19	Tennessee	5-3-0	lost to Mississippi 20-44
20	20	Baylor	6-3-0	beat Rice 45-14
	20	Tulane	8-2-0	bye week
19		Indiana	7-3-0	lost to #12 Purdue 21-37

November 19 Poll — Nov. 24 Games

UP	AP	Team	Record	Result
1	1	Alabama	10-0-0	bye week
3	2	Ohio State	11-0-0	regular season complete
2	3	Nebraska	10-0-0	lost to #8 Oklahoma 14-17
4	4	Southern Cal	9-0-1	beat UCLA 49-14
5	5	Florida State	10-0-0	beat Florida 27-16
6	6	Texas	8-1-0	beat #17 Baylor 13-0
8	7	Arkansas	9-1-0	beat SMU 31-7
7	8	Oklahoma	9-1-0	beat #3 Nebraska 17-14
9	9	Houston	8-1-0	beat Texas Tech 14-10
10	10	Brigham Young	10-0-0	beat San Diego State 63-14
11	11	Pittsburgh	9-1-0	bye week
12	12	Purdue	8-2-0	regular season complete
13	13	Clemson	8-2-0	lost to #19 South Carolina 9-13
PB	14	Auburn	8-2-0	bye week
14	15	Washington	8-3-0	regular season complete
15	16	Michigan	8-3-0	regular season complete
16	17	Baylor	7-3-0	lost to #6 Texas 0-13
17	18	Tulane	8-2-0	beat LSU 24-13
	19	South Carolina	7-3-0	beat #13 Clemson 13-9
	20	Penn State	7-3-0	bye week
18		LSU	6-4-0	lost to Tulane 13-24
19		Indiana	7-4-0	regular season complete
20		North Carolina St.	7-4-0	regular season complete

November 26 Poll — Dec. 1 Games

UP	AP	Team	Record	Result
1	1	Alabama	10-0-0	beat #14 Auburn 25-18
2	2	Southern Cal	10-0-1	regular season complete
3	3	Ohio State	11-0-0	
5	4	Florida State	11-0-0	regular season complete
4	5	Oklahoma	10-1-0	regular season complete
6	6	Texas	9-1-0	lost to Texas A&M 7-13
8	7	Nebraska	10-1-0	regular season complete
7	8	Arkansas	10-1-0	regular season complete
10	9	Brigham Young	11-0-0	regular season complete
9	10	Houston	9-1-0	beat Rice 63-0
11	11	Pittsburgh	9-1-0	beat #19 Penn State 29-14
12	12	Purdue	9-2-0	
13	13	Washington	8-3-0	
PB	14	Auburn	8-2-0	lost to #1 Alabama 18-25
14	15	Michigan	8-3-0	
15	16	Tulane	9-2-0	regular season complete
16	17	South Carolina	8-3-0	regular season complete
17	18	Clemson	8-3-0	regular season complete
20	19	Penn State	7-3-0	lost to #11 Pittsburgh 14-29
18	20	Baylor	7-4-0	regular season complete
19		Temple	9-2-0	regular season complete

December 3 Poll / January 3 Final Poll

UP	AP	Team	Record	Bowl Bid	Date	Bowl Result	RB	UP	AP	January 3 Final Poll	Record
3	1	Ohio State	11-0-0	Rose Bowl	J1	lost to #3 Southern Cal 16-17	1	1	1	Alabama	12-0-0
1	2	Alabama	11-0-0	Sugar Bowl	J1	beat #6 Arkansas 24-9	2	2	2	Southern Cal	11-0-1
2	3	Southern Cal	10-0-1	Rose Bowl	J1	beat #1 Ohio State 17-16	4	3	3	Oklahoma	11-1-0
4	4	Florida State	11-0-0	Orange Bowl	J1	lost to #5 Oklahoma 7-24	7	4	4	Ohio State	11-1-0
5	5	Oklahoma	10-1-0	Orange Bowl	J1	beat #4 Florida State 24-7	3	5	5	Houston	11-1-0
7	6	Arkansas	10-1-0	Sugar Bowl	J1	lost to #2 Alabama 9-24	6	8	6	Florida State	11-1-0
8	7	Nebraska	10-1-0	Cotton Bowl	J1	lost to #8 Houston 14-17	12	6	7	Pittsburgh	11-1-0
6	8	Houston	10-1-0	Cotton Bowl	J1	beat #7 Nebraska 17-14	5	9	8	Arkansas	10-2-0
9	9	Brigham Young	11-0-0	Holiday Bowl	D21	lost to Indiana 37-38	9	7	9	Nebraska	10-2-0
10	10	Pittsburgh	10-1-0	Fiesta Bowl	D25	beat Arizona 16-10	8	10	10	Purdue	10-2-0
11	11	Texas	9-2-0	Sun Bowl	D22	lost to #13 Washington 7-14	10	11	11	Washington	9-3-0
12	12	Purdue	9-2-0	Bluebonnet Bowl	D31	beat Tennessee 27-22	11	13	12	Texas	9-3-0
13	13	Washington	8-3-0	Sun Bowl	D22	beat #11 Texas 14-7	13	12	13	Brigham Young	11-1-0
14	14	Michigan	8-3-0	Gator Bowl	D28	lost to North Carolina 15-17	18	15	14	Baylor	8-4-0
15	15	Tulane	9-2-0	Liberty Bowl	D22	lost to Penn State 6-9	17	14	15	North Carolina	8-3-1
16	16	South Carolina	8-3-0	Hall of Fame Classic	D29	lost to Missouri 14-24	22	PB	16	Auburn	8-3-0
PB	17	Auburn	8-3-0				24	17	17	Temple	10-2-0
17	18	Clemson	8-3-0	Peach Bowl	D31	lost to #19 Baylor 18-24	21	19	18	Michigan	8-4-0
19	19	Baylor	7-4-0	Peach Bowl	D31	beat #18 Clemson 24-18	36	16	19	Indiana	8-4-0
18	20	Temple	9-2-0	Garden State Bowl	D15	beat California 28-17	20	18	20	Penn State	8-4-0
20		Penn State	7-4-0	Liberty Bowl	D22	beat #15 Tulane 9-6	15	20		Missouri	7-5-0

ANNUAL REVIEW

1979

CONSENSUS ALL-AMERICANS

POS	Offense	HT	WT	School	AP	FC	FW	PI
QB	Marc Wilson	6-5	204	Brigham Young	•	•	•	•
RB	Charles White	6-0	185	Southern Cal	•	•	•	•
RB	Billy Sims	6-0	205	Oklahoma	•	•	•	•
RB	Vagas Ferguson	6-1	194	Notre Dame	•	•	•	•
WR	Ken Margerum	6-1	175	Stanford	•	•	•	•
TE	Junior Miller	6-4	222	Nebraska	•	•	•	•
T	Greg Kolenda	6-1	258	Arkansas	•	•	•	•
T	Jim Bunch	6-2	240	Alabama	•	*	•	
G	Brad Budde	6-5	253	Southern Cal	•	•	•	•
G	Ken Fritz	6-3	238	Ohio State	•	•	•	•
C	Jim Ritcher	6-3	245	North Carolina St.	•	•	•	•
PK	Dale Castro	6-1	170	Maryland			•	

OTHERS RECEIVING FIRST-TEAM HONORS

RB	George Rogers	South Carolina	•
WR	Art Monk	Syracuse	•
T	Melvin Jones	Houston	•
T	Tim Foley	Notre Dame	•

FC named Jim Bunch as a G

POS	Defense	HT	WT	School	AP	FC	FW	PI
L	Hugh Green	6-2	220	Pittsburgh	•	•	•	•
L	Steve McMichael	6-2	250	Texas	•	•	•	•
L	Bruce Clark	6-3	255	Penn State	•	•	•	•
L	Jim Stuckey	6-5	241	Clemson	•	•	•	•
MG	Ron Simmons	6-1	235	Florida State	•	•	•	•
LB	George Cumby	6-0	205	Oklahoma	•	•	•	•
LB	Ron Simpkins	6-2	220	Michigan	•	•	•	•
LB	Mike Singletary	6-1	224	Baylor	•	•	•	•
B	Kenny Easley	6-3	204	UCLA	•	•	•	•
B	Johnnie Johnson	6-2	190	Texas	•	•	•	•
B	Roland James	6-2	182	Tennessee			•	
P	Jim Miller	5-11	183	Mississippi			•	

OTHERS RECEIVING FIRST-TEAM HONORS

DL	Curtis Greer	Michigan	•
DL	Jacob Green	Texas A&M	•
LB	David Hodge	Houston	•
LB	Dennis Johnson	Southern Cal	•
B	Mark Haynes	Colorado	•

FC named Simmons as a DL

HEISMAN TROPHY VOTING

	PLAYER	POS	SCHOOL	1ST	2ND	3RD	TOTAL
1	Charles White	TB	Southern Cal	453	144	48	1695
2	Billy Sims	HB	Oklahoma	82	180	167	773
3	Marc Wilson	QB	Brigham Young	72	124	125	589
4	Art Schlichter	QB	Ohio State	19	54	86	251
5	Vagas Ferguson	TB	Notre Dame	12	38	50	162
6	Paul McDonald	QB	Southern Cal	11	18	23	92
7	George Rogers	RB	South Carolina	8	20	17	81
8	Mark Herrmann	QB	Purdue	5	12	15	54
9	Ron Simmons	NG	Florida State	5	8	10	41
10	Steadman Shealy	QB	Alabama	1	10	9	31

AWARD WINNERS

PLAYER	POS	SCHOOL	AWARD NAME
Charles White	RB	Southern Cal	Maxwell
Jim Ritcher	C	North Carolina St.	Outland
Charles White	RB	Southern Cal	Camp
Brad Budde	G	Southern Cal	Lombardi

BOWL GAMES

DATE	GAME	SCORE
D15	Independence	Syracuse 31, McNeese St. 7
D15	Garden State	Temple 28, California 17
D21	Holiday	Indiana 38, Brigham Young 37
D22	Tangerine	LSU 34, Wake Forest 10
D22	Liberty	Penn State 9, Tulane 6
D22	Sun	Washington 14, Texas 7
D25	Fiesta	Pittsburgh 16, Arizona 10
D28	Gator	North Carolina 17, Michigan 15
D29	All-American	Missouri 24, South Carolina 14
D31	Peach	Baylor 24, Clemson 18
D31	Bluebonnet	Purdue 27, Tennessee 22
J1	Sugar	Alabama 24, Arkansas 9
J1	Cotton	Houston 17, Nebraska 14
J1	Orange	Oklahoma 24, Florida State 7
J1	Rose	Southern Cal 17, Ohio State 16

CONFERENCE STANDINGS

ACC

	Conf.			Overall		
	W	L	T	W	L	T
North Carolina St.	5	1	0	7	4	0
Clemson	4	2	0	8	4	0
Maryland	4	2	0	7	4	0
Wake Forest	3	2	0	8	4	0
North Carolina	3	3	0	8	3	1
Virginia	1	4	0	6	5	0
Duke	0	6	0	2	8	1

Big 10

	Conf.			Overall		
	W	L	T	W	L	T
Ohio State	8	0	0	11	1	0
Purdue	7	1	0	10	2	0
Michigan	6	2	0	8	4	0
Indiana	5	3	0	8	4	0
Iowa	4	4	0	5	6	0
Minnesota	3	5	1	4	6	1
Michigan State	3	5	0	5	6	0
Wisconsin	3	5	0	4	7	0
Illinois	1	6	1	2	8	1
Northwestern	0	9	0	1	10	0

Big 8

	Conf.			Overall		
	W	L	T	W	L	T
Oklahoma	7	0	0	11	1	0
Nebraska	6	1	0	10	2	0
Oklahoma State	5	2	0	7	4	0
Missouri	3	4	0	7	5	0
Kansas	2	5	0	3	8	0
Colorado	2	5	0	3	8	0
Iowa State	2	5	0	3	8	0
Kansas State	1	6	0	3	8	0

Big West

	Conf.			Overall		
	W	L	T	W	L	T
Utah State	4	0	1	7	3	1
San Jose State	4	0	1	6	4	1
Long Beach State	3	2	0	7	4	0
Fresno State	3	2	0	5	6	0
Cal-St. Fullerton	1	4	0	3	8	0
Pacific	0	5	0	3	7	0

Ivy

	Conf.			Overall		
	W	L	T	W	L	T
Yale	6	1	0	8	1	0
Brown	5	2	0	6	3	0
Princeton	5	2	0	5	4	0
Cornell	4	3	0	5	4	0
Dartmouth	4	3	0	4	4	1
Harvard	3	4	0	3	6	0
Columbia	1	6	0	1	8	0
Pennsylvania	0	7	0	0	9	0

MAC

	Conf.			Overall		
	W	L	T	W	L	T
Central Michigan	8	0	1	10	0	1
Toledo	7	1	1	7	3	1
Western Michigan	5	4	0	6	5	0
Ball State	4	4	0	6	5	0
Ohio U	4	4	0	6	5	0
Northern Illinois	3	3	1	5	5	1
Miami, Ohio	3	4	0	6	5	0
Bowling Green	3	5	0	4	7	0
Eastern Michigan	1	6	1	2	8	1
Kent State	1	7	0	1	10	0

PAC 10

	Conf.			Overall		
	W	L	T	W	L	T
Southern Cal	6	0	1	11	0	1
Washington	5	2	0	9	3	0
Oregon	4	3	0	6	5	0
Arizona	4	3	0	6	5	1
California	5	4	0	6	6	0
Stanford	3	3	1	5	5	1
Arizona State	3	4	0	6	6	0
UCLA	3	4	0	5	6	0
Washington State	2	6	0	3	8	0
Oregon State	1	7	0	1	10	0

SEC

	Conf.			Overall		
	W	L	T	W	L	T
Alabama	6	0	0	12	0	0
Georgia	5	1	0	6	5	0
Auburn	4	2	0	8	3	0
LSU	4	2	0	7	5	0
Tennessee	3	3	0	7	5	0
Kentucky	3	3	0	5	6	0
Mississippi	3	3	0	4	7	0
Mississippi State	2	4	0	3	8	0
Vanderbilt	0	6	0	1	10	0
Florida	0	6	0	0	10	1

SWC

	Conf.			Overall		
	W	L	T	W	L	T
Houston	7	1	0	11	1	0
Arkansas	7	1	0	10	2	0
Texas	6	2	0	9	3	0
Baylor	5	3	0	8	4	0
Texas A&M	4	4	0	6	5	0
SMU	3	5	0	5	6	0
Texas Tech	2	5	1	3	6	2
TCU	1	6	1	2	8	1
Rice	0	8	0	1	10	0

WAC

	Conf.			Overall		
	W	L	T	W	L	T
Brigham Young	7	0	0	11	1	0
San Diego State	5	2	0	8	3	0
Utah	5	2	0	6	6	0
Hawaii	3	3	0	6	5	0
New Mexico	3	4	0	6	6	0
Colorado State	3	4	0	4	7	1
Wyoming	2	5	0	4	8	0
Texas-El Paso	0	7	0	2	9	0

Independents

	Overall		
	W	L	T
Pittsburgh	11	1	0
Florida State	11	1	0
Temple	10	2	0
Nevada-Las Vegas	9	1	2
Tulane	9	3	0
Rutgers	8	3	0
East Carolina	7	3	1
South Carolina	8	4	0
Penn State	8	4	0
Navy	7	4	0
Notre Dame	7	4	0
Southern Miss	6	4	1
Syracuse	7	5	0
Boston College	5	6	0
Miami, Fla.	5	6	0
North Texas	5	6	0
Memphis	5	6	0
West Virginia	5	6	0
Virginia Tech	5	6	0
Louisville	4	6	1
Georgia Tech	4	6	1
Army	2	8	1
Air Force	2	9	0
Cincinnati	2	9	0

1979 NCAA Major College Statistical Leaders

Individual Leaders

PASSING	G	ATT	COM	PCT	INT	I%	YDS	YPA	TD	TD%	RATING
1 Turk Schonert, Stanford	11	221	148	67.0	6	2.7	1922	8.7	19	8.6	163.0
2 Brian Broomell, Temple	11	214	120	56.1	11	5.1	2103	9.8	22	10.3	162.3
3 Paul McDonald, Southern Cal	11	240	153	63.8	5	2.1	1989	8.3	17	7.1	152.6
4 Marc Wilson, Brigham Young	11	427	250	58.6	15	3.5	3720	8.7	29	6.8	147.1
5 Art Schlichter, Ohio State	11	179	94	52.5	5	2.8	1519	8.5	13	7.3	142.2
6 Eric Hipple, Utah State	10	238	144	60.5	6	2.5	1924	8.1	13	5.5	141.4
7 Rich Campbell, California	11	322	216	67.1	12	3.7	2618	8.1	13	4.0	141.2
8 Sam King, Nevada-Las Vegas	11	188	103	54.8	10	5.3	1594	8.5	12	6.4	136.4
9 Mark Hutsell, East Tennessee State	11	302	186	61.6	14	4.6	2276	7.5	17	5.6	134.2
10 Dan Marino, Pittsburgh	9	193	115	59.6	7	3.6	1508	7.8	9	4.7	133.4

ALL-PURPOSE	G	RUSH	REC	PR	KR	YDS	YPG
1 Charles White, Southern Cal	10	1803	138	0	0	1941	194.1
2 James Brooks, Auburn	11	1208	15	0	577	1800	163.6
3 Joe Morris, Syracuse	11	1372	38	0	313	1723	156.6
4 Anthony Collins, East Carolina	11	1130	92	0	473	1695	154.1
5 Freeman McNeil, UCLA	10	1396	140	0	0	1536	153.6
6 George Rogers, South Carolina	11	1548	122	0	0	1670	151.8
7 Homer Jones, Brigham Young	11	546	404	95	579	1624	147.6
8 Billy Sims, Oklahoma	11	1506	42	0	0	1548	140.7
9 Charlie Wysocki, Maryland	9	1140	26	0	96	1262	140.2
10 Rodney Smith, La. Lafayette	11	782	156	70	506	1514	137.6

RUSHING/Yards Per Game	G	ATT	YDS	TD	AVG	YPG
1 Charles White, Southern Cal	10	293	1803	18	6.2	180.3
2 George Rogers, South Carolina	11	286	1548	8	5.4	140.7
3 Freeman McNeil, UCLA	10	271	1396	6	5.2	139.6
4 Billy Sims, Oklahoma	11	224	1506	22	6.7	136.9
5 Vagas Ferguson, Notre Dame	11	301	1437	17	4.8	130.6
6 Charlie Wysocki, Maryland	9	247	1140	8	4.6	126.7
7 Joe Morris, Syracuse	11	238	1372	7	5.8	124.7
8 James Hadnot, Texas Tech	11	273	1371	1	5.0	124.6
9 Dennis Mosley, Iowa	11	270	1267	12	4.7	115.2
10 Floyd Allen, VMI	11	265	1249	8	4.7	113.5

RUSHING/Yards Per Carry	G	ATT	YDS	YPC
1 Gwain Durden, U.T. Chattanooga	9	114	885	7.8
2 James Brooks, Auburn	11	163	1208	7.4
3 Anthony Collins, East Carolina	11	154	1130	7.3
4 Jarvis Redwine, Nebraska	11	148	1042	7.0
5 Billy Sims, Oklahoma	11	224	1506	6.7
6 Gary Allen, Hawaii	11	162	1032	6.4
7 Charles White, Southern Cal	10	293	1803	6.2
8 Joe Morris, Syracuse	11	238	1372	5.8
9 Tom Vigorito, Virginia	11	184	1044	5.7
10 Stump Mitchell, Citadel	10	165	925	5.6

* Based on top 36 rushers

RECEIVING	G	REC	YDS	TD	YPR	YPG	RPG
1 Rick Beasley, Appalachian State	11	74	1205	12	16.3	109.5	6.7
2 Steve Coury, Oregon State	11	66	842	5	12.8	76.5	6.0
3 James Murphy, Utah State	11	63	1067	6	16.9	97.0	5.7
4 Gerald Harp, Western Carolina	10	57	1009	10	17.7	100.9	5.7
5 Howard Robinson, Lamar	11	59	842	12	14.3	76.5	5.4
6 Mike House, Pacific	10	52	548	2	10.5	54.8	5.2
7 Wayne Baumgardner, Wake Forest	11	55	1000	8	18.2	90.9	5.0
8 Preston Brown, Vanderbilt	11	52	786	3	15.1	71.5	4.7
8 Matt Bouza, California	11	52	717	4	13.8	65.2	4.7
10 Earl Cooper, Rice	10	47	463	2	9.9	46.3	4.7

PUNTING	PUNT	YDS	AVG
1 Clay Brown, Brigham Young	43	1950	45.3
2 Mike Smith, Wyoming	70	3125	44.6
3 Jim Miller, Mississippi	53	2362	44.6
4 David Sims, Clemson	72	3198	44.4
5 Ray Stachowicz, Michigan State	62	2749	44.3
6 Steve Cox, Arkansas	42	1840	43.8
7 Casey Murphy, Temple	40	1718	42.9
8 Greg Cater, U.T. Chattanooga	62	2638	42.5
9 Mike Hubach, Kansas	69	2934	42.5
10 Skip Johnston, Auburn	50	2120	42.4

PUNT RETURNS	PR	YDS	TD	AVG
1 Jeffrey Shockley, Tennessee State	27	456	1	16.9
2 Basil Banks, Oklahoma	17	260	0	15.3
3 Raymond Butler, Southern Cal	21	303	1	14.4
4 Anthony Carter, Michigan	20	265	1	13.2
5 Mark Lee, Washington	21	271	3	12.9
6 Roland James, Tennessee	19	243	1	12.8
7 Ken Smith, Rutgers	14	177	0	12.6
8 Kenny Easley, UCLA	27	336	0	12.4
9 Mike Guess, Ohio State	22	273	0	12.4
10 Marcellus Greene, Arizona	15	183	1	12.2

KICKOFF RETURNS	KR	YDS	TD	AVG
1 Stevie Nelson, Ball State	18	565	1	31.4
2 Derek Hughes, Michigan State	16	497	2	31.1
3 James Brooks, Auburn	21	577	0	27.5
4 Cedric Jones, Duke	20	542	1	27.1
5 Homer Jones, Brigham Young	22	579	0	26.3
6 Jim Stone, Notre Dame	19	493	0	25.9
7 Danny Miller, Citadel	15	383	1	25.5
8 Dwight Robertson, Oregon	25	632	0	25.3
9 Jeff Washington, VMI	19	477	0	25.1
10 Anthony Allen, Washington	15	376	1	25.1

SCORING	TDS	XPT	FG	PTS	PTPG
1 Billy Sims, Oklahoma	22	0	0	132	12.0
2 Mark Bornholdt, Ball State	19	0	0	114	11.4
3 Charles White, Southern Cal	18	0	0	108	10.8
4 Vagas Ferguson, Notre Dame	17	0	0	102	9.3
5 Dennis Mosley, Iowa	16	0	0	96	8.7
6 Joe Cribbs, Auburn	15	4	0	94	8.5
7 Rick Parros, Utah State	15	0	0	90	8.2
8 Vlade Janakievski, Ohio State	0	42	15	87	7.9
9 Wardell Wright, Drake	14	2	0	86	7.8
10 Butch Woolfolk, Michigan	13	0	0	78	7.8

FIELD GOALS	FGA	FGM	PCT	FGG
1 Ish Ordonez, Arkansas	22	18	0.82	1.64
2 Dale Castro, Maryland	21	17	0.81	1.55
2 Bill Adams, Texas Tech	24	17	0.71	1.55
2 John Goodson, Texas	28	17	0.61	1.55
5 Vlade Janakievski. Ohio State	18	15	0.83	1.36
5 Gary Anderson, Syracuse	21	15	0.71	1.36
5 Obed Ariri, Clemson	21	15	0.71	1.36
5 Don Stump, McNeese St.	21	15	0.71	1.36
5 Alan McElroy, Alabama	22	15	0.68	1.36
5 Rex Robinson, Georgia	25	15	0.60	1.36

INTERCEPTIONS	INT	YDS	TD	INT/GM
1 Joe Callan, Ohio U	9	110	0	1.00
2 Sharay Fields, New Mexico	10	67	0	0.83
3 Gene Coleman, Miami, Fla.	9	102	0	0.82
4 Monk Bonasorte, Florida State	8	100	0	0.73
5 Bill Kay, Purdue	7	15	0	0.70
6 Tim Wilbur, Indiana	7	165	2	0.64
6 Ralph Lary, Maryland	7	102	0	0.64
6 Al McCloud, U.T. Chattanooga	7	68	1	0.64
9 Mike Brown, Columbia	5	73	0	0.56
9 Barry Pizor, Dartmouth	5	45	0	0.56
9 Darryl Hemphill, West Texas State	5	35	0	0.56
9 Mike Kachmer, Brown	5	28	0	0.56
9 Chip Kelly, Yale	5	27	0	0.56
9 Dave Chandler, Princeton	5	18	0	0.56

Team Leaders

RUSHING OFFENSE	G	ATT	YDS	AVG	TD	YPG
1 East Carolina	11	692	4053	5.9	47	368.5
2 Oklahoma	11	652	3868	5.9	46	351.6
3 Nebraska	11	715	3796	5.3	35	345.1
4 Alabama	11	763	3792	5.0	38	344.7
5 Texas Arlington	11	650	3315	5.1	33	301.4
6 Auburn	11	579	3279	5.7	31	298.1
7 Houston	11	653	3257	5.0	29	296.1
8 Central Michigan	11	741	3183	4.3	29	289.4
9 Syracuse	11	656	3071	4.7	26	279.2
10 Southern Cal	11	569	3043	5.3	30	276.6

PASSING OFFENSE	G	ATT	COM	INT	PCT	YDS	YPA	TD	I%	YPC	YPG
1 Brigham Young	11	464	276	16	59.5	4051	8.7	33	3.4	14.7	368.3
2 San Jose State	11	421	245	15	58.2	3135	7.4	22	3.6	12.8	285.0
3 California	11	370	245	14	66.2	2974	8.0	15	3.8	12.1	270.4
4 Utah State	11	352	197	12	56.0	2949	8.4	22	3.4	15.0	268.1
5 Tennessee St.	11	382	196	20	51.3	2741	7.2	27	5.2	14.0	249.2
6 Lamar	11	404	237	18	58.7	2729	6.8	24	4.5	11.5	248.1
7 Stanford	11	316	198	9	62.7	2466	7.8	25	2.8	12.5	224.2
8 Tulane	11	387	226	15	58.4	2464	6.4	24	3.9	10.9	224.0
9 Wake Forest	11	375	200	17	53.3	2449	6.5	16	4.5	12.2	222.6
10 Western Carolina	11	320	158	22	49.4	2448	7.7	17	6.9	15.5	222.5

TOTAL OFFENSE	G	P	YDS	AVG	TD	YPG
1 Brigham Young	11	832	5735	6.9	59	521.4
2 East Carolina	11	846	5228	6.2	51	475.3
3 Nevada-Las Vegas	12	957	5664	5.9	51	472.0
4 Southern Cal	11	826	5136	6.2	48	466.9
5 Nebraska	11	899	5113	5.7	46	464.8
6 Temple	11	770	4815	6.3	49	437.7
7 San Jose State	11	836	4795	5.7	42	435.9
8 Utah State	11	825	4727	5.7	45	429.7
9 Alabama	11	875	4715	5.4	44	428.6
10 Oklahoma	11	741	4712	6.4	50	428.4

RUSHING DEFENSE	G	ATT	YDS	AVG	TD	YPG
1 Yale	9	363	675	1.9	5	75.0
2 Nebraska	11	418	1024	2.4	6	93.1
3 Western Michigan	11	435	1091	2.5	7	99.2
4 Michigan	11	443	1092	2.5	8	99.3
5 Alabama	11	393	1121	2.9	2	101.9
6 Texas	11	468	1163	2.5	3	105.7
7 Pittsburgh	11	498	1172	2.4	8	106.5
8 Texas-Arlington	11	471	1213	2.6	10	110.3
9 Central Michigan	11	446	1224	2.7	11	111.3
10 Clemson	11	450	1292	2.9	5	117.5

PASSING DEFENSE	G	ATT	COM	PCT	YPC	INT	I%	YDS	YPA	TD	YPG
1 Western Carolina	11	163	74	45.4	11.5	8	4.9	852	5.2	5	77.5
2 Alabama	11	218	78	35.8	11.0	25	11.5	860	3.9	5	78.2
3 Texas	11	191	75	39.3	11.5	15	7.9	864	4.5	5	78.5
4 Virginia	11	191	84	44.0	11.6	16	8.4	974	5.1	6	88.5
4 Maryland	11	215	92	42.8	10.6	16	7.4	974	4.5	6	88.5
6 La. Monroe	11	188	90	47.9	11.3	18	9.6	1014	5.4	5	92.2
7 East Tennessee State	11	191	89	46.6	11.8	10	5.2	1046	5.5	7	95.1
8 Ohio U	11	185	76	41.1	13.9	17	9.2	1055	5.7	10	95.9
9 Colorado	11	188	76	40.4	14.1	10	5.3	1071	5.7	8	97.4
10 Houston	11	180	84	46.7	13.0	19	10.6	1089	6.1	3	99.0

TOTAL DEFENSE	G	P	YDS	AVG	TD	YPG
1 Yale	9	540	1579	2.9	10	175.4
2 Alabama	11	611	1981	3.2	7	180.1
3 Texas	11	659	2027	3.1	8	184.3
4 Pittsburgh	11	732	2315	3.2	11	210.5
5 Nebraska	11	665	2383	3.6	12	216.6
6 Western Michigan	11	651	2398	3.7	12	218.0
7 Clemson	11	696	2612	3.8	8	237.5
8 Maryland	11	748	2631	3.5	15	239.2
9 Central Michigan	11	689	2646	3.8	17	240.5
10 Florida State	11	715	2669	3.7	18	242.6

SCORING OFFENSE	G	PTS	AVG
1 Brigham Young	11	447	40.6
2 Oklahoma	11	382	34.7
3 East Carolina	11	380	34.5
4 Ohio State	11	374	34.0
5 Southern Cal	11	372	33.8
6 Temple	11	371	33.7
7 Nebraska	11	366	33.3
8 Alabama	11	359	32.6
9 U.T. Chattanooga	11	349	31.7
10 Utah State	11	347	31.5

SCORING DEFENSE	G	PTS	AVG
1 Alabama	11	58	5.3
2 Texas	11	90	8.2
3 Clemson	11	92	8.4
4 Dartmouth	9	86	9.6
5 Pittsburgh	11	106	9.6
6 Arkansas	11	108	9.8
6 McNeese St.	11	108	9.8
8 Ohio State	11	109	9.9
9 Nebraska	11	114	10.4
10 Yale	9	94	10.4

TURNOVER MARGIN	G	FR	INT	TOT	FL	INTL	TOT	MAR
1 Toledo	11	28	18	46	14	6	20	2.4
2 West Texas State	11	28	14	42	13	10	23	1.7
3 Dartmouth	9	13	14	27	6	6	12	1.7
4 Georgia	11	28	21	49	12	20	32	1.5
5 Ohio State	11	14	17	31	10	5	15	1.5
6 Drake	11	25	13	38	12	12	24	1.3
7 Alabama	11	14	25	39	18	8	26	1.2
7 Florida State	11	15	23	38	8	17	25	1.2
7 Southern Miss	11	14	23	37	14	10	24	1.2
7 Stanford	11	18	16	34	12	9	21	1.2

1980 POLL PROGRESSION

Pre-Season 1980 — Sept. 6 Games

UP	AP	Team	Record	Result
1	1	Ohio State	0-0-0	bye week
2	2	Alabama	0-0-0	beat Georgia Tech 26-3
4	3	Pittsburgh	0-0-0	bye week
5	4	Southern Cal	0-0-0	bye week
3	5	Oklahoma	0-0-0	bye week
8	6	Arkansas	0-0-0	lost to # 10 Texas 17-23 S1
7	7	Nebraska	0-0-0	bye week
6	8	Houston	0-0-0	bye week
10	9	Purdue	0-0-0	lost to # 11 Notre Dame 10-31
9	10	Texas	0-0-0	beat # 6 Arkansas 23-17 S1
12	11	Notre Dame	0-0-0	beat # 9 Purdue 31-10
11	12	Michigan	0-0-0	bye week
16	13	Florida State	0-0-0	beat LSU 16-0
17	14	North Carolina	0-0-0	beat Furman 35-13
14	15	Stanford	0-0-0	beat Oregon 35-25
20	16	Georgia	0-0-0	beat Tennessee 16-15
18	17	Missouri	0-0-0	bye week
13	18	Penn State	0-0-0	beat Colgate 54-10
	19	Auburn	0-0-0	bye week
15	20	Washington	0-0-0	bye week
19		Brigham Young	0-0-0	lost to New Mexico 21-25

September 8 Poll — Sept. 13 Games

UP	AP	Team	Record	Result
1	1	Ohio State	0-0-0	beat Syracuse 31-21
2	2	Alabama	1-0-0	bye week
4	3	Pittsburgh	0-0-0	beat Boston College 14-6
3	4	Oklahoma	0-0-0	beat Kentucky 29-7
5	5	Southern Cal	0-0-0	beat Tennessee 20-17
6	6	Texas	1-0-0	bye week
8	7	Notre Dame	1-0-0	bye week
7	8	Nebraska	1-0-0	beat Utah 55-9
9	9	Houston	0-0-0	lost to Arizona State 13-29
11	10	Florida State	1-0-0	beat Louisville 52-0
10	11	Michigan	0-0-0	beat Northwestern 17-10
15	12	Georgia	1-0-0	beat Texas A&M 42-0
14	13	Stanford	1-0-0	beat Tulane 19-14
12	14	Penn State	1-0-0	bye week
13	15	North Carolina	1-0-0	beat Texas Tech 9-3
16	16	Arkansas	0-1-0	bye week
17	17	Missouri	0-0-0	beat New Mexico 47-16
	18	Auburn	0-0-0	beat TCU 10-7
18	19	Washington	0-0-0	beat Air Force 50-7
	20	Purdue	0-1-0	beat Wisconsin 12-6
19		Texas A&M	0-0-0	lost to # 12 Georgia 0-42
20		South Carolina	1-0-0	beat Wichita St. 73-0

September 15 Poll — Sept. 20 Games

UP	AP	Team	Record	Result
1	1	Alabama	1-0-0	beat Mississippi 59-35
2	2	Ohio State	1-0-0	beat Minnesota 47-0
3	3	Oklahoma	1-0-0	bye week
4	4	Southern Cal	1-0-0	beat # 20 South Carolina 23-13
7	5	Pittsburgh	1-0-0	beat Kansas 18-3
6	6	Nebraska	1-0-0	beat Iowa 57-0
5	7	Texas	1-0-0	beat Utah State 35-17
8	8	Notre Dame	1-0-0	beat # 14 Michigan 29-27
10	9	Florida State	2-0-0	beat East Carolina 63-7
9	10	Georgia	2-0-0	beat Clemson 20-16
14	11	Stanford	2-0-0	lost to Boston College 13-30
11	12	Penn State	1-0-0	beat Texas A&M 25-9
13	13	North Carolina	2-0-0	bye week
12	14	Michigan	1-0-0	lost to # 8 Notre Dame 27-29
16	15	Missouri	1-0-0	beat Illinois 52-7
15	16	Washington	1-0-0	beat Northwestern 45-7
20	17	Arkansas	0-1-0	beat Oklahoma State 33-20
19	18	Houston	0-1-0	lost to Miami, Fla. 7-14
	19	Auburn	1-0-0	beat Duke 35-28
18	20	South Carolina	2-0-0	lost to # 4 Southern Cal 13-23
17		UCLA	1-0-0	beat Purdue 23-14

September 22 Poll — Sept. 27 Games

UP	AP	Team	Record	Result
1	1	Alabama	2-0-0	beat Vanderbilt 41-0
2	2	Ohio State	2-0-0	beat # 20 Arizona State 38-21
3	3	Nebraska	2-0-0	beat # 11 Penn State 21-7
4	4	Oklahoma	1-0-0	lost to Stanford 14-31
5	5	Southern Cal	2-0-0	beat Minnesota 24-7
8	6	Pittsburgh	2-0-0	beat Temple 36-2
6	7	Texas	2-0-0	beat Oregon State 35-0
7	8	Notre Dame	2-0-0	bye week
9	9	Florida State	3-0-0	lost to Miami, Fla. 9-10
10	10	Georgia	3-0-0	beat TCU 34-3
11	11	Penn State	2-0-0	lost to # 3 Nebraska 7-21
12	12	Missouri	2-0-0	beat San Diego State 31-7
13	13	Washington	2-0-0	lost to Oregon 10-34
15	14	North Carolina	2-0-0	beat # 19 Maryland 17-3
16	15	Arkansas	1-1-0	beat Tulsa 13-10
14	16	UCLA	2-0-0	beat Wisconsin 35-0
17	17	Michigan	1-1-0	lost to South Carolina 14-17
	18	Auburn	2-0-0	lost to Tennessee 0-42
	19	Maryland	3-0-0	lost to # 14 North Carolina 3-17
18	20	Arizona State	2-0-0	lost to # 2 Ohio State 21-38
19		Miami, Fla.	2-0-0	beat # 9 Florida State 10-9
20		Baylor	2-0-0	beat Texas Tech 11-3

September 29 Poll — Oct. 4 Games

UP	AP	Team	Record	Result
1	1	Alabama	3-0-0	beat Kentucky 45-0 O3
2	2	Ohio State	3-0-0	lost to # 11 UCLA 0-17
3	3	Nebraska	3-0-0	lost to # 16 Florida State 14-18
4	4	Southern Cal	3-0-0	beat Arizona State 23-21
5	5	Texas	3-0-0	beat Rice 41-28
6	6	Pittsburgh	3-0-0	beat Maryland 38-9
7	7	Notre Dame	2-0-0	beat Michigan State 26-21
8	8	Georgia	4-0-0	bye week
9	9	Missouri	3-0-0	lost to # 17 Penn State 21-29
11	10	North Carolina	3-0-0	beat Georgia Tech 33-0
10	11	UCLA	3-0-0	beat # 2 Ohio State 17-0
12	12	Oklahoma	1-1-0	beat Colorado 82-42
13	13	Miami, Fla.	4-0-0	bye week
16	14	Arkansas	2-1-0	beat TCU 44-7
17	15	Stanford	3-1-0	beat San Jose State 35-21
18	16	Florida State	3-1-0	beat # 3 Nebraska 18-14
14	17	Penn State	2-1-0	beat # 9 Missouri 29-21
15	18	South Carolina	3-1-0	beat North Carolina St. 30-10
20	19	Florida	3-0-0	lost to LSU 7-24
19	20	Baylor	3-0-0	beat Houston 24-12

October 6 Poll — Oct. 11 Games

UP	AP	Team	Record	Result
1	1	Alabama	4-0-0	beat Rutgers 17-13
2	2	Southern Cal	4-0-0	beat Arizona 27-10
4	3	Texas	4-0-0	beat # 12 Oklahoma 20-13
3	4	Pittsburgh	4-0-0	lost to # 11 Florida State 22-36
5	5	UCLA	4-0-0	beat # 16 Stanford 35-21
6	6	Georgia	4-0-0	beat Mississippi 28-21
7	7	Notre Dame	3-0-0	beat # 13 Miami, Fla. 32-14
8	8	North Carolina	4-0-0	beat Wake Forest 27-9
11	9	Ohio State	3-1-0	beat Northwestern 63-0
9	10	Nebraska	3-1-0	beat Kansas 54-0
10	11	Florida State	4-1-0	beat # 4 Pittsburgh 36-22
12	12	Oklahoma	2-1-0	lost to # 3 Texas 13-20
13	13	Miami, Fla.	4-0-0	lost to # 7 Notre Dame 14-32
14	14	Penn State	3-1-0	beat Maryland 24-10
18	15	Arkansas	3-1-0	beat Wichita State 27-7
16	16	Stanford	4-1-0	lost to # 5 UCLA 21-35
17	17	South Carolina	4-1-0	beat Duke 20-7
15	18	Baylor	4-0-0	beat # 20 SMU 32-28
19	19	Missouri	3-1-0	beat Oklahoma State 30-7
	20	SMU	4-0-0	beat # 18 Baylor 28-32
20		Iowa State	4-0-0	beat Kansas State 31-7

October 13 Poll — Oct. 18 Games

UP	AP	Team	Record	Result
1	1	Alabama	5-0-0	beat Tennessee 27-0
2	2	Southern Cal	5-0-0	tied Oregon 7-7
3	3	Texas	5-0-0	bye week
4	4	UCLA	5-0-0	bye week
5	5	Notre Dame	4-0-0	beat Army 30-3
6	6	Georgia	5-0-0	beat Vanderbilt 41-0
7	7	Florida State	5-1-0	beat Boston College 41-7
8	8	North Carolina	5-0-0	beat North Carolina St. 28-8
10	9	Ohio State	4-1-0	beat Indiana 27-17
9	10	Nebraska	4-1-0	beat Oklahoma State 48-7
11	11	Pittsburgh	4-1-0	beat West Virginia 42-14
12	12	Penn State	4-1-0	beat Syracuse 24-7
13	13	Baylor	5-0-0	beat Texas A&M 46-7
14	14	Arkansas	4-1-0	bye week
17	15	South Carolina	5-1-0	beat Cincinnati 49-7
16	16	Missouri	4-1-0	beat Colorado 45-7
18	17	Oklahoma	2-2-0	beat Kansas State 35-21
19	18	Miami, Fla.	4-1-0	lost to Mississippi State 31-34
16	19	Iowa State	5-0-0	lost to Kansas 17-28
	20	Stanford	4-2-0	lost to Washington 24-27
20		Brigham Young	4-1-0	beat Utah State 70-46

October 20 Poll — Oct. 25 Games

UP	AP	Team	Record	Result
1	1	Alabama	6-0-0	beat # 20 Southern Miss 42-7
2	2	Texas	5-0-0	lost to SMU 6-20
3	3	UCLA	5-0-0	beat California 32-9
4	4	Notre Dame	5-0-0	beat Arizona 20-3
5	5	Georgia	6-0-0	beat Kentucky 27-0
6	6	Florida State	6-1-0	beat Memphis 24-3
7	7	North Carolina	6-0-0	beat East Carolina 31-3
9	8	Southern Cal	5-0-1	bye week
8	9	Nebraska	5-1-0	beat Colorado 45-7
10	10	Ohio State	5-1-0	beat Wisconsin 21-0
13	11	Baylor	6-0-0	beat TCU 21-6
11	12	Pittsburgh	5-1-0	beat Tennessee 30-6
12	13	Penn State	5-1-0	beat West Virginia 20-15
15	14	South Carolina	6-1-0	bye week
14	15	Arkansas	4-1-0	lost to Houston 17-24
16	16	Missouri	5-1-0	beat Kansas State 13-3
17	17	Oklahoma	3-2-0	beat Iowa State 35-7
19	18	Washington	5-1-0	lost to Navy 10-24
18	19	Brigham Young	5-1-0	beat Hawaii 34-7
20	20	Southern Miss	6-0-0	lost to # 1 Alabama 7-42

October 27 Poll — Nov. 1 Games

UP	AP	Team	Record	Result
1	1	Alabama	7-0-0	lost to Mississippi State 3-6
2	2	UCLA	6-0-0	lost to Arizona 17-23
3	3	Notre Dame	6-0-0	beat Navy 33-0
4	4	Georgia	7-0-0	beat # 14 South Carolina 13-10
5	5	Florida State	7-1-0	beat Tulsa 45-2
6	6	North Carolina	7-0-0	lost to # 16 Oklahoma 7-41
8	7	Southern Cal	5-0-1	beat California 60-7
7	8	Nebraska	6-1-0	beat # 15 Missouri 38-16
9	9	Ohio State	6-1-0	beat Michigan State 48-16
11	10	Baylor	7-0-0	lost to San Jose State 22-30
10	11	Pittsburgh	6-1-0	beat Syracuse 43-6
12	12	Texas	5-1-0	lost to Texas Tech 20-24
13	13	Penn State	6-1-0	beat Miami, Fla. 27-12
14	14	South Carolina	6-1-0	lost to # 4 Georgia 10-13
15	15	Missouri	6-1-0	lost to # 8 Nebraska 16-38
16	16	Oklahoma	4-2-0	beat # 6 North Carolina 41-7
17	17	Brigham Young	6-1-0	beat Texas-El Paso 83-7
18	18	Michigan	5-2-0	beat Indiana 35-0
	19	SMU	5-2-0	beat Texas A&M 27-0
20	20	Purdue	5-2-0	beat Northwestern 52-31
19		Arkansas	4-2-0	lost to Rice 16-17

November 3 Poll

UP	AP	Team	Record	Nov. 8 Games
1	1	Notre Dame	7-0-0	tied Georgia Tech 3-3
2	2	Georgia	8-0-0	beat #20 Florida 26-21
4	3	Florida State	8-1-0	beat Virginia Tech 31-7
3	4	Southern Cal	6-0-1	beat Stanford 34-9
5	5	Nebraska	7-1-0	beat Kansas State 55-0
6	6	Alabama	7-1-0	beat LSU 28-7
7	7	Ohio State	7-1-0	beat Illinois 49-42
9	8	UCLA	6-1-0	lost to Oregon 14-20
8	9	Pittsburgh	7-1-0	beat Louisville 41-23
10	10	Penn State	7-1-0	beat North Carolina St. 21-13
11	11	Oklahoma	5-2-0	beat Kansas 21-19
12	12	Michigan	6-2-0	beat Wisconsin 24-0
16	13	Brigham Young	7-1-0	beat North Texas 41-23
14	14	North Carolina	7-1-0	beat Clemson 24-19
13	15	South Carolina	6-2-0	beat Citadel 45-24
15	16	Baylor	7-1-0	beat Arkansas 42-15
19	17	Purdue	6-2-0	beat Iowa 58-13
	18	SMU	6-2-0	beat Rice 34-14
17	19	Mississippi State	7-2-0	bye week
20	20	Florida	6-1-0	lost to #2 Georgia 21-26
18		Texas	5-2-0	beat Houston 15-13

November 10 Poll

UP	AP	Team	Record	Nov. 15 Games
1	1	Georgia	9-0-0	beat Auburn 31-21
2	2	Southern Cal	7-0-1	lost to Washington 10-20
4	3	Florida State	9-1-0	bye week
3	4	Nebraska	8-1-0	beat Iowa State 35-0
5	5	Alabama	8-1-0	lost to #6 Notre Dame 0-7
7	6	Notre Dame	7-0-1	beat #5 Alabama 7-0
6	7	Ohio State	8-1-0	beat Iowa 41-7
8	8	Pittsburgh	8-1-0	beat Army 45-7
9	9	Penn State	8-1-0	beat Temple 50-7
11	10	Oklahoma	6-2-0	beat Missouri 17-7
12	11	Michigan	7-2-0	beat #16 Purdue 26-0
10	12	Baylor	8-1-0	beat Rice 16-6
13	13	Brigham Young	8-1-0	beat Colorado State 45-14
14	14	South Carolina	7-2-0	beat Wake Forest 39-38
15	15	North Carolina	8-1-0	beat Virginia 26-3
16	16	Purdue	7-2-0	lost to #11 Michigan 0-26
17	17	UCLA	6-2-0	beat Arizona State 23-14
	18	SMU	7-2-0	lost to Texas Tech 0-14
17	19	Mississippi State	7-2-0	beat LSU 55-31
	20	Florida	6-2-0	beat Kentucky 17-15
19		Texas	6-2-0	beat TCU 51-26
20		Washington	7-2-0	beat #2 Southern Cal 20-10

November 17 Poll

UP	AP	Team	Record	Nov. 22 Games
1	1	Georgia	10-0-0	bye week
2	2	Notre Dame	8-0-1	beat Air Force 24-10
4	3	Florida State	9-1-0	bye week
3	4	Nebraska	9-1-0	lost to #9 Oklahoma 17-21
5	5	Ohio State	9-1-0	lost to #10 Michigan 3-9
6	6	Pittsburgh	9-1-0	bye week
7	7	Penn State	9-1-0	bye week
10	8	Alabama	8-2-0	bye week
9	9	Oklahoma	7-2-0	beat #4 Nebraska 21-17
11	10	Michigan	8-2-0	beat #5 Ohio State 9-3
8	11	Baylor	9-1-0	beat #20 Texas 16-0
12	12	Southern Cal	7-1-1	lost to #18 UCLA 17-20
14	13	Brigham Young	9-1-0	beat Utah 56-6
15	14	South Carolina	8-2-0	lost to Clemson 6-27
13	15	North Carolina	9-1-0	beat Duke 44-21
17	16	Washington	8-2-0	beat Washington State 30-23
16	17	Mississippi State	8-2-0	beat Mississippi 19-14
19	18	UCLA	7-2-0	beat #12 Southern Cal 20-17
20	19	Florida	7-2-0	bye week
18	20	Texas	7-2-0	lost to #11 Baylor 0-16

November 24 Poll

UP	AP	Team	Record	Nov. 29 Games
1	1	Georgia	10-0-0	beat Georgia Tech 38-20
2	2	Notre Dame	9-0-1	bye week
3	3	Florida State	9-1-0	bye week
4	4	Pittsburgh	9-1-0	beat #5 Penn State 14-9
5	5	Penn State	9-1-0	lost to #4 Pittsburgh 9-14
6	6	Oklahoma	8-2-0	beat Oklahoma State 63-14
7	7	Michigan	9-2-0	regular season complete
8	8	Baylor	10-1-0	regular season Complete
9	9	Alabama	8-2-0	beat Auburn 34-18
10	10	Nebraska	9-2-0	regular season complete
12	11	Ohio State	9-2-0	regular season complete
13	12	Brigham Young	10-1-0	beat Nevada-Las Vegas 54-14
11	13	North Carolina	10-1-0	regular season complete
14	14	UCLA	8-2-0	beat Oregon State 34-3 N30
15	15	Washington	9-2-0	regular season complete
16	16	Mississippi State	9-2-0	regular season complete
17	17	Southern Cal	7-2-1	bye week
18	18	Florida	7-2-0	lost to Miami, Fla. 7-31
	19	South Carolina	8-3-0	regular season complete
19	20	SMU	8-3-0	regular season complete
20		Texas	7-3-0	lost to Texas A&M 14-24

December 1 Poll

UP	AP	Team	Record	Dec. 6 Games
1	1	Georgia	11-0-0	regular season complete
2	2	Notre Dame	9-0-1	lost to #17 Southern Cal 3-20
3	3	Florida State	9-1-0	beat Florida 17-13
4	4	Pittsburgh	10-1-0	regular season complete
5	5	Oklahoma	9-2-0	regular season complete
6	6	Michigan	9-2-0	
7	7	Baylor	10-1-0	
8	8	Alabama	9-2-0	regular season Complete
9	9	Nebraska	9-2-0	
10	10	Penn State	9-2-0	regular season complete
13	11	Ohio State	9-2-0	
11	12	North Carolina	10-1-0	
14	13	Brigham Young	10-1-0	
12	14	UCLA	9-2-0	regular season complete
15	15	Washington	9-2-0	
16	16	Mississippi State	9-2-0	
17	17	Southern Cal	7-2-1	beat #2 Notre Dame 20-3
18	18	South Carolina	8-3-0	
20	19	SMU	8-3-0	
	20	Miami, Fla.	8-3-0	regular season complete
19		Maryland	8-3-0	regular season complete

December 8 Poll / January 3 Final Poll

UP	AP	December 8 Poll	Record	Bowl Bid	Date	Bowl Result	RB	UP	AP	January 3 Final Poll	Record
1	1	Georgia	11-0-0	Sugar Bowl	J1	beat #7 Notre Dame 17-10	1	1	1	Georgia	12-0-0
2	2	Florida State	10-1-0	Orange Bowl	J1	lost to #4 Oklahoma 17-18	3	2	2	Pittsburgh	11-1-0
3	3	Pittsburgh	10-1-0	Gator Bowl	D29	beat #18 South Carolina 37-9	4	3	3	Oklahoma	10-2-0
4	4	Oklahoma	9-2-0	Orange Bowl	J1	beat #2 Florida State 18-17	9	4	4	Michigan	10-2-0
5	5	Michigan	9-2-0	Rose Bowl	J1	beat #16 Washington 23-6	6	5	5	Florida State	10-2-0
7	6	Baylor	10-1-0	Cotton Bowl	J1	lost to #9 Alabama 2-30	2	6	6	Alabama	10-2-0
8	7	Notre Dame	9-1-1	Sugar Bowl	J1	lost to #1 Georgia 10-17	7	7	7	Nebraska	10-2-0
9	8	Nebraska	9-2-0	Sun Bowl	D27	beat #17 Mississippi State 31-17	11	8	8	Penn State	10-2-0
6	9	Alabama	9-2-0	Cotton Bowl	J1	beat #6 Baylor 30-2	10	10	9	Notre Dame	9-2-1
10	10	Penn State	9-2-0	Fiesta Bowl	D26	beat #11 Ohio State 31-19	5	9	10	North Carolina	11-1-0
14	11	Ohio State	9-2-0	Fiesta Bowl	D26	lost to #10 Penn State 19-31	8	12	11	Southern Cal	8-2-1
13	12	Southern Cal	8-2-1				14	11	12	Brigham Young	12-1-0
11	13	North Carolina	10-1-0	Bluebonnet Bowl	D31	beat Texas 16-7	12	14	13	UCLA	9-2-0
15	14	Brigham Young	11-1-0	Holiday Bowl	D19	beat #19 SMU 46-45	13	13	14	Baylor	10-2-0
12	15	UCLA	9-2-0				16	15	15	Ohio State	9-3-0
16	16	Washington	9-2-0	Rose Bowl	J1	lost to #5 Michigan 6-23	17	17	16	Washington	9-3-0
17	17	Mississippi State	9-2-0	Sun Bowl	D27	lost to #8 Nebraska 17-31	18	16	17	Purdue	9-3-0
18	18	South Carolina	8-3-0	Gator Bowl	D29	lost to #3 Pittsburgh 9-37	19	18	18	Miami, Fla.	9-3-0
19	19	SMU	8-3-0	Holiday Bowl	D19	lost to #14 Brigham Young 45-46	15		19	Mississippi State	9-3-0
	20	Miami, Fla.	8-3-0	Peach Bowl	J2	beat Virginia Tech 20-10	29	20	20	SMU	8-4-0
20		Maryland	8-3-0	Tangerine Bowl	D20	lost to Florida 20-35	27	19		Florida	8-4-0

1980

CONSENSUS ALL-AMERICANS

POS	Offense	HT	WT	School	AP	FC	FW	PI
QB	Mark Herrmann	6-4	187	Purdue	•	•	•	•
RB	George Rogers	6-2	220	South Carolina	•	•	•	•
RB	Herschel Walker	6-2	220	Georgia	•	•	•	•
RB	Jarvis Redwine	5-11	204	Nebraska	•		•	•
WR	Ken Margerum	6-1	175	Stanford	•	•	•	•
TE	Dave Young	6-6	242	Purdue	•		•	•
L	Mark May	6-6	282	Pittsburgh	•	•	•	•
L	Keith Van Horne	6-7	265	Southern Cal	•	•	•	•
L	Nick Eyre	6-5	276	Brigham Young	•		•	•
L	Louis Oubre	6-4	262	Oklahoma	•		•	
L	Randy Schleusener	6-7	242	Nebraska	•			•
C	John Scully	6-5	255	Notre Dame	•	•	•	•

OTHERS RECEIVING FIRST-TEAM HONORS

RB	Freeman McNeil		UCLA	•
WR	Anthony Carter		Michigan	•
L	Bill Dugan		Penn State	•
L	Frank Ditta		Baylor	•
L	Roy Foster		Southern Cal	•
K	Rex Robinson		Georgia	•

POS	Defense	HT	WT	School	AP	FC	FW	PI
L	Hugh Green	6-2	222	Pittsburgh	•	•	•	•
L	E.J. Junior	6-3	227	Alabama	•	•	•	•
L	Kenneth Sims	6-6	265	Texas	•		•	•
L	Leonard Mitchell	6-7	270	Houston	•		•	
MG	Ron Simmons	6-1	230	Florida State	•		•	•
LB	Mike Singletary	6-1	232	Baylor	•		•	•
LB	Lawrence Taylor	6-3	237	North Carolina	•		•	•
LB	David Little	6-1	228	Florida	•		•	
LB	Bob Crable	6-3	222	Notre Dame	•			•
B	Kenny Easley	6-3	206	UCLA	•	•	•	•
B	Ronnie Lott	6-2	200	Southern Cal	•	•	•	•
B	John Simmons	5-11	188	SMU	•		•	•

OTHERS RECEIVING FIRST-TEAM HONORS

L	Derrie Nelson		Nebraska	•
L	Hosea Taylor		Houston	•
L	Scott Zettek		Notre Dame	•
B	Scott Woerner		Georgia	• •
P	Rohn Stark		Florida State	•

FC named Taylor as a DL; AP named Junior as a LB

HEISMAN TROPHY VOTING

	PLAYER	POS	SCHOOL	1ST	2ND	3RD	TOTAL
1	George Rogers	RB	South Carolina	216	179	122	1128
2	Hugh Green	DE	Pittsburgh	179	125	74	861
3	Herschel Walker	TB	Georgia	107	120	122	683
4	Mark Herrmann	QB	Purdue	58	71	89	405
5	Jim McMahon	QB	Brigham Young	30	32	35	189
6	Art Schlichter	QB	Ohio State	18	34	36	158
7	Neil Lomax	QB	Portland State	10	11	17	69
8	Jarvis Redwine	RB	Nebraska	4	16	20	64
9	Ken Easley	DB	UCLA	5	5	19	44
10	Anthony Carter	WR	Michigan	4	6	10	34

AWARD WINNERS

PLAYER	POS	SCHOOL	AWARD NAME
Hugh Green	DE	Pittsburgh	Maxwell
Mark May	OT	Pittsburgh	Outland
Hugh Green	DE	Pittsburgh	Camp
Hugh Green	DE	Pittsburgh	Lombardi

CONFERENCE STANDINGS

ACC	Conf.			Overall		
	W	L	T	W	L	T
North Carolina	6	0	0	11	1	0
Maryland	5	1	0	8	4	0
North Carolina St.	3	3	0	6	5	0
Clemson	2	4	0	6	5	0
Wake Forest	2	4	0	5	6	0
Virginia	2	4	0	4	7	0
Duke	1	5	0	2	9	0

Big 10	Conf.			Overall		
	W	L	T	W	L	T
Michigan	8	0	0	10	2	0
Purdue	7	1	0	9	3	0
Ohio State	7	1	0	9	3	0
Iowa	4	4	0	4	7	0
Minnesota	4	5	0	5	6	0
Indiana	3	5	0	6	5	0
Wisconsin	3	5	0	4	7	0
Illinois	3	5	0	3	7	1
Michigan State	2	6	0	3	8	0
Northwestern	0	9	0	0	11	0

Big 8	Conf.			Overall		
	W	L	T	W	L	T
Oklahoma	7	0	0	10	2	0
Nebraska	6	1	0	10	2	0
Missouri	5	2	0	8	4	0
Kansas	3	3	1	4	5	2
Oklahoma State	2	4	1	3	7	1
Iowa State	2	5	0	6	5	0
Kansas State	1	6	0	3	8	0
Colorado	1	6	0	1	10	0

Big West	Conf.			Overall		
	W	L	T	W	L	T
Long Beach State	5	0	0	8	3	0
Utah State	4	1	0	6	5	0
San Jose State	3	2	0	7	4	0
Fresno State	1	4	0	5	6	0
Cal-St. Fullerton	1	4	0	4	7	0
Pacific	1	4	0	4	8	0

Ivy	Conf.			Overall		
	W	L	T	W	L	T
Yale	6	1	0	8	2	0
Cornell	5	2	0	5	5	0
Harvard	4	3	0	7	3	0
Princeton	4	3	0	6	4	0
Brown	4	3	0	6	4	0
Dartmouth	4	3	0	4	6	0
Pennsylvania	1	6	0	1	9	0
Columbia	0	7	0	1	9	0

MAC	Conf.			Overall		
	W	L	T	W	L	T
Central Michigan	7	2	0	9	2	0
Western Michigan	6	3	0	7	4	0
Northern Illinois	4	3	0	7	4	0
Miami, Ohio	4	3	0	5	6	0
Ohio U	5	4	0	6	5	0
Ball State	5	4	0	6	5	0
Bowling Green	4	4	0	4	7	0
Toledo	3	6	0	4	7	0
Kent State	3	6	0	3	8	0
Eastern Michigan	1	7	0	1	9	0

PAC 10	Conf.			Overall		
	W	L	T	W	L	T
Washington	6	1	0	9	3	0
UCLA	5	2	0	9	2	0
Southern Cal	4	2	1	8	2	1
Arizona State	5	3	0	7	4	0
Oregon	4	3	1	6	3	2
Stanford	3	4	0	6	5	0
Arizona	3	4	0	5	6	0
Washington State	3	4	0	4	7	0
California	3	5	0	3	8	0
Oregon State	0	8	0	0	11	0

SEC	Conf.			Overall		
	W	L	T	W	L	T
Georgia	6	0	0	12	0	0
Alabama*	5	1	0	10	2	0
Mississippi State	2	4	0	9	3	0
Florida	4	2	0	8	4	0
LSU	4	2	0	7	4	0
Tennessee	3	3	0	5	6	0
Mississippi*	2	4	0	3	8	0
Kentucky	1	5	0	3	8	0
Auburn	0	6	0	5	6	0
Vanderbilt	0	6	0	2	9	0

* Alabama-Mississippi game did not count in standings.

SWC	Conf.			Overall		
	W	L	T	W	L	T
Baylor	8	0	0	10	2	0
SMU	5	3	0	8	4	0
Houston	5	3	0	7	5	0
Texas	4	4	0	7	5	0
Rice	4	4	0	5	6	0
Arkansas	3	5	0	7	5	0
Texas Tech	3	5	0	5	6	0
Texas A&M	3	5	0	4	7	0
TCU	1	7	0	1	10	0

WAC	Conf.			Overall		
	W	L	T	W	L	T
Brigham Young	6	1	0	12	1	0
Colorado State	5	1	1	6	4	1
Hawaii	4	3	0	8	3	0
Wyoming	4	4	0	6	5	0
San Diego State	4	4	0	4	8	0
Utah	3	3	1	5	5	1
New Mexico	3	4	0	4	7	0
Air Force	1	6	0	2	9	1
Texas-El Paso	1	6	0	1	11	0

Independents	Overall		
	W	L	T
Pittsburgh	11	1	0
Florida State	10	2	0
Penn State	10	2	0
Notre Dame	9	2	1
Southern Miss	9	3	0
Miami, Fla.	9	3	0
Navy	8	4	0
South Carolina	8	4	0
Virginia Tech	8	4	0
Boston College	7	4	0
Nevada-Las Vegas	7	4	0
Rutgers	7	4	0
Tulane	7	5	0
North Texas	6	5	0
West Virginia	6	6	0
Syracuse	5	6	0
Louisville	5	6	0
East Carolina	4	7	0
Temple	4	7	0
Army	3	7	1
Cincinnati	2	9	0
Memphis	2	9	0
Georgia Tech	1	9	1

BOWL GAMES

DATE	GAME	SCORE
D13	Independence	Southern Miss 16, McNeese State 14
D14	Garden State	Houston 35, Navy 0
D19	Holiday	Brigham Young 46, SMU 45
D20	Tangerine	Florida 35, Maryland 20
D26	Fiesta	Penn State 31, Ohio State 19
D27	All-American	Arkansas 34, Tulane 15
D27	Sun	Nebraska 31, Mississippi State 17
D27	Liberty	Purdue 28, Missouri 25

DATE	GAME	SCORE
D29	Gator	Pittsburgh 37, South Carolina 9
D31	Bluebonnet	North Carolina 16, Texas 7
J1	Sugar	Georgia 17, Notre Dame 10
J1	Cotton	Alabama 30, Baylor 2
J1	Rose	Michigan 23, Washington 6
J1	Orange	Oklahoma 18, Florida State 17
J2	Peach	Miami, Fla. 20, Virginia Tech 10

1980 NCAA Major College Statistical Leaders

Individual Leaders

PASSING	CL	G	ATT	COM	PCT	INT	I%	YDS	YPA	TD	TD%	RATING
1 Jim McMahon, Brigham Young	JR	12	445	284	63.8	18	4.0	4571	10.3	47	10.6	176.9
2 Joe Adams, Tennessee State	SR	10	333	200	60.1	21	6.3	2848	8.6	30	9.0	149.0
3 John Elway, Stanford	SO	11	379	248	65.4	11	2.9	2889	7.6	27	7.1	147.2
4 Steve Woods, U.T. Chattanooga	JR	10	194	100	51.6	13	6.7	1827	9.4	17	8.8	146.2
5 Mark Herrmann, Purdue	SR	10	340	220	64.7	17	5.0	2923	8.6	19	5.6	145.4
6 Larry Gentry, Nevada-Las Vegas	SR	11	209	113	54.1	16	7.7	1691	8.1	22	10.5	141.5
7 Art Schlichter, Ohio State	JR	11	191	102	53.4	8	4.2	1628	8.5	12	6.3	137.4
8 Ricky Hardin, Utah	SR	11	290	179	61.7	19	6.6	2459	8.5	15	5.2	136.9
9 Tom Flick, Washington	SR	11	280	168	60.0	11	3.9	2178	7.8	15	5.4	135.2
10 Kevin Starkey, Long Beach State	SR	11	248	138	55.7	16	6.5	1955	7.9	19	7.7	134.2

ALL-PURPOSE	CL	G	RUSH	REC	PR	KR	YDS	YPG
1 Marcus Allen, Southern Cal	JR	10	1563	231	0	0	1794	179.4
2 Rich Diana, Yale	JR	10	1074	212	145	318	1749	174.9
3 Alvin Lewis, Colorado State	SR	11	1047	335	139	400	1921	174.6
4 Herschel Walker, Georgia	FR	11	1616	70	0	119	1805	164.1
5 George Rogers, South Carolina	SR	11	1781	23	0	0	1804	164.0
6 Gerald Willhite, San Jose State	JR	11	1210	491	0	42	1743	158.5
7 Stump Mitchell, Citadel	SR	11	1647	57	0	0	1704	154.9
8 James Brooks, Auburn	SR	11	1314	63	56	226	1659	150.8
9 Calvin Murray, Ohio State	SR	11	1192	197	0	236	1625	147.7
10 Anthony Collins, East Carolina	SR	11	503	119	0	990	1612	146.5

RUSHING/Yards Per Game	CL	G	ATT	YDS	TD	AVG	YPG
1 George Rogers, South Carolina	SR	11	297	1781	14	6.0	161.9
2 Marcus Allen, Southern Cal	JR	10	354	1563	14	4.4	156.3
3 Stump Mitchell, Citadel	SR	11	291	1647	14	5.7	149.7
4 Herschel Walker, Georgia	FR	11	274	1616	15	5.9	146.9
5 Jarvis Redwine, Nebraska	SR	9	156	1119	9	7.2	124.3
6 Charlie Wysocki, Maryland	JR	11	334	1359	11	4.1	123.5
7 Freeman McNeil, UCLA	SR	9	203	1105	10	5.4	122.8
8 Cyrus Lawrence, Virginia Tech	SO	10	271	1221	8	4.5	122.1
9 James Brooks, Auburn	SR	11	261	1314	9	5.0	119.5
10 Dwayne Crutchfield, Iowa State	JR	11	284	1312	11	4.6	119.3

RUSHING/Yards Per Carry	CL	G	ATT	YDS	YPC
1 Jarvis Redwine, Nebraska	SR	9	156	1119	7.2
2 Calvin Murray, Ohio State	SR	11	185	1192	6.4
3 Dennis Gentry, Baylor	JR	10	147	883	6.0
4 George Rogers, South Carolina	SR	11	297	1781	6.0
5 Herschel Walker, Georgia	FR	11	274	1616	5.9
6 Kelvin Bryant, North Carolina	SO	11	177	1039	5.9
7 Stump Mitchell, Citadel	SR	11	291	1647	5.7
8 Darrin Nelson, Stanford	JR	10	161	889	5.5
9 Freeman McNeil, UCLA	SR	9	203	1105	5.4
10 Garry White, Minnesota	SR	11	177	959	5.4

*-Based on top 38 rushers

RECEIVING	CL	G	REC	YDS	TD	YPR	YPG	RPG
1 Dave Young, Purdue	SR	11	67	917	8	13.7	83.4	6.1
2 James Murphy, Utah State	SR	11	66	966	10	14.6	87.8	6.0
3 Keith Chappelle, Iowa	SR	11	64	1037	6	16.2	94.3	5.8
4 Rainey Meszaros, Pacific	JR	12	68	1062	3	15.6	88.5	5.7
5 Mike Jones, Tennessee State	SO	10	55	934	13	17.0	93.4	5.5
5 Cris Crissy, Princeton	SR	10	55	653	3	11.9	65.3	5.5
7 Bart Burrell, Purdue	SR	11	58	888	6	15.3	80.7	5.3
8 Dave Shula, Dartmouth	SR	10	52	758	3	14.6	75.8	5.2
9 Scott Phillips, Brigham Young	SR	12	60	689	7	11.5	57.4	5.0
9 Gerald Harp, Western Carolina	SR	11	55	854	3	15.5	77.6	5.0
9 Gerald Willhite, San Jose State	JR	11	55	491	3	8.9	44.6	5.0

PUNTING	CL	PUNT	YDS	AVG
1 Steve Cox, Arkansas	SR	47	2186	46.5
2 Ray Stachowicz, Michigan State	SR	71	3278	46.2
3 Rohn Stark, Florida State	JR	57	2576	45.2
4 Eric Kaifes, SMU	JR	68	3034	44.6
5 Jim Arnold, Vanderbilt	SO	72	3180	44.2
6 Bucky Scribner, Kansas	SO	66	2909	44.1
7 Jack Weil, Wyoming	FR	43	1892	44.0
8 Rick Hanschu, Eastern Michigan	SO	57	2487	43.6
9 Steve Streater, North Carolina	SR	59	2560	43.4
10 Mike Black, Arizona State	SO	53	2299	43.4

PUNT RETURNS	CL	PR	YDS	TD	AVG
1 Scott Woerner, Georgia	SR	31	488	1	15.7
2 Fulton Walker, West Virginia	SR	21	307	1	14.6
3 Lonell Phea, Houston	JR	17	232	0	13.6
4 Ray Horton, Washington	SO	18	238	1	13.2
5 John Simmons, SMU	SR	27	330	2	12.2
6 John Holt, West Texas State	SR	14	160	2	11.4
7 Darnell Clash, Wyoming	FR	39	433	0	11.1
8 Dave Martin, Villanova	SR	13	144	1	11.1
9 Mardye McDole, Mississippi State	SR	23	251	1	10.9
10 Eugene Young, Oregon	FR	33	359	0	10.9

KICKOFF RETURNS	CL	KR	YDS	TD	AVG
1 Mike Fox, San Diego State	SO	11	361	0	32.8
2 Anthony Carter, Michigan	SO	14	411	0	29.4
3 Tony Felder, Texas-Arlington	SR	15	424	1	28.3
4 Glen Young, Mississippi State	SO	19	525	1	27.6
5 Willie Gault, Tennessee	SO	24	662	3	27.6
6 Anthony Collins, East Carolina	SR	37	990	2	26.8
7 Carlen Charleston, North Texas	FR	22	587	0	26.7
8 David Toloumu, Hawaii	JR	15	391	0	26.1
9 Peter Lavery, Dartmouth	SO	15	382	1	25.5
10 Johnny Smith, Lamar	SR	17	431	0	25.4

SCORING	CL	TDS	XPT	FG	PTS	PTPG
1 Sammy Winder, Southern Miss	JR	20	0	0	120	10.9
2 J.C. Watts, Oklahoma	SR	18	0	0	108	9.8
3 Bill Capece, Florida State	SR	0	38	22	104	9.5
4 Vlade Janakievski, Ohio State	SR	0	45	15	90	9.0
5 Marcus Allen, Southern Cal	JR	14	0	0	84	8.4
6 Herschel Walker, Georgia	FR	15	0	0	90	8.2
6 Amos Lawrence, North Carolina	SR	15	0	0	90	8.2
6 Roger Craig, Nebraska	SO	15	0	0	90	8.2
9 Obed Ariri, Clemson	SR	0	18	23	87	7.9
10 Stump Mitchell, Citadel	SR	14	2	0	86	7.8
10 Gerald Willhite, San Jose State	JR	14	2	0	86	7.8

FIELD GOALS	CL	FGA	FGM	PCT	FGG
1 Obed Ariri, Clemson	SR	30	23	0.77	2.10
2 Bill Capece, Florida State	SR	30	22	0.73	2.00
3 Harry Oliver, Notre Dame	JR	23	18	0.78	1.64
3 Chuck Nelson, Washington	SO	26	18	0.69	1.64
5 Steve Fehr, Navy	JR	23	17	0.74	1.55
6 Herb Menhardt, Penn State	SR	21	15	0.71	1.50
6 Vlade Janakievski, Ohio State	SR	22	15	0.68	1.50
8 John Cooper, Boston College	JR	21	16	0.76	1.45
8 Rex Robinson, Georgia	SR	22	16	0.73	1.45
8 Jon Poole, Colorado State	FR	22	16	0.73	1.45
8 Rick Anderson, Purdue	JR	23	16	0.70	1.45

INTERCEPTIONS	CL	INT	YDS	TD	INT/GM
1 Ronnie Lott, Southern Cal	SR	8	166	1	0.73
1 Steve McNamee, William & Mary	SR	8	125	0	0.73
1 Greg Benton, Drake	SR	8	119	0	0.73
1 Jeff Hipp, Georgia	SR	8	104	0	0.73
1 Mike Richardson, Arizona State	SO	8	89	2	0.73
1 Vann McElroy, Baylor	JR	8	73	0	0.73
7 Rocky Delgadillo, Harvard	JR	7	130	1	0.70
7 Dave Kimichik, Cornell	JR	7	19	0	0.70
9 Fred Marion, Miami, Fla.	JR	7	85	0	0.64
9 Gill Byrd, San Jose State	SO	7	69	0	0.64
9 John Simmons, SMU	SR	7	62	2	0.64
9 David Morris, North Texas	SR	7	56	0	0.64

Team Leaders

RUSHING OFFENSE	G	ATT	YDS	AVG	TD	YPG
1 Nebraska	11	739	4161	5.6	45	378.3
2 Oklahoma	11	691	3961	5.7	48	360.1
3 Alabama	11	633	3381	5.3	35	307.4
4 South Carolina	11	620	3291	5.3	35	299.2
5 McNeese St.	11	671	3275	4.9	27	297.7
6 Baylor	11	687	3266	4.8	29	296.9
7 Mississippi State	11	651	3135	4.8	28	285.0
8 Citadel	11	641	3066	4.8	32	278.7
9 Furman	11	595	3021	5.1	24	274.6
10 North Carolina	11	633	2977	4.7	26	270.6

PASSING OFFENSE	G	ATT	COM	INT	PCT	YDS	YPA	TD	I%	YPC	YPG
1 Brigham Young	12	498	317	21	63.7	4918	9.9	49	4.2	15.5	409.8
2 Illinois	11	471	250	15	53.1	3227	6.9	20	3.2	12.9	293.4
3 Purdue	11	375	243	17	64.8	3216	8.6	20	4.5	13.2	292.4
4 Tennessee State	10	346	203	24	58.7	2896	8.4	30	6.9	14.3	289.6
5 Pittsburgh	11	378	196	28	51.9	2952	7.8	25	7.4	15.1	268.4
6 Stanford	11	383	251	12	65.5	2921	7.6	27	3.1	11.6	265.5
7 California	11	381	249	17	65.4	2862	7.5	8	4.5	11.5	260.2
8 La. Monroe	11	408	213	25	52.2	2828	6.9	18	6.1	13.3	257.1
9 Appalachian State	11	376	190	17	50.5	2781	7.4	15	4.5	14.6	252.8
10 San Jose State	11	368	186	26	50.5	2712	7.4	18	7.1	14.6	246.5

TOTAL OFFENSE	G	P	YDS	AVG	TD	YPG
1 Brigham Young	12	847	6420	7.6	74	535.0
2 Nebraska	11	913	5576	6.1	59	506.9
3 Oklahoma	11	775	4954	6.4	50	450.4
4 Nevada-Las Vegas	11	825	4908	5.9	50	446.2
5 Purdue	11	845	4856	5.7	35	441.5
6 Baylor	11	901	4848	5.4	41	440.7
7 Stanford	11	846	4759	5.6	41	432.6
8 Ohio State	11	812	4703	5.8	45	427.5
9 Utah	11	827	4617	5.6	33	419.7
10 Drake	11	852	4603	5.4	38	418.5

RUSHING DEFENSE	G	ATT	YDS	AVG	TD	YPG
1 Pittsburgh	11	449	718	1.6	3	65.3
2 Yale	10	428	833	1.9	6	83.3
3 Nebraska	11	454	950	2.1	7	86.4
4 Florida State	11	408	984	2.4	2	89.5
5 Southern Cal	11	413	1064	2.6	6	96.7
6 Virginia Tech	11	473	1126	2.4	4	102.4
7 Baylor	11	460	1160	2.5	7	105.5
8 Notre Dame	11	434	1208	2.8	7	109.8
9 Ohio U	11	481	1269	2.6	11	115.4
10 Navy	11	471	1284	2.7	9	116.7

PASSING DEFENSE	G	ATT	COM	PCT	YPC	INT	I%	YDS	YPA	TD	YPG
1 Kansas State	11	152	75	49.3	13.4	10	6.6	1005	6.6	8	91.4
2 Iowa State	11	242	86	35.5	11.7	11	4.5	1006	4.2	6	91.5
3 Southern Miss	11	196	94	48.0	11.1	11	5.6	1043	5.3	2	94.8
4 Western Michigan	11	219	92	42.0	11.6	13	5.9	1063	4.9	5	96.6
5 Alabama	11	210	93	44.3	11.8	14	6.7	1093	5.2	7	99.4
6 Notre Dame	11	234	108	46.2	10.5	9	3.8	1137	4.9	6	103.4
7 LSU	11	226	91	40.3	12.5	15	6.6	1142	5.1	7	103.8
8 Navy	11	225	109	48.4	10.8	17	7.6	1172	5.2	4	106.5
9 Toledo	11	211	96	45.5	12.4	17	8.1	1189	5.6	5	108.1
9 Northern Illinois	11	199	106	53.3	11.2	13	6.5	1189	6.0	4	108.1

TOTAL DEFENSE	G	P	YDS	AVG	TD	YPG
1 Pittsburgh	11	753	2260	3.0	13	205.5
2 Florida State	11	649	2290	3.5	8	208.2
3 Nebraska	11	713	2300	3.2	10	209.1
4 Notre Dame	11	668	2345	3.5	13	213.2
5 Virginia Tech	11	703	2401	3.4	11	218.3
6 Navy	11	696	2456	3.5	13	223.3
7 Alabama	11	730	2487	3.4	11	226.1
8 Southern Cal	11	651	2577	4.0	15	234.3
9 Yale	10	670	2427	3.6	14	242.7
10 Southern Miss	11	656	2801	4.3	20	254.6

SCORING OFFENSE	G	PTS	AVG
1 Brigham Young	12	560	46.7
2 Nebraska	11	439	39.9
3 Nevada-Las Vegas	11	384	34.9
4 Oklahoma	11	378	34.4
5 Ohio State	11	368	33.5
6 Florida State	11	352	32.0
7 Tennessee State	10	312	31.2
8 Pittsburgh	11	343	31.2
9 South Carolina	11	339	30.8
10 Washington	11	327	29.7

SCORING DEFENSE	G	PTS	AVG
1 Florida State	11	85	7.7
2 Nebraska	11	93	8.5
3 Alabama	11	96	8.7
4 Virginia Tech	11	109	9.9
5 Navy	11	111	10.1
5 Notre Dame	11	111	10.1
7 Pittsburgh	11	121	11.0
8 Michigan	11	123	11.2
8 North Carolina	11	123	11.2
10 Central Michigan	11	127	11.5
10 Georgia	11	127	11.5

TURNOVER MARGIN	G	FR	INT	TOT	FL	INTL	TOT	MAR
1 Georgia	11	20	24	44	11	10	21	2.1
1 Ohio State	11	16	25	41	9	9	18	2.1
3 Missouri	11	21	23	44	14	9	23	1.9
4 Florida State	11	19	18	37	6	11	17	1.8
5 Arizona State	11	21	21	42	15	9	24	1.6
6 Drake	11	16	27	43	14	13	27	1.5
7 Florida	11	20	18	38	9	15	24	1.3
8 Navy	11	14	17	31	11	7	18	1.2
8 Richmond	11	24	13	37	6	18	24	1.2
8 McNeese St.	11	22	23	45	19	13	32	1.2
8 Washington	11	24	16	40	16	11	27	1.2

1981 POLL PROGRESSION

PRE-SEASON 1981 — Sept. 5 Games

UP	AP	Team	Record	Result
1	1	Michigan	0-0-0	bye week
2	2	Oklahoma	0-0-0	bye week
4	3	Notre Dame	0-0-0	bye week
3	4	Alabama	0-0-0	beat LSU 24-7
5	5	Southern Cal	0-0-0	bye week
6	6	Nebraska	0-0-0	bye week
7	7	Penn State	0-0-0	bye week
9	8	Pittsburgh	0-0-0	beat Illinois 26-6
10	9	Texas	0-0-0	bye week
8	10	Georgia	0-0-0	beat Tennessee 44-0
11	11	Ohio State	0-0-0	bye week
14	12	North Carolina	0-0-0	bye week
12	13	UCLA	0-0-0	bye week
15	14	Mississippi State	0-0-0	beat Memphis 20-3
17	15	Washington	0-0-0	bye week
19	16	Brigham Young	0-0-0	beat Long Beach State 31-8
16	17	Florida	0-0-0	lost to Miami, Fla. 20-21
	18	Stanford	0-0-0	bye week
13	19	Florida State	0-0-0	beat Louisville 17-0
PB	20	Arizona State	0-0-0	bye week
18		Houston	0-0-0	beat New Mexico 21-10
20		Baylor		lost to Lamar 17-18

SEPTEMBER 7 POLL — Sept. 12 Games

UP	AP	Team	Record	Result
1	1	Michigan	0-0-0	lost to Wisconsin 14-21
2	2	Alabama	1-0-0	lost to Georgia Tech 21-24
3	3	Oklahoma	1-0-0	beat Wyoming 37-20
4	4	Notre Dame	0-0-0	beat LSU 27-9
5	5	Southern Cal	0-0-0	beat Tennessee 43-7
6	6	Georgia	1-0-0	beat California 27-13
7	7	Nebraska	0-0-0	lost to Iowa 7-10
8	8	Texas	0-0-0	beat Rice 31-3
9	9	Penn State	0-0-0	beat Cincinnati 52-0
10	10	Pittsburgh	1-0-0	bye week
11	11	Ohio State	0-0-0	beat Duke 34-13
12	12	UCLA	0-0-0	beat Arizona 35-18
13	13	North Carolina	0-0-0	beat East Carolina 56-0
14	14	Mississippi State	1-0-0	bye week
15	15	Brigham Young	1-0-0	beat Air Force 45-21
16	16	Miami, Fla.	1-0-0	bye week
17	17	Washington	0-0-0	beat Pacific 34-14
18	18	Florida State	1-0-0	beat Memphis 10-5
19	19	Stanford	0-0-0	lost to Purdue 19-27
20	20	Arizona State	0-0-0	beat Utah 52-10

SEPTEMBER 14 POLL — Sept. 19 Games

UP	AP	Team	Record	Result
1	1	Notre Dame	1-0-0	lost to # 11 Michigan 7-25
2	2	Southern Cal	1-0-0	beat Indiana 21-0
3	3	Oklahoma	1-0-0	bye week
4	4	Georgia	2-0-0	lost to Clemson 3-13
5	5	Penn State	1-0-0	bye week
6	6	Texas	1-0-0	beat North Texas 23-10
7	7	Pittsburgh	1-0-0	beat Cincinnati 38-7
8	8	Ohio State	1-0-0	beat Michigan State 27-13
10	9	UCLA	1-0-0	beat # 20 Wisconsin 31-13
9	10	North Carolina	1-0-0	beat Miami, Ohio 49-7
12	11	Michigan	0-1-0	beat # 1 Notre Dame 25-7
11	12	Alabama	1-1-0	beat Kentucky 19-10
13	13	Brigham Young	2-0-0	beat Texas-El Paso 65-8
14	14	Mississippi State	1-0-0	beat Vanderbilt 29-9
17	15	Washington	1-0-0	beat Kansas State 20-3
15	16	Miami, Fla.	1-0-0	beat Houston 12-7
19	17	Nebraska	0-1-0	beat # 19 Florida State 34-14
PB	18	Arizona State	1-0-0	beat Wichita St. 33-21
16	19	Florida State	2-0-0	lost to # 17 Nebraska 14-34
20	20	Wisconsin	1-0-0	lost to # 9 UCLA 13-31
18		Purdue	1-0-0	lost to Minnesota 13-16

SEPTEMBER 21 POLL — Sept. 26 Games

UP	AP	Team	Record	Result
1	1	Southern Cal	2-0-0	beat # 2 Oklahoma 28-24
2	2	Oklahoma	1-0-0	lost to # 1 Southern Cal 24-28
3	3	Penn State	1-0-0	beat # 15 Nebraska 30-24
4	4	Texas	2-0-0	beat # 14 Miami, Fla. 14-7
5	5	Pittsburgh	2-0-0	bye week
7	6	UCLA	2-0-0	lost to Iowa 7-20
6	7	Michigan	1-1-0	beat Navy 21-16
8	8	Ohio State	2-0-0	beat Stanford 24-19
9	9	North Carolina	2-0-0	beat Boston College 56-14
10	10	Alabama	2-1-0	beat Vanderbilt 28-7
13	11	Brigham Young	3-0-0	beat Colorado 41-20
14	12	Mississippi State	2-0-0	beat Florida 28-7
11	13	Notre Dame	1-1-0	lost to Purdue 14-15
15	14	Miami, Fla.	2-0-0	lost to # 4 Texas 7-14
12	15	Nebraska	1-1-0	lost to # 3 Penn State 24-30
17	16	Washington	2-0-0	beat Oregon 17-3
16	17	Georgia	2-1-0	beat South Carolina 24-0
PB	18	Arizona State	2-0-0	lost to Washington State 21-24
18	19	Clemson	3-0-0	bye week
PB	20	SMU	3-0-0	beat TCU 20-9
19		Florida	2-1-0	lost to # 12 Mississippi State 7-28
20		West Virginia	2-0-0	beat Colorado State 49-3

SEPTEMBER 28 POLL — Oct. 3 Games

UP	AP	Team	Record	Result
1	1	Southern Cal	3-0-0	beat Oregon State 56-22
2	2	Penn State	2-0-0	beat Temple 30-0
3	3	Texas	3-0-0	bye week
4	4	Pittsburgh	2-0-0	beat South Carolina 42-28
5	5	Oklahoma	1-1-0	tied # 20 Iowa State 7-7
6	6	North Carolina	3-0-0	beat Georgia Tech 28-7
7	7	Ohio State	3-0-0	lost to Florida State 27-36
8	8	Michigan	2-1-0	beat Indiana 38-17
9	9	Mississippi State	3-0-0	lost to Missouri 3-14
11	10	Brigham Young	4-0-0	beat Utah State 32-26 O2
10	11	Alabama	3-1-0	beat Mississippi 38-7
13	12	Washington	3-0-0	lost to Arizona State 7-26
12	13	Georgia	3-1-0	bye week
14	14	Clemson	3-0-0	beat Kentucky 21-3
PB	15	SMU	4-0-0	bye week
18	16	UCLA	2-1-0	beat Colorado 27-7
15	17	Miami, Fla.	2-1-0	beat Vanderbilt 48-16
20	18	Iowa	2-1-0	beat Northwestern 64-0
16	19	Arkansas	3-0-0	lost to TCU 24-28
	20	Iowa State	3-0-0	tied # 5 Oklahoma 7-7
17		Missouri	3-0-0	beat # 9 Mississippi State 14-3
19		Nebraska	1-2-0	beat Auburn 17-3

OCTOBER 5 POLL — Oct. 10 Games

UP	AP	Team	Record	Result
1	1	Southern Cal	4-0-0	lost to Arizona 10-13
2	2	Penn State	3-0-0	beat Boston College 38-7
3	3	Texas	3-0-0	beat # 10 Oklahoma 34-14
4	4	Pittsburgh	3-0-0	beat West Virginia 17-0
5	5	North Carolina	4-0-0	beat Wake Forest 48-10
6	6	Michigan	3-1-0	beat Michigan State 38-20
7	7	Alabama	4-1-0	tied Southern Miss 13-13
8	8	Brigham Young	5-0-0	lost to Nevada-Las Vegas 41-45
10	9	Clemson	4-0-0	beat Virginia 27-0
12	10	Oklahoma	1-1-1	lost to # 3 Texas 14-34
9	11	Georgia	3-1-0	beat Mississippi 37-7
14	12	Iowa State	3-0-1	lost to San Diego State 31-52
11	13	Missouri	4-0-0	beat Kansas State 58-13
PB	14	SMU	4-0-0	beat Baylor 37-20
15	15	Iowa	3-1-0	beat Indiana 42-28
13	16	Miami, Fla.	3-1-0	bye week
16	17	UCLA	3-1-0	lost to Stanford 23-26
17	18	Ohio State	3-1-0	lost to Wisconsin 21-24
20	19	Mississippi State	3-1-0	beat Colorado State 37-27
19	20	Florida State	3-1-0	beat Notre Dame 19-13
18		Nebraska	2-2-0	beat Colorado 59-0

OCTOBER 12 POLL — Oct. 17 Games

UP	AP	Team	Record	Result
1	1	Texas	4-0-0	lost to Arkansas 11-42
2	2	Penn State	4-0-0	beat Syracuse 41-16
3	3	Pittsburgh	4-0-0	beat # 11 Florida State 42-14
4	4	North Carolina	5-0-0	beat North Carolina St. 21-10
5	5	Michigan	4-1-0	lost to # 12 Iowa 7-9
7	6	Clemson	5-0-0	beat Duke 38-10
6	7	Southern Cal	4-1-0	beat Stanford 25-17
8	8	Missouri	5-0-0	lost to Iowa State 13-34
9	9	Georgia	4-1-0	beat Vanderbilt 53-21
PB	10	SMU	5-0-0	beat Houston 38-22
10	11	Florida State	4-1-0	lost to # 3 Pittsburgh 14-42
12	12	Iowa	4-1-0	beat # 5 Michigan 9-7
11	13	Miami, Fla.	3-1-0	lost to # 16 Mississippi State 10-14
13	14	Wisconsin	4-1-0	lost to Michigan State 14-33
15	15	Alabama	4-1-1	beat Tennessee 38-19
16	16	Mississippi State	4-1-0	beat # 13 Miami, Fla. 14-10
20	17	Brigham Young	5-1-0	beat San Diego State 27-7
18	18	Washington State	5-1-0	tied UCLA 17-17
14	19	Nebraska	3-2-0	beat Kansas State 49-3
PB	20	Arizona State	4-1-0	beat California 45-17
17		Iowa State	3-1-1	beat # 8 Missouri 34-13
19		Oklahoma	1-2-1	beat Kansas 45-7

OCTOBER 19 POLL — Oct. 24 Games

UP	AP	Team	Record	Result
1	1	Penn State	5-0-0	beat West Virginia 30-7
2	2	Pittsburgh	5-0-0	beat Syracuse 23-10
3	3	North Carolina	6-0-0	lost to South Carolina 13-31
5	4	Clemson	6-0-0	beat North Carolina St. 17-7
4	5	Southern Cal	5-1-0	beat Notre Dame 14-7
7	6	Iowa	5-1-0	lost to Minnesota 10-12
6	7	Georgia	5-1-0	beat Kentucky 21-0
PB	8	SMU	6-0-0	lost to # 10 Texas 7-9
10	9	Mississippi State	5-1-0	beat Auburn 21-17
8	10	Texas	4-1-0	beat # 8 SMU 9-7
9	11	Alabama	5-1-1	beat Rutgers 31-7
13	12	Arkansas	5-1-0	lost to Houston 17-20
15	13	Brigham Young	6-1-0	lost to Wyoming 20-33
12	14	Iowa State	4-1-1	beat Colorado 17-10
11	15	Nebraska	4-2-0	beat # 19 Missouri 6-0
14	16	Washington State	5-0-1	beat Arizona 34-19
PB	17	Arizona State	5-1-0	beat Stanford 62-36
19	18	Michigan	4-2-0	beat Northwestern 38-0
16	19	Missouri	5-1-0	lost to # 15 Nebraska 0-6
20	20	Florida State	4-2-0	beat LSU 38-14
17		Oklahoma	2-2-1	beat Oregon State 42-3
18		Washington	5-1-0	beat Texas Tech 14-7

OCTOBER 26 POLL — Oct. 31 Games

UP	AP	Team	Record	Result
1	1	Penn State	6-0-0	lost to Miami, Fla. 14-17
2	2	Pittsburgh	6-0-0	beat Boston College 29-24
4	3	Clemson	7-0-0	beat Wake Forest 82-24
3	4	Southern Cal	6-1-0	beat # 14 Washington State 41-17
5	5	Georgia	6-1-0	beat Temple 49-3
6	6	Texas	5-1-0	beat Texas Tech 26-9
8	7	Mississippi State	6-1-0	lost to # 8 Alabama 10-13
7	8	Alabama	6-1-1	beat # 7 Mississippi State 13-10
11	9	North Carolina	6-1-0	beat Maryland 17-10
PB	10	Arizona State	6-1-0	beat San Jose State 31-24
10	11	Iowa State	5-1-1	lost to Kansas State 7-10
9	12	Nebraska	5-2-0	beat Kansas 31-15
PB	13	SMU	6-1-0	beat Texas A&M 27-7
12	14	Washington State	6-0-1	lost to # 4 Southern Cal 17-41
14	15	Michigan	5-2-0	beat Minnesota 34-13
16	16	Iowa	5-2-0	lost to Illinois 7-24
17	17	Florida State	5-2-0	beat Western Carolina 56-31
15	18	Washington	6-1-0	beat Stanford 42-31
13	19	Oklahoma	3-2-1	beat Colorado 49-0
20	20	Arkansas	5-2-0	beat Rice 41-7
18		Ohio State	5-2-0	beat Purdue 45-33
19		Miami, Fla.	4-2-0	beat # 1 Penn State 17-14

November 2 Poll — Nov. 7 Games

UP	AP	Team	Record	Result
1	1	Pittsburgh	7-0-0	beat Rutgers 47-3
3	2	Clemson	8-0-0	beat # 8 North Carolina 10-8
2	3	Southern Cal	7-1-0	beat California 21-3
4	4	Georgia	7-1-0	beat Florida 26-21
5	5	Texas	6-1-0	tied Houston 14-14
6	6	Penn State	6-1-0	beat North Carolina St. 22-15
7	7	Alabama	7-1-1	bye week
9	8	North Carolina	7-1-0	lost to # 2 Clemson 8-10
PB	9	Arizona State	6-1-0	bye week
PB	10	SMU	7-1-0	beat Rice 33-12
8	11	Nebraska	6-2-0	beat Oklahoma State 54-7
10	12	Michigan	6-2-0	beat Illinois 70-21
11	13	Miami, Fla.	5-2-0	beat # 14 Florida State 27-19
14	14	Florida State	6-2-0	lost to # 13 Miami, Fla. 19-27
15	15	Mississippi State	6-2-0	lost to # 20 Southern Miss 6-7
12	16	Washington	7-1-0	lost to UCLA 0-31
13	17	Oklahoma	4-2-1	beat Kansas State 28-21
16	18	Ohio State	6-2-0	lost to Minnesota 31-35
17	19	Arkansas	6-2-0	beat Baylor 41-39
18	20	Southern Miss	6-0-1	beat # 15 Mississippi State 7-6
19		Washington State	6-1-1	beat Oregon 39-7
20		Iowa State	5-2-1	lost to Kansas 11-24

November 9 Poll — Nov. 14 Games

UP	AP	Team	Record	Result
1	1	Pittsburgh	8-0-0	beat Army 48-0
2	2	Clemson	9-0-0	beat Maryland 21-7
3	3	Southern Cal	8-1-0	lost to Washington 3-13
4	4	Georgia	8-1-0	beat Auburn 24-13
5	5	Penn State	7-1-0	lost to # 6 Alabama 16-31
6	6	Alabama	7-1-1	beat # 5 Penn State 31-16
7	7	Nebraska	7-2-0	beat Iowa State 31-7
PB	8	SMU	8-1-0	beat Texas Tech 30-6
PB	9	Arizona State	7-1-0	lost to # 18 UCLA 24-34
9	10	Texas	6-1-1	beat TCU 31-15
8	11	Michigan	7-2-0	beat Purdue 28-10
PB	12	Miami, Fla.	6-2-0	beat Virginia Tech 21-14
12	13	North Carolina	7-2-0	beat Virginia 17-14
10	14	Southern Miss	7-0-1	beat # 20 Florida State 58-14
11	15	Oklahoma	5-2-1	lost to Missouri 14-19
13	16	Arkansas	7-2-0	beat Texas A&M 10-7
15	17	Washington State	7-1-1	beat California 19-0
14	18	UCLA	6-2-1	beat # 9 Arizona State 34-24
19	20	Florida State	6-3-0	lost to # 14 Southern Miss 14-58
17		Brigham Young	8-2-0	beat Hawaii 13-3
18		Iowa	6-3-0	beat Wisconsin 17-7
20		Minnesota	6-3-0	lost to Michigan State 36-43

November 16 Poll — Nov. 21 Games

UP	AP	Team	Record	Result
1	1	Pittsburgh	9-0-0	beat Temple 35-0
2	2	Clemson	10-0-0	beat South Carolina 29-13
3	3	Georgia	9-1-0	bye week
4	4	Alabama	8-1-1	bye week
5	5	Nebraska	8-2-0	beat Oklahoma 37-14
PB	6	SMU	9-1-0	beat # 16 Arkansas 32-18
6	7	Michigan	8-2-0	lost Ohio State 9-14
7	8	Texas	7-1-1	beat Baylor 34-12
8	9	Southern Miss	8-0-1	lost to Louisville 10-13
9	10	Southern Cal	8-2-0	beat # 15 UCLA 22-21
PB	11	Miami, Fla.	7-2-0	beat North Carolina St. 14-6
11	12	North Carolina	8-2-0	beat Duke 31-10
14	13	Penn State	7-2-0	beat Notre Dame 24-21
12	14	Washington State	8-1-1	lost to # 17 Washington 10-23
13	15	UCLA	7-2-1	lost to # 10 Southern Cal 21-22
10	16	Arkansas	8-2-0	lost to # 6 SMU 18-32
16	17	Washington	8-2-0	beat # 14 Washington State 23-10
15	18	Brigham Young	9-2-0	beat Utah 56-28
17	19	Iowa	7-3-0	beat Michigan State 36-7
PB	20	Arizona State	7-2-0	beat Colorado State 52-7
18		Ohio State	7-3-0	beat # 7 Michigan 14-9
19		West Virginia	8-2-0	lost to Syracuse 24-27
20		Missouri	7-3-0	lost to Kansas 11-19

November 23 Poll — Nov. 28 Games

UP	AP	Team	Record	Result
1	1	Pittsburgh	10-0-0	lost to # 11 Penn State 14-48
2	2	Clemson	11-0-0	regular season complete
3	3	Georgia	9-1-0	beat Georgia Tech 44-7
4	4	Alabama	8-1-1	beat Auburn 28-17
5	5	Nebraska	9-2-0	regular season complete
PB	6	SMU	10-1-0	regular season complete
6	7	Texas	8-1-1	beat Texas A&M 21-13 (N26)
7	8	Southern Cal	9-2-0	regular season complete
PB	9	Miami, Fla.	8-2-0	beat Notre Dame 37-15 (N27)
8	10	North Carolina	9-2-0	regular season complete
9	11	Penn State	8-2-0	beat # 1 Pittsburgh 48-14
10	12	Washington	9-2-0	regular season complete
11	13	Iowa	8-3-0	regular season complete
12	14	Brigham Young	10-2-0	regular season complete
14	15	Ohio State	8-3-0	regular season complete
13	16	Michigan	8-3-0	regular season complete
15	17	Southern Miss	8-1-1	beat Lamar 45-14
PB	18	Arizona State	8-2-0	beat Arizona 24-13
16	19	UCLA	7-3-1	regular season complete
18	20	Washington State	8-2-1	regular season complete
17		Arkansas	8-3-0	regular season complete
19		Houston	6-3-1	beat Rice 40-3
20		San Jose State	8-2-0	beat North Texas 28-16

November 30 Poll / Bowl Results / January 3 Final Poll

UP	AP	Team	Record	Bowl Bid	Date	Bowl Result	R8	UP	AP	January 3 Final Poll	Record
1	1	Clemson	11-0-0	Orange Bowl	J1	beat # 4 Nebraska 22-15	1	1	1	Clemson	12-0-0
2	2	Georgia	9-1-0	Sugar Bowl	J1	lost to # 10 Pittsburgh 20-24	5	4	2	Texas	10-1-1
3	3	Alabama	9-1-1	Cotton Bowl	J1	lost to # 6 Texas 12-14	3	3	3	Penn State	10-2-0
4	4	Nebraska	9-2-0	Orange Bowl	J1	lost to # 1 Clemson 15-22	2	2	4	Pittsburgh	11-1-0
PB	5	SMU	10-1-0				10	PB	5	SMU	10-1-0
5	6	Texas	9-1-1	Cotton Bowl	J1	beat # 3 Alabama 14-12	7	5	6	Georgia	10-2-0
6	7	Penn State	9-2-0	Fiesta Bowl	J1	beat # 8 Southern Cal 26-10	8	6	7	Alabama	9-2-1
7	8	Southern Cal	9-2-0	Fiesta Bowl	J1	lost to # 7 Penn State 10-26	6	PB	8	Miami, Fla.	9-2-0
PB	9	Miami, Fla.	9-2-0				9	8	9	North Carolina	10-2-0
8	10	Pittsburgh	10-1-0	Sugar Bowl	J1	beat # 2 Georgia 24-20	4	7	10	Washington	10-2-0
9	11	North Carolina	9-2-0	Gator Bowl	D28	beat Arkansas 31-27	13	9	11	Nebraska	9-3-0
10	12	Washington	9-2-0	Rose Bowl	J1	beat # 13 Iowa 28-0	16	10	12	Michigan	9-3-0
11	13	Iowa	8-3-0	Rose Bowl	J1	lost to # 12 Washington 0-28	12	11	13	Brigham Young	11-2-0
12	14	Brigham Young	10-2-0	Holiday Bowl	D18	beat # 20 Washington St. 38-36	11	13	14	Southern Cal	9-3-0
14	15	Ohio State	8-3-0	Liberty Bowl	D30	beat Navy 31-28	15	12	15	Ohio State	9-3-0
13	16	Michigan	8-3-0	Bluebonnet Bowl	D31	beat # 19 UCLA 33-14	14	PB	16	Arizona State	9-2-0
PB	17	Arizona State	9-2-0				21	18	17	West Virginia	9-3-0
15	18	Southern Miss	9-1-1	Tangerine Bowl	D19	lost to Missouri 17-19	30	15	18	Iowa	8-4-0
16	19	UCLA	7-3-1	Bluebonnet Bowl	D31	lost to # 16 Michigan 14-33	20	20	19	Missouri	8-4-0
18	20	Washington State	8-2-1	Holiday Bowl	D18	lost to # 14 Brigham Young 36-38	17	14	20	Oklahoma	7-4-1
17		Arkansas	8-3-0	Gator Bowl	D28	lost to # 11 North Carolina 27-31	27	16		Arkansas	8-3-0
19		Houston	7-3-1	Sun Bowl	D26	lost to Oklahoma 14-40	19	17		Mississippi State	7-4-0
20		San Jose State	9-2-0	California Bowl	D19	lost to Toledo 25-27	24	19		Southern Miss	9-1-1

1981

CONSENSUS ALL-AMERICANS

POS	Offense	HT	WT	School		AP	FC	FW	PI
QB	Jim McMahon	6-0	185	Brigham Young		•	•	•	•
RB	Marcus Allen	6-2	202	Southern Cal		•	•	•	•
RB	Herschel Walker	6-2	222	Georgia		•	•	•	•
WR	Anthony Carter	5-11	161	Michigan		•	•	•	•
TE	Tim Wrightman	6-3	237	UCLA		•	•	•	•
L	Sean Farrell	6-3	266	Penn State		•	•	•	•
L	Roy Foster	6-4	265	Southern Cal		•	•	•	•
L	Terry Crouch	6-1	275	Oklahoma		•	•	•	•
L	Ed Muransky	6-7	275	Michigan		•	•		
L	Terry Tausch	6-4	265	Texas		•	•		
L	Kurt Becker	6-6	260	Michigan		•	•		
C	Dave Rimington	6-3	275	Nebraska		•	•	•	•

	OTHERS RECEIVING FIRST-TEAM HONORS								
QB	Dan Marino			Pittsburgh				•	
RB	Rich Diana			Yale					•
RB	Darrin Nelson			Stanford			•		
RB	Curt Warner			Penn State					•
WR	Stanley Washington			TCU			•		
WR	Julius Dawkins			Pittsburgh				•	
L	David Drechsler			North Carolina					•
K	Bruce Lahay			Arkansas			•		

POS	Defense	HT	WT	School		AP	FC	FW	PI
L	Billy Ray Smith	6-4	228	Arkansas		•	•	•	•
L	Kenneth Sims	6-6	265	Texas		•	•	•	•
L	Andre Tippett	6-4	235	Iowa		•	•	•	•
L	Tim Krumrie	6-3	237	Wisconsin		•	•	•	•
LB	Bob Crable	6-3	225	Notre Dame		•	•	•	•
LB	Jeff Davis	6-0	223	Clemson		•	•	•	•
LB	Sal Sunseri	6-0	220	Pittsburgh		•	•		
DB	Tommy Wilcox	5-11	187	Alabama		•	•	•	•
DB	Mike Richardson	6-1	192	Arizona State		•	•		
DB	Terry Kinard	6-1	183	Clemson		•	•		
DB	Fred Marion	6-3	194	Miami, Fla.		•	•		
P	Reggie Roby	6-3	215	Iowa		•	•	•	•

	OTHERS RECEIVING FIRST-TEAM HONORS								
L	Steve Clark			Utah			•		
L	David Galloway			Florida			•		
L	Harvey Armstrong			SMU			•		
L	Glen Collins			Mississippi State			•		
L	Jimmy Williams			Nebraska			•		
L	Jeff Gaylord			Missouri				•	
L	Lester Williams			Miami, Fla					•
LB	Johnnie Cooks			Mississippi State			•		•
LB	Chip Banks			Southern Cal					•
DB	Johnny Jackson			Air Force			•		
DB	Steve Cordle			Fresno State			•		
DB	Matt Vanden Boom			Wisconsin					•
P	Rohn Stark			Florida State			•		

HEISMAN TROPHY VOTING

	PLAYER	POS	SCHOOL	1ST	2ND	3RD	TOTAL
1	Marcus Allen	TB	Southern Cal	441	204	66	1797
2	Herschel Walker	TB	Georgia	152	278	187	1199
3	Jim McMahon	QB	Brigham Young	91	131	171	706
4	Dan Marino	QB	Pittsburgh	16	51	106	256
5	Art Schlichter	QB	Ohio State	21	15	56	149
6	Darrin Nelson	RB	Stanford	7	7	13	48
7	Anthony Carter	WR	Michigan	2	11	14	42
8	Kenneth Sims	DT	Texas	3	6	13	34
9	Reggie Collier	QB	Southern Miss	2	6	12	30
10	Rich Diana	RB	Yale	3	2	10	23

AWARD WINNERS

PLAYER	POS	SCHOOL	AWARD NAME
Marcus Allen	RB	Southern Cal	Maxwell
Dave Rimington	C	Nebraska	Outland
Marcus Allen	RB	Southern Cal	Camp
Kenneth Sims	DT	Texas	Lombardi
Jim McMahon	QB	Brigham Young	O'Brien

BOWL GAMES

DATE	GAME	SCORE
D12	Independence	Texas A&M 33, Oklahoma State 16
D13	Garden State	Tennessee 28, Wisconsin 21
D18	Holiday	Brigham Young 38, Washington State 36
D19	Tangerine	Missouri 19, Southern Miss 17
D19	California	Toledo 27, San Jose State 25
D26	Sun	Oklahoma 40, Houston 14
D28	Gator	North Carolina 31, Arkansas 27
D30	Liberty	Ohio State 31, Navy 28

CONFERENCE STANDINGS

ACC

	Conf.			Overall		
	W	L	T	W	L	T
Clemson	6	0	0	12	0	0
North Carolina	5	1	0	10	2	0
Maryland	4	2	0	4	6	1
Duke	3	3	0	6	5	0
North Carolina St.	2	4	0	4	7	0
Wake Forest	1	5	0	4	7	0
Virginia	0	6	0	1	10	0

Big 10

	Conf.			Overall		
	W	L	T	W	L	T
Ohio State	6	2	0	9	3	0
Iowa	6	2	0	8	4	0
Michigan	6	3	0	9	3	0
Illinois	6	3	0	7	4	0
Wisconsin	6	3	0	7	5	0
Minnesota	4	5	0	6	5	0
Michigan State	4	5	0	5	6	0
Purdue	3	6	0	5	6	0
Indiana	3	6	0	3	8	0
Northwestern	0	9	0	0	11	0

Big 8

	Conf.			Overall		
	W	L	T	W	L	T
Nebraska	7	0	0	9	3	0
Oklahoma	4	2	1	7	4	1
Kansas	4	3	0	8	4	0
Oklahoma State	4	3	0	7	5	0
Missouri	3	4	0	8	4	0
Iowa State	2	4	1	5	5	1
Colorado	2	5	0	3	8	0
Kansas State	1	6	0	2	9	0

Big West

	Conf.			Overall		
	W	L	T	W	L	T
San Jose State	5	0	0	9	3	0
Utah State	4	1	0	5	5	1
Pacific	2	3	0	5	6	0
Fresno State	2	3	0	5	6	0
Cal-St. Fullerton	1	4	0	3	8	0
Long Beach State	1	4	0	2	8	0

Ivy

	Conf.			Overall		
	W	L	T	W	L	T
Yale	6	1	0	9	1	0
Dartmouth	6	1	0	6	4	0
Princeton	5	1	1	5	4	1
Harvard	4	2	1	5	4	1
Brown	2	5	0	3	7	0
Cornell	2	5	0	3	7	0
Columbia	1	6	0	1	9	0
Pennsylvania	1	6	0	1	9	0

MAC

	Conf.			Overall		
	W	L	T	W	L	T
Toledo	8	1	0	9	3	0
Miami, Ohio	6	1	1	8	2	1
Central Michigan	7	2	0	7	4	0
Bowling Green	5	3	1	5	5	1
Western Michigan	5	4	0	6	5	0
Ohio U	5	4	0	5	6	0
Kent State	3	6	0	4	7	0
Ball State	2	6	0	4	7	0
Northern Illinois	2	7	0	3	8	0
Eastern Michigan	0	9	0	0	11	0

Pac 10

	Conf.			Overall		
	W	L	T	W	L	T
Washington	6	2	0	10	2	0
Arizona State	5	2	0	9	2	0
Southern Cal	5	2	0	9	3	0
Washington State	5	2	1	8	3	1
UCLA	5	2	1	7	4	1
Arizona	4	4	0	6	5	0
Stanford	4	4	0	4	7	0
California	2	6	0	2	9	0
Oregon	1	6	0	2	9	0
Oregon State	0	7	0	1	10	0

SEC

	Conf.			Overall		
	W	L	T	W	L	T
Georgia	6	0	0	10	2	0
Alabama*	6	0	0	9	2	1
Mississippi State	4	2	0	8	4	0
Tennessee	3	3	0	8	4	0
Florida	3	3	0	7	5	0
Auburn	2	4	0	5	6	0
Kentucky	2	4	0	3	8	0
Mississippi*	1	4	1	4	6	1
LSU	1	4	1	3	7	1
Vanderbilt	1	5	0	4	7	0

* Alabama, Mississippi game did not count in standings

SWC

	Conf.			Overall		
	W	L	T	W	L	T
SMU	7	1	0	10	1	0
Texas	6	1	1	10	1	1
Houston	5	2	1	7	4	1
Arkansas	5	3	0	8	4	0
Texas A&M	4	4	0	7	5	0
Baylor	3	5	0	5	6	0
Rice	3	5	0	4	7	0
TCU	1	6	1	2	7	2
Texas Tech	0	7	1	1	9	1

WAC

	Conf.			Overall		
	W	L	T	W	L	T
Brigham Young	7	1	0	11	2	0
Hawaii	6	1	0	9	2	0
Utah	5	1	1	8	2	1
Wyoming	6	2	0	8	3	0
New Mexico	3	4	1	4	7	1
San Diego State	3	5	0	6	5	0
Air Force	2	5	0	4	7	0
Texas-El Paso	1	6	0	1	10	0
Colorado State	0	8	0	0	12	0

Independents

	Overall		
	W	L	T
Pittsburgh	11	1	0
Penn State	10	2	0
Miami, Fla.	9	2	0
Southern Miss	9	2	1
West Virginia	9	3	0
Virginia Tech	7	4	0
Navy	7	4	1
Tulane	6	5	0
Florida State	6	5	0
Cincinnati	6	5	0
South Carolina	6	6	0
Nevada-Las Vegas	6	6	0
Temple	5	5	0
Rutgers	5	6	0
Notre Dame	5	6	0
Boston College	5	6	0
East Carolina	5	6	0
Louisville	5	6	0
Syracuse	4	6	1
Army	3	7	1
North Texas	2	9	0
Memphis	1	10	0
Georgia Tech	1	10	0

DATE	GAME	SCORE
D31	Bluebonnet	Michigan 33, UCLA 14
D31	All-American	Mississippi State 10, Kansas 0
D31	Peach	West Virginia 26, Florida 6
J1	Sugar	Pittsburgh 24, Georgia 20
J1	Orange	Clemson 22, Nebraska 15
J1	Fiesta	Penn State 26, Southern Cal 10
J1	Cotton	Texas 14, Alabama 12
J1	Rose	Washington 28, Iowa 0

1981 NCAA Major College Statistical Leaders

Individual Leaders

	PASSING	CL	G	ATT	COM	PCT	INT	I%	YDS	YPA	TD	TD%	RATING
1	Jim McMahon, Brigham Young	SR	10	423	272	64.3	7	1.7	3555	8.4	30	7.1	155.0
2	Dan Marino, Pittsburgh	JR	10	339	200	59.0	21	6.2	2615	7.7	34	10.0	144.5
3	Buck Belue, Georgia	SR	11	188	114	60.6	9	4.8	1603	8.5	12	6.4	143.8
4	Tony Eason, Illinois	JR	11	406	248	61.1	14	3.5	3360	8.3	20	4.9	140.0
5	Mike Pagel, Arizona State	SR	11	321	171	53.3	14	4.4	2484	7.7	29	9.0	139.4
6	Scott Campbell, Purdue	SO	11	321	185	57.6	13	4.1	2686	8.4	18	5.6	138.3
7	Sam King, Nevada-Las Vegas	SR	12	433	255	58.9	19	4.4	3778	8.7	18	4.2	137.1
8	Bob Holly, Princeton	SR	10	338	206	61.0	9	2.7	2622	7.8	16	4.7	136.4
9	Doug Flutie, Boston College	FR	9	192	105	54.7	8	4.2	1652	8.6	10	5.2	135.8
10	Jim Kelly, Miami, Fla.	JR	11	285	168	59.0	14	4.9	2403	8.4	13	4.6	135.0

	ALL-PURPOSE	CL	G	RUSH	REC	PR	KR	YDS	YPG
1	Marcus Allen, Southern Cal	SR	11	2342	217	0	0	2559	232.6
2	Herschel Walker, Georgia	SO	11	1891	84	0	92	2067	187.9
3	Rich Diana, Yale	SR	10	1442	147	76	205	1870	187.0
4	Darrin Nelson, Stanford	SR	11	1014	846	138	0	1998	181.6
5	Barry Redden, Richmond	SR	10	1629	107	0	0	1736	173.6
6	Larry Van Pelt, Princeton	SR	9	528	400	52	407	1387	154.1
7	Amero Ware, Drake	JR	11	1353	330	0	0	1683	153.0
8	Joe Morris, Syracuse	SR	11	1194	203	0	265	1662	151.1
9	Tim Spencer, Ohio State	JR	11	1121	205	0	307	1633	148.5
10	Buford Jordan, McNeese St.	SO	11	1267	106	0	234	1607	146.1

	RUSHING/Yards Per Game	CL	G	ATT	YDS	TD	AVG	YPG
1	Marcus Allen, Southern Cal	SR	11	403	2342	22	5.8	212.9
2	Herschel Walker, Georgia	SO	11	385	1891	18	4.9	171.9
3	Barry Redden, Richmond	SR	10	335	1629	10	4.9	162.9
4	Rich Diana, Yale	SR	10	293	1442	14	4.9	144.2
5	Eddie Meyers, Navy	SR	10	277	1318	8	4.8	131.8
6	Eric Dickerson, SMU	JR	11	255	1428	19	5.6	129.8
7	Cyrus Lawrence, Virginia Tech	JR	11	325	1403	8	4.3	127.5
8	Amero Ware, Drake	JR	11	290	1353	7	4.7	123.0
9	James Bettis, Cincinnati	SR	10	246	1226	6	5.0	122.6
10	Walter Poole, Southern Illinois	SR	9	229	1092	10	4.8	121.3

	RUSHING/Yards Per Carry	CL	G	ATT	YDS	YPC
1	Del Rogers, Utah	SR	11	170	1127	6.6
2	Stanley Wilson, Oklahoma	JR	10	156	1008	6.5
3	Buford Jordan, McNeese St.	SO	11	205	1267	6.2
4	Roger Craig, Nebraska	JR	11	173	1060	6.1
5	Curt Warner, Penn State	JR	9	171	1044	6.1
6	Danny Miller, Citadel	SR	11	191	1138	6.0
7	Stanford Jennings, Furman	SO	11	197	1168	5.9
8	Marcus Allen, Southern Cal	SR	11	403	2342	5.8
9	Butch Woolfolk, Michigan	SR	11	226	1273	5.6
10	Eric Dickerson, SMU	JR	11	255	1428	5.6

*-Based on top 30 rushers

	RECEIVING	CL	G	REC	YDS	TD	YPR	YPG	RPG
1	Pete Harvey, North Texas	SR	9	57	743	3	13.0	82.6	6.3
2	Darrin Nelson, Stanford	SR	11	67	846	5	12.6	76.9	6.1
3	Darius Durham, San Diego State	JR	11	65	988	7	15.2	89.8	5.9
4	Jim Sandusky, Nevada-Las Vegas	JR	12	68	1346	6	19.8	112.2	5.7
5	Gordon Hudson, Brigham Young	SO	12	67	960	10	14.3	80.0	5.6
6	Herbert Harris, Lamar	JR	11	61	911	7	14.9	82.8	5.5
6	Tim Kearse, San Jose State	JR	11	61	842	7	13.8	76.5	5.5
6	Mark Raugh, West Virginia	JR	11	61	585	3	9.6	53.2	5.5
9	Jeff Champine, Colorado State	SO	12	66	882	10	13.4	73.5	5.5
10	Steve Bryant, Purdue	SR	11	60	971	11	16.2	88.3	5.5
10	Jeff Dean, Western Carolina	SR	11	60	839	2	14	76.3	5.5

	PUNTING	CL	PUNT	YDS	AVG
1	Reggie Roby, Iowa	JR	44	2193	49.8
2	Rohn Stark, Florida State	SR	64	2941	46.0
3	Tom Striegel, Southern Illinois	SR	60	2752	45.9
4	Scott Vernoy, Cal-St. Fullerton	SR	72	3270	45.4
5	Maury Buford, Texas Tech	SR	78	3493	44.8
6	Mike Horan, Long Beach State	SR	63	2814	44.7
7	Larry Martin, West Texas State	SR	62	2766	44.6
8	Guy McClure, Utah State	SR	62	2758	44.5
9	James Gargus, TCU	FR	59	2608	44.2
10	Malcolm Simmons, Alabama	SO	60	2637	43.9

	PUNT RETURNS	CL	PR	YDS	TD	AVG
1	Glen Young, Mississippi State	JR	19	307	2	16.2
2	Keith Humphries, Louisville	FR	16	239	1	14.9
3	John Thomas, TCU	SO	17	244	0	14.4
4	Irving Fryar, Nebraska	SO	24	318	2	13.2
5	Andy Molls, Kentucky	JR	33	420	1	12.7
6	Willie Gault, Tennessee	JR	31	381	1	12.3
7	Fred Fernandes, Utah State	SO	28	342	2	12.2
8	Darnell Clash, Wyoming	SO	28	339	1	12.1
9	Greg Poole, North Carolina	JR	29	349	0	12.0
10	Anthony Allen, Washington	JR	15	178	1	11.9

	KICKOFF RETURNS	CL	KR	YDS	TD	AVG
1	Frank Minnifield, Louisville	JR	11	334	1	30.4
2	Eric Martin, LSU	FR	18	526	1	29.2
3	Anthony Carter, Michigan	JR	15	406	0	27.1
4	James Caver, Missouri	JR	14	378	0	27.0
5	Steve Brown, Oregon	JR	26	694	1	26.7
6	Peter Lavery, Dartmouth	JR	13	331	0	25.5
7	Carl Monroe, Utah	JR	21	528	0	25.1
8	Phil Smith, San Diego State	SO	22	553	0	25.1
9	Kent Hagood, South Carolina	FR	21	519	1	24.7
10	Mark Bridgman, Furman	SO	15	368	0	24.5

	SCORING	CL	TDS	XPT	FG	PTS	PTPG
1	Marcus Allen, Southern Cal	SR	23	0	0	138	12.5
2	Herschel Walker, Georgia	SO	20	0	0	120	10.9
3	Eric Dickerson, SMU	JR	19	0	0	114	10.4
4	Buford Jordan, McNeese St.	SO	18	2	0	110	10.0
5	Dwayne Crutchfield, Iowa State	SR	17	2	0	104	9.5
6	Rich Diana, Yale	SR	15	0	0	90	9.0
7	Darrell Shepard, Oklahoma	SR	13	2	0	80	8.9
8	Darrin Nelson, Stanford	SR	16	0	0	96	8.7
9	Kevin Butler, Georgia	FR	0	37	19	94	8.5
10	Luis Zendejas, Arizona State	FR	0	45	16	93	8.5

	FIELD GOALS	CL	FGA	FGM	PCT	FGG
1	Bruce Lahay, Arkansas	SR	24	19	0.79	1.73
1	Kevin Butler, Georgia	FR	26	19	0.73	1.73
1	Larry Roach, Oklahoma State	FR	28	19	0.68	1.73
4	Gary Anderson, Syracuse	SR	19	18	0.95	1.64
4	Eddie Garcia, SMU	SR	22	18	0.82	1.64
4	Brian Clark, Florida	SR	24	18	0.75	1.64
4	Steve Fehr, Navy	SR	25	18	0.72	1.64
4	Dan Miller, Miami, Fla.	SR	27	18	0.67	1.64
9	Peter Kim, Alabama	JR	20	15	0.75	1.50
10	Luis Zendejas, Arizona State	FR	20	16	0.80	1.45
10	Chuck Nelson, Washington	JR	20	16	0.80	1.45

	INTERCEPTIONS	CL	INT	YDS	TD	INT/GM
1	Sam Shaffer, Temple	SR	9	76	0	0.90
2	Lou King, Iowa	SR	8	62	0	0.73
3	Butch Lacroix, Houston	JR	7	52	0	0.70
4	Eric Williams, North Carolina St.	JR	7	107	0	0.64
4	Russell Carter, SMU	SO	7	102	0	0.64
4	Martin Bayless, Bowling Green	SO	7	55	1	0.64
4	George Radachowsky, Boston College	SO	7	51	0	0.64
4	Reno Hutchins, Tulsa	SR	7	47	0	0.64
4	William Graham, Texas	SR	7	15	0	0.64
10	Andy Fladung, Illinois State	SO	5	32	0	0.62

Team Leaders

	RUSHING OFFENSE	G	ATT	YDS	AVG	TD	YPG
1	Oklahoma	11	656	3677	5.6	36	334.3
2	Nebraska	11	661	3635	5.5	27	330.5
3	Southern Cal	11	605	3293	5.4	27	299.4
4	SMU	11	659	3226	4.9	33	293.3
5	Georgia	11	656	3102	4.7	29	282.0
6	McNeese St.	11	624	3091	5.0	34	281.0
7	Alabama	11	706	3082	4.4	18	280.2
8	North Carolina	11	626	3019	4.8	32	274.5
9	Michigan	11	572	2973	5.2	28	270.3
10	Arizona State	11	581	2933	5.0	20	266.6
10	Southern Miss	11	603	2933	4.9	30	266.6

	PASSING OFFENSE	G	ATT	COM	INT	PCT	YDS	YPA	TD	I%	YPC	YPG
1	Brigham Young	12	538	329	12	61.2	4283	8.0	35	2.2	13.0	356.9
2	Nevada-Las Vegas	12	492	284	22	57.7	4230	8.6	20	4.5	14.9	352.5
3	Illinois	11	409	250	14	61.1	3398	8.3	20	3.4	13.6	308.9
4	San Diego State	11	447	265	15	59.3	3366	7.5	21	3.4	12.7	306.0
5	La. Monroe	11	495	239	17	48.3	3180	6.4	26	3.4	13.3	289.1
6	Princeton	10	371	224	11	60.4	2826	7.6	20	3.0	12.6	282.6
7	Stanford	11	410	241	14	58.8	3066	7.5	22	3.4	12.7	278.7
8	Vanderbilt	11	476	269	20	56.5	3036	6.4	19	4.2	11.3	276.0
9	Wake Forest	11	472	286	24	60.6	2986	6.3	20	5.1	10.4	271.5
10	San Jose State	11	407	209	20	51.4	2969	7.3	27	4.9	14.2	269.9

	TOTAL OFFENSE	G	P	YDS	AVG	TD	YPG
1	Arizona State	11	908	5486	6.0	49	498.7
2	Nevada-Las Vegas	12	935	5867	6.3	44	488.9
3	Brigham Young	12	931	5764	6.2	59	480.3
4	Georgia	11	865	4912	5.7	42	446.5
5	Stanford	11	885	4880	5.5	40	443.6
6	Nebraska	11	842	4812	5.7	41	437.5
7	San Jose State	11	867	4692	5.4	45	426.5
8	Ohio State	11	865	4677	5.4	45	425.2
9	Wichita State	11	861	4674	5.4	34	424.9
10	Appalachian State	11	832	4645	5.6	29	422.3

	RUSHING DEFENSE	G	ATT	YDS	AVG	TD	YPG
1	Pittsburgh	11	406	686	1.7	6	62.4
2	Georgia	11	391	797	2.0	5	72.5
3	San Jose State	11	414	880	2.1	12	80.0
4	Maryland	11	404	923	2.3	4	83.9
5	Iowa	11	421	956	2.3	7	86.9
6	Mississippi State	11	429	968	2.3	6	88.0
7	Clemson	11	421	976	2.3	4	88.7
8	Utah	11	405	995	2.5	13	90.5
9	Ohio State	11	380	1060	2.8	5	96.4
10	Texas	11	477	1062	2.2	9	96.5

	PASSING DEFENSE	G	ATT	COM	PCT	YPC	INT	I%	YDS	YPA	TD	YPG
1	Nebraska	11	215	103	47.9	10.7	19	8.8	1101	5.1	3	100.1
2	Northern Illinois	11	195	91	46.7	12.4	14	7.2	1125	5.8	10	102.3
3	West Virginia	11	248	98	39.5	11.7	22	8.9	1148	4.6	5	104.4
4	Kansas	11	237	110	46.4	10.5	15	6.3	1150	4.9	6	104.5
5	Kent State	11	213	104	48.8	11.5	16	7.5	1195	5.6	4	108.6
6	Columbia	10	182	86	47.3	13.2	4	2.2	1139	6.3	6	113.9
7	Southern Miss	11	241	106	44.0	11.8	11	4.6	1254	5.2	7	114.0
8	Missouri	11	275	134	48.7	9.4	18	6.5	1255	4.6	5	114.1
9	Central Michigan	11	232	121	52.2	10.6	11	4.7	1281	5.5	6	116.5
10	Oklahoma	11	240	113	47.1	12.0	13	5.4	1355	5.6	7	123.2

	TOTAL DEFENSE	G	P	YDS	AVG	TD	YPG
1	Pittsburgh	11	708	2473	3.5	14	224.8
2	Texas	11	756	2584	3.4	16	234.9
3	Houston	11	703	2592	3.7	11	235.6
4	Central Michigan	11	704	2621	3.7	14	238.3
5	Southern Miss	11	711	2629	3.7	10	239.0
6	Nebraska	11	718	2645	3.7	9	240.5
7	Missouri	11	786	2708	3.4	14	246.2
8	Clemson	11	753	2767	3.7	9	251.5
9	Oklahoma State	11	764	2781	3.6	21	252.8
10	Iowa	11	736	2790	3.8	14	253.6

	SCORING OFFENSE	G	PTS	AVG
1	Brigham Young	12	465	38.7
2	Arizona State	11	394	35.8
3	SMU	11	365	33.2
4	Pittsburgh	11	361	32.8
5	Ohio State	11	356	32.4
6	San Jose State	11	355	32.3
7	Georgia	11	352	32.0
8	Nebraska	11	349	31.7
9	Penn State	11	345	31.4
10	North Carolina	11	344	31.3
10	Wyoming	11	344	31.3

	SCORING DEFENSE	G	PTS	AVG
1	Southern Miss	11	89	8.1
2	Clemson	11	90	8.2
3	Georgia	11	98	8.9
4	Nebraska	11	103	9.4
5	North Carolina	11	123	11.2
6	Virginia Tech	11	128	11.6
7	Iowa	11	129	11.7
8	Hawaii	11	130	11.8
9	Central Michigan	11	131	11.9
10	Bowling Green	11	132	12.0

	TURNOVER MARGIN	G	FR	INT	TOT	FL	INTL	TOT	MAR
1	Tulsa	11	23	25	48	18	6	24	2.2
2	Bowling Green	11	19	19	38	4	12	16	2.0
3	SMU	11	17	31	48	17	10	27	1.9
4	Hawaii	11	21	13	34	7	7	14	1.8
4	Wyoming	11	15	22	37	13	4	17	1.8
6	Southern Illinois	11	23	15	38	10	11	21	1.5
7	Penn State	11	22	20	42	10	16	26	1.5
7	Clemson	11	16	23	39	14	9	23	1.5
7	Texas Arlington	11	28	14	42	16	10	26	1.5
10	Harvard	10	11	25	36	14	9	23	1.3

1982 POLL PROGRESSION

Pre-Season 1982 — Sept. 4 Games

UP	AP	Team	Record	Result
1	1	Pittsburgh	0-0-0	bye week
2	2	Washington	0-0-0	bye week
4	3	Alabama	0-0-0	bye week
3	4	Nebraska	0-0-0	bye week
6	5	North Carolina	0-0-0	bye week
11	6	SMU	0-0-0	bye week
7	7	Georgia	0-0-0	beat # 11 Clemson 13-7 (S6)
5	8	Penn State	0-0-0	beat Temple 31-14
8	9	Oklahoma	0-0-0	bye week
PB	10	Southern Cal	0-0-0	bye week
9	11	Clemson	0-0-0	lost to # 7 Georgia 7-13 (S6)
10	12	Michigan	0-0-0	bye week
12	13	Arkansas	0-0-0	bye week
14	14	Ohio State	0-0-0	bye week
15	15	Miami, Fla.	0-0-0	lost to # 16 Florida 14-17
16	16	Florida	0-0-0	beat # 15 Miami, Fla. 17-14
13	17	Texas	0-0-0	bye week
18	18	Notre Dame	0-0-0	bye week
PB	19	Arizona State	0-0-0	beat Oregon 34-3
17	20	UCLA	0-0-0	bye week
19		Brigham Young	0-0-0	beat Nevada-Las Vegas 27-0 (S2)
20		Texas A&M	0-0-0	lost to Boston College 16-38

September 6 Poll — Sept. 11 Games

UP	AP	Team	Record	Result
	1	Pittsburgh	0-0-0	beat #5 North Carolina 7-6 (S9)
	2	Washington	0-0-0	beat Texas-El Paso 55-0
	3	Nebraska	0-0-0	beat Iowa 42-7
	4	Alabama	0-0-0	beat Georgia Tech 45-7
	5	North Carolina	0-0-0	lost to # 1 Pittsburgh 6-7 (S9)
	6	Georgia	1-0-0	beat Brigham Young 17-14
	7	Penn State	1-0-0	beat Maryland 39-31
	8	SMU	0-0-0	beat Tulane 51-7
	9	Oklahoma	0-0-0	lost to West Virginia 27-41
	10	Southern Cal	0-0-0	lost to # 11 Florida 9-17
	11	Florida	1-0-0	beat # 10 Southern Cal 17-9
	12	Michigan	0-0-0	beat Wisconsin 20-9
	13	Arkansas	0-0-0	beat Tulsa 38-0
	14	Ohio State	0-0-0	beat Baylor 21-14
	15	Arizona State	1-0-0	beat Utah 23-10
	16	Clemson	0-1-0	bye week
	17	Texas	0-0-0	bye week
	18	UCLA	0-0-0	beat Long Beach State 41-10
	19	Miami, Fla.	0-1-0	beat Houston 31-12
	20	Notre Dame	0-0-0	bye week

September 13 Poll — Sept. 18 Games

UP	AP	Team	Record	Result
2	1	Washington	1-0-0	beat Arizona 23-13
1	2	Pittsburgh	1-0-0	beat Florida State 37-17
3	3	Nebraska	1-0-0	beat New Mexico State 68-0
4	4	Alabama	1-0-0	beat Mississippi 42-14
7	5	Florida	2-0-0	bye week
6	6	SMU	1-0-0	beat Texas-El Paso
5	7	Georgia	2-0-0	bye week
8	8	Penn State	2-0-0	beat Rutgers 49-14
10	9	Arkansas	1-0-0	beat Navy 29-17
9	10	Michigan	1-0-0	lost to # 20 Notre Dame 17-23
11	11	North Carolina	0-1-0	beat Vanderbilt 34-10
12	12	Ohio State	1-0-0	beat Michigan State 31-10
PB	13	Arizona State	2-0-0	beat Houston 24-10
17	14	UCLA	1-0-0	beat Wisconsin 51-26
16	15	Miami, Fla.	1-1-0	beat Virginia Tech 14-8
13	16	Clemson	0-1-0	tied Boston College 17-17
15	17	West Virginia	1-0-0	beat Maryland 19-18
14	18	Texas	0-0-0	beat Utah 21-12
PB	19	Southern Cal	0-1-0	beat Indiana 28-7
19	20	Notre Dame	0-0-0	beat # 10 Michigan 23-17
18		Mississippi State	2-0-0	beat Memphis 41-17
20		Brigham Young	1-1-0	bye week

September 20 Poll — Sept. 25 Games

UP	AP	Team	Record	Result
3	1	Washington	2-0-0	beat Oregon 37-21
2	2	Nebraska	2-0-0	lost to # 8 Penn State 24-27
1	3	Pittsburgh	2-0-0	beat # 19 Illinois 20-3
4	4	Alabama	2-0-0	beat Vanderbilt 24-21
7	5	Florida	2-0-0	beat Mississippi State 27-17
8	6	SMU	2-0-0	beat TCU 16-13
6	7	Georgia	2-0-0	beat South Carolina 34-18
5	8	Penn State	3-0-0	beat # 2 Nebraska 27-24
9	9	Arkansas	2-0-0	beat Mississippi 14-12
12	10	Notre Dame	1-0-0	beat Purdue 28-14
10	11	North Carolina	1-1-0	beat Army 62-8
13	12	UCLA	2-0-0	beat # 20 Michigan 31-27
11	13	Ohio State	2-0-0	lost to Stanford 20-23
PB	14	Arizona State	3-0-0	beat California 15-0
14	15	West Virginia	2-0-0	beat Richmond 43-10
16	16	Miami, Fla.	2-1-0	beat Michigan State 25-22
15	17	Texas	1-0-0	beat Missouri 21-0
PB	18	Southern Cal	1-1-0	beat Oklahoma 12-0
18	19	Illinois	3-0-0	lost to # 3 Pittsburgh 3-20
	20	Michigan	1-1-0	lost to # 12 UCLA 27-31
17		Mississippi State	3-0-0	lost to # 5 Florida 17-27
19		Boston College	1-0-1	beat Navy 31-0
20		Brigham Young	1-1-0	lost to Air Force 38-39

September 27 Poll — Oct. 2 Games

UP	AP	Team	Record	Result
2	1	Washington	3-0-0	beat San Diego State 46-25
1	2	Pittsburgh	3-0-0	beat # 14 West Virginia 16-13
3	3	Penn State	4-0-0	bye week
5	4	Florida	3-0-0	lost to LSU 13-24
4	5	Alabama	3-0-0	beat Arkansas State 34-7
6	6	Georgia	3-0-0	beat Mississippi State 29-22
7	7	SMU	3-0-0	beat North Texas 38-10
8	8	Nebraska	2-1-0	beat # 20 Auburn 41-7
9	9	UCLA	3-0-0	beat Colorado 34-6
11	10	Arkansas	3-0-0	beat TCU 35-0
12	11	Notre Dame	2-0-0	beat Michigan State 11-3
10	12	North Carolina	2-1-0	beat Georgia Tech 41-0
PB	13	Arizona State	4-0-0	beat Kansas State 30-7
14	14	West Virginia	3-0-0	lost to # 2 Pittsburgh 13-16
13	15	Texas	2-0-0	beat Rice 34-7
PB	16	Southern Cal	2-1-0	beat Oregon 38-7
15	17	Miami, Fla.	3-1-0	beat Louisville 28-6
16	18	Boston College	2-0-1	beat Temple 17-7
20	19	Minnesota	3-0-0	lost to Illinois 24-42
17	20	Auburn	3-0-0	lost to # 8 Nebraska 7-41
18		Mississippi State	3-1-0	lost to # 6 Georgia 22-29
19		Clemson	1-1-1	beat Kentucky 24-6
20		San Jose State	3-0-0	lost to California 7-26

October 4 Poll — Oct. 9 Games

UP	AP	Team	Record	Result
1	1	Washington	4-0-0	beat California 50-7
2	2	Pittsburgh	4-0-0	bye week
3	3	Penn State	4-0-0	lost to # 4 Alabama 21-42
4	4	Alabama	4-0-0	beat # 3 Penn State 42-21
5	5	Georgia	4-0-0	beat Mississippi 33-10
6	6	SMU	4-0-0	beat Baylor 22-19
7	7	Nebraska	3-1-0	beat Colorado 40-14
8	8	UCLA	4-0-0	tied Arizona 24-24
9	9	Arkansas	4-0-0	beat Texas Tech 21-3
11	10	Notre Dame	3-0-0	beat # 17 Miami, Fla. 16-14
PB	11	Arizona State	5-0-0	beat Stanford 21-17
10	12	North Carolina	3-1-0	beat Wake Forest 24-7
12	13	Texas	3-0-0	lost to Oklahoma 22-28
13	14	Florida	3-1-0	lost to Vanderbilt 29-31
PB	15	Southern Cal	3-1-0	bye week
17	16	West Virginia	3-1-0	beat # 19 Boston College 20-13
16	17	Miami, Fla.	4-1-0	lost to # 10 Notre Dame 14-16
14	18	LSU	3-0-0	tied Tennessee 24-24
15	19	Boston College	3-0-1	lost to # 16 West Virginia 13-20
19	20	Illinois	4-1-0	beat Purdue 38-34
18		Stanford	3-1-0	lost to # 11 Arizona State 17-21
20		Clemson	2-1-1	beat Virginia 48-0

October 11 Poll — Oct. 16 Games

UP	AP	Team	Record	Result
1	1	Washington	5-0-0	beat Oregon State 34-17
2	2	Alabama	5-0-0	lost to Tennessee 28-35
3	3	Pittsburgh	4-0-0	beat Temple 38-7
4	4	Georgia	5-0-0	beat Vanderbilt 27-13
5	5	SMU	5-0-0	beat Houston 20-14
6	6	Nebraska	4-1-0	beat Kansas State 42-13
7	7	Arkansas	4-0-0	bye week
10	8	Penn State	4-1-0	beat Syracuse 28-7
9	9	Notre Dame	4-0-0	lost to Arizona 13-16
PB	10	Arizona State	6-0-0	beat Texas-El Paso 37-6
8	11	North Carolina	4-1-0	beat North Carolina St. 41-9
11	12	UCLA	4-0-1	beat Washington State 42-17
12	13	West Virginia	4-1-0	beat Virginia Tech 16-6
PB	14	Southern Cal	3-1-0	beat Stanford 41-21
13	15	Illinois	5-1-0	lost to Ohio State 21-26
14	16	LSU	3-0-1	beat Kentucky 34-10
20	17	Miami, Fla.	4-2-0	beat Mississippi State 31-14
16	18	Texas	3-1-0	bye week
15	19	Florida State	4-1-0	beat East Carolina 56-17
17	20	Clemson	3-1-1	beat Duke 49-14
18		Oklahoma	3-2-0	beat Kansas 38-14
19		Florida	3-2-0	beat West Texas St. 77-14

October 18 Poll — Oct. 23 Games

UP	AP	Team	Record	Result
1	1	Washington	6-0-0	beat Texas Tech 10-3
2	2	Pittsburgh	5-0-0	beat Syracuse 14-0
3	3	Georgia	6-0-0	beat Kentucky 27-14
4	4	SMU	6-0-0	beat # 19 Texas 30-17
5	5	Nebraska	5-1-0	beat Missouri 23-19
6	6	Arkansas	5-0-0	beat Houston 38-3
9	7	Alabama	5-1-0	beat Cincinnati 21-3
PB	8	Arizona State	7-0-0	bye week
8	9	Penn State	5-1-0	beat # 13 West Virginia 24-0
7	10	North Carolina	5-1-0	bye week
10	11	UCLA	5-0-1	beat California 47-31
PB	12	Southern Cal	4-1-0	beat Oregon State 38-0
11	13	West Virginia	5-1-0	lost to # 9 Penn State 0-24
12	14	LSU	4-0-1	beat South Carolina 14-6
13	15	Notre Dame	4-1-1	tied Oregon 13-13
16	16	Miami, Fla.	5-2-0	bye week
14	17	Florida State	5-1-0	bye week
17	18	Clemson	4-1-1	beat North Carolina St. 38-29
15	19	Texas	3-1-0	lost to # 4 SMU 17-30
18	20	Oklahoma	4-2-0	beat Oklahoma State 27-9
19		Michigan	4-2-0	beat Northwestern 49-14
20		Florida	4-2-0	bye week

October 25 Poll — Oct. 30 Games

UP	AP	Team	Record	Result
2	1	Pittsburgh	6-0-0	beat Louisville 63-14
1	2	Washington	7-0-0	lost to Stanford 31-43
3	3	Georgia	7-0-0	beat Memphis 34-3
4	4	SMU	7-0-0	beat Texas A&M 47-9
5	5	Arkansas	6-0-0	beat Rice 24-6
6	6	Nebraska	6-1-0	beat Kansas 52-0
PB	7	Arizona State	7-0-0	beat # 12 Southern Cal 17-10
7	8	Penn State	6-1-0	beat Boston College 52-17
9	9	Alabama	6-1-0	beat Mississippi State 20-12
8	10	North Carolina	5-1-0	lost to Maryland 24-31
10	11	UCLA	6-0-1	beat Oregon 40-12
PB	12	Southern Cal	5-1-0	lost to # 7 Arizona State 10-17
11	13	LSU	5-0-1	beat Mississippi 45-8
12	14	Florida State	5-1-0	beat # 16 Miami, Fla. 24-7
13	15	Clemson	5-1-1	bye week
14	16	Miami, Fla.	5-2-0	lost to # 14 Florida State 7-24
15	17	Oklahoma	5-2-0	beat Colorado 45-10
17	18	West Virginia	6-1-0	beat East Carolina 30-3
18	19	Auburn	6-1-0	lost to Florida 17-19
16	20	Michigan	5-2-0	beat Minnesota 52-14
19		Florida	4-2-0	beat # 19 Auburn 19-17
20		Boston College	5-1-1	lost to # 8 Penn State 17-52

November 1 Poll

UP	AP	Team	Record	Nov. 6 Games
1	1	Pittsburgh	7-0-0	lost to Notre Dame 16-31
3	2	SMU	8-0-0	beat Rice 41-14
2	3	Georgia	8-0-0	beat # 20 Florida 44-0
PB	4	Arizona State	8-0-0	beat Oregon State 30-16
4	5	Arkansas	7-0-0	lost to Baylor 17-24
5	6	Nebraska	7-1-0	beat Oklahoma State 48-10
6	7	Penn State	7-1-0	beat North Carolina St. 54-0
7	8	Alabama	7-1-0	lost to # 11 LSU 10-20
8	9	UCLA	7-0-1	lost to # 10 Washington 7-10
9	10	Washington	7-1-0	beat # 9 UCLA 10-7
10	11	LSU	6-0-1	beat # 8 Alabama 20-10
11	12	Florida State	6-1-0	beat South Carolina 56-26
14	13	Clemson	5-1-1	beat # 18 North Carolina 16-13
12	14	Oklahoma	6-2-0	beat Kansas State 24-10
15	15	Michigan	6-2-0	beat Illinois 16-10
PB	16	Southern Cal	5-2-0	beat California 42-0
16	17	West Virginia	6-2-0	beat Temple 20-17
13	18	North Carolina	5-2-0	lost to # 13 Clemson 13-16
17	19	Maryland	6-2-0	beat Miami, Fla. 18-17
18	20	Florida	5-2-0	lost to # 3 Georgia 0-44
19		Texas	4-2-0	beat Houston 50-0
20		Notre Dame	5-1-1	beat # 1 Pittsburgh 31-16

November 8 Poll

UP	AP	Team	Record	Nov. 13 Games
1	1	Georgia	9-0-0	beat Auburn 19-14
2	2	SMU	9-0-0	beat Texas Tech 34-27
PB	3	Arizona State	9-0-0	lost to # 7 Washington 13-17
3	4	Nebraska	8-1-0	beat Iowa State 48-10
4	5	Penn State	8-1-0	beat # 13 Notre Dame 24-14
5	6	LSU	7-0-1	lost to Mississippi State 24-27
6	7	Washington	8-1-0	beat # 3 Arizona State 17-13
7	8	Pittsburgh	7-1-0	beat Army 24-6
8	9	Florida State	7-1-0	beat Louisville 49-14
9	10	Arkansas	7-1-0	beat Texas A&M 35-0
10	11	Clemson	6-1-1	beat # 18 Maryland 24-22
11	12	UCLA	7-1-1	beat Stanford 38-35
14	13	Notre Dame	6-1-1	lost to # 5 Penn State 14-24
12	14	Michigan	7-2-0	beat Purdue 52-21
11	15	Oklahoma	7-2-0	beat Missouri 41-14
PB	16	Southern Cal	6-2-0	beat Arizona 48-41
15	17	Alabama	7-2-0	lost to Southern Miss 29-38
16	18	Maryland	7-2-0	lost to # 11 Clemson 22-24
17	19	West Virginia	7-2-0	beat Rutgers 44-17 (N11)
18	20	Texas	5-2-0	beat TCU 38-21
19		North Carolina	5-3-0	beat Virginia 27-14
20		Tulsa	8-1-0	beat Indiana St. 48-14

November 15 Poll

UP	AP	Team	Record	Nov. 20 Games
1	1	Georgia	10-0-0	bye week
2	2	SMU	10-0-0	tied # 9 Arkansas 17-17
3	3	Penn State	9-1-0	bye week
4	4	Nebraska	9-1-0	bye week
5	5	Washington	9-1-0	lost to Washington State 20-24
6	6	Pittsburgh	8-1-0	beat Rutgers 52-6
7	7	Florida State	8-1-0	lost to # 12 LSU 21-55
PB	8	Arizona State	9-1-0	bye week
8	9	Arkansas	8-1-0	tied # 2 SMU 17-17
12	10	Clemson	7-1-1	beat South Carolina 24-6
11	11	UCLA	8-1-1	beat # 15 Southern Cal 20-19
13	12	LSU	7-1-1	beat # 7 Florida State 55-21
10	13	Michigan	8-2-0	lost to Ohio State 14-24
9	14	Oklahoma	8-2-0	bye week
PB	15	Southern Cal	7-2-0	lost to # 11 UCLA 19-20
14	16	West Virginia	8-2-0	beat Syracuse 26-0
15	17	Texas	6-2-0	beat Baylor 31-23
16	18	Notre Dame	6-2-1	lost to Air Force 17-30
18	19	Maryland	7-3-0	beat Virginia 45-14
17	20	Tulsa	9-1-0	beat North Texas 38-20
19		North Carolina	6-3-0	lost to Duke 17-23
20		Alabama	7-3-0	bye week
20		New Mexico	9-1-0	beat Hawaii 41-17

November 22 Poll

UP	AP	Team	Record	Nov. 27 Games
1	1	Georgia	10-0-0	beat Georgia Tech 38-18
2	2	Penn State	9-1-0	beat # 5 Pittsburgh 19-10 (N26)
3	3	Nebraska	9-1-0	beat # 11 Oklahoma 28-24 (N26)
4	4	SMU	10-0-1	regular season complete
5	5	Pittsburgh	9-1-0	lost to # 2 Penn State 10-19 (N26)
PB	6	Arizona State	9-1-0	lost to Arizona 18-28
6	7	LSU	8-1-1	lost to Tulane 28-31
8	8	UCLA	9-1-1	regular season complete
7	9	Arkansas	8-1-1	bye week
10	10	Clemson	8-1-1	beat Wake Forest 21-17
9	11	Oklahoma	8-2-0	lost to # 3 Nebraska 24-28 (N26)
11	12	West Virginia	8-2-0	regular season complete
12	13	Washington	9-2-0	regular season complete
13	14	Texas	7-2-0	beat Texas A&M 53-16 (N25)
14	15	Florida State	8-2-0	bye week
15	16	Maryland	8-3-0	regular season complete
PB	17	Southern Cal	7-3-0	beat Notre Dame 17-13
17	18	Ohio State	8-3-0	regular season complete
16	19	Tulsa	10-1-0	regular season complete
18	20	Michigan	8-3-0	regular season complete
19		Brigham Young	8-3-0	regular season complete
20		Alabama	7-3-0	lost to Auburn 22-23
20		New Mexico	10-1-0	regular season complete

November 29 Poll

UP	AP	Team	Record	Dec. 4 Games
1	1	Georgia	11-0-0	regular season complete
2	2	Penn State	10-1-0	regular season complete
3	3	Nebraska	10-1-0	beat Hawaii 37-16
4	4	SMU	10-0-1	
5	5	UCLA	9-1-1	
6	6	Arkansas	8-1-1	lost to # 12 Texas 7-33
7	7	Pittsburgh	9-2-0	regular season complete
PB	8	Clemson	9-1-1	regular season complete
9	9	Washington	9-2-0	
8	10	West Virginia	9-2-0	
12	11	Arizona State	9-2-0	regular season complete
10	12	Texas	8-2-0	beat # 6 Arkansas 33-7
13	13	LSU	8-2-1	regular season complete
11	14	Oklahoma	8-3-0	regular season complete
14	15	Florida State	8-2-0	lost to Florida 10-13
PB	16	Southern Cal	8-3-0	
15	17	Maryland	8-3-0	
16	18	Ohio State	8-3-0	
17	19	Auburn	8-3-0	regular season complete
18	20	Michigan	8-3-0	
19		Tulsa	10-1-0	regular season complete
20		Boston College	8-2-1	regular season complete
20		Brigham Young	8-3-0	

December 6 Poll / January 3 Final Poll

UP	AP	Team	Record	Bowl Bid	Date	Bowl Results	RB	UP	AP	January 3 Final Poll	Record
1	1	Georgia	11-0-0	Sugar Bowl	J1	lost to # 2 Penn State 23-27	1	1	1	Penn State	11-1-0
2	2	Penn State	10-1-0	Sugar Bowl	J1	beat # 1 Georgia 27-23	3	2	2	SMU	11-0-1
3	3	Nebraska	11-1-0	Orange Bowl	J1	beat # 13 LSU 21-20	4	3	3	Nebraska	12-1-0
4	4	SMU	10-0-1	Cotton Bowl	J1	beat # 6 Pittsburgh 7-3	2	4	4	Georgia	11-1-0
5	5	UCLA	9-1-1	Rose Bowl	J1	beat # 19 Michigan 24-14	6	5	5	UCLA	10-1-1
6	6	Pittsburgh	9-2-0	Cotton Bowl	J1	lost to # 4 SMU 3-7	8	6	6	Arizona State	10-2-0
PB	7	Clemson	9-1-1				7	7	7	Washington	10-2-0
7	8	Texas	9-2-0	Sun Bowl	D25	lost to North Carolina 10-26	9	PB	8	Clemson	9-1-1
8	9	Washington	9-2-0	Aloha Bowl	D25	beat # 16 Maryland 21-20	14	8	9	Arkansas	9-2-1
9	10	West Virginia	9-2-0	Gator Bowl	D30	lost to Florida State 12-31	5	9	10	Pittsburgh	9-3-0
11	11	Arizona State	9-2-0	Fiesta Bowl	J1	beat # 12 Oklahoma 32-21	30	11	11	LSU	8-3-1
10	12	Oklahoma	8-3-0	Fiesta Bowl	J1	lost to # 11 Arizona State 21-32	13	12	12	Ohio State	9-3-0
13	13	LSU	8-2-1	Orange Bowl	J1	lost to # 3 Nebraska 20-21	15	10	13	Florida State	9-3-0
12	14	Arkansas	8-2-1	Bluebonnet Bowl	D31	beat Florida 28-24	17	14	14	Auburn	9-3-0
PB	15	Southern Cal	8-3-0				12	PB	15	Southern Cal	8-3-0
14	16	Maryland	8-3-0	Aloha Bowl	D25	lost to # 9 Washington 20-21	22	16	16	Oklahoma	8-4-0
16	17	Ohio State	8-3-0	Holiday Bowl	D17	beat Brigham Young 47-17	11	18	17	Texas	9-3-0
15	18	Auburn	8-3-0	Tangerine Bowl	D18	beat Boston College 33-26	10	13	18	North Carolina	8-4-0
17	19	Michigan	8-3-0	Rose Bowl	J1	lost to # 5 UCLA 14-24	16	19	19	West Virginia	9-3-0
18	20	Tulsa	10-1-0				23	20	20	Maryland	8-4-0
19		Florida	8-3-0	Bluebonnet Bowl	D31	lost to # 14 Arkansas 24-28	20	15		Michigan	8-4-0
20		Florida State	8-3-0	Gator Bowl	D30	beat # 10 West Virginia 31-12	28	17		Alabama	8-4-0

1982

CONSENSUS ALL-AMERICANS

POS	Offense	HT	WT	School	AP	FC	FW	PI
QB	John Elway	6-4	202	Stanford	•	•	•	•
RB	Herschel Walker	6-2	222	Georgia	•	•	•	•
RB	Eric Dickerson	6-2	215	SMU	•	•	•	•
RB	Mike Rozier	5-11	210	Nebraska		•		•
WR	Anthony Carter	5-11	161	Michigan	•	•	•	•
TE	Gordon Hudson	6-4	224	Brigham Young	•	•	•	•
L	Don Mosebar	6-7	270	Southern Cal	•	•	•	•
L	Steve Korte	6-2	270	Arkansas	•	•	•	•
L	Jimbo Covert	6-5	279	Pittsburgh	•	•	•	•
L	Bruce Matthews	6-5	265	Southern Cal		•	•	•
C	Dave Rimington	6-3	290	Nebraska	•	•	•	•
PK	Chuck Nelson	5-11	178	Washington		•	•	

OTHERS RECEIVING FIRST-TEAM HONORS

WR	Kenny Jackson	Penn State	•		
L	David Drechsler	North Carolina		•	
L	Bill Fralic	Pittsburgh	•		

POS	Defense	HT	WT	School	AP	FC	FW	PI
L	Billy Ray Smith	6-3	228	Arkansas	•	•	•	•
L	Vernon Maxwell	6-2	225	Arizona State	•	•		•
L	Mike Pitts	6-5	255	Alabama	•	•		•
L	Wilber Marshall	6-1	230	Florida	•		•	
L	Gabriel Rivera	6-3	270	Texas Tech	•			•
L	Rick Bryan	6-4	260	Oklahoma		•		•
MG	George Achica	6-5	260	Southern Cal	•			•
LB	Darryl Talley	6-4	210	West Virginia	•	•	•	•
LB	Ricky Hunley	6-1	230	Arizona	•	•	•	•
LB	Marcus Marek	6-2	224	Ohio State	•		•	•
DB	Terry Kinard	6-1	189	Clemson	•	•	•	•
DB	Mike Richardson	6-0	190	Arizona State	•	•	•	•
DB	Terry Hoage	6-3	196	Georgia	•	•		•
P	Jim Arnold	6-3	205	Vanderbilt		•	•	

OTHERS RECEIVING FIRST-TEAM HONORS

L	Mike Charles	Syracuse		•	
L	William Fuller	North Carolina		•	
L	Gary Lewis	Oklahoma State	•		
LB	Mark Stewart	Washington		•	
DB	Dave Duerson	Notre Dame			•
DB	Mark Robinson	Penn State			•
DB	Jeremiah Castille	Alabama	•		

FC named Talley as a DL

HEISMAN TROPHY VOTING

	PLAYER	POS	SCHOOL	1ST	2ND	3RD	TOTAL
1	Herschel Walker	TB	Georgia	525	155	41	1926
2	John Elway	QB	Stanford	139	335	144	1231
3	Eric Dickerson	TB	SMU	31	100	172	465
4	Anthony Carter	WR	Michigan	11	27	55	142
5	Dave Rimington	C	Nebraska	13	23	52	137
6	Todd Blackledge	QB	Penn State	4	26	44	108
7	Tom Ramsey	QB	UCLA	2	16	27	65
8	Tony Eason	QB	Illinois	5	6	33	60
9	Dan Marino	QB	Pittsburgh	1	6	32	47
10	Mike Rozier	RB	Nebraska	4	8	12	40
11	Curt Warner	TB	Penn State	2	8	18	40

AWARD WINNERS

PLAYER	POS	SCHOOL	AWARD NAME
Herschel Walker	RB	Georgia	Maxwell
Dave Rimington	C	Nebraska	Outland
Herschel Walker	RB	Georgia	Camp
Dave Rimington	C	Nebraska	Lombardi
Todd Blackledge	QB	Penn State	O'Brien

CONFERENCE STANDINGS

ACC

	CONF. W L T			OVERALL W L T		
Clemson	6	0	0	9	1	1
Maryland	5	1	0	8	4	0
North Carolina	3	3	0	8	4	0
North Carolina St.	3	3	0	6	5	0
Duke	3	3	0	6	5	0
Virginia	1	5	0	2	9	0
Wake Forest	0	6	0	3	8	0

Big 10

	CONF. W L T			OVERALL W L T		
Michigan	8	1	0	8	4	0
Ohio State	7	1	0	9	3	0
Iowa	6	2	0	8	4	0
Illinois	6	3	0	7	5	0
Wisconsin	5	4	0	7	5	0
Indiana	4	5	0	5	6	0
Purdue	3	6	0	3	8	0
Northwestern	2	7	0	3	8	0
Michigan State	2	7	0	2	9	0
Minnesota	1	8	0	3	8	0

Big 8

	CONF. W L T			OVERALL W L T		
Nebraska	7	0	0	12	1	0
Oklahoma	6	1	0	8	4	0
Oklahoma State	3	2	2	4	5	2
Kansas State	3	3	1	6	5	1
Missouri	2	3	2	5	4	2
Iowa State	1	5	1	4	6	1
Kansas	1	5	1	2	7	2
Colorado	1	5	1	2	8	1

Big West

	CONF. W L T			OVERALL W L T		
Fresno State	6	0	0	11	1	0
Long Beach State	5	1	0	6	5	0
San Jose State	4	2	0	8	3	0
Utah State	2	3	0	5	6	0
Pacific	2	4	0	2	9	0
Nevada-Las Vegas	1	5	0	3	8	0
Cal-St. Fullerton	0	6	0	3	9	0

Ivy

	CONF. W L T			OVERALL W L T		
Harvard	5	2	0	7	3	0
Pennsylvania	5	2	0	7	3	0
Dartmouth	5	2	0	5	5	0
Brown	3	4	0	5	5	0
Cornell	3	4	0	4	6	0
Yale	3	4	0	4	6	0
Princeton	3	4	0	3	7	0
Columbia	1	6	0	1	9	0

MAC

	CONF. W L T			OVERALL W L T		
Bowling Green	7	2	0	7	5	0
Western Michigan	5	2	2	7	2	2
Miami, Ohio	5	3	0	7	4	0
Central Michigan	5	3	1	6	4	1
Toledo	5	4	0	6	5	0
Ohio U	5	4	0	6	5	0
Northern Illinois	5	4	0	5	5	0
Ball State	4	4	0	5	6	0
Eastern Michigan	1	7	1	1	9	1
Kent State	0	9	0	0	11	0

Pac 10

	CONF. W L T			OVERALL W L T		
UCLA	5	1	1	10	1	1
Washington	6	2	0	10	2	0
Arizona State	5	2	0	10	2	0
Southern Cal	5	2	0	8	3	0
Arizona	4	3	1	6	4	1
California	4	4	0	7	4	0
Stanford	3	5	0	5	6	0
Washington State	2	4	1	3	7	1
Oregon	2	6	0	2	8	1
Oregon State	0	7	0	1	10	0

SEC

	CONF. W L T			OVERALL W L T		
Georgia	6	0	0	11	1	0
LSU	4	1	1	8	3	1
Auburn	4	2	0	9	3	0
Vanderbilt	4	2	0	8	4	0
Tennessee	3	2	1	6	5	1
Alabama	3	3	0	8	4	0
Florida	3	3	0	8	4	0
Mississippi State	2	4	0	5	6	0
Mississippi	0	6	0	4	7	0
Kentucky	0	6	0	0	10	1

SWC

	CONF. W L T			OVERALL W L T		
SMU	7	0	1	11	0	1
Texas	7	1	0	9	3	0
Arkansas	5	2	1	9	2	1
Houston	4	3	1	5	5	1
Baylor	3	4	1	4	6	1
Texas A&M	3	5	0	5	6	0
Texas Tech	3	5	0	4	7	0
TCU	2	6	0	3	8	0
Rice	0	8	0	0	11	0

WAC

	CONF. W L T			OVERALL W L T		
Brigham Young	7	1	0	8	4	0
New Mexico	6	1	0	10	1	0
Air Force	4	3	0	8	5	0
San Diego State	4	3	0	7	5	0
Hawaii	4	4	0	6	5	0
Utah	3	4	0	5	6	0
Colorado State	3	5	0	4	7	0
Wyoming	2	6	0	5	7	0
Texas-El Paso	1	6	0	2	10	0

Independents

	OVERALL W L T		
Penn State	11	1	0
Florida State	9	3	0
Pittsburgh	9	3	0
West Virginia	9	3	0
Boston College	8	3	1
La. Lafayette	7	3	1
East Carolina	7	4	0
Miami, Fla.	7	4	0
Virginia Tech	7	4	0
Southern Miss	7	4	0
Notre Dame	6	4	1
Navy	6	5	0
Cincinnati	6	5	0
Georgia Tech	6	5	0
Louisville	5	6	0
Rutgers	5	6	0
Tulane	4	7	0
South Carolina	4	7	0
Army	4	7	0
Temple	4	7	0
North Texas	2	9	0
Syracuse	2	9	0
Memphis	1	10	0

BOWL GAMES

DATE	GAME	SCORE
D11	Independence	Wisconsin 14, Kansas State 3
D17	Holiday	Ohio State 47, Brigham Young 17
D18	Tangerine	Auburn 33, Boston College 26
D18	California	Fresno State 29, Bowling Green 28
D25	Sun	North Carolina 26, Texas 10
D25	Aloha	Washington 21, Maryland 20
D29	Liberty	Alabama 21, Illinois 15
D30	Gator	Florida State 31, West Virginia 12
D31	All-American	Air Force 36, Vanderbilt 28
D31	Bluebonnet	Arkansas 28, Florida 24
D31	Peach	Iowa 28, Tennessee 22
J1	Sugar	Penn State 27, Georgia 23
J1	Fiesta	Arizona State 32, Oklahoma 21
J1	Orange	Nebraska 21, LSU 20
J1	Cotton	SMU 7, Pittsburgh 3
J1	Rose	UCLA 24, Michigan 14

1982 ANNUAL REVIEW 1343

1982 NCAA Major College Statistical Leaders

Individual Leaders

Passing

		CL	G	ATT	COM	PCT	INT	I%	YDS	YPA	TD	TD%	RATING
1	Tom Ramsey, UCLA	SR	11	311	191	61.4	10	3.2	2824	9.1	21	6.8	153.5
2	Alan Risher, LSU	SR	11	234	149	63.7	8	3.4	1834	7.8	17	7.3	146.6
3	John Elway, Stanford	SR	11	405	262	64.7	12	3.0	3242	8.0	24	5.9	145.6
4	Wayne Peace, Florida	JR	11	246	174	70.7	10	4.1	2053	8.4	8	3.3	143.4
5	Ben Bennett, Duke	JR	11	374	236	63.1	12	3.2	3033	8.1	20	5.4	142.5
6	Steve Young, Brigham Young	JR	11	367	230	62.7	18	4.9	3100	8.5	18	4.9	140.0
7	Tim Riordan, Temple	JR	11	247	157	63.6	7	2.8	1840	7.5	13	5.3	137.8
8	Jeff Tedford, Fresno State	SR	11	298	153	51.3	18	6.0	2620	8.8	21	7.1	136.4
9	Ken Vierra, Utah	SO	10	166	85	51.2	6	3.6	1315	7.9	13	7.8	136.4
10	Todd Blackledge, Penn State	JR	11	292	161	55.1	14	4.8	2218	7.6	22	7.5	134.2

All-Purpose

		CL	G	RUSH	REC	PR	KR	YDS	YPG
1	Carl Monroe, Utah	SR	11	1507	108	0	421	2036	185.1
2	Sam DeJarnette, Southern Miss	SO	11	1545	32	0	405	1982	180.2
3	Ernest Anderson, Oklahoma State	JR	11	1877	103	0	0	1980	180.0
4	Herschel Walker, Georgia	JR	11	1752	89	0	36	1877	170.6
5	Napoleon McCallum, Navy	SO	10	739	196	379	332	1646	164.6
6	Eric Dickerson, SMU	SR	11	1617	60	0	0	1677	152.5
7	Henry Ellard, Fresno State	SR	11	100	1510	-1	44	1653	150.3
8	Mike Rozier, Nebraska	JR	12	1689	46	0	55	1790	149.2
9	Tim Spencer, Ohio State	SR	11	1371	115	0	117	1603	145.7
10	Robert Lavette, Georgia Tech	SO	11	1208	286	0	76	1570	142.7

Rushing/Yards Per Game

		CL	G	ATT	YDS	TD	AVG	YPG
1	Ernest Anderson, Oklahoma State	JR	11	353	1877	8	5.3	170.6
2	Herschel Walker, Georgia	JR	11	335	1752	16	5.2	159.3
3	Eric Dickerson, SMU	SR	11	232	1617	17	7.0	147.0
4	Mike Rozier, Nebraska	JR	12	242	1689	15	7.0	140.7
5	Sam DeJarnette, Southern Miss	SO	11	311	1545	14	5.0	140.5
6	Carl Monroe, Utah	SR	11	309	1507	4	4.9	137.0
7	Michael Gunter, Tulsa	JR	11	195	1464	11	7.5	133.1
8	Tim Spencer, Ohio State	SR	11	252	1371	12	5.4	124.6
9	Lawrence Ricks, Michigan	SR	11	243	1300	8	5.3	118.2
10	Robert Lavette, Georgia Tech	SO	11	280	1208	19	4.3	109.8

Rushing/Yards Per Carry

		CL	G	ATT	YDS	YPC
1	Michael Gunter, Tulsa	JR	11	195	1464	7.5
2	Marcus Dupree, Oklahoma	FR	11	129	905	7.0
3	Mike Rozier, Nebraska	JR	12	242	1689	7.0
4	Eric Dickerson, SMU	SR	11	232	1617	7.0
5	Tony Baker, East Carolina	FR	10	126	827	6.6
6	Vincent Jackson, Auburn	FR	10	127	829	6.5
7	Allen Harvin, Cincinnati	SR	11	191	1161	6.1
8	Thomas Dendy, South Carolina	FR	10	140	848	6.1
9	Willie Joyner, Maryland	JR	10	177	1039	5.9
10	Ken Lacy, Tulsa	SR	11	199	1097	5.5

*-Based on top 30 rushers

Receiving

		CL	G	REC	YDS	TD	YPR	YPG	RPG
1	Vincent White, Stanford	SR	10	68	677	8	10.0	67.7	6.8
2	Mike Martin, Illinois	SR	11	69	941	5	13.6	85.5	6.3
3	Darren Long, Long Beach State	SR	11	68	749	3	11.0	68.1	6.2
4	Gordon Hudson, Brigham Young	JR	11	67	928	6	13.9	84.4	6.1
5	Henry Ellard, Fresno State	SR	11	62	1510	15	24.4	137.3	5.6
6	Allama Matthews, Vanderbilt	SR	11	61	797	14	13.1	72.5	5.5
7	Darral Hambrick, Nevada-Las Vegas	SR	11	60	1060	8	17.7	96.4	5.5
8	Jeff Simmons, Southern Cal	SR	11	56	973	5	17.4	88.5	5.1
8	Robert Griffin, Tulane	JR	11	56	784	0	14.0	71.3	5.1
8	Norman Jordan, Vanderbilt	SR	11	56	470	3	8.4	42.7	5.1

Punting

		CL	PUNT	YDS	AVG
1	Reggie Roby, Iowa	SR	52	2501	48.1
2	Jimmy Colquitt, Tennessee	SO	46	2157	46.9
3	Bucky Scribner, Kansas	SR	76	3481	45.8
4	Jim Arnold, Vanderbilt	SR	74	3389	45.8
5	Mike Mees, Brigham Young	SR	40	1824	45.6
6	John Kidd, Northwestern	JR	52	2371	45.6
7	Craig James, SMU	SR	66	2963	44.9
8	Ralf Mojsiejenko, Michigan State	SO	77	3434	44.6
9	Mike Black, Arizona State	SR	64	2835	44.3
10	Ron Stowe, Baylor	SR	62	2703	43.6

Punt Returns

		CL	PR	YDS	TD	AVG
1	Lionel James, Auburn	JR	25	394	0	15.8
2	Anthony Carter, Michigan	SR	17	265	1	15.6
3	Irving Fryar, Nebraska	JR	18	277	1	15.4
4	Frank Minnifield, Louisville	SR	11	165	1	15.0
5	Richie Hall, Colorado State	SR	24	320	0	13.3
6	Gerald McNeil, Baylor	JR	16	202	0	12.6
7	Fred Young, New Mexico State	JR	20	244	1	12.2
8	Louis Lipps, Southern Miss	JR	23	280	1	12.2
9	Jack Westbrook, Georgia Tech	JR	21	255	1	12.1
10	Willie Drewrey, West Virginia	SO	25	300	1	12.0

Kickoff Returns

		CL	KR	YDS	TD	AVG
1	Carl Monroe, Utah	SR	14	421	1	30.1
2	Vance Johnson, Arizona	SO	13	353	1	27.2
3	Elton Akins, Army	SO	26	701	2	27.0
4	Harry Roberts, Oklahoma State	FR	14	376	0	26.9
5	Dokie Williams, UCLA	SR	17	449	0	26.4
6	Clarence Verdin, La. Lafayette	SO	12	315	1	26.2
7	Greg Allen, Florida State	SO	20	515	0	25.7
8	Sam DeJarnette, Southern Miss	SO	16	405	1	25.3
9	Allen Pinkett, Notre Dame	FR	14	354	1	25.3
10	Phil Smith, San Diego State	SR	18	450	0	25.0
10	Waymon Aldridge, Nevada-Las Vegas	SR	15	375	0	25.0

Scoring

		CL	TDS	XPT	FG	PTS	PTPG
1	Greg Allen, Florida State	SO	21	0	0	126	11.5
2	Robert Lavette, Georgia Tech	SO	19	0	0	114	10.4
3	Paul Woodside, West Virginia	SO	0	26	28	110	10.0
4	Chuck Nelson, Washington	SR	0	34	25	109	9.9
5	Herschel Walker, Georgia	JR	17	2	0	104	9.5
6	Eric Dickerson, SMU	SR	17	0	0	102	9.3
7	Vincent White, Stanford	SR	15	2	0	92	9.2
8	Fuad Reveiz, Tennessee	SO	0	20	27	101	9.2
8	Mike Bass, Illinois	SR	0	32	23	101	9.2
10	Stu Crum, Tulsa	SR	0	37	21	100	9.1

Field Goals

		CL	FGA	FGM	PCT	FGG
1	Paul Woodside, West Virginia	SO	31	28	0.90	2.55
2	Fuad Reveiz, Tennessee	SO	31	27	0.87	2.45
3	Chuck Nelson, Washington	SR	26	25	0.96	2.27
4	Mike Bass, Illinois	SR	26	23	0.89	2.09
5	Luis Zendejas, Arizona State	SO	28	21	0.75	1.91
5	Stu Crum, Tulsa	SR	29	21	0.72	1.91
7	Brooks Barwick, North Carolina	JR	23	20	0.87	1.82
8	Mike Johnston, Notre Dame	JR	22	19	0.86	1.73
9	Mark Fleetwood, South Carolina	JR	18	17	0.94	1.55
9	Kevin Butler, Georgia	SO	21	17	0.81	1.55
9	Steve Clark, Southern Miss	JR	23	17	0.74	1.55

Interceptions

		CL	INT	YDS	TD	INT/GM
1	Terry Hoage, Georgia	JR	12	51	0	1.20
2	Jeff Sanchez, Georgia	JR	9	49	0	0.82
3	Jeremiah Castille, Alabama	SR	7	60	0	0.78
4	Leonard Coleman, Vanderbilt	JR	8	101	0	0.73
5	Dave Duerson, Notre Dame	SR	7	104	0	0.64
5	Sherman Cocroft, San Jose State	JR	7	72	0	0.64
5	Lendell Jones, Maryland	JR	7	48	0	0.64
8	Johnny Rembert, Clemson	SR	6	128	0	0.60
8	Larry Harris, Florida State	JR	6	49	0	0.60
8	Eric Fox, Fresno State	SO	6	32	0	0.60

Team Leaders

Rushing Offense

		G	ATT	YDS	AVG	TD	YPG
1	Nebraska	12	762	4732	6.2	52	394.3
2	Oklahoma	11	696	3724	5.4	34	338.5
3	Tulsa	11	645	3346	5.2	32	304.2
4	Air Force	12	723	3620	5.0	37	301.7
5	Southern Miss	11	644	3131	4.9	32	284.6
6	SMU	11	619	3041	4.9	26	276.5
7	Georgia	11	647	3023	4.7	28	274.8
8	New Mexico	11	564	2998	5.3	29	272.5
9	Alabama	11	636	2935	4.6	29	266.8
10	Wichita State	11	626	2919	4.7	25	265.4

Passing Offense

		G	ATT	COM	INT	PCT	YDS	YPA	TD	I%	YPC	YPG
1	Long Beach State	11	522	300	23	57.5	3595	6.9	19	4.4	12.0	326.8
2	Duke	11	414	258	16	62.3	3349	8.1	23	3.9	13.0	304.5
3	Stanford	11	422	268	13	63.5	3311	7.8	25	3.1	12.4	301.0
4	Illinois	11	453	279	15	61.6	3254	7.2	17	3.3	11.7	295.8
5	Brigham Young	11	385	240	20	62.3	3188	8.3	19	5.2	13.3	289.8
6	UCLA	11	335	205	12	61.2	3070	9.2	23	3.6	15.0	279.1
7	Nevada-Las Vegas	11	420	216	16	51.4	3008	7.2	17	3.8	13.9	273.5
8	San Diego State	12	455	250	18	54.9	3264	7.2	21	4.0	13.1	272.0
9	Pacific	11	493	244	22	49.5	2931	5.9	14	4.5	12.0	266.5
10	Boston College	11	365	173	20	47.4	2924	8.0	16	5.5	16.9	265.8

Total Offense

		G	P	YDS	AVG	TD	YPG
1	Nebraska	12	976	6223	6.4	65	518.6
2	Brigham Young	11	797	5128	6.4	46	466.2
3	Florida State	11	825	5123	6.2	51	465.7
4	Duke	11	845	4990	5.9	38	453.6
5	New Mexico	11	801	4822	6.0	47	438.4
6	North Carolina	11	901	4768	5.3	37	433.5
7	UCLA	11	836	4757	5.7	46	432.5
8	Long Beach State	11	867	4738	5.5	30	430.7
9	Air Force	12	890	5099	5.7	43	424.9
10	Penn State	11	812	4652	5.7	43	422.9

Rushing Defense

		G	ATT	YDS	AVG	TD	YPG
1	Virginia Tech	11	379	544	1.4	2	49.5
2	San Jose State	11	405	804	2.0	8	73.1
3	Maryland	11	396	959	2.4	12	87.2
4	LSU	11	406	1004	2.5	6	91.3
5	Pittsburgh	11	367	1029	2.8	6	93.5
6	Arizona State	11	488	1046	2.1	7	95.1
7	Southern Cal	11	410	1047	2.6	8	95.2
8	Notre Dame	11	414	1050	2.5	9	95.5
9	Arkansas	11	430	1064	2.5	8	96.7
10	Clemson	11	401	1071	2.7	7	97.4

Passing Defense

		G	ATT	COM	PCT	YPC	INT	I%	YDS	YPA	TD	YPG
1	Missouri	11	277	121	43.7	11.2	14	5.1	1358	4.9	7	123.5
2	Kansas	11	201	87	43.3	16.1	7	3.5	1402	7.0	13	127.5
3	New Mexico State	11	244	111	45.5	12.8	13	5.3	1417	5.8	16	128.8
3	Iowa State	11	233	111	47.6	12.8	13	5.6	1417	6.1	8	128.8
5	Arizona State	11	257	115	44.7	12.8	11	4.3	1472	5.7	5	133.8
6	North Carolina	11	284	141	49.6	10.6	10	3.5	1490	5.2	8	135.5
7	Louisville	11	241	122	50.6	12.3	10	4.1	1498	6.2	10	136.2
8	Kansas State	11	283	137	48.4	11.0	19	6.7	1508	5.3	4	137.1
9	Texas Tech	11	227	109	48.0	14.3	15	6.6	1562	6.9	10	142.0
10	Mississippi State	11	236	132	55.9	12.0	11	4.7	1578	6.7	0	143.5

Total Defense

		G	P	YDS	AVG	TD	YPG
1	Arizona State	11	745	2518	3.4	12	228.9
2	North Carolina	11	692	2602	3.8	16	236.5
3	Pittsburgh	11	683	2681	3.9	12	243.7
4	LSU	11	704	2707	3.8	18	246.1
5	Central Michigan	11	731	2731	3.7	18	248.3
6	Arkansas	11	700	2743	3.9	12	249.4
7	Southern Cal	11	742	2917	3.9	15	265.2
8	Virginia Tech	11	800	3060	3.8	16	278.2
9	Texas	11	767	3081	4.0	18	280.1
10	Notre Dame	11	760	3123	4.1	16	283.9

Scoring Offense

		G	PTS	AVG
1	Nebraska	12	493	41.1
2	Florida State	11	388	35.3
3	UCLA	11	375	34.1
4	New Mexico	11	374	34.0
5	Penn State	11	368	33.5
6	LSU	11	365	33.2
7	Brigham Young	11	358	32.5
8	Maryland	11	353	32.1
9	Fresno State	11	352	32.0
10	SMU	11	347	31.5
10	Texas	11	347	31.5

Scoring Defense

		G	PTS	AVG
1	Arkansas	11	115	10.5
2	Arizona State	11	124	11.3
3	Pittsburgh	11	132	12.0
4	Georgia	11	133	12.1
5	Nebraska	12	147	12.2
6	North Carolina	11	139	12.6
7	Virginia Tech	11	141	12.8
8	Southern Cal	11	143	13.0
9	Texas	11	144	13.1
10	Clemson	11	147	13.4

ANNUAL REVIEW

1983 POLL PROGRESSION

PRE-SEASON 1983 / SEPT. 3 GAMES

UP	AP	Team	Record	Result
1	1	Nebraska	0-0-0	beat #4 Penn State 44-6 (A29)
5	2	Oklahoma	0-0-0	bye week
2	3	Texas	0-0-0	bye week
4	4	Penn State	0-0-0	lost to #1 Nebraska 6-44 (A29)
3	5	Auburn	0-0-0	bye week
8	6	Notre Dame	0-0-0	bye week
7	7	Florida State	0-0-0	beat East Carolina 47-46
PB	8	Southern Cal	0-0-0	bye week
6	9	Ohio State	0-0-0	bye week
9	10	Michigan	0-0-0	bye week
10	11	North Carolina	0-0-0	beat South Carolina 24-8
10	12	LSU	0-0-0	bye week
14	13	Alabama	0-0-0	bye week
PB	14	Arizona	0-0-0	beat Oregon State 50-6
13	15	Georgia	0-0-0	beat #20 UCLA 19-8
20	16	Iowa	0-0-0	bye week
20	17	Maryland	0-0-0	bye week
16	18	Washington	0-0-0	bye week
17	19	SMU	0-0-0	beat Louisville 24-6
12	20	UCLA	0-0-0	lost to #15 Georgia 8-19
15		Pittsburgh	0-0-0	beat Tennessee 13-3
18		Arizona State	0-0-0	bye week
19		Miami, Fla.	0-0-0	lost to Florida 3-28

SEPTEMBER 5 POLL / SEPT 10 GAMES

UP	AP	Team	Record	Result
1	1	Nebraska	1-0-0	beat Wyoming 56-20
4	2	Oklahoma	0-0-0	beat Stanford 27-14
2	3	Texas	0-0-0	bye week
3	4	Auburn	0-0-0	beat Southern Miss 24-3
9	5	Notre Dame	0-0-0	beat Purdue 52-6
5	6	Michigan	0-0-0	beat Washington State 20-17
6	7	Ohio State	0-0-0	beat Oregon 31-6
8	8	North Carolina	1-0-0	beat Memphis 24-10
PB	9	Southern Cal	0-0-0	tied #18 Florida 19-19
7	10	Georgia	1-0-0	bye week
18	11	Arizona State	1-0-0	tied UCLA 26-26
13	12	Florida State	1-0-0	beat #13 LSU 40-35
10	13	LSU	0-0-0	lost to #12 Florida State 35-40
14	14	Alabama	0-0-0	beat Georgia Tech 20-7
16	15	SMU	1-0-0	beat Grambling 20-13
17	16	Iowa	0-0-0	beat Iowa State 51-10
20	17	Maryland	0-0-0	beat Vanderbilt 21-14
12	18	Florida	1-0-0	tied #9 Southern Cal 19-19
	19	Washington	0-0-0	beat Northwestern 34-0
19	20	Penn State	0-1-0	lost to Cincinnati 3-14
11		Pittsburgh	1-0-0	beat Temple 35-0
15		West Virginia	1-0-0	beat Pacific 48-7

SEPTEMBER 12 POLL / SEPT. 17 GAMES

UP	AP	Team	Record	Result
1	1	Nebraska	2-0-0	beat Minnesota 84-13
2	2	Oklahoma	1-0-0	lost to #6 Ohio State 14-24
3	3	Texas	0-0-0	beat #5 Auburn 20-7
5	4	Notre Dame	1-0-0	lost to Michigan State 23-28
4	5	Auburn	1-0-0	lost to #3 Texas 7-20
6	6	Ohio State	1-0-0	beat #2 Oklahoma 24-14
PB	7	Arizona	2-0-0	beat Washington State 45-6
10	8	Michigan	1-0-0	lost to #16 Washington 24-25
9	9	Florida State	2-0-0	lost to Tulane 28-34
8	10	North Carolina	2-0-0	beat Miami, Ohio 48-17
7	11	Georgia	1-0-0	tied Clemson 16-16
11	12	Alabama	1-0-0	beat Mississippi 40-0
12	13	Iowa	1-0-0	beat Penn State 42-34
PB	14	Southern Cal	0-0-1	beat Oregon State 33-10
15	15	Florida	1-0-1	beat Indiana St. 17-13
16	16	Washington	1-0-0	beat #8 Michigan 25-24
19	17	Maryland	1-0-0	lost to #20 West Virginia 21-31
17	18	SMU	2-0-0	bye week
13	19	Pittsburgh	2-0-0	bye week
14	20	West Virginia	2-0-0	beat #17 Maryland 31-21
18		Arizona State	1-0-0	tied UCLA 26-26
20		Boston College	2-0-0	beat Rutgers 42-22

SEPTEMBER 19 POLL / SEPT. 24 GAMES

UP	AP	Team	Record	Result
1	1	Nebraska	3-0-0	beat UCLA 42-10
2	2	Texas	1-0-0	beat North Texas 26-6
3	3	Ohio State	2-0-0	lost to #7 Iowa 14-20
PB	4	Arizona	3-0-0	beat Cal-St. Fullerton 27-10
4	5	North Carolina	3-0-0	beat William & Mary 51-20
5	6	Alabama	2-0-0	beat Vanderbilt 44-24
6	7	Iowa	2-0-0	beat #3 Ohio State 20-14
10	8	Oklahoma	1-1-0	beat Tulsa 28-18
9	9	Washington	2-0-0	lost to LSU 14-40
PB	10	Southern Cal	1-0-1	lost to Kansas 20-26
14	11	Auburn	1-1-0	beat Tennessee 37-14
8	12	West Virginia	3-0-0	beat #19 Boston College 27-17
16	13	Notre Dame	1-1-0	lost to Miami, Fla. 0-20
11	14	Georgia	1-0-1	beat South Carolina 31-13
15	15	Florida	2-0-1	beat Mississippi State 35-12
9	16	Pittsburgh	2-0-0	lost to Maryland 7-13
17	17	Michigan	1-1-0	beat Wisconsin 38-21
12	18	SMU	2-0-0	beat TCU 21-17
15	19	Boston College	3-0-0	lost to #12 West Virginia 17-27
	20	Florida State	2-1-0	bye week
18		Arkansas		lost to Mississippi 10-13
19		Arizona State	1-0-1	beat Wichita St. 44-14
19		Michigan State	2-0-0	lost to Illinois 10-20

SEPTEMBER 26 POLL / OCT. 1 GAMES

UP	AP	Team	Record	Result
1	1	Nebraska	4-0-0	beat Syracuse 63-7
2	2	Texas	2-0-0	beat Rice 42-6
PB	3	Arizona	4-0-0	tied California 33-33
3	4	Iowa	3-0-0	lost to Illinois 0-33
5	5	North Carolina	4-0-0	beat Georgia Tech 38-21
4	6	Alabama	3-0-0	beat Memphis 44-13
6	7	West Virginia	4-0-0	beat Pittsburgh 24-21
11	8	Ohio State	2-1-0	beat Minnesota 69-18
7	9	Oklahoma	2-1-0	beat Kansas State 29-10
10	10	Auburn	2-1-0	beat #17 Florida State 27-24
8	11	Georgia	2-0-1	beat Mississippi State 20-7
12	12	Florida	3-0-1	beat #16 LSU 31-17
13	13	SMU	3-0-0	beat Texas Arlington 34-0
14	14	Michigan	2-1-0	beat Indiana 43-18
15	15	Miami, Fla.	3-1-0	beat Duke 56-17
13	16	LSU	2-1-0	lost to #12 Florida 17-31
	17	Florida State	2-1-0	lost to #10 Auburn 24-27
18	18	Washington	2-1-0	beat Navy 27-10
16	19	Maryland	2-1-0	beat Virginia 23-3
17	20	Arizona State	2-0-1	beat Stanford 29-11
18		Kentucky	4-0-0	bye week
20		Pittsburgh	2-1-0	lost to #7 West Virginia 21-24

OCTOBER 3 POLL / OCT. 8 GAMES

UP	AP	Team	Record	Result
1	1	Nebraska	5-0-0	beat Oklahoma State 14-10
2	2	Texas	3-0-0	beat #8 Oklahoma 28-16
3	3	Alabama	4-0-0	lost to Penn State 28-34
4	4	North Carolina	5-0-0	beat Wake Forest 30-10
5	5	West Virginia	5-0-0	bye week
9	6	Ohio State	3-1-0	beat Purdue 33-22
10	7	Auburn	3-1-0	beat Kentucky 49-21
7	8	Oklahoma	3-1-0	lost to #2 Texas 16-28
6	9	Florida	4-0-1	beat Vanderbilt 29-10
PB	10	Arizona	4-0-1	beat Colorado State 52-21
8	11	Georgia	3-0-1	beat Mississippi 36-11
11	12	Miami, Fla.	4-1-0	beat Louisville 42-14
12	13	SMU	4-0-0	beat Baylor 42-26
13	14	Michigan	3-1-0	beat Michigan State 42-0
15	15	Iowa	3-1-0	beat Northwestern 61-21
14	16	Maryland	3-1-0	beat Syracuse 34-13
18	17	Washington	3-1-0	beat Oregon State 34-7
16	18	Arizona State	3-0-1	bye week
17	19	Illinois		beat Wisconsin 27-15
19	20	Brigham Young	3-1-0	beat Wyoming 41-10
20		Oklahoma State	4-0-0	lost to #1 Nebraska 10-14

OCTOBER 10 POLL / OCT. 15 GAMES

UP	AP	Team	Record	Result
1	1	Nebraska	6-0-0	beat Missouri 34-13
2	2	Texas	4-0-0	beat Arkansas 31-3
3	3	North Carolina	6-0-0	beat North Carolina St. 42-14
4	4	West Virginia	5-0-0	beat Virginia Tech 13-0
8	5	Auburn	4-1-0	beat Georgia Tech 31-13
7	6	Ohio State	4-1-0	lost to #19 Illinois 13-17
5	7	Florida	5-0-1	bye week
6	8	Georgia	4-0-1	beat Vanderbilt 20-13
PB	9	Arizona	5-0-1	lost to Oregon 10-19
12	10	Miami, Fla.	5-1-0	beat Mississippi State 31-7
10	11	Alabama	4-1-0	lost to Tennessee 34-41
9	12	SMU	5-0-0	bye week
11	13	Michigan	4-1-0	beat Northwestern 35-0
13	14	Iowa	4-1-0	beat Purdue 31-14
15	15	Oklahoma	3-2-0	beat Oklahoma State 21-20
15	16	Maryland	4-1-0	beat Wake Forest 36-33
18	17	Washington	4-1-0	beat Stanford 32-15
16	18	Arizona State	3-0-1	beat Southern Cal 34-14
14	19	Illinois		beat #6 Ohio State 17-13
19	20	Brigham Young	4-1-0	beat New Mexico 66-21
20		Oklahoma State	4-1-0	lost to #15 Oklahoma 20-21

OCTOBER 17 POLL / OCT. 22 GAMES

UP	AP	Team	Record	Result
1	1	Nebraska	7-0-0	beat Colorado 69-19
2	2	Texas	5-0-0	beat #9 SMU 15-12
3	3	North Carolina	7-0-0	bye week
4	4	West Virginia	6-0-0	lost to Penn State 23-41
5	5	Auburn	5-1-0	beat Mississippi State 28-13
6	6	Florida	5-0-1	beat East Carolina 24-17
7	7	Georgia	5-0-1	beat Kentucky 47-21
9	8	Miami, Fla.	6-1-0	beat Cincinnati 17-7
8	9	SMU	5-0-0	lost to #2 Texas 12-15
10	10	Michigan	5-1-0	beat #12 Iowa 16-13
11	11	Illinois	5-1-0	beat Purdue 35-21
12	12	Iowa	5-1-0	lost to #10 Michigan 13-16
14	13	Arizona State	4-0-1	lost to Washington State 21-31
15	14	Washington	5-1-0	beat Oregon 32-3
13	15	Maryland	5-1-0	beat Duke 38-3
17	16	Oklahoma	4-2-0	beat Iowa State 49-11
18	17	Ohio State	4-2-0	beat Michigan State 21-11
16	18	Brigham Young	5-1-0	beat San Diego State 47-12
PB	19	Arizona	5-1-1	lost to Stanford 22-31
20	20	Alabama	4-2-0	bye week
19		Pittsburgh	4-2-0	beat Navy 21-14
20		Boston College	5-1-0	bye week

OCTOBER 24 POLL / OCT. 29 GAMES

UP	AP	Team	Record	Result
1	1	Nebraska	8-0-0	beat Kansas State 51-25
2	2	Texas	6-0-0	beat Texas Tech 20-3
3	3	North Carolina	7-0-0	lost to #13 Maryland 26-28
5	4	Auburn	6-1-0	beat #5 Florida 28-21
4	5	Florida	6-0-1	lost to #4 Auburn 21-28
6	6	Georgia	6-0-1	beat Temple 31-14
7	7	Miami, Fla.	7-1-0	beat #12 West Virginia 20-3
8	8	Michigan	6-1-0	lost to #9 Illinois 6-16
9	9	Illinois	6-1-0	beat #8 Michigan 16-6
12	10	SMU	5-1-0	beat Texas A&M 10-7
11	11	Washington	6-1-0	lost to UCLA 24-27
13	12	West Virginia	6-1-0	lost to #7 Miami, Fla. 3-20
10	13	Maryland	6-1-0	beat #3 North Carolina 28-26
14	14	Oklahoma	5-2-0	beat Kansas 45-14
15	15	Brigham Young	6-1-0	beat Utah State 38-34
16	16	Ohio State	5-2-0	beat Wisconsin 45-27
17	17	Iowa	5-2-0	beat Indiana 49-3
19	18	Alabama	5-2-0	beat Mississippi State 35-18
18	19	Boston College	5-1-0	beat Penn State 27-17
	20	Notre Dame	5-2-0	beat Navy 28-12
20		Pittsburgh	5-2-0	beat Syracuse 13-10

October 31 Poll — Nov. 5 Games

UP	AP	Team	Record	Nov. 5 Games
1	1	Nebraska	9-0-0	beat Iowa State 72-29
2	2	Texas	7-0-0	beat Houston 9-3
3	3	Auburn	7-1-0	beat #7 Maryland 35-23
4	4	Georgia	7-0-1	beat #9 Florida 10-9
5	5	Miami, Fla.	8-1-0	beat East Carolina 12-7
6	6	Illinois	7-1-0	beat Minnesota 50-23
7	7	Maryland	7-1-0	lost to #3 Auburn 23-35
8	8	SMU	6-1-0	beat Rice 20-6
10	9	Florida	6-1-1	lost to #4 Georgia 9-10
9	10	North Carolina	7-1-0	lost to Clemson 3-16
11	11	Oklahoma	6-2-0	lost to Missouri 0-10
12	12	Brigham Young	7-1-0	beat #Texas-El Paso 31-9
16	13	Michigan	6-2-0	beat Purdue 42-10
15	14	Ohio State	6-2-0	beat Indiana 56-17
14	15	Iowa	6-2-0	beat Wisconsin 34-14
13	16	Boston College	6-1-0	beat Army 34-14
20	17	West Virginia	6-2-0	beat Temple 27-9
18	18	Notre Dame	6-2-0	lost to Pittsburgh 16-21
17	19	Alabama	5-2-0	beat LSU 32-26
	20	Washington	6-2-0	beat Arizona 23-22
19		West Virginia	6-2-0	beat Temple 27-9

November 7 Poll — Nov. 12 Games

UP	AP	Team	Record	Nov. 12 Games
1	1	Nebraska	10-0-0	beat Kansas 67-13
2	2	Texas	8-0-0	beat TCU 20-14
3	3	Auburn	8-1-0	beat #4 Georgia 13-7
4	4	Georgia	8-0-1	lost to #3 Auburn 7-13
6	5	Illinois	8-1-0	beat Indiana 49-21
5	6	Miami, Fla.	9-1-0	beat Florida State 17-16
7	7	SMU	7-1-0	beat Texas Tech 33-7
10	8	Brigham Young	8-1-0	beat Colorado State 24-6
8	9	Michigan	7-2-0	beat Minnesota 58-10
11	10	Ohio State	7-2-0	beat Northwestern 55-7
17	11	Maryland	7-2-0	lost to #17 Clemson 27-52
9	12	Iowa	7-2-0	beat Michigan State 12-6
12	13	Boston College	7-1-0	lost to Syracuse 10-21
13	14	Florida	6-2-1	beat Kentucky 24-7
15	15	West Virginia	7-2-0	beat Rutgers 35-7
16	16	Alabama	6-2-0	beat Southern Miss 28-16
PB	17	Clemson	7-1-1	beat #11 Maryland 52-27
20	18	Washington	7-2-0	beat Southern Cal 24-0
18	19	North Carolina	7-2-0	lost to Virginia 14-17
14	20	Pittsburgh	7-2-0	beat Army 38-7
19		Tennessee	6-2-0	lost to Mississippi 10-13

November 14 Poll — Nov. 19 Games

UP	AP	Team	Record	Nov. 19 Games
1	1	Nebraska	11-0-0	bye week
2	2	Texas	9-0-0	beat Baylor 24-21
3	3	Auburn	9-1-0	bye week
5	4	Illinois	9-1-0	beat Northwestern 56-24
4	5	Miami, Fla.	10-1-0	regular season complete
6	6	SMU	8-1-0	beat Arkansas 17-0
7	7	Georgia	8-1-1	bye week
8	8	Michigan	8-2-0	beat #10 Ohio State 24-21
9	9	Brigham Young	9-1-0	beat Utah 55-7
10	10	Ohio State	8-2-0	lost to #8 Michigan 21-24
11	11	Iowa	8-2-0	beat Minnesota 61-10
12	12	Florida	7-2-1	bye week
PB	13	Clemson	8-1-1	beat South Carolina 22-13
15	14	West Virginia	8-2-0	lost to Syracuse 16-27
14	15	Washington	8-2-0	lost to Washington State 6-17
16	16	Alabama	7-2-0	bye week
13	17	Pittsburgh	8-2-0	tied Penn State 24-24
19	18	Boston College	7-2-0	beat Holy Cross 47-7
17	19	Missouri	7-3-0	lost to Kansas 27-37
	20	Maryland	7-3-0	beat North Carolina St. 29-6
18		Baylor	7-2-1	lost to #2 Texas 21-24
20		Oklahoma	7-3-0	bye week

November 21 Poll — Nov. 26 Games

UP	AP	Team	Record	Nov. 26 Games
1	1	Nebraska	11-0-0	beat Oklahoma 28-21
2	2	Texas	10-0-0	beat Texas A&M 45-13
3	3	Auburn	9-1-0	bye week
5	4	Illinois	10-1-0	regular season complete
4	5	Miami, Fla.	10-1-0	
6	6	SMU	9-1-0	beat Houston 34-12
7	7	Georgia	8-1-1	beat Georgia Tech 27-24
8	8	Michigan	9-2-0	regular season complete
9	9	Brigham Young	10-1-0	regular season complete
10	10	Iowa	9-2-0	regular season complete
11	11	Florida	7-2-1	bye week
PB	12	Clemson	9-1-1	regular season complete
12	13	Alabama	7-2-0	lost to #15 Boston College 13-20 (N25)
13	14	Ohio State	8-3-0	regular season complete
15	15	Boston College	8-2-0	beat #13 Alabama 20-13 (N25)
14	16	Pittsburgh	8-2-1	regular season complete
17	17	Maryland	8-3-0	regular season complete
18	18	Air Force	8-3-0	bye week
	19	West Virginia	8-3-0	regular season complete
	20	East Carolina	8-3-0	regular season complete
16		Oklahoma	7-3-0	lost to #1 Nebraska 21-28
19		Baylor	7-3-1	regular season complete
20		Virginia Tech	9-2-0	regular season complete

November 28 Poll — Dec. 3 Games

UP	AP	Team	Record	Dec. 3 Games
1	1	Nebraska	12-0-0	regular season complete
2	2	Texas	11-0-0	regular season complete
3	3	Auburn	9-1-0	beat #19 Alabama 23-20
5	4	Illinois	10-1-0	
4	5	Miami, Fla.	10-1-0	
6	6	SMU	10-1-0	regular season complete
7	7	Georgia	9-1-1	regular season complete
8	8	Michigan	9-2-0	
9	9	Brigham Young	10-1-0	
10	10	Iowa	9-2-0	
PB	11	Clemson	9-1-1	
11	12	Florida	7-2-1	beat Florida State 53-14
12	13	Boston College	9-2-0	regular season complete
13	14	Ohio State	8-3-0	
14	15	Pittsburgh	8-2-1	
15	16	Maryland	8-3-0	
16	17	Air Force	8-2-0	beat San Diego State 38-7
19	18	West Virginia	8-3-0	
	19	Alabama	7-3-0	lost to #3 Auburn 20-23
	20	East Carolina	8-3-0	
17		Baylor	7-3-1	regular season complete
18		Virginia Tech	9-2-0	regular season complete
20		Oklahoma	7-4-0	beat Hawaii 21-17

December 5 Poll / Bowls / January 3 Final Poll

UP	AP	December 5 Poll	Record	Bowl Bid	Date	Bowl Result	RB	UP	AP	January 3 Final Poll	Record
1	1	Nebraska	12-0-0	Orange Bowl	J2	lost to #5 Miami, Fla. 30-31	4	1	1	Miami, Fla.	11-1-0
2	2	Texas	11-0-0	Cotton Bowl	J2	lost to #7 Georgia 9-10	5	2	2	Nebraska	12-1-0
3	3	Auburn	10-1-0	Sugar Bowl	J2	beat #8 Michigan 9-7	1	3	3	Auburn	11-1-0
5	4	Illinois	10-1-0	Rose Bowl	J2	lost to UCLA 9-45	2	4	4	Georgia	10-1-1
4	5	Miami, Fla.	10-1-0	Orange Bowl	J2	beat #1 Nebraska 31-30	3	5	5	Texas	11-1-0
6	6	SMU	10-1-0	Sun Bowl	D24	lost to Alabama 7-28	7	6	6	Florida	9-2-1
7	7	Georgia	9-1-1	Cotton Bowl	J2	beat #2 Texas 10-9	9	7	7	Brigham Young	11-1-0
8	8	Michigan	9-2-0	Sugar Bowl	J2	lost to #3 Auburn 7-9	21	9	8	Michigan	9-3-0
9	9	Brigham Young	10-1-0	Holiday Bowl	D23	beat Missouri 21-17	13	8	9	Ohio State	9-3-0
10	10	Iowa	9-2-0	Gator Bowl	D30	lost to #11 Florida 6-14	11	10	10	Illinois	10-2-0
11	11	Florida	8-2-1	Gator Bowl	D30	beat #10 Iowa 14-6	6	PB	11	Clemson	9-1-1
PB	12	Clemson	9-1-1				8	11	12	SMU	10-2-0
12	13	Boston College	9-2-0	Liberty Bowl	D29	lost to Notre Dame 18-19	23	15	13	Air Force	10-2-0
13	14	Ohio State	8-3-0	Fiesta Bowl	J2	beat #15 Pittsburgh 28-23	22	14	14	Iowa	9-3-0
14	15	Pittsburgh	8-2-1	Fiesta Bowl	J2	lost to #14 Ohio State 23-28	24	12	15	Alabama	8-4-0
16	16	Air Force	9-2-0	Independence Bowl	D10	beat Mississippi 9-3	12	16	16	West Virginia	9-3-0
15	17	Maryland	8-3-0	Citrus Bowl	D27	lost to Tennessee 23-30	20	13	17	UCLA	7-4-1
19	18	West Virginia	8-3-0	Hall of Fame Classic	D22	beat Kentucky 20-16	15	19	18	Pittsburgh	8-3-1
	19	East Carolina	8-3-0				30	20	19	Boston College	9-3-0
17	20	Baylor	7-3-1	Bluebonnet Bowl	D31	lost to Oklahoma State 14-24	36		20	East Carolina	8-3-0
20	20	Oklahoma	8-4-0				10	17		Penn State	8-4-1
18		Virginia Tech	9-2-0				34	18		Oklahoma State	8-4-0

ANNUAL REVIEW

1983

CONSENSUS ALL-AMERICANS

POS	OFFENSE	HT	WT	School	AP	CF	FC	FW	PI
QB	Steve Young	6-1	198	Brigham Young	•	•	•	•	•
RB	Mike Rozier	5-11	210	Nebraska	•	•	•	•	•
RB	Bo Jackson	6-1	222	Auburn	•		•	•	•
RB	Greg Allen	6-0	200	Florida State	•				
RB	Napoleon McCallum	6-2	208	Navy		•		•	
WR	Irving Fryar	6-0	200	Nebraska	•	•	•	•	•
TE	Gordon Hudson	6-4	231	Brigham Young	•	•	•	•	•
L	Bill Fralic	6-5	270	Pittsburgh	•	•	•	•	•
L	Terry Long	6-0	280	East Carolina	•	•	•	•	
L	Dean Steinkuhler	6-3	270	Nebraska	•	•	•	•	•
L	Doug Dawson	6-3	263	Texas	•	•	•	•	
C	Tony Slaton	6-4	260	Southern Cal		•	•	•	
PK	Luis Zendejas	5-9	186	Arizona State		•		•	

	OTHERS RECEIVING FIRST-TEAM HONORS								
WR	Gerald McNeil			Baylor	•			•	
L	Stefan Humphries			Michigan			•	•	•
L	Brian Blados			North Carolina	•				
L	Conrad Goode			Missouri					•
C	Tom Dixon			Michigan	•			•	
PK	Bruce Kallmeyer			Kansas			•		

POS	DEFENSE	HT	WT	School	AP	CF	FC	FW	PI
L	Rick Bryan	6-4	260	Oklahoma	•	•	•	•	•
L	Reggie White	6-5	264	Tennessee	•	•	•	•	•
L	William Perry	6-3	320	Clemson	•	•	•	•	•
L	William Fuller	6-4	250	North Carolina	•		•	•	
LB	Ricky Hunley	6-2	230	Arizona	•	•	•	•	•
LB	Wilber Marshall	6-1	230	Florida	•	•	•	•	•
LB	Ron Rivera	6-3	225	California	•	•	•	•	•
LB	Jeff Leiding	6-4	240	Texas	•	•	•	•	
DB	Russell Carter	6-3	193	SMU	•	•	•	•	•
DB	Jerry Gray	6-1	183	Texas	•	•	•	•	•
DB	Terry Hoage	6-3	196	Georgia	•		•	•	•
DB	Don Rogers	6-2	208	UCLA	•	•	•	•	
P	Jack Weil	5-11	171	Wyoming				•	

	OTHERS RECEIVING FIRST-TEAM HONORS								
L	Don Thorp			Illinois			•		
L	Bruce Smith			Virginia Tech			•		
L	Freddie Gilbert			Georgia				•	
L	Ron Faurot			Arkansas				•	
LB	Chip Banks			Southern Cal	•	•			
DB	Mossy Cade			Texas	•	•			
P	Jim Colquitt			Tennessee					•
P	Randall Cunningham			UNLV				•	

AP named Marshall as DL

HEISMAN TROPHY VOTING

	PLAYER	POS	SCHOOL	1ST	2ND	3RD	TOTAL
1	Mike Rozier	RB	Nebraska	482	154	47	1801
2	Steve Young	QB	Brigham Young	153	312	89	1172
3	Doug Flutie	QB	Boston College	23	38	108	253
4	Turner Gill	QB	Nebraska	11	41	75	190
5	Terry Hoage	DB	Georgia	7	25	41	112
6	Napoleon McCallum	HB	Navy	6	18	50	104
7	Jeff Hostetler	QB	West Virginia	5	17	22	71
8	Bill Fralic	OT	Pittsburgh	6	10	28	66
9	Walter Lewis	QB	Alabama	4	13	16	54
10	Boomer Esiason	QB	Maryland	4	11	17	51

AWARD WINNERS

PLAYER	POS	SCHOOL	AWARD NAME
Mike Rozier	RB	Nebraska	Maxwell
Dean Steinkuhler	G	Nebraska	Outland
Mike Rozier	RB	Nebraska	Camp
Dean Steinkuhler	G	Nebraska	Lombardi
Steve Young	QB	Brigham Young	O'Brien

CONFERENCE STANDINGS

ACC

	Conf. W L T			Overall W L T		
Maryland	6	0	0	9	3	0
Clemson	5	2	0	7	4	0
Georgia Tech	3	2	1	6	4	1
Virginia	3	2	2	8	2	2
North Carolina	3	3	1	5	5	1
Wake Forest	3	4	0	6	5	0
North Carolina St.	1	6	0	3	8	0
Duke	1	6	0	2	9	0

Big 10

	Conf. W L T			Overall W L T		
Ohio State	7	2	0	9	3	0
Illinois	6	3	0	7	4	0
Purdue	6	3	0	7	5	0
Iowa	5	3	1	8	4	1
Wisconsin	5	3	1	7	4	1
Michigan State	5	4	0	6	6	0
Michigan	5	4	0	6	6	0
Minnesota	3	6	0	4	7	0
Northwestern	2	7	0	2	9	0
Indiana	0	9	0	0	11	0

Big 8

	Conf. W L T			Overall W L T		
Nebraska	6	1	0	10	2	0
Oklahoma	6	1	0	9	2	1
Oklahoma State	5	2	0	10	2	0
Kansas	4	3	0	5	6	0
Kansas State	2	4	1	3	7	1
Missouri	2	4	1	3	7	1
Colorado	1	6	0	1	10	0
Iowa State	0	5	2	2	7	2

Big West

	Conf. W L T			Overall W L T		
Nevada-Las Vegas	7	0	0	11	2	0
Cal-St. Fullerton	6	1	0	11	1	0
San Jose State	5	2	0	6	5	0
Fresno State	3	4	0	6	6	0
Long Beach State	3	4	0	4	7	0
Pacific	2	5	0	4	7	0
Utah State	1	5	0	1	10	0
New Mexico State	0	6	0	2	9	0

Ivy

	Conf. W L T			Overall W L T		
Pennsylvania	7	0	0	8	1	0
Yale	5	2	0	6	3	0
Harvard	5	2	0	5	4	0
Brown	4	3	0	4	5	0
Princeton	3	4	0	4	5	0
Cornell	2	5	0	2	7	0
Dartmouth	2	5	0	2	7	0
Columbia	0	7	0	0	9	0

MAC

	Conf. W L T			Overall W L T		
Toledo	7	1	1	8	3	1
Bowling Green	7	2	0	8	3	0
Central Michigan	6	2	1	8	2	1
Ohio U	4	4	1	4	6	1
Northern Illinois	3	5	1	4	6	1
Miami, Ohio	3	5	0	4	7	0
Ball State	3	5	0	3	8	0
Western Michigan	3	6	0	5	6	0
Kent State	3	6	0	4	7	0
Eastern Michigan	2	5	2	2	7	2

Pac 10

	Conf. W L T			Overall W L T		
Southern Cal	7	1	0	9	3	0
Washington	6	1	0	11	1	0
UCLA	5	2	0	9	3	0
Arizona	5	2	0	7	4	0
Washington State	4	3	0	6	5	0
Arizona State	3	4	0	5	6	0
Oregon	3	5	0	6	5	0
Stanford	3	5	0	5	6	0
Oregon State	1	7	0	2	9	0
California	1	8	0	2	9	0
UCLA	3	4	0	5	6	0
Washington State	2	6	0	3	8	0
Oregon State	1	7	0	1	10	0

SEC

	Conf. W L T			Overall W L T		
Florida	5	0	1	9	1	1
LSU	4	1	1	8	3	1
Auburn	4	2	0	9	4	0
Georgia	4	2	0	7	4	1
Kentucky	3	3	0	9	3	0
Tennessee	3	3	0	7	4	1
Vanderbilt	2	4	0	5	6	0
Alabama	2	4	0	5	6	0
Mississippi	1	5	0	4	6	1
Mississippi State	1	5	0	4	7	0

SWC

	Conf. W L T			Overall W L T		
SMU	6	2	0	10	2	0
Houston	6	2	0	7	5	0
TCU	5	3	0	8	4	0
Texas	5	3	0	7	4	1
Arkansas	5	3	0	7	4	1
Baylor	4	4	0	5	6	0
Texas A&M	3	5	0	6	5	0
Texas Tech	2	6	0	4	7	0
Rice	0	8	0	1	10	0

WAC

	Conf. W L T			Overall W L T		
Brigham Young	8	0	0	13	0	0
Hawaii	5	2	0	7	4	0
Air Force	4	3	0	8	4	0
Utah	4	3	1	6	5	1
San Diego State	4	3	1	4	7	1
Wyoming	4	4	0	6	6	0
Colorado State	3	5	0	3	8	0
New Mexico	1	7	0	4	8	0
Texas-El Paso	1	7	0	2	9	0

Independents

	Overall W L T		
South Carolina	10	2	0
Boston College	10	2	0
Army	8	3	1
Rutgers	7	3	0
West Virginia	8	4	0
Virginia Tech	8	4	0
Florida State	7	3	2
Miami, Fla.	8	5	0
Notre Dame	7	5	0
Syracuse	6	5	0
Temple	6	5	0
Penn State	6	5	0
La. Lafayette	6	5	0
Memphis	5	5	1
Navy	4	6	1
Southern Miss	4	7	0
Pittsburgh	3	7	1
Tulane	3	8	0
East Carolina	2	9	0
Louisville	2	9	0
Cincinnati	2	9	0

BOWL GAMES

DATE	GAME	SCORE
D10	Independence	Air Force 9, Mississippi 3
D17	California	No. Illinois 20, Cal St.-Fullerton 13
D17	Florida Citrus	Tennessee 30, Maryland 23
D22	All-American	West Virginia 20, Kentucky 16
D23	Holiday	Brigham Young 21, Missouri 17
D24	Sun	Alabama 28, SMU 7
D26	Aloha	Penn State 13, Washington 10
D29	Liberty	Notre Dame 19, Boston College 18
D30	Gator	Florida 14, Iowa 6
D30	Peach	Florida State 28, North Carolina 3
D31	Bluebonnet	Oklahoma State 24, Baylor 14
J2	Sugar	Auburn 9, Michigan 7
J2	Cotton	Georgia 10, Texas 9
J2	Orange	Miami, Fla. 31, Nebraska 30
J2	Fiesta	Ohio State 28, Pittsburgh 23
J2	Rose	UCLA 45, Illinois 9

1983 ANNUAL REVIEW 1347

1983 NCAA Major College Statistical Leaders

Individual Leaders

Passing

		CL	G	ATT	COM	PCT	INT	I%	YDS	YPA	TD	TD%	RATING
1	Steve Young, Brigham Young	SR	11	429	306	71.3	10	2.3	3902	9.1	33	7.7	168.5
2	Chuck Long, Iowa	JR	10	236	144	61.0	8	3.4	2434	10.3	14	5.9	160.4
3	Mike Eppley, Clemson	JR	11	166	99	59.6	9	5.4	1410	8.5	13	7.8	146.0
4	Cody Carlson, Baylor	FR	11	180	98	54.4	7	3.9	1617	9.0	12	6.7	144.1
5	Rick Neuheisel, UCLA	SR	11	236	163	69.1	10	4.2	1947	8.3	9	3.8	142.5
6	Randall Cunningham, Nevada-Las Vegas	JR	11	316	189	59.8	8	2.5	2545	8.1	18	5.7	141.2
7	Marlon Adler, Missouri	JR	11	175	102	58.3	13	7.4	1603	9.2	11	6.3	141.1
8	Brad Baumberger, Wyoming	SR	12	189	112	59.3	7	3.7	1551	8.2	10	5.3	138.2
9	Jack Trudeau, Illinois	SO	11	324	203	62.7	13	4.0	2446	7.6	18	5.6	136.4
10	Raphel Cherry, Hawaii	JR	11	299	170	56.9	15	5.0	2478	8.3	18	6.0	136.3

All-Purpose

		CL	G	RUSH	REC	PR	KR	YDS	YPG
1	Napoleon McCallum, Navy	JR	11	1587	166	272	360	2385	216.8
2	Mike Rozier, Nebraska	SR	12	2148	106	0	232	2486	207.2
3	Shawn Faulkner, Western Michigan	SR	11	1668	221	0	0	1889	171.7
4	Curtis Adams, Central Michigan	JR	11	1431	86	0	234	1751	159.2
5	Jim Sandusky, San Diego State	SR	12	-15	1171	381	340	1877	156.4
6	Allen Pinkett, Notre Dame	SO	11	1394	288	0	0	1682	152.9
7	Ricky Edwards, Northwestern	SR	11	561	570	0	523	1654	150.4
8	Steve Bartalo, Colorado State	FR	10	1113	284	0	0	1397	139.7
9	Keith Byars, Ohio State	SO	11	1126	338	0	37	1501	136.5
10	Mike Grayson, Duke	SR	11	785	582	110	22	1499	136.3

Rushing/Yards Per Game

		CL	G	ATT	YDS	TD	AVG	YPG
1	Mike Rozier, Nebraska	SR	12	275	2148	29	7.8	179.0
2	Shawn Faulkner, Western Michigan	SR	11	394	1668	7	4.2	151.6
3	Napoleon McCallum, Navy	JR	11	331	1587	10	4.8	144.3
4	Curtis Adams, Central Michigan	JR	11	267	1431	15	5.4	130.1
5	Allen Pinkett, Notre Dame	SO	11	252	1394	16	5.5	126.7
6	Kirby Warren, Pacific	SR	12	304	1423	12	4.7	118.6
7	Reggie Dupard, SMU	SO	11	197	1249	9	6.3	113.5
8	Johnnie Jones, Tennessee	JR	10	191	1116	5	5.8	111.6
9	Steve Bartalo, Colorado State	FR	10	292	1113	8	3.8	111.3
10	Bo Jackson, Auburn	SO	11	158	1213	12	7.7	110.3

Rushing/Yards Per Carry

		CL	G	ATT	YDS	YPC
1	Mike Rozier, Nebraska	SR	12	275	2148	7.8
2	Bo Jackson, Auburn	SO	11	158	1213	7.7
3	Earl Johnson, Oklahoma	FR	10	148	945	6.4
4	Reggie Dupard, SMU	SO	11	197	1249	6.3
5	Eric Denson, Wichita State	SO	10	163	1017	6.2
6	Jeff Atkins, SMU	FR	11	154	937	6.1
7	Johnnie Jones, Tennessee	JR	10	191	1116	5.8
8	Tyrone Anthony, North Carolina	SR	11	184	1063	5.8
9	D.J. Dozier, Penn State	FR	12	174	1002	5.8
10	Ricky Moore, Alabama	JR	11	166	947	5.7

*-Based on top 30 rushers

Receiving

		CL	G	REC	YDS	TD	YPR	YPG	RPG
1	Keith Edwards, Vanderbilt	JR	11	97	909	0	9.4	82.6	8.8
2	Ricky Edwards, Northwestern	SR	11	83	570	0	6.9	51.8	7.5
3	Tracy Henderson, Iowa State	SO	11	81	1051	8	13.0	95.5	7.4
4	Chuck Scott, Vanderbilt	JR	11	70	971	9	13.9	88.3	6.4
4	Mark Dowdell, Bowling Green	JR	11	70	679	5	9.7	61.7	6.4
6	Ed Washington, Ohio	SR	11	68	866	5	12.7	78.8	6.2
7	Brian Brennan, Boston College	SR	11	67	1168	8	17.4	106.2	6.1
7	Mike Leuck, Ball State	JR	11	67	667	4	10.0	60.6	6.1
9	Mike Grayson, Duke	SR	11	66	582	2	8.8	52.9	6.0
10	Dave Naumcheff, Ball State	SR	11	65	1065	6	16.4	96.8	5.9

Punting

		CL	PUNT	YDS	AVG
1	Jack Weil, Wyoming	SR	52	2371	45.6
2	Mike Saxon, San Diego State	SR	57	2594	45.5
3	Harry Newsome, Wake Forest	JR	42	1911	45.5
4	Kip Shenefelt, Temple	SO	65	2860	44.0
5	Ralf Mojsiejenko, Michigan State	JR	74	3249	43.9
6	John Teltschik, Texas	SO	63	2753	43.7
7	Dale Hatcher, Clemson	JR	47	2049	43.6
8	Randall Cunningham, Nevada-Las Vegas	JR	56	2436	43.5
9	John Tolish, Duke	JR	53	2300	43.4
10	Paul Calhoun, Kentucky	JR	69	2981	43.2

Punt Returns

		CL	PR	YDS	TD	AVG
1	Jim Sandusky, San Diego State	SR	20	381	1	19.0
2	Tim Gordon, Tulsa	FR	11	171	1	15.5
3	Tim Moffett, Mississippi	JR	17	238	1	14.0
4	Jeff Smith, Nebraska	JR	19	264	1	13.9
5	Leonard Harris, Texas Tech	SR	26	346	1	13.3
6	Norman Jefferson, LSU	FR	18	238	1	13.2
7	Jerry Dunlap, South Carolina	FR	27	354	0	13.1
8	Napoleon McCallum, Navy	JR	21	272	0	13.0
9	Lew Barnes, Oregon	JR	25	323	1	12.9
10	Ed Koban, Syracuse	SR	18	224	0	12.4

Kickoff Returns

		CL	KR	YDS	TD	AVG
1	Henry Williams, East Carolina	JR	19	591	2	31.1
2	Cory Collier, Georgia Tech	FR	12	360	0	30.0
3	Randall Morris, Tennessee	SR	15	447	0	29.8
4	Tim Golden, Long Beach State	SR	15	424	1	28.3
5	Roy Lewis, Cal St. Fullerton	JR	25	690	0	27.6
6	Tony Mayes, Kentucky	FR	14	375	0	26.8
7	Eddie Harris, Toledo	SO	11	290	0	26.4
8	Malcolm Pittman, Virginia	JR	20	486	0	24.3
9	Reggie Sutton, Miami, Fla.	FR	14	332	0	23.7
10	Terrell Smith, Ball State	JR	22	519	0	23.6

Scoring

		CL	TDS	XPT	FG	PTS	PTPG
1	Mike Rozier, Nebraska	SR	29	0	0	174	14.5
2	Keith Byars, Ohio State	SO	20	0	0	120	10.9
3	Luis Zendejas, Arizona State	JR	0	28	28	112	10.2
4	Allen Pinkett, Notre Dame	SO	18	2	0	110	10.0
5	Max Zendejas, Arizona	SO	0	39	20	99	9.0
6	Bruce Kallmeyer, Kansas	SR	0	26	24	98	8.9
7	Curtis Adams, Central Michigan	JR	16	0	0	96	8.7
7	Marty Louthan, Air Force	SR	16	0	0	96	8.7
9	Paul Woodside, West Virginia	JR	0	35	19	92	8.4
10	Bob Bergeron, Michigan	SR	0	30	15	75	8.3

Field Goals

		CL	FGA	FGM	PCT	FGG
1	Luis Zendejas, Arizona State	JR	37	28	0.76	2.55
2	Bruce Kallmeyer, Kansas	SR	29	24	0.83	2.18
3	Randy Pratt, California	SR	27	22	0.82	2.00
4	Jose Oceguera, Long Beach State	JR	29	22	0.76	1.83
5	Bobby Raymond, Florida	JR	23	20	0.87	1.82
5	Max Zendejas, Arizona	SO	25	20	0.80	1.82
5	Jeff Jaeger, Washington	FR	26	20	0.77	1.82
8	Paul Woodside, West Virginia	JR	23	19	0.83	1.73
9	Bob Bergeron, Michigan	SR	17	15	0.88	1.67
10	Bob Pauling, Clemson	SR	20	18	0.90	1.64
10	Rocky Costello, Fresno State	SR	22	18	0.82	1.64
10	Kevin Butler, Georgia	JR	23	18	0.78	1.64
10	Larry Roach, Oklahoma State	JR	26	18	0.69	1.64
10	Alan Smith, Texas A&M	JR	26	18	0.69	1.64

Interceptions

		CL	INT	YDS	TD	INT/GM
1	Martin Bayless, Bowling Green	SR	10	64	0	0.91
2	Mark Brandon, Toledo	JR	9	66	1	0.82
3	Jim Bowman, Central Michigan	JR	8	87	1	0.73
4	Les Miller, Cal-St. Fullerton	JR	7	233	2	0.70
4	Russell Carter, SMU	JR	7	40	0	0.70
6	Scott Case, Oklahoma	SR	8	110	1	0.67
7	Phil Parker, Michigan State	JR	7	203	1	0.64
7	Ricky Hunley, Arizona	SR	7	123	2	0.64
7	Sherman Cocroft, San Jose State	SR	7	76	0	0.64
7	Kevin Young, Ball State	JR	7	72	0	0.64
7	Kirk Perry, Louisville	JR	7	69	0	0.64
7	Mark Collins, Cal-St. Fullerton	SO	7	52	0	0.64
7	Adam Hinds, Oklahoma State	JR	7	37	0	0.64
7	Clarence Baldwin, Maryland	SR	7	5	0	0.64

Team Leaders

Rushing Offense

		G	ATT	YDS	AVG	TD	YPG
1	Nebraska	12	724	4820	6.7	66	401.7
2	Air Force	11	650	3811	5.9	43	346.5
3	Auburn	11	600	3231	5.4	28	293.7
4	Virginia Tech	11	615	3069	5.0	27	279.0
5	Tulsa	11	598	3052	5.1	28	277.5
6	Central Michigan	11	591	3048	5.2	24	277.1
7	North Carolina	11	600	3046	5.1	24	276.9
8	Michigan	11	614	3042	5.0	28	276.5
9	Oklahoma	12	667	3251	4.9	30	270.9
10	Wyoming	12	711	3239	4.6	33	269.9

Passing Offense

		G	ATT	COM	INT	PCT	YDS	YPA	TD	I%	YPC	YPG
1	Brigham Young	11	458	324	11	70.7	4193	9.2	37	2.4	12.9	381.2
2	Bowling Green	11	480	305	17	63.5	3320	6.9	16	3.5	10.9	301.8
3	Vanderbilt	11	519	296	31	57.0	3299	6.4	14	6.0	11.1	299.9
4	Kansas	11	407	216	24	53.1	3146	7.7	16	5.9	14.6	286.0
5	Duke	11	480	305	13	63.5	3132	6.5	17	2.7	10.3	284.7
6	Colorado State	12	444	280	20	63.1	3373	7.6	12	4.5	12.0	281.1
7	Iowa	11	315	181	10	57.5	3072	9.8	20	3.2	17.0	279.3
8	California	11	416	234	22	56.2	3057	7.3	14	5.3	13.1	277.9
9	Boston College	11	385	198	18	51.4	2942	7.6	18	4.7	14.9	267.5
10	Stanford	11	420	210	24	50.0	2802	6.7	15	5.7	13.3	254.7

Total Offense

		G	P	YDS	AVG	TD	YPG
1	Brigham Young	11	865	6426	7.4	65	584.2
2	Nebraska	12	916	6560	7.2	84	546.7
3	Iowa	11	807	5366	6.6	48	487.8
4	Air Force	11	776	5039	6.5	46	458.1
5	Boston College	11	832	4928	5.9	44	448.0
6	Florida State	11	831	4889	5.9	47	444.5
7	North Carolina	11	865	4860	5.6	41	441.8
8	Utah	11	830	4721	5.7	40	429.2
9	Notre Dame	11	799	4713	5.9	37	428.5
10	Alabama	11	823	4665	5.7	37	424.1

Rushing Defense

		G	ATT	YDS	AVG	TD	YPG
1	Virginia Tech	11	367	763	2.1	4	69.4
2	Illinois	11	422	1034	2.5	5	94.0
3	Michigan	11	360	1051	2.9	5	95.5
4	Texas	11	452	1054	2.3	5	95.8
5	Missouri	11	401	1075	2.7	6	97.7
6	Arizona	11	401	1081	2.7	8	98.3
7	West Virginia	11	401	1099	2.7	10	99.9
8	Oklahoma State	11	437	1122	2.6	5	102.0
9	SMU	11	469	1130	2.4	4	102.7
10	Toledo	11	437	1142	2.6	10	103.8

Passing Defense

		G	ATT	COM	PCT	YPC	INT	I%	YDS	YPA	TD	YPG
1	Ohio	11	221	112	50.7	11.3	7	3.2	1268	5.7	5	115.3
2	Texas	11	259	104	40.2	12.3	13	5.0	1278	4.9	5	116.2
3	La. Lafayette	10	205	93	45.4	12.8	11	5.4	1190	5.8	11	119.0
4	TCU	11	208	90	43.3	15.1	11	5.3	1362	6.5	11	123.8
5	Texas A&M	11	228	110	48.2	12.7	9	3.9	1402	6.1	10	127.5
6	Southern Miss	11	267	131	49.1	11.3	14	5.2	1481	5.5	7	134.6
7	Army	11	250	130	52.0	12.0	7	2.8	1566	6.3	12	142.4
8	Wake Forest	11	267	142	53.2	11.1	11	4.1	1580	5.9	7	143.6
9	Eastern Michigan	11	238	138	58.0	11.6	9	3.8	1603	6.7	10	145.7
10	Wisconsin	11	290	140	48.3	11.8	21	7.2	1656	5.7	13	150.5

Total Defense

		G	P	YDS	AVG	TD	YPG
1	Texas	11	711	2332	3.3	10	212.0
2	SMU	11	764	2817	3.7	11	256.1
2	Virginia Tech	11	751	2817	3.8	10	256.1
4	Miami, Fla.	11	770	2853	3.7	12	259.4
5	Michigan	11	683	2937	4.3	17	267.0
6	Southern Miss	11	768	2981	3.9	14	271.0
7	Oklahoma	12	847	3322	3.9	28	276.8
8	Pittsburgh	11	736	3067	4.2	14	278.8
9	Tennessee	11	756	3069	4.1	13	279.0
10	West Virginia	11	745	3105	4.2	18	282.3

Scoring Offense

		G	PTS	AVG
1	Nebraska	12	624	52.0
2	Brigham Young	11	484	44.0
3	Ohio State	11	382	34.7
4	Iowa	11	374	34.0
5	Wisconsin	11	359	32.6
6	Air Force	11	358	32.5
7	Florida State	11	353	32.1
7	Arizona	11	353	32.1
9	Michigan	11	348	31.6
10	Alabama	11	338	30.7
10	Clemson	11	338	30.7
10	Illinois	11	338	30.7

Scoring Defense

		G	PTS	AVG
1	Virginia Tech	11	91	8.3
2	Texas	11	104	9.5
3	Miami, Fla.	11	106	9.6
4	SMU	11	109	9.9
5	Southern Miss	11	128	11.6
6	Central Michigan	11	136	12.4
7	Pittsburgh	11	137	12.5
8	Tennessee	11	142	12.9
9	Oklahoma State	11	148	13.5
10	Georgia	11	149	13.5

ANNUAL REVIEW

1984 POLL PROGRESSION

PRE-SEASON 1984 / SEPT. 1 GAMES

UP	AP	Team	Record	Result
1	1	Auburn	0-0-0	lost to Miami, Fla. 18-20 (A27)
2	2	Nebraska	0-0-0	bye week
7	3	Pittsburgh	0-0-0	lost to Brigham Young 14-20
8	4	Clemson	0-0-0	beat Appalachian St. 40-7
5	5	UCLA	0-0-0	bye week
3	6	Texas	0-0-0	bye week
9	7	Ohio State	0-0-0	bye week
15	8	Notre Dame	0-0-0	bye week
12	9	Alabama	0-0-0	bye week
4	10	Miami, Fla.	0-0-0	beat # 17 Florida 32-20
6	11	Penn State	0-0-0	bye week
14	12	Iowa	0-0-0	bye week
13	13	Arizona State	0-0-0	bye week
10	14	Michigan	0-0-0	bye week
16	15	SMU	0-0-0	bye week
11	16	Oklahoma	0-0-0	bye week
18	17	Florida	0-0-0	lost to # 10 Miami, Fla. 20-32
17	18	Washington	0-0-0	bye week
20	19	Boston College	0-0-0	beat Western Carolina 44-24
	20	Florida State	0-0-0	beat East Carolina 48-17
19		Georgia	0-0-0	bye week

SEPTEMBER 3 POLL / SEPT. 8 GAMES

UP	AP	Team	Record	Result
1	1	Miami, Fla.	2-0-0	lost to # 14 Michigan 14-22
2	2	Nebraska	0-0-0	beat Wyoming 42-7
5	3	Clemson	1-0-0	beat Virginia 55-0
4	4	UCLA	0-0-0	beat San Diego State 18-15
3	5	Texas	0-0-0	bye week
	6	Ohio State	0-0-0	Oregon State 22-14
15	7	Notre Dame	0-0-0	lost to Purdue 21-23
6	8	Auburn	0-1-0	bye week
	9	Alabama	0-0-0	lost to # 18 Boston College 31-38
14	10	Iowa	0-0-0	beat Iowa State 59-21
7	11	Penn State	0-0-0	beat Rutgers 15-12
12	12	Arizona State	0-0-0	lost to Oklahoma State 3-45
13	13	Brigham Young	1-0-0	beat Baylor 47-13
9	14	Michigan	0-0-0	beat # 1 Miami, Fla. 22-14
	15	SMU	0-0-0	bye week
10	16	Oklahoma	0-0-0	beat Stanford 19-7
20	17	Pittsburgh	0-0-0	bye week
16	18	Boston College	1-0-0	beat # 9 Alabama 38-31
18	19	Washington	0-0-0	beat Northwestern 26-0
19	20	Florida State	1-0-0	bye week

SEPTEMBER 10 POLL / SEPT. 15 GAMES

UP	AP	Team	Record	Result
1	1	Nebraska	1-0-0	beat Minnesota 38-7
4	2	Clemson	2-0-0	bye week
2	3	Michigan	1-0-0	lost to Washington 11-20
3	4	Texas	0-0-0	beat # 11 Auburn 35-27
5	5	Iowa	1-0-0	lost to # 12 Penn State 17-20
8	6	Miami, Fla.	2-1-0	beat Purdue 28-17
7	7	UCLA	1-0-0	beat Long Beach State 23-17
6	8	Brigham Young	2-0-0	beat Tulsa 38-15
11	9	Ohio State	1-0-0	beat Washington State 44-0
9	10	Boston College	2-0-0	bye week
10	11	Auburn	0-1-0	lost to # 4 Texas 27-35
13	12	Penn State	1-0-0	beat # 5 Iowa 20-17
14	13	Oklahoma State	1-0-0	beat Bowling Green 31-14
15	14	SMU	0-0-0	beat Louisville 41-7
12	15	Oklahoma	1-0-0	beat # 17 Pittsburgh 42-10
16	16	Washington	1-0-0	beat Michigan 20-11
	17	Pittsburgh	1-0-0	lost to # 15 Oklahoma 10-42
17	18	Florida State	1-0-0	beat Kansas 42-16
20	19	Alabama	0-1-0	lost to Georgia Tech 6-16
18	20	Southern Cal	1-0-0	bye week
19		Georgia	1-0-0	bye week

SEPTEMBER 17 POLL / SEPT. 22 GAMES

UP	AP	Team	Record	Result
1	1	Nebraska	2-0-0	beat # 8 UCLA 42-3
PB	2	Clemson	2-0-0	lost to # 20 Georgia 23-26
2	3	Texas	1-0-0	bye week
9	4	Miami, Fla.	3-1-0	lost to # 15 Florida State 3-38
6	5	Ohio State	2-0-0	beat I# 14 Iowa 45-26
4	6	Brigham Young	3-0-0	beat Hawaii 18-13
5	7	Penn State	2-0-0	beat William & Mary 56-18
10	8	UCLA	2-0-0	lost to # 1 Nebraska 3-42
8	9	Washington	2-0-0	beat Houston 35-7
7	10	Boston College	2-0-0	beat North Carolina 52-20
3	11	Oklahoma	2-0-0	beat Baylor 34-15
11	12	Oklahoma State	2-0-0	beat San Diego State 19-16
12	13	SMU	1-0-0	beat North Texas 24-6
15	14	Iowa	1-1-0	lost to # 5 Ohio State 26-45
13	15	Florida State	2-0-0	beat # 4 Miami, Fla. 38-3
14	16	Michigan	1-1-0	beat Wisconsin 20-14
16	17	Southern Cal	1-0-0	beat Arizona State 6-3
18	18	West Virginia	3-0-0	lost to Maryland 17-20
20	19	Auburn	0-2-0	beat Southern Miss 35-12
17	20	Georgia	1-0-0	beat # 2 Clemson 26-23
19		Tennessee	2-0-0	tied Army 24-24

SEPTEMBER 24 POLL / SEPT. 29 GAMES

UP	AP	Team	Record	Result
1	1	Nebraska	3-0-0	lost to Syracuse 9-17
2	2	Texas	1-0-0	beat # 4 Penn State 28-3
3	3	Ohio State	3-0-0	beat Minnesota 35-22
6	4	Penn State	3-0-0	lost to # 2 Texas 3-28
7	5	Boston College	3-0-0	bye week
5	6	Washington	3-0-0	beat Miami, Ohio 53-7
4	7	Oklahoma	3-0-0	beat Kansas State 24-6
8	8	Brigham Young	4-0-0	bye week
9	9	Florida State	3-0-0	beat Temple 44-27
11	10	Oklahoma State	3-0-0	beat Tulsa 31-7
12	11	SMU	2-0-0	beat TCU 26-17
10	12	Georgia	2-0-0	lost to South Carolina 10-17
PB	13	Clemson	2-1-0	lost to # 18 Georgia Tech 21-28
13	14	Michigan	2-0-0	beat Indiana 14-6
14	15	Southern Cal	2-0-0	lost to LSU 3-23
16	16	Miami, Fla.	3-2-0	beat Rice 38-3
17	17	UCLA	2-0-0	beat Colorado 33-16
	18	Georgia Tech	2-0-0	beat # 13 Clemson 28-21
17	19	Notre Dame	2-1-0	beat Missouri 16-14
19	20	Auburn	1-2-0	beat Tennessee 29-10
18		LSU	2-0-1	beat # 15 Southern Cal 23-3
20		Iowa	1-2-0	beat Illinois 21-16

OCTOBER 1 POLL / OCT. 6 GAMES

UP	AP	Team	Record	Result
1	1	Texas	2-0-0	beat Rice 38-13
2	2	Ohio State	4-0-0	lost to Purdue 23-28
4	3	Washington	4-0-0	beat Oregon State 19-7
5	4	Boston College	3-0-0	bye week
3	5	Oklahoma	4-0-0	bye week
7	6	Florida State	4-0-0	tied Memphis 17-17
6	7	Brigham Young	4-0-0	beat Colorado State 52-9
9	8	Nebraska	3-1-0	beat # 9 Oklahoma 17-3
8	9	Oklahoma State	4-0-0	lost to # 8 Nebraska 3-17
10	10	SMU	3-0-0	bye week
14	11	Penn State	3-1-0	beat Maryland 25-24
12	12	Georgia Tech	3-0-0	lost to North Carolina St. 22-27
11	13	Michigan	3-1-0	lost to Michigan State 7-19
16	14	Miami, Fla.	4-2-0	beat # 16 Notre Dame 31-13
13	15	LSU	3-0-1	bye week
15	16	Notre Dame	3-1-0	lost to # 14 Miami, Fla. 13-31
	17	UCLA	3-1-0	lost to Stanford 21-23
18	18	Auburn	2-2-0	beat Mississippi 17-13
17	19	Vanderbilt	4-0-0	lost to Tulane 23-27
19	20	Georgia	2-1-0	beat Alabama 24-14
20		South Carolina	3-0-0	beat Kansas State 49-17
20		Iowa	2-2-0	beat Northwestern 31-3

OCTOBER 8 POLL / OCT. 13 GAMES

UP	AP	Team	Record	Result
1	1	Texas	3-0-0	tied # 3 Oklahoma 15-15
3	2	Washington	5-0-0	beat Stanford 37-15
2	3	Oklahoma	4-0-0	tied # 1 Texas 15-15
4	4	Boston College	3-0-0	beat Temple 24-10
5	5	Brigham Young	5-0-0	beat Wyoming 41-38
6	6	Nebraska	4-1-0	beat Missouri 33-23
7	7	SMU	3-0-0	beat Baylor 24-20
9	8	Ohio State	4-1-0	beat Illinois 45-38
8	9	Florida State	4-0-1	lost to # 16 Auburn 41-42
11	10	Miami, Fla.	5-2-0	beat Cincinnati 49-25
12	11	Penn State	4-1-0	lost to Alabama 0-6
10	12	LSU	3-0-1	beat Vanderbilt 34-27
13	13	Oklahoma State	4-1-0	bye week
17	14	Purdue	4-1-0	lost to Iowa 3-40
15	15	Georgia	3-1-0	beat Mississippi 18-12
16	16	Auburn	3-2-0	beat # 9 Florida State 42-41
14	17	South Carolina	4-0-0	beat Pittsburgh 45-21
18	18	Florida	3-1-1	beat Tennessee 43-30
20	19	Kentucky	4-0-0	beat Mississippi State 17-13
	20	Georgia Tech	3-1-0	tied Virginia 20-20
19		Iowa	3-2-0	beat # 14 Purdue 40-3

OCTOBER 15 POLL / OCT. 20 GAMES

UP	AP	Team	Record	Result
1	1	Washington	6-0-0	beat Oregon 17-10
2	2	Oklahoma	4-0-1	beat Kansas State 12-10
3	3	Texas	3-0-1	beat Arkansas 24-18
4	4	Boston College	4-0-0	lost to # 20 West Virginia 20-21
6	5	Nebraska	5-1-0	beat Colorado 24-7
7	6	SMU	4-0-0	lost to Houston 20-29
5	7	Brigham Young	6-0-0	beat Air Force 30-25
8	8	Ohio State	5-1-0	beat Michigan State 23-20
10	9	Miami, Fla.	6-2-0	beat Pittsburgh 27-7
9	10	LSU	4-0-1	beat # 16 Kentucky 36-10
11	11	South Carolina	5-0-0	beat Notre Dame 36-32
12	12	Oklahoma State	4-1-0	beat Kansas 47-10
13	13	Auburn	4-2-0	beat Georgia Tech 48-34
14	14	Georgia	4-1-0	beat Vanderbilt 62-35
16	15	Florida State	4-1-1	beat Tulane 27-6
15	16	Kentucky	5-0-0	lost to # 10 LSU 10-36
17	17	Florida	4-1-1	beat Cincinnati 48-17
17	18	Iowa	4-2-0	beat Michigan 26-0
	19	Penn State	4-2-0	beat Syracuse 21-3
19	20	West Virginia	5-1-0	beat # 4 Boston College 21-20
20		Michigan	4-2-0	lost to # 18 Iowa 0-26

OCTOBER 22 POLL / OCT. 27 GAMES

UP	AP	Team	Record	Result
1	1	Washington	7-0-0	beat Arizona 28-12
3	2	Oklahoma	5-0-1	lost to Kansas 11-28
2	3	Texas	4-0-1	beat # 14 SMU 13-7
5	4	Nebraska	6-1-0	beat Kansas State 62-14
4	5	Brigham Young	7-0-0	beat New Mexico 48-0 (O25)
7	6	Ohio State	6-1-0	lost to Wisconsin 14-16
6	7	LSU	5-0-1	lost to Notre Dame 22-30
9	8	Miami, Fla.	7-2-0	bye week
8	9	South Carolina	6-0-0	beat East Carolina 42-20
11	10	Oklahoma State	5-1-0	beat Colorado 20-14
10	11	Boston College	5-1-0	beat Rutgers 35-23
13	12	Auburn	5-2-0	beat Mississippi State 24-21
12	13	Georgia	5-1-0	beat Kentucky 37-7
16	14	SMU	4-1-0	lost to # 3 Texas 7-13
15	15	Florida State	5-1-1	bye week
18	16	Florida	5-1-1	bye week
17	17	Iowa	5-2-0	beat Indiana 24-20
14	18	West Virginia	6-1-0	beat # 19 Penn State 17-14
20	19	Penn State	5-2-0	lost to # 18 West Virginia 14-17
19	20	Southern Cal	5-1-0	beat California 31-7

October 29 Poll — Nov. 3 Games

UP	AP	Team	Record	Nov. 3 Games
1	1	Washington	8-0-0	beat California 44-14
2	2	Texas	5-0-1	beat Texas Tech 13-10
4	3	Nebraska	7-1-0	beat Iowa State 44-0
3	4	Brigham Young	8-0-0	beat Texas-El Paso 42-9
5	5	South Carolina	7-0-0	beat North Carolina St. 35-28
6	6	Miami, Fla.	7-2-0	beat Louisville 38-23
10	7	Oklahoma State	6-1-0	beat Kansas State 34-6
8	8	Georgia	6-1-0	beat Memphis 13-3
7	9	Boston College	5-1-0	lost to Penn State 30-37
12	10	Oklahoma	5-1-1	beat Missouri 49-7
11	11	Auburn	6-2-0	lost to # 13 Florida 3-24
9	12	West Virginia	7-1-0	lost to Virginia 7-27
15	13	Florida	5-1-1	beat # 11 Auburn 24-3
14	14	Florida State	5-1-1	beat Arizona State 52-44
17	15	LSU	5-1-1	beat Mississippi 32-29
18	16	Ohio State	6-2-0	beat Indiana 50-7
13	17	Iowa	6-1-0	tied Wisconsin 10-10
16	18	Southern Cal	6-1-0	beat Stanford 20-11
	19	SMU	4-2-0	beat Texas A&M 28-20
19	20	TCU	6-1-0	beat Houston 21-14
20		Cal-St. Fullerton	9-0-0	beat Fresno State 20-17

November 5 Poll — Nov. 10 Games

UP	AP	Team	Record	Nov. 10 Games
1	1	Washington	9-0-0	lost to # 14 Southern Cal 7-16
3	2	Nebraska	8-1-0	beat Kansas 41-7
2	3	Texas	6-0-1	lost to Houston 15-29
4	4	Brigham Young	9-0-0	beat San Diego State 34-3
5	5	South Carolina	8-0-0	beat # 11 Florida State 38-26
6	6	Miami, Fla.	8-2-0	beat Maryland 40-42
7	7	Oklahoma State	7-1-0	beat Missouri 31-13
8	8	Georgia	7-1-0	lost to # 10 Florida 0-27
9	9	Oklahoma	6-1-1	beat Colorado 42-17
11	10	Florida	6-1-1	beat # 8 Georgia 27-0
10	11	Florida State	6-1-1	lost to # 5 South Carolina 26-38
15	12	LSU	6-1-1	beat Alabama 16-14
13	13	Ohio State	7-2-0	beat Northwestern 52-3
12	14	Southern Cal	8-0-0	beat # 1 Washington 16-7
14	15	TCU	7-1-0	beat Texas Tech 27-16
16	16	Boston College	5-2-0	beat Army 45-31
20	17	SMU	5-2-0	beat Rice 31-17
17	18	Iowa	6-2-1	lost to Michigan State 16-17
18	19	West Virginia	7-2-0	lost to Rutgers 19-23
	20	Auburn	6-3-0	beat Cincinnati 60-0
19		Virginia	6-1-1	beat North Carolina St. 45-0

November 12 Poll — Nov. 17 Games

UP	AP	Team	Record	Nov. 17 Games
1	1	Nebraska	9-1-0	lost to # 6 Oklahoma 7-17
2	2	South Carolina	9-0-0	lost to Navy 21-38
3	3	Brigham Young	10-0-0	beat Utah 24-14
4	4	Oklahoma State	8-1-0	beat Iowa State 16-10
8	5	Florida	7-1-1	beat Kentucky 25-17
6	6	Oklahoma	7-1-1	beat # 1 Nebraska 17-7
7	7	Southern Cal	8-1-0	lost to UCLA 10-29
5	8	Washington	9-1-0	beat Washington State 38-29
12	9	LSU	7-1-1	lost to Mississippi State 14-16
9	10	Texas	6-1-1	beat # 12 TCU 44-23
11	11	Ohio State	8-2-0	beat Michigan 21-6
10	12	TCU	8-1-0	lost to # 10 Texas 23-44
13	13	Boston College	6-2-0	beat Syracuse 24-16
17	14	Miami, Fla.	8-3-0	bye week
15	15	Georgia	7-2-0	lost to # 18 Auburn 12-21
16	16	SMU	6-2-0	beat Texas Tech 31-0
18	17	Florida State	6-2-1	beat U.T. Chattanooga 37-0
19	18	Auburn	7-3-0	beat # 15 Georgia 21-12
14	19	Virginia	7-1-1	tied North Carolina 24-24
PB	20	Clemson	7-2-0	lost to Maryland 23-41
20		Penn State	6-3-0	lost to Notre Dame 7-44

November 19 Poll — Nov. 24 Games

UP	AP	Team	Record	Nov. 24 Games
1	1	Brigham Young	11-0-0	beat Utah State 38-13
3	2	Oklahoma	8-1-1	beat # 3 Oklahoma State 24-14
2	3	Oklahoma State	9-1-0	lost to # 2 Oklahoma 14-24
7	4	Florida	8-1-1	bye week
5	5	Washington	10-1-0	regular season complete
4	6	Texas	7-1-1	lost to Baylor 10-24
8	7	Nebraska	9-2-0	regular season complete
6	8	Ohio State	9-2-0	regular season complete
9	9	South Carolina	9-1-0	beat Clemson 22-21
10	10	Boston College	7-2-0	beat # 12 Miami, Fla. 47-45 (N23)
14	11	SMU	7-2-0	beat Arkansas 31-28
12	12	Miami, Fla.	8-3-0	lost to # 10 Boston College 45-47 (N23)
11	13	Auburn	8-3-0	bye week
12	14	Southern Cal	8-2-0	lost to Notre Dame 7-19
15	15	Florida State	7-2-1	bye week
18	16	LSU	7-2-1	beat Tulane 33-15
16	17	TCU	8-2-0	lost to Texas A&M 21-35
19	18	Maryland	7-3-0	beat Virginia 45-34
	19	UCLA	8-3-0	regular season complete
	20	Georgia	7-3-0	bye week
17		Virginia	7-1-2	lost to # 18 Maryland 34-45
20		Wisconsin	7-3-1	regular season complete

November 26 Poll — Dec. 1 Games

UP	AP	Team	Record	Dec. 1 Games
1	1	Brigham Young	12-0-0	regular season complete
2	2	Oklahoma	9-1-1	regular season complete
7	3	Florida	8-1-1	beat # 12 Florida State 27-17
3	4	Washington	10-1-0	
4	5	Nebraska	9-2-0	
5	6	Ohio State	9-2-0	
6	7	South Carolina	10-1-0	regular season complete
8	8	Boston College	8-2-0	beat Holy Cross 45-10
9	9	Oklahoma State	9-2-0	regular season complete
10	10	SMU	8-2-0	beat Nevada-Las Vegas 38-21
11	11	Auburn	8-3-0	lost to Alabama 15-17
13	12	Florida State	7-2-1	lost to # 3 Florida 17-27
12	13	Texas	7-2-1	lost to Texas A&M 12-37
15	14	LSU	8-2-1	regular season complete
14	15	Maryland	8-3-0	regular season complete
16	16	Miami, Fla.	8-4-0	regular season complete
18	17	UCLA	8-3-0	
	18	Georgia	7-3-0	lost to Georgia Tech 18-35
20	19	Notre Dame	7-4-0	regular season complete
17	20	Southern Cal	8-3-0	regular season complete
19		Wisconsin	7-3-1	

December 3 Poll / Bowls

UP	AP	Team	Record	Bowl Bid	Date	Bowl Result
1	1	Brigham Young	12-0-0	Holiday Bowl	D21	beat Michigan 24-17
2	2	Oklahoma	9-1-1	Orange Bowl	J1	lost to # 4 Washington 17-28
6	3	Florida	9-1-1			
3	4	Washington	10-1-0	Orange Bowl	J1	beat # 2 Oklahoma 28-17
4	5	Nebraska	9-2-0	Sugar Bowl	J1	beat # 11 LSU 28-10
5	6	Ohio State	9-2-0	Rose Bowl	J1	lost to # 18 Southern Cal 17-20
7	7	South Carolina	10-1-0	Gator Bowl	D28	lost to # 9 Oklahoma State 14-21
8	8	Boston College	9-2-0	Cotton Bowl	J1	beat Houston 45-28
9	9	Oklahoma State	9-2-0	Gator Bowl	D28	beat # 7 South Carolina 21-14
10	10	SMU	9-2-0	Aloha Bowl	D29	beat # 17 Notre Dame 27-20
12	11	LSU	8-2-1	Sugar Bowl	J1	lost to # 5 Nebraska 10-28
11	12	Maryland	8-3-0	Sun Bowl	D22	beat Tennessee 28-27
13	13	Miami, Fla.	8-4-0	Fiesta Bowl	J1	lost to # 14 UCLA 37-39
15	14	UCLA	8-3-0	Fiesta Bowl	J1	beat # 13 Miami, Fla. 39-37
16	15	Florida State	7-3-1	Citrus Bowl	D22	tied Georgia 17-17
19	16	Auburn	8-4-0	Liberty Bowl	D27	beat Arkansas 21-15
18	17	Notre Dame	7-4-0	Aloha Bowl	D29	lost to # 10 SMU 20-27
14	18	Southern Cal	8-3-0	Rose Bowl	J1	beat # 6 Ohio State 20-17
20	19	Texas	7-3-1	Freedom Bowl	D26	lost to Iowa 17-55
17	20	Wisconsin	7-3-1	Hall of Fame Classic	D29	lost to Kentucky 19-20

January 3 Final Poll

RB	UP	AP	Team	Record
1	1	1	Brigham Young	13-0-0
3	2	2	Washington	11-1-0
2	7	3	Florida	9-1-1
4	3	4	Nebraska	10-2-0
10	4	5	Boston College	10-2-0
6	6	6	Oklahoma	9-2-1
5	5	7	Oklahoma State	10-2-0
8	8	8	SMU	10-2-0
13	10	9	UCLA	9-3-0
18	9	10	Southern Cal	9-3-0
7	13	11	South Carolina	10-2-0
9	11	12	Maryland	9-3-0
21	12	13	Ohio State	9-3-0
11	14	14	Auburn	9-4-0
32	16	15	LSU	8-3-1
17	15	16	Iowa	8-4-1
14	19	17	Florida State	7-3-2
28		18	Miami, Fla.	8-5-0
15	19	19	Kentucky	9-3-0
25	17	20	Virginia	8-2-2
30	18		West Virginia	8-4-0

ANNUAL REVIEW

1984

CONSENSUS ALL-AMERICANS

POS	Offense	HT	WT	School	AP	CF	FC	FW	PI
QB	Doug Flutie	5-9	177	Boston College	•	•	•	•	•
RB	Keith Byars	6-2	233	Ohio State	•	•	•	•	•
RB	Kenneth Davis	5-11	205	TCU	•	•	•	•	
RB	Rueben Mayes	6-0	200	Washington State				•	•
WR	David Williams	6-3	195	Illinois	•	•	•	•	•
WR	Eddie Brown	6-0	185	Miami, Fla.	•	•			
TE	Jay Novacek	6-4	211	Wyoming				•	•
T	Bill Fralic	6-5	285	Pittsburgh	•	•	•	•	•
T	Lomas Brown	6-5	277	Florida	•	•	•	•	
G	Del Wilkes	6-3	255	South Carolina	•	•	•	•	
G	Jim Lachey	6-6	274	Ohio State					•
G	Bill Mayo	6-3	280	Tennessee					•
C	Mark Traynowicz	6-6	265	Nebraska	•	•	•	•	•
PK	Kevin Butler	6-1	190	Georgia	•	•		•	•

OTHERS RECEIVING FIRST-TEAM HONORS

RB	Greg Allen	Florida State	•	
WR	Jerry Rice	Mississippi Valley State		•
TE	Rob Bennett	West Virginia	•	
TE	Mark Bavaro	Notre Dame	•	
L	Carlton Walker	Utah		•
L	Lance Smith	LSU		•
L	Dan Lynch	Washington State	•	
PK	John Lee	UCLA		•

POS	Defense	HT	WT	School	AP	CF	FC	FW	PI
DL	Bruce Smith	6-4	275	Virginia Tech	•	•	•	•	•
DL	Tony Degrate	6-4	280	Texas	•	•	•	•	
DL	Ron Holmes	6-4	255	Washington		•	•		•
DL	Tony Casillas	6-3	272	Oklahoma	•	•		•	
LB	Gregg Carr	6-2	215	Auburn	•	•			
LB	Jack Del Rio	6-4	235	Southern Cal	•	•		•	
LB	Larry Station	5-11	233	Iowa	•	•	•		•
DB	Jerry Gray	6-1	183	Texas	•	•	•	•	•
DB	Tony Thurman	6-0	179	Boston College	•	•	•		•
DB	Jeff Sanchez	6-0	183	Georgia	•	•	•	•	•
DB	David Fulcher	6-3	220	Arizona State				•	•
DB	Rod Brown	6-3	188	Oklahoma State				•	
P	Ricky Anderson	6-2	190	Vanderbilt	•	•		•	•

OTHERS RECEIVING FIRST-TEAM HONORS

DL	William Perry	Clemson		•
DL	Leslie O'Neal	Oklahoma State	•	
DL	Ray Childress	Texas A&M		•
DL	Fred Nunn	Mississippi		•
LB	Duane Bickett	Southern Cal		•
LB	James Seawright	South Carolina	•	
DB	Bret Clark	Nebraska		•
DB	Richard Johnson	Wisconsin		•
DB	Kyle Morrell	Brigham Young	•	

FC named Del Rio as a DL; AP named Station as a DL.

HEISMAN TROPHY VOTING

	PLAYER	POS	SCHOOL	1ST	2ND	3RD	TOTAL
1	Doug Flutie	QB	Boston College	678	87	32	2240
2	Keith Byars	TB	Ohio State	87	427	136	1251
3	Robbie Bosco	QB	Brigham Young	20	95	193	443
4	Bernie Kosar	QB	Miami, Fla.	9	76	141	320
5	Kenneth Davis	RB	TCU	6	16	36	86
6	Bill Fralic	OT	Pittsburgh	1	24	30	81
7	Chuck Long	QB	Iowa	2	6	19	37
8	Greg Allen	RB	Florida State	0	10	17	37
9	Jerry Rice	WR	Mississippi Valley State	3	9	9	36
10	Rueben Mayes	RB	Washington State	1	7	15	32

AWARD WINNERS

PLAYER	POS	SCHOOL	AWARD NAME
Doug Flutie	QB	Boston College	Maxwell
Bruce Smith	DT	Virginia Tech	Outland
Doug Flutie	QB	Boston College	Camp
Tony Degrate	DT	Texas	Lombardi
Doug Flutie	QB	Boston College	O'Brien

CONFERENCE STANDINGS

ACC

	CONF. W	L	T	OVERALL W	L	T
Maryland	6	0	0	9	3	0
Clemson	5	2	0	7	4	0
Georgia Tech	3	2	1	6	4	1
Virginia	3	2	2	8	2	2
North Carolina	3	3	1	5	5	1
Wake Forest	3	4	0	6	5	0
North Carolina St.	1	6	0	3	8	0
Duke	1	6	0	2	9	0

Big 10

	CONF. W	L	T	OVERALL W	L	T
Ohio State	7	2	0	9	3	0
Illinois	6	3	0	7	4	0
Purdue	6	3	0	7	5	0
Iowa	5	3	1	8	4	1
Wisconsin	5	3	1	7	4	1
Michigan State	5	4	0	6	6	0
Michigan	5	4	0	6	6	0
Minnesota	3	6	0	4	7	0
Northwestern	2	7	0	2	9	0
Indiana	0	9	0	0	11	0

Big 8

	CONF. W	L	T	OVERALL W	L	T
Nebraska	6	1	0	10	2	0
Oklahoma	6	1	0	9	2	1
Oklahoma State	5	2	0	10	2	0
Kansas	4	3	0	5	6	0
Kansas State	2	4	1	3	7	1
Missouri	2	4	1	3	7	1
Colorado	1	6	0	1	10	0
Iowa State	0	5	2	2	7	2

Big West

	CONF. W	L	T	OVERALL W	L	T
Nevada-Las Vegas	7	0	0	11	2	0
Cal-St. Fullerton	6	1	0	11	1	0
San Jose State	5	2	0	6	5	0
Fresno State	3	4	0	6	6	0
Long Beach State	3	4	0	4	7	0
Pacific	2	5	0	4	7	0
Utah State	1	5	0	1	10	0
New Mexico State	0	6	0	2	9	0

Ivy

	CONF. W	L	T	OVERALL W	L	T
Pennsylvania	7	0	0	8	1	0
Yale	5	2	0	6	3	0
Harvard	5	2	0	5	4	0
Brown	4	3	0	4	5	0
Princeton	3	4	0	4	5	0
Cornell	2	5	0	2	7	0
Dartmouth	2	5	0	2	7	0
Columbia	0	7	0	0	9	0

MAC

	CONF. W	L	T	OVERALL W	L	T
Toledo	7	1	1	8	3	1
Bowling Green	7	2	0	8	3	0
Central Michigan	6	2	1	8	2	1
Ohio U.	4	4	1	4	6	1
Northern Illinois	3	5	1	4	6	1
Miami, Ohio	3	5	0	4	7	0
Ball State	3	5	0	3	8	0
Western Michigan	3	6	0	5	6	0
Kent State	3	6	0	4	7	0
Eastern Michigan	2	5	2	2	7	2

Pac 10

	CONF. W	L	T	OVERALL W	L	T
Southern Cal	7	1	0	9	3	0
Washington	6	1	0	11	1	0
UCLA	5	2	0	9	3	0
Arizona	5	2	0	7	4	0
Washington State	4	3	0	6	5	0
Arizona State	3	4	0	5	6	0
Oregon	3	5	0	6	5	0
Stanford	3	5	0	5	6	0
Oregon State	1	7	0	2	9	0
California	1	8	0	2	9	0

SEC

	CONF. W	L	T	OVERALL W	L	T
Florida*	5	0	1	9	1	1
LSU	4	1	1	8	3	1
Auburn	4	2	0	9	4	0
Georgia	4	2	0	7	4	1
Kentucky	3	3	0	9	3	0
Tennessee	3	3	0	7	4	1
Vanderbilt	2	4	0	5	6	0
Alabama	2	4	0	5	6	0
Mississippi	1	5	0	4	6	1
Mississippi State	1	5	0	4	7	0

* Championship vacated

SWC

	CONF. W	L	T	OVERALL W	L	T
SMU	6	2	0	10	2	0
Houston	6	2	0	7	5	0
TCU	5	3	0	8	4	0
Texas	5	3	0	7	4	1
Arkansas	5	3	0	7	4	1
Baylor	4	4	0	5	6	0
Texas A&M	3	5	0	6	5	0
Texas Tech	2	6	0	4	7	0
Rice	0	8	0	1	10	0

WAC

	CONF. W	L	T	OVERALL W	L	T
Brigham Young	8	0	0	13	0	0
Hawaii	5	2	0	7	4	0
Air Force	4	3	0	8	4	0
Utah	4	3	1	6	5	1
San Diego State	4	3	1	4	7	1
Wyoming	4	4	0	6	6	0
Colorado State	3	5	0	3	8	0
New Mexico	1	7	0	4	8	0
Texas-El Paso	1	7	0	2	9	0

Independents

	OVERALL W	L	T
South Carolina	10	2	0
Boston College	10	2	0
Army	8	3	1
Rutgers	7	3	0
West Virginia	8	4	0
Virginia Tech	8	4	0
Florida State	7	3	2
Miami, Fla.	8	5	0
Notre Dame	7	5	0
Syracuse	6	5	0
Temple	6	5	0
Penn State	6	5	0
La. Lafayette	6	5	0
Memphis	5	5	1
Navy	4	6	1
Southern Miss	4	7	0
Pittsburgh	3	7	1
Tulane	3	8	0
East Carolina	2	9	0
Louisville	2	9	0
Cincinnati	2	9	0

BOWL GAMES

DATE	GAME	SCORE
D15	Independence	Air Force 23, Virginia Tech 7
D15	California	Nevada-Las Vegas 30, Toledo 13
D21	Holiday	Brigham Young 24, Michigan 17
D22	Cherry	Army 10, Michigan State 6
D22	Florida Citrus	Florida State 17, Georgia 17
D22	Sun	Maryland 28, Tennessee 27
D26	Freedom	Iowa 55, Texas 17
D27	Liberty	Auburn 21, Arkansas 15
D28	Gator	Oklahoma State 21, South Carolina 14
D29	All-American	Kentucky 20, Wisconsin 19
D29	Aloha	SMU 27, Notre Dame 20
D31	Peach	Virginia 27, Purdue 24
D31	Bluebonnet	West Virginia 31, TCU 14
J1	Sugar	Nebraska 28, LSU 10
J1	Cotton	Boston College 45, Houston 28
J1	Rose	Southern Cal 20, Ohio State 17
J1	Fiesta	UCLA 39, Miami, Fla. 37
J1	Orange	Washington 28, Oklahoma 17

1984 ANNUAL REVIEW 1351

1984 NCAA Major College Statistical Leaders

Individual Leaders

PASSING	CL	G	ATT	COM	PCT	INT	I%	YDS	YPA	TD	TD%	RATING
1 Doug Flutie, Boston College	SR	11	386	233	60.4	11	2.9	3454	9.0	27	7.0	152.9
2 Robbie Bosco, Brigham Young	JR	12	458	283	61.8	11	2.4	3875	8.5	33	7.2	151.8
3 Bernie Kosar, Miami, Fla.	SO	12	416	262	63.0	16	3.9	3642	8.8	25	6.0	148.7
4 Kerwin Bell, Florida	FR	11	184	98	53.3	7	3.8	1614	8.8	16	8.7	148.0
5 Randall Cunningham, Nevada-Las Vegas	SR	12	332	208	62.7	9	2.7	2628	7.9	24	7.2	147.6
6 Frank Reich, Maryland	SR	9	169	108	63.9	5	3.0	1446	8.6	9	5.3	147.4
7 Chuck Long, Iowa	JR	12	283	187	66.1	13	4.6	2410	8.5	16	5.7	147.1
8 John Dewberry, Georgia Tech	JR	11	205	126	61.5	10	4.9	1846	9.0	11	5.4	145.1
9 Bob DeMarco, Central Michigan	SR	11	173	98	56.7	4	2.3	1427	8.3	12	6.9	144.2
10 Doug Gaynor, Long Beach State	JR	10	385	248	64.4	17	4.4	3230	8.4	16	4.2	139.8

ALL-PURPOSE	CL	G	RUSH	REC	PR	KR	YDS	YPG
1 Keith Byars, Ohio State	JR	11	1655	453	0	176	2284	207.6
2 Ronnie Harmon, Iowa	JR	9	907	318	0	262	1487	165.2
3 Kenneth Davis, TCU	JR	11	1611	200	0	0	1811	164.6
4 Rueben Mayes, Washington State	JR	11	1637	113	0	18	1768	160.7
5 George Adams, Kentucky	SR	11	1085	330	0	274	1689	153.5
6 George Swarn, Miami, Ohio	SO	11	1282	187	0	147	1616	146.9
7 Dalton Hilliard, LSU	JR	11	1268	204	0	143	1615	146.8
8 Darryl Clack, Arizona State	JR	10	1052	385	0	18	1455	145.5
9 Curtis Adams, Central Michigan	SR	10	1204	55	0	168	1427	142.7
10 Ethan Horton, North Carolina	SR	11	1247	254	0	0	1501	136.5

RUSHING/Yards Per Game	CL	G	ATT	YDS	TD	AVG	YPG
1 Keith Byars, Ohio State	JR	11	313	1655	22	5.3	150.5
2 Rueben Mayes, Washington State	JR	11	258	1637	11	6.3	148.8
3 Kenneth Davis, TCU	JR	11	211	1611	15	7.6	146.5
4 Curtis Adams, Central Michigan	SR	10	222	1204	13	5.4	120.4
5 Johnnie Jones, Tennessee	SR	11	229	1290	10	5.6	117.3
6 George Swarn, Miami, Ohio	SO	11	269	1282	5	4.8	116.5
7 Dalton Hilliard, LSU	JR	11	254	1268	13	5.0	115.3
8 Ethan Horton, North Carolina	SR	11	238	1247	6	5.2	113.4
9 Robert Lavette, Georgia Tech	SR	11	260	1189	14	4.6	108.1
10 Greg Allen, Florida State	SR	9	133	971	8	7.3	107.9

RUSHING/Yards Per Carry	CL	G	ATT	YDS	YPC
1 Kenneth Davis, TCU	JR	11	211	1611	7.6
2 Greg Allen, Florida State	SR	9	133	971	7.3
3 Doug DuBose, Nebraska	SO	11	156	1040	6.7
4 Rueben Mayes, Washington State	JR	11	258	1637	6.3
5 Reggie Dupard, SMU	JR	11	196	1157	5.9
6 Johnnie Jones, Tennessee	SR	11	229	1290	5.6
7 Curtis Adams, Central Michigan	SR	10	222	1204	5.4
8 Keith Byars, Ohio State	JR	11	313	1655	5.3
9 Jeff Smith, Nebraska	SR	10	177	935	5.3
10 Ethan Horton, North Carolina	SR	11	238	1247	5.2

*-Based on top 23 rushers

RECEIVING	CL	G	REC	YDS	TD	YPR	YPG	RPG
1 David Williams, Illinois	JR	11	101	1278	8	12.7	116.2	9.2
2 Charles Lockett, Long Beach State	SO	11	75	1112	4	14.8	101.1	6.8
3 Larry Willis, Fresno State	SR	12	79	1251	8	15.8	104.3	6.6
4 Gerard Phelan, Boston College	SR	11	64	971	3	15.2	88.3	5.8
4 Tracy Henderson, Iowa State	JR	11	64	941	6	14.7	85.5	5.8
6 Willie Smith, Miami, Fla.	SO	12	66	852	5	12.9	71.0	5.5
7 Steve Griffin, Purdue	JR	11	60	991	4	16.5	90.1	5.5
7 Keith Edwards, Vanderbilt	SR	11	60	576	2	9.6	52.4	5.5
9 Mark Templeton, Long Beach State	SO	11	59	451	4	7.6	41.0	5.4
10 Bernard White, Bowling Green	JR	11	56	400	0	7.1	36.4	5.1

PUNTING	CL	PUNT	YDS	AVG
1 Ricky Anderson, Vanderbilt	SR	58	2796	48.2
2 Bill Smith, Mississippi	SO	44	2099	47.7
3 Randall Cunningham, Nevada-Las Vegas	SR	59	2803	47.5
4 Rick Donnelly, Wyoming	SR	63	2993	47.5
5 Tom Tupa, Ohio State	FR	41	1927	47.0
6 Adam Kelly, Minnesota	JR	59	2726	46.2
7 Lee Johnson, Brigham Young	SR	57	2594	45.5
8 Chip Andrews, Georgia	SR	63	2860	45.4
9 Buzzy Sawyer, Baylor	SR	72	3226	44.8
10 Paul Calhoun, Kentucky	SR	60	2664	44.4

PUNT RETURNS	CL	PR	YDS	TD	AVG
1 Ricky Nattiel, Florida	SO	22	346	1	15.7
2 Jeff Smith, Nebraska	SR	15	225	0	15.0
3 Shane Swanson, Nebraska	SR	19	275	1	14.5
4 Scott Thomas, Air Force	SO	24	304	0	12.7
5 Ron Milus, Washington	JR	17	211	1	12.4
6 Bob Morse, Michigan State	SO	17	204	1	12.0
7 Harold Young, Rutgers	SR	21	251	0	12.0
8 Erroll Tucker, Utah	JR	22	261	1	11.9
9 Bobby Edmonds, Arkansas	JR	25	294	0	11.8
10 Willie Drewrey, West Virginia	SR	30	343	1	11.4

KICKOFF RETURNS	CL	KR	YDS	TD	AVG
1 Keith Henderson, Texas Tech	FR	13	376	1	28.9
2 Joe Rowley, New Mexico State	FR	15	411	1	27.4
3 Willie Drewrey, West Virginia	SR	20	546	1	27.3
4 Curt Duncan, Northwestern	SO	17	464	1	27.3
5 Larry Jackson, Michigan State	SR	20	522	1	26.1
6 Tony Cherry, Oregon	JR	29	751	0	25.9
7 Vai Sikahema, Brigham Young	JR	15	376	0	25.1
8 Sheldon Gaines, Long Beach State	JR	24	575	1	24.0
9 Derrick McAdoo, Baylor	SO	14	335	0	23.9
10 Ronnie Harmon, Iowa	JR	11	262	0	23.8

SCORING	CL	TDS	XP	FG	PTS	PTPG
1 Keith Byars, Ohio State	JR	24	0	0	144	13.1
2 Allen Pinkett, Notre Dame	JR	18	0	0	108	9.8
3 John Lee, UCLA	JR	0	17	29	104	9.5
4 Bobby Raymond, Florida	SR	0	34	23	103	9.4
4 Chris White, Illinois	JR	0	31	24	103	9.4
6 Rick Badanjek, Maryland	JR	16	6	0	102	9.3
6 Kenneth Davis, TCU	JR	17	0	0	102	9.3
8 Reggie Dupard, SMU	JR	16	0	0	96	8.7
8 Jeff Jaeger, Washington	SO	0	30	22	96	8.7
10 Derek Schmidt, Florida State	FR	0	42	17	93	8.5

FIELD GOALS	CL	FGA	FGM	PCT	FGG
1 John Lee, UCLA	JR	33	29	0.88	2.64
2 Chris White, Illinois	JR	28	24	0.86	2.18
2 Mike Prindle, Western Michigan	SR	30	24	0.80	2.18
4 Bobby Raymond, Florida	SR	26	23	0.89	2.09
4 Kevin Butler, Georgia	SR	28	23	0.82	2.09
6 Jeff Jaeger, Washington	SO	28	22	0.79	2.00
7 Max Zendejas, Arizona	JR	27	21	0.78	1.91
7 Richard Spelman, Hawaii	SR	29	21	0.72	1.91
9 Tom Angstadt, Rutgers	SR	28	19	0.68	1.90
10 Fuad Reveiz, Tennessee	SR	23	20	0.87	1.82

INTERCEPTIONS	CL	INT	YDS	TD	INT/GM
1 Tony Thurman, Boston College	SR	12	99	0	1.09
2 Nate Harris, Tulsa	SR	8	131	0	0.73
2 Bryant Gilliard, South Carolina	SR	8	29	0	0.73
2 Sean Thomas, TCU	SR	8	25	0	0.73
5 Ron Cross, Fresno State	JR	8	132	0	0.67
6 Ashley Lee, Virginia Tech	SR	7	155	0	0.64
6 Paul Calhoun, Kentucky	SR	7	91	0	0.64
6 Jerry Gray, Texas	SR	7	67	0	0.64
9 Rod Brown, Oklahoma State *	SR	6	157	1	0.55
9 DeWayne Bowden, Houston *	SR	6	140	1	0.55

*-Eight tied with 0.55; these had the most yards.

Team Leaders

RUSHING OFFENSE	G	ATT	YDS	AVG	TD	YPG
1 Army	11	779	3798	4.9	34	345.3
2 Air Force	11	659	3591	5.4	36	326.5
3 Nebraska	11	695	3422	4.9	39	311.1
4 TCU	11	605	3126	5.2	34	284.2
5 Florida State	11	571	3021	5.3	23	274.6
6 Utah	12	674	3263	4.8	34	271.9
7 Auburn	12	673	3086	4.6	33	257.2
8 Wyoming	12	603	3043	5.0	31	253.6
9 Washington State	11	522	2775	5.3	26	252.3
10 Ohio State	11	574	2772	4.8	35	252.0

PASSING OFFENSE	G	ATT	COM	INT	PCT	YDS	YPA	TD	I%	YPC	YPG
1 Brigham Young	12	496	305	13	61.5	4154	8.4	34	2.6	13.6	346.2
2 Miami, Fla.	12	450	279	17	62.0	3826	8.5	25	3.8	13.7	318.8
3 Boston College	11	392	236	11	60.2	3473	8.9	27	2.8	14.7	315.7
4 Long Beach State	11	431	271	20	62.9	3423	7.9	16	4.6	12.6	311.2
5 Illinois	11	423	276	10	65.2	3130	7.4	22	2.4	11.3	284.5
6 Fresno State	12	432	233	13	53.9	3380	7.8	23	3.0	14.5	281.7
7 Purdue	11	398	229	14	57.5	3019	7.6	15	3.5	13.2	274.5
8 Bowling Green	11	416	265	13	63.7	2960	7.1	21	3.1	11.2	269.1
9 Vanderbilt	11	437	246	16	56.3	2920	6.7	20	3.7	11.9	265.5
10 Louisville	11	428	211	39	49.3	2823	6.6	19	9.1	13.4	256.6

TOTAL OFFENSE	G	P	YDS	AVG	TD	YPG
1 Brigham Young	12	902	5838	6.5	55	486.5
2 Boston College	11	825	5317	6.4	50	483.4
3 TCU	11	835	5103	6.1	47	463.9
4 Florida State	11	807	4959	6.1	42	450.8
5 Miami, Fla.	12	865	5367	6.2	45	447.2
6 Maryland	11	828	4910	5.9	43	446.4
7 Illinois	11	875	4860	5.6	35	441.8
8 Ohio State	11	820	4803	5.9	47	436.6
9 South Carolina	11	794	4797	6.0	46	436.1
10 Washington State	11	803	4762	5.9	40	432.9

RUSHING DEFENSE	G	ATT	YDS	AVG	TD	YPG
1 Oklahoma	11	386	757	2.0	4	68.8
2 Virginia Tech	11	437	787	1.8	7	71.5
3 Arizona	11	383	831	2.2	9	75.5
4 Nebraska	11	438	867	2.0	6	78.8
5 Cal-St. Fullerton	12	426	1183	2.8	8	98.6
6 Iowa	12	439	1193	2.7	7	99.4
7 Central Michigan	11	424	1102	2.6	5	100.2
8 Southern Cal	11	398	1138	2.9	6	103.5
9 Toledo	11	411	1181	2.9	6	107.4
10 Baylor	11	467	1243	2.7	15	113.0

PASSING DEFENSE	G	ATT	COM	PCT	YPC	INT	I%	YDS	YPA	TD	YPG
1 Texas Tech	11	196	89	45.4	14.2	12	6.1	1263	6.4	9	114.8
2 Wichita State	11	221	109	49.3	11.7	9	4.1	1278	5.8	9	116.2
3 Syracuse	11	220	108	49.1	12.1	10	4.5	1312	6.0	4	119.3
4 Memphis State	11	227	95	41.9	14.2	11	4.8	1349	5.9	10	122.6
5 Nebraska	11	256	115	44.9	11.9	16	6.3	1369	5.3	7	124.5
6 La. Lafayette	11	260	116	44.6	12.6	8	3.1	1456	5.6	10	132.4
7 Iowa State	11	222	102	45.9	14.7	8	3.6	1497	6.7	16	136.1
8 Colorado	11	198	114	57.6	13.3	3	1.5	1519	7.7	13	138.1
9 Arizona State	11	275	131	47.6	11.8	12	4.4	1550	5.6	10	140.9
10 California	11	206	105	51.0	14.8	7	3.4	1556	7.6	16	141.5

TOTAL DEFENSE	G	P	YDS	AVG	TD	YPG
1 Nebraska	11	694	2236	3.2	13	203.3
2 Oklahoma	11	726	2477	3.4	13	225.2
3 Virginia Tech	11	772	2574	3.3	14	234.0
4 Central Michigan	11	746	2899	3.9	14	263.5
5 Toledo	11	745	2908	3.9	12	264.4
6 Syracuse	11	698	2967	4.3	14	269.7
7 Iowa	12	790	3239	4.1	20	269.9
8 Oklahoma State	11	774	2989	3.9	14	271.7
9 Washington	11	798	3050	3.8	13	277.3
10 Memphis State	11	734	3060	4.2	22	278.2

SCORING OFFENSE	G	PTS	AVG
1 Boston College	11	404	36.7
2 Brigham Young	12	432	36.0
3 Florida State	11	389	35.4
4 Ohio State	11	374	34.0
5 TCU	11	362	32.9
6 Nebraska	11	359	32.6
7 South Carolina	11	357	32.5
8 Maryland	11	352	32.0
9 Clemson	11	346	31.5
9 Air Force	11	346	31.5

SCORING DEFENSE	G	PTS	AVG
1 Nebraska	11	105	9.5
2 Virginia Tech	11	127	11.5
3 Washington	11	128	11.6
4 Toledo	11	134	12.2
4 Oklahoma State	11	134	12.2
6 Oklahoma	11	136	12.4
7 Arkansas	11	138	12.5
8 Central Michigan	11	141	12.8
9 Syracuse	11	151	13.7
10 Brigham Young	12	166	13.8

ANNUAL REVIEW

1985 POLL PROGRESSION

Pre-Season 1985 — Aug. 31 Games

UP	AP	Team	Record	Result
1	1	Oklahoma	0-0-0	bye week
2	2	Auburn	0-0-0	bye week
PB	3	SMU	0-0-0	bye week
8	4	Iowa	0-0-0	bye week
PB	5	Florida	0-0-0	bye week
5	6	Southern Cal	0-0-0	bye week
9	7	Maryland	0-0-0	bye week
3	8	Ohio State	0-0-0	bye week
4	9	Nebraska	0-0-0	bye week
7	10	Brigham Young	0-0-0	beat Boston College 28-14 (A29)
10	11	Illinois	0-0-0	bye week
6	12	Washington	0-0-0	bye week
11	13	LSU	0-0-0	bye week
12	14	Notre Dame	0-0-0	bye week
16	15	Arkansas	0-0-0	bye week
14	16	Oklahoma State	0-0-0	bye week
18	17	South Carolina	0-0-0	beat Citadel 56-17
17	18	Penn State	0-0-0	bye week
13	19	Florida State	0-0-0	beat Tulane 38-12
15	20	UCLA	0-0-0	bye week
19		Georgia	0-0-0	lost to Alabama 16-20
20		Boston College	0-0-0	lost to # 10 Brigham Young 14-28

September 2 Poll — Sept. 7 Games

AP	Team	Record	Result
1	Oklahoma	0-0-0	bye week
2	Auburn	0-0-0	beat La. Lafayette 49-7
3	SMU	0-0-0	beat Texas-El Paso 35-23
4	Iowa	0-0-0	bye week
5	Florida	0-0-0	beat Miami, Fla. 35-23
6	Southern Cal	0-0-0	beat # 11 Illinois 20-10
7	Maryland	0-0-0	lost to # 19 Penn State 18-20
8	Brigham Young	1-0-0	lost to # 20 UCLA 24-27
9	Ohio State	0-0-0	bye week
10	Nebraska	0-0-0	lost to # 17 Florida State 13-17
11	Illinois	0-0-0	lost to # 6 Southern Cal 10-20
12	Washington	0-0-0	lost to # 16 Oklahoma State 17-31
13	LSU	0-0-0	bye week
14	Notre Dame	0-0-0	bye week
15	Arkansas	0-0-0	bye week
16	Oklahoma State	0-0-0	beat # 12 Washington 31-17
17	Florida State	0-0-0	beat # 10 Nebraska 17-13
18	South Carolina	1-0-0	beat Appalachian St. 20-13
19	Penn State	0-0-0	beat # 7 Maryland 20-18
20	UCLA	0-0-0	beat # 8 Brigham Young 27-24

September 9 Poll — Sept. 14 Games

UP	AP	Team	Record	Result
2	1	Auburn	1-0-0	beat Southern Miss 29-18
1	2	Oklahoma	0-0-0	bye week
PB	3	Florida	1-0-0	tied Rutgers 28-28
3	4	Southern Cal	1-0-0	bye week
7	5	Iowa	0-0-0	beat Drake 58-0
PB	6	SMU	1-0-0	bye week
5	7	Florida State	2-0-0	bye week
6	8	Oklahoma State	1-0-0	beat North Texas 10-9
4	9	Ohio State	1-0-0	beat Pittsburgh 10-7
8	10	UCLA	1-0-0	tied Tennessee 26-26
9	11	Penn State	1-0-0	beat Temple 27-25
10	12	LSU	0-0-0	beat North Carolina 23-13
11	13	Notre Dame	0-0-0	lost to Michigan 12-20
15	14	Arkansas	1-0-0	beat Mississippi 24-19
11	15	South Carolina	2-0-0	bye week
13	16	Brigham Young	1-1-0	beat Washington 31-3
18	17	Maryland	0-1-0	beat Boston College 31-13
14	18	Nebraska	0-1-0	
	19	Illinois	0-1-0	beat So. Illinois 28-25
16	20	Alabama	1-0-0	beat Texas A&M 23-10
17		West Virginia	1-0-0	beat Duke 20-18
19		Pittsburgh	1-0-0	lost to # 9 Ohio State 7-10
20		Texas	0-0-0	bye week

September 16 Poll — Sept. 21 Games

UP	AP	Team	Record	Result
1	1	Auburn	2-0-0	bye week
2	2	Oklahoma	1-0-0	bye week
3	3	Southern Cal	1-0-0	lost to Baylor 13-20
4	4	Iowa	1-0-0	beat No. Illinois 48-20
PB	5	SMU	1-0-0	bye week
6	6	Florida State	2-0-0	beat Memphis 19-10
5	7	Ohio State	1-0-0	beat Colorado 36-13
7	8	Oklahoma State	2-0-0	
9	9	LSU	1-0-0	beat Colorado State 17-3
8	10	Penn State	2-0-0	beat East Carolina 17-10
PB	11	Florida	1-0-1	
13	12	UCLA	1-0-1	beat San Diego State 34-16
10	13	Brigham Young	2-1-0	beat Temple 26-24
14	14	Arkansas	2-0-0	beat Tulsa 24-0
11	15	South Carolina	2-0-0	lost to # 19 Michigan 3-34
12	16	Alabama	2-0-0	beat Cincinnati 45-10
16	17	Maryland	1-1-0	beat West Virginia 28-0
17	18	Nebraska	0-1-0	beat # 20 Illinois 52-25
15	19	Michigan	1-0-0	beat # 15 South Carolina 34-3
	20	Illinois	1-1-0	lost to # 18 Nebraska 25-52
18		West Virginia	2-0-0	lost to # 17 Maryland 0-28
19		Arizona	2-0-0	beat California 23-17
19		Texas	0-0-0	beat Missouri 21-17

September 23 Poll — Sept. 28 Games

UP	AP	Team	Record	Result
1	1	Auburn	2-0-0	lost to Tennessee 20-38
2	2	Oklahoma	0-0-0	beat Minnesota 13-7
3	3	Iowa	2-0-0	beat Iowa State 57-3
5	4	Florida State	3-0-0	beat Kansas 24-20
4	5	Ohio State	2-0-0	beat Washington State 48-32
PB	6	SMU	1-0-0	beat TCU 56-21
7	7	Oklahoma State	2-0-0	beat Miami, Ohio 45-10
8	8	LSU	2-0-0	bye week
6	9	Penn State	3-0-0	beat Rutgers 17-10
13	10	Arkansas	2-0-0	beat New Mexico State 45-13
PB	11	Florida	1-0-1	beat Mississippi State 36-22
9	12	Michigan	2-0-0	beat # 17 Maryland 20-0
11	13	UCLA	2-0-1	lost to Washington 14-21
12	14	Brigham Young	3-1-0	bye week
10	15	Alabama	3-0-0	beat Vanderbilt 40-20
14	16	Nebraska	1-1-0	beat Oregon 63-0
15	17	Maryland	2-1-0	lost to # 12 Michigan 0-20
16	18	Southern Cal	1-1-0	lost to Arizona State 0-24
18	19	Air Force	3-0-0	beat New Mexico 49-12
17	20	Virginia	2-0-0	lost to Navy 13-17
19		Texas	1-0-0	beat Stanford 38-34
20		Kansas	3-0-0	lost to # 4 Florida State 20-24

September 30 Poll — Oct. 5 Games

UP	AP	Team	Record	Result
1	1	Iowa	3-0-0	beat Michigan State 35-31
2	2	Oklahoma	1-0-0	beat Kansas State 41-6
PB	3	SMU	2-0-0	lost to Arizona 6-28
4	4	Florida State	4-0-0	bye week
3	5	Ohio State	3-0-0	lost to Illinois 28-31
6	6	Oklahoma State	3-0-0	beat Tulsa 25-13
5	7	Michigan	3-0-0	beat Wisconsin 33-6
9	8	LSU	2-0-0	lost to # 11 Florida 0-20
7	9	Penn State	4-0-0	bye week
11	10	Arkansas	3-0-0	beat TCU 41-0
PB	11	Florida	2-0-1	beat # 8 LSU 20-0
8	12	Alabama	4-0-0	bye week
10	13	Nebraska	2-1-0	beat New Mexico 38-7
13	14	Auburn	2-1-0	beat Mississippi 41-0
12	15	Brigham Young	3-1-0	beat Colorado State 42-7
14	16	Tennessee	1-0-1	beat Wake Forest 31-29
15	17	Air Force	4-0-0	beat Notre Dame 21-15
18	18	Georgia	3-1-0	bye week
19	19	Baylor	3-1-0	beat Houston 24-21
16	20	Texas	2-0-0	beat Rice 44-16
17		UCLA	2-1-1	beat Arizona State 40-17
20		Indiana	3-0-0	beat Northwestern 26-7

October 7 Poll — Oct. 12 Games

UP	AP	Team	Record	Result
1	1	Iowa	4-0-0	beat Wisconsin 23-13
2	2	Oklahoma	2-0-0	beat # 17 Texas 14-7
3	3	Michigan	4-0-0	beat Michigan State 31-0
4	4	Florida State	4-0-0	lost to # 12 Auburn 27-59
5	5	Oklahoma State	4-0-0	lost to # 9 Nebraska 24-34
7	6	Arkansas	4-0-0	beat Texas Tech 30-7
PB	7	Florida	3-0-1	beat # 14 Tennessee 17-10
6	8	Penn State	4-0-0	beat # 10 Alabama 19-17
9	9	Nebraska	3-1-0	beat # 5 Oklahoma State 34-24
8	10	Alabama	4-0-0	lost to # 8 Penn State 17-19
10	11	Brigham Young	3-1-0	beat San Diego State 28-0
11	12	Auburn	3-1-0	beat # 4 Florida State 59-27
12	13	Air Force	5-0-0	beat Navy 24-7
13	14	Tennessee	2-0-1	lost to # 7 Florida 10-17
15	15	Ohio State	3-1-0	beat Indiana 48-7
PB	16	SMU	2-1-0	lost to # 19 Baylor 14-21
14	17	Texas	3-0-0	lost to # 2 Oklahoma 7-14
17	18	Georgia	3-1-0	beat Mississippi 49-21
18	19	Baylor	4-1-0	beat # 16 SMU 21-14
19	20	LSU	2-1-0	beat Vanderbilt 49-7
16		UCLA	3-1-1	beat Stanford 34-9
20		Indiana	4-0-0	lost to # 15 Ohio State 7-48

October 14 Poll — Oct. 19 Games

UP	AP	Team	Record	Result
1	1	Iowa	5-0-0	beat # 2 Michigan 12-10
3	2	Michigan	5-0-0	lost to # 1 Iowa 10-12
2	3	Oklahoma	3-0-0	lost to Miami, Fla. 14-27
5	4	Arkansas	5-0-0	lost to Texas 13-15
PB	5	Florida	4-0-1	beat La. Lafayette 45-0
4	6	Penn State	5-0-0	beat Syracuse 24-20
6	7	Nebraska	4-1-0	beat Missouri 28-20
7	8	Auburn	4-1-0	beat Georgia Tech 17-14
8	9	Brigham Young	5-1-0	beat New Mexico 45-23
9	10	Air Force	6-0-0	beat Colorado State 35-19
10	11	Ohio State	4-1-0	beat Purdue 41-27
12	12	Oklahoma State	4-1-0	bye week
11	13	Florida State	4-1-0	beat Tulsa 76-14
13	14	Baylor	5-1-0	beat Texas A&M 20-15
14	15	Alabama	4-1-0	lost to # 20 Tennessee 14-16
14	16	Georgia	4-1-0	tied Vanderbilt 13-13
17	17	LSU	3-1-0	beat Kentucky 10-0
16	18	UCLA	4-1-1	beat Washington St. 31-30
20	19	Army	5-0-0	lost to Notre Dame 10-24
19	20	Tennessee	2-1-1	beat # 15 Alabama 16-14
18		Texas	3-1-0	beat # 4 Arkansas 15-13
20		Arizona	4-1-0	beat San Jose State 41-0

October 21 Poll — Oct. 26 Games

UP	AP	Team	Record	Result
1	1	Iowa	6-0-0	beat Northwestern 49-10
PB	2	Florida	5-0-1	beat Virginia Tech 35-18
2	3	Penn State	6-0-0	beat West Virginia 27-0
4	4	Michigan	5-1-0	beat Indiana 42-15
3	5	Nebraska	5-1-0	beat Colorado 17-7
5	6	Auburn	5-1-0	beat Mississippi State 21-9
7	7	Brigham Young	6-1-0	lost to Texas-El Paso 16-23
6	8	Air Force	7-0-0	beat Utah 37-15
8	9	Ohio State	5-1-0	beat # 20 Minnesota 23-19
10	10	Oklahoma	3-1-0	beat Iowa State 59-14
9	11	Florida State	5-1-0	beat North Carolina 20-10
12	12	Oklahoma State	4-1-0	beat Kansas 17-10
11	13	Baylor	6-1-0	beat TCU 45-0
13	14	Arkansas	5-1-0	beat Houston 52-27
14	15	Miami, Fla.	5-1-0	beat Louisville 45-7
16	16	Tennessee	3-1-1	tied Georgia Tech 6-6
15	17	UCLA	5-1-1	beat California 34-7
18	18	LSU	4-1-0	bye week
17	19	Texas	4-1-0	lost to SMU 14-44
20	20	Minnesota	5-1-0	lost to # 9 Ohio State 19-23
19		Arizona	5-1-0	lost to Stanford 17-28

October 28 Poll — Nov. 2 Games

UP	AP	Team	Record	Result
1	1	Iowa	7-0-0	lost to #8 Ohio State 13-22
PB	2	Florida	6-0-1	beat #6 Auburn 14-10
2	3	Penn State	7-0-0	beat Boston College 16-12
4	4	Michigan	6-1-0	tied Illinois 3-3
3	5	Nebraska	6-1-0	beat Kansas State 41-3
5	6	Auburn	6-1-0	lost to #2 Florida 10-14
6	7	Air Force	8-0-0	beat San Diego State 31-10
7	8	Ohio State	6-1-0	beat #1 Iowa 22-13
8	9	Oklahoma	4-1-0	beat Kansas 48-6
9	10	Florida State	6-1-0	lost to #11 Miami, Fla. 27-35
12	11	Miami, Fla.	6-1-0	beat #10 Florida State 35-27
13	12	Oklahoma State	5-1-0	beat Colorado 14-11
10	13	Baylor	7-1-0	bye week
11	14	Arkansas	6-1-0	beat Rice 30-15
14	15	UCLA	6-1-1	bye week
15	16	LSU	4-1-0	beat Mississippi 14-0
16	17	Brigham Young	6-2-0	beat Wyoming 59-0
17	18	Georgia	5-1-1	beat Tulane 58-3
18	19	Tennessee	3-1-2	beat Rutgers 40-0
PB	20	SMU	4-2-0	lost to Texas A&M 17-19
19		Texas A&M	5-2-0	beat #20 SMU 19-17
20		Alabama	5-2-0	beat Mississippi State 44-28

November 4 Poll — Nov. 9 Games

UP	AP	Team	Record	Result
PB	1	Florida	7-0-1	lost to #17 Georgia 3-24
1	2	Penn State	8-0-0	beat Cincinnati 31-10
2	3	Nebraska	7-1-0	beat Iowa State 49-0
3	4	Ohio State	7-1-0	beat Northwestern 35-17
4	5	Air Force	9-0-0	beat Army 45-7
5	6	Iowa	7-1-0	beat Illinois 59-0
5	7	Oklahoma	5-1-0	beat Missouri 51-6
7	8	Miami, Fla.	7-1-0	beat Maryland 29-22
9	9	Michigan	6-1-1	beat Purdue 47-0
11	10	Oklahoma State	6-1-0	beat Kansas State 35-3
8	11	Baylor	7-1-0	lost to #12 Arkansas 14-20
10	12	Arkansas	7-1-0	beat #11 Baylor 20-14
14	13	Auburn	6-2-0	beat East Carolina 35-10
12	14	UCLA	6-1-1	beat Arizona 24-19
13	15	LSU	5-1-0	tied #20 Alabama 14-14
16	16	Florida State	6-2-0	beat South Carolina 56-14
15	17	Georgia	6-1-1	beat #1 Florida 24-3
18	18	Brigham Young	7-2-0	beat Utah State 44-0
17	19	Tennessee	4-1-2	beat Memphis 17-7
20	20	Alabama	6-2-0	tied #15 LSU 14-14
19		Texas A&M	6-2-0	bye week

November 11 Poll — Nov. 16 Games

UP	AP	Team	Record	Result
1	1	Penn State	9-0-0	beat Notre Dame 36-6
2	2	Nebraska	8-1-0	beat Kansas 56-6
3	3	Ohio State	8-1-0	lost to Wisconsin 7-12
4	4	Air Force	10-0-0	lost to #16 Brigham Young 21-28
5	5	Iowa	8-1-0	beat Purdue 27-24
7	6	Miami, Fla.	8-3-0	bye week
6	7	Oklahoma	6-1-0	beat Colorado 31-0
8	8	Michigan	7-1-1	beat Minnesota 48-7
9	9	Arkansas	8-1-0	lost to Texas A&M 6-10
10	10	Oklahoma State	7-1-0	beat Missouri 21-19
PB	11	Florida	7-1-1	beat Kentucky 15-13
12	12	Georgia	7-1-1	lost to #14 Auburn 10-24
11	13	UCLA	7-1-1	beat Oregon State 41-0
13	14	Auburn	7-2-0	beat #12 Georgia 24-10
14	15	Florida State	7-2-0	beat Western Carolina 50-10
15	16	Brigham Young	8-2-0	beat #4 Air Force 28-21
16	17	Baylor	7-2-0	beat Rice 34-10
17	18	Tennessee	5-1-2	beat Mississippi 34-14
18	19	LSU	5-1-1	beat Mississippi State 17-15
	20	Alabama	6-2-1	beat Southern Miss 24-13
19		Texas A&M	6-2-0	beat #9 Arkansas 10-6
20		Texas	6-2-0	beat TCU 20-0

November 18 Poll — Nov. 23 Games

UP	AP	Team	Record	Result
1	1	Penn State	10-0-0	beat Pittsburgh 31-0
2	2	Nebraska	9-1-0	lost to #5 Oklahoma 7-27
4	3	Iowa	9-1-0	beat Minnesota 31-9
5	4	Miami, Fla.	8-1-0	beat Colorado State 24-3
3	5	Oklahoma	7-1-0	beat #2 Nebraska 27-7
6	6	Michigan	8-1-1	beat #12 Ohio State 27-17
7	7	Oklahoma State	8-1-0	lost to Iowa State 10-15
8	8	UCLA	8-1-1	lost to Southern Cal 13-17
PB	9	Florida	8-1-1	bye week
9	10	Auburn	8-2-0	bye week
13	11	Brigham Young	9-2-0	beat Utah 38-28
11	12	Ohio State	8-2-0	lost to #6 Michigan 17-27
10	13	Air Force	10-1-0	beat Hawaii 27-20
12	14	Florida State	8-2-0	bye week
14	15	Baylor	8-2-0	lost to Texas 10-17
15	16	Tennessee	6-1-2	beat Kentucky 42-0
17	17	LSU	6-1-1	beat Notre Dame 10-7
16	18	Arkansas	8-2-0	beat SMU 15-9
18	19	Texas A&M	7-2-0	beat TCU 53-6
	20	Georgia	7-2-1	bye week
19		Texas	7-2-0	beat #15 Baylor 17-10
20		Arizona State	8-2-0	lost to Arizona 13-16

November 25 Poll — Nov. 30 Games

UP	AP	Team	Record	Result
1	1	Penn State	11-0-0	regular season complete
3	2	Iowa	10-1-0	regular season complete
2	3	Oklahoma	8-1-0	beat #17 Oklahoma State 13-0
4	4	Miami, Fla.	9-1-0	beat Notre Dame 58-7
5	5	Michigan	9-1-1	regular season complete
PB	6	Florida	8-1-1	beat #12 Florida State 38-14
6	7	Auburn	8-2-0	lost to Alabama 23-25
8	8	Nebraska	9-2-0	regular season complete
10	9	Brigham Young	10-2-0	bye week
9	10	Tennessee	7-1-2	beat Vanderbilt 30-0
7	11	Air Force	11-1-0	regular season complete
11	12	Florida State	8-2-0	lost to #6 Florida 14-38
12	13	LSU	7-1-1	beat Tulane 31-19
13	14	Arkansas	9-2-0	regular season complete
14	15	Texas A&M	8-2-0	beat #18 Texas 42-10 (N28)
15	16	UCLA	8-2-1	regular season complete
17	17	Oklahoma State	8-2-0	lost to #3 Oklahoma 0-13
16	18	Texas	8-2-0	lost to #15 Texas A&M 10-42 (N28)
18	19	Ohio State	8-3-0	regular season complete
20	20	Georgia	7-2-1	lost to Georgia Tech 16-20
19		Fresno State		regular season complete

December 2 Poll — Dec. 7 Games

UP	AP	Team	Record	Result
1	1	Penn State	11-0-0	
4	2	Miami, Fla.	10-1-0	regular season complete
3	3	Iowa	10-1-0	
2	4	Oklahoma	9-1-0	beat SMU 35-13
5	5	Michigan	9-1-1	
PB	6	Florida	9-1-1	regular season complete
6	7	Nebraska	9-2-0	
7	8	Tennessee	8-1-2	regular season complete
9	9	Brigham Young	10-2-0	beat Hawaii 26-6
8	10	Air Force	11-1-0	
11	11	Texas A&M	9-2-0	regular season complete
10	12	LSU	8-1-1	beat East Carolina 35-15
12	13	Arkansas	9-2-0	
13	14	UCLA	8-2-1	
14	15	Alabama	8-2-1	regular season complete
15	16	Auburn	8-3-0	regular season complete
16	17	Ohio State	8-3-0	
17	18	Florida State	8-3-0	regular season complete
	19	Oklahoma State	8-3-0	regular season complete
	20	Bowling Green	11-0-0	regular season complete
18		Fresno State	10-0-1	
19		Maryland	8-3-0	regular season complete
20		Arizona	8-3-0	regular season complete

December 9 Poll / January 3 Final Poll

UP	AP	December 9 Poll	Record	Bowl Bid	Date	Bowl Result	RB	UP	AP	January 3 Final Poll	Record
1	1	Penn State	11-0-0	Orange Bowl	J1	lost to #3 Oklahoma 10-25	1	1	1	Oklahoma	11-1-0
4	2	Miami, Fla.	10-1-0	Sugar Bowl	J1	lost to #8 Tennessee 7-35	3	2	2	Michigan	10-1-1
2	3	Oklahoma	10-1-0	Orange Bowl	J1	beat #1 Penn State 25-10	2	3	3	Penn State	11-1-0
3	4	Iowa	10-1-0	Rose Bowl	J1	lost to #13 UCLA 28-45	5	4	4	Tennessee	9-1-2
5	5	Michigan	9-1-1	Fiesta Bowl	J1	beat #7 Nebraska 27-23	4	PB	5	Florida	9-1-1
PB	6	Florida	9-1-1				13	7	6	Texas A&M	10-2-0
6	7	Nebraska	9-2-0	Fiesta Bowl	J1	lost to #5 Michigan 23-27	7	6	7	UCLA	9-2-1
8	8	Tennessee	8-1-2	Sugar Bowl	J1	beat #2 Miami, Fla. 35-7	9	5	8	Air Force	12-1-0
9	9	Brigham Young	11-2-0	Citrus Bowl	D28	lost to #17 Ohio State 7-10	6	8	9	Miami, Fla.	10-2-0
7	10	Air Force	11-1-0	Bluebonnet Bowl	D31	beat Texas 24-16	8	9	10	Iowa	10-2-0
11	11	Texas A&M	9-2-0	Cotton Bowl	J1	beat #16 Auburn 36-16	11	10	11	Nebraska	9-3-0
10	12	LSU	9-1-1	Liberty Bowl	D27	lost to Baylor 7-21	18	12	12	Arkansas	10-2-0
13	13	UCLA	8-2-1	Rose Bowl	J1	beat #4 Iowa 45-28	10	14	13	Alabama	9-2-1
12	14	Arkansas	9-2-0	Holiday Bowl	D22	beat Arizona State 18-17	15	11	14	Ohio State	9-3-0
14	15	Alabama	8-2-1	Aloha Bowl	D28	beat Southern Cal 24-3	12	13	15	Florida State	9-3-0
15	16	Auburn	8-3-0	Cotton Bowl	J1	lost to #11 Texas A&M 16-36	16	17	16	Brigham Young	11-3-0
17	17	Ohio State	8-3-0	Citrus Bowl	D28	beat #9 Brigham Young 10-7	22	15	17	Baylor	9-3-0
16	18	Florida State	8-3-0	Gator Bowl	D30	beat #19 Oklahoma State 34-23	20	19	18	Maryland	9-3-0
19	19	Oklahoma State	8-3-0	Gator Bowl	D30	lost to #18 Florida State 23-34	14	18	19	Georgia Tech	9-2-1
	20	Bowling Green	11-0-0	California Bowl	D14	lost to Fresno State 7-51	23	20	20	LSU	9-2-1
	20	Maryland	8-3-0	Cherry Bowl	D21	beat Syracuse 35-16	17	16		Fresno State	11-0-1
18		Fresno State	10-0-1	California Bowl	D14	beat #20 Bowling Green 51-7					
20		Arizona	8-3-0	Sun Bowl	D28	tied Georgia 13-13					

ANNUAL REVIEW

1985

CONSENSUS ALL-AMERICANS

POS	Offense	HT	WT	School	AP	CF	FC	FW	PI
QB	Chuck Long	6-4	213	Iowa	•	•	•	•	•
RB	Bo Jackson	6-1	222	Auburn	•	•	•	•	•
RB	Lorenzo White	5-11	205	Michigan State	•	•	•	•	•
RB	Thurman Thomas	5-11	186	Oklahoma State					•
RB	Reggie Dupard	6-0	201	SMU				•	
RB	Napoleon McCallum	6-2	214	Navy					
WR	David Williams	6-3	195	Illinois	•	•	•	•	•
WR	Tim McGee	5-10	181	Tennessee	•	•	•		•
TE	Willie Smith	6-2	230	Miami, Fla.	•	•	•		•
L	Jim Dombrowski	6-5	280	Virginia	•	•	•	•	•
L	Jeff Bregel	6-4	280	Southern Cal	•	•	•	•	•
L	Brian Jozwiak	6-6	290	West Virginia	•	•	•		•
L	John Rienstra	6-4	280	Temple	•		•	•	
L	J.D. Maarleveld	6-5	300	Maryland		•	•		•
L	Jamie Dukes	6-0	272	Florida State	•		•	•	
C	Pete Anderson	6-3	264	Georgia	•	•	•	•	
PK	John Lee	5-11	187	UCLA	•	•	•		•

OTHERS RECEIVING FIRST-TEAM HONORS

WR	Lew Barnes			Oregon				•	
L	Jeff Zimmerman			Florida					•
L	Don Smith			Army					•
C	Gene Chilton			Texas			•		
C	Bill Lewis			Nebraska					•
KR	Erroll Tucker			Utah					•

POS	Defense	HT	WT	School	AP	CF	FC	FW	PI
L	Tim Green	6-2	246	Syracuse	•	•	•	•	•
L	Leslie O'Neal	6-3	245	Oklahoma State	•	•	•	•	•
L	Tony Casillas	6-3	280	Oklahoma	•	•	•	•	•
L	Mike Ruth	6-2	250	Boston College	•	•	•	•	•
L	Mike Hammerstein	6-4	240	Michigan	•		•	•	•
LB	Brian Bosworth	6-2	234	Oklahoma	•	•	•	•	•
LB	Larry Station	5-11	227	Iowa	•	•	•	•	•
LB	Johnny Holland	6-2	219	Texas A&M	•		•		•
DB	David Fulcher	6-3	228	Arizona State	•	•	•	•	•
DB	Brad Cochran	6-3	219	Michigan	•	•	•		•
DB	Scott Thomas	6-0	185	Air Force		•	•		•
P	Barry Helton	6-3	195	Colorado	•		•		•

OTHERS RECEIVING FIRST-TEAM HONORS

DL	Pat Swilling			Georgia Tech				•	
DL	Jim Skow			Nebraska				•	
LB	Cornelius Bennett			Alabama					•
LB	Pepper Johnson			Ohio State					•
DB	Allan Durden			Arizona		•			
DB	Michael Zordich			Penn State		•		•	
DB	Thomas Everett			Baylor	•				
DB	Mark Moore			Oklahoma State	•				
P	Bill Smith			Mississippi					•
P	Lewis Colbert			Auburn				•	

HEISMAN TROPHY VOTING

	PLAYER	POS	SCHOOL	1ST	2ND	3RD	TOTAL
1	Bo Jackson	TB	Auburn	317	218	122	1509
2	Chuck Long	QB	Iowa	286	254	98	1464
3	Robbie Bosco	QB	Brigham Young	38	95	155	459
4	Lorenzo White	TB	Michigan State	50	63	115	391
5	Vinny Testaverde	QB	Miami, Fla.	41	41	44	249
6	Jim Everett	QB	Purdue	12	11	19	77
7	Napoleon McCallum	HB	Navy	8	11	26	72
8	Allen Pinkett	TB	Notre Dame	9	13	18	71
9	Joe Dudek	HB	Plymouth State	12	4	12	56
10	Brian McClure	QB	Bowling Green	7	10	13	54
	Thurman Thomas	TB	Oklahoma State	1	13	25	54

AWARD WINNERS

PLAYER	POS	SCHOOL	AWARD NAME
Herschel Walker	RB	Georgia	Maxwell
Chuck Long	QB	Iowa	Maxwell
Mike Ruth	NG	Boston College	Outland
Bo Jackson	RB	Auburn	Camp
Tony Casillas	NG	Oklahoma	Lombardi
Chuck Long	QB	Iowa	O'Brien
Brian Bosworth	LB	Oklahoma	Butkus

CONFERENCE STANDINGS

ACC

	CONF. W L T	OVERALL W L T
Maryland	6 0 0	9 3 0
Georgia Tech	5 1 0	9 2 1
Virginia	4 3 0	6 5 0
Clemson	4 3 0	6 6 0
North Carolina	3 4 0	5 6 0
Duke	2 5 0	4 7 0
North Carolina St.	2 5 0	3 8 0
Wake Forest	1 6 0	4 7 0

Big 10

	CONF. W L T	OVERALL W L T
Iowa	7 1 0	10 2 0
Michigan	6 1 1	10 1 1
Illinois	5 2 1	6 5 1
Ohio State	5 3 0	9 3 0
Michigan State	5 3 0	7 5 0
Minnesota	4 4 0	7 5 0
Purdue	3 5 0	5 6 0
Wisconsin	2 6 0	5 6 0
Indiana	1 7 0	4 7 0
Northwestern	1 7 0	3 8 0

Big 8

	CONF. W L T	OVERALL W L T
Oklahoma	7 0 0	11 1 0
Nebraska	6 1 0	9 3 0
Oklahoma State	4 3 0	8 4 0
Colorado	4 3 0	7 5 0
Iowa State	3 4 0	5 6 0
Kansas	2 5 0	6 6 0
Missouri	1 6 0	1 10 0
Kansas State	1 6 0	1 10 0

Big West

	CONF. W L T	OVERALL W L T
Fresno State	7 0 0	11 0 1
Cal-St. Fullerton	5 2 0	6 5 0
Nevada-Las Vegas	4 2 1	5 5 1
Long Beach State	4 3 0	6 6 0
Utah State	3 4 0	3 8 0
San Jose State	2 4 1	2 8 1
Pacific	2 5 0	5 7 0
New Mexico State	0 7 0	1 10 0

Ivy

	CONF. W L T	OVERALL W L T
Pennsylvania	6 1 0	7 2 1
Harvard	5 2 0	7 3 0
Princeton	5 2 0	5 5 0
Brown	4 3 0	5 4 1
Yale	3 3 1	4 4 1
Dartmouth	2 4 1	2 7 1
Cornell	2 5 0	3 7 0
Columbia	0 7 0	0 10 0

MAC

	CONF. W L T	OVERALL W L T
Bowling Green	9 0 0	11 1 0
Miami, Ohio	7 1 1	8 2 1
Central Michigan	6 3 0	7 3 0
Western Michigan	4 4 1	4 6 1
Northern Illinois	4 4 0	4 7 0
Toledo	3 6 0	4 7 0
Eastern Michigan	3 6 0	4 7 0
Ball State	3 6 0	4 7 0
Kent State	2 6 0	3 8 0
Ohio U	2 7 0	2 9 0

Pac 10

	CONF. W L T	OVERALL W L T
UCLA	6 2 0	9 2 1
Arizona	5 2 0	8 3 1
Arizona State	5 2 0	8 4 0
Washington	5 3 0	7 5 0
Southern Cal	5 3 0	6 6 0
Oregon	3 4 0	5 6 0
Stanford	3 5 0	4 7 0
Washington State	3 5 0	4 7 0
Oregon State	2 6 0	3 8 0
California	2 7 0	4 7 0

SEC

	CONF. W L T	OVERALL W L T
Florida*	5 1 0	9 1 1
Tennessee	5 1 0	9 1 2
LSU	4 1 1	9 2 1
Alabama	4 1 1	9 2 1
Georgia	3 2 1	7 3 2
Auburn	3 3 0	8 4 0
Mississippi	2 4 0	4 6 1
Vanderbilt	1 4 1	3 7 1
Kentucky	1 5 0	5 6 0
Mississippi State	0 6 0	5 6 0

* Not eligible for title

SWC

	CONF. W L T	OVERALL W L T
Texas A&M	7 1 0	10 2 0
Arkansas	6 2 0	10 2 0
Baylor	6 2 0	9 3 0
Texas	6 2 0	8 4 0
SMU	5 3 0	6 5 0
Houston	3 5 0	4 7 0
Rice	2 6 0	3 8 0
Texas Tech	1 7 0	4 7 0
TCU	0 8 0	3 8 0

WAC

	CONF. W L T	OVERALL W L T
Air Force	7 1 0	12 1 0
Brigham Young	7 1 0	11 3 0
Utah	5 3 0	8 4 0
Hawaii	4 3 1	4 6 2
Colorado State	4 4 0	5 7 0
San Diego State	3 4 1	5 6 1
New Mexico	2 6 0	3 8 0
Wyoming	2 6 0	3 8 0
Texas-El Paso	1 7 0	1 10 0

Independents

	OVERALL W L T
Penn State	11 1 0
Miami, Fla.	10 2 0
Florida State	9 3 0
Army	9 3 0
West Virginia	7 3 1
Southern Miss	7 4 0
Syracuse	7 5 0
Virginia Tech	6 5 0
Pittsburgh	5 5 1
Notre Dame	5 6 0
South Carolina	5 6 0
Cincinnati	5 6 0
La. Lafayette	4 7 0
Navy	4 7 0
Temple	4 7 0
Boston College	4 8 0
Memphis	2 7 2
Rutgers	2 8 1
Louisville	2 9 0
East Carolina	2 9 0
Tulane	1 10 0

BOWL GAMES

DATE	GAME	SCORE
D14	California	Fresno State 51, Bowling Green 7
D21	Cherry	Maryland 35, Syracuse 18
D21	Independence	Minnesota 20, Clemson 13
D22	Holiday	Arkansas 18, Arizona State 17
D27	Liberty	Baylor 21, LSU 7
D28	Aloha	Alabama 24, Southern Cal 3
D28	Sun	Arizona 13, Georgia 13
D28	Florida Citrus	Ohio State 10, Brigham Young 7
D30	Gator	Florida State 34, Oklahoma State 23
D30	Freedom	Washington 20, Colorado 17
D31	Bluebonnet	Air Force 24, Texas 16
D31	Peach	Army 31, Illinois 29
D31	All-American	Georgia Tech 17, Michigan State 14
J1	Fiesta	Michigan 27, Nebraska 23
J1	Orange	Oklahoma 25, Penn State 10
J1	Cotton	Texas A&M 36, Auburn 16
J1	Rose	UCLA 45, Iowa 28
J1	Sugar	Tennessee 35, Miami, Fla. 7

1985 NCAA Major College Statistical Leaders

Individual Leaders

PASSING	CL	G	ATT	COM	PCT	INT	I%	YDS	YPA	TD	TD%	RATING
1 Jim Harbaugh, Michigan	JR	11	212	139	65.6	6	2.8	1913	9.0	18	8.5	163.7
2 Kerwin Bell, Florida	SO	11	288	180	62.5	8	2.8	2687	9.3	21	7.3	159.4
3 Chuck Long, Iowa	SR	11	351	231	65.8	15	4.3	2978	8.5	26	7.4	153.0
4 Jim Karsatos, Ohio State	JR	11	254	158	62.2	8	3.2	2115	8.3	19	7.5	150.5
5 Mike Shula, Alabama	JR	11	229	138	60.3	8	3.5	2009	8.8	16	7.0	150.0
6 Vinny Testaverde, Miami, Fla.	JR	11	352	216	61.4	15	4.3	3238	9.2	21	6.0	149.8
7 Robbie Bosco, Brigham Young	SR	13	511	338	66.1	24	4.7	4273	8.4	30	5.9	146.4
8 Kevin Sweeney, Fresno State	JR	11	295	177	60.0	7	2.4	2604	8.8	14	4.8	145.1
9 Jim Everett, Purdue	SR	11	450	285	63.3	11	2.4	3651	8.1	23	5.1	143.5
10 Doug Gaynor, Long Beach State	SR	12	452	321	71.0	18	4.0	3563	7.9	19	4.2	143.1

ALL-PURPOSE	CL	G	RUSH	REC	PR	KR	YDS	YPG
1 Napoleon McCallum, Navy	SR	11	1327	358	157	488	2330	211.8
2 Paul Palmer, Temple	JR	9	1516	131	0	96	1743	193.7
3 George Swarn, Miami, Ohio	JR	11	1511	424	0	17	1952	177.5
4 Lorenzo White, Michigan State	SO	11	1908	28	0	0	1936	176.0
5 Bo Jackson, Auburn	SR	11	1786	73	0	0	1859	169.0
6 Ronnie Harmon, Iowa	SR	11	1111	597	0	147	1855	168.6
7 Thurman Thomas, Oklahoma State	SO	11	1553	98	115	15	1781	161.9
8 Ernest Givins, Louisville	SR	11	204	577	154	801	1736	157.8
9 Tony Cherry, Oregon	SR	10	1006	245	0	286	1537	153.7
10 Webster Slaughter, San Diego State	SR	12	58	1071	264	413	1806	150.5

RUSHING/Yards Per Game	CL	G	ATT	YDS	TD	AVG	YPG
1 Lorenzo White, Michigan State	SO	11	386	1908	17	4.9	173.5
2 Paul Palmer, Temple	JR	9	279	1516	9	5.4	168.4
3 Bo Jackson, Auburn	SR	11	278	1786	17	6.4	162.4
4 Thurman Thomas, Oklahoma State	SO	11	302	1553	15	5.1	141.2
5 George Swarn, Miami, Fla.	JR	11	309	1511	12	4.9	137.4
6 Barry Word, Virginia	SR	10	207	1224	6	5.9	122.4
7 Napoleon McCallum, Navy	SR	11	287	1327	14	4.6	120.6
8 Reggie Dupard, SMU	SR	11	235	1278	14	5.4	116.2
9 Doug DuBose, Nebraska	JR	10	203	1161	8	5.7	116.1
10 Steve Bartalo, Colorado State	JR	12	338	1368	12	4.0	114.0

RUSHING/Yards Per Carry	CL	G	ATT	YDS	YPC
1 Chris Hardy, San Diego State	JR	12	158	1150	7.3
2 Gordon Brown, Tulsa	SR	11	169	1201	7.1
3 Bo Jackson, Auburn	SR	11	278	1786	6.4
4 Barry Word, Virginia	SR	10	207	1224	5.9
5 Doug DuBose, Nebraska	JR	10	203	1161	5.7
6 Charles Gladman, Pittsburgh	SO	10	194	1085	5.6
7 Reggie Dupard, SMU	SR	11	235	1278	5.4
8 Paul Palmer, Temple	JR	9	279	1516	5.4
9 Rueben Mayes, Washington State	SR	11	228	1236	5.4
10 Jamelle Holieway, Oklahoma	FR	9	161	861	5.3

* on top 23 rushers

RECEIVING	CL	G	REC	YDS	TD	YPR	YPG	RPG
1 Rodney Carter, Purdue	SR	11	98	1099	4	11.2	99.9	8.9
2 Brad Muster, Stanford	SO	9	78	654	4	8.4	72.7	8.7
3 David Williams, Illinois	SR	11	85	1047	8	12.3	95.2	7.7
4 Webster Slaughter, San Diego State	SR	12	82	1071	10	13.1	89.3	6.8
5 Marc Zeno, Tulane	SO	11	73	1137	3	15.6	103.4	6.6
6 Reggie Bynum, Oregon State	SR	10	61	703	7	11.5	70.3	6.1
7 Loren Richey, Utah	JR	12	73	971	7	13.3	80.9	6.1
8 Richard Estell, Kansas	SR	12	70	1109	4	15.8	92.4	5.8
9 Charles Lockett, Long Beach State	JR	12	69	949	10	13.8	79.1	5.7
10 Mark Bellini, Brigham Young	JR	11	63	1008	14	16.0	91.6	5.7

PUNTING	CL	PUNT	YDS	AVG
1 Mark Simon, Air Force	JR	53	2507	47.3
2 Barry Helton, Colorado	SO	52	2392	46.0
3 Steve Kidd, Rice	JR	55	2525	45.9
4 Lewis Colbert, Auburn	SR	57	2611	45.8
5 Bill Smith, Mississippi	JR	79	3579	45.3
6 John Teltschik, Texas	SR	58	2622	45.2
7 Chris Mohr, Alabama	FR	44	1984	45.1
8 Buzzy Sawyer, Baylor	SR	52	2330	44.8
9 Ray Criswell, Florida	SR	55	2459	44.7
10 Greg Montgomery, Michigan State	SO	69	3084	44.7

PUNT RETURNS	CL	PR	YDS	TD	AVG
1 Erroll Tucker, Utah	SR	16	389	2	24.3
2 Kelvin Martin, Boston College	JR	30	509	1	17.0
3 Scott Schwedes, Syracuse	JR	24	384	2	16.0
4 Stephen Baker, Fresno State	JR	17	243	1	14.3
5 Gilvanni Johnson, Michigan	SR	12	169	1	14.1
6 Tyrone Thurman, Texas Tech	FR	31	419	0	13.5
7 Robb Schnitzler, Nebraska	JR	16	207	0	12.9
8 Tony Brooks, TCU	FR	11	131	0	11.9
9 B.J. Edmonds, Arkansas	SR	40	466	0	11.6
10 Nate Odomes, Wisconsin	JR	14	160	0	11.4

KICKOFF RETURNS	CL	KR	YDS	TD	AVG
1 Erroll Tucker, Utah	SR	24	698	2	29.1
2 Ernest Givins, Louisville	SR	29	801	2	27.6
3 Curtis Duncan, Northwestern	JR	11	299	0	27.2
4 Reggie McKinney, East Carolina	FR	13	332	0	25.5
5 Luther Johnson, Texas-El Paso	JR	29	725	2	25.0
6 Bobby Clair, East Carolina	SR	17	423	0	24.9
7 Joe Redding, La. Lafayette	FR	33	814	1	24.7
8 Jerry Harris, Memphis State	JR	15	369	0	24.6
9 Keith Ross, Florida State	FR	17	418	0	24.6
10 Napoleon McCallum, Navy	SR	20	488	0	24.4

SCORING	CL	TDS	XP	FG	PTS	PTPG
1 Bernard White, Bowling Green	SR	19	0	0	114	10.4
2 Bo Jackson, Auburn	SR	17	0	0	102	9.3
2 Carlos Reveiz, Tennessee	JR	0	30	24	102	9.3
2 Lorenzo White, Michigan State	SO	17	0	0	102	9.3
2 Steve Gage, Tulsa	JR	17	0	0	102	9.3
6 Barry Belli, Fresno State	SO	0	46	18	100	9.1
7 Derek Schmidt, Florida State	SO	0	44	18	98	8.9
8 Rob Houghtlin, Iowa	SO	0	46	17	97	8.8
9 George Swarn, Miami, Ohio	JR	16	0	0	96	8.7
9 Thurman Thomas, Oklahoma State	SO	16	0	0	96	8.7
9 Reggie Dupard, SMU	SR	16	0	0	96	8.7
9 John Lee, UCLA	SR	0	33	21	96	8.7

FIELD GOALS	CL	FGA	FGM	PCT	FGG
1 John Diettrich, Ball State	SR	29	25	0.86	2.27
2 Carlos Reveiz, Tennessee	JR	28	24	0.86	2.18
3 Max Zendejas, Arizona	SR	29	22	0.76	2.00
4 John Lee, UCLA	SR	24	21	0.88	1.91
4 Jeff Jaeger, Washington	JR	24	21	0.88	1.91
4 Massimo Manca, Penn State	SR	26	21	0.81	1.91
7 Jeff Ward, Texas	JR	24	19	0.79	1.73
7 Joe Worley, Kentucky	SO	28	19	0.68	1.73
9 Derek Schmidt, Florida State	SO	25	18	0.72	1.64
9 Gary Gussman, Miami, Ohio	SO	26	18	0.69	1.64
9 Barry Belli, Fresno State	SO	26	18	0.69	1.64

INTERCEPTIONS	CL	INT	YDS	TD	INT/GM
1 Chris White, Tennessee	SR	9	168	1	0.82
1 Kevin Walker, East Carolina	SR	9	155	1	0.82
3 Mike Romero, Cal-St. Fullerton	SR	8	84	1	0.73
4 Tom Rotello, Air Force	JR	8	103	2	0.67
5 Teryl Austin, Pittsburgh	SO	7	186	0	0.64
5 Mark Moore, Oklahoma State	JR	7	176	1	0.64
5 Jay Norvell, Iowa	SR	7	93	0	0.64
5 Doug Pavek, Army	SR	7	80	0	0.64
5 Markus Paul, Syracuse	FR	7	53	0	0.64
5 Lavance Northington, Oregon State	JR	7	39	0	0.64

Team Leaders

RUSHING OFFENSE	G	ATT	YDS	AVG	TD	YPG
1 Nebraska	11	697	4117	5.9	40	374.3
2 Army	11	699	3700	5.3	43	336.4
3 Oklahoma	11	749	3694	4.9	35	335.8
4 Auburn	11	620	3438	5.5	36	312.5
5 Tulsa	11	627	3371	5.4	27	306.5
6 Georgia	11	584	3249	5.6	30	295.4
7 Air Force	12	688	3519	5.1	42	293.2
8 Arkansas	11	685	2922	4.3	29	265.6
9 Colorado	11	647	2858	4.4	23	259.8
10 SMU	11	599	2730	4.6	27	248.2

PASSING OFFENSE	G	ATT	COM	INT	PCT	YDS	YPA	TD	I%	YPC	YPG
1 Brigham Young	13	560	366	24	65.4	4608	8.2	32	4.3	12.6	354.5
2 Purdue	11	471	292	13	62.0	3760	8.0	23	2.8	12.9	341.8
3 Miami, Fla.	11	368	227	16	61.7	3501	9.5	24	4.3	15.4	318.3
4 Iowa	11	382	247	15	64.7	3292	8.6	29	3.9	13.3	299.3
5 Long Beach State	12	456	323	18	70.8	3575	7.8	19	3.9	11.1	297.9
6 New Mexico	11	395	194	24	49.1	3245	8.2	12	6.1	16.7	295.0
7 San Diego State	12	437	269	21	61.6	3447	7.9	24	4.8	12.8	287.2
8 Illinois	11	462	290	17	62.8	2992	6.5	16	3.7	10.3	272.0
9 Boston College	12	455	249	28	54.7	3230	7.1	13	6.2	13.0	269.2
10 Utah	12	449	253	23	56.3	3199	7.1	20	5.1	12.6	266.6

TOTAL OFFENSE	G	P	YDS	AVG	TD	YPG
1 Brigham Young	13	1035	6502	6.3	57	500.2
2 Nebraska	11	841	5197	6.2	46	472.5
3 New Mexico	11	912	5165	5.7	37	469.5
4 Iowa	11	815	5106	6.3	52	464.2
5 Fresno State	11	858	5079	5.9	50	461.7
6 Miami, Fla.	11	828	5076	6.1	46	461.5
7 Washington State	11	836	4851	5.8	41	441.0
8 San Diego State	12	827	5242	6.3	39	436.8
9 Purdue	11	822	4801	5.8	36	436.5
10 Oklahoma	11	860	4697	5.5	42	427.0

RUSHING DEFENSE	G	ATT	YDS	AVG	TD	YPG
1 UCLA	11	370	773	2.1	11	70.3
2 Oklahoma	11	405	988	2.4	4	89.8
3 Georgia	11	440	1095	2.5	9	99.5
4 Syracuse	11	430	1099	2.6	8	99.9
5 Iowa	11	434	1117	2.6	8	101.5
6 Michigan	11	385	1135	2.9	2	103.2
7 Pittsburgh	11	445	1136	2.6	13	103.3
8 LSU	11	388	1178	3.0	6	107.1
9 Arizona	11	434	1196	2.8	12	108.7
10 Air Force	12	466	1307	2.8	8	108.9

PASSING DEFENSE	G	ATT	COM	PCT	YPC	INT	I%	YDS	YPA	TD	YPG
1 Oklahoma	11	245	107	43.7	10.7	18	7.3	1140	4.7	5	103.6
2 Texas Tech	11	184	87	47.3	13.8	9	4.9	1204	6.5	6	109.5
3 Baylor	11	221	96	43.4	13.4	14	6.3	1289	5.8	7	117.2
4 Texas A&M	11	256	106	41.4	13.8	16	6.3	1461	5.7	4	132.8
5 SMU	11	242	116	47.9	12.8	11	4.5	1480	6.1	11	134.5
6 Oklahoma State	11	268	125	46.6	12.1	20	7.5	1512	5.6	7	137.5
7 Central Michigan	10	233	128	54.9	10.8	14	6.0	1377	5.9	2	137.7
8 Western Michigan	11	263	141	53.6	10.8	15	5.7	1520	5.8	7	138.2
9 Toledo	11	301	144	47.8	10.6	17	5.6	1523	5.1	6	138.5
10 Kansas State	11	227	114	50.2	13.7	13	5.7	1557	6.9	6	141.5

TOTAL DEFENSE	G	P	YDS	AVG	TD	YPG
1 Oklahoma	11	650	2128	3.3	9	193.5
2 Michigan	11	689	2790	4.0	5	253.6
3 Toledo	11	763	2880	3.8	17	261.8
4 Central Michigan	10	672	2658	4.0	16	265.8
5 Iowa	11	755	3044	4.0	16	276.7
6 Nebraska	11	765	3070	4.0	16	279.1
7 UCLA	11	733	3100	4.2	20	281.8
8 Texas A&M	11	765	3101	4.1	19	281.9
9 Florida	11	726	3111	4.3	19	282.8
10 Southern Miss	11	722	3169	4.4	18	288.1

SCORING OFFENSE	G	PTS	AVG
1 Fresno State	11	430	39.1
2 Iowa	11	412	37.5
3 Air Force	12	446	37.2
4 Miami, Fla.	11	399	36.3
5 Nebraska	11	398	36.2
6 Utah	12	405	33.7
7 Brigham Young	13	435	33.5
8 Florida State	11	368	33.5
9 Army	11	365	33.2
10 Bowling Green	11	348	31.6

SCORING DEFENSE	G	PTS	AVG
1 Michigan	11	75	6.8
2 Oklahoma	11	93	8.5
3 LSU	11	113	10.3
4 Georgia Tech	11	118	10.7
5 Penn State	11	128	11.6
6 Arkansas	11	129	11.7
7 Tennessee	11	133	12.1
7 Arizona	11	133	12.1
9 Nebraska	11	136	12.4
10 Iowa	11	142	12.9

1986 POLL PROGRESSION

PRE-SEASON 1986 / SEPT. 6 GAMES

UP	AP	Team	Record	Result
1	1	Oklahoma	0-0-0	beat # 4 UCLA 38-3
2	2	Michigan	0-0-0	bye week
7	3	Miami, Fla.	0-0-0	beat # 13 Florida 23-15
4	4	UCLA	0-0-0	lost to # 1 Oklahoma 3-38
6	5	Alabama	0-0-0	beat Vanderbilt 42-10
5	6	Penn State	0-0-0	beat Temple 45-15
3	7	Texas A&M	0-0-0	bye week
8	8	Nebraska	0-0-0	beat # 11 Florida State 34-17
9	9	Ohio State	0-0-0	lost to # 5 Alabama 10-16 (A27)
10	10	Tennessee	0-0-0	beat New Mexico 35-21
11	11	Florida State	0-0-0	lost to # 8 Nebraska 17-34
12	12	Baylor	0-0-0	beat Wyoming 31-28
PB	13	Florida	0-0-0	lost to # 3 Miami, Fla. 15-23
13	14	Auburn	0-0-0	beat U.T. Chatanooga 42-14
19	15	LSU	0-0-0	bye week
15	16	Georgia	0-0-0	bye week
16	17	Washington	0-0-0	bye week
16	18	Brigham Young	0-0-0	beat Utah State 52-0
14	19	Arkansas	0-0-0	bye week
	20	Michigan State	0-0-0	bye week
18		Iowa	0-0-0	bye week
20		Maryland	0-0-0	beat Pittsburgh 10-7 (S1)

SEPTEMBER 8 POLL / SEPT. 13 GAMES

UP	AP	Team	Record	Result
1	1	Oklahoma	1-0-0	bye week
2	2	Miami, Fla.	1-0-0	beat Texas Tech 61-11
3	3	Michigan	0-0-0	beat Notre Dame 24-23
4	4	Alabama	2-0-0	beat Southern Miss 31-17
5	5	Penn State	1-0-0	bye week
6	6	Nebraska	1-0-0	bye week
7	7	Texas A&M	0-0-0	lost to # 14 LSU 17-35
8	8	Tennessee	1-0-0	lost to Mississippi State 23-27
11	9	Auburn	1-0-0	bye week
12	10	Ohio State	0-1-0	lost to # 17 Washington 7-40
9	11	Brigham Young	2-0-0	beat New Mexico 31-30
9	12	Baylor	1-0-0	beat Louisiana Tech 38-7
PB	13	Florida	1-1-0	bye week
17	14	LSU	2-0-0	beat # 7 Texas A&M 35-17
	15	Florida State	1-1-0	bye week
19	16	UCLA	0-1-0	bye week
13	17	Washington	1-0-0	beat # 10 Ohio State 40-7
15	18	Arkansas	0-0-0	beat Mississippi 21-0
14	19	Georgia	0-0-0	beat Duke 31-7
	20	Michigan State	0-0-0	lost to Arizona State 17-20
16		Arizona	1-0-0	beat Colorado State 37-10
18		Maryland	1-0-0	beat Vanderbilt 35-21
20		Iowa	0-0-0	beat Iowa State 43-7

SEPTEMBER 15 POLL / SEPT. 20 GAMES

UP	AP	Team	Record	Result
1	1	Oklahoma	1-0-0	beat Minnesota 63-0
2	2	Miami, Fla.	2-0-0	bye week
3	3	Michigan	1-0-0	beat Oregon State 31-12
4	4	Alabama	3-0-0	beat # 13 Florida 21-7
6	5	Penn State	1-0-0	beat Boston College 26-14
5	6	Nebraska	1-0-0	beat Illinois 59-14
7	7	Washington	1-0-0	beat # 11 Brigham Young 52-21
8	8	LSU	1-0-0	lost to Miami, Ohio 12-21
9	9	Baylor	2-0-0	lost to Southern Cal 14-17
11	10	Auburn	1-0-0	beat East Carolina 45-0
13	11	Brigham Young	2-0-0	lost to # 7 Washington 21-52
12	12	Arkansas	1-0-0	beat Tulsa 34-17
PB	13	Florida	1-1-0	lost to # 4 Alabama 7-21
10	14	Georgia	1-0-0	lost to Clemson 28-31
18	15	Florida State	1-1-0	tied North Carolina 10-10
19	16	Texas A&M	0-1-0	beat North Texas 48-28
15	17	Arizona	2-0-0	beat Oregon 41-17
17	18	Arizona State	1-0-0	beat SMU 30-0
	19	UCLA		beat San Diego State 45-14
	20	Notre Dame	0-1-0	lost to Michigan State 15-20
14		Iowa	1-0-0	beat Northern Illinois 57-3
16		Maryland	2-0-0	beat West Virginia 24-3
20		Southern Cal	1-0-0	beat # 9 Baylor 17-14

SEPTEMBER 22 POLL / SEPT. 27 GAMES

UP	AP	Team	Record	Result
1	1	Oklahoma	2-0-0	lost to # 2 Miami, Fla. 16-28
2	2	Miami, Fla.	3-0-0	beat # 1 Oklahoma 28-16
3	3	Alabama	4-0-0	bye week
5	4	Nebraska	2-0-0	beat Oregon 48-14
4	5	Michigan	2-0-0	beat # 20 Florida State 20-18
7	6	Washington	2-0-0	beat # 12 Southern Cal 10-20
6	7	Penn State	2-0-0	beat East Carolina 42-17
8	8	Auburn	2-0-0	beat Tennessee 34-8
9	9	Arkansas	2-0-0	beat New Mexico State 42-11
10	10	Arizona	3-0-0	beat Colorado 24-21
11	11	Arizona State	2-0-0	tied Washington St. 21-21
12	12	Southern Cal	2-0-0	beat # 6 Washington 20-10
14	13	Maryland	3-0-0	lost to North Carolina St. 16-28
16	14	Texas A&M	1-1-0	beat Southern Miss 16-7
13	15	Iowa	2-0-0	beat Texas-El Paso 69-7
15	16	UCLA	1-1-0	beat Long Beach St. 41-23
17	17	Baylor	2-1-0	beat Texas Tech 45-14
	18	LSU	1-1-0	bye week
18	19	Michigan State	1-1-0	beat Western Michigan 45-10
20	20	Florida State	1-1-1	lost to # 5 Michigan 18-20
19		Fresno State	2-0-0	beat Louisiana Tech 34-10

SEPTEMBER 29 POLL / OCT. 4 GAMES

UP	AP	Team	Record	Result
1	1	Miami, Fla.	4-0-0	beat Northern Illinois 34-0
2	2	Alabama	4-0-0	beat Notre Dame 28-10
3	3	Nebraska	3-0-0	beat South Carolina 27-24
4	4	Michigan	3-0-0	beat Wisconsin 34-17
5	5	Penn State	3-0-0	beat Rutgers 31-6
6	6	Oklahoma	2-1-0	beat Kansas State 56-10
7	7	Auburn	3-0-0	beat Western Carolina 55-6
9	8	Arkansas	3-0-0	beat TCU 34-17
8	8	Southern Cal	3-0-0	beat Oregon 35-21
10	10	Arizona	4-0-0	bye week
11	11	Iowa	3-0-0	beat # 17 Michigan State 24-21
13	12	Washington	2-1-0	beat California 50-18
12	13	Baylor	3-1-0	beat Houston 27-13
14	14	Texas A&M	2-1-0	beat Texas Tech 45-8
17	15	UCLA	2-1-0	lost to # 16 Arizona State 9-16
14	16	Arizona State	2-0-1	beat # 15 UCLA 16-9
16	17	Michigan State	2-1-0	lost to # 11 Iowa 21-24
	18	LSU	1-1-0	beat Florida 28-17
18	19	Fresno State	3-0-0	lost to San Jose State 41-45
19	20	North Carolina St.	3-0-1	bye week
20		Stanford	3-0-0	beat San Diego State 17-10

OCTOBER 6 POLL / OCT. 11 GAMES

UP	AP	Team	Record	Result
1	1	Miami, Fla.	5-0-0	beat West Virginia 58-14
2	2	Alabama	5-0-0	beat Memphis 37-0
5	3	Nebraska	4-0-0	beat Oklahoma State 30-10
3	4	Michigan	4-0-0	beat Michigan State 27-6
4	5	Penn State	4-0-0	beat Cincinnati 23-17
6	6	Oklahoma	3-1-0	beat Texas 47-12
7	7	Auburn	4-0-0	beat Vanderbilt 31-9
10	8	Arkansas	4-0-0	lost to Texas Tech 7-17
8	9	Southern Cal	4-0-0	lost Washington St. 14-34
11	10	Iowa	4-0-0	beat Wisconsin 17-6
9	11	Arizona	4-0-0	lost to UCLA 25-32
12	12	Washington	3-1-0	beat # 18 Stanford 24-14
14	13	Baylor	4-1-0	lost to SMU 21-27
15	14	Texas A&M	3-1-0	beat Houston 19-7
13	15	Arizona State	3-0-1	beat Oregon 37-17
16	16	LSU	2-1-0	beat Georgia 23-14
18	17	North Carolina St.	3-0-1	lost to Georgia Tech 21-59
17	18	Stanford	4-0-0	lost to # 12 Washington 14-24
	19	Mississippi State	4-1-0	beat Arkansas State 24-9
	20	Clemson	3-1-0	beat Virginia 31-17
19		Indiana	4-0-0	lost to Ohio State 22-24
20		North Carolina	3-0-1	beat Wake Forest 40-30

OCTOBER 13 POLL / OCT. 18 GAMES

UP	AP	Team	Record	Result
1	1	Miami, Fla.	6-0-0	beat Cincinnati 45-13
2	2	Alabama	6-0-0	beat Tennessee 56-28
3	3	Nebraska	5-0-0	beat Missouri 48-17
4	4	Michigan	5-0-0	beat # 8 Iowa 20-17
5	5	Oklahoma	4-1-0	beat Oklahoma State 19-0
6	6	Penn State	5-0-0	beat Syracuse 42-3
7	7	Auburn	5-0-0	beat Georgia Tech 31-10
8	8	Iowa	5-0-0	lost to # 4 Michigan 17-20
9	9	Washington	4-1-0	beat Bowling Green 48-0
10	10	Arizona State	4-0-1	beat # 15 Southern Cal 29-20
11	11	Texas A&M	4-1-0	beat # 20 Baylor 31-30
12	12	LSU	3-1-0	beat Kentucky 25-16
15	13	Mississippi State	5-1-0	beat Tulane 34-27
13	14	Arkansas	4-1-0	beat Texas 21-14
16	15	Southern Cal	4-1-0	lost to # 10 Arizona State 20-29
14	16	Arizona	4-1-0	beat Oregon State 23-12
17	17	Clemson	4-1-0	beat Duke 35-3
18	18	North Carolina	4-0-1	lost to North Carolina St. 34-35
19	19	UCLA	3-2-0	beat California 36-10
20	20	Baylor	4-2-0	lost to # 11 Texas A&M 30-31
	20	SMU	4-1-0	beat Houston 10-3

OCTOBER 20 POLL / OCT. 25 GAMES

UP	AP	Team	Record	Result
1	1	Miami, Fla.	7-0-0	bye week
2	2	Alabama	7-0-0	lost to # 6 Penn State 3-23
3	3	Nebraska	6-0-0	lost to Colorado 10-20
4	4	Michigan	6-0-0	beat Indiana 38-14
5	5	Oklahoma	5-1-0	beat Iowa State 38-0
6	6	Penn State	6-0-0	beat # 2 Alabama 23-3
7	7	Auburn	6-0-0	beat # 13 Mississippi State 35-6
8	8	Washington	5-1-0	beat Oregon 38-3
9	9	Arizona State	5-0-1	beat Utah 52-7
10	10	Texas A&M	5-1-0	beat Rice 45-10
12	11	Iowa	5-1-0	beat Northwestern 27-20
11	12	LSU	4-1-0	beat North Carolina 30-3
14	13	Mississippi State	6-1-0	lost to # 7 Auburn 6-35
13	14	Arkansas	5-1-0	beat Houston 30-13
15	15	Arizona	5-1-0	beat California 33-16
16	16	Clemson	5-1-0	lost to North Carolina St. 3-27
17	17	UCLA	4-2-0	beat Washington St. 54-16
	18	SMU	5-1-0	lost to Texas 24-27
17	19	Stanford	5-1-0	lost to Southern Cal 0-10
19	20	North Carolina St.	4-1-1	beat Clemson 27-3
20		Baylor	5-3-0	beat TCU 28-17
20		North Carolina	4-1-1	lost to # 12 LSU 3-30

OCTOBER 27 POLL / NOV. 1 GAMES

UP	AP	Team	Record	Result
1	1	Miami, Fla.	7-0-0	beat # 20 Florida State 41-23
3	2	Penn State	7-0-0	beat West Virginia 19-0
2	3	Michigan	7-0-0	beat Illinois 69-13
4	4	Oklahoma	6-1-0	beat Kansas 64-3
5	5	Auburn	7-0-0	lost to Florida 17-18
6	6	Washington	6-1-0	lost to # 7 Arizona State 21-34
7	7	Arizona State	6-0-1	beat # 6 Washington 34-21
8	8	Alabama	7-1-0	beat # 19 Mississippi State 38-3
9	9	Nebraska	6-1-0	beat Kansas State 38-0
10	10	Texas A&M	6-1-0	beat SMU 39-35
12	11	Iowa	6-1-0	lost to # 17 Ohio State 10-31
11	12	LSU	5-1-0	lost to Mississippi 19-21
13	13	Arkansas	6-1-0	beat Rice 45-14
14	14	Arizona	6-1-0	lost to # 18 Southern Cal 13-20
15	15	UCLA	5-2-0	beat Oregon State 49-0
16	16	North Carolina St.	5-1-1	beat South Carolina 23-22
17	17	Ohio State	6-2-0	beat # 11 Iowa 31-10
19	18	Southern Cal	5-2-0	beat # 14 Arizona 20-13
	19	Mississippi State	6-2-0	lost to # 8 Alabama 3-38
	20	Florida State	4-2-1	lost to # 1 Miami, Fla. 23-41
17		Baylor	5-3-0	bye week

November 3 Poll — Nov. 8 Games

UP	AP	Team	Record	Result
1	1	Miami, Fla.	8-0-0	beat Pittsburgh 37-10
2	2	Penn State	8-0-0	beat Maryland 17-15
3	3	Michigan	8-0-0	beat Purdue 31-7
4	4	Oklahoma	7-1-0	beat Missouri 77-0
5	5	Arizona State	7-0-1	beat California 49-0
6	6	Alabama	8-1-0	lost to # 18 LSU 10-14
7	7	Nebraska	7-1-0	beat Iowa State 35-14
8	8	Texas A&M	7-1-0	bye week
10	9	Auburn	7-1-0	beat Cincinnati 52-7
9	10	Arkansas	7-1-0	lost to Baylor 14-29
11	11	Ohio State	7-2-0	beat Northwestern 30-9
12	12	UCLA	6-2-0	lost to Stanford 23-28
13	13	Washington	6-2-0	beat Oregon State 28-12
15	14	Southern Cal	6-2-0	bye week
14	15	North Carolina St.	6-1-1	lost to Virginia 16-20
16	16	Iowa	6-2-0	lost to Illinois 16-20
17	17	Arizona	6-2-0	beat Washington St. 31-6
18	18	LSU	5-2-0	beat # 6 Alabama 14-10
	19	Georgia	6-2-0	lost to Florida 19-31
	20	Clemson	6-2-0	beat North Carolina 38-10
19		Baylor	5-3-0	beat # 10 Arkansas 29-14
19		Stanford	6-2-0	beat # 12 UCLA 28-23

November 10 Poll — Nov. 15 Games

UP	AP	Team	Record	Result
1	1	Miami, Fla.	9-0-0	beat Tulsa 23-10
2	2	Michigan	9-0-0	lost to Minnesota 17-20
3	3	Penn State	9-0-0	beat Notre Dame 24-19
4	4	Oklahoma	8-1-0	beat Colorado 28-0
5	5	Arizona State	8-0-1	beat Wichita St. 52-6
6	6	Nebraska	8-1-0	beat Kansas 70-0
7	7	Texas A&M	7-1-0	lost to # 17 Arkansas 10-14
8	8	Auburn	8-1-0	lost to Georgia 16-20
9	9	Ohio State	8-2-0	beat Wisconsin 30-17
10	10	Washington	7-2-0	tied # 19 UCLA 17-17
15	11	Alabama	8-2-0	beat Temple 24-14
11	12	LSU	6-2-0	beat Mississippi State 47-0
12	13	Southern Cal	6-2-0	beat California 28-3
13	14	Arizona	7-2-0	bye week
17	15	Clemson	7-2-0	tied Maryland 17-17
14	16	Stanford	7-2-0	bye week
16	17	Arkansas	7-2-0	beat # 7 Texas A&M 14-10
18	18	Baylor	6-3-0	beat Rice 23-17
	19	UCLA	6-3-0	tied # 10 Washington 17-17
	20	Mississippi	6-2-1	lost to Tennessee 10-22
19		Brigham Young	6-2-0	lost to Oregon State 7-10
20		North Carolina St.	6-2-1	beat Duke 29-15

November 17 Poll — Nov. 22 Games

UP	AP	Team	Record	Result
1	1	Miami, Fla.	10-0-0	bye week
2	2	Penn State	10-0-0	beat Pittsburgh 34-14
3	3	Oklahoma	9-1-0	beat # 5 Nebraska 20-17
4	4	Arizona State	9-0-1	lost to # 14 Arizona 17-34
5	5	Nebraska	9-1-0	lost to # 3 Oklahoma 17-20
6	6	Michigan	9-1-0	beat # 7 Ohio State 26-24
7	7	Ohio State	9-2-0	lost to # 6 Michigan 24-26
8	8	LSU	7-2-0	beat Notre Dame 21-19
9	9	Alabama	9-2-0	bye week
10	10	Southern Cal	7-2-0	lost to # 18 UCLA 25-45
13	11	Arkansas	8-2-0	beat SMU 41-0
12	12	Washington	7-2-1	beat Washington St. 44-23
11	13	Texas A&M	7-2-0	beat TCU 74-10
15	14	Arizona	7-2-0	beat # 4 Arizona State 34-17
14	15	Auburn	8-2-0	bye week
16	16	Stanford	7-2-0	lost to California 11-17
17	17	Baylor	7-3-0	beat Texas 18-13
	18	UCLA	6-3-1	beat # 10 Southern Cal 45-25
18	19	Clemson	7-2-1	tied South Carolina 21-21
20	20	Georgia	7-3-0	bye week
19		North Carolina St.	7-2-1	beat Western Carolina 31-18
20		San Jose State	9-2-0	regular season complete

November 24 Poll — Nov. 29 Games

UP	AP	Team	Record	Result
1	1	Miami, Fla.	10-0-0	beat East Carolina 36-10 (N27)
2	2	Penn State	11-0-0	regular season complete
3	3	Oklahoma	10-1-0	regular season complete
4	4	Michigan	10-1-0	regular season complete
6	5	LSU	8-2-0	beat Tulane 37-17
5	6	Nebraska	9-2-0	regular season complete
7	7	Alabama	9-2-0	lost to # 14 Auburn 17-21
8	8	Arizona State	9-1-1	regular season complete
10	9	Arkansas	9-2-0	regular season complete
9	10	Texas A&M	8-2-0	beat Texas 16-3 (N27)
13	11	Ohio State	9-3-0	regular season complete
11	12	Arizona	8-2-0	lost to Stanford 24-29 (N30)
12	13	Washington	8-2-1	regular season complete
14	14	Auburn	8-2-0	beat # 7 Alabama 21-17
16	15	UCLA	7-3-1	regular season complete
15	16	Baylor	8-3-0	regular season complete
17	17	Southern Cal	7-3-0	lost to Notre Dame 37-38
	18	Georgia	7-3-0	beat Georgia Tech 31-24
19	19	North Carolina St.	8-2-1	regular season complete
	20	Iowa	8-3-0	regular season complete
18		Clemson	7-2-2	regular season complete
19		Florida State	6-3-1	lost to Florida 13-17
19		San Jose State	9-2-0	

December 1 Poll / January 3 Final Poll

UP	AP	December 1 Poll	Record	Bowl Bid	Date	Bowl Result	RB	UP	AP	January 3 Final Poll	Record
1	1	Miami, Fla.	11-0-0	Fiesta Bowl	J2	lost to # 2 Penn State 10-14	1	1	1	Penn State	12-0-0
2	2	Penn State	11-0-0	Fiesta Bowl	J2	beat # 1 Miami, Fla. 14-10	2	2	2	Miami, Fla.	11-1-0
3	3	Oklahoma	10-1-0	Orange Bowl	J1	beat # 9 Arkansas 42-8	3	3	3	Oklahoma	11-1-0
4	4	Michigan	10-1-0	Rose Bowl	J1	lost to # 7 Arizona State 15-22	4	5	4	Arizona State	10-1-1
6	5	LSU	9-2-0	Sugar Bowl	J1	lost to # 6 Nebraska 15-30	8	4	5	Nebraska	10-2-0
5	6	Nebraska	9-2-0	Sugar Bowl	J1	beat # 5 LSU 30-15	6	8	6	Auburn	10-2-0
8	7	Arizona State	9-1-1	Rose Bowl	J1	beat # 4 Michigan 22-15	9	6	7	Ohio State	10-3-0
7	8	Texas A&M	9-2-0	Cotton Bowl	J1	lost to # 11 Ohio State 12-28	5	7	8	Michigan	11-2-0
10	9	Arkansas	9-2-0	Orange Bowl	J1	lost to # 3 Oklahoma 8-42	7	9	9	Alabama	10-3-0
9	10	Auburn	9-2-0	Citrus Bowl	J1	beat Southern Cal 16-7	10	11	10	LSU	9-3-0
12	11	Ohio State	9-3-0	Cotton Bowl	J1	beat # 8 Texas A&M 28-12	15	13	11	Arizona	9-3-0
11	12	Washington	8-2-1	Sun Bowl	D25	lost to # 13 Alabama 6-28	14	12	12	Baylor	9-3-0
14	13	Alabama	9-3-0	Sun Bowl	D25	beat # 12 Washington 28-6	13	14	13	Texas A&M	9-3-0
16	14	Baylor	8-3-0	Bluebonnet Bowl	D31	beat Colorado 21-9	11	16	14	UCLA	8-3-1
15	15	UCLA	7-3-1	Freedom Bowl	D30	beat Brigham Young 31-10	12	15	15	Arkansas	9-3-0
13	16	Arizona	8-3-0	Aloha Bowl	D27	beat North Carolina 30-21	20	17	16	Iowa	9-3-0
	17	Georgia	8-3-0	Hall of Fame Bowl	D23	lost to Boston College 24-27	19	17	17	Clemson	8-2-2
	18	North Carolina St.	8-2-1	Peach Bowl	D31	lost to Virginia Tech 24-25	17	18	18	Washington	8-3-1
	19	Iowa	8-3-0	Holiday Bowl	D30	beat San Diego State 39-38	29		19	Boston College	9-3-0
17	20	Stanford	8-3-0	Gator Bowl	D27	lost to Clemson 21-27			20	Virginia Tech	9-2-1
18		Clemson	7-2-2	Gator Bowl	D27	beat # 20 Stanford 27-21	27	20		Florida State	7-4-1
19		San Jose State	9-2-0	California Bowl	D13	beat Miami, Ohio 37-7					

1986

CONSENSUS ALL-AMERICANS

POS	Offense	HT	WT	School	AP	CF	FC	FW	PI
QB	Vinny Testaverde	6-5	218	Miami, Fla.	•	•	•	•	•
RB	Brent Fullwood	5-11	209	Auburn	•	•	•	•	•
RB	Paul Palmer	5-10	180	Temple	•	•	•	•	•
RB	Terrence Flagler	6-1	200	Clemson	•			•	
RB	Brad Muster	6-3	226	Stanford				•	
RB	D.J. Dozier	6-1	204	Penn State					
WR	Cris Carter	6-3	194	Ohio State	•	•	•	•	•
TE	Keith Jackson	6-3	241	Oklahoma	•	•	•	•	•
L	Jeff Bregel	6-4	280	Southern Cal	•	•	•	•	•
L	Randy Dixon	6-4	286	Pittsburgh	•	•		•	•
L	Danny Villa	6-5	284	Arizona State	•	•			
L	John Clay	6-5	285	Missouri	•	•	•	•	•
C	Ben Tamburello	6-3	268	Auburn	•	•	•	•	•
PK	Jeff Jaeger	5-11	191	Washington	•	•	•		

	OTHERS RECEIVING FIRST-TEAM HONORS								
WR	Wendell Davis			LSU				•	
WR	Tim Brown			Notre Dame	•		•		
L	Jeff Zimmerman			Florida	•				
L	Chris Conlin			Penn State				•	
L	Dave Croston			Iowa				•	
L	Paul Kiser			Wake Forest				•	
L	John Elliott			Michigan			•		
L	Randall McDaniel			Arizona State			•		
L	Mark Hutson			Oklahoma	•				
L	Harris Barton			North Carolina	•				
L	John Phillips			Clemson			•		
PK	Marty Zendejas			Nevada			•		
PK	Jeff Ward			Texas			•		

POS	Defense	HT	WT	School	AP	CF	FC	FW	PI
L	Jerome Brown	6-2	285	Miami, Fla.	•	•	•	•	•
L	Danny Noonan	6-4	280	Nebraska	•	•	•	•	•
L	Tony Woods	6-4	240	Pittsburgh			•	•	•
L	Jason Buck	6-6	270	Brigham Young	•	•		•	•
L	Reggie Rogers	6-6	260	Washington		•	•		
LB	Cornelius Bennett	6-4	235	Alabama	•	•	•	•	•
LB	Shane Conlan	6-3	225	Penn State	•	•	•	•	•
LB	Brian Bosworth	6-2	240	Oklahoma	•	•	•	•	•
LB	Chris Spielman	6-2	227	Ohio State	•	•	•	•	•
DB	Thomas Everett	5-9	180	Baylor	•	•	•	•	•
DB	Tim McDonald	6-3	205	Southern Cal	•	•	•	•	•
DB	Bennie Blades	6-0	207	Miami, Fla.	•	•			
DB	Rod Woodson	6-0	195	Purdue	•	•			
DB	Garland Rivers	6-1	187	Michigan	•				
P	Barry Helton	6-4	200	Colorado	•				

	OTHERS RECEIVING FIRST-TEAM HONORS								
DL	Tim Johnson			Penn State		•			
DL	Al Noga			Hawaii	•				
LB	Terry Maki			Air Force			•		
DB	John Little			Georgia				•	
DB	Gordon Lockbaum			Holy Cross	•				
DB	Mark Moore			Oklahoma State	•				
P	Greg Horne			Arkansas			•		
P	Bill Smith			Mississippi		•			
P	Greg Montgomery			Michigan State				•	

FC named Bennett as a DL; FC named Conlan as a DL

HEISMAN TROPHY VOTING

	PLAYER	POS	SCHOOL	1ST	2ND	3RD	TOTAL
1	Vinny Testaverde	QB	Miami, Fla.	678	76	27	2213
2	Paul Palmer	TB	Temple	28	207	174	672
3	Jim Harbaugh	QB	Michigan	25	136	111	458
4	Brian Bosworth	LB	Oklahoma	9	136	96	395
5	Gordie Lockbaum	TB	Holy Cross	32	39	68	242
6	Brent Fullwood	TB	Auburn	4	45	27	129
7	Cornelius Bennett	LB	Alabama	3	29	29	96
8	D.J. Dozier	TB	Penn State	0	23	31	77
9	Kevin Sweeney	QB	Fresno State	6	16	23	73
10	Chris Spielman	LB	Ohio State	5	9	27	60

AWARD WINNERS

PLAYER	POS/SCHOOL	AWARD	PLAYER	POS/SCHOOL	AWARD
Vinny Testaverde	QB Miami, Fla.	Maxwell	Vinny Testaverde	QB Miami, Fla.	O'Brien
Jason Buck	DT Brigham Young	Outland	Brian Bosworth	LB Oklahoma	Butkus
Vinny Testaverde	QB Miami, Fla.	Camp	Thomas Everett	DB Baylor	Thorpe
Cornelius Bennett	LB Alabama	Lombardi			

BOWL GAMES

DATE	GAME	SCORE
D13	California	San Jose State 37, Miami, Ohio 7
D20	Independence	Mississippi 20, Texas Tech 17
D23	Hall of Fame	Boston College 27, Georgia 24
D25	Sun	Alabama 28, Washington 6
D27	Aloha	Arizona 30, North Carolina 21
D27	Gator	Clemson 27, Stanford 21
D29	Liberty	Tennessee 21, Minnesota 14
D30	Holiday	Iowa 39, San Diego State 38
D30	Freedom	UCLA 31, Brigham Young 10
D31	Bluebonnet	Baylor 21, Colorado 9
D31	All-American	Florida State 27, Indiana 13
D31	Peach	Virginia Tech 25, North Carolina St. 24
J1	Rose	Arizona State 22, Michigan 15
J1	Florida Citrus	Auburn 16, Southern Cal 7
J1	Cotton	Ohio State 28, Texas A&M 12
J1	Orange	Oklahoma 42, Arkansas 8
J1	Sugar	Nebraska 30, LSU 15
J2	Fiesta	Penn State 14, Miami, Fla. 10

CONFERENCE STANDINGS

ACC

	Conf. W	L	T	Overall W	L	T
Clemson	5	1	1	8	2	2
North Carolina St.	5	2	0	8	3	1
North Carolina	5	2	0	7	4	1
Georgia Tech	3	3	0	5	5	1
Maryland	2	3	1	5	5	1
Wake Forest	2	5	0	5	6	0
Duke	2	5	0	4	7	0
Virginia	2	5	0	3	8	0

Big 10

	Conf. W	L	T	Overall W	L	T
Michigan	7	1	0	11	2	0
Ohio State	7	1	0	10	3	0
Iowa	5	3	0	9	3	0
Minnesota	5	3	0	6	6	0
Michigan State	4	4	0	6	5	0
Indiana	3	5	0	6	6	0
Illinois	3	5	0	4	7	0
Northwestern	2	6	0	4	7	0
Purdue	2	6	0	3	8	0
Wisconsin	2	6	0	3	9	0

Big 8

	Conf. W	L	T	Overall W	L	T
Oklahoma	7	0	0	11	1	0
Colorado	6	1	0	6	6	0
Nebraska	5	2	0	10	2	0
Oklahoma State	4	3	0	6	5	0
Iowa State	3	4	0	6	5	0
Missouri	2	5	0	3	8	0
Kansas State	1	6	0	2	9	0
Kansas	0	7	0	3	8	0

Big West

	Conf. W	L	T	Overall W	L	T
San Jose State	7	0	0	10	2	0
Fresno State	6	1	0	9	2	0
Long Beach State	4	3	0	6	5	0
Nevada-Las Vegas	3	4	0	6	5	0
Utah State	3	4	0	3	8	0
Pacific	2	5	0	4	7	0
Cal-St. Fullerton	2	5	0	3	9	0
New Mexico State	1	6	0	1	10	0

Ivy

	Conf. W	L	T	Overall W	L	T
Pennsylvania	7	0	0	10	0	0
Cornell	6	1	0	8	2	0
Brown	4	2	1	5	4	1
Dartmouth	3	3	1	3	6	1
Harvard	3	4	0	3	7	0
Yale	2	5	0	3	7	0
Princeton	2	5	0	2	8	0
Columbia	0	7	0	0	10	0

MAC

	Conf. W	L	T	Overall W	L	T
Miami, Ohio	6	2	0	8	4	0
Toledo	5	3	0	7	4	0
Kent State	5	3	0	5	6	0
Bowling Green	5	3	0	5	6	0
Eastern Michigan	4	4	0	6	5	0
Ball State	4	4	0	6	5	0
Central Michigan	4	4	0	5	5	0
Western Michigan	3	5	0	3	8	0
Ohio U	0	8	0	1	10	0

Pac 10

	Conf. W	L	T	Overall W	L	T
Arizona State	5	1	1	10	1	1
Washington	5	2	1	8	3	1
UCLA	5	2	1	8	3	1
Arizona	5	3	0	9	3	0
Stanford	5	3	0	8	4	0
Southern Cal	5	3	0	7	5	0
Oregon	3	5	0	5	6	0
Washington State	2	6	1	3	7	1
California	2	7	0	2	9	0
Oregon State	1	6	0	3	8	0

SEC

	Conf. W	L	T	Overall W	L	T
LSU	5	1	0	9	3	0
Auburn	4	2	0	10	2	0
Alabama	4	2	0	10	3	0
Mississippi	4	2	0	8	3	1
Georgia	4	2	0	8	4	0
Tennessee	3	3	0	7	5	0
Florida	2	4	0	6	5	0
Mississippi State	2	4	0	6	5	0
Kentucky	2	4	0	5	5	1
Vanderbilt	0	6	0	1	10	0

SWC

	Conf. W	L	T	Overall W	L	T
Texas A&M	7	1	0	9	3	0
Baylor	6	2	0	9	3	0
Arkansas	6	2	0	9	3	0
Texas Tech	5	3	0	7	5	0
SMU	5	3	0	6	5	0
Texas	4	4	0	5	6	0
Rice	2	6	0	4	7	0
TCU	1	7	0	3	8	0
Houston	0	8	0	1	10	0

WAC

	Conf. W	L	T	Overall W	L	T
San Diego State	7	1	0	8	4	0
Brigham Young	6	2	0	8	5	0
Air Force	5	2	0	6	5	0
Hawaii	4	4	0	7	5	0
Colorado State	4	4	0	6	5	0
Wyoming	4	4	0	6	6	0
New Mexico	2	5	0	4	8	0
Texas-El Paso	2	6	0	4	8	0
Utah	1	7	0	2	9	0

Independents

	Overall W	L	T
Penn State	12	0	0
Miami, Fla.	11	1	0
Virginia Tech	9	2	1
Boston College	9	3	0
Tulsa	7	4	0
Florida State	7	4	1
La. Lafayette	6	5	0
Temple	6	5	0
Southern Miss	6	5	0
Army	6	5	0
Pittsburgh	5	5	1
Rutgers	5	5	1
Syracuse	5	6	0
Cincinnati	5	6	0
Notre Dame	5	6	0
Tulane	4	7	0
West Virginia	4	7	0
South Carolina	3	6	2
Navy	3	8	0
Louisville	3	8	0
East Carolina	2	9	0
Northern Illinois	2	9	0

1986 NCAA Major College Statistical Leaders

Individual Leaders

PASSING	CL	G	ATT	COM	PCT	INT	I%	YDS	YPA	TD	TD%	RATING
1 Vinny Testaverde, Miami, Fla.	SR	10	276	175	63.4	9	3.3	2557	9.3	26	9.4	165.8
2 Jim Harbaugh, Michigan	SR	12	254	167	65.8	8	3.2	2557	10.1	10	3.9	157.0
3 Dave Yarema, Michigan State	SR	11	297	200	67.3	11	3.7	2581	8.7	16	5.4	150.7
4 Shawn Halloran, Boston College	SR	10	258	159	61.6	6	2.3	2090	8.1	17	6.6	146.8
5 Mark Vlasic, Iowa	SR	9	152	93	61.2	4	2.6	1234	8.1	9	5.9	143.7
6 Tom Hodson, LSU	FR	11	288	175	60.8	8	2.8	2261	7.9	19	6.6	142.9
7 Jeff Francis, Tennessee	SO	11	233	150	64.4	6	2.6	1946	8.4	9	3.9	142.1
8 Lee Saltz, Temple	SR	11	203	117	57.6	7	3.5	1727	8.5	12	5.9	141.7
9 Jeff Van Raaphorst, Arizona State	SR	11	239	144	60.3	11	4.6	1988	8.3	15	6.3	141.6
10 Ned James, New Mexico	SR	11	215	125	58.1	8	3.7	1777	8.3	14	6.5	141.6

ALL-PURPOSE	CL	G	RUSH	REC	PR	KR	YDS	YPG
1 Paul Palmer, Temple	SR	11	1866	110	0	657	2633	239.4
2 Rick Calhoun, Cal. St. Fullerton	SR	12	1398	125	138	522	2183	181.9
3 Tim Brown, Notre Dame	JR	11	254	910	75	698	1937	176.1
4 Bobby Humphrey, Alabama	SO	12	1471	201	0	344	2016	168.0
5 Gary Patton, Eastern Michigan	JR	11	1058	371	0	384	1813	164.8
6 Troy Stradford, Boston College	SR	10	1188	445	0	0	1633	163.3
7 Sterling Sharpe, South Carolina	JR	11	104	1106	190	377	1777	161.6
8 Kelvin Farmer, Toledo	SR	11	1532	203	0	0	1735	157.7
9 Steve Bartalo, Colorado State	SR	11	1419	289	0	0	1708	155.3
10 Chuck Smith, Navy	JR	9	933	280	0	135	1348	149.8

RUSHING/Yards Per Game	CL	G	ATT	YDS	TD	AVG	YPG
1 Paul Palmer, Temple	SR	11	346	1866	15	5.4	169.6
2 Kelvin Farmer, Toledo	SR	11	299	1532	16	5.1	139.3
3 Steve Bartalo, Colorado State	SR	11	366	1419	19	3.9	129.0
4 Brent Fullwood, Auburn	SR	11	167	1391	10	8.3	126.5
5 Derrick Fenner, North Carolina	SO	10	200	1250	6	6.3	125.0
6 Rodney Stevenson, Central Michigan	SO	9	208	1104	14	5.3	122.7
7 Bobby Humphrey, Alabama	SO	12	236	1471	15	6.2	122.6
8 Reggie Taylor, Cincinnati	SR	11	256	1325	11	5.2	120.5
9 Troy Stradford, Boston College	SR	10	218	1188	10	5.4	118.8
10 Rick Calhoun, Cal-St. Fullerton	SR	12	259	1398	11	5.4	116.5

RUSHING/Yards Per Carry	CL	G	ATT	YDS	YPC
1 Brent Fullwood, Auburn	SR	11	167	1391	8.3
2 Tony Jeffery, TCU	JR	9	122	861	7.1
3 Terrence Flagler, Clemson	SR	11	180	1176	6.5
4 Derrick Ellison, Tulsa	SO	11	170	1064	6.3
5 Derrick Fenner, North Carolina	SO	10	200	1250	6.3
6 Bobby Humphrey, Alabama	SO	12	236	1471	6.2
7 Darrell Thompson, Minnesota	FR	11	217	1240	5.7
8 Troy Stradford, Boston College	SR	10	218	1188	5.4
9 Rick Calhoun, Cal. St. Fullerton	SR	12	259	1398	5.4
10 Paul Palmer, Temple	SR	11	346	1866	5.4

RECEIVING	CL	G	REC	YDS	TD	YPR	YPG	RPG
1 Mark Templeton, Long Beach State	SR	11	99	688	2	6.9	62.5	9.0
2 Loren Richey, Utah	SR	9	67	775	6	11.6	86.1	7.4
3 Wendell Davis, LSU	JR	11	80	1244	11	15.6	113.1	7.3
4 Dave Montagne, Oregon State	SR	11	78	862	2	11.1	78.4	7.1
5 Sterling Sharpe, South Carolina	JR	11	74	1106	10	14.9	100.5	6.7
6 Guy Liggins, San Jose State	JR	11	72	983	6	13.7	89.4	6.6
7 Marc Zeno, Tulane	JR	11	68	1033	7	15.2	93.9	6.2
8 James Brim, Wake Forest	SR	11	66	930	5	14.1	84.5	6.0
9 Rod Bernstine, Texas A&M	SR	11	65	710	5	10.9	64.5	5.9
10 Craig McEwen, Utah	SR	11	64	721	7	11.3	65.5	5.8

PUNTING	CL	PUNT	YDS	AVG
1 Greg Horne, Arkansas	SR	49	2313	47.2
2 Alexander Waits, Texas	FR	48	2214	46.1
3 Chris Becker, TCU	SO	59	2717	46.1
4 Barry Helton, Colorado	JR	57	2599	45.6
5 Bill Smith, Mississippi	SR	57	2522	44.3
6 Brian Shulman, Auburn	SO	49	2161	44.1
7 Cris Carpenter, Georgia	SO	41	1808	44.1
8 Mike Preacher, Oregon	SR	49	2141	43.7
9 Mark Simon, Air Force	SR	63	2754	43.7
10 Tom Tupa, Ohio State	JR	50	2180	43.6

PUNT RETURNS	CL	PR	YDS	TD	AVG
1 Rod Smith, Nebraska	JR	12	227	1	18.9
2 Kwante Hampton, Long Beach State	SR	24	363	2	15.1
3 Riccardo Ingram, Georgia Tech	JR	16	233	0	14.6
4 Jeff Joseph, Arizona State	JR	15	212	0	14.1
5 Milt Garner, Kansas	JR	14	193	2	13.8
6 Tyrone Thurman, Texas Tech	SO	33	444	2	13.5
7 Dana Brinson, Nebraska	SO	27	340	0	12.6
8 Kelvin Martin, Boston College	SR	18	222	1	12.3
9 Thomas Henley, Stanford	SR	29	353	1	12.2
10 Andrew Mott, Southern Miss	SR	36	438	1	12.2

KICKOFF RETURNS	CL	KR	YDS	TD	AVG
1 Terrance Roulhac, Clemson	SR	17	561	0	33.0
2 Blair Thomas, Penn State	SO	12	383	1	31.9
3 Tim Brown, Notre Dame	JR	25	698	2	27.9
4 Steve Jones, Washington	SO	15	407	0	27.1
5 Keith Jones, Illinois	SO	15	398	0	26.5
6 Keith Ross, Florida State	SO	22	583	1	26.5
7 Chris Thomas, Miami, Ohio	JR	17	441	1	25.9
8 Vince Delgado, California	JR	11	285	0	25.9
9 Tom Rotello, Air Force	SR	20	518	0	25.9
10 Lonnie White, Southern Cal	SR	26	656	0	25.2

SCORING	CL	TDS	XP	FG	PTS	PTPG
1 Steve Bartalo, Colorado State	SR	19	0	0	114	10.4
2 Rodney Stevenson, Central Michigan	SO	14	0	0	84	9.3
3 Lars Tate, Georgia	JR	17	0	0	102	9.3
4 Scott Slater, Texas A&M	JR	0	37	21	100	9.1
5 Gary Coston, Arizona	FR	0	34	21	97	8.8
6 Tim Lashar, Oklahoma	SR	0	60	12	96	8.7
6 Barry Belli, Fresno State	JR	0	33	21	96	8.7
6 Kelvin Farmer, Toledo	SR	16	0	0	96	8.7
9 Bobby Humphrey, Alabama	SO	17	2	0	104	8.7
10 Chris Kinzer, Virginia Tech	SO	0	27	22	93	8.5
10 Jeff Jaeger, Washington	SR	0	42	17	93	8.5

FIELD GOALS	CL	FGA	FGM	PCT	FGG
1 Chris Kinzer, Virginia Tech	SO	27	22	0.82	2.00
2 Gary Coston, Arizona	FR	24	21	0.88	1.91
2 Scott Slater, Texas A&M	JR	27	21	0.78	1.91
2 John Carney, Notre Dame	SR	28	21	0.75	1.91
2 Barry Belli, Fresno State	JR	31	21	0.68	1.91
6 John Duvic, Northwestern	SR	23	19	0.83	1.73
6 Steve DeLine, Colorado State	SR	24	19	0.79	1.73
8 Jeff Jaeger, Washington	SR	21	17	0.81	1.55
8 John Diettrich, Ball State	SR	23	17	0.74	1.55
8 Joe Worley, Kentucky	JR	25	17	0.68	1.55
8 Bryan Lowe, Boston College	SO	25	17	0.68	1.55

INTERCEPTIONS	CL	INT	YDS	TD	INT/GM
1 Bennie Blades, Miami, Fla.	JR	10	128	0	0.91
2 Teddy Johnson, Oregon State	SO	9	86	0	0.82
3 Toi Cook, Stanford	SR	7	115	0	0.78
4 Ron Francis, Baylor	SR	8	25	0	0.73
4 Elton Slater, La. Lafayette	SR	8	1	0	0.73
6 Jim King, Colorado State	SR	7	83	0	0.64
6 Ed Hulbert, Oregon	SR	7	48	0	0.64
6 Chris Wagner, Western Michigan	FR	7	17	0	0.64
9 Jeff Wilcox, Brigham Young	SR	7	110	0	0.58

Team Leaders

RUSHING OFFENSE	G	ATT	YDS	AVG	TD	YPG
1 Oklahoma	11	719	4452	6.2	51	404.7
2 Nebraska	11	656	3360	5.1	40	305.5
3 Tulsa	11	652	3184	4.9	24	289.5
4 Central Michigan	10	591	2798	4.7	26	279.8
5 Army	11	689	3042	4.4	33	276.5
6 Clemson	11	648	3007	4.6	28	273.4
7 Pacific	11	677	2960	4.4	22	269.1
8 Alabama	12	585	3167	5.4	25	263.9
9 Georgia	11	596	2802	4.7	24	254.7
10 North Carolina	11	553	2777	5.0	16	252.5

PASSING OFFENSE	G	ATT	COM	INT	PCT	YDS	YPA	TD	I%	YPC	YPG
1 San Jose State	11	456	276	23	60.5	3437	7.5	21	5.0	12.5	312.5
2 Wyoming	12	564	305	22	54.1	3523	6.2	30	3.9	11.6	293.6
3 South Carolina	11	356	216	23	60.7	3187	9.0	23	6.5	14.8	289.7
4 Utah	11	451	264	14	58.5	3157	7.0	25	3.1	12.0	287.0
5 Oregon State	11	527	312	22	59.2	3149	6.0	10	4.2	10.1	286.3
6 Miami, Fla.	11	338	209	11	61.8	3095	9.2	30	3.3	14.8	281.4
7 Long Beach State	11	449	259	21	57.7	3069	6.8	21	4.7	11.8	279.0
8 Texas-El Paso	12	437	270	21	61.8	3231	7.4	23	4.8	12.0	269.3
9 Cincinnati	11	374	237	12	63.4	2831	7.6	13	3.2	11.9	257.4
10 San Diego State	11	390	241	12	61.8	2766	7.1	14	3.1	11.5	251.5

TOTAL OFFENSE	G	P	YDS	AVG	TD	YPG
1 San Jose State	11	909	5295	5.8	43	481.4
2 Oklahoma	11	807	5210	6.5	58	473.6
3 Texas A&M	11	895	4842	5.4	39	440.2
4 New Mexico	12	897	5269	5.9	42	439.1
5 Baylor	11	889	4827	5.4	34	438.8
6 North Carolina	11	822	4796	5.8	34	436.0
7 Michigan	12	870	5175	5.9	44	431.3
8 Utah	11	823	4684	5.7	35	425.8
9 Iowa	11	772	4628	6.0	42	420.7
10 Auburn	11	766	4580	6.0	45	416.4

RUSHING DEFENSE	G	ATT	YDS	AVG	TD	YPG
1 Oklahoma	11	408	668	1.6	1	60.7
2 San Jose State	11	387	724	1.9	4	65.8
3 Penn State	11	383	767	2.0	5	69.7
4 Arizona	11	392	928	2.4	9	84.4
5 Baylor	11	396	977	2.5	11	88.8
6 Brigham Young	12	439	1066	2.4	12	88.8
7 Washington	11	400	978	2.4	10	88.9
8 Pittsburgh	11	433	1027	2.4	8	93.4
9 Nebraska	11	442	1051	2.4	7	95.5
10 Fresno State	11	462	1097	2.4	4	99.7

PASSING DEFENSE	G	ATT	COM	PCT	YPC	INT	I%	YDS	YPA	TD	YPG
1 Oklahoma	11	263	128	48.7	9.4	18	6.8	1198	4.6	7	108.9
2 Tennessee	11	203	99	48.8	12.6	13	6.4	1248	6.1	7	113.5
3 Bowling Green	11	221	109	49.3	11.5	20	9.0	1257	5.7	4	114.3
4 Florida	11	227	119	52.4	10.8	16	7.0	1287	5.7	4	117.0
5 Oklahoma State	11	193	105	54.4	12.7	12	6.2	1331	6.9	6	121.0
6 Mississippi State	11	197	103	52.3	13.8	8	4.1	1423	7.2	9	129.4
7 Toledo	11	263	146	55.5	10.0	16	6.1	1464	5.6	8	133.1
8 Mississippi	11	268	127	47.4	11.7	14	5.2	1484	5.5	6	134.9
9 Georgia Tech	11	253	129	51.0	11.7	14	5.5	1506	6.0	9	136.9
9 Miami, Fla.	11	291	130	44.7	11.6	21	7.2	1506	5.2	7	136.9

TOTAL DEFENSE	G	P	YDS	AVG	TD	YPG
1 Oklahoma	11	671	1866	2.8	8	169.6
2 Nebraska	11	700	2590	3.7	17	235.5
3 Baylor	11	707	2727	3.9	23	247.9
4 Texas A&M	11	721	2835	3.9	22	257.7
5 Miami, Fla.	11	777	2886	3.7	13	262.4
6 Hawaii	12	781	3223	4.1	24	268.6
7 Washington	11	728	2982	4.1	19	271.1
8 Iowa	11	717	3031	4.2	18	275.5
9 Pittsburgh	11	758	3046	4.0	23	276.9
10 Brigham Young	12	789	3334	4.2	24	277.8

SCORING OFFENSE	G	PTS	AVG
1 Oklahoma	11	466	42.4
2 Miami, Fla.	11	420	38.2
3 Nebraska	11	416	37.8
4 Auburn	11	379	34.5
5 Washington	11	372	33.8
6 Florida State	11	366	33.3
7 San Jose State	11	360	32.7
7 Texas A&M	11	360	32.7
9 Arizona State	11	357	32.5
10 UCLA	11	354	32.2

SCORING DEFENSE	G	PTS	AVG
1 Oklahoma	11	73	6.6
2 Auburn	11	115	10.5
3 Penn State	11	123	11.2
4 Miami, Fla.	11	136	12.4
5 Arkansas	11	142	12.9
6 Alabama	12	157	13.1
7 Nebraska	11	150	13.6
7 Mississippi	11	150	13.6
7 Fresno State	11	150	13.6
10 Arizona State	11	152	13.8

1987 POLL PROGRESSION

ANNUAL REVIEW

PRE-SEASON 1987 — SEPT. 5 GAMES

AP	Team	Record	Result
1	Oklahoma	0-0-0	beat North Texas 69-14
2	Nebraska	0-0-0	beat Utah State 56-12
3	UCLA	0-0-0	beat San Diego State 47-14
4	Ohio State	0-0-0	bye week
5	Auburn	0-0-0	beat Texas 31-3
6	LSU	0-0-0	beat # 15 Texas A&M 17-3
7	Michigan	0-0-0	bye week
8	Florida State	0-0-0	beat Texas Tech 40-16
9	Clemson	0-0-0	beat Western Carolina 43-0
10	Miami, Fla.	0-0-0	beat # 20 Florida 31-4
11	Penn State	0-0-0	beat Bowling Green 45-19
12	Arkansas	0-0-0	bye week
13	Washington	0-0-0	beat Stanford 31-21
14	Arizona State	0-0-0	
15	Texas A&M	0-0-0	lost to # 6 LSU 3-17
16	Iowa	0-0-0	lost to # 17 Tennessee 22-23 (A30)
17	Tennessee	0-0-0	beat Colorado State 49-3
18	Notre Dame	0-0-0	bye week
19	Southern Cal	0-0-0	lost to Michigan State 13-27 (S7)
20	Florida	0-0-0	lost to # 10 Miami, Fla. 4-31
20	Georgia	0-0-0	beat Virginia 30-22

SEPTEMBER 7 POLL — SEPT. 12 GAMES

UP	AP	Team	Record	Result
1	1	Oklahoma	1-0-0	beat North Carolina 28-0
2	2	Nebraska	1-0-0	beat # 3 UCLA 42-33
3	3	UCLA	1-0-0	lost to # 2 Nebraska 33-42
4	4	Auburn	1-0-0	beat Kansas 49-0
5	5	Ohio State	0-0-0	beat West Virginia 24-3
6	6	LSU	1-0-0	beat Fullerton St. 56-12
7	7	Miami, Fla.	1-0-0	bye week
11	8	Florida State	1-0-0	beat East Carolina 44-3
8	9	Michigan	0-0-0	lost to # 16 Notre Dame 7-26
10	10	Clemson	1-0-0	beat Virginia Tech 22-10
9	11	Penn State	1-0-0	lost to # 19 Alabama 13-24
13	12	Washington	1-0	beat Purdue 28-10
12	13	Arkansas	0-0-0	beat Mississippi 31-10
14	14	Tennessee	2-0-0	beat Mississippi 38-10
15	15	Arizona State	0-0-0	beat Illinois 21-7
16	16	Notre Dame	0-0-0	beat # 9 Michigan 26-7
	17	Michigan State	1-0-0	bye week
18	18	Pittsburgh	1-0-0	beat North Carolina St. 34-0
17	19	Alabama	1-0-0	beat # 11 Penn State 24-13
	20	Georgia	1-0-0	beat Oregon State 41-7
19		North Carolina	1-0-0	lost to # 1 Oklahoma 0-28
20		Southern Cal	0-1-0	bye week

SEPTEMBER 14 POLL — SEPT. 19 GAMES

UP	AP	Team	Record	Result
1	1	Oklahoma	2-0-0	bye week
2	2	Nebraska	2-0-0	bye week
3	3	Auburn	2-0-0	bye week
5	4	LSU	2-0-0	tied # 5 Ohio State 13-13
4	5	Ohio State	1-0-0	tied # 4 LSU 13-13
6	6	Miami, Fla.	1-0-0	bye week
7	7	Florida State	2-0-0	beat Memphis 41-24
8	8	Clemson	2-0-0	beat # 18 Georgia 21-20
9	9	Notre Dame	1-0-0	beat # 17 Michigan State 31-8
12	10	Washington	2-0-0	lost to Texas A&M 12-29
10	11	Alabama	2-0-0	lost to Florida 14-23
11	12	Arkansas	1-0-0	beat Tulsa 30-15
14	13	UCLA	1-1-0	beat Fresno State 17-0
13	14	Tennessee	2-0-0	bye week
15	15	Arizona State	1-0-0	beat Pacific 31-12
16	16	Pittsburgh	2-0-0	lost to Temple 21-24
18	17	Michigan State	1-0-0	lost to # 9 Notre Dame 8-31
17	18	Georgia	2-0-0	lost to # 8 Clemson 20-21
	19	Michigan	0-1-0	beat Washington St. 44-18
20	20	Penn State	1-1-0	beat Cincinnati 41-0
19		Boston College	2-0-0	lost to Southern Cal 17-23

SEPTEMBER 21 POLL — SEPT. 26 GAMES

UP	AP	Team	Record	Result
1	1	Oklahoma	2-0-0	beat Tulsa 65-0
2	2	Nebraska	2-0-0	beat # 12 Arizona State 35-28
3	3	Auburn	2-0-0	tied # 11 Tennessee 20-20
4	4	LSU	3-0-0	beat Rice 49-16
7	5	Miami, Fla.	1-0-0	beat Arkansas 51-7
8	6	Florida State	3-0-0	beat Michigan State 31-3
5	7	Ohio State	2-0-0	beat Oregon 24-14
6	8	Notre Dame	2-0-0	beat Purdue 44-20
9	9	Clemson	3-0-0	beat Georgia Tech 33-12
10	10	Arkansas	2-0-0	lost to Miami, Fla. 7-51
11	11	Tennessee	3-0-0	tied # 3 Auburn 20-20
12	12	Arizona State	2-0-0	lost to # 2 Nebraska 28-35
13	13	UCLA	2-1-0	beat Arizona 34-24
16	14	Michigan	1-1-0	beat Long Beach St. 49-0
14	15	Penn State	2-1-0	beat Boston College 27-17
17	16	Texas A&M	1-1-0	beat Southern Miss 27-14
	17	Alabama	2-1-0	beat Vanderbilt 30-23
20	18	Washington	2-1-0	beat Pacific 31-3
	19	Iowa	2-1-0	beat Kansas State 38-13
19	20	Georgia	2-1-0	beat South Carolina 13-6
15		Florida	2-1-0	beat Mississippi State 38-3
18		Syracuse	3-0-0	beat Virginia Tech 35-21

SEPTEMBER 28 POLL — OCT. 3 GAMES

UP	AP	Team	Record	Result
1	1	Oklahoma	3-0-0	beat Iowa State 56-3
2	2	Nebraska	3-0-0	beat South Carolina 30-21
3	3	Miami, Fla.	2-0-0	beat # 4 Florida State 26-25
4	4	Florida State	4-0-0	lost to # 3 Miami, Fla. 25-26
5	5	Notre Dame	3-0-0	bye week
6	6	Auburn	2-0-1	beat North Carolina 20-10
8	7	LSU	3-0-1	beat # 19 Florida 13-10
7	8	Clemson	3-0-1	bye week
9	9	Ohio State	2-0-1	beat Illinois 10-6
10	10	Tennessee	3-0-1	beat California 38-12
11	11	UCLA	3-1-0	beat Stanford 49-0
14	12	Michigan	2-1-0	beat Wisconsin 49-0
13	13	Arizona State	2-1-0	beat Texas-El Paso 35-16
12	14	Penn State	2-1-0	beat Temple 27-13
19	15	Texas A&M	2-1-0	lost to Texas Tech 21-27
16	16	Washington	3-1	lost to Oregon 22-29
17	17	Alabama	3-1-0	beat La. Lafayette 38-10
	18	Iowa	3-1-0	lost to Michigan State 14-19
18	19	Florida	3-1-0	lost to # 7 LSU 10-13
15	20	Georgia	3-1-0	beat Mississippi 31-14
19		Oklahoma State	4-0-0	bye week

OCTOBER 5 POLL — OCT. 10 GAMES

UP	AP	Team	Record	Result
1	1	Oklahoma	4-0-0	beat Texas 44-9
2	2	Nebraska	4-0-0	beat Kansas 54-2
3	3	Miami, Fla.	3-0-0	beat Maryland 46-16
4	4	Notre Dame	3-0-0	lost to Pittsburgh 22-30
5	5	Auburn	3-0-1	beat Vanderbilt 48-15
8	6	Florida State	4-1-0	beat Southern Miss 61-10
6	7	LSU	4-0-1	beat # 16 Georgia 26-23
7	8	Clemson	4-0-0	beat Virginia 38-21
9	9	Ohio State	3-0-1	lost to Indiana 10-31
10	10	Tennessee	4-1-0	bye week
11	11	UCLA	4-1-0	bye week
12	12	Michigan	3-1-0	lost to Michigan State 11-17
13	13	Arizona State	3-1-0	lost to Washington 14-27
14	14	Penn State	4-1-0	beat Rutgers 35-21
17	15	Alabama	4-1-0	lost to Memphis 10-13
15	16	Georgia	4-0-0	lost to # 7 LSU 23-26
16	17	Syracuse	5-0-0	bye week
19	18	Florida	3-2-0	beat Fullerton St. 65-0
18	19	Oklahoma State	4-0-0	beat Colorado 42-17
	20	Arkansas	3-1-0	beat Texas Tech 31-0
20		Southern Cal	3-1-0	lost to Oregon 27-34

OCTOBER 12 POLL — OCT. 17 GAMES

UP	AP	Team	Record	Result
1	1	Oklahoma	5-0-0	beat Kansas State 59-10
2	2	Nebraska	5-0-0	beat # 12 Oklahoma State 35-0
3	3	Miami, Fla.	4-0-0	bye week
7	4	Florida State	5-1-0	beat Louisville 32-9
4	5	Auburn	4-0-1	beat Georgia Tech 20-10
5	6	LSU	5-0-1	beat Kentucky 34-9
6	7	Clemson	5-0-0	beat Duke 17-10
8	8	Tennessee	4-0-1	lost to Alabama 22-41
9	9	UCLA	4-1-0	beat # 16 Oregon 41-10
10	10	Penn State	5-1-0	lost to # 13 Syracuse 21-48
13	11	Notre Dame	3-1-0	beat Air Force 35-14
12	12	Oklahoma State	5-0-0	lost to # 2 Nebraska 0-35
11	13	Syracuse	5-0-0	beat # 10 Penn State 48-21
14	14	Florida	4-2-0	beat Temple 34-3
15	15	Arkansas	4-1-0	lost to Texas 14-16
18	16	Oregon	4-1-0	lost to # 9 UCLA 10-41
16	17	Ohio State	3-1-1	beat Purdue 20-17
17	18	Georgia	4-2-0	beat Vanderbilt 52-24
20	19	Michigan State	3-2-0	beat Northwestern 38-0
	20	Indiana	4-1-0	beat Minnesota 18-17 (O16)
19		Minnesota	5-0-0	lost to # 20 Indiana 17-18 (O16)

OCTOBER 19 POLL — OCT. 24 GAMES

UP	AP	Team	Record	Result
1	1	Oklahoma	6-0-0	beat Colorado 24-6
2	2	Nebraska	6-0-0	beat Kansas State 56-3
3	3	Miami, Fla.	4-0-0	beat Cincinnati 48-10
5	4	Florida State	6-1-0	bye week
4	5	LSU	6-0-1	bye week
6	6	Auburn	5-0-1	beat Mississippi State 38-7
7	7	Clemson	6-0-0	lost to North Carolina St. 28-30
8	8	UCLA	5-1-0	beat California 42-18
9	9	Syracuse	6-0-0	beat Colgate 52-6
10	10	Notre Dame	4-1-0	beat Southern Cal 26-15
11	11	Florida	5-2-0	bye week
13	12	Georgia	5-2-0	beat Kentucky 17-14
16	13	Tennessee	4-1-1	beat Georgia Tech 29-15
15	14	Michigan State	4-1-0	tied Illinois 14-14
12	15	Indiana	5-1-0	beat # 20 Michigan 14-10
14	16	Ohio State	4-1-1	beat Minnesota 42-9
18	17	Alabama	5-2-0	bye week
	18	Penn State	5-2-0	bye week
19	19	Oklahoma State	5-1-0	beat Missouri 24-20
17	20	Michigan	4-2-0	lost to # 15 Indiana 10-14
20		South Carolina	4-2-0	beat East Carolina 34-12

OCTOBER 26 POLL — OCT. 31 GAMES

UP	AP	Team	Record	Result
1	1	Oklahoma	7-0-0	beat Kansas 71-10
2	2	Nebraska	7-0-0	beat Missouri 42-7
3	3	Miami, Fla.	5-0-0	beat East Carolina 41-3
5	4	Florida State	6-1-0	beat Tulane 73-14
4	5	LSU	6-0-1	beat Mississippi 42-13
6	6	Auburn	6-0-1	beat # 10 Florida 29-6
7	7	UCLA	6-1-0	beat Arizona State 31-23
8	8	Syracuse	7-0-0	beat Pittsburgh 24-10
9	9	Notre Dame	5-1-0	beat Navy 56-13
11	10	Florida	5-2-0	lost to # 6 Auburn 6-29
10	11	Indiana	6-1-0	lost to Iowa 21-29
14	12	Georgia	6-2-0	bye week
13	13	Tennessee	5-1-1	lost to Boston College 18-20
12	14	Clemson	6-1-0	beat Wake Forest 31-17
15	15	Ohio State	5-1-1	lost to # 20 Michigan 7-13
17	16	Alabama	5-2-0	beat Mississippi State 21-18
16	17	Oklahoma State	6-1-0	beat Kansas State 56-7
	18	Penn State	5-2-0	beat West Virginia 25-21
19	19	South Carolina	5-2-0	beat North Carolina St. 48-0
18	20	Michigan State	4-2-1	beat # 15 Ohio State 13-7
20		Arkansas	5-2-0	beat Rice 38-14

November 2 Poll

UP	AP	Team	Record	Nov. 7 Games
1	1	Oklahoma	8-0-0	beat #12 Oklahoma State 29-10
2	2	Nebraska	8-0-0	beat Iowa State 42-3
3	3	Miami, Fla.	6-0-0	beat Miami, Ohio 54-3
4	4	Florida State	7-1-0	beat #6 Auburn 34-6
5	5	LSU	7-0-1	lost to #13 Alabama 10-22
6	6	Auburn	7-0-1	lost to #4 Florida State 6-34
7	7	UCLA	7-1-0	beat Oregon State 52-17
8	8	Syracuse	8-0-0	beat Navy 34-10
9	9	Notre Dame	6-1-0	beat Boston College 32-25
10		Clemson	7-1-0	beat North Carolina 13-10
11	10	Georgia	6-2-0	beat #17 Florida 23-10
12	12	Oklahoma State	7-1-0	lost to #1 Oklahoma 10-29
15	13	Alabama	6-1-0	beat #5 LSU 22-10
14	13	South Carolina	6-2-0	bye week
13	15	Michigan State	5-2-1	beat Purdue 45-3
16	16	Penn State	6-2-0	beat Maryland 21-16
18	17	Florida	5-3-0	lost to #10 Georgia 10-23
17	18	Indiana	6-2-0	beat Illinois 34-22
20	19	Tennessee	5-2-1	beat Louisville 41-10
	20	Texas A&M	6-2-0	bye week
18		Arkansas	6-2-0	beat Baylor 10-7

November 9 Poll

UP	AP	Team	Record	Nov. 14 Games
1	1	Oklahoma	9-0-0	beat Missouri 17-13
2	2	Nebraska	9-0-0	bye week
3	3	Miami, Fla.	7-0-0	beat Virginia Tech 27-13
4	4	Florida State	8-1-0	beat Furman 41-10
5	5	UCLA	8-1-0	beat Washington 47-14
6	6	Syracuse	9-0-0	beat Boston College 45-17
7	7	Notre Dame	7-1-0	beat #11 Alabama 37-6
8	8	Georgia	7-2-0	lost to #12 Auburn 11-27
9	9	Clemson	8-1-0	beat Maryland 45-16
11	10	LSU	7-1-1	beat Mississippi State 34-14
10	11	Alabama	7-2-0	lost to #7 Notre Dame 6-37
12	12	Auburn	7-1-1	beat #8 Georgia 27-11
13	13	Michigan State	6-2-1	beat #16 Indiana 27-3
14	14	South Carolina	6-2-0	beat Wake Forest 30-0
16	15	Penn State	7-2-0	lost to Pittsburgh 0-10
15	16	Indiana	7-2-0	lost to #13 Michigan State 3-27
17	17	Oklahoma State	7-2-0	beat Kansas 49-17
19	18	Tennessee	6-2-1	beat Mississippi 55-13
20	19	Texas A&M	6-2-0	beat #20 Arkansas 14-0
18	20	Arkansas	7-2-0	lost to #19 Texas A&M 0-14

November 16 Poll

UP	AP	Team	Record	Nov. 21 Games
1	1	Nebraska	9-0-0	lost to #2 Oklahoma 7-17
2	2	Oklahoma	10-0-0	beat #1 Nebraska 17-7
3	3	Miami, Fla.	8-0-0	beat Toledo 24-14
4	4	Florida State	9-1-0	bye week
5	5	UCLA	9-1-0	lost to Southern Cal 13-17
6	6	Syracuse	10-0-0	beat West Virginia 32-31
7	7	Notre Dame	8-1-0	lost to Penn State 20-21
8	8	Clemson	9-1-0	lost to #12 South Carolina 7-20
10	9	LSU	8-1-1	beat Tulane 41-36
9	10	Auburn	8-1-1	bye week
11	11	Michigan State	7-2-1	beat Wisconsin 30-9
12	12	South Carolina	7-2-0	beat #8 Clemson 20-7
13	13	Oklahoma State	8-2-0	beat Iowa State 48-27
16	14	Georgia	7-3-0	bye week
15	15	Tennessee	7-2-1	beat Kentucky 24-22
14	16	Texas A&M	7-2-0	beat TCU 42-24
19	17	Alabama	7-3-0	bye week
20	18	Iowa	8-3-0	beat Minnesota 34-20
17	19	Pittsburgh	7-3-0	beat Kent State 28-5
	20	Indiana	7-3-0	beat Purdue 35-14
18		Southern Cal	7-3-0	beat #5 UCLA 17-13

November 23 Poll

UP	AP	Team	Record	Nov. 28 Games
1	1	Oklahoma	11-0-0	regular season complete
2	2	Miami, Fla.	9-0-0	beat #10 Notre Dame 24-0
3	3	Florida State	9-1-0	beat Florida 28-14
4	4	Syracuse	11-0-0	regular season complete
5	5	Nebraska	9-1-0	beat Colorado 24-7
7	6	LSU	9-1-1	regular season complete
6	7	Auburn	8-1-1	beat #18 Alabama 10-0 (N27)
9	8	South Carolina	8-2-0	bye week
8	9	Michigan State	8-2-1	regular season complete
11	10	Notre Dame	8-2-0	lost to #2 Miami, Fla. 0-24
10	11	UCLA	9-2-0	regular season complete
12	12	Oklahoma State	9-2-0	regular season complete
13	13	Clemson	9-2-0	regular season complete
17	14	Georgia	7-3-0	beat Georgia Tech 30-16
15	15	Texas A&M	8-2-0	beat Texas 20-13 N26
16	16	Tennessee	8-2-1	beat Vanderbilt 38-36
14	17	Southern Cal	8-3-0	regular season complete
	18	Alabama	7-3-0	lost to #7 Auburn 0-10 (N27)
	19	Iowa	9-3-0	regular season complete
19	20	Pittsburgh	8-3-0	regular season complete
18		Penn State	8-3-0	regular season complete
20		Indiana	8-3-0	regular season complete

November 30 Poll

UP	AP	Team	Record	Dec. 5 Games
1	1	Oklahoma	11-0-0	
2	2	Miami, Fla.	10-0-0	beat #8 South Carolina 20-16
3	3	Florida State	10-1-0	regular season complete
4	4	Syracuse	11-0-0	
5	5	Nebraska	10-1-0	regular season complete
6	6	Auburn	9-1-1	regular season complete
7	7	LSU	9-1-1	
9	8	South Carolina	8-2-0	lost to #2 Miami, Fla. 16-20
8	9	Michigan State	8-2-1	
11	10	UCLA	9-2-0	
10	11	Oklahoma State	9-2-0	
15	12	Notre Dame	8-3-0	regular season complete
13	13	Clemson	9-2-0	
14	14	Georgia	8-3-0	regular season complete
12	15	Texas A&M	9-2-0	regular season complete
17	16	Tennessee	9-2-1	regular season complete
16	17	Southern Cal	8-3-0	
20	18	Iowa	9-3-0	
18	19	Pittsburgh	8-3-0	
19	20	Penn State	8-3-0	regular season complete

December 7 Poll / January 3 Final Poll

UP	AP	December 7 Poll	Record	Bowl Bid	Date	Bowl Result	RB	UP	AP	January 3 Final Poll	Record
1	1	Oklahoma	11-0-0	Orange Bowl	J1	lost to #2 Miami, Fla. 14-20	1	1	1	Miami, Fla.	12-0-0
2	2	Miami, Fla.	11-0-0	Orange Bowl	J1	beat #1 Oklahoma 20-14	3	2	2	Florida State	11-1-0
3	3	Florida State	10-1-0	Fiesta Bowl	J1	beat #5 Nebraska 31-28	2	3	3	Oklahoma	11-1-0
4	4	Syracuse	11-0-0	Sugar Bowl	J1	tied #6 Auburn 16-16	4	4	4	Syracuse	11-0-1
5	5	Nebraska	10-1-0	Fiesta Bowl	J1	lost to #3 Florida State 28-31	7	5	5	LSU	10-1-1
6	6	Auburn	9-1-1	Sugar Bowl	J1	tied #4 Syracuse 16-16	6	6	6	Nebraska	10-2-0
7	7	LSU	9-1-1	Gator Bowl	D31	beat #9 South Carolina 30-13	5	7	7	Auburn	9-1-2
8	8	Michigan State	8-2-1	Rose Bowl	J1	beat #16 Southern Cal 20-17	9	8	8	Michigan State	9-2-1
9	9	South Carolina	8-3-0	Gator Bowl	D31	lost to #7 LSU 13-30	8	11	9	UCLA	10-2-0
10	10	UCLA	9-2-0	Aloha Bowl	D25	beat Florida 20-16	12	9	10	Texas A&M	10-2-0
11	11	Oklahoma State	9-2-0	Sun Bowl	D25	beat West Virginia 35-33	16	12	11	Oklahoma State	10-2-0
14	12	Notre Dame	8-3-0	Cotton Bowl	J1	lost to #13 Texas A&M 10-35	10	10	12	Clemson	10-2-0
13	13	Texas A&M	9-2-0	Cotton Bowl	J1	beat #12 Notre Dame 35-10	22	14	13	Georgia	9-3-0
12	14	Clemson	9-2-0	Citrus Bowl	J1	beat #20 Penn State 35-10	15	13	14	Tennessee	10-2-1
15	15	Georgia	8-3-0	Liberty Bowl	D29	beat Arkansas 20-17	36	15	15	South Carolina	8-4-0
17	16	Southern Cal	8-3-0	Rose Bowl	J1	lost to #8 Michigan State 17-20	13	15	16	Iowa	10-3-0
16	17	Tennessee	9-2-1	Peach Bowl	J2	beat Indiana 27-22	21		17	Notre Dame	8-4-0
	18	Iowa	9-3-0	Holiday Bowl	D30	beat Wyoming 20-19	11	17	18	Southern Cal	8-4-0
18	19	Pittsburgh	8-3-0	Bluebonnet Bowl	D31	lost to Texas 27-32	17	18	19	Michigan	8-4-0
19	20	Penn State	8-3-0	Citrus Bowl	J1	lost to #14 Clemson 10-35	32		20	Arizona State	7-4-1
20		Indiana	8-3-0	Peach Bowl	J2	lost to #17 Tennessee 22-27	19	19		Texas	7-5-1
							26	20		Indiana	8-4-0

ANNUAL REVIEW

1987

CONSENSUS ALL-AMERICANS

POS	Offense	HT	WT	School		AP	CF	FC	FW	PI
QB	Don McPherson	6-0	182	Syracuse		•	•	•	•	•
RB	Lorenzo White	5-11	211	Michigan State			•	•	•	•
RB	Craig Heyward	6-0	260	Pittsburgh		•		•	•	•
WR	Tim Brown	6-0	195	Notre Dame		•	•	•	•	•
WR	Wendell Davis	6-0	186	LSU		•		•	•	•
TE	Keith Jackson	6-3	248	Oklahoma		•	•	•	•	•
L	Mark Hutson	6-4	282	Oklahoma		•	•	•	•	•
L	Dave Cadigan	6-5	280	Southern Cal		•	•	•	•	•
L	John Elliott	6-7	306	Michigan				•	•	•
L	Randall McDaniel	6-5	261	Arizona State		•		•	•	•
C	Nacho Albergamo	6-2	257	LSU		•	•	•	•	•
PK	David Treadwell	6-1	165	Clemson		•	•		•	

	OTHERS RECEIVING FIRST-TEAM HONORS									
RB	Gaston Green			UCLA			•	•		
RB	Bobby Humphrey			Alabama			•			
RB	Thurman Thomas			Oklahoma State		•				
WR	Sterling Sharpe			South Carolina					•	
WR	Marc Zeno			Tulane			•			
WR	Ernie Jones			Indiana			•			
L	John McCormick			Nebraska			•			
L	Stacy Searels			Auburn			•			
PK	Marty Zendejas			Nevada		•				

FW and AP named Tim Brown as a KR.

POS	Defense	HT	WT	School		AP	CF	FC	FW	PI
L	Daniel Stubbs	6-4	250	Miami, Fla.		•	•	•	•	•
L	Chad Hennings	6-5	260	Air Force		•	•	•	•	•
L	Tracy Rocker	6-3	258	Auburn			•		•	•
L	Ted Gregory	6-1	260	Syracuse		•		•	•	•
L	John Roper	6-2	215	Texas A&M		•			•	
LB	Chris Spielman	6-2	236	Ohio State		•	•	•	•	•
LB	Aundray Bruce	6-6	236	Auburn		•	•	•	•	•
LB	Dante Jones	6-2	235	Oklahoma		•		•	•	
DB	Bennie Blades	6-0	215	Miami, Fla.		•	•	•	•	•
DB	Deion Sanders	6-0	192	Florida State		•	•	•	•	•
DB	Rickey Dixon	5-10	184	Oklahoma		•	•	•	•	
DB	Chuck Cecil	6-0	185	Arizona		•		•	•	•
P	Tom Tupa	6-5	215	Ohio State		•	•	•	•	•

	OTHERS RECEIVING FIRST-TEAM HONORS									
DL	Broderick Thomas			Nebraska			•			
DL	Michael Dean Perry			Clemson				•		
DL	Tony Cherico			Arkansas				•		
DL	Darrell Reed			Oklahoma			•			
LB	Ken Norton			UCLA				•		•
LB	Ezekial Gadson			Pittsburgh				•		
LB	Chris Gaines			Vanderbilt			•			
LB	Kurt Crain			Auburn			•			
LB	Paul McGowan			Florida State			•			
DB	Jarvis Williams			Florida			•			
DB	Donnell Woolford			Clemson			•			

FC named Bruce as a DL

HEISMAN TROPHY VOTING

	PLAYER	POS	SCHOOL	1ST	2ND	3RD	TOTAL
1	Tim Brown	WR	Notre Dame	324	173	124	1442
2	Don McPherson	QB	Syracuse	167	135	60	831
3	Gordie Lockbaum	TB	Holy Cross	108	103	127	657
4	Lorenzo White	TB	Michigan State	89	121	123	632
5	Craig Heyward	RB	Pittsburgh	17	44	31	170
6	Chris Spielman	LB	Ohio State	15	20	25	110
7	Thurman Thomas	TB	Oklahoma State	11	23	20	99
8	Gaston Green	TB	UCLA	4	13	35	73
9	Emmitt Smith	RB	Florida	2	11	42	70
10	Bobby Humphrey	HB	Alabama	5	17	14	63

AWARD WINNERS

PLAYER	POS/SCHOOL	AWARD
Don McPherson	QB Syracuse	Maxwell
Chad Hennings	DT Air Force	Outland
Tim Brown	WR Notre Dame	Camp
Chris Spielman	LB Ohio State	Lombardi

PLAYER	POS/SCHOOL	AWARD
Don McPherson	QB Miami, Fla.	Maxwell
Don McPherson	QB Syracuse	O'Brien
Paul McGowan	LB Florida State	Butkus
Bennie Blades	DB Miami, Fla.	Thorpe
Rickey Dixon	DB Oklahoma	Thorpe
Don McPherson	QB Syracuse	Unitas

BOWL GAMES

DATE	GAME	SCORE
D12	California	Eastern Michigan 30, San Jose State 27
D19	Independence	Washington 24, Tulane 12
D22	All-American	Virginia 22, Brigham Young 16
D25	Sun	Oklahoma State 35, West Virginia 33
D25	Aloha	UCLA 20, Florida 16
D29	Liberty	Georgia 20, Arkansas 17
D30	Freedom	Arizona State 33, Air Force 28
D30	Holiday	Iowa 20, Wyoming 19
D31	Gator	LSU 30, South Carolina 13

DATE	GAME	SCORE
D31	Bluebonnet	Texas 32, Pittsburgh 27
J1	Citrus	Clemson 35, Penn State 10
J1	Fiesta	Florida State 31, Nebraska 28
J1	Orange	Miami, Fla. 20, Oklahoma 14
J1	Rose	Michigan State 20, Southern Cal 17
J1	Cotton	Texas A&M 35, Notre Dame 10
J1	Sugar	Auburn 16, Syracuse 16
J2	Hall of Fame	Michigan 28, Alabama 24
J2	Peach	Tennessee 27, Indiana 22

CONFERENCE STANDINGS

ACC

	CONF. W L T	OVERALL W L T
Clemson	6 1 0	10 2 0
Virginia	5 2 0	8 4 0
Wake Forest	4 3 0	7 4 0
North Carolina St.	4 3 0	4 7 0
Maryland	3 3 0	4 7 0
North Carolina	3 4 0	5 6 0
Duke	2 5 0	5 6 0
Georgia Tech	0 6 0	2 9 0

Big 10

	CONF. W L T	OVERALL W L T
Michigan State	7 0 1	9 2 1
Iowa	6 2 0	10 3 0
Indiana	6 2 0	8 4 0
Michigan	5 3 0	8 4 0
Ohio State	4 4 0	6 4 1
Minnesota	3 5 0	6 5 0
Purdue	3 5 0	3 7 1
Illinois	2 5 1	3 7 1
Northwestern	2 6 0	2 8 1
Wisconsin	1 7 0	3 8 0

Big 8

	CONF. W L T	OVERALL W L T
Oklahoma	7 0 0	11 1 0
Nebraska	6 1 0	10 2 0
Oklahoma State	5 2 0	10 2 0
Colorado	4 3 0	7 4 0
Missouri	3 4 0	5 6 0
Iowa State	2 5 0	3 8 0
Kansas	0 6 1	1 9 1
Kansas State	0 6 1	0 10 1

Big West

	CONF. W L T	OVERALL W L T
San Jose State	7 0 0	10 2 0
Fresno State	4 3 0	6 5 0
Cal-St. Fullerton	4 3 0	6 6 0
Nevada-Las Vegas	4 3 0	5 6 0
Utah State	4 3 0	5 6 0
Pacific	3 4 0	4 7 0
Long Beach State	2 5 0	4 7 0
New Mexico State	0 7 0	2 9 0

Ivy

	CONF. W L T	OVERALL W L T
Harvard	6 1 0	8 2 0
Brown	5 2 0	7 3 0
Yale	5 2 0	7 3 0
Princeton	4 3 0	6 4 0
Cornell	4 3 0	5 5 0
Pennsylvania	3 4 0	4 6 0
Dartmouth	1 6 0	2 8 0
Columbia	0 7 0	0 10 0

MAC

	CONF. W L T	OVERALL W L T
Eastern Michigan	7 1 0	10 2 0
Kent State	5 3 0	7 4 0
Miami, Ohio	5 3 0	5 6 0
Bowling Green	5 3 0	5 6 0
Western Michigan	4 4 0	5 6 0
Central Michigan	3 4 1	5 5 1
Toledo	3 4 1	3 7 1
Ball State	3 5 0	4 7 0
Ohio U	0 8 0	1 10 0

Pac 10

	CONF. W L T	OVERALL W L T
UCLA	7 1 0	10 2 0
Southern Cal	7 1 0	8 4 0
Washington	4 3 1	7 4 1
Oregon	4 4 0	6 5 0
Stanford	4 4 0	5 6 0
Arizona State	3 3 1	7 4 1
Arizona	2 3 3	4 4 3
California	2 3 2	3 6 2
Washington State	1 5 1	3 7 1
Oregon State	0 7 0	2 9 0

SEC

	CONF. W L T	OVERALL W L T
Auburn	5 0 1	9 1 2
LSU	5 1 0	10 1 1
Tennessee	4 1 1	10 2 1
Georgia	4 2 0	9 3 0
Alabama	4 2 0	7 5 0
Florida	3 3 0	6 6 0
Kentucky	1 5 0	5 6 0
Mississippi State	1 5 0	4 7 0
Vanderbilt	1 5 0	4 7 0
Mississippi	1 5 0	3 8 0

SWC

	CONF. W L T	OVERALL W L T
SMU	0 0 0	0 0 0
Rice	0 0 0	2 9 0
Texas A&M	6 1 0	10 2 0
Arkansas	5 2 0	9 4 0
Texas	5 2 0	7 5 0
Texas Tech	3 3 1	6 4 1
Baylor	3 4 0	6 5 0
TCU	3 4 0	5 6 0
Houston	2 4 1	4 6 1

WAC

	CONF. W L T	OVERALL W L T
Wyoming	8 0 0	10 3 0
Brigham Young	7 1 0	9 4 0
Air Force	6 2 0	9 4 0
Texas-El Paso	5 3 0	7 4 0
San Diego State	4 4 0	5 7 0
Hawaii	3 5 0	5 7 0
Utah	2 6 0	5 7 0
Colorado State	1 7 0	1 11 0
New Mexico	0 8 0	0 11 0

Independents

	OVERALL W L T
Miami, Fla.	12 0 0
Syracuse	11 0 1
Florida State	11 1 0
South Carolina	8 4 0
Pittsburgh	8 4 0
Penn State	8 4 0
Notre Dame	8 4 0
Southern Miss	6 5 0
Rutgers	6 5 0
La. Lafayette	6 5 0
Tulane	6 6 0
West Virginia	6 6 0
Memphis	5 5 1
Northern Illinois	5 5 1
Army	5 6 0
East Carolina	5 6 0
Boston College	5 6 0
Cincinnati	4 7 0
Louisville	3 7 1
Temple	3 8 0
Tulsa	3 8 0
Navy	2 9 0
Virginia Tech	2 9 0

1987 NCAA Major College Statistical Leaders

Individual Leaders

PASSING	CL	G	ATT	COM	PCT	INT	I%	YDS	YPA	TD	TD%	RATING
1 Don McPherson, Syracuse	SR	11	229	129	56.3	11	4.8	2341	10.2	22	9.6	164.3
2 Troy Aikman, UCLA	JR	11	243	159	65.4	6	2.5	2354	9.7	16	6.6	163.6
3 Chuck Hartlieb, Iowa	SR	12	299	196	65.6	8	2.7	2855	9.6	19	6.4	161.4
4 Rodney Peete, Southern Cal	JR	11	291	175	60.1	9	3.1	2460	8.5	19	6.5	146.5
5 Eric Jones, Vanderbilt	JR	11	229	139	60.7	11	4.8	1954	8.5	16	7.0	145.8
6 Jeff Burger, Auburn	SR	11	267	178	66.7	9	3.4	2066	7.7	13	4.9	141.0
7 Todd Santos, San Diego State	SR	12	492	306	62.2	15	3.1	3932	8.0	26	5.3	140.7
8 Tom Hodson, LSU	SO	11	265	162	61.1	9	3.4	2125	8.0	15	5.7	140.4
9 Terrence Jones, Tulane	JR	11	319	192	60.2	13	4.1	2551	8.0	20	6.3	139.9
10 Steve Walsh, Miami, Fla.	SO	11	298	176	59.1	7	2.4	2249	7.6	19	6.4	138.8

ALL-PURPOSE	CL	G	RUSH	REC	PR	KR	YDS	YPG
1 Eric Wilkerson, Kent State	JR	11	1221	269	0	584	2074	188.6
2 Thurman Thomas, Oklahoma State	SR	11	1613	184	0	141	1938	176.2
3 Eric Metcalf, Texas	JR	11	1161	238	324	202	1925	175.0
4 Terance Mathis, New Mexico	JR	11	36	1132	16	677	1861	169.2
5 Craig Heyward, Pittsburgh	JR	11	1655	198	0	0	1853	168.5
6 Tim Brown, Notre Dame	SR	11	144	846	401	456	1847	167.9
7 Bobby Humphrey, Alabama	JR	11	1255	170	0	356	1781	161.9
8 Blair Thomas, Penn State	JR	11	1414	300	0	58	1772	161.1
9 Tony Jeffery, TCU	SR	10	1353	257	0	0	1610	161.0
10 Jamie Morris, Michigan	SR	11	1469	126	0	147	1742	158.4

RUSHING/Yards Per Game	CL	G	ATT	YDS	TD	AVG	YPG
1 Elbert Woods, Nevada-Las Vegas	SR	11	259	1658	10	6.4	150.7
2 Craig Heyward, Pittsburgh	JR	11	357	1655	11	4.6	150.5
3 Thurman Thomas, Oklahoma State	SR	11	250	1613	18	6.5	146.6
4 Tony Jeffery, TCU	SR	10	202	1353	10	6.7	135.3
5 Jamie Morris, Michigan	SR	11	259	1469	11	5.7	133.6
6 Lorenzo White, Michigan State	SR	11	322	1459	14	4.5	132.6
7 Blair Thomas, Penn State	JR	11	268	1414	11	5.3	128.6
8 Keith Jones, Nebraska	SR	10	170	1232	13	7.2	123.2
9 Sammie Smith, Florida State	SO	10	172	1230	7	7.2	123.0
10 Emmitt Smith, Florida	FR	11	229	1341	13	5.9	121.9

RUSHING/Yards Per Carry	CL	G	ATT	YDS	YPC
1 Keith Jones, Nebraska	SR	10	170	1232	7.2
2 Sammie Smith, Florida State	SO	10	172	1230	7.2
3 Michael Dowis, Air Force	SO	12	194	1315	6.8
4 Tony Jeffery, TCU	SR	10	202	1353	6.7
5 Mark Higgs, Kentucky	SR	11	193	1278	6.6
6 Thurman Thomas, Oklahoma State	SR	11	250	1613	6.5
7 Elbert Woods, Nevada-Las Vegas	SR	11	259	1658	6.4
8 Emmitt Smith, Florida	FR	11	229	1341	5.9
9 Jamie Morris, Michigan	SR	11	259	1469	5.7
10 Darrell Thompson, Minnesota	SO	11	224	1229	5.5

*-Based on top 23 rushers

RECEIVING	CL	G	REC	YDS	TD	YPR	YPG	RPG
1 Jason Phillips, Houston	JR	11	99	875	3	8.8	79.5	9.0
2 Guy Liggins, San Jose State	SR	11	77	1208	10	15.7	109.8	7.0
2 Marc Zeno, Tulane	SR	11	77	1206	13	15.7	109.6	7.0
4 Ron Jenkins, Fresno State	SR	11	76	985	3	13.0	89.5	6.9
5 Terance Mathis, New Mexico	JR	11	73	1132	8	15.5	102.9	6.6
6 Wendell Davis, LSU	SR	11	72	993	7	13.8	90.3	6.6
7 Kendal Smith, Utah State	JR	11	67	1048	7	15.6	95.3	6.1
8 Shane Hall, New Mexico	SR	11	66	415	0	6.3	37.7	6.0
9 Bill Hoffman, Wyoming	SR	12	68	786	3	11.6	65.5	5.7
10 Roger Boone, Duke	SO	11	62	587	0	9.5	53.4	5.6

PUNTING	CL	PUNT	YDS	AVG
1 Tom Tupa, Ohio State	SR	63	2963	47.0
2 Doug Robison, Stanford	SR	44	2011	45.7
3 Scott Tabor, California	SR	66	2993	45.4
4 Craig Salmon, North Carolina St.	SR	64	2877	45.0
5 Greg Montgomery, Michigan State	SR	62	2772	44.7
6 Chris Becker, TCU	JR	59	2594	44.0
7 Barry Helton, Colorado	SR	40	1758	44.0
8 Tony Rhynes, Nevada-Las Vegas	FR	56	2447	43.7
9 Monte Robbins, Michigan	SR	45	1964	43.6
10 Alex Waits, Texas	SO	43	1873	43.6

PUNT RETURNS	CL	PR	YDS	TD	AVG
1 Alan Grant, Stanford	JR	27	446	2	16.5
2 Barry Sanders, Oklahoma State	SO	15	244	2	16.3
3 Donnell Woolford, Clemson	JR	21	326	2	15.5
4 Nate Lewis, Georgia	JR	14	195	1	13.9
5 James Henry, Southern Miss	JR	41	556	4	13.6
6 Eric Metcalf, Texas	JR	24	324	1	13.5
7 Bernard Hall, Oklahoma	SO	11	145	0	13.2
8 Monty Gilbreath, San Diego State	SO	16	205	0	12.8
9 Joey Hamilton, Louisville	JR	17	209	0	12.3
10 Rodney Taylor, Northern Illinois	JR	23	282	1	12.3

KICKOFF RETURNS	CL	KR	YDS	TD	AVG
1 Barry Sanders, Oklahoma State	SO	14	442	2	31.6
2 Darryl Usher, Illinois	SR	15	445	0	29.7
3 Darrin Greer, California	SO	18	510	0	28.3
4 James Dixon, Houston	JR	33	908	1	27.5
5 Sam Martin, LSU	SR	17	459	0	27.0
6 Brock Smith, Fresno State	SR	19	512	1	27.0
7 Randal Hill, Miami, Fla.	FR	19	497	0	26.2
8 John Hood, Central Michigan	SO	19	489	1	25.7
9 James Saxon, San Jose State	SR	19	488	0	25.7
10 Jon Jeffries, Virginia Tech	FR	22	561	1	25.5

SCORING	CL	TDS	XP	FG	PTS	PTPG
1 Paul Hewitt, San Diego State	JR	24	0	0	144	12.0
2 Derek Schmidt, Florida State	SR	0	47	23	116	10.6
3 Reggie Cobb, Tennessee	FR	20	0	0	120	10.0
3 Thurman Thomas, Oklahoma State	SR	18	2	0	110	10.0
5 John Harvey, Texas-El Paso	JR	18	0	0	108	9.8
6 Collin Mackie, South Carolina	FR	0	37	23	106	9.6
7 Alfredo Velasco, UCLA	SO	0	46	18	100	9.1
8 Bernie Parmalee, Ball State	FR	15	0	0	90	9.0
8 Harold Green, South Carolina	SO	15	0	0	90	9.0
10 Kenny Jackson, San Jose State	SR	16	2	0	98	8.9

FIELD GOALS	CL	FGA	FGM	PCT	FGG
1 Collin Mackie, South Carolina	FR	30	23	0.77	2.09
1 Derek Schmidt, Florida State	SR	31	23	0.74	2.09
3 Jeff Shudak, Iowa State	FR	25	20	0.80	1.82
3 Gary Gussman, Miami, Ohio	SR	25	20	0.80	1.82
5 David Treadwell, Clemson	SR	21	18	0.86	1.80
6 Rob Houghtlin, Iowa	SR	29	21	0.72	1.75
7 Chip Browndyke, Houston	SR	24	19	0.79	1.73
8 Alfredo Velasco, UCLA	SO	22	18	0.82	1.64
8 John Ivanic, Northern Illinois	FR	24	18	0.75	1.64
10 Greg Cox, Miami, Fla.	SR	22	17	0.77	1.55

INTERCEPTIONS	CL	INT	YDS	TD	INT/GM
1 Keith McMeans, Virginia	FR	9	35	0	0.90
2 Todd Krumm, Michigan State	SR	9	129	0	0.82
2 Chuck Cecil, Arizona	SR	9	77	0	0.82
4 Johnny Jackson, Houston	SO	8	218	3	0.73
4 Ricky Dixon, Oklahoma	SR	8	214	1	0.73
4 Eric Allen, Arizona State	SR	8	185	2	0.73
4 Brad Edwards, South Carolina	SR	8	132	2	0.73
4 Kevin Cook, Virginia	SO	8	14	0	0.73
9 Rodney Rice, Brigham Young	JR	6	51	1	0.67
10 Brett Whitley, Northwestern	SR	7	202	0	0.64
10 A.J. Greene, Wake Forest	JR	7	128	2	0.64
10 Falanda Newton, TCU	JR	7	117	0	0.64
10 Todd Sandroni, Mississippi	FR	7	47	0	0.64
10 Brad Humphreys, Stanford	SR	7	22	0	0.64

Team Leaders

RUSHING OFFENSE	G	ATT	YDS	AVG	TD	YPG
1 Oklahoma	11	730	4717	6.5	52	428.8
2 Air Force	12	784	4635	5.9	43	386.3
3 Nebraska	11	673	4108	6.1	40	373.5
4 Colorado	11	665	3370	5.1	28	306.4
5 Army	11	749	3278	4.4	28	298.0
6 Northern Illinois	11	701	3246	4.6	31	295.1
7 TCU	11	618	3241	5.2	24	294.6
8 Georgia	11	596	3019	5.1	27	274.5
9 Florida State	11	530	2995	5.7	34	272.3
10 Arkansas	12	753	3196	4.2	31	266.3

PASSING OFFENSE	G	ATT	COM	INT	PCT	YDS	YPA	TD	I%	YPC	YPG
1 San Jose State	11	450	271	13	60.2	3719	8.3	26	2.9	13.7	338.1
2 San Diego State	12	509	314	16	61.7	3990	7.8	26	3.1	12.7	332.5
3 Utah	12	525	306	21	58.3	3884	7.4	25	4.0	12.7	323.7
4 Duke	11	470	266	20	56.6	3443	7.3	23	4.3	12.9	313.0
5 Wyoming	12	522	282	19	54.0	3703	7.1	27	3.6	13.1	308.6
6 Houston	11	499	283	18	56.7	3265	6.5	15	3.6	11.5	296.8
7 Iowa	12	413	255	13	61.7	3559	8.6	23	3.2	14.0	296.6
8 New Mexico	11	514	284	27	55.3	3230	6.3	17	5.3	11.4	293.6
9 Brigham Young	12	477	276	23	57.9	3501	7.3	18	4.8	12.7	291.8
10 Oregon State	11	489	257	26	52.6	3152	6.4	19	5.3	12.3	286.5

TOTAL OFFENSE	G	P	YDS	AVG	TD	YPG
1 Oklahoma	11	829	5497	6.6	61	499.7
2 Nebraska	11	835	5379	6.4	56	489.0
3 Florida State	11	848	5361	6.3	52	487.4
4 Wyoming	12	951	5655	5.9	49	471.3
5 San Jose State	11	831	5119	6.2	49	465.4
6 UCLA	11	826	4886	5.9	45	444.2
7 Air Force	12	904	5320	5.9	48	443.3
8 LSU	11	747	4843	6.5	42	440.3
8 Syracuse	11	778	4843	6.2	45	440.3
10 San Diego State	12	924	5263	5.7	46	438.6

RUSHING DEFENSE	G	ATT	YDS	AVG	TD	YPG
1 Michigan State	11	360	676	1.9	5	61.5
2 Clemson	11	388	880	2.3	10	80.0
3 San Jose State	11	408	926	2.3	9	84.2
4 UCLA	11	373	936	2.5	7	85.1
5 South Carolina	11	419	1036	2.5	6	94.2
6 Miami, Fla.	11	455	1064	2.3	5	96.7
7 Arkansas	12	393	1208	3.1	9	100.7
8 Oklahoma	11	456	1163	2.6	4	105.7
9 Nebraska	11	423	1177	2.8	10	107.0
10 Texas A&M	11	463	1203	2.6	9	109.4

PASSING DEFENSE	G	ATT	COM	PCT	YPC	INT	I%	YDS	YPA	TD	YPG
1 Oklahoma	11	248	108	43.5	10.4	25	10.1	1126	4.5	3	102.4
2 Illinois	11	185	83	44.9	13.9	9	4.9	1152	6.2	5	104.7
3 Kansas	11	190	95	50.0	12.8	6	3.2	1212	6.4	11	110.2
4 Pittsburgh	11	220	86	39.1	14.8	8	3.6	1273	5.8	5	115.7
5 Navy	11	184	106	57.6	13.2	11	6.0	1399	7.6	10	127.2
6 West Virginia	11	252	131	52.0	11.2	14	5.6	1465	5.8	7	133.2
6 South Carolina	11	295	132	44.7	11.1	23	7.8	1465	5.0	5	133.2
8 Memphis	11	243	124	51.0	12.0	12	4.9	1485	6.1	12	135.0
9 Texas A&M	11	265	116	43.8	12.8	12	4.5	1489	5.6	7	135.4
10 Florida	11	269	128	47.6	11.8	12	4.5	1512	5.6	4	137.5

TOTAL DEFENSE	G	P	YDS	AVG	TD	YPG
1 Oklahoma	11	704	2289	3.3	7	208.1
2 Michigan State	11	676	2482	3.7	13	225.6
3 South Carolina	11	714	2501	3.5	11	227.4
4 Pittsburgh	11	699	2563	3.7	11	233.0
5 Clemson	11	704	2640	3.8	17	240.0
6 Miami, Fla.	11	739	2682	3.6	10	243.8
7 Texas A&M	11	728	2692	3.7	16	244.7
8 Nebraska	11	734	2912	4.0	15	264.7
9 Florida	11	744	2956	4.0	13	268.7
10 Auburn	11	752	3012	4.0	11	273.8

SCORING OFFENSE	G	PTS	AVG
1 Oklahoma	11	479	43.5
2 Florida State	11	450	40.9
3 Nebraska	11	423	38.5
4 UCLA	11	406	36.9
5 Miami, Fla.	11	392	35.6
6 San Jose State	11	390	35.5
7 Oklahoma State	11	374	34.0
8 Wyoming	12	407	33.9
9 Syracuse	11	363	33.0
10 Tennessee	12	395	32.9

SCORING DEFENSE	G	PTS	AVG
1 Oklahoma	11	82	7.5
2 South Carolina	11	111	10.1
2 Miami, Fla.	11	111	10.1
4 Pittsburgh	11	114	10.4
5 Auburn	11	116	10.5
6 Nebraska	11	133	12.1
7 Florida State	11	135	12.3
8 Michigan State	11	136	12.4
9 Michigan	11	148	13.5
10 Syracuse	11	153	13.9

1988 POLL PROGRESSION

Pre-Season 1988 — Sept. 3 Games

UP	AP	Team	Record	Result
1	1	Florida State	0-0-0	lost to # 8 Miami, Fla. 0-31
3	2	Nebraska	0-0-0	beat Utah State 63-13
2	3	Oklahoma	0-0-0	bye week
4	4	Clemson	0-0-0	beat Virginia Tech 40-7
9	5	UCLA	0-0-0	beat San Diego State 59-6
8	6	Southern Cal	0-0-0	beat Boston College 34-7 S1
7	7	Auburn	0-0-0	bye week
5	8	Miami, Fla.	0-0-0	beat # 1 Florida State 31-0
11	9	Iowa	0-0-0	lost to Hawaii 24-27
6	10	Texas A&M	0-0-0	lost to # 18 LSU 0-27
10	11	Michigan	0-0-0	bye week
14	12	Georgia	0-0-0	beat # 17 Tennessee 28-17
12	13	Notre Dame	0-0-0	bye week
19	14	Alabama	0-0-0	bye week
14	15	Michigan State	0-0-0	bye week
	16	West Virginia	0-0-0	beat Bowling Green 62-14
17	17	Tennessee	0-0-0	lost to # 12 Georgia 17-28
13	18	LSU	0-0-0	beat # 10 Texas A&M 27-0
18	19	South Carolina	0-0-0	beat North Carolina 31-10
14	20	Penn State	0-0-0	bye week
20		Texas	0-0-0	bye week

September 5 Poll — Sept. 10 Games

UP	AP	Team	Record	Result
1	1	Miami, Fla.	1-0-0	bye week
2	2	Nebraska	2-0-0	lost to # 5 UCLA 28-41
3	3	Clemson	1-0-0	beat Furman 23-3
4	4	Oklahoma	0-0-0	beat North Carolina 28-0
5	5	UCLA	1-0-0	beat # 2 Nebraska 41-28
6	6	Southern Cal	1-0-0	beat Stanford 24-20
7	7	Auburn	0-0-0	beat Kentucky 20-10
8	8	Georgia	1-0-0	beat TCU 38-10
10	9	Michigan	0-0-0	lost to # 13 Notre Dame 17-19
12	10	Florida State	0-1-0	beat Southern Miss 49-13
9	11	LSU	1-0-0	bye week
13	12	West Virginia	1-0-0	beat Fullerton St. 45-10
11	13	Notre Dame	0-0-0	beat # 9 Michigan 19-17
16	14	Alabama	0-0-0	beat Temple 37-0
14	15	Michigan State	0-0-0	lost to Rutgers 13-17
15	16	South Carolina	1-0-0	beat Western Carolina 38-0
17	17	Iowa	0-1-0	beat Kansas State 45-10
17	18	Penn State	0-0-0	beat Virginia 42-14
	19	Texas	0-0-0	lost to Brigham Young 6-47 (S8)
	20	Washington	0-0-0	beat Purdue 20-6
19		Syracuse	1-0-0	lost to Ohio State 9-26
20		Pittsburgh	1-0-0	bye week

September 12 Poll — Sept. 17 Games

UP	AP	Team	Record	Result
1	1	Miami, Fla.	1-0-0	beat # 15 Michigan 31-30
2	2	UCLA	2-0-0	beat Long Beach St. 56-3
4	3	Clemson	2-0-0	lost to # 10 Florida State 21-24
3	4	Oklahoma	1-0-0	beat Arizona 28-10
5	5	Southern Cal	2-0-0	bye week
7	6	Auburn	1-0-0	beat Kansas 56-7
6	7	Georgia	1-0-0	beat Mississippi State 42-35
9	8	Notre Dame	1-0-0	beat Michigan State 20-3
8	9	LSU	1-0-0	beat Tennessee 34-9
12	10	Florida State	1-1-0	beat # 3 Clemson 24-21
10	11	Nebraska	2-1-0	bye week
11	12	West Virginia	2-0-0	beat Maryland 55-24
13	13	Alabama	1-0-0	bye week
15	14	South Carolina	2-0-0	beat East Carolina 17-0
16	15	Michigan	0-1-0	lost to # 1 Miami, Fla. 30-31
13	16	Penn State	1-0-0	beat Boston College 23-20
19	17	Washington	1-0-0	beat Army 31-17
17	18	Ohio State	1-0-0	lost to Pittsburgh 10-42
	19	Iowa	1-1-0	lost to Colorado 21-24
	20	Oklahoma State	1-0-0	bye week
18		Florida	2-0-0	beat Indiana St. 58-0
20		Pittsburgh	1-0-0	beat # 18 Ohio State 42-10

September 19 Poll — Sept. 24 Games

UP	AP	Team	Record	Result
1	1	Miami, Fla.	2-0-0	beat Wisconsin 23-3
2	2	UCLA	3-0-0	bye week
3	3	Oklahoma	2-0-0	lost to # 5 Southern Cal 7-23
5	4	Auburn	2-0-0	beat Tennessee 38-6
4	5	Southern Cal	2-0-0	beat # 3 Oklahoma 23-7
7	6	Georgia	3-0-0	lost to # 14 South Carolina 10-23
6	7	LSU	2-0-0	lost to Ohio State 33-36
8	8	Notre Dame	2-0-0	beat Purdue 52-7
9	9	Florida State	2-1-0	beat Michigan State 30-7
11	10	Nebraska	2-1-0	beat Arizona State 47-16
10	11	West Virginia	3-0-0	beat # 16 Pittsburgh 31-10
12	12	Clemson	2-1-0	beat Georgia Tech 30-13
16	13	Alabama	1-0-0	beat Vanderbilt 44-10
14	14	South Carolina	3-0-0	beat # 6 Georgia 23-10
13	15	Penn State	2-0-0	lost to Rutgers 16-21
15	16	Pittsburgh	2-0-0	lost to # 11 West Virginia 10-31
17	17	Washington	2-0-0	beat San Jose State 35-31
20	18	Oklahoma State	1-0-0	beat Texas A&M 52-15
	19	Michigan	0-2-0	beat Wake Forest 19-9
18	20	Florida	3-0-0	beat Mississippi State 17-0
19		Wyoming	3-0-0	beat Air Force 48-45

September 26 Poll — Oct. 1 Games

UP	AP	Team	Record	Result
1	1	Miami, Fla.	3-0-0	beat Missouri 55-0
2	2	UCLA	3-0-0	beat # 16 Washington 24-17
3	3	Southern Cal	3-0-0	beat Arizona 38-15
4	4	Auburn	3-0-0	beat North Carolina 47-21
5	5	Notre Dame	3-0-0	beat Stanford 42-14
8	6	Florida State	3-1-0	beat Tulane 48-28
6	7	West Virginia	4-0-0	beat Virginia Tech 22-10
7	8	South Carolina	4-0-0	beat Appalachian St. 35-9
9	9	Nebraska	3-1-0	beat Nevada-Las Vegas 48-6
10	10	Oklahoma	2-1-0	beat Iowa State 35-7
11	11	Clemson	3-1-0	bye week
12	12	Alabama	2-0-0	beat Kentucky 31-27
14	13	Oklahoma State	2-0-0	beat Tulsa 56-35
13	14	LSU	2-1-0	lost to # 17 Florida 6-19
16	15	Georgia	3-1-0	beat Mississippi 36-12
17	16	Washington	3-0-0	lost to # 2 UCLA 17-24
15	17	Florida	4-0-0	beat # 14 LSU 19-6
18	18	Wyoming	4-0-0	beat Fullerton St. 35-16
19	19	Michigan	1-2-0	beat Wisconsin 62-14
	20	Oregon	3-0-0	beat San Diego State 34-13
19		Arkansas	3-0-0	beat TCU 53-10

October 3 Poll — Oct. 8 Games

UP	AP	Team	Record	Result
1	1	Miami, Fla.	4-0-0	bye week
2	2	UCLA	4-0-0	beat Oregon State 38-21
3	3	Southern Cal	4-0-0	beat # 18 Oregon 42-14
4	4	Auburn	4-0-0	lost to LSU 6-7
5	5	Notre Dame	4-0-0	beat Pittsburgh 30-20
7	6	Florida State	4-1-0	beat Georgia Southern 28-10
6	7	West Virginia	5-0-0	beat East Carolina 31-7
8	8	South Carolina	5-0-0	beat Virginia Tech 26-24
9	9	Nebraska	4-1-0	beat Kansas 63-10
10	10	Oklahoma	3-1-0	beat Texas 28-13
12	11	Clemson	3-1-0	beat Virginia 10-7
14	12	Alabama	3-0-0	lost to Mississippi 12-22
13	13	Oklahoma State	3-0-0	beat Colorado 41-21
11	14	Florida	5-0-0	lost to Memphis 11-17
15	15	Georgia	4-1-0	beat Vanderbilt 41-22
16	16	Wyoming	5-0-0	beat San Diego State 55-27
20	17	Michigan	2-2-0	beat Michigan State 17-3
18	18	Oregon	4-0-0	lost to # 3 Southern Cal 14-42
19	19	Washington	3-1-0	beat Arizona State 10-0
17	20	Arkansas	4-0-0	beat Texas Tech 31-10

October 10 Poll — Oct. 15 Games

UP	AP	Team	Record	Result
1	1	Miami, Fla.	4-0-0	lost to # 4 Notre Dame 30-31
2	2	UCLA	5-0-0	beat California 38-21
3	3	Southern Cal	5-0-0	beat # 16 Washington 28-27
4	4	Notre Dame	5-0-0	beat # 1 Miami, Fla. 31-30
6	5	Florida State	5-1-0	beat East Carolina 45-21
5	6	West Virginia	6-0-0	bye week
8	7	Nebraska	5-1-0	beat # 10 Oklahoma State 63-42
7	8	South Carolina	6-0-0	lost to Georgia Tech 0-34
9	9	Oklahoma	4-1-0	beat Kansas State 70-24
10	10	Oklahoma State	4-0-0	lost to # 7 Nebraska 42-63
11	11	Clemson	4-1-0	beat Duke 49-17
12	12	Auburn	4-1-0	beat Akron 42-0
13	13	Georgia	5-1-0	bye week
14	14	Wyoming	6-0-0	beat New Mexico 55-7
17	15	Michigan	3-2-0	tied Iowa 17-17
16	16	Washington	4-1-0	lost to # 3 Southern Cal 27-28
15	17	Arkansas	5-0-0	beat Texas 27-24
18	18	Indiana	4-0-1	beat Minnesota 33-13
19	19	LSU	3-2-0	beat Kentucky 15-12
	20	Florida	5-1-0	lost to Vanderbilt 9-24
20		Syracuse	4-1-0	beat Penn State 24-10
20		Washington St.	4-1-0	lost to Arizona 28-45

October 17 Poll — Oct. 22 Games

UP	AP	Team	Record	Result
1	1	UCLA	6-0-0	beat Arizona 24-3
2	2	Notre Dame	6-0-0	beat Air Force 41-13
3	3	Southern Cal	6-0-0	bye week
4	4	Miami, Fla.	4-1-0	beat Cincinnati 57-3
5	5	Nebraska	6-1-0	beat Kansas State 48-3
6	6	West Virginia	6-0-0	beat Boston College 59-19
7	7	Florida State	6-1-0	beat Louisiana Tech 66-3
8	8	Oklahoma	5-1-0	beat Colorado 17-14
10	9	Clemson	5-1-0	lost to North Carolina St. 3-10
9	10	Auburn	5-1-0	beat Mississippi State 33-0
13	11	Georgia	5-1-0	lost to Kentucky 10-16
12	12	Wyoming	7-0-0	beat Utah 61-18
11	13	Arkansas	6-0-0	beat Houston 26-21
14	14	Indiana	5-0-1	lost to # 20 Michigan 6-31
15	15	Oklahoma State	4-1-0	beat Missouri 49-21
19	16	LSU	4-2-0	bye week
17	17	Washington	4-2-0	lost to Oregon 14-17
17	18	South Carolina	6-1-0	bye week
16	19	Syracuse	5-1-0	beat East Carolina 38-14
	20	Michigan	3-2-1	beat # 14 Indiana 31-6
20		Washington St.	4-2-0	lost to Arizona State 28-31

October 24 Poll — Oct. 29 Games

UP	AP	Team	Record	Result
1	1	UCLA	7-0-0	lost to Washington St. 30-34
2	2	Notre Dame	7-0-0	beat Navy 22-7
3	3	Southern Cal	6-0-0	beat Oregon State 41-20
4	4	Miami, Fla.	5-1-0	beat East Carolina 31-7
5	5	Nebraska	7-1-0	beat Missouri 26-18
7	6	Florida State	7-1-0	bye week
6	7	West Virginia	7-0-0	beat Penn State 51-30
8	8	Oklahoma	6-1-0	beat Kansas 63-14
9	9	Auburn	6-1-0	beat Florida 16-0
10	10	Wyoming	8-0-0	beat Colorado State 48-14
11	11	Arkansas	7-0-0	beat Rice 21-14
12	12	Oklahoma State	5-1-0	beat Kansas State 45-27
15	13	LSU	4-2-0	beat Mississippi 31-20
14	14	Michigan	4-2-1	beat Northwestern 52-7
18	15	Clemson	5-2-0	beat Wake Forest 38-21
13	16	Syracuse	6-1-0	bye week
17	17	South Carolina	6-1-0	beat North Carolina St. 23-7
20	18	Georgia	5-2-0	beat William & Mary 59-24
16	19	Alabama	5-1-0	beat Mississippi State 53-34
19	20	Oregon	6-1-0	lost to Arizona State 20-21

October 31 Poll — Nov. 5 Games

UP	AP	Team	Record	Result
1	1	Notre Dame	8-0-0	beat Rice 54-11
2	2	Southern Cal	7-0-0	beat California 35-3
3	3	Miami, Fla.	6-1-0	beat Tulsa 34-3
4	4	West Virginia	8-0-0	beat Cincinnati 51-13
8	5	Florida State	7-1-0	beat #15 South Carolina 59-0
6	6	UCLA	7-1-0	beat Oregon 16-6
5	7	Nebraska	8-1-0	beat Iowa State 51-16
7	8	Oklahoma	7-1-0	beat #12 Oklahoma State 31-28
9	9	Auburn	7-1-0	beat Southern Miss 38-8
10	10	Wyoming	9-0-0	beat Texas-El Paso 51-6
11	11	Arkansas	8-0-0	beat Baylor 33-3
12	12	Oklahoma State	6-1-0	lost to #8 Oklahoma 28-31
16	13	LSU	5-2-0	beat #18 Alabama 19-18
13	14	Michigan	5-2-0	beat Minnesota 22-7
15	15	South Carolina	7-1-0	lost to #5 Florida State 0-59
14	16	Syracuse	6-1-0	beat Navy 49-21
20	17	Clemson	6-2-0	beat North Carolina 37-14
16	18	Alabama	6-1-0	lost to #13 LSU 18-19
	19	Georgia	6-2-0	beat Florida 26-3
19	20	Brigham Young	7-1-0	lost to San Diego State 15-27
18	20	Indiana	6-1-1	lost to Illinois 20-21

November 7 Poll — Nov. 12 Games

UP	AP	Team	Record	Result
1	1	Notre Dame	9-0-0	bye week
2	2	Southern Cal	8-1-0	beat Arizona State 50-0
3	3	Miami, Fla.	7-1-0	bye week
4	4	West Virginia	9-0-0	beat Rutgers 35-25
5	5	Florida State	8-1-0	beat Virginia Tech 41-14
6	6	UCLA	8-1-0	beat Stanford 27-17
7	7	Nebraska	9-1-0	beat #19 Colorado 7-0
8	8	Oklahoma	8-1-0	beat Missouri 16-7
9	9	Auburn	8-1-0	beat #17 Georgia 20-10
10	10	Wyoming	10-0-0	lost to Houston 10-34
11	11	Arkansas	9-0-0	beat Texas A&M 25-20
14	12	LSU	6-2-0	beat Mississippi State 20-3
12	13	Michigan	6-2-1	beat Illinois 38-9
15	14	Oklahoma State	7-1-0	beat Kansas 63-24
13	15	Syracuse	7-1-0	beat Boston College 45-20
16	16	Clemson	7-2-0	beat Maryland 49-25
17	17	Georgia	7-2-0	lost to #9 Auburn 10-20
19	18	Alabama	6-2-0	beat La. Lafayette 17-0
19	19	Colorado	7-2-0	lost to #7 Nebraska 0-7
	20	Washington State	6-3-0	beat Oregon State 36-27
18		Brigham Young		

November 14 Poll — Nov. 19 Games

UP	AP	Team	Record	Result
1	1	Notre Dame	9-0-0	beat Penn State 21-3
2	2	Southern Cal	9-0-0	beat #6 UCLA 31-22
3	3	Miami, Fla.	7-1-0	beat #11 LSU 44-3
4	4	West Virginia	10-0-0	beat #14 Syracuse 31-9
5	5	Florida State	9-1-0	bye week
6	6	UCLA	9-1-0	lost to #2 Southern Cal 22-31
7	7	Nebraska	10-1-0	beat #9 Oklahoma 7-3
9	8	Auburn	9-1-0	bye week
8	9	Oklahoma	9-1-0	lost to #7 Nebraska 3-7
10	10	Arkansas	10-0-0	bye week
12	11	LSU	7-2-0	lost to #3 Miami, Fla. 3-44
11	12	Michigan	7-2-0	beat Ohio State 34-31
14	13	Oklahoma State	7-2-0	beat Iowa State 49-28
13	14	Syracuse	8-1-0	lost to #4 West Virginia 9-31
15	15	Clemson	8-2-0	beat South Carolina 29-10
16	16	Wyoming	10-1-0	beat Hawaii 28-22
17	17	Houston	7-2-0	beat Texas Tech 30-29
	18	Alabama	7-2-0	bye week
20	19	Washington State	7-3-0	beat Washington 32-31
	20	Georgia	7-3-0	bye week
17		Colorado	7-3-0	beat Kansas State 56-14
19		Brigham Young	8-2-0	lost to Utah 28-57

November 21 Poll — Nov. 26 Games

UP	AP	Team	Record	Result
1	1	Notre Dame	10-0-0	beat #2 Southern Cal 27-10
2	2	Southern Cal	10-0-0	lost to #1 Notre Dame 10-27
3	3	Miami, Fla.	8-1-0	beat #8 Arkansas 18-16
4	4	West Virginia	11-0-0	regular season complete
5	5	Florida State	9-1-0	beat Florida 52-17
6	6	Nebraska	11-1-0	regular season complete
7	7	Auburn	9-1-0	beat #17 Alabama 15-10 (N25)
8	8	Arkansas	10-0-0	lost to #3 Miami, Fla. 16-18
9	9	UCLA	9-2-0	regular season complete
11	10	Oklahoma	9-2-0	regular season complete
10	11	Michigan	8-2-1	regular season complete
12	12	Oklahoma State	8-2-0	bye week
13	13	Clemson	9-2-0	regular season complete
16	14	Houston	8-2-0	beat Rice 45-14
14	15	Wyoming	11-1-0	regular season complete
17	16	LSU	7-3-0	beat Tulane 44-14
15	17	Alabama	7-2-0	lost to #7 Auburn 10-15 (N25)
18	18	Washington State	8-3-0	regular season complete
19	19	Syracuse	8-2-0	bye week
	20	Georgia	7-3-0	beat Georgia Tech 24-3
20		Colorado	8-3-0	regular season complete

November 28 Poll — Dec. 3 Games

UP	AP	Team	Record	Result
1	1	Notre Dame	11-0-0	regular season complete
2	2	Miami, Fla.	9-1-0	beat Brigham Young 41-17
3	3	West Virginia	11-0-0	
4	4	Florida State	10-1-0	regular season complete
6	5	Southern Cal	10-1-0	regular season complete
5	6	Nebraska	11-1-0	
7	7	Auburn	10-1-0	regular season complete
8	8	UCLA	9-2-0	
9	9	Arkansas	10-1-0	regular season complete
10	10	Oklahoma	9-2-0	
11	11	Michigan	8-2-1	
12	12	Oklahoma State	8-2-0	beat Texas Tech 45-42
13	13	Clemson	9-2-0	
15	14	Houston	9-2-0	regular season complete
14	15	Wyoming	11-1-0	
17	16	LSU	8-3-0	regular season complete
18	17	Washington State	8-3-0	
16	18	Syracuse	8-2-0	beat Pittsburgh 24-7
20	19	Georgia	8-3-0	regular season complete
	20	Alabama	7-3-0	beat Texas A&M 30-10 (D1)
19		Colorado	8-3-0	

December 5 Poll

UP	AP	Team	Record	Bowl Bid	Date	Bowl Result	RB	UP	AP	January 3 Final Poll	Record
1	1	Notre Dame	11-0-0	Fiesta Bowl	J2	beat #3 West Virginia 34-21	1	1	1	Notre Dame	12-0-0
2	2	Miami, Fla.	10-1-0	Orange Bowl	J2	beat #6 Nebraska 23-3	2	2	2	Miami, Fla.	11-1-0
3	3	West Virginia	11-0-0	Fiesta Bowl	J2	lost to #1 Notre Dame 21-34	3	3	3	Florida State	11-1-0
4	4	Florida State	10-1-0	Sugar Bowl	J2	beat #7 Auburn 13-7	5	4	4	Michigan	9-2-1
5	5	Southern Cal	10-1-0	Rose Bowl	J2	lost to #11 Michigan 14-22	8	5	5	West Virginia	11-1-0
6	6	Nebraska	11-1-0	Orange Bowl	J2	lost to #2 Miami, Fla. 3-23	7	6	6	UCLA	10-2-0
7	7	Auburn	10-1-0	Sugar Bowl	J2	lost to #4 Florida State 7-13	6	9	7	Southern Cal	10-2-0
8	8	Arkansas	10-1-0	Cotton Bowl	J2	lost to #9 UCLA 3-17	9	7	8	Auburn	10-2-0
9	9	UCLA	10-1-0	Cotton Bowl	J2	beat #8 Arkansas 17-3	12	8	9	Clemson	10-2-0
10	10	Oklahoma	9-2-0	Citrus Bowl	J2	lost to #13 Clemson 6-13	4	10	10	Nebraska	11-2-0
11	11	Michigan	8-2-1	Rose Bowl	J2	beat #5 Southern Cal 22-14	11	11	11	Oklahoma State	10-2-0
12	12	Oklahoma State	9-2-0	Holiday Bowl	D30	beat #15 Wyoming 62-14	14	13	12	Arkansas	10-2-0
13	13	Clemson	9-2-0	Citrus Bowl	J2	beat #10 Oklahoma 13-6	10	12	13	Syracuse	10-2-0
14	14	Houston	9-2-0	Aloha Bowl	D25	lost to #18 Washington St. 22-24	13	14	14	Oklahoma	9-3-0
15	15	Wyoming	11-1-0	Holiday Bowl	D30	lost to #12 Oklahoma State 14-62	23	15	15	Georgia	9-3-0
17	16	LSU	8-3-0	Hall of Fame Bowl	J2	lost to #17 Syracuse 10-23	17	16	16	Washington State	9-3-0
16	17	Syracuse	9-2-0	Hall of Fame Bowl	J2	beat #16 LSU 23-10	16	17	17	Alabama	9-3-0
18	18	Washington State	8-3-0	Aloha Bowl	D25	beat #14 Houston 24-22	19		18	Houston	9-3-0
19	19	Georgia	8-3-0	Gator Bowl	J1	beat Michigan State 34-27	15		19	LSU	8-4-0
20	20	Alabama	8-3-0	Sun Bowl	D24	beat Army 29-28	24	19	20	Indiana	8-3-1
20		Colorado	8-3-0	Freedon Bowl	D29	lost to Brigham Young 17-20	28	17		North Carolina St.	8-3-1
							18	20		Wyoming	11-2-0

1988

CONSENSUS ALL-AMERICANS

POS	Offense	HT	WT	School	AP	CF	FC	FW	PI
QB	Steve Walsh	6-3	195	Miami, Fla.	•			•	
QB	Troy Aikman	6-4	217	UCLA					•
RB	Barry Sanders	5-8	197	Oklahoma State	•	•	•	•	•
RB	Anthony Thompson	6-0	205	Indiana		•	•		•
RB	Tim Worley	6-2	216	Georgia	•			•	
WR	Jason Phillips	5-9	175	Houston	•	•	•	•	•
WR	Hart Lee Dykes	6-4	220	Oklahoma State	•	•			•
TE	Marv Cook	6-4	243	Iowa	•				•
L	Tony Mandarich	6-6	315	Michigan State	•	•	•	•	•
L	Anthony Phillips	6-3	286	Oklahoma	•	•	•	•	•
L	Mike Utley	6-6	302	Washington State	•		•	•	•
L	Mark Stepnoski	6-3	265	Pittsburgh		•	•	•	•
C	Jake Young	6-5	260	Nebraska	•			•	
C	John Vitale	6-1	273	Michigan		•		•	•
PK	Kendall Trainor	6-2	205	Arkansas	•	•		•	•

	OTHERS RECEIVING FIRST-TEAM HONORS	
QB	Rodney Peete	Southern Cal
RB	Darren Lewis	Texas A&M	•
WR	Clarkston Hines	Duke
WR	Erik Affholter	Southern Cal
TE	Troy Sadowski	Georgia	•
TE	Wesley Walls	Mississippi	•
L	Pat Tomberlin	Florida State	•
L	Steve Wisniewski	Penn State
L	Andy Heck	Notre Dame	•
PK	Chris Jacke	Texas-El Paso	•
RS	Tyrone Thurman	Texas Tech	•

POS	Defense	HT	WT	School	AP	CF	FC	FW	PI
L	Mark Messner	6-3	244	Michigan	•	•	•	•	•
L	Tracy Rocker	6-3	278	Auburn	•	•	•	•	•
L	Wayne Martin	6-5	263	Arkansas	•	•		•	•
L	Frank Stams	6-4	237	Notre Dame	•	•	•	•	•
L	Bill Hawkins	6-6	260	Miami, Fla.			•	•	
LB	Derrick Thomas	6-4	230	Alabama	•	•	•	•	•
LB	Broderick Thomas	6-3	235	Nebraska	•	•		•	•
LB	Michael Stonebreaker	6-1	228	Notre Dame	•	•		•	
DB	Deion Sanders	6-0	195	Florida State	•	•	•	•	•
DB	Donnell Woolford	5-10	195	Clemson	•	•	•	•	•
DB	Louis Oliver	6-2	222	Florida	•	•	•	•	•
DB	Darryl Henley	5-10	165	UCLA	•		•	•	•
P	Keith English	6-3	215	Colorado	•	•			

	OTHERS RECEIVING FIRST-TEAM HONORS	
L	Dave Haight	Iowa	•
L	Tim Ryan	Southern Cal	•
LB	Carnell Lake	UCLA	•
LB	Britt Hager	Texas	•
LB	Jerry Olsavsky	Pittsburgh	•
LB	Keith DeLong	Tennessee	• •
DB	Markus Paul	Syracuse	•
DB	Mark Carrier	Southern Cal	•
P	Pat Thompson	Brigham Young	• •

FC named Broderick Thomas as a DL; FC named Derrick Thomas as a DL

HEISMAN TROPHY VOTING

	PLAYER	POS	SCHOOL	1ST	2ND	3RD	TOTAL
1	Barry Sanders	TB	Oklahoma State	559	77	47	1878
2	Rodney Peete	QB	Southern Cal	70	264	174	912
3	Troy Aikman	QB	UCLA	31	149	191	582
4	Steve Walsh	QB	Miami, Fla.	16	108	77	341
5	Major Harris	QB	West Virginia	27	60	79	280
6	Tony Mandarich	OT	Michigan State	3	9	25	52
7	Timm Rosenbach	QB	Washington State	6	6	14	44
8	Deion Sanders	CB	Florida State	0	3	16	22
9	Anthony Thompson	TB	Indiana	0	4	13	21
10	Derrick Thomas	LB	Alabama	3	2	7	20

AWARD WINNERS

PLAYER	POS/SCHOOL	AWARD	PLAYER	POS/SCHOOL	AWARD
Barry Sanders	RB Oklahoma State	Maxwell	Troy Aikman	QB UCLA	O'Brien
Tracy Rocker	DT Auburn	Outland	Derrick Thomas	LB Alabama	Butkus
Barry Sanders	RB Oklahoma State	Camp	Deion Sanders	DB Florida State	Thorpe
Tracy Rocker	DT Auburn	Lombardi	Rodney Peete	QB Southern Cal	Unitas

BOWL GAMES

DATE	GAME	SCORE
D10	California	Fresno State 35, Western Michigan 30
D23	Independence	Southern Miss 38, Texas-El Paso 18
D24	Sun	Alabama 29, Army 28
D25	Aloha	Washington State 24, Houston 22
D28	Liberty	Indiana 34, South Carolina 10
D29	Freedom	Brigham Young 20, Colorado 17
D29	All-American	Florida 14, Illinois 10
D30	Holiday	Oklahoma State 62, Wyoming 14

DATE	GAME	SCORE
D31	Peach	North Carolina St. 28, Iowa 23
J1	Gator	Georgia 34, Michigan State 27
J2	Citrus	Clemson 13, Oklahoma 6
J2	Orange	Miami, Fla. 23, Nebraska 3
J2	Rose	Michigan 22, Southern Cal 14
J2	Fiesta	Notre Dame 34, West Virginia 21
J2	Hall of Fame	Syracuse 23, LSU 10
J2	Cotton	UCLA 17, Arkansas 3
J2	Sugar	Florida State 13, Auburn 7

CONFERENCE STANDINGS

ACC

	Conf. W L T	Overall W L T
Clemson	6 1 0	10 2 0
Virginia	5 2 0	7 4 0
North Carolina St.	4 2 1	8 3 1
Wake Forest	4 3 0	6 4 1
Maryland	4 3 0	5 6 0
Duke	3 3 1	7 3 1
North Carolina	1 6 0	1 10 0
Georgia Tech	0 7 0	3 8 0

Big 10

	Conf. W L T	Overall W L T
Michigan	7 0 1	9 2 1
Michigan State	6 1 1	6 5 1
Illinois	5 2 1	6 5 1
Iowa	4 1 3	6 4 3
Indiana	5 3 0	8 3 1
Purdue	3 5 0	4 7 0
Ohio State	2 5 1	4 6 1
Northwestern	2 5 1	2 8 1
Wisconsin	1 7 0	1 10 0
Minnesota	0 6 2	2 7 2

Big 8

	Conf. W L T	Overall W L T
Nebraska	7 0 0	11 2 0
Oklahoma	6 1 0	9 3 0
Oklahoma State	5 2 0	10 2 0
Colorado	4 3 0	8 4 0
Iowa State	3 4 0	5 6 0
Missouri	2 5 0	3 7 1
Kansas	1 6 0	1 10 0
Kansas State	0 7 0	0 11 0

Big West

	Conf. W L T	Overall W L T
Fresno State	7 0 0	10 2 0
Cal-St. Fullerton	5 2 0	5 6 0
Utah State	4 3 0	4 7 0
San Jose State	4 3 0	4 8 0
Nevada-Las Vegas	3 4 0	4 7 0
Long Beach State	3 4 0	3 9 0
Pacific	2 5 0	2 9 0
New Mexico State	0 7 0	1 10 0

Ivy

	Conf. W L T	Overall W L T
Pennsylvania	6 1 0	9 1 0
Cornell	6 1 0	7 2 1
Princeton	4 3 0	6 4 0
Dartmouth	4 3 0	5 5 0
Yale	3 3 1	3 6 1
Harvard	2 5 0	2 8 0
Columbia	2 5 0	2 8 0
Brown	0 6 1	0 9 1

MAC

	Conf. W L T	Overall W L T
Western Michigan	7 1 0	9 3 0
Eastern Michigan	5 2 1	6 3 1
Ball State	5 3 0	8 3 0
Central Michigan	5 3 0	7 4 0
Ohio U	4 3 1	4 6 1
Toledo	4 4 0	6 5 0
Kent State	3 5 0	5 6 0
Bowling Green	1 6 1	2 8 1
Miami, Ohio	0 7 1	0 10 1

Pac 10

	Conf. W L T	Overall W L T
Southern Cal	8 0 0	10 2 0
UCLA	6 2 0	10 2 0
Washington State	5 3 0	9 3 0
Arizona	5 3 0	7 4 0
Arizona State	3 4 0	6 5 0
Washington	3 5 0	6 5 0
Oregon	3 5 0	6 6 0
Oregon State	2 5 1	4 6 1
Stanford	1 5 2	3 6 2
California	1 5 1	5 5 1

SEC

	Conf. W L T	Overall W L T
Auburn	6 1 0	10 2 0
LSU	6 1 0	8 4 0
Georgia	5 2 0	9 3 0
Alabama	4 3 0	9 3 0
Florida	4 3 0	7 5 0
Tennessee	3 4 0	5 6 0
Mississippi	3 4 0	5 6 0
Kentucky	2 5 0	5 6 0
Vanderbilt	2 5 0	3 8 0
Mississippi State	0 7 0	1 10 0

SWC

	Conf. W L T	Overall W L T
SMU	0 0 0	0 0 0
Rice	0 0 0	0 11 0
Arkansas	7 0 0	10 2 0
Texas A&M	6 1 0	7 5 0
Houston	5 2 0	9 3 0
Texas Tech	4 3 0	5 6 0
Baylor	2 5 0	6 5 0
Texas	2 5 0	4 7 0
TCU	2 5 0	4 7 0

WAC

	Conf. W L T	Overall W L T
Wyoming	8 0 0	11 2 0
Texas-El Paso	6 2 0	10 3 0
Hawaii	5 3 0	9 3 0
Brigham Young	5 3 0	9 4 0
Utah	4 4 0	6 5 0
Air Force	3 5 0	5 7 0
San Diego State	3 5 0	3 8 0
New Mexico	1 7 0	2 10 0
Colorado State	1 7 0	1 10 0

Independents

	Overall W L T
Notre Dame	12 0 0
Florida State	11 1 0
Miami, Fla.	11 1 0
West Virginia	11 1 0
Southern Miss	10 2 0
Syracuse	10 2 0
Army	9 3 0
Louisville	8 3 0
South Carolina	8 4 0
Northern Illinois	7 4 0
La. Lafayette	6 5 0
Pittsburgh	6 5 0
Memphis	6 5 0
Rutgers	5 6 0
Penn State	5 6 0
Tulane	5 6 0
Louisiana Tech	4 7 0
Tulsa	4 7 0
Temple	4 7 0
Boston College	3 8 0
East Carolina	3 8 0
Virginia Tech	3 8 0
Cincinnati	3 8 0
Navy	3 8 0

1988 ANNUAL REVIEW 1367

1988 NCAA Major College Statistical Leaders

Individual Leaders

PASSING	CL	G	ATT	COM	PCT	INT	I%	YDS	YPA	TD	TD%	RATING
1 Timm Rosenbach, Washington State	JR	11	302	199	65.9	10	3.3	2791	9.2	23	7.6	162.0
2 Mike Gundy, Oklahoma State	JR	11	236	153	64.8	12	5.1	2163	9.2	19	8.1	158.2
3 Chip Ferguson, Florida State	SR	10	194	122	62.9	11	5.7	1714	8.8	16	8.3	153.0
4 Troy Aikman, UCLA	SR	11	327	209	63.9	8	2.5	2599	8.0	23	7.0	149.0
5 Todd Philcox, Syracuse	SR	11	234	141	60.3	11	4.7	2076	8.9	16	6.9	147.9
6 Steve Walsh, Miami, Fla.	JR	11	390	233	59.7	12	3.1	3115	8.0	29	7.4	145.2
7 Warren Jones, Hawaii	SR	12	259	138	53.3	11	4.3	2268	8.8	19	7.3	142.6
8 Scott Mitchell, Utah	SO	11	533	323	60.6	15	2.8	4322	8.1	29	5.4	141.0
9 Randy Welniak, Wyoming	SR	12	324	184	56.8	9	2.8	2627	8.1	21	6.5	140.7
10 Rodney Peete, Southern Cal	SR	11	338	208	61.5	10	3.0	2654	7.9	18	5.3	139.2

ALL-PURPOSE	CL	G	RUSH	REC	PR	KR	YDS	YPG
1 Barry Sanders, Oklahoma State	JR	11	2628	106	95	421	3250	295.5
2 Johnny Johnson, San Jose State	JR	12	1219	668	0	315	2202	183.5
3 Eric Wilkerson, Kent State	SR	11	1325	73	0	502	1900	172.7
4 Tony Boles, Michigan	JR	10	1359	64	0	302	1725	172.5
5 Kendal Smith, Utah State	SR	11	25	1196	141	525	1887	171.6
6 Michael Pierce, Tulane	JR	10	345	534	0	765	1644	164.4
7 Andrew Greer, Ohio U	JR	11	863	114	0	810	1787	162.5
8 Anthony Thompson, Indiana	JR	11	1546	219	0	0	1765	160.5
9 Eric Metcalf, Texas	SR	10	932	333	192	117	1574	157.4
10 Darren Lewis, Texas A&M	SO	11	1692	13	0	0	1705	155.0

RUSHING/Yards Per Game	CL	G	ATT	YDS	TD	AVG	YPG
1 Barry Sanders, Oklahoma State	JR	11	344	2628	37	7.6	238.9
2 Darren Lewis, Texas A&M	SO	11	306	1692	7	5.5	153.8
3 Anthony Thompson, Indiana	JR	11	329	1546	24	4.7	140.6
4 Tony Boles, Michigan	JR	10	248	1359	9	5.5	135.9
5 Ken Clark, Nebraska	JR	12	232	1497	12	6.5	124.8
6 Eric Bieniemy, Colorado	SO	10	219	1243	10	5.7	124.3
7 Blake Ezor, Michigan State	JR	11	290	1358	10	4.7	123.5
8 Eric Wilkerson, Kent State	SR	11	247	1325	14	5.4	120.5
9 Steve Broussard, Washington State	JR	10	189	1141	11	6.0	114.1
10 Don Riley, Central Michigan	JR	11	215	1238	7	5.8	112.6

RUSHING/Yards Per Carry	CL	G	ATT	YDS	YPC
1 Barry Sanders, Oklahoma State	JR	11	344	2628	7.6
2 Ken Clark, Nebraska	JR	12	232	1497	6.5
3 Tim Worley, Georgia	JR	11	191	1216	6.4
4 Steve Broussard, Washington State	JR	10	189	1141	6.0
5 Kennard Martin, North Carolina	SO	11	193	1146	5.9
6 Curvin Richards, Pittsburgh	FR	11	207	1228	5.9
7 Don Riley, Central Michigan	JR	11	215	1238	5.8
8 Terry Allen, Clemson	SO	11	199	1139	5.7
9 Eric Bieniemy, Colorado	SO	10	219	1243	5.7
10 Darren Lewis, Texas A&M	SO	11	306	1692	5.5

*-Based on top 23 rushers

RECEIVING	CL	G	REC	YDS	TD	YPR	YPG	RPG
1 Jason Phillips, Houston	SR	11	108	1444	15	13.4	131.3	9.8
2 James Dixon, Houston	SR	11	102	1103	11	10.8	100.3	9.3
3 Boo Mitchell, Vanderbilt	SR	11	78	1213	5	15.6	110.3	7.1
4 Hart Lee Dykes, Oklahoma State	SR	11	74	1278	14	17.3	116.2	6.7
5 Roger Boone, Duke	JR	11	73	630	2	8.6	57.3	6.6
6 Tom Waddle, Boston College	SR	11	70	902	5	12.9	82.0	6.4
7 Greg Washington, Kansas State	JR	11	69	928	9	13.4	84.4	6.3
8 Clarkston Hines, Duke	JR	11	68	1067	10	15.7	97.0	6.2
9 Marv Cook, Iowa	SR	9	55	645	3	11.7	71.7	6.1
10 Kevin Evans, San Jose State	JR	10	61	887	4	14.5	88.7	6.1

PUNTING	CL	PUNT	YDS	AVG
1 Keith English, Colorado	SR	51	2297	45.0
2 Pat Thompson, Brigham Young	SR	49	2195	44.8
3 Kent Elmore, Tennessee	JR	41	1818	44.3
4 Tony Rhynes, Nevada-Las Vegas	JR	66	2905	44.0
5 Martin Bailey, Wake Forest	SR	46	2012	43.7
6 Bill Rudison, Akron	JR	58	2511	43.3
7 Chris Mohr, Alabama	SR	58	2475	42.7
8 Tom Kilpatrick, Wyoming	SR	50	2131	42.6
9 Jim Sirois, Cal-St. Fullerton	SR	59	2513	42.6
10 Bobby Lilljedahl, Texas	JR	61	2598	42.6

PUNT RETURNS	CL	PR	YDS	TD	AVG
1 Deion Sanders, Florida State	SR	33	503	1	15.2
2 Marcus Cherry, Boston College	SR	15	206	1	13.7
3 James Henry, Southern Miss	SR	23	309	2	13.4
4 Ricky Watters, Notre Dame	SO	19	253	2	13.3
5 Darryl Henley, UCLA	SR	21	279	2	13.3
6 Carl Platt, South Carolina	SO	21	266	0	12.7
7 Chuck Carswell, Georgia	FR	31	388	0	12.5
8 Kimble Anders, Houston	JR	17	205	0	12.1
9 Larry Hargrove, Ohio U	JR	21	253	1	12.1
10 John Miller, Michigan State	SR	15	179	0	11.9

KICKOFF RETURNS	CL	KR	YDS	TD	AVG
1 Raghib Ismail, Notre Dame	FR	12	433	2	36.1
2 Chris Oldham, Oregon	JR	26	764	1	29.4
3 Erik Mortensen, Brigham Young	FR	14	398	1	28.4
4 Carlos Snow, Ohio State	SO	19	513	1	27.0
5 Larry Khan-Smith, Hawaii	SO	32	852	1	26.6
6 Chris Williams, North Carolina St.	SO	18	468	0	26.0
7 Tim Frager, Boston College	SO	19	491	0	25.8
8 Patrick Rowe, San Diego State	SO	31	799	0	25.8
9 Quinton McCracken, Duke	FR	19	483	1	25.4
10 Tony Boles, Michigan	JR	12	302	0	25.2

SCORING	CL	TDS	XP	FG	PTS	PTPG
1 Barry Sanders, Oklahoma State	JR	39	0	0	234	21.3
2 Anthony Thompson, Indiana	JR	24	0	0	144	13.1
3 Chris Jacke, Texas-El Paso	SR	0	48	25	123	10.3
4 Charlie Baumann, West Virginia	SR	0	58	18	112	10.2
5 Roman Anderson, Houston	FR	0	51	19	108	9.8
5 Tim Worley, Georgia	JR	18	0	0	108	9.8
7 Carlos Huerta, Miami, Fla.	FR	0	44	21	107	9.7
8 Johnny Johnson, San Jose State	JR	19	2	0	116	9.7
9 Kendall Trainor, Arkansas	SR	0	30	24	102	9.3
10 Cary Blanchard, Oklahoma State	SO	0	67	11	100	9.1

FIELD GOALS	CL	FGA	FGM	PCT	FGG
1 Kendall Trainor, Arkansas	SR	27	24	0.89	2.18
2 Chris Jacke, Texas-El Paso	SR	27	25	0.93	2.08
3 Rob Keen, California	SO	25	21	0.84	1.91
3 Carlos Huerta, Miami, Fla.	FR	27	21	0.78	1.91
5 David Browndyke, LSU	JR	23	19	0.83	1.73
5 John Hopkins, Stanford	SO	24	19	0.79	1.73
5 Roman Anderson, Houston	FR	25	19	0.76	1.73
5 Philip Doyle, Alabama	SO	31	19	0.61	1.73
9 Kenny Stucker, Ball State	FR	23	18	0.78	1.64
9 Pat O'Morrow, Ohio State	JR	23	18	0.78	1.64
9 Collin Mackie, South Carolina	SO	24	18	0.75	1.64
9 Charlie Baumann, West Virginia	SR	25	18	0.72	1.64
9 John Langeloh, Michigan State	SO	26	18	0.69	1.64
9 Steve Loop, Fresno State	JR	27	18	0.67	1.64

INTERCEPTIONS	CL	INT	YDS	TD	INT/GM
1 Kurt Larson, Michigan State	SR	8	78	1	0.73
1 Andy Logan, Kent State	SR	8	54	0	0.73
3 Todd Sandroni, Mississippi	SO	7	33	1	0.70
4 Greg Jackson, LSU	SR	7	221	2	0.64
4 Eddie Moore, Memphis	JR	7	51	0	0.64
4 Tony McCorvey, Bowling Green	SR	7	33	0	0.64
7 Deion Sanders, Florida State	SR	5	116	2	0.56
8 Stanley Richards, Texas *	SO	6	92	0	0.55
8 Adrian Jones, Missouri *	JR	6	84	0	0.55
8 Lavon Edwards, Utah *	FR	6	74	0	0.55
8 Patrick Williams, Arkansas *	JR	6	57	1	0.55
8 David Johnson, Central Michigan *	SO	6	56	0	0.55

*-Nine tied with 0.55; these had the most yards.

Team Leaders

RUSHING OFFENSE	G	ATT	YDS	AVG	TD	YPG
1 Nebraska	12	735	4588	6.2	47	382.3
2 Air Force	12	734	4530	6.2	48	377.5
3 Army	11	786	3813	4.9	35	346.6
4 Oklahoma	11	668	3777	5.7	36	343.4
5 Oklahoma State	11	561	3492	6.2	47	317.5
6 West Virginia	11	621	3228	5.2	40	293.5
7 Colorado	11	614	3095	5.0	34	281.4
8 Kent State	11	624	3073	4.9	28	279.4
9 Clemson	11	625	3054	4.9	32	277.6
10 Texas A&M	12	653	3102	4.8	33	258.5

PASSING OFFENSE	G	ATT	COM	INT	PCT	YDS	YPA	TD	I%	YPC	YPG
1 Utah	11	543	327	20	60.2	4355	8.0	29	3.7	13.3	395.9
2 Houston	11	580	344	15	59.3	4153	7.2	38	2.6	12.1	377.5
3 Duke	11	496	292	20	58.9	3868	7.8	24	4.0	13.2	351.6
4 Brigham Young	12	475	258	20	54.3	3874	8.2	26	4.2	15.0	322.8
5 Miami, Fla.	11	441	260	13	59.0	3503	7.9	35	3.0	13.5	318.5
6 Utah State	11	455	248	21	54.5	3278	7.2	19	4.6	13.2	298.0
7 Iowa	12	419	260	10	62.1	3324	7.9	15	2.4	12.8	277.0
8 Texas Tech	11	364	194	11	53.3	2917	8.0	20	3.0	15.0	265.2
9 Oregon State	11	445	275	9	61.8	2896	6.5	18	2.0	10.5	263.3
10 Western Michigan	11	397	221	18	55.7	2863	7.2	22	4.5	13.0	260.3

TOTAL OFFENSE	G	P	YDS	AVG	TD	YPG
1 Utah	11	901	5795	6.4	48	526.8
2 Oklahoma State	11	803	5667	7.1	66	515.2
3 Washington State	11	854	5439	6.4	49	494.5
4 Houston	11	832	5331	6.4	55	484.6
5 West Virginia	11	816	5310	6.5	56	482.7
6 Wyoming	12	922	5741	6.2	62	478.4
7 Nebraska	12	898	5735	6.4	59	477.9
8 Duke	11	868	5111	5.9	39	464.6
9 Southern Cal	11	911	5077	5.6	45	461.6
10 Brigham Young	12	909	5483	6.0	47	456.9

RUSHING DEFENSE	G	ATT	YDS	AVG	TD	YPG
1 Auburn	11	334	695	2.1	3	63.2
2 Southern Cal	11	313	843	2.7	7	76.6
3 Miami, Fla.	11	419	908	2.2	4	82.5
4 Arkansas	11	394	1010	2.6	12	91.8
5 Alabama	11	401	1053	2.6	8	95.7
6 North Carolina St.	11	451	1140	2.5	5	103.6
7 Central Michigan	11	441	1165	2.6	10	105.9
8 UCLA	11	416	1173	2.8	10	106.6
9 Wyoming	12	437	1314	3.0	14	109.5
10 Notre Dame	11	403	1236	3.1	6	112.4

PASSING DEFENSE	G	ATT	COM	PCT	YPC	INT	I%	YDS	YPA	TD	YPG
1 Baylor	11	237	97	40.9	13.4	9	3.8	1296	5.5	11	117.8
2 Pittsburgh	11	208	87	41.8	15.0	13	6.3	1308	6.3	7	118.9
3 Florida	11	254	121	47.6	11.2	16	6.3	1360	5.4	10	123.6
4 Purdue	11	232	93	40.1	15.4	16	6.9	1430	6.2	10	130.0
5 Florida State	11	278	110	39.6	13.1	18	6.5	1443	5.2	10	131.2
6 Nebraska	12	282	123	43.6	13.2	16	5.7	1618	5.7	10	134.8
7 Navy	11	212	105	49.5	14.1	7	3.3	1484	7.0	8	134.9
8 Georgia Tech	11	252	129	51.2	11.8	14	5.6	1528	6.1	8	138.9
9 Eastern Michigan	10	212	124	58.5	11.3	11	5.2	1395	6.6	7	139.5
10 Kentucky	11	250	134	53.6	11.5	10	4.0	1535	6.1	11	139.5

TOTAL DEFENSE	G	P	YDS	AVG	TD	YPG
1 Auburn	11	666	2399	3.6	9	218.1
2 Miami, Fla.	11	726	2662	3.7	11	242.0
3 Florida	11	710	2726	3.8	18	247.8
4 Pittsburgh	11	697	2796	4.0	20	254.2
5 Baylor	11	686	2835	4.1	24	257.7
6 Ball State	11	664	2887	4.3	18	262.5
7 Nebraska	12	743	3153	4.2	20	262.8
8 North Carolina St.	11	783	2907	3.7	11	264.3
9 Fresno State	11	738	2909	3.9	17	264.5
10 Southern Cal	11	655	2958	4.5	19	268.9

SCORING OFFENSE	G	PTS	AVG
1 Oklahoma State	11	522	47.5
2 West Virginia	11	472	42.9
3 Wyoming	12	497	41.4
4 Houston	11	452	41.1
5 Florida State	11	442	40.2
6 Nebraska	12	474	39.5
7 Utah	11	399	36.3
8 Miami, Fla.	11	395	35.9
9 Texas-El Paso	12	427	35.6
10 Washington State	11	391	35.5

SCORING DEFENSE	G	PTS	AVG
1 Auburn	11	79	7.2
2 Miami, Fla.	11	113	10.3
3 Notre Dame	11	135	12.3
4 Fresno State	11	139	12.6
5 North Carolina St.	11	142	12.9
6 Michigan State	11	143	13.0
7 Oklahoma	11	147	13.4
8 Clemson	11	151	13.7
9 Michigan	11	153	13.9
10 Alabama	11	160	14.5

ANNUAL REVIEW

1989 POLL PROGRESSION

AP	Pre-Season 1989		Sept. 2 Games
1	Michigan	0-0-0	bye week
2	Notre Dame	0-0-0	beat Virginia 36-13 (A31)
3	Nebraska	0-0-0	bye week
4	Miami, Fla.	0-0-0	bye week
5	Southern Cal	0-0-0	lost to # 22 Illinois 13-14 (S4)
6	Florida State	0-0-0	lost to Southern Miss 26-30
7	LSU	0-0-0	lost to Texas A&M 16-28
8	Auburn	0-0-0	bye week
9	UCLA	0-0-0	bye week
10	Arkansas	0-0-0	bye week
11	Penn State	0-0-0	bye week
12	Clemson	0-0-0	bye week
13	Syracuse	0-0-0	bye week
14	Colorado	0-0-0	beat Texas 27-6 (S4)
15	Oklahoma	0-0-0	beat New Mexico State 73-3
16	Alabama	0-0-0	bye week
17	West Virginia	0-0-0	beat Ball State 35-10
18	Arizona	0-0-0	beat Stanford 19-3
19	Brigham Young	0-0-0	beat New Mexico 24-3
20	Pittsburgh	0-0-0	beat Pacific 38-3
21	Houston	0-0-0	beat Nevada-Las Vegas 69-0
22	Illinois	0-0-0	beat # 5 Southern Cal 14-13 (S4)
23	Iowa	0-0-0	bye week
24	North Carolina St.	0-0-0	beat Maryland 10-6
25	Ohio State	0-0-0	bye week

UP	AP	September 4 Poll		Sept. 9 Games
1	1	Notre Dame	1-0-0	bye week
6	2	Michigan	0-0-0	bye week
5	3	Miami, Fla.	0-0-0	beat Wisconsin 51-3
2	4	Nebraska	0-0-0	beat Northern Illinois 48-17
4	5	Auburn	0-0-0	beat Pacific 55-0
7	6	UCLA	0-0-0	lost to Tennessee 6-24
8	7	Arkansas	0-0-0	bye week
PB	8	Oklahoma	1-0-0	beat Baylor 33-7
11	9	Colorado	1-0-0	beat Colorado State 45-20
9	10	Clemson	1-0-0	beat # 16 Florida State 34-23
	11	Illinois	1-0-0	bye week
10	12	Penn State	0-0-0	lost to Virginia 6-14
3	13	Southern Cal	0-1-0	bye week
15	14	Syracuse	0-0-0	beat Temple 43-3
12	15	Texas A&M	1-0-0	lost to Washington 6-19
16	16	Florida State	0-1-0	lost to # 10 Clemson 23-34
13	17	West Virginia	1-0-0	beat Maryland 14-10
18	18	Southern Miss	1-0-0	lost to Mississippi State 23-26
14	19	Alabama	0-0-0	bye week
	20	Arizona	1-0-0	lost to Texas Tech 14-24
19	21	LSU	0-1-0	bye week
PB	22	Houston	1-0-0	bye week
	23	Pittsburgh	1-0-0	beat Boston College 29-10
17	24	Brigham Young	1-0-0	lost to Washington St. 41-46
	25	North Carolina St.	1-0-0	beat Georgia Tech 38-28
20		Georgia	0-0-0	bye week

UP	AP	September 11 Poll		Sept. 16 Games
1	1	Notre Dame	1-0-0	beat # 2 Michigan 24-19
5	2	Michigan	0-0-0	lost to # 1 Notre Dame 19-24
2	3	Miami, Fla.	1-0-0	beat California 31-3
3	4	Nebraska	1-0-0	beat Utah 42-30
4	5	Auburn	1-0-0	beat Southern Miss 24-3
PB	6	Oklahoma	2-0-0	lost to Arizona 3-6
6	7	Clemson	2-0-0	beat Virginia Tech 27-7
7	8	Colorado	2-0-0	beat # 10 Illinois 38-7
8	9	Arkansas	0-0-0	beat Tulsa 26-7
11	10	Illinois	1-0-0	lost to # 8 Colorado 7-38
10	11	Syracuse	1-0-0	beat Army 10-7
9	12	West Virginia	2-0-0	beat South Carolina 45-21
16	13	Southern Cal	0-1-0	beat Utah State 66-10
14	14	Pittsburgh	2-0-0	bye week
12	15	Washington	1-0-0	beat Purdue 38-9
13	16	Alabama	0-0-0	beat Memphis 35-7
17	17	Tennessee	2-0-0	beat Duke 28-6
PB	18	Houston	1-0-0	bye week
15	19	North Carolina St.	2-0-0	beat Wake Forest 27-17
20	20	UCLA	0-1-0	beat San Diego State 28-25
	21	LSU	0-1-0	lost to Florida State 21-31
	22	Texas A&M	1-1-0	beat TCU 44-7
	23	Washington State	2-0-0	beat Oregon State 41-3
	24	Iowa	0-0-0	bye week
	25	Mississippi State	2-0-0	lost to Georgia 6-23
19		Georgia	0-0-0	beat Baylor 15-3

UP	AP	September 18 Poll		Sept. 23 Games
1	1	Notre Dame	2-0-0	beat Michigan State 21-13
2	2	Miami, Fla.	2-0-0	beat Missouri 38-7
3	3	Nebraska	2-0-0	beat Minnesota 48-0
3	4	Auburn	2-0-0	bye week
7	5	Michigan	0-1-0	beat # 24 UCLA 24-23
5	6	Colorado	3-0-0	bye week
6	7	Clemson	3-0-0	beat Maryland 31-7
8	8	Arkansas	1-0-0	beat Mississippi 24-17
9	9	West Virginia	3-0-0	beat Louisville 30-21
13	10	Syracuse	2-0-0	lost to # 13 Pittsburgh 23-30
10	11	Washington	2-0-0	lost to Arizona 17-20
15	12	Southern Cal	1-1-0	beat # 25 Ohio State 42-3
14	13	Pittsburgh	2-0-0	beat # 10 Syracuse 30-23
11	14	Tennessee	3-0-0	bye week
12	15	Alabama	1-0-0	beat Kentucky 15-3
PB	16	Oklahoma	2-1-0	bye week
PB	17	Houston	1-0-0	beat Arizona State 36-7
16	18	North Carolina St.	3-0-0	beat North Carolina 40-6
17	19	Washington State	3-0-0	beat Wyoming 29-23
	20	Illinois	1-1-0	beat Utah State 41-2
	21	Texas A&M	2-1-0	bye week
18	22	Oregon	2-0-0	lost to Stanford 17-18
	23	Arizona	2-1-0	beat Washington 20-17
	24	UCLA	1-1-0	lost to # 5 Michigan 23-24
20	25	Ohio State	1-0-0	lost to # 12 Southern Cal 3-42
19		Air Force	3-0-0	beat Texas-El Paso 43-26
20		Georgia	1-0-0	beat Mississippi State 23-6

UP	AP	September 25 Poll		Sept. 30 Games
1	1	Notre Dame	3-0-0	beat Purdue 40-7
2	2	Miami, Fla.	3-0-0	beat Michigan State 26-20
3	3	Nebraska	3-0-0	beat Oregon State 35-7
4	4	Auburn	2-0-0	lost to # 12 Tennessee 14-21
5	5	Colorado	3-0-0	beat # 21 Washington 45-28
7	6	Michigan	1-1-0	beat Maryland 41-21
6	7	Clemson	4-0-0	lost to Duke 17-21
8	8	Arkansas	2-0-0	beat Texas-El Paso 39-7
9	9	West Virginia	4-0-0	tied # 10 Pittsburgh 31-31
10	10	Pittsburgh	3-0-0	tied # 9 West Virginia 31-31
11	11	Southern Cal	2-1-0	beat # 19 Washington St. 18-17
12	12	Tennessee	3-0-0	beat # 4 Auburn 21-14
13	13	Alabama	2-0-0	beat Vanderbilt 20-14
PB	14	Houston	2-0-0	beat Temple 65-7
14	15	North Carolina St.	4-0-0	beat Kent State 42-22
PB	16	Oklahoma	2-1-0	beat Kansas 45-6
15	17	Arizona	3-1-0	lost to Oregon 10-16
	18	Syracuse	2-1-0	bye week
16	19	Washington State	4-0-0	lost to # 11 Southern Cal 17-18
	20	Illinois	2-1-0	bye week
17	21	Washington	2-1-0	lost to # 5 Colorado 28-45
	22	Texas A&M	2-1-0	beat Southern Miss 31-14
18	23	Georgia	2-0-0	lost to South Carolina 20-24
19	24	Air Force	4-0-0	beat Colorado State 46-21
20	25	Florida State	2-2-0	bye week

UP	AP	October 2 Poll		Oct. 7 Games
1	1	Notre Dame	4-0-0	beat Stanford 27-17
2	2	Miami, Fla.	4-0-0	beat Cincinnati 56-0
4	3	Colorado	4-0-0	beat Missouri 49-3
3	4	Nebraska	4-0-0	beat Kansas State 58-7
7	5	Michigan	2-1-0	beat Wisconsin 24-0
5	6	Tennessee	4-0-0	beat Georgia 17-14
6	7	Arkansas	3-0-0	beat TCU 41-19
12	8	Pittsburgh	3-0-1	beat Temple 27-3
9	9	Southern Cal	3-1-0	beat Washington 24-16
8	9	West Virginia	4-0-1	lost to Virginia Tech 10-12
10	11	Auburn	2-1-0	beat Kentucky 24-12
PB	12	Houston	3-0-0	beat Baylor 66-10
10	13	Alabama	3-0-0	beat Mississippi 62-27
13	14	North Carolina St.	5-0-0	beat Middle Tennessee 35-14
14	15	Clemson	4-1-0	beat Virginia 34-20
PB	16	Oklahoma	3-1-0	beat Oklahoma State 37-15
19	17	Syracuse	2-1-0	lost to # 22 Florida State 10-41
17	18	Illinois	2-1-0	beat Ohio State 34-14
18	19	Texas A&M	3-1-0	lost to Texas Tech 24-27
15	20	Air Force	5-0-0	beat Navy 35-7
16	21	Washington State	4-1-0	beat # 23 Oregon 51-38
20	22	Florida State	2-2-0	beat # 17 Syracuse 41-10
	23	Oregon	3-1-0	lost to # 21 Washington State 38-51
	24	Michigan State	1-2-0	beat Iowa 17-14
	25	UCLA	2-2-0	beat Arizona State 33-14

UP	AP	October 9 Poll		Oct. 14 Games
1	1	Notre Dame	5-0-0	beat # 17 Air Force 41-27
2	2	Miami, Fla.	5-0-0	beat San Jose State 48-16
4	3	Colorado	5-0-0	beat Iowa State 52-17
3	4	Nebraska	5-0-0	beat Missouri 50-7
7	5	Michigan	3-1-0	beat # 21 Michigan State 10-7
5	6	Tennessee	5-0-0	bye week
6	7	Arkansas	4-0-0	beat Texas Tech 45-13
PB	8	Houston	4-0-0	lost to Texas A&M 13-17
9	9	Pittsburgh	4-0-1	beat Navy 31-14
10	10	Southern Cal	4-1-0	beat California 31-15
8	11	Alabama	4-0-0	beat La. Lafayette 24-17
11	12	Auburn	3-1-0	beat LSU 10-6
12	13	North Carolina St.	6-0-0	bye week
13	14	Clemson	5-1-0	lost to Georgia Tech 14-30
PB	15	Oklahoma	4-1-0	lost to Texas 24-28
15	16	Illinois	3-1-0	beat Purdue 14-2
14	17	Air Force	6-0-0	lost to # 1 Notre Dame 27-41
16	18	Washington State	5-1-0	beat Stanford 31-13
16	19	Florida State	3-2-0	beat Virginia Tech 41-7
18	20	West Virginia	4-1-1	bye week
19	21	Michigan State	2-2-0	lost to # 5 Michigan 7-10
	22	UCLA	3-2-0	lost to Arizona 7-42
	23	Penn State	4-1-0	beat Syracuse 34-12
	24	South Carolina	4-1-1	bye week
	25	Brigham Young	4-1-0	beat Colorado State 45-16
	26	Florida	4-1-0	beat Vanderbilt 34-11
19		Hawaii	5-1-0	bye week

UP	AP	October 16 Poll		Oct. 21 Games
1	1	Notre Dame	6-0-0	beat # 9 Southern Cal 28-24
2	2	Miami, Fla.	6-0-0	bye week
3	3	Colorado	6-0-0	beat Kansas 49-17
4	4	Nebraska	6-0-0	beat Oklahoma State 48-23
7	5	Michigan	4-1-0	beat Iowa 26-12
5	6	Tennessee	5-0-0	lost to # 10 Alabama 30-47
6	7	Arkansas	5-0-0	lost to Texas 20-24
9	8	Pittsburgh	5-0-1	bye week
10	9	Southern Cal	5-1-0	lost to # 1 Notre Dame 24-28
8	10	Alabama	5-0-0	beat # 6 Tennessee 47-30
11	11	Auburn	4-1-0	lost to # 14 Florida State 14-22
12	12	North Carolina St.	6-0-0	lost to Clemson 10-30
15	13	Illinois	4-1-0	beat Michigan State 14-10
13	14	Florida State	4-2-0	beat # 11 Auburn 22-14
14	15	Washington State	6-1-0	lost to # 22 Arizona 21-23
PB	16	Houston	4-1-0	beat SMU 95-21
16	17	Penn State	5-1-0	bye week
18	18	West Virginia	4-1-1	beat Cincinnati 69-3
17	19	Air Force	6-1-0	lost to TCU 9-27
	20	Florida	5-1-0	beat New Mexico 27-21
20	21	Brigham Young	5-1-0	beat Texas-El Paso 49-24
19	22	Arizona	4-2-0	beat # 15 Washington St. 23-21
	23	Texas A&M	4-2-0	beat Baylor 14-11
	24	South Carolina	4-1-1	beat Western Carolina 24-3
PB	25	Oklahoma	4-2-0	beat Iowa State 43-40

UP	AP	October 23 Poll		Oct. 28 Games
1	1	Notre Dame	7-0-0	beat # 7 Pittsburgh 45-7
2	2	Miami, Fla.	6-0-0	lost to # 9 Florida State 10-24
3	3	Colorado	7-0-0	beat Oklahoma 20-3
4	4	Nebraska	7-0-0	beat Iowa State 49-17
6	5	Michigan	5-1-0	beat Indiana 38-10
5	6	Alabama	6-0-0	beat # 14 Penn State 17-16
7	7	Pittsburgh	5-0-1	lost to # 1 Notre Dame 7-45
8	8	Illinois	5-1-0	beat Wisconsin 32-9
9	9	Florida State	5-2-0	beat # 2 Miami, Fla. 24-10
10	10	Southern Cal	5-2-0	beat Stanford 19-0
12	11	Tennessee	5-1-0	beat LSU 45-39
PB	12	Houston	5-1-0	lost to # 13 Arkansas 39-45
11	13	Arkansas	5-1-0	beat # 12 Houston 45-39
13	14	Penn State	5-1-0	lost to # 6 Alabama 16-17
14	15	West Virginia	5-1-1	beat Boston College 44-30
15	16	Auburn	4-2-0	beat Mississippi State 14-0
16	17	Arizona	5-2-0	beat Pacific 38-14
18	18	Brigham Young	6-1-0	lost to Hawaii 14-56
20	19	Florida	6-1-0	bye week
17	20	North Carolina St.	6-1-0	beat # 25 South Carolina 20-10
	21	Texas A&M	5-2-0	beat Rice 45-7
19	22	Clemson	6-2-0	beat Wake Forest 44-10
	23	Washington State	6-2-0	lost to Arizona State 39-44
	24	Texas	4-2-0	bye week
	25	South Carolina	5-1-1	lost to # 20 North Carolina St. 10-20

October 30 Poll

UP	AP	Team	Record	Nov. 4 Games
1	1	Notre Dame	8-0-0	beat Navy 41-0
2	2	Colorado	8-0-0	beat #3 Nebraska 27-21
3	3	Nebraska	8-0-0	lost to #2 Colorado 21-27
7	4	Michigan	6-1-0	beat Purdue 42-27
4	5	Alabama	7-0-0	beat Mississippi 23-10
5	6	Florida State	6-2-0	beat South Carolina 35-10
6	7	Miami, Fla.	6-1-0	beat East Carolina 40-10
8	8	Illinois	6-1-0	beat Iowa 31-7
9	9	Southern Cal	6-2-0	beat Oregon State 48-6
10	10	Tennessee	6-1-0	bye week
11	11	Arkansas	6-1-0	beat Rice 38-17
13	12	Auburn	5-2-0	beat #19 Florida 10-7
12	13	West Virginia	6-1-1	lost to #16 Penn State 9-19
14	14	Pittsburgh	5-1-1	bye week
16	15	Arizona	6-2-0	lost to California 28-29
17	16	Penn State	5-2-0	beat #13 West Virginia 19-9
	17	Houston	5-2-0	beat TCU 55-10
15	18	North Carolina St.	7-1-0	lost to #24 Virginia 9-20
	19	Florida	6-1-0	lost to #12 Auburn 7-10
19	20	Texas A&M	6-2-0	beat SMU 63-14
18	21	Clemson	7-2-0	beat North Carolina 35-3
19	22	Texas	4-2-0	lost to Texas Tech 17-24
	23	Brigham Young	6-2-0	beat Oregon 45-41
	24	Virginia	7-2-0	beat #18 North Carolina St. 20-9
	25	Fresno State	8-0-0	beat San Jose State 31-30

November 6 Poll

UP	AP	Team	Record	Nov. 11 Games
1	1	Notre Dame	9-0-0	beat SMU 59-6
2	2	Colorado	9-0-0	beat Oklahoma State 41-17
5	3	Michigan	7-1-0	beat #8 Illinois 24-10
3	4	Alabama	8-0-0	beat LSU 32-16
4	5	Florida State	7-2-0	bye week
6	6	Nebraska	8-1-0	beat Kansas 51-14
7	7	Miami, Fla.	6-1-0	beat #14 Pittsburgh 24-3
8	8	Illinois	7-1-0	lost to #3 Michigan 10-24
9	9	Southern Cal	7-2-0	beat #25 Arizona 24-3
11	10	Arkansas	6-1-0	beat Baylor 19-10
10	11	Tennessee	6-1-0	beat Akron 52-9
12	12	Auburn	6-2-0	beat Louisiana Tech 38-23
13	13	Penn State	6-2-0	tied Maryland 13-13
14	14	Pittsburgh	5-1-1	lost to #7 Miami, Fla. 3-24
PB	15	Houston	6-2-0	beat Texas 47-9
16	16	Texas A&M	7-2-0	bye week
15	17	Clemson	8-2-0	bye week
17	18	Virginia	8-2-0	beat Virginia Tech 32-25
19	19	West Virginia	6-2-1	beat Rutgers 21-20
	20	Florida	6-2-0	lost to Georgia 10-17
18	21	Brigham Young	7-2-0	beat Air Force 44-35
	22	North Carolina St.	7-2-0	beat Duke 26-35
19	23	Texas Tech	6-2-0	beat TCU 37-7
	24	Fresno State	9-0-0	beat New Mexico State 45-5
	25	Arizona	6-3-0	lost to #9 Southern Cal 3-24

November 13 Poll

UP	AP	Team	Record	Nov. 18 Games
1	1	Notre Dame	10-0-0	beat #17 Penn State 34-23
2	2	Colorado	10-0-0	beat Kansas State 59-11
4	3	Michigan	8-1-0	beat Minnesota 49-15
3	4	Alabama	9-0-0	beat Southern Miss 37-14
5	5	Florida State	7-2-0	beat Memphis 57-20
6	6	Nebraska	9-1-0	beat Oklahoma 42-25
7	7	Miami, Fla.	7-1-0	beat San Diego State 42-6
8	8	Southern Cal	8-2-0	tied UCLA 10-10
10	9	Tennessee	7-1-0	beat Mississippi 33-21
9	10	Arkansas	8-1-0	bye week
11	11	Auburn	7-2-0	beat Georgia 20-3
12	12	Illinois	7-2-0	beat Indiana 41-28
PB	13	Houston	7-2-0	bye week
15	14	Texas A&M	7-2-0	bye week
13	15	Clemson	8-2-0	beat South Carolina 45-0
14	16	Virginia	9-2-0	beat Maryland 48-21
16	17	Penn State	6-2-1	lost to #1 Notre Dame 23-34
20	18	West Virginia	7-2-1	bye week
18	19	Pittsburgh	5-2-1	beat East Carolina 47-42
19	20	Texas Tech	7-2-0	beat SMU 48-24
17	21	Brigham Young	8-2-0	beat Utah 70-31
	22	Ohio State	7-2-0	beat Wisconsin 42-22
	23	Fresno State	10-0-0	lost to New Mexico 22-45
	24	Hawaii	8-2-0	bye week
	25	Duke	7-3-0	beat North Carolina 41-0

November 20 Poll

UP	AP	Team	Record	Nov. 25 Games
1	1	Notre Dame	11-0-0	lost to #7 Miami, Fla. 10-27
2	2	Colorado	11-0-0	regular season complete
4	3	Michigan	9-1-0	beat #20 Ohio State 28-10
3	4	Alabama	10-0-0	bye week
5	5	Florida State	8-2-0	bye week
6	6	Nebraska	10-1-0	regular season complete
7	7	Miami, Fla.	9-1-0	beat #1 Notre Dame 27-10
8	8	Tennessee	8-1-0	beat Kentucky 31-10
9	9	Arkansas	8-1-0	beat #14 Texas A&M 23-22 (N24)
10	10	Auburn	8-2-0	bye week
11	11	Illinois	8-2-0	beat Northwestern 63-14
12	12	Southern Cal	8-2-1	regular season complete
PB	13	Houston	7-2-0	beat #18 Texas Tech 40-24
15	14	Texas A&M	7-2-0	lost to #9 Arkansas 22-23 (N24)
13	15	Clemson	9-2-0	regular season complete
14	16	Virginia	10-2-0	regular season complete
19	17	West Virginia	7-2-1	beat Syracuse 24-17 (N23)
17	18	Texas Tech	8-2-0	lost to #13 Houston 24-40
20	19	Pittsburgh	6-2-1	lost to Penn State 13-16
18	20	Ohio State	8-2-0	lost to #3 Michigan 18-28
16	21	Brigham Young	9-2-0	beat San Diego State 48-27
	22	Penn State	6-3-1	beat Pittsburgh 16-13
	23	Duke	8-3-0	regular season complete
	24	Hawaii	8-2-0	beat Oregon State 23-21
	25	Michigan State	6-4-0	beat Wisconsin 31-3

November 27 Poll

UP	AP	Team	Record	Dec. 2 Games
1	1	Colorado	11-0-0	
2	2	Alabama	10-0-0	lost to #11 Auburn 20-30
4	3	Michigan	10-1-0	regular season complete
3	4	Miami, Fla.	10-1-0	regular season complete
5	5	Notre Dame	11-1-0	regular season complete
6	6	Florida State	8-2-0	beat Florida 24-17
7	7	Nebraska	10-1-0	
8	8	Tennessee	9-1-0	beat Vanderbilt 17-10
9	9	Arkansas	9-1-0	beat SMU 38-24
11	10	Illinois	9-2-0	regular season complete
10	11	Auburn	8-2-0	beat #2 Alabama 30-20
12	12	Southern Cal	8-2-1	
PB	13	Houston	8-2-0	beat Rice 64-0
13	14	Clemson	9-2-0	
14	15	Virginia	10-2-0	
16	16	Texas A&M	7-3-0	beat Texas 21-10
16	17	West Virginia	8-2-1	regular season complete
18	18	Penn State	7-3-1	regular season complete
15	19	Brigham Young	10-2-0	regular season complete
	20	Duke	8-3-0	
20	21	Ohio State	8-3-0	regular season complete
	22	Michigan State	7-4-0	regular season complete
19	23	Hawaii	9-2-0	regular season complete
	24	Pittsburgh	6-3-1	beat Rutgers 46-29
	25	Texas Tech	8-3-0	regular season complete
20		Arizona	7-4-0	regular season complete

December 4 Poll

UP	AP	Team	Record	Bowl Bid	Date	Bowl Result	RB	UP	AP	January 2 Final Poll	Record
1	1	Colorado	11-0-0	Orange Bowl	J1	lost to #4 Notre Dame 6-21	1	1	1	Miami, Fla.	11-1-0
2	2	Miami, Fla.	10-1-0	Sugar Bowl	J1	beat #7 Alabama 33-25	2	3	2	Notre Dame	12-1-0
3	3	Michigan	10-1-0	Rose Bowl	J1	lost to #12 Southern Cal 10-17	4	2	3	Florida State	10-2-0
4	4	Notre Dame	11-1-0	Orange Bowl	J1	beat #1 Colorado 21-6	6	4	4	Colorado	11-1-0
5	5	Florida State	9-2-0	Fiesta Bowl	J1	beat #6 Nebraska 41-17	5	5	5	Tennessee	11-1-0
6	6	Nebraska	10-1-0	Fiesta Bowl	J1	lost to #5 Florida State 17-41	3	6	6	Auburn	10-2-0
7	7	Alabama	10-1-0	Sugar Bowl	J1	lost to #2 Miami, Fla. 25-33	9	8	7	Michigan	10-2-0
8	8	Tennessee	10-1-0	Cotton Bowl	J1	beat #10 Arkansas 31-27	8	9	8	Southern Cal	9-2-1
10	9	Auburn	9-2-0	Hall of Fame Bowl	J1	beat #21 Ohio State 31-14	7	7	9	Alabama	10-2-0
9	10	Arkansas	10-1-0	Cotton Bowl	J1	lost to #8 Tennessee 27-31	12	10	10	Illinois	10-2-0
11	11	Illinois	9-2-0	Citrus Bowl	J1	beat #15 Virginia 31-21	10	12	11	Nebraska	10-2-0
12	12	Southern Cal	8-2-1	Rose Bowl	J1	beat #3 Michigan 17-10	13	11	12	Clemson	10-2-0
PB	13	Houston	9-2-0					11	13	Arkansas	10-2-0
13	14	Clemson	9-2-0	Gator Bowl	D30	beat #17 West Virginia 27-7	14	PB	14	Houston	9-2-0
14	15	Virginia	10-2-0	Citrus Bowl	J1	lost to #11 Illinois 21-31	15	14	15	Penn State	8-3-1
15	16	Texas A&M	8-3-0	Sun Bowl	D30	lost to #24 Pittsburgh 28-31	26	16	16	Michigan State	8-4-0
17	17	West Virginia	8-2-1	Gator Bowl	D30	lost to #14 Clemson 7-27	16	19	17	Pittsburgh	8-3-1
18	18	Penn State	7-3-1	Holiday Bowl	D29	beat #19 Brigham Young 50-39	18	15	18	Virginia	10-3-0
16	19	Brigham Young	10-2-0	Holiday Bowl	D29	lost to #18 Penn State 39-50	21	16	19	Texas Tech	9-3-0
	20	Duke	8-3-0	All-American Bowl	D28	lost to #25 Texas Tech 21-49	20		20	Texas A&M	8-4-0
	21	Ohio State	8-3-0	Hall of Fame Bowl	J1	lost to #9 Auburn 14-31	17		21	West Virginia	8-3-1
	22	Michigan State	7-4-0	Aloha Bowl	D25	beat #23 Hawaii 33-13	23	18	22	Brigham Young	10-3-0
19	23	Hawaii	9-2-0	Aloha Bowl	D25	lost to #22 Michigan State 13-33	25	20	23	Washington	8-4-0
	24	Pittsburgh	7-3-1	Sun Bowl	D30	beat #16 Texas A&M 31-28	33		24	Ohio State	8-4-0
19	25	Texas Tech	8-3-0	All-American Bowl	D28	beat #20 Duke 49-21	19		25	Arizona	8-4-0

1989

CONSENSUS ALL-AMERICANS

POS	Offense	HT	WT	School	AP	CF	FC	FW	PI
QB	Andre Ware	6-2	205	Houston	•	•	•	•	•
RB	Anthony Thompson	6-0	209	Indiana	•	•	•	•	•
RB	Emmitt Smith	5-10	201	Florida	•	•	•	•	•
WR	Clarkston Hines	6-1	170	Duke	•	•	•	•	•
WR	Terance Mathis	5-9	167	New Mexico	•		•		•
TE	Mike Busch	6-5	252	Iowa State		•	•	•	
L	Jim Mabry	6-4	262	Arkansas	•	•	•	•	•
L	Bob Kula	6-4	282	Michigan State	•	•			
L	Mohammed Elewonibi	6-5	290	Brigham Young			•	•	•
L	Joe Garten	6-3	280	Colorado	•			•	•
L	Eric Still	6-3	283	Tennessee	•	•	•	•	•
C	Jake Young	6-4	270	Nebraska		•	•		•
PK	Jason Hanson	6-0	164	Washington State	•			•	

Others receiving first-team honors

QB	Major Harris	West Virginia				•	
RB	Blair Thomas	Penn State		•			
RB	Johnny Bailey	Texas A&T-Kingsville				•	
WR	Emmanuel Hazard	Houston			•		
L	Chris Port	Duke				•	
L	Doug Glaser	Nebraska			•		
L	Ed King	Auburn			•		
C	Michael Tanks	Florida State	•			•	
KR	Raghib Ismail	Notre Dame	•			•	

POS	Defense	HT	WT	School	AP	CF	FC	FW	PI
L	Chris Zorich	6-1	268	Notre Dame	•	•		•	•
L	Greg Mark	6-4	255	Miami, Fla.	•		•	•	•
L	Tim Ryan	6-5	260	Southern Cal	•	•	•	•	•
L	Moe Gardner	6-2	250	Illinois	•	•	•	•	•
LB	Percy Snow	6-3	240	Michigan State	•	•	•	•	•
LB	Keith McCants	6-5	256	Alabama	•	•	•	•	•
LB	Alfred Williams	6-6	230	Colorado	•	•	*	•	•
DB	Todd Lyght	6-1	181	Notre Dame	•	•	•	•	•
DB	Mark Carrier	6-1	185	Southern Cal	•	•	•	•	•
DB	Tripp Welborne	6-1	193	Michigan	•	•	•	•	•
DB	LeRoy Butler	6-0	194	Florida State	•	•		•	
P	Tom Rouen	6-3	220	Colorado	•	•		•	

Others receiving first-team honors

L	Odell Haggins	Florida State		•		•	
L	Ray Savage	Virginia				•	
LB	Kanavis McGhee	Colorado		•			
LB	Andre Collins	Penn State				•	
LB	James Francis	Baylor	•			•	
DB	Chris Oldham	Oregon			•		
P	Robbie Keen	California				•	

FC named Alfred Williams as a DL

HEISMAN TROPHY VOTING

	PLAYER	POS	SCHOOL	1ST	2ND	3RD	TOTAL
1	Andre Ware	QB	Houston	242	132	83	1073
2	Anthony Thompson	TB	Indiana	185	170	108	1003
3	Major Harris	QB	West Virginia	115	115	134	709
4	Tony Rice	QB	Notre Dame	72	101	105	523
5	Darian Hagan	QB	Colorado	52	42	52	292
6	Dee Dowis	QB	Air Force	15	31	38	145
7	Emmitt Smith	RB	Florida	13	29	43	140
8	Percy Snow	LB	Michigan State	7	15	19	70
9	Ty Detmer	QB	Brigham Young	3	13	14	49
10	Raghib Ismail	WR	Notre Dame	3	11	17	48
	Blair Thomas	TB	Penn State	4	12	12	48

AWARD WINNERS

PLAYER	POS/SCHOOL	AWARD
Anthony Thompson	RB Indiana	Maxwell
Mohammed Elewonibi	G Brigham Young	Outland
Anthony Thompson	RB Indiana	Camp
Percy Snow	LB Michigan State	Lombardi

PLAYER	POS/SCHOOL	AWARD
Andre Ware	QB Houston	O'Brien
Percy Snow	LB Michigan State	Butkus
Mark Carrier	DB Southern Cal	Thorpe
Tony Rice	QB Notre Dame	Unitas

CONFERENCE STANDINGS

ACC

	CONF. W L T			OVERALL W L T		
Virginia	6	1	0	10	3	0
Duke	6	1	0	8	4	0
Clemson	5	2	0	10	2	0
Georgia Tech	4	3	0	7	4	0
North Carolina St.	4	3	0	7	5	0
Maryland	2	5	0	3	7	1
Wake Forest	1	6	0	2	8	1
North Carolina	0	7	0	1	10	0

Big 10

	CONF. W L T			OVERALL W L T		
Michigan	8	0	0	10	2	0
Illinois	7	1	0	10	2	0
Michigan State	6	2	0	8	4	0
Ohio State	6	2	0	8	4	0
Minnesota	4	4	0	6	5	0
Indiana	3	5	0	5	6	0
Iowa	3	5	0	5	6	0
Purdue	2	6	0	3	8	0
Wisconsin	1	7	0	2	9	0
Northwestern	0	8	0	0	11	0

Big 8

	CONF. W L T			OVERALL W L T		
Colorado	7	0	0	11	1	0
Nebraska	6	1	0	10	2	0
Oklahoma	5	2	0	7	4	0
Iowa State	4	3	0	6	5	0
Oklahoma State	3	4	0	4	7	0
Kansas	2	5	0	4	7	0
Missouri	1	6	0	2	9	0
Kansas State	0	7	0	1	10	0

Big West

	CONF. W L T			OVERALL W L T		
Fresno State	7	0	0	11	1	0
Cal-St. Fullerton	5	2	0	6	4	1
San Jose State	5	2	0	6	5	0
Utah State	4	3	0	4	7	0
Nevada-Las Vegas	3	4	0	4	7	0
Long Beach State	2	5	0	4	8	0
Pacific	2	5	0	2	10	0
New Mexico State	0	7	0	0	11	0

Ivy

	CONF. W L T			OVERALL W L T		
Yale	6	1	0	8	2	0
Princeton	6	1	0	7	2	1
Harvard	5	2	0	5	5	0
Dartmouth	4	3	0	5	5	0
Cornell	2	5	0	4	6	0
Pennsylvania	2	5	0	4	6	0
Brown	2	5	0	2	8	0
Columbia	1	6	0	1	9	0

MAC

	CONF. W L T			OVERALL W L T		
Ball State	6	1	1	7	3	2
Eastern Michigan	6	2	0	7	3	1
Toledo	6	2	0	6	5	0
Central Michigan	5	2	1	5	5	1
Bowling Green	5	3	0	5	6	0
Western Michigan	3	5	0	5	6	0
Miami, Ohio	2	5	1	2	8	1
Ohio U.	1	6	1	1	9	1
Kent State	0	8	0	0	11	0

Pac 10

	CONF. W L T			OVERALL W L T		
Southern Cal	6	0	1	9	2	1
Washington	5	3	0	8	4	0
Oregon	5	3	0	8	4	0
Arizona	5	3	0	8	4	0
Arizona State	3	3	1	6	4	1
Oregon State	3	4	1	4	7	1
Washington State	3	5	0	6	5	0
Stanford	3	5	0	3	8	0
UCLA	2	5	1	3	7	1
California	2	6	0	4	7	0

SEC

	CONF. W L T			OVERALL W L T		
Tennessee	6	1	0	11	1	0
Alabama	6	1	0	10	2	0
Auburn	6	1	0	10	2	0
Mississippi	4	3	0	8	4	0
Florida	4	3	0	7	5	0
Georgia	4	3	0	6	6	0
Kentucky	2	5	0	6	5	0
LSU	2	5	0	4	7	0
Mississippi State	1	6	0	5	6	0
Vanderbilt	0	7	0	1	10	0

SWC

	CONF. W L T			OVERALL W L T		
Arkansas	7	1	0	10	2	0
Houston	6	2	0	9	2	0
Texas A&M	6	2	0	8	4	0
Texas Tech	5	3	0	9	3	0
Texas	4	4	0	5	6	0
Baylor	4	4	0	5	6	0
TCU	2	6	0	4	7	0
Rice	2	6	0	2	8	1
SMU	0	8	0	2	9	0

WAC

	CONF. W L T			OVERALL W L T		
Brigham Young	7	1	0	10	3	0
Air Force	5	1	1	8	4	1
Hawaii	5	2	1	9	3	1
Wyoming	5	3	0	5	6	0
San Diego State	4	3	0	6	5	1
Colorado State	4	3	0	5	5	1
Utah	2	6	0	4	8	0
Texas-El Paso	1	7	0	2	10	0
New Mexico	0	7	0	2	10	0

Independents

	OVERALL W L T		
Notre Dame	12	1	0
Miami, Fla.	11	1	0
Florida State	10	2	0
Northern Illinois	9	2	0
West Virginia	8	3	1
Pittsburgh	8	3	1
Penn State	8	3	1
Syracuse	8	4	0
La. Lafayette	7	4	0
Virginia Tech	6	4	1
South Carolina	6	4	1
Louisiana Tech	5	4	1
Army	6	5	0
Louisville	6	5	0
Tulsa	6	6	0
East Carolina	5	5	1
Southern Miss	5	6	0
Tulane	4	8	0
Navy	3	8	0
Rutgers	2	7	2
Memphis	2	9	0
Boston College	2	9	0
Cincinnati	1	9	1
Temple	1	10	0

BOWL GAMES

DATE	GAME	SCORE
D9	California	Fresno State 27, Ball State 6
D16	Independence	Oregon 27, Tulsa 24
D25	Aloha	Michigan State 33, Hawaii 13
D28	Liberty	Mississippi 42, Air Force 29
D28	All-American	Texas Tech 49, Duke 21
D29	Holiday	Penn State 50, Brigham Young 39
D30	Gator	Clemson 27, West Virginia 7
D30	Sun	Pittsburgh 31, Texas A&M 28
D30	Peach	Syracuse 19, Georgia 18

DATE	GAME	SCORE
D30	Freedom	Washington 34, Florida 7
D31	Copper	Arizona 17, North Carolina St. 10
J1	Hall of Fame	Auburn 31, Ohio State 14
J1	Fiesta	Florida State 41, Nebraska 17
J1	Citrus	Illinois 31, Virginia 21
J1	Orange	Notre Dame 21, Colorado 6
J1	Rose	Southern Cal 17, Michigan 10
J1	Cotton	Tennessee 31, Arkansas 27
J1	Sugar	Miami, Fla. 33, Alabama 25

1989 NCAA Major College Statistical Leaders

Individual Leaders

	PASSING	CL	G	ATT	COM	PCT	INT	I%	YDS	YPA	TD	TD%	RATING
1	Ty Detmer, Brigham Young	SO	12	412	265	64.3	15	3.6	4560	11.1	32	7.8	175.6
2	David Brown, Duke	SO	9	163	104	63.8	6	3.7	1479	9.1	14	8.6	161.0
3	Dan Speltz, Cal St Fullerton	SR	11	309	214	69.3	11	3.6	2671	8.6	20	6.5	156.1
4	Shawn Moore, Virginia	JR	11	221	125	56.6	7	3.2	2078	9.4	18	8.1	156.1
5	Andre Ware, Houston	JR	11	578	365	63.2	15	2.6	4699	8.1	46	8.0	152.5
6	Bill Scharr, Syracuse	JR	11	169	107	63.3	8	4.7	1625	9.6	9	5.3	152.2
7	Peter Tom Willis, Florida State	SR	11	346	211	61.0	9	2.6	3124	9.0	20	5.8	150.7
8	Major Harris, West Virginia	JR	11	224	131	58.5	10	4.5	1939	8.7	16	7.1	145.8
9	Greg Frey, Ohio State	JR	11	215	128	59.5	7	3.3	1900	8.8	12	5.6	145.7
10	Bret Oberg, Iowa State	SR	11	245	152	62.0	9	3.7	2242	9.2	9	3.7	143.7

	ALL-PURPOSE	CL	G	RUSH	REC	PR	KR	YDS	YPG
1	Mike Pringle, Cal-St. Fullerton	SR	11	1727	249	0	714	2690	244.6
2	Sheldon Canley, San Jose State	JR	11	1201	353	0	959	2513	228.5
3	Chuck Weatherspoon, Houston	JR	11	1146	735	415	95	2391	217.4
4	Anthony Thompson, Indiana	SR	11	1793	201	0	394	2388	217.1
5	Terance Mathis, New Mexico	SR	12	38	1315	0	785	2138	178.2
6	Emmitt Smith, Florida	JR	11	1599	207	0	0	1806	164.2
7	Steve Broussard, Washington State	SR	11	1237	326	0	227	1790	162.7
8	Andrew Greer, Ohio	SR	11	903	227	0	598	1728	157.1
9	Blaise Bryant, Iowa State	JR	11	1516	202	0	0	1718	156.2
10	Emmanuel Hazard, Houston	JR	11	0	1689	0	0	1689	153.6

	RUSHING/Yards Per Game	CL	G	ATT	YDS	TD	AVG	YPG
1	Anthony Thompson, Indiana	SR	11	358	1793	24	5.0	163.0
2	Mike Pringle, Cal-St. Fullerton	SR	11	296	1727	16	5.8	157.0
3	Emmitt Smith, Florida	JR	11	284	1599	14	5.6	145.4
4	Blaise Bryant, Iowa State	JR	11	299	1516	19	5.1	137.8
5	James Gray, Texas Tech	SR	11	263	1509	18	5.7	137.2
6	Stacey Robinson, Northern Illinois	JR	11	223	1443	19	6.5	131.2
7	Blake Ezor, Michigan State	SR	9	226	1120	16	5.0	124.4
8	Derrick Douglas, Louisiana Tech	SR	10	281	1232	11	4.4	123.2
9	Jerry Mays, Georgia Tech	SR	11	249	1349	8	5.4	122.6
10	Blair Thomas, Penn State	SR	11	264	1341	5	5.1	121.9

	RUSHING/Yards Per Carry	CL	G	ATT	YDS	YPC
1	Dee Dowis, Air Force	SR	12	172	1286	7.5
2	J.J. Flannigan, Colorado	SR	11	164	1187	7.2
3	Stacey Robinson, Northern Illinois	JR	11	223	1443	6.5
4	Ken Clark, Nebraska	SR	10	198	1196	6.0
5	Chuck Webb, Tennessee	FR	11	209	1236	5.9
6	Mike Pringle, Cal-St. Fullerton	SR	11	296	1727	5.8
7	James Gray, Texas Tech	SR	11	263	1509	5.7
8	Emmitt Smith, Florida	JR	11	284	1599	5.6
9	Aaron Craver, Fresno State	JR	11	225	1248	5.5
10	Brian Mitchell, La. Lafayette	SR	11	237	1311	5.5

*-Based on top 23 rushers

	RECEIVING	CL	G	REC	YDS	TD	YPR	YPG	RPG
1	Emmanuel Hazard, Houston	JR	11	142	1689	22	11.9	153.5	12.9
2	Richard Buchanan, Northwestern	JR	11	94	1115	9	11.9	101.4	8.6
3	Eric Henley, Rice	SO	11	81	900	5	11.1	81.8	7.4
4	Terance Mathis, New Mexico	SR	12	88	1315	13	14.9	109.6	7.3
5	Monty Gilbreath, San Diego State	SR	12	80	903	4	11.3	75.3	6.7
6	Dan Bitson, Tulsa	JR	11	73	1425	16	19.5	129.5	6.6
7	Michael Smith, Kansas State	SO	11	70	816	2	11.7	74.2	6.4
8	Rocky Palamara, Cal-St. Fullerton	SR	11	69	1024	10	14.8	93.1	6.3
9	Brad Gaines, Vanderbilt	JR	11	67	634	2	9.5	57.6	6.1
10	Dennis Smith, Utah	SR	12	73	1089	18	14.9	90.8	6.1

	PUNTING	CL	PUNT	YDS	AVG
1	Tom Rouen, Colorado	SO	36	1651	45.9
2	Kirk Maggio, UCLA	SR	45	2036	45.2
3	Rob Myers, Washington State	SR	52	2326	44.7
4	Shawn McCarthy, Purdue	SR	69	3075	44.6
5	Daren Parker, South Carolina	JR	49	2170	44.3
6	Pete Rutter, Baylor	SR	57	2496	43.8
7	Robbie Keen, California	JR	59	2565	43.5
8	Tim Luke, Colorado State	JR	51	2199	43.1
9	Greg Hertzog, West Virginia	JR	40	1718	43.0
10	Chris Gardocki, Clemson	SR	44	1878	42.7

	PUNT RETURNS	CL	PR	YDS	TD	AVG
1	Larry Hargrove, Ohio U	SR	17	309	2	18.2
2	Herb Jackson, Ball State	JR	16	262	0	16.4
3	Dwight Pickens, Fresno State	SR	30	470	1	15.7
4	Jeff Sydner, Hawaii	FR	19	293	1	15.4
5	Tyrone Hughes, Nebraska	FR	15	227	0	15.1
6	Dee Smith, Louisville	SR	14	207	0	14.8
7	O.J. McDuffie, Penn State	SO	19	278	1	14.6
8	Jeff Campbell, Colorado	SR	25	365	0	14.6
9	Terrell Buckley, Florida State	FR	22	313	1	14.2
10	Troy Vincent, Wisconsin	SO	17	235	1	13.8

	KICKOFF RETURNS	CL	KR	YDS	TD	AVG
1	Tony Smith, Southern Miss	SO	14	455	2	32.5
2	Mike Bellamy, Illinois	SR	14	432	0	30.9
3	Chris Oldham, Oregon	SR	14	402	0	28.7
4	Kelvin Means, Fresno State	SO	18	509	0	28.3
5	Arthur Marshall, Georgia	SO	16	445	0	27.8
6	Ron Gray, Air Force	SO	21	571	0	27.2
7	Deral Boykin, Kansas	SO	14	365	0	26.1
8	Raymond Patterson, Northern Illinois	FR	15	390	0	26.0
9	Alan Grant, Stanford	SR	16	412	0	25.8
10	Kurt Johnson, Kentucky	FR	21	537	1	25.6

	SCORING	CL	TDS	XP	FG	PTS	PTPG
1	Anthony Thompson, Indiana	SR	25	4	0	154	14.0
2	Emmanuel Hazard, Houston	JR	22	2	0	134	12.2
3	Roman Anderson, Houston	SO	0	65	22	131	11.9
4	James Gray, Texas Tech	SR	20	0	0	120	10.9
4	Blaise Bryant, Iowa State	JR	19	6	0	120	10.9
6	Blake Ezor, Michigan State	SR	16	0	0	96	10.7
7	Mike Pringle, Cal-St. Fullerton	SR	19	2	0	116	10.6
7	Jamal Farmer, Hawaii	FR	19	2	0	116	10.6
9	Brian Mitchell, La. Lafayette	SR	19	0	0	114	10.4
9	Stacey Robinson, Northern Illinois	JR	19	0	0	114	10.4

	FIELD GOALS	CL	FGA	FGM	PCT	FGG
1	Philip Doyle, Alabama	JR	25	22	0.88	2.00
1	Gregg McCallum, Oregon	SO	29	22	0.76	2.00
1	Roman Anderson, Houston	SO	34	22	0.65	2.00
4	Mickey Thomas, Virginia Tech	FR	25	21	0.84	1.91
4	Jason Hanson, Washington State	SO	27	21	0.78	1.91
6	David Fuess, Tulsa	SR	23	20	0.87	1.82
6	Todd Wright, Arkansas	FR	23	20	0.87	1.82
6	Kevin Nicholl, Central Michigan	SR	24	20	0.83	1.82
6	Chris Gardocki, Clemson	SR	26	20	0.77	1.82
6	Cary Blanchard, Oklahoma State	JR	26	20	0.77	1.82

	INTERCEPTIONS	CL	INT	YDS	TD	INT/GM
1	Cornelius Price, Houston	JR	12	187	2	1.09
1	Bob Navarro, Eastern Michigan	JR	12	73	0	1.09
3	Ben Smith, Georgia	SR	10	54	0	0.91
4	Kevin Smith, Texas A&M	SO	9	75	1	0.82
5	Walter Briggs, Hawaii	SR	9	116	1	0.75
6	Tracy Saul, Texas Tech	FR	8	157	0	0.73
6	Robert Blackmon, Baylor	SR	8	150	2	0.73
8	Todd Lyght, Notre Dame	JR	8	42	0	0.67
8	Greg Koperek, Pacific	SR	6	50	0	0.67
10	Leroy Butler, Florida State*	SR	7	139	1	0.64
10	Robert O'Neil, Clemson*	FR	7	96	0	0.64
10	Rob Thomson, Syracuse*	JR	7	74	1	0.64

*-Six tied with 0.64; these had the most yards.

Team Leaders

	RUSHING OFFENSE	G	ATT	YDS	AVG	TD	YPG
1	Nebraska	11	641	4128	6.4	40	375.3
2	Colorado	11	666	4090	6.1	54	371.8
3	Air Force	12	736	4272	5.8	50	356.0
4	Army	11	738	3813	5.2	37	346.6
5	Oklahoma	11	684	3679	5.4	39	334.5
6	Northern Illinois	11	680	3638	5.3	40	330.7
7	Arkansas	11	680	3456	5.1	34	314.2
8	Notre Dame	12	673	3452	5.1	42	287.7
9	Fresno State	11	581	2918	5.0	38	265.3
10	Hawaii	11	555	2760	5.0	31	250.9

	PASSING OFFENSE	G	ATT	COM	INT	PCT	YDS	YPA	TD	I%	YPC	YPG
1	Houston	11	694	434	16	62.5	5624	8.1	55	2.3	13.0	511.3
2	Brigham Young	12	433	279	15	64.4	4732	10.9	33	3.5	17.0	394.3
3	Utah	12	556	298	21	53.6	4064	7.3	39	3.8	13.6	338.7
4	Duke	11	439	279	20	63.6	3553	8.1	29	4.6	12.7	323.0
5	Florida State	11	387	230	11	59.4	3448	8.9	25	2.8	15.0	313.5
6	New Mexico	12	532	290	22	54.5	3732	7.0	23	4.1	12.9	311.0
7	Miami, Fla.	11	465	254	22	54.6	3406	7.3	24	4.7	13.4	309.6
8	San Diego State	12	449	262	20	58.4	3697	8.2	16	4.5	14.1	308.1
9	SMU	11	551	303	22	55.0	3047	5.5	14	4.0	10.1	277.0
10	Washington State	11	332	205	15	61.7	2972	9.0	20	4.5	14.5	270.2

	TOTAL OFFENSE	G	P	YDS	AVG	TD	YPG
1	Houston	11	904	6874	7.6	70	624.9
2	Brigham Young	12	852	6485	7.6	61	540.4
3	Nebraska	11	809	5646	7.0	63	513.3
4	Duke	11	866	5519	6.4	46	501.7
5	Air Force	12	886	5753	6.5	59	493.3
6	Colorado	11	768	5201	6.8	59	472.8
7	San Diego State	12	951	5610	5.9	46	467.5
8	Southern Cal	11	864	5029	5.8	39	457.2
9	Miami, Fla.	11	898	4995	5.6	46	454.1
10	Florida State	11	779	4965	6.4	46	451.4

	RUSHING DEFENSE	G	ATT	YDS	AVG	TD	YPG
1	Southern Cal	11	322	676	2.1	5	61.5
2	Miami, Fla.	11	391	760	1.9	4	69.1
3	Virginia Tech	11	401	914	2.3	9	83.1
4	Florida	11	397	975	2.5	8	88.6
5	Clemson	11	336	1041	3.1	7	94.6
6	Hawaii	12	428	1152	2.7	16	96.0
7	Fresno State	11	376	1081	2.9	10	98.3
8	Louisville	11	416	1098	2.6	7	99.8
9	San Jose State	11	436	1105	2.5	10	100.5
10	Alabama	11	376	1107	2.9	11	100.6

	PASSING DEFENSE	G	ATT	COM	PCT	YPC	INT	I%	YDS	YPA	TD	YPG
1	Kansas State	11	156	95	60.9	15.0	7	4.5	1422	9.1	11	129.3
2	Illinois	11	259	127	49.0	12.2	18	7.0	1545	6.0	3	140.5
3	Navy	11	198	105	53.0	14.8	9	4.5	1554	7.8	10	141.3
4	Mississippi State	11	288	148	51.4	10.8	12	4.2	1599	5.6	10	145.4
5	Miami, Fla.	11	318	153	48.1	10.6	21	6.6	1621	5.1	4	147.4
6	Baylor	11	273	141	51.6	11.6	22	8.1	1634	6.0	8	148.5
7	Indiana	11	217	123	56.7	13.4	9	4.2	1654	7.6	15	150.4
8	Auburn	11	278	141	50.7	12.0	11	4.0	1686	6.1	3	153.3
8	Florida	11	286	154	53.8	10.9	17	5.9	1686	5.9	10	153.3
10	Boston College	11	230	116	50.4	14.7	17	7.4	1707	7.4	9	155.2

	TOTAL DEFENSE	G	P	YDS	AVG	TD	YPG
1	Miami, Fla.	11	709	2381	3.4	8	216.5
2	Southern Cal	11	635	2627	4.1	14	238.8
3	Florida	11	683	2661	3.9	18	241.9
4	Virginia Tech	11	705	2671	3.8	19	242.8
5	Clemson	11	690	2947	4.3	14	267.9
6	Auburn	11	686	2956	4.3	11	268.7
7	Eastern Michigan	11	740	3014	4.1	20	274.0
8	Nebraska	11	727	3015	4.1	21	274.1
9	Baylor	11	749	3077	4.1	20	279.7
10	Illinois	11	721	3136	4.3	15	285.1

	SCORING OFFENSE	G	PTS	AVG
1	Houston	11	589	53.5
2	Nebraska	11	492	44.7
3	Colorado	11	452	41.1
4	Brigham Young	12	484	40.3
5	Hawaii	12	457	38.1
6	Air Force	11	411	37.4
7	Fresno State	12	446	37.2
8	Miami, Fla.	11	393	35.7
9	Florida State	11	383	34.8
10	Oklahoma	11	380	34.5

	SCORING DEFENSE	G	PTS	AVG
1	Miami, Fla.	11	102	9.3
2	Auburn	11	117	10.6
3	Southern Cal	11	122	11.1
4	Penn State	11	130	11.8
5	Clemson	11	131	11.9
6	Michigan State	11	150	13.6
6	Colorado	11	150	13.6
6	Houston	11	150	13.6
9	Texas A&M	11	161	14.6
9	Illinois	11	161	14.6

1990 Poll Progression

AP	Pre-Season 1990		Sept. 1 Games
1	Miami, Fla.	0-0-0	bye week
2	Notre Dame	0-0-0	bye week
3	Auburn	0-0-0	bye week
4	Florida State	0-0-0	bye week
5	Colorado	0-0-0	tied # 8 Tennessee 31-31 (A26)
6	Michigan	0-0-0	bye week
7	Nebraska	0-0-0	beat Baylor 13-0
8	Tennessee	0-0-0	beat Pacific 55-7
9	Southern Cal	0-0-0	beat Syracuse 34-16 (A31)
10	Clemson	0-0-0	beat Long Beach St. 59-0
11	Illinois	0-0-0	bye week
12	Alabama	0-0-0	bye week
13	Texas A&M	0-0-0	beat Hawaii 28-13
14	Arkansas	0-0-0	bye week
15	Virginia	0-0-0	beat Kansas 59-10
16	Brigham Young	0-0-0	beat Texas-El Paso 30-10
17	Ohio State	0-0-0	bye week
18	Pittsburgh	0-0-0	beat Ohio U. 35-3
19	UCLA	0-0-0	bye week
20	Washington	0-0-0	bye week
21	Penn State	0-0-0	bye week
22	Oklahoma	0-0-0	bye week
23	Michigan State	0-0-0	bye week
24	Houston	0-0-0	bye week
25	West Virginia	0-0-0	beat Kent State 35-24

UP	AP	September 3 Poll		Sept. 8 Games
1	1	Miami, Fla.	0-0-0	lost to # 16 Brigham Young 21-28
2	2	Notre Dame	0-0-0	bye week
4	3	Auburn	0-0-0	beat Fullerton St. 38-17
3	4	Florida State	0-0-0	beat East Carolina 45-24
6	5	Michigan	0-0-0	bye week
7	6	Colorado	0-0-1	beat Stanford 21-17 (S6)
5	7	Southern Cal	1-0-0	bye week
8	8	Tennessee	1-0-1	beat Mississippi State 40-7
10	9	Clemson	1-0-0	lost to # 14 Virginia 7-20
9	10	Nebraska	1-0-0	beat Northern Illinois 60-14
12	11	Illinois	0-0-0	lost to Arizona 16-28
11	12	Texas A&M	1-0-0	bye week
17	13	Alabama	0-0-0	lost to Southern Miss 24-27
13	14	Virginia	1-0-0	beat # 9 Clemson 20-7
15	15	Arkansas	0-0-0	bye week
18	16	Brigham Young	1-0-0	beat # 1 Miami, Fla. 28-21
19	17	Pittsburgh	1-0-0	beat Boston College 29-6
14	18	Ohio State	0-0-0	beat Texas Tech 17-10
21	19	UCLA	0-0-0	lost to # 23 Oklahoma 14-34
16	20	Washington	0-0-0	beat San Jose State 20-17
20	21	Penn State	0-0-0	lost to Texas 13-17
	22	Michigan State	0-0-0	bye week
	23	Oklahoma	0-0-0	beat # 19 UCLA 34-14
	24	Houston	0-0-0	beat Nevada-Las Vegas 37-9
	25	West Virginia	1-0-0	lost to Maryland 10-14
22		Fresno State	1-0-0	beat New Mexico 24-17
23		Florida	0-0-0	beat Oklahoma State 50-7
23		Texas	0-0-0	beat # 21 Penn State 17-13

UP	AP	September 10 Poll		Sept. 15 Games
1	1	Notre Dame	0-0-0	beat # 4 Michigan 28-24
3	2	Auburn	1-0-0	beat Mississippi 24-10
2	3	Florida State	1-0-0	beat Georgia Southern 48-6
5	4	Michigan	0-0-0	lost to # 1 Notre Dame 24-28
7	5	Brigham Young	2-0-0	beat Washington St. 50-36
4	6	Southern Cal	1-0-0	beat Penn State 19-14
6	7	Tennessee	2-0-1	beat Texas-El Paso 56-0
8	8	Nebraska	2-0-0	bye week
9	9	Colorado	1-0-1	lost to # 21 Illinois 22-23
10	10	Miami, Fla.	0-1-0	beat California 52-24
11	11	Virginia	2-0-0	beat Navy 56-14
12	12	Texas A&M	1-0-0	beat La. Lafayette 63-14
13	13	Pittsburgh	2-0-0	lost to # 14 Oklahoma 10-52
PB	14	Oklahoma	1-0-0	beat # 13 Pittsburgh 52-10
15	15	Arkansas	0-0-0	beat Tulsa 28-3
19	16	Clemson	1-1-0	beat Maryland 18-17
14	17	Ohio State	1-0-0	beat Boston College 31-10
PB	18	Houston	1-0-0	beat Texas Tech 51-35 (S13)
22	19	Michigan State	0-0-0	tied Syracuse 23-23
16	20	Arizona	1-0-0	beat New Mexico 25-10
17	21	Illinois	0-1-0	beat # 9 Colorado 23-22
20	22	Washington	1-0-0	beat Purdue 20-14
17	23	Texas	1-0-0	bye week
21	24	Florida	1-0-0	beat Alabama 17-13
24	25	Arizona State	1-0-0	beat Colorado State 31-20
23		Fresno State	2-0-0	beat Utah 31-7
25		Georgia Tech	1-0-0	bye week

UP	AP	September 17 Poll		Sept. 22 Games
1	1	Notre Dame	1-0-0	beat # 24 Michigan State 20-19
2	2	Florida State	2-0-0	beat Tulane 31-13
3	3	Auburn	2-0-0	bye week
4	4	Brigham Young	3-0-0	beat San Diego State 62-34
5	5	Southern Cal	2-0-0	lost to # 21 Washington 0-31
6	6	Tennessee	3-0-1	bye week
10	7	Michigan	0-1-0	beat UCLA 38-15
7	8	Nebraska	2-0-0	beat Minnesota 56-0
8	9	Miami, Fla.	1-1-0	bye week
9	10	Virginia	3-0-0	beat Duke 59-0
PB	11	Oklahoma	2-0-0	beat Tulsa 52-10
11	12	Texas A&M	2-0-0	beat North Texas 40-8
13	13	Arkansas	1-0-0	lost to Mississippi 17-21
PB	14	Houston	2-0-0	bye week
17	15	Illinois	1-1-0	beat So. Illinois 56-21
12	16	Ohio State	2-0-0	bye week
19	17	Clemson	2-1-0	beat Appalachian St. 48-0
14	18	Arizona	2-0-0	beat Oregon 22-17
15	19	Florida	2-0-0	beat Furman 27-3
18	20	Colorado	1-1-1	beat # 22 Texas 29-22
16	21	Washington	2-0-0	beat # 5 Southern Cal 31-0
20	22	Texas	1-0-0	lost to # 20 Colorado 22-29
21	23	Arizona State	2-0-0	bye week
23	24	Michigan State	0-0-1	lost to # 1 Notre Dame 19-20
	25	Pittsburgh	2-1-0	tied Syracuse 20-20
21		Fresno State	3-0-0	beat New Mexico State 42-3
23		Oregon	2-0-0	lost to # 18 Arizona 17-22
25		Syracuse	1-1-1	tied # 25 Pittsburgh 20-20

UP	AP	September 24 Poll		Sept. 29 Games
1	1	Notre Dame	2-0-0	beat Purdue 37-11
2	2	Florida State	3-0-0	beat Virginia Tech 39-28
3	3	Auburn	2-0-0	tied # 5 Tennessee 26-26
4	4	Brigham Young	4-0-0	lost to Oregon 16-32
5	5	Tennessee	3-0-1	tied # 3 Auburn 26-26
7	6	Michigan	1-1-0	beat Maryland 45-17
8	7	Virginia	4-0-0	beat William & Mary 63-35
6	8	Nebraska	3-0-0	beat Oregon State 31-7
PB	9	Oklahoma	3-0-0	beat Kansas 31-17
9	10	Miami, Fla.	1-1-0	beat Iowa 48-21
10	11	Texas A&M	3-0-0	lost to LSU 8-17
11	12	Washington	3-0-0	lost to # 20 Colorado 14-20
PB	13	Houston	2-0-0	beat Rice 24-22
15	14	Illinois	2-1-0	bye week
12	15	Ohio State	2-0-0	lost to # 18 Southern Cal 26-35
13	16	Arizona	3-0-0	lost to California 25-30
17	17	Florida	3-0-0	beat Mississippi State 34-21
14	18	Southern Cal	2-1-0	beat # 15 Ohio State 35-26
18	19	Clemson	3-1-0	beat Duke 26-7
16	20	Colorado	2-1-1	beat # 12 Washington 20-14
23	21	Arizona State	2-0-0	lost to Missouri 9-30
20	22	Michigan State	0-1-1	beat Rutgers 34-10
21	23	Arkansas	1-1-0	beat Colorado State 31-20
19	24	Fresno State	4-0-0	beat Fullerton St. 38-3
	25	South Carolina	3-0-0	lost to Georgia Tech 6-27
21		Mississippi	2-1-0	beat Tulane 31-21
23		Wyoming	4-0-0	beat Utah 28-10
25		Iowa	2-0-0	lost to # 10 Miami, Fla. 21-48

UP	AP	October 1 Poll		Oct. 6 Games
1	1	Notre Dame	3-0-0	lost to Stanford 31-36
2	2	Florida State	4-0-0	lost to # 9 Miami, Fla. 22-31
4	3	Michigan	2-1-0	beat Wisconsin 41-3
5	4	Virginia	5-0-0	bye week
6	5	Auburn	2-0-1	beat Louisiana Tech 16-14
7	6	Tennessee	3-0-2	bye week
PB	7	Oklahoma	4-0-0	beat Oklahoma State 31-17
3	8	Nebraska	4-0-0	beat Kansas State 45-8
8	9	Miami, Fla.	2-1-0	beat # 2 Florida State 31-22
PB	10	Florida	4-0-0	beat LSU 34-8
10	11	Brigham Young	4-1-0	bye week
9	12	Colorado	3-1-1	beat Missouri 33-31
PB	13	Houston	3-0-0	beat Baylor 31-15
12	14	Illinois	2-1-0	beat # 20 Ohio State 31-20
11	15	Southern Cal	3-1-0	beat Washington State 30-17
13	16	Clemson	4-1-0	beat Georgia 34-3
14	17	Washington	3-1-0	beat Arizona State 42-14
19	18	Michigan State	1-1-1	lost to Iowa 7-12
15	19	Texas A&M	3-1-0	beat Texas Tech 28-24
25	20	Ohio State	2-1-0	lost to # 13 Illinois 20-31
16	21	Arkansas	2-1-0	lost to TCU 26-54
17	22	Oregon	3-1-0	beat Utah State 52-7
18	23	Georgia Tech	3-0-0	beat Maryland 31-3
20	24	Fresno State	5-0-0	lost to Northern Illinois 18-73
21	25	Arizona	3-1-0	beat UCLA 28-21
22		Indiana	3-0-0	beat Northwestern 42-0
23		Mississippi	3-1-0	beat Kentucky 35-29
24		Wyoming	5-0-0	beat San Diego State 52-51

UP	AP	October 8 Poll		Oct. 13 Games
1	1	Michigan	3-1-0	lost to Michigan State 27-28
3	2	Virginia	5-0-0	beat North Carolina St. 31-0
4	3	Miami, Fla.	3-1-0	beat Kansas 34-0
PB	4	Oklahoma	5-0-0	lost to Texas 13-14
5	5	Tennessee	3-0-2	beat # 9 Florida 45-3
6	6	Auburn	3-0-1	beat Vanderbilt 56-6
2	7	Nebraska	5-0-0	beat Missouri 69-21
7	8	Notre Dame	3-1-0	beat Air Force 57-27
PB	9	Florida	5-0-0	lost to # 5 Tennessee 3-45
8	10	Florida State	4-1-0	bye week
12	11	Illinois	3-1-0	beat Purdue 34-0
PB	12	Houston	4-0-0	beat # 20 Texas A&M 36-31
9	13	Brigham Young	4-1-0	beat Colorado State 52-9
11	14	Colorado	4-1-1	beat Iowa State 28-12
14	15	Clemson	5-1-0	lost to # 18 Georgia Tech 19-21
10	16	Southern Cal	4-1-0	beat Stanford 37-22
13	17	Washington	4-1-0	beat # 19 Oregon 38-17
15	18	Georgia Tech	4-0-0	beat # 15 Clemson 21-19
17	19	Oregon	4-1-0	lost to # 17 Washington 17-38
16	20	Texas A&M	4-1-0	lost to # 12 Houston 31-36
20	21	Arizona	4-1-0	lost to Oregon State 21-35
18	22	Indiana	4-0-0	tied Ohio State 27-27
19	23	Wyoming	6-0-0	beat New Mexico 25-22
20	24	Mississippi	4-1-0	beat Georgia 28-12
24	25	Iowa	3-1-0	beat Wisconsin 30-10
22		Texas	2-1-0	beat # 4 Oklahoma 14-13
23		Arkansas	2-2-0	lost to Texas Tech 44-49
25		TCU	4-1-0	beat Rice 38-28

UP	AP	October 15 Poll		Oct. 20 Games
1	1	Virginia	6-0-0	beat Wake Forest 49-14
2	2	Miami, Fla.	4-1-0	lost to # 6 Notre Dame 20-29
4	3	Tennessee	4-0-2	lost to Alabama 6-9
3	4	Nebraska	6-0-0	beat Oklahoma State 31-3
5	5	Auburn	4-0-1	beat # 7 Florida State 20-17
6	6	Notre Dame	4-1-0	beat # 2 Miami, Fla. 29-20
7	7	Florida State	4-1-0	lost to # 5 Auburn 17-20
9	8	Illinois	4-1-0	beat # 24 Michigan State 15-13
PB	9	Houston	5-0-0	beat SMU 44-17
8	10	Michigan	3-2-0	lost to # 22 Iowa 23-24
11	11	Georgia Tech	5-0-0	tied North Carolina 13-13
10	12	Brigham Young	5-1-0	bye week
12	13	Washington	5-1-0	beat Stanford 52-16
14	14	Colorado	5-1-1	beat Kansas 41-10
13	15	Southern Cal	5-1-0	lost to Arizona 26-35
PB	16	Oklahoma	5-1-0	lost to Iowa State 31-33
PB	17	Florida	5-1-0	beat Akron 59-0
18	18	Mississippi	5-1-0	beat Arkansas St. 42-13
15	19	Texas	3-1-0	beat Arkansas 49-17
16	20	Indiana	4-0-1	lost to Minnesota 0-12
17	21	Wyoming	7-0-0	beat Weber St. 21-12
22	22	Clemson	5-2-0	beat North Carolina St. 24-17
19	23	Iowa	4-1-0	beat # 10 Michigan 24-23
23	24	Michigan State	2-2-1	lost to # 8 Illinois 13-15
21	25	Texas A&M	4-2-0	tied Baylor 20-20
19		TCU	5-1-0	bye week
24		Oregon	4-2-0	beat Arizona State 27-7
25		Louisville	5-1-1	beat Pittsburgh 27-20

UP	AP	October 22 Poll		Oct. 27 Games
1	1	Virginia	7-0-0	bye week
3	2	Auburn	5-0-1	beat Mississippi State 17-16
4	3	Notre Dame	5-1-0	beat Pittsburgh 31-22
2	4	Nebraska	7-0-0	beat Iowa State 45-13
5	5	Illinois	5-1-0	beat Wisconsin 21-3
PB	6	Houston	6-0-0	beat Arkansas 62-28
6	7	Washington	6-1-0	beat California 46-7
9	8	Miami, Fla.	4-2-0	beat Texas Tech 45-10
7	9	Brigham Young	5-1-0	beat New Mexico 55-31
8	10	Colorado	6-1-1	beat # 22 Oklahoma 32-23
10	11	Tennessee	4-1-2	bye week
11	12	Florida State	4-2-0	beat LSU 42-3
14	13	Texas	4-1-0	beat SMU 52-3
PB	14	Florida	6-1-0	bye week
13	15	Iowa	5-1-0	beat Northwestern 56-14
12	16	Georgia Tech	5-0-1	beat Duke 48-31
15	17	Mississippi	6-1-0	beat Vanderbilt 14-13
16	18	Wyoming	8-0-0	beat Texas-El Paso 17-10
17	19	Clemson	6-2-0	beat Wake Forest 24-6
18	20	Michigan	3-3-0	beat Indiana 45-19
20	21	Southern Cal	5-2-0	beat Arizona State 13-6
PB	22	Oklahoma	5-2-0	lost to # 10 Colorado 23-32
21	23	Arizona	5-2-0	beat Washington St. 42-34
19	24	TCU	5-1-0	lost to Baylor 21-27
22	25	Oregon	5-2-0	beat Stanford 31-0
23		Louisville	6-1-1	beat Western Kentucky 41-7
24		Penn State	4-2-0	beat Alabama 9-0
25		Texas A&M	4-2-1	beat Rice 41-15

October 29 Poll / Nov. 3 Games

UP	AP	Team	Record	Result
1	1	Virginia	7-0-0	lost to #16 Georgia Tech 38-41
3	2	Notre Dame	6-1-0	beat Navy 52-31
2	3	Nebraska	8-0-0	lost to #9 Colorado 12-27
4	4	Auburn	6-0-1	lost to #5 Florida 7-48
6	5	Illinois	6-1-0	lost to #13 Iowa 28-54
PB	6	Houston	7-0-0	beat TCU 56-35
5	7	Washington	7-1-0	beat #23 Arizona 54-10
8	8	Miami, Fla.	5-2-0	beat Pittsburgh 45-0
7	9	Colorado	7-1-1	beat #3 Nebraska 27-12
9	10	Brigham Young	6-1-0	beat Air Force 54-7
10	11	Tennessee	4-1-2	beat Temple 41-20
11	12	Florida State	5-2-0	beat South Carolina 41-10
13	13	Iowa	6-1-0	beat #5 Illinois 54-28
12	14	Texas	5-1-0	beat Texas Tech 41-22
PB	15	Florida	6-1-0	beat #4 Auburn 48-7
14	16	Georgia Tech	6-0-1	beat #1 Virginia 41-38
15	17	Mississippi	7-1-0	beat LSU 19-10
17	18	Clemson	7-2-0	beat North Carolina 20-3
16	19	Wyoming	9-0-0	lost to Colorado State 8-17
18	20	Michigan	4-3-0	beat Purdue 38-13
23	21	Southern Cal	6-2-0	tied California 31-31
20	22	Oregon	6-2-0	beat UCLA 28-24
19	23	Arizona	6-2-0	lost to #7 Washington 10-54
21	24	Penn State	5-2-0	beat West Virginia 31-19
22	25	Louisville	7-1-1	beat Cincinnati 41-16
24		Texas A&M	5-2-1	beat SMU 38-17
24		North Carolina	5-2-1	lost to Clemson 3-20

November 5 Poll / Nov. 10 Games

UP	AP	Team	Record	Result
1	1	Notre Dame	7-1-0	beat #9 Tennessee 34-29
2	2	Washington	8-1-0	lost to UCLA 22-25
PB	3	Houston	8-0-0	lost to #14 Texas 24-45
3	4	Colorado	8-1-0	beat Oklahoma State 41-22
4	5	Miami, Fla.	6-2-0	bye week
5	6	Iowa	7-1-0	lost to Ohio State 26-27
7	7	Georgia Tech	7-0-1	beat Virginia Tech 6-3
6	8	Brigham Young	7-1-0	beat #25 Wyoming 45-14
8	9	Tennessee	5-1-2	lost to #1 Notre Dame 29-34
PB	10	Florida	7-1-0	beat Georgia 38-7
9	11	Virginia	7-1-0	beat North Carolina 24-10
11	12	Florida State	6-2-0	beat Cincinnati 70-21
10	13	Nebraska	8-1-0	beat Kansas 41-9
12	14	Texas	6-1-0	beat #3 Houston 45-24
13	15	Auburn	6-1-1	lost to Southern Miss 12-13
14	16	Mississippi	8-1-0	bye week
15	17	Illinois	6-2-0	lost to #19 Michigan 17-22
16	18	Clemson	8-2-0	bye week
17	19	Michigan	5-3-0	beat #17 Illinois 22-17
18	20	Oregon	7-2-0	lost to California 3-28
19	21	Penn State	6-2-0	beat Maryland 24-10
20	22	Louisville	7-1-1	beat Boston College 17-10
	23	Southern Cal	6-2-1	beat Oregon State 56-7
	24	Michigan State	4-3-1	beat Minnesota 28-16
21	25	Wyoming	9-1-0	lost to #8 Brigham Young 14-45
22		Texas A&M	6-2-1	bye week
23		Fresno State	7-1-1	beat Pacific 48-17
24		Ohio State	5-2-1	beat #6 Iowa 27-26
24		Arizona	6-3-0	lost to Stanford 10-23

November 12 Poll / Nov. 17 Games

UP	AP	Team	Record	Result
1	1	Notre Dame	8-1-0	lost to #18 Penn State 21-24
2	2	Colorado	9-1-0	beat Kansas State 64-3
3	3	Miami, Fla.	6-2-0	beat Boston College 42-12
5	4	Georgia Tech	8-0-1	beat Wake Forest 42-7
4	5	Brigham Young	8-1-0	beat Utah 45-22
PB	6	Florida	8-1-0	beat Kentucky 47-15
6	7	Texas	7-1-0	beat TCU 38-10
7	8	Virginia	8-1-0	lost to Maryland 30-35
10	9	Florida State	7-2-0	beat Memphis 35-3
8	10	Washington	8-2-0	beat Washington St. 55-10
9	11	Nebraska	9-1-0	bye week
PB	12	Houston	8-1-0	beat Ea. Washington 84-21
12	13	Iowa	7-2-0	beat Purdue 38-9
13	14	Tennessee	5-2-2	beat #15 Mississippi 22-13
11	15	Mississippi	8-1-0	lost to #14 Tennessee 13-22
16	16	Michigan	6-3-0	beat Minnesota 35-18
15	17	Clemson	8-2-0	beat South Carolina 24-15
14	18	Penn State	7-2-0	beat #1 Notre Dame 24-21
19	19	Southern Cal	7-2-1	beat UCLA 45-42
17	20	Louisville	9-1-1	regular season complete
18	21	Ohio State	6-2-1	beat Wisconsin 35-10
24	22	Illinois	6-3-0	beat Indiana 24-10
21	23	Michigan State	5-3-1	beat Northwestern 29-22
21	24	Auburn	6-2-1	beat Georgia 33-10
25	25	Southern Miss	8-3-0	regular season complete
20		Texas A&M	6-2-1	beat Arkansas 20-16
23		Fresno State	8-1-1	lost to San Jose State 7-42
25		California	6-3-1	lost to Stanford 25-27

November 19 Poll / Nov. 24 Games

UP	AP	Team	Record	Result
1	1	Colorado	10-1-1	regular season complete
2	2	Miami, Fla.	7-2-0	beat Syracuse 33-7
3	3	Georgia Tech	9-0-1	bye week
4	4	Brigham Young	9-1-0	beat Utah State 45-10
PB	5	Florida	9-1-0	bye week
5	6	Texas	8-1-0	beat Baylor 23-13
8	7	Notre Dame	8-2-0	beat #18 Southern Cal 10-6
9	8	Florida State	8-2-0	bye week
7	9	Washington	9-2-0	regular season complete
6	10	Nebraska	9-1-0	lost to Oklahoma 10-45 (N23)
10	11	Penn State	8-2-0	beat Pittsburgh 22-17
PB	12	Houston	9-1-0	bye week
11	13	Iowa	8-2-0	lost to Minnesota 24-31
12	14	Tennessee	6-2-2	beat Kentucky 42-28
15	15	Michigan	7-3-0	beat #19 Ohio State 16-13
13	16	Clemson	9-2-0	regular season complete
14	17	Virginia	8-2-0	lost to Virginia Tech 13-38
16	18	Southern Cal	8-2-1	lost to #7 Notre Dame 6-10
17	19	Ohio State	7-2-1	lost to #15 Michigan 13-16
19	20	Louisville	9-1-1	
17	21	Mississippi	8-2-0	beat Mississippi State 21-9
20	22	Illinois	7-3-0	beat Northwestern 28-23
21	23	Auburn	7-2-1	bye week
23	24	Michigan State	6-3-1	beat Wisconsin 14-9
	24	Southern Miss	8-3-0	
22		Texas A&M	7-2-1	beat TCU 56-10
23		San Jose State	8-2-1	regular season complete
25		Baylor	6-3-1	lost to #6 Texas 13-23

November 26 Poll / Dec. 1 Games

UP	AP	Team	Record	Result
1	1	Colorado	10-1-1	
3	2	Georgia Tech	9-0-1	beat Georgia 40-23
2	3	Miami, Fla.	8-2-0	beat San Diego State 30-28
4	4	Brigham Young	10-1-0	lost to Hawaii 28-59
4	5	Texas	9-1-0	beat Texas A&M 28-27
PB	6	Florida	9-1-0	lost to #8 Florida State 30-45
6	7	Notre Dame	9-2-0	regular season complete
8	8	Florida State	8-2-0	beat #6 Florida 45-30
7	9	Washington	9-2-0	
9	10	Penn State	9-2-0	regular season complete
PB	11	Houston	9-1-0	beat Arizona State 62-45 (D2)
10	12	Tennessee	7-2-2	beat Vanderbilt 49-20
12	13	Michigan	8-3-0	regular season complete
11	14	Clemson	9-2-0	
13	15	Mississippi	9-2-0	regular season complete
19	16	Illinois	8-3-0	regular season complete
16	17	Louisville	9-1-1	
15	18	Iowa	8-3-0	regular season complete
14	19	Nebraska	9-2-0	regular season complete
20	20	Auburn	7-2-1	lost to Alabama 7-16
18	21	Southern Cal	8-3-1	regular season complete
PB	22	Oklahoma	8-3-0	regular season complete
21	23	Michigan State	7-3-1	regular season complete
23	24	Southern Miss	8-3-0	
22	25	Ohio State	7-3-1	regular season complete
17		Texas A&M	8-2-1	lost to #5 Texas 27-28
23		Virginia	8-3-0	regular season complete
25		San Jose State	8-2-1	
25		Oregon	8-3-0	regular season complete

December 3 Poll / Bowls / January 2 Final Poll

UP	AP	December 3 Poll	Record	Bowl Bid	Date	Bowl Result	RB	UP	AP	January 2 Final Poll	Record
1	1	Colorado	10-1-1	Orange Bowl	J1	beat #5 Notre Dame 10-9	1	2	1	Colorado	11-1-1
2	2	Georgia Tech	10-0-1	Citrus Bowl	J1	beat #19 Nebraska 45-21	2	1	2	Georgia Tech	11-0-1
3	3	Texas	10-1-0	Cotton Bowl	J1	lost to #4 Miami, Fla. 3-46	3	3	3	Miami, Fla.	10-2-0
4	4	Miami, Fla.	9-2-0	Cotton Bowl	J1	beat #3 Texas 46-3	5	4	4	Florida State	10-2-0
6	5	Notre Dame	9-2-0	Orange Bowl	J1	lost to #1 Colorado 9-10	8	5	5	Washington	10-2-0
5	6	Florida State	9-2-0	Blockbuster Bowl	D28	beat #7 Penn State 24-17	10	6	6	Notre Dame	9-3-0
8	7	Penn State	9-2-0	Blockbuster Bowl	D28	lost to #6 Florida State 17-24	11	8	7	Michigan	9-3-0
7	8	Washington	9-2-0	Rose Bowl	J1	beat #17 Iowa 46-34	6	7	8	Tennessee	9-2-2
PB	9	Houston	10-1-0				9	9	9	Clemson	10-2-0
10	10	Tennessee	8-2-2	Sugar Bowl	J1	beat Virginia 23-22	4	PB	10	Houston	10-1-0
PB	11	Florida	9-2-0				19	10	11	Penn State	9-3-0
12	12	Michigan	8-3-0	Gator Bowl	J1	beat #15 Mississippi 35-3	7	11	12	Texas	10-2-0
9	13	Brigham Young	10-2-0	Holiday Bowl	D29	lost to Texas A&M 14-65	12	PB	13	Florida	9-2-0
11	14	Clemson	9-2-0	Hall of Fame Bowl	J1	beat #16 Illinois 30-0	13	12	14	Louisville	10-1-1
14	15	Mississippi	9-2-0	Gator Bowl	J1	lost to #12 Michigan 3-35	18	13	15	Texas A&M	9-3-1
17	16	Illinois	8-3-0	Hall of Fame Bowl	J1	lost to #14 Clemson 0-30	16	14	16	Michigan State	8-3-1
15	17	Iowa	8-3-0	Rose Bowl	J1	lost to #8 Washington 34-46	28	15	17	Oklahoma	8-3-0
16	18	Louisville	9-1-1	Fiesta Bowl	J1	beat #25 Alabama 34-7	30	16	18	Iowa	8-4-0
13	19	Nebraska	9-2-0	Citrus Bowl	J1	lost to #2 Georgia Tech 21-45	14	19	19	Auburn	8-3-1
PB	20	Oklahoma	8-3-0				23	22	20	Southern Cal	
18	21	Southern Cal	8-3-1	Sun Bowl	D31	lost to #22 Michigan State 16-17	17	23	21	Mississippi	9-3-0
20	22	Michigan State	7-3-1	Sun Bowl	D31	beat #21 Southern Cal 17-16	21	17	22	Brigham Young	10-3-0
24	23	Southern Miss	8-3-0	All-American Bowl	D28	lost to North Carolina St. 27-31	24	15	23	Virginia	8-4-0
20	24	Ohio State	7-3-1	Liberty Bowl	D27	lost to Air Force 11-23	15	17	24	Nebraska	9-3-0
22	25	Alabama	7-4-0	Fiesta Bowl	J1	lost to #18 Louisville 7-34	22	24	25	Illinois	8-4-0
19		Texas A&M	8-3-1	Holiday Bowl	D29	beat #13 Brigham Young 65-14	29	20		San Jose State	9-2-1
							26	21		Syracuse	7-4-2
							31	25		Virginia Tech	6-5-0

1990

CONSENSUS ALL-AMERICANS

POS	Offense	HT	WT	School	AP	CF	FC	FW	PI
QB	Ty Detmer	6-0	175	Brigham Young	•	•	•	•	•
RB	Eric Bieniemy	5-7	195	Colorado	•	•	•	•	•
RB	Darren Lewis	6-0	220	Texas A&M	•	•	•	•	•
WR	Raghib Ismail	5-10	175	Notre Dame	•	•	•	•	•
WR	Herman Moore	6-5	197	Virginia	•		•	•	•
TE	Chris Smith	6-4	230	Brigham Young	•	•	•	•	•
OL	Antone Davis	6-4	310	Tennessee	•	•	•	•	•
OL	Joe Garten	6-3	280	Colorado	•	•	•	•	•
OL	Ed King	6-4	284	Auburn	•	•	•	•	•
OL	Stacy Long	6-2	275	Clemson	•	•	•	•	•
C	John Flannery	6-4	301	Syracuse	•	•	•	•	•
PK	Philip Doyle	6-1	190	Alabama	•	•	•	•	•

OTHERS RECEIVING FIRST-TEAM HONORS

QB	Shawn Moore	Virginia			•	•		•	•
RB	Greg Lewis	Washington				•			
RB	Mike Mayweather	Army							
WR	Lawrence Dawsey	Florida State			•				
WR	Ed McCaffrey	Stanford					•		
OL	Greg Skrepenak	Michigan				•			
OL	Dean Dingman	Michigan					•		
C	Mike Arthur	Texas A&M						•	

FW named Ismail as KR

POS	Defense	HT	WT	School	AP	CF	FC	FW	PI
DL	Russell Maryland	6-2	273	Miami, Fla.	•	•	•	•	•
DL	Chris Zorich	6-1	266	Notre Dame	•	•	•	•	•
DL	Moe Gardner	6-2	258	Illinois		•	•	•	•
DL	David Rocker	6-4	264	Auburn		•	•	•	•
LB	Alfred Williams	6-6	236	Colorado	•	•	•		•
LB	Michael Stonebreaker	6-1	228	Notre Dame	•	•	•		•
LB	Maurice Crum	6-0	222	Miami, Fla.	•	•	•	•	•
DB	Tripp Welborne	6-1	201	Michigan	•	•	•	•	•
DB	Darryll Lewis	5-9	186	Arizona	•	•	•	•	•
DB	Ken Swilling	6-3	230	Georgia Tech	•	•	•	•	•
DB	Todd Lyght	6-1	184	Notre Dame	•	•	•		•
P	Brian Greenfield	6-1	210	Pittsburgh		•	•		•

OTHERS RECEIVING FIRST-TEAM HONORS

DL	Mitch Donahue	Wyoming						•	
DL	Kenny Walker	Nebraska				•		•	
DL	Huey Richardson	Florida						•	
LB	Scott Ross	Southern Cal						•	
DB	Will White	Florida						•	
DB	Stanley Richard	Texas				•			
P	Cris Shale	Bowling Green				•			

FC named Alfred Williams as a DL

HEISMAN TROPHY VOTING

	PLAYER	POS	SCHOOL	1ST	2ND	3RD	TOTAL
1	Ty Detmer	QB	Brigham Young	316	208	118	1482
2	Raghib Ismail	WR	Notre Dame	237	174	118	1177
3	Eric Bieniemy	TB	Colorado	114	153	150	798
4	Shawn Moore	QB	Virginia	46	96	135	465
5	David Klingler	QB	Houston	7	27	50	125
6	Herman Moore	WR	Virginia	6	14	22	68
7	Greg Lewis	TB	Washington	4	5	19	41
8	Craig Erickson	QB	Miami, Fla.	0	6	19	31
	Darren Lewis	RB	Texas A&M	0	9	13	31
10	Mike Mayweather	HB	Army	3	4	3	20

AWARD WINNERS

PLAYER	POS/SCHOOL	AWARD
Ty Detmer	QB Brigham Young	Maxwell
Russell Maryland	DT Miami, Fla.	Outland
Raghib Ismail	WR Notre Dame	Camp
Chris Zorich	NT Notre Dame	Lombardi

PLAYER	POS/SCHOOL	AWARD
Ty Detmer	QB Brigham Young	O'Brien
Alfred Williams	LB Colorado	Butkus
Darryll Lewis	DB Arizona	Thorpe
Craig Erickson	QB Miami, Fla.	Unitas
Greg Lewis	RB Washington	Walker

CONFERENCE STANDINGS

ACC

	Conf. W L T			Overall W L T		
Georgia Tech	6	0	1	11	0	1
Clemson	5	2	0	10	2	0
Virginia	5	2	0	8	4	0
Maryland	4	3	0	6	5	1
North Carolina	3	3	1	6	4	1
North Carolina St.	3	4	0	7	5	0
Duke	1	6	0	4	7	0
Wake Forest	0	7	0	3	8	0

Big 10

	Conf. W L T			Overall W L T		
Michigan	6	2	0	9	3	0
Michigan State	6	2	0	8	3	1
Illinois	6	2	0	8	4	0
Iowa	6	2	0	8	4	0
Ohio State	5	2	1	7	4	1
Minnesota	5	3	0	6	5	0
Indiana	3	4	1	6	5	1
Purdue	1	7	0	2	9	0
Northwestern	1	7	0	2	9	0
Wisconsin	0	8	0	1	10	0

Big 8

	Conf. W L T			Overall W L T		
Colorado	7	0	0	11	1	1
Nebraska	5	2	0	9	3	0
Oklahoma	5	2	0	8	3	0
Iowa State	2	4	1	4	6	1
Kansas	2	4	1	3	7	1
Kansas State	2	5	0	5	6	0
Missouri	2	5	0	4	7	0
Oklahoma State	2	5	0	4	7	0

Big West

	Conf. W L T			Overall W L T		
San Jose State	7	0	0	9	2	1
Fresno State	5	1	1	8	2	1
Utah State	5	1	1	5	5	1
Long Beach State	4	3	0	6	5	0
Nevada-Las Vegas	3	4	0	4	7	0
Pacific	2	5	0	4	7	0
New Mexico State	1	6	0	1	10	0
Cal-St. Fullerton	0	7	0	1	11	0

Ivy

	Conf. W L T			Overall W L T		
Dartmouth	6	1	0	7	2	1
Cornell	6	1	0	7	3	0
Yale	5	2	0	6	4	0
Harvard	3	4	0	5	5	0
Pennsylvania	3	4	0	3	7	0
Princeton	2	5	0	3	7	0
Brown	2	5	0	2	8	0
Columbia	1	6	0	1	9	0

MAC

	Conf. W L T			Overall W L T		
Toledo	7	1	0	9	2	0
Central Michigan	7	1	0	8	3	1
Western Michigan	5	3	0	7	4	0
Ball State	5	3	0	7	4	0
Miami, Ohio	4	3	1	5	5	1
Bowling Green	2	4	2	3	5	2
Kent State	2	6	0	2	9	0
Eastern Michigan	2	6	0	2	9	0
Ohio U	0	7	1	1	9	1

Pac 10

	Conf. W L T			Overall W L T		
Washington	7	1	0	10	2	0
Southern Cal	5	2	1	8	4	1
Oregon	4	3	0	8	4	0
California	4	3	1	7	4	1
Arizona	5	4	0	7	5	0
Stanford	4	4	0	5	6	0
UCLA	4	4	0	5	6	0
Arizona State	2	5	0	4	7	0
Washington State	2	6	0	3	8	0
Oregon State	1	6	0	1	10	0

SEC

	Conf. W L T			Overall W L T		
Florida	6	1	0	9	2	0
Tennessee	5	1	1	9	2	2
Mississippi	5	2	0	9	3	0
Alabama	5	2	0	7	5	0
Auburn	4	2	1	8	3	1
Kentucky	3	4	0	4	7	0
LSU	2	5	0	5	6	0
Georgia	2	5	0	4	7	0
Mississippi State	1	6	0	5	6	0
Vanderbilt	1	6	0	1	10	0

SWC

	Conf. W L T			Overall W L T		
Texas	8	0	0	10	2	0
Houston	7	1	0	10	1	0
Texas A&M	5	2	1	9	3	1
Baylor	5	2	1	6	4	1
Rice	3	5	0	5	6	0
TCU	3	5	0	5	6	0
Texas Tech	3	5	0	4	7	0
Arkansas	1	7	0	3	8	0
SMU	0	8	0	1	10	0

WAC

	Conf. W L T			Overall W L T		
Brigham Young	7	1	0	10	3	0
Colorado State	6	1	0	9	4	0
San Diego State	5	2	0	6	5	0
Wyoming	5	3	0	9	4	0
Hawaii	4	4	0	7	5	0
Air Force	3	4	0	7	5	0
Utah	2	6	0	4	7	0
New Mexico	1	6	0	2	10	0
Texas-El Paso	1	7	0	3	8	0

Independents

	Overall W L T		
Louisville	10	1	1
Miami, Fla.	10	2	0
Florida State	10	2	0
Notre Dame	9	3	0
Penn State	9	3	0
Louisiana Tech	8	3	1
Southern Miss	8	4	0
Temple	7	4	0
Syracuse	7	4	2
South Carolina	6	5	0
Virginia Tech	6	5	0
Army	6	5	0
Northern Illinois	6	5	0
Navy	5	6	0
East Carolina	5	6	0
La. Lafayette	5	6	0
Memphis	4	6	1
Boston College	4	7	0
Tulane	4	7	0
West Virginia	4	7	0
Pittsburgh	3	7	1
Arkansas State	3	7	1
Akron	3	7	1
Rutgers	3	8	0
Tulsa	3	8	0
Cincinnati	1	10	0

BOWL GAMES

DATE	GAME	SCORE
D8	California	San Jose State 48, Central Michigan 24
D15	Independence	Louisiana Tech 34, Maryland 34
D25	Aloha	Syracuse 28, Arizona 0
D27	Liberty	Air Force 23, Ohio State 11
D28	Blockbuster	Florida State 24, Penn State 17
D28	All-American	North Carolina St. 31, Southern Miss 27
D29	Peach	Auburn 27, Indiana 23
D29	Freedom	Colorado State 32, Oregon 31
D29	Holiday	Texas A&M 65, Brigham Young 14
D31	Copper	California 17, Wyoming 15

DATE	GAME	SCORE
J1	Hall of Fame	Clemson 30, Illinois 0
J1	Orange	Colorado 10, Notre Dame 9
J1	Citrus	Georgia Tech 45, Nebraska 21
J1	Fiesta	Louisville 34, Alabama 7
J1	Cotton	Miami, Fla. 46, Texas 3
J1	Gator	Michigan 35, Mississippi 3
J1	Rose	Washington 46, Iowa 34
J1	Sugar	Tennessee 23, Virginia 22

1990 ANNUAL REVIEW 1375

1990 NCAA Major College Statistical Leaders

Individual Leaders

PASSING	CL	G	ATT	COM	PCT	INT	I%	YDS	YPA	TD	TD%	RATING
1 Shawn Moore, Virginia	SR	10	241	144	59.8	8	3.3	2262	9.4	21	8.7	160.7
2 Ty Detmer, Brigham Young	JR	12	562	361	64.2	28	5.0	5188	9.2	41	7.3	155.9
3 Casey Weldon, Florida State	JR	11	182	112	61.5	4	2.2	1600	8.8	12	6.6	152.7
4 Dan McGwire, San Diego State	SR	11	449	270	60.1	7	1.6	3833	8.5	27	6.0	148.6
5 David Klingler, Houston	JR	11	643	374	58.2	20	3.1	5140	8.0	54	8.4	146.8
6 Craig Erickson, Miami, Fla.	SR	11	393	225	57.3	7	1.8	3363	8.6	22	5.6	144.0
7 Shane Matthews, Florida	SO	11	378	229	60.6	12	3.2	2952	7.8	23	6.1	139.9
8 Garrett Gabriel, Hawaii	SR	12	320	165	51.6	16	5.0	2752	8.6	25	7.8	139.6
9 Troy Kopp, Pacific	SO	9	428	243	56.8	14	3.3	3311	7.7	31	7.2	139.1
10 Rick Mirer, Notre Dame	SO	11	200	110	55.0	6	3.0	1824	9.1	8	4.0	138.8

ALL-PURPOSE	CL	G	RUSH	REC	PR	KR	YDS	YPG
1 Glyn Milburn, Stanford	SO	11	729	632	267	594	2222	202.0
2 Sheldon Canley, San Jose State	SR	11	1248	386	5	574	2213	201.2
3 Chuck Weatherspoon, Houston	SR	11	1097	560	196	185	2038	185.3
4 Eric Bieniemy, Colorado	SR	11	1628	159	0	31	1818	165.3
5 Jeff Sydner, Hawaii	SO	12	390	820	483	265	1958	163.2
6 Greg Lewis, Washington	SR	10	1279	345	0	0	1624	162.4
7 Russell White, California	SO	11	1000	127	0	629	1756	159.6
8 Dwayne Owens, Oregon State	FR	9	364	49	0	1014	1427	158.6
9 Raghib Ismail, Notre Dame	JR	11	537	702	151	336	1726	156.9
10 Dion Johnson, East Carolina	JR	9	266	90	167	879	1402	155.8

RUSHING/Yards Per Game	CL	G	ATT	YDS	TD	AVG	YPG
1 Gerald Hudson, Oklahoma State	SR	11	279	1642	10	5.9	149.3
2 Eric Bieniemy, Colorado	SR	11	288	1628	17	5.7	148.0
3 Darren Lewis, Texas A&M	SR	12	291	1691	18	5.8	140.9
4 Greg Lewis, Washington	SR	10	229	1279	8	5.6	127.9
5 Tico Duckett, Michigan State	SO	11	249	1376	10	5.5	125.1
6 Roger Grant, Utah State	JR	11	266	1370	8	5.2	124.6
7 Mike Mayweather, Army	SR	11	274	1338	10	4.9	121.6
8 Trevor Cobb, Rice	SO	11	283	1325	10	4.7	120.5
9 Sheldon Canley, San Jose State	SR	11	296	1248	12	4.2	113.5
10 Stacey Robinson, Northern Illinois	SR	11	193	1238	19	6.4	112.6

RUSHING/Yards Per Carry	CL	G	ATT	YDS	YPC
1 Chuck Weatherspoon, Houston	SR	11	158	1097	6.9
2 Robert Smith, Ohio State	FR	11	164	1064	6.5
3 Stacey Robinson, No. Illinois	SR	11	193	1238	6.4
4 Leodis Flowers, Nebraska	JR	9	149	940	6.3
5 Jon Vaughn, Michigan	SO	11	201	1236	6.1
6 Gerald Hudson, Oklahoma State	SR	11	279	1642	5.9
7 Darren Lewis, Texas A&M	SR	12	291	1691	5.8
8 Tony Thompson, Tennessee	SR	12	219	1261	5.8
9 Howard Griffith, Illinois	SR	11	186	1056	5.7
10 Eric Bieniemy, Colorado	SR	11	288	1628	5.7

*-Based on top 22 rushers

RECEIVING	CL	G	REC	YDS	TD	RPG	YPR	YPG
1 Patrick Rowe, San Diego State	JR	11	71	1392	8	6.5	19.6	126.6
2 Aaron Turner, Pacific	SO	11	66	1264	11	6.0	19.2	114.9
3 Herman Moore, Virginia	JR	11	54	1190	13	4.9	22.0	108.2
4 Andy Boyce, Brigham Young	SR	12	79	1241	13	6.6	15.7	103.4
5 Dennis Arey, San Diego State	SR	11	68	1118	10	6.2	16.4	101.6
6 Chris Smith, Brigham Young	SR	12	68	1156	2	5.7	17.0	96.3
7 Keenan McCardell, Nevada-Las Vegas	SR	11	68	1046	8	6.2	15.4	95.1
8 Manny Hazard, Houston	SR	10	78	946	9	7.8	12.1	94.6
9 Ed McCaffrey, Stanford	SR	10	61	917	8	6.1	15.0	91.7
10 Lawrence Dawsey, Florida State	SR	11	65	999	7	5.9	15.4	90.8

PUNTING	CL	PUNT	YDS	AVG
1 Cris Shale, Bowling Green	SR	66	3087	46.8
2 Brian Greenfield, Pittsburgh	SR	50	2280	45.6
3 Jason Hanson, Washington State	JR	59	2679	45.4
4 Chris Gardocki, Clemson	JR	53	2350	44.3
5 Greg Hertzog, West Virginia	SR	62	2697	43.5
6 Scott McAlister, North Carolina	JR	79	3433	43.5
7 Brad Williams, Arizona State	SR	56	2422	43.3
8 Klaus Wilmsmeyer, Louisville	JR	48	2062	43.0
9 Todd Rawsthorne, Western Michigan	JR	35	1502	42.9
10 Trent Thompson, Temple	JR	42	1795	42.7

PUNT RETURNS	CL	PR	YDS	TD	AVG
1 Dave McCloughan, Colorado	SR	32	524	2	16.4
2 Beno Bryant, Washington	SO	36	560	3	15.6
3 Jeff Graham, Ohio State	SR	22	327	2	14.9
4 Tony James, Mississippi State	SO	23	341	2	14.8
5 Tripp Welborne, Michigan	SR	31	455	0	14.7
6 Terrell Buckley, Florida State	SO	24	350	2	14.6
7 George Coghill, Wake Forest	SO	19	275	1	14.5
8 Rob Turner, Indiana	JR	27	373	2	13.8
9 Tony Smith, Southern Miss	JR	38	507	2	13.3
10 Joey Smith, Louisville	SR	29	382	0	13.2

KICKOFF RETURNS	CL	KR	YDS	TD	AVG
1 Dale Carter, Tennessee	JR	17	507	1	29.8
2 Desmond Howard, Michigan	JR	16	472	1	29.5
3 Tyrone Hughes, Nebraska	SO	18	523	1	29.0
4 Ray Washington, New Mexico State	JR	22	638	1	29.0
5 Randy Jones, Duke	SR	24	678	2	28.3
6 Andre Hastings, Georgia	FR	15	422	1	28.1
7 Milt Stegall, Miami, Ohio	JR	18	497	1	27.6
8 Russell White, California	SO	24	629	1	26.2
9 Dion Johnson, East Carolina	JR	34	879	1	25.9
10 Dexter Pointer, Utah State	JR	30	769	0	25.6

SCORING	CL	TDS	XP	FG	PTS	PTPG
1 Stacey Robinson, Northern Illinois	SR	19	6	0	120	10.9
2 Aaron Craver, Fresno State	SR	18	0	0	108	10.8
3 Roman Anderson, Houston	JR	0	58	19	115	10.5
4 Amp Lee, Florida State	SO	18	0	0	108	9.8
5 Andy Trakas, San Diego State	SO	0	53	18	107	9.7
6 Darren Lewis, Texas A&M	SR	19	0	0	114	9.5
7 Eric Bieniemy, Colorado	SR	17	0	0	102	9.3
8 Carlos Huerta, Miami, Fla.	JR	0	50	17	101	9.2
9 Michale Pollak, Texas	SR	0	39	20	99	9.0
10 Greg Burke, Tennessee	SR	0	50	19	107	8.9

FIELD GOALS	CL	FGA	FGM	PCT	FGG
1 Philip Doyle, Alabama	SR	29	24	0.83	2.18
2 Clint Gwaltney, North Carolina	JR	27	21	0.78	1.91
3 Michale Pollak, Texas	SR	26	20	0.77	1.82
4 Chris Gardocki, Clemson	JR	24	19	0.79	1.73
4 John Kasay, Georgia	SR	24	19	0.79	1.73
4 Roman Anderson, Houston	JR	25	19	0.76	1.73
4 Bob Wright, Temple	SR	25	19	0.76	1.73
4 Jeff Shudak, Iowa State	SR	27	19	0.70	1.73
9 Andy Trakas, San Diego State	SO	26	18	0.69	1.64
9 Rusty Hanna, Toledo	SO	29	18	0.62	1.64

INTERCEPTIONS	CL	INT	YDS	TD	INT/GM
1 Jerry Parks, Houston	JR	8	124	1	0.73
2 Will White, Florida	SO	7	116	0	0.70
3 Darryl Lewis, Arizona	SR	7	192	2	0.64
3 Shawn Vincent, Akron	SR	7	191	0	0.64
3 Ron Carpenter, Miami, Ohio	JR	7	164	1	0.64
3 Darren Perry, Penn State	SR	7	125	1	0.64
3 Mike Welch, Baylor	SR	7	80	0	0.64
3 Ozzie Jackson, Akron	SR	7	50	0	0.64
9 Jaime Mendez, Kansas State	FR	6	154	1	0.60
9 Dave Bielinski, Bowling Green	SO	6	63	0	0.60

Team Leaders

RUSHING OFFENSE	G	ATT	YDS	AVG	TD	YPG
1 Northern Illinois	11	619	3791	6.1	36	344.6
2 Nebraska	11	641	3740	5.8	36	340.0
3 Army	11	746	3647	4.9	30	331.5
4 Texas A&M	12	661	3829	5.8	37	319.1
5 Oklahoma	11	637	3182	5.0	41	289.3
6 Colorado	12	629	3254	5.2	33	271.2
7 Air Force	11	653	2942	4.5	28	267.5
8 Virginia	11	520	2831	5.4	31	257.4
9 Clemson	11	623	2808	4.5	24	255.3
10 Michigan State	11	590	2793	4.7	34	253.9

PASSING OFFENSE	G	ATT	COM	INT	PCT	YDS	YPA	TD	I%	YPC	YPG
1 Houston	11	659	386	20	58.6	5213	7.9	54	3.0	13.5	473.9
2 Brigham Young	12	580	373	29	64.3	5379	9.3	41	5.0	14.4	448.3
3 San Diego State	11	485	287	8	59.2	4086	8.4	29	1.7	14.2	371.5
4 Pacific	11	535	303	16	56.6	4051	7.6	40	3.0	13.4	368.3
5 Miami, Fla.	11	434	246	8	56.7	3573	8.2	22	1.8	14.5	324.8
6 Missouri	11	404	246	19	60.9	3248	8.0	18	4.7	13.2	295.3
7 TCU	11	511	258	20	50.5	3237	6.3	24	3.9	12.5	294.3
8 San Jose State	11	393	219	15	55.7	3208	8.2	27	3.8	14.6	291.6
9 Florida	11	415	246	16	59.3	3197	7.7	25	3.9	13.0	290.6
10 New Mexico	12	510	237	23	46.5	3221	6.3	18	4.5	13.6	268.4

TOTAL OFFENSE	G	P	YDS	AVG	TD	YPG
1 Houston	11	905	6455	7.1	63	586.8
2 Brigham Young	12	968	6788	7.0	64	565.7
3 San Diego State	11	927	5798	6.3	57	527.1
4 Virginia	11	804	5516	6.9	55	501.5
5 Miami, Fla.	11	842	5312	6.3	49	482.9
6 Texas A&M	12	875	5653	6.5	50	471.1
7 San Jose State	11	872	5116	5.9	51	465.1
8 Pacific	11	835	5080	6.1	47	461.8
9 Fresno State	11	868	5026	5.8	45	456.9
10 Florida	11	855	4978	5.8	44	452.6

RUSHING DEFENSE	G	ATT	YDS	AVG	TD	YPG
1 Washington	11	392	735	1.9	10	66.8
2 Clemson	11	369	789	2.1	5	71.7
3 Miami, Fla.	11	387	877	2.3	7	79.7
4 San Jose State	11	410	916	2.2	9	83.3
5 Florida	11	386	941	2.4	8	85.5
6 Alabama	11	402	1007	2.5	6	91.5
7 Penn State	11	401	1040	2.6	8	94.5
8 Iowa	11	392	1095	2.8	14	99.5
9 Central Michigan	11	392	1097	2.8	2	99.7
10 Ball State	11	461	1120	2.4	8	101.8

PASSING DEFENSE	G	ATT	COM	PCT	INT	I%	YDS	YPA	TD	TD%	RAT
1 Alabama	11	309	141	45.6	15	4.9	1516	4.9	5	1.6	82.5
2 Central Michigan	11	289	129	44.6	15	5.2	1462	5.1	6	2.1	83.6
3 Ball State	11	247	116	47.0	17	6.9	1329	5.4	4	1.6	83.7
4 Miami, Ohio	11	244	106	43.4	15	6.2	1327	5.4	8	3.3	87.7
5 Texas	11	314	129	41.1	13	4.1	1780	5.7	7	2.2	87.8
6 Clemson	11	309	149	48.2	14	4.5	1597	5.2	5	1.6	87.9
7 Tennessee	12	336	163	48.5	24	7.1	1737	5.2	12	3.6	89.4
8 Louisville	11	279	141	50.5	19	6.8	1641	5.9	4	1.4	91.1
9 Fresno State	11	346	144	41.6	11	3.2	2109	6.1	5	1.5	91.2
10 Penn State	11	361	178	49.3	23	6.4	2023	5.6	9	2.5	91.9

TOTAL DEFENSE	G	P	YDS	AVG	TD	YPG
1 Clemson	11	678	2386	3.5	10	216.9
2 Ball State	11	708	2449	3.5	12	222.6
3 Alabama	11	711	2523	3.5	11	229.4
4 Central Michigan	11	681	2559	3.8	8	232.6
5 Florida	11	708	2834	4.0	17	257.6
6 Louisville	11	737	2855	3.9	13	259.5
7 Nebraska	11	724	2898	4.0	16	263.5
8 Auburn	11	738	3002	4.1	22	272.9
9 Miami, Ohio	11	765	3036	4.0	26	276.0
10 North Carolina St.	11	772	3054	4.0	17	277.6

SCORING OFFENSE	G	PTS	AVG
1 Houston	11	511	46.5
2 Brigham Young	12	510	42.5
3 San Diego State	11	459	41.7
4 Virginia	11	442	40.2
5 Florida State	11	435	39.5
6 Nebraska	11	413	37.5
7 Tennessee	12	442	36.8
8 Miami, Fla.	11	401	36.5
8 Oklahoma	11	401	36.5
10 Washington	11	394	35.8

SCORING DEFENSE	G	PTS	AVG
1 Central Michigan	11	98	8.9
2 Clemson	11	109	9.9
3 Ball State	11	121	11.0
4 Alabama	11	127	11.5
5 Southern Miss	11	141	12.8
6 Louisville	11	142	12.9
7 Nebraska	11	147	13.4
8 Washington	11	150	13.6
9 Penn State	11	155	14.1
10 North Carolina St.	11	162	14.7

ANNUAL REVIEW

1991 Poll Progression

AP	Pre-Season 1991		Aug. 31 Games
1	Florida State	0-0-0	beat # 19 Brigham Young 44-28 (A29)
2	Michigan	0-0-0	bye week
3	Miami, Fla.	0-0-0	beat Arkansas 31-3
4	Washington	0-0-0	bye week
5	Florida	0-0-0	bye week
6	Notre Dame	0-0-0	bye week
7	Penn State	0-0-0	beat # 8 Georgia Tech 34-22 (A28)
8	Georgia Tech	0-0-0	lost to # 7 Penn State 22-34 (A28)
9	Clemson	0-0-0	bye week
10	Oklahoma	0-0-0	bye week
11	Tennessee	0-0-0	bye week
12	Houston	0-0-0	beat Louisiana Tech 73-3
13	Colorado	0-0-0	bye week
14	Texas	0-0-0	bye week
15	Nebraska	0-0-0	bye week
16	Southern Cal	0-0-0	bye week
17	Auburn	0-0-0	beat Geo. Southern 32-17
18	Iowa	0-0-0	bye week
19	Brigham Young	0-0-0	lost to # 1 Florida State 28-44 (A29)
20	Michigan State	0-0-0	bye week
21	Texas A&M	0-0-0	bye week
22	Alabama	0-0-0	bye week
23	Ohio State	0-0-0	bye week
24	UCLA	0-0-0	bye week
25	Syracuse	0-0-0	bye week

AP	September 2 Poll		Sept. 7 Games
1	Florida State	1-0-0	beat Tulane 38-11
2	Michigan	0-0-0	beat Boston College 35-13
3	Miami, Fla.	1-0-0	bye week
4	Washington	0-0-0	beat Stanford 42-7
5	Penn State	1-0-0	beat Cincinnati 81-0
6	Florida	0-0-0	beat San Jose State 59-21
7	Notre Dame	0-0-0	beat Indiana 49-27
8	Clemson	0-0-0	beat Appalachian St. 34-0
9	Oklahoma	0-0-0	bye week
10	Houston	1-0-0	bye week
11	Tennessee	0-0-0	beat Louisville 28-11 S5
12	Colorado	0-0-0	beat Wyoming 30-13
13	Texas	0-0-0	lost to Mississippi State 6-13
14	Nebraska	0-0-0	beat Utah State 59-28
15	Iowa	0-0-0	beat Hawaii 53-10
16	Southern Cal	0-0-0	lost to Memphis 10-24 S2
17	Georgia Tech	0-1-0	bye week
18	Auburn	1-0-0	bye week
19	Michigan State	0-0-0	bye week
20	Alabama	0-0-0	beat Temple 41-3
21	Texas A&M	0-0-0	bye week
22	Ohio State	0-0-0	beat Arizona 38-14
23	UCLA	0-0-0	beat # 25 Brigham Young 27-23
24	Syracuse	0-0-0	beat Vanderbilt 37-10
25	Brigham Young	0-1-0	lost to # 23 UCLA 23-27

AP	September 9 Poll		Sept. 14 Games
1	Florida State	2-0-0	beat Western Michigan 58-0
2	Miami, Fla.	1-0-0	beat # 10 Houston 40-10 (S12)
3	Michigan	1-0-0	beat # 7 Notre Dame 24-14
4	Washington	1-0-0	bye week
5	Penn State	2-0-0	lost to Southern Cal 10-21
6	Florida	1-0-0	beat # 16 Alabama 35-0
7	Notre Dame	1-0-0	lost to # 3 Michigan 14-24
8	Clemson	1-0-0	bye week
9	Oklahoma	0-0-0	beat North Texas 40-2
10	Houston	1-0-0	lost to # 2 Miami, Fla. 10-40 (S12)
11	Tennessee	1-0-0	beat # 21 UCLA 30-16
12	Colorado	1-0-0	lost to # 23 Baylor 14-16
13	Nebraska	1-0-0	beat Colorado State 71-14
14	Iowa	1-0-0	beat Iowa State 29-10
15	Auburn	1-0-0	beat Mississippi 23-13
16	Alabama	1-0-0	lost to # 6 Florida 0-35
17	Georgia Tech	0-1-0	beat Boston College 30-14
18	Michigan State	0-0-0	lost to Central Michigan 3-20
19	Ohio State	1-0-0	beat Louisville 23-15
20	Texas A&M	0-0-0	beat LSU 45-7
21	UCLA	1-0-0	lost to # 11 Tennessee 16-30
22	Syracuse	1-0-0	beat Maryland 31-17
23	Baylor	1-0-0	beat # 12 Colorado 16-14
24	Pittsburgh	2-0-0	beat Temple 26-7
25	Mississippi State	2-0-0	beat Tulane 48-0

AP	September 16 Poll		Sept. 21 Games
1	Florida State	3-0-0	bye week
2	Miami, Fla.	2-0-0	bye week
3	Michigan	2-0-0	bye week
4	Washington	1-0-0	beat # 9 Nebraska 36-21
5	Florida	2-0-0	lost to # 18 Syracuse 21-38
6	Tennessee	2-0-0	beat # 23 Mississippi State 26-24
7	Oklahoma	1-0-0	beat Utah State 55-21
8	Clemson	1-0-0	beat Temple 37-7
9	Nebraska	2-0-0	lost to # 4 Washington 21-36
10	Iowa	2-0-0	bye week
11	Notre Dame	1-1-0	beat Michigan State 49-10
12	Penn State	2-1-0	beat Brigham Young 33-7
13	Auburn	2-0-0	beat Texas 14-10
14	Baylor	2-0-0	beat Missouri 47-21
15	Texas A&M	1-0-0	lost to Tulsa 34-35
16	Ohio State	2-0-0	beat Washington St. 33-19
17	Georgia Tech	1-1-0	beat Virginia 24-21
18	Syracuse	2-0-0	beat # 5 Florida 38-21
19	Colorado	1-1-0	beat Minnesota 58-0
20	Pittsburgh	3-0-0	bye week
21	Houston	1-1-0	lost to Illinois 10-51
22	Southern Cal	1-1-0	lost to Arizona State 25-32
23	Mississippi State	3-0-0	lost to # 6 Tennessee 24-26
24	California	2-0-0	beat Arizona 23-21
25	Georgia	2-0-0	lost to Alabama 0-10

UP	AP	September 23 Poll		Sept. 28 Games
1	1	Florida State	3-0-0	beat # 3 Michigan 51-31
2	2	Miami, Fla.	2-0-0	beat Tulsa 34-10
3	3	Michigan	2-0-0	lost to # 1 Florida State 31-51
4	4	Washington	2-0-0	beat Kansas State 56-3
5	5	Tennessee	3-0-0	beat # 13 Auburn 30-21
6	6	Oklahoma	2-0-0	beat Virginia Tech 27-17
7	7	Clemson	2-0-0	beat # 19 Georgia Tech 9-7
9	8	Notre Dame	2-1-0	beat Purdue 45-20
8	9	Iowa	2-0-0	beat Northern Illinois 58-7
11	10	Penn State	3-1-0	beat Boston College 28-21
10	11	Syracuse	3-0-0	beat Tulane 24-0
14	12	Baylor	3-0-0	beat SMU 45-7
12	13	Auburn	3-0-0	lost to # 5 Tennessee 21-30
15	14	Florida	2-1-0	beat # 21 Mississippi State 29-7
13	15	Ohio State	3-0-0	bye week
16	16	Nebraska	2-1-0	beat # 24 Arizona State 18-9
17	17	Colorado	2-1-0	lost to Stanford 21-28
19	18	Pittsburgh	3-0-0	beat Minnesota 14-13
18	19	Georgia Tech	2-1-0	lost to # 7 Clemson 7-9
20	20	California	3-0-0	bye week
21	21	Mississippi State	3-1-0	lost to # 14 Florida 7-29
22	22	Alabama	2-1-0	beat Vanderbilt 48-17
	23	North Carolina	2-0-0	lost to North Carolina St. 7-24
24	24	Arizona State	2-0-0	lost to # 16 Nebraska 9-18
	24	Illinois	2-1-0	bye week
23		Texas A&M	1-1-0	beat La. Lafayette 34-7
25		North Carolina St.	3-0-0	beat # 23 North Carolina 24-7

UP	AP	September 30 Poll		Oct. 5 Games
1	1	Florida State	4-0-0	beat # 10 Syracuse 46-14
2	2	Miami, Fla.	3-0-0	beat Oklahoma State 40-3
3	3	Washington	3-0-0	beat Arizona 54-0
4	4	Tennessee	4-0-0	bye week
5	5	Oklahoma	3-0-0	beat Iowa State 29-8
6	6	Clemson	3-0-0	lost to Georgia 12-27
8	7	Michigan	2-1-0	beat # 9 Iowa 43-24
9	8	Notre Dame	3-1-0	beat Stanford 42-26
7	9	Iowa	3-0-0	lost to # 7 Michigan 24-43
10	10	Syracuse	4-0-0	lost to # 1 Florida State 14-46
12	11	Baylor	4-0-0	beat Houston 38-21
11	12	Penn State	4-1-0	beat Temple 24-7
14	13	Florida	3-1-0	beat LSU 16-0
13	14	Ohio State	3-0-0	beat Wisconsin 31-16
15	15	Nebraska	3-1-0	bye week
16	16	Auburn	3-1-0	lost to Southern Miss 9-10
17	17	Pittsburgh	4-0-0	beat Maryland 24-20
18	18	California	3-0-0	beat # 24 UCLA 27-24
20	19	North Carolina St.	4-0-0	beat # 21 Georgia Tech 28-21
19	20	Alabama	3-1-0	beat U.T. Chattanooga 53-7
21	21	Georgia Tech	2-2-0	lost to # 19 North Carolina St. 21-28
22	22	Illinois	2-1-0	beat Minnesota 24-3
23	23	Texas A&M	2-1-0	beat Texas Tech 37-14
24	24	UCLA	2-1-0	lost to # 18 California 24-27
	25	Colorado	2-2-0	bye week
25		Arizona State	2-1-0	beat Utah 21-15

UP	AP	October 7 Poll		Oct. 12 Games
1	1	Florida State	5-0-0	beat Virginia Tech 33-20
2	2	Miami, Fla.	4-0-0	beat # 9 Penn State 26-20
3	3	Washington	4-0-0	beat Toledo 48-0
4	4	Tennessee	4-0-0	lost to # 10 Florida 18-35
6	5	Michigan	3-1-0	beat Michigan State 45-28
5	6	Oklahoma	4-0-0	lost to Texas 7-10
7	7	Notre Dame	4-1-0	beat # 12 Pittsburgh 42-7
8	8	Baylor	5-0-0	lost to Rice 17-20
10	9	Penn State	5-1-0	lost to # 2 Miami, Fla. 20-26
11	10	Florida	4-1-0	beat # 4 Tennessee 35-18
9	11	Ohio State	4-0-0	lost to # 20 Illinois 7-10
12	12	Pittsburgh	5-0-0	lost to # 7 Notre Dame 7-42
14	13	California	4-0-0	beat Oregon 45-7
13	14	Nebraska	3-1-0	beat Oklahoma State 49-15
17	15	Syracuse	4-1-0	lost to East Carolina 20-23
15	16	North Carolina St.	5-0-0	bye week
18	17	Iowa	3-1-0	beat Wisconsin 10-6
16	18	Clemson	3-1-0	tied Virginia 20-20
19	19	Alabama	4-1-0	beat Tulane 62-0
20	20	Illinois	3-1-0	beat # 11 Ohio State 10-7
21	21	Texas A&M	3-1-0	bye week
22	22	Georgia	4-1-0	beat # 23 Mississippi 37-17
25	23	Mississippi	5-1-0	lost to # 22 Georgia 17-37
23	24	Auburn	3-2-0	beat Vanderbilt 24-22
24	25	Colorado	2-2-0	beat Missouri 55-7

UP	AP	October 14 Poll		Oct. 19 Games
1	1	Florida State	6-0-0	beat Middle Tennessee 39-10
2	2	Miami, Fla.	5-0-0	beat Long Beach St. 55-0
3	3	Washington	5-0-0	beat # 7 California 24-17
4	4	Michigan	4-1-0	beat Indiana 24-16
5	5	Notre Dame	5-1-0	beat Air Force 28-15
6	6	Florida	5-1-0	beat Northern Illinois 41-10
7	7	California	5-0-0	lost to # 3 Washington 17-24
9	8	Tennessee	4-1-0	lost to # 14 Alabama 19-24
8	9	Nebraska	4-1-0	beat Kansas State 38-31
13	10	Penn State	5-2-0	beat Rutgers 37-17
10	11	North Carolina St.	5-0-0	beat Marshall 15-14
14	12	Oklahoma	4-1-0	lost to # 22 Colorado 17-34
15	13	Illinois	4-1-0	lost to # 15 Iowa 21-24
11	14	Alabama	5-1-0	beat # 8 Tennessee 24-19
12	15	Iowa	4-1-0	beat # 13 Illinois 24-21
16	16	Baylor	5-1-0	lost to # 19 Texas A&M 12-34
18	17	Georgia	5-1-0	lost to Vanderbilt 25-27
17	18	Ohio State	4-1-0	beat Northwestern 34-3
19	19	Texas A&M	3-1-0	beat # 16 Baylor 34-12
20	20	Pittsburgh	5-1-0	lost to # 24 Syracuse 27-31
21	21	Clemson	3-1-1	bye week
22	22	Colorado	3-2-0	beat # 12 Oklahoma 34-17
	23	East Carolina	5-1-0	bye week
23	24	Syracuse	4-2-0	beat # 20 Pittsburgh 31-27
25	25	Arizona State	4-1-0	lost to Washington St. 3-17
24		Auburn	4-2-0	bye week

UP	AP	October 21 Poll		Oct. 26 Games
1	1	Florida State	7-0-0	beat LSU 27-16
2	2	Miami, Fla.	6-0-0	beat Arizona 36-9
3	3	Washington	6-0-0	beat Oregon 29-7
4	4	Michigan	5-1-0	beat Minnesota 52-6 (O25)
5	5	Notre Dame	6-1-0	beat Southern Cal 24-20
6	6	Florida	6-1-0	bye week
7	7	Alabama	6-1-0	bye week
9	8	Penn State	6-2-0	beat West Virginia 51-6
8	9	Nebraska	5-1-0	beat Missouri 63-6
11	10	California	5-1-0	beat San Jose State 41-20
10	11	Iowa	5-1-0	beat Purdue 31-21
12	12	North Carolina St.	6-0-0	lost to # 19 Clemson 19-29
14	13	Texas A&M	4-1-0	beat Houston 27-18
13	14	Ohio State	5-1-0	beat Michigan State 27-17
15	15	Tennessee	4-2-0	bye week
16	16	Colorado	4-2-0	beat Kansas State 10-0
17	17	Illinois	4-2-0	lost to Northwestern 11-17
18	18	Syracuse	5-2-0	beat Rutgers 21-7
19	19	Clemson	3-1-1	beat # 12 North Carolina St. 29-19
21	20	East Carolina	5-1-0	beat # 23 Pittsburgh 24-23
20	21	Oklahoma	4-2-0	beat Kansas 41-3
22	22	Baylor	5-2-0	beat TCU 26-9
23	23	Pittsburgh	5-2-0	lost to # 20 East Carolina 23-24
25	24	Georgia	5-2-0	beat Kentucky 49-27
	25	Arkansas	5-2-0	bye week
24		Auburn	4-2-0	lost to Mississippi State 17-24

October 28 Poll

UP	AP	Team	Record	Nov. 2 Games
1	1	Florida State	8-0-0	beat Louisville 40-15
2	2	Miami, Fla.	7-0-0	bye week
3	3	Washington	7-0-0	beat Arizona State 44-16
4	4	Michigan	6-1-0	beat Purdue 42-0
5	5	Notre Dame	7-1-0	beat Navy 38-0
6	6	Florida	6-1-0	beat Auburn 31-10
7	7	Alabama	6-1-0	beat Mississippi State 13-7
9	8	Penn State	7-2-0	bye week
8	9	Nebraska	6-1-0	tied #15 Colorado 19-19
10	10	California	6-1-0	beat Southern Cal 52-30
11	11	Iowa	6-1-0	beat #13 Ohio State 16-9
13	12	Texas A&M	5-1-0	beat Rice 38-21
12	13	Ohio State	6-1-0	lost to #11 Iowa 9-16
14	14	Tennessee	4-2-0	beat Memphis 52-24
15	15	Colorado	5-2-0	tied #9 Nebraska 19-19
16	16	Clemson	4-1-0	beat Wake Forest 28-10
18	17	East Carolina	6-1-0	beat Tulane 38-28
17	18	Syracuse	6-2-0	beat Temple 27-6
20	19	North Carolina St.	6-1-0	beat South Carolina 38-21
19	20	Oklahoma	6-1-0	beat Kansas State 28-7
21	21	Baylor	6-2-0	beat #24 Arkansas 9-5
22	22	Georgia	6-2-0	bye week
24	23	UCLA	5-2-0	beat Washington St. 44-3
23	24	Arkansas	5-2-0	lost to #21 Baylor 5-9
25	25	Fresno State	7-0-0	lost to Utah State 19-20

November 4 Poll

UP	AP	Team	Record	Nov. 9 Games
1	1	Florida State	9-0-0	beat South Carolina 38-10
3	2	Miami, Fla.	7-0-0	beat West Virginia 24-3
2	2	Washington	8-0-0	beat Southern Cal 14-3
4	4	Michigan	7-1-0	beat Northwestern 59-14
5	5	Notre Dame	8-1-0	lost to #13 Tennessee 34-35
6	6	Florida	7-1-0	beat #23 Georgia 45-13
8	7	California	7-1-0	beat Oregon State 27-14
7	8	Alabama	7-1-0	beat LSU 20-17
9	9	Penn State	7-2-0	beat Maryland 47-7
10	10	Iowa	7-1-0	beat #25 Indiana 38-21
11	11	Nebraska	6-1-1	beat Kansas 59-23
12	12	Texas A&M	6-1-0	beat TCU 44-7
13	13	Tennessee	5-2-0	beat #5 Notre Dame 35-34
15	14	Colorado	5-2-1	beat Oklahoma State 16-12
14	15	Clemson	5-1-1	beat North Carolina 21-6
16	16	East Carolina	7-1-0	beat Southern Miss 48-20
17	17	Syracuse	7-2-0	bye week
18	18	North Carolina St.	7-1-0	lost to #24 Virginia 10-42
20	19	Ohio State	6-2-0	beat Minnesota 35-6
19	20	Oklahoma	6-2-0	beat Missouri 56-16
21	21	Baylor	7-2-0	bye week
23	22	UCLA	6-2-0	lost to Stanford 10-27
22	23	Georgia	6-2-0	lost to #6 Florida 13-45
24	24	Virginia	6-2-1	beat #18 North Carolina St. 42-10
	24	Indiana	5-2-1	lost to #10 Iowa 21-38
	25	Arkansas	5-3-0	lost to Texas Tech 21-38

November 11 Poll

UP	AP	Team	Record	Nov. 16 Games
1	1	Florida State	10-0-0	lost to #2 Miami, Fla. 16-17
3	2	Miami, Fla.	8-0-0	beat #1 Florida State 17-16
2	3	Washington	9-0-0	beat Oregon State 58-6
4	4	Michigan	8-1-0	beat #25 Illinois 20-0
5	5	Florida	8-1-0	beat Kentucky 35-26
6	6	California	8-1-0	beat Arizona State 25-6
7	7	Alabama	8-1-0	beat Memphis 10-7
9	8	Penn State	8-2-0	beat #12 Notre Dame 35-13
8	9	Iowa	8-1-0	beat Northwestern 24-10
10	10	Tennessee	6-2-0	beat Mississippi 36-25
12	11	Nebraska	7-1-1	beat Iowa State 38-13
11	12	Notre Dame	8-2-0	lost to #8 Penn State 13-35
13	13	Texas A&M	7-1-0	beat Arkansas 13-3
16	14	East Carolina	8-1-0	beat Virginia Tech 24-17
14	15	Clemson	6-1-1	beat Maryland 40-7
15	16	Colorado	6-2-1	beat Kansas 30-24
17	17	Syracuse	7-2-0	beat Boston College 38-16
19	18	Oklahoma	7-2-0	beat Oklahoma State 21-6
18	19	Ohio State	7-2-0	beat Indiana 20-16
20	20	Baylor	7-2-0	lost to Texas Tech 24-31
21	21	Virginia	7-2-1	bye week
23	22	Stanford	6-3-0	beat Washington St. 49-14
24	23	Brigham Young	7-3-0	tied San Diego State 52-52
22	24	North Carolina St.	7-2-0	beat Duke 32-31
25	25	Illinois	6-3-0	lost to #4 Michigan 0-20

November 18 Poll

UP	AP	Team	Record	Nov. 23 Games
1	1	Miami, Fla.	9-0-0	beat Boston College 19-14
2	2	Washington	10-0-0	beat Washington State 56-21
3	3	Florida State	10-1-0	bye week
4	4	Michigan	9-1-0	beat #18 Ohio State 31-3
5	5	Florida	9-1-0	bye week
6	6	California	9-1-0	lost to #21 Stanford 21-38
7	7	Penn State	9-2-0	bye week
9	8	Alabama	9-1-0	bye week
8	9	Iowa	9-1-0	beat Minnesota 23-0
10	10	Tennessee	7-2-0	beat Kentucky 16-7
11	11	Nebraska	8-1-1	bye week
12	12	Texas A&M	8-1-0	beat SMU 65-6
14	13	East Carolina	9-1-0	beat Cincinnati 30-19
13	14	Clemson	7-1-1	beat South Carolina 41-24
15	15	Colorado	7-2-1	beat Iowa State 17-14
16	16	Syracuse	8-2-0	beat West Virginia 16-10
19	17	Notre Dame	8-3-0	bye week
18	18	Ohio State	8-2-0	lost to #4 Michigan 3-31
17	19	Oklahoma	8-2-0	bye week
20	20	Virginia	7-2-1	beat Virginia Tech 38-0
21	21	Stanford	7-3-0	beat #6 California 38-21
22	22	North Carolina St.	8-2-0	beat Maryland 20-17
	23	Tulsa	7-2-0	beat Ohio U. 45-13
23	24	Georgia	7-3-0	bye week
24	25	UCLA	7-3-0	beat Southern Cal 24-21
25		Brigham Young	7-3-0	beat Utah 48-17

November 25 Poll

UP	AP	Team	Record	Nov. 30 Games
2	1	Miami, Fla.	10-0-0	beat San Diego State 39-12
1	2	Washington	11-0-0	regular season complete
3	3	Florida State	10-1-0	lost to #5 Florida 9-14
4	4	Michigan	10-1-0	regular season complete
5	5	Florida	9-1-0	beat #3 Florida State 14-9
6	6	Penn State	9-2-0	beat Pittsburgh 32-20 (N28)
7	7	Iowa	10-1-0	regular season complete
8	8	Alabama	9-1-0	beat Auburn 13-6
9	9	Tennessee	8-2-0	beat Vanderbilt 45-0
10	10	Texas A&M	9-1-0	beat Texas 31-14 (N28)
11	11	Nebraska	8-1-1	beat #19 Oklahoma 19-14 (N29)
14	12	East Carolina	10-1-0	regular season complete
12	13	Clemson	8-1-1	beat Duke 33-21
13	14	California	9-2-0	regular season complete
15	15	Colorado	8-2-1	regular season complete
16	16	Syracuse	9-2-0	regular season complete
19	17	Stanford	8-3-0	regular season complete
18	18	Notre Dame	8-3-0	beat Hawaii 48-42
17	19	Oklahoma	8-2-0	lost to #11 Nebraska 14-19 (N29)
20	20	Virginia	8-2-1	regular season complete
21	21	North Carolina St.	9-2-0	regular season complete
25	22	Tulsa	8-2-0	beat SMU 31-26
23	23	UCLA	8-3-0	regular season complete
22	24	Ohio State	8-3-0	regular season complete
24	25	Georgia	7-3-0	beat Georgia Tech 18-15

December 2 Poll / January 2 Final Poll

UP	AP	December 2 Poll	Record	Bowl Bid	Date	Bowl Result	RR	UP	AP	January 2 Final Poll	Record
2	1	Miami, Fla.	11-0-0	Orange Bowl	J1	beat #11 Nebraska 22-0	1	2	1	Miami, Fla.	12-0-0
1	2	Washington	11-0-0	Rose Bowl	J1	beat #4 Michigan 34-14	2	1	2	Washington	12-0-0
4	3	Florida	10-1-0	Sugar Bowl	J1	lost to #18 Notre Dame 28-39	8	3	3	Penn State	11-2-0
3	4	Michigan	10-1-0	Rose Bowl	J1	lost to #2 Washington 14-34	4	4	4	Florida State	11-2-0
6	5	Florida State	10-2-0	Cotton Bowl	J1	beat #9 Texas A&M 10-2	3	5	5	Alabama	11-1-0
5	6	Penn State	10-2-0	Fiesta Bowl	J1	beat #10 Tennessee 42-17	7	6	6	Michigan	10-2-0
7	7	Iowa	10-1-0	Holiday Bowl	D30	tied Brigham Young 13-13	6	7	7	Florida	10-2-0
8	8	Alabama	10-1-0	Blockbuster Bowl	D28	beat #15 Colorado 30-25	14	8	8	California	10-2-0
9	9	Texas A&M	10-1-0	Cotton Bowl	J1	lost to #5 Florida State 2-10	16	9	9	East Carolina	11-1-0
10	10	Tennessee	9-2-0	Fiesta Bowl	J1	lost to #6 Penn State 17-42	12	10	10	Iowa	10-1-1
11	11	Nebraska	9-1-1	Orange Bowl	J1	lost to #1 Miami, Fla. 0-22	11	11	11	Syracuse	10-2-0
13	12	East Carolina	10-1-0	Peach Bowl	J1	beat #21 North Carolina St. 37-34	13	13	12	Texas A&M	10-2-0
12	13	Clemson	9-1-1	Citrus Bowl	J1	lost to #14 California 13-37	5	12	13	Notre Dame	10-3-0
14	14	California	9-2-0	Citrus Bowl	J1	beat #13 Clemson 37-13	9	14	14	Tennessee	9-3-0
15	15	Colorado	8-2-1	Blockbuster Bowl	D28	lost to #8 Alabama 25-30	10	15	15	Nebraska	9-2-1
16	16	Syracuse	9-2-0	Hall of Fame Bowl	J1	beat #25 Ohio State 24-17	22	16	16	Oklahoma	9-3-0
17	17	Stanford	8-3-0	Aloha Bowl	D25	lost to Georgia Tech 17-18	25	20	17	Georgia	9-3-0
18	18	Notre Dame	9-3-0	Sugar Bowl	J1	beat #3 Florida 39-28	15	17	18	Clemson	9-2-1
19	19	Virginia	8-2-1	Gator Bowl	D29	lost to #20 Oklahoma 14-48	28	19	19	UCLA	9-3-0
20	20	Oklahoma	8-3-0	Gator Bowl	D29	beat #19 Virginia 48-14	17	18	20	Colorado	8-3-1
21	21	North Carolina St.	9-2-0	Peach Bowl	J1	lost to #12 East Carolina 34-37	30	21	21	Tulsa	10-2-0
23	22	UCLA	8-3-0	Sun Bowl	D31	beat Illinois 6-3	19	22	22	Stanford	8-4-0
25	23	Tulsa	9-2-0	Freedom Bowl	D30	beat San Diego State 28-17	20	24	23	Brigham Young	8-3-2
24	24	Georgia	8-3-0	Independence Bowl	D29	beat Arkansas 24-15	26	23	24	North Carolina St.	9-3-0
22	25	Ohio State	8-3-0	Hall of Fame Bowl	J1	lost to #16 Syracuse 17-24	32		25	Air Force	10-3-0
								27	25	Ohio State	8-4-0

1991

CONSENSUS ALL-AMERICANS

Offense

POS	Offense	HT	WT	School	AP	CF	FC	FW	PI
QB	Ty Detmer	6-0	175	Brigham Young	•		•	•	•
RB	Vaughn Dunbar	6-0	207	Indiana	•	•	•	•	•
RB	Trevor Cobb	5-9	180	Rice			•	•	
RB	Russell White	6-0	210	California		•		•	•
WR	Desmond Howard	5-9	176	Michigan	•	•	•	•	•
WR	Mario Bailey	5-9	167	Washington	•			•	
TE	Kelly Blackwell	6-2	242	TCU	•	•	•	•	
OL	Greg Skrepenak	6-8	322	Michigan	•	•	•	•	•
OL	Bob Whitfield	6-7	300	Stanford	•	•	•		
OL	Jeb Flesch	6-3	266	Clemson	•	•		•	
OL	Jerry Ostroski	6-4	305	Tulsa	•		•		
OL	Mirko Jurkovic	6-4	289	Notre Dame		•		•	
C	Jay Leeuwenburg	6-3	265	Colorado	•	•	•	•	•
PK	Carlos Huerta	5-9	186	Miami, Fla.	•	•		•	

Others receiving first-team honors

POS		School	
QB	Casey Weldon	Florida State	•
RB	Amp Lee	Florida State	•
RB	Marshall Faulk	San Diego State	•
WR	Carl Pickens	Tennessee	•
TE	Derek Brown	Notre Dame	•
TE	Mark Chmura	Boston College	•
OL	Eugene Chung	Virginia Tech	•
OL	Leon Searcy	Miami, Fla	•
OL	Troy Auzenne	California	•
OL	Ray Roberts	Virginia	•
OL	Tim Simpson	Illinois	•
K	Jason Hanson	Washington State	•
KR	Qadry Ismail	Syracuse	•

Defense

POS	Defense	HT	WT	School	AP	CF	FC	FW	PI
DL	Steve Emtman	6-4	280	Washington	•	•	•	•	•
DL	Santana Dotson	6-5	264	Baylor	•	•	•	•	
DL	Brad Culpepper	6-2	263	Florida	•	•	•	•	
DL	Leroy Smith	6-2	214	Iowa	•		•		
LB	Robert Jones	6-3	234	East Carolina	•	•	•	•	
LB	Marvin Jones	6-2	220	Florida State	•	•	•	•	•
LB	Levan Kirkland	6-2	245	Clemson	•	•		•	
DB	Terrell Buckley	5-10	175	Florida State	•	•	•	•	•
DB	Dale Carter	6-2	182	Tennessee	•	•	•	•	•
DB	Kevin Smith	6-0	180	Texas A&M	•	•	•	•	
DB	Darryl Williams	6-2	190	Miami, Fla.	•	•	•	•	
P	Mark Bounds	5-11	185	Texas Tech	•	•	•		

Others receiving first-team honors

POS		School	
DL	Joel Steed	Colorado	•
DL	Shane Dronett	Texas	•
DL	Rob Bodine	Clemson	•
DL	Robert Stewart	Alabama	•
LB	Marco Coleman	Georgia Tech	•
LB	David Hoffman	Washington	•
LB	Steve Tovar	Ohio State	•
LB	Joe Bowden	Oklahoma	•
LB	Darrin Smith	Miami, Fla	•
LB	Erick Anderson	Michigan	•
DB	Darren Perry	Penn State	•
DB	Troy Vincent	Wisconsin	•
DB	Matt Darby	UCLA	•
PR	Kevin Williams	Miami, Fla	•

FC named Kirkland as a DL

HEISMAN TROPHY VOTING

	PLAYER	POS	SCHOOL	1ST	2ND	3RD	TOTAL
1	Desmond Howard	WR	Michigan	640	68	21	2077
2	Casey Weldon	QB	Florida State	19	175	96	503
3	Ty Detmer	QB	Brigham Young	19	129	130	445
4	Steve Emtman	DT	Washington	29	100	70	357
5	Shane Matthews	QB	Florida	11	72	69	246
6	Vaughn Dunbar	TB	Indiana	6	51	53	173
7	Jeff Blake	QB	East Carolina	7	29	35	114
8	Terrell Buckley	CB	Florida State	1	24	51	102
9	Marshall Faulk	RB	San Diego State	0	10	32	52
10	Bucky Richardson	QB	Texas A&M	6	9	9	45

AWARD WINNERS

PLAYER	POS/SCHOOL	AWARD
Desmond Howard	WR Michigan	Maxwell
Steve Emtman	DT Washington	Outland
Desmond Howard	WR Michigan	Camp
Steve Emtman	DT Washington	Lombardi

PLAYER	POS/SCHOOL	AWARD
Ty Detmer	QB Brigham Young	O'Brien
Erick Anderson	LB Michigan	Butkus
Terrell Buckley	DB Florida State	Thorpe
Casey Weldon	QB Florida State	Unitas
Trevor Cobb	RB Rice	Walker

BOWL GAMES

DATE	GAME	SCORE
D14	California	Bowling Green 28, Fresno State 21
D25	Aloha	Georgia Tech 18, Stanford 17
D28	Blockbuster	Alabama 30, Colorado 25
D29	Liberty	Air Force 38, Mississippi State 15
D29	Independence	Georgia 24, Arkansas 15
D29	Gator	Oklahoma 48, Virginia 14
D30	Holiday	Brigham Young 13, Iowa 13

CONFERENCE STANDINGS

ACC

	Conf. W L T			Overall W L T		
Clemson	6	0	1	9	2	1
North Carolina St.	5	2	0	9	3	0
Georgia Tech	5	2	0	8	5	0
Virginia	4	2	1	8	3	1
North Carolina	3	4	0	7	4	0
Maryland	2	5	0	2	9	0
Duke	1	6	0	4	6	1
Wake Forest	1	6	0	3	8	0

Big 10

	Conf. W L T			Overall W L T		
Michigan	8	0	0	10	2	0
Iowa	7	1	0	10	1	1
Ohio State	5	3	0	8	4	0
Indiana	5	3	0	7	4	1
Illinois	4	4	0	6	6	0
Purdue	3	5	0	4	7	0
Michigan State	3	5	0	3	8	0
Wisconsin	2	6	0	5	6	0
Northwestern	2	6	0	3	8	0
Minnesota	1	7	0	2	9	0

Big 8

	Conf. W L T			Overall W L T		
Nebraska	6	0	1	9	2	1
Colorado	6	0	1	8	3	1
Oklahoma	5	2	0	9	3	0
Kansas State	4	3	0	7	4	0
Kansas	3	4	0	6	5	0
Iowa State	1	5	1	3	7	1
Missouri	1	6	0	3	7	1
Oklahoma State	0	6	1	0	10	1

Big East

	Conf. W L T			Overall W L T		
Syracuse	5	0	0	10	2	0
Miami, Fla.	2	0	0	12	0	0
Virginia Tech	1	0	0	5	6	0
Pittsburgh	3	2	0	6	5	0
West Virginia	3	4	0	6	5	0
Rutgers	2	3	0	6	5	0
Boston College	2	4	0	4	7	0
Temple	0	5	0	2	9	0

Big West

	Conf. W L T			Overall W L T		
Fresno State	6	1	0	10	2	0
San Jose State	6	1	0	6	4	1
Utah State	5	2	0	5	6	0
Pacific	4	3	0	5	7	0
Nevada-Las Vegas	2	5	0	4	7	0
New Mexico State	2	5	0	2	9	0
Long Beach State	2	5	0	2	9	0
Cal-St. Fullerton	1	6	0	2	9	0

Ivy

	Conf. W L T			Overall W L T		
Dartmouth	6	0	1	7	2	1
Princeton	5	2	0	8	2	0
Harvard	4	2	1	4	5	1
Yale	4	3	0	6	4	0
Cornell	4	3	0	5	5	0
Pennsylvania	2	5	0	1	9	0
Columbia	1	6	0	1	9	0
Brown	1	6	0	1	9	0

MAC

	Conf. W L T			Overall W L T		
Bowling Green	8	0	0	11	1	0
Central Michigan	3	1	4	6	1	4
Miami, Ohio	4	3	1	6	4	1
Toledo	4	3	1	5	5	1
Ball State	4	4	0	6	5	0
Western Michigan	4	4	0	6	5	0
Eastern Michigan	3	4	1	3	7	1
Ohio U	1	6	1	2	8	1
Kent State	1	7	0	1	10	0

Pac 10

	Conf. W L T			Overall W L T		
Washington	8	0	0	12	0	0
California	6	2	0	10	2	0
UCLA	6	2	0	9	3	0
Stanford	6	2	0	8	4	0
Arizona State	4	4	0	6	5	0
Washington State	3	5	0	4	7	0
Arizona	3	5	0	4	7	0
Southern Cal	2	6	0	3	8	0
Oregon	1	7	0	3	8	0
Oregon State	1	7	0	1	10	0

SEC

	Conf. W L T			Overall W L T		
Florida	7	0	0	10	2	0
Alabama	6	1	0	11	1	0
Tennessee	5	2	0	9	3	0
Georgia	4	3	0	9	3	0
Mississippi State	4	3	0	7	5	0
LSU	3	4	0	5	6	0
Vanderbilt	3	4	0	5	6	0
Auburn	2	5	0	5	6	0
Mississippi	1	6	0	5	6	0
Kentucky	0	7	0	3	8	0

SWC

	Conf. W L T			Overall W L T		
Texas A&M	8	0	0	10	2	0
Baylor	5	3	0	8	4	0
Texas Tech	5	3	0	6	5	0
Arkansas	5	3	0	6	6	0
TCU	4	4	0	7	4	0
Texas	4	4	0	5	6	0
Houston	3	5	0	4	7	0
Rice	2	6	0	4	7	0
SMU	0	8	0	1	10	0

WAC

	Conf. W L T			Overall W L T		
Brigham Young	7	0	1	8	3	2
San Diego State	6	1	1	8	4	1
Air Force	6	2	0	10	3	0
Utah	4	4	0	7	5	0
Hawaii	3	5	0	4	7	1
Wyoming	2	5	1	4	6	1
Texas-El Paso	2	5	1	4	7	1
Colorado State	2	6	0	3	8	0
New Mexico	2	6	0	3	9	0

Independents

	Overall W L T		
East Carolina	11	1	0
Florida State	11	2	0
Penn State	11	2	0
Tulsa	10	2	0
Louisiana Tech	8	1	2
Notre Dame	10	3	0
Akron	5	6	0
Memphis	5	6	0
Army	4	7	0
Southern Miss	4	7	0
Cincinnati	4	7	0
South Carolina	3	6	2
La. Lafayette	2	8	1
Louisville	2	9	0
Northern Illinois	2	9	0
Arkansas State	1	10	0
Tulane	1	10	0
Navy	1	10	0

DATE	GAME	SCORE
D30	Freedom	Tulsa 28, San Diego State 17
D31	Copper	Indiana 24, Baylor 0
D31	Sun	UCLA 6, Illinois 3
J1	Citrus	California 37, Clemson 13
J1	Peach	East Carolina 37, North Carolina St. 34
J1	Cotton	Florida State 10, Texas A&M 2
J1	Orange	Miami, Fla. 22, Nebraska 0
J1	Fiesta	Penn State 42, Tennessee 17
J1	Hall of Fame	Syracuse 24, Ohio State 17
J1	Rose	Washington 34, Michigan 14
J1	Sugar	Notre Dame 39, Florida 28

1991 ANNUAL REVIEW 1379

1991 NCAA Major College Statistical Leaders

Individual Leaders

PASSING	CL	G	ATT	COM	PCT	INT	I%	YDS	YPA	TD	TD%	RATING
1 Elvis Grbac, Michigan	JR	11	228	152	66.7	5	2.2	1955	8.6	24	10.5	169.0
2 Ty Detmer, Brigham Young	SR	12	403	249	61.8	12	3.0	4031	10.0	35	8.7	168.5
3 Jeff Garcia, San Jose State	SO	9	160	99	61.9	5	3.1	1519	9.5	12	7.5	160.1
4 Matt Blundin, Virginia	SR	9	224	135	60.3	0	0.0	1902	8.5	19	8.5	159.6
5 Troy Kopp, Pacific	JR	12	449	275	61.3	16	3.6	3767	8.4	37	8.2	151.8
6 Steve Stenstrom, Stanford	SO	9	197	119	60.4	7	3.6	1683	8.5	15	7.6	150.2
7 Tony Sacca, Penn State	SR	12	292	169	57.9	5	1.7	2488	8.5	21	7.2	149.8
8 Rick Mirer, Notre Dame	JR	12	234	132	56.4	10	4.3	2116	9.0	18	7.7	149.2
9 Shane Matthews, Florida	JR	11	361	218	60.4	18	5.0	3130	8.7	28	7.8	148.8
10 Keithen McCant, Nebraska	SR	11	168	97	57.7	8	4.8	1454	8.7	13	7.7	146.5

ALL-PURPOSE	CL	G	RUSH	REC	PR	KR	YDS	YPG
1 Ryan Benjamin, Pacific	JR	12	1581	612	4	798	2995	249.6
2 Vaughn Dunbar, Indiana	SR	11	1699	252	0	262	2213	201.2
3 Marshall Faulk, San Diego State	FR	9	1429	201	0	33	1663	184.8
4 Trevor Cobb, Rice	JR	11	1692	136	0	16	1844	167.6
5 Corey Harris, Vanderbilt	SR	11	1103	283	0	445	1831	166.5
6 Tony Smith, Southern Miss	SR	9	998	97	115	271	1481	164.6
7 Desmond Howard, Michigan	JR	11	165	950	261	373	1749	159.0
7 Chris Hughley, Tulsa	JR	10	1326	74	0	190	1590	159.0
9 Russell White, California	JR	11	1177	139	0	408	1724	156.7
10 Dion Johnson, East Carolina	SR	11	255	743	162	513	1673	152.1

RUSHING/Yards Per Game	CL	G	ATT	YDS	TD	AVG	YPG
1 Marshall Faulk, San Diego State	FR	9	201	1429	21	7.1	158.8
2 Vaughn Dunbar, Indiana	SR	11	336	1699	11	5.1	154.5
3 Trevor Cobb, Rice	JR	11	360	1692	14	4.7	153.8
4 Jason Davis, Louisiana Tech	JR	10	244	1351	14	5.5	135.1
5 Chris Hughley, Tulsa	JR	10	267	1326	8	5.0	132.6
6 Ryan Benjamin, Pacific	JR	12	226	1581	13	7.0	131.8
7 Tony Sands, Kansas	SR	11	273	1442	9	5.3	131.1
8 Billy Smith, Central Michigan	SR	11	374	1440	6	3.9	130.9
9 Derek Brown, Nebraska	SO	11	230	1313	14	5.7	119.4
10 Mike Gaddis, Oklahoma	SR	11	221	1240	14	5.6	112.7

RUSHING/Yards Per Carry	CL	G	ATT	YDS	YPC
1 Ron Rivers, Fresno State	SO	10	134	984	7.3
2 Marshall Faulk, San Diego State	FR	9	201	1429	7.1
3 Ryan Benjamin, Pacific	JR	12	226	1581	7.0
4 Kevin Williams, UCLA	JR	10	168	1089	6.5
5 Derek Brown, Nebraska	SO	11	230	1313	5.7
6 Mike Gaddis, Oklahoma	SR	11	221	1240	5.6
7 Jason Davis, Louisiana Tech	JR	10	244	1351	5.5
8 Brian Copeland, Colorado State	SR	10	190	1028	5.4
9 Lamont Warren, Colorado	FR	9	157	830	5.3
10 Tony Sands, Kansas	SR	11	273	1442	5.3

*-Based on top 30 rushers

RECEIVING	CL	G	REC	YDS	TD	RPG	YPR	YPG
1 Aaron Turner, Pacific	JR	11	92	1604	18	8.4	17.4	145.8
2 Marcus Grant, Houston	JR	11	78	1262	10	7.1	16.2	114.7
3 Greg Primus, Colorado State	JR	11	67	1081	8	6.1	16.1	98.3
3 Ryan Yarborough, Wyoming	SO	11	53	1081	13	4.8	20.4	98.3
5 Carl Winston, New Mexico	SO	12	76	1177	7	6.3	15.5	98.1
6 Mario Bailey, Washington	SR	11	62	1037	17	5.6	16.7	94.3
7 Sean LaChapelle, UCLA	JR	11	68	987	11	6.2	14.5	89.7
8 Wilbert Ursin, Tulane	SO	11	70	969	9	6.4	13.8	88.1
9 Fred Gilbert, Houston	JR	11	106	957	7	9.6	9.0	87.0
10 Desmond Howard, Michigan	JR	11	61	950	19	5.5	15.6	86.4

PUNTING	CL	PUNT	YDS	AVG
1 Mark Bounds, Texas Tech	SR	53	2481	46.8
2 Jason Christ, Air Force	SR	50	2283	45.7
3 Pete Raether, Arkansas	SO	65	2836	43.6
4 Shayne Edge, Florida	FR	46	1991	43.3
5 Charles Langston, Houston	SR	52	2246	43.2
6 Eric Bruun, Purdue	SR	59	2548	43.2
7 Garret Henson, New Mexico State	SR	54	2326	43.1
8 Rusty Carlsen, Utah State	SR	56	2410	43.0
9 Ray Magana, Long Beach State	SR	57	2446	42.9
10 David Lawrence, Vanderbilt	JR	54	2308	42.7

PUNT RETURNS	CL	PR	YDS	TD	AVG
1 Bo Campbell, Virginia Tech	JR	15	273	0	18.2
2 Desmond Howard, Michigan	JR	15	261	1	17.4
3 David Palmer, Alabama	FR	24	386	3	16.1
4 Kevin Williams, Miami, Fla.	SO	36	560	3	15.6
5 James McMillion, Iowa State	SO	17	251	0	14.8
6 Kevin Smith, Texas A&M	SR	19	275	2	14.5
7 Michael James, Arkansas	SR	19	272	1	14.3
8 Darnell Stephens, Clemson	FR	25	352	1	14.1
9 Brad Clark, Brigham Young	JR	20	269	1	13.5
10 Marshall Roberts, Rutgers	SR	34	454	0	13.4

KICKOFF RETURNS	CL	KR	YDS	TD	AVG
1 Fred Montgomery, New Mexico State	JR	25	734	1	29.4
2 Ronald Rice, Eastern Michigan	FR	11	319	0	29.0
3 Jeff Sydner, Hawaii	JR	18	495	0	27.5
4 Courtney Hawkins, Michigan State	SR	20	548	0	27.4
5 Eric Blount, North Carolina	SR	25	679	1	27.2
6 Andre Hastings, Georgia	SO	14	380	0	27.1
7 Floyd Foreman, Utah State	SR	27	730	0	27.0
8 Gary Melton, Rutgers	SR	17	435	1	25.6
9 Charles Levy, Arizona	FR	27	682	0	25.3
10 Donovan Moore, Oregon	JR	13	327	0	25.2

SCORING	CL	TDS	XP	FG	PTS	PTPG
1 Marshall Faulk, San Diego State	FR	23	2	0	140	15.6
2 Desmond Howard, Michigan	JR	23	0	0	138	12.6
3 Tommy Vardell, Stanford	SR	20	0	0	120	10.9
4 Jerome Bettis, Notre Dame	SO	20	0	0	120	10.0
5 Aaron Turner, Pacific	JR	18	0	0	108	9.8
6 Mario Bailey, Washington	SR	17	0	0	102	9.3
7 Russell White, California	JR	16	2	0	98	8.9
7 Doug Brien, California	SO	0	41	19	98	8.9
9 Derek Mahoney, Fresno State	SO	0	63	11	96	8.7
10 Jason Davis, Louisiana Tech	JR	14	0	0	84	8.4
10 Calvin Jones, Nebraska	FR	14	0	0	84	8.4

FIELD GOALS	CL	FGA	FGM	PCT	FGG
1 Doug Brien, California	SO	28	19	0.68	1.73
2 Dan Eichloff, Kansas	SO	24	18	0.75	1.64
3 Jason Elam, Hawaii	JR	24	19	0.79	1.58
4 Carlos Huerta, Miami, Fla.	SR	21	17	0.81	1.55
4 John Biskup, Syracuse	JR	22	17	0.77	1.55
4 Nelson Welch, Clemson	FR	26	17	0.65	1.55
4 Lin Elliott, Texas Tech	SR	26	17	0.65	1.55
8 Eric Lange, Tulsa	JR	18	16	0.89	1.45
9 Joe Wood, Air Force	SR	22	17	0.77	1.42
9 Craig Fayak, Penn State	SO	26	17	0.65	1.42

INTERCEPTIONS	CL	INT	YDS	TD	INT/GM
1 Terrell Buckley, Florida State	JR	12	238	2	1.00
2 Carlton Gray, UCLA	JR	10	119	1	0.91
3 Willie Clay, Georgia Tech	SR	9	66	1	0.75
4 Ray Buchanan, Louisville	JR	8	89	0	0.73
4 Tracy Saul, Texas Tech	JR	8	79	0	0.73
6 Richard Palmer, Eastern Michigan	SO	7	219	1	0.64
6 Ron Carpenter, Miami, Ohio	JR	7	197	1	0.64
6 Ron Edwards, Utah State	SR	7	146	2	0.64
6 Walter Bailey, Washington	JR	7	114	2	0.64
6 Willie Lindsey, Northwestern	JR	7	52	0	0.64

Team Leaders

RUSHING OFFENSE	G	ATT	YDS	AVG	TD	YPG
1 Nebraska	11	595	3885	6.5	45	353.2
2 Air Force	12	760	4057	5.3	34	338.1
3 Fresno State	11	613	3303	5.4	42	300.3
4 Army	11	701	3222	4.6	23	292.9
5 Hawaii	12	626	3416	5.5	32	284.7
6 Notre Dame	12	584	3229	5.5	37	269.1
7 Texas A&M	11	633	2850	4.5	34	259.1
8 Clemson	11	614	2813	4.6	28	255.7
9 Alabama	11	557	2772	5.0	24	252.0
10 Oklahoma	11	606	2752	4.5	33	250.2

PASSING OFFENSE	G	ATT	COM	INT	PCT	YDS	YPA	TD	I%	YPC	YPG
1 Houston	11	591	330	24	55.8	4101	6.9	33	4.1	12.4	372.8
2 Brigham Young	12	420	257	14	61.2	4125	9.8	35	3.3	16.1	343.8
3 Pacific	12	500	300	18	60.0	4114	8.2	42	3.6	13.7	342.8
4 Florida	11	390	235	19	60.3	3393	8.7	32	4.9	14.4	308.5
5 East Carolina	11	414	229	10	55.3	3379	8.2	30	2.4	14.8	307.2
6 San Jose State	11	374	211	14	56.4	3338	8.9	21	3.7	15.8	303.5
7 New Mexico	12	518	246	24	47.5	3584	6.9	20	4.6	14.6	298.7
8 Wyoming	11	400	227	10	56.7	3264	8.2	24	2.5	14.4	296.7
9 Miami, Fla.	11	396	223	11	56.3	3244	8.2	20	2.8	14.5	294.9
10 Washington State	11	395	218	16	55.2	3028	7.7	19	4.1	13.9	275.3

TOTAL OFFENSE	G	P	YDS	AVG	TD	YPG
1 Fresno State	11	922	5961	6.5	62	541.9
2 Pacific	12	871	6135	7.0	61	511.3
3 Nebraska	11	800	5571	7.0	60	506.5
4 San Jose State	11	813	5279	6.5	47	479.9
5 Brigham Young	12	837	5754	6.9	54	479.5
6 San Diego State	12	955	5739	6.0	52	478.3
7 Washington	11	861	5191	6.0	60	471.9
8 Tennessee	11	878	5145	5.9	36	467.7
9 Florida	11	787	5028	6.4	45	457.1
10 UCLA	11	831	5019	6.0	39	456.3

RUSHING DEFENSE	G	ATT	YDS	AVG	TD	YPG
1 Clemson	11	360	587	1.6	5	53.4
2 Washington	11	390	738	1.9	6	67.1
3 Florida State	12	398	994	2.5	9	82.8
4 Texas A&M	11	393	946	2.4	13	86.0
5 Penn State	12	408	1120	2.7	9	93.3
6 Florida	11	399	1103	2.8	7	100.3
7 Louisiana Tech	11	386	1105	2.9	8	100.5
8 UCLA	11	403	1110	2.8	13	100.9
9 Oklahoma	11	403	1140	2.8	5	103.6
10 Michigan	11	397	1142	2.9	7	103.8

PASSING DEFENSE	G	ATT	COM	PCT	INT	I%	YDS	YPA	TD	TD%	RAT
1 Texas	11	304	115	37.8	15	4.9	1513	5.0	7	2.3	77.4
2 Texas A&M	11	290	129	44.5	14	4.8	1500	5.2	6	2.1	85.1
3 Washington	11	340	156	45.9	21	6.2	1870	5.5	6	1.8	85.6
4 Miami, Fla.	11	346	175	50.6	19	5.5	1724	5.0	7	2.0	88.1
5 Penn State	12	397	172	43.3	26	6.6	2246	5.7	13	3.3	88.6
6 Virginia	11	267	137	51.3	12	4.5	1512	5.7	1	0.4	91.1
7 Arizona State	11	290	143	49.3	23	7.9	1676	5.8	9	3.1	92.2
8 Tulsa	11	275	129	46.9	18	6.6	1586	5.8	10	3.6	94.3
9 Georgia Tech	12	369	178	48.2	18	4.9	1989	5.4	12	3.3	94.5
10 Oklahoma	11	328	161	49.1	25	7.6	2004	6.1	10	3.1	95.2

TOTAL DEFENSE	G	P	YDS	AVG	TD	YPG
1 Texas A&M	11	683	2446	3.6	19	222.4
2 Washington	11	730	2608	3.6	12	237.1
3 Texas	11	769	2848	3.7	15	258.9
4 Clemson	11	718	2895	4.0	17	263.2
5 Miami, Ohio	11	747	2980	4.0	15	270.9
6 Iowa	11	712	2987	4.2	20	271.5
7 Central Michigan	11	741	3001	4.0	16	272.8
8 Georgia Tech	12	831	3333	4.0	22	277.8
9 Penn State	12	805	3366	4.2	22	280.5
10 Florida State	12	776	3375	4.3	22	281.3

SCORING OFFENSE	G	PTS	AVG
1 Fresno State	11	486	44.2
2 Washington	11	461	41.9
3 Nebraska	11	454	41.3
4 California	11	406	36.9
4 Michigan	11	406	36.9
6 Florida State	12	439	36.6
7 Texas A&M	11	402	36.5
8 Pacific	12	435	36.3
9 Penn State	12	432	36.0
10 Notre Dame	12	426	35.5

SCORING DEFENSE	G	PTS	AVG
1 Miami, Fla.	11	100	9.1
2 Washington	11	101	9.2
3 Alabama	11	118	10.7
4 Virginia	11	119	10.8
5 Miami, Ohio	11	140	12.7
6 Oklahoma	11	143	13.0
7 Texas A&M	11	144	13.1
8 Texas	11	145	13.2
9 Bowling Green	11	147	13.4
10 Clemson	11	148	13.5

ANNUAL REVIEW

1992 Poll Progression

AP	Pre-Season 1992		Aug. 29 Games
1	Miami, Fla.	0-0-0	
2	Washington	0-0-0	
3	Notre Dame	0-0-0	
4	Florida	0-0-0	
5	Florida State	0-0-0	
6	Michigan	0-0-0	
7	Texas A&M	0-0-0	beat # 17 Stanford 10-7
8	Penn State	0-0-0	
9	Alabama	0-0-0	
10	Syracuse	0-0-0	
11	Nebraska	0-0-0	
12	Colorado	0-0-0	
13	Clemson	0-0-0	
14	Georgia	0-0-0	
15	Oklahoma	0-0-0	
16	Iowa	0-0-0	lost to North Carolina St. 14-24
17	Stanford	0-0-0	lost to # 7 Texas A&M 7-10
18	UCLA	0-0-0	
19	Ohio State	0-0-0	
20	California	0-0-0	
21	Tennessee	0-0-0	
22	Mississippi State	0-0-0	
23	Georgia Tech	0-0-0	
24	Brigham Young	0-0-0	
25	Texas	0-0-0	

AP	August 30 Poll		Sept. 5 Games
1	Miami, Fla.	0-0-0	beat # 23 Iowa 24-7
2	Washington	0-0-0	beat Arizona State 31-7
3	Notre Dame	0-0-0	beat Northwestern 42-7
4	Florida State	0-0-0	beat Duke 48-21
5	Michigan	0-0-0	bye week
6	Florida	0-0-0	bye week
7	Texas A&M	1-0-0	beat LSU 31-22
8	Penn State	0-0-0	beat Cincinnati 24-20
9	Alabama	0-0-0	beat Vanderbilt 25-8
10	Syracuse	0-0-0	beat East Carolina 42-21
11	Nebraska	0-0-0	beat Utah 49-22
12	Colorado	0-0-0	beat Colorado State 37-17
13	Clemson	0-0-0	beat Ball State 24-10
14	Georgia	0-0-0	beat South Carolina 28-6
15	Oklahoma	0-0-0	beat Texas Tech 34-9 (S3)
16	UCLA	0-0-0	bye week
17	Ohio State	0-0-0	beat Louisville 20-19
18	North Carolina St.	1-0-0	beat Appalachian St. 35-10
19	California	0-0-0	beat San Jose State 46-16
20	Stanford	0-1-0	bye week
21	Mississippi State	0-0-0	beat Texas 28-10
22	Tennessee	0-0-0	beat La. Lafayette 38-3
23	Iowa	0-1-0	lost to # 1 Miami, Fla. 7-24
24	Georgia Tech	0-0-0	bye week
25	Virginia	0-0-0	beat Maryland 28-15

UP	AP	September 7 Poll		Sept. 12 Games
1	1	Miami, Fla.	1-0-0	bye week
2	2	Washington	1-0-0	beat Wisconsin 27-10
3	3	Notre Dame	1-0-0	tied # 6 Michigan 17-17
6	4	Florida	0-0-0	beat Kentucky 35-19
4	5	Florida State	1-0-0	beat # 15 Clemson 24-20
5	6	Michigan	0-0-0	tied # 3 Notre Dame 17-17
7	7	Texas A&M	2-0-0	beat Tulsa 19-9
8	8	Alabama	1-0-0	beat Southern Miss 17-10
9	9	Syracuse	1-0-0	beat Texas 31-21
10	10	Penn State	1-0-0	beat Temple 49-8
11	11	Nebraska	1-0-0	beat Middle Tennessee 48-7
13	12	Colorado	1-0-0	beat Baylor 57-38
12	13	Oklahoma	1-0-0	beat Arkansas State 61-0
15	14	Georgia	1-0-0	lost to Tennessee 31-34
14	15	Clemson	1-0-0	lost to # 5 Florida State 20-24
18	16	UCLA	0-0-0	beat Fullerton St. 37-14
20	17	California	1-0-0	lost to Purdue 14-41
19	18	Mississippi State	1-0-0	lost to LSU 3-24
16	19	North Carolina St.	2-0-0	beat Maryland 14-10
17	20	Tennessee	1-0-0	beat Georgia 34-21
25	21	Stanford	0-1-0	beat Oregon 21-7
21	22	Ohio State	1-0-0	beat Bowling Green 17-6
23	23	Virginia	1-0-0	beat Navy 53-0
24	24	Georgia Tech	0-0-0	beat Western Carolina 37-19
22	25	Brigham Young	1-0-0	lost to San Diego State 38-45 (S10)

UP	AP	September 14 Poll		Sept. 19 Games
1	1	Miami, Fla.	1-0-0	beat Florida A&M 38-0
2	2	Washington	2-0-0	beat # 12 Nebraska 29-14
3	3	Florida State	2-0-0	beat # 16 North Carolina St. 34-13
4	4	Florida	1-0-0	lost to # 14 Tennessee 14-31
5	5	Texas A&M	3-0-0	beat Missouri 26-13
6	6	Michigan	0-0-1	beat Oklahoma State 35-3
7	7	Notre Dame	1-0-1	beat Michigan State 52-31
10	8	Syracuse	2-0-0	lost to # 21 Ohio State 12-35
9	9	Alabama	2-0-0	beat Arkansas 38-11
8	10	Penn State	2-0-0	beat Eastern Michigan 52-7
13	11	Colorado	2-0-0	beat Minnesota 21-20
11	12	Nebraska	2-0-0	lost to # 2 Washington 14-29
12	13	Oklahoma	2-0-0	lost to Southern Cal 10-20
14	14	Tennessee	2-0-0	beat # 4 Florida 31-14
16	15	UCLA	1-0-0	beat Brigham Young 17-10
15	16	North Carolina St.	3-0-0	lost to # 3 Florida State 13-34
17	17	Clemson	1-1-0	bye week
22	18	Stanford	1-1-0	beat Northwestern 35-24
23	19	Georgia	1-1-0	beat Fullerton St. 56-0
19	20	Virginia	2-0-0	beat # 22 Georgia Tech 55-24
18	21	Ohio State	2-0-0	beat # 8 Syracuse 35-12
20	22	Georgia Tech	1-0-0	lost to # 20 Virginia 24-55
21	23	San Diego State	1-0-1	bye week
	24	Mississippi State	1-1-0	beat Memphis 20-16
24	25	Mississippi	2-0-0	lost to Vanderbilt 9-31
25		Illinois	2-0-0	lost to Houston 13-31

UP	AP	September 21 Poll		Sept. 26 Games
1	1	Miami, Fla.	2-0-0	beat Arizona 8-7
2	2	Washington	3-0-0	bye week
3	3	Florida State	3-0-0	beat Wake Forest 35-7
5	4	Michigan	1-0-1	beat Houston 61-7
4	5	Texas A&M	4-0-0	bye week
6	6	Notre Dame	2-0-1	beat Purdue 48-0
8	7	Alabama	3-0-0	beat Louisiana Tech 13-0
9	8	Tennessee	3-0-0	beat Cincinnati 40-0
7	9	Penn State	3-0-0	beat Maryland 49-13
10	10	Colorado	3-0-0	beat Iowa 28-12
12	11	UCLA	2-0-0	beat San Diego State 35-7
11	12	Ohio State	3-0-0	bye week
13	13	Florida	1-1-0	bye week
14	14	Virginia	3-0-0	beat Duke 55-28
15	15	Nebraska	2-1-0	beat Arizona State 45-24
16	16	Clemson	1-1-0	lost to Georgia Tech 16-20
17	17	Syracuse	2-1-0	bye week
18	18	Georgia	2-1-0	beat Mississippi 37-11
19	19	Stanford	2-1-0	beat San Jose State 37-13
20	20	Oklahoma	2-1-0	bye week
21	21	San Diego State	1-0-1	lost to UCLA 7-35
22	22	Southern Cal	1-0-1	bye week
23	23	North Carolina St.	3-1-0	beat North Carolina 27-20
24	24	Kansas	3-0-0	lost to California 23-27 (S24)
	25	Boston College	3-0-0	beat Michigan State 14-0
25		North Carolina	3-0-0	lost to # 23 North Carolina St. 20-27

UP	AP	September 28 Poll		Oct. 3 Games
1	1	Washington	3-0-0	beat # 20 Southern Cal 17-10
2	2	Miami, Fla.	3-0-0	beat # 3 Florida State 19-16
3	3	Florida State	4-0-0	lost to # 2 Miami, Fla. 16-19
4	4	Michigan	2-0-1	beat Iowa 52-28
5	5	Texas A&M	4-0-0	beat Texas Tech 19-17
7	6	Notre Dame	3-0-1	lost to # 18 Stanford 16-33
8	7	Tennessee	4-0-0	beat LSU 20-0
6	8	Penn State	4-0-0	beat Rutgers 38-24
9	9	Alabama	4-0-0	beat South Carolina 48-7
10	10	Colorado	4-0-0	bye week
11	11	UCLA	3-0-0	lost to Arizona 3-23
12	12	Ohio State	3-0-0	lost to Wisconsin 16-20
15	13	Florida	1-1-0	lost to # 24 Mississippi State 6-30 (O1)
13	14	Virginia	4-0-0	beat Wake Forest 31-17
14	15	Nebraska	3-1-0	bye week
16	16	Georgia	3-1-0	beat Arkansas 27-3
17	17	Syracuse	2-1-0	beat Louisville 15-9
19	18	Stanford	3-1-0	beat # 6 Notre Dame 33-16
20	19	Oklahoma	2-1-0	beat Iowa State 17-3
21	20	Southern Cal	1-0-1	lost to # 1 Washington 10-17
18	21	North Carolina St.	4-1-0	lost to # 23 Georgia Tech 13-16
22	22	Boston College	4-0-0	tied West Virginia 24-24
23	23	Georgia Tech	2-1-0	beat # 21 North Carolina St. 16-13
	24	Mississippi State	2-1-0	beat # 13 Florida 30-6 (O1)
24	25	Clemson	1-2-0	beat U.T. Chattanooga 54-3
25		West Virginia	3-0-1	tied # 22 Boston College 24-24

UP	AP	October 5 Poll		Oct. 10 Games
1	1	Washington	4-0-0	beat # 24 California 35-16
2	2	Miami, Fla.	4-0-0	beat # 7 Penn State 17-14
3	3	Michigan	3-0-1	beat Michigan State 35-10
6	4	Tennessee	5-0-0	lost to Arkansas 24-25
4	5	Texas A&M	5-0-0	bye week
7	6	Alabama	5-0-0	beat Tulane 37-0
5	7	Penn State	5-0-0	lost to # 2 Miami, Fla. 14-17
8	8	Florida State	4-1-0	beat North Carolina 36-13
9	9	Colorado	4-0-0	beat Missouri 6-0 (O8)
10	10	Virginia	5-0-0	lost to # 25 Clemson 28-29
12	11	Stanford	4-1-0	beat # 19 UCLA 19-7
13	12	Georgia	4-1-0	beat Georgia Southern 34-7
14	13	Notre Dame	3-1-1	beat Pittsburgh 52-21
11	14	Nebraska	3-1-0	beat Oklahoma State 55-0
15	15	Syracuse	3-1-0	beat Rutgers 50-28
16	16	Oklahoma	3-1-0	lost to Texas 24-34
17	17	Georgia Tech	3-1-0	beat Maryland 28-26
19	18	Mississippi State	3-1-0	beat Auburn 14-7
18	19	UCLA	3-1-0	lost to # 11 Stanford 7-19
	20	Southern Cal	1-1-1	beat Oregon 32-10
21	21	Boston College	4-0-1	bye week
20	22	Ohio State	3-1-0	lost to Illinois 16-18
24	23	Florida	1-2-0	beat LSU 28-21
23	24	California	3-1-0	lost to # 1 Washington 16-35
22	25	Clemson	2-2-0	beat # 10 Virginia 29-28
	25	North Carolina St.	4-2-0	beat Texas Tech 48-13
24		West Virginia	3-0-2	bye week

UP	AP	October 12 Poll		Oct. 17 Games
2	1	Washington	5-0-0	beat Oregon 24-3
1	2	Miami, Fla.	5-0-0	beat TCU 45-10
3	3	Michigan	4-0-1	beat Indiana 31-3
5	4	Alabama	6-0-0	beat # 13 Tennessee 17-10
4	5	Texas A&M	5-0-0	beat Rice 35-9
6	6	Florida State	5-1-0	beat # 16 Georgia Tech 29-24
7	7	Colorado	5-0-0	tied Oklahoma 24-24
10	8	Stanford	5-1-0	lost to Arizona 6-21
9	9	Penn State	5-1-0	lost to # 20 Boston College 32-35
11	10	Georgia	5-1-0	beat Vanderbilt 30-20
8	11	Nebraska	4-1-0	bye week
12	12	Notre Dame	4-1-1	bye week
13	13	Tennessee	5-1-0	lost to # 4 Alabama 10-17
14	14	Syracuse	4-1-0	beat # 24 West Virginia 20-17
17	15	Mississippi State	4-1-0	lost to South Carolina 6-21
15	16	Georgia Tech	4-1-0	lost to # 6 Florida State 24-29
16	17	Virginia	5-1-0	lost to North Carolina 7-27
22	18	Southern Cal	2-1-1	beat California 27-24
19	19	Clemson	3-2-0	beat Duke 21-6
18	20	Boston College	4-0-1	beat # 9 Penn State 35-32
20	21	North Carolina St.	5-2-0	tied Virginia Tech 13-13
21	22	Washington State	5-0-0	beat UCLA 30-17
23	23	Florida	2-2-0	beat Auburn 24-9
24	24	West Virginia	3-0-2	lost to # 14 Syracuse 17-20
25	25	Kansas	4-1-0	beat Iowa State 50-47

UP	AP	October 19 Poll		Oct. 24 Games
1	1	Miami, Fla.	6-0-0	beat Virginia Tech 43-23
2	1	Washington	6-0-0	beat Pacific 31-7
3	3	Michigan	5-0-1	beat Minnesota 63-13
4	4	Alabama	7-0-0	beat Mississippi 31-10
5	5	Texas A&M	6-0-0	beat Baylor 19-13
6	6	Florida State	6-1-0	bye week
8	7	Georgia	6-1-0	beat Kentucky 40-7
7	8	Nebraska	4-1-0	beat Missouri 34-24
9	9	Colorado	5-0-1	beat Kansas State 54-7
10	10	Notre Dame	4-1-1	beat Brigham Young 42-16
12	11	Boston College	5-0-1	beat Tulane 17-13
11	12	Syracuse	5-1-0	beat Temple 38-7
13	13	Washington State	6-0-0	lost to # 15 Southern Cal 21-31
14	14	Penn State	5-2-0	beat West Virginia 40-26
18	15	Southern Cal	3-1-1	beat # 13 Washington State 31-21
17	16	Stanford	5-2-0	beat Oregon State 27-21
16	17	Tennessee	5-2-0	bye week
15	18	Clemson	4-2-0	lost to # 23 North Carolina St. 6-20
19	19	Georgia Tech	4-2-0	lost to North Carolina 14-26
20	20	Florida	3-2-0	beat Louisville 31-17
22	21	Arizona	3-2-1	beat California 24-17
21	22	Kansas	5-1-0	beat Oklahoma 27-10
23	23	North Carolina St.	5-2-1	beat # 18 Clemson 20-6
24	24	Virginia	5-2-0	beat William & Mary 33-7
	25	Mississippi State	4-2-0	beat Arkansas State 56-6
25		Oklahoma	3-2-1	lost to # 22 Kansas 10-27

1992 ANNUAL REVIEW 1381

UP	AP	October 26 Poll		Oct. 31 Games
1	1	**Miami, Fla.**	7-0-0	beat West Virginia 35-23
2	2	**Washington**	7-0-0	beat # 15 Stanford 41-7
3	3	**Michigan**	6-0-1	beat Purdue 24-17
4	4	**Alabama**	8-0-0	bye week
5	5	**Texas A&M**	7-0-0	beat SMU 41-7
6	6	**Florida State**	6-1-0	beat # 23 Virginia 13-3
8	7	**Georgia**	7-1-0	lost to # 20 Florida 24-26
9	8	**Colorado**	6-0-1	lost to # 8 Nebraska 7-52
7	8	**Nebraska**	5-1-0	beat # 8 Colorado 52-7
10	10	**Notre Dame**	5-1-1	beat Navy 38-7
12	11	**Boston College**	6-0-1	beat Temple 45-6
11	12	**Syracuse**	6-1-0	beat Pittsburgh 41-10
14	13	**Southern Cal**	4-1-1	beat Arizona State 23-13
13	14	**Penn State**	6-2-0	lost to Brigham Young 17-30
17	15	**Stanford**	6-2-0	lost to # 2 Washington 7-41
15	16	**Tennessee**	5-2-0	lost to South Carolina 23-24
19	17	**Arizona**	4-2-1	beat New Mexico State 30-0
16	18	**Kansas**	6-1-0	beat Oklahoma State 26-18
18	19	**Washington State**	6-1-0	lost to Oregon 17-34
20	20	**Florida**	4-2-0	beat # 7 Georgia 26-24
21	21	**North Carolina St.**	6-2-1	bye week
23	22	**North Carolina**	6-2-0	beat Maryland 31-24
22	23	**Virginia**	6-2-0	lost to # 6 Florida State 3-13
24	24	**Mississippi State**	5-2-0	beat Kentucky 37-36
	25	**Texas**	4-2-0	beat Texas Tech 44-33
25		**Clemson**	4-3-0	lost to Wake Forest 15-18

UP	AP	November 2 Poll		Nov. 7 Games
	1	**Washington**	8-0-0	lost to # 12 Arizona 3-16
	2	**Miami, Fla.**	8-0-0	bye week
	3	**Alabama**	8-0-0	beat LSU 31-11
	4	**Michigan**	7-0-1	beat Northwestern 40-7
	5	**Texas A&M**	8-0-0	beat Louisville 40-18
	6	**Florida State**	7-1-0	beat Maryland 69-21
	7	**Nebraska**	6-1-0	beat # 13 Kansas 49-7
	8	**Notre Dame**	6-1-1	beat # 9 Boston College 54-7
	9	**Boston College**	7-0-1	lost to # 8 Notre Dame 7-54
	10	**Syracuse**	7-1-0	beat Virginia Tech 28-9
	11	**Southern Cal**	5-1-1	lost to # 21 Stanford 9-23
	12	**Arizona**	5-2-1	beat # 1 Washington 16-3
	13	**Kansas**	7-1-0	lost to # 7 Nebraska 7-49
	14	**Florida**	5-2-0	beat Southern Miss 24-20
	15	**Georgia**	7-2-0	bye week
	16	**Colorado**	6-1-1	beat Oklahoma State 28-0
	17	**North Carolina St.**	6-2-1	beat Virginia 31-7
	18	**North Carolina**	7-2-0	lost to Clemson 7-40
	19	**Mississippi State**	6-2-0	beat Arkansas 10-3
	20	**Texas**	5-2-0	lost to TCU 14-23
	21	**Stanford**	6-3-0	beat # 11 Southern Cal 23-9
	22	**Ohio State**	6-2-0	beat Minnesota 17-0
	23	**Penn State**	6-3-0	bye week
	24	**Tennessee**	5-3-0	bye week
	25	**Washington State**	6-2-0	beat Arizona State 20-18

UP	AP	November 9 Poll		Nov. 14 Games
1	1	**Miami, Fla.**	8-0-0	beat Temple 48-0
2	2	**Alabama**	9-0-0	beat # 16 Mississippi State 30-21
3	3	**Michigan**	8-0-1	tied Illinois 22-22
4	4	**Texas A&M**	9-0-0	beat Houston 38-30 (N12)
5	5	**Florida State**	8-1-0	beat Tulane 70-7
7	6	**Washington**	8-1-0	beat Oregon State 45-16
5	7	**Nebraska**	7-1-0	lost to Iowa State 10-19
8	8	**Notre Dame**	7-1-1	beat # 22 Penn State 17-16
10	9	**Arizona**	6-2-1	lost to # 18 Southern Cal 7-14
9	10	**Syracuse**	8-1-0	beat Boston College 27-10
13	11	**Florida**	6-2-0	beat South Carolina 14-9
12	12	**Georgia**	7-2-0	beat Auburn 14-10
11	13	**Colorado**	7-1-1	beat # 20 Kansas 25-18
14	14	**North Carolina St.**	7-2-1	beat Duke 45-27
17	15	**Stanford**	7-3-0	beat # 21 Washington State 40-3
16	16	**Mississippi State**	7-2-0	lost to # 2 Alabama 21-30
15	17	**Boston College**	7-1-1	lost to Syracuse 10-27
20	18	**Southern Cal**	5-2-1	beat # 9 Arizona 14-7
18	19	**Ohio State**	7-2-0	beat Indiana 27-10
19	20	**Kansas**	7-2-0	lost to # 13 Colorado 18-25
22	21	**Washington State**	7-2-0	lost to # 15 Stanford 3-40
21	22	**Penn State**	6-3-0	lost to # 8 Notre Dame 16-17
24	23	**Tennessee**	5-3-0	beat Memphis 26-21
23	24	**Hawaii**	7-1-0	lost to San Diego State 28-52
25	25	**North Carolina**	7-3-0	bye week

UP	AP	November 16 Poll		Nov. 21 Games
1	1	**Miami, Fla.**	9-0-0	beat # 8 Syracuse 16-10
2	2	**Alabama**	10-0-0	bye week
4	3	**Florida State**	9-1-0	bye week
3	4	**Texas A&M**	10-0-0	beat TCU 37-10
5	5	**Washington**	9-1-0	lost to Washington State 23-42
8	6	**Michigan**	8-0-2	tied # 17 Ohio State 13-13
6	7	**Notre Dame**	8-1-1	bye week
7	8	**Syracuse**	9-1-0	lost to # 1 Miami, Fla. 10-16
11	9	**Florida**	7-2-0	beat Vanderbilt 41-21
10	10	**Georgia**	8-2-0	bye week
9	11	**Colorado**	8-1-1	beat Iowa State 31-10
12	12	**Nebraska**	7-2-0	bye week
13	13	**North Carolina St.**	8-2-1	beat # 25 Wake Forest 42-14
15	14	**Stanford**	8-3-0	beat California 41-21
14	15	**Southern Cal**	6-2-1	lost to UCLA 37-38
17	16	**Arizona**	6-3-1	lost to Arizona State 6-7
16	17	**Ohio State**	8-2-0	tied # 6 Michigan 13-13
18	18	**Mississippi State**	7-3-0	bye week
19	19	**Boston College**	7-2-1	beat Army 41-24
20	20	**Tennessee**	6-3-0	beat Kentucky 34-13
22	21	**North Carolina**	7-3-0	beat Duke 31-28
21	22	**Kansas**	7-3-0	lost to Missouri 17-22
23	23	**Penn State**	6-4-0	beat Pittsburgh 57-13
24	24	**Mississippi**	7-3-0	bye week
	25	**Wake Forest**	7-3-0	lost to # 13 North Carolina St. 14-42
25		**Hawaii**	7-2-0	beat Wyoming 42-18
25		**Washington State**	7-3-0	beat # 5 Washington 42-23

UP	AP	November 23 Poll		Nov. 28 Games
1	1	**Miami, Fla.**	10-0-0	beat San Diego State 63-17
2	2	**Alabama**	10-0-0	beat Auburn 17-0 (N26)
4	3	**Florida State**	9-1-0	beat # 6 Florida 45-24
3	4	**Texas A&M**	11-0-0	beat Texas 34-13 (N26)
5	5	**Notre Dame**	8-1-1	beat # 19 Southern Cal 31-23
10	6	**Florida**	8-2-0	lost to # 3 Florida State 24-45
8	7	**Michigan**	8-0-3	regular season complete
9	8	**Syracuse**	9-2-0	regular season complete
7	9	**Georgia**	8-2-0	beat Georgia Tech 31-17
6	10	**Colorado**	9-1-1	regular season complete
13	11	**Washington**	9-2-0	regular season complete
12	12	**Nebraska**	7-2-0	beat Oklahoma 33-9 (N27)
11	13	**North Carolina St.**	9-2-1	regular season complete
14	14	**Stanford**	9-3-0	regular season complete
15	15	**Ohio State**	8-2-1	regular season complete
17	16	**Mississippi State**	7-3-0	lost to # 24 Mississippi 10-17
16	17	**Boston College**	8-2-1	regular season complete
18	18	**Tennessee**	7-3-0	beat Vanderbilt 29-25
23	19	**Southern Cal**	6-3-1	lost to # 5 Notre Dame 23-31
19	20	**North Carolina**	8-3-0	regular season complete
20	21	**Washington State**	8-3-0	regular season complete
21	22	**Penn State**	7-4-0	regular season complete
22	23	**Arizona**	6-4-1	regular season complete
24	24	**Mississippi**	7-3-0	beat # 16 Mississippi State 17-10
25	25	**Brigham Young**	8-4-0	regular season complete

UP	AP	November 30 Poll		Dec. 5 Games
1	1	**Miami, Fla.**	11-0-0	regular season complete
2	2	**Alabama**	11-0-0	beat # 12 Florida 28-21 (SEC CH.)
4	3	**Florida State**	10-1-0	regular season complete
3	4	**Texas A&M**	12-0-0	regular season complete
5	5	**Notre Dame**	9-1-1	regular season complete
9	6	**Syracuse**	9-2-0	
7	7	**Michigan**	8-0-3	
8	8	**Georgia**	9-2-0	regular season complete
6	9	**Colorado**	9-1-1	
11	10	**Washington**	9-2-0	
10	11	**Nebraska**	8-2-0	beat Kansas State 38-24
15	12	**Florida**	8-3-0	lost to # 2 Alabama 21-28
12	13	**North Carolina St.**	9-2-1	
13	14	**Stanford**	9-3-0	
14	15	**Ohio State**	8-2-1	
16	16	**Boston College**	8-2-1	
17	17	**Tennessee**	8-3-0	regular season complete
19	18	**Washington State**	8-3-0	
20	19	**Mississippi**	8-3-0	regular season complete
18	20	**North Carolina**	8-3-0	
21	21	**Penn State**	7-4-0	
22	22	**Arizona**	6-4-1	
24	23	**Southern Cal**	6-4-1	regular season complete
	24	**Mississippi State**	7-4-0	regular season complete
23	25	**Brigham Young**	8-4-0	
25		**Hawaii**		

UP	AP	December 7 Poll	Record	Bowl Bid	Date	Bowl Result	RB	UP	AP	January 2 Final Poll	Record
1	1	**Miami, Fla.**	11-0-0	Sugar Bowl	J1	lost to # 2 Alabama 13-34	1	1	1	**Alabama**	13-0-0
2	2	**Alabama**	12-0-0	Sugar Bowl	J1	beat # 1 Miami, Fla. 34-13	3	2	2	**Florida State**	11-1-0
4	3	**Florida State**	10-1-0	Orange Bowl	J1	beat # 11 Nebraska 27-14	2	3	3	**Miami, Fla.**	11-1-0
3	4	**Texas A&M**	12-0-0	Cotton Bowl	J1	lost to # 5 Notre Dame 3-28	4	4	4	**Notre Dame**	10-1-1
5	5	**Notre Dame**	9-1-1	Cotton Bowl	J1	beat # 4 Texas A&M 28-3	6	5	5	**Michigan**	9-0-3
9	6	**Syracuse**	9-2-0	Fiesta Bowl	J1	beat # 10 Colorado 26-22	7	7	6	**Syracuse**	10-2-0
7	7	**Michigan**	8-0-3	Rose Bowl	J1	beat # 9 Washington 38-31	5	6	7	**Texas A&M**	12-1-0
8	8	**Georgia**	9-2-0	Citrus Bowl	J1	beat # 15 Ohio State 21-14	10	8	8	**Georgia**	10-2-0
11	9	**Washington**	9-2-0	Rose Bowl	J1	lost to # 7 Michigan 31-38	11	9	9	**Stanford**	10-3-0
6	10	**Colorado**	9-1-1	Fiesta Bowl	J1	lost to # 6 Syracuse 22-26	12	11	10	**Florida**	9-4-0
10	11	**Nebraska**	9-2-0	Orange Bowl	J1	lost to # 3 Florida State 14-27	8	10	11	**Washington**	9-3-0
12	12	**North Carolina St.**	9-2-1	Gator Bowl	D31	lost to # 14 Florida 10-27	14	12	12	**Tennessee**	9-3-0
13	13	**Stanford**	9-3-0	Blockbuster Bowl	J1	beat # 21 Penn State 24-3	9	13	13	**Colorado**	9-2-1
15	14	**Florida**	8-4-0	Gator Bowl	D31	beat # 12 North Carolina St. 27-10	15	14	14	**Nebraska**	9-3-0
14	15	**Ohio State**	8-2-1	Citrus Bowl	J1	lost to # 8 Georgia 14-21	19	17	15	**Washington State**	9-3-0
16	16	**Boston College**	8-2-1	Hall of Fame Bowl	J1	lost to # 17 Tennessee 23-38	23	16	16	**Mississippi**	9-3-0
17	17	**Tennessee**	8-3-0	Hall of Fame Bowl	J1	beat # 16 Boston College 38-33	17	15	17	**North Carolina St.**	9-3-1
18	18	**Washington State**	8-3-0	Copper Bowl	D29	beat Utah 31-28	16	19	18	**Ohio State**	8-3-1
20	19	**North Carolina**	8-3-0	Peach Bowl	J2	beat # 24 Mississippi State 21-17	18	18	19	**North Carolina**	9-3-0
19	20	**Mississippi**	8-3-0	Liberty Bowl	D31	beat Air Force 13-0	21	20	20	**Hawaii**	11-2-0
21	21	**Penn State**	7-4-0	Blockbuster Bowl	J1	lost to # 13 Stanford 3-24	20	21	21	**Boston College**	8-3-1
22	22	**Arizona**	6-4-1	Sun Bowl	D31	lost to Baylor 15-20	22	23	22	**Kansas**	8-4-0
25	23	**Southern Cal**	6-4-1	Freedom Bowl	D29	lost to Fresno State 7-24	32		23	**Mississippi State**	7-5-0
	24	**Mississippi State**	7-4-0	Peach Bowl	J2	lost to # 19 North Carolina 17-21	27	22	24	**Fresno State**	9-4-0
23	25	**Brigham Young**	8-4-0	Aloha Bowl	D25	lost to Kansas 20-23	26	25	25	**Wake Forest**	8-4-0
24		**Hawaii**	10-2-0	Holiday Bowl	D30	beat Illinois 27-17					

ANNUAL REVIEW

1992

CONSENSUS ALL-AMERICANS

POS	OFFENSE	HT	WT	School	AP	CF	FC	FW	PI
QB	Gino Toretta	6-3	205	Miami, Fla.	•	•	•	•	•
RB	Marshall Faulk	5-10	200	San Diego State	•	•	•	•	•
RB	Garrison Hearst	5-11	202	Georgia	•	•	•	•	•
WR	O.J. McDuffie	5-11	185	Penn State	•	•	•	•	•
WR	Sean Dawkins	6-4	205	California	•	•	•	•	•
TE	Chris Gedney	6-5	256	Syracuse	•	•	•	•	•
OL	Lincoln Kennedy	6-7	325	Washington	•	•	•	•	•
OL	Will Shields	6-1	305	Nebraska	•	•	•	•	•
OL	Aaron Taylor	6-4	294	Notre Dame	•	•			
OL	Willie Roaf	6-5	300	Louisiana Tech	•		•	•	
OL	Everett Lindsay	6-5	290	Mississippi	•				
C	Mike Compton	6-7	289	West Virginia	•	•	•	•	•
PK	Joe Allison	6-0	184	Memphis			•		

OTHERS RECEIVING FIRST-TEAM HONORS

WR	Ryan Yarborough			Wyoming				•	
WR	Lloyd Hill			Texas Tech		•			•
OL	Tony Boselli			Southern Cal			•		
OL	Ben Coleman			Wake Forest					•
C	Mike Devlin			Iowa				•	•
PK	Scott Sisson			Georgia Tech		•			
PK	Jason Elam			Hawaii					•
KR	Curtis Conway			Southern Cal				•	

POS	DEFENSE	HT	WT	School	AP	CF	FC	FW	PI
DL	Eric Curry	6-6	265	Alabama	•	•	•	•	•
DL	John Copeland	6-3	261	Alabama	•	•	•	•	•
DL	Chris Slade	6-5	235	Virginia	•	•	•	•	•
DL	Rob Waldrop	6-2	265	Arizona	•	•	•	•	•
LB	Marcus Buckley	6-4	230	Texas A&M	•	•	•	•	•
LB	Marvin Jones	6-2	235	Florida State	•	•	•	•	•
LB	Micheal Barrow	6-2	230	Miami, Fla.	•	•	•	•	•
DB	Carlton McDonald	6-0	185	Air Force	•	•	•	•	•
DB	Carlton Gray	6-0	194	UCLA	•	•	•	•	•
DB	Deon Figures	6-1	195	Colorado	•	•	•	•	•
DB	Ryan McNeil	6-2	185	Miami, Fla.	•		•	•	•
P	Sean Snyder	6-1	190	Kansas State			•		

OTHERS RECEIVING FIRST-TEAM HONORS

DL	Coleman Rudolph			Georgia Tech		•			
DL	Chris Hutchinson			Michigan					•
DL	Travis Hill			Nebraska				•	
LB	David Hoffman			Washington				•	
LB	Steve Tovar			Ohio State				•	
LB	Darrin Smith			Miami, Fla.				•	
DB	Patrick Bates			Texas A&M				•	•
DB	Lance Gunn			Texas				•	
P	Ed Bunn			UTEP		•			
P	Josh Miller			Arizona				•	

FC named Buckley as a DL

HEISMAN TROPHY VOTING

	PLAYER	POS	SCHOOL	1ST	2ND	3RD	TOTAL
1	Gino Torretta	QB	Miami, Fla.	310	179	112	1400
2	Marshall Faulk	RB	San Diego State	164	207	174	1080
3	Garrison Hearst	RB	Georgia	140	196	170	982
4	Marvin Jones	LB	Florida State	81	51	47	392
5	Reggie Brooks	RB	Notre Dame	42	53	62	294
6	Charlie Ward	QB	Florida State	18	18	36	126
7	Micheal Barrow	LB	Miami, Fla.	10	10	14	64
8	Drew Bledsoe	QB	Washington State	6	18	14	48
9	Glyn Milburn	RB	Stanford	5	11	10	47
10	Eric Curry	DE	Alabama	3	13	12	47

AWARD WINNERS

PLAYER	POS/SCHOOL	AWARD		PLAYER	POS/SCHOOL	AWARD
Gino Torretta	QB Miami, Fla.	Maxwell		Marvin Jones	LB Florida State	Butkus
Will Shields	G Nebraska	Outland		Deon Figures	DB Colorado	Thorpe
Gino Torretta	QB Miami, Fla.	Camp		Gino Torretta	QB Miami, Fla.	Unitas
Marvin Jones	LB Florida State	Lombardi		Garrison Hearst	RB Georgia	Walker
Gino Torretta	QB Miami, Fla.	O'Brien		Joe Allison	K Memphis	Groza

BOWL GAMES

DATE	GAME	SCORE
D18	Las Vegas	Bowling Green 35, Nevada 34
D25	Aloha	Kansas 23, Brigham Young 20
D29	Freedom	Fresno State 24, Southern Cal 7
D29	Copper	Washington State 31, Utah 28
D30	Holiday	Hawaii 27, Illinois 17
D31	Sun	Baylor 20, Arizona 15
D31	Gator	Florida 27, North Carolina St. 10
D31	Liberty	Mississippi 13, Air Force 0
D31	Independence	Wake Forest 39, Oregon 35

CONFERENCE STANDINGS

ACC

	Conf. W L T			Overall W L T		
Florida State	8	0	0	11	1	0
North Carolina St.	6	2	0	9	3	1
North Carolina	5	3	0	9	3	0
Wake Forest	4	4	0	8	4	0
Virginia	4	4	0	7	4	0
Georgia Tech	4	4	0	5	6	0
Clemson	3	5	0	5	6	0
Maryland	2	6	0	3	8	0
Duke	0	8	0	2	9	0

Big 10

	Conf. W L T			Overall W L T		
Michigan	6	0	2	9	0	3
Ohio State	5	2	1	8	3	1
Michigan State	5	3	0	5	6	0
Illinois	4	3	1	6	5	1
Iowa	4	4	0	5	7	0
Indiana	3	5	0	5	6	0
Wisconsin	3	5	0	5	6	0
Purdue	3	5	0	4	7	0
Northwestern	3	5	0	3	8	0
Minnesota	2	6	0	2	9	0

Big 8

	Conf. W L T			Overall W L T		
Nebraska	6	1	0	9	3	0
Colorado	5	1	1	9	2	1
Kansas	4	3	0	8	4	0
Oklahoma	3	2	2	5	4	2
Oklahoma State	2	4	1	4	6	1
Kansas State	2	5	0	5	6	0
Iowa State	2	5	0	4	7	0
Missouri	2	5	0	3	8	0

Big East

	Conf. W L T			Overall W L T		
Miami, Fla.	4	0	0	11	1	0
Syracuse	6	1	0	10	2	0
Rutgers	4	2	0	7	4	0
Boston College	2	1	1	8	3	1
West Virginia	2	3	1	5	4	2
Pittsburgh	1	3	0	3	9	0
Virginia Tech	1	4	0	2	8	1
Temple	0	6	0	1	10	0

Big West

	Conf. W L T			Overall W L T		
Nevada	5	1	0	7	5	0
San Jose State	4	2	0	7	4	0
Utah State	4	2	0	5	6	0
New Mexico State	3	3	0	6	5	0
Nevada-Las Vegas	3	3	0	6	5	0
Pacific	2	4	0	3	8	0
Cal-St. Fullerton	0	6	0	2	9	0

Ivy

	Conf. W L T			Overall W L T		
Dartmouth	6	1	0	8	2	0
Princeton	6	1	0	8	2	0
Pennsylvania	5	2	0	7	3	0
Cornell	4	3	0	7	3	0
Harvard	3	4	0	3	7	0
Yale	2	5	0	4	6	0
Columbia	2	5	0	3	7	0
Brown	0	7	0	0	10	0

MAC

	Conf. W L T			Overall W L T		
Bowling Green	8	0	0	10	2	0
Western Michigan	6	3	0	7	3	1
Toledo	5	3	0	8	3	0
Akron	5	3	0	7	3	1
Miami, Ohio	5	3	0	6	4	1
Ball State	5	4	0	5	6	0
Central Michigan	4	5	0	5	6	0
Kent State	2	7	0	2	9	0
Ohio U	1	7	0	1	10	0
Eastern Michigan	1	7	0	1	10	0

Pac 10

	Conf. W L T			Overall W L T		
Stanford	6	2	0	10	3	0
Washington	6	2	0	9	3	0
Washington State	5	3	0	9	3	0
Southern Cal	5	3	0	6	5	1
Arizona	4	3	1	6	5	1
Arizona State	4	4	0	6	5	0
Oregon	4	4	0	6	6	0
UCLA	3	5	0	6	5	0
California	2	6	0	4	7	0
Oregon State	0	7	1	1	9	1

SEC

	Conf. W L T			Overall W L T		
EAST						
Florida	6	2	0	9	4	0
Georgia	6	2	0	10	2	0
Tennessee	5	3	0	9	3	0
South Carolina	3	5	0	5	6	0
Vanderbilt	2	6	0	4	7	0
Kentucky	2	6	0	4	7	0
WEST						
Alabama	8	0	0	13	0	0
Mississippi	5	3	0	9	3	0
Mississippi State	4	4	0	7	5	0
Arkansas	3	4	1	3	7	1
Auburn	2	5	1	5	5	1
LSU	1	7	0	2	9	0

Championship Game **Alabama 28 Florida 21**

SWC

	Conf. W L T			Overall W L T		
Texas A&M	7	0	0	12	1	0
Baylor	4	3	0	7	5	0
Rice	4	3	0	6	5	0
Texas	4	3	0	6	5	0
Texas Tech	4	3	0	5	6	0
SMU	2	5	0	5	6	0
Houston	2	5	0	4	7	0
TCU	1	6	0	2	8	1

WAC

	Conf. W L T			Overall W L T		
Hawaii	6	2	0	11	2	0
Fresno State	6	2	0	9	4	0
Brigham Young	6	2	0	8	5	0
San Diego State	5	3	0	5	5	1
Air Force	4	4	0	7	5	0
Utah	4	4	0	6	6	0
Wyoming	3	5	0	5	7	0
Colorado State	3	5	0	5	7	0
New Mexico	2	6	0	3	8	0
Texas-El Paso	1	7	0	1	10	0

Independents

	Overall W L T		
Notre Dame	10	1	1
Southern Miss	7	4	0
Penn State	7	5	0
Memphis	6	5	0
Northern Illinois	5	6	0
East Carolina	5	6	0
Army	5	6	0
Louisiana Tech	5	6	0
Louisville	5	6	0
Tulsa	4	7	0
Cincinnati	3	8	0
Tulane	2	9	0
La. Lafayette	2	9	0
Arkansas State	2	9	0
Navy	1	10	0

DATE	GAME	SCORE
J1	Orange	Florida State 27, Nebraska 14
J1	Citrus	Georgia 21, Ohio State 14
J1	Rose	Michigan 38, Washington 31
J1	Cotton	Notre Dame 28, Texas A&M 3
J1	Blockbuster	Stanford 24, Penn State 3
J1	Fiesta	Syracuse 26, Colorado 22
J1	Hall of Fame	Tennessee 38, Boston College 23
J1	Sugar	Alabama 34, Miami, Fla. 13
J2	Peach	North Carolina 21, Mississippi State 17

1992 NCAA Major College Statistical Leaders

Individual Leaders

PASSING	CL	G	ATT	COM	PCT	INT	I%	YDS	YPA	TD	TD%	RATING
1 Elvis Grbac, Michigan	SR	9	169	112	66.3	12	7.1	1465	8.7	15	8.9	154.2
2 Marvin Graves, Syracuse	JR	11	242	146	60.3	12	5.0	2296	9.5	14	5.8	149.2
3 Ryan Hancock, Brigham Young	SO	9	288	165	57.3	13	4.5	2635	9.2	17	5.9	144.6
4 Bert Emanuel, Rice	JR	11	179	94	52.5	6	3.4	1558	8.7	11	6.2	139.2
5 Kordell Stewart, Colorado	SO	9	252	151	59.9	9	3.6	2109	8.4	12	4.8	138.8
6 Eric Zeier, Georgia	SO	11	258	151	58.5	12	4.7	2248	8.7	12	4.7	137.8
7 Jimmy Klingler, Houston	SO	11	504	303	60.1	18	3.6	3818	7.6	32	6.4	137.6
8 Bobby Goodman, Virginia	SR	11	232	130	56.0	12	5.2	1707	7.4	21	9.1	137.4
9 Joe Youngblood, Central Michigan	JR	11	278	161	57.9	13	4.7	2209	8.0	18	6.5	136.7
10 Trent Dilfer, Fresno State	SO	12	331	174	52.6	14	4.2	2828	8.5	20	6.0	135.8

ALL-PURPOSE	CL	G	RUSH	REC	PR	KR	YDS	YPG
1 Ryan Benjamin, Pacific	SR	11	1441	434	96	626	2597	236.1
2 Glyn Milburn, Stanford	SR	12	851	405	573	292	2121	176.8
3 Marshall Faulk, San Diego State	SO	10	1630	128	0	0	1758	175.8
4 Garrison Hearst, Georgia	JR	11	1547	324	0	39	1910	173.6
5 Henry Bailey, Nevada-Las Vegas	SO	11	15	832	219	817	1883	171.2
6 O.J. McDuffie, Penn State	SR	11	133	977	398	323	1831	166.5
7 Chuckie Dukes, Boston College	SR	11	1387	194	0	225	1806	164.2
8 Curtis Conway, Southern Cal	JR	11	37	764	324	652	1777	161.6
9 Tyrone Wheatley, Michigan	SO	10	1122	141	0	260	1523	152.3
10 Trevor Cobb, Rice	SR	11	1386	283	0	0	1669	151.7
10 Darnay Scott, San Diego State	SO	11	20	1150	0	499	1669	151.7

RUSHING/Yards Per Game	CL	G	ATT	YDS	TD	AVG	YPG
1 Marshall Faulk, San Diego State	SO	10	265	1630	15	6.2	163.0
2 Garrison Hearst, Georgia	JR	11	228	1547	19	6.8	140.6
3 Ryan Benjamin, Pacific	SR	11	231	1441	13	6.2	131.0
4 Chuckie Dukes, Boston College	SR	11	238	1387	10	5.8	126.1
5 Trevor Cobb, Rice	SR	11	279	1386	11	5.0	126.0
6 Travis Sims, Hawaii	SR	12	220	1498	9	6.8	124.8
7 Reggie Brooks, Notre Dame	SR	11	167	1343	13	8.0	122.1
8 LeShon Johnson, Northern Illinois	JR	11	265	1338	6	5.0	121.6
9 Byron Morris, Texas Tech	SO	11	242	1279	10	5.3	116.3
10 Deland McCullough, Miami, Ohio	FR	9	227	1026	6	4.5	114.0

RUSHING/Yards Per Carry	CL	G	ATT	YDS	YPC
1 Reggie Brooks, Notre Dame	SR	11	167	1343	8.0
2 Calvin Jones, Nebraska	SO	11	168	1210	7.2
3 Travis Sims, Hawaii	SR	12	220	1498	6.8
4 Garrison Hearst, Georgia	JR	11	228	1547	6.8
5 Tyrone Wheatley, Michigan	SO	10	170	1122	6.6
6 Napoleon Kaufman, Washington	SO	11	162	1045	6.5
7 Ryan Benjamin, Pacific	SR	11	231	1441	6.2
8 Marshall Faulk, San Diego State	SO	10	265	1630	6.2
9 Anthony Barbour, North Carolina St.	SR	12	199	1204	6.1
10 Derek Brown, Nebraska	JR	10	170	1015	6.0

*-Based on top 25 rushers

RECEIVING	CL	G	REC	YDS	TD	RPG	YPR	YPG
1 Lloyd Hill, Texas Tech	JR	11	76	1261	12	6.9	16.6	114.6
2 Marcus Badgett, Maryland	SR	11	75	1240	9	6.8	16.5	112.7
3 Ryan Yarborough, Wyoming	JR	12	86	1351	12	7.2	15.7	112.6
4 Victor Bailey, Missouri	SR	11	75	1210	6	6.8	16.1	110.0
5 Aaron Turner, Pacific	SR	11	79	1171	11	7.2	14.8	106.5
6 Darnay Scott, San Diego State	SO	11	68	1150	9	6.2	16.9	104.6
7 Charles Johnson, Colorado	JR	11	57	1149	5	5.2	20.2	104.5
8 Bryan Reeves, Nevada	JR	11	81	1114	10	7.4	13.8	101.3
9 Sean Dawkins, California	JR	11	65	1070	14	5.9	16.5	97.3
10 Michael Westbrook, Colorado	SO	11	76	1060	8	6.9	13.9	96.4

PUNTING	CL	PUNT	YDS	AVG
1 Ed Bunn, Texas-El Paso	SR	41	1955	47.7
2 Mitch Berger, Colorado	JR	53	2493	47.0
3 Brian Parvin, Nevada-Las Vegas	SR	57	2637	46.3
4 Sean Snyder, Kansas State	SR	80	3572	44.6
5 Jeff Buffaloe, Memphis	SR	52	2317	44.6
6 Jason Elam, Hawaii	SR	49	2179	44.5
7 Todd Sauerbrun, West Virginia	SO	53	2348	44.3
8 Jim DiGuilio, Indiana	SO	53	2347	44.3
9 David Davis, Texas A&M	SR	70	3067	43.8
10 Todd Jordan, Mississippi State	JR	52	2267	43.6

PUNT RETURNS	CL	PR	YDS	TD	AVG
1 Lee Gissendaner, Northwestern	JR	15	327	1	21.8
2 James McMillion, Iowa State	JR	23	435	3	18.9
3 Glyn Milburn, Stanford	SR	31	573	3	18.5
4 Jamie Mouton, Houston	SR	18	278	1	15.4
5 Corey Sawyer, Florida State	SO	33	488	1	14.8
6 Henry Bailey, Nevada-Las Vegas	SO	15	219	1	14.6
7 Napoleon Kaufman, Washington	SO	19	269	0	14.2
8 Marc Baxter, Temple	FR	12	167	0	13.9
9 Derrick Alexander, Michigan	SR	25	343	2	13.7
10 O.J. McDuffie, Penn State	SR	30	398	0	13.3

KICKOFF RETURNS	CL	KR	YDS	TD	AVG
1 Fred Montgomery, New Mexico State	SR	14	457	0	32.6
2 Leroy Gallman, Duke	SR	14	433	0	30.9
3 Lew Lawhorn, Temple	SO	20	600	2	30.0
4 Chris Singleton, Nevada	JR	17	497	0	29.2
5 Brad Breedlove, Duke	SR	15	438	0	29.2
6 Craig Thompson, Eastern Michigan	JR	18	490	1	27.2
7 Polee Banks, Cal-St. Fullerton	JR	14	370	0	26.4
8 John Lewis, Minnesota	SR	29	755	1	26.0
9 Courtney Burton, Ohio	JR	21	545	1	26.0
10 Eric Redmon, Louisiana Tech	SO	12	310	0	25.8

SCORING	CL	TDS	XP	FG	PTS	PTPG
1 Garrison Hearst, Georgia	JR	21	0	0	126	11.5
2 Richie Anderson, Penn State	SR	19	2	0	116	10.6
3 Marshall Faulk, San Diego State	SO	15	2	0	92	9.2
4 Joe Allison, Memphis	JR	0	32	23	101	9.2
5 Greg Hill, Texas A&M	SO	17	0	0	102	8.5
6 Tyrone Wheatley, Michigan	SO	14	0	0	84	8.4
7 Trevor Cobb, Rice	SR	15	2	0	92	8.4
8 Calvin Jones, Nebraska	SO	15	0	0	90	8.2
8 Craig Thomas, Michigan State	JR	15	0	0	90	8.2
10 Rusty Hanna, Toledo	SR	0	26	21	89	8.1
10 Nelson Welch, Clemson	SO	0	23	22	89	8.1

FIELD GOALS	CL	FGA	FGM	PCT	FGG
1 Joe Allison, Memphis	JR	25	23	0.92	2.10
2 Scott Ethridge, Auburn	SO	28	22	0.79	2.00
2 Nelson Welch, Clemson	SO	28	22	0.79	2.00
2 Rich Thompson, Wisconsin	SR	32	22	0.69	2.00
5 Rusty Hanna, Toledo	SR	29	21	0.72	1.90
6 Tommy Thompson, Oregon	JR	31	20	0.65	1.80
7 Eric Lange, Tulsa	SR	23	19	0.83	1.70
7 Scott Sisson, Georgia Tech	SR	24	19	0.79	1.70
9 Sean Jones, Utah State	SR	24	18	0.75	1.60
9 Daron Alcorn, Akron	SR	26	18	0.69	1.60

INTERCEPTIONS	CL	INT	YDS	TD	INT/GM
1 Carlton McDonald, Air Force	SR	8	109	1	0.73
2 C.J. Masters, Kansas State	SR	7	152	2	0.64
2 Tyronne Drakeford, Virginia Tech	JR	7	121	1	0.64
2 Greg Evans, TCU	JR	7	121	0	0.64
2 Joe Bair, Bowling Green	JR	7	51	0	0.64
2 Chris Owens, Akron	SR	7	49	0	0.64
2 Corey Sawyer, Florida State	SO	7	0	0	0.64
8 Deon Figures, Colorado	SR	6	21	0	0.60
8 Herman O'Berry, Oregon	SO	6	3	0	0.60
10 Terryl Ulmer, Southern Miss *	JR	6	132	0	0.55
10 Rico Wesley, TCU *	JR	6	125	0	0.55
10 Jaime Mendez, Kansas State *	JR	6	121	0	0.55
10 Greg Grandison, East Carolina *	SR	6	104	0	0.55
10 Charlie Brennan, Boston College *	SR	6	88	0	0.55

*-Eleven tied with 0.55; these had the most yards.

Team Leaders

RUSHING OFFENSE	G	ATT	YDS	AVG	TD	YPG
1 Nebraska	11	618	3610	5.8	40	328.2
2 Hawaii	12	630	3519	5.6	32	293.3
3 Notre Dame	11	555	3090	5.6	34	280.9
4 Army	11	667	2934	4.4	23	266.7
5 Michigan	11	531	2909	5.5	28	264.5
6 Clemson	11	580	2828	4.9	21	257.1
7 Air Force	11	610	2665	4.4	26	242.3
8 Baylor	11	570	2641	4.6	24	240.1
9 Colorado State	12	571	2881	5.0	25	240.1
10 Virginia	11	513	2589	5.0	19	235.4

PASSING OFFENSE	G	ATT	COM	INT	PCT	YDS	YPA	TD	I%	YPC	YPG
1 Houston	11	619	368	24	59.5	4478	7.2	36	3.9	12.2	407.1
2 Maryland	11	514	304	23	59.1	3628	7.1	18	4.5	11.9	329.8
3 Miami, Fla.	11	457	259	7	56.7	3476	7.6	23	1.5	13.4	316.0
4 Nevada	11	497	268	27	53.9	3328	6.7	23	5.4	12.4	302.5
5 Brigham Young	12	405	222	19	54.8	3575	8.8	27	4.7	16.1	297.9
6 Colorado	11	398	232	20	58.3	3271	8.2	22	5.0	14.1	297.4
7 Missouri	11	442	258	12	58.4	3223	7.3	13	2.7	12.5	293.0
8 Pittsburgh	12	455	266	20	58.5	3483	7.7	23	4.4	13.1	290.3
9 Florida	12	503	290	18	57.7	3440	6.8	25	3.6	11.9	286.7
10 East Carolina	11	437	272	27	54.7	3085	6.2	27	5.4	11.3	280.5

TOTAL OFFENSE	G	P	YDS	AVG	TD	YPG
1 Houston	11	842	5714	6.8	48	519.5
2 Fresno State	12	881	5791	6.6	61	482.6
3 Notre Dame	11	808	5174	6.4	52	470.4
4 Maryland	11	945	5131	5.4	37	466.5
5 Michigan	11	806	5120	6.4	51	465.5
6 Florida State	11	851	5080	6.0	49	461.8
7 Brigham Young	12	879	5517	6.3	44	459.8
8 Pittsburgh	12	919	5429	5.9	35	452.4
9 Georgia	11	732	4954	6.8	41	450.4
10 Boston College	11	817	4822	5.9	41	438.4

RUSHING DEFENSE	G	ATT	YDS	AVG	TD	YPG
1 Alabama	12	395	660	1.7	5	55.0
2 Arizona	11	384	716	1.9	4	65.1
3 Mississippi	11	413	895	2.2	10	81.4
4 Michigan	11	369	985	2.7	6	89.5
5 Syracuse	11	339	1007	3.0	10	91.5
6 Florida State	11	400	1103	2.8	3	100.3
7 Memphis	11	447	1107	2.5	9	100.6
8 Miami, Fla.	11	406	1118	2.8	4	101.6
9 Notre Dame	11	399	1222	3.1	9	111.1
10 Toledo	11	466	1248	2.7	8	113.5

PASSING DEFENSE	G	ATT	COM	PCT	INT	I%	YDS	YPA	TD	TD%	RAT
1 Western Michigan	11	283	121	42.8	15	5.3	1522	5.4	5	1.8	83.2
2 Alabama	12	330	164	49.7	22	6.7	1670	5.1	6	1.8	84.9
3 Colorado	11	257	105	40.9	18	7.0	1461	5.7	8	3.1	84.9
4 Stanford	12	354	161	45.5	18	5.1	1869	5.3	10	2.8	89.0
5 Miami, Fla.	11	358	173	48.3	18	5.0	1861	5.2	10	2.8	91.2
6 Auburn	11	270	117	43.3	16	5.9	1565	5.8	10	3.7	92.4
7 Mississippi	11	362	169	46.7	17	4.7	2014	5.6	10	2.8	93.1
8 Southern Miss	11	297	143	48.2	19	6.4	1692	5.7	9	3.0	93.2
9 Toledo	11	325	148	45.5	13	4.0	1880	5.8	7	2.2	93.2
10 Georgia	11	302	151	50.0	12	4.0	1699	5.6	5	1.7	94.8

TOTAL DEFENSE	G	P	YDS	AVG	TD	YPG
1 Alabama	12	725	2330	3.2	11	194.2
2 Arizona	11	747	2783	3.7	9	253.0
3 Memphis	11	766	2788	3.6	20	253.5
4 Louisiana Tech	11	698	2822	4.0	15	256.5
5 Auburn	11	699	2837	4.1	20	257.9
6 Mississippi	11	775	2909	3.8	20	264.5
7 Arizona State	11	734	2957	4.0	18	268.8
8 Miami, Fla.	11	764	2979	3.9	14	270.8
9 Colorado	11	731	3058	4.2	19	278.0
10 Stanford	12	821	3369	4.1	23	280.8

SCORING OFFENSE	G	PTS	AVG
1 Fresno State	12	486	40.5
2 Nebraska	11	427	38.8
3 Florida State	11	419	38.1
4 Notre Dame	11	409	37.2
5 Michigan	11	393	35.7
6 Penn State	11	388	35.3
7 Houston	11	378	34.4
8 Hawaii	12	394	32.8
9 Miami, Fla.	11	356	32.4
10 Georgia	11	352	32.0

SCORING DEFENSE	G	PTS	AVG
1 Arizona	11	98	8.9
2 Alabama	12	109	9.1
3 Miami, Fla.	11	127	11.5
4 Ohio State	11	137	12.5
5 Michigan	11	140	12.7
6 Georgia	11	141	12.8
7 Washington	11	148	13.5
8 Toledo	11	153	13.9
9 Texas A&M	12	168	14.0
10 Louisiana Tech	11	167	15.2

TURNOVER MARGIN	G	FR	INT	TOT	FL	INTL	TOT	MAR
1 Nebraska	11	14	16	30	5	7	12	1.6
2 Akron	11	10	24	34	7	11	18	1.5
2 Miami, Fla.	11	11	18	29	6	7	13	1.5
4 Alabama	12	15	22	37	10	10	20	1.4
5 Rice	11	12	18	30	8	8	16	1.3
5 Southern Miss	11	11	19	30	6	10	16	1.3
5 Tennessee	11	14	11	25	7	4	11	1.3
8 Wake Forest	11	15	13	28	7	9	16	1.1
9 Stanford	12	16	18	34	12	9	21	1.1
10 Arizona	11	10	16	26	8	7	15	1.0

1993 Poll Progression

AP	Pre-Season 1993		Aug. 28 Games
1	Florida State	0-0-0	beat Kansas 42-0
2	Alabama	0-0-0	bye week
3	Michigan	0-0-0	bye week
4	Texas A&M	0-0-0	bye week
5	Miami, Fla.	0-0-0	bye week
6	Syracuse	0-0-0	bye week
7	Notre Dame	0-0-0	bye week
8	Nebraska	0-0-0	bye week
9	Florida	0-0-0	bye week
10	Tennessee	0-0-0	bye week
11	Colorado	0-0-0	bye week
12	Washington	0-0-0	bye week
13	Georgia	0-0-0	bye week
14	Arizona	0-0-0	bye week
15	Stanford	0-0-0	bye week
16	Penn State	0-0-0	bye week
17	Ohio State	0-0-0	bye week
18	Southern Cal	0-0-0	lost to # 20 North Carolina 9-31 (A29)
19	Brigham Young	0-0-0	bye week
20	North Carolina	0-0-0	beat # 18 Southern Cal 31-9 (A29)
21	Boston College	0-0-0	bye week
22	Oklahoma	0-0-0	bye week
23	Clemson	0-0-0	bye week
24	Mississippi State	0-0-0	bye week
25	North Carolina St.	0-0-0	bye week

CNN	AP	August 30 Poll		Sept. 4 Games
1	1	Florida State	1-0-0	beat Duke 45-7
2	2	Alabama	0-0-0	beat Tulane 31-17
4	3	Miami, Fla.	0-0-0	beat # 20 Boston College 23-7
3	3	Michigan	0-0-0	beat Washington State 41-14
5	5	Texas A&M	0-0-0	beat LSU 24-0
7	6	Syracuse	0-0-0	beat Ball State 35-12
6	7	Notre Dame	0-0-0	beat Northwestern 27-12
9	8	Florida	0-0-0	beat Arkansas State 44-6
8	9	Nebraska	0-0-0	beat North Texas 76-14
11	10	Tennessee	0-0-0	beat Louisiana Tech 50-0
10	11	Colorado	0-0-0	beat Texas 36-14
PB	12	Washington	0-0-0	beat Stanford 31-14
15	13	Arizona	0-0-0	beat Texas-El Paso 24-6
13	14	Georgia	0-0-0	lost to South Carolina 21-23
14	15	Stanford	0-0-0	lost to Washington 14-31
18	16	North Carolina	1-0-0	beat Ohio U. 44-3
12	17	Penn State	0-0-0	beat Minnesota 38-20
16	18	Ohio State	0-0-0	beat Rice 34-7
20	19	Brigham Young	0-0-0	beat New Mexico 34-31
23	20	Boston College	0-0-0	lost to # 3 Miami, Fla. 7-23
19	21	Oklahoma	0-0-0	beat TCU 35-3
21	22	Clemson	0-0-0	beat Nevada-Las Vegas 24-14
25	23	Mississippi State	0-0-0	lost to Memphis 35-45
22	24	North Carolina St.	0-0-0	beat Purdue 20-7
	25	Fresno State	0-0-0	lost to Baylor 39-42
17		Southern Cal	0-1-0	beat Houston 49-7
24		Texas	0-0-0	lost to # 11 Colorado 14-36

CNN	AP	September 6 Poll		Sept. 11 Games
1	1	Florida State	2-0-0	beat # 21 Clemson 57-0
3	2	Alabama	1-0-0	beat Vanderbilt 17-6
2	3	Michigan	1-0-0	lost to # 11 Notre Dame 23-27
4	4	Miami, Fla.	1-0-0	bye week
5	5	Texas A&M	1-0-0	lost to # 17 Oklahoma 14-44
6	6	Syracuse	1-0-0	beat East Carolina 41-22
8	7	Florida	1-0-0	beat Kentucky 24-20
11	8	Tennessee	1-0-0	beat # 22 Georgia 38-6
7	9	Nebraska	1-0-0	beat Texas Tech 50-27
9	10	Colorado	1-0-0	beat # 24 Baylor 45-21
10	11	Notre Dame	1-0-0	beat # 3 Michigan 27-23
PB	12	Washington	1-0-0	lost to # 16 Ohio State 12-21
13	13	Arizona	1-0-0	beat Pacific 16-13
15	14	North Carolina	2-0-0	beat Maryland 59-42
12	15	Penn State	1-0-0	beat Southern Cal 21-20
14	16	Ohio State	1-0-0	beat # 12 Washington 21-12
16	17	Oklahoma	1-0-0	beat # 5 Texas A&M 44-14
18	18	North Carolina St.	1-0-0	beat Wake Forest 34-16
20	19	South Carolina	1-0-0	lost to Arkansas 17-18
19	20	Brigham Young	1-0-0	beat Hawaii 41-38
17	21	Clemson	1-0-0	lost to # 1 Florida State 0-57
21	22	Georgia	0-1-0	lost to # 8 Tennessee 6-38
22	23	Stanford	0-1-0	beat San Jose State 31-28
25	24	Baylor	1-0-0	lost to # 10 Colorado 21-45
	25	Boston College	0-1-0	bye week
23		Southern Cal	1-1-0	lost to # 15 Penn State 20-21
24		Arizona State	1-0-0	bye week

CNN	AP	September 13 Poll		Sept. 18 Games
1	1	Florida State	3-0-0	beat # 13 North Carolina 33-7
2	2	Alabama	2-0-0	beat Arkansas 43-3
3	3	Miami, Fla.	1-0-0	beat Virginia Tech 21-2
5	4	Notre Dame	2-0-0	beat Michigan State 36-14
7	5	Tennessee	2-0-0	lost to # 9 Florida 34-41
4	6	Syracuse	2-0-0	tied Texas 21-21
8	7	Colorado	2-0-0	lost to # 20 Stanford 37-41
6	8	Nebraska	2-0-0	beat UCLA 14-13
9	9	Florida	2-0-0	beat # 5 Tennessee 41-34
10	10	Michigan	1-1-0	bye week
11	11	Ohio State	2-0-0	beat Pittsburgh 63-28
13	12	Oklahoma	2-0-0	bye week
14	13	North Carolina	3-0-0	lost to # 1 Florida State 7-33
12	14	Penn State	2-0-0	beat Iowa 31-0
15	15	Arizona	2-0-0	beat Illinois 16-14
16	16	Texas A&M	1-1-0	beat Missouri 73-0
17	17	North Carolina St.	2-0-0	bye week
PB	18	Washington	1-1-0	bye week
18	19	Brigham Young	2-0-0	beat Colorado State 27-22
19	20	Stanford	1-1-0	beat # 7 Colorado 41-37
21	21	California	2-0-0	beat Temple 58-0
24	22	Boston College	0-1-0	lost to Northwestern 21-22
20	23	Arizona State	1-0-0	lost to Louisville 17-35
25	24	Wisconsin	2-0-0	beat Iowa State 28-7
23	25	Virginia	2-0-0	beat Georgia Tech 35-14 S16
22		Iowa	2-0-0	lost to # 14 Penn State 0-31

CNN	AP	September 20 Poll		Sept. 25 Games
1	1	Florida State	4-0-0	bye week
2	2	Alabama	3-0-0	beat Louisiana Tech 56-3
3	3	Miami, Fla.	2-0-0	beat # 13 Colorado 35-29
4	4	Notre Dame	3-0-0	beat Purdue 17-0
6	5	Florida	3-0-0	bye week
5	6	Nebraska	3-0-0	beat Colorado State 48-13
7	7	Ohio State	3-0-0	bye week
9	8	Michigan	1-1-0	beat Houston 42-21
8	9	Penn State	3-0-0	beat Rutgers 31-7
10	10	Oklahoma	2-0-0	beat Tulsa 41-20
13	11	Tennessee	2-1-0	beat LSU 42-20
11	12	Syracuse	2-0-1	beat Cincinnati 24-21
12	13	Colorado	2-1-0	lost to # 3 Miami, Fla. 29-35
15	14	Texas A&M	2-1-0	bye week
14	15	Arizona	3-0-0	beat Oregon State 33-0
PB	16	Washington	1-1-0	beat East Carolina 35-0
20	17	Stanford	2-1-0	lost to UCLA 25-28
19	18	North Carolina	3-1-0	beat # 19 North Carolina St. 35-14
16	19	North Carolina St.	2-0-0	lost to # 18 North Carolina 14-35
18	20	California	3-0-0	beat San Jose State 46-13
17	21	Brigham Young	3-0-0	beat Air Force 30-3
21	22	Virginia	3-0-0	beat Duke 35-0
22	23	Wisconsin	3-0-0	beat Indiana 27-15
23	24	Louisville	3-0-0	beat Texas 41-10
PB	25	Auburn	3-0-0	beat Southern Miss 35-24
24		West Virginia	2-0-0	beat Missouri 35-3
25		Fresno State	2-1-0	beat Utah State 30-14

CNN	AP	September 27 Poll		Oct. 2 Games
1	1	Florida State	4-0-0	beat Georgia Tech 51-0
2	2	Alabama	4-0-0	beat South Carolina 17-6
3	3	Miami, Fla.	3-0-0	beat Georgia Southern 30-7
4	4	Notre Dame	4-0-0	beat Stanford 48-20
6	5	Florida	3-0-0	beat Mississippi State 38-24
5	6	Nebraska	4-0-0	bye week
7	7	Ohio State	3-0-0	beat Northwestern 51-3
10	8	Michigan	2-1-0	beat Iowa 24-7
8	9	Penn State	4-0-0	beat Maryland 70-7
9	10	Oklahoma	3-0-0	beat Iowa State 24-7
12	11	Tennessee	3-1-0	beat Duke 52-19
11	12	Arizona	4-0-0	beat Southern Cal 38-7
13	13	Syracuse	3-0-1	lost to Boston College 29-33
14	14	Texas A&M	2-1-0	beat Texas Tech 31-6
PB	15	Washington	2-1-0	beat San Jose State 52-17
16	16	North Carolina	4-1-0	beat Texas-El Paso 45-39
15	17	California	4-0-0	beat Oregon 42-41
19	18	Louisville	4-0-0	beat Pittsburgh 29-7
21	19	Colorado	2-2-0	bye week
17	20	Brigham Young	4-0-0	bye week
18	21	Virginia	4-0-0	beat Ohio U. 41-7
20	22	Wisconsin	4-0-0	bye week
PB	23	Auburn	4-0-0	beat Vanderbilt 14-10
23	24	North Carolina St.	2-1-0	lost to Clemson 14-20
22	25	West Virginia	3-0-0	beat Virginia Tech 14-13
24		Fresno State	3-1-0	bye week
25		Mississippi	3-1-0	lost to Kentucky 0-21

CNN	AP	October 4 Poll		Oct. 9 Games
1	1	Florida State	5-0-0	beat # 3 Miami, Fla. 28-10
2	2	Alabama	5-0-0	bye week
3	3	Miami, Fla.	4-0-0	lost to # 1 Florida State 10-28
4	4	Notre Dame	5-0-0	beat Pittsburgh 44-0
6	5	Florida	4-0-0	beat LSU 58-3
7	6	Ohio State	4-0-0	beat Illinois 20-12
5	7	Nebraska	4-0-0	beat Oklahoma State 27-13 O7
8	8	Penn State	5-0-0	bye week
10	9	Michigan	3-1-0	lost to Michigan State 7-17
9	10	Oklahoma	4-0-0	beat Texas 38-17
12	11	Tennessee	4-1-0	beat Arkansas 28-14
11	12	Arizona	5-0-0	bye week
PB	13	Washington	3-1-0	beat # 16 California 24-23
13	14	Texas A&M	3-1-0	beat Houston 34-10
15	15	North Carolina	5-1-0	beat Wake Forest 45-35
14	16	California	5-0-0	lost to # 13 Washington 23-24
17	17	Louisville	5-0-0	lost to West Virginia 34-36
16	18	Virginia	5-0-0	bye week
18	19	Brigham Young	4-0-0	lost to # 25 UCLA 14-68
21	20	Colorado	2-2-0	beat Missouri 30-18
19	21	Wisconsin	4-0-0	beat Northwestern 53-14
PB	22	Auburn	5-0-0	beat Mississippi State 31-17
22	23	Syracuse	3-1-1	bye week
20	24	West Virginia	4-0-0	beat Louisville 36-34
	25	UCLA	2-2-0	beat # 19 Brigham Young 68-14
23		Fresno State	3-1-0	lost to Colorado State 32-34
24		Clemson	3-1-0	beat Duke 13-10
25		Indiana	4-1-0	beat Iowa 16-10

CNN	AP	October 11 Poll		Oct. 16 Games
1	1	Florida State	6-0-0	beat # 15 Virginia 40-14
2	2	Alabama	5-0-0	tied # 10 Tennessee 17-17
3	3	Notre Dame	6-0-0	beat Brigham Young 45-20
4	4	Florida	5-0-0	lost to # 19 Auburn 35-38
6	5	Ohio State	5-0-0	beat # 25 Michigan State 28-21
5	6	Nebraska	5-0-0	beat Kansas State 45-28
7	7	Penn State	5-0-0	lost to # 18 Michigan 13-21
9	8	Miami, Fla.	4-1-0	bye week
8	9	Oklahoma	5-0-0	lost to # 20 Colorado 10-27
11	10	Tennessee	5-1-0	tied # 2 Alabama 17-17
10	11	Arizona	5-0-0	beat Stanford 27-24
PB	12	Washington	4-1-0	lost to # 22 UCLA 25-39
12	13	Texas A&M	4-1-0	beat Baylor 34-17
13	14	North Carolina	6-1-0	beat Georgia Tech 41-3
14	15	Virginia	5-0-0	lost to # 1 Florida State 14-40
16	16	Wisconsin	5-0-0	beat Purdue 42-28
15	17	West Virginia	5-0-0	bye week
17	18	Michigan	3-2-0	beat # 7 Penn State 21-13
PB	19	Auburn	6-0-0	beat # 4 Florida 38-35
18	20	Colorado	3-2-0	beat # 9 Oklahoma 27-10
20	21	California	5-1-0	lost to Washington St. 7-34
23	22	UCLA	3-2-0	beat # 12 Washington 39-25
21	23	Louisville	5-1-0	beat Southern Miss 35-27
19	24	Syracuse	3-1-1	beat Pittsburgh 24-21
25	25	Michigan State	3-1-0	lost to # 5 Ohio State 21-28
22		Indiana	5-1-0	bye week
24		Kansas State	5-0-0	lost to # 6 Nebraska 28-45

CNN	AP	October 18 Poll		Oct. 23 Games
1	1	Florida State	7-0-0	bye week
2	2	Notre Dame	7-0-0	beat Southern Cal 31-13
4	3	Ohio State	6-0-0	beat Purdue 45-24
5	4	Alabama	5-0-1	beat Mississippi 19-14
3	5	Nebraska	6-0-0	beat Missouri 49-7
6	6	Miami, Fla.	4-1-0	beat # 23 Syracuse 49-0
7	7	Arizona	6-0-0	beat # 25 Washington St. 9-6
8	8	Tennessee	5-1-1	bye week
10	9	Florida	5-1-0	bye week
PB	10	Auburn	7-0-0	bye week
9	11	Texas A&M	5-1-0	beat Rice 38-10
11	12	North Carolina	7-1-0	lost to # 21 Virginia 10-17
14	13	Michigan	4-2-0	lost to Illinois 21-24
13	14	Penn State	5-1-0	bye week
12	15	Wisconsin	6-0-0	lost to Minnesota 21-28
16	16	Colorado	4-2-0	tied Kansas State 16-16
17	17	Oklahoma	5-1-0	beat Kansas 38-23
15	18	West Virginia	5-0-0	beat Pittsburgh 42-21
18	19	UCLA	4-2-0	beat Oregon State 20-17
19	20	Louisville	6-1-0	beat Navy 28-0
20	21	Virginia	5-1-0	beat # 12 North Carolina 17-10
PB	22	Washington	4-2-0	beat Oregon 21-6
21	23	Syracuse	4-1-1	lost to # 6 Miami, Fla. 0-49
23	24	Michigan State	3-2-0	beat Iowa 24-10
24	25	Washington State	5-2-0	lost to # 7 Arizona 6-9
22		Indiana	5-1-0	beat Northwestern 24-0
25		Kansas State	5-1-0	tied # 16 Colorado 16-16

1993 ANNUAL REVIEW 1385

CNN	AP	October 25 Poll		Oct. 30 Games
1	1	Florida State	7-0-0	beat Wake Forest 54-0
2	2	Notre Dame	8-0-0	beat Navy 58-27
3	3	Ohio State	7-0-0	beat # 12 Penn State 24-6
6	4	Miami, Fla.	5-1-0	beat Temple 42-7
5	5	Alabama	6-0-1	beat Southern Miss 40-0
4	6	Nebraska	7-0-0	beat # 20 Colorado 21-17
7	7	Arizona	7-0-0	lost to # 15 UCLA 17-37
9	8	Tennessee	5-1-1	beat South Carolina 55-3
PB	9	Auburn	7-0-0	beat Arkansas 31-21
10	10	Florida	5-1-0	beat Georgia 33-26
8	11	Texas A&M	6-1-0	beat SMU 37-13
12	12	Penn State	5-1-0	lost to # 3 Ohio State 6-24
11	13	West Virginia	6-0-0	beat Syracuse 43-0
13	14	Oklahoma	6-1-0	lost to # 25 Kansas State 7-21
15	15	UCLA	5-2-0	beat # 7 Arizona 37-17
14	16	Virginia	6-1-0	lost to North Carolina St. 29-34
16	17	Louisville	7-1-0	bye week
19	18	North Carolina	7-2-0	bye week
PB	19	Washington	5-2-0	lost to Arizona State 17-32
18	20	Colorado	4-2-1	lost to # 6 Nebraska 17-21
20	21	Wisconsin	6-1-0	beat # 24 Michigan 13-10
21	22	Michigan State	4-2-0	lost to # 23 Indiana 0-10
17	23	Indiana	6-1-0	beat # 22 Michgan State 10-0
23	24	Michigan	4-3-0	lost to # 21 Wisconsin 10-13
22	25	Kansas State	5-1-1	beat # 14 Oklahoma 21-7
24		Virginia Tech	5-2-0	beat East Carolina 31-12
25		Wyoming	6-1-0	beat Fresno State 32-28

CNN	AP	November 1 Poll		Nov. 6 Games
1	1	Florida State	8-0-0	beat Maryland 49-20
2	2	Notre Dame	9-0-0	bye week
3	3	Ohio State	8-0-0	tied # 15 Wisconsin 14-14
6	4	Miami, Fla.	6-1-0	beat Pittsburgh 35-7
5	5	Alabama	7-0-1	lost to LSU 13-17
4	6	Nebraska	8-0-0	beat Kansas 21-20
7	7	Tennessee	6-1-1	beat # 13 Louisville 45-10
PB	8	Auburn	8-0-0	beat New Mexico State 55-14
10	9	Florida	6-1-0	beat La. Lafayette 61-14
8	10	Texas A&M	7-1-0	bye week
9	11	West Virginia	7-0-0	beat Rutgers 58-22
11	12	UCLA	6-2-0	beat Washington State 40-27
15	13	Louisville	7-1-0	lost to # 7 Tennessee 10-45
12	14	Arizona	7-1-0	beat Oregon 31-10
14	15	Wisconsin	7-1-0	tied # 3 Ohio State 14-14
18	16	North Carolina	7-2-0	beat Clemson 24-0
13	17	Indiana	7-1-0	lost to # 19 Penn State 31-38
17	18	Kansas State	6-1-1	lost to Iowa State 23-27
16	19	Penn State	5-2-0	beat # 17 Indiana 38-31
20	20	Oklahoma	6-2-0	beat Missouri 42-23
19	21	Virginia	6-2-0	beat Wake Forest 21-9
22	22	North Carolina St.	6-2-0	lost to Duke 20-21
24	23	Colorado	4-3-1	beat Oklahoma State 31-14
21	24	Wyoming	7-1-0	bye week
23	25	Virginia Tech	6-2-0	lost to Boston College 34-48
25		Boston College	5-2-0	beat # 25 Virginia Tech 48-34

CNN	AP	November 8 Poll		Nov. 13 Games
1	1	Florida State	9-0-0	lost to # 2 Notre Dame 24-31
2	2	Notre Dame	9-0-0	beat # 1 Florida State 31-24
4	3	Miami, Fla.	7-1-0	beat Rutgers 31-17
3	4	Nebraska	9-0-0	beat Iowa State 49-17
5	5	Ohio State	8-0-1	beat # 19 Indiana 23-17
6	6	Tennessee	7-1-1	bye week
PB	7	Auburn	9-0-0	beat Georgia 42-28
9	8	Florida	7-1-0	beat South Carolina 37-26
7	9	West Virginia	8-0-0	beat Temple 49-7
10	10	UCLA	7-2-0	lost to Arizona State 3-9
8	11	Texas A&M	7-1-0	beat # 20 Louisville 42-7
11	12	Alabama	7-1-1	beat Mississippi State 36-25
12	13	Arizona	8-1-0	lost to California 20-24
13	14	Wisconsin	7-1-1	bye week
15	15	North Carolina	8-2-0	beat Tulane 42-10
14	16	Penn State	6-2-0	beat Illinois 28-14
17	17	Oklahoma	7-2-0	beat Oklahoma State 31-0
16	18	Virginia	7-2-0	lost to Clemson 14-23
18	19	Indiana	7-2-0	lost to # 5 Ohio State 17-23
20	20	Louisville	7-2-0	lost to # 11 Texas A&M 7-42
22	21	Colorado	5-3-1	beat Kansas 38-14
21	22	Boston College	6-2-0	beat Pittsburgh 33-0
19	23	Wyoming	7-1-0	lost to New Mexico 7-10
23	24	Kansas State	6-2-1	beat Missouri 31-21
	25	Washington	6-3-0	lost to Southern Cal 17-22
24		Southern Cal	6-4-0	beat # 25 Washington 22-17
25		Michigan State	5-3-0	beat Purdue 27-24

*CNN	AP	November 15 Poll		Nov. 20 Games
1	1	Notre Dame	10-0-0	lost to # 17 Boston College 39-41
3	2	Florida State	9-1-0	beat North Carolina St. 62-3
2	3	Nebraska	10-0-0	bye week
4	4	Miami, Fla.	8-1-0	lost to # 9 West Virginia 14-17
5	5	Ohio State	9-0-1	lost to Michigan 0-28
PB	6	Auburn	10-0-0	beat # 11 Alabama 22-14
7	7	Tennessee	7-1-1	beat Kentucky 48-0
9	8	Florida	8-1-0	beat Vanderbilt 52-0
6	9	West Virginia	9-0-0	beat # 4 Miami, Fla. 17-14
8	10	Texas A&M	8-1-0	beat TCU 59-3
10	11	Alabama	8-1-1	lost to # 6 Auburn 14-22
11	12	Wisconsin	7-1-1	beat Illinois 35-10
13	13	North Carolina	9-2-0	bye week
12	14	Penn State	7-2-0	beat Northwestern 43-21
14	15	Oklahoma	8-2-0	bye week
15	16	UCLA	7-3-0	beat # 22 Southern Cal 27-21
16	17	Boston College	7-2-0	beat # 1 Notre Dame 41-39
18	18	Colorado	6-3-1	beat Iowa State 21-16
17	19	Arizona	8-2-0	bye week
20	20	Kansas State	7-2-1	beat Oklahoma State 21-17
21	21	Indiana	7-3-0	beat Purdue 24-17
19	22	Southern Cal	7-4-0	lost to # 16 UCLA 21-27
22	23	Virginia	7-3-0	lost to # 25 Virginia Tech 17-20
25	24	Clemson	7-3-0	beat South Carolina 16-13
23	25	Virginia Tech	7-3-0	beat # 23 Virginia 20-17
24		Michigan State	6-3-0	bye week

CNN	AP	November 22 Poll		Nov. 27 Games
2	1	Florida State	10-1-0	beat # 7 Florida 33-21
1	2	Nebraska	10-0-0	beat # 16 Oklahoma 21-7 (N26)
PB	3	Auburn	11-0-0	regular season complete
4	4	Notre Dame	10-1-0	regular season complete
3	5	West Virginia	10-0-0	beat # 11 Boston College 17-14
5	6	Tennessee	8-1-1	beat Vanderbilt 62-14
6	7	Florida	9-1-0	lost to # 1 Florida State 21-33
6	8	Texas A&M	9-1-0	beat Texas 18-9 (N25)
9	9	Miami, Fla.	8-2-0	beat Memphis 41-17
8	10	Wisconsin	8-1-1	bye week
12	11	Boston College	8-2-0	lost to # 5 West Virginia 14-17
10	12	Ohio State	9-1-1	regular season complete
13	13	North Carolina	9-2-0	beat Duke 38-24 (N26)
11	14	Penn State	8-2-0	beat # 25 Michigan State 38-37
14	15	UCLA	8-3-0	regular season complete
15	16	Oklahoma	8-2-0	lost to # 2 Nebraska 7-21 (N26)
17	17	Alabama	8-2-1	bye week
18	18	Colorado	7-3-1	regular season complete
16	19	Arizona	8-2-0	beat Arizona State 34-20 (N26)
19	20	Kansas State	8-2-1	regular season complete
21	21	Indiana	8-3-0	regular season complete
20	22	Virginia Tech	8-3-0	regular season complete
22	23	Michigan	7-4-0	regular season complete
23	24	Clemson	8-3-0	regular season complete
24	25	Michigan State	6-3-0	lost to # 14 Penn State 37-38
25		Southern Cal	7-5-0	regular season complete

CNN	AP	November 29 Poll		Dec. 4 Games
3	1	Florida State	11-1-0	regular season complete
1	2	Nebraska	11-0-0	regular season complete
2	3	West Virginia	11-0-0	regular season complete
PB	4	Auburn	11-0-0	
4	5	Notre Dame	10-1-0	
5	6	Tennessee	9-1-1	regular season complete
6	7	Texas A&M	10-1-0	regular season complete
8	8	Miami, Fla.	9-2-0	regular season complete
9	9	Florida	9-2-0	beat # 16 Alabama 28-13 (SEC CH)
7	10	Wisconsin	8-1-1	beat # 25 Michigan State 41-20
10	11	Ohio State	9-1-1	
11	12	North Carolina	10-2-0	regular season complete
12	13	Penn State	9-2-0	regular season complete
13	14	UCLA	8-3-0	
16	15	Boston College	8-3-0	regular season complete
15	16	Alabama	8-2-1	lost to # 9 Florida 13-28 (SEC CH)
14	17	Arizona	9-2-0	regular season complete
18	18	Colorado	7-3-1	
17	19	Oklahoma	8-3-0	regular season complete
19	20	Kansas State	8-2-1	
21	21	Indiana	8-3-0	
20	22	Virginia Tech	8-3-0	
22	23	Michigan	7-4-0	
23	24	Clemson	8-3-0	
	25	Michigan State	6-4-0	lost to # 10 Wisconsin 20-41
24		Fresno State	8-3-0	regular season complete
25		Louisville	8-3-0	regular season complete

CNN	AP	December 6 Poll	Record	Bowl Bid	Date	Bowl Result	RB	CNN	AP	January 3 Final Poll	Record
3	1	Florida State	11-1-0	Orange Bowl	J1	beat # 2 Nebraska 18-16	1	1	1	Florida State	12-1-0
1	2	Nebraska	11-0-0	Orange Bowl	J1	lost to # 1 Florida State 16-18	2	2	2	Notre Dame	11-1-0
2	3	West Virginia	11-0-0	Sugar Bowl	J1	lost to # 8 Florida 7-41	4	3	3	Nebraska	11-1-0
4	4	Notre Dame	10-1-0	Cotton Bowl	J1	beat # 7 Texas A&M 24-21	3	PB	4	Auburn	11-0-0
PB	5	Auburn	11-0-0				6	4	5	Florida	11-2-0
5	6	Tennessee	9-1-1	Citrus Bowl	J1	lost to # 13 Penn State 13-31	12	5	6	Wisconsin	10-1-1
6	7	Texas A&M	10-1-0	Cotton Bowl	J1	lost to # 4 Notre Dame 21-24	7	6	7	West Virginia	11-1-0
8	8	Florida	10-2-0	Sugar Bowl	J1	beat # 3 West Virginia 41-7	10	7	8	Penn State	10-2-0
7	9	Wisconsin	9-1-1	Rose Bowl	J1	beat # 14 UCLA 21-16	13	8	9	Texas A&M	10-2-0
9	10	Miami, Fla.	9-2-0	Fiesta Bowl	J1	lost to # 16 Arizona 0-29	8	9	10	Arizona	10-2-0
10	11	Ohio State	9-1-1	Holiday Bowl	D30	beat Brigham Young 28-21	5	10	11	Ohio State	10-1-1
11	12	North Carolina	10-2-0	Gator Bowl	D31	lost to # 18 Alabama 10-24	11	11	12	Tennessee	9-2-1
12	13	Penn State	9-2-0	Citrus Bowl	J1	beat # 6 Tennessee 31-13	14	12	13	Boston College	9-3-0
13	14	UCLA	8-3-0	Rose Bowl	J1	lost to # 9 Wisconsin 16-21	15	13	14	Alabama	9-3-1
15	15	Boston College	8-3-0	Carquest Bowl	J1	beat Virginia 31-13	9	15	15	Miami, Fla.	9-3-0
14	16	Arizona	9-2-0	Fiesta Bowl	J1	beat # 10 Miami, Fla. 29-0	18	16	16	Colorado	8-3-1
17	17	Colorado	7-3-1	Aloha Bowl	D25	beat # 25 Fresno State 41-30	22	14	17	Oklahoma	9-3-0
18	18	Alabama	8-3-1	Gator Bowl	D31	beat # 12 North Carolina 24-10	16	17	18	UCLA	8-4-0
16	19	Oklahoma	8-3-0	Sun Bowl	D24	beat Texas Tech 41-10	17	21	19	North Carolina	10-3-0
19	20	Kansas State	8-2-1	Copper Bowl	D29	beat Wyoming 52-17	25	18	20	Kansas State	9-2-1
20	21	Indiana	8-3-0	Independence Bowl	D31	lost to # 22 Virginia Tech 20-45	20	19	21	Michigan	8-4-0
20	22	Virginia Tech	8-3-0	Independence Bowl	D31	beat # 21 Indiana 45-20	26	20	22	Virginia Tech	9-3-0
22	23	Michigan	7-4-0	Hall of Fame Bowl	J1	beat North Carolina St. 42-7	21	22	23	Clemson	9-3-0
23	24	Clemson	8-3-0	Peach Bowl	D31	beat Kentucky 14-13	24	23	24	Louisville	9-3-0
24	25	Fresno State	8-3-0	Aloha Bowl	D25	lost to # 17 Colorado 30-41	28	24	25	California	9-4-0
25	26	Louisville	8-3-0	Liberty Bowl	D28	beat Michigan State 18-7	27	25		Southern Cal	8-5-0

ANNUAL REVIEW

1993

CONSENSUS ALL-AMERICANS

POS	Offense	HT	WT	School	AP	CF	FC	FN	FW	PI	SN
QB	Charlie Ward	6-2	190	Florida State	•	•	•	•	•	•	•
RB	Marshall Faulk	5-10	200	San Diego State	•	•	•	•	•	•	•
RB	LeShon Johnson	6-0	201	Northern Illinois	•	•	•	•	•	•	•
WR	J.J. Stokes	6-5	214	UCLA	•	•	•		•	•	•
WR	Johnnie Morton	6-0	190	Southern Cal	•	•		•			
OL	Mark Dixon	6-4	283	Virginia	•	•	•	•	•		
OL	Stacy Seegars	6-4	320	Clemson	•	•	•	•			
OL	Aaron Taylor	6-4	299	Notre Dame	•	•	•	•	•	•	•
OL	Wayne Gandy	6-5	275	Auburn	•						
C	Jim Pyne	6-2	280	Virginia Tech	•	•	•	•		•	
PK	Bjorn Merten	6-0	203	UCLA	•						
KR	David Palmer	5-9	170	Alabama		•	•		•	•	

OTHERS RECEIVING FIRST-TEAM HONORS

POS		School							
RB	Errict Rhett	Florida							
WR	Ryan Yarborough	Wyoming		•		•			
TE	Carlester Crumpler	East Carolina							
TE	Pete Mitchell	Boston College					•	•	
OL	Korey Stringer	Ohio State		•	•				
OL	Marcus Spears	Northwestern State							•
OL	Rich Braham	West Virginia		•		•			
OL	Todd Steussie	California						•	
OL	Bernard Williams	Georgia						•	
K	John Becksvoort	Tennessee		•					
K	John Stewart	SMU		•					

FC named Palmer as a WR

POS	Defense	HT	WT	School	AP	CF	FC	FN	FW	PI	SN
DL	Rob Waldrop	6-2	275	Arizona	•	•	•	•	•	•	•
DL	Dan Wilkinson	6-5	300	Ohio State	•	•	•	•	•	•	•
DL	Sam Adams	6-4	269	Texas A&M	•	•	•	•		•	•
LB	Trev Alberts	6-4	240	Nebraska	•	•	•	•	•	•	•
LB	Derrick Brooks	6-1	225	Florida State	•	•	•	•	•	•	•
LB	Jamir Miller	6-4	233	UCLA	•	•	•	•	•		
DB	Antonio Langham	6-1	170	Alabama	•	•	•	•	•	•	•
DB	Aaron Glenn	5-10	182	Texas A&M	•	•	•	•		•	•
DB	Jeff Burris	6-0	204	Notre Dame	•	•	•	•			
DB	Corey Sawyer	5-11	171	Florida State	•	•	•		•		•
P	Terry Daniel	6-1	226	Auburn	•		•	•			

OTHERS RECEIVING FIRST-TEAM HONORS

POS		School							
DL	Lou Benfatti	Penn State							
DL	Derrick Alexander	Florida State							
DL	Shante Carver	Arizona State							
DL	Kevin Patrick	Miami, Fla.	•		•		•		
DL	Bryant Young	Notre Dame			•				
LB	Barron Wortham	Texas-El Paso							
LB	Dana Howard	Illinois							
DB	Bobby Taylor	Notre Dame					•	•	
DB	Bracey Walker	North Carolina			•		•		
DB	Jaime Mendez	Kansas State	•		•				

FC named Trev Alberts as a DL

HEISMAN TROPHY VOTING

	PLAYER	POS	SCHOOL	1ST	2ND	3RD	TOTAL
1	Charlie Ward	QB	Florida State	740	39	12	2310
2	Heath Shuler	QB	Tennessee	10	274	110	688
3	David Palmer	RB	Alabama	16	78	88	292
4	Marshall Faulk	RB	San Diego State	7	74	81	250
5	Glenn Foley	QB	Boston College	5	47	71	180
6	LeShon Johnson	RB	Northern Illinois	5	51	59	176
7	J.J. Stokes	WR	UCLA	3	37	48	131
8	Tyrone Wheatley	RB	Michigan	2	31	32	100
9	Trent Dilfer	QB	Fresno State	2	28	29	91
10	Eric Zeier	QB	Georgia	0	24	37	85

AWARD WINNERS

PLAYER	POS/SCHOOL	AWARD	PLAYER	POS/SCHOOL	AWARD
Charlie Ward	QB Florida State	Maxwell	Trev Alberts	LB Nebraska	Butkus
Rob Waldrop	NG Arizona	Outland	Antonio Langham	DB Alabama	Thorpe
Charlie Ward	QB Florida State	Camp	Charlie Ward	QB Florida State	Unitas
Aaron Taylor	OT Notre Dame	Lombardi	Byron Morris	RB Texas Tech	Walker
Charlie Ward	QB Florida State	O'Brien	Judd Davis	K Florida	Groza
			Rob Waldrop	NG Arizona	Nagurski

BOWL GAMES

DATE	GAME	SCORE
D17	Las Vegas	Utah State 42, Ball State 33
D24	Sun	Oklahoma 41, Texas Tech 10
D25	Aloha	Colorado 41, Fresno State 30
D28	Liberty	Louisville 18, Michigan State 7
D29	Copper	Kansas State 52, Wyoming 17
D30	Holiday	Ohio State 28, Brigham Young 21
D30	Freedom	Southern Cal 28, Utah 21
D31	Gator	Alabama 24, North Carolina 10
D31	Alamo	California 37, Iowa 3

CONFERENCE STANDINGS

ACC

	CONF. W L T	OVERALL W L T
Florida State	8 0 0	12 1 0
North Carolina	6 2 0	10 3 0
Clemson	5 3 0	9 3 0
Virginia	5 3 0	7 5 0
North Carolina St.	4 4 0	7 5 0
Georgia Tech	3 5 0	5 6 0
Duke	2 6 0	3 8 0
Maryland	2 6 0	2 9 0
Wake Forest	1 7 0	2 9 0

Big 10

	CONF. W L T	OVERALL W L T
Ohio State	6 1 1	10 1 1
Wisconsin	6 1 1	10 1 1
Penn State	6 2 0	10 2 0
Indiana	5 3 0	8 4 0
Michigan	5 3 0	8 4 0
Illinois	5 3 0	5 6 0
Michigan State	4 4 0	6 6 0
Iowa	3 5 0	6 6 0
Minnesota	3 5 0	4 7 0
Northwestern	0 8 0	2 9 0
Purdue	0 8 0	1 10 0

Big 8

	CONF. W L T	OVERALL W L T
Nebraska	7 0 0	11 1 0
Colorado	5 1 1	8 3 1
Kansas State	4 2 1	9 2 1
Oklahoma	4 3 0	9 3 0
Kansas	3 4 0	5 7 0
Missouri	2 5 0	3 7 1
Iowa State	2 5 0	3 8 0
Oklahoma State	0 7 0	3 8 0

Big East

	CONF. W L T	OVERALL W L T
West Virginia	7 0 0	11 1 0
Miami, Fla.	6 1 0	9 3 0
Boston College	5 2 0	9 3 0
Virginia Tech	4 3 0	9 3 0
Syracuse	3 4 0	6 4 1
Pittsburgh	2 5 0	3 8 0
Rutgers	1 6 0	4 7 0
Temple	0 7 0	1 10 0

Big West

	CONF. W L T	OVERALL W L T
La. Lafayette	5 1 0	8 3 0
Utah State	5 1 0	7 5 0
Nevada	5 2 0	7 4 0
New Mexico State	4 3 0	5 6 0
Northern Illinois	3 3 0	4 7 0
Pacific	2 4 0	3 8 0
Nevada-Las Vegas	2 4 0	3 8 0
Louisiana Tech	2 4 0	2 9 0
San Jose State	2 4 0	2 9 0
Arkansas State	1 5 0	2 8 1

Ivy

	CONF. W L T	OVERALL W L T
Pennsylvania	7 0 0	10 0 0
Dartmouth	6 1 0	7 3 0
Princeton	5 2 0	8 2 0
Brown	3 4 0	4 6 0
Cornell	3 4 0	4 6 0
Yale	2 5 0	3 7 0
Harvard	1 6 0	3 7 0
Columbia	1 6 0	2 8 0

MAC

	CONF. W L T	OVERALL W L T
Ball State	7 0 1	8 3 1
Western Michigan	6 1 1	7 3 1
Bowling Green	5 1 2	6 3 2
Central Michigan	5 4 0	5 6 0
Akron	4 4 0	5 6 0
Ohio U	4 5 0	4 7 0
Eastern Michigan	3 5 0	4 7 0
Toledo	3 5 0	4 7 0
Miami, Ohio	3 6 0	4 7 0
Kent State	0 9 0	0 11 0

Pac 10

	CONF. W L T	OVERALL W L T
Arizona	6 2 0	10 2 0
UCLA	6 2 0	8 4 0
Southern Cal	6 2 0	8 5 0
Washington	5 3 0	7 4 0
California	4 4 0	9 4 0
Arizona State	4 4 0	6 5 0
Washington State	3 5 0	5 6 0
Oregon	2 6 0	5 6 0
Oregon State	2 6 0	4 7 0
Stanford	2 6 0	4 7 0

SEC

	CONF. W L T	OVERALL W L T
EAST		
Florida	7 1 0	11 2 0
Tennessee	6 1 1	9 2 1
Kentucky	4 4 0	6 6 0
Georgia	2 6 0	5 6 0
South Carolina	2 6 0	4 7 0
Vanderbilt	1 7 0	4 7 0
WEST		
Auburn*	8 0 0	11 0 0
Alabama**	5 2 1	9 3 1
Arkansas	3 4 1	5 5 1
Mississippi	3 5 0	5 6 0
LSU	3 5 0	5 6 0

Championship Game **Florida 28 Alabama 13**

* not eligible for title   **later forfeited to 0-8-0

SWC

	CONF. W L T	OVERALL W L T
Texas A&M	7 0 0	10 2 0
Texas	5 2 0	5 5 1
Texas Tech	5 2 0	6 6 0
Rice	3 4 0	6 5 0
Baylor	3 4 0	5 6 0
TCU	2 5 0	4 7 0
SMU	1 5 1	2 7 2
Houston	1 5 1	1 9 1

WAC

	CONF. W L T	OVERALL W L T
Wyoming	6 2 0	8 4 0
Fresno State	6 2 0	8 4 0
Brigham Young	6 2 0	6 6 0
Utah	5 3 0	7 6 0
Colorado State	5 3 0	5 6 0
New Mexico	4 4 0	6 5 0
San Diego State	4 4 0	6 6 0
Hawaii	3 5 0	6 6 0
Air Force	1 7 0	4 8 0
Texas-El Paso	0 8 0	1 11 0

Independents

	OVERALL W L T
Notre Dame	11 1 0
Louisville	9 3 0
Cincinnati	8 3 0
Army	6 5 0
Memphis	6 5 0
Tulsa	4 6 1
Navy	4 7 0
Tulane	3 9 0
Southern Miss	2 8 1
East Carolina	2 9 0

DATE	GAME	SCORE
D31	Peach	Clemson 14, Kentucky 13
D31	Independence	Virginia Tech 45, Indiana 20
J1	Fiesta	Arizona 29, Miami, Fla. 0
J1	Carquest	Boston College 31, Virginia 13
J1	Orange	Florida State 18, Nebraska 16
J1	Hall of Fame	Michigan 42, North Carolina St. 7
J1	Cotton	Notre Dame 24, Texas A&M 21
J1	Citrus	Penn State 31, Tennessee 13
J1	Rose	Wisconsin 21, UCLA 16
J1	Sugar	Florida 41, West Virginia 7

1993 NCAA Major College Statistical Leaders

Individual Leaders

PASSING		CL	G	ATT	COM	PCT	INT	I%	YDS	YPA	TD	TD%	RATING
1	Trent Dilfer, Fresno State	JR	11	333	217	65.2	4	1.2	3276	9.8	28	8.4	173.1
2	Dave Barr, California	JR	11	275	187	68.0	12	4.4	2619	9.5	21	7.6	164.5
3	Darrell Bevell, Wisconsin	SO	11	256	177	69.1	10	3.9	2294	9.0	19	7.4	161.1
4	Charlie Ward, Florida State	SR	11	380	264	69.5	4	1.1	3032	8.0	27	7.1	157.8
5	Maurice DeShazo, Virginia Tech	JR	11	230	129	56.1	7	3.0	2080	9.0	22	9.6	157.5
6	Heath Shuler, Tennessee	JR	11	285	184	64.6	8	2.8	2354	8.3	25	8.8	157.3
7	Glenn Foley, Boston College	SR	11	363	222	61.2	10	2.8	3397	9.4	25	6.9	157.0
8	Chris Vargas, Nevada	SR	11	490	331	67.6	18	3.7	4265	8.7	34	6.9	156.2
9	John Walsh, Brigham Young	SO	11	397	244	61.5	15	3.8	3727	9.4	28	7.1	156.0
10	Rob Johnson, Southern Cal	JR	12	405	278	68.6	5	1.2	3285	8.1	26	6.4	155.5

ALL-PURPOSE		CL	G	RUSH	REC	PR	KR	YDS	YPG
1	LeShon Johnson, Northern Illinois	SR	11	1976	106	0	0	2082	189.3
2	Terrell Willis, Rutgers	FR	11	1261	61	0	704	2026	184.2
3	Marshall Faulk, San Diego State	JR	12	1530	644	0	0	2174	181.2
4	Byron Morris, Texas Tech	JR	11	1752	150	0	0	1902	172.9
5	Mike Adams, Texas	SO	11	68	908	256	622	1854	168.6
6	Napoleon Kaufman, Washington	JR	11	1299	139	25	388	1851	168.3
7	David Palmer, Alabama	JR	12	278	1000	244	439	1961	163.4
8	Tyrone Wheatley, Michigan	JR	9	1005	152	0	246	1403	155.9
9	Chris Penn, Tulsa	SR	11	2	1578	134	0	1714	155.8
10	John Leach, Wake Forest	SR	11	1089	340	9	253	1691	153.7

RUSHING/Yards Per Game		CL	G	ATT	YDS	TD	AVG	YPG
1	LeShon Johnson, Northern Illinois	SR	11	327	1976	12	6.0	179.6
2	Byron Morris, Texas Tech	JR	11	298	1752	22	5.9	159.3
3	Brent Moss, Wisconsin	JR	11	276	1479	14	5.4	134.5
4	Ron Rivers, Fresno State	SR	11	216	1440	14	6.7	130.9
5	Marshall Faulk, San Diego State	JR	12	300	1530	21	5.1	127.5
6	Junior Smith, East Carolina	JR	11	278	1352	9	4.9	122.9
7	Napoleon Kaufman, Washington	JR	11	226	1299	14	5.7	118.1
8	David Small, Cincinnati	SR	10	223	1180	17	5.3	118.0
9	Calvin Jones, Nebraska	JR	9	185	1043	12	5.6	115.9
10	Terrell Willis, Rutgers	FR	11	195	1261	13	6.5	114.6

RUSHING/Yards Per Carry		CL	G	ATT	YDS	YPC
1	Charlie Garner, Tennessee	SR	11	159	1161	7.3
2	Ron Rivers, Fresno State	SR	11	216	1440	6.7
3	Ki-Jana Carter, Penn State	SO	9	155	1026	6.6
4	Terrell Willis, Rutgers	FR	11	195	1261	6.5
5	Lee Becton, Notre Dame	JR	10	164	1044	6.4
6	James Bostic, Auburn	JR	11	199	1205	6.1
7	LeShon Johnson, Northern Illinois	SR	11	327	1976	6.0
8	Robert Walker, West Virginia	SO	11	201	1191	5.9
9	Byron Morris, Texas Tech	JR	11	298	1752	5.9
10	Napoleon Kaufman, Washington	JR	11	226	1299	5.7

*-Based on top 21 rushers

RECEIVING		CL	G	REC	YDS	TD	RPG	YPR	YPG
1	Chris Penn, Tulsa	SR	11	105	1578	12	9.5	15.0	143.5
2	Ryan Yarborough, Wyoming	SR	11	67	1512	16	6.1	22.6	137.5
3	Bryan Reeves, Nevada	SR	10	91	1362	17	9.1	15.0	136.2
4	Darnay Scott, San Diego State	JR	11	75	1262	10	6.8	16.8	114.7
5	Johnnie Morton, Southern Cal	SR	12	78	1373	12	6.5	17.6	114.4
6	Charles Johnson, Colorado	SR	11	57	1082	9	5.2	19.0	98.4
7	Demond Thompkins, Nevada-Las Vegas	JR	11	62	1068	8	5.6	17.2	97.1
8	Michael Stephens, Nevada	SR	11	80	1062	7	7.3	13.3	96.6
9	Isaac Bruce, Memphis	SR	11	74	1054	10	6.7	14.2	95.8
10	Brian Oliver, Ball State	JR	11	62	1010	10	5.6	16.3	91.8

PUNTING		CL	PUNT	YDS	AVG
1	Chris MacInnis, Air Force	SR	49	2303	47.0
2	Terry Daniel, Auburn	JR	51	2393	46.9
3	Mike Nesbitt, New Mexico	SR	53	2387	45.0
4	Brad Faunce, Nevada-Las Vegas	JR	61	2745	45.0
5	Pat O'Neill, Syracuse	SR	44	1950	44.3
6	Scott Milanovich, Maryland	SO	50	2189	43.8
7	Bryne Diehl, Alabama	JR	56	2441	43.6
8	Scott Tyner, Oklahoma State	SR	75	3249	43.3
9	Alan Boardman, Brigham Young	FR	56	2415	43.1
10	Stephen Wilson, Hawaii	JR	46	1976	43.0

PUNT RETURNS		CL	PR	YDS	TD	AVG
1	Aaron Glenn, Texas A&M	SR	17	339	2	19.9
2	Shawn Summers, Tennessee	SO	18	255	1	14.2
3	Lee Gissendaner, Northwestern	SR	16	223	0	13.9
4	Scott Gumina, Mississippi State	JR	13	180	1	13.9
5	Andre Coleman, Kansas State	SR	27	362	1	13.4
6	Eddie Kennison, LSU	FR	20	266	0	13.3
7	Todd Dixon, Wake Forest	SR	13	167	1	12.9
8	James Dye, Utah State	SO	21	256	1	12.2
9	Bobby Engram, Penn State	SO	33	402	0	12.2
10	Greg Myers, Colorado State	SO	27	325	0	12.0

KICKOFF RETURNS		CL	KR	YDS	TD	AVG
1	Leeland McElroy, Texas A&M	FR	15	590	3	39.3
2	Chris Hewitt, Cincinnati	FR	14	441	1	31.5
3	Tyler Anderson, Brigham Young	SR	19	568	1	29.9
4	Andre Coleman, Kansas State	SR	15	434	0	28.9
5	Jack Jackson, Florida	SO	17	480	1	28.2
6	Polee Banks, New Mexico State	SR	14	394	1	28.1
7	Demond Thompkins, Nevada-Las Vegas	JR	16	442	0	27.6
8	Steve Mehl, Pacific	JR	15	410	0	27.3
9	Mike Adams, Texas	SO	23	622	0	27.0
10	Dondra Jolly, Army	JR	19	510	0	26.8

SCORING		CL	TDS	XP	FG	PTS	PTPG
1	Byron Morris, Texas Tech	JR	22	2	0	134	12.2
2	Marshall Faulk, San Diego State	JR	24	0	0	144	12.0
3	Darnell Campbell, Boston College	SR	21	0	0	126	11.5
4	Bryan Reeves, Nevada	SR	17	0	0	102	10.2
4	David Small, Cincinnati	SR	17	0	0	102	10.2
6	Lindsey Chapman, California	SR	17	0	0	102	9.3
6	J.J. Stokes, UCLA	JR	17	0	0	102	9.3
8	Ryan Yarborough, Wyoming	SR	16	2	0	98	8.9
9	Calvin Jones, Nebraska	JR	13	0	0	78	8.7
10	John Becksvoort, Tennessee	JR	0	59	12	95	8.6

FIELD GOALS		CL	FGA	FGM	PCT	FGG
1	Michael Proctor, Alabama	SO	29	22	0.76	1.83
2	Bjorn Merten, UCLA	FR	25	20	0.80	1.82
3	Nathan Morreale, Utah State	FR	27	19	0.70	1.73
3	Kanon Parkman, Georgia	SO	27	19	0.70	1.73
5	Jon Baker, Arizona State	JR	26	18	0.69	1.64
6	Tom Dallen, Cincinnati	JR	22	17	0.77	1.55
6	Tom Burke, Mississippi State	SR	23	17	0.74	1.55
6	Aaron Price, Washington State	SR	31	17	0.55	1.55
9	Tommy Thompson, Oregon	SR	21	16	0.76	1.45
9	Chris Boniol, Louisiana Tech	SR	22	16	0.73	1.45
9	Scott Szeredy, Texas	SR	22	16	0.73	1.45

INTERCEPTIONS		CL	INT	YDS	TD	INT/GM
1	Orlanda Thomas, La. Lafayette	JR	9	84	1	0.82
2	Anthony Bridges, Louisville	JR	7	184	2	0.64
2	Alundis Brice, Mississippi	JR	7	98	2	0.64
2	Antonio Langham, Alabama	SR	7	67	1	0.64
2	Troy Jensen, San Jose State	SR	7	60	0	0.64
6	Ernest Boyd, Utah	JR	6	126	1	0.60
7	Orlando Watters, Arkansas	SR	6	185	2	0.55
7	Marvin Goodwin, UCLA	JR	6	136	0	0.55
7	Nathan Bennett, Rice	SR	6	123	1	0.55
7	Tony Bouie, Arizona	JR	6	100	0	0.55
7	David Thomas, Miami, Ohio	JR	6	63	0	0.55
7	Walt Harris, Mississippi State	SO	6	59	0	0.55
7	Marcus Jenkins, Kentucky	SR	6	45	0	0.55
7	Jeff Messenger, Wisconsin	JR	6	41	0	0.55

Team Leaders

RUSHING OFFENSE		G	ATT	YDS	AVG	TD	YPG
1	Army	11	660	3283	5.0	35	298.5
2	Oregon State	11	675	3254	4.8	25	295.8
3	Nebraska	11	589	3167	5.4	39	287.9
4	Air Force	12	713	3419	4.8	29	284.9
5	Hawaii	12	569	3247	5.7	35	270.6
6	Notre Dame	11	561	2868	5.1	37	260.7
7	North Carolina	12	628	3036	4.8	39	253.0
8	Wisconsin	11	557	2759	5.0	26	250.8
9	West Virginia	11	542	2684	5.0	28	244.0
10	Virginia Tech	11	582	2671	4.6	28	242.8

PASSING OFFENSE		G	ATT	COM	INT	PCT	YDS	YPA	TD	I%	YPC	YPG
1	Nevada	11	516	343	19	66.5	4373	8.5	34	3.7	12.7	397.5
2	Brigham Young	11	458	278	18	60.7	4060	8.9	31	3.9	14.6	369.1
3	Maryland	11	473	302	21	63.8	3823	8.1	26	4.4	12.7	347.5
4	Florida	12	488	284	21	58.2	4072	8.3	41	4.3	14.3	339.3
5	Stanford	11	474	308	14	65.0	3709	7.8	27	3.0	12.0	337.2
6	Florida State	12	469	327	6	69.7	3909	8.3	37	1.3	12.0	325.8
7	Utah	12	433	278	10	64.2	3891	9.0	22	2.3	14.0	324.3
8	Georgia	11	432	272	7	63.0	3552	8.2	24	1.6	13.1	322.9
9	San Diego State	12	465	269	14	57.8	3836	8.2	28	3.0	14.3	319.7
10	Fresno State	11	350	225	5	64.3	3425	9.8	29	1.4	15.2	311.4

TOTAL OFFENSE		G	P	YDS	AVG	TD	YPG
1	Nevada	11	955	6260	6.6	56	569.1
2	Florida State	12	939	6576	7.0	63	548.0
3	Fresno State	11	808	5863	7.3	53	533.0
4	Boston College	11	827	5570	6.7	51	506.4
5	Utah	12	906	5815	6.4	43	484.6
6	Tennessee	11	762	5286	6.9	58	480.6
7	Florida	12	888	5719	6.4	59	476.6
8	Texas Tech	11	854	5225	6.1	51	475.0
9	Brigham Young	11	853	5222	6.1	51	474.7
10	Colorado	11	841	5175	6.2	40	470.5

RUSHING DEFENSE		G	ATT	YDS	AVG	TD	YPG
1	Arizona	11	368	331	0.9	5	30.1
2	Washington State	11	438	949	2.2	11	86.3
3	La. Lafayette	11	378	975	2.6	12	88.6
4	Notre Dame	11	331	985	3.0	8	89.5
5	Florida State	12	397	1182	3.0	6	98.5
6	Mississippi	11	463	1127	2.4	8	102.5
7	North Carolina	12	410	1230	3.0	10	102.5
8	Michigan	11	379	1179	3.1	6	107.2
9	Florida	12	417	1334	3.2	9	111.2
10	Illinois	11	444	1265	2.8	10	115.0

PASSING DEFENSE		G	ATT	COM	PCT	INT	I%	YDS	YPA	TD	TD%	RAT
1	Texas A&M	11	292	116	39.7	13	4.5	1339	4.6	5	1.7	75.0
2	Alabama	12	310	144	46.5	22	7.1	1539	5.0	9	2.9	83.5
3	Mississippi	11	264	117	44.3	15	5.7	1453	5.5	5	1.9	85.4
4	Miami, Fla.	11	288	138	47.9	17	5.9	1517	5.3	6	2.1	87.2
5	Tennessee	11	347	167	48.1	18	5.2	2105	6.1	7	2.0	95.4
6	Iowa	11	291	143	49.1	18	6.2	1798	6.2	6	2.1	95.5
7	Central Michigan	11	302	151	50.0	13	4.3	1730	5.7	6	2.0	96.1
8	Florida State	12	376	181	48.1	15	4.0	2232	5.9	9	2.4	97.9
9	Auburn	11	349	153	43.8	15	4.3	2039	5.8	15	4.3	98.5
10	Cincinnati	11	315	164	52.1	14	4.4	1867	5.9	7	2.2	100.3

TOTAL DEFENSE		G	P	YDS	AVG	TD	YPG
1	Mississippi	11	727	2580	3.5	13	234.5
2	Arizona	11	739	2606	3.5	14	236.9
3	Texas A&M	11	740	2724	3.7	10	247.6
4	Miami, Fla.	11	723	2814	3.9	15	255.8
5	Alabama	12	738	3104	4.2	19	258.7
6	Florida State	12	773	3414	4.4	15	284.5
7	Bowling Green	11	715	3285	4.6	22	298.6
8	Washington State	11	773	3287	4.3	27	298.8
9	Ohio State	11	744	3293	4.4	19	299.4
10	Indiana	11	747	3336	4.5	18	303.3

SCORING OFFENSE		G	PTS	AVG
1	Florida State	12	518	43.2
2	Tennessee	11	471	42.8
3	Fresno State	11	437	39.7
4	Florida	12	472	39.3
5	Nebraska	11	421	38.3
6	Nevada	11	419	38.1
7	Texas Tech	11	409	37.2
8	Texas A&M	11	404	36.7
9	Notre Dame	11	403	36.6
10	West Virginia	11	401	36.5

SCORING DEFENSE		G	PTS	AVG
1	Florida State	12	113	9.4
2	Texas A&M	11	119	10.8
3	Miami, Fla.	11	138	12.5
4	Mississippi	11	142	12.9
5	Tennessee	11	144	13.1
6	Alabama	12	158	13.2
7	Indiana	11	152	13.8
8	Michigan	11	153	13.9
9	Arizona	11	161	14.6
10	West Virginia	11	171	15.5

TURNOVER MARGIN		G	FR	INT	TOT	FL	INTL	TOT	MAR
1	UCLA	11	21	18	39	13	7	20	1.7
2	Fresno State	11	15	16	31	9	5	14	1.6
3	Cincinnati	11	13	14	27	5	7	12	1.4
4	Tennessee	11	15	18	33	11	9	20	1.2
4	Texas A&M	11	19	13	32	7	12	19	1.2
4	Mississippi	11	15	15	30	3	14	17	1.2
4	Penn State	11	11	21	32	6	13	19	1.2
4	Colorado	11	13	13	26	6	7	13	1.2
9	Notre Dame	11	10	12	22	5	5	10	1.1
9	Texas Tech	11	16	14	30	11	7	18	1.1
9	Clemson	11	11	17	28	9	7	16	1.1

1994 Poll Progression

Pre-Season 1994 — Aug. 29 Games

CNN	AP	Team	Record	Result
1	1	Florida	0-0-0	bye week
4	2	Notre Dame	0-0-0	bye week
2	3	Florida State	0-0-0	bye week
3	4	Nebraska	0-0-0	beat # 24 West Virginia 31-0 (A28)
5	5	Michigan	0-0-0	bye week
6	6	Miami, Fla.	0-0-0	bye week
8	7	Arizona	0-0-0	bye week
7	8	Colorado	0-0-0	bye week
9	9	Penn State	0-0-0	bye week
11	10	Wisconsin	0-0-0	bye week
PB	11	Auburn	0-0-0	bye week
10	12	Alabama	0-0-0	bye week
12	13	Tennessee	0-0-0	bye week
15	14	UCLA	0-0-0	bye week
PB	15	Texas A&M	0-0-0	bye week
13	16	Oklahoma	0-0-0	bye week
14	17	Southern Cal	0-0-0	bye week
18	18	Texas	0-0-0	bye week
17	19	North Carolina	0-0-0	bye week
16	20	Ohio State	0-0-0	beat Fresno State 34-10
22	21	Illinois	0-0-0	bye week
19	22	Virginia Tech	0-0-0	bye week
PB	23	Washington	0-0-0	bye week
23	24	West Virginia	0-0-0	lost to # 4 Nebraska 0-31 (A28)
21	25	Clemson	0-0-0	bye week
20		Brigham Young	0-0-0	bye week
24		Georgia	0-0-0	bye week
25		Virginia	0-0-0	bye week

August 30 Poll — Sept. 3 Games

AP	Team	Record	Result
1	Florida	0-0-0	beat New Mexico State 70-21
2	Nebraska	1-0-0	bye week
3	Notre Dame	0-0-0	beat Northwestern 42-15
4	Florida State	0-0-0	beat Virginia 41-17
5	Michigan	0-0-0	beat Boston College 34-26
6	Miami, Fla.	0-0-0	beat Georgia Southern 56-0
7	Arizona	0-0-0	beat Georgia Tech 19-14 (S1)
8	Colorado	0-0-0	beat La. Monroe 48-13
9	Penn State	0-0-0	beat Minnesota 56-3
10	Wisconsin	0-0-0	bye week
11	Alabama	0-0-0	beat U.T. Chattanooga 42-13
12	Auburn	0-0-0	beat Mississippi 22-17
13	Tennessee	0-0-0	lost to # 14 UCLA 23-25
14	UCLA	0-0-0	beat # 13 Tennessee 25-23
15	Texas A&M	0-0-0	beat LSU 18-13
16	Oklahoma	0-0-0	beat Syracuse 30-29
17	Southern Cal	0-0-0	beat # 23 Washington 24-17
18	North Carolina	0-0-0	beat TCU 27-17
19	Texas	0-0-0	beat Pittsburgh 30-28
20	Ohio State	1-0-0	bye week
21	Virginia Tech	0-0-0	beat Arkansas State 34-7
22	Illinois	0-0-0	lost to Washington State 9-10 (S1)
23	Washington	0-0-0	lost to # 17 Southern Cal 17-24
24	Clemson	0-0-0	beat Furman 27-6
25	Stanford	0-0-0	bye week

September 5 Poll — Sept. 10 Games

CNN	AP	Team	Record	Result
1	1	Nebraska	1-0-0	beat Texas Tech 42-16 S8
2	2	Florida	1-0-0	beat Kentucky 73-7
4	3	Notre Dame	1-0-0	lost to # 6 Michigan 24-26
3	4	Florida State	1-0-0	beat Maryland 52-20
6	5	Miami, Fla.	1-0-0	beat Arizona State 47-10
5	6	Michigan	1-0-0	beat # 3 Notre Dame 26-24
7	7	Colorado	1-0-0	bye week
8	8	Penn State	1-0-0	beat # 14 Southern Cal 38-14
9	9	Arizona	1-0-0	beat New Mexico State 44-0
11	10	Wisconsin	0-0-0	beat Eastern Michigan 56-0
10	11	Alabama	1-0-0	beat Vanderbilt 17-7
PB	12	Auburn	1-0-0	beat La. Monroe 44-12
12	13	UCLA	1-0-0	beat SMU 17-10
13	14	Southern Cal	1-0-0	lost to # 8 Penn State 14-38
15	15	Oklahoma	1-0-0	lost to # 16 Texas A&M 14-36
PB	16	Texas A&M	1-0-0	beat # 15 Oklahoma 36-14
16	17	North Carolina	1-0-0	bye week
14	18	Ohio State	1-0-0	lost to # 25 Washington 16-25
19	19	Tennessee	0-1-0	beat # 23 Georgia 41-23
17	20	Texas	1-0-0	beat Louisville 30-16
18	21	Virginia Tech	1-0-0	beat Southern Miss 24-14
20	22	Clemson	1-0-0	lost to North Carolina St. 12-29
22	23	Georgia	1-0-0	lost to # 19 Tennessee 23-41
25	24	Stanford	0-0-0	tied Northwestern 41-41
PB	25	Washington	0-1-0	beat # 18 Ohio State 25-16
21		Brigham Young	1-0-0	beat Air Force 45-21
23		California	0-0-0	lost to San Diego State 20-22
24		Kansas State	1-0-0	bye week

September 12 Poll — Sept. 17 Games

CNN	AP	Team	Record	Result
2	1	Florida	2-0-0	beat # 15 Tennessee 31-0
1	2	Nebraska	2-0-0	beat # 13 UCLA 49-21
4	3	Florida State	2-0-0	beat Wake Forest 56-14
3	4	Michigan	2-0-0	bye week
6	5	Miami, Fla.	2-0-0	bye week
5	6	Penn State	2-0-0	beat Iowa 61-21
7	7	Colorado	1-0-0	beat # 10 Wisconsin 55-17
9	8	Notre Dame	1-1-0	beat Michigan State 21-20
8	9	Arizona	2-0-0	bye week
10	10	Wisconsin	1-0-0	lost to # 7 Colorado 17-55
PB	11	Auburn	2-0-0	beat LSU 30-26
11	12	Alabama	2-0-0	beat Arkansas 13-6
12	13	UCLA	2-0-0	lost to # 2 Nebraska 21-49
PB	14	Texas A&M	2-0-0	bye week
14	15	Tennessee	1-1-0	lost to # 1 Florida 0-31
13	16	North Carolina	1-0-0	beat Tulane 49-0
15	17	Texas	2-0-0	bye week
16	18	Virginia Tech	2-0-0	beat Boston College 12-7
PB	19	Washington	1-1-0	bye week
20	20	Southern Cal	1-1-0	bye week
19	21	Oklahoma	1-1-0	beat Texas Tech 17-11
17	22	Brigham Young	2-0-0	lost to Colorado State 21-28
18	23	Ohio State	1-1-0	beat Pittsburgh 27-3
22	24	Washington State	2-0-0	bye week
24	25	North Carolina St.	2-0-0	bye week
21		Kansas State	1-0-0	beat Rice 27-18
23		Kansas	2-0-0	lost to TCU 21-31
25		Indiana	2-0-0	beat Kentucky 59-29

September 19 Poll — Sept. 24 Games

CNN	AP	Team	Record	Result
2	1	Florida	3-0-0	bye week
1	2	Nebraska	3-0-0	beat Pacific 70-21
3	3	Florida State	3-0-0	beat # 13 North Carolina 31-18
4	4	Michigan	2-0-0	lost to # 7 Colorado 26-27
5	5	Penn State	3-0-0	beat Rutgers 55-27
6	6	Miami, Fla.	2-0-0	lost to # 17 Washington 20-38
7	7	Colorado	2-0-0	beat # 4 Michigan 27-26
8	8	Arizona	2-0-0	beat Stanford 34-10
9	9	Notre Dame	2-1-0	beat Purdue 39-31
PB	10	Auburn	3-0-0	beat E. Tennessee St. 38-0
10	11	Alabama	3-0-0	beat Tulane 20-10
PB	12	Texas A&M	2-0-0	beat Southern Miss 41-17
11	13	North Carolina	2-0-0	lost to # 3 Florida State 18-31
12	14	Virginia Tech	3-0-0	beat West Virginia 34-6 (S22)
13	15	Texas	2-0-0	beat TCU 34-18
15	16	Wisconsin	1-1-0	beat # 25 Indiana 62-13
PB	17	Washington	1-1-0	beat # 6 Miami, Fla. 38-20
20	18	UCLA	2-1-0	lost to # 22 Washington State 0-21
19	19	Southern Cal	1-1-0	beat Baylor 37-27
14	20	Ohio State	2-1-0	beat Houston 52-0
16	21	Oklahoma	2-1-0	bye week
18	22	Washington State	2-0-0	beat # 18 UCLA 21-0
23	23	Tennessee	1-2-0	lost to Mississippi State 21-24
22	24	North Carolina St.	2-0-0	beat Western Carolina 38-13
21	25	Indiana	3-0-0	lost to # 16 Wisconsin 13-62
17		Kansas State	2-0-0	beat Minnesota 35-0
24		Baylor	3-0-0	lost to # 19 Southern Cal 27-37
25		Colorado State	3-0-0	beat San Diego State 19-17

September 26 Poll — Oct. 1 Games

CNN	AP	Team	Record	Result
2	1	Florida	3-0-0	beat Mississippi 38-14
1	2	Nebraska	4-0-0	beat Wyoming 42-32
3	3	Florida State	4-0-0	bye week
4	4	Penn State	4-0-0	beat Temple 48-21
5	5	Colorado	3-0-0	beat # 16 Texas 34-31
6	6	Arizona	3-0-0	beat Oregon State 30-10
8	7	Michigan	2-1-0	beat Iowa 29-14
7	8	Notre Dame	3-1-0	beat Stanford 34-15
PB	9	Auburn	4-0-0	beat Kentucky 41-14 (S29)
PB	10	Texas A&M	3-0-0	beat Texas Tech 23-17
9	11	Alabama	4-0-0	beat Georgia 29-28
PB	12	Washington	2-1-0	beat UCLA 37-10
12	13	Miami, Fla.	2-1-0	beat Rutgers 24-3
10	14	Virginia Tech	4-0-0	lost to Syracuse 20-28
14	15	Wisconsin	2-1-0	lost to Michigan State 10-29
11	16	Texas	3-0-0	lost to # 5 Colorado 31-34
15	17	Washington State	3-0-0	lost to Tennessee 9-10
18	18	North Carolina	2-1-0	beat SMU 28-24
19	19	Southern Cal	2-1-0	lost to Oregon 7-22
13	20	Ohio State	3-1-0	beat Northwestern 17-15
17	21	Oklahoma	2-1-0	beat Iowa State 34-6
20	22	North Carolina St.	3-0-0	beat Georgia Tech 21-13
16	23	Kansas State	3-0-0	bye week
21	24	Colorado State	4-0-0	beat New Mexico 38-31
24	25	Illinois	2-1-0	lost to Purdue 16-22
22		Syracuse	3-1-0	beat # 14 Virginia Tech 28-20
23		Utah	4-0-0	bye week
25		Brigham Young	3-1-0	beat Utah State 34-6 (S30)

October 3 Poll — Oct. 8 Games

CNN	AP	Team	Record	Result
1	1	Florida	4-0-0	beat LSU 42-18
2	2	Nebraska	5-0-0	beat Oklahoma State 32-3
3	3	Florida State	4-0-0	lost to # 13 Miami, Fla. 20-34
4	4	Penn State	5-0-0	bye week
5	5	Colorado	4-0-0	beat Missouri 38-23
6	6	Arizona	4-0-0	lost to # 23 Colorado State 16-21
8	7	Michigan	3-1-0	beat Michigan State 40-20
7	8	Notre Dame	4-1-0	lost to Boston College 11-30
PB	9	Auburn	5-0-0	beat Mississippi State 42-18
PB	10	Texas A&M	4-0-0	beat Houston 38-7
9	11	Alabama	5-0-0	beat Southern Miss 14-6
PB	12	Washington	3-1-0	beat San Jose State 34-20
10	13	Miami, Fla.	3-1-0	beat # 3 Florida State 34-20
14	14	North Carolina	3-1-0	beat Georgia Tech 31-24
15	15	Texas	3-1-0	beat # 16 Oklahoma 17-10
12	16	Oklahoma	3-1-0	lost to # 15 Texas 10-17
11	17	Ohio State	4-1-0	lost to Illinois 10-24
16	18	North Carolina St.	4-0-0	lost to Louisville 14-35
13	19	Kansas State	3-0-0	beat Kansas 21-13 O6
17	20	Virginia Tech	4-1-0	beat Temple 41-13
19	21	Syracuse	4-1-0	beat Pittsburgh 31-7
20	22	Washington State	3-1-0	beat Oregon 21-7
18	23	Colorado State	5-0-0	beat # 6 Arizona 21-16
22	24	Wisconsin	2-2-0	beat Northwestern 46-14
21	25	Utah	4-0-0	beat San Diego State 38-22
23		Baylor	4-1-0	beat SMU 44-10
24		Duke	5-0-0	bye week
25		Brigham Young	4-1-0	beat Fresno State 32-30

October 10 Poll — Oct. 15 Games

CNN	AP	Team	Record	Result
1	1	Florida	5-0-0	lost to # 6 Auburn 33-36
2	2	Nebraska	6-0-0	beat # 16 Kansas State 17-6
3	3	Penn State	5-0-0	beat # 5 Michigan 31-24
4	4	Colorado	5-0-0	beat # 22 Oklahoma 45-7
5	5	Michigan	4-1-0	lost to # 3 Penn State 24-31
PB	6	Auburn	6-0-0	beat # 1 Florida 36-33
PB	7	Texas A&M	5-0-0	beat Baylor 41-21
7	8	Miami, Fla.	4-1-0	bye week
PB	9	Washington	4-1-0	beat Arizona State 35-14
6	10	Alabama	6-0-0	beat Tennessee 17-13
8	11	Florida State	4-1-0	bye week
9	12	Texas	4-1-0	lost to Rice 17-19 (O16)
13	13	Colorado State	6-0-0	beat Texas-El Paso 47-9
10	14	Arizona	4-1-0	beat # 20 Washington State 10-7
12	15	North Carolina	4-1-0	beat Maryland 41-17
11	16	Kansas State	4-0-0	lost to # 2 Nebraska 6-17
16	17	Notre Dame	4-2-0	lost to Brigham Young 14-21
15	18	Syracuse	5-1-0	bye week
14	19	Virginia Tech	5-1-0	beat East Carolina 27-20
17	20	Washington State	4-1-0	lost to # 14 Arizona 7-10
18	21	Utah	5-0-0	beat Hawaii 14-3
21	22	Oklahoma	3-2-0	lost to # 4 Colorado 7-45
20	23	Wisconsin	3-2-0	tied Purdue 27-27
	24	Boston College	2-2-0	beat Temple 45-28
23	25	Duke	5-0-0	beat Clemson 19-13
19		Baylor	5-1-0	lost to # 7 Texas A&M 21-41
22		Ohio State	4-2-0	beat Michigan State 23-7
24		North Carolina St.	4-1-0	beat Wake Forest 34-3
25		Brigham Young	5-1-0	beat # 17 Notre Dame 21-14

October 17 Poll — Oct. 22 Games

CNN	AP	Team	Record	Result
1	1	Penn State	6-0-0	bye week
3	2	Colorado	6-0-0	beat # 19 Kansas State 35-21
2	3	Nebraska	7-0-0	beat Missouri 42-7
PB	4	Auburn	7-0-0	bye week
6	5	Florida	5-1-0	bye week
PB	6	Texas A&M	6-0-0	beat Rice 7-0
4	7	Miami, Fla.	4-1-0	beat West Virginia 38-6
5	8	Alabama	7-0-0	beat Mississippi 21-10
PB	9	Washington	5-1-0	lost to Oregon 20-31
7	10	Florida State	4-1-0	beat Clemson 17-0
12	11	Michigan	4-2-0	beat Illinois 19-14
11	12	Colorado State	7-0-0	lost to Utah 31-45
9	13	Texas	4-1-0	beat SMU 42-20
8	14	Arizona	5-1-0	beat UCLA 34-24
10	15	North Carolina	5-1-0	lost to Virginia 10-34
14	16	Syracuse	5-1-0	beat Temple 49-42
13	17	Virginia Tech	6-1-0	beat Pittsburgh 45-7
15	18	Utah	6-0-0	beat Colorado State 45-31
16	19	Kansas State	4-1-0	lost to # 2 Colorado 21-35
17	20	Duke	6-0-0	beat Wake Forest 51-26
18	21	Brigham Young	6-1-0	beat Texas-El Paso 34-28
23	22	Boston College	3-2-0	tied Rutgers 7-7
20	23	Washington State	4-2-0	beat Arizona State 28-21
19	24	Ohio State	5-2-0	beat Purdue 48-14
22	25	Virginia	5-1-0	beat North Carolina St. 34-10
21		North Carolina St.	5-1-0	bye week
24		Indiana	5-1-0	lost to Northwestern 7-20
25		Illinois	4-2-0	lost to # 11 Michigan 14-19

CNN	AP	October 24 Poll		Oct. 29 Games
1	1	Penn State	6-0-0	beat #21 Ohio State 63-14
3	2	Colorado	7-0-0	lost to #3 Nebraska 7-24
2	3	Nebraska	8-0-0	beat #2 Colorado 24-7
PB	4	Auburn	7-0-0	beat Arkansas 31-14
6	5	Florida	5-1-0	beat Georgia 52-14
4	6	Miami, Fla.	5-1-0	beat #13 Virginia Tech 24-3
PB	7	Texas A&M	7-0-0	tied SMU 21-21
5	8	Alabama	8-0-0	bye week
7	9	Florida State	5-1-0	beat #16 Duke 59-20
9	10	Michigan	5-2-0	lost to Wisconsin 19-31
8	11	Arizona	6-1-0	lost to Oregon 9-10
11	12	Utah	7-0-0	beat Texas-El Paso 52-7
10	13	Virginia Tech	7-1-0	lost to #6 Miami, Fla. 3-24
12	14	Syracuse	6-1-0	bye week
PB	15	Washington	5-2-0	beat Oregon State 24-10
13	16	Duke	7-0-0	lost to #9 Florida State 20-59
18	17	Colorado State	7-1-0	bye week
16	18	Virginia	6-1-0	bye week
15	19	Texas	5-2-0	lost to Texas Tech 9-33
17	20	Brigham Young	7-1-0	lost to Arizona State 15-36
14	21	Ohio State	6-2-0	lost to #1 Penn State 14-63
19	22	Washington State	5-2-0	beat California 26-23
21	23	Kansas State	4-2-0	beat Oklahoma 37-20
20	24	North Carolina	5-2-0	beat North Carolina St. 31-17
23	25	Southern Cal	5-2-0	bye week
22		North Carolina St.	5-1-0	lost to #24 North Carolina 17-31
24		Oregon	5-3-0	beat #11 Arizona 10-9
25		Oklahoma	4-3-0	lost to #23 Kansas State 20-37

CNN	AP	October 31 Poll		Nov. 5 Games
2	1	Nebraska	9-0-0	beat Kansas 45-17
1	2	Penn State	7-0-0	beat Indiana 35-29
PB	3	Auburn	8-0-0	beat East Carolina 38-21
5	4	Florida	6-1-0	beat Southern Miss 55-17
3	5	Miami, Fla.	6-1-0	beat #10 Syracuse 27-6
4	6	Alabama	8-0-0	beat LSU 35-17
7	7	Colorado	7-1-0	beat Oklahoma State 17-3
6	8	Florida State	6-1-0	beat Georgia Tech 41-10
8	9	Utah	8-0-0	lost to New Mexico 21-23
9	10	Syracuse	6-1-0	lost to #5 Miami, Fla. 6-27
PB	11	Texas A&M	7-0-1	beat Texas 34-10
PB	12	Washington	6-2-0	lost to Stanford 28-46
10	13	Virginia	6-1-0	lost to #23 Duke 25-28
11	14	Colorado State	7-1-0	beat Wyoming 35-24
15	15	Kansas State	5-2-0	beat Iowa State 38-20
14	16	Washington State	6-2-0	lost to #22 Southern Cal 10-23
16	17	Virginia Tech	7-2-0	bye week
13	18	Arizona	6-2-0	beat California 13-6
12	19	North Carolina	6-2-0	lost to Clemson 17-28
18	20	Michigan	5-3-0	beat Purdue 45-23
17	21	Oregon	6-3-0	beat Arizona State 34-10
20	22	Southern Cal	5-2-0	beat #16 Washington State 23-10
19	23	Duke	7-1-0	beat #13 Virginia 28-25
22	24	Mississippi State	6-2-0	beat Arkansas 17-7
21	25	Brigham Young	7-2-0	beat La. Monroe 24 10
23		Illinois	5-3-0	beat Minnesota 21-17
24		Ohio State	6-3-0	beat Wisconsin 24-3
25		Notre Dame	5-3-0	bye week

CNN	AP	November 7 Poll		Nov. 12 Games
1	1	Nebraska	10-0-0	beat Iowa State 28-12
2	2	Penn State	8-0-0	beat Illinois 35-31
PB	3	Auburn	9-0-0	tied Georgia 23-23
5	4	Florida	7-1-0	beat South Carolina 48-17
3	5	Miami, Fla.	7-1-0	beat Pittsburgh 17-12
4	6	Alabama	9-0-0	beat #20 Mississippi State 29-25
7	7	Colorado	8-1-0	beat Kansas 51-26
6	8	Florida State	7-1-0	beat Notre Dame 23-16
PB	9	Texas A&M	8-0-1	beat Louisville 26-10
10	10	Colorado State	8-1-0	beat Arkansas State 48-3
9	11	Kansas State	6-2-0	beat Missouri 21-18
14	12	Utah	8-1-0	lost to Air Force 33-40
8	13	Arizona	7-2-0	lost to #17 Southern Cal 28-45
15	14	Syracuse	6-2-0	lost to #25 Boston College 0-31
11	15	Oregon	7-3-0	beat Stanford 55-21
12	16	Virginia Tech	7-2-0	beat Rutgers 41-34
16	17	Southern Cal	6-2-0	beat #13 Arizona 45-28
13	18	Duke	8-1-0	lost to North Carolina St. 23-24
17	19	Michigan	6-3-0	beat Minnesota 38-22
20	20	Mississippi State	7-2-0	lost to #6 Alabama 25-29
18	21	Virginia	6-2-0	beat Maryland 46-21
PB	22	Washington	6-3-0	beat California 31-19
19	23	Brigham Young	8-2-0	beat San Diego State 35-28 (N10)
22	24	Washington State	6-3-0	lost to Oregon State 3-21
24	25	Boston College	5-2-1	beat #14 Syracuse 31-0
21		Ohio State	7-3-0	beat Indiana 32-17
23		North Carolina	6-3-0	beat Wake Forest 50-0
25		Illinois	6-3-0	lost to #2 Penn State 31-35

CNN	AP	November 14 Poll		Nov. 19 Games
1	1	Nebraska	11-0-0	bye week
2	2	Penn State	9-0-0	beat Northwestern 45-17
5	3	Florida	8-1-0	beat Vanderbilt 24-7
3	4	Alabama	10-0-0	beat #6 Auburn 21-14
4	5	Miami, Fla.	8-1-0	beat Temple 38-14
PB	6	Auburn	9-0-1	lost to #4 Alabama 14-21
7	7	Colorado	9-1-0	beat Iowa State 41-20
6	8	Florida State	8-1-0	beat #25 North Carolina St. 34-3
PB	9	Texas A&M	9-0-1	beat TCU 34-17
10	10	Colorado State	9-1-0	beat Fresno State 44-42
8	11	Kansas State	7-2-0	beat Oklahoma State 23-6
9	12	Oregon	8-3-0	beat Oregon State 17-13
12	13	Southern Cal	7-2-0	lost to UCLA 19-31
11	14	Virginia Tech	8-2-0	lost to #16 Virginia 23-42
13	15	Michigan	7-3-0	lost to #22 Ohio State 6-22
14	16	Virginia	7-2-0	beat #14 Virginia Tech 42-23
17	17	Boston College	6-2-1	lost to West Virginia 20-21
PB	18	Washington	7-3-0	lost to Washington State 6-23
18	19	Arizona	7-3-0	bye week
15	20	Brigham Young	9-2-0	lost to #21 Utah 31-34
20	21	Utah	8-2-0	beat #20 Brigham Young 34-31
16	22	Ohio State	8-3-0	beat #15 Michigan 22-6
23	23	Mississippi State	7-3-0	bye week
19	24	Duke	8-2-0	lost to North Carolina 40-41
22	25	North Carolina St.	7-2-0	lost to #8 Florida State 3-34
21		North Carolina	7-3-0	beat #24 Duke 41-40
24		Syracuse	6-3-0	beat Maryland 21-16
25		Baylor	7-3-0	bye week

CNN	AP	November 21 Poll		Nov. 26 Games
1	1	Nebraska	11-0-0	beat Oklahoma 13-3 (N25)
2	2	Penn State	10-0-0	beat Michigan State 59-21
3	3	Alabama	11-0-0	bye week
4	4	Florida	9-1-0	tied #7 Florida State 31-31
5	5	Miami, Fla.	9-1-0	beat #25 Boston College 23-7
7	6	Colorado	10-1-0	regular season complete
6	7	Florida State	9-1-0	tied #4 Florida 31-31
PB	8	Texas A&M	10-0-1	regular season complete
PB	9	Auburn	9-1-1	regular season complete
10	10	Colorado State	10-1-0	regular season complete
8	11	Kansas State	8-2-0	beat Nevada-Las Vegas 42-3
9	12	Oregon	9-3-0	regular season complete
11	13	Virginia	8-2-0	lost to North Carolina St. 27-30 (N25)
12	14	Ohio State	9-3-0	regular season complete
13	15	Utah	9-2-0	regular season complete
15	16	Arizona	7-3-0	beat Arizona State 28-27 (N25)
17	17	Southern Cal	7-3-0	tied Notre Dame 17-17
16	18	Virginia Tech	8-3-0	regular season complete
18	19	Mississippi State	7-3-0	beat Mississippi 21-17
21	20	Michigan	7-4-0	regular season complete
14	21	North Carolina	8-3-0	regular season complete
20	22	Syracuse	7-3-0	lost to West Virginia 0-13 (N24)
19	23	Brigham Young	9-3-0	regular season complete
24	24	Washington State	7-4-0	regular season complete
25	25	Boston College	6-3-1	lost to #5 Miami, Fla. 7-23
22		Duke	8-3-0	regular season complete
23		Baylor	7-3-0	lost to Texas 35-63 (N24)

CNN	AP	November 28 Poll		Dec. 3 Games
1	1	Nebraska	12-0-0	regular season complete
2	2	Penn State	11-0-0	regular season complete
3	3	Alabama	11-0-0	lost to #6 Florida 23-24 (SEC CH)
4	4	Miami, Fla.	10-1-0	regular season complete
5	5	Colorado	10-1-0	
6	6	Florida	9-1-1	beat #3 Alabama 24-23 (SEC CH)
7	7	Florida State	9-1-1	regular season complete
PB	8	Texas A&M	10-0-1	
PB	9	Auburn	9-1-1	
10	10	Colorado State	10-1-0	
8	11	Kansas State	9-2-0	regular season complete
9	12	Oregon	9-3-0	
11	13	Ohio State	9-3-0	
12	14	Utah	9-2-0	
13	15	Arizona	8-3-0	regular season complete
17	16	Mississippi State	8-3-0	regular season complete
15	17	Virginia Tech	8-3-0	
14	18	North Carolina	8-3-0	
16	19	Virginia	8-3-0	regular season complete
19	20	Michigan	7-4-0	
22	21	Southern Cal	7-3-1	regular season complete
18	22	Brigham Young	9-3-0	
21	23	North Carolina St.	8-3-0	regular season complete
23	24	Washington State	7-4-0	
20	25	Duke	8-3-0	regular season complete
24		Tennessee	7-4-0	regular season complete
25		Boston College	6-4-1	regular season complete

CNN	AP	December 5 Poll	Record	Bowl Bid	Date	Bowl Result
1	1	Nebraska	12-0-0	Orange Bowl	J1	beat #3 Miami, Fla. 24-17
2	2	Penn State	11-0-0	Rose Bowl	J2	beat #12 Oregon 38-20
3	3	Miami, Fla.	10-1-0	Orange Bowl	J1	lost to #1 Nebraska 17-24
5	4	Colorado	10-1-0	Fiesta Bowl	J2	beat Notre Dame 41-24
4	5	Florida	10-1-1	Sugar Bowl	J2	lost to #7 Florida State 17-23
6	6	Alabama	11-1-0	Citrus Bowl	J2	beat #13 Ohio State 24-17
7	7	Florida State	9-1-1	Sugar Bowl	J2	beat #5 Florida 23-17
PB	8	Texas A&M	10-0-1			
PB	9	Auburn	9-1-1			
10	10	Colorado State	10-1-0	Holiday Bowl	D30	lost to #20 Michigan 14-24
8	11	Kansas State	9-2-0	Aloha Bowl	D25	lost to Boston College 7-12
9	12	Oregon	9-3-0	Rose Bowl	J2	lost to #2 Penn State 20-38
11	13	Ohio State	9-3-0	Citrus Bowl	J2	lost to #6 Alabama 17-24
12	14	Utah	9-2-0	Freedom Bowl	D27	beat #15 Arizona 16-13
13	15	Arizona	8-3-0	Freedom Bowl	D27	lost to #14 Utah 13-16
17	16	Mississippi State	8-3-0	Peach Bowl	J1	lost to #23 North Carolina St. 24-28
15	17	Virginia Tech	8-3-0	Gator Bowl	D30	lost to Tennessee 23-45
16	18	Virginia	8-3-0	Independence Bowl	D28	beat TCU 20-10
14	19	North Carolina	8-3-0	Sun Bowl	D30	lost to Texas 31-35
18	20	Michigan	7-4-0	Holiday Bowl	D30	beat #10 Colorado State 24-14
22	21	Southern Cal	7-3-1	Cotton Bowl	J2	beat Texas Tech 55-14
19	22	Brigham Young	9-3-0	Copper Bowl	D29	beat Oklahoma 31-6
20	23	North Carolina St.	8-3-0	Peach Bowl	J1	beat #16 Mississippi State 28-24
23	24	Washington State	7-4-0	Alamo Bowl	D31	beat Baylor 10-3
21	25	Duke	8-3-0	Hall of Fame Bowl	J2	lost to Wisconsin 20-34
24		Tennessee	7-4-0	Gator Bowl	D30	beat #17 Virginia Tech 45-23
25		Boston College	6-4-1	Aloha Bowl	D25	beat #11 Kansas State 12-7

RB	CNN	AP	January 3 Fianl Poll	Record
1	1	1	Nebraska	13-0-0
2	2	2	Penn State	12-0-0
5	3	3	Colorado	11-1-0
4	5	4	Florida State	10-1-1
3	4	5	Alabama	12-1-0
6	6	6	Miami, Fla.	10-2-0
8	7	7	Florida	10-2-1
7	PB	8	Texas A&M	10-0-1
9	PB	9	Auburn	9-1-1
15	8	10	Utah	10-2-0
10	11	11	Oregon	9-4-0
11	12	12	Michigan	8-4-0
23	15	13	Southern Cal	8-3-1
20	9	14	Ohio State	9-4-0
21	13	15	Virginia	9-3-0
12	14	16	Colorado State	10-2-0
19	17	17	North Carolina St.	9-3-0
25	10	18	Brigham Young	10-3-0
17	16	19	Kansas State	9-3-0
18	20	20	Arizona	8-4-0
22	19	21	Washington State	8-4-0
14	18	22	Tennessee	8-4-0
13	22	23	Boston College	7-4-1
34	25	24	Mississippi State	8-4-0
29	23	25	Texas	8-4-0
31	21		North Carolina	8-4-0

1994

CONSENSUS ALL-AMERICANS

POS	Offense	HT	WT	School	AP	CF	FC	FN	FW	PI	SN
QB	Kerry Collins	6-5	235	Penn State	•	•	•		•	•	•
RB	Rashaan Salaam	6-1	210	Colorado	•	•	•	•	•	•	•
RB	Ki-Jana Carter	5-10	212	Penn State	•	•	•	•	•	•	•
WR	Jack Jackson	5-9	171	Florida	•		•	•	•	•	•
WR	Michael Westbrook	6-4	210	Colorado	•		•		•		•
TE	Pete Mitchell	6-2	238	Boston College	•	•			•		•
OL	Zach Wiegert	6-5	300	Nebraska	•	•	•	•	•	•	•
OL	Tony Boselli	6-8	305	Southern Cal	•		•		•	•	
OL	Korey Stringer	6-5	315	Ohio State	•	•	•	•	•	•	•
OL	Brenden Stai	6-4	300	Nebraska	•	•		•	•	•	•
C	Cory Raymer	6-4	290	Wisconsin	•	•	•	•	•	•	•
PK	Steve McLaughlin	6-1	175	Arizona						•	
KR	Leeland McElroy	5-11	200	Texas A&M						•	

OTHERS RECEIVING FIRST-TEAM HONORS

POS		School			CF						
QB	Eric Zeier	Georgia			•						
WR	Bobby Engram	Penn State					•				
WR	Frank Sanders	Auburn			•				•		
WR	Kevin Jordan	UCLA						•			
TE	Kyle Brady	Penn State					•				
TE	Jamie Asher	Louisville						•	•		
OL	Jeff Hartings	Penn State			•		•				
OL	Blake Brockermeyer	Texas						•	•		
OL	Reuben Brown	Pittsburgh						•			
C	Clay Shiver	Florida State					•				
PK	Remy Hamilton	Michigan					•				
KR	Michael Proctor	Alabama					•				

POS	Defense	HT	WT	School	AP	CF	FC	FN	FW	PI	SN
DL	Warren Sapp	6-3	284	Miami, Fla.	•	•	•	•	•	•	•
DL	Tedy Bruschi	6-1	255	Arizona	•	•	•	•	•		•
DL	Luther Elliss	6-6	288	Utah	•		•		•		•
DL	Kevin Carter	6-6	265	Florida	•		•	•	•		•
LB	Dana Howard	6-0	235	Illinois	•	•	•	•	•	•	•
LB	Ed Stewart	6-1	215	Nebraska	•	•	•	•	•		•
LB	Derrick Brooks	6-1	226	Florida State	•	•	•		•	•	•
DB	Clifton Abraham	5-9	185	Florida State	•	•	•	•	•	•	•
DB	Bobby Taylor	6-3	201	Notre Dame	•	•	•		•	•	•
DB	Chris Hudson	5-11	195	Colorado	•		•		•		•
DB	Brian Robinson	6-3	194	Auburn	•				•	•	
DB	Tony Bouie	5-10	183	Arizona			•		•	•	
P	Todd Sauerbrun	6-0	205	West Virginia	•	•	•		•		•

OTHERS RECEIVING FIRST-TEAM HONORS

POS		School			CF		FN			PI	SN
DL	Derrick Alexander	Florida State			•	•					•
DL	Simeon Rice	Illinois					•				
DL	DeWayne Patterson	Washington State					•				
LB	Zach Thomas	Texas Tech				•					
LB	Antonio Armstrong	Texas A&M	•								
DB	Ty Law	Michigan			•						
DB	Greg Myers	Colorado State					•			•	
DB	Herman O'Berry	Oregon					•				
DB	Chris Shelling	Auburn					•				
DB	Orlando Thomas	Southwestern Louisiana					•				
DB	C.J. Richardson	Miami, Fla	•								

FC named Brooks as a DL; FN named Rice as a LB

HEISMAN TROPHY VOTING

	PLAYER	POS	SCHOOL	1ST	2ND	3RD	TOTAL
1	Rashaan Salaam	RB	Colorado	400	229	85	1743
2	Ki-Jana Carter	RB	Penn State	115	205	146	901
3	Steve McNair	QB	Alcorn State	111	85	152	655
4	Kerry Collins	QB	Penn State	101	117	102	639
5	Jay Barker	QB	Alabama	36	58	71	295
6	Warren Sapp	DT	Miami, Fla.	17	37	67	192
7	Eric Zeier	QB	Georgia	7	15	32	83
8	Lawrence Phillips	RB	Nebraska	1	8	21	40
9	Napolean Kaufman	RB	Washington	3	3	12	27
10	Zach Wiegert	OT	Nebraska	1	7	10	27

AWARD WINNERS

PLAYER	POS/SCHOOL	AWARD
Kerry Collins	QB Penn State	Maxwell
Zach Wiegert	OT Nebraska	Outland
Rashaan Salaam	RB Colorado	Camp
Warren Sapp	DT Miami, Fla.	Lombardi
Kerry Collins	QB Penn State	O'Brien
Dana Howard	LB Ilinois	Butkus

PLAYER	POS/SCHOOL	AWARD
Chris Hudson	DB Colorado	Thorpe
Jay Barker	QB Alabama	Unitas
Rashaan Salaam	RB Colorado	Walker
Steve McLaughlin	K Arizona	Groza
Warren Sapp	DT Miami, Fla.	Nagurski
Bobby Engram	WR, Penn State	Biletnikoff

BOWL GAMES

DATE	GAME	SCORE
D15	Las Vegas	Nevada-Las Vegas 52, Central Michigan 24
D25	Aloha	Boston College 12, Kansas State 7
D27	Freedom	Utah 16, Arizona 13
D28	Independence	Virginia 20, TCU 10
D29	Copper	Brigham Young 31, Oklahoma 6
D30	Holiday	Michigan 24, Colorado State 14
D30	Gator	Tennessee 45, Virginia Tech 23
D30	Sun	Texas 35, North Carolina 31

CONFERENCE STANDINGS

ACC

	Conf. W L T	Overall W L T
Florida State	8 0 0	10 1 1
North Carolina St.	6 2 0	9 3 0
Virginia	5 3 0	9 3 0
North Carolina	5 3 0	8 4 0
Duke	5 3 0	8 4 0
Clemson	4 4 0	5 6 0
Maryland	2 6 0	4 7 0
Wake Forest	1 7 0	3 8 0
Georgia Tech	0 8 0	1 10 0

Big 10

	Conf. W L T	Overall W L T
Penn State	8 0 0	12 0 0
Ohio State	6 2 0	9 4 0
Michigan	5 3 0	8 4 0
Wisconsin	4 3 1	7 4 1
Illinois	4 4 0	7 5 0
Michigan State	4 4 0	5 6 0
Iowa	3 4 1	5 5 1
Indiana	3 5 0	6 5 0
Purdue	2 4 2	4 5 2
Northwestern	2 6 0	3 7 1
Minnesota	1 7 0	3 8 0

Big 8

	Conf. W L T	Overall W L T
Nebraska	7 0 0	13 0 0
Colorado	6 1 0	11 1 0
Kansas State	5 2 0	9 3 0
Oklahoma	4 3 0	6 6 0
Kansas	3 4 0	6 5 0
Missouri	2 5 0	3 8 1
Oklahoma State	0 6 1	3 7 1
Iowa State	0 6 1	0 10 1

Big East

	Conf. W L T	Overall W L T
Miami, Fla.	7 0 0	10 2 0
Virginia Tech	5 2 0	8 4 0
Syracuse	4 3 0	7 4 0
West Virginia	4 3 0	7 6 0
Boston College	3 3 1	7 4 1
Rutgers	2 4 1	5 5 1
Pittsburgh	2 5 0	3 8 0
Temple	0 7 0	2 9 0

Big West

	Conf. W L T	Overall W L T
Nevada	6 1 0	9 2 0
Nevada-Las Vegas	5 1 0	7 5 0
La. Lafayette	5 1 0	6 5 0
Pacific	4 2 0	6 5 0
Northern Illinois	3 3 0	4 7 0
San Jose State	3 3 0	3 8 0
Utah State	2 4 0	3 8 0
New Mexico State	2 5 0	3 8 0
Louisiana Tech	1 5 0	3 8 0
Arkansas State	0 6 0	1 10 0

Ivy

	Conf. W L T	Overall W L T
Pennsylvania	7 0 0	9 0 0
Princeton	4 3 0	7 3 0
Brown	4 3 0	7 3 0
Cornell	3 4 0	6 4 0
Columbia	3 4 0	5 4 1
Yale	3 4 0	5 5 0
Dartmouth	2 5 0	4 6 0
Harvard	2 5 0	4 6 0

MAC

	Conf. W L T	Overall W L T
Central Michigan	8 1 0	9 3 0
Bowling Green	7 1 0	9 2 0
Western Michigan	5 3 0	7 4 0
Miami, Ohio	5 3 0	5 5 1
Ball State	5 3 1	5 5 1
Toledo	4 3 1	5 5 1
Eastern Michigan	5 4 0	5 6 0
Kent State	2 7 0	2 9 0
Akron	1 8 0	1 10 0
Ohio U	0 9 0	0 11 0

DATE	GAME	SCORE
D31	Liberty	Illinois 30, East Carolina 0
D31	Alamo	Washington State 10, Baylor 3\
J1	Orange	Nebraska 24, Miami, Fla. 17
J1	Peach	North Carolina St. 28, Mississippi State 24
J2	Citrus	Alabama 24, Ohio State 17
J2	Fiesta	Colorado 41, Notre Dame 24
J2	Rose	Penn State 38, Oregon 20
J2	Carquest	South Carolina 24, West Virginia 21
J2	Cotton	Southern Cal 55, Texas Tech 14
J2	Hall of Fame	Wisconsin 34, Duke 20
J2	Sugar	Florida State 23, Florida 17

Pac 10

	Conf. W L T	Overall W L T
Oregon	7 1 0	9 4 0
Southern Cal	6 2 0	8 3 1
Arizona	6 2 0	8 4 0
Washington State	5 3 0	8 4 0
Washington	4 4 0	7 4 0
UCLA	3 5 0	5 6 0
California	3 5 0	4 7 0
Oregon State	2 6 0	4 7 0
Stanford	2 6 0	3 7 1
Arizona State	2 6 0	3 8 0

SEC

EAST

	Conf. W L T	Overall W L T
Florida	7 1 0	10 2 1
Tennessee	5 3 0	8 4 0
South Carolina	4 4 0	7 5 0
Georgia	3 4 1	6 4 1
Vanderbilt	2 6 0	5 6 0
Kentucky	0 8 0	1 10 0

WEST

	Conf. W L T	Overall W L T
Alabama	8 0 0	12 1 0
Auburn	6 1 1	9 1 1
Mississippi State	5 3 0	8 4 0
LSU	3 5 0	4 7 0
Arkansas	2 6 0	4 7 0
Mississippi	2 6 0	4 7 0

Championship Game Florida 24 Alabama 23

SWC

	Conf. W L T	Overall W L T
Texas A&M	6 0 1	10 0 1
Texas	4 3 0	8 4 0
TCU	4 3 0	7 5 0
Baylor	4 3 0	7 5 0
Texas Tech	4 3 0	6 6 0
Rice	4 3 0	5 6 0
Houston	1 6 0	1 10 0
SMU	0 6 1	1 9 1

WAC

	Conf. W L T	Overall W L T
Colorado State	7 1 0	10 2 0
Utah	6 2 0	10 2 0
Brigham Young	6 2 0	10 3 0
Air Force	6 2 0	8 4 0
Wyoming	4 4 0	6 6 0
New Mexico	4 4 0	5 7 0
Fresno State	3 4 1	5 7 1
San Diego State	2 6 0	4 7 0
Texas-El Paso	1 6 1	3 7 1
Hawaii	0 8 0	3 8 1

Independents

	Overall W L T
East Carolina	7 5 0
Southern Miss	6 5 0
Louisville	6 5 0
Memphis	6 5 0
Notre Dame	6 5 1
Army	4 7 0
Navy	3 8 0
La. Monroe	3 8 0
Tulsa	3 8 0
Cincinnati	2 8 1
Tulane	1 10 0

1994 NCAA Major College Statistical Leaders

Individual Leaders

PASSING	CL	G	ATT	COM	PCT	INT	I%	YDS	YPA	TD	TD%	RATING
1 Kerry Collins, Penn State	SR	11	264	176	66.7	7	2.7	2679	10.2	21	8.0	172.9
2 Terry Dean, Florida	JR	10	180	109	60.6	10	5.6	1492	8.3	20	11.1	155.7
3 Jay Barker, Alabama	SR	12	226	139	61.5	5	2.2	1996	8.8	14	6.2	151.7
4 Danny Wuerffel, Florida	SO	12	212	132	62.3	9	4.3	1754	8.3	18	8.5	151.3
5 Rob Johnson, Southern Cal	SR	9	255	170	66.7	6	2.4	2210	8.7	12	4.7	150.3
6 Mike McCoy, Utah	SR	11	381	247	64.8	11	2.9	3035	8.0	28	7.4	150.2
7 Max Knake, TCU	JR	11	316	184	58.2	7	2.2	2624	8.3	24	7.6	148.6
8 Steve Stenstrom, Stanford	SR	9	333	217	65.2	6	1.8	2822	8.5	16	4.8	148.6
9 Todd Collins, Michigan	SR	11	264	172	65.2	7	2.7	2356	8.9	11	4.2	148.6
10 Ryan Henry, Bowling Green	SO	11	293	174	59.4	11	3.8	2368	8.1	25	8.5	147.9

ALL-PURPOSE	CL	G	RUSH	REC	PR	KR	YDS	YPG
1 Rashaan Salaam, Colorado	JR	11	2055	294	0	0	2349	213.6
2 Brian Pruitt, Central Michigan	SR	11	1890	69	0	330	2289	208.1
3 Andre Davis, TCU	JR	11	1494	522	0	0	2016	183.3
4 Napoleon Kaufman, Washington	SR	11	1390	199	8	229	1826	166.0
5 Ki-Jana Carter, Penn State	JR	11	1539	123	0	81	1743	158.5
6 Chris Darkins, Minnesota	JR	11	1443	299	0	0	1742	158.4
7 Lawrence Phillips, Nebraska	SO	12	1722	172	0	0	1894	157.8
8 Terrell Fletcher, Wisconsin	SR	11	1235	172	0	314	1721	156.5
9 Alex Van Dyke, Nevada	JR	11	1	1246	5	451	1703	154.8
10 Terrell Willis, Rutgers	SO	11	1080	71	0	546	1697	154.3

RUSHING/Yards Per Game	CL	G	ATT	YDS	TD	AVG	YPG
1 Rashaan Salaam, Colorado	JR	11	298	2055	24	6.9	186.8
2 Brian Pruitt, Central Michigan	SR	11	292	1890	20	6.5	171.8
3 Lawrence Phillips, Nebraska	SO	12	286	1722	16	6.0	143.5
4 Ki-Jana Carter, Penn State	JR	11	198	1539	23	7.8	139.9
5 Andre Davis, TCU	JR	11	260	1494	7	5.7	135.8
6 Alex Smith, Indiana	FR	11	265	1475	10	5.6	134.1
7 Chris Darkins, Minnesota	JR	11	277	1443	11	5.2	131.2
8 Napoleon Kaufman, Washington	SR	11	255	1390	9	5.5	126.4
9 Billy West, Pittsburgh	SO	11	252	1358	6	5.4	123.5
10 Ryan Christopherson, Wyoming	SR	12	300	1455	10	4.8	121.3

RUSHING/Yards Per Carry	CL	G	ATT	YDS	YPC
1 Ki-Jana Carter, Penn State	JR	11	198	1539	7.8
2 Rashaan Salaam, Colorado	JR	11	298	2055	6.9
3 Brian Pruitt, Central Michigan	SR	11	292	1890	6.5
4 Terrell Fletcher, Wisconsin	SR	11	205	1235	6.0
5 Lawrence Phillips, Nebraska	SO	12	286	1722	6.0
6 Mike Alstott, Purdue	JR	11	202	1188	5.9
7 Sharmon Shah, UCLA	SO	11	210	1227	5.8
8 Andre Davis, TCU	JR	11	260	1494	5.7
9 Stephen Davis, Auburn	JR	11	221	1263	5.7
10 Marcellus Chrishon, Nevada	SR	9	189	1076	5.7

*-Based on top 30 rushers

RECEIVING	CL	G	REC	YDS	TD	RPG	YPR	YPG
1 Marcus Harris, Wyoming	SO	12	71	1431	11	5.9	20.2	119.3
2 Keyshawn Johnson, Southern Cal	JR	10	58	1140	6	5.8	19.7	114.0
3 Alex Van Dyke, Nevada	JR	11	98	1246	10	8.9	12.7	113.3
4 Kevin Jordan, UCLA	JR	11	73	1228	7	6.6	16.8	111.6
5 Randy Gatewood, Nevada-Las Vegas	SR	11	88	1203	6	8.0	13.7	109.4
6 Stepfret Williams, La. Monroe	JR	11	57	1106	10	5.2	19.4	100.6
7 Justin Armour, Stanford	SR	11	67	1092	7	6.1	16.3	99.3
8 Amani Toomer, Michigan	JR	11	49	1033	5	4.5	21.1	93.9
9 Bobby Engram, Penn State	JR	11	52	1029	7	4.7	19.8	93.6
10 Lucious Davis, New Mexico State	JR	11	54	985	11	4.9	18.2	89.6

PUNTING	CL	PUNT	YDS	AVG
1 Todd Sauerbrun, West Virginia	SR	72	3486	48.4
2 Jason Bender, Georgia Tech	SR	55	2503	45.5
3 Brad Maynard, Ball State	JR	59	2684	45.5
4 Brian Lambert, La. Monroe	SR	55	2479	45.1
5 Gary Layton, Miami, Ohio	SR	55	2477	45.0
6 Terry Daniel, Auburn	SR	53	2358	44.5
7 Darren Schager, UCLA	SR	53	2342	44.2
8 John Stonehouse, Southern Cal	JR	61	2693	44.2
9 Greg Ivy, Oklahoma State	JR	64	2818	44.0
10 Jeff Beckley, Boston College	SR	58	2545	43.9

PUNT RETURNS	CL	PR	YDS	TD	AVG
1 Steve Clay, Eastern Michigan	JR	14	278	1	19.9
2 Nilo Silvan, Tennessee	JR	15	272	0	18.1
3 Ray Peterson, San Diego State	JR	12	190	2	15.8
4 Kevin Alexander, Utah State	JR	14	199	1	14.2
5 Eddie Kennison, LSU	SO	36	439	1	12.2
6 Antonio Freeman, Virginia Tech	SR	39	467	1	12.0
7 Parrish Foster, New Mexico State	SR	14	167	0	11.9
8 Greg Myers, Colorado State	JR	25	294	0	11.8
9 Ryan Roskelly, Memphis	JR	40	468	1	11.7
10 Dane Johnson, Texas Tech	FR	27	313	1	11.6

KICKOFF RETURNS	CL	KR	YDS	TD	AVG
1 Eric Moulds, Mississippi State	JR	13	426	0	32.8
2 David Dunn, Fresno State	SR	35	1013	0	28.9
3 Marcus Wall, North Carolina	JR	27	743	1	27.5
4 Parrish Foster, New Mexico State	SR	14	385	0	27.5
5 Derrick Mason, Michigan State	SO	36	966	1	26.8
6 Joey Galloway, Ohio State	SR	15	401	1	26.7
7 Ashaundai Smith, Kansas	JR	17	448	1	26.4
8 Ben Bronson, Baylor	SR	18	470	1	26.1
9 Seth Smith, Michigan	FR	18	468	1	26.0
9 Brian Davis, Memphis	JR	16	416	0	26.0
9 Jack Jackson, Florida	JR	15	390	0	26.0

SCORING	CL	TDS	XP	FG	PTS	PTPG
1 Rashaan Salaam, Colorado	JR	24	0	0	144	13.1
2 Ki-Jana Carter, Penn State	JR	23	0	0	138	12.6
3 Brian Pruitt, Central Michigan	SR	22	0	0	132	12.0
4 Brian Leaver, Bowling Green	SR	0	42	21	105	9.6
5 Judd Davis, Florida	SR	0	65	14	107	8.9
6 Rodney Thomas, Texas A&M	SR	16	0	0	96	8.7
7 Tyrone Wheatley, Michigan	SR	13	0	0	78	8.7
8 Remy Hamilton, Michigan	SO	0	23	24	95	8.6
8 Steve McLaughlin, Arizona	SR	0	26	23	95	8.6
10 Brett Conway, Penn State	SO	0	62	10	92	8.4

FIELD GOALS	CL	FGA	FGM	PCT	FGG
1 Remy Hamilton, Michigan	SO	29	24	0.83	2.18
2 Steve McLaughlin, Arizona	SR	29	23	0.79	2.09
3 Brian Leaver, Bowling Green	SR	24	21	0.88	1.91
3 Nick Garritano, Nevada-Las Vegas	SR	26	21	0.81	1.91
5 Ryan Williams, Virginia Tech	SR	21	17	0.81	1.70
5 Mike Chalberg, Minnesota	JR	23	17	0.74	1.70
7 John Wales, Washington	SO	25	18	0.72	1.64
8 Kanon Parkman, Georgia	JR	22	17	0.77	1.55
8 Rafael Garcia, Virginia	SO	22	17	0.77	1.55
8 Jon Baker, Arizona State	SR	24	17	0.71	1.55
8 Marty Kent, Louisiana Tech	FR	24	17	0.71	1.55
8 Kyle Bryant, Texas A&M	FR	25	17	0.68	1.55

INTERCEPTIONS	CL	INT	YDS	TD	INT/GM
1 Aaron Beasley, West Virginia	JR	10	133	2	0.83
2 Brian Robinson, Auburn	JR	8	140	1	0.73
2 Ronde Barber, Virginia	FR	8	56	0	0.73
4 Demetrice Martin, Michigan State	JR	7	41	0	0.64
5 Carlos Yancy, Georgia	SR	6	154	1	0.55
5 Kareem Leary, Utah	SR	6	140	2	0.55
5 Bart Thomas, Texas Tech	SR	6	91	0	0.55
5 Ray Jackson, Colorado State	JR	6	71	0	0.55
5 Joe Crocker, Virginia	JR	6	54	1	0.55
5 Ernest Boyd, Utah	SR	6	41	0	0.55
5 Walt Harris, Mississippi State	JR	6	41	1	0.55
5 Brian Watkins, Air Force	SR	6	28	0	0.55
5 Denorse Mosley, Pittsburgh	SO	6	27	0	0.55
5 Orlanda Thomas, La. Lafayette	SR	6	25	0	0.55

Team Leaders

RUSHING OFFENSE	G	ATT	YDS	AVG	TD	YPG
1 Nebraska	12	687	4080	5.9	44	340.0
2 Air Force	12	720	3657	5.1	36	304.8
3 Colorado	11	517	3206	6.2	40	291.5
4 Central Michigan	11	571	3132	5.5	37	284.7
5 Oregon State	11	640	3072	4.8	24	279.3
6 Penn State	11	450	2760	6.1	45	250.9
7 Army	11	619	2738	4.4	22	248.9
8 Kansas	11	558	2718	4.9	31	247.1
9 Toledo	11	509	2667	5.2	28	242.5
10 Wisconsin	11	497	2649	5.3	23	240.8

PASSING OFFENSE	G	ATT	COM	INT	PCT	YDS	YPA	TD	I%	YPC	YPG
1 Georgia	11	462	276	14	59.7	3721	8.1	24	3.0	13.5	338.3
2 Nevada	11	463	279	16	60.3	3625	7.8	29	3.5	13.0	329.5
3 Brigham Young	12	475	287	14	60.4	3755	7.9	29	3.0	13.1	312.9
4 Florida	12	435	267	21	61.4	3740	8.6	43	4.8	14.0	311.7
5 Stanford	11	422	255	12	60.4	3358	8.0	18	2.8	13.2	305.3
6 San Diego State	11	410	257	16	62.7	3244	7.9	27	3.9	12.6	294.9
7 Florida State	11	441	264	18	59.9	3234	7.3	21	4.1	12.3	294.0
8 Wyoming	12	409	225	19	55.0	3367	8.2	21	4.7	15.0	280.6
9 Utah	11	387	249	11	64.3	3061	7.9	28	2.8	12.3	278.3
10 Maryland	11	428	291	13	68.0	3037	7.1	23	3.0	10.4	276.1

TOTAL OFFENSE	G	P	YDS	AVG	TD	YPG
1 Penn State	11	749	5722	7.6	68	520.2
2 Nevada	11	901	5581	6.2	55	507.4
3 Colorado	11	773	5448	7.0	52	495.3
4 Florida State	11	853	5314	6.2	52	483.1
5 Nebraska	12	897	5734	6.4	59	477.8
6 New Mexico	12	937	5664	6.0	51	472.0
7 Georgia	11	754	5135	6.8	41	466.8
8 Florida	12	851	5553	6.5	62	462.8
9 Brigham Young	12	955	5489	5.7	45	457.4
10 Wyoming	12	929	5468	5.9	38	455.7

RUSHING DEFENSE	G	ATT	YDS	AVG	TD	YPG
1 Virginia	11	323	700	2.2	9	63.6
2 Arizona	11	369	715	1.9	6	65.0
3 Washington State	11	418	812	1.9	4	73.8
4 Nebraska	12	401	951	2.4	8	79.3
5 Florida	12	387	1015	2.6	9	84.6
6 Texas A&M	11	440	1016	2.3	11	92.4
7 Miami, Fla.	11	409	1065	2.6	4	96.8
8 Florida State	11	378	1077	2.8	6	97.9
9 Utah	11	410	1163	2.8	11	105.7
10 Memphis	11	419	1172	2.8	8	106.5

PASSING DEFENSE	G	ATT	COM	PCT	INT	I%	YDS	YPA	TD	TD%	RAT
1 Miami, Fla.	11	293	143	48.8	18	6.1	1365	4.7	5	1.7	81.3
2 La. Lafayette	11	309	135	43.7	19	6.2	1626	5.3	10	3.2	86.3
3 Texas Tech	11	283	122	43.1	17	6.0	1623	5.7	8	2.8	88.6
4 Florida State	11	376	180	47.9	15	4.0	1860	5.0	13	3.5	92.9
5 Washington State	11	314	140	44.6	10	3.2	1707	5.4	9	2.9	93.3
6 Mississippi	11	300	134	44.7	19	6.3	1708	5.7	13	4.3	94.1
7 Kansas State	11	279	130	46.6	12	4.3	1596	5.7	7	2.5	94.3
8 Virginia Tech	11	354	168	47.5	15	4.2	1945	5.5	10	2.8	94.5
9 Memphis	11	310	162	52.3	13	4.2	1602	5.2	7	2.3	94.7
10 Nebraska	12	364	172	47.3	17	4.7	2155	5.9	10	2.8	96.7

TOTAL DEFENSE	G	P	YDS	AVG	TD	YPG
1 Miami, Fla.	11	702	2430	3.5	9	220.9
2 Washington State	11	732	2519	3.4	13	229.0
3 Memphis	11	729	2774	3.8	15	252.2
4 Nebraska	12	765	3106	4.1	18	258.8
5 Texas A&M	11	758	2920	3.9	17	265.5
6 Boston College	11	697	2927	4.2	19	266.1
7 Florida State	11	754	2937	3.9	19	267.0
8 Western Michigan	11	726	3047	4.2	23	277.0
9 Illinois	11	700	3138	4.5	16	285.3
10 Arizona	11	688	3140	4.6	19	285.5

SCORING OFFENSE	G	PTS	AVG
1 Penn State	11	526	47.8
2 Florida	12	521	43.4
3 Nevada	11	414	37.6
4 Utah	11	410	37.3
5 Florida State	11	405	36.8
6 Nebraska	12	435	36.3
7 Colorado	11	398	36.2
8 Bowling Green	11	391	35.5
9 Colorado State	11	386	35.1
10 Central Michigan	11	376	34.2

SCORING DEFENSE	G	PTS	AVG
1 Miami, Fla.	11	119	10.8
2 Nebraska	12	145	12.1
3 Washington State	11	133	12.1
4 Texas A&M	11	147	13.4
5 Kansas State	11	156	14.2
5 Illinois	11	156	14.2
7 Alabama	12	173	14.4
8 Memphis	11	159	14.5
9 Boston College	11	162	14.7
10 Ohio State	12	187	15.6

TURNOVER MARGIN	G	FR	INT	TOT	FL	INTL	TOT	MAR
1 Clemson	11	13	16	29	2	10	12	1.6
2 Duke	11	12	17	29	4	9	13	1.5
3 Auburn	11	11	22	33	11	7	18	1.4
4 Mississippi	11	13	19	32	13	6	19	1.2
4 SMU	11	20	9	29	6	10	16	1.2
4 Kansas State	11	12	12	24	5	6	11	1.2
7 Penn State	11	12	11	23	4	7	11	1.1
8 Utah	11	13	19	32	10	11	21	1.0
8 East Carolina	11	11	22	33	7	15	22	1.0
8 Northern Illinois	11	16	15	31	13	7	20	1.0
8 Mississippi State	11	13	22	35	16	8	24	1.0
8 Virginia	11	9	27	36	13	12	25	1.0
8 Southern Cal	11	9	16	25	8	6	14	1.0
8 Southern Miss	11	15	25	40	8	21	29	1.0
8 Air Force	12	11	21	32	16	4	20	1.0

1995 Poll Progression

CNN	AP	Pre-Season 1995		Aug. 26 Games
1	1	**Florida State**	0-0-0	bye week
2	2	**Nebraska**	0-0-0	bye week
3	3	**Texas A&M**	0-0-0	bye week
4	4	**Penn State**	0-0-0	bye week
5	5	**Florida**	0-0-0	bye week
7	6	**Auburn**	0-0-0	bye week
6	7	**Southern Cal**	0-0-0	bye week
11	8	**Tennessee**	0-0-0	bye week
8	9	**Notre Dame**	0-0-0	bye week
14	10	**Alabama**	0-0-0	bye week
9	11	**Miami, Fla.**	0-0-0	bye week
10	12	**Ohio State**	0-0-0	beat # 22 Boston College 38-6 (A27)
13	13	**Colorado**	0-0-0	bye week
12	14	**Michigan**	0-0-0	beat # 17 Virginia 18-17
17	15	**Oklahoma**	0-0-0	bye week
15	16	**UCLA**	0-0-0	bye week
16	17	**Virginia**	0-0-0	lost to # 14 Michigan 17-18
18	18	**Texas**	0-0-0	bye week
19	19	**Arizona**	0-0-0	bye week
20	20	**North Carolina**	0-0-0	bye week
22	21	**Wisconsin**	0-0-0	bye week
23	22	**Boston College**	0-0-0	lost to # 12 Ohio State 6-38 (A27)
	23	**West Virginia**	0-0-0	bye week
	24	**Virginia Tech**	0-0-0	bye week
21	24	**Washington**	0-0-0	bye week
24		**Illinois**	0-0-0	bye week
25		**North Carolina St.**	0-0-0	bye week

AP	August 28 Poll		Sept. 2 Games
1	**Florida State**	0-0-0	beat Duke 70-26
2	**Nebraska**	0-0-0	beat Oklahoma State 64-21 (A31)
3	**Texas A&M**	0-0-0	beat LSU 33-17
4	**Penn State**	0-0-0	bye week
5	**Florida**	0-0-0	beat Houston 45-21
6	**Auburn**	0-0-0	beat Mississippi 46-13
7	**Southern Cal**	0-0-0	bye week
8	**Tennessee**	0-0-0	beat East Carolina 27-7
9	**Notre Dame**	0-0-0	lost to Northwestern 15-17
10	**Ohio State**	1-0-0	bye week
11	**Alabama**	0-0-0	beat Vanderbilt 33-25
12	**Miami, Fla.**	0-0-0	lost to # 15 UCLA 8-31
13	**Michigan**	1-0-0	beat Illinois 38-14
14	**Colorado**	0-0-0	beat # 21 Wisconsin 43-7
15	**UCLA**	0-0-0	beat # 12 Miami, Fla. 31-8
16	**Oklahoma**	0-0-0	bye week
17	**Virginia**	0-1-0	beat William & Mary 40-16
18	**Texas**	0-0-0	beat Hawaii 38-17
19	**Arizona**	0-0-0	beat Pacific 41-9
20	**North Carolina**	0-0-0	lost to Syracuse 9-20
21	**Wisconsin**	0-0-0	lost to # 14 Colorado 7-43
22	**Washington**	0-0-0	beat Arizona State 23-20
23	**West Virginia**	0-0-0	lost to Purdue 24-26
24	**Virginia Tech**	0-0-0	bye week
25	**Illinois**	0-0-0	bye week

CNN	AP	September 4 Poll		Sept. 9 Games
1	1	**Florida State**	1-0-0	beat Clemson 45-26
2	2	**Nebraska**	1-0-0	beat Michigan State 50-10
3	3	**Texas A&M**	1-0-0	bye week
4	4	**Penn State**	0-0-0	beat Texas Tech 24-23
5	5	**Florida**	1-0-0	beat Kentucky 42-7
6	6	**Auburn**	1-0-0	beat U.T. Chattanooga 76-10
7	7	**Southern Cal**	0-0-0	beat San Jose State 45-7
11	8	**Tennessee**	1-0-0	beat Georgia 30-27
8	9	**Ohio State**	1-0-0	bye week
10	10	**Colorado**	1-0-0	beat Colorado State 42-14
9	11	**Michigan**	2-0-0	beat Memphis 24-7
12	12	**UCLA**	1-0-0	beat Brigham Young 23-9
16	13	**Alabama**	1-0-0	beat Southern Miss 24-20
14	14	**Oklahoma**	0-0-0	beat San Diego State 38-22
13	15	**Texas**	1-0-0	bye week
18	16	**Virginia**	1-1-0	beat # 23 North Carolina St. 29-24
15	17	**Arizona**	1-0-0	beat Georgia Tech 20-19 (S7)
17	18	**Washington**	1-0-0	bye week
21	19	**Miami, Fla.**	0-1-0	beat Florida A&M 49-3
22	20	**Virginia Tech**	0-0-0	lost to Boston College 14-20 (S7)
23	21	**Kansas State**	1-0-0	beat Cincinnati 23-21
20	22	**Syracuse**	1-0-0	lost to East Carolina 24-27
19	23	**North Carolina St.**	1-0-0	lost to # 16 Virginia 24-29
	24	**Oregon**	1-0-0	beat Illinois 34-31
	25	**Notre Dame**	0-1-0	beat Purdue 35-28
24		**Georgia**	1-0-0	lost to # 8 Tennessee 27-30
25		**Air Force**	1-0-0	beat Wyoming 34-10

CNN	AP	September 11 Poll		Sept. 16 Games
1	1	**Florida State**	2-0-0	beat North Carolina St. 77-17
2	2	**Nebraska**	2-0-0	beat Arizona State 77-28
3	3	**Texas A&M**	1-0-0	beat Tulsa 52-9
4	4	**Florida**	2-0-0	beat # 8 Tennessee 62-37
6	5	**Auburn**	2-0-0	lost to LSU 6-12
5	6	**Southern Cal**	1-0-0	beat Houston 45-10
7	7	**Penn State**	1-0-0	beat Temple 66-14
12	8	**Tennessee**	2-0-0	lost to # 4 Florida 37-62
10	9	**Colorado**	2-0-0	beat La. Monroe 66-14
8	10	**Ohio State**	1-0-0	beat # 18 Washington 30-20
9	11	**Michigan**	3-0-0	beat Boston College 23-13
11	12	**UCLA**	2-0-0	lost to # 20 Oregon 31-38
18	13	**Alabama**	2-0-0	lost to Arkansas 19-20
14	14	**Oklahoma**	1-0-0	beat SMU 24-10
13	15	**Texas**	1-0-0	beat Pittsburgh 38-27
17	16	**Virginia**	2-1-0	beat Georgia Tech 41-14
16	17	**Arizona**	2-0-0	lost to Illinois 7-9
15	18	**Washington**	1-0-0	lost to # 10 Ohio State 20-30
20	19	**Miami, Fla.**	1-1-0	bye week
22	20	**Oregon**	2-0-0	beat # 12 UCLA 38-31
19	21	**Air Force**	2-0-0	lost to Colorado State 20-27
21	22	**Kansas State**	2-0-0	bye week
23	23	**Georgia**	1-1-0	beat New Mexico State 40-13
24	24	**Notre Dame**	1-1-0	beat Vanderbilt 41-0
	25	**Northwestern**	1-0-0	lost to Miami, Ohio 28-30
25		**Boston College**	1-1-1	lost to # 11 Michigan 13-23

CNN	AP	September 18 Poll		Sept. 23 Games
1	1	**Florida State**	3-0-0	beat Central Florida 46-14
2	2	**Nebraska**	3-0-0	beat Pacific 49-7
3	3	**Texas A&M**	2-0-0	lost to # 7 Colorado 21-29
4	4	**Florida**	3-0-0	bye week
5	5	**Southern Cal**	2-0-0	beat # 25 Arizona 31-10
6	6	**Penn State**	2-0-0	beat Rutgers 59-34
8	7	**Colorado**	3-0-0	beat # 3 Texas A&M 29-21
7	8	**Ohio State**	2-0-0	beat Pittsburgh 54-14
9	9	**Michigan**	4-0-0	bye week
11	10	**Oklahoma**	2-0-0	beat North Texas 51-10
14	11	**Virginia**	3-1-0	beat Clemson 22-3
13	12	**Oregon**	3-0-0	lost to Stanford 21-28
10	13	**Texas**	2-0-0	lost to # 21 Notre Dame 27-55
12	14	**Auburn**	2-1-0	bye week
16	15	**Tennessee**	2-1-0	beat Mississippi State 52-14
15	16	**UCLA**	2-1-0	lost to Washington State 15-24
17	17	**Miami, Fla.**	1-1-0	lost to Virginia Tech 7-13
20	18	**LSU**	2-1-0	beat Rice 52-7
19	19	**Kansas State**	2-0-0	beat Akron 67-0
18	20	**Georgia**	2-1-0	lost to Mississippi 10-18
21	21	**Notre Dame**	2-1-0	beat # 13 Texas 55-27
22	22	**Washington**	1-1-0	beat Army 21-13
23	23	**Alabama**	2-1-0	bye week
25	24	**Maryland**	3-0-0	beat Duke 41-28
24	25	**Arizona**	2-1-0	lost to # 5 Southern Cal 10-31

CNN	AP	September 25 Poll		Sept. 30 Games
1	1	**Florida State**	4-0-0	bye week
2	2	**Nebraska**	4-0-0	beat Washington State 35-21
3	3	**Florida**	3-0-0	beat Mississippi 28-10
5	4	**Colorado**	4-0-0	beat # 10 Oklahoma 38-17
4	5	**Southern Cal**	3-0-0	beat Arizona State 31-0
7	6	**Penn State**	3-0-0	lost to Wisconsin 9-17
6	7	**Ohio State**	3-0-0	beat # 15 Notre Dame 45-26
8	8	**Michigan**	4-0-0	beat Miami, Ohio 38-19
10	9	**Texas A&M**	2-1-0	bye week
9	10	**Oklahoma**	3-0-0	lost to # 4 Colorado 17-38
11	11	**Virginia**	4-1-0	beat Wake Forest 35-17
13	12	**Tennessee**	3-1-0	beat Oklahoma State 31-0
12	13	**Auburn**	2-1-0	beat Kentucky 42-21
16	14	**LSU**	3-1-0	tied South Carolina 20-20
14	15	**Notre Dame**	3-1-0	lost to # 7 Ohio State 26-45
15	16	**Kansas State**	3-0-0	beat Northern Illinois 44-0
17	17	**Maryland**	4-0-0	lost to Georgia Tech 3-31 (S28)
18	18	**Washington**	2-1-0	beat Oregon State 26-16
20	19	**Oregon**	3-1-0	bye week
21	20	**Alabama**	2-1-0	beat Georgia 31-0
19	21	**Texas**	2-1-0	beat SMU 35-10
23	22	**Stanford**	3-0-1	bye week
24	23	**Arkansas**	3-1-0	beat Vanderbilt 35-7
	24	**Texas Tech**	1-1-0	lost to Baylor 7-9
22	25	**Kansas**	4-0-0	bye week
25		**UCLA**	2-2-0	beat Fresno State 45-21

CNN	AP	October 2 Poll		Oct. 7 Games
1	1	**Florida State**	4-0-0	beat Miami, Fla. 41-17
2	2	**Nebraska**	5-0-0	bye week
3	3	**Florida**	4-0-0	beat # 21 LSU 28-10
6	4	**Colorado**	5-0-0	lost to # 24 Kansas 24-40
5	5	**Ohio State**	4-0-0	beat # 12 Penn State 28-25
4	5	**Southern Cal**	4-0-0	beat California 26-16
7	7	**Michigan**	5-0-0	lost to # 25 Northwestern 13-19
8	8	**Texas A&M**	2-1-0	lost to Texas Tech 7-14
9	9	**Virginia**	5-1-0	lost to North Carolina 17-22
11	10	**Tennessee**	4-1-0	beat # 18 Arkansas 49-31
10	11	**Auburn**	3-1-0	beat Mississippi State 48-20
12	12	**Penn State**	3-1-0	lost to # 5 Ohio State 25-28
13	13	**Kansas State**	4-0-0	beat Missouri 30-0
14	14	**Oklahoma**	3-1-0	beat Iowa State 39-26
15	15	**Washington**	3-1-0	lost to # 23 Notre Dame 21-29
17	16	**Alabama**	3-1-0	beat North Carolina St. 27-11
18	17	**Oregon**	3-1-0	beat Pacific 45-7
21	18	**Arkansas**	4-1-0	lost to # 10 Tennessee 31-49
20	19	**Stanford**	3-0-1	beat Arizona State 30-28
16	20	**Texas**	3-1-0	beat Rice 37-13
22	21	**LSU**	3-1-1	lost to # 3 Florida 10-28
	22	**Wisconsin**	2-1-1	bye week
23	23	**Notre Dame**	3-2-0	beat # 15 Washington 29-21
19	24	**Kansas**	4-0-0	beat # 4 Colorado 40-24
	25	**Northwestern**	3-1-0	beat # 7 Michigan 19-13
24		**Baylor**	3-1-0	bye week
25		**UCLA**	3-2-0	bye week

CNN	AP	October 9 Poll		Oct. 14 Games
1	1	**Florida State**	5-0-0	beat Wake Forest 72-13
2	2	**Nebraska**	5-0-0	beat Missouri 57-0
3	3	**Florida**	5-0-0	beat # 7 Auburn 49-38
4	4	**Ohio State**	5-0-0	beat # 21 Wisconsin 27-16
5	5	**Southern Cal**	5-0-0	beat Washington State 26-14
7	6	**Tennessee**	5-1-0	beat # 11 Alabama 41-14
6	7	**Auburn**	4-1-0	lost to # 3 Florida 38-49
8	8	**Kansas State**	5-0-0	beat Oklahoma State 23-17
10	9	**Colorado**	5-1-0	bye week
9	10	**Kansas**	5-0-0	beat Iowa State 34-7
14	11	**Alabama**	4-1-0	lost to # 6 Tennessee 14-41
11	12	**Michigan**	5-1-0	bye week
12	13	**Oklahoma**	4-1-0	tied # 18 Texas 24-24
17	14	**Northwestern**	4-1-0	beat Minnesota 27-17
15	15	**Oregon**	4-1-0	beat California 52-30
19	16	**Stanford**	4-0-1	lost to Washington 28-38
21	17	**Notre Dame**	4-2-0	beat Army 28-27
13	18	**Texas**	4-1-0	tied # 13 Oklahoma 24-24
16	19	**Virginia**	5-2-0	beat Duke 44-30
20	20	**Penn State**	3-2-0	beat Purdue 26-23
25	21	**Wisconsin**	2-1-1	lost to # 4 Ohio State 16-27
18	22	**Texas A&M**	2-2-0	beat SMU 20-17
22	23	**Iowa**	4-0-0	beat Indiana 22-13
	24	**Washington**	3-2-0	beat Stanford 38-28
	25	**Texas Tech**	2-2-0	beat Arkansas State 63-25
23		**Baylor**	3-1-0	beat Houston 47-7
24		**Syracuse**	4-1-0	beat Eastern Michigan 52-24

CNN	AP	October 16 Poll		Oct. 21 Games
1	1	**Florida State**	6-0-0	beat Georgia Tech 42-10
2	2	**Nebraska**	6-0-0	beat # 8 Kansas State 49-25
3	3	**Florida**	6-0-0	bye week
4	4	**Ohio State**	6-0-0	beat Purdue 28-0
5	5	**Southern Cal**	6-0-0	lost to # 17 Notre Dame 10-38
6	6	**Tennessee**	6-1-0	bye week
7	7	**Kansas**	6-0-0	beat # 15 Oklahoma 38-17
8	8	**Kansas State**	6-0-0	lost to # 2 Nebraska 25-49
9	9	**Colorado**	5-1-0	beat Iowa State 50-28
10	10	**Michigan**	5-1-0	beat Indiana 34-17
11	11	**Northwestern**	5-1-0	beat # 24 Wisconsin 35-0
12	12	**Oregon**	5-1-0	beat Washington State 26-7
13	13	**Auburn**	4-2-0	beat Western Michigan 34-13
15	14	**Virginia**	6-2-0	lost to # 16 Texas 16-17
14	15	**Oklahoma**	4-1-1	lost to # 7 Kansas 17-38
16	16	**Texas**	4-1-1	beat # 14 Virginia 17-16
22	17	**Notre Dame**	5-2-0	beat # 5 Southern Cal 38-10
17	18	**Iowa**	5-0-0	lost to # 19 Penn State 27-41
18	19	**Penn State**	4-2-0	beat # 18 Iowa 41-27
23	20	**Washington**	4-2-0	beat Arizona 31-17
24	21	**Alabama**	4-2-0	beat Mississippi 23-9
19	22	**Texas A&M**	3-2-0	beat Baylor 24-9
25	23	**Stanford**	4-1-1	lost to UCLA 28-42
	24	**Wisconsin**	2-2-1	lost to # 11 Northwestern 0-35
	25	**Texas Tech**	3-2-0	beat Rice 31-26
20		**Syracuse**	5-1-0	beat West Virginia 22-0
21		**Baylor**	4-1-0	lost to # 22 Texas A&M 9-24

CNN	AP	October 23 Poll		Oct. 28 Games
1	1	Florida State	7-0-0	bye week
2	2	Nebraska	7-0-0	beat # 7 Colorado 44-21
3	3	Florida	6-0-0	beat Georgia 52-17
4	4	Ohio State	7-0-0	beat # 25 Iowa 56-35
5	5	Tennessee	6-1-0	beat South Carolina 56-21
6	6	Kansas	7-0-0	lost to # 14 Kansas State 7-41
7	7	Colorado	6-1-0	lost to # 2 Nebraska 21-44
8	8	Northwestern	6-1-0	beat Illinois 17-14
9	9	Michigan	6-1-0	beat Minnesota 52-17
12	10	Oregon	6-1-0	lost to Arizona State 24-35
11	11	Auburn	5-2-0	lost to Arkansas 28-30
15	12	Notre Dame	6-2-0	beat Boston College 20-10
10	13	Southern Cal	6-1-0	tied # 17 Washington 21-21
14	14	Kansas State	6-1-0	beat # 6 Kansas 41-7
13	15	Texas	5-1-1	bye week
16	16	Penn State	5-2-0	beat Indiana 45-21
19	17	Washington	5-2-0	tied # 13 Southern Cal 21-21
22	18	Alabama	5-2-0	beat North Texas 38-19
18	19	Texas A&M	4-2-0	beat Houston 31-7
20	20	Virginia	6-3-0	bye week
17	21	Syracuse	6-1-0	bye week
25	22	Texas Tech	4-2-0	beat New Mexico 34-7
21	23	Oklahoma	4-2-1	beat Missouri 13-9
24	24	UCLA	5-2-0	beat California 33-16
23	25	Iowa	5-1-0	lost to # 4 Ohio State 35-56

CNN	AP	October 30 Poll		Nov. 4 Games
1	1	Nebraska	8-0-0	beat Iowa State 73-14
2	2	Florida State	7-0-0	lost to # 24 Virginia 28-33 (N2)
3	3	Florida	7-0-0	beat Northern Illinois 58-20
4	4	Ohio State	8-0-0	beat Minnesota 49-21
5	5	Tennessee	7-1-0	beat Southern Miss 42-0
6	6	Northwestern	7-1-0	beat # 12 Penn State 21-10
7	7	Michigan	7-1-0	lost to Michigan State 25-28
10	8	Notre Dame	7-2-0	beat Navy 35-17
8	9	Kansas State	7-1-0	beat # 25 Oklahoma 49-10
12	10	Colorado	6-2-0	beat Oklahoma State 45-32
14	11	Kansas	7-1-0	beat Missouri 42-23
13	12	Penn State	6-2-0	lost to # 6 Northwestern 10-21
9	13	Texas	5-1-1	beat # 23 Texas Tech 48-7
11	14	Southern Cal	6-1-1	beat Stanford 31-30
17	15	Washington	5-2-1	lost to Oregon 22-24
22	16	Alabama	6-2-0	beat LSU 10-3
16	17	Texas A&M	5-2-0	bye week
18	18	Arkansas	6-2-0	beat Mississippi State 26-21
19	19	Oregon	6-2-0	beat Washington 24-22
15	20	Syracuse	6-1-0	lost to Virginia Tech 7-31
23	21	Auburn	5-3-0	beat La. Monroe 38-14
21	22	UCLA	6-2-0	lost to Arizona State 33-37
24	23	Texas Tech	5-2-0	lost to # 13 Texas 7-48
20	24	Virginia	6-3-0	beat # 2 Florida State 33-28 (N2)
25	25	Oklahoma	5-2-1	lost to # 9 Kansas State 10-49

CNN	AP	November 6 Poll		Nov. 11 Games
1	1	Nebraska	9-0-0	beat # 10 Kansas 41-3
2	2	Ohio State	9-0-0	beat Illinois 41-3
3	3	Florida	8-0-0	beat South Carolina 63-7
4	4	Tennessee	8-1-0	bye week
5	5	Northwestern	8-1-0	beat Iowa 31-20
6	6	Florida State	7-1-0	beat North Carolina 28-12
7	7	Kansas State	8-1-0	beat Iowa State 49-7
9	8	Notre Dame	8-2-0	bye week
10	9	Colorado	7-2-0	beat Missouri 21-0
12	10	Kansas	8-1-0	lost to # 1 Nebraska 3-41
8	11	Texas	6-1-1	beat Houston 52-20
10	12	Southern Cal	7-1-1	beat Oregon State 28-10
15	13	Michigan	7-2-0	beat Purdue 5-0
13	14	Virginia	7-3-0	beat Maryland 21-18
16	15	Arkansas	7-2-0	beat La. Lafayette 24-13
18	16	Alabama	7-2-0	beat Mississippi State 14-9
17	17	Oregon	7-2-0	beat Arizona 17-13
14	18	Texas A&M	5-2-0	beat Rice 17-10 (N9)
21	19	Penn State	6-3-0	bye week
20	20	Auburn	6-3-0	beat Georgia 37-31
19	21	Virginia Tech	7-2-0	beat Temple 38-16
23	22	Washington	5-3-1	beat UCLA 38-14
22	23	Syracuse	6-2-0	beat Pittsburgh 42-10
25	24	Clemson	6-3-0	beat Duke 34-17
	25	San Diego State	7-2-0	lost to Wyoming 31-34
24		UCLA	6-3-0	lost to Washington 14-38

CNN	AP	November 13 Poll		Nov. 18 Games
1	1	Nebraska	10-0-0	bye week
2	2	Ohio State	10-0-0	beat Indiana 42-3
3	3	Florida	9-0-0	beat Vanderbilt 38-7
4	4	Tennessee	8-1-0	beat Kentucky 34-31
5	5	Northwestern	9-1-0	beat Purdue 23-8
6	6	Florida State	8-1-0	beat Maryland 59-17
7	7	Kansas State	9-1-0	lost to # 9 Colorado 17-27
10	8	Notre Dame	8-2-0	beat Air Force 44-14
9	9	Colorado	8-2-0	beat # 7 Kansas State 27-17
8	10	Texas	7-1-1	beat TCU 27-19
11	11	Southern Cal	8-1-1	lost to UCLA 20-24
14	12	Michigan	8-2-0	lost to # 19 Penn State 17-27
12	13	Virginia	8-3-0	lost to # 20 Virginia Tech 29-36
13	14	Arkansas	8-2-0	lost to LSU 0-28
17	15	Kansas	8-2-0	beat Oklahoma State 22-17
16	16	Oregon	8-2-0	beat Oregon State 12-10
19	17	Alabama	8-2-0	lost to # 21 Auburn 27-31
15	18	Texas A&M	6-2-0	beat Middle Tennessee 56-14
21	19	Penn State	6-3-0	beat # 12 Michigan 27-17
18	20	Virginia Tech	8-2-0	beat # 13 Virginia 36-29
20	21	Auburn	7-3-0	beat # 17 Alabama 31-27
23	22	Washington	6-3-1	beat Washington State 33-30
22	23	Syracuse	7-2-0	beat Boston College 58-29
24	24	Clemson	7-3-0	beat South Carolina 38-17
	25	Miami, Fla.	6-3-0	beat West Virginia 17-12
25		Brigham Young	6-3-0	lost to Utah 17-34

CNN	AP	November 20 Poll		Nov. 25 Games
1	1	Nebraska	10-0-0	beat Oklahoma 37-0 (N24)
2	2	Ohio State	11-0-0	lost to # 18 Michigan 23-31
3	3	Florida	10-0-0	beat # 6 Florida State 35-24
4	4	Northwestern	10-1-0	regular season complete
5	5	Tennessee	9-1-0	beat Vanderbilt 12-7
6	6	Florida State	9-1-0	lost to # 3 Florida 24-35
9	7	Notre Dame	9-2-0	regular season complete
8	8	Colorado	9-2-0	regular season complete
7	9	Texas	8-1-1	beat Baylor 21-13 (N23)
10	10	Kansas State	9-2-0	regular season complete
14	11	Kansas	9-2-0	regular season complete
12	12	Oregon	9-2-0	regular season complete
11	13	Virginia Tech	9-2-0	regular season complete
16	14	Penn State	7-3-0	beat Michigan State 24-20
13	15	Texas A&M	7-2-0	beat TCU 38-6
15	16	Auburn	8-3-0	regular season complete
17	17	Southern Cal	8-2-1	regular season complete
20	18	Michigan	8-3-0	beat # 2 Ohio State 31-23
19	19	Virginia	8-4-0	regular season complete
21	20	Washington	7-3-1	regular season complete
23	21	Alabama	8-3-0	regular season complete
18	22	Syracuse	8-2-0	lost to # 25 Miami, Fla. 24-35
24	23	Arkansas	8-3-0	bye week
22	24	Clemson	8-3-0	regular season complete
25	25	Miami, Fla.	7-3-0	beat # 22 Syracuse 35-24

CNN	AP	November 27 Poll		Dec. 2 Games
1	1	Nebraska	11-0-0	regular season complete
2	2	Florida	11-0-0	beat # 23 Arkansas 34-3 (SEC CH)
3	3	Northwestern	10-1-0	
4	4	Tennessee	10-1-0	regular season complete
5	5	Ohio State	11-1-0	regular season complete
9	6	Notre Dame	9-2-0	
7	7	Colorado	9-2-0	
8	8	Florida State	9-2-0	regular season complete
6	9	Texas	9-1-1	beat # 16 Texas A&M 16-6
10	10	Kansas State	9-2-0	
14	11	Kansas	9-2-0	
12	12	Oregon	9-2-0	
11	13	Virginia Tech	9-2-0	
15	14	Michigan	9-3-0	regular season complete
17	15	Penn State	8-3-0	
13	16	Texas A&M	8-2-0	lost to # 9 Texas 6-16
16	17	Auburn	8-3-0	
18	18	Southern Cal	8-2-1	
19	19	Virginia	8-4-0	
20	20	Washington	7-3-1	
23	21	Alabama	8-3-0	
21	22	Miami, Fla.	8-3-0	regular season complete
24	23	Arkansas	8-3-0	lost to # 2 Florida 3-34 (SEC CH)
22	24	Clemson	8-3-0	
	25	Toledo	10-0-1	regular season complete
25		Syracuse	8-3-0	regular season complete

CNN	AP	December 4 Poll	Record	Bowl Bid	Date	Bowl Result
1	1	Nebraska	11-0-0	Fiesta Bowl	J2	beat # 2 Florida 62-24
2	2	Florida	12-0-0	Fiesta Bowl	J2	lost to # 1 Nebraska 24-62
3	3	Northwestern	10-1-0	Rose Bowl	J1	lost to # 17 Southern Cal 32-41
5	4	Ohio State	11-1-0	Citrus Bowl	J1	lost to # 4 Tennessee 14-20
4	4	Tennessee	10-1-0	Citrus Bowl	J1	beat # 4 Ohio State 20-14
9	6	Notre Dame	9-2-0	Orange Bowl	J1	lost to # 8 Florida State 26-31
7	7	Colorado	9-2-0	Cotton Bowl	J1	beat # 12 Oregon 38-6
8	8	Florida State	9-2-0	Orange Bowl	J1	beat # 6 Notre Dame 31-26
6	9	Texas	10-1-1	Sugar Bowl	D31	lost to # 13 Virginia Tech 10-28
10	10	Kansas State	9-2-0	Holiday Bowl	D29	beat Colorado State 54-21
13	11	Kansas	9-2-0	Aloha Bowl	D25	beat UCLA 51-30
12	12	Oregon	9-2-0	Cotton Bowl	J1	lost to # 7 Colorado 6-38
11	13	Virginia Tech	9-2-0	Sugar Bowl	D31	beat # 9 Texas 28-10
14	14	Michigan	9-3-0	Alamo Bowl	D28	lost to # 19 Texas A&M 20-22
16	15	Penn State	8-3-0	Outback Bowl	J1	beat # 16 Auburn 43-14
15	16	Auburn	8-3-0	Outback Bowl	J1	lost to # 15 Penn State 14-43
17	17	Southern Cal	8-2-1	Rose Bowl	J1	beat # 3 Northwestern 41-32
19	18	Virginia	8-4-0	Peach Bowl	D30	beat Georgia 34-27
18	19	Texas A&M	8-3-0	Alamo Bowl	D28	beat # 14 Michigan 22-20
20	20	Washington	7-3-1	Sun Bowl	D29	lost to Iowa 18-38
	21	Alabama	8-3-0			
	22	Miami, Fla.	8-3-0			
21	23	Clemson	8-3-0	Gator Bowl	J1	lost to Syracuse 0-41
23	24	Arkansas	8-4-0	Carquest Bowl	D30	lost to North Carolina 10-20
	25	Toledo	10-0-1	Las Vegas Bowl	D14	beat Nevada 40-37
22		Syracuse	8-3-0	Gator Bowl	J1	beat # 23 Clemson 41-0
24		UCLA	7-4-0	Aloha Bowl	D25	lost to # 11 Kansas 30-51
25		Texas Tech	8-3-0	Copper Bowl	D27	beat Air Force 55-41

RB	CNN	AP	January 3 Final Poll	Record
1	1	1	Nebraska	12-0-0
2	3	2	Florida	12-1-0
3	2	3	Tennessee	11-1-0
6	5	4	Florida State	10-2-0
5	4	5	Colorado	10-2-0
4	8	6	Ohio State	11-2-0
11	6	7	Kansas State	10-2-0
9	7	8	Northwestern	10-2-0
7	10	9	Kansas	10-2-0
12	9	10	Virginia Tech	10-2-0
16	13	11	Notre Dame	9-3-0
8	11	12	Southern Cal	9-2-1
10	12	13	Penn State	9-3-0
17	14	14	Texas	10-2-1
14	15	15	Texas A&M	9-3-0
27	17	16	Virginia	9-4-0
15	19	17	Michigan	9-4-0
13	18	18	Oregon	9-3-0
26	16	19	Syracuse	9-3-0
21	PB	20	Miami, Fla.	8-3-0
18	PB	21	Alabama	8-3-0
20	21	22	Auburn	8-4-0
31	20	23	Texas Tech	9-3-0
19	24	24	Toledo	11-0-1
24	22	25	Iowa	8-4-0
23	23		East Carolina	9-3-0
25	25		LSU	7-4-1

1995

CONSENSUS ALL-AMERICANS

POS	Offense	HT	WT	School	AP	CF	FC	FN	FW	PI	SN
QB	Tommie Frazier	6-2	205	Nebraska	•	•	•	•	•	•	•
RB	Eddie George	6-3	230	Ohio State	•	•	•	•	•	•	•
RB	Troy Davis	5-8	182	Iowa State	•	•	•	•	•	•	•
WR	Terry Glenn	5-11	185	Ohio State	•	•	•	•	•	•	•
WR	Keyshawn Johnson	6-4	210	Southern Cal	•	•	•	•	•	•	•
TE	Marco Battaglia	6-3	240	Rutgers	•	•	•	•	•	•	•
OL	Jonathan Ogden	6-8	310	UCLA	•	•	•	•	•	•	•
OL	Jason Odom	6-5	291	Florida	•	•	•	•	•	•	•
OL	Orlando Pace	6-6	320	Ohio State	•	•	•	•	•	•	•
OL	Jeff Hartings	6-3	278	Penn State	•	•	•		•		•
C	Clay Shiver	6-2	285	Florida State	•	•	•	•	•	•	•
C	Bryan Stoltenberg	6-2	280	Colorado		•				•	
PK	Michael Reeder	6-0	160	TCU				•	•		•

OTHERS RECEIVING FIRST-TEAM HONORS

QB	Danny Wuerffel	Florida		•	
RB	Karim Abdul-Jabbar	UCLA		•	
WR	Marcus Harris	Wyoming		•	
OL	Dan Neil	Texas		•	
OL	Aaron Graham	Nebraska	•	•	
OL	Heath Irwin	Colorado	•		
PK	Sam Valenzisi	Northwestern		•	
KR	Marvin Harrison	Syracuse		•	

POS	Defense	HT	WT	School	AP	CF	FC	FN	FW	PI	SN
DL	Tedy Bruschi	6-1	253	Arizona	•	•	•	•	•	•	•
DL	Cornell Brown	6-2	240	Virginia Tech	•			•		•	
DL	Marcus Jones	6-6	270	North Carolina	•	•	•		•		
DL	Tony Brackens	6-4	250	Texas		•		•		•	•
LB	Zach Thomas	6-0	232	Texas Tech	•	•	•	•		•	•
LB	Kevin Hardy	6-4	243	Illinois	•	•	•	•	•	•	•
LB	Pat Fitzgerald	6-4	228	Northwestern	•	•			•		•
DB	Chris Canty	5-10	190	Kansas State	•		•	•	•	•	•
DB	Lawyer Milloy	6-2	200	Washington	•	•	•	•		•	•
DB	Aaron Beasley	6-0	190	West Virginia	•	•		•	•		
DB	Greg Myers	6-2	191	Colorado State	•	•	•		•		•
P	Brad Maynard	6-1	175	Ball State						•	

OTHERS RECEIVING FIRST-TEAM HONORS

DL	Tim Colston	Kansas State		•	•	
DL	Brandon Mitchell	Texas A&M	•			
DL	Cedric Jones	Oklahoma			•	•
DL	Jason Horn	Michigan			•	
DL	Jared Tomich	Nebraska	•			
DL	Mike Vrabel	Ohio State			•	
LB	Simeon Rice	Illinois		•	•	
LB	Ray Lewis	Miami, Fla.	•			
LB	Duane Clemons	California			•	
DB	Ray Mickens	Texas A&M	•			
DB	Kevin Abrams	Syracuse				•
DB	Marcus Coleman	Texas Tech	•			
DB	Alex Molden	Oregon			•	
DB	Adrian Robinson	Baylor			•	
DB	Percy Ellsworth	Virginia				•
P	Will Brice	Virginia			•	

HEISMAN TROPHY VOTING

	PLAYER	POS	SCHOOL	1ST	2ND	3RD	TOTAL
1	Eddie George	RB	Ohio State	268	248	160	1460
2	Tommie Frazier	QB	Nebraska	218	192	158	1196
3	Danny Wuerffel	QB	Florida	185	152	128	987
4	Darnell Autry	RB	Northwestern	87	78	118	535
5	Troy Davis	RB	Iowa State	41	80	119	402
6	Peyton Manning	QB	Tennessee	10	21	37	109
7	Keyshawn Johnson	WR	Southern Cal	9	10	12	59
8	Tim Biakabutuka	RB	Michigan	1	11	6	31
9	Warrick Dunn	RB	Florida State	2	3	17	29
10	Bobby Hoying	QB	Ohio State	0	9	10	28

AWARD WINNERS

PLAYER	POS/SCHOOL	AWARD		PLAYER	POS/SCHOOL	AWARD
Eddie George	RB Ohio State	Maxwell		Greg Myers	DB Colorado State	Thorpe
Jonathan Ogden	OT UCLA	Outland		Tommie Frazier	QB Nebraska	Unitas
Eddie George	RB Ohio State	Camp		Eddie George	RB Ohio State	Walker
Orlando Pace	OT Ohio State	Lombardi		Michael Reeder	K TCU	Groza
Danny Wuerffel	QB Florida	O'Brien		Pat Fitzgerald	LB Northwestern	Nagurski
Kevin Hardy	LB Illinois	Butkus		Terry Glenn	WR Ohio State	Biletnikoff
				Pat Fitzgerald	LB Northwestern	Bednarik

BOWL GAMES

DATE	GAME	SCORE
D14	Las Vegas	Toledo 40, Nevada 37 OT
D25	Aloha	Kansas 51, UCLA 30
D27	Copper	Texas Tech 55, Air Force 41
D28	Alamo	Texas A&M 22, Michigan 20
D29	Sun	Iowa 38, Washington 18
D29	Holiday	Kansas State 54, Colorado State 21
D29	Independence	LSU 45, Michigan State 26
D30	Liberty	East Carolina 19, Stanford 13
D30	Carquest	North Carolina 20, Arkansas 10

CONFERENCE STANDINGS

ACC

	Conf.			Overall		
	W	L	T	W	L	T
Florida State	7	1	0	10	2	0
Virginia	7	1	0	9	4	0
Clemson	6	2	0	8	4	0
Georgia Tech	5	3	0	6	5	0
North Carolina	4	4	0	7	5	0
Maryland	4	4	0	6	5	0
North Carolina St.	2	6	0	3	8	0
Duke	1	7	0	3	8	0
Wake Forest	0	8	0	1	10	0

Big 10

	Conf.			Overall		
	W	L	T	W	L	T
Northwestern	8	0	0	10	2	0
Ohio State	7	1	0	11	2	0
Penn State	5	3	0	9	3	0
Michigan	5	3	0	9	4	0
Michigan State	4	3	1	6	5	1
Iowa	4	4	0	8	4	0
Illinois	3	4	1	5	5	1
Wisconsin	3	4	1	4	5	2
Purdue	2	5	1	4	6	1
Minnesota	1	7	0	3	8	0
Indiana	0	8	0	2	9	0

Big 8

	Conf.			Overall		
	W	L	T	W	L	T
Nebraska	7	0	0	12	0	0
Kansas	5	2	0	10	2	0
Colorado	5	2	0	10	2	0
Kansas State	5	2	0	10	2	0
Oklahoma	2	5	0	5	5	1
Oklahoma State	2	5	0	4	8	0
Missouri	1	6	0	3	8	0
Iowa State	1	6	0	3	8	0

Big East

	Conf.			Overall		
	W	L	T	W	L	T
Virginia Tech	6	1	0	10	2	0
Miami, Fla.	6	1	0	8	3	0
Syracuse	5	2	0	9	3	0
West Virginia	4	3	0	5	6	0
Boston College	4	3	0	4	8	0
Rutgers	2	5	0	4	7	0
Temple	1	6	0	1	10	0
Pittsburgh	0	7	0	2	9	0

Big West

	Conf.			Overall		
	W	L	T	W	L	T
Nevada	7	0	0	9	3	0
La. Lafayette	4	2	0	6	5	0
Utah State	4	3	0	4	7	0
Arkansas State	3	3	0	6	5	0
Northern Illinois	3	3	0	3	8	0
New Mexico State	3	4	0	4	7	0
San Jose State	3	4	0	3	8	0
Pacific	3	4	0	3	8	0
Louisiana Tech	2	4	0	5	6	0
Nevada-Las Vegas	1	5	0	2	9	0

Ivy

	Conf.			Overall		
	W	L	T	W	L	T
Princeton	5	1	1	8	1	1
Pennsylvania	5	2	0	7	3	0
Cornell	5	2	0	6	4	0
Dartmouth	4	2	1	7	2	1
Columbia	3	4	0	3	6	1
Yale	2	5	0	3	7	0
Brown	2	5	0	3	7	0
Harvard	1	6	0	2	8	0

MAC

	Conf.			Overall		
	W	L	T	W	L	T
Toledo	7	0	1	11	0	1
Miami, Ohio	6	1	1	8	2	1
Ball State	6	2	0	7	4	0
Western Michigan	6	2	0	7	4	0
Eastern Michigan	5	3	0	6	5	0
Bowling Green	3	5	0	5	6	0
Central Michigan	2	6	0	4	7	0
Akron	2	6	0	2	9	0
Ohio U	1	6	1	2	8	1
Kent State	0	7	1	1	9	1

Pac 10

	Conf.			Overall		
	W	L	T	W	L	T
Southern Cal	6	1	1	9	2	1
Washington	6	1	1	7	4	1
Oregon	6	2	0	9	3	0
Stanford	5	3	0	7	4	1
UCLA	4	4	0	7	5	0
Arizona	4	4	0	6	5	0
Arizona State	4	4	0	6	5	0
Washington State	2	6	0	3	8	0
California	2	6	0	3	8	0
Oregon State	0	8	0	1	10	0

SEC

	Conf.			Overall		
	W	L	T	W	L	T
EAST						
Florida	8	0	0	12	1	0
Tennessee	7	1	0	11	1	0
Georgia	3	5	0	6	6	0
South Carolina	2	5	1	4	6	1
Kentucky	2	6	0	4	7	0
Vanderbilt	1	7	0	2	9	0
WEST						
Arkansas	6	2	0	8	5	0
Alabama	5	3	0	8	3	0
Auburn	5	3	0	8	4	0
LSU	4	3	1	7	4	1
Mississippi	3	5	0	6	5	0
Mississippi State	1	7	0	3	8	0

Championship Game **Florida 34 Arkansas 3**

SWC

	Conf.			Overall		
	W	L	T	W	L	T
Texas	7	0	0	10	2	1
Texas Tech	5	2	0	9	3	0
Texas A&M	5	2	0	9	3	0
Baylor	5	2	0	7	4	0
TCU	3	4	0	6	5	0
Houston	2	5	0	2	9	0
Rice	1	6	0	2	8	1
SMU	0	7	0	1	10	0

WAC

	Conf.			Overall		
	W	L	T	W	L	T
Colorado State	6	2	0	8	4	0
Utah	6	2	0	7	4	0
Brigham Young	6	2	0	7	4	0
Air Force	6	2	0	8	5	0
San Diego State	5	3	0	8	4	0
Wyoming	4	4	0	6	5	0
Fresno State	2	6	0	5	7	0
New Mexico	2	6	0	4	7	0
Hawaii	2	6	0	4	8	0
Texas-El Paso	1	7	0	2	10	0

Independents

	Overall		
	W	L	T
Notre Dame	9	3	0
East Carolina	9	3	0
Louisville	7	4	0
Southern Miss	6	5	0
Cincinnati	6	5	0
Army	5	5	1
Navy	5	6	0
Tulsa	4	7	0
Memphis	3	8	0
La. Monroe	2	9	0
North Texas	2	9	0
Tulane	2	9	0

DATE	GAME	SCORE
D30	Peach	Virginia 34, Georgia 27
D31	Sugar	Virginia Tech 28, Texas 10
J1	Cotton	Colorado 38, Oregon 6
J1	Orange	Florida State 31, Notre Dame 26
J1	Outback	Penn State 43, Auburn 14
J1	Rose	Southern Cal 41, Northwestern 32
J1	Gator	Syracuse 41, Clemson 0
J1	Citrus	Tennessee 20, Ohio State 14
J2	Fiesta	Nebraska 62, Florida 24

1995 NCAA Major College Statistical Leaders

Individual Leaders

PASSING	CL	G	ATT	COM	PCT	INT	I%	YDS	YPA	TD	TD%	RATING
1 Danny Wuerffel, Florida	JR	11	325	210	64.6	10	3.1	3266	10.1	35	10.8	178.4
2 Bobby Hoying, Ohio State	SR	12	303	192	63.4	11	3.6	3023	10.0	28	9.2	170.4
3 Donovan McNabb, Syracuse	FR	11	207	128	61.8	6	2.9	1991	9.6	16	7.7	162.3
4 Mike Maxwell, Nevada	SR	9	409	277	67.7	17	4.2	3611	8.8	33	8.1	160.2
5 Matt Miller, Kansas State	SR	11	240	154	64.2	11	4.6	2059	8.6	22	9.2	157.3
6 Steve Taneyhill, South Carolina	SR	11	389	261	67.1	9	2.3	3094	8.0	29	7.5	153.9
7 Jim Arellanes, Fresno State	JR	9	172	102	59.3	6	3.5	1539	9.0	13	7.6	152.4
8 Donald Sellers, New Mexico	JR	10	195	121	62.1	3	1.5	1693	8.7	11	5.6	150.5
9 Steve Sarkisian, Brigham Young	JR	11	385	250	64.9	14	3.6	3437	8.9	20	5.2	149.8
10 Josh Wallwork, Wyoming	JR	10	271	163	60.2	13	4.8	2363	8.7	21	7.8	149.4

ALL-PURPOSE	CL	G	RUSH	REC	PR	KR	YDS	YPG
1 Troy Davis, Iowa State	SO	11	2010	159	0	297	2466	224.2
2 Alex Van Dyke, Nevada	SR	11	6	1854	0	583	2443	222.1
3 Wasean Tait, Toledo	JR	11	1905	183	0	0	2088	189.8
4 Eddie George, Ohio State	SR	12	1826	399	0	0	2225	185.4
5 Abu Wilson, Utah State	SR	11	1476	375	0	153	2004	182.2
6 Winslow Oliver, New Mexico	SR	11	915	228	101	666	1910	173.6
7 Corey Walker, Arkansas St.	JR	11	1013	411	0	459	1883	171.2
8 Leeland McElroy, Texas A&M	JR	10	1122	379	0	208	1709	170.9
9 Darnell Autry, Northwestern	SO	11	1675	130	0	45	1850	168.2
10 Byron Hanspard, Texas Tech	SO	11	1374	474	0	0	1848	168.0

RUSHING/YARDS PER GAME	CL	G	ATT	YDS	TD	AVG	YPG
1 Troy Davis, Iowa State	SO	11	345	2010	15	5.8	182.7
2 Wasean Tait, Toledo	JR	11	357	1905	20	5.3	173.2
3 George Jones, San Diego State	JR	12	305	1842	23	6.0	153.5
4 Darnell Autry, Northwestern	SO	11	355	1675	14	4.7	152.3
5 Eddie George, Ohio State	SR	12	303	1826	23	6.0	152.2
6 Deland McCullough, Miami, Ohio	SR	11	321	1627	14	5.1	147.9
7 Moe Williams, Kentucky	JR	11	294	1600	17	5.4	145.5
8 Tim Biakabutuka, Michigan	JR	12	279	1724	12	6.2	143.7
9 Karim Abdul-Jabbar, UCLA	JR	10	270	1419	11	5.3	141.9
10 Charles Talley, Northern Illinois	JR	11	285	1540	7	5.4	140.0

RUSHING/YARDS PER CARRY	CL	G	ATT	YDS	YPC
1 Warrick Dunn, Florida State	JR	11	166	1242	7.5
2 Denvis Manns, New Mexico State	FR	11	157	1120	7.1
3 Tim Biakabutuka, Michigan	JR	12	279	1724	6.2
4 Jerald Moore, Oklahoma	JR	10	165	1001	6.1
5 George Jones, San Diego State	JR	12	305	1842	6.0
6 Eddie George, Ohio State	SR	12	303	1826	6.0
7 Mike Alstott, Purdue	SR	11	243	1436	5.9
8 David Thompson, Oklahoma State	JR	12	256	1509	5.9
9 Troy Davis, Iowa State	SO	11	345	2010	5.8
10 Raymond Priester, Clemson	SO	11	223	1286	5.8

*-Based on top 30 rushers

RECEIVING	CL	G	REC	YDS	TD	RPG	YPR	YPG
1 Alex Van Dyke, Nevada	SR	11	129	1854	16	11.7	14.4	168.6
2 Marcus Harris, Wyoming	JR	11	78	1423	14	7.1	18.2	129.4
3 Kevin Alexander, Utah State	SR	11	92	1400	6	8.4	15.2	127.3
4 Terry Glenn, Ohio State	JR	11	57	1316	17	5.2	23.1	119.6
5 Chad Mackey, Louisiana Tech	JR	11	90	1255	9	8.2	13.9	114.1
6 Keyshawn Johnson, Southern Cal	SR	11	90	1218	6	8.2	13.5	110.7
7 Will Blackwell, San Diego State	SO	11	86	1207	8	7.8	14.0	109.7
8 Marvin Harrison, Syracuse	SR	11	56	1131	8	5.1	20.2	102.8
9 Brandon Stokley, La. Lafayette	FR	11	75	1121	9	6.8	14.9	101.9
10 Bobby Engram, Penn State	SR	11	63	1084	11	5.7	17.2	98.6

PUNTING	CL	PUNT	YDS	AVG
1 Brad Maynard, Ball State	JR	66	3071	46.5
2 Brian Gragert, Wyoming	SR	40	1808	45.2
3 Greg Ivy, Oklahoma State	SR	66	2947	44.7
4 Chad Kessler, LSU	SO	47	2072	44.1
5 Sean Liss, Florida State	JR	49	2153	43.9
6 Darrin Simmons, Kansas	SR	51	2233	43.8
7 Tucker Phillips, Rice	JR	57	2487	43.6
8 John Stonehouse, Southern Cal	SR	44	1918	43.6
9 Sean Terry, Texas A&M	SR	60	2598	43.3
10 Steve Carr, Air Force	SR	45	1946	43.2

PUNT RETURNS	CL	PR	YDS	TD	AVG
1 James Dye, Brigham Young	JR	20	438	2	21.9
2 Brian Roberson, Fresno State	JR	19	346	1	18.2
3 Marvin Harrison, Syracuse	SR	22	369	2	16.8
4 Greg Myers, Colorado State	SR	35	555	3	15.9
5 Paul Guidry, UCLA	JR	24	370	1	15.4
6 Ray Peterson, San Diego State	SR	22	320	0	14.6
7 Kenyatta Watson, Boston College	JR	17	245	2	14.4
8 Dane Johnson, Texas Tech	SO	15	214	0	14.3
9 Brian Musso, Northwestern	JR	28	393	1	14.0
10 Mike Fullman, Nebraska	JR	21	285	1	13.6

KICKOFF RETURNS	CL	KR	YDS	TD	AVG
1 Robert Tate, Cincinnati	JR	15	515	1	34.3
2 Winslow Oliver, New Mexico	SR	21	666	1	31.7
3 Damon Dunn, Stanford	SO	19	539	1	28.4
4 Steve Clay, Eastern Michigan	SR	14	395	1	28.2
5 Emmett Mosley, Notre Dame	JR	15	419	0	27.9
6 Marlon Evans, Stanford	SR	16	446	1	27.9
7 Silas Massey, Central Michigan	FR	16	434	0	27.1
8 Chris Buckhalter, Southern Miss	SR	14	377	0	26.9
9 Vertis McKinney, North Texas	SR	14	373	0	26.6
10 Derrick Mason, Michigan State	JR	31	815	1	26.3

SCORING	CL	TDS	XP	FG	PTS	PTPG
1 Eddie George, Ohio State	SR	24	0	0	144	12.0
2 George Jones, San Diego State	JR	23	0	0	138	11.5
3 Wasean Tait, Toledo	JR	20	0	0	120	10.9
4 Scott Greene, Michigan State	SR	17	2	0	104	10.4
5 Byron Hanspard, Texas Tech	SO	18	0	0	108	9.8
6 Leeland McElroy, Texas A&M	JR	16	0	0	96	9.6
7 Beau Morgan, Air Force	JR	19	0	0	114	9.5
8 Terry Glenn, Ohio State	JR	17	2	0	104	9.5
9 Stephen Davis, Auburn	SR	17	0	0	102	9.3
9 Moe Williams, Kentucky	JR	17	0	0	102	9.3

FIELD GOALS	CL	FGA	FGM	PCT	FGG
1 Michael Reeder, TCU	SO	25	23	0.92	2.09
2 Rafael Garcia, Virginia	JR	27	20	0.74	1.67
3 Dan Pulsipher, Utah	JR	22	17	0.77	1.55
4 Eric Abrams, Stanford	SR	18	16	0.89	1.45
4 Brett Conway, Penn State	JR	24	16	0.67	1.45
4 Eric Richards, Cincinnati	SO	24	16	0.67	1.45
4 Jeff Hall, Tennessee	FR	25	16	0.64	1.45
8 Remy Hamilton, Michigan	JR	25	17	0.68	1.42
9 Josh Smith, Oregon	FR	21	14	0.67	1.40
10 Jeff Sauve, Clemson	SR	20	15	0.75	1.36

INTERCEPTIONS	CL	INT	YDS	TD	INT/GM
1 Willie Smith, Louisiana Tech	JR	8	65	0	0.80
2 Chris Canty, Kansas State	SO	8	117	2	0.73
2 Sean Andrews, Navy	SO	8	30	0	0.73
4 Sam Madison, Louisville	JR	7	136	0	0.64
5 Plez Atkins, Iowa	SO	6	97	2	0.60
5 Harold Lusk, Utah	JR	6	40	0	0.60
5 Kevin Abrams, Syracuse	JR	6	13	0	0.60
8 Emmanuel McDaniel, East Carolina *	SR	6	111	1	0.55
8 Sam Garnes, Cincinnati *	JR	6	101	0	0.55
8 Jeremy Bunch, Tulsa *	JR	6	76	1	0.55

*-Nine tied with 0.55; these had the most yards.

Team Leaders

RUSHING OFFENSE	G	ATT	YDS	AVG	TD	YPG
1 Nebraska	11	627	4398	7.0	51	399.8
2 Air Force	12	672	3989	5.9	36	332.4
3 Army	11	699	3632	5.2	36	330.2
4 Clemson	11	611	2855	4.7	24	259.5
5 Toledo	11	564	2690	4.8	32	244.5
6 Notre Dame	11	562	2572	4.6	29	233.8
7 Navy	11	574	2570	4.5	21	233.6
8 Purdue	11	522	2567	4.9	25	233.4
9 Iowa State	11	506	2513	5.0	23	228.5
10 Northern Illinois	11	546	2497	4.6	18	227.0

PASSING OFFENSE	G	ATT	COM	INT	PCT	YDS	YPA	TD	I%	YPC	YPG
1 Nevada	11	509	337	22	66.2	4579	9.0	39	4.3	13.6	416.3
2 Florida	12	457	287	12	62.8	4330	9.5	48	2.6	15.1	360.8
3 Florida State	11	465	297	14	63.9	3616	7.8	36	3.0	12.2	328.7
4 New Mexico State	11	454	260	20	57.3	3540	7.8	30	4.4	13.6	321.8
5 Brigham Young	11	388	252	14	64.9	3469	8.9	20	3.6	13.8	315.4
6 South Carolina	11	420	282	10	67.1	3373	8.0	32	2.4	12.0	306.6
7 Eastern Michigan	11	441	254	19	57.6	3323	7.5	23	4.3	13.1	302.1
8 Colorado	11	366	222	11	60.7	3269	8.9	28	3.0	14.7	297.2
9 Fresno State	12	432	247	17	57.2	3483	8.1	25	3.9	14.1	290.3
10 Wake Forest	11	483	289	18	59.8	3073	6.4	19	3.7	10.6	279.4

TOTAL OFFENSE	G	P	YDS	AVG	TD	YPG
1 Nevada	11	917	6263	6.8	63	569.4
2 Nebraska	11	855	6119	7.2	69	556.3
3 Florida State	11	885	6067	6.9	71	551.6
4 Florida	12	867	6413	7.4	72	534.4
5 Ohio State	12	865	5887	6.8	60	490.6
6 Colorado	11	809	5353	6.6	48	486.6
7 San Diego State	12	883	5785	6.6	51	482.1
8 New Mexico State	11	811	5248	6.5	46	477.1
9 Auburn	11	788	5049	6.4	54	459.0
10 Fresno State	12	899	5479	6.1	47	456.6

RUSHING DEFENSE	G	ATT	YDS	AVG	TD	YPG
1 Virginia Tech	11	429	851	2.0	7	77.4
2 Nebraska	11	341	862	2.5	6	78.4
3 Michigan	12	419	1081	2.6	12	90.1
4 Georgia Tech	11	372	1003	2.7	17	91.2
5 Arkansas	12	424	1251	3.0	15	104.3
6 Alabama	11	380	1158	3.0	9	105.3
7 Oregon	11	416	1163	2.8	15	105.7
8 Texas A&M	11	444	1164	2.6	8	105.8
9 Oklahoma	11	424	1200	2.8	11	109.1
10 Virginia	12	424	1310	3.1	15	109.2

PASSING DEFENSE	G	ATT	COM	PCT	INT	I%	YDS	YPA	TD	TD%	RAT
1 Miami, Ohio	11	303	137	45.2	22	7.3	1544	5.1	11	3.6	85.5
2 Texas A&M	11	329	150	45.6	13	4.0	1671	5.1	8	2.4	88.4
3 Texas Tech	11	372	153	41.1	15	4.0	2020	5.4	14	3.8	91.1
4 Ball State	11	303	128	42.2	10	3.3	1469	4.9	14	4.6	91.6
5 Baylor	11	310	148	47.7	13	4.2	1661	5.4	7	2.3	91.8
6 LSU	11	343	158	46.1	13	3.8	1907	5.6	8	2.3	92.9
7 East Carolina	11	332	157	47.3	19	5.7	1988	6.0	7	2.1	93.1
8 Cincinnati	11	347	162	46.7	20	5.8	2011	5.8	11	3.2	94.3
9 Louisville	11	350	175	50.0	24	6.9	2130	6.1	8	2.3	95.0
10 Miami, Fla.	11	302	145	48.0	12	4.0	1631	5.4	10	3.3	96.4

TOTAL DEFENSE	G	P	YDS	AVG	TD	YPG
1 Kansas State	11	673	2759	4.1	16	250.8
2 Miami, Ohio	11	738	2764	3.7	15	251.3
3 Texas A&M	11	773	2835	3.7	16	257.7
4 Ball State	11	712	2850	4.0	22	259.1
5 Baylor	11	709	2903	4.1	19	263.9
6 North Carolina	11	729	2940	4.0	25	267.3
7 Arizona	11	739	2976	4.0	19	270.5
8 Western Michigan	11	686	3092	4.5	23	281.1
9 Alabama	11	727	3125	4.3	21	284.1
10 Virginia Tech	11	782	3145	4.0	18	285.9

SCORING OFFENSE	G	PTS	AVG
1 Nebraska	11	576	52.4
2 Florida State	11	532	48.4
3 Florida	12	534	44.5
4 Nevada	11	484	44.0
5 Auburn	11	424	38.5
6 Ohio State	12	461	38.4
7 Tennessee	11	411	37.4
8 Colorado	11	406	36.9
9 Kansas State	11	402	36.5
10 South Carolina	11	401	36.5

SCORING DEFENSE	G	PTS	AVG
1 Northwestern	11	140	12.7
2 Kansas State	11	145	13.2
3 Texas A&M	11	148	13.5
4 Nebraska	11	150	13.6
5 Virginia Tech	11	155	14.1
6 LSU	11	160	14.5
7 Louisville	11	165	15.0
7 Miami, Ohio	11	165	15.0
9 Baylor	11	166	15.1
10 Clemson	11	178	16.2

TURNOVER MARGIN	G	FR	INT	TOT	FL	INTL	TOT	MAR
1 Toledo	11	16	18	34	6	6	12	2.0
2 Louisville	11	17	24	41	12	8	20	1.9
3 Northwestern	11	16	16	32	6	6	12	1.8
4 Florida State	11	18	16	34	6	14	20	1.3
5 Nebraska	11	8	20	28	9	6	15	1.2
5 Washington	11	12	16	28	9	6	15	1.2
7 Miami, Ohio	11	9	22	31	8	11	19	1.1
8 Virginia	12	8	25	33	9	11	20	1.1
9 Louisiana Tech	11	19	20	39	14	14	28	1.0
9 Missouri	11	13	16	29	9	9	18	1.0
9 Tennessee	11	7	16	23	8	4	12	1.0

1996 Poll Progression

CNN	AP	Pre-Season 1996		Aug. 24 Games
1	1	Nebraska	0-0	bye week
2	2	Tennessee	0-0	bye week
3	3	Florida State	0-0	bye week
4	4	Florida	0-0	bye week
5	5	Colorado	0-0	bye week
7	6	Notre Dame	0-0	bye week
6	7	Southern Cal	0-0	lost to # 11 Penn State 7-24 (A25)
9	8	Texas	0-0	bye week
10	9	Ohio State	0-0	bye week
13	10	Syracuse	0-0	bye week
8	11	Penn State	0-0	beat # 7 Southern Cal 24-7 (A25)
16	12	Miami, Fla.	0-0	bye week
12	13	Texas A&M	0-0	lost to Brigham Young 37-41
11	14	Michigan	0-0	bye week
14	15	Alabama	0-0	bye week
15	16	Virginia Tech	0-0	bye week
17	17	Auburn	0-0	bye week
19	18	Northwestern	0-0	bye week
20	19	LSU	0-0	bye week
	20	Arizona State	0-0	bye week
18	21	Kansas State	0-0	bye week
25	22	Iowa	0-0	bye week
21	23	Virginia	0-0	bye week
24	24	Kansas	0-0	bye week
23	25	Clemson	0-0	bye week
22		Washington	0-0	bye week

AP	August 26 Poll		Aug. 31 Games
1	Nebraska	0-0	bye week
2	Tennessee	0-0	beat Nevada-Las Vegas 62-3
3	Florida State	0-0	bye week
4	Florida	0-0	beat La. Lafayette 55-21 (A30)
5	Colorado	0-0	beat Washington State 37-19
6	Notre Dame	0-0	bye week
7	Penn State	1-0	bye week
8	Texas	0-0	beat Missouri 40-10
9	Ohio State	0-0	bye week
10	Syracuse	0-0	bye week
11	Miami, Fla.	0-0	beat Memphis 30-7
12	Michigan	0-0	beat Illinois 20-0
13	Alabama	0-0	beat Bowling Green 21-7
14	Virginia Tech	0-0	bye week
15	Northwestern	0-0	bye week
16	Auburn	0-0	beat UAB 29-0
17	Southern Cal	0-1	bye week
18	LSU	0-0	bye week
19	Brigham Young	1-0	beat Arkansas State 58-9
20	Arizona State	0-0	bye week
21	Kansas State	0-0	beat Texas Tech 21-14
22	Iowa	0-0	bye week
23	Texas A&M	0-1	bye week
24	Virginia	0-0	bye week
25	Kansas	0-0	beat Ball State 35-10 (A29)

CNN	AP	September 2 Poll		Sept. 7 Games
1	1	Nebraska	0-0	beat Michigan State 55-14
2	2	Tennessee	1-0	beat UCLA 35-20
3	3	Florida State	0-0	beat Duke 44-7
4	4	Florida	1-0	beat Georgia Southern 62-14
5	5	Colorado	1-0	beat Colorado State 48-34
7	6	Notre Dame	0-0	beat Vanderbilt 14-7 S5
6	7	Penn State	1-0	beat Louisville 24-7
8	8	Texas	1-0	beat New Mexico State 41-7
11	9	Syracuse	0-0	lost to North Carolina 10-27
9	10	Ohio State	0-0	beat Rice 70-7
12	11	Miami, Fla.	1-0	beat Citadel 52-6
10	12	Michigan	1-0	bye week
18	13	Northwestern	0-0	lost to Wake Forest 27-28
13	14	Alabama	1-0	beat Southern Miss 20-10
14	15	Virginia Tech	0-0	beat Akron 21-18
16	16	Brigham Young	2-0	bye week
19	17	LSU	0-0	beat Houston 35-34
17	18	Auburn	1-0	beat Fresno State 62-0
21	19	Southern Cal	0-1	beat Illinois 55-3
	20	Arizona State	0-0	beat Washington 45-42
15	21	Kansas State	1-0	beat Indiana St. 59-3
	22	Iowa	0-0	beat Arizona 21-20
20	23	Virginia	0-0	beat Central Michigan 55-21
22	24	North Carolina	1-0	beat Syracuse 27-10
25	25	Texas A&M	0-1	bye week
23		Washington	0-0	lost to # 20 Arizona State 42-45
24		Kansas	1-0	bye week

CNN	AP	September 9 Poll		Sept. 14 Games
1	1	Nebraska	1-0	bye week
2	2	Tennessee	2-0	bye week
3	3	Florida State	1-0	bye week
4	4	Florida	2-0	bye week
5	5	Colorado	2-0	lost to # 11 Michigan 13-20
6	6	Penn State	2-0	beat Northern Illinois 49-0
8	7	Texas	2-0	bye week
7	8	Ohio State	1-0	bye week
10	9	Notre Dame	1-0	beat Purdue 35-0
11	10	Miami, Fla.	2-0	beat Rutgers 33-0 (S12)
9	11	Michigan	1-0	beat # 5 Colorado 20-13
13	12	North Carolina	2-0	bye week
12	13	Alabama	2-0	beat Vanderbilt 36-26
15	14	Brigham Young	2-0	lost to Washington 17-29
16	15	Auburn	2-0	beat Mississippi 45-28
18	16	Southern Cal	1-1	beat Oregon State 46-17
14	17	Kansas State	2-0	beat Cincinnati 35-0
23	18	Arizona State	1-0	beat North Texas 52-7
19	19	Virginia Tech	1-0	beat Boston College 45-7
20	20	LSU	1-0	bye week
21	21	Iowa	1-0	beat Iowa State 38-13
17	22	Virginia	1-0	beat Maryland 21-3
24	23	Syracuse	0-1	bye week
22	24	Kansas	1-0	bye week
25	25	Texas A&M	0-1	lost to La. Lafayette 22-29

CNN	AP	September 16 Poll		Sept. 21 Games
1	1	Nebraska	1-0	lost to # 17 Arizona State 0-19
2	2	Tennessee	2-0	lost to # 4 Florida 29-35
3	3	Florida State	1-0	beat North Carolina St. 51-17 (S19)
4	4	Florida	2-0	beat # 2 Tennessee 35-29
5	5	Penn State	3-0	beat Temple 41-0
8	6	Texas	2-0	lost to # 9 Notre Dame 24-27
6	7	Ohio State	1-0	beat Pittsburgh 72-0
7	8	Michigan	2-0	beat Boston College 20-14
9	9	Notre Dame	2-0	beat # 6 Texas 27-24
10	10	Miami, Fla.	3-0	bye week
13	11	North Carolina	2-0	beat Georgia Tech 16-0
12	12	Colorado	2-1	bye week
11	13	Alabama	3-0	beat Arkansas 17-7
15	14	Auburn	3-0	lost to # 21 LSU 15-19
18	15	Southern Cal	2-1	beat Houston 26-9
14	16	Kansas State	3-0	beat Rice 34-7
22	17	Arizona State	2-0	beat # 1 Nebraska 19-0
16	18	Virginia Tech	2-0	beat Rutgers 30-14
19	19	Iowa	2-0	lost to Tulsa 20-27
17	20	Virginia	2-0	beat Wake Forest 42-7
21	21	LSU	1-0	beat # 14 Auburn 19-15
20	22	Kansas	2-0	beat TCU 52-17
24	23	Syracuse	0-1	lost to Minnesota 33-35
23	24	Washington	1-1	beat Arizona 31-17
	25	Oregon	3-0	lost to Washington State 44-55
25		Brigham Young	2-1	beat New Mexico 17-14

CNN	AP	September 23 Poll		Sept. 28 Games
1	1	Florida	3-0	beat Kentucky 65-0
2	2	Florida State	2-0	beat # 11 North Carolina 13-0
3	3	Penn State	4-0	beat Wisconsin 23-20
4	4	Ohio State	2-0	beat # 5 Notre Dame 29-16
5	5	Notre Dame	3-0	lost to # 4 Ohio State 16-29
12	6	Arizona State	3-0	beat Oregon 48-27
6	7	Michigan	3-0	beat UCLA 38-9
7	8	Nebraska	1-1	beat Colorado State 65-9
8	9	Tennessee	2-1	bye week
9	10	Miami, Fla.	3-0	beat Pittsburgh 45-0
11	11	North Carolina	3-0	lost to # 2 Florida State 0-13
15	12	Colorado	2-1	beat Texas A&M 24-10
14	13	Texas	2-1	lost to # 19 Virginia 13-37
10	14	Alabama	4-0	bye week
18	15	Southern Cal	3-1	bye week
13	16	Kansas State	4-0	bye week
19	17	LSU	2-0	beat New Mexico State 63-7
16	18	Virginia Tech	3-0	lost to Syracuse 21-52
17	19	Virginia	3-0	beat # 13 Texas 37-13
20	20	Kansas	2-0	bye week
21	21	Washington	2-1	bye week
22	22	Auburn	3-1	bye week
23	23	West Virginia	4-0	beat Maryland 13-0
24	24	Brigham Young	3-1	beat SMU 31-3
	25	Northwestern	2-1	beat Indiana 35-17
25		Iowa	2-1	bye week

CNN	AP	September 30 Poll		Oct. 5 Games
1	1	Florida	4-0	beat Arkansas 42-7
2	2	Florida State	3-0	beat Clemson 34-3
3	3	Ohio State	3-0	beat # 4 Penn State 38-7
4	4	Penn State	5-0	lost to # 3 Ohio State 7-38
7	5	Arizona State	4-0	beat Boise State 56-7
5	6	Michigan	4-0	lost to # 22 Northwestern 16-17
6	7	Nebraska	2-1	beat # 16 Kansas State 39-3
8	8	Miami, Fla.	4-0	bye week
9	9	Tennessee	2-1	beat Mississippi 41-3 (O3)
13	10	Colorado	3-1	bye week
14	11	Notre Dame	3-1	bye week
11	12	Virginia	4-0	lost to Georgia Tech 7-13
10	13	Alabama	4-0	beat Kentucky 35-7
15	14	LSU	3-0	beat Vanderbilt 35-0
17	15	North Carolina	3-1	beat Wake Forest 45-6
12	16	Kansas State	4-0	lost to # 7 Nebraska 3-39
16	17	Southern Cal	3-1	lost to California 15-22
18	18	Washington	2-1	beat Stanford 27-6
19	19	West Virginia	5-0	beat Boston College 34-17
20	20	Auburn	3-1	beat South Carolina 28-24
21	21	Brigham Young	4-1	beat Utah State 45-17 (O4)
	22	Northwestern	3-1	beat # 6 Michigan 17-16
23	23	Texas	2-2	beat Oklahoma State 71-14
24	24	Utah	4-1	beat Texas El Paso 34-27
25	25	Wyoming	5-0	beat San Jose State 45-22
22		Virginia Tech	3-1	bye week

CNN	AP	October 7 Poll		Oct. 12 Games
1	1	Florida	5-0	beat # 12 LSU 56-13
2	2	Ohio State	4-0	beat Wisconsin 17-14
3	3	Florida State	4-0	beat # 6 Miami, Fla. 34-16
5	4	Arizona State	5-0	beat UCLA 42-34
4	5	Nebraska	3-1	beat Baylor 49-0
6	6	Miami, Fla.	4-0	lost to # 3 Florida State 16-34
7	7	Tennessee	3-1	beat Georgia 29-17
8	8	Alabama	5-0	beat North Carolina St. 24-19
10	9	Colorado	3-1	beat Oklahoma State 35-13
9	10	Penn State	5-1	beat Purdue 31-14
12	11	Notre Dame	3-1	beat # 16 Washington 54-20
11	12	LSU	4-0	lost to # 1 Florida 13-56
14	13	North Carolina	4-1	beat Maryland 38-7
13	14	Michigan	4-1	bye week
18	15	Northwestern	4-1	beat Minnesota 26-24
16	16	Washington	3-1	lost to # 11 Notre Dame 20-54
15	17	West Virginia	6-0	bye week
19	18	Auburn	4-1	beat Mississippi State 49-15
20	19	Brigham Young	5-1	beat Nevada-Las Vegas 63-28
17	20	Virginia	4-1	bye week
22	21	California	5-0	bye week
21	22	Kansas State	4-1	beat Missouri 35-10
	23	Georgia Tech	4-1	bye week
24	24	Wyoming	6-0	beat Western Michigan 42-28
25	25	Texas	3-2	lost to Oklahoma 27-30
23		Virginia Tech	3-1	beat Temple 38-0

CNN	AP	October 14 Poll		Oct. 19 Games
1	1	Florida	6-0	beat # 16 Auburn 51-10
3	2	Ohio State	5-0	beat Purdue 42-14
2	3	Florida State	5-0	bye week
5	4	Arizona State	6-0	beat Southern Cal 48-35
4	5	Nebraska	4-1	beat Texas Tech 24-10
6	6	Tennessee	4-1	bye week
7	7	Alabama	6-0	beat Mississippi 37-0
9	8	Notre Dame	4-1	lost to Air Force 17-20
10	9	Colorado	4-1	beat Kansas 20-7
8	10	Penn State	6-1	lost to Iowa 20-21
11	11	North Carolina	5-1	bye week
13	12	Miami, Fla.	4-1	lost to East Carolina 6-31
12	13	Michigan	4-1	beat Indiana 27-20
15	14	Northwestern	5-1	beat Wisconsin 34-30
14	15	West Virginia	6-0	beat Temple 30-10
16	16	Auburn	5-1	lost to # 1 Florida 10-51
18	17	LSU	4-1	beat Kentucky 41-14
20	18	Brigham Young	6-1	beat Tulsa 55-30
21	19	California	5-0	lost to Washington State 18-21
17	20	Virginia	4-1	beat North Carolina St. 62-14
19	21	Kansas State	5-1	beat Texas A&M 23-20
24	22	Georgia Tech	4-1	lost to Clemson 25-28
22	23	Wyoming	7-0	beat Fresno State 42-21
25	24	Utah	5-1	beat TCU 21-7
	25	Washington	3-2	beat UCLA 41-21
23		Virginia Tech	4-1	bye week

CNN	AP	October 21 Poll		Oct. 26 Games
1	1	**Florida**	7-0	bye week
3	2	**Ohio State**	6-0	beat # 20 Iowa 38-26
2	3	**Florida State**	5-0	beat # 14 Virginia 31-24
4	4	**Arizona State**	7-0	beat Stanford 41-9
5	5	**Nebraska**	5-1	beat Kansas 63-7
7	6	**Tennessee**	4-1	beat # 7 Alabama 20-13
6	7	**Alabama**	7-0	lost to # 6 Tennessee 13-20
8	8	**Colorado**	5-1	beat Texas 28-24
9	9	**North Carolina**	5-1	beat Houston 42-14
10	10	**Michigan**	5-1	beat Minnesota 44-10
12	11	**Northwestern**	6-1	beat Illiniois 27-24
11	12	**West Virginia**	7-0	lost to # 25 Miami, Fla. 7-10
15	13	**LSU**	5-1	beat Mississippi State 28-20
13	14	**Virginia**	5-1	lost to # 3 Florida State 24-31
16	15	**Brigham Young**	7-1	beat TCU 45-21
14	16	**Kansas State**	6-1	beat Oklahoma 42-35
17	17	**Penn State**	6-2	beat Indiana 48-26
18	18	**Wyoming**	8-0	bye week
20	19	**Notre Dame**	4-2	bye week
19	20	**Iowa**	5-1	lost to # 2 Ohio State 26-38
22	21	**Utah**	6-1	beat Tulsa 45-19
	22	**Auburn**	5-2	bye week
24	23	**Washington**	4-2	beat Oregon 33-14
	24	**Southern Miss**	6-1	beat Tulane 31-28
23	25	**Miami, Fla.**	4-2	beat # 12 West Virginia 10-7
21		**Virginia Tech**	4-1	beat Pittsburgh 34-17
25		**California**	5-1	lost to UCLA 29-38

CNN	AP	October 28 Poll		Nov. 2 Games
1	1	**Florida**	7-0	beat Georgia 47-7
3	2	**Ohio State**	7-0	beat Minnesota 45-0
2	3	**Florida State**	6-0	beat Georgia Tech 49-3
4	4	**Arizona State**	8-0	beat Oregon State 29-14
5	5	**Nebraska**	6-1	beat Oklahoma 73-21
6	6	**Tennessee**	5-1	beat South Carolina 31-14
7	7	**Colorado**	6-1	beat Missouri 41-13
8	8	**North Carolina**	6-1	beat North Carolina St. 52-20
9	9	**Michigan**	6-1	beat Michigan State 45-29
11	10	**Alabama**	7-1	bye week
10	11	**Northwestern**	7-1	lost to # 15 Penn State 9-34
13	12	**LSU**	6-1	bye week
14	13	**Brigham Young**	8-1	beat Texas-El Paso 40-18
12	14	**Kansas State**	7-1	bye week
15	15	**Penn State**	7-2	beat # 11 Northwestern 34-9
18	16	**Virginia**	5-2	beat Duke 27-3
16	17	**Wyoming**	8-0	beat SMU 59-17
17	18	**West Virginia**	7-1	lost to Syracuse 7-30
21	19	**Notre Dame**	4-2	beat Navy 54-27
19	20	**Utah**	7-1	lost to Rice 10-51
23	21	**Washington**	5-2	beat Southern Cal 21-10
22	22	**Miami, Fla.**	5-2	beat Temple 57-26
24	23	**Southern Miss**	7-1	beat Cincinnati 21-17
25	24	**Auburn**	5-2	beat Arkansas 28-7
	25	**Iowa**	5-2	beat Illiniois 31-21
20		**Virginia Tech**	5-1	beat La. Lafayette 47-16

CNN	AP	November 4 Poll		Nov. 9 Games
1	1	**Florida**	7-0	beat Vanderbilt 28-21
3	2	**Ohio State**	8-0	beat Illinois 48-0
2	3	**Florida State**	7-0	beat Wake Forest 44-7
4	4	**Arizona State**	9-0	beat California 35-7
5	5	**Nebraska**	7-1	beat Missouri 51-7
6	6	**Tennessee**	6-1	lost to Memphis 17-21
7	7	**Colorado**	7-1	beat Iowa State 49-42
8	8	**North Carolina**	7-1	beat Louisville 28-10
9	9	**Michigan**	7-1	lost to Purdue 3-9
10	10	**Alabama**	7-1	beat # 11 LSU 26-0
13	11	**LSU**	7-1	lost to # 10 Alabama 0-26
12	12	**Brigham Young**	9-1	beat Rice 49-0
11	13	**Kansas State**	8-1	beat Kansas 38-12
14	14	**Penn State**	8-2	bye week
16	15	**Virginia**	6-2	lost to Clemson 16-24
15	16	**Wyoming**	9-0	lost to San Diego State 24-28
19	17	**Notre Dame**	5-2	beat Boston College 48-21
18	18	**Northwestern**	7-2	beat # 23 Iowa 40-13
20	19	**Washington**	6-2	beat Oregon State 42-3
22	20	**Southern Miss**	8-1	lost to Houston 49-56
21	21	**Miami, Fla.**	6-2	bye week
24	22	**Auburn**	6-2	beat La. Monroe 28-24
25	23	**Iowa**	6-2	lost to # 18 Northwestern 13-40
23	24	**Syracuse**	5-2	beat Tulane 31-7
17	25	**Virginia Tech**	6-1	beat East Carolina 35-14

CNN	AP	November 11 Poll		Nov. 16 Games
1	1	**Florida**	9-0	beat South Carolina 52-25
2	2	**Ohio State**	9-0	beat Indiana 27-17
3	3	**Florida State**	8-0	beat # 25 Southern Miss 54-14
4	4	**Arizona State**	10-0	bye week
5	5	**Nebraska**	8-1	beat Iowa State 49-14
6	6	**Colorado**	8-1	beat # 9 Kansas State 12-0
7	6	**North Carolina**	8-1	lost to # 24 Virginia 17-20
8	8	**Alabama**	8-1	lost to Mississippi State 16-17
9	9	**Kansas State**	8-1	lost to # 6 Colorado 0-12
10	10	**Brigham Young**	10-1	beat Hawaii 45-14
11	11	**Penn State**	8-2	beat # 16 Michigan 29-17
12	12	**Tennessee**	6-2	beat Arkansas 55-14
14	13	**Northwestern**	8-2	beat Purdue 27-24
15	14	**Notre Dame**	6-2	beat Pittsburgh 60-6
17	15	**Washington**	7-2	beat San Jose State 53-10
16	16	**Michigan**	7-2	lost to # 11 Penn State 17-29
20	17	**LSU**	6-2	beat Mississippi 39-7
18	18	**Miami, Fla.**	6-2	lost to # 21 Virginia Tech 7-21
19	19	**Syracuse**	6-2	beat Army 42-17
21	20	**Auburn**	7-2	lost to Georgia 49-56
13	21	**Virginia Tech**	7-1	beat # 18 Miami, Fla. 21-7
23	22	**Army**	9-0	lost to Syracuse 17-42
22	23	**Wyoming**	9-1	beat Colorado State 25-24
25	24	**Virginia**	6-3	beat # 6 North Carolina 20-17
	25	**Southern Miss**	8-2	lost to # 3 Florida State 14-54
24		**West Virginia**	8-2	bye week

CNN	AP	November 18 Poll		Nov. 23 Games
1	1	**Florida**	10-0	bye week
2	2	**Ohio State**	10-0	lost to # 21 Michigan 9-13
3	3	**Florida State**	9-0	beat Maryland 48-10
4	4	**Arizona State**	10-0	beat Arizona 56-14
5	5	**Nebraska**	9-1	bye week
6	6	**Colorado**	9-1	bye week
8	7	**Penn State**	9-2	beat Michigan State 32-29
7	8	**Brigham Young**	11-1	beat Utah 37-17
10	9	**Tennessee**	7-2	beat Kentucky 56-10
13	10	**Notre Dame**	7-2	beat Rutgers 62-0
11	11	**Northwestern**	9-2	regular season complete
15	12	**Washington**	8-2	beat Washington State 31-24
14	13	**North Carolina**	8-2	beat Duke 27-10
16	14	**Kansas State**	8-2	beat Iowa State 35-20
12	15	**Alabama**	8-2	beat Auburn 24-23
17	16	**Syracuse**	7-2	beat Temple 36-15
9	17	**Virginia Tech**	8-1	beat # 23 West Virginia 31-14
18	18	**LSU**	7-2	beat Tulane 35-17
19	19	**Virginia**	7-3	bye week
19	20	**Wyoming**	10-1	bye week
22	21	**Michigan**	7-3	beat # 2 Ohio State 13-9
24	22	**Clemson**	7-3	lost to South Carolina 31-34
21	23	**West Virginia**	8-2	lost to # 17 Virginia Tech 14-31
23	24	**Iowa**	7-3	beat Minnesota 43-24
25	25	**Miami, Fla.**	6-3	beat Boston College 43-26

CNN	AP	November 25 Poll		Nov. 30 Games
1	1	**Florida**	10-0	lost to # 2 Florida State 21-24
2	2	**Florida State**	10-0	beat # 1 Florida 24-21
3	3	**Arizona State**	11-0	regular season complete
4	4	**Nebraska**	9-1	beat # 5 Colorado 17-12 (N29)
5	5	**Colorado**	9-1	lost to # 4 Nebraska 12-17 (N29)
6	6	**Ohio State**	10-1	regular season complete
7	7	**Brigham Young**	12-1	regular season complete
8	8	**Penn State**	10-2	regular season complete
10	9	**Tennessee**	8-2	beat Vanderbilt 14-7
13	10	**Notre Dame**	8-2	lost to Southern Cal 20-27
11	11	**Northwestern**	9-2	
15	12	**Washington**	9-2	regular season complete
14	13	**North Carolina**	9-2	regular season complete
16	14	**Kansas State**	9-2	regular season complete
12	15	**Alabama**	9-2	bye week
17	16	**Syracuse**	8-2	lost to # 23 Miami, Fla. 31-38
9	17	**Virginia Tech**	9-1	beat # 20 Virginia 26-9 (N29)
19	18	**Michigan**	8-3	regular season complete
18	19	**LSU**	8-2	beat Arkansas 17-7 (N29)
21	20	**Virginia**	7-3	lost to # 17 Virginia Tech 9-26 (N29)
20	21	**Wyoming**	10-1	
22	22	**Iowa**	8-3	regular season complete
23	23	**Miami, Fla.**	7-3	beat # 16 Syracuse 38-31
24	24	**Army**	9-1	bye week
25	25	**West Virginia**	8-3	regular season complete

CNN	AP	December 2 Poll		Dec. 7 Games
1	1	**Florida State**	11-0	regular season complete
2	2	**Arizona State**	11-0	
3	3	**Nebraska**	10-1	lost to Texas 27-37 (B12 CH)
4	4	**Florida**	10-1	beat # 11 Alabama 45-30 (SEC CH)
5	5	**Ohio State**	10-1	
6	6	**Brigham Young**	12-1	beat Wyoming 28-25 (WAC CH)
8	7	**Colorado**	9-2	regular season complete
7	8	**Penn State**	10-2	
10	9	**Tennessee**	9-2	regular season complete
12	10	**Northwestern**	9-2	
11	11	**Alabama**	9-2	lost to # 4 Florida 30-45 (SEC CH)
13	12	**Washington**	9-2	
14	13	**North Carolina**	9-2	
15	14	**Kansas State**	9-2	
9	15	**Virginia Tech**	9-2	regular season complete
17	16	**Michigan**	8-3	
16	17	**LSU**	9-2	regular season complete
18	18	**Notre Dame**	8-3	regular season complete
20	19	**Miami, Fla.**	8-3	regular season complete
19	20	**Wyoming**	10-1	lost to Brigham Young 25-28 (WAC CH)
21	21	**Iowa**	8-3	
22	22	**Syracuse**	8-3	regular season complete
23	23	**Army**	9-1	beat Navy 28-24
24	24	**West Virginia**	8-3	
25	25	**Virginia**	7-4	regular season complete

CNN	AP	December 9 Poll	Record	Bowl Bid	Date	Bowl Result
1	1	**Florida State**	11-0	Sugar Bowl	J2	lost to # 3 Florida 20-52
2	2	**Arizona State**	11-0	Rose Bowl	J1	lost to # 4 Ohio State 17-20
3	3	**Florida**	11-1	Sugar Bowl	J2	beat # 1 Florida State 52-20
4	4	**Ohio State**	10-1	Rose Bowl	J1	beat # 2 Arizona State 20-17
5	5	**Brigham Young**	13-1	Cotton Bowl	J1	beat # 14 Kansas State 19-15
6	6	**Nebraska**	10-2	Orange Bowl	D31	beat # 10 Virginia Tech 41-21
7	7	**Penn State**	10-2	Fiesta Bowl	J1	beat # 20 Texas 38-15
8	8	**Colorado**	9-2	Holiday Bowl	D30	beat # 13 Washington 33-21
10	9	**Tennessee**	9-2	Citrus Bowl	J1	beat # 11 Northwestern 48-28
9	10	**Virginia Tech**	10-1	Orange Bowl	J1	lost to # 6 Nebraska 21-41
11	11	**Northwestern**	9-2	Citrus Bowl	J1	lost to # 9 Tennessee 28-48
13	12	**North Carolina**	9-2	Gator Bowl	J1	beat # 25 West Virginia 20-13
12	13	**Washington**	9-2	Holiday Bowl	D30	lost to # 8 Colorado 21-33
14	14	**Kansas State**	9-2	Cotton Bowl	J1	lost to # 5 Brigham Young 15-19
17	15	**Michigan**	8-3	Outback Bowl	J1	lost to # 16 Alabama 14-17
15	16	**Alabama**	9-3	Outback Bowl	J1	beat # 15 Michigan 17-14
16	17	**LSU**	9-2	Peach Bowl	D28	beat Clemson 10-7
18	18	**Notre Dame**	8-3			
19	19	**Miami, Fla.**	8-3	Carquest Bowl	D27	beat Virginia 31-21
20	20	**Texas**	8-4	Fiesta Bowl	J1	lost to # 7 Penn State 15-38
21	21	**Iowa**	8-3	Alamo Bowl	D29	beat Texas Tech 27-0
23	22	**Wyoming**	10-2			
22	23	**Syracuse**	8-3	Liberty Bowl	D27	beat Houston 30-17
24	24	**Army**	10-1	Independence Bowl	D31	lost to Auburn 29-32
25	25	**West Virginia**	8-3	Gator Bowl	J1	lost to # 12 North Carolina 13-20

RB	CNN	AP	January 3 Final Poll	Record
1	1	1	**Florida**	12-1
2	2	2	**Ohio State**	11-1
3	3	3	**Florida State**	11-1
4	4	4	**Arizona State**	11-1
9	5	5	**Brigham Young**	14-1
5	6	6	**Nebraska**	11-2
6	7	7	**Penn State**	11-2
7	8	8	**Colorado**	10-2
8	9	9	**Tennessee**	10-2
20	10	10	**North Carolina**	10-2
13	11	11	**Alabama**	10-3
14	13	12	**LSU**	10-2
10	12	13	**Virginia Tech**	10-2
11	14	14	**Miami, Fla.**	9-3
16	16	15	**Northwestern**	9-3
18	15	16	**Washington**	9-3
12	17	17	**Kansas State**	9-3
19	18	18	**Iowa**	9-3
24	21	19	**Notre Dame**	8-3
15	20	20	**Michigan**	8-4
17	19	21	**Syracuse**	9-3
27	22	22	**Wyoming**	10-2
21	23	23	**Texas**	8-5
22	24	24	**Auburn**	8-4
23	25	25	**Army**	10-2

1996

CONSENSUS ALL-AMERICANS

Offense

POS	Offense	HT	WT	CL	School	AP	CF	FC	FN	FW	SN
QB	Danny Wuerffel	6-2	209	Sr.	Florida	•	•	•	•	•	•
RB	Byron Hanspard	6-0	193	Jr.	Texas Tech	•	•	•	•	•	•
RB	Troy Davis	5-8	185	Jr.	Iowa State	•	•	•	•	•	•
WR	Marcus Harris	6-2	216	Sr.	Wyoming	•	•	•	•	•	•
WR	Ike Hilliard	5-11	182	Jr.	Florida	•		•	•		•
WR	Reidel Anthony	6-0	181	Jr.	Florida	•			•	•	•
TE	Tony Gonzalez	6-6	235	Jr.	California	•	•	•	•	•	•
OL	Orlando Pace	6-6	330	Jr.	Ohio State	•	•	•	•	•	•
OL	Juan Roque	6-8	319	Sr.	Arizona State	•	•	•	•		•
OL	Chris Naeole	6-4	310	Sr.	Colorado	•	•	•	•		•
OL	Dan Neil	6-2	283	Sr.	Texas	•	•		•		•
OL	Benji Olson	6-4	310	So.	Washington	•			•		
C	Aaron Taylor	6-1	305	Jr.	Nebraska		•		•		•
PK	Marc Primanti	5-7	171	Sr.	North Carolina St.	•	•		•		•

OTHERS RECEIVING FIRST-TEAM HONORS

POS		School	AP	CF	FC	FN	FW	SN
QB	Jake Plummer	Arizona State						•
RB	Warrick Dunn	Florida State						•
RB	Darnell Autry	Northwestern			•			
WR	Rae Carruth	Colorado						•
TE	David LaFleur	LSU		•				
TE	Itula Mili	Brigham Young			•			
TE	Pat Fitzgerald	Texas		•				
OL	Steve Scifres	Wyoming						•
OL	Scott Sanderson	Washington State						•
OL	Billy Conaty	Virginia Tech						•
C	Rod Payne	Michigan			•			
C	K.C. Jones	Miami, Fla.	•					
PK	Cory Wedel	Wyoming					•	•
KR	Tim Dwight	Iowa						•
AP	Kevin Faulk	LSU		•				

Defense

POS	Defense	HT	WT	CL	School	AP	CF	FC	FN	FW	SN
DL	Grant Wistrom	6-5	250	Jr.	Nebraska	•		•	•	•	•
DL	Peter Boulware	6-5	255	Sr.	Florida State	•	•		•		•
DL	Reinard Wilson	6-2	255	Sr.	Florida State	•	•	•	•		
DL	Derrick Rodgers	6-2	220	Jr.	Arizona State	•			•		•
DL	Mike Vrabel	6-4	260	Sr.	Ohio State		•	•	•		
LB	Canute Curtis	6-2	250	Sr.	West Virginia	•		•	•	•	•
LB	Pat Fitzgerald	6-2	243	Sr.	Northwestern	•	•	•	•	•	•
LB	Matt Russell	6-2	245	Sr.	Colorado	•	•	•	•		•
LB	Jarrett Irons	6-2	234	Sr.	Michigan	•	•		•		•
DB	Chris Canty	5-10	190	Jr.	Kansas State	•	•		•	•	•
DB	Kevin Jackson	6-2	206	Sr.	Alabama	•	•	•	•		•
DB	Dre' Bly	5-10	180	Fr.	North Carolina	•	•	•	•	•	•
DB	Shawn Springs	6-0	188	Jr.	Ohio State	•	•	•	•		•
P	Brad Maynard	6-1	176	Sr.	Ball State	•	•		•		

OTHERS RECEIVING FIRST-TEAM HONORS

POS		School	AP	CF	FC	FN	FW	SN
DL	Cornell Brown	Virginia Tech			•			
DL	Jared Tornich	Nebraska						•
DL	Tarek Saleh	Wisconsin				•		
DL	Michael Myers	Alabama					•	
LB	Dwayne Rudd	Alabama			•			
LB	Jason Chorak	Washington						•
LB	Keith Mitchell	Texas A&M						•
LB	Anthony Simmons	Clemson						•
DB	Charles Woodson	Michigan	•	•		•		
DB	Kevin Abrams	Syracuse			•			
DB	Sam Madison	Louisville						•
DB	Kim Herring	Penn State					•	
P	Noel Prefontaine	San Diego State	•	•				

FC named Curtis as a DL; AP named Rodgers as a LB

HEISMAN TROPHY VOTING

	PLAYER	POS	SCHOOL	1ST	2ND	3RD	TOTAL
1	Danny Wuerffel	QB	Florida	300	158	147	1363
2	Troy Davis	RB	Iowa State	209	206	135	1174
3	Jake Plummer	QB	Arizona State	116	113	111	685
4	Orlando Pace	OT	Ohio State	87	101	136	599
5	Warrick Dunn	RB	Florida State	40	76	69	341
6	Byron Hanspard	RB	Texas Tech	15	68	70	251
7	Darnell Autry	RB	Northwestern	9	19	20	85
8	Peyton Manning	QB	Tennessee	4	23	23	81
9	Marcus Harris	WR	Wyoming	7	7	18	53
10	Beau Morgan	QB	Air Force	3	3	11	26

AWARD WINNERS

Danny Wuerffel QB, Florida. Maxwell, O'Brien, Unitas, Camp, **Orlando Pace** OT, Ohio State, Outland, Lombardi, **Matt Russell** LB, Colorado, Butkus **Lawrence Wright** DB, Florida, Thorpe, **Byron Hanspard** RB, Texas Tech, Walker **Marc Primanti** K, North Carolina St., Groza **Pat Fitzgerald** LB, Northwestern, Nagurski, Bednarik **Marcus Harris** WR, Wyoming, Biletnikoff

CONFERENCE STANDINGS

ACC

	CONF. W L T			OVERALL W L T		
Florida State	8	0	0	11	1	0
North Carolina	6	2	0	10	2	0
Clemson	6	2	0	7	5	0
Virginia	5	3	0	7	5	0
Georgia Tech	4	4	0	5	6	0
Maryland	3	5	0	5	6	0
North Carolina St.	3	5	0	3	8	0
Wake Forest	1	7	0	3	8	0
Duke	0	8	0	0	11	0

Big 10

	CONF. W L T			OVERALL W L T		
Ohio State	7	1	0	11	1	0
Northwestern	7	1	0	9	3	0
Penn State	6	2	0	11	2	0
Iowa	6	2	0	9	3	0
Michigan	5	3	0	8	4	0
Michigan State	5	3	0	6	6	0
Wisconsin	3	5	0	8	5	0
Purdue	2	6	0	3	8	0
Minnesota	1	7	0	4	7	0
Indiana	1	7	0	3	8	0
Illinois	1	7	0	2	9	0

Big 12

	CONF. W L T			OVERALL W L T		
NORTH						
Nebraska	8	0	0	11	2	0
Colorado	7	1	0	10	2	0
Kansas State	6	2	0	9	3	0
Missouri	3	5	0	5	6	0
Kansas	2	6	0	4	7	0
Iowa State	1	7	0	2	9	0
SOUTH						
Texas	6	2	0	8	5	0
Texas Tech	5	3	0	7	5	0
Texas A&M	4	4	0	6	6	0
Oklahoma	3	5	0	3	8	0
Oklahoma State	2	6	0	5	6	0
Baylor	1	7	0	4	7	0

Championship Game **Texas 37 Nebraska 27**

Big East

	CONF. W L T			OVERALL W L T		
Virginia Tech	6	1	0	10	2	0
Syracuse	6	1	0	9	3	0
Miami, Fla.	6	1	0	9	3	0
West Virginia	4	3	0	8	4	0
Pittsburgh	3	4	0	4	7	0
Boston College	2	5	0	5	7	0
Rutgers	1	6	0	2	9	0
Temple	0	7	0	1	10	0

Big West

	CONF. W L T			OVERALL W L T		
Nevada	4	1	0	9	3	0
Utah State	4	1	0	6	5	0
Idaho	3	2	0	6	5	0
North Texas	3	2	0	5	6	0
Boise State	1	4	0	2	10	0
New Mexico State	0	5	0	1	10	0

C-USA

	CONF. W L T			OVERALL W L T		
Southern Miss	4	1	0	8	3	0
Houston	4	1	0	7	5	0
Cincinnati	2	3	0	6	5	0
Louisville	2	3	0	5	6	0
Memphis	2	3	0	4	7	0
Tulane	1	4	0	2	9	0

Ivy

	CONF. W L T			OVERALL W L T		
Dartmouth	7	0	0	10	0	0
Columbia	5	2	0	8	2	0
Brown	4	3	0	5	5	0
Cornell	4	3	0	4	6	0
Pennsylvania	3	4	0	5	5	0
Harvard	2	5	0	4	6	0
Princeton	2	5	0	3	7	0

MAC

	CONF. W L T			OVERALL W L T		
Ball State	7	1	0	8	4	0
Toledo	6	2	0	7	4	0
Miami, Ohio	6	2	0	6	5	0
Ohio U	5	3	0	6	6	0
Central Michigan	4	4	0	5	6	0
Akron	3	5	0	4	7	0
Bowling Green	3	5	0	4	7	0
Eastern Michigan	3	5	0	3	8	0
Western Michigan	2	6	0	2	9	0
Kent State	1	7	0	2	9	0

Pac 10

	CONF. W L T			OVERALL W L T		
Arizona State	8	0	0	11	1	0
Washington	7	1	0	9	3	0
Stanford	5	3	0	7	5	0
UCLA	4	4	0	5	6	0
Oregon	3	5	0	6	5	0
California	3	5	0	6	6	0
Southern Cal	3	5	0	6	6	0
Arizona	3	5	0	5	6	0
Washington State	3	5	0	5	6	0
Oregon State	1	7	0	2	9	0

SEC

	CONF. W L T			OVERALL W L T		
EAST						
Florida	8	0	0	12	1	0
Tennessee	7	1	0	10	2	0
South Carolina	4	4	0	6	5	0
Georgia	3	5	0	5	6	0
Kentucky	3	5	0	4	7	0
Vanderbilt	0	8	0	2	9	0
WEST						
Alabama	6	2	0	10	3	0
LSU	6	2	0	10	2	0
Auburn	4	4	0	8	4	0
Mississippi State	3	5	0	5	6	0
Mississippi	2	6	0	5	6	0
Arkansas	2	6	0	4	7	0

Championship Game **Florida 35 Alabama 30**

WAC

	CONF. W L T			OVERALL W L T		
MOUNTAIN						
Brigham Young	10	0	0	14	1	0
Utah	6	2	0	8	4	0
Rice	6	2	0	7	4	0
SMU	4	4	0	5	6	0
New Mexico	3	5	0	6	5	0
TCU	3	5	0	4	7	0
Tulsa	2	6	0	4	7	0
Texas-El Paso	0	8	0	2	9	0
PACIFIC						
Wyoming	7	1	0	10	2	0
San Diego State	6	2	0	8	3	0
Colorado State	6	2	0	7	5	0
Air Force	5	3	0	6	5	0
Fresno State	3	5	0	4	7	0
San Jose State	3	5	0	3	9	0
Hawaii	1	7	0	2	10	0
Nevada-Las Vegas	1	8	0	1	11	0

Championship game **Brigham Young 28 Wyoming 17**

Independents

	OVERALL W L T		
Army	10	2	0
Navy	9	3	0
East Carolina	8	3	0
Notre Dame	8	3	0
Louisiana Tech	6	5	0
La. Monroe	5	6	0
La. Lafayette	5	6	0
UAB	5	6	0
Central Florida	5	6	0
Arkansas State	4	7	0
Northern Illinois	1	10	0

BOWL GAMES

D19, **Las Vegas**, Nevada 18, Ball State 15, D25, **Aloha**, Navy 42, California 38, D27, **Carquest**, Miami, Fla. 31, Virginia 21, D27, **Liberty**, Syracuse 30, Houston 17, D27, **Copper**, Wisconsin 38, Utah 10, D28, **Peach**, LSU 10, Clemson 7, D29, **Alamo**, Iowa 27, Texas Tech 0, D30, **Holiday** Colorado 33, Washington 21, D31, **Independence**, Auburn 32, Army 29, D31, **Orange**, Nebraska 41, Virginia Tech 21, D31, **Sun**, Stanford 38, Michigan State 0, J1, **Outback**, Alabama 17, Michigan 14, J1, **Cotton**, Brigham Young 19, Kansas State 15, J1, **Gator**, North Carolina 20, West Virginia 13, J1, **Rose**, Ohio State 20, Arizona State 17, J1, **Fiesta**, Penn State 38, Texas 15, J1, **Florida Citrus**, Tennessee 48, Northwestern 28, J2, **Sugar**, Florida 52, Florida State 20

1996 NCAA Major College Statistical Leaders

Individual Leaders

PASSING	CL	G	ATT	COM	PCT	INT	I%	YDS	YPA	TD	TD%	RATING
1 Steve Sarkisian, Brigham Young	SR	14	404	278	68.8	12	3.0	4027	10.0	33	8.2	173.6
2 Danny Wuerffel, Florida	SR	12	360	207	57.5	13	3.6	3625	10.1	39	10.8	170.6
3 Billy Blanton, San Diego State	SR	11	344	227	66.0	5	1.5	3221	9.4	29	8.4	169.6
4 Josh Wallwork, Wyoming	SR	12	458	286	62.5	15	3.3	4090	8.9	33	7.2	154.7
5 John Dutton, Nevada	SO	11	334	222	66.5	6	1.8	2750	8.2	22	6.6	153.8
6 Pat Barnes, California	SR	11	420	250	59.5	8	1.9	3499	8.3	31	7.4	150.1
7 Peyton Manning, Tennessee	JR	11	380	243	64.0	12	3.2	3287	8.7	20	5.3	147.7
8 Mike Fouts, Utah	SR	11	302	177	58.6	7	2.3	2526	8.4	21	7.0	147.2
9 Ryan Clement, Miami, Fla.	JR	11	246	148	60.2	6	2.4	1983	8.1	18	7.3	147.1
10 Brent Baldwin, Ball State	SR	11	205	121	59.0	5	2.4	1703	8.3	14	6.8	146.5

ALL-PURPOSE	CL	G	RUSH	REC	PR	KR	YDS	YPG
1 Troy Davis, Iowa State	JR	11	2185	61	0	118	2364	214.9
2 Byron Hanspard, Texas Tech	JR	11	2084	192	0	0	2276	206.9
3 Corey Dillon, Washington	JR	11	1555	273	0	357	2185	198.6
4 Kevin Faulk, LSU	SO	11	1282	134	375	313	2104	191.3
5 Silas Massey, Central Michigan	SO	10	1544	103	0	159	1806	180.6
6 June Henley, Kansas	SR	10	1349	215	0	209	1773	177.3
7 Scott Harley, East Carolina	SO	11	1745	199	0	0	1944	176.7
8 Tiki Barber, Virginia	SR	11	1360	258	241	0	1859	169.0
9 Leon Johnson, North Carolina	SR	11	913	381	191	347	1832	166.6
10 Ron Dayne, Wisconsin	FR	12	1863	133	0	0	1996	166.3

RUSHING/Yards Per Game	CL	G	ATT	YDS	TD	AVG	YPG
1 Troy Davis, Iowa State	JR	11	402	2185	21	5.4	198.6
2 Byron Hanspard, Texas Tech	JR	11	339	2084	13	6.1	189.5
3 Scott Harley, East Carolina	SO	11	307	1745	14	5.7	158.6
4 Ron Dayne, Wisconsin	FR	12	295	1863	18	6.3	155.3
5 Silas Massey, Central Michigan	SO	10	312	1544	16	4.9	154.4
6 Corey Dillon, Washington	JR	11	271	1555	22	5.7	141.4
7 Darnell Autry, Northwestern	JR	10	263	1386	15	5.3	138.6
8 David Thompson, Oklahoma State	SR	11	293	1524	13	5.2	138.6
9 Beau Morgan, Air Force	SR	11	225	1494	18	6.6	135.8
10 June Henley, Kansas	SR	10	302	1349	17	4.5	134.9

RUSHING/Yards Per Carry	CL	G	ATT	YDS	YPC
1 Carl Sanders, UAB	JR	11	168	1154	6.9
2 Beau Morgan, Air Force	SR	11	225	1494	6.6
3 Damon Washington, Colorado State	SO	10	162	1075	6.6
4 Demond Parker, Oklahoma	FR	11	180	1184	6.6
5 Terry Battle, Arizona State	SR	11	160	1043	6.5
6 Ron Dayne, Wisconsin	FR	12	295	1863	6.3
7 Warrick Dunn, Florida State	SR	11	189	1179	6.2
8 Ricky Williams, Texas	SO	12	205	1272	6.2
9 Byron Hanspard, Texas Tech	JR	11	339	2084	6.1
10 Antowain Smith, Houston	SR	11	202	1239	6.1

*-Based on top 50 rushers

RECEIVING	CL	G	REC	YDS	TD	RPG	YPR	YPG
1 Marcus Harris, Wyoming	SR	12	109	1650	13	9.1	15.1	137.5
2 Chad Mackey, Louisiana Tech	SR	11	85	1466	10	7.7	17.2	133.3
3 Geoffery Noisy, Nevada	SO	11	98	1435	9	8.9	14.6	130.5
4 Nakia Jenkins, Utah State	JR	11	82	1397	8	7.5	17.0	127.0
5 Reggie Allen, Central Michigan	SO	10	66	1229	9	6.6	18.6	122.9
6 Brian Roberson, Fresno State	SR	11	78	1248	5	7.1	16.0	113.5
7 Will Blackwell, San Diego State	JR	9	60	1000	11	6.7	16.7	111.1
8 Eugene Baker, Kent	SO	11	69	1215	13	6.3	17.6	110.5
9 Antonio Wilson, Idaho	JR	11	65	1203	7	5.9	18.5	109.4
10 Reidel Anthony, Florida	JR	12	72	1293	18	6.0	18.0	107.8

PUNTING	CL	PUNT	YDS	AVG
1 Bill Marinangel, Vanderbilt	SR	77	3586	46.6
2 Noel Prefontaine, San Diego State	SR	48	2234	46.5
3 Andy Russ, Mississippi State	SR	53	2466	46.5
4 Ty Atteberry, Baylor	SR	60	2781	46.4
5 Tucker Phillips, Rice	SR	53	2433	45.9
6 Brad Maynard, Ball State	SR	59	2705	45.9
7 Jim Wren, Southern Cal	JR	66	3006	45.6
8 Marc Harris, Iowa State	SR	51	2312	45.3
9 Ryan Longwell, California	SR	60	2714	45.2
10 John Krueger, Duke	SR	58	2619	45.2

PUNT RETURNS	CL	PR	YDS	TD	AVG
1 Allen Rossum, Notre Dame	JR	15	344	3	22.9
2 Tim Dwight, Iowa	JR	22	417	2	19.0
3 James Dye, Brigham Young	SR	20	352	2	17.6
4 Kevin Faulk, LSU	SO	24	375	1	15.6
5 Keijuan Douglas, Eastern Michigan	FR	12	183	1	15.3
6 Leandrew Childs, San Diego State	JR	22	332	0	15.1
7 Chad Smith, New Mexico	SO	14	200	1	14.3
8 Terry Fair, Tennessee	JR	29	400	2	13.8
9 Brian Roberson, Fresno State	SR	24	330	1	13.8
10 Tremayne Banks, Miami, Ohio	SR	29	395	0	13.6

KICKOFF RETURNS	CL	KR	YDS	TD	AVG
1 Tremain Mack, Miami, Fla.	JR	13	514	1	39.5
2 Terry Battle, Arizona State	JR	17	528	2	31.1
3 Pat Johnson, Oregon	JR	12	368	1	30.7
4 Eric Booth, Southern Miss	JR	12	352	0	29.3
5 Cedric Johnson, Texas-El Paso	SR	25	729	1	29.2
6 Rodnick Phillips, SMU	FR	22	618	1	28.1
7 John Avery, Mississippi	JR	17	473	2	27.8
8 Tony Knox, Western Michigan	SR	25	690	1	27.6
9 Jim Turner, Syracuse	JR	23	633	1	27.5
10 Tremayne Banks, Miami, Ohio	SR	19	518	1	27.3

SCORING	CL	TDS	XP	FG	PTS	PTPG
1 Corey Dillon, Washington	JR	23	0	0	138	12.6
2 Troy Davis, Iowa State	JR	21	0	0	126	11.5
3 Calvin Branch, Colorado State	SR	22	0	0	132	11.0
4 Terry Battle, Arizona State	JR	20	0	0	120	10.9
4 Skip Hicks, UCLA	JR	20	0	0	120	10.9
6 June Henley, Kansas	SR	18	0	0	108	10.8
7 Damon Shea, Nevada	SO	0	55	20	115	10.5
8 Beau Morgan, Air Force	SR	18	0	0	108	9.8
8 Sedrick Irvin, Michigan State	FR	18	0	0	108	9.8
10 Silas Massey, Central Michigan	SO	16	2	0	98	9.8

FIELD GOALS	CL	FGA	FGM	PCT	FGG
1 Rafael Garcia, Virginia	SR	27	21	0.78	1.91
2 Marc Primanti, North Carolina St.	SR	20	20	1.00	1.82
2 Damon Shea, Nevada	SO	22	20	0.91	1.82
2 James Anderson, Tulsa	JR	28	20	0.71	1.82
5 Cory Wedel, Wyoming	JR	27	20	0.74	1.67
6 J. Parker, Army	SR	21	18	0.86	1.64
7 John Matich, Boston College	FR	23	16	0.70	1.60
8 Phil Dawson, Texas	JR	24	19	0.79	1.58
9 Chris Gardner, Michigan State	JR	22	17	0.77	1.55
10 Kyle Bryant, Texas A&M	JR	23	18	0.78	1.50
10 Brett Conway, Penn State	SR	24	18	0.75	1.50

INTERCEPTIONS	CL	INT	YDS	TD	INT/GM
1 Dre' Bly, North Carolina	FR	11	141	1	1.00
2 Brian Lee, Wyoming	JR	8	68	0	0.67
3 Kim Herring, Penn State	SR	7	64	0	0.58
3 Kevin Jackson, Alabama	SR	7	44	1	0.58
5 Chris McAlister, Arizona	JR	6	103	1	0.55
5 Damien Robinson, Iowa	JR	6	99	0	0.55
5 Delmonico Montgomery, Houston	SR	6	87	0	0.55
5 Harold Lusk, Utah	SR	6	86	0	0.55
5 Ramos McDonald, New Mexico	JR	6	78	1	0.55
5 Patrick Surtain, Southern Miss	JR	6	77	0	0.55
5 Sam Madison, Louisville	SR	6	50	1	0.55
5 Darnell Hasson, Nevada	SR	6	25	1	0.55

Team Leaders

RUSHING OFFENSE	G	ATT	YDS	AVG	TD	YPG
1 Army	11	740	3812	5.2	33	346.5
2 Air Force	11	618	3618	5.9	37	328.9
3 Rice	11	637	3360	5.3	34	305.5
4 Nebraska	12	691	3503	5.1	45	291.9
5 Navy	11	628	3120	5.0	31	283.6
6 Ohio	12	685	3286	4.8	29	273.8
7 Texas Tech	11	573	3008	5.2	27	273.5
8 Notre Dame	11	567	2965	5.2	34	269.5
9 Missouri	11	553	2758	5.0	24	250.7
10 Arizona State	11	538	2734	5.1	30	248.5

PASSING OFFENSE	G	ATT	COM	INT	PCT	YDS	YPA	TD	I%	YPC	YPG
1 Wyoming	12	486	299	17	61.5	4310	8.9	35	3.5	14.4	359.2
2 Nevada	11	480	307	11	64.0	3907	8.1	34	2.3	12.7	355.2
3 Louisiana Tech	11	475	279	17	58.7	3778	8.0	35	3.6	13.5	343.5
4 Idaho	11	460	270	12	58.7	3772	8.2	29	2.6	14.0	342.9
5 Florida	12	412	234	16	56.8	4007	9.7	42	3.9	17.1	333.9
6 California	11	427	253	8	59.3	3536	8.3	32	1.9	14.0	321.5
7 Utah State	11	422	233	23	55.2	3493	8.3	15	5.5	15.0	317.5
8 Tennessee	11	399	255	12	63.9	3396	8.5	20	3.0	13.3	308.7
9 Nevada-Las Vegas	12	530	287	17	54.2	3685	7.0	26	3.2	12.8	307.1
10 Colorado	11	390	221	14	56.7	3338	8.6	22	3.6	15.1	303.5

TOTAL OFFENSE	G	P	YDS	AVG	TD	YPG
1 Nevada	11	915	5800	6.3	57	527.3
2 Florida	12	854	6047	7.1	67	503.9
3 Wyoming	12	905	5987	6.6	54	498.9
4 Arizona State	11	874	5417	6.2	54	492.5
5 Idaho	11	848	5294	6.2	48	481.3
6 Brigham Young	14	1004	6692	6.7	67	478.0
7 Central Michigan	11	871	5252	6.0	45	477.5
8 San Diego State	11	803	5241	6.5	51	476.5
9 Utah State	11	835	5110	6.1	43	464.6
10 Notre Dame	11	817	5096	6.2	49	463.3

RUSHING DEFENSE	G	ATT	YDS	AVG	TD	YPG
1 Florida State	11	418	649	1.6	5	59.0
2 West Virginia	11	364	677	1.9	5	61.5
3 North Carolina	11	334	813	2.4	5	73.9
4 Louisville	11	437	892	2.0	9	81.1
5 Nebraska	12	447	1006	2.3	7	83.8
6 Army	11	325	979	3.0	12	89.0
7 Alabama	12	392	1110	2.8	9	92.5
8 Southern Miss	11	384	1069	2.8	12	97.2
9 Ohio State	11	398	1074	2.7	7	97.6
10 Arizona State	11	407	1078	2.6	10	98.0

PASSING DEFENSE	G	ATT	COM	PCT	INT	I%	YDS	YPA	TD	TD%	RAT
1 Ohio State	11	309	140	45.3	20	6.5	1602	5.2	5	1.6	81.3
2 Miami, Ohio	11	260	104	40.0	11	4.2	1323	5.1	6	2.3	81.9
3 North Carolina	11	326	148	45.4	20	6.1	1669	5.1	7	2.2	83.2
4 Kansas State	11	299	126	42.1	13	4.4	1509	5.1	9	3.0	85.8
5 West Virginia	11	348	157	45.1	16	4.6	1715	4.9	10	2.9	86.8
6 Florida State	11	358	162	45.3	11	3.1	1875	5.2	9	2.5	91.4
7 Nebraska	12	329	149	45.3	23	7.0	2059	6.3	8	2.4	91.9
8 Tennessee	11	285	134	47.0	14	4.9	1434	5.0	12	4.2	93.4
9 Alabama	12	319	132	41.4	17	5.3	1957	6.1	11	3.5	93.6
10 Notre Dame	11	292	131	44.9	13	4.5	1656	5.7	9	3.1	93.8

TOTAL DEFENSE	G	P	YDS	AVG	TD	YPG
1 West Virginia	11	712	2392	3.4	15	217.5
2 North Carolina	11	660	2482	3.8	12	225.6
3 Florida State	11	776	2524	3.3	14	229.5
4 Louisville	11	765	2594	3.4	20	235.8
5 Tennessee	11	708	2602	3.7	16	236.5
6 Ohio State	11	707	2676	3.8	12	243.3
7 Nebraska	12	776	3065	3.9	15	255.4
8 Alabama	12	711	3067	4.3	20	255.6
9 Army	11	626	2819	4.5	23	256.3
10 Syracuse	11	725	2875	4.0	17	261.4

SCORING OFFENSE	G	PTS	AVG
1 Florida	12	559	46.6
2 Nevada	11	497	45.2
3 Arizona State	11	471	42.8
4 Nebraska	12	512	42.7
5 Brigham Young	14	571	40.8
6 Ohio State	11	435	39.5
7 San Diego State	11	428	38.9
8 Florida State	11	426	38.7
9 Wyoming	12	464	38.7
10 Syracuse	11	407	37.0
10 Notre Dame	11	407	37.0

SCORING DEFENSE	G	PTS	AVG
1 North Carolina	11	110	10.0
2 Ohio State	11	114	10.4
3 Florida State	11	122	11.1
4 West Virginia	11	136	12.4
5 Nebraska	12	153	12.8
6 Tennessee	11	157	14.3
7 Alabama	12	181	15.1
8 Michigan	11	167	15.2
9 Virginia Tech	11	168	15.3
9 Miami, Ohio	11	168	15.3

TURNOVER MARGIN	G	FR	INT	TOT	FL	INTL	TOT	MAR
1 North Carolina	11	14	20	34	6	6	12	2.0
2 Auburn	11	14	22	36	9	13	22	1.3
2 Southern Miss	11	16	18	34	5	15	20	1.3
2 West Virginia	11	8	16	24	4	6	10	1.3
2 East Carolina	11	23	13	36	6	16	22	1.3
2 Ohio State	11	10	20	30	7	9	16	1.3
7 Arizona	11	13	16	29	9	7	16	1.2
8 Navy	11	15	13	28	10	6	16	1.1
9 Kansas	11	11	12	23	4	8	12	1.0
9 Bowling Green	11	13	13	26	1	14	15	1.0
9 Arizona State	11	15	11	26	5	10	15	1.0

1997 Poll Progression

ESPN	AP	Pre-Season 1997		Aug. 23 Games
2	1	Penn State	0-0	bye week
1	2	Florida	0-0	bye week
4	3	Florida State	0-0	bye week
3	4	Washington	0-0	bye week
5	5	Tennessee	0-0	bye week
6	6	Nebraska	0-0	bye week
8	7	North Carolina	0-0	bye week
7	8	Colorado	0-0	bye week
9	9	Ohio State	0-0	bye week
11	10	LSU	0-0	bye week
12	11	Notre Dame	0-0	bye week
10	12	Texas	0-0	bye week
14	13	Miami, Fla.	0-0	bye week
13	14	Michigan	0-0	bye week
15	15	Alabama	0-0	bye week
19	16	Auburn	0-0	bye week
16	17	Syracuse	0-0	beat # 24 Wisconsin 34-0 (A24)
18	18	Stanford	0-0	bye week
17	19	Brigham Young	0-0	bye week
21	20	Clemson	0-0	bye week
20	21	Iowa	0-0	bye week
22	22	Southern Cal	0-0	bye week
23	23	Kansas State	0-0	bye week
24	24	Wisconsin	0-0	lost to # 17 Syracuse 0-34 (A24)
	25	Michigan State	0-0	bye week
25		Virginia Tech	0-0	bye week

AP	August 25 Poll		Aug. 30 Games
1	Penn State	0-0	bye week
2	Florida	0-0	beat Southern Miss 21-6
3	Florida State	0-0	bye week
4	Washington	0-0	bye week
5	Tennessee	0-0	beat Texas Tech 52-17
6	Nebraska	0-0	beat Akron 59-14
7	North Carolina	0-0	bye week
8	Colorado	0-0	bye week
9	Ohio State	0-0	beat Wyoming 24-10 (A28)
10	LSU	0-0	bye week
11	Notre Dame	0-0	bye week
12	Texas	0-0	bye week
13	Syracuse	1-0	lost to North Carolina St. 31-32
14	Miami, Fla.	0-0	beat Baylor 45-14
15	Michigan	0-0	bye week
16	Alabama	0-0	beat Houston 42-17
17	Auburn	0-0	bye week
18	Stanford	0-0	bye week
19	Brigham Young	0-0	bye week
20	Clemson	0-0	bye week
21	Iowa	0-0	bye week
22	Kansas State	0-0	bye week
23	Southern Cal	0-0	bye week
24	Northwestern	1-0	bye week
25	Michigan State	0-0	bye week

ESPN	AP	September 1 Poll		Sept. 6 Games
2	1	Penn State	0-0	beat Pittsburgh 34-17
1	2	Florida	1-0	beat Central Michigan 82-6
3	3	Tennessee	1-0	beat UCLA 30-24
4	4	Washington	0-0	beat # 19 Brigham Young 42-20
5	5	Florida State	0-0	beat # 23 Southern Cal 14-7
6	6	Nebraska	1-0	bye week
8	7	North Carolina	0-0	beat Indiana 23-6
7	8	Colorado	0-0	beat # 24 Colorado State 31-21
9	9	Ohio State	1-0	bye week
11	10	LSU	0-0	beat Texas-El Paso 55-3
13	11	Notre Dame	0-0	beat Georgia Tech 17-13
10	12	Texas	0-0	beat Rutgers 48-14
12	13	Miami, Fla.	1-0	bye week
14	14	Michigan	0-0	bye week
15	15	Alabama	1-0	bye week
18	16	Auburn	0-0	beat Virginia 28-17 (S4)
17	17	Stanford	0-0	beat San Jose State 28-12
	18	Air Force	1-0	beat Rice 41-12
16	19	Brigham Young	0-0	lost to # 4 Washington 20-42
19	20	Iowa	0-0	beat No. Iowa 66-0
23	21	Kansas State	0-0	beat No. Illinois 47-7
24	21	Northwestern	1-0	lost to Wake Forest 20-27
21	23	Southern Cal	0-0	lost to # 5 Florida State 7-14
25	24	Colorado State	1-0	lost to # 8 Colorado 21-31
	25	Michigan State	0-0	beat Western Michigan 42-10
20		Clemson	0-0	beat Appalachian St. 23-12
22		Virginia Tech	1-0	bye week

ESPN	AP	September 8 Poll		Sept. 13 Games
2	1	Penn State	1-0	beat Temple 52-10
1	2	Florida	2-0	bye week
3	3	Washington	1-0	beat San Diego State 36-3
4	4	Tennessee	2-0	bye week
6	5	Florida State	1-0	beat Maryland 50-7
5	6	Nebraska	1-0	beat Central Florida 38-24
8	7	North Carolina	1-0	beat Stanford 28-17
7	8	Colorado	1-0	lost to # 14 Michigan 3-27
9	9	Ohio State	1-0	beat Bowling Green 44-13
11	10	LSU	1-0	beat Mississippi State 24-9
10	11	Texas	1-0	lost to UCLA 3-66
15	12	Notre Dame	1-0	lost to Purdue 17-28
12	13	Miami, Fla.	1-0	lost to # 24 Arizona State 12-23
13	14	Michigan	0-0	beat # 8 Colorado 27-3
14	15	Alabama	1-0	beat Vanderbilt 20-0 (S11)
16	16	Auburn	1-0	beat Mississippi 19-9
18	17	Stanford	1-0	lost to North Carolina 17-28
17	18	Iowa	1-0	beat Tulsa 54-16
21	19	Clemson	1-0	beat North Carolina St. 19-17
20	20	Kansas State	1-0	beat Ohio U 23-20
23	21	Michigan State	1-0	beat Memphis 51-21
19	22	Virginia Tech	1-0	beat Syracuse 31-3
22	23	Southern Cal	0-1	lost to Washington State 21-28
	24	Arizona State	1-0	beat # 13 Miami, Fla. 23-12
	25	Colorado State	1-1	beat Utah State 35-24
24		West Virginia	2-0	lost to Boston College 24-31
25		North Carolina St.	2-0	lost to # 19 Clemson 17-19

ESPN	AP	September 15 Poll		Sept. 20 Games
2	1	Penn State	2-0	beat Louisville 57-21
3	2	Washington	2-0	lost to # 7 Nebraska 14-27
1	3	Florida	2-0	beat # 4 Tennessee 33-20
4	4	Tennessee	2-0	lost to # 3 Florida 20-33
5	5	Florida State	2-0	beat # 16 Clemson 35-28
7	6	North Carolina	2-0	beat Maryland 40-14
6	7	Nebraska	2-0	beat # 2 Washington 27-14
9	8	Michigan	1-0	beat Baylor 38-3
8	9	Ohio State	2-0	beat Arizona 28-20
10	10	LSU	2-0	lost to # 12 Auburn 28-31
11	11	Alabama	2-0	lost to Arkansas 16-17
12	12	Auburn	2-0	beat # 10 LSU 31-28
13	13	Iowa	2-0	beat Iowa State 63-20
17	14	Arizona State	2-0	lost to Brigham Young 10-13
16	15	Colorado	1-1	bye week
15	16	Clemson	2-0	lost to # 5 Florida State 28-35
18	17	Michigan State	2-0	beat Notre Dame 23-7
14	18	Virginia Tech	2-0	beat Temple 23-13
20	19	Washington State	2-0	beat Illinois 35-22
19	20	Kansas State	2-0	bye week
23	21	Stanford	1-1	beat Oregon State 27-24
21	22	Miami, Fla.	1-1	lost to Pittsburgh 17-21 (S18)
	23	Colorado State	2-1	lost to Air Force 0-24
	24	UCLA	1-2	bye week
25	25	Georgia	2-0	beat La. Monroe 42-3
22		Texas A&M	1-0	beat La. Lafayette 66-0
24		Texas	1-1	bye week

ESPN	AP	September 22 Poll		Sept. 27 Games
1	1	Florida	3-0	beat Kentucky 55-28
2	2	Penn State	3-0	bye week
3	3	Nebraska	3-0	bye week
4	4	Florida State	3-0	bye week
5	5	North Carolina	3-0	beat Virginia 48-20
6	6	Michigan	2-0	beat Notre Dame 21-14
7	7	Ohio State	3-0	beat Missouri 31-10
8	8	Auburn	3-0	beat Central Florida 41-14
10	9	Tennessee	2-1	bye week
11	10	Washington	2-1	bye week
9	11	Iowa	3-0	beat Illinois 38-10
13	12	Michigan State	3-0	bye week
15	13	LSU	2-1	beat Akron 56-0
12	14	Virginia Tech	3-0	beat Arkansas State 50-0
14	15	Washington State	3-0	beat Boise State 58-0
16	16	Colorado	1-1	beat Wyoming 20-19
21	17	Clemson	2-1	lost to Georgia Tech 20-23
17	18	Kansas State	2-0	beat Bowling Green 58-0
20	19	Georgia	3-0	bye week
22	20	Stanford	2-1	beat Oregon 58-49
19	21	Alabama	2-1	beat Southern Miss 27-13
18	22	Texas A&M	2-0	beat North Texas 36-10
24	23	Brigham Young	1-1	beat SMU 19-16
	24	UCLA	1-2	beat Arizona 40-27
23	25	Arizona State	2-1	beat Oregon State 13-10
25		Air Force	4-0	beat San Diego State 24-18

ESPN	AP	September 29 Poll		Oct. 4 Games
1	1	Florida	4-0	beat Arkansas 56-7
2	2	Penn State	3-0	beat Illinois 41-6
3	3	Nebraska	3-0	beat # 17 Kansas State 56-26
4	4	Florida State	3-0	beat Miami, Fla. 47-0
5	5	North Carolina	4-0	beat TCU 31-10
6	6	Michigan	3-0	beat Indiana 37-0
7	7	Ohio State	4-0	beat # 11 Iowa 23-7
9	8	Auburn	4-0	beat South Carolina 23-6
10	9	Tennessee	2-1	beat Mississippi 31-17
11	10	Washington	2-1	beat # 25 Arizona State 26-14
8	11	Iowa	4-0	lost to # 7 Ohio State 7-23
13	12	Michigan State	3-0	beat Minnesota 31-10
14	13	LSU	3-1	beat Vanderbilt 7-6
12	14	Virginia Tech	4-0	lost to Miami, Ohio 17-24
15	15	Washington State	4-0	beat Oregon 24-13
18	16	Colorado	2-1	lost to # 21 Texas A&M 10-16
16	17	Kansas State	3-0	lost to # 3 Nebraska 26-56
19	18	Georgia	3-0	beat Mississippi State 47-0
21	19	Stanford	3-1	beat Notre Dame 33-15
20	20	Alabama	3-1	lost to Kentucky 34-40
17	21	Texas A&M	3-0	beat # 16 Colorado 16-10
25	22	UCLA	2-2	beat Houston 66-10
23	23	Air Force	5-0	beat Citadel 17-3
24	24	Brigham Young	2-1	beat Utah State 42-35 (O3)
22	25	Arizona State	3-1	lost to # 10 Washington 14-26

ESPN	AP	October 6 Poll		Oct. 11 Games
1	1	Florida	5-0	lost to # 14 LSU 21-28
2	2	Penn State	4-0	beat # 7 Ohio State 31-27
3	3	Nebraska	4-0	beat Baylor 49-21
4	4	Florida State	4-0	beat Duke 51-27
5	5	North Carolina	5-0	beat Wake Forest 30-12
6	6	Michigan	4-0	beat Northwestern 23-6
7	7	Ohio State	5-0	lost to # 2 Penn State 27-31
8	8	Auburn	5-0	beat Louisiana Tech 49-13
10	9	Tennessee	3-1	beat # 13 Georgia 38-13
9	10	Washington	3-1	beat California 30-3
11	11	Michigan State	4-0	beat Indiana 38-6
12	12	Washington State	5-0	bye week
15	13	Georgia	4-0	lost to # 9 Tennessee 13-38
14	14	LSU	4-1	beat # 1 Florida 28-21
13	15	Texas A&M	4-0	beat Iowa State 56-17
17	16	Stanford	4-1	lost to Arizona 22-28
16	17	Iowa	4-1	bye week
19	18	UCLA	3-2	beat Oregon 39-31
18	19	Air Force	6-0	beat Navy 10-7
20	20	Oklahoma State	5-0	beat # 24 Colorado 33-29
22	21	Brigham Young	3-1	lost to Rice 14-27
23	22	Kansas State	3-1	beat Missouri 41-11
20	23	Virginia Tech	4-1	beat Boston College 17-7
25	24	Colorado	2-2	lost to # 20 Oklahoma State 29-33
	25	Georgia Tech	3-1	beat North Carolina St. 27-17
24		West Virginia	4-1	beat Maryland 31-14

ESPN	AP	October 13 Poll		Oct. 18 Games
1	1	Penn State	5-0	beat Minnesota 16-15
2	2	Nebraska	5-0	beat Texas Tech 29-0
3	3	Florida State	5-0	beat # 21 Georgia Tech 38-0
4	4	North Carolina	6-0	beat North Carolina St. 20-7
5	5	Michigan	5-0	beat # 15 Iowa 28-24
7	6	Auburn	6-0	lost to # 7 Florida 10-24
6	7	Florida	5-1	beat # 6 Auburn 24-10
10	8	LSU	5-1	lost to Mississippi 21-36
9	9	Tennessee	4-1	beat Alabama 38-21
8	10	Washington	4-1	beat Arizona 58-28
12	11	Ohio State	5-1	beat Indiana 31-0
11	12	Michigan State	5-0	lost to Northwestern 17-19
13	13	Washington State	5-0	beat California 63-37
14	14	Texas A&M	5-0	lost to # 20 Kansas State 17-36
15	15	Iowa	4-1	lost to # 5 Michigan 24-28
16	16	Oklahoma State	6-0	bye week
18	17	UCLA	4-2	beat Oregon State 34-10
17	18	Air Force	7-0	lost to Fresno State 17-20
21	19	Georgia	4-1	beat Vanderbilt 34-13
20	20	Kansas State	4-1	beat # 14 Texas A&M 36-17
25	21	Georgia Tech	4-1	lost to # 3 Florida State 0-38
19	22	Virginia Tech	5-1	bye week
22	23	West Virginia	5-1	bye week
24	24	Wisconsin	6-1	lost to Purdue 20-45
23	25	Stanford	4-2	lost to Arizona State 14-31

ESPN	AP	October 20 Poll		Oct. 25 Games
1	1	**Nebraska**	6-0	beat Kansas 35-0
2	2	**Penn State**	6-0	bye week
3	3	**Florida State**	6-0	beat Virginia 47-21
4	4	**North Carolina**	7-0	bye week
5	5	**Michigan**	6-0	beat # 15 Michigan State 23-7
6	6	**Florida**	6-1	bye week
7	7	**Washington**	5-1	beat Oregon State 45-17
8	8	**Tennessee**	5-1	bye week
9	9	**Ohio State**	6-1	beat Northwestern 49-6
10	10	**Washington State**	6-0	beat Arizona 35-34
11	11	**Auburn**	6-1	beat Arkansas 26-21
12	12	**Oklahoma State**	6-0	lost to Missouri 50-51
16	13	**UCLA**	5-2	beat California 35-17
13	14	**Kansas State**	5-1	beat Oklahoma 26-7
14	15	**Michigan State**	5-1	lost to # 5 Michigan 7-23
18	16	**Georgia**	5-1	beat Kentucky 23-13
15	17	**LSU**	5-2	bye week
19	18	**Iowa**	4-2	beat Indiana 62-0
17	19	**Virginia Tech**	5-1	lost to # 21 West Virginia 17-30
21	20	**Texas A&M**	5-1	lost to Texas Tech 13-16
20	21	**West Virginia**	5-1	beat # 19 Virginia Tech 30-17
23	22	**Purdue**	5-1	beat Illinois 48-3
22	23	**Arizona State**	5-2	bye week
	24	**Toledo**	6-0	beat Bowling Green 35-20
	25	**Mississippi**	4-2	lost to Alabama 20-29
24		**Air Force**	7-1	lost to San Jose State 22-25
25		**Syracuse**	5-3	bye week

ESPN	AP	October 27 Poll		Nov. 1 Games
1	1	**Nebraska**	7-0	beat Oklahoma 69-7
2	2	**Penn State**	6-0	beat Northwestern 30-27
3	3	**Florida State**	7-0	beat North Carolina St. 48-35
4	4	**Michigan**	7-0	beat Minnesota 24-3
5	5	**North Carolina**	7-0	beat Georgia Tech 16-13 (030)
6	6	**Florida**	6-1	lost to # 14 Georgia 17-37
7	7	**Washington**	6-1	beat Southern Cal 27-0
8	8	**Tennessee**	5-1	beat South Carolina 22-7
9	9	**Ohio State**	7-1	beat # 21 Michigan State 37-13
10	10	**Washington State**	7-0	lost to # 20 Arizona State 31-44
11	11	**Auburn**	7-1	lost to Mississippi State 0-20
13	12	**UCLA**	6-2	beat Stanford 27-7
12	13	**Kansas State**	6-1	beat Texas Tech 13-2
15	14	**Georgia**	6-1	beat # 6 Florida 37-17
16	15	**Iowa**	5-2	beat # 18 Purdue 35-17
14	16	**LSU**	5-2	beat Kentucky 63-28
17	17	**West Virginia**	6-1	lost to Syracuse 10-40
18	18	**Purdue**	6-1	lost to # 15 Iowa 17-35
19	19	**Oklahoma State**	6-1	lost to # 25 Texas A&M 25-28
21	20	**Arizona State**	5-2	beat # 10 Washington State 44-31
20	21	**Michigan State**	5-2	lost to # 9 Ohio State 13-37
23	22	**Toledo**	7-0	beat Miami, Ohio 35-28
22	23	**Virginia Tech**	5-2	beat UAB 37-0
	24	**Southern Miss**	5-2	beat Cincinnati 24-17
	25	**Texas A&M**	5-2	beat # 19 Oklahoma State 28-25
24		**Syracuse**	5-3	beat West Virginia 40-10
25		**Brigham Young**	5-2	lost to Texas-El Paso 3-14

ESPN	AP	November 3 Poll		Nov. 8 Games
1	1	**Nebraska**	8-0	beat Missouri 45-38
3	2	**Penn State**	7-0	lost to # 4 Michigan 8-34
2	3	**Florida State**	8-0	beat # 5 North Carolina 20-3
4	4	**Michigan**	8-0	beat # 2 Penn State 34-8
5	5	**North Carolina**	8-0	lost to # 3 Florida State 3-20
6	6	**Washington**	7-1	lost to Oregon 28-31
8	7	**Ohio State**	8-1	beat Minnesota 31-3
7	8	**Tennessee**	6-1	beat # 24 Southern Miss 44-20
9	9	**Georgia**	7-1	bye week
11	10	**UCLA**	7-2	bye week
10	11	**Kansas State**	7-1	beat Kansas 48-16
14	12	**Iowa**	6-2	lost to Wisconsin 10-13
13	13	**Florida**	6-2	beat Vanderbilt 20-7
12	14	**LSU**	6-2	beat Alabama 27-0
16	15	**Arizona State**	6-2	beat California 28-21
15	16	**Washington State**	7-1	beat La. Lafayette 77-7
17	17	**Auburn**	7-2	bye week
20	18	**Toledo**	8-0	lost to Ball State 3-35
	19	**Mississippi State**	6-2	bye week
18	20	**Virginia Tech**	6-2	beat Miami, Fla. 27-25
21	21	**Texas A&M**	6-2	beat Baylor 38-10
19	22	**Syracuse**	6-3	beat Boston College 20-13
24	23	**Purdue**	6-2	beat Michigan State 22-21
25	24	**Southern Miss**	6-2	lost to # 8 Tennessee 20-44
23	25	**Oklahoma State**	6-2	beat Oklahoma 30-7
22		**West Virginia**	6-2	bye week

ESPN	AP	November 10 Poll		Nov. 15 Games
2	1	**Michigan**	9-0	beat # 23 Wisconsin 26-16
1	2	**Florida State**	9-0	beat Wake Forest 58-7
3	3	**Nebraska**	9-0	beat Iowa State 77-14
4	4	**Ohio State**	9-1	beat Illinois 41-6
5	5	**Tennessee**	7-1	beat Arkansas 30-22
6	6	**Penn State**	7-1	beat # 19 Purdue 42-17
7	7	**Georgia**	7-1	lost to # 16 Auburn 34-45
9	8	**North Carolina**	8-1	beat Clemson 17-10
10	9	**UCLA**	7-2	beat Washington 52-28
8	10	**Kansas State**	8-1	beat Colorado 37-20
11	11	**LSU**	7-2	lost to Notre Dame 6-24
12	12	**Florida**	7-2	beat South Carolina 48-21
14	13	**Washington**	7-2	lost to UCLA 28-52
13	14	**Washington State**	8-1	beat Stanford 38-28
15	15	**Arizona State**	7-2	beat Oregon 52-31
16	16	**Auburn**	7-2	beat # 7 Georgia 45-34
25	17	**Mississippi State**	6-2	beat Alabama 32-20
18	18	**Texas A&M**	7-2	beat Oklahoma 51-7
20	19	**Purdue**	7-2	lost to # 6 Penn State 17-42
17	19	**Virginia Tech**	7-2	bye week
19	21	**Syracuse**	7-3	beat Pittsburgh 32-27
22	22	**Iowa**	6-3	lost to Northwestern 14-15
24	23	**Wisconsin**	8-2	lost to # 1 Michigan 16-26
21	24	**Oklahoma State**	7-2	lost to Texas Tech 3-27
	25	**Missouri**	6-4	beat Baylor 42-24
23		**West Virginia**	6-2	beat Temple 41-21

ESPN	AP	November 17 Poll		Nov. 22 Games
2	1	**Michigan**	10-0	beat # 4 Ohio State 20-14
1	2	**Florida State**	10-0	lost to # 10 Florida 29-32
3	3	**Nebraska**	10-0	bye week
4	4	**Ohio State**	10-1	lost to # 1 Michigan 14-20
5	5	**Tennessee**	8-1	beat Kentucky 59-31
6	6	**Penn State**	8-1	beat # 24 Wisconsin 35-10
9	7	**UCLA**	8-2	beat Southern Cal 31-24
8	8	**North Carolina**	9-1	beat Duke 50-14
7	9	**Kansas State**	9-1	beat Iowa State 28-3
10	10	**Florida**	8-2	beat # 2 Florida State 32-29
11	11	**Washington State**	9-1	beat # 17 Washington 41-35
12	12	**Arizona State**	8-2	bye week
13	13	**Auburn**	8-2	beat Alabama 18-17
14	14	**Georgia**	7-2	beat Mississippi 21-14
19	15	**Mississippi State**	7-2	lost to Arkansas 7-17
16	16	**Texas A&M**	8-2	bye week
20	17	**Washington**	7-3	lost to # 11 Washington State 35-41
17	18	**Syracuse**	8-3	bye week
15	19	**Virginia Tech**	7-2	lost to Pittsburgh 23-30
18	20	**LSU**	7-3	bye week
23	21	**Missouri**	7-4	regular season complete
21	22	**West Virginia**	7-2	lost to Notre Dame 14-21
25	23	**Purdue**	7-3	beat Indiana 56-7
24	24	**Wisconsin**	8-3	lost to # 6 Penn State 10-35
22	25	**Colorado State**	8-2	beat San Diego State 38-17

ESPN	AP	November 24 Poll		Nov. 29 Games
1	1	**Michigan**	11-0	regular season complete
2	2	**Nebraska**	10-0	beat Colorado 27-24 (N28)
3	3	**Tennessee**	9-1	beat Vanderbilt 17-10
4	4	**Penn State**	9-1	lost to Michigan State 14-49
5	5	**Florida State**	10-1	regular season complete
7	6	**UCLA**	9-2	regular season complete
8	7	**Florida**	9-2	regular season complete
6	8	**North Carolina**	10-1	regular season complete
11	9	**Ohio State**	10-2	regular season complete
10	10	**Washington State**	10-1	regular season complete
9	11	**Kansas State**	10-1	regular season complete
12	12	**Arizona State**	8-2	lost to Arizona 16-28 (N28)
13	13	**Auburn**	9-2	bye week
14	14	**Georgia**	8-2	beat Georgia Tech 27-24
15	15	**Texas A&M**	8-2	beat Texas 27-16 (N28)
16	16	**Syracuse**	8-3	beat Miami, Fla. 33-13
17	17	**LSU**	7-3	beat Arkansas 31-21 (N28)
18	18	**Purdue**	8-3	regular season complete
20	19	**Missouri**	7-4	
19	20	**Colorado State**	9-2	bye week
22	21	**Washington**	7-4	regular season complete
	22	**Mississippi State**	7-3	lost to Mississippi 14-15
24	23	**Southern Miss**	8-3	regular season complete
23	24	**Air Force**	10-2	regular season complete
25	25	**Oklahoma State**	8-3	regular season complete
21		**Virginia Tech**	7-3	lost to Virginia 20-34

ESPN	AP	December 1 Poll		Dec. 6 Games
1	1	**Michigan**	11-0	
2	2	**Nebraska**	11-0	beat # 14 Texas A&M 54-14 (Big 12 CH)
3	3	**Tennessee**	10-1	beat # 11 Auburn 30-29 (SEC CH)
4	4	**Florida State**	10-1	
6	5	**UCLA**	9-2	
8	6	**Florida**	9-2	
5	7	**North Carolina**	10-1	
7	8	**Washington State**	10-1	
10	9	**Ohio State**	10-2	
9	10	**Kansas State**	10-1	
11	11	**Auburn**	9-2	lost to # 3 Tennessee 29-30 (SEC CH)
12	12	**Penn State**	9-2	regular season complete
13	13	**Georgia**	9-2	regular season complete
14	14	**Texas A&M**	9-2	lost to # 2 Nebraska 15-54 (Big 12 CH)
15	15	**Syracuse**	9-3	regular season complete
16	16	**LSU**	8-3	regular season complete
19	17	**Arizona State**	8-3	regular season complete
17	18	**Purdue**	8-3	
20	19	**Missouri**	7-4	
18	20	**Colorado State**	9-2	beat New Mexico 41-13 (WAC CH)
22	21	**Washington**	7-4	
23	22	**Southern Miss**	8-3	
21	23	**Air Force**	10-2	
24	24	**Oklahoma State**	8-3	
	25	**Michigan State**	7-4	regular season complete
25		**New Mexico**	9-2	lost to # 20 Colorado State 13-41 (WAC CH)

ESPN	AP	December 8 Poll	Record	Bowl Bid	Date	Bowl Result	RB	ESPN	AP	January 3 Final Poll	Record
1	1	**Michigan**	11-0	Rose Bowl	J1	beat # 8 Washington State 21-16	2	2	1	**Michigan**	12-0
2	2	**Nebraska**	12-0	Orange Bowl	J2	beat # 3 Tennessee 42-17	1	1	2	**Nebraska**	13-0
3	3	**Tennessee**	11-1	Orange Bowl	J2	lost to # 2 Nebraska 17-42	4	3	3	**Florida State**	11-1
4	4	**Florida State**	10-1	Sugar Bowl	J1	beat # 9 Ohio State 31-14	3	6	4	**Florida**	10-2
6	5	**UCLA**	9-2	Cotton Bowl	J1	beat # 20 Texas A&M 29-23	9	5	5	**UCLA**	10-2
8	6	**Florida**	9-2	Citrus Bowl	J1	beat # 11 Penn State 21-6	7	4	6	**North Carolina**	11-1
5	7	**North Carolina**	10-1	Gator Bowl	J1	beat Virginia Tech 42-3	5	8	7	**Tennessee**	11-2
7	8	**Washington State**	10-1	Rose Bowl	J1	lost to # 1 Michigan 16-21	6	7	8	**Kansas State**	11-1
10	9	**Ohio State**	10-2	Sugar Bowl	J1	lost to # 4 Florida State 14-31	13	9	9	**Washington State**	10-2
9	10	**Kansas State**	10-1	Fiesta Bowl	D31	beat # 14 Syracuse 35-18	12	10	10	**Georgia**	10-2
12	11	**Penn State**	9-2	Citrus Bowl	J1	lost to # 6 Florida 6-21	11	11	11	**Auburn**	10-3
11	12	**Georgia**	9-2	Outback Bowl	J1	beat Wisconsin 33-6	8	12	12	**Ohio State**	10-3
13	13	**Auburn**	9-3	Peach Bowl	J2	beat Clemson 21-17	17	13	13	**LSU**	9-3
14	14	**Syracuse**	9-3	Fiesta Bowl	D31	lost to # 10 Kansas State 18-35	14	14	14	**Arizona State**	9-3
15	15	**LSU**	8-3	Independence Bowl	D28	beat Notre Dame 27-9	24	15	15	**Purdue**	9-3
18	16	**Arizona State**	8-3	Sun Bowl	D31	beat Iowa 17-7	10	17	16	**Penn State**	9-3
16	17	**Purdue**	8-3	Alamo Bowl	D30	beat # 24 Oklahoma State 33-20	16	16	17	**Colorado State**	11-2
17	18	**Colorado State**	10-2	Holiday Bowl	D29	beat # 19 Missouri 35-24	15	18	18	**Washington**	8-4
20	19	**Missouri**	7-4	Holiday Bowl	D29	lost to # 18 Colorado State 24-35	20	19	19	**Southern Miss**	9-3
19	20	**Texas A&M**	9-3	Cotton Bowl	J1	lost to # 5 UCLA 23-29	25	21	20	**Texas A&M**	9-4
23	21	**Washington**	7-4	Aloha Bowl	D25	beat # 25 Michigan State 51-23	22	20	21	**Syracuse**	9-4
22	22	**Southern Miss**	8-3	Liberty Bowl	D31	beat Pittsburgh 41-7	21	22	22	**Mississippi**	8-4
21	23	**Air Force**	10-2	Las Vegas Bowl	D20	lost to Oregon 13-41	29	23	23	**Missouri**	7-5
24	24	**Oklahoma State**	8-3	Alamo Bowl	D30	lost to # 17 Purdue 20-33	32	24	24	**Oklahoma State**	8-4
25	25	**Michigan State**	7-4	Aloha Bowl	D25	lost to # 21 Washington 23-51	38		25	**Georgia Tech**	7-5

1997

Consensus All-Americans

POS	Offense	HT	WT	CL	School	AP	CF	FC	FN	FW	SN
QB	**Peyton Manning**	6-5	222	Sr.	Tennessee	•	•	•	•	•	
RB	**Ricky Williams**	6-0	220	Jr.	Texas	•	•	•	•	•	•
RB	**Curtis Enis**	6-1	233	Jr.	Penn State	•	•			•	
WR	**Randy Moss**	6-5	210	So.	Marshall	•	•	•	•	•	•
WR	**Jacquez Green**	5-9	168	Jr.	Florida	•	•			•	
TE	**Alonzo Mayes**	6-6	265	Sr.	Oklahoma State	•	•	•		•	•
OL	**Aaron Taylor**	6-1	305	Sr.	Nebraska	•	•	•	•	•	•
OL	**Alan Faneca**	6-5	310	Jr.	LSU	•	•		•	•	•
OL	**Kyle Turley**	6-6	305	Sr.	San Diego State			•	•	•	•
OL	**Chad Overhauser**	6-6	304	Sr.	UCLA	•				•	•
C	**Olin Kreutz**	6-4	290	Jr.	Washington	•	•		•		•
PK	**Martin Gramatica**	5-9	170	Jr.	Kansas State	•				•	
KR	**Tim Dwight**	5-9	185	Sr.	Iowa	•		•		•	•

Others receiving first-team honors

POS	Name	School	AP	CF	FC	FN	FW	SN
QB	Ryan Leaf	Washington State						•
RB	Skip Hicks	UCLA			•			•
RB	Ron Dayne	Wisconsin				•		
WR	Jerome Pathon	Washington			•			
WR	Brian Alford	Purdue				•		
WR	Bobby Shaw	California						•
TE	Jerame Tuman	Michigan				•		
OL	Flozell Adams	Michigan State		•				
OL	Benji Olson	Washington	•	•				
OL	Victor Riley	Auburn			•			
OL	Matt Stinchcomb	Georgia			•			
OL	Rob Murphy	Ohio State				•		
C	Ben Fricke	Houston					•	
C	Kevin Long	Florida State			•			
PK	Chris Sailer	UCLA		•	•			
P	Chris Sailer	UCLA					•	

POS	Defense	HT	WT	CL	School	AP	CF	FC	FN	FW	SN
DL	**Grant Wistrom**	6-5	255	Sr.	Nebraska	•	•	•		•	•
DL	**Andre Wadsworth**	6-4	282	Sr.	Florida State	•	•	•	•		•
DL	**Greg Ellis**	6-6	265	Sr.	North Carolina	•	•	•	•		
DL	**Jason Peter**	6-5	285	Sr.	Nebraska	•	•			•	•
LB	**Andy Katzenmoyer**	6-4	260	So.	Ohio State	•	•	•	•	•	
LB	**Sam Cowart**	6-3	239	Sr.	Florida State	•			•	•	•
LB	**Anthony Simmons**	6-1	225	Jr.	Clemson	•		•	•		•
LB	**Brian Simmons**	6-4	230	Sr.	North Carolina	•	•				
DB	**Charles Woodson**	6-1	198	Jr.	Michigan	•	•	•	•	•	•
DB	**Dre' Bly**	5-10	185	So.	North Carolina	•	•		•	•	
DB	**Fred Weary**	5-10	180	Sr.	Florida		•	•	•		•
DB	**Brian Lee**	6-2	200	Sr.	Wyoming	•	•		•	•	
P	**Chad Kessler**	6-1	197	Sr.	LSU	•	•	•			

Others receiving first-team honors

POS	Name	School	AP	CF	FC	FN	FW	SN
DL	Lamanzer Williams	Minnesota					•	
DL	Jeremy Staat	Arizona State					•	
DL	Glen Steele	Michigan			•			
DL	Kailee Wong	Stanford				•		
LB	Leonard Little	Tennessee		•				
LB	Jamie Duncan	Vanderbilt			•		•	
LB	Ron Warner	Kansas				•		
LB	Takeo Spikes	Auburn						•
LB	Pat Tillman	Arizona State						•
DB	Anthony Poindexter	Virginia						•
DB	Antoine Winfield	Ohio State			•		•	
DB	Donovin Darins	Syracuse	•		•			•

Heisman Trophy Voting

	Player	POS	School	1st	2nd	3rd	Total
1	**Charles Woodson**	CB	Michigan	433	209	98	1815
2	**Peyton Manning**	QB	Tennessee	281	263	174	1543
3	**Ryan Leaf**	QB	Washington State	70	203	241	861
4	**Randy Moss**	WR	Marshall	17	56	90	253
5	**Ricky Williams**	RB	Texas	4	31	61	135
6	**Curtis Enis**	RB	Penn State	3	18	20	65
7	**Tim Dwight**	WR	Iowa	5	3	11	32
8	**Cade McNown**	QB	UCLA	0	7	12	26
9	**Tim Couch**	QB	Kentucky	0	5	12	22
10	**Amos Zereoue**	RB	West Virginia	3	1	10	21

Award Winners

Peyton Manning, QB, Tennessee, Maxwell, O'Brien, Unitas **Aaron Taylor**, OG, Nebraska, Outland, **Charles Woodson**, DB, Michigan, Camp, Nagurski, Bednarik, Thorpe **Grant Wistrom**, DE, Nebraska, Lombardi, **Andy Katzenmoyer**, LB, Ohio State, Butkus, **Ricky Williams, RB**, Texas, Walker, **Martin Gramatica**, K, Kansas State, Groza, **Randy Moss**, WR, Marshall, Biletnikoff, **Brock Olivo**, RB, Missouri, Tatupu

Conference Standings

ACC	Conf. W	L	T	Overall W	L	T
Florida State	8	0	0	11	1	0
North Carolina	7	1	0	11	1	0
Virginia	5	3	0	7	4	0
Georgia Tech	5	3	0	7	5	0
Clemson	4	4	0	7	5	0
North Carolina St.	3	5	0	6	5	0
Wake Forest	3	5	0	5	6	0
Maryland	1	7	0	2	9	0
Duke	0	8	0	2	9	0

Big 10	Conf. W	L	T	Overall W	L	T
Michigan	8	0	0	12	0	0
Ohio State	6	2	0	10	3	0
Purdue	6	2	0	9	3	0
Penn State	6	2	0	9	3	0
Wisconsin	5	3	0	8	5	0
Iowa	4	4	0	7	5	0
Michigan State	4	4	0	7	5	0
Northwestern	3	5	0	5	7	0
Minnesota	1	7	0	3	9	0
Indiana	1	7	0	2	9	0
Illinois	0	8	0	0	11	0

Big 12	Conf. W	L	T	Overall W	L	T
NORTH						
Nebraska	8	0	0	13	0	0
Kansas State	7	1	0	11	1	0
Missouri	5	3	0	7	5	0
Kansas	3	5	0	5	6	0
Colorado	3	5	0	5	6	0
Iowa State	1	7	0	1	10	0
SOUTH						
Texas A&M	6	2	0	9	4	0
Oklahoma State	5	3	0	8	4	0
Texas Tech	5	3	0	6	5	0
Texas	2	6	0	4	7	0
Oklahoma	2	6	0	4	8	0
Baylor	1	7	0	2	9	0

Championship **Nebraska 54 Texas A&M 15**

Big East	Conf. W	L	T	Overall W	L	T
Syracuse	6	1	0	9	4	0
Virginia Tech	5	2	0	7	5	0
West Virginia	4	3	0	7	5	0
Pittsburgh	4	3	0	6	6	0
Miami, Fla.	3	4	0	5	6	0
Boston College	3	4	0	4	7	0
Temple	3	4	0	3	8	0
Rutgers	0	7	0	0	11	0

Big West	Conf. W	L	T	Overall W	L	T
Utah State	4	1	0	6	6	0
Nevada	4	1	0	5	6	0
Boise State	3	2	0	4	7	0
Idaho	2	3	0	5	6	0
North Texas	2	3	0	4	7	0
New Mexico State	0	5	0	2	9	0

C-USA	Conf. W	L	T	Overall W	L	T
Southern Miss	6	0	0	9	3	0
Tulane	5	1	0	7	4	0
East Carolina	4	2	0	5	6	0
Cincinnati	2	4	0	8	4	0
Memphis	2	4	0	4	7	0
Houston	2	4	0	3	8	0
Louisville	0	6	0	1	10	0

Ivy	Conf. W	L	T	Overall W	L	T
Harvard	7	0	0	9	1	0
Dartmouth	6	1	0	8	2	0
Pennsylvania	5	2	0	6	4	0
Brown	3	4	0	6	4	0
Cornell	3	4	0	5	5	0
Princeton	2	5	0	5	5	0
Columbia	2	5	0	3	7	0
Yale	0	7	0	1	9	0

MAC	Conf. W	L	T	Overall W	L	T
EAST						
Marshall	7	1	0	10	3	0
Miami, Ohio	6	2	0	8	3	0
Ohio U	6	2	0	8	3	0
Kent State	3	5	0	3	8	0
Bowling Green	3	5	0	3	8	0
Akron	2	7	0	2	9	0
WEST						
Toledo	7	1	0	9	3	0
Western Michigan	6	2	0	8	3	0
Ball State	4	4	0	5	6	0
Eastern Michigan	4	5	0	4	7	0
Central Michigan	1	7	0	2	9	0
Northern Illinois	0	8	0	0	11	0

Championship **Marshall 34 Toledo 14**

Pac 10	Conf. W	L	T	Overall W	L	T
Washington State	7	1	0	10	2	0
UCLA	7	1	0	10	2	0
Arizona State	6	2	0	9	3	0
Washington	5	3	0	8	4	0
Arizona	4	4	0	7	5	0
Southern Cal	4	4	0	6	5	0
Oregon	3	5	0	7	5	0
Stanford	3	5	0	5	6	0
California	1	7	0	3	8	0
Oregon State	0	8	0	3	8	0

SEC	Conf. W	L	T	Overall W	L	T
EAST						
Tennessee	7	1	0	11	2	0
Georgia	6	2	0	10	2	0
Florida	6	2	0	10	2	0
South Carolina	3	5	0	5	6	0
Kentucky	2	6	0	5	6	0
Vanderbilt	0	8	0	3	8	0
WEST						
Auburn	6	2	0	10	3	0
LSU	6	2	0	9	3	0
Mississippi	4	4	0	8	4	0
Mississippi State	4	4	0	7	4	0
Alabama	2	6	0	4	7	0
Arkansas	2	6	0	4	7	0

Championship **Tennessee 30 Auburn 29**

WAC	Conf. W	L	T	Overall W	L	T
MOUNTAIN						
New Mexico	6	2	0	9	4	0
Rice	5	3	0	7	4	0
Utah	5	3	0	6	5	0
SMU	5	3	0	6	5	0
Brigham Young	4	4	0	6	5	0
Texas-El Paso	3	5	0	4	7	0
Tulsa	2	6	0	2	9	0
TCU	1	7	0	1	10	0
PACIFIC						
Colorado State	7	1	0	11	2	0
Air Force	6	2	0	10	3	0
Fresno State	5	3	0	6	6	0
Wyoming	4	4	0	7	6	0
San Diego State	4	4	0	5	7	0
San Jose State	4	4	0	4	7	0
Nevada-Las Vegas	2	6	0	3	8	0
Hawaii	1	7	0	3	9	0

Independents	Overall W	L	T
Louisiana Tech	9	2	0
Navy	7	4	0
Notre Dame	7	6	0
UAB	5	6	0
Central Florida	5	6	0
La. Monroe	5	7	0
Army	4	7	0
Arkansas State	2	9	0
La. Lafayette	1	10	0

Bowl Games

D20, **Las Vegas**, Oregon 41, Air Force 13, D25, **Aloha**, Washington 51, Michigan State 23, D26, **Motor City**, Mississippi 34, Marshall 31, D27, **Copper**, Arizona 20, New Mexico 14, D28, **Independence**, LSU 27, Notre Dame 9, D29, **Humanitarian**, Cincinnati 35, Utah State 19, D29, **Holiday**, Colorado State 35, Missouri 24, D29, **Carquest**, Georgia Tech 35, West Virginia 30, D30, **Alamo**, Purdue 33, Oklahoma State 20, D31, **Sun**, Arizona State 17, Iowa 7, D31, **Fiesta**, Kansas State 35, Syracuse 18, D31, **Liberty**, Southern Miss 41, Pittsburgh 7, J1, **Florida Citrus**, Florida 21, Penn State 6, J1, **Outback**, Georgia 33, Wisconsin 6, J1, **Rose**, Michigan 21, Washington State 16, J1, **Gator**, North Carolina 42, Virginia Tech 3, J1, **Cotton**, UCLA 29, Texas A&M 23, J1, **Sugar**, Florida State 31, Ohio State 14, J2, **Peach**, Auburn 21, Clemson 17, J2, **Orange**, Nebraska 42, Tennessee 17

1997 NCAA Major College Statistical Leaders

Individual Leaders

PASSING		CL	G	ATT	COM	PCT	INT	I%	YDS	YPA	TD	TD%	RATING
1	Cade McNown, UCLA	JR	11	283	173	61.1	5	1.8	2877	10.2	22	7.8	168.6
2	Ryan Leaf, Washington State	JR	11	375	210	56.0	10	2.7	3637	9.7	33	8.8	161.2
3	Joe Germaine, Ohio State	SR	12	184	119	64.7	7	3.8	1674	9.1	15	8.2	160.4
4	John Dutton, Nevada	SR	11	367	225	61.3	6	1.6	3526	9.6	20	5.5	156.7
5	Brock Huard, Washington	SO	10	244	146	59.8	10	4.1	2140	8.8	23	9.4	156.4
6	Mike Bobo, Georgia	SR	11	306	199	65.0	8	2.6	2751	9.0	19	6.2	155.8
7	Donovan McNabb, Syracuse	JR	12	265	145	54.7	6	2.3	2488	9.4	20	7.6	154.0
8	Graham Leigh, New Mexico	JR	12	276	166	60.1	8	2.9	2318	8.4	24	8.7	153.6
9	Moses Moreno, Colorado State	SR	12	257	157	61.1	9	3.5	2257	8.8	20	7.8	153.5
10	Chad Pennington, Marshall	SO	12	428	253	59.1	12	2.8	3480	8.1	39	9.1	151.9

ALL-PURPOSE		CL	G	RUSH	REC	PR	KR	YDS	YPG
1	Troy Edwards, Louisiana Tech	JR	11	190	1707	6	241	2144	194.9
2	Ricky Williams, Texas	JR	11	1893	150	0	0	2043	185.7
3	Kevin Faulk, LSU	JR	9	1144	93	192	217	1646	182.9
4	Randy Moss, Marshall	SO	12	2	1647	266	263	2178	181.5
5	Michael Perry, Rice	JR	10	1034	44	26	680	1784	178.4
6	Tutu Atwell, Minnesota	SR	12	77	924	296	776	2073	172.8
7	Jerome Pathon, Washington	SR	11	0	1245	209	386	1840	167.3
8	Tavian Banks, Iowa	SR	11	1639	200	0	0	1839	167.2
9	Ahman Green, Nebraska	JR	12	1877	105	0	0	1982	165.2
10	Sedrick Irvin, Michigan State	SO	11	1211	339	263	0	1813	164.8

RUSHING/Yards Per Game		CL	G	ATT	YDS	TD	AVG	YPG
1	Ricky Williams, Texas	JR	11	279	1893	25	6.8	172.1
2	Ahman Green, Nebraska	JR	12	278	1877	22	6.8	156.4
3	Amos Zereoue, West Virginia	SO	10	264	1505	16	5.7	150.5
4	Tavian Banks, Iowa	SR	11	246	1639	17	6.7	149.0
5	Ron Dayne, Wisconsin	SO	10	249	1421	15	5.7	142.1
6	Travis Prentice, Miami, Ohio	SO	11	296	1549	25	5.2	140.8
7	Dwayne Harris, Toledo	JR	10	254	1278	10	5.0	127.8
8	Kevin Faulk, LSU	JR	9	205	1144	15	5.6	127.1
9	Demond Parker, Oklahoma	SO	9	194	1143	6	5.9	127.0
10	Chris McCoy, Navy	SR	11	246	1370	20	5.6	124.6

RUSHING/Yards Per Carry		CL	G	ATT	YDS	YPC
1	Kevin McDougal, Colorado State	SO	12	150	1111	7.4
2	Ricky Williams, Texas	JR	11	279	1893	6.8
3	Ahman Green, Nebraska	JR	12	278	1877	6.8
4	Tavian Banks, Iowa	SR	11	246	1639	6.7
5	Mike Cloud, Boston College	JR	10	137	886	6.5
6	Michael Perry, Rice	JR	10	162	1034	6.4
7	Scott Frost, Nebraska	SR	12	176	1095	6.2
8	Damon Washington, Colorado State	JR	12	180	1112	6.2
9	J.R. Redmond, Arizona State	SO	10	142	865	6.1
10	Fred Taylor, Florida	SR	11	214	1292	6.0

*-Based on top 50 rushers

RECEIVING		CL	G	REC	YDS	TD	RPG	YPR	YPG
1	Troy Edwards, Louisiana Tech	JR	11	102	1707	13	9.3	16.7	155.2
2	Eugene Baker, Kent	JR	11	103	1549	18	9.4	15.0	140.8
3	Randy Moss, Marshall	SO	12	90	1647	25	7.5	18.3	137.3
4	Jerome Pathon, Washington	SR	11	69	1245	8	6.3	18.0	113.2
5	Troy Walters, Stanford	JR	11	86	1206	8	7.8	14.0	109.6
6	Geoff Noisy, Nevada	SR	11	86	1184	5	7.8	13.8	107.6
7	Brian Alford, Purdue	SR	11	59	1167	9	5.4	19.8	106.1
8	Trevor Insley, Nevada	SO	11	59	1151	6	5.4	19.5	104.6
9	Pascal Volz, New Mexico	SR	12	69	1229	13	5.8	17.8	102.4
10	Siaha Burley, Central Florida	JR	11	77	1106	7	7.0	14.4	100.6

PUNTING		CL	PUNT	YDS	AVG
1	Chad Kessler, LSU	SR	39	1961	50.3
2	John Baker, North Texas	SO	62	2925	47.2
3	Shane Lechler, Texas A&M	SO	56	2631	47.0
4	Brad Hill, Tulane	SR	42	1940	46.2
5	Chad Shrout, Hawaii	SO	68	3133	46.1
6	Rodney Williams, Georgia Tech	JR	47	2145	45.6
7	Jeff Walker, Mississippi State	SO	45	2049	45.5
8	Aron Langley, Wyoming	JR	79	3568	45.2
9	Brent Bartholomew, Ohio State	JR	65	2934	45.1
10	Jimmy Kibble, Virginia Tech	SO	50	2255	45.1

PUNT RETURNS		CL	PR	YDS	TD	AVG
1	Tim Dwight, Iowa	SR	19	367	3	19.3
2	R.W. McQuarters, Oklahoma State	JR	32	521	1	16.3
3	Steve Smith, Utah State	SR	22	344	2	15.6
4	Nod Washington, Miami, Ohio	JR	12	185	0	15.4
5	Geoff Turner, Colorado State	SR	20	304	1	15.2
6	Dee Feaster, Florida State	JR	14	210	0	15.0
7	Quinton Spotwood, Syracuse	SO	31	463	4	14.9
8	Tinker Keck, Cincinnati	JR	39	575	4	14.7
9	Steve Neal, Western Michigan	SO	14	204	1	14.6
10	Jacquez Green, Florida	JR	27	392	2	14.5

KICKOFF RETURNS		CL	KR	YDS	TD	AVG
1	Eric Booth, Southern Miss	SR	22	766	2	34.8
2	Ben Kelly, Colorado	FR	25	777	1	31.1
3	Pat McGrew, Navy	SR	15	441	0	29.4
4	Boo Williams, South Carolina	SO	18	527	2	29.3
5	Pat Johnson, Oregon	SR	16	462	0	28.9
6	Allen Rossum, Notre Dame	SR	20	570	2	28.5
7	Ketrick Sanford, Houston	SO	19	530	0	27.9
8	Tony Horne, Clemson	SR	18	491	0	27.3
9	Damon Dunn, Stanford	SR	21	566	0	27.0
10	Tyrone Carter, Minnesota	SO	17	455	0	26.8

SCORING		CL	TDS	XP	FG	PTS	PTPG
1	Ricky Williams, Texas	JR	25	2	0	152	13.8
2	Skip Hicks, UCLA	SR	25	0	0	150	13.6
2	Travis Prentice, Miami, Ohio	SO	25	0	0	150	13.6
4	Randy Moss, Marshall	SO	25	2	0	152	12.7
5	Curtis Enis, Penn State	JR	20	2	0	122	11.1
6	Ahman Green, Nebraska	JR	22	0	0	132	11.0
7	Chris McCoy, Navy	SR	20	0	0	120	10.9
8	Tavian Banks, Iowa	SR	19	0	0	114	10.4
8	Chris Lemon, Nevada	SO	19	0	0	114	10.4
10	Eugene Baker, Kent	JR	18	2	0	110	10.0
10	Kevin Faulk, LSU	JR	15	0	0	90	10.0

FIELD GOALS		CL	FGA	FGM	PCT	FGG
1	Brad Palazzo, Tulane	JR	28	23	0.82	2.09
2	Colby Cason New Mexico	SR	30	21	0.70	1.75
3	Martin Gramatica, Kansas State	JR	20	19	0.95	1.73
3	Shayne Graham, Virginia Tech	SO	23	19	0.83	1.73
3	Chris Sailer, UCLA	JR	24	19	0.79	1.73
6	Brian Gowins, Northwestern	SR	27	20	0.74	1.67
7	Kris Brown, Nebraska	JR	21	18	0.86	1.50
7	Kyle Bryant, Texas A&M	SR	22	18	0.82	1.50
9	Sims Lenhardt, Duke	SO	20	16	0.80	1.45
9	Sebastian Janikowski, Florida State	FR	21	16	0.76	1.45
9	Sebastian Villarreal, Houston	SR	21	16	0.76	1.45
9	Robert Nycz, Arizona State	SR	23	16	0.70	1.45
9	Brian Hazelwood, Mississippi State	JR	26	16	0.62	1.45

INTERCEPTIONS		CL	INT	YDS	TD	INT/GM
1	Brian Lee, Wyoming	SR	8	103	1	0.73
2	Cedric Donaldson, LSU	SR	7	192	2	0.64
2	John Noel, Louisiana Tech	SR	7	93	0	0.64
2	Omarr Smith, San Jose State	JR	7	80	0	0.64
2	Tevell Jones, Ohio	SR	7	36	0	0.64
2	Samari Rolle, Florida State	SR	7	32	0	0.64
2	Charles Woodson, Michigan	JR	7	7	0	0.64
8	Donovin Darius, Syracuse	SR	7	56	0	0.58
9	Paul Jackson, Maryland	JR	5	14	0	0.56
10	Patrick Surtain, Southern Miss *	SR	6	127	0	0.55
10	Efrain Guizar, Fresno State *	JR	6	114	2	0.55
10	Fred Weary, Florida *	SR	6	113	0	0.55
10	Kevin Williams, Oklahoma State *	SR	6	107	1	0.55
10	Arturo Freeman, South Carolina *	JR	6	95	1	0.55

* Ten tied with 0.55; these had the most yards.

Team Leaders

RUSHING OFFENSE		G	ATT	YDS	AVG	TD	YPG
1	Nebraska	12	755	4711	6.2	66	392.6
2	Rice	11	690	3660	5.3	38	332.7
3	Navy	11	618	3370	5.5	36	306.4
4	Ohio	11	649	3321	5.1	32	301.9
5	Army	11	670	3247	4.8	24	295.2
6	Missouri	11	592	2899	4.9	35	263.5
7	LSU	11	521	2823	5.4	34	256.6
8	Iowa	11	492	2585	5.3	25	235.0
9	Air Force	12	688	2791	4.1	22	232.6
10	Oklahoma State	11	592	2486	4.2	25	226.0

PASSING OFFENSE		G	ATT	COM	INT	PCT	YDS	YPA	TD	I%	YPC	YPG
1	Nevada	11	443	265	11	59.8	4072	9.2	21	2.5	15.4	370.2
2	Kentucky	11	562	374	19	66.5	4019	7.2	37	3.4	10.7	365.4
3	Louisiana Tech	11	495	301	11	60.8	3965	8.0	34	2.2	13.2	360.5
4	Washington State	11	400	223	12	55.8	3789	9.5	34	3.0	17.0	344.5
5	Florida State	11	440	262	11	59.5	3740	8.5	30	2.5	14.3	340.0
6	Tennessee	12	492	296	12	60.2	3981	8.1	37	2.4	13.4	331.8
7	Marshall	12	450	264	13	58.7	3688	8.2	41	2.9	14.0	307.3
8	Eastern Michigan	11	438	250	11	57.1	3314	7.6	23	2.5	13.3	301.3
9	Louisville	11	473	276	14	58.4	3282	6.9	19	3.0	11.9	298.4
10	Kent	11	451	235	16	52.1	3243	7.2	35	3.6	13.8	294.8

TOTAL OFFENSE		G	P	YDS	AVG	TD	YPG
1	Nebraska	12	937	6164	6.6	71	513.7
2	Washington State	11	808	5524	6.8	60	502.2
3	Louisiana Tech	11	813	5456	6.7	48	496.0
4	Tennessee	12	890	5794	6.5	50	482.8
5	Nevada	11	796	5272	6.6	45	479.3
6	Kentucky	11	876	5214	6.0	45	474.0
7	Purdue	11	794	5056	6.4	42	459.6
8	Florida State	11	784	4973	6.3	49	452.1
9	Utah State	11	835	4933	5.9	45	448.5
10	Marshall	12	832	5339	6.4	58	444.9

RUSHING DEFENSE		G	ATT	YDS	AVG	TD	YPG
1	Florida State	11	379	571	1.5	10	51.9
2	Florida	11	362	778	2.1	12	70.7
3	Nebraska	12	407	881	2.2	12	73.4
4	North Carolina	11	371	857	2.3	5	77.9
5	Cincinnati	11	338	930	2.8	10	84.5
6	Clemson	11	362	971	2.7	10	88.3
7	Michigan	11	368	1001	2.7	6	91.0
8	Tennessee	12	382	1119	2.9	11	93.3
9	Southern Cal	11	381	1032	2.7	12	93.8
10	Wake Forest	11	364	1057	2.9	11	96.1

PASSING DEFENSE		G	ATT	COM	PCT	INT	I%	YDS	YPA	TD	TD%	RAT
1	Michigan	11	292	145	49.7	22	7.5	1275	4.4	4	1.4	75.8
2	Ohio State	12	360	160	44.4	19	5.3	1724	4.8	6	1.7	79.6
3	North Carolina	11	322	148	46.0	15	4.7	1445	4.5	7	2.2	81.5
4	Iowa	11	325	146	44.9	22	6.8	1766	5.4	12	3.7	89.2
5	Kansas State	11	239	99	41.4	5	2.1	1396	5.8	4	1.7	91.8
6	Wyoming	13	374	169	45.2	24	6.4	2358	6.3	11	2.9	95.0
7	Marshall	12	322	146	45.3	15	4.7	1948	6.1	8	2.5	95.0
8	New Mexico	12	333	153	46.0	16	4.8	1989	6.0	10	3.0	96.4
9	UAB	11	337	159	47.2	17	5.0	1912	5.7	12	3.6	96.5
10	Florida State	11	338	164	48.5	22	6.5	2084	6.2	12	3.6	99.0

TOTAL DEFENSE		G	P	YDS	AVG	TD	YPG
1	Michigan	11	660	2276	3.4	10	206.9
2	North Carolina	11	693	2302	3.3	12	209.3
3	Florida State	11	717	2655	3.7	22	241.4
4	Kansas State	11	702	2825	4.0	17	256.8
5	Nebraska	12	717	3088	4.3	25	257.3
6	Navy	11	642	2863	4.5	24	260.3
7	Iowa	11	733	2927	4.0	18	266.1
8	Ohio State	12	820	3215	3.9	13	267.9
9	Vanderbilt	11	704	3026	4.3	22	275.1
10	Air Force	12	756	3471	4.6	16	289.3

SCORING OFFENSE		G	PTS	AVG
1	Nebraska	12	565	47.1
2	Washington State	11	467	42.5
3	UCLA	11	448	40.7
4	Florida State	11	437	39.7
5	Marshall	12	453	37.8
6	Miami, Ohio	11	412	37.5
7	Florida	11	409	37.2
8	Colorado State	12	442	36.8
9	Iowa	11	404	36.7
10	Navy	11	398	36.2

SCORING DEFENSE		G	PTS	AVG
1	Michigan	11	98	8.9
2	Ohio State	12	139	11.6
3	Air Force	12	149	12.4
4	Iowa	11	142	12.9
5	North Carolina	11	143	13.0
6	Kansas State	11	159	14.5
7	Colorado State	12	179	14.9
8	Florida State	11	167	15.2
9	Syracuse	12	191	15.9
10	Ohio	11	177	16.1

TURNOVER MARGIN		G	FR	INT	TOT	FL	INTL	TOT	MAR
1	Colorado State	12	20	18	38	4	9	13	2.1
2	UCLA	11	18	21	39	14	5	19	1.8
3	Texas A&M	12	22	11	33	1	14	15	1.5
4	Florida State	11	10	22	32	6	11	17	1.4
5	Tulane	11	8	26	34	6	14	20	1.3
6	SMU	11	12	15	27	7	7	14	1.2
6	Oklahoma State	11	14	15	29	8	8	16	1.2
6	Navy	11	13	14	27	6	8	14	1.2
9	Texas Tech	11	13	13	26	8	6	14	1.1
9	Purdue	11	11	20	31	5	14	19	1.1
9	LSU	11	12	14	26	7	7	14	1.1

1998 Poll Progression

Pre-Season 1998 — Sept. 5 Games

AP	Team	Record	Result
1	Ohio State	0-0	beat # 11 West Virginia 34-17
2	Florida State	0-0	bye week
3	Florida	0-0	beat Citadel 49-10
4	Nebraska	0-0	beat UAB 38-7
5	Michigan	0-0	lost to # 22 Notre Dame 20-36
6	Kansas State	0-0	beat Indiana St. 66-0
7	UCLA	0-0	bye week
8	Arizona State	0-0	lost to # 18 Washington 38-42
9	LSU	0-0	bye week
10	Tennessee	0-0	beat # 17 Syracuse 34-33
11	West Virginia	0-0	lost to # 1 Ohio State 17-34
12	North Carolina	0-0	lost to Miami, Ohio 10-13
13	Penn State	0-0	beat # 21 Southern Miss 34-6
14	Texas A&M	0-0	bye week
15	Colorado State	0-0	lost to Colorado 14-42
16	Virginia	0-0	beat # 25 Auburn 19-0 (S3)
17	Syracuse	0-0	lost to # 10 Tennessee 33-34
18	Washington	0-0	beat # 8 Arizona State 42-28
19	Georgia	0-0	beat Kent State 56-3
20	Wisconsin	0-0	beat San Diego State 26-14
21	Southern Miss	0-0	lost to # 13 Penn State 6-34
22	Notre Dame	0-0	beat # 5 Michigan 36-20
23	Michigan State	0-0	lost to Oregon 14-48
24	Arizona	0-0	beat Hawaii 27-6 (S3)
25	Auburn	0-0	lost to # 16 Virginia 0-19 (S3)

September 6 Poll — Sept. 12 Games

ESPN	AP	Team	Record	Result
1	1	Ohio State	1-0	beat Toledo 49-0
2	2	Florida State	1-0	lost to North Carolina St. 7-24
4	3	Florida	1-0	beat La. Monroe 42-10
3	4	Nebraska	2-0	beat California 24-3
5	5	Kansas State	1-0	beat No. Illinois 73-7
6	6	UCLA	0-0	beat # 23 Texas 49-31
8	7	LSU	0-0	beat Arkansas State 42-6
7	8	Tennessee	1-0	bye week
9	9	Penn State	1-0	beat Bowling Green 48-3
11	10	Notre Dame	1-0	lost to Michigan State 23-45
10	11	Washington	1-0	bye week
12	12	Virginia	1-0	beat Maryland 31-19
14	13	Michigan	0-1	lost to # 19 Syracuse 28-38
15	14	Arizona State	0-1	lost to Brigham Young 6-26
13	15	Georgia	1-0	beat South Carolina 17-3
16	16	Colorado	1-0	beat Fresno State 29-21
17	17	Wisconsin	1-0	beat Ohio U 45-0
19	18	Texas A&M	0-1	beat Louisiana Tech 28-7
18	19	Syracuse	0-1	beat # 13 Michigan 38-28
20	20	West Virginia	0-1	bye week
21	21	Arizona	1-0	beat Stanford 31-14
23	22	Southern Cal	1-0	beat San Diego State 35-6
22	23	Texas	1-0	lost to # 6 UCLA 31-49
	24	Oregon	1-0	beat Texas-El Paso 33-26
25	25	Missouri	1-0	beat Kansas 41-23
24		North Carolina	0-1	bye week

September 13 Poll — Sept. 19 Games

ESPN	AP	Team	Record	Result
1	1	Ohio State	2-0	beat # 21 Missouri 35-14
2	2	Florida	2-0	lost to # 6 Tennessee 17-20
3	3	Nebraska	3-0	bye week
5	4	UCLA	1-0	beat Houston 42-24
4	5	Kansas State	2-0	beat Texas 48-7
6	6	Tennessee	1-0	beat # 2 Florida 20-17
7	7	LSU	1-0	beat Auburn 31-19
8	8	Penn State	2-0	beat Pittsburgh 20-13
9	9	Washington	1-0	beat Brigham Young 20-10
10	10	Virginia	2-0	beat Clemson 20-18
11	11	Florida State	1-1	beat Duke 62-13
12	12	Georgia	2-0	beat Wyoming 16-9
13	13	Syracuse	1-1	beat Rutgers 70-14
14	14	Wisconsin	2-0	beat Nevada-Las Vegas 52-7
15	15	Colorado	2-0	beat Utah State 25-6
17	16	Arizona	2-0	beat Iowa 35-11
18	17	Texas A&M	1-1	beat Southern Miss 24-6
16	18	Southern Cal	2-0	beat Oregon State 40-20
20	19	West Virginia	0-1	beat Maryland 42-20
24	20	North Carolina St.	2-0	lost to Baylor 30-33
19	21	Missouri	2-0	lost to # 1 Ohio State 14-35
23	22	Oregon	2-0	beat San Jose State 58-3
25	23	Notre Dame	1-1	bye week
22	24	Alabama	2-0	bye week
	25	Mississippi State	2-0	lost to Oklahoma State 23-42
21		Virginia Tech	2-0	beat Miami, Fla. 27-20

September 20 Poll — Sept. 26 Games

ESPN	AP	Team	Record	Result
1	1	Ohio State	3-0	bye week
2	2	Nebraska	3-0	beat # 9 Washington 55-7
5	3	UCLA	2-0	bye week
4	4	Tennessee	2-0	beat Houston 42-7
3	5	Kansas State	3-0	beat La. Monroe 62-7
6	6	LSU	2-0	beat Idaho 53-20
7	7	Penn State	3-0	bye week
9	8	Florida	2-1	beat Kentucky 51-35
8	9	Washington	2-0	lost to # 2 Nebraska 7-55
11	10	Florida State	2-1	beat # 18 Southern Cal 30-10
10	11	Virginia	3-0	beat Duke 24-0
13	12	Syracuse	2-1	bye week
12	13	Georgia	3-0	bye week
14	14	Wisconsin	3-0	beat Northwestern 38-7
15	15	Colorado	3-0	beat Baylor 18-16
16	16	Arizona	3-0	beat San Diego State 35-16 (S24)
18	17	Texas A&M	2-1	beat North Texas 28-9
17	18	Southern Cal	3-0	lost to # 10 Florida State 10-30
20	19	West Virginia	1-1	beat Tulsa 44-21
21	20	Oregon	3-0	beat Stanford 63-28
19	21	Virginia Tech	3-0	beat Pittsburgh 27-7
22	22	Alabama	2-0	lost to Arkansas 6-42
23	23	Air Force	3-0	lost to TCU 34-35
	24	Notre Dame	1-1	beat Purdue 31-30
24	25	Missouri	2-1	bye week
25		Kentucky	3-0	lost to # 8 Florida 35-51

September 27 Poll — Oct. 3 Games

ESPN	AP	Team	Record	Result
1	1	Ohio State	3-0	beat # 7 Penn State 28-9
2	2	Nebraska	4-0	beat Oklahoma State 24-17
5	3	Tennessee	3-0	beat Auburn 17-9
4	4	UCLA	2-0	beat Washington State 49-17
3	5	Kansas State	4-0	bye week
6	6	LSU	3-0	lost to # 12 Georgia 27-28
7	7	Penn State	3-0	lost to # 1 Ohio State 9-28
8	8	Florida	3-1	beat Alabama 16-10
10	9	Florida State	3-1	beat Maryland 24-10
9	10	Virginia	4-0	beat San Jose State 52-14
11	11	Syracuse	2-1	lost to North Carolina St. 17-38 (O1)
12	12	Georgia	3-0	beat # 6 LSU 28-27
13	13	Wisconsin	4-0	beat Indiana 24-20
14	14	Arizona	4-0	beat # 20 Washington 31-28
15	15	Colorado	4-0	beat Oklahoma 27-25
17	16	West Virginia	2-1	beat Navy 45-24
17	17	Oregon	4-0	bye week
18	18	Texas A&M	3-1	beat Kansas 24-21
16	19	Virginia Tech	4-0	bye week
20	20	Washington	2-1	lost to # 14 Arizona 28-31
22	21	Southern Cal	3-1	beat Arizona State 35-24
24	22	Arkansas	3-0	beat Kentucky 27-20
21	23	Missouri	2-1	beat Northwestern St. 35-14
23	24	Notre Dame	2-1	beat Stanford 35-17
	25	Michigan	2-2	beat Iowa 12-9
25		Tulane	3-0	beat Southern Miss 21-7

October 4 Poll — Oct. 10 Games

ESPN	AP	Team	Record	Result
1	1	Ohio State	4-0	beat Illinois 41-0
2	2	Nebraska	5-0	lost to # 18 Texas A&M 21-28
3	3	UCLA	3-0	beat # 10 Arizona 52-28
5	4	Tennessee	4-0	beat # 7 Georgia 22-3
4	5	Kansas State	4-0	beat # 14 Colorado 16-9
6	6	Florida	4-1	beat # 11 LSU 22-10
7	7	Georgia	4-0	lost to # 4 Tennessee 3-22
9	8	Florida State	4-1	beat Miami, Fla. 26-14
8	9	Virginia	5-0	bye week
11	10	Arizona	5-0	lost to # 3 UCLA 28-52
12	11	LSU	3-1	lost to # 6 Florida 10-22
10	12	Wisconsin	5-0	beat Purdue 31-24
13	13	Penn State	3-1	beat Minnesota 27-17
14	14	Colorado	5-0	lost to # 5 Kansas State 9-16
16	15	Oregon	4-0	beat Washington State 51-29
17	16	West Virginia	3-1	beat Temple 37-7
15	17	Virginia Tech	4-0	beat Boston College 17-0 (O8)
18	18	Texas A&M	4-1	beat # 2 Nebraska 28-21
20	19	Southern Cal	4-1	lost to California 31-32
19	20	Arkansas	4-0	beat Memphis 23-9
21	21	Missouri	3-1	beat Iowa State 35-19
22	22	Notre Dame	3-1	beat Arizona State 28-9
23	23	North Carolina St.	3-1	lost to Georgia Tech 24-47
24	24	Syracuse	2-2	beat Cincinnati 63-21
25	25	Tulane	4-0	bye week

October 11 Poll — Oct. 17 Games

ESPN	AP	Team	Record	Result
1	1	Ohio State	5-0	beat Minnesota 45-15
2	2	UCLA	4-0	beat # 11 Oregon 41-38
4	3	Tennessee	5-0	bye week
3	4	Kansas State	5-0	beat Oklahoma State 52-20
5	5	Florida	5-1	beat Auburn 24-3
7	6	Florida State	5-1	beat Clemson 48-0
6	7	Virginia	5-0	lost to # 25 Georgia Tech 38-41
8	8	Nebraska	5-1	beat Kansas 41-0
9	9	Wisconsin	6-0	beat Illinois 37-3
13	10	Texas A&M	5-1	beat Baylor 35-14
12	11	Oregon	5-0	lost to # 2 UCLA 38-41
11	12	Penn State	4-1	beat Purdue 31-13
14	13	Georgia	4-1	beat Vanderbilt 31-6
10	14	Virginia Tech	5-0	lost to Temple 24-28
15	15	West Virginia	4-1	bye week
17	16	Arizona	5-1	beat Oregon State 28-7
16	17	Arkansas	5-0	beat South Carolina 41-28
20	18	Notre Dame	4-1	bye week
18	19	Colorado	5-1	beat # 22 Texas Tech 19-17
19	20	Missouri	4-1	beat Oklahoma 20-6
21	21	LSU	3-2	lost to Kentucky 36-39
23	22	Texas Tech	6-0	lost to # 19 Colorado 17-19
22	23	Syracuse	3-2	beat Boston College 42-25
24	24	Tulane	4-0	beat Louisville 28-22
25	25	Georgia Tech	4-1	beat # 7 Virginia 41-38

October 18 Poll — Oct. 24 Games

ESPN	AP	Team	Record	Result
1	1	Ohio State	6-0	beat Northwestern 36-10
2	2	UCLA	5-0	beat California 28-16
4	3	Tennessee	5-0	beat Alabama 35-18
3	4	Kansas State	6-0	beat Iowa State 52-7
5	5	Florida	6-1	bye week
6	6	Florida State	6-1	beat # 20 Georgia Tech 34-7
7	7	Nebraska	6-1	beat # 19 Missouri 20-13
10	8	Texas A&M	6-1	beat # 25 Texas Tech 17-10
8	9	Wisconsin	7-0	beat Iowa 31-0
9	10	Penn State	5-1	bye week
11	11	Georgia	5-1	beat Kentucky 28-26
14	12	Oregon	5-1	beat Southern Cal 17-13
13	13	West Virginia	4-1	lost to Miami, Fla. 31-34
16	14	Arizona	6-1	beat La. Monroe 45-7
12	15	Arkansas	6-0	bye week
15	16	Virginia	5-1	beat North Carolina St. 23-13
17	17	Colorado	6-1	lost to Kansas 17-33
20	18	Notre Dame	4-1	beat Army 20-17
18	19	Missouri	5-1	lost to # 7 Nebraska 13-20
19	20	Georgia Tech	5-1	lost to # 6 Florida State 7-34
22	21	Syracuse	4-2	bye week
23	22	Tulane	5-0	beat Rutgers 52-24
21	23	Virginia Tech	5-1	beat UAB 41-0
24	24	Mississippi State	5-1	lost to LSU 6-41
25	25	Texas Tech	6-1	lost to # 8 Texas A&M 10-17

October 25 Poll — Oct. 31 Games

ESPN	AP	Team	Record	Result
1	1	Ohio State	7-0	beat Indiana 38-7
2	2	UCLA	6-0	beat Stanford 28-24
4	3	Tennessee	6-0	beat South Carolina 49-14
3	4	Kansas State	7-0	beat Kansas 54-6
6	5	Florida State	7-1	beat North Carolina 39-13
5	6	Florida	6-1	beat # 11 Georgia 38-7
7	7	Nebraska	7-1	lost to Texas 16-20
9	8	Texas A&M	7-1	beat Oklahoma State 17-6
8	9	Wisconsin	8-0	bye week
10	10	Penn State	5-1	beat Illinois 27-0
11	11	Georgia	6-1	lost to # 6 Florida 7-38
13	12	Oregon	6-1	lost to # 13 Arizona 3-38
15	13	Arizona	7-1	beat # 12 Oregon 38-3
12	14	Arkansas	6-0	beat Auburn 24-21
14	15	Virginia	6-1	beat Wake Forest 38-17
16	16	Notre Dame	5-1	beat Baylor 27-3
19	17	Syracuse	4-2	beat Pittsburgh 45-28
21	18	Missouri	5-2	beat Texas Tech 28-26
18	19	Tulane	6-0	beat La. Lafayette 72-20
17	20	Virginia Tech	6-1	beat # 21 West Virginia 27-13
20	21	West Virginia	4-2	lost to # 20 Virginia Tech 13-27
22	22	Michigan	5-2	beat Minnesota 15-10
24	23	Georgia Tech	5-2	beat Maryland 31-14
25	24	Colorado	6-2	bye week
	25	Miami, Fla.	4-2	beat Boston College 35-17
23		Air Force	6-1	beat SMU 31-7

November 1 Poll — Nov. 7 Games

ESPN	AP	Team	Record	Nov. 7 Games
1	1	Ohio State	8-0	lost to Michigan State 24-28
3	2	Tennessee	7-0	beat UAB 37-13
4	3	UCLA	7-0	beat Oregon State 41-34
2	4	Kansas State	8-0	beat Baylor 49-6
5	5	Florida	7-1	beat Vanderbilt 45-13
6	6	Florida State	8-1	beat # 12 Virginia 45-14
8	7	Texas A&M	8-1	beat Oklahoma 29-0
7	8	Wisconsin	8-0	beat Minnesota 26-7
9	9	Penn State	6-1	lost to # 22 Michigan 0-27
11	10	Arizona	8-1	beat Washington State 41-7
10	11	Arkansas	7-0	beat Mississippi 34-0
12	12	Virginia	7-1	lost to # 6 Florida State 14-45
13	13	Notre Dame	6-1	beat Boston College 31-26
15	14	Nebraska	7-2	beat Iowa State 42-7
17	15	Syracuse	5-2	lost to West Virginia 28-35
16	16	Tulane	7-0	beat Memphis 41-31
14	17	Virginia Tech	7-1	bye week
19	18	Missouri	6-2	beat Colorado 38-14
18	19	Georgia	6-2	bye week
23	20	Texas	6-2	beat Oklahoma State 37-24
20	21	Oregon	6-2	beat Washington 27-22
22	22	Michigan	6-2	beat # 9 Penn State 27-0
24	23	Georgia Tech	6-2	bye week
	24	Miami, Fla.	5-2	bye week
21	25	Air Force	7-1	beat Army 35-7
25		Colorado	6-2	lost to # 18 Missouri 14-38

November 8 Poll — Nov. 14 Games

ESPN	AP	Team	Record	Nov. 14 Games
1	1	Tennessee	8-0	beat # 10 Arkansas 28-24
1	2	Kansas State	9-0	beat # 11 Nebraska 40-30
3	3	UCLA	8-0	beat Washington 36-24
4	4	Florida	8-1	beat South Carolina 33-14
5	5	Florida State	9-1	beat Wake Forest 24-7
8	6	Texas A&M	9-1	beat # 13 Missouri 17-14
7	7	Ohio State	8-1	beat Iowa 45-14
6	8	Wisconsin	9-0	beat # 15 Michigan 10-27
9	9	Arizona	9-1	beat California 27-23
10	10	Arkansas	8-0	lost to # 1 Tennessee 24-28
11	11	Nebraska	8-2	lost to # 2 Kansas State 30-40
13	12	Notre Dame	7-1	beat Navy 30-0
15	13	Missouri	7-2	lost to # 6 Texas A&M 14-17
14	14	Tulane	8-0	beat Army 49-35
16	15	Michigan	7-2	beat # 8 Wisconsin 27-10
12	16	Virginia Tech	7-1	lost to Syracuse 26-28
18	17	Georgia	6-2	beat Auburn 28-17
17	18	Texas	7-2	lost to Texas Tech 35-42
21	19	Penn State	6-2	beat Northwestern 41-10
19	20	Oregon	7-2	beat Arizona State 51-19
22	21	Virginia	7-2	beat North Carolina 30-13
23	22	Georgia Tech	6-2	beat Clemson 24-21 (N12)
20	23	Air Force	8-1	beat # 25 Wyoming 10-3
24	24	Miami, Fla.	5-2	beat Temple 42-7
25	25	Wyoming	8-1	lost to # 23 Air Force 3-10
25		Syracuse	5-3	beat # 16 Virginia Tech 28-26

November 15 Poll — Nov. 21 Games

ESPN	AP	Team	Record	Nov. 21 Games
2	1	Tennessee	9-0	beat Kentucky 59-21
1	2	Kansas State	10-0	beat # 19 Missouri 31-25
3	3	UCLA	9-0	beat Southern Cal 34-17
4	4	Florida	9-1	lost to # 5 Florida State 12-23
5	5	Florida State	10-1	beat # 4 Florida 23-12
7	6	Texas A&M	10-1	bye week
6	7	Ohio State	9-1	beat # 11 Michigan 31-16
8	8	Arizona	10-1	bye week
9	9	Arkansas	8-1	lost to Mississippi State 21-22
10	10	Notre Dame	8-1	beat LSU 39-36
11	11	Michigan	8-2	lost to # 7 Ohio State 16-31
13	12	Tulane	9-0	beat Houston 48-20
12	13	Wisconsin	9-1	beat # 16 Penn State 24-3
15	14	Georgia	7-2	beat Mississippi 24-17
16	15	Oregon	8-2	lost to Oregon State 41-44
14	16	Penn State	7-2	lost to # 13 Wisconsin 3-24
19	17	Nebraska	8-3	bye week
18	18	Virginia	8-2	bye week
23	19	Missouri	7-3	lost to # 2 Kansas State 25-31
17	20	Air Force	9-1	beat Rice 22-16
21	21	Georgia Tech	7-2	beat Wake Forest 63-35
22	22	Miami, Fla.	6-2	beat Pittsburgh 38-10 (N19)
20	23	Virginia Tech	7-2	beat Rutgers 47-7
24	24	Syracuse	6-3	beat Temple 38-7
	25	Texas	7-3	bye week
25		Kentucky	7-3	lost to # 1 Tennessee 21-59

November 22 Poll — Nov. 28 Games

ESPN	AP	Team	Record	Nov. 28 Games
2	1	Tennessee	10-0	beat Vanderbilt 41-0
1	2	Kansas State	11-0	bye week
3	3	UCLA	10-0	bye week
4	4	Florida State	11-1	regular season complete
5	5	Ohio State	10-1	regular season complete
6	6	Texas A&M	10-1	lost to Texas 24-26 (N27)
7	7	Arizona	10-1	beat Arizona State 50-42 (N27)
8	8	Florida	9-2	regular season complete
10	9	Notre Dame	9-1	lost to Southern Cal 0-10
9	10	Wisconsin	10-1	regular season complete
11	11	Tulane	10-0	beat Louisiana Tech 63-30 (N26)
12	12	Georgia	8-2	lost to # 17 Georgia Tech 19-21
13	13	Arkansas	8-2	beat LSU 41-14 (N27)
17	14	Nebraska	8-3	beat Colorado 16-14 (N27)
16	15	Michigan	8-3	beat Hawaii 48-17
15	16	Virginia	8-2	beat # 20 Virginia Tech 36-32
18	17	Georgia Tech	8-2	beat # 12 Georgia 21-19
14	18	Air Force	10-1	regular season complete
20	19	Miami, Fla.	7-2	lost to # 21 Syracuse 13-66
19	20	Virginia Tech	8-3	lost to # 16 Virginia 32-36
22	21	Syracuse	7-3	beat # 19 Miami, Fla. 66-13
23	22	Oregon	8-3	regular season complete
21	23	Penn State	7-3	beat Michigan State 51-28
25		Missouri	7-4	regular season complete
24	25	Mississippi State	7-3	beat Mississippi 28-6 (N26)

November 29 Poll — Dec. 5 Games

ESPN	AP	Team	Record	Dec. 5 Games
2	1	Tennessee	11-0	beat # 23 Mississippi State 24-14 (SEC CH)
1	2	Kansas State	11-0	lost to # 10 Texas A&M 33-36 (Big 12 CH)
3	3	UCLA	10-0	lost to Miami, Fla. 45-49
4	4	Florida State	11-1	
5	5	Ohio State	10-1	
6	6	Arizona	11-1	regular season complete
7	7	Florida	9-2	
8	8	Wisconsin	10-1	
9	9	Tulane	11-0	regular season complete
10	10	Texas A&M	10-2	beat # 2 Kansas State 36-33 (Big 12 CH)
11	11	Arkansas	9-2	regular season complete
14	12	Georgia Tech	9-2	regular season complete
17	13	Nebraska	9-3	regular season complete
12	14	Virginia	9-2	regular season complete
15	15	Michigan	9-3	regular season complete
16	16	Notre Dame	9-2	regular season complete
13	17	Air Force	10-1	beat Brigham Young 20-13 (WAC CH)
18	18	Syracuse	8-3	regular season complete
19	19	Georgia	8-3	regular season complete
23	20	Texas	8-3	regular season complete
21	21	Oregon	8-3	
20	22	Penn State	8-3	regular season complete
	23	Mississippi State	8-3	lost to # 1 Tennessee 14-24 (SEC CH)
	24	Missouri	7-4	
24	25	Virginia Tech	8-3	regular season complete
25		West Virginia	8-3	regular season complete

December 6 Poll

ESPN	AP	December 6 Poll	RECORD	BOWL BID	DATE	BOWL RESULT	RB	ESPN	AP	January 5 Final Poll	RECORD
1	1	Tennessee	12-0	Fiesta Bowl	J4	beat # 2 Florida State 23-16	1	1	1	Tennessee	13-0
2	2	Florida State	11-1	Fiesta Bowl	J4	lost to # 1 Tennessee 16-23	2	2	2	Ohio State	11-1
3	3	Ohio State	10-1	Sugar Bowl	J1	beat # 8 Texas A&M 24-14	3	3	3	Florida State	11-2
4	4	Kansas State	11-1	Alamo Bowl	D29	lost to Purdue 34-37	4	4	4	Arizona	12-1
6	5	Arizona	11-1	Holiday Bowl	D30	beat # 14 Nebraska 23-20	8	6	5	Florida	10-2
5	6	UCLA	10-1	Rose Bowl	J1	lost to # 9 Wisconsin 31-38	5	5	6	Wisconsin	11-1
7	7	Florida	9-2	Orange Bowl	J2	beat # 18 Syracuse 31-10	13	7	7	Tulane	12-0
9	8	Texas A&M	11-2	Sugar Bowl	J1	lost to # 3 Ohio State 14-24	6	8	8	UCLA	10-2
8	9	Wisconsin	10-1	Rose Bowl	J1	beat # 6 UCLA 38-31	10	11	9	Georgia Tech	10-2
10	10	Tulane	11-0	Liberty Bowl	D31	beat Brigham Young 41-27	9	9	10	Kansas State	11-2
11	11	Arkansas	9-2	Citrus Bowl	J1	lost to # 15 Michigan 31-45	7	13	11	Texas A&M	11-3
14	12	Georgia Tech	9-2	Gator Bowl	J1	beat # 17 Notre Dame 35-28	11	12	12	Michigan	10-3
12	13	Virginia	9-2	Peach Bowl	D31	lost to # 19 Georgia 33-35	14	10	13	Air Force	12-1
16	14	Nebraska	9-3	Holiday Bowl	D30	lost to # 5 Arizona 20-23	12	14	14	Georgia	9-3
15	15	Michigan	9-3	Citrus Bowl	J1	beat # 11 Arkansas 45-31	21	16	15	Texas	9-3
13	16	Air Force	11-1	Oahu Bowl	D25	beat Washington 45-25	20	17	16	Arkansas	9-3
18	17	Notre Dame	9-2	Gator Bowl	J1	lost to # 12 Georgia Tech 28-35	15	15	17	Penn State	9-3
17	18	Syracuse	8-3	Orange Bowl	J2	lost to # 7 Florida 10-31	18	18	18	Virginia	9-3
19	19	Georgia	8-3	Peach Bowl	D31	beat # 13 Virginia 35-33	17	20	19	Nebraska	9-4
22	20	Texas	8-3	Cotton Bowl	J1	beat # 25 Mississippi State 38-11	26	21	20	Miami, Fla.	9-3
21	21	Oregon	8-3	Aloha Bowl	D25	lost to Colorado 43-51	25	25	21	Missouri	8-4
20	22	Penn State	8-3	Outback Bowl	J1	beat Kentucky 26-14	24	22	22	Notre Dame	9-3
	23	Missouri	7-4	Insight.com Bowl	D26	beat West Virginia 34-31	32	19	23	Virginia Tech	9-3
	24	Miami, Fla.	8-3	Micron PC Bowl	D29	beat North Carolina St. 46-23	22	23	24	Purdue	9-4
23	25	Mississippi State	8-4	Cotton Bowl	J1	lost to # 20 Texas 11-38	34	24	25	Syracuse	8-4
24		Virginia Tech	8-3	Music City Bowl	D29	beat Alabama 38-7					
25		West Virginia	8-3	Insight.com Bowl	D26	lost to # 23 Missouri 31-34					

1998

Consensus All-Americans

POS	Offense	HT	WT	CL	School	AP	CF	FC	FN	FW	SN
QB	**Cade McNown**	6-1	214	Sr.	UCLA	•		•			
QB	**Michael Bishop**	6-1	205	Sr.	Kansas State				•		•
QB	**Tim Couch**	6-5	225	Jr.	Kentucky		•			•	
RB	**Ricky Williams**	6-0	225	Sr.	Texas	•	•	•	•	•	•
RB	**Mike Cloud**	5-11	201	Sr.	Boston College	•		•		•	
WR	**Torry Holt**	6-2	188	Sr.	North Carolina St.	•		•	•	•	•
WR	**Peter Warrick**	6-0	190	Jr.	Florida State	•	•				•
WR	**Troy Edwards**	5-10	195	Sr.	Louisiana Tech		•	•		•	
TE	**Rufus French**	6-4	245	Jr.	Mississippi	•	•	•	•		•
OL	**Kris Farris**	6-9	310	Jr.	UCLA	•	•		•	•	•
OL	**Aaron Gibson**	6-7	372	Sr.	Wisconsin	•	•	•	•	•	
OL	**Matt Stinchcomb**	6-6	291	Sr.	Georgia	•	•	•	•		
OL	**Rob Murphy**	6-5	300	Jr.	Ohio State	•			•		•
C	**Craig Page**	6-3	288	Sr.	Georgia Tech	•				•	•
PK	**Sebastian Janikowski**	6-2	255	So.	Florida State	•				•	
KR	**David Allen**	5-9	185	So.	Kansas State	•				•	

Others receiving first-team honors

POS	Name	School	AP	CF	FC	FN	FW	SN
RB	Ron Dayne	Wisconsin		•				
RB	Devin West	Missouri				•		•
WR	David Boston	Ohio State				•	•	
OL	Mike Rosenthal	Notre Dame		•				
OL	Ben Adams	Texas					•	
OL	Doug Brzezinski	Boston College						•
OL	Jay Humphrey	Texas						•
OL	Brandon Bulsworth	Arkansas				•		
OL	Jason Whitaker	Florida State					•	
OL	Jon Jansen	Michigan			•			
OL	Anthony Cesario	Colorado State			•			
C	Grey Ruegamer	Arizona State		•				
C	Todd McClure	LSU			•			
PK	Martin Gramatica	Kansas State		•	•			
KR	Kevin Johnson	Syracuse			•			

POS	Defense	HT	WT	CL	School	AP	CF	FC	FN	FW	SN
DL	**Tom Burke**	6-4	249	Sr.	Wisconsin	•	•	•	•	•	•
DL	**Montae Reagor**	6-2	254	Sr.	Texas Tech	•	•	•		•	•
DL	**Jared DeVries**	6-4	284	Sr.	Iowa		•	•			•
LB	**Chris Claiborne**	6-3	250	Jr.	Southern Cal	•	•	•	•	•	•
LB	**Dat Nguyen**	6-0	216	Sr.	Texas A&M	•	•	•	•	•	•
LB	**Jeff Kelly**	6-0	250	Sr.	Kansas State	•			•	•	
LB	**Al Wilson**	6-0	226	Sr.	Tennessee	•		•		•	
DB	**Chris McAlister**	6-2	185	Sr.	Arizona	•	•	•	•	•	•
DB	**Antoine Winfield**	5-9	180	Sr.	Ohio State	•	•	•	•	•	•
DB	**Champ Bailey**	6-1	186	Jr.	Georgia	•	•	•	•	•	
DB	**Anthony Poindexter**	6-1	220	Sr.	Virginia	•				•	•
P	**Joe Kristosik**	6-3	220	Jr.	UNLV	•	•	•		•	

Others receiving first-team honors

POS	Name	School	AP	CF	FC	FN	FW	SN
DL	Robaire Smith	Michigan State		•				
DL	Patrick Kerney	Virginia				•	•	
DL	Corey Moore	Virginia Tech			•			
DL	Corey Simon	Florida State	•					
DL	Anthony McFarland	LSU	•			•		
LB	Jevon Kearse	Florida		•		•		
LB	Adalius Thomas	Southern Miss			•			
LB	LaVar Arrington	Penn State						•
DB	Dre' Bly	North Carolina		•				
DB	Tyrone Carter	Minnesota				•		
DB	Damon Moore	Ohio State						•

Heisman Trophy Voting

	PLAYER	POS	SCHOOL	1ST	2ND	3RD	TOTAL
1	**Ricky Williams**	RB	Texas	714	91	31	2355
2	**Michael Bishop**	QB	Kansas State	41	250	169	792
3	**Cade McNown**	QB	UCLA	28	217	178	696
4	**Tim Couch**	QB	Kentucky	26	153	143	527
5	**Donovan McNabb**	QB	Syracuse	13	54	85	232
6	**Daunte Culpepper**	QB	Central Florida	5	11	30	67
7	**Champ Bailey**	DB	Georgia	6	8	21	55
8	**Torry Holt**	WR	North Carolina St.	2	8	32	44
9	**Joe Germaine**	QB	Ohio State	2	11	15	43
10	**Shaun King**	QB	Tulane	1	11	13	38

Award Winners

Ricky Williams, RB, Texas, Maxwell, Camp, Walker, **Kris Farris,** OT, UCLA, Outland, **Dat Nguyen**, LB, Texas A&M, Lombardi, Bednarik, **Michael Bishop,** QB, Kansas State, O'Brien, **Chris Claiborne,** LB, Southern Cal, Butkus, **Antoine Winfield,** DB, Ohio State, Thorpe, **Cade McNown,** QB, UCLA, Unitas, **Sebastian Janikowski,** K, Florida State, Groza, **Champ Bailey,** DB, Georgia, Nagurski, **Troy Edwards,** WR, Louisiana Tech, Biletnikoff, **Chris McAlister,** CB, Arizona, Tatupu

Bowl Games

D19, **Las Vegas**, North Carolina 20, San Diego State 13, D23, **Motor City**, Marshall 48, Louisville 29, D25, **Oahu**, Air Force 45, Washington 25, D25, **Aloha**, Colorado 51, Oregon 43, D26, **Insight.com**, Missouri 34, West Virginia 31, D29, **Micron PC**, Miami, Fla. 46, North Carolina St. 23, D29, **Alamo**, Purdue 37, Kansas State 34, D29, **Music City**, Virginia Tech 38, Alabama 7, D30, **Holiday**, Arizona 23, Nebraska 20, D30, **Humanitarian**, Idaho 42, Southern Miss 35, D31, **Peach**, Georgia 35, Virginia 33, D31, **Independence**, Mississippi 35, Texas Tech 18, D31, **Sun**, TCU 28, Southern Cal 19, D31, **Liberty**, Tulane 41, Brigham Young 27, J1, **Gator**, Georgia Tech 35, Notre Dame 28, J1, **Florida Citrus**, Michigan 45, Arkansas 31, J1, **Outback**, Penn State 26, Kentucky 14, J1, **Cotton**, Texas 38, Mississippi State 11, J1, **Rose**, Wisconsin 38, UCLA 31, J1, **Sugar**, Ohio State 24, Texas A&M 14, J2, **Orange**, Florida 31, Syracuse 10, J4, **Fiesta**, Tennessee 26, Florida State 16

Conference Standings

ACC	Conf. W	L	T	Overall W	L	T
Florida State	7	1	0	11	2	0
Georgia Tech	7	1	0	10	2	0
Virginia	6	2	0	9	3	0
North Carolina St.	5	3	0	7	5	0
North Carolina	5	3	0	7	5	0
Duke	2	6	0	4	7	0
Wake Forest	2	6	0	3	8	0
Clemson	1	7	0	3	8	0
Maryland	1	7	0	3	8	0

Big 10	Conf. W	L	T	Overall W	L	T
Ohio State	7	1	0	11	1	0
Wisconsin	7	1	0	11	1	0
Michigan	7	1	0	10	3	0
Purdue	6	2	0	9	4	0
Penn State	5	3	0	9	3	0
Michigan State	4	4	0	6	6	0
Minnesota	2	6	0	5	6	0
Indiana	2	6	0	4	7	0
Iowa	2	6	0	3	8	0
Illinois	2	6	0	3	8	0
Northwestern	0	8	0	3	9	0

Big 12	Conf. W	L	T	Overall W	L	T
NORTH						
Kansas State	8	0	0	11	2	0
Nebraska	5	3	0	9	4	0
Missouri	5	3	0	8	4	0
Colorado	4	4	0	8	4	0
Kansas	1	7	0	4	7	0
Iowa State	1	7	0	3	8	0
SOUTH						
Texas A&M	7	1	0	11	3	0
Texas	6	2	0	9	3	0
Texas Tech	4	4	0	7	5	0
Oklahoma State	3	5	0	5	6	0
Oklahoma	3	5	0	5	6	0
Baylor	1	7	0	2	9	0

Championship **Texas A&M 36 Kansas State 33**

Big East	Conf. W	L	T	Overall W	L	T
Syracuse	6	1	0	8	4	0
Virginia Tech	5	2	0	9	3	0
Miami, Fla.	5	2	0	9	3	0
West Virginia	5	2	0	8	4	0
Boston College	3	4	0	4	7	0
Rutgers	2	5	0	5	6	0
Temple	2	5	0	2	9	0
Pittsburgh	0	7	0	2	9	0

Big West	Conf. W	L	T	Overall W	L	T
Idaho	4	1	0	9	3	0
Nevada	3	2	0	6	5	0
North Texas	3	2	0	3	8	0
Boise State	2	3	0	6	5	0
Utah State	2	3	0	3	8	0
New Mexico State	1	4	0	3	8	0

C-USA	Conf. W	L	T	Overall W	L	T
Tulane	6	0	0	12	0	0
Southern Miss	5	1	0	7	5	0
Louisville	4	2	0	7	5	0
East Carolina	3	3	0	6	5	0
Army	2	4	0	3	8	0
Houston	2	4	0	3	8	0
Cincinnati	1	5	0	2	9	0
Memphis	1	5	0	2	9	0

Ivy	Conf. W	L	T	Overall W	L	T
Pennsylvania	6	1	0	8	2	0
Brown	5	2	0	7	3	0
Yale	5	2	0	6	4	0
Princeton	4	3	0	5	5	0
Columbia	3	4	0	4	6	0
Harvard	3	4	0	4	6	0
Cornell	1	6	0	4	6	0
Dartmouth	1	6	0	2	8	0

MAC	Conf. W	L	T	Overall W	L	T
EAST						
Marshall	7	1	0	12	1	0
Miami, Ohio	7	1	0	10	1	0
Ohio U	5	3	0	5	6	0
Bowling Green	5	3	0	5	6	0
Akron	3	6	0	4	7	0
Kent State	0	8	0	0	11	0
WEST						
Toledo	6	2	0	7	5	0
Western Michigan	5	3	0	7	4	0
Central Michigan	5	3	0	6	5	0
Eastern Michigan	3	6	0	3	8	0
Northern Illinois	2	6	0	2	9	0
Ball State	1	7	0	1	10	0

Championship **Marshall 23 Toledo 17**

Pac 10	Conf. W	L	T	Overall W	L	T
UCLA	8	0	0	10	2	0
Arizona	7	1	0	12	1	0
Oregon	5	3	0	8	4	0
Southern Cal	5	3	0	8	5	0
Washington	4	4	0	6	6	0
Arizona State	4	4	0	5	6	0
California	3	5	0	5	6	0
Oregon State	2	6	0	5	6	0
Stanford	2	6	0	3	8	0
Washington State	0	8	0	3	8	0

SEC	Conf. W	L	T	Overall W	L	T
EAST						
Tennessee	8	0	0	13	0	0
Florida	7	1	0	10	2	0
Georgia	6	2	0	9	3	0
Kentucky	4	4	0	7	5	0
Vanderbilt	1	7	0	2	9	0
South Carolina	0	8	0	1	10	0
WEST						
Mississippi State	6	2	0	8	5	0
Arkansas	6	2	0	9	3	0
Alabama	4	4	0	7	5	0
Mississippi	3	5	0	7	5	0
LSU	2	6	0	4	7	0
Auburn	1	7	0	3	8	0

Championship **Tennessee 24 Mississippi State 14**

WAC	Conf. W	L	T	Overall W	L	T
MOUNTAIN						
Air Force	7	1	0	12	1	0
Wyoming	6	2	0	8	3	0
Colorado State	5	3	0	8	4	0
Rice	5	3	0	5	6	0
TCU	4	4	0	7	5	0
SMU	4	4	0	5	7	0
Tulsa	2	6	0	4	7	0
Nevada-Las Vegas	0	8	0	0	11	0
PACIFIC						
Brigham Young	7	1	0	9	5	0
San Diego State	7	1	0	7	5	0
Utah	5	3	0	7	4	0
Fresno State	5	3	0	5	6	0
San Jose State	3	5	0	4	8	0
Texas-El Paso	3	5	0	3	8	0
New Mexico	1	7	0	3	9	0
Hawaii	0	8	0	0	12	0

Championship **Air Force 20 Brigham Young 13**

Independents	Overall W	L	T
Central Florida	9	2	0
Notre Dame	9	3	0
Louisiana Tech	6	6	0
La. Monroe	5	6	0
UAB	4	7	0
Arkansas State	4	8	0
Navy	3	8	0
La. Lafayette	2	9	0

1998 NCAA Major College Statistical Leaders

Individual Leaders

PASSING	CL	G	ATT	COM	PCT	INT	I%	YDS	YPA	TD	TD%	RATING
1 Shaun King, Tulane	SR	11	328	223	68.0	6	1.8	3232	9.9	36	11.0	183.3
2 Akili Smith, Oregon	SR	11	325	191	58.8	7	2.2	3307	10.2	30	9.2	170.4
3 Daunte Culpepper, Central Florida	SR	11	402	296	73.6	7	1.7	3690	9.2	28	7.0	170.2
4 Tim Rattay, Louisiana Tech	JR	12	559	380	68.0	13	2.3	4943	8.8	46	8.2	164.8
5 David Neill, Nevada	FR	9	344	199	57.9	9	2.6	3249	9.4	29	8.4	159.8
6 Michael Bishop, Kansas State	SR	12	295	164	55.6	4	1.4	2844	9.6	23	7.8	159.6
7 Donovan McNabb, Syracuse	SR	11	251	157	62.6	5	2.0	2134	8.5	22	8.8	158.9
8 Marc Bulger, West Virginia	JR	11	369	240	65.0	8	2.2	3178	8.6	27	7.3	157.2
9 Cade McNown, UCLA	SR	11	323	188	58.2	10	3.1	3130	9.7	23	7.1	156.9
10 Joe Germaine, Ohio State	SR	11	346	209	60.4	7	2.0	3108	9.0	24	6.9	154.7

ALL-PURPOSE	CL	G	RUSH	REC	PR	KR	YDS	YPG
1 Troy Edwards, Louisiana Tech	SR	12	227	1996	235	326	2784	232.0
2 Ricky Williams, Texas	SR	11	2124	262	0	0	2386	216.9
3 Kevin Faulk, LSU	SR	11	1279	287	265	278	2109	191.7
4 Torry Holt, North Carolina St.	SR	11	102	1604	273	0	1979	179.9
5 Jaime Kimbrough, Fresno State	SR	11	1168	391	0	393	1952	177.5
6 Amos Zereoue, West Virginia	JR	10	1430	175	0	168	1773	177.3
7 Mike Cloud, Boston College	SR	11	1726	198	0	0	1924	174.9
8 Travis Prentice, Miami, Ohio	JR	11	1787	107	0	0	1894	172.2
9 Craig Yeast, Kentucky	SR	11	87	1311	33	410	1841	167.4
10 Kevin Johnson, Syracuse	SR	11	105	894	145	690	1834	166.7

RUSHING/Yards Per Game	CL	G	ATT	YDS	TD	AVG	YPG
1 Ricky Williams, Texas	SR	11	361	2124	27	5.9	193.1
2 Travis Prentice, Miami, Ohio	JR	11	365	1787	19	4.9	162.5
3 Mike Cloud, Boston College	SR	11	308	1726	14	5.6	156.9
4 Ricky Williams, Texas Tech	SO	11	306	1582	13	5.2	143.8
5 Devin West, Missouri	SR	11	283	1578	17	5.6	143.5
6 Amos Zereoue, West Virginia	JR	10	261	1430	13	5.5	143.0
7 Denvis Manns, New Mexico State	SR	11	269	1469	6	5.5	133.6
8 Edgerrin James, Miami, Fla.	JR	11	242	1416	17	5.9	128.7
9 Ron Dayne, Wisconsin	JR	10	268	1279	11	4.8	127.9
10 Steve Hookfin, Ohio U	SR	11	273	1315	11	4.8	119.6

RUSHING/Yards Per Carry	CL	G	ATT	YDS	YPC
1 Trung Canidate, Arizona	JR	11	166	1225	7.4
2 Basil Mitchell, TCU	JR	11	166	1111	6.7
3 Michael Wiley, Ohio State	JR	11	182	1147	6.3
4 Ricky Williams, Texas	SR	11	361	2124	5.9
5 James Johnson, Mississippi State	SR	12	236	1383	5.9
6 Edgerrin James, Miami, Fla.	JR	11	242	1416	5.9
7 Chrys Chukwuma, Arkansas	JR	10	149	870	5.8
8 Mike Cloud, Boston College	SR	11	308	1726	5.6
9 Kevin Faulk, LSU	SR	11	229	1279	5.6
10 Devin West, Missouri	SR	11	283	1578	5.6

*-Based on top 50 rushers

RECEIVING	CL	G	REC	YDS	TD	RPG	YPR	YPG
1 Troy Edwards, Louisiana Tech	SR	12	140	1996	27	11.7	14.3	166.3
2 Torry Holt, North Carolina St.	SR	11	88	1604	11	8.0	18.2	145.8
3 Geoff Noisy, Nevada	SR	11	94	1405	7	8.6	14.9	127.7
4 Travis McGriff, Florida	SR	11	70	1357	10	6.4	19.4	123.4
5 David Boston, Ohio State	JR	11	74	1330	13	6.8	18.0	120.9
6 Craig Yeast, Kentucky	SR	11	85	1311	14	7.7	15.4	119.2
7 Trevor Insley, Nevada	JR	11	69	1220	11	6.3	17.7	110.9
8 Sherrod Gideon, Southern Miss	JR	11	66	1186	13	6.0	18.0	107.8
9 P.J. Franklin, Tulane	JR	11	74	1174	11	6.7	15.9	106.7
10 Brandon Stokley, La. Lafayette	SR	11	65	1173	8	5.9	18.0	106.6

PUNTING	CL	PUNT	YDS	AVG
1 Joe Kristosik, Nevada-Las Vegas	SR	76	3509	46.2
2 Josh Bidwell, Oregon	SR	47	2153	45.8
3 Stephen Baker, Arizona State	FR	56	2561	45.7
4 Dave Zastudil, Ohio U	FR	50	2266	45.3
5 Bill Lafleur, Nebraska	SR	52	2337	44.9
6 Andy Pollock, Bowling Green	SR	50	2243	44.9
7 Deone Horinek, Colorado State	JR	52	2331	44.8
8 Brian Schmitz, North Carolina	JR	75	3357	44.8
9 Graham White, Army	JR	47	2101	44.7
10 Kevin Stemke, Wisconsin	SO	67	2949	44.0

PUNT RETURNS	CL	PR	YDS	TD	AVG
1 David Allen, Kansas State	SO	33	730	4	22.1
2 Damon Gourdine, San Diego State	JR	16	294	2	18.4
3 Nick Davis, Wisconsin	FR	27	424	2	15.7
4 David Boston, Ohio State	JR	18	268	1	14.9
5 Payton Williams, Fresno State	JR	24	343	1	14.3
6 Charlie Rogers, Georgia Tech	SR	30	425	2	14.2
7 Siaha Burley, Central Florida	SR	21	293	1	14.0
8 Peter Warrick, Florida State	JR	15	208	0	13.9
9 Gari Scott, Michigan State	JR	32	440	0	13.8
10 J.R. Redmond, Arizona State	JR	18	246	1	13.7

KICKOFF RETURNS	CL	KR	YDS	TD	AVG
1 Broderick McGrew, North Texas	JR	18	587	1	32.6
2 Dee Moronkola, Washington State	SR	16	504	2	31.5
3 Kevin Johnson, Syracuse	SR	23	690	2	30.0
4 Tim Alexander, Oregon State	SR	27	799	1	29.6
5 Craig Yeast, Kentucky	SR	14	410	1	29.3
6 Toure Butler, Washington	SO	22	626	1	28.5
7 Deltha O'Neal, California	JR	22	624	0	28.4
8 Sam Simmons, Northwestern	FR	22	607	0	27.6
9 Russell Harvey, Illinois	FR	15	406	0	27.1
10 Antwan Edwards, Clemson	SR	13	350	0	26.9

SCORING	CL	TDS	XP	FG	PTS	PTPG
1 Troy Edwards, Louisiana Tech	SR	31	2	0	188	15.7
2 Ricky Williams, Texas	SR	28	0	0	168	15.3
3 Martin Gramatica, Kansas State	SR	0	69	22	135	11.3
4 Travis Prentice, Miami, Ohio	JR	20	0	0	120	10.9
5 Leroy Collins, Louisville	JR	19	2	0	116	10.6
6 Edgerrin James, Miami, Fla.	JR	19	0	0	114	10.4
7 Sebastian Janikowski, Florida State	SO	0	42	27	123	10.3
8 Nathan Villegas, Oregon	JR	0	52	20	112	10.2
9 Devin West, Missouri	SR	18	0	0	108	9.8
10 Shayne Graham, Virginia Tech	JR	0	37	22	103	9.4

FIELD GOALS	CL	FGA	FGM	PCT	FGG
1 Sebastian Janikowski, Florida State	SO	32	27	0.84	2.25
2 Brad Bohn, Utah State	SO	28	24	0.86	2.18
3 Paul Edinger, Michigan State	JR	26	22	0.85	2.00
3 Shayne Graham, Virginia Tech	JR	32	22	0.69	2.00
5 Derek Franz, Colorado State	SR	26	21	0.81	1.91
6 Martin Gramatica, Kansas State	SR	31	22	0.71	1.83
7 Nathan Villegas, Oregon	JR	22	20	0.91	1.82
7 Travis Forney, Penn State	JR	29	20	0.69	1.82
9 Todd Latourette, Arkansas	SR	24	17	0.71	1.70
10 Matt Davenport, Wisconsin	SR	20	18	0.90	1.64
10 Brad Selent, Western Michigan	SO	26	18	0.69	1.64

INTERCEPTIONS	CL	INT	YDS	TD	INT/GM
1 Jamar Fletcher, Wisconsin	FR	6	99	2	0.67
2 Pat Dennis, La. Monroe	SO	7	196	2	0.64
2 Lloyd Harrison, North Carolina St.	JR	7	51	0	0.64
4 Hank Poteat, Pittsburgh	JR	6	53	0	0.60
5 Wade Perkins, Missouri	SR	6	129	1	0.55
5 David Macklin, Penn State	JR	6	120	1	0.55
5 Tim Smith, Stanford	SR	6	69	0	0.55
8 Chris Claiborne, Southern Cal	JR	6	159	2	0.50
8 Daninelle Derricott, Marshall	JR	6	118	0	0.50
8 Mario Edwards, Florida State	FR	6	109	0	0.50
8 Chappell Mitchell, Arkansas State	SR	6	41	0	0.50

Team Leaders

RUSHING OFFENSE	G	ATT	YDS	AVG	TD	YPG
1 Army	11	610	3232	5.3	25	293.8
2 Ohio	11	680	3044	4.5	27	276.7
3 Air Force	12	648	3201	4.9	39	266.8
4 Navy	11	580	2874	5.0	25	261.3
5 Rice	11	624	2829	4.5	25	257.2
6 Nebraska	12	636	3045	4.8	37	253.8
7 New Mexico State	11	579	2790	4.8	18	253.6
8 TCU	11	542	2630	4.9	21	239.1
9 Missouri	11	546	2552	4.7	28	232.0
10 Syracuse	11	521	2512	4.8	34	228.4

PASSING OFFENSE	G	ATT	COM	INT	PCT	YDS	YPA	TD	I%	YPC	YPG
1 Louisiana Tech	12	600	402	13	67.0	5185	8.6	48	2.2	12.9	432.1
2 Kentucky	11	574	414	16	72.1	4534	7.9	39	2.8	11.0	412.2
3 Louisville	11	515	338	15	65.6	4498	8.7	33	2.9	13.3	408.9
4 Nevada	11	458	265	18	57.9	3992	8.7	32	3.9	15.1	362.9
5 Florida	11	417	238	15	57.1	3807	9.1	35	3.6	16.0	346.1
6 Central Florida	11	411	302	7	73.5	3771	9.2	29	1.7	12.5	342.8
7 Purdue	12	541	352	17	65.1	3978	7.4	40	3.1	11.3	331.5
8 Stanford	11	513	263	8	51.3	3516	6.9	22	1.6	13.4	319.6
9 Western Michigan	11	409	238	16	58.2	3414	8.3	24	3.9	14.3	310.4
10 North Carolina St.	11	405	210	11	51.9	3401	8.4	20	2.7	16.2	309.2

TOTAL OFFENSE	G	P	YDS	AVG	TD	YPG
1 Louisville	11	883	6156	7.0	62	559.6
2 Louisiana Tech	12	894	6479	7.2	66	539.9
3 Kentucky	11	911	5876	6.5	50	534.2
4 Tulane	11	816	5578	6.8	64	507.1
5 Nevada	11	869	5577	6.4	49	507.0
6 Ohio State	11	853	5539	6.5	46	503.6
7 Central Florida	11	789	5365	6.8	50	487.7
8 UCLA	11	785	5309	6.8	56	482.6
9 Kansas State	12	887	5742	6.5	65	478.5
10 Oregon	11	785	5260	6.7	49	478.2

RUSHING DEFENSE	G	ATT	YDS	AVG	TD	YPG
1 Ohio State	11	348	741	2.1	5	67.4
2 Florida State	12	412	958	2.3	5	79.8
3 Wisconsin	11	377	986	2.6	4	89.6
4 Florida	11	393	998	2.5	6	90.7
5 Brigham Young	13	444	1186	2.7	12	91.2
6 Tennessee	12	420	1127	2.7	5	93.9
7 Arkansas	11	390	1050	2.7	6	95.5
8 Penn State	11	407	1070	2.6	7	97.3
9 Utah	11	344	1071	3.1	9	97.4
10 Kansas State	12	433	1179	2.7	3	98.3

PASSING DEFENSE	G	ATT	COM	PCT	INT	I%	YDS	YPA	TD	TD%	RAT
1 Florida State	12	335	138	41.2	18	5.4	1620	4.8	9	2.7	79.9
2 Ohio State	11	414	197	47.6	17	4.1	2094	5.1	7	1.7	87.4
3 Southern Cal	12	455	225	49.5	24	5.3	2248	4.9	14	3.1	90.6
4 Colorado	11	290	138	47.6	11	3.8	1633	5.6	4	1.4	91.9
5 Miami, Ohio	11	298	142	47.7	13	4.4	1659	5.6	6	2.0	92.3
6 Wisconsin	11	337	182	54.0	18	5.3	1987	5.9	5	1.5	97.8
7 Florida	11	380	197	51.8	13	3.4	2155	5.7	9	2.4	100.5
8 Penn State	11	362	188	51.9	17	4.7	2170	6.0	9	2.5	101.1
9 Kansas State	12	326	141	43.3	16	4.9	2041	6.3	15	4.6	101.2
10 Michigan State	12	385	188	48.8	13	3.4	2298	6.0	11	2.9	101.6

TOTAL DEFENSE	G	P	YDS	AVG	TD	YPG
1 Florida State	12	747	2578	3.5	14	214.8
2 Ohio State	11	762	2835	3.7	12	257.7
3 Kansas State	12	759	3220	4.2	18	268.3
4 Wisconsin	11	714	2973	4.2	9	270.3
5 Brigham Young	13	830	3561	4.3	29	273.9
6 Oklahoma	11	694	3067	4.4	24	278.8
7 Virginia Tech	11	710	3134	4.4	18	284.9
8 Texas Tech	11	710	3135	4.4	21	285.0
9 Florida	11	773	3153	4.1	15	286.6
10 Texas A&M	13	871	3761	4.3	21	289.3

SCORING OFFENSE	G	PTS	AVG
1 Kansas State	12	576	48.0
2 Tulane	11	499	45.4
3 Syracuse	11	468	42.5
4 Louisiana Tech	12	493	41.1
5 UCLA	11	445	40.5
6 Louisville	11	444	40.4
7 Oregon	11	430	39.1
8 Kentucky	11	417	37.9
9 Ohio State	11	406	36.9
10 Miami, Fla.	11	402	36.5

SCORING DEFENSE	G	PTS	AVG
1 Wisconsin	11	112	10.2
2 Florida State	12	138	11.5
3 Ohio State	11	130	11.8
4 Miami, Ohio	11	142	12.9
4 Virginia Tech	11	142	12.9
6 Kansas State	12	160	13.3
6 Air Force	12	160	13.3
8 Florida	11	155	14.1
9 Tennessee	12	173	14.4
10 Texas A&M	13	190	14.6

TURNOVER MARGIN	G	FR	INT	TOT	FL	INTL	TOT	MAR
1 Wisconsin	11	13	18	31	4	5	9	2.00
2 La. Monroe	11	21	18	39	12	11	23	1.45
2 UCLA	11	21	12	33	6	11	17	1.45
4 Air Force	12	14	16	30	7	6	13	1.42
5 Tulane	11	12	14	26	5	6	11	1.36
6 Tennessee	12	17	16	33	10	7	17	1.33
7 Texas A&M	13	16	15	31	10	5	15	1.23
8 Syracuse	11	13	11	24	5	6	11	1.18
9 Kansas State	12	17	16	33	14	5	19	1.17
10 Fresno State	11	13	12	25	10	4	14	1.00
10 Arkansas	11	15	17	32	13	8	21	1.00

1999 Poll Progression

ESPN	AP	Pre-Season 1999		Aug. 28 Games
1	1	Florida State	0-0	beat Louisiana Tech 41-7
2	2	Tennessee	0-0	bye week
4	3	Penn State	0-0	beat # 4 Arizona 41-7
3	4	Arizona	0-0	lost to # 3 Penn State 7-41
5	5	Florida	0-0	bye week
6	6	Nebraska	0-0	bye week
8	7	Texas A&M	0-0	bye week
7	8	Michigan	0-0	bye week
9	9	Ohio State	0-0	lost to # 12 Miami, Fla. 12-23 (A29)
10	10	Wisconsin	0-0	bye week
11	11	Georgia Tech	0-0	bye week
12	12	Miami, Fla.	0-0	beat # 9 Ohio State 23-12 (A29)
14	13	Virginia Tech	0-0	bye week
13	14	Georgia	0-0	bye week
17	15	Colorado	0-0	bye week
15	16	UCLA	0-0	bye week
16	17	Texas	0-0	lost to North Carolina St. 20-23
18	18	Notre Dame	0-0	beat Kansas 48-13
21	19	Southern Cal	0-0	bye week
20	20	Alabama	0-0	bye week
19	20	Kansas State	0-0	bye week
22	22	Arkansas	0-0	bye week
23	23	Purdue	0-0	bye week
24	24	Virginia	0-0	bye week
25	25	Arizona State	0-0	bye week

AP	August 29 Poll		Sept. 4 Games
1	Florida State	1-0	bye week
2	Penn State	1-0	beat Akron 70-24
3	Tennessee	0-0	beat Wyoming 42-17
4	Florida	0-0	beat Western Michigan 55-26
5	Nebraska	0-0	beat Iowa 42-7
6	Texas A&M	0-0	beat Louisiana Tech 37-17
7	Michigan	0-0	beat # 16 Notre Dame 26-22
8	Miami, Fla.	1-0	beat Florida A&M 57-3
9	Wisconsin	0-0	beat Murray St. 49-10
10	Georgia Tech	0-0	beat Navy 49-14
11	Virginia Tech	0-0	beat James Madison 47-0
12	Georgia	0-0	beat Utah State 38-7
13	Ohio State	0-1	bye week
14	Colorado	0-0	lost to Colorado State 14-41
15	Arizona	0-1	beat TCU 35-31 (S5)
16	Notre Dame	1-0	lost to # 7 Michigan 22-26
17	UCLA	0-0	beat Boise State 38-7
18	Arkansas	0-0	beat SMU 26-0
19	Kansas State	0-0	bye week
20	Alabama	0-0	beat Vanderbilt 28-17
21	Southern Cal	0-0	beat Hawaii 62-7
22	Purdue	0-0	beat Central Florida 47-13
23	Virginia	0-0	beat North Carolina 20-17
24	North Carolina St.	1-0	beat South Carolina 10-0
25	Arizona State	0-0	bye week

ESPN	AP	September 5 Poll		Sept. 11 Games
1	1	Florida State	1-0	beat # 10 Georgia Tech 41-35
2	2	Penn State	2-0	beat Pittsburgh 20-17
3	3	Tennessee	1-0	bye week
4	4	Florida	1-0	beat Central Florida 58-27
6	5	Nebraska	1-0	beat California 45-0
5	6	Michigan	1-0	beat Rice 37-3
6	7	Texas A&M	1-0	bye week
9	8	Miami, Fla.	2-0	bye week
8	9	Wisconsin	1-0	beat Ball St. 50-10
10	10	Georgia Tech	1-0	lost to # 1 Florida State 35-41
11	11	Virginia Tech	1-0	beat UAB 31-10
12	12	Georgia	1-0	beat South Carolina 24-9
14	13	Ohio State	0-1	beat # 14 UCLA 42-20
13	14	UCLA	1-0	lost to # 13 Ohio State 20-42
17	15	Arkansas	1-0	bye week
21	16	Notre Dame	1-1	lost to # 20 Purdue 23-28
18	17	Kansas State	0-0	beat Temple 40-0
20	18	Southern Cal	1-0	bye week
15	19	Arizona	1-1	beat Middle Tennessee 34-19
16	20	Purdue	1-0	beat # 16 Notre Dame 28-23
22	21	Alabama	1-0	beat Houston 37-10
19	22	Virginia	1-0	lost to Clemson 14-33
24	23	North Carolina St.	2-0	beat William & Mary 38-9
	24	Colorado State	1-0	beat Nevada 38-33
25	25	Arizona State	0-0	beat Texas Tech 31-13 S6
23		Texas	1-1	beat Rutgers 38-21

ESPN	AP	September 12 Poll		Sept. 18 Games
1	1	Florida State	2-0	beat # 20 North Carolina St. 42-11
2	2	Tennessee	1-0	lost to # 4 Florida 21-23
3	3	Penn State	3-0	beat # 8 Miami, Fla. 27-23
4	4	Florida	2-0	beat # 2 Tennessee 23-21
6	5	Nebraska	2-0	beat Southern Miss 20-13
5	6	Michigan	2-0	beat Syracuse 18-13
7	7	Texas A&M	1-0	beat Tulsa 62-13
9	8	Miami, Fla.	2-0	lost to # 3 Penn State 23-27
8	9	Wisconsin	2-0	lost Cincinnati 12-17
10	10	Virginia Tech	2-0	bye week
11	11	Georgia	2-0	bye week
13	12	Georgia Tech	1-1	beat Central Florida 41-10
12	13	Ohio State	1-1	beat Ohio U 40-16
14	14	Purdue	2-0	beat Central Michigan 58-16
15	15	Arkansas	1-0	beat La. Monroe 44-6
16	16	Kansas State	1-0	beat Texas-El Paso 40-7
19	17	Southern Cal	1-0	beat San Diego State 24-21
18	18	Alabama	2-0	lost to Louisiana Tech 28-29
17	19	Arizona	2-1	lost to Stanford 22-50
20	20	North Carolina St.	3-0	lost to # 1 Florida State 11-42
21	21	UCLA	1-1	beat Fresno State 35-21
23	22	Arizona State	1-0	lost to New Mexico State 7-35
24	23	Colorado State	2-0	lost to # 25 Brigham Young 13-34 (S16)
	24	Notre Dame	1-2	lost to Michigan State 13-23
	25	Brigham Young	1-0	beat # 23 Colorado State 34-13 (S16)
22		Texas	2-1	beat Rice 18-13
25		Marshall	2-0	beat Bowling Green 35-16

ESPN	AP	September 19 Poll		Sept. 25 Games
1	1	Florida State	3-0	beat North Carolina 42-10
2	2	Penn State	4-0	beat Indiana 45-24
3	3	Florida	3-0	beat Kentucky 38-10
4	4	Michigan	3-0	beat # 20 Wisconsin 21-16
6	5	Texas A&M	2-0	beat Southern Miss 23-6
5	6	Nebraska	3-0	beat Missouri 40-10
7	7	Tennessee	1-1	beat Memphis 17-16
8	8	Virginia Tech	2-0	beat Clemson 31-11 (S23)
13	9	Miami, Fla.	2-1	lost to East Carolina 23-27
12	10	Georgia Tech	2-1	bye week
9	11	Georgia	2-0	beat Central Florida 24-23
10	12	Ohio State	2-1	beat Cincinnati 34-20
11	13	Purdue	3-0	beat Northwestern 31-23
14	14	Arkansas	2-0	lost to Alabama 28-35
15	15	Kansas State	2-0	beat Iowa State 35-28
16	16	Southern Cal	2-0	lost to Oregon 30-33
19	17	Brigham Young	2-0	lost to Virginia 40-45
18	18	UCLA	2-1	lost to Stanford 32-42
21	19	Michigan State	3-0	beat Illinois 27-10
17	20	Wisconsin	2-1	lost to # 4 Michigan 16-21
22	21	Marshall	3-0	beat Temple 34-0
20	22	Texas	3-1	beat Baylor 62-0
23	23	Mississippi State	3-0	beat South Carolina 17-0
25	24	Air Force	2-0	lost to Wyoming 7-10
24	25	North Carolina St.	3-1	lost to Wake Forest 7-31

ESPN	AP	September 26 Poll		Oct. 2 Games
1	1	Florida State	4-0	beat Duke 51-23
2	2	Penn State	5-0	bye week
3	3	Florida	4-0	lost to # 21 Alabama 39-40
4	4	Michigan	4-0	beat # 11 Purdue 38-12
6	5	Texas A&M	3-0	lost to Texas Tech 19-21
5	6	Nebraska	4-0	beat Oklahoma State 38-14
8	7	Tennessee	2-1	beat Auburn 24-0
7	8	Virginia Tech	3-0	beat # 24 Virginia 31-7
12	9	Georgia Tech	2-1	beat Maryland 49-31 (S30)
11	10	Georgia	3-0	beat LSU 23-22
10	11	Purdue	4-0	lost to # 4 Michigan 12-38
9	12	Ohio State	3-1	lost to Wisconsin 17-42
13	13	Kansas State	3-0	beat # 15 Texas 35-17
14	14	Michigan State	4-0	beat Iowa 49-3
15	15	Texas	4-1	lost to # 13 Kansas State 17-35
	16	Mississippi State	4-0	beat Vanderbilt 42-14
17	17	Marshall	4-0	beat Miami, Ohio
20	18	Miami, Fla.	2-2	bye week
21	19	East Carolina	4-0	beat Army 33-14
18	20	Arkansas	2-1	lost to Kentucky 20-31
22	21	Alabama	3-1	beat # 3 Florida 40-39
19	22	Syracuse	3-1	beat Tulane 47-17
25	23	Oklahoma	3-0	lost to Notre Dame 30-34
24	24	Virginia	3-1	lost to # 8 Virginia Tech 7-31
	25	Oregon	3-1	lost to Washington 20-34
23		Southern Cal	2-1	beat Oregon State 37-29

ESPN	AP	October 3 Poll		Oct. 9 Games
1	1	Florida State	5-0	beat # 19 Miami, Fla. 31-21
2	2	Penn State	5-0	beat Iowa 31-7
3	3	Michigan	5-0	lost to # 11 Michigan State 31-34
4	4	Nebraska	5-0	beat Iowa State 49-14
5	5	Virginia Tech	4-0	beat Rutgers 58-20
6	6	Tennessee	3-1	beat # 10 Georgia 37-20
8	7	Georgia Tech	3-1	beat North Carolina 31-24
7	8	Florida	4-1	beat LSU 31-40
10	9	Kansas State	4-0	beat Kansas 50-9
9	10	Georgia	4-0	lost to # 6 Tennessee 20-37
11	11	Michigan State	5-0	beat # 3 Michigan 34-31
14	12	Alabama	4-1	bye week
12	13	Texas A&M	3-1	beat Baylor 45-13
13	14	Mississippi State	5-0	beat Auburn 18-16
15	15	Marshall	5-0	bye week
18	16	East Carolina	5-0	lost to Southern Miss 22-39
15	17	Purdue	4-1	lost to # 21 Ohio State 22-25
17	18	Syracuse	4-1	beat Pittsburgh 24-17 (O7)
21	19	Miami, Fla.	2-2	lost to # 1 Florida State 21-31
20	20	Wisconsin	3-2	beat # 25 Minnesota 20-17
19	21	Ohio State	3-2	beat # 17 Purdue 25-22
22	22	Southern Cal	3-1	lost to Arizona 24-31
23	23	Texas	4-2	beat Oklahoma 38-28
24	24	Brigham Young	3-1	beat California 38-28
	25	Minnesota	4-0	lost to # 20 Wisconsin 17-20
25		Mississippi	4-1	beat Tulane 20-13

ESPN	AP	October 10 Poll		Oct. 16 Games
1	1	Florida State	6-0	beat Wake Forest 33-10
2	2	Penn State	6-0	beat # 18 Ohio State 23-10
3	3	Nebraska	6-0	bye week
4	4	Virginia Tech	5-0	beat # 16 Syracuse 62-0
7	5	Michigan State	6-0	lost to # 20 Purdue 28-52
5	6	Tennessee	4-1	bye week
6	7	Florida	5-1	beat Auburn 32-14
9	8	Georgia Tech	4-1	beat Duke 38-31
8	9	Kansas State	5-0	beat Utah State 40-0
10	10	Michigan	5-1	bye week
13	11	Alabama	4-1	beat Mississippi 30-24
12	12	Mississippi State	6-0	bye week
11	13	Texas A&M	4-1	beat Kansas 34-17
14	14	Georgia	4-1	beat Vanderbilt 27-17
16	15	Marshall	5-0	beat Toledo 38-13 (O14)
15	16	Syracuse	5-1	lost to # 4 Virginia Tech 0-62
18	17	Wisconsin	4-2	beat Indiana 59-0
17	18	Ohio State	4-2	lost to # 2 Penn State 10-23
19	19	Texas	5-2	bye week
21	20	Purdue	4-2	beat # 5 Michigan State 52-28
20	21	Brigham Young	4-1	beat New Mexico 31-7
22	22	Mississippi	5-1	lost to Alabama 24-30
23	23	East Carolina	5-1	bye week
24	24	Miami, Fla.	2-3	bye week
	25	Southern Miss	3-2	beat Army 24-0
25		Air Force	4-1	lost to Utah 15-21

ESPN	AP	October 17 Poll		Oct. 23 Games
1	1	Florida State	7-0	beat Clemson 17-14
2	2	Penn State	7-0	beat # 16 Purdue 31-25
3	3	Nebraska	6-0	lost to # 18 Texas 20-24
4	4	Virginia Tech	6-0	bye week
5	5	Tennessee	4-1	beat # 10 Alabama 21-7
6	6	Florida	6-1	bye week
7	7	Kansas State	6-0	beat Oklahoma State 44-21
8	8	Georgia Tech	5-1	bye week
9	9	Michigan	5-1	lost to Ilinois 29-35
12	10	Alabama	5-1	lost to # 5 Tennessee 7-21
13	11	Michigan State	6-1	lost to # 17 Wisconsin 10-40
11	12	Mississippi State	6-0	beat LSU 17-16
10	13	Texas A&M	5-1	lost to Oklahoma 6-51
14	14	Georgia	5-1	beat Kentucky 49-34
15	15	Marshall	6-0	beat Buffalo 59-3
17	16	Purdue	5-2	lost to # 2 Penn State 25-31
16	17	Wisconsin	5-2	beat # 11 Michigan State 40-10
18	18	Texas	5-2	beat # 3 Nebraska 24-20
19	19	Brigham Young	5-1	beat Nevada-Las Vegas 29-0
20	20	East Carolina	5-1	beat Tulane 52-7
21	21	Southern Miss	4-2	beat Cincinnati 28-20
22	22	Ohio State	4-3	beat # 24 Minnesota 20-17
23	23	Miami, Fla.	2-3	beat Boston College 31-28
25	24	Minnesota	5-1	lost to # 22 Ohio State 17-20
	25	Mississippi	5-2	bye week
24		Syracuse	5-2	bye week

October 24 Poll — Oct. 30 Games

ESPN	AP	Team	Record	Oct. 30 Games
1	1	Florida State	8-0	beat Virginia 35-10
2	2	Penn State	8-0	beat Illinois 27-7
3	3	Virginia Tech	6-0	beat Pittsburgh 30-17
4	4	Tennessee	5-1	beat South Carolina 30-7
5	5	Florida	6-1	beat # 10 Georgia 30-14
6	6	Kansas State	7-0	beat Baylor 48-7
7	7	Georgia Tech	5-1	beat North Carolina St. 48-21
8	8	Mississippi State	7-0	bye week
9	9	Nebraska	6-1	beat Kansas 24-17
10	10	Georgia	6-1	lost to # 5 Florida 14-30
11	11	Wisconsin	6-2	beat Northwestern 35-19
12	12	Texas	6-2	beat Iowa State 44-41
13	13	Marshall	7-0	beat No. Illinois 41-9
16	14	Alabama	5-2	beat # 20 Southern Miss 35-14
14	15	Michigan	5-2	beat Indiana 34-31
15	16	Brigham Young	6-1	beat Air Force 27-20
17	17	East Carolina	6-1	beat Houston 19-3
22	18	Purdue	5-3	beat Minnesota 33-28
20	19	Michigan State	6-2	bye week
19	20	Southern Miss	5-2	lost to # 14 Alabama 14-35
21	21	Ohio State	5-3	beat Iowa 41-11
18	22	Texas A&M	5-2	beat Oklahoma State 21-3
23	23	Miami, Fla.	3-3	beat West Virginia 28-20
	24	Oklahoma	4-2	lost to Colorado 24-38
	25	Mississippi	5-2	beat LSU 42-23
24		Syracuse	5-2	lost to Boston College 23-24
25		Stanford	5-2	lost to Washington 30-35

October 31 Poll — Nov. 6 Games

ESPN	AP	Team	Record	Nov. 6 Games
1	1	Florida State	9-0	bye week
2	2	Penn State	9-0	lost to Minnesota 23-24
3	3	Virginia Tech	7-0	beat West Virginia 22-20
4	4	Tennessee	6-1	beat #24 Notre Dame 38-14
5	5	Florida	7-1	beat Vanderbilt 13-6
6	6	Kansas State	8-0	beat Colorado 20-14
7	7	Georgia Tech	6-1	lost to Virginia 38-45
8	8	Mississippi State	7-0	beat Kentucky 23-22 (N4)
9	9	Nebraska	7-1	beat # 21 Texas A&M 37-0
10	10	Wisconsin	7-2	beat # 17 Purdue 28-21
11	11	Texas	7-2	beat Oklahoma State 34-21
14	12	Alabama	6-2	beat LSU 23-17
12	13	Marshall	8-0	beat Kent State 28-16
16	14	Georgia	6-2	bye week
13	15	Brigham Young	7-1	beat San Diego State 30-7
15	16	Michigan	6-2	beat Northwestern 37-3
21	17	Purdue	6-3	lost to # 10 Wisconsin 21-28
17	18	East Carolina	7-1	lost to UAB 17-36
19	19	Michigan State	6-2	beat # 20 Ohio State 23-7
20	20	Ohio State	6-3	lost to #19 Michigan State 7-23
18	21	Texas A&M	6-2	lost to # 9 Nebraska 0-37
22	22	Miami, Fla.	4-3	beat Pittsburgh 33-3
23	23	Mississippi	6-2	beat Arkansas 38-16
	24	Notre Dame	5-3	lost to # 4 Tennessee 14-38
25	25	Southern Miss	5-3	beat Memphis 20-5
24		Arkansas	5-2	lost to # 23 Mississippi 16-38

November 7 Poll — Nov. 13 Games

ESPN	AP	Team	Record	Nov. 13 Games
1	1	Florida State	9-0	beat Maryland 49-10
2	2	Virginia Tech	8-0	beat # 19 Miami, Fla. 43-10
3	3	Tennessee	7-1	lost to Arkansas 24-28
4	4	Florida	8-1	beat South Carolina 20-3
5	5	Kansas State	9-0	lost to # 7 Nebraska 15-41
8	6	Penn State	9-1	lost to # 16 Michigan 27-31
6	7	Nebraska	8-1	beat # 5 Kansas State 41-15
7	8	Mississippi State	8-0	lost to # 11 Alabama 7-19
9	9	Wisconsin	8-2	beat Iowa 41-3
10	10	Texas	8-2	beat Texas Tech 58-7
13	11	Alabama	7-2	beat # 8 Mississippi State 19-7
11	12	Marshall	9-0	beat Western Michigan 31-17
14	13	Georgia Tech	6-2	beat Clemson 45-42
16	14	Georgia	6-2	lost to Auburn 21-38
12	15	Brigham Young	8-1	lost to Wyoming 17-31
15	16	Michigan	7-2	beat # 6 Penn State 31-27
17	17	Michigan State	7-2	beat Northwestern 34-0
18	18	Mississippi	7-2	bye week
19	19	Miami, Fla.	5-3	lost to # 2 Virginia Tech 10-43
21	20	Minnesota	6-3	beat Indiana 44-20
20	21	Southern Miss	6-3	beat La. Lafayette 48-0
	22	Purdue	6-4	bye week
22	23	Washington	6-3	lost to UCLA 20-23
24	24	East Carolina	7-2	beat Cincinnati 48-34
	25	Ohio State	6-4	lost to Illinois 20-46
23		Texas A&M	6-3	beat Missouri 51-14
25		Boston College	6-2	beat West Virginia 34-17

November 14 Poll — Nov. 20 Games

ESPN	AP	Team	Record	Nov. 20 Games
1	1	Florida State	10-0	beat # 3 Florida 30-23
2	2	Virginia Tech	9-0	beat Temple 62-7
3	3	Florida	9-1	lost to # 1 Florida State 23-30
4	4	Nebraska	9-1	bye week
5	5	Wisconsin	9-2	regular season complete
6	6	Texas	9-2	bye week
7	7	Tennessee	7-2	beat Kentucky 56-21
8	8	Alabama	8-2	beat Auburn 28-17
9	9	Kansas State	9-1	beat Missouri 66-0
10	10	Michigan	8-2	beat Ohio State 24-17
11	11	Marshall	10-0	bye week
15	12	Mississippi State	8-1	lost to # 22 Arkansas 9-14
13	13	Penn State	9-2	lost to # 15 Michigan State 28-35
12	14	Georgia Tech	7-2	lost to Wake Forest 23-26
14	15	Michigan State	8-2	beat # 13 Penn State 35-28
16	16	Mississippi	7-2	lost to # 21 Georgia 17-20
18	17	Minnesota	7-3	beat Iowa 25-21
17	18	Southern Miss	7-3	beat Louisville 30-27
19	19	Brigham Young	8-2	lost to Utah 17-20
25	20	Purdue	6-4	beat Indiana 30-24
23	21	Georgia	6-3	beat # 16 Mississippi 20-17
24	22	Arkansas	6-3	beat # 12 Mississippi State 14-9
21	23	East Carolina	8-2	beat North Carolina St. 23-6
20	24	Texas A&M	7-3	bye week
22	25	Boston College	7-2	beat Notre Dame 31-29

November 21 Poll — Nov. 27 Games

ESPN	AP	Team	Record	Nov. 27 Games
1	1	Florida State	11-0	regular season complete
2	2	Virginia Tech	10-0	beat # 22 Boston College 38-14 (N26)
3	3	Nebraska	9-1	beat Colorado 33-30 (N26)
4	4	Wisconsin	9-2	
6	5	Florida	9-2	bye week
7	6	Tennessee	8-2	beat Vanderbilt 38-10
5	7	Texas	9-2	lost to # 24 Texas A&M 16-20 (N26)
9	8	Alabama	9-2	bye week
8	9	Kansas State	10-1	regular season complete
10	10	Michigan	9-2	regular season complete
11	11	Michigan State	9-2	regular season complete
12	12	Marshall	10-0	beat Ohio U 34-3 (N26)
14	13	Minnesota	8-3	regular season complete
13	14	Southern Miss	8-3	regular season complete
15	15	Penn State	9-3	regular season complete
21	16	Georgia	7-3	lost to # 20 Georgia Tech 48-51
22	17	Arkansas	7-3	lost to LSU 10-35 (N26)
19	18	Mississippi State	8-2	beat # 23 Mississippi 23-20 (N25)
23	19	Purdue	7-4	regular season complete
16	20	Georgia Tech	7-3	beat # 16 Georgia 51-48
18	21	East Carolina	9-2	regular season complete
20	22	Boston College	8-2	lost to # 2 Virginia Tech 14-38 (N26)
24	23	Mississippi	7-3	lost to # 18 Mississippi State 20-23
17	24	Texas A&M	7-3	beat # 7 Texas 20-16 (N26)
	25	Louisiana Tech	8-2	lost to Southern Cal 19-45 (N26)
25		Stanford	7-3	beat Notre Dame 40-37

November 28 Poll — Dec. 4 Games

ESPN	AP	Team	Record	Dec. 4 Games
1	1	Florida State	11-0	
2	2	Virginia Tech	11-0	regular season complete
3	3	Nebraska	10-1	beat # 12 Texas 22-6 (Big 12 CH)
4	4	Wisconsin	9-2	
5	5	Florida	9-2	lost to # 7 Alabama 7-34 (SEC CH)
6	6	Tennessee	9-2	regular season complete
8	7	Alabama	9-2	beat # 5 Florida 34-7 (SEC CH)
7	8	Kansas State	10-1	
9	9	Michigan	9-2	
10	10	Michigan State	9-2	
11	11	Marshall	11-0	beat Western Michigan 34-30 (MAC CH D3)
12	12	Texas	9-3	lost to # 3 Nebraska 6-22 (Big 12 CH)
13	13	Minnesota	8-3	
17	14	Penn State	9-3	
15	15	Southern Miss	8-3	
18	16	Mississippi State	9-2	regular season complete
16	17	Georgia Tech	8-3	regular season complete
14	18	Texas A&M	8-3	regular season complete
20	19	Purdue	7-4	
19	20	East Carolina	9-2	
23	21	Georgia	7-4	regular season complete
21	22	Stanford	8-3	regular season complete
24	23	Miami, Fla.	7-4	beat Temple 55-0
	24	Arkansas	7-4	regular season complete
22	25	Boston College	8-3	regular season complete
25		Brigham Young	8-3	regular season complete

December 5 Poll

ESPN	AP	Team	Record	Bowl Bid	Date	Bowl Result
1	1	Florida State	11-0	Sugar Bowl	J4	beat # 2 Virginia Tech 46-29
2	2	Virginia Tech	11-0	Sugar Bowl	J4	lost to # 1 Florida State 29-46
3	3	Nebraska	11-1	Fiesta Bowl	J2	beat # 6 Tennessee 31-21
4	4	Wisconsin	9-2	Rose Bowl	J1	beat # 22 Stanford 17-9
6	5	Alabama	10-2	Orange Bowl	J1	lost to # 8 Michigan 34-35
5	6	Tennessee	9-2	Fiesta Bowl	J2	lost to # 3 Nebraska 21-31
7	7	Kansas State	10-1	Holiday Bowl	D29	beat Washington 24-20
8	8	Michigan	9-2	Orange Bowl	J1	beat # 5 Alabama 35-34
9	9	Michigan State	9-2	Citrus Bowl	J1	beat # 10 Florida 37-34
10	10	Florida	9-3	Citrus Bowl	J1	lost to # 9 Michigan State 34-37
11	11	Marshall	12-0	Motor City Bowl	D27	beat Brigham Young 21-3
12	12	Minnesota	8-3	Sun Bowl	D31	lost to Oregon 20-24
17	13	Penn State	9-3	Alamo Bowl	D28	beat # 18 Texas A&M 24-0
18	14	Texas	9-4	Cotton Bowl	J1	lost to # 24 Arkansas 6-27
16	15	Mississippi State	9-2	Peach Bowl	D30	beat Clemson 17-7
14	16	Southern Miss	8-3	Liberty Bowl	D31	beat Colorado State 23-17
15	17	Georgia Tech	8-3	Gator Bowl	J1	lost to # 23 Miami, Fla. 13-28
13	18	Texas A&M	8-3	Alamo Bowl	D28	lost to # 13 Penn State 0-24
20	19	Purdue	7-4	Outback Bowl	J1	lost to # 21 Georgia 25-28
19	20	East Carolina	9-2	Mobile Bowl	D22	lost to TCU 14-28
24	21	Georgia	7-4	Outback Bowl	J1	beat # 19 Purdue 28-25
21	22	Stanford	8-3	Rose Bowl	J1	lost to # 4 Wisconsin 9-17
23	23	Miami, Fla.	8-4	Gator Bowl	J1	beat # 17 Georgia Tech 28-13
	24	Arkansas	7-4	Cotton Bowl	J1	beat # 14 Texas 27-6
22	25	Boston College	8-3	Insight.com Bowl	D31	lost to Colorado 28-62
25		Brigham Young	8-3	Motor City Bowl	D27	lost to # 11 Marshall 3-21

January 5 Final Poll

RB	ESPN	AP	Team	Record
1	1	1	Florida State	12-0
5	3	2	Virginia Tech	11-1
2	2	3	Nebraska	12-1
8	4	4	Wisconsin	10-2
3	5	5	Michigan	10-2
4	6	6	Kansas State	11-1
7	7	7	Michigan State	10-2
11	8	8	Alabama	10-3
10	9	9	Tennessee	9-3
6	10	10	Marshall	13-0
9	11	11	Penn State	10-3
12	14	12	Florida	9-4
13	12	13	Mississippi State	10-2
15	13	14	Southern Miss	9-3
19	15	15	Miami, Fla.	9-4
16	16	16	Georgia	8-4
17	19	17	Arkansas	8-4
26	17	18	Minnesota	8-4
14	18	19	Oregon	9-3
27	21	20	Georgia Tech	8-4
33	23	21	Texas	9-5
29	22	22	Mississippi	8-4
21	20	23	Texas A&M	8-4
18	25	24	Illinois	8-4
20		25	Purdue	7-5
28	24		Stanford	8-4

1999

Consensus All-Americans

POS	Offense	HT	WT	CL	School	AP	CF	FC	FN	FW	SN
QB	**Joe Hamilton**	5-10	189	Sr.	Georgia Tech	•	•	•		•	•
RB	**Ron Dayne**	5-10	254	Sr.	Wisconsin	•	•	•	•	•	•
RB	**Thomas Jones**	5-10	205	Sr.	Virginia	•	•		•	•	•
WR	**Troy Walters**	5-8	170	Sr.	Stanford	•	•		•	•	•
WR	**Peter Warrick**	6-0	195	Sr.	Florida State	•	•	•	•	•	•
TE	**James Whalen**	6-4	231	Sr.	Kentucky	•	•			•	
OL	**Chris McIntosh**	6-7	310	Sr.	Wisconsin	•	•	•	•	•	•
OL	**Chris Samuels**	6-6	291	Sr.	Alabama	•	•	•	•	•	•
OL	**Cosey Coleman**	6-5	315	Jr.	Tennessee	•	•	•	•	•	
OL	**Jason Whitaker**	6-5	300	Sr.	Florida State	•	•	•	•		
C	**Ben Hamilton**	6-5	271	Jr.	Minnesota	•					•
C	**Rob Riti**	6-3	289	Sr.	Missouri		•	•			
PK	**Sebastian Janikowski**	6-2	255	Jr.	Florida State	•	•	•		•	
AP	**Dennis Northcutt**	5-11	178	Sr.	Arizona	•		*		•	

OTHERS RECEIVING FIRST-TEAM HONORS

POS	Name	School	AP	CF	FC	FN	FW	SN
QB	Michael Vick	Virginia Tech				•		
RB	Shaun Alexander	Alabama			•			
TE	Ibn Green	Louisville			•			
TE	Bubba Franks	Miami, Fla.				•		•
OL	Brad Bedell	Colorado					•	
OL	Mike Malano	San Diego State					•	
OL	Marvel Smith	Arizona State				•		
OL	Richard Mercier	Miami, Fla.						•
OL	Noel LaMontagne	Virginia						•
AP	David Allen	Kansas State			•			

FC named Northcutt as a WR

POS	Defense	HT	WT	CL	School	AP	CF	FC	FN	FW	SN
DL	**Courtney Brown**	6-5	270	Sr.	Penn State	•	•	•	•	•	•
DL	**Corey Moore**	6-0	225	Sr.	Virginia Tech	•	•	•	•	•	•
DL	**Corey Simon**	6-4	275	Sr.	Florida State	•	•	•		•	•
LB	**LaVar Arrington**	6-3	242	Jr.	Penn State	•	•	•	•	•	•
LB	**Mark Simoneau**	6-0	240	Sr.	Kansas State	•	•	•		•	•
LB	**Brandon Short**	6-3	252	Sr.	Penn State	•	•			•	
DB	**Tyrone Carter**	5-9	184	Sr.	Minnesota	•	•	•		•	•
DB	**Brian Urlacher**	6-4	240	Sr.	New Mexico	•	•	•		•	
DB	**Ralph Brown**	5-10	180	Sr.	Nebraska		•		•		•
DB	**Deon Grant**	6-3	205	Sr.	Tennessee		•	•	•		•
DB	**Deltha O'Neal**	5-11	195	Sr.	California	•		•		•	
P	**Andrew Bayes**	6-3	200	Sr.	East Carolina		•	•		•	

OTHERS RECEIVING FIRST-TEAM HONORS

POS	Name	School	AP	CF	FC	FN	FW	SN
DL	Alex Brown	Florida		•		•		
DL	Casey Hampton	Texas	•				•	
DL	Chris Hovan	Boston College			•			
DL	Rob Renes	Michigan						•
LB	Raynoch Thompson	Tennessee	•		•			
LB	Keith Adams	Clemson				•		
LB	Julian Peterson	Michigan State				•		
LB	Na'il Diggs	Ohio State				•		
LB	Barrin Simpson	Mississippi State						•
DB	Mike Brown	Nebraska	•				•	
DB	Jamar Fletcher	Wisconsin				•		•
DB	Ben Kelly	Colorado				•		
P	Shane Lechler	Texas A&M	•					

Heisman Trophy Voting

	PLAYER	POS	SCHOOL	1ST	2ND	3RD	TOTAL
1	**Ron Dayne**	RB	Wisconsin	586	121	42	2042
2	**Joe Hamilton**	QB	Georgia Tech	96	285	136	994
3	**Michael Vick**	QB	Virginia Tech	25	72	100	319
4	**Drew Brees**	QB	Purdue	3	89	121	308
5	**Chad Pennington**	QB	Marshall	21	45	94	247
6	**Peter Warrick**	WR	Florida State	14	50	61	203
7	**Shaun Alexander**	RB	Alabama	11	42	52	171
8	**Thomas Jones**	RB	Virginia	10	32	46	140
9	**LaVar Arrington**	LB	Penn State	3	14	17	54
10	**Tim Rattay**	QB	Louisiana Tech	1	5	16	29

Award Winners

Ron Dayne, RB, Wisconsin, Maxwell, Camp, Walker, **Chris Samuels**, OT, Alabama, Outland, **Corey Moore**, DE, Virginia Tech, Lombardi, Nagurski, **Joe Hamilton**, QB, Georgia Tech, O'Brien, **LaVar Arrington**, LB, Penn State, Butkus, Bednarik, **Tyrone Carter**, DB, Minnesota, Thorpe, **Chris Redman**, QB, Louisville, Unitas, **Sebastian Janikowski**, K, Florida State, Groza, **Troy Walters**, WR, Stanford, Biletnikoff, **Deltha O'Neal**, CB, California, Tatupu

Bowl Games

D18, **Las Vegas**, Utah 17, Fresno State 16, D22, **GMAC**, TCU 28, East Carolina 14, D25, **Oahu**, Hawaii 23, Oregon State 17, D25, **Aloha**, Wake Forest 23, Arizona State 3, D27**Motor City**, Marshall 21, Brigham Young 3, D28, **Alamo**, Penn State 24, Texas A&M 0, D29, **Holiday**, Kansas State 24, Washington 20, D29**Music City**, Syracuse 20, Kentucky 13, D30, **Humanitarian**, Boise State 34, Louisville 31, D30, **Micron PC**, Illinois 63, Virginia 21, D30, **Peach**, Mississippi State 17, Clemson 7, D31, **Insight.com**, Colorado 62, Boston College 28, D31, **Independence**, Mississippi 27, Oklahoma 25, D31, **Sun**, Oregon 24, Minnesota 20, D31, **Liberty**, Southern Miss 23, Colorado State 17, J1, **Cotton**, Arkansas 27, Texas 6, J1, **Outback**, Georgia 28, Purdue 25, OT, J1, **Gator**, Miami, Fla. 28, Georgia Tech 13, J1, **Orange**, Michigan 35, Alabama 34, OT, J1, **Florida Citrus**, Michigan State 37, Florida 34, J1, **Rose**, Wisconsin 17, Stanford 9, J2, **Fiesta**, Nebraska 31, Tennessee 21, J4, **Sugar**, Florida State 46, Virginia Tech 29

Conference Standings

ACC	Conf. W	Conf. L	Conf. T	Overall W	Overall L	Overall T
Florida State	8	0	0	12	0	0
Georgia Tech	5	3	0	8	4	0
Virginia	5	3	0	7	5	0
Clemson	5	3	0	6	6	0
Wake Forest	3	5	0	7	5	0
North Carolina St.	3	5	0	6	6	0
Duke	3	5	0	3	8	0
Maryland	2	6	0	5	6	0
North Carolina	2	6	0	3	8	0

Big 10	Conf. W	Conf. L	Conf. T	Overall W	Overall L	Overall T
Wisconsin	7	1	0	10	2	0
Michigan State	6	2	0	10	2	0
Michigan	6	2	0	10	2	0
Penn State	5	3	0	10	3	0
Minnesota	5	3	0	8	4	0
Illinois	4	4	0	8	4	0
Purdue	4	4	0	7	5	0
Ohio State	3	5	0	6	6	0
Indiana	3	5	0	4	7	0
Northwestern	1	7	0	3	8	0
Iowa	0	8	0	1	10	0

Big 12	Conf. W	Conf. L	Conf. T	Overall W	Overall L	Overall T
NORTH						
Nebraska	7	1	0	12	1	0
Kansas State	7	1	0	11	1	0
Colorado	5	3	0	7	5	0
Kansas	3	5	0	5	7	0
Iowa State	1	7	0	4	7	0
Missouri	1	7	0	4	7	0
SOUTH						
Texas	6	2	0	9	5	0
Texas A&M	5	3	0	8	4	0
Oklahoma	5	3	0	7	5	0
Texas Tech	5	3	0	6	5	0
Oklahoma State	3	5	0	5	6	0
Baylor	0	8	0	1	10	0

Championship **Nebraska 22 Texas 6**

Big East	Conf. W	Conf. L	Conf. T	Overall W	Overall L	Overall T
Virginia Tech	7	0	0	11	1	0
Miami, Fla.	6	1	0	9	4	0
Boston College	4	3	0	8	4	0
Syracuse	3	4	0	7	5	0
West Virginia	3	4	0	4	7	0
Pittsburgh	2	5	0	5	6	0
Temple	2	5	0	2	9	0
Rutgers	1	6	0	1	10	0

Big West	Conf. W	Conf. L	Conf. T	Overall W	Overall L	Overall T
Boise State	5	1	0	10	3	0
Idaho	4	2	0	7	4	0
New Mexico State	3	2	0	6	5	0
Utah State	3	3	0	4	7	0
Arkansas State	2	3	0	4	7	0
Nevada	2	4	0	3	8	0
North Texas	1	5	0	2	9	0

C-USA	Conf. W	Conf. L	Conf. T	Overall W	Overall L	Overall T
Southern Miss	6	0	0	9	3	0
East Carolina	4	2	0	9	3	0
Louisville	4	2	0	7	5	0
UAB	4	2	0	5	6	0
Memphis	4	2	0	5	6	0
Houston	3	3	0	7	4	0
Tulane	1	5	0	3	8	0
Army	1	5	0	3	8	0
Cincinnati	0	6	0	3	8	0

Ivy	Conf. W	Conf. L	Conf. T	Overall W	Overall L	Overall T
Yale	6	1	0	9	1	0
Brown	6	1	0	9	1	0
Cornell	5	2	0	7	3	0
Pennsylvania	4	3	0	7	5	0
Harvard	3	4	0	5	5	0
Darmouth	2	5	0	2	8	0
Columbia	1	6	0	3	7	0
Princeton	1	6	0	3	7	0

MAC	Conf. W	Conf. L	Conf. T	Overall W	Overall L	Overall T
EAST						
Marshall	8	0	0	13	0	0
Miami, Ohio	6	2	0	7	4	0
Akron	5	3	0	7	4	0
Ohio U	5	3	0	5	6	0
Bowling Green	3	5	0	5	6	0
Kent State	2	6	0	2	9	0
Buffalo	0	8	0	0	11	0
WEST						
Western Michigan	6	2	0	7	5	0
Toledo	5	3	0	6	5	0
Northern Illinois	5	3	0	5	6	0
Eastern Michigan	4	4	0	4	7	0
Central Michigan	3	5	0	4	7	0
Ball State	0	8	0	0	11	0

Championship **Marshall 34 Western Michigan 30**

MWC	Conf. W	Conf. L	Conf. T	Overall W	Overall L	Overall T
Utah	5	2	0	9	3	0
Colorado State	5	2	0	8	4	0
Brigham Young	5	2	0	8	4	0
Wyoming	4	3	0	7	4	0
San Diego State	3	4	0	5	6	0
New Mexico	3	4	0	4	7	0
Air Force	2	5	0	6	5	0
Nevada-Las Vegas	1	6	0	3	8	0

Pac 10	Conf. W	Conf. L	Conf. T	Overall W	Overall L	Overall T
Stanford	7	1	0	8	4	0
Oregon	6	2	0	9	3	0
Washington	6	2	0	7	5	0
Arizona State	5	3	0	6	6	0
Oregon State	4	4	0	7	5	0
Southern Cal	3	5	0	6	6	0
Arizona	3	5	0	6	6	0
California	3	5	0	4	7	0
UCLA	2	6	0	4	7	0
Washington State	1	7	0	3	9	0

SEC	Conf. W	Conf. L	Conf. T	Overall W	Overall L	Overall T
EAST						
Florida	7	1	0	9	4	0
Tennessee	6	2	0	9	3	0
Georgia	5	3	0	8	4	0
Kentucky	4	4	0	6	6	0
Vanderbilt	2	6	0	5	6	0
South Carolina	0	8	0	0	11	0
WEST						
Alabama	7	1	0	10	3	0
Mississippi State	6	2	0	10	2	0
Arkansas	4	4	0	8	4	0
Mississippi	4	4	0	8	4	0
Auburn	2	6	0	5	6	0
LSU	1	7	0	3	8	0

Championship **Alabama 34 Florida 7**

WAC	Conf. W	Conf. L	Conf. T	Overall W	Overall L	Overall T
Hawaii	5	2	0	9	4	0
TCU	5	2	0	8	4	0
Fresno State	5	2	0	8	5	0
Rice	4	3	0	5	6	0
SMU	3	3	0	4	6	0
Texas-El Paso	3	4	0	5	7	0
San Jose State	1	5	0	3	7	0
Tulsa	1	6	0	2	9	0

Independents	Overall W	Overall L	Overall T
Louisiana Tech	8	3	0
La. Monroe	5	6	0
Notre Dame	5	7	0
Navy	5	7	0
Central Florida	4	7	0
Middle Tennessee	3	8	0
La. Lafayette	2	9	0

1999 NCAA Major College Statistical Leaders

Individual Leaders

	PASSING	CL	G	ATT	COM	PCT	INT	I%	YDS	YPA	TD	TD%	RATING
1	Michael Vick, Virginia Tech	SO	10	152	90	59.2	5	3.3	1840	12.1	12	7.9	180.4
2	Joe Hamilton, Georgia Tech	SR	11	305	203	66.6	11	3.6	3060	10.0	29	9.5	175.0
3	Chad Pennington, Marshall	SR	12	405	275	67.9	11	2.7	3799	9.4	37	9.1	171.4
4	Billy Volek, Fresno State	SR	12	355	235	66.2	3	0.9	2559	7.2	30	8.5	152.9
5	Tim Rattay, Louisiana Tech	SR	10	516	342	66.3	12	2.3	3922	7.6	35	6.8	147.9
6	Jay Stuckey, Texas-El Paso	SR	12	225	145	64.4	13	5.8	1918	8.5	15	6.7	146.5
7	Chris Weinke, Florida State	JR	11	377	232	61.5	14	3.7	3103	8.2	25	6.6	145.1
8	Dan Ellis, Virginia	JR	10	258	156	60.5	10	3.9	2050	8.0	20	7.8	145.0
9	Jeff Kelly, Southern Miss	SO	11	260	153	58.9	11	4.2	2062	7.9	21	8.1	143.7
10	Tim Lester, Western Michigan	SR	12	470	282	60.0	13	2.8	3639	7.7	34	7.2	143.4

	ALL-PURPOSE	CL	G	RUSH	REC	PR	KR	YDS	YPG
1	Trevor Insley, Nevada	SR	11	5	2060	111	0	2176	197.8
2	Dennis Northcutt, Arizona	SR	12	200	1422	436	191	2249	187.4
3	Thomas Jones, Virginia	SR	11	1798	239	17	0	2054	186.7
4	LaDainian Tomlinson, TCU	JR	11	1850	55	0	69	1974	179.5
5	Travis Prentice, Miami, Ohio	SR	11	1659	270	0	0	1929	175.4
6	Troy Walters, Stanford	SR	11	6	1456	131	284	1877	170.6
7	Deuce McAllister, Mississippi	JR	10	809	201	30	652	1692	169.2
8	Ron Dayne, Wisconsin	SR	11	1834	9	0	0	1843	167.6
9	Lamont Jordan, Maryland	JR	11	1632	208	0	0	1840	167.3
10	Demario Brown, Utah State	SR	11	1536	282	0	0	1818	165.3

	RUSHING/Yards Per Game	CL	G	ATT	YDS	TD	AVG	YPG
1	LaDainian Tomlinson, TCU	JR	11	268	1850	18	6.9	168.2
2	Ron Dayne, Wisconsin	SR	11	303	1834	19	6.1	166.7
3	Thomas Jones, Virginia	SR	11	334	1798	16	5.4	163.5
4	Travis Prentice, Miami, Ohio	SR	11	354	1659	17	4.7	150.8
5	Lamont Jordan, Maryland	JR	11	266	1632	16	6.1	148.4
6	Demario Brown, Utah State	SR	11	279	1536	14	5.5	139.6
7	Trung Canidate, Arizona	SR	12	253	1602	11	6.3	133.5
8	Frank Moreau, Louisville	SR	10	233	1289	17	5.5	128.9
9	Darren Davis, Iowa State	SR	11	287	1388	14	4.8	126.2
10	Shaun Alexander, Alabama	SR	11	302	1383	19	4.6	125.7

	RUSHING/Yards Per Carry	CL	G	ATT	YDS	YPC
1	LaDainian Tomlinson, TCU	JR	11	268	1850	6.9
2	Chester Taylor, Toledo	JR	11	182	1176	6.5
3	Trung Canidate, Arizona	SR	12	253	1602	6.3
4	Lamont Jordan, Maryland	JR	11	266	1632	6.1
5	Ron Dayne, Wisconsin	SR	11	303	1834	6.1
6	Mike Green, Houston	JR	10	142	838	5.9
7	Clinton Portis, Miami, Fla.	FR	10	143	838	5.9
8	Kevin McDougal, Colorado State	SR	10	207	1164	5.6
9	Deoncé Whitaker, San Jose State	JR	9	137	769	5.6
10	Jamie Wilson, East Carolina	JR	11	156	865	5.5

*-Based on top 50 rushers

	RECEIVING	CL	G	REC	YDS	TD	RPG	YPR	YPG
1	Trevor Insley, Nevada	SR	11	134	2060	13	12.2	15.4	187.3
2	Troy Walters, Stanford	SR	11	74	1456	10	6.7	19.7	132.4
3	Dennis Northcutt, Arizona	SR	12	88	1422	8	7.3	16.2	118.5
4	Arnold Jackson, Louisville	SR	11	101	1209	9	9.2	12.0	109.9
5	Drew Haddad, Buffalo	SR	11	85	1158	6	7.7	13.6	105.3
6	Jajuan Dawson, Tulane	SR	10	96	1051	8	9.6	10.9	105.1
7	Dwight Carter, Hawaii	SR	12	77	1253	9	6.4	16.3	104.4
8	Peter Warrick, Florida State	SR	9	71	934	8	7.9	13.2	103.8
9	Chris Daniels, Purdue	SR	11	109	1133	5	9.9	10.4	103.0
9	Charles Lee, Central Florida	SR	11	87	1133	5	7.9	13.0	103.0

	PUNTING	CL	PUNT	YDS	AVG
1	Andrew Bayes, East Carolina	SR	47	2871	48.1
2	Brian Schmitz, North Carolina	SR	74	3538	47.8
3	Shane Lechler, Texas A&M	SR	60	2787	46.5
4	Ray Cheetany, Nevada-Las Vegas	JR	65	2950	45.4
5	Dan Hadenfeldt, Nebraska	SR	65	2924	45.0
6	Drew Hagan, Indiana	SR	44	1971	44.8
7	Nick Harris, California	JR	85	3795	44.7
8	Ryan Smith, Arkansas State	SR	42	1864	44.4
9	Casey Roussel, Tulane	SO	55	2429	44.2
10	Tim Morgan, San Jose State	SR	57	2510	44.0

	PUNT RETURNS	CL	PR	YDS	TD	AVG
1	Dennis Northcutt, Arizona	SR	23	436	2	19.0
2	Bobby Newcombe, Nebraska	JR	16	294	1	18.4
3	Vinny Sutherland, Purdue	JR	17	295	2	17.4
4	Rodregis Brooks, UAB	JR	19	325	0	17.1
5	Stevonne Smith, Utah	JR	29	495	3	17.1
6	Dallas Davis, Colorado State	JR	32	541	2	16.9
7	Hank Poteat, Pittsburgh	SR	19	307	1	16.2
8	Keith Stokes, East Carolina	JR	26	404	1	15.5
9	Emmett White, Utah State	SO	24	361	0	15.0
10	Terance Richardson, Oklahoma State	SR	40	591	1	14.8

	KICKOFF RETURNS	CL	KR	YDS	TD	AVG
1	James Williams, Marshall	SR	15	493	1	32.9
2	Brandon Daniels, Oklahoma	SR	16	508	1	31.8
3	John Stone, Wake Forest	SO	13	389	1	29.9
4	Deltha O'Neal, California	SR	19	555	1	29.2
5	Ben Kelly, Colorado	JR	19	547	2	28.8
6	Sonny Cook, Oregon	JR	14	402	0	28.7
7	Deoncé Whitaker, San Jose State	JR	14	396	1	28.3
8	Scottie Montgomery, Duke	JR	21	587	1	28.0
9	Chris Lacy, Idaho	SO	15	419	1	27.9
10	Ryan Wells, Stanford	SO	15	412	0	27.5

	SCORING	CL	TDS	XP	FG	PTS	PTPG
1	Shaun Alexander, Alabama	SR	24	0	0	144	13.1
2	Travis Prentice, Miami, Ohio	SR	21	0	0	126	11.5
3	Sebastian Janikowski, Florida State	JR	0	47	23	116	10.6
4	Ron Dayne, Wisconsin	SR	19	0	0	114	10.4
5	Frank Moreau, Louisville	SR	17	0	0	102	10.2
6	LaDainian Tomlinson, TCU	JR	18	0	0	108	9.8
7	Shayne Graham, Virginia Tech	SR	0	56	17	107	9.7
8	Ken Simonton, Oregon State	SO	17	4	0	106	9.6
9	Travis Zachery, Clemson	SO	16	0	0	96	9.6
10	Jamie Rheem, Kansas State	JR	0	41	18	95	9.5

	FIELD GOALS	CL	FGA	FGM	PCT	FGG
1	Sebastian Janikowski, Florida State	JR	30	23	0.77	2.09
2	Neil Rackers, Illinois	SR	25	20	0.80	1.82
3	Jamie Rheem, Kansas State	JR	21	18	0.86	1.80
4	Jeff Chandler, Florida	JR	24	21	0.88	1.75
4	Travis Forney, Penn State	SR	26	21	0.81	1.75
6	Paul Edinger, Michigan State	SR	22	18	0.82	1.64
6	Scott Westerfield, Mississippi State	JR	24	18	0.75	1.64
6	Owen Pochman, Brigham Young	JR	25	18	0.72	1.64
6	Todd France, Toledo	SO	26	18	0.69	1.64
6	Travis Dorsch, Purdue	SO	28	18	0.64	1.64

	INTERCEPTIONS	CL	INT	YDS	TD	INT/GM
1	Deltha O'Neal, California	SR	9	280	4	0.82
1	Deon Grant, Tennessee	JR	9	167	1	0.82
1	Rodregis Brooks, UAB	JR	9	152	1	0.82
4	Erik Olson, Colorado State	SR	6	93	1	0.67
5	Jamar Fletcher, Wisconsin	SO	7	135	2	0.64
5	Mike James, Houston	SR	7	57	1	0.64
7	Anthony Vontoure, Washington	SO	6	99	2	0.60
7	Kevin Harvey, Temple	SR	6	55	1	0.60
9	Quincy Lejay, Hawaii	SR	7	151	3	0.58
10	Tim Smith, Stanford *	SR	6	86	0	0.55
10	Robert Carswell, Clemson *	JR	6	72	0	0.55
10	Perlo Bastien, West Virginia *	SR	6	62	0	0.55

*-Seven tied with 0.55; these had the most yards.

Team Leaders

	RUSHING OFFENSE	G	ATT	YDS	AVG	TD	YPG
1	Navy	12	680	3506	5.2	30	292.2
2	Air Force	11	635	3140	4.9	25	285.5
3	Wisconsin	11	583	3075	5.3	34	279.5
4	Nebraska	12	633	3191	5.0	37	265.9
5	Army	11	636	2915	4.6	24	265.0
6	Ohio	11	624	2883	4.6	26	262.1
7	Rice	11	655	2835	4.3	22	257.7
8	Virginia Tech	11	559	2793	5.0	35	253.9
9	TCU	11	518	2640	5.1	26	240.0
10	Toledo	11	492	2631	5.3	21	239.2

	PASSING OFFENSE	G	ATT	COM	INT	PCT	YDS	YPA	TD	I%	YPC	YPG
1	Louisiana Tech	11	566	372	12	65.7	4434	7.8	38	2.1	11.9	403.1
2	Louisville	11	501	322	13	64.3	3687	7.4	29	2.6	11.5	335.2
3	Hawaii	12	577	297	19	51.5	3944	6.8	28	3.3	13.3	328.7
4	Purdue	11	508	306	12	60.2	3608	7.1	23	2.4	11.8	328.0
5	Tulane	11	556	326	25	58.6	3600	6.5	25	4.5	11.0	327.3
6	Nevada	11	457	263	9	57.5	3590	7.9	20	2.0	13.7	326.4
7	Marshall	12	427	286	11	67.0	3901	9.1	37	2.6	13.6	325.1
8	Brigham Young	11	458	280	16	61.1	3567	7.8	25	3.5	12.7	324.3
9	Oklahoma	11	512	319	15	62.3	3539	6.9	31	2.9	11.1	321.7
10	Stanford	11	385	219	12	56.9	3448	9.0	25	3.1	15.7	313.5

	TOTAL OFFENSE	G	P	YDS	AVG	TD	YPG
1	Georgia Tech	11	822	5599	6.8	58	509.0
2	Nevada	11	843	5192	6.2	39	472.0
3	Arizona	12	870	5663	6.5	42	471.9
4	Louisiana Tech	11	822	5181	6.3	50	471.0
5	Stanford	11	793	5138	6.5	47	467.1
6	Louisville	11	851	5136	6.0	48	466.9
7	Marshall	12	841	5584	6.6	57	465.3
8	Purdue	11	859	5016	5.8	38	456.0
9	Virginia Tech	11	758	4970	6.6	49	451.8
10	Oregon State	11	857	4774	5.6	41	434.0

	RUSHING DEFENSE	G	ATT	YDS	AVG	TD	YPG
1	Mississippi State	11	403	736	1.8	7	66.9
2	Alabama	12	335	904	2.7	6	75.3
3	Virginia Tech	11	388	835	2.2	5	75.9
4	Mississippi	11	369	846	2.3	10	76.9
5	Michigan State	11	376	847	2.3	7	77.0
6	Nebraska	12	427	928	2.2	6	77.3
7	Tennessee	11	364	986	2.7	3	89.6
8	Southern Miss	11	403	1006	2.5	6	91.5
9	Florida	12	416	1099	2.6	15	91.6
10	Florida State	11	387	1087	2.8	6	98.8

	PASSING DEFENSE	G	ATT	COM	PCT	INT	I%	YDS	YPA	TD	TD%	RAT
1	Kansas State	11	315	118	37.5	21	6.7	1364	4.3	5	1.6	65.7
2	Nebraska	12	388	165	42.5	18	4.6	2094	5.4	11	2.8	87.9
3	Marshall	12	432	226	52.3	24	5.6	2308	5.3	8	1.9	92.2
4	Mississippi State	11	331	172	52.0	15	4.5	1712	5.2	7	2.1	93.3
5	Wisconsin	11	351	176	50.1	16	4.6	1994	5.7	8	2.3	96.3
6	Utah	11	359	179	49.9	16	4.5	2113	5.9	7	2.0	96.8
7	Virginia Tech	11	344	166	48.3	10	2.9	1885	5.5	10	2.9	98.1
8	Minnesota	11	340	159	46.8	8	2.4	1921	5.7	9	2.7	98.3
9	Oregon State	11	355	174	49.0	13	3.7	2104	5.9	8	2.3	98.9
10	East Carolina	11	389	200	51.4	17	4.4	2305	5.9	10	2.6	100.9

	TOTAL DEFENSE	G	P	YDS	AVG	TD	YPG
1	Mississippi State	11	734	2448	3.3	14	222.5
2	Kansas State	11	693	2585	3.7	18	235.0
3	Virginia Tech	11	732	2720	3.7	15	247.3
4	Nebraska	12	815	3022	3.7	17	251.8
5	TCU	11	729	3129	4.3	24	284.5
6	Texas	13	876	3727	4.3	28	286.7
7	Marshall	12	882	3516	4.0	11	293.0
8	Southern Miss	11	754	3235	4.3	14	294.1
9	Alabama	12	749	3568	4.8	26	297.3
10	Oklahoma State	11	683	3273	4.8	30	297.5

	SCORING OFFENSE	G	PTS	AVG
1	Virginia Tech	11	455	41.4
2	Georgia Tech	11	448	40.7
3	Kansas State	11	433	39.4
4	Louisville	11	412	37.5
4	Florida State	11	412	37.5
6	Stanford	11	409	37.2
7	Marshall	12	442	36.8
8	Oklahoma	11	405	36.8
9	Wisconsin	11	392	35.6
10	Louisiana Tech	11	389	35.4

	SCORING DEFENSE	G	PTS	AVG
1	Virginia Tech	11	116	10.5
2	Marshall	12	134	11.2
3	Nebraska	12	150	12.5
4	Kansas State	11	144	13.1
5	Wisconsin	11	145	13.2
6	Mississippi State	11	149	13.5
7	Tennessee	11	163	14.8
8	Southern Miss	11	172	15.6
8	Minnesota	11	172	15.6
10	Florida State	11	174	15.8

	TURNOVER MARGIN	G	FR	INT	TOT	FL	INTL	TOT	MAR
1	Kansas State	11	17	21	38	12	9	21	1.6
2	Illinois	11	11	14	25	7	5	12	1.2
3	Southern Cal	12	18	21	39	11	14	25	1.2
4	Marshall	12	6	24	30	6	11	17	1.1
5	Wisconsin	11	6	16	22	8	3	11	1.0
6	Stanford	11	13	17	30	8	12	20	0.9
6	Southern Miss	11	15	15	30	6	14	20	0.9
6	Michigan	11	12	10	22	4	8	12	0.9
9	Texas	13	23	10	33	12	10	22	0.9
10	Boise State	12	15	14	29	5	14	19	0.8

2000 Poll Progression

ESPN	AP	Pre-Season 2000		Aug. 26 Games
1	1	Nebraska	0-0	bye week
2	2	Florida State	0-0	beat Brigham Young 29-3
3	3	Alabama	0-0	bye week
5	4	Wisconsin	0-0	bye week
6	5	Miami, Fla.	0-0	bye week
4	6	Michigan	0-0	bye week
8	7	Texas	0-0	bye week
9	8	Kansas State	0-0	beat Iowa 27-7
7	9	Florida	0-0	bye week
11	10	Georgia	0-0	bye week
10	11	Virginia Tech	0-0	bye week
12	12	Tennessee	0-0	bye week
14	13	Washington	0-0	bye week
13	14	Purdue	0-0	bye week
16	15	Southern Cal	0-0	beat # 22 Penn State 29-5 (A27)
15	16	Ohio State	0-0	bye week
19	17	Clemson	0-0	bye week
18	18	Mississippi	0-0	bye week
20	19	Oklahoma	0-0	bye week
23	20	TCU	0-0	bye week
21	21	Illinois	0-0	bye week
17	22	Penn State	0-0	lost to # 15 Southern Cal 5-29 (A27)
25	23	Southern Miss	0-0	bye week
	24	Colorado	0-0	bye week
22	25	Michigan State	0-0	bye week
25		Texas A&M	0-0	bye week

ESPN	AP	August 27 Poll		Sept. 2 Games
1	1	Nebraska	0-0	beat San Jose State 49-13
2	2	Florida State	1-0	bye week
3	3	Alabama	0-0	lost to UCLA 24-35
5	4	Wisconsin	0-0	beat Western Michigan 19-7 (A31)
6	5	Miami, Fla.	0-0	beat Mc Neese St. 61-14 (A31)
4	6	Michigan	0-0	beat Bowling Green 42-7
8	7	Texas	0-0	bye week
9	8	Kansas State	1-0	beat Louisiana Tech 54-10
7	9	Florida	0-0	beat Ball State 40-19
11	10	Georgia	0-0	beat Georgia Southern 29-7
10	11	Virginia Tech	0-0	beat Akron 52-23
13	12	Southern Cal	1-0	bye week
12	13	Tennessee	0-0	beat # 22 Southern Miss 19-16
15	14	Washington	0-0	beat Idaho 44-20
14	15	Purdue	0-0	beat Central Michigan 48-0
16	16	Ohio State	0-0	beat Fresno State 43-10
18	17	Clemson	0-0	beat Citadel 38-0
17	18	Mississippi	0-0	beat Tulane 49-20
19	19	Oklahoma	0-0	beat Texas-El Paso 55-14
21	20	TCU	0-0	bye week
20	21	Illinois	0-0	beat Middle Tennessee 35-6
24	22	Southern Miss	0-0	lost to # 13 Tennessee 16-19
25	23	Colorado	0-0	lost to Colorado State 24-28
22	24	Michigan State	0-0	bye week
23	25	Texas A&M	0-0	bye week

ESPN	AP	September 3 Poll		Sept. 9 Games
1	1	Nebraska	1-0	beat # 23 Notre Dame 27-24
2	2	Florida State	1-0	beat Georgia Tech 26-21
3	3	Michigan	1-0	beat Rice 38-7
4	4	Miami, Fla.	1-0	lost to # 15 Washington 29-34
6	5	Wisconsin	1-0	beat Oregon 27-23
8	6	Texas	0-0	beat La. Lafayette 52-10
7	7	Kansas State	2-0	bye week
5	8	Florida	1-0	beat Middle Tennessee 55-0
10	9	Georgia	1-0	lost to South Carolina 10-21
9	10	Virginia Tech	1-0	beat East Carolina 45-28 (S7)
12	11	Southern Cal	1-0	beat Colorado 17-14
11	12	Tennessee	1-0	bye week
14	13	Alabama	0-1	beat Vanderbilt 28-10
13	14	Purdue	1-0	beat Kent State 45-10
15	15	Washington	1-0	beat # 4 Miami, Fla. 34-29
17	16	UCLA	1-0	beat Fresno State 24-21
19	17	Clemson	1-0	beat Missouri 62-9
16	18	Ohio State	1-0	beat Arizona 27-17
18	19	Mississippi	1-0	lost to Auburn 27-35
20	20	Oklahoma	1-0	beat Arkansas State 45-7
21	21	Illinois	1-0	beat San Diego State 49-13
22	22	TCU	0-0	beat Nevada 41-10
25	23	Notre Dame	1-0	lost to # 1 Nebraska 24-27
23	24	Michigan State	0-0	beat Marshall 34-24
24	25	Southern Miss	0-1	bye week

ESPN	AP	September 10 Poll		Sept. 16 Games
1	1	Nebraska	2-0	bye week
2	2	Florida State	2-0	beat North Carolina 63-14
3	3	Michigan	2-0	lost to # 14 UCLA 20-23
5	4	Wisconsin	2-0	beat Cincinnati 28-25
6	5	Texas	1-0	lost to Stanford 24-27
4	6	Florida	2-0	beat # 11 Tennessee 27-23
7	7	Kansas State	2-0	beat Ball State 76-0
8	8	Virginia Tech	2-0	beat Rutgers 49-0
10	9	Washington	2-0	beat Colorado 17-14
11	10	Southern Cal	2-0	bye week
9	11	Tennessee	1-0	lost to # 6 Florida 23-27
14	12	Miami, Fla.	1-1	bye week
12	13	Purdue	2-0	lost to # 21 Notre Dame 21-23
17	14	UCLA	2-0	beat # 3 Michigan 23-20
13	15	Alabama	1-1	lost to # 25 Southern Miss 0-21
16	16	Clemson	2-0	beat Wake Forest 55-7
15	17	Ohio State	2-0	beat Miami, Ohio 27-16
18	18	Oklahoma	2-0	bye week
19	19	Illinois	2-0	beat California 17-15
21	20	TCU	1-0	beat Northwestern 41-14
23	21	Notre Dame	1-1	beat # 13 Purdue 23-21
20	22	Michigan State	1-0	beat Missouri 13-10
22	23	Georgia	1-1	bye week
24	24	Auburn	2-0	beat LSU 34-17
	25	Southern Miss	0-1	beat # 15 Alabama 21-0
25		Colorado State	2-0	lost to Arizona State 10-13

ESPN	AP	September 17 Poll		Sept. 23 Games
1	1	Nebraska	2-0	beat Iowa 42-13
2	2	Florida State	3-0	beat Louisville 31-0
3	3	Florida	3-0	beat Kentucky 59-31
5	4	Kansas State	3-0	beat North Texas 55-10
4	5	Virginia Tech	3-0	bye week
8	6	UCLA	3-0	lost to Oregon 10-29
6	7	Wisconsin	3-0	lost to Northwestern 44-47
7	8	Washington	3-0	bye week
9	9	Southern Cal	2-0	beat San Jose State 34-24
10	10	Michigan	2-1	beat # 19 Illinois 35-31
11	11	Clemson	3-0	beat Virginia 31-10
14	12	Miami, Fla.	1-1	beat West Virginia 47-10
13	13	Tennessee	1-1	beat La. Monroe 70-3
12	14	Ohio State	3-0	beat Penn State 45-6
15	15	Texas	1-1	beat Houston 48-0
18	16	Notre Dame	2-1	lost to # 23 Michigan State 21-27
16	17	Oklahoma	2-0	beat Rice 42-14
19	18	TCU	2-0	beat Arkansas State 52-3
17	19	Illinois	3-0	lost to # 10 Michigan 31-35
22	20	Auburn	3-0	beat No. Illinois 31-14
21	21	Purdue	2-1	beat Minnesota 38-24
23	22	Southern Miss	1-1	beat Oklahoma State 28-6
20	23	Michigan State	2-0	beat # 16 Notre Dame 27-21
24	24	Georgia	1-1	beat New Mexico State 37-0
25	25	Mississippi State	2-0	lost to South Carolina 19-23

ESPN	AP	September 24 Poll		Sept. 30 Games
1	1	Nebraska	3-0	beat Missouri 42-24
2	2	Florida State	4-0	beat Maryland 59-7 (S28)
3	3	Florida	4-0	lost to Mississippi State 35-47
4	4	Virginia Tech	3-0	beat Boston College 48-34
5	5	Kansas State	4-0	beat Colorado 44-21
6	6	Washington	3-0	lost to # 20 Oregon 16-23
8	7	Clemson	4-0	beat Duke 52-22
7	8	Southern Cal	3-0	lost to Oregon State 21-31
9	9	Michigan	3-1	beat # 17 Wisconsin 13-10
12	10	Miami, Fla.	2-1	beat Rutgers 64-6
11	11	Tennessee	2-1	lost to LSU 31-38
10	12	Ohio State	4-0	bye week
13	13	Texas	2-1	beat Oklahoma State 42-7
16	14	Oklahoma	3-0	beat Kansas 34-16
17	15	UCLA	3-1	beat Arizona State 38-31
18	16	TCU	3-0	beat Navy 24-0
14	17	Wisconsin	3-1	lost to # 9 Michigan 10-13
15	18	Michigan State	3-0	lost to Northwestern 17-37
20	19	Auburn	4-0	beat Vanderbilt 33-0
25	20	Oregon	3-1	beat # 6 Washington 23-16
21	21	Southern Miss	2-1	beat Memphis 24-3
19	22	Purdue	3-1	lost to Penn State 20-22
23	23	South Carolina	4-0	lost to Alabama 17-27
22	24	Illinois	3-1	lost to Minnesota 10-44
24	25	Georgia	2-1	beat Arkansas 38-7

ESPN	AP	October 1 Poll		Oct. 7 Games
2	1	Florida State	5-0	lost to # 7 Miami, Fla. 24-27
1	2	Nebraska	4-0	beat Iowa State 49-27
3	3	Virginia Tech	4-0	beat Temple 35-13
4	4	Kansas State	5-0	beat Kansas 52-13
5	5	Clemson	5-0	beat North Carolina St. 34-27
6	6	Michigan	4-1	lost to Purdue 31-32
8	7	Miami, Fla.	3-1	beat # 1 Florida State 27-24
7	8	Ohio State	4-0	beat # 24 Wisconsin 23-7
15	9	Oregon	4-1	bye week
12	10	Oklahoma	4-0	beat # 11 Texas 63-14
10	11	Texas	3-1	lost to # 10 Oklahoma 14-63
9	12	Florida	4-1	beat LSU 41-9
11	13	Washington	3-1	beat # 23 Oregon State 33-30
14	14	TCU	4-0	beat Hawaii 41-21
13	15	Auburn	5-0	lost to Mississippi State 10-17
17	16	UCLA	4-1	bye week
18	17	Southern Miss	3-1	beat South Florida 41-7
16	18	Southern Cal	3-1	lost to Arizona 15-31
19	19	Georgia	3-1	beat # 21 Tennessee 21-10
20	20	Mississippi State	3-1	beat Auburn 17-10
21	21	Tennessee	2-2	lost to # 19 Georgia 10-21
24	22	Northwestern	4-1	beat Indiana 52-33
23	23	Oregon State	4-0	lost to # 13 Washington 30-33
22	24	Wisconsin	3-2	lost to # 8 Ohio State 7-23
	25	Notre Dame	2-2	beat Stanford 20-14
25		Michigan State	3-1	lost to Iowa 16-21

ESPN	AP	October 8 Poll		Oct. 14 Games
1	1	Nebraska	5-0	beat Texas Tech 56-3
3	2	Kansas State	6-0	lost to # 8 Oklahoma 31-41
2	3	Virginia Tech	5-0	beat West Virginia 48-20 (O12)
6	4	Miami, Fla.	4-1	bye week
4	5	Clemson	6-0	beat Maryland 35-14
5	6	Ohio State	5-0	lost to Minnesota 17-29
7	7	Florida State	5-1	beat Duke 63-14
8	8	Oklahoma	5-0	beat # 2 Kansas State 41-31
12	9	Oregon	4-1	beat Southern Cal 28-17
9	10	Florida	5-1	beat # 19 Auburn 38-7
10	11	Washington	4-1	beat Arizona State 21-15
11	12	TCU	5-0	bye week
15	13	UCLA	4-1	lost to California 38-46
13	14	Georgia	4-1	beat Vanderbilt 29-19
14	15	Mississippi State	4-1	bye week
16	16	Southern Miss	4-1	beat Tulane 56-24
18	17	Northwestern	5-1	lost to # 21 Purdue 28-41
17	18	Michigan	4-2	beat Indiana 58-0
19	19	Auburn	5-1	lost to # 10 Florida 7-38
	20	Notre Dame	3-2	beat Navy 45-14
21	21	Purdue	4-2	beat # 17 Northwestern 41-28
22	22	Arizona	4-1	beat Washington State 53-47
20	23	Oregon State	4-1	beat Stanford 38-6
24	24	South Carolina	5-1	beat Arkansas 27-7
23	25	Texas	3-2	beat Colorado 28-14
25		Mississippi	4-1	lost to Alabama 7-45

ESPN	AP	October 15 Poll		Oct. 21 Games
1	1	Nebraska	6-0	beat Baylor 59-0
2	2	Virginia Tech	6-0	beat Syracuse 22-14
4	3	Oklahoma	6-0	bye week
5	4	Miami, Fla.	4-1	beat Temple 45-17
3	5	Clemson	7-0	beat North Carolina 38-24
6	6	Florida State	6-1	beat Virginia 37-3
11	7	Oregon	5-1	beat # 21 Arizona 14-10
7	8	Florida	6-1	bye week
9	9	Washington	5-1	beat California 36-24
8	10	Kansas State	6-1	beat Texas Tech 28-23
10	11	TCU	5-0	beat Tulsa 17-3
12	12	Georgia	5-1	beat Kentucky 34-30
14	13	Mississippi State	4-1	lost to LSU 38-45
13	14	Ohio State	5-1	beat Iowa 38-10
15	15	Southern Miss	5-1	bye week
16	16	Michigan	5-2	beat Michigan State 14-0
17	17	Purdue	5-2	beat Wisconsin 30-24
19	18	South Carolina	6-1	beat Vanderbilt 30-14
18	19	Oregon State	5-1	beat # 23 UCLA 44-38
22	20	Notre Dame	4-2	beat West Virginia 42-28
20	21	Arizona	5-1	lost to # 7 Oregon 10-14
23	22	Minnesota	5-2	lost to Indiana 43-51
24	23	UCLA	4-2	lost to # 19 Oregon State 38-44
25	24	North Carolina St.	5-1	bye week
	25	Northwestern	5-2	bye week
21		Texas	4-2	beat Missouri 46-12

ANNUAL REVIEW

October 22 Poll / Oct. 28 Games

ESPN	AP	Team	Record	Oct. 28 Games
1	1	Nebraska	7-0	lost to #3 Oklahoma 14-31
2	2	Virginia Tech	7-0	beat Pittsburgh 37-34
3	3	Oklahoma	6-0	beat #1 Nebraska 31-14
5	4	Miami, Fla.	5-1	beat Louisiana Tech 42-31
4	5	Clemson	8-0	lost to Georgia Tech 28-31
6	6	Florida State	7-1	beat #21 North Carolina St. 58-14
10	7	Oregon	6-1	beat Arizona State 56-55
7	8	Florida	6-1	beat #13 Georgia 34-23
9	9	Washington	6-1	beat Stanford 31-28
8	10	Kansas State	7-1	lost to Texas A&M 10-26
11	11	TCU	6-0	beat Rice 37-0
13	12	Ohio State	6-1	lost to #16 Purdue 27-31
12	13	Georgia	6-1	lost to #8 Florida 23-34
14	14	Southern Miss	5-1	beat Houston 6-3
15	15	Michigan	6-2	bye week
16	16	Purdue	6-2	beat #12 Ohio State 31-27
18	17	South Carolina	7-1	lost to Tennessee 14-17
17	18	Oregon State	6-1	beat Washington State 38-9
19	19	Notre Dame	5-2	beat Air Force 34-31
21	20	Mississippi State	4-2	beat Middle Tennessee 61-35
22	21	North Carolina St.	5-1	lost to #6 Florida State 14-58
20	22	Texas	5-2	beat Baylor 48-14
	23	Northwestern	5-2	beat Minnesota 41-35
23	24	Arizona	5-2	lost to UCLA 24-27
25	25	Auburn	6-2	beat Arkansas 21-19
24		Colorado State	6-1	beat San Diego State 34-22

October 29 Poll / Nov. 4 Games

ESPN	AP	Team	Record	Nov. 4 Games
1	1	Oklahoma	7-0	beat Baylor 56-7
2	2	Virginia Tech	8-0	lost to #3 Miami, Fla. 21-41
3	3	Miami, Fla.	6-1	beat #2 Virginia Tech 41-21
4	4	Florida State	8-1	beat #10 Clemson 54-7
5	5	Nebraska	7-1	beat Kansas 56-17
5	6	Florida	7-1	beat Vanderbilt 43-20
8	7	Oregon	7-1	beat Washington State 27-24
7	8	Washington	7-1	beat Arizona 35-32
9	9	TCU	7-0	lost to San Jose State 24-27
10	10	Clemson	8-1	lost to #4 Florida State 7-54
13	11	Purdue	7-2	bye week
12	12	Michigan	6-2	lost to #21 Northwestern 51-54
11	13	Southern Miss	6-1	lost to Louisville 28-49
14	14	Oregon State	7-1	beat California 38-32
16	15	Notre Dame	6-2	bye week
	16	Ohio State	6-2	beat Michigan State 27-13
17	17	Georgia	6-2	bye week
18	18	Mississippi State	5-2	beat Kentucky 35-17
15	19	Kansas State	7-2	beat Iowa State 56-10
20	20	Texas	6-2	beat Texas Tech 29-17
23	21	Northwestern	6-2	beat #12 Michigan 54-51
24	22	South Carolina	7-2	bye week
22	23	Auburn	7-2	bye week
	25	Texas A&M	6-2	beat Oklahoma State 21-16
21		Colorado State	7-1	beat Brigham Young 45-21 (N2)

November 5 Poll / Nov. 11 Games

ESPN	AP	Team	Record	Nov. 11 Games
1	1	Oklahoma	8-0	beat #23 Texas A&M 35-31
2	2	Miami, Fla.	7-1	beat Pittsburgh 35-7
3	3	Florida State	9-1	beat Wake Forest 35-6
5	4	Nebraska	8-1	lost to #16 Kansas State 28-29
4	5	Florida	8-1	beat #21 South Carolina 41-21
7	6	Oregon	8-1	beat California 25-17
6	7	Washington	8-1	beat UCLA 35-28
8	8	Virginia Tech	8-1	beat Central Florida 44-21
9	9	Purdue	7-2	lost to Michigan 10-30
10	10	Oregon State	8-1	beat Arizona 33-9
11	11	Notre Dame	6-2	beat Boston College 28-16
18	12	Northwestern	7-2	lost to Iowa 17-27
14	13	Ohio State	7-2	beat Illinois 24-21
13	14	Georgia	6-2	lost to #22 Auburn 26-29
16	15	Mississippi State	6-2	beat Alabama 29-7
11	16	Kansas State	8-2	beat #4 Nebraska 29-28
15	17	Clemson	8-2	bye week
17	18	TCU	7-1	beat Fresno State 24-7
19	19	Texas	7-2	beat Kansas 51-16
21	20	Michigan	6-3	beat Penn State 33-11
25	25	South Carolina	7-2	lost to #5 Florida 21-41
23	22	Auburn	7-2	beat #14 Georgia 29-26
24	23	Texas A&M	7-2	lost to #1 Oklahoma 31-35
	24	Georgia Tech	6-2	beat Virginia 35-0 (N9)
22	25	Southern Miss	6-2	beat UAB 33-30
20		Colorado State	8-1	lost to Air Force 40-44

November 12 Poll / Nov. 18 Games

ESPN	AP	Team	Record	Nov. 18 Games
1	1	Oklahoma	9-0	beat Texas Tech 27-13
2	2	Miami, Fla.	8-1	beat Syracuse 26-0
3	3	Florida State	10-1	beat #4 Florida 30-7
4	4	Florida	9-1	lost to #3 Florida State 7-30
6	5	Oregon	9-1	lost to #8 Oregon State 13-23
5	6	Washington	9-1	beat Washington State 51-3
7	7	Virginia Tech	9-1	bye week
8	8	Oregon State	9-1	beat #5 Oregon 23-13
9	9	Kansas State	9-2	beat Missouri 28-24
10	10	Nebraska	8-2	bye week
11	11	Notre Dame	7-2	beat Rutgers 45-17
12	12	Ohio State	8-2	lost to #19 Michigan 26-38
13	13	Mississippi State	7-2	lost to Arkansas 10-17
15	14	Texas	8-2	bye week
16	15	TCU	8-1	beat Texas-El Paso 47-14
14	16	Clemson	8-2	beat #25 South Carolina 16-14
17	17	Purdue	7-3	beat Indiana 41-13
19	18	Auburn	8-2	beat Alabama 9-0
18	19	Michigan	7-3	beat #12 Ohio State 38-26
22	20	Georgia Tech	7-2	beat Maryland 35-22
23	21	Texas A&M	7-3	bye week
21	22	Georgia	6-3	beat Mississippi 32-14
24	23	Northwestern	7-3	beat Illinois 61-23
20	24	Southern Miss	7-2	lost to Cincinnati 24-27
	25	South Carolina	7-3	lost to #16 Clemson 14-16
25		Tennessee	6-3	beat Kentucky 59-20

November 19 Poll / Nov. 25 Games

ESPN	AP	Team	Record	Nov. 25 Games
1	1	Oklahoma	10-0	beat Oklahoma State 12-7
2	2	Miami, Fla.	9-1	beat Boston College 52-6
3	3	Florida State	11-1	regular season complete
4	4	Washington	10-1	regular season complete
5	5	Oregon State	10-1	regular season complete
6	6	Virginia Tech	9-1	beat Virginia 42-21
9	7	Florida	9-2	bye week
7	8	Kansas State	10-2	bye week
8	9	Nebraska	8-2	beat Colorado 34-32 (N24)
11	10	Oregon	9-2	regular season complete
10	11	Notre Dame	8-2	beat Southern Cal 38-21
13	12	Texas	8-2	beat #22 Texas A&M 43-17 (N24)
15	13	TCU	9-1	beat SMU 62-7 (N24)
14	14	Purdue	8-3	regular season complete
12	15	Clemson	9-2	regular season complete
16	16	Michigan	8-3	regular season complete
17	17	Auburn	8-2	bye week
19	18	Georgia Tech	8-2	beat #19 Georgia 27-15
18	19	Georgia	7-3	lost to #18 Georgia Tech 15-27
21	20	Northwestern	8-3	regular season complete
20	21	Ohio State	8-3	regular season complete
22	22	Texas A&M	7-3	lost to #12 Texas 17-43 (N24)
23	23	Mississippi State	7-3	lost to Mississippi 30-45 (N23)
	24	LSU	7-3	lost to Arkansas 3-14 (N24)
24	25	Tennessee	7-3	beat Vanderbilt 28-26
25		Colorado State	9-2	regular season complete

November 26 Poll / Dec. 2 Games

ESPN	AP	Team	Record	Dec. 2 Games
1	1	Oklahoma	11-0	beat #8 Kansas State 27-24 (Big 12 CH)
2	2	Miami, Fla.	10-1	regular season complete
3	3	Florida State	11-1	
4	4	Washington	10-1	
5	5	Oregon State	10-1	
5	6	Virginia Tech	10-1	regular season complete
8	7	Florida	9-2	beat #18 Auburn 28-6 (SEC CH)
7	8	Kansas State	10-2	lost to #1 Oklahoma 24-27 (Big 12 CH)
11	9	Oregon	9-2	
9	10	Nebraska	9-2	regular season complete
10	11	Notre Dame	9-2	regular season complete
12	12	Texas	9-2	regular season complete
15	13	TCU	10-1	regular season complete
14	14	Purdue	8-3	
13	15	Clemson	9-2	
16	16	Michigan	8-3	
18	17	Georgia Tech	9-2	regular season complete
17	18	Auburn	9-2	lost to #7 Florida 6-28 (SEC CH)
)20	19	Northwestern	8-3	
19	20	Ohio State	8-3	
21	21	Tennessee	8-3	regular season complete
23	22	Louisville	9-2	
22	23	Colorado State	9-2	regular season complete
24	24	Georgia	7-4	regular season complete
25	25	Toledo	10-1	regular season complete

December 3 Poll / Bowl Results

ESPN	AP	Team	Record	Bowl Bid	Date	Bowl Result
1	1	Oklahoma	12-0	Orange Bowl	J3	beat #3 Florida State 13-2
2	2	Miami, Fla.	10-1	Sugar Bowl	J2	beat #7 Florida 37-20
3	3	Florida State	11-1	Orange Bowl	J3	lost to #1 Oklahoma 2-13
4	4	Washington	10-1	Rose Bowl	J1	beat #14 Purdue 34-24
6	5	Oregon State	10-1	Fiesta Bowl	J1	beat #10 Notre Dame 41-9
5	6	Virginia Tech	10-1	Gator Bowl	J1	beat #16 Clemson 41-20
7	7	Florida	10-2	Sugar Bowl	J2	lost to #2 Miami, Fla. 20-37
11	8	Oregon	9-2	Holiday Bowl	D29	beat #12 Texas 35-30
8	9	Nebraska	9-2	Alamo Bowl	D30	beat #18 Northwestern 66-17
10	10	Notre Dame	9-2	Fiesta Bowl	J1	lost to #5 Oregon State 9-41
9	11	Kansas State	10-3	Cotton Bowl	J1	beat #21 Tennessee 35-21
12	12	Texas	9-2	Holiday Bowl	D29	lost to #8 Oregon 30-35
16	13	TCU	10-1	Mobile Bowl	D20	lost to Southern Miss 21-28
14	14	Purdue	8-3	Rose Bowl	J1	lost to #4 Washington 24-34
17	15	Georgia Tech	9-2	Peach Bowl	D29	lost to LSU 14-28
13	16	Clemson	9-2	Gator Bowl	J1	lost to #6 Virginia Tech 20-41
15	17	Michigan	8-3	Citrus Bowl	J1	beat #20 Auburn 31-28
19	18	Northwestern	8-3	Alamo Bowl	D30	lost to #9 Nebraska 17-66
18	19	Ohio State	8-3	Outback Bowl	J1	lost to South Carolina 7-24
20	20	Auburn	9-3	Citrus Bowl	J1	lost to #17 Michigan 28-31
21	21	Tennessee	8-3	Cotton Bowl	J1	lost to #11 Kansas State 21-35
23	22	Louisville	9-2	Liberty Bowl	D29	lost to #23 Colorado State 17-22
22	23	Colorado State	9-2	Liberty Bowl	D29	beat #22 Louisville 22-17
24	24	Georgia	7-4	Oahu Bowl	D24	beat Virginia 37-14
25	25	Toledo	10-1			

January 6 Final Poll

RB	ESPN	AP	Team	Record
1	1	1	Oklahoma	13-0
2	2	2	Miami, Fla.	11-1
5	3	3	Washington	11-1
6	5	4	Oregon State	11-1
3	4	5	Florida State	11-2
4	6	6	Virginia Tech	11-1
7	9	7	Oregon	10-2
8	7	8	Nebraska	10-2
9	8	9	Kansas State	11-3
10	11	10	Florida	10-3
11	10	11	Michigan	9-3
25	12	12	Texas	9-3
27	13	13	Purdue	8-4
20	15	14	Colorado State	10-2
14	16	15	Notre Dame	9-3
16	14	16	Clemson	9-3
13	19	17	Georgia Tech	9-3
28	20	18	Auburn	9-4
22	21	19	South Carolina	8-4
21	17	20	Georgia	8-4
31	18	21	TCU	10-2
12		22	LSU	8-4
18	24	23	Wisconsin	9-4
26	22	24	Mississippi State	8-4
35	23	25	Iowa State	9-3
15	25		Tennessee	8-4

ANNUAL REVIEW

2000

Consensus All-Americans

POS	Offense	HT	WT	CL	School	AP	CF	FC	FN	FW	SN
QB	**Josh Heupel**	6-2	214	Sr.	Oklahoma		•	•		•	•
RB	**LaDainian Tomlinson**	5-11	220	Sr.	TCU	•	•	•	•	•	•
RB	**Damien Anderson**	5-11	202	Jr.	Northwestern	•	•		•	•	•
WR	**Marvin Minnis**	6-1	185	Sr.	Florida State	•		•	•	•	•
WR	**Antonio Bryant**	6-2	185	So.	Pittsburgh	•				•	
WR	**Fred Mitchell**	6-0	188	Jr.	UCLA		•				•
TE	**Brian Natkin**	6-4	245	Sr.	Texas-El Paso	•	•	•	•	•	•
OL	**Steve Hutchinson**	6-5	299	Sr.	Michigan	•	•	•	•	•	•
OL	**Ben Hamilton**	6-5	285	Sr.	Minnesota		•	•	•		•
OL	**Chris Brown**	6-6	315	Sr.	Georgia Tech	•		•		•	
OL	**Leonard Davis**	6-6	365	Sr.	Texas	•	•		•	•	•
C	**Dominic Raiola**	6-2	300	Jr.	Nebraska	•	•	•	•	•	
PK	**Jonathan Ruffin**	5-10	184	So.	Cincinnati	•	•			•	
AP	**Santana Moss**	5-10	180	Sr.	Miami, Fla.	•	•	*	•	•	•

Others receiving first-team honors

POS	Player	School	AP	CF	FC	FN	FW	SN
QB	Chris Weinke	Florida State	•					•
RB	Ken Simonton	Oregon State			•			
OL	Tarlos Thomas	Florida State		•				
OL	Joaquin Gonzalez	Miami, Fla.					•	
OL	Paul Zukauskas	Boston College			•			
OL	Chad Ward	Washington	•					•
OL	Russ Hochstein	Nebraska						•
PK	Jamie Rheem	Kansas State			•			
AP	Andre Davis	Virginia Tech			•			

FC named Moss as a WR

POS	Defense	HT	WT	CL	School	AP	CF	FC	FN	FW	SN
DL	**Jamal Reynolds**	6-4	254	Sr.	Florida State	•	•	•	•	•	•
DL	**Andre Carter**	6-5	265	Sr.	California	•	•	•	•	•	•
DL	**Casey Hampton**	6-1	310	Sr.	Texas	•	•	•	•		•
DL	**John Henderson**	6-7	290	Jr.	Tennessee	•			•	•	
LB	**Dan Morgan**	6-3	245	Sr.	Miami, Fla.	•	•	•	•	•	•
LB	**Rocky Calmus**	6-3	240	Jr.	Oklahoma	•	•	•	•	•	•
LB	**Keith Adams**	5-11	220	Jr.	Clemson	•	•		•		•
DB	**Dwight Smith**	5-11	205	Sr.	Akron	•	•	•		•	•
DB	**Jamar Fletcher**	5-10	175	Jr.	Wisconsin	•	•	•		•	•
DB	**Fred Smoot**	6-1	179	Sr.	Mississippi State	•	•		•		•
DB	**Tay Cody**	5-11	180	Sr.	Florida State			•			•
DB	**Edward Reed**	6-0	190	Jr.	Miami, Fla.	•				•	
DB	**J.T. Thatcher**	6-0	225	Sr.	Oklahoma				•		
P	**Nick Harris**	6-3	225	Sr.	California	•	•	•			

Others receiving first-team honors

POS	Player	School	AP	CF	FC	FN	FW	SN
DL	Richard Seymour	Georgia		•	•			
DL	Justin Smith	Missouri					•	
DL	Mario Fatafeni	Kansas State				•		
LB	Levar Fisher	North Carolina St.				•	•	
LB	Carlos Polk	Nebraska	•		•			
DB	Anthony Floyd	Louisville		•				•
DB	Lito Sheppard	Florida					•	
DB	Sheldon Brown	South Carolina			•			
DB	Mike Doss	Ohio State				•		
P	Brian Morton	Duke					•	

Heisman Trophy Voting

	Player	POS	School	1st	2nd	3rd	Total
1	**Chris Weinke**	QB	Florida State	369	216	89	1628
2	**Josh Heupel**	QB	Oklahoma	286	290	114	1552
3	**Drew Brees**	QB	Purdue	69	107	198	619
4	**LaDainian Tomlinson**	RB	TCU	47	110	205	566
5	**Damien Anderson**	RB	Northwestern	6	20	43	101
6	**Michael Vick**	QB	Virginia Tech	7	14	34	83
7	**Santana Moss**	WR	Miami, Fla.	3	9	28	55
8	**Marques Tuiasosopo**	QB	Washington	5	8	10	41
9	**Ken Simonton**	RB	Oregon State	1	5	12	25
10	**Rudi Johnson**	RB	Auburn	3	1	9	20

Award Winners

Drew Brees, QB, Purdue, Maxwell, **John Henderson,** DL, Tennessee, Outland, **Josh Heupel,** QB, Oklahoma, Camp, **Jamal Reynolds,** DE, Florida State, Lombardi, **Chris Weinke,** QB, Florida State, O'Brien Unitas, **Dan Morgan,** LB, Miami, Fla., Butkus, Bednarik, Nagurski, **Jamar Fletcher,** DB, Wisconsin, Thorpe, **LaDainian Tomlinson,** RB, TCU, Walker, **Jonathan Ruffin,** K, Cincinnati, Groza, **Antonio Bryant,** WR, Pittsburgh, Biletnikoff, **J.T. Thatcher,** FS, Oklahoma, Tatupu, **Kevin Stemke,** P, Wisconsin, Guy, **Tim Stratton,** TE, Purdue, Mackey, **Dominic Raiola,** C, Nebraska, Rimington

Bowl Games

D20, **GMAC**, Southern Miss 28, TCU 21, D21, **Las Vegas**, Nevada-Las Vegas 31, Arkansas 14, D24, **Oahu**, Georgia 37, Virginia 14, D25, **Aloha**, Boston College 31, Arizona State 17, D27, **Galleryfurniture.com**, East Carolina 40, Texas Tech 27, D27, **Motor City**, Marshall 25, Cincinnati 14, D28, **Humanitarian**, Boise State 38, Texas-El Paso 23, D28, **Insight.com**, Iowa State 37, Pittsburgh 29, D28, **Micron PC**, North Carolina St. 38, Minnesota 30, D28, **Music City**, West Virginia 49, Mississippi 38, D29, **Liberty**, Colorado State 22, Louisville 17, D29, **Peach**, LSU 28, Georgia Tech 14, D29, **Holiday**, Oregon 35, Texas 30, D29, **Sun**, Wisconsin 21, UCLA 20, D30, **Alamo**, Nebraska 66, Northwestern 17, D31, **Silicon Valley**, Air Force 37, Fresno State 34, D31, **Independence**, Mississippi State 43, Texas A&M 41, OT, J1, **Cotton**, Kansas State 35, Tennessee 21, J1, **Florida Citrus**, Michigan 31, Auburn 28, J1, **Fiesta**, Oregon State 41, Notre Dame 9, J1, **Outback**, South Carolina 24, Ohio State 7, J1, **Gator**, Virginia Tech 41, Clemson 20, J1, **Rose**, Washington 34, Purdue 24, J2, **Sugar**, Miami, Fla. 37, Florida 20, J3, **Orange**, Oklahoma 13, Florida State 2,

Conference Standings

ACC	Conf. W	L	T	Overall W	L	T
Florida State	8	0	0	11	2	0
Georgia Tech	6	2	0	9	3	0
Clemson	6	2	0	9	3	0
Virginia	5	3	0	6	6	0
North Carolina St.	4	4	0	8	4	0
North Carolina	3	5	0	6	5	0
Maryland	3	5	0	5	6	0
Wake Forest	1	7	0	2	9	0
Duke	0	8	0	0	11	0

Big 10	Conf. W	L	T	Overall W	L	T
Michigan	6	2	0	9	3	0
Northwestern	6	2	0	8	4	0
Purdue	6	2	0	8	4	0
Ohio State	5	3	0	8	4	0
Wisconsin	4	4	0	9	4	0
Minnesota	4	4	0	6	6	0
Penn State	4	4	0	5	7	0
Iowa	3	5	0	3	9	0
Michigan State	2	6	0	5	6	0
Illinois	2	6	0	5	6	0
Indiana	2	6	0	3	8	0

Big 12	Conf. W	L	T	Overall W	L	T
NORTH						
Kansas State	6	2	0	11	3	0
Nebraska	6	2	0	10	2	0
Iowa State	5	3	0	9	3	0
Colorado	3	5	0	3	8	0
Kansas	2	6	0	4	7	0
Missouri	2	6	0	3	8	0
SOUTH						
Oklahoma	8	0	0	13	0	0
Texas	7	1	0	9	3	0
Texas A&M	5	3	0	7	5	0
Texas Tech	3	5	0	7	6	0
Oklahoma State	1	7	0	3	8	0
Baylor	0	8	0	2	9	0

Championship **Oklahoma 27 Kansas State 24**

Big East	Conf. W	L	T	Overall W	L	T
Miami, Fla.	7	0	0	11	1	0
Virginia Tech	6	1	0	11	1	0
Pittsburgh	4	3	0	7	5	0
Syracuse	4	3	0	6	5	0
Boston College	3	4	0	7	5	0
West Virginia	3	4	0	7	5	0
Temple	1	6	0	4	7	0
Rutgers	0	7	0	3	8	0

Big West	Conf. W	L	T	Overall W	L	T
Boise State	5	0	0	10	2	0
Utah State	4	1	0	5	6	0
Idaho	3	2	0	5	6	0
North Texas	1	4	0	3	8	0
New Mexico State	1	4	0	3	8	0
Arkansas State	1	4	0	1	10	0

C-USA	Conf. W	L	T	Overall W	L	T
Louisville	6	1	0	9	3	0
East Carolina	5	2	0	8	4	0
Cincinnati	5	2	0	7	5	0
Southern Miss	4	3	0	8	4	0
UAB	3	3	0	7	4	0
Tulane	3	4	0	6	5	0
Memphis	2	5	0	4	7	0
Houston	2	5	0	3	8	0
Army	1	6	0	1	10	0

Ivy	Conf. W	L	T	Overall W	L	T
Brown	6	1	0	9	1	0
Pennsylvania	6	1	0	7	3	0
Cornell	5	2	0	5	5	0
Yale	4	3	0	7	3	0
Harvard	4	3	0	5	5	0
Princeton	3	4	0	3	7	0
Columbia	1	6	0	3	7	0
Dartmouth	1	6	0	2	8	0

MAC	Conf. W	L	T	Overall W	L	T
EAST						
Marshall	5	3	0	8	5	0
Ohio U	5	3	0	7	4	0
Miami, Ohio	5	3	0	6	5	0
Akron	5	3	0	6	5	0
Buffalo	2	6	0	2	9	0
Bowling Green	2	6	0	2	9	0
Kent State	1	7	0	1	10	0
WEST						
Western Michigan	7	1	0	9	3	0
Toledo	6	1	0	10	1	0
No. Illinois	4	3	0	6	5	0
Ball State	4	3	0	5	6	0
Eastern Michigan	2	5	0	3	8	0
Central Michigan	2	6	0	2	9	0

Championship **Marshall 19 Western Michigan 14**

MWC	Conf. W	L	T	Overall W	L	T
Colorado State	6	1	0	10	2	0
Air Force	5	2	0	9	3	0
Nevada-Las Vegas	4	3	0	8	5	0
Brigham Young	4	3	0	6	6	0
New Mexico	3	4	0	5	7	0
Utah	3	4	0	4	7	0
San Diego State	3	4	0	3	8	0
Wyoming	0	7	0	1	10	0

Pac 10	Conf. W	L	T	Overall W	L	T
Oregon State	7	1	0	11	1	0
Washington	7	1	0	11	1	0
Oregon	7	1	0	10	2	0
Stanford	4	4	0	5	6	0
UCLA	3	5	0	6	6	0
Arizona State	3	5	0	6	6	0
Arizona	3	5	0	5	6	0
Southern Cal	2	6	0	5	7	0
Washington State	2	6	0	4	7	0
California	2	6	0	3	8	0

SEC	Conf. W	L	T	Overall W	L	T
EAST						
Florida	7	1	0	10	3	0
Tennessee	5	3	0	8	4	0
South Carolina	5	3	0	8	4	0
Georgia	5	3	0	8	4	0
Vanderbilt	1	7	0	3	8	0
Kentucky	0	8	0	2	9	0
WEST						
Auburn	6	2	0	9	4	0
LSU	5	3	0	8	4	0
Mississippi State	4	4	0	8	4	0
Mississippi	4	4	0	7	5	0
Arkansas	3	5	0	6	6	0
Alabama	3	5	0	3	8	0

Championship **Florida 28 Auburn 6**

WAC	Conf. W	L	T	Overall W	L	T
TCU	7	1	0	10	2	0
Texas-El Paso	7	1	0	8	4	0
Fresno State	6	2	0	7	5	0
San Jose State	5	3	0	7	5	0
Tulsa	4	4	0	5	7	0
Rice	2	6	0	3	8	0
Hawaii	2	6	0	3	9	0
SMU	2	6	0	3	9	0
Nevada	1	7	0	2	10	0

Independents	Overall W	L	T
Notre Dame	9	3	0
Central Florida	7	4	0
Middle Tennessee	6	5	0
Connecticut	3	8	0
Louisiana Tech	3	9	0
La. Monroe	1	10	0
Navy	1	10	0

ANNUAL REVIEW

2000 ANNUAL REVIEW 1415

2000 NCAA Major College Statistical Leaders

Individual Leaders

PASSING	POS	CL	G	ATT	COM	PCT	INT	I%	YDS	YPA	TD	TD%	RATING
1 Bart Hendricks, Boise State	QB	SR	11	347	210	60.5	8	2.3	3364	9.7	35	10.1	170.6
2 Chris Weinke, Florida State	QB	SR	12	431	266	61.7	11	2.6	4167	9.7	33	7.7	163.1
3 Rex Grossman, Florida	QB	FR	11	212	131	61.8	7	3.3	1866	8.8	21	9.9	161.8
4 Casey Printers, TCU	QB	SO	11	176	102	58.0	6	3.4	1584	9.0	16	9.1	156.7
5 Ken Dorsey, Miami, Fla.	QB	SO	11	322	188	58.4	5	1.6	2737	8.5	25	7.8	152.3
6 George Godsey, Georgia Tech	QB	JR	11	349	222	63.6	6	1.7	2906	8.3	23	6.6	151.9
7 John Turman, Pittsburgh	QB	SR	11	233	128	54.9	7	3.0	2135	9.2	18	7.7	151.4
8 Rocky Perez, Texas-El Paso	QB	SR	11	338	200	59.2	6	1.8	2661	7.9	26	7.7	147.1
9 Mike Thiessen, Air Force	QB	SR	11	195	112	57.4	5	2.6	1687	8.7	13	6.7	147.0
10 Ryan Schneider, Central Florida	QB	FR	9	286	177	61.9	11	3.9	2334	8.2	21	7.3	147.0

ALL-PURPOSE	POS	CL	G	RUSH	REC	PR	KR	YDS	YPG
1 Emmett White, Utah State	HB	JR	11	1322	592	183	531	2628	238.9
2 LaDainian Tomlinson, TCU	TB	SR	11	2158	40	0	0	2198	199.8
3 Robert Kilow, Arkansas State	WR	SR	10	42	1002	133	724	1901	190.1
4 Damien Anderson, Northwestern	RB	SR	11	1914	120	0	0	2034	184.9
5 Justin McCareins, No. Illinois	FL	SR	11	73	1168	362	411	2014	183.1
6 Brock Forsey, Boise State	RB	SO	10	914	399	0	517	1830	183.0
7 Deoncé Whitaker, San Jose State	TB	SR	10	1577	37	0	151	1765	176.5
8 Hodges Mitchell, Texas	RB	SR	11	1118	386	427	0	1931	175.6
9 Michael Bennett, Wisconsin	TB	JR	10	1598	23	0	94	1715	171.5
10 Koren Robinson, North Carolina St.	WR	SO	11	95	1061	218	506	1880	170.9

RUSHING/Yards Per Game	POS	CL	G	ATT	YDS	TD	AVG	YPG
1 LaDainian Tomlinson, TCU	TB	SR	11	369	2158	22	5.9	196.2
2 Damien Anderson, Northwestern	RB	SR	11	293	1914	22	6.5	174.0
3 Michael Bennett, Wisconsin	TB	JR	10	294	1598	10	5.4	159.8
4 Deoncé Whitaker, San Jose State	TB	SR	10	224	1577	15	7.0	157.7
5 Anthony Thomas, Michigan	HB	SR	11	287	1551	16	5.4	141.0
6 Ken Simonton, Oregon State	TB	JR	11	266	1474	18	5.5	134.0
7 Chester Taylor, Toledo	TB	SR	11	250	1470	18	5.9	133.6
8 Robert Sanford, Western Michigan	TB	SR	12	293	1571	18	5.4	130.9
9 Rudi Johnson, Auburn	TB	JR	12	324	1567	13	4.8	130.6
10 Ennis Haywood, Iowa State	RB	JR	10	230	1237	8	5.4	123.7

RUSHING/Yards Per Carry	POS	CL	G	ATT	YDS	YPC
1 Keith Kenton, New Mexico State	RB	JR	11	109	849	7.8
2 Levron Williams, Indiana	RB	SR	10	116	821	7.1
3 Correll Buckhalter, Nebraska	IB	SR	11	106	750	7.1
4 Deoncé Whitaker, San Jose State	TB	SR	10	224	1577	7.0
5 James Mungro, Syracuse	RB	JR	10	115	797	6.9
6 Dwone Hicks, Middle Tennessee	TB	SO	11	186	1277	6.9
7 Chris Barnes, New Mexico State	RB	SR	11	171	1131	6.6
8 Damien Anderson, Northwestern	RB	SR	11	293	1914	6.5
9 Dan Alexander, Nebraska	IB	SR	11	182	1154	6.3
10 Dicenzo Miller, Mississippi State	TB	JR	11	160	1005	6.3

*-Based on top 50 rushers

RECEIVING	POS	CL	G	REC	YDS	TD	RPG	YPR	YPG
1 Antonio Bryant, Pittsburgh	WR	SO	10	68	1302	11	6.8	19.2	130.2
2 Freddie Mitchell, UCLA	FL	JR	11	68	1314	8	6.2	19.3	119.5
3 Marvin Minnis, Florida State	FL	SR	12	63	1340	11	5.3	21.3	111.7
4 Justin McCareins, No. Illinois	FL	SR	11	66	1168	10	6.0	17.7	106.2
5 Aaron Jones, Utah State	WR	SR	11	63	1159	11	5.7	18.4	105.4
6 Josh Reed, LSU	SE	SO	11	65	1127	10	5.9	17.3	102.5
7 Robert Kilow, Arkansas State	WR	SR	10	72	1002	3	7.2	13.9	100.2
8 Lee Mays, Texas-El Paso	WR	JR	11	70	1098	15	6.4	15.7	99.8
9 Don Shoals, Tulsa	WR	JR	12	80	1195	5	6.7	14.9	99.6
10 Tyson Hinshaw, Central Florida	WR	SR	11	89	1089	13	8.1	12.2	99.0

PUNTING	POS	CL	PUNT	YDS	AVG
1 Preston Gruening, Minnesota	P	SO	46	2080	45.2
2 Brian Morton, Duke	P	SR	77	3478	45.2
3 Kevin Stemke, Wisconsin	P	SR	65	2915	44.9
4 Brooks Barnard, Maryland	P	SO	49	2191	44.7
5 Dave Zastudil, Ohio U	P	JR	47	2084	44.3
6 Casey Roussel, Tulane	P	JR	59	2609	44.2
7 Jeff Ferguson, Oklahoma	K	JR	48	2108	43.9
8 Dan Hadenfeldt, Nebraska	P	SR	39	1708	43.8
9 Alan Rhine, Florida	P	SR	47	2035	43.3
10 Aaron Edmonds, Brigham Young	K	JR	67	2898	43.3

PUNT RETURNS	POS	CL	PR	YDS	TD	AVG
1 Aaron Lockett, Kansas State	WR	JR	22	501	3	22.8
2 Andre Davis, Virginia Tech	WR	JR	18	396	3	22.0
3 Justin McCareins, No. Illinois	FL	SR	19	362	1	19.1
4 Santana Moss, Miami, Fla.	WR	SR	36	655	4	18.2
5 Jemeel Powell, California	DB	SO	12	218	1	18.2
6 Pete Rebstock, Colorado State	WR	JR	28	469	1	16.8
7 Troy Mason, Nevada-Las Vegas	WR	SO	23	378	1	16.4
8 Joey Getherall, Notre Dame	FL	SR	24	392	2	16.3
9 J.T. Thatcher, Oklahoma	DB	SR	38	599	2	15.8
10 Don Shoals, Tulsa	WR	JR	17	266	2	15.7

KICKOFF RETURNS	POS	CL	KR	YDS	TD	AVG
1 LaTarence Dunbar, TCU	WR	SO	15	506	2	33.7
2 Zek Parker, Louisville	WR	SR	26	752	0	28.9
3 David Mikell, Boise State	RB	FR	16	459	1	28.7
4 Julius Jones, Notre Dame	TB	SO	15	427	1	28.5
5 Ken-Yon Rambo, Ohio State	FL	SR	17	478	0	28.1
6 Kahlil Hill, Iowa	WR	JR	25	680	1	27.2
7 Robert Kilow, Arkansas State	WR	SR	27	724	0	26.8
8 Shawn Terry, West Virginia	WR	JR	27	720	2	26.7
9 Kyle Moore, Duke	WR	JR	13	335	0	25.8
10 James Hickenbocham, Arkansas State	WR	SO	17	435	1	25.6

SCORING	POS	CL	TDS	XP	FG	PTS	PTPG
1 Lee Suggs, Virginia Tech	RB	SO	28	0	0	168	15.3
2 LaDainian Tomlinson, TCU	TB	SR	22	0	0	132	12.0
2 Damien Anderson, Northwestern	RB	SR	22	0	0	132	12.0
4 Dwone Hicks, Middle Tennessee	TB	SO	21	0	0	126	11.5
5 Eric Crouch, Nebraska	QB	JR	20	0	0	120	10.9
6 Thomas Hammock, No. Illinois	TB	SO	16	0	0	96	10.7
7 Chester Taylor, Toledo	TB	SR	19	0	0	114	10.4
8 Ken Simonton, Oregon State	TB	JR	18	0	0	110	10.0
9 Deoncé Whitaker, San Jose State	TB	SR	16	0	0	98	9.8
10 Kris Stockton, Texas	K	SR	0	41	22	107	9.7

FIELD GOALS	POS	CL	FGA	FGM	PCT	FGG
1 Jonathan Ruffin, Cincinnati	K	SO	29	26	0.90	2.36
2 Dan Nystrom, Minnesota	K	SO	34	22	0.65	2.00
2 Kris Stockton, Texas	K	SR	26	22	0.85	2.00
4 Rhett Gallego, UAB	K	SO	24	19	0.79	1.73
4 Dave Adams, Air Force	K	SR	24	19	0.79	1.73
4 Dan Stultz, Ohio State	K	SR	23	19	0.83	1.73
7 Alex Walls, Tennessee	K	SO	20	18	0.90	1.64
8 Owen Pochman, Brigham Young	K	SR	24	19	0.79	1.58
9 Steve Azar, No. Illinois	K	FR	15	14	0.93	1.56
10 Jeff Reed, North Carolina	K	SR	20	16	0.80	1.45
10 Chris Kaylakie, TCU	K	SR	18	16	0.89	1.45
10 Seth Marler, Tulane	K	SO	21	16	0.76	1.45

INTERCEPTIONS	POS	CL	INT	YDS	TD	INT/GM
1 Dwight Smith, Akron	DB	SR	10	208	2	0.91
1 Anthony Floyd, Louisville	DB	SO	10	152	1	0.91
3 Ed Reed, Miami, Fla.	DB	JR	8	92	2	0.73
4 J.T. Thatcher, Oklahoma	DB	SR	8	162	1	0.67
4 Jamar Fletcher, Wisconsin	DB	JR	6	159	0	0.67
6 Dan Dawson, Rice	LB	JR	7	206	1	0.64
7 Nate Jackson, Hawaii	DB	JR	7	57	0	0.58
8 Tim Wansley, Georgia	DB	JR	6	148	2	0.55
8 Alex Ardley, Clemson	DB	JR	6	61	0	0.55
8 Rashad Holman, Louisville	DB	SR	6	32	0	0.55
8 Lenny Walls, Boston College	DB	JR	6	29	1	0.55
8 Willie Pile, Virginia Tech	DB	SO	6	22	1	0.55
8 Charles Tillman, La. Lafayette	DB	SO	6	15	0	0.55
8 Todd Howard, Michigan	DB	JR	6	1	0	0.55
8 Shawn Robinson, Pittsburgh	DB	SO	6	-6	0	0.55

Team Leaders

RUSHING OFFENSE	G	ATT	YDS	AVG	TD	YPG
1 Nebraska	11	636	3842	6.0	45	349.3
2 Ohio U	11	646	3553	5.5	32	323.0
3 Air Force	11	647	3244	5.0	33	294.9
4 TCU	11	588	3032	5.2	33	275.6
5 Virginia Tech	11	570	2975	5.2	44	270.5
6 New Mexico State	11	535	2972	5.6	16	270.2
7 Indiana	11	505	2930	5.8	34	266.4
8 Northwestern	11	565	2830	5.0	36	257.3
9 Toledo	11	514	2792	5.4	29	253.8
10 Clemson	11	557	2600	4.7	33	236.4

PASSING OFFENSE	G	ATT	COM	INT	PCT	YDS	YPA	TD	I%	YPC	YPG
1 Florida State	12	469	290	14	61.8	4608	9.8	36	3.0	15.9	384.0
2 Kentucky	11	564	322	21	57.1	3689	6.5	19	3.7	11.5	335.4
3 Tulane	11	506	288	16	56.9	3569	7.1	28	3.2	12.4	324.5
4 Hawaii	12	609	309	23	50.7	3875	6.4	25	3.8	12.5	322.9
5 Boise State	11	372	225	8	60.5	3537	9.5	37	2.2	15.7	321.5
6 Purdue	11	489	292	12	59.7	3438	7.0	26	2.5	11.8	312.5
7 Louisiana Tech	12	546	357	28	65.4	3715	6.8	30	5.1	10.4	309.6
8 Florida	12	466	265	12	56.9	3698	7.9	34	2.6	14.0	308.2
9 Idaho	11	428	265	19	61.9	3357	7.8	24	4.4	12.7	305.2
10 Marshall	12	483	293	10	60.7	3584	7.4	24	2.1	12.2	298.7

TOTAL OFFENSE	G	P	YDS	AVG	TD	YPG
1 Florida State	12	924	6588	7.1	67	549.0
2 Boise State	11	812	5459	6.7	64	496.3
3 Northwestern	11	911	5232	5.7	56	475.6
4 Purdue	11	904	5183	5.7	47	471.2
5 Miami, Fla.	11	774	5069	6.6	63	460.8
6 Nebraska	11	808	5059	6.3	63	459.9
7 Tulane	11	897	4989	5.6	40	453.6
8 Idaho	11	846	4985	5.9	42	453.2
9 Air Force	11	852	4971	5.8	47	451.9
10 Clemson	11	853	4911	5.8	53	446.5

RUSHING DEFENSE	G	ATT	YDS	AVG	TD	YPG
1 Memphis	11	346	800	2.3	6	72.7
2 Florida State	12	387	887	2.3	6	73.9
3 Tennessee	11	338	817	2.4	7	74.3
4 Louisville	11	395	879	2.2	12	79.9
5 Toledo	11	365	897	2.5	10	81.5
6 UAB	11	386	919	2.4	9	83.5
7 TCU	11	395	928	2.4	3	84.4
8 Arizona	11	393	973	2.5	12	88.5
9 Ohio State	11	396	1008	2.6	10	91.6
10 Oregon State	11	385	1024	2.7	9	93.1

PASSING DEFENSE	G	ATT	COM	PCT	INT	I%	YDS	YPA	TD	TD%	RAT
1 Texas	11	379	171	45.1	17	4.5	2027	5.4	8	2.1	88.0
2 Oklahoma	12	397	196	49.4	22	5.5	2049	5.2	9	2.3	89.2
3 TCU	11	323	143	44.3	15	4.6	1767	5.5	10	3.1	91.2
4 Southern Miss	11	370	186	50.3	14	3.8	1788	4.8	9	2.4	91.4
5 Florida State	12	447	220	49.2	19	4.3	2437	5.5	7	1.6	91.7
6 Kansas State	13	399	204	51.1	20	5.0	2241	5.6	8	2.0	94.9
7 Nebraska	11	393	179	45.6	14	3.6	2291	5.8	10	2.5	95.7
8 Miami, Fla.	11	428	216	50.5	23	5.4	2427	5.7	11	2.6	95.9
9 Mississippi	11	341	160	46.9	18	5.3	2064	6.1	9	2.6	95.9
10 Texas Tech	12	343	177	51.6	15	4.4	1969	5.7	7	2.0	97.8

TOTAL DEFENSE	G	P	YDS	AVG	TD	YPG
1 TCU	11	718	2695	3.8	13	245.0
2 Southern Miss	11	784	2950	3.8	21	268.2
3 Toledo	11	703	2959	4.2	16	269.0
4 Kansas State	13	872	3517	4.0	29	270.5
5 Memphis	11	755	3028	4.0	20	275.3
6 Florida State	12	834	3324	4.0	15	277.0
7 Texas	11	766	3061	4.0	26	278.3
8 Oklahoma	12	809	3347	4.1	25	278.9
9 Western Michigan	12	803	3399	4.2	16	283.3
10 Utah	11	735	3171	4.3	24	288.3

SCORING OFFENSE	G	PTS	AVG
1 Boise State	11	494	44.9
2 Miami, Fla.	11	469	42.6
3 Florida State	12	509	42.4
4 Nebraska	11	456	41.5
5 Virginia Tech	11	443	40.3
6 Kansas State	13	514	39.5
7 Oklahoma	12	468	39.0
8 Texas	11	425	38.6
9 Northwestern	11	424	38.6
10 Florida	12	448	37.3

SCORING DEFENSE	G	PTS	AVG
1 TCU	11	106	9.6
2 Florida State	12	123	10.3
3 Toledo	11	125	11.4
4 Western Michigan	12	139	11.6
5 Miami, Fla.	11	170	15.5
6 South Carolina	11	174	15.8
7 Oklahoma	12	192	16.0
8 Southern Miss	11	182	16.5
9 UAB	11	192	17.5
10 Texas A&M	11	196	17.8

TURNOVER MARGIN	G	FR	INT	TOT	FL	INTL	TOT	MAR
1 Toledo	11	16	15	31	5	4	9	2.00
2 Georgia Tech	11	15	15	30	6	6	12	1.64
3 Florida	12	16	24	40	9	12	21	1.58
4 Oregon State	11	10	22	32	9	7	16	1.45
5 Notre Dame	11	9	13	22	4	4	8	1.27
6 Cincinnati	11	15	19	34	9	13	22	1.09
6 Miami, Fla.	11	10	23	33	16	5	21	1.09
6 Northwestern	11	13	12	25	6	7	13	1.09
6 Louisville	11	11	27	38	14	12	26	1.09
10 Arizona State	11	23	13	36	13	12	25	1.00
10 Michigan	11	12	14	26	10	5	15	1.00
10 Boston College	11	10	16	26	3	12	15	1.00

ANNUAL REVIEW

2001 Poll Progression

ESPN	AP	Pre-Season 2001		Aug. 25 Games
1	1	Florida	0-0	bye week
2	2	Miami, Fla.	0-0	bye week
3	3	Oklahoma	0-0	beat North Carolina 41-27
4	4	Nebraska	0-0	beat TCU 21-7
6	5	Texas	0-0	bye week
5	6	Florida State	0-0	bye week
8	7	Oregon	0-0	bye week
7	8	Tennessee	0-0	bye week
9	9	Virginia Tech	0-0	bye week
13	10	Georgia Tech	0-0	beat Syracuse 13-7 (A26)
12	11	Oregon State	0-0	bye week
10	12	Michigan	0-0	bye week
11	13	Kansas State	0-0	bye week
17	14	LSU	0-0	bye week
14	15	Washington	0-0	bye week
20	16	Northwestern	0-0	bye week
15	17	UCLA	0-0	bye week
16	18	Notre Dame	0-0	bye week
18	19	Clemson	0-0	bye week
19	20	Mississippi State	0-0	bye week
22	21	South Carolina	0-0	bye week
23	22	Wisconsin	0-0	beat Virginia 26-17
21	23	Ohio State	0-0	bye week
24	24	Colorado State	0-0	bye week
25	25	Alabama	0-0	bye week

ESPN	AP	August 26 Poll		Sept. 1 Games
1	1	Florida	0-0	beat Marshall 49-14
2	2	Miami, Fla.	0-0	beat Penn State 33-7
3	3	Oklahoma	1-0	beat Air Force 44-3
4	4	Nebraska	1-0	beat Troy State 42-14
6	5	Texas	0-0	beat New Mexico State 41-7
5	6	Florida State	0-0	beat Duke 55-13
7	7	Oregon	0-0	beat # 22 Wisconsin 31-28
8	8	Tennessee	0-0	beat Syracuse 33-9
9	9	Virginia Tech	0-0	beat Connecticut 52-10
12	10	Oregon State	0-0	lost to Fresno State 24-44 (S2)
14	11	Georgia Tech	1-0	beat Citadel 35-7
10	12	Michigan	0-0	beat Miami, Ohio 31-13
11	13	Kansas State	0-0	bye week
16	14	LSU	0-0	beat Tulane 48-17
13	15	Washington	0-0	bye week
20	16	Northwestern	0-0	bye week
15	17	UCLA	0-0	beat # 25 Alabama 20-17
17	18	Notre Dame	0-0	bye week
18	19	Clemson	0-0	beat Central Florida 21-13
19	20	Mississippi State	0-0	bye week
22	21	South Carolina	0-0	beat Boise State 32-13
23	22	Wisconsin	1-0	lost to # 7 Oregon 28-31
21	23	Ohio State	0-0	bye week
24	24	Colorado State	0-0	lost to Colorado 14-41
25	25	Alabama	0-0	lost to # 17 UCLA 17-20

ESPN	AP	September 2 Poll		Sept. 8 Games
2	1	Miami, Fla.	1-0	beat Rutgers 61-0
1	2	Florida	1-0	beat La. Monroe 55-6
3	3	Oklahoma	2-0	beat North Texas 37-10
6	4	Texas	1-0	beat North Carolina 44-14
4	5	Nebraska	2-0	beat # 17 Notre Dame 27-10
5	6	Florida State	1-0	beat UAB 29-7
8	7	Oregon	1-0	beat Utah 24-10
7	8	Tennessee	1-0	beat Arkansas 13-3
9	9	Virginia Tech	1-0	beat Western Michigan 31-0
13	10	Georgia Tech	2-0	beat Navy 70-7
10	11	Michigan	1-0	lost to # 15 Washington 18-23
11	12	Kansas State	0-0	beat Southern Cal 10-6
16	13	LSU	1-0	beat Utah State 31-14
14	14	UCLA	1-0	beat Kansas 41-17
15	15	Washington	0-0	beat # 11 Michigan 23-18
20	16	Northwestern	0-0	beat Nevada-Las Vegas 37-28 (S7)
17	17	Notre Dame	0-0	lost to # 5 Nebraska 10-27
18	18	Mississippi State	1-0	beat Memphis 30-10 (S3)
	19	Fresno State	2-0	beat # 23 Wisconsin 32-20
19	20	Clemson	1-0	beat Wofford 38-14
21	21	South Carolina	1-0	beat # 25 Georgia 14-9
12	22	Oregon State	0-1	beat New Mexico State 27-22
23	23	Wisconsin	1-1	lost to # 19 Fresno State 20-32
22	24	Ohio State	0-0	beat Akron 28-14
24	25	Georgia	1-0	lost to # 21 South Carolina 9-14
25		Purdue	1-0	bye week

ESPN	AP	September 9 Poll		Sept. 22 Games
1	1	Miami, Fla.	2-0	bye week
2	2	Florida	2-0	beat Kentucky 44-10
3	3	Oklahoma	3-0	bye week
4	4	Nebraska	3-0	beat Rice 48-3 (S20)
6	5	Texas	2-0	beat Houston 52-26
5	6	Florida State	2-0	lost to North Carolina 9-41
7	7	Oregon	2-0	beat Southern Cal 24-22
8	8	Tennessee	2-0	bye week
9	9	Virginia Tech	2-0	beat Rutgers 50-0
11	10	Georgia Tech	3-0	bye week
15	11	Fresno State	3-0	beat Tulsa 37-18
10	12	Kansas State	1-0	beat New Mexico State 64-0
13	13	Washington	1-0	beat Idaho 53-3
12	14	UCLA	2-0	beat # 21 Ohio State 13-6
14	15	LSU	2-0	bye week
19	16	Northwestern	1-0	beat Duke 44-7
16	17	Mississippi State	1-0	lost to # 18 South Carolina 14-16 (S20)
20	18	South Carolina	2-0	beat # 17 Mississippi State 16-14 (S20)
18	19	Clemson	2-0	lost to Virginia 24-26
17	20	Michigan	1-1	beat Western Michigan 38-21
21	21	Ohio State	1-0	lost to # 14 UCLA 6-13
22	22	Oregon State	1-1	bye week
23	23	Notre Dame	0-1	lost to Michigan State 10-17
25	24	Brigham Young	3-0	bye week
	25	Louisville	3-0	lost to Illinois 10-34
24		Purdue	1-0	beat Akron 33-14

ESPN	AP	September 23 Poll		Sept. 29 Games
1	1	Miami, Fla.	2-0	beat Pittsburgh 43-21 (S27)
2	2	Florida	3-0	beat # 21 Mississippi State 52-0
3	3	Oklahoma	3-0	beat # 11 Kansas State 38-37
4	4	Nebraska	4-0	beat Missouri 36-3
5	5	Texas	3-0	beat Texas Tech 42-7
6	6	Oregon	3-0	beat Utah State 38-21
8	7	Tennessee	2-0	beat # 14 LSU 26-18
7	8	Virginia Tech	3-0	beat Central Florida 46-14
11	9	Georgia Tech	3-0	lost to Clemson 44-47
13	10	Fresno State	4-0	beat Louisiana Tech 38-28
9	11	Kansas State	2-0	lost to # 3 Oklahoma 37-38
10	12	UCLA	3-0	beat # 19 Oregon State 38-7
12	13	Washington	2-0	beat California 31-28
14	14	LSU	2-0	lost to # 7 Tennessee 18-26
16	15	South Carolina	3-0	beat Alabama 37-36
18	16	Northwestern	2-0	beat # 23 Michigan State 27-26
17	17	Michigan	2-1	beat # 22 Illinois 45-20
15	18	Florida State	2-1	beat Wake Forest 48-24
19	19	Oregon State	1-1	lost to # 12 UCLA 7-38
20	20	Brigham Young	3-0	beat Nevada-Las Vegas 35-31
22	21	Mississippi State	1-1	lost to # 2 Florida 0-52
23	22	Illinois	3-0	lost to # 17 Michigan 20-45
24	23	Michigan State	2-0	lost to # 16 Northwestern 26-27
21	24	Purdue	2-0	beat Minnesota 35-28
	25	Toledo	3-0	beat No. Illinois 41-20
25		Clemson	2-1	beat # 9 Georgia Tech 47-44

ESPN	AP	September 30 Poll		Oct. 6 Games
1	1	Miami, Fla.	3-0	beat Troy State 38-7
2	2	Florida	4-0	beat # 18 LSU 44-15
3	3	Oklahoma	4-0	beat # 5 Texas 14-3
4	4	Nebraska	5-0	beat Iowa State 48-14
5	5	Texas	4-0	lost to # 3 Oklahoma 3-14
7	6	Tennessee	3-0	lost to Georgia 24-26
8	7	Oregon	4-0	beat Arizona 63-28
6	8	Virginia Tech	4-0	beat West Virginia 35-0
9	9	UCLA	4-0	bye week
11	10	Fresno State	5-0	bye week
10	11	Washington	3-0	beat Southern Cal 27-24
13	12	Kansas State	2-1	lost to Colorado 6-16
12	13	South Carolina	4-0	beat Kentucky 42-6
16	14	Northwestern	3-0	lost to Ohio State 20-38
15	15	Michigan	3-1	beat Penn State 20-0
14	16	Florida State	3-1	bye week
17	17	Georgia Tech	3-1	beat Duke 37-10
20	18	LSU	2-1	lost to # 2 Florida 15-44
21	19	Clemson	3-1	bye week
18	20	Brigham Young	4-0	beat Utah State 54-34 (O5)
18	21	Purdue	3-0	beat Iowa 23-14
24	22	Stanford	3-0	bye week
23	23	Toledo	4-0	beat Ohio U 48-41
22	24	Texas A&M	4-0	beat Baylor 16-10
25	25	Maryland	4-0	beat Virginia 41-21

ESPN	AP	October 7 Poll		Oct. 13 Games
2	1	Florida	5-0	lost to Auburn 20-23
1	2	Miami, Fla.	4-0	beat # 14 Florida State 49-27
3	3	Oklahoma	5-0	beat Kansas 38-10
4	4	Nebraska	6-0	beat Baylor 48-7
6	5	Oregon	5-0	beat California 48-7
5	6	Virginia Tech	5-0	beat Boston College 34-20
7	7	UCLA	4-0	beat # 10 Washington 35-13
10	8	Fresno State	5-0	beat Colorado State 25-22
9	9	South Carolina	5-0	lost to Arkansas 7-10
8	10	Washington	4-0	lost to # 7 UCLA 13-35
11	11	Texas	4-1	beat Oklahoma State 45-17
12	12	Michigan	4-1	beat # 17 Purdue 24-10
14	13	Tennessee	3-1	bye week
13	14	Florida State	3-1	lost to # 2 Miami, Fla. 27-49
15	15	Georgia Tech	4-1	lost to # 22 Maryland 17-20 (O11)
18	16	Clemson	3-1	beat North Carolina St. 45-37
16	17	Purdue	4-0	lost to # 12 Michigan 10-24
17	18	Brigham Young	5-0	beat New Mexico 24-20
	19	Georgia	3-1	beat Vanderbilt 30-14
	20	Colorado	4-1	beat # 25 Texas A&M 31-21
25	21	Ohio State	3-1	lost to Wisconsin 17-20
20	22	Maryland	5-0	beat # 15 Georgia Tech 20-17 (O11)
22	23	Stanford	3-0	lost to Washington State 39-45
21	24	Kansas State	2-2	lost to Texas Tech 19-38
19	25	Texas A&M	5-0	lost to # 20 Colorado 21-31
23		Toledo	5-0	bye week
24		Northwestern	3-1	beat Minnesota 23-17

ESPN	AP	October 14 Poll		Oct. 20 Games
1	1	Miami, Fla.	5-0	bye week
2	2	Oklahoma	6-0	beat Baylor 33-17
3	3	Nebraska	7-0	beat Texas Tech 41-31
6	4	UCLA	5-0	beat California 56-17
5	5	Oregon	6-0	lost to Stanford 42-49
4	6	Virginia Tech	6-0	bye week
7	7	Florida	5-1	bye week
10	8	Fresno State	6-0	lost to Boise State 30-35 (O19)
8	9	Texas	5-1	beat # 14 Colorado 41-7
9	10	Michigan	5-1	bye week
11	11	Tennessee	3-1	beat Alabama 35-24
14	12	Maryland	6-0	beat Duke 59-17
15	13	Clemson	4-1	lost to North Carolina 3-38
17	14	Colorado	5-1	lost to # 9 Texas 7-41
12	15	Washington	4-1	beat Arizona 31-28
16	16	South Carolina	5-1	beat Vanderbilt 46-14
19	17	Georgia	4-1	beat Kentucky 43-29
13	18	Brigham Young	6-0	beat Air Force 63-33
18	19	Washington State	6-0	beat Montana St. 53-28 (O18)
21	20	Auburn	5-1	beat Louisiana Tech 48-41
22	21	Florida State	3-2	beat Virginia 43-7
20	22	Northwestern	4-1	lost to Penn State 35-38
25	23	Georgia Tech	4-2	beat North Carolina St. 27-17
24	24	Purdue	4-1	bye week
23	25	Toledo	5-0	lost to Ball State 20-24

ESPN	AP	October 21 Poll		Oct. 27 Games
1	1	Miami, Fla.	5-0	beat West Virginia 45-3 (O25)
2	2	Oklahoma	7-0	lost to # 3 Nebraska 10-20
3	3	Nebraska	8-0	beat # 2 Oklahoma 20-10
5	4	UCLA	6-0	lost to # 20 Stanford 28-38
4	5	Virginia Tech	6-0	lost to Syracuse 14-22
6	6	Florida	5-1	beat # 15 Georgia 24-10
7	7	Texas	6-1	beat Missouri 35-16
8	8	Michigan	5-1	beat Iowa 32-26
9	9	Tennessee	4-1	beat # 12 South Carolina 17-10
12	10	Maryland	7-0	lost to # 19 Florida State 31-52
13	11	Oregon	6-1	beat # 14 Washington State 24-17
14	12	South Carolina	6-1	lost to # 9 Tennessee 10-17
11	13	Washington	5-1	beat Arizona State 33-31
15	14	Washington State	7-0	lost to # 11 Oregon 17-24
16	15	Georgia	5-1	lost to # 6 Florida 10-24
10	16	Brigham Young	7-0	beat San Diego State 59-21
17	17	Auburn	6-1	lost to Arkansas 17-42
19	18	Fresno State	6-1	lost to Hawaii 34-38 (O26)
18	19	Florida State	4-2	beat # 10 Maryland 52-31
22	20	Stanford	4-1	beat # 4 UCLA 38-28
21	21	Georgia Tech	5-2	bye week
23	22	Illinois	6-1	bye week
	23	North Carolina	5-3	bye week
20	24	Purdue	4-1	beat Northwestern 32-27
	25	Colorado	5-2	beat Oklahoma State 22-19
24		Texas A&M	6-1	beat Iowa State 24-21
25		Clemson	4-2	beat Wake Forest 21-14

October 28 Poll

ESPN	AP	Team	Record	Nov. 3 Games
1	1	Miami, Fla.	6-0	beat Temple 38-0
2	2	Nebraska	9-0	beat Kansas 51-7
4	3	Oklahoma	7-1	beat Tulsa 58-0
3	4	Florida	6-1	beat Vanderbilt 71-13
5	5	Texas	7-1	beat Baylor 49-10
6	6	Michigan	6-1	lost to Michigan State 24-26
7	7	Tennessee	5-1	beat Notre Dame 28-18
9	8	Oregon	7-1	beat Arizona State 42-24
11	9	UCLA	6-1	lost to # 16 Washington State 14-20
13	10	Stanford	5-1	lost to # 11 Washington 28-42
10	11	Washington	6-1	beat # 10 Stanford 42-28
12	12	Virginia Tech	6-1	lost to Pittsburgh 7-38
8	13	Brigham Young	8-0	beat Colorado State 56-34 (N1)
14	14	Florida State	5-2	beat Clemson 41-27
16	15	Maryland	7-1	beat Troy State 47-14
19	16	Washington State	7-1	beat # 9 UCLA 20-14
20	17	South Carolina	6-2	beat Wofford 38-14
23	18	Georgia	5-2	bye week
22	19	Syracuse	7-2	bye week
15	20	Purdue	5-1	lost to # 21 Illinois 13-38
18	21	Illinois	6-1	beat # 20 Purdue 38-13
	22	North Carolina	5-3	lost to # 23 Georgia Tech 21-28 (N1)
21	23	Georgia Tech	5-2	beat # 21 North Carolina 28-21 (N1)
17	24	Texas A&M	7-1	lost to Texas Tech 0-12
25	25	Colorado	6-2	beat Missouri 38-24
24		Clemson	5-2	lost to # 14 Florida State 27-41

November 4 Poll

ESPN	AP	Team	Record	Nov. 10 Games
1	1	Miami, Fla.	7-0	beat Boston College 18-7
2	2	Nebraska	10-0	beat Kansas State 31-21
4	3	Oklahoma	8-1	beat Texas A&M 31-10
3	4	Florida	7-1	beat # 14 South Carolina 54-17
5	5	Texas	8-1	beat Kansas 59-0
6	6	Tennessee	6-1	beat Memphis 49-28
7	7	Oregon	8-1	beat # 17 UCLA 21-20
8	8	Washington	7-1	lost to Oregon State 24-49
9	9	Brigham Young	9-0	beat Wyoming 41-34
10	10	Florida State	6-2	lost to North Carolina St. 28-34
12	11	Washington State	8-1	beat Arizona State 28-16
13	12	Michigan	6-2	beat Minnesota 31-10
11	13	Maryland	8-1	beat Clemson 37-20
15	14	South Carolina	7-2	lost to # 4 Florida 17-54
14	15	Illinois	7-1	beat Penn State 33-28
19	16	Stanford	5-2	beat Arizona 51-37
16	17	UCLA	6-2	lost to # 7 Oregon 20-21
18	18	Syracuse	7-2	beat West Virginia 24-13
21	19	Georgia	5-2	lost to # 24 Auburn 17-24
17	20	Georgia Tech	6-2	lost to Virginia 38-39
20	21	Colorado	7-2	beat Iowa State 40-27
23	22	Michigan State	5-2	lost to Indiana 28-37
22	23	Virginia Tech	6-2	beat Temple 35-0
	24	Auburn	6-2	beat # 19 Georgia 24-17
25	25	Louisville	8-1	beat Houston 34-10
24		Purdue	5-2	lost to Ohio State 9-35

November 11 Poll

ESPN	AP	Team	Record	Nov. 17 Games
2	1	Miami, Fla.	8-0	beat Syracuse 59-0
1	2	Nebraska	11-0	bye week
4	3	Oklahoma	9-1	beat Texas Tech 30-13
3	4	Florida	8-1	beat # 21 Florida State 37-13
5	5	Texas	9-1	bye week
6	6	Tennessee	7-1	beat Kentucky 38-35
7	7	Oregon	9-1	bye week
8	8	Brigham Young	10-0	beat Utah 24-21
10	9	Washington State	9-1	lost to # 16 Washington 14-26
9	10	Maryland	9-1	beat North Carolina St. 23-19
11	11	Michigan	7-2	beat Wisconsin 20-17
12	12	Illinois	8-1	beat Ohio State 34-22
15	13	Stanford	6-2	beat California 35-28
13	14	Syracuse	8-2	lost to Miami, Fla. 0-59
16	15	Colorado	8-2	bye week
14	16	Washington	7-2	beat # 9 Washington State 26-14
18	17	Auburn	7-2	lost to Alabama 7-31
17	18	Virginia Tech	7-2	beat Virginia 31-17
19	19	Louisville	9-1	beat East Carolina 39-34 (N15)
21	20	UCLA	6-3	lost to Southern Cal 0-27
20	21	Florida State	6-3	lost to # 4 Florida 13-37
22	22	South Carolina	7-3	beat Clemson 20-15
	23	Georgia	5-3	beat Mississippi 35-15
24	24	Marshall	8-1	beat Ohio U 42-18
	25	Ohio State	6-3	lost to Illinois 22-34
23		Georgia Tech	6-3	beat Wake Forest 38-33
25		Fresno State	8-2	beat Nevada 61-14

November 18 Poll

ESPN	AP	Team	Record	Nov. 24 Games
1	1	Miami, Fla.	9-0	beat # 12 Washington 65-7
2	2	Nebraska	11-0	lost to # 14 Colorado 36-62 (N23)
3	3	Florida	9-1	bye week
4	4	Oklahoma	10-1	lost to Oklahoma State 13-16
5	5	Texas	9-1	beat Texas A&M 21-7 (N23)
7	6	Oregon	9-1	bye week
6	7	Tennessee	8-1	beat Vanderbilt 38-0
9	8	Maryland	10-1	regular season complete
8	9	Brigham Young	11-0	bye week
10	10	Illinois	9-1	beat Northwestern 34-28 (N22)
11	11	Michigan	8-2	lost to Ohio State 20-26
12	12	Washington	8-2	lost to # 1 Miami, Fla. 7-65
13	13	Stanford	7-2	beat Notre Dame 17-13
14	14	Colorado	8-2	beat # 2 Nebraska 62-36 (N23)
16	15	Washington State	9-2	regular season complete
15	16	Virginia Tech	8-2	bye week
17	17	Louisville	10-1	lost to TCU 22-37 (N23)
18	18	South Carolina	8-3	regular season complete
23	19	Georgia	6-3	beat # 21 Georgia Tech 31-17
20	20	Marshall	9-1	beat Youngstown St. 38-24
19	21	Georgia Tech	7-3	lost to # 19 Georgia 17-31
21	22	Syracuse	8-3	beat # 25 Boston College 39-28
22	23	Fresno State	9-2	beat San Jose State 40-21 (N23)
25	24	Arkansas	7-3	lost to LSU 38-41 (N23)
	25	Boston College	7-3	lost to # 22 Syracuse 28-39
24		Auburn	7-3	bye week

November 25 Poll

ESPN	AP	Team	Record	Dec. 1 Games
1	1	Miami, Fla.	10-0	beat # 14 Virginia Tech 26-24
2	2	Florida	9-1	lost to # 5 Tennessee 32-34
3	3	Texas	10-1	lost to # 9 Colorado 37-39 (Big 12 CH)
5	4	Oregon	9-1	beat Oregon State 17-14
4	5	Tennessee	9-1	beat # 2 Florida 34-32
6	6	Nebraska	11-1	regular season complete
7	7	Maryland	10-1	regular season complete
9	8	Illinois	10-1	regular season complete
10	9	Colorado	9-2	beat # 3 Texas 39-37 (Big 12 CH)
7	10	Brigham Young	11-0	beat Mississippi State 41-38
11	11	Oklahoma	10-2	regular season complete
12	12	Stanford	8-2	beat San Jose State 41-14
14	13	Washington State	9-2	
13	14	Virginia Tech	8-2	lost to # 1 Miami, Fla. 24-26
15	15	South Carolina	8-3	
19	16	Georgia	7-3	beat Houston 35-7
17	17	Michigan	8-3	regular season complete
18	18	Syracuse	9-3	regular season complete
20	19	Washington	8-3	regular season complete
18	20	Marshall	10-1	lost to Toledo 29-41 (N30)
21	21	Fresno State	10-2	beat Utah State 70-21
24	22	LSU	7-3	beat # 25 Auburn 27-14
25	23	Ohio State	7-4	regular season complete
23	24	Louisville	10-2	regular season complete
22	25	Auburn	7-3	lost to # 22 LSU 14-27

December 2 Poll

ESPN	AP	Team	Record	Dec. 8 Games
1	1	Miami, Fla.	11-0	regular season complete
2	2	Tennessee	10-1	lost to # 21 LSU 20-31 (SEC CH)
3	3	Oregon	10-1	regular season complete
5	4	Colorado	10-2	regular season complete
4	5	Nebraska	11-1	
6	6	Florida	9-2	regular season complete
7	7	Maryland	10-1	
8	8	Illinois	10-1	
8	9	Brigham Young	12-0	lost to Hawaii 45-72
10	10	Texas	10-2	regular season complete
11	11	Oklahoma	10-2	
12	12	Stanford	9-2	regular season complete
13	13	Washington State	9-2	
14	14	South Carolina	8-3	
16	15	Virginia Tech	8-3	regular season complete
18	16	Georgia	8-3	regular season complete
15	17	Michigan	8-3	
17	18	Syracuse	9-3	
21	19	Fresno State	11-2	regular season complete
19	20	Washington	8-3	
20	21	LSU	8-3	beat # 2 Tennessee 31-20 (SEC CH)
23	22	Ohio State	7-4	
22	23	Louisville	10-2	
24	24	Florida State	7-4	regular season complete
	25	Toledo	9-2	regular season complete
25		Marshall	10-2	regular season complete

December 9 Poll / January 4 Final Poll

ESPN	AP	December 9 Poll	RECORD	BOWL BID	DATE	BOWL RESULT	RB	ESPN	AP	January 4 Final Poll	RECORD
1	1	Miami, Fla.	11-0	Rose Bowl	J3	beat # 4 Nebraska 37-14	1	1	1	Miami, Fla.	12-0
2	2	Oregon	10-1	Fiesta Bowl	J1	beat # 3 Colorado 38-16	2	2	2	Oregon	11-1
3	3	Colorado	10-2	Fiesta Bowl	J1	lost to # 2 Oregon 16-38	5	3	3	Florida	10-2
4	4	Nebraska	11-1	Rose Bowl	J3	lost to # 1 Miami, Fla. 14-37	7	4	4	Tennessee	11-2
5	5	Florida	9-2	Orange Bowl	J1	beat # 6 Maryland 56-23	9	5	5	Texas	11-2
6	6	Maryland	10-1	Orange Bowl	J2	lost to # 5 Florida 23-56	4	6	6	Oklahoma	11-2
7	7	Illinois	10-1	Sugar Bowl	J1	lost to # 12 LSU 34-47	6	8	7	LSU	10-3
8	8	Tennessee	10-2	Capital One Bowl	J1	beat # 17 Michigan 45-17	3	7	8	Nebraska	11-2
9	9	Texas	10-2	Holiday Bowl	D28	beat # 21 Washington 47-43	8	9	9	Colorado	10-3
10	10	Oklahoma	10-2	Cotton Bowl	J1	beat Arkansas 10-3	10	11	10	Washington State	10-2
11	11	Stanford	9-2	Seattle Bowl	D27	lost to Georgia Tech 14-24	12	10	11	Maryland	10-2
12	12	LSU	9-3	Sugar Bowl	J1	beat # 7 Illinois 47-34	11	12	12	Illinois	10-2
13	13	Washington State	9-2	Sun Bowl	D31	beat Purdue 33-27	15	13	13	South Carolina	9-3
14	14	South Carolina	8-3	Outback Bowl	J1	beat # 22 Ohio State 31-28	24	14	14	Syracuse	10-3
16	15	Virginia Tech	8-3	Gator Bowl	J1	lost to # 24 Florida State 17-30	20	15	15	Florida State	8-4
19	16	Georgia	8-3	Music City Bowl	D28	lost to Boston College 16-20	13	17	16	Stanford	9-3
15	17	Michigan	8-3	Capital One Bowl	J1	lost to # 8 Tennessee 17-45	18	16	17	Louisville	11-2
18	18	Syracuse	9-3	Insight.com Bowl	D29	beat Kansas State 26-3	26	18	18	Virginia Tech	8-4
17	19	Brigham Young	12-1	Liberty Bowl	D31	lost to # 23 Louisville 10-28	14	19	19	Washington	8-4
21	20	Fresno State	11-2	Silicon Valley Classic	D28	lost to Michigan State 35-44	22	20	20	Michigan	8-4
20	21	Washington	8-3	Holiday Bowl	D28	lost to # 9 Texas 43-47	27	23	21	Boston College	8-4
23	22	Ohio State	7-4	Outback Bowl	J1	lost to # 14 South Carolina 28-31	29	25	22	Georgia	8-4
22	23	Louisville	10-2	Liberty Bowl	D31	beat # 19 Brigham Young 28-10	16	22	23	Toledo	10-2
24	24	Florida State	7-4	Gator Bowl	J1	beat # 15 Virginia Tech 30-17	34		24	Georgia Tech	8-5
	25	Toledo	9-2	Motor City Bowl	D29	beat Cincinnati 23-16	19	24	25	Brigham Young	12-2
25		Marshall	10-2	GMAC Bowl	D19	beat East Carolina 64-61	21	21		Marshall	11-2

2001

Consensus All-Americans

POS	Offense	HT	WT	CL	School	AP	CF	CN	FC	FN	FW	SN
QB	**Rex Grossman**	6-1	223	So.	Florida	•	•	•		•		
RB	**Luke Staley**	6-2	225	So.	Brigham Young	•	•	•	•	•	•	•
RB	**William Green**	6-1	217	Jr.	Boston College		•		•	•		•
WR	**Jabar Gaffney**	6-1	197	So.	Florida	•	•	•	•	•	•	•
WR	**Josh Reed**	5-11	205	Jr.	LSU	•	•	•			•	•
TE	**Dan Graham**	6-3	245	Sr.	Colorado	•	•		•	•	•	•
OL	**Bryant McKinnie**	6-9	335	Sr.	Miami, Fla.	•	•	•	•	•	•	•
OL	**Toniu Fonoti**	6-4	340	Jr.	Nebraska	•	•	•		•	•	•
OL	**Andre Gurode**	6-4	320	Sr.	Colorado	•		•				•
OL	**Mike Williams**	6-6	339	Sr.	Texas		•		•	•		
OL	**Mike Pearson**	6-7	300	Jr.	Florida	•					•	•
OL	**Terrence Metcalf**	6-4	315	Sr.	Mississippi		•		•	•		•
C	**LeCharles Bentley**	6-2	300	Sr.	Ohio State	•	•		•		•	•
PK	**Damon Duval**	6-1	186	Jr.	Auburn	•	•		•			
	OTHERS RECEIVING FIRST-TEAM HONORS											
QB	Antwaan Randle El				Indiana						•	
QB	Eric Crouch				Nebraska	•			•			•
RB	Travis Stephens				Tennessee	•		•			•	
RB	Bruce Perry				Maryland							•
WR	Marquise Walker				Michigan				•			
WR	Lee Evans				Wisconsin					•		
WR	Kevin Curtis				Utah State							•
TE	Jeremy Shockey				Miami, Fla.			•				
OL	Joaquin Gonzalez				Miami, Fla.			•			•	
OL	Eric Heitmann				Stanford				•			
OL	Frank Romero				Oklahoma			•				•
OL	Melvin Fowler				Maryland							•
PK	Seth Marler				Tulane						•	
PK	Todd Sievers				Miami, Fla.			•				
KR	Herb Haygood				Michigan State		•	•				
KR	Luke Powell				Stanford						•	
KR	Bernard Berrian				Fresno State				•			
PR	Roman Hollowell				Colorado			•				

AP named Crouch as all-purpose.

POS	Defense	HT	WT	CL	School	AP	CF	CN	FC	FN	FW	SN
DL	**Alex Brown**	6-4	254	Sr.	Florida	•	•	•			•	
DL	**Dwight Freeney**	6-1	250	Sr.	Syracuse	•	•	•	•	•	•	•
DL	**John Henderson**	6-7	290	Sr.	Tennessee	•	•		•		•	•
DL	**Julius Peppers**	6-6	285	Jr.	North Carolina	•	•	•	•	•	•	•
LB	**Rocky Calmus**	6-3	235	Sr.	Oklahoma	•	•	•	•		•	•
LB	**Robert Thomas**	6-2	237	Sr.	UCLA	•	•			•	•	•
LB	**E.J. Henderson**	6-2	238	Jr.	Maryland	•	•	•		•	•	•
DB	**Quentin Jammer**	6-1	200	Sr.	Texas	•		•	•	•	•	•
DB	**Edward Reed**	6-0	198	Sr.	Miami, Fla.	•	•	•	•	•	•	•
DB	**Roy Williams**	6-0	215	Jr.	Oklahoma	•	•	•	•	•	•	•
P	**Travis Dorsch**	6-6	222	Jr.	Purdue		•	•	•			
	OTHERS RECEIVING FIRST-TEAM HONORS											
DL	Wendell Bryant				Wisconsin			•	•	•		
DL	Kenyon Coleman				UCLA							•
DL	Terrell Suggs				Arizona State							•
LB	Jermaine Petty				Arkansas				•			
LB	Levar Fisher				North Carolina St.		•			•		
LB	Larry Foote				Michigan					•		
LB	Lawrence Flugence				Texas Tech							•
LB	Andra Davis				Florida			•				
DB	Mike Doss				Ohio State		•					
DB	Troy Polamalu				Southern Cal						•	
DB	Tank Williams				Stanford				•			
DB	Lamont Thompson				Washington State	•						•
DB	Keyou Craver				Nebraska			•				
P	Dave Zastudil				Ohio						•	

Heisman Trophy Voting

	PLAYER	POS	SCHOOL	1ST	2ND	3RD	TOTAL
1	**Eric Crouch**	QB	Nebraska	162	98	88	770
2	**Rex Grossman**	QB	Florida	137	105	87	708
3	**Ken Dorsey**	QB	Miami, Fla.	109	122	67	638
4	**Joey Harrington**	QB	Oregon	54	68	66	364
5	**David Carr**	QB	Fresno State	34	60	58	280
6	**Antwaan Randel El**	QB	Indiana	46	39	51	267
7	**Roy Williams**	DB	Oklahoma	13	36	35	146
8	**Bryant McKinnie**	OL	Miami, Fla.	26	12	14	116
9	**Dwight Freeney**	DL	Syracuse	2	6	24	42
10	**Julius Peppers**	DL	North Carolina	2	10	15	41

Award Winners

Ken Dorsey, QB, Miami, Fla., Maxwell, **Bryant McKinnie**, OT, Miami, Fla., Outland, **Eric Crouch**, QB, Nebraska, Camp, **Julius Peppers**, DE, North Carolina, Lombardi, Bednarik, **Eric Crouch**, QB, Nebraska, O'Brien, **Rocky Calmus**, LB, Oklahoma, Butkus, **Roy Williams**, DB, Oklahoma, Thorpe, Nagurski, **David Carr**, QB, Fresno State, Unitas, **Luke Staley**, RB, Brigham Young, Walker, **Seth Marler**, K, Tulane, Groza, **Josh Reed**, WR, LSU, Biletnikoff, **Kahlil Hill**, WR, Iowa, Tatupu, **Travis Dorsch**, P, Purdue, Guy, **Dan Graham**, TE, Colorado, Mackey, **LeCharles Bentley**, C, Ohio State, Rimington

Conference Standings

ACC	Conf. W	L	T	Overall W	L	T
Maryland	7	1	0	10	2	0
Florida State	6	2	0	8	4	0
North Carolina	5	3	0	8	5	0
Georgia Tech	4	4	0	8	5	0
Clemson	4	4	0	7	5	0
North Carolina St.	4	4	0	7	5	0
Wake Forest	3	5	0	6	5	0
Virginia	3	5	0	5	7	0
Duke	0	8	0	0	11	0

Big 10	Conf. W	L	T	Overall W	L	T
Illinois	7	1	0	10	2	0
Michigan	6	2	0	8	4	0
Ohio State	5	3	0	7	5	0
Iowa	4	4	0	7	5	0
Purdue	4	4	0	6	6	0
Penn State	4	4	0	5	6	0
Indiana	4	4	0	5	6	0
Michigan State	3	5	0	7	5	0
Wisconsin	3	5	0	5	7	0
Minnesota	2	6	0	4	7	0
Northwestern	2	6	0	4	7	0

Big 12	Conf. W	L	T	Overall W	L	T
NORTH						
Nebraska	7	1	0	11	2	0
Colorado	7	1	0	10	3	0
Iowa State	4	4	0	7	5	0
Kansas State	3	5	0	6	6	0
Missouri	3	5	0	4	7	0
Kansas	1	7	0	3	8	0
SOUTH						
Texas	6	2	0	11	2	0
Oklahoma	6	2	0	11	2	0
Texas A&M	4	4	0	8	4	0
Texas Tech	4	4	0	7	5	0
Oklahoma State	2	6	0	4	7	0
Baylor	0	8	0	3	8	0

Championship **Colorado 39 Texas 37**

Big East	Conf. W	L	T	Overall W	L	T
Miami, Fla.	7	0	0	12	0	0
Syracuse	6	1	0	10	3	0
Boston College	4	3	0	8	4	0
Virginia Tech	4	3	0	8	4	0
Pittsburgh	4	3	0	7	5	0
Temple	2	5	0	4	7	0
West Virginia	1	6	0	3	8	0
Rutgers	0	7	0	2	9	0

C-USA	Conf. W	L	T	Overall W	L	T
Louisville	6	1	0	11	2	0
Cincinnati	5	2	0	7	5	0
UAB	5	2	0	6	5	0
East Carolina	5	2	0	6	6	0
Southern Miss	4	3	0	6	5	0
TCU	4	3	0	6	6	0
Memphis	3	4	0	5	6	0
Army	2	5	0	3	8	0
Tulane	1	6	0	3	9	0
Houston	0	7	0	0	11	0

Ivy	Conf. W	L	T	Overall W	L	T
Harvard	7	0	0	9	0	0
Pennsylvania	6	1	0	8	1	0
Brown	5	2	0	6	3	0
Princeton	3	4	0	3	6	0
Columbia	3	4	0	3	7	0
Cornell	2	5	0	2	7	0
Yale	1	6	0	3	6	0
Dartmouth	1	6	0	1	8	0

MAC	Conf. W	L	T	Overall W	L	T
EAST						
Marshall	8	0	0	11	2	0
Miami, Ohio	6	2	0	7	5	0
Bowling Green	5	3	0	8	3	0
Kent State	5	3	0	6	5	0
Akron	4	4	0	4	7	0
Buffalo	1	7	0	3	8	0
Ohio U	1	7	0	1	10	0
WEST						
Toledo	5	2	0	10	2	0
Northern Illinois	4	3	0	6	5	0
Ball State	4	3	0	5	6	0
Western Michigan	4	4	0	5	6	0
Central Michigan	2	6	0	3	8	0
Eastern Michigan	1	6	0	2	9	0

Championship **Toledo 41 Marshall 36**

MWC	Conf. W	L	T	Overall W	L	T
Brigham Young	7	0	0	12	2	0
Colorado State	5	2	0	7	5	0
Utah	4	3	0	8	4	0
New Mexico	4	3	0	6	5	0
Air Force	3	4	0	6	6	0
Nevada-Las Vegas	3	4	0	4	7	0
San Diego State	2	5	0	3	8	0
Wyoming	0	7	0	2	9	0

Pac 10	Conf. W	L	T	Overall W	L	T
Oregon	7	1	0	11	1	0
Washington State	6	2	0	10	2	0
Stanford	6	2	0	9	3	0
Washington	6	2	0	8	4	0
Southern Cal	5	3	0	6	6	0
UCLA	4	4	0	7	4	0
Oregon State	3	5	0	5	6	0
Arizona	2	6	0	5	6	0
Arizona State	1	7	0	4	7	0
California	0	8	0	1	10	0

SEC	Conf. W	L	T	Overall W	L	T
EAST						
Tennessee	6	2	0	11	2	0
Florida	6	2	0	10	2	0
South Carolina	5	3	0	9	3	0
Georgia	5	3	0	8	4	0
Kentucky	1	7	0	2	9	0
Vanderbilt	0	8	0	2	9	0
WEST						
LSU	5	3	0	10	3	0
Auburn	5	3	0	7	5	0
Mississippi	4	4	0	7	4	0
Arkansas	4	4	0	7	5	0
Alabama	4	4	0	7	5	0
Mississippi State	2	6	0	3	8	0

Championship **LSU 31 Tennessee 20**

Sun Belt	Conf. W	L	T	Overall W	L	T
Middle Tennessee	5	1	0	8	3	0
North Texas	5	1	0	5	7	0
New Mexico State	4	2	0	5	7	0
La. Lafayette	2	4	0	3	8	0
Arkansas State	2	4	0	2	9	0
La. Monroe	2	4	0	2	9	0
Idaho	1	5	0	1	10	0

WAC	Conf. W	L	T	Overall W	L	T
Louisiana Tech	7	1	0	7	5	0
Fresno State	6	2	0	11	3	0
Boise State	6	2	0	8	4	0
Hawaii	5	3	0	9	3	0
Rice	5	3	0	8	4	0
SMU	4	4	0	4	7	0
Nevada	3	5	0	3	8	0
San Jose State	3	5	0	3	9	0
Texas-El Paso	1	7	0	2	9	0
Tulsa	0	8	0	1	10	0

Independents	Overall W	L	T
South Florida	8	3	0
Troy State	7	4	0
Central Florida	6	5	0
Notre Dame	5	6	0
Utah State	4	7	0
Connecticut	2	9	0
Navy	0	10	0

Bowl Games

D18, **New Orleans**, Colorado State 45, North Texas 20, D19, **GMAC**, Marshall 64, East Carolina 61, 2 OT, D20, **Tangerine**, Pittsburgh 34, North Carolina St. 19, D25, **Las Vegas**, Utah 10, Southern Cal 6, D27, **Seattle**, Georgia Tech 24, Stanford 14, D27, **Independence**, Alabama 14, Iowa State 13, D28, **Galleryfurniture.com**, Texas A&M 28, TCU 9, D28, **Music City**, Boston College 20, Georgia 16, D28, **Holiday**, Texas 47, Washington 43, D29, **Motor City**, Toledo 23, Cincinnati 16, D29, **Alamo**, Iowa 19, Texas Tech 16, D29, **Insight.com**, Syracuse 26, Kansas State 3, D31, **Humanitarian**, Clemson 49, Louisiana Tech 24, D31, **Sun**, Washington State 33, Purdue 27, D31, **Silicon Valley Classic**, Michigan State 44, Fresno State 35, D31, **Liberty**, Louisville 28, Brigham Young 10, D31, **Peach**, North Carolina 16, Auburn 10, J1, **Cotton**, Oklahoma 10, Arkansas 3, J1, **Outback**, South Carolina 31, Ohio State 28, J1, **Gator**, Florida State 30, Virginia Tech 17, J1, **Florida Citrus**, Tennessee 45, Michigan 17, J1, **Fiesta**, Oregon 38, Colorado 16, J1, **Sugar**, LSU 47, Illinois 34, J2, **Orange**, Florida 56, Maryland 23, J3, **Rose**, Miami, Fla. 37, Nebraska 14

2001 NCAA Major College Statistical Leaders

Individual Leaders

PASSING	POS	CL	G	ATT	COM	PCT	INT	I%	YDS	YPA	TD	TD%	RATING
1 Rex Grossman, Florida	QB	SO	11	395	259	65.6	12	3.0	3896	9.86	34	8.6	170.8
2 David Carr, Fresno State	QB	SR	13	476	308	64.7	7	1.5	4299	9.03	42	8.8	166.7
3 Wes Counts, Middle Tennessee	QB	SR	11	259	188	72.6	4	1.5	2327	8.98	17	6.6	166.6
4 Ryan Dinwiddie, Boise State	QB	SO	11	322	201	62.4	11	3.4	3043	9.45	29	9.0	164.7
5 Byron Leftwich, Marshall	QB	JR	12	470	315	67.0	7	1.5	4132	8.79	38	8.1	164.6
6 Jeff Smoker, Michigan State	QB	SO	10	230	144	62.6	7	3.0	2203	9.58	18	7.8	162.8
7 Brandon Doman, Brigham Young	QB	SR	13	408	261	64.0	8	2.0	3542	8.68	33	8.1	159.7
8 Chris Rix, Florida State	QB	FR	11	286	165	57.7	13	4.6	2734	9.56	24	8.4	156.6
9 Jeff Krohn, Arizona State	QB	SO	10	213	115	54.0	7	3.3	1942	9.12	19	8.9	153.4
10 Nick Rolovich, Hawaii	QB	SR	10	405	233	57.5	9	2.2	3361	8.30	34	8.4	150.5

ALL-PURPOSE	POS	CL	G	RUSH	REC	PR	KR	YDS	YPG
1 Levron Williams, Indiana	RB	SR	11	1401	289	0	511	2201	200.1
2 Bernard Berrian, Fresno State	WR	JR	13	101	1270	552	668	2591	199.3
3 Mewelde Moore, Tulane	RB	SO	12	1421	756	0	82	2259	188.3
4 Luke Staley, Brigham Young	RB	JR	11	1582	334	0	102	2018	183.5
5 Emmett White, Utah State	RB	SR	11	1361	408	125	120	2014	183.1
6 William Green, Boston College	RB	JR	10	1559	260	0	0	1819	181.9
7 Chris Douglas, Duke	TB	SO	11	841	233	0	775	1849	168.1
8 Chance Kretschmer, Nevada	RB	FR	11	1732	55	0	0	1787	162.5
9 Brock Forsey, Boise State	RB	JR	12	1207	369	0	362	1938	161.5
10 Bruce Perry, Maryland	TB	SO	11	1242	359	0	117	1718	156.2

RUSHING/Yards Per Game	POS	CL	G	ATT	YDS	TD	AVG	YPG
1 Chance Kretschmer, Nevada	RB	FR	11	302	1732	15	5.7	157.5
2 William Green, Boston College	RB	JR	10	265	1559	15	5.9	155.9
3 Luke Staley, Brigham Young	RB	JR	11	196	1582	24	8.1	143.8
4 Larry Ned, San Diego State	RB	SR	11	311	1549	15	5.0	140.8
5 Anthony Davis, Wisconsin	RB	FR	11	291	1466	11	5.0	133.3
6 Leonard Henry, East Carolina	RB	SR	11	184	1432	16	7.8	130.2
7 Chester Taylor, Toledo	TB	JR	11	268	1430	20	5.3	130.0
8 Levron Williams, Indiana	RB	SR	11	212	1401	17	6.6	127.4
9 Dameon Hunter, Utah	RB	SR	11	257	1396	9	5.4	126.9
10 Marcus Merriweather, Ball State	TB	SR	10	268	1244	12	4.6	124.4

RUSHING/Yards Per Carry	POS	CL	G	ATT	YDS	YPC
1 Santonio Beard, Alabama	TB	JR	9	77	633	8.2
2 Luke Staley, Brigham Young	RB	JR	11	196	1582	8.1
3 Leonard Henry, East Carolina	RB	SR	11	184	1432	7.8
4 Reshard Lee, Middle Tennessee	RB	SO	11	108	790	7.3
5 Levron Williams, Indiana	RB	SR	11	212	1401	6.6
6 ShanDerrick Charles, SMU	RB	FR	11	134	860	6.4
7 Marion Barber, Minnesota	RB	FR	11	118	742	6.3
8 Onterrio Smith, Oregon	TB	SO	11	161	1007	6.3
9 Joshua Cribbs, Kent State	QB	FR	11	164	1019	6.2
10 Dwone Hicks, Middle Tennessee	TB	JR	11	191	1144	6.0

RECEIVING	POS	CL	G	REC	YDS	TD	RPG	YPR	YPG
1 Josh Reed, LSU	SE	JR	12	94	1740	7	7.8	18.5	145.0
2 Ashley Lelie, Hawaii	WR	JR	12	84	1713	19	7.0	20.4	142.8
3 Kevin Curtis, Utah State	WR	JR	11	100	1531	10	9.1	15.3	139.2
4 Lee Evans, Wisconsin	WR	JR	12	75	1545	9	6.3	20.6	128.8
5 Edell Shepherd, San Jose State	WR	SR	12	83	1500	14	6.9	18.1	125.0
6 Darius Watts, Marshall	WR	SO	12	91	1417	18	7.6	15.6	118.1
7 Charles Rogers, Michigan State	WR	SO	11	57	1200	12	5.2	21.1	109.1
8 Jabar Gaffney, Florida	WR	SO	11	67	1191	13	6.1	17.8	108.3
9 Rodney Wright, Fresno State	WR	SR	13	91	1331	10	7.0	14.6	102.4
10 Shaun McDonald, Arizona State	WR	SO	11	47	1104	10	4.3	23.5	100.4

PUNTING	POS	CL	PUNT	YDS	AVG
1 Travis Dorsch, Purdue	K	SR	49	2370	48.4
2 Dave Zastudil, Ohio	P	SR	50	2280	45.6
3 Andy Groom, Ohio State	DT	SR	44	1981	45.0
4 Steve Mullins, Utah State	P	JR	50	2241	44.8
5 John Skaggs, Navy	P	SO	48	2151	44.8
6 Glenn Pakulak, Kentucky	P	JR	56	2492	44.5
7 Brooks Barnard, Maryland	P	JR	54	2401	44.5
8 Dan MacElroy, Army	P	SR	51	2264	44.4
9 Curtis Head, Marshall	P	JR	45	1996	44.4
10 Nate Fikse, UCLA	P	JR	53	2342	44.2

PUNT RETURNS	POS	CL	PR	YDS	TD	AVG
1 Roman Hollowell, Colorado	WR	SR	29	522	2	18.0
2 Luke Powell, Stanford	FL	JR	19	304	0	16.0
3 DeAndrew Rubin, South Florida	WR	JR	26	406	1	15.6
4 Ronnie Hamilton, Duke	CB	SR	20	311	1	15.6
5 Dexter Wynn, Colorado State	DB	SO	14	214	0	15.3
6 Nathan Vasher, Texas	DB	SO	37	554	1	15.0
7 Phillip Buchanon, Miami, Fla.	DB	JR	31	464	2	15.0
8 Keenan Howry, Oregon	WR	JR	32	465	2	14.5
9 DeJuan Groce, Nebraska	DB	JR	33	469	1	14.2
10 Bernard Berrian, Fresno State	WR	JR	39	552	1	14.2

KICKOFF RETURNS	POS	CL	KR	YDS	TD	AVG
1 Chris Massey, Oklahoma State	DB	JR	15	522	1	34.8
2 Chad Owens, Hawaii	WR	FR	24	807	2	33.6
3 Derrick Hamilton, Clemson	WR	FR	15	476	1	31.7
4 Tom Pace, Arizona State	TB	SR	17	537	1	31.6
5 Corey Parchman, Ball State	WR	SR	15	465	2	31.0
6 Roc Alexander, Washington	CB	SO	19	555	1	29.2
7 David Mikell, Boise State	RB	SO	25	709	1	28.4
8 Aaron Lockett, Kansas State	WR	SR	14	397	1	28.4
9 Herb Haygood, Michigan State	WR	SR	19	524	2	27.6
9 Jason Armstead, Mississippi	WR	JR	19	524	1	27.6

SCORING	POS	CL	TDS	XP	FG	PTS	PTPG
1 Luke Staley, Brigham Young	RB	JR	28	0	0	170	15.5
2 Dwone Hicks, Middle Tennessee	TB	JR	24	0	0	148	13.5
3 Chester Taylor, Toledo	TB	JR	23	0	0	138	12.6
4 Todd Sievers, Miami, Fla.	K	JR	0	56	21	119	10.8
5 Levron Williams, Indiana	RB	SR	19	0	0	114	10.4
6 Jeff Chandler, Florida	PK	SR	0	46	19	103	10.3
7 William Green, Boston College	RB	JR	17	0	0	102	10.2
8 Leonard Henry, East Carolina	RB	SR	18	0	0	108	9.8
8 Ricky Williams, Texas Tech	TB	SR	18	0	0	108	9.8
10 Eric Crouch, Nebraska	QB	SR	19	0	0	116	9.7

FIELD GOALS	POS	CL	FGA	FGM	PCT	FGG
1 Todd Sievers, Miami, Fla.	K	JR	26	21	0.81	1.91
2 Jeff Chandler, Florida	PK	SR	22	19	0.86	1.90
3 Travis Dorsch, Purdue	K	SR	25	20	0.80	1.82
3 Jarvis Wallum, Wyoming	K	JR	23	20	0.87	1.82
3 Steve Azar, Northern Illinois	K	SO	26	20	0.77	1.82
6 Asen Asparuhov, Fresno State	K	JR	30	23	0.77	1.77
7 Tim Duncan, Oklahoma	PK	SR	28	20	0.71	1.67
8 Josh Scobee, Louisiana Tech	K	SO	22	18	0.82	1.64
8 Jeremy Flores, Colorado	K	SR	24	18	0.75	1.64
10 Luke Manget, Georgia Tech	K	JR	28	19	0.68	1.58
10 Justin Ayat, Hawaii	K	FR	29	19	0.66	1.58

INTERCEPTIONS	POS	CL	INT	YDS	TD	INT/GM
1 Ed Reed, Miami, Fla.	DB	SR	9	206	2	0.82
2 Lamont Thompson, Washington State	FS	SR	8	96	1	0.73
3 Derek Ross, Ohio State	DB	SR	7	194	1	0.64
3 Kevin Thomas, Nevada-Las Vegas	DB	SR	7	213	3	0.64
5 Nathan Vasher, Texas	DB	SO	7	17	0	0.58
6 Jonas Buckles, North Texas	DB	SO	5	9	0	0.56
7 Stuart Schweigert, Purdue	DB	SO	6	110	0	0.55
7 Steve Smith, Oregon	DB	SR	6	104	1	0.55
7 Glenn Sumter, Memphis	DB	JR	6	61	0	0.55
7 Stephen Persley, New Mexico	DB	SR	6	36	1	0.55
7 Eugene Wilson, Illinois	CB	JR	6	29	0	0.55
7 Tony Jackson, Maryland	SS	SR	6	6	0	0.55

Team Leaders

RUSHING OFFENSE	G	ATT	YDS	AVG	TD	YPG
1 Nebraska	12	672	3776	5.6	47	314.7
2 Rice	12	751	3378	4.5	30	281.5
3 Air Force	12	677	3279	4.8	36	273.3
4 Indiana	11	541	2964	5.5	33	269.5
5 Kansas State	11	606	2835	4.7	34	257.7
6 Ohio U	11	567	2641	4.7	20	240.1
7 Middle Tennessee	11	471	2615	5.6	32	237.7
8 Colorado	12	575	2742	4.8	27	228.5
9 Alabama	11	472	2490	5.3	19	226.4
10 Wake Forest	11	609	2438	4.0	27	221.6

PASSING OFFENSE	G	ATT	COM	INT	PCT	YDS	YPA	TD	I%	YPC	YPG
1 Florida	11	464	299	13	64.4	4457	9.6	43	3.0	14.9	405.2
2 Hawaii	12	570	327	16	57.4	4576	8.0	41	3.7	14.0	381.3
3 Marshall	12	477	319	7	66.9	4201	8.8	40	3.2	13.2	350.1
4 Idaho	11	497	309	15	62.2	3826	7.7	28	3.8	12.4	347.8
5 Texas Tech	11	569	390	11	68.5	3710	6.5	27	2.2	9.5	337.3
6 Fresno State	13	483	311	8	64.4	4336	9.0	42	2.5	13.9	333.5
7 Brigham Young	13	486	315	9	64.8	4225	8.7	39	5.1	13.4	325.0
8 Louisiana Tech	11	482	283	14	58.7	3443	7.1	30	2.6	12.2	313.0
9 Central Florida	11	407	230	12	56.5	3391	8.3	21	4.4	14.7	308.3
10 Washington State	11	393	214	12	54.5	3310	8.4	30	2.1	15.5	300.9

TOTAL OFFENSE	G	P	YDS	AVG	TD	YPG
1 Brigham Young	13	991	7057	7.1	82	542.9
2 Florida	11	788	5803	7.4	61	527.6
3 Marshall	12	880	6060	6.9	61	505.0
4 Fresno State	13	983	6464	6.6	65	497.2
5 Middle Tennessee	11	781	5296	6.9	56	481.5
6 Idaho	11	872	5113	5.9	42	464.8
7 Hawaii	12	855	5552	6.5	61	462.7
8 Miami, Fla.	11	762	5003	6.6	59	454.8
9 Nevada	11	871	4993	5.7	35	453.9
10 Stanford	11	840	4967	5.9	54	451.6

RUSHING DEFENSE	G	ATT	YDS	AVG	TD	YPG
1 UAB	11	333	630	1.9	6	57.3
2 Virginia Tech	11	371	788	2.1	7	71.6
3 Tennessee	12	384	1024	2.7	8	85.3
4 Bowling Green	11	372	949	2.6	5	86.3
5 New Mexico	11	383	961	2.5	9	87.4
6 Texas	12	385	1074	2.8	13	89.5
7 Oklahoma	12	430	1079	2.5	5	89.9
8 Michigan	11	391	996	2.6	9	90.5
9 Maryland	11	387	997	2.6	5	90.6
10 TCU	11	376	1032	2.7	12	93.8

PASSING DEFENSE	G	ATT	COM	PCT	INT	I%	YDS	YPA	TD	TD%	RAT
1 Miami, Fla.	11	290	129	44.5	27	9.3	1520	5.2	5	1.7	75.6
2 Nebraska	12	395	171	43.3	19	4.8	2043	5.2	8	2.0	83.8
3 Virginia Tech	11	354	161	45.5	19	5.4	1829	5.2	8	2.3	85.6
4 Texas	12	369	187	50.7	15	4.0	1760	4.8	6	1.6	88.0
5 Oklahoma	12	383	177	46.2	20	5.2	2075	5.4	9	2.4	89.0
6 Kansas State	11	320	152	47.5	18	5.6	1825	5.7	11	3.4	95.5
7 North Carolina	12	403	203	50.4	8	2.0	2166	5.4	9	2.2	99.0
8 West Virginia	11	251	122	48.6	11	4.4	1504	6.0	7	2.8	99.4
9 Texas A&M	11	369	206	55.8	14	3.8	1987	5.4	7	1.9	99.7
10 Boston College	11	313	154	49.2	18	5.8	1911	6.1	11	3.5	100.6

TOTAL DEFENSE	G	P	YDS	AVG	TD	YPG
1 Texas	12	754	2834	3.76	22	236.2
2 Virginia Tech	11	725	2617	3.61	17	237.9
3 Kansas State	11	684	2886	4.22	21	262.4
4 Oklahoma	12	813	3154	3.88	18	262.8
5 UAB	11	719	2925	4.07	24	265.9
6 Miami, Fla.	11	758	2980	3.93	14	270.9
7 Pittsburgh	11	786	3131	3.98	29	284.6
8 Nebraska	12	813	3446	4.24	24	287.2
9 Florida	11	712	3192	4.48	19	290.2
10 Texas A&M	11	798	3234	4.05	24	294.0

SCORING OFFENSE	G	PTS	AVG
1 Brigham Young	13	608	46.8
2 Florida	11	482	43.8
3 Miami, Fla.	11	475	43.2
4 Fresno State	13	525	40.4
5 Hawaii	12	483	40.3
6 Texas	12	470	39.2
7 Nebraska	12	449	37.4
8 Marshall	12	448	37.3
9 Middle Tennessee	11	408	37.1
9 Stanford	11	408	37.1

SCORING DEFENSE	G	PTS	AVG
1 Miami, Fla.	11	103	9.4
2 Virginia Tech	11	147	13.4
3 Texas	12	164	13.7
4 Oklahoma	12	166	13.8
5 Florida	11	155	14.1
6 Nebraska	12	189	15.8
7 Kansas State	11	179	16.3
8 Southern Miss	11	186	16.9
9 Michigan	11	192	17.5
10 Louisville	12	213	17.8

TURNOVER MARGIN	G	FR	INT	TOT	FL	INTL	TOT	MAR
1 Miami, Fla.	11	18	27	45	10	9	19	2.4
2 Fresno State	13	13	23	36	5	8	13	1.8
3 Bowling Green	11	17	18	35	5	13	18	1.6
4 Maryland	11	10	24	34	9	9	18	1.5
5 Oregon	11	7	18	25	6	5	11	1.3
5 Southern Cal	11	14	19	33	7	12	19	1.3
7 Syracuse	12	17	13	30	7	8	15	1.3
8 Iowa State	11	8	18	26	2	12	14	1.1
8 Purdue	11	18	18	36	11	13	24	1.1
10 Ohio State	11	10	19	29	8	10	18	1.0
10 Washington State	11	13	22	35	12	12	24	1.0

2002 Poll Progression

ESPN	AP	Pre-Season 2002		Aug. 24 Games
1	1	Miami, Fla.	0-0	bye week
3	2	Oklahoma	0-0	bye week
4	3	Florida State	0-0	beat Iowa State 38-31
2	4	Texas	0-0	bye week
5	5	Tennessee	0-0	bye week
7	6	Florida	0-0	bye week
6	7	Colorado	0-0	bye week
11	8	Georgia	0-0	bye week
9	9	Washington	0-0	bye week
8	10	Nebraska	0-0	beat Arizona State 48-10
14	11	Washington State	0-0	bye week
10	12	Michigan	0-0	bye week
12	13	Ohio State	0-0	beat Texas Tech 45-21
13	14	LSU	0-0	bye week
15	15	Oregon	0-0	bye week
16	16	Virginia Tech	0-0	beat Arkansas State 63-7 (A25)
17	17	Louisville	0-0	bye week
18	17	Michigan State	0-0	bye week
21	18	Marshall	0-0	bye week
19	20	Southern Cal	0-0	bye week
20	21	Maryland	0-0	bye week
22	22	South Carolina	0-0	bye week
	23	Texas A&M	0-0	bye week
24	24	Penn State	0-0	bye week
23	25	Wisconsin	0-0	beat Fresno State 23-21 (A23)
25		North Carolina St.	0-0	beat New Mexico 34-14

ESPN	AP	August 26 Poll		Aug. 31 Games
1	1	Miami, Fla.	0-0	beat Florida A&M 63-17
3	1	Oklahoma	0-0	beat Tulsa 37-0 A30
2	3	Texas	0-0	beat North Texas 27-0
4	4	Tennessee	0-0	beat Wyoming 47-7
5	5	Florida State	1-0	beat Virginia 40-19
7	6	Florida	0-0	beat UAB 51-3
6	7	Colorado	0-0	lost to Colorado State 14-19
12	8	Georgia	0-0	beat Clemson 31-28
8	9	Nebraska	1-0	beat Troy State 31-16
11	10	Ohio State	1-0	bye week
9	11	Washington	0-0	lost to # 13 Michigan 29-31
13	12	Washington State	0-0	beat Nevada 31-7
10	13	Michigan	0-0	beat # 11 Washington 31-29
14	14	LSU	0-0	lost to # 16 Virginia Tech 8-26 (S1)
15	15	Oregon	0-0	beat Mississippi State 36-13
16	16	Virginia Tech	1-0	beat # 14 LSU 26-8 (S1)
18	17	Louisville	0-0	lost to Kentucky 17-22
17	18	Michigan State	0-0	beat Eastern Michigan 56-7
22	19	Marshall	0-0	beat Appalachian St. 50-17
19	20	Southern Cal	0-0	bye week
20	21	Maryland	0-0	lost to Notre Dame 0-22
21	22	South Carolina	0-0	beat New Mexico State 34-24
	23	Texas A&M	0-0	beat La. Lafayette 31-7
23	24	Penn State	0-0	beat Central Florida 27-24
24	25	North Carolina St.	1-0	beat E. Tenn. St. 34-0
25		Wisconsin	1-0	beat Nevada-Las Vegas 27-7

ESPN	AP	September 1 Poll		Sept. 7 Games
1	1	Miami, Fla.	1-0	beat # 6 Florida 41-16
3	2	Oklahoma	1-0	beat Alabama 37-27
2	3	Texas	1-0	bye week
4	4	Tennessee	1-0	beat Middle Tennessee 26-3
5	5	Florida State	2-0	bye week
6	6	Florida	1-0	lost to # 1 Miami, Fla. 16-41
7	7	Michigan	1-0	beat Western Michigan 35-12
9	8	Ohio State	1-0	beat Kent State 51-17
8	9	Nebraska	2-0	beat Utah State 44-13
11	10	Georgia	1-0	bye week
12	11	Washington State	1-0	beat Idaho 49-14
10	12	Virginia Tech	2-0	bye week
13	13	Oregon	1-0	beat Fresno State 28-24
14	14	Washington	0-1	beat San Jose State 34-10
15	15	Michigan State	1-0	beat Rice 27-10
18	16	Marshall	1-0	bye week
17	17	Colorado	0-1	beat San Diego State 34-14
16	18	Southern Cal	0-0	beat Auburn 24-17 (S2)
20	19	Colorado State	2-0	lost to UCLA 19-30
	20	Texas A&M	1-0	beat Pittsburgh 14-12
22	21	North Carolina St.	2-0	beat Navy 65-19
19	22	South Carolina	1-0	lost to Virginia 21-34
24	23	Notre Dame	1-0	beat Purdue 24-17
23	24	LSU	0-1	beat Citadel 35-10
21	25	Wisconsin	2-0	beat West Virginia 34-17
25		Penn State	1-0	bye week

ESPN	AP	September 8 Poll		Sept. 14 Games
1	1	Miami, Fla.	2-0	beat Temple 44-21
3	2	Oklahoma	2-0	beat Texas-El Paso 68-0
2	3	Texas	1-0	beat North Carolina 52-21
4	4	Tennessee	2-0	bye week
5	5	Florida State	2-0	beat Maryland 37-10
8	6	Ohio State	2-0	beat # 10 Washington State 25-7
6	7	Michigan	2-0	lost to # 20 Notre Dame 23-25
7	8	Nebraska	3-0	lost to Penn State 7-40
10	9	Georgia	1-0	beat South Carolina 13-7
11	10	Washington State	2-0	lost to # 6 Ohio State 7-25
9	11	Virginia Tech	2-0	beat # 16 Marshall 47-21 (S12)
13	12	Florida	1-1	beat Ohio U 34-6
12	13	Oregon	2-0	beat Idaho 58-21
14	14	Washington	1-1	bye week
15	15	Michigan State	2-0	lost to California 22-46
17	16	Marshall	1-0	lost to # 11 Virginia Tech 21-47 (S12)
16	17	Southern Cal	1-0	beat # 18 Colorado 40-3
19	18	Colorado	1-1	lost to # 17 Southern Cal 3-40
20	19	North Carolina St.	3-0	beat Wake Forest 32-13
21	20	Notre Dame	2-0	beat # 7 Michigan 25-23
23	21	Texas A&M	2-0	bye week
18	22	Wisconsin	3-0	beat No. Illinois 24-21
	23	UCLA	1-0	beat Oklahoma State 38-24
	24	Colorado State	2-1	beat Louisville 36-33
22	25	LSU	1-1	beat Miami, Ohio 33-7
24		Brigham Young	2-0	lost to Nevada 28-31
25		Penn State	1-0	beat # 8 Nebraska 40-7

ESPN	AP	September 15 Poll		Sept. 21 Games
1	1	Miami, Fla.	3-0	beat Boston College 38-6
3	2	Oklahoma	3-0	bye week
2	3	Texas	2-0	beat Houston 41-11
4	4	Tennessee	2-0	lost to # 10 Florida 13-30
5	5	Florida State	3-0	beat Duke 48-17
6	6	Ohio State	3-0	beat Cincinnati 23-19
7	7	Virginia Tech	3-0	beat # 19 Texas A&M 13-3
8	8	Georgia	2-0	beat Northwestern St. 45-7
9	9	Oregon	3-0	beat Portland St. 41-0
10	10	Florida	2-1	beat # 4 Tennessee 30-13
11	11	Southern Cal	2-0	lost to # 25 Kansas State 20-27
12	12	Notre Dame	3-0	beat Michigan State 21-17
13	13	Washington	1-1	beat Wyoming 38-7
14	14	Michigan	2-1	beat Utah 10-7
15	15	Penn State	2-0	beat Louisiana Tech 49-17
18	16	Washington State	2-1	beat Montana St. 45-28
16	17	North Carolina St.	4-0	beat Texas Tech 51-48
19	18	Nebraska	3-1	bye week
21	19	Texas A&M	2-0	lost to # 7 Virginia Tech 3-13
22	20	UCLA	2-0	lost to Colorado 17-31
24	21	Iowa State	3-1	beat Troy State 42-12
17	22	Wisconsin	4-0	beat Arizona 31-10
	23	California	3-0	lost to Air Force 21-23
20	24	LSU	2-1	bye week
23	25	Kansas State	3-0	beat # 11 Southern Cal 27-20
25		Colorado State	3-1	bye week

ESPN	AP	September 22 Poll		Sept. 28 Games
1	1	Miami, Fla.	4-0	bye week
3	2	Oklahoma	3-0	beat South Florida 31-14
2	3	Texas	3-0	beat Tulane 49-0
4	4	Florida State	4-0	lost to Louisville 20-26 (S26)
5	5	Virginia Tech	4-0	beat Western Michigan 30-0
6	6	Ohio State	4-0	beat Indiana 45-17
9	7	Florida	3-1	beat Kentucky 41-34
7	8	Georgia	3-0	beat New Mexico State 41-10
8	9	Oregon	4-0	bye week
10	10	Notre Dame	4-0	bye week
11	11	Tennessee	2-1	beat Rutgers 35-14
12	12	Penn State	3-0	lost to Iowa 35-42
13	13	Washington	2-1	beat Idaho 41-27
14	14	Michigan	3-1	beat Illinois 45-28
17	15	Kansas State	4-0	bye week
18	16	Washington State	3-1	beat California 48-38
15	17	North Carolina St.	5-0	beat Massachusetts 56-24
22	18	Southern Cal	2-1	beat # 23 Oregon State 22-0
21	19	Iowa State	4-1	beat # 20 Nebraska 36-14
19	20	Nebraska	3-1	lost to # 19 Iowa State 14-36
16	21	Wisconsin	5-0	bye week
20	22	LSU	2-1	beat Mississippi State 31-13
24	23	Oregon State	4-0	lost to # 18 Southern Cal 0-22
	24	Texas A&M	2-1	beat Louisiana Tech 31-3
23	25	Colorado State	3-1	beat Nevada 32-28
25		Auburn	3-1	beat Syracuse 37-34

ESPN	AP	September 29 Poll		Oct. 5 Games
1	1	Miami, Fla.	4-0	beat Connecticut 48-14
2	2	Texas	4-0	beat Oklahoma State 17-15
3	3	Oklahoma	4-0	beat Missouri 31-24
4	4	Virginia Tech	5-0	bye week
5	5	Ohio State	5-0	beat Northwestern 27-16
8	6	Florida	4-1	lost to Mississippi 14-17
6	7	Georgia	4-0	beat # 22 Alabama 27-25
7	8	Oregon	4-0	beat Arizona 31-14
9	9	Notre Dame	4-0	beat Stanford 31-7
10	10	Tennessee	3-1	beat Arkansas 41-38
11	11	Florida State	4-1	beat Clemson 48-31 (O3)
12	12	Washington	3-1	lost to California 27-34
16	13	Kansas State	4-0	lost to Colorado 31-35
13	14	Michigan	4-1	bye week
18	15	Iowa State	5-1	bye week
14	16	North Carolina St.	6-0	bye week
17	17	Washington State	4-1	beat # 18 Southern Cal 30-27
20	18	Southern Cal	3-1	lost to # 17 Washington State 27-30
15	19	Wisconsin	5-0	lost to # 20 Penn State 31-34
21	20	Penn State	3-1	beat # 19 Wisconsin 34-31
19	21	LSU	3-1	beat La. Lafayette 48-0
PB	22	Alabama	4-1	lost to # 7 Georgia 25-27
23	23	Texas A&M	3-1	lost to Texas Tech 47-48
	24	Iowa	4-1	beat Purdue 31-28
22	25	Colorado State	4-1	lost to Fresno State 30-32 (O4)
24		Auburn	4-1	bye week
25		Air Force	4-0	beat Navy 48-7

ESPN	AP	October 6 Poll		Oct. 12 Games
1	1	Miami, Fla.	5-0	beat # 9 Florida State 28-27
3	2	Oklahoma	5-0	beat # 3 Texas 35-24
2	3	Texas	5-0	lost to # 2 Oklahoma 24-35
4	4	Virginia Tech	5-0	beat Boston College 28-23 (O10)
5	5	Ohio State	6-0	beat San Jose State 50-7
6	6	Georgia	5-0	beat # 10 Tennessee 18-13
7	7	Oregon	5-0	beat UCLA 31-30
8	8	Notre Dame	5-0	beat Pittsburgh 14-6
12	9	Florida State	5-1	lost to # 1 Miami, Fla. 27-28
9	10	Tennessee	4-1	lost to # 6 Georgia 13-18
14	11	Iowa State	5-1	beat Texas Tech 31-17
13	12	Washington State	5-1	beat Stanford 36-11
10	13	Michigan	4-1	beat # 15 Penn State 27-24
11	14	North Carolina St.	6-0	beat North Carolina 34-17
17	15	Penn State	4-1	lost to # 13 Michigan 24-27
16	16	Florida	4-2	lost to # 18 LSU 7-36
20	17	Iowa	5-1	beat Michigan State 44-16
15	18	LSU	4-1	beat # 16 Florida 36-7
23	19	Kansas State	4-1	beat Oklahoma State 44-9
24	20	Southern Cal	3-2	beat California 30-28
19	21	Air Force	5-0	beat Brigham Young 52-9
18	22	Washington	3-2	beat Arizona 32-28
22	23	Wisconsin	5-1	lost to Indiana 29-32
21	24	Auburn	4-1	lost to Arkansas 17-38
	25	Mississippi	4-1	beat Arkansas State 52-17
25		UCLA	4-1	lost to # 7 Oregon 30-31

ESPN	AP	October 13 Poll		Oct. 19 Games
1	1	Miami, Fla.	6-0	bye week
2	2	Oklahoma	6-0	beat # 9 Iowa State 49-3
3	3	Virginia Tech	6-0	beat Rutgers 35-14
4	4	Ohio State	7-0	beat Wisconsin 19-14
5	5	Georgia	6-0	beat Vanderbilt 48-17
6	6	Oregon	6-0	lost to Arizona State 42-45
7	7	Notre Dame	6-0	beat # 18 Air Force 21-14
8	8	Texas	5-1	beat # 17 Kansas State 17-14
13	9	Iowa State	6-1	lost to # 2 Oklahoma 3-49
11	10	Washington State	6-1	bye week
9	11	Michigan	5-1	beat Purdue 23-21
14	12	Florida State	5-2	bye week
10	13	North Carolina St.	7-0	beat Duke 24-22
12	14	LSU	5-1	beat South Carolina 38-14
16	15	Iowa	6-1	beat Indiana 24-8
18	16	Tennessee	4-2	bye week
19	17	Kansas State	5-1	lost to # 8 Texas 14-17
15	18	Air Force	6-0	lost to # 7 Notre Dame 14-21
20	19	Southern Cal	4-2	beat # 22 Washington 41-21
21	20	Penn State	4-2	beat Northwestern 49-0
22	21	Mississippi	5-1	lost to # 24 Alabama 7-42
17	22	Washington	4-2	lost to # 19 Southern Cal 21-41
25	23	Colorado	4-2	beat Baylor 34-0
PB	24	Alabama	4-2	beat # 21 Mississippi 42-7
23	25	Bowling Green	5-0	beat Western Michigan 48-45
24		Florida	4-3	beat Auburn 30-23

ESPN	AP	October 20 Poll		Oct. 26 Games
1	1	Miami, Fla.	6-0	beat West Virginia 40-23
2	2	Oklahoma	7-0	bye week
3	3	Virginia Tech	7-0	beat Temple 20-10
4	4	Ohio State	8-0	beat # 18 Penn State 13-7
5	5	Georgia	7-0	beat Kentucky 52-24
6	6	Notre Dame	7-0	beat # 11 Florida State 34-24
7	7	Texas	6-1	beat # 17 Iowa State 21-10
8	8	Michigan	6-1	lost to # 13 Iowa 9-34
11	9	Washington State	6-1	beat Arizona 21-13
10	10	LSU	6-1	lost to Auburn 7-31
13	11	Florida State	5-2	lost to # 6 Notre Dame 24-34
9	12	North Carolina St.	8-0	beat Clemson 38-6 (O24)
14	13	Iowa	7-1	beat # 8 Michigan 34-9
12	14	Oregon	6-1	lost to # 15 Southern Cal 33-44
16	15	Southern Cal	5-2	beat # 14 Oregon 44-33
15	16	Tennessee	4-2	lost to # 19 Alabama 14-34
18	17	Iowa State	6-2	lost to # 7 Texas 10-21
17	18	Penn State	5-2	lost to # 4 Ohio State 7-13
PB	19	Alabama	5-2	beat # 16 Tennessee 34-14
21	20	Kansas State	5-2	beat Baylor 44-10
20	21	Colorado	5-2	beat Texas Tech 37-13
19	22	Air Force	6-1	lost to Wyoming 26-34
25	23	Arizona State	6-2	beat Washington 27-16
22	24	Bowling Green	6-0	beat Ball State 38-20
24	25	Minnesota	7-1	bye week
23		Florida	5-3	bye week
25		Marshall	5-1	beat Central Michigan 23-18

ESPN	AP	October 27 Poll		Nov. 2 Games
1	1	Miami, Fla.	7-0	beat Rutgers 42-17
2	2	Oklahoma	7-0	beat # 13 Colorado 27-11
3	3	Virginia Tech	8-0	lost to Pittsburgh 21-28
6	4	Notre Dame	8-0	lost to Boston College 7-14
5	5	Georgia	8-0	lost to Florida 13-20
4	6	Ohio State	9-0	beat # 23 Minnesota 34-3
7	7	Texas	7-1	beat Nebraska 27-24
9	8	Washington State	7-1	beat # 16 Arizona State 44-22
10	9	Iowa	8-1	beat Wisconsin 20-3
8	10	North Carolina St.	9-0	lost to Georgia Tech 17-24
11	11	Southern Cal	6-2	bye week
PB	12	Alabama	6-2	beat Vanderbilt 30-8
12	13	Colorado	6-2	lost to # 2 Oklahoma 11-27
14	14	Kansas State	6-2	beat Kansas 64-0
13	15	Michigan	6-2	beat Michigan State 49-3
17	16	Arizona State	7-2	lost to # 8 Washington State 22-44
15	17	LSU	6-2	bye week
20	18	Florida State	5-3	beat Wake Forest 34-21
16	19	Oregon	6-2	beat Stanford 41-14
21	20	Penn State	5-3	beat Illinois 18-7
18	21	Bowling Green	7-0	beat Kent State 45-14
23	22	Iowa State	6-3	beat Missouri 42-35
19	23	Minnesota	7-1	lost to # 6 Ohio State 3-34
24	24	Colorado State	7-2	beat Air Force 31-12 (O31)
	25	Tennessee	4-3	beat South Carolina 18-10
22		Florida	5-3	beat # 5 Georgia 20-13
25		Marshall	6-1	lost to Akron 20-34

ESPN	AP	November 3 Poll		Nov. 9 Games
2	1	Oklahoma	8-0	lost to Texas A&M 26-30
1	2	Miami, Fla.	8-0	beat Tennessee 26-3
3	3	Ohio State	10-0	beat Purdue 10-6
4	4	Texas	8-1	beat Baylor 41-0
5	5	Washington State	8-1	beat # 15 Oregon 32-21
6	6	Iowa	9-1	beat Northwestern 62-10
8	7	Georgia	8-1	beat Mississippi 31-17
7	8	Virginia Tech	8-1	lost to Syracuse 42-50
10	9	Notre Dame	8-1	beat Navy 30-23
9	10	Southern Cal	6-2	beat Stanford 49-17
PB	11	Alabama	7-2	beat Mississippi State 28-14
12	12	Kansas State	7-2	beat # 21 Iowa State 58-7
11	13	Michigan	7-2	beat Minnesota 41-24
13	14	North Carolina St.	9-1	lost to Maryland 21-24
15	15	Oregon	7-2	lost to # 5 Washington State 21-32
14	16	LSU	6-2	beat Kentucky 33-30
18	17	Florida State	6-3	beat Georgia Tech 21-13
21	18	Colorado	6-3	beat Missouri 42-35
19	19	Penn State	6-3	beat Virginia 35-14
16	20	Bowling Green	8-0	lost to No. Illinois 17-26
22	21	Iowa State	7-3	lost to # 12 Kansas State 7-58
23	22	Pittsburgh	7-2	beat Temple 29-22
17	23	Florida	6-3	beat Vanderbilt 21-17
20	24	Colorado State	8-2	bye week
24	25	Arizona State	7-3	lost to California 38-55
25		Maryland	7-2	beat # 14 North Carolina St. 24-21

ESPN	AP	November 10 Poll		Nov. 16 Games
1	1	Miami, Fla.	9-0	bye week
2	2	Ohio State	11-0	beat Illinois 23-16
4	3	Washington State	9-1	bye week
6	4	Oklahoma	8-1	beat Baylor 49-9
3	4	Texas	9-1	lost to Texas Tech 38-42
5	6	Iowa	10-1	beat Minnesota 45-21
7	7	Georgia	9-1	beat # 24 Auburn 24-21
8	8	Southern Cal	7-2	beat Arizona State 34-13
9	9	Notre Dame	9-1	bye week
PB	10	Alabama	8-2	beat # 14 LSU 31-0
11	11	Kansas State	8-2	beat Nebraska 49-13
10	12	Michigan	8-2	beat Wisconsin 21-14
13	13	Virginia Tech	8-2	bye week
12	14	LSU	7-2	lost to # 10 Alabama 0-31
15	15	Florida State	7-3	beat North Carolina 40-14
16	16	Penn State	7-3	beat Indiana 58-25
17	17	Colorado	7-3	beat Iowa State 41-27
21	18	Pittsburgh	8-2	bye week
19	19	Maryland	8-2	beat Clemson 30-12
14	20	Florida	7-3	beat South Carolina 28-7
17	21	Colorado State	8-2	beat San Diego State
20	22	North Carolina St.	9-2	lost to Virginia 9-14
22	23	Oregon	7-3	lost to Washington 14-42
	24	Auburn	7-3	lost to # 7 Georgia 21-24
24	25	TCU	8-1	bye week
23		Boise State	9-1	beat Louisiana Tech 36-10
25		Bowling Green	8-1	lost to South Florida 7-29

ESPN	AP	November 17 Poll		Nov. 23 Games
1	1	Miami, Fla.	9-0	beat # 17 Pittsburgh 28-21 (N21)
2	2	Ohio State	12-0	beat # 12 Michigan 14-9
3	3	Washington State	9-1	lost to Washington 26-29
5	4	Oklahoma	9-1	beat # 24 Texas Tech 60-15
4	5	Iowa	11-1	regular season complete
6	6	Georgia	10-1	bye week
7	7	Southern Cal	8-2	beat # 25 UCLA 52-21
8	8	Notre Dame	9-1	beat Rutgers 42-0
PB	9	Alabama	9-2	lost to Auburn 7-17
10	10	Kansas State	9-2	beat Missouri 38-0
11	11	Texas	9-2	bye week
9	12	Michigan	9-2	lost to # 2 Ohio State 9-14
12	13	Virginia Tech	8-2	lost to West Virginia 18-21 (N20)
14	14	Florida State	8-3	lost to North Carolina St. 7-17
16	15	Penn State	8-3	beat Michigan State 61-7
17	16	Colorado	8-3	bye week
19	17	Pittsburgh	8-2	lost to # 1 Miami, Fla. 21-28 (N21)
18	18	Maryland	9-2	lost to Virginia 13-48
13	19	Florida	8-3	bye week
15	20	Colorado State	9-2	beat New Mexico 22-14
20	21	LSU	7-3	beat Mississippi 14-13
22	22	TCU	8-1	lost to East Carolina 28-31
21	23	Boise State	10-1	beat Nevada 44-7
23	24	Texas Tech	8-4	lost to # 4 Oklahoma 15-60
24	25	UCLA	7-3	lost to # 7 Southern Cal 21-52
25		Hawaii	8-2	beat Cincinnati 20-19

ESPN	AP	November 24 Poll		Nov. 30 Games
1	1	Miami, Fla.	10-0	beat Syracuse 49-7
2	2	Ohio State	13-0	regular season complete
4	3	Oklahoma	10-1	lost to Oklahoma State 28-38
3	4	Iowa	11-1	
5	5	Georgia	10-1	beat Georgia Tech 51-7
6	6	Southern Cal	9-2	beat # 7 Notre Dame 44-13
7	7	Notre Dame	10-1	lost to # 6 Southern Cal 13-44
8	8	Kansas State	10-2	regular season complete
9	9	Washington State	9-2	bye week
10	10	Texas	9-2	beat Texas A&M 50-20 (N29)
12	11	Penn State	9-3	regular season complete
14	12	Michigan	9-3	regular season complete
15	13	Colorado	8-3	beat Nebraska 28-13 (N29)
PB	14	Alabama	9-3	beat Hawaii 21-16
11	15	Florida	8-3	lost to # 23 Florida State 14-31
13	16	Colorado State	10-2	lost to Nevada-Las Vegas 33-36
18	17	Pittsburgh	8-3	lost to # 24 West Virginia 17-24
17	18	LSU	8-3	lost to Arkansas 20-21 (N29)
16	19	Boise State	11-1	regular season complete
25	20	Auburn	8-4	regular season complete
20	21	North Carolina St.	10-3	regular season complete
19	22	Virginia Tech	8-3	beat Virginia 21-9
22	23	Florida State	8-4	beat # 15 Florida 31-14
21	24	West Virginia	8-3	beat # 17 Pittsburgh 24-17
23	25	Maryland	9-3	beat Wake Forest 32-14
24		Hawaii	9-2	lost to # 14 Alabama 16-21

ESPN	AP	December 1 Poll		Dec. 7 Games
1	1	Miami, Fla.	11-0	beat # 18 Virginia Tech 56-45
2	2	Ohio State	13-0	
3	3	Iowa	11-1	
4	4	Georgia	11-1	beat # 22 Arkansas 30-3 (SEC CH)
5	5	Southern Cal	10-2	regular season complete
6	6	Kansas State	10-2	
7	7	Washington State	9-2	beat UCLA 48-27
9	8	Oklahoma	10-2	beat # 12 Colorado 29-7 (Big 12 CH)
8	9	Texas	10-2	regular season complete
10	10	Penn State	9-3	
13	11	Notre Dame	10-2	regular season complete
12	12	Colorado	9-3	lost to # 8 Oklahoma 7-29 (Big 12 CH)
11	13	Michigan	9-3	
PB	14	Alabama	10-3	regular season complete
16	15	West Virginia	9-3	regular season complete
18	16	Florida State	9-4	regular season complete
17	17	North Carolina St.	10-3	
14	18	Virginia Tech	9-3	lost to # 1 Miami, Fla. 45-56
15	19	Boise State	11-1	
23	20	Auburn	8-4	
19	21	Maryland	10-3	regular season complete
22	22	Arkansas	9-3	lost to # 4 Georgia 3-30 (SEC CH)
20	23	Florida	8-4	regular season complete
21	24	Colorado State	10-3	regular season complete
24	25	Pittsburgh	8-4	regular season complete
25		LSU	8-4	regular season complete

ESPN	AP	December 8 Poll	Record	Bowl Bid	Date	Bowl Result
1	1	Miami, Fla.	12-0	Fiesta Bowl	J3	lost to # 2 Ohio State 24-31
2	2	Ohio State	13-0	Fiesta Bowl	J3	beat # 1 Miami, Fla. 31-24
3	3	Iowa	11-1	Orange Bowl	J2	lost to # 5 Southern Cal 17-38
4	4	Georgia	12-1	Sugar Bowl	J1	beat # 16 Florida State 26-13
5	5	Southern Cal	10-2	Orange Bowl	J2	beat # 3 Iowa 38-17
6	6	Kansas State	10-2	Holiday Bowl	D27	beat Arizona State 34-27
7	7	Washington State	10-2	Rose Bowl	J1	lost to # 8 Oklahoma 14-34
8	8	Oklahoma	11-2	Rose Bowl	J1	beat # 7 Washington State 34-14
9	9	Texas	10-2	Cotton Bowl	J1	beat LSU 35-20
10	10	Penn State	9-3	Capital One Bowl	J1	lost to # 19 Auburn 9-13
12	11	Notre Dame	10-2	Gator Bowl	J1	lost to # 17 North Carolina St. 6-28
11	12	Michigan	9-3	Outback Bowl	J1	beat # 22 Florida 38-30
PB	13	Alabama	10-3			
14	14	Colorado	9-4	Alamo Bowl	D28	lost to Wisconsin 28-31
13	15	West Virginia	9-3	Continental Bowl	D28	lost to Virginia 22-48
16	16	Florida State	9-4	Sugar Bowl	J1	lost to # 4 Georgia 13-26
17	17	North Carolina St.	10-3	Gator Bowl	J1	beat # 11 Notre Dame 28-6
15	18	Boise State	11-1	Humanitarian Bowl	D31	beat Iowa State 34-16
22	19	Auburn	8-4	Capital One Bowl	J1	beat # 10 Penn State 13-9
18	20	Maryland	10-3	Peach Bowl	D31	beat Tennessee 30-3
19	21	Virginia Tech	9-4	San Francisco Bowl	D31	beat Air Force 20-13
20	22	Florida	8-4	Outback Bowl	J1	lost to # 12 Michigan 30-38
21	23	Colorado State	10-3	Liberty Bowl	D31	lost to TCU 3-17
23	24	Pittsburgh	8-4	Insight Bowl	D26	beat Oregon State 38-13
	25	Arkansas	9-4	Music City Bowl	D30	lost to Minnesota 14-29
24		Marshall	10-2	GMAC Bowl	D18	beat Louisville 38-15
25		LSU	8-4	Cotton Bowl	J1	lost to # 9 Texas 20-35

RB	ESPN	AP	January 4 Final Poll	Record
1	1	1	Ohio State	14-0
2	2	2	Miami, Fla.	12-1
3	3	3	Georgia	13-1
5	4	4	Southern Cal	11-2
4	5	5	Oklahoma	12-2
6	7	6	Texas	11-2
12	6	7	Kansas State	11-2
7	8	8	Iowa	11-2
10	9	9	Michigan	10-3
9	10	10	Washington State	10-3
15	PB	11	Alabama	10-3
8	11	12	North Carolina St.	11-3
17	13	13	Maryland	11-3
13	16	14	Auburn	9-4
14	12	15	Boise State	12-1
20	15	16	Penn State	9-4
11	17	17	Notre Dame	10-3
19	14	18	Virginia Tech	10-4
24	18	19	Pittsburgh	9-4
28	21	20	Colorado	9-5
22	23	21	Florida State	9-5
16	25	22	Virginia	9-5
39	22	23	TCU	10-2
25	19	24	Marshall	11-2
18	20	25	West Virginia	9-4
30	24		Florida	8-4

ANNUAL REVIEW

2002

CONSENSUS ALL-AMERICANS

POS	Offense	HT	WT	CL	School	AP	CF	FC	FW	SN
QB	Carson Palmer	6-5	225	Sr.	Southern Cal	•			•	•
RB	Larry Johnson	6-2	222	Sr.	Penn State	•	•	•	•	•
RB	Willis McGahee	6-1	224	So.	Miami, Fla.	•	•	•	•	•
WR	Charles Rogers	6-4	205	Jr.	Michigan State	•	•	•	•	•
WR	Reggie Williams	6-4	200	So.	Washington	•				•
WR	Rashaun Woods	6-2	187	Jr.	Oklahoma State		•		•	
TE	Dallas Clark	6-4	244	Jr.	Iowa	•	•	•	•	•
OL	Shawn Andrews	6-5	345	So.	Arkansas	•	•	•	•	•
OL	Eric Steinbach	6-7	284	Sr.	Iowa	•	•		•	•
OL	Derrick Dockery	6-6	345	Sr.	Texas	•	•		•	•
OL	Jordan Gross	6-5	306	Sr.	Utah	•			•	•
C	Brett Romberg	6-3	290	Sr.	Miami, Fla.	•	•		•	•
PK	Mike Nugent	5-10	170	So.	Ohio State	•	•		•	•
AP	Derek Abney	5-10	175	Jr.	Kentucky	•	•	•	•	•

OTHERS RECEIVING FIRST-TEAM HONORS

QB	Ken Dorsey		Miami, Fla.	•	•
QB	Brad Banks		Iowa	•	
RB	Chris Brown		Colorado		•
WR	Nate Burleson		Nevada		•
OL	Bruce Nelson		Iowa		•
OL	Jon Stinchcomb		Georgia		•
OL	Brett Williams		Florida State		• •
OL	Wayne Lucier		Colorado		•
OL	Jeff Faine		Notre Dame		•
OL	Derrick Roche		Washington State		• •
PK	Nate Kaeding		Iowa		•
AP	DeJuan Groce		Nebraska		•

POS	Defense	HT	WT	CL	School	AP	CF	FC	FW	SN
DL	Terrell Suggs	6-3	251	Jr.	Arizona State	•	•	•	•	•
DL	David Pollack	6-2	275	So.	Georgia	•	•		•	•
DL	Rien Long	6-6	287	Jr.	Washington State	•	•		•	•
DL	Tommie Harris	6-3	280	So.	Oklahoma	•	•	•		•
LB	E.J. Henderson	6-2	250	Sr.	Maryland	•	•	•	•	•
LB	Teddy Lehman	6-2	235	Jr.	Oklahoma	•	•		•	•
LB	Matt Wilhelm	6-5	245	Sr.	Ohio State	•	•		•	•
DB	Mike Doss	5-11	204	Sr.	Ohio State	•	•	•	•	•
DB	Terence Newman	5-11	185	Sr.	Kansas State	•	•	•	•	•
DB	Shane Walton	5-11	185	Sr.	Notre Dame	•	•		•	•
DB	Troy Polamalu	5-10	215	Sr.	Southern Cal	•	•	•		•
P	Mark Mariscal	6-2	200	Sr.	Colorado	•	•	•	•	•

OTHERS RECEIVING FIRST-TEAM HONORS

DL	Michael Haynes		Penn State		•
DL	Jimmy Kennedy		Penn State		• •
DL	Cory Redding		Texas		•
DL	Jerome McDougle		Miami, Fla.		•
DL	Calvin Pace		Wake Forest		•
LB	Boss Bailey		Georgia		• •
LB	Bradie James		LSU		• •
DB	Terrence Holt		North Carolina St.		• •
DB	Brandon Everage		Oklahoma		•
P	Andy Groom		Ohio State		•

HEISMAN TROPHY VOTING

	PLAYER	POS	SCHOOL	1ST	2ND	3RD	TOTAL
1	Carson Palmer	QB	Southern Cal	242	224	154	1328
2	Brad Banks	QB	Iowa	199	173	152	1095
3	Larry Johnson	RB	Penn State	108	130	142	726
4	Willis McGahee	RB	Miami, Fla.	101	118	121	660
5	Ken Dorsey	QB	Miami, Fla.	122	89	99	643
6	Byron Leftwich	QB	Marshall	22	26	34	152
7	Jason Gesser	QB	Washington State	5	22	15	74
8	Chris Brown	RB	Colorado	5	11	11	48
9	Kliff Klingsbury	QB	Texas Tech	6	2	11	33
10	Quentin Griffin	RB	Oklahoma	1	8	9	28

AWARD WINNERS

Larry Johnson, RB, Penn State, Maxwell, Camp, Walker, **Rien Long**, DT, Washington State, Outland, **Terrell Suggs**, DE, Arizona State, Lombardi, Nagurski, Hendricks, **Brad Banks**, QB, Iowa, O'Brien, **E.J. Henderson**, LB, Maryland, Butkus, Bednarik, **Terence Newman**, DB, Kansas State, Thorpe, **Carson Palmer**, QB, Southern Cal, Unitas, **Nate Kaeding**, K, Iowa, Groza, **Charles Rogers**, WR, Michigan State, Biletnikoff, **Glenn Pakulak**, P, Kentucky, Tatupu, **Mark Mariscal**, P, Colorado, Guy, **Dallas Clark**, TE, Iowa, Mackey, **Brett Romberg**, C, Miami, Fla., Rimington

BOWL GAMES

D17, **New Orleans**, North Texas 24 Cincinnati 19, D18, **GMAC**, Marshall 38, Louisville 15, D23, **Tangerine**, Texas Tech 55, Clemson 15, D25, **Las Vegas**, UCLA 27, New Mexico 13, D25, **Hawaii**, Tulane 36, Hawaii 28, D26, **Motor City**, Boston College 51, Toledo 25, D26, **Insight**, Pittsburgh 38, Oregon State 13, D27, **Houston**, Oklahoma State 33, Southern Miss 23, D27, **Independence**, Mississippi 27, Nebraska 23, D27, **Holiday**, Kansas State 34, Arizona State 27, D28, **Continental Tire**, Virginia 48, West Virginia 22, D28, **Alamo**, Wisconsin 31, Colorado 28, OT, D30 **Music City** Minnesota 29, Arkansas 14, D30, **Seattle**, Wake Forest 38, Oregon 17, D31, **Humanitarian**, Boise State 34, Iowa State 16, D31, **Sun**, Purdue 34, Washington 24, D31, **Liberty**, TCU 17, Colorado State 3, D31, **Silicon Valley Classic**, Fresno State 30, Georgia Tech 21,

CONFERENCE STANDINGS

ACC

	Conf. W L T	Overall W L T
Florida State	7 1 0	9 5 0
Maryland	6 2 0	11 3 0
Virginia	6 2 0	9 5 0
North Carolina St.	5 3 0	11 3 0
Clemson	4 4 0	7 6 0
Georgia Tech	4 4 0	7 6 0
Wake Forest	3 5 0	7 6 0
North Carolina	1 7 0	3 9 0
Duke	0 8 0	2 10 0

Big 10

	Conf. W L T	Overall W L T
Ohio State	8 0 0	14 0 0
Iowa	8 0 0	11 2 0
Michigan	6 2 0	10 3 0
Penn State	5 3 0	9 4 0
Purdue	4 4 0	7 6 0
Illinois	4 4 0	5 7 0
Minnesota	3 5 0	8 5 0
Wisconsin	2 6 0	8 6 0
Michigan State	2 6 0	4 8 0
Northwestern	1 7 0	3 9 0
Indiana	1 7 0	3 9 0

Big 12

NORTH	Conf. W L T	Overall W L T
Colorado	7 1 0	9 5 0
Kansas State	6 2 0	11 2 0
Iowa State	4 4 0	7 7 0
Nebraska	3 5 0	7 7 0
Missouri	2 6 0	5 7 0
Kansas	0 8 0	2 10 0
SOUTH		
Oklahoma	6 2 0	12 2 0
Texas	6 2 0	11 2 0
Texas Tech	5 3 0	9 5 0
Oklahoma State	5 3 0	8 5 0
Texas A&M	3 5 0	6 6 0
Baylor	1 7 0	3 9 0

Championship **Oklahoma 29 Colorado 7**

Big East

	Conf. W L T	Overall W L T
Miami, Fla.	7 0 0	12 1 0
West Virginia	6 1 0	9 4 0
Pittsburgh	5 2 0	9 4 0
Virginia Tech	3 4 0	10 4 0
Boston College	3 4 0	9 4 0
Temple	2 5 0	4 8 0
Syracuse	2 5 0	4 8 0
Rutgers	0 7 0	1 11 0

C-USA

	Conf. W L T	Overall W L T
TCU	6 2 0	10 2 0
Cincinnati	6 2 0	7 7 0
Southern Miss	5 3 0	7 6 0
Louisville	5 3 0	7 6 0
Tulane	4 4 0	8 5 0
UAB	4 4 0	5 7 0
East Carolina	4 4 0	4 8 0
Houston	3 5 0	5 7 0
Memphis	2 6 0	3 9 0
Army	1 7 0	1 11 0

Ivy

	Conf. W L T	Overall W L T
Pennsylvania	7 0 0	9 1 0
Harvard	6 1 0	7 3 0
Princeton	4 3 0	6 4 0
Yale	4 3 0	6 4 0
Cornell	3 4 0	4 6 0
Dartmouth	2 5 0	3 7 0
Brown	2 5 0	2 8 0
Columbia	0 7 0	1 9 0

MAC

EAST	Conf. W L T	Overall W L T
Marshall	7 1 0	11 2 0
Central Florida	6 2 0	7 5 0
Miami, Ohio	5 3 0	7 5 0
Ohio U	4 4 0	4 8 0
Akron	3 5 0	4 8 0
Kent State	1 7 0	3 9 0
Buffalo	0 8 0	1 11 0

MAC

WEST	Conf. W L T	Overall W L T
Northern Illinois	7 1 0	8 4 0
Toledo	7 1 0	9 5 0
Bowling Green	6 2 0	9 3 0
Ball State	4 4 0	6 6 0
Western Michigan	3 5 0	4 8 0
Central Michigan	2 6 0	4 8 0
Eastern Michigan	1 7 0	3 9 0

Championship **Marshall 49 Toledo 45**

MWC

	Conf. W L T	Overall W L T
Colorado State	6 1 0	10 4 0
New Mexico	5 2 0	7 7 0
Air Force	4 3 0	8 5 0
San Diego State	4 3 0	4 9 0
Utah	3 4 0	5 6 0
Nevada-Las Vegas	3 4 0	5 7 0
Brigham Young	2 5 0	5 7 0
Wyoming	1 6 0	2 10 0

Pac 10

	Conf. W L T	Overall W L T
Southern Cal	7 1 0	11 2 0
Washington State	7 1 0	10 3 0
Arizona State	5 3 0	8 6 0
UCLA	4 4 0	8 5 0
Oregon State	4 4 0	8 5 0
California	4 4 0	7 5 0
Washington	4 4 0	7 6 0
Oregon	3 5 0	7 6 0
Arizona	1 7 0	4 8 0
Stanford	1 7 0	2 9 0

SEC

EAST	Conf. W L T	Overall W L T
Georgia	7 1 0	13 1 0
Florida	6 2 0	8 5 0
Tennessee	5 3 0	8 5 0
Kentucky	3 5 0	7 5 0
South Carolina	3 5 0	5 7 0
Vanderbilt	0 8 0	2 10 0
WEST		
Alabama*	6 2 0	10 3 0
Arkansas	5 3 0	9 5 0
Auburn	5 3 0	9 4 0
LSU	5 3 0	8 5 0
Mississippi	3 5 0	7 6 0
Mississippi State	0 8 0	3 9 0

Championship **Georgia 30 Arkansas 3**
* Not eligible for title

Sun Belt

	Conf. W L T	Overall W L T
North Texas	6 0 0	8 5 0
New Mexico State	5 1 0	7 5 0
Arkansas State	3 3 0	6 7 0
Middle Tennessee	2 4 0	4 8 0
La. Monroe	2 4 0	3 9 0
La. Lafayette	2 4 0	3 9 0
Idaho	1 5 0	2 10 0

WAC

	Conf. W L T	Overall W L T
Boise State	8 0 0	12 1 0
Hawaii	7 1 0	10 4 0
Fresno State	6 2 0	9 5 0
San Jose State	4 4 0	6 7 0
Nevada	4 4 0	5 7 0
Rice	3 5 0	4 7 0
Louisiana Tech	3 5 0	4 8 0
SMU	3 5 0	3 9 0
Texas-El Paso	1 7 0	2 10 0
Tulsa	1 7 0	1 11 0

Independents

	Overall W L T
South Florida	9 2 0
Notre Dame	10 3 0
Connecticut	6 6 0
Utah State	4 7 0
Troy State	4 8 0
Navy	2 10 0

D31, **Peach**, Maryland 30, Tennessee 3, D31, **San Francisco**, Virginia Tech 20, Air Force 13, J1, **Cotton**, Texas 35, LSU 20, J1**Gator**, North Carolina St. 28, Notre Dame 6, J1, **Capital One**, Auburn 13, Penn State 9, J1, **Rose**, Oklahoma 34, Washington State 14, J1, **Sugar**, Georgia 26, Florida State 13, J2, **Orange**, Southern Cal 38, Iowa 17, J3, **Fiesta**, Ohio State 31, Miami, Fla. 24, 2 OT

2002 NCAA Major College Statistical Leaders

Individual Leaders

PASSING		POS	CL	G	ATT	COM	PCT	INT	I%	YDS	YPA	TD	TD%	RATING
1	Brad Banks, Iowa	QB	SR	13	294	170	57.8	5	1.7	2573	8.8	26	8.8	157.1
2	Byron Leftwich, Marshall	QB	SR	12	491	331	67.4	10	2.0	4268	8.7	30	6.1	156.5
3	Brian Jones, Toledo	QB	SR	14	423	297	70.2	9	2.1	3446	8.2	23	5.4	152.3
4	Ryan Schneider, Central Florida	QB	JR	12	430	265	61.6	16	3.7	3770	8.8	31	7.2	151.6
5	Carson Palmer, Southern Cal	QB	SR	13	489	309	63.2	10	2.0	3942	8.1	33	6.8	149.1
6	Matt Schaub, Virginia	QB	JR	14	418	288	68.9	7	1.7	2976	7.1	28	6.7	147.5
7	Jason Gesser, Washington State	QB	SR	13	402	236	58.7	13	3.2	3408	8.5	28	7.0	146.4
8	Ken Dorsey, Miami, Fla.	QB	SR	13	393	222	56.5	12	3.1	3369	8.6	28	7.1	145.9
9	Kliff Kingsbury, Texas Tech	QB	SR	14	712	479	67.3	13	1.8	5017	7.1	45	6.3	143.7
10	Bryan Randall, Virginia Tech	QB	SO	14	248	158	63.7	11	4.4	2134	8.6	12	4.8	143.1

ALL-PURPOSE		POS	CL	G	RUSH	REC	PR	KR	YDS	YPG
1	Larry Johnson, Penn State	TB	SR	13	2087	349	0	219	2655	204.2
2	Michael Turner, No. Illinois	RB	JR	12	1915	100	0	269	2284	190.3
3	Robbie Mixon, Central Michigan	RB	SR	12	1361	253	0	524	2138	178.2
4	Jason Wright, Northwestern	WR	JR	12	1234	266	0	513	2013	167.8
5	Brock Forsey, Boise State	RB	SR	13	1611	282	0	234	2127	163.6
6	Domanick Davis, LSU	RB	SR	13	931	130	499	560	2120	163.1
7	Bobby Wade, Arizona	WR	SR	12	4	1389	224	332	1949	162.4
8	Willis McGahee, Miami, Fla.	RB	SO	13	1753	355	0	0	2108	162.2
9	Charley Pauley, San Jose State	WR	SR	13	67	804	237	978	2086	160.5
10	Derek Abney, Kentucky	WR	JR	12	5	569	544	804	1922	160.2

RUSHING/Yards Per Game		POS	CL	G	ATT	YDS	TD	AVG	YPG
1	Larry Johnson, Penn State	TB	SR	13	271	2087	20	7.7	160.5
2	Michael Turner, No. Illinois	RB	JR	12	338	1915	19	5.7	159.6
3	Chris Brown, Colorado	RB	JR	12	303	1841	19	6.1	153.4
4	Willis McGahee, Miami, Fla.	RB	SO	13	282	1753	28	6.2	134.9
5	Marcus Merriweather, Ball State	RB	SR	12	332	1618	12	4.9	134.8
6	Quentin Griffin, Oklahoma	RB	SR	14	287	1884	15	6.6	134.6
7	Avon Cobourne, West Virginia	RB	SR	13	335	1710	17	5.1	131.5
8	Steven Jackson, Oregon State	RB	SO	13	319	1690	15	5.3	130.0
9	Joffrey Reynolds, Houston	RB	SR	12	316	1545	11	4.9	128.8
10	Terry Caulley, Connecticut	RB	FR	10	220	1247	15	5.7	124.7

RUSHING/Yards Per Carry		POS	CL	G	ATT	YDS	YPC
1	Joshua Cribbs, Kent State	QB	SO	10	137	1057	7.7
2	Larry Johnson, Penn State	TB	SR	13	271	2087	7.7
3	Shaud Williams, Alabama	RB	JR	13	130	921	7.1
4	DeWhitt Betterson, Troy State	RB	SO	11	101	711	7.0
5	DeAngelo Williams, Memphis	RB	FR	11	103	684	6.6
6	Joe Alls, Bowling Green	RB	SR	10	122	801	6.6
7	Quentin Griffin, Oklahoma	RB	SR	14	287	1884	6.6
8	Quincy Wilson, West Virginia	RB	JR	13	140	901	6.4
9	Tatum Bell, Oklahoma State	RB	JR	11	175	1096	6.3
10	Walter Reyes, Syracuse	RB	SO	12	182	1135	6.2

RECEIVING		POS	CL	G	REC	YDS	TD	RPG	YPR	YPG
1	J.R. Tolver, San Diego State	WR	SR	13	128	1785	13	9.9	14.0	137.3
2	Nate Burleson, Nevada	WR	SR	12	138	1629	12	11.5	11.8	135.8
3	Rashaun Woods, Oklahoma State	WR	JR	13	107	1695	17	8.2	15.8	130.4
4	Kassim Osgood, San Diego State	WR	SR	13	108	1552	8	8.3	14.4	119.4
5	Bobby Wade, Arizona	WR	SR	12	93	1389	8	7.8	14.9	115.8
6	Kevin Curtis, Utah State	WR	SR	11	74	1258	9	6.7	17.0	114.4
7	Kevin Walter, Eastern Michigan	WR	SR	12	93	1368	9	7.8	14.7	114.0
8	Charles Rogers, Michigan State	WR	JR	12	68	1351	13	5.7	19.9	112.6
9	Reggie Williams, Washington	WR	SO	13	94	1454	11	7.2	15.5	111.9
10	Doug Gabriel, Central Florida	WR	SR	12	75	1237	11	6.3	16.5	103.1

PUNTING		POS	CL	PUNT	YDS	AVG
1	Matt Payne, Brigham Young	K	SO	51	2427	47.6
2	Mark Mariscal, Colorado	K	SR	67	3186	47.6
3	Glenn Pakulak, Kentucky	P	SR	66	3008	45.6
4	Andy Groom, Ohio State	P	SR	60	2697	45.0
5	Donnie Jones, LSU	P	JR	64	2813	44.0
6	Greg Johnson, Vanderbilt	P	FR	66	2892	43.8
7	Cody Scates, Texas A&M	P	JR	67	2931	43.8
8	Dustin Colquitt, Tennessee	P	SO	65	2833	43.6
9	Jarad Preston, East Carolina	P	SR	73	3170	43.4
10	Damon Duval, Auburn	P	SR	54	2344	43.4

PUNT RETURNS		POS	CL	PR	YDS	TD	AVG
1	Dan Sheldon, No. Illinois	WR	SO	21	477	3	22.7
2	Aris Comeaux, Army	WR	SR	12	233	2	19.4
3	Cody Cardwell, SMU	WR	SR	27	467	1	17.3
4	DeJuan Groce, Nebraska	DB	SR	43	732	4	17.0
5	Lynaris Elpheage, Tulane	DB	JR	28	463	1	16.5
6	Dexter Wynn, Colorado State	DB	JR	35	567	1	16.2
7	DeAngelo Hall, Virginia Tech	DB	SO	22	352	2	16.0
7	Craig Bragg, UCLA	WR	SO	16	256	1	16.0
9	Damien Dorsey, Louisville	WR	SR	33	508	1	15.4
10	Kendrick Mosley, Western Michigan	WR	SR	29	440	2	15.2

KICKOFF RETURNS		POS	CL	KR	YDS	TD	AVG
1	Charles Pauley, San Jose State	WR	SR	31	978	2	31.6
2	Broderick Clark, Louisville	WR	FR	31	897	2	28.9
3	LaShaun Ward, California	WR	SR	28	809	1	28.9
4	Jason Wright, Northwestern	WR	JR	18	513	1	28.5
5	Nathan Jones, Rutgers	DB	JR	26	736	2	28.3
6	LaTarence Dunbar, TCU	WR	SR	18	501	1	27.8
7	Jerome Dennis, Utah State	DB	SO	14	388	0	27.7
8	Vontez Duff, Notre Dame	DB	JR	19	526	1	27.7
9	Makonnen Fenton, Temple	RB	JR	14	380	1	27.1
10	Derek Abney, Kentucky	WR	JR	30	804	2	26.8
10	DeAndrew Rubin, South Florida	WR	SR	15	402	1	26.8

SCORING		POS	CL	TDS	XP	FG	PTS	PTPG
1	Brock Forsey, Boise State	RB	SR	32	0	0	192	14.8
2	Willis McGahee, Miami, Fla.	RB	SO	28	0	0	168	12.9
3	Josh Harris, Bowling Green	QB	JR	22	0	0	134	11.2
4	Larry Johnson, Penn State	TB	SR	23	0	0	140	10.8
5	Lee Suggs, Virginia Tech	RB	SR	24	0	0	144	10.3
6	Art Brown, East Carolina	RB	JR	17	0	0	102	10.2
7	Chance Harridge, Air Force	QB	JR	22	0	0	132	10.2
8	Michael Turner, No. Illinois	RB	JR	20	0	0	120	10.0
9	Maurice Clarett, Ohio State	RB	FR	18	0	0	108	9.8
10	Terry Caulley, Connecticut	RB	FR	16	0	0	96	9.6
10	Nick Calaycay, Boise State	K	SR	0	63	11	96	9.6

FIELD GOALS		POS	CL	FGA	FGM	PCT	FGG
1	Nick Browne, TCU	K	JR	30	23	0.77	1.92
2	Billy Bennett, Georgia	K	JR	33	26	0.79	1.86
3	Mike Nugent, Ohio State	K	SO	28	25	0.89	1.79
4	Sandro Sciortino, Boston College	K	JR	32	23	0.72	1.77
5	Nick Novak, Maryland	K	SO	28	24	0.86	1.71
5	Jeff Babcock, Colorado State	K	SO	32	24	0.76	1.71
7	John Anderson, Washington	K	SR	34	22	0.65	1.69
7	Drew Dunning, Washington State	K	JR	33	22	0.67	1.69
9	Mike Barth, Arizona State	K	SR	33	23	0.70	1.64
9	Asen Asparuhov, Fresno State	K	SR	30	23	0.77	1.64

INTERCEPTIONS		POS	CL	INT	YDS	TD	INT/GM
1	Jim Leonhard, Wisconsin	DB	SO	11	115	0	0.79
2	Jason David, Washington State	DB	JR	7	101	0	0.70
3	Gerald Jones, San Jose State	DB	JR	8	116	1	0.67
3	Jason Goss, TCU	DB	SR	8	27	0	0.67
5	Gabe Franklin, Boise State	DB	SO	8	70	0	0.62
5	Lynaris Elpheage, Tulane	DB	JR	8	133	1	0.62
5	Justin Miller, Clemson	DB	FR	8	70	0	0.62
8	Randee Drew, No. Illinois	DB	JR	7	103	0	0.58
9	Vince Thompson, No. Illinois	DB	SR	5	4	0	0.56
10	Bop White, Ohio U	DB	SR	6	52	0	0.55
10	Bobby Walker, Kansas State	DB	SR	6	177	3	0.55
10	J.R. Reed, South Florida	DB	JR	6	34	1	0.55

Team Leaders

RUSHING OFFENSE		G	ATT	YDS	AVG	TD	YPG
1	Air Force	13	786	4001	5.1	41	307.8
2	West Virginia	13	714	3687	5.2	39	283.6
3	Navy	12	652	3249	5.0	34	270.8
4	Nebraska	14	724	3762	5.2	29	268.7
5	Kansas State	13	655	3433	5.2	53	264.1
6	Rice	11	606	2725	4.5	24	247.7
7	Wake Forest	13	718	3135	4.4	33	241.2
8	Ohio	12	649	2878	4.4	30	239.8
9	Colorado	14	652	3259	5.0	28	232.8
10	Penn State	13	526	2972	5.7	36	228.6

PASSING OFFENSE		G	ATT	COM	INT	PCT	YDS	YPA	TD	I%	YPC	YPG
1	Texas Tech	14	770	515	15	66.9	5444	7.1	50	2.0	10.6	388.9
2	Hawaii	14	731	407	26	55.7	5406	7.4	35	3.6	13.3	386.1
3	Marshall	13	575	383	15	66.6	4804	8.4	35	2.6	12.5	369.5
4	Washington	13	621	372	14	59.9	4501	7.3	28	2.3	12.1	346.2
5	San Diego State	13	584	352	10	60.3	4302	7.4	24	1.7	12.2	330.9
6	Central Florida	12	442	270	17	61.1	3837	8.7	31	3.9	14.2	319.8
7	Utah State	11	487	258	16	53.0	3388	7.0	21	3.3	13.1	308.0
8	Southern Cal	13	494	313	10	63.4	3988	8.1	33	2.0	12.7	306.8
9	Arizona State	14	558	306	16	54.8	4254	7.6	31	2.9	13.9	303.9
10	Louisiana Tech	12	527	305	19	57.9	3633	6.9	19	3.6	11.9	302.8

TOTAL OFFENSE		G	P	YDS	AVG	TD	YPG
1	Boise State	13	950	6519	6.9	79	501.5
2	Hawaii	14	1039	6939	6.7	66	495.6
3	Marshall	13	991	6439	6.5	59	495.3
4	Texas Tech	14	1155	6835	5.9	71	488.2
5	Toledo	14	1033	6611	6.4	66	472.2
6	Miami, Fla.	13	887	6056	6.8	70	465.9
7	Purdue	13	1034	5879	5.7	51	452.2
8	Southern Cal	13	1009	5840	5.8	60	449.2
9	Bowling Green	12	898	5387	6.0	65	448.9
10	Illinois	12	915	5356	5.9	43	446.3

RUSHING DEFENSE		G	ATT	YDS	AVG	TD	YPG
1	TCU	12	393	778	2.0	9	64.8
2	Kansas State	13	446	904	2.0	7	69.5
3	Ohio State	14	418	1088	2.6	5	77.7
4	Alabama	13	390	1042	2.7	10	80.2
5	Iowa	13	416	1065	2.6	17	81.9
6	Southern Cal	13	388	1081	2.8	9	83.2
7	South Florida	11	420	959	2.3	8	87.2
8	Washington State	13	453	1134	2.5	11	87.2
9	Oregon State	13	479	1225	2.6	13	94.2
10	Notre Dame	13	439	1238	2.8	11	95.2

PASSING DEFENSE		G	ATT	COM	PCT	INT	I%	YDS	YPA	TD	TD%	RAT
1	Miami, Fla.	13	353	163	46.2	12	3.4	1556	4.4	8	2.3	83.9
2	TCU	12	406	158	38.9	22	5.4	2105	5.2	16	3.9	84.6
3	Kansas State	13	418	191	45.7	20	4.8	2333	5.6	11	2.6	91.7
4	Southern Miss	13	379	177	46.7	16	4.2	2195	5.8	6	1.6	92.1
5	LSU	13	361	163	45.2	17	4.7	1985	5.5	13	3.6	93.9
6	Oregon State	13	456	222	48.7	20	4.4	2591	5.7	10	2.2	94.9
7	Texas	13	400	192	48.0	22	5.5	2147	5.4	17	4.3	96.1
8	Marshall	13	366	175	47.8	15	4.1	2099	5.7	10	2.7	96.8
9	Oklahoma	14	432	206	47.7	24	5.6	2594	6.0	13	3.0	97.0
10	Notre Dame	13	452	223	49.3	21	4.7	2662	5.9	12	2.7	98.2

TOTAL DEFENSE		G	P	YDS	AVG	TD	YPG
1	TCU	12	799	2883	3.6	27	240.3
2	Kansas State	13	864	3237	3.8	19	249.0
3	Alabama	13	764	3345	4.4	24	257.3
4	Troy State	12	784	3322	4.2	31	276.8
5	Tennessee	13	840	3703	4.4	24	284.9
6	Southern Cal	13	842	3704	4.4	27	284.9
7	Miami, Fla.	13	935	3705	4.0	31	285.0
8	LSU	13	825	3728	4.5	30	286.8
9	North Texas	13	870	3778	4.3	23	290.6
10	Oklahoma	14	928	4104	4.4	27	293.1

SCORING OFFENSE		G	PTS	AVG
1	Boise State	13	593	45.6
2	Kansas State	13	582	44.8
3	Bowling Green	12	490	40.8
4	Miami, Fla.	13	527	40.5
5	Oklahoma	14	541	38.6
6	Texas Tech	14	537	38.4
7	Iowa	13	484	37.2
8	Hawaii	14	502	35.9
9	Southern Cal	13	465	35.8
10	California	12	427	35.6

SCORING DEFENSE		G	PTS	AVG
1	Kansas State	13	154	11.8
2	Ohio State	14	183	13.1
3	North Texas	13	192	14.8
4	Georgia	14	212	15.1
5	Alabama	13	200	15.4
6	Oklahoma	14	216	15.4
7	Maryland	14	228	16.3
8	Texas	13	212	16.3
9	Notre Dame	13	217	16.7
10	North Carolina St.	14	238	17.0

TURNOVER MARGIN		G	FR	INT	TOT	FL	INTL	TOT	MAR
1	South Florida	11	14	22	36	10	5	15	1.9
2	Tulane	13	21	22	43	11	10	21	1.7
3	California	12	21	15	36	8	10	18	1.5
4	West Virginia	13	15	19	34	6	9	15	1.5
5	Southern Cal	13	19	17	36	8	10	18	1.4
5	Wake Forest	13	21	13	34	10	6	16	1.4
7	Oklahoma	14	12	24	36	6	11	17	1.4
8	Texas	13	13	22	35	6	12	18	1.3
9	Wisconsin	14	13	22	35	9	8	17	1.3
10	TCU	12	20	22	42	14	13	27	1.3

2003 Poll Progression

ESPN	AP	Pre-Season 2003		Aug. 30 Games
1	1	Oklahoma	0-0	beat North Texas 37-3
2	2	Ohio State	0-0	beat #17 Washington 28-9
3	3	Miami, Fla.	0-0	beat Louisiana Tech 48-9 (A28)
7	4	Michigan	0-0	beat Central Michigan 45-7
4	5	Texas	0-0	beat New Mexico State 66-7 (A31)
6	6	Auburn	0-0	lost to #8 Southern Cal 0-23
5	7	Kansas State	0-0	beat Troy State 41-5
8	8	Southern Cal	0-0	beat # 6 Auburn 23-0
10	9	Virginia Tech	0-0	beat Central Florida 49-28 (A31)
11	10	Pittsburgh	0-0	bye week
9	11	Georgia	0-0	beat Clemson 30-0
16	12	Tennessee	0-0	beat Fresno State 24-6
12	13	Florida State	0-0	beat North Carolina 37-0
15	14	LSU	0-0	beat La. Monroe 49-7
13	15	Maryland	0-0	lost to Northern Illinois 13-20 (A28)
14	16	North Carolina St.	0-0	beat Western Carolina 59-26
19	17	Washington	0-0	lost to #2 Ohio State 9-28
17	18	Virginia	0-0	beat Duke 27-0
22	19	Purdue	0-0	bye week
18	20	Notre Dame	0-0	bye week
20	21	Wisconsin	0-0	beat West Virginia 24-17
23	22	Arizona State	0-0	bye week
25	23	Colorado State	0-0	lost to Colorado 35-42
24	24	Oklahoma State	0-0	lost to Nebraska 7-17
	25	TCU	0-0	beat Tulane 38-35 (S1)
25		Penn State	0-0	beat Temple 23-10

ESPN	AP	September 1 Poll		Sept. 6 Games
1	1	Oklahoma	1-0	beat Alabama 20-13
2	2	Ohio State	1-0	beat San Diego State 16-13
3	3	Miami, Fla.	1-0	beat #21 Florida 38-33
5	4	Southern Cal	1-0	beat Brigham Young 35-18
7	5	Michigan	1-0	beat Houston 50-3
4	6	Texas	1-0	bye week
6	7	Kansas State	2-0	beat McNeese St. 55-14
8	8	Georgia	1-0	beat Middle Tennessee 29-10
9	9	Virginia Tech	1-0	beat James Madison 43-0
12	10	Pittsburgh	0-0	beat Kent State 43-3
10	11	Florida State	1-0	beat Maryland 35-10
14	12	Tennessee	1-0	beat Marshall 34-24
13	13	LSU	1-0	beat Arizona 59-13
11	14	North Carolina St.	1-0	lost to Wake Forest 24-38
15	15	Virginia	1-0	lost to South Carolina 7-31
20	16	Purdue	0-0	lost to Bowling Green 26-27
19	17	Auburn	0-1	lost to Georgia Tech 3-17
17	18	Wisconsin	1-0	beat Akron 48-31
16	19	Notre Dame	0-0	beat Washington State 29-26
21	20	Arizona State	0-0	beat No. Arizona 34-14
18	21	Florida	1-0	lost to # 3 Miami, Fla. 33-38
	22	Washington	0-1	beat Indiana 38-13
24	23	Nebraska	1-0	beat Utah State 31-7
22	24	Colorado	1-0	beat UCLA 16-14
	25	TCU	0-0	beat Navy 17-3
23		Iowa	1-0	beat Buffalo 56-7
25		Penn State	1-0	lost to Boston College 14-27

ESPN	AP	September 7 Poll		Sept. 13 Games
1	1	Oklahoma	2-0	beat Fresno State 52-28
2	2	Miami, Fla.	2-0	beat East Carolina 38-3
3	3	Ohio State	2-0	beat # 24 North Carolina St. 44-38
4	4	Southern Cal	2-0	beat Hawaii 61-32
7	5	Michigan	2-0	beat # 15 Notre Dame 38-0
5	6	Texas	2-0	lost to Arkansas 28-38
6	7	Kansas State	3-0	beat Massachusetts 38-7
8	8	Georgia	2-0	beat # 25 South Carolina 31-7
9	9	Virginia Tech	2-0	bye week
10	10	Florida State	2-0	beat Georgia Tech 14-13
12	11	Pittsburgh	2-0	beat Ball State 42-21
11	12	LSU	1-0	beat Western Illinois 35-7
13	13	Tennessee	2-0	bye week
15	14	Wisconsin	1-0	lost to Nevada-Las Vegas 5-23
14	15	Notre Dame	1-0	lost to # 5 Michigan 0-38
16	16	Arizona State	1-0	beat Utah State 26-16
17	17	Colorado	2-0	lost to Washington State 26-47
18	18	Nebraska	2-0	beat Penn State 18-10
21	20	Wake Forest	2-0	lost to Purdue 10-16
20	21	Florida	1-1	beat Florida A&M 63-3
24	21	Washington	1-1	bye week
23	22	TCU	2-0	bye week
19	23	Iowa	2-0	beat Iowa State 40-21
22	24	North Carolina St.	1-1	lost to # 3 Ohio State 38-44
	25	South Carolina	2-0	lost to # 8 Georgia 7-31
25		Texas A&M	2-0	bye week

ESPN	AP	September 14 Poll		Sept. 20 Games
1	1	Oklahoma	3-0	beat UCLA 59-24
2	2	Miami, Fla.	3-0	beat Boston College 33-14
5	3	Michigan	3-0	lost to # 22 Oregon 27-31
3	4	Southern Cal	3-0	bye week
4	5	Ohio State	3-0	beat Bowling Green 24-17
6	6	Kansas State	4-0	lost to Marshall 20-27
7	7	Georgia	3-0	lost to # 11 LSU 10-17
8	8	Virginia Tech	2-0	beat Texas A&M 35-19 S18
11	9	Pittsburgh	2-0	lost to Toledo 31-35
9	10	Florida State	3-0	beat Colorado 47-7
10	11	LSU	3-0	beat # 7 Georgia 17-10
12	12	Tennessee	2-0	beat # 17 Florida 24-10
13	13	Texas	1-1	beat Rice 48-7
18	14	Arkansas	2-0	beat North Texas 31-7
15	15	Nebraska	3-0	bye week
16	16	Arizona State	2-0	lost to Iowa 2-21
17	17	Florida	2-1	lost to # 12 Tennessee 10-24
14	18	Iowa	3-0	beat Arizona State 21-2
21	19	Washington	1-1	beat Idaho 45-14
19	20	TCU	2-0	beat Vanderbilt 30-14
PB	21	Alabama	2-1	lost to Northern Illinois 16-19
22	22	Oregon	3-0	beat # 3 Michigan 31-27
	23	Missouri	3-0	beat Middle Tennessee 41-40
25	24	Washington State	2-1	beat New Mexico 23-13
	25	Purdue	1-1	beat Arizona 59-7
23		Notre Dame	3-0	lost to Michigan State 16-22
24		Minnesota	1-1	beat La. Lafayette 48-14

ESPN	AP	September 21 Poll		Sept. 27 Games
1	1	Oklahoma	4-0	bye week
2	2	Miami, Fla.	4-0	bye week
3	3	Southern Cal	3-0	lost to California 31-34
4	4	Ohio State	4-0	beat Northwestern 20-0
5	5	Virginia Tech	3-0	beat Connecticut 47-13
6	6	Florida State	4-0	beat Duke 56-7
7	7	LSU	4-0	beat Mississippi State 41-6
8	8	Tennessee	3-0	beat South Carolina 23-20
14	9	Arkansas	3-0	beat Alabama 34-31
15	10	Oregon	4-0	lost to # 21 Washington State 16-55
10	11	Michigan	3-1	beat Indiana 31-17
12	12	Georgia	3-1	bye week
9	13	Iowa	4-0	lost to Michigan State 10-20
13	14	Texas	2-1	beat Tulane 63-18
11	15	Nebraska	3-0	beat Southern Miss 38-14 (S25)
16	16	Kansas State	4-1	bye week
19	17	Pittsburgh	2-1	beat Texas A&M 37-26
18	18	Washington	2-1	beat Stanford 28-17
17	19	TCU	3-0	beat Arizona 13-10
22	20	Northern Illinois	3-0	beat Iowa State 24-16
21	21	Washington State	3-1	beat # 10 Oregon 55-16
	22	Purdue	2-1	beat Notre Dame 23-10
23	23	Missouri	4-0	lost to Kansas 14-35
20	24	Minnesota	4-0	beat Penn State 20-14
25	25	Florida	2-2	beat Kentucky 24-21
24		Arizona State	2-1	lost to Oregon State 17-45

ESPN	AP	September 28 Poll		Oct. 4 Games
1	1	Oklahoma	4-0	beat Iowa State 53-7
2	2	Miami, Fla.	4-0	beat West Virginia 22-20 (O2)
3	3	Ohio State	5-0	bye week
4	4	Virginia Tech	4-0	beat Rutgers 48-22
5	5	Florida State	5-0	bye week
6	6	LSU	5-0	bye week
7	7	Tennessee	4-0	lost to Auburn 21-28
9	8	Arkansas	4-0	bye week
11	9	Michigan	4-1	lost to # 23 Iowa 27-30
10	10	Southern Cal	3-1	beat Arizona State 37-17
12	11	Georgia	3-1	beat Alabama 37-23
8	12	Nebraska	4-0	beat Troy State 30-0
13	13	Texas	3-1	beat # 16 Kansas State 24-20
15	14	Washington State	4-1	beat Arizona 30-7
18	15	Pittsburgh	3-1	bye week
14	16	Kansas State	4-1	lost to # 13 Texas 20-24
20	17	Northern Illinois	4-0	beat Ohio U 30-23
17	18	Washington	3-1	lost to UCLA 16-46
22	19	Oregon	4-1	lost to Utah 13-17 (O3)
21	20	TCU	4-0	beat Army 27-0
16	21	Minnesota	5-0	beat Northwestern 42-17
23	22	Purdue	3-1	beat Illinois 43-10
19	23	Iowa	4-1	beat # 9 Michigan 30-27
24	24	Florida	3-2	lost to Mississippi 17-20
	25	Michigan State	4-1	beat Indiana 31-3
25		Air Force	5-0	lost to Navy 25-28

ESPN	AP	October 5 Poll		Oct. 11 Games
1	1	Oklahoma	5-0	beat # 11 Texas 65-13
2	2	Miami, Fla.	5-0	beat # 5 Florida State 22-14
3	3	Ohio State	5-0	lost to # 23 Wisconsin 10-17
4	4	Virginia Tech	5-0	beat Syracuse 51-7
5	5	Florida State	5-0	lost to # 2 Miami, Fla. 14-22
6	6	LSU	5-0	lost to Florida 7-19
8	7	Arkansas	4-0	lost to Auburn 3-10
10	8	Georgia	4-1	beat # 13 Tennessee 41-14
9	9	Southern Cal	4-1	beat Stanford 44-21
7	10	Nebraska	5-0	lost to Missouri 24-41
11	11	Texas	4-1	lost to # 1 Oklahoma 13-65
12	12	Washington State	5-1	bye week
14	13	Tennessee	4-1	lost to # 8 Georgia 14-41
15	14	Iowa	5-1	bye week
16	15	Pittsburgh	3-1	lost to Notre Dame 14-20
18	16	Northern Illinois	5-0	beat Central Michigan 40-24
13	17	Minnesota	6-0	lost to # 20 Michigan 35-38 (O10)
20	18	Purdue	4-1	beat Penn State 28-14
17	19	TCU	5-0	beat South Florida 13-10 (O10)
18	20	Michigan	4-2	beat # 17 Minnesota 38-35 (O10)
23	21	Michigan State	5-1	beat Illinois 49-14
21	22	Kansas State	4-2	lost to Oklahoma State 34-38
22	23	Wisconsin	5-1	beat # 3 Ohio State 17-10
25	24	Oregon State	5-1	bye week
24	25	Virginia	4-1	lost to Clemson 27-30

ESPN	AP	October 12 Poll		Oct. 18 Games
1	1	Oklahoma	6-0	beat # 24 Missouri 34-13
2	2	Miami, Fla.	6-0	beat Temple 52-14
3	3	Virginia Tech	6-0	bye week
5	4	Georgia	5-1	beat Vanderbilt 27-8
4	5	Southern Cal	5-1	beat Notre Dame 45-14
6	6	Washington State	5-1	beat Stanford 24-14
7	7	Florida State	5-1	beat Virginia 19-14
8	8	Ohio State	5-1	beat # 9 Iowa 19-10
9	9	Iowa	5-1	lost to # 8 Ohio State 10-19
10	10	LSU	5-1	beat South Carolina 33-7
11	11	Arkansas	4-1	lost to Florida 28-33
16	12	Northern Illinois	6-0	beat Western Michigan 37-10
15	13	Purdue	5-1	beat # 14 Wisconsin 26-23
12	14	Wisconsin	6-1	lost to # 13 Purdue 23-26
18	15	Michigan State	6-1	beat # 25 Minnesota 44-38
13	16	TCU	6-0	beat UAB 27-24
17	17	Michigan	5-2	beat Illinois 56-14
25	18	Auburn	4-2	beat Mississippi State 45-13
14	19	Nebraska	5-1	beat Texas A&M 48-12
20	20	Texas	4-2	beat Iowa State 40-19
22	21	Tennessee	4-2	bye week
21	22	Oregon State	5-1	lost to Washington 17-38
24	23	Oklahoma State	5-1	beat Texas Tech 51-49
	24	Missouri	5-1	lost to # 1 Oklahoma 13-34
18	25	Minnesota	6-1	lost to # 15 Michigan State 38-44
23		Texas Tech	5-1	lost to # 23 Oklahoma State 49-51

ESPN	AP	October 19 Poll		Oct. 25 Games
1	1	Oklahoma	7-0	beat Colorado 34-20
2	2	Miami, Fla.	7-0	bye week
3	3	Virginia Tech	6-0	lost to West Virginia 7-28 (O22)
5	4	Georgia	6-1	beat UAB 16-13
4	5	Southern Cal	6-1	beat Washington 43-23
7	6	Florida State	6-1	beat Wake Forest 48-24
6	7	Washington State	6-1	beat Oregon State 36-30
8	8	Ohio State	6-1	beat Indiana 35-6
9	9	LSU	6-1	beat # 17 Auburn 31-7
10	10	Purdue	6-1	lost to # 13 Michigan 3-31
12	11	Michigan State	7-1	bye week
14	12	Northern Illinois	7-0	lost to # 23 Bowling Green 18-34
15	13	Michigan	6-2	beat # 10 Purdue 31-3
11	14	Nebraska	6-1	beat Iowa State 28-0
13	15	TCU	7-0	beat Houston 62-55
16	16	Iowa	5-2	beat Penn State 26-14
21	17	Auburn	5-2	lost to # 9 LSU 7-31
18	18	Oklahoma State	6-1	beat Texas A&M 38-10
18	19	Texas	5-2	beat Baylor 56-0
17	20	Wisconsin	6-2	lost to Northwestern 7-16
20	21	Arkansas	4-2	lost to Mississippi 7-19
22	22	Tennessee	4-2	beat Alabama 51-43
	23	Bowling Green	6-1	beat # 12 Northern Illinois 34-18
23	24	Utah	6-1	lost to New Mexico 35-47
25	25	Florida	5-3	bye week
24		Minnesota	6-2	beat Illinois 36-10

October 26 Poll / Nov. 1 Games

ESPN	AP	Team	Record	Game
1	1	Oklahoma	8-0	beat #14 Oklahoma State 52-9
2	2	Miami, Fla.	7-0	lost to #10 Virginia Tech 7-31
3	3	Southern Cal	7-1	beat #6 Washington State 43-16
4	4	Georgia	7-1	lost to #23 Florida 13-16
5	5	Florida State	7-1	beat Notre Dame 37-0
6	6	Washington State	7-1	lost to #3 Southern Cal 16-43
8	7	LSU	7-1	beat Louisiana Tech 49-10
7	8	Ohio State	7-1	beat Penn State 21-20
10	9	Michigan State	7-1	lost to #11 Michigan 20-27
11	10	Virginia Tech	6-1	beat #2 Miami, Fla. 31-7
12	11	Michigan	7-2	beat Michigan State 27-20
9	12	Nebraska	7-1	lost to #16 Texas 7-31
14	13	Iowa	6-2	beat Illinois 41-10
15	14	Oklahoma State	7-1	lost to #1 Oklahoma 9-52
13	15	TCU	8-0	bye week
16	16	Texas	6-2	beat #12 Nebraska 31-7
20	17	Bowling Green	7-1	bye week
17	18	Purdue	6-2	beat Northwestern 34-14
18	19	Tennessee	5-2	beat Duke 23-6
	20	Mississippi	6-2	beat South Carolina 43-40
24	21	Missouri	6-2	bye week
22	22	Northern Illinois	7-1	beat Ball State 48-23
21	23	Florida	5-3	beat Georgia 16-13
19	24	Minnesota	7-2	beat Indiana 55-7
23	25	Pittsburgh	5-2	beat Boston College 24-13
25		Louisville	7-1	bye week

November 2 Poll / Nov. 8 Games

ESPN	AP	Team	Record	Game
1	1	Oklahoma	9-0	beat Texas A&M 77-0
2	2	Southern Cal	8-1	bye week
3	3	Florida State	8-1	lost to Clemson 10-26
4	4	LSU	8-1	bye week
5	5	Virginia Tech	7-1	lost to #25 Pittsburgh 28-31
7	6	Miami, Fla.	7-1	lost to #18 Tennessee 6-10
6	7	Ohio State	8-1	beat #14 Michigan State 33-23
8	8	Michigan	8-2	bye week
9	9	Georgia	7-2	bye week
10	10	Iowa	7-2	lost to #16 Purdue 14-27
11	11	Texas	8-1	beat #21 Oklahoma State 55-16
13	12	Washington State	7-2	beat UCLA 31-13
12	13	TCU	8-0	beat Louisville 31-28 (N5)
15	14	Michigan State	7-2	beat South Carolina 34-17
20	15	Bowling Green	7-1	lost to Miami, Ohio 10-33 (N4)
14	16	Purdue	7-2	beat #10 Iowa 27-14
19	17	Florida	6-3	beat Vanderbilt 35-17
17	18	Tennessee	6-2	beat #6 Miami, Fla. 10-6
16	19	Nebraska	7-2	beat Kansas 24-3
24	20	Mississippi	7-2	beat Auburn 24-20
22	21	Oklahoma State	7-2	lost to #11 Texas 16-55
	22	Missouri	6-2	lost to Colorado 16-21
23	23	Northern Illinois	8-1	beat Buffalo 40-9
18	24	Minnesota	8-2	beat Wisconsin 37-34
21	25	Pittsburgh	6-2	beat #5 Virginia Tech 31-28
25		Louisville	7-1	lost to #13 TCU 28-31 (N5)

November 9 Poll / Nov. 15 Games

ESPN	AP	Team	Record	Game
1	1	Oklahoma	10-0	beat Baylor 41-3
2	2	Southern Cal	7-1	beat Arizona 45-0
3	3	LSU	8-1	beat Alabama 27-3
4	4	Ohio State	9-1	beat #11 Purdue 16-13
5	5	Michigan	8-2	beat Northwestern 41-10
7	6	Texas	8-2	beat Texas Tech 43-40
6	7	Georgia	6-2	beat Auburn 26-7
8	8	Washington State	8-2	beat Arizona State 34-19
13	9	Tennessee	7-2	beat Mississippi State 59-21
9	10	TCU	9-0	beat Cincinnati 43-10
10	11	Purdue	8-2	lost to #4 Ohio State 13-16
12	12	Virginia Tech	7-2	beat Temple 24-23
11	13	Florida State	8-2	beat North Carolina St. 50-44
14	14	Miami, Fla.	7-2	beat Syracuse 17-10
18	15	Florida	6-3	beat South Carolina 24-22
16	16	Pittsburgh	7-2	lost to West Virginia 31-52
19	17	Mississippi	8-2	bye week
15	18	Nebraska	8-2	lost to Kansas State 9-38
17	19	Minnesota	9-2	lost to #20 Iowa 22-40
20	20	Iowa	9-1	beat #19 Minnesota 40-22
22	21	Michigan State	7-3	lost to Wisconsin 21-56
21	22	Northern Illinois	9-1	lost to Toledo 30-49
24	23	Miami, Ohio	8-1	beat Marshall 45-6 (N12)
23	24	Boise State	8-1	beat Texas-El Paso 51-21
	25	Bowling Green	7-2	beat Kent State 42-33
25		Kansas State	8-3	beat #18 Nebraska 38-9

November 16 Poll / Nov. 22 Games

ESPN	AP	Team	Record	Game
1	1	Oklahoma	11-0	beat Texas Tech 56-25
2	2	Southern Cal	9-1	beat UCLA 47-22
3	3	LSU	9-1	beat #15 Mississippi 17-14
4	4	Ohio State	10-1	lost to #5 Michigan 21-35
5	5	Michigan	9-2	beat #4 Ohio State 35-21
6	6	Georgia	8-2	beat Kentucky 30-10
7	7	Texas	9-2	bye week
8	8	Washington State	8-2	lost to Washington 19-27
11	9	Tennessee	8-2	beat Vanderbilt 48-0
9	10	TCU	10-0	lost to Southern Miss 28-40 (N20)
10	11	Florida State	8-2	bye week
12	12	Virginia Tech	8-2	lost to Boston College 27-34
14	13	Florida	8-3	bye week
13	14	Miami, Fla.	8-3	beat Rutgers 34-10
15	15	Mississippi	8-2	lost to #3 LSU 14-17
16	16	Purdue	8-3	beat Indiana 24-16
17	17	Iowa	8-3	beat Wisconsin 27-21
19	18	Miami, Ohio	9-1	beat Ohio U 49-31
18	19	Kansas State	9-3	beat Missouri 24-14
20	20	Boise State	9-1	beat Fresno State 31-17 (N21)
22	21	Pittsburgh	7-3	beat Temple 30-16
25	22	Bowling Green	8-2	beat Ball State 41-14
23	23	Nebraska	8-3	bye week
24	24	Oklahoma State	8-3	beat Kansas 44-21
	25	West Virginia	6-4	beat Syracuse 34-23
21		Minnesota	9-3	regular season complete

November 23 Poll / Nov. 29 Games

ESPN	AP	Team	Record	Game
1	1	Oklahoma	12-0	bye week
2	2	Southern Cal	10-1	bye week
3	3	LSU	10-1	beat Arkansas 55-24
4	4	Michigan	10-2	regular season complete
5	5	Georgia	9-2	beat Georgia Tech 34-17
6	6	Texas	9-2	beat Texas A&M 46-15 (N28)
7	7	Tennessee	9-2	beat Kentucky 20-7
8	8	Ohio State	10-2	regular season complete
9	9	Florida State	9-2	beat #11 Florida 38-34
10	10	Miami, Fla.	9-2	beat #20 Pittsburgh 28-14
11	11	Florida	8-3	lost to #9 Florida State 34-38
13	12	Purdue	9-3	regular season complete
12	13	Iowa	9-3	regular season complete
15	14	Kansas State	9-3	bye week
16	15	Miami, Ohio	10-1	beat Central Florida 56-21 (N28)
13	16	Washington State	9-3	regular season complete
17	17	Mississippi	8-3	beat Mississippi State (N27)
18	18	Boise State	10-1	beat Nevada 56-3
17	19	TCU	10-1	beat SMU 20-13
21	20	Pittsburgh	8-3	lost to #10 Miami, Fla. 14-28
20	21	Virginia Tech	8-3	lost to Virginia 21-35
25	22	Bowling Green	9-2	beat Toledo 31-23 (N28)
24	23	Oklahoma State	9-3	beat Baylor 38-21
	24	West Virginia	7-4	beat Temple 45-28
23	25	Nebraska	8-3	beat Colorado 31-22 (N28)
22		Minnesota	9-3	

November 30 Poll / Dec. 6 Games

ESPN	AP	Team	Record	Game
1	1	Oklahoma	12-0	lost to #13 Kansas State 7-35 (Big 12 CH)
2	2	Southern Cal	10-1	beat Oregon State 52-28
3	3	LSU	11-1	beat #5 Georgia 34-13 (SEC CH)
4	4	Michigan	10-2	
5	5	Georgia	10-2	lost to #3 LSU 13-34 (SEC CH)
6	6	Texas	10-2	regular season complete
8	7	Tennessee	10-2	regular season complete
7	8	Ohio State	10-2	
9	9	Florida State	10-2	regular season complete
10	10	Miami, Fla.	10-2	regular season complete
12	11	Purdue	9-3	
11	12	Iowa	9-3	
13	13	Kansas State	10-3	beat #1 Oklahoma 35-7 (Big 12 CH)
14	14	Miami, Ohio	11-1	beat #20 Bowling Green 49-27 (MAC CH)
13	15	Washington State	9-3	
16	16	Florida	8-4	regular season complete
17	17	Mississippi	9-3	regular season complete
18	18	Boise State	11-1	beat Hawaii 45-28
19	19	TCU	11-1	regular season complete
23	20	Bowling Green	10-2	lost to #14 Miami, Ohio 27-49 (MAC CH)
24	21	West Virginia	8-4	regular season complete
22	22	Oklahoma State	9-3	regular season complete
21	23	Nebraska	9-3	regular season complete
25	24	Maryland	9-3	regular season complete
20	25	Minnesota	9-3	regular season complete

December 7 Poll

ESPN	AP	Team	RECORD	BOWL BID	DATE	BOWL RESULT	RB	ESPN	AP
1	1	Southern Cal	11-1	Rose Bowl	J1	beat #4 Michigan 28-14	2	2	1
2	2	LSU	12-1	Sugar Bowl	J4	beat #3 Oklahoma 21-14	1	1	2
3	3	Oklahoma	12-1	Sugar Bowl	J4	lost to #2 LSU 14-21	3	3	3
4	4	Michigan	10-2	Rose Bowl	J1	lost to #1 Southern Cal 14-28	5	4	4
5	5	Texas	10-2	Holiday Bowl	D30	lost to #15 Washington State 20-28	4	5	5
7	6	Tennessee	10-2	Peach Bowl	J2	lost to Clemson 14-27	7	7	6
6	7	Ohio State	10-2	Fiesta Bowl	J2	beat #8 Kansas State 35-28	9	6	7
10	8	Kansas State	11-3	Fiesta Bowl	J2	lost to #7 Ohio State 28-35	10	8	8
8	9	Florida State	10-2	Orange Bowl	J1	lost to #10 Miami, Fla. 14-16	12	9	9
9	10	Miami, Fla.	10-2	Orange Bowl	J1	beat #9 Florida State 16-14	6	12	10
11	11	Georgia	10-3	Capital One Bowl	J1	beat #12 Purdue 34-27	11	10	11
13	12	Purdue	9-3	Capital One Bowl	J1	lost to #11 Georgia 27-34	13	11	12
12	13	Iowa	9-3	Outback Bowl	J1	beat #17 Florida 37-17	16	14	13
15	14	Miami, Ohio	11-1	GMAC Bowl	D18	beat Louisville 49-28	19	13	14
13	15	Washington State	9-3	Holiday Bowl	D30	beat #5 Texas 28-20	15	16	15
18	16	Mississippi	9-3	Cotton Bowl	J2	beat #21 Oklahoma State 31-28	8	15	16
17	17	Florida	8-4	Outback Bowl	J1	lost to #13 Iowa 17-37	23	20	17
16	18	Boise State	12-1	Fort Worth Bowl	D23	beat #19 TCU 34-31	22	19	18
18	19	TCU	11-1	Fort Worth Bowl	D23	lost to #18 Boise State 31-34	25	18	19
23	20	West Virginia	8-4	Gator Bowl	J1	lost to #23 Maryland 7-41	21	23	20
22	21	Oklahoma State	9-3	Cotton Bowl	J2	lost to #16 Mississippi 28-31	18	21	21
21	22	Nebraska	9-3	Alamo Bowl	D29	beat Michigan State 17-3	14	22	22
24	23	Maryland	9-3	Gator Bowl	J1	beat #20 West Virginia 41-7	24	23	23
20	24	Minnesota	9-3	Sun Bowl	D31	beat Oregon 31-30	20	25	24
25	25	Utah	9-2	Liberty Bowl	D31	beat Southern Miss 17-0	17	24	25

January 5 Final Poll

Rank	Team	RECORD
1	Southern Cal	12-1
2	LSU	13-1
3	Oklahoma	12-2
4	Ohio State	11-2
5	Miami, Fla.	11-2
6	Michigan	10-3
7	Georgia	11-3
8	Iowa	10-3
9	Washington State	10-3
10	Miami, Ohio	13-1
11	Florida State	10-3
12	Texas	10-3
13	Mississippi	10-3
14	Kansas State	11-4
15	Tennessee	10-3
16	Boise State	13-1
17	Maryland	10-3
18	Purdue	9-4
19	Nebraska	10-3
20	Minnesota	10-3
21	Utah	10-2
22	Clemson	9-4
23	Bowling Green	11-3
24	Florida	8-5
25	TCU	11-2

ANNUAL REVIEW

2003

CONSENSUS ALL-AMERICANS

POS	Offense	HT	WT	CL	School	AP	CF	FC	FW	SN
QB	Jason White	6-3	221	Jr.	Oklahoma	•	•	•	•	•
RB	Chris Perry	6-1	218	Jr.	Michigan	•	•	•	•	
RB	Kevin Jones	6-0	221	Sr.	Virginia Tech		•	•	•	•
WR	Larry Fitzgerald	6-3	225	So.	Pittsburgh	•	•	•	•	•
WR	Mike Williams	6-5	230	So.	Southern Cal	•	•	•	•	•
TE	Kellen Winslow	6-5	250	Jr.	Miami, Fla.	•	•	•	•	•
OL	Shawn Andrews	6-6	353	Jr.	Arkansas	•	•	•	•	•
OL	Robert Gallery	6-7	321	Sr.	Iowa	•	•	•	•	•
OL	Jacob Rogers	6-6	305	Sr.	Southern Cal	•	•	•	•	•
OL	Alex Barron	6-6	316	Jr.	Florida State	•	•	•		
C	Jake Grove	6-3	300	Sr.	Virginia Tech	•	•	•	•	
PK	Nate Kaeding	6-0	180	Sr.	Iowa	•	•		•	
PK	Nick Browne	5-10	172	Sr.	TCU	•		•		
AP	Antonio Perkins	6-0	188	Jr.	Oklahoma	•	•			

OTHERS RECEIVING FIRST-TEAM HONORS

POS		School						
RB	Darren Sproles	Kansas State	•					
WR	Rashaun Woods	Oklahoma State	•					
WR	Mark Clayton	Oklahoma		•				
OL	Jammal Brown	Oklahoma		•				
OL	Stephen Peterman	LSU					•	
OL	Shannon Snell	Florida					•	
PK	Drew Dunning	Washington State					•	

POS	Defense	HT	WT	CL	School	AP	CF	FC	FW	SN
DL	Dave Ball	6-6	269	Sr.	UCLA	•	•	•	•	•
DL	Tommie Harris	6-3	289	Jr.	Oklahoma	•	•	•	•	•
DL	Chad Lavalais	6-3	292	Sr.	LSU	•	•	•	•	•
DL	Kenechi Udeze	6-4	285	Jr.	Southern Cal	•	•	•	•	•
LB	Teddy Lehman	6-2	243	Sr.	Oklahoma	•	•	•	•	•
LB	Derrick Johnson	6-4	230	Jr.	Texas	•	•	•	•	•
LB	Grant Wiley	6-1	235	Sr.	West Virginia	•	•	•	•	
DB	Derrick Strait	5-11	195	Sr.	Oklahoma	•	•	•	•	•
DB	Sean Taylor	6-3	230	Jr.	Miami, Fla.	•	•	•	•	•
DB	Keiwan Ratliff	5-10	178	Sr.	Florida	•	•	•	•	•
DB	Will Allen	6-2	190	Sr.	Ohio State	•	•		•	
P	Dustin Colquitt	6-2	196	Jr.	Tennessee	•	•		•	•

OTHERS RECEIVING FIRST-TEAM HONORS

POS		School		
DL	David Pollack	Georgia	•	
DL	Will Smith	Ohio State	•	
LB	Jonathan Vilma	Miami, Fla.	•	•
LB	Karlos Dansby	Auburn	•	
LB	Josh Buhl	Kansas State		•
DB	Corey Webster	LSU	•	
DB	Sean Jones	Georgia	•	
DB	Josh Bullocks	Nebraska		•
P	Kyle Larson	Nebraska	•	

HEISMAN TROPHY VOTING

	PLAYER	POS	SCHOOL	1ST	2ND	3RD	TOTAL
1	Jason White	QB	Oklahoma	319	204	116	1481
2	Larry Fitzgerald	WR	Pittsburgh	253	233	128	1353
3	Eli Manning	QB	Mississippi	95	132	161	710
4	Chris Perry	RB	Michigan	27	66	128	341
5	Darren Sproles	RB	Kansas State	15	30	29	134
6	Matt Leinart	QB	Southern Cal	5	27	58	127
7	Philip Rivers	QB	North Carolina St.	18	20	24	118
8	Mike Williams	WR	Southern Cal	12	12	18	78
9	Ben Roethlisberger	QB	Miami, Ohio	5	9	14	47
10	B.J. Symons	QB	Texas Tech	1	7	21	38

AWARD WINNERS

Eli Manning, QB, Mississippi, Maxwell, Unitas, Robert Gallery, OL, Iowa, Outland, Larry Fitzgerald, WR, Pittsburgh, Camp, Biletnikoff, Tommie Harris, DT, Oklahoma, Lombardi, Jason White, QB, Oklahoma, O'Brien, Teddy Lehman, LB, Oklahoma, Butkus, Bednarik, Derrick Strait, DB, Oklahoma, Thorpe, Nagurski, Chris Perry, RB, Michigan, Walker, Jonathan Nichols, K, Mississippi, Groza, Wes Welker, KR, Texas Tech, Tatupu, B.J. Sander, P, Ohio State, Guy, Kellen Winslow II, TE, Miami, Mackey, Jake Grove, C, Virginia Tech, Rimington, David Pollack, DE, Georgia, Hendricks

BOWL GAMES

D16, **New Orleans**, Memphis 27, North Texas 17, D18, **GMAC**, Miami, Ohio 49, Louisville 28, D22, **Tangerine** , North Carolina St. 56, Kansas 26, D23, **Fort Worth**, Boise State 34, TCU 31, D24, **Las Vegas**, Oregon State 55, New Mexico 14, D25, **Hawaii**, Hawaii 54, Houston 48, 3 OT, D26, **Motor City**, Bowling Green 28, Northwestern 24, D26, **Insight**, California 52, Virginia Tech 49, D27, **Continental Tire**, Virginia 23, Pittsburgh 16, D29, **Alamo**, Nebraska 17, Michigan State 3, D30, **Houston**, Texas Tech 38, Navy 14, D30, **Holiday**, Washington State 28, Texas 20, D30, **Silicon Valley Classic**, Fresno State 17, UCLA 9, D31, **Music City**, Auburn 28, Wisconsin 14, D31, **Sun**, Minnesota 31, Oregon 30, D31, **Liberty**, Utah 17, Southern Miss 0, D31, **Independence**, Arkansas 27, Missouri 14, D31, **San Francisco** , Boston College 35, Colorado State 21, J1, **Outback**, Iowa 37, Florida 17, J1, **Gator**, Maryland 41, West Virginia 7, J1, **Capital One**, Georgia 34, Purdue 27, OT, J1, **Rose**, Southern Cal 28, Michigan 14, J1, **Orange**, Miami 16, Florida State 14, J2, **Fiesta**, Ohio State 35, Kansas State 28, J2, **Cotton**, Mississippi 31, Oklahoma State 28, J2, **Peach**, Clemson 27, Tennessee 14, J3, **Humanitarian**, Georgia Tech 52, Tulsa 10, J4, **Sugar**, LSU 21, Oklahoma 14

CONFERENCE STANDINGS

ACC

	CONF. W L T			OVERALL W L T		
Florida State	7	1	0	10	3	0
Maryland	6	2	0	10	3	0
Clemson	5	3	0	9	4	0
North Carolina St.	4	4	0	8	5	0
Virginia	4	4	0	8	5	0
Georgia Tech	4	4	0	7	6	0
Wake Forest	3	5	0	5	7	0
Duke	2	6	0	4	8	0
North Carolina	1	7	0	2	10	0

Big 10

	CONF. W L T			OVERALL W L T		
Michigan	7	1	0	10	3	0
Ohio State	6	2	0	11	2	0
Purdue	6	2	0	9	4	0
Iowa	5	3	0	10	3	0
Minnesota	5	3	0	10	3	0
Michigan State	5	3	0	8	5	0
Wisconsin	4	4	0	7	6	0
Northwestern	4	4	0	6	7	0
Penn State	1	7	0	3	9	0
Indiana	1	7	0	2	10	0
Illinois	0	8	0	1	11	0

Big 12

	CONF. W L T			OVERALL W L T		
NORTH						
Kansas State	6	2	0	11	4	0
Nebraska	5	3	0	10	3	0
Missouri	4	4	0	8	5	0
Kansas	3	5	0	6	7	0
Colorado	3	5	0	5	7	0
Iowa State	0	8	0	2	10	0
SOUTH						
Oklahoma	8	0	0	12	2	0
Texas	7	1	0	10	3	0
Oklahoma State	5	3	0	9	4	0
Texas Tech	4	4	0	8	5	0
Texas A&M	2	6	0	4	8	0
Baylor	1	7	0	3	9	0

Championship **Kansas State 35 Oklahoma 7**

Big East

	CONF. W L T			OVERALL W L T		
Miami, Fla.	6	1	0	11	2	0
West Virginia	6	1	0	8	5	0
Pittsburgh	5	2	0	8	5	0
Virginia Tech	4	3	0	8	5	0
Boston College	3	4	0	8	5	0
Syracuse	2	5	0	6	6	0
Rutgers	2	5	0	5	7	0
Temple	0	7	0	1	11	0

C-USA

	CONF. W L T			OVERALL W L T		
Southern Miss	8	0	0	9	4	0
TCU	7	1	0	11	2	0
Memphis	5	3	0	9	4	0
Louisville	5	3	0	9	4	0
South Florida	5	3	0	7	4	0
Houston	4	4	0	7	6	0
UAB	4	4	0	5	7	0
Tulane	3	5	0	5	7	0
Cincinnati	2	6	0	5	7	0
East Carolina	1	7	0	1	11	0
Army	0	8	0	0	13	0

Ivy

	CONF. W L T			OVERALL W L T		
Pennsylvania	7	0	0	10	0	0
Harvard	4	3	0	7	3	0
Yale	4	3	0	6	4	0
Brown	4	3	0	5	5	0
Dartmouth	4	3	0	5	5	0
Columbia	3	4	0	4	6	0
Princeton	2	5	0	2	8	0
Cornell	0	7	0	1	9	0

MAC

	CONF. W L T			OVERALL W L T		
EAST						
Miami, Ohio	8	0	0	13	1	0
Marshall	6	2	0	8	4	0
Akron	5	3	0	7	5	0
Kent State	4	4	0	5	7	0

	CONF. W L T			OVERALL W L T		
Central Florida	2	6	0	3	9	0
Ohio U	1	7	0	2	10	0
Buffalo	1	7	0	1	11	0
WEST						
Bowling Green	7	1	0	11	3	0
Northern Illinois	6	2	0	10	2	0
Toledo	6	2	0	8	4	0
Western Michigan	4	4	0	5	7	0
Ball State	3	5	0	4	8	0
Eastern Michigan	2	6	0	3	9	0
Central Michigan	1	7	0	3	9	0

Championship Miami, Ohio 49 Bowling Green 27

MWC

	CONF. W L T			OVERALL W L T		
Utah	6	1	0	10	2	0
New Mexico	5	2	0	8	5	0
Colorado State	4	3	0	7	6	0
Air Force	3	4	0	7	5	0
San Diego State	3	4	0	6	6	0
Brigham Young	3	4	0	4	8	0
Nevada-Las Vegas	2	5	0	6	6	0
Wyoming	2	5	0	4	8	0

Pac 10

	CONF. W L T			OVERALL W L T		
Southern Cal	7	1	0	12	1	0
Washington State	6	2	0	10	3	0
Oregon	5	3	0	8	5	0
California	5	3	0	8	6	0
Oregon State	4	4	0	8	5	0
Washington	4	4	0	6	6	0
UCLA	4	4	0	6	7	0
Arizona State	2	6	0	5	7	0
Stanford	2	6	0	4	7	0
Arizona	1	7	0	2	10	0

SEC

	CONF. W L T			OVERALL W L T		
EAST						
Georgia	6	2	0	11	3	0
Tennessee	6	2	0	10	3	0
Florida	6	2	0	8	5	0
South Carolina	2	6	0	5	7	0
Kentucky	1	7	0	4	8	0
Vanderbilt	1	7	0	2	10	0
WEST						
LSU	7	1	0	13	1	0
Mississippi	7	1	0	10	3	0
Auburn	5	3	0	8	5	0
Arkansas	4	4	0	9	4	0
Alabama	2	6	0	4	9	0
Mississippi State	1	7	0	2	10	0

Championship LSU 34 Georgia 13

Sun Belt

	CONF. W L T			OVERALL W L T		
North Texas	7	0	0	9	4	0
La. Lafayette	3	2	0	4	8	0
Arkansas State	3	3	0	5	7	0
Middle Tennessee	3	3	0	4	8	0
Utah State	3	3	0	3	9	0
Idaho	3	4	0	3	9	0
New Mexico State	2	5	0	3	9	0
La. Monroe	1	5	0	1	11	0

WAC

	CONF. W L T			OVERALL W L T		
Boise State	8	0	0	13	1	0
Fresno State	6	2	0	9	5	0
Tulsa	6	2	0	8	5	0
Hawaii	5	3	0	9	5	0
Rice	5	3	0	5	7	0
Nevada	4	4	0	6	6	0
Louisiana Tech	3	5	0	5	7	0
San Jose State	2	6	0	3	8	0
Texas-El Paso	1	7	0	2	11	0
SMU	0	8	0	0	12	0

Independents

	OVERALL W L T		
Connecticut	9	3	0
Navy	8	5	0
Troy State	6	6	0
Notre Dame	5	7	0

2003 NCAA Major College Statistical Leaders

Individual Leaders

PASSING	POS	CL	G	ATT	COM	PCT	INT	I%	YDS	YPA	TD	TD%	RATING
1 Philip Rivers, North Carolina St.	QB	SR	13	483	348	72.1	7	1.5	4491	9.3	34	7.0	170.5
2 Ben Roethlisberger, Miami, Ohio	QB	JR	14	495	342	69.1	10	2.0	4486	9.1	37	7.5	165.8
3 Matt Leinart, Southern Cal	QB	SO	13	402	255	63.4	9	2.2	3556	8.9	38	9.5	164.5
4 Ryan Dinwiddie, Boise State	QB	SR	14	446	276	61.9	7	1.6	4356	9.8	31	7.0	163.7
5 Asad Abdul-Khaliq, Minnesota	QB	SR	13	250	158	63.2	5	2.0	2401	9.6	17	6.8	162.3
6 Bruce Gradkowski, Toledo	QB	SO	12	389	277	71.2	7	1.8	3210	8.3	29	7.5	161.5
7 Jason White, Oklahoma	QB	SR	14	451	278	61.6	10	2.2	3846	8.5	40	8.9	158.1
8 Rod Rutherford, Pittsburgh	QB	SR	13	413	247	59.8	14	3.4	3679	8.9	37	9.0	157.4
9 Bill Whittemore, Kansas	QB	SR	10	263	159	60.5	6	2.3	2385	9.1	18	6.8	154.7
10 Kevin Kolb, Houston	QB	FR	13	360	220	61.1	6	1.7	3131	8.7	25	6.9	153.8

ALL-PURPOSE	POS	CL	G	RUSH	REC	PR	KR	YDS	YPG
1 DeAngelo Williams, Memphis	RB	SO	11	1430	384	0	299	2113	192.1
2 Darren Sproles, Kansas State	RB	JR	15	1986	287	190	272	2735	182.3
3 Jerry Seymour, Central Michigan	RB	FR	9	1117	103	0	330	1550	172.2
4 Howard Jackson, Texas-El Paso	RB	JR	13	1146	391	0	609	2146	165.1
5 Michael Turner, Northern Ilinois	RB	SR	12	1648	230	0	58	1936	161.3
6 Patrick Cobbs, North Texas	RB	JR	11	1680	43	8	40	1771	161.0
7 Lance Moore, Toledo	WR	JR	12	26	1194	219	456	1895	157.9
8 Chris Perry, Michigan	RB	SR	13	1674	367	0	0	2041	157.0
9 Steven Jackson, Oregon State	RB	JR	13	1545	470	0	0	2015	155.0
10 Anthony Sherrell, Eastern Michigan	RB	JR	12	1531	304	0	0	1835	152.9

RUSHING/Yards Per Game	POS	CL	G	ATT	YDS	TD	AVG	YPG
1 Patrick Cobbs, North Texas	RB	JR	11	307	1680	19	5.5	152.7
2 Michael Turner, Northern Illinois	RB	SR	12	310	1648	14	5.3	137.3
3 Darren Sproles, Kansas State	RB	JR	15	306	1986	16	6.5	132.4
4 Derrick Knight, Boston College	RB	SR	13	321	1721	11	5.4	132.4
5 DeAngelo Williams, Memphis	RB	SO	11	243	1430	10	5.9	130.0
6 Chris Perry, Michigan	RB	SR	13	338	1674	18	5.0	128.8
7 Anthony Sherrell, Eastern Michigan	RB	JR	12	338	1531	12	4.5	127.6
8 Kevin Jones, Virginia Tech	RB	JR	13	281	1647	21	5.9	126.7
9 Jerry Seymour, Central Michigan	RB	FR	9	205	1117	8	5.5	124.1
10 Steven Jackson, Oregon State	RB	JR	13	350	1545	19	4.4	118.9

RUSHING/Yards Per Carry	POS	CL	G	ATT	YDS	YPC
1 Vince Young, Texas	QB	FR	12	135	998	7.4
2 Thomas Lott, Rice	RB	SO	11	98	714	7.3
3 Laurence Maroney, Minnesota	RB	FR	13	162	1121	6.9
4 Vernand Morency, Oklahoma State	RB	FR	13	135	918	6.8
5 Brad Smith, Missouri	QB	SO	13	212	1406	6.6
6 Ryan Moats, Louisiana Tech	RB	SO	12	199	1300	6.5
7 Justin Vincent, LSU	RB	FR	14	154	1001	6.5
8 Darren Sproles, Kansas State	RB	JR	15	306	1986	6.5
9 Tatum Bell, Oklahoma State	RB	SR	11	213	1286	6.0
10 DeAngelo Williams, Memphis	RB	SO	11	243	1430	5.9

RECEIVING	POS	CL	G	REC	YDS	TD	RPG	YPR	YPG
1 Larry Fitzgerald, Pittsburgh	WR	SO	13	92	1672	22	7.1	18.2	128.6
2 Geoff McArthur, California	WR	JR	13	85	1504	10	6.5	17.7	115.7
3 James Newson, Oregon State	WR	SR	12	81	1306	3	6.8	16.1	108.8
4 Martin Nance, Miami, Ohio	WR	JR	14	90	1498	11	6.4	16.6	107.0
5 Kerry Wright, Middle Tennessee	WR	JR	12	73	1280	9	6.1	17.5	106.7
6 Jerricho Cotchery, North Carolina St.	WR	SR	13	86	1369	10	6.6	15.9	105.3
7 Rashaun Woods, Oklahoma State	WR	SR	13	77	1367	15	5.9	17.8	105.2
8 Chad Owens, Hawaii	WR	JR	11	85	1134	9	7.7	13.3	103.1
9 Mark Clayton, Oklahoma	WR	JR	14	83	1425	15	5.9	17.2	101.8
10 Mike Williams, Southern Cal	WR	SO	13	95	1314	16	7.3	13.8	101.1

PUNTING	POS	CL	PUNT	YDS	AVG
1 Matt Prater, Central Florida	K	SO	58	2781	48.0
2 Brandon Fields, Michigan State	P	SO	62	2878	46.4
3 Joel Stelly, La. Monroe	K	SO	67	3099	46.3
4 Jared Scruggs, Rice	P	FR	51	2341	45.9
5 Ryan Plackemeier, Wake Forest	K	SO	57	2600	45.6
6 Dustin Colquitt, Tennessee	P	JR	68	3081	45.3
7 Kyle Larson, Nebraska	P	SR	66	2978	45.1
8 Eric Wilbur, Florida	P	FR	66	2954	44.8
9 Ryan Dougherty, East Carolina	P	FR	64	2846	44.5
10 Steve Weatherford, Illinois	P	SO	46	2045	44.5

PUNT RETURNS	POS	CL	PR	YDS	TD	AVG
1 Skyler Green, LSU	WR	SO	25	462	2	18.5
2 Ryne Robinson, Miami, Ohio	WR	FR	38	654	3	17.2
3 Mark Jones, Tennessee	WR	SR	20	303	1	15.2
4 Gabe Lindsay, Oklahoma State	WR	SR	26	393	1	15.1
5 DeAngelo Hall, Virginia Tech	DB	JR	33	487	3	14.8
6 Marcus James, Missouri	WR	SR	26	377	0	14.5
7 Marion Barber III, Minnesota	RB	SO	28	405	0	14.5
8 Jim Leonhard, Wisconsin	DB	JR	34	470	2	13.8
9 Steve Breaston, Michigan	WR	SO	45	619	2	13.8
10 Marvin Young, Southern Miss	WR	JR	33	450	1	13.6

KICKOFF RETURNS	POS	CL	KR	YDS	TD	AVG
1 Michael Waddell, North Carolina	CB	SR	15	475	1	31.7
1 J.R. Reed, South Florida	DB	SR	18	570	1	31.7
3 Mike Imoh, Virginia Tech	RB	SO	18	549	1	30.5
4 John Eubanks, Southern Miss	DB	SO	17	499	1	29.4
5 Dexter Wynn, Colorado State	DB	SR	27	782	0	29.0
6 Devin Hester, Miami, Fla.	WR	FR	18	517	1	28.7
7 Senterrio Landrum, Duke	WR	JR	25	709	0	28.4
8 Kendrick Starling, San Jose State	WR	SR	20	562	0	28.1
9 Charles Estes, La. Monroe	WR	JR	36	988	1	27.4
10 Reggie Bush, Southern Cal	RB	FR	18	492	1	27.3

SCORING	POS	CL	TDS	XP	FG	PTS	PTPG
1 Patrick Cobbs, North Texas	RB	JR	21	0	0	126	11.5
2 Cedric Benson, Texas	RB	JR	22	0	0	134	11.2
3 Walter Reyes, Syracuse	RB	JR	21	0	0	128	10.7
4 Larry Fitzgerald, Pittsburgh	WR	SO	22	0	0	132	10.2
4 Steven Jackson, Oregon State	RB	JR	22	0	0	132	10.2
6 Jason Wright, Northwestern	RB	SR	21	0	0	126	9.7
6 Kevin Jones, Virginia Tech	RB	JR	21	0	0	126	9.7
6 DonTrell Moore, New Mexico	RB	SO	21	0	0	126	9.7
9 Nick Browne, TCU	K	SR	0	38	28	124	9.5
9 Jonathan Nichols, Mississippi	K	JR	0	49	25	124	9.5

FIELD GOALS	POS	CL	FGA	FGM	PCT	FGG
1 Billy Bennett, Georgia	K	SR	38	31	0.82	2.21
2 Nick Browne, TCU	K	SR	33	28	0.85	2.15
3 Drew Dunning, Washington State	K	SR	31	27	0.87	2.08
4 Ben Jones, Purdue	K	SO	30	25	0.83	1.92
4 Jonathan Nichols, Mississippi	K	JR	29	25	0.86	1.92
6 Nick Novak, Maryland	K	JR	32	24	0.75	1.85
7 Connor Hughes, Virginia	OL	SO	25	23	0.92	1.77
8 Steve Azar, Northern Illinois	K	SR	26	21	0.81	1.75
8 Josh Scobee, Louisiana Tech	K	SR	31	21	0.68	1.75
10 Jon Peattie, Miami, Fla.	P	FR	28	22	0.79	1.69
10 David Rayner, Michigan State	K	JR	29	22	0.76	1.69

INTERCEPTIONS	POS	CL	INT	YDS	TD	INT/GM
1 Sean Taylor, Miami, Fla.	DB	JR	10	184	3	0.83
2 Josh Bullocks, Nebraska	DB	SO	10	154	0	0.77
3 Jonathan Burke, Arkansas State	DB	SR	9	120	0	0.75
3 Derrick Ansley, Troy State	DB	JR	9	74	1	0.75
5 Keiwan Ratliff, Florida	DB	SR	9	182	2	0.69
6 J.R. Reed, South Florida	DB	SR	7	45	0	0.64
7 Gerald Jones, San Jose State	DB	SR	6	178	2	0.55
8 Jim Leonhard, Wisconsin	DB	JR	7	98	0	0.54
8 Will Poole, Southern Cal	DB	SO	7	70	1	0.54
8 Erik Coleman, Washington State	DB	SR	7	22	0	0.54

Team Leaders

RUSHING OFFENSE	G	ATT	YDS	AVG	TD	YPG
1 Navy	13	760	4202	5.5	44	323.2
2 Rice	12	687	3800	5.5	35	316.7
3 Minnesota	13	683	3759	5.5	46	289.2
4 Air Force	12	716	3367	4.7	31	280.6
5 Arkansas	13	626	3145	5.0	34	241.9
6 Missouri	13	551	3087	5.6	38	237.5
7 Nebraska	13	716	3063	4.3	28	235.6
8 Texas	13	587	3023	5.2	41	232.5
9 Kansas State	15	688	3429	5.0	42	228.6
10 Louisville	13	518	2966	5.7	35	228.2

PASSING OFFENSE	G	ATT	COM	INT	PCT	YDS	YPA	TD	I%	YPC	YPG
1 Texas Tech	13	780	506	23	64.9	6179	7.9	53	3.0	12.2	475.3
2 Hawaii	14	754	444	27	58.9	5382	7.1	42	3.6	12.1	384.4
3 North Carolina St.	13	496	357	7	72.0	4580	9.2	35	1.4	12.8	352.3
4 Miami, Ohio	14	535	363	11	67.9	4772	8.9	38	2.1	13.2	340.9
5 Boise State	14	489	295	9	60.3	4708	9.6	33	1.8	16.0	336.3
6 Oregon State	13	534	274	25	51.3	4265	8.0	25	4.7	15.6	328.1
7 Akron	12	449	287	10	63.9	3736	8.3	22	2.2	13.0	311.3
8 Western Michigan	12	450	272	20	60.4	3701	8.2	31	4.4	13.6	308.4
9 Bowling Green	14	528	345	13	65.3	4206	8.0	32	2.5	12.2	300.4
10 Connecticut	12	483	283	14	58.6	3575	7.4	33	2.9	12.6	297.9

TOTAL OFFENSE	G	P	YDS	AVG	TD	YPG
1 Texas Tech	13	1088	7576	7.0	76	582.8
2 Miami, Ohio	14	1053	7016	6.7	82	501.1
3 Bowling Green	14	1111	6954	6.3	61	496.7
4 Minnesota	13	970	6430	6.6	66	494.6
5 Louisville	13	913	6355	7.0	58	488.9
6 Hawaii	14	1072	6834	6.4	63	488.1
7 Boise State	14	1061	6809	6.4	77	486.4
8 Connecticut	12	946	5730	6.1	54	477.5
9 Akron	12	923	5643	6.1	55	470.3
10 Oregon State	13	1060	6019	5.7	53	463.0

RUSHING DEFENSE	G	ATT	YDS	AVG	TD	YPG
1 Southern Cal	13	425	782	1.8	9	60.2
2 Ohio State	13	415	810	2.0	12	62.3
3 LSU	14	400	938	2.4	5	67.0
4 Oregon State	13	447	1097	2.5	11	84.4
5 New Mexico	13	428	1119	2.6	11	86.1
6 Washington State	13	441	1181	2.7	8	90.8
7 Auburn	13	440	1204	2.7	8	92.6
8 Iowa	13	480	1205	2.5	10	92.7
9 TCU	13	443	1218	2.8	13	93.7
10 Purdue	13	467	1260	2.7	9	96.9

PASSING DEFENSE	G	ATT	COM	PCT	INT	I%	YDS	YPA	TD	TD%	RAT
1 Nebraska	13	430	218	50.7	32	7.4	2312	5.38	10	2.3	88.7
2 LSU	14	477	213	44.7	21	4.4	2590	5.43	12	2.5	89.8
3 Oklahoma	14	419	218	52.0	22	5.3	2050	4.89	11	2.6	91.3
4 Miami, Fla.	13	328	167	50.9	19	5.8	1866	5.69	9	2.7	96.2
5 Washington State	13	547	263	48.1	24	4.4	2960	5.41	19	3.5	96.2
6 Oregon State	13	467	206	44.1	20	4.3	2656	5.69	22	4.7	98.9
7 Boise State	14	614	302	49.2	21	3.4	3470	5.65	17	2.8	99.0
8 South Florida	11	352	173	49.2	13	3.7	1979	5.62	14	4.0	102.1
9 Michigan	13	411	221	53.8	14	3.4	2347	5.71	9	2.2	102.2
10 San Diego State	12	345	176	51.0	12	3.5	1923	5.57	12	3.5	102.3

TOTAL DEFENSE	G	P	YDS	AVG	TD	YPG
1 LSU	14	877	3528	4.0	19	252.0
2 Miami, Fla.	13	786	3348	4.3	23	257.5
3 Oklahoma	14	881	3635	4.1	27	259.6
4 Georgia	14	880	3876	4.4	23	276.9
5 Auburn	13	802	3661	4.6	25	281.6
6 Kansas State	15	996	4246	4.3	31	283.1
7 Oregon State	13	914	3753	4.1	38	288.7
8 San Diego State	12	813	3477	4.3	22	289.8
9 Memphis	13	879	3845	4.4	32	295.8
10 Ohio State	13	930	3859	4.2	28	296.9

SCORING OFFENSE	G	PTS	AVG
1 Boise State	14	602	43.0
1 Miami, Ohio	14	602	43.0
3 Oklahoma	14	601	42.9
4 Texas Tech	13	552	42.5
5 Southern Cal	13	534	41.1
6 Texas	13	533	41.0
7 Minnesota	13	503	38.7
8 North Carolina St.	13	489	37.6
9 Kansas State	15	549	36.6
10 Akron	12	435	36.3

SCORING DEFENSE	G	PTS	AVG
1 LSU	14	154	11.0
2 Nebraska	13	188	14.5
3 Georgia	14	203	14.5
4 Miami, Fla.	13	196	15.1
5 Oklahoma	14	214	15.3
6 Maryland	13	206	15.8
7 Iowa	13	210	16.2
8 Kansas State	15	244	16.3
9 Auburn	13	212	16.3
10 Florida State	13	217	16.7

TURNOVER MARGIN	G	FR	INT	TOT	FL	INTL	TOT	MAR
1 Nebraska	13	15	32	47	14	10	24	1.8
2 Southern Cal	13	20	22	42	13	9	22	1.5
3 Miami, Ohio	14	18	21	39	8	11	19	1.4
4 West Virginia	13	15	21	36	12	8	20	1.2
5 Oklahoma	14	12	22	34	6	11	17	1.2
6 Northern Illinois	12	8	23	31	7	10	17	1.2
7 UNLV	12	19	16	35	12	11	23	1.0
8 Purdue	13	14	14	28	9	7	16	0.9
9 Toledo	12	10	15	25	6	8	14	0.9
10 Arkansas	13	16	17	33	13	9	22	0.9
10 Missouri	13	15	9	24	5	8	13	0.9
10 North Texas	13	15	18	33	13	9	22	0.9
10 Michigan State	13	14	15	29	3	15	18	0.9

2004 Poll Progression

ESPN	AP	Pre-Season 2004		Sept. 4 Games
1	1	Southern Cal	0-0	beat Virginia Tech 24-13 (A28)
2	2	Oklahoma	0-0	beat Bowling Green 40-24
4	3	Georgia	0-0	beat Georgia So. 48-28
3	4	LSU	0-0	beat Oregon State 22-21
6	5	Florida State	0-0	bye week
5	6	Miami, Fla.	0-0	bye week
8	7	Texas	0-0	beat North texas 65-0
7	8	Michigan	0-0	beat Miami, Ohio 43-10
9	9	Ohio State	0-0	beat Cincinnati 27-6
11	10	West Virginia	0-0	beat East Carolina 56-23
10	11	Florida	0-0	bye week
13	12	Kansas State	0-0	beat W. Kentucky 27-13
15	13	California	0-0	beat Air Force 56-14
14	14	Tennessee	0-0	beat Nevada-Las Vegas 42-17 (S5)
16	15	Clemson	0-0	beat Wake Forest 37-30
19	16	Virginia	0-0	beat Temple 44-14
18	17	Auburn	0-0	beat La. Monroe 31-0
17	18	Missouri	0-0	beat Arkansas State 52-20
12	19	Iowa	0-0	beat Kent State 39-7
21	20	Utah	0-0	beat Texas A&M 41-21 (S2)
22	21	Wisconsin	0-0	beat Central Florida 34-6
20	22	Maryland	0-0	beat Northern Illinois 23-20
25	23	Oregon	0-0	bye week
23	24	Purdue	0-0	beat Syracuse 51-0 (S5)
23	25	Minnesota	0-0	beat Toledo 63-21

ESPN	AP	September 5 Poll		Sept. 11 Games
1	1	Southern Cal	1-0	beat Colorado State 49-0
2	2	Oklahoma	1-0	beat Houston 63-13
3	3	Georgia	1-0	beat South Carolina 20-16
6	4	Florida State	0-0	lost to #5 Miami, Fla. 10-16 (S10)
5	5	Miami, Fla.	0-0	beat #4 Florida State 16-10 (S10)
4	6	LSU	1-0	beat Arkansas State 53-3
8	7	Texas	1-0	beat Arkansas 22-20
7	8	Michigan	1-0	lost to Notre Dame 20-28
9	9	Ohio State	1-0	beat Marshall 24-21
10	10	West Virginia	1-0	beat Central Florida 45-20
11	11	Florida	0-0	beat Eastern Michigan 49-10
13	12	California	1-0	beat New Mexico State 41-14
14	13	Kansas State	1-0	lost to Fresno State 21-45
15	14	Tennessee	0-0	bye week
20	15	Virginia	1-0	beat North Carolina 56-24
12	16	Iowa	1-0	beat Iowa State 17-10
16	17	Utah	1-0	beat Arizona 23-6
19	18	Auburn	1-0	beat Mississippi State 43-14
17	19	Missouri	1-0	lost to Troy State 14-24 S9
18	20	Clemson	1-0	lost to Georgia Tech 24-28
22	21	Wisconsin	1-0	beat Nevada-Las Vegas 18-3
24	22	Minnesota	1-0	beat Illinois St. 37-21
21	23	Maryland	1-0	beat Temple 45-22
25	24	Oregon	0-0	lost to Indiana 24-30
23	25	Purdue	0-0	beat Ball State 59-7

ESPN	AP	September 12 Poll		Sept. 18 Games
1	1	Southern Cal	2-0	beat Brigham Young 42-10
2	2	Oklahoma	2-0	beat Oregon 31-7
3	3	Georgia	2-0	beat Marshall 13-3
5	4	Miami, Fla.	1-0	beat Louisiana Tech 48-0
4	5	LSU	2-0	lost to # 13 Auburn 9-10
6	6	Texas	2-0	bye week
8	7	West Virginia	2-0	beat # 21 Maryland 19-16
11	8	Florida State	0-1	beat UAB 34-7
7	9	Ohio State	2-0	beat North Carolina St. 22-14
10	10	California	2-0	bye week
9	11	Florida	1-0	lost to # 14 Tennessee 28-30
16	12	Virginia	2-0	beat Akron 51-0
15	13	Auburn	2-0	beat # 5 LSU 10-9
13	14	Tennessee	1-0	beat # 11 Florida 30-28
14	15	Utah	2-0	beat Utah State 48-6
12	16	Iowa	2-0	lost to Arizona State 7-44
17	17	Michigan	1-1	beat San Diego State 24-21
21	18	Fresno State	2-0	beat Portland St. 27-17
18	19	Purdue	2-0	bye week
21	20	Wisconsin	2-0	beat Arizona 9-7
20	21	Maryland	2-0	lost to # 7 West Virginia 16-19
22	22	Minnesota	2-0	beat Colorado State 34-16
23	23	Boise State	2-0	beat Texas-El Paso 47-31
24	24	Louisville	2-0	bye week
	25	Memphis	2-0	beat Arkansas State 47-35
25		Clemson	1-1	lost to Texas A&M 6-27

ESPN	AP	September 19 Poll		Sept 25 Games
1	1	Southern Cal	3-0	beat Stanford 31-28
2	2	Oklahoma	3-0	bye week
3	3	Georgia	3-0	bye week
4	4	Miami, Fla.	2-0	beat Houston 38-13 (S23)
5	5	Texas	2-0	beat Rice 35-13
7	6	West Virginia	3-0	beat James Madison 45-10
6	7	Ohio State	3-0	bye week
11	8	Florida State	1-1	beat Clemson 41-22
10	9	Auburn	3-0	beat Citadel 33-3
9	11	California	2-0	bye week
8	12	Tennessee	2-0	beat Louisiana Tech 42-17
12	13	Virginia	3-0	beat Syracuse 31-10
13	14	LSU	2-1	beat Mississippi State 51-0
14	15	Utah	3-0	beat Air Force 49-35
15	16	Purdue	2-0	beat Illinois 38-30
16	17	Florida	1-1	beat Kentucky 20-3
17	18	Fresno State	3-0	bye week
18	19	Michigan	2-1	beat Iowa 17-30
19	19	Minnesota	3-0	beat Northwestern 43-17
20	20	Wisconsin	3-0	beat Penn State 16-3
21	21	Boise State	3-0	beat Brigham Young 28-27
	22	Arizona State	3-0	beat Oregon State 27-14
23	23	Maryland	2-1	beat Duke 55-21
22	24	Louisville	2-0	beat North Carolina 34-0
25	25	Oklahoma State	3-0	bye week
24		Iowa	2-1	lost to # 19 Michigan 17-30

ESPN	AP	September 26 Poll		Oct. 2 Games
1	1	Southern Cal	4-0	bye week
2	2	Oklahoma	3-0	beat Texas Tech 28-13
3	3	Georgia	3-0	beat # 13 LSU 45-16
4	4	Miami, Fla.	3-0	beat Georgia Tech 27-3
5	5	Texas	3-0	beat Baylor 44-14
7	6	West Virginia	4-0	lost to Virginia Tech 13-19
6	7	Ohio State	3-0	lost to Northwestern 27-33
9	8	Auburn	4-0	beat # 11 Tennessee 34-10
11	9	Florida State	2-1	beat North Carolina 38-16
10	10	California	2-0	beat Oregon State 49-7
8	11	Tennessee	3-0	lost to # 8 Auburn 10-34
12	12	Virginia	4-0	bye week
13	13	LSU	3-1	lost to # 3 Georgia 16-45
14	14	Utah	4-0	beat New Mexico 28-7 (O1)
16	15	Purdue	3-0	beat Notre Dame 41-16
16	16	Florida	2-1	beat Arkansas 45-30
17	17	Fresno State	3-0	lost to Louisiana Tech 21-28
19	18	Minnesota	4-0	beat Penn State 16-7
18	19	Michigan	3-1	beat Indiana 35-14
20	20	Wisconsin	4-0	beat Illinois 24-7
25	21	Arizona State	4-0	beat Oregon 28-13
22	22	Louisville	3-0	beat East Carolina 59-7
21	23	Boise State	4-0	beat SMU 38-20
23	24	Maryland	3-1	bye week
24	25	Oklahoma State	3-0	beat Iowa State 36-7

ESPN	AP	October 3 Poll		Oct. 9 Games
1	1	Southern Cal	4-0	beat # 7 California 23-17
2	2	Oklahoma	4-0	beat # 5 Texas 12-0
3	3	Georgia	4-0	lost to # 17 Tennessee 14-19
4	4	Miami, Fla.	4-0	bye week
5	5	Texas	4-0	lost to # 2 Oklahoma 0-12
6	6	Auburn	5-0	beat Louisiana Tech 52-7
7	7	California	3-0	lost to # 1 Southern Cal 17-23
8	8	Florida State	3-1	beat Syracuse 17-13
10	9	Purdue	4-0	beat Penn State 20-13
9	10	Virginia	4-0	beat Clemson 30-10
11	11	Utah	5-0	bye week
12	12	Florida	3-1	lost to # 24 LSU 21-24
13	13	Minnesota	5-0	lost to # 14 Michigan 24-27
14	14	Michigan	4-1	beat # 13 Minnesota 27-24
16	15	Wisconsin	5-0	beat # 18 Ohio State 24-13
18	16	West Virginia	4-1	bye week
17	17	Tennessee	3-1	beat # 3 Georgia 19-14
15	18	Ohio State	3-1	lost to # 15 Wisconsin 13-24
22	19	Arizona State	5-0	bye week
20	20	Louisville	4-0	bye week
19	21	Boise State	5-0	bye week
21	22	Oklahoma State	4-0	beat Colorado 42-14
23	23	Maryland	3-1	lost to Georgia Tech 7-20
24	24	LSU	3-2	beat # 12 Florida 24-21
	26	South Carolina	4-1	lost to Mississippi 28-31
25		North Carolina St.	3-1	lost to North Carolina 24-30

ESPN	AP	October 10 Poll		Oct. 16 Games
1	1	Southern Cal	5-0	beat # 15 Arizona State 45-7
2	2	Oklahoma	5-0	beat Kansas State 31-21
3	3	Miami, Fla.	4-0	beat # 18 Louisville 41-38
4	4	Auburn	6-0	beat Arkansas 38-20
5	5	Purdue	5-0	lost to # 10 Wisconsin 17-20
6	6	Virginia	5-0	lost to # 7 Florida State 3-36
7	7	Florida State	4-1	beat # 6 Virginia 36-3
9	8	California	3-1	beat UCLA 45-28
11	9	Texas	4-1	beat Missouri 28-20
12	10	Wisconsin	6-0	beat # 5 Purdue 20-17
10	11	Utah	5-0	beat North Carolina 46-16
8	12	Georgia	4-1	beat Vanderbilt 33-3
14	13	Tennessee	4-1	beat Mississippi 21-17
13	14	Michigan	5-1	beat Illinois 30-19
19	15	Arizona State	5-0	lost to # 1 Southern Cal 7-45
15	16	Oklahoma State	5-0	lost to # 23 Texas A&M 20-36
16	17	West Virginia	4-1	beat Connecticut 31-19 (O13)
17	18	Louisville	4-0	lost to # 3 Miami, Fla. 38-41 (O14)
20	19	Minnesota	5-1	lost to Michigan State 17-51
21	20	LSU	4-2	bye week
18	21	Boise State	5-0	beat Tulsa 45-42
22	22	Florida	3-2	beat Middle Tennessee 52-16
	23	Texas A&M	4-1	beat # 16 Oklahoma State 36-20
25	24	Southern Miss	4-0	lost to Alabama 3-27
23	25	Ohio State	3-2	lost to Iowa 7-33
24		Missouri	4-1	lost to # 9 Texas 20-28

ESPN	AP	October 17 Poll		Oct 23 Games
1	1	Southern Cal	6-0	beat Washington 38-0
2	2	Oklahoma	6-0	beat Kansas 41-10
4	3	Auburn	7-0	beat Kentucky 42-10
3	4	Miami, Fla.	5-0	beat North Carolina St. 45-31
5	5	Florida State	5-1	beat Wake Forest 20-17
7	6	Wisconsin	7-0	beat Northwestern 24-12
8	7	California	4-1	beat Arizona 38-0
9	8	Texas	5-1	beat Texas Tech 51-21
10	9	Utah	6-0	beat Nevada-Las Vegas 63-28
6	10	Georgia	5-1	beat Arkansas 20-14
13	11	Tennessee	5-1	beat Alabama 17-13
12	12	Purdue	5-1	lost to Michigan 14-16
11	13	Michigan	6-1	beat Purdue 16-14
15	14	Virginia	5-1	beat Duke 37-16
14	15	West Virginia	5-1	beat Syracuse 27-6
18	16	Louisville	4-1	beat South Florida 41-9
20	17	Texas A&M	5-1	beat Colorado 29-26
17	18	LSU	4-2	beat Troy State 24-20
16	19	Boise State	6-0	beat Fresno State 33-16
19	20	Florida	4-2	lost to Mississippi State 31-38
23	21	Arizona State	5-1	beat UCLA 48-42
21	22	Oklahoma State	5-1	beat Missouri 20-17
22	23	Virginia Tech	5-2	bye week
25	24	Notre Dame	5-2	lost to Boston College 23-24
	25	Iowa	4-2	beat Penn State 6-4
24		Texas Tech	4-2	lost to # 8 Texas 21-51

ESPN	AP	October 24 Poll		Oct 30 Games
1	1	Southern Cal	7-0	beat Washington State 42-12
2	2	Oklahoma	7-0	beat #21 Oklahoma State 38-35
4	3	Auburn	8-0	beat Mississippi State 35-14
3	4	Miami, Fla.	6-0	lost to North Carolina 28-31
5	5	Florida State	6-1	lost to Maryland 17-20
6	6	Wisconsin	8-0	bye week
8	7	California	5-1	beat # 20 Arizona State 27-0
9	8	Texas	6-1	beat Colorado 31-7
10	9	Utah	7-0	beat San Diego State 51-28
7	10	Georgia	6-1	beat Florida 31-24
12	11	Tennessee	6-1	beat South Carolina 43-29
11	12	Michigan	7-1	beat Michigan State 45-37
14	13	Virginia	6-1	bye week
16	14	Louisville	5-1	bye week
13	15	West Virginia	6-1	beat Rutgers 35-30
17	16	Texas A&M	6-1	lost to Baylor 34-35
19	17	Purdue	5-2	lost to Northwestern 10-13
15	18	Boise State	7-0	beat Hawaii 69-3
18	19	LSU	5-2	beat Vanderbilt 24-7
21	20	Arizona State	6-1	lost to # 7 California 0-27
20	21	Oklahoma State	6-1	lost to # 2 Oklahoma 35-38
22	22	Virginia Tech	5-2	beat Georgia Tech 34-20 (O28)
24	23	Iowa	5-2	beat Illinois 23-13
23	24	Minnesota	6-2	lost to Indiana 21-30
25	25	Southern Miss	5-1	bye week

October 31 Poll — Nov. 6 Games

ESPN	AP	Team		Result
1	1	Southern Cal	8-0	beat Oregon State 28-20
2	2	Oklahoma	8-0	beat #22 Texas A&M 42-35
3	3	Auburn	9-0	bye week
6	4	California	6-1	beat Oregon 28-27
4	5	Wisconsin	8-0	beat Minnesota 38-14
7	6	Texas	7-1	beat #19 Oklahoma State 56-35
8	7	Utah	8-0	beat Colorado State 63-31
5	8	Georgia	7-1	beat Kentucky 62-17
11	9	Tennessee	7-1	lost to Notre Dame 13-17
9	10	Michigan	8-1	bye week
10	11	Miami, Fla.	6-1	lost to Clemson 17-24
13	12	Virginia	6-1	beat Maryland 16-0
14	13	Florida State	6-2	beat Duke 29-7
16	14	Louisville	5-1	beat Memphis 56-49 (N4)
12	15	West Virginia	7-1	beat Temple 42-21
15	16	Boise State	8-0	bye week
17	17	LSU	6-2	bye week
18	18	Virginia Tech	6-2	beat North Carolina 27-24
19	19	Oklahoma State	6-2	lost to #6 Texas 35-56
20	20	Iowa	6-2	beat Purdue 23-21
21	21	Southern Miss	5-1	lost to Cincinnati 24-52
22	22	Texas A&M	6-2	lost to #2 Oklahoma 35-42
23	23	Arizona State	6-2	beat Stanford 34-31
25	24	Boston College	5-2	beat Rutgers 21-10
	25	Texas-El Paso	6-2	bye week
24		Northern Illinois	7-2	bye week

November 7 Poll — Nov. 13 Games

ESPN	AP	Team		Result
1	1	Southern Cal	9-0	beat Arizona 49-9
2	2	Oklahoma	9-0	beat Nebraska 30-3
3	3	Auburn	9-0	beat #8 Georgia 24-6
4	4	Wisconsin	9-0	lost to Michigan State 19-49
5	5	California	7-1	beat Washington 42-12
7	6	Texas	8-1	beat Kansas 27-23
8	7	Utah	9-0	beat Wyoming 45-28
5	8	Georgia	8-1	lost to #3 Auburn 6-24
9	9	Michigan	8-1	beat Northwestern 42-20
11	10	Virginia	7-1	lost to #18 Miami, Fla. 21-31
12	11	Florida State	7-2	beat North Carolina St. 17-10
14	12	Louisville	6-1	beat TCU 55-28
10	13	West Virginia	8-1	lost to #21 Boston College 17-36
13	14	Boise State	8-0	beat San Jose State 56-49
18	15	Tennessee	7-2	bye week
16	16	Virginia Tech	7-2	bye week
15	17	LSU	6-2	beat Alabama 26-10
17	18	Miami, Fla.	6-2	beat #10 Virginia 31-21
19	19	Iowa	7-2	beat Minnesota 29-27
20	20	Arizona State	7-2	beat Washington State 45-28
21	21	Boston College	6-2	beat #13 West Virginia 36-17
23	22	Texas A&M	6-3	beat Texas Tech 32-25
	23	Texas-El Paso	6-2	beat Rice 35-28
	24	Notre Dame	6-3	lost to Pittsburgh 38-41
24	25	Oklahoma State	6-3	beat Baylor 49-21
22		Northern Illinois	7-2	lost to Toledo 17-31
25		Texas Tech	6-3	lost to #22 Texas A&M 25-32

November 14 Poll — Nov. 20 Games

ESPN	AP	Team		Result
1	1	Southern Cal	10-0	bye week
2t	2	Oklahoma	10-0	beat Baylor 35-0
3t	3	Auburn	10-0	beat Alabama 21-13
4	4	California	8-1	beat Stanford 41-6
6	5	Utah	10-0	beat Brigham Young 52-21
5	6	Texas	9-1	bye week
7	7	Michigan	9-1	lost to Ohio State 21-37
11	8	Louisville	7-1	beat Houston 65-27
9	9	Wisconsin	9-1	lost to #17 Iowa 7-30
8	10	Florida State	8-2	lost to Florida 13-20
10	11	Georgia	8-2	bye week
13	12	Miami, Fla.	7-2	beat Wake Forest 52-7
12	13	Boise State	9-0	beat Louisiana Tech 55-14
14	14	LSU	7-2	beat Mississippi 27-24
16	15	Tennessee	7-2	beat Vanderbilt 38-33
15	16	Virginia Tech	7-2	beat Maryland 55-6 (N18)
17	17	Iowa	8-2	beat #9 Wisconsin 30-7
18	18	Virginia	8-2	beat Georgia Tech 30-10
19	19	Boston College	7-2	beat Temple 34-17
20	20	Arizona State	8-2	bye week
20	21	West Virginia	8-2	bye week
22	22	Texas A&M	7-3	bye week
23	23	Oklahoma State	7-3	bye week
25	24	Texas-El Paso	7-2	beat SMU 57-27
24	25	Bowling Green	8-2	bye week

November 21 Poll — Nov. 27 Games

ESPN	AP	Team		Result
1	1	Southern Cal	10-0	beat Notre Dame 41-10
2	2	Oklahoma	11-0	bye week
3	3	Auburn	11-0	bye week
4	4	California	9-1	bye week
6	5	Utah	11-0	regular season complete
5	6	Texas	9-1	beat #22 Texas A&M 26-13 (N26)
8	7	Louisville	8-1	beat Cincinnati 70-7
7	8	Georgia	8-2	beat Georgia Tech 19-13
9	9	Miami, Fla.	8-2	bye week
10	10	Boise State	10-0	beat Nevada 58-21
11	11	Virginia Tech	8-2	beat #16 Virginia 24-10
14	12	Iowa	9-2	regular season complete
13	13	Michigan	9-2	regular season complete
12	14	LSU	8-2	beat Arkansas 43-14 (N26)
15	15	Tennessee	8-2	beat Kentucky 37-31
16	16	Virginia	8-2	lost to #11 Virginia Tech 10-24
19	17	Boston College	8-2	lost to Syracuse 17-43
20	18	Arizona State	8-2	lost to Arizona 27-34 (N26)
17	19	Florida State	8-3	regular season complete
18	20	Wisconsin	9-2	regular season complete
21	21	West Virginia	8-2	lost to Pittsburgh 13-16 (N25)
22	22	Texas A&M	7-3	lost to #6 Texas 13-26 (N26)
23	23	Oklahoma State	7-3	lost to Texas Tech 15-31
25	24	Texas-El Paso	8-2	lost to Tulsa 35-37
	25	Florida	7-4	regular season complete
24		Bowling Green	8-2	lost to Toledo 41-49 (N23)

November 28 Poll — Dec. 4 Games

ESPN	AP	Team		Result
1	1	Southern Cal	11-0	beat UCLA 29-24
2	2	Oklahoma	11-0	beat Colorado 42-3 (Big 12 CH)
3	3	Auburn	11-0	beat #15 Tennessee 38-28 (SEC CH)
4	4	California	9-1	beat Southern Miss 26-16
6	5	Utah	11-0	
5	6	Texas	10-1	
8	7	Louisville	9-1	beat Tulane 55-7
7	8	Georgia	9-2	
9	9	Miami, Fla.	8-2	lost to #10 Virginia Tech 10-16
11	10	Virginia Tech	9-2	beat #9 Miami, Fla. 16-10
10	11	Boise State	11-0	
14	12	Iowa	9-2	
12	13	LSU	9-2	
13	14	Michigan	9-2	
15	15	Tennessee	9-2	lost to #3 Auburn 28-38 (SEC CH)
16	16	Florida State	8-3	
17	17	Wisconsin	9-2	
18	18	Virginia	8-3	
21	19	Pittsburgh	7-3	beat South Florida 43-14
19	20	Florida	7-4	
23	21	Arizona State	8-3	
25	22	Texas A&M	7-4	
	23	Boston College	8-3	
20	24	Texas Tech	7-4	
22	25	Ohio State	7-4	
24		West Virginia	8-3	

December 4 Poll / Bowl Results / January 5 Final Poll

ESPN	AP	Team	RECORD	BOWL BID	DATE	BOWL RESULT	RB	ESPN	AP	JANUARY 5 FINAL POLL	RECORD
1	1	Southern Cal	12-0	Orange Bowl	J4	beat #2 Oklahoma 55-19	1	1	1	Southern Cal	13-0
2	2	Oklahoma	12-0	Orange Bowl	J4	lost to #1 Southern Cal 19-55	2	2	2	Auburn	13-0
3	3	Auburn	12-0	Sugar Bowl	J3	beat #9 Virginia Tech 16-13	3	3	3	Oklahoma	12-1
4	4	California	10-1	Holiday Bowl	D30	lost to #23 Texas Tech 31-45	5	5	4	Utah	12-0
6	5	Utah	11-0	Fiesta Bowl	J1	beat #19 Pittsburgh 35-7	4	4	5	Texas	11-1
5	6	Texas	10-1	Rose Bowl	J1	beat #13 Michigan 38-37	8	7	6	Louisville	11-1
8	7	Louisville	10-1	Liberty Bowl	D31	beat #10 Boise State 44-40	6	6	7	Georgia	10-2
7	8	Georgia	9-2	Outback Bowl	J1	beat #16 Wisconsin 24-21	7	8	8	Iowa	10-2
9	9	Virginia Tech	10-2	Sugar Bowl	J3	lost to #3 Auburn 13-16	15	9	9	California	10-2
10	10	Boise State	11-0	Liberty Bowl	D31	lost to #7 Louisville 40-44	10	10	10	Virginia Tech	10-3
13	11	Iowa	9-2	Capital One Bowl	J1	beat #12 LSU 30-25	13	11	11	Miami, Fla.	9-3
11	12	LSU	9-2	Capital One Bowl	J1	lost to #11 Iowa 25-30	9	12	12	Boise State	11-1
12	13	Michigan	9-2	Rose Bowl	J1	lost to #6 Texas 37-38	14	15	13	Tennessee	10-3
14	14	Miami, Fla.	8-3	Peach Bowl	D31	beat #20 Florida 27-10	15	14	14	Michigan	9-3
17	15	Tennessee	9-3	Cotton Bowl	J1	beat #22 Texas A&M 38-7	19	14	15	Florida State	9-3
16	16	Wisconsin	9-2	Outback Bowl	J1	lost to #8 Georgia 21-24	12	16	16	LSU	9-3
15	17	Florida State	8-3	Gator Bowl	J1	beat West Virginia 30-18	18	18	17	Wisconsin	9-3
18	18	Virginia	8-3	MPC Computers Bowl	D27	lost to Fresno St. 34-37	17	17	18	Texas Tech	8-4
20	19	Pittsburgh	8-3	Fiesta Bowl	J1	lost to #5 Utah 7-35	21	20	19	Arizona State	9-3
19	20	Florida	7-4	Peach Bowl	D31	lost to #14 Miami, Fla. 10-27	16	19	20	Ohio State	8-4
24	21	Arizona State	8-3	Sun Bowl	D31	beat Purdue 27-23	23	21	21	Boston College	9-3
25	22	Texas A&M	7-4	Cotton Bowl	J1	lost to #15 Tennessee 7-38	46	22	22	Fresno State	9-3
21	23	Texas Tech	7-4	Holiday Bowl	D30	beat #4 California 45-31	47	23	23	Virginia	8-4
22	24	Ohio State	7-4	Alamo Bowl	D29	beat Oklahoma State 33-7	25	24	24	Navy	10-2
	25	Boston College	8-3	Continental Tire Bowl	D30	beat North Carolina 37-24	22		25	Pittsburgh	8-4
23		West Virginia	8-3	Gator Bowl	J1	lost to #17 Florida State 18-30	28	25		Florida	7-5

2004

Consensus All-Americans

POS	Offense	HT	WT	CL	School	AP	CF	FC	FN	FW
QB	Matt Leinart	6-5	225	Jr.	Southern Cal	•	•	•		
RB	Adrian Peterson	6-2	210	Fr.	Oklahoma	•	•	•	•	•
RB	J.J. Arrington	5-10	210	Sr.	California	•		•	•	•
WR	Braylon Edwards	6-3	208	Sr.	Michigan	•	•	•	•	•
WR	Taylor Stubblefield	6-1	182	Sr.	Purdue	•	•	•		•
TE	Heath Miller	6-5	255	Jr.	Virginia	•	•	•	•	•
OL	Jammal Brown	6-6	313	Sr.	Oklahoma	•	•	•	•	•
OL	Elton Brown	6-6	338	Sr.	Virginia	•	•	•	•	•
OL	David Baas	6-5	323	Sr.	Michigan	•	•		•	•
OL	Alex Barron	6-6	308	Sr.	Florida State	•	•	•	•	•
OL	Michael Munoz	6-6	315	Sr.	Tennessee	•				
OL	Ben Wilkerson	6-4	297	Sr.	LSU			•	•	
PK	Mike Nugent	5-10	180	Sr.	Ohio State	•	•	•	•	•
AP	Reggie Bush	6-0	200	So.	Southern Cal	•		•		•

Others receiving first-team honors

QB	Alex Smith		Utah				•	•
RB	Carnell Williams		Auburn				•	
RB	Cedric Benson		Texas		•			
WR	Mark Clayton		Oklahoma				•	
OL	Sam Mayes		Oklahoma State					•
OL	Chris Kemoeatu		Utah				•	
OL	Greg Eslinger		Minnesota				•	
OL	Vince Carter		Oklahoma		•			
KR	Devin Hester		Miami, Fla.		•			•

POS	Defense	HT	WT	CL	School	AP	CF	FC	FN	FW
DL	David Pollack	6-3	261	Sr.	Georgia	•	•	•	•	•
DL	Erasmus James	6-4	263	Sr.	Wisconsin	•	•	•	•	•
DL	Shaun Cody	6-4	295	Sr.	USC	•	•	•		
DL	Marcus Spears	6-4	298	Sr.	LSU	•	•	•	•	•
LB	Matt Grootegoed	5-11	215	Sr.	Southern Cal	•	•	•	•	•
LB	Derrick Johnson	6-4	235	Sr.	Texas	•	•	•	•	•
LB	A.J. Hawk	6-1	238	Jr.	Ohio State	•	•	•	•	
DB	Antrel Rolle	6-1	202	Sr.	Miami	•	•	•	•	•
DB	Marlin Jackson	6-1	196	Sr.	Michigan	•	•	•	•	•
DB	Carlos Rogers	6-1	194	Sr.	Auburn	•	•	•	•	•
DB	Ernest Shazor	6-4	229	Sr.	Michigan	•	•	•	•	
DB	Thomas Davis	6-1	230	Jr.	Georgia	•	•	•		•
P	Brandon Fields	6-6	234	So.	Michigan State	•	•	•	•	

Others receiving first-team honors

DL	Ryan Riddle		California				•	
DL	Mathias Kiwanuka		Boston College				•	
DL	Mike Patterson		Southern Cal					•
DL	Jesse Mahelona		Tennessee					•
DL	Dan Cody		Oklahoma		•			
DL	Jonathan Goddard		Marshall					•
LB	Ahmad Brooks		Virginia				•	
LB	Kevin Burnett		Tennessee					•
LB	Michael Boley		Southern Mississippi				•	
DB	Corey Webster		LSU				•	•
P	Matt Payne		Brigham Young					•

Heisman Trophy Voting

	PLAYER	POS	SCHOOL	1ST	2ND	3RD	TOTAL
1	Matt Leinart	QB	Southern Cal	267	211	102	1,325
2	Adrian Peterson	RB	Oklahoma	154	180	175	997
3	Jason White	QB	Oklahoma	171	149	146	957
4	Alex Smith	QB	Utah	98	112	117	635
5	Reggie Bush	TB	Southern Cal	118	80	83	597
6	Cedric Benson	RB	Texas	12	41	69	187
7	Jason Campbell	QB	Auburn	21	24	51	162
8	J.J. Arrington	RB	California	10	33	19	115
9	Aaron Rodgers	QB	California	8	14	15	67
10	Braylon Edwards	WR	Michigan	3	13	27	62

Award Winners

Jason White, QB, Oklahoma, Maxwell, Unitas, **Jammal Brown**, OL, Oklahoma, Outland, **Matt Leinart**, QB, Southern Cal, Camp, **David Pollack**, DE, Georgia, Lombardi, Bednarik, Hendricks, **Derrick Johnson**, LB, Texas, Butkus, **Carlos Rogers**, DB, Auburn, Thorpe, **Cedric Benson**, RB, Texas, Walker, **Mike Nugent**, K, Ohio State, Groza, **Derrick Johnson**, LB, Texas, Nagurski, **Braylon Edwards**, WR, Michigan, Biletnikoff, **Chad Owens**, AP, Hawaii, Tatupu, **Daniel Sepulveda**, P, Baylor, Guy, **Heath Miller**, TE, Virginia, Mackey, **Ben Wilkerson**, C, LSU, Rimington, **David Baas**, OL, Michigan

Bowl Games

D14, **New Orleans**, Southern Miss 31, North Texas 10, D21, **Champs Sports**, Georgia Tech 51, Syracuse 14, D22, **GMAC**, Bowling Green 52, Memphis 35, D23, **Fort Worth**, Cinncinnati 32, Marshall 14, D23, **Las Vegas**, Wyoming 24, UCLA 21, D24, **Hawaii**, Hawaii 59, UAB 40, D27, **Motor City**, Connecticut 39, Toledo 10, D27, **MPC Computers**, Fresno State 37, Virginia 34, D28, **Independence**, Iowa State 17, Miami, Ohio 13, D28, **Insight**, Oregon State 38, Notre Dame 21, D29, **Alamo**, Ohio State 33, Oklahoma State 7, D29, **Houston**, Colorado 33, UTEP 28, D30, **Continental Tire**, Boston College 37, North Carolina 24, D30, **Emerald**, Navy 34, New Mexico 19, D30, **Holiday**, Texas Tech 45, California 31, D30, **Silicon Valley Classic**, Northern Illinois 34, Troy 21, D31, **Sun**, Arizona State 27, Purdue 23, D31, **Liberty**, Louisville 44, Boise State 40, D31, **Music City**, Minnesota 20, Alabama 16, D31, **Peach**, Miami, Fla. 27, Florida 10, J1, **Outback** Georgia 24, Wisconsin 21, J1, **Cotton**, Tennessee 38, Texas A&M 7, J1, **Gator**, Florida State 30, West Virginia 18, J1, **Capital One**, Iowa 30, Louisiana State 25, J1, **Rose**, Texas 38, Michigan 37, J1, **Fiesta**, Utah 35, Pittsburgh 7, J3, **Sugar**, Auburn 16, Virginia Tech 13, J4, **Orange**, Southern Cal 55, Oklahoma 19

Conference Standings

ACC

	Conf. W	L	Overall W	L
Virginia Tech	7	1	10	3
Florida State	6	2	9	3
Miami, Fla.	5	3	9	3
Virginia	5	3	8	4
North Carolina	5	3	6	6
Clemson	4	4	6	5
Georgia Tech	4	4	7	5
North Carolina St.	3	5	5	6
Maryland	3	5	5	6
Duke	1	7	2	9
Wake Forest	1	7	4	7

Big 10

	Conf. W	L	Overall W	L
Michigan	7	1	9	3
Iowa	7	1	10	2
Wisconsin	6	2	9	3
Northwestern	5	3	6	6
Purdue	4	4	7	5
Ohio State	4	4	8	4
Michigan State	4	4	5	7
Minnesota	3	5	7	5
Penn State	2	6	4	7
Illinois	1	7	3	8
Indiana	1	7	3	8

Big 12

	Conf. W	L	Overall W	L
NORTH				
Colorado	4	4	8	5
Iowa State	4	4	7	5
Nebraska	3	5	5	6
Missouri	3	5	5	6
Kansas	2	6	4	7
Kansas State	2	6	4	7
SOUTH				
Oklahoma	8	0	12	1
Texas	7	1	11	1
Texas A&M	5	3	7	5
Texas Tech	5	3	8	4
Oklahoma State	4	4	7	5
Baylor	1	7	3	8

Championship **Oklahoma 42 Colorado 3**

Big East

	Conf. W	L	Overall W	L
Pittsburgh	4	2	8	4
Boston College	4	2	9	3
West Virginia	4	2	8	4
Syracuse	4	2	6	6
Connecticut	3	3	8	4
Rutgers	1	5	4	7
Temple	1	5	2	9

C-USA

	Conf. W	L	Overall W	L
Louisville	8	0	11	1
UAB	5	3	7	5
Cincinnati	5	3	7	5
Memphis	5	3	8	4
Southern Miss	5	3	7	5
South Florida	3	5	4	7
Houston	3	5	3	8
Tulane	3	5	5	6
TCU	3	5	5	6
East Carolina	2	6	2	9
Army	2	6	2	9

MAC

	Conf. W	L	Overall W	L
EAST				
Miami, Ohio	7	1	8	5
Akron	6	2	6	5
Marshall	6	2	6	6
Kent State	4	4	5	6
Ohio U	2	6	4	7
Buffalo	2	6	2	8
Central Florida	0	8	0	11

MAC

	Conf. W	L	Overall W	L
WEST				
Toledo	7	1	9	4
Northern Illinois	7	1	9	3
Bowling Green	6	2	9	3
Eastern Michigan	4	4	4	7
Central Michigan	3	5	4	7
Ball State	2	6	2	9
Western Michigan	0	8	1	10

Championship **Toledo 35 Miami, Ohio 27**

MWC

	Conf. W	L	Overall W	L
Utah	7	0	12	0
New Mexico	5	2	7	5
Brigham Young	4	3	5	6
Wyoming	3	4	7	5
Air Force	3	4	5	6
Colorado State	3	4	4	7
San Diego State	2	5	4	7
Nevada-Las Vegas	1	6	2	9

Pac 10

	Conf. W	L	Overall W	L
Southern Cal	8	0	13	0
California	7	1	10	2
Arizona State	5	3	9	3
Oregon State	5	3	7	5
UCLA	4	4	6	6
Oregon	4	4	5	6
Washington State	3	5	5	6
Stanford	2	6	4	7
Arizona	2	6	3	8
Washington	0	8	1	10

SEC

	Conf. W	L	Overall W	L
EAST				
Tennessee	7	1	10	3
Georgia	6	2	10	2
Florida	4	4	7	5
South Carolina	4	4	6	5
Kentucky	1	7	2	9
Vanderbilt	1	7	2	9
WEST				
Auburn	8	0	13	0
LSU	6	2	9	3
Arkansas	3	5	5	6
Alabama	3	5	6	6
Mississippi	3	5	4	7
Mississippi State	2	6	3	8

Championship **Auburn 38 Tennessee 28**

Sun Belt

	Conf. W	L	Overall W	L
North Texas	7	0	7	5
Troy State	4	2	7	5
Middle Tennessee	4	4	5	6
New Mexico State	3	2	5	6
La. Monroe	3	3	5	6
Arkansas State	3	4	3	8
Utah State	2	5	3	8
Idaho	2	5	3	9
La. Lafayette	2	5	4	7

WAC

	Conf. W	L	Overall W	L
Boise State	8	0	11	1
Texas-El Paso	6	2	8	4
Fresno State	5	3	9	3
Louisiana Tech	5	3	6	6
Hawaii	4	4	8	5
SMU	3	5	3	8
Nevada	3	5	5	7
Tulsa	3	5	4	8
Rice	2	6	3	8
San Jose State	1	7	2	9

Independents

	Overall W	L
Notre Dame	6	6
Navy	10	2

2004 NCAA Major College Statistical Leaders

Individual Leaders

PASSING	POS	CL	G	ATT	COM	PCT	INT	I%	YDS	YPA	TD	TD%	RATING
1 Stefan Lefors, Louisville	QB	SR	12	257	189	73.5	3	1.2	2596	10.1	20	7.9	181.7
2 Alex Smith, Utah	QB	JR	12	317	214	67.5	4	1.3	2952	9.3	32	10.1	176.5
3 Jason Campbell, Auburn	QB	SR	13	270	188	69.6	7	2.6	2700	10.0	20	7.4	172.9
4 Omar Jacobs, Bowling Green	QB	SO	12	462	309	66.9	4	0.9	4002	8.7	41	8.9	167.2
5 Bruce Gradkowski, Toledo	QB	JR	13	399	280	70.2	8	2.0	3518	8.8	27	6.8	162.6
6 Jason White, Oklahoma	QB	SR	13	390	255	65.4	9	2.3	3205	8.2	35	9.0	159.4
7 Matt Leinart, Southern Cal	QB	JR	13	412	269	65.3	6	1.5	3322	8.1	33	8.0	156.5
8 Aaron Rodgers, California	QB	JR	12	316	209	66.1	8	2.5	2566	8.1	24	7.6	154.3
9 Lester Ricard, Tulane	QB	SO	9	231	143	61.9	9	3.9	1881	8.1	21	9.1	152.5
10 Kyle Orton, Purdue	QB	SR	11	389	236	60.7	5	1.3	3090	7.9	31	8.0	151.1

ALL-PURPOSE	POS	CL	G	RUSH	REC	PR	KR	YDS	YPG
1 Darren Sproles, Kansas State	RB	SR	11	1318	223	34	492	2067	187.9
2 DeAngelo Williams, Memphis	RB	JR	12	1948	210	0	72	2230	185.8
3 Garrett Wolfe, Northern Illinois	RB	SO	11	1656	117	0	231	2004	182.2
4 Jamario Thomas, North Texas	RB	FR	10	1801	14	0	0	1815	181.5
5 Reggie Bush, Southern Cal	RB	SO	13	908	509	376	537	2330	179.2
6 J.J. Arrington, California	RB	SR	12	2018	121	0	0	2139	178.3
7 Cedric Benson, Texas	RB	SR	12	1834	179	0	0	2013	167.8
8 Andre Hall, South Florida	RB	JR	11	1357	149	0	332	1838	167.1
9 Jerry Seymour, Central Michigan	RB	SO	11	1284	413	0	105	1802	163.8
10 Cory Rodgers, TCU	WR	SO	11	35	836	183	723	1777	161.6

RUSHING/Yards Per Game	POS	CL	G	ATT	YDS	TD	AVG	YPG
1 Jamario Thomas, North Texas	RB	FR	10	285	1801	17	6.3	180.1
2 J.J. Arrington, California	RB	SR	12	289	2018	15	7.0	168.2
3 DeAngelo Williams, Memphis	RB	JR	12	313	1948	22	6.2	162.3
4 Cedric Benson, Texas	RB	SR	12	326	1834	19	5.6	152.8
5 Garrett Wolfe, Northern Illinois	RB	SO	11	256	1656	18	6.5	150.6
6 Adrian Peterson, Oklahoma	RB	FR	13	339	1925	15	5.7	148.1
7 Ryan Moats, Louisiana Tech	RB	JR	12	288	1774	18	6.2	147.8
8 Vernand Morency, Oklahoma State	RB	JR	11	258	1474	12	5.7	134.0
9 Andre Hall, South Florida	RB	JR	11	210	1357	11	6.5	123.4
10 Michael Hart, Michigan	RB	FR	12	282	1455	9	5.2	121.3

RUSHING/Yards Per Carry	POS	CL	G	ATT	YDS	YPC
1 Drew Stanton, Michigan State	QB	JR	10	96	687	7.2
2 J.J. Arrington, California	RB	SR	12	289	2018	7.0
3 Leon Washington, Florida State	RB	JR	10	138	951	6.9
4 Wendell Mathis, Fresno State	RB	JR	11	146	995	6.8
5 Garrett Wolfe, Northern Illinois	RB	SO	11	256	1656	6.5
5 Andre Hall, South Florida	RB	JR	11	210	1357	6.5
5 Vince Young, Texas	QB	SO	12	167	1079	6.5
8 Eric Shelton, Louisville	RB	JR	12	146	938	6.4
8 Reggie Bush, Southern Cal	RB	SO	13	143	908	6.4
10 Jamario Thomas, North Texas	RB	FR	10	285	1801	6.3

RECEIVING	POS	CL	G	REC	YDS	TD	RPG	YPG	YPG
1 Dante Ridgeway, Ball State	WR	JR	11	105	1399	8	9.6	13.3	127.2
2 Roddy White, UAB	WR	SR	12	71	1452	14	5.9	20.5	121.0
3 Mike Hass, Oregon State	WR	JR	12	86	1379	7	7.2	16.0	114.9
4 Eric Deslauriers, Eastern Michigan	WR	JR	11	84	1257	13	7.6	15.0	114.3
5 Braylon Edwards, Michigan	WR	SR	12	97	1330	15	8.1	13.7	110.8
6 Greg Lee, Pittsburgh	WR	SO	12	68	1297	10	5.7	19.1	108.1
7 Derek Hagan, Arizona State	WR	JR	12	83	1248	10	6.9	15.0	104.0
8 Greg Jennings, Western Michigan	WR	SR	11	74	1092	11	6.7	14.8	99.3
9 Chad Owens, Hawaii	WR	SR	13	102	1290	17	7.9	12.7	99.2
10 Jarrett Hicks, Texas Tech	WR	SO	12	76	1177	13	6.3	15.5	98.1

PUNTING	POS	CL	PUNT	YDS	AVG
1 Brandon Fields, Michigan State	P	JR	50	2394	47.9
2 John Torp, Colorado	P	JR	72	3351	46.5
3 Daniel Sepulveda, Baylor	P	SO	62	2850	46.0
4 Steve Weatherford, Illinois	P	JR	57	2589	45.4
5 Matt Payne, Brigham Young	K	SR	62	2808	45.3
6 Joel Stelly, La. Monroe	P	JR	62	2796	45.1
7 Bryce Benekos, Texas-El Paso	P	SR	62	2732	44.1
8 Ryan Plackemeier, Wake Forest	K	JR	64	2809	43.9
9 Tom Malone, Southern Cal	P	JR	49	2144	43.8
10 Adam Podlesh, Maryland	P	SO	63	2756	43.8

PUNT RETURNS	POS	CL	PR	YDS	TD	AVG
1 Ted Ginn Jr., Ohio State	DB	FR	15	384	4	25.6
2 Kevin Robinson, Utah State	WR	FR	17	382	2	22.5
3 Darrell Blackmon, North Carolina St.	RB	FR	12	214	1	17.8
4 Travis Williams, East Carolina	CB	FR	20	354	1	17.7
5 Domenik Hixon, Akron	WR	JR	16	275	1	17.2
6 Devin Hester, Miami, Fla.	WR	SO	19	326	3	17.2
7 Dan Sheldon, Northern Illinois	WR	SR	24	394	1	16.4
8 Roscoe Parrish, Miami, Fla.	WR	JR	20	324	2	16.2
9 Reggie Bush, Southern Cal	RB	SO	24	376	2	15.7
10 Jahmal Fenner, Texas-El Paso	DB	SR	21	324	1	15.4

KICKOFF RETURNS	POS	CL	KR	YDS	TD	AVG
1 Justin Miller, Clemson	DB	JR	20	661	2	33.1
2 Larry Taylor, Connecticut	RB	FR	12	376	1	31.3
3 Ashlan Davis, Tulsa	WR	JR	37	1131	5	30.6
4 Lance Bennett, Indiana	RB	SO	20	599	1	30.0
5 John Eubanks, Southern Miss	DB	JR	21	618	1	29.4
6 T.J. Rushing, Stanford	DB	JR	23	653	1	28.4
7 Asante White, Central Michigan	WR	FR	12	336	0	28.0
8 Will Blackmon, Boston College	DB	JR	28	762	1	27.2
9 Diamond Ferri, Syracuse	DB	SR	24	653	0	27.2
10 Pierre Thomas, Illinois	RB	SO	25	677	1	27.1

SCORING	POS	CL	TDS	XP	FG	PTS	PTPG
1 Tyler Jones, Boise State	K	SR	0	69	24	141	11.8
2 DeAngelo Williams, Memphis	RB	JR	23	0	0	138	11.5
3 Garrett Wolfe, Northern Illinois	RB	SO	21	0	0	126	11.5
4 P.J. Pope, Bowling Green	RB	JR	21	0	0	126	10.5
5 Jamario Thomas, North Texas	RB	FR	17	0	0	102	10.2
6 Chad Owens, Hawaii	WR	SR	22	0	0	132	10.2
7 Eric Shelton, Louisville	RB	JR	20	0	0	120	10.0
7 Cedric Benson, Texas	RB	SR	20	0	0	120	10.0
9 Ryan Moats, Louisiana Tech	RB	JR	19	0	0	114	9.5
10 Carlton Jones, Army	RB	JR	17	0	0	104	9.5

FIELD GOALS	POS	CL	FGA	FGM	PCT	FGG
1 Mike Nugent, Ohio State	K	SR	27	24	0.89	2.00
1 Tyler Jones, Boise State	K	SR	27	24	0.89	2.00
3 Andrew Wellock, Eastern Michigan	K	SO	23	21	0.91	1.91
4 David Rayner, Michigan State	K	SR	31	22	0.71	1.83
5 Jonathan Nichols, Mississippi	K	SR	27	20	0.74	1.82
6 Mason Crosby, Colorado	K	SO	29	23	0.79	1.77
7 Kyle Schlicher, Iowa	K	SO	26	21	0.81	1.75
8 Stephen Gostkowski, Memphis	K	JR	24	20	0.83	1.67
8 Matt Nuzie, Connecticut	K	JR	28	20	0.71	1.67
10 Brandon Pace, Virginia Tech	K	SO	27	21	0.78	1.62

INTERCEPTIONS	POS	CL	INT	YDS	TD	INT/GM
1 Charles Gordon, Kansas	CB	SO	7	52	0	0.64
1 Chris Harris, La. Monroe	DB	SR	7	11	0	0.64
3 Ko Simpson, South Carolina	DB	FR	6	94	1	0.55
4 Keon Newson, Bowling Green	DB	SR	6	107	2	0.50
4 Chris Royal, Marshall	DB	JR	6	103	1	0.50
4 Morgan Scalley, Utah	DB	SR	6	79	0	0.50
4 Brandon Payne, New Mexico	DB	SR	6	69	0	0.50
4 Kerry Rhodes, Louisville	DB	SR	6	56	1	0.50
4 Ray Henderson, Boston College	LB	JR	6	52	0	0.50
4 Mitch Meeuwsen, Oregon State	DB	SR	6	12	0	0.50

Team Leaders

RUSHING OFFENSE	G	ATT	YDS	AVG	TD	YPG
1 Rice	11	688	3372	4.9	30	306.6
2 Texas	12	615	3590	5.8	41	299.2
3 Navy	12	689	3474	5.0	36	289.5
4 Air Force	11	648	3051	4.7	32	277.4
5 Minnesota	12	572	3082	5.4	29	256.8
6 California	12	509	3081	6.1	30	256.8
7 West Virginia	12	590	3034	5.1	23	252.8
8 Louisville	12	534	3005	5.6	47	250.4
9 Virginia	12	550	2914	5.3	34	242.8
10 Michigan State	12	500	2862	5.7	22	238.5

PASSING OFFENSE	G	ATT	COM	INT	PCT	YDS	YPA	TD	I%	YPC	YPG
1 Texas Tech	12	651	426	18	65.4	4796	7.4	34	2.8	11.3	399.7
2 Hawaii	13	636	370	18	58.2	4402	6.9	38	2.8	11.9	338.6
3 Bowling Green	12	472	313	4	66.3	4057	8.6	41	0.9	13.0	338.1
4 Purdue	12	486	297	8	61.1	3854	7.9	38	1.7	13.0	321.1
5 Arizona State	12	502	289	10	57.6	3808	7.6	35	2.0	13.2	317.3
6 Rutgers	11	473	303	20	64.1	3416	7.2	19	4.2	11.3	310.5
7 Oregon State	12	532	287	17	54.0	3706	7.0	29	3.2	12.9	308.8
8 Toledo	13	449	308	10	68.6	3879	8.6	28	2.2	12.6	298.4
9 Louisville	12	359	256	5	71.3	3463	9.7	27	1.4	13.5	288.6
10 Connecticut	12	464	292	15	62.9	3376	7.3	23	3.2	11.6	281.3

TOTAL OFFENSE	G	P	YDS	AVG	TD	YPG
1 Louisville	12	893	6468	7.2	80	539.0
2 Bowling Green	12	904	6076	6.7	69	506.3
3 Utah	12	869	5997	6.9	75	499.8
4 Boise State	12	951	5912	6.2	74	492.7
5 California	12	840	5909	7.0	59	492.4
6 Texas Tech	12	944	5900	6.3	59	491.7
7 Texas	12	890	5573	6.3	55	464.4
8 Oklahoma	13	971	6007	6.2	61	462.1
9 Memphis	12	903	5524	6.1	53	460.3
10 Michigan State	12	899	5520	6.1	41	460.0

RUSHING DEFENSE	G	ATT	YDS	AVG	TD	YPG
1 Southern Cal	13	394	1032	2.6	5	79.4
2 California	12	368	990	2.7	7	82.5
3 Florida State	12	418	997	2.4	5	83.1
4 Notre Dame	12	399	1058	2.7	6	88.2
5 Iowa	12	392	1110	2.8	8	92.5
6 Oklahoma	13	402	1230	3.1	10	94.6
7 LSU	12	410	1197	2.9	7	99.8
8 Troy	12	444	1211	2.7	12	100.9
9 North Carolina St.	11	429	1126	2.6	6	102.4
10 Boise State	12	373	1247	3.3	17	103.9

PASSING DEFENSE	G	ATT	COM	PCT	INT	I%	YDS	YPA	TD	TD%	RAT
1 North Carolina St.	11	272	118	43.4	9	3.3	1309	4.8	12	4.4	91.8
2 Alabama	12	242	105	43.4	12	5.0	1357	5.6	9	3.7	92.9
3 Fresno State	12	362	185	51.1	16	4.4	2097	5.8	9	2.5	99.1
4 Penn State	11	310	175	56.5	16	5.2	1785	5.8	5	1.6	99.9
5 Wisconsin	12	369	180	48.8	11	3.0	2007	5.4	13	3.5	100.2
6 Troy	12	406	217	53.5	25	6.2	2521	6.2	9	2.2	100.6
7 Virginia Tech	13	332	180	54.2	19	5.7	1986	6.0	8	2.4	101.0
8 Oregon State	12	424	186	43.9	19	4.5	2352	5.6	25	5.9	101.0
9 Southern California	13	457	246	53.8	22	4.8	2599	5.7	13	2.8	101.3
10 LSU	12	333	160	48.1	14	4.2	1886	5.7	16	4.8	103.0

TOTAL DEFENSE	G	P	YDS	AVG	TD	YPG
1 North Carolina St.	11	701	2435	3.5	23	221.4
2 Alabama	12	726	2946	4.1	23	245.5
3 LSU	12	743	3083	4.2	25	256.9
4 Virginia Tech	13	794	3484	4.4	18	268.0
5 Auburn	13	780	3609	4.6	19	277.6
6 Southern Cal	13	851	3631	4.3	20	279.3
7 Florida State	12	798	3406	4.3	18	283.8
8 Georgia	12	747	3467	4.6	23	288.9
9 Wisconsin	12	756	3495	4.6	22	291.3
10 Penn State	11	753	3207	4.3	18	291.6

SCORING OFFENSE	G	PTS	AVG
1 Louisville	12	597	49.8
2 Boise State	12	587	48.9
3 Utah	12	544	45.3
4 Bowling Green	12	532	44.3
5 Fresno State	12	482	40.2
6 Southern Cal	13	496	38.2
7 California	12	441	36.8
8 Texas Tech	12	434	36.2
9 Hawaii	13	467	35.9
10 Memphis	12	430	35.8

SCORING DEFENSE	G	PTS	AVG
1 Auburn	13	147	11.3
2 Virginia Tech	13	167	12.8
3 Southern Cal	13	169	13.0
4 Florida State	12	169	14.1
5 Penn State	11	168	15.3
6 Wisconsin	12	185	15.4
7 Alabama	12	189	15.8
8 California	12	192	16.0
9 Georgia	12	198	16.5
10 Troy	12	200	16.7

TURNOVER MARGIN	G	FR	INT	TOT	FL	INTL	TOT	MAR
1 Southern Cal	13	16	22	38	12	7	19	1.5
2 Oklahoma State	12	15	11	26	4	5	9	1.4
3 Utah	12	13	16	29	9	5	14	1.3
3 Bowling Green	12	11	14	25	6	4	10	1.3
5 Miami, Fla.	12	14	13	27	7	6	13	1.2
6 Iowa	12	15	17	32	5	14	19	1.1
6 Pittsburgh	12	9	17	26	6	7	13	1.1
6 North Texas	12	12	14	26	9	4	13	1.1
9 Virginia Tech	13	13	19	32	10	9	19	1.0
10 Louisville	12	10	17	27	11	5	16	0.9
10 Troy	12	7	25	32	10	11	21	0.9

THE BOWLS

What follows is the most complete list of bowl game summaries ever compiled, along with—for the first time anywhere—a record of the pre- and (when available) postgame national rankings for each team. When possible, we have also included the MVPs cited in media guides, on the bowls' websites or in reported accounts of the game.

The summaries were assembled from a variety of sources, including bowl records, local libraries, newspapers, media guides, books and the Pro Football Hall of Fame (for the College All-Star Game). If a scoring summary does not appear, we were unable to piece one together through published accounts of the game.

Bowls currently certified by the NCAA are listed in chronological order based on the date of their inaugural game. Defunct bowls—excluding unsanctioned games involving lesser quality opponents or squads of servicemen—appear in alphabetical order along with the College All-Star Game, which used to pit the defending champs of pro football against a first-rate team of recent grads each summer at Soldier Field in Chicago.

The Second Season

How the Rise of the Bowls Shaped College Football

By Todd Jones

Sit in the Rose Bowl on a glorious afternoon, with the San Gabriel Mountains rising above the rim of the historic stadium …

Watch as the huge bowl slowly fills up with people, a jostling, revved, buzzing 100,000 of them, crammed together elbow to elbow in harmony as kickoff time nears …

Feel the crisp air, warm yourself in the Southern California sunshine, marvel at the surrounding colors, all as vivid as a painting by Monet …

Revel in how the grass field, a magic carpet in perfect green, sits poised to whisk you away from lingering thoughts of a cold winter …

Bask in the cleansing lightness that bathes the day from kickoff to final whistle, never relenting until the sun begins to set and deepen the hues of the afternoon shade …

Welcome the incoming darkness as, soon after game's end, it begins to surround the day, accompanied by a gentle but persistent fog that promises to transform the San Gabriel Valley into a far-off place of wonder …

Finally, walk among the exiting crowd—still jostling, still revved, still buzzing—and tilt an ear in the cool air.

You will barely, if at all, be able to hear the war drums beaten by those demanding a playoff system for Division I-A college football.

COLLEGE BOWL GAMES WERE NOT INVENTED TO determine the best team in college football.

College bowl games came into being to serve one simple goal: entice people to take midwinter vacations. The promise of fun was at their core. Organizers figured fans would travel to the host town to cheer on their favorite team, and please the local chamber of commerce by spending money during the holiday season. Sure, fans would see a good football game. But bowl games were mainly about parties and parades and pageantry and—above all—fun.

The essence of the bowl game has remained the same throughout college football's evolution, even as the number of postseason games has grown to today's bloated total of 28,

and despite the hunger for an undisputed national champion that has led to the Bowl Championship Series. The bowls have carried on, year after year, decade after decade, while their increased commercialization and financial texture have laid bare the system's venal side. Even minor bowl games, some struggling with money and attendance problems, continue to be held, their creators working against long odds to create a romantic, exciting atmosphere that will lift them to a higher place in the game's mythology.

Reality, of course, can be a cold, miserly corrective to marketing dreams. That's why bowl games come and go, and why even the ones with staying power change their first names from time to time. (The Holiday Bowl, for instance, has had five title sponsors—and counting—since its inception in 1986: Sea World, 1986-90; Thrifty Car Rental, 1991-94; Plymouth, 1995-97; Culligan, 1998-2001; and Pacific Life, since 2002.)

Still, the promise of something different—a special trip, a special game, a special brand of fun, a special celebration of the end of another special season—has been enough to weave bowls into the fabric of college football.

The Rose Bowl, first played on Jan. 1, 1902, set the gold standard of what a bowl game could and should be. Its historical success, buoyed by the eventual rise of the Sugar, Orange and Cotton Bowls, led to a second football season— lasting exactly one day—on Jan. 1. Over time, those second seasons became so ingrained that maintaining the "integrity of the bowl system" became a mantra of their proponents.

To this day, hucksters clad in garish blazers travel the country to speak of the valuable exposure, positive feelings and recruiting advantages provided to schools that agree to play in their bowls. The sales pitch is compelling, in great measure because it's so lucrative. Sponsors and television networks offer ever-growing pots of cash for the affiliation rights to the bowls.

The financial rewards vary for schools and conferences, of course, and yet all the games, at least idealistically, remain true to the spirit of their creation. They're set up to give people a reason to leave home in the middle of winter and go to a place they might not normally visit—to have fun.

The seed that would become the Rose Bowl was planted during a blizzard. Back in 1889, with New York buried in a snowstorm, two farsighted members of the Valley Hunt Club in Pasadena hit on the idea that Easterners might be persuaded to come West for some warm weather. And, once

there, perhaps they might purchase a little land. Pasadena, with a population of 5,000, was eager to grow. Dr. Francis Rowland and professor Charles Frederick Holder thought a parade featuring the beauty of blooming roses could lure people, and their money, from the colder climes to California.

The first Tournament of Roses was held in 1890. Besides a parade, the event included foot-races, tug-of-war matches, jousts and an old Spanish game called tourney of rings. The event made a profit of $229.30.

The Tournament's sports, which later included polo matches, didn't draw much attention over the next 12 years. But in the fall of 1901, the Tournament of Roses elected James Wagner as its president. He was from the East and enjoyed football. Wagner suggested holding a game, with a team from the West taking on a team from another part of the country. He reasoned that a school located in a cold climate would bring its fans along to sunny Pasadena.

Michigan coach Fielding Yost accepted an invitation to take his Wolverines to Pasadena to play California. Cal declined the offer, but Stanford accepted the challenge. On Jan. 1, 1902, the first Rose Bowl was played, although it wasn't yet known as the Rose Bowl. Michigan defeated Stanford 49-0 in the first East-West college football game before a crowd of 8,000. Stanford's players quit playing with eight minutes left. Both schools were paid $3,500 and the Tournament of Roses made a profit of $3,161.86.

Tournament officials, however, fearing Michigan's dominance would deter West Coast teams from participating, replaced the football game the following year with a chariot race. For the next 12 years, the Tournament of Roses tried chariot races, auto races, ostrich races and, in 1913, a race between an elephant and a camel. (The elephant won.) Not surprisingly, interest waned. Finally, on the eve of war, Tournament organizers returned to football.

A crowd of 7,000 saw Washington State beat Brown 14-0 in Pasadena on New Year's Day 1916. The next year, more than 25,000 turned out to see Oregon beat Penn 14-0. Crowds continued to grow each year at the football game, played at rickety Tournament Park. In response, William L. Leishman, the Tournament of Roses president, announced in 1921 that a new stadium would be built. A 57,000-seat

Bowl games were mainly about parties and parades and pageantry. And—above all— fun.

horseshoe, modeled after the Yale Bowl, was completed the following fall in an area of Pasadena called Arroyo Seco. The first football game (between California and USC) was played at the new stadium on Oct. 28, 1922. Harlan "Dusty" Hall, a sportswriter, called the new stadium the Rose Bowl.

The name stuck.

In the first New Year's Day game played in the Rose Bowl, on Jan. 1, 1923, Southern California beat Penn State 14-3. Four years later, NBC aired the first transcontinental radio broadcast of a sporting event at the Rose Bowl. A surging demand for tickets led organizers to enclose the stadium's south end, upping capacity to 76,000 for the 1928 Rose Bowl (Stanford 7, Pittsburgh 6).

Soon enough, civic boosters in other cities began to smell the roses. And in the 1930s, despite the Depression, bowls began to pop up all over the Sunbelt.

On Jan. 1, 1935, the first Orange Bowl and Sugar Bowl games were played. The Sun Bowl kicked off a year later in El Paso, Texas. The first Cotton Bowl was played in 1937. Dozens of other postseason games, not called bowls, were held during the 1930s to raise money for various charities. The Rose Bowl no longer had New Year's Day to itself.

Creation of the new bowls sparked immediate—and immediately intense—competition to attract the best teams. And nobody embodied the spirit of salesmanship driving that competition more than Earnie Seiler, the cigar-chomping, city-boosting force behind the Orange Bowl.

The Miami recreation director was known as the Mad Genius, and he lived up to his moniker during the 1938 season. The Sugar Bowl and Cotton Bowl were offering undefeated Oklahoma twice as much money as the Orange Bowl could pay. Three years earlier, the Orange Bowl had drawn just 5,134 fans (many of them talked in off the streets) in its inaugural game between Bucknell and Miami. Seiler wasn't deterred. He went to Norman, Okla., and acted like a candidate soliciting votes. He took chalk and wrote "On to Miami!" on the sidewalks. He strolled through campus with huge posters featuring photos of girls on Miami Beach. He lobbied players, coaches and school officials. And his persistence paid off. On Jan. 1, 1939, a crowd of 32,191 turned out to see Tennessee beat Oklahoma 17-0 in a game heard nationwide on CBS radio.

Soon, the Orange Bowl stadium was expanded and a way of doing business took root in the evolving bowl system. Groups such as the Mid-Winter Sports Association in New Orleans, which created and ran the Sugar Bowl, eventually gained a huge role in college football by producing matchups on New Year's Day. Men such as Jim "Hoss" Brock, boss of the Cotton Bowl, became legends. Brock once dismissed the University of Houston from consideration for the game in Dallas by saying, "I don't care if Houston is 9–0 or 99–0, they ain't going to the Cotton Bowl." The bowls, not the participants, called the shots.

The Rose Bowl, of course, led the way in controlling who would play in its game. Beginning in 1947, the Rose Bowl had an exclusive agreement with the Big Ten and Pacific Coast Conference (later to be known as the Pacific-8 and eventually the Pac-10). Other alliances between conferences and individual bowls soon followed. The Southwest Conference champion went to the Cotton Bowl to play a foe determined by Brock and his friends. The Sugar Bowl took the Southeastern Conference champ. The Big Eight sent its champ to the Orange Bowl.

A sense of familiarity developed over time in the biggest games on New Year's Day. Fans became used to seeing certain schools, and their coaches, in the same games. John McKay of USC made the Rose Bowl his home eight times. Ohio State's Woody Hayes and Michigan's Bo Schembechler would bring big, strong, physical Big Ten teams to Pasadena and often leave town muttering in defeat. Alabama coach Bear Bryant spent so much time at the Sugar Bowl that he should have been charged rent. Nebraska's Tom Osborne and Oklahoma's Barry Switzer seemed to trade off trips to the Orange Bowl. Some players even became synonymous with certain games. Archie Griffin of Ohio State started in four straight Rose Bowls. Billy Sims played in four Orange Bowls for Oklahoma.

A sense of royalty generated by the familiarity offset the occasional strain in the bowl system from the failure of lesser bowls. Many postseason games commenced and quickly withered away in the aftermath of World War II. The Gotham Bowl. The Aviation Bowl. The Cherry Bowl. The Harbor Bowl. The Dixie Bowl. The Delta Bowl. The Oil Bowl. The Raisin Bowl. And, yes, even the Salad Bowl.

New Year's Day solidified itself as a national football holiday in the post WWII era with the big four bowls: the Rose, Orange, Sugar and Cotton. In the early 1950s, television began to beam those marquee games into the nation's living rooms, eventually making them feel as much a part of the local New Year's celebrations as "Auld Lang Syne" and hangovers. In 1965, NBC scheduled the Orange Bowl in prime time and 40 million tuned in to see Texas play Alabama, led by a cannon-armed quarterback named Joe Namath.

But another fateful decision in 1965 had an even greater impact on the bowls. That year, the Associated Press began conducting its final poll vote after the bowls were played instead of before. The media and fans soon became increasingly fixated on how the New Year's Day results affected the crowning of a mythical national champion—and not everybody in the world of college football was happy about it. "It takes too much pressure when bowls are used for it," Bryant complained in 1976. "It takes all the fun out of the bowls." It was as if the old Bear could sense the passing of an age, one soon to be overwhelmed by the forthcoming corporate commercialization and creation of the domineering Bowl Coalition, then Bowl Alliance and, eventually, the BCS.

Money drove the expansion of the bowl system and its importance to schools. Notre Dame had refused to participate in bowls for 45 years, but changed its policy in 1969 as available revenues became too big to ignore. The Big Ten changed a policy too, in 1975, and allowed its members who failed to win the league title to accept invitations to bowl games besides the Rose. Michigan, which had not gone to a bowl in 1972-74 despite going 30–2–1, gladly accepted a berth in the 1976 Orange Bowl after Ohio State earned the Rose Bowl trip.

As bowl money paid to participating schools grew, so, naturally, did the cost to the games' organizers. Run as non-profit groups, they needed new ways to raise money to stage their events. The Tangerine Bowl in Orlando created a different revenue stream in 1983. It accepted money from Florida's citrus growers, renamed the game the Citrus Bowl and, in the process, created the era of title sponsorship. The Fiesta Bowl took on the name the Sunkist Fiesta Bowl in 1986, and the $1 million paid by Sunkist provided the funds necessary to propel the game into the upper echelon of bowls. The USF&G Sugar Bowl came to life two years later. The Cotton Bowl became the Mobil Cotton Bowl (and then the Southwestern Bell Cotton Bowl, and then the SBC Cotton Bowl …) and eventually the Orange Bowl became the FedEx Orange Bowl. Only the Rose Bowl among the majors holds onto its original, unsponsored name.

Lesser bowl games were also used to spread big brand names. The holidays came to be decorated with the Blockbuster Bowl, the GMAC Bowl, the Continental Tire Bowl, the Sylvania Alamo Bowl, the Poulan/Weed Eater

Independence Bowl and, for a period of time, several bowls with .com or .net in their names. By the turn of the 21st century, the number of bowls had grown to 28. A postseason system that had paid out $30.6 million in 1990 was generating $187 million in 2003. That year, the Big Ten had eight teams in bowl games, earning a total of $30.8 million. Eight teams from the Big 12 garnered $27.8 million for the conference. The Southeastern Conference took in $28.9 million with seven bowl teams in 2003.

Bowl revenues continued to escalate because of television's willingness to pay whatever it cost to broadcast a postseason game that could produce a "true" national champion. Ironically, the desire for such a clear conclusion to the season empowered critics of the bowls, who began to demand that the system be scrapped in favor of a Division I-A playoff.

The BCS is the latest attempt by college football's various power entities to appease both the bowls and playoff proponents. First came the Bowl Coalition in 1992, which included the Cotton, Fiesta, Orange and Sugar bowls, as well as five major conferences and Notre Dame. Three years later, the Bowl Coalition morphed into the Bowl Alliance, which included the Fiesta, Orange, Sugar, five conferences and Notre Dame. The system didn't produce an undisputed national champion as planned because of the Rose Bowl's alliance with the Big Ten and Pac-10. Finally, the Rose Bowl turned its back on its own tradition, allowing for the creation of the BCS before the 1998 season. The Cotton Bowl was dropped in favor of the Rose, while the Fiesta, Orange and Sugar remained part of the new format, along with the top six conferences and Notre Dame.

ABC outbid other networks for BCS rights fees, eventually signing a second deal for $900 million through 2006. Payouts for each BCS bowl reached $14-17 million, but the big checks couldn't hide the system's inherent flaws. The convoluted formula for determining the BCS teams has been "tweaked" every year in confusing attempts to appease critics.

Lower-profile conferences, in an attempt to tap into the money flow, prevailed on the Senate Judiciary Committee to hold a hearing to examine the BCS in 2003 for possible restraint-of-trade violations. The BCS offered a modest concession by creating a fifth BCS game to be played beginning in January 2007.

As the BCS debate rages, the bowl games go on and on—and on. Between Dec. 16, 2003, and Jan. 4, 2004, at least one bowl game was played every day but one. Fluctuating attendance figures, flattened or declining TV ratings and bowl teams with average records have strained the "integrity of the bowl system" while strengthening the playoff argument. Yet university presidents show no desire do away with such an integral part of college football.

And who can blame them? The bowls, after all, have produced many of the sport's most thrilling moments and showcased its most illustrious names. Wrong Way Riegels, Howard Jones, Herschel Walker … Al Hudson returning an interception 89 yards to win the Orange Bowl … O.J. Simpson and Johnny Rodgers running wild … Dan Marino beating the blitz and Joe Montana being revived by chicken soup … Nebraska going for two and losing a national title—and Alabama winning one with a furious goal-line stand … Charles White willing USC down the field, and BYU scoring 21 points in the final three minutes … Woody Hayes making his Buckeyes stay in a monastery, and Vince Dooley shaving his head to honor his Georgia defense … Sam "Bam" Cunningham over the top and Jake "The Snake" slithering through the middle … Penn State's defense rising up in the desert against Miami, and Ohio State doing the same in a double-OT game for the ages.

The bowls are John McKay saying, "We didn't come to play for a tie." The bowls are parties, parades and magical performances, played out in thrilling fashion, a canvas of color and excitement, all unfolding like game day at the Rose Bowl.

The bowls *are* college football.

ROSE BOWL

PROFILE

Site: Pasadena, Calif.
Stadium: Rose Bowl
Capacity: 92,542
Surface: Grass

PLAYING SITES

Tournament Park, Pasadena, 1902, 1916-22
Rose Bowl, 1923-41
Duke Stadium, Durham, N.C., 1942
Rose Bowl, since 1943

NAME CHANGES

Rose Bowl, 1902-1999
Rose Bowl Presented by AT&T, 1999-2002
Rose Bowl Presented by Playstation 2, 2003
Rose Bowl Presented by Citi, since 2004

SEASON	DATE	PRE-GAME RANK	TEAMS	SCORE	FINAL RANK	MOST VALUABLE PLAYERS	ATT.
1901	Jan. 1, 1902		Michigan	49		Neil Snow, Michigan, FB	8,000
			Stanford	0			
1915	Jan. 1, 1916		Washington State	14		Carl Dietz, Washington State, FB	7,000
			Brown	0			
1916	Jan. 1, 1917		Oregon	14		John Beckett, Oregon, T	26,000
			Pennsylvania	0			
1917	Jan. 1, 1918		Mare Island	19		Hollis Huntington, Mare Island, FB	NA
			Camp Lewis	7			
1918	Jan. 1, 1919		Great Lakes	17		George Halas, Great Lakes, E	NA
			Mare Island	0			
1919	Jan. 1, 1920		Harvard	7		Edward Casey, Harvard, HB	30,000
			Oregon	6			
1920	Jan. 1, 1921		California	28		Harold "Brick" Muller, California, E	42,000
			Ohio State	0			
1921	Jan. 2, 1922		California	0		Russell Stein, Washington & Jefferson, T	40,000
			Washington & Jefferson	0			
1922	Jan. 1, 1923		Southern Cal	14		Leo Calland, Southern Cal, G	43,000
			Penn State	3			
1923	Jan. 1, 1924		Navy	14		Ira McKee, Navy, QB	40,000
			Washington	14			
1924	Jan. 1, 1925		Notre Dame	27		Elmer Layden, Notre Dame, FB	53,000
			Stanford	10		Ernie Nevers, Stanford, FB	
1925	Jan. 1, 1926		Alabama	20		Johnny Mack Brown, Alabama, HB	50,000
			Washington	19		George Wilson, Washington, HB	
1926	Jan. 1, 1927		Alabama	7		Fred Pickhard, Alabama, T	57,417
			Stanford	7			
1927	Jan. 2, 1928		Stanford	7		Clifford Hoffman, Stanford, FB	65,000
			Pittsburgh	6			
1928	Jan. 1, 1929		Georgia Tech	8		Benjamin Lom, California, HB	66,604
			California	7			
1929	Jan. 1, 1930		Southern Cal	47		Russell Saunders, Southern Cal, QB	72,000
			Pittsburgh	14			
1930	Jan. 1, 1931		Alabama	24		John "Monk" Campbell, Alabama, QB	60,000
			Washington State	0			
1931	Jan. 1, 1932		Southern Cal	21		Ernie Pinckert, Southern Cal, HB	75,562
			Tulane	12			
1932	Jan. 2, 1933		Southern Cal	35		Homer Griffith, Southern Cal, QB	78,874
			Pittsburgh	0			
1933	Jan. 1, 1934		Columbia	7		Cliff Montgomery, Columbia, QB	35,000
			Stanford	0			
1934	Jan. 1, 1935		Alabama	29		Millard "Dixie" Howell, Alabama, HB	84,474
			Stanford	13			
1935	Jan. 1, 1936		Stanford	7		James "Monk" Moscrip, Stanford, E	84,474
			SMU	0		Keith Topping, Stanford, E	
1936	Jan. 1, 1937	3	Pittsburgh	21		William Daddio, Pittsburgh, E	87,196
		5	Washington	0			
1937	Jan. 1, 1938	2	California	13		Victor Bottari, California, HB	90,000
		4	Alabama	0			
1938	Jan. 2, 1939	7	Southern Cal	7		Doyle Nave, Southern Cal, QB	89,452
		3	Duke	3		Alvin Krueger, Southern Cal, E	
1939	Jan. 1, 1940	3	Southern Cal	14		Ambrose Schindler, Southern Cal, QB	92,200
		2	Tennessee	0			
1940	Jan. 1, 1941	2	Stanford	21		Peter Kmetovic, Stanford, HB	91,500
		7	Nebraska	13			
1941	Jan. 1, 1942	12	Oregon State	20		Donald Durdan, Oregon State, HB	56,000
		2	Duke	16			
1942	Jan. 1, 1943	2	Georgia	9		Charles Trippi, Georgia, HB	93,000
		13	UCLA	0			
1943	Jan. 1, 1944		Southern Cal	29		Norman Verry, Southern Cal, G	68,000
		12	Washington	0			
1944	Jan. 1, 1945	7	Southern Cal	25		James Hardy, Southern Cal, QB	91,000
		12	Tennessee	0			
1945	Jan. 1, 1946		Alabama	34		Harry Gilmer, Alabama, HB	93,000
			Southern Cal	14			
1946	Jan. 1, 1947	5	Illinois	45		Claude "Buddy" Young, Illinois, HB	90,000
		4	UCLA	14		Julius Rykovich, Illinois, HB	
1947	Jan. 1, 1948	2	Michigan	49		Robert Chappuis, Michigan, HB	93,000
		8	Southern Cal	0			
1948	Jan. 1, 1949	7	Northwestern	20		Frank Aschenbrenner, Northwestern, HB	93,000
		4	California	14			
1949	Jan. 2, 1950	6	Ohio State	17		Fred Morrison, Ohio State, FB	100,963
		3	California	14			
1950	Jan. 1, 1951	9	Michigan	14		Donald Dufek, Michigan, FB	98,939
		5	California	6			
1951	Jan. 1, 1952	7	Illinois	40		William Tate, Illinois, HB	96,825
		4	Stanford	7			
1952	Jan. 1, 1953	5	Southern Cal	7		Rudy Bukich, Southern Cal, QB	101,500
		11	Wisconsin	0			
1953	Jan. 1, 1954	3	Michigan State	28		Billy Wells, Michigan State, HB	101,000
		5	UCLA	20			
1954	Jan. 1, 1955	1	Ohio State	20		Dave Leggett, Ohio State, QB	89,191
		17	Southern Cal	7			
1955	Jan. 2, 1956	2	Michigan State	17		Walter Kowalczyk, Michigan State, HB	100,809
		4	UCLA	14			
1956	Jan. 1, 1957	3	Iowa	35		Kenneth Ploen, Iowa, QB	97,126
		10	Oregon State	19			
1957	Jan. 1, 1958	2	Ohio State	10		Jack Crabtree, Oregon, QB	98,202
			Oregon	7			
1958	Jan. 1, 1959	2	Iowa	38		Bob Jeter, Iowa, HB	98,297
		16	California	12			
1959	Jan. 1, 1960	8	Washington	44		Bob Schloredt, Washington, QB	100,809
		6	Wisconsin	8		George Fleming, Washington, HB	
1960	Jan. 2, 1961	6	Washington	17		Bob Schloredt, Washington, QB	97,314
		1	Minnesota	7			

SEASON	DATE	PRE-GAME RANK	TEAMS	SCORE	FINAL RANK	MOST VALUABLE PLAYERS	ATT.
1961	Jan. 1, 1962	6	**Minnesota**	21		Sandy Stephens, Minnesota, QB	98,214
		16	**UCLA**	3			
1962	Jan. 1, 1963	1	**Southern Cal**	42		Pete Beathard, Southern Cal, QB	98,698
		2	**Wisconsin**	37		Ron Vander Kelen, Wisconsin, QB	
1963	Jan. 1, 1964	3	**Illinois**	17		Jim Grabowski, Illinois, FB	96,957
			Washington	7			
1964	Jan. 1, 1965	4	**Michigan**	34		Mel Anthony, Michigan, FB	100,423
		8	**Oregon State**	7			
1965	Jan. 1, 1966	5	**UCLA**	14	4	Bob Stiles, UCLA, DB	100,087
		1	**Michigan State**	12	2		
1966	Jan. 2, 1967	7	**Purdue**	14		John Charles, Purdue, DB	100,807
			Southern Cal	13			
1967	Jan. 1, 1968	1	**Southern Cal**	14		O.J. Simpson, Southern Cal, TB	102,946
		4	**Indiana**	3			
1968	Jan. 1, 1969	1	**Ohio State**	27	1	Rex Kern, Ohio State, QB	102,063
		2	**Southern Cal**	16	4		
1969	Jan. 1, 1970	5	**Southern Cal**	10	3	Bob Chandler, Southern Cal, FL	103,878
		7	**Michigan**	3	9		
1970	Jan. 1, 1971	12	**Stanford**	27	8	Jim Plunkett, Stanford, QB	103,839
		2	**Ohio State**	17	5		
1971	Jan. 1, 1972	16	**Stanford**	13	10	Don Bunce, Stanford, QB	103,154
		4	**Michigan**	12	6		
1972	Jan. 1, 1973	1	**Southern Cal**	42	1	Sam Cunningham, Southern Cal, FB	106,869
		3	**Ohio State**	17	9		
1973	Jan. 1, 1974	4	**Ohio State**	42	2	Cornelius Greene, Ohio State, QB	105,267
		7	**Southern Cal**	21	8		
1974	Jan. 1, 1975	5	**Southern Cal**	18	2	Pat Haden, Southern Cal, QB	106,721
		3	**Ohio State**	17	4	John McKay Jr., Southern Cal, SE	
1975	Jan. 1, 1976	11	**UCLA**	23	5	John Sciarra, UCLA, QB	105,464
		1	**Ohio State**	10	4		
1976	Jan. 1, 1977	3	**Southern Cal**	14	2	Vince Evans, Southern Cal, QB	106,182
		2	**Michigan**	6	3		
1977	Jan. 2, 1978	13	**Washington**	27	10	Warren Moon, Washington, QB	105,312
		4	**Michigan**	20	9		
1978	Jan. 1, 1979	3	**Southern Cal**	17	2	Charles White, Southern Cal, TB	105,629
		5	**Michigan**	10	5	Rick Leach, Michigan, QB	
1979	Jan. 1, 1980	3	**Southern Cal**	17	2	Charles White, Southern Cal, TB	105,526
		1	**Ohio State**	16	4		
1980	Jan. 1, 1981	5	**Michigan**	23	4	Butch Woolfolk, Michigan, RB	104,863
		16	**Washington**	6	16		
1981	Jan. 1, 1982	12	**Washington**	28	10	Jacque Robinson, Washington, RB	105,611
		13	**Iowa**	0	18		
1982	Jan. 1, 1983	5	**UCLA**	24	5	Don Rogers, UCLA, FS	104,991
		19	**Michigan**	14		Tom Ramsey, UCLA, QB	
1983	Jan. 2, 1984		**UCLA**	45	17	Rick Neuheisel, UCLA, QB	103,217
		4	**Illinois**	9	10		
1984	Jan. 1, 1985	18	**Southern Cal**	20	10	Tim Green, Southern Cal, QB	102,594
		6	**Ohio State**	17	13	Jack Del Rio, Southern Cal, LB	
1985	Jan. 1, 1986	13	**UCLA**	45	7	Eric Ball, UCLA, TB	103,292
		4	**Iowa**	28	10		
1986	Jan. 1, 1987	7	**Arizona State**	22	4	Jeff Van Raaphorst, Arizona State, QB	103,168
		4	**Michigan**	15	8		
1987	Jan. 1, 1988	8	**Michigan State**	20	8	Percy Snow, Michigan State, LB	103,847
		16	**Southern Cal**	17	18		
1988	Jan. 2, 1989	11	**Michigan**	22	4	Leroy Hoard, Michigan, FB	101,688
		5	**Southern Cal**	14	7		
1989	Jan. 1, 1990	12	**Southern Cal**	17	8	Ricky Ervins, Southern Cal, TB	103,450
		3	**Michigan**	10	7		
1990	Jan. 1, 1991	8	**Washington**	46	2	Mark Brunell, Washington, QB	101,273
		17	**Iowa**	34	18		
1991	Jan. 1, 1992	2	**Washington**	34	2	Steve Emtman, Washington, DT	103,566
		4	**Michigan**	14	6	Billy Joe Hobert, Washington, QB	
1992	Jan. 1, 1993	7	**Michigan**	38	5	Tyrone Wheatley, Michigan, RB	94,236
		9	**Washington**	31	11		
1993	Jan. 1, 1994	9	**Wisconsin**	21	6	Brent Moss, Wisconsin, TB	101,237
		14	**UCLA**	16	18		
1994	Jan. 2, 1995	2	**Penn State**	38	2	Danny O'Neil, Oregon, QB	102,247
		12	**Oregon**	20	11	Ki-Jana Carter, Penn State, RB	
1995	Jan. 1, 1996	3	**Southern Cal**	41	8	Keyshawn Johnson, Southern Cal, WR	100,102
		17	**Northwestern**	32	12		
1996	Jan. 1, 1997	4	**Ohio State**	20	2	Joe Germaine, Ohio State, QB	100,635
		2	**Arizona State**	17	4		
1997	Jan. 1, 1998	1	**Michigan**	21	1	Brian Griese, Michigan, QB	101,219
		8	**Washington State**	16	9		
1998	Jan. 1, 1999	9	**Wisconsin**	38	6	Ron Dayne, Wisconsin, RB	93,872
		6	**UCLA**	31	8		
1999	Jan. 1, 2000	4	**Wisconsin**	17	4	Ron Dayne, Wisconsin, RB	93,731
		22	**Stanford**	9			
2000	Jan. 1, 2001	4	**Washington**	34	3	Marques Tuiasosopo, Washington, QB	94,392
		14	**Purdue**	24	13		
2001	Jan. 3, 2002	1	**Miami (Fla.)**	37	1	Ken Dorsey, Miami, QB	93,781
		4	**Nebraska**	14	8	Andre Johnson, Miami, WR	
2002	Jan. 1, 2003	8	**Oklahoma**	34	5	Nate Hybl, Oklahoma, QB	86,848
		7	**Washington State**	14	10		
2003	Jan. 1, 2004	1	**Southern Cal**	28	1	Matt Leinart, Southern Cal, QB	93,849
		4	**Michigan**	14	6		
2004	Jan. 1, 2005	6	**Texas**	38	5	Vince Young, Texas, QB	93,465
		13	**Michigan**	37	14		

JANUARY 1, 1902
MICHIGAN 49, STANFORD 0

	1ST	2ND	3RD	4TH	FINAL
MICH	0	17	0	32	49
STAN	0	0	0	0	0

SCORING SUMMARY

MICH	FG Sweely 20
MICH	Redden 25 punt return (Short kick)
MICH	Snow 2 run (kick failed)
MICH	Redden 25 fumble return (Short kick)
MICH	Snow 8 run (kick failed)
MICH	Snow 17 run (kick failed)
MICH	Snow 4 run (Short kick)
MICH	Herrenstein 21 run (kick failed)

MICH	TEAM STATISTICS	STAN
27	First Downs	5
527	Rushing Yards	67
21-38.9	Punts - Average	16-34.9
1	Fumbles Lost	9
10	Penalty Yards	15

JANUARY 1, 1916
WASHINGTON STATE 14, BROWN 0

	1ST	2ND	3RD	4TH	FINAL
WSU	0	0	7	7	14
Brown	0	0	0	0	0

SCORING SUMMARY

WSU	Boone 3 run (Durham kick)
WSU	Dietz 4 run (Durham kick)

WSU	TEAM STATISTICS	BROWN
19	First Downs	6
313	Rushing Yards	74
0-2-2	Passing	1-3-1
0	Passing Yards	12
313	Total Yards	86
7-37.0	Punts - Average	13-29.3
2	Fumbles Lost	1
55	Penalty Yards	10

JANUARY 1, 1917
OREGON 14, PENNSYLVANIA 0

	1ST	2ND	3RD	4TH	FINAL
ORE	0	0	7	7	14
PENN	0	0	0	0	0

SCORING SUMMARY

ORE	Tegert 15 pass from Huntington (Huntington kick)
ORE	Huntington 1 run (Huntington kick)

ORE	TEAM STATISTICS	PENN
13	First Downs	8
111	Rushing Yards	198
12-27-5	Passing	2-9-2
131	Passing Yards	32
242	Total Yards	230
10-41.8	Punts - Average	16-35.7
1-1	Fumbles - Lost	1-1
6-95	Penalties - Yards	4-37

JANUARY 1, 1918
MARE ISLAND 19, CAMP LEWIS 7

	1ST	2ND	3RD	4TH	FINAL
MARE	0	9	0	10	19
CL	0	7	0	0	7

SCORING SUMMARY

MARE	FG Ambrose 31
CL	Romney 6 run (Sharpe kick)
MARE	Brown 5 run (Kick failed)
MARE	Huntington 1 run (Ambrose kick)
MARE	FG Ambrose 33

MARE	TEAM STATISTICS	CL
12	First Downs	9
224	Rushing Yards	115
3-6-0	Passing	1-3-0
49	Passing Yards	6
273	Total Yards	121
6-36.0	Punts - Average	6-34.6
1	Fumbles Lost	1
30	Penalty Yards	5

JANUARY 1, 1919
GREAT LAKES 17, MARE ISLAND 0

	1ST	2ND	3RD	4TH	FINAL
GL	3	7	7	0	17
MARE	0	0	0	0	0

SCORING SUMMARY

GL	FG Driscoll 30
GL	Reeves 3 run (Blacklock kick)
GL	Halas 32 pass from Driscoll (kick good)

GL	TEAM STATISTICS	MARE
8	First Downs	9
71	Rushing Yards	119
6-13-1	Passing	4-21-5
120	Passing Yards	66
191	Total Yards	185
12-34.0	Punts - Average	13-33.5
1	Fumbles Lost	1
55	Penalty Yards	0

JANUARY 1, 1920
HARVARD 7, OREGON 6

	1ST	2ND	3RD	4TH	FINAL
HAR	0	7	0	0	7
ORE	0	6	0	0	6

SCORING SUMMARY

ORE	FG Steers 25
HAR	Church 13 run (Horween kick)
ORE	FG Manerud 30

HAR	TEAM STATISTICS	ORE
9	First Downs	18
146	Rushing Yards	272
4-6-0	Passing	0-2-0
59	Passing Yards	0
205	Total Yards	272
8-28.9	Punts - Average	7-30.8
3-2	Fumbles - Lost	3-1
4-34	Penalties - Yards	5-59

INDIVIDUAL LEADERS

RUSHING
HAR: Horween 19-75.
ORE: Huntington 29-122; Steers 15-75 1 TD.

PASSING
HAR: Murray 2-2-0, 40 yards.

JANUARY 1, 1921
CALIFORNIA 28, OHIO STATE 0

	1ST	2ND	3RD	4TH	FINAL
CAL	7	14	0	7	28
OSU	0	0	0	0	0

SCORING SUMMARY

CAL	Sprott 1 run (Toomey kick)
CAL	Stephens 37 pass from Muller (Toomey kick)
CAL	Sprott 5 run (Erb kick)
CAL	Deeds 1 run (Toomey kick)

CAL	TEAM STATISTICS	OSU
17	First Downs	11
244	Rushing Yards	105
6-9-1	Passing	11-24-4
102	Passing Yards	133
346	Total Yards	238
10-37.6	Punts - Average	7-43.3
52	Penalty Yards	0

INDIVIDUAL LEADERS

RUSHING
CAL: Sprott 20-94, 2 TD; Toomey 7-61.
OSU: Stinchcomb 11-82; Blair 6-11.

JANUARY 2, 1922
CALIFORNIA 0, WASH & JEFF 0

	1ST	2ND	3RD	4TH	FINAL
CAL	0	0	0	0	0
W&J	0	0	0	0	0

CAL	TEAM STATISTICS	W&J
2	First Downs	8
49	Rushing Yards	114
2-6-1	Passing	1-4-1
0	Passing Yards	23
49	Total Yards	137
13-39.1	Punts - Average	15-27.1
2-2	Fumbles - Lost	3-3
30	Penalty Yards	25

JANUARY 1, 1923
SOUTHERN CAL 14, PENN STATE 3

	1ST	2ND	3RD	4TH	FINAL
USC	0	7	7	0	14
PSU	3	0	0	0	3

SCORING SUMMARY

PSU	FG Palm 20
USC	Campbell 1 run (Hawkins kick)
USC	Baker 1 run (Hawkins kick)

USC	TEAM STATISTICS	PSU
13	First Downs	5
254	Rushing Yards	98
6-12-1	Passing	5-11-3
39	Passing Yards	6
293	Total Yards	104
6-1	Fumbles - Lost	2-1
3-35	Penalties - Yards	2-10

INDIVIDUAL LEADERS

RUSHING
USC: Baker 29-123, 1 TD; Campbell 17-52, 1 TD.
PSU: Wilson 20-55; Palm 16-25.

PASSING
USC: Galloway 1-3-1, 23 yards.
PSU: Wilson 2-5-0, 5 yards.

RECEIVING
USC: Pythian 1-23; Campbell 2-8.
PSU: Palm 2-5; Wilson 3-1.

JANUARY 1, 1924
NAVY 14, WASHINGTON 14

	1ST	2ND	3RD	4TH	FINAL
NAVY	0	14	0	0	14
WASH	0	7	0	7	14

SCORING SUMMARY

NAVY	Cullen 20 pass from McKee (McKee kick)
WASH	Wilson 14 run (Sherman kick)
NAVY	Cullen 7 pass from McKee (McKee kick)
WASH	Bryan 12 pass from Abel (Sherman kick)

NAVY	TEAM STATISTICS	WASH
15	First Downs	9
187	Rushing Yards	137
16-20-2	Passing	3-8-2
175	Passing Yards	65
362	Total Yards	202
5-33.8	Punts - Average	9-33.0
0-0	Fumbles - Lost	0-0
2-10	Penalties - Yards	4-20

JANUARY 1, 1925
NOTRE DAME 27, STANFORD 10

	1ST	2ND	3RD	4TH	FINAL
ND	0	13	7	7	27
STAN	3	0	7	0	10

SCORING SUMMARY

STAN	FG Cuddeback 27
ND	Layden 3 run (kick failed)
ND	Layden 78 interception return (Crowley kick)
ND	Hunsinger 20 fumble return (Crowley kick)
STAN	Shipkey 7 pass from Walker (Cuddeback kick)
ND	Layden 70 interception return (Crowley kick)

ND	TEAM STATISTICS	STAN
7	First Downs	17
130	Rushing Yards	178
3-7-3	Passing	12-17-5
56	Passing Yards	138
186	Total Yards	316
48.5	Punt Returns - Yards	42.5
1	Fumbles Lost	3
4-30	Penalties - Yards	1-15

JANUARY 1, 1926
ALABAMA 20, WASHINGTON 19

	1ST	2ND	3RD	4TH	FINAL
ALA	0	0	20	0	20
WASH	6	6	0	7	19

SCORING SUMMARY
WASH Paton 1 run (kick failed)
WASH Cole 20 pass from Wilson (kick failed)
ALA Hubert 8 run (Buckler kick)
ALA Brown 61 pass from Hubert (Buckler kick)
ALA Brown 5 run (kick failed)
WASH Guttormsen 27 pass from Wilson (Cook kick)

ALA	TEAM STATISTICS	WASH
15	First Downs	13
220	Rushing Yards	220
4-14-3	Passing	7-16-2
141	Passing Yards	94
361	Total Yards	314
5-40.8	Punts - Average	6-37.5
0-0	Fumbles - Lost	1-1
0-0	Penalties - Yards	1-15

INDIVIDUAL LEADERS
RUSHING
ALA: Hubert 15-97, 1 TD; Brown 12-76, 1 TD.
WASH: Wilson 15-139; Paton 11-43, 1 TD.

JANUARY 1, 1927
ALABAMA 7, STANFORD 7

	1ST	2ND	3RD	4TH	FINAL
ALA	0	0	0	7	7
STAN	7	0	0	0	7

SCORING SUMMARY
STAN Walker 20 pass from Bogue (Bogue kick)
ALA Johnson 1 run (Caldwell kick)

ALA	TEAM STATISTICS	STAN
6	First Downs	12
83	Rushing Yards	134
6-14-2	Passing	13-17-1
9	Passing Yards	177
92	Total Yards	311
8-32.6	Punts - Average	6-32.2
2	Fumbles Lost	3
5	Penalty Yards	55

JANUARY 2, 1928
STANFORD 7, PITTSBURGH 6

	1ST	2ND	3RD	4TH	FINAL
STAN	0	0	7	0	7
PITT	0	0	6	0	6

SCORING SUMMARY
PITT Hagen 20 fumble return (kick failed)
STAN Wilton 3 pass from Hoffman (Hoffman kick)

STAN	TEAM STATISTICS	PITT
14	First Downs	7
171	Rushing Yards	121
3-13-3	Passing	2-13-2
35	Passing Yards	22
206	Total Yards	143
6-48.0	Punts - Average	9-45.0
1	Fumbles Lost	1
5-52	Penalties - Yards	8-82

JANUARY 1, 1929
GEORGIA TECH 8, CALIFORNIA 7

	1ST	2ND	3RD	4TH	FINAL
GT	0	2	6	0	8
CAL	0	0	0	7	7

SCORING SUMMARY
GT Saftey
GT R. Thomason 14 run (kick failed)
CAL Phillips 10 pass from Lom (Barr kick)

GT	TEAM STATISTICS	CAL
5	First Downs	11
166	Rushing Yards	204
1-3-0	Passing	4-12-1
23	Passing Yards	67
189	Total Yards	271
12-31.1	Punts - Average	12-35.7
2	Fumbles Lost	2
35	Penalty Yards	10

JANUARY 1, 1930
SOUTHERN CAL 47, PITTSBURGH 14

	1ST	2ND	3RD	4TH	FINAL
USC	13	13	14	7	47
PITT	0	0	7	7	14

USC	TEAM STATISTICS	PITT
10	First Downs	7
146	Rushing Yards	220
8-16-3	Passing	4-19-3
279	Passing Yards	87
425	Total Yards	307
2-2	Fumbles - Lost	4-2

INDIVIDUAL LEADERS
RUSHING
USC: Saunders 21-64.
PITT: Toby Uansa 11-84.

JANUARY 1, 1931
ALABAMA 24, WASHINGTON STATE 0

	1ST	2ND	3RD	4TH	FINAL
ALA	0	21	3	0	24
WSU	0	0	0	0	0

SCORING SUMMARY
ALA Suther 62 pass from Moore (Campbell kick)
ALA Campbell 1 run (Campbell kick)
ALA Campbell 43 run (Campbell kick)
ALA FG Whitworth 40

ALA	TEAM STATISTICS	WSU
9	First Downs	11
261	Rushing Yards	145
2-7-0	Passing	7-17-3
98	Passing Yards	71
359	Total Yards	216
11-40.1	Punts - Average	12-37.0
2-1	Fumbles - Lost	3-2

INDIVIDUAL LEADERS
RUSHING
ALA: Campbell 12-109, 2 TD; Holley 6-45.
WSU: Lainhart 7-70; Schwartz 12-42.

JANUARY 1, 1932
SOUTHERN CAL 21, TULANE 12

	1ST	2ND	3RD	4TH	FINAL
USC	0	7	14	0	21
TUL	0	0	6	6	12

SCORING SUMMARY
USC Sparling 6 run (Baker kick)
USC Pinckert 28 run (Baker kick)
USC Pinckert 23 run (Baker kick)
TUL Haynes 7 pass from Zimmerman (kick blocked)
TUL Glover 3 run (pass failed)

USC	TEAM STATISTICS	TUL
9	First Downs	18
183	Rushing Yards	280
1-6-2	Passing	5-19-2
23	Passing Yards	61
206	Total Yards	341
2-1	Fumbles - Lost	3-2
4-20	Penalties - Yards	6-30

INDIVIDUAL LEADERS
RUSHING
USC: Shaver 14-73; Pinckert 5-63, 2 TD.
TUL: Glover 13-123, 1TD; Zimmerman 21-92.

JANUARY 2, 1933
SOUTHERN CAL 35, PITTSBURGH 0

	1ST	2ND	3RD	4TH	FINAL
USC	7	0	7	21	35
PITT	0	0	0	0	0

SCORING SUMMARY
USC Palmer 35 pass from Griffith (Smith kick)
USC Griffith 2 pass from Bright (Smith kick)
USC Warburton 6 interception return (Smith kick)
USC Warburton 10 run (Smith kick)
USC Barber 2 run (Lady kick)

USC	TEAM STATISTICS	PITT
18	First Downs	8
156	Rushing Yards	82
2-4-0	Passing	4-14-2
35	Passing Yards	50
201	Total Yards	132
8-41	Punts - Average	7-39
1-0	Fumbles - Lost	3-3
3-25	Penalties - Yards	3-25

INDIVIDUAL LEADERS
RUSHING
USC: Warburton 18-76, 1TD; Sparling 6-56.
PITT: Weisenbaugh 2-32; Heller 13-24.

JANUARY 1, 1934
COLUMBIA 7, STANFORD 0

	1ST	2ND	3RD	4TH	FINAL
COLU	0	7	0	0	7
STAN	0	0	0	0	0

SCORING SUMMARY
COLU Barabas 17 run (Wilder kick)

COLU	TEAM STATISTICS	STAN
6	First Downs	16
76	Rushing Yards	227
1-2-0	Passing	2-12-1
28	Passing Yards	45
104	Total Yards	272
14-37.0	Punts - Average	9-36.0
4-2	Fumbles - Lost	7-2
4-20	Penalties - Yards	8-70

JANUARY 1, 1935
ALABAMA 29, STANFORD 13

	1ST	2ND	3RD	4TH	FINAL
STAN	7	0	6	0	13
ALA	0	22	0	7	29

SCORING SUMMARY
STAN Grayson 1 run (Moscrip kick)
ALA Howell 5 run (kick failed)
ALA FG Smith 27
ALA Howell 67 run (Smith kick)
ALA Huston 46 pass from Riley (kick failed)
STAN VanDellen 12 run
ALA Huston 59 pass from Howell (Smith good)

STAN	TEAM STATISTICS	ALA
14	First Downs	12
204	Rushing Yards	167
5-23-4	Passing	10-13-1
86	Passing Yards	216
290	Total Yards	383
6-38.0	Punts - Average	6-44.0
0	Fumbles Lost	4
4-40	Penalties - Yards	4-40

JANUARY 1, 1936
STANFORD 7, SMU 0

	1ST	2ND	3RD	4TH	FINAL
STAN	7	0	0	0	7
SMU	0	0	0	0	0

SCORING SUMMARY
STAN Paulman 1 run (Moscrip kick)

STAN	TEAM STATISTICS	SMU
6	First Downs	9
75	Rushing Yards	38
2-6-1	Passing	11-31-6
42	Passing Yards	105
117	Total Yards	143
16-38.0	Punts - Average	9-39.0
3-0	Fumbles - Lost	1-1
4-25	Penalties - Yards	1-20

INDIVIDUAL LEADERS
RUSHING
STAN: Grayson 17-28; Hamilton 15-23.
SMU: Wilson 11-23; Shuford 5-12.

JANUARY 1, 1937
PITTSBURGH 21, WASHINGTON 0

	1ST	2ND	3RD	4TH	FINAL
PITT	7	0	7	7	21
WASH	0	0	0	0	0

SCORING SUMMARY
PITT Patrick 1 run (Daddio kick)
PITT Patrick 5 run (Daddio kick)
PITT Daddio 71 interception (Daddio kick)

PITT	TEAM STATISTICS	WASH
11	First Downs	8
254	Rushing Yards	57
2-4-2	Passing	7-18-4
46	Passing Yards	96
300	Total Yards	153
5-39.6	Punts - Average	6-29.7
1-0	Fumbles - Lost	0-0
2-20	Penalties - Yards	0-0

INDIVIDUAL LEADERS
RUSHING
PITT: LaRue 15-109; Patrick 11-42, 2 TD.
WASH: Haines 8-26.

JANUARY 1, 1938
CALIFORNIA 13, ALABAMA 0

	1ST	2ND	3RD	4TH	FINAL
CAL	0	7	6	0	13
ALA	0	0	0	0	0

SCORING SUMMARY
CAL   Bottari 3 run (Chapman kick)
CAL   Bottari 4 run (kick failed)

CAL	TEAM STATISTICS	ALA
10	First Downs	11
192	Rushing Yards	140
2-9-2	Passing	3-12-4
16	Passing Yards	40
208	Total Yards	180

INDIVIDUAL LEADERS
RUSHING
CAL: Bottari 32-146, 2 TD; Chapman 12-65.
ALA: Holm 14-60; Kilgrow 16-50.

JANUARY 2, 1939
SOUTHERN CAL 7, DUKE 3

	1ST	2ND	3RD	4TH	FINAL
USC	0	0	0	7	7
DUKE	0	0	0	3	3

SCORING SUMMARY
DUKE   FG Ruffa 23
USC   Krueger 19 pass from Nave (Gaspar kick)

USC	TEAM STATISTICS	DUKE
13	First Downs	8
135	Rushing Yards	86
13-31-2	Passing	6-13-1
84	Passing Yards	53
219	Total Yards	139
16-40.8	Punts - Average	15-40.5

INDIVIDUAL LEADERS
RUSHING
USC: Lansdell 12-97; Anderson 6-27.
DUKE: Tipton 16-65; O'Mara 8-19.

JANUARY 1, 1940
SOUTHERN CAL 14, TENNESSEE 0

	1ST	2ND	3RD	4TH	FINAL
USC	0	7	0	7	14
TENN	0	0	0	0	0

SCORING SUMMARY
USC   Schindler 1 run (Jones kick)
USC   Krueger 1 pass from Schindler (Gaspar kick)

USC	TEAM STATISTICS	TENN
18	First Downs	9
229	Rushing Yards	71
7-14-1	Passing	6-14-2
43	Passing Yards	70
272	Total Yards	141
8-40.1	Punts - Average	11-39.2
1-0	Fumbles - Lost	1-1

INDIVIDUAL LEADERS
RUSHING
USC: Schindler 19-75, 1 TD; Lansdell 18-68.
TENN: Butler 5-40; Coffman 3-15.

JANUARY 1, 1941
STANFORD 21, NEBRASKA 13

	1ST	2ND	3RD	4TH	FINAL
STAN	7	7	7	0	21
NEB	7	6	0	0	13

SCORING SUMMARY
NEB   Francis 2 run (Francis kick)
STAN   Gallarneau 10 run (Albert kick)
NEB   Zikmund 33 pass from Rohrig (kick blocked)
STAN   Gallarneau 40 pass from Albert (Albert kick)
STAN   Kmetovic 40 punt return (Albert kick)

STAN	TEAM STATISTICS	NEB
14	First Downs	9
254	Rushing Yards	56
7-14-1	Passing	3-14-4
98	Passing Yards	72
352	Total Yards	128
35	Punts - Average	37
2	Fumbles Lost	0
58	Penalty Yards	28

INDIVIDUAL LEADERS
RUSHING
STAN: Kmetovic 14-129; Gallarneau 17-84, 1 TD.
NEB: Francis 9-51, 1 TD; Hopp 5-15.

JANUARY 1, 1942
OREGON STATE 20, DUKE 16

	1ST	2ND	3RD	4TH	FINAL
OSU	7	0	13	0	20
DUKE	0	7	7	2	16

SCORING SUMMARY
OSU   Durdan 15 run (Simas kick)
DUKE   Lach 4 run (Gantt kick)
OSU   Zellick 31 pass from Dethman (Simas kick)
DUKE   Siegfried 1 run (Prothro kick)
OSU   Gray 68 pass from Dethman (kick failed)
DUKE   Saftey

OSU	TEAM STATISTICS	DUKE
14	First Downs	15
154	Rushing Yards	222
5-15-2	Passing	5-16-4
148	Passing Yards	73
302	Total Yards	295
47.8	Punts - Average	46.4
1-1	Fumbles - Lost	3-3
2-20	Penalties - Yards	3-25

INDIVIDUAL LEADERS
RUSHING
OSU: Durdan 17-43, 1 TD; Dethman 11-42.
DUKE: Lach 12-124, 1 TD; Davis 12-80.
PASSING
OSU: Dethman 6-7-0, 148 yards, 2 TD.
DUKE: Rute 3-8-1, 81 yards.
RECEIVING
OSU: Gray 1-68, 1 TD; Zellick 1-32, 1 TD.
DUKE: Gantt 4-93; Smith 1-18.

JANUARY 1, 1943
GEORGIA 9, UCLA 0

	1ST	2ND	3RD	4TH	FINAL
UGA	0	0	0	9	9
UCLA	0	0	0	0	0

SCORING SUMMARY
UGA   Saftey blocked punt
UGA   Sinkwich 1 run (Costa kick)

UGA	TEAM STATISTICS	UCLA
24	First Downs	5
212	Rushing Yards	97
12-30-2	Passing	4-15-4
161	Passing Yards	62
373	Total Yards	159

INDIVIDUAL LEADERS
RUSHING
UGA: Trippi 27-115; Sinkwich 11-33, 1 TD.
UCLA: Snelling 5-41.

JANUARY 1, 1944
SOUTHERN CAL 29, WASHINGTON 0

	1ST	2ND	3RD	4TH	FINAL
USC	0	7	13	9	29
WASH	0	0	0	0	0

SCORING SUMMARY
USC   Callahan 11 pass from Hardy (Jamison kick)
USC   Callahan 10 pass from Hardy (Jamison kick)
USC   Gray 21 pass from Hardy (kick failed)
USC   Saftey
USC   Gray 15 pass from Bell (Jamison kick)

USC	TEAM STATISTICS	WASH
8	First Downs	7
117	Rushing Yards	134
9-16-0	Passing	5-22-3
113	Passing Yards	51
230	Total Yards	185
10-37.5	Punts - Average	7-35.9
2-0	Fumbles - Lost	2-0
3-25	Penalties - Yards	1-10

INDIVIDUAL LEADERS
RUSHING
USC: Callahan 6-46; Saenz 10-26.
WASH: Akins 9-41; Robinson 9-35.

JANUARY 1, 1945
SOUTHERN CAL 25, TENNESSEE 0

	1ST	2ND	3RD	4TH	FINAL
TENN	0	0	0	0	0
USC	6	6	0	13	25

SCORING SUMMARY
USC   Callahan 11 blocked punt (kick failed)
USC   Salata 19 pass from Hardy (kick failed)
USC   Hardy 9 run (West kick)
USC   MacLachan 7 run (kick failed)

TENN	TEAM STATISTICS	USC
8	First Downs	15
152	Rushing Yards	262
3-14-1	Passing	5-15-0
17	Passing Yards	43
169	Total Yards	305
13-32.2	Punts - Average	11-32.6
2-1	Fumbles - Lost	1-1
5-35	Penalties - Yards	4-25

INDIVIDUAL LEADERS
RUSHING
TENN: Stephens 15-89; Manning 5-28.
USC: Burnside 13-114.

JANUARY 1, 1946
ALABAMA 34, SOUTHERN CAL 14

	1ST	2ND	3RD	4TH	FINAL
ALA	7	13	7	7	34
USC	0	0	0	14	14

ALA	TEAM STATISTICS	USC
18	First Downs	3
292	Rushing Yards	6
4-12-1	Passing	2-11-2
59	Passing Yards	35
351	Total Yards	41
4-19.5	Punts - Average	6-48.0
3-1	Fumbles - Lost	6-3
5-35	Penalties - Yards	3-15

INDIVIDUAL LEADERS
RUSHING
ALA: Gilmer 16-116, 1 TD; Corbitt 8-48.
USC: Tannehill 7-15; Morris 5-8.
PASSING
ALA: Gilmer 4-12-1, 59 yards.
USC: Lillywhite 1-6-1, 20 yards, 1 TD.

JANUARY 1, 1947
ILLINOIS 45, UCLA 14

	1ST	2ND	3RD	4TH	FINAL
ILL	6	19	0	20	45
UCLA	7	7	0	0	14

SCORING SUMMARY
ILL   Rykovich 1 run (kick failed)
UCLA   Case 1 run (Case kick)
ILL   Young 2 run (Maechtle kick)
ILL   Patterson 4 run (kick failed)
ILL   Moss 1 run (kick blocked)
UCLA   Hoisch 100 kick return (Case kick)
ILL   Young 1 run (Maechtle kick)
ILL   Steger 68 interception return (kick failed)
ILL   Green 81 interception return (Maechtle kick)

ILL	TEAM STATISTICS	UCLA
23	First Downs	12
320	Rushing Yards	62
4-15-2	Passing	13-29-4
78	Passing Yards	176
398	Total Yards	238

INDIVIDUAL LEADERS
RUSHING
ILL: Young 20-103, 2 TD; Rykovich 18-103, 1 TD.
UCLA: Hoisch 4-27; Rossi 10-25.
PASSING
ILL: Moss 3-8-0, 85 yards.
UCLA: Case 11-24-2, 165 yards.
RECEIVING
ILL: Rykovich 1-44; Huber 2-21.
UCLA: Baldwin 3-57; Dobrow 2-28.

JANUARY 1, 1948
MICHIGAN 49, SOUTHERN CAL 0

	1ST	2ND	3RD	4TH	FINAL
MICH	7	14	7	21	49
USC	0	0	0	0	0

SCORING SUMMARY

MICH	Weisenburger 1 run (Brieske kick)
MICH	Weisenburger 1 run (Brieske kick)
MICH	Elliott 11 pass from Chappuis (Brieske kick)
MICH	Yerges 18 pass from Chappuis (Brieske kick)
MICH	Weisenburger 1 run (Brieske kick)
MICH	Derricotte 45 pass from Fonde (Brieske kick)
MICH	Rifenburg 29 pass from Yerges (Brieske kick)

MICH	TEAM STATISTICS	USC
21	First Downs	10
268	Rushing Yards	91
17-27-1	Passing	6-11-1
223	Passing Yards	42
491	Total Yards	133
4-38.3	Punts - Average	8-43.8
2-1	Fumbles - Lost	4-2
4-40	Penalties - Yards	1-10

INDIVIDUAL LEADERS

RUSHING
MICH: Weisenburger 20-91, 3 TD; Chappuis 13-91.
USC: Garlin 5-25.

PASSING
MICH: Chappuis 14-24-0, 139 yards, 2 TD.
USC: Powers 4-5-0, 22 yards.

JANUARY 1, 1949
NORTHWESTERN 20, CALIFORNIA 14

	1ST	2ND	3RD	4TH	FINAL
NU	7	6	0	7	20
CAL	7	0	7	0	14

SCORING SUMMARY

NU	Aschenbrenner 73 run (Farrar kick)
CAL	Jensen 67 run (Cullom kick)
NU	Marakowski 1 run (kick failed)
CAL	Swaner run (Cullom kick)
NU	Tunnicliff 43 run (Farrar kick)

NU	TEAM STATISTICS	CAL
6	First Downs	12
273	Rushing Yards	173
1-4-0	Passing	6-16-4
17	Passing Yards	83
290	Total Yards	256
6-43.0	Punts - Average	4-33.0
3-2	Fumbles - Lost	3-1
3-15	Penalties - Yards	2-5

INDIVIDUAL LEADERS

RUSHING
NU: Aschenbrenner 11-119, 1 TD.
CAL: Swaner 17-79, 1 TD.

PASSING
NU: Aschenbrenner 1-1-0, 17 yards.
CAL: Celeri 3-8-2, 50 yards.

JANUARY 2, 1950
OHIO STATE 17, CALIFORNIA 14

	1ST	2ND	3RD	4TH	FINAL
CAL	0	7	7	0	14
OSU	0	0	14	3	17

CAL	TEAM STATISTICS	OSU
11	First Downs	19
133	Rushing Yards	221
3-13-4	Passing	4-13-1
106	Passing Yards	34
239	Total Yards	255
5-25.4	Punts - Average	4-39.8
0-0	Fumbles - Lost	4-1
9-45	Penalties - Yards	7-50

INDIVIDUAL LEADERS

RUSHING
CAL: Monachino 14-90; Brunk 9-38.
OSU: Morrison 24-127; Krall 24-50.

PASSING
CAL: Celeri 3-11-3, 106 yards.
OSU: Krall 3-8-0, 20 yards.

JANUARY 1, 1951
MICHIGAN 14, CALIFORNIA 6

	1ST	2ND	3RD	4TH	FINAL
MICH	0	0	0	14	14
CAL	0	6	0	0	6

SCORING SUMMARY

CAL	Cummings 39 pass from Marinos (kick failed)
MICH	Dufek 1 run (Allis kick)
MICH	Dufek 7 run (Allis kick)

MICH	TEAM STATISTICS	CAL
17	First Downs	12
145	Rushing Yards	175
15-21-2	Passing	4-8-0
146	Passing Yards	69
291	Total Yards	244
2-32.5	Punts - Average	4-35.7
2-2	Fumbles - Lost	2-2
2-20	Penalties - Yards	6-50

INDIVIDUAL LEADERS

RUSHING
MICH: Dufek 23-113, 2 TD; Koceski 7-19.
CAL: Olszewski 16-58; Schabarum 15-57.

PASSING
MICH: Ortmann 15-19-1, 146 yards.
CAL: Marinos 4-7-0, 69 yards, 1 TD.

JANUARY 1, 1952
ILLINOIS 40, STANFORD 7

	1ST	2ND	3RD	4TH	FINAL
ILL	6	0	7	27	40
STAN	7	0	0	0	7

SCORING SUMMARY

ILL	Bachourus 6 run (kick failed)
STAN	Hugasian 1 run (Kerkorian kick)
ILL	Tate 5 run (Rebecca kick)
ILL	Karras 8 run (Rebecca kick)
ILL	Tate 8 run (Rebecca kick)
ILL	Stevens 7 run (kick blocked)
ILL	Ryan 6 pass from Engels (Rebecca kick)

ILL	TEAM STATISTICS	STAN
19	First Downs	16
361	Rushing Yards	53
7-15-1	Passing	14-29-3
73	Passing Yards	180
434	Total Yards	233
2-10	Punt Returns - Yards	0-0
2-28	Kickoff Returns - Yards	7-88
2-50.1	Punts - Average	6-30.3
0-0	Fumbles - Lost	2-0
4-43	Penalties - Yards	6-50

INDIVIDUAL LEADERS

RUSHING
ILL: Tate 20-150, 2 TD; Bachouros 15-86.
STAN: Hugasian 14-41, 1 TD.

PASSING
ILL: O'Connell 6-14-1, 67yards.
STAN: Kerkorian 11-22-2, 166 yards.

RECEIVING
ILL: Bachouros 3-36.
STAN: McColl 4-62; Hugasian 4-49.

JANUARY 1, 1953
SOUTHERN CAL 7, WISCONSIN 0

	1ST	2ND	3RD	4TH	FINAL
WISC	0	0	0	0	0
USC	0	0	7	0	7

SCORING SUMMARY

USC	Carmichael 22 pass from Bukich (Tsagalakis kick)

WISC	TEAM STATISTICS	USC
19	First Downs	16
211	Rushing Yards	48
11-26-2	Passing	18-27-2
142	Passing Yards	185
353	Total Yards	233
5-39.2	Punts - Average	8-51.4
2-1	Fumbles - Lost	1-0
2-20	Penalties - Yards	6-62

INDIVIDUAL LEADERS

RUSHING
WISC: Ameche 28-133; Witt 10-47.
USC: Haw 6-28; Dandoy 5-18.

PASSING
WISC: Haluska 11-26-2, 142 yards.
USC: Bukich 12-20-2, 137, yards, 1 TD.

RECEIVING
WISC: Witt 2-46; Andrykowski 3-32.
USC: Nickoloff 7-73; Stillwell 3-35.

JANUARY 1, 1954
MICHIGAN STATE 28, UCLA 20

	1ST	2ND	3RD	4TH	FINAL
MSU	0	7	14	7	28
UCLA	7	7	0	6	20

SCORING SUMMARY

UCLA	Stits 13 pass from Cameron (Hermann kick)
UCLA	Cameron 2 run (Hermann kick)
MSU	Duckett 6 blocked punt return (Slonac kick)
MSU	Bolden 1 run (Slonac kick)
MSU	Wells 2 run (Slonac kick)
UCLA	Loudd 28 pass from Cameron (kick failed)
MSU	Wells 62 punt return (Slonac kick)

MSU	TEAM STATISTICS	UCLA
14	First Downs	16
195	Rushing Yards	90
2-10-1	Passing	9-24-2
11	Passing Yards	152
206	Total Yards	242
5-80	Punt Returns - Yards	3-31
4-60	Kickoff Returns - Yards	4-100
5-35.4	Punts - Average	6-38.7
4-4	Fumbles - Lost	4-3
2-15	Penalties - Yards	4-30

INDIVIDUAL LEADERS

RUSHING
MSU: Wells 14-80-1; Bolden 14-52, 1 TD.
UCLA: Stits 5-25; davenport 8-22.

PASSING
MSU: Yewcic 2-8-1, 11 yards.
UCLA: Cameron 9-22-1, 152 yards, 2 TD.

RECEIVING
MSU: Bolden 1-18.
UCLA: Stits 2-46, 1 TD; Heydenfeldt 1-33.

JANUARY 1, 1955
SOUTHERN CAL 7, OHIO STATE 20

	1ST	2ND	3RD	4TH	FINAL
USC	0	7	0	0	7
OSU	0	14	0	6	20

SCORING SUMMARY

OSU	Leggett 3 run (Weed kick)
OSU	Watkins 21 pass from Leggett (Watkins good)
USC	Dandoy 86 punt return
OSU	Harkrader 9 run

USC	TEAM STATISTICS	OSU
6	First Downs	22
177	Rushing Yards	295
3-8-0	Passing	6-11-1
29	Passing Yards	63
206	Total Yards	358
5-46.4	Punts - Average	4-38.2
3	Fumbles Lost	0
60	Penalty Yards	40

INDIVIDUAL LEADERS

RUSHING
USC: Arnett 9-123; Duvall 5-23.
OSU: Cassady 21-92; Leggett 16-67, 1 TD.

PASSING
USC: Hall 1-4-0, 23 yards.
OSU: Leggett 6-11-1, 63 yards, 1 TD.

RECEIVING
USC: Bordier 1-23.
OSU: Watkins 3-43.

THE BOWLS

JANUARY 2, 1956

MICHIGAN STATE 17, UCLA 14

	1ST	2ND	3RD	4TH	FINAL
MSU	0	7	0	10	17
UCLA	7	0	0	7	14

SCORING SUMMARY

UCLA	Davenport 2 run (Decker kick)
MSU	Peaks 13 pass from Morrall (Planutis kick)
MSU	Lewis 67 yard pass from Peaks (Planutis kick)
UCLA	Peters 1 run (Decker kick)
MSU	FG Kaiser 41

MSU	TEAM STATISTICS	UCLA
18	First Downs	13
251	Rushing Yards	136
6-18-2	Passing	2-10-2
130	Passing Yards	61
381	Total Yards	197
6-8	Punt Returns - Yards	2-12
3-61	Kickoff Returns - Yards	2-58
2-40.0	Punts - Average	7-39.6
4-1	Fumbles - Lost	2-0
10-98	Penalties - Yards	8-60

INDIVIDUAL LEADERS

RUSHING
MSU: Kowalczyk 13-88; Planutis 12-66.
UCLA: Brown 14-63; Davenport 10-26, 1 TD.

PASSING
MSU: Morrall 4-15-2, 38 yards, 1 TD.
UCLA: Knox 2-8-1, 61 yards.

RECEIVING
MSU: Lewis 1-67, 1 TD; Peaks 3-40, 1 TD.
UCLA: Decker 1-47; Loudd 1-14.

JANUARY 1, 1957

IOWA 35, OREGON STATE 19

	1ST	2ND	3RD	4TH	FINAL
IA	14	7	7	7	35
OSU	0	6	6	7	19

SCORING SUMMARY

IA	Ploen 49 run (Prescott kick)
IA	Hagler 9 run (Prescott kick)
OSU	Berry 3 run (kick failed)
IA	Happel 5 run (Prescott kick)
IA	Hagler 66 run (Prescott kick)
OSU	Beamer 1 run (kick failed)
IA	Gibbons 16 pass from Ploen (Prescott kick)
OSU	Hammack 35 pass from Francis (Beamer run)

IA	TEAM STATISTICS	OSU
16	First Downs	16
301	Rushing Yards	166
11-15-1	Passing	10-14-0
107	Passing Yards	130
408	Total Yards	296
2-36.0	Punts - Average	3-35.0
3-3	Fumbles - Lost	4-3
5-50	Penalties - Yards	6-60

INDIVIDUAL LEADERS

RUSHING
IA: Hagler 10-85, 2 TD; Dobrino 4-64.
OSU: Francis 15-73; Beamer 7-31, 1 TD.

PASSING
IA: Ploen 9-10-0, 83 yards, 1 TD.
OSU: Francis 10-12-0, 130 yards, 1 TD.

RECEIVING
IA: Gibbons 5-61, 1 TD; Harris 2-21.
OSU: Hammack 4-65, 1 TD; Beamer 2-31.

JANUARY 1, 1958

OHIO STATE 10, OREGON 7

	1ST	2ND	3RD	4TH	FINAL
ORE	0	7	0	0	7
OSU	0	0	0	3	10

SCORING SUMMARY

OSU	Kremblas 1 run (Kremblas kick)
ORE	Shanley 5 run (Morris kick)
OSU	FG Sutherlin 34

ORE	TEAM STATISTICS	OSU
21	First Downs	19
160	Rushing Yards	245
14-21-2	Passing	2-6-0
191	Passing Yards	59
351	Total Yards	304
0-0	Punts - Average	2-19.0
3-2	Fumbles - Lost	0-0
3-25	Penalties - Yards	3-15

INDIVIDUAL LEADERS

RUSHING
ORE: Morris 11-60; Shanley 11-59, 1 TD.
OSU: White 25-93; Clark 14-82.

PASSING
ORE: Crabtree 10-17-2, 135 yards.
OSU: Kremblas 2-6-0, 59 yards.

RECEIVING
ORE: Stover 10-144; Tourville 2-27.
OSU: Houston 2-59.

JANUARY 1, 1959

IOWA 38, CALIFORNIA 12

	1ST	2ND	3RD	4TH	FINAL
IA	7	13	12	6	38
CAL	0	0	6	6	12

SCORING SUMMARY

IA	Duncan 2 run (Prescott kick)
IA	Langston 7 pass from Duncan (Prescott kick)
IA	Horn 4 run (kick failed)
CAL	Hart 1 run (pass failed)
IA	Fleming 37 run (pass failed)
IA	Jeter 81 run (pass failed)
IA	Fleming 7 run (pass failed)
CAL	Hart 17 pass from Kapp (run failed)

IA	TEAM STATISTICS	CAL
24	First Downs	20
429	Rushing Yards	214
9-14-0	Passing	9-20-2
87	Passing Yards	130
516	Total Yards	344
3-41.0	Punts - Average	5-37.0
3-1	Fumbles - Lost	2-2
5-55	Penalties - Yards	5-35

INDIVIDUAL LEADERS

RUSHING
IA: Jeter 9-194, 1 TD; Fleming 9-85, 2 TD.
CAL: Olguin 9-62; Patton 9-45.

PASSING
IA: Ogiego 4-5-0, 37 yards.
CAL: Kapp 8-17-1, 126 yards, 1 TD.

RECEIVING
IA: Prescott 3-31.
CAL: Hart 4-61, 1TD; Garvin 1-31.

JANUARY 1, 1960

WASHINGTON 44, WISCONSIN 8

	1ST	2ND	3RD	4TH	FINAL
WISC	0	8	0	0	8
WASH	17	7	7	13	44

SCORING SUMMARY

WASH	McKeta 6 run (Fleming kick)
WASH	FG Fleming 36
WASH	Fleming 53 punt return (Fleming kick)
WISC	Wiesner 4 run (Schoonover pass from Hackbart)
WASH	Folkins 23 pass from Schloredt (Fleming kick)
WASH	Jackson 2 run (Fleming kick)
WASH	Schloredt 3 run (Fleming kick)
WASH	Millich 1 pass from Hivner (pass failed)

WISC	TEAM STATISTICS	WASH
13	First Downs	16
123	Rushing Yards	215
14-32-0	Passing	7-13-0
153	Passing Yards	137
276	Total Yards	352
6-36.8	Punts - Average	6-36.0
4-4	Fumbles - Lost	2-0
3-18	Penalties - Yards	7-85

INDIVIDUAL LEADERS

RUSHING
WISC: Hobbs 7-32.
WASH: Schloredt 21-81, 1 TD; Jackson 12-61, 1 TD.

PASSING
WISC: Hackbart 11-25-0, 145 yards.
WASH: Schloredt 4-7-0, 102 yards, 1 TD.

RECEIVING
WISC: Schoonover 3-57.
WASH: Fleming 1-65.

JANUARY 2, 1961

WASHINGTON 17, MINNESOTA 7

	1ST	2ND	3RD	4TH	FINAL
WASH	3	14	0	0	17
MINN	0	0	7	0	7

SCORING SUMMARY

WASH	FG Fleming 34
WASH	Wooten 4 pass from Schloredt (Fleming kick)
WASH	Schloredt 1 run (Fleming kick)
MINN	Munsey 18 run (Rogers kick)

WASH	TEAM STATISTICS	MINN
11	First Downs	14
177	Rushing Yards	202
2-5-0	Passing	5-18-3
16	Passing Yards	51
193	Total Yards	253
3-2	Fumbles - Lost	0-0
6-50	Penalties - Yards	3-35

INDIVIDUAL LEADERS

RUSHING
WASH: Schloredt 5-68, 1 TD; Jackson 13-60.
MINN: Stephens 10-51; Hagberg 11-44.

PASSING
WASH: Schloredt 2-4-0, 16 yards, 1 TD.
MINN: Stephens 2-10-3, 21 yards.

RECEIVING
WASH: Jackson 1-12; Wooten 1-4, 1 TD.
MINN: Hagberg 1-18; Hall 1-15.

JANUARY 1, 1962

MINNESOTA 21, UCLA 3

	1ST	2ND	3RD	4TH	FINAL
MINN	7	7	0	7	21
UCLA	3	0	0	0	3

SCORING SUMMARY

UCLA	FG Smith 28
MINN	Stephens 1 run (Loechler kick)
MINN	Munsey 3 run (Loechler kick)
MINN	Stephens 2 run (Loechler kick)

MINN	TEAM STATISTICS	UCLA
21	First Downs	8
222	Rushing Yards	55
7-11-0	Passing	5-8-0
75	Passing Yards	52
297	Total Yards	107
3-2	Fumbles - Lost	2-2
6-70	Penalties - Yards	1-5

INDIVIDUAL LEADERS

RUSHING
MINN: Stephens 12-46, 2 TD; Dickson 12-45.
UCLA: Alexander 10-48.

PASSING
MINN: Stephens 7-11-0, 75 yards.
UCLA: Smith 2-5-0, 22 yards.

RECEIVING
MINN: Cairns 2-24.
UCLA: Alexander 3-26.

January 1, 1963
Southern Cal 42, Wisconsin 37

	1st	2nd	3rd	4th	FINAL
WISC	7	0	7	23	37
USC	7	14	14	7	42

SCORING SUMMARY
USC — Butcher 13 pass from Beathard (Lupo kick)
WISC — Kurek 1 run (Kroner kick)
USC — Wilson 1 run (Lupo kick)
USC — Heller 25 run (Lupo kick)
USC — Bedsole 57 pass from Beathard (Lupo kick)
WISC — Vander Kelen 17 run (Kroner kick)
USC — Bedsole 23 pass from Beathard (Lupo kick)
USC — Hill 13 pass from Beathard (Lupo Kick)
WISC — Holland 13 run (Kroner kick)
WISC — Kroner 4 pass from Vander Kelen (Kroner kick)
WISC — Safety
WISC — Richter 18 pass from Vander Kelen (Kroner kick)

WISC	TEAM STATISTICS	USC
32	First Downs	15
67	Rushing Yards	114
34-49-3	Passing	10-20-0
419	Passing Yards	253
486	Total Yards	367
4-40.3	Punts - Average	5-40.4
6-0	Fumbles - Lost	2-2
7-77	Penalties - Yards	12-93

INDIVIDUAL LEADERS
RUSHING
WISC: Vander Kelen 9-30, 1 TD; Holland 4-27, 1 TD.
USC: Wilson 17-57, 1 TD; Heller 4-32, 1 TD.
PASSING
WISC: Vander Kelen 33-48-3, 401 yards, 2 TD.
USC: Beathard 8-12-0, 190 yards, 4 TD.
RECEIVING
WISC: Richter 11-163, 1 TD; Holland 8-72.
USC: Brown 3-108; Bedsole 4-101, 2 TD.

January 1, 1964
Illinois 17, Washington 7

	1st	2nd	3rd	4th	FINAL
ILL	0	3	7	7	17
WASH	0	7	0	0	7

SCORING SUMMARY
WASH — Kopay 7 run (Medved kick)
ILL — FG Plankenhorn 32
ILL — Warren 2 run (Plankenhorn kick)
ILL — Grabowski 10 run (Plankenhorn kick)

ILL	TEAM STATISTICS	WASH
22	First Downs	12
291	Rushing Yards	114
6-15-0	Passing	8-19-3
59	Passing Yards	69
350	Total Yards	183
5-3	Fumbles - Lost	5-3
6-64	Penalties - Yards	5-25

INDIVIDUAL LEADERS
RUSHING
ILL : Grabowski 23-125, 1 TD; Price 10-55.
WASH: Kopay 4-29, 1TD.
PASSING
ILL : Custardo 4-7-0, 43 yards.
WASH: Siler 6-17-3, 46 yards.
RECEIVING
ILL : Fearn 3-24.
WASH: Libke 3-19.

January 1, 1965
Michigan 34, Oregon State 7

	1st	2nd	3rd	4th	FINAL
MICH	0	12	15	7	34
OSU	0	7	0	0	7

SCORING SUMMARY
OSU — McDougal 5 pass from Brothers (Clark kick)
MICH — Anthony 84 run (kick failed)
MICH — Ward 43 run (pass failed)
MICH — Anthony 1 run (Timberlake run)
MICH — Anthony 7 run (Timberlake kick)
MICH — Timberlake 24 run (Timberlake kick)

MICH	TEAM STATISTICS	OSU
18	First Downs	14
332	Rushing Yards	64
8-11-0	Passing	19-33-0
83	Passing Yards	179
415	Total Yards	243
5-33.6	Punts - Average	9-43.5
2-1	Fumbles - Lost	1-1
6-55	Penalties - Yards	5-57

INDIVIDUAL LEADERS
RUSHING
MICH: Anthony 13-123, 3 TD; Ward 10-88, 1 TD.
OSU: Shaw 4-28; Watkins 8-24.
PASSING
MICH: Timberlake 7-10-0, 77 yards.
OSU: Brothers 9-17-0, 89 yards, 1 TD; Queen 10-16-0, 90 yards.
RECEIVING
MICH: Henderson 4-34; Defuller 1-30.
OSU: Watkins 3-43; Grim 3-42.

January 1, 1966
UCLA 14, Michigan State 12

	1st	2nd	3rd	4th	FINAL
MSU	0	0	0	12	12
UCLA	0	14	0	0	14

SCORING SUMMARY
UCLA — Beban 1 run (Zimmerman kick)
UCLA — Beban 1 run (Zimmerman kick)
MSU — Apisa 38 run (pass failed)
MSU — Juday 1 run (run failed)

MSU	TEAM STATISTICS	UCLA
13	First Downs	10
204	Rushing Yards	65
8-22-3	Passing	8-20-0
110	Passing Yards	147
314	Total Yards	212
4-3	Punt Returns - Yards	2-2
2-23	Kickoff Returns - Yards	3-49
5-42.4	Punts - Average	11-39.9
3-2	Fumbles - Lost	3-2
1-14	Penalties - Yards	9-86

INDIVIDUAL LEADERS
RUSHING
MSU: Jones 20-113; Apisa 4-49, 1 TD.
UCLA: Farr 10-36; Beban 25-14, 2 TD.
PASSING
MSU: Steve Juday 6-18-3, 80 yards.
UCLA: Gary Beban 8-20-0, 147 yards.
RECEIVING
MSU: Washington 4-81; Lee 3-23.
UCLA: Altenberg 3-55; Nelson 2-29.

January 2, 1967
Purdue 14, Southern Cal 13

	1st	2nd	3rd	4th	FINAL
PU	0	7	7	0	14
USC	0	7	0	6	13

SCORING SUMMARY
PU — Williams 1 run (Griese kick)
USC — McCall 1 run (Russovich kick)
PU — Williams 2 run (Griese kick)
USC — Sherman 19 pass from Winslow (pass failed)

PU	TEAM STATISTICS	USC
11	First Downs	18
105	Rushing Yards	149
10-18-0	Passing	12-17-0
139	Passing Yards	174
244	Total Yards	323
4-38.75	Punts - Average	3-34.00
1-1	Fumbles - Lost	2-2
2-10	Penalties - Yards	2-16

INDIVIDUAL LEADERS
RUSHING
PU: Williams 20-61, 2 TD; Baltzell 11-25.
USC: McCall 22-92, 1 TD; Hull 7-53.
PASSING
PU: Griese 10-18-0, 139 yards.
USC: Winslow 12-17-0, 174 yards, 1 TD.
RECEIVING
PU: Beirne 4-69; Hurst 2-27.
USC: Sherman 7-102, 1 TD; Lawrence 3-52.

January 1, 1968
Southern Cal 14, Indiana 3

	1st	2nd	3rd	4th	FINAL
IND	0	3	0	0	3
USC	7	0	7	0	14

SCORING SUMMARY
USC — Simpson 2 run (Aldridge kick)
IND — FG Koronwa 17
USC — Simpson 3 run (Aldridge kick)

IND	TEAM STATISTICS	USC
13	First Downs	20
79	Rushing Yards	248
9-25-1	Passing	5-9-1
110	Passing Yards	69
189	Total Yards	317
4-41.0	Punts - Average	4-41.3
2-1	Fumbles - Lost	3-1
4-29	Penalties - Yards	8-65

INDIVIDUAL LEADERS
RUSHING
IND: Isenbarger 12-38; Cole 10-21.
USC: Simpson 25-128, 2 TD; Scott 18-85.
PASSING
IND: Gonso 9-25-1, 110 yards.
USC: Sogge 4-7-1, 57 yards.
RECEIVING
IND: Gage 6-67; Butcher 3-43.
USC: Rake 3-46.

January 1, 1969
Ohio State 27, Southern Cal 16

	1st	2nd	3rd	4th	FINAL
OSU	0	10	3	14	27
USC	0	10	0	6	16

SCORING SUMMARY
USC — FG Ayala 21
USC — Simpson 80 run (Ayala kick)
OSU — Otis 1 run (Roman kick)
OSU — FG Roman 26
OSU — FG Roman 25
OSU — Hayden 4 pass from Kern (Roman kick)
OSU — Gillian 16 pass from Kern (Roman kick)
USC — Dickerson 19 pass from Sogge (pass failed)

OSU	TEAM STATISTICS	USC
21	First Downs	19
260	Rushing Yards	177
9-15-0	Passing	19-32-2
101	Passing Yards	189
361	Total Yards	366
7-45.6	Punts - Average	6-36.9
1-0	Fumbles - Lost	3-3
6-53	Penalties - Yards	3-51

INDIVIDUAL LEADERS
RUSHING
OSU: Otis 30-101, 1 TD; Hayden 15-90.
USC: Simpson 28-171, 1 TD.
PASSING
OSU: Kern 9-15-0, 101 yards, 2 TD.
USC: Sogge 19-30-1, 189 yards, 1 TD.
RECEIVING
OSU: Gillian 4-69, 1 TD; White 1-17.
USC: Simpson 8-85; Dickerson 3-50, 1 TD.

January 1, 1970
Southern Cal 10, Michigan 3

	1st	2nd	3rd	4th	FINAL
USC	3	0	7	0	10
MICH	0	3	0	0	3

SCORING SUMMARY
USC — FG Ayala 25
MICH — FG Killian 20
USC — Chandler 33 pass from Jones (Ayala kick)

USC	TEAM STATISTICS	MICH
16	First Downs	20
195	Rushing Yards	162
10-17-0	Passing	14-32-1
128	Passing Yards	127
323	Total Yards	289
5-40.6	Punts - Average	6-36.2
2-0	Fumbles - Lost	1-0
6-38	Penalties - Yards	2-20

INDIVIDUAL LEADERS
RUSHING
USC: Davis 15-76; Berry 23-65.
MICH: Moorhead 18-60; Taylor 18-56.
PASSING
USC: Jones 10-17-0, 128 yards, 1 TD.
MICH: Moorhead 14-32-1, 127 yards.
RECEIVING
USC: Chandler 3-78, 1 TD; Debrah 3-27.
MICH: Mandich 8-79; Oldham 2-19.

JANUARY 1, 1971
STANFORD 27, OHIO STATE 17

	1ST	2ND	3RD	4TH	FINAL
STAN	10	0	3	14	27
OSU	7	7	3	0	17

SCORING SUMMARY

STAN	Brown 4 run (Horowitz kick)
STAN	FG Horowitz 37
OSU	Brockington 1 run (Schram kick)
OSU	Brockington 1 run (Schram kick)
STAN	FG Horowitz 48
OSU	FG Schram 32
STAN	Brown 1 run (Horowitz kick)
STAN	Vataha 10 pass from Plunkett (Horowitz kick)

STAN	TEAM STATISTICS	OSU
21	First Downs	22
143	Rushing Yards	380
20-30-1	Passing	7-20-1
265	Passing Yards	75
408	Total Yards	455
3-33	Punts - Average	2-28
3-2	Fumbles - Lost	2-0
3-46	Penalties - Yards	6-64

INDIVIDUAL LEADERS

RUSHING
STAN: Brown 10-41, 2 TD; Cross 1-41.
OSU: Kern 20-129; Brockington 21-101, 2 TD.

PASSING
STAN: Plunkett 20-30-1, 265 yards, 1 TD.
OSU: Kern 4-13-1, 40 yards.

RECEIVING
STAN: Moore 5-113; Washington 6-80.
OSU: White 4-28; Zelina 2-27.

JANUARY 1, 1972
STANFORD 13, MICHIGAN 12

	1ST	2ND	3RD	4TH	FINAL
STAN	0	0	3	10	13
MICH	0	3	0	9	12

SCORING SUMMARY

MICH	FG Coin 30
STAN	FG Garcia 42
MICH	Seyferth 1 run (Coin kick)
STAN	Brown 24 run (Garcia kick)
MICH	Safety
STAN	FG Garcia 31

STAN	TEAM STATISTICS	MICH
22	First Downs	16
93	Rushing Yards	264
24-44-0	Passing	3-11-1
290	Passing Yards	26
383	Total Yards	290
4-30	Punt Returns - Yards	2-14
3-35	Kickoff Returns - Yards	5-108
4-41.5	Punts - Average	7-38.9
4-4	Fumbles - Lost	2-1
3-14	Penalties - Yards	2-23

INDIVIDUAL LEADERS

RUSHING
STAN: Brown 6-60, 1 TD; Sanderson 5-16.
MICH: Taylor 32-82; Shuttlesworth 13-62.

PASSING
STAN: Bunce 24-44-0, 290 yards.
MICH: Slade 3-10-1, 26 yards.

RECEIVING
STAN: Winesberry 8-112; Scott 5-55.
MICH: Doughty 2-13; Seymour 1-13.

JANUARY 1, 1973
SOUTHERN CAL 42, OHIO STATE 17

	1ST	2ND	3RD	4TH	FINAL
OSU	0	7	3	7	17
USC	7	0	21	14	42

SCORING SUMMARY

USC	Swann 10 pass from Rae (Roe kick)
OSU	Keith 1 run (Conway kick)
USC	Cunningham 2 run (Roe kick)
OSU	FG Conway 21
USC	Davis 20 run (Roe kick)
USC	Cunningham 1 run (Roe kick)
USC	Cunningham 1 run (Roe kick)
USC	Cunningham 1 run (Roe kick)
OSU	Bledsoe 5 run (Conway kick)

OSU	TEAM STATISTICS	USC
21	First Downs	24
285	Rushing Yards	207
5-11-2	Passing	19-27-0
81	Passing Yards	244
366	Total Yards	451
5-36.2	Punts - Average	4-41.3
2-1	Fumbles - Lost	2-1
2-7	Penalties - Yards	6-48

INDIVIDUAL LEADERS

RUSHING
OSU: Griffin 20-95; Keith 15-59, 1 TD.
USC: Davis 23-157, 1 TD; Cunningham 11-38, 4 TD.

PASSING
OSU: Hare 4-8-1, 64 yards.
USC: Rae 18-25-0, 229 yards, 1 TD.

RECEIVING
OSU: Holycross 2-37; Griffin 2-27.
USC: Swann 6-108, 1 TD; Young 6-82.

JANUARY 1, 1974
OHIO STATE 42, SOUTHERN CAL 21

	1ST	2ND	3RD	4TH	FINAL
OSU	7	7	13	15	42
USC	3	11	7	0	21

SCORING SUMMARY

USC	FG Limahelu 47
OSU	Johnson 1 run (Conway kick)
USC	FG Limahelu 42
USC	McKay 10 pass from Davis (McKay pass from Haden)
OSU	Johnson 1 run (Conway kick)
USC	Davis 1 run (Limahelu kick)
OSU	Johnson 4 run (kick failed)
OSU	Greene 1 run (Conway kick)
OSU	Elia 2 run (Greene run)
OSU	Griffin 47 run (Conway kick)

OSU	TEAM STATISTICS	USC
20	First Downs	27
320	Rushing Yards	167
6-8-1	Passing	22-40-0
129	Passing Yards	239
449	Total Yards	406
2-41.0	Punts - Average	3-36.0
2-1	Fumbles - Lost	2-1
7-59	Penalties - Yards	6-40

INDIVIDUAL LEADERS

RUSHING
OSU: Griffin 22-149, 1 TD; Johnson 21-94, 3 TD.
USC: Davis 16-74, 1 TD; McNeill 8-46.

PASSING
OSU: Greene 6-8-1, 129 yards.
USC: Haden 21-39-0, 229 yards.

RECEIVING
OSU: Pagac 4-89; Bashnagel 1-25.
USC: McKay 6-83, 1 TD; Swann 5-47.

JANUARY 1, 1975
SOUTHERN CAL 18, OHIO STATE 17

	1ST	2ND	3RD	4TH	FINAL
OSU	0	7	0	10	17
USC	3	0	0	15	18

SCORING SUMMARY

USC	FG Limahelu 30
OSU	Henson 2 run (Klaban kick)
USC	Obradovich 8 pass from Haden (Limahelu kick)
OSU	Greene 3 run (Klaban kick)
OSU	FG Klaban 32
USC	McKay 38 pass from Haden (Diggs pass from Haden)

OSU	TEAM STATISTICS	USC
14	First Downs	24
193	Rushing Yards	280
8-14-1	Passing	12-22-2
93	Passing Yards	181
286	Total Yards	461
3-47.6	Punts - Average	2-14.5
4-2	Fumbles - Lost	2-2
3-25	Penalties - Yards	2-21

INDIVIDUAL LEADERS

RUSHING
OSU: Griffin 20-75; Greene 11-52, 1 TD.
USC: Carter 18-75; Davis 13-67; Farmer 7-67.

PASSING
OSU: Greene 8-14-1, 93 yards.
USC: Haden 12-22-2, 181 yards, 2 TD.

RECEIVING
OSU: France 2-28; Griffin 2-25.
USC: McKay 5-104, 1 TD; Obradovich 4-75, 1 TD.

JANUARY 1, 1976
UCLA 23, OHIO STATE 10

	1ST	2ND	3RD	4TH	FINAL
OSU	3	0	0	7	10
UCLA	0	0	16	7	23

SCORING SUMMARY

OSU	FG Klaban 42
UCLA	FG White 33
UCLA	Henry 16 pass from Sciarra (kick failed)
UCLA	Henry 67 pass from Sciarra (White kick)
OSU	Johnson 3 run (Klaban kick)
UCLA	Tyler 54 run (White kick)

OSU	TEAM STATISTICS	UCLA
20	First Downs	19
208	Rushing Yards	202
7-18-2	Passing	13-19-2
90	Passing Yards	212
298	Total Yards	414
5-47.2	Punts - Average	5-39.4
3-1	Fumbles - Lost	2-1
3-25	Penalties - Yards	4-30

INDIVIDUAL LEADERS

RUSHING
OSU: Griffin 17-93; Johnson 19-70, 1 TD.
UCLA: Tyler 21-172, 1 TD; Ayers 12-36.

PASSING
OSU: Greene 7-18-2, 90 yards.
UCLA: Sciarra 13-19-2, 212 yards, 2 TD.

RECEIVING
OSU: Baschnagel 3-26; Kain 1-19.
UCLA: Henry 5-113, 2 TD; Anderson 3-39.

JANUARY 1, 1977
SOUTHERN CAL 14, MICHIGAN 6

	1ST	2ND	3RD	4TH	FINAL
MICH	0	6	0	0	6
USC	0	7	0	7	14

SCORING SUMMARY

MICH	Lytle 1 run (kick failed)
USC	Evans 1 run (Walker kick)
USC	White 7 run (Walker kick)

MICH	TEAM STATISTICS	USC
12	First Downs	19
155	Rushing Yards	200
4-12-0	Passing	14-20-1
76	Passing Yards	181
231	Total Yards	381
5-45.0	Punts - Average	3-29.7
4-2	Fumbles - Lost	2-1
24:03	Possession Time	35:57

INDIVIDUAL LEADERS

RUSHING
MICH: Lytle 18-67, 1 TD; Davis 10-39.
USC: White 32-114, 1 TD; Tatupu 7-60.

PASSING
MICH: Leach 4-12-0, 76 yards.
USC: Evans 14-20-1, 181 yards.

RECEIVING
MICH: Smith 2-52; Johnson 2-24.
USC: Diggs 8-98; Robinson 2-42.

JANUARY 2, 1978
WASHINGTON 27, MICHIGAN 20

	1ST	2ND	3RD	4TH	FINAL
MICH	0	0	7	13	20
WASH	7	10	10	0	27

SCORING SUMMARY
WASH   Moon 2 run (Robbins kick)
WASH   FG Robbins 30
WASH   Moon 1 run (Robbins kick)
WASH   Gaines 28 pass from Moon (Robbins kick)
MICH   Stephenson 76 pass from Leach (Willner kick)
WASH   FG Robbins 18
MICH   Davis 2 run (Willner kick)
MICH   Edwards 32 pass from Leach (kick failed)

MICH	TEAM STATISTICS	WASH
22	First Downs	17
149	Rushing Yards	164
14-27-2	Passing	13-24-2
239	Passing Yards	234
388	Total Yards	398
4-42.5	Punts - Average	5-39.0
2-1	Fumbles - Lost	0-0
3-11	Penalties - Yards	6-47

INDIVIDUAL LEADERS
RUSHING
MICH: Davis 18-79, 1 TD; Edwards 15-74.
WASH: Steele 13-77; Gipson 15-48.
PASSING
MICH: Leach 14-27-2, 239 yards, 2 TD.
WASH: Moon 12-23-2, 188 yards, 1 TD.
RECEIVING
MICH: Clayton 5-84; Stephenson 1-76, 1 TD.
WASH: Gaines 4-122, 1 TD; Stevens 1-46.

JANUARY 1, 1979
SOUTHERN CAL 17, MICHIGAN 10

	1ST	2ND	3RD	4TH	FINAL
MICH	0	3	7	0	10
USC	7	10	0	0	17

SCORING SUMMARY
USC   Brenner 9 pass from McDonald (Jordan kick)
MICH   FG Willner 36
USC   White 3 run (Jordan kick)
USC   FG Jordan 35
MICH   Smith 44 pass from Leach (Willner kick)

MICH	TEAM STATISTICS	USC
12	First Downs	14
99	Rushing Yards	134
10-22-2	Passing	4-9-0
137	Passing Yards	23
236	Total Yards	157
8-29.5	Punts - Average	9-38.6
2-0	Fumbles - Lost	2-1
4-30	Penalties - Yards	2-21

INDIVIDUAL LEADERS
RUSHING
MICH: Huckleby 9-28; Davis 8-28.
USC: White 32-99, 1; Cain 14-90.
PASSING
MICH: Leach 10-21-2, 137 yards, 1 TD.
USC: McDonald 4-9-0, 23 yards, 1 TD.
RECEIVING
MICH: Smith 4-58, 1 TD; Clayton 2-40.
USC: Garcia 1-12; Brenner 1-9, 1 TD.

JANUARY 1, 1980
SOUTHERN CAL 17, OHIO STATE 16

	1ST	2ND	3RD	4TH	FINAL
OSU	0	10	3	3	16
USC	3	7	0	7	17

SCORING SUMMARY
USC   FG Hipp 41
USC   Williams 53 pass from McDonald (Hipp kick)
OSU   FG Janakievski 35
OSU   Williams 53 pass from Schlichter (Janakievski kick)
OSU   FG Janakievski 37
OSU   FG Janakievski 24
USC   White 1 run (Hipp kick)

OSU	TEAM STATISTICS	USC
16	First Downs	23
115	Rushing Yards	285
11-21-1	Passing	11-24-1
297	Passing Yards	234
412	Total Yards	519
3-43.3	Punts - Average	1-52
1-1	Fumbles - Lost	2-1
2-18	Penalties - Yards	3-33
28:13	Possession Time	31:47

INDIVIDUAL LEADERS
RUSHING
OSU: Murray 18-73.
USC: White 39-242-1 TD; Pillen 9-43.
PASSING
OSU: Schlichter 11-21-1, 297 yards, 1 TD.
USC: McDonald 11-24-1, 234 yards, 1 TD.
RECEIVING
OSU: Williams 3-131, 1 TD; Donley 4-110.
USC: Williams 2-70, 1 TD; Garcia 2-57.

JANUARY 1, 1981
MICHIGAN 23, WASHINGTON 6

	1ST	2ND	3RD	4TH	FINAL
MICH	0	7	10	6	23
WASH	0	6	0	0	6

SCORING SUMMARY
WASH   FG Nelson 35
MICH   Woolfolk 6 run (Haji-Sheikh kick)
WASH   FG Nelson 26
MICH   FG Haji-Sheikh 25
MICH   Carter 7 pass from Wangler (Haji-Sheikh kick)
MICH   Edwards 1 run (kick failed)

MICH	TEAM STATISTICS	WASH
23	First Downs	20
292	Rushing Yards	92
12-20-0	Passing	23-39-2
145	Passing Yards	282
437	Total Yards	374
6-47.3	Punts - Average	5-39.2
0-0	Fumbles - Lost	2-1
3-37	Penalties - Yards	5-32

INDIVIDUAL LEADERS
RUSHING
MICH: Woolfolk 26-182, 1 TD; Edwards 19-68, 1 TD.
WASH: Stevens 17-59; Tyler 10-45.
PASSING
MICH: Wangler 12-20-0, 145 yards, 1 TD.
WASH: Flick 23-39-2, 282 yards.
RECEIVING
MICH: Carter 5-68, 1 TD; B. Mitchell 2-36.
WASH: Allen 6-101; Bayle 6-45.

JANUARY 1, 1982
WASHINGTON 28, IOWA 0

	1ST	2ND	3RD	4TH	FINAL
WASH	0	13	0	15	28
IA	0	0	0	0	0

SCORING SUMMARY
WASH   Robinson 1 run (Nelson kick)
WASH   Coby 1 run (pass failed)
WASH   Robinson 34 run (Skansi pass from Pelluer)
WASH   Cowan 3 run (Nelson kick)

WASH	TEAM STATISTICS	IA
22	First Downs	14
186	Rushing Yards	180
15-29-1	Passing	10-21-3
142	Passing Yards	84
328	Total Yards	264
7-35.6	Punts - Average	5-47.0
0-0	Fumbles - Lost	2-2
3-28	Penalties - Yards	6-73

INDIVIDUAL LEADERS
RUSHING
WASH: Robinson 20-142, 2 TD.
IA: Granger 13-80; Bohannon 10-44.
PASSING
WASH: Pulluer 15-29-1, 142 yards.
IA: Bohannon 6-14-2, 33 yards.
RECEIVING
WASH: Skansi 4-69; Allen 5-68.
IA: Brown 6-52.

JANUARY 1, 1983
UCLA 24, MICHIGAN 14

	1ST	2ND	3RD	4TH	FINAL
MICH	0	0	7	7	14
UCLA	7	3	7	7	24

SCORING SUMMARY
UCLA   Ramsey 1 run (Lee kick)
UCLA   FG Lee 39
MICH   Garrett 1 pass from Hall (Haji-Sheikh kick)
UCLA   Andrews 9 run (Lee kick)
UCLA   Montgomery 11 interception return (Lee kick)
MICH   Rice 4 pass from Hall (Haji-Sheikh kick)

MICH	TEAM STATISTICS	UCLA
19	First Downs	19
110	Rushing Yards	181
19-34-3	Passing	18-25-0
209	Passing Yards	162
319	Total Yards	343
6-40.3	Punts - Average	6-32.2
1-1	Fumbles - Lost	1-0
3-17	Penalties - Yards	2-10

INDIVIDUAL LEADERS
RUSHING
MICH: Ricks 23-88; Smith 3-15.
UCLA: Nelson 11-48; Cephous 8-46.
PASSING
MICH: Hall 13-24-2, 155 yards, 2 TD.
UCLA: Ramsey 18-25-0, 162 yards.
RECEIVING
MICH: Dunaway 5-110, 1 TD; Carter 5-59.
UCLA: Bergmann 6-48; Townsell 4-45.

JANUARY 2, 1984
UCLA 45, ILLINOIS 9

	1ST	2ND	3RD	4TH	FINAL
ILL	0	3	0	6	9
UCLA	7	21	10	7	45

SCORING SUMMARY
UCLA   Bergmann 3 pass from Neuheisel (Lee kick)
ILL   FG White 41
UCLA   Nelson 28 run (Lee kick)
UCLA   Dorrell 16 pass from Neuheisel (Lee kick)
UCLA   Young 53 pass from Neuheisel (Lee kick)
UCLA   Dorrell 15 pass from Neuheisel (Lee kick)
UCLA   FG Lee 29
ILL   Rooks 5 pass from Trudeau (pass failed)
UCLA   Wiley 8 run (Lee kick)

ILL	TEAM STATISTICS	UCLA
16	First Downs	27
0	Rushing Yards	213
25-47-4	Passing	22-31-0
205	Passing Yards	298
205	Total Yards	511

INDIVIDUAL LEADERS
RUSHING
ILL: Beverly 4-22; Rooks 8-21.
UCLA: Cephous 12-86; Nelson 18-69, 1 TD.
PASSING
ILL: Trudeau 23-39-3, 178 yards, 1 TD.
UCLA: Neuheisel 22-31-0, 298 yards, 4 TD.
RECEIVING
ILL: Williams 10-88; Brewster 5-60.
UCLA: Young 5-129, 1 TD; Dorrell 5-61, 2 TD.

JANUARY 1, 1985
SOUTHERN CAL 20, OHIO STATE 17

	1ST	2ND	3RD	4TH	FINAL
OSU	3	3	3	8	17
USC	10	7	3	0	20

SCORING SUMMARY
OSU FG Spangler 21
USC FG Jordan 51
USC Cormier 3 pass from Green (Jordan kick)
USC Ware 19 pass from Green (Jordan kick)
OSU FG Spangler 46
OSU FG Spangler 52
USC FG Jordan 51
OSU Carter 18 pass from Tomczak (Tomczak run)

OSU	TEAM STATISTICS	USC
19	First Downs	16
113	Rushing Yards	133
24-37-3	Passing	13-25-0
290	Passing Yards	128
403	Total Yards	261
4-47.8	Punts - Average	7-42.1
4-1	Fumbles - Lost	2-1
4-46	Penalties - Yards	4-38
28:49	Possession Time	31:11

INDIVIDUAL LEADERS
RUSHING
OSU: Byars 23-109.
USC: Crutcher 21-72; Pola 9-52.
PASSING
OSU: Tomczak 24-37-3, 290 yards, 1 TD.
USC: Green 13-24-0, 128 yards, 2 TD.
RECEIVING
OSU: Carter 9-172, 1 TD; Lanese 3-33.
USC: Ware 3-56, 1 TD; Cormier 3-19, 1 TD.

JANUARY 1, 1986
UCLA 45, IOWA 28

	1ST	2ND	3RD	4TH	FINAL
IA	7	3	7	11	28
UCLA	10	14	7	14	45

SCORING SUMMARY
IA Hudson 1 run (Houghtlin kick)
UCLA Ball 30 run (Lee kick)
UCLA FG Lee 42
IA FG Houghtlin 24
UCLA Ball 40 run (Lee kick)
UCLA Ball 6 run (Lee kick)
IA Long 4 run (Houghtlin kick)
UCLA Sherrard 6 pass from Stevens (Lee kick)
UCLA Ball 32 run (Lee kick)
IA FG Houghtlin 52 field goal
UCLA Stevens 1 run (Lee kick)
IA Happel 11 pass from Long (Harmon run)

IA	TEAM STATISTICS	UCLA
25	First Downs	29
82	Rushing Yards	299
29-38-1	Passing	16-26-1
319	Passing Yards	189
401	Total Yards	488
2-32.0	Punts - Average	2-38.0
4-4	Fumbles - Lost	3-2
5-40	Penalties - Yards	6-36

INDIVIDUAL LEADERS
RUSHING
IA: Harmon 14-55; Hudson 13-53, 1 TD.
UCLA: Ball 22-227, 4 TD; Green 13-46.
PASSING
IA: Long 29-37-1, 319 yards, 1 TD.
UCLA: Stevens 16-26-1, 189 yards, 1 TD.
RECEIVING
IA: Harmon 11-102; Happel 6-89, 1 TD.
UCLA: Dorrell 3-59; Sherrard 4-48, 1 TD.

JANUARY 1, 1987
ARIZONA STATE 22, MICHIGAN 15

	1ST	2ND	3RD	4TH	FINAL
MICH	8	7	0	0	15
ASU	0	13	6	3	22

SCORING SUMMARY
MICH Morris 18 run (White pass from Gillette)
ASU FG Bostrom 37
MICH Harbaugh 2 run (Gillette kick)
ASU FG Bostrom 27
ASU Hill 4 pass from Van Raaphorst (Bostrom kick)
ASU Hill 1 pass from Van Raaphorst (pass failed)
ASU FG Bostrom 25

MICH	TEAM STATISTICS	ASU
13	First Downs	22
59	Rushing Yards	188
13-23-3	Passing	16-30-0
172	Passing Yards	193
231	Total Yards	381
6-40.8	Punts - Average	4-39.0
3-0	Fumbles - Lost	1-0
6-42	Penalties - Yards	6-26

INDIVIDUAL LEADERS
RUSHING
MICH: Morris 16-47, 1 TD.
ASU: Harris 23-109; Williams 18-69.
PASSING
MICH: Harbaugh 13-23-3, 172 yards.
ASU: Van Raaphorst 16-30-0, 193 yards, 2 TD.
RECEIVING
MICH: McMurtry 3-59; Morris 4-47.
ASU: Cox 6-104; Harris 3-34.

JANUARY 1, 1988
MICHIGAN STATE 20, SOUTHERN CAL 17

	1ST	2ND	3RD	4TH	FINAL
USC	3	0	7	7	17
MSU	7	7	0	6	20

SCORING SUMMARY
USC FG Rodriguez 34
MSU White 5 run (Langeloh kick)
MSU White 3 run (Langeloh kick)
USC Henry 33 pass from Peete (Rodriguez kick)
MSU FG Langeloh 40
USC Henry 22 pass from Peete (Rodriguez kick)
MSU FG Langeloh 36

USC	TEAM STATISTICS	MSU
21	First Downs	11
161	Rushing Yards	148
22-42-4	Passing	4-7-0
249	Passing Yards	128
410	Total Yards	276
4-45.0	Punts - Average	8-47.1
4-1	Fumbles - Lost	0-0
4-20	Penalties - Yards	5-32
27:13	Possession Time	32:47

INDIVIDUAL LEADERS
RUSHING
USC: Peete 11-54; Holt 10-44.
MSU: White 35-113, 2 TD.
PASSING
USC: Peete 22-41-3, 249 yards, 2 TD.
MSU: McAllister 4-7-0, 128 yards.
RECEIVING
USC: Henry 3-66, 2 TD; Green 7-58.
MSU: Rison 2-91; Bouyer 1-29.

JANUARY 2, 1989
MICHIGAN 22, SOUTHERN CAL 14

	1ST	2ND	3RD	4TH	FINAL
MICH	3	0	6	13	22
USC	0	14	0	0	14

SCORING SUMMARY
MICH FG Gillette 49
USC Peete 1 run (Rodriguez kick)
USC Peete 4 run (Rodriguez kick)
MICH Calloway 6 pass from Brown (run failed)
MICH Hoard 1 run (pass failed)
MICH Hoard 1 run (Gillette kick)

MICH	TEAM STATISTICS	USC
19	First Downs	15
208	Rushing Yards	138
11-24-0	Passing	15-21-2
144	Passing Yards	158
352	Total Yards	296
4-34.8	Punts - Average	4-50.3
1-1	Fumbles - Lost	3-3
4-20	Penalties - Yards	11-83
31:01	Possession Time	28:59

INDIVIDUAL LEADERS
RUSHING
MICH: Hoard 19-142, 2 TD; Boles 14-49.
USC: Emanuel 16-55; Peete 9-42, 2 TD.
PASSING
MICH: Brown 11-24-0, 144 yards, 1 TD.
USC: Peete 15-21-2, 158 yards.
RECEIVING
MICH: Walker 3-54; Kolesar 3-49.
USC: Affholter 5-56; Wellman 2-47.

JANUARY 1, 1990
SOUTHERN CAL 17, MICHIGAN 10

	1ST	2ND	3RD	4TH	FINAL
MICH	0	3	7	0	10
USC	0	10	0	7	17

SCORING SUMMARY
USC Marinovich 1 run (Rodriguez kick)
MICH FG Carlson 19
USC FG Rodriguez 34
MICH Jefferson 2 run (Carlson kick)
USC Ervins 14 run (Rodriguez kick)

MICH	TEAM STATISTICS	USC
11	First Downs	23
119	Rushing Yards	181
10-20-0	Passing	22-31-1
115	Passing Yards	178
234	Total Yards	359
7-35.9	Punts - Average	4-39.3
2-0	Fumbles - Lost	0-0
8-62	Penalties - Yards	8-87
27:20	Possession Time	32:40

INDIVIDUAL LEADERS
RUSHING
MICH: Hoard 17-108.
USC: Ervins 30-126, 1 TD; Holt 8-35.
PASSING
MICH: Taylor 10-19-0, 116 yards.
USC: Marinovich 22-31-1, 178 yards.
RECEIVING
MICH: McMurty 4-56; Calloway 2-33.
USC: Jackson 5-56; Ervins 5-44.

WASHINGTON 46, IOWA 34

	1ST	2ND	3RD	4TH	FINAL
IA	0	7	7	20	34
WASH	10	23	6	7	46

SCORING SUMMARY
WASH FG Hanson 23
WASH Hall 27 blocked punt return (Hanson kick)
IA Bell 15 run (Skillet kick)
WASH FG Hanson 38
WASH Mincy 37 interception return (pass failed)
WASH Brunell 5 run (Hanson kick)
WASH M. Bailey 22 pass from Brunell (Hanson kick)
IA Rodgers 7 run (Skillett kick)
WASH Brunell 20 run (run failed)
IA Rodgers 9 run (run failed)
IA Bell 20 run (pass failed)
WASH M. Bailey 31 pass from Brunell (Hanson kick)
IA Saunders 12 pass from Rodgers (Velicer pass from Rodgers)

IA	TEAM STATISTICS	WASH
19	First Downs	19
139	Rushing Yards	222
17-37-4	Passing	14-25-2
315	Passing Yards	163
454	Total Yards	385
6-33.3	Punts - Average	4-41.8
4-1	Fumbles - Lost	3-1
8-55	Penalties - Yards	5-45
29:30	Possession Time	30:30

INDIVIDUAL LEADERS
RUSHING
IA: Bell 11-64, 2 TD; Montgomery 4-26.
WASH: Lewis 19-128; Bryant 3-47.
PASSING
IA: Rodgers 15-34-3, 196 yards, 1 TD.
WASH: Brunell 14-22-1, 163 yards, 2 TD.
RECEIVING
IA: Saunders 5-99, 1 TD; Bell 3-85.
WASH: Bailey 2-53, 2 TD; Turner 3-36.

WASHINGTON 34, MICHIGAN 14

	1ST	2ND	3RD	4TH	FINAL
WASH	0	13	8	13	34
MICH	0	7	0	7	14

SCORING SUMMARY
WASH Hobert 2 run (Hanson kick)
MICH Smith 9 pass from Grbac (Carlson kick)
WASH FG Hanson 24
WASH FG Handon 23
WASH Bruener 5 pass from Hobert (Pierce from Hobert)
WASH Pierce 2 pass from Hobert (kick failed)
WASH Bailey 38 pass from Brunell (Hanson kick)
MICH Wheatley 53 run (Carlson kick)

WASH	TEAM STATISTICS	MICH
19	First Downs	10
123	Rushing Yards	72
25-42-2	Passing	14-28-1
281	Passing Yards	133
404	Total Yards	205
6-41.8	Punts - Average	10-37.8
0-0	Fumbles - Lost	3-0
6-50	Penalties - Yards	8-62

INDIVIDUAL LEADERS
RUSHING
WASH: Bryant 15-38; Barry 13-37.
MICH: Wheatley 9-68, 1 TD; Johnson 4-30.
PASSING
WASH: Hobert 18-34-2, 192 yards, 2 TD; Brunell 7-8-0, 89 yards, 1 TD.
MICH: Grbac 13-26-1, 130 yards, 1 TD.
RECEIVING
WASH: M. Bailey 6-126, 1 TD; Pierce 7-86, 1 TD.
MICH: Howard 1-35; Wheatley 3-30.

MICHIGAN 38, WASHINGTON 31

	1ST	2ND	3RD	4TH	FINAL
MICH	10	7	14	7	38
WASH	7	14	10	0	31

SCORING SUMMARY
MICH FG Elezovic 41
WASH Turner 1 run (Hanson kick)
MICH McGee 49 pass from Grbac (Elezovic kick)
MICH Wheatley 56 run (Elezovic kick)
WASH Shelley 64 pass from Brunell (Hanson kick)
WASH Bruener 18 pass from Brunell (Hanson kick)
MICH Wheatley 88 run (Elezovic kick)
WASH Kaufman 1 run (Hanson kick)
WASH FG Hanson 44
MICH Wheatley 24 run (Elezovic kick)
MICH McGee 15 pass from Grbac (Elezovic kick)

MICH	TEAM STATISTICS	WASH
16	First Downs	19
308	Rushing Yards	105
17-30-0	Passing	18-31-0
175	Passing Yards	308
483	Total Yards	413
6-37.0	Punts - Average	5-39.2
1-0	Fumbles - Lost	1-1
8-72	Penalties - Yards	5-43
28:12	Possession Time	31:48

INDIVIDUAL LEADERS
RUSHING
MICH: Wheatley 15-235, 3 TD; Davis 9-35.
WASH: Kaufman 20-39, 1 TD.
PASSING
MICH: Grbac 17-30-0, 175 yards, 2 TD.
WASH: Brunell 18-30-0, 308 yards, 2 TD.
RECEIVING
MICH: McGee 6-117, 2 TD.
WASH: Shelley 3-100, 1 TD; Bruener 4-85, 1 TD.

WISCONSIN 21, UCLA 16

	1ST	2ND	3RD	4TH	FINAL
UCLA	3	0	0	13	16
WISC	7	7	0	7	21

SCORING SUMMARY
UCLA FG Merten 27
WISC Moss 3 run (Schnetzky kick)
WISC Moss 1 run (Schnetzky kick)
UCLA Davis 12 run (Merten kick)
WISC Bevell 21 run (Schnetzky kick)
UCLA Nguyen five pass from Cook (pass failed)

UCLA	TEAM STATISTICS	WISC
31	First Downs	21
212	Rushing Yards	250
28-43-1	Passing	10-20-1
288	Passing Yards	96
500	Total Yards	346
2-35.0	Punts - Average	6-38.0
5-5	Fumbles - Lost	2-0
9-95	Penalties - Yards	12-89

INDIVIDUAL LEADERS
RUSHING
UCLA: Davis 13-88, 1 TD; Hicks 8-67.
WISC: Moss 36-158, 2 TD; Fletcher 7-64.
PASSING
UCLA: Bevell 10-20-1, 96 yards.
WISC: Cook 28-43-1, 288 yards, 1 TD.
RECEIVING
UCLA: Stokes 14-176; Allen 4-32.
WISC: Dawkins 4-33.

PENN STATE 38, OREGON 20

	1ST	2ND	3RD	4TH	FINAL
ORE	7	0	7	6	20
PSU	7	7	14	10	38

SCORING SUMMARY
PSU Carter 83 run (Conway kick)
ORE Wilcox 1 pass from O'Neil (Belden kick)
PSU Milne 1 run (Conway kick)
ORE McLemore 17 pass from O'Neil (Belden kick)
PSU Carter 17 run (Conway kick)
PSU Carter 3 run (Conway kick)
PSU FG Conway 43
PSU Witman 9 run (Baminger kick)
ORE Whittle 3 run (pass failed)

ORE	TEAM STATISTICS	PSU
27	First Downs	22
45	Rushing Yards	228
41-61-2	Passing	20-31-1
456	Passing Yards	202
501	Total Yards	430
6-42.8	Punts - Average	6-41.7
1-0	Fumbles - Lost	1-1
6-52	Penalties - Yards	5-37

INDIVIDUAL LEADERS
RUSHING
ORE: Whittle 12-45, 1 TD; Philyaw 4-14.
PSU: Carter 21-156, 3 TD; Milne 9-36, 1 TD.
PASSING
ORE: O'Neil 41-61-2, 456 yards, 2 TD.
PSU: K. Collins 19-30-1, 200 yards.
RECEIVING
ORE: Wilcox 11-135, 1 TD; McLemore 10-90, 1 TD.
PSU: Engram 5-52; Scott 4-41

SOUTHERN CAL 41, NORTHWESTERN 32

	1ST	2ND	3RD	4TH	FINAL
USC	7	17	7	10	41
NU	7	3	16	6	32

SCORING SUMMARY
USC L. Woods 1 run (Abrams kick)
NU D. Autry 3 run (Gowins kick)
USC Barnum 21 pass from Otton (Abrams kick)
USC FG Abrams 30
USC McCutcheon 53 fumble return (Abrams kick)
NU FG Gowins 29
NU FG Gowins 28
NU D. Autry 9 run (pass failed)
USC K. Johnson 56 pass from Otton (Abrams kick)
NU Schnur 1 run (Gowins kick)
NU D. Autry 2 run (pass failed)
USC FG Abrams 46
USC Washington 2 run (Abrams kick)

USC	TEAM STATISTICS	NU
22	First Downs	23
29	Rushing Yards	139
29-44-0	Passing	23-39-1
391	Passing Yards	336
420	Total Yards	475
2-18	Punt Returns - Yards	0-0
3-31	Kickoff Returns - Yards	8-225
2-44.5	Punts - Average	2-38.5
1-1	Fumbles - Lost	1-1
11-86	Penalties - Yards	7-72
29:47	Possession Time	30:13

INDIVIDUAL LEADERS
RUSHING
USC: Washington 16-51, 1 TD.
NU: D. Autry 32-110, 3 TD; Schnur 3-13, 1 TD.
PASSING
USC: Otton 29-44-0, 391 yards, 2 TD.
NU: Schnur 23-39-1, 336 yards.
RECEIVING
USC: Johnson 12-216, 1 TD; C Miller 3-50, Barnum 4-42, 1 TD.
NU: Bates 7-145; Musso 5-91.

JANUARY 1, 1997
OHIO STATE 20, ARIZONA STATE 17

	1ST	2ND	3RD	4TH	FINAL
ASU	0	7	3	7	17
OSU	7	0	7	6	20

SCORING SUMMARY
OSU   Boston 9 pass from S. Jackson (J. Jackson kick)
ASU   Boyer 25 pass from Plummer (Nycz kick)
ASU   FG Nycz 37
OSU   Stanley 72 pass from Germaine (J. Jackson kick)
ASU   Plummer 11 run (Nycz kick)
OSU   Boston 5 pass from Germaine (kick failed)

ASU	TEAM STATISTICS	OSU
18	First Downs	18
75	Rushing Yards	133
19-35-1	Passing	15-31-0
201	Passing Yards	190
276	Total Yards	323
1-0	Fumbles - Lost	1-0
9-85	Penalties - Yards	10-75
33:17	Possession Time	26:43

INDIVIDUAL LEADERS
RUSHING
ASU: Battle 18-34; Redmond 8-26.
OSU: Pearson 13-114; Wiley 7-32.

PASSING
ASU: Plummer 19-35-1, 201 yards, 1 TD.
OSU: Germaine 9-17-0, 131 yards, 2 TD.

RECEIVING
ASU: L. Jackson 5-71; Bush 3-41.
OSU: Stanley 5-124, 1 TD; Keller 3-24.

JANUARY 1, 1998
MICHIGAN 21, WASHINGTON STATE 16

	1ST	2ND	3RD	4TH	FINAL
WSU	7	0	6	3	16
MICH	0	7	7	7	21

SCORING SUMMARY
WSU   McKenzie 15 pass from Leaf (Lindell kick)
MICH   Streets 53 pass from Griese (Baker kick)
WSU   Tims 14 reverse (kick blocked)
MICH   Streets 58 pass from Griese (Baker kick)
MICH   Tuman 23 pass from Griese (Baker kick)
WSU   FG Lindell 48

WSU	TEAM STATISTICS	MICH
18	First Downs	22
67	Rushing Yards	128
17-35-1	Passing	18-30-1
331	Passing Yards	251
398	Total Yards	379
6-40.3	Punts - Average	6-30.5
2-0	Fumbles - Lost	0-0
4-43	Penalties - Yards	4-40
27:46	Possession Time	32:14

INDIVIDUAL LEADERS
RUSHING
WSU: Black 7-24; Gilmore 8-20.
MICH: Howard 19-70; Thomas 7-20.

PASSING
WSU: Leaf 17-35-1, 331 yards, 1 TD.
MICH: Griese 18-30-1, 251 yards, 3 TD.

RECEIVING
WSU: Jackson 5-89; McKenzie 5-78, 1 TD.
MICH: Streets 4-127, 2 TD; Shaw 6-49.

JANUARY 1, 1999
WISCONSIN 38, UCLA 31

	1ST	2ND	3RD	4TH	FINAL
WISC	7	17	7	7	38
UCLA	7	14	7	3	31

SCORING SUMMARY
WISC   Dayne 54 run (Davenport kick)
UCLA   Lewis 38 pass from McNown (Sailer kick)
WISC   Dayne 7 run (Davenport kick)
UCLA   Price 61 pass from Mitchell (Sailer kick)
UCLA   Farmer 41 pass from McNown (Sailer kick)
WISC   Dayne 10 run (Davenport kick)
WISC   FG Davenport 40
WISC   Dayne 22 run (Davenport kick)
UCLA   Lewis 10 run (Sailer kick)
WISC   Fletcher 46 interception return (Davenport kick)
UCLA   FG Sailer 30

WISC	TEAM STATISTICS	UCLA
22	First Downs	25
343	Rushing Yards	120
9-17-0	Passing	21-36-1
154	Passing Yards	418
497	Total Yards	538
5-41.0	Punts - Average	3-47.0
2-1	Fumbles - Lost	1-1
7-45	Penalties - Yards	9-94
29:15	Possession Time	30:45

INDIVIDUAL LEADERS
RUSHING
WISC: Dayne 27-246, 4 TD; Samuel 13-65.
UCLA: Lewis 10-50, 1 TD; Foster 10-38.

PASSING
WISC: Samuel 9-17-0, 154 yards.
UCLA: McNown 19-34-1, 340 yards, 2 TD.

RECEIVING
WISC: Davis 3-57.
UCLA: Farmer 7-142, 1 TD; Price 3-102, 1 TD.

JANUARY 1, 2000
WISCONSIN 17, STANFORD 9

	1ST	2ND	3RD	4TH	FINAL
STAN	0	9	0	0	9
WISC	0	3	7	7	17

SCORING SUMMARY
STAN   FG Biselli 28
WISC   FG Pisetsky 31
STAN   K. Carter 1 run (run failed)
WISC   Dayne 4 run (Pisetsky kick)
WISC   Bollinger 1 run (Pisetsky kick)

STAN	TEAM STATISTICS	WISC
14	First Downs	16
-5	Rushing Yards	226
18-35-0	Passing	7-14-0
264	Passing Yards	105
259	Total Yards	331
8-38.3	Punts - Average	8-43.4
2-0	Fumbles - Lost	0-0
7-50	Penalties - Yards	8-72
26:32	Possession Time	33:28

INDIVIDUAL LEADERS
RUSHING
STAN: Wire 5-6; Allen 6-4; K.Carter 6-3, 1 TD.
WISC: Dayne 34-200, 1 TD.

PASSING
STAN: Husak 17-34-0, 258 yards.
WISC: Bollinger 7-14-0, 105 yards.

RECEIVING
STAN: Pitts 6-81; Uso 3-60.
WISC: Chambers 5-76; Sigmund 2-29.

JANUARY 1, 2001
WASHINGTON 34, PURDUE 24

	1ST	2ND	3RD	4TH	FINAL
PU	0	10	7	7	24
WASH	14	0	6	14	34

SCORING SUMMARY
WASH   Cleman 1 run (Anderson kick)
WASH   Tuiasosopo 5 run (Anderson Kick)
PU   Sutherland 5 pass from Brees (Dorsch kick)
PU   FG Dorsch 26
WASH   FG Anderson 47
PU   Sutherland 24 pass from Brees (Dorsch kick)
WASH   FG Anderson 42
WASH   Elstrom 8 pass from Tuiasosopo (Anderson kick)
WASH   Hurst 8 run (Anderson kick)
PU   Brown 42 run (Dorsch kick)

PU	TEAM STATISTICS	WASH
19	First Downs	23
76	Rushing Yards	268
23-39-0	Passing	18-24-0
275	Passing Yards	149
351	Total Yards	417
4-41.0	Punts - Average	3-37.7
3-1	Fumbles - Lost	2-1
11-69	Penalties - Yards	6-48
24:07	Possession Time	35:53

INDIVIDUAL LEADERS
RUSHING
PU: Lowe 20-79; Brown 3-52, 1 TD.
WASH: Alexis 10-78; Tuiasosopo 15-75, 1 TD.

PASSING
PU: Brees 23-39-0, 275 yards, 2 TD.
WASH: Tuiasosopo 16-22-0, 138 yards, 1 TD.

RECEIVING
PU: Sutherland 7-88, 2 TD; Standeford 5-67.
WASH: Stevens 5-51; Elstrom 4-24, 1 TD.

JANUARY 3, 2002
MIAMI (FLA.) 37, NEBRASKA 14

	1ST	2ND	3RD	4TH	FINAL
MIA	7	27	0	3	37
NEB	0	0	7	7	14

SCORING SUMMARY
MIA   Johnson 49 pass from Dorsey (Sievers kick)
MIA   Portis 39 run (Sievers kick)
MIA   Lewis 47 interception return (Sievers kick)
MIA   Shockey 21 pass from Dorsey (kick failed)
MIA   Johnson 8 pass from Dorsey (Sievers kick)
NEB   Davies 16 run (Brown kick)
NEB   Groce 71 punt return (Brown kick)
MIA   FG Sievers 37

MIA	TEAM STATISTICS	NEB
18	First Downs	16
110	Rushing Yards	197
22-35-1	Passing	5-15-1
362	Passing Yards	62
472	Total Yards	259
4-35.8	Punts - Average	5-40.6
2-0	Fumbles - Lost	4-2
12-85	Penalties - Yards	4-26
25:33	Possession Time	34:27

INDIVIDUAL LEADERS
RUSHING
MIA: Portis 20-104, 1 TD.
NEB: Crouch 22-114; Diedrick 15-47; Davies 5-16, 1 TD.

PASSING
MIA: Dorsey 22-35-1, 362 yards, 3 TD.
NEB: Crouch 5-15-1, 62 yards.

RECEIVING
MIA: Johnson 7-199, 2 TD; Shockey 5-85, 1 TD.
NEB: Thomas 3-36; Winstrom 2-26.

JANUARY 1, 2003
OKLAHOMA 34, WASHINGTON STATE 14

	1ST	2ND	3RD	4TH	FINAL
OK	3	14	3	14	34
WSU	0	0	0	14	14

SCORING SUMMARY

OK	FG DiCarlo 45
OK	Savage 12 pass from Hybl (DiCarlo kick)
OK	Perkins 51 punt return (DiCarlo kick)
OK	FG DiCarlo 30
OK	Fagan 9 pass from Hybl (DiCarlo kick)
WSU	Riley 37 pass from Gesser (Dunning kick)
OK	Griffin 19 run (DiCarlo kick)
WSU	Moore 89 kickoff return (Dunning kick)

OK	TEAM STATISTICS	WSU
19	First Downs	11
146	Rushing Yards	4
19-29-0	Passing	17-34-2
240	Passing Yards	239
386	Total Yards	243
4-90	Punt Returns - Yards	2-10
1-22	Kickoff Returns - Yards	5-114
5-26.2	Punts - Average	6-46.0
2-1	Fumbles - Lost	3-1
4-28	Penalties - Yards	9-52
37:14	Possession Time	22:46

INDIVIDUAL LEADERS

RUSHING
OK: Griffin 30-144, 1 TD.
WSU: Green 8-45.

PASSING
OK: Hybl 19-29-0, 240 yards, 2 TD
WSU: Gesser 17-34-2, 239 yards, 1 TD

RECEIVING
OK: Peoples 3-80; Savage 4-52, 1 TD.
WSU: Riley 9-139, 1 TD; Darling 5-75

JANUARY 1, 2004
SOUTHERN CAL 28, MICHIGAN 14

	1ST	2ND	3RD	4TH	FINAL
USC	7	7	14	0	28
MICH	0	0	7	7	14

SCORING SUMMARY

USC	Colbert 25 pass from Leinart (Killeen kick)
USC	White 6 pass from Leinart (Killeen kick)
USC	Colbert 47 pass from Leinart (Killeen kick)
MICH	Massaquoi 5 pass from Navarre (Rivas kick)
USC	Leinart 15 pass from Williams (Killeen kick)
MICH	Perry 2 run (Rivas kick)

USC	TEAM STATISTICS	MICH
19	First Downs	25
68	Rushing Yards	49
24-35-0	Passing	27-46-1
342	Passing Yards	271
410	Total Yards	320
2-4	Punt Returns - Yards	2-45
1-0	Kickoff Returns - Yards	2-48
3-46.7	Punts - Average	4-44.0
2-1	Fumbles - Lost	3-0
3-22	Penalties - Yards	2-10
25:34	Possession Time	34:26

INDIVIDUAL LEADERS

RUSHING
USC: Bush 8-41; White 8-26.
MICH: Perry 23-85, 1 TD.

PASSING
USC: Leinart 23-34-0, 327 yards, 3 TD.
MICH: Navarre 27-46-1, 271 yards, 1 TD.

RECEIVING
USC: Colbert 6-149, 2 TD; Williams 8-88.
MICH: Edwards 10-107; Breaston 6-61; Avant 4-61.

JANUARY 1, 2005
TEXAS 38, MICHIGAN 37

	1ST	2ND	3RD	4TH	FINAL
TEX	7	7	7	17	38
MICH	0	14	17	6	37

SCORING SUMMARY

TEX	Young 20 run (Mangum kick)
MICH	Edwards 39 pass from Henne (Rivas kick)
TEX	Thomas 11 pass from Young (Mangum kick)
MICH	Edwards 8 pass from Henne (Rivas kick)
TEX	Young 60 run (Mangum kick)
MICH	Breaston 50 pass from Henne (Rivas kick)
MICH	Edwards 9 pass from Henne (Rivas kick)
MICH	FG Rivas 44
TEX	Young 10 run (Mangum kick)
MICH	FG Rivas 32
TEX	Young 23 run (Mangum kick)
MICH	FG Rivas 42
TEX	FG Mangum 37

TEX	TEAM STATISTICS	MICH
25	First Downs	17
264	Rushing Yards	125
16-28-1	Passing	18-34-0
180	Passing Yards	227
444	Total Yards	352
4-9	Punt Returns - Yards	1-2
8-214	Kickoff Returns - Yards	6-221
4-39.8	Punts - Average	5-42
1-1	Fumbles - Lost	1-0
5-40	Penalties - Yards	9-67
32:40	Possession Time	27:20

INDIVIDUAL LEADERS

RUSHING
TEX: Young 21-192, 4 TD.
MICH: Hart 21-83.

PASSING
TEX: Young 16-28-1, 180 yards, 1 TD.
MICH: Henne 18-34-0, 227 yards, 4 TD.

RECEIVING
TEX: Scaife 5-68; Thomas 4-54, 1 TD.
MICH: Edwards 10-109, 3 TD.

THE BOWLS

ORANGE BOWL

PROFILE

Site: Miami
Stadium: Dolphins Stadium
Capacity: 72,319
Surface: Prescription Athletic Turf

PLAYING SITES

Miami Field Stadium, 1935-37
Orange Bowl, 1938-95, 1999
Pro Player Stadium, renamed
  Dolphins Stadium in 2005, 1996-
  98, since 2000

NAME CHANGES

Orange Bowl, 1935-88
Federal Express Orange Bowl,
  1989-1994
FedEx Orange Bowl, since 1995

SEASON	DATE	PRE-GAME RANK	TEAMS	SCORE	FINAL RANK	MOST VALUABLE PLAYERS	ATT.
1934	Jan. 1, 1935		Bucknell	26			5,134
			Miami (Fla.)	0			
1935	Jan. 1, 1936		Catholic	20			6,568
			Mississippi	19			
1936	Jan. 1, 1937	14	Duquesne	13			9,210
			Mississippi State	12			
1937	Jan. 1, 1938		Auburn	6			18,972
			Michigan State	0			
1938	Jan. 2, 1939	2	Tennessee	17			32,191
		4	Oklahoma	0			
1939	Jan. 1, 1940	16	Georgia Tech	21			29,278
		6	Missouri	7			
1940	Jan. 1, 1941	9	Mississippi State	14			29,554
		13	Georgetown	7			
1941	Jan. 1, 1942	14	Georgia	40			35,786
			TCU	26			
1942	Jan. 1, 1943	10	Alabama	37			25,166
		8	Boston College	21			
1943	Jan. 1, 1944		LSU	19			25,203
			Texas A&M	14			
1944	Jan. 1, 1945		Tulsa	26			23,279
		13	Georgia Tech	12			
1945	Jan. 1, 1946		Miami (Fla.)	13			35,709
			Holy Cross	6			
1946	Jan. 1, 1947	10	Rice	8			36,152
		7	Tennessee	0			
1947	Jan. 1, 1948	10	Georgia Tech	20			59,578
		12	Kansas	14			
1948	Jan. 1, 1949		Texas	41			60,523
		8	Georgia	28			
1949	Jan. 2, 1950	15	Santa Clara	21			64,816
		11	Kentucky	13			
1950	Jan. 1, 1951	10	Clemson	15			65,181
		15	Miami (Fla.)	14			
1951	Jan. 1, 1952	5	Georgia Tech	17			65,839
		9	Baylor	14			
1952	Jan. 1, 1953	9	Alabama	61			66,280
		14	Syracuse	6			
1953	Jan. 1, 1954	4	Oklahoma	7			68,640
		1	Maryland	0			
1954	Jan. 1, 1955	14	Duke	34			68,750
			Nebraska	7			
1955	Jan. 2, 1956	1	Oklahoma	20			76,561
		3	Maryland	6			
1956	Jan. 1, 1957	20	Colorado	27			73,280
		19	Clemson	21			
1957	Jan. 1, 1958	4	Oklahoma	48			76,561
		16	Duke	21			
1958	Jan. 1, 1959	5	Oklahoma	21			75,281
		9	Syracuse	6			
1959	Jan. 1, 1960	5	Georgia	14			72,186
		18	Missouri	0			
1960	Jan. 2, 1961	5	Missouri	21			72,212
		4	Navy	14			
1961	Jan. 1, 1962	4	LSU	25			68,150
		7	Colorado	7			
1962	Jan. 1, 1963	5	Alabama	17			72,880
		8	Oklahoma	0			
1963	Jan. 1, 1964	5	Nebraska	13			72,647
		6	Auburn	7			
1964	Jan. 1, 1965	5	Texas	21		Joe Namath, Alabama, QB	72,647
		1	Alabama	17			
1965	Jan. 1, 1966	4	Alabama	39	1	Steve Sloan, Alabama, QB	72,214
		3	Nebraska	28	5		
1966	Jan. 2, 1967		Florida	27		Larry Smith, Florida, TB	72,426
		8	Georgia Tech	12			
1967	Jan. 1, 1968	3	Oklahoma	26		Bob Warmack, Oklahoma, QB	77,993
		2	Tennessee	24			
1968	Jan. 1, 1969	3	Penn State	15	2	Donnie Shanklin, Kansas, HB	77,719
		6	Kansas	14	7		
1969	Jan. 1, 1970	2	Penn State	10	2	Chuck Burkhart, Penn State, QB	77,282
		6	Missouri	3	6	Mike Reid, Penn State, DT	
1970	Jan. 1, 1971	3	Nebraska	17	1	Jerry Tagge, Nebraska, QB	80,699
		5	LSU	12	7	Willie Harper, Nebraska, DE	
1971	Jan. 1, 1972	1	Nebraska	38	1	Jerry Tagge, Nebraska, QB	78,151
		2	Alabama	6	4	Rich Glover, Nebraska, DG	
1972	Jan. 1, 1973	9	Nebraska	40	4	Johnny Rodgers, Nebraska, WB	80,010
		12	Notre Dame	6	14	Rich Glover, Nebraska, DG	
1973	Jan. 1, 1974	6	Penn State	16	5	Tom Shuman, Penn State, QB	60,477
		13	LSU	9	13	Randy Crowder, Penn State, DT	
1974	Jan. 1, 1975	9	Notre Dame	13	6	Wayne Bullock, Notre Dame, FB	71,801
		2	Alabama	11	5	Leroy Cook, Alabama, DE	
1975	Jan. 1, 1976	3	Oklahoma	14	1	Steve Davis, Oklahoma, QB	80,307
		5	Michigan	6	8	Lee Roy Selmon, Oklahoma, DT	
1976	Jan. 1, 1977	11	Ohio State	27	6	Rod Gerald, Ohio State, QB	65,537
		12	Colorado	10	16	Tom Cousineau, Ohio State, LB	
1977	Jan. 2, 1978	6	Arkansas	31	3	Roland Sales, Arkansas, RB	60,987
		2	Oklahoma	6	7	Reggie Freeman, Arkansas, NG	
1978	Jan. 1, 1979	4	Oklahoma	31	3	Billy Sims, Oklahoma, RB	66,365
		6	Nebraska	24	8	Reggie Kinlaw, Oklahoma, NG	
1979	Jan. 1, 1980	5	Oklahoma	24	3	J.C. Watts, Oklahoma, QB	66,714
		4	Florida State	7	6	Bud Hebert, Oklahoma, FS	
1980	Jan. 1, 1981	4	Oklahoma	18	3	J.C. Watts, Oklahoma, QB	71,043
		2	Florida State	17	5	Jarvis Coursey, Florida State, DE	

SEASON	DATE	PRE-GAME RANK	TEAMS	SCORE	FINAL RANK	MOST VALUABLE PLAYERS	ATT.
1981	Jan. 1, 1982	1	Clemson	22	1	Homer Jordan, Clemson, QB	72,748
		4	Nebraska	15	11	Jeff Davis, Clemson, LB	
1982	Jan. 1, 1983	3	Nebraska	21	3	Turner Gill, Nebraska, QB	68,713
		13	LSU	20	11	Dave Rimington, Nebraska, C	
1983	Jan. 2, 1984	5	Miami (Fla.)	31	1	Bernie Kosar, Miami (Fla.), QB	72,549
		1	Nebraska	30	2	Jack Fernandez, Miami (Fla.), LB	
1984	Jan. 1, 1985	4	Washington	28	2	Jacque Robinson, Washington, TB	56,294
		2	Oklahoma	17	6	Ron Holmes, Washington, DT	
1985	Jan. 1, 1986	3	Oklahoma	25	1	Sonny Brown, Oklahoma, DB	74,178
		1	Penn State	10	3	Tim Lashar, Oklahoma, K	
1986	Jan. 1, 1987	3	Oklahoma	42	3	Spencer Tillman, Oklahoma, HB	52,717
		9	Arkansas	8	15	Dante Jones, Oklahoma, LB	
1987	Jan. 1, 1988	2	Miami (Fla.)	20	1	Bernard Clark, Miami (Fla.), LB	74,760
		1	Oklahoma	14	3	Darrell Reed, Oklahoma, DE	
1988	Jan. 2, 1989	2	Miami (Fla.)	23	2	Steve Walsh, Miami (Fla.), QB	79,480
		6	Nebraska	3	10	Charles Fryar, Nebraska, CB	
1989	Jan. 1, 1990	4	Notre Dame	21	2	Raghib Ismail, Notre Dame, WR	81,190
		1	Colorado	6	4	Darian Hagan, Colorado, QB	
1990	Jan. 1, 1991	1	Colorado	10	1	Charles Johnson, Colorado, QB	77,062
		5	Notre Dame	9	6	Chris Zorich, Notre Dame, NG	
1991	Jan. 1, 1992	1	Miami (Fla.)	22	1	Larry Jones, Miami, RB	77,747
		11	Nebraska	0	15	Tyrone Leggett, Nebraska, CB	
1992	Jan. 1, 1993	3	Florida State	27	2	Charlie Ward, Florida State, QB	57,324
		11	Nebraska	14	14	Corey Dixon, Nebraska, SE	
1993	Jan. 1, 1994	1	Florida State	18	1	Charlie Ward, Florida State, QB	81,536
		2	Nebraska	16	3	Tommie Frazier, Nebraska, QB	
1994	Jan. 1, 1995	1	Nebraska	24	1	Tommie Frazier, Nebraska, QB	81,753
		3	Miami (Fla.)	17	6	Chris T. Jones, Miami (Fla.) WR	
1995	Jan. 1, 1996	8	Florida State	31	4	Andre Cooper, Florida State, WR	72,198
		6	Notre Dame	26	11	Derrick Mayes, Notre Dame, WR	
1996	Dec. 31, 1996	6	Nebraska	41	6	Damon Benning, Nebraska, RB	63,297
		10	Virginia Tech	21	13	Ken Oxendine, Virginia Tech, RB	
1997	Jan. 2, 1998	2	Nebraska	42	2	Ahman Green, Nebraska, RB	74,002
		3	Tennessee	17	7		
1998	Jan. 2, 1999	7	Florida	31	5	Travis Taylor, Florida, WR	67,919
		18	Syracuse	10	25		
1999	Jan. 1, 2000	8	Michigan	35 OT	5	David Terrell, Michigan, WR	70,461
		5	Alabama	34	8		
2000	Jan. 3, 2001	1	Oklahoma	13	1	Torrance Marshall, Oklahoma, LB	76,835
		3	Florida State	2	5		
2001	Jan. 2, 2002	5	Florida	56	3	Taylor Jacobs, Florida, WR	73,640
		6	Maryland	23	11		
2002	Jan. 2, 2003	5	Southern Cal	38	4	Carson Palmer, Southern Cal, QB	75,971
		3	Iowa	17	8		
2003	Jan. 1, 2004	10	Miami (Fla.)	16	5	Jarrett Payton, Miami (Fla.) RB	76,739
		9	Florida State	14	11		
2004	Jan. 4, 2005	1	Southern Cal	55	1	Matt Leinart, Southern Cal, QB	75,192
		2	Oklahoma	19	3		

JANUARY 1, 1935
BUCKNELL 26, MIAMI (FLA.) 0

	1ST	2ND	3RD	4TH	FINAL
BUCK	0	7	6	13	26
MIA	0	0	0	0	0

SCORING SUMMARY
BUCK	Smith 23 pass from Jenkins (Dobie kick)
BUCK	Miller 4 run (kick failed)
BUCK	Smith 8 run (Dobie kick)
BUCK	Reznichak 10 run (kick failed)

BUCK	TEAM STATISTICS	MIA
12	First Downs	8
215	Rushing Yards	15
3-13-1	Passing	3-14-5
63	Passing Yards	13
278	Total Yards	28
6-41.7	Punts - Average	13-29.6
2-1	Fumbles - Lost	4-1
4-30	Penalties - Yards	1-15

JANUARY 1, 1936
CATHOLIC 20, MISSISSIPPI 19

	1ST	2ND	3RD	4TH	FINAL
CA	7	6	7	0	20
MISS	0	6	0	13	19

SCORING SUMMARY
CA	Adamaitis 2 yard run (Milligan kick)
CA	Foley 48 pass from Adamaitis (kick failed)
MISS	Peters 67 run (kick failed)
CA	Rydewski 24 blocked punt return (Makofske kick)
MISS	Bernard 3 run (kick failed)
MISS	Poole 24 pass from Baumsten (Richardson kick)

CA	TEAM STATISTICS	MISS
7	First Downs	15
124	Rushing Yards	212
1-3-2	Passing	3-12-4
48	Passing Yards	53
172	Total Yards	265
13-41.0	Punts - Average	11-38.0
1-1	Fumbles - Lost	3-2
1-10	Penalties - Yards	3-30

INDIVIDUAL LEADERS
RUSHING
CA: Makofske 12-46; Carroll 12-45.
MISS: Peters 11-89, 1 TD; Rogers 16-50.
PASSING
CA: Adamaitis 1-3-2, 48 yards, 1 TD.
MISS: Baumsten 3-12-4, 53 yards, 1 TD.
RECEIVING
CA: Foley 1-48, 1 TD.
MISS: Poole 1-24, 1 TD.

JANUARY 1, 1937
DUQUESNE 13, MISSISSIPPI STATE 12

	1ST	2ND	3RD	4TH	FINAL
DUQ	0	7	0	6	13
MSU	6	6	0	0	12

SCORING SUMMARY
MSU	Pickle 10 run (kick failed)
DUQ	Brumbaugh 1 run (Brumbaugh kick)
MSU	Walters 40 pass from Armstrong (kick failed)
DUQ	Hefferle 72 pass from Brumbaugh (kick failed)

DUQ	TEAM STATISTICS	MSU
14	First Downs	12
184	Rushing Yards	133
3-13-0	Passing	5-18-4
98	Passing Yards	150
282	Total Yards	283
9-24.7	Punts - Average	6-43.0
0-0	Fumbles - Lost	0-0
1-5	Penalties - Yards	1-5

JANUARY 1, 1938
AUBURN 6, MICHIGAN STATE 0

	1ST	2ND	3RD	4TH	FINAL
AUB	0	6	0	0	6
MSU	0	0	0	0	0

SCORING SUMMARY
AUB	O'Gwynne 2 run (kick failed)

AUB	TEAM STATISTICS	MSU
12	First Downs	2
197	Rushing Yards	40
4-12-2	Passing	2-9-3
81	Passing Yards	25
278	Total Yards	65
10-33.7	Punts - Average	12-35.2
0-0	Fumbles - Lost	0-0
50	Penalty Yards	35

JANUARY 2, 1939
TENNESSEE 17, OKLAHOMA 0

	1ST	2ND	3RD	4TH	FINAL
TENN	7	3	0	7	17
OKLA	0	0	0	0	0

SCORING SUMMARY

TENN	Foxx 8 run (Wyatt kick)
TENN	FG Wyatt 22
TENN	Wood 19 run (Foxx Kick)

TENN	TEAM STATISTICS	OKLA
16	First Downs	5
217	Rushing Yards	25
5-16-0	Passing	9-26-1
51	Passing Yards	56
268	Total Yards	81
12-37.1	Punts - Average	13-40.6
2-2	Fumbles - Lost	2-2
17-157	Penalties - Yards	9-85

INDIVIDUAL LEADERS

RUSHING
TENN: Coffman 12-56; Cafego 13-45.
OKLA: McCullough 9-9.

PASSING
TENN: Wood 2-5-0, 40 yards.
OKLA: McCullough 7-19-1, 37 yards.

RECEIVING
TENN: Cifers 1-23.
OKLA: Clark 3-30.

JANUARY 1, 1940
GEORGIA TECH 21, MISSOURI 7

	1ST	2ND	3RD	4TH	FINAL
GT	7	7	7	0	21
MO	7	0	0	0	7

SCORING SUMMARY

MO	Christman 1 run (Cunningham kick)
GT	Ector 1 run (Goree kick)
GT	Ison 31 run (Goree kick)
GT	Wheby 59 run (Goree kick)

GT	TEAM STATISTICS	MO
12	First Downs	14
210	Rushing Yards	151
8-14-1	Passing	8-26-1
91	Passing Yards	76
301	Total Yards	227
7-33.0	Punts - Average	7-33.0
6-3	Fumbles - Lost	2-1
6-36	Penalties - Yards	3-15

JANUARY 1, 1941
MISSISSIPPI STATE 14, GEORGETOWN 7

	1ST	2ND	3RD	4TH	FINAL
MSU	7	7	0	0	14
GEO	0	0	7	0	7

SCORING SUMMARY

MSU	Tripson blocked punt recovery (Dees kick)
MSU	Jefferson 2 run (Bruce kick)
GEO	Castiglia 2 run (Lio kick)

MSU	TEAM STATISTICS	GEO
8	First Downs	14
69	Rushing Yards	117
5-11-3	Passing	9-22-0
50	Passing Yards	104
119	Total Yards	221
11-36.8	Punts - Average	8-28.2
2-2	Fumbles - Lost	1-1
11-71	Penalties - Yards	9-90

JANUARY 1, 1942
GEORGIA 40, TCU 26

	1ST	2ND	3RD	4TH	FINAL
UGA	19	14	7	0	40
TCU	7	0	7	12	26

SCORING SUMMARY

UGA	Keuper 2 run (Costa kick)
UGA	Conger 61 pass from Sinkwich (kick failed)
UGA	Kimsey 60 pass from Sinkwich (kick failed)
TCU	Gillespie 4 run (Medanich kick)
UGA	Davis 15 pass from Sinkwich (Costa kick)
UGA	Davis 23 pass from Todd (Costa kick)
UGA	Sinkwich 43 run (Costa kick)
TCU	Alford 20 pass from Nix (Roach kick)
TCU	Alford 15 pass from Nix (run failed)
TCU	Kring 53 pass from Gillespie (run failed)

UGA	TEAM STATISTICS	TCU
12	First Downs	8
218	Rushing Yards	71
12-24-4	Passing	9-24-6
281	Passing Yards	137
499	Total Yards	208
4-22.2	Punts - Average	7-37.0
3-3	Fumbles - Lost	1-0
7-54	Penalties - Yards	2-24

JANUARY 1, 1943
ALABAMA 37, BOSTON COLLEGE 21

	1ST	2ND	3RD	4TH	FINAL
ALA	0	22	6	9	37
BC	14	7	0	0	21

SCORING SUMMARY

BC	Holovak 65 run (Connolly kick)
BC	Holovak 35 run (Connolly kick)
ALA	Leeth 14 pass from Mosley (Hecht kick)
ALA	Cook 18 pass from August (kick failed)
ALA	Jenkins 40 run (kick failed)
BC	Holovak 2 run (Connolly kick)
ALA	FG Hecht 25
ALA	August 15 run (kick failed)
ALA	Jenkins 1 run (Hecht kick)
ALA	Safety

ALA	TEAM STATISTICS	BC
13	First Downs	13
244	Rushing Yards	202
9-15-2	Passing	11-20-1
97	Passing Yards	170
341	Total Yards	372
5-39.0	Punts - Average	4-33.7
1-0	Fumbles - Lost	5-2
4-20	Penalties - Yards	3-11

JANUARY 1, 1944
LSU 19, TEXAS A&M 14

	1ST	2ND	3RD	4TH	FINAL
LSU	12	0	7	0	19
A&M	7	0	7	0	14

SCORING SUMMARY

LSU	Van Buren 11 run (kick failed)
LSU	Goode 24 pass from Van Buren (kick failed)
A&M	Burditt 21 pass from Hallmark (Burditt kick)
LSU	Van Buren 63 run (Van Buren kick)
A&M	Settegast 18 pass from Hallmark (Burditt kick)

LSU	TEAM STATISTICS	A&M
7	First Downs	7
207	Rushing Yards	4
4-12-0	Passing	14-32-5
172	Passing Yards	199
379	Total Yards	203
10-40.3	Punts - Average	9-41.8
3-3	Fumbles - Lost	5-2
7-81	Penalties - Yards	4-35

JANUARY 1, 1945
TULSA 26, GEORGIA TECH 12

	1ST	2ND	3RD	4TH	FINAL
UT	14	0	12	0	26
GT	0	0	6	6	12

SCORING SUMMARY

UT	Shedlosky 14 pass from Moss (Moss kick)
UT	Shedlosky 3 run (Moss kick)
UT	White 35 run (kick failed)
GT	McIntosh 51 pass from Broyles (kick failed)
UT	Wilson 90 kickoff return (kick failed)
GT	Taylor 2 run (kick failed)

UT	TEAM STATISTICS	GT
14	First Downs	17
180	Rushing Yards	36
6-16-0	Passing	19-34-2
137	Passing Yards	304
317	Total Yards	340
6-38.8	Punts - Average	4-25.7
2-1	Fumbles - Lost	6-3
4-41	Penalties - Yards	1-15

JANUARY 1, 1946
MIAMI (FLA.) 13, HOLY CROSS 6

	1ST	2ND	3RD	4TH	FINAL
MIA	0	6	0	7	13
HC	0	6	0	0	6

SCORING SUMMARY

MIA	Krull 1 run (kick failed)
HC	Brennan 16 pass from Koslowski (kick failed)
MIA	Hudson 89 interception return (Ghaul kick)

MIA	TEAM STATISTICS	HC
7	First Downs	13
185	Rushing Yards	169
0-10-2	Passing	9-19-4
0	Passing Yards	70
185	Total Yards	239
10-36.4	Punts - Average	9-38.5
0-0	Fumbles - Lost	1-1
7-42	Penalties - Yards	1-5

JANUARY 1, 1947
RICE 8, TENNESSEE 0

	1ST	2ND	3RD	4TH	FINAL
RICE	8	0	0	0	8
TENN	0	0	0	0	0

SCORING SUMMARY

RICE	Safety (Murphy blocks punt out of endzone)
RICE	Kenney 50 run (kick failed)

RICE	TEAM STATISTICS	TENN
9	First Downs	5
208	Rushing Yards	105
0-4-2	Passing	4-19-4
0	Passing Yards	32
208	Total Yards	137
13-44.0	Punts - Average	15-38.8
4-3	Fumbles - Lost	2-0
4-40	Penalties - Yards	6-67

JANUARY 1, 1948
GEORGIA TECH 20, KANSAS 14

	1ST	2ND	3RD	4TH	FINAL
GT	0	7	13	0	20
KU	0	7	0	7	14

SCORING SUMMARY

GT	Patton 26 pass from Still (Bowen kick)
KU	Evans 12 run (Fambrough kick)
GT	Queen 15 pass from Still (kick failed)
GT	Patton 5 pass from Still (Bowen kick)
KU	Evans 13 pass from Hogan (Fambrough kick)

GT	TEAM STATISTICS	KU
9	First Downs	14
99	Rushing Yards	93
11-19-1	Passing	10-19-1
109	Passing Yards	148
208	Total Yards	241
9-39.7	Punts - Average	7-34.3
1-1	Fumbles - Lost	4-1
10-67.5	Penalties - Yards	5-37.5

JANUARY 1, 1949
TEXAS 41, GEORGIA 28

	1ST	2ND	3RD	4TH	FINAL
TEX	13	7	7	14	41
UGA	7	7	7	7	28

SCORING SUMMARY

UGA	Bodine 71 interception return (Geri kick)
TEX	Borneman 4 run (Clay kick)
TEX	Landry 14 run (kick failed)
UGA	Geri 1 run (Geri kick)
TEX	Samuels 21 run (Clay kick)
TEX	Proctor 24 pass from Campbell (Clay kick)
UGA	Geri 6 run (Geri kick)
UGA	Walston 37 pass from Rauch (Geri kick)
TEX	Clay 2 run (Clay kick)
TEX	Clay 4 run (Clay kick)

TEX	TEAM STATISTICS	UGA
19	First Downs	9
332	Rushing Yards	56
5-10-0	Passing	11-17-2
70	Passing Yards	161
402	Total Yards	217
5-40.0	Punts - Average	5-41.0
2-1	Fumbles - Lost	1-1
5-55	Penalties - Yards	6-50

INDIVIDUAL LEADERS

RUSHING
TEX: Landry 17-117, 1 TD; Pyle 11-76; Clay 13-70, 2 TD.
UGA: Geri 15-45, 2 TD.

PASSING
TEX: Campbell 5-10-0, 70 yards, 1 TD.
UGA: Rauch 11-17-2, 161 yards, 1 TD.

JANUARY 2, 1950
SANTA CLARA 21, KENTUCKY 13

	1ST	2ND	3RD	4TH	FINAL
SC	0	0	14	7	21
UK	0	7	0	6	13

SCORING SUMMARY

UK	Jamerson 2 run (Brooks kick)
SC	Pasco 2 run (Vargas kick)
SC	Haynes 2 run (Vargas kick)
UK	Clark 52 pass from Parilli (kick failed)
SC	Vogel 17 run (Vargas kick)

SC	TEAM STATISTICS	UK
8	First Downs	18
144	Rushing Yards	184
3-12-1	Passing	6-11-2
79	Passing Yards	122
223	Total Yards	306
7-41.2	Punts - Average	9-38.5
2-2	Fumbles - Lost	1-1
4-30	Penalties - Yards	4-22.5

JANUARY 1, 1951
CLEMSON 15, MIAMI (FLA.) 14

	1ST	2ND	3RD	4TH	FINAL
CLEM	0	7	6	2	15
MIA	0	0	14	0	14

SCORING SUMMARY
CLEM   Cone 1 run (Radcliff kick)
CLEM   Smith 21 pass from Hair (kick failed)
MIA   Mallios 5 run (Watson kick)
MIA   F. Smith 17 pass from Hackett (Watson kick)
CLEM   Safety (F. Smith tackled by S. Smith in endzone)

CLEM	TEAM STATISTICS	MIA
19	First Downs	7
144	Rushing Yards	112
9-18-4	Passing	5-15-3
178	Passing Yards	100
322	Total Yards	212
4-29.4	Punts - Average	5-40.2
3-1	Fumbles - Lost	0-0
2-20	Penalties - Yards	4-55

INDIVIDUAL LEADERS
RUSHING
CLEM: Cone 31-81, 1 TD; Hair 10-48.
MIA: Smith 15-87.
PASSING
CLEM: Hair 9-16-3, 178 yards, 1 TD.
MIA: Schneidenbach 3-9-3, 78 yards.
RECEIVING
CLEM: Smith 6-93, 1 TD; Hudson 1-46.
MIA: Lutes 1-78; F. Smith 2-19, 1 TD.

JANUARY 1, 1952
GEORGIA TECH 17, BAYLOR 14

	1ST	2ND	3RD	4TH	FINAL
GT	7	0	0	10	17
BU	7	7	0	0	14

SCORING SUMMARY
BU   Parma 1 run (Brocato kick)
GT   Hardeman 3 run (Rodgers kick)
BU   Coody 4 run (Brocato kick)
GT   Martin 22 pass from Crawford (Rodgers kick)
GT   FG Rodgers 16

GT	TEAM STATISTICS	BU
9	First Downs	17
107	Rushing Yards	206
6-14-1	Passing	7-18-3
84	Passing Yards	93
191	Total Yards	299
7-35.3	Punts - Average	6-34.3
1-1	Fumbles - Lost	3-0
6-60	Penalties - Yards	7-85

INDIVIDUAL LEADERS
RUSHING
GT: Hardeman 17-44, 1 TD; Crawford 9-36.
BU: Parma 19-107, 1 TD; Carpenter 15-65.
PASSING
GT: Crawford 6-14-1, 84 yards, 1 TD.
BU: Isbell 8-18-3, 93 yards.
RECEIVING
GT: Martin 4-49, 1 TD.
BU: Riley 3-35; Williams 3-32.

JANUARY 1, 1953
ALABAMA 61, SYRACUSE 6

	1ST	2ND	3RD	4TH	FINAL
ALA	7	14	20	20	61
SYR	6	0	0	0	6

SCORING SUMMARY
ALA   Luna 28 pass from Hobson (Luna kick)
SYR   Szombathy 15 pass from Stark (kick failed)
ALA   Marlow 2 run (Luna kick)
ALA   Tharp 50 pass from Hobson (Luna kick)
ALA   Luna 38 run (Luna kick)
ALA   Lewis 4 run (Luna kick)
ALA   Lewis 30 run (kick failed)
ALA   Cummings 22 pass from Starr (kick failed)
ALA   Ingram 80 punt return (Luna kick)
ALA   Hill 60 interception return (Luna kick)

ALA	TEAM STATISTICS	SYR
25	First Downs	15
286	Rushing Yards	75
22-34-2	Passing	17-34-5
300	Passing Yards	157
586	Total Yards	232
3-30.0	Punts - Average	8-35.0
3-2	Fumbles - Lost	0-0
5-45	Penalties - Yards	5-42

INDIVIDUAL LEADERS
RUSHING
ALA: Lewis 11-77, 2 TD; Tharp 11-62, 1 TD; Luna 4-51, 1 TD.
SYR: Leberman 14-36.
PASSING
ALA: Hobson 14-22-2, 207 yards, 2 TD; Starr 8-12-0, 93 yards, 1 TD.
SYR: Stark 17-33-4, 157 yards, 1 TD.
RECEIVING
ALA: Curtis 8-65; Cummings 2-61, 1 TD.
SYR: Szombathy 5-45, 1 TD; Hoffman 5-43.

JANUARY 1, 1954
OKLAHOMA 7, MARYLAND 0

	1ST	2ND	3RD	4TH	FINAL
OKLA	0	7	0	0	7
MD	0	0	0	0	0

SCORING SUMMARY
OKLA   Griggs 25 run (Leake kick)

OKLA	TEAM STATISTICS	MD
10	First Downs	13
208	Rushing Yards	176
4-6-0	Passing	5-12-1
22	Passing Yards	36
230	Total Yards	212
7-31.3	Punts - Average	5-29.0
2-2	Fumbles - Lost	2-1
7-45	Penalties - Yards	2-10

INDIVIDUAL LEADERS
RUSHING
OKLA: Griggs 13-89, 1 TD.
MD: Felton 10-51.
PASSING
OKLA: Calame 4-4-0, 22 yards.
MD: Boxold 3-9-1, 42 yards.
RECEIVING
OKLA: Burris 3-17.
MD: Holan 2-31.

JANUARY 1, 1955
DUKE 34, NEBRASKA 7

	1ST	2ND	3RD	4TH	FINAL
DUKE	0	14	6	14	34
NEB	0	0	7	0	7

SCORING SUMMARY
DUKE   Pascal 7 run (Nelson kick)
DUKE   Kocourek 5 pass from Barger (Nelson kick)
DUKE   Sorrell 5 pass from Barger (kick failed)
NEB   Comstock 3 run (Smith kick)
DUKE   McKeithan 1 run (Nelson kick)
DUKE   Eberdt 3 run (Nelson kick)

DUKE	TEAM STATISTICS	NEB
23	First Downs	6
288	Rushing Yards	84
7-13-0	Passing	1-9-2
82	Passing Yards	26
370	Total Yards	110
5-23.6	Punts - Average	7-28.9
2-1	Fumbles - Lost	0-0
2-30	Penalties - Yards	2-20

INDIVIDUAL LEADERS
RUSHING
DUKE: Pascal 9-91, 1 TD; McKeithan 8-48, 1 TD.
NEB: Smith 5-22; Comstock 3-20, 1 TD.
PASSING
DUKE: Barger 7-9-0, 82 yards, 2 TD.
NEB: Greenlaw 1-9-2, 26 yards.
RECEIVING
DUKE: Sorrell 3-53, 1 TD.
NEB: Korinek 1-26.

JANUARY 2, 1956
OKLAHOMA 20, MARYLAND 6

	1ST	2ND	3RD	4TH	FINAL
OKLA	0	0	14	6	20
MD	0	6	0	0	6

SCORING SUMMARY
MD   Vereb 15 run (kick failed)
OKLA   McDonald 4 run (Pricer kick)
OKLA   O'Neal 1 run (Pricer kick)
OKLA   Dodd 82 interception return (kick failed)

OKLA	TEAM STATISTICS	MD
16	First Downs	9
202	Rushing Yards	187
4-10-1	Passing	3-10-3
53	Passing Yards	46
255	Total Yards	233
8-34.5	Punts - Average	7-61.0
1-1	Fumbles - Lost	3-2
3-35	Penalties - Yards	7-61

INDIVIDUAL LEADERS
RUSHING
OKLA: Harris 9-50.
MD: Vereb 8-108, 1 TD.
PASSING
OKLA: Harris 3-5-0, 34 yards.
MD: Beightol 2-7-2, 35 yards.
RECEIVING
OKLA: Burris 2-28.
MD: Cooke 1-21.

JANUARY 1, 1957
COLORADO 27, CLEMSON 21

	1ST	2ND	3RD	4TH	FINAL
COLO	0	20	0	7	27
CLEM	0	0	14	7	21

SCORING SUMMARY
COLO   Bayuk 2 run (Indorf kick)
COLO   Dowler 6 run (Cook kick)
COLO   Cook 26 run (kick failed)
CLEM   Wells 3 run (Bussey kick)
CLEM   Wells 58 run (Bussey kick)
CLEM   Spooner 1 run (Bussey kick)
COLO   Bayuk 1 run (Indorf kick)

COLO	TEAM STATISTICS	CLEM
16	First Downs	14
279	Rushing Yards	217
2-4-0	Passing	3-8-2
27	Passing Yards	25
306	Total Yards	242
5-36.6	Punts - Average	7-37.9
8-3	Fumbles - Lost	0-0
5-55	Penalties - Yards	4-40

INDIVIDUAL LEADERS
RUSHING
COLO: Bayuk 23-121, 2 TD; Stransky 7-59.
CLEM: Wells 18-125, 2 TD; Spooner 18-65, 1 TD.
PASSING
COLO: Morley 1-1-0, 18 yards.
CLEM: Bussey 3-8-2, 9 yards.
RECEIVING
COLO: Clark 1-18; Dowler 1-9.
CLEM: Lawrence 1-16; Smith 1-16.

JANUARY 1, 1958
OKLAHOMA 48, DUKE 21

	1ST	2ND	3RD	4TH	FINAL
OKLA	7	7	7	27	48
DUKE	0	7	7	7	21

SCORING SUMMARY

OKLA	Baker 94 interception (Dodd kick)
OKLA	Thomas 13 run (Dodd kick)
DUKE	McElhaney 1 run (Carlton kick)
OKLA	Dodd 1 run (Dodd kick)
DUKE	Dutrow 8 run (Carlton kick)
OKLA	Sandefer 4 run (Dodd kick)
OKLA	Baker 29 pass from Hobby (Boyd kick)
OKLA	Hobby 9 pass from Baker (kick failed)
DUKE	McElhaney 4 run (Carlton kick)
OKLA	Carpenter 73 interception return (McDaniel kick)

OKLA	TEAM STATISTICS	DUKE
11	First Downs	16
165	Rushing Yards	231
9-18-3	Passing	8-13-2
114	Passing Yards	97
279	Total Yards	328
7-34.7	Punts - Average	10-28.1
2-1	Fumbles - Lost	3-2
12-150	Penalties - Yards	3-25

INDIVIDUAL LEADERS

RUSHING
OKLA: Thomas 13-62, 1 TD.
DUKE: Carlton 15-84.

PASSING
OKLA: Hobby 3-4-0, 48 yards, 1 TD.
DUKE: Brodhead 4-6-1, 53 yards.

RECEIVING
OKLA: Baker 1-29, 1 TD.
DUKE: Latimore 3-33.

JANUARY 1, 1959
OKLAHOMA 21, SYRACUSE 6

	1ST	2ND	3RD	4TH	FINAL
OKLA	14	0	7	0	21
SYR	0	0	0	6	6

SCORING SUMMARY

OKLA	Gautt 42 run (run failed)
OKLA	Coyle 79 pass from Hobby (Sandefer to Hobby)
OKLA	Hobby 40 punt return (Boyd kick)
SYR	Weber 15 run (run failed)

OKLA	TEAM STATISTICS	SYR
12	First Downs	18
152	Rushing Yards	239
3-4-0	Passing	10-25-2
93	Passing Yards	72
245	Total Yards	311
8-37.0	Punts - Average	8-31.2
2-1	Fumbles - Lost	2-2
3-35	Penalties - Yards	4-20

INDIVIDUAL LEADERS

RUSHING
OKLA: Gautt 6-94, 1 TD.
SYR: Stephens 15-77; Anderson 12-58.

PASSING
OKLA: Hobby 1-1-0, 79 yards, 1 TD.
SYR: Zimmerman 10-22-1, 72 yards.

RECEIVING
OKLA: Coyle 1-79, 1 TD.
SYR: Stephens 5-43.

JANUARY 1, 1960
GEORGIA 14, MISSOURI 0

	1ST	2ND	3RD	4TH	FINAL
UGA	7	0	0	7	14
MO	0	0	0	0	0

SCORING SUMMARY

UGA	McKenny 29 pass from Tarkenton (Pennington kick)
UGA	Box 33 pass from Tarkenton (Pennington kick)

UGA	TEAM STATISTICS	MO
14	First Downs	17
88	Rushing Yards	80
9-21-2	Passing	14-24-3
128	Passing Yards	180
216	Total Yards	260
7-46.9	Punts - Average	6-38.7
1-0	Fumbles - Lost	3-0
7-44	Penalties - Yards	7-72

INDIVIDUAL LEADERS

RUSHING
UGA: Brown 10-39.
MO: West 9-37; Smith 14-21.

PASSING
UGA: Tarkenton 9-16-1, 128 yards, 2 TD.
MO: Snowden 11-17-1, 152 yards.

RECEIVING
UGA: Box 1-33, 1 TD; Brown 3-29.
MO: Sloan 6-73; Smith 3-35.

JANUARY 2, 1961
MISSOURI 21, NAVY 14

	1ST	2ND	3RD	4TH	FINAL
MO	7	7	0	7	21
NAVY	6	0	0	8	14

SCORING SUMMARY

NAVY	Mather 98 fumble return (kick failed)
MO	Beal 90 interception return (Tobin kick)
MO	Smith 4 run (Tobin kick)
MO	Taylor 1 run (Tobin kick)
NAVY	Bellino 27 pass from Spooner (Luper pass from Spooner)

MO	TEAM STATISTICS	NAVY
19	First Downs	9
296	Rushing Yards	-8
1-6-0	Passing	13-23-4
5	Passing Yards	176
301	Total Yards	168
5-40.0	Punts - Average	3-37.0
5-3	Fumbles - Lost	2-0
1-15	Penalties - Yards	1-4

INDIVIDUAL LEADERS

RUSHING
MO: West 21-108; Smith 16-93, 1 TD.
NAVY: Prichard 1-9.

PASSING
MO: Taylor 1-6-0, 5 yards.
NAVY: Spooner 13-21-4, 176 yards, 1 TD.

RECEIVING
MO: West 1-5.
NAVY: Prichard 4-69; Bellino 3-37, 1 TD.

JANUARY 1, 1962
LSU 25, COLORADO 7

	1ST	2ND	3RD	4TH	FINAL
LSU	5	6	14	0	25
COLO	0	7	0	0	7

SCORING SUMMARY

LSU	FG Harris 30
LSU	Safety (blocked punt)
COLO	Schweninger 59 interception return (Hillebrand kick)
LSU	Crawford 1 run (run failed)
LSU	Field 9 run (Harris kick)
LSU	Sykes recovered blocked punt in end zone (Harris kick)

LSU	TEAM STATISTICS	COLO
19	First Downs	7
206	Rushing Yards	24
8-18-3	Passing	12-39-0
109	Passing Yards	105
315	Total Yards	129
4-33.8	Punts - Average	8-22.1
2-1	Fumbles - Lost	2-1
65	Penalty Yards	35

INDIVIDUAL LEADERS

RUSHING
LSU: Gros 10-55; Field 8-36, 1 TD.
COLO: Schweninger 5-9.

PASSING
LSU: Amedee 6-12-2, 88 yards.
COLO: Weidner 11-36-0, 98 yards.

RECEIVING
LSU: Wilkins 3-58; Campbell 3-30.
COLO: Hillebrand 4-52; Meadows 3-24.

JANUARY 1, 1963
ALABAMA 17, OKLAHOMA 0

	1ST	2ND	3RD	4TH	FINAL
ALA	7	7	3	0	17
OKLA	0	0	0	0	0

SCORING SUMMARY

ALA	Williamson 25 pass from Namath (Davis kick)
ALA	Clark 15 run (Davis kick)
ALA	FG Davis 19

ALA	TEAM STATISTICS	OKLA
15	First Downs	10
174	Rushing Yards	154
9-17-1	Passing	4-8-0
86	Passing Yards	106
260	Total Yards	260
8-40.5	Punts - Average	10-34.0
1-1	Fumbles - Lost	2-2
1-12	Penalties - Yards	1-5

INDIVIDUAL LEADERS

RUSHING
ALA: Versprille 14-52.
OKLA: Grisham 28-107.

PASSING
ALA: Namath 9-17-1, 86 yards, 1 TD.
OKLA: Fletcher 1-1-0, 56 yards.

RECEIVING
ALA: Williamson 4-58, 1 TD.
OKLA: Bumgardner 1-56.

JANUARY 1, 1964
NEBRASKA 13, AUBURN 7

	1ST	2ND	3RD	4TH	FINAL
NEB	10	3	0	0	13
AUB	0	0	7	0	7

SCORING SUMMARY

NEB	Claridge 68 run (Theisen kick)
NEB	FG Theisen 31
NEB	FG Theisen 26
AUB	Sidle 13 run (Woodall kick)

NEB	TEAM STATISTICS	AUB
11	First Downs	17
204	Rushing Yards	126
4-9-0	Passing	14-27-1
30	Passing Yards	157
234	Total Yards	283
7-38.3	Punts - Average	6-35.2
2-1	Fumbles - Lost	3-1
6-65	Penalties - Yards	5-39

INDIVIDUAL LEADERS

RUSHING
NEB: Claridge 14-108, 1 TD.
AUB: Sidle 25-96, 1 TD.

PASSING
NEB: Claridge 4-9-0, 30 yards.
AUB: Sidle 12-25-0, 141 yards.

RECEIVING
NEB: Duepke 1-13.
AUB: Simpson 4-39.

JANUARY 1, 1965
TEXAS 21, ALABAMA 17

	1ST	2ND	3RD	4TH	FINAL
TEX	7	14	0	0	21
ALA	0	7	7	3	17

SCORING SUMMARY

TEX	Koy 79 run (Conway kick)
TEX	Sauer 69 pass from Hudson (Conway kick)
ALA	Trimble 7 pass from Namath (Ray kick)
TEX	Koy 1 run (Conway kick)
ALA	Perkins 20 pass from Namath (Ray kick)
ALA	FG Ray 24

TEX	TEAM STATISTICS	ALA
15	First Downs	18
212	Rushing Yards	49
4-17-1	Passing	20-44-2
101	Passing Yards	298
313	Total Yards	347
9-36.8	Punts - Average	5-43.4
2-1	Fumbles - Lost	3-1
3-25	Penalties - Yards	4-46

INDIVIDUAL LEADERS

RUSHING
TEX: Koy 24-133, 2 TD; Philipp 10-44.
ALA: Bowman 10-23.

PASSING
TEX: Hudson 4-13-0, 101 yards, 1 TD.
ALA: Namath 18-37-2, 255 yards, 2 TD.

RECEIVING
TEX: Sauer 3-96, 1 TD.
ALA: Perkins 5-85, 1 TD; Ogden 3-69; Trimble 4-44, 1 TD.

JANUARY 1, 1966
ALABAMA 39, NEBRASKA 28

	1ST	2ND	3RD	4TH	FINAL
ALA	7	17	8	7	39
NEB	0	7	6	15	28

SCORING SUMMARY
ALA	Perkins 32 pass from Sloan (Ray kick)
NEB	Jeter 33 pass from Churchich (Wachholtz kick)
ALA	Kelley 4 run (Ray kick)
ALA	Perkins 11 pass from Sloan (Ray kick)
ALA	FG Ray 18
NEB	Gregory 49 pass from Churchich (pass failed)
ALA	Bowman 1 run (Perkins pass from Sloan)
NEB	Churchich 1 run (Wachholtz kick)
ALA	Bowman 3 run (Ray kick)
NEB	Jeter 14 pass from Churchich (Gregory pass from Churchich)

ALA	TEAM STATISTICS	NEB
29	First Downs	17
222	Rushing Yards	145
20-29-2	Passing	12-19-1
296	Passing Yards	232
518	Total Yards	377
5-31.2	Punts - Average	3-41.7
0-0	Fumbles - Lost	4-4
8-62	Penalties - Yards	8-86

INDIVIDUAL LEADERS
RUSHING
ALA: Kelley 26-118, 1 TD; Bowman 21-85, 2 TD.
NEB: Kirkland 7-67.
PASSING
ALA: Sloan 20-28-1, 296 yards, 2 TD.
NEB: Churchich 12-17, 232 yards, 3 TD.
RECEIVING
ALA: Perkins 9-159, 2 TD.
NEB: Jeter 3-73, 2 TD.

JANUARY 2, 1967
FLORIDA 27, GEORGIA TECH 12

	1ST	2ND	3RD	4TH	FINAL
UF	0	7	7	13	27
GT	6	0	0	6	12

SCORING SUMMARY
GT	Baynham 10 pass from King (run failed)
UF	McKeel 1 run (Barfield kick)
UF	Smith 94 run (Barfield kick)
UF	McKeel 1 run (Barfield kick)
GT	Good 25 run (pass failed)
UF	Coons 5 pass from Wages (pass failed)

UF	TEAM STATISTICS	GT
22	First Downs	17
289	Rushing Yards	197
15-32-1	Passing	16-22-4
165	Passing Yards	128
454	Total Yards	325
7-36.1	Punts - Average	6-42.3
1-1	Fumbles - Lost	2-1
4-32	Penalties - Yards	5-42

INDIVIDUAL LEADERS
RUSHING
UF: Smith 23-187, 1 TD; McKeel 3-50, 2 TD.
GT: Snow 24-110; Good 3-24, 1 TD.
PASSING
UF: Spurrier 14-30-1, 160 yards.
GT: Good 3-6-1, 86 yards; King 3-16-3, 42 yards, 1 TD.
RECEIVING
UF: Trapp 5-43; Coons 3-35, 1 TD.
GT: Snow 1-52; Smith 2-32.

JANUARY 1, 1968
OKLAHOMA 26, TENNESSEE 24

	1ST	2ND	3RD	4TH	FINAL
OKLA	7	12	0	7	26
TENN	0	0	14	10	24

SCORING SUMMARY
OKLA	Warmack 7 run (Vachon kick)
OKLA	Hinton 20 pass from Warmack (kick failed)
OKLA	Owens 1 run (run failed)
TENN	Glover 36 interception return (Kremser kick)
TENN	Fulton 5 run (Kremser kick)
OKLA	Stephenson 25 interception return (Vachon kick)
TENN	FG Kremser 26
TENN	Warren 1 run (Kremser kick)

OKLA	TEAM STATISTICS	TENN
18	First Downs	18
203	Rushing Yards	172
9-18-2	Passing	12-24-3
107	Passing Yards	160
310	Total Yards	332
5-47.0	Punts - Average	2-32.0
0-0	Fumbles - Lost	1-1
2-10	Penalties - Yards	4-27

INDIVIDUAL LEADERS
RUSHING
OKLA: Warmack 17-81, 1 TD; Owens 17-61, 1 TD.
TENN: Chadwick 12-72.
PASSING
OKLA: Warmack, 9-18-2, 107 yards, 1 TD.
TENN: Warren 12-23-2. 160 yards.
RECEIVING
OKLA: Hinton 5-87, 1 TD.
TENN: Flowers 4-59; DeLong 4-53.

JANUARY 1, 1969
PENN STATE 15, KANSAS 14

	1ST	2ND	3RD	4TH	FINAL
PSU	0	7	0	8	15
KU	7	0	0	7	14

SCORING SUMMARY
KU	Reeves 2 run (Bell kick)
PSU	Pittman 13 run (Garthwaite kick)
KU	Riggins 1 run (Bell kick)
PSU	Burkhart 3 run (Campbell run)

PSU	TEAM STATISTICS	KU
17	First Downs	16
207	Rushing Yards	76
12-23-1	Passing	9-18-2
154	Passing Yards	165
361	Total Yards	241
9-38.0	Punts - Average	10-38.3
2-2	Fumbles - Lost	2-0
1-15	Penalties - Yards	2-11

INDIVIDUAL LEADERS
RUSHING
PSU: Campbell 18-101; Pittman 14-58, 1 TD.
KU: Riggins 18-47, 1 TD.
PASSING
PSU: Burkhart 12-23-2, 154 yards.
KU: Douglass 9-17-1, 165 yards.
RECEIVING
PSU: Kwalick 6-74; Campbell 2-55.
KU: Mosier 5-77; Shanklin 1-42.

JANUARY 1, 1970
PENN STATE 10, MISSOURI 3

	1ST	2ND	3RD	4TH	FINAL
PSU	10	0	0	0	10
MO	0	3	0	0	3

SCORING SUMMARY
PSU	FG Reitz 29
PSU	Mitchell 28 pass from Burkhart (Rietz kick)
MO	FG Brown 33

PSU	TEAM STATISTICS	MO
12	First Downs	13
57	Rushing Yards	189
11-26-1	Passing	6-26-7
187	Passing Yards	117
244	Total Yards	306
12-43.1	Punts - Average	6-44.7
0-0	Fumbles - Lost	4-2
5-40	Penalties - Yards	3-25

INDIVIDUAL LEADERS
RUSHING
PSU: Harris 17-46.
MO: Staggers 9-69; Moore 19-62.
PASSING
PSU: Burkhart 11-26-1, 187 yards, 1 TD.
MO: McMillan 4-17-5, 73 yards; Roper 2-9-2, 44 yards.
RECEIVING
PSU: Mitchell 5-81, 1 TD.
MO: Henley 2-44; Shryock 3-33.

JANUARY 1, 1971
NEBRASKA 17, LSU 12

	1ST	2ND	3RD	4TH	FINAL
NEB	10	0	0	7	17
LSU	0	3	9	0	12

SCORING SUMMARY
NEB	FG Rogers 26
NEB	Orduna 3 run (Rogers kick)
LSU	FG Lumpkin 36
LSU	FG Lumpkin 25
LSU	Coffee 31 pass from Lee (kick failed)
NEB	Tagge 1 run (Rogers kick)

NEB	TEAM STATISTICS	LSU
18	First Downs	20
132	Rushing Yards	54
14-28-2	Passing	17-32-1
161	Passing Yards	227
293	Total Yards	281
6-37.7	Punts - Average	8-32.5
4-3	Fumbles - Lost	4-3
8-67	Penalties - Yards	4-27

INDIVIDUAL LEADERS
RUSHING
NEB: Orduna 63, 1 TD.
LSU: Jones 8-54.
PASSING
NEB: Tagge 12-25, 153 yards.
LSU: Lee 17-32-1, 182 yards, 1 TD.
RECEIVING
NEB: List 4-63.
LSU: Hamilton 9-146.

JANUARY 1, 1972
NEBRASKA 38, ALABAMA 6

	1ST	2ND	3RD	4TH	FINAL
NEB	14	14	3	7	38
ALA	0	0	6	0	6

SCORING SUMMARY
NEB	Kinney 2 run (kick failed)
NEB	Rodgers 77 punt return (Damkroger pass from Tagge)
NEB	Tagge 1 run (Sanger kick)
NEB	Dixon 2 run (Sanger kick)
ALA	Davis 3 run (run failed)
NEB	FG Sanger 21
NEB	Van Brownson 1 run (Sanger kick)

NEB	TEAM STATISTICS	ALA
15	First Downs	16
183	Rushing Yards	241
11-20-0	Passing	3-13-2
159	Passing Yards	47
342	Total Yards	288
5-42.2	Punts - Average	7-43.3
3-2	Fumbles - Lost	5-2
4-50	Penalties - Yards	4-58

INDIVIDUAL LEADERS
RUSHING
NEB: Kinney 20-99, 1 TD.
ALA: Musso 15-79.
PASSING
NEB: Tagge 11-19-0, 159 yards.
ALA: Davis 3-9, 47 yards.
RECEIVING
NEB: Rodgers 4-84.
ALA: Wheeler 2-22.

THE BOWLS

JANUARY 1, 1973

NEBRASKA 40, NOTRE DAME 6

	1ST	2ND	3RD	4TH	FINAL
NEB	7	13	20	0	40
ND	0	0	0	6	6

SCORING SUMMARY

NEB   Rodgers 8 run (Sanger kick)
NEB   Dixon 1 run (Sanger kick)
NEB   Anderson 52 pass from Rodgers (kick failed)
NEB   Rodgers 4 run (pass failed)
NEB   Rodgers 5 run (Sanger kick)
NEB   Rodgers 50 pass from Humm (Sanger kick)
ND   Demmerle 5 pass from Clements (pass failed)

NEB	TEAM STATISTICS	ND
30	First Downs	13
300	Rushing Yards	124
19-26-1	Passing	9-23-3
260	Passing Yards	103
560	Total Yards	227
2-3	Punt Returns - Yards	2-18
2-34	Kickoff Returns - Yards	6-84
4-38.3	Punts - Average	6-37.2
1-1	Fumbles - Lost	3-0
5-68	Penalties - Yards	1-15

INDIVIDUAL LEADERS

RUSHING
NEB: Rodgers 15-81, 3 TD; Dixon 9-69, 1 TD.
ND: Penick 8-48.

PASSING
NEB: Humm 13-19-0, 185 yards, 1 TD.
ND: Clements 9-23-3, 103 yards, 1 TD.

RECEIVING
NEB: Rodgers 3-71, 1 TD; Revelle 3-62.
ND: Dewan 3-46.

JANUARY 1, 1974

PENN STATE 16, LSU 9

	1ST	2ND	3RD	4TH	FINAL
PSU	3	13	0	0	16
LSU	7	0	2	0	9

SCORING SUMMARY

LSU   Rogers 3 run (Jackson kick)
PSU   FG Bahr 44
PSU   Herd 72 pass from Shuman (Bahr kick)
PSU   Cappelletti 1 run (kick failed)
LSU   Safety (Shuman fumbled snap in end zone)

PSU	TEAM STATISTICS	LSU
9	First Downs	19
28	Rushing Yards	205
6-17-1	Passing	8-20-1
157	Passing Yards	69
185	Total Yards	274
7-34.7	Punts - Average	8-46.8
1-0	Fumbles - Lost	3-1
3-37	Penalties - Yards	3-30

INDIVIDUAL LEADERS

RUSHING
PSU: Cappelletti 26-50, 1 TD.
LSU: Davis 19-70; Robiskie 10-58.

PASSING
PSU: Shuman 6-17-1, 157 yards, 1 TD.
LSU: Miley 8-18-1, 69 yards.

RECEIVING
PSU: Herd 1-72, 1 TD; Hayman 3-35.
LSU: Davis 6-20.

JANUARY 1, 1975

NOTRE DAME 13, ALABAMA 11

	1ST	2ND	3RD	4TH	FINAL
ND	7	6	0	0	13
ALA	0	0	3	8	11

SCORING SUMMARY

ND   Bullock 4 run (Reeve kick)
ND   McLane 9 run (kick failed)
ALA   FG Ridgeway 21
ALA   Schamun 48 pass from Todd (Pugh pass from Todd)

ND	TEAM STATISTICS	ALA
15	First Downs	14
185	Rushing Yards	62
4-8-2	Passing	15-29-2
19	Passing Yards	223
204	Total Yards	285
0-0	Punt Returns - Yards	5-34
3-54	Kickoff Returns - Yards	2-32
6-38.0	Punts - Average	7-40.0
1-1	Fumbles - Lost	5-2
1-15	Penalties - Yards	1-5

INDIVIDUAL LEADERS

RUSHING
ND: Bullock 24-83, 1 TD; McLane 8-30, 1 TD.
ALA: Culliver 11-60.

PASSING
ND: Clements 4-7-1, 19 yards.
ALA: Todd 13-24-2, 194 yards, 1 TD.

RECEIVING
ND: Demmerle 2-12.
ALA: Schamun 5-126, 1 TD; Newsome 6-68.

JANUARY 1, 1976

OKLAHOMA 14, MICHIGAN 6

	1ST	2ND	3RD	4TH	FINAL
OKLA	0	7	0	7	14
MICH	0	0	0	6	6

SCORING SUMMARY

OKLA   Brooks 39 run (DiRienzo kick)
OKLA   Davis 9 run (DiRienzo kick)
MICH   G. Bell 2 run (run failed)

OKLA	TEAM STATISTICS	MICH
16	First Downs	12
282	Rushing Yards	169
3-5-0	Passing	2-20-3
63	Passing Yards	33
345	Total Yards	202
9-34.9	Punts - Average	10-38.6
4-3	Fumbles - Lost	1-0
9-90	Penalties - Yards	5-24

INDIVIDUAL LEADERS

RUSHING
OKLA: Washington 17-73; Culbreath 11-63.
MICH: Leach 13-62; G. Bell 18-53, 1 TD.

PASSING
OKLA: Davis 3-5-0, 63 yards.
MICH: Leach 2-15-3, 30 yards.

RECEIVING
OKLA: Owens 3-63.
MICH: Bell 1-17.

JANUARY 1, 1977

OHIO STATE 27, COLORADO 10

	1ST	2ND	3RD	4TH	FINAL
OSU	7	10	3	7	27
COLO	10	0	0	0	10

SCORING SUMMARY

COLO   FG Zetterberg 26
COLO   Moorehead 11 pass from Knapple (Zetterberg kick)
OSU   Logan 36 run (Skladany kick)
OSU   FG Skladany 28
OSU   Johnson 3 run (Skladany kick)
OSU   FG Skladany 20
OSU   Gerald 4 run (Skladany kick)

OSU	TEAM STATISTICS	COLO
21	First Downs	12
271	Rushing Yards	134
2-7-0	Passing	8-23-2
59	Passing Yards	137
330	Total Yards	271
3-42.2	Punts - Average	7-35.2
4-4	Fumbles - Lost	1-0
4-37	Penalties - Yards	8-60
34:29	Possession Time	25:31

INDIVIDUAL LEADERS

RUSHING
OSU: Springs 23-98; Gerald 14-81, 1 TD; Logan 14-79, 1 TD.
COLO: Reed 22-58.

PASSING
OSU: Gerald 2-6-0, 59 yards.
COLO: Knapple 8-22-2, 137 yards, 1 TD.

RECEIVING
OSU: Harrell 2-59.
COLO: Moorehead 4-68, 1 TD; Reed 2-51.

JANUARY 2, 1978

ARKANSAS 31, OKLAHOMA 6

	1ST	2ND	3RD	4TH	FINAL
ARK	14	0	10	7	31
OKLA	0	0	0	6	6

SCORING SUMMARY

ARK   Sales 1 run (Little kick)
ARK   Calcagni 1 run (Little kick)
ARK   FG Little 32
ARK   Sales 4 run (Little kick)
OKLA   Hicks 8 pass from Blevins (run failed)
ARK   White 20 run (Little kick)

ARK	TEAM STATISTICS	OKLA
15	First Downs	14
317	Rushing Yards	230
7-12-1	Passing	7-14-0
90	Passing Yards	80
407	Total Yards	310
4-40.5	Punts - Average	5-44.4
2-1	Fumbles - Lost	4-3
7-50	Penalties - Yards	5-25

INDIVIDUAL LEADERS

RUSHING
ARK: Sales 22-205, 2 TD.
OKLA: Peacock 15-117; King 5-49.

PASSING
ARK: Calcagni 7-11-1, 90 yards.
OKLA: Lott 4-7-0, 42 yards.

RECEIVING
ARK: Sales 4-52.
OKLA: Rhodes 3-46.

JANUARY 1, 1979

OKLAHOMA 31, NEBRASKA 24

	1ST	2ND	3RD	4TH	FINAL
OKLA	7	7	17	0	31
NEB	7	0	3	14	24

SCORING SUMMARY

NEB   Smith 21 pass from Sorley (Todd kick)
OKLA   Sims 3 run (Von Schamann kick)
OKLA   Lott 3 run (Von Schamann kick)
OKLA   Sims 11 run (Von Schamann kick)
OKLA   FG Von Schamann 26
NEB   FG Todd 31
OKLA   Lott 2 run (Von Schamann kick)
NEB   Berns 1 run (Todd kick)
NEB   Miller 2 pass from Sorley (Todd kick)

OKLA	TEAM STATISTICS	NEB
17	First Downs	27
292	Rushing Yards	217
2-3-0	Passing	18-31-2
47	Passing Yards	220
339	Total Yards	437
3-39.3	Punts - Average	2-37.5
1-1	Fumbles - Lost	0-0
6-50	Penalties - Yards	8-96

INDIVIDUAL LEADERS

RUSHING
OKLA: Sims 25-134, 2 TD.
NEB: Berns 19-99, 1 TD.

PASSING
OKLA: Lott 2-3-0, 47 yards.
NEB: Sorley 18-31-2, 220 yards, 2 TD.

RECEIVING
OKLA: Rhodes 1-38.
NEB: Smith 3-62, 1 TD.

JANUARY 1, 1980
OKLAHOMA 24, FLORIDA STATE 7

	1ST	2ND	3RD	4TH	FINAL
OKLA	0	17	0	7	24
FSU	7	0	0	0	7

SCORING SUMMARY
FSU Whiting 1 run (Cappelen kick)
OKLA Watts 61 run (Keeling kick)
OKLA Wilson 5 run (Keeling kick)
OKLA FG Keeling 24
OKLA Sims 22 run (Keeling kick)

OKLA	TEAM STATISTICS	FSU
23	First Downs	12
411	Rushing Yards	82
2-4-0	Passing	8-27-3
36	Passing Yards	100
447	Total Yards	182
4-25.0	Punts - Average	9-42.2
5-4	Fumbles - Lost	1-0
3-27	Penalties - Yards	4-20
32:38	Possession Time	27:22

INDIVIDUAL LEADERS
RUSHING
OKLA: Sims 24-164, 1 TD; Watts 15-127, 1 TD.
FSU: Whiting 13-40, 1 TD; Lyles 13-40.
PASSING
OKLA: Watts 2-4-0, 36 yards.
FSU: Jordan 6-16-1, 76 yards.
RECEIVING
OKLA: Nixon 2-36.
FSU: King 2-24; Childers 2-24.

JANUARY 1, 1981
OKLAHOMA 18, FLORIDA STATE 17

	1ST	2ND	3RD	4TH	FINAL
OKLA	0	3	7	8	18
FSU	0	7	3	7	17

SCORING SUMMARY
FSU Williams 10 run (Capece kick)
OKLA FG Keeling 53
OKLA Overstreet 4 run (Keeling kick)
FSU FG Capece 19
FSU Butler fumble recovery (Capece kick)
OKLA Rhodes 11 pass from Watts (Valora pass from Watts)

OKLA	TEAM STATISTICS	FSU
18	First Downs	23
156	Rushing Yards	212
7-12-0	Passing	11-15-0
128	Passing Yards	51
284	Total Yards	263
2-37.0	Punts - Average	4-42.5
7-5	Fumbles - Lost	1-0
4-32	Penalties - Yards	5-58
26:32	Possession Time	33:28

INDIVIDUAL LEADERS
RUSHING
OKLA: Watts 25-48.
FSU: Williams 19-99, 1 TD.
PASSING
OKLA: Watts 7-12-0, 128 yards, 1 TD.
FSU: Stockstill 11-15-0, 51 yards.
RECEIVING
OKLA: Rhodes 2-53, 1 TD.
FSU: Williams 2-27.

JANUARY 1, 1982
CLEMSON 22, NEBRASKA 15

	1ST	2ND	3RD	4TH	FINAL
CLEM	6	6	10	0	22
NEB	7	0	0	8	15

SCORING SUMMARY
CLEM FG Igwebuike 41
NEB Steels 25 pass from Rozier (Seibel kick)
CLEM FG Igwebuike 37
CLEM Austin 2 run (pass failed)
CLEM Tuttle 13 pass from Jordan (Paulling kick)
CLEM FG Igwebuike 36
NEB Craig 26 run (Craig run)

CLEM	TEAM STATISTICS	NEB
17	First Downs	13
155	Rushing Yards	193
11-22-1	Passing	6-17-0
134	Passing Yards	63
289	Total Yards	256
4-18.0	Punts - Average	6-43.0
3-0	Fumbles - Lost	3-2
7-57	Penalties - Yards	8-64
32:06	Possession Time	27:54

INDIVIDUAL LEADERS
RUSHING
CLEM: McCall 12-48; Jordan 16-46.
NEB: Craig 10-87, 1 TD; Rozier 15-75.
PASSING
CLEM: Jordan 11-22-1, 134 yards, 1 TD.
NEB: Mauer 5-15-0, 38 yards; Rozier 1-1-0, 38 yards, 1 TD.
RECEIVING
CLEM: Tuttle 5-56, 1 TD; Magwood 1-42.
NEB: Steels 1-25, 1 TD; Rozier 1-11.

JANUARY 1, 1983
NEBRASKA 21, LSU 20

	1ST	2ND	3RD	4TH	FINAL
NEB	7	0	7	7	21
LSU	7	7	3	3	20

SCORING SUMMARY
NEB Schellen 5 run (Seibel kick)
LSU Hilliard 1 run (Betanzos kick)
LSU Hilliard 1 run (Betanzos kick)
LSU FG Betanzos 28
NEB Rozier 11 pass from Gill (Seibel kick)
NEB Gill 1 run (Seibel kick)
LSU FG Betanzos 49

NEB	TEAM STATISTICS	LSU
22	First Downs	12
219	Rushing Yards	38
13-22-2	Passing	14-30-2
184	Passing Yards	173
403	Total Yards	211
1-31.0	Punts - Average	6-39.2
4-4	Fumbles - Lost	1-0
4-25	Penalties - Yards	8-54
34:32	Possession Time	25:28

INDIVIDUAL LEADERS
RUSHING
NEB: Rozier 26-118.
LSU: Hilliard 18-29, 2 TD.
PASSING
NEB: Gill 13-22-2, 184 yards, 1 TD.
LSU: Risher 14-30-2, 173 yards.
RECEIVING
NEB: Fryar 5-84.
LSU: Hilliard 5-82.

JANUARY 2, 1984
MIAMI (FLA.) 31, NEBRASKA 30

	1ST	2ND	3RD	4TH	FINAL
MIA	17	0	14	0	31
NEB	0	14	3	13	30

SCORING SUMMARY
MIA Dennison 2 pass from Kosar (Davis kick)
MIA FG Davis 45
MIA Dennison 22 pass from Kosar (Davis kick)
NEB Steinkuhler 19 run (Livingston kick)
NEB Gill 1 run (Livingston kick)
NEB FG Livingston 34
MIA Highsmith 1 run (Davis kick)
MIA Bentley 7 run (Davis kick)
NEB Smith 1 run (Livingston kick)
NEB Smith 24 run (pass failed)

MIA	TEAM STATISTICS	NEB
22	First Downs	24
130	Rushing Yards	247
19-35-1	Passing	16-30-1
300	Passing Yards	172
430	Total Yards	419
4-41.8	Punts - Average	3-37.3
1-1	Fumbles - Lost	6-1
13-101	Penalties - Yards	4-51
27:53	Possession Time	32:07

INDIVIDUAL LEADERS
RUSHING
MIA: Highsmith 7-50, 1 TD; Bentley 10-46, 1 TD.
NEB: Rozier 24-147; Smith 9-99, 2 TD.
PASSING
MIA: Kosar 19-35-1, 300 yards, 2 TD.
NEB: Gill 16-30-1, 172 yards.
RECEIVING
MIA: Brown 6-115; Shakespeare 3-63; Dennison 3-44, 2 TD.
NEB: Fryar 5-61.

JANUARY 1, 1985
WASHINGTON 28, OKLAHOMA 17

	1ST	2ND	3RD	4TH	FINAL
WASH	14	0	0	14	28
OKLA	0	14	0	3	17

SCORING SUMMARY
WASH Greene 29 pass from Sicuro (Jaeger kick)
WASH Robinson 1 run (Jaeger kick)
OKLA Bradley 1 run (Lashar kick)
OKLA Shepard 61 pass from Bradley (Lashar kick)
OKLA FG Lashar 35
WASH Pattison 12 pass from Millen (Jaeger kick)
WASH Fenney 6 run (Jaeger kick)

WASH	TEAM STATISTICS	OKLA
17	First Downs	17
192	Rushing Yards	162
9-21-3	Passing	6-21-1
119	Passing Yards	124
311	Total Yards	286
6-37.7	Punts - Average	7-34.6
3-1	Fumbles - Lost	6-2
5-25	Penalties - Yards	8-60
28:56	Possession Time	31:04

INDIVIDUAL LEADERS
RUSHING
WASH: Robinson 28-135, 1 TD.
OKLA: Carr 10-63.
PASSING
WASH: Sicuro 7-17-3, 78 yards, 1 TD.
OKLA: Bradley 6-21-1, 124 yards, 1TD.
RECEIVING
WASH: Greene 4-97, 1 TD.
OKLA: Shepard 3-87, 1 TD.

THE BOWLS

JANUARY 1, 1986
OKLAHOMA 25, PENN STATE 10

	1ST	2ND	3RD	4TH	FINAL
OKLA	0	16	3	6	25
PSU	7	3	0	0	10

SCORING SUMMARY
PSU	Manoa 1 run (Manca kick)
OKLA	FG Lashar 21
OKLA	K. Jackson 71 pass from Holieway (Lashar kick)
OKLA	FG Lashar 31
OKLA	FG Lashar 26
PSU	FG Manca 27
OKLA	FG Lashar 22
OKLA	Carr 61 run (kick failed)

OKLA	TEAM STATISTICS	PSU
12	First Downs	14
228	Rushing Yards	103
3-6-0	Passing	18-34-4
91	Passing Yards	164
319	Total Yards	267
5-42.6	Punts - Average	6-46.3
5-1	Fumbles - Lost	2-1
7-45	Penalties - Yards	6-49
28:37	Possession Time	31:23

INDIVIDUAL LEADERS
RUSHING
OKLA: Carr 19-148, 1 TD.
PSU: Dozier 12-39.
PASSING
OKLA: Holieway 3-6-0, 91 yards, 1 TD.
PSU: Knizer 8-11-1, 90 yards; Shaffer 10-22-3, 74 yards.
RECEIVING
OKLA: K. Jackson 2-83, 1 TD.
PSU: Dimidio 6-50.

JANUARY 1, 1987
OKLAHOMA 42, ARKANSAS 8

	1ST	2ND	3RD	4TH	FINAL
OKLA	0	14	14	14	42
ARK	0	0	0	8	8

SCORING SUMMARY
OKLA	Tillman 77 run (Lashar kick)
OKLA	Tillman 21 run (Lashar kick)
OKLA	Holieway 2 run (Lashar kick)
OKLA	Holieway 4 run (Lashar kick)
OKLA	Stafford 13 run (Lashar kick)
OKLA	Parham 49 run (Lashar kick)
ARK	Thomas 2 run (Shibest pass from Bland)

OKLA	TEAM STATISTICS	ARK
11	First Downs	17
366	Rushing Yards	48
2-5-0	Passing	16-33-5
47	Passing Yards	192
413	Total Yards	240
5-47.6	Punts - Average	9-41.1
3-2	Fumbles - Lost	2-0
4-40	Penalties - Yards	3-25
24:31	Possession Time	35:29

INDIVIDUAL LEADERS
RUSHING
OKLA: Tillman 7-109, 2 TD.
ARK: Thomas 22-59, 1 TD.
PASSING
OKLA: Holieway 2-3-0, 47 yards.
ARK: Thomas 13-26-4, 129 yards.
RECEIVING
OKLA: Shepard 1-36.
ARK: Shibest 4-83.

JANUARY 1, 1988
MIAMI (FLA.) 20, OKLAHOMA 14

	1ST	2ND	3RD	4TH	FINAL
MIA	7	0	10	3	20
OKLA	0	7	0	7	14

SCORING SUMMARY
MIA	Bratton 30 pass from Walsh (Cox kick)
OKLA	Stafford 1 run (Lashar kick)
MIA	FG Cox 56
MIA	Irvin 23 pass from Walsh (Cox kick)
MIA	FG Cox 48
OKLA	Hutson 29 run (Lashar kick)

MIA	TEAM STATISTICS	OKLA
15	First Downs	13
72	Rushing Yards	179
18-30-1	Passing	5-13-0
209	Passing Yards	76
281	Total Yards	255
6-44.7	Punts - Average	8-39.0
0-0	Fumbles - Lost	4-2
8-85	Penalties - Yards	5-39
32:08	Possession Time	27:52

INDIVIDUAL LEADERS
RUSHING
MIA: Williams 19-41.
OKLA: Collins 10-50.
PASSING
MIA: Walsh 18-30-1, 209 yards, 2 TD.
OKLA: Thompson 4-12-0, 56 yards.
RECEIVING
MIA: Bratton 9-102, 1 TD.
OKLA: Jackson 3-45.

JANUARY 2, 1989
MIAMI (FLA.) 23, NEBRASKA 3

	1ST	2ND	3RD	4TH	FINAL
MIA	7	13	0	3	23
NEB	0	0	3	0	3

SCORING SUMMARY
MIA	Conley 22 pass from Walsh (Huerta kick)
MIA	FG Huerta 18
MIA	Conley 42 pass from Walsh (Huerta kick)
MIA	FG Huerta 37
NEB	FG Barrios 50
MIA	FG Huerta 37

MIA	TEAM STATISTICS	NEB
20	First Downs	10
69	Rushing Yards	80
23-48-3	Passing	8-22-3
285	Passing Yards	55
354	Total Yards	135
4-39.5	Punts - Average	9-37.2
47	Return Yards	31
1-0	Fumbles - Lost	0-0
7-60	Penalties - Yards	5-45
30:16	Possession Time	29:44

INDIVIDUAL LEADERS
RUSHING
MIA: Conley 10-40; Crowell 5-23.
NEB: Clark 14-36; Carpenter 5-15.
PASSING
MIA: Walsh 21-44-3, 277 yards, 2 TD.
NEB: Taylor 8-21-2, 55 yards.
RECEIVING
MIA: Conley 4-94, 2 TD; Chudzinski 5-81.
NEB: Bell 2-39.

JANUARY 1, 1990
NOTRE DAME 21, COLORADO 6

	1ST	2ND	3RD	4TH	FINAL
ND	0	0	14	7	21
COLO	0	0	6	0	6

SCORING SUMMARY
ND	A. Johnson 4 run (Hentrich kick)
ND	Ismail 35 run (Hentrich kick)
COLO	Hagan 39 run (kick failed)
ND	A. Johnson 7 run (Hentrich kick)

ND	TEAM STATISTICS	COLO
18	First Downs	16
279	Rushing Yards	217
5-9-0	Passing	4-13-2
99	Passing Yards	65
378	Total Yards	282
0-0	Punt Returns - Yards	3-36
2-24	Kickoff Returns - Yards	3-43
5-40.1	Punts - Average	3-39.3
0-0	Fumbles - Lost	1-1
3-35	Penalties - Yards	1-5
32:43	Possession Time	27:17

INDIVIDUAL LEADERS
RUSHING
ND: Ismail 16-108, 1 TD; A. Johnson 15-89, 2 TD.
COLO: Hagan 19-106, 1 TD; Bieniemy 11-66.
PASSING
ND: Rice 5-9-0, 99 yards.
COLO: Hagan 4-13-2, 65 yards.
RECEIVING
ND: Eilers 2-47; Smith 1-27.
COLO: Kissick 2-33; Pritchard 1-16.

JANUARY 1, 1991
COLORADO 10, NOTRE DAME 9

	1ST	2ND	3RD	4TH	FINAL
COLO	0	3	7	0	10
ND	0	6	3	0	9

SCORING SUMMARY
COLO	FG Harper 22
ND	Watters 2 run (kick blocked)
ND	FG Hentrich 24
COLO	Bieniemy 1 run (Harper kick)

COLO	TEAM STATISTICS	ND
19	First Downs	18
186	Rushing Yards	123
9-19-0	Passing	13-31-3
109	Passing Yards	141
295	Total Yards	264
0-0	Punt Returns - Yards	4-68
3-49	Kickoff Returns - Yards	3-53
7-40.4	Punts - Average	3-51.0
2-1	Fumbles - Lost	2-2
6-50	Penalties - Yards	3-45
35:36	Possession Time	24:24

INDIVIDUAL LEADERS
RUSHING
COLO: Bieniemy 26-86, 1 TD; Hemingway 14-76.
ND: Brooks 9-46; Watters 9-44, 1 TD.
PASSING
COLO: Hagan 4-12-0, 29 yards; C.S. Johnson 5-6-0, 80 yards.
ND: Mirer 13-31-3, 141 yards.
RECEIVING
COLO: Pritchard 3-45; S. Brown 2-23.
ND: Ismail 6-57; D. Brown 4-56.

JANUARY 1, 1992
MIAMI (FLA.) 22, NEBRASKA 0

	1ST	2ND	3RD	4TH	FINAL
MIA	13	0	9	0	22
NEB	0	0	0	0	0

SCORING SUMMARY

MIA	Williams 8 pass from Torretta (Huerta kick)
MIA	FG Huerta 24
MIA	FG Huerta 24
MIA	Jones 1 run (Pass failed)
MIA	FG Huerta 54

MIA	TEAM STATISTICS	NEB
25	First Downs	9
192	Rushing Yards	122
19-41-2	Passing	7-19-2
257	Passing Yards	89
449	Total Yards	211
5-33.0	Punts - Average	8-36.6
3-0	Fumbles - Lost	3-2
12-143	Penalties - Yards	6-36
34:29	Possession Time	25:31

INDIVIDUAL LEADERS

RUSHING
MIA: Jones 30-144, 1 TD; Marucci 8-23.
NEB: Jones 15-69; Joseph 2-18.
PASSING
MIA: Torretta 19-41-2, 257 yards, 1 TD.
NEB: McCant 6-18-2, 80 yards.
RECEIVING
MIA: Williams 8-126, 1 TD; Thomas 5-73.
NEB: Mitchell 3-57; Muhammed 1-16.

JANUARY 1, 1993
FLORIDA STATE 27, NEBRASKA 14

	1ST	2ND	3RD	4TH	FINAL
FSU	7	13	7	0	27
NEB	0	7	0	7	14

SCORING SUMMARY

FSU	Vanover 25 pass from Ward (Mowrey kick)
FSU	FG Mowrey 40
FSU	McCorvey 4 pass from Ward (Mowry kick)
FSU	FG Mowrey 24
NEB	Dixon 41 pass from Frazier (Bennett kick)
FSU	Jackson 11 run (Mowrey kick)
NEB	Armstrong 1 pass from Frazier (Bennett kick)

FSU	TEAM STATISTICS	NEB
23	First Downs	13
221	Rushing Yards	144
16-31-1	Passing	10-22-2
215	Passing Yards	146
436	Total Yards	290
6-35.8	Punts - Average	4-44.8
3-0	Fumbles - Lost	5-1
6-71	Penalties - Yards	6-50
36:53	Possession Time	23:07

INDIVIDUAL LEADERS

RUSHING
FSU: Jackson 17-101, 1 TD; Vanover 3-50.
NEB: Jones 19-76; Lewis 3-19.
PASSING
FSU: Ward 15-30-1, 187 yards, 2 TD.
NEB: Frazier 10-21-2, 146 yards, 2 TD.
RECEIVING
FSU: Jackson 4-61; Vanover 3-40, 1 TD.
NEB: Dixon 5-123, 1 TD; Hawkins 2-18.

JANUARY 1, 1994
FLORIDA STATE 18, NEBRASKA 16

	1ST	2ND	3RD	4TH	FINAL
FSU	0	6	9	3	18
NEB	0	7	0	9	16

SCORING SUMMARY

FSU	FG Bentley 34
NEB	Baul 34 pass from Frazier (Bennett kick)
FSU	FG Bentley 25
FSU	Floyd 1 run (pass failed)
FSU	FG Bentley 39
NEB	Phillips 12 run (run failed)
NEB	FG Bennett 27
FSU	FG Bentley 22

FSU	TEAM STATISTICS	NEB
22	First Downs	20
47	Rushing Yards	183
24-43-0	Passing	13-25-2
286	Passing Yards	206
333	Total Yards	389
6-45.2	Punts - Average	7-38.4
0-0	Fumbles - Lost	2-0
10-69	Penalties - Yards	11-115
27:03	Possession Time	32:57

INDIVIDUAL LEADERS

RUSHING
FSU: Floyd 7-53, 1 TD.
NEB: Frazier 14-77; Phillips 13-64, 1 TD.
PASSING
FSU: Ward 24-43-0, 286 yards.
NEB: Frazier 13-24-2, 206 yards, 1 TD.
RECEIVING
FSU: Knox 5-99; McCorvey 5-70; Vanover 6-48.
NEB: Bell 4-75; Dixon 3-50; Johnson 3-40.

JANUARY 1, 1995
NEBRASKA 24, MIAMI (FLA.) 17

	1ST	2ND	3RD	4TH	FINAL
NEB	0	7	2	15	24
MIA	10	0	7	0	17

SCORING SUMMARY

MIA	FG Prewitt 44
MIA	Jones 35 pass from Costa (Prewitt kick)
NEB	Gilman 19 run (Berringer (Sieler kick)
MIA	Harris 44 pass from Costa (Prewitt kick)
NEB	Safety (Costa sacked in end zone)
NEB	Schlesinger 15 run (Alford pass from Frazier)
NEB	Schlesinger 14 run (Sieler kick)

NEB	TEAM STATISTICS	MIA
20	First Downs	14
199	Rushing Yards	29
11-20-2	Passing	18-35-1
106	Passing Yards	248
305	Total Yards	277
7-41.1	Punts - Average	7-39.7
17	Return Yards	-6
2-1	Fumbles - Lost	2-0
3-20	Penalties - Yards	11-92
32:32	Possession Time	27:28

INDIVIDUAL LEADERS

RUSHING
NEB: Phillips 19-96; Schlesinger 6-48, 2 TD; Frazier 7-31.
MIA: Stewart 17-72.
PASSING
NEB: Berringer 8-15-1, 81 yards, 1 TD.
MIA: Costa 18-35-1, 248 yards, 2 TD.
RECEIVING
NEB: Muhammad 4-60; Phillips 4-13.
MIA: Jones 6-63, 1 TD; Harris 1-44, 1 TD; German 3-22.

JANUARY 1, 1996
FLORIDA STATE 31, NOTRE DAME 26

	1ST	2ND	3RD	4TH	FINAL
FSU	7	7	0	17	31
ND	10	0	7	9	26

SCORING SUMMARY

ND	Mayes 39 pass from Krug (Cengia kick)
FSU	Cooper 15 pass from Kanell (Bentley kick)
ND	FG Cengia 20
FSU	Cooper 10 pass from Kanell (Bentley kick)
ND	Mayes 33 pass from Krug (Cengia kick)
ND	Safety (Kanell steps out of end zone)
ND	Chryplewicz 5 pass from Krug (Cengiakick)
FSU	Green 11 pass from Kanell (Bentley kick)
FSU	Cooper 3 pass from Kanell (Cooper pass from Kannell)
FSU	Safety (Krug intentional grounding in end zone)

FSU	TEAM STATISTICS	ND
26	First Downs	17
188	Rushing Yards	256
20-33-2	Passing	15-26-1
290	Passing Yards	169
478	Total Yards	425
3-44.0	Punts - Average	5-42.4
1-0	Fumbles - Lost	2-1
7-59	Penalties - Yards	7-55
28.13	Possession Time	31:47

INDIVIDUAL LEADERS

RUSHING
FSU: Dunn 22-151; Preston 6-55.
ND: Farmer 7-93; Denson 11-67; Edwards 14-55.
PASSING
FSU: Kanell 20-32-2, 290 yards, 4 TD.
ND: Krug 14-24-1, 140 yards, 3 TD.
RECEIVING
FSU: Messam 6-103; Green 5-99, 1 TD; Cooper 4-38, 3 TD.
ND: Mayes 6-96, 2 TD; Chryplewicz 3-18, 1 TD.

DECEMBER 31, 1996
NEBRASKA 41, VIRGINIA TECH 21

	1ST	2ND	3RD	4TH	FINAL
NEB	0	17	14	10	41
VT	7	7	7	0	21

SCORING SUMMARY

VT	Parker 19 pass from Druckenmiller (Graham kick)
NEB	FG Brown 25
NEB	Frost 5 run (Brown kick)
NEB	Peter 31 fumble return (Brown kick)
VT	Scales 6 pass from Druckenmiller (Graham kick)
NEB	Benning 33 run (Brown kick)
VT	White 33 pass from Druckenmiller (Graham kick)
NEB	Benning 6 run (Brown kick)
NEB	FG Brown 37
NEB	Frost 22 run (Brown kick)

NEB	TEAM STATISTICS	VT
25	First Downs	22
279	Rushing Yards	193
11-22-0	Passing	16-33-0
136	Passing Yards	214
415	Total Yards	407
2-44.5	Punts - Average	5-34.2
1-0	Fumbles - Lost	1-1
3-16	Penalties - Yards	5-89
28:58	Possession Time	31:02

INDIVIDUAL LEADERS

RUSHING
NEB: Benning 19-95, 2 TD; Frost 9-62, 2 TD; Green 7-52.
VT: Oxendine 20-150; Parker 8-22.
PASSING
NEB: Frost 11-22-0, 136 yards.
VT: Druckenmiller 16-33-0, 214 yards, 3 TD.
RECEIVING
NEB: Wiggins 3-36; Lake 2-27.
VT: Oxendine 3-60; Jennings 4-58.

JANUARY 2, 1998
Nebraska 42, Tennessee 17

	1ST	2ND	3RD	4TH	FINAL
NEB	7	7	21	7	42
TENN	0	3	6	8	17

SCORING SUMMARY
NEB	Green 5 run (Brown kick)
NEB	Wiggins 10 run (Brown kick)
TENN	FG Hall 44
NEB	Frost 1 run (Brown kick)
NEB	Frost 11 run (Brown kick)
TENN	Price 5 pass from Manning (pass failed)
NEB	Green 22 run (Brown kick)
NEB	Frost 9 run (Brown kick)
TENN	McCullough 3 pass from Martin (Stephens pass from Martin)

NEB	TEAM STATISTICS	TENN
30	First Downs	16
409	Rushing Yards	128
9-12-0	Passing	25-35-1
125	Passing Yards	187
534	Total Yards	315
4-39.0	Punts - Average	6-52.3
3-2	Fumbles - Lost	2-2
8-63	Penalties - Yards	5-37
36:03	Possession Time	23:57

INDIVIDUAL LEADERS

RUSHING
NEB: Green 29-206, 2 TD; Makovicka 9-61; Frost 17-60, 3 TD.
TENN: Lewis 14-90; Levine 2-30.

PASSING
NEB: Frost 9-12-0, 125 yards.
TENN: Manning 21-31-1, 134 yards, 1 TD.

RECEIVING
NEB: K. Jackson 4-56; Green 3-31.
TENN: Nash 5-53; McCullough 3-50, 1 TD.

JANUARY 2, 1999
Florida 31, Syracuse 10

	1ST	2ND	3RD	4TH	FINAL
FLA	14	14	0	3	31
SYR	0	3	0	7	10

SCORING SUMMARY
FLA	Taylor 51 pass from Johnson (Chandler kick)
FLA	Taylor 26 pass from Johnson (Chandler kick)
SYR	FG Trout 36
FLA	Kinney 4 pass from Palmer (Chandler kick)
FLA	Palmer 2 run (Chandler kick)
FLA	FG Chandler 32
SYR	M. Jackson 62 pass from McNabb (Trout kick)

FLA	TEAM STATISTICS	SYR
18	First Downs	18
133	Rushing Yards	129
22-31-0	Passing	14-30-1
308	Passing Yards	192
441	Total Yards	321
7-36.9	Punts - Average	5-43.0
0-0	Fumbles - Lost	3-3
11-76	Penalties - Yards	2-20
31:48	Possession Time	28:12

INDIVIDUAL LEADERS

RUSHING
FLA: Jackson 21-108; Taylor 2-16.
SYR: McNabb 20-72; Brown 5-31.

PASSING
FLA: Johnson 12-17-0, 195 yards, 2 TD; Palmer 10-14-0, 113 yards, 1 TD.
SYR: McNabb 14-30-1, 192 yards, 1 TD.

RECEIVING
FLA: Taylor 7-159, 2 TD; Karim 4-79.
SYR: M.Jackson 1-62, 1 TD; K. Johnson 4-49.

JANUARY 1, 2000
Michigan 35, Alabama 34

	1ST	2ND	3RD	4TH	OT	FINAL
MICH	0	7	21	0	7	35
ALA	0	14	14	0	6	34

SCORING SUMMARY
ALA	Alexander 5 run (Pflugner kick)
ALA	Alexander 6 run (Pflugner kick)
MICH	Terrell 27 pass from Brady (Epstein kick)
MICH	Terrell 57 pass from Brady (Epstein kick)
ALA	Alexander 50 run (Pflugner kick)
ALA	Milons 62 punt return (Pflugner kick)
MICH	Terrell 20 pass from Brady (Epstein kick)
MICH	A.Thomas 3 run (Epstein kick)
MICH	Thompson 25 pass from Brady (Epstein kick)
ALA	Carter 21 pass from Zow (kick failed)

MICH	TEAM STATISTICS	ALA
18	First Downs	12
37	Rushing Yards	184
35-47-0	Passing	13-20-1
369	Passing Yards	111
406	Total Yards	295
8-43.4	Punts - Average	9-34.4
2-1	Fumbles - Lost	1-0
10-115	Penalties - Yards	18-132
32:08	Possession Time	27:52

INDIVIDUAL LEADERS

RUSHING
MICH: A. Thomas 18-40, 1 TD.
ALA: Alexander 25-161, 3 TD, Watts 4-15.

PASSING
MICH: Brady 34-46-0, 369 yards, 4 TD.
ALA: Zow 7-14-0, 86 yards, 1 TD.

RECEIVING
MICH: Terrell 10-150, 3 TD; Shea 7-50; Thompson 3-47, 1 TD.
ALA: Carter 4-38, 1 TD; Alexander 2-21.

JANUARY 3, 2001
Oklahoma 13, Florida State 2

	1ST	2ND	3RD	4TH	FINAL
OKLA	3	3	0	7	13
FSU	0	0	0	2	2

SCORING SUMMARY
OKLA	FG Duncan 27
OKLA	FG Duncan 42
OKLA	Griffin 10 run (Duncan kick)
FSU	Safety

OKLA	TEAM STATISTICS	FSU
12	First Downs	14
56	Rushing Yards	27
25-39-1	Passing	25-52-2
214	Passing Yards	274
270	Total Yards	301
8-41.1	Punts - Average	10-44.7
2-1	Fumbles - Lost	3-1
7-45	Penalties - Yards	6-38
36:33	Possession Time	23:27

INDIVIDUAL LEADERS

RUSHING
OKLA: Griffin 11-40, 1 TD.
FSU: Minor 13-20.

PASSING
OKLA: Heupel 25-39-1, 214 yards.
FSU: Weinke 25-51-2, 274 yards.

RECEIVING
OKLA: Norman 3-49; Woolfolk 3-41.
FSU: Bell 7-137; Boldin 3-31.

JANUARY 2, 2002
Florida 56, Maryland 23

	1ST	2ND	3RD	4TH	FINAL
FLA	14	14	21	7	56
MD	7	3	0	13	23

SCORING SUMMARY
FLA	Graham 1 run (Chandler kick)
FLA	Jacobs 46 pass from Berlin (Chandler kick)
MD	J. Williams 64 pass from Hill (Novak kick)
MD	FG Novak 20
FLA	Jacobs 15 pass from Grossman (Chandler kick)
FLA	Gaffney 4 pass from Grossman (Chandler kick)
FLA	Graham 6 run (Chandler kick)
FLA	Gillespie 11 run (Chandler kick)
FLA	Gaffney 33 pass from Grossman (Chandler kick)
MD	Riley 1 run (pass failed)
FLA	Perez 10 pass from Grossman (Chandler kick)
MD	Riley 10 run (Novak kick)

FLA	TEAM STATISTICS	MD
30	First Downs	19
203	Rushing Yards	103
33-49-2	Passing	23-39-1
456	Passing Yards	257
659	Total Yards	360
2-1	Fumbles - Lost	0-0
6-43	Penalties - Yards	4-20
28:26	Possession Time	31:34

INDIVIDUAL LEADERS

RUSHING
FLA: Graham 16-149, 2 TD; Gillespie 4-63, 1 TD.
MD: Hill 11-31; Riley 9-23, 2 TD.

PASSING
FLA: Grossman 20-28-0, 248 yards, 4 TD; Berlin 11-19-2, 196 yards, 1 TD.
MD: Hill 23-39-1, 257 yards, 1 TD.

RECEIVING
FLA: Jacobs 10-170, 2 TD; Gaffney 7-118, 2 TD; Caldwell 4-47.
MD: J. Williams 4-91, 1 TD; Murphy 5-42.

JANUARY 2, 2003
Southern Cal 38, Iowa 17

	1ST	2ND	3RD	4TH	FINAL
USC	7	3	14	14	38
IOWA	10	0	0	7	17

SCORING SUMMARY
IOWA	Jones 100 kick return (Kaeding kick)
USC	Fargas 4 run (Killeen kick)
IOWA	FG Kaeding 35
USC	FG Killeen 35
USC	Williams 18 pass from Palmer (Killeen kick)
USC	Fargas 50 run (Killeen kick)
USC	McCullough 5 run (Killeen kick)
USC	Byrd 6 run (Killeen kick)
IOWA	Brown 18 pass from Banks (Kaeding kick)

USC	TEAM STATISTICS	IOWA
30	First Downs	18
247	Rushing Yards	119
21-31-0	Passing	15-36-1
303	Passing Yards	204
550	Total Yards	323
4-49	Punt Returns - Yards	0-0
2-33	Kickoff Returns - Yards	7-224
2-37.5	Punts - Average	5-42.6
2-0	Fumbles - Lost	2-1
6-45	Penalties - Yards	13-85
38:06	Possession Time	21:54

INDIVIDUAL LEADERS

RUSHING
USC: Fargas 20-122, 2 TD; McCullough 12-77, 1 TD.
IOWA: Russell 9-45; Banks 8-36.

PASSING
USC: Palmer 21-31-0, 303 yards, 1 TD.
IOWA: Banks 15-36-1, 204 yards, 1 TD.

RECEIVING
USC: Williams 6-99, 1 TD; Colbert 6-81; Kelly 3-74.
IOWA: Clark 4-97; Brown 6-63, 1 TD.

MIAMI (FLA.) 16, FLORIDA STATE 14

	1ST	2ND	3RD	4TH	FINAL
MIA	3	10	3	0	16
FSU	0	14	0	0	14

SCORING SUMMARY

MIA	FG Peattie 32
FSU	Booker 9 run (Beitia kick)
FSU	Henshaw 7 pass from Rix (Beitia kick)
MIA	Moss 3 run (Peattie kick)
MIA	FG Peattie 44
MIA	FG Peattie 51

MIA	TEAM STATISTICS	FSU
16	First Downs	10
218	Rushing Yards	110
14-29-2	Passing	6-19-1
157	Passing Yards	96
375	Total Yards	206
3-23	Punt Returns - Yards	1-6
3-63	Kickoff Returns - Yards	4-66
5-25.2	Punts - Average	7-43.6
2-1	Fumbles - Lost	2-1
5-40	Penalties - Yards	10-85
36:08	Possession Time	23:52

INDIVIDUAL LEADERS

RUSHING
MIA: Payton 22-131; Moss 15-31, 1 TD.
FSU: Jones 6-38; Booker 8-25, 1 TD.

PASSING
MIA: Berlin 14-29-2, 157 yards.
FSU: Rix 6-19-1, 96 yards, 1 TD.

RECEIVING
MIA: Moore 3-52; Winslow 5-48.
FSU: Stovall 4-79; Sam 1-10.

SOUTHERN CAL 55, OKLAHOMA 19

	1ST	2ND	3RD	4TH	FINAL
USC	14	24	10	7	55
OKLA	7	3	0	9	19

SCORING SUMMARY

OKLA	Wilson 5 pass from White (Hartley kick)
USC	Byrd 33 pass from Leinart (Killeen kick)
USC	White 6 run (Killeen kick)
USC	Jarrett 54 pass from Leinart (Kalil kick)
USC	Smith 5 pass from Leinart (Killeen kick)
OKLA	FG Hartley 29
USC	Smith 33 pass from Leinart (Killeen kick)
USC	FG Killeen 44
USC	Smith 4 pass from Leinart (Killeen kick)
USC	FG Killeen 42
USC	White 8 run (Killeen kick)
OKLA	Saftey
OKLA	Wilson 9 pass from White (Hartley kick)

USC	TEAM STATISTICS	OKLA
20	First Downs	19
193	Rushing Yards	128
18-35-0	Passing	24-36-3
332	Passing Yards	244
525	Total Yards	372
1-7	Punt Returns - Yards	1-3
2-36	Kickoff Returns - Yards	3-51
4-43.5	Punts - Average	4-44.5
1-0	Fumbles - Lost	3-2
9-75	Penalties - Yards	3-30
35:06	Possession Time	24:54

INDIVIDUAL LEADERS

RUSHING
USC: White 15-118, 2 TD; Bush 6-75.
OKLA: Peterson 24-82; Wolfe 7-40.

PASSING
USC: Leinart 18-35-0, 332 yards, 5 TD.
OKLA: White 24-36-3, 244 yards, 2 TD.

RECEIVING
USC: Jarrett 5-115, 1 TD; Smith 7-113, 3 TD; Byrd 3-58, 1 TD.
OKLA: Bradley 2-66; Wilson 7-59, 2 TD.

SUGAR BOWL

PROFILE

Site: New Orleans
Stadium: Louisiana Superdome
Capacity: 72,003
Surface: Momentum Turf

PLAYING SITES

Tulane Stadium, 1935-74
Louisiana Superdome, since 1975

NAME CHANGES

Sugar Bowl Football Classic,
  1935-87
USF&G Sugar Bowl, 1988-95
Nokia Sugar Bowl, since 1996

SEASON	DATE	PRE-GAME RANK	TEAMS	SCORE	FINAL RANK	MOST VALUABLE PLAYERS	ATT.
1934	Jan. 1, 1935		Tulane	20			22,026
			Temple	14			
1935	Jan. 1, 1936		TCU	3			35,000
			LSU	2			
1936	Jan. 1, 1937	6	Santa Clara	21			38,483
		2	LSU	14			
1937	Jan. 1, 1938	9	Santa Clara	6			40,000
		8	LSU	0			
1938	Jan. 2, 1939	1	TCU	15			44,308
		6	Carnegie Tech	7			
1939	Jan. 1, 1940	1	Texas A&M	14			73,000
		5	Tulane	13			
1940	Jan. 1, 1941	5	Boston College	19			68,486
		4	Tennessee	13			
1941	Jan. 1, 1942	6	Fordham	2			68,154
		7	Missouri	0			
1942	Jan. 1, 1943	7	Tennessee	14			58,361
		4	Tulsa	7			
1943	Jan. 1, 1944	13	Georgia Tech	20			69,134
		15	Tulsa	18			
1944	Jan. 1, 1945	11	Duke	29			66,822
			Alabama	26			
1945	Jan. 1, 1946		Oklahoma State	33			75,000
			St. Mary's (Cal.)	13			
1946	Jan. 1, 1947	3	Georgia	20			68,936
		9	North Carolina	10			
1947	Jan. 1, 1948	5	Texas	27		Bobby Layne, Texas, QB	73,000
		6	Alabama	7			
1948	Jan. 1, 1949	5	Oklahoma	14		Jack Mitchell, Oklahoma, QB	80,383
		3	North Carolina	6			
1949	Jan. 2, 1950	2	Oklahoma	35		Leon Heath, Oklahoma, FB	82,000
		9	LSU	0			
1950	Jan. 1, 1951	7	Kentucky	13		Walt Yowarsky, Kentucky, T	80,206
		1	Oklahoma	7			
1951	Jan. 1, 1952	3	Maryland	28		Ed Modzelewski, Maryland, FB	80,187
		1	Tennessee	13			
1952	Jan. 1, 1953	2	Georgia Tech	24		Leon Hardemann, Georgia Tech, HB	80,205
		7	Mississippi	7			
1953	Jan. 1, 1954	8	Georgia Tech	42		"Pepper" Rodgers, Georgia Tech, QB	80,187
		10	West Virginia	19			
1954	Jan. 1, 1955	5	Navy	21		Joe Gattuso, Navy, FB	80,205
		6	Mississippi	0			
1955	Jan. 2, 1956	7	Georgia Tech	7		Franklin Brooks, Georgia Tech, G	71,666
		11	Pittsburgh	0			
1956	Jan. 1, 1957	11	Baylor	13		Del Shofner, Baylor, HB	80,190
		2	Tennessee	7			
1957	Jan. 1, 1958	7	Mississippi	39		Raymond Brown, Mississippi, QB	76,535
		11	Texas	7			
1958	Jan. 1, 1959	1	LSU	7		Billy Cannon, LSU, HB	78,084
		12	Clemson	0			
1959	Jan. 1, 1960	2	Mississippi	21		Bobby Franklin, Mississippi, QB	77,484
		3	LSU	0			
1960	Jan. 2, 1961	2	Mississippi	14		Jake Gibbs, Mississippi, QB	80,331
			Rice	6			
1961	Jan. 1, 1962	1	Alabama	10		Mike Fracchia, Alabama, FB	81,141
		9	Arkansas	3			
1962	Jan. 1, 1963	3	Mississippi	17		Glynn Griffin, Mississippi, QB	79,707
		6	Arkansas	13			
1963	Jan. 1, 1964	8	Alabama	12		Tim Davis, Alabama, K	82,910
		7	Mississippi	7			
1964	Jan. 1, 1965	7	LSU	13		Doug Moreau, LSU, FL	80,096
			Syracuse	10			
1965	Jan. 1, 1966	6	Missouri	20	6	Steve Spurrier, Florida, QB	73,024
			Florida	18			
1966	Jan. 2, 1967	3	Alabama	34		Kenny Stabler, Alabama, QB	60,322
		6	Nebraska	7			
1967	Jan. 1, 1968		LSU	20		Glenn Smith, LSU, HB	61,346
		6	Wyoming	13			
1968	Jan. 1, 1969	9	Arkansas	16	6	Chuck Dicus, Arkansas, FL	82,000
		4	Georgia	2	8		
1969	Jan. 1, 1970	13	Mississippi	27	8	Archie Manning, Mississippi, QB	72,858
		3	Arkansas	22	7		
1970	Jan. 1, 1971	4	Tennessee	34	4	Bobby Scott, Tennessee, QB	82,113
		11	Air Force	13	16		
1971	Jan. 1, 1972	3	Oklahoma	40	2	Jack Mildren, Oklahoma, QB	80,096
		5	Auburn	22	12		
1972	Dec. 31, 1972	2	Oklahoma	14	2	Tinker Owens, Oklahoma, FL	80,123
		5	Penn State	0	10		
1973	Dec. 31, 1973	3	Notre Dame	24	1	Tom Clements, Notre Dame, QB	85,161
		1	Alabama	23	4		
1974	Dec. 31, 1974	8	Nebraska	13	9	Tony Davis, Nebraska, FB	68,890
		18	Florida	10	15		
1975	Dec. 31, 1975	4	Alabama	13	3	Richard Todd, Alabama, QB	74,331
		8	Penn State	6	10		
1976	Jan. 1, 1977	1	Pittsburgh	27	1	Matt Cavanaugh, Pittsburgh, QB	75,212
		5	Georgia	3	10		
1977	Jan. 2, 1978	3	Alabama	35	2	Jeff Rutledge, Alabama, QB	76,811
		9	Ohio State	6	11		
1978	Jan. 1, 1979	2	Alabama	14	1	Barry Krauss, Alabama, LB	76,824
		1	Penn State	7	4		
1979	Jan. 1, 1980	2	Alabama	24	1	Major Ogilvie, Alabama, RB	77,484
		6	Arkansas	9	8		
1980	Jan. 1, 1981	1	Georgia	17	1	Herschel Walker, Georgia, RB	77,895
		7	Notre Dame	10	9		

SEASON	DATE	PRE-GAME RANK	TEAMS	SCORE	FINAL RANK	MOST VALUABLE PLAYERS	ATT.
1981	Jan. 1, 1982	10	Pittsburgh	24	4	Dan Marino, Pittsburgh, QB	77,224
		2	Georgia	20	6		
1982	Jan. 1, 1983	2	Penn State	27	1	Todd Blackledge, Penn State, QB	78,124
		1	Georgia	23	4		
1983	Jan. 2, 1984	3	Auburn	9	3	Bo Jackson, Auburn, RB	77,893
		8	Michigan	7	8		
1984	Jan. 1, 1985	5	Nebraska	28	4	Craig Sundberg, Nebraska, QB	75,608
		11	LSU	10	5		
1985	Jan. 1, 1986	8	Tennessee	35	4	Daryl Dickey, Tennessee, QB	77,432
		2	Miami (Fla.)	7	9		
1986	Jan. 1, 1987	6	Nebraska	30	5	Steve Taylor, Nebraska, QB	76,234
		5	LSU	15	10		
1987	Jan. 1, 1988	6	Auburn	16	7	Don McPherson, Syracuse, QB	75,495
		4	Syracuse	16	4		
1988	Jan. 2, 1989	4	Florida State	13	3	Sammie Smith, Florida State, RB	75,098
		7	Auburn	7	8		
1989	Jan. 1, 1990	2	Miami (Fla.)	33	1	Craig Erickson, Miami (Fla.), QB	77,452
		7	Alabama	25	9		
1990	Jan. 1, 1991	10	Tennessee	23	8	Andy Kelly, Tennessee, QB	75,132
			Virginia	22	23		
1991	Jan. 1, 1992	18	Notre Dame	39	13	Jerome Bettis, Notre Dame, FB	76,447
		3	Florida	28	7		
1992	Jan. 1, 1993	2	Alabama	34	1	Derrick Lassic, Alabama, RB	76,789
		1	Miami (Fla.)	13	3		
1993	Jan. 1, 1994	8	Florida	41	5	Errict Rhett, Florida, RB	75,437
		3	West Virginia	7	7		
1994	Jan. 2, 1995	7	Florida State	23	4	Warrick Dunn, Florida State, RB	76,224
		5	Florida	17	7		
1995	Dec. 31, 1995	13	Virginia Tech	28	10	Bryan Still, Virginia Tech, WR	70,283
		9	Texas	10	14		
1996	Jan. 2, 1997	3	Florida	52	1	Danny Wuerffel, Florida, QB	78,347
		1	Florida State	20	3		
1997	Jan. 1, 1998	4	Florida State	31	3	E.G. Green, Florida State, WR	67,289
		9	Ohio State	14	12		
1998	Jan. 1, 1999	3	Ohio State	24	2	David Boston, Ohio State, WR	76,503
		8	Texas A&M	14	11		
1999	Jan. 4, 2000	1	Florida State	46	1	Peter Warrick, Florida State, WR	79,280
		2	Virginia Tech	29	2		
2000	Jan. 2, 2001	2	Miami (Fla.)	37	2	Ken Dorsey, Miami (Fla.), QB	64,407
		7	Florida	20	10		
2001	Jan. 1, 2002	12	LSU	47	7	Rohan Davey, LSU, QB	77,688
		7	Illinois	34	12		
2002	Jan. 1, 2003	4	Georgia	26	3	Musa Smith, Georgia, TB	74,269
		16	Florida State	13	21		
2003	Jan. 4, 2004	2	LSU	21	2	Justin Vincent, LSU, RB	79,342
		3	Oklahoma	14	3		
2004	Jan. 3, 2005	3	Auburn	16	2	Jason Campbell, Auburn, QB	77,349
		9	Va. Tech	13	10		

JANUARY 1, 1935
TULANE 20, TEMPLE 14

	1ST	2ND	3RD	4TH	FINAL
TUL	0	7	7	6	20
TEM	7	7	0	0	14

SCORING SUMMARY
TEM Tester 7 pass from Smukler (Smukler kick)
TEM Smukler 3 run (Smukler kick)
TUL Simons 85 kickoff return (Mintz kick)
TUL Hardy 11 pass from Bryan (Mintz kick)
TUL Hardy 25 pass from Mintz (kick failed)

TUL	TEAM STATISTICS	TEM
10	First Downs	13
140	Rushing Yards	182
8-16-1	Passing	3-13-1
88	Passing Yards	19
228	Total Yards	201
3-2	Fumbles - Lost	2-1
2-20	Penalties - Yards	2-7

JANUARY 1, 1936
TCU 3, LSU 2

	1ST	2ND	3RD	4TH	FINAL
TCU	0	3	0	0	3
LSU	0	2	0	0	2

SCORING SUMMARY
LSU Safety (Baugh fumbles in end zone)
TCU FG Manton 26

TCU	TEAM STATISTICS	LSU
6	First Downs	9
121	Rushing Yards	120
3-8-1	Passing	3-21-3
54	Passing Yards	59
175	Total Yards	179
14-46.0	Punts - Average	13-44.7
2-1	Fumbles - Lost	3-2
4-20	Penalties - Yards	3-33

INDIVIDUAL LEADERS
RUSHING
TCU: Lawrence 6-54; Baugh 22-45.
LSU: Crass 15-34; Reed 6-29.
PASSING
TCU: Baugh 2-7-1, 29 yards.
LSU: Mickal 2-14-3, 36 yards.
RECEIVING
TCU: Walls 1-25, Meyer 1-18.
LSU: Barrett 3-59.

JANUARY 1, 1937
SANTA CLARA 21, LSU 14

	1ST	2ND	3RD	4TH	FINAL
SCL	14	0	7	0	21
LSU	0	7	0	7	14

SCORING SUMMARY
SCL Gomez 26 pass from Falaschi (Pellegrini kick)
SCL Finney 30 pass from Pellegrini (Pellegrini kick)
LSU Tinsley 50 pass from Crass (Crass kick)
SCL Falaschi 1 run (Smith from Gomez)
LSU Reed 10 pass from Crass (Milner kick)

SCL	TEAM STATISTICS	LSU
10	First Downs	7
108	Rushing Yards	44
6-12-4	Passing	7-21-2
74	Passing Yards	125
182	Total Yards	169

JANUARY 1, 1938
SANTA CLARA 6, LSU 0

	1ST	2ND	3RD	4TH	FINAL
SCL	0	6	0	0	6
LSU	0	0	0	0	0

SCORING SUMMARY
SCL Coughlan 1 pass from Pellegrini (kick failed)

SCL	TEAM STATISTICS	LSU
5	First Downs	10
34	Rushing Yards	106
5-13-3	Passing	8-21-0
67	Passing Yards	95
101	Total Yards	201

THE BOWLS

JANUARY 2, 1939
TCU 15, Carnegie Tech 7

	1ST	2ND	3RD	4TH	FINAL
TCU	0	6	6	3	15
CT	0	7	0	0	7

SCORING SUMMARY
TCU Sparks 1 run (kick failed)
CT Muha 37 pass from Moroz (Muha kick)
TCU Horner 44 pass from O'Brien (kick failed)
TCU FG O'Brien 19

TCU	TEAM STATISTICS	CT
17	First Downs	10
142	Rushing Yards	129
17-28-0	Passing	3-8-2
225	Passing Yards	59
367	Total Yards	188
1-40.0	Punts - Average	6-40.0
0-0	Fumbles - Lost	0-0

INDIVIDUAL LEADERS
RUSHING
TCU: Hall 6-47; Sparks 14-37, 1 TD.
CT: Muha 16-69; Condit 10-31.
PASSING
TCU: O'Brien 17-27-0, 224 yards, 1 TD.
CT: Moroz 1-2-0, 38 yards, 1 TD.

JANUARY 1, 1940
Texas A&M 14, Tulane 13

	1ST	2ND	3RD	4TH	FINAL
A&M	7	0	0	7	14
TUL	0	0	7	6	13

SCORING SUMMARY
A&M Kimbrough 1 run (Price kick)
TUL Kellogg 75 punt return (Thibaut kick)
TUL Butler 2 run (kick blocked)
A&M Kimbrough 18 pass from Smith (Price kick)

A&M	TEAM STATISTICS	TUL
18	First Downs	8
244	Rushing Yards	193
8-15-1	Passing	0-4-0
62	Passing Yards	0
306	Total Yards	193
2-2	Fumbles - Lost	1-0
2-30	Penalties - Yards	2-20

INDIVIDUAL LEADERS
RUSHING
A&M: Kimbrough 25-159, 1 TD; Connatser 9-31.
TUL: Butler 10-55, 1 TD; Cassibry 11-42.
PASSING
A&M: Price 8-15-1, 62 yards.
TUL: Kellogg 0-2-0, 0 yards.

JANUARY 1, 1941
Boston College 19, Tennessee 13

	1ST	2ND	3RD	4TH	FINAL
BC	0	0	13	6	19
TENN	7	0	6	0	13

SCORING SUMMARY
TENN Thompson 4 run (Foxx kick)
BC Connally 13 run (Maznicki kick)
TENN Warren 2 run (kick failed)
BC Holovak 1 run (kick failed)
BC O'Rourke 24 run (kick failed)

BC	TEAM STATISTICS	TENN
11	First Downs	13
142	Rushing Yards	124
6-14-3	Passing	9-22-2
106	Passing Yards	121
248	Total Yards	245
6-35.0	Punts - Average	7-36.0
1-1	Fumbles - Lost	1-1
3-25	Penalties - Yards	4-36

INDIVIDUAL LEADERS
RUSHING
BC: O'Rourke 7-52, 1 TD.
TENN: Fozz 7-41; Thompson 11-40, 1 TD.
PASSING
BC: O'Rourke 5-11-2, 85 yards.
TENN: Thompson 4-9-1, 42 yards.
RECEIVING
BC: Zabilski 2-39.
TENN: Coleman 3-49.

JANUARY 1, 1942
Fordham 2, Missouri 0

	1ST	2ND	3RD	4TH	FINAL
FORD	2	0	0	0	2
MO	0	0	0	0	0

SCORING SUMMARY
FORD Safety (Santilli blocked punt out of endzone)

10	First Downs	MO
137	Rushing Yards	8
0-4-0	Passing	148
0	Passing Yards	2-5-2
137	Total Yards	21
3-1	Fumbles - Lost	169
		3-2

JANUARY 1, 1943
Tennessee 14, Tulsa 7

	1ST	2ND	3RD	4TH	FINAL
TENN	0	6	2	6	14
TUL	0	7	0	0	7

SCORING SUMMARY
TUL Purdin 9 pass from Dobbs (LaForce kick)
TENN Gold 3 run (kick failed)
TENN Safey (Crawford blocked punt out of end zone)
TENN Fuson 1 run (kick failed)

TENN	TEAM STATISTICS	TUL
14	First Downs	10
208	Rushing Yards	-39
7-17-0	Passing	17-27-2
88	Passing Yards	168
296	Total Yards	129
2-2	Fumbles - Lost	0-0

JANUARY 1, 1944
Georgia Tech 20, Tulsa 18

	1ST	2ND	3RD	4TH	FINAL
GT	0	7	6	7	20
TUL	6	12	0	0	18

JANUARY 1, 1945
Duke 29, Alabama 26

	1ST	2ND	3RD	4TH	FINAL
DUKE	7	6	7	9	29
ALA	12	7	0	7	26

SCORING SUMMARY
DUKE Clark 15 run (Raether kick)
ALA Hodges 1 run (kick failed)
ALA Hodges 2 run (kick failed)
ALA Jones 13 pass from Gilmer (Morrow kick)
DUKE Davis 1 run (kick failed)
DUKE Davis 1 run (Raether kick)
ALA Morrow 80 interception (Morrow kick)
DUKE Safety
DUKE Clark 20 run (Raether kick)

DUKE	TEAM STATISTICS	ALA
19	First Downs	8
336	Rushing Yards	102
5-8-1	Passing	8-8-0
47	Passing Yards	142
383	Total Yards	244
4-34.0	Punts - Average	5-35.0
6-1	Fumbles - Lost	1-1
1-5	Penalties - Yards	2-6

INDIVIDUAL LEADERS
RUSHING
DUKE: Clark 14-123, 2 TD; Davis 27-101, 2 TD.
ALA: Gilmer 14-63; Hodges 8-29, 2 TD.
PASSING
DUKE: Lewis 4-7-1, 40 yards.
ALA: Gilmer 8-8-0, 142 yards, 1 TD.
RECEIVING
DUKE: Carver 4-35.
ALA: Jones 4-136, 1 TD.

JANUARY 1, 1946
Oklahoma St 33, St. Mary's 13

	1ST	2ND	3RD	4TH	FINAL
OKST	7	7	6	13	33
ST.M	7	6	0	0	13

SCORING SUMMARY
ST.M O'Connor 46 pass from Wedemeyer (Wedemeyer kick)
OKST Hankins 29 pass from Fenimore (Reynolds kick)
OKST Fenimore 1 run (Reynolds kick)
ST.M DeSalvo 20 run (kick failed)
OKST Fenimore 1 run (kick failed)
OKST Reynolds 1 run (kick failed)
OKST Thomas 10 pass from Reynolds (Reynolds kick)

OKST	TEAM STATISTICS	ST.M
15	First Downs	8
217	Rushing Yards	61
4-13-4	Passing	11-24-2
112	Passing Yards	177
339	Total Yards	238
4-47.2	Punts - Average	5-43.0
0-0	Fumbles - Lost	2-2

JANUARY 1, 1947
Georgia 20, North Carolina 10

	1ST	2ND	3RD	4TH	FINAL
UGA	0	0	13	7	20
UNC	0	7	3	0	10

SCORING SUMMARY
UNC Pupa 4 run (Cox kick)
UGA Rauch 4 run (Jernigan kick)
UNC FG Cox 27
UGA Edwards 67 pass from Trippi (kick blocked)
UGA Rauch 13 run (Jernigan kick)

UGA	TEAM STATISTICS	UNC
12	First Downs	17
175	Rushing Yards	166
3-14-1	Passing	8-14-1
81	Passing Yards	99
256	Total Yards	265
7-32.7	Punts - Average	6-38.0
0-0	Fumbles Lost	1-1

INDIVIDUAL LEADERS
RUSHING
UGA: Trippi 15-77.
UNC: Justice 18-37.

JANUARY 1, 1948
Texas 27, Alabama 7

	1ST	2ND	3RD	4TH	FINAL
TEX	7	0	7	13	27
ALA	0	7	0	0	7

SCORING SUMMARY
TEX Blount 5 pass from Layne (Guess kick)
ALA White 8 pass from Gilmer (Morrow kick)
TEX Vasicek fumble recovery (Guess kick)
TEX Holder 18 interception return (Guess kick)
TEX Layne 1 run (kick failed)

JANUARY 1, 1949
Oklahoma 14, North Carolina 6

	1ST	2ND	3RD	4TH	FINAL
OKLA	7	0	7	0	14
UNC	6	0	0	0	6

SCORING SUMMARY
OKLA Mitchell 1 run (Ming kick)
UNC Rodgers 2 run (kick failed)
OKLA Pearson 8 run (Ming kick)

OKLA	TEAM STATISTICS	UNC
15	First Downs	12
186	Rushing Yards	128
1-4-0	Passing	8-21-2
43	Passing Yards	82
229	Total Yards	210
5-36.8	Punts - Average	7-38.0
1-1	Fumbles - Lost	0-0
40	Penalty Yards	30

INDIVIDUAL LEADERS
RUSHING
OKLA: Heath 12-58; Thomas 19-51.
UNC: Justice 16-84; Rodgers 12-25, 1 TD.
PASSING
OKLA: Royal 1-1-0, 43 yards.
UNC: Justice 6-13-1, 57 yards.
RECEIVING
OKLA: Anderson 1-43.
UNC: Weiner 3-35; Kennedy 4-25.

JANUARY 2, 1950
OKLAHOMA 35, LSU 0

	1ST	2ND	3RD	4TH	FINAL
OKLA	0	14	7	14	35
LSU	0	0	0	0	0

SCORING SUMMARY
OKLA — Heath 86 run (Tipps kick)
OKLA — Heath 34 run (Tipps kick)
OKLA — Thomas 34 pass from Pearson (Tipps kick)
OKLA — Thomas 5 run (Tipps kick)
OKLA — Royal 5 run (Tipps kick)

OKLA	TEAM STATISTICS	LSU
10	First Downs	8
286	Rushing Yards	38
2-11-4	Passing	9-20-2
74	Passing Yards	121
360	Total Yards	159
7-37.4	Punts - Average	8-33.6
4-4	Fumbles - Lost	4-4
8-40	Penalties - Yards	6-40

INDIVIDUAL LEADERS
RUSHING
OKLA: Heath 15-170, 2 TD.
LSU: West 5-26.
PASSING
OKLA: Pearson 2-7-0, 74 yards, 1 TD.
LSU: Pevy 5-11-0, 82 yards.
RECEIVING
OKLA: Goad 1-40.
LSU: Baggett 4-50.

JANUARY 1, 1951
KENTUCKY 13, OKLAHOMA 7

	1ST	2ND	3RD	4TH	FINAL
UK	7	6	0	0	13
OKLA	0	0	0	7	7

SCORING SUMMARY
UK — Jamerson 22 pass from Parilli (Gain kick)
UK — Jamerson 1 run (kick failed)
OKLA — Green 17 pass from Vessels (Weatherall kick)

INDIVIDUAL LEADERS
RUSHING
UK: Jamerson 15-58, 1 TD.
OKLA: Heath 20-121.
PASSING
UK: Parilli 9-12-0, 105 yards, 1 TD.
OKLA: Arnold 2-5-0, 21 yards.
RECEIVING
UK: Bruno 3-57.
OKLA: Vessels 2-21.

JANUARY 1, 1952
MARYLAND 28, TENNESSEE 13

	1ST	2ND	3RD	4TH	FINAL
MARY	7	14	7	0	28
TENN	0	6	0	7	13

SCORING SUMMARY
MARY — Fullerton 2 run (Decker kick)
MARY — Shemonski 6 pass from Fullerton (Decker kick)
MARY — Scarbath 1 run (Decker kick)
TENN — Rechichar 4 pass from Payne (kick failed)
MARY — Fullerton 46 interception (Decker kick)
TENN — Payne 2 run (Rechichar kick)

MARY	TEAM STATISTICS	TENN
18	First Downs	12
289	Rushing Yards	81
7-13-1	Passing	9-19-4
62	Passing Yards	75
351	Total Yards	156
8-38.8	Punts - Average	7-43.0
7-3	Fumbles-Lost	2-2
12-120	Penalty Yards	2-20

INDIVIDUAL LEADERS
RUSHING
MARY: Modzelewski 28-153.
TENN: Payne 11-54, 1 TD; Kozar 9-29.
PASSING
MARY: Scarbath 6-9-0, 57 yards.
TENN: Payne 7-14-1, 61 yards, 1 TD.
RECEIVING
MARY: Shemonski 3-19, 1 TD.
TENN: Rechichar 3-27, 1 TD.

JANUARY 1, 1953
GEORGIA TECH 24, MISSISSIPPI 7

	1ST	2ND	3RD	4TH	FINAL
GT	0	10	7	7	24
MISS	7	0	0	0	7

SCORING SUMMARY
MISS — Dillard 4 run (Lear kick)
GT — Brigman 1 run (Rodgers kick)
GT — FG Rodgers 25
GT — Hardemann 6 run (Rodgers kick)
GT — Knox 26 pass from Rodgers (Rodgers kick)

GT	TEAM STATISTICS	MISS
16	First Downs	15
194	Rushing Yards	137
10-18-1	Passing	11-23-3
101	Passing Yards	150
295	Total Yards	287
6-41.8	Punts - Average	7-35.4
5-2	Fumbles - Lost	5-3
5-42	Penalties - Yards	6-60

INDIVIDUAL LEADERS
RUSHING
GT: Hardemann 14-76, 1 TD; Turner 20-56.
MISS: Dillard 17-39, 1 TD; Westerman 7-36.
PASSING
GT: Brigman 5-7-1, 39 yards; Rodgers 4-9-0, 55 yards, 1 TD.
MISS: Lear 8-19-3, 122 yards.
RECEIVING
GT: Hardemann 2-24; Marks 2-14.
MISS: Slay 1-45; Bridges 2-25.

JANUARY 1, 1954
GEORGIA TECH 42, WEST VIRGINIA 19

	1ST	2ND	3RD	4TH	FINAL
GT	14	6	9	13	42
WVU	0	6	0	13	19

SCORING SUMMARY
GT — Hensley 24 pass from Rodgers (Rodgers kick)
GT — Durham 2 pass from Rodgers (Rodgers kick)
WVU — Williams 5 run (kick failed)
GT — Hair 5 pass from Rodgers (kick failed)
GT — FG Rodgers 18
GT — Hardeman 23 run (kick failed)
WVU — Marconi 1 run (Allman kick)
GT — Ruffin 43 run (kick blocked)
WVU — Allman 1 run (kick failed)
GU — Teas 9 run (Turner kick)

GT	TEAM STATISTICS	WVU
19	First Downs	19
170	Rushing Yards	223
20-35-2	Passing	7-18-2
268	Passing Yards	78
438	Total Yards	301
1-36.0	Punts - Average	2-28.5
3-1	Fumbles - Lost	5-4
7-45	Penalties - Yards	5-35

INDIVIDUAL LEADERS
RUSHING
GT: Ruffin 3-58, 1 TD; Teas 9-32, 1 TD.
WVU: Anderson 13-57; Moss 5-36.
PASSING
GT: Rodgers 16-26-2, 195 yards, 3 TD.
WVU: Wyant 4-15-2, 29 yards; Anderson 3-3-0, 49 yards.

JANUARY 1, 1955
NAVY 21, MISSISSIPPI 0

	1ST	2ND	3RD	4TH	FINAL
MISS	0	0	0	0	0
NAVY	7	0	14	0	21

SCORING SUMMARY
NAVY — Gattuso 3 run (Weaver kick)
NAVY — Weaver 16 pass from Welsh (Weaver kick)
NAVY — Gattuso 1 run (Weaver kick)

MISS	TEAM STATISTICS	NAVY
5	First Downs	20
78	Rushing Yards	295
5-18-0	Passing	12-28-4
43	Passing Yards	147
121	Total Yards	442
9-36.1	Punts - Average	4-33.8
2-1	Fumbles - Lost	1-0
6-50	Penalties - Yards	1-15

INDIVIDUAL LEADERS
RUSHING
MISS: Cothren 7-24.
NAVY: Weaver 16-106; Gattuso 16-11, 2 TD.
PASSING
MISS: Day 2-9-0, 16 yards; Patton 3-6-0, 27 yards.
NAVY: Welsh 8-14-0, 76 yards, 1 TD.
RECEIVING
MISS: Muirhead 2-16.
NAVY: Weaver 3-39, 1 TD; Beagle 3-19.

JANUARY 2, 1956
GEORGIA TECH 7, PITTSBURGH 0

	1ST	2ND	3RD	4TH	FINAL
GT	7	0	0	0	7
PITT	0	0	0	0	0

SCORING SUMMARY
GT — Mitchell 1 run (Mitchell kick)

GT	TEAM STATISTICS	PITT
10	First Downs	19
142	Rushing Yards	217
0-3-1	Passing	8-18-1
0	Passing Yards	94
142	Total Yards	311
6-33.8	Punts - Average	4-38.7
2-0	Fumbles - Lost	4-2
1-15	Penalties - Yards	8-72

INDIVIDUAL LEADERS
RUSHING
GT: Owen 7-29; Mattison 7-27.
PITT: Grier 6-51; Cimarolli 11-37.

JANUARY 1, 1957
BAYLOR 13, TENNESSEE 7

	1ST	2ND	3RD	4TH	FINAL
BU	0	6	0	7	13
TENN	0	0	7	0	7

SCORING SUMMARY
BU — Marcontell 12 pass from Jones (kick failed)
TENN — Majors 1 run (Burklow kick)
BU — Humphrey 1 run (Berry kick)

BU	TEAM STATISTICS	TENN
13	First Downs	10
275	Rushing Yards	146
3-11-0	Passing	1-10-4
24	Passing Yards	16
299	Total Yards	162
8-32.6	Punts - Average	5-41.6
60	Penalty Yards	55

INDIVIDUAL LEADERS
RUSHING
BU : Shofner 14-88.
TENN: Majors 15-59, 1 TD; Bronson 8-56.
PASSING
BU : Jones 2-4-0, 19 yards, 1 TD.
TENN: Majors 1-7-2, 16 yards.
RECEIVING
BU : Marcontell 3-24, 1 TD.
TENN: Urbano 1-16.

JANUARY 1, 1958
MISSISSIPPI 39, TEXAS 7

	1ST	2ND	3RD	4TH	FINAL
MISS	6	13	7	13	39
TEX	0	0	0	7	7

SCORING SUMMARY
MISS — Brown 1 run (kick failed)
MISS — Williams 3 pass from Brown (Khayat kick)
MISS — Lovelace 9 run (Khayat kick)
MISS — Franklin 3 run (Khayat kick)
TEX — Blanch 1 run (Lackey kick)
MISS — Brown 92 run (Khayat kick)
MISS — Taylor 12 pass from Brewer (kick failed)

MISS	TEAM STATISTICS	TEX
18	First Downs	13
304	Rushing Yards	192
7-16-0	Passing	2-11-4
71	Passing Yards	14
375	Total Yards	206
7-34.7	Punts - Average	5-38.2
5-2	Fumbles - Lost	7-4
9-95	Penalties - Yards	6-30

INDIVIDUAL LEADERS
RUSHING
MISS: Brown 15-157 yards, 2 TD; Franklin 9-64, 1 TD.
TEX: Blanch 11-58, 1 TD; Allen 8-43; Fondren 8-39.
PASSING
MISS: Brown 3-8-0, 24 yards, 1 TD.
TEX: Lackey 2-5-2, 14 yards.
RECEIVING
MISS: Taylor 2-20, 1 TD; Willaims 2-15, 1 TD.
TEX: Ramirez 1-3.

JANUARY 1, 1959
LSU 7, Clemson 0

	1ST	2ND	3RD	4TH	FINAL
LSU	0	0	7	0	7
CLEM	0	0	0	0	0

SCORING SUMMARY
LSU   Mangham 9 pass from Cannon (Cannon kick)

LSU	TEAM STATISTICS	CLEM
9	First Downs	12
114	Rushing Yards	168
4-11-0	Passing	2-4-0
68	Passing Yards	23
182	Total Yards	191
6-41.7	Punts - Average	6-32.8
4-2	Fumbles - Lost	3-2
5-35	Penalties - Yards	2-20

INDIVIDUAL LEADERS
RUSHING
LSU: Cannon 13-51; Davis 2-17.
CLEM: Hayes 17-55; Usry 10-29.

JANUARY 1, 1960
Mississippi 21, LSU 0

	1ST	2ND	3RD	4TH	FINAL
MISS	0	7	7	7	21
LSU	0	0	0	0	0

SCORING SUMMARY
MISS   Woodruff 43 pass from Gibbs (Franklin kick)
MISS   Granthan 18 pass from Franklin (Khayat kick)
MISS   Blair 9 pass from Franklin (Khayat kick)

MISS	TEAM STATISTICS	LSU
19	First Downs	6
140	Rushing Yards	-15
15-27-2	Passing	9-25-2
223	Passing Yards	89
363	Total Yards	74
6-37.5	Punts - Average	12-34.3
4-2	Fumbles - Lost	2-0
7-65	Penalties - Yards	4-30

INDIVIDUAL LEADERS
RUSHING
MISS: Flowers 19-60; Blair 8-26.
LSU: Cannon 6-8.
PASSING
MISS: Franklin 10-15-1, 148 yards, 2 TD; Gibbs 4-10-1, 65 yards, 1 TD.
LSU: Rabb 4-15-0, 36 yards.
RECEIVING
MISS: Flowers 4-64.
LSU: Cannon 3-39; McClain 3-31.

JANUARY 2, 1961
Mississippi 14, Rice 6

	1ST	2ND	3RD	4TH	FINAL
MISS	7	0	0	7	14
RICE	0	0	6	0	6

SCORING SUMMARY
MISS   Gibbs 8 run (Green kick)
RICE   Blume 2 run (kick failed)
MISS   Gibbs 3 run (Green kick)

MISS	TEAM STATISTICS	RICE
13	First Downs	19
143	Rushing Yards	103
5-15-0	Passing	14-28-4
43	Passing Yards	178
186	Total Yards	281
5-42.4	Punts - Average	3-34.0
1-1	Fumbles - Lost	2-0
2-10	Penalties - Yards	6-30

INDIVIDUAL LEADERS
RUSHING
MISS: Anderson 15-59; Doty 4-25.
RICE: Blume 7-54, 1 TD.
PASSING
MISS: Gibbs 5-15-0, 43 yards.
RICE: Cox 11-20-1, 143 yards.
RECEIVING
MISS: Crespini 2-21; Blair 2-18.
RICE: Webb 3-31.

JANUARY 1, 1962
Alabama 10, Arkansas 3

	1ST	2ND	3RD	4TH	FINAL
ALA	7	3	0	0	10
ARK	0	0	3	0	3

SCORING SUMMARY
ALA   Trammell 12 run (Davis kick)
ALA   FG Davis 32
ARK   FG Cissell 23

JANUARY 1, 1963
Mississippi 17, Arkansas 13

	1ST	2ND	3RD	4TH	FINAL
MISS	0	10	7	0	17
ARK	0	3	10	0	13

SCORING SUMMARY
MISS   FG Irwin 30
ARK   FG McKnelly 30
MISS   Guy 33 pass from Griffin (Irwin kick)
ARK   Branch 5 pass from Moore (McKnelly kick)
MISS   Griffin 1 run (Irwin kick)
ARK   FG McKnelly 22

MISS	TEAM STATISTICS	ARK
22	First Downs	7
160	Rushing Yards	47
18-28-1	Passing	6-18-2
269	Passing Yards	123
429	Total Yards	170
2-36.0	Punts - Average	4-38.3
2-1	Fumbles - Lost	2-0
4-40	Penalties - Yards	2-13

INDIVIDUAL LEADERS
RUSHING
MISS: Jennings 9-39; Weatherly 9-36.
ARK: Branch 7-21.
PASSING
MISS: Griffin 14-23-1, 242 yards, 1 TD.
ARK: Moore 5-10-0, 55 yards, 1 TD.
RECEIVING
MISS: Guy 5-107, 1 TD; Morris 5-62.
ARK: Lamb 3-107; Branch 3-16, 1 TD.

JANUARY 1, 1964
Alabama 12, Mississippi 7

	1ST	2ND	3RD	4TH	FINAL
ALA	3	6	3	0	12
MISS	0	0	0	7	7

SCORING SUMMARY
ALA   FG Davis 46
ALA   FG Davis 31
ALA   FG Davis 34
ALA   FG Davis 48
MISS   Smith 5 pass from Dunn (Irwin kick)

ALA	TEAM STATISTICS	MISS
14	First Downs	9
165	Rushing Yards	77
3-11-1	Passing	11-21-3
29	Passing Yards	171
194	Total Yards	248
5-36.8	Punts - Average	4-44.0
6-3	Fumbles - Lost	11-6
3-15	Penalties - Yards	5-45

INDIVIDUAL LEADERS
RUSHING
ALA: Sloan 16-51; Nelson 16-47.
MISS: Dennis 7-37; Dunn 6-24.
PASSING
ALA: Sloan 3-10-1, 29 yards.
MISS: Dunn 8-10-0, 125 yards, 1 TD.
RECEIVING
ALA: Stephens 1-15.
MISS: Wells 4-76.

JANUARY 1, 1965
LSU 13, Syracuse 10

	1ST	2ND	3RD	4TH	FINAL
LSU	2	0	8	3	13
SYR	10	0	0	0	10

SCORING SUMMARY
SYR   FG Smith 23
LSU   Safety
SYR   Clarke 28 blocked punt return (Smith kick)
LSU   Moreau 57 pass from Ezell
          (Labruzzo pass from Ezell)
LSU   FG Moreau 28

LSU	TEAM STATISTICS	SYR
11	First Downs	10
161	Rushing Yards	151
6-15-1	Passing	8-20-1
114	Passing Yards	52
275	Total Yards	203
9-36.2	Punts - Average	6-37.5
4-0	Fumbles - Lost	3-1
4-46	Penalties - Yards	5-55

INDIVIDUAL LEADERS
RUSHING
LSU: Schwab 17-81.
SYR: Nance 15-70; Little 8-46.
PASSING
LSU: Ezell 2-5-0, 67 yards, 1 TD.
SYR: King 6-15-0, 41 yards.
RECEIVING
LSU: Moreau 2-54, 1 TD; Labruzzo 2-45.
SYR: Cripps 2-18; Mahle 3-15.

JANUARY 1, 1966
Missouri 20, Florida 18

	1ST	2ND	3RD	4TH	FINAL
MO	0	17	3	0	20
UF	0	0	0	18	18

SCORING SUMMARY
MO   Brown 16 run (Bates kick)
MO   Denny 11 pass from Roland (Bates kick)
MO   FG Bates 27
MO   FG Bates 34
UF   Harper 22 pass from Spurrier (pass failed)
UF   Casey 21 pass from Spurrier (pass failed)
UF   Spurrier 2 run (pass failed)

MO	TEAM STATISTICS	UF
18	First Downs	18
257	Rushing Yards	-2
5-14-1	Passing	22-45-1
50	Passing Yards	352
307	Total Yards	350
6-32.0	Punts - Average	8-44.0
2-2	Fumbles - Lost	1-1

INDIVIDUAL LEADERS
RUSHING
MO: Brown 23-121, 1 TD; Lane 19-76.
UF: Poe 2-11.
PASSING
MO: Lane 4-13-1, 39 yards.
UF: Spurrier 22-45-1, 352 yards, 2 TD.
RECEIVING
MO: Phelps 2-11.
UF: Casey 5-108, 1 TD; Brown 9-88; Harper 4-66, 1 TD.

JANUARY 2, 1967
Alabama 34, Nebraska 7

	1ST	2ND	3RD	4TH	FINAL
ALA	17	7	3	7	34
NEB	0	0	0	7	7

SCORING SUMMARY
ALA   Kelley 1 run (Davis kick)
ALA   Stabler 14 run (Davis kick)
ALA   FG Davis 30
ALA   Trimble 6 run (Davis kick)
ALA   FG Davis 40
NEB   Davis 15 pass from Churchich (Wachholtz kick)
ALA   Perkins 45 pass from Stabler (Davis kick)

ALA	TEAM STATISTICS	NEB
19	First Downs	16
157	Rushing Yards	84
15-26-1	Passing	22-38-5
279	Passing Yards	213
436	Total Yards	297

JANUARY 1, 1968

LSU 20, Wyoming 13

	1ST	2ND	3RD	4TH	FINAL
LSU	0	0	7	13	20
WYO	0	13	0	0	13

SCORING SUMMARY

WYO	Kiick 1 run (DePoyster kick)
WYO	FG DePoyster 24
WYO	FG DePoyster 49
LSU	Smith 1 run (Hurd kick)
LSU	Morel 8 pass from Stokely (kick failed)
LSU	Morel 14 pass from Stokely (Hurd kick)

LSU	TEAM STATISTICS	WYO
12	First Downs	20
151	Rushing Yards	167
6-20-0	Passing	14-24-4
91	Passing Yards	239
242	Total Yards	406
9-31.1	Punts - Average	4-49.0
0	Fumbles Lost	1-1
3-25	Penalties - Yards	5-65

INDIVIDUAL LEADERS

RUSHING
LSU: Smith 16-74, 1 TD; Allen 16-41.
WYO: Kiick 19-75, 1 TD; Williams 16-64.

JANUARY 1, 1969

Arkansas 16, Georgia 2

	1ST	2ND	3RD	4TH	FINAL
ARK	0	10	0	6	16
UGA	0	2	0	0	2

SCORING SUMMARY

ARK	Dicus 27 pass from Montgomery (White kick)
UGA	Safety
ARK	FG White 34
ARK	FG White 24
ARK	FG White 31

ARK	TEAM STATISTICS	UGA
13	First Downs	13
40	Rushing Yards	75
17-39-3	Passing	11-31-1
185	Passing Yards	117
225	Total Yards	192
10-33.6	Punts - Average	10-38.6
2-2	Fumbles - Lost	5-5
4-31	Penalties - Yards	4-25

INDIVIDUAL LEADERS

RUSHING
ARK: Burnett 2-31.
UGA: Johnson 12-45.

PASSING
ARK: Montgomery 17-39-1, 185 yards, 1 TD.
UGA: Cavan 9-22-1, 103 yards.

RECEIVING
ARK: Dicus 12-169, 1 TD; Peacock 3-15.
UGA: Whittemore 5-56; Lawrence 3-54.

JANUARY 1, 1970

Mississippi 27, Arkansas 22

	1ST	2ND	3RD	4TH	FINAL
MISS	14	10	3	0	27
ARK	0	12	3	7	22

SCORING SUMMARY

MISS	Bowen 69 run (King kick)
MISS	Manning 18 run (King kick)
ARK	Burnett 12 run (kick failed)
MISS	FG Hinton 52
MISS	Studdard 30 pass from Manning (King kick)
ARK	Dicus 47 pass from Montgomery (pass failed)
MISS	FG Hinton 36
ARK	FG McClard 35
ARK	Maxwell 6 pass from Montgomery (McClard kick)

MISS	TEAM STATISTICS	ARK
24	First Downs	21
154	Rushing Yards	189
21-35-2	Passing	17-35-2
273	Passing Yards	338
427	Total Yards	527
2-30.5	Punts - Average	6-37.6
1-1	Fumbles - Lost	0
3-22	Penalties - Yards	11-101

INDIVIDUAL LEADERS

RUSHING
MISS: Bowen 12-94, 1 TD; Manning 13-39, 1 TD.
ARK: Maxwell 8-108; Burnett 17-59, 1 TD.

PASSING
MISS: Manning 21-35-2, 273 yards, 1 TD.
ARK: Montgomery 17-34-1, 338 yards, 2 TD.

RECEIVING
MISS: Studdard 5-109, 1 TD; Reed 2-22.
ARK: Dicus 6-171, 1 TD; Maxwell 9-137, 1 TD.

JANUARY 1, 1971

Tennessee 34, Air Force 13

	1ST	2ND	3RD	4TH	FINAL
TENN	24	0	7	3	34
AFA	7	0	6	0	13

SCORING SUMMARY

TENN	McLeary 5 run (Hunt kick)
TENN	FG Hunt 30
TENN	McLeary 20 run (Hunt kick)
TENN	Theiler 10 pass from Scott (Hunt kick)
AFA	Haas fumble recovery (Barry kick)
TENN	Majors 57 punt return (Hunt kick)
AFA	Bassa 27 pass from Parker (kick failed)
TENN	FG Hunt 33

TENN	TEAM STATISTICS	AFA
24	First Downs	15
86	Rushing Yards	-12
24-46-2	Passing	23-46-4
306	Passing Yards	239
392	Total Yards	227
5-31.4	Punts - Average	8-34.5
7-3	Fumbles - Lost	7-4
8-74	Penalties - Yards	0

INDIVIDUAL LEADERS

RUSHING
TENN: Watson 14-57; McLeary 14-39, 2 TD.
AFA: Bream 16-16.

PASSING
TENN: Scott 22-40-2, 288 yards, 1 TD.
AFA: Parker 23-46-4, 239 yards, 1 TD.

RECEIVING
TENN: Thompson 9-125.
AFA: Bassa 10-114, 1 TD; Bolen 6-60.

JANUARY 1, 1972

Oklahoma 40, Auburn 22

	1ST	2ND	3RD	4TH	FINAL
OKLA	19	12	3	6	40
AUB	0	0	7	15	22

SCORING SUMMARY

OKLA	Crosswhite 4 run (kick failed)
OKLA	Mildren 5 run (Carroll kick)
OKLA	Wylie 71 punt return (pass failed)
OKLA	Mildren 4 run (run failed)
OKLA	Mildren 7 run (pass failed)
OKLA	FG Carroll 53
AUB	Unger 1 run (Jett kick)
OKLA	Pruitt 2 run (kick failed)
AUB	Cannon 11 pass from Sullivan (Jett kick)
AUB	Unger 1 run (Beck run)

OKLA	TEAM STATISTICS	AUB
28	First Downs	15
439	Rushing Yards	40
1-4-0	Passing	20-45-2
11	Passing Yards	250
450	Total Yards	290
5-35.4	Punts - Average	5-45.2
5-2	Fumbles - Lost	4-1
3-12	Penalties - Yards	0-0

INDIVIDUAL LEADERS

RUSHING
OKLA: Mildren 30-149, 3 TD; Pruitt 18-95, 1 TD; Crosswhite 17-78, 1 TD.
AUB: Unger 6-38, 2 TD; Lowry 5-12.

PASSING
OKLA: Mildren 1-4-0, 11 yards.
AUB: Sullivan 20-44-1, 250 yards, 1 TD.

RECEIVING
OKLA: Chandler 1-11.
AUB: Beasley 6-117; Unger 5-36.

DECEMBER 31, 1972

Oklahoma 14, Penn State 0

	1ST	2ND	3RD	4TH	FINAL
OKLA	0	7	0	7	14
PSU	0	0	0	0	0

SCORING SUMMARY

OKLA	Owens 27 pass from Robertson (Fulcher kick)
OKLA	Crosswhite 1 run (Fulcher kick)

OKLA	TEAM STATISTICS	PSU
20	First Downs	11
278	Rushing Yards	49
7-12-0	Passing	12-31-1
175	Passing Yards	147
453	Total Yards	196
8-32.8	Punts - Average	10-42.9
8-5	Fumbles - Lost	6-4
3-55	Penalties - Yards	3-15

INDIVIDUAL LEADERS

RUSHING
OKLA: Pruitt 21-86; Crosswhite 22-82, 1 TD.
PSU: Nagle 10-22; Addie 7-18.

PASSING
OKLA: Robertson 3-6-0, 88 yards, 1 TD.
PSU: Hufnagel 12-31-1, 147 yards.

RECEIVING
OKLA: Owens 5-132, 1 TD; Pruitt 2-43.
PSU: Scott 3-59; Bland 3-39.

DECEMBER 31, 1973

Notre Dame 24, Alabama 23

	1ST	2ND	3RD	4TH	FINAL
ND	6	8	7	3	24
ALA	0	10	7	6	23

SCORING SUMMARY

ND	Bullock 6 run (kick failed)
ALA	Billingsley 6 run (Davis kick)
ND	Hunter 93 kickoff return (Demmerle pass from Clements)
ALA	FG Davis 39
ALA	Jackson 5 run (Davis kick)
ND	Penick 12 run (Thomas kick)
ALA	Todd 25 pass from Stock (kick failed)
ND	FG Thomas 19

ND	TEAM STATISTICS	ALA
20	First Downs	23
252	Rushing Yards	190
7-12-0	Passing	10-15-1
169	Passing Yards	127
421	Total Yards	317
7-35.8	Punts - Average	6-46.3
4-3	Fumbles - Lost	5-2
5-45	Penalties - Yards	3-32

INDIVIDUAL LEADERS

RUSHING
ND: Bullock 19-79, 1 TD; Clements 15-74.
ALA: Jackson 11-62, 1 TD; Billingsley 7-54, 1 TD.

PASSING
ND: Clements 7-12-0, 169 yards.
ALA: Rutledge 7-12-1, 88 yards.

RECEIVING
ND: Casper 3-75; Demmerle 3-59.
ALA: Pugh 2-28; Jackson 2-22.

DECEMBER 31, 1974

Nebraska 13, Florida 10

	1ST	2ND	3RD	4TH	FINAL
NEB	0	0	0	13	13
UF	7	3	0	0	10

SCORING SUMMARY

UF	Green 21 run (Posey kick)
UF	FG Posey 40
NEB	Anthony 2 run (Coyle kick)
NEB	FG Coyle 37
NEB	FG Coyle 39

NEB	TEAM STATISTICS	UF
18	First Downs	13
304	Rushing Yards	178
2-14-4	Passing	5-10-1
16	Passing Yards	97
320	Total Yards	275
3-1	Fumbles - Lost	3-1
2-17	Penalties - Yards	5-41

INDIVIDUAL LEADERS

RUSHING
NEB: Davis 17-126; Anthony 15-64, 1 TD.
UF: Dubose 17-84; Green 14-73, 1 TD.

PASSING
NEB: Humm 2-12-4, 16 yards.
UF: Gaffney 5-10-1, 97 yards.

RECEIVING
NEB: Westbrook 2-16.
UF: McGriff 2-52, Darby 1-32.

December 31, 1975
Alabama 13, Penn State 6

	1st	2nd	3rd	4th	Final
ALA	3	3	7	0	13
PSU	0	0	3	3	6

SCORING SUMMARY
ALA FG Ridgeway 25
PSU FG Bahr 42
ALA Stock 14 run (Ridgeway kick)
PSU FG Bahr 37
ALA FG Ridgeway 28

ALA	TEAM STATISTICS	PSU
14	First Downs	12
106	Rushing Yards	157
10-12-0	Passing	8-14-1
210	Passing Yards	57
316	Total Yards	214
5-40.8	Punts - Average	4-48.5
1-0	Fumbles - Lost	1-0
3-22	Penalties - Yards	0

INDIVIDUAL LEADERS
RUSHING
ALA: Shelby 8-45; Davis 12-32.
PSU: Geise 8-46; Taylor 12-36.
PASSING
ALA: Todd 10-12-0, 210 yards.
PSU: Andress 8-14-1, 57 yards.
RECEIVING
ALA: Newsome 4-97; Harris 2-69.
PSU: Cefalo 2-18; Petchel 2-13.

January 1, 1977
Pittsburgh 27, Georgia 3

	1st	2nd	3rd	4th	Final
PITT	7	14	3	3	27
UGA	0	0	3	0	3

SCORING SUMMARY
PITT Cavanaugh 6 run (Long kick)
PITT Jones 59 pass from Cavanaugh (Long kick)
PITT Dorsett 11 run (Long kick)
UGA FG Leavitt 25
PITT FG Long 42
PITT FG Long 31

PITT	TEAM STATISTICS	UGA
24	First Downs	14
288	Rushing Yards	135
10-18-0	Passing	3-22-4
192	Passing Yards	46
480	Total Yards	181
5-36.8	Punts - Average	8-47.1
2-1	Fumbles - Lost	4-2
6-66	Penalties - Yards	4-30

INDIVIDUAL LEADERS
RUSHING
PITT: Dorsett 32-202, 1 TD.
UGA: Goff 17-76.
PASSING
PITT: Cavanaugh 10-18-0, 192 yards, 1 TD.
UGA: Robinson 2-15-2, 33 yards.

January 2, 1978
Alabama 35, Ohio State 6

	1st	2nd	3rd	4th	Final
ALA	0	13	8	14	35
OSU	0	0	0	6	6

SCORING SUMMARY
ALA Nathan 1 run (Chapman kick)
ALA Bolton 27 pass from Rutledge (kick failed)
ALA Neal 3 pass from Rutledge
(Nathan pass from Rutledge)
OSU Harrell 38 pass from Gerald (run failed)
ALA Ogilvie 1 run (Chapman kick)
ALA Davis 5 run (Chapman kick)

ALA	TEAM STATISTICS	OSU
25	First Downs	13
286	Rushing Yards	179
8-11-0	Passing	7-17-3
109	Passing Yards	103
395	Total Yards	282
1-33.0	Punts - Average	4-37.5
1-5	Penalties - Yards	4-40

INDIVIDUAL LEADERS
RUSHING
ALA: Davis 24-95, 1 TD; Crow 5-46.
OSU: Springs 10-74; Logan 13-57.
PASSING
ALA: Rutledge 8-11-0, 109 yards, 2 TD.
OSU: Gerald 7-17-3, 103 yards, 1 TD.
RECEIVING
ALA: Newsom 2-45; Ferguson 2-28.
OSU: Hunter 2-25; Springs 2-6.

January 1, 1979
Alabama 14, Penn State 7

	1st	2nd	3rd	4th	Final
ALA	0	7	7	0	14
PSU	0	0	7	0	7

SCORING SUMMARY
ALA Bolton 30 pass from Rutledge (McElroy kick)
PSU Fitzkee 17 pass from Fusina (Bahr kick)
ALA Ogilvie 8 run (McElroy kick)

ALA	TEAM STATISTICS	PSU
12	First Downs	12
208	Rushing Yards	19
8-15-2	Passing	15-30-4
91	Passing Yards	163
299	Total Yards	182
10-38.8	Punts - Average	10-38.7
2-1	Fumbles - Lost	2-0
11-75	Penalties - Yards	8-51

INDIVIDUAL LEADERS
RUSHING
ALA: Nathan 21-127; Whitman 11-51.
PSU: Suhey 10-48; Guman 9-22.
PASSING
ALA: Rutledge 8-15-2, 91 yards, 1 TD.
PSU: Fusina 15-30-4, 163 yards, 1 TD.
RECEIVING
ALA: Bolton 2-46, 1 TD; Whitman 2-27.
PSU: Guman 5-59; Fitzkee 3-38, 1 TD.

January 1, 1980
Alabama 24, Arkansas 9

	1st	2nd	3rd	4th	Final
ALA	14	3	0	7	24
ARK	3	0	6	0	9

SCORING SUMMARY
ARK FG Ordonez 34
ALA Ogilvie 22 run (McElroy kick)
ALA Ogilvie 1 run (McElroy kick)
ALA FG McElroy 25
ARK Farrell 3 pass from Scanlon (run failed)
ALA Whitman 12 run (McElroy kick)

ALA	TEAM STATISTICS	ARK
18	First Downs	21
284	Rushing Yards	97
4-7-2	Passing	22-40-2
70	Passing Yards	245
354	Total Yards	342
8-36.2	Punts - Average	7-36.2
7-61	Penalties - Yards	1-15

INDIVIDUAL LEADERS
RUSHING
ALA: Jackson 13-120; Ogilvie 14-67, 2 TD; Whitman 6-37, 1 TD.
ARK: Bowles 15-46; Anderson 6-28.
PASSING
ALA: Shealy 4-7-0, 70 yards.
ARK: Scanlon 22-39-1, 245 yards, 1 TD.
RECEIVING
ALA: Jackson 3-62.
ARK: Anderson 7-53; Farrell 3-51, 1 TD.

January 1, 1981
Georgia 17, Notre Dame 10

	1st	2nd	3rd	4th	Final
UGA	10	7	0	0	17
ND	3	0	7	0	10

SCORING SUMMARY
ND FG Oliver 50
UGA FG Robinson 46
UGA Walker 1 run (Robinson kick)
UGA Walker 3 run (Robinson kick)
ND Carter 1 run (Oliver kick)

UGA	TEAM STATISTICS	ND
10	First Downs	17
120	Rushing Yards	190
1-13-0	Passing	14-28-3
7	Passing Yards	138
127	Total Yards	328
11-38.5	Punts - Average	5-42.0
0	Fumbles Lost	1-1
6-32	Penalties - Yards	8-69

INDIVIDUAL LEADERS
RUSHING
UGA: Walker 36-150, 2 TD.
ND: Carter 27-109, 1 TD.
PASSING
UGA: Belue 1-12-0, 7 yards.
ND: Kiel 14-27-3, 138 yards.
RECEIVING
UGA: Arnold 1-7.
ND: Holohan 4-44.

January 1, 1982
Pittsburgh 24, Georgia 20

	1st	2nd	3rd	4th	Final
PITT	0	3	7	14	24
UGA	0	7	6	7	20

SCORING SUMMARY
UGA Walker 8 run (Butler kick)
PITT FG Everett 41
PITT Dawkins 30 pass from Marino (Everett kick)
UGA Walker 10 run (kick failed)
PITT Brown 6 pass from Marino (Everett kick)
UGA Kay 6 pass from Belue (Butler kick)
PITT Brown 33 pass from Marino (Everett kick)

PITT	TEAM STATISTICS	UGA
27	First Downs	11
208	Rushing Yards	141
26-41-2	Passing	8-15-2
261	Passing Yards	83
469	Total Yards	224
2-44.5	Punts - Average	6-39.5
5-3	Fumbles - Lost	2-2
14-96	Penalties - Yards	5-35

INDIVIDUAL LEADERS
RUSHING
PITT: Thomas 26-129; DiBartola 13-68.
UGA: Walker 25-84, 2 TD.
PASSING
PITT: Marino 26-41-2, 261 yards, 3 TD.
UGA: Belue 8-15-2, 83 yards.
RECEIVING
PITT: Dawkins 6-77, 1 TD; DiBartola 8-64; Brown 6-62, 2 TD.
UGA: Walker 3-53.

January 1, 1983
Penn State 27, Georgia 23

	1st	2nd	3rd	4th	Final
PSU	7	13	0	7	27
UGA	3	7	7	6	23

SCORING SUMMARY
PSU Warner 2 run (Gancitano kick)
UGA FG Butler 27
PSU FG Gancitano 38
PSU Warner 9 run (Gancitano kick)
PSU FG Grancitano 45
UGA Archie 10 pass from Lastinger (Butler kick)
UGA Walker 1 run (Butler kick)
PSU Garrity 47 pass from Blackledge (Gancitano kick)
UGA Kay 9 pass from Lastinger (run failed)

PSU	TEAM STATISTICS	UGA
19	First Downs	19
139	Rushing Yards	160
13-23-0	Passing	12-28-2
228	Passing Yards	166
367	Total Yards	326
7-42.5	Punts - Average	8-41.7
2-1	Fumbles - Lost	3-0
7-39	Penalties - Yards	7-42

INDIVIDUAL LEADERS
RUSHING
PSU: Warner 18-117, 2 TD.
UGA: Walker 28-103, 1 TD.
PASSING
PSU: Blackledge 13-23-0, 228 yards, 1 TD.
UGA: Lastinger 12-27-2, 166 yards, 2 TD.
RECEIVING
PSU: Garrity 4-116, 1 TD.
UGA: Kay 5-61, 1 TD.

JANUARY 2, 1984
Auburn 9, Michigan 7

	1ST	2ND	3RD	4TH	FINAL
AUB	0	0	3	6	9
MICH	7	0	0	0	7

SCORING SUMMARY
MICH Smith 4 run (Bergeron kick)
AUB FG Del Greco 31
AUB FG Del Greco 32
AUB FG Del Greco 19

AUB	TEAM STATISTICS	MICH
21	First Downs	12
301	Rushing Yards	118
2-6-1	Passing	9-25-1
21	Passing Yards	125
322	Total Yards	243
4-42.0	Punts - Average	8-38.3
4-3	Fumbles - Lost	2-1
3-15	Penalties - Yards	6-49

INDIVIDUAL LEADERS
RUSHING
AUB: Jackson 22-130; Agee 16-93.
MICH: Rogers 17-86; Garrett 5-18.
PASSING
AUB: Campbell 2-6-1, 21 yards.
MICH: Smith 9-25-1, 125 yards.
RECEIVING
AUB: James 1-15.
MICH: Markray 3-68; Bean 3-37.

JANUARY 1, 1985
Nebraska 28, LSU 10

	1ST	2ND	3RD	4TH	FINAL
NEB	0	7	7	14	28
LSU	3	7	0	0	10

SCORING SUMMARY
LSU FG Lewis 37
LSU Hilliard 2 run (Lewis kick)
NEB DuBose 31 pass from Sundberg (Klein kick)
NEB Sundberg 9 run (Klein kick)
NEB Frain 24 pass from Sundberg (Klein kick)
NEB Frain 17 pass from Sundberg (Klein kick)

NEB	TEAM STATISTICS	LSU
23	First Downs	21
280	Rushing Yards	183
10-18-3	Passing	20-38-5
143	Passing Yards	221
423	Total Yards	404

INDIVIDUAL LEADERS
RUSHING
NEB : DuBose 102 yards.
LSU: Hilliard 16-86, 1 TD.
PASSING
NEB : Sundberg 10-15-3, 143 yards, 3 TD.
LSU: Wickersham 20-37-5, 221 yards.
RECEIVING
NEB : Frain 4-53, 2 TD.
LSU: James 4-25.

JANUARY 1, 1986
Tennessee 35, Miami (Fla.) 7

	1ST	2ND	3RD	4TH	FINAL
TENN	0	14	14	7	35
MIA	7	0	0	0	7

SCORING SUMMARY
MIA Irvin 18 pass from Testaverde (Cox kick)
TENN Smith 6 pass from Dickey (Reveiz kick)
TENN McGee fumble recovery (Reveiz kick)
TENN Henderson 1 run (Reveiz kick)
TENN Powell 60 run (Reveiz kick)
TENN Wilson 6 run (Reveiz kick)

TENN	TEAM STATISTICS	MIA
16	First Downs	22
211	Rushing Yards	95
15-25-1	Passing	23-44-4
131	Passing Yards	237
342	Total Yards	332
6-39.1	Punts - Average	6-37.6
2-1	Fumbles - Lost	5-2
11-125	Penalties - Yards	15-120
31:01	Possession Time	28:59

INDIVIDUAL LEADERS
RUSHING
TENN: Powell 11-104, 1 TD.
MIA: Williams 8-45.
PASSING
TENN: Dickey 15-25-1, 131 yards, 1 TD.
MIA: Testaverde 20-36-3, 217 yards, 1 TD.
RECEIVING
TENN: McGee 7-94.
MIA: Irvin 5-91, TD; Perriman 5-43.

JANUARY 1, 1987
Nebraska 30, LSU 15

	1ST	2ND	3RD	4TH	FINAL
NU	0	10	7	13	30
LSU	7	0	0	8	15

SCORING SUMMARY
LSU Williams 1 run (Browndyke kick)
NU FG Klein 42
NU Taylor 2 run (Klein kick)
NU Knox 1 run (Klein kick)
NU Millikan 3 pass from Taylor (Klein kick)
NU Knox 1 run (kick failed)
LSU Moss 24 pass from Hodson (Lee pass from Hodson)

NU	TEAM STATISTICS	LSU
22	First Downs	10
242	Rushing Yards	32
11-20-0	Passing	14-30-1
110	Passing Yards	159
352	Total Yards	191

INDIVIDUAL LEADERS
RUSHING
NU: Knox 16-84 yards, 2 TD.
LSU: Williams 12-48, 1 TD.
PASSING
NU: Taylor 11-19-0, 110 yards, 1 TD.
LSU: Hodson 14-30-1, 159 yards, 1 TD.
RECEIVING
NU: Banderas 4-42.
LSU: Davis 3-63.

JANUARY 1, 1988
Auburn 16, Syracuse 16

	1ST	2ND	3RD	4TH	FINAL
AUB	7	3	0	6	16
SYR	0	7	3	6	16

SCORING SUMMARY
AUB Tillman 17 pass from Burger (Lyle kick)
SYR Glover 12 pass from McPherson (Vesling kick)
AUB FG Lyle 40
SYR FG Vesling 27
AUB FG Lyle 41
SYR FG Vesling 32
SYR FG Vesling 38
AUB FG Lyle 30

AUB	TEAM STATISTICS	SYR
14	First Downs	23
41	Rushing Yards	174
25-34-1	Passing	11-21-0
229	Passing Yards	140
270	Total Yards	314
6-44.8	Punts - Average	5-35.6
1-0	Fumbles - Lost	2-0
5-43	Penalties - Yards	2-20
22:25	Possession Time	37:35

INDIVIDUAL LEADERS
RUSHING
AUB: Danley 13-42.
SYR: Drummon 17-82; Johnston 14-50.
PASSING
AUB: Burger 24-33-1, 171 yards, 1 TD.
SYR: McPherson 11-21-0, 140 yards, 1 TD.
RECEIVING
AUB: Tillman 6-125, 1 TD; Danley 7-34.
SYR: Glover 6-91, 1 TD; Kane 2-30.

JANUARY 2, 1989
Florida State 13, Auburn 7

	1ST	2ND	3RD	4TH	FINAL
FSU	10	3	0	0	13
AUB	0	7	0	0	7

SCORING SUMMARY
FSU Williams 2 run (Andrews kick)
FSU FG Mason 35
FSU FG Mason 31
AUB Reeves 20 pass from Slack (Lyle kick)

FSU	TEAM STATISTICS	AUB
21	First Downs	18
148	Rushing Yards	108
14-27-1	Passing	19-33-3
157	Passing Yards	162
305	Total Yards	270
4-35.0	Punts - Average	4-35.8
2-1	Fumbles - Lost	3-2
6-45	Penalties - Yards	5-65
33:35	Possession Time	26:25

INDIVIDUAL LEADERS
RUSHING
FSU: Smith 24-115; Carter 7-25.
AUB: Danley 19-68; Joseph 8-47.
PASSING
FSU: Ferguson 14-26-1, 157 yards.
AUB: Slack 19-33-3, 162 yards, 1 TD.
RECEIVING
FSU: Anthony 3-47; O'Malley 2-31.
AUB: Tillman 4-48; Taylor 5-35.

JANUARY 1, 1990
Miami (Fla.) 33, Alabama 25

	1ST	2ND	3RD	4TH	FINAL
MIA	7	13	6	7	33
ALA	0	17	0	8	25

SCORING SUMMARY
MIA McGuire 3 run (Huerta kick)
ALA Battle 4 pass from Hollingsworth (Doyle kick)
MIA Carroll 19 pass from Erickson (kick blocked)
ALA FG Doyle 45
MIA Johnson 3 run (Huerta kick)
ALA Russell 7 pass from Hollingsworth (Doyle kick)
MIA Chudzinski 11 pass from Erickson (pass failed)
MIA Bethel 12 pass from Erickson (Huerta kick)
ALA Wembley 9 pass from Hollingsworth
(Russell pass from Hollingsworth)

JANUARY 1, 1991
Tennessee 23, Virginia 22

	1ST	2ND	3RD	4TH	FINAL
TENN	0	0	3	20	23
UVA	9	7	0	6	22

SCORING SUMMARY
UVA Steele 10 run (kick blocked)
UVA FG McInerney 22
UVA Kirby 1 run (McInerney kick)
TENN FG Burke 27
TENN Thompson 7 run (Burke kick)
UVA FG McInerney 43
TENN Pickens 15 pass from Kelly (Burke kick)
UVA FG McInerney 44
TENN Thompson 1 run (pass failed)

TENN	TEAM STATISTICS	UVA
28	First Downs	25
191	Rushing Yards	287
24-35-2	Passing	9-24-3
273	Passing Yards	62
464	Total Yards	349
2-20.0	Punts - Average	1-48.0
1-1	Fumbles - Lost	1-0
5-65	Penalties - Yards	5-30
23:32	Possession Time	36:28

INDIVIDUAL LEADERS
RUSHING
TENN: Thompson 25-154, 2 TD.
UVA: Fisher 15-90; Moore 11-76; Kirby 21-75, 1 TD.
PASSING
TENN: Kelly 24-35-2, 273 yards, 1 TD.
UVA: Moore 9-22-2, 62 yards.
RECEIVING
TENN: Moore 7-97; Pickens 6-87, 1 TD.
UVA: Kirby 4-27.

THE BOWLS

January 1, 1992
Notre Dame 39, Florida 28

	1ST	2ND	3RD	4TH	FINAL
ND	0	7	10	22	39
UF	10	6	0	12	28

SCORING SUMMARY

UF	Jackson 15 pass from Matthews (Czyzewski kick)
UF	FG Czyzewski 26
UF	FG Czyzewski 24
ND	Dawson 40 pass from Mirer (Hentrich kick)
UF	FG Czyzewski 36
ND	FG Pendergast 23
ND	Smith 4 pass from Mirer (Hentrich kick)
UF	FG Czyzewski 37
UF	FG Czyzewski 24
ND	Bettis 3 run (Brooks pass from Mirer)
ND	Bettis 49 run (Pendergast kick)
UF	Houston 36 pass from Matthews (pass failed)
ND	Bettis 39 run (Pendergast kick)

ND	TEAM STATISTICS	UF
23	First Downs	29
279	Rushing Yards	141
14-19-1	Passing	28-58-2
154	Passing Yards	370
433	Total Yards	511
4-3	Fumbles - Lost	0-0
3-15	Penalties - Yards	4-40
29:00	Possession Time	31:00

INDIVIDUAL LEADERS

RUSHING
ND: Bettis 16-150, 3 TD; Culver 13-93; Brooks 13-68.
UF: Rhett 15-63; McClendon 7-34.

PASSING
ND: Mirer 14-19-1, 154 yards, 2 TD.
UF: Matthews 28-58-2, 370 yards, 2 TD.

RECEIVING
ND: Smith 7-75; Dawson 2-49, 1 TD.
UF: Jackson 8-148, 1 TD; Houston 3-52, 1 TD; Sullivan 4-47.

January 1, 1993
Alabama 34, Miami (Fla.) 13

	1ST	2ND	3RD	4TH	FINAL
ALA	3	10	14	7	34
MIA	3	3	0	7	13

SCORING SUMMARY

ALA	FG Proctor 19
MIA	FG Prewitt 49
ALA	FG Proctor 23
ALA	Williams 2 run (Proctor kick)
MIA	FG Prewitt 42
ALA	Lassic 1 run (Proctor kick)
ALA	Teague 31 interception return (Proctor kick)
MIA	Williams 78 punt return (Prewitt kick)
ALA	Lassic 4 run (Proctor kick)

ALA	TEAM STATISTICS	MIA
15	First Downs	16
290	Rushing Yards	75
4-13-2	Passing	24-56-3
18	Passing Yards	278
308	Total Yards	353
6-44.5	Punts - Average	5-41.6
0-0	Fumbles - Lost	4-1
7-46	Penalties - Yards	6-37
36:04	Possession Time	23:56

INDIVIDUAL LEADERS

RUSHING
ALA: Lassic 28-135, 2 TD; Lynch 5-39; Williams 7-23, 1 TD.
MIA: Jones 5-28; Bennett 3-26.

PASSING
ALA: Barker 4-13-2, 18 yards.
MIA: Torretta 24-56-3, 278 yards.

RECEIVING
ALA: Wimbley 2-11.
MIA: Jones 3-64; Thomas 6-52; Williams 3-49.

January 1, 1994
Florida 41, West Virginia 7

	1ST	2ND	3RD	4TH	FINAL
UF	7	14	14	6	41
WVU	7	0	0	0	7

SCORING SUMMARY

WVU	Kearney 32 pass from Kelchner (Mazzone kick)
UF	Rhett 3 run (Davis kick)
UF	Wright 52 interception return (Davis kick)
UF	Jackson 39 pass from Dean (Davis kick)
UF	Rhett 2 run (Davis kick)
UF	Rhett 1 run (Davis kick)
UF	FG Davis 43
UF	FG Davis 26

UF	TEAM STATISTICS	WVU
30	First Downs	16
201	Rushing Yards	122
24-39-1	Passing	16-40-1
280	Passing Yards	143
481	Total Yards	265
2-1	Fumbles - Lost	2-1
5-43	Penalties - Yards	8-71
33:22	Possession Time	26:38

INDIVIDUAL LEADERS

RUSHING
UF: Rhett 25-105, 3 TD; Foy 10-53.
WVU: Walker 13-59; Woodard 2-18.

PASSING
UF: Dean 22-37-1, 244 yards, 1 TD.
WVU: Kelchner 13-27-0, 123 yards, 1 TD.

RECEIVING
UF: W. Jackson 9-131; J. Jackson 3-32.
WVU: Kearney 4-59, 1 TD; Baker 4-46.

January 2, 1995
Florida State 23, Florida 17

	1ST	2ND	3RD	4TH	FINAL
FSU	3	17	3	0	23
UF	3	7	0	7	17

SCORING SUMMARY

FSU	FG Mowrey 21
UF	FG Davis 22
FSU	Ellison 73 pass from Dunn (Mowrey kick)
FSU	McCorvey 16 pass from Kanell (Mowrey kick)
UF	Hilliard 82 pass from Wuerffel (Davis kick)
FSU	FG Mowrey 24
FSU	FG Mowrey 45
UF	Wuerffel 1 run (Davis kick)

FSU	TEAM STATISTICS	UF
21	First Downs	23
76	Rushing Yards	5
24-41-0	Passing	30-43-1
325	Passing Yards	449
401	Total Yards	454
4-39.0	Punts - Average	3-45.7
0-0	Fumbles - Lost	2-2
0-0	Penalties - Yards	2-2
27:56	Possession Time	32:04

INDIVIDUAL LEADERS

RUSHING
FSU: Dunn 14-58; Crockett 5-19.
UF: Williams 10-27; Taylor 8-18.

PASSING
FSU: Kanell 23-40-0, 252 yards, 1 TD.
UF: Wuerffel 28-39-1, 394 yards, 1 TD.

RECEIVING
FSU: Ellison 4-102, 1 TD; McCorvey 4-84, 1 TD.
UF: Jackson 6-128; Hilliard 3-119, 1 TD.

December 31, 1995
Virginia Tech 28, Texas 10

	1ST	2ND	3RD	4TH	FINAL
VT	0	7	7	14	28
TEX	7	3	0	0	10

SCORING SUMMARY

TEX	Fitzgerald 4 pass from Brown (Dawson kick)
TEX	FG Dawson 52
VT	Still 60 punt return (Larsen kick)
VT	Parker 2 run (Larsen kick)
VT	Still 54 pass from Druckenmiller (Larsen kick)
VT	Baron 20 fumble return (Larsen kick)

VT	TEAM STATISTICS	TEX
20	First Downs	15
105	Rushing Yards	78
18-24-1	Passing	14-37-3
266	Passing Yards	148
371	Total Yards	226
8-37.0	Punts - Average	9-40.0
5-2	Fumbles - Lost	2-1
11-99	Penalties - Yards	9-91
30:25	Possession Time	29:35

INDIVIDUAL LEADERS

RUSHING
VT: Thomas 15-62; Oxendine 8-31.
TEX: Williams 12-62; Mitchell 15-59.

PASSING
VT: Druckenmiller 18-34-1, 266 yards, 1 TD.
TEX: Brown 14-36-3, 148 yards, 1 TD.

RECEIVING
VT: Still 6-119, 1 TD; Jennings 6-77.
TEX: Adams 6-92; Fitzgerald 3-21, 1 TD.

January 2, 1997
Florida 52, Florida State 20

	1ST	2ND	3RD	4TH	FINAL
UF	10	14	14	14	52
FSU	3	14	3	0	20

SCORING SUMMARY

UF	Hilliard 5 pass from Wuerffel (Edmiston kick)
FSU	FG Bentley 43
UF	FG Edmiston 32
UF	Taylor 2 run (Edmiston kick)
FSU	Green 29 pass from Busby (Bentley kick)
UF	Hilliard 31 pass from Wuerffel (Edmiston kick)
FSU	Dunn 12 run (Bentley kick)
FSU	FG Bentley 45
UF	Hilliard 8 pass from Wuerffel (Edmiston kick)
UF	Wuerffel 16 run (Edmiston kick)
UF	Jackson 42 run (Edmiston kick)
UF	Jackson 1 run (Edmiston kick)

UF	TEAM STATISTICS	FSU
26	First Downs	13
203	Rushing Yards	70
18-34-1	Passing	17-42-2
306	Passing Yards	271
509	Total Yards	341
7-48.1	Punts - Average	8-46.4
1-0	Fumbles - Lost	0-0
15-102	Penalties - Yards	14-115
36:27	Possession Time	23:33

INDIVIDUAL LEADERS

RUSHING
UF: Jackson 12-118, 2 TD; Taylor 18-60, 1 TD.
FSU: Dunn 9-29, 1 TD.

PASSING
UF: Wuerffel 18-34-1, 306 yards, 3 TD.
FSU: Busby 17-41-1, 271 yards, 1 TD.

RECEIVING
UF: Hilliard 7-150, 3 TD; Green 5-79; Anthony 4-50.
FSU: Green 3-86, 1 TD; Cooper 4-82.

JANUARY 1, 1998
FLORIDA STATE 31, OHIO STATE 14

	1ST	2ND	3RD	4TH	FINAL
FSU	7	14	0	10	31
OSU	3	0	5	6	14

SCORING SUMMARY
OSU   FG Stultz 40
FSU   Green 27 pass from Busby (Janikowski kick)
FSU   Busby 9 run (Janikowski kick)
FSU   McCray 1 run (Janikowski kick)
OSU   FG Stultz 34
OSU   Safety
FSU   FG Janikowski 35
OSU   Lumpkin 50 pass from Germaine (pass failed)
FSU   McCray 1 run (Janikowski kick)

FSU	TEAM STATISTICS	OSU
18	First Downs	21
60	Rushing Yards	118
22-33-2	Passing	16-36-3
334	Passing Yards	207
394	Total Yards	325
0-0	Fumbles - Lost	1-0
9-74	Penalties - Yards	10-70
24:56	Possession Time	35:04

INDIVIDUAL LEADERS
RUSHING
FSU: Minor 12-53; Feaster 2-10.
OSU: Pearson 22-60; Keller 6-20.
PASSING
FSU: Busby 22-33-2, 334 yards, 1 TD.
OSU: Germaine 10-26-2, 173 yards, 1 TD.
RECEIVING
FSU: Green 7-176, 1 TD; Warrick 3-82.
OSU: Miller 6-79; Lumpkin 2-61, 1 TD.

JANUARY 1, 1999
OHIO STATE 24, TEXAS A&M 14

	1ST	2ND	3RD	4TH	FINAL
OSU	21	3	0	0	24
A&M	7	0	7	0	14

SCORING SUMMARY
A&M   Hall 9 run (Bynum kick)
OSU   Germany 18 pass from Germaine (Stultz kick)
OSU   Montgomery 10 run (Stultz kick)
OSU   Griffin 16 blocked punt return (Stultz kick)
OSU   FG Stultz 31
A&M   Hodge 7 pass from Stewart (Bynum kick)

OSU	TEAM STATISTICS	A&M
25	First Downs	17
210	Rushing Yards	96
21-38-0	Passing	22-39-0
222	Passing Yards	187
432	Total Yards	283
6-38.3	Punts - Average	10-39.8
3-0	Fumbles - Lost	1-1
6-61	Penalties - Yards	6-43
31:42	Possession Time	28:18

INDIVIDUAL LEADERS
RUSHING
OSU: Montgomery 9-96, 1 TD; Wiley 16-88.
A&M: Toombs 10-62; Hall 11-53, 1 TD.
PASSING
OSU: Germaine 21-38-0, 222 yards, 1 TD.
A&M: Stewart 22-39-0, 187 yards, 1 TD.
RECEIVING
OSU: Boston 11-105; Wiley 5-40.
A&M: Taylor 5-52; Spiller 5-43.

JANUARY 4, 2000
FLORIDA STATE 46, VIRGINIA TECH 29

	1ST	2ND	3RD	4TH	FINAL
FSU	14	14	0	18	46
VT	7	7	15	0	29

SCORING SUMMARY
FSU   Warrick 64 pass from Weinke (Janikowski kick)
FSU   Chaney 6 blocked punt return (Janikowski kick)
VT   Davis 49 pass from Vick (Graham kick)
FSU   Dugans 63 pass from Weinke (Janikowski kick)
FSU   Warrick 59 punt return (Janikowski kick)
VT   Vick 3 run (Graham kick)
VT   FG Graham 23
VT   Kendrick 29 run (pass failed)
VT   Kendrick 6 run (pass failed)
FSU   Dugans 14 pass from Weinke
       (Warrick pass from Weinke)
FSU   FG Janikowski 32
FSU   Warrick 43 pass from Weinke (Janikowski kick)

FSU	TEAM STATISTICS	VT
15	First Downs	24
30	Rushing Yards	278
20-34-1	Passing	15-29-0
329	Passing Yards	225
359	Total Yards	503
4-80	Punt Returns - Yards	4-88
4-75	Kickoff Returns - Yards	4-134
7-44.3	Punts - Average	6-29.3
2-0	Fumbles - Lost	3-3
7-59	Penalties - Yards	6-65
23:35	Possession Time	36:25

INDIVIDUAL LEADERS
RUSHING
FSU: Chaney 4-43; Minor 9-35.
VT: Vick 23-97, 1 TD; Kendrick 12-69, 2 TD; Stith 11-68.
PASSING
FSU: Weinke 20-34-1, 329 yards, 4 TD.
VT: Vick 15-20-0, 225 yards, 1 TD.
RECEIVING
FSU: Warrick 6-163, 2 TD; Dugans 5-99, 1 TD.
VT: Davis 7-108, 1 TD; Hawkins 2-49.

JANUARY 2, 2001
MIAMI (FLA.) 37, FLORIDA 20

	1ST	2ND	3RD	4TH	FINAL
MIA	10	3	14	10	37
UF	7	3	7	3	20

SCORING SUMMARY
UF   Wells 23 pass from Grossman (Chandler kick)
MIA   FG Sievers 44
MIA   Shockey 8 pass from Dorsey (Sievers kick)
MIA   FG Sievers 29
UF   FG Chandler 51
UF   Graham 36 run (Chandler kick)
MIA   Williams 19 pass from Dorsey (Sievers kick)
MIA   Davenport 2 pass from Dorsey (Sievers kick)
UF   FG Chandler 26
MIA   FG Sievers 29
MIA   Davenport 3 run (Sievers kick)

MIA	TEAM STATISTICS	UF
28	First Downs	25
184	Rushing Yards	140
22-40-2	Passing	24-51-3
270	Passing Yards	312
454	Total Yards	452
2-44.0	Punts - Average	5-46.8
157	Return Yards	120
0	Fumbles Lost	0
11-109	Penalties - Yards	9-79
35:19	Possession Time	24:41

INDIVIDUAL LEADERS
RUSHING
MIA: Portis 18-97; Jackson 12-62.
UF: Graham 15-136, 1 TD.
PASSING
MIA: Dorsey 22-40-2, 270 yards, 3 TD.
UF: Grossman 18-41-3, 312 yards, 1 TD.
RECEIVING
MIA: Moss 6-89; Shockey 4-47, 1 TD.
UF: Caldwell 6-100; Gaffney 7-75.

JANUARY 1, 2002
LSU 47, ILLINOIS 34

	1ST	2ND	3RD	4TH	FINAL
LSU	7	27	7	6	47
ILL	0	7	14	13	34

SCORING SUMMARY
LSU   Davis 4 run (Corbello kick)
LSU   Davis 25 run (Corbello kick)
LSU   Davis 16 run (Corbello kick)
LSU   Reed 5 pass from Davey (Corbello kick)
ILL   Hodges 2 pas from Kittner (Christofilakos kick)
LSU   Royal 7 pass from Davey (Corbello kick)
ILL   Lloyd 17 pass from Kittner (Christofilakos kick)
LSU   Reed 32 pass from Davey (Corbello kick)
ILL   Lloyd 10 pass from Kittner (Christofilakos kick)
ILL   Young 17 pass from Kittner (Christofilakos kick)
LSU   Davis 4 run (pass failed)
ILL   Young 40 pass from Lloyd (pass failed)

LSU	TEAM STATISTICS	ILL
32	First Downs	14
151	Rushing Yards	61
31-53-0	Passing	15-36-1
444	Passing Yards	302
595	Total Yards	363
3-36	Punt Returns - Yards	2-9
6-147	Kickoff Returns - Yards	5-89
8-39.4	Punts - Average	9-40.4
2-1	Fumbles - Lost	1-1
13-113	Penalties - Yards	4-39
39:16	Possession Time	20:44

INDIVIDUAL LEADERS
RUSHING
LSU: Davis 28-129, 4 TD; Henderson 13-55.
ILL: Harvey 9-42.
PASSING
LSU: Davey 31-53-0, 444 yards, 3 TD.
ILL: Kittner 14-35-1, 262 yards, 4 TD.
RECEIVING
LSU: Reed 14-239, 2 TD; Clayton 8-120.
ILL: Young 6-178, 2 TD; Lloyd 5-56, 2 TD.

JANUARY 1, 2003
GEORGIA 26, FLORIDA STATE 13

	1ST	2ND	3RD	4TH	FINAL
UGA	3	14	6	3	26
FSU	0	7	6	0	13

SCORING SUMMARY
UGA   FG Bennett 23
FSU   Boldin 5 pass from Walker (Beitia kick)
UGA   Thornton 71 interception return (Bennett kick)
UGA   Edwards 37 pass from Shockley (Bennett kick)
UGA   FG Bennett 42
UGA   FG Bennett 25
FSU   Thorpe 40 pass from Boldin (run failed)
UGA   FG Bennett 35

UGA	TEAM STATISTICS	FSU
11	First Downs	18
151	Rushing Yards	115
10-15-0	Passing	13-26-2
125	Passing Yards	147
276	Total Yards	262
4-48.2	Punts - Average	5-40.4
1-1	Fumbles - Lost	2-1
6-59	Penalties - Yards	5-37
26:09	Possession Time	33:51

INDIVIDUAL LEADERS
RUSHING
GEO: Smith 23-145; Milton 5-13.
FSU: Washington 10-48; Boldin 13-34.
PASSING
GEO: Greene 9-14-0, 88 yards.
FSU: Boldin 6-14-0, 78 yards, 1 TD.
RECEIVING
GEO: Edwards 3-60, 1 TD; Johnson 1-34.
FSU: Thorpe 1-40, 1 TD; Boldin 3-34, 1 TD.

THE BOWLS

JANUARY 4, 2004

LSU 21, OKLAHOMA 14

	1ST	2ND	3RD	4TH	FINAL
LSU	7	7	7	0	21
OU	0	7	0	7	14

SCORING SUMMARY
LSU Green 24 run (Gaudet kick)
OU Jones 1 run (DiCarlo kick)
LSU Vincent 18 run (Gaudet kick)
LSU Spears 20 interception return (Gaudet kick)
OU Jones 1 run (DiCarlo kick)

LSU	TEAM STATISTICS	OU
13	First Downs	12
159	Rushing Yards	52
14-24-2	Passing	13-37-2
153	Passing Yards	102
312	Total Yards	154
3-26	Punt Returns - Yards	5-36
0-0	Kickoff Returns - Yards	2-24
8-34.0	Punts - Average	8-45.9
1-1	Fumbles - Lost	2-0
8-65	Penalties - Yards	11-70
31:19	Possession Time	28:41

INDIVIDUAL LEADERS
RUSHING
LSU: Vincent 16-117, 1 TD; Mauck 14-27.
OU: Jones 20-59, 2 TD; Clayton 4-38.
PASSING
LSU: Mauck 13-22-2, 124 yards.
OU: White 13-37-2, 102 yards.
RECEIVING
LSU: Jones 3-54; Clayton 4-38.
OU: Clayton 4-32; Wilson 3-31.

JANUARY 3, 2005

AUBURN 16, VIRGINIA TECH 13

	1ST	2ND	3RD	4TH	FINAL
AU	6	3	7	0	16
VT	0	0	0	13	13

SCORING SUMMARY
AU FG Vaughn 23
AU FG Vaughn 19
AU FG Vaughn 24
AU Aromashodu 5 pass from Campbell (Vaughn kick)
VT Morgan 29 pass from Randall (conversion failed)
VT Morgan 80 pass from Randall (Pace kick)

AU	TEAM STATISTICS	VT
14	First Downs	19
110	Rushing Yards	76
11-16-1	Passing	21-38-2
189	Passing Yards	299
299	Total Yards	375
2-17	Punt Returns - Yards	1-(-5)
1-22	Kickoff Returns - Yards	2-76
4-42.0	Punts - Average	5-35.2
1-1	Fumbles - Lost	0-0
4-35	Penalties - Yards	7-57
33:34	Possession Time	26:26

INDIVIDUAL LEADERS
RUSHING
AU: Brown 15-68; Williams 19-61.
VT: Randall 9-45; Imoh 6-16.
PASSING
AU: Campbell 11-16-1, 189 yards, 1 TD.
VT: Randall 21-38-2, 299 yards, 2 TD.
RECEIVING
AU: Taylor 5-87; Mix 2-68.
VT: Morgan 3-126, 2 TD; Hyman 5-71.

SUN BOWL

PROFILE

Site: El Paso, Texas
Stadium: Sun Bowl Stadium
Capacity: 52,000
Surface: AstroPlay

PLAYING SITES

El Paso High School Stadium, 1935-37
Kidd Field, 1938-62
Sun Bowl Stadium, since 1963

NAME CHANGES

Sun Bowl, 1935-85
John Hancock Sun Bowl, 1986-89
John Hancock Bowl, 1990-93
Sun Bowl, 1994-95
Norwest Sun Bowl, 1996-98
Wells Fargo Sun Bowl, 1999-2003
Vitalis Sun Bowl, since 2004

SEASON	DATE	PRE-GAME RANK	TEAMS	SCORE	FINAL RANK	MOST VALUABLE PLAYERS	ATT.
1934	Jan. 1, 1935		El Paso	25			3,000
			Ranger	21			
1935	Jan. 1, 1936		Hardin-Simmons	14			11,000
			New Mexico State	14			
1936	Jan. 1, 1937		Hardin-Simmons	34			10,000
			UTEP	6			
1937	Jan. 1, 1938		West Virginia	7			12,000
			Texas Tech	6			
1938	Jan. 2, 1939		Utah	26			13,000
			New Mexico	0			
1939	Jan. 1, 1940		Arizona State	0			12,000
			Catholic	0			
1940	Jan. 1, 1941		Western Reserve	26			14,000
			Arizona State	13			
1941	Jan. 1, 1942		Tulsa	6			14,000
			Texas Tech	0			
1942	Jan. 1, 1943		Second Air Force	13			16,000
			Hardin-Simmons	7			
1943	Jan. 1, 1944		Southwestern	7			18,000
			New Mexico	0			
1944	Jan. 1, 1945		Southwestern	35			13,000
			University of Mexico	0			
1945	Jan. 1, 1946		New Mexico	34			15,000
			Denver	24			
1946	Jan. 1, 1947		Cincinnati	18			10,000
			Virginia Tech	6			
1947	Jan. 1, 1948		Miami (Ohio)	13			18,000
			Texas Tech	12			
1948	Jan. 1, 1949		West Virginia	21			13,000
			UTEP	12			
1949	Jan. 2, 1950		UTEP	33		Harvey Gabrel, UTEP, HB	15,000
			Georgetown	20			
1950	Jan. 1, 1951		West Texas A&M	14		Bill Cross, West Texas A&M, E	16,000
			Cincinnati	13			
1951	Jan. 1, 1952		Texas Tech	25		Junior Arteburn, Texas Tech, QB	17,000
			Pacific	14			
1952	Jan. 1, 1953		Pacific	26		Tom McCormick, Pacific (Cal.), HB	11,000
			Southern Miss	7			
1953	Jan. 1, 1954		UTEP	37		Dick Shinaut, UTEP, QB	9,500
			Southern Miss	14			
1954	Jan. 1, 1955		UTEP	47		Jesse Whittenton, UTEP, QB	14,000
			Florida State	20			
1955	Jan. 2, 1956		Wyoming	21		Jim Crawford, Wyoming, HB	14,500
			Texas Tech	14			
1956	Jan. 1, 1957	17	George Washington	13		Claude Austin, George Washington, RB	13,500
			UTEP	0			
1957	Jan. 1, 1958		Louisville	34		Ken Porco, Louisville, RB	12,000
			Drake	20			
1958	Dec. 31, 1958		Wyoming	14		Leonard Kucewski, Wyoming, G	13,000
			Hardin-Simmons	6			
1959	Dec. 31, 1959		New Mexico State	28		Charley Johnson, New Mexico State, QB	14,000
			North Texas	8			
1960	Dec. 31, 1960	17	New Mexico State	20		Charley Johnson, New Mexico State, QB	16,000
			Utah State	13			
1961	Dec. 30, 1961		Villanova	17		Billy Joe, Villanova, FB	15,000
			Wichita State	9		Richie Ross, Villanova, G	
1962	Dec. 31, 1962		West Texas A&M	15		Jerry Logan, West Texas A&M, HB	16,000
			Ohio	14		Don Hoovler, Ohio U., G	
1963	Dec. 31, 1963		Oregon	21		Bob Berry, Oregon, QB	26,500
			SMU	14		John Hughes, SMU, G	
1964	Dec. 26, 1964		Georgia	7		Preston Ridlehuber, Georgia, QB	28,500
			Texas Tech	0		Jim Wilson, Georgia, T	
1965	Dec. 31, 1965		UTEP	13		Billy Stevens, UTEP, QB	27,450
			TCU	12		Ronny Nixon, TCU, T	
1966	Dec. 24, 1966		Wyoming	28		Jim Kiick, Wyoming, TB	24,381
			Florida State	20		Jerry Durling, Wyoming, MG	
1967	Dec. 30, 1967		UTEP	14		Billy Stevens, UTEP, QB	34,685
			Mississippi	7		Fred Carr, UTEP, LB	
1968	Dec. 28, 1968		Auburn	34	16	Buddy McClinton, Auburn, DB	32,307
			Arizona	10		David Campbell, Auburn, T	
1969	Dec. 20, 1969	14	Nebraska	45	11	Paul Rogers, Nebraska, HB	29,723
			Georgia	6		Jerry Murtaugh, Nebraska, LB	
1970	Dec. 19, 1970	13	Georgia Tech	17	13	Rock Perdoni, Georgia Tech, DT	30,512
		19	Texas Tech	9		Bill Flowers, Georgia Tech, LB	
1971	Dec. 18, 1971	11	LSU	33	11	Bert Jones, LSU, QB	33,503
			Iowa State	15		Matt Blair, Iowa State, LB	
1972	Dec. 30, 1972	16	North Carolina	32	12	George Smith, Texas Tech, HB	31,312
			Texas Tech	28		Ecomet Burley, Texas Tech, DT	
1973	Dec. 29, 1973		Missouri	34	17	Ray Bybee, Missouri, FB	30,127
			Auburn	17		John Kelsey, Missouri, TE	
1974	Dec. 28, 1974		Mississippi State	26	17	Terry Vitrano, Mississippi State, FB	30,131
			North Carolina	24		Jimmy Webb, Mississippi State, DT	
1975	Dec. 26, 1975	20	Pittsburgh	33	15	Robert Haygood, Pittsburgh, QB	33,240
		19	Kansas	19		Al Romano, Pittsburgh, MG	
1976	Jan. 2, 1977	10	Texas A&M	37	7	Tony Franklin, Texas A&M, K	33,252
			Florida	14		Edgar Fields, Texas A&M, DT	
1977	Dec. 31, 1977		Stanford	24	15	Charles Alexander, LSU, TB	31,318
			LSU	14		Gordy Ceresino, Stanford, LB	
1978	Dec. 23, 1978	14	Texas	42	9	Johnny "Ham" Jones, Texas, RB	33,122
		13	Maryland	0	20	Dwight Jefferson, Texas, DE	
1979	Dec. 22, 1979	13	Washington	14	11	Paul Skansi, Washington, WR	33,412
		11	Texas	7		Doug Martin, Washington, DT	
1980	Dec. 27, 1980	8	Nebraska	31	7	Jeff Quinn, Nebraska, QB	34,723
		17	Mississippi State	17	19	Jimmy Williams, Nebraska, DE	

SEASON	DATE	PRE-GAME RANK	TEAMS	SCORE	FINAL RANK	MOST VALUABLE PLAYERS	ATT.
1981	Dec. 26, 1981		Oklahoma	40	20	Darrell Shepard, Oklahoma, QB	33,816
		14	Houston	14		Rick Bryan, Oklahoma, DT	
1982	Dec. 25, 1982		North Carolina	26	18	Ethan Horton, North Carolina, TB	31,359
		8	Texas	10	17	Ronnie Mullins, Texas, DE	
1983	Dec. 24, 1983		Alabama	28	15	Walter Lewis, Alabama, QB	41,412
		6	SMU	7	12	Wes Neighbors, Alabama, C	
1984	Dec. 22, 1984	12	Maryland	28	12	Rick Badanjek, Maryland, FB	50,126
			Tennessee	27		Carl Zander, Tennessee, LB	
1985	Dec. 28, 1985		Arizona	13		Max Zendejas, Arizona, K	52,203
			Georgia	13		Peter Anderson, Georgia, C	
1986	Dec. 25, 1986	13	Alabama	28	9	Cornelius Bennett, Alabama, DE	48,722
		12	Washington	6	18	Steve Alvord, Washington, MG	
1987	Dec. 25, 1987	11	Oklahoma State	35	11	Thurman Thomas, Oklahoma State, RB	43,240
			West Virginia	33		Darnell Warren, West Virginia, LB	
1988	Dec. 24, 1988	20	Alabama	29	17	David Smith, Alabama, QB	48,719
			Army	28		Derrick Thomas, Alabama, LB	
1989	Dec. 30, 1989	24	Pittsburgh	31	17	Alex Van Pelt, Pittsburgh, QB	44,887
		16	Texas A&M	28	20	Anthony Williams, Texas A&M, LB	
1990	Dec. 31, 1990	22	Michigan State	17	16	Courtney Hawkins, Michigan State, WR	50,562
		21	Southern Cal	16	20	Craig Hartsuyker, Southern Cal, LB	
1991	Dec. 31, 1991	22	UCLA	6	19	Arnold Ale, UCLA, LB	42,281
			Illinois	3		Mike Poloskey, Illinois, LB	
1992	Dec. 31, 1992		Baylor	20		Melvin Bonner, Baylor, WR	41,622
		22	Arizona	15			
1993	Dec. 24, 1993	19	Oklahoma	41	17	Jerald Moore, Oklahoma, RB	43,848
			Texas Tech	10			
1994	Dec. 30, 1994		Texas	35	25	Priest Holmes, RB, Blake Brockermeyer, OL,Texas	50,612
		19	North Carolina	31		Marcus Wall, North Carolina, WR	
1995	Dec. 29, 1995		Iowa	38	25	Sedrick Shaw, Iowa, RB	49,116
		20	Washington	18		Jared DeVries, DT, Brion Hurley, K, Iowa	
1996	Dec. 31, 1996		Stanford	38		Troy Walters, WR , Chad Hutchinson, QB, Stanford	42,721
			Michigan State	0		Kailee Wong, Stanford, DE	
1997	Dec. 31, 1997	16	Arizona State	17	14	Mike Martin, Arizona State, RB	49,104
			Iowa	7			
1998	Dec. 31, 1998		TCU	28		Basil Mitchell, TB, London Dunlap, DE, TCU	46,612
			Southern Cal	19		Adam Abrams, Southern Cal, K	
1999	Dec. 31, 1999		Oregon	24	19	Billy Cockerham, Minnesota, QB	48,757
		12	Minnesota	20	18	Dyron Russ, T, Ryan Rindels, P, Minnesota	
2000	Dec. 29, 2000		Wisconsin	21	23	Freddie Mitchell, WR, Oscar Cabrera, OL, UCLA	49,093
			UCLA	20		Michael Bennett, Wisconsin, RB	
2001	Dec. 31, 2001	13	Washington State	33	10	Lamont Thompson, S, Drew Dunning, K, Washington State	47,812
			Purdue	27		Akin Ayodele, Purdue, DE	
2002	Dec. 31, 2002		Purdue	34		Kyle Orton, Purdue, QB	48,917
			Washington	24		Shaun Phillips, DE, Anthony Chambers, WR, Purdue	
2003	Dec. 31, 2003	24	Minnesota	31		Samie Parker, Oregon, WR	49,894
			Oregon	30		Junior Siavii, DT, Jared Siegel, K, Oregon	
2004	Dec. 31, 2004	21	Arizona State	27	19	Sam Keller, Arizona State, QB	51,288
			Purdue	23			

JANUARY 1, 1935
EL PASO ALL-STARS 25, RANGER 21

	1ST	2ND	3RD	4TH	FINAL
El Paso	6	0	19	0	25
RANGER	0	7	0	14	21

SCORING SUMMARY
EL PASO Salcedo 65 pass from Heineman (kick failed)
RANGER Britt 45 run (Anderson kick)
EL PASO Heineman 7 run (kick failed)
EL PASO Crysler 30 pass from Heineman (Heineman kick)
EL PASO Heineman 70 interception return (kick failed)
RANGER Anderson 1 run (Anderson kick)
RANGER Anderson 3 run (Anderson kick)

EL PASO	TEAM STATISTICS	RANGER
10	First Downs	8
145	Rushing Yards	166
9-22-2	Passing	6-18-3
212	Passing Yards	58
357	Total Yards	224
5-37.2	Punts - Average	6-57.0
3-1	Fumbles - Lost	1-1
3-15	Penalties - Yards	2-10

JANUARY 1, 1936
HARDIN-SIMMONS 14, NEW MEXICO ST. 14

	1ST	2ND	3RD	4TH	FINAL
HS	0	7	7	0	14
NMS	0	0	7	7	14

SCORING SUMMARY
HS Scroggins 15 pass from Tyler (Calloway kick)
NMS Spanogle 1 run (A. Apodaca kick)
HS Cherry 1 run (Green kick)
NMS L. Apodaca 35 run (A. Apodaca kick)

HS	TEAM STATISTICS	NMS
15	First Downs	8
210	Rushing Yards	83
9-18-1	Passing	12-27-4
92	Passing Yards	121
302	Total Yards	204
13-45.2	Punts - Average	16-38.4
7-5	Fumbles - Lost	3-1
10-86	Penalties - Yards	8-75

JANUARY 1, 1937
HARDIN-SIMMONS 34, UTEP 6

	1ST	2ND	3RD	4TH	FINAL
HS	7	6	14	7	34
UTEP	0	6	0	0	6

SCORING SUMMARY
HS Addington 13 run (Selfridge kick)
UTEP Arnold 40 pass from May (kick failed)
HS Tyler 1 run (kick failed)
HS Cherry 1 run (Calloway kick)
HS Tyler 1 run (Selfridge kick)
HS White 9 run (Hinrichs kick)

HS	TEAM STATISTICS	UTEP
19	First Downs	7
400	Rushing Yards	46
5-15-2	Passing	7-20-3
67	Passing Yards	63
467	Total Yards	109
5-41.8	Punts - Average	8-36.3
1-1	Fumbles - Lost	4-2
7-95	Penalties - Yards	3-45

INDIVIDUAL LEADERS
RUSHING
HS: Addington 16-142, 1 TD; Cherry 19-83, 1 TD; Tyler 14-62, 2 TD.
UTEP: D. Balenti 7-30; Barrett 5-12.
PASSING
HS: Emory 2-5-1, 34 yards.
UTEP: May 4-5-0, 54 yards, 1 TD; Barrett 3-9-1, 43 yards.
RECEIVING
HS: Fletcher 2-34; Yeary 1-22.
UTEP: Arnold 2-55, 1 TD; M. Balenti 1-15.

JANUARY 1, 1938
WEST VIRGINIA 7, TEXAS TECH 6

	1ST	2ND	3RD	4TH	FINAL
WVU	0	7	0	0	7
TT	0	6	0	0	6

SCORING SUMMARY
WVU Isaac 3 run (Moan kick)
TT Calhoun 1 run (kick blocked)

WVU	TEAM STATISTICS	TT
9	First Downs	14
185	Rushing Yards	175
0-7-0	Passing	7-21-0
0	Passing Yards	74
185	Total Yards	249
8-32.0	Punts - Average	5-34.8
1-0	Fumbles - Lost	3-2
9-90	Penalties - Yards	6-57

JANUARY 2, 1939
UTAH 26, NEW MEXICO 0

	1ST	2ND	3RD	4TH	FINAL
UT	14	6	0	6	26
UNM	0	0	0	0	0

SCORING SUMMARY
UT Pace 15 run (McGarry kick)
UT Peterson 64 interception return (McGarry kick)
UT Peterson 9 run (kick failed)
UT Gehrke 10 run (kick failed)

UT	TEAM STATISTICS	UNM
16	First Downs	12
366	Rushing Yards	153
1-4-1	Passing	4-11-4
18	Passing Yards	59
384	Total Yards	212
8-30.5	Punts - Average	9-40.8
1-1	Fumbles - Lost	3-1
9-55	Penalties - Yards	6-35

THE BOWLS

JANUARY 1, 1940
CATHOLIC 0, ARIZONA STATE 0

	1ST	2ND	3RD	4TH	FINAL
CATH	0	0	0	0	0
ASU	0	0	0	0	0

CATH	TEAM STATISTICS	ASU
6	First Downs	11
182	Rushing Yards	205
3-15-0	Passing	0-7-2
16	Passing Yards	0
198	Total Yards	205
3-12	Punt Returns - Yards	3-18
0-0	Kickoff Returns - Yards	1-35
12-35.0	Punts - Average	11-37.0
1-1	Fumbles - Lost	4-3
6-50	Penalties - Yards	7-65

JANUARY 1, 1941
WESTERN RESERVE 26, ARIZONA STATE 13

	1ST	2ND	3RD	4TH	FINAL
WRA	7	0	6	13	26
ASU	0	13	0	0	13

SCORING SUMMARY
WRA Belichick 1 run (Belichick kick)
ASU Pitts 14 pass from Hernandez (kick failed)
ASU Henshaw 94 run (Hernandez kick)
WRA Waggle 3 block punt return (kick failed)
WRA Ries 13 run (Skoczen kick)
WRA Ries 3 run (kick failed)

WRA	TEAM STATISTICS	ASU
6	First Downs	9
176	Rushing Yards	230
2-5-1	Passing	7-16-4
59	Passing Yards	95
235	Total Yards	325
2-16	Punt Returns - Yards	3-25
4-54	Kickoff Returns - Yards	1-16
8-44.0	Punts - Average	8-38.0
3-2	Fumbles - Lost	4-2
7-55	Penalties - Yards	5-30

JANUARY 1, 1942
TULSA 6, TEXAS TECH 0

	1ST	2ND	3RD	4TH	FINAL
TUL	0	0	0	6	6
TT	0	0	0	0	0

SCORING SUMMARY
TUL Judd 25 pass from Dobbs (kick failed)

TUL	TEAM STATISTICS	TT
15	First Downs	4
96	Rushing Yards	62
24-39-2	Passing	2-10-1
239	Passing Yards	42
335	Total Yards	104
2-75	Punt Returns - Yards	5-126
13-37.0	Punts - Average	12-43.0
0-0	Fumbles - Lost	5-2
6-60	Penalties - Yards	8-90

JANUARY 1, 1943
2ND AIR FORCE 13, HARDIN-SIMMONS 7

	1ST	2ND	3RD	4TH	FINAL
SAFA	0	0	6	7	13
HS	0	7	0	0	7

SCORING SUMMARY
HS Wilson 19 run (Ryan kick)
SAFA Spadaccini 1 run (kick failed)
SAFA VanEverly 3 run (Bodney kick)

SAFA	TEAM STATISTICS	HS
12	First Downs	9
117	Rushing Yards	148
8-21-2	Passing	3-13-1
176	Passing Yards	41
293	Total Yards	189
30	Penalty Yards	70

JANUARY 1, 1944
SOUTHWESTERN 7, NEW MEXICO 0

	1ST	2ND	3RD	4TH	FINAL
SU	0	0	0	7	7
UNM	0	0	0	0	0

SCORING SUMMARY
SU Macgruder 34 pass from Cooper (Collins kick)

SU	TEAM STATISTICS	UNM
12	First Downs	4
214	Rushing Yards	38
7-10-1	Passing	3-10-0
65	Passing Yards	10
279	Total Yards	48
4-66	Punt Returns - Yards	2-7
1-30	Kickoff Returns - Yards	1-17
5-35.0	Punts - Average	11-38.0
1-1	Fumbles - Lost	1-0
4-20	Penalties - Yards	4-20

JANUARY 1, 1945
SOUTHWESTERN 35, MEXICO 0

	1ST	2ND	3RD	4TH	FINAL
SU	7	7	14	7	35
MEX	0	0	0	0	0

SCORING SUMMARY
SU Blodzinsky recovers blocked punt in end zone (Francis kick)
SU Bare 24 pass from Brechtel (Francis kick)
SU Ullrey 15 run after lateral from Means (Francis kick)
SU McDonald 6 run (Francis kick)
SU Flores 20 run (Francis kick)

SU	TEAM STATISTICS	MEX
14	First Downs	4
212	Rushing Yards	29
12-26-2	Passing	2-9-3
196	Passing Yards	-50
408	Total Yards	-21
6-11	Punt Returns - Yards	3-3
1-14	Kickoff Returns - Yards	6-23
5-37.0	Punts - Average	14-36.0
2-2	Fumbles - Lost	0-0
8-109	Penalties - Yards	2-20

JANUARY 1, 1946
NEW MEXICO 34, DENVER 24

	1ST	2ND	3RD	4TH	FINAL
UNM	0	13	0	21	34
DEN	10	0	7	7	24

SCORING SUMMARY
DEN Karamigios 21 run (Redding kick)
DEN FG Miller 28
UNM Krall 65 interception return (kick failed)
UNM Rumley 9 run (Doar kick)
DEN Adams 2 run (Redding kick)
UNM Moser 37 pass from Rumley (Doar kick)
UNM Moser 47 pass from Rumley (Doar kick)
UNM McDonald 28 pass from Rumley (Doar kick)
DEN Karamigios 35 pass from Cochran (Redding kick)

UNM	TEAM STATISTICS	DEN
15	First Downs	13
208	Rushing Yards	244
8-12-1	Passing	3-16-1
207	Passing Yards	39
415	Total Yards	283
5-111	Kickoff Returns - Yards	7-113
1-1	Fumbles - Lost	1-0
90	Penalty Yards	25

JANUARY 1, 1947
CINCINNATI 18, VIRGINIA TECH 6

	1ST	2ND	3RD	4TH	FINAL
CIN	0	0	12	6	18
VT	0	0	0	6	6

SCORING SUMMARY
CIN Johnson 13 run (kick failed)
CIN Sabato 1 run (kick failed)
VT Beard 3 run (kick failed)
CIN McMillan 3 run (kick failed)

CIN	TEAM STATISTICS	VT
16	First Downs	13
369	Rushing Yards	34
5-18-3	Passing	4-15-2
94	Passing Yards	85
463	Total Yards	119
6-19.0	Punts - Average	7-40.6
0-0	Fumbles - Lost	0-0
9-100	Penalties - Yards	3-25

JANUARY 1, 1948
MIAMI (OHIO) 13, TEXAS TECH 12

	1ST	2ND	3RD	4TH	FINAL
MIA	6	0	0	7	13
TT	0	6	0	6	12

SCORING SUMMARY
MIA Parseghian 1 run (kick failed)
TT Conley 3 run (kick failed)
MIA Shoults 1 run (Speelman kick)
TT Winkler 30 interception return (kick blocked)

MIA	TEAM STATISTICS	TT
21	First Downs	5
294	Rushing Yards	194
11-22-2	Passing	5-14-2
120	Passing Yards	83
414	Total Yards	277
6-11	Punt Returns - Yards	1-33
3-11	Kickoff Returns - Yards	2-35
7-35.0	Punts - Average	7-25.0
1-1	Fumbles - Lost	1-0
9-65	Penalties - Yards	6-50

JANUARY 1, 1949
WEST VIRGINIA 21, UTEP 12

	1ST	2ND	3RD	4TH	FINAL
WVU	0	7	14	0	21
UTEP	0	6	0	6	12

SCORING SUMMARY
UTEP Gabrel 1 run (kick failed)
WVU Cox 25 pass from Walthall (Simmons kick)
WVU Devonshire 14 run (Simmons kick)
WVU Devonshire 3 run (Simmons kick)
UTEP Wendt 60 run (kick blocked)

WVU	TEAM STATISTICS	UTEP
13	First Downs	12
183	Rushing Yards	245
7-16-1	Passing	4-9-0
122	Passing Yards	57
305	Total Yards	302
3-24	Punt Returns - Yards	3-18
3-27	Kickoff Returns - Yards	2-34
9-27.0	Punts - Average	5-41.0
1-0	Fumbles - Lost	4-4
6-50	Penalties - Yards	3-25

INDIVIDUAL LEADERS
RUSHING
WVU: Devonshire 14-78, 2 TD; Murphy 2-31.
UTEP: Wendt 15-92, 1 TD; Fraser 9-91.
PASSING
WVU: Walthall 7-16-1, 122 yards, 1 TD.
UTEP: Bowden 4-9-0, 57 yards.
RECEIVING
WVU: Lester 3-60; Cox 2-45, 1 TD.
UTEP: Bowden 2-30; Gabrel 2-27.

JANUARY 2, 1950
UTEP 33, GEORGETOWN 20

	1ST	2ND	3RD	4TH	FINAL
UTEP	0	13	7	13	33
GTOWN	0	0	7	13	20

SCORING SUMMARY
UTEP Chesak 1 run (kick failed)
UTEP Gabrel 1 run (McWilliams pass to Chesak)
UTEP Fraser 31 run (Davis kick)
GTOWN Kivus 5 run (Haesler kick)
UTEP Gabrel 19 run (kick blocked)
GTOWN Schmitt 14 pass from Mattingly (kick blocked)
UTEP Hansen 53 kickoff return (Davis kick)
GTOWN Fornaciari 43 pass from Deacon (Haesler kick)

UTEP	TEAM STATISTICS	GTOWN
14	First Downs	13
348	Rushing Yards	82
5-9-0	Passing	12-31-3
24	Passing Yards	226
372	Total Yards	308
5-36.0	Punts - Average	10-33.0
2-2	Fumbles - Lost	2-1
11-95	Penalties - Yards	7-65

INDIVIDUAL LEADERS
RUSHING
UTEP: Cargile 12-96; Gabrel 11-85, 2 TD.
GTOWN: Conn 8-30; Kivus 8-20, 1 TD.
PASSING
UTEP: Brewster 5-9-0, 24 yards.
GTOWN: Mattingly 8-20-3, 118 yards, 1 TD; Deacon 4 -11-0, 108 yards, 1 TD.
RECEIVING
UTEP: Campbell 2-17; Wilkinson 1-6.
GTOWN: Fornaciari 4-114, 1 TD; Conn 3-54.

January 1, 1951
West Texas A&M 14, Cincinnati 13

	1ST	2ND	3RD	4TH	FINAL
WT A&M	0	7	7	0	14
CIN	0	6	7	0	13

SCORING SUMMARY
WT A&M — Cross 4 run (Dunn kick)
CIN — McKeever 3 run (kick failed)
CIN — Stratton 17 pass from Rossi (Shalonsky kick)
WT A&M — Cross 62 pass from Mayfield (Dunn kick)

WT A&M	TEAM STATISTICS	CIN
19	First Downs	12
238	Rushing Yards	106
6-15-3	Passing	14-30-3
123	Passing Yards	170
361	Total Yards	276
4-44.0	Punts - Average	5-30.0
3-0	Fumbles - Lost	3-0
8-80	Penalties - Yards	8-70

INDIVIDUAL LEADERS
RUSHING
WT A&M: Wright 23-135; Cross 15-53.
CIN: Stratton 8-59; McKeever 9-40, 1 TD.
PASSING
WT A&M: Mayfield 5-14-3, 103 yards, 1 TD.
CIN: Rossi 14-29-3, 170 yards, 1 TD.

January 1, 1952
Texas Tech 25, Pacific 14

	1ST	2ND	3RD	4TH	FINAL
TT	13	6	6	0	25
PAC	7	7	0	0	14

SCORING SUMMARY
TT — Turner 39 run (Whittaker kick)
PAC — Myers 4 run (DeCristofaro kick)
TT — Crossley 19 pass from Johnson (kick failed)
TT — Arterburn 5 run (kick failed)
PAC — Cobb 1 run (DeCristofaro kick)
TT — Welton 11 run (kick failed)

TT	TEAM STATISTICS	PAC
12	First Downs	18
274	Rushing Yards	278
5-9-0	Passing	3-14-3
79	Passing Yards	38
353	Total Yards	316
5-41.0	Punts - Average	3-32.0
2-0	Fumbles - Lost	5-4
12-90	Penalties - Yards	3-25

January 1, 1953
Pacific 26, Southern Miss 7

	1ST	2ND	3RD	4TH	FINAL
PAC	6	7	7	6	26
SMU	0	0	0	7	7

SCORING SUMMARY
PAC — McCormick 2 run (kick failed)
PAC — Berndt 9 pass from Ottoson (Mendonca kick)
PAC — McCormick 5 run (Mendonca kick)
PAC — McCormick 2 run (pass failed)
SMU — Pepper 1 run (Davenport kick)

PAC	TEAM STATISTICS	SMU
16	First Downs	7
166	Rushing Yards	126
10-17-0	Passing	5-15-0
101	Passing Yards	89
267	Total Yards	215
8-40.0	Punts - Average	7-38.0
2-1	Fumbles - Lost	5-4
3-45	Penalties - Yards	5-35

January 1, 1954
UTEP 37, Southern Miss 14

	1ST	2ND	3RD	4TH	FINAL
UTEP	14	16	7	0	37
USM	0	7	7	0	14

SCORING SUMMARY
UTEP — Howle recovers fumble in end zone (Shinaut kick)
UTEP — Whittenton 25 pass from Shinaut (Shinaut kick)
UTEP — FG Shinaut 14
UTEP — Howle 49 pass from Shinaut (Shinaut kick)
UTEP — McCormick 2 run (kick blocked)
USM — Woods 12 pass from Jerrell (McElroy kick)
USM — Smallwood 14 run (Davenport kick)
UTEP — Riley 43 run (Shinaut kick)

UTEP	TEAM STATISTICS	USM
15	First Downs	13
245	Rushing Yards	166
11-20-0	Passing	0-8-0
158	Passing Yards	145
403	Total Yards	311
5-28.0	Punts - Average	4-28.0
4-2	Fumbles - Lost	4-3
4-40	Penalties - Yards	3-13

INDIVIDUAL LEADERS
RUSHING
UTEP: Riley 12-112, 1 TD; Coleman 2-39.
USM: Pepper 14-57; McElroy 11-50.
PASSING
UTEP: Shinaut 11-17-0, 158 yards, 2 TD.
USM: Jerrell 6-18-0, 134 yards, 1 TD.
RECEIVING
UTEP: Howle 4-76, 1 TD; Odell 5-43.
USM: Waters 3-76; Woods 4-52, 1 TD.

January 1, 1955
UTEP 47, Florida State 20

	1ST	2ND	3RD	4TH	FINAL
UTEP	7	27	13	0	47
FSU	7	0	6	7	20

SCORING SUMMARY
FSU — Massey 1 run (Graham kick)
UTEP — Rutledge 56 pass from Whittenton (Whittenton kick)
UTEP — Whittenton 7 run (kick failed)
UTEP — B. Forrest 45 run (Whittenton kick)
UTEP — D. Forrest 19 pass from Whittenton (Whittenton kick)
UTEP — Rutledge 16 pass from Whittenton (Whittenton kick)
UTEP — B. Forrest 11 run (Whittenton kick)
FSU — Feamster 57 pass from Swantic (kick blocked)
UTEP — Whittenton 2 run (kick failed)
FSU — Odom 16 pass from Massey (Graham kick)

UTEP	TEAM STATISTICS	FSU
17	First Downs	13
253	Rushing Yards	139
8-15-0	Passing	12-21-2
149	Passing Yards	155
402	Total Yards	294
4-44.0	Punts - Average	6-26.0
3-2	Fumbles - Lost	2-2
7-65	Penalties - Yards	3-25

INDIVIDUAL LEADERS
RUSHING
UTEP: B. Forrest 5-72, 2 TD; Rutledge 6-56.
FSU: Corso 2-50; Reynolds 7-35.
PASSING
UTEP: Whittenton 7-13-0, 138 yards, 3 TD.
FSU: Massey 8-17-2, 107 yards, 1 TD.
RECEIVING
UTEP: Rutledge 3-88, 2 TD; Howle 2-35.
FSU: Feamster 4-68, 1 TD; Graham 1-27.

January 2, 1956
Wyoming 21, Texas Tech 14

	1ST	2ND	3RD	4TH	FINAL
WYO	0	7	0	14	21
TT	0	0	7	7	14

SCORING SUMMARY
WYO — Watts 53 pass from Zowada (Kutches kick)
TT — Herr 2 run (Williams kick)
TT — Fewin 1 run (Williams kick)
WYO — Marshall 13 pass from Zowada (Kutches kick)
WYO — Stapleton 1 run (Kutches kick)

WYO	TEAM STATISTICS	TT
12	First Downs	13
129	Rushing Yards	202
8-12-1	Passing	6-14-1
172	Passing Yards	57
301	Total Yards	259
7-30.0	Punts - Average	4-34.0
1-0	Fumbles - Lost	5-3
10-82	Penalties - Yards	3-35

INDIVIDUAL LEADERS
RUSHING
TT: Crawford 18-103; Stapleton 9-36, 1 TD.
TT: Schmidt 12-60; Sides 10-56.
PASSING
WYO: Zowada 6-10-1, 112 yards, 2 TD.
TT: Williams 6-14-1, 57 yards.

January 1, 1957
George Washington 13, UTEP 0

	1ST	2ND	3RD	4TH	FINAL
GWU	6	0	0	7	13
UTEP	0	0	0	0	0

SCORING SUMMARY
GWU — Thompson 30 pass from Looney (kick blocked)
GWU — Spera 3 run (Spera kick)

GWU	TEAM STATISTICS	UTEP
14	First Downs	10
257	Rushing Yards	146
4-9-0	Passing	3-16-3
61	Passing Yards	22
318	Total Yards	168
7-33.0	Punts - Average	8-34.0
3-2	Fumbles - Lost	3-3
7-55	Penalties - Yards	3-45

INDIVIDUAL LEADERS
RUSHING
GWU: Austin 18-98; Spera 9-47, 1 TD.
UTEP: Forrest 14-49; Maynard 6-24.
PASSING
GWU: Looney 4-9-0, 61 yards, 1 TD.
UTEP: Forrest 2-7-1, 22 yards.
RECEIVING
GWU: Thompson 3-46, 1 TD; Harman 1-15.
UTEP: Bevers 1-16; Watkins 1-8.

January 1, 1958
Louisville 34, Drake 20

	1ST	2ND	3RD	4TH	FINAL
LOU	7	14	7	6	34
DRAKE	7	7	0	6	20

SCORING SUMMARY
DRAKE — LaBrasca 7 run (Leeman kick)
LOU — Cain 40 pass from Orem (Young kick)
LOU — Young 32 pass from Orem (Young kick)
DRAKE — Newell 1 run (Leeman kick)
LOU — Bryant 4 run (Young kick)
LOU — Porco 3 run (Young kick)
LOU — Young 20 pass from Bryant (kick failed)
DRAKE — Kinzel 55 pass from LaBrasca (kick failed)

LOU	TEAM STATISTICS	DRAKE
14	First Downs	16
228	Rushing Yards	176
6-10-0	Passing	10-33-1
148	Passing Yards	140
376	Total Yards	316
5-34.0	Punts - Average	4-26.0
1-0	Fumbles - Lost	3-2
5-75	Penalties - Yards	5-51

THE BOWLS

December 31, 1958
Wyoming 14, Hardin-Simmons 6

	1st	2nd	3rd	4th	FINAL
WYO	0	14	0	0	14
HS	0	0	6	0	6

SCORING SUMMARY
WYO	Smolinski 22 run (McGill kick)
WYO	Snyder 3 run (McGill kick)
HS	Lipsey 22 pass from Stephens (pass failed)

WYO	TEAM STATISTICS	HS
11	First Downs	15
164	Rushing Yards	153
3-9-1	Passing	11-23-1
24	Passing Yards	82
188	Total Yards	235
8-35.0	Punts - Average	3-27.0
4-1	Fumbles - Lost	5-3

INDIVIDUAL LEADERS
RUSHING
WYO: Smolinski 12-52, 1 TD; Sawyer 9-45.
HS: Hart 20- 73; Allen 9-53.

PASSING
WYO: Wilkinson 1-2-0, 23 yards.
HS: Stephens 7-13-1, 54 yards, 1 TD.

December 31, 1959
New Mexico St. 28, North Texas St. 8

	1st	2nd	3rd	4th	FINAL
NMS	14	7	0	7	28
NTSU	0	0	8	0	8

SCORING SUMMARY
NMS	Atkins 57 pass from Johnson (Gaiters run)
NMS	Locklin recovers fumble in endzone (run failed)
NMS	Kelly 15 pass from Johnson (Villanueva kick)
NTSU	Christle 51 punt return (Perkins pass from Duty)
NMS	Gaiters 44 run (Villanueva kick)

NMS	TEAM STATISTICS	NTSU
18	First Downs	20
206	Rushing Yards	152
8-16-0	Passing	15-31-2
136	Passing Yards	182
342	Total Yards	334
7-39.0	Punts - Average	4-38.0
4-2	Fumbles - Lost	8-6
8-69	Penalties - Yards	5-35

December 31, 1960
New Mexico St. 20, Utah State 13

	1st	2nd	3rd	4th	FINAL
NMS	0	7	7	6	20
USU	7	6	0	0	13

SCORING SUMMARY
USU	Larscheid 13 run (Miller kick)
NMS	Atkins 3 pass from Johnson (Atkins kick)
USU	Camilli 11 run (kick failed)
NMU	Gaiters 32 run (Atkins kick)
NMU	Sims 7 pass from Johnson (kick failed)

NMS	TEAM STATISTICS	USU
15	First Downs	15
44	Rushing Yards	268
18-26-1	Passing	0-4-0
180	Passing Yards	0
224	Total Yards	268
3-37.0	Punts - Average	4-31.0
1-1	Fumbles - Lost	2-1
2-16	Penalties - Yards	4-32

December 30, 1961
Villanova 17, Wichita State 9

	1st	2nd	3rd	4th	FINAL
NOVA	7	0	10	0	17
WICH	0	3	0	6	9

SCORING SUMMARY
NOVA	Joe 9 run (Gruneisen kick)
WICH	FG Seigle 36
NOVA	Rettino 1 run (Gruneisen kick)
NOVA	FG Gruneisen 26
WICH	Zyskowski 7 run (pass failed)

NOVA	TEAM STATISTICS	WICH
14	First Downs	9
225	Rushing Yards	111
4-12-1	Passing	5-19-4
50	Passing Yards	71
275	Total Yards	182
4-41.0	Punts - Average	5-32.0
6-45	Penalties - Yards	3-15

December 31, 1962
West Texas A&M 15, Ohio 14

	1st	2nd	3rd	4th	FINAL
WT A&M	0	7	0	8	15
OHIO	0	3	8	3	14

SCORING SUMMARY
OHIO	FG McGee 52
WT A&M	Logan 13 pass from Dawson (Gibson kick)
OHIO	Hoovler 91 interception return (Smith pass from Babbitt)
OHIO	FG McGee 24
WT A&M	Richardson 32 pass from Dawson (Ostander pass from Dawson)

WT A&M	TEAM STATISTICS	OHIO
18	First Downs	14
343	Rushing Yards	167
7-10-0	Passing	12-29-0
105	Passing Yards	157
448	Total Yards	324
5-41.0	Punts - Average	4-41.0
6-4	Fumbles - Lost	1-0
97	Penalty Yards	40

December 31, 1963
Oregon 21, SMU 14

	1st	2nd	3rd	4th	FINAL
ORE	7	14	0	0	21
SMU	0	0	0	14	14

SCORING SUMMARY
ORE	Keller 9 run (Corey kick)
ORE	Imwalle 23 pass from Berry (Meister kick)
ORE	Burleson 20 pass from Berry (Meister kick)
SMU	Roderick 3 pass from Thomas (pass failed)
SMU	Roderick 7 pass from White (White run)

ORE	TEAM STATISTICS	SMU
16	First Downs	20
153	Rushing Yards	145
12-28-1	Passing	18-34-4
166	Passing Yards	232
319	Total Yards	377
7-36.0	Punts - Average	4-39.0
79	Penalty Yards	38

December 26, 1964
Georgia 7, Texas Tech 0

	1st	2nd	3rd	4th	FINAL
UGA	0	7	0	0	7
TT	0	0	0	0	0

SCORING SUMMARY
UGA	Lankewicz 2 run (Etter kick)

UGA	TEAM STATISTICS	TT
17	First Downs	7
245	Rushing Yards	32
5-9-0	Passing	11-24-1
84	Passing Yards	96
329	Total Yards	128
2-6	Punt Returns - Yards	3-26
2-33	Kickoff Returns - Yards	2-50
4-38.0	Punts - Average	8-37.0
3-3	Fumbles - Lost	1-0
7-45	Penalties - Yards	8-37

INDIVIDUAL LEADERS
RUSHING
UGA: Ridlehuber 19-87.
TT: Agan 5-20.

PASSING
UGA: Ridlehuber 4-5-0, 77 yards.
TT: Wilson 11-24-1, 96 yards.

RECEIVING
UGA: Barber 1-52; Brown 3-29.
TT: Agan 3-11.

December 31, 1965
UTEP 13, TCU 12

	1st	2nd	3rd	4th	FINAL
UTEP	0	0	10	3	13
TCU	0	10	0	2	12

SCORING SUMMARY
TCU	FG Alford 35
TCU	Smith 11 pass from Nix (Alford kick)
UTEP	Hughes 34 pass from Stevens (Cook kick)
UTEP	FG Cook 21
UTEP	FG Cook 18
TCU	Safety (Stevens intentionally downs ball in end zone)

UTEP	TEAM STATISTICS	TCU
14	First Downs	18
12	Rushing Yards	100
21-34-3	Passing	15-28-3
208	Passing Yards	148
220	Total Yards	248
5-39.0	Punts - Average	4-48.0
2-0	Fumbles - Lost	4-3
45	Penalty Yards	35

INDIVIDUAL LEADERS
RUSHING
UTEP: Davis 14-41; Harrell 1-9.
TCU: Post 22-76; Landon 15-28.

PASSING
UTEP: Stevens 21-34-3, 208 yards, 1 TD.
TCU: Nix 15-27-3, 148 yards, 1 TD.

RECEIVING
UTEP: Hughes 7-115, 1 TD; Anderson 4-45.
TCU: Campbell 6-74; Smith 5-39, 1 TD.

December 24, 1966
Wyoming 28, Florida State 20

	1st	2nd	3rd	4th	FINAL
WYO	7	0	14	7	28
FSU	0	14	0	6	20

SCORING SUMMARY
WYO	Kiick 1 run (DePoyster kick)
FSU	Sellers 49 pass from Hammond (Loner kick)
FSU	Wetherell 59 pass from Hammond (Loner kick)
WYO	Marion 39 pass from Egloff (DePoyster kick)
WYO	Kiick 43 run (DePoyster kick)
WYO	Egloff 14 run (DePoyster kick)
FSU	Sellers 23 pass from Hammond (pass failed)

WYO	TEAM STATISTICS	FSU
14	First Downs	13
229	Rushing Yards	(-21)
9-27-0	Passing	17-35-2
135	Passing Yards	293
364	Total Yards	272
2-42	Punt Returns - Yards	4-23
3-22	Kickoff Returns - Yards	2-40
8-37.0	Punts - Average	9-40.0
3-2	Fumbles - Lost	4-2
4-50	Penalties - Yards	10-102

INDIVIDUAL LEADERS
RUSHING
WYO: Kiick 25-135, 2 TD; Egloff 5-42, 1 TD.
FSU: Moreman 13-11, Mankins 6-10.

PASSING
WYO: Egloff 9-16-0, 135 yards, 1 TD.
FSU: Hammond 9-15-1, 215 yards, 2 TD.

December 30, 1967
UTEP 14, Mississippi 7

	1st	2nd	3rd	4th	FINAL
UTEP	0	0	0	14	14
MISS	0	7	0	0	7

SCORING SUMMARY
MISS	Newell 1 run (Brown kick)
UTEP	Karns 5 pass from Stevens (Waddles kick)
UTEP	McHenry 4 run (Waddles kick)

UTEP	TEAM STATISTICS	MISS
16	First Downs	6
75	Rushing Yards	38
16-35-1	Passing	12-23-1
201	Passing Yards	71
276	Total Yards	109
6-25	Punt Returns - Yards	8-75
1-7	Kickoff Returns - Yards	4-98
12-39.0	Punts - Average	11-42.0
0-0	Fumbles - Lost	4-3
9-92	Penalties - Yards	5-33

INDIVIDUAL LEADERS
RUSHING
UTEP: McHenry 13-73, 1 TD; White 17-72.
MISS: Hindman 15-53.

PASSING
UTEP: Stevens 13-26-1, 155 yards, 1 TD.
MISS: Newell 12-23-1, 71 yards.

RECEIVING
UTEP: Wallace 6-83; Karns 5-56, 1 TD.
MISS: Matthews 4-25; Haik 3-24.

December 28, 1968
AUBURN 34, ARIZONA 10

	1ST	2ND	3RD	4TH	FINAL
AUB	10	0	14	10	34
ARIZ	0	10	0	0	10

SCORING SUMMARY
AUB FG Riley 52
AUB Zofko 6 pass from Carter (Riley kick)
ARIZ FG Hurley 37
ARIZ Arnason 11 pass from Lee (Hurley kick)
AUB Taylor 9 run (Riley kick)
AUB McClinton 32 interception return (Riley kick)
AUB Christian 43 pass from Carter (Riley kick)
AUB FG Riley 41

AUB	TEAM STATISTICS	ARIZ
12	First Downs	16
147	Rushing Yards	70
7-28-4	Passing	13-44-8
156	Passing Yards	164
303	Total Yards	234
5-35	Punt Returns - Yards	11-34
0-0	Kickoff Returns - Yards	3-51
7-26.0	Punts - Average	11-34.0
3-2	Fumbles - Lost	2-1
4-36	Penalties - Yards	4-38

INDIVIDUAL LEADERS
RUSHING
AUB: Hurston 14-49; Currier 11-29.
ARIZ: Fuimaono 18-48; Hustead 16-35.
PASSING
AUB: Carter 7-28-3, 156 yards, 2 TD.
ARIZ: Lee 6-24-6 89 yards, 1 TD; Driscoll 7-20-2, 75 yards.
RECEIVING
AUB: Zofko 1-65, 1 TD; Christian 3-62, 1 TD.
ARIZ: Gardin 5-74; Sherwood 2-40.

December 20, 1969
NEBRASKA 45, GEORGIA 6

	1ST	2ND	3RD	4TH	FINAL
NEB	18	0	14	13	45
UGA	0	0	0	6	6

SCORING SUMMARY
NEB FG Rogers 50
NEB FG Rogers 32
NEB Kinney 10 run (pass failed)
NEB FG Rogers 42
NEB FG Rogers 37
NEB Green 7 pass from Brownson (Rogers kick)
NEB Brownson 1 run (Rogers kick)
NEB Schneiss 1 run (kick failed)
UGA Gilbert 6 run (kick failed)
NEB Tagge 2 run (Rogers kick)

NEB	TEAM STATISTICS	UGA
17	First Downs	11
190	Rushing Yards	55
18-35-2	Passing	11-35-6
165	Passing Yards	130
355	Total Yards	185
3-38	Punt Returns - Yards	2-11
7-35.0	Punts - Average	10-42.0
1-0	Fumbles - Lost	2-2
6-50	Penalties - Yards	3-31

INDIVIDUAL LEADERS
RUSHING
NEB: Green 13-46.
UGA Paine 13-41.
PASSING
NEB: Brownson 11-18, 109 yards, 1 TD.
UGA: Gilbert 10-30, 116 yards.
RECEIVING
NEB: Ingles 4-55.
UGA: Whittemore 5-86.

December 19, 1970
GEORGIA TECH 17, TEXAS TECH 9

	1ST	2ND	3RD	4TH	FINAL
GT	7	3	0	7	17
TT	0	0	9	0	9

SCORING SUMMARY
GT Healy 2 run (Thigpen kick)
GT FG Moore 21
TT McCutchen 7 run (Ingram kick)
TT Safety (blocked punt out of end zone)
GT McNamara 2 run (Thigpen kick)

GT	TEAM STATISTICS	TT
18	First Downs	13
186	Rushing Yards	215
13-19-1	Passing	3-11-3
138	Passing Yards	28
324	Total Yards	243
2-36	Punt Returns - Yards	1-1
2-15	Kickoff Returns - Yards	4-62
7-34.0	Punts - Average	4-41.0
0-0	Fumbles - Lost	6-3
7-66	Penalties - Yards	4-40

INDIVIDUAL LEADERS
RUSHING
GT: Healy 20-59, 1 TD; Cunningham 14-42.
TT: Hargrave 8-83; McCutchen 22-81, 1 TD.
PASSING
GT: Williams 11-14-1, 123 yards.
TT: Napper 3-11-3, 28 yards.
RECEIVING
GT: Pallman 3-42; Macy 3-37.
TT: Odom 2-23.

December 18, 1971
LSU 33, IOWA STATE 15

	1ST	2ND	3RD	4TH	FINAL
LSU	6	0	13	14	33
ISU	0	3	6	6	15

SCORING SUMMARY
LSU FG Michaelson 39
LSU FG Michaelson 39
ISU FG Shoemaker 32
LSU Hamilton 37 pass from Jones (Michaelson kick)
LSU Kelgley 21 pass from Jones (kick failed)
ISU Marquardt 30 pass from Carlson (pass failed)
ISU Krepfle 1 pass from Carlson (pass failed)
LSU Michaelson 6 pass from Jones (Michaelson kick)
LSU Jones 6 run (Michaelson kick)

LSU	TEAM STATISTICS	ISU
13	First Downs	16
187	Rushing Yards	83
12-23-1	Passing	19-35-1
227	Passing Yards	249
414	Total Yards	332
5-29.0	Punts - Average	9-34.0
60	Penalty Yards	61

INDIVIDUAL LEADERS
RUSHING
LSU: Shoreu 12-68; Walker 9-37.
ISU: Amundson 15-56.
PASSING
LSU: Jones 12-18-0, 227 yards, 3 TD.
ISU: Carlson 18-32-2, 230 yards, 2 TD.
RECEIVING
LSU: Hamilton 6-165, 1 TD.
ISU: Krepfle 6-88, 1 TD; Amundson 4-46.

December 30, 1972
NORTH CAROLINA 32, TEXAS TECH 28

	1ST	2ND	3RD	4TH	FINAL
UNC	3	6	16	7	32
TT	0	7	14	7	28

SCORING SUMMARY
UNC FG Alexander 32
UNC Oliver 22 run (kick failed)
TT Tillman 14 pass from Barnes (Grimes kick)
TT Smith 65 run (Grimes kick)
TT Smith 46 run (Grimes kick)
UNC Leverenz 62 pass from Vidnovic (Alexander kick)
UNC Hite 3 run (Leverenz pass from Vidnovic)
TT Smith 5 run (Grimes kick)
UNC Leverenz 13 pass from Vidnovic (kick failed)
UNC Safety (Barnes tackled in end zone by Chapman)

UNC	TEAM STATISTICS	TT
24	First Downs	13
238	Rushing Yards	293
14-26-1	Passing	9-16-1
215	Passing Yards	94
453	Total Yards	387
9-38.0	Punts - Average	6-35.0
3-0	Fumbles - Lost	3-2
7-55	Penalties - Yards	4-39

INDIVIDUAL LEADERS
RUSHING
UNC: Oglesby 16-71; Johnson 13-52.
TT: Smith 14-172, 3 TD; Hoskins 13-60.
PASSING
UNC: Vidnovic 14-26-1, 215 yards, 2 TD.
TT: Barnes 9-16-0, 94 yards, 1 TD.
RECEIVING
UNC: Leverenz 5-95, 2 TD; Bethea 3-34.
TT: Samford 3-34; Tillman 2-31, 1 TD.

December 29, 1973
MISSOURI 34, AUBURN 17

	1ST	2ND	3RD	4TH	FINAL
MO	0	28	6	0	34
AUB	0	10	7	0	17

SCORING SUMMARY
AUB FG Pruett 35
MO Kelsey 35 pass from Link (Hill kick)
MO Bybee 2 run (Hill kick)
MO Kelsey 2 pass from Smith (Hill kick)
AUB Gossom 17 pass from Gargis (Pruett kick)
MO Mosley 84 kickoff return (Hill kick)
MO Sharp 15 pass from Smith (kick failed)
AUB Gossom 32 pass from Gargis (Pruett kick)

MO	TEAM STATISTICS	AUB
20	First Downs	11
295	Rushing Yards	113
8-14-1	Passing	7-15-1
95	Passing Yards	120
390	Total Yards	233
6-37.0	Punts - Average	6-46.0
4-1	Fumbles - Lost	5-4
2-29	Penalties - Yards	1-5

INDIVIDUAL LEADERS
RUSHING
MO: Bybee 27-127, 1 TD; Reamon 23-110.
AUB: McIntyre 10-46; Neel 7-26.
PASSING
MO: Smith 7-12-0, 60 yards, 2 TD; Link 1-2-1 35 yards, 1 TD.
AUB: Gargis 7-15-1, 120 yards, 2 TD.
RECEIVING
MO: Kelsey 2-37, 2 TD; Sharp 2-26, 1 TD.
AUB: Stivey 3-56; Gossom 2-49, 2 TD.

THE BOWLS

December 28, 1974
Mississippi State 26, North Carolina 24

	1st	2nd	3rd	4th	FINAL
MSU	7	3	10	6	26
UNC	7	0	14	3	24

SCORING SUMMARY

MSU	Packer 1 run (Nichels kick)
UNC	Betterson 1 run (Alexander kick)
MSU	FG Nichels 24
UNC	Betterson 6 run (Alexander kick)
MSU	Packer 16 run (Nichels kick)
UNC	Jerome 28 pass from Kupec (Alexander kick)
MSU	FG Nichels 32
UNC	FG Alexander 26
MSU	Vitrano 2 run (kick failed)

MSU	TEAM STATISTICS	UNC
25	First Downs	22
455	Rushing Yards	277
3-8-0	Passing	5-15-1
44	Passing Yards	125
499	Total Yards	402
3-35.0	Punts - Average	4-38.0
1-1	Fumbles - Lost	3-0
5-45	Penalties - Yards	2-30

INDIVIDUAL LEADERS

RUSHING
MSU: Packer 24-183, 2 TD; Vitrano 20-164, 1 TD.
UNC: Voight 17-90; Betterson 19-84, 2 TD.

PASSING
MSU: Felker 2-7-0, 33 yards.
UNC: Kupec 5-15-1, 125 yards, 1 TD.

RECEIVING
MSU: Lewis 2-27; Barkum 1-17.
UNC: Norton 2-61; Jerome 2-42, 1 TD.

December 26, 1975
Pittsburgh 33, Kansas 19

	1st	2nd	3rd	4th	FINAL
PITT	7	12	0	14	33
KU	0	0	7	12	19

SCORING SUMMARY

PITT	Walker 60 run (Long kick)
PITT	Dorsett 8 run (kick failed)
PITT	Dorsett 2 run (pass failed)
KU	Smith 55 run (Swift kick)
PITT	Walker 2 run (Long kick)
KU	Smith 17 run (kick failed)
PITT	Jones 7 pass from Haygood (Long kick)
KU	Sharp 38 pass from McMichael (run failed)

PITT	TEAM STATISTICS	KU
16	First Downs	19
372	Rushing Yards	342
8-13-2	Passing	4-14-2
60	Passing Yards	76
432	Total Yards	418
5-35.0	Punts - Average	5-36.0
1-0	Fumbles - Lost	6-2
10-95	Penalties - Yards	5-25

INDIVIDUAL LEADERS

RUSHING
PITT: Dorsett 27-142, 2 TD; Walker 11-123, 2 TD.
KU: Smith 16-124, 2 TD; Cromwell 24-99.

PASSING
PITT: Haygood 8-11-2, 60 yards, 1 TD.
KU: McMichael 4 -8, 76 yards, 1 TD.

RECEIVING
PITT: Jones 4 -26 yards, 1 TD; Corbett 3-25.
KU: Sharp 1-38, 1 TD; Fender 1-16.

January 2, 1977
Texas A&M 37, Florida 14

	1st	2nd	3rd	4th	FINAL
A&M	3	13	8	13	37
FLA	0	0	7	7	14

SCORING SUMMARY

A&M	FG Franklin 39
A&M	Walker 9 run (Franklin kick)
A&M	FG Franklin 62
A&M	FG Franklin
A&M	Woodard 1 run (Woodard run)
FLA	Chandler 29 run (Posey kick)
A&M	Woodard 4 run (Franklin kick)
FLA	LeCount 1 run (Posey kick)
A&M	Woodard 15 pass from Walker (kick failed)

A&M	TEAM STATISTICS	FLA
20	First Downs	14
243	Rushing Yards	172
11-19-1	Passing	7-24-1
122	Passing Yards	50
365	Total Yards	222
5-34.0	Punts - Average	9-39.0
4-3	Fumbles - Lost	4-4
6-33	Penalties - Yards	4-26

INDIVIDUAL LEADERS

RUSHING
A&M: Woodard 25-125, 2 TD; Dickey 15-54.
FLA: Brinson 10-64; Chandler 2-38, 1 TD.

PASSING
A&M: Walker 11-18-1, 122 yards, 1 TD.
FLA: Fisher 5-13-1, 42 yards.

RECEIVING
A&M: Haack 3-42; Woodard 4 -24, 1 TD.
FLA: Chandler 2-29; Green 1-8.

December 31, 1977
Stanford 24, LSU 14

	1st	2nd	3rd	4th	FINAL
STAN	0	10	7	7	24
LSU	7	7	0	0	14

SCORING SUMMARY

LSU	Quintela 3 pass from Ensminger (Conway kick)
STAN	Lofton 49 pass from Benjamin (Nabor kick)
STAN	FG Nabor 36
LSU	Alexander 7 run (Conway kick)
STAN	Lofton 2 pass from Benjamin (Nabor kick)
STAN	Nelson 35 pass from Benjamin (Nabor kick)

STAN	TEAM STATISTICS	LSU
21	First Downs	21
103	Rushing Yards	307
23-36-0	Passing	7-23-3
269	Passing Yards	68
372	Total Yards	375
2-(-2)	Punt Returns - Yards	1-0
2-39	Kickoff Returns - Yards	2-25
6-36.0	Punts - Average	4-35.0
0-0	Fumbles - Lost	2-1
7-65	Penalties - Yards	5-45

INDIVIDUAL LEADERS

RUSHING
STAN: Nelson 11-36; Finley 7-30.
LSU: Alexander 31-197, 1 TD; Simmons 11-47.

PASSING
STAN: Benjamin 23-36, 269 yards, 3 TD.
LSU: Ensminger 7-21, 55 yards, 1 TD.

RECEIVING
STAN: Lofton 4 -79, 2 TD; Nelson 6-77, 1 TD.
LSU: Simmons 2-26; Quintela 2-11, 1 TD.

December 23, 1978
Texas 42, Maryland 0

	1st	2nd	3rd	4th	FINAL
TEX	21	7	14	0	42
MD	0	0	0	0	0

SCORING SUMMARY

TEX	L. Jones 7 run (Erxleben kick)
TEX	J. Jones 1 run (Erxleben kick)
TEX	L. Jones 29 pass from McBath (Erxleben kick)
TEX	McBath 2 run (Erxleben kick)
TEX	J. Jones 14 run (Erxleben kick)
TEX	H. Jones 32 run (Erxleben kick)

TEX	TEAM STATISTICS	MD
18	First Downs	20
224	Rushing Yards	34
2-7-0	Passing	17-43-4
45	Passing Yards	214
269	Total Yards	248
3-22	Punt Returns - Yards	1-6
0-0	Kickoff Returns - Yards	0-0
7-41.0	Punts - Average	8-37.0
3-1	Fumbles - Lost	2-1
7-42	Penalties - Yards	5-35

INDIVIDUAL LEADERS

RUSHING
TEX: H. Jones 14 -104, 1TD; J. Jones 19-100, 2 TD.
MD: Atkins 10-15; Wysocki 2-15.

PASSING
TEX: McBath 2-5-0, 45 yards, 1 TD.
MD: O'Hare 12-27, 146 yards; Trice 5-16, 68 yards.

RECEIVING
TEX: L. Jones 2-45, 1 TD.
MD: Richards 5-52; Carinci 4-52.

December 22, 1979
Washington 14, Texas 7

	1st	2nd	3rd	4th	FINAL
WASH	0	14	0	0	14
TEX	0	7	0	0	7

SCORING SUMMARY

WASH	Skansi 18 pass from Flick (Lansford kick)
WASH	Mackey 4 run (Lansford kick)
TEX	Beck 5 pass from Little (Goodson kick)

WASH	TEAM STATISTICS	TEX
11	First Downs	15
98	Rushing Yards	199
7-15-1	Passing	4-15-1
67	Passing Yards	37
165	Total Yards	236
1-6	Punt Returns - Yards	3-11
2-30	Kickoff Returns - Yards	0-0
7-39.0	Punts - Average	4-39.0
1-1	Fumbles - Lost	3-3
4-30	Penalties - Yards	4-38

INDIVIDUAL LEADERS

RUSHING
WASH: Tyler 19-70; Coby 7-26.
TEX: Beck 16-98; Clark 19-61.

PASSING
WASH: Flick 6-14-1, 57 yards, 1 TD.
TEX: McIvor 3-11-1, 32 yards.

RECEIVING
WASH: Skansi 5-52, 1 TD; Bayle 1-11.
TEX: Koenning 2-18; Beck 1-5, 1 TD.

DECEMBER 27, 1980
NEBRASKA 31, MISSISSIPPI STATE 17

	1ST	2ND	3RD	4TH	FINAL
NEB	7	10	7	7	31
MSU	0	0	3	14	17

SCORING SUMMARY
NEB	Brown 23 run (Seibel kick)
NEB	FG Seibel 22
NEB	Finn 8 pass from Quinn (Seibel kick)
MSU	FG Moore 47
NEB	Franklin 2 run (Seibel kick)
MSU	Bond 1 run (Morgan kick)
NEB	McCrady 52 pass from Quinn (Seibel kick)
MSU	Haddix 3 pass from Bond (Morgan kick)

NEB	TEAM STATISTICS	MSU
16	First Downs	15
159	Rushing Yards	93
9-19-1	Passing	7-19-2
159	Passing Yards	102
318	Total Yards	195
3-32	Punt Returns - Yards	1-(-3)
2-39	Kickoff Returns - Yards	4-116
8-42.0	Punts - Average	5-50.0
1-1	Fumbles - Lost	5-4
4-37	Penalties - Yards	4-30

INDIVIDUAL LEADERS

RUSHING
NEB: Franklin 17-67, 1 TD; Redwine 13-42.
MSU: King 23-96; Haddix 4-14.

PASSING
NEB: Quinn 9-19-2, 159 yards, 2 TD.
MSU: Bond 7-19-1, 102 yards, 1 TD.

RECEIVING
NEB: McCrady 2-107, 1 TD; Brown 2-16.
MSU: McDole 4-69; Price 1-25.

DECEMBER 26, 1981
OKLAHOMA 40, HOUSTON 14

	1ST	2ND	3RD	4TH	FINAL
OKLA	7	0	3	30	40
HOU	0	7	0	7	14

SCORING SUMMARY
OKLA	Shepard 34 run (Keeling kick)
HOU	Wilson 1 run (Clendenen kick)
OKLA	FG Keeling 32
OKLA	Shepard 1 run (Keeling kick)
OKLA	FG Keeling 49
OKLA	Sims 30 run (Keeling kick)
HOU	Jordan 6 run (Clendenen kick)
OKLA	Mills 2 run (kick failed)
OKLA	Truitt 28 interception return (Keeling kick)

OKLA	TEAM STATISTICS	HOU
15	First Downs	26
409	Rushing Yards	157
1-5-1	Passing	18-29-1
-2	Passing Yards	228
407	Total Yards	385
0-0	Punt Returns - Yards	4-13
0-0	Kickoff Returns - Yards	3-59
5-38.0	Punts - Average	6-37.0
2-1	Fumbles - Lost	4-3
7-48	Penalties - Yards	2-27

INDIVIDUAL LEADERS

RUSHING
OKLA: Sims 15-181, 1 TD; Shepard 17-107, 2 TD.
HOU: Polk 19-74; Franklin 4-29.

PASSING
OKLA: Shepard 1-5-1, -2 yards.
HOU: L. Wilson 17-28-1, 216 yards.

RECEIVING
OKLA: Ross 1-(-2).
HOU: Durham 1-60; Ford 6-52.

DECEMBER 25, 1982
NORTH CAROLINA 26, TEXAS 10

	1ST	2ND	3RD	4TH	FINAL
UNC	0	3	0	23	26
TEX	7	3	0	0	10

SCORING SUMMARY
TEX	Mullins recovers blocked punt in endzone (Allegre kick)
UNC	FG Rogers 53
TEX	FG Allegre 24
UNC	FG Rogers 47
UNC	FG Barwick 24
UNC	FG Barwick 42
UNC	Horton 3 run (Barwick kick)
UNC	Wilcher recovers fumble in endzone (Barwick kick)

UNC	TEAM STATISTICS	TEX
15	First Downs	10
224	Rushing Yards	80
3-11-0	Passing	6-23-1
10	Passing Yards	50
234	Total Yards	130
0-0	Punt Returns - Yards	1-0
2-30	Kickoff Returns - Yards	1-17
6-26.0	Punts - Average	5-32.0
3-3	Fumbles - Lost	2-2
4-20	Penalties - Yards	2-20

INDIVIDUAL LEADERS

RUSHING
UNC: Horton 27-119, 1 TD; Bryant 15-45.
TEX: Clark 14-56; Luck 7-32.

PASSING
UNC: Stankavage 3-11-0, 10 yards.
TEX: Dodge 6-22-1, 50 yards.

RECEIVING
UNC: Anthony 1-4; Bryant 1-3.
TEX: Micho 2-18; Mullins 1-14.

DECEMBER 24, 1983
ALABAMA 28, SMU 7

	1ST	2ND	3RD	4TH	FINAL
ALA	14	14	0	0	28
SMU	0	0	7	0	7

SCORING SUMMARY
ALA	Moore 1 run (Tiffin kick)
ALA	Moore 11 run (Tiffin kick)
ALA	Lewis 1 run (Tiffin kick)
ALA	Jones 19 pass from Lewis (Tiffin kick)
SMU	Pleasant 15 pass from McIlhenny (Herrell kick)

ALA	TEAM STATISTICS	SMU
23	First Downs	13
251	Rushing Yards	194
9-14-0	Passing	14-27-2
148	Passing Yards	148
399	Total Yards	342
2-21	Punt Returns - Yards	1-6
1-34	Kickoff Returns - Yards	3-43
6-40.0	Punts - Average	4-41.0
1-1	Fumbles - Lost	3-3
3-25	Penalties - Yards	0-0

INDIVIDUAL LEADERS

RUSHING
ALA: Moore 28-113, 2 TD; Goode 7-59.
SMU: Atkins 9-116; Dupard 13-51.

PASSING
ALA: Lewis 9-14-0, 148 yards, 1 TD.
SMU: McIlhenny 14-27-2, 148 yards, 1 TD.

RECEIVING
ALA: Jones 2-36 yards, 1 TD; Richardson 1-32.
SMU: Pleasant 3-67, 1 TD; Morris 5-63.

DECEMBER 22, 1984
MARYLAND 28, TENNESSEE 27

	1ST	2ND	3RD	4TH	FINAL
MD	0	0	22	6	28
TENN	10	11	6	0	27

SCORING SUMMARY
TENN	Jones 2 run (Reveiz kick)
TENN	FG Reveiz 24
TENN	FG Reveiz 52
TENN	McGee 6 pass from Robinson (McGee pass from Robinson)
MD	Neal 57 run (pass failed)
MD	FG Atkinson 23
MD	Badanjek 1 run (run failed)
MD	Edmunds 40 pass from Reich (Atkinson kick)
TENN	Panuska 100 kickoff return (pass failed)
MD	Badanjek 1 run (pass failed)

MD	TEAM STATISTICS	TENN
22	First Downs	13
229	Rushing Yards	148
17-28-1	Passing	15-24-0
201	Passing Yards	132
430	Total Yards	280
4-56	Punt Returns - Yards	3-24
4-47.0	Punts - Average	5-42.0
2-2	Fumbles - Lost	1-0
8-63	Penalties - Yards	6-49
35:57	Possession Time	24:03

INDIVIDUAL LEADERS

RUSHING
MD: Neal 12-107, 1 TD; Badanjek 21-90, 2 TD.
TENN: Jones 16-69, 1 TD; Robinson 8-43.

PASSING
MD: Reich 17-28-1, 201 yards, 1 TD.
TENN: Robinson 15-24 -0, 132 yards, 1 TD.

RECEIVING
MD : Hill 4-69; Edmunds 3-53, 1 TD.
TENN: McGee 6-66, 1 TD; Howard 3-22.

DECEMBER 28, 1985
GEORGIA 13, ARIZONA 13

	1ST	2ND	3RD	4TH	FINAL
UGA	0	3	0	10	13
ARIZ	0	3	10	0	13

SCORING SUMMARY
UGA	FG Crumley 37
ARIZ	FG Zendejas 22
ARIZ	FG Zendejas 52
ARIZ	Rudolph 35 interception return (Zendejas kick)
UGA	FG Jacobs 44
UGA	Tate 2 run (Jacobs kick)

UGA	TEAM STATISTICS	ARIZ
18	First Downs	11
211	Rushing Yards	99
5-8-2	Passing	13-22-0
51	Passing Yards	133
262	Total Yards	232
1-3	Punt Returns - Yards	0-0
2-31	Kickoff Returns - Yards	3-63
2-27.0	Punts - Average	4-40.0
1-1	Fumbles - Lost	2-2
4-20	Penalties - Yards	4-40

INDIVIDUAL LEADERS

RUSHING
UGA: Tate 22-71, 1 TD; Henderson 12-59.
ARIZ: Adams 13-51; Jenkins 6-22.

PASSING
UGA: Jackson 4 -7-2, 42 yards.
ARIZ: Jenkins 13-22-0, 133 yards.

RECEIVING
UGA : Tate 2-16; Sadowski 1-15.
ARIZ: Fairholm 4-40; Adams 3-33.

DECEMBER 25, 1986
ALABAMA 28, WASHINGTON 6

	1ST	2ND	3RD	4TH	FINAL
ALA	0	7	14	7	28
WASH	0	6	0	0	6

SCORING SUMMARY
ALA Humphrey 64 run (Tiffin kick)
WASH FG Jaeger 31
WASH FG Jaeger 34
ALA Richardson 32 pass from Shula (Tiffin kick)
ALA Humphrey 18 pass from Shula (Tiffin kick)
ALA Humphrey 3 run (Tiffin kick)

ALA	TEAM STATISTICS	WASH
13	First Downs	16
215	Rushing Yards	102
15-26-0	Passing	20-43-2
176	Passing Yards	189
391	Total Yards	291
3-24	Punt Returns - Yards	5-68
9-45.0	Punts - Average	8-35.0
0-0	Fumbles - Lost	4-1

INDIVIDUAL LEADERS
RUSHING
ALA: Humphrey 28-159, 2 TD; Wright 4 -32.
WASH: Weathersby 9-28 yards; Fenney 11-19.
PASSING
ALA: Shula 15-26-0, 176 yards, 2 TD.
WASH: Chandler 20-43-2, 189 yards.
RECEIVING
ALA: Richardson 2-59, 1 TD; Humphrey 5-43, 1 TD.
WASH: Hill 5-77; Weathersby 5-45.

DECEMBER 25, 1987
OKLAHOMA STATE 35, WEST VIRGINIA 33

	1ST	2ND	3RD	4TH	FINAL
OKST	14	0	14	7	35
WVU	7	17	3	6	33

SCORING SUMMARY
OKST Thomas 5 run (Blanchard kick)
WVU Brown 1 run (Baumann kick)
OKST Thomas 9 run (Blanchard kick)
WVU Brown 5 run (Baumann kick)
WVU FG Baumann 33
WVU Warren 23 pass interception (Baumann kick)
OKST Thomas 4 run (Blanchard kick)
WVU FG Baumann 38
OKST Dillard 6 pass from Gundy (Blanchard kick)
OKST Thomas 4 run (Blanchard kick)
WVU Taylor 6 run (pass failed)

OKST	TEAM STATISTICS	WVU
23	First Downs	22
185	Rushing Yards	331
12-18-2	Passing	2-7-1
161	Passing Yards	54
346	Total Yards	385
3-29	Punt Returns - Yards	0-0
2-33.0	Punts - Average	3-41.0
0-0	Fumbles - Lost	1-0

INDIVIDUAL LEADERS
RUSHING
OKST: Thomas 33-157, 4 TD; Sanders 6-19.
WVU: Brown 32-167, 2 TD; Harris 24-103.
PASSING
OKST: Gundy 12-18-2, 161 yards, 1 TD.
WVU: Harris 7-21-1, 54 yards.
RECEIVING
OKST: Dykes 3-72; Thomas 3-20.
WVU: Bell 1-45; Winn 1-9.

DECEMBER 24, 1988
ALABAMA 29, ARMY 28

	1ST	2ND	3RD	4TH	FINAL
ALA	3	10	7	9	29
ARMY	7	7	14	0	28

SCORING SUMMARY
ARMY Mayweather 1 run (Walker kick)
ALA FG Doyle 37
ARMY McWilliams 30 run (Walker kick)
ALA FG Doyle 22
ALA Battle 7 pass from Smith (Doyle kick)
ALA Payne 23 pass from Smith (Doyle kick)
ARMY Mayweather 3 run (Walker kick)
ARMY Miller 57 interception return (Walker kick)
ALA FG Doyle 32
ALA Casteal 2 run (run failed)

ALA	TEAM STATISTICS	ARMY
29	First Downs	19
95	Rushing Yards	350
33-52-1	Passing	0-6-1
412	Passing Yards	0
507	Total Yards	350
3-32	Punt Returns - Yards	1-14
4-45.0	Punts - Average	5-39.0
1-0	Fumbles - Lost	1-0

INDIVIDUAL LEADERS
RUSHING
ALA: Hall 12-57; Shaw 7-38.
ARMY: Barnett 14-177; Mayweather 19-80, 2 TD.
PASSING
ALA: Smith 33-52-1, 412 yards, 2 TD.
ARMY: Mayweather 0-6-1, 0 yards.

DECEMBER 30, 1989
PITTSBURGH 31, TEXAS A&M 28

	1ST	2ND	3RD	4TH	FINAL
PITT	7	10	7	7	31
A&M	7	3	12	6	28

SCORING SUMMARY
PITT Richards 12 run (Frazier kick)
A&M Pavlas 9 run (Talbot kick)
PITT FG Frazier 24
A&M FG Talbot 39
PITT Redmond 8 pass from Van Pelt (Frazier kick)
PITT Van Pelt 1 run (Frazier kick)
A&M McAfee 31 run (run failed)
A&M McAfee 1 run (pass failed)
A&M Simmons 5 run (run failed)
PITT Tuten 44 pass from Van Pelt (Frazier kick)

PITT	TEAM STATISTICS	A&M
22	First Downs	21
176	Rushing Yards	252
20-40-1	Passing	16-33-3
354	Passing Yards	196
530	Total Yards	448
4-33	Punt Returns - Yards	2-5
5-42	Punts - Average	4-46
2-1	Fumbles - Lost	1-0

INDIVIDUAL LEADERS
RUSHING
PITT: Richards 23-156, 1 TD; Walker 8-29.
A&M: Wilson 16-145; McAfee 15-94, 2 TD.
PASSING
PITT: Van Pelt 20-40-1, 354 yards, 2 TD.
A&M: Pavlas 10-20, 152 yards.
RECEIVING
PITT: Truitt 4-124; Tuten 4-96, 1 TD.
A&M: Waddle 6-105; Wilson 2-31.

DECEMBER 31, 1990
MICHIGAN STATE 17, SOUTHERN CAL 16

	1ST	2ND	3RD	4TH	FINAL
MSU	0	7	10	0	17
USC	7	0	3	6	16

SCORING SUMMARY
USC Wellman 7 pass from Marinovich (Rodriguez kick)
MSU Hickson 18 run (Langeloh kick)
USC FG Rodriguez 20
MSU Hawkins 21 pass from Enos (Rodriguez kick)
MSU FG Langeloh 52
USC FG Rodriguez 54
USC FG Rodriguez 43

MSU	TEAM STATISTICS	USC
12	First Downs	21
84	Rushing Yards	156
9-17-1	Passing	19-32-3
131	Passing Yards	180
215	Total Yards	336
1-7	Punt Returns - Yards	2-27
5-38.0	Punts - Average	1-50.0
1-1	Fumbles - Lost	2-1

INDIVIDUAL LEADERS
RUSHING
MSU: Hickson 14-68, 1 TD; Duckett 8-18.
USC: Royster 32-125; Lockwood 5-18.
PASSING
MSU: Enos 9-17-1, 131 yards, 1 TD.
USC: Marinovich 18-30-3, 174 yards, 1 TD.
RECEIVING
MSU: Hawkins 6-106, 1 TD; Roy 2-14.
USC: Lockwood 5-41; Morton 3-36.

DECEMBER 31, 1991
UCLA 6, ILLINOIS 3

	1ST	2ND	3RD	4TH	FINAL
UCLA	3	0	0	3	6
ILL	0	0	3	0	3

SCORING SUMMARY
UCLA FG Perez 32
ILL FG Richardson 27
UCLA FG Perez 19

UCLA	TEAM STATISTICS	ILL
14	First Downs	19
92	Rushing Yards	119
17-28-1	Passing	17-38-3
176	Passing Yards	189
268	Total Yards	308
4-58	Punt Returns - Yards	2-2
6-40.0	Punts - Average	7-34.0
1-1	Fumbles - Lost	2-1

INDIVIDUAL LEADERS
RUSHING
UCLA: Williams 23-52; Carter 6-22.
ILL: Feagin 12-71; Bell 6-22.
PASSING
UCLA: Maddox 17-28-1, 176 yards.
ILL: Verduzco 17-38-3, 189 yards.
RECEIVING
UCLA: LaChapelle 5-69; Davis 4-41.
ILL: Wright 9-94; Turner 1-53.

December 31, 1992
Baylor 20, Arizona 15

	1ST	2ND	3RD	4TH	FINAL
BU	0	7	7	6	20
ARIZ	3	10	0	2	15

SCORING SUMMARY
ARIZ   FG McLaughlin 22
ARIZ   Malauulu 7 run (McLaughlin kick)
BU   Bonner 61 pass from Jackson (Weir kick)
ARIZ   FG McLaughlin 20
BU   Bonner 69 pass from Joe (Delaney kick)
BU   FG Weir 32
BU   FG Weir 35
ARIZ   Safety (Delaney intentionally downs ball in end zone)

BU	TEAM STATISTICS	ARIZ
12	First Downs	23
47	Rushing Yards	136
20-38-0	Passing	8-24-0
202	Passing Yards	282
249	Total Yards	418
1-1	Punt Returns - Yards	4-36
6-39.0	Punts - Average	5-33.0
4-0	Fumbles - Lost	2-2

INDIVIDUAL LEADERS
RUSHING
BU: Strait 10-23; Bell 4 -17.
ARIZ: Carter 15-49; Malauulu 11-47, 1 TD.
PASSING
BU: Joe 7-23-0, 141 yards, 1 TD.
ARIZ: Malauulu 20-38-0, 282 yards.
RECEIVING
BU: Bonner 5-166, 2 TD; McKenzie 1-14.
ARIZ: Dickey 9-108; Levy 4-85.

December 24, 1993
Oklahoma 41, Texas Tech 10

	1ST	2ND	3RD	4TH	FINAL
OKLA	14	14	0	13	41
TT	0	3	7	0	10

SCORING SUMMARY
OKLA   Chandler 2 run (Blanton kick)
OKLA   Brady 9 pass from Gundy (Blanton kick)
TT   FG Davis 22
OKLA   Warren 34 pass from Gundy (Blanton kick)
OKLA   Brady 15 pass from Gundy (Blanton kick)
TT   Morris 2 run (Davis kick)
OKLA   Moore 32 run (Blanton kick)
OKLA   Moore 6 run

OKLA	TEAM STATISTICS	TT
21	First Downs	18
177	Rushing Yards	116
15-26-1	Passing	19-37-4
215	Passing Yards	199
392	Total Yards	315
5-60	Punt Returns - Yards	2-17
7-48.0	Punts - Average	4-2.0
4-2	Fumbles - Lost	0-0

INDIVIDUAL LEADERS
RUSHING
OKLA: Moore 15-85, 2 TD; Brown 3-63.
TT: Morris 27-95, 1 TD; Hall 5-19.
PASSING
OKLA: Gundy 15-26-1, 215 yards, 3 TD.
TT: Hall 19-37-4, 199 yards.
RECEIVING
OKLA: Warren 4-93, 1 TD; Allen 3-40.
TT: Mitchell 6-86; Baker 3-27.

December 30, 1994
Texas 35, North Carolina 31

	1ST	2ND	3RD	4TH	FINAL
TEX	7	14	0	14	35
UNC	7	10	0	14	31

SCORING SUMMARY
UNC   C. Johnson 11 run (Pignetti kick)
TEX   Holmes 1 run (Dawson kick)
TEX   Watkins 8 fumble return (Dawson kick)
UNC   FG Pignetti 25
TEX   Holmes 1 run (Dawson kick)
UNC   Wall 8 pass from Thomas (Pignetti kick)
UNC   Wall 82 punt return (Pignetti kick)
UNC   Barnes 50 pass from Thomas (Pignetti kick)
TEX   Holmes 9 run (Dawson kick)
TEX   Holmes 5 run (Dawson kick)

TEX	TEAM STATISTICS	UNC
26	First Downs	25
229	Rushing Yards	180
15-32-1	Passing	23-40-1
196	Passing Yards	298
425	Total Yards	478
5-175	Punt Returns - Yards	6-136
6-35.0	Punts - Average	5-35.0
3-1	Fumbles - Lost	2-1

INDIVIDUAL LEADERS
RUSHING
TEX: Holmes 27-165, 4 TD; Brown 7-43.
UNC: C. Johnson 17-70, 1 TD; L. Johnson 15-70.
PASSING
TEX: Brown 15-31-1, 196 yards.
UNC: Thomas 23-39-1, 298 yards, 2 TD.
RECEIVING
TEX: Fitzgerald 6-60; Holmes 2-44.
UNC: Barnes 9-165, 1 TD; Wall 7-82, 1 TD.

December 29, 1995
Iowa 38, Washington 18

	1ST	2ND	3RD	4TH	FINAL
IOWA	10	11	10	7	38
WASH	0	0	6	12	18

SCORING SUMMARY
IOWA   Shaw 58 run (Bromert kick)
IOWA   FG Hurley 49
IOWA   Safety (Washington punt snap out of end zone)
IOWA   FG Bromert 33
IOWA   FG Bromert 34
IOWA   FG Hurley 47
IOWA   FG Hurley 50
WASH   Pathon 30 pass from Fortney (pass failed)
IOWA   Burger 8 run (Bromert kick)
IOWA   Burger 1 run (Bromert kick)
WASH   Coleman 3 pass from Huard (pass failed)
WASH   Conwell 20 pass from Huard (run failed)

IOWA	TEAM STATISTICS	WASH
18	First Downs	14
286	Rushing Yards	96
11-26-2	Passing	19-37-0
135	Passing Yards	250
421	Total Yards	346
7-22	Punt Returns - Yards	5-3
5-39.0	Punts - Average	7-27.0
1-0	Fumbles - Lost	3-3

INDIVIDUAL LEADERS
RUSHING
IOWA: Shaw 21-135, 1 TD; Banks 13-122.
WASH: Neal 9-65; Shehee 8-38.
PASSING
IOWA: Sherman 11-24 -1, 135 yards.
WASH: Huard 14 -26-0, 194 yards, 2 TD.
RECEIVING
IOWA: Slutzker 4-66; Dwight 3-40.
WASH: Conwell 4 -71, 1 TD; Pathon 4-62, 1 TD.

December 31, 1996
Stanford 38, Michigan State 0

	1ST	2ND	3RD	4TH	FINAL
STAN	7	14	10	7	38
MSU	0	0	0	0	0

SCORING SUMMARY
STAN   Pruitt 50 lateral return of an interception by Madsen (Miller kick)
STAN   Ritchie 8 pass from Hutchinson (Miller kick)
STAN   Salina 1 run (Miller kick)
STAN   FG Miller 25
STAN   Dunn 27 run (Miller kick)
STAN   Allen 9 run of blocked punt (Miller kick)

STAN	TEAM STATISTICS	MSU
25	First Downs	13
257	Rushing Yards	68
23-30-1	Passing	13-33-3
238	Passing Yards	151
495	Total Yards	219
7-94	Punt Returns - Yards	2-19
2-52.5	Punts - Average	9-41.9
3-1	Fumbles - Lost	3-2

INDIVIDUAL LEADERS
RUSHING
STAN: Bookman 11-103; Mitchell 16-74.
MSU: Goldbourne 12-51; Irvin 9-31.
PASSING
STAN: Hutchinson 22-28-1, 135 yards, 1 TD.
MSU: Schultz 8-21-2, 68 yards; Burke 4-7-0, 71 yards.
RECEIVING
STAN: Dunn 4 -63; Manning 3-42.
MSU: Long 2-46; Mason 4-43.

December 31, 1997
Arizona State 17, Iowa 7

	1ST	2ND	3RD	4TH	FINAL
ASU	0	10	7	0	17
IOWA	0	0	0	7	7

SCORING SUMMARY
ASU   Jackson 35 pass from Campbell (Nycz kick)
ASU   FG Nycz 20
ASU   Martin 1 run (Nycz kick)
IOWA   Carter 26 pass from Reiners (Bromert kick)

ASU	TEAM STATISTICS	IOWA
18	First Downs	10
268	Rushing Yards	19
5-11-0	Passing	12-27-0
109	Passing Yards	190
377	Total Yards	209
4-26	Punt Returns - Yards	4-16
9-36.1	Punts - Average	8-48.9
2-0	Fumbles - Lost	2-1

INDIVIDUAL LEADERS
RUSHING
ASU: Martin 27-169, 1 TD; Redmond 13-50.
IOWA: Banks 14-52; Thein 3-5.
PASSING
ASU: Campbell 5-11-0, 109 yards, 1 TD.
IOWA: Sherman 8-22-0, 120 yards; Reiners 4 -5-0, 70 yards, 1 TD.
RECEIVING
ASU: Jackson 2-44, 1 TD; Mitchell 1-41.
IOWA: Gibson 3-79; Dwight 3-51.

December 31, 1998
TCU 28, Southern Cal 19

	1ST	2ND	3RD	4TH	FINAL
TCU	14	7	7	0	28
USC	0	3	13	3	19

SCORING SUMMARY

TCU	Mitchell 3 run (Kaylakie kick)
TCU	Mitchell 60 run (Kaylakie kick)
TCU	Batteaux 8 run (Kaylakie kick)
USC	FG Abrams 34
TCU	Batteaux 3 run (Kaylakie kick)
USC	Miller 23 pass from Palmer (Abrams kick)
USC	Papadakis 1 run (pass failed)
USC	FG Abrams 46

TCU	TEAM STATISTICS	USC
18	First Downs	12
314	Rushing Yards	-23
4-6-0	Passing	17-28-0
51	Passing Yards	280
365	Total Yards	257
3-19	Punt Returns - Yards	1-(-6)
5-37.8	Punts - Average	6-45.8
0-0	Fumbles - Lost	1-0

INDIVIDUAL LEADERS

RUSHING
TCU: Mitchell 19-185, 2 TD; Batteaux 28-94, 2 TD.
USC: Morton 11-18; Papadakis 3-5, 1 TD.

PASSING
TCU: Batteaux 4-5-0, 51 yards.
USC: Palmer 17-28-0, 280 yards, 1 TD.

RECEIVING
TCU: Tomlinson 1-25; Maiden 1-22.
USC: Parker 4-104; Miller 3-67, 1 TD.

December 31, 1999
Oregon 24, Minnesota 20

	1ST	2ND	3RD	4TH	FINAL
ORE	0	7	10	7	24
MINN	7	0	6	7	20

SCORING SUMMARY

MINN	Johnson 1 pass from Cockerham (Nystrom kick)
ORE	Harrington 5 run (Villegas kick)
MINN	Bruce 38 pass from Cockerham (kick failed)
ORE	Harrington 3 run (Villegas kick)
ORE	FG Villegas 37
MINN	Johnson 7 pass from Cockerham (Nystrom kick)
ORE	Howry 10 pass from Harrington (Villegas kick)

ORE	TEAM STATISTICS	MINN
22	First Downs	19
156	Rushing Yards	96
20-43-0	Passing	19-37-2
232	Passing Yards	257
388	Total Yards	353
4-40	Punt Returns - Yards	3-20
8-40.6	Punts - Average	7-46.1
2-1	Fumbles - Lost	1-1
35:25	Possession Time	24:35

INDIVIDUAL LEADERS

RUSHING
ORE: Droughns 21-95; Ho-Ching 9-56.
MINN: Hamner 20-64; Cockerham 12-26.

PASSING
ORE: Harrington 20-43-0, 232 yards, 1 TD.
MINN: Cockerham 19-37-2, 257 yards, 3 TD.

RECEIVING
ORE: Hartley 7-113; Howry 3-54, 1 TD.
MINN: Leverson 6-126; Johnson 7-54, 2 TD.

December 29, 2000
Wisconsin 21, UCLA 20

	1ST	2ND	3RD	4TH	FINAL
WISC	7	0	7	7	21
UCLA	10	7	3	0	20

SCORING SUMMARY

WISC	Evans 54 pass from Bollinger (Pisetsky kick)
UCLA	Mitchell 64 pass from Paus (Griffith kick)
UCLA	FG Griffith 31
UCLA	Foster 7 run (Griffith kick)
UCLA	FG Griffith 25
WISC	Chambers 3 pass from Bollinger (Pisetsky kick)
WISC	Bennett 6 run (Pisetsky kick)

WISC	TEAM STATISTICS	UCLA
18	First Downs	20
177	Rushing Yards	114
9-18-1	Passing	20-33-1
130	Passing Yards	282
307	Total Yards	396
2-12	Punt Returns - Yards	0-0
5-37.2	Punts - Average	3-45.7
0-0	Fumbles - Lost	0-0
29:38	Possession Time	30:22

INDIVIDUAL LEADERS

RUSHING
WISC: Bennett 16-83, 1 TD; Bollinger 16-55.
UCLA: Foster 26-107, 1 TD; Lewis 4 -8.

PASSING
WISC: Bollinger 8-16-0, 107 yards, 2 TD.
UCLA: McEwan 12-18-1, 135 yards; Paus 8-15-0, 147 yards, 1 TD.

RECEIVING
WISC: Evans 3-86, 1 TD; Chambers 4 -30, 1 TD.
UCLA: Mitchell 9-180, 1 TD; Poli-Dixon 7-50.

December 31, 2001
Washington State 33, Purdue 27

	1ST	2ND	3RD	4TH	FINAL
WSU	14	3	13	3	33
PU	0	20	0	7	27

SCORING SUMMARY

WSU	David 45 interception return (Dunning kick)
WSU	Bush 46 pass from Gesser (Dunning kick)
PU	Lowe 1 run (Dorsch kick)
PU	FG Dorsch 28
WSU	FG Dunning 47
PU	Stubblefield 3 pass from Orton (Dorsch kick)
PU	FG Dorsch 51
WSU	FG Dunning 34
WSU	Gesser 1 run (Dunning kick)
WSU	FG Dunning 30
WSU	FG Dunning 37
PU	Stubblefield 51 pass from Orton (Dorsch kick)

WSU	TEAM STATISTICS	PU
15	First Downs	28
81	Rushing Yards	55
15-41-3	Passing	38-75-4
281	Passing Yards	419
362	Total Yards	474
5-29	Punt Returns - Yards	4-31
6-44.3	Punts - Average	6-38.8
2-1	Fumbles - Lost	2-1
26:08	Possession Time	33:52

INDIVIDUAL LEADERS

RUSHING
WSU: Minnich 17-51; Cox 1-20.
PU: Lowe 17-45, 1 TD; Harris 5-27.

PASSING
WSU: Gesser 15-40-3, 281 yards, 1 TD.
PU: Orton 38-74 -4, 419 yards, 2 TD.

RECEIVING
WSU: McElrath 5-116; Riley 6-65.
PU: Stubblefield 9-196, 2 TD; Standeford 12-103.

December 31, 2002
Purdue 34, Washington 24

	1ST	2ND	3RD	4TH	FINAL
PU	0	14	17	3	34
WASH	17	0	0	7	24

SCORING SUMMARY

WASH	Reddick 7 pass from Pickett (Anderson kick)
WASH	Cooper 31 fumble recovery (Anderson kick)
WASH	FG Anderson 38
PU	Standeford 7 pass from Orton (Lacevic kick)
PU	Williams fumble recovery in end zone (Lacevic kick)
PU	FG Lacevic 22
PU	Harris 10 run (Lacevic kick)
PU	Gardner 19 fumble recovery (Lacevic kick)
PU	FG Lacevic 29
WASH	Reddick 12 pass from Pickett (Anderson kick)

PU	TEAM STATISTICS	WASH
24	First Downs	23
117	Rushing Yards	44
25-37-0	Passing	25-54-1
283	Passing Yards	272
400	Total Yards	316
4-39.2	Punts - Average	5-36.4
13-118	Penalties - Yards	5-44

INDIVIDUAL LEADERS

RUSHING
PU: Harris 23-93, 1 TD; Jones 9-28.
WASH: Alexis 7-18; Cleman 7-13.

PASSING
PU: Orton 25-37-0, 283 yards, 2 TD.
WASH: Pickett 25-54-1, 272 yards, 2 TD.

RECEIVING
PU: Standeford 10-105, 1 TD; Stubblefield 7-92.
WASH: Williams 5-64; Reddick 6-63, 2 TD.

December 31, 2003
Minnesota 31, Oregon 30

	1ST	2ND	3RD	4TH	FINAL
MINN	0	14	14	3	31
ORE	0	17	7	6	30

SCORING SUMMARY

ORE	Rosario 9 pass from Clemens (Siegel kick)
MINN	Tapeh 1 run (Lloyd kick)
ORE	Parker 18 pass from Clemens (Siegel kick)
MINN	Tapeh 1 run (Lloyd kick)
ORE	FG Siegel 30
MINN	Tapeh 6 run (Lloyd kick)
ORE	Parker 40 pass from Clemens (Siegel kick)
MINN	Maroney 22 run (Lloyd kick)
ORE	FG Siegel 32
ORE	FG Siegel 47
MINN	FG Lloyd 42

MINN	TEAM STATISTICS	ORE
23	First Downs	25
241	Rushing Yards	77
12-21-0	Passing	33-44-1
172	Passing Yards	376
413	Total Yards	453
1-4	Punt Returns - Yards	2-47
2-47	Kickoff Returns - Yards	5-97
3-38.7	Punts - Average	4-29.0
2-1	Fumbles - Lost	0-0
3-19	Penalties - Yards	5-40
31:33	Possession Time	28:27

INDIVIDUAL LEADERS

RUSHING
MINN: Maroney 15-131, 1 TD; Tapeh 13-40, 3 TD.
ORE: Whitehead 6-35; Washington 6-28.

PASSING
MINN: Abdul-Khaliq 12-21-0, 172 yards.
ORE: Clemens 32-42-1, 363 yards, 3 TD.

RECEIVING
MINN: Hosack 6-107; Patterson 3-33.
ORE: Parker 16-200, 2 TD; Williams 4-49.

DECEMBER 31, 2004

ARIZONA STATE 27, PURDUE 23

	1ST	2ND	3RD	4TH	FINAL
ASU	3	0	7	17	27
PU	0	2	7	14	23

SCORING SUMMARY

ASU	FG Ainsworth 22
PU	Saftey
PU	Hare 80 pass from Orton (Jones kick)
ASU	Hagan 27 pass from Keller (Ainsworth kick)
PU	Stubblefield 5 pass from Orton (Jones kick)
ASU	FG Ainsworth 34
ASU	Burgess 41 pass from Keller (Ainsworth kick)
PU	Davis 6 pass from Orton (Jones kick)
ASU	Burgess 19 pass from Keller (Ainsworth kick)

ASU	TEAM STATISTICS	PU
26	First Downs	15
158	Rushing Yards	66
25-45-0	Passing	23-47-0
370	Passing Yards	281
528	Total Yards	347
2-1	Fumbles - Lost	2-2
9-66	Penalties - Yards	6-55
32:19	Possession Time	27:41

INDIVIDUAL LEADERS

RUSHING
ASU: Burgess 20-125; Jones 9-35.
PU: Jones 5-30.

PASSING
ASU: Keller 25-45-0, 370 yards, 3 TD.
PU: Orton 23-47-0, 281 yards, 3 TD.

RECEIVING
ASU: Hagan 9-182, 1 TD; Burgess 3-64, 2 TD.
PU: Hare 3-97, 1 TD; Stubblefield 7-81, 1 TD.

COTTON BOWL

PROFILE

Site: Dallas
Stadium: Cotton Bowl
Capacity: 68,252
Surface: Grass

PLAYING SITES

Fair Park Stadium, 1937
Cotton Bowl, since 1938

NAME CHANGES

Cotton Bowl Classic, 1937-88
Mobil Cotton Bowl Classic, 1989-95
Cotton Bowl Classic, 1996
Southwestern Bell Cotton Bowl Classic, 1997-2000
SBC Cotton Bowl Classic, since 2001

SEASON	DATE	PRE-GAME RANK	TEAMS	SCORE	FINAL RANK	MOST VALUABLE PLAYERS	ATT.
1936	Jan. 1, 1937	16	TCU	16		Ki Aldrich, TCU, C	17,000
		20	Marquette	6		Sammy Baugh, TCU, QB, L.D. Meyer, TCU, E	
1937	Jan. 1, 1938	18	Rice	28		Ernie Lain, Rice, HB	37,000
		17	Colorado	14		Byron "Whizzer" White, Colorado, QB	
1938	Jan. 2, 1939		St. Mary's Coll.	20		Jerry Dowd, St. Mary's Coll., C	40,000
		11	Texas Tech	13		Elmer Tarbox, Texas Tech, HB	
1939	Jan. 1, 1940	12	Clemson	6		Banks McFadden, Clemson, B	20,000
		11	Boston College	3			
1940	Jan. 1, 1941	6	Texas A&M	13		Charles Henke, G, John Kimbrough, FB, Chip Routt, T, Texas A&M	45,500
		12	Fordham	12		Lou DeFilippo, C Joe Ungerer, T, Fordham	
1941	Jan. 1, 1942	20	Alabama	29		Jimmy Nelson, HB, Holt Rast, E, Don Whitmire, T, Alabama	38,000
		9	Texas A&M	21		Martin Ruby, Texas A&M, T	
1942	Jan. 1, 1943	11	Texas	14		Jack Freeman, G, Roy McKay, B, Stanley Mauldin, T, Texas	36,000
		5	Georgia Tech	7		Harvey Hardy, G, Jack Marshall, E, Georgia Tech	
1943	Jan. 1, 1944		Randolph Field	7		Martin Ruby, T, Glenn Dobbs, QB, Randolph Field	15,000
		14	Texas	7		Joe Parker, Texas, E	
1944	Jan. 1, 1945		Oklahoma State	34		Neill Armstrong, E, Bob Fenimore, RB, Oklahoma State	37,000
			TCU	0		Ralph Foster, DT, Oklahoma State	
1945	Jan. 1, 1946		Texas	40		Hub Bechtol, E, Bobby Layne, B, Texas	45,000
			Missouri	27		Jim Kekeris, Missouri, T	
1946	Jan. 1, 1947	16	Arkansas	0		Alton Baldwin, Arkansas, E	38,000
		8	LSU	0		Y.A. Tittle, LSU, QB	
1947	Jan. 1, 1948	4	Penn State	13		Steve Suhey, Penn State, G	43,000
		3	SMU	13		Doak Walker, SMU, RB	
1948	Jan. 1, 1949	10	SMU	21		Kyle Rote, RB, Doak Walker, RB, SMU	69,000
		9	Oregon	13		Brad Ecklund, C, Norm Van Brocklin, QB, Oregon	
1949	Jan. 2, 1950	5	Rice	27		Billy Burkhalter, HB, Joe Watson, C, James Williams, E, Rice	75,347
		16	North Carolina	13			
1950	Jan. 1, 1951	4	Tennessee	20		Andy Kozar, FB, Hank Lauricella, HB, Horace "Bud" Sherrod, DE, Tennessee	75,349
		3	Texas	14		Bud McFadin, Texas, G	
1951	Jan. 1, 1952	15	Kentucky	20		Emery Clark, HB, Ray Correll, G, Vito "Babe" Parilli, QB, Kentucky	75,347
		11	TCU	7		Keith Flowers, TCU, FB	
1952	Jan. 1, 1953	10	Texas	16		Richard Ochoa, FB, Harley Sewell, G, Texas	75,504
		8	Tennessee	0		Bob Griesbach, Tennessee, LB	
1953	Jan. 1, 1954	6	Rice	28		Richard Chapman, T, Dan Hart, E, Dicky Maegle, HB, Rice	75,504
		13	Alabama	6			
1954	Jan. 1, 1955		Georgia Tech	14		George Humphreys, Georgia Tech, FB	75,504
		10	Arkansas	6		Bud Brooks, Arkansas, G	
1955	Jan. 2, 1956	10	Mississippi	14		Buddy Alliston, Mississippi, G	75,504
		6	TCU	13		Eagle Day, Mississippi, QB	
1956	Jan. 1, 1957	14	TCU	28		Norman Hamilton, TCU, T	68,000
		8	Syracuse	27		Jim Brown, Syracuse, HB	
1957	Jan. 1, 1958	5	Navy	20		Tom Forrestal, Navy, QB	75,504
		8	Rice	7		Tony Stremic, Navy, G	
1958	Jan. 1, 1959	6	Air Force	0		Dave Phillips, Air Force, T	75,504
		10	TCU	0		Jack Spikes, TCU, FB	
1959	Jan. 1, 1960	1	Syracuse	23		Ernie Davis, Syracuse, HB	75,504
		4	Texas	14		Maurice Doke, Texas, G	
1960	Jan. 2, 1961	10	Duke	7		Dwight Bumgarner, Duke, T	74,000
		7	Arkansas	6		Lance Alworth, Arkansas, HB	
1961	Jan. 1, 1962	3	Texas	12		Mike Cotten, Texas, QB	75,504
		5	Mississippi	7		Bob Moses, Texas, E	
1962	Jan. 1, 1963	7	LSU	13		Lynn Amedee, LSU, QB	75,504
		4	Texas	0		Johnny Treadwell, Texas, G	
1963	Jan. 1, 1964	1	Texas	28		Scott Appleton, Texas, T	75,504
		2	Navy	6		Duke Carlisle, Texas, QB	
1964	Jan. 1, 1965	2	Arkansas	10		Ronnie Caveness, Arkansas, LB	75,504
		6	Nebraska	7		Fred Marshall, Arkansas, QB	
1965	Jan. 1, 1966		LSU	14	8	Joe Labruzzo, LSU, TB	76,200
		2	Arkansas	7	3	David McCormick, LSU, T	
1966	Dec. 31, 1966	4	Georgia	24		Kent Lawrence, Georgia, TB	75,400
		10	SMU	9		George Patton, Georgia, T	
1967	Jan. 1, 1968		Texas A&M	20		Grady Allen, DE, Edd Hargett, QB,	75,504
		9	Alabama	16		Bill Hobbs, LB, Texas A&M	
1968	Jan. 1, 1969	5	Texas	36	3	Tom Campbell, LB, Charles "Cotton" Speyrer, WR,	72,000
		8	Tennessee	13	13	James Street, QB, Texas	
1969	Jan. 1, 1970	1	Texas	21	1	Steve Worster, Texas, FB	73,000
		9	Notre Dame	17	5	Bob Olson, Notre Dame, LB	
1970	Jan. 1, 1971	6	Notre Dame	24	2	Clarence Ellis, Notre Dame, CB	72,000
		1	Texas	11	3	Eddie Phillips, Texas, QB	
1971	Jan. 1, 1972	10	Penn State	30	5	Bruce Bannon, Penn State, DE	72,000
		12	Texas	6	18	Lydell Mitchell, Penn State, RB	
1972	Jan. 1, 1973	7	Texas	17	3	Randy Braband, Texas, LB	72,000
		4	Alabama	13	7	Alan Lowry, Texas, QB	
1973	Jan. 1, 1974	12	Nebraska	19	7	Tony Davis, Nebraska, TB	67,500
		8	Texas	3	14	Wade Johnston, Texas, LB	
1974	Jan. 1, 1975	7	Penn State	41	7	Tom Shuman, Penn State, QB	67,500
		12	Baylor	20	14	Ken Quesenberry, Baylor, S	
1975	Jan. 1, 1976	18	Arkansas	31	7	Ike Forte, Arkansas, RB	74,500
		12	Georgia	10	19	Hal McAfee, Arkansas, LB	
1976	Jan. 1, 1977	6	Houston	30	4	Alois Blackwell, Houston, RB	54,500
		4	Maryland	21	8	Mark Mohr, Houston, CB	
1977	Jan. 2, 1978	5	Notre Dame	38	1	Vagas Ferguson, Notre Dame, RB	76,601
		1	Texas	10	4	Bob Golic, Notre Dame, LB	
1978	Jan. 1, 1979	10	Notre Dame	35	7	Joe Montana, Notre Dame, QB	32,500
		9	Houston	34	10	David Hodge, Houston, LB	
1979	Jan. 1, 1980	8	Houston	17	5	Terry Elston, Houston, QB	72,032
		7	Nebraska	14	9	David Hodge, Houston, LB	
1980	Jan. 1, 1981	9	Alabama	30	6	Warren Lyles, Alabama, NG	74,281
		6	Baylor	2	14	Major Ogilvie, Alabama, RB	
1981	Jan. 1, 1982	6	Texas	14	2	Robert Brewer, Texas, QB	73,243
		3	Alabama	12	7	Robbie Jones, Alabama, LB	
1982	Jan. 1, 1983	4	SMU	7	2	Wes Hopkins, SMU, SS	60,359
		6	Pittsburgh	3	10	Lance McIlhenny, SMU, QB	

SEASON	DATE	PRE-GAME RANK	TEAMS	SCORE	FINAL RANK	MOST VALUABLE PLAYERS	ATT.
1983	Jan. 2, 1984	7	Georgia	10	4	John Lastinger, Georgia, QB	67,891
		2	Texas	9	5	Jeff Leiding, Texas, LB	
1984	Jan. 1, 1985	8	Boston College	45	5	Bill Romanowski, Boston College, LB	56,522
			Houston	28		Steve Strachan, Boston College, FB	
1985	Jan. 1, 1986	11	Texas A&M	36	6	Domingo Bryant, Texas A&M, SS	73,137
		16	Auburn	16		Bo Jackson, Auburn, TB	
1986	Jan. 1, 1987	11	Ohio State	28	7	Chris Spielman, Ohio State, LB	74,188
		8	Texas A&M	12	13	Roger Vick, Texas A&M, FB	
1987	Jan. 1, 1988	13	Texas A&M	35	10	Adam Bob, Texas A&M, LB	73,006
		12	Notre Dame	10	17	Bucky Richardson, Texas A&M, QB	
1988	Jan. 2, 1989	9	UCLA	17	6	Troy Aikman, UCLA, QB	74,304
		8	Arkansas	3	12	LaSalle Harper, Arkansas, LB	
1989	Jan. 1, 1990	8	Tennessee	31	5	Carl Pickens, Tennessee, FS	74,358
		10	Arkansas	27	13	Chuck Webb, Tennessee, TB	
1990	Jan. 1, 1991	4	Miami (Fla.)	46	3	Craig Erickson, Miami (Fla.), QB	73,521
		3	Texas	3	12	Russell Maryland, Miami (Fla.), DL	
1991	Jan. 1, 1992	5	Florida State	10	4	Sean Jackson, Florida State, RB	73,728
		9	Texas A&M	2	12	Chris Crooms, Texas A&M, S	
1992	Jan. 1, 1993	5	Notre Dame	28	4	Rick Mirer, Notre Dame, QB	71,615
		4	Texas A&M	3	7	Devon McDonald, Notre Dame, DE	
1993	Jan. 1, 1994	4	Notre Dame	24	2	Lee Becton, Notre Dame, RB	69,855
		7	Texas A&M	21	9	Antonio Shorter, Texas A&M, LB	
1994	Jan. 2, 1995	21	Southern Cal	55	13	Keyshawn Johnson, Southern Cal, WR	70,218
			Texas Tech	14		John Herpin, Southern Cal, CB	
1995	Jan. 1, 1996	7	Colorado	38	5	Herchell Troutman, Colorado, RB	58,214
		12	Oregon	6	18	Marcus Washington, Colorado, DB	
1996	Jan. 1, 1997	5	BYU	19	5	Steve Sarkisian, QB, Shay Muirbrook, LB, BYU	71,928
		14	Kansas State	15	17	Kevin Lockett, Kansas State, WR	
1997	Jan. 1, 1998	5	UCLA	29	5	Cade McNown, UCLA, QB	59,215
		20	Texas A&M	23	20	Dat Nguyen, Texas A&M, LB	
1998	Jan. 1, 1999	20	Texas	38	15	Ricky Williams, Texas, RB	72,611
		25	Mississippi State	11		Aaron Babino, Texas, LB	
1999	Jan. 1, 2000	24	Arkansas	27	17	Cedric Cobbs, Arkansas, RB	72,723
		14	Texas	6	21	D.J. Cooper, Arkansas, LB	
2000	Jan. 1, 2001	11	Kansas State	35	9	Jonathan Beasley, Kansas State, QB	63,465
		21	Tennessee	21		Chris Johnson, Kansas State, DE	
2001	Jan. 1, 2002	10	Oklahoma	10	6	Quentin Griffin, Oklahoma, RB	72,955
			Arkansas	3		Roy Williams, Oklahoma, DB	
2002	Jan. 1, 2003	9	Texas	35	6	Roy Williams, Texas, WR	70,817
			LSU	20		Cory Redding, Texas, DE	
2003	Jan. 2, 2004	16	Mississippi	31	13	Eli Manning, Mississippi, QB	73,928
		21	Oklahoma State	28		Josh Cooper, Mississippi, DE	
2004	Jan. 1, 2005	15	Tennessee	38	13	Rick Clausen, Tennessee, QB	75,704
		22	Texas A&M	7		Justin Harrell, Tennessee, DT	

JANUARY 1, 1937
TCU 16, MARQUETTE 6

	1ST	2ND	3RD	4TH	FINAL
MARQ	6	0	0	0	6
TCU	10	6	0	0	16

SCORING SUMMARY
TCU FG Meyer 33
MARQ Guepe 60 punt return (kick failed)
TCU Meyer 55 pass from Baugh (Meyer kick)
TCU Meyer 18 pass from Montgomery (kick failed)

MARQ	TEAM STATISTICS	TCU
10	First Downs	16
55	Rushing Yards	169
11-21-3	Passing	9-20-3
134	Passing Yards	149
189	Total Yards	318
6-39.5	Punts - Average	4-32.5
1-0	Fumbles - Lost	1-0
3-25	Penalties - Yards	5-35

INDIVIDUAL LEADERS
RUSHING
MARQ: Guepe 12-31; Cuff 7-30.
TCU: McClure 5-48; Roberts 11-46.
PASSING
MARQ: Buivid 9-18-3, 111 yards.
TCU: Baugh 5-13-2, 100 yards, 1 TD.
RECEIVING
MARQ: Guepe 1-41; Cuff 3-30.
TCU: Meyer 3-79, 2 TD; McCall 2-32.

JANUARY 1, 1938
RICE 28, COLORADO 14

	1ST	2ND	3RD	4TH	FINAL
COLO	14	0	0	0	14
RICE	0	21	7	0	28

SCORING SUMMARY
COLO Antonio 9 pass from White (White kick)
COLO White 47 interception return (White kick)
RICE Schuehle 13 pass from Lain (Vestal kick)
RICE Lain 3 run (Vestal kick)
RICE Cordill 37 pass from Lain (Vestal kick)
RICE Steen 11 pass from Lain (Vestal kick)

COLO	TEAM STATISTICS	RICE
6	First Downs	20
87	Rushing Yards	257
1-9-2	Passing	11-20-1
8	Passing Yards	158
95	Total Yards	415
9-41.0	Punts - Average	4-38.0
3-15	Penalties - Yards	9-65

INDIVIDUAL LEADERS
RUSHING
COLO: White 23-62; Cheney 9-21.
RICE: Lain 14-78, 1 TD; Vickers 13-59.
PASSING
COLO: White 1-5-2, 9 yards, 1 TD.
RICE: Lain 8-12-1, 123 yards, 3 TD.
RECEIVING
COLO: Antonio 1-9, 1 TD.
RICE: Cordill 3-60, 1 TD; Steen 4-57, 1 TD.

JANUARY 2, 1939
ST. MARY'S 20, TEXAS TECH 13

	1ST	2ND	3RD	4TH	FINAL
STM	7	7	6	0	20
TT	0	0	0	13	13

SCORING SUMMARY
STM Heffernan 9 run (Perrie kick)
STM Klotovich 1 run (Marefos kick)
STM Smith 24 interception return (kick failed)
TT Tarbox 33 pass from Barnett (Marek kick)
TT McKnight 31 pass from Barnett (kick failed)

STM	TEAM STATISTICS	TT
11	First Downs	7
180	Rushing Yards	73
2-15-2	Passing	11-31-5
22	Passing Yards	210
202	Total Yards	283
11-47.5	Punts - Average	11-34.3
8-65	Penalties - Yards	5-30

JANUARY 1, 1940
CLEMSON 6, BOSTON COLLEGE 3

	1ST	2ND	3RD	4TH	FINAL
CLEM	0	6	0	0	6
BC	0	3	0	0	3

SCORING SUMMARY
BC   FG Lukachik 36
CLEM   Timmons 1 run (kick failed)

CLEM	TEAM STATISTICS	BC
11	First Downs	9
204	Rushing Yards	111
2-4-1	Passing	4-23-1
35	Passing Yards	73
239	Total Yards	184
11-42.6	Punts - Average	10-39.3
5-3	Fumbles - Lost	3-2
8-80	Penalties - Yards	8-90

INDIVIDUAL LEADERS
RUSHING
CLEM: Timmons 27-115, 1 TD; Bryant 14-56.
BC: Ananis 11-43; O'Rourke 8-41.
PASSING
CLEM: McFadden 2-3-0, 35 yards.
BC: Toczlowski 4-23-1, 73 yards.

JANUARY 1, 1941
TEXAS A&M 13, FORDHAM 12

	1ST	2ND	3RD	4TH	FINAL
FORD	0	6	0	6	12
A&M	0	0	13	0	13

SCORING SUMMARY
FORD   Filipowicz 2 run (kick blocked)
A&M   Smith 62 pass from Pugh (kick failed)
A&M   Kimbrough 1 run (Pugh kick)
FORD   Blumenstock 15 run (kick blocked)

FORD	TEAM STATISTICS	A&M
13	First Downs	8
118	Rushing Yards	52
5-23-3	Passing	6-18-1
62	Passing Yards	101
180	Total Yards	153
8-30.4	Punts - Average	10-32.9
1	Fumbles - Lost	3
2-29	Penalties - Yards	3-25

INDIVIDUAL LEADERS
RUSHING
FORD: Eshmont 16-48; Blumenstock 12-42, 1 TD.
A&M: Kimbrough 18-66, 1 TD; Thomason 1-10.
PASSING
FORD: Filipowicz 5-20-3, 62 yards.
A&M: Pugh 5-14-1, 97 yards, 1 TD.
RECEIVING
FORD: Blumenstock 1-17.
A&M: Smith 1-62, 1 TD.

JANUARY 1, 1942
ALABAMA 29, TEXAS A&M 21

	1ST	2ND	3RD	4TH	FINAL
ALA	0	7	13	9	29
A&M	0	7	0	14	21

SCORING SUMMARY
A&M   Cowley 12 pass from Daniels (Webster kick)
ALA   Craft 8 run (Hecht kick)
ALA   Nelson 72 punt return (kick blocked)
ALA   Nelson 21 run (Hecht kick)
ALA   FG Hecht 31
ALA   Rast 10 interception return (kick failed)
A&M   Webster 1 run (Webster kick)
A&M   Sterling 35 pass from Moser (Webster kick)

ALA	TEAM STATISTICS	A&M
1	First Downs	13
59	Rushing Yards	115
1-7-0	Passing	14-41-7
16	Passing Yards	194
75	Total Yards	309
16-36.3	Punts - Average	7-36.4
2-1	Fumbles - Lost	6-5
8-81	Penalties - Yards	1-5

INDIVIDUAL LEADERS
RUSHING
ALA: Nelson 9-38, 1 TD; Hughes 3-6.
A&M: Webster 12-52, 1 TD; Moser 16-31.
PASSING
ALA: Nelson 1-7-0, 16 yards.
A&M: Daniels 6-19-2, 87 yards, 1 TD; Moser 5-23-4, 107 yards, 1 TD.
RECEIVING
ALA: Rast 1-16.
A&M: Sterling 5-112, 1 TD; Cowley 4-39, 1 TD.

JANUARY 1, 1943
TEXAS 14, GEORGIA TECH 7

	1ST	2ND	3RD	4TH	FINAL
GT	0	0	0	7	7
TEX	7	0	7	0	14

SCORING SUMMARY
TEX   Minor 4 pass from McKay (Field kick)
TEX   Field 60 punt return (McKay kick)
GT   Eldredge 4 run (Jordan kick)

GT	TEAM STATISTICS	TEX
10	First Downs	15
57	Rushing Yards	201
8-20-1	Passing	5-9-1
138	Passing Yards	23
195	Total Yards	224
8-31.4	Punts - Average	7-30.6
2	Fumbles Lost	2
4-20	Penalties - Yards	2-20

JANUARY 1, 1944
RANDOLPH FIELD 7, TEXAS 7

	1ST	2ND	3RD	4TH	FINAL
RAND	7	0	0	0	7
TEX	0	7	0	0	7

SCORING SUMMARY
RAND   Aulds 16 pass from Dobbs (West kick)
TEX   McCall 35 pass from Ellsworth (Calahan kick)

RAND	TEAM STATISTICS	TEX
7	First Downs	3
99	Rushing Yards	73
3-16-3	Passing	3-10-1
51	Passing Yards	37
150	Total Yards	110
10-39..9	Punts - Average	8-33.1
4-20	Penalties - Yards	0-0

JANUARY 1, 1945
OKLAHOMA STATE 34, TCU 0

	1ST	2ND	3RD	4TH	FINAL
OKST	14	0	7	13	34
TCU	0	0	0	0	0

SCORING SUMMARY
OKST   Fenimore 1 run (Creager kick)
OKST   Spavital 52 run (Creager kick)
OKST   Fenimore 8 run (Creager kick)
OKST   Thomas 1 run (Creager kick)
OKST   Creager 1 run (kick failed)

OKST	TEAM STATISTICS	TCU
20	First Downs	5
295	Rushing Yards	74
9-17-1	Passing	3-10-1
199	Passing Yards	31
494	Total Yards	105
6-26.3	Punts - Average	8-34.3
1-1	Fumbles - Lost	2-1
7-75	Penalties - Yards	5-25

INDIVIDUAL LEADERS
RUSHING
OKST: Spavital 18-120, 1 TD; Fenimore 16-63, 2 TD.
TCU: Ruff 7-35; Mason 8-26.
PASSING
OKST: Fenimore 6-13-1, 136 yards.
TCU: Hadaway 3-6-1, 31 yards.
RECEIVING
OKST: Hankins 4-103; Creager 2-54.
TCU: Jackson 1-34.

JANUARY 1, 1946
TEXAS 40, MISSOURI 27

	1ST	2ND	3RD	4TH	FINAL
MO	7	7	0	13	27
TEX	14	7	6	13	40

SCORING SUMMARY
TEX   Baumgardner 48 pass from Layne (Layne kick)
MO   Oakes 51 pass from Dellastatious (Kekeris kick)
TEX   Layne 1 run (Layne kick)
MO   Dellastatious 3 run (Kekeris kick)
TEX   Layne 10 run (Layne kick)
TEX   Baumgardner 15 pass from Layne (Layne kick blocked)
MO   Bennett 21 run (Kekeris kick)
TEX   Layne 50 pass from Ellsworth (pass failed)
MO   Hopkins 1 run (kick blocked)
TEX   Layne 2 run (Layne kick)

MO	TEAM STATISTICS	TEX
22	First Downs	19
408	Rushing Yards	202
4-17-1	Passing	13-14-0
106	Passing Yards	234
514	Total Yards	436
2-37.0	Punts - Average	2-41.5
4-30	Penalties - Yards	5-35

JANUARY 1, 1947
LSU 0, ARKANSAS 0

	1ST	2ND	3RD	4TH	FINAL
LSU	0	0	0	0	0
ARK	0	0	0	0	0

LSU	TEAM STATISTICS	ARK
15	First Downs	1
255	Rushing Yards	54
5-17-0	Passing	0-4-1
16	Passing Yards	0
271	Total Yards	54
9-30.4	Punts - Average	11-36.0
2	Fumbles Lost	3
8-50	Penalties - Yards	1-5

JANUARY 1, 1948
PENN STATE 13, SMU 13

	1ST	2ND	3RD	4TH	FINAL
PSU	0	7	6	0	13
SMU	7	6	0	0	13

SCORING SUMMARY
SMU   Page 53 pass from Walker (Walker kick)
SMU   Walker 2 run (kick failed)
PSU   Larry Cooney 38 pass from Petchel (Czekaj kick)
PSU   Triplett 6 pass from Petchel (kick failed)

PSU	TEAM STATISTICS	SMU
12	First Downs	12
165	Rushing Yards	92
7-15-1	Passing	11-25-1
93	Passing Yards	114
258	Total Yards	206
2	Fumbles Lost	1
3-15	Penalties - Yards	1-5

INDIVIDUAL LEADERS
RUSHING
PSU: Rogel 25-95.
SMU: Walker 18-56, 1 TD.
PASSING
PSU: Petchel 7-16, 91 yards, 2 TD.
SMU: Walker 5-9, 69 yards, 1 TD.

JANUARY 1, 1949
SMU 21, OREGON 13

	1ST	2ND	3RD	4TH	FINAL
ORE	0	0	0	13	13
SMU	7	0	7	7	21

SCORING SUMMARY
SMU   Walker 1 run (Walker kick)
SMU   Rote 36 run (Walker kick)
ORE   Wilkins 24 pass from Van Brocklin (kick failed)
SMU   Roberts 8 run (Ethridge kick)
ORE   Sanders 1 run (Daniels kick)

ORE	TEAM STATISTICS	SMU
19	First Downs	19
242	Rushing Yards	226
8-19-0	Passing	10-20-2
145	Passing Yards	111
387	Total Yards	337
3-31.0	Punts - Average	3-68.7
1	Fumbles Lost	0
6-30	Penalties - Yards	1-5

INDIVIDUAL LEADERS
RUSHING
ORE: Bell 17-93; Lewis 12-63; Sanders 12-63, 1 TD.
SMU: Rote 16-93, 1 TD; Walker 14-66, 1 TD.
PASSING
ORE: Van Brocklin 8-19-0, 145 yards, 1 TD.
SMU: Walker 6-10-1, 79 yards; Johnson 4-10-1, 32 yards.
RECEIVING
ORE: Wilkins 4-57, 1 TD; Robinson 3-56.
SMU: Rote 4-55; McKissack 2-21.

JANUARY 2, 1950
RICE 27, NORTH CAROLINA 13

	1ST	2ND	3RD	4TH	FINAL
UNC	0	0	0	13	13
RICE	0	14	7	6	27

SCORING SUMMARY
RICE   Burkhalter 44 pass from Rote (Williams kick)
RICE   Lantrip 3 run (Williams kick)
RICE   Williams 17 pass from Rote (Williams kick)
RICE   Burkhalter 12 run (kick failed)
UNC   Rizzo 2 pass from Justice (kick failed)
UNC   Rizzo 2 run (Williams kick)

UNC	TEAM STATISTICS	RICE
16	First Downs	18
174	Rushing Yards	226
9-22-1	Passing	11-19-1
80	Passing Yards	152
254	Total Yards	378
6-38.0	Punts - Average	4-42.8
3-1	Fumbles - Lost	2-1
4-30	Penalties - Yards	3-26

INDIVIDUAL LEADERS
RUSHING
UNC: Hayes 19-107; Justice 16-59.
RICE: Burkhalter 16-74, 1 TD; Lantrip 14-63, 1 TD.
PASSING
UNC: Justice 7-14-0, 63 yards, 1 TD.
RICE: Rote 9-17, 140 yards, 2 TD.
RECEIVING
UNC: Weiner 5-41; Powell 2-24;
RICE: Williams 4-55, 1 TD; Burkhalter 1-44, 1 TD.

JANUARY 1, 1951
TENNESSEE 20, TEXAS 14

	1ST	2ND	3RD	4TH	FINAL
TENN	7	0	0	13	20
TEX	0	14	0	0	14

SCORING SUMMARY
TENN   Gruble 5 pass from Payne (Shires kick)
TEX   Townsend 5 run (Tompkins kick)
TEX   Dawson 35 pass from Tompkins (Tompkins kick)
TENN   Kozar 5 run (kick failed)
TENN   Kozar 1 run (Shires kick)

TENN	TEAM STATISTICS	TEX
18	First Downs	12
295	Rushing Yards	146
3-8-2	Passing	5-14-1
45	Passing Yards	97
340	Total Yards	243
6-32.8	Punts - Average	7-29.3
4-1	Fumbles - Lost	1-1
4-35	Penalties - Yards	5-55

INDIVIDUAL LEADERS
RUSHING
TENN: Lauricella 16-131; Kozar 20-92, 2 TD.
TEX: Townsend 23-105, 1 TD; Dawson 8-42.
PASSING
TENN: Lauricella 1-6-2, 23 yards; Rechichar 1-1-0, 18 yards.
TEX: Tompkins 5-14-1, 97 yards, 1 TD.
RECEIVING
TENN: Rechichar 1-23; Lauricella 1-18.
TEX: Dawson 2-65, 1 TD; Stolhandske 3-32.

JANUARY 1, 1952
KENTUCKY 20, TCU 7

	1ST	2ND	3RD	4TH	FINAL
UK	7	6	0	7	20
TCU	0	0	7	0	7

SCORING SUMMARY
UK   Clark 5 pass from Parilli (Jones kick)
UK   Clark 12 pass from Parilli (kick failed)
TCU   Floyd 43 run (Flowers kick)
UK   Hamilton 4 run (Jones kick)

UK	TEAM STATISTICS	TCU
13	First Downs	15
213	Rushing Yards	201
8-20-1	Passing	5-17-1
85	Passing Yards	99
298	Total Yards	300
6-34.7	Punts - Average	5-40.8
0-0	Fumbles - Lost	2-1
6-40	Penalties - Yards	7-32

INDIVIDUAL LEADERS
RUSHING
UK: Fillion 10-73; Jones 11-42.
TCU: Floyd 14-115, 1 TD; McKown 16-42.
PASSING
UK: Parilli 8-20-1, 85 yards, 2 TD.
TCU: McKown 1-8-0, 51 yards.
RECEIVING
UK: Meilinger 3-61; Clark 2-17, 2 TD.
TCU: Vaught 1-51; Medanich 3-43.

JANUARY 1, 1953
TEXAS 16, TENNESSEE 0

	1ST	2ND	3RD	4TH	FINAL
TENN	0	0	0	0	0
TEX	2	7	0	7	16

SCORING SUMMARY
TEX   Safety (Griffith tackled by Massey in end zone)
TEX   Dawson 4 run (Dawson kick)
TEX   Quinn 1 run (Dawson kick)

TENN	TEAM STATISTICS	TEX
6	First Downs	20
-14	Rushing Yards	269
3-6-0	Passing	2-8-1
46	Passing Yards	32
32	Total Yards	301
7-40.9	Punts - Average	5-35.4
5-3	Fumbles - Lost	5-3
3-30	Penalties - Yards	5-55

INDIVIDUAL LEADERS
RUSHING
TENN: Schwanger 5-22; Wade 7-4.
TEX: Ochoa 26-108; Quinn 19-67, 1 TD.
PASSING
TENN: Shires 2-4-0, 23 yards.
TEX: Jones 2-5-1, 32 yards.
RECEIVING
TENN: Morgan 2-23; Kolenik 1-23.
TEX: Quinn 1-23; Spring 1-9.

JANUARY 1, 1954
RICE 28, ALABAMA 6

	1ST	2ND	3RD	4TH	FINAL
ALA	6	0	0	0	6
RICE	0	14	7	7	28

SCORING SUMMARY
ALA   Lewis 1 run (kick blocked)
RICE   Maegle 79 run (Fenstemaker kick)
RICE   Maegle awarded 95 run after bench tackle by Lewis
RICE   Maegle 34 run (Fenstemaker kick)
RICE   Grantham 7 run (Burk kick)

ALA	TEAM STATISTICS	RICE
11	First Downs	14
188	Rushing Yards	379
7-16-0	Passing	4-10-2
67	Passing Yards	59
255	Total Yards	438
7-42.7	Punts - Average	8-25.1
4-4	Fumbles - Lost	1-0
6-65	Penalties - Yards	8-89

INDIVIDUAL LEADERS
RUSHING
ALA: Oliver 2-56; Starr 11-54.
RICE: Maegle 11-265, 3 TD; Kellogg 14-32.
PASSING
ALA: Starr 7-16-0, 67 yards.
RICE: Grantham 3-5-0, 43 yards.
RECEIVING
ALA: Cummings 2-37; Stone 2-20.
RICE: Holland-2-28; Bridges 1-16.

JANUARY 1, 1955
GEORGIA TECH 14, ARKANSAS 6

	1ST	2ND	3RD	4TH	FINAL
GT	0	0	7	7	14
ARK	0	6	0	0	6

SCORING SUMMARY
ARK   Walker 3 run (kick failed)
GT   Rotenberry 3 run (Mitchell kick)
GT   Mitchell 1 run (Mitchell kick)

GT	TEAM STATISTICS	ARK
19	First Downs	10
285	Rushing Yards	141
4-15-0	Passing	7-10-1
31	Passing Yards	86
316	Total Yards	227
4-30.0	Punts - Average	4-28.0
1-0	Fumbles - Lost	0-0
4-30	Penalties - Yards	4-30

INDIVIDUAL LEADERS
RUSHING
GT: Humphreys 19-99; Thompson 12-63.
ARK: Moore 16-86; Walker 11-34, 1 TD.
PASSING
GT: Mitchell 4-10-0, 31 yards.
ARK: Walker 3-5-1, 51 yards.
RECEIVING
GT: Durham 2-20; Hair 2-11.
ARK: Lyons 2-34; Thomason 1-22.

JANUARY 2, 1956
MISSISSIPPI 14, TCU 13

	1ST	2ND	3RD	4TH	FINAL
MISS	0	7	0	7	14
TCU	7	6	0	0	13

SCORING SUMMARY
TCU   Swink 1 run (Pollard kick)
TCU   Swink 39 run (kick failed)
MISS   Cothren 3 run (Cothren kick)
MISS   Lott 5 run (Cothren kick)

MISS	TEAM STATISTICS	TCU
12	First Downs	11
92	Rushing Yards	233
10-21-0	Passing	2-5-2
137	Passing Yards	20
229	Total Yards	253
6-42.7	Punts - Average	5-28.8
1-1	Fumbles - Lost	2-1
6-80	Penalties - Yards	8-80

INDIVIDUAL LEADERS
RUSHING
MISS: Cothren 12-79, 1 TD; Kinard 3-7.
TCU: Swink 19-107, 2 TD; Taylor 10-76.
PASSING
MISS: Day 10-21-0, 137 yards.
TCU: Finney 1-3-2, 13 yards.
RECEIVING
MISS: Kinard 6-83; Blair 1-28.
TCU: Williams 1-13; Nikkel 1-7.

JANUARY 1, 1957
TCU 28, SYRACUSE 27

	1ST	2ND	3RD	4TH	FINAL
SYR	0	14	0	13	27
TCU	7	7	7	7	28

SCORING SUMMARY
TCU   Nikkel 6 pass from Curtis (Pollard kick)
TCU   Shofner 8 pass from Curtis (Pollard kick)
SYR   Brown 2 run (Brown kick)
SYR   Brown 4 run (Brown kick)
TCU   Curtis 7 run (Pollard kick)
TCU   Swink 3 run (Pollard kick)
SYR   Brown 1 run (kick blocked)
SYR   Ridlon 27 pass from Zimmerman (Brown kick)

SYR	TEAM STATISTICS	TCU
16	First Downs	15
235	Rushing Yards	133
3-7-1	Passing	13-16-0
63	Passing Yards	202
298	Total Yards	335
2-46.5	Punts - Average	4-37.5
3-3	Fumbles - Lost	3-2
1-5	Penalties - Yards	4-40

INDIVIDUAL LEADERS
RUSHING
SYR: Brown 26-132, 3 TD; Cann 8-28.
TCU: Dike 11-54; Swink 12-41, 1 TD.
PASSING
SYR: Zimmerman 1-3-0, 22 yards, 1 TD; Brown 1-2-1, 20 yards.
TCU: Curtis 12-15-0, 174 yards, 2 TD.
RECEIVING
SYR: Ridlon 2-48, 1 TD; Massey 1-15.
TCU: Swink 4-60; Nikkel 3-57, 1 TD.

JANUARY 1, 1958
NAVY 20, RICE 7

	1ST	2ND	3RD	4TH	FINAL
NAVY	6	7	7	0	20
RICE	0	0	7	0	7

SCORING SUMMARY
NAVY   Tranchini 1 run (kick failed)
NAVY   Hurst 13 run (Oldham kick)
NAVY   Oldham 19 run (Oldham kick)
RICE   Williams 8 pass from Ryan (Hill kick)

NAVY	TEAM STATISTICS	RICE
21	First Downs	14
222	Rushing Yards	137
13-27-1	Passing	14-27-1
153	Passing Yards	164
375	Total Yards	301
3-36.6	Punts - Average	5-42.0
5-3	Fumbles - Lost	5-5
9-65	Penalties - Yards	7-53

INDIVIDUAL LEADERS
RUSHING
NAVY: Hurst 10-50, 1 TD; Oldham 8-50, 1 TD.
RICE: Ryan 17-69; Speer 4-16.
PASSING
NAVY: Forrestal 13-24-1, 153 yards.
RICE: Ryan 13-22-1, 151 yards, 1 TD.
RECEIVING
NAVY: Ruth 5-62; Jokanovich 4-47.
RICE: Dial 7-80; Jones 3-30.

THE BOWLS

Air Force 0, TCU 0

JANUARY 1, 1959

	1ST	2ND	3RD	4TH	FINAL
AFA	0	0	0	0	0
TCU	0	0	0	0	0

AFA	TEAM STATISTICS	TCU
13	First Downs	9
140	Rushing Yards	190
12-23-2	Passing	3-11-0
91	Passing Yards	37
231	Total Yards	227
7-38.1	Punts - Average	9-38.4
5-3	Fumbles - Lost	8-3
3-15	Penalties - Yards	8-61

INDIVIDUAL LEADERS

RUSHING
AFA: Galios 13-52; Quinlan 7-33.
TCU: Spikes 17-108; Harris 7-24.

PASSING
AFA: Mayo 9-19-2, 70 yards.
TCU: Lasater 1-1-0, 37 yards.

RECEIVING
AFA: Lane 4-27; Bickey 1-19.
TCU: Meyer 1-37; Gilmore 1-5.

Syracuse 23, Texas 14

JANUARY 1, 1960

	1ST	2ND	3RD	4TH	FINAL
SYR	7	8	8	0	23
TEX	0	0	6	8	14

SCORING SUMMARY

SYR	Davis 87 pass from Schwedes (Yates kick)
SYR	Davis 1 run (Davis pass from Sarette)
TEX	Collins 69 pass from Lackey (run failed)
SYR	Schwedes 3 run (Davis pass from Sarette)
TEX	Lackey 1 run (Shulte pass from Lackey)

SYR	TEAM STATISTICS	TEX
12	First Downs	10
133	Rushing Yards	145
9-12-1	Passing	4-15-1
181	Passing Yards	99
314	Total Yards	244
9	Punt Returns - Yards	31
51	Kickoff Returns - Yards	100
6-33.3	Punts - Average	5-42.4
4-3	Fumbles - Lost	1-1
6-67	Penalties - Yards	7-61.5

INDIVIDUAL LEADERS

RUSHING
SYR: Davis 8-57, 1 TD; Baker 6-26.
TEX: Branch 11-71; Ramirez 9-36.

PASSING
SYR: Schwedes 2-2-0, 97 yards, 1 TD.
TEX: Lackey 3-9-0, 92 yards, 1 TD.

RECEIVING
SYR: Davis 1-87, 1 TD; Erickson 2-49.
TEX: Collins 1-69, 1 TD; Ramirez 2-23.

Duke 7, Arkansas 6

JANUARY 2, 1961

	1ST	2ND	3RD	4TH	FINAL
DUKE	0	0	0	7	7
ARK	0	0	6	0	6

SCORING SUMMARY

ARK	Alworth 49 punt return (kick blocked)
DUKE	Moorman 9 pass from Altman (Browning kick)

DUKE	TEAM STATISTICS	ARK
10	First Downs	12
96	Rushing Yards	148
13-17-1	Passing	5-13-1
93	Passing Yards	71
189	Total Yards	219
8-36.9	Punts - Average	6-30.8
2-2	Fumbles - Lost	1-1
3-15	Penalties - Yards	4-40

INDIVIDUAL LEADERS

RUSHING
DUKE: Wilson 12-32; Wright 9-26.
ARK: Alberty 13-44; Alworth 11-33.

PASSING
DUKE: Altman 12-15-0, 83 yards, 1 TD.
ARK: McKinney 4-10-1, 58 yards.

RECEIVING
DUKE: Moorman 8-45, 1 TD; Wilson 3-30.
ARK: Alworth 3-41; Collier 2-30.

Texas 12, Mississippi 7

JANUARY 1, 1962

	1ST	2ND	3RD	4TH	FINAL
MISS	0	0	7	0	7
TEX	6	6	0	0	12

SCORING SUMMARY

TEX	Saxton 1 run (kick blocked)
TEX	Collins 24 pass from Cotten (run failed)
MISS	Davis 20 pass from Griffing (Sullivan kick)

MISS	TEAM STATISTICS	TEX
17	First Downs	12
127	Rushing Yards	123
15-37-5	Passing	6-13-3
192	Passing Yards	60
319	Total Yards	183
4-32.5	Punts - Average	5-40.2
1-1	Fumbles - Lost	2-1
4-30	Penalties - Yards	3-35

INDIVIDUAL LEADERS

RUSHING
MISS: Griffing 10-45; Doty 5-29.
TEX: Poage 11-54; Cotten 11-25.

PASSING
MISS: Griffing 12-29-3, 163 yards, 1 TD.
TEX: Cotten 6-13-3, 60 yards, 1 TD.

RECEIVING
MISS: Guy 4-43; Doty 4-41.
TEX: Collins 2-30, 1 TD; Saxton 3-18.

LSU 13, Texas 0

JANUARY 1, 1963

	1ST	2ND	3RD	4TH	FINAL
LSU	0	3	7	3	13
TEX	0	0	0	0	0

SCORING SUMMARY

LSU	FG Amedee 23
LSU	Field 22 run (Amedee kick)
LSU	FG Amedee 37

LSU	TEAM STATISTICS	TEX
17	First Downs	9
126	Rushing Yards	80
13-21-0	Passing	8-22-3
133	Passing Yards	92
259	Total Yards	172
9-41.8	Punts - Average	8-46.8
0-0	Fumbles - Lost	2-2
1-15	Penalties - Yards	4-44

INDIVIDUAL LEADERS

RUSHING
LSU: Stovall 12-36; LeBlanc 6-23.
TEX: Cook 10-39; Wade 3-17.

PASSING
LSU: Amedee 9-13-0, 94 yards.
TEX: Genung 5-9-0, 59 yards; Wade 3-13-3, 33 yards.

RECEIVING
LSU: Truax 3-49; Cranford 2-16.
TEX: Green 1-18; Dixon 1-17.

Texas 28, Navy 6

JANUARY 1, 1964

	1ST	2ND	3RD	4TH	FINAL
NAVY	0	0	0	6	6
TEX	7	14	7	0	28

SCORING SUMMARY

TEX	Harris 58 pass from Carlisle (Crosby kick)
TEX	Harris 63 pass from Carlisle (Crosby kick)
TEX	Carlisle 9 run (Crosby kick)
TEX	Philipp 2 run (Crosby kick)
NAVY	Staubach 2 run (pass failed)

NAVY	TEAM STATISTICS	TEX
16	First Downs	18
-14	Rushing Yards	168
22-34-1	Passing	8-21-1
227	Passing Yards	234
213	Total Yards	402
6-36.5	Punts - Average	3-43.3
2-2	Fumbles - Lost	2-1
2-35	Penalties - Yards	8-72

INDIVIDUAL LEADERS

RUSHING
NAVY: Donnelly 8-12; Ownsworth 1-8.
TEX: Carlisle 11-54, 1 TD; Ford 9-39.

PASSING
NAVY: Staubach 21-31-1, 228 yards; Wade 1-2-0, 21 yards.
TEX: Carlisle 7-19-1, 213 yards, 2 TD.

RECEIVING
NAVY: Orr 9-112; Sjuggerud 4-52.
TEX: Harris 3-157, 2 TD; Lammons 2-30.

Arkansas 10, Nebraska 7

JANUARY 1, 1965

	1ST	2ND	3RD	4TH	FINAL
NEB	0	7	0	0	7
ARK	3	0	0	7	10

SCORING SUMMARY

ARK	FG McKnelly 31
NEB	Wilson 1 run (Drum kick)
ARK	Burnett 3 run (McKnelly kick)

NEB	TEAM STATISTICS	ARK
11	First Downs	11
100	Rushing Yards	45
8-16-2	Passing	11-19-1
68	Passing Yards	131
168	Total Yards	176
6-33.3	Punts - Average	6-40.2
0-0	Fumbles - Lost	2-2
5-25	Penalties - Yards	6-50

INDIVIDUAL LEADERS

RUSHING
NEB: Wilson 12-84, 1 TD; Solich 11-34.
ARK: Burnett 11-23, 1 TD; Lindsey 3-14.

PASSING
NEB: Churchich 8-15-2, 68 yards.
ARK: Marshall 11-19-1, 131 yards.

RECEIVING
NEB: Wilson 1-36; White 2-18.
ARK: Lindsey 3-54; Burnett 5-44.

LSU 14, Arkansas 7

JANUARY 1, 1966

	1ST	2ND	3RD	4TH	FINAL
LSU	0	14	0	0	14
ARK	7	0	0	0	7

SCORING SUMMARY

ARK	Crockett 19 pass from Brittenum (South kick)
LSU	Labruzzo 3 run (Moreau kick)
LSU	Labruzzo 1 run (Moreau kick)

LSU	TEAM STATISTICS	ARK
15	First Downs	22
166	Rushing Yards	129
8-11-0	Passing	15-24-1
100	Passing Yards	177
266	Total Yards	306
6-42.2	Punts - Average	3-34.0
0-0	Fumbles - Lost	2-1
4-62	Penalties - Yards	2-10

INDIVIDUAL LEADERS

RUSHING
LSU: Labruzzo 21-69, 2 TD; Dousay 14-38.
ARK: Jones 10-79; Burnett 12-44.

PASSING
LSU: Screen 7-10-0, 82 yards.
ARK: Brittenum 15-24-1, 177 yards, 1 TD.

RECEIVING
LSU: Masters 4-45; Labruzzo 1-19.
ARK: Crockett 10-129, 1 TD; Jones 2-26.

Georgia 24, SMU 9

DECEMBER 31, 1966

	1ST	2ND	3RD	4TH	FINAL
UGA	10	7	0	7	24
SMU	3	6	0	0	9

SCORING SUMMARY

UGA	Lawrence 74 run (Etter kick)
SMU	FG Partee 22
UGA	FG Etter 28
UGA	Payne 20 pass from Moore (Etter kick)
SMU	Richardson 1 run (kick failed)
UGA	Jenkins 4 run (Etter kick)

UGA	TEAM STATISTICS	SMU
17	First Downs	11
284	Rushing Yards	40
6-14-1	Passing	10-20-3
79	Passing Yards	165
363	Total Yards	205
4-28.5	Punts - Average	4-36.5
2-1	Fumbles - Lost	1-1
3-37	Penalties - Yards	7-45

INDIVIDUAL LEADERS

RUSHING
UGA: Lawrence 16-149, 1 TD; Jenkins 23-88, 1 TD.
SMU: Jernigan 9-28; Richardson 11-24, 1 TD.

PASSING
UGA: Moore 6-11-1, 79 yards, 1 TD.
SMU: White 9-17-1, 160 yards.

RECEIVING
UGA: Payne 3-49, 1 TD; Johnson 2-27.
SMU: Levias 3-62; Richardson 3-45.

THE BOWLS

JANUARY 1, 1968
TEXAS A&M 20, ALABAMA 16

	1ST	2ND	3RD	4TH	FINAL
ALA	7	3	6	0	16
A&M	7	6	7	0	20

SCORING SUMMARY

ALA	Stabler 3 run (Davis kick)
A&M	Stegent 13 pass from Hargett (Riggs kick)
ALA	FG Davis 36
A&M	Maxwell 7 pass from Hargett (kick failed)
A&M	Housley 20 run (Riggs kick)
ALA	Stabler 2 run (run failed)

ALA	TEAM STATISTICS	A&M
14	First Downs	13
135	Rushing Yards	114
16-26-3	Passing	11-22-0
179	Passing Yards	143
314	Total Yards	257
6-37.5	Punts - Average	10-41.0
5-2	Fumbles - Lost	3-1
4-37	Penalties - Yards	7-83

INDIVIDUAL LEADERS

RUSHING
ALA: Chatwood 12-62; Martin 5-36.
A&M: Housley 10-59, 1 TD; Stegent 18-56.

PASSING
ALA: Stabler 16-26-3, 179 yards.
A&M: Hargett 11-22-0, 143 yards, 2 TD.

RECEIVING
ALA: Homan 6-90; Willis 4-39.
A&M: Stegent 4-51, 1 TD; Harris 2-38.

JANUARY 1, 1969
TEXAS 36, TENNESSEE 13

	1ST	2ND	3RD	4TH	FINAL
TENN	0	0	7	6	13
TEX	13	15	8	0	36

SCORING SUMMARY

TEX	Worster 14 run (Feller kick)
TEX	Speyrer 78 pass from Street (kick failed)
TEX	Koy 9 run (Feller kick)
TEX	Gilbert 5 run (Speyrer pass from Street)
TENN	Kreis 17 pass from Scott (Kremser kick)
TEX	Speyrer 79 pass from Street (Bradley run)
TENN	Price 3 pass from Scott (pass failed)

TENN	TEAM STATISTICS	TEX
16	First Downs	22
83	Rushing Yards	279
16-41-3	Passing	8-14-1
192	Passing Yards	234
275	Total Yards	513
8-42.1	Punts - Average	7-40.7
5-0	Fumbles - Lost	3-2
4-17	Penalties - Yards	5-60

INDIVIDUAL LEADERS

RUSHING
TENN: Pearce 2-26; Pickens 8-20.
TEX: Worster 10-85, 1 TD; Gilbert 13-82, 1 TD.

PASSING
TENN: Scott 11-30-3, 159 yards, 2 TD.
TEX: Street 7-13-1, 200 yards, 2 TD.

RECEIVING
TENN: Kreis 3-77, 1 TD; McClain 3-57.
TEX: Speyrer 5-161, 2 TD; Bradley 1-34.

JANUARY 1, 1970
TEXAS 21, NOTRE DAME 17

	1ST	2ND	3RD	4TH	FINAL
ND	3	7	0	7	17
TEX	0	7	0	14	21

SCORING SUMMARY

ND	FG Hempel 26
ND	Gatewood 54 pass from Theismann (Hempel kick)
TEX	Bertelsen 1 run (Feller kick)
TEX	Koy 3 run (Feller kick)
ND	Yoder 24 pass from Theismann (Hempel kick)
TEX	Dale 1 run (Feller kick)

ND	TEAM STATISTICS	TEX
25	First Downs	25
189	Rushing Yards	331
17-27-2	Passing	6-11-1
231	Passing Yards	107
420	Total Yards	438
7-36.6	Punts - Average	4-39.8
0-0	Fumbles - Lost	2-1
2-10	Penalties - Yards	1-5

INDIVIDUAL LEADERS

RUSHING
ND: Barz 10-49; Theismann 11-48.
TEX: Worster 20-155; Bertelsen 18-81, 1 TD.

PASSING
ND: Theismann 17-27-2, 231 yards, 2 TD.
TEX: Street 6-11-1, 107 yards.

RECEIVING
ND: Gatewood 6-112, 1 TD; Allan 3-43.
TEX: Speyrer 4-70; Bertelsen 1-21.

JANUARY 1, 1971
NOTRE DAME 24, TEXAS 11

	1ST	2ND	3RD	4TH	FINAL
ND	14	10	0	0	24
TEX	3	8	0	0	11

SCORING SUMMARY

TEX	FG Feller 23
ND	Gatewood 26 pass from Theismann (Hempel kick)
ND	Theismann 3 run (Hempel kick)
ND	Theismann 15 run (Hempel kick)
TEX	Bertelsen 2 run (Lester pass from Phillips)
ND	FG Hempel 36

ND	TEAM STATISTICS	TEX
16	First Downs	20
146	Rushing Yards	216
10-19-1	Passing	10-27-1
213	Passing Yards	210
359	Total Yards	426
8-45.8	Punts - Average	5-32.6
1-1	Fumbles - Lost	9-5
5-52	Penalties - Yards	3-33

INDIVIDUAL LEADERS

RUSHING
ND: Cieszkowski 13-52; Parker 13-48.
TEX: Phillips 23-164; Worster 16-42.

PASSING
ND: Theismann 9-16-1, 176 yards, 1 TD.
TEX: Phillips 9-17-0, 199 yards.

RECEIVING
ND: Yoder 2-96; Gatewood 2-43, 1 TD.
TEX: Bertelsen 3-85; Comer 4-67.

JANUARY 1, 1972
PENN STATE 30, TEXAS 6

	1ST	2ND	3RD	4TH	FINAL
PSU	0	3	17	10	30
TEX	3	3	0	0	6

SCORING SUMMARY

TEX	FG Valek 29
PSU	FG Vitiello 21
TEX	FG Valek 40
PSU	Mitchell 1 run (Vitiello kick)
PSU	Skarzynski 65 pass from Hufnagel (Vitiello kick)
PSU	FG Vitiello 37
PSU	FG Vitiello 22
PSU	Hufnagel 4 run (Vitiello kick)

PSU	TEAM STATISTICS	TEX
18	First Downs	15
239	Rushing Yards	159
7-13-1	Passing	5-14-0
137	Passing Yards	83
376	Total Yards	242
5-36.0	Punts - Average	5-33.0
1-0	Fumbles - Lost	5-3
2-30	Penalties - Yards	1-5

INDIVIDUAL LEADERS

RUSHING
PSU: Mitchell 27-146, 1 TD; Harris 11-47.
TEX: Bertelsen 14-58; Ladd 8-45.

PASSING
PSU: Hufnagel 7-12-1, 137 yards, 1 TD.
TEX: Phillips 3-8-0, 59 yards.

RECEIVING
PSU: Skarzynski 2-81, 1 TD; Parson 3-48.
TEX: Burrisk 3-45; Kelly 2-38.

JANUARY 1, 1973
TEXAS 17, ALABAMA 13

	1ST	2ND	3RD	4TH	FINAL
ALA	10	3	0	0	13
TEX	0	3	7	7	17

SCORING SUMMARY

ALA	FG Gantt 50
ALA	Jackson 31 run (Davis kick)
TEX	FG Schott 24
ALA	FG Davis 30
TEX	Lowry 3 run (Schott kick)
TEX	Lowry 34 run (Schott kick)

ALA	TEAM STATISTICS	TEX
15	First Downs	20
138	Rushing Yards	317
11-18-2	Passing	5-11-2
186	Passing Yards	61
324	Total Yards	378
5-29.4	Punts - Average	2-44.0
1-0	Fumbles - Lost	0-0
4-30	Penalties - Yards	0-0

INDIVIDUAL LEADERS

RUSHING
ALA: Jackson 10-64, 1 TD; Bisceglia 11-30.
TEX: Leaks 15-120; Lowry 16-117, 2 TD.

PASSING
ALA: Davis 10-17-2, 174 yards.
TEX: Lowry 5-11-2, 61 yards.

RECEIVING
ALA: Wood 5-81; Wheeler 2-57.
TEX: Moore 2-24; Kelly 1-20.

THE BOWLS

JANUARY 1, 1974
NEBRASKA 19, TEXAS 3

	1ST	2ND	3RD	4TH	FINAL
NEB	0	3	13	3	19
TEX	3	0	0	0	3

SCORING SUMMARY

TEX	FG Schott 22
NEB	FG Sanger 24
NEB	Bahe 12 run (Sanger kick)
NEB	Davis 3 run (kick blocked)
NEB	FG Sanger 43

NEB	TEAM STATISTICS	TEX
21	First Downs	11
240	Rushing Yards	106
7-17-2	Passing	7-17-2
91	Passing Yards	90
331	Total Yards	196
3-40.0	Punts - Average	4-39.8
3-1	Fumbles - Lost	6-3
4-51	Penalties - Yards	2-30

INDIVIDUAL LEADERS

RUSHING
NEB: Davis 28-106, 1 TD; Humm 6-29.
TEX: Leaks 13-48; Akins 15-44.

PASSING
NEB: Humm 5-13-2, 75 yards.
TEX: Presley 7-13-1, 90 yards.

RECEIVING
NEB: Bahe 2-35; Anderson 1-20.
TEX: Alford 3-32; Moore 1-20.

JANUARY 1, 1975
PENN STATE 41, BAYLOR 20

	1ST	2ND	3RD	4TH	FINAL
PSU	0	3	14	24	41
BU	7	0	7	6	20

SCORING SUMMARY

BU	Beaird 4 run (Hicks kick)
PSU	FG Bahr 25
PSU	Donchez 1 run (Reihner kick)
BU	Thompson 35 pass from Jeffrey (Hicks kick)
PSU	Cefalo 49 pass from Shuman (Reihner kick)
PSU	Cefalo 3 run (Reihner kick)
PSU	FG Bahr 33
PSU	Shuman 2 run (Reihner kick)
BU	Thompson 11 pass from Jackson (pass failed)
PSU	Jackson 50 kickoff return (Reihner kick)

PSU	TEAM STATISTICS	BU
23	First Downs	20
265	Rushing Yards	138
10-20-0	Passing	10-23-2
226	Passing Yards	175
491	Total Yards	313
2-36.5	Punts - Average	6-34.0
3-2	Fumbles - Lost	4-0
8-70	Penalties - Yards	7-45

INDIVIDUAL LEADERS

RUSHING
PSU: Donchez 25-116, 1 TD; Hutton 12-79.
BU: Beaird 21-84, 1 TD; McNeil 8-36.

PASSING
PSU: Shuman 10-20-0, 226 yards, 1 TD.
BU: Jeffrey 7-19-2, 135 yards, 1 TD.

RECEIVING
PSU: Cefalo 3-102, 1 TD; Natale 3-74.
BU: Thompson 3-62, 2 TD; Harper 3-45.

JANUARY 1, 1976
ARKANSAS 31, GEORGIA 10

	1ST	2ND	3RD	4TH	FINAL
UGA	3	7	0	0	10
ARK	0	10	0	21	31

SCORING SUMMARY

UGA	FG Leavitt 35
UGA	Washington 21 pass from Robinson (Leavitt kick)
ARK	FG Little 39
ARK	Forte 1 run (Little kick)
ARK	Fuchs 5 run (Little kick)
ARK	Forrest 1 run (Little kick)
ARK	Forte 6 run (Little kick)

UGA	TEAM STATISTICS	ARK
13	First Downs	20
102	Rushing Yards	235
8-18-2	Passing	5-14-0
91	Passing Yards	89
193	Total Yards	324
6-38.7	Punts - Average	4-43.0
3-2	Fumbles - Lost	6-1
3-15	Penalties - Yards	5-35

INDIVIDUAL LEADERS

RUSHING
UGA: Harrison 14-44; Goff 16-32.
ARK: Forte 24-119, 2 TD; Fuchs 16-71, 1 TD.

PASSING
UGA: Robinson 7-15-2, 85 yards, 1 TD.
ARK: Bull 5-13-0, 89 yards.

RECEIVING
UGA: Wilson 1-29; Washington 1-21.
ARK: Douglas 2-54; Daily 1-13.

JANUARY 1, 1977
HOUSTON 30, MARYLAND 21

	1ST	2ND	3RD	4TH	FINAL
MD	0	7	7	7	21
HOU	21	6	0	3	30

SCORING SUMMARY

HOU	Thomas 11 run (Coplin kick)
HOU	Blackwell 33 run (Coplin kick)
HOU	Blackwell 1 run (Coplin kick)
MD	Manges 6 run (Loncar kick)
HOU	Bass 33 pass from Davis (kick failed)
MD	Sievers 11 pass from Manges (Sochko kick)
MD	Wilson 1 run (Sochko kick)
HOU	FG Coplin 28

MD	TEAM STATISTICS	HOU
17	First Downs	20
120	Rushing Yards	320
17-32-0	Passing	5-8-0
179	Passing Yards	108
299	Total Yards	428
6-43.7	Punts - Average	4-35.8
1-1	Fumbles - Lost	4-3
8-80	Penalties - Yards	5-22

INDIVIDUAL LEADERS

RUSHING
MD: Scott 11-47; Manges 14-32, 1 TD.
HOU: Blackwell 22-149, 2 TD; Thomas 14-104, 1 TD.

PASSING
MD: Manges 17-32-0, 179, 1 TD.
HOU: Davis 5-8-0, 108 yards, 1 TD.

RECEIVING
MD: Kinney 5-72; Richards 3-39.
HOU: Foster 3-62; Bass 1-33, 1 TD.

JANUARY 2, 1978
NOTRE DAME 38, TEXAS 10

	1ST	2ND	3RD	4TH	FINAL
ND	3	21	7	7	38
TEX	3	7	0	0	10

SCORING SUMMARY

ND	FG Reeve 47
TEX	FG Erxleben 42
ND	Eurick 6 run (Reeve kick)
ND	Eurick 10 run (Reeve kick)
ND	Ferguson 17 pass from Montana (Reeve kick)
TEX	Lockett 13 pass from McEachern (Erxleben kick)
ND	Ferguson 3 run (Reeve kick)
ND	Ferguson 26 run (Reeve kick)

ND	TEAM STATISTICS	TEX
26	First Downs	16
243	Rushing Yards	131
14-32-1	Passing	11-24-3
156	Passing Yards	160
399	Total Yards	291
5-30.4	Punts - Average	3-40.0
1-0	Fumbles - Lost	3-3
4-37	Penalties - Yards	1-5

INDIVIDUAL LEADERS

RUSHING
ND: Heavens 22-101; Ferguson 21-100, 2 TD.
TEX: Campbell 29-116; Jones 11-63.

PASSING
ND: Montana 10-25-1, 111 yards, 1 TD.
TEX: McEachern 11-24-3, 160 yards, 1 TD.

RECEIVING
ND: MacAfee 4-45; Waymer 3-38.
TEX: Harris 4-57; Jones 1-34.

JANUARY 1, 1979
NOTRE DAME 35, HOUSTON 34

	1ST	2ND	3RD	4TH	FINAL
ND	12	0	0	23	35
HOU	7	13	14	0	34

SCORING SUMMARY

ND	Montana 3 run (kick failed)
ND	Buchanan 1 run (pass failed)
HOU	Adams 15 pass from Davis (Hatfield kick)
HOU	Love 1 run (Hatfield kick)
HOU	FG Hatfield 21
HOU	FG Hatfield 34
HOU	Davis 2 run (Hatfield kick)
HOU	Davis 5 run (Hatfield kick)
ND	Cichy 33 return of blocked punt (Ferguson pass from Montana)
ND	Montana 2 run (Haines pass from Montana)
ND	Haines 8 pass from Montana (Unis kick)

ND	TEAM STATISTICS	HOU
13	First Downs	16
131	Rushing Yards	229
13-37-4	Passing	4-13-0
163	Passing Yards	60
294	Total Yards	289
7-26.3	Punts - Average	10-25.5
3-3	Fumbles - Lost	6-3
8-74	Penalties - Yards	6-39

INDIVIDUAL LEADERS

RUSHING
ND: Heavens 16-71; Montana 7-26, 2 TD.
HOU: Davis 19-76, 2 TD; King 21-74.

PASSING
ND: Montana 13-34-4, 163 yards, 1 TD.
HOU: Davis 4-12-0, 60 yards, 1 TD.

RECEIVING
ND: Heavens 4-60; Masztak 3-49.
HOU: Adams 2-35, 1 TD; Herring 2-25.

JANUARY 1, 1980
HOUSTON 17, NEBRASKA 14

	1ST	2ND	3RD	4TH	FINAL
NEB	7	0	0	7	14
HOU	0	7	0	10	17

SCORING SUMMARY

NEB	Redwine 9 run (Sukup kick)
HOU	Elston 8 run (Hatfield kick)
HOU	FG Hatfield 41
NEB	Finn 6 pass from Quinn (Sukup kick)
HOU	Herring 6 pass from Elston (Hatfield kick)

NEB	TEAM STATISTICS	HOU
13	First Downs	18
136	Rushing Yards	206
11-22-1	Passing	9-19-0
91	Passing Yards	119
227	Total Yards	325
10-40.6	Punts - Average	7-42.0
1-1	Fumbles - Lost	7-3
7-90	Penalties - Yards	2-22

INDIVIDUAL LEADERS

RUSHING
NEB: Redwine 17-58, 1 TD; Franklin 12-40.
HOU: Elston 22-87, 1 TD; Newhouse 14-61.

PASSING
NEB: Quinn 10-19-1, 78 yards, 1 TD.
HOU: Elston 9-16-0, 119 yards, 1 TD.

RECEIVING
NEB: Brown 5-30; Miller 2-26.
HOU: Herring 5-51, 1 TD; Phea 2-47.

JANUARY 1, 1981
ALABAMA 30, BAYLOR 2

	1ST	2ND	3RD	4TH	FINAL
ALA	6	7	3	14	30
BU	2	0	0	0	2

SCORING SUMMARY

ALA	FG Kim 29
ALA	FG Kim 28
BU	Safety (Lewis tackled by Tabor in end zone)
ALA	Ogilvie 1 run (Kim kick)
ALA	FG Kim 42
ALA	Jacobs 1 run (Kim kick)
ALA	Nix 3 run (Mardini kick)

ALA	TEAM STATISTICS	BU
17	First Downs	13
241	Rushing Yards	54
5-12-0	Passing	12-27-3
98	Passing Yards	104
339	Total Yards	158
6-37.2	Punts - Average	7-35.9
5-1	Fumbles - Lost	5-4
5-89	Penalties - Yards	6-59
36:22	Possession Time	23:38

INDIVIDUAL LEADERS

RUSHING
ALA: Ogilvie 15-74, 1 TD; Carter 4-71.
BU: Jeffrey 8-18; Gentry 11-17.

PASSING
ALA: Jacobs 5-12-0, 98 yards.
BU: Jeffrey 8-19-2, 55 yards; Mangrum 4-8-1, 49 yards.

RECEIVING
ALA: Bendross 1-49; Jackson 1-20; Brown 1-20.
BU: Hold 3-41; Gentry 5-26.

JANUARY 1, 1982
TEXAS 14, ALABAMA 12

	1ST	2ND	3RD	4TH	FINAL
ALA	0	7	0	5	12
TEX	0	0	0	14	14

SCORING SUMMARY

ALA	Bendross 6 pass from Lewis (Kim kick)
ALA	FG Kim 24
TEX	Brewer 30 run (Allegre kick)
TEX	Orr 8 run (Allegre kick)
ALA	Safety (Goodson steps out of end zone)

ALA	TEAM STATISTICS	TEX
15	First Downs	21
163	Rushing Yards	158
8-13-1	Passing	12-22-0
144	Passing Yards	201
307	Total Yards	359
5-45.2	Punts - Average	6-36.8
1-1	Fumbles - Lost	0-0
1-5	Penalties - Yards	4-17
27:58	Possession Time	32:02

INDIVIDUAL LEADERS

RUSHING
ALA: Lewis 24-79; Carter 6-44.
TEX: Clark 7-58; Jones 16-57.

PASSING
ALA: Lewis 7-12-1, 122 yards, 1 TD.
TEX: Brewer 12-21-0, 201 yards.

RECEIVING
ALA: Bendross 5-78, 1 TD; Krout 3-66.
TEX: Little 7-92; Sampleton 2-56.

JANUARY 1, 1983
SMU 7, PITTSBURGH 3

	1ST	2ND	3RD	4TH	FINAL
PITT	0	0	3	0	3
SMU	0	0	0	7	7

SCORING SUMMARY

PITT	FG Schubert 43
SMU	McIlhenny 9 run (Harrell kick)

PITT	TEAM STATISTICS	SMU
17	First Downs	22
104	Rushing Yards	153
19-37-1	Passing	5-9-0
181	Passing Yards	101
285	Total Yards	254
3-44.7	Punts - Average	4-38.0
1-1	Fumbles - Lost	4-2
8-74	Penalties - Yards	2-30

INDIVIDUAL LEADERS

RUSHING
PITT: Thomas 13-69; McCall 9-16.
SMU: Dickerson 27-124; James 14-54.

PASSING
PITT: Marino 19-37-1, 183 yards.
SMU: McIlhenny 5-8-0, 101 yards.

RECEIVING
PITT: McCall 5-58; Compton 4-42.
SMU: Leach 2-62; James 3-39.

JANUARY 2, 1984
GEORGIA 10, TEXAS 9

	1ST	2ND	3RD	4TH	FINAL
UGA	3	0	0	7	10
TEX	3	0	6	0	9

SCORING SUMMARY

TEX	FG Ward 22
UGA	FG Butler 43
TEX	FG Ward 40
TEX	FG Ward 27
UGA	Lastinger 17 run (Butler kick)

UGA	TEAM STATISTICS	TEX
13	First Downs	14
149	Rushing Yards	110
6-20-1	Passing	8-26-2
66	Passing Yards	168
215	Total Yards	278
9-41.2	Punts - Average	7-46.7
2-1	Fumbles - Lost	4-2
3-25	Penalties - Yards	6-52

INDIVIDUAL LEADERS

RUSHING
UGA: Montgomery 11-40; Lane 1-35.
TEX: Robinson 28-88; Orr 7-19.

PASSING
UGA: Lastinger 6-19-1, 66 yards.
TEX: McIvor 8-26-2, 168 yards.

RECEIVING
UGA: Harris 2-33; Wisham 1-14.
TEX: Micho 2-59; Epps 1-44.

JANUARY 1, 1985
BOSTON COLLEGE 45, HOUSTON 28

	1ST	2ND	3RD	4TH	FINAL
BC	17	14	0	14	45
HOU	7	7	14	0	28

SCORING SUMMARY

BC	Martin 63 pass from Flutie (Snow kick)
BC	Stradford 8 pass from Flutie (Snow kick)
HOU	Allen 98 kickoff return (Clendenen kick)
BC	FG Snow 31
BC	Phelan 13 pass from Flutie (Snow kick)
BC	Strachan 2 run (Snow kick)
HOU	Sheperd 15 pass from Landry (Clendenen kick)
HOU	Tate 2 run (Clendenen kick)
HOU	McMillian 25 interception return (Clendenen kick)
BC	Strachan 4 run (Snow kick)
BC	Stradford 18 run (Snow kick)

BC	TEAM STATISTICS	HOU
22	First Downs	15
353	Rushing Yards	167
13-37-2	Passing	9-29-2
180	Passing Yards	154
533	Total Yards	321
8-29.9	Punts - Average	10-33.0
2-1	Fumbles - Lost	3-2
7-64	Penalties - Yards	7-66

INDIVIDUAL LEADERS

RUSHING
BC: Stradford 20-196, 1 TD; Strachan 23-91, 2 TD.
HOU: Tate 10-71, 1 TD; Landry 22-66.

PASSING
BC: Flutie 13-37-2, 180 yards, 3 TD.
HOU: Landry 9-29-2, 154 yards, 1 TD.

RECEIVING
BC: Phelan 7-94, 1 TD; Martin 1-63, 1 TD.
HOU: Hilton 5-97; Shepherd 2-47, 1 TD.

JANUARY 1, 1986
TEXAS A&M 36, AUBURN 16

	1ST	2ND	3RD	4TH	FINAL
AU	7	6	3	0	16
A&M	12	3	6	15	36

SCORING SUMMARY

AU	Jackson 5 run (Johnson kick)
A&M	Johnson 11 run (kick failed)
A&M	Woodside 22 run (pass failed)
AU	Jackson 73 pass from Washington (run failed)
A&M	FG Slater 26
A&M	Toney 21 run (pass failed)
AU	FG Johnson 26
A&M	Woodside 9 pass from Murray (Bernstine run)
A&M	Toney 1 run (Slater kick)

AU	TEAM STATISTICS	A&M
16	First Downs	21
198	Rushing Yards	186
7-17-2	Passing	16-26-1
154	Passing Yards	292
352	Total Yards	478
5-43.8	Punts - Average	5-45.0
2-1	Fumbles - Lost	1-1
1-5	Penalties - Yards	5-45

INDIVIDUAL LEADERS

RUSHING
AU: Jackson 31-129, 1 TD; Agee 5-36.
A&M: Vick 15-67; Woodside 3-32, 1 TD.

PASSING
AU: Washington 2-7-0, 82 yards, 1 TD; Burger 5-10-2, 72 yards.
A&M: Murray 16-26-1, 292 yards, 1 TD.

RECEIVING
AU: Jackson 2-73, 1 TD; Parks 2-32.
A&M: Bernstine 6-108; Woodside 3-88, 1 TD.

THE BOWLS

JANUARY 1, 1987
OHIO STATE 28, TEXAS A&M 12

	1ST	2ND	3RD	4TH	FINAL
OSU	0	7	14	7	28
A&M	3	3	0	6	12

SCORING SUMMARY

A&M	FG Slater 30
OSU	Karsatos 3 run (Frantz kick)
A&M	FG Slater 44
OSU	Spielman 24 interception return (Frantz kick)
OSU	Workman 8 run (Frantz kick)
A&M	Vick 2 run (pass failed)
OSU	Kee 49 interception return (Frantz kick)

OSU	TEAM STATISTICS	A&M
16	First Downs	18
85	Rushing Yards	160
13-29-3	Passing	13-33-5
218	Passing Yards	136
303	Total Yards	296
6-35.2	Punts - Average	6-42.2
1-0	Fumbles - Lost	1-0
11-70	Penalties - Yards	3-15

INDIVIDUAL LEADERS

RUSHING
OSU: Cooper 13-55; Workman 13-45, 1 TD.
A&M: Vick 24-113, 1 TD; Woodside 11-32.

PASSING
OSU: Karsatos 10-21-2, 195 yards.
A&M: Murray 12-31-5, 143 yards.

RECEIVING
OSU: Harris 6-105; Carter 4-61.
A&M: Bernstine 4-59; Walker 3-35.

JANUARY 1, 1988
TEXAS A&M 35, NOTRE DAME 10

	1ST	2ND	3RD	4TH	FINAL
ND	7	3	0	0	10
A&M	3	15	7	10	35

SCORING SUMMARY

ND	Brown 17 pass from Andrysiak (Gradel kick)
A&M	FG Slater 26
ND	FG Gradel 36
A&M	Thompson 24 pass from Lewis (Slater kick)
A&M	Horton 2 run (Hartley run)
A&M	Richardson 1 run (Slater kick)
A&M	FG Slater 25
A&M	Richardson 8 run (Slater kick)

ND	TEAM STATISTICS	A&M
16	First Downs	24
74	Rushing Yards	294
15-28-2	Passing	8-17-0
203	Passing Yards	116
277	Total Yards	410
5-31.4	Punts - Average	4-42.2
2-2	Fumbles - Lost	1-1
6-64	Penalties - Yards	6-55

INDIVIDUAL LEADERS

RUSHING
ND: Johnson 8-20; Andrysiak 11-15.
A&M: Richardson 13-96, 2 TD; Woodside 17-73.

PASSING
ND: Andrysiak 15-25-1, 203 yards, 1 TD.
A&M: Pavlas 5-7-0, 77 yards.

RECEIVING
ND: Brown 6-105, 1 TD; Ward 2-37.
A&M: Oliver 1-33; Thompson 1-24, 1 TD.

JANUARY 2, 1989
UCLA 17, ARKANSAS 3

	1ST	2ND	3RD	4TH	FINAL
UCLA	0	14	0	3	17
ARK	0	0	3	0	3

SCORING SUMMARY

UCLA	Estwick 1 run (Velasco kick)
UCLA	Anthony 1 pass from Aikman (Velasco kick)
ARK	FG Trainor 49
UCLA	FG Velasco 32

UCLA	TEAM STATISTICS	ARK
22	First Downs	4
199	Rushing Yards	21
19-27-1	Passing	4-14-1
172	Passing Yards	21
371	Total Yards	42
3-36.0	Punts - Average	6-49.2
3-2	Fumbles - Lost	0-0
7-74	Penalties - Yards	7-61
42:43	Possession Time	17:17

INDIVIDUAL LEADERS

RUSHING
UCLA: Willis 18-120; Brown 16-56.
ARK: Grovey 7-19; Foster 6-16.

PASSING
UCLA: Aikman 19-27-1, 172 yards, 1 TD.
ARK: Grovey 2-7-0, 10 yards.

RECEIVING
UCLA: Farr 4-48; Arbuckle 1-35.
ARK: Jackson 1-8; Harshaw 1-7.

JANUARY 1, 1990
TENNESSEE 31, ARKANSAS 27

	1ST	2ND	3RD	4TH	FINAL
TENN	3	14	14	0	31
ARK	6	0	7	14	27

SCORING SUMMARY

TENN	FG Burke 23
ARK	Foster 1 run (run failed)
TENN	Morgan 84 pass from Kelly (Burke kick)
TENN	Webb 1 run (Burke kick)
TENN	Amsler 1 pass from Kelly (Burke kick)
ARK	Rouse 1 run (Wright kick)
TENN	Webb 78 run (Burke kick)
ARK	Foster 1 run (Foster run)
ARK	Winston 67 pass from Grovey (pass failed)

TENN	TEAM STATISTICS	ARK
16	First Downs	31
320	Rushing Yards	361
9-23-2	Passing	12-22-1
150	Passing Yards	207
470	Total Yards	568
5-39.0	Punts - Average	3-44.3
0-0	Fumbles - Lost	3-2
4-36	Penalties - Yards	3-20
22:17	Possession Time	37:43

INDIVIDUAL LEADERS

RUSHING
TENN: Webb 26-250, 2 TD; Moore 1-36.
ARK: Rouse 22-134, 1 TD; Foster 22-103, 2 TD.

PASSING
TENN: Kelly 9-23-2, 150 yards, 2 TD.
ARK: Grovey 12-22-1, 207 yards, 1 TD.

RECEIVING
TENN: Morgan 2-96, 1 TD; Harper 2-28.
ARK: Russell 7-105; Winston 4-94, 1 TD.

JANUARY 1, 1991
MIAMI (FLA.) 46, TEXAS 3

	1ST	2ND	3RD	4TH	FINAL
MIA	12	7	14	13	46
TEX	0	3	0	0	3

SCORING SUMMARY

MIA	FG Huerta 28
MIA	FG Huerta 50
MIA	Carroll 12 pass from Erickson (pass failed)
TEX	FG Pollak 29
MIA	Carroll 24 pass from Erickson (Huerta kick)
MIA	Smith 34 interception return (Huerta kick)
MIA	Hill 48 pass from Erickson (Huerta kick)
MIA	Bethel 4 pass from Erickson (kick blocked)
MIA	Conley 26 run (Huerta kick)

MIA	TEAM STATISTICS	TEX
16	First Downs	20
67	Rushing Yards	150
17-28-0	Passing	8-18-3
272	Passing Yards	55
339	Total Yards	205
5-38.4	Punts - Average	5-40.6
1-0	Fumbles - Lost	2-2
16-202	Penalties - Yards	8-68
25:08	Possession Time	24:52

INDIVIDUAL LEADERS

RUSHING
MIA: Conley 3-38, 1 TD; McGuire 9-33.
TEX: Hadnot 17-101; Samuels 8-30.

PASSING
MIA: Erickson 17-26-0, 272 yards, 4 TD.
TEX: Gardere 7-16-3, 40 yards.

RECEIVING
MIA: Carroll 8-135, 2 TD; Hill 1-48, 1 TD.
TEX: Samuels 3-24; Davis 1-15.

JANUARY 1, 1992
FLORIDA STATE 10, TEXAS A&M 2

	1ST	2ND	3RD	4TH	FINAL
FSU	7	0	0	3	10
A&M	2	0	0	0	2

SCORING SUMMARY

A&M	Safety (Weldon tackled by Coryatt in end zone)
FSU	Weldon 4 run (Thomas kick)
FSU	FG Thomas 27

FSU	TEAM STATISTICS	A&M
17	First Downs	12
188	Rushing Yards	123
14-32-4	Passing	6-24-2
92	Passing Yards	57
280	Total Yards	180
8-43.3	Punts - Average	9-39.7
3-1	Fumbles - Lost	7-6
11-77	Penalties - Yards	6-50
33:59	Possession Time	26:01

INDIVIDUAL LEADERS

RUSHING
FSU: Jackson 27-119; Bennett 11-47.
A&M: Hill 14-71; Carter 7-22.

PASSING
FSU: Weldon 14-32-4, 92 yards.
A&M: Richardson 6-24-2, 57 yards.

RECEIVING
FSU: Baker 4-44; Jackson 3-20.
A&M: Harrison 2-27; Hill 2-17.

JANUARY 1, 1993
NOTRE DAME 28, TEXAS A&M 3

	1ST	2ND	3RD	4TH	FINAL
ND	0	7	14	7	28
A&M	0	0	0	3	3

SCORING SUMMARY

ND	Dawson 40 pass from Mirer (Hentrich kick)
ND	Bettis 26 pass from Mirer (Hentrich kick)
ND	Bettis 1 run (Hentrich kick)
A&M	FG Venetoulias 41
ND	Bettis 4 run (Hentrich kick)

ND	TEAM STATISTICS	A&M
28	First Downs	11
290	Rushing Yards	78
9-18-0	Passing	7-18-0
149	Passing Yards	87
439	Total Yards	165
9	Punt Returns - Yards	8
13	Kickoff Returns - Yards	98
4-38.0	Punts - Average	6-40.5
3-3	Fumbles - Lost	2-2
3-30	Penalties - Yards	7-42
38:01	Possession Time	21:59

INDIVIDUAL LEADERS

RUSHING
ND: Brooks 22-115; Bettis 20-75, 2 TD.
A&M: Thomas 20-50; Mitchell 1-12.

PASSING
ND: Mirer 8-16-0, 119 yards, 2 TD.
A&M: Pullig 7-18-0, 87 yards.

RECEIVING
ND: Dawson 2-46, 1 TD; Smith 3-38.
A&M: Harrison 3-59; Schorp 2-14.

JANUARY 1, 1994
NOTRE DAME 24, TEXAS A&M 21

	1ST	2ND	3RD	4TH	FINAL
ND	7	0	14	3	24
A&M	7	7	7	0	21

SCORING SUMMARY

ND	McDougal 19 run (Pendergast kick)
A&M	Hill 8 run (Venetoulias kick)
A&M	Smith 15 pass from Pullig (Venetoulias kick)
ND	Zellars 2 run (Pendergast kick)
A&M	Thomas 1 run (Venetoulias kick)
ND	Edwards 2 run (Pendergast kick)
ND	FG Pendergast 31

ND	TEAM STATISTICS	A&M
19	First Downs	20
206	Rushing Yards	103
7-15-0	Passing	17-31-1
105	Passing Yards	238
311	Total Yards	341
7-38.0	Punts - Average	4-37.3
1-0	Fumbles - Lost	4-2
5-34	Penalties - Yards	3-15

INDIVIDUAL LEADERS

RUSHING
ND: Becton 26-138; Zellars 9-25, 1 TD.
A&M: McElroy 4-45; Hill 16-38, 1 TD.

PASSING
ND: McDougal 7-15-0, 105 yards.
A&M: Pullig 17-31-1, 238 yards, 1 TD.

RECEIVING
ND: Dawson 2-41; Mayes 2-27.
A&M: Schorp 3-53; Harrison 3-52.

JANUARY 2, 1995
SOUTHERN CAL 55, TEXAS TECH 14

	1ST	2ND	3RD	4TH	FINAL
USC	28	6	14	7	55
TT	0	0	7	7	14

SCORING SUMMARY

USC	Walters 11 run (Ford kick)
USC	Barnum 19 pass from R. Johnson (Ford kick)
USC	Herpin 26 interception return (Ford kick)
USC	K. Johnson 12 pass from R. Johnson (Ford kick)
USC	FG Ford 39
USC	FG Ford 42
USC	K. Johnson 22 pass from R. Johnson (Ford kick)
USC	K. Johnson 86 pass from Otton (Ford kick)
TT	Lethridge 5 run (Davis kick)
USC	Diltz pass from Otton (Ford kick)
TT	Mitchell 45 pass from Cavazos (Davis kick)

USC	TEAM STATISTICS	TT
21	First Downs	14
143	Rushing Yards	55
24-35-0	Passing	15-37-2
435	Passing Yards	205
578	Total Yards	260
4-43.0	Punts - Average	10-38.0
1-1	Fumbles - Lost	4-2
12-133	Penalties - Yards	2-20

INDIVIDUAL LEADERS

RUSHING
USC: Walters 14-82, 1 TD; Sermons 12-32.
TT: Hanspard 9-36; Crain 2-22.

PASSING
USC: R. Johnson 16-21-0, 289 yards, 3 TD; Otton 8-14-0, 146 yards, 2 TD.
TT: Lethridge 12-29-2, 134 yards; Cavazos 3-5-0, 71 yards, 1 TD.

RECEIVING
USC: K. Johnson 8-222, 3 TD; Hervey 3-99.
TT: Darden 6-79; Mitchell 1-45, 1 TD.

JANUARY 1, 1996
COLORADO 38, OREGON 6

	1ST	2ND	3RD	4TH	FINAL
ORE	6	0	0	0	6
COLO	0	13	19	6	38

SCORING SUMMARY

ORE	FG Smith 25
ORE	FG Smith 33
COLO	Hessler 1 run (Voskeritchian kick)
COLO	Washington 95 interception return (kick failed)
COLO	Lepsis 2 pass from Hessler (Voskeritchian kick)
COLO	Troutman 6 run (kick failed)
COLO	Savoy 12 pass from Hessler (kick blocked)
COLO	Abdul-Rahmaan 5 run (kick blocked)

ORE	TEAM STATISTICS	COLO
16	First Downs	16
105	Rushing Yards	170
21-44-2	Passing	12-27-2
162	Passing Yards	143
267	Total Yards	313
5-38.4	Punts - Average	4-28.5
4-3	Fumbles - Lost	2-1
8-67	Penalties - Yards	6-41
30:01	Possession Time	29:59

INDIVIDUAL LEADERS

RUSHING
ORE: Whittle 12-50; Parker 3-43.
COLO: Troutman 13-100, 1 TD; Henry 7-38.

PASSING
ORE: Graziani 19-37-2, 113 yards.
COLO: Hessler 11-26-2, 115 yards, 2 TD.

RECEIVING
ORE: Hodge 2-33; McLemore 3-26.
COLO: Kidd 2-73; Savoy 3-29, 1 TD.

JANUARY 1, 1997
BYU 19, KANSAS STATE 15

	1ST	2ND	3RD	4TH	FINAL
BYU	5	0	0	14	19
KSU	0	8	7	0	15

SCORING SUMMARY

BYU	Safety (Kavanagh tackled by Muirbrook in end zone)
BYU	FG Pochman 39
KSU	Anderson 41 pass from Kavanagh (Lawrence run)
KSU	Lockett 72 pass from Kavanagh (Rheem kick)
BYU	Dye 32 pass from Sarkisian (Pochman kick)
BYU	Kealaluhi 28 pass from Sarkisian (Pochman kick)

BYU	TEAM STATISTICS	KSU
21	First Downs	14
59	Rushing Yards	41
21-36-1	Passing	14-28-2
291	Passing Yards	233
350	Total Yards	274
5-38.8	Punts - Average	7-46.0
1-0	Fumbles - Lost	1-0
8-59	Penalties - Yards	7-55
33:21	Possession Time	26:39

INDIVIDUAL LEADERS

RUSHING
BYU: Johnson 6-38; McKenzie 9-17.
KSU: Lawrence 23-54; Anderson 1-5.

PASSING
BYU: Sarkisian 21-36-1, 291 yards, 2 TD.
KSU: Kavanagh 14-28-2, 233 yards, 2 TD.

RECEIVING
BYU: Lewis 5-79; Dye 4-70, 1 TD.
KSU: Lockett 7-135, 1 TD; Anderson 2-50, 1 TD.

JANUARY 1, 1998
UCLA 29, TEXAS A&M 23

	1ST	2ND	3RD	4TH	FINAL
UCLA	0	7	14	8	29
A&M	7	9	7	0	23

SCORING SUMMARY

A&M	Jennings 64 interception return (Bryant kick)
A&M	Safety (McNown tackled by Rollins in end zone)
A&M	Hall 74 run (Bryant kick)
UCLA	McElroy 22 pass from McNown (Sailer kick)
UCLA	Hicks 41 pass from McNown (Sailer kick)
A&M	Cole 43 run (Bryant kick)
UCLA	McNown 20 run (Sailer kick)
UCLA	Neufeld 5 run (McNown run)

UCLA	TEAM STATISTICS	A&M
23	First Downs	10
154	Rushing Yards	192
16-30-1	Passing	7-14-1
239	Passing Yards	55
393	Total Yards	247
8-43.6	Punts - Average	9-45.3
3-0	Fumbles - Lost	1-0
7-73	Penalties - Yards	4-38
33:04	Possession Time	26:56

INDIVIDUAL LEADERS

RUSHING
UCLA: Hicks 31-140, 1 TD.
A&M: Hall 7-93, 1 TD; Parker 11-40.

PASSING
UCLA: McNown 16-29-1, 239 yards, 2 TD.
A&M: Stewart 4-8-0, 30 yards; McCown 3-6-1, 25 yards.

RECEIVING
UCLA: McElroy 5-84, 1 TD; Hicks 3-53, 1 TD.
A&M: Cole 4-32; Oliver 3-23.

THE BOWLS

JANUARY 1, 1999
TEXAS 38, MISSISSIPPI STATE 11

	1ST	2ND	3RD	4TH	FINAL
MSU	0	3	0	8	11
TEX	7	7	24	0	38

SCORING SUMMARY

TEX	McGarity 59 pass from Applewhite (Stockton kick)
TEX	McGarity 52 pass from Applewhite (Stockton kick)
MSU	FG Hazelwood 39
TEX	Williams 37 run (Stockton kick)
TEX	FG Stockton 47
TEX	Williams 2 run (Stockton kick)
TEX	Cavil 18 pass from Applewhite (Stockton kick)
MSU	Grant 5 pass from Wyatt (Johnson run)

MSU	TEAM STATISTICS	TEX
18	First Downs	27
87	Rushing Yards	238
16-40-1	Passing	15-26-0
205	Passing Yards	225
292	Total Yards	463
7-41.0	Punts - Average	6-37.2
2-1	Fumbles - Lost	1-0
9-89	Penalties - Yards	5-55
27:59	Possession Time	32:01

INDIVIDUAL LEADERS

RUSHING
MSU: Johnson 22-112; McKinley 2-7.
TEX: Williams 30-203, 2 TD; Mitchell 7-26.

PASSING
MSU: Wyatt 12-24-0, 156 yards, 1 TD; Madkin 4-16-1, 49 yards.
TEX: Applewhite 15-26-0, 225 yards 3 TD.

RECEIVING
MSU: Grant 4-62, 1 TD; Cooper 4-38.
TEX: McGarity 4-132, 2 TD; Williams 5-45.

JANUARY 1, 2000
ARKANSAS 27, TEXAS 6

	1ST	2ND	3RD	4TH	FINAL
TEX	0	3	3	0	6
ARK	3	0	7	17	27

SCORING SUMMARY

ARK	FG Dodson 25
TEX	FG Stockton 35
ARK	Cobbs 30 pass from Stoerner (Dodson kick)
TEX	FG Stockton 22
ARK	Jenkins 42 run (Dodson kick)
ARK	Cobbs 37 run (Dodson kick)
ARK	FG Dodson 27

TEX	TEAM STATISTICS	ARK
14	First Downs	17
-27	Rushing Yards	191
24-39-0	Passing	12-23-0
212	Passing Yards	194
185	Total Yards	385
9-39.7	Punts - Average	4-39.0
0-0	Fumbles - Lost	0-0
7-40	Penalties - Yards	4-36
31:30	Possession Time	28:30

INDIVIDUAL LEADERS

RUSHING
TEX: Mitchell 13-36.
ARK: Cobbs 15-98, 1 TD; Jenkins 16-82, 1 TD.

PASSING
TEX: Applewhite 15-21-0, 121 yards; Simms 9-18-0, 91 yards.
ARK: Stoerner 12-23-2, 194 yards, 1 TD.

RECEIVING
TEX: Flowers 5-62; Nunez 6-48.
ARK: Williams 2-47; Davenport 2-25.

JANUARY 1, 2001
KANSAS STATE 35, TENNESSEE 21

	1ST	2ND	3RD	4TH	FINAL
TENN	0	14	0	7	21
KSU	7	14	14	0	35

SCORING SUMMARY

KSU	Beasley 14 run (Rheem kick)
TENN	Martin 17 pass from Clausen (Walls kick)
KSU	Morgan 56 pass from Beasley (Rheem kick)
KSU	Morgan 10 pass from Beasley (Rheem kick)
TENN	Greer 78 interception return (Walls kick)
KSU	Scobey 12 run (Rheem kick)
KSU	Scobey 6 run (Rheem kick)
TENN	Henry 81 run (Walls kick)

TENN	TEAM STATISTICS	KSU
12	First Downs	25
178	Rushing Yards	297
7-25-3	Passing	13-27-1
120	Passing Yards	210
298	Total Yards	507
8-29.2	Punts - Average	5-34.0
1-0	Fumbles - Lost	1-1
5-40	Penalties - Yards	7-44
21:34	Possession Time	38:26

INDIVIDUAL LEADERS

RUSHING
TENN: Henry 17-180, 1 TD.
KSU: Scobey 28-147, 2 TD; Beasley 17-98, 1 TD.

PASSING
TENN: Clausen 7-25-3, 120 yards, 1 TD.
KSU: Beasley 13-27-1, 210 yards, 2 TD.

RECEIVING
TENN: Wilson 3-54; Parker 1-27.
KSU: Morgan 7-145, 2 TD; Lockett 3-22.

JANUARY 1, 2002
OKLAHOMA 10, ARKANSAS 3

	1ST	2ND	3RD	4TH	FINAL
OKLA	7	0	3	0	10
ARK	0	0	0	3	3

SCORING SUMMARY

OKLA	Hybl 1 run (Duncan kick)
OKLA	FG Duncan 32
ARK	FG O'Donohoe 32

OKLA	TEAM STATISTICS	ARK
11	First Downs	6
56	Rushing Yards	37
24-32-0	Passing	2-13-1
175	Passing Yards	13
231	Total Yards	50
9-34.9	Punts - Average	8-40.5
2-1	Fumbles - Lost	1-1
9-76	Penalties - Yards	6-54
33:34	Possession Time	26:26

INDIVIDUAL LEADERS

RUSHING
OKLA: Griffin 19-56; Works 2-4.
ARK: Holmes 8-27; Jones 15-23.

PASSING
OKLA: Hybl 24-32-0, 175 yards.
ARK: Clark 2-12-1, 13 yards.

RECEIVING
OKLA: Norman 7-74; Smith 5-39.
ARK: Wilson 1-7; Pierce 1-6.

JANUARY 1, 2003
TEXAS 35, LSU 20

	1ST	2ND	3RD	4TH	FINAL
TEX	7	14	7	7	35
LSU	10	7	0	3	20

SCORING SUMMARY

LSU	FG Corbello 26
TEX	Jackson 46 fumble recovery for TD (Mangum kick)
LSU	Toefield 20 pass from Randall (Corbello kick)
LSU	Davis 10 run (Corbello kick)
TEX	R. Williams 51 pass from Simms (Mangum kick)
TEX	Benson 1 run (Mangum kick)
TEX	R. Williams 39 run (Mangum kick)
TEX	I. Williams 8 pass from Simms (Mangum kick)
LSU	FG Corbello 39

TEX	TEAM STATISTICS	LSU
15	First Downs	25
113	Rushing Yards	248
15-28-1	Passing	19-46-1
269	Passing Yards	193
382	Total Yards	441
1-14	Punt Returns - Yards	1-0
4-77	Kickoff Returns - Yards	5-109
7-37.3	Punts - Average	4-48.8
0-0	Fumbles - Lost	3-2
6-60	Penalties - Yards	4-28
23:09	Possession Time	36:51

INDIVIDUAL LEADERS

RUSHING
TEX: Young 11-49; Benson 12-46, 1 TD.
LSU: Davis 13-85, 1 TD; Randall 11-78.

PASSING
TEX: Simms 15-28-1, 269 yards 2 TD.
LSU: Randall 19-45-1, 193 yards, 1 TD.

RECEIVING
TEX: R. Williams 4-142, 1 TD; Thomas 4-59.
LSU: Clayton 6-88; Davis 3-31.

JANUARY 2, 2004
MISSISSIPPI 31, OKLAHOMA STATE 28

	1ST	2ND	3RD	4TH	FINAL
MISS	7	10	7	7	31
OSU	7	7	0	14	28

SCORING SUMMARY

MISS	Turner 16 pass from Manning (Nichols kick)
OSU	Morency 4 run (Phillips kick)
OSU	Bell 3 run (Phillips kick)
MISS	Espy 25 pass from Manning (Nichols kick)
MISS	FG Nichols 33
MISS	Turner 2 run (Nichols kick)
MISS	Manning 1 run (Nichols kick)
OSU	Morency 1 run (Phillips kick)
OSU	R. Woods 17 pass from Fields (Phillips kick)

MISS	TEAM STATISTICS	OSU
24	First Downs	22
190	Rushing Yards	110
22-31-1	Passing	21-33-0
259	Passing Yards	307
449	Total Yards	417
3-57	Punt Returns - Yards	1-15
0-0	Kickoff Returns - Yards	3-57
3-38.0	Punts - Average	3-37.7
1-0	Fumbles - Lost	1-0
2-20	Penalties - Yards	6-49
31:29	Possession Time	28:31

INDIVIDUAL LEADERS

RUSHING
MISS: Turner 20-133, 1 TD; Pearson 12-42.
OSU: Morency 15-59, 2 TD; Bell 14-46, 1 TD.

PASSING
MISS: Manning 22-31-1, 259 yards, 2 TD.
OSU: Fields 21-33-0, 307 yards, 1 TD.

RECEIVING
MISS: Collins 8-75; Johnson 3-53; Espy 2-47, 1 TD.
OSU: R. Woods 11-223, 1 TD; D. Woods 4-51.

JANUARY 1, 2005

TENNESSEE 38, TEXAS A&M 7

	1ST	2ND	3RD	4TH	FINAL
TENN	14	14	10	0	38
A&M	0	0	0	7	7

SCORING SUMMARY

TENN	Fayton 57 pass from Clausen (Wilhoit kick)
TENN	Anderson 12 pass from Clausen (Wilhoit kick)
TENN	Houston 8 run (Wilhoit kick)
TENN	Brown 13 pass from Clausen (Wilhoit kick)
TENN	Riggs 9 run (Wilhoit kick)
TENN	FG Wilhoit 37
A&M	Taylor 5 pass from McNeal (Pegram kick)

TENN	TEAM STATISTICS	A&M
32	First Downs	17
241	Rushing Yards	77
19-31-0	Passing	23-38-1
233	Passing Yards	241
474	Total Yards	318
3-20	Punt Returns - Yards	1-(-6)
0-0	Kickoff Returns - Yards	3-47
4-34.0	Punts - Average	5-43.2
1-0	Fumbles - Lost	4-4
9-100	Penalties - Yards	7-65
40:22	Possession Time	19:38

INDIVIDUAL LEADERS

RUSHING
TENN: Riggs 18-102, 1 TD; Houston 13-62, 1 TD.
A&M: Thomas 1-54.

PASSING
TENN: Clausen 18-27-0, 222 yards, 3 TD.
A&M: McNeal 23-38-1, 241 yards, 1 TD.

RECEIVING
TENN: Fayton 3-94, 1 TD.
A&M: Mobley 5-70; Taylor 5-39, 1 TD.

GATOR BOWL

PROFILE

Site: Jacksonville, Fla.
Stadium: Alltel Stadium
Capacity: 76,976
Surface: Grass

PLAYING SITES

Gator Bowl, 1946-93
Florida Field, 1994
Jacksonville Municipal Stadium, renamed Alltel Stadium in 1997, since 1995

NAME CHANGES

Gator Bowl, 1946-85
Mazda Gator Bowl, 1986-90
Gator Bowl, 1991
Outback Steakhouse Gator Bowl, 1992-94
Toyota Gator Bowl, since 1995

SEASON	DATE	PRE-GAME RANK	TEAMS	SCORE	FINAL RANK	MOST VALUABLE PLAYERS	ATT.
1945	Jan. 1, 1946		Wake Forest	26		Nick Sacrinty, Wake Forest, QB	7,362
			South Carolina	14			
1946	Jan. 1, 1947		Oklahoma	34		Joe Golding, Oklahoma, HB	10,134
			North Carolina State	13			
1947	Jan. 1, 1948		Georgia	20		Lu Gambino, Maryland, HB	16,666
			Maryland	20			
1948	Jan. 1, 1949	11	Clemson	24		Bobby Gage, Clemson, HB	32,939
			Missouri	23			
1949	Jan. 2, 1950	14	Maryland	20		Bob Ward, Maryland, G	18,409
		20	Missouri	7			
1950	Jan. 1, 1951	12	Wyoming	20		Eddie Talboom, Wyoming, HB	19,834
		18	Washington & Lee	7			
1951	Jan. 1, 1952		Miami (Fla.)	14		Jim Dooley, Miami (Fla.), HB	34,577
		19	Clemson	0			
1952	Jan. 1, 1953	15	Florida	14		John Hall, Florida, RB	30,015
		12	Tulsa	13		Marv Matuszak, Tulsa, T	
1953	Jan. 1, 1954	12	Texas Tech	35		Bobby Cavazos, Texas Tech, RB	28,641
		17	Auburn	13		Vince Dooley, Auburn, QB	
1954	Dec. 31, 1954	13	Auburn	33		Joe Childress, Auburn, FB	28,426
		18	Baylor	13		Billy Hooper, Baylor, QB	
1955	Dec. 31, 1955		Vanderbilt	25		Don Orr, Vanderbilt, QB	32,174
		8	Auburn	13		Joe Childress, Auburn, FB	
1956	Dec. 29, 1956	4	Georgia Tech	21		Wade Mitchell, Georgia Tech, QB	36,256
		13	Pittsburgh	14		Corny Salvaterra, Pittsburgh, QB	
1957	Dec. 28, 1957	13	Tennessee	3		Bobby Gordon, Tennessee, TB	41,160
		9	Texas A&M	0		John David Crow, Texas A&M, HB	
1958	Dec. 27, 1958	11	Mississippi	7		Bobby Franklin, Mississippi, QB	41,312
		14	Florida	3		Dave Hudson, Florida, E	
1959	Jan. 2, 1960	9	Arkansas	14		Jim Mooty, Arkansas, HB	45,104
			Georgia Tech	7		Maxie Baughan, Georgia Tech, LB	
1960	Dec. 31, 1960	12	Florida	13		Larry Libertore, Florida, QB	50,112
		18	Baylor	12		Bobby Ply, Baylor, QB	
1961	Dec. 30, 1961	17	Penn State	30		Galen Hall, Penn State, QB	50,202
		13	Georgia Tech	15		Joe Auer, Georgia Tech, HB	
1962	Dec. 29, 1962		Florida	17		Tom Shannon, Florida, QB	50,026
		9	Penn State	7		Dave Robinson, Penn State, E	
1963	Dec. 28, 1963		North Carolina	35		Ken Willard, North Carolina, RB	50,018
			Air Force	0		David Sicks, Air Force, C	
1964	Jan. 2, 1965		Florida State	36		Fred Biletnikoff, SE, Steve Tensi, QB, Florida State	50,408
			Oklahoma	19		Carl McAdams, Oklahoma, LB	
1965	Dec. 31, 1965		Georgia Tech	31		Lenny Snow, Georgia Tech, TB	60,127
		10	Texas Tech	21		Donny Anderson, Texas Tech, RB	
1966	Dec. 31, 1966		Tennessee	18		Dewey Warren, Tennessee, QB	60,312
			Syracuse	12		Floyd Little, Syracuse, HB	
1967	Dec. 30, 1967		Florida State	17		Kim Hammond, Florida State, QB	68,019
		10	Penn State	17		Tom Sherman, Penn State, QB	
1968	Dec. 28, 1968	16	Missouri	35	9	Terry McMillan, Missouri, QB	68,011
		12	Alabama	10	17	Mike Hall, Alabama, LB	
1969	Dec. 27, 1969	15	Florida	14	14	Mike Kelley, Florida, LB	72,248
		11	Tennessee	13	15	Curt Watson, Tennessee, FB	
1970	Jan. 2, 1971	10	Auburn	35	10	Pat Sullivan, Auburn. QB	71,136
			Mississippi	28	20	Archie Manning, Mississippi, QB	
1971	Dec. 31, 1971	6	Georgia	7	7	Jimmy Poulos, Georgia, TB	71,208
			North Carolina	3		James Webster, North Carolina, LB	
1972	Dec. 30, 1972	6	Auburn	24	5	Wade Whatley, Auburn, QB	71,114
		13	Colorado	3	16	Mark Cooney, Colorado, LB	
1973	Dec. 29, 1973	11	Texas Tech	28	11	Joe Barnes, Texas Tech. QB	62,109
		20	Tennessee	19	19	Haskell Stanback, Tennessee, TB	
1974	Dec. 30, 1974	6	Auburn	27	8	Phil Gargis, Auburn, QB	63,811
		11	Texas	3	17	Earl Campbell, Texas, RB	
1975	Dec. 29, 1975	17	Maryland	13	13	Steve Atkins, Maryland, TB	64,012
		13	Florida	0		Sammy Green, Florida, LB	
1976	Dec. 27, 1976	15	Notre Dame	20	12	Al Hunter, Notre Dame, HB	67,827
		20	Penn State	9		Jim Cefalo, Penn State, WR	
1977	Dec. 30, 1977	10	Pittsburgh	34	8	Matt Cavanaugh, Pittsburgh, QB	72,289
		11	Clemson	3	19	Jerry Butler, Clemson, SE	
1978	Dec. 29, 1978	7	Clemson	17	6	Steve Fuller, Clemson, QB	72,011
		20	Ohio State	15		Art Schlichter, Ohio State, QB	
1979	Dec. 28, 1979		North Carolina	17	15	Matt Kupec, QB, Amos Lawrence, RB, North Carolina	70,407
		14	Michigan	15	18	John Wangler QB, Anthony Carter, WR, Michigan	
1980	Dec. 29, 1980	3	Pittsburgh	37	2	Rick Trocano, Pittsburgh, QB	72,297
		18	South Carolina	9		George Rogers, South Carolina, RB	
1981	Dec. 28, 1981	11	North Carolina	31	9	Kelvin Bryant TB, Ethan Horton, TB, North Carolina	71,009
			Arkansas	27		Gary Anderson, Arkansas, RB	
1982	Dec. 30, 1982		Florida State	31	13	Greg Allen, Florida State, TB	80,913
		10	West Virginia	12	19	Paul Woodside, West Virginia, K	
1983	Dec. 30, 1983	11	Florida	14	6	Tony Lilly, Florida, S	81,293
		10	Iowa	6	14	Owen Gill, Iowa, FB	
1984	Dec. 28, 1984	9	Oklahoma State	21	7	Thurman Thomas, Oklahoma State, RB	82,138
		7	South Carolina	14	11	Mike Hold, South Carolina, QB	
1985	Dec. 30, 1985	18	Florida State	34	15	Chip Ferguson, Florida State, QB	79,417
		19	Oklahoma State	23		Thurman Thomas, Oklahoma State, RB	
1986	Dec. 27, 1986		Clemson	27	17	Rodney Williams, Clemson, QB	80,104
		20	Stanford	21		Brad Muster, Stanford, RB	
1987	Dec. 31, 1987	7	LSU	30	5	Wendell Davis, LSU, SE	82,119
		9	South Carolina	13	15	Harold Green, South Carolina, RB	
1988	Jan. 1, 1989	19	Georgia	34	15	Wayne Johnson, Georgia, QB	76,236
			Michigan State	27		Andre Rison, Michigan State, WR	
1989	Dec. 30, 1989	14	Clemson	27	12	Levon Kirkland, Clemson, LB	82,911
		17	West Virginia	7	21	Mike Fox, West Virginia, DT	
1990	Jan. 1, 1991	12	Michigan	35	7	Michigan offensive line*	68,927
		15	Mississippi	3	21	Tyrone Ashley, Mississippi, DB	
1991	Dec. 29, 1991	20	Oklahoma	48	16	Cale Gundy, Oklahoma, QB	62,003
		19	Virginia	14		Tyrone Davis, Virginia, DB	

SEASON	DATE	PRE-GAME RANK	TEAMS	SCORE	FINAL RANK	MOST VALUABLE PLAYERS	ATT.
1992	Dec. 31, 1992	14	Florida	27	10	Errict Rhett, Florida, RB	71,233
		12	North Carolina State	10	17	Reggie Lawrence, North Carolina State, WR	
1993	Dec. 31, 1993	18	Alabama	24	14	Brian Burgdorf, Alabama, QB	67,205
		12	North Carolina	10	19	Corey Holliday, North Carolina, WR	
1994	Dec. 30, 1994		Tennessee	45	22	James Stewart, Tennessee, TB	62,200
		17	Virginia Tech	23		Maurice DeShazo, Virginia Tech, QB	
1995	Jan. 1, 1996		Syracuse	41	19	Donovan McNabb, Syracuse, QB	45,202
		23	Clemson	0		Peter Ford, Clemson, CB	
1996	Jan. 1, 1997	12	North Carolina	20	10	Oscar Davenport, North Carolina, QB	52,103
		25	West Virginia	13		David Saunders, West Virginia, WR	
1997	Jan. 1, 1998	7	North Carolina	42	6	Chris Keldorf, North Carolina, QB	54,116
			Virginia Tech	3		Nick Sorenson, Virginia Tech, QB	
1998	Jan. 1, 1999	12	Georgia Tech	35	9	Dez White, WR, Joe Hamilton , QB, Georgia Tech	70,791
		17	Notre Dame	28	22	Autry Denson, Notre Dame, RB	
1999	Jan. 1, 2000	23	Miami (Fla.)	28	15	Nate Webster, Miami (Fla.), LB	43,416
		17	Georgia Tech	13	20	Joe Hamilton, Georgia Tech, QB	
2000	Jan. 1, 2001	6	Virginia Tech	41	6	Michael Vick, Virginia Tech, QB	68,741
		16	Clemson	20	16	Rod Gardner, Clemson, WR	
2001	Jan. 1, 2002	24	Florida State	30	15	Javon Walker, Florida State, WR	72,202
		15	Virginia Tech	17	18	Andre Davis, Virginia Tech, WR	
2002	Jan. 1, 2003	17	North Carolina State	28	12	Philip Rivers, North Carolina State, QB	73,491
		11	Notre Dame	6	17	Cedric Hillard, Notre Dame, NG	
2003	Jan. 1, 2004		Maryland	41		Scott McBrien, Maryland, QB	78,892
			West Virginia	7		Brian King, West Virginia, DB	
2004	Jan. 1, 2005		Florida State	30		Leon Washington, Florida State, RB	70,112
			West Virginia	18		Kay-Jay Harris, West Virginia, RB	

JANUARY 1, 1946
WAKE FOREST 26, SOUTH CAROLINA 14

	1ST	2ND	3RD	4TH	FINAL
WFU	6	0	6	14	26
SC	0	7	0	7	14

SCORING SUMMARY
WFU	Sacrinty 3 run (kick failed)
SC	Giles 1 run (Brembs kick)
WFU	Brinkley 3 run (kick blocked)
WFU	Brinkley 1 run (Sacrinty kick)
WFU	Smathers 25 run (Sacrinty kick)
SC	Brembs 90 interception return (Brembs kick)

WFU	TEAM STATISTICS	SC
24	First Downs	7
378	Rushing Yards	88
1-6-2	Passing	4-11-1
18	Passing Yards	69
396	Total Yards	157
3-24	Kickoff Returns - Yards	5-63
3-27.0	Punts - Average	7-37.0
3-1	Fumbles - Lost	3-1
8-70	Penalties - Yards	1-5

JANUARY 1, 1947
OKLAHOMA 34, NC STATE 13

	1ST	2ND	3RD	4TH	FINAL
OKLA	7	20	0	7	34
NCST	7	0	6	0	13

SCORING SUMMARY
OKLA	Davis 1 run (Wallace kick)
NCST	Phillips 63 pass from Turner (Byler kick)
OKLA	Davis 7 run (Wallace kick)
OKLA	Wallace 5 run (kick failed)
OKLA	Golding 5 run (Wallace kick)
NCST	Palmer 8 run (kick failed)
OKLA	Owens 15 pass from Sarratt (Wallace kick)

OKLA	TEAM STATISTICS	NCST
12	First Downs	13
195	Rushing Yards	136
3-9-2	Passing	7-18-3
75	Passing Yards	103
270	Total Yards	239
5-31.0	Punts - Average	4-36.0
4-3	Fumbles - Lost	2-1
7-35	Penalties - Yards	3-13

INDIVIDUAL LEADERS
RUSHING
OKLA: Golding 12-91, 1 TD; Mitchell 9-36.
NCST: Palmer 10-70, 1 TD; Roseman 8-37.
PASSING
OKLA: Sarratt 3-9-2, 75 yards, 1 TD.
NCST: Turner 7-18-3, 103 yards, 1 TD.

JANUARY 1, 1948
MARYLAND 20, GEORGIA 20

	1ST	2ND	3RD	4TH	FINAL
MD	0	7	13	0	20
UGA	0	0	7	13	20

SCORING SUMMARY
MD	Gambino 35 run (McHugh kick)
UGA	Rauch 1 run (Geri kick)
MD	Gambino 1 run (kick failed)
MD	Gambino 24 pass from Baroni (McHugh kick)
UGA	Geri 4 run (kick failed)
UGA	Donaldson 9 pass from Rauch (Geri kick)

MD	TEAM STATISTICS	UGA
16	First Downs	19
247	Rushing Yards	219
7-14-1	Passing	12-20-1
127	Passing Yards	187
374	Total Yards	406
5-44.2	Punts - Average	4-40.0
0-0	Fumbles - Lost	2-1
5-66	Penalties - Yards	4-80

INDIVIDUAL LEADERS
RUSHING
MD: Gambino 22-165, 2 TD; Idzik 2-32.
UGA: Donaldson 10-69; Geri 7-56, 1 TD.
PASSING
MD: Tucker 4-5-0; Baroni 2-3-0, 1 TD.
UGA: Rauch 12-20-1, 187 yards, 1 TD.
RECEIVING
MD: Gambino 2-69, 1 TD; Evans 4-45.
UGA: Henderson 1-62; Edwards 3-44.

JANUARY 1, 1949
CLEMSON 24, MISSOURI 23

	1ST	2ND	3RD	4TH	FINAL
CLEM	14	0	7	3	24
MO	0	14	2	7	23

SCORING SUMMARY
CLEM	Cone 1 run (Miller kick)
CLEM	Cone 1 run (Miller kick)
MO	Entsminger 23 run (Dawson kick)
MO	Entsminger 1 run (Dawson kick)
CLEM	Poulos 9 pass from Gage (Miller kick)
MO	Safety (Gage pass grounded in end zone)
CLEM	FG Miller 32
MO	Bounds 20 pass from Braznell (Dawson kick)

CLEM	TEAM STATISTICS	MO
19	First Downs	16
186	Rushing Yards	225
10-23-1	Passing	4-8-0
112	Passing Yards	73
298	Total Yards	298
1-35.0	Punts - Average	3-31.0
1-0	Fumbles - Lost	3-2
2-10	Penalties - Yards	4-42

INDIVIDUAL LEADERS
RUSHING
CLEM: Mathews 11-74; Cone 14-72, 2 TD.
MO: Entsminger 17-77, 2 TD; Carras 12-73.
PASSING
CLEM: Gage 10-23-1, 112 yards, 1 TD.
MO: Braznell 1-1-0, 37 yards, 1 TD.
RECEIVING
CLEM: Thompson 4-48; Poulos 3-28, 1 TD.
MO: Bounds 2-57, 1 TD.

JANUARY 2, 1950
MARYLAND 20, MISSOURI 7

	1ST	2ND	3RD	4TH	FINAL
MD	7	13	0	0	20
MO	0	0	0	7	7

SCORING SUMMARY
MD	Shemonski 11 run (Dean kick)
MD	Modzelewski 3 run (Dean kick)
MD	Shemonski 6 run (kick failed)
MO	Klein 5 run (Glorioso kick)

MD	TEAM STATISTICS	MO
11	First Downs	13
266	Rushing Yards	100
2-17-1	Passing	11-29-3
16	Passing Yards	167
282	Total Yards	267
7-39.0	Punts - Average	3-38.0
2-1	Fumbles - Lost	5-5
63	Penalty Yards	10

INDIVIDUAL LEADERS
RUSHING
MD: Shemonski 9-72, 2 TD.
MO: Klein 9-30, 1 TD.

JANUARY 1, 1951
WYOMING 20, WASHINGTON & LEE 7

	1ST	2ND	3RD	4TH	FINAL
WYO	0	13	7	0	20
W&L	0	0	0	7	7

SCORING SUMMARY
WYO	Campbell 8 pass from Talboom (kick failed)
WYO	Talboom 2 run (Talboom kick)
WYO	Melton 25 run (Talboom kick)
W&L	Bocetti 3 run (Brewer kick)

WYO	TEAM STATISTICS	W&L
14	First Downs	19
147	Rushing Yards	252
10-16-2	Passing	3-13-0
141	Passing Yards	31
288	Total Yards	283
5-39.0	Punts - Average	6-29.5
1-1	Fumbles - Lost	7-4
6-75	Penalties - Yards	2-31

INDIVIDUAL LEADERS
RUSHING
WYO: Geldien 11-56; Melton 12-49, 1 TD.
W&L: Holt 21-107; Broyles 12-89.
PASSING
WYO: Talboom 10-16-0, 141 yards, 1 TD.
W&L: Bocetti 3-12-1, 31 yards.

THE BOWLS

JANUARY 1, 1952
MIAMI (FLA.) 14, CLEMSON 0

	1ST	2ND	3RD	4TH	FINAL
MIA	7	7	0	0	14
CLEM	0	0	0	0	0

SCORING SUMMARY
MIA Mallios 11 run (Tremont kick)
MIA Mallios 2 run (Tremont kick)

MIA	TEAM STATISTICS	CLEM
5	First Downs	14
119	Rushing Yards	145
2-2-0	Passing	6-20-4
55	Passing Yards	88
174	Total Yards	233
9-44.5	Punts - Average	4-30.5
0-0	Fumbles - Lost	4-1
4-30	Penalties - Yards	0-0

INDIVIDUAL LEADERS
RUSHING
MIA: Mallios 20-50, 2 TD; Bow 13-33.
CLEM: Gressette 16-64; Hair 12-35.
PASSING
MIA: Hackett 2-2-0, 55 yards.
CLEM: Hair 6-20-4, 88 yards.
RECEIVING
MIA: Lutes 1-40.
CLEM: Smith 4-55; Kempson 1-31.

JANUARY 1, 1953
FLORIDA 14, TULSA 13

	1ST	2ND	3RD	4TH	FINAL
UF	7	7	0	0	14
UT	0	0	7	6	13

SCORING SUMMARY
UF Casares 2 run (Casares kick)
UF Hall 37 pass from Robinson (Casares kick)
UT Roberts 3 run (Miner kick)
UT Waugh 2 run (kick failed)

UF	TEAM STATISTICS	UT
20	First Downs	17
233	Rushing Yards	182
7-11-1	Passing	10-16-1
101	Passing Yards	132
334	Total Yards	314
1-38.0	Punts - Average	4-31.0
5-4	Fumbles - Lost	3-1
4-34	Penalties - Yards	11-84

INDIVIDUAL LEADERS
RUSHING
UF: Hall 17-94; Casares 21-86, 1 TD.
UT: Kercher 16-71; Waugh 15-64, 1 TD.
PASSING
UF: Dickey 4-5-0, 65 yards; Robinson 3-6-1, 35 yards, 1 TD.
UT: Morris 10-16-1, 132 yards.
RECEIVING
UF: Hall 2-66, 1 TD; O'Brien 2-22.
UT: Miner 6-77; Roberts 3-41.

JANUARY 1, 1954
TEXAS TECH 35, AUBURN 13

	1ST	2ND	3RD	4TH	FINAL
TT	0	7	14	14	35
AUB	7	6	0	0	13

SCORING SUMMARY
AUB Duke 1 run (Davis kick)
TT Cavazos 6 run (Kirkpatrick kick)
AUB Dooley 10 run (kick failed)
TT Erwin 52 pass from Kirkpatrick (Kirkpatrick kick)
TT Lewis fumble recovery in end zone (Kirkpatrick kick)
TT Cavazos 59 run (Kirkpatrick kick)
TT Cavazos 2 run (Kirkpatrick kick)

TT	TEAM STATISTICS	AUB
11	First Downs	12
226	Rushing Yards	195
6-12-1	Passing	6-16-2
145	Passing Yards	72
371	Total Yards	267
6-33.1	Punts - Average	6-30.5
2-0	Fumbles - Lost	2-2
6-83	Penalties - Yards	5-66

INDIVIDUAL LEADERS
RUSHING
TT: Cavazos 13-141, 3 TD; Jones 2-44.
AUB: Dooley 14-56, 1 TD; Duke 4-37, 1 TD.
PASSING
TT: Kirkpatrick 3-4-0, 95 yards, 1 TD.
AUB: Dooley 4-8-0, 49 yards.

DECEMBER 31, 1954
AUBURN 33, BAYLOR 13

	1ST	2ND	3RD	4TH	FINAL
AUB	7	14	12	0	33
BU	7	0	6	0	13

SCORING SUMMARY
AUB Childress 7 run (Childress kick)
BU Saage 1 run (Smith kick)
AUB James 43 run (Childress kick)
AUB Long 4 pass from Freeman (Childress kick)
AUB Childress 3 run (kick failed)
BU Dupre 38 (kick blocked)
AUB Freeman 5 run (kick failed)

AUB	TEAM STATISTICS	BU
25	First Downs	16
423	Rushing Yards	105
3-7-0	Passing	10-18-1
53	Passing Yards	134
476	Total Yards	239
2-41.0	Punts - Average	3-42.0
2-2	Fumbles - Lost	3-2
5-52	Penalties - Yards	3-25

INDIVIDUAL LEADERS
RUSHING
AUB: Childress 20-134, 2 TD; Freeman 12-80, 1 TD.
BU: Dupre 8-69, 1 TD; Jones 8-27.
PASSING
AUB: Freeman 3-7-0, 53 yards, 1 TD.
BU: Hooper 9-15-0, 112 yards.
RECEIVING
AUB: Hall 1-33; Pyburn 1-16.
BU: J.R. Smith 2-49; C. Smith 4-48.

DECEMBER 31, 1955
VANDERBILT 25, AUBURN 13

	1ST	2ND	3RD	4TH	FINAL
VAN	7	6	6	6	25
AUB	0	7	0	6	13

SCORING SUMMARY
VAN Stephenson 8 pass from Orr (Jalufka kick)
AUB James 38 pass from Tubbs (Tubbs kick)
VAN Orr 3 run (kick failed)
VAN King 1 run (kick failed)
VAN Horton 1 run (kick blocked)
AUB Phillips 4 pass from Cook (kick failed)

VAN	TEAM STATISTICS	AUB
15	First Downs	15
177	Rushing Yards	159
5-8-1	Passing	7-13-0
94	Passing Yards	142
271	Total Yards	301
4-31.7	Punts - Average	3-29.0
1-1	Fumbles - Lost	5-5
5-54	Penalties - Yards	6-59

INDIVIDUAL LEADERS
RUSHING
VAN: Horton 13-57, 1 TD; Orr 10-43, 1 TD.
AUB: Childress 15-58; James 9-42.
PASSING
VAN: Orr 4-6-1, 67 yards, 1 TD.
AUB: Tubbs 4-9-0, 101 yards, 1 TD.
RECEIVING
VAN: Scalen 2-44; Stephenson 2-23, 1 TD.
AUB: James 2-51, 1 TD; Elliott 2-41.

DECEMBER 29, 1956
GEORGIA TECH 21, PITTSBURGH 14

	1ST	2ND	3RD	4TH	FINAL
GT	7	7	7	0	21
PITT	0	7	7	0	14

SCORING SUMMARY
GT Owen 2 run (Mitchell kick)
GT Nabors 6 pass from Volkert (Mitchell kick)
PITT Bowan 42 pass from Salvaterra (Walton pass from Salvaterra)
GT Rotenberry 5 run (Mitchell kick)
PITT Salvaterra 1 run (Bagamery kick)

GT	TEAM STATISTICS	PITT
10	First Downs	16
162	Rushing Yards	246
3-3-0	Passing	3-11-2
45	Passing Yards	67
207	Total Yards	313
5-41.2	Punts - Average	3-36.0
1-1	Fumbles - Lost	2-2
1-13	Penalties - Yards	0-0

INDIVIDUAL LEADERS
RUSHING
GT: Flowers 4-63; Mattison 11-43.
PITT: Jelic 10-66; Passodelis 10-38.
PASSING
GT: Mitchell 2-2-0, 39 yards; Volkert 1-1-0, 6 yards, 1 TD.
PITT: Salvaterra 3-10-2, 67 yards, 1 TD.
RECEIVING
GT: Nabors 2-32, 1 TD; Rotenberry 1-13.
PITT: Bowan 1-42, 1 TD; Walton 1-21.

DECEMBER 28, 1957
TENNESSEE 3, TEXAS A&M 0

	1ST	2ND	3RD	4TH	FINAL
TENN	0	0	3	0	3
A&M	0	0	0	0	0

SCORING SUMMARY
TENN FG Burklow 17

TENN	TEAM STATISTICS	A&M
14	First Downs	8
135	Rushing Yards	142
4-6-0	Passing	3-8-0
56	Passing Yards	27
191	Total Yards	169
8-36.0	Punts - Average	7-38.0
2-1	Fumbles - Lost	2-2
3-30	Penalties - Yards	3-35

INDIVIDUAL LEADERS
RUSHING
TENN: Gordon 32-60; Bronson 11-31.
A&M: Crow 14-46; Osborne 12-31.
PASSING
TENN: Gordon 4-6-0, 56 yards.
A&M: Milstead 2-5-0, 16 yards.
RECEIVING
TENN: Darty 2-26; Anderson 1-20.
A&M: Smith 1-11; Marks 1-11.

DECEMBER 27, 1958
MISSISSIPPI 7, FLORIDA 3

	1ST	2ND	3RD	4TH	FINAL
MISS	7	0	0	0	7
UF	3	0	0	0	3

SCORING SUMMARY
MISS Anderson 1 run (Khayat kick)
UF FG Booker 17

MISS	TEAM STATISTICS	UF
9	First Downs	12
157	Rushing Yards	157
2-7-0	Passing	5-11-1
27	Passing Yards	58
184	Total Yards	215
10-34.4	Punts - Average	7-44.1
5-2	Fumbles - Lost	5-3
2-10	Penalties - Yards	3-35

INDIVIDUAL LEADERS
RUSHING
MISS: Anderson 9-62, 1 TD; Lovelace 7-28.
UF: Newbern 5-59; Milby 10-35.
PASSING
MISS: Franklin 2-7-0, 27 yards.
UF: Dunn 5-11-1, 58 yards.
RECEIVING
MISS: Grantham 1-15; Daniels 1-12.
UF: Hudson 2-22; Dilts 1-13.

ARKANSAS 14, GEORGIA TECH 7
JANUARY 2, 1960

	1ST	2ND	3RD	4TH	FINAL
ARK	0	7	7	0	14
GT	7	0	0	0	7

SCORING SUMMARY
GT   Tibbetts 51 run (Faucette kick)
ARK Alberty 1 run (Akers kick)
ARK Mooty 19 run (Akers kick)

ARK	TEAM STATISTICS	GT
15	First Downs	13
218	Rushing Yards	172
2-6-1	Passing	8-18-1
21	Passing Yards	64
239	Total Yards	236
4-36.5	Punts - Average	4-40.7
1-1	Fumbles - Lost	0-0
5-56	Penalties - Yards	3-15

INDIVIDUAL LEADERS
RUSHING
ARK: Mooty 18-99, 1 TD; Alworth 9-40; Alberty 12-38, 1 TD.
GT: Tibbetts 3-59, 1 TD; Anderson 12-38.
PASSING
ARK: Monroe 2-4-0, 21 yards.
GT: Braselton 8-18-1, 64 yards.
RECEIVING
ARK: Mooty 1-12.
GT: Graning 3-19.

FLORIDA 13, BAYLOR 12
DECEMBER 31, 1960

	1ST	2ND	3RD	4TH	FINAL
UF	0	13	0	0	13
BU	0	0	0	12	12

SCORING SUMMARY
UF   Goodman 3 run (Cash kick)
UF   Travis fumble recovery in end zone (kick failed)
BU   Goodwin 12 pass from Ply (kick failed)
BU   Bull 3 run (pass failed)

UF	TEAM STATISTICS	BU
11	First Downs	15
176	Rushing Yards	40
5-8-0	Passing	13-27-0
57	Passing Yards	211
233	Total Yards	251
7-37.0	Punts - Average	5-33.0
3-1	Fumbles - Lost	4-3
6-70	Penalties - Yards	1-5

INDIVIDUAL LEADERS
RUSHING
UF: Libertore 14-61; Goodman 10-28, 1 TD.
BU: Bull 14-53, 1 TD.
PASSING
UF: Libertore 2-3-0, 36 yards.
BU: Ply 12-24-0, 161 yards, 1 TD.
RECEIVING
UF: Infante 3-47.
BU: Goodwin 7-129, 1 TD; Davis 3-33.

PENN STATE 30, GEORGIA TECH 15
DECEMBER 31, 1961

	1ST	2ND	3RD	4TH	FINAL
PSU	0	14	6	10	30
GT	2	7	0	6	15

SCORING SUMMARY
GT   Safety (Hall intentional grounding in end zone)
GT   Auer 68 run (Lothridge kick)
PSU Gursky 13 pass from Hall (Jonas kick)
PSU Kochman 27 pass from Hall (Jonas kick)
PSU Powell 35 pass from Hall (kick failed)
GT   Auer 14 run (run failed)
PSU FG Jonas 23
PSU Torris 1 run (Jonas kick)

PSU	TEAM STATISTICS	GT
13	First Downs	19
138	Rushing Yards	211
12-22-0	Passing	12-24-2
175	Passing Yards	201
313	Total Yards	412
8-41.0	Punts - Average	5-27.6
1-1	Fumbles - Lost	6-3
6-63	Penalties - Yards	2-14

INDIVIDUAL LEADERS
RUSHING
PSU: Kochman 13-76; Torris 12-27, 1 TD.
GT: Auer 10-98, 2 TD; Williamson 11-44.
RECEIVING
PSU: Robinson 4-40; Anderson 3-40.
GT: Williamson 4-102; Martin 3-36.

FLORIDA 17, PENN STATE 7
DECEMBER 29, 1962

	1ST	2ND	3RD	4TH	FINAL
UF	3	7	0	7	17
PSU	0	7	0	0	7

SCORING SUMMARY
UF   FG Hall 43
UF   Dupree 7 pass from Shannon (Hall kick)
PSU Liske 1 run (Coates kick)
UF   Clarke 19 pass from Shannon (Hall kick)

UF	TEAM STATISTICS	PSU
14	First Downs	8
162	Rushing Yards	89
8-13-1	Passing	5-21-2
86	Passing Yards	58
248	Total Yards	147
6-23.8	Punts - Average	6-40.8
4-1	Fumbles - Lost	4-3
5-42	Penalties - Yards	2-10

INDIVIDUAL LEADERS
RUSHING
UF: Dupree 25-66; Mack 10-33.
PSU: Kochman 6-51; Hayes 10-25.
PASSING
UF: Shannon 7-9-1, 79 yards, 2 TD.
PSU: Liske 5-18-1, 58 yards.
RECEIVING
UF: Clarke 2-27, 1 TD; Brown 3-25.
PSU: Powell 4-40; Yost 1-18.

NORTH CAROLINA 35, AIR FORCE 0
DECEMBER 28, 1963

	1ST	2ND	3RD	4TH	FINAL
UNC	6	14	8	7	35
AFA	0	0	0	0	0

SCORING SUMMARY
UNC Willard 1 run (kick failed)
UNC Edge 6 run (pass failed)
UNC Robinson 5 pass from Black (Robinson pass from Black)
UNC Kesler 1 run (Lacey pass from Edge)
UNC Black 5 run (Chapman kick)

UNC	TEAM STATISTICS	AFA
23	First Downs	14
251	Rushing Yards	95
12-21-0	Passing	14-36-5
119	Passing Yards	165
370	Total Yards	260
4-40.0	Punts - Average	4-40.0
2-0	Fumbles - Lost	3-2
3-42	Penalties - Yards	3-35

INDIVIDUAL LEADERS
RUSHING
UNC: Willard 18-94, 1 TD; Kesler 9-32, 1 TD.
AFA: Isaacson 3-44; Amdor 4-12.
PASSING
UNC: Black 6-6-0, 71 yards, 1 TD.
AFA: Isaacson 9-23-3, 85 yards.
RECEIVING
UNC: Lacey 3-35; Hammett 3-34.
AFA: Puster 2-46; Greth 3-35.

FLORIDA STATE 36, OKLAHOMA 19
JANUARY 2, 1965

	1ST	2ND	3RD	4TH	FINAL
FSU	6	18	6	6	36
OKLA	7	0	6	6	19

SCORING SUMMARY
FSU   Ehler 69 interception return (kick failed)
OKLA Kennedy 1 run (Metcalf kick)
FSU   Biletnikoff 15 pass from Tensi (pass failed)
FSU   Biletnikoff 14 pass from Tensi (pass failed)
FSU   Biletnikoff 10 pass from Tensi (pass failed)
OKLA Pannell 2 run (pass failed)
FSU   Floyd 14 pass from Tensi (pass failed)
OKLA Hart 95 pass from Fletcher (pass failed)
FSU   Biletnikoff 6 pass from Tensi (kick failed)

FSU	TEAM STATISTICS	OKLA
29	First Downs	13
217	Rushing Yards	71
23-36-4	Passing	10-22-1
303	Passing Yards	209
520	Total Yards	280
1-26.0	Punts - Average	6-38.0
2-2	Fumbles - Lost	1-1
52	Penalty Yards	35

INDIVIDUAL LEADERS
RUSHING
FSU: Spooner 27-125; Giardino 7-82.
OKLA: Ringer 7-41; Kennedy 13-32, 1 TD.
PASSING
FSU: Tensi 23-36-4, 303 yards, 5 TD.
OKLA: Fletcher 3-7-0, 117 yards; Page 7-15-1, 92 yards.
RECEIVING
FSU: Biletnikoff 13-192, 4 TD; Floyd 5-52, 1 TD.
OKLA: Hart 6-165, 1 TD.

GEORGIA TECH 31, TEXAS TECH 21
DECEMBER 31, 1965

	1ST	2ND	3RD	4TH	FINAL
GT	0	9	15	15	31
TT	7	0	14	0	21

SCORING SUMMARY
TT   Agan 4 pass from Wilson (Gill kick)
GT   Smith 2 run (Henry kick)
GT   Safety
GT   Snow 1 run (Henry kick)
TT   Anderson 1 run (Gill kick)
TT   Shipley 15 pass from Wilson (Gill kick)
GT   Priestley 1 run (Priestley run)
GT   Varner 13 run (Henry kick)

GT	TEAM STATISTICS	TT
27	First Downs	17
364	Rushing Yards	113
5-10-1	Passing	22-40-2
77	Passing Yards	283
441	Total Yards	396
4-32.5	Punts - Average	3-41.6
2-1	Fumbles - Lost	3-3
5-57	Penalties - Yards	2-25

INDIVIDUAL LEADERS
RUSHING
GT: Snow 35-136, 1 TD; Smith 15-73, 1 TD.
TT: Anderson 13-85, 1 TD; Agan 4-21.
PASSING
GT: King 4-7-1, 58 yards.
TT: Wilson 22-40-2, 283 yards, 2 TD.
RECEIVING
GT: Baynham 2-52; Gautier 1-19.
TT: Anderson 9-138; Shipley 5-64, 1 TD.

December 31, 1966
Tennessee 18, Syracuse 12

	1ST	2ND	3RD	4TH	FINAL
TENN	3	15	0	0	18
SYR	0	0	6	6	12

SCORING SUMMARY
TENN	FG Wright 36
TENN	FG Wright 38
TENN	Denney 24 pass from Warren (pass failed)
TENN	Flowers 2 pass from Warren (kick failed)
SYR	Csonka 8 run (run failed)
SYR	Little 3 run (run failed)

TENN	TEAM STATISTICS	SYR
14	First Downs	20
85	Rushing Yards	348
17-29-1	Passing	2-7-3
244	Passing Yards	16
329	Total Yards	364
3-43.0	Punts - Average	2-39.5
2-2	Fumbles - Lost	3-1
4-44	Penalties - Yards	7-79

INDIVIDUAL LEADERS

RUSHING
TENN: Chadwick 12-47; Pickens 6-36.
SYR: Little 29-216, 1 TD; Csonka 18-114, 1 TD.

PASSING
TENN: Warren 17-29-1, 244 yards, 2 TD.
SYR: Cassata 2-7-3, 16 yards.

RECEIVING
TENN: Mills 8-86; Flowers 5-80, 1 TD.
SYR: Little 2-16.

December 30, 1967
Florida State 17, Penn State 17

	1ST	2ND	3RD	4TH	FINAL
FSU	0	0	14	3	17
PSU	3	14	0	0	17

SCORING SUMMARY
PSU	FG Sherman 27
PSU	Curry 9 pass from Sherman (Sherman kick)
PSU	Kwalick 12 pass from Sherman (Sherman kick)
FSU	Sellers 20 pass from Hammond (Guthrie kick)
FSU	Hammond 1 run (Guthrie kick)
FSU	FG Guthrie 26

FSU	TEAM STATISTICS	PSU
23	First Downs	12
55	Rushing Yards	175
38-55-4	Passing	7-19-2
363	Passing Yards	69
418	Total Yards	244
4-29.8	Punts - Average	7-39.9
1-0	Fumbles - Lost	3-2
4-40	Penalties - Yards	1-5

INDIVIDUAL LEADERS

RUSHING
FSU: Green 12-34; Hammond 9-28, 1 TD.
PSU: Pittman 19-128; Sherman 6-27.

PASSING
FSU: Hammond 37-53-4, 362 yards, 1 TD.
PSU: Sherman 9-17-2, 69 yards, 2 TD.

RECEIVING
FSU: Sellers 14-145, 1 TD; Moremen 12-106.
PSU: Kwalick 2-25, 1 TD; Curry 2-22, 1 TD.

December 28, 1968
Missouri 35, Alabama 10

	1ST	2ND	3RD	4TH	FINAL
MO	7	7	0	21	35
ALA	0	7	0	3	10

SCORING SUMMARY
MO	McMillian 4 run (Sangster kick)
ALA	Sutton 38 interception return (Dean kick)
MO	McMillian 5 run (Sangster kick)
ALA	FG Dean 25
MO	McMillian 2 run (Sangster kick)
MO	Cook 37 run (Sangster kick)
MO	Poppe 47 interception return (Sangster kick)

MO	TEAM STATISTICS	ALA
21	First Downs	6
402	Rushing Yards	-45
0-6-2	Passing	7-27-2
0	Passing Yards	77
402	Total Yards	32
5-36.0	Punts - Average	10-42.0
4-2	Fumbles - Lost	1-0
5-29	Penalties - Yards	2-14

INDIVIDUAL LEADERS

RUSHING
MO: Cook 27-179, 1 TD; McMillian 18-76, 3 TD.
ALA: Jilleba 5-20; Moore 5-10.

PASSING
MO: McMillian 0-6-2, 0 yards.
ALA: Hunter 7-25-1, 68 yards.

December 27, 1969
Florida 14, Tennessee 13

	1ST	2ND	3RD	4TH	FINAL
UF	7	0	7	0	14
TENN	0	10	0	3	13

SCORING SUMMARY
UF	Kelley 8 blocked punt return (Franco kick)
TENN	FG Hunt 20
TENN	McClain 12 pass from Scott (Hunt kick)
UF	Alvarez 9 pass from Reaves (Franco kick)
TENN	FG Hunt 26

UF	TEAM STATISTICS	TENN
15	First Downs	23
90	Rushing Yards	214
15-27-0	Passing	12-34-2
161	Passing Yards	174
251	Total Yards	388
7-31.3	Punts - Average	2-15.0
1-1	Fumbles - Lost	1-1
2-58	Penalties - Yards	3-24

INDIVIDUAL LEADERS

RUSHING
UF: Murrance 22-62; Walker 10-33.
TENN: Watson 25-121; Patterson 8-40.

PASSING
UF: Reaves 15-26-0, 161 yards, 1 TD.
TENN: Scott 12-34-2, 174 yards, 1 TD.

RECEIVING
UF: Maliska 6-54; Alvarez 4-51, 1 TD.
TENN: Kreis 4-82; DeLong 5-50.

January 2, 1971
Auburn 35, Mississippi 28

	1ST	2ND	3RD	4TH	FINAL
AUB	14	7	14	0	35
MISS	0	14	7	7	28

SCORING SUMMARY
AUB	Beasley 12 pass from Sullivan (Jett kick)
AUB	Bresler 7 pass from Sullivan (Jett kick)
AUB	Sullivan 37 run (Jett kick)
MISS	Manning 1 run (Poole kick)
MISS	Franks 34 pass from Manning (Poole kick)
AUB	Zofko 6 run (Jett kick)
MISS	Poole 23 pass from Chumbler (Poole kick)
AUB	Willingham 55 punt return (Jett kick)
MISS	Chumbler 1 run (Poole kick)

AUB	TEAM STATISTICS	MISS
23	First Downs	21
208	Rushing Yards	209
27-44-1	Passing	23-39-1
351	Passing Yards	256
559	Total Yards	465
4-40.5	Punts - Average	6-47.3
5-3	Fumbles - Lost	3-2
6-63	Penalties - Yards	2-13

INDIVIDUAL LEADERS

RUSHING
AUB: Clark 14-108; Sullivan 10-35, 1 TD.
MISS: Manning 11-95, 1 TD; Ainsworth 11-68.

PASSING
AUB: Sullivan 27-43-1, 351 yards, 2 TD.
MISS: Manning 19-28-1, 180 yards, 1 TD; Chumbler 4-11-0, 76 yards, 1 TD.

RECEIVING
AUB: Beasley 8-143, 1 TD; Bresler 4-102, 1 TD.
MISS: Poole 9-111, 1 TD; Franks 7-78, 1 TD.

December 31, 1971
Georgia 7, North Carolina 3

	1ST	2ND	3RD	4TH	FINAL
UGA	0	0	7	0	7
UNC	0	0	3	0	3

SCORING SUMMARY
UNC	FG Craven 35
UGA	Poulos 25 run (Braswell kick)

UGA	TEAM STATISTICS	UNC
13	First Downs	9
238	Rushing Yards	115
6-17-0	Passing	6-14-1
84	Passing Yards	66
322	Total Yards	181
10-34.8	Punts - Average	10-46.6
2-1	Fumbles - Lost	2-1
5-29	Penalties - Yards	3-15

INDIVIDUAL LEADERS

RUSHING
UGA: Poulos 20-161, 1 TD; Johnson 19-50.
UNC: Jolley 20-77; Hamlin 5-17.

PASSING
UGA: Johnson 6-13-0, 84 yards.
UNC: Miller 6-14-1, 66 yards.

RECEIVING
UGA: Hunnicut 4-58; Greene 1-26.
UNC: Sigler 2-32; Cowell 1-19.

December 30, 1972
Auburn 24, Colorado 3

	1ST	2ND	3RD	4TH	FINAL
AUB	0	10	7	7	24
COL	0	0	0	3	3

SCORING SUMMARY
AUB	FG Jett 27
AUB	Whatley 1 run (Jett kick)
AUB	Spivey 22 pass from Fuller (Jett kick)
COL	FG Lima 33
AUB	Nugent 16 pass from Beck (Jett kick)

AUB	TEAM STATISTICS	COL
13	First Downs	14
153	Rushing Yards	63
5-8-0	Passing	20-33-2
80	Passing Yards	204
233	Total Yards	267
7-40.7	Punts - Average	5-39.8
3-1	Fumbles - Lost	3-2
4-30	Penalties - Yards	5-47

INDIVIDUAL LEADERS

RUSHING
AUB: Fuller 12-72; Linderman 15-37.
COL: Matthews 8-34; Davis 14-12.

PASSING
AUB: Whatley 3-6-0, 42 yards.
COL: Johnson 17-29-2, 169 yards.

RECEIVING
AUB: Spivey 1-22, 1 TD; Cannon 1-17; Nugent 1-16, 1 TD.
COL: Keyworth 3-55; Elwood 3-49.

December 29, 1973
Texas Tech 28, Tennessee 19

	1ST	2ND	3RD	4TH	FINAL
TT	7	7	7	7	28
TENN	0	3	10	6	19

SCORING SUMMARY
TT	Barnes 7 run (Grimes kick)
TT	Williams 79 pass from Barnes (Grimes kick)
TENN	FG Townsend 30
TENN	Stanback 5 run (Townsend kick)
TT	Tillman 7 pass from Barnes (Grimes kick)
TENN	FG Townsend 37
TENN	Stanback 7 pass from Holloway (pass failed)
TT	Isaac 3 run (Grimes kick)

TT	TEAM STATISTICS	TENN
19	First Downs	18
276	Rushing Yards	153
8-11-0	Passing	17-28-1
154	Passing Yards	190
430	Total Yards	343
6-40.9	Punts - Average	4-40.5
3-1	Fumbles - Lost	1-1
5-55	Penalties - Yards	1-3

INDIVIDUAL LEADERS

RUSHING
TT: Mosley 8-85; Barnes 16-73, 1 TD.
TENN: Stanback 19-95, 1 TD; Chancey 11-53.

PASSING
TT: Barnes 8-11-0, 154 yards, 2 TD.
TENN: Holloway 17-27-1, 190 yards, 1 TD.

RECEIVING
TT: Williams 3-94, 1 TD; Tillman 2-30, 1 TD.
TENN: Yarbrough 4-28; Howard 3-18.

December 30, 1974
AUBURN 27, TEXAS 3

	1ST	2ND	3RD	4TH	FINAL
AUB	14	2	0	11	27
TEX	3	0	0	0	3

SCORING SUMMARY
AUB   Butler 7 pass from Gargis (Wilson kick)
AUB   Jackson 2 run (Wilson kick)
TEX   FG Schott 35
AUB   Safety (McKinney blocked punt out of end zone)
AUB   Butler 14 pass from Gargis (Nugent pass from Gargis)
AUB   FG Wilson 28

AUB	TEAM STATISTICS	TEX
19	First Downs	14
256	Rushing Yards	203
7-13-2	Passing	10-21-3
70	Passing Yards	98
326	Total Yards	301
2-45.5	Punts - Average	4-28.8
7-5	Fumbles - Lost	5-4
6-70	Penalties - Yards	5-37

INDIVIDUAL LEADERS
RUSHING
AUB: McIntyre 19-89; Jackson 10-64, 1 TD.
TEX: Campbell 23-91; Atkins 11-40.
PASSING
AUB: Gargis 6-11-2, 60 yards, 2 TD.
TEX: Atkins 9-16-1, 70 yards.
RECEIVING
AUB: Nugent 2-22; Butler 2-21, 2 TD.
TEX: Thompson 1-28; Ingram 2-17.

December 29, 1975
MARYLAND 13, FLORIDA 0

	1ST	2ND	3RD	4TH	FINAL
MD	7	3	0	3	13
UF	0	0	0	0	0

SCORING SUMMARY
MD   Hoover 19 pass from Dick (Sochko kick)
MD   FG Sochko 20
MD   FG Sochko 27

MD	TEAM STATISTICS	UF
15	First Downs	14
209	Rushing Yards	182
7-16-0	Passing	3-19-3
82	Passing Yards	28
291	Total Yards	210
7-39.8	Punts - Average	7-38.5
0-0	Fumbles - Lost	1-1
5-47	Penalties - Yards	6-48

INDIVIDUAL LEADERS
RUSHING
MD: Atkins 20-127; Jennings 9-53.
UF: DuBose 18-95; Green 13-31.
PASSING
MD: Dick 5-13-0, 67 yards, 1 TD.
UF: Fisher 2-12-1, 33 yards.
RECEIVING
MD: Hoover 2-24, 1 TD; Wilson 2-21.
UF: LeCount 1-25; Enclade 1-8.

December 27, 1976
NOTRE DAME 20, PENN STATE 9

	1ST	2ND	3RD	4TH	FINAL
ND	7	13	0	0	20
PSU	3	0	0	6	9

SCORING SUMMARY
PSU   FG Capozzolli 26
ND   Hunter 1 run (Reeve kick)
ND   FG Reeve 23
ND   Hunter 1 run (Reeve kick)
ND   FG Reeve 23
PSU   Suhey 8 pass from Fusina (run failed)

ND	TEAM STATISTICS	PSU
17	First Downs	16
132	Rushing Yards	156
10-20-0	Passing	14-33-2
141	Passing Yards	118
273	Total Yards	274
5-33.2	Punts - Average	5-29.2
2-0	Fumbles - Lost	4-1
5-62	Penalties - Yards	6-55

INDIVIDUAL LEADERS
RUSHING
ND: Hunter 26-102, 2 TD; Ferguson 10-22.
PSU: Torrey 12-63; Suhey 9-40.
PASSING
ND: Slager 10-19-0, 141 yards.
PSU: Fusina 14-33-2, 118 yards, 1 TD.
RECEIVING
ND: MacAfee 5-78; Kelleher 3-46.
PSU: Cefalo 5-60; Mauti 1-21; Suhey 2-17, 1 TD.

December 30, 1977
PITTSBURGH 34, CLEMSON 3

	1ST	2ND	3RD	4TH	FINAL
PITT	10	7	7	10	34
CLEM	0	3	0	0	3

SCORING SUMMARY
PITT   Walker 39 pass from Cavanaugh (Schubert kick)
PITT   FG Schubert 24
PITT   Walker 10 pass from Cavanaugh (Schubert kick)
CLEM   FG Ariri 49
PITT   Jones 10 pass from Cavanaugh (Schubert kick)
PITT   FG Schubert 21
PITT   Walker 25 pass from Cavanaugh (Schubert kick)

PITT	TEAM STATISTICS	CLEM
30	First Downs	14
179	Rushing Yards	110
23-37-1	Passing	10-23-4
387	Passing Yards	158
566	Total Yards	268
3-43.5	Punts - Average	4-33.3
5-1	Fumbles - Lost	1-0
10-91	Penalties - Yards	3-24

INDIVIDUAL LEADERS
RUSHING
PITT: Walker 15-53; Hawkins 2-43.
CLEM: Fuller 13-34; Callicutt 7-32.
PASSING
PITT: Cavanaugh 23-36-0, 387 yards, 4 TD.
CLEM: Fuller 10-23-4, 158 yards.
RECEIVING
PITT: Jones 10-163, 1 TD; Walker 6-121, 3 TD.
CLEM: Butler 4-64; Weddington 2-57.

December 29, 1978
CLEMSON 17, OHIO STATE 15

	1ST	2ND	3RD	4TH	FINAL
CLEM	0	10	7	0	17
OSU	0	9	0	6	15

SCORING SUMMARY
OSU   FG Atha 27
CLEM   Fuller 4 run (Ariri kick)
OSU   Schlichter 4 run (kick failed)
CLEM   FG Ariri 47
CLEM   Austin 1 run (Ariri kick)
OSU   Schlichter 1 run (run failed)

CLEM	TEAM STATISTICS	OSU
20	First Downs	16
207	Rushing Yards	150
9-20-0	Passing	16-20-1
123	Passing Yards	205
330	Total Yards	355
6-38.3	Punts - Average	4-41.5
5-1	Fumbles - Lost	1-0
7-65	Penalties - Yards	7-83

INDIVIDUAL LEADERS
RUSHING
CLEM: Perry 14-54; Ratchford 10-54; Fuller 17-38, 1 TD.
OSU: Schlichter 18-70, 2 TD; Springs 10-42.
PASSING
CLEM: Fuller 9-20-0, 123 yards.
OSU: Schlichter 16-20-1, 205 yards.
RECEIVING
CLEM: Butler 4-44; Tuttle 3-41.
OSU: Barwig 2-51; Hunter 2-49.

December 28, 1979
NORTH CAROLINA 17, MICHIGAN 15

	1ST	2ND	3RD	4TH	FINAL
UNC	0	7	7	3	17
MICH	0	9	0	6	15

SCORING SUMMARY
MICH   FG Virgil 20
MICH   Carter 53 pass from Wangler (kick failed)
UNC   Paschal 1 run (Hayes kick)
UNC   Farris 12 pass from Kupec (Hayes kick)
UNC   FG Hayes 32
MICH   Carter 30 pass from Dickey (pass failed)

UNC	TEAM STATISTICS	MICH
20	First Downs	18
169	Rushing Yards	152
19-28-0	Passing	17-26-2
161	Passing Yards	328
330	Total Yards	480
6-45.4	Punts - Average	6-35.1
3-2	Fumbles - Lost	2-2
6-74	Penalties - Yards	8-87

INDIVIDUAL LEADERS
RUSHING
UNC: Lawrence 23-118; Paschal 14-49, 1 TD.
MICH: Woolfolk 16-63; Smith 8-51.
PASSING
UNC: Kupec 18-28-0, 161 yards, 1 TD.
MICH: Wangler 6-8-0, 203 yards, 1 TD; Dickey 11-18-2, 125 yards, 1 TD.
RECEIVING
UNC: Lawrence 5-38; Chatham 5-37; Farris 2-34, 1 TD.
MICH: Carter 4-141, 2 TD; Clayton 1-50.

December 29, 1980
PITTSBURGH 37, SOUTH CAROLINA 9

	1ST	2ND	3RD	4TH	FINAL
PITT	10	7	17	3	37
SC	0	3	0	6	9

SCORING SUMMARY
PITT   Trocano 1 run (Trout kick)
PITT   FG Trout 35
SC   FG Leopard 39
PITT   Collier 3 pass from Marino (Trout kick)
PITT   FG Trout 25
PITT   McMillan 3 run (Trout kick)
PITT   McMillan 42 pass from Trocano (Trout kick)
PITT   FG Trout 29
SC   Gillespie 14 pass from Beckham (kick failed)

PITT	TEAM STATISTICS	SC
22	First Downs	17
165	Rushing Yards	116
17-35-3	Passing	11-27-3
233	Passing Yards	168
398	Total Yards	284
3-30.3	Punts - Average	7-30.0
1-1	Fumbles - Lost	3-2
11-73	Penalties - Yards	3-12

INDIVIDUAL LEADERS
RUSHING
PITT: McMillan 13-59, 1 TD; Hawkins 9-50; Trocano 8-41, 1 TD.
SC: Rogers 27-113; Wright 4-23.
PASSING
PITT: Trocano 10-21-2, 155 yards, 1 TD; Marino 7-13-0, 78 yards, 1 TD.
SC: Harper 7-16-1, 116 yards; Beckham 4-10-1, 52 yards, 1 TD.
RECEIVING
PITT: Collier 5-57, 1 TD; Collins 3-50; McMillan 2-46, 1 TD.
SC: Scott 7-109; Gillespie 2-32, 1 TD.

DECEMBER 28, 1981
NORTH CAROLINA 31, ARKANSAS 27

	1ST	2ND	3RD	4TH	FINAL
UNC	3	7	14	7	31
ARK	7	3	0	17	27

SCORING SUMMARY

UNC	FG Barwick 31
ARK	Holloway 66 pass from Taylor (Lahay kick)
UNC	Bryant 1 run (Hayes kick)
ARK	FG Lahay 28
UNC	Horton 1 run (Hayes kick)
UNC	Elkins 1 run (Hayes kick)
UNC	Horton 4 run (Hayes kick)
ARK	Clark 3 run (Clark pass from Taylor)
ARK	Mason 7 pass from Taylor (Lahay kick)
ARK	Safety (Hayes ran out of end zone)

UNC	TEAM STATISTICS	ARK
21	First Downs	16
283	Rushing Yards	89
7-17-0	Passing	14-21-1
53	Passing Yards	307
336	Total Yards	396
6-41.9	Punts - Average	6-36.5
3-1	Fumbles - Lost	2-1
8-55	Penalties - Yards	3-44

INDIVIDUAL LEADERS

RUSHING
UNC: Bryant 27-148, 1 TD; Horton 27-144, 2 TD.
ARK: Clark 10-40, 1 TD; Tolbert 5-27.

PASSING
UNC: Elkins 7-17-0, 53 yards.
ARK: Taylor 14-21-1, 307 yards, 2 TD.

RECEIVING
UNC: Bryant 3-24; Richardson 2-15.
ARK: Holloway 4-171, 1 TD; Anderson 5-85.

DECEMBER 30, 1982
FLORIDA STATE 31, WEST VIRGINIA 12

	1ST	2ND	3RD	4TH	FINAL
FSU	3	14	14	0	31
WVU	0	6	0	6	12

SCORING SUMMARY

FSU	FG Hall 20
WVU	FG Woodside 48
FSU	Allen 95 kickoff return (Hall kick)
WVU	FG Woodside 48
FSU	McKinnon 27 pass from Williams (Hall kick)
FSU	Allen 29 run (Hall kick)
FSU	Allen 1 run (Hall kick)
WVU	Miller 26 pass from White (pass failed)

FSU	TEAM STATISTICS	WVU
23	First Downs	22
259	Rushing Yards	155
16-32-1	Passing	14-34-2
204	Passing Yards	208
463	Total Yards	363
4-36.8	Punts - Average	4-30.5
1-0	Fumbles - Lost	2-0
11-100	Penalties - Yards	5-57

INDIVIDUAL LEADERS

RUSHING
FSU: Allen 15-138, 2 TD; McKinnon 1-65.
WVU: Mullen 2-42; Wolfley 7-32.

PASSING
FSU: Williams 16-30-0, 202 yards, 1 TD.
WVU: Hostetler 10-28-2, 118 yards.

RECEIVING
FSU: Thompson 2-41; McKinnon 2-36, 1 TD.
WVU: Miller 5-100, 1 TD; Raugh 4-60.

DECEMBER 30, 1983
FLORIDA 14, IOWA 6

	1ST	2ND	3RD	4TH	FINAL
UF	7	7	0	0	14
IA	0	3	3	0	6

SCORING SUMMARY

UF	Anderson 1 run (Raymond kick)
IA	FG Nichol 32
UF	Drew fumble recovery in end zone (Raymond kick)
IA	FG Nichol 31

UF	TEAM STATISTICS	IA
14	First Downs	16
168	Rushing Yards	114
9-23-2	Passing	13-30-4
92	Passing Yards	167
260	Total Yards	281
7-37.5	Punts - Average	2-40.0
0-0	Fumbles - Lost	2-1
12-105	Penalties - Yards	7-44

INDIVIDUAL LEADERS

RUSHING
UF: Anderson 17-84, 1 TD; Williams 10-68.
IA: Gill 10-83; Granger 9-37.

PASSING
UF: Peace 9-22-2, 92 yards.
IA: Long 13-29-4, 167 yards.

RECEIVING
UF: Dixon 5-55.
IA: Harmon 6-90.

DECEMBER 28, 1984
OKLAHOMA STATE 21, SOUTH CAROLINA 14

	1ST	2ND	3RD	4TH	FINAL
OKST	7	6	0	8	21
SC	0	0	14	0	14

SCORING SUMMARY

OKST	Thomas 1 run (Roach kick)
OKST	Hilger 6 pass from Thomas (kick failed)
SC	Wade 24 pass from Lewis (Hagler kick)
SC	Hillary 57 pass from Hold (Hagler kick)
OKST	Hanna 25 pass from Hilger (Harris pass from Hilger)

OKST	TEAM STATISTICS	SC
21	First Downs	15
165	Rushing Yards	104
25-42-1	Passing	8-21-1
211	Passing Yards	194
376	Total Yards	298
5-35.4	Punts - Average	7-41.7
2-0	Fumbles - Lost	6-3
3-21	Penalties - Yards	5-38

INDIVIDUAL LEADERS

RUSHING
OKST: Thomas 32-155, 1 TD.
SC: Lewis 6-36; Hold 18-33.

PASSING
OKST: Hilger 21-41-1, 205 yards, 1 TD.
SC: Hold 7-20-1, 170 yards, 1 TD; Lewis 1-1-0, 24 yards, 1 TD.

RECEIVING
OKST: Hanna 8-92, 1 TD; Lewis 3-33.
SC: Hillary 2-75, 1 TD; Poole 1-45; Wade 1-24, 1 TD.

DECEMBER 30, 1985
FLORIDA STATE 34, OKLAHOMA STATE 23

	1ST	2ND	3RD	4TH	FINAL
FSU	3	10	14	7	34
OKST	0	0	17	6	23

SCORING SUMMARY

FSU	FG Schmidt 23
FSU	Gainer 39 pass from Ferguson (Schmidt kick)
FSU	FG Schmidt 39
OKST	FG Dennis 33
FSU	Jones 3 run (Schmidt kick)
FSU	Gainer 19 pass from Ferguson (Schmidt kick)
OKST	Thomas 29 pass from Williams (Dennis kick)
OKST	Williams 12 pass from Thomas (Dennis kick)
FSU	Ferguson 1 run (Schmidt kick)
OKST	Dykes 31 pass from Williams (pass failed)

FSU	TEAM STATISTICS	OKST
31	First Downs	23
259	Rushing Yards	142
20-43-1	Passing	22-42-2
338	Passing Yards	263
597	Total Yards	405
4-47.5	Punts - Average	7-35.9
3-2	Fumbles - Lost	1-0
9-110	Penalties - Yards	3-27

INDIVIDUAL LEADERS

RUSHING
FSU: Smith 24-201; Jones 6-18, 1 TD.
OKST: Thomas 26-97; Williams 6-12.

PASSING
FSU: Ferguson 20-43-1, 338 yards, 2 TD.
OKST: Williams 21-43-2, 251 yards, 2 TD.

RECEIVING
FSU: Gainer 7-148, 2 TD; White 4-87.
OKST: Dykes 8-104, 1 TD; Riley 3-49.

DECEMBER 27, 1986
CLEMSON 27, STANFORD 21

	1ST	2ND	3RD	4TH	FINAL
CLEM	7	20	0	0	27
STAN	0	0	7	14	21

SCORING SUMMARY

CLEM	Lancaster 5 run (Treadwell kick)
CLEM	Ray Williams 1 run (Treadwell kick)
CLEM	FG Treadwell 22
CLEM	Rod Williams 14 run (Treadwell kick)
CLEM	FG Treadwell 46
STAN	Muster 1 run (Sweeney kick)
STAN	Muster 13 pass from Ennis (Sweeney kick)
STAN	Muster 37 pass from Ennis (Sweeney kick)

CLEM	TEAM STATISTICS	STAN
19	First Downs	18
238	Rushing Yards	114
12-19-1	Passing	20-40-1
135	Passing Yards	168
373	Total Yards	282
6-33.7	Punts - Average	5-43.0
4-0	Fumbles - Lost	1-1
5-49	Penalties - Yards	3-28

INDIVIDUAL LEADERS

RUSHING
CLEM: Flagler 12-82; Flowers 14-67.
STAN: Muster 17-70, 1 TD; Dillard 3-13.

PASSING
CLEM: Rod Williams 12-19-1, 135 yards.
STAN: Ennis 20-40-1, 168 yards, 2 TD.

RECEIVING
CLEM: Hooper 2-44; Flagler 3-25.
STAN: Muster 4-53, 2 TD; Snelson 4-42.

December 31, 1987
LSU 30, South Carolina 13

	1ST	2ND	3RD	4TH	FINAL
LSU	14	6	7	3	30
SC	3	3	0	7	13

SCORING SUMMARY

LSU	Davis 39 pass from Hodson (Browndyke kick)
LSU	Davis 12 pass from Hodson (Browndyke kick)
SC	FG Mackie 44
LSU	FG Browndyke 27
SC	FG Mackie 39
LSU	FG Browndyke 18
LSU	Davis 25 pass from Hodson (Browndyke kick)
SC	Green 10 run (Mackie kick)
LSU	FG Browndyke 23

LSU	TEAM STATISTICS	SC
17	First Downs	21
122	Rushing Yards	25
20-32-0	Passing	28-47-4
224	Passing Yards	304
346	Total Yards	329
3-37.6	Punts - Average	2-40.5
5-3	Fumbles - Lost	2-1
10-107	Penalties - Yards	6-49

INDIVIDUAL LEADERS

RUSHING
LSU: Fuller 14-48; Martin 8-38.
SC: Green 15-72, 1 TD; Bethea 1-9.
PASSING
LSU: Hodson 20-32-0, 224 yards, 3 TD.
SC: Ellis 28-47-4, 304 yards.
RECEIVING
LSU: Davis 9-132, 3 TD; Martin 3-43.
SC: Smith 4-79; Bethea 4-69; Sharpe 6-53.

January 1, 1989
Georgia 34, Michigan State 27

	1ST	2ND	3RD	4TH	FINAL
UGA	7	10	10	7	34
MSU	0	7	6	14	27

SCORING SUMMARY

UGA	Hampton 6 pass from Johnson (Kasay kick)
UGA	FG Crumley 39
UGA	Hampton 30 pass from Johnson (Kasay kick)
MSU	Rison 4 pass from McAllister (Langeloh kick)
UGA	Warner 18 pass from Johnson (Kasay kick)
MSU	Rison 55 pass from McAllister (kick failed)
UGA	FG Crumley 36
MSU	Ezor 3 run (Langeloh kick)
UGA	Hampton 32 run (Kasay kick)
MSU	Rison 50 pass from McAllister (Langeloh kick)

UGA	TEAM STATISTICS	MSU
22	First Downs	22
182	Rushing Yards	158
15-27-0	Passing	14-24-0
227	Passing Yards	288
409	Total Yards	446
4-34.0	Punts - Average	6-42.8
0-0	Fumbles - Lost	1-0
5-25	Penalties - Yards	8-102

INDIVIDUAL LEADERS

RUSHING
UGA: Hampton 10-109, 1 TD; Johnson 14-30.
MSU: Ezor 33-146, 1 TD; Selzer 5-13.
PASSING
UGA: Johnson 15-27-0, 227 yards, 3 TD.
MSU: McAllister 14-24-0, 228, 3 TD.
RECEIVING
UGA: Hampton 4-71, 2 TD; Worley 3-36.
MSU: Rison 9-252, 3 TD; Montgomery 4-21.

December 30, 1989
Clemson 27, West Virginia 7

	1ST	2ND	3RD	4TH	FINAL
CLEM	0	10	0	17	27
WVU	7	0	0	0	7

SCORING SUMMARY

WVU	Jett 12 pass from Harris (Carroll kick)
CLEM	FG Gardocki 27
CLEM	McFadden 1 run (Gardocki kick)
CLEM	Henderson 4 run (Gardocki kick)
CLEM	McGlockton fumble recovery in end zone (Gardocki kick)
CLEM	FG Gardocki 24

CLEM	TEAM STATISTICS	WVU
21	First Downs	13
257	Rushing Yards	118
6-11-0	Passing	11-25-1
91	Passing Yards	119
348	Total Yards	237
4-46.0	Punts - Average	6-43.2
0-0	Fumbles - Lost	3-3
4-30	Penalties - Yards	4-37

INDIVIDUAL LEADERS

RUSHING
CLEM: Henderson 22-92, 1 TD; Morocco 11-65.
WVU: Ford 8-45; Napoleon 6-24.
PASSING
CLEM: Morocco 5-9-0, 57 yards.
WVU: Harris 11-21-1, 119 yards, 1 TD.
RECEIVING
CLEM: Fletcher 3-66; Cooper 2-15.
WVU: Rembert 4-57; Dykes 2-27.

January 1, 1991
Michigan 35, Mississippi 3

	1ST	2ND	3RD	4TH	FINAL
MICH	7	7	21	0	35
MISS	0	3	0	0	3

SCORING SUMMARY

MICH	Howard 63 pass from Grbac (Carlson kick)
MISS	FG Lee 51
MICH	Bunch 7 pass from Grbac (Carlson kick)
MICH	Howard 50 pass from Grbac (Carlson kick)
MICH	Bunch 5 run (Carlson kick)
MICH	Alexander 33 pass from Grbac (Carlson kick)

MICH	TEAM STATISTICS	MISS
35	First Downs	20
391	Rushing Yards	93
20-32-1	Passing	18-32-4
324	Passing Yards	240
715	Total Yards	333
2-24.5	Punts - Average	5-38.0
2-1	Fumbles - Lost	4-2
6-69	Penalties - Yards	4-49

INDIVIDUAL LEADERS

RUSHING
MICH: Vaughn 15-128; Powers 14-112; Bunch 11-54, 1 TD.
MISS: Baldwin 8-53; Thigpen 6-32.
PASSING
MICH: Grbac 16-25-1, 296 yards, 4 TD.
MISS: Shows 13-21-3, 175 yards.
RECEIVING
MICH: Howard 6-167, 2 TD; Alexander 2-50, 1 TD.
MISS: Brownlee 5-71; Roberts 4-67.

December 29, 1991
Oklahoma 48, Virginia 14

	1ST	2ND	3RD	4TH	FINAL
OKLA	7	27	14	0	48
UVA	0	7	0	7	14

SCORING SUMMARY

OKLA	Mickey 10 pass from Gundy (Blanton kick)
OKLA	Gaddis 2 run (Blanton kick)
OKLA	Gaddis 8 run (Blanton kick)
OKLA	Jones 4 blocked punt return (Blanton kick)
OKLA	Mickey 13 pass from Gundy (kick blocked)
UVA	Davis 22 pass from Blundin (Husted kick)
OKLA	Rasheed 7 run (Blanton kick)
OKLA	Gaddis 7 run (Blanton kick)
UVA	Tomlin 23 pass from Blundin (Husted kick)

OKLA	TEAM STATISTICS	UVA
36	First Downs	13
261	Rushing Yards	101
27-36-0	Passing	12-29-1
357	Passing Yards	142
618	Total Yards	243
3-40.3	Punts - Average	8-34.8
1-1	Fumbles - Lost	4-1
12-128	Penalties - Yards	6-48

INDIVIDUAL LEADERS

RUSHING
OKLA: Gaddis 20-104, 3 TD; Brewer 12-58.
UVA: Kirby 13-66; Fisher 6-39.
PASSING
OKLA: Gundy 25-31-0, 329 yards, 2 TD.
UVA: Blundin 12-26-1, 142 yards, 2 TD.
RECEIVING
OKLA: Warren 5-110; Mickey 5-55, 2 TD.
UVA: Mundy 3-44; Holmes 3-31.

December 31, 1992
Florida 27, NC State 10

	1ST	2ND	3RD	4TH	FINAL
UF	0	10	10	7	27
NCST	0	0	3	7	10

SCORING SUMMARY

UF	FG Davis 26
UF	Matthews 1 run (Davis kick)
UF	Jackson 17 pass from Matthews (Davis kick)
NCST	FG Videtich 23
UF	FG Davis 42
NCST	Shaw 11 pass from Jordan (Videtich kick)
UF	Houston 34 pass from Matthews (Davis kick)

UF	TEAM STATISTICS	NCST
26	First Downs	13
221	Rushing Yards	82
19-38-0	Passing	22-42-2
247	Passing Yards	213
468	Total Yards	295
5-41.0	Punts - Average	11-39.3
3-2	Fumbles - Lost	2-1
6-44	Penalties - Yards	1-10

INDIVIDUAL LEADERS

RUSHING
UF: Rhett 30-182; Matthews 8-8, 1 TD.
NCST: Barbour 11-50.
PASSING
UF: Matthews 19-38-0, 247 yards, 2 TD.
NCST: Jordan 22-42-2, 213 yards, 1 TD.
RECEIVING
UF: Rhett 7-60; Jackson 3-42, 1 TD; Houston 2-40, 1 TD.
NCST: Lawrence 5-77; Auer 5-48; Shaw 5-33, 1 TD.

THE BOWLS

DECEMBER 31, 1993
ALABAMA 24, NORTH CAROLINA 10

	1ST	2ND	3RD	4TH	FINAL
ALA	3	7	7	7	24
UNC	0	10	0	0	10

SCORING SUMMARY
ALA FG Proctor 22
UNC Henderson 1 run (Pignetti kick)
ALA Burgdorf 33 run (Proctor kick)
UNC FG Pignetti 23
ALA Lynch 8 pass from Burgdorf (Proctor kick)
ALA Key 10 pass from Burgdorf (Proctor kick)

ALA	TEAM STATISTICS	UNC
21	First Downs	14
164	Rushing Yards	42
15-23-0	Passing	19-35-0
166	Passing Yards	225
330	Total Yards	267
6-40.0	Punts - Average	7-30.1
3-0	Fumbles - Lost	1-1
4-34	Penalties - Yards	1-15

INDIVIDUAL LEADERS
RUSHING
ALA: Williams 18-94; Burgdorf 6-48, 1 TD.
UNC: C. Johnson 6-27; L. Johnson 2-24.
PASSING
ALA: Burgdorf 15-23-0, 166 yards, 2 TD.
UNC: Stanicek 19-35-0, 225 yards.
RECEIVING
ALA: Palmer 5-62; T. Johnson 2-40.
UNC: Holliday 9-125; F. Jones 2-55.

DECEMBER 30, 1994
TENNESSEE 45, VIRGINIA TECH 23

	1ST	2ND	3RD	4TH	FINAL
TENN	14	21	0	10	45
VT	0	10	6	7	23

SCORING SUMMARY
TENN Stewart 1 run (Becksvoort kick)
TENN Nash 36 pass from Manning (Becksvoort kick)
TENN Graham 1 run (Becksvoort kick)
VT Thomas 1 run (Williams kick)
TENN Stewart 1 run (Becksvoort kick)
TENN Jones 19 pass from Stewart (Becksvoort kick)
VT FG Williams 28
VT DeShazo 7 run (kick failed)
TENN Stewart 5 run (Becksvoort kick)
TENN FG Becksvoort 19
VT Still 9 pass from Druckenmiller (Williams kick)

TENN	TEAM STATISTICS	VT
18	First Downs	22
245	Rushing Yards	189
16-23-0	Passing	23-38-2
250	Passing Yards	237
495	Total Yards	426
5-43.6	Punts - Average	5-43.4
0-0	Fumbles - Lost	5-1
7-58	Penalties - Yards	3-25

INDIVIDUAL LEADERS
RUSHING
TENN: Stewart 22-85, 3 TD; Jones 1-76.
VT: Thomas 19-102, 1 TD; DeShazo 11-39, 1 TD.
PASSING
TENN: Manning 12-19-0, 189 yards, 1 TD.
VT: DeShazo 17-30-2, 140 yards.
RECEIVING
TENN: Kent 6-119; Nash 3-54, 1 TD.
VT: Still 5-79, 1 TD; Holmes 5-45.

JANUARY 1, 1996
SYRACUSE 41, CLEMSON 0

	1ST	2ND	3RD	4TH	FINAL
SYR	20	0	14	7	41
CLEM	0	0	0	0	0

SCORING SUMMARY
SYR Thomas 1 run (Mare kick)
SYR McNabb 5 run (kick failed)
SYR Harrison 38 pass from McNabb (Mare kick)
SYR Thomas 2 run (Mare kick)
SYR Harrison 56 pass from McNabb (Mare kick)
SYR Sinceno 15 pass from McNabb (Mare kick)

SYR	TEAM STATISTICS	CLEM
21	First Downs	12
208	Rushing Yards	124
13-23-1	Passing	11-24-2
309	Passing Yards	69
517	Total Yards	193
4-43.5	Punts - Average	6-49.3
1-0	Fumbles - Lost	1-0
7-65	Penalties - Yards	1-16

INDIVIDUAL LEADERS
RUSHING
SYR: Thomas 14-71, 2 TD; Downing 6-37.
CLEM: Priester 15-36; Smith 6-30.
PASSING
SYR: McNabb 13-23-1, 309 yards, 3 TD.
CLEM: Greene 9-19-2, 63 yards.
RECEIVING
SYR: Harrison 7-173, 2 TD; Wilson 2-70; Sinceno 2-47, 1 TD.
CLEM: Wyatt 3-21; Priester 2-16.

JANUARY 1, 1997
NORTH CAROLINA 20, WEST VIRGINIA 13

	1ST	2ND	3RD	4TH	FINAL
UNC	0	17	3	0	20
WVU	0	3	7	3	13

SCORING SUMMARY
UNC Barnes 18 pass from Davenport (McGee kick)
UNC FG McGee 22
WVU FG Taylor 47
UNC Davenport 5 run (McGee kick)
WVU Saunders 34 pass from Johnston (Taylor kick)
UNC FG McGee 20
WVU FG Taylor 47

UNC	TEAM STATISTICS	WVU
21	First Downs	19
114	Rushing Yards	66
14-26-0	Passing	17-34-3
175	Passing Yards	197
289	Total Yards	263
7-38.3	Punts - Average	3-41.0
3-1	Fumbles - Lost	1-1
9-63	Penalties - Yards	4-52

INDIVIDUAL LEADERS
RUSHING
UNC: Johnson 25-79; Davenport 14-31, 1 TD.
WVU: Zereoue 21-63; White 6-16.
PASSING
UNC: Davenport 14-26-0, 175 yards, 1 TD.
WVU: Johnston 17-34-3, 197 yards, 1 TD.
RECEIVING
UNC: Brown 3-62; Johnson 3-33.
WVU: Saunders 9-130, 1 TD; Vanterpool 5-56.

JANUARY 1, 1998
NORTH CAROLINA 42, VIRGINIA TECH 3

	1ST	2ND	3RD	4TH	FINAL
UNC	16	6	6	14	42
VT	0	0	3	0	3

SCORING SUMMARY
UNC FG McGee 29
UNC Barnes 62 pass from Keldorf (McGee kick)
UNC Bly 6 blocked punt return (kick failed)
UNC Ellis fumble recovery in end zone (pass failed)
UNC Linton 1 run (kick failed)
VT FG Graham 40
UNC Barnes 14 pass from Keldorf (McGee kick)
UNC Carrick 4 pass from Keldorf (McGee kick)

UNC	TEAM STATISTICS	VT
18	First Downs	14
109	Rushing Yards	95
18-29-0	Passing	13-25-0
318	Passing Yards	90
427	Total Yards	185
3-40.3	Punts - Average	6-30.8
0-0	Fumbles - Lost	6-3
6-61	Penalties - Yards	4-36

INDIVIDUAL LEADERS
RUSHING
UNC: Linton 20-68, 1 TD; Geter 7-25.
VT: Oxendine 10-39; Scales 1-29.
PASSING
UNC: Keldorf 17-28-0, 290 yards, 3 TD.
VT: Clark 9-17-0, 66 yards.
RECEIVING
UNC: Barnes 3-89, 2 TD; Linton 6-81.
VT: Parker 4-32; Steuwe 2-24.

JANUARY 1, 1999
GEORGIA TECH 35, NOTRE DAME 28

	1ST	2ND	3RD	4TH	FINAL
GT	7	14	7	7	35
ND	7	0	13	8	28

SCORING SUMMARY
GT Hamilton 5 pass from Burns (Chambers kick)
ND Denson 9 run (Sanson kick)
GT Rogers 2 run (Chambers kick)
GT Sheridan 9 pass from Hamilton (Chambers kick)
ND Denson 1 run (Sanson kick)
ND Jackson 2 run (kick blocked)
GT White 44 pass from Hamilton (Chambers kick)
ND Denson 1 run (Brown pass from Jackson)
GT White 55 pass from Hamilton (Chambers kick)

GT	TEAM STATISTICS	ND
23	First Downs	20
194	Rushing Yards	150
14-21-0	Passing	13-24-0
242	Passing Yards	159
436	Total Yards	309
3-34.7	Punts - Average	5-36.6
2-1	Fumbles - Lost	2-1
7-53	Penalties - Yards	6-30
30:47	Possession Time	29:13

INDIVIDUAL LEADERS
RUSHING
GT: C. Rogers 13-82, 1 TD; P. Rogers 10-28.
ND: Denson 26-130, 3 TD; Jackson 12-12, 1 TD.
PASSING
GT: Hamilton 13-20-0, 237 yards, 3 TD.
ND: Jackson 13-24-0, 150 yards.
RECEIVING
GT: White 4-129, 2 TD; Rogers 4-52.
ND: Johnson 5-43; Brown 2-42.

JANUARY 1, 2000
MIAMI (FLA.) 28, GEORGIA TECH 13

	1ST	2ND	3RD	4TH	FINAL
MIA	7	14	0	7	28
GT	0	7	6	0	13

SCORING SUMMARY
MIA	Jackson 8 run (Crosland kick)
MIA	King 15 pass from Kelly (Crosland kick)
GT	Hamilton 17 run (Manget kick)
MIA	Portis 73 run (Crosland kick)
GT	FG Manget 25
GT	FG Manget 36
MIA	Wayne 17 pass from Dorsey (Crosland kick)

MIA	TEAM STATISTICS	GT
22	First Downs	29
220	Rushing Yards	176
16-32-1	Passing	20-40-2
208	Passing Yards	245
428	Total Yards	421
5-42.6	Punts - Average	6-26.2
1-1	Fumbles - Lost	1-0
9-90	Penalties - Yards	7-65
27:40	Possession Time	32:20

INDIVIDUAL LEADERS
RUSHING
MIA: Portis 12-117, 1 TD; Jackson 21-107, 1 TD.
GT: Gregory 16-64; Hamilton 22-49, 1 TD.
PASSING
MIA: Kelly 9-17-1, 127 yards, 1 TD; Dorsey 7-15-0, 81 yards, 1 TD.
GT: Hamilton 20-40-2, 245 yards.
RECEIVING
MIA: Franks 3-72; Moss 3-53; Wayne 4-44, 1 TD.
GT: White 8-100; Campbell 3-39.

JANUARY 1, 2001
VIRGINIA TECH 41, CLEMSON 20

	1ST	2ND	3RD	4TH	FINAL
VT	14	7	13	7	41
CLEM	0	10	3	7	20

SCORING SUMMARY
VT	Ferguson 23 pass from Vick (Warley kick)
VT	Vick 6 run (Warley kick)
CLEM	Zachery 3 pass from Dantzler (Hunt kick)
CLEM	FG Hunt 28
VT	Suggs 3 run (Warley kick)
VT	Suggs 1 run (kick failed)
CLEM	FG Hunt 26
VT	Ferguson 5 run (Warley kick)
CLEM	Gardner 23 pass from Simmons (Hunt kick)
VT	Suggs 5 run (Warley kick)

VT	TEAM STATISTICS	CLEM
19	First Downs	21
211	Rushing Yards	88
10-18-1	Passing	21-44-2
205	Passing Yards	243
416	Total Yards	331
2-32.0	Punts - Average	5-38.4
2-2	Fumbles - Lost	2-0
2-20	Penalties - Yards	7-50
31:36	Possession Time	28:24

INDIVIDUAL LEADERS
RUSHING
VT: Suggs 20-73, 3 TD; Kendrick 4-52.
CLEM: Dantzler 18-81; Zachery 5-15.
PASSING
VT: Vick 10-18-1, 205 yards, 1 TD.
CLEM: Dantzler 15-32-1, 180 yards, 1 TD.
RECEIVING
VT: Davis 2-70; Kendrick 2-55.
CLEM: Gardner 7-94, 1 TD; Watts 4-59.

JANUARY 1, 2002
FLORIDA STATE 30, VIRGINIA TECH 17

	1ST	2ND	3RD	4TH	FINAL
FSU	0	10	3	17	30
VT	3	0	14	0	17

SCORING SUMMARY
VT	FG Warley 36
FSU	Rix 1 run (Beitia kick)
FSU	FG Beitia 50
VT	K. Jones 5 run (Warley kick)
FSU	FG Beitia 47
VT	Davis 55 pass from Noel (Warley kick)
FSU	Walker 77 pass from Rix (Beitia kick)
FSU	FG Beitia 35
FSU	Walker 23 pass from Rix (Beitia kick)

FSU	TEAM STATISTICS	VT
19	First Downs	16
104	Rushing Yards	43
12-25-1	Passing	15-29-1
326	Passing Yards	269
430	Total Yards	312
2-13	Punt Returns - Yards	1-14
4-40.5	Punts - Average	7-29.9
1-1	Fumbles - Lost	2-1
4-25	Penalties - Yards	4-30
28:51	Possession Time	31:09

INDIVIDUAL LEADERS
RUSHING
FSU: G. Jones 23-120.
VT: K. Jones 23-55, 1 TD.
PASSING
FSU: Rix 12-25-1, 326 yards, 2 TD.
VT: Noel 15-27-0, 269 yards, 1 TD.
RECEIVING
FSU: Walker 4-195, 2 TD; Thorpe 2-48.
VT: Davis 5-158, 1 TD; Slowikowski 2-36.

JANUARY 1, 2003
NC STATE 28, NOTRE DAME 6

	1ST	2ND	3RD	4TH	FINAL
NCST	0	21	0	7	28
ND	3	0	3	0	6

SCORING SUMMARY
ND	FG Setta 23
NCST	McLendon 2 run (Kiker kick)
NCST	McLendon 3 run (Kiker kick)
NCST	Cotchery 9 pass from Rivers (Kiker kick)
ND	FG Setta 41
NCST	Berton 7 pass from Rivers (Kiker kick)

NCST	TEAM STATISTICS	ND
21	First Downs	23
62	Rushing Yards	86
25-41-0	Passing	23-44-3
255	Passing Yards	200
317	Total Yards	286
5-43.2	Punts - Average	4-30.3
1-0	Fumbles - Lost	0-0
10-87	Penalties - Yards	9-90
26:57	Possession Time	33:03

INDIVIDUAL LEADERS
RUSHING
NCST: Rivers 7-22; McLendon 11-18, 2 TD.
ND: Grant 21-68; Powers-Neal 5-16.
PASSING
NCST: Rivers 23-37-0, 228 yards, 2 TD.
ND: Dillingham 19-37-3, 166 yards.
RECEIVING
NCST: Cotchery 10-127, 1 TD; Berton 5-40, 1 TD.
ND: Battle 10-84; Jenkins 3-42.

JANUARY 1, 2004
MARYLAND 41, WEST VIRGINIA 7

	1ST	2ND	3RD	4TH	FINAL
MARY	10	14	10	7	41
WVU	0	0	7	0	7

SCORING SUMMARY
MARY	FG Novak 26
MARY	Williams 31 pass from McBrien (Novak kick)
MARY	Suter 76 punt return (Novak kick)
MARY	Williams 22 pass from McBrien (Novak kick)
MARY	McBrien 2 run (Novak kick)
WVU	Marshall 15 run (Cooper kick)
MARY	FG Novak 24
MARY	Walker 14 pass from McBrien (Novak kick)

MARY	TEAM STATISTICS	WVU
26	First Downs	9
141	Rushing Yards	155
21-33-0	Passing	11-19-0
381	Passing Yards	86
522	Total Yards	241
4-94	Punt Returns - Yards	2-9
1-20	Kickoff Returns - Yards	7-156
2-33.5	Punts - Average	7-42.4
5-0	Fumbles - Lost	2-2
6-45	Penalties - Yards	6-40
38:59	Possession Time	21:01

INDIVIDUAL LEADERS
RUSHING
MARY: Perry 20-67; Humber 4-29.
WVU: Harris 6-56; Wilson 12-49.
PASSING
MARY: McBrien 21-33-0, 381 yards, 3 TD.
WVU: Marshall 10-16-0, 87 yards.
RECEIVING
MARY: Suter 4-84; Williams 4-65, 2 TD.
WVU: Henry 3-46; Pennington 2-19.

JANUARY 1, 2005
FLORIDA STATE 30, WEST VIRGINIA 18

	1ST	2ND	3RD	4TH	FINAL
FSU	10	3	10	7	30
WVU	12	0	3	3	18

SCORING SUMMARY
FSU	Washington 69 run (Beitia kick)
FSU	FG Beitia 32
WVU	Harris 36 pass from Marshall (kick failed)
WVU	Harris 1 run (kick failed)
FSU	FG Beitia 28
FSU	FG Beitia 28
WVU	FG Good 44
FSU	Thorpe 14 pass from Rix (Beitia kick)
WVU	FG Good 34
FSU	Coleman 1 run (Beitia kick)

FSU	TEAM STATISTICS	WVU
22	First Downs	26
301	Rushing Yards	238
16-31-2	Passing	13-30-2
157	Passing Yards	191
458	Total Yards	429
1-8	Punt Returns - Yards	1-11
1-21	Kickoff Returns - Yards	0-0
4-41.8	Punts - Average	2-39.5
3-1	Fumbles - Lost	2-2
17-174	Penalties - Yards	11-121
32:08	Possession Time	27:52

INDIVIDUAL LEADERS
RUSHING
FSU: Washington 12-195, 1 TD; Booker 20-101.
WVU: Harris 25-134, 1 TD; Marshall 11-71.
PASSING
FSU: Rix 16-31-2, 157 yards, 1 TD.
WVU: Marshall 11-23-1, 131 yards, 1 TD.
RECEIVING
FSU: Thorpe 5-73, 1 TD; Davis 3-39.
WVU: Henry 3-61; Harris 4-50, 1 TD.

CAPITAL ONE BOWL

PROFILE

Site: Orlando, Fla.
Stadium: Florida Citrus Bowl
Capacity: 70,000
Surface: Grass

PLAYING SITES

Tangerine Bowl, 1947-72
Florida Field, 1973
Tangerine Bowl, now Florida Citrus Bowl, 1974-82
Orlando Stadium, now Florida Citrus Bowl, 1983-85
Florida Citrus Bowl, since 1986

NAME CHANGES

Tangerine Bowl, 1947-82
Florida Citrus Bowl, 1983-93
CompUSA Florida Citrus Bowl, 1994-99
OurHouse.com Florida Citrus Bowl, 2000
Capital One/Florida Citrus Bowl, 2001-02
Capital One Bowl, since 2003

SEASON	DATE	PRE-GAME RANK	TEAMS	SCORE	FINAL RANK	MOST VALUABLE PLAYERS	ATT.
1946	Jan. 1, 1947		Catawba	31			9,000
			Maryville (Tenn.)	6			
1947	Jan. 1, 1948		Catawba	7			9,000
			Marshall	0			
1948	Jan. 1, 1949		Murray State	21		Dale McDaniels, Murray State	9,000
			Sul Ross State	21		Ted Scown, Sul Ross State	
1949	Jan. 2, 1950		St. Vincent	7		Don Heinigan, St. Vincent	10,000
			Emory & Henry	6		Chick Davis, Emory & Henry	
1950	Jan. 1, 1951		Morris Harvey	35		Pete Anania, Morris Harvey	10,000
			Emory & Henry	14		Charles Hubbard, Morris Harvey	
1951	Jan. 1, 1952		Stetson	35		Bill Johnson, Stetson	12,500
			Arkansas State	20		Dave Laude, Stetson	
1952	Jan. 1, 1953		East Texas State	33		Marvin Brown, East Texas State	12,340
			Tennessee Tech	0			
1953	Jan. 1, 1954		Arkansas State	7		Billy Ray Norris, East Texas State	12,976
			East Texas State	7		Bobby Spann, Arkansas State	
1954	Jan. 1, 1955		Omaha	7		Bill Englehardt, Omaha	12,759
			Eastern Kentucky	6			
1955	Jan. 2, 1956		Juniata	6		Pat Tarquinio, Juniata	10,000
			Missouri Valley	6			
1956	Jan. 1, 1957		West Texas State	20		Ron Mills, West Texas State	11,000
			Southern Miss	13			
1957	Jan. 1, 1958		East Texas State	10		Garry Berry, East Texas State	11,000
			Southern Miss	9		Neal Hinson, East Texas State	
1958	Dec. 27, 1958		East Texas State	26		Sam McCord, East Texas State	4,000
			Missouri Valley	7			
1959	Jan. 1, 1960		Middle Tennessee State	21		Bucky Pitts, Middle Tennessee	12,500
			Presbyterian	12		Bob Waters, Presbyterian	
1960	Dec. 30, 1960		Citadel	27		Jerry Nettles, Citadel	13,000
			Tennessee Tech	0			
1961	Dec. 29, 1961		Lamar	21		Win Herbert, Lamar	6,000
			Middle Tennessee State	14			
1962	Dec. 22, 1962		Houston	49		Joe Lopasky, Houston	7,500
			Miami (Ohio)	21		Billy Roland, Houston	
1963	Dec. 28, 1963		Western Kentucky	27		Sharon Miller, Western Kentucky	7,500
			Coast Guard	0			
1964	Dec. 12, 1964		East Carolina	14		Bill Cline, East Carolina	8,000
			Massachusetts	13		Jerry Whelchel, Massachusetts	
1965	Dec. 11, 1965		East Carolina	31		Dave Alexander, East Carolina	8,350
			Maine	0			
1966	Dec. 10, 1966		Morgan State	14		Willie Lanier, Morgan State	7,138
			West Chester State	6			
1967	Dec. 16, 1967		Tennessee-Martin	25		Errol Hook, Tennessee-Martin	5,500
			West Chester	8		Gordon Lambert, Tennessee-Martin	
1968	Dec. 27, 1968		Richmond	49		Buster O'Brien, Richmond, B	16,114
		15	Ohio U.	42	20	Walker Gillette, Richmond, L	
1969	Dec. 26, 1969	20	Toledo	56		Chuck Ealey, Toledo, QB	16,311
			Davidson	33		Dan Crockett, Toledo, L	
1970	Dec. 28, 1970	15	Toledo	40	12	Chuck Ealey, Toledo, QB	15,164
			William & Mary	12		Vince Hublen, William & Mary, L	
1971	Dec. 28, 1971	14	Toledo	28	14	Chuck Ealey, Toledo, QB	16,750
			Richmond	3		Mel Long, Toledo, L	
1972	Dec. 29, 1972		Tampa	21		Freddie Solomon, Tampa, B	20,062
			Kent State	18		Jack Lambert, Kent State, L	
1973	Dec. 22, 1973	15	Miami (Ohio)	16	15	Chuck Varner, Miami, B	37,234
			Florida	7		Brad Cousino, Miami, L	
1974	Dec. 21, 1974	15	Miami (Ohio)	21	10	Sherman Smith, Miami, B	15,897
			Georgia	10		Brad Cousino and John Roudebush, Miami, L	
1975	Dec. 20, 1975	16	Miami (Ohio)	20	12	Rob Carpenter, Miami, B	20,247
			South Carolina	7		Jeff Kelly, Miami, L	
1976	Dec. 18, 1976	14	Oklahoma State	49	14	Terry Miller, Oklahoma State, B	37,812
			BYU	21		Phillip Dokes, Oklahoma State, L	
1977	Dec. 23, 1977	19	Florida State	40	14	Jimmy Jordan, Florida State, QB	41,150
			Texas Tech	17			
1978	Dec. 23, 1978		North Carolina State	30	18	Ted Brown, North Carolina State, RB	28,075
			Pittsburgh	17			
1979	Dec. 22, 1979		LSU	34		David Woodley, LSU, QB	38,142
			Wake Forest	10			
1980	Dec. 20, 1980		Florida	35		Cris Collinsworth, Florida, WR	52,541
			Maryland	20			
1981	Dec. 19, 1981		Missouri	19	19	Jeff Gaylord, Missouri, LB	50,466
		18	Southern Miss	17			
1982	Dec. 18, 1982	18	Auburn	33	14	Randy Campbell, Auburn, QB	51,296
			Boston College	26			
1983	Dec. 17, 1983		Tennessee	30		Johnnie Jones, Tennessee, RB	50,183
		16	Maryland	23			
1984	Dec. 22, 1984	15	Florida State	17	17	James Jackson, Georgia, QB	51,821
			Georgia	17			
1985	Dec. 28, 1985	17	Ohio State	10	14	Larry Kolic, Ohio State, LB	50,920
		19	BYU	7	16		
1986	Jan. 1, 1987	10	Auburn	16	6	Aundray Bruce, Auburn, LB	51,113
			Southern Cal	7			
1987	Jan. 1, 1988	14	Clemson	35	12	Rodney Williams, Clemson, QB	53,152
		20	Penn State	10			
1988	Jan. 2, 1989	13	Clemson	13	9	Terry Allen, Clemson, TB	53,571
		10	Oklahoma	6	14		
1989	Jan. 1, 1990	11	Illinois	31	10	Jeff George, Illinois, QB	60,016
		15	Virginia	21	18		
1990	Jan. 1, 1991	2	Georgia Tech	45	1	Shawn Jones, Georgia Tech, QB	72,328
		19	Nebraska	21	24		
1991	Jan. 1, 1992	14	California	37	8	Mike Pawlawski, California, QB	64,192
		13	Clemson	13	18		
1992	Jan. 1, 1993	8	Georgia	21	8	Garrison Hearst, Georgia, RB	65,861
		15	Ohio State	14	18		

SEASON	DATE	PRE-GAME RANK	TEAMS	SCORE	FINAL RANK	MOST VALUABLE PLAYERS	ATT.
1993	Jan. 1, 1994	13	Penn State	31	8	Bobby Engram, Penn State, WR	72,456
		6	Tennessee	13	12		
1994	Jan. 2, 1995	6	Alabama	24	5	Sherman Williams, Alabama, RB	71,195
		13	Ohio State	17	14		
1995	Jan. 1, 1996	4T	Tennessee	20	3	Jay Graham, Tennessee, RB	70,797
		4T	Ohio State	14	6		
1996	Jan. 1, 1997	9	Tennessee	48	9	Peyton Manning, Tennessee, QB	63,467
		11	Northwestern	28	15		
1997	Jan. 1, 1998	6	Florida	21	4	Fred Taylor, Florida, TB	72,940
		11	Penn State	6	16		
1998	Jan. 1, 1999	15	Michigan	45	12	Anthony Thomas, Michigan, RB	63,584
		11	Arkansas	31	16		
1999	Jan. 1, 2000	9	Michigan State	37	7	Plaxico Burress, Michigan State, WR	62,011
		10	Florida	34	12		
2000	Jan. 1, 2001	17	Michigan	31	11	Anthony Thomas, Michigan, RB	66,928
		20	Auburn	28	18		
2001	Jan. 1, 2002	8	Tennessee	45	4	Casey Clausen, Tennessee, QB	59,693
		17	Michigan	17	20		
2002	Jan. 1, 2003	19	Auburn	13	14	Ronnie Brown, Auburn, TB	66,334
		10	Penn State	9	16		
2003	Jan. 1, 2004	11	Georgia	34	7	David Greene, Gerogia, QB	64,565
		12	Purdue	27	18		
2004	Jan. 1, 2005	11	Iowa	30	8	JaMarcus Russell, LSU, QB	70,227
		12	LSU	25	16		

JANUARY 1, 1947
CATAWBA 31, MARYVILLE 6

	1ST	2ND	3RD	4TH	FINAL
CAT	0	18	7	6	31
MARY	0	0	0	6	6

SCORING SUMMARY
CAT	Georganio 11 run (kick failed)
CAT	Hanley 6 pass from Bowen (kick failed)
CAT	Bowen 35 interception return (kick failed)
CAT	Bowen 10 run (Dorton kick)
MARY	Spears 2 run (pass failed)
CAT	Greene 20 pass from Bowen (kick failed)

JANUARY 1, 1948
CATAWBA 7, MARSHALL 0

	1ST	2ND	3RD	4TH	FINAL
CAT	0	0	0	7	7
MAR	0	0	0	0	0

SCORING SUMMARY
CAT	Spears 2 run (Dorton kick)

CAT	TEAM STATISTICS	MAR
6	First Downs	12
54	Rushing Yards	109
2-5-1	Passing	5-10-1
38	Passing Yards	54
92	Total Yards	163
8-36.0	Punts - Average	6-40.5

JANUARY 1, 1949
MURRAY STATE 21, SUL ROSS STATE 21

	1ST	2ND	3RD	4TH	FINAL
MSU	0	7	7	7	21
SRS	7	14	0	0	21

SCORING SUMMARY
SRS	Scown 1 run (Barton kick)
SRS	Scown 5 pass from Laffon (Barton kick)
SRS	Scown 12 run (Barton kick)
MSU	Bronson 85 kickoff return (Sanders kick)
MSU	McDaniels 7 run (Sanders kick)
MSU	Bronson 2 run (Sanders kick)

JANUARY 2, 1950
ST. VINCENT 7, EMORY & HENRY 6

	1ST	2ND	3RD	4TH	FINAL
SV	0	7	0	0	7
E&H	0	6	0	0	6

SCORING SUMMARY
SV	Heinigan 1 run (Heimbeucher kick)
E&H	Howard 9 pass from Davis (kick failed)

JANUARY 1, 1951
MORRIS HARVEY 35, EMORY & HENRY 14

	1ST	2ND	3RD	4TH	FINAL
MH	0	14	14	7	35
E&H	7	0	7	0	14

SCORING SUMMARY
E&H	Spurgeon 5 run (Cubine kick)
MH	Hubbard 7 pass from Anania (Denton kick)
MH	Hubbard 10 pass from Anania (Denton kick)
MH	Hubbard 14 pass from Anania (Denton kick)
E&H	Miller 95 kickoff return (Cubine kick)
MH	Romine 18 run (Denton kick)
MH	Brown 22 pass from Anania (Denton kick)

JANUARY 1, 1952
STETSON 35, ARKANSAS STATE 20

	1ST	2ND	3RD	4TH	FINAL
STET	0	7	21	7	35
ASU	7	6	0	7	20

SCORING SUMMARY
ASU	Greenwald 5 run (LaPlante kick)
STET	Laude 2 pass from Johnson (Martin kick)
ASU	Greenwald 4 run (kick failed)
STET	Laude 23 pass from Johnson (Martin kick)
STET	Laude 30 pass from Johnson (Martin kick)
STET	Marks 5 run (Martin kick)
ASU	Koldus 9 pass from Dinges (LaPlante kick)
STET	Gallagher 4 run (Martin kick)

JANUARY 1, 1953
EAST TEXAS ST 33, TENNESSEE TECH 0

	1ST	2ND	3RD	4TH	FINAL
ETS	13	0	0	20	33
TT	0	0	0	0	0

SCORING SUMMARY
ETS	Brown 25 run (Corder kick)
ETS	McCormick 16 pass from Gray (kick failed)
ETS	Brown 67 pass from Gray (Corder kick)
ETS	Johnson 75 interception return (pass failed)
ETS	Parks 9 run (Corder kick)

JANUARY 1, 1954
EAST TEXAS ST 7, ARKANSAS STATE 7

	1ST	2ND	3RD	4TH	FINAL
ETS	0	0	0	7	7
ASU	7	0	0	0	7

SCORING SUMMARY
ASU	Turley 20 pass from Spann (Sechrest kick)
ETS	Norris 20 run (Riley kick)

JANUARY 1, 1955
OMAHA 7, EASTERN KENTUCKY 6

	1ST	2ND	3RD	4TH	FINAL
OMA	7	0	0	0	7
EKU	0	6	0	0	6

SCORING SUMMARY
OMA	Rotella 20 pass from Engelhardt (Engelhardt kick)
EKU	Green 9 pass from Lenderman (kick failed)

JANUARY 2, 1956
JUNIATA 6, MISSOURI VALLEY 6

	1ST	2ND	3RD	4TH	FINAL
JUN	6	0	0	0	6
MV	6	0	0	0	6

SCORING SUMMARY
JUN	Drexler 30 pass from Tarquinio (pass failed)
MV	Gibler 11 pass from Seates (run failed)

95	Rushing Yards	152
15-26-1	Passing	6-12-1
216	Passing Yards	114
311	Total Yards	266

INDIVIDUAL LEADERS
RUSHING
JUN: Sill 19-44; Pheasant 6-29.
MV: Lehman 11-47; Montgomery 7-39.
PASSING
JUN: Tarquinio 15-26-1, 216 yards, 1 TD.
MV: Portell 3-5-0, 59 yards; Seates 3-5-1, 55 yards, 1 TD.

JANUARY 1, 1957
WEST TEXAS ST 20, SOUTHERN MISS 13

	1ST	2ND	3RD	4TH	FINAL
WTS	0	0	6	14	20
MSO	0	13	0	0	13

SCORING SUMMARY
MSO	Barfield 1 run (kick failed)
MSO	Taylor 58 pass from Hughes (Whitfield kick)
WTS	Mills 75 interception return (kick failed)
WTS	Mills 2 run (Coffey kick)
WTS	Hillman 19 run (Coffey kick)

170	Rushing Yards	200
4-8-0	Passing	11-22-2
42	Passing Yards	156
212	Total Yards	356

INDIVIDUAL LEADERS
RUSHING
WTS: Mills 15-70, 1 TD; Hillman 7-31, 1 TD.
MSO: Arban 9-77; Whitfield 9-45; Barfield 5-29, 1 TD.
PASSING
WTS: Hillman 3-6-0, 38 yards.
MSO: Hughes 8-13-1, 148 yards, 1 TD.
RECEIVING
WTS: Ratliff 1-18; Ballard 1-11.
MSO: Taylor 2-66, 1 TD; Meeks 2-35.

JANUARY 1, 1958
EAST TEXAS ST 10, SOUTHERN MISS 9

	1ST	2ND	3RD	4TH	FINAL
ETS	7	0	0	3	10
MSO	0	7	2	0	9

SCORING SUMMARY
ETS	Berry 3 run (Hinson kick)
MSO	Sekul 6 run (Lance kick)
MSO	Safety (QB tackled in end zone)
ETS	FG Hinson 31

58	Rushing Yards	140
4-9-0	Passing	9-17-1
56	Passing Yards	55
114	Total Yards	195

INDIVIDUAL LEADERS
RUSHING
ETS: Hinson 9-35; McCord 20-32.
MSO: Dickinson 12-38; Sekul 8-35, 1 TD.
PASSING
ETS: Williams 1-2-0, 24 yards.
MSO: Sekul 8-13-1, 48 yards.
RECEIVING
ETS: Ewell 1-24; Berry 1-14.
MSO: Yencho 3-24; Juneau 3-19.

DECEMBER 27, 1958
EAST TEXAS ST 26, MISS VALLEY 7

	1ST	2ND	3RD	4TH	FINAL
ETS	0	12	0	14	26
MV	0	7	0	0	7

SCORING SUMMARY
ETS	Harbour 2 run (kick failed)
MV	Rogers 1 run (Mosley kick)
ETS	Berry recovered fumble in end zone (kick failed)
ETS	Malone 3 pass from McCord (Roberts pass from McCord)
ETS	Mandum 53 interception return (pass failed)

THE BOWLS

JANUARY 1, 1960
MIDDLE TENN ST 21, PRESBYTERIAN 12

	1ST	2ND	3RD	4TH	FINAL
MTSU	7	7	0	7	21
PRES	0	6	6	0	12

SCORING SUMMARY
MTSU	Pitts 53 punt return (Adams kick)
MTSU	Purvis 5 run (Adams kick)
PRES	Pate 47 pass from Waters (pass failed)
PRES	Pate 42 pass from Waters (kick failed)
MTSU	Pitts 20 run (Adams kick)

MTSU	TEAM STATISTICS	PRES
10	First Downs	15
240	Rushing Yards	129
0-6-0	Passing	13-30-2
0	Passing Yards	197
240	Total Yards	326
1-34.4	Punts - Average	8-30.0

DECEMBER 30, 1960
CITADEL 27, TENNESSEE TECH 0

	1ST	2ND	3RD	4TH	FINAL
CIT	7	0	13	7	27
TT	0	0	0	0	0

SCORING SUMMARY
CIT	Allen 6 pass from Nettles (Gilgo kick)
CIT	Edwards 56 run (kick failed)
CIT	Gilgo 16 pass from Nettles (Gilgo kick)
CIT	Mitchell 1 run (Gilgo kick)

CIT	TEAM STATISTICS	TT
25	First Downs	11
236	Rushing Yards	71
11-20-0	Passing	3-11-2
167	Passing Yards	30
403	Total Yards	101
4-39.0	Punts - Average	1-31.0

INDIVIDUAL LEADERS
RUSHING
CIT: Edwards 7-84, 1 TD; Eastburn 14-78.
TT: Jaquess 4-24; Broyles 5-19.
PASSING
CIT: Nettles 8-14-0, 137 yards, 2 TD.
TT: Mason 3-9-1, 30 yards.

DECEMBER 29, 1961
LAMAR TECH 21, MIDDLE TENN ST 14

	1ST	2ND	3RD	4TH	FINAL
LT	7	7	0	7	21
MTSU	0	0	6	8	14

SCORING SUMMARY
LT	Hebert 52 run (Smith kick)
LT	King fumble recovery in end zone (Smith kick)
MTSU	Dykes 32 pass from Pearson (pass failed)
LT	McManus 3 pass from Hebert (Smith kick)
MTSU	Pearson 1 run (Dykes pass from Pearson)

LT	TEAM STATISTICS	MTSU
8	First Downs	6
193	Rushing Yards	121
8-17-0	Passing	6-14-2
88	Passing Yards	94
281	Total Yards	215
5-40.2	Punts - Average	3-37.0
12-115	Penalties - Yards	5-73

DECEMBER 22, 1962
HOUSTON 49, MIAMI (OHIO) 21

	1ST	2ND	3RD	4TH	FINAL
HOU	7	28	7	7	49
MIA	7	0	7	7	21

SCORING SUMMARY
MIA	Myers 9 pass from Kellerman (Jencks kick)
HOU	Lopasky 3 run (McMillan kick)
HOU	Brezena 1 run (McMillan kick)
HOU	Brezena 44 pass from Roland (McMillan kick)
HOU	Lopasky 70 punt return (McMillan kick)
HOU	McMillan 5 pass from Roland (McMillan kick)
MIA	Kellerman 1 run (Jencks kick)
HOU	Lopasky 4 run (McMillan kick)
MIA	Neumeier 10 run (Jencks kick)
HOU	Lopasky 13 pass from Roland (McMillan kick)

HOU	TEAM STATISTICS	MIA
17	First Downs	18
207	Rushing Yards	54
13-19-1	Passing	17-40-2
206	Passing Yards	265
413	Total Yards	319
3-41.3	Punts - Average	5-38.8
7-83	Penalties - Yards	7-65

INDIVIDUAL LEADERS
RUSHING
HOU: Brezena 11-55, 1 TD; Roland 7-48.
MIA: Longsworth 6-27; Neumeier 3-14, 1 TD.
PASSING
HOU: Roland 11-17-1, 199 yards, 3 TD.
MIA: Kellermann 17-40-2, 265 yards, 1 TD.
RECEIVING
HOU: Lopasky 3-81, 1 TD; Brewer 2-58.
MIA: Jencks 5-75; Myers 5-75.

DECEMBER 28, 1963
WESTERN KENTUCKY 27, COAST GUARD 0

	1ST	2ND	3RD	4TH	FINAL
WKU	0	14	6	7	27
CG	0	0	0	0	0

SCORING SUMMARY
WKU	Miller 12 run (Clark kick)
WKU	Mutchler 20 pass from Miller (Clark kick)
WKU	Napper 56 pass from Miller (kick failed)
WKU	Jim Burt 14 run (Clark kick)

WKU	TEAM STATISTICS	CG
12	First Downs	14
147	Rushing Yards	-1
3-16-0	Passing	14-40-4
79	Passing Yards	195
226	Total Yards	194
8-38.0	Punts - Average	5-28.6
12-120	Penalties - Yards	6-60

INDIVIDUAL LEADERS
RUSHING
WKU: Jim Burt 9-40, 1 TD; John Burt 10-36.
PASSING
WKU: Miller 3-6-0, 79 yards, 2 TD; Jim Burt 0-3-0, 0 yards.
RECEIVING
WKU: Napper 1-56; Mutchler 1-20.

DECEMBER 12, 1964
EAST CAROLINA 14, UMASS 13

	1ST	2ND	3RD	4TH	FINAL
ECU	0	0	6	8	14
MASS	0	7	6	0	13

SCORING SUMMARY
MASS	Palm 12 pass from Whelchel (Whelchel kick)
MASS	Palm 61 pass from Whelchel (kick failed)
ECU	Richardson 2 run (pass failed)
ECU	Cline 9 run (Crane pass from Cline)

ECU	TEAM STATISTICS	MASS
14	First Downs	14
153	Rushing Yards	135
10-19-1	Passing	9-15-2
192	Passing Yards	153
345	Total Yards	288
4-33.6	Punts - Average	5-43.8
3-3	Fumbles - Lost	1-1
6-45	Penalties - Yards	10-81

INDIVIDUAL LEADERS
RUSHING
ECU: Richardson 14-69, 1 TD; Cline 12-39, 1 TD.
MASS: Ross 7-55; Whelchel 14-35.
PASSING
ECU: Cline 8-16-1, 178 yards.
MASS: Whelchel 9-14-1, 153 yards, 2 TD.
RECEIVING
ECU: Bumgarner 5-69; Mills 2-45.
MASS: Palm 3-84, 2 TD; DeRose 2-36.

DECEMBER 11, 1965
EAST CAROLINA 31, MAINE 0

	1ST	2ND	3RD	4TH	FINAL
ECU	0	10	14	7	31
UM	0	0	0	0	0

SCORING SUMMARY
ECU	FG Kriz 24
ECU	Abernathy 35 pass from Richardson (Kriz kick)
ECU	Alexander 1 run (Kriz kick)
ECU	Grimes 5 pass from Alexander (Kriz kick)
ECU	Alexander 54 run (Kriz kick)

ECU	TEAM STATISTICS	UM
172	Rushing Yards	66
13-26-1	Passing	7-26-4
175	Passing Yards	86
347	Total Yards	152

INDIVIDUAL LEADERS
RUSHING
ECU: Alexander 31-170, 2 TD; Bailey 8-27.
UM: Belisle 11-40; Harney 7-25.
PASSING
ECU: Richardson 9-17-1, 118 yards, 1 TD.
UM: Platter 5-19-2, 61 yards.
RECEIVING
ECU: Swindell 2-40; Odom 3-37.
UM: Harney 1-44; Doyle 2-27 .

DECEMBER 10, 1966
MORGAN STATE 14, WEST CHESTER ST 6

	1ST	2ND	3RD	4TH	FINAL
MSU	0	7	0	7	14
WCS	0	0	0	6	6

SCORING SUMMARY
MSU	Savage 1 run (Johnson kick)
MSU	Queen 11 interception return (Johnson kick)
WCS	Wilkinson 31 pass from Haynie (pass failed)

DECEMBER 16, 1967
TENN. MARTIN 25, WEST CHESTER ST 8

	1ST	2ND	3RD	4TH	FINAL
UTM	9	9	0	7	25
WCS	0	8	0	0	8

SCORING SUMMARY
UTM	Wiggins 2 run (Mayo kick)
UTM	Safety (Haynie tackled in end zone)
UTM	Hook 4 run (Mayo kick)
UTM	Safety (Haynie tackled in end zone)
WCS	Dunkleberger 74 punt return (Wilkinson pass from Haynie)
UTM	Capers 20 pass from Cox (Mayo kick)

UTM	TEAM STATISTICS	WCS
20	First Downs	14
145	Rushing Yards	17
12-32-1	Passing	18-35-2
145	Passing Yards	169
290	Total Yards	186
7-42.0	Punts - Average	7-35.0

DECEMBER 27, 1968
RICHMOND 49, OHIO 42

	1ST	2ND	3RD	4TH	FINAL
UR	7	21	14	7	49
OU	7	14	13	8	42

SCORING SUMMARY
OU	Snyder 40 pass from Bryant (Pataki kick)
UR	Livesay 24 pass from O'Brien (Dussault kick)
UR	O'Brien 31 run (Dussault kick)
OU	Bryant 7 run (Pataki kick)
UR	Kellum 1 run (Dussault kick)
UR	Gillette 5 pass from O'Brien (Dussault kick)
OU	Snyder 2 pass from Bryant (Pataki kick)
UR	Kellum 9 run (Dussault kick)
UR	Crenshaw 12 pass from O'Brien (Dussault kick)
OU	LeVeck 1 run (run failed)
UR	Snyder 4 pass from Bryant (Pataki kick)
UR	Livesay 15 pass from O'Brien (Dussault kick)
OU	Houmard 3 pass from Bryant (LeVeck run)

INDIVIDUAL LEADERS
RUSHING
UR: O'Brien 7-39, 1 TD; Kellum 15-36, 2 TD.
OU: LeVeck 20-85, 1 TD; Bryant 17-74, 1 TD.
PASSING
UR: O'Brien 39-58-1, 447 yards, 4 TD.
OU: Bryant 17-33-2, 233 yards, 4 TD.
RECEIVING
UR: Gillette 20-242, 1 TD; Livesay 10-127, 2 TD.
OU: Snyder 11-214, 3 TD; Swindell 3-28.

DECEMBER 26, 1969
TOLEDO 56, DAVIDSON 33

	1ST	2ND	3RD	4TH	FINAL
TOL	14	28	0	14	56
DAV	7	0	14	12	33

SCORING SUMMARY
TOL	Ealey 52 run (Crots kick)
DAV	Zaharov 1 run (Terry kick)
TOL	Cole 1 run (Crots kick)
TOL	Seymour 10 pass from Ealey (Crots kick)
TOL	Crockett 34 pass from Ealey (Crots kick)
TOL	Seymour 5 pass from Ealey (Crots kick)
TOL	Cole 11 run (Crots kick)
DAV	Hannen 12 pass from Slade (kick failed)
DAV	Hannen 16 pass from Slade (Mikolayunas pass from Slade)
DAV	Hannen 8 pass from Slade (pass failed)
TOL	Cole 16 run (Crots kick)
DAV	Lyon 29 pass from Slade (pass failed)
TOL	Aschliman recovered fumble in end zone (Crots kick)

TOL	TEAM STATISTICS	DAV
22	First Downs	24
334	Rushing Yards	101
11-14-0	Passing	22-38-0
147	Passing Yards	305
481	Total Yards	406
4-28.0	Punts - Average	5-36.0
6-65	Penalties - Yards	2-17

DECEMBER 28, 1970
TOLEDO 40, WILLIAM & MARY 12

	1ST	2ND	3RD	4TH	FINAL
TOL	0	7	13	20	40
W&M	6	0	0	6	12

SCORING SUMMARY
W&M	Bushnell 10 run (kick failed)
TOL	Cole 1 run (Duncan kick)
TOL	Harris 15 run (Duncan kick)
TOL	Schwartz 9 run (kick failed)
TOL	Fair 4 pass from Ealey (Duncan kick)
TOL	Ealey 3 run (Duncan kick)
TOL	Niezgoda 52 interception return (kick failed)
W&M	Regan 2 run (pass failed)

TOL	TEAM STATISTICS	W&M
26	First Downs	15
326	Rushing Yards	139
12-22-0	Passing	13-22-2
128	Passing Yards	127
454	Total Yards	266
2-38.5	Punts - Average	7-38.4
9-100	Penalties - Yards	7-66

DECEMBER 28, 1971
TOLEDO 28, RICHMOND 3

	1ST	2ND	3RD	4TH	FINAL
TOL	0	14	0	14	28
UR	3	0	0	0	3

SCORING SUMMARY
UR	FG Clark 27
TOL	Long recovered fumble in end zone (Keim kick)
TOL	Schwartz 1 run (Keim kick)
TOL	Ealey 1 run (Keim kick)
TOL	Schwartz 3 run (Keim kick)

TOL	TEAM STATISTICS	UR
25	First Downs	7
206	Rushing Yards	114
15-24-0	Passing	2-11-2
189	Passing Yards	24
395	Total Yards	138
4-34.7	Punts - Average	7-46.4
1-1	Fumbles - Lost	1-1
5-51	Penalties - Yards	10-70

INDIVIDUAL LEADERS
RUSHING
TOL: Schwartz 20-51, 2 TD; Ealey 12-38, 1 TD.
UR: Meyers 13-32; Smith 10-51.
PASSING
TOL: Ealey 14-23-0, 176 yards.
UR: Nichols 2-11-2, 24 yards.
RECEIVING
TOL: Fair 8-100; Baker 2-37.
UR: Popovich 1-12; Smith 1-12.

DECEMBER 29, 1972
TAMPA 21, KENT STATE 18

	1ST	2ND	3RD	4TH	FINAL
TAM	14	7	0	0	21
KENT	0	0	6	12	18

SCORING SUMMARY
TAM	Orndorff 15 pass from Carter (Cooper kick)
TAM	Orndorff 35 pass from Carter (Cooper kick)
TAM	Solomon 2 run (Cooper kick)
KENT	Tinker 76 pass from Kokal (kick failed)
KENT	Dooner 10 pass from Kokal (run failed)
KENT	Harmon 78 punt return (kick failed)

DECEMBER 22, 1973
MIAMI (OHIO) 16, FLORIDA 7

	1ST	2ND	3RD	4TH	FINAL
MIA	3	0	10	3	16
UF	0	0	0	7	7

SCORING SUMMARY
MIA	FG Draudt 26
MIA	FG Draudt 45
MIA	Varner 3 run (Draudt kick)
UF	Moore 1 run (Williams kick)
MIA	FG Draudt 27

MIA	TEAM STATISTICS	UF
14	First Downs	12
239	Rushing Yards	90
1-8-0	Passing	9-21-4
6	Passing Yards	99
245	Total Yards	189
10-33.3	Punts - Average	6-34.3
2-1	Fumbles - Lost	4-3
3-39	Penalties - Yards	3-27

INDIVIDUAL LEADERS
RUSHING
MIA: Varner 28-157, 1 TD; Hitchens 20-62.
UF: Moore 16-101, 1 TD; Richards 7-49.
PASSING
MIA: Sanna 1-8-0, 6 yards.
UF: Bowden 5-9-1, 66 yards.
RECEIVING
MIA: Williams 1-6.
UF: Moore 3-30; Foldberg 2-25.

DECEMBER 21, 1974
MIAMI (OHIO) 21, GEORGIA 10

	1ST	2ND	3RD	4TH	FINAL
MIA	14	7	0	0	21
UGA	3	0	7	0	10

SCORING SUMMARY
MIA	Carpenter 1 run (Draudt kick)
UGA	FG Leavitt 20
MIA	Taylor 7 pass from Smith (Draudt kick)
MIA	Smith 8 run (Draudt kick)
UGA	Goff 1 run (Leavitt kick)

MIA	TEAM STATISTICS	UGA
18	First Downs	17
228	Rushing Yards	74
3-8-0	Passing	11-24-0
39	Passing Yards	200
267	Total Yards	274
5-36.0	Punts - Average	4-30.0
3-3	Fumbles - Lost	5-2
3-25	Penalties - Yards	20-24

INDIVIDUAL LEADERS
RUSHING
MIA: Carpenter 30-114, 1 TD; Smith 22-90, 1 TD.
UGA: Harrison 17-69.
PASSING
MIA: Smith 1-2-0, 7 yards; Sanna 2-24-0, 22 yards.
UGA: Robinson 11-24-0, 190 yards.
RECEIVING
MIA: Schulte 1-15; Taylor 1-7, 1 TD.
UGA: Appleby 6-102; Wilson 3-45.

DECEMBER 20, 1975
MIAMI (OHIO) 20, SOUTH CAROLINA 7

	1ST	2ND	3RD	4TH	FINAL
MIA	7	7	3	3	20
USC	0	0	7	0	7

SCORING SUMMARY
MIA	Carpenter 5 run (Johnson kick)
MIA	Carpenter 1 run (Johnson kick)
MIA	FG Johnson 47
USC	Amrein 3 run (Marino kick)
MIA	FG Johnson 33

MIA	TEAM STATISTICS	USC
19	First Downs	17
238	Rushing Yards	56
10-13-1	Passing	18-29-1
137	Passing Yards	228
375	Total Yards	284
4-35.8	Punts - Average	6-44.8
0-0	Fumbles - Lost	1-0
5-35	Penalties - Yards	3-24

INDIVIDUAL LEADERS
RUSHING
MIA: Carpenter 29-120, 2 TD; Smith 17-64.
USC: Williams 9-57; Long 11-19.
PASSING
MIA: Smith 10-13-1, 137 yards.
USC: Grantz 18-29-1, 228 yards.
RECEIVING
MIA: Joecken 3-68; Walker 4-44.
USC: Logan 9-109; Stephens 4-51.

DECEMBER 18, 1976
OKLAHOMA STATE 49, BYU 21

	1ST	2ND	3RD	4TH	FINAL
OKST	7	21	21	0	49
BYU	0	14	7	0	21

SCORING SUMMARY
OKST	Dawson 36 interception return (Daigle kick)
BYU	Christensen 1 run (Taylor kick)
OKST	Weatherbie 1 run (Daigle kick)
OKST	Miller 3 run (Daigle kick)
BYU	Thompson 37 pass from Nielsen (Taylor kick)
OKST	Miller 78 run (Daigle kick)
BYU	Lowry 102 kickoff return (Taylor kick)
OKST	Turner 1 run (kick failed)
OKST	Miller 6 run (Lisle pass from Weatherbie)
OKST	Miller 1 run (Daigle kick)

OKST	TEAM STATISTICS	BYU
18	First Downs	14
375	Rushing Yards	46
2-10-0	Passing	23-34-4
27	Passing Yards	209
402	Total Yards	255
5-40.8	Punts - Average	5-34.4
4-2	Fumbles - Lost	3-1
7-56	Penalties - Yards	6-67

INDIVIDUAL LEADERS
RUSHING
OKST: Miller 23-173, 4 TD; Turner 22-80, 1 TD.
BYU: Blanc 8-31; Nielson 6-6.
PASSING
OKST: Weatherbie 1-9-0, 27 yards.
BYU: Nielsen 23-34-4, 209 yards, 1 TD.
RECEIVING
OKST: Lisle 2-27.
BYU: Thompson 3-63, 1 TD; Christensen 6-53.

December 23, 1977
Florida State 40, Texas Tech 17

	1ST	2ND	3RD	4TH	FINAL
FSU	3	13	11	13	40
TT	0	3	6	8	17

SCORING SUMMARY

FSU	FG Cappelen 23
TT	FG Mock 24
FSU	Key 93 kickoff return (Cappelen kick)
FSU	King 37 pass from Jordan (kick failed)
FSU	Shumann 40 pass from Jordan (King pass from Jordan)
FSU	FG Cappelen 22
TT	Nelson 44 pass from Allison (pass failed)
FSU	Overby 15 pass from Woodham (kick failed)
TT	Taylor 21 run (Taylor pass from Allison)
FSU	Sanders 44 pass from Woodham (Cappelen kick)

FSU	TEAM STATISTICS	TT
22	First Downs	21
85	Rushing Yards	99
25-35-0	Passing	18-28-2
455	Passing Yards	279
540	Total Yards	378
3-35.6	Punts - Average	7-29.6
2-2	Fumbles - Lost	3-2
10-130	Penalties - Yards	3-50

INDIVIDUAL LEADERS

RUSHING
FSU: Key 21-83; Lyles 10-36.
TT: Taylor 19-60, 1 TD; Hadnot 3-15.

PASSING
FSU: Jordan 18-25-0, 311 yards, 2 TD; Woodham 7-10-0, 144 yards, 1 TD.
TT: Allison 17-27-2, 243 yards, 1 TD.

RECEIVING
FSU: Key 6-100; Shumann 4-99, 1 TD; King 6-85, 1 TD.
TT: Nelson 4-99, 1 TD; Hadnot 4-62.

December 23, 1978
NC State 30, Pittsburgh 17

	1ST	2ND	3RD	4TH	FINAL
NCSU	7	10	3	10	30
PITT	0	0	3	14	17

SCORING SUMMARY

NCSU	Brown 1 run (Ritter kick)
NCSU	FG Ritter 51
NCSU	Jukes 55 pass from Isley (Ritter kick)
PITT	FG Schubert 37
NCSU	FG Ritter 29
NCSU	FG Ritter 23
PITT	Jacobs 1 run (Schubert kick)
NCSU	Nall 66 interception return (Ritter kick)
PITT	Carter 1 run (Schubert kick)

207	Rushing Yards	110
6-9-0	Passing	32-48-4
103	Passing Yards	268
310	Total Yards	378
5-36.0	Punts - Average	6-41.0
3-2	Fumbles - Lost	2-0
8-60	Penalties - Yards	7-70

December 22, 1979
LSU 34, Wake Forest 10

	1ST	2ND	3RD	4TH	FINAL
LSU	14	10	0	10	34
WFU	0	3	7	0	10

SCORING SUMMARY

LSU	Woodley 13 run (Barthel kick)
LSU	Woodley 3 run (Barthel kick)
LSU	Murphree 19 pass from Woodley (Barthel kick)
LSU	FG Barthel 31
WFU	FG Denfeld 43
WFU	Baumgardner 34 pass from Venuto (Harnish kick)
LSU	FG Barthel 41
LSU	Ensminger 4 run (Barthel kick)

LSU	TEAM STATISTICS	WFU
24	First Downs	16
258	Rushing Yards	30
16-26-1	Passing	15-30-4
273	Passing Yards	233
531	Total Yards	263
2-38.5	Punts - Average	7-36.9
2-2	Fumbles - Lost	4-1
6-44	Penalties - Yards	4-30

INDIVIDUAL LEADERS

RUSHING
LSU: Woodley 10-68, 2 TD; Hernandez 14-58.
WFU: McDougald 15-54; Ventresca 2-19.

PASSING
LSU: Woodley 11-19-1, 199 yards, 1 TD.
WFU: Venuto 10-20-3, 165 yards, 1 TD.

RECEIVING
LSU: Carson 3-76; Porter 3-73.
WFU: Baumgardner 6-128, 1 TD; McDougald 2-30.

December 20, 1980
Florida 35, Maryland 20

	1ST	2ND	3RD	4TH	FINAL
UF	0	14	14	7	35
MD	3	6	11	0	20

SCORING SUMMARY

MD	FG Castro 35
UF	Collinsworth 24 pass from Peace (Clark kick)
MD	FG Castro 27
MD	FG Castro 27
UF	Jones 2 run (Clark kick)
MD	Wysocki 1 run (Tice run)
MD	FG Castro 43
UF	Peace 1 run (Clark kick)
UF	Collinsworth 21 pass from Peace (Clark kick)
UF	Brown 2 run (Clark kick)

UF		MD
16	First Downs	9
108	Rushing Yards	177
20-34-1	Passing	12-26-3
271	Passing Yards	155
379	Total Yards	332
6-33.7	Punts - Average	4-39.0
1-0	Fumbles - Lost	4-2
11-108	Penalties - Yards	6-44

INDIVIDUAL LEADERS

RUSHING
UF: Brown 6-71, 1 TD; Peace 6-12, 1 TD.
MD: Wysocki 39-159, 1 TD; Fasano 3-13.

PASSING
UF: Peace 20-34-1, 271 yards, 2 TD.
MD: Tice 11-23-3, 129 yards.

RECEIVING
UF: Collinsworth 8-166, 2 TD; Young 8-66.
MD: Havener 4-83; Sievers 3-24.

December 19, 1981
Missouri 19, Southern Miss 17

	1ST	2ND	3RD	4TH	FINAL
MO	7	6	3	3	19
USM	0	3	7	7	17

SCORING SUMMARY

MO	Meyer 3 run (Lucchesi kick)
USM	FG Clark 37
MO	FG Lucchesi 45
MO	FG Lucchesi 41
USM	Winder 4 run (Clark kick)
MO	FG Lucchesi 30
MO	FG Lucchesi 28
USM	Lipps 74 pass from Sellers (Clark kick)

MO		USM
15	First Downs	15
164	Rushing Yards	133
10-22-1	Passing	6-20-0
141	Passing Yards	128
305	Total Yards	261
7-35.9	Punts - Average	8-34.5
1-0	Fumbles - Lost	2-1
7-50	Penalties - Yards	6-58

INDIVIDUAL LEADERS

RUSHING
MO: Meyer 20-96, 1 TD; B. White 18-62.
USM: Winder 13-50, 1 TD; Terrell 9-44.

PASSING
MO: Perry 10-22-1, 141 yards.
USM: Collier 5-17-0, 54 yards; Sellers 1-3-0, 74 yards, 1 TD.

RECEIVING
MO: Caver 4-65; Meyer 3-11.
USM: Lipps 1-74, 1 TD; Powell 2-26.

December 18, 1982
Auburn 33, Boston College 26

	1ST	2ND	3RD	4TH	FINAL
AU	3	20	10	0	33
BC	7	3	0	16	26

SCORING SUMMARY

BC	Flutie 5 run (Snow kick)
AU	FG Del Greco 19
AU	Jackson 1 run (Del Greco kick)
AU	Howell 2 run (Del Greco kick)
BC	FG Snow 34
AU	Jackson 6 run (pass failed)
AU	FG Del Greco 23
AU	Pratt 15 run (Del Greco kick)
BC	Nizolek 2 pass from Flutie (Nizolek pass from Flutie)
BC	Brennan 16 pass from Flutie (Flutie run)

AU		BC
27	First Downs	24
313	Rushing Yards	115
10-16-1	Passing	22-38-2
177	Passing Yards	299
490	Total Yards	414
2-32.0	Punts - Average	3-34.3
4-1	Fumbles - Lost	3-3
3-30	Penalties - Yards	2-38

INDIVIDUAL LEADERS

RUSHING
AU: James 17-101; Jackson 14-64, 2 TD.
BC: Stradford 15-67; Krystoforski 3-19.

PASSING
AU: Campbell 10-16-1, 177 yards.
BC: Flutie 22-38-2, 299 yards, 2 TD.

RECEIVING
AU: Woods 3-67; Edwards 3-55.
BC: Brennan 7-149, 1 TD; Phelan 4-69.

December 17, 1983
Tennessee 30, Maryland 23

	1ST	2ND	3RD	4TH	FINAL
TENN	7	3	6	14	30
MD	3	6	11	3	23

SCORING SUMMARY

MD	FG Atkinson 18
TENN	Taylor 12 pass from Cockrell (Reveiz kick)
MD	FG Atkinson 48
MD	FG Atkinson 31
TENN	FG Reveiz 25
MD	FG Atkinson 22
TENN	Henderson 19 run (pass failed)
MD	Badanjek 3 run (Badanjek run)
TENN	Jones 1 run (Reveiz kick)
TENN	Jones 2 run (Reveiz kick)
MD	FG Atkinson 26

TENN	TEAM STATISTICS	MD
25	First Downs	17
201	Rushing Yards	95
16-23-1	Passing	18-28-1
185	Passing Yards	253
386	Total Yards	348
1-47.0	Punts - Average	0-0.0
1-1	Fumbles - Lost	3-1
1-5	Penalties - Yards	6-32

INDIVIDUAL LEADERS

RUSHING
TENN: Jones 29-154, 2 TD; Henderson 11-57, 1 TD.
MD: Joyner 17-58; Badanjek 14-44, 1 TD.

PASSING
TENN: Cockrell 16-23-1, 185 yards, 1 TD.
MD: Reich 14-22-1, 192 yards; Esiason 4-6-0, 61 yards.

RECEIVING
TENN: Duncan 6-59; Taylor 4-68, 1 TD.
MD: Davis 4-66; Joyner 4-65.

DECEMBER 22, 1984
FLORIDA STATE 17, GEORGIA 17

	1ST	2ND	3RD	4TH	FINAL
FSU	0	0	3	14	17
UGA	0	14	0	3	17

SCORING SUMMARY

UGA	Tate 4 run (Butler kick)
UGA	Tate 2 run (Butler kick)
FSU	FG Schmidt 32
FSU	Smith 1 run (run failed)
UGA	FG Butler 36
FSU	Wessel 14 blocked punt return (Holloman run)

FSU	TEAM STATISTICS	UGA
18	First Downs	15
161	Rushing Yards	189
10-26-2	Passing	9-18-1
85	Passing Yards	178
246	Total Yards	367
8-38.6	Punts - Average	8-37.1
3-1	Fumbles - Lost	5-1
8-65	Penalties - Yards	6-42

INDIVIDUAL LEADERS

RUSHING
FSU: Smith 10-65, 1 TD; Snipes 8-60.
UGA: Tate 11-75, 2 TD; T. Jackson 12-46.
PASSING
FSU: Thomas 10-26-2, 85 yards.
UGA: J. Jackson 7-16-1, 159 yards.
RECEIVING
FSU: Hester 3-26; Carter 2-15.
UGA: Lane 2-64; S. Williams 2-45.

DECEMBER 28, 1985
OHIO STATE 10, BYU 7

	1ST	2ND	3RD	4TH	FINAL
OSU	0	3	7	0	10
BYU	0	7	0	0	7

SCORING SUMMARY

OSU	FG Spangler 47
BYU	Miles 38 pass from Bosco (Webster kick)
OSU	Kolic 14 interception return (Spangler kick)

OSU	TEAM STATISTICS	BYU
20	First Downs	19
133	Rushing Yards	88
19-36-0	Passing	26-50-4
196	Passing Yards	261
329	Total Yards	349
8-38.6	Punts - Average	7-45.3
2-2	Fumbles - Lost	3-2
10-61	Penalties - Yards	6-54

INDIVIDUAL LEADERS

RUSHING
OSU: Woolridge 25-92; Workman 5-23.
BYU: Tuipulotu 9-43; Sikahema 5-23.
PASSING
OSU: Karsatos 19-35-0, 196 yards.
BYU: Bosco 26-50-4, 261 yards, 1 TD.
RECEIVING
OSU: Carter 5-71; Cooper 5-48.
BYU: Bellini 5-87; Heimuli 10-77.

JANUARY 1, 1987
AUBURN 16, SOUTHERN CAL 7

	1ST	2ND	3RD	4TH	FINAL
AU	0	14	0	2	16
USC	7	0	0	0	7

SCORING SUMMARY

USC	Cotton 24 interception return (Shafer kick)
AU	Reeves 3 pass from Burger (Knapp kick)
AU	Fullwood 4 run (Knapp kick)
AU	Safety (Peete tackled by Rocker in end zone)

AU	TEAM STATISTICS	USC
19	First Downs	10
200	Rushing Yards	44
8-18-2	Passing	12-31-4
90	Passing Yards	113
290	Total Yards	157
8-37.9	Punts - Average	4-41.5
2-2	Fumbles - Lost	1-1
9-84	Penalties - Yards	6-40

INDIVIDUAL LEADERS

RUSHING
AU: Fullwood 28-152, 1 TD; Harris 12-31.
USC: Holt 9-34; Knight 8-9.
PASSING
AU: Burger 8-18-2, 90 yards, 1 TD.
USC: Peete 12-30-4, 113 yards.
RECEIVING
AU: Gainous 2-40; Reeves 3-23, 1 TD.
USC: Affholter 6-66; White 1-17.

JANUARY 1, 1988
CLEMSON 35, PENN STATE 10

	1ST	2ND	3RD	4TH	FINAL
CLEM	7	7	7	14	35
PSU	7	0	3	0	10

SCORING SUMMARY

CLEM	Johnson 7 run (Treadwell kick)
PSU	Alexander 39 pass from Knizner (Etze kick)
CLEM	Johnson 6 run (Treadwell kick)
PSU	FG Etze 27
CLEM	Johnson 1 run (Treadwell kick)
CLEM	Allen 25 run (Treadwell kick)
CLEM	Henderson 4 run (Treadwell kick)

CLEM	TEAM STATISTICS	PSU
25	First Downs	12
285	Rushing Yards	111
15-24-0	Passing	14-23-2
214	Passing Yards	194
499	Total Yards	305
5-39.0	Punts - Average	5-51.0
0-0	Fumbles - Lost	2-1
8-44	Penalties - Yards	4-26

INDIVIDUAL LEADERS

RUSHING
CLEM: Allen 11-105, 1 TD; Johnson 18-88, 3 TD.
PSU: Thompson 6-55; Brown 13-51.
PASSING
CLEM: Williams 15-24-0, 214 yards.
PSU: Knizner 13-22-2, 148 yards, 1 TD.
RECEIVING
CLEM: Jennings 7-110; Cooper 4-56.
PSU: Timpson 4-81; Thompson 3-19.

JANUARY 2, 1989
CLEMSON 13, OKLAHOMA 6

	1ST	2ND	3RD	4TH	FINAL
CLEM	0	6	0	7	13
OKLA	3	0	3	0	6

SCORING SUMMARY

OKLA	FG Lashar 35
CLEM	FG Gardocki 20
CLEM	FG Gardocki 46
OKLA	FG Lashar 30
CLEM	Allen 4 run (Seyle kick)

CLEM	TEAM STATISTICS	OKLA
12	First Downs	17
187	Rushing Yards	116
5-11-0	Passing	10-24-1
57	Passing Yards	138
244	Total Yards	254
7-44.3	Punts - Average	5-38.6
1-0	Fumbles - Lost	4-1
7-76	Penalties - Yards	5-50

INDIVIDUAL LEADERS

RUSHING
CLEM: McFadden 9-55; Allen 17-53, 1 TD.
OKLA: Perry 12-52; Gaddis 12-37.
PASSING
CLEM: R. Williams 5-11-0, 57 yards.
OKLA: Holieway 10-24-1, 138 yards.
RECEIVING
CLEM: Allen 4-47; Hooper 1-10.
OKLA: Ca. Cabbiness 3-78; Guess 2-25.

JANUARY 1, 1990
ILLINOIS 31, VIRGINIA 21

	1ST	2ND	3RD	4TH	FINAL
ILL	7	10	7	7	31
UVA	0	7	7	7	21

SCORING SUMMARY

ILL	Williams 35 pass from George (Higgins kick)
UVA	Finkelston 30 pass from S. Moore (McInerney kick)
ILL	Donovan 1 pass from George (Higgins kick)
ILL	FG Higgins 34
ILL	Griffith 3 run (Higgins kick)
UVA	Wilson 2 run (McInerney kick)
ILL	Bellamy 24 pass from George (Higgins kick)
UVA	H. Moore 3 pass from S. Moore (McInerney kick)

ILL	TEAM STATISTICS	UVA
29	First Downs	18
176	Rushing Yards	110
26-38-1	Passing	19-30-2
321	Passing Yards	212
497	Total Yards	322
3-38.0	Punts - Average	6-41.3
3-3	Fumbles - Lost	2-1
4-35	Penalties - Yards	6-40

INDIVIDUAL LEADERS

RUSHING
ILL: Griffith 18-93, 1 TD; Feagin 10-54.
UVA: Kirby 8-64; S. Moore 15-34.
PASSING
ILL: George 26-38-1, 321 yards, 3 TD.
UVA: S. Moore 17-27-2, 191 yards, 2 TD.
RECEIVING
ILL: Bellamy 8-166, 1 TD; Williams 4-45, 1 TD.
UVA: Finkelston 3-69, 1 TD; H. Moore 5-56, 1 TD.

JANUARY 1, 1991
GEORGIA TECH 45, NEBRASKA 21

	1ST	2ND	3RD	4TH	FINAL
GT	7	7	7	14	45
NEB	0	14	7	0	21

SCORING SUMMARY

GT	Scotten 2 run (Sisson kick)
GT	Merchant 22 pass from Jones (Sisson kick)
GT	Bell 2 pass from Jones (Sisson kick)
NEB	Mitchell 30 pass from Haase (Barrios kick)
NEB	Brown 50 run (Barrios kick)
GT	FG Sisson 37
GT	Jones 1 run (Sisson kick)
NEB	Washington 21 pass from Haase (Barrios kick)
GT	Bell 6 run (Sisson kick)
GT	Bell 57 run (Sisson kick)

GT	TEAM STATISTICS	NEB
19	First Downs	14
190	Rushing Yards	126
16-23-1	Passing	14-25-0
277	Passing Yards	209
467	Total Yards	335
6-40.2	Punts - Average	8-39.2
2-1	Fumbles - Lost	3-2
5-50	Penalties - Yards	6-69

INDIVIDUAL LEADERS

RUSHING
GT: Bell 16-127, 2 TD; Jones 11-41, 1 TD.
NEB: Brown 11-99, 1 TD; Turner 2-21.
PASSING
GT: Jones 16-23-1, 277 yards, 2 TD.
NEB: Haase 14-21-0, 209 yards.
RECEIVING
GT: Bell 4-53, 1 TD; Rodriguez 3-66.
NEB: Mitchell 5-138, 1 TD; Turner 3-24.

JANUARY 1, 1992
CALIFORNIA 37, CLEMSON 13

	1ST	2ND	3RD	4TH	FINAL
CAL	17	10	10	0	37
CLEM	3	7	3	0	13

SCORING SUMMARY

CAL	Zomalt 1 run (Brien kick)
CAL	FG Brien 31
CAL	Treggs 72 punt return (Brien kick)
CLEM	FG Welch 32
CAL	White 2 run (Brien kick)
CLEM	Cameron 62 run (Welch kick)
CAL	FG Brien 33
CLEM	FG Welch 36
CAL	FG Brien 34
CAL	Dawkins 23 pass from Pawlawski (Brien kick)

CAL	TEAM STATISTICS	CLEM
22	First Downs	19
146	Rushing Yards	206
21-33-0	Passing	15-36-3
230	Passing Yards	123
376	Total Yards	329
6-45.2	Punts - Average	8-42.2
3-0	Fumbles - Lost	1-0
8-60	Penalties - Yards	6-62

INDIVIDUAL LEADERS

RUSHING
CAL: White 22-103, 1 TD; Chapman 5-25.
CLEM: Harris 14-83; Cameron 12-66, 1 TD.
PASSING
CAL: Pawlawski 21-32-0, 230 yards, 1 TD.
CLEM: Cameron 15-33-1, 123 yards.
RECEIVING
CAL: Dawkins 5-55, 1 TD; Zomalt 6-41.
CLEM: Smith 7-71; Blunt 3-28.

THE BOWLS

JANUARY 1, 1993
GEORGIA 21, OHIO STATE 14

	1ST	2ND	3RD	4TH	FINAL
UGA	7	0	7	7	21
OSU	0	7	7	0	14

SCORING SUMMARY

UGA	Hearst 1 run (Peterson kick)
OSU	Smith 1 run (Williams kick)
UGA	Hearst 5 run (Peterson kick)
OSU	Smith 5 run (Williams kick)
UGA	Harvey 1 run (Peterson kick)

UGA	TEAM STATISTICS	OSU
26	First Downs	18
202	Rushing Yards	179
21-31-0	Passing	8-24-1
242	Passing Yards	110
444	Total Yards	289
6-39.0	Punts - Average	8-37.1
2-2	Fumbles - Lost	1-1
3-30	Penalties - Yards	5-35

INDIVIDUAL LEADERS

RUSHING
UGA: Hearst 28-163, 2 TD; Davis 7-42.
OSU: Smith 25-112, 2 TD; Harris 7-38.

PASSING
UGA: Zeier 21-31-0, 242 yards.
OSU: Herbstreit 8-24-1, 110 yards.

RECEIVING
UGA: Hastings 8-113; Mitchell 2-39.
OSU: Smith 2-49; Stablein 2-31.

JANUARY 1, 1994
PENN STATE 31, TENNESSEE 13

	1ST	2ND	3RD	4TH	FINAL
PSU	7	10	7	7	31
TENN	10	3	0	0	13

SCORING SUMMARY

TENN	FG Becksvoort 46
TENN	Fleming 19 pass from Shuler (Becksvoort kick)
PSU	Carter 3 run (Fayak kick)
PSU	FG Fayak 19
TENN	FG Becksvoort 50
PSU	Carter 14 run (Fayak kick)
PSU	Brady 7 pass from Collins (Fayak kick)
PSU	Engram 15 pass from Collins (Fayak kick)

PSU	TEAM STATISTICS	TENN
20	First Downs	16
209	Rushing Yards	135
15-24-1	Passing	23-44-1
162	Passing Yards	213
371	Total Yards	348
6-32.0	Punts - Average	6-44.2
0-0	Fumbles - Lost	0-0
4-30	Penalties - Yards	10-79

INDIVIDUAL LEADERS

RUSHING
PSU: Carter 19-93, 2 TD; Archie 13-69.
TENN: Garner 16-89; Williams 1-38.

PASSING
PSU: Collins 15-24-1, 162 yards, 2 TD.
TENN: Shuler 22-42-1, 205 yards, 1 TD.

RECEIVING
PSU: Engram 7-107, 1 TD; O'Neal 2-19.
TENN: Fleming 7-101, 1 TD; Phillips 3-23.

JANUARY 2, 1995
ALABAMA 24, OHIO STATE 17

	1ST	2ND	3RD	4TH	FINAL
ALA	0	14	0	10	24
OSU	0	14	0	3	17

SCORING SUMMARY

ALA	Lynch 9 run (Proctor kick)
OSU	Galloway 69 pass from Hoying (Jackson kick)
OSU	Galloway 11 pass from Hoying (Jackson kick)
ALA	Williams 7 run (Proctor kick)
OSU	FG Jackson 34
ALA	FG Proctor 27
ALA	Williams 50 pass from Barker (Proctor kick)

ALA	TEAM STATISTICS	OSU
28	First Downs	15
204	Rushing Yards	96
18-37-0	Passing	11-27-1
317	Passing Yards	180
521	Total Yards	276
4-24.0	Punts - Average	7-36.1
3-3	Fumbles - Lost	4-1
4-45	Penalties - Yards	6-43

INDIVIDUAL LEADERS

RUSHING
ALA: Williams 27-166, 1 TD; Lynch 13-35.
OSU: George 15-89; Sualua 6-44.

PASSING
ALA: Barker 18-37-0, 317 yards, 1 TD.
OSU: Hoying 11-27-1, 180 yards, 2 TD.

RECEIVING
ALA: Williams 8-155, 1 TD; Malone 3-70.
OSU: Galloway 8-146, 2 TD; Dudley 2-26.

JANUARY 1, 1996
TENNESSEE 20, OHIO STATE 14

	1ST	2ND	3RD	4TH	FINAL
TENN	0	7	7	6	20
OSU	7	0	0	7	14

SCORING SUMMARY

OSU	George 2 run (Jackson kick)
TENN	Graham 69 run (Hall kick)
TENN	Kent 47 pass from Manning (Hall kick)
OSU	Dudley 32 pass from Hoying (Jackson kick)
TENN	FG Hall 29
TENN	FG Hall 25

TENN	TEAM STATISTICS	OSU
15	First Downs	17
145	Rushing Yards	89
20-35-0	Passing	19-38-1
182	Passing Yards	246
327	Total Yards	335
9-34.2	Punts-Average	7-48.1
1-1	Fumbles-Lost	5-3
8-43	Penalties-Yards	6-57
30:39	Possession Time	29:21

INDIVIDUAL LEADERS

RUSHING
TENN: Graham 26-168, 1 TD.
OSU: George 25-107, 1 TD.

PASSING
TENN: Manning 20-35-0, 182 yards, 1 TD.
OSU: Hoying 19-38-1, 246 yards, 1 TD.

RECEIVING
TENN: Kent 7-109, 1 TD.
OSU: Glenn 7-95; Dudley 5-106, 1 TD.

JANUARY 1, 1997
TENNESSEE 48, NORTHWESTERN 28

	1ST	2ND	3RD	4TH	FINAL
TENN	21	10	7	10	48
NU	0	21	0	7	28

SCORING SUMMARY

TENN	Price 43 pass from Manning (Hall kick)
TENN	Manning 10 run (Hall kick)
TENN	Kent 11 pass from Manning (Hall kick)
NU	D. Autry 2 run (Gowins kick)
NU	Musso 20 pass from Schnur (Gowins kick)
NU	D. Autry 28 run (Gowins kick)
TENN	Kent 67 pass from Manning (Hall kick)
TENN	FG Hall 19
TENN	Hines 30 interception return (Hall kick)
TENN	FG Hall 28
NU	Bates 22 pass from Schnur (Gowins kick)
TENN	Moore 6 pass from Manning (Hall kick)

TENN	TEAM STATISTICS	NU
29	First Downs	22
115	Rushing Yards	43
27-39-0	Passing	27-51-4
408	Passing Yards	242
523	Total Yards	285
4-35.8	Punts - Average	6-37.3
4-2	Fumbles - Lost	1-1
13-112	Penalties - Yards	5-40

INDIVIDUAL LEADERS

RUSHING
TENN: Graham 14-79; Levine 7-33.
NU: D. Autry 17-66, 2 TD; Gooch 2-10.

PASSING
TENN: Manning 27-39-0, 408 yards, 4 TD.
NU: Schnur 25-45-3, 228 yards, 2 TD.

RECEIVING
TENN: Kent 5-122, 2 TD; Price 6-110, 1 TD.
NU: Bates 10-97, 1 TD; Musso 10-91, 1 TD.

JANUARY 1, 1998
FLORIDA 21, PENN STATE 6

	1ST	2ND	3RD	4TH	FINAL
UF	14	0	0	7	21
PSU	0	3	3	0	6

SCORING SUMMARY

UF	Brindise 1 run (Cooper kick)
UF	Green 35 pass from Johnson (Cooper kick)
PSU	FG Forney 42
PSU	FG Jackson 30
UF	Green 37 pass from Palmer (Cooper kick)

UF	TEAM STATISTICS	PSU
23	First Downs	9
254	Rushing Yards	47
9-19-2	Passing	10-32-3
143	Passing Yards	92
397	Total Yards	139
5-36.4	Punts - Average	7-42.1
2-1	Fumbles - Lost	0-0
5-46	Penalties - Yards	1-5

INDIVIDUAL LEADERS

RUSHING
UF: Taylor 43-234; Carroll 9-28.
PSU: Eberly 14-53; Watson 4-5.

PASSING
UF: Johnson 5-12-1, 77 yards, 1 TD; Brindise 3-6-1, 29 yards.
PSU: McQuery 10-32-3, 92 yards.

RECEIVING
UF: Green 2-72, 2 TD; Taylor 1-19.
PSU: Brown 3-25; Natasi 2-26.

JANUARY 1, 1999
MICHIGAN 45, ARKANSAS 31

	1ST	2ND	3RD	4TH	FINAL
MICH	3	21	0	21	45
ARK	0	10	14	7	31

SCORING SUMMARY

MICH	FG Feely 43
ARK	Williams 35 pass from Stoerner (Latourette kick)
MICH	Thomas 2 run (Feely kick)
MICH	Gold 46 interception return (Feely kick)
ARK	FG Latourette 42
MICH	Thomas 5 run (Feely kick)
ARK	Chukwuma 2 run (Latourette kick)
ARK	Chukwuma 1 run (Latourette kick)
ARK	Davenport 9 pass from Stoerner (Latourette kick)
MICH	Thomas 1 run (Feely kick)
MICH	Johnson 21 pass from Brady (Feely kick)
MICH	Whitley 26 interception return (Feely kick)

MICH	TEAM STATISTICS	ARK
21	First Downs	20
204	Rushing Yards	116
16-30-2	Passing	17-42-2
230	Passing Yards	232
434	Total Yards	348
5-40.0	Punts - Average	7-33.9
78	Return Yards	81
1-1	Fumbles - Lost	0-0
12-104	Penalties - Yards	4-31
31:17	Possession Time	28:43

INDIVIDUAL LEADERS

RUSHING
MICH: Thomas 21-132, 3 TD; Williams 19-72.
ARK: Chukwuma 17-56, 2 TD; Hill 13-35.

PASSING
MICH: Brady 14-27-2, 209 yards, 1 TD.
ARK: Stoerner 17-42-2, 232 yards, 2 TD.

RECEIVING
MICH: Streets 7-129; Williams 2-15.
ARK: Williams 7-90, 1 TD; Lucas 3-63.

January 1, 2000
Michigan State 37, Florida 34

	1st	2nd	3rd	4th	FINAL
MSU	3	17	6	11	37
UF	7	14	6	7	34

SCORING SUMMARY
MSU — FG Edinger 46
UF — Taylor 12 pass from Johnson (Chandler kick)
MSU — Burress 37 pass from Burke (Edinger kick)
MSU — Turner 24 fumble return (Edinger kick)
UF — Taylor 8 pass from Johnson (Chandler kick)
MSU — FG Edinger 20
UF — Johnson 1 run (Chandler kick)
MSU — Burress 21 pass from Burke (pass failed)
UF — Taylor 39 pass from Johnson (pass failed)
UF — Gillespie 2 run (Chandler kick)
MSU — Burress 30 pass from Burke (Scott pass from Burke)
MSU — FG Edinger 39

MSU	TEAM STATISTICS	UF
25	First Downs	27
143	Rushing Yards	67
21-35-2	Passing	25-51-0
257	Passing Yards	300
400	Total Yards	367
3-43.3	Punts - Average	6-35.5
3-1	Fumbles - Lost	4-2
7-80	Penalties - Yards	10-100
32:49	Possession Time	27:11

INDIVIDUAL LEADERS
RUSHING
MSU: Clemons 20-105; Duckett 14-77.
UF: Gilespie 15-74, 1 TD; Carroll 5-14.
PASSING
MSU: Burke 21-35-2, 257 yards, 3 TD.
UF: Johnson 24-50-0, 288 yards, 3 TD.
RECEIVING
MSU: Burress 13-185, 3 TD; Baker 2-21.
UF: Taylor 11-156, 3 TD; Jackson 5-61.

January 1, 2001
Michigan 31, Auburn 28

	1st	2nd	3rd	4th	FINAL
MICH	7	14	10	0	31
AU	0	14	7	7	28

SCORING SUMMARY
MICH — Terrell 31 pass from Henson (Epstein kick)
AU — Daniels 19 pass from Leard (Duval kick)
AU — Robinson 20 pass from Leard (Duval kick)
MICH — Askew 4 pass from Henson (Epstein kick)
MICH — Thomas 11 run (Epstein kick)
MICH — Thomas 25 run (Epstein kick)
AU — Johnson 12 run (Duval kick)
MICH — FG Epstein 41
AU — Green 21 pass from Leard (Duval kick)

MICH	TEAM STATISTICS	AU
21	First Downs	23
159	Rushing Yards	92
15-21-0	Passing	28-37-2
294	Passing Yards	394
453	Total Yards	486
4-43.5	Punts - Average	3-42.7
2-1	Fumbles - Lost	2-1
2-20	Penalties - Yards	7-60
29:57	Possession Time	30:03

INDIVIDUAL LEADERS
RUSHING
MICH: Thomas 32-182, 2 TD; Bellamy 3-13.
AU: Johnson 25-85, 1 TD; Evans 3-16.
PASSING
MICH: Henson 15-20-0, 294 yards, 2 TD.
AU: Leard 28-37-2, 394 yards, 3 TD.
RECEIVING
MICH: Terrell 4-136, 1 TD; Walker 4-100.
AU: Daniels 7-98, 1 TD; Willis 5-69.

January 1, 2002
Tennessee 45, Michigan 17

	1st	2nd	3rd	4th	FINAL
TENN	10	14	7	14	45
MICH	0	10	0	7	17

SCORING SUMMARY
TENN — FG Walls 32
TENN — Washington 3 pass from Clausen (Walls kick)
TENN — Clausen 1 run (Walls kick)
MICH — Askew 14 pass from Navarre (Epstein kick)
TENN — Clausen 1 run (Walls kick)
MICH — FG Epstein 28
TENN — Witten 64 pass from Clausen (Walls kick)
TENN — Washington 37 pass from Clausen (Walls kick)
TENN — Stephens 3 run (Walls kick)
MICH — Bell 24 pass from Navarre (Epstein kick)

TENN	TEAM STATISTICS	MICH
22	First Downs	20
97	Rushing Yards	103
27-35-0	Passing	21-39-1
406	Passing Yards	240
503	Total Yards	343
4-36	Punt Returns - Yards	3-14
3-67	Kickoff Returns - Yards	8-125
5-31.8	Punts - Average	7-39.6
3-32	Penalties - Yards	6-42
34:13	Possession Time	25:47

INDIVIDUAL LEADERS
RUSHING
TENN: Stallworth 2-44; Stephens 16-38, 1 TD.
MICH: Askew 9-76; Perry 17-41.
PASSING
TENN: Clausen 26-34-0, 393 yards, 3 TD.
MICH: Navarre 21-39-1, 240 yards, 2 TD.
RECEIVING
TENN: Witten 6-125, 1 TD; Stallworth 8-119; Washington 6-70, 2 TD.
MICH: Walker 5-100; Joppru 5-45.

January 1, 2003
Auburn 13, Penn State 9

	1st	2nd	3rd	4th	FINAL
AU	0	0	7	6	13
PSU	3	3	0	3	9

SCORING SUMMARY
PSU — FG Gould 21
PSU — FG Gould 27
AU — Brown 1 run (Duval kick)
PSU — FG Gould 31
AU — Brown 17 run (pass failed)

AU	TEAM STATISTICS	PSU
15	First Downs	15
200	Rushing Yards	170
10-17-1	Passing	10-27-1
78	Passing Yards	98
278	Total Yards	268
4-48.2	Punts - Average	5-38.2
1-1	Fumbles - Lost	3-0
9-84	Penalties - Yards	7-68

INDIVIDUAL LEADERS
RUSHING
AU: Brown 37-184, 2 TD; Smith 5-10.
PSU: L. Johnson 20-72; Mills 9-56.
PASSING
AU: Campbell 10-17-1, 78 yards.
PSU: Mills 8-24-1, 67 yards.
RECEIVING
AU: Aromashodu 2-18; Johnson 2-17.
PSU: T. Johnson 2-54; Kranchick 2-15.

January 1, 2004
Georgia 34, Purdue 27

	1st	2nd	3rd	4th	OT	FINAL
GEO	14	10	0	3	7	34
PUR	0	10	17	0	0	27

SCORING SUMMARY
GEO — Gibson 6 pass from Greene (Bennett kick)
GEO — Gibson 4 pass from Greene (Bennett kick)
GEO — FG Bennett 28
GEO — Brown 11 pass from Greene (Bennett kick)
PUR — Orton 17 run (Jones kick)
PUR — FG Jones 27
PUR — Orton 2 run (Jones kick)
GEO — FG Bennett 40
PUR — Chambers 3 pass from Orton (Jones kick)
PUR — FG Jones 44
GEO — Lumpkin 1 run (Bennett kick)

GEO	TEAM STATISTICS	PUR
23	First Downs	15
113	Rushing Yards	59
27-37-0	Passing	20-35-1
327	Passing Yards	230
440	Total Yards	289
4-34	Punt Returns - Yards	5-53
2-48	Kickoff Returns - Yards	6-163
6-44.7	Punts - Average	9-44.4
34	Return Yards	53
2-2	Fumbles - Lost	1-0
10-90	Penalties - Yards	10-69
35:29	Possession Time	24:31

INDIVIDUAL LEADERS
RUSHING
GEO: Lumpkin 27-90, 1 TD.
PUR: Void 15-63.
PASSING
GEO: Greene 27-37-0, 327 yards, 3 TD.
PUR: Orton 20-34-1, 230 yards, 1 TD.
RECEIVING
GEO: Brown 5-99, 1 TD; Gary 2-53; Browning 2-48.
PUR: Standeford 7-102; Stubblefield 8-99.

January 1, 2005
Iowa 30, LSU 25

	1st	2nd	3rd	4th	FINAL
IA	7	0	3	13	30
LSU	0	12	0	13	25

SCORING SUMMARY
IA — Solomon 57 pass from Tate (Schlicher kick)
LSU — FG Jackson 29
LSU — FG Jackson 47
IA — Considine 7 blocked punt return (Schlicher kick)
LSU — Broussard 74 run (kick failed)
IA — FG Schlicher 19
IA — Simmons 4 run (Schlicher kick)
LSU — Green 22 pass from Russell (Jackson kick)
LSU — Green 3 pass from Russell (kick failed)
IA — Holloway 56 pass from Tate

IA	TEAM STATISTICS	LSU
16	First Downs	19
47	Rushing Yards	118
20-32-2	Passing	23-35-1
287	Passing Yards	228
334	Total Yards	346
5-45	Punt Returns - Yards	4-42
5-76	Kickoff Returns - Yards	5-134
6-49.2	Punts - Average	6-30.2
1-0	Fumbles - Lost	1-0
9-50	Penalties - Yards	5-42
25:48	Possession Time	34:12

INDIVIDUAL LEADERS
RUSHING
IA: Simmons 13-35, 1 TD.
LSU: Broussard 13-109, 1 TD.
PASSING
IA: Tate 20-32-2, 287 yards, 2 TD.
LSU: Russell 12-15-0, 128 yards, 2 TD.
RECEIVING
IA: Hinkel 10-93; Solomon 4-81, 1 TD.
LSU: Bowe 8-122; Green 6-59, 2 TD.

LIBERTY BOWL

PROFILE

Site: Memphis
Stadium: Liberty Bowl Memorial Stadium
Capacity: 62,338
Surface: FieldTurf

PLAYING SITES

Municipal Stadium, 1959-1963
Atlantic City Convention Hall, 1964
Liberty Bowl Memorial Stadium, since 1965

NAME CHANGES

Liberty Bowl Classic, 1959-92
St. Jude Liberty Bowl, 1993-96
AXA Liberty Bowl, 1997-2003
AutoZone Liberty Bowl, since 2004

SEASON	DATE	PRE-GAME RANK	TEAMS	SCORE	FINAL RANK	MOST VALUABLE PLAYERS	ATT.
1959	Dec. 19, 1959	12	Penn State	7		Jay Huffman, Penn State, C	36,211
		10	Alabama	0			
1960	Dec. 17, 1960	16	Penn State	41		Dick Hoak, Penn State, RB	16,624
			Oregon	12			
1961	Dec. 16, 1961	14	Syracuse	15		Ernie Davis, Syracuse, RB	15,712
			Miami (Fla.)	14			
1962	Dec. 15, 1962		Oregon State	6		Terry Baker, Oregon State, QB	17,048
			Villanova	0			
1963	Dec. 21, 1963		Mississippi State	16		Ode Burrell, Mississippi State, HB	8,309
			North Carolina State	12			
1964	Dec. 19, 1964		Utah	32		Ernest Allen, Utah, QB	6,059
			West Virginia	6			
1965	Dec. 18, 1965		Mississippi	13		Tom Bryan, Auburn, FB	38,607
			Auburn	7			
1966	Dec. 10, 1966	9	Miami (Fla.)	14		Jimmy Cox, Miami (Fla.), SE	39,101
			Virginia Tech	7			
1967	Dec. 16, 1967		North Carolina State	14		Jim Donnan, North Carolina St., QB	35,045
			Georgia	7			
1968	Dec. 14, 1968		Mississippi	34		Steve Hindman, Mississippi, TB	46,206
			Virginia Tech	17			
1969	Dec. 13, 1969		Colorado	47	16	Bob Anderson, Colorado, TB	50,042
			Alabama	33			
1970	Dec. 12, 1970		Tulane	17	17	Dave Abercrombie, Tulane, TB	44,640
			Colorado	3			
1971	Dec. 20, 1971	9	Tennessee	14	9	Joe Ferguson, Arkansas, QB	51,410
		18	Arkansas	13	16		
1972	Dec. 18, 1972		Georgia Tech	31	20	Jim Stevens, Georgia Tech, QB	50,021
			Iowa State	30			
1973	Dec. 17, 1973	16	North Carolina State	31	16	Stan Fritts, North Carolina State, FB	50,011
		19	Kansas	18	18		
1974	Dec. 16, 1974		Tennessee	7	20	Randy White, Maryland, DT	51,284
		10	Maryland	3	13		
1975	Dec. 22, 1975		Southern Cal	20	17	Ricky Bell, Southern Cal, RB	52,129
		2	Texas A&M	0	11		
1976	Dec. 20, 1976	16	Alabama	36	11	Barry Krauss, Alabama, LB	52,736
		7	UCLA	6	15		
1977	Dec. 19, 1977	12	Nebraska	21	12	Matt Kupec, North Carolina, QB	49,456
		14	North Carolina	17	17		
1978	Dec. 23, 1978	18	Missouri	20	15	James, Wilder, Missouri, RB	53,064
			LSU	15			
1979	Dec. 22, 1979		Penn State	9		Roch Hontas, Tulane, QB	50,021
		15	Tulane	6			
1980	Dec. 27, 1980		Purdue	28	17	Mark Herrmann, Purdue, QB	53,667
			Missouri	25			
1981	Dec. 30, 1981	15	Ohio State	31	15	Eddie Meyers, Navy, TB	43,216
			Navy	28			
1982	Dec. 29, 1982		Alabama	21		Jeremiah Castille, Alabama, DB	54,123
			Illinois	15			
1983	Dec. 29, 1983		Notre Dame	19		Doug Flutie, Boston College, QB	38,229
		13	Boston College	18	19		
1984	Dec. 27, 1984	16	Auburn	21	14	Bo Jackson, Auburn, RB	50,108
			Arkansas	15			
1985	Dec. 27, 1985		Baylor	21	17	Cody Carlson, Baylor, QB	40,186
		12	LSU	7	20		
1986	Dec. 29, 1986		Tennessee	21		Jeff Francis, Tennessee, QB	51,327
			Minnesota	14			
1987	Dec. 29, 1987	15	Georgia	20	13	Greg Thomas, Arkansas, QB	53,249
			Arkansas	17			
1988	Dec. 28, 1988		Indiana	34	20	Dave Schnell, Indiana, QB	39,210
			South Carolina	10			
1989	Dec. 28, 1989		Mississippi	42		Randy Baldwin, Mississippi, RB	60,128
			Air Force	29			
1990	Dec. 27, 1990		Air Force	23		Rob Perez, Air Force, QB	13,144
		24	Ohio State	11			
1991	Dec. 29, 1991		Air Force	38	25	Rob Perez, Air Force, QB	61,497
			Mississippi State	15			
1992	Dec. 31, 1992	20	Mississippi	13	16	Cassius Ware, Mississippi, LB	32,107
			Air Force	0			
1993	Dec. 28, 1993	25	Louisville	18	24	Jeff Brohm, Louisville, QB	21,097
			Michigan State	7			
1994	Dec. 31, 1994		Illinois	30		Johnny Johnson, Illinois, QB	33,280
			East Carolina	0			
1995	Dec. 30, 1995		East Carolina	19		Kwame Ellis, Stanford, CB	47,398
			Stanford	13			
1996	Dec. 27, 1996	23	Syracuse	30	21	Malcolm Thomas, Syracuse, RB	49,163
			Houston	17			
1997	Dec. 31, 1997	22	Southern Miss	41	19	Sherrod Gideon, Southern Miss, WR	50,209
			Pittsburgh	7			
1998	Dec. 31, 1998	10	Tulane	41	7	Shaun King, Tulane, QB	52,192
			BYU	27			
1999	Dec. 31, 1999	16	Southern Miss	23	14	Adalius Thomas, Southern Miss, DE	54,866
			Colorado State	17			
2000	Dec. 29, 2000	23	Colorado State	22	14	Cecil Sapp, Colorado State, RB	58,302
		22	Louisville	17			
2001	Dec. 31, 2001	23	Louisville	28	17	Dave Ragone, Louisville, QB	58,968
		19	BYU	10	25		
2002	Dec. 31, 2002		TCU	17	23	LaTarence Dunbar, TCU, WR	55,207
		23	Colorado State	3			
2003	Dec. 31, 2003	25	Utah	17	21	Brandon Warfield, Utah, RB	55,989
			Southern Miss	0			
2004	Dec. 31,2004	7	Louisville	44	6	Stefan LeFors, Louisville, QB	58,355
		10	Boise State	40	12		

December 19, 1959
Penn State 7, Alabama 0

	1ST	2ND	3RD	4TH	FINAL
PSU	0	7	0	0	7
ALA	0	0	0	0	0

SCORING SUMMARY
PSU   Kochman 18 pass from Hall (Stellatella kick)

PSU	TEAM STATISTICS	ALA
18	First Downs	8
278	Rushing Yards	104
2-10-0	Passing	2-8-0
41	Passing Yards	27
319	Total Yards	131
6-29.0	Punts - Average	8-34.4
4-4	Fumbles - Lost	7-4
4-45	Penalties - Yards	3-45

INDIVIDUAL LEADERS
RUSHING
PSU: Lucas 9-54.
ALA: Trammel 13-37.
PASSING
PSU: Lucas 1-4-0, 23 yards; Hall 1-6-0, 18 yards, 1 TD.
ALA: Trammel 1-4-0, 20 yards.

December 17, 1960
Penn State 41, Oregon 12

	1ST	2ND	3RD	4TH	FINAL
PSU	0	21	0	20	41
ORE	6	0	6	0	12

SCORING SUMMARY
ORE   Grosz 1 run (kick failed)
PSU   Jonas 1 run (Opperman kick)
PSU   Gursky 2 run (Opperman kick)
PSU   Hoak 6 run (Opperman kick)
ORE   Grayson 10 run (pass failed)
PSU   Caye 1 run (Opperman kick)
PSU   Hoak 11 run (kick failed)
PSU   Pae 33 pass from Hoak (Jonas kick)

PSU	TEAM STATISTICS	ORE
25	First Downs	17
301	Rushing Yards	187
8-14-0	Passing	10-16-2
119	Passing Yards	173
420	Total Yards	360
4-25.0	Punts - Average	4-34.0
2-1	Fumbles - Lost	4-2
6-40	Penalties - Yards	2-12

INDIVIDUAL LEADERS
RUSHING
PSU: Hoak 9-61, 2 TD; Jonas 13-40, 1 TD.
ORE: Grayson 10-93, 1 TD.
PASSING
PSU: Hall 4-7-0, 47 yards.
ORE: Grosz 9-15-2, 178 yards.
RECEIVING
PSU: Opperman 4-49.
ORE: Bruce 4-90.

December 16, 1961
Syracuse 15, Miami (Fla.) 14

	1ST	2ND	3RD	4TH	FINAL
SYR	0	0	8	7	15
MIA	6	8	0	0	14

SCORING SUMMARY
MIA   Vollenweider 12 run (kick failed)
MIA   Spinelli 60 punt return (Miller pass from Mira)
SYR   E. Davis 1 run (Easterly pass from Sarette)
SYR   Easterly 7 pass from Sarette (Erickson kick)

SYR	TEAM STATISTICS	MIA
21	First Downs	11
221	Rushing Yards	109
13-27-0	Passing	7-21-0
148	Passing Yards	94
369	Total Yards	203
5-14	Punt Returns - Yards	6-78
4-60	Kickoff Returns - Yards	2-32
7-31.4	Punts - Average	9-30.3
3-2	Fumbles - Lost	3-1
5-35	Penalties - Yards	3-29

INDIVIDUAL LEADERS
RUSHING
SYR: E. Davis 30-140, 1 TD.
MIA: Vollenweider 11-67, 1 TD.
PASSING
SYR: Sarette 13-26-0, 148 yards.
MIA: Mira 7-21-0, 94 yards.
RECEIVING
SYR: Easterly 4-50, 1 TD; Mackey 4-49.
MIA: Wilson 3-53.

December 15, 1962
Oregon State 6, Villanova 0

	1ST	2ND	3RD	4TH	FINAL
OSU	6	0	0	0	6
VIL	0	0	0	0	0

SCORING SUMMARY
OSU   Baker 99 run (pass failed)

OSU	TEAM STATISTICS	VIL
11	First Downs	20
176	Rushing Yards	246
9-21-0	Passing	6-10-2
123	Passing Yards	63
299	Total Yards	309
3-1	Fumbles - Lost	4-4
6-80	Penalties - Yards	5-42

INDIVIDUAL LEADERS
RUSHING
OSU: Baker 13-137, 1 TD.
VIL: Joe 14-66; Rettino, 12-49.
PASSING
OSU: Baker 9-21-0, 123 yards.
VIL: Aceto 5-8-1, 61 yards.
RECEIVING
OSU: Frketich 3-43.
VIL: Delane 1-22.

December 21, 1963
Mississippi State 16, NC State 12

	1ST	2ND	3RD	4TH	FINAL
MSU	13	3	0	0	16
NCSU	0	6	0	6	12

SCORING SUMMARY
MSU   Inman 11 blocked kick return (Canale kick)
MSU   Fisher 3 run (kick failed)
MSU   FG Canale 43
NCSU Rossi 1 run (pass failed)
NCSU Barlow 5 pass from Rossi (pass failed)

MSU	TEAM STATISTICS	NCSU
16	First Downs	15
275	Rushing Yards	176
3-6-1	Passing	5-12-0
28	Passing Yards	58
303	Total Yards	234
2-1	Fumbles - Lost	2-2
11-122	Penalties - Yards	3-25

INDIVIDUAL LEADERS
RUSHING
MSU: Grainger 13-94.
NCSU: Rossi 18-67, 1 TD.
PASSING
MSU: Ficher 2-5-1, 10 yards.
NCSU: Rossi 5-12-0, 58 yards.

December 19, 1964
Utah 32, West Virginia 6

	1ST	2ND	3RD	4TH	FINAL
UTAH	3	16	6	7	32
WVU	0	0	0	6	6

SCORING SUMMARY
UTAH   FG Jefferson 29
UTAH   Allen 1 run (Jefferson kick)
UTAH   FG Jefferson 32
UTAH   Coleman 53 run (pass failed)
UTAH   Ireland 47 run (run failed)
WVU   Clegg 6 pass from McCune (pass failed)
UTAH   Morely 33 pass from Allen (Pullman kick)

UTAH	TEAM STATISTICS	WVU
25	First Downs	12
323	Rushing Yards	105
11-23-0	Passing	13-28-4
143	Passing Yards	123
466	Total Yards	228
1-43.0	Punts - Average	4-25.0
3	Fumbles Lost	1

INDIVIDUAL LEADERS
RUSHING
UTAH: Coleman 15-154, 1 TD.
WVU: LeFridge 11-73.
PASSING
UTAH: Allen 5-11-2, 72 yards, 1 TD.
WVU: McCune 13-28-4, 123 yards, 1 TD.

December 18, 1965
Mississippi 13, Auburn 7

	1ST	2ND	3RD	4TH	FINAL
MISS	0	3	7	3	13
AU	0	7	0	0	7

SCORING SUMMARY
MISS   FG Keyes 42
AU   Bryan 44 run (Lewis kick)
MISS   Cunningham 6 pass from Graves (Keyes kick)
MISS   FG Keyes 30

MISS	TEAM STATISTICS	AU
12	First Downs	15
189	Rushing Yards	156
4-12-0	Passing	11-24-1
24	Passing Yards	112
213	Total Yards	268
8-39.0	Punts - Average	9-34.8
0-0	Fumbles - Lost	0-0
5-25	Penalties - Yards	4-29

INDIVIDUAL LEADERS
RUSHING
AU: Bryan 19-111, 1 TD.
MISS: Dennis 15-75; Heidel 16-72.
PASSING
AU: Bowden 11-24-1, 112 yards.
MISS: Graves 2-10-0, 15 yards, 1 TD.
RECEIVING
AU: Hardy 4-46.
MISS: Matthews 2-9.

December 10, 1966
Miami (Fla.) 14, Virginia Tech 7

	1ST	2ND	3RD	4TH	FINAL
MIA	0	0	7	7	14
VT	7	0	0	0	7

SCORING SUMMARY
VT   Francisco 1 run (Utin kick)
MIA   Mira 7 pass from Miller (Harris kick)
MIA   McGee 1 run (Harris kick)

MIA	TEAM STATISTICS	VT
11	First Downs	7
55	Rushing Yards	36
10-28-0	Passing	6-16-1
108	Passing Yards	75
163	Total Yards	111
1	Fumbles Lost	2
7-80	Penalties - Yards	6-57

INDIVIDUAL LEADERS
RUSHING
MIA: McGee 12-36, 1 TD.
VT: Francisco 21-55, 1 TD.
PASSING
MIA: Miller 9-26-0, 99 yards, 1 TD.
VT: Stafford 4-13-1, 59 yards.

December 16, 1967
NC State 14, Georgia 7

	1ST	2ND	3RD	4TH	FINAL
NCST	0	7	0	7	14
UGA	0	7	0	0	7

SCORING SUMMARY
NCST   Martell 6 pass from Donnan (Warren kick)
UGA   Jenkins 1 run (McCullough kick)
NCST   Barchuk 1 run (Warren kick)

NCST	TEAM STATISTICS	UGA
14	First Downs	14
79	Rushing Yards	140
17-25-1	Passing	11-23-1
128	Passing Yards	136
207	Total Yards	276
6-41.6	Punts - Average	5-35.6
2-1	Fumbles - Lost	2-0
3-45	Penalties - Yards	6-67

INDIVIDUAL LEADERS
RUSHING
NCST: Bowers 10-35; Barchuk 13-20, 1 TD.
UGA: Jenkins 16-33, 1 TD.
PASSING
NCST: Donnan 15-24-1, 121 yards, 1 TD.
UGA: Moore 10-22-0, 124 yards.
RECEIVING
NCST: Martell 7-69, 1 TD.
UGA: Hughes 6-86.

THE BOWLS

December 14, 1968
Mississippi 34, Virginia Tech 17

	1ST	2ND	3RD	4TH	FINAL
MISS	0	14	7	13	34
VT	17	0	0	0	17

SCORING SUMMARY
VT	Edwards 58 run (Simsack kick)
VT	Smoot 7 run (Simsack kick)
VT	FG Simsack 29
MISS	Shows 21 pass from Manning (Brown kick)
MISS	Felts 23 pass from Manning (Brown kick)
MISS	Hindman 79 run (Brown kick)
MISS	Bailey 70 interception return (Brown kick)
MISS	FG Brown 46
MISS	FG Brown 26

MISS	TEAM STATISTICS	VT
7	First Downs	14
185	Rushing Yards	330
12-28-1	Passing	1-7-0
141	Passing Yards	2
326	Total Yards	332
5-37.4	Punts - Average	7-40.7
3-2	Fumbles - Lost	5-3
4-30	Penalties - Yards	12-120

INDIVIDUAL LEADERS
RUSHING
MISS: Hindman 15-121, 1 TD; Bowen 19-65.
VT: Edwards 12-119, 1 TD, Smoot 21-91, 1 TD.
PASSING
MISS: Manning 12-28-0, 141 yards, 2 TD.
VT: Humphries 1-3-0, 2 yards.

December 13, 1969
Colorado 47, Alabama 33

	1ST	2ND	3RD	4TH	FINAL
COLO	10	21	7	9	47
ALA	0	19	14	0	33

SCORING SUMMARY
COLO	Walsh 13 run (Haney kick)
COLO	FG Haney 30
COLO	Anderson 3 run (Haney kick)
ALA	Hunter 31 run (Buck kick)
ALA	Ranager 6 run (pass failed)
COLO	Walsh 15 run (Haney kick)
ALA	Musso 2 run (pass failed)
COLO	Engel 91 kickoff return (Haney kick)
ALA	Langston 55 pass from Hayden (Buck kick)
ALA	Musso 10 pass from Hayden (Buck kick)
COLO	Anderson 2 run (Haney kick)
COLO	Safety (Hayden tackled in end zone)
COLO	Anderson 3 run (Haney kick)

COLO	TEAM STATISTICS	ALA
29	First Downs	24
473	Rushing Yards	155
6-16-3	Passing	14-34-0
212	Passing Yards	90
685	Total Yards	245
2-37.5	Punts - Average	7-41
18	Return Yards	5
3-2	Fumbles - Lost	2-0
8-94	Penalties - Yards	2-24
30:57	Possession Time	29:03

INDIVIDUAL LEADERS
RUSHING
COLO: Anderson 13-254, 3 TD; Bratten 19-111.
ALA: Musso 23-107, 1 TD.
PASSING
COLO: Bratten 3-11-3, 49 yards; Anderson 3-4-0, 41 yards.
ALA: Hayden 8-21-0, 164 yards, 2 TD; Hunter 6-13-0, 48 yards.
RECEIVING
COLO: Masten 2-35; Dal Porto 2-29.
ALA: Bailey 3-43, Musso 3-22, 1 TD.

December 12, 1970
Tulane 17, Colorado 3

	1ST	2ND	3RD	4TH	FINAL
TUL	3	0	7	7	17
COLO	0	3	0	0	3

SCORING SUMMARY
TUL	FG Gibson 19
COLO	FG Haney 33
TUL	Abercrombie 2 run (Gibson kick)
TUL	Abercrombie 4 run (Gibson kick)

TUL	TEAM STATISTICS	COLO
15	First Downs	13
213	Rushing Yards	155
3-9-1	Passing	3-7-1
28	Passing Yards	20
241	Total Yards	175
6-38.5	Punts - Average	7-42.9
56	Return Yards	28
4-0	Fumbles - Lost	4-1
5-39	Penalties - Yards	5-52
27:52	Possession Time	32:08

INDIVIDUAL LEADERS
RUSHING
TUL: Abercrombie 25-128, 2 TD; Marshall 13-87.
COLO: Tarver 29-65.
PASSING
TUL: Walker 3-8-1, 28 yards.
COLO: Arendt 3-7-1, 20 yards.
RECEIVING
TUL: Barrios 2-34.
COLO: Dal Porto 2-17.

December 20, 1971
Tennessee 14, Arkansas 13

	1ST	2ND	3RD	4TH	FINAL
TENN	7	0	0	7	14
ARK	0	7	0	6	13

SCORING SUMMARY
TENN	Rudder 2 run (Hunt kick)
ARK	Hodge 36 pass from Ferguson (McClard kick)
ARK	FG McClard 19
ARK	FG McClard 30
TENN	Watson 17 run (Hunt kick)

TENN	TEAM STATISTICS	ARK
15	First Downs	22
97	Rushing Yards	167
11-21-3	Passing	18-28-3
142	Passing Yards	200
239	Total Yards	367
5-43.8	Punts - Average	3-43.6
1-1	Fumbles - Lost	2-2
7-73	Penalties - Yards	6-85

INDIVIDUAL LEADERS
RUSHING
TENN: Watson 11-39, 1 TD; Chauncey 12-34.
ARK: Saint 17-71.
PASSING
TENN: Maxwell 20-30-3, 120 yards.
ARK: Ferguson 18-28-3, 200 yards, 1 TD.
RECEIVING
TENN: Theiler 3-53.
ARK: Hodge 6-75, 1 TD.

December 18, 1972
Georgia Tech 31, Iowa State 30

	1ST	2ND	3RD	4TH	FINAL
GT	3	14	7	7	31
ISU	14	7	3	6	30

SCORING SUMMARY
GT	FG Bonifay 32
ISU	Harris 13 pass from Amundson (Goedjen kick)
ISU	Moore 1 run (Goedjen kick)
GT	Robinson 9 pass from Stevens (kick failed)
GT	Faulkner 19 interception return (Thigpen kick)
ISU	Jones 93 kickoff return (Goedjen kick)
GT	Healy 22 pass from Stevens (Thigpen kick)
ISU	FG Goedjen 30
GT	McNamara 3 pass from Stevens (Thigpen kick)
ISU	Harris pass from Amundson (pass failed)

GT	TEAM STATISTICS	ISU
18	First Downs	18
123	Rushing Yards	185
12-15-1	Passing	10-19-2
157	Passing Yards	153
278	Total Yards	338
5-2	Fumbles - Lost	3-2
1-5	Penalties - Yards	4-39

INDIVIDUAL LEADERS
RUSHING
GT: Southall 22-48; Healy 11-46.
ISU: Amundson 13-78; Moore 19-50, 1 TD.
PASSING
GT: Stevens 12-15-1, 157 yards, 3 TD.
ISU: Amundson 10-19-2, 153 yards, 2 TD.
RECEIVING
GT: Oven 3-38; Robinson 3-29, 1 TD.
ISU: Harris 4-46, 2 TD; Jones 2-65.

December 17, 1973
NC State 31, Kansas 18

	1ST	2ND	3RD	4TH	FINAL
NCSU	7	3	7	14	31
KU	0	10	0	8	18

SCORING SUMMARY
NCSU	Fritts 2 run (Sewell kick)
KU	Miller 12 pass from Jaynes (Lowe kick)
NCSU	FG Sewell 33
KU	FG Lowe 18
NCSU	Fritts 18 run (Sewell kick)
NCSU	Young 12 run (Sewell kick)
NCSU	Henderson 31 interception return (Sewell kick)
KU	Miller 12 run (Adams pass from Jaynes)

NCSU	TEAM STATISTICS	KU
17	First Downs	24
188	Rushing Yards	130
7-14-1	Passing	24-33-2
86	Passing Yards	218
274	Total Yards	348
5-38.0	Punts - Average	4-37.0
2-0	Fumbles - Lost	2-1
4-35	Penalties - Yards	4-37

INDIVIDUAL LEADERS
RUSHING
NCSU: Fritts 18-83, 2 TD; Young 12-55, 1TD.
KU: Miller 15-104, 1 TD.
PASSING
NCSU: Shaw 5-8-1, 71 yards.
KU: Jaynes 24-36-2, 218 yards, 1 TD.
RECEIVING
NCSU: Gargano 4-48.
KU: Adams 8-73.

DECEMBER 16, 1974
TENNESSEE 7, MARYLAND 3

	1ST	2ND	3RD	4TH	FINAL
TENN	0	0	0	7	7
MARY	0	3	0	0	3

SCORING SUMMARY
MARY FG Mayer 28
TENN Seivers 11 pass from Wallace (Townsend kick)

TENN	TEAM STATISTICS	MARY
15	First Downs	16
173	Rushing Yards	108
7-16-0	Passing	15-24-2
65	Passing Yards	158
238	Total Yards	266
7-39.1	Punts - Average	6-41.0
4-2	Fumbles - Lost	3-3
8-69	Penalties - Yards	4-63

INDIVIDUAL LEADERS
RUSHING
TENN: Gayles 17-106.
MARY: Carter 22-65.
PASSING
TENN: Holloway 6-15-0, 54 yards.
MARY: Avellini 15-22-2, 158 yards.
RECEIVING
TENN: Seivers 4-38, 1 TD.
MARY: Carter 6-68.

DECEMBER 22, 1975
SOUTHERN CAL 20, TEXAS A&M 0

	1ST	2ND	3RD	4TH	FINAL
USC	3	17	0	0	20
A&M	0	0	0	0	0

SCORING SUMMARY
USC FG Walker 45
USC Tatupu 1 run (Walker kick)
USC FG Walker 40
USC Bell 76 pass from Evans (Walker kick)

USC	TEAM STATISTICS	S&M
13	First Downs	15
141	Rushing Yards	148
6-16-1	Passing	6-14-2
174	Passing Yards	99
315	Total Yards	247
7-36	Punts - Average	7-36
1-0	Fumbles - Lost	4-2
7-65	Penalties - Yards	6-49

INDIVIDUAL LEADERS
RUSHING
USC: Bell 28-82, 1 TD; Evans 10-41.
S&M: Bean 16-80; Woodard 13-50.
PASSING
USC: Evans 6-16-1, 174 yards.
S&M: Jay 6-14-2, 99 yards.
RECEIVING
USC: Simkin 3-82; Bell 1-76.
S&M: Roache 3-57; Hartman 2-25.

DECEMBER 20, 1976
ALABAMA 36, UCLA 6

	1ST	2ND	3RD	4TH	FINAL
ALA	17	7	3	9	36
UCLA	0	0	0	6	6

SCORING SUMMARY
ALA FG Berrey 37
ALA Krauss 44 interception return (Berrey kick)
ALA Davis 2 run (Berrey kick)
ALA O'Rear 20 pass from Nathan (Berrey kick)
ALA FG Berrey 25
ALA FG Berrey 28
UCLA Brown 61 run (kick failed)
ALA Watson 1 run (pass failed)

ALA	TEAM STATISTICS	UCLA
23	First Downs	17
268	Rushing Yards	233
8-11-0	Passing	10-18-3
104	Passing Yards	147
372	Total Yards	380

INDIVIDUAL LEADERS
RUSHING
ALA: Nathan 9-67; Davis 11-59, 1 TD.
UCLA: Brown 16-102, 1 TD; Tyler 17-59.
PASSING
ALA: Rutledge 6-7-0, 53 yards.
UCLA: Dankworth 10-17-3, 147 yards.
RECEIVING
ALA: Neal 2-45.
UCLA: Walker 2-44; Brown 3-24.

DECEMBER 19, 1977
NEBRASKA 21, NORTH CAROLINA 17

	1ST	2ND	3RD	4TH	FINAL
NEB	0	7	0	14	21
UNC	0	14	3	0	17

SCORING SUMMARY
UNC Williams 12 pass from Kupec (Biddle kick)
NEB Donnell 15 run (Todd kick)
UNC Loomis 10 pass from Kupec (Biddle kick)
UNC FG Biddle 47
NEB Craig 10 pass from Garcia (Todd kick)
NEB T. Smith 34 pass from Garcia (Todd kick)

NEB	TEAM STATISTICS	UNC
21	First Downs	17
206	Rushing Yards	169
14-17-0	Passing	8-13-1
161	Passing Yards	93
367	Total Yards	262
3-37.0	Punts - Average	3-40.3
-1	Return Yards	0
4-2	Fumbles - Lost	3-2
2-10	Penalties - Yards	5-35

INDIVIDUAL LEADERS
RUSHING
NEB: Donnell 9-59, 1 TD; Hipp 18-52.
UNC: Paschal 16-77; Lawrence 8-35.
PASSING
NEB: Sorley 11-13-0, 105 yards; Garcia 3-3-0, 56 yards, 1 TD.
UNC: Kupec 7-11-1, 52 yards, 2 TD.
RECEIVING
NEB: T. Smith 4-78, 1 TD; Craig 4-53, 1 TD.
UNC: Williams 4-44.

DECEMBER 23, 1978
MISSOURI 20, LSU 15

	1ST	2ND	3RD	4TH	FINAL
MO	7	13	0	0	20
LSU	3	0	6	6	15

SCORING SUMMARY
MO Grant 13 run (Brockhaus kick)
LSU FG Conway 37
MO Winslow 16 pass from Bradley (Brockhaus kick)
MO Wilder 3 run (kick failed)
LSU Alexander 1 run (kick failed)
LSU Woodley 1 run (pass failed)

MO	TEAM STATISTICS	LSU
18	First Downs	12
200	Rushing Yards	194
11-21-1	Passing	14-31-4
117	Passing Yards	170
317	Total Yards	364
6-38.3	Punts - Average	4-36.5
0-0	Fumbles - Lost	2-1
8-75	Penalties - Yards	6-49

INDIVIDUAL LEADERS
RUSHING
MO: Wilder 28-115, 1 TD; Gant 8-46.
LSU: Alexander 24-133, 1 TD.
PASSING
MO: Bradley 11-21-1, 117 yards, 1 TD.
LSU: Woodley 9-22-2, 123 yards.
RECEIVING
MO: Wilder 4-20.
LSU: Quintella 6-81; Carson 6-77.

DECEMBER 22, 1979
PENN STATE 9, TULANE 6

	1ST	2ND	3RD	4TH	FINAL
PSU	0	6	0	3	9
TUL	0	0	0	6	6

SCORING SUMMARY
PSU FG Menhardt 33
PSU FG Menhardt 27
TUL FG Murray 26
TUL FG Murray 26
PSU FG Menhardt 20

PSU	TEAM STATISTICS	TUL
27	First Downs	10
242	Rushing Yards	-8
6-11-2	Passing	21-39-0
95	Passing Yards	210
337	Total Yards	202
2-2	Fumbles - Lost	1-0
1-5	Penalties - Yards	5-40

INDIVIDUAL LEADERS
RUSHING
PSU: Suhey 19-112; Warner 14-57.
TUL: Christian 6-12.
PASSING
PSU: Rocco 5-10-2, 56 yards.
TUL: Hontas 21-39-0, 210 yards.
RECEIVING
PSU: Donovan 2-53.
TUL: Alexis 7-77; Griffin 3-50.

DECEMBER 27, 1980
PURDUE 28, MISSOURI 25

	1ST	2ND	3RD	4TH	FINAL
PUR	7	14	7	0	28
MO	0	12	3	10	25

SCORING SUMMARY
PUR Burrell 8 pass from Herrmann (Anderson kick)
PUR Bryant 43 pass from Herrmann (Anderson kick)
MO Fellows 92 kickoff return (kick failed)
MO Wilder 1 run (pass failed)
PUR Young 5 pass from Herrmann (Anderson kick)
PUR Burrell 27 pass from Herrmann (Anderson kick)
MO FG Verrelli 45
MO Safety (Herrmann tackled in end zone)
MO Hill 1 run (Hornof pass from Bradley)

PUR	TEAM STATISTICS	MO
18	First Downs	17
124	Rushing Yards	103
22-28-0	Passing	16-29-1
289	Passing Yards	210
413	Total Yards	313
6-34.0	Punts - Average	6-43.8
1-1	Fumbles - Lost	2-1
5-31	Penalties - Yards	1-5

INDIVIDUAL LEADERS
RUSHING
PUR: McCall 17-85; Macon 16-69.
MO: Hill 9-54, 1 TD; Wilder 16-49, 1 TD.
PASSING
PUR: Herrmann 22-28-0, 289 yards, 4 TD.
MO: Bradley 16-29-1, 210 yards.
RECEIVING
PUR: Burrell 8-113, 2 TD.
MO: Blair 3-62.

DECEMBER 30, 1981
OHIO STATE 31, NAVY 28

	1ST	2ND	3RD	4TH	FINAL
OSU	10	7	7	7	31
NAVY	7	6	7	8	28

SCORING SUMMARY

OSU	FG Atha 35
OSU	Williams 50 pass from Schlichter (Atha kick)
NAVY	Papajohn 1 pass from Pagnanelli (Fehr kick)
NAVY	FG Fehr 23
OSU	Gayle 1 run (Atha kick)
NAVY	FG Fehr 23
NAVY	Olson 20 blocked kick return (Fehr kick)
OSU	Gayle 2 run (Atha kick)
OSU	Anderson 9 pass from Schlichter (Atha kick)
NAVY	Papajohn 1 pass from Pagnanelli (Papajohn pass from Pagnanelli)

OSU	TEAM STATISTICS	NAVY
19	First Downs	19
173	Rushing Yards	75
11-26-1	Passing	15-29-1
159	Passing Yards	240
332	Total Yards	315
6-32.6	Punts - Average	5-22.8
3-2	Fumbles - Lost	2-1
9-76	Penalties - Yards	2-20

INDIVIDUAL LEADERS

RUSHING
OSU: Spencer 22-96; Gayle 15-88, 2 TD.
NAVY: Meyers 30-117.

PASSING
OSU: Schlichter 11-26-1, 159 yards, 2 TD.
NAVY: Pagnanelli 14-27-1, 201 yards, 2 TD.

RECEIVING
OSU: Williams 2-61; Anderson 5-57.
NAVY: Weller 2-50; Papajohn 4-41, 2 TD.

DECEMBER 29, 1982
ALABAMA 21, ILLINOIS 15

	1ST	2ND	3RD	4TH	FINAL
ALA	7	0	7	7	21
ILL	0	6	0	9	15

SCORING SUMMARY

ALA	Moore 4 run (Kim kick)
ILL	Curtis 1 run (kick failed)
ALA	Bendross 8 run (Kim kick)
ILL	Williams 2 pass from Eason (pass failed)
ILL	FG Bass 23
ALA	Turner 1 run (Kim kick)

ALA	TEAM STATISTICS	ILL
19	First Downs	21
217	Rushing Yards	21
7-13-2	Passing	35-58-2
130	Passing Yards	423
347	Total Yards	444

INDIVIDUAL LEADERS

RUSHING
ALA: Moore 13-65, 1 TD; Turner 11-36, 1 TD.
ILL: Curtis 7-13, 1 TD.

PASSING
ALA: Lewis 7-13-2, 130 yards.
ILL: Eason 35-55-4, 423 yards, 1 TD.

RECEIVING
ALA: Jones 2-60; Bendross 3-51.
ILL: Martin 8-127; Williams 7-84, 1 TD.

DECEMBER 29, 1983
NOTRE DAME 19, BOSTON COLLEGE 18

	1ST	2ND	3RD	4TH	FINAL
ND	7	12	0	0	19
BC	6	6	6	0	18

SCORING SUMMARY

BC	Brennan 17 pass from Flutie (kick failed)
ND	Pinkett 1 run (Johnston kick)
ND	Miller 15 pass from Kiel (kick failed)
ND	Pinkett 3 run (kick failed)
BC	Phelan 28 pass from Flutie (pass failed)
BC	Gieselman 3 pass from Flutie (pass failed)

ND	TEAM STATISTICS	BC
19	First Downs	15
225	Rushing Yards	93
11-19-1	Passing	16-38-2
151	Passing Yards	287
376	Total Yards	380
2-7	Punt Returns - Yards	1-0
4-55	Kickoff Returns - Yards	4-83
6-17.0	Punts - Average	16-28.0
62	Return Yards	83
3-1	Fumbles - Lost	1-0
5-47	Penalties - Yards	7-55

INDIVIDUAL LEADERS

RUSHING
ND: Pinkett 28-111, 2 TD; Smith 18-104.
BC: Stradford 16-51; Flutie 5-32.

PASSING
ND: Kiel 11-19-1, 151 yards, 1 TD.
BC: Flutie 16-37-2, 287 yards, 3 TD.

RECEIVING
ND: Bavaro 5-52; Howard 3-31.
BC: Brennan 4-91, 1 TD; Phelan 4-52, 1 TD.

DECEMBER 27, 1984
AUBURN 21, ARKANSAS 15

	1ST	2ND	3RD	4TH	FINAL
AUB	14	0	0	7	21
ARK	3	0	0	12	15

SCORING SUMMARY

ARK	FG Horne 31
AUB	Jackson 2 run (kick failed)
AUB	Porter 35 interception return (Washington kick)
ARK	Foreman 1 run (pass failed)
AUB	Jackson 39 run (Knapp kick)
ARK	Shibest 25 pass from Taylor (kick failed)

AUB	TEAM STATISTICS	ARK
13	First Downs	20
168	Rushing Yards	130
5-15-0	Passing	19-40-4
84	Passing Yards	226
252	Total Yards	356
9-37.9	Punts - Average	4-38.3
1	Fumbles Lost	0
8-56	Penalties - Yards	8-60

INDIVIDUAL LEADERS

RUSHING
AUB: Jackson 18-88, 2 TD.
ARK: Foreman 15-62, 1 TD; Thomas 9-56.

PASSING
AUB: Washington 5-12-0, 84 yards.
ARK: Taylor 18-34-2, 201 yards, 1 TD.

RECEIVING
AUB: Jackson 1-25.
ARK: Shibest 5-84, 1 TD; Edmonds 10-68.

DECEMBER 27, 1985
BAYLOR 21, LSU 7

	1ST	2ND	3RD	4TH	FINAL
BU	7	3	3	8	21
LSU	7	0	0	0	7

SCORING SUMMARY

LSU	Jefferson 79 punt return (Lewis kick)
BU	Clark 5 pass from Carlson (Syler kick)
BU	FG Syler 23
BU	FG Syler 35
BU	Simpson 15 pass from Carlson (Clark pass from Carlson)

BU	TEAM STATISTICS	LSU
26	First Downs	9
215	Rushing Yards	91
18-30-0	Passing	13-27-1
274	Passing Yards	101
489	Total Yards	192
6-31.5	Punts - Average	8-40.6
6-40	Penalties - Yards	5-41
37:14	Possession Time	22:46

INDIVIDUAL LEADERS

RUSHING
BU: Perry 7-45, Rutledge 10-36.
LSU: Hilliard 20-66.

PASSING
BU: Carlson 9-12-0, 161 yards, 2 TD.
LSU: Wickersham 11-24-1, 95 yards.

RECEIVING
BU: Simpson 3-117, 1 TD; Clark 3-31, 1 TD.
LSU: James 4-25.

DECEMBER 29, 1986
TENNESSEE 21, MINNESOTA 14

	1ST	2ND	3RD	4TH	FINAL
TENN	7	7	0	7	21
MINN	0	3	8	3	14

SCORING SUMMARY

TENN	Clinkscales 18 pass from Francis (Reveiz kick)
TENN	Howard 23 pass from Francis (Reveiz kick)
MINN	FG Lohmiller 27
MINN	Foggie 11 run (Thompson run)
MINN	FG Lohmiller 25
TENN	Clinkscales 15 pass from Francis (Reveiz kick)

TENN	TEAM STATISTICS	MINN
17	First Downs	20
81	Rushing Yards	238
22-31-0	Passing	10-25-0
243	Passing Yards	136
324	Total Yards	374
5-38.4	Punts - Average	3-39.7
4-1	Fumbles - Lost	2-2
5-49	Penalties - Yards	5-30
28:40	Possession Time	31:20

INDIVIDUAL LEADERS

RUSHING
TENN: Howard 16-63.
MINN: Thompson 25-136.

PASSING
TENN: Francis 22-31-0, 243 yards, 3 TD.
MINN: Foggie 10-25-0, 136 yards.

RECEIVING
TENN: Clinkscales 7-72, 2 TD; Miller 6-72.
MINN: Anderson 3-31.

DECEMBER 29, 1987
GEORGIA 20, ARKANSAS 17

	1ST	2ND	3RD	4TH	FINAL
UGA	0	7	0	13	20
ARK	3	7	7	0	17

SCORING SUMMARY
ARK	FG Trainor 43
UGA	Tate 1 run (Kasay kick)
ARK	Thomas 10 run (Trainor kick)
ARK	Thomas 1 run (Trainor kick)
UGA	FG Kasay 24
UGA	Jackson 5 run (Kasay kick)
UGA	FG Kasay 39

UGA	TEAM STATISTICS	ARK
20	First Downs	19
202	Rushing Yards	258
15-25-2	Passing	7-17-2
148	Passing Yards	86
350	Total Yards	344
3-32.7	Punts - Average	3-32.7
68	Return Yards	95
2-1	Fumbles - Lost	0-0
4-45	Penalties - Yards	5-50

INDIVIDUAL LEADERS
RUSHING
UGA: Jackson 10-72, 1 TD.
ARK: Thomas 13-79, 2 TD.

PASSING
UGA: Jackson 15-25-2, 148 yards.
ARK: Thomas 7-17-2, 86 yards.

RECEIVING
UGA: Thomas 7-76.
ARK: Winston 2-36.

DECEMBER 28, 1988
INDIANA 34, SOUTH CAROLINA 10

	1ST	2ND	3RD	4TH	FINAL
IND	7	10	3	14	34
SC	0	0	10	0	10

SCORING SUMMARY
IND	Thompson 7 run (Stoyanovich kick)
IND	Miller 10 pass from Schnell (Stoyanovich kick)
IND	FG Stoyanovich 28
SC	Tolbert 34 block punt return (Mackie kick)
IND	FG Stoyanovich 19
SC	FG Mackie 43
IND	Turner 88 pass from Schnell (Stoyanovich kick)
IND	Thompson 8 run (Stoyanovich kick)

IND	TEAM STATISTICS	SC
23	First Downs	12
185	Rushing Yards	23
17-32-1	Passing	15-37-3
390	Passing Yards	130
575	Total Yards	153
6-26.0	Punts - Average	9-38.0
1-0	Fumbles - Lost	1-1
6-40	Penalties - Yards	2-15

INDIVIDUAL LEADERS
RUSHING
IND: Thompson 26-140, 2 TD.
SC: Green 11-41.

PASSING
IND: Schnell 16-31-1, 378 yards, 2 TD.
SC: Ellis 15-37-3, 130 yards.

RECEIVING
IND: Turner 5-182, 1 TD; Thompson 2-14, 2 TD.
SC: Brooks 2-35.

DECEMBER 28, 1989
MISSISSIPPI 42, AIR FORCE 29

	1ST	2ND	3RD	4TH	FINAL
MISS	14	14	7	7	42
AFA	9	0	6	14	29

SCORING SUMMARY
MISS	Hines 23 pass from Darnell (Hogue kick)
AFA	FG Woods 37
MISS	Baldwin 23 run (Hogue kick)
AFA	Dowis 2 run (pass failed)
MISS	Baldwin 21 run (Hogue kick)
MISS	Coleman 58 punt return (Hogue kick)
AFA	Johnson 3 run (run failed)
MISS	Coleman 11 run (Hogue kick)
MISS	Thigpen 8 pass from Shows (Hogue kick)
AFA	Senn 35 pass from McDowell (pass failed)
AFA	Senn 21 pass from McDowell (Durham run)

MISS	TEAM STATISTICS	AFA
30	First Downs	25
225	Rushing Yards	259
21-37-0	Passing	14-24-2
285	Passing Yards	233
510	Total Yards	492
5-38.2	Punts - Average	4-43.3
2-2	Fumbles - Lost	3-2
7-45	Penalties - Yards	2-12
27:15	Possession Time	32:45

INDIVIDUAL LEADERS
RUSHING
MISS: Baldwin 15-177, 2 TD.
AFA: Dowis 18-92, 1 TD; Johnson 10-48, 1 TD.

PASSING
MISS: Darnell 19-33-0, 261 yards, 1 TD.
AFA: McDowell 7-8-2, 147 yards, 2 TD.

RECEIVING
MISS: Green 5-72; Hines 3-69, 1 TD.
AFA: Senn 7-150, 2 TD; Van Hulzen 5-57.

DECEMBER 27, 1990
AIR FORCE 23, OHIO STATE 11

	1ST	2ND	3RD	4TH	FINAL
AFA	0	6	7	10	23
OSU	5	0	0	6	11

SCORING SUMMARY
OSU	Safety (punter tackled in end zone)
OSU	FG Williams 28
AFA	Perez 1 run (run failed)
AFA	Perez 1 run (Wood kick)
OSU	Smith 29 run (pass failed)
AFA	FG Wood 46
AFA	McDonald 40 interception return (Wood kick)

AFA	TEAM STATISTICS	OSU
16	First Downs	14
254	Rushing Yards	80
1-3-1	Passing	12-32-2
11	Passing Yards	134
265	Total Yards	214
6-60.0	Punts - Average	6-42.0
3-2	Fumbles - Lost	1-0
6-60	Penalties - Yards	6-42
33:23	Possession Time	26:37

INDIVIDUAL LEADERS
RUSHING
AFA: Perez 26-93, 2 TD; Lewis 12-74.
OSU: Smith 13-62, 1 TD.

PASSING
AFA: Perez 1-3-1, 11 yards.
OSU: Frey 10-27-3, 110 yards.

RECEIVING
AFA: Mott 1-11.
OSU: Olive 4-63.

DECEMBER 29,1991
AIR FORCE 38, MISSISSIPPI STATE 15

	1ST	2ND	3RD	4TH	FINAL
AFA	14	7	3	14	38
MSU	0	7	0	8	15

SCORING SUMMARY
AFA	Jones 1 run (Wood kick)
AFA	Perez 1 run (Wood kick)
AFA	Yates 35 fumble return (Wood kick)
MSU	Edwards 4 pass from Robinson (Garnderk kick)
AFA	FG Wood 20
AFA	Hufford 31 run (Wood kick)
MSU	Davis 7 run (Jordan pass from Robinson)
AFA	Simpson fumble recovery in end zone (Wood kick)

AFA	TEAM STATISTICS	MSU
19	First Downs	18
318	Rushing Yards	163
1-2-1	Passing	13-24-1
10	Passing Yards	121
328	Total Yards	284
4-48.3	Punts - Average	4-37.8
2-0	Fumbles - Lost	3-2
4-31	Penalties - Yards	5-35

INDIVIDUAL LEADERS
RUSHING
AFA: Perez 26-114, 1 TD.
MSU: Roberts 8-66.

PASSING
AFA: Perez 1-2-1, 10 yards.
MSU: Robinson 6-12-0, 49 yards, 1 TD.

RECEIVING
AFA: Wilkie 1-10.
MSU: Roberts 4-28.

DECEMBER 31, 1992
MISSISSIPPI 13, AIR FORCE 0

	1ST	2ND	3RD	4TH	FINAL
MISS	7	3	0	3	13
AFA	0	0	0	0	0

SCORING SUMMARY
MISS	Innocent 2 run (Lee kick)
MISS	FG Lee 24
MISS	FG Lee 29

MISS	TEAM STATISTICS	AFA
13	First Downs	14
168	Rushing Yards	104
9-19-0	Passing	10-17-2
163	Passing Yards	81
331	Total Yards	185
5-33	Punts - Average	5-20.2
2-1	Fumbles - Lost	2-1
7-57	Penalties - Yards	6-53

INDIVIDUAL LEADERS
RUSHING
MISS: Innocent 16-62, 1 TD.
AFA: Pastorello 13-49.

PASSING
MISS: Shows 9-19-0, 163 yards.
AFA: Teigen 5-8-1, 55 yards.

RECEIVING
MISS: Courtney 4-63.
AFA: Hufford 2-18.

THE BOWLS

December 28, 1993
Louisville 18, Michigan State 7

	1ST	2ND	3RD	4TH	FINAL
LOU	3	0	0	15	18
MSU	7	0	0	0	7

SCORING SUMMARY
MSU   Goulborne 1 run (Stoyanovich kick)
LOU   FG Akers 31
LOU   Ferguson 25 pass from Brohm (Akers kick)
LOU   Safety (Thomas tackled in end zone)
LOU   Dawkins 11 run (kick failed)

LOU	TEAM STATISTICS	MSU
20	First Downs	18
172	Rushing Yards	114
19-31-0	Passing	15-28-1
197	Passing Yards	193
369	Total Yards	307
1-25	Punt Returns - Yards	1-3
2-48	Kickoff Returns - Yards	4-59
5-36.2	Punts - Average	5-29.0
1-0	Fumbles - Lost	0-0
6-45	Penalties - Yards	5-60

INDIVIDUAL LEADERS
RUSHING
LOU: Dawkins 14-88, 1 TD; Shelman 17-59.
MSU: Goulborne 19-63, 1 TD; Thomas 10-57.
PASSING
LOU: Brohm 19-29-0, 197 yards, 1 TD.
MSU: Miller 15-28-1, 193 yards.
RECEIVING
LOU: Dawkins 8-68; Ferguson 3-68.
MSU: Coleman 6-100; Greene 4-49.

December 31, 1994
Illinois 30, East Carolina 0

	1ST	2ND	3RD	4TH	FINAL
ILL	14	10	6	0	30
ECU	0	0	0	0	0

SCORING SUMMARY
ILL   Dilger 17 pass from Johnson (Richardson kick)
ILL   Strong 73 pass from Johnson (Richardson kick)
ILL   FG Richardson 21
ILL   Dulick 5 pass from Johnson (Richardson kick)
ILL   Douthard 9 pass from Johnson (Richardson kick)

ILL	TEAM STATISTICS	ECU
18	First Downs	17
134	Rushing Yards	92
20-34-0	Passing	20-41-4
255	Passing Yards	179
389	Total Yards	271
15-164	Penalties - Yards	6-40

INDIVIDUAL LEADERS
RUSHING
ILL: Douthard 13-52; Holcome 12-46.
ECU: Smith 15-46.
PASSING
ILL: Johnson 18-30-0, 250 yards, 4 TD.
ECU: Crandell 20-41-4, 179 yards.
RECEIVING
ILL: Strong 3-96, 1 TD; Dilger 7-60, 1 TD.
ECU: Nichols 6-55; Richards 4-25.

December 30, 1995
East Carolina 19, Stanford 13

	1ST	2ND	3RD	4TH	FINAL
ECU	7	9	0	3	19
STAN	0	7	6	0	13

SCORING SUMMARY
ECU   Hart 39 interception return (Holcomb kick)
ECU   FG Holcomb 46
STAN   Salina 1 run (Abrams kick)
ECU   FG Holcomb 26
ECU   FG Holcomb 41
STAN   Ellis 2 blocked punt return (kick failed)
ECU   FG Holcomb 34

ECU	TEAM STATISTICS	STAN
18	First Downs	11
129	Rushing Yards	72
19-46-1	Passing	15-27-2
218	Passing Yards	139
347	Total Yards	211
2-14	Punt Returns - Yards	3-46
1-34	Kickoff Returns - Yards	6-188
6-28.5	Punts - Average	7-36.9
4-25	Penalties - Yards	3-18

INDIVIDUAL LEADERS
RUSHING
ECU: McPhail 27-92.
STAN: Bookman 13-46; Mitchell 8-30.
PASSING
ECU: Cradell 19-46-1, 218 yards.
STAN: Butterfield 15-27-2, 139 yards.
RECEIVING
ECU: Galloway 4-70; Richards 5-59.
STAN: Manning 3-43.

December 27, 1996
Syracuse 30, Houston 17

	1ST	2ND	3RD	4TH	FINAL
SYR	7	9	0	14	30
HOU	7	7	0	3	17

SCORING SUMMARY
SYR   McNabb 1 run (Trout kick)
HOU   Smith 21 pass from Clements (Villarreal kick)
SYR   Konrad 2 run (Trout kick)
SYR   Safety
HOU   Smith 3 run (Villarreal kick)
SYR   McNabb 2 run (Trout kick)
HOU   FG Villarreal 23
SYR   Thomas 6 run (Trout kick)

SYR	TEAM STATISTICS	HOU
25	First Downs	13
396	Rushing Yards	124
4-10-0	Passing	14-28-1
76	Passing Yards	217
472	Total Yards	341
1-2	Punt Returns - Yards	2-10
4-78	Kickoff Returns - Yards	5-138
4-42.5	Punts - Average	3-35.0
4-4	Fumbles - Lost	7-4
5-41	Penalties - Yards	5-30

INDIVIDUAL LEADERS
RUSHING
SYR: Thomas 24-201, 1 TD.
HOU: Smith 19-119, 1 TD.
PASSING
SYR: McNabb 4-10-0, 76 yards.
HOU: Clements 14-28-1, 217 yards, 1 TD.
RECEIVING
SYR: Maddox 2-47.
HOU: Smith 5-44, 1 TD.

December 31, 1997
Southern Miss 41, Pittsburgh 7

	1ST	2ND	3RD	4TH	FINAL
USM	7	7	14	13	41
PITT	0	7	0	0	7

SCORING SUMMARY
USM   Gideon 31 pass from Roberts (Hardaway kick)
USM   Gideon 8 pass from Roberts (Hardaway kick)
PITT   Hoffart 89 pass from Gonzalez (Ferencik kick)
USM   Phenix 16 fumble return (Hardaway kick)
USM   Gideon 5 pass from Roberts (Hardaway kick)
USM   Thomas 26 interception return (kick failed)
USM   Parrish 63 interception return (kick failed)

USM	TEAM STATISTICS	PITT
15	First Downs	16
125	Rushing Yards	150
18-27-1	Passing	16-41-2
227	Passing Yards	190
352	Total Yards	340
7-36.3	Punts - Average	7-40.3
0-0	Fumbles - Lost	1-1
6-40	Penalties - Yards	8-72
27:05	Possession Time	32:55

INDIVIDUAL LEADERS
RUSHING
USM: Shaw 17-62; Booth 7-49.
PITT: Barlow 9-68; West 19-56.
PASSING
USM: Roberts 18-26-1, 227 yards, 3 TD.
PITT: Gonzalez 13-29-2, 172 yards, 1 TD.
RECEIVING
USM: Gideon 7-111, 3 TD; Hardy 4-43.
PITT: Hoffart 5-121, 1 TD; J. Williams 4-21.

December 31, 1998
Tulane 41, BYU 27

	1ST	2ND	3RD	4TH	FINAL
TUL	10	10	14	7	41
BYU	6	0	0	21	27

SCORING SUMMARY
BYU   Horton 11 pass from Feterik (kick failed)
TUL   FG Palazzo 31
TUL   Jordan 79 interception return (Palazzo kick)
TUL   King 3 run (Palazzo kick)
TUL   FG Palazzo 23
TUL   Cook 60 pass from King (Palazzo kick)
TUL   Dartez 13 pass from King (Palazzo kick)
BYU   Cupp 3 run (Pochman kick)
TUL   Converse 5 run (Palazzo kick)
BYU   Cupp 18 pass from Feterik (Pochman kick)
BYU   Mahe 3 run (Pochman kick)

TUL	TEAM STATISTICS	BYU
28	First Downs	20
252	Rushing Yards	54
23-38-0	Passing	27-44-1
276	Passing Yards	267
528	Total Yards	321
4-41.5	Punts - Average	7-33.6
2-0	Fumbles - Lost	3-0
8-59	Penalties - Yards	10-110
31:15	Possession Time	28:45

INDIVIDUAL LEADERS
RUSHING
TUL: King 16-109, 1 TD; Converse 18-103, 1 TD.
BYU: Mahe 16-70, 1 TD.
PASSING
TUL: King 23-38-0, 276 yards, 2 TD.
BYU: Feterik 27-44-1, 267 yards, 2 TD.
RECEIVING
TUL: Dawson 6-83.
BYU: Horton 6-67, 1 TD; Sitake 5-77.

December 31, 1999
Southern Miss 23, Colorado State 17

	1st	2nd	3rd	4th	Final
USM	13	7	3	0	23
CSU	3	14	0	0	17

SCORING SUMMARY
USM	Williams 5 fumble return (Hanna kick)
CSU	FG Hurst 35
USM	Frances blocked punt recovered in end zone (kick failed)
CSU	Rice 2 run (Hurst kick)
CSU	Woolstenhulme 38 pass from Newton (Hurst kick)
USM	Nix 3 run (Hannah kick)
CSU	FG Hannah 25

USM	TEAM STATISTICS	CSU
11	First Downs	15
62	Rushing Yards	40
13-30-1	Passing	20-46-1
125	Passing Yards	228
187	Total Yards	268
1-11	Punt Returns - Yards	4-21
3-57	Kickoff Returns - Yards	5-88
9-34.3	Punts - Average	5-31.8
2-1	Fumbles - Lost	3-2
11-59	Penalties - Yards	8-71
24:58	Possession Time	35:02

INDIVIDUAL LEADERS
RUSHING
USM: Nix 17-55, 1 TD.
CSU: McDougal 25-59.
PASSING
USM: Kelly 13-30-1, 125 yards.
CSU: Newton 20-46-1, 158 yards, 1 TD.
RECEIVING
USM: Pinkston 4-49; Gideon 3-39.
CSU: Davis 6-82; Rebstock 7-69.

December 29, 2000
Colorado State 22, Louisville 17

	1st	2nd	3rd	4th	Final
CSU	3	13	3	3	22
LOU	7	3	0	7	17

SCORING SUMMARY
CSU	FG Hurst 23
LOU	Dorsey 58 pass from Ragone (Smith kick)
LOU	FG Smith 23
CSU	Sapp 2 run (Hurst kick)
CSU	Rice 16 run (kick failed)
CSU	FG Hurst 21
LOU	Branch 14 pass from Ragone (Smith kick)
CSU	FG Hurst 23

CSU	TEAM STATISTICS	LOU
22	First Downs	17
157	Rushing Yards	76
13-28-1	Passing	24-37-0
158	Passing Yards	321
315	Total Yards	397
4-47	Punt Returns - Yards	1-2
4-87	Kickoff Returns - Yards	4-38
5-44.8	Punts - Average	5-39.2
3-1	Fumbles - Lost	3-3
3-39	Penalties - Yards	6-55
32:25	Possession Time	24:35

INDIVIDUAL LEADERS
RUSHING
CSU: Sapp 36-160, 1 TD; Rice 2-39, 1 TD.
LOU: Stallings 15-63.
PASSING
CSU: Newton 13-28-1, 158 yards.
LOU: Ragone 24-37-0, 321, 2 TD.
RECEIVING
CSU: Layne 2-46; Rebstock 3-34.
LOU: Branch 10-170, 1 TD; Dorsey 1-58, 1 TD.

December 31, 2001
Louisville 28, BYU 10

	1st	2nd	3rd	4th	Final
LOU	7	7	7	7	28
BYU	0	7	3	0	10

SCORING SUMMARY
LOU	Miller 1 run (Smith kick)
BYU	Rykert 10 run (Payne kick)
LOU	Mattingly 1 pass from Ragone (Smith kick)
BYU	FG Payne 29
LOU	Branch 34 pass from Ragone (Smith kick)
LOU	Ghent 27 pass from Ragone (Smith kick)

LOU	TEAM STATISTICS	BYU
17	First Downs	17
58	Rushing Yards	84
19-28-1	Passing	18-38-3
228	Passing Yards	192
286	Total Yards	276
6-36.5	Punts - Average	4-36.8
2-0	Fumbles - Lost	0-0
8-64	Penalties - Yards	4-40

INDIVIDUAL LEADERS
RUSHING
LOU: Patterson 21-45.
BYU: P. Peterson 15-73.
PASSING
LOU: Ragone 19-28-1, 228 yards, 3 TD.
BYU: Doman 18-37-2, 192 yards.
RECEIVING
LOU: Branch 6-88, 1 TD; Ghent 4-62, 1 TD.
BYU: Ord 4-62.

December 31, 2002
TCU 17, Colorado State 3

	1st	2nd	3rd	4th	Final
TCU	0	7	0	10	17
CSU	0	0	3	0	3

SCORING SUMMARY
TCU	Dunbar 2 pass from Stilley (Browne kick)
CSU	FG Babcock 46
TCU	FG Browne 25
TCU	Madison 3 run (Browne kick)

TCU	TEAM STATISTICS	CSU
19	First Downs	8
197	Rushing Yards	89
16-28-1	Passing	6-28-3
141	Passing Yards	50
338	Total Yards	139
2-10	Punt Returns - Yards	4-64
1-11	Kickoff Returns - Yards	3-45
8-36.6	Punts - Average	8-36.9
2-1	Fumbles - Lost	5-3
9-70	Penalties - Yards	7-49
22:47	Possession Time	26:13

INDIVIDUAL LEADERS
RUSHING
TCU: Madison 19-111, 1 TD; Hobbs 20-77.
CSU: Sapp 19-106.
PASSING
TCU: Stilley 16-28-1, 141 yards, 1 TD.
CSU: Van Pelt 4-19-1, 24 yards; Holland 2-8-2, 26 yards.
RECEIVING
TCU: Dunbar 6-71, 1 TD.
CSU: Pittman 4-33.

December 31, 2003
Utah 17, Southern Miss 0

	1st	2nd	3rd	4th	Final
UTAH	0	7	0	10	17
USM	0	0	0	0	0

SCORING SUMMARY
UTAH	Warfield 5 run (Borreson kick)
UTAH	FG Borreson 19
UTAH	Scalley 74 fumble return (Borreson kick)

UTAH	TEAM STATISTICS	USM
12	First Downs	11
104	Rushing Yards	69
8-19-1	Passing	13-39-0
124	Passing Yards	144
228	Total Yards	213
7-31	Punt Returns - Yards	3-20
0-0	Kickoff Returns - Yards	3-56
9-37.9	Punts - Average	8-45.8
6-2	Fumbles - Lost	4-4
12-85	Penalties - Yards	12-92
33:24	Possession Time	26:36

INDIVIDUAL LEADERS
RUSHING
UTAH: Warfield 27-91, 1 TD; Smith 13-42.
USM: Harris 14-70.
PASSING
UTAH: Smith 8-19-1, 124 yards.
USM: Almond 11-33-0, 122 yards.
RECEIVING
UTAH: Warren 5-72; Savoy 1-41.
USM: Courington 2-34; Browden 2-33.

December 31, 2004
Louisville 44, Boise State 40

	1st	2nd	3rd	4th	Final
LOU	14	7	14	9	44
BSU	10	21	3	6	40

SCORING SUMMARY
BSU	FG Jones 48
LOU	Barnidge 7 pass from LeFors (Carmody kick)
BSU	Avalos 92 Interception return (Jones kick)
LOU	Douglas 65 run (Carmody kick)
LOU	Clark 30 pass from Brohm (Carmody kick)
BSU	Lau Recovered fumble in end zone (Jones Kick)
BSU	Acree 19 pass from Zabransky (Jones kick)
BSU	Zabransky 1 run (Jones kick)
BSU	FG Jones 42
LOU	Russell 14 pass from LeFors (Carmody kick)
LOU	LeFors 1 run (Carmody kick)
BSU	Helmandollar 2 run (pass failed)
LOU	Shelton 1 run (pass failed)
BSU	FG Carmody 19

LOU	TEAM STATISTICS	BSU
29	First Downs	15
329	Rushing Yards	88
21-31-2	Passing	15-31-1
235	Passing Yards	196
564	Total Yards	284
4-36	Punt Returns - Yards	1-14
6-139	Kickoff Returns - Yards	8-186
2-24.0	Punts - Average	6-39.7
2-2	Fumbles - Lost	1-0
5-34	Penalties - Yards	6-55
33:35	Possession Time	26:25

INDIVIDUAL LEADERS
RUSHING
LOU: Bush 12-96; Shelton 18-76, 1 TD.
BSU: Marks 15-66.
PASSING
LOU: LeFors 18-26-1, 193 yards, 2 TD.
BSU: Zabransky 14-29-1, 199 yards, 1 TD.
RECEIVING
LOU: Russell 6-59, 1 TD; McCauley 4-58.
BSU: Acree 4-57, 1 TD; Schouman 3-53.

PEACH BOWL

THE BOWLS

PROFILE

Site: Atlanta
Stadium: Georgia Dome
Capacity: 71,500
Surface: FieldTurf

PLAYING SITES

Grant Field, 1968-70
Atlanta-Fulton County Stadium, 1971-92
Georgia Dome, since 1993

NAME CHANGES

Peach Bowl, 1968-96
Chick-fil-A Peach Bowl, since 1997

SEASON	DATE	PRE-GAME RANK	TEAMS	SCORE	FINAL RANK	MOST VALUABLE PLAYERS	ATT.
1968	Dec. 30, 1968		LSU	31	19	Mike Hillman, LSU, QB	35,545
		19	Florida State	27		Buddy Millican, LSU, DE	
1969	Dec. 30, 1969		West Virginia	14		Ed Williams, West Virginia, FB	48,452
			South Carolina	3		Carl Crennel, West Virginia, MG	
1970	Dec. 30, 1970		Arizona State	48		Monroe Eley, Arizona State, HB	52,126
			North Carolina	26		Junior Ah You, Arizona State, DE	
1971	Dec. 30, 1971	17	Mississippi	41	15	Norris Weese, Mississippi, QB	36,771
			Georgia Tech	18		Crowell Armstrong, Mississippi, LB	
1972	Dec. 29, 1972		North Carolina State	49	17	Dave Buckey, North Carolina State, QB	52,761
			West Virginia	13		George Bell, North Carolina State, DT	
1973	Dec. 28, 1973		Georgia	17		Louis Carter, Maryland, TB	38,107
		18	Maryland	16	20	Sylvester Boler, Georgia, LB	
1974	Dec. 28, 1974		Texas Tech	6		Larry Isaac, Texas Tech, TB	31,695
			Vanderbilt	6		Dennis Harrison, Vanderbilt, DT	
1975	Dec. 31, 1975		West Virginia	13	20	Dan Kendra, West Virginia, QB	45,134
			North Carolina State	10		Ray Marshall, West Virginia, LB	
1976	Dec. 31, 1976		Kentucky	21	18	Rod Stewart, Kentucky, TB	54,132
		19	North Carolina	0		Mike Martin, Kentucky, LB	
1977	Dec. 31, 1977		North Carolina State	24		Johnny Evans, North Carolina State, QB	36,733
			Iowa State	14		Richard Carter, North Carolina State, DB	
1978	Dec. 25, 1978	17	Purdue	41	13	Mark Herrmann, Purdue, QB	20,277
			Georgia Tech	21		Calvin Clark, Purdue, DT	
1979	Dec. 31, 1979	19	Baylor	24	14	Mike Brannan, Baylor, QB	57,321
		18	Clemson	18		Andrew Melontree, Baylor, DE	
1980	Jan. 2, 1981	20	Miami (Fla.)	20	18	Jim Kelly, Miami (Fla.), QB	45,384
			Virginia Tech	10		Jim Burt, Miami (Fla.), MG	
1981	Dec. 31, 1981		West Virginia	26	17	Mickey Walczak, West Virginia, RB	37,582
			Florida	6		Don Stemple, West Virginia, DB	
1982	Dec. 31, 1982		Iowa	28		Chuck Long, Iowa, QB	50,134
			Tennessee	22		Clay Uhlenhake, Iowa, DT	
1983	Dec. 28, 1983		Florida State	28		Eric Thomas, Florida State, QB	25,648
			North Carolina	3		Alphonso Carreker, Florida State, DT	
1984	Dec. 31, 1984		Virginia	27	20	Howard Petty, Virginia, TB	41,107
			Purdue	24		Ray Daly, Virginia, DB	
1985	Dec. 31, 1985		Army	31		Rob Healy, Army, QB	29,857
			Illinois	29		Peel Chronister, Army, S	
1986	Dec. 31, 1986		Virginia Tech	25	20	Erik Kramer, North Carolina State, QB	53,668
		18	North Carolina State	24		Derrick Taylor, North Carolina State, CB	
1987	Jan. 2, 1988	17	Tennessee	27	14	Reggie Cobb, Tennessee, TB	58,737
			Indiana	22		Van Waiters, Indiana, LB	
1988	Dec. 31, 1988		North Carolina State	28		Shane Montgomery, North Carolina State, QB	44,635
			Iowa	23		Michael Brooks, North Carolina St., FS	
1989	Dec. 30, 1989		Syracuse	19		Michael Owens, RB, Terry Wooden, LB, Syracuse	44,991
			Georgia	18		Rodney Hampton, RB, Morris Lewis, LB, Georgia	
1990	Dec. 29, 1990		Auburn	27	19	Stan White, ,QB Darrel Crawford,LB, Auburn	38,962
			Indiana	23		Vaughn Dunbar, RB, Mike Dumas, FS, Indiana	
1991	Jan. 1, 1992	12	East Carolina	37	9	Jeff Blake, QB Robert Jones, LB, East Carolina	59,322
		21	North Carolina State	34	24	Terry Jordan, QB, Billy Ray Haynes, DB, North Carolina State	
1992	Jan. 2, 1993	19	North Carolina	21	19	Natrone Means, RB Bracey Walker, DB, North Carolina	69,125
		24	Mississippi State	17	23	Greg Plump, QB Marc Woodard, LB, Mississippi State	
1993	Dec. 31, 1993	24	Clemson	14	23	Emory Smith, RB Brentson Buckner, DE, Clemson	63,416
			Kentucky	13		Pookie Jones, QB Zane Beehn, LB, Kentucky	
1994	Jan. 1, 1995	23	North Carolina State	28	17	Tremayne Stephens, RB, Damien Covington, ILB, Carl Reeves, DT, North Carolina State	64,902
		16	Mississippi State	24	24	Tim Rogers, K, Larry Williams, DL, Mississippi State	
1995	Dec. 30, 1995	18	Virginia	34	16	Tiki Barber, RB, Skeet Jones, LB, Virginia	70,284
			Georgia	27		Hines Ward, QB, Whit Marshall, LB, Georgia	
1996	Dec. 28, 1996	17	LSU	10	12	Herb Tyler, QB, Anthony McFarland, DL, LSU	63,622
			Clemson	7		Raymond Priester, DE, Trevor Pryce, LB, Clemson	
1997	Jan. 2, 1998	13	Auburn	21	11	Dameyune Craig, QB, Takeo Spikes, LB, Auburn	71,212
			Clemson	17		Raymond Priester, DE, Rahim Abdullah, LB, Clemson	
1998	Dec. 31, 1998	19	Georgia	35	14	Olandis Gary, RB, Champ Bailey, DB, Georgia	72,876
		13	Virginia	33	18	Aaron Brooks, QB, Wally Rainer, LB, Virginia	
1999	Dec. 30, 1999	15	Mississippi State	17	13	Wayne Madkin, Mississippi State, QB	73,315
			Clemson	7		Keith Adams, Clemson, LB	
2000	Dec. 29, 2000		LSU	28	22	Rohan Davey, LSU, QB	73,614
		15	Georgia Tech	14	17	Bradie James, LSU, LB	
2001	Dec. 31, 2001		North Carolina	16		Ronald Curry, North Carolina, QB	71,827
			Auburn	10		Ryan Sims, North Carolina, DL	
2002	Dec. 31, 2002	20	Maryland	30	13	Scott McBrien, Maryland, QB	68,330
			Tennessee	3		E.J. Henderson, Maryland, LB	
2003	Jan. 2, 2004		Clemson	27	15	Chad Jasmin, Clemson, RB	75,125
			Tennessee	14	22	LeRoy Hill, Clemson, LB	
2004	Dec. 31, 2004	14	Miami (Fla.)	27	11	Roscoe Parrish, Miami (Fla.), WR	69,322
		20	Florida	10		Devin Hester, Miami (Fla.), CB	

December 30, 1968
LSU 31, Florida State 27

	1ST	2ND	3RD	4TH	FINAL
LSU	0	10	14	7	31
FSU	7	6	0	14	27

SCORING SUMMARY

FSU	Bailey 36 run (Guthrie kick)
FSU	Gunter 75 pass from Cappleman (kick failed)
LSU	Burns 39 punt return (Lumpkin kick)
LSU	FG Lumpkin 32
LSU	Hamlett 11 pass from Hillman (Lumpkin kick)
LSU	Stobler 11 pass from Hillman (Lumpkin kick)
FSU	Sellers 7 pass from Cappleman (pass failed)
FSU	Sellers 4 pass from Cappleman (Glass pass from Cappleman)
LSU	LeBlanc 3 run (Lumpkin kick)

LSU	TEAM STATISTICS	FSU
22	First Downs	19
151	Rushing Yards	92
17-30-1	Passing	21-41-1
233	Passing Yards	221
384	Total Yards	313
4-41.5	Punts - Average	9-34.6
5-4	Fumbles - Lost	1-0
7-70	Penalties - Yards	8-90

INDIVIDUAL LEADERS

RUSHING
LSU: LeBlanc 14-97, 1 TD; Matte 5-20.
FSU: Bailey 11-75, 1 TD; Gunter 8-30.

PASSING
LSU: Hillman 16-29-1, 229 yards, 2 TD.
FSU: Cappleman 21-41-1, 221 yards, 3 TD.

RECEIVING
LSU: West 2-144; Morel 6-103.
FSU: Sellers 8-75, 2 TD; Tyson 1-31.

December 30, 1969
West Virginia 14, South Carolina 3

	1ST	2ND	3RD	4TH	FINAL
WVU	7	0	0	7	14
SC	0	3	0	0	3

SCORING SUMMARY

WVU	Gresham 10 run (Braxton kick)
SC	FG DuPre 37
WVU	Braxton 1 run (Braxton kick)

WVU	TEAM STATISTICS	SC
21	First Downs	11
356	Rushing Yards	64
1-2-0	Passing	11-23-2
3	Passing Yards	126
359	Total Yards	190
9-28.8	Punts - Average	6-39.3

INDIVIDUAL LEADERS

RUSHING
WVU: Williams 35-208; Gresham 16-98, 1 TD.
SC: Muir 18-52; Holloman 7-18.

PASSING
WVU: Sherwood 1-2-0, 3 yards.
SC: Suggs 9-17-1, 98 yards.

RECEIVING
WVU: Braxton 1-3.
SC: Hamrick 4-64; Holloman 5-33.

December 30, 1970
Arizona State 48, North Carolina 26

	1ST	2ND	3RD	4TH	FINAL
ASU	7	14	20	7	48
UNC	0	26	0	0	26

SCORING SUMMARY

ASU	Thomas 8 run (Ekstrand kick)
ASU	Thomas 33 run (Ekstrand kick)
UNC	McCauley 1 run (Craven kick)
ASU	Hill 67 pass from Spagnola (Ekstrand kick)
UNC	Blanchard 36 pass from Miller (Craven kick)
UNC	McCauley 17 run (kick failed)
UNC	McCauley 4 run (pass failed)
ASU	Eley 8 run (Ekstrand kick)
ASU	Holden 13 run (kick failed)
ASU	Eley 5 run (Ekstrand kick)
ASU	Thomas 2 run (Ekstrand kick)

ASU	TEAM STATISTICS	UNC
22	First Downs	13
306	Rushing Yards	131
9-24-2	Passing	6-17-2
145	Passing Yards	123
451	Total Yards	254
3-42.3	Punts - Average	10-27.3
4-2	Fumbles - Lost	2-1
1-5	Penalties - Yards	4-45

INDIVIDUAL LEADERS

RUSHING
ASU: Eley 23-173, 2 TD; Thomas 22-124, 3 TD.
UNC: McCauley 36-143, 3 TD; Hamlin 4-17.

PASSING
ASU: Spagnola 8-23-2, 155 yards, 1 TD.
UNC: Mansfield 3-12-2, 26 yards; Miller 3-5-0, 97 yards, 1 TD.

RECEIVING
ASU: Hill 3-101, 1 TD; Petty 2-38.
UNC: Lanier 2-50; Blanchard 1-36, 1 TD.

December 30, 1971
Mississippi 41, Georgia Tech 18

	1ST	2ND	3RD	4TH	FINAL
MISS	10	28	0	3	41
GT	0	6	6	6	18

SCORING SUMMARY

MISS	Weese 1 run (Hinton kick)
MISS	FG Hinton 25
MISS	Porter 2 run (Hinton kick)
MISS	Porter 10 run (Hinton kick)
MISS	Felts 15 pass from Lyons (Hinton kick)
MISS	Myers 11 pass from Weese (Hinton kick)
GT	Healy 2 run (run failed)
GT	Healy 1 run (pass failed)
GT	Healy 1 run (run failed)
MISS	FG Hinton 30

MISS	TEAM STATISTICS	GT
17	First Downs	16
179	Rushing Yards	166
9-18-1	Passing	13-26-2
139	Passing Yards	151
318	Total Yards	317
5-37.4	Punts - Average	5-31.2
2-1	Fumbles - Lost	3-3
5-25	Penalties - Yards	8-38

INDIVIDUAL LEADERS

RUSHING
MISS: Ainsworth 28-119; Porter 8-26, 2 TD.
GT: Hennessey 6-57; Cunningham 5-30.

PASSING
MISS: Weese 7-14-0, 23 yards, 1 TD.
GT: McAshan 13-26-2, 151 yards.

RECEIVING
MISS: Myers 2-49, 1 TD; Barry 3-39.
GT: Owings 5-87; Oven 3-26.

December 29, 1972
NC State 49, West Virginia 13

	1ST	2ND	3RD	4TH	FINAL
NCST	7	7	21	14	49
WVU	13	0	0	0	13

SCORING SUMMARY

WVU	FG Nester 27
WVU	FG Nester 39
NCST	Don Buckey 37 pass from Dave Buckey (Sewell kick)
WVU	Buggs 4 pass from Galiffa (Nester kick)
NCST	Fritts 1 run (Sewell kick)
NCST	Don Buckey 2 run (Sewell kick)
NCST	Fritts 1 run (Sewell kick)
NCST	Fritts 4 run (Sewell kick)
NCST	Hovance 14 pass from Dave Buckey (Sewell kick)
NCST	Burden 7 run (Sewell kick)

NCST	TEAM STATISTICS	WVU
27	First Downs	15
337	Rushing Yards	91
11-21-2	Passing	16-34-0
198	Passing Yards	134
535	Total Yards	225
2-34.5	Punts - Average	5-33.2
1-1	Fumbles - Lost	2-2
2-10	Penalties - Yards	6-61

INDIVIDUAL LEADERS

RUSHING
NCST: Burden 20-116, 1 TD; Young 10-90.
WVU: Marbury 13-69; Lee 11-42.

PASSING
NCST: Dave Buckey 8-13-1, 139 yards, 2 TD.
WVU: Galiffa 16-32-0, 184 yards, 1 TD.

RECEIVING
NCST: Don Buckey 4-70, 1 TD; Kennedy 3-52.
WVU: Buggs 2-51, 1 TD; Stephens 2-32.

December 28, 1973
Georgia 17, Maryland 16

	1ST	2ND	3RD	4TH	FINAL
UGA	0	10	7	0	17
MARY	0	10	0	6	16

SCORING SUMMARY

UGA	Poulos 62 pass from Johnson (Leavitt kick)
MARY	White 68 pass from Carter (Mayer kick)
MARY	FG Mayer 36
UGA	FG Leavitt 26
UGA	Johnson 1 run (Leavitt kick)
MARY	FG Mayer 25
MARY	FG Mayer 28

UGA	TEAM STATISTICS	MARY
11	First Downs	15
170	Rushing Yards	219
5-16-1	Passing	8-18-1
114	Passing Yards	242
284	Total Yards	461
8-41.3	Punts - Average	6-31.8
2-2	Fumbles - Lost	4-3
1-5	Penalties - Yards	5-63

INDIVIDUAL LEADERS

RUSHING
UGA: King 16-57.
MARY: Carter 29-126.

PASSING
UGA: Johnson 5-16-1, 114 yards, 1 TD.
MARY: Kinard 4-8-1, 113 yards.

RECEIVING
UGA: Poulos 2-62, 1 TD.
MARY: White 2-106, 1 TD.

DECEMBER 28, 1974
TEXAS TECH 6, VANDERBILT 6

	1ST	2ND	3RD	4TH	FINAL
TT	0	0	3	3	6
VANDY	0	3	0	3	6

SCORING SUMMARY
VANDY FG Adams 31
TT FG Hall 26
VANDY FG Adams 26
TT FG Hall 35

TT	TEAM STATISTICS	VANDY
19	First Downs	10
306	Rushing Yards	140
3-10-1	Passing	5-17-1
35	Passing Yards	60
341	Total Yards	200
6-36.0	Punts - Average	8-40.0
3-2	Fumbles - Lost	1-1
1-14	Penalties - Yards	1-5

INDIVIDUAL LEADERS
RUSHING
TT: Hoskins 13-116; Isaac 20-101.
VANDY: O'Rourke 17-76; Sadler 8-31.
PASSING
TT: Dunevin 3-8-0, 35 yards.
VANDY: Lee 5-14-1, 60 yards.
RECEIVING
TT: Felux 2-21; Williams 1-14.
VANDY: Burton 2-36; O'Rourke 2-15.

DECEMBER 31, 1975
WEST VIRGINIA 13, NC STATE 10

	1ST	2ND	3RD	4TH	FINAL
WVU	0	6	0	7	13
NCST	7	3	0	0	10

SCORING SUMMARY
NCST Adams 1 run (Sherrill kick)
NCST FG Sherrill 21
WVU Owens 39 pass from Kendra (kick failed)
WVU MacDonald 50 pass from Kendra (McKenzie kick)

WVU	TEAM STATISTICS	NCST
20	First Downs	23
210	Rushing Yards	223
11-25-1	Passing	12-29-0
103	Passing Yards	202
313	Total Yards	425
8-42.0	Punts - Average	6-40.0
1-1	Fumbles - Lost	1-1
8-80	Penalties - Yards	7-59

INDIVIDUAL LEADERS
RUSHING
WVU: Owens 19-96; Lee 15-76.
NCST: Brown 21-159; Adams 11-46, 1 TD.
PASSING
WVU: Kendra 12-28-0, 202 yards, 2 TD.
NCST: Buckey 11-23-1, 103 yards.
RECEIVING
WVU: MacDonald 5-110, 1 TD; Owens 3-61, 1 TD.
NCST: Buckey 5-64; Brown 2-19.

DECEMBER 31, 1976
KENTUCKY 21, NORTH CAROLINA 0

	1ST	2ND	3RD	4TH	FINAL
UK	0	0	7	14	21
UNC	0	0	0	0	0

SCORING SUMMARY
UK Stewart 1 run (Pierce kick)
UK Stewart 13 run (Pierce kick)
UK Stewart 3 run (Pierce kick)

UK	TEAM STATISTICS	UNC
19	First Downs	5
318	Rushing Yards	84
2-9-1	Passing	3-15-3
16	Passing Yards	24
334	Total Yards	108
8-34.6	Punts - Average	7-33.7
4-2	Fumbles - Lost	3-2
7-55	Penalties - Yards	2-10

INDIVIDUAL LEADERS
RUSHING
UK: Stewart 19-104, 3 TD; Brooks 8-66.
UNC: Paschal 11-41.
PASSING
UK: Ramsey 2-8-0, 16 yards.
UNC: Kupec 3-15-3, 24 yards.
RECEIVING
UK: Hill 1-13.
UNC: Mabry 1-11.

DECEMBER 31, 1977
NC STATE 24, IOWA STATE 14

	1ST	2ND	3RD	4TH	FINAL
NCST	7	14	0	3	24
ISU	0	0	0	14	14

SCORING SUMMARY
NCST Hall 77 pass from Evans (Sherrill kick)
NCST Brown 5 pass from Evans (Sherrill kick)
NCST Evans 32 run (Sherrill kick)
ISU Quinn 1 run (Kollman kick)
NCST FG Sherrill 42
ISU Meckstroth 10 pass from Quinn (Kollman kick)

NCST	TEAM STATISTICS	ISU
20	First Downs	27
172	Rushing Yards	178
14-23-0	Passing	19-32-2
249	Passing Yards	227
421	Total Yards	405
6-44.6	Punts - Average	4-42.7
1-0	Fumbles - Lost	4-3
11-103	Penalties - Yards	6-64

INDIVIDUAL LEADERS
RUSHING
NCST: Brown 25-114; Evans 11-62, 1 TD.
ISU: Green 29-172.
PASSING
NCST: Evans 12-21-0, 202 yards, 2 TD.
ISU: Rubley 10-12-0, 133 yards; Quinn 9-20-2, 94 yards, 1 TD.
RECEIVING
NCST: Marshall 3-75; Brown 7-66, 1 TD.
ISU: Cerrato 3-64; Hixon 3-45

DECEMBER 25, 1978
PURDUE 41, GEORGIA TECH 21

	1ST	2ND	3RD	4TH	FINAL
PUR	21	13	0	7	41
GT	0	7	0	14	21

SCORING SUMMARY
PUR Jones 3 run (Savereen kick)
PUR Jones 8 run (Savereen kick)
PUR Smith 10 pass from Herrmann (Savereen kick)
PUR Herrmann 2 run (Savereen kick)
GT Lee 1 run (Smith kick)
PUR Macon 1 run (kick failed)
PUR Burrell 12 pass from Herrmann (Savereen kick)
GT Moore 3 pass from Kelley (Hill run)
GT Hill 31 pass from Kelley (pass failed)

PUR	TEAM STATISTICS	GT
24	First Downs	14
157	Rushing Yards	12
12-27-2	Passing	17-38-2
166	Passing Yards	168
323	Total Yards	180
5-36.6	Punts - Average	7-36.7
3-1	Fumbles - Lost	2-2
9-78	Penalties - Yards	5-48

INDIVIDUAL LEADERS
RUSHING
PUR: Macon 19-66, 1 TD; Jones 13-50, 2 TD.
GT: Lee 6-24, 1 TD.
PASSING
PUR: Herrmann 12-24-2, 166 yards, 2 TD.
GT: Kelley 17-38-2, 168 yards, 2 TD.
RECEIVING
PUR: Burrell 4-55, 1 TD; Harris 2-38.
GT: Hill 5-77, 1 TD; Hardie 4-40.

DECEMBER 31, 1979
BAYLOR 24, CLEMSON 18

	1ST	2ND	3RD	4TH	FINAL
BU	0	14	10	0	24
CLEM	7	0	3	8	18

SCORING SUMMARY
CLEM Brown 1 run (Ariri kick)
BU Taylor 3 pass from Brannan (Bledsoe kick)
BU Holt 24 pass from Brannan (Bledsoe kick)
CLEM FG Ariri 40
BU FG Bledsoe 29
BU Cockrell 7 pass from Elam (Bledsoe kick)
CLEM McSwain 1 run (McCall pass from Lott)

BU	TEAM STATISTICS	CLEM
11	First Downs	20
62	Rushing Yards	67
8-17-0	Passing	17-34-3
172	Passing Yards	204
234	Total Yards	271
9-40.7	Punts - Average	9-31.5
4-2	Fumbles - Lost	1-0
4-30	Penalties - Yards	7-47

INDIVIDUAL LEADERS
RUSHING
BU: Abercrombie 12-32.
CLEM: Brown 25-76, 1 TD.
PASSING
BU: Elam 4-11-0, 86 yards, 1 TD.
CLEM: Lott 17-34-3, 213 yards.
RECEIVING
BU: Abercrombie 1-63. Holt 2-52, 1 TD.
CLEM: Tuttle 8-108; Gaillard 4-48.

JANUARY 2, 1981
MIAMI (FLA.) 20, VIRGINIA TECH 10

	1ST	2ND	3RD	4TH	FINAL
MIA	7	7	3	3	20
VT	0	3	7	0	10

SCORING SUMMARY
MIA Brodsky 15 pass from Kelly (Miller kick)
MIA Hobbs 12 run (Miller kick)
VT FG Laury 42
VT Lawrence 1 run (Laury kick)
MIA FG Miller 31
MIA FG Miller 37

MIA	TEAM STATISTICS	VT
19	First Downs	19
163	Rushing Yards	180
11-22-1	Passing	9-24-2
179	Passing Yards	119
342	Total Yards	299
5-37.0	Punts - Average	6-38.1
4-1	Fumbles - Lost	3-0
6-66	Penalties - Yards	7-72

INDIVIDUAL LEADERS
RUSHING
MIA: Roan 16-86; Hobbs 10-66, 1 TD.
VT: Lawrence 27-134, 1 TD.
PASSING
MIA: Kelly 11-22-1, 179 yards, 1 TD.
VT: Casey 9-23-1, 119 yards.
RECEIVING
MIA: Brodsky 4-80, 1 TD; Baratta 2-34.
VT: Purdham 2-56.

December 31, 1981
West Virginia 26, Florida 6

	1ST	2ND	3RD	4TH	FINAL
WVU	7	9	3	7	26
FLA	0	0	0	6	6

SCORING SUMMARY

WVU	Walczak 7 pass from Luck (Woodside kick)
WVU	FG Woodside 36
WVU	FG Woodside 42
WVU	FG Woodside 49
WVU	FG Woodside 24
WVU	Walczak 1 run (Woodside kick)
FLA	Faulkner 22 pass from Hewko (pass failed)

WVU	TEAM STATISTICS	FLA
19	First Downs	10
194	Rushing Yards	-30
14-23-1	Passing	11-20-2
107	Passing Yards	135
301	Total Yards	105
5-33.0	Punts - Average	6-40.0
1-0	Fumbles - Lost	6-4
4-17	Penalties - Yards	4-39

INDIVIDUAL LEADERS

RUSHING
WVU: Cornwell 26-97; Beck 8-37.
FLA: Jones 9-25.

PASSING
WVU: Luck 14-23-1, 107 yards, 1 TD.
FLA: Hewko 5-7-0, 88 yards, 1 TD.

RECEIVING
WVU: Walczak 8-75, 1 TD.
FLA: Mularkey 2-36.

December 31, 1982
Iowa 28, Tennessee 22

	1ST	2ND	3RD	4TH	FINAL
IA	0	21	7	0	28
TENN	7	0	12	3	22

SCORING SUMMARY

TENN	Cockrell 6 run (Reveiz kick)
IA	Moritz 57 pass from Long (Nichol kick)
IA	Harmon 18 pass from Long (Nichol kick)
IA	Harmon 8 pass from Long (Nichol kick)
TENN	Coleman 10 run (kick failed)
IA	Phillips 2 run (Nichol kick)
TENN	Gault 19 pass from Cockrell (pass failed)
TENN	FG Reveiz 27

IA	TEAM STATISTICS	TENN
24	First Downs	23
110	Rushing Yards	154
19-26-1	Passing	22-41-0
304	Passing Yards	221
414	Total Yards	375
5-35.0	Punts - Average	5-45.0
1-1	Fumbles - Lost	2-1
3-30	Penalties - Yards	7-47

INDIVIDUAL LEADERS

RUSHING
IA: Gill 16-70; Phillips 10-34, 1 TD.
TENN: Coleman 11-103, 1 TD; Fumas 12-52.

PASSING
IA: Long 19-26-1, 304 yards, 3 TD.
TENN: Cockrell 22-41-0, 221 yards, 1 TD.

RECEIVING
IA: Moritz 8-168, 1 TD; Harmon 3-44, 2 TD.
TENN: Wilson 7-62; Duncan 3-52.

December 28, 1983
Florida State 28, North Carolina 3

	1ST	2ND	3RD	4TH	FINAL
FSU	14	7	0	7	28
UNC	0	0	0	3	3

SCORING SUMMARY

FSU	Thompson 15 pass from Thomas (Hall kick)
FSU	Thompson 18 pass from Thomas (Hall kick)
FSU	Snipes 1 run (Hall kick)
UNC	FG Barwick 36
FSU	Thomas 1 run (Hall kick)

FSU	TEAM STATISTICS	UNC
23	First Downs	16
265	Rushing Yards	32
7-13-1	Passing	18-40-0
99	Passing Yards	166
364	Total Yards	198
6-38.8	Punts - Average	6-45.2
3-0	Fumbles - Lost	4-1
6-34	Penalties - Yards	7-60
33:48	Possession Time	26:12

INDIVIDUAL LEADERS

RUSHING
FSU: Allen 17-97; Jones 20-79.
UNC: Horton 9-30.

PASSING
FSU: Thomas 7-13-1, 99 yards, 2 TD.
UNC: Stankavage 17-39-0, 150 yards.

RECEIVING
FSU: Panton 3-48; Thompson 2-33, 2 TD.
UNC: Winfield 4-55; Franklin 3-34.

December 31, 1984
Virginia 27, Purdue 24

	1ST	2ND	3RD	4TH	FINAL
UVA	7	7	7	6	27
PUR	10	14	0	0	24

SCORING SUMMARY

UVA	Petty 11 run (Stadlin kick)
PUR	FG Rendina 24
PUR	Griffin 23 pass from Everett (Rendina kick)
UVA	Zimmerlink 3 pass from Majkowski (Stadlin kick)
PUR	Price 17 pass from Everett (Rendina kick)
PUR	Scott 12 pass from Everett (Rendina kick)
UVA	Majkowski 1 run (Stadlin kick)
UVA	FG Stadlin 19
UVA	FG Stadlin 22

UVA	TEAM STATISTICS	PUR
24	First Downs	20
274	Rushing Yards	75
8-17-2	Passing	22-42-3
118	Passing Yards	253
392	Total Yards	328
3-34.0	Punts - Average	4-43.0
1-0	Fumbles - Lost	1-1
3-20	Penalties - Yards	5-45
36:34	Possession Time	23:26

INDIVIDUAL LEADERS

RUSHING
UVA: Petty 21-114, 1 TD; Word 17-86.
PUR: Carter 8-33; King 6-29.

PASSING
UVA: Majkowski 8-17-2, 118 yards, 1 TD.
PUR: Everett 22-42-3, 253 yards, 3 TD.

RECEIVING
UVA: Zimmerlink 3-35, 1 TD; Merrick 2-32.
PUR: Griffin 4-69, 1 TD; Scott 4-50, 1 TD.

December 31, 1985
Army 31, Illinois 29

	1ST	2ND	3RD	4TH	FINAL
ARMY	7	14	7	3	31
ILL	3	13	7	6	29

SCORING SUMMARY

ARMY	Healy 22 run (Stopa kick)
ILL	FG White 45
ILL	Boso 1 pass from Trudeau (White kick)
ARMY	Black 1 run (Stopa kick)
ARMY	White 33 pass from Lampley (Stopa kick)
ILL	Williams 15 pass from Trudeau (pass failed)
ILL	Wilson 1 run (White kick)
ARMY	Spellmon 26 pass from Jones (Stopa kick)
ARMY	FG Stopa 39
ILL	Williams 54 pass from Trudeau (pass failed)

ARMY	TEAM STATISTICS	ILL
20	First Downs	26
291	Rushing Yards	77
5-7-1	Passing	38-55-2
94	Passing Yards	401
385	Total Yards	478
5-36.0	Punts - Average	3-45.0
0-0	Fumbles - Lost	2-2
3-35	Penalties - Yards	8-67
30:14	Possession Time	29:46

INDIVIDUAL LEADERS

RUSHING
ARMY: Healy 23-107, 1 TD; Lampley 16-76.
ILL: Rooks 10-35; Wilson 8-31, 1 TD.

PASSING
ARMY: Healy 3-6-1, 35 yards.
ILL: Trudeau 38-55-2, 401 yards, 3 TD.

RECEIVING
ARMY: Spellmon 2-43, 1 TD.
ILL: Williams 7-109, 2 TD; Pierce 6-92.

December 31, 1986
Virginia Tech 25, NC State 24

	1ST	2ND	3RD	4TH	FINAL
VT	10	0	6	9	25
NCST	7	14	0	3	24

SCORING SUMMARY

VT	Hunter 1 run (Kinzer kick)
NCST	Bulluck blocked punt recovered (Cofer kick)
VT	FG Kinzer 46
NCST	Worthen 25 pass from Kramer (Cofer kick)
NCST	Britt 5 pass from Kramer (Cofer kick)
VT	Williams 1 run (pass failed)
VT	Johnson 6 pass from Chapman (run failed)
NCST	FG Cofer 33
VT	FG Kinzer 40

VT	TEAM STATISTICS	NCST
29	First Downs	16
287	Rushing Yards	132
20-30-2	Passing	12-19-0
200	Passing Yards	155
487	Total Yards	287
2-34.0	Punts - Average	5-42.0
1-1	Fumbles - Lost	2-2
5-51	Penalties - Yards	3-25
36:06	Possession Time	23:54

INDIVIDUAL LEADERS

RUSHING
VT: Williams 16-129, 1 TD; Hunter 22-113, 1 TD.
NCST: Crite 14-101; Crumpler 9-21.

PASSING
VT: Chapman 20-30-2, 200 yards, 1 TD.
NCST: Kramer 12-19-0, 155 yards, 2 TD.

RECEIVING
VT: Johnson 6-54, 1 TD; Williams 4-39.
NCST: Worthen 5-70, 1 TD; Jeffires 3-44.

THE BOWLS

JANUARY 2, 1988
TENNESSEE 27, INDIANA 22

	1ST	2ND	3RD	4TH	FINAL
TENN	14	7	0	6	27
IU	3	7	6	6	22

SCORING SUMMARY

TENN	Cobb 6 run (Reich kick)
IU	FG Stoyanovich 52
TENN	Miller 45 pass from Francis (Reich kick)
TENN	Cleveland 15 pass from Francis (Reich kick)
IU	Jones 43 pass from Schnell (Stoyanovich kick)
IU	Thompson 12 run (pass failed)
IU	Jorden 12 run (pass failed)
TENN	Cobb 9 run (pass failed)

TENN	TEAM STATISTICS	IU
26	First Downs	16
244	Rushing Yards	96
21-27-0	Passing	18-33-2
230	Passing Yards	218
474	Total Yards	314
2-36.0	Punts - Average	6-30.0
2-2	Fumbles - Lost	0-0
5-35	Penalties - Yards	4-37
33:19	Possession Time	26:41

INDIVIDUAL LEADERS

RUSHING
TENN: Cobb 21-146, 2 TD; Davis 9-51.
IU: Thompson 18-67, 1 TD.

PASSING
TENN: Francis 20-26-0, 225 yards, 2 TD.
IU: Schnell 18-33-2, 218 yards, 1 TD.

RECEIVING
TENN: Miller 5-78, 1 TD; Woods 4-43.
IU: Jones 7-150, 1 TD; Thompson 6-28.

DECEMBER 31, 1988
NC STATE 28, IOWA 23

	1ST	2ND	3RD	4TH	FINAL
NCST	7	21	0	0	28
IA	3	7	7	6	23

SCORING SUMMARY

NCST	Davenport 1 run (Hartman kick)
IA	FG Murphy 30
NCST	Peebles 75 pass from Montgomery (Hartman kick)
NCST	Jackson 2 run (Hartman kick)
NCST	Jackson 30 run (Hartman kick)
IA	Harberts 8 pass from Hartlieb (Murphy kick)
IA	Harberts 22 pass from Hartlieb (Murphy kick)
IA	S. Smith 7 pass from Hartlieb (pass failed)

NCST	TEAM STATISTICS	IA
24	First Downs	21
236	Rushing Yards	19
11-23-2	Passing	30-51-4
195	Passing Yards	428
431	Total Yards	447
8-5	Fumbles - Lost	4-3
4-40	Penalties - Yards	4-44
5-36.0	Possession Time	6-36.3

INDIVIDUAL LEADERS

RUSHING
NCST: Jackson 17-86, 2 TD.
IA: Saunders 6-22.

PASSING
NCST: Montgomery 7-10-1, 152 yards, 1 TD.
IA: Hartlieb 30-51-4, 428 yards, 3 TD.

RECEIVING
NCST: Peebles 2-91, 1 TD.
IA: Cook 8-122; Harberts 6-101, 2 TD.

DECEMBER 30, 1989
SYRACUSE 19, GEORGIA 18

	1ST	2ND	3RD	4TH	FINAL
SYR	7	0	3	9	19
UGA	7	3	8	0	18

SCORING SUMMARY

UGA	Warner 5 pass from Talley (Kasay kick)
SYR	Owens 1 run (Biskup kick)
UGA	FG Kasay 20
UGA	Safety
UGA	Hampton 4 pass from Talley (pass failed)
SYR	FG Biskup 32
SYR	Moore 19 pass from McDonald (pass failed)

SYR	TEAM STATISTICS	UGA
27	First Downs	12
245	Rushing Yards	113
22-34-3	Passing	10-19-1
224	Passing Yards	88
469	Total Yards	201
3-41.0	Punts - Average	7-41.0
3-1	Fumbles - Lost	1-0
2-10	Penalties - Yards	3-30

INDIVIDUAL LEADERS

RUSHING
SYR: Owens 14-112, 1 TD.
UGA: Hampton 14-32.

PASSING
SYR: Scharr 12-21-3, 100 yards; McDonald 10-13-0, 135 yards, 1 TD.
UGA: Talley 8-14-1, 93 yards, 2 TD.

RECEIVING
SYR: Hampton 7-62, 1 TD.
UGA: Owens 5-62; Moore 4-60, 1 TD.

DECEMBER 29, 1990
AUBURN 27, INDIANA 23

	1ST	2ND	3RD	4TH	FINAL
AUB	7	10	3	7	27
IND	7	3	0	13	23

SCORING SUMMARY

AUB	White 6 run (Von Wyl kick)
IND	Green 3 run (Bonnell kick)
AUB	Smith 11 pass from White (Von Wyl kick)
IND	FG Bonnell 42
AUB	FG Von Wyl 26
AUB	FG Von Wyl 43
IND	Green 2 run (run failed)
IND	Green 11 run (Bonnell kick)
AUB	White 1 run (Von Wyl kick)

AUB	TEAM STATISTICS	IND
24	First Downs	15
89	Rushing Yards	121
31-48-0	Passing	10-19-0
351	Passing Yards	99
440	Total Yards	220
3-23.0	Punts - Average	5-41.4
2-2	Fumbles - Lost	1-1
12-75	Penalties - Yards	6-55
28:09	Possession Time	31:51

INDIVIDUAL LEADERS

RUSHING
AUB: Williams 12-52; Smith 5-24.
IND: Dunbar 21-81.

PASSING
AUB: White 31-48-0, 351 yards, 1 TD.
IND: Green 10-19-0, 99 yards.

RECEIVING
AUB: Casey 7-159; Hall 9-74.
IND: Thomas 3-43; Turner 3-26.

JANUARY 1, 1992
EAST CAROLINA 37, NC STATE 34

	1ST	2ND	3RD	4TH	FINAL
ECU	7	10	0	20	37
NCST	7	7	13	7	34

SCORING SUMMARY

NCST	Downs 2 run (Hartman kick)
ECU	Van Buren 5 pass from Blake (Brenner kick)
NCST	Harrison 4 pass from Jordan (Hartman kick)
ECU	FG Brenner 27
ECU	Gallimore 55 pass from Blake (Brenner kick)
NCST	Hinton 14 pass from Jordan (Hartman kick)
NCST	Manior 1 run (kick blocked)
NCST	Davenport 52 pass from George (Hartman kick)
ECU	Blake 2 run (Brenner kick)
ECU	Johnson 17 pass from Blake (run failed)
ECU	Fisher 22 pass from Blake (Brenner kick)

ECU	TEAM STATISTICS	NCST
24	First Downs	20
42	Rushing Yards	186
31-51-3	Passing	16-24-1
378	Passing Yards	197
420	Total Yards	383
4-41.5	Punts - Average	8-35.8
4-1	Fumbles - Lost	1-1
8-45	Penalties - Yards	5-34
23:53	Possession Time	36:07

INDIVIDUAL LEADERS

RUSHING
ECU: Van Buren 11-65.
NCST: Barbour 23-90; Downs 10-63, 1 TD.

PASSING
ECU: Blake 31-51-3, 378 yards, 4 TD.
NCST: Jordan 15-23-1, 145 yards, 2 TD.

RECEIVING
ECU: Fisher 12-144, 1 TD; Gallimore 5-113, 1 TD.
NCST: Davenport 6-118, 1 TD; Hinton 2-37, 1 TD.

JANUARY 2, 1993
NORTH CAROLINA 21, MISSISSIPPI STATE 17

	1ST	2ND	3RD	4TH	FINAL
UNC	0	0	14	7	21
MSU	14	0	0	3	17

SCORING SUMMARY

MSU	Truitt 2 pass from Plump (Gardner kick)
MSU	Roberts 22 run (Gardner kick)
UNC	Means 1 run (Pignetti kick)
UNC	Walker 24 blocked punt return (Pignetti kick)
UNC	Baskerville 44 interception return (Pignetti kick)
MSU	FG Gardner 46

UNC	TEAM STATISTICS	MSU
13	First Downs	24
149	Rushing Yards	144
7-17-2	Passing	25-45-2
106	Passing Yards	296
255	Total Yards	440
6-38.2	Punts - Average	3-36.7
1-1	Fumbles - Lost	1-0
4-36	Penalties - Yards	9-87
25:27	Possession Time	34:33

INDIVIDUAL LEADERS

RUSHING
UNC: Means 21-128, 1 TD.
MSU: Roberts 9-64, 1 TD; Davis 10-32.

PASSING
UNC: Thomas 7-16-2, 106 yards.
MSU: Plump 24-40-2, 287 yards, 1 TD.

RECEIVING
UNC: Brooks 2-60; Jerry 2-20.
MSU: Harris 8-127; Roberts 5-49.

CLEMSON 14, KENTUCKY 13

	1ST	2ND	3RD	4TH	FINAL
CLEM	7	0	0	7	14
UK	0	3	0	10	13

SCORING SUMMARY
CLEM	Smith 1 run (Welch kick)
UK	FG Nickles 34
UK	Chatman 5 pass from Jones (Nickles kick)
UK	FG Nickles 26
CLEM	T. Smith 21 pass from Sapp (Welch kick)

CLEM	TEAM STATISTICS	UK
14	First Downs	20
119	Rushing Yards	139
8-16-3	Passing	16-32-0
129	Passing Yards	154
248	Total Yards	293
6-38.8	Punts - Average	5-40.6
1-0	Fumbles - Lost	2-2
10-75	Penalties - Yards	4-35
31:09	Possession Time	28:51

INDIVIDUAL LEADERS
RUSHING
CLEM: Blunt 15-59; Smith 8-45, 1 TD.
UK: Williams 13-58; Hood 8-36.
PASSING
CLEM: Sapp 5-9-1, 109 yards, 1 TD.
UK: Jones 16-32-0, 154 yards, 1 TD.
RECEIVING
CLEM: E. Smith 1-57; T. Smith 4-56, 1 TD.
UK: Calvert 2-32; Wyatt 4-28.

NC STATE 28, MISSISSIPPI STATE 24

	1ST	2ND	3RD	4TH	FINAL
NCST	7	6	8	7	28
MSU	6	7	8	3	24

SCORING SUMMARY
MSU	FG Rogers 37
NCST	Stephens 2 run (Videtich kick)
MSU	FG Rogers 21
NCST	FG Videtich 45
MSU	Davis 11 run (Rogers kick)
NCST	FG Videtich 36
MSU	Safety
MSU	FG Rogers 29
MSU	FG Rogers 36
NCST	Dickerson 3 pass from Harvey (Harvey run)
NCST	King 11 run (Videtich kick)
MSU	FG Rogers 30

NCST	TEAM STATISTICS	MSU
20	First Downs	16
172	Rushing Yards	117
14-25-1	Passing	14-29-0
164	Passing Yards	185
336	Total Yards	302
3-48.0	Punts - Average	3-53.0
2-1	Fumbles - Lost	0-0
2-15	Penalties - Yards	6-53
33:11	Possession Time	26:49

INDIVIDUAL LEADERS
RUSHING
NCST: Stephens 21-105, 1 TD; King 6-38, 1 TD.
MSU: Davis 13-51, 1 TD; Bouie 12-51.
PASSING
NCST: Harvey 11-18-0, 139 yards, 1 TD.
MSU: Taite 13-28-0, 141 yards.
RECEIVING
NCST: Grissett 2-68; Dickerson 3-31, 1 TD.
MSU: McGee 2-62; Jones 3-39.

VIRGINIA 34, GEORGIA 27

	1ST	2ND	3RD	4TH	FINAL
UVA	14	10	3	7	34
UGA	3	11	3	10	27

SCORING SUMMARY
UVA	Barber 1 run (Garcia kick)
UVA	Brooks 5 run (Garcia kick)
UGA	FG 36 Parkman
UGA	FG 37 Parkman
UVA	FG 36 Garcia
UVA	Allen 82 pass from Groh (Garcia kick)
UGA	Ward 1 run (Hunter run)
UGA	FG 20 Parkman
UVA	FG 36 Parkman
UGA	FG 42 Parkman
UGA	Fergerson 10 fumble return (Parkman kick)
UVA	Allen 83 kickoff return (Garcia kick)

UVA	TEAM STATISTICS	UGA
10	First Downs	20
100	Rushing Yards	112
10-20-1	Passing	31-59-2
156	Passing Yards	413
256	Total Yards	525
8-42.4	Punts - Average	5-33.0
4-2	Fumbles - Lost	1-1
3-30	Penalties - Yards	6-40
25:35	Possession Time	34:25

INDIVIDUAL LEADERS
RUSHING
UVA: Barber 20-103, 1 TD; Brooks 7-23, 1 TD.
UGA: Ward 9-56, 1 TD; Kirtsey 16-43.
PASSING
UVA: Groh 10-20-1, 156 yards, 1 TD.
UGA: Ward 31-59-2, 413 yards.
RECEIVING
UVA: Allen 5-111, 1 TD; Jeffers 4-47.
UGA: Bowie 10-156; Hunter 7-67; Allen 4-48.

LSU 10, CLEMSON 7

	1ST	2ND	3RD	4TH	FINAL
LSU	0	10	0	0	10
CLEM	7	0	0	0	7

SCORING SUMMARY
CLEM	Greene 5 run (Padgett kick)
LSU	Faulk 3 run (Richey kick)
LSU	FG Richey 22

LSU	TEAM STATISTICS	CLEM
17	First Downs	12
124	Rushing Yards	192
14-21-0	Passing	6-20-0
163	Passing Yards	66
287	Total Yards	258
7-42.3	Punts - Average	10-38.2
3-1	Fumbles - Lost	3-2
7-43	Penalties - Yards	7-69
30:15	Possession Time	29:45

INDIVIDUAL LEADERS
RUSHING
LSU: Faulk 23-64, 1 TD; Tyler 12-38.
CLEM: Priester 25-151; Smith 9-40.
PASSING
LSU: Tyler 14-21-0, 163 yards.
CLEM: Greene 6-20-0, 66 yards.
RECEIVING
LSU: LaFleur 4-63; Savoie 2-40.
CLEM: Smith 2-25; Woods 1-22.

AUBURN 21, CLEMSON 17

	1ST	2ND	3RD	4TH	FINAL
AUB	3	3	0	15	21
CLEM	0	7	10	0	17

SCORING SUMMARY
AUB	FG Holmes 52
CLEM	Speck 18 block punt return (Richardson kick)
AUB	FG Holmes 24
CLEM	Witherspoon 2 run (Richardson kick)
CLEM	FG Richardson 48
AUB	Craig 22 run (pass failed)
AUB	Williams 7 run (pass failed)
AUB	FG Holmes 22

AUB	TEAM STATISTICS	CLEM
18	First Downs	4
108	Rushing Yards	60
15-45-0	Passing	11-25-1
258	Passing Yards	86
366	Total Yards	146
6-25.8	Punts - Average	9-43.7
1-1	Fumbles - Lost	1-0
7-63	Penalties - Yards	5-59
32:01	Possession Time	27:59

INDIVIDUAL LEADERS
RUSHING
AUB: Willliams 18-71, 1 TD; Craig 9-26, 1 TD.
CLEM: Priester 19-62.
PASSING
AUB: Craig 15-45-0, 258 yards.
CLEM: Greene 11-25-1, 86 yards.
RECEIVING
AUB: Bailey 4-119; Goodson 4-64.
CLEM: Austin 3-32; Gardner 1-27.

GEORGIA 35, VIRGINIA 33

	1ST	2ND	3RD	4TH	FINAL
UGA	0	7	14	14	35
UVA	0	21	6	6	33

SCORING SUMMARY
UVA	Southern 2 run (Braverman kick)
UVA	Wilkins 43 pass from Brooks (Braverman kick)
UVA	Jones 24 pass from Brooks (Braverman kick)
UGA	Small 11 pass from Carter (Hines kick)
UGA	Bailey 14 pass from Carter (Hines kick)
UGA	Gary 15 run (Hines kick)
UVA	Wilkins 67 pass from Brooks (kick failed)
UGA	Gary 2 run (Hines kick)
UGA	Carter 1 run (Hines kick)
UVA	Brooks 30 run (pass failed)

UGA	TEAM STATISTICS	UVA
19	First Downs	21
159	Rushing Yards	198
18-33-3	Passing	13-35-1
222	Passing Yards	236
381	Total Yards	434
0-0	Fumbles - Lost	3-1
8-74	Penalties - Yards	9-71
28:01	Possession Time	31:59

INDIVIDUAL LEADERS
RUSHING
UGA: Gary 19-110, 2 TD; Carter 14-41, 1 TD.
UVA: Jones 23-96; Brooks 14-88, 1 TD.
PASSING
UGA: Carter 18-33-3, 222 yards, 2 TD.
UVA: Brooks 12-32-1, 226 yards, 3 TD.
RECEIVING
UGA: Bailey 3-73, 1 TD; Greer 2-60.
UVA: Wilkins 6-161, 2 TD; Jones 4-46, 1 TD.

December 30, 1999
Mississippi State 17, Clemson 7

	1ST	2ND	3RD	4TH	FINAL
MSU	0	0	3	14	17
CLEM	0	0	0	7	7

SCORING SUMMARY
MSU FG Westerfield 39
MSU Madkin 2 run (Westerfield kick)
CLEM Streeter 1 run (Lazzara kick)
MSU Walker 15 pass from Madkin (Westerfield kick)

MSU	TEAM STATISTICS	CLEM
16	First Downs	24
89	Rushing Yards	85
17-38-0	Passing	25-56-5
176	Passing Yards	306
265	Total Yards	391
2-1	Fumbles - Lost	1-1
21-188	Penalties - Yards	8-82
30:41	Possession Time	29:19

INDIVIDUAL LEADERS
RUSHING
MSU: Madkin 5-37, 1 TD; Miller 10-24.
CLEM: Rambert 18-70.
PASSING
MSU: Madkin 17-38-0, 176 yards, 1 TD.
CLEM: Streeter 24-50-4, 301 yards.
RECEIVING
MSU: Miller 3-54, Sirmones 2-21.
CLEM: Wofford 6-147; Gardner 7-75.

December 29, 2000
LSU 28, Georgia Tech 14

	1ST	2ND	3RD	4TH	FINAL
LSU	3	0	6	19	28
GT	7	7	0	0	14

SCORING SUMMARY
LSU FG Corbello 32
GT Burns 32 run (Manget kick)
GT Hatch 9 run (Manget kick)
LSU Banks 3 pass from Davey (Corbello kick)
LSU Reed 9 pass from Davey (Reed pass from Davey)
LSU FG Corbello 49
LSU Banks 3 pass from Davey (Robinson pass from Davey)

LSU	TEAM STATISTICS	GT
21	First Downs	19
90	Rushing Yards	140
25-44-0	Passing	19-38-2
284	Passing Yards	177
374	Total Yards	317
8-40.8	Punts - Average	5-48.2
3-1	Fumbles - Lost	7-4
7-59	Penalties - Yards	6-45
37:10	Possession Time	22:50

INDIVIDUAL LEADERS
RUSHING
LSU: Toefield 22-78; Davis 8-25.
GT: Burns 17-96, 1 TD; Hatch 6-45, 1 TD.
PASSING
LSU: Davey 17-25-0, 174 yards, 3 TD; Booty 8-19-0, 110 yards.
GT: Godsey 19-36-2, 177 yards.
RECEIVING
LSU: Reed 9-96, 1 TD; Banks 7-71, 2 TD.
GT: Watkins 3-45; Campbell 5-31.

December 31, 2001
North Carolina 16, Auburn 10

	1ST	2ND	3RD	4TH	FINAL
UNC	7	3	6	0	16
AUB	0	0	0	10	10

SCORING SUMMARY
UNC Parker 10 run (Reed kick)
UNC FG Reed 22
UNC Curry 62 run (kick failed)
AUB FG Duval 34
AUB Diamond 12 pass from Cobb (Duval kick)

UNC	TEAM STATISTICS	AUB
12	First Downs	12
174	Rushing Yards	31
13-21-1	Passing	18-28-2
114	Passing Yards	145
288	Total Yards	176
8-39.8	Punts - Average	9-49.3
2-1	Fumbles - Lost	5-1
9-73	Penalties - Yards	4-26
32:02	Possession Time	27:58

INDIVIDUAL LEADERS
RUSHING
UNC: Parker 19-131, 1 TD; Curry 10-67, 1 TD.
AUB: Brown 6-28; Butler 8-22.
PASSING
UNC: Durant 7-14-1-76 yards; Curry 5-6-0-25 yards.
AUB: Campbell 12-18-1-74 yards; Cobb 6-10-1, 71 yards, 1 TD.
RECEIVING
UNC: Aiken 7-73; Parker 3-24.
AUB: Daniels 3-21; Carter 1-21.

December 31, 2002
Maryland 30, Tennessee 3

	1ST	2ND	3RD	4TH	FINAL
MARY	7	10	3	10	30
TENN	0	3	0	0	3

SCORING SUMMARY
MARY McBrien 1 run (Novak kick)
MARY Cox 54 interception return (Novak kick)
TENN FG Walls 38
MARY FG Novak 48
MARY FG Novak 44
MARY McBrien 6 run (Novak kick)
TENN FG Novak 25

MARY	TEAM STATISTICS	TENN
17	First Downs	18
154	Rushing Yards	45
11-19-0	Passing	23-37-1
120	Passing Yards	242
274	Total Yards	287
3-50.3	Punts - Average	6-47.7
2-1	Fumbles - Lost	1-1
2-10	Penalties - Yards	8-68

INDIVIDUAL LEADERS
RUSHING
MARY: Perry 15-50.
TENN: Houston 9-34.
PASSING
MARY: McBrien 11-19-0, 120 yards.
TENN: Clausen 23-37-1, 242 yards.
RECEIVING
MARY: Harrison 4-74.
TENN: Brown 5-75.

January 2, 2004
Clemson 27, Tennessee 14

	1ST	2ND	3RD	4TH	FINAL
CLEM	10	14	0	3	27
TENN	7	7	0	0	14

SCORING SUMMARY
CLEM Coleman 8 run (Hunt kick)
CLEM FG Hunt 23
TENN Hannon 19 pass from Clausen (Wilhoit kick)
CLEM Jasmin 15 run (Hunt kick)
TENN Jones 30 pass from Clausen (Wilhoit kick)
CLEM Browning 8 run (Hunt kick)
CLEM FG Hunt 28

CLEM	TEAM STATISTICS	TENN
25	First Downs	28
153	Rushing Yards	38
22-40-1	Passing	31-56-0
246	Passing Yards	384
399	Total Yards	422
4-67	Punt Returns - Yards	1-5
0-0	Kickoff Returns - Yards	2-46
5-42.0	Punts - Average	8-38.5
1-0	Fumbles - Lost	1-1
6-45	Penalties - Yards	10-119
27:51	Possession Time	32:09

INDIVIDUAL LEADERS
RUSHING
CLEM: Jasmin 15-130, 1 TD; Hamilton 4-23.
TENN: Houston 6-24; Riggs 2-10.
PASSING
CLEM: Whitehurst 22-40-1, 246 yards.
TENN: Clausen 31-55-0, 384 yards, 2 TD.
RECEIVING
CLEM: Hamilton 5-69; Youngblood 3-64.
TENN: Jones 5-66, 1 TD; Hannon 4-57, 1 TD.

December 31, 2004
Miami (Fla.) 27, Florida 10

	1ST	2ND	3RD	4TH	FINAL
MIA	7	10	7	3	27
UF	0	3	7	0	10

SCORING SUMMARY
MIA Hester 78 blocked field goal (Peattie kick)
UF FG Leach 34
MIA FG Peattie 47
MIA Parrish 72 punt return (Peattie kick)
MIA Moore 20 pass from Berlin (Peattie kick)
UF Cornelius 45 pass from Leak (Leach kick)
MIA FG Peattie 32

MIA	TEAM STATISTICS	UF
16	First Downs	22
106	Rushing Yards	144
13-24-1	Passing	19-39-2
171	Passing Yards	262
277	Total Yards	406
4-81	Punt Returns - Yards	2-17
2-31	Kickoff Returns - Yards	2-34
6-33.3	Punts - Average	7-40.9
2-1	Fumbles - Lost	1-0
4-30	Penalties - Yards	8-74
28:51	Possession Time	31:09

INDIVIDUAL LEADERS
RUSHING
MIA: Gore 25-80; Moss 4-18.
UF: Fason 17-94; Leak 14-38.
PASSING
MIA: Berlin 13-24-1, 171 yards, 1 TD,
UF: Leak 19-39-2, 262 yards, 1 TD.
RECEIVING
MIA: Parrish 4-63; Leggett 2-41.
UF: Small 8-92; Cornelius 1-45, 1 TD.

FIESTA BOWL

SEASON	DATE	PRE-GAME RANK	TEAMS	SCORE	FINAL RANK	MOST VALUABLE PLAYERS	ATT.
1971	Dec. 27, 1971	8	Arizona State	45	8	Gary Huff, Florida State, QB	51,098
			Florida State	38		Junior Ah You, Arizona State, DE	
1972	Dec. 23, 1972	15	Arizona State	49	13	Woody Green, Arizona State, HB	51,318
			Missouri	35		Mike Fink, Missouri, DB	
1973	Dec. 21, 1973	10	Arizona State	28	9T	Greg Hudson, Arizona State, SE	50,878
			Pittsburgh	7		Mike Haynes, Arizona State, CB	
1974	Dec. 28, 1974		Oklahoma State	16		Kenny Walker, Oklahoma State, RB	50,879
			BYU	6		Phil Dokes, Oklahoma State, DT	
1975	Dec. 26, 1975	7	Arizona State	17	2	John Jefferson, Arizona State, WR	51,396
		6	Nebraska	14	9	Larry Gordon, Arizona State, LB	
1976	Dec. 25, 1976	8	Oklahoma	41	5	Thomas Lott, Oklahoma QB	48,174
			Wyoming	7		Terry Peters, Oklahoma, CB	
1977	Dec. 25, 1977	8	Penn State	42	5	Matt Millen, Penn State, LB	57,727
		15	Arizona State	30	18	Dennis Sproul, Arizona State, QB	
1978	Dec. 25, 1978	8	Arkansas	10	11	James Owens, UCLA, RB	55,227
		15	UCLA	10	14	Jimmy Walker, Arkansas, DT	
1979	Dec. 25, 1979	10	Pittsburgh	16	7	Mark Schubert, Pittsburgh, K	55,347
			Arizona	10		Dave Liggins, Arizona, S	
1980	Dec. 26, 1980	10	Penn State	31	8	Curt Warner, Penn State, RB	66,738
		11	Ohio State	19	15	Frank Case, Penn State, DE	
1981	Jan. 1, 1982	7	Penn State	26	3	Curt Warner, Penn State, RB	71,053
		8	Southern Cal	10	14	Leo Wisniewski, Penn State, NT	
1982	Jan. 1, 1983	11	Arizona State	32	6	Marcus Dupree, Oklahoma, RB	70,553
		12	Oklahoma	21	16	Jim Jeffcoat, Arizona State, DL	
1983	Jan. 2, 1984	14	Ohio State	28	9	John Congemi, Pittsburgh, QB	66,484
		15	Pittsburgh	23	18	Rowland Tatum, Ohio State, LB	
1984	Jan. 1, 1985	14	UCLA	39	9	Gaston Green, UCLA, TB	60,310
		13	Miami (Fla.)	37	18	James Washington, UCLA, DB	
1985	Jan. 1, 1986	5	Michigan	27	2	Jamie Morris, Michigan, RB	72,454
		7	Nebraska	23	11	Mark Messner, Michigan, DT	
1986	Jan. 2, 1987	2	Penn State	14	1	D.J. Dozier, Penn State, RB	73,098
		1	Miami (Fla.)	10	2	Shane Conlan, Penn State, LB	
1987	Jan. 1, 1988	3	Florida State	31	2	Danny McManus, Florida State, QB	72,112
		5	Nebraska	28	6	Neil Smith, Nebraska, DL	
1988	Jan. 2, 1989	1	Notre Dame	34	1	Tony Rice, Notre Dame, QB	74,911
		3	West Virginia	21	5	Frank Stams, Notre Dame, DE	
1989	Jan. 1, 1990	5	Florida State	41	3	Peter Tom Willis, Florida State, QB	73,953
		6	Nebraska	17	11	Odell Haggins, Florida State, NG	
1990	Jan. 1, 1991	18	Louisville	34	14	Browning Nagle, Louisville, QB	69,098
		25	Alabama	7		Ray Buchanan, Louisville, FS	
1991	Jan. 1, 1992	6	Penn State	42	3	O.J. McDuffie, Penn State, WR	71,133
		10	Tennessee	17	14	Reggie Givens, Penn State, OLB	
1992	Jan. 1, 1993	6	Syracuse	26	6	Marvin Graves, Syracuse, QB	70,224
		10	Colorado	22	13	Kevin Mitchell, Syracuse, NG	
1993	Jan. 1, 1994	16	Arizona	29	10	Chuck Levy, Arizona, RB	72,260
		10	Miami (Fla.)	0	15	Tedy Bruschi, Arizona, DE	
1994	Jan. 2, 1995	4	Colorado	41	3	Kordell Stewart, Colorado, QB	73,968
			Notre Dame	24		Shannon Clavelle, Colorado, DT	
1995	Jan. 2, 1996	1	Nebraska	62	1	Tommie Frazier, Nebraska, QB	79,864
		2	Florida	24	2	Michael Booker, Nebraska, CB	
1996	Jan. 1, 1997	7	Penn State	38	7	Curtis Enis, Penn State, TB	65,106
		20	Texas	15	23	Brandon Noble, Penn State, DT	
1997	Dec. 31, 1997	10	Kansas State	35	8	Michael Bishop, Kansas State, QB	69,336
		14	Syracuse	18	21	Travis Ochs, Kansas State, LB	
1998	Jan. 4, 1999	1	Tennessee	23	1	Peerless Price, Tennessee, WR	80,470
		2	Florida State	16	3	Dwayne Goodrich, Tennessee, CB	
1999	Jan. 2, 2000	3	Nebraska	31	3	Eric Crouch, Nebraska, QB	71,526
		6	Tennessee	21	9	Mike Brown, Nebraska, DB	
2000	Jan. 1, 2001	5	Oregon State	41	4	Jonathan Smith, Oregon State, QB	75,428
		10	Notre Dame	9	15	Darnell Robinson, Oregon State, LB	
2001	Jan. 1, 2002	2	Oregon	38	2	Joey Harrington, Oregon, QB	74,118
		3	Colorado	16	9	Steve Smith, Oregon, DB	
2002	Jan. 3, 2003	2	Ohio State	31	2OT 1	Craig Krenzel, Ohio State, QB	77,502
		1	Miami (Fla.)	24	2	Mike Doss, Ohio State, DB	
2003	Jan. 2, 2004	7	Ohio State	35	4	Craig Krenzel, Ohio State, QB	73,425
		8	Kansas State	28	14	A.J. Hawk, Ohio State, CB	
2004	Jan. 1, 2005	5	Utah	35	4	Alex Smith, QB, Paris Warren, WR, Utah	73,519
		19	Pittsburgh	7	25	Steve Fifita, Utah, NG	

December 27, 1971
Arizona State 45, Florida State 38

	1ST	2ND	3RD	4TH	FINAL
ASU	7	14	10	14	45
FSU	10	18	0	10	38

SCORING SUMMARY
ASU	Demery 21 pass from White (Eckstrand kick)
FSU	Magalski 1 run (Fontes kick)
FSU	FG Fontes 30
ASU	Green 1 run (Eckstrand kick)
FSU	FG Fontes 25
FSU	Dawson 14 pass from Gaydos (Dawson pass from Huff)
ASU	Holden 54 pass from White (Eckstrand kick)
FSU	Dawson 10 pass from Huff (Fontes kick)
ASU	FG Eckstrand 34
ASU	Green 2 run (Eckstrand kick)
FSU	FG Fontes 42
ASU	Holden 58 punt return (Eckstrand kick)
FSU	Dawson 25 pass from Huff (Fontes kick)
ASU	Green 2 run (Eckstrand kick)

ASU	TEAM STATISTICS	FSU
26	First Downs	20
200	Rushing Yards	72
15-30-0	Passing	26-47-2
250	Passing Yards	361
450	Total Yards	433
6-37.0	Punts - Average	7-42.2
5-2	Fumbles - Lost	2-0
4-37	Penalties - Yards	8-91

INDIVIDUAL LEADERS
RUSHING
ASU: Green 24-101, 3 TD; Malone 17-60.
FSU: Jarrett 8-48; Magalski 17-42, 1 TD.
PASSING
ASU: White 15-30-0, 250 yards, 2 TD.
FSU: Huff 25-46-2, 347 yards, 2 TD.
RECEIVING
ASU: Demery 4-55, 1 TD; Holden 2-66, 1 TD.
FSU: Smith 8-143; Dawson 8-108, 3 TD; Gaydos 5-101.

December 23, 1972
Arizona State 49, Missouri 35

	1ST	2ND	3RD	4TH	FINAL
ASU	14	14	0	21	49
MO	0	7	14	14	35

SCORING SUMMARY
ASU	Green 2 run (Cruz kick)
ASU	Green 12 run (Cruz kick)
MO	Johnson 1 run (Hill kick)
ASU	McClanahan 1 run (Cruz kick)
ASU	Beverly 34 pass from White (Cruz kick)
MO	Link 48 pass from Cherry (kick failed)
MO	Link 4 pass from Cherry (Link pass from Cherry)
ASU	Green 17 run (Cruz kick)
MO	Fink 100 kickoff return (Hill kick)
ASU	Beverly 53 pass from White (Cruz kick)
ASU	Green 21 run (Cruz kick)
MO	Reamon 31 run (Hill kick)

ASU	TEAM STATISTICS	MO
33	First Downs	16
452	Rushing Yards	229
13-24-3	Passing	12-27-3
266	Passing Yards	182
718	Total Yards	411
3-43.6	Punts - Average	6-37.8
2-1	Fumbles - Lost	1-0
6-50	Penalties - Yards	2-10

INDIVIDUAL LEADERS
RUSHING
ASU: Green 25-202, 4 TD; McClanahan 26-171, 1 TD.
MO: Reamon 17-155, 1 TD; Johnson 12-41, 1 TD.
PASSING
ASU: White 13-23-3, 266 yards, 2 TD.
MO: Cherry 12-27-3, 182 yards, 2 TD.
RECEIVING
ASU: Beverly 3-103, 2 TD; Petty 5-85.
MO: Link 5-80, 2 TD; Bastable 3-63.

December 21, 1973
Arizona State 28, Pittsburgh 7

	1ST	2ND	3RD	4TH	FINAL
ASU	7	0	3	18	28
PITT	7	0	0	0	7

SCORING SUMMARY
PITT	Dorsett 3 run (Long kick)
ASU	Green 3 run (Kush kick)
ASU	FG Kush 30
ASU	Hudson 38 pass from White (kick failed)
ASU	Green 23 run (kick failed)
ASU	Green 1 run (kick failed)

ASU	TEAM STATISTICS	PITT
18	First Downs	12
164	Rushing Yards	151
14-20-3	Passing	7-23-4
269	Passing Yards	57
433	Total Yards	208
5-46.0	Punts - Average	8-34.4
3-1	Fumbles - Lost	5-4
9-66	Penalties - Yards	12-84

INDIVIDUAL LEADERS
RUSHING
ASU: Green 25-131, 3 TD; Malone 15-57.
PITT: Dorsett 30-100, 1 TD; Block 2-30.
PASSING
ASU: White 14-19-3, 269 yards, 1 TD.
PITT: Daniels 7-20-3, 57 yards.
RECEIVING
ASU: Hudson 8-186, 1 TD; Owens 2-68.
PITT: Farley 1-22; Dorsett 2-7.

December 28, 1974
Oklahoma State 16, BYU 6

	1ST	2ND	3RD	4TH	FINAL
OKST	0	7	3	6	16
BYU	6	0	0	0	6

SCORING SUMMARY
BYU	FG Uselman 30
BYU	FG Uselman 43
OKST	Walker 12 run (Daigle kick)
OKST	FG Daigle 42
OKST	Bain 40 pass from Thompson (kick failed)

OKST	TEAM STATISTICS	BYU
14	First Downs	17
147	Rushing Yards	120
7-18-0	Passing	15-31-3
77	Passing Yards	181
224	Total Yards	301
7-41.9	Punts - Average	6-41.8
6-0	Fumbles - Lost	3-1
12-84	Penalties - Yards	9-66

INDIVIDUAL LEADERS
RUSHING
OKST: Walker 7-35, 1 TD; Nelms 6-32.
BYU: Blanc 19-55; Giles 10-33.
PASSING
OKST: Weatherbie 4-13-0, 21 yards.
BYU: Giles 11-26-3, 138 yards.
RECEIVING
OKST: Bain 2-48, 1 TD; Boyer 2-12.
BYU: LaBue 3-50; Blanc 4-36.

December 26, 1975
Arizona State 17, Nebraska 14

	1ST	2ND	3RD	4TH	FINAL
ASU	3	3	0	11	17
NEB	0	7	7	0	14

SCORING SUMMARY
ASU	FG Kush 27
NEB	Anthony 1 run (Coyle kick)
ASU	FG Kush 33
NEB	Anthony 4 run (Coyle kick)
ASU	Jefferson 10 pass from Mortensen (Mucker pass from Mortensen)
ASU	FG Kush 29

ASU	TEAM STATISTICS	NEB
20	First Downs	20
162	Rushing Yards	198
15-37-2	Passing	12-23-1
173	Passing Yards	90
335	Total Yards	288
5-37.2	Punts - Average	7-39.4
0-0	Fumbles - Lost	2-2
6-54	Penalties - Yards	4-38

INDIVIDUAL LEADERS
RUSHING
ASU: Williams 18-111; Robinson 8-30.
NEB: Anthony 22-94, 2 TD; Davis 17-60.
PASSING
ASU: Sproul 14-35-1, 163 yards.
NEB: Luck 12-22-0, 90 yards.
RECEIVING
ASU: Jefferson 8-113, 1 TD; Mucker 3-39.
NEB: Thomas 6-44; Shamblin 2-13.

December 25, 1976
Oklahoma 41, Wyoming 7

	1ST	2ND	3RD	4TH	FINAL
OKLA	14	6	7	14	41
WYO	0	0	0	7	7

SCORING SUMMARY
OKLA	Peacock 3 run (Von Schamann kick)
OKLA	Ivory 4 run (Von Schamann kick)
OKLA	FG Von Schamann 32
OKLA	FG Von Schamann 50
OKLA	Peacock 15 run (Von Schamann kick)
OKLA	Cumby 4 run (Von Schamann kick)
OKLA	Shephard 8 run (Von Schamann kick)
WYO	Jones 1 run (Christopulos kick)

OKLA	TEAM STATISTICS	WYO
24	First Downs	14
415	Rushing Yards	153
3-5-0	Passing	6-19-5
23	Passing Yards	51
438	Total Yards	204
0-0.0	Punts - Average	5-25.2
6-3	Fumbles - Lost	5-1
2-20	Penalties - Yards	4-30

INDIVIDUAL LEADERS
RUSHING
OKLA: Shephard 7-85, 1 TD; Lott 13-79, Peacock 8-77, 2 TD.
WYO: Jones 14-68, 1 TD; Wright 13-46.
PASSING
OKLA: Blevins 2-3-0, 14 yards.
WYO: Clayton 5-14-4, 54 yards.
RECEIVING
OKLA: Hatcher 2-14; Hoover 1-9.
WYO: Howard 3-45; Combs 1-7.

December 25, 1977
Penn State 42, Arizona State 30

	1ST	2ND	3RD	4TH	FINAL
PSU	14	3	7	18	42
ASU	0	14	0	16	30

SCORING SUMMARY
PSU	Lally 21 blocked punt return (Bahr kick)
PSU	Torrey 3 pass from Fusina (Bahr kick)
ASU	Lane 11 pass from Sproul (Hicks kick)
PSU	FG Bahr 23
ASU	Washington 13 pass from Sproul (Hicks kick)
PSU	Geise 18 run (Bahr kick)
PSU	Suhey 3 run (Bahr kick)
ASU	Washington 30 pass from Sproul (Hicks kick)
PSU	FG Bahr 32
ASU	Perry 1 run (Hicks kick)
PSU	Suhey 3 run (Geise run)
ASU	Safety (Fitzkee tackled in end zone)

PSU	TEAM STATISTICS	ASU
18	First Downs	29
268	Rushing Yards	90
9-23-0	Passing	23-47-2
83	Passing Yards	336
351	Total Yards	426
7-40.0	Punts - Average	5-34.8
1-0	Fumbles - Lost	1-1
12-126	Penalties - Yards	5-33

INDIVIDUAL LEADERS
RUSHING
PSU: Geise 26-111, 1 TD; Torrey 9-107; Suhey 13-76, 2 TD.
ASU: Harris 20-56; Sproul 15-16.
PASSING
PSU: Fusina 9-23-0, 83 yards, 1 TD.
ASU: Sproul 23-47-2, 336 yards, 3 TD.
RECEIVING
PSU: Cefalo 3-39; Fitzkee 1-24.
ASU: DeFrance 7-123; Washington 4-76, 2 TD.

DECEMBER 25, 1978
ARKANSAS 10, UCLA 10

	1ST	2ND	3RD	4TH	FINAL
ARK	0	10	0	0	10
UCLA	0	0	3	7	10

SCORING SUMMARY
ARK   Sales 4 run (Ordonez kick)
ARK   FG Ordonez 37
UCLA   FG Boermeester 41
UCLA   Bukich 15 run (Boermeester kick)

ARK	TEAM STATISTICS	UCLA
19	First Downs	14
200	Rushing Yards	255
13-24-2	Passing	4-11-2
78	Passing Yards	61
278	Total Yards	316
8-37.3	Punts - Average	6-41.3
2-0	Fumbles - Lost	2-1
4-50	Penalties - Yards	7-67

INDIVIDUAL LEADERS
RUSHING
ARK: Cowins 24-89; Eckwood 8-44.
UCLA: Owens 17-121; Brown 11-84.
PASSING
ARK: Calcagni 11-16-0, 49 yards.
UCLA: Bukich 4-11-2, 61 yards.
RECEIVING
ARK: Farrell 2-25; Stiggers 2-33.
UCLA: Reece 2-56; McNeil 1-3.

DECEMBER 25, 1979
PITTSBURGH 16, ARIZONA 10

	1ST	2ND	3RD	4TH	FINAL
PITT	3	3	7	4	16
ARIZ	0	0	3	7	10

SCORING SUMMARY
PITT   FG Schubert 46
PITT   FG Schubert 36
ARIZ   FG Weber 38
PITT   Pryor 12 pass from Marino (Schubert kick)
PITT   FG Schubert 46
ARIZ   Oliver 1 run (Zivic kick)

PITT	TEAM STATISTICS	ARIZ
20	First Downs	20
127	Rushing Yards	91
15-29-2	Passing	18-35-3
172	Passing Yards	226
299	Total Yards	317
5-34.2	Punts - Average	4-39.8
1-0	Fumbles - Lost	2-1
10-89	Penalties - Yards	7-85

INDIVIDUAL LEADERS
RUSHING
PITT: McMillin 19-81; Jacobs 7-44.
ARIZ: Heater 13-37; Oliver 12-35, 1 TD.
PASSING
PITT: Marino 15-29-2, 172 yards, 1 TD.
ARIZ: Krohn 17-34-3, 180 yards.
RECEIVING
PITT: Dombrowski 3-61; Still 3-38.
ARIZ: Jackson 5-89; Holmes 7-84.

DECEMBER 26, 1980
PENN STATE 31, OHIO STATE 19

	1ST	2ND	3RD	4TH	FINAL
PSU	7	3	7	14	31
OSU	6	13	0	0	19

SCORING SUMMARY
PSU   Warner 64 run (Menhardt kick)
OSU   Donley 23 pass from Schlichter (kick failed)
OSU   Williams 33 pass from Schlichter (run failed)
OSU   Donley 19 pass from Schlichter (Atha kick)
PSU   FG Menhardt 38
PSU   Blackledge 3 run (Menhardt kick)
PSU   Williams 4 run (Menhardt kick)
PSU   Moore 37 run (Menhardt kick)

PSU	TEAM STATISTICS	OSU
22	First Downs	23
351	Rushing Yards	110
8-22-0	Passing	20-35-1
117	Passing Yards	302
468	Total Yards	412
5-40.8	Punts - Average	7-38.7
1-1	Fumbles - Lost	1-0
1-10	Penalties - Yards	2-30

INDIVIDUAL LEADERS
RUSHING
PSU: Warner 18-155, 1 TD; Moore 10-76, 1 TD.
OSU: Murray 10-75; Gayle 11-39.
PASSING
PSU: Blackledge 8-22-0, 117 yards.
OSU: Schlichter 20-35-1, 302 yards, 3 TD.
RECEIVING
PSU: Baugh 3-53; Scovill 3-42.
OSU: Donley 5-112, 2 TD; Williams 7-112, 1 TD.

JANUARY 1, 1982
PENN STATE 26, SOUTHERN CAL 10

	1ST	2ND	3RD	4TH	FINAL
PSU	7	10	9	0	26
USC	7	0	3	0	10

SCORING SUMMARY
PSU   Warner 17 run (Franco kick)
USC   Banks 20 interception return (Jordan kick)
PSU   Garrity 52 pass from Blackledge (Franco kick)
PSU   FG Franco 21
PSU   Warner 21 run (Franco kick)
USC   FG Jordan 37
PSU   Safety

PSU	TEAM STATISTICS	USC
20	First Downs	19
218	Rushing Yards	60
11-24-2	Passing	16-32-3
175	Passing Yards	202
393	Total Yards	262
4-50.8	Punts - Average	5-40.2
3-2	Fumbles - Lost	3-2
7-70	Penalties - Yards	7-49

INDIVIDUAL LEADERS
RUSHING
PSU: Warner 26-145, 2 TD; Meade 9-60.
USC: Allen 30-85; Spencer 3-16.
PASSING
PSU: Blackledge 11-24-2, 175 yards, 1 TD.
USC: Mazur 11-23-2, 123 yards.
RECEIVING
PSU: Jackson 3-55; Garrity 1-52, 1 TD.
USC: Ware 4-75; Simmons 3-51.

JANUARY 1, 1983
ARIZONA STATE 32, OKLAHOMA 21

	1ST	2ND	3RD	4TH	FINAL
ASU	0	11	7	14	32
OKLA	7	6	8	0	21

SCORING SUMMARY
OKLA   Wilson 1 run (Keeling kick)
ASU   FG Zendejas 32
ASU   Safety (Phelps tackled in end zone)
ASU   FG Zendejas 22
OKLA   Wilson 1 run (run failed)
ASU   FG Zendejas 54
ASU   Clack 15 run (Zendejas kick)
OKLA   Sims 19 run (Fontenette pass from Phelps)
ASU   Moore 1 run (Zendejas kick)
ASU   Brown 52 pass from Hons (Zendejas kick)

ASU	TEAM STATISTICS	OKLA
25	First Downs	19
100	Rushing Yards	417
17-35-2	Passing	4-10-1
329	Passing Yards	40
429	Total Yards	457
6-43.5	Punts - Average	4-29.5
3-0	Fumbles - Lost	6-4
7-64	Penalties - Yards	8-68

INDIVIDUAL LEADERS
RUSHING
ASU: Moore 20-64, 1 TD; Clack 11-29, 1 TD.
OKLA: Dupree 17-242; Wilson 17-48, 2 TD.
PASSING
ASU: Hons 17-35-2, 329 yards, 1 TD.
OKLA: Phelps 4-10-1, 40 yards.
RECEIVING
ASU: Moore 3-88.
OKLA: Lewis 2-23; Winters 1-14.

JANUARY 2, 1984
OHIO STATE 28, PITTSBURGH 23

	1ST	2ND	3RD	4TH	FINAL
OSU	7	7	0	14	28
PITT	0	7	0	16	23

SCORING SUMMARY
OSU   Tomczak 3 run (Spangler kick)
PITT   Wilson 6 pass from Congemi (Everett kick)
OSU   Byars 11 run (Spangler kick)
PITT   Wilson fumble recovery in end zone (Everett kick)
OSU   Byars 99 kickoff return (Spangler kick)
PITT   Collins 11 pass from Congemi (pass failed)
PITT   FG Everett 37
OSU   Jemison 39 pass from Tomczak (Spangler kick)

OSU	TEAM STATISTICS	PITT
27	First Downs	27
184	Rushing Yards	146
15-32-1	Passing	31-46-2
226	Passing Yards	341
410	Total Yards	487
4-37.3	Punts - Average	3-39.0
3-1	Fumbles - Lost	2-1
8-70	Penalties - Yards	8-60

INDIVIDUAL LEADERS
RUSHING
OSU: Byars 15-73, 1 TD; Broadnax 6-38.
PITT: McCall 26-115; Congemi 6-20.
PASSING
OSU: Tomczak 15-32-1, 226 yards, 1 TD.
PITT: Congemi 31-44-2, 341 yards, 2 TD.
RECEIVING
OSU: Jemison 8-131, 1 TD; Frank 4-57.
PITT: Wallace 8-97; McCall 6-75; Collins 7-72, 1 TD.

JANUARY 1, 1985
UCLA 39, MIAMI (FLA.) 37

	1ST	2ND	3RD	4TH	FINAL
UCLA	7	15	7	10	39
MIA	14	7	3	13	37

SCORING SUMMARY
UCLA   Green 6 run (Lee kick)
MIA   Oliver 34 run (Cox kick)
MIA   Brown 68 punt return (Cox kick)
MIA   Blades 48 pass from Kosar (Cox kick)
UCLA   Green 72 run (Lee kick)
UCLA   Safety (Tuten tackled in end zone)
UCLA   FG Lee 51
UCLA   FG Lee 33
MIA   FG Cox 31
UCLA   Sherrard 10 pass from Bono (Lee kick)
UCLA   Young 33 pass from Bono (Lee kick)
MIA   Bratton 19 run (pass failed)
MIA   Bratton 3 pass from Kosar (Cox kick)
UCLA   FG Lee 23

UCLA	TEAM STATISTICS	MIA
20	First Downs	23
161	Rushing Yards	129
18-27-0	Passing	31-44-1
243	Passing Yards	294
404	Total Yards	423
7-37.6	Punts - Average	6-37.0
2-0	Fumbles - Lost	3-1
5-35	Penalties - Yards	10-68

INDIVIDUAL LEADERS
RUSHING
UCLA: Green 21-144, 2 TD; Wiley 8-28.
MIA: Oliver 8-75, 1 TD; Bratton 12-56, 1 TD.
PASSING
UCLA: Bono 18-27-0, 243 yards, 2 TD.
MIA: Kosar 31-44-1, 294 yards, 2 TD.
RECEIVING
UCLA: Sherrard 5-94, 1 TD; Young 4-57, 1 TD.
MIA: Blades 4-66, 1 TD; Smith 8-61.

JANUARY 1, 1986
MICHIGAN 27, NEBRASKA 23

	1ST	2ND	3RD	4TH	FINAL
MICH	3	0	24	0	27
NEB	0	14	0	9	23

SCORING SUMMARY
MICH	FG Moons 42
NEB	DuBose 5 pass from Clayton (Klein kick)
NEB	DuBose 3 run (Klein kick)
MICH	White 1 run (Moons kick)
MICH	Harbaugh 1 run (Moons kick)
MICH	FG Moons 19
MICH	Harbaugh 2 run (Moons kick)
NEB	Taylor 1 run (Klein kick)
NEB	Safety

MICH	TEAM STATISTICS	NEB
16	First Downs	20
171	Rushing Yards	304
6-16-0	Passing	6-15-1
63	Passing Yards	66
234	Total Yards	370
5-43.8	Punts - Average	3-40.3
2-0	Fumbles - Lost	6-3
8-43	Penalties - Yards	7-46

INDIVIDUAL LEADERS
RUSHING
MICH: Morris 22-156; White 13-38, 1 TD.
NEB: Dubose 17-99, 1 TD; Taylor 10-76, 1 TD; Clayton 14-68.
PASSING
MICH: Harbaugh 6-15-0, 63 yards.
NEB: Clayton 4-6-0, 51 yards, 1 TD.
RECEIVING
MICH: Kattus 3-38; Morris 2-10.
NEB: Frain 3-46; Smith 1-8.

JANUARY 2, 1987
PENN STATE 14, MIAMI (FLA.) 10

	1ST	2ND	3RD	4TH	FINAL
PSU	0	7	0	7	14
MIA	0	7	0	3	10

SCORING SUMMARY
MIA	Bratton 1 run (Cox kick)
PSU	Shaffer 4 run (Manca kick)
MIA	FG Seelig 38
PSU	Dozier 6 run (Manca kick)

PSU	TEAM STATISTICS	MIA
8	First Downs	22
109	Rushing Yards	160
5-16-1	Passing	26-50-5
53	Passing Yards	285
162	Total Yards	445
9-43.4	Punts - Average	4-46.0
5-2	Fumbles - Lost	4-2
4-39	Penalties - Yards	9-62

INDIVIDUAL LEADERS
RUSHING
PSU: Dozier 20-99, 1 TD; Manoa 8-36.
MIA: Highsmith 18-119; Bratton 11-31, 1 TD.
PASSING
PSU: Shaffer 5-16-1, 53 yards.
MIA: Testaverde 26-50-5, 285 yards.
RECEIVING
PSU: Dozier 2-12; Hamilton 1-23.
MIA: Blades 5-81; Irvin 5-55.

JANUARY 1, 1988
FLORIDA STATE 31, NEBRASKA 28

	1ST	2ND	3RD	4TH	FINAL
FSU	0	21	3	7	31
NEB	14	0	14	0	28

SCORING SUMMARY
NEB	Jones 2 run (Drennan kick)
NEB	Brinson 52 punt return (Drennan kick)
FSU	Gainer 10 pass from McManus (Schmidt kick)
FSU	Williams 4 run (Schmidt kick)
FSU	Gainer 25 pass from McManus (Schmidt kick)
NEB	Taylor 2 run (Drennan kick)
FSU	FG Schmidt 32
NEB	Knox 4 run (Drennan kick)
FSU	Lewis 15 pass from McManus (Schmidt kick)

FSU	TEAM STATISTICS	NEB
26	First Downs	20
82	Rushing Yards	242
28-51-1	Passing	7-14-1
375	Passing Yards	142
457	Total Yards	384
4-29.5	Punts - Average	4-35.5
2-1	Fumbles - Lost	4-2
2-20	Penalties - Yards	9-78

INDIVIDUAL LEADERS
RUSHING
FSU: Smith 9-28; McManus 5-26.
NEB: Jones 15-80, 1 TD; Taylor 20-75, 1 TD; Knox 13-62, 1 TD.
PASSING
FSU: McManus 28-51-1, 375 yards, 3 TD.
NEB: Taylor 7-14-1, 142 yards.
RECEIVING
FSU: Gainer 5-89, 2 TD; Carter 4-89.
NEB: Gregory 3-49; Banderas 1-48.

JANUARY 2, 1989
NOTRE DAME 34, WEST VIRGINIA 21

	1ST	2ND	3RD	4TH	FINAL
ND	9	14	3	8	34
WVU	0	6	7	8	21

SCORING SUMMARY
ND	FG Hackett 45
ND	Johnson 1 run (run failed)
ND	Culver 5 run (Ho kick)
WVU	FG Baumann 29
ND	Ismail 29 pass from Rice (Ho kick)
WVU	FG Baumann 31
ND	FG Ho 32
WVU	Bell 17 pass from Harris (Baumann kick)
ND	Jacobs 3 run (Rice run)
WVU	Rembert 3 run (Jones pass from Rembert)

ND	TEAM STATISTICS	WVU
19	First Downs	19
242	Rushing Yards	108
7-11-1	Passing	14-30-1
213	Passing Yards	174
455	Total Yards	282
4-36.8	Punts - Average	7-45.1
2-0	Fumbles - Lost	0-0
11-102	Penalties - Yards	3-38

INDIVIDUAL LEADERS
RUSHING
ND: Rice 13-75; Green 13-62.
WVU: Brown 11-49; Tyler 2-21.
PASSING
ND: Rice 7-11-1, 213 yards, 2 TD.
WVU: Harris 13-26-1, 166 yards, 1 TD.
RECEIVING
ND: Brown 2-70; Watters 1-57; Ismail 1-29, 1 TD.
WVU: Bell 4-44, 1 TD; Rembert 2-40.

JANUARY 1, 1990
FLORIDA STATE 41, NEBRASKA 17

	1ST	2ND	3RD	4TH	FINAL
FSU	0	21	20	0	41
NEB	7	3	0	7	17

SCORING SUMMARY
NEB	Gregory 9 pass from Gdowski (Barrios kick)
FSU	Anthony 14 pass from Willis (Andrews kick)
NEB	FG Drennan 39
FSU	Johnson 5 pass from Willis (Andrews kick)
FSU	Carter 10 pass from Willis (Andrews kick)
FSU	Moore 1 run (kick failed)
FSU	Johnson 8 pass from Willis (Andrews kick)
FSU	Anthony 24 pass from Willis (Andrews kick)
NEB	Joseph 2 run (Drennan kick)

FSU	TEAM STATISTICS	NEB
18	First Downs	18
72	Rushing Yards	115
25-41-0	Passing	15-26-2
422	Passing Yards	207
494	Total Yards	322
3-35.7	Punts - Average	3-34.3
0-0	Fumbles - Lost	5-3
13-135	Penalties - Yards	6-48

INDIVIDUAL LEADERS
RUSHING
FSU: Carter 13-72.
NEB: Clark 16-86; Flowers 4-25.
PASSING
FSU: Willis 25-40-0, 422 yards, 5 TD.
NEB: Gdowski 13-23-2, 154 yards, 1 TD.
RECEIVING
FSU: Lewis 5-106; Anthony 6-88, 2 TD.
NEB: Gregory 4-67, 1 TD; Bell 3-46.

JANUARY 1, 1991
LOUISVILLE 34, ALABAMA 7

	1ST	2ND	3RD	4TH	FINAL
LOU	25	0	7	2	34
ALA	0	7	0	0	7

SCORING SUMMARY
LOU	Ware 70 pass from Nagle (Wilmsmeyer kick)
LOU	Dawkins 5 run (kick failed)
LOU	Cummings 37 pass from Nagle (pass failed)
LOU	Buchanan recovered blocked punt in end zone (pass failed)
ALA	Gardner 49 interception return (Doyle kick)
LOU	Cummings 19 pass from Nagle (Bell kick)
LOU	Safety (Woodson intentional grounding)

LOU	TEAM STATISTICS	ALA
25	First Downs	10
113	Rushing Yards	95
21-39-3	Passing	12-35-2
458	Passing Yards	94
571	Total Yards	189
3-41.0	Punts - Average	8-40.2
3-1	Fumbles - Lost	3-1
10-87	Penalties - Yards	7-40

INDIVIDUAL LEADERS
RUSHING
LOU: Bynm 8-48; Dawkins 5-38, 1 TD.
ALA: Turner 6-49; Anderson 7-26.
PASSING
LOU: Nagle 20-33-1, 451 yards, 3 TD.
ALA: Hollingsworth 10-23-1, 59 yards.
RECEIVING
LOU: McKay 5-110; Jones 2-89; Cummings 3-69, 2 TD.
ALA: Turner 4-35; Lassic 2-35.

JANUARY 1, 1992
PENN STATE 42, TENNESSEE 17

	1ST	2ND	3RD	4TH	FINAL
PSU	7	0	14	21	42
TENN	10	0	7	0	17

SCORING SUMMARY

PSU	Gash 10 pass from Sacca (Fayak kick)
TENN	Stewart 1 run (Becksvoort kick)
TENN	FG Becksvoort 24
TENN	Fleming 44 pass from Kelly (Becksvoort kick)
PSU	LaBarca 3 pass from Sacca (Fayak kick)
PSU	Brady 13 pass from Sacca (Fayak kick)
PSU	Anderson 2 run (Fayak kick)
PSU	Givens 23 fumble return (Fayak kick)
PSU	McDuffie 37 pass from Sacca (Fayak kick)

PSU	TEAM STATISTICS	TENN
12	First Downs	25
76	Rushing Yards	171
11-28-0	Passing	21-43-1
150	Passing Yards	270
226	Total Yards	441
9-47.9	Punts - Average	6-36.3
0-0	Fumbles - Lost	5-3
3-36	Penalties - Yards	3-34

INDIVIDUAL LEADERS

RUSHING
PSU: Anderson 17-57, 1 TD; Gash 7-15.
TENN: Stewart 15-84, 1 TD; Hayden 13-56.

PASSING
PSU: Sacca 11-28-0, 150 yards, 4 TD.
TENN: Kelly 20-40-1, 273 yards, 1 TD.

RECEIVING
PSU: McDuffie 4-78, 1 TD; Drayton 3-35.
TENN: Pickens 8-100; Fleming 2- 68, 1 TD.

JANUARY 1, 1993
SYRACUSE 26, COLORADO 22

	1ST	2ND	3RD	4TH	FINAL
SYR	3	3	20	0	26
COLO	0	7	9	6	22

SCORING SUMMARY

SYR	FG Biskup 46
SYR	FG Biskup 34
COLO	Embree 7 pass from Stewart (Berger kick)
SYR	Walker 13 run (pass failed)
COLO	FG Berger 38
SYR	Graves 28 run (Biskup kick)
COLO	Johnson 16 pass from Stewart (kick failed)
SYR	Dar Dar 100 kickoff return (Biskup kick)
COLO	Warren 6 run (kick failed)

SYR	TEAM STATISTICS	COLO
15	First Downs	19
201	Rushing Yards	153
5-12-1	Passing	17-43-3
64	Passing Yards	217
265	Total Yards	370
5-45.0	Punts - Average	3-48.3
0-0	Fumbles - Lost	0-0
5-30	Penalties - Yards	8-37

INDIVIDUAL LEADERS

RUSHING
SYR: Walker 16-80, 1 TD; Richardson 7-63.
COLO: Hill 11-109; Stewart 8-29.

PASSING
SYR: Graves 5-12-1, 64 yards.
COLO: Stewart 17-41-3, 217 yards, 2 TD.

RECEIVING
SYR: Lee 1-38; Ferrell 1-12.
COLO: Westbrook 6-83; Johnson 3-46, 1 TD.

JANUARY 1, 1994
ARIZONA 29, MIAMI (FLA.) 0

	1ST	2ND	3RD	4TH	FINAL
ARIZ	9	7	6	7	29
MIA	0	0	0	0	0

SCORING SUMMARY

ARIZ	Dickey 13 pass from White (kick failed)
ARIZ	FG McLaughlin 39
ARIZ	Levy 68 run (McLaughlin kick)
ARIZ	FG McLaughlin 31
ARIZ	FG McLaughlin 21
ARIZ	Dickey 14 pass from White (McLaughlin kick)

ARIZ	TEAM STATISTICS	MIA
24	First Downs	13
257	Rushing Yards	35
12-24-2	Passing	15-44-3
152	Passing Yards	147
409	Total Yards	182
5-36.0	Punts - Average	10-37.0
2-0	Fumbles - Lost	2-1
2-25	Penalties - Yards	6-40

INDIVIDUAL LEADERS

RUSHING
ARIZ: Levy 17-142, 1 TD; Carter 17-63.
MIA: Stewart 7-35; Bennett 6-32.

PASSING
ARIZ: White 11-23-2, 138 yards, 2 TD.
MIA: Collins 5-15-2, 50 yards.

RECEIVING
ARIZ: Dickey 4-62, 2 TD; Vaughn 2-41.
MIA: Jones 6-98; Harris 1-15.

JANUARY 2, 1995
COLORADO 41, NOTRE DAME 24

	1ST	2ND	3RD	4TH	FINAL
COLO	10	21	3	7	41
ND	3	7	7	7	24

SCORING SUMMARY

COLO	FG Voskeritchian 33
COLO	Fauria 1 pass from Stewart (Voskeritchian kick)
ND	FG Cengia 29
COLO	Stewart 9 run (Voskeritchian kick)
COLO	Salaam 1 run (Voskeritchian kick)
COLO	Salaam 1 run (Voskeritchian kick)
ND	Mayes 7 pass from Powlus (Cengia kick)
ND	Mayes 40 pass from Powlus (Cengia kick)
COLO	FG Voskeritchian 48
COLO	Salaam 5 run (Voskeritchian kick)
ND	Wallace 7 pass from Powlus (Schroffner kick)

COLO	TEAM STATISTICS	ND
18	First Downs	22
246	Rushing Yards	149
12-21-0	Passing	18-35-1
226	Passing Yards	259
472	Total Yards	408
4-36.0	Punts - Average	5-33.0
0-0	Fumbles - Lost	2-0
4-35	Penalties - Yards	3-25

INDIVIDUAL LEADERS

RUSHING
COLO: Stewart 7-143, 1 TD; Salaam 27-83, 3 TD.
ND: Becton 17-81; Zellars 5-21.

PASSING
COLO: Stewart 11-20-0, 205 yards, 1 TD.
ND: Powlus 18-34-1, 259 yards, 3 TD.

RECEIVING
COLO: Westbrook 4-70; Kidd 2-83.
ND: Mayes 4-93, 2 TD; Becton 3-60.

JANUARY 2, 1996
NEBRASKA 62, FLORIDA 24

	1ST	2ND	3RD	4TH	FINAL
NEB	6	29	14	13	62
UF	10	0	8	6	24

SCORING SUMMARY

UF	FG Edmiston 23
NEB	Phillips 16 pass from Frazier (kick blocked)
UF	Wuerffel 1 run (Edmiston kick)
NEB	Phillips 42 run (Brown kick)
NEB	Safety (Wuerffel sacked in end zone)
NEB	Green 1 run (Brown kick)
NEB	FG Brown 26
NEB	Booker 42 interception return (Brown kick)
NEB	FG Brown 24
NEB	Frazier 35 run (Brown kick)
UF	Hilliard 35 pass from Wuerffel (Anthony pass from Wuerffel)
NEB	Frazier 75 run (Brown kick)
NEB	Phillips 15 run (kick blocked)
NEB	Berringer 1 run (Retzlaff kick)
UF	Anthony 93 kickoff return (run failed)

NEB	TEAM STATISTICS	UF
27	First Downs	15
524	Rushing Yards	-28
6-15-2	Passing	20-38-3
105	Passing Yards	297
629	Total Yards	269
1-36.0	Punts - Average	4-41.3
1-0	Fumbles - Lost	1-1
4-30	Penalties - Yards	9-78

INDIVIDUAL LEADERS

RUSHING
NEB: Frazier 16-199, 2 TD; Phillips 25-165, 3 TD; Green 9-68, 1 TD.
UF: Williams 6-6.

PASSING
NEB: Frazier 6-14-2, 105 yards, 1 TD.
UF: Wuerffel 17-31-3, 255 yards, 1 TD.

RECEIVING
NEB: Johnson 2-43; Holbein 1-33.
UF: Doering 8-123; Hilliard 6-100, 1 TD.

JANUARY 1, 1997
PENN STATE 38, TEXAS 15

	1ST	2ND	3RD	4TH	FINAL
PSU	7	0	21	10	38
TEX	3	9	3	0	15

SCORING SUMMARY

PSU	Enis 4 pass from Richardson (Conway kick)
TEX	FG Dawson 28
TEX	FG Dawson 28
TEX	Williams 7 run (pass failed)
PSU	Harris 5 run (Enis pass from Richardson)
TEX	FG Dawson 48
PSU	Enis 2 run (Conway kick)
PSU	Cleary 1 run (kick failed)
PSU	FG Conway 23
PSU	Enis 12 run (Conway kick)

PSU	TEAM STATISTICS	TEX
19	First Downs	19
330	Rushing Yards	73
12-20-0	Passing	27-43-1
95	Passing Yards	287
425	Total Yards	360
5-35.6	Punts - Average	6-37.7
0-0	Fumbles - Lost	2-1
4-49	Penalties - Yards	8-57

INDIVIDUAL LEADERS

RUSHING
PSU: Enis 16-95, 2 TD; Fields 1-84.
TEX: Williams 11-48, 1 TD; Mitchell 7-24.

PASSING
PSU: Richardson 12-20-0, 95 yards, 1 TD.
TEX: Brown 26-42-1, 254 yards.

RECEIVING
PSU: Brown 3-32; Jurevicius 2-22.
TEX: Adams 4-73; Davis 5-72.

December 31, 1997
Kansas State 35, Syracuse 18

	1st	2nd	3rd	4th	FINAL
KSU	0	21	0	14	35
SYR	3	12	0	3	18

SCORING SUMMARY
SYR	FG Trout 27
KSU	McDonald 19 pass from Bishop (Gramatica kick)
KSU	Bishop 12 run (Gramatica kick)
KSU	Swift 28 pass from Bishop (Gramatica kick)
SYR	Brown 24 run (Trout kick)
SYR	Safety (Ball snapped out of end zone)
SYR	FG Trout 33
KSU	McDonald 77 pass from Bishop (Gramatica kick)
SYR	FG Trout 40
KSU	McDonald 41 pass from Bishop (Gramatica kick)

KSU	TEAM STATISTICS	SYR
21	First Downs	24
140	Rushing Yards	176
14-23-1	Passing	16-39-1
317	Passing Yards	271
457	Total Yards	447
3-44.0	Punts - Average	5-43.0
0-0	Fumbles - Lost	1-1
7-58	Penalties - Yards	8-68

INDIVIDUAL LEADERS
RUSHING
KSU: Bishop 15-73, 1 TD; Hickson 7-26.
SYR: McNabb 16-81; Brown 6-47, 1 TD.

PASSING
KSU: Bishop 14-23-1, 317 yards, 4 TD.
SYR: McNabb 16-39-1, 271 yards.

RECEIVING
KSU: McDonald 7-206, 3 TD; Swift 5-98, 1 TD.
SYR: Johnson 4-101; Turner 2-59.

January 4, 1999
Tennessee 23, Florida State 16

	1st	2nd	3rd	4th	FINAL
TENN	0	14	0	9	23
FSU	0	9	0	7	16

SCORING SUMMARY
TENN	Bryson 4 pass from Martin (Hall kick)
TENN	Goodrich 54 interception return (Hall kick)
FSU	McCray 1 run (kick failed)
FSU	FG Janikowski 34
TENN	Price 79 pass from Martin (kick failed)
TENN	FG Hall 23
FSU	Outzen 7 run (Janikowksi kick)

TENN	TEAM STATISTICS	FSU
16	First Downs	13
114	Rushing Yards	108
11-19-2	Passing	9-22-2
278	Passing Yards	145
392	Total Yards	253
5-38.0	Punts - Average	9-39.8
3-2	Fumbles - Lost	4-1
9-55	Penalties - Yards	12-110

INDIVIDUAL LEADERS
RUSHING
TENN: Stephens 13-60; Henry 19-28.
FSU: Minor 15-83; Warrick 1-11.

PASSING
TENN: Martin 11-18-2, 278 yards, 2 TD.
FSU: Outzen 9-22-2, 145 yards.

RECEIVING
TENN: Price 4-199, 1 TD; Bryson 3-34, 1 TD.
FSU: Dugans 6-135; McCray 1-11.

January 2, 2000
Nebraska 31, Tennessee 21

	1st	2nd	3rd	4th	FINAL
NEB	14	3	7	7	31
TENN	0	7	7	7	21

SCORING SUMMARY
NEB	Alexander 7 run (Brown kick)
NEB	Newcombe 60 punt return (Brown kick)
NEB	FG Brown 31
TENN	Stallworth 9 pass from Martin (Walls kick)
TENN	Henry 4 run (Walls kick)
NEB	Golliday 13 pass from Crouch (Brown kick)
NEB	Buckhalter 2 run (Brown kick)
TENN	Stallworth 44 pass from Wilson (Walls kick)

NEB	TEAM STATISTICS	TENN
23	First Downs	17
321	Rushing Yards	44
9-15-0	Passing	20-35-2
148	Passing Yards	267
469	Total Yards	311
6-39.5	Punts - Average	7-43.1
1-1	Fumbles - Lost	1-0
8-59	Penalties - Yards	5-41

INDIVIDUAL LEADERS
RUSHING
NEB: Alexander 21-108, 1 TD; Miller 8-87.
TENN: Henry 10-31, 1 TD; Lewis 8-19.

PASSING
NEB: Crouch 9-15-0, 148 yards, 1 TD.
TENN: Martin 19-34-2, 223 yards, 1 TD.

RECEIVING
NEB: Davison 2-68; Bowling 2-45.
TENN: Stallworth 8-108, 2 TD; Wilson 7-75.

January 1, 2001
Oregon State 41, Notre Dame 9

	1st	2nd	3rd	4th	FINAL
OSU	3	9	29	0	41
ND	0	3	0	6	9

SCORING SUMMARY
OSU	FG Cesca 32
OSU	FG Cesca 29
OSU	Johnson 74 pass from Smith (pass failed)
ND	FG Setta 29
OSU	Houshmandzadeh 23 pass from Smith (Cesca kick)
OSU	Roberts 45 punt return (Prescott pass from Smith)
OSU	Johnson 4 pass from Smith (Cesca kick)
OSU	Simonton 4 run (Cesca kick)
ND	Fisher 1 run (run failed)

OSU	TEAM STATISTICS	ND
20	First Downs	18
127	Rushing Yards	17
17-25-0	Passing	13-33-2
319	Passing Yards	138
446	Total Yards	155
3-39.0	Punts - Average	6-41.5
3-1	Fumbles - Lost	2-1
18-174	Penalties - Yards	7-42

INDIVIDUAL LEADERS
RUSHING
OSU: Simonton 18-85, 1 TD; Battle 8-32.
ND: Jones 13-30; Howard 8-28.

PASSING
OSU: Smith 16-24-0, 305 yards, 3 TD.
ND: LoVecchio 13-33-2, 138 yards.

RECEIVING
OSU: Johnson 4-93, 2 TD; Maurer 3-82; Houshmandzadeh 6-74, 1 TD.
ND: Hunter 3-57; O'Leary 2-36.

January 1, 2002
Oregon 38, Colorado 16

	1st	2nd	3rd	4th	FINAL
ORE	7	14	10	7	38
COLO	7	0	0	9	16

SCORING SUMMARY
COLO	Drumm 1 run (Brougham kick)
ORE	Howry 28 pass from Harrington (Siegel kick)
ORE	Parker 79 pass from Harrington (Siegel kick)
ORE	Smith 6 pass from Harrington (Siegel kick)
ORE	Morris 49 run (Siegel kick)
ORE	FG Siegel 47
ORE	Peelle 4 pass from Harrington (Siegel kick)
COLO	FG Flores 39
COLO	Graham 4 pass from Ochs (kick failed)

ORE	TEAM STATISTICS	COLO
22	First Downs	20
150	Rushing Yards	49
28-42-1	Passing	24-47-3
350	Passing Yards	279
500	Total Yards	328
3-4	Punt Returns - Yards	3-25
3-49	Kickoff Returns - Yards	7-159
5-36.2	Punts - Average	5-40.8
0-0	Fumbles - Lost	0-0
8-74	Penalties - Yards	8-55
31:05	Possession Time	28:55

INDIVIDUAL LEADERS
RUSHING
ORE: Morris 11-89, 1 TD; Smith 14-51.
COLO: Brown 9-30; Johnson 8-24.

PASSING
ORE: Harrington 28-42-1, 350 yards, 4 TD.
COLO: Ochs 13-20-1, 140 yards, 1 TD.

RECEIVING
ORE: Parker 9-162, 1 TD; Peelle 5-66, 1 TD.
COLO: Graham 10-89, 1 TD; McCoy 5-66.

January 3, 2003
Ohio State 31, Miami (Fla.) 24

	1st	2nd	3rd	4th	OT	OT	FINAL
OSU	0	14	3	7	7		31
MIA	7	0	7	3	7	0	24

SCORING SUMMARY
MIA	Parrish 25 pass from Dorsey (Sievers kick)
OSU	Krenzel 1 run (Nugent kick)
OSU	Clarett 7 run (Nugent kick)
OSU	FG Nugent 44
MIA	McGahee 9 run (Sievers kick)
MIA	FG Sievers 40
MIA	Winslow 7 pass from Dorsey (Sievers kick)
OSU	Krenzel 1 run (Nugent kick)
OSU	Clarett 5 run (Nugent kick)

OSU	TEAM STATISTICS	MIA
14	First Downs	19
145	Rushing Yards	65
7-21-2	Passing	29-44-2
122	Passing Yards	304
267	Total Yards	369
1-1	Punt Returns - Yards	2-56
1-15	Kickoff Returns - Yards	1-39
6-47.7	Punts - Average	4-43.2
0-0	Fumbles - Lost	3-3
9-49	Penalties - Yards	6-30
31:27	Possession Time	28:33

INDIVIDUAL LEADERS
RUSHING
OSU: Krenzel 19-81, 2 TD; Clarett 23-47, 2 TD.
MIA: McGahee 20-67, 1 TD; Payton 8-17.

PASSING
OSU: Krenzel 7-21-2, 122 yards.
MIA: Dorsey 28-43-2, 296 yards, 2 TD.

RECEIVING
OSU: Gamble 2-69; Jenkins 4-45.
MIA: Winslow 11-122, 1 TD; Parrish 5-70, 1 TD; Johnson 4-54.

JANUARY 2, 2004
OHIO STATE 35, KANSAS STATE 28

	1ST	2ND	3RD	4TH	FINAL
OSU	14	7	14	0	35
KSU	0	7	7	14	28

SCORING SUMMARY
OSU	Hollins 7 blocked punt return (Nugent kick)
OSU	Holmes 6 pass from Krenzel (Nugent kick)
OSU	Jenkins 17 pass from Krenzel (Nugent kick)
KSU	Sproles 6 run (Rheem kick)
KSU	Roberson 14 run (Rheem kick)
OSU	Jenkins 8 pass from Krenzel (Nugent kick)
OSU	Holmes 31 pass from Krenzel (Nugent kick)
KSU	Saba 3 run (Rheem kick)
KSU	Roberson 1 run (Rheem kick)

OSU	TEAM STATISTICS	KSU
15	First Downs	25
148	Rushing Yards	84
11-24-2	Passing	20-52-1
189	Passing Yards	294
337	Total Yards	378
5-48	Punt Returns - Yards	4-10
3-60	Kickoff Returns - Yards	5-79
7-40.1	Punts - Average	8-40.0
0-0	Fumbles - Lost	0-0
9-63	Penalties - Yards	8-51
31:28	Possession Time	28:32

INDIVIDUAL LEADERS
RUSHING
OSU: Ross 20-82; Joe 11-46.
KSU: Sproles 13-38, 1 TD; Roberson 16-32, 2 TD.

PASSING
OSU: Krenzel 11-24-2, 189 yards, 4 TD.
KSU: Roberson 20-51-1, 294 yards.

RECEIVING
OSU: Jenkins 5-96, 2 TD; Childress 2-44.
KSU: Dennis 7-113; Moreira 3-59.

JANUARY 1, 2005
UTAH 35, PITTSBURGH 7

	1ST	2ND	3RD	4TH	FINAL
UT	7	7	21	0	35
PITT	0	0	7	0	7

SCORING SUMMARY
UT	Ganther 4 run (Carroll kick)
UT	Madsen 6 pass from Smith (Carroll kick)
UT	Johnson 18 pass from Smith (Carroll kick)
UT	Warren 23 pass from Smith (Carroll kick)
PITT	Lee 31 pass from Palko (Cummings kick)
UT	Warren 18 pass from Smith (Carroll kick)

UT	TEAM STATISTICS	PITT
25	First Downs	19
139	Rushing Yards	17
29-37-0	Passing	29-37-0
328	Passing Yards	251
467	Total Yards	268
1-10	Punt Returns - Yards	0-0
2-42	Kickoff Returns - Yards	5-180
1-28	Punts - Average	5-36
1-1	Fumbles - Lost	0-0
7-51	Penalties - Yards	3-30
28:43	Possession Time	31-17

INDIVIDUAL LEADERS
RUSHING
UT: Smith 15-68, Ganther 6-34, 1 TD.
PITT: Murphy 12-37.

PASSING
UT: Smith 29-37-0, 328 yards, 4 TD.
PITT: Palko 22-40-0, 251 yards, 1 TD.

RECEIVING
UT: Warren 15-198, 2 TD.
PITT: DelSardo 9-109; Lee 7-93, 1 TD.

THE BOWLS

INDEPENDENCE BOWL

PROFILE

Site: Shreveport, La.
Stadium: Independence Stadium
Capacity: 50,459
Surface: Grass

PLAYING SITES

Independence Stadium, since 1976

NAME CHANGES

Independence Bowl, 1976-90
Poulan/Weed Eater Independence Bowl, 1991-97
Sanford Independence Bowl, 1998-2000
MainStay Independence Bowl, 2001-03
Independence Bowl, since 2004

SEASON	DATE	PRE-GAME RANK	TEAMS	SCORE	FINAL RANK	MOST VALUABLE PLAYERS	ATT.
1976	Dec. 13, 1976		McNeese State	20		Terry McFarland, McNeese State, QB	15,542
			Tulsa	16		Terry Clark, Tulsa, CB	
1977	Dec. 17, 1977		Louisiana Tech	24		Keith Thibodeaux, Louisiana Tech, QB	18,500
			Louisville	14		Otis Wilson, Louisville, LB	
1978	Dec. 16, 1978		East Carolina	35		Theodore Sutton, East Carolina, FB	18,200
			Louisiana Tech	13		Zack Valentine, East Carolina, DE	
1979	Dec. 15, 1979		Syracuse	31		Joe Morris, Syracuse, RB	27,234
			McNeese State	7		Clay Carroll, McNeese State, DT	
1980	Dec. 13, 1980		Southern Miss	16		Stephan Starring, McNeese State, QB	45,000
			McNeese State	14		Jerald Baylis, Southern Miss, NG	
1981	Dec. 12, 1981		Texas A&M	33		Gary Kubiak, Texas A&M, QB	47,300
			Oklahoma State	16		Mike Green, Oklahoma State, LB	
1982	Dec. 11, 1982		Wisconsin	14		Randy Wright, Wisconsin, QB	49,503
			Kansas State	3		Tim Krumrie, Wisconsin, NG	
1983	Dec. 10, 1983	16	Air Force	9	13	Marty Louthan, Air Force, QB	41,274
			Mississippi	3		Andre Townsend, Mississippi, DT	
1984	Dec. 15, 1984		Air Force	23		Bart Weiss, Air Force, QB	41,000
			Virginia Tech	7		Scott Thomas, Air Force, S	
1985	Dec. 21, 1985		Minnesota	20		Rickey Foggie, Minnesota, QB	42,800
			Clemson	13		Bruce Holmes, Minnesota, LB	
1986	Dec. 20, 1986		Mississippi	20		Mark Young, Mississippi, QB	46,369
			Texas Tech	17		James Mosley, Texas Tech, DE	
1987	Dec. 19, 1987		Washington	24		Chris Chandler, Washington, QB	44,683
			Tulane	12		David Rill, Washington, LB	
1988	Dec. 23, 1988		Southern Miss	38		James Henry, Southern Miss, PR-CB	20,242
			UTEP	18			
1989	Dec. 16, 1989		Oregon	27		Bill Musgrave, Oregon, QB	44,621
			Tulsa	24		Chris Oldham, Oregon, DB	
1990	Dec. 15, 1990		Louisiana Tech	34		Mike Richardson, Louisiana Tech, RB	48,325
			Maryland	34		Lorenza Baker, Louisiana Tech, LB	
1991	Dec. 29, 1991	24	Georgia	24	17	Andre Hastings, Georgia, FL	46,932
			Arkansas	15		Torrey Evans, Georgia, LB	
1992	Dec. 31, 1992		Wake Forest	39	25	Todd Dixon, Wake Forest, SE	31,337
			Oregon	35		Herman O'Berry, Oregon, CB	
1993	Dec. 31, 1993	22	Virginia Tech	45	22	Maurice DeShazo, Virginia Tech, QB	33,819
		21	Indiana	20		Antonio Banks, Virginia Tech, S	
1994	Dec. 28, 1994	18	Virginia	20	15	Mike Groh, Virginia, QB	36,192
			TCU	10		Mike Frederick, Virginia, DE	
1995	Dec. 29, 1995		LSU	45		Kevin Faulk, LSU, RB	48,835
			Michigan State	26		Gabe Northern, LSU, DE	
1996	Dec. 31, 1996		Auburn	32	24	Dameyune Craig, Auburn, QB	41,366
		24	Army	29	25	Takeo Spikes, LB, Rickey Neal, LB, Auburn	
1997	Dec. 28, 1997	15	LSU	27	13	Rondell Mealey, LSU, RB	50,459
			Notre Dame	9		Arnold Miller, LSU, DE	
1998	Dec. 31, 1998		Mississippi	35		Romaro Miller, Mississippi, QB	46,862
			Texas Tech	18		Kendrick Clancy, Mississippi, DL	
1999	Dec. 31, 1999		Mississippi	27	22	Tim Strickland, Mississippi, CB	49,873
			Oklahoma	25		Josh Heupel, Oklahoma, QB	
2000	Dec. 31, 2000		Mississippi State	43 OT	24	Ja'Mar Toombs, Texas A&M, RB	36,974
			Texas A&M	41		Willie Blade, Mississippi State, DT	
2001	Dec. 27, 2001		Alabama	14		Seneca Wallace, QB, Matt Word, LB, Iowa State	45,627
			Iowa State	13		Waine Bacon, Alabama, S	
2002	Dec. 27, 2002		Mississippi	27		Eli Manning, Mississippi, QB	46,096
			Nebraska	23		Chris Kelsay, Nebraska, DE	
2003	Dec. 31, 2003		Arkansas	27		Cedric Cobbs, Arkansas, RB	49,625
			Missouri	14		Caleb Miller, Arkansas, LB	
2004	Dec. 28, 2004		Iowa State	17		Bret Meyer, Iowa State, QB	43,000
			Miami (Ohio)	13		Nick Moser, Iowa State, DB	

DECEMBER 13, 1976
McNEESE STATE 20, TULSA 16

	1ST	2ND	3RD	4TH	FINAL
MSU	3	3	8	6	20
TUL	7	0	6	3	16

SCORING SUMMARY
TUL — Bailey 1 run (Cox kick)
MSU — FG Peebles 42
MSU — FG Peebles 34
MSU — McArthur 1 run (McFarland run)
TUL — McGowen 65 blocked FG return (kick blocked)
TUL — FG Cox 38
MSU — Hadnot 25 run (pass failed)

MSU	TEAM STATISTICS	TUL
11	First Downs	17
152	Rushing Yards	108
5-18-1	Passing	13-30-1
57	Passing Yards	172
209	Total Yards	280
9-38.9	Punts - Average	5-29.6
3-1	Fumbles - Lost	7-3
11-105	Penalties - Yards	16-100

INDIVIDUAL LEADERS
RUSHING
MSU: McFarland 17-71; Hadnot 13-57, 1 TD.
TUL: Bailey 16-60, 1 TD.
PASSING
MSU: McFarland 4-15-1, 29 yards.
TUL: Hickerson 8-20-0, 127 yards.
RECEIVING
MSU: Heisser 2-35; Ellender 2-19.
TUL: Powell 3-70; Webster 3-39.

DECEMBER 17, 1977
LOUISIANA TECH 24, LOUISVILLE 14

	1ST	2ND	3RD	4TH	FINAL
LT	21	3	0	0	24
LOU	7	0	7	0	14

SCORING SUMMARY
LOU — Miller 60 punt return (Posadas kick)
LT — Lewis 1 run (Swilley kick)
LT — Pree 41 pass from Thibodeaux (run failed)
LT — McCartney 8 pass from Thibodeaux (Lewis run)
LT — FG Swilley 21
LOU — Miller 13 run (Posadas kick)

LT	TEAM STATISTICS	LOU
25	First Downs	11
48	Rushing Yards	100
19-39-2	Passing	9-23-1
287	Passing Yards	61
335	Total Yards	161
6-32.0	Punts - Average	8-38.0
6-3	Fumbles - Lost	8-3
4-36	Penalties - Yards	8-92

INDIVIDUAL LEADERS
RUSHING
LT: Lewis 17-59, 1 TD.
LOU: Poole 17-50.
PASSING
LT: Thibodeaux 19-39-2, 287 yards, 2 TD.
LOU: Stram 7-18-1, 61 yards.
RECEIVING
LT: Foppe 4-78; McCartney 5-71, 1 TD.
LOU: Besanceney 2-25; Mitchell 3-17.

DECEMBER 16, 1978
EAST CAROLINA 35, LOUISIANA TECH 13

	1ST	2ND	3RD	4TH	FINAL
ECU	14	7	7	7	35
LT	0	10	3	0	13

SCORING SUMMARY
ECU — Collins 3 run (Lamm kick)
ECU — Green 1 run (Lamm kick)
ECU — Collins 1 run (Lamm kick)
LT — Spruiell 32 pass from Thibodeaux (Swilley kick)
LT — FG Swilley 36
LT — FG Swilley 36
ECU — Sutton 45 run (Lamm kick)
ECU — Hicks 3 run (Lamm kick)

ECU	TEAM STATISTICS	LT
17	First Downs	18
278	Rushing Yards	12
4-13-0	Passing	18-53-3
54	Passing Yards	263
332	Total Yards	275
7-36.4	Punts - Average	5-41.6
2-2	Fumbles - Lost	4-4
7-65	Penalties - Yards	0-0

INDIVIDUAL LEADERS
RUSHING
ECU : Sutton 17-143, 1 TD; Green 17-41.
LT: Clark 6-28; Yates 12-19.
PASSING
ECU : Green 4-13-0, 54 yards.
LT: Barkley 12-39-3, 160 yards.
RECEIVING
ECU : Gallagher 3-33.
LT: Spruiell 7-130, 1 TD.

DECEMBER 15, 1979
SYRACUSE 31, McNEESE STATE 7

	1ST	2ND	3RD	4TH	FINAL
SYR	0	3	7	21	31
MSU	0	0	7	0	7

SCORING SUMMARY
SYR	FG Anderson 40
SYR	Mandeville 1 run (Anderson kick)
MSU	Millett 4 run (Stump kick)
SYR	Monk 9 pass from Hurley (Anderson kick)
SYR	Hurley 1 run (Anderson kick)
SYR	Matichak 6 run (Anderson kick)

SYR	TEAM STATISTICS	MSU
23	First Downs	13
276	Rushing Yards	127
5-10-0	Passing	5-17-3
51	Passing Yards	102
327	Total Yards	229
4-36.0	Punts - Average	3-43.7
1-0	Fumbles - Lost	5-1
2-10	Penalties - Yards	1-3

INDIVIDUAL LEADERS
RUSHING
SYR: Morris 33-155; Hartman 18-57.
MSU: Shankle 16-85; Hadnot 5-24.
PASSING
SYR: Hurley 5-10-0, 51 yards, 1 TD.
MSU: Millett 5-17-3, 102 yards.
RECEIVING
SYR: Zambuto 2-27; Sidor 2-17; Monk 1-7, 1 TD.
MSU: Price 2-55; Branch 2-33.

DECEMBER 13, 1980
SOUTHERN MISS 16, McNEESE ST. 14

	1ST	2ND	3RD	4TH	FINAL
USM	10	0	0	6	16
MSU	0	7	7	0	14

SCORING SUMMARY
USM	FG Walker 36
USM	Terrell 14 run (Walker kick)
MSU	Jordan 1 run (Stump kick)
MSU	Starring 4 run (Stump kick)
USM	Woodard 1 run (kick failed)

USM	TEAM STATISTICS	MSU
14	First Downs	14
181	Rushing Yards	262
8-18-1	Passing	6-12-0
69	Passing Yards	139
250	Total Yards	401
8-44.5	Punts - Average	5-37.4
1-1	Fumbles - Lost	4-4
8-75	Penalties - Yards	4-35

INDIVIDUAL LEADERS
RUSHING
USM: Collier 14-63; Winder 18-48.
MSU: McClendon 20-97; Starring 23-82, 1 TD.
PASSING
USM: Collier 8-17-1, 69 yards.
MSU: Starring 6-12-0, 139 yards.
RECEIVING
USM: Harvey 3-24; Horn 2-23.
MSU: Barrouse 2-69; McClendon 2-31.

DECEMBER 12, 1981
TEXAS A&M 33, OKLAHOMA STATE 16

	1ST	2ND	3RD	4TH	FINAL
A&M	3	17	3	10	33
OKST	10	0	0	6	16

SCORING SUMMARY
OKST	Anderson 1 run (Roach kick)
OKST	FG Roach 42
A&M	FG Hardy 33
A&M	FG Hardy 32
A&M	Williams 50 pass from Kubiak (Hardy kick)
A&M	Williams 38 pass from Kubiak (Hardy kick)
A&M	FG Hardy 50
A&M	FG Hardy 18
A&M	Hector 4 run (Hardy kick)
OKST	Orange 5 run (pass failed)

A&M	TEAM STATISTICS	OKST
23	First Downs	16
223	Rushing Yards	70
15-21-0	Passing	16-35-1
225	Passing Yards	187
448	Total Yards	257
3-40.0	Punts - Average	6-40.3
4-1	Fumbles - Lost	3-1
6-60	Penalties - Yards	3-34

INDIVIDUAL LEADERS
RUSHING
A&M: Jackson 22-123; Hector 18-45, 1 TD.
OKST: Jones 14-37; Anderson 5-20, 1 TD.
PASSING
A&M: Kubiak 15-20-0, 225 yards, 2 TD.
OKST: Hilger 14-35-1, 187 yards.
RECEIVING
A&M: Williams 5-118, 2 TD; Whitnall 3-43.
OKST: Cramer 5-73; Young 4-45.

DECEMBER 11, 1982
WISCONSIN 14, KANSAS STATE 3

	1ST	2ND	3RD	4TH	FINAL
WISC	0	7	7	0	14
KSU	0	3	0	0	3

SCORING SUMMARY
KSU	FG Willis 29
WISC	Jones 16 pass from Wright (Rohde kick)
WISC	Stracka 87 pass from Wright (Rohde kick)

WISC	TEAM STATISTICS	KSU
14	First Downs	12
131	Rushing Yards	65
9-24-0	Passing	13-35-1
183	Passing Yards	127
314	Total Yards	192
6-40.7	Punts - Average	8-36.8
4-3	Fumbles - Lost	2-1
5-40	Penalties - Yards	9-75

INDIVIDUAL LEADERS
RUSHING
WISC: Williams 11-57; Ellerson 13-47.
KSU: Taluao 10-31; Fergimo 11-25.
PASSING
WISC: Wright 9-24-0, 183 yards, 2 TD.
KSU: Dickey 13-35-1, 127 yards.
RECEIVING
WISC: Stracka 187, 1 TD; Keeling 4-64.
KSU: Wallace 3-51; Dageforde 4-30.

DECEMBER 10, 1983
AIR FORCE 9, MISSISSIPPI 3

	1ST	2ND	3RD	4TH	FINAL
AFA	3	3	3	0	9
MISS	0	3	0	0	3

SCORING SUMMARY
AFA	FG Pavlich 44
AFA	FG Pavlich 39
MISS	FG Teevan 39
AFA	FG Pavlich 27

AFA	TEAM STATISTICS	MISS
18	First Downs	11
277	Rushing Yards	106
6-7-1	Passing	11-27-2
71	Passing Yards	138
348	Total Yards	244
3-30.3	Punts - Average	5-43.6
3-3	Fumbles - Lost	1-0
4-19	Penalties - Yards	4-20

INDIVIDUAL LEADERS
RUSHING
AFA: Brown 12-91; Louthan 25-67.
MISS: McGee 22-111; Humphrey 6-15.
PASSING
AFA: Louthan 6-7-0, 71 yards.
MISS: Powell 11-27-2, 138 yards.
RECEIVING
AFA: Kirby 3-49.
MISS: Moffett 6-96.

DECEMBER 15, 1984
AIR FORCE 23, VIRGINIA TECH 7

	1ST	2ND	3RD	4TH	FINAL
AFA	3	7	0	13	23
VT	7	0	0	0	7

SCORING SUMMARY
AFA	FG Mateos 35
VT	Williams 3 run (Wade kick)
AFA	Simmons 3 run (Mateos kick)
AFA	Brown 2 run (Mateos kick)
AFA	Weiss 13 run (kick failed)

AFA	TEAM STATISTICS	VT
15	First Downs	17
221	Rushing Yards	207
6-7-0	Passing	11-26-2
49	Passing Yards	102
270	Total Yards	309
6-42.5	Punts - Average	4-40.0
2-0	Fumbles - Lost	2-2
4-30	Penalties - Yards	11-112

INDIVIDUAL LEADERS
RUSHING
AFA: Weiss 29-120, 1 TD; Evans 15-58.
VT: Hunter 12-75; Williams 12-62, 1 TD.
PASSING
AFA: Weiss 6-7-0, 49 yards.
VT: Cox 6-17-1, 50 yards; Greenwood 3-5-0, 52 yards.
RECEIVING
AFA: Coleman 1-16; Fleming 1-14.
VT: Rider 4-45; Nelson 3-24.

DECEMBER 21, 1985
MINNESOTA 20, CLEMSON 13

	1ST	2ND	3RD	4TH	FINAL
MINN	3	7	0	10	20
CLEM	0	6	7	0	13

SCORING SUMMARY
MINN	FG Lohmiller 22
MINN	Anderson 9 pass from Foggie (Lohmiller kick)
CLEM	FG Treadwell 39
CLEM	FG Treadwell 21
CLEM	Jennings 3 pass from Driver (Treadwell kick)
MINN	FG Lohmiller 19
MINN	Baylor 1 run (Lohmiller kick)

MINN	TEAM STATISTICS	CLEM
20	First Downs	18
257	Rushing Yards	211
9-22-0	Passing	10-29-1
123	Passing Yards	162
380	Total Yards	373
6-37.5	Punts - Average	4-41.5
1-1	Fumbles - Lost	5-3
7-55	Penalties - Yards	5-51
28:22	Possession Time	31:38

INDIVIDUAL LEADERS
RUSHING
MINN: Baylor 13-98, 1 TD; Puk 15-69.
CLEM: Flowers 27-148; Driver 13-37.
PASSING
MINN: Foggie 9-22-0, 123 yards, 1 TD.
CLEM: Rodney Williams 9-23-1, 159 yards.
RECEIVING
MINN: Anderson 4-34, 1 TD.
CLEM: Ray Williams 5-58.

THE BOWLS

DECEMBER 20, 1986
MISSISSIPPI 20, TEXAS TECH 17

	1ST	2ND	3RD	4TH	FINAL
MISS	7	10	0	3	20
TT	0	7	7	3	17

SCORING SUMMARY
MISS   Goodloe 1 run (Owen kick)
MISS   Mickles 9 run (Owen kick)
MISS   FG Owen 21
TT   Gray 1 run (Segrist kick)
TT   Scurlark 33 interception return (Segrist kick)
TT   FG Segrist 19
MISS   FG Owen 48

MISS	TEAM STATISTICS	TT
26	First Downs	18
60	Rushing Yards	175
31-50-1	Passing	17-40-1
343	Passing Yards	181
403	Total Yards	356
6-45.5	Punts - Average	8-41.5
1-1	Fumbles - Lost	2-0
5-33	Penalties - Yards	5-60

INDIVIDUAL LEADERS
RUSHING
MISS: Myers 4-69; Mickles 10-53, 1 TD.
TT: Farris 17-99.
PASSING
MISS: Young 31-50-1, 343 yards.
TT: Tolliver 17-40-1, 181 yards.
RECEIVING
MISS: Ambrose 8-102.
TT: Price 9-74; Walker 3-71.

DECEMBER 19, 1987
WASHINGTON 24, TULANE 12

	1ST	2ND	3RD	4TH	FINAL
WASH	7	14	0	3	24
TUL	0	10	0	2	12

SCORING SUMMARY
WASH   Covington 3 run (Brownlee kick)
TUL   Price 44 punt return (Wiggins kick)
TUL   FG Wiggins 21
WASH   Ames 5 pass from Chandler (Brownlee kick)
WASH   Franklin 5 pass from Chandler (Brownlee kick)
WASH   FG Wyles 41
TUL   Safety (Chandler kneeled in end zone)

WASH	TEAM STATISTICS	TUL
22	First Downs	21
147	Rushing Yards	131
16-32-3	Passing	17-40-1
249	Passing Yards	248
396	Total Yards	379
4-32.8	Punts - Average	6-43.7
1-0	Fumbles - Lost	2-1
10-67	Penalties - Yards	7-73

INDIVIDUAL LEADERS
RUSHING
WASH: Weathersby 14-84.
TUL: Jones 18-91.
PASSING
WASH: Chandler 15-30-3, 234 yards, 2 TD.
TUL: Jones 17-40-1, 248 yards.
RECEIVING
WASH: Weathersby 5-64; Franklin 4-61, 1 TD.
TUL: Zeno 7-116; Pierce 2-56.

DECEMBER 23, 1988
SOUTHERN MISS 38, UTEP 18

	1ST	2ND	3RD	4TH	FINAL
USM	3	7	21	7	38
UTEP	7	0	3	8	18

SCORING SUMMARY
UTEP   Barrett 30 pass from Hegarty (Jacke kick)
USM   FG Seroka 26
USM   Warnsley 3 pass from Favre (Seroka kick)
USM   Henry 65 punt return (Seroka kick)
USM   Gandy 1 run (Seroka kick)
USM   Henry 45 punt return (Seroka kick)
UTEP   FG Jacke 37
USM   Gandy 7 run (Seroka run)
UTEP   Fuller 2 pass from Flores (Fuller pass from Flores)

USM	TEAM STATISTICS	UTEP
17	First Downs	19
168	Rushing Yards	53
15-26-2	Passing	23-44-0
157	Passing Yards	308
325	Total Yards	361
6-32.2	Punts - Average	6-39.2
2-0	Fumbles - Lost	3-0
5-45	Penalties - Yards	10-95

INDIVIDUAL LEADERS
RUSHING
USM: Gandy 22-134, 2 TD.
UTEP: Fuller 9-31.
PASSING
USM: Favre 15-26-2, 157 yards, 1 TD.
UTEP: Hegarty 14-27-0, 203 yards, 1 TD; Flores 9-17-0, 105 yards, 1 TD.
RECEIVING
USM: Tillman 2-44; Williams 2-28.
UTEP: Barrett 9-119, 1 TD; Adkson 4-55.

DECEMBER 16, 1989
OREGON 27, TULSA 24

	1ST	2ND	3RD	4TH	FINAL
ORE	3	7	7	10	27
TUL	7	10	7	0	24

SCORING SUMMARY
TUL   Adams 1 run (Fuess kick)
ORE   FG McCallum 29
ORE   Hargain 20 pass from Musgrave (McCallum kick)
TUL   FG Fuess 26
TUL   Williams 21 blocked punt return (Fuess kick)
TUL   Adams 1 run (Fuess kick)
ORE   Reitzug 9 pass from Musgrave (McCallum kick)
ORE   Musgrave 1 run (McCallum kick)
ORE   FG McCallum 20

ORE	TEAM STATISTICS	TUL
16	First Downs	14
140	Rushing Yards	70
23-40-2	Passing	17-34-2
320	Passing Yards	183
460	Total Yards	253
3-23.5	Punts - Average	5-34.8
2-1	Fumbles - Lost	3-1
5-49	Penalties - Yards	1-15

INDIVIDUAL LEADERS
RUSHING
ORE: Loville 20-82.
TUL: Adams 26-72, 2 TD.
PASSING
ORE: Musgrave 22-37-2, 320 yards, 2 TD.
TUL: Rubley 17-34-2, 183 yards.
RECEIVING
ORE: Reitzug 6-121, 1 TD; Hargain 5-100, 1 TD.
TUL: Treat 3-50; McVey 4-47.

DECEMBER 15, 1990
MARYLAND 34, LOUISIANA TECH 34

	1ST	2ND	3RD	4TH	FINAL
MD	14	0	6	14	34
LT	0	14	14	6	34

SCORING SUMMARY
MD   Jackson 1 run (DeArmas kick)
MD   Jackson 2 run (DeArmas kick)
LT   Richardson 5 run (Boniol kick)
LT   Davis 3 run (Boniol kick)
LT   Richardson 1 run (Boniol kick)
LT   Slaughter 7 pass from Johnson (Boniol kick)
MD   Jackson 11 run (kick failed)
LT   FG Boniol 36
LT   FG Boniol 29
MD   Mason 28 pass from Zolak (DeArmas kick)
MD   Johnson 15 pass from Zolak (DeArmas kick)

MD	TEAM STATISTICS	LT
25	First Downs	16
150	Rushing Yards	191
18-29-3	Passing	11-18-1
254	Passing Yards	115
404	Total Yards	306
1-34.0	Punts - Average	4-37.2
3-1	Fumbles - Lost	1-1
6-53	Penalties - Yards	9-88
28:46	Possession Time	38:14

INDIVIDUAL LEADERS
RUSHING
MD: Mason 15-93; Jackson 17-50, 3 TD.
LT: Richardson 27-81, 2 TD; Davis 12-72, 1 TD.
PASSING
MD: Zolak 17-28-3, 215 yards, 2 TD.
LT: Johnson 7-8, 70 yards, 1 TD.
RECEIVING
MD : Johnson 5-107, 1 TD.
LT: Slaughter 5-66, 1 TD.

DECEMBER 29, 1991
GEORGIA 24, ARKANSAS 15

	1ST	2ND	3RD	4TH	FINAL
UGA	14	3	7	0	24
ARK	0	7	0	8	15

SCORING SUMMARY
UGA   Marshall 7 pass from Zeier (Peterson kick)
UGA   Hastings 27 pass from Zeier (Peterson kick)
UGA   FG Parkman 39
ARK   Jackson 7 run (Wright kick)
UGA   Hastings 53 run (Peterson kick)
ARK   Jackson 1 run (Jackson run)

UGA	TEAM STATISTICS	ARK
15	First Downs	22
125	Rushing Yards	188
20-31-0	Passing	12-31-5
237	Passing Yards	122
362	Total Yards	310
6-32.5	Punts - Average	4-45.3
1-0	Fumbles - Lost	1-1
10-75	Penalties - Yards	7-43

INDIVIDUAL LEADERS
RUSHING
UGA: Hastings 1-53, 1 TD; Strong 8-36.
ARK: Jackson 28-112, 2 TD; Jeffrey 9-44.
PASSING
UGA : Zeier 18-28-0, 228 yards, 2 TD.
ARK: Hill 12-31-5, 122 yards.
RECEIVING
UGA : Hastings 4-94, 1 TD.
ARK: Keith 3-38.

WAKE FOREST 39, OREGON 35
DECEMBER 31, 1992

	1ST	2ND	3RD	4TH	FINAL
WFU	7	3	14	15	39
ORE	13	9	7	6	35

SCORING SUMMARY
WFU	Leach 1 run (Green kick)
ORE	Burwell 40 run (Thompson kick)
ORE	O'Berry 24 fumble recovery (kick failed)
WFU	FG Green 38
ORE	Ferry 4 pass from O'Neil (kick blocked)
ORE	FG Thompson 48
ORE	Molden 8 interception return (Thompson kick)
WFU	Moultrie 1 run (Green kick)
WFU	Dixon 30 pass from West (Green kick)
WFU	Dixon 61 pass from Jones (Leach pass from West)
WFU	Leach 6 run (Green kick)
ORE	Harris 10 pass from O'Neil (kick failed)

WFU	TEAM STATISTICS	ORE
18	First Downs	23
193	Rushing Yards	112
16-29-3	Passing	24-40-1
323	Passing Yards	227
516	Total Yards	339
4-39.5	Punts - Average	7-35.9
3-3	Fumbles - Lost	0-0
11-108	Penalties - Yards	6-55

INDIVIDUAL LEADERS
RUSHING
WFU: Leach 21-116, 2 TD; Moultrie 11-60, 1 TD.
ORE: Burwell 11-48, 1 TD; Whittle 7-27.
PASSING
WFU : West 15-27-3, 262 yards, 1 TD; Jones 1-1-0, 61 yards, 1 TD.
ORE: O'Neil 24-40-1, 227 yards, 2 TD.
RECEIVING
WFU: Dixon 5-166, 2 TD; Mills 4-83.
ORE: Harris 6-74, 1 TD; Jones 4-56.

VIRGINIA TECH 45, INDIANA 20
DECEMBER 31, 1993

	1ST	2ND	3RD	4TH	FINAL
VT	7	21	0	17	45
IND	7	6	0	7	20

SCORING SUMMARY
IND	Lewis 75 pass from Paci (Manolopoulos kick)
VT	Thomas 13 pass from DeShazo (Williams kick)
VT	Swarm 6 run (Williams kick)
VT	Lewis 20 fumble return (Williams kick)
VT	Banks 80 blocked FG return (Williams kick)
IND	FG Manolopoulos 26
IND	FG Manolopoulos 40
VT	Freeman 42 pass from DeShazo (Williams kick)
VT	Edwards 5 run (Williams kick)
VT	FG Williams 42
IND	Lewis 42 pass from Dittoe (Manolopoulos kick)

VT	TEAM STATISTICS	IND
17	First Downs	11
125	Rushing Yards	20
19-33-2	Passing	17-37-2
193	Passing Yards	276
318	Total Yards	296
8-39.1	Punts - Average	7-38.4
2-1	Fumbles - Lost	2-2
8-84	Penalties - Yards	7-55
32:48	Possession Time	27:12

INDIVIDUAL LEADERS
RUSHING
VT: Thomas 24-65.
IND: Thurman 1-37.
PASSING
VT: DeShazo 19-33-2, 193 yards, 2 TD.
IND: Paci 10-22-1, 171 yards, 1 TD; Dittoe 7-14-1, 105 yards, 1 TD.
RECEIVING
VT: Freeman 5-66, 1 TD.
IND: Lewis 6-177, 2 TD.

VIRGINIA 20, TCU 10
DECEMBER 28, 1994

	1ST	2ND	3RD	4TH	FINAL
UVA	0	10	10	0	20
TCU	0	3	0	7	10

SCORING SUMMARY
UVA	FG Garcia 20
UVA	Way 6 run (Garcia kick)
TCU	FG Reeder 43
UVA	Davis 37 pass from Groh (Garcia kick)
UVA	FG Garcia 32
TCU	Collins 1 pass from Knake (Reeder kick)

UVA	TEAM STATISTICS	TCU
20	First Downs	11
237	Rushing Yards	126
14-23-2	Passing	8-24-1
199	Passing Yards	65
436	Total Yards	191
4-38.5	Punts - Average	8-37.3
1-0	Fumbles - Lost	2-1
9-66	Penalties - Yards	6-39

INDIVIDUAL LEADERS
RUSHING
UVA: Brooks 17-114; Way 24-90, 1 TD.
TCU: Davis 24-97.
PASSING
UVA: Groh 14-23-2, 199 yards, 1 TD.
TCU: Knake 8-24-1, 65 yards, 1 TD.
RECEIVING
UVA: Jeffers 3-60; Neely 3-55.
TCU: Oliver 1-22; Collins 2-14, 1 TD.

LSU 45, MICHIGAN STATE 26
DECEMBER 29, 1995

	1ST	2ND	3RD	4TH	FINAL
LSU	7	14	21	3	45
MSU	7	17	0	2	26

SCORING SUMMARY
MSU	Muhammed 78 pass from Banks (Gardner kick)
LSU	Cleveland 6 run (LaFleur kick)
MSU	Greene 3 run (kick blocked)
MSU	Mason 100 kick return (Greene run)
MSU	FG Gardner 37
LSU	Kennison 92 kick return (LaFleur kick)
LSU	Faulk 51 run (LaFleur kick)
LSU	Faulk 5 run (LaFleur kick)
LSU	Northern 37 fumble return (LaFleur kick)
LSU	Kennison 27 pass from Tyler (LaFleur kick)
LSU	FG Richey 48
MSU	Safety

LSU	TEAM STATISTICS	MSU
17	First Downs	23
272	Rushing Yards	100
10-20-1	Passing	22-44-3
164	Passing Yards	348
436	Total Yards	448
4-150	Kickoff Returns - Yards	7-158
4-44.5	Punts - Average	6-37.5
2-1	Fumbles - Lost	4-3
5-42	Penalties - Yards	9-80

INDIVIDUAL LEADERS
RUSHING
LSU: Faulk 25-234, 2 TD.
MSU: Renaud 16-79.
PASSING
LSU: Tyler 10-20-1, 164 yards, 1 TD.
MSU: Banks 22-44-3, 348 yards, 1 TD.
RECEIVING
LSU: Kennison 5-124, 1 TD.
MSU: Muhammed 9-171, 1 TD.

AUBURN 32, ARMY 29
DECEMBER 31, 1996

	1ST	2ND	3RD	4TH	FINAL
AU	10	10	12	0	32
ARMY	0	7	0	22	29

SCORING SUMMARY
AU	FG Holmes 31
AU	Goodson 30 pass from Craig (Holmes kick)
AU	Gosha 7 pass from Craig (Holmes kick)
AU	FG Holmes 49
ARMY	B. Williams 3 run (Parker kick)
AU	Craig 33 run (pass failed)
AU	R. Williams 18 run (pass failed)
ARMY	Perry 12 run (Parker kick)
ARMY	B. Williams 1 run (Parker kick)
ARMY	Richardson 30 pass from McAda (B. Williams run)

AU	TEAM STATISTICS	ARMY
27	First Downs	18
195	Rushing Yards	264
24-40-1	Passing	10-16-0
372	Passing Yards	148
567	Total Yards	412
2-41.5	Punts - Average	6-43.0
3-3	Fumbles - Lost	1-1
5-47	Penalties - Yards	3-20
29:53	Possession Time	30:07

INDIVIDUAL LEADERS
RUSHING
AU: Craig 13-75, 1 TD; R. Williams 12-72, 1 TD.
ARMY: B. Williams 12-82, 2 TD; Perry 19-81, 1 TD.
PASSING
AU: Craig 24-40-1, 372 yards, 2 TD.
ARMY: McAda 10-16-0, 148 yards, 1 TD.
RECEIVING
AU: Gosha 10-132, 1 TD; Baker 5-104.
ARMY: Williams 3-74; Richardson 2-59, 1 TD.

LSU 27, NOTRE DAME 9
DECEMBER 28, 1997

	1ST	2ND	3RD	4TH	FINAL
LSU	0	3	10	14	27
ND	3	3	0	3	9

SCORING SUMMARY
ND	FG Cengia 33
LSU	FG Richey 33
ND	FG Cengia 21
LSU	FG Richey 42
LSU	Booty 12 pass from Tyler (Richey kick)
ND	FG Cengia 33
LSU	Mealey 2 run (Richey kick)
LSU	Mealey 1 run (Richey kick)

LSU	TEAM STATISTICS	ND
19	First Downs	19
265	Rushing Yards	128
5-12-0	Passing	13-25-0
61	Passing Yards	115
326	Total Yards	243
3-38	Punt Returns - Yards	2-23
2-34	Kickoff Returns - Yards	4-61
4-35.8	Punts - Average	5-45.0
0-0	Fumbles - Lost	1-1
5-55	Penalties - Yards	5-30

INDIVIDUAL LEADERS
RUSHING
LSU: Mealey 34-222, 2 TD.
ND: Denson 20-101.
PASSING
LSU: Tyler 5-12-0, 61 yards, 1 TD.
ND: Powlus 8-18-0, 66 yards.
RECEIVING
LSU: Booty 5-61, 1 TD.
ND: Johnson 5-49.

THE BOWLS

December 31, 1998
Mississippi 35, Texas Tech 18

	1ST	2ND	3RD	4TH	FINAL
MISS	7	7	0	21	35
TT	7	3	0	8	18

SCORING SUMMARY

TT	Dorris 22 pass from Peters (Birkholz kick)
MISS	Lucas 33 pass from Miller (McGee kick)
MISS	McAllister 32 pass from Miller (McGee kick)
TT	FG Birkholz 49
MISS	Peterson 26 pass from Miller (McGee kick)
MISS	McAllister 4 run (McGee kick)
TT	McCullar 14 fumble return (Winn pass from Tittle)
MISS	McAllister 43 kickoff return (McGee kick)

MISS	TEAM STATISTICS	TT
19	First Downs	18
139	Rushing Yards	82
14-23-1	Passing	16-30-2
216	Passing Yards	203
355	Total Yards	285
5-32.4	Punts - Average	6-30.8
3-2	Fumbles - Lost	2-1
7-86	Penalties - Yards	5-55
34:47	Possession Time	25:13

INDIVIDUAL LEADERS

RUSHING
MISS: McAllister 27-83, 1 TD.
TT: Williams 23-95.

PASSING
MISS: Miller 14-23-1, 216, 3 TD.
TT: Tittle 11-19-2, 134 yards; Peters 5-11-0, 69 yards, 1 TD.

RECEIVING
MISS: McAllister 2-55, 1 TD; Peterson 3-54.
TT: Dorris 5-66, 1 TD; Hart 4-50.

December 31, 1999
Mississippi 27, Oklahoma 25

	1ST	2ND	3RD	4TH	FINAL
MISS	7	14	0	6	27
OKLA	3	0	15	7	25

SCORING SUMMARY

MISS	McAllister 25 pass from Miller (Binkley kick)
OKLA	FG Duncan 34
MISS	Bettis 9 pass from Miller (Binkley kick)
MISS	McAllister 80 run (Binkley kick)
OKLA	Jackson 3 pass from Heupel (Duncan kick)
OKLA	Daniels 41 pass from Heupel (Hammons pass from Heupel)
MISS	FG Binkley 29
OKLA	Griffin 17 pass from Heupel (Duncan kick)
MISS	FG Binkley 39

MISS	TEAM STATISTICS	OKLA
19	First Downs	27
159	Rushing Yards	91
18-29-2	Passing	39-54-1
202	Passing Yards	390
361	Total Yards	481
5-39.4	Punts - Average	1-10.0
1-0	Fumbles - Lost	3-3
3-13	Penalties - Yards	4-35
29:24	Possession Time	30:36

INDIVIDUAL LEADERS

RUSHING
MISS: McAllister 17-121, 1 TD.
OKLA: Griffin 12-86.

PASSING
MISS: Miller 18-28-2, 202 yards, 2 TD.
OKLA: Heupel 39-53-1, 390 yards, 3 TD.

RECEIVING
MISS: McAllister 3-55, 1 TD; Peterson 5-51.
OKLA: Daniels 6-109, 1 TD; Jackson 10-76, 1 TD.

December 31, 2000
Mississippi State 43, Texas A&M 41

	1ST	2ND	3RD	4TH	OT	FINAL
MSU	0	14	7	14	8	43
A&M	14	6	0	15	6	41

SCORING SUMMARY

A&M	Whitaker 9 run (Kitchens kick)
A&M	Toombs 4 run (Kitchens kick)
MSU	Walker 40 run (Westerfield kick)
MSU	Miller 4 pass from Madkin (Westerfield kick)
A&M	Ferguson 42 pass from Farris (kick blocked)
MSU	Walker 1 run (Westerfield kick)
MSU	Johnson 35 pass from Farris (Whitaker run)
A&M	Toombs 13 run (Kitchens kick)
MSU	Walker 32 run (Westerfield kick)
MSU	Lee 3 pass from Madkin (Westerfield kick)
A&M	Toombs 25 run (kick blocked)
MSU	Griffith blocked PAT return
MSU	Madkin 6 run

MSU	TEAM STATISTICS	A&M
16	First Downs	14
246	Rushing Yards	209
9-19-0	Passing	9-11-1
71	Passing Yards	133
317	Total Yards	342
7-37.1	Punts - Average	7-34.3
4-1	Fumbles - Lost	1-1
6-45	Penalties - Yards	7-71

INDIVIDUAL LEADERS

RUSHING
MSU: Walker 16-143, 3 TD.
A&M: Toombs 35-193, 3 TD.

PASSING
MSU: Madkin 9-19-0, 71 yards, 2 TD.
A&M: Farris 9-11-1, 133 yards, 2 TD.

RECEIVING
MSU: Miller 4-30, 1 TD.
A&M: Ferguson 3-54, 1 TD.

December 27, 2001
Alabama 14, Iowa State 13

	1ST	2ND	3RD	4TH	FINAL
ALA	0	7	0	7	14
ISU	3	7	3	0	13

SCORING SUMMARY

ISU	FG Yelk 36
ISU	Woodley 1 run (Yelk kick)
ALA	Zow 8 run (Thomas kick)
ISU	FG Yelk 41
ALA	Jones 27 pass from Zow (Thomas kick)

ALA	TEAM STATISTICS	ISU
15	First Downs	23
188	Rushing Yards	199
11-19-1	Passing	25-42-0
119	Passing Yards	284
307	Total Yards	483
2-14	Punt Returns - Yards	3-22
1-16	Kickoff Returns - Yards	3-48
7-39.9	Punts - Average	4-35.5
0-0	Fumbles - Lost	1-0
2-20	Penalties - Yards	4-32
29:22	Possession Time	30:38

INDIVIDUAL LEADERS

RUSHING
ALA: Galloway 16-90.
ISU: Haywood 20-125.

PASSING
ALA: Zow 11-19-1, 119 yards, 1 TD.
ISU: Wallace 25-42-0, 284 yards.

RECEIVING
ALA: Jones Jr. 2-44, 1 TD; Milons 3-32.
ISU: Campbell 7-109; Danielsen 5-57.

December 27, 2002
Mississippi 27, Nebraska 23

	1ST	2ND	3RD	4TH	FINAL
MISS	0	14	10	3	27
NEB	3	14	3	3	23

SCORING SUMMARY

NEB	FG Brown 29
NEB	Herian 41 pass from Lord (Brown kick)
MISS	Johnson 11 pass from Manning (Nichols kick)
NEB	Groce 60 punt return (Brown kick)
MISS	Sanford 1 run (Nichols kick)
MISS	FG Nichols 37
NEB	FG Brown 23
MISS	Sanford 1 run (Nichols kick)
NEB	FG Brown 29
MISS	FG Nichols 43

MISS	TEAM STATISTICS	NEB
20	First Downs	17
52	Rushing Yards	266
25-44-0	Passing	7-17-2
313	Passing Yards	93
365	Total Yards	359
3-23	Punt Returns - Yards	8-102
5-80	Kickoff Returns - Yards	5-105
8-43.8	Punts - Average	6-43.8
1-0	Fumbles - Lost	0-0
6-41	Penalties - Yards	6-70
30:31	Possession Time	29:29

INDIVIDUAL LEADERS

RUSHING
MISS: McClendon 12-36.
NEB: Diedrick 13-92; Lord 17-83.

PASSING
MISS: Manning 25-44-1, 313 yards, 1 TD.
NEB: Lord 7-16-2, 93 yards, 1 TD.

RECEIVING
MISS: Flowers 6-76.
NEB: Herian 1-41, 1 TD.

December 31, 2003
Arkansas 27, Missouri 14

	1ST	2ND	3RD	4TH	FINAL
ARK	3	18	3	3	27
MO	7	0	7	0	14

SCORING SUMMARY

ARK	FG Balseiro 33
MO	Abron 1 run (Matheny kick)
ARK	FG Balseiro 28
ARK	Jones 1 run (Wilson pass from Jones)
ARK	Cobbs 41 run (Balseiro kick)
ARK	FG Balseiro 25
MO	Smith 5 run (Matheny kick)
ARK	FG Balseiro 24

ARK	TEAM STATISTICS	MO
19	First Downs	25
300	Rushing Yards	252
9-18-0	Passing	17-31-2
85	Passing Yards	155
385	Total Yards	407
1-14	Punt Returns - Yards	1--2
3-87	Kickoff Returns - Yards	6-120
4-30.0	Punts - Average	3-25.0
0-0	Fumbles - Lost	2-1
3-26	Penalties - Yards	5-35
30:24	Possession Time	29:36

INDIVIDUAL LEADERS

RUSHING
ARK: Cobbs 27-141, 1 TD; Birmingham 10-85; Jones 7-74, 1 TD.
MO: Abron 19-137, 1 TD; Smith 20-96, 1 TD.

PASSING
ARK: Jones 6-14-0, 49 yards.
MO: Smith 17-30-1, 155 yards.

RECEIVING
ARK: Smith 3-29; Wilson 3-25.
MO: Coffey 4-68; Omboga 8-63.

December 28, 2004
Iowa State 17, Miami (Ohio) 13

	1ST	2ND	3RD	4TH	FINAL
ISU	7	3	0	7	17
MIA	0	7	6	0	13

SCORING SUMMARY

ISU	Hicks 4 run (Culbertson kick)
ISU	FG Culbertson 23
MIA	Clemens 28 pass from Betts (Parseghian kick)
MIA	Smith 2 run (kick failed)
ISU	Kock 1 run (Culbertson kick)

ISU	TEAM STATISTICS	MIA
22	First Downs	18
295	Rushing Yards	60
10-28-0	Passing	20-44-1
114	Passing Yards	240
409	Total Yards	300
3-34	Punt Returns - Yards	3-72
1-21	Kickoff Returns - Yards	3-22
7-37.9	Punts - Average	8-45.4
0-0	Fumbles - Lost	1-0
7-71	Penalties - Yards	7-48
30:33	Possession Time	29:27

INDIVIDUAL LEADERS

RUSHING
ISU: Hicks 27-159, 1 TD; Meyer 23-122.
MIA: Smith 9-46, 1 TD.

PASSING
ISU: Meyer 10-28-0, 114 yards.
MIA: Betts 20-44-1, 240 yards, 1 TD.

RECEIVING
ISU: Blythe 3-42; Davis 3-30.
MIA: Robinson 7-101.

HOLIDAY BOWL

PROFILE

Site: San Diego
Stadium: Qualcomm Stadium
Capacity: 71,400
Surface: Grass

PLAYING SITES

San Diego Jack Murphy Stadium, renamed Qualcomm Stadium in 1997, since 1978

NAME CHANGES

Holiday Bowl, 1978-85
Sea World Holiday Bowl, 1986-91
Thrifty Car Rental Holiday Bowl, 1992-94
Plymouth Holiday Bowl, 1995-97
Culligan Holiday Bowl, 1998-2001
Holiday Bowl, 2002
Pacific Life Holiday Bowl, since 2002

SEASON	DATE	PRE-GAME RANK	TEAMS	SCORE	FINAL RANK	MOST VALUABLE PLAYERS	ATT.
1978	Dec. 22, 1978		Navy	23		Phil McConkey, Navy, WR	52,500
			BYU	16			
1979	Dec. 21, 1979		Indiana	38	19	Marc Wilson, BYU, QB	52,200
		9	BYU	37	13	Tim Wilbur, Indiana, CB	
1980	Dec. 19, 1980	14	BYU	46	12	Jim McMahon, BYU, QB	50,214
		19	SMU	45	20	Craig James, SMU, RB	
1981	Dec. 18, 1981	14	BYU	38	13	Jim McMahon, BYU, QB	52,419
		20	Washington State	36		Kyle Whittingham, BYU, LB	
1982	Dec. 17, 1982		Ohio State	47		Tim Spencer, Ohio State, RB	52,533
			BYU	17		Garcia Lane, Ohio State, CB	
1983	Dec. 23, 1983	9	BYU	21	7	Steve Young, BYU, QB	51,480
			Missouri	17		Bobby Bell, Missouri, DE	
1984	Dec. 21, 1984	1	BYU	24	1	Robbie Bosco, BYU, QB	61,243
			Michigan	17		Leon White, BYU, LB	
1985	Dec. 22, 1985	14	Arkansas	18	12	Bobby Joe Edmonds, Arkansas, RB	42,324
			Arizona State	17		Greg Battle, Arizona State, LB	
1986	Dec. 30, 1986	19	Iowa	39	16	Mark Vlasic, Iowa, QB, Todd Santos, San Diego State, QB	59,473
			San Diego State	38		Richard Brown, San Diego State, LB	
1987	Dec. 30, 1987	18	Iowa	20	16	Craig Burnett, Wyoming, QB	61,892
			Wyoming	19		Anthony Wright, Iowa, CB	
1988	Dec. 30, 1988	12	Oklahoma State	62	11	Barry Sanders, Oklahoma State, RB	60,718
		15	Wyoming	14		Sim Drain, Oklahoma State, LB	
1989	Dec. 29, 1989	18	Penn State	50	15	Blair Thomas, Penn State, RB	61,113
		19	BYU	39	22	Ty Detmer, BYU, QB	
1990	Dec. 29, 1990		Texas A&M	65	15	Bucky Richardson, Texas A&M, QB	61,441
		13	BYU	14	22	William Thomas, Texas A&M, LB	
1991	Dec. 30, 1991		BYU	13	23	Ty Detmer, QB, Josh Arnold, DB, BYU	60,646
		7	Iowa	13	10	Carlos James, Iowa, DB	
1992	Dec. 30, 1992		Hawaii	27	20	Michael Carter, Hawaii, QB	44,457
			Illinois	17		Junior Tagoai, Hawaii, DT	
1993	Dec. 30, 1993	11	Ohio State	28	11	Raymont Harris, Lorenzo Styles, Ohio State	52,108
			BYU	21		John Walsh, BYU, QB	
1994	Dec. 30, 1994	20	Michigan	24	12	Todd Collins, QB, Matt Dyson, LB, Michigan	59,453
		10	Colorado State	14	16	Anthoney Hill, Colorado State, QB	
1995	Dec. 29, 1995	10	Kansas State	54	7	Brian Kavanagh, Kansas State, QB	51,051
			Colorado State	21		Mario Smith, Kansas State, DB	
1996	Dec. 30, 1996	8	Colorado	33	8	Koy Detmer, Colorado, QB	54,749
		13	Washington	21	16	Nick Ziegler, Colorado, DE	
1997	Dec. 29, 1997	18	Colorado State	35	17	Moses Moreno, Colorado State, QB	50,761
		19	Missouri	24	23	Darran Hall, Colorado State, WR	
1998	Dec. 30, 1998	5	Arizona	23	4	Keith Smith, Arizona, QB	65,354
		14	Nebraska	20	19	Chris McAlister, Arizona, CB	
1999	Dec. 29, 1999	7	Kansas State	24	6	Jonathan Beasley, Kansas State, QB	57,118
			Washington	20		Darren Howard, Kansas State, LB	
2000	Dec. 29, 2000	8	Oregon	35	7	Joey Harrington, Oregon, QB	63,278
		12	Texas	30	12		
2001	Dec. 28, 2001	9	Texas	47	5	Major Applewhite, Texas, QB, Willie Hurst, Washington, TB	60,548
		21	Washington	43	19	Derrick Johnson, Texas, LB	
2002	Dec. 27, 2002	6	Kansas State	34	7	Ell Roberson, Kansas State, QB	58,717
			Arizona State	27		Terrell Suggs, Arizona State, DE	
2003	Dec. 30, 2003	15	Washington State	28	9	Kyle Basler, Washington State, P	61,102
		5	Texas	20	12		
2004	Dec. 30, 2004	23	Texas Tech	45	18	Sonny Cumbie, Texas Tech, QB	63,711
		4	California	31	9	Adell Duckett, Texas Tech, DE	

NAVY 23, BYU 16
DECEMBER 22, 1978

	1ST	2ND	3RD	4TH	FINAL
NAVY	0	3	7	13	23
BYU	3	6	7	0	16

SCORING SUMMARY
BYU   FG Johnson 33
NAVY   FG Tata 40
BYU   Chronister 10 pass from McMahon (kick failed)
BYU   McMahon 2 run (Johnson kick)
NAVY   Tolbert 4 run (Tata kick)
NAVY   FG Tata 28
NAVY   McConkey 65 pass from Leszczynski (Tata kick)
NAVY   FG Tata 27

NAVY	TEAM STATISTICS	BYU
20	First Downs	16
214	Rushing Yards	74
8-14-0	Passing	16-34-2
138	Passing Yards	181
352	Total Yards	255
2-0	Punt Returns - Yards	2-18
3-70	Kickoff Returns - Yards	6-80
3-38.7	Punts - Average	5-37.0
2-2	Fumbles - Lost	0-0
3-37	Penalties - Yards	12-91
32:03	Possession Time	27:57

INDIVIDUAL LEADERS
RUSHING
NAVY: Sherlock 19-62; Tolbert 14-50, 1 TD.
BYU: Wingard 7-37; McMahon 12-17, 1 TD.
PASSING
NAVY: Leszczynski 7-13-0, 123 yards, 1 TD.
BYU: McMahon 9-18-1, 133 yards, 1 TD.
RECEIVING
NAVY: McConkey 4-88, 1 TD; Gallahan 2-24.
BYU: Chronister 3-60, 1 TD; Davis 2-38.

INDIANA 38, BYU 37
DECEMBER 21, 1979

	1ST	2ND	3RD	4TH	FINAL
IND	14	7	10	7	38
BYU	14	3	17	3	37

SCORING SUMMARY
BYU   Lane 1 run (Johnson kick)
IND   Stephenson 38 pass from Clifford (Kellogg kick)
IND   Clifford 1 run (Kellogg kick)
BYU   M. Wilson 3 run (Johnson kick)
BYU   FG Johnson 40
IND   Clifford 1 run (Kellogg kick)
BYU   H. Jones 13 pass from M. Wilson (Johnson kick)
IND   Harkrader 1 run (Kellogg kick)
IND   FG Kellogg 26
BYU   FG Johnson 29
BYU   Lane 15 pass from M. Wilson (Johnson kick)
BYU   FG Johnson 28
IND   Wilbur 62 punt return (Kellogg kick)

IND	TEAM STATISTICS	BYU
21	First Downs	31
183	Rushing Yards	140
11-30-1	Passing	28-43-3
171	Passing Yards	380
354	Total Yards	520
2-66	Punt Returns - Yards	5-30
6-114	Kickoff Returns - Yards	7-126
6-41.3	Punts - Average	2-38.0
1-0	Fumbles - Lost	1-1
7-70	Penalties - Yards	1-15
35:07	Possession Time	24:53

INDIVIDUAL LEADERS
RUSHING
IND: Johnson 21-76; Harkrader 24-71, 1 TD.
BYU: H. Jones 8-55, 1 TD; Phillips 4-31.
PASSING
IND: Clifford 11-29-1, 171 yards, 1 TD.
BYU: M. Wilson 28-3-3, 380 yards, 2 TD.
RECEIVING
IND: Stephenson 5-91, 1 TD; Friede 2-43.
BYU: C. Brown 9-142; Lane 9-79, 1 TD.

BYU 46, SMU 45
DECEMBER 19, 1980

	1ST	2ND	3RD	4TH	FINAL
BYU	7	6	6	27	46
SMU	19	10	9	7	45

SCORING SUMMARY
SMU	Dickerson 15 run (Garcia kick)
SMU	James 45 run (Garcia kick)
SMU	Safety (Snap out of end zone)
SMU	FG Garcia 42
BYU	Brown 64 pass from McMahon (Gunther kick)
SMU	James 3 pass from McIlhenny (Garcia kick)
SMU	FG Garcia 44
BYU	Sikahema 83 punt return (pass failed)
SMU	Dickerson 1 run (pass failed)
BYU	Brown 13 pass from McMahon (pass failed)
SMU	FG Garcia 42
BYU	Phillips 1 run (pass failed)
SMU	James 42 run (Garcia kick)
BYU	Braga 15 pass from McMahon (pass failed)
BYU	Phillips 1 run (McMahon pass to Phillips)
BYU	Brown 41 pass from McMahon (Gunther kick)

BYU	TEAM STATISTICS	SMU
23	First Downs	25
-2	Rushing Yards	393
32-49-1	Passing	6-11-0
446	Passing Yards	53
444	Total Yards	446
3-98	Punt Returns - Yards	1-0
4-65	Kickoff Returns - Yards	4-85
5-32.6	Punts - Average	4-38.8
2-0	Fumbles - Lost	2-0
8-80	Penalties - Yards	7-65

INDIVIDUAL LEADERS
RUSHING
BYU: Phillips 8-18, 2 TD.
SMU: James 23-225, 2 TD; Dickerson 23-110, 2 TD.
PASSING
BYU: McMahon 32-49-1, 446 yards, 4 TD.
SMU: McIlhenny 6-11-0, 53 yards, 1 TD.
RECEIVING
BYU: Brown 5-155, 3 TD; Phillips 10-81; Braga 5-77, 1 TD.
SMU: Bennett 1-20; James 2-13, 1 TD.

BYU 38, Washington State 36
DECEMBER 18, 1981

	1ST	2ND	3RD	4TH	FINAL
BYU	7	17	7	7	38
WSU	0	7	21	8	36

SCORING SUMMARY
BYU	Plater 35 pass from McMahon (Gunther kick)
BYU	Hudson 7 pass from McMahon (Gunther kick)
WSU	Turner 2 run (Leland kick)
BYU	FG Gunther 20
BYU	Hamilton 1 run (Gunther kick)
BYU	Holmoe 35 interception return (Gunther kick)
WSU	LaBomme 18 run (Beech pass from Casper)
WSU	Williams 5 run (pass failed)
WSU	Turner 13 run (Leland kick)
BYU	Pettis 11 pass from McMahon (Gunther kick)
WSU	Martin 1 run (Turner run)

BYU	TEAM STATISTICS	WSU
22	First Downs	23
69	Rushing Yards	245
28-44-0	Passing	8-25-2
368	Passing Yards	106
437	Total Yards	351
3-16	Punt Returns - Yards	6-39
4-26	Kickoff Returns - Yards	4-106
8-36.9	Punts - Average	8-40.9
5-0	Fumbles - Lost	0-0
9-86	Penalties - Yards	5-45
27:59	Possession Time	32:01

INDIVIDUAL LEADERS
RUSHING
BYU: Hamilton 9-52, 1 TD; Pettis 7-28.
WSU: Turner 12-92, 2 TD; LaBomme 14-79, 1 TD; Williams 11-48, 1 TD.
PASSING
BYU: McMahon 27-43-0, 342 yards, 3 TD.
WSU: Casper 6-16-2, 69 yards.
RECEIVING
BYU: Hudson 7-126, 1 TD; Pettis 8-73, 1 TD.
WSU: Beach 2-57; Keller 4-40.

Ohio State 47, BYU 17
DECEMBER 17, 1982

	1ST	2ND	3RD	4TH	FINAL
OSU	3	14	17	13	47
BYU	0	10	0	7	17

SCORING SUMMARY
OSU	FG Spangler 47
BYU	Balholm 7 pass from Young (Gunther kick)
OSU	Spencer 61 run (Spangler kick)
OSU	Tomczak 3 run (Spangler kick)
BYU	FG Gunther 39
OSU	Broadnax 1 run (Spangler kick)
OSU	Spencer 18 run (Spangler kick)
OSU	FG Spangler 37
OSU	Gayle 1 run (Spangler kick)
BYU	Hudson 13 pass from Young (Gunther kick)
OSU	Gayle 5 run (kick failed)

OSU	TEAM STATISTICS	BYU
24	First Downs	21
329	Rushing Yards	19
11-19-0	Passing	28-46-1
132	Passing Yards	352
461	Total Yards	371
4-41	Punt Returns - Yards	0-0
4-55	Kickoff Returns - Yards	7-124
3-37.7	Punts - Average	5-34.8
1-1	Fumbles - Lost	1-1
12-109	Penalties - Yards	9-75
34:33	Possession Time	25:27

INDIVIDUAL LEADERS
RUSHING
OSU: Spencer 21-167, 2 TD; Gayle 17-80, 2 TD; Broadnax 15-58, 1 TD.
BYU: Hamilton 3-14; Tiumalu 3-13.
PASSING
OSU: Tomczak 11-19-0, 132 yards.
BYU: Young 27-45-1, 341 yards, 2 TD.
RECEIVING
OSU: Williams 5-63; Spencer 1-23.
BYU: Hudson 7-81, 1 TD; Balholm 3-58, 1 TD.

BYU 21, Missouri 17
DECEMBER 23, 1983

	1ST	2ND	3RD	4TH	FINAL
BYU	0	7	7	7	21
MO	7	3	0	7	17

SCORING SUMMARY
MO	Drain 2 run (Burditt kick)
BYU	Young 10 run (Johnson kick)
MO	FG Burditt 37
BYU	Stinnett 33 pass from Young (Johnson kick)
MO	Drain 2 run (Burditt kick)
BYU	Young 14 pass from Stinnett (Johnson kick)

BYU	TEAM STATISTICS	MO
23	First Downs	19
42	Rushing Yards	252
25-37-3	Passing	7-16-2
328	Passing Yards	86
370	Total Yards	338
3-20	Punt Returns - Yards	1-3
3-51	Kickoff Returns - Yards	2-19
3-42.7	Punts - Average	5-36.8
3-2	Fumbles - Lost	2-2
3-25	Penalties - Yards	6-78
22:53	Possession Time	37:07

INDIVIDUAL LEADERS
RUSHING
BYU: Tiumalu 11-57.
MO: Drain 27-115, 2 TD; Redd 16-68.
PASSING
BYU: Young 24-36-3, 314 yards; Stinnett 1-1-0, 14 yards, 1 TD.
MO: Seitz 4-7-1, 49 yards; Adler 3-9-1, 37 yards.
RECEIVING
BYU: Eddo 2-70; Stinnett 5-60; Haysbert 3-53.
MO: Shorthouse 4-50; Drain 1-21.

BYU 24, Michigan 17
DECEMBER 21, 1984

	1ST	2ND	3RD	4TH	FINAL
BYU	0	10	0	14	24
MICH	0	7	7	3	17

SCORING SUMMARY
BYU	Smith 5 run (Johnson kick)
MICH	Rogers 5 run (Bergeron kick)
BYU	FG Johnson 31
MICH	Perryman 10 pass from Zurbrugg (Bergeron kick)
MICH	FG Bergeron 32
BYU	Kozlowski 7 pass from Bosco (Johnson kick)
BYU	Smith 13 pass from Bosco (Johnson kick)

BYU	TEAM STATISTICS	MICH
32	First Downs	13
112	Rushing Yards	120
35-49-3	Passing	7-15-1
371	Passing Yards	82
483	Total Yards	202
2-(-6)	Punt Returns - Yards	0-0
3-24	Kickoff Returns - Yards	2-23
1-45.0	Punts - Average	7-39.1
4-3	Fumbles - Lost	2-0
9-82	Penalties - Yards	11-112
28:59	Possession Time	31:01

INDIVIDUAL LEADERS
RUSHING
BYU: Heimuli 16-82; Bosco 6-16.
MICH: Perryman 13-110; Rogers 19-60, 1 TD.
PASSING
BYU: Bosco 30-42-3, 343 yards, 2 TD.
MICH: Zurbrugg 7-15-1, 82 yards, 1 TD.
RECEIVING
BYU: Mills 11-103; Smith 10-88, 1 TD.
MICH: Bean 3-46; Perryman 2-15, 1 TD.

Arkansas 18, Arizona State 17
DECEMBER 22, 1985

	1ST	2ND	3RD	4TH	FINAL
ARK	7	0	0	11	18
ASU	3	11	0	3	17

SCORING SUMMARY
ASU	FG Bostrom 47
ARK	D. Thomas 9 run (Trainor kick)
ASU	FG Bostrom 22
ASU	Cox 16 pass from Van Raaphorst (Amoia pass from Van Raaphorst)
ARK	Edmonds 17 run (Calcagni run)
ASU	FG Bostrom 28
ARK	FG Trainor 37

ARK	TEAM STATISTICS	ASU
21	First Downs	20
260	Rushing Yards	195
10-18-0	Passing	14-27-1
117	Passing Yards	167
377	Total Yards	362
1-10	Punt Returns - Yards	0-0
4-67	Kickoff Returns - Yards	3-81
5-37.0	Punts - Average	5-32.8
1-1	Fumbles - Lost	0-0
2-10	Penalties - Yards	2-21
32:44	Possession Time	27:16

INDIVIDUAL LEADERS
RUSHING
ARK: Rouse 15-76; Calcagni 16-45; Edmonds 7-43, 1 TD.
ASU: Crawford 18-103; Amoia 13-56.
PASSING
ARK: Calcagni 10-17-0, 117 yards.
ASU: Van Raaphorst 14-27-1, 167 yards, 1 TD.
RECEIVING
ARK: Edmonds 7-93; Centers 1-17.
ASU: Cox 3-67, 1 TD; Gallimore 4-36.

Iowa 39, San Diego State 38
December 30, 1986

	1ST	2ND	3RD	4TH	FINAL
IOWA	7	6	8	18	39
SDSU	6	15	7	10	38

SCORING SUMMARY
IOWA Bayless 5 run (Houghtlin kick)
SDSU Hardy 6 pass from Santos (kick failed)
SDSU Jackson 44 pass from Santos (Hardy run)
IOWA Vlasic 1 run (kick failed)
SDSU Gilbreath 28 pass from Santos (Rahill kick)
SDSU Gilmore 1 run (Rahill kick)
IOWA Hudson 1 run (Smith pass from Vlasic)
SDSU Hardy 6 run (Rahill kick)
IOWA Cook 29 pass from Vlasic (Flagg pass from Vlasic)
IOWA Flagg 4 pass from Vlasic (Houghtlin kick)
SDSU FG Rahill 21
IOWA FG Houghtlin 41

IOWA	TEAM STATISTICS	SDSU
21	First Downs	17
141	Rushing Yards	117
15-29-1	Passing	21-33-2
222	Passing Yards	298
363	Total Yards	415
3-6	Punt Returns - Yards	3-12
7-161	Kickoff Returns - Yards	6-98
4-42.5	Punts - Average	5-47.0
2-1	Fumbles - Lost	0-0
4-17	Penalties - Yards	7-70

INDIVIDUAL LEADERS
RUSHING
IOWA: Bayless 19-110, 1 TD; Hudson 9-43, 1 TD.
SDSU: Hardy 26-83, 1 TD; Gilmore 7-35, 1 TD.
PASSING
IOWA: Vlasic 15-28-1, 222 yards, 2 TD.
SDSU: Santos 21-33-2, 298 yards, 3 TD.
RECEIVING
IOWA: Flagg 4-66, 1 TD; Early 3-57; Cook 2-51, 1 TD.
SDSU: Jackson 2-89, 1 TD; Gilbreath 5-87, 1 TD; Gilmore 9-70.

Iowa 20, Wyoming 19
December 30, 1987

	1ST	2ND	3RD	4TH	FINAL
IOWA	0	7	0	13	20
WYO	12	7	0	0	19

SCORING SUMMARY
WYO FG Worker 43
WYO FG Worker 38
WYO Loving 15 pass from Burnett (pass failed)
IOWA Hess 10 blocked punt return (Houghtlin kick)
WYO Abraham 3 run (Worker kick)
IOWA Wright 33 interception return (Houghtlin kick)
IOWA Hudson 1 run (pass failed)

IOWA	TEAM STATISTICS	WYO
17	First Downs	19
94	Rushing Yards	43
21-35-0	Passing	28-51-1
237	Passing Yards	332
331	Total Yards	375
4-19	Punt Returns - Yards	5-27
5-92	Kickoff Returns - Yards	4-63
8-42.0	Punts - Average	6-30.0
1-1	Fumbles - Lost	0-0
6-57	Penalties - Yards	7-61
30:34	Possession Time	29:26

INDIVIDUAL LEADERS
RUSHING
IOWA: Harmon 12-47; Hudson 10-43, 1 TD.
WYO: Abraham 14-39, 1 TD; Bena 4-14.
PASSING
IOWA: Hartlieb 21-35-0, 237 yards.
WYO: Burnett 28-51-1, 332 yards, 1 TD.
RECEIVING
IOWA: Flagg 6-93; Watkins 4-72.
WYO: Sargent 8-106; Loving 5-63, 1 TD.

Oklahoma State 62, Wyoming 14
December 30, 1988

	1ST	2ND	3RD	4TH	FINAL
OKST	7	10	28	17	62
WYO	7	0	7	0	14

SCORING SUMMARY
OKST Sanders 33 run (Blanchard kick)
WYO Welniak 6 pass from (Fleming kick)
OKST Sanders 2 run (Blanchard kick)
OKST FG Blanchard 33
OKST Parker 12 pass from Gundy (Blanchard kick)
WYO Welniak 4 pass from (Fleming kick)
OKST Sanders 67 run (Blanchard kick)
OKST Sanders 10 run (Blanchard kick)
OKST FG Blanchard 19
OKST Dykes 25 pass from Gundy (Blanchard kick)
OKST Smith 5 run (Blanchard kick)

OKST	TEAM STATISTICS	WYO
34	First Downs	14
320	Rushing Yards	33
24-29-0	Passing	16-32-2
378	Passing Yards	171
698	Total Yards	204
2-7	Punt Returns - Yards	0-0
3-35	Kickoff Returns - Yards	10-205
0-0.0	Punts - Average	6-37.2
1-1	Fumbles - Lost	1-0
3-39	Penalties - Yards	4-30

INDIVIDUAL LEADERS
RUSHING
OKST: Sanders 29-222, 5 TD; Gundy 6-38.
WYO: Gunn 7-19; Jones 2-19.
PASSING
OKST: Gundy 20-24-0, 315 yards, 2 TD.
WYO: Welniak 15-30-2, 164 yards.
RECEIVING
OKST: Dykes 10-163, 1 TD; Hudson 1-42.
WYO: Gibson 4-37; Dussett 3-31.

Penn State 50, BYU 39
December 29, 1989

	1ST	2ND	3RD	4TH	FINAL
PSU	3	9	17	21	50
BYU	3	10	13	13	39

SCORING SUMMARY
PSU FG Tarasi 30
BYU FG Chaffetz 20
PSU Smith 24 pass from Sacca (kick failed)
BYU Detmer 1 run (Chaffetz kick)
PSU FG Tarasi 36
BYU FG Chaffetz 22
PSU FG Tarasi 51
PSU Thompson 16 run (Tarasi kick)
BYU Detmer 1 run (kick failed)
PSU Thompson 14 run (Tarasi kick)
BYU Boyce 12 pass from Detmer (Chaffetz kick)
PSU Thomas 7 run (run failed)
PSU Daniels 52 pass from Sacca (pass failed)
BYU Whittingham 10 run (Chaffetz kick)
BYU Nyberg 3 pass from Detmer (pass failed)
PSU Collins 2 point conversion interception return
PSU Brown 53 fumble return (Tarasi kick)

PSU	TEAM STATISTICS	BYU
26	First Downs	35
249	Rushing Yards	75
11-21-1	Passing	42-59-2
215	Passing Yards	576
464	Total Yards	651
1-7	Punt Returns - Yards	1-3
7-167	Kickoff Returns - Yards	9-177
2-38.0	Punts - Average	1-39.0
0-0	Fumbles - Lost	3-1
10-93	Penalties - Yards	10-88
31:04	Possession Time	28:56

INDIVIDUAL LEADERS
RUSHING
PSU: Thomas 35-186, 1 TD; Thompson 14-68, 2 TD.
BYU: Whittingham 9-39, 1 TD; Detmer 8-18, 2 TD.
PASSING
PSU: Sacca 10-19-1, 206 yards, 2 TD.
BYU: Detmer 42-59-2, 576 yards, 2 TD.
RECEIVING
PSU: Thomas 2-46; McDuffie 2-36.
BYU: Boyce 8-127, 1 TD; Bellini 10-124; Nyberg 8-117, 1 TD.

Texas A&M 65, BYU 14
December 29, 1990

	1ST	2ND	3RD	4TH	FINAL
A&M	14	23	7	21	65
BYU	7	0	7	0	14

SCORING SUMMARY
A&M Wilson 1 run (Talbot kick)
BYU Smith 8 pass from Detmer (Kauffman kick)
A&M Lewis 6 run (Talbot kick)
A&M Richardson 6 run (Talbot kick)
A&M Safety
A&M Richardson 22 pass from Lewis (Talbot kick)
A&M Garrett 6 pass from Richardson (Talbot kick)
BYU Clark 1 pass from Evans (Kauffman kick)
A&M Richardson 27 run (Talbot kick)
A&M Lewis 3 run (Talbot kick)
A&M Patterson 14 pass from Pavlas (Talbot kick)
A&M Krahl 9 pass from Pavlas (Talbot kick)

A&M	TEAM STATISTICS	BYU
28	First Downs	15
356	Rushing Yards	-12
16-18-0	Passing	15-32-1
324	Passing Yards	197
680	Total Yards	185
1-13	Punt Returns - Yards	1-3
10-204	Kickoff Returns - Yards	9-164
1-35.0	Punts - Average	4-35.7
1-1	Fumbles - Lost	5-3
11-111	Penalties - Yards	6-39
38:28	Possession Time	21:32

INDIVIDUAL LEADERS
RUSHING
A&M: Richardson 12-119, 2 TD; Lewis 25-104, 2 TD; Wilson 9-51, 1 TD.
BYU: Tuipulotu 5-44; Salido 4-18.
PASSING
A&M: Richardson 9-11-0, 203 yards, 1 TD; Pavlas 5-5-0, 60 yards, 2 TD.
BYU: Detmer 11-23-1, 120 yards, 1 TD; Evans 4-9-0, 77 yards, 1 TD.
RECEIVING
A&M: Patterson 2-69, 1 TD; Oliver 4-65; Garrett 4-57, 1 TD.
BYU: Smith 5-96, 1 TD; Matsuzaki 2-39; Boyce 2-30.

BYU 13, Iowa 13
December 30, 1991

	1ST	2ND	3RD	4TH	FINAL
BYU	0	6	0	7	13
IOWA	6	7	0	0	13

SCORING SUMMARY
IOWA Saunders 13 run (kick failed)
IOWA Saunders 5 run (Skillett kick)
BYU Tuipulotu 9 pass from Detmer (kick failed)
BYU Anderson 26 pass from Detmer (Kauffman kick)

BYU	TEAM STATISTICS	IOWA
26	First Downs	20
80	Rushing Yards	125
29-44-1	Passing	19-28-1
350	Passing Yards	221
430	Total Yards	346
1-14	Punt Returns - Yards	0-0
3-50	Kickoff Returns - Yards	3-38
2-44.0	Punts - Average	4-34.8
1-1	Fumbles - Lost	0-0
7-60	Penalties - Yards	7-61
32:23	Possession Time	27:37

INDIVIDUAL LEADERS
RUSHING
BYU: Willis 13-61; Tuipulotu 12-44.
IOWA: Saunders 19-103, 2 TD; Montgomery 7-35.
PASSING
BYU: Detmer 29-44-1, 350 yards, 2 TD.
IOWA: Rodgers 19-28-1, 221 yards.
RECEIVING
BYU: Tuipulotu 8-85, 1 TD; Rex 6-71; Drage 5-62.
IOWA: Filloon 7-107; Hughes 5-48.

December 30, 1992
Hawaii 27, Illinois 17

	1ST	2ND	3RD	4TH	FINAL
HAW	0	7	10	10	27
ILL	7	3	0	7	17

SCORING SUMMARY
ILL	Wright 14 pass from Verduzco (Richardson kick)
HAW	Sims 6 run (Elam kick)
ILL	FG Richardson 19
HAW	Sims 1 run (Elam kick)
HAW	FG Elam 45
HAW	FG Elam 37
HAW	Branch 53 pass from Carter (Elam kick)
ILL	Wright 18 pass from Verduzco (Richardson kick)

HAW	TEAM STATISTICS	ILL
23	First Downs	23
287	Rushing Yards	108
6-17-2	Passing	26-34-1
115	Passing Yards	239
402	Total Yards	347
1-11	Punt Returns - Yards	1-5
3-45	Kickoff Returns - Yards	5-82
2-41.0	Punts - Average	3-46.0
2-0	Fumbles - Lost	2-1
3-26	Penalties - Yards	3-25
32:33	Possession Time	27:27

INDIVIDUAL LEADERS
RUSHING
HAW: Sims 29-113, 2 TD; Carter 21-105.
ILL: Boyer 11-39; Feagin 7-31.
PASSING
HAW: Carter 6-16-2, 115 yards, 1 TD.
ILL: Verduzco 26-34-1, 248 yards, 2 TD.
RECEIVING
HAW: Branch 1-53, 1 TD; Gordon 2-23.
ILL: Wright 7-82, 2 TD; Klein 3-59; Strong 5-55.

December 30, 1993
Ohio State 28, BYU 21

	1ST	2ND	3RD	4TH	FINAL
OSU	14	7	7	0	28
BYU	0	14	0	0	21

SCORING SUMMARY
OSU	Patillo 4 punt return (Williams kick)
BYU	Willis 27 pass from Walsh (Herrick kick)
OSU	Harris 2 run (Williams kick)
OSU	Harris 2 run (Williams kick)
BYU	Lewis 8 run (Herrick kick)
BYU	Doman 27 pass from Walsh (Herrick kick)
OSU	Harris 1 run (Williams kick)

OSU	TEAM STATISTICS	BYU
21	First Downs	24
330	Rushing Yards	50
6-13-0	Passing	25-44-1
61	Passing Yards	389
391	Total Yards	439
1-4	Punt Returns - Yards	2-24
2-24	Kickoff Returns - Yards	5-139
6-36.3	Punts - Average	2-20.5
0-0	Fumbles - Lost	2-1
7-45	Penalties - Yards	5-25
32:23	Possession Time	27:37

INDIVIDUAL LEADERS
RUSHING
OSU: Harris 39-235, 3 TD; By'not'e 9-61.
BYU: Hall 11-42; Heimuli 6-21.
PASSING
OSU: Hoying 5-11-0, 55 yards.
BYU: Walsh 25-44-1, 389 yards, 3 TD.
RECEIVING
OSU: Galloway 2-19; Tillman 1-17.
BYU: Doman 3-82, 1 TD; Willis 2-72, 1 TD.

December 30, 1994
Michigan 24, Colorado State 14

	1ST	2ND	3RD	4TH	FINAL
MICH	10	7	7	0	24
CSU	7	0	0	7	14

SCORING SUMMARY
MICH	Toomer 4 pass from Collins (Hamilton kick)
CSU	Turner 32 pass from Hill (McDougal kick)
MICH	FG Hamilton 34
MICH	Hayes 16 pass from Collins (Hamilton kick)
MICH	Wheatley 3 run (Hamilton kick)
CSU	Burkett 18 pass from Hill (McDougal kick)

MICH	TEAM STATISTICS	CSU
18	First Downs	20
179	Rushing Yards	51
14-24-3	Passing	22-40-2
162	Passing Yards	289
341	Total Yards	340
0-0	Punt Returns - Yards	2-15
2-61	Kickoff Returns - Yards	5-102
5-28.0	Punts - Average	4-35.5
0-0	Fumbles - Lost	2-2
11-97	Penalties - Yards	8-72
27:40	Possession Time	32:20

INDIVIDUAL LEADERS
RUSHING
MICH: Wheatley 16-80, 1 TD; Biakabutuka 9-70.
CSU: Watson 17-47; Ward 1-8.
PASSING
MICH: Collins 14-24-3, 162 yards, 2 TD.
CSU: Hill 22-40-2, 289 yards, 2 TD.
RECEIVING
MICH: Toomer 5-63, 1 TD; Hayes 3-41, 1 TD.
CSU: Shull 3-101; Burkett 5-62, 1 TD; Turner 4-62, 1 TD.

December 29, 1995
Kansas State 54, Colorado State 21

	1ST	2ND	3RD	4TH	FINAL
KSU	7	19	21	7	54
CSU	7	0	14	0	21

SCORING SUMMARY
KSU	Hickson 4 run (Gramatica kick)
CSU	Blake 2 run (McDougal kick)
KSU	Lawrence 5 run (kick failed)
KSU	Kelly 18 run (pass failed)
KSU	Lojka 12 pass from Kavanagh (Gramatica kick)
KSU	Schwieger 18 pass from Kavanagh (Gramatica kick)
CSU	Watson 3 run (McDougal kick)
KSU	Lawrence 5 run (Gramatica kick)
CSU	Washington 12 run (McDougal kick)
KSU	Lockett 4 pass from Kavanagh (Gramatica kick)
KSU	Running 33 pass from Kavanagh (Gramatica kick)

KSU	TEAM STATISTICS	CSU
30	First Downs	14
212	Rushing Yards	169
24-32-1	Passing	6-30-3
324	Passing Yards	132
536	Total Yards	301
3-7	Punt Returns - Yards	0-0
3-67	Kickoff Returns - Yards	7-136
3-45.0	Punts - Average	8-28.4
0-0	Fumbles - Lost	2-1
12-124	Penalties - Yards	11-95
36:17	Possession Time	23:43

INDIVIDUAL LEADERS
RUSHING
KSU: Hickson 20-103, 1 TD; Lawrence 7-33, 2 TD.
CSU: Washingon 10-101, 1 TD; Blake 11-41, 1 TD.
PASSING
KSU: Kavanagh 18-24-1, 242 yards, 4 TD.
CSU: Moreno 5-24-2, 91 yards.
RECEIVING
KSU: Running 6-126, 1 TD; Hickson 6-55; Schwieger 4-47, 1 TD.
CSU: Antoine 1-41; Turner 1-35.

December 30, 1996
Colorado 33, Washington 21

	1ST	2ND	3RD	4TH	FINAL
COLO	7	17	3	6	33
WASH	14	7	0	0	21

SCORING SUMMARY
WASH	Dillon 2 run (Jones kick)
WASH	Dillon 12 run (Jones kick)
COLO	Carruth 76 pass from Detmer (Aldrich kick)
COLO	Ziegler 31 interception return (Aldrich kick)
WASH	Pathon 86 kickoff return (Jones kick)
COLO	Chiaverini 7 pass from Detmer (Aldrich kick)
COLO	FG Aldrich 42
COLO	FG Aldrich 36
COLO	Carruth 4 pass from Detmer (pass failed)

COLO	TEAM STATISTICS	WASH
24	First Downs	18
43	Rushing Yards	138
25-45-0	Passing	21-37-1
371	Passing Yards	203
414	Total Yards	341
4-32	Punt Returns - Yards	3-11
4-19	Kickoff Returns - Yards	5-179
5-34.6	Punts - Average	7-37.1
3-1	Fumbles - Lost	1-0
5-39	Penalties - Yards	7-75
29:36	Possession Time	30:24

INDIVIDUAL LEADERS
RUSHING
COLO: Troutman 9-22; Henry 11-14.
WASH: Dillon 30-140, 2 TD.
PASSING
COLO: Detmer 25-45-0, 371 yards, 3 TD.
WASH: Huard 21-37-1, 203 yards.
RECEIVING
COLO: Carruth 7-162, 2 TD; Chiaverini 7-94, 1 TD.
WASH: Pathon 5-96; Coleman 5-38.

December 29, 1997
Colorado State 35, Missouri 24

	1ST	2ND	3RD	4TH	FINAL
CSU	7	7	14	7	35
MO	3	14	7	0	24

SCORING SUMMARY
CSU	Hall 14 run (Franz kick)
MO	FG Knickman 32
MO	C. Jones 4 run (Knickman kick)
CSU	McCoy 22 pass from Moreno (Franz kick)
MO	Blackwell 7 run (Knickman kick)
CSU	Hall 85 punt return (Franz kick)
CSU	Davis 47 pass from Moreno (Franz kick)
MO	Olivo 3 run (Knickman kick)
CSU	Eslinger 23 run (Franz kick)

CSU	TEAM STATISTICS	MO
22	First Downs	17
214	Rushing Yards	314
18-24-0	Passing	7-17-1
206	Passing Yards	68
420	Total Yards	382
1-85	Punt Returns - Yards	0-0
5-111	Kickoff Returns - Yards	6-94
5-30.6	Punts - Average	4-44.3
1-1	Fumbles - Lost	3-2
5-59	Penalties - Yards	5-39
32:42	Possession Time	27:18

INDIVIDUAL LEADERS
RUSHING
CSU: McDougal 18-110; Washington 16-83.
MO: Jones 20-143, 1 TD; West 11-104.
PASSING
CSU: Moreno 18-24-0, 206 yards, 2 TD.
MO: C. Jones 7-17-1, 68 yards.
RECEIVING
CSU: Davis 6-115, 1 TD; McCoy 2-33, 1 TD.
MO: Brooks 2-26; Layman 1-22.

THE BOWLS

DECEMBER 30, 1998
ARIZONA 23, NEBRASKA 20

	1ST	2ND	3RD	4TH	FINAL
ARIZ	6	3	0	14	23
NEB	0	13	0	7	20

SCORING SUMMARY

ARIZ	FG McDonald 38
ARIZ	FG McDonald 25
ARIZ	FG McDonald 48
NEB	FG Brown 25
NEB	Wiggins 45 pass from Crouch (Brown kick)
NEB	FG Brown 23
ARIZ	Brennan 15 pass from Smith (McDonald kick)
NEB	Wistrom 4 pass from Crouch (Brown kick)
ARIZ	Eafon 1 run (McDonald kick)

ARIZ	TEAM STATISTICS	NEB
16	First Downs	12
107	Rushing Yards	87
12-23-0	Passing	12-28-2
158	Passing Yards	193
265	Total Yards	280
3-28	Punt Returns - Yards	3-6
4-71	Kickoff Returns - Yards	5-88
7-36.0	Punts - Average	6-39.2
4-3	Fumbles - Lost	4-2
7-5	Penalties - Yards	2-6
32:34	Possession Time	27:26

INDIVIDUAL LEADERS

RUSHING
ARIZ: Canidate 22-101; Smith 11-25; Eafon 5-14, 1 TD.
NEB: Crouch 15-28; Makovicka 5-26; Buckhalter 8-22.

PASSING
ARIZ: Smith 11-19-0, 143 yards, 1 TD.
NEB: Crouch 12-28-2, 193 yards, 2 TD.

RECEIVING
ARIZ: Brennan 2-78, 1 TD; Northcutt 4-47.
NEB: Davison 3-64; Wiggins 1-45, 1 TD; Wistrom 3-41, 1 TD.

DECEMBER 29, 1999
KANSAS STATE 24, WASHINGTON 20

	1ST	2ND	3RD	4TH	FINAL
KSU	7	3	7	7	24
WASH	6	7	7	0	20

SCORING SUMMARY

WASH	FG Anderson 39
KSU	Beasley 1 run (Rheem kick)
WASH	FG Anderson 47
KSU	FG Rheem 41
WASH	Conniff 3 run (Anderson kick)
KSU	Beasley 11 run (Rheem kick)
WASH	Shaw 5 run (Anderson kick)
KSU	Beasley 1 run (Rheem kick)

KSU	TEAM STATISTICS	WASH
21	First Downs	16
138	Rushing Yards	75
5-31-1	Passing	18-27-1
197	Passing Yards	197
335	Total Yards	272
1-0	Punt Returns - Yards	3-45
5-98	Kickoff Returns - Yards	3-77
5-30.8	Punts - Average	2-31.0
3-0	Fumbles - Lost	0-0
11-75	Penalties - Yards	7-49
33:12	Possession Time	26:48

INDIVIDUAL LEADERS

RUSHING
KSU: Beasley 20-48, 3 TD; Murphy 8-42; Hall 11-40.
WASH: Tuiasosopo 11-30; Arnold 5-27.

PASSING
KSU: Beasley 15-31-1, 216 yards.
WASH: Tuiasosopo 18-27-1, 197 yards.

RECEIVING
KSU: Morgan 7-75; Murphy 3-67.
WASH: Looker 4-72; Conniff 4-57.

DECEMBER 29, 2000
OREGON 35, TEXAS 30

	1ST	2ND	3RD	4TH	FINAL
ORE	14	0	7	14	35
TEX	0	21	0	9	30

SCORING SUMMARY

ORE	Peelle 1 pass from Harrington (Frankel kick)
ORE	Harrington 18 pass from Howry (Frankel kick)
TEX	Mitchell 3 run (Stockton kick)
TEX	Simms 4 run (Stockton kick)
TEX	Brown 23 interception return (Stockton kick)
ORE	Morris 55 pass from Harrington (Frankel kick)
ORE	Harrington 9 run (Frankel kick)
TEX	Ike 93 kickoff return (Stockton kick)
ORE	Willis 4 run (Frankel kick)
TEX	Safety

ORE	TEAM STATISTICS	TEX
21	First Downs	19
129	Rushing Yards	54
20-32-1	Passing	17-33-4
291	Passing Yards	245
420	Total Yards	299
1-1	Punt Returns - Yards	3-22
5-111	Kickoff Returns - Yards	6-186
5-32.4	Punts - Average	3-42.3
1-1	Fumbles - Lost	3-1
6-50	Penalties - Yards	6-55
31:51	Possession Time	28:09

INDIVIDUAL LEADERS

RUSHING
ORE: Morris 26-82; Amundson 5-48.
TEX: Mitchell 17-41, 1 TD; Simms 9-10, 1 TD.

PASSING
ORE: Harrington 19-30-1, 273 yards, 2 TD.
TEX: Simms 17-33-4, 245 yards.

RECEIVING
ORE: Morris 5-104, 1 TD; Howry 5-59; Peelle 4-48, 1 TD.
TEX: Healy 5-98; Williams 2-44; Johnson 4-42.

DECEMBER 28, 2001
TEXAS 47, WASHINGTON 43

	1ST	2ND	3RD	4TH	FINAL
TEX	0	14	6	27	47
WASH	0	23	13	7	43

SCORING SUMMARY

WASH	FG Anderson 43
WASH	FG Anderson 43
WASH	Johnson 38 interception return (Anderson kick)
TEX	Johnson 43 pass from Applewhite (Mangum kick)
TEX	I. Williams 25 pass from Applewhite (Mangum kick)
WASH	Collier 4 pass from Pickett (Anderson kick)
WASH	Stevens 17 pass from Pickett (Anderson kick)
TEX	FG Mangum 26
WASH	Hurst 4 run (pass failed)
TEX	FG Mangum 24
TEX	Trissel 2 pass from Applewhite (pass failed)
TEX	I. Williams 1 run (Mangum kick)
TEX	Scaife 4 pass from Applewhite (Mangum kick)
WASH	Hurst 34 run (Anderson kick)
TEX	I. Williams 3 run (Mangum kick)

TEX	TEAM STATISTICS	WASH
29	First Downs	22
119	Rushing Yards	151
37-55-3	Passing	27-54-2
473	Passing Yards	293
592	Total Yards	444
2-9	Punt Returns - Yards	1-12
3-70	Kickoff Returns - Yards	8-144
5-37.8	Punts - Average	6-37.3
0-0	Fumbles - Lost	2-0
2-9	Penalties - Yards	7-44
31:55	Possession Time	28:05

INDIVIDUAL LEADERS

RUSHING
TEX: I. Williams 14-59, 2 TD; Ike 10-21.
WASH: Hurst 16-137, 2 TD; Pickett 7-8.

PASSING
TEX: Applewhite 37-55-3, 473 yards, 4 TD.
WASH: Pickett 27-54-2, 293 yards, 2 TD.

RECEIVING
TEX: Johnson 6-157, 1 TD; R. Williams 11-134, 1 TD; Scaife 7-84, 1 TD.
WASH: Stevens 9-109, 1 TD; Williams 5-62; Elstrom 4-49.

DECEMBER 27, 2002
KANSAS STATE 34, ARIZONA STATE 27

	1ST	2ND	3RD	4TH	FINAL
KSU	0	14	0	20	34
ASU	0	20	0	7	27

SCORING SUMMARY

ASU	Taplin 6 pass from Walter (Barth kick)
ASU	FG Barth 26
KSU	Sproles 41 run (Rheem kick)
ASU	Hill 9 run (Barth kick)
ASU	FG Barth 39
KSU	Roberson 32 run (Rheem kick)
KSU	Roberson 3 run (run failed)
ASU	Williams 10 pass from Walter (Barth kick)
KSU	Roberson 1 run (Rheem kick)
KSU	Evans 10 pass from Roberson (Rheem kick)

KSU	TEAM STATISTICS	ASU
19	First Downs	19
224	Rushing Yards	17
11-28-0	Passing	28-57-1
215	Passing Yards	293
439	Total Yards	310
5-39	Punt Returns - Yards	7-37
4-67	Kickoff Returns - Yards	6-124
8-34.5	Punts - Average	7-39.4
2-2	Fumbles - Lost	1-0
5-40	Penalties - Yards	4-20
28:33	Possession Time	31:27

INDIVIDUAL LEADERS

RUSHING
KSU: Sproles 21-118, 1 TD; Roberson 18-63, 3 TD; Newman 2-26.
ASU: Hill 11-39, 1 TD; Williams 9-7.

PASSING
KSU: Roberson 11-28-0, 215 yards, 1 TD.
ASU: Walter 28-57-1, 293 yards, 2 TD.

RECEIVING
KSU: Terry 5-90; Newman 3-47; Evans 2-37, 1 TD.
ASU: McDonald 11-114; Taplin 4-38, 1 TD; Williams 2-25, 1 TD.

DECEMBER 30, 2003
WASHINGTON STATE 28, TEXAS 20

	1ST	2ND	3RD	4TH	FINAL
WSU	0	7	19	2	28
TEX	0	10	0	10	20

SCORING SUMMARY

TEX	Benson 1 run (Pino kick)
WSU	Moore 12 pass from Kegel (Dunning kick)
TEX	FG Pino 39
WSU	Moore 54 pass from Kegel (kick failed)
WSU	Smith 12 run (Dunning kick)
WSU	David 18 fumble return (kick failed)
TEX	FG Pino 19
WSU	Safety
TEX	Williams 30 pass from Mock (Pino kick)

WSU	TEAM STATISTICS	TEX
19	First Downs	22
157	Rushing Yards	131
18-32-2	Passing	20-49-0
203	Passing Yards	196
360	Total Yards	327
4-68	Punt Returns - Yards	1-20
5-59	Kickoff Returns - Yards	5-105
7-40.1	Punts - Average	6-42.2
0-0	Fumbles - Lost	5-3
6-68	Penalties - Yards	4-24
20:41	Possession Time	39:19

INDIVIDUAL LEADERS

RUSHING
WSU: Smith 21-110, 1 TD; Bruhn 10-44.
TEX: Benson 22-83, 1 TD; V. Young 9-50.

PASSING
WSU: Kegel 18-32-2, 203 yards, 2 TD.
TEX: Mock 14-35-0, 181 yards, 1 TD.

RECEIVING
WSU: Moore 2-66, 2 TD; Smith 5-51.
TEX: Williams 9-97, 1 TD; Johnson 3-41.

DECEMBER 30, 2004

TEXAS TECH 45, CALIFORNIA 31

	1ST	2ND	3RD	4TH	FINAL
TT	7	17	14	7	45
CAL	14	0	3	14	31

SCORING SUMMARY

TT	Hicks 9 pass from Cumbie (Trlica kick)
CAL	Arrington 2 run (Schneider kick)
CAL	Lynch 5 run (Schneider kick)
TT	FG Trlica 21
TT	Hicks 5 pass from Cumbie (Trlica kick)
TT	Henderson 2 run (Trlica kick)
TT	Filani 60 pass from Cumbie (Trlica kick)
CAL	FG Schneider 29
TT	Mack 11 run (Trlica kick)
CAL	Cross 11 pass from Rodgers (Schneider kick)
TT	Henderson 1 run (Trlica kick)
CAL	Rodgers 1 run (Schneider kick)

TT	TEAM STATISTICS	CAL
30	First Downs	27
77	Rushing Yards	221
39-60-0	Passing	24-42-1
520	Passing Yards	246
597	Total Yards	467
2-11	Punt Returns - Yards	2-11
5-96	Kickoff Returns - Yards	7-126
3-46.0	Punts - Average	7-38.4
8-50	Penalties - Yards	5-59
28:41	Possession Time	31:19

INDIVIDUAL LEADERS

RUSHING
TT: Henderson 10-35, 2 TD; Mack 7-31, 1 TD.
CAL: Arrington 25-173, 1 TD; Lynch 5-26, 1 TD.

PASSING
TT: Cumbie 39-60-0, 520, 3 TD.
CAL: Rodgers 24-42-1, 246, 1 TD.

RECEIVING
TT: Haverty 8-147, Filani 5-144, 1 TD, Hicks 9-69, 2 TD.
CAL: Makonnen 8-99, Jordan 5-36.

OUTBACK BOWL

PROFILE

Site: Tampa, Fla.
Stadium: Raymond James Stadium
Capacity: 65,657
Surface: Grass

PLAYING SITES

Tampa Stadium, renamed Houlihan's Stadium in 1997, 1986-97
Tampa Community Stadium, 1998
Raymond James Stadium, since 1999

NAME CHANGES

Hall of Fame Bowl, 1986-95
Outback Bowl, since 1996

SEASON	DATE	PRE-GAME RANK	TEAMS	SCORE	FINAL RANK	MOST VALUABLE PLAYERS	ATT.
1986	Dec. 23, 1986		Boston College	27	19	James Jackson, QB, Georgia	25,368
		17	Georgia	24		Gary Moss, CB, Georgia	
1987	Jan. 2, 1988		Michigan	28	19	Jamie Morris, Michigan, TB	60,156
			Alabama	24		Bobby Humphrey, Alabama, TB	
1988	Jan. 2, 1989	17	Syracuse	23	13	Robert Drummond, Syracuse, RB	51,112
		16	LSU	10	19		
1989	Jan. 1, 1990	9	Auburn	31	6	Reggie Slack, Auburn, QB	52,535
		21	Ohio State	14	24		
1990	Jan. 1, 1991	14	Clemson	30	9	DeChane Cameron, Clemson, QB	63,154
		16	Illinois	0	25		
1991	Jan. 1, 1992	16	Syracuse	24	11	Marvin Graves, Syracuse, QB	57,789
		25	Ohio State	17			
1992	Jan. 1, 1993	17	Tennessee	38	12	Heath Shuler, Tennessee, QB	52,056
		16	Boston College	23	21		
1993	Jan. 1, 1994	23	Michigan	42	21	Tyrone Wheatley, Michigan, RB	52,649
			North Carolina State	7			
1994	Jan. 2, 1995		Wisconsin	34		Terrell Fletcher, Wisconsin, RB	61,384
		25	Duke	20			
1995	Jan. 1, 1996	15	Penn State	43	13	Bobby Engram, Penn State, WR	65,313
		16	Auburn	14	22		
1996	Jan. 1, 1997	16	Alabama	17	11	Dwayne Rudd, Alabama, LB	53,161
		15	Michigan	14	20		
1997	Jan. 1, 1998	12	Georgia	33	10	Mike Bobo, Georgia, QB	56,186
			Wisconsin	6			
1998	Jan. 1, 1999	22	Penn State	26	17	Courtney Brown, Penn State, DE	66,005
			Kentucky	14			
1999	Jan. 1, 2000	21	Georgia	28 OT	16	Drew Brees, Purdue, QB	54,059
		19	Purdue	25	25		
2000	Jan. 1, 2001		South Carolina	24	19	Ryan Brewer, South Carolina, WR	65,229
		19	Ohio State	7			
2001	Jan. 1, 2002	14	South Carolina	31	13	Phil Petty, South Carolina, QB	66,249
		22	Ohio State	28			
2002	Jan. 1, 2003	12	Michigan	38	9	Chris Perry, Michigan, TB	65,101
		22	Florida	30			
2003	Jan. 1, 2004	13	Iowa	37	8	Fred Russell, Iowa, RB	65,657
		17	Florida	17	24		
2004	Jan. 1, 2005	8	Georgia	24	7	David Pollack, Georgia, DE	62,414
		16	Wisconsin	21	17		

DECEMBER 23, 1986
BOSTON COLLEGE 27, GEORGIA 24

	1ST	2ND	3RD	4TH	FINAL
BC	3	17	0	7	27
UGA	7	0	10	7	24

SCORING SUMMARY
UGA Jackson 7 run (Crumley kick)
BC FG Lowe 23
BC Casparriello 4 pass from Halloran (Lowe kick)
BC Stradford 1 run (Lowe kick)
BC FG Lowe 37
UGA FG Jacobs 28
UGA Moss 81 interception return (Crumley kick)
UGA Jackson 5 run (Crumley kick)
BC Martin 5 pass from Halloran (Lowe kick)

BC	TEAM STATISTICS	UGA
26	First Downs	18
111	Rushing Yards	94
31-52-2	Passing	21-13-0
316	Passing Yards	178
427	Total Yards	272
4-63	Punt Returns - Yards	1-2
5-51	Kickoff Returns - Yards	6-112
8-33.8	Punts - Average	7-44.9
3-0	Fumbles - Lost	4-2
6-45	Penalties - Yards	3-30
31:00	Possession Time	29:00

INDIVIDUAL LEADERS
RUSHING
BC: Stradford 20-122, 1 TD; Halloran 9-22.
UGA: Tate 17-63; Jackson 13-6, 2 TD.
PASSING
BC: Halloran 31-52-2, 316 yards, 2 TD.
UGA: Jackson 13-21-0, 178 yards.
RECEIVING
BC: Martin 9-98, 1 TD; Casparriello 7-75, 1 TD.
UGA: Thomas 7-75; Tate 2-52.

JANUARY 2, 1988
MICHIGAN 28, ALABAMA 24

	1ST	2ND	3RD	4TH	FINAL
MICH	0	14	7	7	28
ALA	3	0	6	15	24

SCORING SUMMARY
ALA FG Doyle 51
MICH Morris 25 run (Gillette kick)
MICH Morris 14 run (Gillette kick)
MICH Morris 77 run (Gillette kick)
ALA Cross 16 pass from Dunn (run failed)
ALA Humphrey 1 run (Doyle kick)
ALA Humphrey 17 run (Whitehurst pass from Dunn)
MICH Kolesar 20 pass from Brown (Gillette kick)

MICH	TEAM STATISTICS	ALA
12	First Downs	28
278	Rushing Yards	191
6-17-0	Passing	23-40-1
68	Passing Yards	269
346	Total Yards	460
6-42.5	Punts - Average	4-42.5
0-0	Fumbles - Lost	1-1
4-30	Penalties - Yards	1-5
21:42	Possession Time	38:18

INDIVIDUAL LEADERS
RUSHING
MICH: Morris 23-234, 3 TD; Bunch 3-16.
ALA: Humphrey 27-149, 2 TD; Goode 6-14.
PASSING
MICH: Brown 4-13-0, 72 yards, 1 TD.
ALA: Dunn 23-40-1, 269 yards, 1 TD.
RECEIVING
MICH: McMurtry 1-31; Kolesar 1-20, 1 TD.
ALA: Whitehurst 6-85; Cross 6-81, 1 TD.

JANUARY 2, 1989
SYRACUSE 23, LSU 10

	1ST	2ND	3RD	4TH	FINAL
SYR	7	3	7	6	23
LSU	0	7	3	0	10

SCORING SUMMARY
SYR Drummond 2 run (Greene kick)
SYR FG Greene 38
LSU Windom 19 run (Browndyke kick)
LSU FG Browndyke 35
SYR Drummond 1 run (Greene kick)
SYR Glover 4 pass from Philcox (kick failed)

SYR	TEAM STATISTICS	LSU
24	First Downs	14
208	Rushing Yards	76
16-23-0	Passing	18-35-3
130	Passing Yards	221
338	Total Yards	297
0-0	Punt Returns - Yards	2-6
3-47	Kickoff Returns - Yards	4-69
5-39.6	Punts - Average	3-32.0
1-0	Fumbles - Lost	0-0
4-37	Penalties - Yards	5-48
34:08	Possession Time	25:52

INDIVIDUAL LEADERS
RUSHING
SYR: Drummond 23-122, 2 TD; Johnston 19-74.
LSU: Windom 7-32, 1 TD; Jones 4-25.
PASSING
SYR: Philcox 16-23-0, 130 yards, 1 TD.
LSU: Hodson 16-33-3, 192 yards.
RECEIVING
SYR: Moore 6-56; Glover 4-41, 1 TD.
LSU: Moss 5-96; Fuller 5-53.

JANUARY 1, 1990
AUBURN 31, OHIO STATE 14

	1ST	2ND	3RD	4TH	FINAL
AU	3	7	7	14	31
OSU	7	7	0	0	14

SCORING SUMMARY
OSU Snow 1 run (O'Morrow kick)
AU FG Lyle 19
OSU Stablein 9 pass from Frey (O'Morrow kick)
AU Taylor 11 pass from Slack (Lyle kick)
AU Taylor 4 pass from Slack (Lyle kick)
AU Slack 5 run (Lyle kick)
AU Casey 2 pass from Slack (Lyle kick)

AU	TEAM STATISTICS	OSU
21	First Downs	18
171	Rushing Yards	66
16-23-2	Passing	16-31-1
141	Passing Yards	232
312	Total Yards	298
3-72	Punt Returns - Yards	4-25
2-57	Kickoff Returns - Yards	6-121
5-40.8	Punts - Average	7-41.1
1-0	Fumbles - Lost	1-0
2-15	Penalties - Yards	5-33
31:47	Possession Time	28:13

INDIVIDUAL LEADERS
RUSHING
AU: Danley 20-85; Williams 10-46.
OSU: S. Graham 12-53; Snow 13-42, 1 TD.
PASSING
AU: Slack 16-22-2, 141 yards, 3 TD.
OSU: Frey 16-31-1, 232 yards, 1 TD.
RECEIVING
AU: Wright 4-59; Taylor 4-33, 2 TD.
OSU: J. Graham 5-103; Snow 3-30.

JANUARY 1, 1991
CLEMSON 30, ILLINOIS 0

	1ST	2ND	3RD	4TH	FINAL
CLEM	10	14	3	3	30
ILL	0	0	0	0	0

SCORING SUMMARY
CLEM FG Gardocki 18
CLEM Thomas 14 pass from Cameron (Gardocki kick)
CLEM Hall 17 pass from Cameron (Gardocki kick)
CLEM Nunn 34 interception return (Gardocki kick)
CLEM FG Gardocki 26
CLEM FG Gardocki 43

CLEM	TEAM STATISTICS	ILL
18	First Downs	14
148	Rushing Yards	62
16-24-0	Passing	18-36-2
157	Passing Yards	185
305	Total Yards	247
6-72	Punt Returns - Yards	3-18
1-26	Kickoff Returns - Yards	4-77
5-46.0	Punts - Average	7-34.6
1-0	Fumbles - Lost	2-2
10-75	Penalties - Yards	2-28

INDIVIDUAL LEADERS
RUSHING
CLEM: Cameron 17-76; Williams 14-27.
ILL: Griffith 15-59; Feagin 5-28.
PASSING
CLEM: Cameron 14-19-0, 141 yards, 2 TD.
ILL: Verduzco 13-25-2, 121 yards.
RECEIVING
CLEM: Thomas 5-57, 1 TD; Smith 3-43.
ILL: Wax 6-77; Mueller 3-76.

JANUARY 1, 1992
SYRACUSE 24, OHIO STATE 17

	1ST	2ND	3RD	4TH	FINAL
SYR	14	0	3	7	24
OSU	0	3	7	7	17

SCORING SUMMARY
SYR Hill 50 pass from Graves (Biskup kick)
SYR Graves 3 run (Biskup kick)
OSU FG Williams 34
SYR FG Biskup 32
OSU Snow 2 run (Williams kick)
OSU Paul blocked punt recovery in end zone (Williams kick)
SYR Johnson 60 pass from Graves (Biskup kick)

SYR	TEAM STATISTICS	OSU
16	First Downs	17
99	Rushing Yards	93
18-31-1	Passing	14-33-0
309	Passing Yards	174
408	Total Yards	267
4-13	Punt Returns - Yards	3-23
3-65	Kickoff Returns - Yards	4-147
7-40.0	Punts - Average	7-40.9
3-0	Fumbles - Lost	0-0
9-49	Penalties - Yards	5-45
32:01	Possession Time	27:59

INDIVIDUAL LEADERS
RUSHING
SYR: Walker 14-60; Ferrell 1-24.
OSU: Snow 10-56, 1 TD; Harris 7-28.
PASSING
SYR: Graves 18-31-1, 309 yards, 2 TD.
OSU: Herbstreit 14-32-0, 174 yards.
RECEIVING
SYR: Johnson 4-85, 1 TD; Hill 3-62, 1 TD.
OSU: Galloway 6-88; Saunders 1-28.

JANUARY 1, 1993
TENNESSEE 38, BOSTON COLLEGE 23

	1ST	2ND	3RD	4TH	FINAL
TENN	14	0	17	7	38
BC	0	7	0	16	23

SCORING SUMMARY
TENN Shuler 1 run (Becksvoort kick)
TENN Fleming 27 pass from Shuler (Becksvoort kick)
BC Mitchell 12 from Foley (Gordon kick)
TENN Shuler 14 run (Becksvoort kick)
TENN FG Becksvoort 25
TENN Phillips 69 pass from Shuler (Becksvoort kick)
TENN Fleming 48 pass from Colquitt (Becksvoort kick)
BC Mitchell 17 pass from Foley (Mitchell pass from Foley)
BC Campbell 7 run (Boyd pass from Foley)

TENN	TEAM STATISTICS	BC
20	First Downs	22
157	Rushing Yards	103
19-26-0	Passing	23-47-1
293	Passing Yards	268
450	Total Yards	371
2-18	Punt Returns - Yards	2-2
2-48	Kickoff Returns - Yards	3-52
4-41.3	Punts - Average	5-37.0
1-1	Fumbles - Lost	1-0
5-40	Penalties - Yards	5-25
29:31	Possession Time	30:29

INDIVIDUAL LEADERS
RUSHING
TENN: Garner 10-45; Hayden 7-33; Shuler 6-31, 2 TD.
BC: Dukes 15-83; Campbell 11-42, 1 TD.
PASSING
TENN: Shuler 18-23-0, 245 yards, 2 TD.
BC: Foley 23-46-1, 268 yards, 2 TD.
RECEIVING
TENN: Fleming 5-102, 2 TD; Phillips 3-88, 1 TD.
BC: Mitchell 9-100, 2 TD; Cannon 3-63.

JANUARY 1, 1994
MICHIGAN 42, NC STATE 7

	1ST	2ND	3RD	4TH	FINAL
MICH	0	21	21	0	42
NCST	0	0	7	0	7

SCORING SUMMARY
MICH Wheatley 26 run (Elezovic kick)
MICH Alexander 79 punt return (Elezovic kick)
MICH Toomer 31 pass from Collins (Elezovic kick)
MICH Thompson 43 interception return (Elezovic kick)
MICH Wheatley 18 run (Elezovic kick)
NCST Fitzgerald 12 pass from Bender (Videtich kick)
MICH Powers 16 run (Elezovic kick)

MICH	TEAM STATISTICS	NCST
21	First Downs	18
265	Rushing Yards	117
12-23-0	Passing	19-38-4
201	Passing Yards	195
466	Total Yards	312
3-92	Punt Returns - Yards	1-5
2-48	Kickoff Returns - Yards	6-110
6-47.0	Punts - Average	6-42.0
1-0	Fumbles - Lost	4-2
5-35	Penalties - Yards	3-15
27:29	Possession Time	32:31

INDIVIDUAL LEADERS
RUSHING
MICH: Wheatley 18-124, 2 TD; Davis 7-36.
NCST: Downs 13-102; George 3-21.
PASSING
MICH: Collins 11-22-0, 189 yards, 1 TD.
NCST: Harvey 13-27-2, 108 yards; Bender 6-10-2, 87 yards, 1 TD.
RECEIVING
MICH: Jones 2-65; Smith 3-48.
NCST: Goines 7-72; Downs 4-34.

JANUARY 2, 1995
WISCONSIN 34, DUKE 20

	1ST	2ND	3RD	4TH	FINAL
WISC	13	0	7	14	34
DUKE	0	10	3	7	20

SCORING SUMMARY
WISC Messenger 19 interception return (Schnetzky kick)
WISC FG Hall 48
WISC FG Hall 43
DUKE Baldwin 7 run (Cochran kick)
DUKE FG Cochran 30
DUKE FG Cochran 30
WISC Fletcher 1 run (Schnetzky kick)
WISC Burns 11 pass from Bevell (Fletcher pass from Bevell)
DUKE Baldwin 2 run (Cochran kick)
WISC Fletcher 49 run (Schnetzky kick)

WISC	TEAM STATISTICS	DUKE
19	First Downs	23
278	Rushing Yards	68
11-20-1	Passing	28-46-4
161	Passing Yards	314
439	Total Yards	382
4-49	Punt Returns - Yards	0-0
5-75	Kickoff Returns - Yards	4-61
1-38.0	Punts - Average	4-42.5
2-2	Fumbles - Lost	0-0
12-86	Penalties - Yards	5-40
30:46	Possession Time	29:14

INDIVIDUAL LEADERS
RUSHING
WISC: Fletcher 39-241, 2 TD; Burns 6-45.
DUKE: Baldwin 21-70, 2 TD; Fischer 6-15.
PASSING
WISC: Bevell 11-20-1, 161 yards 1 TD.
DUKE: Fischer 28-46-4, 314 yards.
RECEIVING
WISC: Simmons 1-52; Dawkins 3-29.
DUKE: Khayat 11-109; Jensen 6-97.

THE BOWLS

JANUARY 1, 1996
PENN STATE 43, AUBURN 14

	1ST	2ND	3RD	4TH	FINAL
PSU	3	13	27	0	43
AU	0	7	0	7	14

SCORING SUMMARY
PSU FG Conway 19
AU Baker 25 pass from Nix (Hawkins kick)
PSU FG Conway 22
PSU FG Conway 38
PSU Archie 8 pass from Richardson (Conway kick)
PSU Engram 9 pass from Richardson (Conway kick)
PSU Pitts 4 pass from Richardson (pass failed)
PSU Enis 1 run (Conway kick)
PSU Engram 20 pass from Richardson (Conway kick)
AU McLeod 12 run (Hawkins kick)

PSU	TEAM STATISTICS	AU
22	First Downs	19
266	Rushing Yards	220
14-29-2	Passing	8-33-2
221	Passing Yards	94
487	Total Yards	314
4-33	Punt Returns - Yards	2-10
1-37	Kickoff Returns - Yards	5-101
4-35.7	Punts - Average	8-39.1
2-1	Fumbles - Lost	5-2
6-35	Penalties - Yards	5-59
32:11	Possession Time	27:49

INDIVIDUAL LEADERS
RUSHING
PSU: Pitts 15-115; Milne 12-82.
AU: Davis 12-119; Morrow 10-39.
PASSING
PSU: Richardson 13-24-1, 217 yards, 4 TD.
AU: Nix 5-25-2, 48 yards, 1 TD.
RECEIVING
PSU: Engram 4-113, 2 TD; Jurevicius 1-43.
AU: Bailey 1-32; Baker 1-25, 1 TD.

JANUARY 1, 1997
ALABAMA 17, MICHIGAN 14

	1ST	2ND	3RD	4TH	FINAL
ALA	3	0	7	7	17
MICH	0	6	0	8	14

SCORING SUMMARY
ALA FG Brock 43
MICH FG Hamilton 44
MICH FG Hamilton 22
ALA Rudd 88 interception return (Brock kick)
ALA Alexander 46 run (Brock kick)
MICH Shaw 9 pass from Griese (Floyd run)

ALA	TEAM STATISTICS	MICH
13	First Downs	22
182	Rushing Yards	124
9-18-1	Passing	22-38-1
65	Passing Yards	291
247	Total Yards	415
0-0	Punt Returns - Yards	4-17
1-9	Kickoff Returns - Yards	1-22
6-46.5	Punts - Average	7-26.1
2-1	Fumbles - Lost	3-0
8-42	Penalties - Yards	6-47
25:28	Possession Time	34:32

INDIVIDUAL LEADERS
RUSHING
ALA: Alexander 9-99, 1 TD; Riddle 13-58.
MICH: Williams 12-58; Floyd 6-35.
PASSING
ALA: Kitchens 9-18-1, 65 yards.
MICH: Griese 21-37-1, 287 yards, 1 TD.
RECEIVING
ALA: Vaughn 2-27; Rutledge 1-13.
MICH: Williams 5-113; Shaw 6-84, 1 TD.

JANUARY 1, 1998
GEORGIA 33, WISCONSIN 6

	1ST	2ND	3RD	4TH	FINAL
UGA	12	7	7	7	33
WISC	0	0	0	6	6

SCORING SUMMARY
UGA Edwards 2 run (kick blocked)
UGA Edwards 40 run (pass failed)
UGA Gary 3 run (Hines kick)
UGA Edwards 13 run (Hines kick)
UGA Allen 7 pass from Bobo (Hines kick)
WISC Retzlaff 12 pass from Kavanagh (kick failed)

UGA	TEAM STATISTICS	WISC
25	First Downs	18
207	Rushing Yards	74
26-29-0	Passing	14-36-2
235	Passing Yards	160
442	Total Yards	234
1-0	Punt Returns - Yards	2-0
1-16	Kickoff Returns - Yards	5-104
3-35.7	Punts - Average	5-43.6
2-1	Fumbles - Lost	0-0
5-59	Penalties - Yards	7-71
34:05	Possession Time	25:55

INDIVIDUAL LEADERS
RUSHING
UGA: Edwards 22-110, 3 TD; Gary 4-61, 1 TD.
WISC: McCullough 4-37; Dayne 14-36.
PASSING
UGA: Bobo 26-28-0, 235 yards, 1 TD.
WISC: Samuel 8-27-2, 84 yards; Kavanagh 6-9-0, 76 yards, 1 TD.
RECEIVING
UGA: Ward 12-122; Allen 3-22, 1 TD.
WISC: Chambers 4-46; Hayes 5-44.

JANUARY 1, 1999
PENN STATE 26, KENTUCKY 14

	1ST	2ND	3RD	4TH	FINAL
PSU	3	10	6	7	26
UK	14	0	0	0	14

SCORING SUMMARY
UK Mickelsen 36 pass from Couch (Hanson kick)
PSU FG Forney 43
UK White 16 pass from Couch (Hanson kick)
PSU Nastasi 56 pass from Thompson (Forney kick)
PSU FG Forney 26
PSU FG Forney 21
PSU FG Forney 25
PSU Fields 19 run (Forney kick)

PSU	TEAM STATISTICS	UK
24	First Downs	24
233	Rushing Yards	105
14-27-0	Passing	30-48-2
187	Passing Yards	336
420	Total Yards	441
2-25	Punt Returns - Yards	0-0
3-64	Kickoff Returns - Yards	4-126
3-30.3	Punts - Average	3-17.0
1-1	Fumbles - Lost	1-1
8-58	Penalties - Yards	14-103
27:07	Possession Time	32:53

INDIVIDUAL LEADERS
RUSHING
PSU: McCoo 21-105; Harris 13-54.
UK: White 8-61; Homer 12-26.
PASSING
PSU: Thompson 14-27-0, 187 yards, 1 TD.
UK: Couch 30-48-2, 336 yards, 2 TD.
RECEIVING
PSU: Stewart 7-71; Nastasi 2-70, 1 TD.
UK: Mickelsen 3-65, 1 TD; Homer 7-64.

JANUARY 1, 2000
GEORGIA 28, PURDUE 25

	1ST	2ND	3RD	4TH	OT	FINAL
UGA	0	10	8	7	3	28
PU	19	6	0	0	0	25

SCORING SUMMARY
PU Daniels 3 pass from Brees (Dorsch kick)
PU Daniels 11 pass from Brees (kick failed)
PU Sutherland 21 pass from Brees (pass failed)
PU James 32 pass from Brees (pass failed)
UGA Edwards 74 run (Hines kick)
UGA FG Hines 32
UGA Carter 8 run (Pass run)
UGA McMichael 8 pass from Carter (Hines kick)
UGA FG Hines 21

UGA	TEAM STATISTICS	PU
21	First Downs	30
154	Rushing Yards	150
20-33-0	Passing	36-60-1
243	Passing Yards	378
397	Total Yards	528
2-24	Punt Returns - Yards	1-1
3-63	Kickoff Returns - Yards	2-31
3-48.0	Punts - Average	3-45.3
2-2	Fumbles - Lost	2-1
10-55	Penalties - Yards	14-153
25:11	Possession Time	34:49

INDIVIDUAL LEADERS
RUSHING
UGA: Edwards 2-70, 1 TD; Carter 16-41, 1 TD.
PU: Lowe 15-87; Sutherland 2-65.
PASSING
UGA: Carter 20-33-0, 243 yards, 1 TD.
PU: Brees 36-60-1, 378 yards, 4 TD.
RECEIVING
UGA: Edwards 8-97; Greer 5-86.
PU: Daniels 12-103, 2 TD; James 4-65, 1 TD.

JANUARY 1, 2001
SOUTH CAROLINA 24, OHIO STATE 7

	1ST	2ND	3RD	4TH	FINAL
SC	0	3	7	14	24
OSU	0	0	7	0	7

SCORING SUMMARY
SC FG Corse 23
SC Brewer 7 run (Corse kick)
OSU Gurr fumble recovery in end zone (Stultz kick)
SC Brewer 28 pass from Petty (Corse kick)
SC Brewer 2 run (Corse kick)

SC	TEAM STATISTICS	OSU
18	First Downs	16
218	Rushing Yards	85
9-19-1	Passing	16-28-2
175	Passing Yards	173
393	Total Yards	258
2-18	Punt Returns - Yards	3-43
2-33	Kickoff Returns - Yards	5-100
4-46.8	Punts - Average	6-37.5
1-0	Fumbles - Lost	3-1
7-50	Penalties - Yards	9-65
33:33	Possession Time	26:27

INDIVIDUAL LEADERS
RUSHING
SC: Brewer 19-109, 2 TD; Pinnock 11-33.
OSU: Wells 14-52; Combs 8-25.
PASSING
SC: Petty 9-19-1, 175 yards, 1 TD.
OSU: Bellisari 14-25-1, 157 yards.
RECEIVING
SC: Brewer 3-92, 1 TD; Kelly 3-43.
OSU: Rambo 2-65; Sanders 5-47.

JANUARY 1, 2002
SOUTH CAROLINA 31, OHIO STATE 28

	1ST	2ND	3RD	4TH	FINAL
SC	0	14	14	3	31
OSU	0	0	7	21	28

SCORING SUMMARY

SC	Pinnock 1 run (Weaver kick)
SC	Scott 7 pass from Petty (Weaver kick)
SC	Gause 50 pass from Petty (kick failed)
SC	Pinnock 10 run (Watson pass from Petty)
OSU	Bellisari 2 run (Nugent kick)
OSU	Sanders 16 pass from Bellisari (Nugent kick)
OSU	Wells 1 run (Nugent kick)
OSU	Sanders 9 pass from Bellisari (Nugent kick)
SC	FG Weaver 42

SC	TEAM STATISTICS	OSU
17	First Downs	21
120	Rushing Yards	64
19-37-1	Passing	22-37-1
227	Passing Yards	324
347	Total Yards	388
2-16	Punt Returns - Yards	4-20
4-66	Kickoff Returns - Yards	4-101
6-47.7	Punts - Average	5-44.6
2-1	Fumbles - Lost	2-2
8-43	Penalties - Yards	6-40
31:23	Possession Time	28:37

INDIVIDUAL LEADERS

RUSHING
SC: Brewer 5-61; Pinnock 12-49, 2 TD.
OSU: Wells 19-37, 1 TD; Ross 1-13.

PASSING
SC: Petty 19-37-1, 227 yards, 2 TD.
OSU: Bellisari 21-35-1, 320 yards, 2 TD.

RECEIVING
SC: Scott 7-83, 1 TD; Gause 3-72, 1 TD.
OSU: Jenkins 8-152; Vance 5-61; Sanders 5-56, 2 TD.

JANUARY 1, 2003
MICHIGAN 38, FLORIDA 30

	1ST	2ND	3RD	4TH	FINAL
MICH	7	14	14	3	38
UF	0	16	7	7	30

SCORING SUMMARY

MICH	Perry 4 run (Finley kick)
UF	Graham 2 run (Leach kick)
UF	Graham`1 run (run failed)
MICH	Perry 1 run (Finley kick)
UF	FG Leach 29
MICH	Bellamy 8 pass from Navarre (Finley kick)
UF	Ratliff 33 pass from Grossman (Leach kick)
MICH	Perry 7 run (Finley kick)
MICH	Perry 12 run (Finley kick)
UF	Walker 3 pass from Grossman (Leach kick)
MICH	FG Finley 33

MICH	TEAM STATISTICS	UF
17	First Downs	28
104	Rushing Yards	183
21-37-0	Passing	21-42-1
319	Passing Yards	323
423	Total Yards	506
3-29	Punt Returns - Yards	3-10
2-45	Kickoff Returns - Yards	5-101
9-38.6	Punts - Average	8-32.1
1-0	Fumbles - Lost	2-2
3-23	Penalties - Yards	6-38
32:39	Possession Time	27:21

INDIVIDUAL LEADERS

RUSHING
MICH: Perry 28-85, 4 TD; Bellamy 2-20.
UF: Graham 22-120, 2 TD; Carthon 6-56.

PASSING
MICH: Navarre 21-36-0, 319 yards, 1 TD.
UF : Grossman 21-41-0, 323 yards, 2 TD.

RECEIVING
MICH: Perry 6-108; Edwards 4-110.
UF : Jacobs 7-88; Carthon 3-65.

JANUARY 1, 2004
IOWA 37, FLORIDA 17

	1ST	2ND	3RD	4TH	FINAL
UI	7	13	14	3	37
UF	7	0	3	7	17

SCORING SUMMARY

UF	Kight 70 pass from Leak (Leach kick)
UI	Brown 3 pass from Chandler (Kaeding kick)
UI	FG Kaeding 47
UI	Chandler 5 run (Kaeding kick)
UI	Melloy recovered blocked punt (Kaeding kick)
UF	FG Leach 48
UI	Russell 34 run (Kaeding kick)
UI	FG Kaeding 38
UF	Baker 25 pass from Leak (Leach kick)

UI	TEAM STATISTICS	UF
22	First Downs	16
238	Rushing Yards	57
13-26-0	Passing	22-41-1
170	Passing Yards	268
408	Total Yards	325
5-71	Punt Returns - Yards	3-26
3-54	Kickoff Returns - Yards	5-66
7-42.6	Punts - Average	10-40.1
1-0	Fumbles - Lost	1-0
3-15	Penalties - Yards	4-43
34:10	Possession Time	25:50

INDIVIDUAL LEADERS

RUSHING
UI: Russell 21-150, 1 TD; Lewis 12-45.
UF: Carthon 10-44; Fason 4-23.

PASSING
UI : Chandler 13-25-0, 170 yards, 1 TD.
UF: Leak 22-41-1, 268 yards, 1 TD.

RECEIVING
UI : Brown 6-96, 1 TD; Hinkel 3-44.
UF: Kight 2-75, 1 TD; Perez 7-70.

JANUARY 1, 2005
GEORGIA 24, WISCONSIN 21

	1ST	2ND	3RD	4TH	FINAL
UGA	3	7	14	0	24
WISC	3	3	7	8	21

SCORING SUMMARY

UGA	FG Coutu 20
WISC	FG Allen 46
WISC	FG Allen 44
UGA	Gibson 19 pass from Greene (Coutu kick)
UGA	Thomas 24 pass from Greene (Coutu kick)
UGA	Brown 29 run (Coutu kick)
WISC	Charles 19 pass from Stocco (Allen kick)
WISC	Crooks 11 Interception return (Orr pass from Stocco)

UGA	TEAM STATISTICS	WISC
21	First Downs	14
196	Rushing Yards	60
19-41-2	Passing	12-27-0
264	Passing Yards	170
460	Total Yards	230
5-45	Punt Returns - Yards	3-34
4-49	Kickoff Returns - Yards	5-49
6-33.2	Punts - Average	7-44.3
1-1	Fumbles - Lost	2-2
8-85	Penalties - Yards	7-45
29:05	Possession Time	30:55

INDIVIDUAL LEADERS

RUSHING
UGA: Brown 16-111, 1 TD; Ware 12-61.
WISC: Davis 21-79; Donovan 2-15.

PASSING
UGA: Greene 19-38-2, 264 yards, 2 TD.
WISC: Stocco 12-27-0, 170 yards, 1 TD.

RECEIVING
UGA: Pope 3-65; Brown 4-44.
WISC: Williams 3-56; Charles 3-52, 1 TD.

THE BOWLS

INSIGHT BOWL

PROFILE

Site: Phoenix
Stadium: Bank One Ballpark
Capacity: 42,915
Surface: Grass

PLAYING SITES

Arizona Stadium, 1989-99
Bank One Ballpark, since 2000

NAME CHANGES

Copper Bowl, 1989
Domino's Pizza Copper Bowl, 1990-91
Weiser Lock Copper Bowl, 1992-95
Copper Bowl, 1996
Insight.com Bowl, 1997-2001
Insight Bowl, since 2002

SEASON	DATE	PRE-GAME RANK	TEAMS	SCORE	FINAL RANK	MOST VALUABLE PLAYERS	ATT.
1989	Dec. 31, 1989		Arizona	17	25	Shane Montgomery, North Carolina State, QB	37,237
			North Carolina State	10		Scott Geyer, Arizona, DB	
1990	Dec. 31, 1990		California	17		Mike Pawlawski, California, QB	36,340
			Wyoming	15		Robert Midgett, Wyoming, LB	
1991	Dec. 31, 1991		Indiana	24		Vaughn Dunbar, Indiana, TB	35,752
			Baylor	0		Mark Hagen, Indiana, LB	
1992	Dec. 29, 1992	18	Washington State	31	15	Drew Bledsoe, QB, Phillip Bobo, WR, Washington State	40,876
			Utah	28		Kareem Leary, Utah, DB	
1993	Dec. 29, 1993	20	Kansas State	52	20	Andre Coleman, Kansas State, WR	49,075
			Wyoming	17		Kenny McEntyre, Kansas State, CB	
1994	Dec. 29, 1994	22	BYU	31	18	John Walsh, QB, Jamal Willis, RB, BYU	45,122
			Oklahoma	6		Broderick Simpson, Oklahoma, LB	
1995	Dec. 27, 1995		Texas Tech	55	23	Byron Hanspard, RB, Zebbie Lethridge, QB, Texas Tech	41,004
			Air Force	41		Mickey Dalton, Air Force, CB	
1996	Dec. 27, 1996		Wisconsin	38		Ron Dayne, Wisconsin, RB	42,122
			Utah	10		Tarek Saleh, Wisconsin, LB	
1997	Dec. 27, 1997		Arizona	20		Trung Canidate, Arizona, RB	49,385
			New Mexico	14		Jimmy Sprotte, Arizona, LB	
1998	Dec. 26, 1998	23	Missouri	34	21	Mark Bulger, West Virginia, QB	36,147
			West Virginia	31		Jeff Marriott, Missouri, DT	
1999	Dec. 31, 1999		Colorado	62		Cortlen Johnson, Colorado, RB	35,762
			25 Boston College	28		Jashon Sykes, Colorado, LB	
2000	Dec. 28, 2000		Iowa State	37	25	Sage Rosenfels, Iowa State, QB	41,813
			Pittsburgh	29		Reggie Hayward, Iowa State, DE	
2001	Dec. 29, 2001	18	Syracuse	26	14	James Mungro, Syracuse, RB	40,028
			Kansas State	3		Clifton Smith, Syracuse, LB	
2002	Dec. 26, 2002	24	Pittsburgh	38	19	Brandon Miree, Pittsburgh, TB	40,533
			Oregon State	13		Claude Harriott, Pittsburgh, DL	
2003	Dec. 26, 2003		California	52		Aaron Rodgers, California, QB	42,364
			Virginia Tech	49		Ryan Gutierrez, California, FS	
2004	Dec. 28, 2004		Oregon State	38		Derek Anderson, Oregon State, QB	45,917
			Notre Dame	21		Trent Bray, Oregon State, LB	

DECEMBER 31, 1989
ARIZONA 17, NC STATE 10

	1ST	2ND	3RD	4TH	FINAL
ARIZ	7	10	0	0	17
NCST	0	7	3	0	10

SCORING SUMMARY
ARIZ   Ogunfiditimi 37 pass from Veal (Coston kick)
ARIZ   Geyer 85 interception return (Coston kick)
NCST   Varn 4 pass from Montgomery (Hartman kick)
ARIZ   FG Coston 34
NCST   FG Hartman 43

ARIZ	TEAM STATISTICS	NCST
8	First Downs	23
50	Rushing Yards	88
5-15-1	Passing	21-47-2
80	Passing Yards	222
130	Total Yards	310
10-41.7	Punts - Average	7-37.7
3-2	Fumbles - Lost	2-2
5-47	Penalties - Yards	6-49
21:54	Possession Time	38:06

INDIVIDUAL LEADERS
RUSHING
ARIZ: McGill 14-49; Veal 10-14.
NCST: Barbour 16-41; Shaw 9-26.
PASSING
ARIZ: Veal 5-15-1, 80 yards, 1 TD.
NCST: Montgomery 21-46-1, 222 yards, 1 TD.
RECEIVING
ARIZ: Ogunfiditimi 1-37, 1 TD; McGill 2-23.
NCST: Byrd 6-67; Harrison 2-43.

DECEMBER 31, 1990
CALIFORNIA 17, WYOMING 15

	1ST	2ND	3RD	4TH	FINAL
CAL	0	7	3	7	17
WYO	0	3	0	12	15

SCORING SUMMARY
CAL   Treggs 25 pass from Pawlawski (Keen kick)
WYO   FG Fleming 26
CAL   FG Keen 46
CAL   Zomalt 4 run (Keen kick)
WYO   Daffer 11 run (pass failed)
WYO   Rivers 70 punt return (run failed)

CAL	TEAM STATISTICS	WYO
14	First Downs	18
89	Rushing Yards	129
15-26-1	Passing	20-39-2
172	Passing Yards	226
261	Total Yards	355
9-41.9	Punts - Average	8-35.5
0-0	Fumbles - Lost	0-0
8-57	Penalties - Yards	1-5

INDIVIDUAL LEADERS
RUSHING
CAL: Wallace 17-76.
WYO: Timmer 6-34.
PASSING
CAL: Pawlawski 15-26-1, 172 yards, 1 TD.
WYO: Corontzos 20-39-2, 226 yards.

DECEMBER 31, 1991
INDIANA 24, BAYLOR 0

	1ST	2ND	3RD	4TH	FINAL
IND	7	10	0	7	24
BU	0	0	0	0	0

SCORING SUMMARY
IND   Green 1 run (Bonnell kick)
IND   FG Bonnell 27
IND   Dunbar 5 run (Bonnell kick)
IND   Green 4 run (Bonnell kick)

IND	TEAM STATISTICS	BU
20	First Downs	17
147	Rushing Yards	138
12-22-0	Passing	10-27-1
176	Passing Yards	131
323	Total Yards	269
6-49.0	Punts - Average	6-34.8
2-0	Fumbles - Lost	4-1
6-59	Penalties - Yards	4-29
32:55	Possession Time	27:05

INDIVIDUAL LEADERS
RUSHING
IND: Dunbar 28-106, 1 TD; Law 6-38.
BU: Strait 15-72, Mims 9-49.
PASSING
IND: Green 11-21-0, 165 yards.
BU: Joe 10-26-1, 131 yards.
RECEIVING
IND: McGowan 3-63; Thomas 4-58.
BU: Miles 2-41; Pierce 3-32; Bonner 3-32.

DECEMBER 29, 1992
WASHINGTON STATE 31, UTAH 28

	1ST	2ND	3RD	4TH	FINAL
WSU	21	7	0	3	31
UTAH	0	14	14	0	28

SCORING SUMMARY
WSU   Wright-Fair 3 run (Price kick)
WSU   Bobo 87 pass from Bledsoe (Price kick)
WSU   Wright-Fair 3 run (Price kick)
UTAH   S. Williams 10 pass from Dolce (Yergensen kick)
UTAH   K. Williams 25 run (Yergensen kick)
WSU   Bobo 48 pass from Bledsoe (Price kick)
UTAH   Lusk 49 pass from Dolce (kick blocked)
UTAH   Jones 8 run (Murry pass from Dolce)
WSU   FG Price 22

WSU	TEAM STATISTICS	UTAH
28	First Downs	20
144	Rushing Yards	179
32-38-1	Passing	21-40-0
492	Passing Yards	316
636	Total Yards	495
2-(-2)	Punt Returns - Yards	3-17
1-7	Kickoff Returns - Yards	6-73
6-36.5	Punts - Average	6-43.0
4-2	Fumbles - Lost	3-1
18-136	Penalties - Yards	7-55
29:52	Possession Time	30:08

INDIVIDUAL LEADERS
RUSHING
WSU: Wright-Fair 27-123, 2 TD; Bobo 2-26.
UTAH: K.Williams 13-112, 1 TD; Jones 11-43, 1 TD.
PASSING
WSU: Bledsoe 30-46-1, 476 yards, 2 TD.
UTAH: Dolce 21-40-0, 316 yards, 2 TD.
RECEIVING
WSU: Bobo 7-212, 2 TD; Davis 8-134.
UTAH: S. Williams 7-121, 1 TD; Hooks 5-75.

DECEMBER 29, 1993
KANSAS STATE 52, WYOMING 17

	1ST	2ND	3RD	4TH	FINAL
KSU	9	15	14	14	52
WYO	3	7	0	7	17

SCORING SUMMARY

WYO	FG Sorenson 35
KSU	Smith 2 run (kick failed)
KSU	FG Wright 22
KSU	May 2 run (Wright kick)
WYO	Christopherson 3 run (Sorenson kick)
KSU	Coleman 68 punt return (May run)
KSU	Coleman 61 pass from May (Wright kick)
KSU	Lockett 30 pass from May (Wright kick)
WYO	Pratt 14 pass from Gustin (Sorenson kick)
KSU	Edwards 13 run (Claassen kick)
KSU	McEntyre 37 interception return (Wright kick)

KSU	TEAM STATISTICS	WYO
22	First Downs	20
227	Rushing Yards	36
19-28-0	Passing	31-51-2
275	Passing Yards	266
502	Total Yards	302
3-83	Punt Returns - Yards	1-34
4-81	Kickoff Returns - Yards	6-94
3-23.3	Punts - Average	5-44.2
0-0	Fumbles - Lost	2-1
5-40	Penalties - Yards	8-70
30:01	Possession Time	29:59

INDIVIDUAL LEADERS

RUSHING
KSU: Smith 20-133, 1 TD; Edwards 9-65, 1 TD.
WYO: Christopherson 15-28, 1 TD; Gragert 1-8.

PASSING
KSU: May 19-28-0, 275 yards, 2 TD.
WYO: Hughes 28-43-0, 237 yards.

RECEIVING
KSU: Coleman 8-144, 1 TD; Running 5-50.
WYO: Yarborough 8-72; Pratt 3-52, 1 TD.

DECEMBER 29, 1994
BYU 31, OKLAHOMA 6

	1ST	2ND	3RD	4TH	FINAL
BYU	7	10	7	7	31
OKLA	0	0	0	6	6

SCORING SUMMARY

BYU	Doman 7 pass from Walsh (Lauder kick)
BYU	FG Lauder 22
BYU	Johnston 25 pass from Walsh (Lauder kick)
BYU	Johnston 4 pass from Walsh (Lauder kick)
OKLA	Moore 2 run (kick failed)
BYU	Doman 28 pass from Walsh (Lauder kick)

BYU	TEAM STATISTICS	OKLA
28	First Downs	16
71	Rushing Yards	72
32-46-0	Passing	13-30-1
485	Passing Yards	163
556	Total Yards	235
4-37.0	Punts - Average	8-37.1
0-0	Fumbles - Lost	0-0
6-48	Penalties - Yards	7-44
35:16	Possession Time	24:44

INDIVIDUAL LEADERS

RUSHING
BYU: Willis 11-41.
OKLA: Moore 9-41, 1 TD.

PASSING
BYU: Walsh 31-45-0, 454 yards, 4 TD.
OKLA: Brown 13-30-1, 163 yards.

RECEIVING
BYU: Willis 7-103.
OKLA: Hall 5-75.

DECEMBER 27, 1995
TEXAS TECH 55, AIR FORCE 41

	1ST	2ND	3RD	4TH	FINAL
TT	21	10	7	17	55
AFA	7	6	15	13	41

SCORING SUMMARY

TT	Mitchell 38 pass from Lethridge (Rogers kick).
AFA	Addison 2 run (Thompson kick)
TT	Hanspard 2 run (Rogers kick)
TT	Hanspard 2 run (Rogers kick)
TT	Lethridge 1 run (Rogers kick)
AFA	Johnson 71 run (kick failed)
TT	FG Rogers 24
AFA	Campbell 7 run (Addison run)
AFA	Johnson 60 run (Roberts kick)
TT	Hanspard 2 run (Rogers kick)
TT	Lethridge 3 run (Rogers kick)
TT	FG Rogers 31
AFA	Morgan 1 run (Roberts kick)
TT	Hanspard 29 run (Rogers kick)
AFA	Addison 7 run (run failed)

TT	TEAM STATISTICS	AFA
28	First Downs	25
374	Rushing Yards	449
22-41-1	Passing	7-13-0
245	Passing Yards	83
619	Total Yards	532
3-43.3	Punts - Average	3-39.3
1-0	Fumbles - Lost	3-1
11-90	Penalties - Yards	5-51

INDIVIDUAL LEADERS

RUSHING
TT: Hanspard 24-260, 4 TD.
AFA: Johnson 5-148, 2 TD.

PASSING
TT: Lethridge 22-41-1, 245 yards, 1 TD.
AFA: Morgan 5-11-0, 51 yards.

RECEIVING
TT: Darden 7-47.
AFA: Campbell 4-43.

DECEMBER 27, 1996
WISCONSIN 38, UTAH 10

	1ST	2ND	3RD	4TH	FINAL
WISC	14	17	0	7	38
UTAH	3	0	7	0	10

SCORING SUMMARY

WISC	Samuel 38 run (Hall kick)
UTAH	FG Pulsipher 24
WISC	Dayne 40 run (Hall kick)
WISC	Weems 82 interception return (Hall kick)
WISC	FG Hall 38
WISC	Dayne 3 run (Hall kick)
UTAH	Johnson 1 run (Pulsipher kick)
WISC	Dayne 1 run (Hall kick)

WISC	TEAM STATISTICS	UTAH
16	First Downs	26
349	Rushing Yards	103
2-6-0	Passing	27-49-4
16	Passing Yards	327
365	Total Yards	430
0-0	Punt Returns - Yards	1-8
3-59	Kickoff Returns - Yards	2-46
2-41.0	Punts - Average	2-31.0
2-1	Fumbles - Lost	1-0
3-31	Penalties - Yards	2-11
25:42	Possession Time	34:18

INDIVIDUAL LEADERS

RUSHING
WISC: Dayne 30-246, 3 TD; Samuel 5-44, 1 TD.
UTAH: Johnson 20-88, 1 TD; Bacon 4-9.

PASSING
WISC: Samuel 2-6-0, 16 yards.
UTAH: Fouts 27-49-4, 327 yards.

RECEIVING
WISC: Hayes 1-9; Brown 1-7.
UTAH: Keehan 6-100; Dyson 6-95.

DECEMBER 27, 1997
ARIZONA 20, NEW MEXICO 14

	1ST	2ND	3RD	4TH	FINAL
ARIZ	7	6	7	0	20
UNM	0	7	7	0	14

SCORING SUMMARY

ARIZ	Eafon 15 run (McDonald kick)
UNM	Thomas 15 pass from Leigh (Cason kick)
ARIZ	Canidate 3 run (kick failed)
ARIZ	Eafon 1 run (McDonald kick)
UNM	Leigh 4 run (Cason kick)

ARIZ	TEAM STATISTICS	UNM
19	First Downs	16
209	Rushing Yards	140
7-22-2	Passing	12-32-4
89	Passing Yards	150
298	Total Yards	290
9-38.7	Punts - Average	7-40.7
0-0	Fumbles - Lost	0-0
5-39	Penalties - Yards	9-60
35:45	Possession Time	24:15

INDIVIDUAL LEADERS

RUSHING
ARIZ: Canidate 24-97, 1 TD; Eafon 19-75, 2 TD.
UNM: Leigh 17-79, 1 TD; Gordon 3-42.

PASSING
ARIZ: Batten 7-17-0, 89 yards.
UNM: Leigh 12-35-4, 150 yards, 1 TD.

RECEIVING
ARIZ: Lucky 2-37; Brennan 3-33.
UNM: Volz 5-51; Thomas 3-39, 1 TD.

DECEMBER 26, 1998
MISSOURI 34, WEST VIRGINIA 31

	1ST	2ND	3RD	4TH	FINAL
MO	14	10	7	3	34
WVU	0	3	14	14	31

SCORING SUMMARY

MO	Posey 70 blocked field goal return (Long kick)
MO	Jones 9 run (McDonald kick)
WVU	FG Taylor 28
MO	Safety (Jones blocked punt out of end zone)
MO	Jones 3 run (Layman pass from Jones)
WVU	Saunders 9 pass from Bulger (Taylor kick)
MO	Jones 11 run (Long kick)
WVU	Ivy 8 pass from Bulger (Taylor kick)
WVU	Zereoue 9 pass from Bulger (Taylor kick)
MO	FG Long 18
WVU	Saunders 1 pass from Bulger (Taylor kick)

MO	TEAM STATISTICS	WVU
21	First Downs	27
197	Rushing Yards	39
8-12-0	Passing	35-51-2
130	Passing Yards	452
327	Total Yards	491
5-32.6	Punts - Average	2-25.5
3-1	Fumbles - Lost	0-0
4-29	Penalties - Yards	6-60
32:19	Possession Time	27:41

INDIVIDUAL LEADERS

RUSHING
MO: West 31-125; Jones 18-51, 3 TD.
WVU: Zereoue 22-32; Greene 1-12.

PASSING
MO: Jones 8-12-0, 130 yards.
WVU: Bulger 34-50-2, 429 yards, 4 TD.

RECEIVING
MO: Dausman 3-44; Wise 2-27.
WVU: Forbes 11-189; Saunders 8-95, 2 TD.

December 31, 1999
Colorado 62, Boston College 28

	1ST	2ND	3RD	4TH	FINAL
COLO	21	24	10	7	62
BC	0	7	7	14	28

SCORING SUMMARY
COLO Johnson 10 run (Aldrich kick)
COLO Moschetti 2 run (Aldrich kick)
COLO Sykes 29 interception return (Aldrich kick)
COLO Barnes 21 interception return (Aldrich kick)
COLO Kelly 88 punt return (Aldrich kick)
BC   White 78 interception return (Matich kick)
COLO Johnson 2 run (Aldrich kick)
COLO FG Aldrich 26
COLO FG Aldrich 21
BC   Arndt recovered fumble in end zone (Matich kick)
COLO Hollowell 18 pass from Moschetti (Mariscal kick)
COLO Colvin 4 run (Mariscal kick)
BC   Burke 2 pass from Hasselbeck (Matich kick)
BC   Bessette 9 blocked punt return (Matich kick)

COLO	TEAM STATISTICS	BC
29	First Downs	12
347	Rushing Yards	96
16-27-1	Passing	14-35-3
176	Passing Yards	159
523	Total Yards	255
3-27.7	Punts - Average	6-41.0
1-0	Fumbles - Lost	2-1
5-40	Penalties - Yards	6-62
31:38	Possession Time	28:22

INDIVIDUAL LEADERS
RUSHING
COLO: Johnson 15-201, 2 TD; Stiggers 4-24.
BC: Green 11-32; Washington 16-30.
PASSING
COLO: Moschetti 15-25-1, 167 yards, 1 TD.
BC: Hasselbeck 13-32-2, 146 yards, 1 TD.
RECEIVING
COLO: Graham 3-51; Stiggers 3-41.
BC: DeWalt 4-70; Burch 4-47.

December 28, 2000
Iowa State 37, Pittsburgh 29

	1ST	2ND	3RD	4TH	FINAL
ISU	7	20	0	10	37
PITT	7	0	13	9	29

SCORING SUMMARY
PITT Bryant 72 pass from Turman (Lotz kick)
ISU   Anthony 23 pass from Rosenfels (Gomez kick)
ISU   Woodley 1 run (run failed)
ISU   Haywood 3 run (Gomez kick)
ISU   Anthony 9 pass from Rosenfels (Gomez kick)
PITT Rutherford 2 run (Lotz kick)
PITT Bryant 44 pass from Turman (kick failed)
ISU   Billups 72 punt return (Gomez kick)
PITT FG Lotz 25
PITT Barlow 3 run (pass failed)
ISU   FG Gomez 41

ISU	TEAM STATISTICS	PITT
22	First Downs	23
67	Rushing Yards	144
23-34-0	Passing	20-36-1
308	Passing Yards	347
375	Total Yards	491
4-42.0	Punts - Average	5-35.6
1-1	Fumbles - Lost	2-0
2-10	Penalties - Yards	8-55
29:09	Possession Time	30:51

INDIVIDUAL LEADERS
RUSHING
ISU: Haywood 21-74, 1 TD.
PITT: Barlow 22-114, 1 TD; Turman 10-17.
PASSING
ISU: Rosenfels 23-34-0, 308 yards, 2 TD.
PITT: Turman 20-36-1, 347 yards, 2 TD.
RECEIVING
ISU: Anthony 5-71, 2 TD; Moses 5-63; Campbell 5-62.
PITT: Bryant 5-155, 2 TD; Grim 4-73.

December 29, 2001
Syracuse 26, Kansas State 3

	1ST	2ND	3RD	4TH	FINAL
SYR	7	12	0	7	26
KSU	3	0	0	0	3

SCORING SUMMARY
SYR Mungro 65 run (Barber kick)
KSU FG Rheem 29
SYR Mungro 1 run (kick blocked)
SYR Mungro 1 run (kick blocked)
SYR Morant 52 pass from Anderson (Barber kick)

SYR	TEAM STATISTICS	KSU
8	First Downs	15
109	Rushing Yards	33
5-14-1	Passing	14-40-2
113	Passing Yards	221
222	Total Yards	254
11-44.8	Punts - Average	9-46.3
1-0	Fumbles - Lost	4-2
6-44	Penalties - Yards	6-38
29:27	Possession Time	30:33

INDIVIDUAL LEADERS
RUSHING
SYR: Mungro 19-112, 3 TD; Davis 2-11.
KSU: Scobey 10-46; Roberson 9-9.
PASSING
SYR: Anderson 5-14-1, 113 yards, 1 TD.
KSU: Dunn 12-25-1, 151 yards.
RECEIVING
SYR: Morant 2-93, 1 TD; Davis 1-8.
KSU: Lockett 4-83; Warren 2-42.

December 26, 2002
Pittsburgh 38, Oregon State 13

	1ST	2ND	3RD	4TH	FINAL
PITT	7	3	14	14	38
OSU	7	3	3	0	13

SCORING SUMMARY
PITT Fitzgerald 40 pass from Rutherford (Abdul kick)
OSU   Newson 65 pass from Anderson (Yliniemi kick)
OSU   FG Yliniemi 50
PITT FG Abdul 45
PITT Rutherford 1 run (Abdul kick)
PITT Robinson 66 punt return (Abdul kick)
OSU   FG Yliniemi 31
PITT Miree 7 run (Abdul kick)
PITT Palko 8 run (Abdul kick)

PITT	TEAM STATISTICS	OSU
21	First Downs	20
117	Rushing Yards	8
13-26-0	Passing	21-45-1
183	Passing Yards	319
300	Total Yards	327
4-83	Punt Returns - Yards	4-26
4-61	Kickoff Returns - Yards	6-152
7-41.0	Punts - Average	6-40.2
0-0	Fumbles - Lost	2-1
7-55	Penalties - Yards	9-90
30:20	Possession Time	29:40

INDIVIDUAL LEADERS
RUSHING
PITT: Miree 20-113, 1 TD; Polite 3-11.
OSU: Jackson 19-34; Wright 7-22.
PASSING
PITT: Rutherford 13-26-0, 183 yards, 1 TD.
OSU: Anderson 21-45-1, 319 yards, 1 TD.
RECEIVING
PITT: Fitzgerald 5-88, 1 TD; Slade 3-36.
OSU: Newson 10-165, 1 TD; Euhus 3-72.

December 26, 2003
California 52, Virginia Tech 46

	1ST	2ND	3RD	4TH	FINAL
CAL	7	14	21	10	52
VT	21	7	0	21	49

SCORING SUMMARY
CAL Rodgers 1 run (Fredrickson kick)
VT   Randall 2 run (Warley kick)
VT   Willis 3 pass from Randall (Warley kick)
VT   Vick 36 pass from Randall (Warley kick)
CAL Lyman 33 pass from Rodgers (Fredrickson kick)
VT   Jones 11 run (Warley kick)
CAL Arrington 13 pass from Rodgers (Fredrickson kick)
CAL Manderino 3 run (Fredrickson kick)
CAL Echemandu 9 run (Fredrickson kick)
CAL Rodgers 8 run (Fredrickson kick)
VT   Willis 22 pass from Randall (Pace kick)
CAL Strang 13 run (Fredrickson kick)
VT   Shreve 28 pass from Randall (Pace kick)
VT   Hall 52 punt return (Warley kick)
CAL FG Fredrickson 35

CAL	TEAM STATISTICS	VT
27	First Downs	27
136	Rushing Yards	153
27-35-0	Passing	24-36-0
394	Passing Yards	398
530	Total Yards	551
1-14	Punt Returns - Yards	3-53
5-71	Kickoff Returns - Yards	5-156
4-39.8	Punts - Average	2-41.0
1-0	Fumbles - Lost	0-0
4-25	Penalties - Yards	6-40
37:15	Possession Time	22:45

INDIVIDUAL LEADERS
RUSHING
CAL: Arrington 11-37; Echemandu 13-34, 1 TD.
VT: Jones 16-153, 1 TD.
PASSING
CAL: Rodgers 27-35-0, 394 yards, 2 TD.
VT: Randall 24-34-0, 398 yards, 4 TD.
RECEIVING
CAL: Lyman 5-149, 1 TD; Toler 6-84.
VT: Wilford 8-110; Shreve 3-93, 1 TD; Vick 4-82, 1 TD.

December 28, 2004
Oregon State 38, Notre Dame 21

	1ST	2ND	3RD	4TH	FINAL
OSU	14	7	3	14	38
ND	0	7	7	7	21

SCORING SUMMARY
OSU Gillett 12 pass from Anderson (Serna kick)
OSU Newton 11 pass from Anderson (Serna kick)
OSU Haines 11 pass from Anderson (Serna kick)
ND   Fasano 13 pass from Quinn (Fitzpatrick kick)
OSU FG Serna 38
ND   Walker 5 run (Fitzpatrick kick)
OSU Newton 1 pass from Anderson (Serna kick)
ND   McKnight 18 pass from Quinn (Fitzpatrick kick)
OSU Wright 2 run (Serna kick)

OSU	TEAM STATISTICS	ND
19	First Downs	17
20	Rushing Yards	59
28-45-0	Passing	18-33-1
358	Passing Yards	217
378	Total Yards	276
5-77	Punt Returns - Yards	1-7
3-34	Kickoff Returns - Yards	6-109
4-35.3	Punts - Average	8-31.9
1-0	Fumbles - Lost	0-0
5-45	Penalties - Yards	2-10
25:42	Possession Time	34:18

INDIVIDUAL LEADERS
RUSHING
OSU: Wright 9-24, 1 TD.
ND: Walker 13-43, 1 TD; Grant 14-19.
PASSING
OSU: Anderson 28-45-0, 358 yards, 4 TD.
ND: Quinn 17-29-1, 214 yards, 2 TD.
RECEIVING
OSU: Hass 5-105; Newton 7-85, 2 TD.
ND: McKnight 4-90, 1 TD; Samardzija 5-89.

CHAMPS SPORTS BOWL

PROFILE

Site: Orlando, Fla.
Stadium: Florida Citrus Bowl
Capacity: 70,000
Surface: Grass

PLAYING SITES

Joe Robbie Stadium, renamed Pro Player Stadium in 1996, 1990-2000

Florida Citrus Bowl Stadium, since 2001

NAME CHANGES

Blockbuster Bowl, 1990-93
Carquest Bowl, 1994-97
Micron PC Bowl, 1998-99
MicronPC.com Bowl, 2000
Visit Florida Tangerine Bowl, 2001
Mazda Tangerine Bowl, 2002-03
Champs Sports Bowl, since 2004

SEASON	DATE	PRE-GAME RANK	TEAMS	SCORE	FINAL RANK	MOST VALUABLE PLAYERS	ATT.
1990	Dec. 28, 1990	6	Florida State	24	4	Amp Lee, Florida State, RB	74,021
		7	Penn State	17	11		
1991	Dec. 28, 1991	8	Alabama	30	5	David Palmer, Alabama, WR	46,123
		15	Colorado	25	20		
1992	Jan. 1, 1993	13	Stanford	24	9	Darrien Gordon, Stanford, CB	45,554
		21	Penn State	3			
1993	Jan. 1, 1994	15	Boston College	31	13	Glenn Foley, Boston College, QB	38,516
			Virginia	13			
1994	Jan. 2, 1995		South Carolina	24		Steve Taneyhill, South Carolina, QB	50,833
			West Virginia	21			
1995	Dec. 30, 1995		North Carolina	20		Leon Johnson, North Carolina, RB	34,428
		24	Arkansas	10			
1996	Dec. 27, 1996	19	Miami (Fla.)	31	14	Tremain Mack, Miami, SS	46,418
			Virginia	21			
1997	Dec. 29, 1997		Georgia Tech	35	25	Joe Hamilton, Georgia Tech, QB	28,262
			West Virginia	30			
1998	Dec. 29, 1998	24	Miami (Fla.)	46	20	Scott Covington, Miami, QB	44,387
			North Carolina State	23			
1999	Dec. 30, 1999		Illinois	63	24	Kurt Kittner, Illinois, QB	31,089
			Virginia	21			
2000	Dec. 28, 2000		North Carolina State	38		Philip Rivers, North Carolina St., QB	28,359
			Minnesota	30			
2001	Dec. 20, 2001		Pittsburgh	34		Antonio Bryant, Pittsburgh, WR	28,562
			North Carolina State	19			
2002	Dec. 23, 2002		Texas Tech	55		Kliff Kingsbury, Texas Tech, QB	21,689
			Clemson	15			
2003	Dec. 22, 2003		North Carolina State	56		Philip Rivers, North Carolina St., QB	26,482
			Kansas	26			
2004	Dec. 21, 2004		Georgia Tech	51		Reggie Ball, Georgia Tech, QB	28,237
			Syracuse	14			

DECEMBER 28, 1990
FLORIDA STATE 24, PENN STATE 17

	1ST	2ND	3RD	4TH	FINAL
FSU	10	7	7	0	24
PSU	7	0	3	7	17

SCORING SUMMARY
FSU   FG Andrews 41
FSU   Lee 1 run (Andrews kick)
PSU   Daniels 56 pass from Sacca (Fayak kick)
FSU   Lee 7 run (Andrews Kick)
FSU   Weldon 5 run (Andrews kick)
PSU   T. Smith 37 pass from Bill (Fayak kick)

FSU	TEAM STATISTICS	PSU
19	First Downs	17
152	Rushing Yards	122
22-36-2	Passing	15-32-3
248	Passing Yards	278
400	Total Yards	400
43	Punt Returns - Yards	72
7-37.6	Punts - Average	6-36.3
0-0	Fumbles - Lost	2-0
4-35	Penalties - Yards	6-46
33:47	Possession Time	26:13

INDIVIDUAL LEADERS
RUSHING
FSU: Lee 21-86, 2 TD; Bennett 7-30.
PSU: Brown 14-46; Thompson 8-33.
PASSING
FSU: Weldon 22-36-2, 248 yards.
PSU: Sacca 12-25-2, 194 yards, 1 TD; Bill 3-7-1, 84 yards, 1 TD.
RECEIVING
FSU: Dawsey 8-107; Bennett 4-49.
PSU: Daniels 7-154, 1TD; T. Smith 5-100, 1 TD.

DECEMBER 28, 1991
ALABAMA 30, COLORADO 25

	1ST	2ND	3RD	4TH	FINAL
ALA	7	3	13	7	30
COLO	7	5	7	6	25

SCORING SUMMARY
ALA   Palmer 52 punt return (Wethington kick)
COLO   Phillips 1 run (Harper kick)
COLO   Safety (Houston tackled in end zone)
ALA   FG Wethington 25
COLO   FG Harper 33
ALA   Stacy 13 pass from Barker (pass failed)
COLO   Westbrook 62 pass from Hagan (Harper kick)
ALA   Lee 12 pass from Barker (Wethington kick)
ALA   Palmer 5 pass from Barker (Wethington kick)
COLO   Johnson 13 pass from Hagan (pass failed)

ALA	TEAM STATISTICS	COLO
19	First Downs	8
153	Rushing Yards	-11
12-17-1	Passing	11-30-1
154	Passing Yards	210
307	Total Yards	199
7-39.8	Punts - Average	12-41.0
4-1	Fumbles - Lost	2-0
6-33	Penalties - Yards	6-60
38:10	Possession Time	21:50

INDIVIDUAL LEADERS
RUSHING
ALA: Turner 9-43; Stacy 26-11.
COLO: Hagan 14-12.
PASSING
ALA: Barker 12-16-1, 154 yards, 3 TD.
COLO: Hagan 11-30-1, 210 yards, 2 TD.
RECEIVING
ALA: Stacy 4-59, 1 TD; Lee 2-39, 1 TD.
COLO: Westbrook 3-87, 1 TD; Johnson 2-38, 1 TD.

JANUARY 1, 1993
STANFORD 24, PENN STATE 3

	1ST	2ND	3RD	4TH	FINAL
STAN	7	7	10	0	24
PSU	3	0	0	0	3

SCORING SUMMARY
STAN   Wetnight 2 pass from Stenstrom (Abrams kick)
PSU   FG Muscillo 33
STAN   Lasley 5 run (Abrams kick)
STAN   FG Abrams 28
STAN   Milburn 40 pass from Stenstrom (Abrams kick)

STAN	TEAM STATISTICS	PSU
16	First Downs	12
155	Rushing Yards	107
17-29-2	Passing	13-40-2
210	Passing Yards	156
365	Total Yards	263
7-42.4	Punts - Average	11-38.4
2-1	Fumbles - Lost	0-0
5-41	Penalties - Yards	3-25

INDIVIDUAL LEADERS
RUSHING
STAN: Roberts 17-98; Lasley 4-19, 1 TD.
PSU: Anderson 13-40; O'Neal 11-38.
PASSING
STAN: Stenstrom 17-28-1, 210 yards, 2 TD.
PSU: Collins 12-30-1, 145 yards.
RECEIVING
STAN: Wetnight 5-71, 1 TD; Cook 4-55.
PSU: McDuffie 6-111; Drayton 3-21.

January 1, 1994
Boston College 31, Virginia 13

	1ST	2ND	3RD	4TH	FINAL
BC	3	14	7	7	31
VIR	7	6	0	0	13

SCORING SUMMARY

VIR	Washington 8 run (Kirkeirde kick)
BC	FG Gordon 19
BC	Cannon 78 pass from Foley (Gordon kick)
VIR	Way 7 run (kick failed)
BC	Cannon 5 pass from Foley (Gordon kick)
BC	Miller 46 pass from Foley (Gordon kick)
BC	Campbell 12 run (Gordon kick)

BC	TEAM STATISTICS	VIR
27	First Downs	16
166	Rushing Yards	85
25-36-2	Passing	21-36-0
391	Passing Yards	213
557	Total Yards	298
2-39.5	Punts - Average	6-40.8
2-1	Fumbles - Lost	1-0
4-33	Penalties - Yards	3-35
32:54	Possession Time	27:06

INDIVIDUAL LEADERS

RUSHING
BC: Campbell 22-99, 1 TD; Green 10-73.
VIR: Washington 9-40, 1 TD; Brooks 4-22.

PASSING
BC: Foley 25-36-2, 391 yards, 3 TD.
VIR: Willis 19-34-0, 207 yards.

RECEIVING
BC: Cannon 3-109, 2 TD; Mitchell 7-82.
VIR: Holmes 8-93; Mundy 6-60.

January 2, 1995
South Carolina 24, West Virginia 21

	1ST	2ND	3RD	4TH	FINAL
SC	7	10	7	0	24
WVU	0	7	14	0	21

SCORING SUMMARY

SC	Foster 2 pass from Taneyhill (Morton kick)
SC	FG Morton 47
WVU	Walker 24 run (Baumann kick)
SC	Taneyhill 4 run (Morton kick)
WVU	Purnell 6 pass from Johnston (Baumann kick)
SC	Pritchett 1 run (Morton kick)
WVU	Purnell 7 pass from Johnston (Baumann kick)

SC	TEAM STATISTICS	WVU
21	First Downs	16
148	Rushing Yards	150
26-36-0	Passing	19-32-1
227	Passing Yards	240
375	Total Yards	390
4-35.2	Punts - Average	2-54.0
6-2	Fumbles - Lost	3-2
6-38	Penalties - Yards	7-55

December 30, 1995
North Carolina 20, Arkansas 10

	1ST	2ND	3RD	4TH	FINAL
UNC	7	0	13	0	20
ARK	7	0	3	0	10

SCORING SUMMARY

ARK	Lucas 25 pass from Lunney (Latourette kick)
UNC	Ashford 18 pass from Thomas (Welch kick)
ARK	FG Latourette 26
UNC	L. Johnson 28 run (Welch kick)
UNC	Stevens 87 pass from Thomas (conversion failed)

UNC	TEAM STATISTICS	ARK
20	First Downs	26
242	Rushing Yards	162
10-23-0	Passing	16-35-2
177	Passing Yards	227
419	Total Yards	389
4-32.5	Punts - Average	4-38.8
0-0	Fumbles - Lost	1-1
4-31	Penalties - Yards	3-36
29:07	Possession Time	30:03

INDIVIDUAL LEADERS

RUSHING
UNC: L. Johnson 29-195, 1 TD.
ARK: M. Johnson 19-136.

PASSING
UNC: Thomas 10-23-0, 177 yards, 2 TD.
ARK: Lunney 16-35-2, 227 yards, 1 TD.

RECEIVING
UNC: Stevens 1-87, 1 TD; Ashford 3-38, 1 TD.
ARK: Meadors 7-101; Eubanks 3-45.

December 27, 1996
Miami (Fla.) 31, Virginia 21

	1ST	2ND	3RD	4TH	FINAL
MIA	14	10	0	7	31
VIR	7	0	7	7	21

SCORING SUMMARY

MIA	Green 70 pass from Clement (Crosland kick)
MIA	Mack recovered fumble (Crosland kick)
VIR	Crowell 29 pass from Brooks (Garcia kick)
MIA	FG Crosland 20
MIA	Mack 42 interception return (Crosland kick)
VIR	Brooks 1 run (Garcia kick)
MIA	T. Jones 2 run (Crosland kick)
VIR	T. Jones 3 run (Garcia kick)

December 29, 1997
Georgia Tech 35, West Virginia 30

	1ST	2ND	3RD	4TH	FINAL
GT	14	14	0	7	35
WVU	7	7	10	6	30

SCORING SUMMARY

GT	Wilder 1 run (Chambers kick)
WVU	Zereoue 14 run (Taylor kick)
GT	Hamilton 30 run (Chambers kick)
GT	Lillie 3 pass from Hamilton (Chambers kick)
WVU	Porter 21 pass from Bulger (Taylor kick)
GT	Hamilton 9 run (Chambers kick)
WVU	Zereoue 19 run (Taylor kick)
WVU	FG Taylor 21
GT	Wiley 5 run (Chambers kick)
WVU	Porter 74 pass from Bulger (pass failed)

GT	TEAM STATISTICS	WVU
28	First Downs	24
210	Rushing Yards	56
19-36-0	Passing	25-40-1
274	Passing Yards	353
484	Total Yards	409
4-42.0	Punts - Average	3-43.3
1-1	Fumbles - Lost	1-1
10-86	Penalties - Yards	9-75
35:02	Possession Time	24:58

INDIVIDUAL LEADERS

RUSHING
GT: Hamilton 14-82, 2 TD; Rogers 16-75.
WVU: Zereoue 17-84, 2 TD.

PASSING
GT: Hamilton 19-36-0, 274 yards, 1 TD.
WVU: Bulger 25-40-1, 353 yards, 2 TD.

RECEIVING
GT: Steagall 7-112, Middleton 4-45.
WVU: Porter 4-124, 2 TD; Foreman 12-110.

December 29, 1998
Miami (Fla.) 46, NC State 23

	1ST	2ND	3RD	4TH	FINAL
MIA	20	7	3	16	46
NCST	7	3	7	6	23

SCORING SUMMARY

MIA	King 4 pass from Covington (Crosland kick)
NCST	Barnette 1 run (Deskevich kick)
MIA	James 5 run (Crosland kick)
MIA	Moss 80 pass from Covington (kick blocked)
NCST	FG Deskevich 28
MIA	James 2 run (Crosland kick)
MIA	FG 31 Crosland
NCST	Spikes 30 run (Deskevich kick)
MIA	Jackson 13 run (pass failed)
MIA	Jackson 25 run (Crosland kick)
NCST	Coleman 7 pass from Barnette (run failed)
MIA	FG Gaitan 29

MIA	TEAM STATISTICS	NCST
27	First Downs	31
269	Rushing Yards	297
18-27-0	Passing	22-44-5
325	Passing Yards	201
594	Total Yards	498
2-34.5	Punts - Average	3-29.3
2-2	Fumbles - Lost	3-1
7-75	Penalties - Yards	3-88
29:07	Possession Time	30:53

INDIVIDUAL LEADERS

RUSHING
MIA: James 20-156, 2 TD; Jackson 11-99, 2 TD.
NCST: Spikes 24-176, 1 TD; Barnette 8-81, 1 TD.

PASSING
MIA: Covington 17-24-0, 320 yards, 2 TD.
NCST: Barnette 22-41-3, 201 yards, 1 TD.

RECEIVING
MIA: Moss 5-141, 1 TD; Franks 4-72.
NCST: Coleman 6-98, 1 TD; Holt 7-52.

December 30, 1999
Illinois 63, Virginia 21

	1ST	2ND	3RD	4TH	FINAL
ILL	14	28	7	14	63
VIR	7	0	7	7	21

SCORING SUMMARY

ILL	Kittner 1 run (Rackers kick)
VIR	Jones 7 run (Braverman kick)
ILL	Harvey 47 run (Rackers kick)
ILL	Kittner 30 pass from Lloyd (Rackers kick)
ILL	Cook 61 pass from Kittner (Rackers kick)
ILL	Havard 2 run (Rackers kick)
ILL	Cook 1 pass from Kittner (Rackers kick)
VIR	Coffey 5 pass from Ellis (Braverman kick)
ILL	Havard 2 run (Rackers kick)
ILL	Harvey 9 run (Rackers kick)
ILL	Johnson 1 run (Rackers kick)
VIR	Thompson 55 pass from Rivers (Braverman kick)

ILL	TEAM STATISTICS	VIR
26	First Downs	20
325	Rushing Yards	172
16-26-1	Passing	17-35-1
286	Passing Yards	208
611	Total Yards	380
0-0	Punts - Average	6-36.7
2-1	Fumbles - Lost	1-1
5-39	Penalties - Yards	5-25
33:23	Possession Time	26:37

INDIVIDUAL LEADERS

RUSHING
ILL: Harvey 10-122, 2 TD; Havard 15-75, 2 TD.
VIR: Jones 23-110, 1 TD.

PASSING
ILL: Kittner 14-24-1, 254 yards, 2 TD.
VIR: Ellis 15-32-1, 146 yards, 1 TD.

RECEIVING
ILL: Cook 4-88, 2 TD; Lloyd 3-57.
VIR: Jones 5-31; McMullen 3-31.

December 28, 2000
NC State 38, Minnesota 30

	1ST	2ND	3RD	4TH	FINAL
NCST	0	8	17	13	38
MINN	21	3	0	6	30

SCORING SUMMARY

MINN	Redmon 12 run (Nystrom kick)
MINN	Redmon 3 run (Nystrom kick)
MINN	Cole 2 run (Nystrom kick)
MINN	FG Nystrom 27
NCST	Vanderveer 2 pass from Rivers (Robinson pass from Cole)
NCST	K Robinson 19 run (Leak pass from Cole)
NCST	FG Passingham 37
NCST	R. Robinson 3 run (pass failed)
MINN	FG Nystrom 23
NCST	K. Robinson 23 pass from Rivers (conversion failed)
MINN	FG Nystrom 29
NCST	R. Robinson 8 run (Passingham kick)

NCST	TEAM STATISTICS	MINN
22	First Downs	31
109	Rushing Yards	300
24-39-2	Passing	16-30-1
310	Passing Yards	202
419	Total Yards	502
5-44.6	Punts - Average	5-28.4
2-0	Fumbles - Lost	2-1
7-75	Penalties - Yards	14-107
24:27	Possession Time	35:33

INDIVIDUAL LEADERS

RUSHING
NCST: R. Robinson 15-74, 2 TD; K. Robinson 1-19, 1 TD.
MINN: Redmon 42-246, 2 TD.

PASSING
NCST: Rivers 24-39-2, 310 yards, 2 TD.
MINN: Cole 16-29-0, 202 yards.

RECEIVING
NCST: K. Robinson 7-157, 1 TD; Leak 4-76.
MINN: Keller 5-51; Patterson 4-30.

DECEMBER 20, 2001
PITTSBURGH 34, NC STATE 19

	1ST	2ND	3RD	4TH	FINAL
NCST	3	7	0	9	19
PITT	3	21	3	7	34

SCORING SUMMARY
PITT   FG Lotz 27
NCST   FG Kiker 32
PITT   Bryant 15 pass from Priestley (Lotz kick)
PITT   Bryant 2 pass from Priestley (Lotz kick)
NCST   Golden 90 kick return (Kiker kick)
PITT   Rutherford 1 run (Lotz kick)
PITT   FG Lotz 33
NCST   Edwards 5 pass from Rivers (kick failed)
NCST   FG Kiker 19
PITT   Young 16 fumble return (Lotz kick)

NCST	TEAM STATISTICS	PITT
19	First Downs	20
105	Rushing Yards	136
26-40-1	Passing	18-32-0
189	Passing Yards	271
294	Total Yards	407
5-40.2	Punts - Average	6-44.2
2-1	Fumbles - Lost	1-0
4-28	Penalties - Yards	10-75
26:59	Possession Time	33:01

INDIVIDUAL LEADERS
RUSHING
NCST: Robinson 10-51; Jackson 2-31.
PITT: Polite 9-63; Furman 7-33.
PASSING
NCST: Rivers 26-40-1, 189 yards, 1 TD.
PITT: Priestley 18-32-0, 271 yards, 2 TD.
RECEIVING
NCST: Wright 8-61; Edwards 8-47, 1 TD.
PITT: Bryant 7-101, 2 TD; English 5-76.

DECEMBER 23, 2002
TEXAS TECH 55, CLEMSON 15

	1ST	2ND	3RD	4TH	FINAL
TT	17	17	7	14	55
CLEM	0	2	7	6	15

SCORING SUMMARY
TT   FG Treece 29
TT   Glover 46 pass from Kingsbury (Treece kick)
TT   Peters 19 pass from Kingsbury (Treece kick)
TT   Henderson 10 run (Treece kick)
CLEM   Safety
TT   Welker 59 punt return (Treece kick)
TT   FG Treece 40
CLEM   Hall 10 pass from Whitehurst (Hunt kick)
TT   Francis 2 pass from Symons (Bishop kick)
CLEM   Jasmin 2 run (pass failed)
TT   Welker 9 pass from Kingsbury (Bishop kick)
TT   Henderson 26 pass from Symons (Bishop kick)

TT	TEAM STATISTICS	CLEM
28	First Downs	20
91	Rushing Yards	41
39-52-1	Passing	25-56-4
464	Passing Yards	319
555	Total Yards	360
3-29.7	Punts - Average	6-38.3
0-0	Fumbles - Lost	2-0
8-79	Penalties - Yards	7-55
29:29	Possession Time	30:31

INDIVIDUAL LEADERS
RUSHING
TT: Henderson 10-60, 1 TD; Welker 4-30.
CLEM: Hill 5-16.
PASSING
TT: Kingsbury 32-43-1, 375 yards, 3 TD; Symons 7-9-0, 89 yards, 2 TD.
CLEM: Whitehurst 20-48-4, 263 yards, 1 TD.
RECEIVING
TT: Glover 8-121, 1 TD; Francis 6-88, 1 TD.
CLEM: Youngblood 7-134; Hamilton 4-72.

DECEMBER 22, 2003
NC STATE 56, KANSAS 26

	1ST	2ND	3RD	4TH	FINAL
NCST	21	7	14	14	56
KAN	7	3	10	6	26

SCORING SUMMARY
NCST   Washington 45 pass from Rivers (Kiker kick)
KAN   Gordon 23 pass from Whittemore (Brooks kick)
NCST   Washington 14 pass from Rivers (Kiker kick)
NCST   McLendon 1 run (Kiker kick)
KAN   FG Brooks 28
NCST   McLendon 3 pass from Rivers (Kiker kick)
KAN   Green 11 pass from Whittemore (Brooks kick)
NCST   Clark 40 pass from Rivers (Kiker kick)
NCST   Davis 10 run (Kiker kick)
KAN   FG Beck 39
KAN   Whittemore 9 run (pass failed)
NCST   Cotchery 21 pass from Rivers (Kiker kick)
NCST   McLendon 26 run (Kiker kick)

NCST	TEAM STATISTICS	KAN
34	First Downs	28
172	Rushing Yards	220
38-46-0	Passing	20-42-2
481	Passing Yards	243
653	Total Yards	463
1-(-2)	Punt Returns - Yards	1-13
5-108	Kickoff Returns - Yards	9-210
1-53.0	Punts - Average	4-28.8
0-0	Fumbles - Lost	0-0
9-86	Penalties - Yards	9-75
26:05	Possession Time	33:55

INDIVIDUAL LEADERS
RUSHING
NCST: McLendon 7-72, 2 TD; Hall 3-40.
KAN: Green 14-87; Whittemore 17-84, 1 TD.
PASSING
NCST: Rivers 37-45-0, 475 yards, 5 TD.
KAN: Whittemore 20-41-2, 243 yards, 2 TD.
RECEIVING
NCST: Cotchery 13-171, 1 TD; Washington 7-97, 2 TD.
KAN: Rideau 9-109; Gordon 4-73, 1 TD.

DECEMBER 21, 2004
GEORGIA TECH 51, SYRACUSE 14

	1ST	2ND	3RD	4TH	FINAL
GT	21	14	14	2	51
SYR	6	0	0	8	14

SCORING SUMMARY
GT   Reis 20 interception return (Bell kick)
SYR   Patterson 21 run (kick failed)
GT   Johnson 10 pass from Ball (Bell kick)
GT   Curry 80 pass from Ball (Bell kick)
GT   Daniels 2 run (Bell kick)
GT   Johnson 5 run (Bell kick)
GT   Ball 11 run (Bell kick)
GT   Daniels 1 run (Bell kick)
SYR   Gregory 25 pass from Patterson (Rhodes pass to Darlington)
GT   Safety

GT	TEAM STATISTICS	SYR
28	First Downs	20
286	Rushing Yards	51
13-20-1	Passing	22-39-2
228	Passing Yards	230
514	Total Yards	281
2-7	Punt Returns - Yards	2-8
3-75	Kickoff Returns - Yards	4-100
2-35.5	Punts - Average	7-34.4
3-2	Fumbles - Lost	1-1
5-38	Penalties - Yards	7-45
35:50	Possession Time	24:10

INDIVIDUAL LEADERS
RUSHING
GT: Daniels 17-119, 2 TD; Ball 9-38, 1 TD.
SYR: Gregory 1-16; Rhodes 9-14.
PASSING
GT: Ball 12-19-1, 207 yards 2 TD.
SYR: Patterson 21-34-1, 219 yards, 1 TD.
RECEIVING
GT: Curry 3-105, 1 TD; Johnson 2-61, 1 TD.
SYR: Gregory 5-66, 1 TD; Jones 6-61.

LAS VEGAS BOWL

PROFILE

Site: Las Vegas
Stadium: Sam Boyd Stadium
Capacity: 36,800
Surface: TurfTech

PLAYING SITES

Sam Boyd Stadium, since 1992

NAME CHANGES

Las Vegas Bowl, 1992-98
EA Sports Las Vegas Bowl, 1999
Las Vegas Bowl, 2000
Sega Sports Las Vegas Bowl,
  2001-2002
Las Vegas Bowl, 2003
Pioneer PureVision Las Vegas
  Bowl, since 2004

SEASON	DATE	PRE-GAME RANK	TEAMS	SCORE	FINAL RANK	MOST VALUABLE PLAYERS	ATT.
1992	Dec. 18, 1992		Bowling Green	35		Erik White, Bowling Green, QB	15,476
			Nevada	34			
1993	Dec. 17, 1993		Utah State	42		Anthony Calvillo, Utah State, QB	15,508
			Ball State	33			
1994	Dec. 15, 1994		UNLV	52		Henry Bailey, UNLV, WR	17,562
			Central Michigan	24			
1995	Dec. 14, 1995	25	Toledo	40 OT	24	Wasean Tait, Toledo, RB	11,127
			Nevada	37			
1996	Dec. 18, 1996		Nevada	18		Mike Crawford, Nevada, LB	10,118
			Ball State	15			
1997	Dec. 20, 1997		Oregon	41		Pat Johnson, Oregon, WR	21,514
		23	Air Force	13			
1998	Dec. 19, 1998		North Carolina	20		Ronald Curry, North Carolina, QB	21,429
			San Diego State	13			
1999	Dec. 18, 1999		Utah	17		Mike Anderson, Utah, RB	28,227
			Fresno State	16			
2000	Dec. 21, 2000		UNLV	31		Jason Thomas, UNLV, QB	29,113
			Arkansas	14			
2001	Dec. 25, 2001		Utah	10		Dameon Hunter, Utah, RB	30,894
			Southern Cal	6			
2002	Dec. 25, 2002		UCLA	27		Craig Bragg, UCLA, WR	30,324
			New Mexico	13			
2003	Dec. 24, 2003		Oregon State	55		Steven Jackson, Oregon State, RB	25,437
			New Mexico	14			
2004	Dec. 23, 2004		Wyoming	24		Corey Bramlet, Wyoming, QB	27,784
			UCLA	21			

DECEMBER 18, 1992
BOWLING GREEN 35, NEVADA 34

	1ST	2ND	3RD	4TH	FINAL
BG	14	14	0	7	35
NEV	3	0	21	10	34

SCORING SUMMARY
BG   Smith 10 pass from White (Leaver kick)
NEV FG Terelak 30
BG   Jackson 4 run (Leaver kick)
BG   White 8 pass from Smith (Leaver kick)
BG   Jackson 17 run (Leaver kick)
NEV Senior 5 pass from Vargas (Terelak kick)
NEV Holmes 5 run (Terelak kick)
NEV Matter 3 pass from Vargas (Terelak kick)
NEV Reeves 3 run (Terelak kick)
NEV FG Terelak 19
BG   Hankins 3 pass from White (Leaver kick)

BG	TEAM STATISTICS	NEV
21	First Downs	25
157	Rushing Yards	94
25-41-0	Passing	29-49-0
253	Passing Yards	344
410	Total Yards	438
5-43.2	Punts - Average	4-36.7
0-0	Fumbles - Lost	3-2
5-56	Penalties - Yards	3-10
33:35	Possession Time	26:25

INDIVIDUAL LEADERS
RUSHING
BG: Jackson 22-113, 2 TD; Smith 12-27.
NEV: Holmes 18-62, 1 TD; Vargas 4-22.
PASSING
BG: White 24-40-0, 245 yards, 2 TD; Smith 1-1-0, 8 yards, 1 TD.
NEV: Vargas 24-40-0, 283 yards, 2 TD.
RECEIVING
BG: Smith 7-68, 1 TD; Szlachcic 5-51.
NEV: Reeves 8-92; King 5-88.

DECEMBER 17, 1993
UTAH STATE 42, BALL STATE 33

	1ST	2ND	3RD	4TH	FINAL
USU	14	7	14	7	42
BSU	0	0	17	16	33

SCORING SUMMARY
USU McMahon 22 pass from Calvillo (Morrealle kick)
USU Grier 3 run (Morrealle kick)
USU Thompson 3 pass from Calvillo (Morrealle kick)
BSU McCray 7 pass from Neu (Swart kick)
BSU FG Swart 31
USU Grier 15 run (Morrealle kick)
USU Lee 16 pass from Calvillo (Morrealle kick)
BSU Blair 2 pass from Neu (Swart kick)
BSU Safety (Calvillo forced out of end zone)
USU Toomer 32 interception return (Morrealle kick)
BSU Nibbs 2 run (Oliver pass from Neu)
BSU Oliver 2 pass from Neu (pass failed)

USU	TEAM STATISTICS	BSU
25	First Downs	14
205	Rushing Yards	73
25-39-2	Passing	21-38-2
286	Passing Yards	241
491	Total Yards	314
3-39.3	Punts - Average	5-41.0
2-1	Fumbles - Lost	1-1
15-150	Penalties - Yards	5-30
35:11	Possession Time	24:49

INDIVIDUAL LEADERS
RUSHING
USU: Grier 33-142, 2 TD; Calvillo 8-50.
BSU: Kent 1-27; Nibbs 6-18, 1 TD.
PASSING
USU: Calvillo 25-29-2, 286 yards, 3 TD.
BSU: Neu 20-37-2, 239 yards, 3 TD.
RECEIVING
USU: Jenkins 5-94; McMahon 4-54, 1 TD.
BSU: Oliver 5-114, 1 TD; Blair 10-66, 1 TD.

DECEMBER 15, 1994
UNLV 52, CENTRAL MICHIGAN 24

	1ST	2ND	3RD	4TH	FINAL
UNLV	14	17	14	7	52
CMU	10	0	0	14	24

SCORING SUMMARY
UNLV Bailey 46 pass from Brown (Garritano kick)
UNLV Bailey 1 run (Garritano kick)
CMU   FG Blasy 20
CMU   McMillan 53 pass from Timpf (Blasy kick)
UNLV Bailey 49 run (Garritano kick)
UNLV Washington 15 fumble return (Garritano kick)
UNLV FG Garritano 38
UNLV Bailey 1 run (Garritano kick)
UNLV Keener 33 pass from Brown (Garritano kick)
UNLV Gatewood 45 pass from Davis (Garritano kick)
CMU   McMillan 24 pass from Darnell (Blasy kick)
CMU   Tolbert 4 run (Blasy kick)

UNLV	TEAM STATISTICS	CMU
26	First Downs	22
301	Rushing Yards	152
15-27-0	Passing	13-25-2
288	Passing Yards	224
589	Total Yards	376
2-45.0	Punts - Average	5-41.2
3-1	Fumbles - Lost	5-2
8-89	Penalties - Yards	6-50
23:29	Possession Time	36:34

INDIVIDUAL LEADERS
RUSHING
UNLV: Branch 13-125; Bailey 7-79, 3 TD.
CMU: Tolbert 11-79, 1 TD; King 6-51.
PASSING
UNLV: Brown 11-21-0, 195 yards, 2 TD.
CMU: Timpf 7-12-1, 122 yards, 1 TD.
RECEIVING
UNLV: Gatewood 6-104, 1 TD; Bailey 5-101, 1 TD.
CMU: McMillan 4-100, 2 TD; Korytkowski 3-44.

December 14, 1995
Toledo 40, Nevada 37

	1ST	2ND	3RD	4TH	OT	FINAL
TOL	7	14	6	7	6	40
NEV	7	7	10	10	3	37

SCORING SUMMARY

TOL	Huzjak 31 run (Spring kick)
NEV	Minor 2 run (Shea kick)
TOL	Tait 18 run (Spring kick)
TOL	Tait 31 run (Spring kick)
NEV	Minor 1 run (Shea kick)
NEV	FG Shea 34
TOL	Harris 16 run (kick failed)
NEV	Bennett 4 run (Shea kick)
TOL	Tait 26 run (Spring kick)
NEV	Minor 1 run (Shea kick)
NEV	FG Shea 26
NEV	FG Shea 22
TOL	Tait 2 run

TOL	TEAM STATISTICS	NEV
33	First Downs	23
307	Rushing Yards	83
23-41-1	Passing	27-51-0
254	Passing Yards	330
561	Total Yards	413
3-37.3	Punts - Average	5-49.8
4-3	Fumbles - Lost	2-0
9-84	Penalties - Yards	3-15
34:29	Possession Time	25:31

INDIVIDUAL LEADERS

RUSHING
TOL: Tait 31-185, 4 TD; Huzjak 13-59, 1 TD.
NEV: Minor 16-38, 3 TD; Wilson 10-34.

PASSING
TOL: Huzjak 23-41-1, 254 yards.
NEV: Maxwell 27-49-0, 330 yards.

RECEIVING
TOL: Tait 6-53; Kreitzburg 4-49.
NEV: Van Dyke 14-176; West 4-46.

December 18, 1996
Nevada 18, Ball State 15

	1ST	2ND	3RD	4TH	FINAL
NEV	9	3	0	6	18
BSU	0	7	0	8	15

SCORING SUMMARY

NEV	Wilkins 16 pass from Dutton (kick blocked)
NEV	FG Shea 22
BSU	Moore 62 run (Locklear kick)
NEV	FG Shea 33
NEV	Wilkins 11 pass from Bennett (pass failed)
BSU	Reese 27 pass from Baldwin (Abernathy pass from Baldwin)

NEV	TEAM STATISTICS	BSU
24	First Downs	12
84	Rushing Yards	112
26-48-2	Passing	11-31-1
376	Passing Yards	106
460	Total Yards	218
6-39.0	Punts - Average	12-41.1
1-0	Fumbles - Lost	1-0
6-51	Penalties - Yards	7-49

INDIVIDUAL LEADERS

RUSHING
NEV: Lemon 24-96.
BSU: Moore 8-74, 1 TD; Blair 14-44.

PASSING
NEV: Dutton 18-33-2, 224, 1 TD; Bennett 8-15-0, 152, 1 TD.
BSU: Baldwin 11-31-1, 106 yards, 1 TD.

December 20, 1997
Oregon 41, Air Force 13

	1ST	2ND	3RD	4TH	FINAL
ORE	13	13	8	7	41
AFA	0	0	13	0	13

SCORING SUMMARY

ORE	Johnson 69 pass from Smith (Frankel kick)
ORE	McCullough 76 run (kick failed)
ORE	Parker block punt recovered for TD (kick failed)
ORE	Hartley 7 pass from Maas (Smith kick)
AFA	Morgan 1 run (Wright kick)
ORE	Hartley 21 pass from Maas (Spence pass from Maas)
AFA	Fisher 45 fumble recovery (pass failed)
ORE	Johnson 78 pass from Maas (Smith kick)

ORE	TEAM STATISTICS	AFA
22	First Downs	11
266	Rushing Yards	152
16-30-1	Passing	6-21-1
317	Passing Yards	59
583	Total Yards	211
6-38.7	Punts - Average	10-36.6
3-2	Fumbles - Lost	1-1
19-166	Penalties - Yards	7-57
30:22	Possession Time	29:38

INDIVIDUAL LEADERS

RUSHING
ORE: McCullough 17-150, 1 TD; Maas 5-40.
AFA: Singleton 13-66; Ruff 7-27.

PASSING
ORE: Maas 9-15-0, 188 yards, 3 TD; Smith 4-10-1, 87 yards, 1 TD.
AFA: Morgan 6-19-1, 59 yards.

RECEIVING
ORE: Johnson 5-169, 2 TD; Spence 2-59.
AFA: Newman 2-29; Rillos 1-13.

December 19, 1998
North Carolina 20, San Diego St. 13

	1ST	2ND	3RD	4TH	FINAL
UNC	12	8	0	0	20
SDSU	7	3	0	3	13

SCORING SUMMARY

SDSU	Mitchell 60 yard run (Tandberg kick)
UNC	FG McGee 32
UNC	FG McGee 23
UNC	Curry 48 run (kick failed)
UNC	Bomar block punt recovered for TD (Bailey pass from Curry)
SDSU	FG Tandberg 32
SDSU	FG Tandberg 38

UNC	TEAM STATISTICS	SDSU
8	First Downs	20
163	Rushing Yards	193
4-13-0	Passing	11-23-1
33	Passing Yards	102
196	Total Yards	295
5-44.0	Punts - Average	7-24.1
1-1	Fumbles - Lost	3-0
6-73	Penalties - Yards	4-36
26:13	Possession Time	33:47

INDIVIDUAL LEADERS

RUSHING
UNC: Curry 10-93, 1 TD; Saunders 17-39.
SDSU: Lewis 25-61; Mitchell 1-60, 1 TD.

PASSING
UNC: Davenport 3-11-0, 30 yards.
SDSU: Russell 10-22-1, 99 yards.

RECEIVING
UNC: Brown 3-18; Harris 1-15.
SDSU: Gourdine 3-31; Ned 2-18.

December 18, 1999
Utah 17, Fresno State 16

	1ST	2ND	3RD	4TH	FINAL
UTAH	7	0	7	3	17
FRES	7	0	3	6	16

SCORING SUMMARY

FRES	Williams 75 blocked field goal return (Hanna kick)
UTAH	Anderson 34 run (Truhe kick)
FRES	FG Hanna 27
UTAH	Anderson 5 run (Truhe kick)
FRES	Ward 2 run (kick blocked)
UTAH	FG Truhe 33

UTAH	TEAM STATISTICS	FRES
25	First Downs	16
334	Rushing Yards	132
11-24-1	Passing	14-28-0
214	Passing Yards	147
548	Total Yards	279
3-(-7)	Punt Returns - Yards	2-15
3-57	Kickoff Returns - Yards	3-74
4-39.0	Punts - Average	5-37.2
15-151	Penalties - Yards	6-59
35:54	Possession Time	24:06

INDIVIDUAL LEADERS

RUSHING
UTAH: Anderson 34-254, 2 TD; Bacon 8-91.
FRES: Ward 15-63, 1 TD; Gaines 8-34.

PASSING
UTAH: Arceneaux 8-15-0, 94 yards; Croshaw 3-9-1, 120 yards.
FRES: Volek 14-28-0, 147 yards.

RECEIVING
UTAH: Russell 5-96; Bendinger 2-70.
FRES: Wright 6-55; Smith 4-53.

December 21, 2000
UNLV 31, Arkansas 14

	1ST	2ND	3RD	4TH	FINAL
UNLV	0	14	7	10	31
ARK	7	7	0	0	14

SCORING SUMMARY

ARK	Stinson 7 pass from Hampton (O'Donohoe kick)
UNLV	Turner 19 pass from Thomas (Pieffer kick)
ARK	Williams 25 pass from Hampton (O'Donohoe kick)
UNLV	Turner 5 pass from Thomas (Pieffer kick)
UNLV	Mason 54 pass from Thomas (Pieffer kick)
UNLV	FG Pieffer 26
UNLV	Brown 18 run (Pieffer kick)

UNLV	TEAM STATISTICS	ARK
19	First Downs	15
314	Rushing Yards	127
12-17-0	Passing	18-40-0
217	Passing Yards	183
531	Total Yards	310
5-51	Punt Returns - Yards	0-0
2-33	Kickoff Returns - Yards	5-79
4-40.3	Punts - Average	7-46.1
6-1	Fumbles - Lost	0-0
12-119	Penalties - Yards	6-76
30:25	Possession Time	29:35

INDIVIDUAL LEADERS

RUSHING
UNLV: Rudolf 14-110; Brown 13-80, 1 TD.
ARK: Holmes 26-104; Howard 1-12.

PASSING
UNLV: Thomas 12-17-0, 217 yards, 3 TD.
ARK: Hampton 18-40-0, 183 yards, 2 TD.

RECEIVING
UNLV: Turner 8-126, 2 TD; Mason 3-89, 1 TD.
ARK: Williams 7-97, 1 TD; Hamilton 2-33.

DECEMBER 25, 2001
UTAH 10, SOUTHERN CAL 6

	1ST	2ND	3RD	4TH	FINAL
UTAH	7	3	0	0	10
USC	0	0	6	0	6

SCORING SUMMARY

UTAH	Tate 3 run (Kaneshiro kick)
UTAH	FG Kaneshiro 26
USC	Byrd 2 run (kick failed)

UTAH	TEAM STATISTICS	USC
20	First Downs	12
222	Rushing Yards	1
12-21-1	Passing	15-26-0
136	Passing Yards	150
358	Total Yards	151
4-8	Punt Returns - Yards	2-27
0-0	Kickoff Returns - Yards	2-33
6-38.0	Punts - Average	8-37.8
1-1	Fumbles - Lost	1-0
10-95	Penalties - Yards	6-47
38:01	Possession Time	21:59

INDIVIDUAL LEADERS

RUSHING
UTAH: Tate 23-103, 1 TD; Hunter 17-94.
USC: Byrd 10-31, 1 TD; Howard 3-14.

PASSING
UTAH: Rice 12-21-1, 136 yards.
USC: Palmer 15-26-0, 150 yards.

RECEIVING
UTAH: Lyman 4-41; Richardson 3-35.
USC: Colbert 2-38; Kelly 3-33.

DECEMBER 25.2002
UCLA 27, NEW MEXICO 13

	1ST	2ND	3RD	4TH	FINAL
UCLA	3	3	7	14	27
UNM	6	0	0	7	13

SCORING SUMMARY

UCLA	FG Fikse 49
UNM	Black 55 interception return (kick blocked)
UCLA	FG Fikse 39
UCLA	Bragg 74 punt return (Fikse kick)
UCLA	Page 29 interception return (Griffith kick)
UCLA	Ebell 1 run (Fikse kick)
UNM	Manning 11 pass from Kelly (Byrd kick)

UCLA	TEAM STATISTICS	UNM
9	First Downs	15
73	Rushing Yards	45
12-22-1	Passing	18-35-1
94	Passing Yards	237
167	Total Yards	282
3-96	Punt Returns - Yards	6-18
2-50	Kickoff Returns - Yards	5-100
8-44.9	Punts - Average	6-38.5
1-0	Fumbles - Lost	4-2
10-108	Penalties - Yards	9-68
31:13	Possession Time	28:47

INDIVIDUAL LEADERS

RUSHING
UCLA: Ebell 25-70, 1 TD; White 9-23.
UNM: Moore 14-17; Brody 4-17.

PASSING
UCLA: Moore 9-16-0, 80 yards.
UNM: Kelly 18-32-1, 237 yards, 1 TD.

RECEIVING
UCLA: Bragg 4-38; Taylor 4-19.
UNM: Counter 5-78; Farrel 4-78.

DECEMBER 24, 2003
OREGON STATE 55, NEW MEXICO 14

	1ST	2ND	3RD	4TH	FINAL
OKST	17	14	10	14	55
UNM	7	0	0	7	14

SCORING SUMMARY

OKST	Jackson 34 pass from Anderson (Yliniemi kick)
OKST	FG Yliniemi 21
UNM	Baskett 27 pass from Kelly (Zunker kick)
OKST	Hass 42 pass from Anderson (Yliniemi kick)
OKST	Jackson 3 run (Yliniemi kick)
OKST	Jackson 11 run (Yliniemi kick)
OKST	Jackson 6 run (Yliniemi kick)
OKST	FG Yliniemi 31
OKST	Jackson 1 run (Yliniemi kick)
UNM	Counter 17 pass from McKamey (Zunker kick)
OKST	Hawkins 19 pass from Rothenfluh (Yliniemi kick)

OKST	TEAM STATISTICS	UNM
29	First Downs	7
154	Rushing Yards	6
27-41-1	Passing	10-23-1
386	Passing Yards	121
540	Total Yards	127
5-16	Punt Returns - Yards	1-0
3-65	Kickoff Returns - Yards	8-175
3-37.3	Punts - Average	10-39.1
1-1	Fumbles - Lost	1-1
10-94	Penalties - Yards	13-103
29:16	Possession Time	30:44

INDIVIDUAL LEADERS

RUSHING
OKST: Jackson 28-149, 4 TD.
UNM: Byrd 2-13.

PASSING
OKST: Anderson 21-32-1, 322 yards, 2 TD.
UNM: Kelly 4-12-0, 32 yards.

RECEIVING
OKST: Euhus 7-121; Hass 6-88, 1 TD.
UNM: Counter 2-63, 1 TD; Baskett 1-27, 1 TD.

DECEMBER 23, 2004
WYOMING 24, UCLA 21

	1ST	2ND	3RD	4TH	FINAL
WYO	10	0	0	14	24
UCLA	0	14	7	0	21

SCORING SUMMARY

WYO	FG Yaussi 39
WYO	Holden 10 pass from Bramlet (Yaussi kick)
UCLA	Taylor 29 pass from Olson (Medlock kick)
UCLA	Bragg 17 pass from Koral (Medlock kick)
UCLA	Bragg 25 pass from Koral (Medlock kick)
WYO	Raterink 22 pass from Bouknight (Yaussi kick)
WYO	Wadkowski 12 pass from Bramlet (Yaussi kick)

WYO	TEAM STATISTICS	UCLA
19	First Downs	19
76	Rushing Yards	126
21-38-1	Passing	13-24-0
329	Passing Yards	185
405	Total Yards	311
0-0	Punt Returns - Yards	3-31
5-81	Kickoff Returns - Yards	4-82
7-31.9	Punts - Average	6-44.0
1-0	Fumbles - Lost	6-2
11-114	Penalties - Yards	10-84
30:11	Possession Time	29:49

INDIVIDUAL LEADERS

RUSHING
WYO: Harris 13-27; Harrison 5-16.
UCLA: Drew 25-126; Markey 5-20.

PASSING
WYO: Bramlet 20-34-1, 307 yards, 2 TD.
UCLA: Olson 6-12-0, 96 yards, 1 TD; Koral 7-12-0, 89 yards, 2 TD.

RECEIVING
WYO: Holden 4-115, 1 TD; Bouknight 5-107.
UCLA: Bragg 7-95, 2 TD; Lewis 2-41.

ALAMO BOWL

PROFILE

Site: San Antonio, Texas
Stadium: Alamodome
Capacity: 65,000
Surface: SportField

PLAYING SITES

Alamodome, since 1993

NAME CHANGES

Builders Square Alamo Bowl, 1993-98
Sylvania Alamo Bowl, 1999-2001
Alamo Bowl presented by MasterCard, 2002
MasterCard Alamo Bowl, since 2003

SEASON	DATE	PRE-GAME RANK	TEAMS	SCORE	FINAL RANK	MOST VALUABLE PLAYERS	ATT.
1993	Dec. 31, 1993		**California**	37	25	Dave Barr, California, QB	45,716
		3	Iowa	3		Jerrott Willard, California, LB	
1994	Dec. 31, 1994	24	**Washington State**	10	21	Chad Davis, Washington State, QB	44,106
			Baylor	3		Ron Childs, Washington State, LB	
1995	Dec. 28, 1995	19	**Texas A&M**	22	15	Kyle Bryant, Texas A&M, K	64,597
		14	Michigan	20	17	Keith Mitchell, Texas A&M, LB	
1996	Dec. 29, 1996	21	**Iowa**	27	18	Sedrick Shaw, Iowa, RB	55,677
			Texas Tech	0		Jared DeVries, Iowa, DL	
1997	Dec. 30, 1997	17	**Purdue**	33	15	Billy Dicken, Purdue, QB	55,552
		24	Oklahoma State	20		Adrian Beasley, Purdue, S	
1998	Dec. 29, 1998		**Purdue**	37	24	Drew Brees, Purdue, QB	60,780
		4	Kansas State	34	10	Rosevelt Colvin, Purdue, DE	
1999	Dec. 28, 1999	13	**Penn State**	24	11	Rashard Casey, Penn State, QB	65,380
		18	Texas A&M	0	23	LaVar Arrington, Penn State, LB	
2000	Dec. 30, 2000	9	**Nebraska**	66	8	Dan Alexander, Nebraska, RB	60,028
		18	Northwestern	17		Kyle Vanden Bosch, Nebraska, DL	
2001	Dec. 29, 2001		**Iowa**	19		Aaron Greving, Iowa, RB	65,232
			Texas Tech	16		Derrick Pickens, Iowa, DL	
2002	Dec. 28, 2002		**Wisconsin**	31	OT	Brooks Bollinger, Wisconsin, QB	50,690
		14	Colorado	28		Jeff Mack, Wisconsin, LB	
2003	Dec. 29, 2003		**Nebraska**	17		Jammal Lord, Nebraska, QB	56,229
			Michigan State	3		Trevor Johnson, Nebraska, DL	
2004	Dec. 29, 2004	24	**Ohio State**	33	20	Ted Ginn Jr., Ohio State, FL	65,265
			Oklahoma State	7		Simon Fraser, Ohio State, DE	

DECEMBER 31, 1993
CALIFORNIA 37, IOWA 3

	1ST	2ND	3RD	4TH	FINAL
CAL	6	17	7	7	37
IOWA	0	0	3	0	3

SCORING SUMMARY
CAL — FG Brien 37
CAL — FG Brien 20
CAL — FG Brien 30
CAL — Caldwell 6 pass from Barr (Brien kick)
CAL — Willard 61 interception return (Brien kick)
IOWA — FG Hurley 42
CAL — Uwaezuoke 34 pass from Barr (Brien kick)
CAL — Remington 12 pass from Barr (Brien kick)

CAL	TEAM STATISTICS	IOWA
28	First Downs	5
179	Rushing Yards	20
21-28-0	Passing	6-17-1
266	Passing Yards	70
445	Total Yards	90
2-42.0	Punts - Average	8-43.0
3-1	Fumbles - Lost	1-0
5-35	Penalties - Yards	10-74
43:14	Possession Time	16:46

INDIVIDUAL LEADERS
RUSHING
CAL: Chapman 24-89; Edwards 6-42.
IOWA: Kahl 5-27; King 5-19.
PASSING
CAL: Barr 21-28-0, 266 yards, 3 TD.
IOWA : Burmeister 6-17-1, 70 yards.
RECEIVING
CAL: Caldwell 5-80, 1 TD; Uwaezuoke 2-55, 1 TD.
IOWA : Jasper 4-55; Dean 2-15.

DECEMBER 31, 1994
WASHINGTON STATE 10, BAYLOR 3

	1ST	2ND	3RD	4TH	FINAL
WSU	7	3	0	0	10
BU	0	0	3	0	3

SCORING SUMMARY
WSU — Hicks 1 run (Truant kick)
WSU — FG Truant 37
BU — FG Van Dyke 36

WSU	TEAM STATISTICS	BU
14	First Downs	8
7	Rushing Yards	74
27-35-0	Passing	8-23-2
286	Passing Yards	77
293	Total Yards	151
7-33.7	Punts - Average	6-35.0
3-1	Fumbles - Lost	0-0
6-17	Penalties - Yards	3-15
32:02	Possession Time	27:58

INDIVIDUAL LEADERS
RUSHING
WSU: Sparks 8-20; Hicks 10-12, 1 TD.
BU: Douglas 13-42; B. Lewis 9-34.
PASSING
WSU: Davis 27-35-0, 286 yards.
BU: Watson 8-22-2, 77 yards.
RECEIVING
WSU: Carpenter 5-91; E. Moore 5-38.
BU: Muhammad 2-34; Douglas 2-16.

DECEMBER 28, 1995
TEXAS A&M 22, MICHIGAN 20

	1ST	2ND	3RD	4TH	FINAL
A&M	10	3	3	6	22
MICH	7	3	3	7	20

SCORING SUMMARY
A&M — Bernard 9 run (Bryant kick)
MICH — Toomer 41 pass from Griese (Hamilton kick)
A&M — FG Bryant 27
MICH — FG Hamilton 28
A&M — FG Bryant 49
A&M — FG Bryant 47
MICH — FG Hamilton 26
A&M — FG Bryant 31
A&M — FG Bryant 37
MICH — Toomer 44 pass from Griese (Hamilton kick)

A&M	TEAM STATISTICS	MICH
17	First Downs	19
130	Rushing Yards	129
12-22-0	Passing	9-23-1
136	Passing Yards	182
266	Total Yards	311
5-43.0	Punts - Average	7-36.0
2-1	Fumbles - Lost	2-1
11-110	Penalties - Yards	6-60
31:07	Possession Time	28:53

INDIVIDUAL LEADERS
RUSHING
A&M: Parker 21-56; Hardeman 6-41; Bernard 15-40, 1 TD.
MICH: Biakabutuka 24-94; Wlliams 7-36.
PASSING
A&M: Pullig 12-22-0, 136 yards.
MICH: Griese 9-23-1, 182 yards, 2 TD.
RECEIVING
A&M: Hardeman 3-41; Connell 3-36.
MICH: Toomer 5-135, 2 TD; Hayes 2-35.

DECEMBER 29, 1996
IOWA 27, TEXAS TECH 0

	1ST	2ND	3RD	4TH	FINAL
IOWA	6	11	0	10	27
TT	0	0	0	0	0

SCORING SUMMARY
IOWA — Sherman 1 run (run failed)
IOWA — Shaw 20 run (Knipper pass from Sherman)
IOWA — FG Bromert 36
IOWA — FG Bromert 26
IOWA — Filer 14 run (Bromert kick)

IOWA	TEAM STATISTICS	TT
23	First Downs	13
217	Rushing Yards	61
10-17-1	Passing	14-32-1
139	Passing Yards	145
356	Total Yards	206
5-52.0	Punts - Average	4-45.8
8-78	Penalties - Yards	7-68
34:56	Possession Time	25:04

INDIVIDUAL LEADERS
RUSHING
IOWA: Shaw 20-113, 1 TD; Filer 4-41, 1 TD.
TT: Hanspard 18-64.
PASSING
IOWA : Sherman 9-16-0, 126 yards.
TT: Lethridge 13-28-1, 139 yards.
RECEIVING
IOWA : Dwight 6-105; Knipper 1-17.
TT: Hart 4-46; McKenzie 3-38.

DECEMBER 30, 1997
PURDUE 33, OKLAHOMA STATE 20

	1ST	2ND	3RD	4TH	FINAL
PUR	7	3	20	3	33
OKST	3	3	7	7	20

SCORING SUMMARY
OKST — FG Sydnes 34
PUR — Alford 18 pass from Dicken (Ryan kick)
OKST — FG Sydnes 22
PUR — FG Ryan 42
PUR — Dicken 1 run (kick failed)
OKST — Fobbs 21 run (Sydnes kick)
PUR — Sutherland 16 run (Ryan kick)
PUR — Daniels 69 pass from Dicken (Ryan kick)
PUR — FG Ryan 37
OKST — McQuarters 17 pass from Lindsay (Sydnes kick)

PUR	TEAM STATISTICS	OKST
20	First Downs	24
129	Rushing Yards	162
18-36-3	Passing	17-35-3
325	Passing Yards	206
454	Total Yards	368
2-45.0	Punts - Average	4-45.0
1-0	Fumbles - Lost	2-1
9-81	Penalties - Yards	8-70
25:35	Possession Time	34:25

INDIVIDUAL LEADERS
RUSHING
PUR: Watson 13-45; Dicken 8-43, 1 TD; Sutherland 2-38, 1 TD.
OKST: Fobbs 11-82, 1 TD; Lindsay 12-61.
PASSING
PUR: Dicken 18-34-3, 325 yards, 2 TD.
OKST: Lindsay 9-18-2, 111 yards, 1 TD; Chaloupka 8-17-1, 95 yards.
RECEIVING
PUR: Watson 5-102; Daniels 1-69, 1 TD; Alford 4-61, 1 TD.
OKST: G. Brown 4-52; McQuarters 4-43, 1 TD.

December 29, 1998
Purdue 37, Kansas State 34

	1ST	2ND	3RD	4TH	FINAL
PUR	0	17	10	10	37
KSU	0	7	6	21	34

SCORING SUMMARY

PUR	Daniels 5 pass from Brees (Dorsch kick)
PUR	FG Dorsch 25
KSU	McDonald 1 pass from Bishop (Gramatica kick)
PUR	Jones 30 pass from Brees (Dorsch kick)
KSU	Havick recovered fumble in end zone (kick failed)
PUR	Nugent recovered fumble in end zone (Dorsch kick)
PUR	FG Dorsch 26
KSU	Allen 3 run (Gramatica kick)
PUR	FG Dorsch 37
KSU	McDonald 88 pass from Bishop (Gramatica kick)
KSU	Swift 2 pass from Bishop (Gramatica kick)
PUR	Jones 24 pass from Brees (Dorsch kick)

PUR	TEAM STATISTICS	KSU
19	First Downs	12
5	Rushing Yards	126
25-53-3	Passing	9-24-4
230	Passing Yards	182
235	Total Yards	308
7-38.3	Punts - Average	7-44.1
2-1	Fumbles - Lost	3-3
7-35	Penalties - Yards	14-125
28:58	Possession Time	31:02

INDIVIDUAL LEADERS

RUSHING
PUR: Crabtree 12-46; Brees 10-25.
KSU: Allen 13-83, 1 TD; Hickson 7-35.

PASSING
PUR: Brees 25-53-3, 230 yards, 3 TD.
KSU: Bishop 9-24-4, 182 yards, 3 TD.

RECEIVING
PUR: Jones 11-98, 2 TD; Daniels 6-47, 1 TD.
KSU: McDonald 5-124, 2 TD; Peries 1-52.

December 28, 1999
Penn State 24, Texas A&M 0

	1ST	2ND	3RD	4TH	FINAL
PSU	7	7	0	10	24
A&M	0	0	0	0	0

SCORING SUMMARY

PSU	Fox 34 interception return (Forney kick)
PSU	Drummond 45 pass from Casey (Forney kick)
PSU	Casey 4 run (Forney kick)
PSU	FG Forney 39

PSU	TEAM STATISTICS	A&M
17	First Downs	16
175	Rushing Yards	80
8-17-1	Passing	15-28-4
146	Passing Yards	122
321	Total Yards	202
2-35	Punt Returns - Yards	2-9
0-0	Kickoff Returns - Yards	4-70
4-45.5	Punts - Average	3-52.0
0-0	Fumbles - Lost	2-1
7-74	Penalties - Yards	2-27
29:23	Possession Time	30:37

INDIVIDUAL LEADERS

RUSHING
PSU: McCoo 6-43; Johnson 6-30; Casey 7-27, 1 TD.
A&M: Toombs 19-70; Hardeman 10-41.

PASSING
PSU: Casey 8-16-1, 146 yards, 1 TD.
A&M: McCown 13-22-4, 105 yards.

RECEIVING
PSU: Drummond 1-45, 1 TD; Stewart 2-27.
A&M: Bumgardner 5-59; Taylor 6-38.

December 30, 2000
Nebraska 66, Northwestern 17

	1ST	2ND	3RD	4TH	FINAL
NEB	7	31	21	7	66
NU	3	14	0	0	17

SCORING SUMMARY

NEB	Alexander 15 run (Brown kick)
NU	FG Long 44
NU	Johnson 10 pass from Kustok (Long kick)
NEB	Crouch 50 run (Brown kick)
NEB	Alexander 2 run (Brown kick)
NEB	Buckhalter 2 run (Brown kick)
NEB	FG Brown 51
NU	Anderson 69 run (Long kick)
NEB	Newcombe 58 pass from Crouch (Brown kick)
NEB	Davison 11 pass from Crouch (Brown kick)
NEB	Crouch 2 run (Brown kick)
NEB	Davison 69 pass from Newcombe (Brown kick)
NEB	Diedrick 9 run (Brown kick)

NEB	TEAM STATISTICS	NU
28	First Downs	14
476	Rushing Yards	232
6-14-1	Passing	17-43-1
160	Passing Yards	151
636	Total Yards	383
3-44.3	Punts - Average	10-35.7
2-1	Fumbles - Lost	1-0
4-67	Penalties - Yards	7-46
33:37	Possession Time	26:23

INDIVIDUAL LEADERS

RUSHING
NEB: Alexander 20-240, 2 TD; Crouch 15-90, 2 TD; Buckhalter 12-58, 1 TD.
NU: Anderson 18-149, 1 TD; Kustok 14-55.

PASSING
NEB: Crouch 5-13-1, 91 yards, 2 TD; Newcombe 1-1-0, 69 yards, 1 TD.
NU: Kustok 15-35-0, 138 yards, 1 TD.

RECEIVING
NEB: Davison 3-85, 2 TD; Newcombe 1-58, 1 TD.
NU: Johnson 4-53, 1 TD; Anderson 4-12.

December 29, 2001
Iowa 19, Texas Tech 16

	1ST	2ND	3RD	4TH	FINAL
IOWA	3	7	3	6	19
TT	0	3	7	6	16

SCORING SUMMARY

IOWA	FG Kaeding 36
IOWA	Greving 1 run (Kaeding kick)
TT	FG Greathouse 50
TT	Welker 20 pass from Kingsbury (Treece kick)
IOWA	FG Kaeding 31
IOWA	FG Kaeding 46
TT	FG Treece 23
TT	FG Treece 37
IOWA	FG Kaeding 47

IOWA	TEAM STATISTICS	TT
20	First Downs	20
178	Rushing Yards	80
19-26-0	Passing	29-49-3
161	Passing Yards	309
339	Total Yards	389
0-0	Punt Returns - Yards	4-13
4-82	Kickoff Returns - Yards	5-76
5-36.0	Punts - Average	5-37.2
1-0	Fumbles - Lost	0-0
5-26	Penalties - Yards	5-35
35:03	Possession Time	24:57

INDIVIDUAL LEADERS

RUSHING
IOWA: Greving 25-115, 1 TD; Allen 7-36.
TT: Kingsbury 9-42; Williams 9-30.

PASSING
IOWA: McCann 19-26-0, 161 yards.
TT: Kingsbury 29-49-3, 309 yards, 1 TD.

RECEIVING
IOWA: Hill 6-49; Clark 4-30.
TT: Glover 6-77; Welker 6-62, 1 TD; Peters 8-60.

December 28, 2002
Wisconsin 31, Colorado 28

	1ST	2ND	3RD	4TH	OT	FINAL
WISC	7	14	0	7	3	31
COLO	14	0	14	0	0	28

SCORING SUMMARY

COLO	Strickland 91 interception return (Brougham kick)
WISC	A. Davis 4 run (Allen kick)
COLO	Hackett 10 pass from Hodge (Brougham kick)
WISC	Williams 10 pass from Bollinger (Allen kick)
WISC	Charles 7 pass from Bollinger (Allen kick)
COLO	Brown 4 run (Brougham kick)
COLO	Hackett 11 pass from Colvin (Brougham kick)
WISC	Bollinger 1 run (Allen kick)
WISC	FG Allen 37

WISC	TEAM STATISTICS	COLO
21	First Downs	13
193	Rushing Yards	123
12-24-1	Passing	9-18-3
163	Passing Yards	77
356	Total Yards	200
3-30	Punt Returns - Yards	3-8
4-84	Kickoff Returns - Yards	3-49
5-36.0	Punts - Average	6-40.8
3-3	Fumbles - Lost	1-0
6-64	Penalties - Yards	9-71
30:37	Possession Time	29:23

INDIVIDUAL LEADERS

RUSHING
WISC: A. Davis 25-99, 1 TD; Bollinger 20-82, 1 TD.
COLO: Brown 28-97, 1 TD; Calhoun 9-16.

PASSING
WISC: Bollinger 12-24-1, 163 yards, 2 TD.
COLO: Hodge 6-13-3, 62 yards, 1 TD; Colvin 3-5-0, 15 yards, 1 TD.

RECEIVING
WISC: Williams 5-83, 1 TD; Charles 5-67, 1 TD.
COLO: Hackett 3-30, 2 TD; Monteilh 1-20.

December 29, 2003
Nebraska 17, Michigan State 3

	1ST	2ND	3RD	4TH	FINAL
NEB	3	14	0	0	17
MSU	3	0	0	0	3

SCORING SUMMARY

NEB	FG Dyches 29
MSU	FG Rayner 46
NEB	Ross 2 run (Dyches kick)
NEB	Ross 6 run (Dyches kick)

NEB	TEAM STATISTICS	MSU
20	First Downs	13
229	Rushing Yards	18
8-17-0	Passing	21-39-3
160	Passing Yards	156
389	Total Yards	174
4-28	Punt Returns - Yards	2-3
0-0	Kickoff Returns - Yards	3-47
7-42.9	Punts - Average	8-46.4
1-0	Fumbles - Lost	0-0
8-69	Penalties - Yards	5-53
30:29	Possession Time	29:31

INDIVIDUAL LEADERS

RUSHING
NEB: Ross 37-138, 2 TD; Lord 10-79.
MSU: Dortch 9-31; Hayes 6-13.

PASSING
NEB: Lord 8-17-0, 160 yards.
MSU: Smoker 21-39-3, 156 yards.

RECEIVING
NEB: Fluellen 4-84; Pilkington 3-70.
MSU: Alexander 8-63; Brown 4-41.

DECEMBER 29, 2004

OHIO STATE 33, OKLAHOMA STATE 7

	1ST	2ND	3RD	4TH	FINAL
OSU	13	10	7	3	33
OKST	0	0	0	7	7

SCORING SUMMARY

OSU	Gonzalez 23 pass from Zwick (Nugent kick)
OSU	FG Nugent 37
OSU	FG Nugent 35
OSU	Ross 1 run (Nugent kick)
OSU	FG Nugent 41
OSU	Ginn Jr. 5 run (Nugent kick)
OSU	FG Nugent 37
OKST	Willis 4 run (Ricks kick)

OSU	TEAM STATISTICS	OKST
19	First Downs	15
214	Rushing Yards	149
17-27-0	Passing	15-35-1
189	Passing Yards	137
403	Total Yards	286
3-17	Punt Returns - Yards	2-1
1-26	Kickoff Returns - Yards	1-15
4-42.3	Punts - Average	7-41.9
1-1	Fumbles - Lost	1-1
2-25	Penalties - Yards	6-45
34:51	Possession Time	25:09

INDIVIDUAL LEADERS

RUSHING
OSU: Ross 12-99, 1 TD; Branden 13-57.
OKST: Woods 12-72; Elliott 3-39.

PASSING
OSU: Zwick 17-27-0, 189 yards, 1 TD.
OKST: Woods 15-34-1, 137 yards.

RECEIVING
OSU: Ginn Jr. 6-78; Holmes 5-47.
OKST: Woods 4-40; Bajema 2-29.

MOTOR CITY BOWL

PROFILE

Site: Detroit
Stadium: Ford Field
Capacity: 65,000
Surface: FieldTurf

PLAYING SITES

Pontiac Silverdome, 1997-2001
Ford Field, since 2002

NAME CHANGES

Motor City Bowl, since 1997

SEASON	DATE	PRE-GAME RANK	TEAMS	SCORE	FINAL RANK	MOST VALUABLE PLAYERS	ATT.
1997	Dec. 26, 1997		**Mississippi**	34	22	Stewart Patridge, Mississippi, QB	43,340
			Marshall	31			
1998	Dec. 23, 1998		**Marshall**	48		Chad Pennington, Marshall, QB	32,206
			Louisville	29			
1999	Dec. 27, 1999	11	**Marshall**	21	10	Doug Chapman, Marshall, RB	44,449
			BYU	3			
2000	Dec. 27, 2000		**Marshall**	25		Byron Leftwich, Marshall, QB	44,911
			Cincinnati	14			
2001	Dec. 29, 2001	25	**Toledo**	23	23	Chester Taylor, Toledo, RB	44,164
			Cincinnati	16			
2002	Dec. 26, 2002		**Boston College**	51		Brian St. Pierre, Boston College, QB	45,761
			Toledo	25			
2003	Dec. 26, 2003		**Bowling Green**	28	23	Josh Harris, Bowling Green, QB	51,286
			Northwestern	24		Jason Wright, Northwestern, RB	
2004	Dec. 27, 2004		**Connecticut**	39		Dan Orlovsky, Connecticut, QB	52,552
			Toledo	10			

DECEMBER 26, 1997
MISSISSIPPI 34, MARSHALL 31

	1ST	2ND	3RD	4TH	FINAL
MISS	7	0	14	13	34
MAR	10	7	0	14	31

SCORING SUMMARY

MISS	Avery 1 run (Lindsey kick)
MAR	Moss 80 pass from Pennington (Malashevich kick)
MAR	FG Malashevich 36
MAR	Colclough 19 pass from Pennington (Malashevich kick)
MISS	Rone 13 pass from Patridge (Lindsey kick)
MISS	McAllister 20 pass from Patridge (Lindsey kick)
MAR	Chapman 6 pass from Pennington (Malashevich kick)
MISS	Heard 19 pass from Patridge (kick failed)
MAR	Chapman 9 run (Malashevich kick)
MISS	McAllister 1 run (Lindsey kick)

MISS	TEAM STATISTICS	MAR
29	First Downs	23
179	Rushing Yards	170
29-48-1	Passing	23-45-0
332	Passing Yards	337
511	Total Yards	507
4-41.8	Punts - Average	7-39.7
0-0	Fumbles - Lost	3-2
7-71	Penalties - Yards	10-93
34:21	Possession Time	25:39

INDIVIDUAL LEADERS

RUSHING
MISS: Avery 27-110, 1 TD; McAllister 8-71, 1 TD.
MAR: Chapman 19-152, 1 TD.

PASSING
MISS: Patridge 29-47-1, 332 yards, 3 TD.
MAR: Pennington 23-45-0, 337 yards, 3 TD.

RECEIVING
MISS: Heard 3-81, 1 TD; Peterson 7-66.
MAR: Moss 6-173, 1 TD; Colclough 8-84, 1 TD.

DECEMBER 23, 1998
MARSHALL 48, LOUISVILLE 29

	1ST	2ND	3RD	4TH	FINAL
LOU	0	21	0	8	29
MAR	7	14	17	10	48

SCORING SUMMARY

MAR	Williams 29 pass from Pennington (Malashevich kick)
LOU	Collins 2 run (Hilbert kick)
MAR	Washington 14 pass from Pennington (Malashevich kick)
LOU	Sheffield 21 pass from Redman (Hilbert kick)
MAR	Williams 26 pass from Pennington (Malashevich kick)
LOU	Collins 13 run (Hilbert kick)
MAR	Long 50 pass from Pennington (Malashevich kick)
MAR	Chapman 1 run (Malashevich kick)
MAR	FG Malashevich 22
MAR	Chapman 1 run (Malashevich kick)
LOU	Collins 1 run (Hilbert kick)
MAR	FG Malashevich 32

LOU	TEAM STATISTICS	MAR
26	First Downs	27
66	Rushing Yards	202
35-54-1	Passing	18-24-0
336	Passing Yards	411
402	Total Yards	613
0-0	Punt Returns - Yards	4-62
4-78	Kickoff Returns - Yards	2-38
4-49.3	Punts - Average	1-58.0
3-0	Fumbles - Lost	2-0
13-109	Penalties - Yards	14-123
28:49	Possession Time	31:11

INDIVIDUAL LEADERS

RUSHING
LOU: Collins 14-94, 3 TD.
MAR: Turner 13-94; Chapman 26-76, 2 TD.

PASSING
LOU: Redman 35-54-1, 336 yards, 1 TD.
MAR: Pennington 18-24-0, 411 yards, 4 TD.

RECEIVING
LOU: Jackson 8-96; Boyd 8-84; Sheffield 8-75, 1 TD.
MAR: Chapman 2-69; Williams 3-68, 2 TD; Cooper 5-67.

DECEMBER 27, 1999
MARSHALL 21, BYU 3

	1ST	2ND	3RD	4TH	FINAL
BYU	3	0	0	0	3
MAR	0	7	7	7	21

SCORING SUMMARY

BYU	FG Pochman 28
MAR	Chapman 30 pass from Pennington (Malashevich kick)
MAR	Chapman 87 run (Malashevich kick)
MAR	Chapman 1 run (Malashevich kick)

BYU	TEAM STATISTICS	MAR
12	First Downs	14
-16	Rushing Yards	147
16-29-2	Passing	17-28-1
220	Passing Yards	207
204	Total Yards	354
7-48.3	Punts - Average	5-42.8
2-2	Fumbles - Lost	0-0
8-81	Penalties - Yards	11-84
30:31	Possession Time	29:29

INDIVIDUAL LEADERS

RUSHING
BYU: Atuaia 4-35.
MAR: Chapman 14-133, 2 TD; Turner 7-15.

PASSING
BYU: Feterik 6-11-0, 125 yards; Peterson 4-7-1, 50 yards.
MAR: Pennington 17-28-1, 207 yards, 1 TD.

RECEIVING
BYU: Hooks 4-108; Atuaia 4-25.
MAR: Williams 5-95; Chapman 4-40, 1 TD.

December 27, 2000
MARSHALL 25, CINCINNATI 14

	1ST	2ND	3RD	4TH	FINAL
CIN	7	7	0	0	14
MAR	9	0	13	3	25

SCORING SUMMARY

MAR	Watts 77 pass from Leftwich (Jenkins kick)
CIN	McCleskey 2 run (Ruffin kick)
MAR	Safety (Jackson tackled by Owens in end zone)
CIN	McCleskey 2 run (Ruffin kick)
MAR	Leftwich 1 run (pass failed)
MAR	Wallace 4 run (Jenkins kick)
MAR	FG Jenkins 25

CIN	TEAM STATISTICS	MAR
24	First Downs	13
96	Rushing Yards	101
19-39-2	Passing	17-30-1
189	Passing Yards	221
285	Total Yards	322
5-29.8	Punts - Average	6-37.5
1-0	Fumbles - Lost	1-1
11-80	Penalties - Yards	14-110
35:59	Possession Time	24:01

INDIVIDUAL LEADERS

RUSHING
CIN: McCleskey 20-72, 2 TD; Jackson 14-61.
MAR: Wallace 20-78, 1 TD; Leftwich 9-21, 1 TD.

PASSING
CIN: Kenner 19-39-2, 189 yards.
MAR: Leftwich 17-30-1, 221 yards, 1 TD.

RECEIVING
CIN: Collins-Baker 4-55; Chatman 3-42; Vann 3-42.
MAR: Watts 3-90, 1 TD; Poole 3-65.

December 29, 2001
TOLEDO 23, CINCINNATI 16

	1ST	2ND	3RD	4TH	FINAL
CIN	0	13	0	3	16
TOL	3	0	10	10	23

SCORING SUMMARY

TOL	FG France 28
CIN	FG Ruffin 29
CIN	Walker 28 pass from Guidugli (Ruffin kick)
CIN	FG Ruffin 46
TOL	FG France 42
TOL	Bolden 28 run (France kick)
TOL	FG France 30
CIN	FG Ruffin 25
TOL	Taylor 24 run (France kick)

CIN	TEAM STATISTICS	TOL
19	First Downs	24
13	Rushing Yards	322
29-47-0	Passing	14-28-1
283	Passing Yards	135
296	Total Yards	457
7-49.1	Punts - Average	4-39.3
1-0	Fumbles - Lost	0-0
6-48	Penalties - Yards	8-75
25:44	Possession Time	34:16

INDIVIDUAL LEADERS

RUSHING
CIN: McClesky 11-18.
TOL: Taylor 31-190, 1 TD; Bolden 7-99, 1 TD.

PASSING
CIN: Guidugli 29-46-0, 283 yards, 1 TD.
TOL: Bolden 14-28-1, 135 yards.

RECEIVING
CIN: Vann 8-78; Keith 9-63.
TOL: Ford 5-73.

December 26, 2002
BOSTON COLLEGE 51, TOLEDO 25

	1ST	2ND	3RD	4TH	FINAL
BC	14	28	6	3	51
TOL	3	15	7	0	25

SCORING SUMMARY

BC	Knight 2 run (Sciortino kick)
BC	Adams 17 pass from St. Pierre (Sciortino kick)
TOL	FG Robbins 35
BC	Hazard 40 pass from St. Pierre (Sciortino kick)
TOL	Dawson 2 run (Robbins kick)
BC	Dodd 5 run (Sciortino kick)
BC	Adams 40 pass from St. Pierre (Sciortino kick)
BC	Brokaw 1 run (Sciortino kick)
TOL	Ford 9 pass from Jones (Dawson run)
BC	FG Sciortino 23
BC	FG Sciortino 35
TOL	Johnson 30 pass from Jones (Robbins kick)
BC	FG Sciortino 45

BC	TEAM STATISTICS	TOL
30	First Downs	21
149	Rushing Yards	102
25-35-0	Passing	27-41-2
342	Passing Yards	331
491	Total Yards	433
1-3	Punt Returns - Yards	1-2
5-112	Kickoff Returns - Yards	8-173
1-39.0	Punts - Average	3-23.3
0-0	Fumbles - Lost	3-0
4-26	Penalties - Yards	11-96
29:59	Possession Time	30:01

INDIVIDUAL LEADERS

RUSHING
BC: Knight 19-65, 1 TD; Dodd 7-33, 1 TD; Brokaw 7-20, 1 TD.
TOL: Jones 9-32; Martin 6-31; Dawson 10-28, 1 TD.

PASSING
BC: St. Pierre 25-35-0, 342 yards, 3 TD.
TOL: Jones 27-41-2, 331 yards, 2 TD.

RECEIVING
BC: Adams 5-92, 2 TD; Hemmings 4-71; Hazard 5-66, 1 TD.
TOL: Ford 10-112, 1 TD; Greene 4-63; Johnson 3-49, 1 TD.

December 26, 2003
BOWLING GREEN 28, NORTHWESTERN 24

	1ST	2ND	3RD	4TH	FINAL
BG	0	7	7	14	28
NU	7	3	7	7	24

SCORING SUMMARY

NU	Herron 40 run (Huffman kick)
NU	FG Huffman 31
BG	Harris 4 run (Suisham kick)
NU	Wright 77 run (Huffman kick)
BG	Magner 7 pass from Harris (Suisham kick)
BG	Sanders 11 pass from Harris (Suisham kick)
NU	Herron 2 run (Huffman kick)
BG	Magner 3 pass from Harris (Suisham kick)

BG	TEAM STATISTICS	NU
30	First Downs	16
88	Rushing Yards	357
38-51-3	Passing	7-15-0
386	Passing Yards	58
474	Total Yards	415
2-21	Punt Returns - Yards	2-3
3-46.0	Punts - Average	5-34.4
0-0	Fumbles - Lost	2-2
1-15	Penalties - Yards	3-40
34:08	Possession Time	25:52

INDIVIDUAL LEADERS

RUSHING
BG: Harris 21-68, 1 TD; Pope 11-23.
NU: Wright 21-237, 1 TD; Herron 12-80, 2 TD.

PASSING
BG: Harris 38-50-2, 386 yards, 3 TD.
NU: Basanez 7-15-0, 58 yards.

RECEIVING
BG: Magner 12-97, 2 TD; Sharon 7-93; Sanders 5-74, 1 TD.
NU: Philmore 3-43; Wright 2-11.

December 27, 2004
CONNECTICUT 39, TOLEDO 10

	1ST	2ND	3RD	4TH	FINAL
UCONN	17	13	3	6	39
TOL	0	7	3	0	10

SCORING SUMMARY

UCONN	FG Nuzie 35
UCONN	Williams 32 pass from Orlovsky (Nuzie kick)
UCONN	Taylor 68 punt return (Nuzie kick)
TOL	Gradkowski 1 run (Robbins kick)
UCONN	Sparks 7 pass from Orlovsky (Nuzie kick)
UCONN	FG Nuzie 37
UCONN	FG Nuzie 25
TOL	FG Robbins 27
UCONN	FG Nuzie 36
UCONN	Lawrence 11 run (kick failed)

UCONN	TEAM STATISTICS	TOL
20	First Downs	20
159	Rushing Yards	78
20-41-1	Passing	22-40-2
239	Passing Yards	203
398	Total Yards	281
2-69	Punt Returns - Yards	1-7
3-101	Kickoff Returns - Yards	5-83
3-30.3	Punts - Average	6-32.3
0-0	Fumbles - Lost	2-1
5-44	Penalties - Yards	4-35
28:18	Possession Time	31:42

INDIVIDUAL LEADERS

RUSHING
UCONN: Brockington 15-72; Bellamy 9-55.
TOL: Dawson 19-78.

PASSING
UCONN: Orlovsky 20-41-1, 239 yards, 2 TD.
TOL: Council 16-28-2, 160 yards.

RECEIVING
UCONN: Henry 9-109; Cutaia 2-47.
TOL: Moore 5-48; Holmes 4-47.

THE BOWLS

MPC COMPUTERS BOWL

PROFILE

Site: Boise, Idaho
Stadium: Bronco Stadium
Capacity: 30,000
Surface: Blue Astroplay

PLAYING SITES

Bronco Stadium, since 1997

NAME CHANGES

Sports Humanitarian Bowl, 1997
Humanitarian Bowl, 1998
Crucial.com Humanitarian Bowl,
1999-2003
MPC Computers Bowl, since 2004

SEASON	DATE	PRE-GAME RANK	TEAMS	SCORE	FINAL RANK	MOST VALUABLE PLAYERS	ATT.
1997	Dec. 29, 1997		Cincinnati	35		Steve Smith, Utah State, WR	16,131
			Utah State	19		Chad Plummer, Cincinnati, QB	
1998	Dec. 30, 1998		Idaho	42		Lee Roberts, Southern Miss, QB	19,664
			Southern Miss	35		John Welsh, Idaho, QB	
1999	Dec. 30, 1999		Boise State	34		Brock Forsey, Boise State, RB	29,283
			Louisville	31		Chris Redman, Louisville, QB	
2000	Dec. 28, 2000		Boise State	38		Bart Hendricks, Boise State, QB	26,203
			UTEP	23		Chris Porter, UTEP, RB	
2001	Dec. 31, 2001		Clemson	49		Woodrow Dantzler, Clemson, QB	23,472
			Louisiana Tech	24		Delwyn Daigre, Louisiana Tech, WR	
2002	Dec. 31, 2002	18	Boise State	34	15	Bobby Hammer, Boise State, DT	30,446
			Iowa State	16		Anthony Forrest, Iowa State, DB	
2003	Jan. 3, 2004		Georgia Tech	52		P.J. Daniels, Georgia Tech, RB	23,118
			Tulsa	10		Cort Moffitt, Tulsa, P	
2004	Dec. 27, 2004		Fresno State	37 OT		Paul Pinegar, Fresno St., QB	28,516
			Virginia	34		Marques Hagans, Virginia, QB	

DECEMBER 29, 1997
CINCINNATI 35, UTAH STATE 19

	1ST	2ND	3RD	4TH	FINAL
CIN	7	14	14	0	35
USU	0	0	13	6	19

SCORING SUMMARY
CIN — Bonner 14 pass from Plummer (Judge kick)
CIN — Bonner 14 pass from Kenner (Judge kick)
CIN — Smith 1 run (Judge kick)
CIN — Plummer 15 run (Judge kick)
USU — S. Smith 75 pass from Sauk (Bohn kick)
CIN — O. Smith 7 run (Judge kick)
USU — Blue 3 run (kick failed)
USU — Passey 10 fumble return (pass failed)

CIN	TEAM STATISTICS	USU
23	First Downs	15
225	Rushing Yards	63
15-25-0	Passing	12-30-3
186	Passing Yards	253
411	Total Yards	316
4-65	Punt Returns - Yards	2-26
4-83	Kickoff Returns - Yards	2-58
5-36.8	Punts - Average	6-32.3
2-1	Fumbles - Lost	1-1
7-84	Penalties - Yards	3-13
42:17	Possession Time	17:43

INDIVIDUAL LEADERS
RUSHING
CIN: O. Smith 15-78, 1 TD; Plummer 15-53, 1 TD.
USU: Brown 12-56; Smith 2-11.
PASSING
CIN: Kenner 10-16-0, 124 yards, 1 TD; Plummer 5-9-0, 62 yards, 1 TD.
USU: Sauk 12-30-3, 253 yards, 1 TD.
RECEIVING
CIN: Bonner 4-48, 2 TD; Plummer 4-64.
USU: S. Smith 4-136, 1 TD; Jenkins 4-80.

DECEMBER 30, 1998
IDAHO 42, SOUTHERN MISS 35

	1ST	2ND	3RD	4TH	FINAL
IDA	7	21	7	7	42
USM	13	8	0	14	35

SCORING SUMMARY
USM — Gideon 2 pass from Roberts (Hardaway kick)
IDA — Thomas 98 kick return (Davis kick)
USM — Nix 8 run (kick failed)
USM — Nix 1 run (Gideon pass from Roberts)
IDA — Townsley 12 pass from Welsh (Davis kick)
IDA — Roberg 21 pass from Welsh (Davis kick)
IDA — Moody 2 pass from Welsh (Davis kick)
IDA — Thomas 1 run (Davis kick)
USM — Gideon 7 pass from Roberts (Hardaway kick)
USM — Nix 15 run (Hardaway kick)
IDA — Prestimonico 28 pass from Welsh (Davis kick)

IDA	TEAM STATISTICS	USM
26	First Downs	25
130	Rushing Yards	117
24-41-0	Passing	31-52-0
291	Passing Yards	362
421	Total Yards	479
2-60	Punt Returns - Yards	2-19
6-187	Kickoff Returns - Yards	4-78
5-39.0	Punts - Average	4-43.5
3-3	Fumbles - Lost	6-5
9-59	Penalties - Yards	5-44
28:37	Possession Time	31:23

INDIVIDUAL LEADERS
RUSHING
IDA: Thomas 22-86, 1 TD; Welsh 11-48.
USM: Nix 29-122, 3 TD; Woods 3-15.
PASSING
IDA: Welsh 24-41-0, 291 yards, 4 TD.
USM: Roberts 30-51-0, 342 yards, 2 TD.
RECEIVING
IDA: Townsley 4-62, 1 TD; Prestimonico 5-61, 1 TD.
USM: Gideon 12-117, 2 TD; Pinkston 7-101.

DECEMBER 30, 1999
BOISE STATE 34, LOUISVILLE 31

	1ST	2ND	3RD	4TH	FINAL
BSU	14	7	6	7	34
LOU	17	7	0	7	31

SCORING SUMMARY
LOU — FG Hilbert 40
BSU — Hendricks 3 run (Calaycay kick)
LOU — Jackson 54 pass from Redman (Hilbert kick)
BSU — Swan 4 pass from Hendricks (Calaycay kick)
LOU — Parker 91 kickoff return (Hilbert kick)
BSU — Harts 80 interception return (Calaycay kick)
LOU — Dorsey 8 pass from Redman (Hilbert kick)
BSU — FG Calaycay 26
BSU — FG Calaycay 46
LOU — Moreau 3 run (Hilbert kick)
BSU — Malaythong 5 run (Calaycay kick)

BSU	TEAM STATISTICS	LOU
28	First Downs	26
198	Rushing Yards	89
20-39-0	Passing	26-47-3
335	Passing Yards	314
533	Total Yards	403
4-18	Punt Returns - Yards	1-15
3-96	Kickoff Returns - Yards	7-188
2-38.5	Punts - Average	5-39.8
3-2	Fumbles - Lost	1-0
5-61	Penalties - Yards	14-120
31:24	Possession Time	28:36

INDIVIDUAL LEADERS
RUSHING
BSU: Forsey 23-152; Hendricks 10-26, 1 TD.
LOU: Moreau 24-111, 1 TD.
PASSING
BSU: Hendricks 20-39-0, 335 yards, 1 TD.
LOU: Redman 26-47-3, 314 yards, 2 TD.
RECEIVING
BSU: Fanucchi 3-80; Swillie 4-70; Forsey 2-50.
LOU: Jackson 9-109, 1 TD; Green 6-97; Boyd 6-73.

December 28, 2000
Boise State 38, UTEP 23

	1st	2nd	3rd	4th	Final
BSU	7	10	7	14	38
UTEP	0	10	3	10	23

SCORING SUMMARY

BSU	Swillie 28 pass from Hendricks (Calaycay kick)
BSU	FG Calaycay 41
UTEP	Knapp 9 pass from Perez (Bishop kick)
UTEP	FG Bishop 28
BSU	Hendricks 12 run (Calaycay kick)
BSU	Hendricks 77 run (Calaycay kick)
UTEP	FG Bishop 43
BSU	Forsey 41 run (Calaycay kick)
UTEP	FG Bishop 47
UTEP	Porter 3 run (Bishop kick)
BSU	Hendricks 11 pass from Banks (Calaycay kick)

BSU	TEAM STATISTICS	UTEP
18	First Downs	22
175	Rushing Yards	118
18-30-1	Passing	17-38-1
258	Passing Yards	201
433	Total Yards	319
3-15	Punt Returns - Yards	5-91
6-118	Kickoff Returns - Yards	5-66
7-42.6	Punts - Average	5-48.8
2-0	Fumbles - Lost	4-2
6-59	Penalties - Yards	4-35
27:05	Possession Time	32:55

INDIVIDUAL LEADERS

RUSHING
BSU: Forsey 10-68, 1 TD; Hendricks 13-57, 2 TD.
UTEP: Porter 26-134, 1 TD; Austin 3-10.

PASSING
BSU: Hendricks 17-29-1, 247 yards, 1 TD.
UTEP: Perez 17-38-1, 201 yards, 1 TD.

RECEIVING
BSU: Forsey 4-56; Swillie 4-50, 1 TD.
UTEP: Mays 7-91; Natkin 4-69.

December 31, 2001
Clemson 49, Louisiana Tech 24

	1st	2nd	3rd	4th	Final
CLEM	7	7	28	7	49
LT	3	7	0	14	24

SCORING SUMMARY

LT	FG Scobee 29
CLEM	Bailey 10 pass from Dantzler (Hunt kick)
LT	McCown 11 run (Scobee kick)
CLEM	Crosby 53 pass from Dantzler (Hunt kick)
CLEM	Hall 5 pass from Dantzler (Hunt kick)
CLEM	Rambert 62 pass from Dantzler (Hunt kick)
CLEM	Rambert 21 run (Hunt kick)
CLEM	Currie 19 run (Hunt kick)
CLEM	Hamilton 57 pass from Simmons (Hunt kick)
LT	Daigre 34 pass from McCown (Simmons pass from McCown)
LT	Smith 2 run (kick failed)

CLEM	TEAM STATISTICS	LT
28	First Downs	25
273	Rushing Yards	49
16-29-1	Passing	29-59-3
275	Passing Yards	401
548	Total Yards	450
2-12	Punt Returns - Yards	1-3
3-24	Kickoff Returns - Yards	7-150
6-32.7	Punts - Average	7-34.3
1-0	Fumbles - Lost	0-0
5-34	Penalties - Yards	8-80
31:03	Possession Time	28:57

INDIVIDUAL LEADERS

RUSHING
CLEM: Rambert 16-101, 1 TD; Jasmin 16-83; Dantzler 15-57.
LT: Smith 14-57, 1 TD.

PASSING
CLEM: Dantzler 15-23-0, 218 yards, 4 TD.
LT: McCown 25-52-3, 328 yards, 1 TD.

RECEIVING
CLEM: Hamilton 4-94, 1 TD; Rambert 3-77, 1 TD; Crosby 4-69, 1 TD.
LT: Daigre 10-178, 1 TD; Simon 7-96.

December 31, 2002
Boise State 34, Iowa State 16

	1st	2nd	3rd	4th	Final
BSU	0	7	14	13	34
ISU	3	7	0	6	16

SCORING SUMMARY

ISU	FG Benike 30
BSU	Forsey 4 run (Calaycay kick)
ISU	Montgomery 6 pass from Wallace (Benike kick)
BSU	Forsey 2 run (Calaycay kick)
BSU	Dinwiddie 1 run (Calaycay kick)
BSU	Forsey 9 run (kick failed)
ISU	Danielsen 4 run (kick failed)
BSU	Fanucchi 3 pass from Dinwiddie (Calaycay kick)

BSU	TEAM STATISTICS	ISU
19	First Downs	17
157	Rushing Yards	145
17-32-0	Passing	15-42-0
160	Passing Yards	130
317	Total Yards	275
5-57	Punt Returns - Yards	5-38
3-84	Kickoff Returns - Yards	4-77
8-31.5	Punts - Average	7-38.1
0-0	Fumbles - Lost	3-1
5-34	Penalties - Yards	6-47
29:31	Possession Time	30:29

INDIVIDUAL LEADERS

RUSHING
BSU: Forsey 24-78, 3 TD; Mikell 8-41.
ISU: Wallace 12-83; Wagner 12-41.

PASSING
BSU: Dinwiddie 17-32-0, 160 yards, 1 TD.
ISU: Wallace 13-38-0, 107 yards, 1 TD.

RECEIVING
BSU: Wingfield 5-64; Forsey 3-25.
ISU: Danielsen 4-47; Young 3-23.

January 3, 2004
Georgia Tech 52, Tulsa 10

	1st	2nd	3rd	4th	Final
GT	7	3	21	21	52
TUL	0	3	0	7	10

SCORING SUMMARY

GT	Daniels 9 run (Burnett kick)
TUL	FG DeVault 22
GT	FG Burnett 29
GT	Daniels 1 run (Burnett kick)
GT	Woods 2 run (Burnett kick)
GT	Daniels 33 run (Burnett kick)
GT	Daniels 38 run (Schroeder kick)
GT	Hatch 1 run (Schroeder kick)
TUL	Mills 18 pass from Smith (DeVault kick)
GT	Hatch 7 run (Schroeder kick)

GT	TEAM STATISTICS	TUL
15	First Downs	10
371	Rushing Yards	-56
7-13-0	Passing	17-27-0
19	Passing Yards	200
390	Total Yards	144
4-20	Punt Returns - Yards	2-13
2-57	Kickoff Returns - Yards	6-91
5-42.8	Punts - Average	7-45.0
1-1	Fumbles - Lost	7-6
5-45	Penalties - Yards	6-35
35:07	Possession Time	24:53

INDIVIDUAL LEADERS

RUSHING
GT: Daniels 31-307, 4 TD; Woods 10-40, 1 TD; Hatch 8-33, 2 TD.
TUL: Richardson 7-13.

PASSING
GT: Ball 4-10-0, 16 yards.
TUL: Kilian 11-21-0, 97 yards; Smith 6-6-0, 103 yards, 1 TD.

RECEIVING
GT: Smith 3-14.
TUL: Blankenship 3-76; Landrum 3-55; Mills 3-27, 1 TD.

December 27, 2004
Fresno State 37, Virginia 34

	1st	2nd	3rd	4th	OT	Final
FRES	7	3	7	14	6	37
UVA	14	3	7	7	3	34

SCORING SUMMARY

UVA	Pearman 13 run (Hughes kick)
FRES	Jennings 13 pass from Pinegar (Visintainer kick)
UVA	McGrew 7 pass from Hagans (Hughes kick)
UVA	Hagans 8 run (Hughes kick)
FRES	FG Visintainer 49
FRES	Jamison 22 pass from Pinegar (Visintainer kick)
UVA	FG Hughes 33
FRES	Wood 22 pass from Pinegar (Visintainer kick)
UVA	Lundy 20 run (Hughes kick)
FRES	Fairman 3 pass from Pinegar (Visintainer kick)
UVA	FG Hughes 28
FRES	Pach 25 pass from Pinegar

FRES	TEAM STATISTICS	UVA
25	First Downs	21
222	Rushing Yards	260
23-38-0	Passing	18-31-0
235	Passing Yards	162
457	Total Yards	422
0-0	Punt Returns - Yards	0-0
3-67	Kickoff Returns - Yards	3-97
5-35.6	Punts - Average	4-32.0
0-0	Fumbles - Lost	0-0
7-64	Penalties - Yards	10-82
32:48	Possession Time	27:12

INDIVIDUAL LEADERS

RUSHING
FRES: Mathis 12-126; Sumlin 21-94.
UVA: Hagans 7-85, 1 TD; Lundy 14-63, 1 TD.

PASSING
FRES: Pinegar 23-36-0, 235 yards, 5 TD.
UVA: Hagans 18-30-0, 162 yards, 1 TD.

RECEIVING
FRES: Fernandez 5-72; Jamison 4-46, 1 TD.
UVA: Miller 5-66; McGrew 4-30, 1 TD.

MUSIC CITY BOWL

PROFILE

Site: Nashville
Stadium: The Coliseum
Capacity: 67,000
Surface: Grass

PLAYING SITES

Vanderbilt Stadium, 1998
Adelphia Coliseum, renamed
The Coliseum in 2002, since 1999

NAME CHANGES

Music City Bowl, 1998
HomePoint.com Music City Bowl,
1999
Music City Bowl, 2000-01
Gaylord Hotels Music City Bowl,
2002-03
Gaylord Hotels Music City Bowl
Presented By Bridgestone,
since 2004

SEASON	DATE	PRE-GAME RANK	TEAMS	SCORE	FINAL RANK	MOST VALUABLE PLAYERS	ATT.
1998	Dec. 29, 1998		**Virginia Tech**	38	23	Corey Moore, Virginia Tech, DE	41,248
			Alabama	7			
1999	Dec. 29, 1999		**Syracuse**	20		James Mungro, Syracuse, RB	59,221
			Kentucky	13			
2000	Dec. 28, 2000		**West Virginia**	49		Brad Lewis, West Virginia, QB	47,119
			Mississippi	38			
2001	Dec. 28, 2001		**Boston College**	20	21	William Green, Boston College, RB	46,125
		16	Georgia	16	22		
2002	Dec. 30, 2002		**Minnesota**	29		Dan Nystrom, Minnesota, K	39,183
		25	Arkansas	14			
2003	Dec. 31 2003		**Auburn**	28		Jason Campbell, Auburn, QB	55,109
			Wisconsin	14			
2004	Dec. 31, 2004		**Minnesota**	20		Marion Barber, Minnesota, RB	66,089
			Alabama	16			

DECEMBER 29, 1998
VIRGINIA TECH 38, ALABAMA 7

	1ST	2ND	3RD	4TH	FINAL
VT	7	3	14	14	38
ALA	0	7	0	0	7

SCORING SUMMARY

VT	Clark 43 run (Graham kick)
ALA	Vaughn 5 pass from Zow (Pflugner kick)
VT	FG Graham 44
VT	Pegues 1 run (Graham kick)
VT	Stith 4 run (Graham kick)
VT	Pegues 1 run (Graham kick)
VT	Midget 27 interception return (Graham kick)

VT	TEAM STATISTICS	ALA
15	First Downs	15
207	Rushing Yards	50
7-14-1	Passing	19-35-3
71	Passing Yards	224
278	Total Yards	274
4-30	Punt Returns - Yards	1-(-3)
1-44	Kickoff Returns - Yards	6-67
3-46.7	Punts - Average	6-29.0
0-0	Fumbles - Lost	2-1
5-31	Penalties - Yards	10-94
23:43	Possession Time	36:17

INDIVIDUAL LEADERS

RUSHING
VT: Stith 10-71, 1 TD; Clark 9-55, 1 TD; Pegues 15-41, 2 TD.
ALA: Alexander 21-55.

PASSING
VT: Clark 7-14-1, 71 yards.
ALA: Zow 19-35-3, 224 yards, 1 TD.

RECEIVING
VT: Hall 1-20; Harrison 2-11.
ALA: Alexander 8-87; Vaughn 3-55, 1 TD.

DECEMBER 29, 1999
SYRACUSE 20, KENTUCKY 13

	1ST	2ND	3RD	4TH	FINAL
SYR	0	7	0	13	20
UK	10	0	0	3	13

SCORING SUMMARY

UK	Shanklin 3 run (Samuel kick)
UK	FG Samuel 22
SYR	Johnson 2 run (Trout kick)
UK	FG Samuel 35
SYR	Mungro 32 run (Trout kick)
SYR	Mungro 20 run (run failed)

SYR	TEAM STATISTICS	UK
19	First Downs	18
276	Rushing Yards	57
11-15-0	Passing	30-45-1
128	Passing Yards	308
404	Total Yards	365
2-29	Punt Returns - Yards	0-0
4-78	Kickoff Returns - Yards	4-54
3-33.0	Punts - Average	4-45.0
3-2	Fumbles - Lost	3-1
3-20	Penalties - Yards	4-20
31:24	Possession Time	28:36

INDIVIDUAL LEADERS

RUSHING
SYR: Mungro 12-162, 2 TD; Brown 22-87.
UK: Homer 1-24; Bonner 9-16.

PASSING
SYR: Nunes 11-15-0, 128 yards.
UK: Bonner 30-45-1, 308 yards.

RECEIVING
SYR: Spotwood 5-77; Woodcock 2-37.
UK: White 8-85; Smith 5-56; Shanklin 5-34.

DECEMBER 28, 2000
WEST VIRGINIA 49, MISSISSIPPI 38

	1ST	2ND	3RD	4TH	FINAL
MISS	3	6	7	22	38
WVU	7	28	14	0	49

SCORING SUMMARY

WVU	Ours 40 pass from Lewis (Rauh kick)
MISS	FG Binkley 23
WVU	Ivy 11 pass from Lewis (Rauh kick)
MISS	FG Binkley 47
WVU	Brown 35 pass from Lewis (Rauh kick)
MISS	FG Binkley 26
WVU	Brown 60 pass from Lewis (Rauh kick)
WVU	Ours 1 run (Rauh kick)
WVU	Terry 99 kickoff return (Rauh kick)
WVU	Ivy 10 pass from Lewis (Rauh Kick)
MISS	Miller 7 run (Binkley kick)
MISS	Armstrong 23 pass from Manning (Binkley kick)
MISS	Rayford 18 pass from Manning (Binkley kick)
MISS	Sanford 16 pass from Manning (Taylor pass from Miller)

MISS	TEAM STATISTICS	WVU
28	First Downs	19
96	Rushing Yards	114
28-51-3	Passing	15-21-1
388	Passing Yards	318
484	Total Yards	432
2-18	Punt Returns - Yards	0-0
4-83	Kickoff Returns - Yards	5-171
3-29.3	Punts - Average	2-39.0
1-0	Fumbles - Lost	0-0
12-93	Penalties - Yards	8-77
35:16	Possession Time	24:44

INDIVIDUAL LEADERS

RUSHING
MISS: Gunn 8-34; Miller 7-32, 1 TD.
WVU: Cobourne 27-125.

PASSING
MISS: Miller 16-31-2, 221 yards; Manning 12-20-1, 167 yards, 3 TD.
WVU: Lewis 15-21-1, 318 yards, 5 TD.

RECEIVING
MISS: Collins 5-65; Rayford 2-61, 1 TD; Armstrong 3-59, 1 TD.
WVU: Brown 6-156, 2 TD; Ivy 6-99, 2 TD.

December 28, 2001
Boston College 20, Georgia 16

	1ST	2ND	3RD	4TH	FINAL
BC	3	10	0	7	20
UGA	7	3	6	0	16

SCORING SUMMARY
UGA	Gibson 15 pass from Greene (Bennett kick)
BC	FG Sciortino 25
BC	Dewalt 10 pass from St. Pierre (Sciortino kick)
BC	FG Sciortino 26
UGA	FG Bennett 24
UGA	Haynes 1 run (kick failed)
BC	Green 7 run (Sciortino kick)

BC	TEAM STATISTICS	UGA
16	First Downs	23
197	Rushing Yards	122
9-25-0	Passing	22-39-2
109	Passing Yards	288
306	Total Yards	410
0-0	Punt Returns - Yards	3-7
3-28	Kickoff Returns - Yards	5-177
6-37.5	Punts - Average	3-43.7
2-0	Fumbles - Lost	2-2
4-20	Penalties - Yards	9-74
35:02	Possession Time	24:58

INDIVIDUAL LEADERS
RUSHING
BC: Green 35-149, 1 TD; St. Pierre 8-44.
UGA: Haynes 27-132, 1 TD.
PASSING
BC: St. Pierre 9-25-0, 109 yards, 1 TD.
UGA: Greene 22-38-2, 288 yards, 1 TD.
RECEIVING
BC: Dewalt 3-62, 1 TD.
UGA: Gibson 6-109, 1 TD; Mitchell 4-54; McMichael 4-47.

December 30, 2002
Minnesota 29, Arkansas 14

	1ST	2ND	3RD	4TH	FINAL
ARK	7	0	0	7	14
MINN	6	6	7	10	29

SCORING SUMMARY
ARK	Wilson 2 pass from Jones (Carlton kick)
MINN	FG Nystrom 24
MINN	FG Nystrom 45
MINN	FG Nystrom 21
MINN	FG Nystrom 22
MINN	Utecht 19 pass from Abdul-Khaliq (Nystrom kick)
MINN	FG Nystrom 29
MINN	Tapeh 33 run (Nystrom kick)
ARK	Smith 10 pass from Sorahan (Carlton kick)

ARK	TEAM STATISTICS	MINN
19	First Downs	21
80	Rushing Yards	168
18-40-3	Passing	17-32-0
208	Passing Yards	266
288	Total Yards	434
2-15	Punt Returns - Yards	4-3
8-128	Kickoff Returns - Yards	2-42
5-34.2	Punts - Average	2-32.5
2-1	Fumbles - Lost	0-0
6-44	Penalties - Yards	9-71
21:45	Possession Time	38:15

INDIVIDUAL LEADERS
RUSHING
ARK: Talley 14-33; Jones 7-14.
MINN: Tapeh 19-99, 1 TD; Jackson II 16-37.
PASSING
ARK: Jones 12-24-2, 119 yards, 1 TD; Sorahan 6-15-1, 89 yards, 1 TD.
MINN: Abdul-Khaliq 16-31-0, 216 yards, 1 TD.
RECEIVING
ARK: Wilson 8-111, 1 TD; Smith 5-65, 1 TD.
MINN: Burns 4-88; Utecht 5-77, 1 TD.

December 31, 2003
Auburn 28, Wisconsin 14

	1ST	2ND	3RD	4TH	FINAL
AUB	0	7	7	14	28
WIS	0	6	0	8	14

SCORING SUMMARY
WIS	FG Allen 20
AUB	Brown 1 run (Vaughn kick)
WIS	FG Allen 35
AUB	Williams 1 run (Vaughn kick)
WIS	Evans 12 pass from Sorgi (Daniels pass from Sorgi)
AUB	Brown 2 run (Vaughn kick)
AUB	Williams 1 run (Vaughn kick)

AUB	TEAM STATISTICS	WIS
15	First Downs	18
197	Rushing Yards	58
11-23-1	Passing	17-29-1
157	Passing Yards	203
354	Total Yards	261
5-99	Punt Returns - Yards	3-35
4-64	Kickoff Returns - Yards	2-6
5-45.2	Punts - Average	4-38.5
0-0	Fumbles - Lost	2-1
8-66	Penalties - Yards	4-25
29:00	Possession Time	31:00

INDIVIDUAL LEADERS
RUSHING
AUB: Williams 18-68, 2 TD; Campbell 9-67; Brown 13-62, 2 TD.
WIS: Davis 17-77; Evans 3-19.
PASSING
AUB: Campbell 10-22-1, 138 yards.
WIS: Sorgi 13-22-1, 169 yards, 1 TD.
RECEIVING
AUB: McIntyre 3-74; Daniels 3-40.
WIS: Williams 6-57; Evans 4-51, 1 TD.

December 31, 2004
Minnesota 20, Alabama 16

	1ST	2ND	3RD	4TH	FINAL
MINN	7	10	3	0	20
ALA	7	7	0	2	16

SCORING SUMMARY
ALA	McClain 2 pass from Pennington (Bostick kick)
MINN	Lipka 1 fumble return (Lloyd kick)
MINN	Barber 5 run (Lloyd kick)
MINN	FG Lloyd 27
ALA	McClain 1 run (Bostick kick)
MINN	FG Lloyd 24
ALA	Saftey

MINN	TEAM STATISTICS	ALA
23	First Downs	13
276	Rushing Yards	21
5-13-2	Passing	22-36-0
75	Passing Yards	243
351	Total Yards	264
4-10	Punt Returns - Yards	2-10
1-18	Kickoff Returns - Yards	5-76
4-37.8	Punts - Average	7-37.1
2-1	Fumbles - Lost	2-2
11-84	Penalties - Yards	4-35
37:54	Possession Time	22:06

INDIVIDUAL LEADERS
RUSHING
MINN: Barber 37-187, 1 TD; Maroney 29-105.
ALA: Brown 1-17.
PASSING
MINN: Cupito 5-12-1, 75 yards.
ALA: Pennington 22-36-0, 243 yards, 1 TD.
RECEIVING
MINN: Ellerson 3-51.
ALA: Prothro 4-82; Brown 3-56.

GMAC BOWL

PROFILE

Site: Mobile, Ala.
Stadium: Ladd-Peebles Stadium
Capacity: 40,686
Surface: FieldTurf

PLAYING SITES

Ladd-Peebles Stadium, since 1999

NAME CHANGES

Mobile Alabama Bowl, 1999
GMAC Mobile Alabama Bowl,
   2000
GMAC Bowl, since 2001

SEASON	DATE	PRE-GAME RANK	TEAMS	SCORE	FINAL RANK	MOST VALUABLE PLAYERS	ATT.
1999	Dec. 22, 1999		TCU	28		Casey Printers, TCU, QB	34,200
			East Carolina	14			
2000	Dec. 20, 2000		Southern Miss	28		LaDainian Tomlinson, TCU, RB	40,300
			TCU	21			
2001	Dec. 19, 2001		Marshall	64	2 OT	Byron Leftwich, Marshall, QB	40,139
			East Carolina	61			
2002	Dec. 18, 2002		Marshall	38	24	Byron Leftwich, Marshall, QB	40,646
			Louisville	15			
2003	Dec. 18, 2003	14	Miami (Ohio)	49	10	Ben Roethlisberger, Miami (Ohio), QB	40,620
			Louisville	28			
2004	Dec. 22, 2004		Bowling Green	52		Omar Jacobs, Bowling Green, QB	40,160
			Memphis	35			

DECEMBER 22, 1999
TCU 28, EAST CAROLINA 14

	1ST	2ND	3RD	4TH	FINAL
TCU	7	14	0	7	28
ECU	7	0	7	0	14

SCORING SUMMARY

ECU	Powell 58 pass from Garrard (Miller kick)
TCU	Tomlinson 2 run (Kaylakie kick)
TCU	Scarborough 21 pass from Printers (Kaylakie kick)
TCU	Tomlinson 3 run (Kaylakie kick)
ECU	Wilson 13 run (Miller kick)
TCU	Gary 32 interception return (Kaylakie kick)

TCU	TEAM STATISTICS	ECU
16	First Downs	12
186	Rushing Yards	-16
13-19-1	Passing	20-37-1
174	Passing Yards	239
360	Total Yards	223
3-49	Punt Returns - Yards	1-25
1-20	Kickoff Returns - Yards	5-115
6-31.7	Punts - Average	7-38.1
1-1	Fumbles - Lost	0-0
8-80	Penalties - Yards	3-15
35:20	Possession Time	24:40

INDIVIDUAL LEADERS

RUSHING
TCU: Tomlinson 36-124, 2 TD; Batteaux 6-37.
ECU: Henry 4-22; Wilson 9-16, 1 TD.

PASSING
TCU: Printers 13-19-1, 174 yards, 1 TD.
ECU: Garrard 19-35-1, 191 yards, 1 TD.

RECEIVING
TCU: Scarborough 2-49, 1 TD; Maiden 2-41.
ECU: Chappell 5-116; Powell 2-67, 1 TD.

DECEMBER 20, 2000
SOUTHERN MISS 28, TCU 21

	1ST	2ND	3RD	4TH	FINAL
TCU	7	0	14	0	21
USM	7	0	7	14	28

SCORING SUMMARY

TCU	Layne 3 pass from Printers (Kaylakie kick)
USM	Barnes 50 interception return (Hanna kick)
USM	Handy 9 pass from Kelly (Hanna kick)
TCU	Tomlinson 7 run (Kaylakie kick)
TCU	Tomlinson 33 run (Kaylakie kick)
USM	Handy 56 pass from Kelly (Hanna kick)
USM	Johnson 29 pass from Kelly (Hanna kick)

TCU	TEAM STATISTICS	USM
16	First Downs	15
150	Rushing Yards	158
10-22-2	Passing	11-23-0
115	Passing Yards	159
265	Total Yards	317
3-48	Punt Returns - Yards	1-3
3-94	Kickoff Returns - Yards	3-40
6-33.3	Punts - Average	4-40.5
2-0	Fumbles - Lost	0-0
8-68	Penalties - Yards	5-35
32:41	Possession Time	27:19

INDIVIDUAL LEADERS

RUSHING
TCU: Tomlinson 28-118, 2 TD; Layne 7-31.
USM: Nance 16-104; Kelly 11-43.

PASSING
TCU: Printers 10-22-2, 115 yards, 1 TD.
USM: Kelly 11-23-0, 159 yards, 3 TD.

RECEIVING
TCU: Dunbar 2-42; Brown 3-37.
USM: Handy 5-84, 2 TD; Garner 3-42.

DECEMBER 19, 2001
MARSHALL 64, EAST CAROLINA 61

	1ST	2ND	3RD	4TH	OT	OT	FINAL
MAR	0	8	28	15	7	6	64
ECU	21	17	3	10	7	3	61

SCORING SUMMARY

ECU	Hunt 12 interception return (Miller kick)
ECU	Steward 43 fumble return (Miller kick)
ECU	Garrard 9 run (Miller kick)
ECU	FG Miller 25
MAR	Watts 35 pass from Leftwich (Buggs run)
ECU	Henry 7 run (Miller kick)
ECU	Garrard 6 run (Miller kick)
MAR	Street 25 interception return (Head kick)
MAR	Leftwich 9 run (Head kick)
ECU	FG Miller 22
MAR	Tarpley 25 interception return (Head kick)
MAR	Wallace 15 run (Head kick)
ECU	FG Miller 32
MAR	Marriott 30 pass from Leftwich (pass failed)
ECU	Henry 55 run (Miller kick)
MAR	FG Head 27
MAR	Watts 11 pass from Leftwich (kick failed)
MAR	Wallace 2 run (Head kick)
ECU	Leonard 25 run (Miller kick)
ECU	FG Miller 37
MAR	Davis 8 pass from Leftwich

MAR	TEAM STATISTICS	ECU
36	First Downs	23
73	Rushing Yards	331
41-70-2	Passing	11-23-2
576	Passing Yards	161
649	Total Yards	492
1-5	Punt Returns - Yards	2-12
6-88	Kickoff Returns - Yards	2-(-3)
4-35.5	Punts - Average	4-38.3
3-2	Fumbles - Lost	1-1
7-59	Penalties - Yards	5-32
46:49	Possession Time	28:11

INDIVIDUAL LEADERS

RUSHING
MAR: Wallace 17-86, 2 TD.
ECU: Henry 29-195, 2 TD; Alston 6-91; Garrard 14-40, 2 TD.

PASSING
MAR: Leftwich 41-70-2, 576 yards, 4 TD.
ECU: Garrard 11-23-2, 161 yards.

RECEIVING
MAR: Marriott 15-234, 1 TD; Watts 7-133, 2 TD; Davis 8-87, 1 TD.
ECU: Collier 4-75; Alston 2-44.

DECEMBER 18, 2002
MARSHALL 38, LOUISVILLE 15

	1ST	2ND	3RD	4TH	FINAL
LOU	0	7	0	8	15
MAR	7	10	7	14	38

SCORING SUMMARY

MAR	Marriott 9 pass from Leftwich (Head kick)
MAR	FG Head 23
MAR	Doss 8 pass from Leftwich (Head kick)
LOU	Patterson 2 run (Smith kick)
MAR	Doss 12 pass from Leftwich (Head kick)
MAR	Marriott 26 pass from Leftwich (Head kick)
MAR	Wallace 15 run (Head kick)
LOU	Jones 11 pass from Ragone (Jones pass from Ragone)

LOU	TEAM STATISTICS	MAR
20	First Downs	23
56	Rushing Yards	99
21-48-1	Passing	22-44-1
205	Passing Yards	249
261	Total Yards	348
2-15	Punt Returns - Yards	3-5
6-76	Kickoff Returns - Yards	2-24
7-43.7	Punts - Average	6-50.2
4-2	Fumbles - Lost	0-0
10-88	Penalties - Yards	17-147
26:59	Possession Time	33:01

INDIVIDUAL LEADERS

RUSHING
LOU: Ragone 9-31; Patterson 6-19, 1 TD.
MAR: Wallace 14-75, 1 TD; Carey 9-15.

PASSING
LOU: Ragone 20-45-1, 193 yards, 1 TD.
MAR: Leftwich 22-44-1, 249 yards, 4 TD.

RECEIVING
LOU: Owens 5-39; Glenn 2-26; Jones 2-25, 1 TD.
MAR: Marriott 10-137, 2 TD; Watts 3-32; Doss 3-26, 2 TD.

DECEMBER 18, 2003
MIAMI (OHIO) 49, LOUISVILLE 28

	1ST	2ND	3RD	4TH	FINAL
MIA	21	14	0	14	49
LOU	0	21	7	0	28

SCORING SUMMARY

MIA	Larkin 28 pass from Roethlisberger (Parseghian kick)
MIA	Murray 2 run (Parseghian kick)
MIA	Nance 12 pass from Roethlisberger (Parseghian kick)
LOU	Gates 1 run (Smith kick)
MIA	Brandt 16 pass from Roethlisberger (Parseghian kick)
MIA	Larkin 26 pass from Roethlisberger (Parseghian kick)
LOU	Russell 31 pass from Bush (Smith kick)
LOU	Russell 2 pass from LeFors (Smith kick)
LOU	Russell 24 pass from LeFors (Smith kick)
MIA	Smith 3 run (Parseghian kick)
MIA	Pusateri 35 interception return (Parseghian kick)

MIA	TEAM STATISTICS	LOU
28	First Downs	22
221	Rushing Yards	237
21-33-0	Passing	18-27-3
376	Passing Yards	255
597	Total Yards	492
4-17	Punt Returns - Yards	2-18
4-36	Kickoff Returns - Yards	7-92
4-30.0	Punts - Average	4-42.3
2-0	Fumbles - Lost	1-0
8-73	Penalties - Yards	5-58
30:52	Possession Time	29:08

INDIVIDUAL LEADERS

RUSHING
MIA: Murray 15-142, 1 TD; Smith 12-82, 1 TD.
LOU: Gates 12-128, 1 TD; LeFors 8-49.

PASSING
MIA: Roethlisberger 21-33-0, 376 yards, 4 TD.
LOU: LeFors 17-26-3, 224 yards, 2 TD.

RECEIVING
MIA: Nance 9-169 ,1 TD; Larkin 5-88, 2 TD.
LOU: Russell 7-144, 3 TD; Ghent 2-45.

DECEMBER 22, 2004
BOWLING GREEN 52, MEMPHIS 35

	1ST	2ND	3RD	4TH	FINAL
BG	21	14	7	10	52
MEM	7	21	0	7	35

SCORING SUMMARY

BG	Pope 1 run (Suisham kick)
BG	Sharon 18 pass from Jacobs (Gostkowski kick)
MEM	Doucette 42 pass from Wimprine (Gostkowski kick)
BG	Sharon 36 pass from Jacobs (Suisham kick)
MEM	Kelley 60 pass from Wimprine (Gostkowski kick)
BG	Sanders 31 pass from Jacobs (Suisham kick)
MEM	Avery 38 pass from Wimprine (Gostkowski kick)
MEM	Williams 31 run (Gostkowski kick)
BG	Sanders 17 pass from Jacobs (Suisham kick)
BG	Pope 13 pass from Jacobs (Suisham kick)
BG	FG Suisham 37
BG	Pope 1 run (Suisham kick)
MEM	Doucette 14 pass from Wimprine (Gostkowski kick)

BG	TEAM STATISTICS	MEM
29	First Downs	21
193	Rushing Yards	90
26-44-1	Passing	26-39-1
365	Passing Yards	324
558	Total Yards	414
2-0	Punt Returns - Yards	2-11
1-26	Kickoff Returns - Yards	3-57
4-31.8	Punts - Average	6-32.8
1-1	Fumbles - Lost	2-1
2-14	Penalties - Yards	4-28
33:23	Possession Time	26:37

INDIVIDUAL LEADERS

RUSHING
BG: Pope 28-151, 2 TD; Lane 5-36.
MEM: Williams 18-120, 1 TD.

PASSING
BG: Jacobs 26-44-1, 365 yards, 5 TD.
MEM: Wimprine 26-39-1, 324 yards, 4 TD.

RECEIVING
BG: Sanders 7-123, 2 TD; Sharon 5-117, 2 TD.
MEM: Kelley 4-108, 1 TD; Doucette 2-56, 2 TD.

THE BOWLS

HOUSTON BOWL

PROFILE

Site: Houston, Texas
Stadium: Reliant Stadium
Capacity: 69,500
Surface: Grass

PLAYING SITES

Reliant Astrodome, 2000-01
Reliant Stadium, since 2002

NAME CHANGES

galleryfurniture.com Bowl,
  2000-01
Houston Bowl, 2002
EV1.net Houston Bowl, since 2003

SEASON	DATE	PRE-GAME RANK	TEAMS	SCORE	FINAL RANK	MOST VALUABLE PLAYERS	ATT.
2000	Dec. 27, 2000		**East Carolina**	40		David Garrard, East Carolina, QB	33,899
			Texas Tech	27		Bernard Williams, East Carolina, DT	
2001	Dec. 28, 2001		**Texas A&M**	28		Byron Jones, Texas A&M, DB	53,480
			TCU		9	Joe Weber, Texas A&M, RB	
2002	Dec. 27, 2002		**Oklahoma State**	33		Rashaun Woods, Oklahoma State, WR	44,687
			Southern Miss	23		Kevin Williams, Oklahoma State, DT	
2003	Dec. 30, 2003		**Texas Tech**	38		B.J. Symons, Texas Tech, QB	51,068
			Navy	14		Adell Duckett, Texas Tech, DL	
2004	Dec. 29, 2004		**Colorado**	33		Joel Klatt, Colorado, QB	27,235
			UTEP	28		Tom Hubbard, Colorado, S	

DECEMBER 27, 2000
EAST CAROLINA 40, TEXAS TECH 27

	1ST	2ND	3RD	4TH	FINAL
ECU	20	14	6	0	40
TT	0	7	7	13	27

SCORING SUMMARY

ECU	Garrard 6 run (kick blocked)
ECU	Stokes 71 punt return (Miller kick)
ECU	Henry 1 run (Miller kick)
ECU	Collier 44 pass from Garrard (Miller kick)
ECU	Henry 1 run (Miller kick)
TT	Dorris 7 pass from Kingsbury (Birkholz kick)
TT	Jones 65 yard pass from Kingsbury (Birkholz kick)
ECU	FG Miller 36
ECU	FG Miller 35
TT	Roberts 17 pass from Kingsbury (Birkholz kick)
TT	Dorris 3 pass from Kingsbury (pass failed)

ECU	TEAM STATISTICS	TT
25	First Downs	18
252	Rushing Yards	62
17-27-2	Passing	31-49-2
229	Passing Yards	307
481	Total Yards	369
3-82	Punt Returns - Yards	3-41
5-105	Kickoff Returns - Yards	4-78
3-34.0	Punts - Average	6-41.0
4-3	Fumbles - Lost	1-0
4-40	Penalties - Yards	4-23
33:08	Possession Time	26:52

INDIVIDUAL LEADERS

RUSHING
ECU: Henry 20-92, 2 TD; Burns 6-52; Garrard 13-33, 1 TD.
TT: R.Williams 9-55; S.Williams 2-18.

PASSING
ECU: Garrard 17-27-2, 229 yards, 1 TD.
TT: Kingsbury 31-49-2, 307 yards, 4 TD.

RECEIVING
ECU: Harris 3-76; Stokes 5-46.
TT: Jones 6-147, 1 TD; Dorris 7-53, 2 TD.

DECEMBER 28, 2001
TEXAS A&M 28, TCU 9

	1ST	2ND	3RD	4TH	FINAL
A&M	0	14	7	7	28
TCU	0	7	0	2	9

SCORING SUMMARY

A&M	Farris 1 run (Scates kick)
TCU	Owens 89 fumble return (Browne kick)
A&M	Weber 2 run (Scates kick)
A&M	Weber 14 run (Scates kick)
A&M	Jones 82 pass from Farris (Scates kick)
TCU	Safety

A&M	TEAM STATISTICS	TCU
17	First Downs	11
104	Rushing Yards	-26
9-20-0	Passing	15-30-4
191	Passing Yards	144
295	Total Yards	118
3-13	Punt Returns - Yards	5-18
2-53	Kickoff Returns - Yards	3-89
7-41.7	Punts - Average	6-49.8
1-1	Fumbles - Lost	2-1
4-25	Penalties - Yards	11-87
37:22	Possession Time	22:38

INDIVIDUAL LEADERS

RUSHING
A&M: Weber 9-59, 2 TD; Farmer 17-33.
TCU: Madison 11-29; Holts 3-9.

PASSING
A&M: Farris 9-19-0, 191 yards, 1 TD.
TCU: Printers 15-30-4, 144 yards.

RECEIVING
A&M: Jones 1-82, 1 TD; Carriger 2-57.
TCU: Madise 7-65; Dunbar 4-36.

DECEMBER 27, 2002
OKLAHOMA STATE 33, SOUTHERN MISS 23

	1ST	2ND	3RD	4TH	FINAL
OKST	10	10	0	13	33
USM	3	10	10	0	23

SCORING SUMMARY

OKST	Denard 3 pass from Fields (Phillips kick)
OKST	FG Phillips 46
USM	FG Jones 38
USM	Almond 13 run (Jones kick)
OKST	FG Phillips 52
USM	FG Jones 24
OKST	Woods 51 pass from Fields (Phillips kick)
USM	Walley 2 run (Jones kick)
USM	FG Jones 30
OKST	FG Phillips 28
OKST	Bell 22 run (Phillips kick)
OKST	FG Phillips 24

OKST	TEAM STATISTICS	USM
21	First Downs	17
194	Rushing Yards	148
21-40-1	Passing	11-28-1
310	Passing Yards	173
504	Total Yards	321
5-32	Punt Returns - Yards	3-55
4-117	Kickoff Returns - Yards	5-126
4-41.5	Punts - Average	7-44.1
1-1	Fumbles - Lost	1-0
10-97	Penalties - Yards	8-57
29:28	Possession Time	30:32

INDIVIDUAL LEADERS

RUSHING
OSU: Bell 13-160, 1 TD; Shaw 12-37.
USM: Walley 21-74, 1 TD; Almond 17-54, 1 TD.

PASSING
OSU: Fields 21-40-1, 310 yards, 2 TD.
USM: Almond 11-27-0, 173 yards.

RECEIVING
OSU: Woods 9-164, 1 TD; Johnson 3-47.
USM: Johnson 5-67; Walley 2-45.

DECEMBER 30, 2003
TEXAS TECH 38, NAVY 14

	1ST	2ND	3RD	4TH	FINAL
TT	0	14	10	14	38
NAVY	0	0	7	7	14

SCORING SUMMARY

TT	Peters 4 pass from Symons (Toogood kick)
TT	Glover 17 pass from Symons (Toogood kick)
NAVY	Candeto 2 run (Rolfs kick)
TT	Henderson 4 run (Toogood kick)
TT	FG Toogood 21
NAVY	Candeto 1 run (Rolfs kick)
TT	Hicks 13 pass from Symons (Toogood kick)
TT	Peters 4 pass from Symons (Toogood kick)

TT	TEAM STATISTICS	NAVY
30	First Downs	17
64	Rushing Yards	289
41-53-1	Passing	3-13-0
497	Passing Yards	40
561	Total Yards	329
0-0.0	Punts - Average	2-46.0
1-0	Fumbles - Lost	3-1
11-127	Penalties - Yards	6-78
29:31	Possession Time	30:29

INDIVIDUAL LEADERS

RUSHING
TT: Henderson 11-43, 1 TD.
NAVY: Candeto 23-90, 2 TD; Eckel 14-71.

PASSING
TT: Symons 41-53-1, 497 yards, 4 TD.
NAVY: Candeto 2-9-0, 33 yards.

RECEIVING
TT: Glover 9-116, 1 TD; Welker 7-107; Francis 6-90.
NAVY: Jenkins 2-33.

DECEMBER 29, 2004
COLORADO 33, UTEP 28

	1ST	2ND	3RD	4TH	FINAL
COLO	3	10	6	14	33
UTEP	14	7	0	7	28

SCORING SUMMARY

COLO	FG Crosby 26
UTEP	Jackson 7 run (Schneider kick)
UTEP	Chamois 1 run (Schneider kick)
COLO	Charles 1 run (Crosby kick)
COLO	FG Crosby 54
UTEP	Boyd 17 pass from Palmer (Schneider kick)
COLO	FG Crosby 37
COLO	FG Crosby 20
UTEP	Higgins Jr. 3 pass from Palmer (Schneider kick)
COLO	Klopfenstein 78 pass from Klatt (Crosby kick)
COLO	Judge 39 pass from Klatt (Crosby kick)

COLO	TEAM STATISTICS	UTEP
23	First Downs	19
157	Rushing Yards	34
24-33-0	Passing	22-42-2
333	Passing Yards	328
490	Total Yards	362
2-2	Punt Returns - Yards	2-11
5-83	Kickoff Returns - Yards	1-16
4-50.0	Punts - Average	5-45.0
0-0	Fumbles - Lost	1-1
10-83	Penalties - Yards	4-43
37:09	Possession Time	22:51

INDIVIDUAL LEADERS

RUSHING
COLO: Purify 22-80; Charles 7-51, 1 TD.
UTEP: Jackson 16-37, 1 TD.

PASSING
COLO: Klatt 24-33-0, 333 yards, 2 TD.
UTEP: Palmer 22-42-2, 328 yards, 2 TD.

RECEIVING
COLO: Klopfenstein 5-134, 1 TD; Judge 2-50, 1 TD.
UTEP: Boyd 7-140, 1 TD; Higgins Jr. 7-122, 1 TD.

NEW ORLEANS BOWL

Site: New Orleans
Stadium: Louisiana Superdome
Capacity: 69,767
Surface: MomentumTurf

Louisiana Superdome, since 2001

New Orleans Bowl, 2001-2003
Wyndham New Orleans Bowl,
  since 2004

SEASON	DATE	PRE-GAME RANK	TEAMS	SCORE	FINAL RANK	MOST VALUABLE PLAYERS	ATT.
2001	Dec. 18, 2001		Colorado State	45		Justin Gallimore, Colorado State, DB	27,004
			North Texas	20			
2002	Dec. 17, 2002		North Texas	24		Kevin Galbreath, North Texas, RB	19,024
			Cincinnati	19			
2003	Dec. 16, 2003		Memphis	27		Danny Wimprine, Memphis, QB	25,184
			North Texas	17			
2004	Dec. 14, 2004		Southern Miss	31		Michael Boley, Southern Miss, LB	27,253
			North Texas	10			

DECEMBER 18, 2001
COLORADO STATE 45, NORTH TEXAS 20

	1ST	2ND	3RD	4TH	FINAL
CSU	17	7	7	14	45
NT	0	14	0	6	20

SCORING SUMMARY
CSU   Svoboda 2 run (Naughton kick)
CSU   FG Naughton 46
CSU   Ochoa 8 pass from Van Pelt (Naughton kick)
NT   Dean 5 pass from Hall (Ball kick)
CSU   Van Pelt 6 run (Naughton kick)
NT   Branch 42 pass from Hall (Ball kick)
CSU   Gallimore recovered blocked punt in end zone
      (Naughton kick)
CSU   Dixon 2 run (Naughton kick)
CSU   Vomhof 20 run (Naughton kick)
NT   Blount 13 pass from Bridges (pass failed)

CSU	TEAM STATISTICS	NT
20	First Downs	19
246	Rushing Yards	133
8-17-2	Passing	15-34-1
129	Passing Yards	196
375	Total Yards	329
4-31	Punt Returns - Yards	1-15
3-59	Kickoff Returns - Yards	5-79
3-32.3	Punts - Average	5-27.2
1-1	Fumbles - Lost	1-1
6-41	Penalties - Yards	10-78
33:45	Possession Time	26:15

INDIVIDUAL LEADERS
RUSHING
CSU: Childs 12-97; Ruff 12-60; Vomhof 9-51, 1 TD.
NT: Galbreath 22-106; Cobbs 7-50.
PASSING
CSU: Van Pelt 5-14-2, 106 yards, 1 TD.
NT: Hall 13-30-1, 185 yards, 2 TD.
RECEIVING
CSU: Rebstock 2-73; Ochoa 2-18, 1 TD.
NT: Branch 3-58, 1 TD; Marshall 4-53.

DECEMBER 17, 2002
NORTH TEXAS 24, CINCINNATI 19

	1ST	2ND	3RD	4TH	FINAL
NT	3	14	7	0	24
CIN	7	0	6	6	19

SCORING SUMMARY
CIN   Keith 6 pass from Guidugli (Ruffin kick)
NT   FG Bazaldua 30
NT   Cobbs 27 run (Bazaldua kick)
NT   Pearl 20 interception return (Bazaldua kick)
NT   Galbreath 35 run (Bazaldua kick)
CIN   FG Ruffin 29
CIN   FG Ruffin 33
CIN   Callicott 43 fumble return (pass failed)

NT	TEAM STATISTICS	CIN
15	First Downs	15
192	Rushing Yards	85
9-22-1	Passing	19-34-5
126	Passing Yards	224
318	Total Yards	309
1-11	Punt Returns - Yards	2-2
5-154	Kickoff Returns - Yards	4-70
7-46.0	Punts - Average	4-42.8
3-1	Fumbles - Lost	0-0
10-92	Penalties - Yards	10-78
30:28	Possession Time	29:32

INDIVIDUAL LEADERS
RUSHING
NT: Galbreath 28-130, 1 TD; Cobbs 4-29, 1 TD.
CIN: McCleskey 23-85.
PASSING
NT: Smith 9-22-1, 126 yards.
CIN: Guidugli 19-34-5, 224 yards, 1 TD.
RECEIVING
NT: Howard 5-78; Branch 3-27.
CIN: Olinger 4-107; Keith 4-44, 1 TD.

DECEMBER 16, 2003
MEMPHIS 27, NORTH TEXAS 17

	1ST	2ND	3RD	4TH	FINAL
MEM	7	10	0	10	27
NT	3	0	7	7	17

SCORING SUMMARY
NT   FG Bazaldua 47
MEM   Wimprine 7 run (Gostkowski kick)
MEM   Kelley 10 pass from Wimprine (Gostkowski kick)
MEM   FG Gostkowski 21
NT   Cobbs 35 run (Bazaldua kick)
MEM   Cole 5 run (Gostkwoski kick)
NT   Cobbs 2 run (Bazaldua kick)
MEM   FG Gostkowski 42

MEM	TEAM STATISTICS	NT
15	First Downs	11
88	Rushing Yards	122
17-24-0	Passing	9-21-0
254	Passing Yards	152
342	Total Yards	274
1-2	Punt Returns - Yards	2 (-3)
4-69	Kickoff Returns - Yards	4-61
6-38.7	Punts - Average	8-37.3
0-0	Fumbles - Lost	1-1
9-57	Penalties - Yards	6-61
34:08	Possession Time	25:52

INDIVIDUAL LEADERS
RUSHING
MEM: Cole 27-62, 1 TD.
NT: Cobbs 23-110, 2 TD.
PASSING
MEM: Wimprine 17-23-0, 254 yards, 1 TD.
NT: Hall 9-21-0, 152 yards.
RECEIVING
MEM: Garcia 2-109; Pratcher 2-62.
NT: Quinn 4-56; Branch 3-50.

DECEMBER 14, 2004
SOUTHERN MISS 31, NORTH TEXAS 10

	1ST	2ND	3RD	4TH	FINAL
USM	14	3	0	14	31
NT	0	3	0	7	10

SCORING SUMMARY
USM   Graves 37 pass from Almond (McCaleb kick)
USM   Almond 1 run (McCaleb kick)
NT   FG Bazaldua 24
USM   FG McCaleb 45
USM   Boley 62 interception return (McCaleb kick)
USM   Moore 1 run (McCaleb kick)
NT   Quinn 11 pass from Hall (Bazaldua kick)

USM	TEAM STATISTICS	NT
17	First Downs	17
156	Rushing Yards	78
16-30-1	Passing	15-30-2
247	Passing Yards	134
403	Total Yards	212
5-22	Punt Returns - Yards	2-(-8)
2-64	Kickoff Returns - Yards	4-51
3-46	Punts - Average	8-43
3-2	Fumbles - Lost	2-1
9-60	Penalties - Yards	1-0
27:32	Possession Time	32:28

INDIVIDUAL LEADERS
RUSHING
USM: Harris 14-104; Moore 10-33, 1 TD.
NT: Thomas 29-92.
PASSING
USM: Almond 16-30-1, 247 yards, 1 TD.
NT: Hall 15-30-2, 134 yards, 1 TD.
RECEIVING
USM: Graves 3-58, 1 TD; Courington 5-57.
NT: Quinn 8-92, 1 TD; Blount 3-13.

HAWAII BOWL

PROFILE

Site: Honolulu
Stadium: Aloha Stadium
Capacity: 50,000
Surface: FieldTurf

PLAYING SITES

Aloha Stadium, since 2002

NAME CHANGES

ConAgra Foods Hawaii Bowl, 2002
Sheraton Hawaii Bowl, since 2003

SEASON	DATE	PRE-GAME RANK	TEAMS	SCORE	FINAL RANK	MOST VALUABLE PLAYERS	ATT.
2002	Dec. 25, 2002		**Tulane**	36		Lynaris Elpheage, Tulane, CB	31,535
			Hawaii	28			
2003	Dec. 25, 2003		Hawaii	54	3OT	Timmy Chang, Hawaii, QB	29,005
			Houston	48			
2004	Dec. 24, 2004		Hawaii	59		Chad Owens, Hawaii, WR	38,322
			UAB	40		Timmy Chang, Hawaii, QB	

DECEMBER 25, 2002

TULANE 36, HAWAII 28

	1ST	2ND	3RD	4TH	FINAL
TUL	0	6	20	10	36
HAW	7	7	0	14	28

SCORING SUMMARY

HAW	Mitchell 1 run (Ayat kick)
HAW	Galeai 2 run (Ayat kick)
TUL	FG Marler 23
TUL	FG Marler 37
TUL	Elpheage 60 punt return (pass failed)
TUL	Losman 1 run (Losman run)
TUL	Moore 25 run (pass failed)
HAW	Colbert 57 pass from Withy-Allen (Ayat kick)
TUL	Losman 3 run (Davis pass from Losman)
HAW	Colbert 31 pass from Withy-Allen (Ayat kick)
TUL	Safety

TUL	TEAM STATISTICS	HAW
25	First Downs	23
144	Rushing Yards	66
20-39-0	Passing	32-52-1
240	Passing Yards	363
384	Total Yards	429
4-143	Punt Returns - Yards	1-13
2-57	Kickoff Returns - Yards	4-75
4-47.0	Punts - Average	5-53.8
3-1	Fumbles - Lost	5-2
6-64	Penalties - Yards	12-88
31:49	Possession Time	28:11

INDIVIDUAL LEADERS

RUSHING
TUL: Moore 30-116, 1 TD; Losman 12-21, 2 TD.
HAW: Mitchell 5-38, 1 TD; Withy-Allen 9-21.

PASSING
TUL: Losman 20-39-0, 240 yards.
HAW: Withy-Allen 18-31-1, 239 yards, 2 TD; Chang 14-21-0, 124 yards.

RECEIVING
TUL: Moore 6-80; Narcisse 5-64.
HAW: Colbert 9-158, 2 TD; Cockheran 9-87.

DECEMBER 25, 2003

HAWAII 54, HOUSTON 48

	1ST	2ND	3RD	4TH	OT	OT	OT	FINAL
HAW	3	10	14	7	7	7	6	54
HOU	10	10	0	14	7	7	0	48

SCORING SUMMARY

HOU	McCullar 34 pass from Kolb (Bell kick)
HOU	FG Bell 21
HAW	FG Miranda 19
HAW	Herbert 48 pass from Chang (Miranda kick)
HOU	Battle 2 run (Bell kick)
HOU	FG Bell 35
HAW	FG Miranda 29
HAW	Brewster 1 run (Miranda kick)
HAW	Rivers 7 pass from Chang (Miranda kick)
HOU	Battle 2 run (Bell kick)
HAW	Rivers 4 pass from Chang (Miranda kick)
HOU	Marshall 81 pass from Kolb (Bell kick)
HAW	Komine 11 pass from Chang (Miranda kick)
HOU	Evans 6 run (Bell kick)
HOU	Battle 4 run (Bell kick)
HAW	Rivers 18 pass from Chang (Miranda kick)
HAW	Brewster 8 run (pass failed)

HAW	TEAM STATISTICS	HOU
26	First Downs	21
114	Rushing Yards	185
29-47-1	Passing	19-34-2
527	Passing Yards	332
641	Total Yards	517
4-22	Punt Returns - Yards	3-83
2-29	Kickoff Returns - Yards	4-108
4-41.0	Punts - Average	5-46.6
2-1	Fumbles - Lost	2-0
5-45	Penalties - Yards	10-105
30:10	Possession Time	29:50

INDIVIDUAL LEADERS

RUSHING
HAW: Brewster 14-79, 2 TD; West 6-33.
HOU: Battle 19-124, 3 TD; Evans 22-66, 1 TD.

PASSING
HAW: Chang 26-42-1, 475 yards, 5 TD.
HOU: Kolb 19-34-2, 332 yards, 2 TD.

RECEIVING
HAW: Cockheran 5-162; Rivers 7-143, 3 TD.
HOU: Marshall 7-157, 1 TD; McCullar 5-103, 1 TD.

DECEMBER 24, 2004

HAWAII 59, UAB 40

	1ST	2ND	3RD	4TH	FINAL
HAW	21	7	17	14	59
UAB	13	13	7	7	40

SCORING SUMMARY

UAB	White 51 pass from Hackney (kick failed)
HAW	Rivers 74 pass from Chang (Ayat kick)
UAB	Burks 4 run (Hayes kick)
HAW	Keliikipi 4 run (Ayat kick)
HAW	Welch 29 pass from Chang (Ayat kick)
UAB	FG Hayes 22
HAW	Owens 13 pass from Chang (Ayat kick)
UAB	Drinkard 10 run (Hayes kick)
UAB	FG Hayes 36
HAW	Owens 15 pass from Chang (Ayat kick)
HAW	Owens 59 punt return (Ayat kick)
HAW	FG Ayat 43
UAB	Hackney 4 run (Hayes kick)
HAW	Chang 4 run (Ayat kick)
UAB	Rhodes 17 pass from Hackney (Hayes kick)
HAW	Komine 42 kickoff return (Ayat kick)

HAW	TEAM STATISTICS	UAB
23	First Downs	31
84	Rushing Yards	173
31-47-0	Passing	31-54-1
405	Passing Yards	417
489	Total Yards	590
5-90	Punt Returns - Yards	3-14
7-163	Kickoff Returns - Yards	5-142
4-42.8	Punts - Average	6-40.8
1-1	Fumbles - Lost	1-1
6-43	Penalties - Yards	12-104
26:32	Possession Time	33:28

INDIVIDUAL LEADERS

RUSHING
HAW: Brewster 7-60; Keliikipi 6-27, 1 TD.
UAB: Burks 14-55, 1 TD; White 8-53.

PASSING
HAW: Chang 31-46-0, 405 yards, 4 TD.
UAB: Hackney 31-54-1, 417 yards, 2 TD.

RECEIVING
HAW: Rivers 11-148, 1 TD; Owens 8-114, 2 TD.
UAB: White 6-113, 1 TD; Chavez 5-81.

MEINEKE CAR CARE BOWL

Site: Charlotte, N.C.
Stadium: Bank of America Stadium
Capacity: 73,367
Surface: Grass

PLAYING SITES

Ericsson Stadium, renamed Bank of America Stadium in 2004, since 2002

NAME CHANGES

Continental Tire Bowl, 2002-04
Meineke Car Care Bowl, since 2005

SEASON	DATE	PRE-GAME RANK	TEAMS	SCORE	FINAL RANK	MOST VALUABLE PLAYERS	ATT.
2002	Dec. 28, 2002		**Virginia**	**48**	22	Wali Lundy, Virginia, TB	73,535
		15	**West Virginia**	**22**	25		
2003	Dec. 27, 2003		**Virginia**	**23**		Matt Schaub, Virginia, QB	51,236
			Pittsburgh	**16**			
2004	Dec. 30, 2004	25	**Boston College**	**37**	21	Paul Peterson, Boston College, QB	70,412
			North Carolina	**`24**			

DECEMBER 28, 2002
VIRGINIA 48, WEST VIRGINIA 22

	1ST	2ND	3RD	4TH	FINAL
WVU	10	0	6	6	22
VIR	7	21	10	10	48

SCORING SUMMARY

WVU	FG James 27
VIR	Lundy 14 pass from Hagans (Hughes kick)
WVU	Cobourne 6 run (James kick)
VIR	Schaub 1 run (Hughes kick)
VIR	Hagans 69 punt return (Hughes kick)
VIR	Lundy 4 run (Hughes kick)
VIR	Lundy 48 pass from Schaub (Hughes kick)
VIR	FG Hughes 27
WVU	Marshall 1 run (kick blocked)
VIR	FG Hughes 30
WVU	Cobourne 1 run (run failed)
VIR	Lundy 31 run (Hughes kick)

WVU	TEAM STATISTICS	VIR
21	First Downs	20
244	Rushing Yards	195
12-20-2	Passing	17-23-0
215	Passing Yards	196
459	Total Yards	391
2-44.0	Punts - Average	1-27.0
6-39	Penalties - Yards	2-9
31:34	Possession Time	28:26

INDIVIDUAL LEADERS
RUSHING
WVU: Cobourne 25-117, 2 TD; Marshall 12-48, 1 TD.
VIR: Lundy 22-127, 2 TD; Schaub 7-39, 1 TD.
PASSING
WVU: Marshall 12-18-1, 215 yards.
VIR : Schaub 16-22-0, 182 yards, 1 TD.
RECEIVING
WVU: Braxton 4-108; Henderson 2-75.
VIR : Lundy 5-76, 2 TD; Sawyer 4-41.

DECEMBER 27, 2003
VIRGINIA 23, PITTSBURGH 16

	1ST	2ND	3RD	4TH	FINAL
VIR	7	10	3	3	23
PITT	0	13	3	0	16

SCORING SUMMARY

VIR	Miller 52 pass from Schaub (Hughes kick)
PITT	Brockenbrough 13 pass from Rutherford (Abdul kick)
VIR	Lundy 1 run (Hughes kick)
PITT	Miree 17 pass from Rutherford (kick failed)
VIR	FG Hughes 44
VIR	FG Hughes 30
PITT	FG Gibboney 28
VIR	FG Hughes 39

VIR	TEAM STATISTICS	PITT
21	First Downs	27
196	Rushing Yards	148
20-31-1	Passing	18-26-1
244	Passing Yards	246
440	Total Yards	394
1-8	Punt Returns - Yards	2-7
4-154	Kickoff Returns - Yards	5-109
3-36.3	Punts - Average	2-49.5
0-0	Fumbles - Lost	2-1
5-60	Penalties - Yards	1-5
22:55	Possession Time	37:05

INDIVIDUAL LEADERS
RUSHING
VIR: Pearman 7-104; Lundy 23-90, 1 TD.
PITT: Miree 22-110; Polite 7-15.
PASSING
VIR : Schaub 20-31-1, 244 yards, 1 TD.
PITT: Rutherford 18-26-1, 246 yards, 2 TD.
RECEIVING
VIR : Miller 4-84, 1 TD; Sawyer 3-45.
PITT: Fitzgerald 5-77; Wilson 2-54; Brockenbrough 4-53, 1 TD.

DECEMBER 30, 2004
BOSTON COLLEGE 37, NORTH CAROLINA 24

	1ST	2ND	3RD	4TH	FINAL
BC	14	7	0	16	37
UNC	7	14	3	0	24

SCORING SUMMARY

BC	Whitworth 3 run (Ohliger kick)
UNC	McGill 12 pass from Durant (Barth kick)
BC	Adams 2 pass from Peterson (Ohliger kick)
UNC	Wright 5 pass from Durant (Barth kick)
UNC	Mitchell 51 pass from Durant (Barth kick)
BC	Kashetta 1 pass from Peterson (Ohliger kick)
UNC	FG Barth 27
BC	Callender 1 run (kick failed)
BC	Ohliger 21 run (Troost kick)
BC	FG Troost 18

BC	TEAM STATISTICS	UNC
20	First Downs	22
228	Rushing Yards	105
25-35-0	Passing	23-41-0
249	Passing Yards	259
477	Total Yards	364
4-32	Punt Returns - Yards	1-10
4-37.3	Punts - Average	7-41.4
2-1	Fumbles - Lost	0-0
3-20	Penalties - Yards	5-40
33:58	Possession Time	26:02

INDIVIDUAL LEADERS
RUSHING
BC: Callender 26-174, 1 TD; Whitworth 10-30, 1 TD.
UNC: McGill 8-53; Scott 16-49.
PASSING
BC: Peterson 24-33-0, 236 yards, 2 TD.
UNC: Durant 23-41-0, 259 yards, 3 TD.
RECEIVING
BC: Hazard 5-81; Adams 5-53, 1 TD.
UNC: Mitchell 7-116, 1 TD; Holley 5-66.

EMERALD BOWL

PROFILE

Site: San Francisco
Stadium: SBC Park
Capacity: 37,000
Surface: Grass

PLAYING SITES

Pacific Bell Park, renamed SBC
Park in 2003, since 2002

NAME CHANGES

**Diamond Walnut San Francisco
Bowl,** 2002-03
Emerald Bowl, since 2004

SEASON	DATE	PRE-GAME RANK	TEAMS	SCORE	FINAL RANK	MOST VALUABLE PLAYERS	ATT.
2002	Dec. 31, 2002	21	**Virginia Tech**	**20**	18	Bryan Randall, Virginia Tech, QB	25,966
			Air Force	13		Anthony Schlegel, Air Force, LB	
2003	Jan. 1, 2004		**Boston College**	**35**		Derrick Knight, Boston College, RB	25,621
			Colorado State	21		T.J. Stancil, Boston College, FS	
2004	Dec. 30, 2004		**New Mexico**	**34**		Aaron Polanco, Navy, QB	30,563
			Navy	19		Vaughn Kelley, Navy, CB	

DECEMBER 31, 2002
VIRGINIA TECH 20, AIR FORCE 13

	1ST	2ND	3RD	4TH	FINAL
VT	7	3	7	3	20
AFA	10	0	0	3	13

SCORING SUMMARY
AFA   Ward 15 run (Ashcroft kick)
AFA   FG Ashcroft 45
VT   Suggs 16 run (Warley kick)
VT   FG Warley 23
VT   Suggs 2 run (Warley kick)
AFA   FG Ashcroft 21
VT   FG Warley 37

VT	TEAM STATISTICS	AFA
21	First Downs	17
101	Rushing Yards	227
18-23-0	Passing	4-19-2
177	Passing Yards	91
278	Total Yards	318
3-52	Kickoff Returns - Yards	5-82
3-40.0	Punts - Average	3-30.7
2-1	Fumbles - Lost	1-0
3-25	Penalties - Yards	7-73
29:35	Possession Time	30:25

INDIVIDUAL LEADERS
RUSHING
VT: Suggs 19-70, 2 TD; Jones 11-35.
AFA: Butler 17-75; Harridge 18-70.
PASSING
VT: Randall 18-23-0, 177 yards.
AFA: Harridge 4-19-2, 91 yards.
RECEIVING
VT: Wilford 5-50; Witten 4-48.
AFA: Park 1-47; Waller 1-20.

JANUARY 1, 2004
BOSTON COLLEGE 35, COLORADO STATE 21

	1ST	2ND	3RD	4TH	FINAL
BC	21	0	0	14	35
CSU	0	7	7	7	21

SCORING SUMMARY
BC   Knight 5 run (Sciortino kick)
BC   Lester 50 pass from Peterson (Sciortino kick)
BC   Knight 3 run (Sciortino kick)
CSU   Green 7 run (Babcock kick)
CSU   Anderson 40 pass from Van Pelt (Babcock kick)
BC   Lester 20 pass from Peterson (Sciortino kick)
BC   Knight 28 run (Sciortino kick)
CSU   Van Pelt 1 run (Babcock kick)

BC	TEAM STATISTICS	CSU
19	First Downs	21
137	Rushing Yards	146
16-25-1	Passing	22-37-5
224	Passing Yards	242
361	Total Yards	388
1-16	Punt Returns - Yards	1-3
4-90	Kickoff Returns - Yards	6-159
5-33.8	Punts - Average	3-40.3
2-0	Fumbles - Lost	1-0
5-56	Penalties - Yards	4-35
28:49	Possession Time	31:11

INDIVIDUAL LEADERS
RUSHING
BC: Knight 30-122, 3 TD.
CSU: Green 20-74, 1 TD; Van Pelt 11-65, 1 TD.
PASSING
BC: Peterson 16-25-1, 224 yards, 2 TD.
CSU: Van Pelt 14-25-3, 163 yards, 1 TD.
RECEIVING
BC: Lester 2-69, 2 TD; Adams 5-47.
CSU: Anderson 10-134, 1 TD; Bartz 2-37.

DECEMBER 30, 2004
NEW MEXICO 34, NAVY 19

	1ST	2ND	3RD	4TH	FINAL
NAVY	7	12	0	0	19
UNM	14	10	7	3	34

SCORING SUMMARY
UNM   Hail 17 pass from McKamey (Zunker kick)
NAVY   Polanco 14 run (Blumenfeld kick)
NAVY   Polanco 1 run (Blumenfeld kick)
NAVY   Dryden 61 pass from Polanco (Blumenfeld kick)
UNM   Ferguson 4 run (kick failed)
NAVY   FG Blumenfeld 27
UNM   McKamey 3 run
NAVY   Polanco 27 run (Blumenfeld kick)
UNM   FG Blumenfeld 22

UMN	TEAM STATISTICS	NAVY
23	First Downs	22
212	Rushing Yards	269
15-24-2	Passing	5-8-0
207	Passing Yards	124
419	Total Yards	393
1-2	Punt Returns - Yards	0-0
7-127	Kickoff Returns - Yards	2-11
1-27.0	Punts - Average	2-39.0
1-1	Fumbles - Lost	1-0
9-85	Penalties - Yards	6-53
27:39	Possession Time	32:21

INDIVIDUAL LEADERS
RUSHING
NAVY: Polanco 26-136, 3 TD; Eckel 24-85.
UNM: McKamey 19-138, 1 TD; Cox 11-32.
PASSING
NAVY: Polanco 3-6-0, 101 yards, 1 TD.
UNM: McKamey 15-24-2, 207 yards, 1 TD.
RECEIVING
NAVY: Dryden 1-61, 1 TD; Roberts 1-35.
UNM: Baskett 5-115; Hail 2-23, 1 TD.

FORT WORTH BOWL

PROFILE

Site: Fort Worth, Texas
Stadium: Amon G. Carter
Capacity: 46,000
Surface: Grass

PLAYING SITES

Amon G. Carter Stadium, since 2003

NAME CHANGES

PlainsCapital Fort Worth Bowl, since 2003

SEASON	DATE	PRE-GAME RANK	TEAMS	SCORE	FINAL RANK	MOST VALUABLE PLAYERS	ATT.
2003	Dec. 23, 2003	18	**Boise State**	**34**	16	Ryan Dinwiddie, Boise State, QB	38,028
		19	**TCU**	**31**	25	Brandon Hassel, TCU, QB	
2004	Dec. 23, 2004		**Cincinnati**	**32**		Gino Guidugli, Cincinnati, QB	27,902
			Marshall	**14**		Josh Davis, Marshall, WR	

DECEMBER 23, 2003
BOISE STATE 34, TCU 31

	1ST	2ND	3RD	4TH	FINAL
BSU	7	17	3	7	34
TCU	14	10	7	0	31

SCORING SUMMARY

TCU	Rodgers 3 run (Browne kick)
BSU	Acree 27 pass from Dinwiddie (Jones kick)
TCU	Rodgers 22 pass from Hassell (Browne kick)
TCU	Hassell 21 run (Browne kick)
BSU	Carpenter 54 pass from Dinwiddie (Jones kick)
BSU	Mikell 75 run (Jones kick)
TCU	FG Browne 32
BSU	FG Jones 23
BSU	FG Jones 37
TCU	Hobbs 7 run (Browne kick)
BSU	Schouman 18 pass from Dinwiddie (Jones kick)

BSU	TEAM STATISTICS	TCU
19	First Downs	26
117	Rushing Yards	280
19-35-2	Passing	15-29-1
325	Passing Yards	214
442	Total Yards	494
3-34	Punt Returns - Yards	2-8
6-127	Kickoff Returns - Yards	4-65
5-36.8	Punts - Average	4-40.8
0-0	Fumbles - Lost	2-2
6-70	Penalties - Yards	6-57
25:55	Possession Time	34:05

INDIVIDUAL LEADERS

RUSHING
BSU: Mikell 16-101, 1 TD.
TCU: Hobbs 23-117, 1 TD; Hassell 19-110, 1 TD.

PASSING
BSU: Dinwiddie 19-35-2, 325 yards, 3 TD.
TCU: Hassell 13-26-1, 160 yards, 1 TD.

RECEIVING
BSU: Acree 8-150, 1 TD; Carpenter 1-54, 1 TD.
TCU: Harrell 6-107; Rodgers 4-51, 1 TD.

DECEMBER 23, 2004
CINCINNATI 32, MARSHALL 14

	1ST	2ND	3RD	4TH	FINAL
CIN	10	14	0	8	32
MAR	14	0	0	0	14

SCORING SUMMARY

CIN	Giddens 9 blocked punt return (Lovell kick)
CIN	FG Lovell 23
MAR	Davis 14 pass from Hill (O'Connor kick)
MAR	Smith 32 interception return (O'Connor kick)
CIN	Celek 15 pass from Guidugli (Lovell kick)
CIN	Jackson 8 pass from Guidugli (Lovell kick)
CIN	FG Lovell 19
CIN	FG Lovell 35

CIN	TEAM STATISTICS	MAR
24	First Downs	11
168	Rushing Yards	(-3)
24-39-2	Passing	14-32-1
231	Passing Yards	137
399	Total Yards	134
3-53	Punt Returns - Yards	1-8
2-41	Kickoff Returns - Yards	7-133
2-40.0	Punts - Average	5-25.6
1-0	Fumbles - Lost	2-1
6-60	Penalties - Yards	1-5
38:27	Possession Time	21:33

INDIVIDUAL LEADERS

RUSHING
CIN: Hall 23-62; Glatthaar 10-48.
MAR: Charles 7-9; Hill 5-4.

PASSING
CIN: Guidugli 24-36-1, 231 yards, 2 TD.
MAR: Hill 14-30-1, 137 yards, 1 TD.

RECEIVING
CIN: Thomas 9-102; Hall 5-38.
MAR: Davis 5-67, 1 TD; Deifel 1-30.

THE BOWLS

DEFUNCT BOWLS

ALAMO BOWL (1947)

PROFILE

Site: San Antonio, Texas
Stadium: Alamo Stadium
Capacity: 23,000
Surface: Grass

SEASON	DATE	PRE-GAME RANK	TEAMS	SCORE	FINAL RANK	MOST VALUABLE PLAYERS	ATT.
1946	Jan. 4, 1947		**Hardin-Simmons**	20			3,730
			Denver	0			

JANUARY 4, 1947
HARDIN-SIMMONS 20, DENVER 0

	1ST	2ND	3RD	4TH	FINAL
HS	0	6	7	7	20
DEN	0	0	0	0	0

SCORING SUMMARY
HS   Mobley 34 run (kicked failed)
HS   Boles pass from Johnson (Poulus kick)
HS   Mobley 17 run (Poulos kick)

HS	TEAM STATISTICS	DEN
14	First Downs	9
267	Rushing Yards	131
6-13-2	Passing	5-17-2
86	Passing Yards	48
353	Total Yards	179

ALL-AMERICAN BOWL

PROFILE

Site: Birmingham
Stadium: Legion Field
Capacity: 75,952
Surface: AstroTurf

PLAYING SITES

Legion Field, 1977-90

NAME CHANGES

Hall of Fame Classic, 1977-85
All-American Bowl, 1986-90

SEASON	DATE	PRE-GAME RANK	TEAMS	SCORE	FINAL RANK	MOST VALUABLE PLAYERS	ATT.
1977	Dec. 22, 1977		**Maryland**	17		Chuck White, Maryland, SE	47,000
			Minnesota	7		Charles Johnson, Maryland, DT	
1978	Dec. 20, 1978		**Texas A&M**	28	19	Curtis Dickey, Texas A&M, RB	41,500
		19	Iowa State	12			
1979	Dec. 29, 1979		**Missouri**	24		Phil Bradley, Missouri, QB	62,785
		16	South Carolina	14			
1980	Dec. 27, 1980		**Arkansas**	34		Gary Anderson, Arkansas, RB	30,000
			Tulane	15		Billy Ray Smith, Arkansas, LB	
1981	Dec. 31, 1981		**Mississippi State**	10		John Bond, Mississippi St. QB	41,672
			Kansas	0		Johnie Cooks, Mississippi St., LB	
1982	Dec. 31, 1982		**Air Force**	36		Carl Dieudonne, Air Force, DE	75,000
			Vanderbilt	28		Whit Taylor, Vanderbilt, QB	
1983	Dec. 22, 1983	18	**West Virginia**	20	16	Jeff Hostetler, West Virginia, QB	42,000
			Kentucky	16			
1984	Dec. 29, 1984		**Kentucky**	20	19	Mark Logan, Kentucky, RB	47,300
		20	Wisconsin	19		Todd Gregoire, Wisconsin, K	
1985	Dec. 31, 1985		**Georgia Tech**	17	19	Mark Ingram, Michigan State, WR	45,000
			Michigan State	14			
1986	Dec. 31, 1986		**Florida State**	27		Sammie Smith, Florida State, RB	30,000
			Indiana	13			
1987	Dec. 22, 1987		**Virginia**	22		Scott Secules, Virginia, QB	37,000
			Brigham Young	16			
1988	Dec. 29, 1988		**Florida**	14		Emmitt Smith, Florida, RB	48,218
			Illinois	10			
1989	Dec. 28, 1989	25	**Texas Tech**	49	19	Jerry Gray, Texas Tech, RB	47,750
		20	Duke	21			
1990	Dec. 28, 1990		**North Carolina St.**	31			44,000
		23	**Southern Miss**	27		Brett Favre, Southern Miss, QB	

DECEMBER 22, 1977
MARYLAND 17, MINNESOTA 7

	1ST	2ND	3RD	4TH	FINAL
MARY	3	14	0	0	17
MINN	7	0	0	0	7

SCORING SUMMARY
MINN   Barber 1 run (Rogind kick)
MARY   FG Sochko 32
MARY   Scott 2 run (Sochko kick)
MARY   Scott 1 run (Sochko kick)

MARY	TEAM STATISTICS	MINN
15	First Downs	17
120	Rushing Yards	113
12-23-1	Passing	13-26-0
211	Passing Yards	155
331	Total Yards	268
2-3	Punt Returns - Yards	2-6
2-34	Kickoff Returns - Yards	4-70
5-36.8	Punts - Average	9-27.7
3-2	Fumbles - Lost	3-2
12-80	Penalties - Yards	6-54

INDIVIDUAL LEADERS
RUSHING
MARY: Scott 24-75, 2 TD; Maddox 2-17.
MINN: Kitzmann 24-76; Thompson 4-11.
PASSING
MARY: Dick 12-20-0, 211 yards.
MINN: Avery 12-23-0, 130 yards.
RECEIVING
MARY: White 8-126; Sievers 1-57.
MINN: Barber 4-58; Anhorn 5-49.

DECEMBER 20, 1978
TEXAS A&M 28, IOWA STATE 12

	1ST	2ND	3RD	4TH	FINAL
A&M	0	14	0	14	28
ISU	0	6	6	0	12

SCORING SUMMARY
ISU   Green 5 pass from Grant (kick failed)
A&M   Brothers 1 run (Franklin kick)
A&M   Carter 4 pass from Mosley (Franklin kick)
ISU   Green 28 pass (pass failed)
A&M   Dickey 19 run (Franklin kick)
A&M   Armstrong 5 run (Franklin kick)

A&M	TEAM STATISTICS	ISU
18	First Downs	20
322	Rushing Yards	220
5-10-0	Passing	9-29-0
44	Passing Yards	115
366	Total Yards	335
1-0	Punt Returns - Yards	4-8
4-88	Kickoff Returns - Yards	3-84
8-42.4	Punts - Average	7-34.9
2-1	Fumbles - Lost	3-2
5-71	Penalties - Yards	2-32

INDIVIDUAL LEADERS
RUSHING
A&M: Dickey 34-276, 1 TD.
ISU: Green 21-148, 1 TD.
PASSING
A&M: Mosley 5-10-0, 44 yards, 1 TD.
ISU: Grant 9-29-0, 115 yards, 1 TD.
RECEIVING
A&M: Carter 2-18, 1 TD.
ISU: Hardee 1-29; Preston 2-28.

DECEMBER 29, 1979
MISSOURI 24, SOUTH CAROLINA 14

	1ST	2ND	3RD	4TH	FINAL
MO	0	17	7	0	24
SC	6	0	8	0	14

SCORING SUMMARY
SC   McKinney 20 pass from Harper (run failed)
MO   FG Verrilli 22
MO   Newman 28 pass from Bradley (Verrilli kick)
MO   Bradley 1 run (Verrilli kick)
SC   Harper 11 run (McKinney pass from Harper)
MO   Ellis 12 run (Verrilli kick)

MO	TEAM STATISTICS	SC
17	First Downs	20
209	Rushing Yards	142
7-11-0	Passing	13-20-1
72	Passing Yards	121
281	Total Yards	263
2-(-2)	Punt Returns - Yards	1-(-1)
2-41	Kickoff Returns - Yards	4-79
6-44.3	Punts - Average	6-35.0
2-1	Fumbles - Lost	1-1
5-50	Penalties - Yards	2-16

INDIVIDUAL LEADERS
RUSHING
MO: Wilder 24-95; Ellis 12-81, 1 TD.
SC: Rogers 25-133; Clark 10-48.
PASSING
MO: Bradley 7-11-0, 72 yards, 1 TD.
SC: Harper 13-19-1, 121 yards, 1 TD.
RECEIVING
MO: Newman 1-28, 1 TD; Blair 2-22.
SC: McKinney 6-87, 1 TD; Rogers 3-18.

DECEMBER 27, 1980
ARKANSAS 34, TULANE 15

	1ST	2ND	3RD	4TH	FINAL
ARK	14	14	3	3	34
TUL	0	0	0	15	15

SCORING SUMMARY
ARK	Tolbert 1 run (Ordonez kick)
ARK	Anderson 80 punt return (Ordonez kick)
ARK	Clyde 9 pass from Jones (Ordonez kick)
ARK	Anderson 46 run (Ordonez kick)
ARK	FG Ordonez 40
TUL	Anderson 62 pass from Hall (Manalla kick)
ARK	FG Ordonez 27
TUL	Robinson 1 run (Hall run)

ARK	TEAM STATISTICS	TUL
22	First Downs	18
383	Rushing Yards	157
5-13-1	Passing	16-37-2
83	Passing Yards	241
466	Total Yards	398
2-80	Punt Returns - Yards	1-10
1-21	Kickoff Returns - Yards	5-122
4-42.5	Punts - Average	7-34.6
0-0	Fumbles - Lost	3-2
1-19	Penalties - Yards	3-15

INDIVIDUAL LEADERS
RUSHING
ARK: Anderson 11-156, 1 TD; Douglas 10-83.
TUL: Lewis 5-45; Robinson 6-44, 1 TD.
PASSING
ARK: Jones 5-13-1, 83 yards, 1 TD.
TUL: Hall 16-37-2, 241 yards, 1 TD.
RECEIVING
ARK: Walters 1-36; Holloway 1-23.
TUL: Anderson 2-88, 1 TD; Griffin 2-59.

DECEMBER 31, 1981
MISSISSIPPI STATE 10, KANSAS 0

	1ST	2ND	3RD	4TH	FINAL
MSU	7	3	0	0	10
KU	0	0	0	0	0

SCORING SUMMARY
MSU	Bond 17 run (Morgan kick)
MSU	FG Moore 14

MSU	TEAM STATISTICS	KU
12	First Downs	14
236	Rushing Yards	35
5-16-0	Passing	15-31-2
51	Passing Yards	171
287	Total Yards	206
4-38	Punt Returns - Yards	4-19
1-15	Kickoff Returns - Yards	3-68
9-49.1	Punts - Average	9-45.2
5-1	Fumbles - Lost	1-1
10-65	Penalties - Yards	7-82

INDIVIDUAL LEADERS
RUSHING
MSU: Bond 17-79, 1 TD; King 14-38.
KU: Taylor 20-61; Jones 7-20.
PASSING
MSU: Bond 5-16-0, 51 yards.
KU: Smith 8-22-2, 61 yards; Frederick 7-9-0, 110 yards.
RECEIVING
MSU: Haddix 2-16; Price 1-15.
KU: Capers 2-57; Taylor 7-41.

DECEMBER 31, 1982
AIR FORCE 36, VANDERBILT 28

	1ST	2ND	3RD	4TH	FINAL
AFA	7	7	3	19	36
VAN	7	14	7	0	28

SCORING SUMMARY
VAN	Jordan 28 pass from Taylor (Anderson kick)
AFA	Louthan 1 run (Pavlich kick)
AFA	Brown 19 run (Pavlich kick)
VAN	Roach 15 pass from Taylor (Anderson kick)
VAN	Jordan 4 pass from Taylor (Anderson kick)
AFA	FG Pavlich 21
VAN	Jordan 4 pass from Taylor (Anderson kick)
AFA	Sundquist 3 run (pass failed)
AFA	Kershner 3 run (pass failed)
AFA	Louthan 46 run (Pavlich kick)

AFA	TEAM STATISTICS	VAN
23	First Downs	26
331	Rushing Yards	35
11-17-0	Passing	38-51-3
136	Passing Yards	456
467	Total Yards	491
0-0	Punt Returns - Yards	2-7
4-84	Kickoff Returns - Yards	6-102
5-36.0	Punts - Average	2-32.5
1-0	Fumbles - Lost	2-2
8-75	Penalties - Yards	4-39
39:18	Possession Time	20:42

INDIVIDUAL LEADERS
RUSHING
AFA: Kershner 32-132, 1 TD; Louthan 16-74, 2 TD.
VAN: Edwards 5-21; Matthews 1-13.
PASSING
AFA: Louthan 11-17-0, 136 yards.
VAN: Taylor 38-51-3, 452 yards, 4 TD.
RECEIVING
AFA: Greenwood 6-77; Kirby 2-30.
VAN: Jordan 20-173, 3 TD; Scott 5-93.

DECEMBER 22, 1983
WEST VIRGINIA 20, KENTUCKY 16

	1ST	2ND	3RD	4TH	FINAL
WVU	3	0	7	10	20
UK	0	10	0	6	16

SCORING SUMMARY
WVU	FG Woodside 39
UK	Jenkins 26 pass from Mayes (Hutcherson kick)
UK	FG Hutcherson 32
WVU	Hollins 16 pass from Hostetler (Woodside kick)
WVU	Bennett 2 pass from Hostetler (Woodside kick)
WVU	FG Woodside 23
UK	Phillips 13 pass from Ransdell (kick failed)

WVU	TEAM STATISTICS	UK
18	First Downs	19
231	Rushing Yards	123
10-23-1	Passing	19-34-1
88	Passing Yards	216
319	Total Yards	339
1-15	Punt Returns - Yards	3-63
4-29	Kickoff Returns - Yards	3-62
6-39.7	Punts - Average	4-34.5
1-0	Fumbles - Lost	2-1
1-5	Penalties - Yards	1-15
30:48	Possession Time	29:12

INDIVIDUAL LEADERS
RUSHING
WVU: Gray 32-149; Hostetler 6-30.
UK: Adams 19-69; Lee 6-25.
PASSING
WVU: Hostetler 10-23-1, 88 yards, 2 TD.
UK: Jenkins 9-17-1, 73 yards; Ransdell 9-15-0, 117 yards, 1 TD.
RECEIVING
WVU: Hollins 3-22, 1 TD; Bennett 3-28, 1 TD.
UK: Phillips 6-78, 1 TD; Pitts 3-37.

DECEMBER 29, 1984
KENTUCKY 20, WISCONSIN 19

	1ST	2ND	3RD	4TH	FINAL
UK	0	7	10	3	20
WISC	10	6	3	0	19

SCORING SUMMARY
WISC	FG Gregoire 40
WISC	McFadden 3 pass from Howard (Gregoire kick)
WISC	FG Gregoire 27
UK	Logan 9 run (Worley kick)
WISC	FG Gregoire 20
UK	FG Worley 22
WISC	FG Gregoire 40
UK	Logan 27 pass from Ransdell (Worley kick)
UK	FG Worley 52

UK	TEAM STATISTICS	WISC
19	First Downs	17
124	Rushing Yards	181
18-34-0	Passing	19-30-2
188	Passing Yards	203
312	Total Yards	384
3-(-1)	Punt Returns - Yards	3-78
4-133	Kickoff Returns - Yards	5-100
6-37.5	Punts - Average	5-41.4
1-0	Fumbles - Lost	0-0
6-49	Penalties - Yards	13-133
28:57	Possession Time	31:03

INDIVIDUAL LEADERS
RUSHING
UK: Adams 18-62; Higgs 9-39.
WISC: Armentrout 15-105; Harrison 14-52.
PASSING
UK: Ransdell 18-34-0, 188 yards, 1 TD.
WISC: Howard 19-29-1, 203 yards, 1 TD.
RECEIVING
UK: Phillips 6-55; Adams 5-34.
WISC: Pearson 5-55; Toon 4-48.

DECEMBER 31, 1985
GEORGIA TECH 17, MICHIGAN STATE 14

	1ST	2ND	3RD	4TH	FINAL
GT	0	0	7	10	17
MSU	0	7	7	0	14

SCORING SUMMARY
MSU	Ingram 6 pass from Yarema (Caudell kick)
GT	Rampley 1 run (Bell kick)
MSU	Ingram 27 pass from Yarema (Caudell kick)
GT	FG Bell 40
GT	King 5 run (Bell kick)

GT	TEAM STATISTICS	MSU
16	First Downs	14
182	Rushing Yards	148
12-23-1	Passing	6-15-1
99	Passing Yards	85
281	Total Yards	233
1-11	Punt Returns - Yards	2-14
2-30	Kickoff Returns - Yards	4-47
6-37.8	Punts - Average	6-36.7
2-0	Fumbles - Lost	2-1
5-47	Penalties - Yards	3-28
35:03	Possession Time	24:57

INDIVIDUAL LEADERS
RUSHING
GT: King 16-122, 1 TD; Kelsey 8-30.
MSU: White 33-158; Morse 2-8.
PASSING
GT: Rampley 12-23-1, 99 yards.
MSU: Yarema 6-15-1, 85 yards, 2 TD.
RECEIVING
GT: Massey 2-23; Mayes 3-22.
MSU: Ingram 3-70, 2 TD; Rison 1-18.

December 31, 1986
Florida State 27, Indiana 13

	1ST	2ND	3RD	4TH	FINAL
FSU	6	7	7	7	27
IU	3	0	7	3	13

SCORING SUMMARY
IU	FG Stoyanovich 35
FSU	Smith 4 run (kick failed)
FSU	Smith 9 run (Schmidt kick)
FSU	Holloman 8 run (Schmidt kick)
IU	Powell 2 run (Stoyanovich kick)
IU	FG Stoyanovich 30
FSU	Holloman 10 run (Schmidt kick)

FSU	TEAM STATISTICS	IU
20	First Downs	23
288	Rushing Yards	215
6-14-1	Passing	11-25-1
54	Passing Yards	168
342	Total Yards	383
1-12	Punt Returns - Yards	1-7
4-97	Kickoff Returns - Yards	5-70
2-35.0	Punts - Average	2-35.0
2-1	Fumbles - Lost	1-0
6-50	Penalties - Yards	10-88
22:41	Possession Time	37:19

INDIVIDUAL LEADERS
RUSHING
FSU: Smith 25-205, 2 TD; Holloman 6-36, 2 TD.
IU: Thompson 28-127; Powell 6-38, 1 TD.
PASSING
FSU: McManus 6-14-1, 54 yards.
IU: Kramme 11-25-1, 168 yards.
RECEIVING
FSU: O'Malley 2-20; Gainer 1-19.
IU: Dawsey 5-74; Lilja 2-44.

December 22, 1987
Virginia 22, Brigham Young 16

	1ST	2ND	3RD	4TH	FINAL
UVA	7	7	0	8	22
BYU	3	0	6	7	16

SCORING SUMMARY
BYU	FG Chitty 20
UVA	Secules 2 run (Inderlied kick)
UVA	Morgan 25 run (Inderlied kick)
BYU	Whittingham 8 run (pass failed)
UVA	Ford 22 pass from Secules (Secules pass to Wilson)
BYU	Whittingham 1 pass from Covey (Chitty kick)

UVA	TEAM STATISTICS	BYU
22	First Downs	27
187	Rushing Yards	95
10-19-2	Passing	37-61-1
162	Passing Yards	394
349	Total Yards	489
1-8	Punt Returns - Yards	1-0
4-90	Kickoff Returns - Yards	3-57
3-42.7	Punts - Average	1-36.0
2-1	Fumbles - Lost	2-0
2-15	Penalties - Yards	7-64
25:47	Possession Time	34:13

INDIVIDUAL LEADERS
RUSHING
UVA: Morgan 10-82, 1 TD; Wilson 15-77.
BYU: Whittingham 10-53, 1 TD; Salito 7-31.
PASSING
UVA: Secules 10-19-2, 162 yards, 1 TD.
BYU: Covey 37-61-1, 394 yards, 1 TD.
RECEIVING
UVA: Ford 4-54 1 TD; Mattioli 2-43.
BYU: Miles 10-188; Bellini 9-59.

December 29, 1988
Florida 14, Illinois 10

	1ST	2ND	3RD	4TH	FINAL
FLA	7	0	0	7	14
ILL	0	7	0	3	10

SCORING SUMMARY
FLA	Smith 55 run (Francis kick)
ILL	Jones 30 run (Higgins kick)
ILL	FG Higgins 44
FLA	Smith 2 run (Francis kick)

FLA	TEAM STATISTICS	ILL
12	First Downs	17
187	Rushing Yards	55
8-16-2	Passing	20-38-2
69	Passing Yards	194
256	Total Yards	249
3-10	Punt Returns - Yards	0-0
3-90	Kickoff Returns - Yards	3-60
4-29.8	Punts - Average	7-35.3
1-1	Fumbles - Lost	1-1
5-36	Penalties - Yards	8-59
26:38	Possession Time	33:22

INDIVIDUAL LEADERS
RUSHING
FLA: Smith 28-159, 2 TD; McClendon 9-34.
ILL: Jones 18-88, 1 TD; Griffith 5-8.
PASSING
FLA: Morris 6-12-2, 50 yards.
ILL: George 20-37-2, 194 yards.
RECEIVING
FLA: Barber 4-29; Smith 2-19.
ILL: Bellamy 5-49; Williams 5-49.

December 28, 1989
Texas Tech 49, Duke 21

	1ST	2ND	3RD	4TH	FINAL
TT	14	14	14	7	49
DUKE	0	14	0	7	21

SCORING SUMMARY
TT	Gray 2 run (kick failed)
TT	Price 36 pass from Gill (Gill pass to Talkington)
TT	Gray 54 run (Elliott kick)
TT	Gray 18 run (Elliott kick)
DUKE	Zuberer 30 pass from Brown (Gardner kick)
DUKE	Colonna 25 pass from Brown (Gardner kick)
TT	Lynn 1 run (Elliott kick)
TT	Gill 1 run (Elliott kick)
DUKE	Colonna 16 pass from Brown (Gardner kick)
TT	Gray 32 run (Elliott kick)

TT	TEAM STATISTICS	DUKE
22	First Downs	19
349	Rushing Yards	67
6-14-0	Passing	25-42-2
174	Passing Yards	349
523	Total Yards	416
3-21	Punt Returns - Yards	1-0
3-42	Kickoff Returns - Yards	7-105
5-37.6	Punts - Average	5-36.4
0-0	Fumbles - Lost	3-2
6-40	Penalties - Yards	4-40
41:25	Possession Time	18:35

INDIVIDUAL LEADERS
RUSHING
TT: Gray 33-280, 4 TD; Lynn 13-64, 1 TD.
DUKE: Cuthbert 5-32; Boone 2-24.
PASSING
TT: Gill 6-13-0, 174 yards, 1 TD.
DUKE: Brown 17-30-1, 268 yards, 3 TD; Ray 7-11-1, 69 yards.
RECEIVING
TT: Price 3-89, 1 TD; Lynn 2-57.
DUKE: Hines 6-112; Colonna 5-63, 2 TD.

December 28, 1990
NC State 31, Southern Miss 27

	1ST	2ND	3RD	4TH	FINAL
NCSU	14	3	7	7	31
USM	6	8	7	6	27

SCORING SUMMARY
USM	Montgomery 10 pass from Favre (kick failed)
NCSU	Jordan 10 run (Fowble kick)
NCSU	Downs 2 run (Fowble kick)
USM	Montgomery 13 pass from Favre (Favre pass to Welch)
NCSU	FG Fowble 22
USM	Smith 1 run (Taylor kick)
NCSU	Jurgens 12 pass from Jordan (Fowble kick)
NCSU	Manior 41 run (Fowble kick)
USM	Welch 5 run (pass failed)

NCSU	TEAM STATISTICS	USM
23	First Downs	19
193	Rushing Yards	44
15-25-1	Passing	28-39-1
166	Passing Yards	341
359	Total Yards	385
2-18	Punt Returns - Yards	4-16
5-62	Kickoff Returns - Yards	5-48
7-26.0	Punts - Average	5-34.6
2-0	Fumbles - Lost	4-2
7-67	Penalties - Yards	9-73
32:36	Possession Time	27:24

INDIVIDUAL LEADERS
RUSHING
NCSU: Manior 10-71, 1 TD; Downs 9-53, 1 TD.
USM: Smith 9-35, 1 TD; Welch 2-11, 1 TD.
PASSING
NCSU: Jordan 15-25-1, 166 yards, 1 TD.
USM: Favre 28-39-1, 341 yards, 2 TD.
RECEIVING
NCSU: Davenport 5-37; Harrison 2-29.
USM: Jackson 4-116; Montgomery 5-85, 2 TD.

ALOHA BOWL

PROFILE

Site: Honolulu
Stadium: Aloha Stadium
Capacity: 50,000
Surface: AstroTurf

PLAYING SITES

Aloha Stadium, 1982-2000

NAME CHANGES

Aloha Bowl, 1982-84
Eagle Aloha Bowl, 1985-88
Jeep Eagle Aloha Bowl, 1989-96
Eagle Aloha Bowl Football Classic, 1997
Jeep Aloha Christmas Football Classic, 1998-2000

SEASON	DATE	PRE-GAME RANK	TEAMS	SCORE	FINAL RANK	MOST VALUABLE PLAYERS	ATT.
1982	Dec. 25, 1982	9	Washington	21	7	Tim Cowan, Washington, QB	30,055
		16	Maryland	20	20	Tony Caldwell, Washington, LB	
1983	Dec. 26, 1983		Penn State	13		George Reynolds, Penn State, P	37,212
			Washington	10		Danny Greene, Washington, WR	
1984	Dec. 29, 1984	10	SMU	27	8	Jeff Atkins, SMU, RB	41,777
		17	Notre Dame	20		Jerry Ball, SMU, NG	
1985	Dec. 28, 1985	15	Alabama	24	13	Gene Jelks, Alabama, RB	35,183
			Southern Cal	3		Cornelius Bennett, Alabama, LB	
1986	Dec. 27, 1986	16	Arizona	30	11	Alfred Jenkins, Arizona, QB	26,743
			North Carolina	21		Chuck Cecil, Arizona, S	
1987	Dec. 25, 1987	10	UCLA	20	9	Troy Aikman, UCLA, QB	24,839
			Florida	16		Emmitt Smith, Florida, RB	
1988	Dec. 25, 1988	18	Washington State	24	16	Victor Wood, Washington State, WR	35,132
		14	Houston	22	18	David Dacus, Houston, QB	
1989	Dec. 25, 1989	22	Michigan State	33	16	Blake Ezor, Michigan State, TB	50,000
		23	Hawaii	13		Chris Roscoe, Hawaii, WR	
1990	Dec. 25, 1990		Syracuse	28		Marvin Graves, Syracuse, QB	14,185
			Arizona	0		Todd Burden, Arizona, CB	
1991	Dec. 25, 1991		Georgia Tech	18		Shawn Jones, Georgia Tech, QB	34,433
		17	Stanford	17	22	Tommy Vardell, Stanford, RB	
1992	Dec. 25, 1992		Kansas	23	22	Dana Stubblefield, Kansas, DT	42,933
		25	Brigham Young	20		Tom Young, Brigham Young, QB	
1993	Dec. 25, 1993	17	Colorado	41	16	Rashaan Salaam, Colorado, TB	44,009
		25T	Fresno State	30		Trent Dilfer, Fresno State, QB	
1994	Dec. 25, 1994		Boston College	12	23	David Green, RB and Mike Mamula, DE, Boston College	44,862
		11	Kansas State	7	19	Joe Gordon, Kansas State, CB	
1995	Dec. 25, 1995	11	Kansas	51	9	Mark Williams, Kansas, QB	41,111
			UCLA	30		Karim Abdul-Jabbar, UCLA, RB	
1996	Dec. 25, 1996		Navy	42		Chris McCoy, Navy, QB	43,380
			California	38		Pat Barnes, California, QB	
1997	Dec. 25, 1997	21	Washington	51	18	Rashaan Shehee, Washington, RB	44,598
		25	Michigan State	23			
1998	Dec. 25, 1998		Colorado	51		Mike Moschetti, Colorado, QB	46,451
		21	Oregon	43		Akili Smith, Oregon, QB	
1999	Dec. 25, 1999		Wake Forest	23		Ben Sankey, Wake Forest, QB	40,974
			Arizona State	3			
2000	Dec. 25, 2000		Boston College	31		Tim Hasselbeck, Boston College, QB	24,397
			Arizona State	17			

DECEMBER 25, 1982
WASHINGTON 21, MARYLAND 20

	1ST	2ND	3RD	4TH	FINAL
WASH	7	7	0	7	21
MD	0	6	6	8	20

SCORING SUMMARY
WASH Allen 27 pass from Cowan (Nelson kick)
MD D'Addio 6 pass from Esiason (kick failed)
WASH Allen 71 pass from Cowan (Nelson kick)
MD Tice 36 pass from Esiason (run failed)
MD Nash 2 run (Tice pass from Esiason)
WASH Allen 11 pass from Cowan (Nelson kick)

WASH	TEAM STATISTICS	MD
20	First Downs	17
63	Rushing Yards	68
35-56-0	Passing	19-32-1
369	Passing Yards	251
432	Total Yards	319
5-45.4	Punts - Average	7-38.4
4-4	Fumbles - Lost	2-1
7-50	Penalties - Yards	8-55

INDIVIDUAL LEADERS
RUSHING
WASH: Robinson 16-50.
MD: Nash 11-41, 1 TD.
PASSING
WASH: Cowan 33-53-0, 350 yards, 3 TD.
MD: Esiason 19-32-1, 251 yards, 2 TD.
RECEIVING
WASH: Allen 8-152, 3 TD; Skansi 10-87.
MD: Tice 6-85, 1 TD; D'Addio 4-30, 1 TD.

DECEMBER 26, 1983
PENN STATE 13, WASHINGTON 10

	1ST	2ND	3RD	4TH	FINAL
PSU	3	0	0	10	13
WASH	0	10	0	0	10

SCORING SUMMARY
PSU FG Gancitano 23
WASH Greene 57 punt return (Jaeger kick)
WASH FG Jaeger 39
PSU FG Gancitano 49
PSU Dozier 2 run (Gancitano kick)

PSU	TEAM STATISTICS	WASH
15	First Downs	18
95	Rushing Yards	126
14-34-1	Passing	19-40-0
118	Passing Yards	153
213	Total Yards	279
8-46.8	Punts - Average	9-39.6
0-0	Fumbles - Lost	0-0
7-6	Penalties - Yards	6-50

INDIVIDUAL LEADERS
RUSHING
PSU: Williams 12-48; Dozier 15-37, 1 TD.
WASH: Jackson 7-34.
PASSING
PSU: Strang 14-34-1, 118 yards.
WASH: Pelluer 19-40-0, 153 yards.
RECEIVING
PSU: DiMidio 4-35.
WASH: Pattison 6-55; Wroten 4-25.

DECEMBER 29, 1984
SMU 27, NOTRE DAME 20

	1ST	2ND	3RD	4TH	FINAL
SMU	7	10	0	10	27
ND	0	10	7	3	20

SCORING SUMMARY
SMU Atkins 7 run (Brownlee kick)
SMU Morrison 12 pass from King (Brownlee kick)
ND Pinkett 17 pass from Beuerlein (Carney kick)
ND FG Carney 51
SMU FG Brownlee 47
ND Brooks 11 run (Carney kick)
SMU FG Brownlee 30
SMU Dupard 2 run (Brownlee kick)
ND FG Carney 31

SMU	TEAM STATISTICS	ND
26	First Downs	22
226	Rushing Yards	218
9-17-0	Passing	11-23-0
153	Passing Yards	144
379	Total Yards	362
2-25	Punt Returns - Yards	4-42
2-55	Kickoff Returns - Yards	4-105
5-41.0	Punts - Average	4-41.5
4-0	Fumbles - Lost	0-0
5-55	Penalties - Yards	5-44

INDIVIDUAL LEADERS
RUSHING
SMU: Atkins 17-112, 1 TD; Dupard 23-103, 1 TD.
ND: Pinkett 24-136; Jefferson 9-60.
PASSING
SMU: King 9-17-0, 153 yards, 1 TD.
ND: Beuerlein 11-23-0, 144 yards, 1 TD.
RECEIVING
SMU: Dupard 1-39; Atkins 2-31.
ND: Jefferson 2-37; Howard 2-24.

December 28, 1985
Alabama 24, Southern Cal 3

	1ST	2ND	3RD	4TH	FINAL
ALA	3	0	7	14	24
USC	0	3	0	0	3

SCORING SUMMARY

ALA	FG Tiffin 48
USC	FG Shafer 24
ALA	Turner 1 run (Tiffin kick)
ALA	Whitehurst 24 pass from Shula (Tiffin kick)
ALA	Bell 14 run (Tiffin kick)

December 27, 1986
Arizona 30, North Carolina 21

	1ST	2ND	3RD	4TH	FINAL
ARIZ	0	13	17	0	30
UNC	0	0	7	14	21

SCORING SUMMARY

ARIZ	FG Coston 31
ARIZ	Adams 1 run (Coston kick)
ARIZ	FG Coston 38
ARIZ	FG Valder 52
ARIZ	Horton 13 pass from Jenkins (Coston kick)
ARIZ	Greathouse 5 run (Coston kick)
UNC	Dorn 58 run (Gliarmis kick)
UNC	Marriott 6 pass from Maye (Gliarmis kick)
UNC	Maye 2 run (Gliarmis kick)

ARIZ	TEAM STATISTICS	UNC
15	First Downs	18
137	Rushing Yards	197
12-23-1	Passing	18-35-0
187	Passing Yards	178
324	Total Yards	375
7-31.4	Punts - Average	6-36.5
3-1	Fumbles - Lost	5-5
6-45	Penalties - Yards	3-25

INDIVIDUAL LEADERS

RUSHING
ARIZ: Adams 23-81, 1 TD; Greathouse 6-18, 1 TD.
UNC: Dorn 7-101, 1 TD; Starr 19-54.

PASSING
ARIZ: Jenkins 12-23-1, 187 yards, 1 TD.
UNC: Maye 17-34-0, 171 yards, 1 TD.

RECEIVING
ARIZ: Adams 3-77; Lotti 1-25.
UNC: Starr 7-53; Streater 2-39.

December 25, 1987
UCLA 20, Florida 16

	1ST	2ND	3RD	4TH	FINAL
UCLA	3	7	7	3	20
UF	7	3	0	6	16

SCORING SUMMARY

UCLA	FG Velasco 34
UF	Simmons 7 pass from Bell (McGinty kick)
UF	FG McGinty 32
UCLA	Brown 1 run (Velasco kick)
UCLA	Thompson 5 pass from Aikman (Velasco kick)
UCLA	FG Velasco 32
UF	Williams 14 pass from Bell (kick failed)

UCLA	TEAM STATISTICS	UF
15	First Downs	24
48	Rushing Yards	185
19-30-2	Passing	19-38-0
173	Passing Yards	188
221	Total Yards	373

INDIVIDUAL LEADERS

RUSHING
UCLA: Ball 23-49; Brown 10-29, 1 TD.
UF: Smith 17-128; Williams 8-43.

PASSING
UCLA: Aikman 19-30-0, 173 yards, 1 TD.
UF: Bell 19-38-0, 188 yards, 2 TD.

RECEIVING
UCLA: Anderson 4-52; Pickert 3-37.
UF: Snead 3-62; Smith 4-19.

December 25, 1988
Washington State 24, Houston 22

	1ST	2ND	3RD	4TH	FINAL
WSU	0	24	0	0	24
HOU	3	6	6	7	22

SCORING SUMMARY

HOU	FG Anderson 27
WSU	Wood 9 fumble return (Hanson kick)
WSU	Wood 15 pass from Rosenbach (Hanson kick)
WSU	FG Hanson 33
HOU	Weatherspoon 1 run (kick failed)
WSU	Rosenbach 1 run (Hanson kick)
HOU	Mason 53 pass from Dacus (pass failed)
HOU	Weatherspoon 2 pass from Dacus (Anderson kick)

WSU	TEAM STATISTICS	HOU
23	First Downs	13
154	Rushing Yards	68
19-36-1	Passing	17-40-2
306	Passing Yards	241
460	Total Yards	309
6-46.0	Punts - Average	8-45.4
2-1	Fumbles - Lost	2-1
11-95	Penalties - Yards	9-58

INDIVIDUAL LEADERS

RUSHING
WSU: Broussard 33-139.
HOU: Weatherspoon 14-80, 1 TD.

PASSING
WSU: Rosenbach 19-36-1, 306 yards, 1 TD.
HOU: Dacus 8-11-0, 153 yards, 2 TD; Ware 8-28-2, 44 yards.

RECEIVING
WSU: Stallworth 8-120.
HOU: Mason 2-83, 1 TD; Dixon 4-52.

December 25, 1989
Michigan State 33, Hawaii 13

	1ST	2ND	3RD	4TH	FINAL
MSU	6	13	0	14	33
HAW	0	0	6	7	13

SCORING SUMMARY

MSU	Ezor 3 run (kick blocked)
MSU	Ezor 2 run (Langeloh kick)
MSU	FG Langeloh 30
MSU	FG Langeloh 34
HAW	Roscoe 11 pass from Gabriel (kick blocked)
MSU	Hickson 1 run (Langeloh kick)
HAW	McArthur 23 pass from Gabriel (Khan kick)
MSU	Ezor 26 run (Langeloh kick)

MSU	TEAM STATISTICS	HAW
21	First Downs	19
225	Rushing Yards	82
7-12-2	Passing	20-33-4
116	Passing Yards	198
341	Total Yards	280
0-0	Punt Returns - Yards	2-31
1-2	Kickoff Returns - Yards	7-174
3-50.7	Punts - Average	1-27.0
0-0	Fumbles - Lost	7-4
9-85	Penalties - Yards	3-30

INDIVIDUAL LEADERS

RUSHING
MSU: Ezor 41-179, 3 TD; Hawkins 1-31.
HAW: McArthur 2-34; Ahuna 3-21.

PASSING
MSU: Enos 7-12-2, 116 yards.
HAW: Gabriel 19-31-3, 197 yards, 2 TD.

RECEIVING
MSU: Bradley 4-85; Hickson 1-13.
HAW: Roscoe 6-71, 1 TD; Lau 2-34.

December 25, 1990
Syracuse 28, Arizona 0

	1ST	2ND	3RD	4TH	FINAL
SYR	7	7	0	14	28
ARIZ	0	0	0	0	0

SCORING SUMMARY

SYR	Graves 5 run (Biskup kick)
SYR	Richardson 47 pass from Graves (Biskup kick)
SYR	Gedney 6 pass from Graves (Biskup kick)
SYR	Graves 5 run (Biskup kick)

SYR	TEAM STATISTICS	ARIZ
20	First Downs	14
207	Rushing Yards	149
10-20-2	Passing	10-23-0
145	Passing Yards	77
352	Total Yards	226
3-40.0	Punts - Average	7-31.7
1-0	Fumbles - Lost	0-0
3-20	Penalties - Yards	5-40
30:01	Possession Time	29:59

INDIVIDUAL LEADERS

RUSHING
SYR: Graves 11-45, 2 TD; Walker 10-44.
ARIZ: Hampton 3-27; Veal 8-26.

PASSING
SYR: Graves 10-19-1, 145 yards, 2 TD.
ARIZ: Malauulu 7-14-0, 55 yards.

RECEIVING
SYR: Richardson 1-47, 1 TD; Gedney 2-30, 1 TD.
ARIZ: Vaughn 3-38; Jan 2-20.

December 25, 1991
Georgia Tech 18, Stanford 17

	1ST	2ND	3RD	4TH	FINAL
GT	10	0	0	8	18
STAN	7	10	0	0	17

SCORING SUMMARY

STAN	Vardell 6 run (Mills kick)
GT	Smith 2 pass from Jones (Sisson kick)
GT	FG Sisson 24
STAN	FG Mills 38
STAN	Vardell 2 run (Mills kick)
GT	Jones 1 run (Lincoln run)

GT	TEAM STATISTICS	STAN
14	First Downs	19
198	Rushing Yards	159
14-30-1	Passing	16-32-1
61	Passing Yards	170
259	Total Yards	329
7-47.4	Punts - Average	6-42.3
3-2	Fumbles - Lost	2-1
6-50	Penalties - Yards	6-49

INDIVIDUAL LEADERS

RUSHING
GT: Jones 10-48, 1 TD; Smith 7-47.
STAN: Vardell 21-104, 2 TD; Milburn 12-56.

PASSING
GT: Jones 14-29-1, 61 yards, 1 TD.
STAN: Stenstrom 16-32-1, 170 yards.

RECEIVING
GT: Wilkerson 3-25; Lester 3-20; Smith 3-17, 1 TD.
STAN: Walsh 5-61; Lasley 5-33.

December 25, 1992
Kansas 23, Brigham Young 20

	1ST	2ND	3RD	4TH	FINAL
KU	9	3	0	11	23
BYU	7	7	6	0	20

SCORING SUMMARY

BYU	Heimuli 94 kickoff return (Lauder kick)
KU	Harris 74 pass from Gay (Eichloff kick)
KU	Safety (Willis tackled in end zone)
BYU	Willis 29 run (Lauder kick)
KU	FG Eichloff 42
BYU	Sterling 10 pass from Young (pass failed)
KU	Hilleary 1 run (Hilleary run)
KU	FG Eichloff 48

KU	TEAM STATISTICS	BYU
18	First Downs	19
172	Rushing Yards	142
12-24-0	Passing	15-31-1
200	Passing Yards	262
372	Total Yards	404
8-48.3	Punts - Average	4-48.3
0-0	Fumbles - Lost	1-0
7-55	Penalties - Yards	7-73

INDIVIDUAL LEADERS

PASSING
KU: Hilleary 11-23-0, 126 yards; Gay 1-1-0, 74 yards, 1 TD.
BYU: Young 15-31-1, 262 yards, 1 TD.

DECEMBER 25, 1993
COLORADO 41, FRESNO STATE 30

	1ST	2ND	3RD	4TH	FINAL
COLO	10	10	14	7	41
FRES	0	10	14	6	30

SCORING SUMMARY
COLO   Salaam 2 run (Berger kick)
COLO   FG Berger 44
COLO   Hill 7 run (Berger kick)
FRES   FG Mahoney 27
COLO   FG Berger 49
FRES   Seabron 68 fumble return (Mahoney kick)
COLO   Salaam 40 run (Berger kick)
FRES   Daigle 1 run (kick failed)
COLO   Leomiti 28 fumble return (Berger kick)
FRES   Winans 8 pass from Dilfer (Daigle pass from Dilfer)
COLO   Salaam 4 run (Berger kick)
FRES   Winans 11 pass from Dilfer (pass failed)

COLO	TEAM STATISTICS	FRES
19	First Downs	34
271	Rushing Yards	3
8-15-0	Passing	37-63-1
124	Passing Yards	523
395	Total Yards	526
4-43.3	Punts - Average	3-31.3
1-1	Fumbles - Lost	5-4
7-84	Penalties - Yards	9-88

INDIVIDUAL LEADERS
RUSHING
COLO: Salaam 23-135, 3 TD; Warren 10-68.
FRES: Rivers 14-37; Daigle 5-14, 1 TD.
PASSING
COLO: Stewart 8-15-0, 124 yards.
FRES: Dilfer 37-63-1, 523 yards, 2 TD.
RECEIVING
COLO: Westbrook 1-43; Johnson 3-27.
FRES: Dunn 9-149; Harris 5-87.

DECEMBER 25, 1994
BOSTON COLLEGE 12, KANSAS STATE 7

	1ST	2ND	3RD	4TH	FINAL
BC	7	2	0	3	12
KSU	7	0	0	0	7

SCORING SUMMARY
BC   Smith 2 run (Gordon kick)
KSU   Sublette recovered blocked punt in end zone (Gramatica kick)
BC   Safety (May tackled in end zone)
BC   FG Gordon 35

BC	TEAM STATISTICS	KSU
13	First Downs	7
149	Rushing Yards	-61
12-29-1	Passing	13-31-2
168	Passing Yards	185
317	Total Yards	124
8-40.6	Punts - Average	11-45.5
0-0	Fumbles - Lost	0-0
7-84	Penalties - Yards	9-56
35:42	Possession Time	24:18

INDIVIDUAL LEADERS
RUSHING
BC: Green 28-127; Smith 16-22, 1 TD.
KSU: Smith 9-18; Edwards 4-7.
PASSING
BC: Hartsell 12-29-1, 168 yards.
KSU: May 13-31-2, 185 yards.
RECEIVING
BC: Watson 2-80; Mitchell 2-32.
KSU: Lockett 5-99; Running 3-39.

DECEMBER 25, 1995
KANSAS 51, UCLA 30

	1ST	2ND	3RD	4TH	FINAL
KU	7	10	20	14	51
UCLA	0	0	7	23	30

SCORING SUMMARY
KU   Moore 9 pass from Williams (McCord kick)
KU   Henley 49 run (McCord kick)
KU   FG McCord 27
KU   Henley 2 run (kick failed)
UCLA   Melsby 8 pass from McNown (Merten kick)
KU   Byrd 77 pass from Williams (McCord kick)
KU   Carter 27 pass from Williams (McCord kick)
UCLA   Jordan 8 pass from McNown (Merten kick)
UCLA   Abdul-Jabbar 5 run (Melsby pass from McNown)
KU   Williams 6 run (McCord kick)
UCLA   Melsby 7 pass from McNown (Abdul-Jabbar run)
KU   Vann 67 run (McCord kick)

KU	TEAM STATISTICS	UCLA
21	First Downs	21
277	Rushing Yards	286
19-28-1	Passing	15-38-0
292	Passing Yards	136
569	Total Yards	422
2-48.0	Punts - Average	4-44.8
0-0	Fumbles - Lost	1-1
4-32	Penalties - Yards	6-37

INDIVIDUAL LEADERS
RUSHING
KU: Henley 13-107, 2 TD; Vann 5-78, 1 TD.
UCLA: Abdul-Jabbar 26-152, 1 TD; McNown 11-82.
PASSING
KU: Williams 18-27-1, 288 yards, 3 TD.
UCLA: McNown 13-34-0, 121 yards, 3 TD.
RECEIVING
KU: Byrd 4-116, 1 TD; Henley 3-41.
UCLA: Melsby 5-35, 2 TD; Abdul-Jabbar 4-34.

DECEMBER 25, 1996
NAVY 42, CALIFORNIA 38

	1ST	2ND	3RD	4TH	FINAL
NAVY	7	21	0	14	42
CAL	13	22	0	3	38

SCORING SUMMARY
CAL   O'Neal 100 kickoff return (kick failed)
NAVY   Cannada 7 run (Vanderhorst kick)
CAL   Shaw 6 pass from Barnes (Longwell kick)
NAVY   McCoy 1 run (Vanderhorst kick)
NAVY   Scott 4 run (Vanderhorst kick)
CAL   Bullard 8 pass from Barnes (Benjamin pass from Barnes)
CAL   O'Neal 31 run (Longwell kick)
NAVY   McCoy 2 run (Vanderhorst kick)
CAL   Shaw 20 pass from Barnes (Longwell kick)
CAL   FG Longwell 41
NAVY   Fay 3 run (Vanderhorst kick)
NAVY   Fay 10 run (Vanderhorst kick)

NAVY	TEAM STATISTICS	CAL
25	First Downs	24
251	Rushing Yards	121
14-21-1	Passing	27-38-0
395	Passing Yards	313
646	Total Yards	434
2-43.0	Punts - Average	4-52.8
1-1	Fumbles - Lost	1-1
4-21	Penalties - Yards	5-40

INDIVIDUAL LEADERS
RUSHING
NAVY: Nelson 15-119; McCoy 19-61, 2 TD.
CAL: O'Neal 22-78, 1 TD; Benjamin 1-32.
PASSING
NAVY: McCoy 9-13-1, 277 yards; Fay 5-8-0, 118 yards.
CAL: Barnes 27-38-0, 313 yards, 3 TD.
RECEIVING
NAVY: Schemm 5-194; Plaskonos 2-58.
CAL: Benjamin 8-95; Gonzalez 9-69.

DECEMBER 25, 1997
WASHINGTON 51, MICHIGAN STATE 23

	1ST	2ND	3RD	4TH	FINAL
WASH	14	17	13	7	51
MSU	7	3	7	6	23

SCORING SUMMARY
WASH   Shehee 33 run (Lentz kick)
WASH   Coleman 15 pass from Huard (Lentz kick)
MSU   Scott 12 pass from Schultz (Edinger kick)
WASH   Coleman 22 pass from Huard (Lentz kick)
WASH   FG Lentz 41
MSU   FG Edinger 43
WASH   Parrish 56 interception return (Lentz kick)
WASH   Shehee 15 run (Lentz kick)
MSU   Scott 28 pass from Schultz (Edinger kick)
WASH   Reed 64 run (kick failed)
WASH   Towns 66 interception return (Lentz kick)
MSU   Richardson 21 pass from Burke (kick failed)

WASH	TEAM STATISTICS	MSU
23	First Downs	15
298	Rushing Yards	47
18-30-0	Passing	20-35-3
179	Passing Yards	296
477	Total Yards	343
2-7	Punt Returns - Yards	4-70
1-25	Kickoff Returns - Yards	8-217
6-39.8	Punts - Average	3-30.0
2-1	Fumbles - Lost	6-2
13-126	Penalties - Yards	4-28

INDIVIDUAL LEADERS
RUSHING
WASH: Shehee 29-193, 2 TD; Reed 2-70, 1 TD.
MSU: Irvin 15-59; McFadden 2-10.
PASSING
WASH: Huard 18-30-0, 179 yards, 2 TD.
MSU: Schultz 14-24-3, 220 yards, 2 TD; Burke 6-10-0, 76 yards, 1 TD.
RECEIVING
WASH: Coleman 5-68, 2 TD; Pathon 4-54.
MSU: Scott 5-114, 2 TD; Richardson 3-42, 1 TD.

DECEMBER 25, 1998
COLORADO 51, OREGON 43

	1ST	2ND	3RD	4TH	FINAL
COLO	17	20	7	7	51
ORE	0	14	7	22	43

SCORING SUMMARY
COLO   Kelly 93 kickoff return (Aldrich kick)
COLO   FG Aldrich 48
COLO   Green 5 pass from Moschetti (Aldrich kick)
ORE   Latimer 11 run (Villegas kick)
COLO   Stiggers 58 pass from Moschetti (Aldrich kick)
ORE   Latimer 4 run (Villegas kick)
COLO   FG Aldrich 41
COLO   Chiaverini 72 pass from Moschetti (Aldrich kick)
COLO   FG Aldrich 23
COLO   Wheeler 52 interception return (Aldrich kick)
ORE   Weaver 9 pass from Smith (Villegas kick)
ORE   Latimer 1 run (Villegas kick)
COLO   Graham 20 pass from Moschetti (Aldrich kick)
ORE   Smith 1 run (Villegas kick)
ORE   Haynes 42 pass from Smith (Nero pass from Smith)

COLO	TEAM STATISTICS	ORE
13	First Downs	27
176	Rushing Yards	71
12-24-0	Passing	24-45-1
221	Passing Yards	456
397	Total Yards	527
3-1	Punt Returns - Yards	3-56
4-114	Kickoff Returns - Yards	7-138
6-51.5	Punts - Average	4-48.3
3-1	Fumbles - Lost	5-5
8-75	Penalties - Yards	4-30
26:42	Possession Time	33:18

INDIVIDUAL LEADERS
RUSHING
COLO: Cherrington 10-92; Stiggers 1-28.
ORE: Latimer 19-74, 3 TD; Chance 1-4.
PASSING
COLO: Moschetti 11-23-0, 213 yards, 4 TD.
ORE: Smith 24-45-1, 456 yards, 2 TD.
RECEIVING
COLO: Chiaverini 3-96, 1 TD; Stiggers 3-81, 1 TD.
ORE: Haynes 7-148, 1 TD; Griffin 8-146.

DECEMBER 25, 1999
WAKE FOREST 23, ARIZONA STATE 3

	1ST	2ND	3RD	4TH	FINAL
WFU	3	0	10	10	23
ASU	0	3	0	0	3

SCORING SUMMARY
WFU	FG Burdick 22
ASU	FG Barth 46
WFU	FG Burdick 24
WFU	Caldwell 56 pass from Sankey (Burdick kick)
WFU	Kane 1 run (Burdick kick)
WFU	FG Burdick 43

WFU	TEAM STATISTICS	ASU
15	First Downs	11
162	Rushing Yards	94
13-22-1	Passing	15-26-0
188	Passing Yards	70
350	Total Yards	164
6-36.0	Punts - Average	9-35.0
0-0	Fumbles - Lost	3-2
1-15	Penalties - Yards	3-21
34:14	Possession Time	25:46

INDIVIDUAL LEADERS
RUSHING
WFU: Kane 20-83, 1 TD; Sankey 15-56.
ASU: Redmond 17-93; Green 7-28.
PASSING
WFU: Sankey 13-22-1, 188 yards, 1 TD.
ASU: Goodman 10-16-0, 42 yards.
RECEIVING
WFU: Caldwell 1-56, 1 TD; Deese 3-38.
ASU: Heap 5-39; Jennings 1-11.

DECEMBER 25, 2000
BOSTON COLLEGE 31, ARIZONA STATE 17

	1ST	2ND	3RD	4TH	FINAL
BC	10	0	14	7	31
ASU	7	3	0	7	17

SCORING SUMMARY
ASU	Pace 14 run (Barth kick)
BC	Washington 10 run (Sutphin kick)
BC	FG Sutphin 50
ASU	FG Barth 28
BC	Dewalt 58 pass from Hasselbeck (Sutphin kick)
BC	Read 40 pass from Hasselbeck (Sutphin kick)
BC	Washington 11 run (Sutphin kick)
ASU	Dennard 31 pass from Cooper (Barth kick)

BC	TEAM STATISTICS	ASU
14	First Downs	20
180	Rushing Yards	140
9-22-1	Passing	17-34-2
209	Passing Yards	220
389	Total Yards	360
4-17	Punt Returns - Yards	5-19
4-29	Kickoff Returns - Yards	3-60
6-43.7	Punts - Average	6-43.8
2-1	Fumbles - Lost	4-3
6-62	Penalties - Yards	3-30
24:27	Possession Time	35:33

INDIVIDUAL LEADERS
RUSHING
BC: Washington 22-109, 2 TD; Hasselbeck 2-68.
ASU: Pace 25-139, 1 TD; Hightower 7-34.
PASSING
BC: Hasselbeck 9-21-1, 209 yards, 2 TD.
ASU: Goodman 9-19-1, 73 yards; Krohn 6-10-0, 74 yards.
RECEIVING
BC: Dewalt 2-88, 1 TD; Read 2-42, 1 TD.
ASU: Williams 6-78; McDonald 4-61.

AVIATION BOWL

PROFILE

Site: Dayton, Ohio
Stadium: Welcome Stadium
Capacity: 10,000
Surface: Grass

SEASON	DATE	PRE-GAME RANK	TEAMS	SCORE	FINAL RANK	MOST VALUABLE PLAYERS	ATT.
1961	Dec. 9, 1961		**New Mexico**	**28**		Bobby Santiago, New Mexico, RB	3,694
			Western Michigan	**12**		Chuck Cummings, New Mexico, G	

DECEMBER 9, 1961
NEW MEXICO 28, WESTERN MICHIGAN 12

	1ST	2ND	3RD	4TH	FINAL
UNM	14	0	14	0	28
WMU	6	0	0	6	12

SCORING SUMMARY
UNM	Cromartie 2 run (kick failed)
UNM	Santiago 10 run (Morgan run)
WMU	White 4 run (run failed)
UNM	Morgan 10 run (run failed)
UNM	Cummings 43 interception return (Bradford run)
WMU	Cooke 5 pass from Chlebeck (pass failed)

UNM	TEAM STATISTICS	WMU
20	First Downs	18
339	Rushing Yards	96
0-4-0	Passing	18-33-2
0	Passing Yards	207
339	Total Yards	303
7-33.0	Punts - Average	4-36.0

INDIVIDUAL LEADERS
RUSHING
UNM: Santiago 10-83, 1 TD.
WMU: White 10-43, 1 TD.

BACARDI BOWL

PROFILE

Site: Havana, Cuba
Stadium: Tropical Stadium
Surface: Grass

SEASON	DATE	PRE-GAME RANK	TEAMS	SCORE	FINAL RANK	MOST VALUABLE PLAYERS	ATT.
1936	Jan. 1, 1937		**Auburn**	**7**			12,000
			Villanova	**7**			

JANUARY 1, 1937
AUBURN 7, VILLANOVA 7

	1ST	2ND	3RD	4TH	FINAL
AUB	7	0	0	0	7
NOVA	0	0	0	7	7

AUB	TEAM STATISTICS	NOVA
9	First Downs	7
152	Rushing Yards	129
2-12-2	Passing	2-6-1
29	Passing Yards	24
181	Total Yards	153

BLUEBONNET BOWL

PROFILE

Site: Houston
Stadium: Astrodome
Capacity: 60,000
Surface: AstroTurf

PLAYING SITES

Rice Stadium, 1959-67 and 1985
Astrodome, 1964-84 and 1986-87

NAME CHANGES

Bluebonnet Bowl, 1959-67 and 1977-87
Astro-Bluebonnet Bowl, 1968-76

SEASON	DATE	PRE-GAME RANK	TEAMS	SCORE	FINAL RANK	MOST VALUABLE PLAYERS	ATT.
1959	Dec. 19, 1959	7	Clemson	23		Lowndes Shingler, Clemson, QB	55,000
		11	TCU	7		Bob Lilly, TCU, DT	
1960	Dec. 17, 1960	9	Alabama	3		Lee Roy Jordan, Alabama, LB	68,000
			Texas	3		James Saxton, Texas, QB	
1961	Dec. 16, 1961		Kansas	33		Ken Coleman, Kansas, FB	52,000
		17	Rice	7		Elvin Basham, Kansas, G	
1962	Dec. 22, 1962		Missouri	14		Bill Tobin, Missouri, B	55,000
			Georgia Tech	10		Conrad Hitchler, Missouri, E	
1963	Dec. 21, 1963		Baylor	14		Don Trull, Baylor, QB	50,000
			LSU	7		James Ingram, Baylor, E	
1964	Dec. 19, 1964		Tulsa	14		Jerry Rhome, Tulsa, QB	50,000
			Mississippi	7		Willy Townes, Tulsa, DT	
1965	Dec. 18, 1965	7	Tennessee	27	7	Dewey Warren, Tennessee, QB	40,000
			Tulsa	6		Frank Emanuel, Tennessee, LB	
1966	Dec. 17, 1966		Texas	19		Chris Gilbert, Texas, RB	67,000
			Mississippi	0		Fred Edwards, Texas, LB	
1967	Dec. 23, 1967		Colorado	31		Bob Anderson, Colorado, QB	30,156
			Miami, Fla.	21		Ted Hendricks, Miami, Fla., DE	
1968	Dec. 31, 1968	20	SMU	28	14	Joe Pearce, Oklahoma, CB	53,543
		10	Oklahoma	27	11	Rufus Cormier, SMU, DG	
1969	Dec. 31, 1969	17	Houston	36	12	Jim Strong, Houston, HB	55,203
		12	Auburn	7	20	Jerry Drones, Houston, DE	
1970	Dec. 31, 1970		Alabama	24		Jeff Rouzie, Alabama, LB	53,829
		20	Oklahoma	24	20	Greg Pruitt, Oklahoma, HB	
1971	Dec. 31, 1971	7	Colorado	29	3	Charlie Davis, Colorado, TB	54,720
		15	Houston	17	17	Butch Brezina, Houston, DL	
1972	Dec. 30, 1972	11	Tennessee	24	8	Condredge Holloway, Tennessee, QB	52,961
		10	LSU	17	11	Carl Johnson, Tennessee, DE	
1973	Dec. 29, 1973	14	Houston	47	9-t	D.C. Nobles, Houston, QB	44,358
		17	Tulane	7	20-t	Deryl McGallion, Houston, LB	
1974	Dec. 23, 1974		Houston	31		John Housmann, Houston, RB	35,122
		13	North Carolina St.	31	11	Mack Mitchell, Houston, DE	
1975	Dec. 27, 1975	9	Texas	38	6	Earl Campbell, Texas, RB	52,748
		10	Colorado	21	16	Tim Campbell, Texas, DE	
1976	Dec. 31, 1976	13	Nebraska	27	9	Chuck Malito, Nebraska, SE	48,618
		9	Texas Tech	24	13	Rodney Allison, Texas Tech, QB	
1977	Dec. 31, 1977	20	Southern Cal	47	13	Rob Hertel, Southern Cal, QB	52,842
		17	Texas A&M	28		Walt Underwood, Southern Cal, DT	
1978	Dec. 31, 1978		Stanford	25	17	Steve Dils, Stanford, QB	34,084
		11	Georgia	22	16	Gordy Ceresino, Stanford, LB	
1979	Dec. 31, 1979	12	Purdue	27	10	Mark Herrmann, Purdue, QB	40,542
			Tennessee	22		Roland James, Tennessee, DB	
1980	Dec. 31, 1980	13	North Carolina	16	10	Amos Lawrence, North Carolina, HB	36,667
			Texas	7		Steve Streater, North Carolina, DB	
1981	Dec. 31, 1981	16	Michigan	33	12	Butch Woolfolk, Michigan, RB	40,309
		19	UCLA	14		Ben Needham, Michigan, LB	
1982	Dec. 31, 1982	14	Arkansas	28	9	Gary Anderson, Arkansas, RB	31,557
			Florida	24		Dwayne Dixon, Florida, WR	
1983	Dec. 31, 1983		Oklahoma State	24		Rusty Hilger, Oklahoma St., QB	50,090
		20	Baylor	14		Alfred Anderson, Baylor, RB	
1984	Dec. 31, 1984		West Virginia	31		Willie Drewrey, West Virginia, WR	43,260
			TCU	14			
1985	Dec. 31, 1985	10	Air Force	24	8	Pat Evans, Air Force, FB	42,000
			Texas	16		James McKinney, Texas, DE	
1986	Dec. 31, 1986	14	Baylor	21	12	Ray Berry, Baylor, LB	40,476
			Colorado	9		Mark Hatcher, Colorado, QB	
1987	Dec. 31, 1987		Texas	32		Tony Jones, Texas, WR	23,282
		19	Pittsburgh	27		Zeke Gadson, Pittsburgh, LB	

CLEMSON 23, TCU 7
DECEMBER 19, 1959

	1ST	2ND	3RD	4TH	FINAL
CLEM	0	3	0	20	23
TCU	0	7	0	0	7

SCORING SUMMARY

CLEM	FG Armstrong 22
TCU	Moreland 19 pass from Reding (Dodson kick)
CLEM	Barnes 68 pass from White (Armstrong kick)
CLEM	King 23 pass from Shingler (kick failed)
CLEM	Scrudato 1 run (Armstrong kick)

CLEM	TEAM STATISTICS	TCU
16	First Downs	12
203	Rushing Yards	89
6-13-1	Passing	7-17-4
103	Passing Yards	70
306	Total Yards	159
3-37.0	Punts - Average	5-32.0
3-1	Fumbles - Lost	1-0
3-23	Penalties - Yards	5-35

INDIVIDUAL LEADERS

RUSHING
CLEM: Shingler 3-65; Daigneault 12-50.
TCU: Spikes 11-33; Harris 8-29.

PASSING
CLEM: White 4-9-1, 69 yards, 1 TD; Shingler 2-4-0, 34 yards, 1 TD.
TCU: George 3-7-2, 37 yards; Reding 1-2-0, 19 yards, 1 TD.

RECEIVING
CLEM: Barnes 1-68, 1 TD; King 1-23, 1 TD.
TCU: Moreland 2-37, 1 TD; Harris 2-17.

ALABAMA 3, TEXAS 3
DECEMBER 17, 1960

	1ST	2ND	3RD	4TH	FINAL
ALA	0	0	3	0	3
TEX	0	0	0	3	3

SCORING SUMMARY

ALA	FG Brooker 30
TEX	FG Petty 20

ALA	TEAM STATISTICS	TEX
4	First Downs	11
65	Rushing Yards	124
8-14-0	Passing	7-17-1
90	Passing Yards	108
155	Total Yards	232
7-40.4	Punts - Average	8-39.8
1-1	Fumbles - Lost	1-0
2-49	Penalties - Yards	2-20

INDIVIDUAL LEADERS

RUSHING
ALA: Trammell 9-29; Fracchia 6-20.
TEX: Poage 14-56; Saxton 13-48.

PASSING
ALA: Skelton 8-12-0, 90 yards.
TEX: Cotten 5-11-1, 79 yards; Collins 2-4-0, 39 yards.

RECEIVING
ALA: Rice 1-49; Abruzzese 3-15.
TEX: Collins 4-41; Saxton 1-38.

KANSAS 33, RICE 7
DECEMBER 16, 1961

	1ST	2ND	3RD	4TH	FINAL
KU	6	6	13	8	33
RICE	7	0	0	0	7

SCORING SUMMARY

KU	Coleman 1 run (kick failed)
RICE	Burrell 5 pass from Kerbow (Blume kick)
KU	Coleman 1 run (pass failed)
KU	McClinton 6 run (Barnes kick)
KU	McFarland 13 run (kick failed)
KU	McFarland 12 run (Boydston pass from Hadl)

KU	TEAM STATISTICS	RICE
21	First Downs	11
293	Rushing Yards	58
7-10-2	Passing	11-20-0
64	Passing Yards	163
357	Total Yards	221
3-37.0	Punts - Average	6-31.0
0	Fumbles Lost	3

Missouri 14, Georgia Tech 10

December 22, 1962

	1ST	2ND	3RD	4TH	FINAL
MO	7	0	7	0	14
GT	0	7	3	0	10

SCORING SUMMARY
MO   Johnson 21 run (Leistritz kick)
GT   Auer 6 run (Lothridge kick)
MO   Tobin 77 run (Leistritz kick)
GT   FG Lothridge 26

MO	TEAM STATISTICS	GT
10	First Downs	13
258	Rushing Yards	169
0-7-2	Passing	5-15-4
0	Passing Yards	68
258	Total Yards	237
5-39.6	Punts - Average	6-38.5
2-2	Fumbles - Lost	0-0
4-35	Penalties - Yards	1-5

INDIVIDUAL LEADERS
RUSHING
MO: Tobin 11-114, 1 TD; Johnson 8-66, 1 TD.
GT: Auer 10-67, 1 TD; McNames 13-57.
PASSING
MO: Johnson 0-5-1, 0 yards.
GT: Lothridge 5-15-4, 68 yards.

Baylor 14, LSU 7

December 21, 1963

	1ST	2ND	3RD	4TH	FINAL
BU	0	0	0	14	14
LSU	7	0	0	0	7

SCORING SUMMARY
LSU   Soefker 8 run (Moreau kick)
BU   Ingram 7 pass from Trull (Davies kick)
BU   Ingram 13 pass from Trull (Davies kick)

BU	TEAM STATISTICS	LSU
27	First Downs	4
130	Rushing Yards	95
26-37-1	Passing	1-5-0
255	Passing Yards	13
385	Total Yards	108
4-34.0	Punts - Average	7-37.3
1-1	Fumbles - Lost	1-0
2-30	Penalties - Yards	2-10

INDIVIDUAL LEADERS
RUSHING
BU: Hoffman 15-70; Mitchell 10-32.
LSU: Ezell 9-30; Schwab 7-25.
PASSING
BU: Trull 26-37-1, 255 yards, 2 TD.
LSU: Ezell 1-5-0, 13 yards.
RECEIVING
BU: Ingram 11-163, 2 TD; Elkins 7-66.
LSU: Truax 1-13.

Tulsa 14, Mississippi 7

December 19, 1964

	1ST	2ND	3RD	4TH	FINAL
TUL	0	7	7	0	14
MISS	0	7	0	0	7

SCORING SUMMARY
MISS   Weatherly 1 run (Irwin kick)
TUL   Rhome 1 run (Twilley kick)
TUL   Fletcher 35 pass from Rhome (Twilley kick)

TUL	TEAM STATISTICS	MISS
19	First Downs	10
71	Rushing Yards	104
22-36-1	Passing	16-24-2
252	Passing Yards	113
323	Total Yards	217
7-31.6	Punts - Average	8-31.1
1-0	Fumbles - Lost	2-0
4-30	Penalties - Yards	4-50

INDIVIDUAL LEADERS
RUSHING
TUL: Daugherty 6-32; Rhome 22-29, 1 TD.
MISS: Dennis 17-73.
PASSING
TUL: Rhome 22-36-1, 252 yards, 1 TD.
MISS: Weatherly 16-24-2, 113 yards.
RECEIVING
TUL: Roberts 8-108; Daugherty 9-80.
MISS: Dennis 9-114.

Tennessee 27, Tulsa 6

December 18, 1965

	1ST	2ND	3RD	4TH	FINAL
TENN	6	14	7	0	27
TUL	6	0	0	0	6

SCORING SUMMARY
TENN   Wantland 4 pass from Warren (kick failed)
TUL   McDermott 1 run (kick failed)
TENN   Warren 1 run (Leake kick)
TENN   Warren 1 run (Leake kick)
TENN   Mitchell 11 run (Leake kick)

TENN	TEAM STATISTICS	TUL
11	First Downs	16
181	Rushing Yards	73
3-7-1	Passing	23-47-4
37	Passing Yards	250
218	Total Yards	323
6-42.8	Punts - Average	5-35.0
4-2	Fumbles - Lost	3-3
8-80	Penalties - Yards	1-15

INDIVIDUAL LEADERS
RUSHING
TENN: Warren 18-39, 2 TD; Mitchell 7-49, 1 TD.
TUL: McDermott 7-37, 1 TD; Lakusiak 9-18.
PASSING
TENN: Warren 3-7-1, 37 yards, 1 TD.
TUL: Anderson 23-47-4, 250 yards.
RECEIVING
TENN: Wantland 2-24, 1 TD.
TUL: Twilley 8-78; McDermott 7-74.

Texas 19, Mississippi 0

December 17, 1966

	1ST	2ND	3RD	4TH	FINAL
TEX	6	0	6	7	19
MISS	0	0	0	0	0

SCORING SUMMARY
TEX   Bradley 25 run (kick failed)
TEX   Gilbert 1 run (pass failed)
TEX   Bradley 4 run (Conway kick)

TEX	TEAM STATISTICS	MISS
19	First Downs	7
285	Rushing Yards	143
5-17-4	Passing	10-26-4
95	Passing Yards	65
380	Total Yards	208
3-42.0	Punts - Average	7-28.4
3-3	Fumbles - Lost	0-0
4-34	Penalties - Yards	8-84

INDIVIDUAL LEADERS
RUSHING
TEX: Gilbert 26-156, 1 TD; Bradley 20-105, 2 TD.
MISS: Cunningham 12-60; Street 6-39.
PASSING
TEX: Bradley 4-12-2, 49 yards; White 1-5-2, 46 yards.
MISS: Newell 9-20-2, 54 yards.
RECEIVING
TEX: Higgins 1-46; Gennusa 2-30.
MISS: Matthews 3-24; Cunningham 3-17.

Colorado 31, Miami (Fla.) 21

December 23, 1967

	1ST	2ND	3RD	4TH	FINAL
COLO	7	3	7	14	31
MIA	0	14	0	7	21

SCORING SUMMARY
COLO   Plantz 7 run (Farler kick)
MIA   Mira 2 run (Harris kick)
MIA   Dye 77 interception return (Harris kick)
COLO   Farler 31 FG
COLO   Anderson 2 run (Bartelt kick)
MIA   Daanen 9 pass from Miller (Harris kick)
COLO   Anderson 38 run (Farler kick)
COLO   Cooks 2 run (Farler kick)

COLO	TEAM STATISTICS	MIA
21	First Downs	14
283	Rushing Yards	120
10-21-1	Passing	10-28-2
82	Passing Yards	113
365	Total Yards	233
3-32.5	Punts - Average	7-37.7
2-0	Fumbles - Lost	2-1
2-10	Penalties - Yards	9-75

INDIVIDUAL LEADERS
RUSHING
COLO: Anderson 17-108, 2 TD; Cooks 17-74, 1 TD.
MIA: Acuff 8-38; Opalsky 12-38.
PASSING
COLO: Kelly 5-11-1, 33 yards; Anderson 5-10-0, 49 yards.
MIA: Miller 5-14-2, 75 yards, 1 TD; Olivo 5-14-0, 38 yards.
RECEIVING
COLO: Huber 6-52; Pruitt 2-26.
MIA: Daanen 4-56, 1 TD; Cox 2-29.

SMU 28, Oklahoma 27

December 31, 1968

	1ST	2ND	3RD	4TH	FINAL
SMU	0	0	6	22	28
OKLA	7	0	14	6	27

SCORING SUMMARY
OKLA   Warmack 3 run (Derr kick)
SMU   Richardson 1 run (kick failed)
OKLA   Barr 21 pass from Owens (Derr kick)
SMU   LeVias 11 pass from Hixson (Clements pass from Hixson)
SMU   Richardson 18 run (Lesser kick)
OKLA   Denton 22 pass from Ripley (Derr kick)
SMU   Fleming 19 pass from Hixson (Lesser kick)
OKLA   Barr 21 pass from Ripley (run failed)

SMU	TEAM STATISTICS	OKLA
22	First Downs	23
72	Rushing Yards	176
22-43-3	Passing	18-37-2
281	Passing Yards	294
353	Total Yards	470
7-41.0	Punts - Average	6-38.2
2-2	Fumbles - Lost	1-1
4-34	Penalties - Yards	6-55

INDIVIDUAL LEADERS
RUSHING
SMU: Richardson 18-76, 2 TD.
OKLA: Owens 36-113.
PASSING
SMU: Hixson 22-43-2, 281 yards, 2 TD.
OKLA: Ripley 10-22-2, 153 yards, 2 TD.
RECEIVING
SMU: LeVias 8-112, 1 TD.
OKLA: Barr 8-138, 2 TD.

Houston 36, Auburn 7

December 31, 1969

	1ST	2ND	3RD	4TH	FINAL
HOU	7	9	6	14	36
AUB	0	7	0	0	7

SCORING SUMMARY
HOU   Mullins 1 run (Lopez kick)
HOU   FG Lopez 27
HOU   Strong 1 run (kick failed)
AUB   Frederick 36 pass from Zofko (Riley kick)
HOU   Heiskell 1 run (pass failed)
HOU   Srong 12 run (Lopez kick)
HOU   Mozisek 20 pass from Clark (Lopez kick)

HOU	TEAM STATISTICS	AUB
25	First Downs	14
376	Rushing Yards	1
10-19-2	Passing	13-37-2
140	Passing Yards	188
516	Total Yards	189
2-42.5	Punts - Average	6-39.8
2-1	Fumbles - Lost	1-1
6-63	Penalties - Yards	4-26

INDIVIDUAL LEADERS
RUSHING
HOU: Strong 32-184, 2 TD; Heiskell 10-70, 1 TD.
AUB: Zofko 12-31; Clark 7-32.
PASSING
HOU: Mullins 9-17-2, 120 yards.
AUB: Sullivan 10-30-1, 132 yards.
RECEIVING
HOU: Wright 4-62; Thomas 2-35.
AUB: Beasley 6-76; Fredericks 3-59, 1 TD.

December 31, 1970
Alabama 24, Oklahoma 24

	1ST	2ND	3RD	4TH	FINAL
ALA	7	7	3	7	24
OKLA	7	14	0	3	24

SCORING SUMMARY
OKLA — Pruitt 58 run (Derr kick)
ALA — Moore 4 pass from Hunter (Clemmy kick)
OKLA — Pruitt 25 run (Derr kick)
ALA — Bailey 5 pass from Hunter (Clemmy kick)
OKLA — Wylie 2 run (Derr kick)
ALA — FG Clemmy 21
ALA — Hunter 25 pass from Musso (Clemmy kick)
OKLA — FG Derr 42

ALA	TEAM STATISTICS	OKLA
21	First Downs	19
229	Rushing Yards	349
14-27-0	Passing	5-7-0
199	Passing Yards	66
428	Total Yards	415
4-37.0	Punts - Average	5-37.0
2-1	Fumbles - Lost	3-2
7-50	Penalties - Yards	3-42

INDIVIDUAL LEADERS
RUSHING
ALA: Musso 27-138.
OKLA: Crosswhite 20-111.
PASSING
ALA: Hunter 13-26-1, 174 yards, 2 TD.
OKLA: Mildren 5-7-0, 66 yards.
RECEIVING
ALA: Bailey 4-86, 1 TD.
OKLA: Harrison 2-45.

December 31, 1971
Colorado 29, Houston 17

	1ST	2ND	3RD	4TH	FINAL
COLO	7	16	0	6	29
HOU	14	0	3	0	17

SCORING SUMMARY
COLO — Davis 27 run (Dean kick)
HOU — Newhouse 2 run (Terrell kick)
HOU — Newhouse 3 run (Terrell kick)
COLO — Brunson 5 pass from Johnson (kick failed)
COLO — FG Dean 32
COLO — Davis 1 run (Dean kick)
HOU — FG Terrell 29
COLO — Johnson 1 run (pass failed)

COLO	TEAM STATISTICS	HOU
24	First Downs	19
333	Rushing Yards	219
7-17-1	Passing	11-25-1
62	Passing Yards	173
395	Total Yards	392
3-32.0	Punts - Average	2-37.5
4-0	Fumbles - Lost	2-2
7-52	Penalties - Yards	2-47

INDIVIDUAL LEADERS
RUSHING
COLO: Davis 37-202, 2 TD; Johnson 16-81, 1 TD.
HOU: Newhouse 35-168, 2 TD; Mozisek 11-43.
PASSING
COLO: Johnson 6-16-1, 51 yards, 1 TD.
HOU: Mullins 11-25-1, 173 yards.
RECEIVING
COLO: Nichols 2-28; Brunson 2-16, 1 TD.
HOU: Orchin 6-94; Odoms 4-51.

December 30, 1972
Tennessee 24, LSU 17

	1ST	2ND	3RD	4TH	FINAL
TENN	14	10	0	0	24
LSU	3	0	7	7	17

SCORING SUMMARY
LSU — FG Jackson 29
TENN — Young 6 pass from Holloway (Townsend kick)
TENN — Holloway 15 run (Townsend kick)
TENN — FG Townsend 33
TENN — Holloway 10 run (Townsend kick)
LSU — Jones 2 run (Jackson kick)
LSU — Davis 1 run (Jackson kick)

TENN	TEAM STATISTICS	LSU
17	First Downs	18
179	Rushing Yards	187
11-19-1	Passing	7-20-1
94	Passing Yards	90
273	Total Yards	277
6-41.2	Punts - Average	5-37.0
0-0	Fumbles - Lost	1-0
4-35	Penalties - Yards	3-35

INDIVIDUAL LEADERS
RUSHING
TENN: Holloway 19-74, 2 TD; Chancey 13-73.
LSU: Davis 16-88, 1 TD.
PASSING
TENN: Holloway 11-19-1, 94 yards, 1 TD.
LSU: Jones 7-19-0, 90 yards.
RECEIVING
TENN: Stanback 4-41.
LSU: Boyd 2-33.

December 29, 1973
Houston 47, Tulane 7

	1ST	2ND	3RD	4TH	FINAL
HOU	7	14	14	12	47
TUL	0	7	0	0	7

SCORING SUMMARY
HOU — Johnson 75 run (Terrell kick)
HOU — Parker 1 run (Terrell kick)
HOU — Parker 3 run (Terrell kick)
TUL — Forner 32 pass from Gilbert (Falgoust kick)
HOU — Nobles 3 run (Terrell kick)
HOU — McGraw 1 run (Terrell kick)
HOU — McGraw 32 run (kick failed)
HOU — Husmann 7 run (kick failed)

HOU	TEAM STATISTICS	TUL
26	First Downs	10
402	Rushing Yards	102
12-29-1	Passing	6-24-4
253	Passing Yards	71
655	Total Yards	173
3-43.3	Punts - Average	9-39.2
6-4	Fumbles - Lost	2-1
5-55	Penalties - Yards	4-26

INDIVIDUAL LEADERS
RUSHING
HOU: Johnson 5-114, 1 TD; McGraw 13-108, 2 TD; Parker 12-47, 2 TD.
TUL: Bynum 12-40; Treuting 2-27.
PASSING
HOU: Nobles 8-13-0, 201 yards; Husman 4-6-1, 52 yards.
TUL: Foley 4-16-4, 32 yards; Gilbert 2-5-0, 39 yards, 1 TD.
RECEIVING
HOU: Willingham 3-105; Bassler 1-60.
TUL: Forner 1-32, 1 TD; Thibodeaux 2-19.

December 23, 1974
NC State 31, Houston 31

	1ST	2ND	3RD	4TH	FINAL
NCSU	3	7	7	14	31
HOU	0	3	7	21	31

SCORING SUMMARY
NCSU — FG Huff 37
HOU — FG Coplin 21
NCSU — Hooks 11 run (Huff kick)
HOU — Housmann 1 run (Coplin kick)
NCSU — Fritts 7 pass from Buckey (Huff kick)
HOU — Johnson 10 run (Coplin kick)
HOU — Foster 73 pass from McGallion (Coplin kick)
HOU — Housmann 5 run (Coplin kick)
NCSU — London 9 run (pass failed)
NCSU — Buckey 1 run (Fritts run)

NCSU	TEAM STATISTICS	HOU
20	First Downs	25
154	Rushing Yards	343
18-30-2	Passing	8-14-2
200	Passing Yards	179
354	Total Yards	522
6-36.0	Punts - Average	2-44.5
5-1	Fumbles - Lost	5-3
1-15	Penalties - Yards	3-35

INDIVIDUAL LEADERS
RUSHING
NCSU: Fritts 16-89; Hooks 8-29, 1 TD.
HOU: Housmann 21-134, 2 TD; McGraw 10-62.
PASSING
NCSU: Buckey 18-28-2, 200 yards, 1 TD.
HOU: McGallion 8-14-2, 178 yards, 1 TD.
RECEIVING
NCSU: Hovance 3-78; Fritts 5-33, 1 TD.
HOU: Bass 5-92; Foster 1-73, 1 TD.

December 27, 1975
Texas 38, Colorado 21

	1ST	2ND	3RD	4TH	FINAL
TEX	0	7	24	7	38
COLO	7	14	0	0	21

SCORING SUMMARY
COLO — Kunz 1 run (MacKenzie kick)
COLO — Logan 4 pass from Williams (MacKenzie kick)
TEX — Jackson 21 pass from Akins (Erxleben kick)
COLO — Hasselbeck 25 pass from Williams (MacKenzie kick)
TEX — Walker 3 run (kick blocked)
TEX — T. Campbell 25 blocked punt return (E. Campbell pass from Akins)
TEX — FG Erxleben 55
TEX — Jones 4 run (Erxleben kick)
TEX — Jones 7 run (Erxleben kick)

TEX	TEAM STATISTICS	COLO
15	First Downs	21
171	Rushing Yards	117
4-5-0	Passing	17-26-3
66	Passing Yards	177
237	Total Yards	294
2-40.0	Punts - Average	4-24.0
2-2	Fumbles - Lost	3-2
5-35	Penalties - Yards	6-50
25:04	Possession Time	34:56

INDIVIDUAL LEADERS
RUSHING
TEX: E. Campbell 19-95; Jones 8-33, 2 TD.
COLO: Reed 14-41; Moorehead 9-39.
PASSING
TEX: Akins 4-5-0, 66 yards, 1 TD.
COLO: Williams 17-25-2, 177 yards, 2 TD.
RECEIVING
TEX: Jackson 2-31, 1 TD; Jones 1-30.
COLO: Hasselbeck 5-84, 1 TD; Moorehead 3-25.

December 31, 1976
Nebraska 27, Texas Tech 24

	1ST	2ND	3RD	4TH	FINAL
NEB	7	7	13	0	27
TT	3	14	7	0	24

SCORING SUMMARY

NEB	Berns 1 run (Eveland kick)
TT	FG Hall 28
TT	Taylor 14 pass from Allison (Hall kick)
TT	Taylor 11 pass from Allison (Hall kick)
NEB	Dufresne 22 pass from Ferragamo (Eveland kick)
TT	Taylor 8 run (Hall kick)
NEB	Berns 18 run (kick failed)
NEB	Malito 23 pass from Ferragamo (Eveland kick)

NEB	TEAM STATISTICS	TT
21	First Downs	24
164	Rushing Yards	191
14-24-0	Passing	15-23-0
232	Passing Yards	193
396	Total Yards	384

December 31, 1977
Southern Cal 47, Texas A&M 28

	1ST	2ND	3RD	4TH	FINAL
USC	7	13	14	13	47
A&M	14	0	0	14	28

SCORING SUMMARY

A&M	Woodard 3 run (Franklin kick)
A&M	Mosley 44 run (Franklin kick)
USC	Sweeney 29 pass from Hertel (Jordan kick)
USC	White 25 pass from Hertel (Jordan kick)
USC	FG Jordan 22
USC	FG Jordan 29
USC	Sweeney 40 pass from Hertel (Burns pass from Hertel)
USC	Simmrin 14 pass from Hertel (kick failed)
A&M	Woodard 1 run (Franklin kick)
USC	Ford 94 run (run failed)
USC	Tatupu 8 run (Jordan kick)
A&M	Armstrong 4 run (Franklin kick)

December 31, 1978
Stanford 25, Georgia 22

	1ST	2ND	3RD	4TH	FINAL
STAN	0	0	22	3	25
UGA	3	12	7	0	22

SCORING SUMMARY

UGA	FG Robinson 31
UGA	Prince 22 pass from Belue (kick failed)
UGA	Prince 8 pass from Pyburn (kick failed)
UGA	Pyburn 1 run (Robinson kick)
STAN	Margerum 32 pass from Dils (pass failed)
STAN	Nelson 20 pass from Dils (Naber run)
STAN	Margerum 14 pass from Dils (Nelson pass from Dils)
STAN	FG Naber 24

STAN	TEAM STATISTICS	UGA
20	First Downs	27
128	Rushing Yards	315
17-28-0	Passing	11-18-1
210	Passing Yards	189
338	Total Yards	504
1-6	Punt Returns - Yards	4-38
2-45	Kickoff Returns - Yards	4-81
8-41.6	Punts - Average	1-35.0
2-1	Fumbles - Lost	6-5
2-34	Penalties - Yards	5-43

INDIVIDUAL LEADERS

RUSHING
STAN: Nelson 16-100; Francis 11-67.
UGA: McClendon 30-115; Womack 13-60.

PASSING
STAN: Dils 17-28-0, 210 yards, 3 TD.
UGA: Pyburn 6-12-1, 87 yards, 1 TD; Belue 4-4-0, 59 yards, 1 TD.

RECEIVING
STAN: Margerum 5-87, 2 TD; Francis 5-48.
UGA: Scott 5-67; Prince 2-30, 1 TD.

December 31, 1979
Purdue 27, Tennessee 22

	1ST	2ND	3RD	4TH	FINAL
PUR	0	14	7	6	27
TENN	0	0	6	16	22

SCORING SUMMARY

PUR	McCall 6 run (Seibel kick)
PUR	Burrell 12 pass from Herrmann (Seibel kick)
PUR	Young 12 pass from Herrmann (Seibel kick)
TENN	Ford 8 pass from Streater (pass failed)
TENN	Berry 15 pass from Ingram (Simpson run)
TENN	Simpson 1 run (Simpson pass from Streater)
PUR	Young 17 pass from Herrmann (pass failed)

PUR	TEAM STATISTICS	TENN
31	First Downs	19
180	Rushing Yards	146
21-39-0	Passing	17-36-3
303	Passing Yards	234
483	Total Yards	380
7-43.6	Punts - Average	6-38.0
2-1	Fumbles - Lost	3-2
3-25	Penalties - Yards	7-56

INDIVIDUAL LEADERS

RUSHING
PUR: McCall 18-91, 1 TD.
TENN: Simpson 16-47, 1 TD.

PASSING
PUR: Herrmann 21-39-0, 303 yards, 3 TD.
TENN: Streater 16-34-3, 219 yards, 1 TD.

RECEIVING
PUR: Burrell 8-144, 1 TD.
TENN: Gault 4-22.

December 31, 1980
North Carolina 16, Texas 7

	1ST	2ND	3RD	4TH	FINAL
UNC	6	7	3	0	16
TEX	0	7	0	0	7

SCORING SUMMARY

UNC	Lawrence 59 run (run failed)
TEX	Luck 1 run (Goodson kick)
UNC	Bryant 1 run (Hayes kick)
UNC	FG Hayes 31

UNC	TEAM STATISTICS	TEX
16	First Downs	13
234	Rushing Yards	132
11-19-0	Passing	11-27-1
121	Passing Yards	128
355	Total Yards	260
5-37.0	Punts - Average	5-43.6
0-0	Fumbles - Lost	4-1
5-35	Penalties - Yards	3-35

INDIVIDUAL LEADERS

RUSHING
UNC: Lawrence 18-104, 1 TD; Bryant 15-82, 1 TD.
TEX: Clark 11-47; Walls 1-42.

PASSING
UNC: Elkins 11-18-0, 121 yards; Lawrence 0-1-0, 0 yards.
TEX: McIvor 11-27-1, 128 yards.

RECEIVING
UNC: Chatham 4-54, Bryant 4-31.
TEX: Koenning 3-51; Sampleton 4-49.

December 31, 1981
Michigan 33, UCLA 14

	1ST	2ND	3RD	4TH	FINAL
MICH	10	0	3	20	33
UCLA	0	0	7	7	14

SCORING SUMMARY

MICH	FG Haji-Sheikh 24
MICH	Carter 50 pass from Smith (Haji-Sheikh kick)
UCLA	Townsell 17 pass from Ramsey (Johnson kick)
MICH	FG Haji-Sheikh 47
MICH	Woolfolk 1 run (run failed)
UCLA	Wrightman 9 pass from Ramsey (Johnson kick)
MICH	Smith 9 run (Haji-Sheikh kick)
MICH	Dickey 5 run (Haji-Sheikh kick)

MICH	TEAM STATISTICS	UCLA
25	First Downs	14
320	Rushing Yards	33
10-16-0	Passing	12-26-2
168	Passing Yards	162
488	Total Yards	195
5-39.6	Punts - Average	8-47.8
1-1	Fumbles - Lost	1-0
14-148	Penalties - Yards	9-94

INDIVIDUAL LEADERS

RUSHING
MICH: Woolfolk 27-186, 1 TD; Smith 10-64, 1 TD.
UCLA: Nelson 18-33.

PASSING
MICH: Smith 9-15-0, 152 yards, 1 TD.
UCLA: Ramsey 12-25-1, 162 yards, 2 TD.

RECEIVING
MICH: Carter 6-127, 1 TD; Bean 2-33.
UCLA: Carney 5-89; Townsell 3-37, 1 TD.

December 31, 1982
Arkansas 28, Florida 24

	1ST	2ND	3RD	4TH	FINAL
ARK	7	0	7	14	28
FLA	7	10	7	0	24

SCORING SUMMARY

ARK	Anderson 16 run (Smith kick)
FLA	Dixon 3 pass from Hewko (Raymond kick)
FLA	FG Raymond 34
FLA	Dixon 13 pass from Hewko (Raymond kick)
ARK	Anderson 1 run (Smith kick)
FLA	Dixon 17 pass from Hewko (Raymond kick)
ARK	Clark 5 pass from Jones (Smith kick)
ARK	Jones 1 run (Smith kick)

ARK	TEAM STATISTICS	FLA
28	First Downs	23
356	Rushing Yards	171
7-12-1	Passing	19-29-1
122	Passing Yards	234
478	Total Yards	405
3-43.3	Punts - Average	4-45.8
5-36	Penalties - Yards	6-50

INDIVIDUAL LEADERS

RUSHING
ARK: Anderson 26-161, 2 TD; Clark 17-77.
FLA: Jones 12-89; Hampton 21-61.

PASSING
ARK: Taylor 5-7-1, 123 yards; Jones 2-5-0, minus-1 yards, 1 TD.
FLA: Hewko 19-28-0, 234 yards, 3 TD; Jones 0-1-1, 0 yards.

RECEIVING
ARK: White 1-40; Anderson 3-37.
FLA: Dixon 8-106, 3 TD; Hampton 2-37.

December 31, 1983
Oklahoma State 24, Baylor 14

	1ST	2ND	3RD	4TH	FINAL
OSU	6	18	0	0	24
BU	0	7	0	7	14

Scoring Summary
OSU	Lewis 12 pass from Hilger (kick blocked)
OSU	Anderson 1 run (Lewis pass from Hilger)
OSU	Harris 26 pass from Hilger (Roach kick)
BU	McNeil 12 pass from Carlson (Jimmerson kick)
OSU	FG Roach 44
BU	McNeil 28 pass from Anderson (Jimmerson kick)

OSU	TEAM STATISTICS	BU
19	First Downs	18
178	Rushing Yards	134
17-30-1	Passing	16-32-2
187	Passing Yards	245
365	Total Yards	379
6-39.0	Punts - Average	5-42.0
1-1	Fumbles - Lost	1-1
4-40	Penalties - Yards	7-55

Individual Leaders
RUSHING
OSU: Anderson 27-143, 1 TD; Jones 13-32.
BU: Anderson 21-103; Rice 4-28.
PASSING
OSU: Hilger 12-17-0, 137 yards, 2 TD; Jackson 5-13-1, 50 yards.
BU: Muecke 8-14-1, 152 yards; Carlson 7-17-1, 65 yards, 1 TD.
RECEIVING
OSU: Harris 3-69, 1 TD; Chesley 5-54.
BU: McNeil 10-163, 2 TD; Davis 4-64.

December 31, 1984
West Virginia 31, TCU 14

	1ST	2ND	3RD	4TH	FINAL
WVU	14	17	0	0	31
TCU	0	7	0	7	14

Scoring Summary
WVU	Gay 2 pass from White (Woodside kick)
TCU	Sharp 5 pass from Gulley (Ozee kick)
WVU	Mullen 62 pass from White (Woodside kick)
WVU	Holifield 1 run (Woodside kick)
WVU	Wolfley 5 pass from White (Woodside kick)
WVU	FG Woodside 21
TCU	Burnett 20 pass from Gulley (Ozee kick)

WVU	TEAM STATISTICS	TCU
23	First Downs	15
200	Rushing Yards	92
17-31-1	Passing	12-22-1
302	Passing Yards	187
502	Total Yards	279
4-37.0	Punts - Average	6-47.5
2-2	Fumbles - Lost	2-2
5-45	Penalties - Yards	2-15

Individual Leaders
RUSHING
WVU: Holifield 13-84, 1 TD; Wolfley 7-53.
TCU: Jeffery 10-37; Gulley 13-34.
PASSING
WVU: White 16-30-1, 280 yards, 3 TD.
TCU: Gulley 9-14-0, 150 yards, 2 TD; Sciaraffa 3-8-1, 37 yards.
RECEIVING
WVU: Drewery 6-152; Wolfley 3-36, 1 TD.
TCU: Maness 5-90; Burnett 3-65, 1 TD.

December 31, 1985
Air Force 24, Texas 16

	1ST	2ND	3RD	4TH	FINAL
AFA	14	0	7	3	24
TEX	7	0	3	6	16

Scoring Summary
TEX	Harris 34 pass from Stafford (Ward kick)
AFA	Pshsniak 1 run (Ruby kick)
AFA	Weiss 1 run (Ruby kick)
TEX	FG Ward 24
AFA	Evans 19 run (Ruby kick)
TEX	FG Ward 31
TEX	FG Ward 28
AFA	FG Ruby 40

AFA	TEAM STATISTICS	TEX
9	First Downs	14
189	Rushing Yards	214
1-5-0	Passing	9-18-2
5	Passing Yards	88
194	Total Yards	302
11-49.2	Punts - Average	6-44.5
1-0	Fumbles - Lost	0-0
6-45	Penalties - Yards	8-67

RUSHING
AFA: Evans 18-129, 1 TD; Weiss 21-41, 1 TD.
TEX: Stafford 9-63; Hunter 16-58.
PASSING
AFA: Weiss 1-5-0, 5 yards.
TEX: Stafford 9-18-2, 88 yards, 1 TD.
RECEIVING
AFA: Pittman 1-5.
TEX: Harris 3-65, 1 TD; Gay 1-18.

December 31, 1986
Baylor 21, Colorado 9

	1ST	2ND	3RD	4TH	FINAL
BU	7	7	7	0	21
COLO	0	3	6	0	9

Scoring Summary
BU	McAdoo 1 run (Syler kick)
COLO	FG DeLine 36
BU	Chase 2 pass from Carlson (Syler kick)
BU	McAdoo 1 run (Syler kick)
COLO	Hatcher 31 run (run failed)

BU	TEAM STATISTICS	COLO
12	First Downs	12
114	Rushing Yards	83
14-28-2	Passing	7-14-1
165	Passing Yards	111
279	Total Yards	194
7-31.1	Punts - Average	5-37.6
2-0	Fumbles - Lost	7-3
7-58	Penalties - Yards	4-25
31:09	Possession Time	28:51

Individual Leaders
RUSHING
BU: McAdoo 8-36, 2 TD; Murray 11-35.
COLO: Kissick 9-37; Oliver 11-36.
PASSING
BU: Carlson 11-22-2, 136 yards, 1 TD.
COLO: Walters 5-8-1, 71 yards; Hatcher 2-5-0, 40 yards.
RECEIVING
BU: Clark 3-58, Chase 2-23, 1 TD.
COLO: Embree 3-57; Oliver 1-19.

December 31, 1987
Texas 32, Pittsburgh 27

	1ST	2ND	3RD	4TH	FINAL
TEX	14	3	3	12	32
PITT	7	0	7	13	27

Scoring Summary
TEX	Jones 77 pass from Stafford (Clements kick)
PITT	Heyward 4 run (Van Horne kick)
TEX	Jones 40 pass from Stafford (Clements kick)
TEX	FG Clements 33
PITT	Heard 40 pass from Wanke (Van Horne kick)
TEX	FG Clements 49
TEX	Johnson 14 pass from Stafford (pass failed)
TEX	Metcalf 24 run (run failed)
PITT	Stewart 43 pass from Wanke (Van Horne kick)
PITT	Osborn 15 pass from Wanke (pass failed)

TEX	TEAM STATISTICS	PITT
20	First Downs	17
116	Rushing Yards	117
20-34-1	Passing	14-34-3
368	Passing Yards	273
484	Total Yards	390
4-44.0	Punts - Average	8-33.1
6-3	Fumbles - Lost	0-0
5-55	Penalties - Yards	6-53
28:32	Possession Time	31:28

Individual Leaders
RUSHING
TEX: Metcalf 18-95, 1 TD; Norris 8-40.
PITT: Heyward 30-136, 1 TD; Riddick 3-1.
PASSING
TEX: Stafford 20-34-1, 368 yards, 3 TD.
PITT: Wanke 8-20-3, 172, 3 TD; Dickerson 5-13-0, 56 yards.
RECEIVING
TEX: Jones 8-242, 2 TD; Metcalf 4-51.
PITT: Williams 4-79; Tuten 2-47.

BLUEGRASS BOWL

Site: Louisville
Stadium: Fairgrounds Stadium
Capacity: 20,000
Surface: Grass

SEASON	DATE	PRE-GAME RANK	TEAMS	SCORE	FINAL RANK	MOST VALUABLE PLAYERS	ATT.
1958	Dec. 13, 1958	19	Oklahoma State	15		Forrest Campbell, Oklahoma State, RB	7,000
			Florida State	6			

DECEMBER 13, 1958
OKLAHOMA STATE 15, FLORIDA STATE 6

	1ST	2ND	3RD	4TH	FINAL
OSU	0	7	8	0	15
FSU	0	0	0	6	6

SCORING SUMMARY
OSU D. Wood 17 run (J. Wood kick)
OSU D. Wood 1 run (D. Wood pass from Soergel)
FSU Meyer 39 pass from Majors (run failed)

OSU	TEAM STATISTICS	FSU
23	First Downs	12
298	Rushing Yards	100
6-12-1	Passing	9-22-4
77	Passing Yards	185
375	Total Yards	285
5-30.0	Punts - Average	2-30.0
1-1	Fumbles - Lost	2-2
6-65	Penalties - Yards	3-25

INDIVIDUAL LEADERS
RUSHING
OSU: Campbell 26-130; D. Wood 17-81, 2 TD.
FSU: Pickard 14-44; Prinzi 7-30.
PASSING
OSU: Soergel 6-12-1, 77 yards.
FSU: Majors 5-9-1, 116 yards, 1 TD.
RECEIVING
OSU: Wiggins 2-38; D. Wood 2-23.
FSU: Romeo 3-62; Renn 2-48.

CALIFORNIA BOWL

Site: Fresno, Calif.
Stadium: Bulldog Stadium
Capacity: 30,000
Surface: Grass

SEASON	DATE	PRE-GAME RANK	TEAMS	SCORE	FINAL RANK	MOST VALUABLE PLAYERS	ATT.
1981	Dec. 19, 1981		Toledo	27		Arnold Smiley, Toledo, RB	15,565
			San Jose State	25		Marlin Russell, Toledo, LB	
1982	Dec. 18, 1982		Fresno State	29		Chip Otten, Bowling Green, TB	30,000
			Bowling Green	28		Jac Tomasello, Bowling Green, DB	
1983	Dec. 17, 1983		No. Illinois	20		Lou Wicks, No. Illinois, FB	20,464
			Cal. St. Fullerton	13		James Pruitt, Cal. St. Fullerton, WR	
1984	Dec. 15, 1984		Nevada-Las Vegas	30		Randall Cunningham, Nevada-Las Vegas, QB	21,741
			Toledo *	13		Steve Morgan, Toledo, TB	
1985	Dec. 14, 1985		Fresno State	51		Mike Mancini, Fresno State, P	32,554
		20	Bowling Green	7		Greg Meehan, Bowling Green, FL	
1986	Dec. 13, 1986		San Jose State	37		Mike Perez, San Jose State, QB	10,743
			Miami (Ohio)	7		Andrew Marlatt, Miami, Ohio, DT	
1987	Dec. 12, 1987		Eastern Michigan	30		Gary Patton, Eastern Michigan, TB	24,000
			San Jose State	27		Mike Perez, San Jose State, QB	
1988	Dec. 10, 1988		Fresno State	35		Darrell Rosette, Fresno State, RB	31,272
			Western Michigan	30		Tony Kimbrough, Western Michigan, QB	
1989	Dec. 9, 1989		Fresno State	27		Ron Cox, Fresno State, LB	31,610
			Ball State	6		Sean Jones, Ball State, WR	
1990	Dec. 8, 1990		San Jose State	48		Sheldon Canley, San Jose State, TB	25,431
			Central Michigan	24		Ken Ealy, Central Michigan, WR	
1991	Dec. 14, 1991		Bowling Green	28		Mark Szlachcic, Bowling Green, WR	34,825
			Fresno State	21		Mark Barsotti, Fresno State, QB	

* UNLV won by forfeit

DECEMBER 19, 1981
TOLEDO 27, SAN JOSE STATE 25

	1ST	2ND	3RD	4TH	FINAL
TOL	7	7	7	6	27
SJSU	0	3	8	14	25

SCORING SUMMARY
TOL Achter 45 run (Lee kick)
SJSU FG Berg 24
TOL Smiley 7 run (Lee kick)
TOL Schafer 12 pass from Hall (Lee kick)
SJSU Fernandez 12 pass from Clarkson (Fernandez pass from Clarkson)
TOL FG Lee 27
SJSU Fernandez 22 pass from Clarkson (kick blocked)
SJSU Fernandez 35 pass from Clarkson (Taylor pass from Willhite)
TOL FG Lee 41

TOL	TEAM STATISTICS	SJSU
21	First Downs	29
221	Rushing Yards	54
11-22-1	Passing	43-63-5
265	Passing Yards	467
486	Total Yards	521
3-39.3	Punts - Average	2-47.0
7-2	Fumbles - Lost	4-1
3-25	Penalties - Yards	10-85

DECEMBER 18, 1982
FRESNO STATE 29, BOWLING GREEN 28

	1ST	2ND	3RD	4TH	FINAL
FRES	0	0	7	22	29
BG	0	14	14	0	28

SCORING SUMMARY
BG Otten 4 run (Youssef kick)
BG Meek 1 pass from McClure (Youssef kick)
BG Potts 5 pass from McClure (Youssef kick)
FRES Paige 11 pass from Tedford (Darrow kick)
BG Potts 6 fumble recovery (Youssef kick)
FRES Paige 4 run (Darrow kick)
FRES Paige 27 pass from Tedford (Carter pass from Tedford)
FRES Wesson 2 pass from Tedford (Darrow kick)

FRES	TEAM STATISTICS	BG
27	First Downs	17
80	Rushing Yards	126
31-50-4	Passing	22-32-1
373	Passing Yards	246
453	Total Yards	372
2-39.5	Punts - Average	7-39.9
4-3	Fumbles - Lost	2-0
24:20	Possession Time	35:40

INDIVIDUAL LEADERS
RUSHING
FRES: Thomas 5-48; Carter 6-41.
BG: Otten 31-136, 1 TD; Wagner 5-18.
PASSING
FRES: Tedford 31-50-4, 373 yards, 3 TD.
BG: McClure 22-32-1, 246 yards, 2 TD.
RECEIVING
FRES: Paige 15-246, 2 TD; Griever 4-43.
BG: Otten 11-76; Taylor 3-74.

December 17, 1983
No. Illinois 20, Cal St. Fullerton 13

	1ST	2ND	3RD	4TH	FINAL
NIU	3	7	7	3	20
CSF	3	7	0	3	13

SCORING SUMMARY
NIU	FG Scott 23
CSF	FG Steinke 26
NIU	Richardson 3 run (Scott kick)
CSF	Redick 25 pass from Allen (Steinke kick)
NIU	Richardson 4 run (Scott kick)
NIU	FG Scott 42
CSF	FG Steinke 40

NIU	TEAM STATISTICS	CSF
15	First Downs	15
253	Rushing Yards	146
10-18-0	Passing	18-32-0
119	Passing Yards	233
372	Total Yards	379
3-42.0	Punts - Average	3-36.3
1-0	Fumbles - Lost	2-0
9-75	Penalties - Yards	9-85
33:33	Possession Time	26:27

INDIVIDUAL LEADERS

RUSHING
NIU: Wicks 14-117, Richardson 21-67, 2TD.
CSF: Calhoun 5-55.

PASSING
NIU : Tyrell 10-18-0, 119 yards.
CSF : Allen 18-32-0, 323 yards, 1 TD.

RECEIVING
SJSU: Sims 4-42
CSF: Pruitt 6-133, Pitts 6-60.

December 15, 1984
UNLV 30, Toledo 13*

	1ST	2ND	3RD	4TH	FINAL
UNLV	7	6	17	0	30
TOL	3	3	7	0	13

* UNLV won by forfeit

SCORING SUMMARY
UNLV	Gladney 19 pass from Cunningham (DiGiovanna kick)
TOL	FG Walker 22
UNLV	Jones 7 pass from Cunningham (kick failed)
TOL	FG Walker 36
UNLV	FG DiGiovanna 44
TOL	Poure 38 pass from Sager (Walker kick)
UNLV	Woods 16 run (DiGiovanna kick)
UNLV	Cunningham 10 run (DiGiovanna kick)

UNLV	TEAM STATISTICS	TOL
18	First Downs	20
127	Rushing Yards	203
18-28-1	Passing	12-31-0
270	Passing Yards	137
397	Total Yards	340
3-27.7	Punts - Average	5-34.6
2-2	Fumbles - Lost	3-1
8-77	Penalties - Yards	6-40

December 14, 1985
Fresno State 51, Bowling Green 7

	1ST	2ND	3RD	4TH	FINAL
FRES	7	16	14	14	51
BG	0	0	0	7	7

SCORING SUMMARY
FRES	Williams 10 run (Belli kick)
FRES	Mosley 1 run (Belli kick)
FRES	Taylor 33 pass from Sweeney (Belli kick)
FRES	Safety (McClure tackled in end zone)
FRES	Taylor 53 pass from Sweeney (Belli kick)
FRES	Skipper 29 run (Belli kick)
BG	Davis 18 run (Silvi kick)
FRES	Baker 40 pass from Sweeney (Belli kick)
FRES	Skipper 13 run (Belli kick)

FRES	TEAM STATISTICS	BG
15	First Downs	21
225	Rushing Yards	89
10-20-1	Passing	23-48-3
194	Passing Yards	259
419	Total Yards	348
7-47.4	Punts - Average	6-35.3
2-1	Fumbles - Lost	6-5
27:51	Possession Time	32:09

INDIVIDUAL LEADERS

RUSHING
FRES: Williams 18-94, 1 TD; Skipper 7-77, 2 TD.
BG: Davis 7-78, 1 TD; Story 9-41.

PASSING
FRES: Sweeney 9-19-1, 185 yards, 3 TD.
BG: McClure 22-42-3, 254 yards.

RECEIVING
FRES: Taylor 2-86, 2 TD; Baker 2-49, 1 TD.
BG: Schmelzle 7-84; Meehan 7-65.

December 13, 1986
San Jose State 37, Miami (Ohio) 7

	1ST	2ND	3RD	4TH	FINAL
SJSU	3	14	7	13	37
MIA	7	0	0	0	7

SCORING SUMMARY
SJSU	FG Olivarez 45
MIA	Stofa 20 pass from Morris (Gussman kick)
SJSU	Saxon 1 run (Olivarez kick)
SJSU	Liggins 36 pass from Perez (Olivarez kick)
SJSU	Malauulu 4 run (Olivarez kick)
SJSU	Liggins 31 pass from Perez (Olivarez kick)
SJSU	Alexander 39 interception return (kick failed)

SJSU	TEAM STATISTICS	MIA
23	First Downs	22
113	Rushing Yards	24
22-40-0	Passing	18-41-5
313	Passing Yards	208
426	Total Yards	232
4-29.3	Punts - Average	5-34.4
6-1	Fumbles - Lost	1-1
14-163	Penalties - Yards	10-101

INDIVIDUAL LEADERS

RUSHING
SJSU: Saxon 25-92, 1 TD; Jackson 6-18.
MIA: Swarn 12-46; Morris 6-12.

PASSING
SJSU: Perez 21-37-0, 291 yards, 3 TD.
MIA: Morris 15-33-4, 166 yards, 1 TD.

RECEIVING
SJSU: Liggins 8-133, 2 TD; McCloud 2-41.
MIA: Stofa 5-71, 1 TD; Marhofer 5-69.

December 12, 1987
Eastern Michigan 30, San Jose St 27

	1ST	2ND	3RD	4TH	FINAL
EMU	10	7	0	13	30
SJSU	7	7	7	6	27

SCORING SUMMARY
EMU	Foster 1 run (Henneghan kick)
SJSU	Jackson 6 run (Olivarez kick)
EMU	FG Henneghan 42
EMU	Foster 1 run (Henneghan kick)
SJSU	Klump 1 pass from Saxon (Olivarez kick)
SJSU	Johnson 12 pass from Perez (Olivarez kick)
EMU	Patton 15 run (kick failed)
SJSU	Saxon 16 run (pass failed)
EMU	Ostrander 32 pass from Adams (Henneghan kick)

December 10, 1988
Fresno St 35, Western Michigan 30

	1ST	2ND	3RD	4TH	FINAL
FRES	7	7	21	0	35
WMU	0	17	7	6	30

SCORING SUMMARY
FRES	Alexander 55 pass from Barsotti (Loop kick)
FRES	Alexander 38 pass from Barsotti (Loop kick)
WMU	Oliver 31 pass from Kimbrough (Creek kick)
WMU	Davis 51 run (Creek kick)
WMU	FG Creek 29
FRES	Rosette 65 run (Loop kick)
WMU	Davis 15 pass from Kimbrough (Creek kick)
FRES	Rosette 4 run (Loop kick)
FRES	Jones 26 run (Loop kick)
WMU	Kimbrough 6 run (pass failed)

FRES	TEAM STATISTICS	WMU
17	First Downs	24
200	Rushing Yards	137
15-29-3	Passing	24-57-0
240	Passing Yards	366
440	Total Yards	503
9-36.0	Punts - Average	10-37.0
1-1	Fumbles - Lost	3-2
20-166	Penalties - Yards	8-65
32:34	Possession Time	27:26

INDIVIDUAL LEADERS

RUSHING
FRES: Rosette 23-149, 2 TD; Jones 6-69, 1 TD.
WMU: Davis 15-71, 1 TD; Kimbrough 17-65, 1 TD.

PASSING
FRES : Barsotti 15-29-3, 240 yards, 2 TD.
WMU: Kimbrough 24-57-0, 366 yards, 2 TD.

RECEIVING
FRES : Alexander 3-103, 2 TD; Jones 5-76.
WMU: Boyko 5-120; Oliver 7-119, 1 TD.

December 9, 1989
Fresno State 27, Ball State 6

	1ST	2ND	3RD	4TH	FINAL
FRES	0	10	3	14	27
BSU	0	6	0	0	6

SCORING SUMMARY
FRES	FG Loop 34
BSU	Barbee 1 run (kick failed)
FRES	Shelley 91 pass from Barsotti (Loop kick)
FRES	FG Loop 27
FRES	Cox 58 interception return (Loop kick)
FRES	Thornton 5 pass from Buechele (Loop kick)

FRES	TEAM STATISTICS	BSU
18	First Downs	16
116	Rushing Yards	61
17-28-0	Passing	15-32-4
309	Passing Yards	160
425	Total Yards	221
2-2	Punt Returns - Yards	3-10
2-19	Kickoff Returns - Yards	6-149
6-31.7	Punts - Average	7-34.0
0-0	Fumbles - Lost	0-0
9-57	Penalties - Yards	4-30
31:41	Possession Time	29:18

INDIVIDUAL LEADERS

RUSHING
FRES: Craver 22-65; Cooks 8-31.
BSU: Parmalee 21-77; Hammersley 1-3.

PASSING
FRES: Barsotti 14-23-0, 246 yards, 1 TD.
BSU: Riley 13-29-3, 138 yards.

RECEIVING
FRES: Jones 7-70; Pickens 2-66.
BSU: Wilson 5-46; Parmalee 4-18.

December 8, 1990
San Jose St 48, Central Michigan 24

	1ST	2ND	3RD	4TH	FINAL
SJSU	7	19	15	7	48
CMU	0	7	3	14	24

SCORING SUMMARY
SJSU	Canley 5 run (Bowen kick)
SJSU	FG Bowen 37
CMU	Ealy 55 pass from Bender (Nicholl kick)
SJSU	Canley 22 run (Bowen kick)
SJSU	Blackmon 25 pass from Marrini (run failed)
SJSU	FG Bowen 25
CMU	FG Nicholl 27
SJSU	Canley 59 run (Blackmon pass from Marrini)
SJSU	Canley 5 run (Bowen kick)
SJSU	Canley 5 pass from Marrini (Bowen kick)
CMU	Ealy 48 pass from Bender (Nicholl kick)
CMU	Ealy 17 pass from Bender (Nicholl kick)

SJSU	TEAM STATISTICS	CMU
28	First Downs	13
200	Rushing Yards	63
32-43-1	Passing	14-25-1
442	Passing Yards	220
642	Total Yards	283
2-1	Fumbles - Lost	1-1
12-118	Penalties - Yards	4-30
37:11	Possession Time	22:49

INDIVIDUAL LEADERS

RUSHING
SJSU: Canley 23-164, 4 TD; Barbosa 8-16.
CMU: Smith 20-37; Rush 3-10.

PASSING
SJSU: Marrini 27-36-1, 404 yards, 2 TD.
CMU: Bender 14-25-1, 220 yards, 3 TD.

RECEIVING
SJSU: Blakes 4-95; Jackson 4-69.
CMU: Ealy 7-161, 3 TD; Kench 4-36.

DECEMBER 14, 1991
BOWLING GREEN 28, FRESNO STATE 21

	1ST	2ND	3RD	4TH	FINAL
BG	14	7	0	7	28
FRES	7	7	0	7	21

SCORING SUMMARY

BG	Landman 5 pass from Smith (Leaver kick)
BG	Szlachcic 29 pass from White (Leaver kick)
FRES	Barsotti 3 run (Mahoney kick)
BG	Szlachcic 9 pass from White (Leaver kick)
FRES	Daigle 57 run (Mahoney kick)
BG	Smith 1 run (Leaver kick)
FRES	Thompson 5 pass from Barsotti (Mahoney kick)

BG	TEAM STATISTICS	FRES
22	First Downs	24
115	Rushing Yards	198
19-31-1	Passing	25-36-1
268	Passing Yards	286
383	Total Yards	484
4-31.6	Punts - Average	3-32.0
2-1	Fumbles - Lost	2-2
3-36	Penalties - Yards	11-86
30:46	Possession Time	29:14

INDIVIDUAL LEADERS

RUSHING
BG: Jackson 16-59; Smith 13-46, 1 TD.
FRES: Neal 14-78; Daigle 8-77, 1 TD.
PASSING
BG: White 18-30-1, 263 yards, 2 TD.
FRES: Barsotti 25-36-1, 286 yards, 1 TD.
RECEIVING
BG: Szlachcic 11-189, 2 TD; Redd 2-47.
FRES: Rivers 6-84; Winans 3-66.

CAMELLIA BOWL

PROFILE

Site: Lafayette, La.
Surface: Grass
Stadium: McNasty Stadium

SEASON	DATE	TEAMS	PRE-GAME RANK	SCORE	FINAL RANK	MOST VALUABLE PLAYERS	ATT.
1948	Dec. 30, 1948	Hardin-Simmons		49			4,500
		Wichita State		12			

DECEMBER 30, 1948
HARDIN-SIMMONS 49, WICHITA STATE 12

	1ST	2ND	3RD	4TH	FINAL
HS	0	14	14	21	49
WICH	6	0	6	0	12

HS	TEAM STATISTICS	WICH
547	Total Yards	361

CHERRY BOWL

PROFILE

Site: Pontiac, Mich.
Stadium: Pontiac Silverdome
Capacity: 80,311
Surface: AstroTurf

YEAR	DATE	TEAMS	GAME RANK	SCORE	FINAL RANK	MOST VALUABLE PLAYERS	ATT.
1984	Dec. 22, 1984	Army		10		Nate Sassaman, Army, QB	70,332
		Michigan State		6			
1985	Dec. 21, 1985	Maryland	20	35	18	Stan Gelbaugh, Maryland, QB	51,858
		Syracuse		18			

DECEMBER 22, 1984
ARMY 10, MICHIGAN STATE 6

	1ST	2ND	3RD	4TH	FINAL
ARMY	0	7	0	3	10
MSU	0	0	0	6	6

SCORING SUMMARY

ARMY	Jones 4 run (Stopa kick)
ARMY	FG Stopa 38
MSU	Wasczenski 36 pass from Yarema (pass failed)

ARMY	TEAM STATISTICS	MSU
15	First Downs	13
256	Rushing Yards	89
1-2-1	Passing	11-25-3
10	Passing Yards	155
266	Total Yards	244
2-18	Punt Returns - Yards	6-23
0-0	Kickoff Returns - Yards	2-29
7-36.7	Punts - Average	4-55.8
2-1	Fumbles - Lost	3-2
1-7	Penalties - Yards	4-26

INDIVIDUAL LEADERS
RUSHING
ARMY: Sassaman 28-136; Black 22-57; Jones 10-41, 1 TD.
MSU: White 23-103.
PASSING
ARMY: Sassaman 1-2-1, 10 yards.
MSU: Yarema 11-25-3, 155 yards, 1 TD.
RECEIVING
ARMY: Hollingsworth 1-10.
MSU: Rolle 5-65; Wasczenski 2-54, 1 TD.

DECEMBER 21, 1985
MARYLAND 35, SYRACUSE 18

	1ST	2ND	3RD	4TH	FINAL
MD	6	22	7	0	35
SYR	3	7	8	0	18

SCORING SUMMARY

SYR	FG McAulay 26
MD	Gelbaugh 4 run (kick failed)
SYR	Drummond 10 run (McAulay kick)
MD	Knight 3 pass from Gelbaugh (Badajnek run)
MD	Tye 8 fumble return (Plocki kick)
MD	Blount 20 run (Plocki kick)
MD	Abdur-Ra'oof 6 pass from Gelbaugh (Plocki kick)
SYR	McPherson 17 run (Schwedes pass from McPherson)

MD	TEAM STATISTICS	SYR
22	First Downs	28
244	Rushing Yards	241
14-20-1	Passing	18-30-3
223	Passing Yards	204
467	Total Yards	445
1-10	Punt Returns - Yards	2-18
3-71	Kickoff Returns - Yards	6-111
3-38.7	Punts - Average	1-52.0
0-0	Fumbles - Lost	3-2
5-54	Penalties - Yards	3-26

INDIVIDUAL LEADERS
RUSHING
MD: Blount 24-132, 1 TD.
SYR: McPherson 21-111, 1 TD; Drummond 10-93, 1 TD.
PASSING
MD: Gelbaugh 14-20-1, 223 yards, 2 TD.
SYR: McPherson 18-30-3, 204 yards.
RECEIVING
MD: Abdur-Ra'oof 5-86, 1 TD.
SYR: Schwedes 4-69; Siano 5-60.

COLLEGE ALL-STAR GAME

PROFILE

Site: Chicago
Stadium: Soldier Field (except 1943-44, Dyche Stadium, Evanston, Ind.)
Capacity: 100,000
Surface: Grass

SEASON	DATE	PRE-GAME RANK	TEAMS	SCORE	FINAL RANK	MOST VALUABLE PLAYERS	ATT.
1934	Aug. 31, 1934		Chicago Bears	0			79,432
			All-Stars	0			
1935	Aug. 29, 1935		Chicago Bears	5			77,450
			All-Stars	0			
1936	Sept. 2, 1936		Detroit Lions	7			76,301
			All-Stars	7			
1937	Sept. 1, 1937		All-Stars	6			84,560
			Green Bay Packers	0			
1938	Aug. 31, 1938		All-Stars	28			74,250
			Washington Redskins	16		Cecil Isbell, Purdue, HB	
1939	Aug. 30, 1939		New York Giants	9			81,456
			All-Stars	0		Bill Osmanski, Holy Cross, HB	
1940	Aug. 29, 1940		Green Bay Packers	45			84,567
			All-Stars	28		Ambrose Schindler, USC, QB	
1941	Aug. 28, 1941		Chicago Bears	37			98,203
			All-Stars	13		George Franck, Minnesota, HB	
1942	Aug. 28, 1942		Chicago Bears	21			101,103
			All-Stars	0		Bruce Smith, Minnesota, HB	
1943	Aug. 25, 1943		All-Stars	27		Pat Harder, Wisconsin, FB	48,437
			Washington Redskins	7			
1944	Aug. 30, 1944		Chicago Bears	24			49,246
			All-Stars	21		Glenn Dobbs, Tulsa, FB	
1945	Aug. 30, 1945		Green Bay Packers	19			92,753
			All-Stars	7		Charles Trippi, Georgia, HB	
1946	Aug. 23, 1946		All-Stars	16		Elroy Hirsch, Wisconsin, HB	97,380
			Los Angeles Rams	0			
1947	Aug. 22, 1947		All-Stars	16		Claude "Buddy" Young, Illinois, HB	105,840
			Chicago Bears	0			
1948	Aug. 20, 1948		Chicago Cardinals	28			101,220
			All-Stars	0		Jay Rhodemyre, Kentucky, C	
1949	Aug. 12, 1949		Philadelphia Eagles	38			93,780
			All-Stars	0		Bill Fischer, Notre Dame, G	
1950	Aug. 11, 1950		All-Stars	17		Charles Justice, North Carolina, HB	88,885
			Philadelphia Eagles	7			
1951	Aug. 17, 1951		Cleveland Browns	33			92,180
			All-Stars	0		Lewis "Bud" McFodin, Texas, G	
1952	Aug. 15, 1952		Los Angeles Rams	10			88,316
			All-Stars	7		Vito "Babe" Parilli, Kentucky, QB	
1953	Aug. 14, 1953		Detroit Lions	24			93,818
			All-Stars	10		Gib Dawson, Texas, HB	
1954	Aug. 13, 1954		Detroit Lions	31			93,470
			All-Stars	6		Carlton Massey, Texas, E	
1955	Aug. 12, 1955		All-Stars	30		Ralph Gugliemi, Notre Dame, QB	75,000
			Cleveland Browns	27			
1956	Aug. 10, 1956		Cleveland Browns	26			75,000
			All-Stars	0		Bob Pellegrini, Maryland, C	
1957	Aug. 9, 1957		New York Giants	22			75,000
			All-Stars	12		John Brodie, Stanford, QB	
1958	Aug. 15, 1958		All-Stars	35		Bob Mitchell, Illinois HB and Jim Ninowski, Michigan State QB	70,000
			Detroit Lions	19			
1959	Aug. 14, 1959		Baltimore Colts	29			70,000
			All-Stars	0		Bob Ptacek, Michigan, QB	
1960	Aug. 12, 1960		Baltimore Colts	32			70,000
			All-Stars	7		Jim Leo, Cincinnati, E	
1961	Aug. 4, 1961		Philadelphia Eagles	28			66,000
			All-Stars	14		Bill Kilmer, UCLA, QB	
1962	Aug. 3, 1962		Green Bay Packers	42			65,000
			All-Stars	20		John Hadl, Kansas, QB	
1963	Aug. 2, 1963		All-Stars	20		Ron VanderKelen, Wisconsin, QB	65,000
			Green Bay Packers	17			
1964	Aug. 7, 1964		Chicago Bears	28			65,000
			All-Stars	17		Charles Taylor, Arizona State , QB	
1965	Aug. 6, 1965		Cleveland Browns	24			68,000
			All-Stars	16		John Huarte, Notre Dame, QB	
1966	Aug. 5, 1966		Green Bay Packers	38			72,000
			All-Stars	0		Gary Lane, Missouri, QB	
1967	Aug. 4, 1967		Green Bay Packers	27			70,934
			All-Stars	0		Charles "Bubba" Smith, Michigan State, T	
1968	Aug. 2, 1968		Green Bay Packers	34			69,917
			All-Stars	17		Larry Csonka, Syracuse, HB	
1969	Aug. 1, 1969		New York Jets	26			74,208
			All-Stars	24		Greg Cook, Cincinnati, QB	
1970	Jul. 31, 1970		Kansas City Chiefs	24			69,940
			All-Stars	3		Bruce Taylor, Boston, DB	
1971	Jul. 30, 1971		Baltimore	24			52,289
			All-Stars	17		Richard Harris, Grambling, DE	
1972	Jul. 28, 1972		Dallas Cowboys	20			54,162
			All-Stars	7		Pat Sullivan, Auburn, QB	
1973	Jul. 27, 1973		Miami Dolphins	14			54,103
			All-Stars	3		Ray Guy, Southern Mississippi, K	
*							
1975	Aug. 1, 1975		Pittsburgh Steelers	21			54,562
			All-Stars	14		Steve Bartkowski, California, QB	
1976 #	Jul. 23, 1976		Pittsburgh Steelers	24			52,895
			All-Stars	0			

* No game due to NFL players strike
# Bad weather prevented completion of game

August 31, 1934
Chicago Bears 0, All-Stars 0

	1st	2nd	3rd	4th	final
CHB	0	0	0	0	0
CAS	0	0	0	0	0

CHB	TEAM STATISTICS	CAS
3	First Downs	6
57	Rushing Yards	136
3-12-4	Passing	1-13-4
66	Passing Yards	7
123	Total Yards	143
3-25	Punt Returns - Yards	3-33
1-22	Kickoff Returns - Yards	1-33
12-31.8	Punts - Average	11-34.1
4-2	Fumbles - Lost	2-2
5-45	Penalties - Yards	4-30

August 29, 1935
Chicago Bears 5, All-Stars 0

	1st	2nd	3rd	4th	final
CHB	3	0	0	2	5
CAS	0	0	0	0	0

SCORING SUMMARY
CHB FG Manders 27
CHB Safety (Shepherd tackled in end zone)

CHB	TEAM STATISTICS	CAS
9	First Downs	5
157	Rushing Yards	49
4-13-0	Passing	5-10-1
11	Passing Yards	13
168	Total Yards	62
5-37	Punt Returns - Yards	1-0
1-8	Kickoff Returns - Yards	1-28
14-43.2	Punts - Average	14-37.1
2-1	Fumbles - Lost	2-1
9-94	Penalties - Yards	1-5

September 2, 1936
Detroit Lions 7, All-Stars 7

	1st	2nd	3rd	4th	final
DET	0	0	0	7	7
CAS	0	7	0	0	7

SCORING SUMMARY
CAS LeVoir 17 run (Fromhart kick)
DET Caddel 8 run (Clark kick)

DET	TEAM STATISTICS	CAS
5	First Downs	9
124	Rushing Yards	117
1-5-1	Passing	4-8-0
4	Passing Yards	49
128	Total Yards	166
4-29	Punt Returns - Yards	4-56
2-48	Kickoff Returns - Yards	1-25
9-33.5	Punts - Average	10-32.0
1-0	Fumbles - Lost	3-1
1-33	Penalties - Yards	4-50

September 1, 1937
All-Stars 6, Green Bay Packers 0

	1st	2nd	3rd	4th	final
CAS	6	0	0	0	6
GB	0	0	0	0	0

SCORING SUMMARY
CAS Tinsley 47 pass from Baugh (kick failed)

CAS	TEAM STATISTICS	GB
8	First Downs	17
65	Rushing Yards	126
7-13-0	Passing	14-38-3
115	Passing Yards	202
180	Total Yards	328
4-58	Punt Returns - Yards	4-34
0-0	Kickoff Returns - Yards	1-28
12-39.1	Punts - Average	8-39.0
1-0	Fumbles - Lost	1-0
7-45	Penalties - Yards	2-10

INDIVIDUAL LEADERS
PASSING
CAS: Baugh 7-13-0, 115 yards, 1 TD.
GB: Herber 14-38-3, 202 yards.

August 31, 1938
All-Stars 28, Washington Redskins 16

	1st	2nd	3rd	4th	final
CAS	3	0	12	13	28
WASH	7	3	0	6	16

SCORING SUMMARY
CAS FG McDonald 15
WASH Krause 4 run (Smith kick)
WASH FG Smith 30
CAS Kovatch 40 pass from Isbell (kick failed)
CAS Dougherty 40 interception return (kick failed)
CAS Davis 4 run (kick blocked)
WASH Karamatic 2 run (kick failed)
CAS Uram 47 interception return (Patrick kick)

CAS	TEAM STATISTICS	WASH
7	First Downs	13
23	Rushing Yards	103
8-19-1	Passing	11-24-5
159	Passing Yards	147
182	Total Yards	250
3-10	Punt Returns - Yards	2-20
1-29	Kickoff Returns - Yards	6-138
4-32.0	Punts - Average	7-28.0
4-1	Fumbles - Lost	3-1
5-25	Penalties - Yards	8-50

August 30, 1939
New York Giants 9, All-Stars 0

	1st	2nd	3rd	4th	final
NYG	3	3	0	3	9
CAS	0	0	0	0	0

SCORING SUMMARY
NYG FG Cuff 34
NYG FG Strong 22
NYG FG Strong 41

NYG	TEAM STATISTICS	CAS
9	First Downs	10
135	Rushing Yards	63
5-12-1	Passing	9-17-5
54	Passing Yards	89
189	Total Yards	152
3-34	Punt Returns - Yards	3-16
1-18	Kickoff Returns - Yards	3-45
6-42.0	Punts - Average	6-44.0
1-0	Fumbles - Lost	3-2
5-39	Penalties - Yards	3-15

August 29, 1940
Green Bay Packers 45, All-Stars 28

	1st	2nd	3rd	4th	final
GB	14	14	7	10	45
CAS	7	14	0	7	28

SCORING SUMMARY
CAS Schindler 1 run (Kinnick kick)
GB Hutson 61 pass from Isbell (Smith kick)
GB Mulloneaux 26 pass from Isbell (Smith kick)
CAS Washington 1 run (Kellogg kick)
GB Uram 60 pass from Herber (Engebratsen kick)
GB Hutson 35 pass from Isbell (Smith kick)
CAS McFadden 56 pass from Kinnick (Kinnick kick)
GB Hutson 29 pass from Herber (Smith kick)
CAS Schindler 1 run (Kinnick kick)
GB FG Smith 34
GB Isbell 4 run (Hurson kick)

GB	TEAM STATISTICS	CAS
9	First Downs	9
50	Rushing Yards	92
11-20-2	Passing	7-23-1
306	Passing Yards	134
356	Total Yards	226
7-24	Punt Returns - Yards	5-59
2-72	Kickoff Returns - Yards	7-184
7-38.5	Punts - Average	9-31.5
1-0	Fumbles - Lost	3-1
2-20	Penalties - Yards	5-45

August 28, 1941
Chicago Bears 37, All-Stars 13

	1st	2nd	3rd	4th	final
CHB	6	7	3	21	37
CAS	6	0	0	7	13

SCORING SUMMARY
CHB Kavanaugh 34 pass from Luckman (kick blocked)
CAS Franck 22 pass from Harmon (kick blocked)
CHB Clark 1 run (Manders kick)
CHB FG Arloe 46
CAS Robinson 46 pass from O'Rourke (Lio kick)
CHB Clark 1 run (Manders kick)
CHB McAfee 25 pass from Luckman (Manders kick)
CHB Nowaskey 9 pass from Bussey (Manders kick)

CHB	TEAM STATISTICS	CAS
19	First Downs	14
176	Rushing Yards	120
17-29-1	Passing	9-19-1
286	Passing Yards	172
462	Total Yards	292
1-8	Punt Returns - Yards	2-23
3-63	Kickoff Returns - Yards	5-109
4-43.0	Punts - Average	4-46.2
3-1	Fumbles - Lost	3-1
14-82	Penalties - Yards	5-39

August 28, 1942
Chicago Bears 21, All-Stars 0

	1st	2nd	3rd	4th	final
CHB	7	7	7	0	21
CAS	0	0	0	0	0

SCORING SUMMARY
CHB Gallarneau 4 run (Stydahar kick)
CHB Pool 24 pass from Bussey (Stydahar kick)
CHB Gallarneau 8 run (Stydahar kick)

CHB	TEAM STATISTICS	CAS
18	First Downs	7
239	Rushing Yards	44
7-17-3	Passing	8-29-2
195	Passing Yards	81
434	Total Yards	125
6-66	Punt Returns - Yards	3-108
1-18	Kickoff Returns - Yards	1-20
4-44.7	Punts - Average	7-46.7
3-3	Fumbles - Lost	3-1
7-57	Penalties - Yards	1-5

August 25, 1943
All-Stars 27, Washington Redskins 7

	1st	2nd	3rd	4th	final
CAS	7	7	6	7	27
WASH	0	7	0	0	7

SCORING SUMMARY
CAS Steuber 50 punt return (Harder kick)
WASH Aguirre 6 pass from Baugh (Masterson kick)
CAS Harder 37 pass from Dobbs (Harder kick)
CAS Graham 97 interception return (kick blocked)
CAS Harder 33 run (Graham kick)

CAS	TEAM STATISTICS	WASH
10	First Downs	15
103	Rushing Yards	40
9-15-0	Passing	22-46-3
116	Passing Yards	273
219	Total Yards	313
2-67	Punt Returns - Yards	2-4
1-24	Kickoff Returns - Yards	4-113
8-40.1	Punts - Average	7-35.8
5-2	Fumbles - Lost	6-1
2-10	Penalties - Yards	6-60

August 30, 1944
Chicago Bears 24, All-Stars 21

	1st	2nd	3rd	4th	final
CHB	0	14	7	3	24
CAS	14	0	7	0	21

SCORING SUMMARY
CAS Miller 4 pass from Dobbs (Saban kick)
CAS Tavener 12 fumble return (Saban kick)
CHB Famiglietti 3 run (Gudauskas kick)
CHB Benton 12 pass from Luckman (Gudauskas kick)
CAS Saban 1 run (Saban kick)
CHB McLeon 19 run (Gudauskas kick)
CHB FG Gudauskas 13

CHB	TEAM STATISTICS	CAS
13	First Downs	10
149	Rushing Yards	74
12-22-1	Passing	14-28-3
129	Passing Yards	147
278	Total Yards	221
3-48	Punt Returns - Yards	3-36
1-19	Kickoff Returns - Yards	4-59
7-36.7	Punts - Average	7-39.1
2-1	Fumbles - Lost	6-1
8-60	Penalties - Yards	9-65

August 30, 1945
Green Bay Packers 19, All-Stars 7

	1ST	2ND	3RD	4TH	FINAL
GB	3	9	0	7	19
CAS	0	7	0	0	7

SCORING SUMMARY
GB	FG Hutson 12
GB	Safety
GB	McKay 20 pass from Rohrig (Hutson kick)
CAS	Scollard 63 pass from Kennedy (Harmon kick)
GB	Hutson 85 interception return (Hutson kick)

GB	TEAM STATISTICS	CAS
15	First Downs	12
259	Rushing Yards	135
8-24-5	Passing	9-22-5
85	Passing Yards	162
344	Total Yards	297
1-3	Punt Returns - Yards	1-5
3-48	Kickoff Returns - Yards	3-66
4-39.7	Punts - Average	4-49.2
2-2	Fumbles - Lost	5-4
8-55	Penalties - Yards	6-40

August 23, 1946
All-Stars 16, Los Angeles Rams 0

	1ST	2ND	3RD	4TH	FINAL
CAS	7	0	7	2	16
LA	0	0	0	0	0

SCORING SUMMARY
CAS	Hirsch 68 run (Harder kick)
CAS	Hirsch 62 pass from Graham (Harder kick)
CAS	Safety (Washington tackled in end zone)

CAS	TEAM STATISTICS	LA
6	First Downs	6
110	Rushing Yards	58
6-13-2	Passing	8-27-3
121	Passing Yards	98
231	Total Yards	156
3-59	Punt Returns - Yards	4-52
1-15	Kickoff Returns - Yards	3-52
5-40.6	Punts - Average	6-42.6
6-4	Fumbles - Lost	2-0
7-50	Penalties - Yards	8-80

August 22, 1947
All-Stars 16, Chicago Bears 0

	1ST	2ND	3RD	4TH	FINAL
CAS	13	0	3	0	16
CHB	0	0	0	0	0

SCORING SUMMARY
CAS	Mello 6 run (kick blocked)
CAS	Zilly 46 pass from Ratterman (Case kick)
CAS	FG Case 21

CAS	TEAM STATISTICS	CHB
11	First Downs	8
189	Rushing Yards	35
8-12-1	Passing	8-22-0
151	Passing Yards	81
340	Total Yards	116
4-57	Punt Returns - Yards	2-20
1-12	Kickoff Returns - Yards	4-61
4-38.8	Punts - Average	6-39.1
2-0	Fumbles - Lost	5-4
9-91	Penalties - Yards	5-50

August 20, 1948
Chicago Cardinals 28, All-Stars 0

	1ST	2ND	3RD	4TH	FINAL
CHC	7	7	0	14	28
CAS	0	0	0	0	0

SCORING SUMMARY
CHC	Angsman 2 run (Harder kick)
CHC	Schwall 14 run (Harder kick)
CHC	Banonis 31 interception return (Harder kick)
CHC	Trippi 13 pass from Mallouf (Harder kick)

CHC	TEAM STATISTICS	CAS
18	First Downs	12
200	Rushing Yards	102
11-24-1	Passing	9-27-1
133	Passing Yards	132
333	Total Yards	234
2-36	Punt Returns - Yards	0-0
1-6	Kickoff Returns - Yards	4-71
3-25.3	Punts - Average	6-34.7
4-3	Fumbles - Lost	2-1
4-30	Penalties - Yards	2-20

August 12, 1949
Philadelphia Eagles 38, All-Stars 0

	1ST	2ND	3RD	4TH	FINAL
PHI	0	17	7	14	38
CAS	0	0	0	0	0

SCORING SUMMARY
PHI	Van Buren 1 run (Patton kick)
PHI	FG Patton 14
PHI	Craft 4 run (Patton kick)
PHI	Pinos 7 pass from Thompson (Patton kick)
PHI	Doss 4 run (Patton kick)
PHI	Armstrong 13 pass from Mackrides (Patton kick)

PHI	TEAM STATISTICS	CAS
19	First Downs	5
228	Rushing Yards	116
12-31-1	Passing	3-15-3
130	Passing Yards	-3
358	Total Yards	113
2-19	Punt Returns - Yards	0-0
1-24	Kickoff Returns - Yards	5-95
3-29.0	Punts - Average	7-26.6
1-0	Fumbles - Lost	3-3
1-5	Penalties - Yards	3-25

August 11, 1950
All-Stars 17, Philadelphia 7

	1ST	2ND	3RD	4TH	FINAL
CAS	7	7	0	3	17
PHI	0	0	0	7	7

SCORING SUMMARY
CAS	Pasquariello 1 run (Soltau kick)
CAS	Justice 35 pass from LeBaron (Soltau kick)
PHI	Van Buren 1 run (Patton kick)
CAS	FG Soltau 23

CAS	TEAM STATISTICS	PHI
9	First Downs	14
221	Rushing Yards	85
2-9-0	Passing	15-28-3
75	Passing Yards	131
296	Total Yards	216
2-22	Punt Returns - Yards	2-18
2-18	Kickoff Returns - Yards	2-48
3-40.0	Punts - Average	3-34.0
4-3	Fumbles - Lost	2-1
3-25	Penalties - Yards	1-5

August 17, 1951
Cleveland Browns 33, All-Stars 0

	1ST	2ND	3RD	4TH	FINAL
CLE	2	10	7	14	33
CAS	0	0	0	0	0

SCORING SUMMARY
CLE	Safety (Williams tackled in end zone)
CLE	Jones 2 run (Groza kick)
CLE	FG Groza 17
CLE	Jones 3 run (Groza kick)
CLE	Lavelli 14 pass from Graham (Groza kick)
CLE	Cole 5 pass from Graham (Groza kick)

CLE	TEAM STATISTICS	CAS
20	First Downs	5
132	Rushing Yards	83
20-33-2	Passing	5-15-3
293	Passing Yards	43
425	Total Yards	126
5-59	Punt Returns - Yards	1-0
4-35.3	Punts - Average	9-31.7
1-1	Fumbles - Lost	2-0
7-73	Penalties - Yards	3-33

August 15, 1952
Los Angeles Rams 10, All-Stars 7

	1ST	2ND	3RD	4TH	FINAL
LAR	0	0	0	10	10
CAS	0	7	0	0	7

SCORING SUMMARY
CAS	Janowicz 3 run (Janowicz kick)
LAR	Younger 3 pass from Van Brocklin (Waterfield kick)
LAR	FG Waterfield 24

LAR	TEAM STATISTICS	CAS
18	First Downs	13
107	Rushing Yards	178
15-37-2	Passing	7-15-3
170	Passing Yards	104
277	Total Yards	282
5-15	Punt Returns - Yards	1-12
1-25	Kickoff Returns - Yards	2-38
7-41.1	Punts - Average	7-41.7
2-0	Fumbles - Lost	7-5
6-60	Penalties - Yards	8-71

August 14, 1953
Detroit Lions 24, All-Stars 10

	1ST	2ND	3RD	4TH	FINAL
DET	7	3	7	7	24
CAS	0	3	0	7	10

SCORING SUMMARY
DET	Hoernschemeyer 5 run (Harder kick)
DET	FG Walker 10
CAS	FG Dawson 23
DET	Box 8 pass from Layne (Harder kick)
DET	Hoernschemeyer 2 run (Harder kick)
CAS	Dawson 17 run (Samuels kick)

DET	TEAM STATISTICS	CAS
21	First Downs	14
134	Rushing Yards	109
24-33-1	Passing	9-28-1
339	Passing Yards	80
473	Total Yards	189
1-2	Punt Returns - Yards	2-37
4-74	Kickoff Returns - Yards	3-122
4-41.5	Punts - Average	5-25.4
2-1	Fumbles - Lost	1-1
10-112	Penalties - Yards	4-20

August 13, 1954
Detroit 31, All-Stars 6

	1ST	2ND	3RD	4TH	FINAL
DET	17	0	7	7	31
CAS	0	0	6	0	6

SCORING SUMMARY
DET	FG Martin 46
DET	Walker 5 run (Walker kick)
DET	Carpenter 4 run (Girard kick)
CAS	Lattner 4 run (kick blocked)
DET	Carpenter 1 run (Martin kick)
DET	Doran 34 fumble return (Walker kick)

DET	TEAM STATISTICS	CAS
20	First Downs	11
250	Rushing Yards	62
11-16-1	Passing	11-26-2
111	Passing Yards	82
361	Total Yards	144
3-42	Punt Returns - Yards	0-0
2-42	Kickoff Returns - Yards	5-92
2-36.5	Punts - Average	6-42.7
2-2	Fumbles - Lost	7-3
7-60	Penalties - Yards	2-10

August 12, 1955
All-Stars 30, Cleveland Browns 27

	1ST	2ND	3RD	4TH	FINAL
CAS	3	14	3	10	30
CLE	7	13	0	7	27

SCORING SUMMARY
CAS	FG Weed 21
CLE	Ratterman 1 run (Groza kick)
CAS	Eidorn 2 run (Weed kick)
CLE	Renfro 18 run (Groza kick)
CAS	Hair 5 pass from Guglielmi (Weed kick)
CLE	Renfro 25 pass from Ratterman (kick blocked)
CAS	FG Weed 19
CAS	Triplett 1 run (Leggett run)
CAS	FG Weed 41
CLE	Morrison 5 run (Groza kick)

CAS	TEAM STATISTICS	CLE
20	First Downs	15
200	Rushing Yards	163
10-19-2	Passing	9-18-1
129	Passing Yards	162
329	Total Yards	325
1-3	Punt Returns - Yards	0-0
4-100	Kickoff Returns - Yards	4-75
1-27.0	Punts - Average	4-42.8
3-0	Fumbles - Lost	1-1
2-10	Penalties - Yards	0-0

THE BOWLS

AUGUST 10, 1956
CLEVELAND BROWNS 26, ALL-STARS 0

	1ST	2ND	3RD	4TH	FINAL
CLE	7	6	6	7	26
CAS	0	0	0	0	0

SCORING SUMMARY

CLE	Morrison 13 pass from Ratterman (Groza kick)
CLE	FG Groza 38
CLE	FG Groza 30
CLE	FG Groza 24
CLE	FG Groza 27
CLE	Filipski 3 run (Groza kick)

CLE	TEAM STATISTICS	CAS
18	First Downs	5
191	Rushing Yards	121
8-18-0	Passing	2-10-2
88	Passing Yards	12
279	Total Yards	133
5-35	Punt Returns - Yards	2-4
1-23	Kickoff Returns - Yards	5-103
3-46.7	Punts - Average	6-39.2
0-0	Fumbles - Lost	3-2
6-61	Penalties - Yards	3-35

AUGUST 9, 1957
NEW YORK GIANTS 22, ALL-STARS 12

	1ST	2ND	3RD	4TH	FINAL
NYG	3	7	7	5	22
CAS	6	3	0	3	12

SCORING SUMMARY

CAS	Barnes 2 run (kick failed)
NYG	FG Agajanian 33
NYG	McAfee 36 pass from Conerly (Agajanian kick)
CAS	FG Cothren 12
NYG	McAfee 10 pass from Conerly (Agajanian kick)
NYG	FG Agajanian 45
CAS	FG Cothren 33
NYG	Safety (Woodson tackled in end zone)

NYG	TEAM STATISTICS	CAS
14	First Downs	16
121	Rushing Yards	87
12-24-0	Passing	13-27-0
160	Passing Yards	133
281	Total Yards	220
4-6	Punt Returns - Yards	4-17
5-99	Kickoff Returns - Yards	4-103
5-41.4	Punts - Average	5-41.2
2-1	Fumbles - Lost	3-1
7-82	Penalties - Yards	5-75

AUGUST 15, 1958
ALL-STARS 35, DETROIT LIONS 19

	1ST	2ND	3RD	4TH	FINAL
CAS	0	20	2	13	35
DET	7	0	6	6	19

SCORING SUMMARY

DET	Doran 24 pass from Rote (Layne kick)
CAS	FG Conrad 19
CAS	Mitchell 84 pass from Ninowski (Conrad kick)
CAS	Mitchell 18 pass from Ninowski (Conrad kick)
CAS	FG Conrad 33
CAS	Safety (Rote tackled in end zone)
DET	Gedman 9 run (kick blocked)
CAS	FG Conrad 24
CAS	FG Conrad 24
CAS	Howley 29 interception return (Conrad kick)
DET	Pleller 1 run (kick blocked)

CAS	TEAM STATISTICS	DET
11	First Downs	22
3	Rushing Yards	179
16-26-3	Passing	16-37-5
293	Passing Yards	193
296	Total Yards	372
1-28	Punt Returns - Yards	2-5
3-34	Kickoff Returns - Yards	7-159
3-46.3	Punts - Average	2-39.5
2-0	Fumbles - Lost	3-1
5-60	Penalties - Yards	9-99

AUGUST 14, 1959
BALTIMORE COLTS 29, ALL-STARS 0

	1ST	2ND	3RD	4TH	FINAL
BAL	8	21	0	0	29
CAS	0	0	0	0	0

SCORING SUMMARY

BAL	Safety (James snapped ball out of end zone)
BAL	Berry 3 pass from Unitas (kick failed)
BAL	Mutscheller 29 pass from Unitas (Rechichar kick)
BAL	Dupre 13 pass from Unitas (Rechichar kick)
BAL	Davis 38 interception return (Rechichar kick)

BAL	TEAM STATISTICS	CAS
18	First Downs	19
155	Rushing Yards	21
14-28-0	Passing	15-41-5
211	Passing Yards	186
366	Total Yards	207
2-9	Punt Returns - Yards	2-5
1-42	Kickoff Returns - Yards	3-38
5-38.0	Punts - Average	6-39.7
1-1	Fumbles - Lost	1-1
15-137	Penalties - Yards	0-0

AUGUST 12, 1960
BALTIMORE COLTS 32, ALL-STARS 7

	1ST	2ND	3RD	4TH	FINAL
BAL	7	17	5	3	32
CAS	0	0	0	7	7

SCORING SUMMARY

BAL	Moore 4 pass from Unitas (Myhra kick)
BAL	Moore 3 pass from Unitas (Myhra kick)
BAL	FG Myhra 38
BAL	Moore 14 pass from Unitas (Myhra kick)
BAL	Safety (Izo tackled in end zone)
BAL	FG Myhra 27
CAS	Gault 60 pass from Meredith (Khayat kick)
BAL	FG Myhra 26

BAL	TEAM STATISTICS	CAS
19	First Downs	10
133	Rushing Yards	13
22-42-1	Passing	9-27-3
281	Passing Yards	108
414	Total Yards	121
4-47	Punt Returns - Yards	1-4
3-93	Kickoff Returns - Yards	6-145
3-49.3	Punts - Average	6-40.7
2-0	Fumbles - Lost	2-1
5-75	Penalties - Yards	1-3

AUGUST 4, 1961
PHILADELPHIA EAGLES 28, ALL-STARS 14

	1ST	2ND	3RD	4TH	FINAL
PHI	14	7	0	7	28
CAS	0	0	0	14	14

SCORING SUMMARY

PHI	McDonald 27 pass from Jurgensen (Walston kick)
PHI	Retzlaff 25 pass from Jurgensen (Walston kick)
PHI	McDonald 24 pass from Hill (Walston kick)
PHI	McDonald 24 pass from Jurgensen (Walston kick)
CAS	Gregory 18 pass from Kilmer (Fleming kick)
CAS	Grecni 57 interception return (Fleming kick)

PHI	TEAM STATISTICS	CAS
17	First Downs	16
123	Rushing Yards	0
19-32-3	Passing	19-38-1
278	Passing Yards	271
401	Total Yards	271
3-46	Punt Returns - Yards	2-12
2-27	Kickoff Returns - Yards	3-83
4-38.0	Punts - Average	4-44.0
0-0	Fumbles - Lost	2-1
5-52	Penalties - Yards	3-40

AUGUST 3, 1962
GREEN BAY PACKERS 42, ALL-STARS 20

	1ST	2ND	3RD	4TH	FINAL
GB	7	7	7	21	42
CAS	7	3	10	0	20

SCORING SUMMARY

CAS	Gros 1 run (Mather kick)
GB	Dowler 22 pass from Starr (Hornung kick)
CAS	FG Mather 26
GB	Kramer 4 pass from Starr (Hornung kick)
CAS	Bryant 21 pass from Hadl (Mather kick)
GB	Dowler 22 pass from Starr (Hornung kick)
CAS	FG Mather 15
GB	McGee 20 pass from Starr (Hornung kick)
GB	McGee 38 pass from Starr (Hornung kick)
GB	Pitts 3 run (Hornung kick)

GB	TEAM STATISTICS	CAS
16	First Downs	11
125	Rushing Yards	16
13-25-1	Passing	14-26-1
255	Passing Yards	201
380	Total Yards	217
2-40	Punt Returns - Yards	0-0
5-108	Kickoff Returns - Yards	3-57
4-41.2	Punts - Average	6-47.8
2-2	Fumbles - Lost	3-1
6-70	Penalties - Yards	1-15

AUGUST 2, 1963
ALL-STARS 20, GREEN BAY PACKERS 17

	1ST	2ND	3RD	4TH	FINAL
CAS	3	7	0	10	20
GB	7	3	0	7	17

SCORING SUMMARY

GB	Taylor 2 run (Kramer kick)
CAS	FG Jencks 20
CAS	Ferguson 6 run (Jencks kick)
GB	FG Kramer 21
CAS	FG Jencks 33
CAS	Richter 73 pass from VanderKelen (Jencks kick)
GB	Taylor 1 run (Kramer kick)

CAS	TEAM STATISTICS	GB
16	First Downs	16
140	Rushing Yards	139
15-21-1	Passing	19-33-1
183	Passing Yards	169
323	Total Yards	308
0-0	Punt Returns - Yards	1-10
4-65	Kickoff Returns - Yards	5-107
2-30.5	Punts - Average	2-48.5
2-1	Fumbles - Lost	2-1
2-13	Penalties - Yards	5-77

AUGUST 7, 1964
CHICAGO BEARS 28, ALL-STARS 17

	1ST	2ND	3RD	4TH	FINAL
CHB	0	7	14	7	28
CAS	0	10	0	7	17

SCORING SUMMARY

CAS	FG Van Raaphorst 14
CHB	Ditka 13 pass from Wade (Jencks kick)
CAS	Davis 14 pass from Taylor (Van Raaphorst kick)
CHB	Wade 1 run (Jencks kick)
CHB	Barnes 20 pass from Wade (Jencks kick)
CHB	Bivins 30 pass from Bukich (Jencks kick)
CAS	Taylor 5 pass from Mira (Van Raaphorst kick)

CHB	TEAM STATISTICS	CAS
20	First Downs	17
84	Rushing Yards	142
20-33-3	Passing	13-27-2
287	Passing Yards	147
371	Total Yards	289
1-1	Punt Returns - Yards	1-6
0-0	Kickoff Returns - Yards	4-61
1-40.0	Punts - Average	3-38.0
1-1	Fumbles - Lost	5-2
7-75	Penalties - Yards	10-55

AUGUST 6, 1965
CLEVELAND BROWNS 24, ALL-STARS 16

	1ST	2ND	3RD	4TH	FINAL
CLE	7	10	7	0	24
CAS	0	3	6	7	16

SCORING SUMMARY

CLE	Brown 7 run (Groza kick)
CAS	FG Mercein 36
CLE	Sczurek blocked punt recovered in end zone (Groza kick)
CLE	FG Groza 30
CLE	Collins 10 pass from Ryan (Groza kick)
CAS	Mercein 5 pass from Huarte (kick failed)
CAS	Rentzal 5 pass from Huarte (Mercein kick)

CLE	TEAM STATISTICS	CAS
17	First Downs	15
165	Rushing Yards	23
9-24-1	Passing	16-24-0
123	Passing Yards	192
288	Total Yards	215
6-144	Punt Returns - Yards	2-7
3-43	Kickoff Returns - Yards	4-70
3-52.0	Punts - Average	8-40.0
0-0	Fumbles - Lost	1-0
11-137	Penalties - Yards	2-20

AUGUST 5, 1966
GREEN BAY PACKERS 38, ALL-STARS 0

	1ST	2ND	3RD	4TH	FINAL
GB	7	21	10	0	38
CAS	0	0	0	0	0

SCORING SUMMARY

GB	Dowler 10 pass from Starr (Chandler kick)
GB	Anderson 13 pass from Starr (Chandler kick)
GB	Taylor 1 run (Chandler kick)
GB	Adderley 36 interception return (Chandler kick)
GB	FG Chandler 17
GB	Taylor 13 run (Chandler kick)

GB	TEAM STATISTICS	CAS
24	First Downs	8
166	Rushing Yards	84
16-32-0	Passing	14-23-2
222	Passing Yards	73
388	Total Yards	157
2-82	Punt Returns - Yards	0-0
1-19	Kickoff Returns - Yards	6-108
1-41.0	Punts - Average	6-39.5
2-1	Fumbles - Lost	4-3
4-38	Penalties - Yards	7-65

AUGUST 4, 1967
GREEN BAY PACKERS 27, ALL-STARS 0

	1ST	2ND	3RD	4TH	FINAL
GB	6	14	0	7	27
CAS	0	0	0	0	0

SCORING SUMMARY

GB	FG Chandler 13
GB	FG Chandler 14
GB	Dowler 11 pass from Starr (Chandler kick)
GB	Long 22 pass from Starr (Chandler kick)
GB	Grabowski 22 run (Chandler kick)

GB	TEAM STATISTICS	CAS
27	First Downs	10
121	Rushing Yards	33
24-35-1	Passing	12-28-1
304	Passing Yards	103
425	Total Yards	136
1-40	Punt Returns - Yards	0-0
1-37	Kickoff Returns - Yards	3-58
2-40.0	Punts - Average	6-39.0
2-2	Fumbles - Lost	3-2
6-53	Penalties - Yards	5-50

AUGUST 2, 1968
GREEN BAY PACKERS 34, ALL-STARS 17

	1ST	2ND	3RD	4TH	FINAL
GB	7	17	0	10	34
CAS	0	3	7	7	17

SCORING SUMMARY

GB	Anderson 1 run (Kramer kick)
GB	Dale 20 pass from Starr (Kramer kick)
GB	Dale 36 pass from Starr (Kramer kick)
CAS	FG DePoyster 22
GB	FG Traynham 30
CAS	McCullouch 7 pass from Beban (DePoyster kick)
GB	Dale 23 pass from Starr (Kramer kick)
GB	FG Kramer 47
CAS	McCullouch 24 pass from Landry (DePoyster kick)

GB	TEAM STATISTICS	CAS
20	First Downs	17
89	Rushing Yards	206
18-26-0	Passing	10-20-3
292	Passing Yards	106
381	Total Yards	312
2-12	Punt Returns - Yards	1-1
2-47	Kickoff Returns - Yards	4-70
3-42.0	Punts - Average	4-42.0
1-1	Fumbles - Lost	2-1
6-40	Penalties - Yards	6-33

AUGUST 1, 1969
NEW YORK JETS 26, ALL-STARS 24

	1ST	2ND	3RD	4TH	FINAL
NYJ	6	7	10	3	26
CAS	0	0	17	7	24

SCORING SUMMARY

NYJ	FG Turner 43
NYJ	FG Turner 16
NYJ	Snell 3 run (Turner kick)
NYJ	FG Turner 42
CAS	Washington 17 pass from Cook (Gerela kick)
CAS	FG Gerela 28
NYJ	Snell 35 run (Turner kick)
CAS	Klein 12 pass from Cook (Gerela kick)
NYJ	FG Turner 18
CAS	LeVias 19 pass from Cook (Gerela kick)

NYJ	TEAM STATISTICS	CAS
28	First Downs	8
181	Rushing Yards	16
18-36-3	Passing	13-31-1
282	Passing Yards	244
463	Total Yards	260
1-33	Kickoff Returns - Yards	6-172
1-38.0	Punts - Average	7-41.0
3-1	Fumbles - Lost	0-0
3-47	Penalties - Yards	8-93

JULY 31, 1970
KANSAS CITY CHIEFS 24, ALL-STARS 3

	1ST	2ND	3RD	4TH	FINAL
KC	10	14	0	0	24
CAS	0	0	3	0	3

SCORING SUMMARY

KC	Pitts 25 pass from Dawson (Stenerud kick)
KC	FG Stenerud 43
KC	McVea 3 run (Stenerud kick)
KC	Kearney 65 interception return (Stenerud kick)
CAS	FG Delaney 26

KC	TEAM STATISTICS	CAS
16	First Downs	6
120	Rushing Yards	43
19-24-0	Passing	7-25-3
177	Passing Yards	46
297	Total Yards	89
2-24	Punt Returns - Yards	3-81
2-42	Kickoff Returns - Yards	4-96
2-39.0	Punts - Average	7-50.0
2-1	Fumbles - Lost	0-0
7-61	Penalties - Yards	2-20

JULY 30, 1971
BALTIMORE COLTS 24, ALL-STARS 17

	1ST	2ND	3RD	4TH	FINAL
BAL	7	7	3	7	24
CAS	0	10	0	7	17

SCORING SUMMARY

BAL	Perkins 24 pass from Morrall (O'Brien kick)
CAS	Brockington 1 run (Pastorini kick)
BAL	Matte 15 pass from Morrall (O'Brien kick)
CAS	FG Jacobs 40
BAL	FG O'Brien 22
BAL	Mitchell 44 pass from Morrall (O'Brien kick)
CAS	Ham 47 fumble return (Jacobs kick)

BAL	TEAM STATISTICS	CAS
18	First Downs	11
60	Rushing Yards	72
21-32-0	Passing	8-24-2
343	Passing Yards	78
403	Total Yards	150
5-20	Punt Returns - Yards	2-30
4-74	Kickoff Returns - Yards	4-60
4-39.0	Punts - Average	15-34.0
4-1	Fumbles - Lost	2-0
9-120	Penalties - Yards	8-78

JULY 28, 1972
DALLAS COWBOYS 20, ALL-STARS 7

	1ST	2ND	3RD	4TH	FINAL
DAL	3	7	7	3	20
CAS	0	0	0	7	7

SCORING SUMMARY

DAL	FG Clark 31
DAL	Sellers 16 pass from Morton (Clark kick)
DAL	Hayes 24 pass from Morton (Fritsch kick)
DAL	FG Fritsch 33
CAS	Newhouse 1 run (Marcol kick)

DAL	TEAM STATISTICS	CAS
16	First Downs	16
108	Rushing Yards	77
10-25-1	Passing	16-35-1
154	Passing Yards	156
262	Total Yards	233
1-11	Punt Returns - Yards	1-13
1-6	Kickoff Returns - Yards	2-16
6-41.0	Punts - Average	5-36.0
0-0	Fumbles - Lost	3-2
7-75	Penalties - Yards	8-70

JULY 27, 1973
MIAMI DOLPHINS 14, ALL-STARS 3

	1ST	2ND	3RD	4TH	FINAL
MIA	7	0	0	7	14
CAS	0	3	0	0	3

SCORING SUMMARY

MIA	Csonka 3 run (Yepremian kick)
CAS	FG Guy 19
MIA	Csonka 7 run (Yepremian kick)

MIA	TEAM STATISTICS	CAS
16	First Downs	9
173	Rushing Yards	79
9-13-0	Passing	9-20-1
78	Passing Yards	54
251	Total Yards	133
5-10	Punt Returns - Yards	2-18
2-58	Kickoff Returns - Yards	2-42
7-43.0	Punts - Average	9-44.0
4-1	Fumbles - Lost	2-1
5-60	Penalties - Yards	3-15

1974: NO GAME, NFLPA STRIKE

AUGUST 1, 1975
PITTSBURGH STEELERS 21, ALL-STARS 14

	1ST	2ND	3RD	4TH	FINAL
PITT	0	7	0	14	21
CAS	7	7	0	0	14

SCORING SUMMARY

CAS	McInally 28 pass from Bartkowski (Mike-Mayer kick)
PITT	Grossman 2 pass from Bradshaw (Gerela kick)
CAS	Livers 66 punt return (Mike-Mayer kick)
PITT	Bleier 6 pass from Gilliam (Gerela kick)
PITT	Lewis 21 pass from Gilliam (Gerela kick)

PITT	TEAM STATISTICS	CAS
20	First Downs	4
127	Rushing Yards	19
19-30-1	Passing	7-19-1
160	Passing Yards	104
287	Total Yards	123
4-20	Punt Returns - Yards	7-105
3-30	Kickoff Returns - Yards	3-75
7-43.0	Punts - Average	7-42.0
2-1	Fumbles - Lost	4-0
7-12	Penalties - Yards	9-100

JULY 23, 1976
PITTSBURGH STEELERS 24, ALL-STARS 0*

	1ST	2ND	3RD	4TH	FINAL
PITT	3	6	15	x	24
CAS	0	0	0	x	0

*Bad weather prevented completion of game

SCORING SUMMARY

PITT	FG Gerela 29
PITT	FG Gerela 32
PITT	FG Gerela 23
PITT	Safety (Pinney snapped ball out of end zone)
PITT	Harris 21 run (Gerela kick)
PITT	Reamon 2 run (kick failed)

PITT	TEAM STATISTICS	CAS
11	First Downs	3
70	Rushing Yards	36
12-28-2	Passing	6-12-1
168	Passing Yards	22
238	Total Yards	58
5-31.0	Punts - Average	7-31.0
1-0	Fumbles - Lost	6-30
5-40	Penalties - Yards	5-26

DELTA BOWL

PROFILE

Site: Memphis
Stadium: Crump Stadium
Capacity: 28,800
Surface: Grass

SEASON	DATE	PRE-GAME RANK	TEAMS	SCORE	FINAL RANK	MOST VALUABLE PLAYERS	ATT.
1947	Jan. 1, 1948	13	Mississippi	13		Charlie Conerly, Mississippi, QB	28,120
			TCU	9			
1948	Jan. 1, 1949	17	William & Mary	20			15,069
			Oklahoma State	0			

JANUARY 1, 1948
MISSISSIPPI 13, TCU 9

	1ST	2ND	3RD	4TH	FINAL
MISS	0	0	0	13	13
TCU	0	9	0	0	9

SCORING SUMMARY

TCU	Berry 30 interception return (Pitcock kick)
TCU	Safety (Conerly blocked punt out of end zone)
MISS	Johnson 30 pass from Conerly (kick failed)
MISS	Howell 13 pass from Conerly (Oswalt kick)

MISS	TEAM STATISTICS	TCU
15	First Downs	15
111	Rushing Yards	141
12-30-4	Passing	6-11-2
186	Passing Yards	55
297	Total Yards	196
3-40.6	Punts - Average	5-42.8
1-1	Fumbles - Lost	2-2
7-35	Penalties - Yards	5-45

INDIVIDUAL LEADERS

RUSHING
MISS: Salmon 6-48; Harrell 6-18.
TCU: Stout 15-73; McKelvey 7-26.

PASSING
MISS: Conerly 12-28-3, 186 yards, 2 TD.
TCU: Berry 3-5-1, 32 yards.

RECEIVING
MISS: Johnson 3-79, 1 TD; Howell 2-25, 1 TD.
TCU: Bailey 3-23; Stout 1-13.

JANUARY 1, 1949
WILLIAM & MARY 20, OKLAHOMA STATE 0

	1ST	2ND	3RD	4TH	FINAL
W&M	0	0	6	14	20
A&M	0	0	0	0	0

SCORING SUMMARY

W&M	Hoitsma 12 pass from Korczowski (kick failed)
W&M	Bruce 22 pass from Korczowski (Lex kick)
W&M	Creekmur 70 interception return (Lex kick)

W&M	TEAM STATISTICS	A&M
7	First Downs	10
161	Rushing Yards	161
5-12-0	Passing	6-27-2
50	Passing Yards	68
211	Total Yards	229
12-43.0	Punts - Average	9-43.0

DIXIE BOWL

PROFILE

Site: Birmingham
Stadium: Legion Field
Capacity: 35,000
Surface: Grass

SEASON	DATE	PRE-GAME RANK	TEAMS	SCORE	FINAL RANK	MOST VALUABLE PLAYERS	ATT.
1947	Jan. 1, 1948		Arkansas	21			22,000
		14	William & Mary	19			
1948	Jan. 1, 1949		Baylor	20			20,000
		20	Wake Forest	7			

JANUARY 1, 1948
ARKANSAS 21, WILLIAM & MARY 19

	1ST	2ND	3RD	4TH	FINAL
ARK	0	14	0	7	21
W&M	7	6	6	0	19

SCORING SUMMARY
W&M Cloud 1 run (Magdziak kick)
W&M Cloud 2 run (kick failed)
ARK Pritchard 59 pass from Holland (Fowler kick)
ARK McGaha 70 interception return (Fowler kick)
W&M Bland 6 pass from Magdziak (kick failed)
ARK Campbell 7 run (Fowler kick)

ARK	TEAM STATISTICS	W&M
9	First Downs	14
103	Rushing Yards	243
5-14-1	Passing	3-12-3
134	Passing Yards	47
237	Total Yards	290

JANUARY 1, 1949
BAYLOR 20, WAKE FOREST 7

	1ST	2ND	3RD	4TH	FINAL
BU	6	14	0	0	20
WFU	0	0	7	0	7

SCORING SUMMARY
BU Pierce 1 run (kick failed)
BU Mangrum 1 run (Dickerson kick)
BU Riley 12 pass from Painter (Dickerson kick)
WFU Sprock run (George kick)

BU	TEAM STATISTICS	WFU
11	First Downs	17
136	Rushing Yards	191
6-15-2	Passing	10-24-0
76	Passing Yards	86
212	Total Yards	277

DIXIE CLASSIC

PROFILE

Site: Dallas
Stadium: Fair Park Stadium
Surface: Grass

SEASON	DATE	PRE-GAME RANK	TEAMS	SCORE	FINAL RANK	MOST VALUABLE PLAYERS	ATT.
1921	Jan. 2, 1922		Texas A&M	22			12,000
			Centre	14			
1924	Jan. 1, 1925		West Va. Wesleyan	9			7,000
			SMU	7			
1933	Jan. 1, 1934		Arkansas	7			12,000
			Centenary	7			

JANUARY 2, 1922
TEXAS A&M 22, CENTRE 14

	1ST	2ND	3RD	4TH	FINAL
A&M	2	0	14	6	22
CEN	0	0	7	7	14

SCORING SUMMARY
A&M Safety (Bartlett tackled by Wilson in end zone)
CEN Snoddy 3 run (Roberts kick)
A&M Evans 15 pass from Wilson (McMillan kick)
A&M Wilson 5 run (McMillan kick)
A&M Winn 45 interception return (kick failed)
CEN Covington 2 pass from McMillin (Roberts kick)

JANUARY 1, 1925
WEST VIRGINIA WESLEYAN 9, SMU 7

	1ST	2ND	3RD	4TH	FINAL
WVW	0	0	3	6	9
SMU	0	0	7	0	7

SCORING SUMMARY
SMU Watters recoverd fumble in end zone (Stollenwerck kick)
WVW FG King 30
WVW Bullman pass from De Long (conversion failed)

JANUARY 1, 1934
ARKANSAS 7, CENTENARY 7

	1ST	2ND	3RD	4TH	FINAL
ARK	0	7	0	0	7
CEN	0	7	0	0	7

SCORING SUMMARY
ARK Geiser 27 pass from Murphy (Geiser kick)
CEN Oslin 20 pass from Smith (Weidman kick)

FORT WORTH CLASSIC

PROFILE

Site: Fort Worth, Texas
Surface: Grass

SEASON	DATE	PRE-GAME RANK	TEAMS	SCORE	FINAL RANK	MOST VALUABLE PLAYERS	ATT.
1920	Jan. 1, 1921		Centre	63			9,000
			TCU	7			

JANUARY 1, 1921
CENTRE 63, TCU 7

	1ST	2ND	3RD	4TH	FINAL
Centre	21	7	20	15	63
TCU	7	0	0	0	7

SCORING SUMMARY
TCU Jackson 90 interception return (Acker kick)
Centre Tanner 5 run (Weaver kick)
Centre Robb block punt return (Weaver kick)
Centre McMillin 8 run (Weaver kick)
Centre Armstrong 10 run (Weaver kick)
Centre Snoddy run (Weaver kicked)
Centre Harris fumble retuen (Weaver kick)
Centre McMillin run (Weaver kick)
Centre McMillin 60 run (Weaver kick)
Centre McMillin 20 run (Weaver kicked)

FREEDOM BOWL

PROFILE

Site: Anaheim, Calif.
Stadium: Anaheim Stadium
Capacity: 69,008
Surface: Grass

SEASON	DATE	PRE-GAME RANK	TEAMS	SCORE	FINAL RANK	MOST VALUABLE PLAYERS	ATT.
1984	Dec. 26, 1984		**Iowa**	**55**	16	Chuck Long, Iowa, QB	24,093
		19	Texas	17		William Harris, Texas, TE	
1985	Dec. 30, 1985		**Washington**	**20**		Chris Chandler, Washington, QB	30,961
			Colorado	17		Barry Helton, Colorado, P	
1986	Dec. 30, 1986	15	**UCLA**	**31**	14	Gaston Green, UCLA, TB	55,422
			Brigham Young	10		Shane Shumway, Brigham Young, DB	
1987	Dec. 30, 1987		**Arizona State**	**33**	20	Daniel Ford, Arizona State, QB	33,261
			Air Force	28		Chad Hennings, Air Force, DT	
1988	Dec. 29, 1988		**Brigham Young**	**20**		Ty Detmer, Brigham Young, QB	35,941
			Colorado	17		Eric Bieniemy, Colorado, HB	
1989	Dec. 30, 1989		**Washington**	**34**	23	Cary Conklin, Washington, QB	33,858
			Florida	7		Huey Richardson, Florida, LB	
1990	Dec. 29, 1990		**Colorado State**	**32**		Todd Yert, Colorado State, RB	41,450
			Oregon	31		Bill Musgrave, Oregon, QB	
1991	Dec. 30, 1991	23	**Tulsa**	**28**	21	Marshall Faulk, San Diego State, RB	34,217
			San Diego State	17		Ron Jackson, Tulsa, RB	
1992	Dec. 29, 1992		**Fresno State**	**24**	24	Lorenzo Neal, Fresno State, FB	50,745
		23	Southern Cal	7		Estrus Crayton, Southern Cal, TB	
1993	Dec. 30, 1993		**Southern Cal**	**28**		Johnnie Morton, Southern Cal, WR	37,203
			Utah	21		Henry Lusk, Utah, WR	
1994	Dec. 27, 1994	14	**Utah**	**16**	10	Tedy Bruschi, Arizona, DE	27,477
		15	Arizona	13	20	Cal Beck, Utah, KR	

DECEMBER 26, 1984
IOWA 55, TEXAS 17

	1ST	2ND	3RD	4TH	FINAL
IOWA	14	10	31	0	55
TEX	0	17	0	0	17

SCORING SUMMARY
IOWA Hayes 6 pass from Long (Nichol kick)
IOWA Flagg 11 pass from Long (Nichol kick)
TEX Bryant 11 pass from Dodge (Ward kick)
IOWA Bush 1 run (Nichol kick)
TEX Harris 1 pass from Dodge (Ward kick)
TEX FG Ward 46
IOWA FG Nichol 27
IOWA FG Nichol 35
IOWA Happel 33 pass from Long (Nichol kick)
IOWA Smith 49 pass from Long (Nichol kick)
IOWA Helverson 4 pass from Long (Nichol kick)
IOWA Hayes 15 pass from Long (Nichol kick)

IOWA	TEAM STATISTICS	TEX
28	First Downs	15
91	Rushing Yards	115
30-40-0	Passing	17-34-2
469	Passing Yards	185
560	Total Yards	300
4-42.0	Punts - Average	5-43.0
5-2	Fumbles - Lost	3-3
4-27	Penalties - Yards	6-50
33:32	Possession Time	26:28

INDIVIDUAL LEADERS
RUSHING
IOWA: Gill 17-61; Long 7-20.
TEX: Orr 12-67; Johnson 8-56.

PASSING
IOWA: Long 29-39-0, 461 yards, 6 TD.
TEX: Dodge 16-32-2, 180, 2 TD.

RECEIVING
IOWA: Smith 4-115, 1 TD; Happel 8-104, 1 TD.
TEX: Bryant 3-50, 1 TD; Duhon 1-47.

DECEMBER 30, 1985
WASHINGTON 20, COLORADO 17

	1ST	2ND	3RD	4TH	FINAL
WASH	3	7	7	3	20
COLO	0	7	3	7	17

SCORING SUMMARY
WASH FG Jaeger 30
COLO Weatherspoon 1 run (Eckel kick)
WASH Toy 3 run (Jaeger kick)
COLO FG Eckel 33
WASH Covington 1 run (Jaeger kick)
WASH FG Jaeger 46
COLO Embree 31 pass from Helton (Eckel kick)

WASH	TEAM STATISTICS	COLO
20	First Downs	15
207	Rushing Yards	190
15-26-1	Passing	2-10-0
141	Passing Yards	44
348	Total Yards	234
6-40.0	Punts - Average	5-39.0
1-0	Fumbles - Lost	1-1
13-88	Penalties - Yards	4-20
29:38	Possession Time	30:22

INDIVIDUAL LEADERS
RUSHING
WASH: Chandler 7-72; Weathersby 11-56.
COLO: Marquez 10-80; Hatcher 12-36.

PASSING
WASH: Chandler 15-26-1, 141 yards.
COLO: Hatcher 1-8-0, 13 yards; Helton 1-1-0, 31 yards, 1 TD.

RECEIVING
WASH: Hill 4-48; Jones 3-39.
COLO: Embree 1-31, 1 TD; Ferrando 1-13.

DECEMBER 30, 1986
UCLA 31, BRIGHAM YOUNG 10

	1ST	2ND	3RD	4TH	FINAL
UCLA	7	0	17	7	31
BYU	3	0	0	7	10

SCORING SUMMARY
BYU FG Chitty 32
UCLA Green 3 run (Franey kick)
UCLA Green 1 run (Franey kick)
UCLA FG Franey 49
UCLA Green 79 run (Franey kick)
UCLA Dorrell 13 pass from Green (Franey kick)
BYU Hansen 3 run (Chitty kick)

UCLA	TEAM STATISTICS	BYU
19	First Downs	18
423	Rushing Yards	73
8-21-1	Passing	25-43-3
95	Passing Yards	221
518	Total Yards	294

INDIVIDUAL LEADERS
RUSHING
UCLA: Green 33-266, 3 TD; Greenwood 5-104.
BYU: Heimuli 11-40; Hansen 8-36, 1 TD.

PASSING
UCLA: Stevens 7-20-1, 82 yards; Green 1-1-0, 13 yards, 1 TD.
BYU: Jensen 18-31-3, 124 yards.

RECEIVING
UCLA: Dorrell 6-83, 1 TD.
BYU: Heimuli 8-66; Parker 5-27.

DECEMBER 30, 1987
ARIZONA STATE 33, AIR FORCE 28

	1ST	2ND	3RD	4TH	FINAL
ASU	0	24	3	6	33
AFA	7	7	0	14	28

SCORING SUMMARY
AFA Johnson 12 run (Yarbrough kick)
ASU Williams 2 run (Zendejas kick)
ASU Harris 2 run (Zendejas kick)
ASU FG Zendejas 36
AFA Booker 3 run (Yarbrough kick)
ASU Cox 61 pass from Ford (Zendejas kick)
ASU FG Zendejas 20
ASU Wendorf 20 run (kick failed)
AFA Senn 10 pass from McDowell (run failed)
AFA Senn 18 pass from McDowell (McDowell run)

ASU	TEAM STATISTICS	AFA
22	First Downs	21
187	Rushing Yards	309
16-30-1	Passing	8-16-2
272	Passing Yards	117
459	Total Yards	426
4-44.5	Punts - Average	7-35.0
2-2	Fumbles - Lost	2-1
10-86	Penalties - Yards	5-65

INDIVIDUAL LEADERS
RUSHING
ASU: Harris 13-93, 1 TD.
AFA: Letnich 16-90.

PASSING
ASU: Ford 16-30-1, 272 yards, 1 TD.
AFA: McDowell 5-7-0, 66 yards, 2 TD.

RECEIVING
ASU: Cox 4-110, 1 TD.
AFA: Senn 3-45, 2 TD.

December 29, 1988
Brigham Young 20, Colorado 17

	1ST	2ND	3RD	4TH	FINAL
BYU	7	0	7	6	20
COLO	7	7	0	3	17

SCORING SUMMARY

COLO	Bieniemy 1 run (Blottiaux kick)
BYU	Salido 19 pass from Covey (Chaffetz kick)
COLO	Bieniemy 1 run (Blottiaux kick)
BYU	Cutler 14 pass from Detmer (Chaffetz kick)
COLO	FG Blottiaux 19
BYU	FG Chaffetz 31
BYU	FG Chaffetz 35

BYU	TEAM STATISTICS	COLO
23	First Downs	20
152	Rushing Yards	273
15-28-1	Passing	5-16-2
168	Passing Yards	64
320	Total Yards	337
4-33.5	Punts - Average	2-39.0
3-1	Fumbles - Lost	1-0
4-33	Penalties - Yards	9-81
30:15	Possession Time	29:45

INDIVIDUAL LEADERS

RUSHING
BYU: Bellini 8-78; Salido 9-62.
COLO: Bieniemy 33-144, 2 TD; Aunese 14-49.

PASSING
BYU: Detmer 11-17-0, 129 yards, 1 TD; Covey 4-10-1, 39 yards, 1 TD.
COLO: Aunese 4-13-1, 46 yards.

RECEIVING
BYU: Handley 3-42; Bellini 4-41.
COLO: Bieniemy 2-30; Kissick 2-23.

December 30, 1989
Washington 34, Florida 7

	1ST	2ND	3RD	4TH	FINAL
WASH	17	10	0	7	34
UF	7	0	0	0	7

SCORING SUMMARY

WASH	Bailey 21 pass from Conklin (McCallum kick)
UF	Douglas 67 run (Francis kick)
WASH	FG McCallum 21
WASH	Riley 10 pass from Conklin (McCallum kick)
WASH	Fields recovered blocked punt in end zone (McCallum kick)
WASH	FG McCallum 32
WASH	Brunell 20 run (Jolley kick)

WASH	TEAM STATISTICS	UF
28	First Downs	10
191	Rushing Yards	83
24-44-0	Passing	11-28-1
242	Passing Yards	148
433	Total Yards	231
7-37.0	Punts - Average	8-32.9
0-0	Fumbles - Lost	7-3
9-86	Penalties - Yards	9-85

INDIVIDUAL LEADERS

RUSHING
WASH: Lewis 27-97; Turner 7-38.
UF: Douglas 9-65, 1 TD; Smith 7-17.

PASSING
WASH: Conklin 21-39-0, 217 yards, 2 TD.
UF: Douglas 8-18-1, 91 yards.

RECEIVING
WASH: McKay 5-83; Lewis 6-44.
UF: Barber 2-41.

December 29, 1990
Colorado State 32, Oregon 31

	1ST	2ND	3RD	4TH	FINAL
CSU	7	7	5	13	32
ORE	7	10	0	14	31

SCORING SUMMARY

CSU	Gimenez 1 run (Brown kick)
ORE	Jones 16 pass from Musgrave (McCallum kick)
ORE	FG McCallum 23
CSU	Alford 1 run (Brown kick)
ORE	Burwell 3 pass from Musgrave (McCallum kick)
CSU	Safety (fumble recovered in end zone)
CSU	FG Brown 35
ORE	McClelland 44 pass from Musgrave (Burwell pass from Musgrave)
CSU	Primus 49 pass from Gimenez (Brown kick)
CSU	Yert 52 run (kick failed)
ORE	Burwell 1 run (pass failed)

CSU	TEAM STATISTICS	ORE
16	First Downs	21
196	Rushing Yards	7
8-15-1	Passing	29-47-0
108	Passing Yards	392
304	Total Yards	399
6-34.7	Punts - Average	3-38.3
2-0	Fumbles - Lost	5-3
5-47	Penalties - Yards	7-60

INDIVIDUAL LEADERS

RUSHING
CSU: Yert 12-94, 1 TD; Copeland 8-44.
ORE: Burwell 12-20, 1 TD; Kelemeni 5-7.

PASSING
CSU: Gimenez 5-10-1, 73 yards, 1 TD.
ORE: Musgrave 29-47-0, 392 yards, 3 TD.

RECEIVING
CSU: Primus 2-63, 1 TD; Yert 2-18.
ORE: McClelland 9-148, 1 TD; Jones 2-35, 1 TD.

December 30, 1991
Tulsa 28, San Diego State 17

	1ST	2ND	3RD	4TH	FINAL
TUL	7	7	7	7	28
SDSU	7	7	0	3	17

SCORING SUMMARY

SDSU	Faulk 2 run (Trakas kick)
TUL	Jackson 10 run (Lange kick)
TUL	Jackson 6 run (Lange kick)
SDSU	Lowery 4 run (Trakas kick)
TUL	Jackson 3 run (Lange kick)
SDSU	FG Trakas 26
TUL	Jackson 4 run (Lange kick)

TUL	TEAM STATISTICS	SDSU
23	First Downs	21
256	Rushing Yards	189
9-17-0	Passing	19-37-0
122	Passing Yards	164
378	Total Yards	353
5-34.0	Punts - Average	5-35.0
4-1	Fumbles - Lost	3-2
2-20	Penalties - Yards	6-38
31:20	Possession Time	28:40

INDIVIDUAL LEADERS

RUSHING
TUL: Jackson 46-211, 4 TD; Rubley 6-31.
SDSU: Faulk 30-157, 1 TD; Pittman 5-20.

PASSING
TUL: Rubley 9-17-0, 122 yards.
SDSU: Lowery 19-37-0, 164 yards.

RECEIVING
TUL: Penn 6-86; Jackson 1-14.
SDSU: Faulk 9-42; Tate 3-40.

December 29, 1992
Fresno State 24, Southern Cal 7

	1ST	2ND	3RD	4TH	FINAL
FRES	0	7	3	14	24
USC	0	7	0	0	7

SCORING SUMMARY

USC	Strother 1 run (Ford kick)
FRES	Neal 1 run (Mahoney kick)
FRES	FG Mahoney 43
FRES	Daigle 2 run (Mahoney kick)
FRES	Rivers 5 run (Mahoney kick)

FRES	TEAM STATISTICS	USC
24	First Downs	14
241	Rushing Yards	88
13-28-0	Passing	7-18-3
164	Passing Yards	96
405	Total Yards	184

December 30, 1993
Southern Cal 28, Utah 21

	1ST	2ND	3RD	4TH	FINAL
USC	20	8	0	0	28
UU	0	0	13	8	21

SCORING SUMMARY

USC	Morton 31 pass from Johnson (Ford kick)
USC	Morton 9 pass from Johnson (Ford kick)
USC	Dotson 2 run (kick failed)
USC	McWilliams 5 pass from Johnson (Banta pass from Johnson)
UU	Lusk 59 pass from McCoy (Yergensen kick)
UU	Anderson 34 run (kick failed)
UU	Williams 1 run (Anderson pass from McCoy)

USC	TEAM STATISTICS	UU
20	First Downs	17
91	Rushing Yards	64
30-44-1	Passing	23-40-3
345	Passing Yards	286
436	Total Yards	350
1-31	Punt Returns - Yards	3-28
3-68	Kickoff Returns - Yards	1-20
6-36.7	Punts - Average	8-34.1
2-1	Fumbles - Lost	2-0
10-96	Penalties - Yards	5-51
32:14	Possession Time	27:45

INDIVIDUAL LEADERS

RUSHING
USC: Walters 19-70; Strother 9-50.
UU: Anderson 16-67, 1 TD.

PASSING
USC: Johnson 30-44-1, 345 yards, 3 TD.
UU: McCoy 23-40-3, 286 yards, 1 TD.

RECEIVING
USC: Morton 10-147, 2 TD; Strother 6-63.
UU: Lusk 6-140, 1 TD; Anderson 7-61.

December 27, 1994
Utah 16, Arizona 13

	1ST	2ND	3RD	4TH	FINAL
UT	0	7	0	9	16
ARIZ	0	7	0	6	13

SCORING SUMMARY

ARIZ	Carter 23 pass from White (McLaughlin kick)
UT	Brown 6 run (Pulsipher kick)
ARIZ	FG McLaughlin 44
ARIZ	FG McLaughlin 20
UT	Safety (Peyton stepped out of end zone)
UT	Dyson 5 pass from McCoy (Pulsipher kick)

UT	TEAM STATISTICS	ARIZ
5	First Downs	14
6	Rushing Yards	45
11-25-2	Passing	13-27-1
69	Passing Yards	139
75	Total Yards	184
2-6	Punt Returns - Yards	4-28
5-173	Kickoff Returns - Yards	3-59
10-41.0	Punts - Average	6-36.8
0-0	Fumbles - Lost	2-2
9-94	Penalties - Yards	4-35
27:33	Possession Time	32:27

INDIVIDUAL LEADERS

RUSHING
UT: Brown 16-44, 1 TD; Johnson 4-6.
ARIZ: Carter 19-44; Myles 9-12.

PASSING
UT: McCoy 11-25-2, 69 yards, 1 TD.
ARIZ: White 13-27-1, 139 yards, 1 TD.

RECEIVING
UT: Tucker 4-28; Marsh 3-25.
ARIZ: Dice 7-65; Carter 4-50, 1 TD.

GARDEN STATE BOWL

PROFILE

Site: East Rutherford, N.J.
Stadium: Giants Stadium
Capacity: 77,716
Surface: AstroTurf

SEASON	DATE	PRE-GAME RANK	TEAMS	SCORE	FINAL RANK	MOST VALUABLE PLAYERS	ATT.
1978	Dec. 16, 1978		Arizona State	34		John Mistler, Arizona State, WR	33,402
			Rutgers	18			
1979	Dec. 15, 1979	20	Temple	28	17	Mark Bright, Temple, RB	55,493
			California	17			
1980	Dec. 14, 1980		Houston	35		Terald Clark, Houston, RB	41,417
			Navy	0			
1981	Dec. 13, 1981		Tennessee	28		Steve Alatorre, QB and Anthony Hancock, Tennessee, WR	38,782
			Wisconsin	21		Randy Wright, Wisconsin, QB	

DECEMBER 16, 1978
ARIZONA STATE 34, RUTGERS 18

	1ST	2ND	3RD	4TH	FINAL
ASU	0	7	14	13	34
RU	10	0	0	8	18

SCORING SUMMARY
RU   Dorn 47 run (Startzell kick)
RU   FG Startzell 46
ASU Weathers 14 pass from Malone (Hicks kick)
ASU Mistler 26 pass from Malone (Hicks kick)
ASU DeFrance 53 pass from Malone (Hicks kick)
ASU Malone 1 run (Hicks kick)
RU   Blackwell 5 run (Blackwell pass from McMichael)
ASU Malone 4 run (kick failed)

ASU	TEAM STATISTICS	RU
18	First Downs	14
111	Rushing Yards	163
13-31-4	Passing	11-22-3
268	Passing Yards	115
379	Total Yards	278
5-47	Punt Returns - Yards	0-0
3-48	Kickoff Returns - Yards	6-95
8-34.1	Punts - Average	8-44.5
2-2	Fumbles - Lost	3-2
5-45	Penalties - Yards	5-61

INDIVIDUAL LEADERS
RUSHING
ASU: Malone 21-46, 2 TD; Moore 10-38.
RU: Kehler 23-87; Dorn 6-48, 1 TD.
PASSING
ASU: Malone 13-31-4, 268 yards, 3 TD.
RU: McMichael 8-12-0, 86 yards.
RECEIVING
ASU: Mistler 7-148, 1 TD; DeFrance 2-63, 1 TD.
RU: Blackwell 5-51; Dorn 1-26.

DECEMBER 15, 1979
TEMPLE 28, CALIFORNIA 17

	1ST	2ND	3RD	4TH	FINAL
TU	21	0	0	7	28
CAL	0	14	0	3	17

SCORING SUMMARY
TU   Duckett 8 run (Fioravanti kick)
TU   Duckett 4 run (Fioravanti kick)
TU   Pitts 7 pass from Broomell (Fioravanti kick)
CAL Bouza 12 pass from Campbell (Luckhurst kick)
CAL Rose 14 pass from Campbell (Luckhurst kick)
CAL FG Luckhurst 34
TU   Lucear 5 pass from Broomell (Fioravanti kick)

TU	TEAM STATISTICS	CAL
21	First Downs	15
300	Rushing Yards	23
9-20-0	Passing	25-39-1
81	Passing Yards	241
381	Total Yards	264
6-34.2	Punts - Average	6-37.0
1-1	Fumbles - Lost	3-1

INDIVIDUAL LEADERS
RUSHING
TU: Bright 19-112; Duckett 22-92, 2 TD.
CAL: Jones 14-49; Campbell 6-29.
PASSING
TU: Broomell 9-20-0, 81 yards, 2 TD.
CAL: Campbell 25-38-1, 241 yards, 2 TD.
RECEIVING
TU: Lucear 3-41, 1 TD; Wesnak 1-20.
CAL: Bouza 7-114, 1 TD; Rose 8-62, 1 TD.

DECEMBER 14, 1980
HOUSTON 35, NAVY 0

	1ST	2ND	3RD	4TH	FINAL
HOU	14	14	7	0	35
NAVY	0	0	0	0	0

SCORING SUMMARY
HOU Clark 1 run (Shaffer kick)
HOU Elston 1 run (Shaffer kick)
HOU Barrett 14 run (kick failed)
HOU Clark 26 run (Elston run)
HOU Clark 2 run (Shaffer kick)

HOU	TEAM STATISTICS	NAVY
24	First Downs	12
405	Rushing Yards	135
3-7-1	Passing	7-25-1
45	Passing Yards	65
450	Total Yards	200
2-35.5	Punts - Average	6-29.7
8-3	Fumbles - Lost	4-2
4-39	Penalties - Yards	2-26

INDIVIDUAL LEADERS
RUSHING
HOU: Clark 26-163, 3 TD; Polk 17-76.
NAVY: Tolbert 7-53; Sherlock 15-41.
PASSING
HOU: Elston 1-4-0, 28 yards.
NAVY: Reitzel 5-12-1, 42 yards.
RECEIVING
HOU: Miller 1-28; Phea 1-11.
NAVY: Papajohn 3-36; Dent 2-23.

DECEMBER 13, 1981
TENNESSEE 28, WISCONSIN 21

	1ST	2ND	3RD	4TH	FINAL
TENN	13	8	0	7	28
WISC	7	0	0	14	21

SCORING SUMMARY
TENN FG Reveiz 22
WISC Cole 3 run (Doran kick)
TENN Gault 87 kickoff return (Reveiz kick)
TENN FG Reveiz 44
TENN Hancock 43 pass from Alatorre (Cofer pass from Alatorre)
WISC Nault 6 pass from Wright (Doran kick)
TENN Alatorre 6 run (Reveiz kick)
WISC McFadden 11 pass from Wright (Doran kick)

TENN	TEAM STATISTICS	WISC
27	First Downs	22
89	Rushing Yards	177
24-42-0	Passing	14-37-3
315	Passing Yards	212
404	Total Yards	389
6-45.2	Punts - Average	6-36.7
4-0	Fumbles - Lost	1-1
8-84	Penalties - Yards	6-73

INDIVIDUAL LEADERS
RUSHING
TENN: Berry 10-44; Morris 10-39.
WISC: Davis 6-44; Cole 9-39, 1 TD.
PASSING
TENN: Alatorre 24-42-0, 315 yards, 1 TD.
WISC: Wright 9-21-1, 123 yards, 2 TD.
RECEIVING
TENN: Hancock 11-196, 1 TD; Miller 4-42.
WISC: Nault 5-85, 1 TD; McFadden 3-74, 1 TD.

GOTHAM BOWL

Site: New York
Stadium: Yankee Stadium
Capacity: 67,000
Surface: Grass

SEASON	DATE	PRE-GAME RANK	TEAMS	SCORE	FINAL RANK	MOST VALUABLE PLAYERS	ATT.
1961	Dec. 9, 1961		Baylor	24		Don Trull, Baylor, QB	15,123
		10	Utah State	9			
1962	Dec. 15, 1962		Nebraska	36		Willie Ross, Nebraska, RB	6,166
			Miami (Fla.)	34		George Mira, Miami (Fla.), QB	

DECEMBER 9, 1961
BAYLOR 24, UTAH STATE 9

	1ST	2ND	3RD	4TH	FINAL
BU	7	3	7	7	24
USU	0	0	3	6	9

SCORING SUMMARY
BU   Bull 14 run (Choate kick)
BU   FG Choate 22
USU   FG Turner 36
BU   Trull 2 run (Choate kick)
BU   Plumb 38 pass from Trull (Choate kick)
USU   Munson 4 run (kick failed)

BU	TEAM STATISTICS	USU
14	First Downs	10
113	Rushing Yards	153
14-30-3	Passing	3-14-1
153	Passing Yards	41
266	Total Yards	194
6-31.0	Punts - Average	5-36.6
5-2	Fumbles - Lost	6-5
3-16	Penalties - Yards	2-32

INDIVIDUAL LEADERS
RUSHING
BU: Bull 13-61, 1 TD; Whorton 6-14.
USU: Montalbo 4-35; Prince 8-28.
PASSING
BU: Trull 11-16-0, 116 yards, 1 TD.
USU: Munson 1-8-2, 24 yards.
RECEIVING
BU: Plumb 3-59, 1 TD; Lane 2-30.
USU: McNaughton 3-41.

DECEMBER 15, 1962
NEBRASKA 36, MIAMI (FLA) 34

	1ST	2ND	3RD	4TH	FINAL
NEB	6	14	8	8	36
MIA	6	14	7	7	34

SCORING SUMMARY
NEB   Thornton 2 run (run failed)
MIA   Rizzo 10 pass from Mira (kick failed)
MIA   Spinnelli 30 pass from Mira (pass failed)
NEB   Ross 92 kickoff return (Johnson kick)
MIA   Ryder 1 run (Ryder pass from Mira)
NEB   Eger 6 pass from Claridge (Johnson kick)
MIA   Bennett 3 run (Wilson kick)
NEB   Thornton 1 run (Claridge run)
NEB   Ross 1 run (Thornton run)
MIA   Ryder 1 run (Wilson kick)

NEB	TEAM STATISTICS	MIA
12	First Downs	34
150	Rushing Yards	181
9-14-2	Passing	24-46-0
146	Passing Yards	321
296	Total Yards	502

GREAT LAKES BOWL

Site: Cleveland
Stadium: Cleveland Municipal
Stadium
Capacity: 78,000
Surface: Grass

SEASON	DATE	PRE-GAME RANK	TEAMS	SCORE	FINAL RANK	MOST VALUABLE PLAYERS	ATT.
1947	Dec. 6, 1947		Kentucky	24			14,908
			Villanova	14			

DECEMBER 6, 1947
KENTUCKY 24, VILLANOVA 14

	1ST	2ND	3RD	4TH	FINAL
UK	3	0	7	14	24
NOVA	0	0	0	14	14

SCORING SUMMARY
UK   FG Blanda 27
UK   Howe 29 run (Blanda kick)
UK   Boller 15 run (Blanda kick)
UK   Boller 49 interception return (Blanda kick)
NOVA   Pasquariello 10 run (Siano kick)
NOVA   Sheahan 9 pass from Gordon (Siano kick)

UK	TEAM STATISTICS	NOVA
14	First Downs	10
177	Rushing Yards	90
14-25-1	Passing	12-18-1
107	Passing Yards	138
284	Total Yards	228
7-38.0	Punts - Average	9-33.0
1-0	Fumbles - Lost	2-0
2-10	Penalties - Yards	2-30

HARBOR BOWL

Site: San Diego
Surface: Grass

SEASON	DATE	PRE-GAME RANK	TEAMS	SCORE	FINAL RANK	MOST VALUABLE PLAYERS	ATT.
1946	Jan. 1, 1947		Montana St.	13		Bill Nelson, Montana State, RB	7,000
			New Mexico State	13		Bryan Brock, New Mexico, QB	
1947	Jan. 1, 1948		Hardin-Simmons	53			12,000
			San Diego State	0			
1948	Jan. 1, 1949		Villanova	27			20,000
			Nevada	7			

JANUARY 1, 1947
NEW MEXICO ST. 13, MONTANA STATE 13

	1ST	2ND	3RD	4TH	FINAL
UNM	6	0	0	7	13
MSU	0	13	0	0	13

SCORING SUMMARY
UNM Cullen 26 pass from Hackett (kick failed)
MSU Brooks 48 run (Borudet run)
MSU Card 7 pass from Bourdet (kick failed)
UNM Brock 2 run (Hackett kick)

UNM	TEAM STATISTICS	MSU
12	First Downs	12
182	Rushing Yards	155
4-13-3	Passing	7-16-3
83	Passing Yards	180
265	Total Yards	335

JANUARY 1, 1948
HARDIN-SIMMONS 53, SAN DIEGO ST 0

	1ST	2ND	3RD	4TH	FINAL
HS	14	13	14	12	53
SDSU	0	0	0	0	0

HS	TEAM STATISTICS	SDSU
11	First Downs	11
470	Rushing Yards	66
3-5-0	Passing	5-20-1
75	Passing Yards	60
545	Total Yards	126

JANUARY 1, 1949
VILLANOVA 27, NEVADA 7

	1ST	2ND	3RD	4TH	FINAL
NOVA	13	0	14	0	27
NEV	0	0	7	0	7

LOS ANGELES CHRISTMAS FESTIVAL

Site: Los Angeles
Stadium: Los Angeles Coliseum
Capacity: 74,000
Surface: Grass

SEASON	DATE	PRE-GAME RANK	TEAMS	SCORE	FINAL RANK	MOST VALUABLE PLAYERS	ATT.
1924	Dec. 25, 1924		Southern Cal	20			47,000
			Missouri	7			

DECEMBER 25, 1924
SOUTHERN CAL 20, MISSOURI 7

	1ST	2ND	3RD	4TH	FINAL
USC	0	0	20	0	20
MO	0	0	0	7	7

MERCY BOWL

Site: Los Angeles
Stadium: Memorial Coliseum
Capacity: 94,000
Surface: Grass

SEASON	DATE	PRE-GAME RANK	TEAMS	SCORE	FINAL RANK	MOST VALUABLE PLAYERS	ATT.
1961	Nov. 23, 1961		Fresno State	36		Beau Carter, Fresno State, QB	33,145
			Bowling Green	6			

NOVEMBER 23, 1961
FRESNO STATE 36, BOWLING GREEN 6

	1ST	2ND	3RD	4TH	FINAL
FRES	3	7	20	6	36
BG	0	6	0	0	6

SCORING SUMMARY
FRES FG Masich 29
BG Bell 2 run (kick failed)
FRES Barrett 45 pass from Carter (Masich kick)
FRES Seifert 1 run (Masich kick)
FRES Barrett 23 pass from Carter (Masich kick)
FRES Carter 4 run (Masich kick)
FRES Carter 8 run (Masich kick)

FRES	TEAM STATISTICS	BG
23	First Downs	17
100	Rushing Yards	111
22-43-1	Passing	11-22-3
368	Passing Yards	208
468	Total Yards	319
4-32.0	Punts - Average	4-34.0
1-0	Fumbles - Lost	5-3
7-75	Penalties - Yards	4-20

OIL BOWL

Site: Houston
Stadium: Rice Stadium
Capacity: 37,000
Surface: Grass

SEASON	DATE	PRE-GAME RANK	TEAMS	SCORE	FINAL RANK	MOST VALUABLE PLAYERS	ATT.
1945	Jan. 1, 1946		**Georgia**	20			27,000
			Tulsa	6			
1946	Jan. 1, 1947	11	**Georgia Tech**	41			23,000
			St. Mary's	19			

GEORGIA 20, TULSA 6 — JANUARY 1, 1946

	1ST	2ND	3RD	4TH	FINAL
UGA	7	0	0	13	20
TUL	0	6	0	0	6

SCORING SUMMARY

UGA	Smith 3 run (Jernigan kick)
TUL	Wilson 1 run (kick failed)
UGA	Donaldson 54 pass from Trippi (Jernigan kick)
UGA	Trippi 69 punt return (kick failed)

UGA	TEAM STATISTICS	TUL
14	First Downs	7
178	Rushing Yards	69
5-15-1	Passing	6-21-0
110	Passing Yards	79
288	Total Yards	148

GEORGIA TECH 41, ST. MARY'S 19 — JANUARY 1, 1947

	1ST	2ND	3RD	4TH	FINAL
GT	7	20	7	7	41
STM	0	7	6	6	19

PASADENA BOWL

Site: Pasadena, Calif.
Stadium: Rose Bowl
Capacity: 96,576
Surface: Grass

NAME CHANGES

Junior Rose Bowl, 1967
Pasadena Bowl, 1969-71

SEASON	DATE	PRE-GAME RANK	TEAMS	SCORE	FINAL RANK	MOST VALUABLE PLAYERS	ATT.
1967	Dec. 2, 1967		**West Texas State**	35		Mercury Morris, West Texas State, RB	28,802
			Cal. St. Northridge	13		Albie Owens, West Texas A&M	
1969	Dec. 6, 1969		**San Diego State**	28		John Featherstone, San Diego State, WR	41,276
			Boston University	7			
1970	Dec. 19, 1970		**Long Beach St.**	24		Leon Burns, Long Beach St., FB	20,472
			Louisville	24		Paul Mattingly, Louisville, LB	
1971	Dec. 18, 1971		**Memphis**	28		Tom Carlsen, Memphis, DB	15,244
			San Jose State	9		Dornell Harris, Memphis, RB	

WEST TEXAS STATE 35, VALLEY STATE 13 — DECEMBER 2, 1967

	1ST	2ND	3RD	4TH	FINAL
WTS	7	7	7	14	35
VS	7	0	6	0	13

SAN DIEGO STATE 28, BOSTON UNIVERSITY 7 — DECEMBER 6, 1969

	1ST	2ND	3RD	4TH	FINAL
SDSU	0	14	7	7	28
BU	7	0	0	0	7

SCORING SUMMARY

BU	Jewett 6 pass from Hollo (McNeilly kick)
SDSU	Kafka 2 run (Limahelu kick)
SDSU	Featherstone 34 pass from Shaw (Limahelu kick)
SDSU	Featherstone 57 pass from Sipe (Limahelu kick)
SDSU	Sipe 1 run (Limahelu kick)

SDSU	TEAM STATISTICS	BU
24	First Downs	12
191	Rushing Yards	110
18-32-3	Passing	7-17-3
294	Passing Yards	57
485	Total Yards	167
3-37.0	Punts - Average	9-35.0

LOUISVILLE 24, LONG BEACH STATE 24 — DECEMBER 19, 1970

	1ST	2ND	3RD	4TH	FINAL
UL	14	7	3	0	24
LBSU	7	7	2	8	24

SCORING SUMMARY

LBSU	Burns 4 run (Logue kick)
UL	Madeya 4 run (Marcus kick)
UL	Welch 65 interception return (Marcus kick)
UL	Madeya 1 run (Marcus kick)
LBSU	Burns 2 run (Logue kick)
UL	FG Marcus 24
LBSU	Safety (Gatti tackled in end zone)
LBSU	Burns 4 run (Matthews pass from Graves)

UL	TEAM STATISTICS	LBSU
20	First Downs	16
174	Rushing Yards	191
12-27-1	Passing	9-17-1
148	Passing Yards	90
322	Total Yards	281
8-39.0	Punts - Average	6-30.0

MEMPHIS 28, SAN JOSE STATE 9 — DECEMBER 18, 1971

	1ST	2ND	3RD	4TH	FINAL
MEM	7	7	0	14	28
SJSU	3	0	0	6	9

SCORING SUMMARY

SJSU	FG Barnes 33
MEM	Carlsen blocked punt recovered in end zone (McGeorge kick)
MEM	Harris 9 run (McGeorge kick)
MEM	Gowen 18 run (McGeorge kick)
MEM	Taylor 1 run (McGeorge kick)
SJSU	Motheana 1 run (kick failed)

MEM	TEAM STATISTICS	SJSU
15	First Downs	11
195	Rushing Yards	187
3-13-2	Passing	6-19-4
41	Passing Yards	81
236	Total Yards	268
7-39.0	Punts - Average	6-36.0

PRESIDENTIAL CUP

PROFILE

Site: College Park, Md.
Stadium: Byrd Stadium
Capacity: 34,680
Surface: Grass

SEASON	DATE	PRE-GAME RANK	TEAMS	SCORE	FINAL RANK	MOST VALUABLE PLAYERS	ATT.
1950	Dec. 9, 1950		**Texas A&M**	**40**		Bob Smith, Texas A&M, RB	12,245
			Georgia	**20**		Zippy Morocco, Georgia, HB	

DECEMBER 9, 1950
TEXAS A&M 40, GEORGIA 20

	1ST	2ND	3RD	4TH	FINAL
A&M	20	13	7	0	40
UGA	0	0	7	13	20

SCORING SUMMARY

A&M	Smith 100 kickoff return (Hooper kick)
A&M	Lippman 2 run (kick failed)
A&M	Smith 81 run (Hooper kick)
A&M	Tidwell 6 run (Hooper kick)
A&M	Tidwell 6 run (Hooper kick)
A&M	Tidwell 36 run (kick failed)
UGA	Morocco 30 run (Durand kick)
UGA	Morocco 65 punt return (Durand kick)
UGA	Hargrove 1 run (kick failed)

RAISIN BOWL

PROFILE

Site: Fresno, Calif.
Stadium: Ratcliffe Stadium
Capacity: 13,000
Surface: Grass

SEASON	DATE	PRE-GAME RANK	TEAMS	SCORE	FINAL RANK	MOST VALUABLE PLAYERS	ATT.
1945	Jan. 1, 1946		**Drake**	**13**			10,000
			Fresno State	**12**			
1946	Jan. 1, 1947		**San Jose State**	**20**			13,000
			Utah State	**0**			
1947	Jan. 1, 1948		**Pacific**	**26**			13,000
			Wichita State	**14**			
1948	Jan. 1 1949		**Occidental**	**21**			10,000
			Colorado State	**20**			
1949	Dec. 31, 1949		**San Jose State**	**20**			9,000
			Texas Tech	**13**			

JANUARY 1, 1946
DRAKE 13, FRESNO STATE 12

	1ST	2ND	3RD	4TH	FINAL
DU	6	0	0	7	13
FSU	0	6	0	6	12

JANUARY 1, 1947
SAN JOSE STATE 20, UTAH STATE 0

	1ST	2ND	3RD	4TH	FINAL
SJSU	0	7	13	0	20
USU	0	0	0	0	0

JANUARY 1, 1948
PACIFIC 26, WICHITA STATE 14

	1ST	2ND	3RD	4TH	FINAL
PA	6	7	0	13	26
WICH	7	0	0	7	14

JANUARY 1, 1949
OCCIDENTAL 21, COLORADO 20

	1ST	2ND	3RD	4TH	FINAL
OCC	0	0	7	14	21
COLO	0	13	0	7	20

DECEMBER 31, 1949
SAN JOSE STATE 20, TEXAS TECH 13

	1ST	2ND	3RD	4TH	FINAL
SJSU	0	7	13	0	20
TT	7	0	0	6	13

SJSU	TEAM STATISTICS	TT
170	Rushing Yards	254
9-16-1	Passing	4-12-3
131	Passing Yards	88
301	Total Yards	342
5-33.8	Punts - Average	4-39.7

SALAD BOWL

PROFILE

Site: Phoenix
Stadium: Montgomery Stadium
Surface: Grass

SEASON	DATE	PRE-GAME RANK	TEAMS	SCORE	FINAL RANK	MOST VALUABLE PLAYERS	ATT.
1947	Jan. 1, 1948		**Nevada**	13			12,500
			North Texas		6		
1948	Jan. 1, 1949		**Drake**	14			17,500
			Arizona		13		
1949	Jan. 1, 1950		**Xavier**	33		Bob McQuade, Xavier, QB	18,500
			Arizona State	21		Wilford White, Arizona State, HB	
1950	Jan. 1, 1951		**Miami (Ohio)**	34		Jim Bailey, Miami (Ohio), RB	23,000
			Arizona State	21			
1951	Jan. 1, 1952		**Houston**	26		Gene Shannon, Houston, RB	17,000
			Dayton	21			

288	Rushing Yards	215
6-14-1	Passing	11-25-1
54	Passing Yards	168
342	Total Yards	383
1-12	Punt Returns - Yards	1-7
4-97	Kickoff Returns - Yards	5-70
2-35.0	Punts - Average	2-35.0
2-1	Fumbles - Lost	1-0
6-50	Penalties - Yards	10-88
22:41	Possession Time	37:19

INDIVIDUAL LEADERS

RUSHING
FSU: Smith 25-205, 2 TD; Holloman 6-36, 2 TD.
IU: Thompson 28-127; Powell 6-38, 1 TD.

PASSING
FSU: McManus 6-14-1, 54 yards.
IU: Kramme 11-25-1, 168 yards.

RECEIVING
FSU: O'Malley 2-20; Gainer 1-19.
IU: Dawsey 5-74; Lilja 2-44.

DECEMBER 22, 1987
Virginia 22, Brigham Young 16

	1ST	2ND	3RD	4TH	FINAL
UVA	7	7	0	8	22
BYU	3	0	6	7	16

SCORING SUMMARY
BYU	FG Chitty 20
UVA	Secules 2 run (Inderlied kick)
UVA	Morgan 25 run (Inderlied kick)
BYU	Whittingham 8 run (pass failed)
UVA	Ford 22 pass from Secules (Secules pass to Wilson)
BYU	Whittingham 1 pass from Covey (Chitty kick)

UVA	TEAM STATISTICS	BYU
22	First Downs	27
187	Rushing Yards	95
10-19-2	Passing	37-61-1
162	Passing Yards	394
349	Total Yards	489
1-8	Punt Returns - Yards	1-0
4-90	Kickoff Returns - Yards	3-57
3-42.7	Punts - Average	1-36.0
2-1	Fumbles - Lost	2-0
2-15	Penalties - Yards	7-64
25:47	Possession Time	34:13

INDIVIDUAL LEADERS
RUSHING

UVA: Morgan 10-82, 1 TD; Wilson 15-77.
BYU: Whittingham 10-53, 1 TD; Salito 7-31.
PASSING
UVA: Secules 10-19-2, 162 yards, 1 TD.
BYU: Covey 37-61-1, 394 yards, 1 TD.
RECEIVING
UVA: Ford 4-54 1 TD; Mattioli 2-43.
BYU: Miles 10-188; Bellini 9-59.

DECEMBER 29, 1988
Florida 14, Illinois 10

	1ST	2ND	3RD	4TH	FINAL
FLA	7	0	0	7	14
ILL	0	7	0	3	10

SCORING SUMMARY
FLA	Smith 55 run (Francis kick)
ILL	Jones 30 run (Higgins kick)
ILL	FG Higgins 44
FLA	Smith 2 run (Francis kick)

FLA	TEAM STATISTICS	ILL
12	First Downs	17
187	Rushing Yards	55
8-16-2	Passing	20-38-2
69	Passing Yards	194
256	Total Yards	249
3-10	Punt Returns - Yards	0-0
3-90	Kickoff Returns - Yards	3-60
4-29.8	Punts - Average	7-35.3
1-1	Fumbles - Lost	1-1
5-36	Penalties - Yards	8-59
26:38	Possession Time	33:22

INDIVIDUAL LEADERS
RUSHING

JANUARY 1, 1952
Houston 26, Dayton 21

	1ST	2ND	3RD	4TH	FINAL
HOUS	6	7	13	0	26
DAY	7	14	0	0	21

SCORING SUMMARY
DAY	Recker 7 run (Spakowski kick)
HOUS	Shannon 15 run (kick failed)
DAY	Recker 25 pass from Siggins (Spakowski kick)
HOUS	Shannon 19 run (Owens kick)
DAY	Currin 36 pass from Siggins (Spakowski kick)
HOUS	Shannon 1 run (Owens kick)
HOUS	Shannon 10 run (kick failed)

HOUS	TEAM STATISTICS	DAY
31	First Downs	11
344	Rushing Yards	124
4-7-1	Passing	10-22-2
124	Passing Yards	183
468	Total Yards	307
4-34.7	Punts - Average	6-45.8
6-3	Fumbles - Lost	3-1
7-35	Penalties - Yards	5-45

SAN DIEGO EAST-WEST CHRISTMAS CLASSIC

PROFILE

Site: San Diego, Calif.
Stadium: Balboa Stadium
Surface: Grass

SEASON	DATE	PRE-GAME RANK	TEAMS	SCORE	FINAL RANK	MOST VALUABLE PLAYERS	ATT.
1921	Dec. 26, 1921		**Centre**	38			5,000
			Arizona	0			
1922	Dec. 25, 1922		**West Virginia**	21			5,000
			Gonzaga	13			

DECEMBER 22, 1977
Maryland 17, Minnesota 7

	1ST	2ND	3RD	4TH	FINAL
MARY	3	14	0	0	17
MINN	7	0	0	0	7

SCORING SUMMARY
MINN	Barber 1 run (Rogind kick)
MARY	FG Sochko 32
MARY	Scott 2 run (Sochko kick)
MARY	Scott 1 run (Sochko kick)

MARY	TEAM STATISTICS	MINN
15	First Downs	17
120	Rushing Yards	113
12-23-1	Passing	13-26-0
211	Passing Yards	155
331	Total Yards	268
2-3	Punt Returns - Yards	2-6
2-34	Kickoff Returns - Yards	4-70
5-36.8	Punts - Average	9-27.7
3-2	Fumbles - Lost	3-2
12-80	Penalties - Yards	6-54

SEATTLE BOWL

PROFILE

Site: Seattle
Stadium: Seahawks Stadium
Capacity: 67,000
Surface: Grass

PLAYING SITES

Aloha Stadium, Honolulu
  1998-2000
Safeco Field, Seattle, 2001
Seahawks Stadium, since 2002

NAME CHANGES

Jeep O'ahu Bowl, 1998-2000
Seattle Bowl, 2001-2002

SEASON	DATE	PRE-GAME RANK	TEAMS	SCORE	FINAL RANK	MOST VALUABLE PLAYERS	ATT.
1998	Dec. 25, 1998		**Air Force**	45		Blane Morgan, Air Force, QB	46,451
			Washington	25			
1999	Dec. 25, 1999		**Hawaii**	23		Avion Weaver, Hawaii, RB	40,974
			Oregon State	17			
2000	Dec. 24, 2000		**Georgia**	37		Terrence Edwards, Georgia, WR	24,187
			Virginia	14			
2001	Dec. 27, 2001		**Georgia Tech**	24	24	George Godsey, Georgia Tech, QB	30,144
		11	Stanford	14	16		
2002	Dec. 30, 2002		**Wake Forest**	38		James MacPherson, Wake Forest, QB	38,241
			Oregon	17			

DECEMBER 25, 1998
AIR FORCE 45, WASHINGTON 25

	1ST	2ND	3RD	4TH	FINAL
AFA	7	15	16	7	45
UW	0	13	0	12	25

SCORING SUMMARY
AFA Singleton 12 run (conversion good)
AFA Singleton 2 run (Whiting kick)
UW Cleman 3 run (Jarzynka kick)
AFA McKay 15 run (Morgan run)
UW Cleman 2 run (pass failed)
AFA FG Whiting 42
AFA Gilliam 4 run (Whiting kick)
AFA Farmer 79 pass from Morgan (run failed)
UW Tuiasosopo 7 run (pass failed)
UW Austin 11 pass from Tuiasosopo (kick failed)

AFA	TEAM STATISTICS	UW
26	First Downs	21
232	Rushing Yards	107
12-16-0	Passing	28-40-3
267	Passing Yards	310
499	Total Yards	417
2-46.0	Punts - Average	2-41.0
3-1	Fumbles - Lost	3-0
6-45	Penalties - Yards	5-31
37:47	Possession Time	22:13

INDIVIDUAL LEADERS
RUSHING
AFA: Morgan 20-50; Gilliam 8-34, 1 TD.
UW: Hurst 9-66; Cleman 9-16, 2 TD.
PASSING
AFA: Morgan 12-16-0, 267 yards, 1 TD.
UW: Huard 23-32-3, 267 yards.
RECEIVING
AFA: Farmer 4-109, 1 TD; McKay 4-77.
UW: Looker 8-100; Jarzynke 4-39.

DECEMBER 25, 1999
HAWAII 23, OREGON STATE 17

	1ST	2ND	3RD	4TH	FINAL
HAW	0	10	10	3	23
OSU	7	3	0	7	17

SCORING SUMMARY
OSU Simonton 1 run (Cesca kick)
HAW FG Hannum 26
HAW Harris 9 pass from Robinson (Hannum kick)
OSU FG Cesca 37
HAW Harris 30 pass from Robinson (Hannum kick)
HAW FG Hannum 22
HAW FG Hannum 35
OSU Simonton 13 run (Cesca kick)

HAW	TEAM STATISTICS	OSU
83	Rushing Yards	169
23-40-1	Passing	19-40-0
266	Passing Yards	269
349	Total Yards	438
3-1	Fumbles - Lost	3-1
9-88	Penalties - Yards	14-138
28:51	Possession Time	31:09

INDIVIDUAL LEADERS
RUSHING
HAW: Weaver 18-84.
OSU: Simonton 18-157, 2 TD.
PASSING
HAW: Robinson 23-40-1, 266 yards, 2 TD.
OSU: Smith 19-40-0, 269 yards.
RECEIVING
HAW: Harris 5-81, 2 TD; Weaver 5-65.
OSU: Percoats 5-67; Prescott 4-61.

DECEMBER 24, 2000
GEORGIA 37, VIRGINIA 14

	1ST	2ND	3RD	4TH	FINAL
GA	17	7	0	13	37
UVA	0	7	7	0	14

SCORING SUMMARY
GA FG Bennett 35
GA Edwards 40 run (Bennett kick)
GA Curry fumble recovery (Bennett kick)
UVA Dotson 14 run (Greene kick)
GA Haynes 3 run (Bennett good)
UVA Thweatt 58 fumble return (Greene kick)
GA Gary 21 pass from Phillips (Bennett kick)
GA Burnett 4 fumble return (kick failed)

GA	TEAM STATISTICS	UVA
21	First Downs	20
157	Rushing Yards	144
25-39-1	Passing	22-36-2
241	Passing Yards	226
398	Total Yards	370
5-42.6	Punts - Average	5-44.8
1-1	Fumbles - Lost	4-2
4-20	Penalties - Yards	4-29
29:57	Possession Time	30:03

INDIVIDUAL LEADERS
RUSHING
GA: Edwards 5-97, 1 TD.
UVA: Womack 15-48.
PASSING
GA: Phillips 22-35-1, 213 yards, 1 TD.
UVA: Spinner 14-22-2, 153 yards.
RECEIVING
GA: Edwards 8-79.
UVA: McGrew 4-40.

DECEMBER 27, 2001
GEORGIA TECH 24, STANFORD 14

	1ST	2ND	3RD	4TH	FINAL
GT	7	10	0	7	24
STAN	0	3	3	8	14

SCORING SUMMARY
GT Glover 5 run (Manget kick)
STAN FG Biselli 35
GT Campbell 34 pass from Godsey (Manget kick)
GT FG Manget 20
STAN FG Biselli 26
STAN Johnson 4 pass from Lewis (Wells pass from Lewis)
GT Campbell 2 run (Manget kick)

GT	TEAM STATISTICS	STAN
20	First Downs	20
137	Rushing Yards	125
23-38-0	Passing	17-34-0
266	Passing Yards	225
403	Total Yards	350
4-44.3	Punts - Average	4-35.0
0-0	Fumbles - Lost	0-0
3-35	Penalties - Yards	4-20
29:37	Possession Time	30:23

INDIVIDUAL LEADERS
RUSHING
GT: Gregory 19-91; Hall 7-32.
STAN: Allen 10-41; Carter 11-37.
PASSING
GT: Godsey 23-37-0, 266 yards, 1 TD.
STAN: Fasani 11-21-0, 115 yards.
RECEIVING
GT: Campbell 10-106, 1 TD; Smith 4-58.
STAN: Johnson 6-45, 1 TD; Powell 5-94.

DECEMBER 30, 2002
WAKE FOREST 38, OREGON 17

	1ST	2ND	3RD	4TH	FINAL
WAKE	7	14	10	7	38
ORE	3	7	7	0	17

SCORING SUMMARY
ORE FG Siegel 45
WAKE Mughelli 1 run (Wisnosky kick)
WAKE Anderson 57 pass from MacPherson (Wisnosky kick)
WAKE MacPherson 1 run (Wisnosky kick)
ORE Parker 7 pass from Clemens (Siegel kick)
WAKE FG Wisnosky 43
ORE Floberg 1 run (Siegel kick)
WAKE Anderson 63 pass from MacPherson (Wisnosky kick)
WAKE Barclay 12 run (Wisnosky kick)

WAKE	TEAM STATISTICS	ORE
23	First Downs	13
256	Rushing Yards	125
9-16-0	Passing	20-41-0
241	Passing Yards	165
497	Total Yards	290
5-48.4	Punts - Average	6-50.0
3-0	Fumbles - Lost	1-1
3-15	Penalties - Yards	2-10
34:34	Possession Time	25:26

INDIVIDUAL LEADERS
RUSHING
WAKE: Barclay 19-82, 1 TD; Davis 9-65.
ORE: Smith 18-62.
PASSING
WAKE: MacPherson 9-16-0, 241 yards, 2 TD.
ORE: Clemens 19-31-0, 161 yards, 1 TD.
RECEIVING
WAKE: Anderson 3-157, 2 TD; Landfried 3-45.
ORE: Howry 5-50; Parker 4-43, 1 TD.

SHRINE BOWL

PROFILE

Site: Little Rock, Ark.
Stadium: Arkansas War Memorial Stadium
Capacity: 31,500
Surface: Grass

SEASON	DATE	PRE-GAME RANK	TEAMS	SCORE	FINAL RANK	MOST VALUABLE PLAYERS	ATT.
1948	Dec. 18, 1948		Hardin-Simmons	40			5,000
			Ouachita Baptist	12			

DECEMBER 18, 1948
HARDIN-SIMMONS 40, OUACHITA BAP.12

	1ST	2ND	3RD	4TH	FINAL
HS	0	6	14	20	40
OUA	0	12	0	0	12

SILICON VALLEY CLASSIC

PROFILE

Site: San Jose, Calif.
Stadium: Spartan Stadium
Capacity: 31,500
Surface: Grass

PLAYING SITES

Spartan Stadium, since 2000

NAME CHANGES

Silicon Valley Football Classic, since 2000

SEASON	DATE	PRE-GAME RANK	TEAMS	SCORE	FINAL RANK	MOST VALUABLE PLAYERS	ATT.
2000	Dec. 31, 2000		Air Force	37		Mike Thiessen and Dave Adams,	26,542
			Fresno State	34		Air Force; Asen Asparuhov, Fresno State	
2001	Dec. 31, 2001		Michigan State	44		Nick Myers and Charles Rogers, Michigan State	30,456
		20	Fresno State	35		Bryce McGill, Fresno State	
2002	Dec. 31, 2002		Fresno State	30		Rodney Davis, Jason Stewart, Fresno State	10,142
			Georgia Tech	21		Asen Asparuhov, Fresno State	
2003	Dec. 30, 2003		Fresno State	17		Rodney Davis, Fresno State, RB	20,126
			UCLA	9			
2004	Dec. 30, 2004		No. Illinois	34		DeWitt Betterson, No. Illinois, RB	21,456
			Troy State	21			

DECEMBER 31, 2000
AIR FORCE 37, FRESNO STATE 34

	1ST	2ND	3RD	4TH	FINAL
AFA	19	15	3	0	37
FRES	7	0	13	14	34

SCORING SUMMARY
AFA FG Adams 37
AFA McKay 29 pass from Thiessen (Adams kick)
AFA FG Adams 46
AFA McKay 13 pass from Thiessen (run failed)
FRES Gaines 73 pass from Carr (Asparuhov kick)
AFA Thiessen 1 run (Adams kick)
AFA Thiessen 9 run (Jessop pass from Thiessen)
FRES Greco 2 pass from Carr (Asparuhov kick)
AFA FG Adams 24
FRES Burch 8 pass from Carr (pass failed)
FRES Berrian 47 pass from Carr (Asparuhov kick)
FRES Berrian 51 pass from Carr (Asparuhov kick)

AFA	TEAM STATISTICS	FRES
28	First Downs	18
267	Rushing Yards	59
12-24-0	Passing	22-38-1
204	Passing Yards	391
471	Total Yards	450
3-26.0	Punts - Average	5-40.2
0-0	Fumbles - Lost	2-1
4-41	Penalties - Yards	9-82
38:17	Possession Time	21:43

INDIVIDUAL LEADERS
RUSHING
AFA: Thiessen 18-99, 2 TD; Palmer 4-56.
FRES: Ward 5-27; Gaines 5-16.
PASSING
AFA: Thiessen 12-24-0, 204 yards, 2 TD.
FRES: Carr 22-33-1, 391 yards, 5 TD.
RECEIVING
AFA: Labasco 3-68; McKay 4-56, 2 TD.
FRES: Berrian 7-162, 2 TD; Gaines 4-102, 1 TD.

December 31, 2001
Michigan State 44, Fresno State 35

	1ST	2ND	3RD	4TH	FINAL
MSU	17	20	0	7	44
FRES	14	7	7	7	35

SCORING SUMMARY

FRES	Spach 5 pass from Carr (Asparuhov kick)
MSU	Rogers 72 pass from Smoker (Rayner kick)
MSU	Wedlow fumble recovery in end zone (Rayner kick)
FRES	Wright 36 pass from Carr (Asparuhov kick)
MSU	FG Rayner 41
MSU	Duckett 5 run (Rayner kick)
FRES	Wright 79 pass from Carr (Asparuhov kick)
MSU	Duckett 39 run (Rayner kick)
MSU	Rogers 69 pass from Smoker (kick failed)
FRES	Gaines 2 run (Asparuhov kick)
FRES	Gaines 15 pass from Carr (Asparuhov kick)
MSU	McCoy 5 pass from Smoker (Rayner kick)

MSU	TEAM STATISTICS	FRES
23	First Downs	25
210	Rushing Yards	29
22-32-1	Passing	35-58-2
376	Passing Yards	531
586	Total Yards	560
2-3	Punt Returns - Yards	3-27
5-108	Kickoff Returns - Yards	6-115
6-38.7	Punts - Average	5-39.6
0-0	Fumbles - Lost	0-0
8-64	Penalties - Yards	6-30
34:43	Possession Time	25:17

INDIVIDUAL LEADERS

RUSHING
MSU: Duckett 27-184, 2 TD; Smoker 9-17.
FRES: Gaines 10-26, 1 TD; Wright 2-19.

PASSING
MSU: Smoker 22-32-1, 376 yards, 3 TD.
FRES: Carr 35-56-2, 531 yards, 4 TD.

RECEIVING
MSU: Rogers 10-270, 2 TD; Haygood 5-49.
FRES: Wright 13-299, 2 TD; Berrian 9-94.

December 31, 2002
Fresno State 30, Georgia Tech 21

	1ST	2ND	3RD	4TH	FINAL
GT	7	0	14	0	21
FRES	3	10	7	10	30

SCORING SUMMARY

FRES	FG Asparuhov 22
GT	Watkins 35 pass from Suggs (Manget kick)
FRES	FG Asparuhov 42
FRES	Meza 48 interception return (Asparuhov kick)
GT	Bilbo 1 run (Manget kick)
FRES	Davis 3 run (Asparuhov kick)
GT	Smith 42 pass from Bilbo (Manget kick)
FRES	FG Asparuhov 33
FRES	Davis 28 run (Asparuhov kick)

GT	TEAM STATISTICS	FRES
16	First Downs	20
130	Rushing Yards	186
9-27-6	Passing	16-31-0
218	Passing Yards	188
348	Total Yards	374
4-59	Punt Returns - Yards	3-7
3-54	Kickoff Returns - Yards	2-72
5-38.6	Punts - Average	7-37.3
2-1	Fumbles - Lost	3-2
5-53	Penalties - Yards	10-94
21:54	Possession Time	38:06

INDIVIDUAL LEADERS

RUSHING
GT: Eziemefe 3-38; Smith 7-35.
FRES: Davis 37-153, 2 TD; Pinegar 9-20.

PASSING
GT: Bilbo 7-20-4, 178 yards, 1 TD.
FRES: Pinegar 16-31-0, 188 yards.

RECEIVING
GT: Bridges 3-94; Watkins 5-82, 1 TD.
FRES: Gilbert 4-84; Jamison 5-50.

December 30, 2003
Fresno State 17, UCLA 9

	1ST	2ND	3RD	4TH	FINAL
FRES	14	3	0	0	17
UCLA	0	7	2	0	9

SCORING SUMMARY

FRES	Sumlin 1 run (Visintainer kick)
FRES	Sumlin 44 pass from Pinegar (Visintainer kick)
FRES	FG Visintainer 36
UCLA	Bragg 27 pass from Olson (Medlock kick)
UCLA	Safety

FRES	TEAM STATISTICS	UCLA
20	First Downs	11
156	Rushing Yards	68
12-26-1	Passing	11-31-1
133	Passing Yards	96
289	Total Yards	164
4-75	Punt Returns - Yards	2-12
4-31	Kickoff Returns - Yards	1-12
7-32.9	Punts - Average	9-44.3
2-0	Fumbles - Lost	2-0
8-71	Penalties - Yards	5-55
35:58	Possession Time	24:02

INDIVIDUAL LEADERS

RUSHING
FRES Davis 13-77; Wright 13-58.
UCLA: Drew 17-65.

PASSING
FRES: Pinegar 12-26-1, 133 yards, 1 TD.
UCLA: Olson 11-31-1, 96 yards, 1 TD.

RECEIVING
FRES: Sumlin 1-44, 1 TD; Wood 3-33.
UCLA: Bragg 5-71, 1 TD; Cowan 3-16.

December 30, 2004
Northern Illinois 34, Troy State 21

	1ST	2ND	3RD	4TH	FINAL
NI	14	10	3	7	34
TS	14	0	0	7	21

SCORING SUMMARY

TS	McDowell 1 run (Whibbs kick)
TS	Richardson 23 pass from McDowell (Whibbs kick)
NI	Wolfe 50 run (Nendick kick)
NI	Haldi 1 run (Nendick kick)
NI	FG Nendick 30
NI	Haldi 1 run (Nendick kick)
NI	FG Nendick 39
NI	Harris 3 run (Nendick kick)
TS	McDowell 4 run (whibbs kick)

NI	TEAM STATISTICS	TS
17	First Downs	13
213	Rushing Yards	170
8-24-0	Passing	6-22-1
146	Passing Yards	122
359	Total Yards	292
0	Fumbles Lost	0
4-40	Penalties - Yards	4-29
32:8	Possession Time	27:52

INDIVIDUAL LEADERS

RUSHING
NI: Harris 23-120, 1 TD; Wolfe 15-84, 1 TD.
TS: Betterson 25-150; McDowell 13-18, 2 TD.

PASSING
NI: Haldi 8-24-0, 146 yards.
TS: McDowell 6-20-1, 122 yards, 1 TD.

RECEIVING
NI: Powers 1-47; Cieslak 2-35.
TS: Samples 3-87; Richardson 1-23, 1 TD.

POSTGAME WRAP-UP

ACKNOWLEDGMENTS

Talking about football games, Woody Hayes once said, "You win with people."

If the ESPN College Football Encyclopedia is a winner, it further proves the Hayes maxim, because this book wouldn't have been possible without the help of a countless number of talented, committed people. But let me try to count them anyway.

The two people most responsible for the finished product—the offensive and defensive coordinators, if you will—are ESPN The Magazine editorial research director Craig Winston and BCS pollster Richard Billingsley. This is their book as much as it is mine.

Winston is living proof that if you need something done, you should ask a busy person. In addition to his already extensive duties with The Magazine, he threw himself into this project and directed virtually every aspect of the book's production from New York, acting as my conduit for all editorial page flow. But he didn't stop there. He visited both the NCAA national headquarters and the College Football Hall of Fame to help us unearth some of the extensive statistical treasures that appear in this book, and he personally tracked down many of the missing pieces over our three-plus years of producing the book. When someone had a question about style or page flow or production in New York—and every day brought more people with more questions—they lined up outside Craig's office.

It was Billingsley's exhaustive database that we used to start our reporting on the all-time scores for the 119 Division I-A schools and the Ivy League. But in addition to presiding over and inputting those 111,000 game results, Richard also constructed the one-of-a-kind poll progression charts dating back to 1936, and offered invaluable assistance on the Annual Review pages. His conscientious attention to detail was an inspiration to us all throughout the project. My friend Pat Porter's invaluable computer expertise was crucial in getting Richard's massive database on speaking terms with the designers' QuarkXPress publishing program.

The major editing work came from Vahe Gregorian and Glen Waggoner, a pair of accomplished, award-winning writers in their own right. Vahe helped me wade through the first pass of the lengthy manuscript, and communicated with our team of more than 20 different writers. Glen applied his bright, rigorous editing eye to the copy once it got to New York, and saved us all from numerous errors in the process.

The first writer I asked to help me was Dan Jenkins, in the belief that any book about college football needed to have not only his blessing, but also his active participation. I want to thank Dan and all the writers who followed for spending so much of the past few years working so hard on my behalf. I'm especially grateful to Seth Wickersham, Dan Galvin, Chris Pepus and Ryan Hockensmith, all of whom were called in late to help us finish the daunting job of chronicling the histories of the schools.

The ESPN College GameDay crew of Chris Fowler, Lee Corso and Kirk Herbstreit was involved throughout the production, and it will be my pleasure to hand the book off to them to bring around to college campuses this fall. They were joined in the Elevens section by such luminaries as Keith Jackson, Edwin Pope, Blackie Sherrod, Furman Bisher and Bill Curry. Thanks also to Mark Gross for all his help along the way.

The book's crisp, handsome design was realized in collaboration with Ellen Scordato at the Stonesong Press and Peter Romeo at Mada Design, Inc. The wonderful cover design is the work of Eric Baker. The helmets on the cover and in the 16-page center section were researched and carefully drawn by Carey Chiselbrook, founder of the Helmet Project, whose knowledge of the subject is the very definition of "encyclopedic." Helping on design-related issues through Stonesong were Beth Adelman, Marcella Durand, Kelsey Goss and Chris Orr. At Mada Design, we worked with founder Stan Madaloni, along with Alan Fiore, Cindy Chan and Jasmine Marcin, for design and typesetting. We're also grateful to the Collegiate Licensing Company for helping us gain approval for use of the helmet images.

The multitasking Lesley McCullough oversaw the Profile boxes in each team's history—even as she was working on her master's degree at Northwestern—synthesizing information from a variety of sources. And in addition to his writing, Hockensmith tracked down 135 years of All-America teams, and then put together the consensus All-American charts that are a featured part of the annual review section.

In the research phase, we relied heavily on the work of Roger Jackson, who knows of what he speaks when it comes to college football, as well as Mike Ogle, Gueorgui Milkov, Jordan G. Brenner and Jonathan Wank, each of whom spent a ridiculous amount of time overseeing different aspects of the book. They received extensive assistance from Gregory

Michael Blanco, John Boell, Dale Brauner, Simon Brennan, Matthew A. Cole, Shauna DeGeorge, Terence Egan, Eric Eichelsdorfer, Chris Fallica, Raymond A. Franklin, Robert Gallance, Dan Galvin, Chris Gasiewski, Shawn Geraghty, Nigel Goodman, Ian Gordon, David Hyde, Ted Keith, Daniel Kim, Lindsay Krasnoff, Jennifer Levine-Smith, Evan Markfield, Douglas McIntyre, Matthew Meyers, David Mikesell, Douglas Mittler, Mike Mott, Amy K. Nelson, David Ortiz, Shekar Sathyanarayana, Howie Schwab, Russell Slaton, Tim Sultan, Darrell Trimble, Luke Waltzer, Matthew Wong and Michael J. Woods. I also received invaluable research help along the way from Rob Minter, Kevin Lyttle and Michael Point, as well as Larry Kindbom, head football coach at Washington University in St. Louis.

The copy received a thorough polish from Michael J. Agovino, Tim Carroll, Andrew Chaikivsky, John Cochran, Steve Horne, Ethan Lipton, Andrew Littell, Jonathan A. Malki, Mark Miller, J.B. Morris, Anna Moschovakis, Adrienne Onofri, Michael Rubin, Peter Rubin, Michael Solomon, Lauren Spencer and David Sutter. Mike Ogle lent a hand here, too.

Helping with the production and operations of the big book were Perry L. van der Meer, managing editor of The Magazine, and editorial operations manager Christian Sean Rogers, who helped us pull together an army of copy editing and production people. Gavin Aghamore, Lee Berman, Jed Davis, Mark Decker, Sabina Eberle, Pakij Kent Ochjaroen and Alan Sikiric all helped out along the way. Jon Bergh and Tony Gentile shared their considerable wisdom on systems technology.

On the promotions side, we received help from Sandy DeShong, Ellie Seifert and Kim Willis. I want to also thank Maria Delgado, for handling my travel arrangements, and Judy Mezi, Laurie Chamberlain and Grace Gallo, for helping me navigate the ESPN universe. Grace also helped with the questionnaires we sent to all of the schools we featured in the text.

At the NCAA, director of information Rick Campbell was our point man for the endless stream of informational requests and clarifications. We are also indebted to Bo Carter, Big 12 Conference; Therese Gonzalez, Great Lakes (Ill.) Naval Museum; Michael Kotlanger, University of San Francisco archivist; Bernie McCarty's *All-America: The Complete Roster of Football's Heroes*; George K. Rugg, special collections, Notre Dame University; Kent Stephens, College Football Hall of Fame; Heidi Wiseman, Mishawaka-Penn-Harris Public Library, Mishawaka, Ind.; Russell Slaton, and Keith Meador, SoonerStats.com, as well as the sports information directors of each school we wrote about.

Presiding over the big-picture issues were Gretchen Young of Hyperion and, later, Chris Raymond of ESPN Books. Both are book people with a passion for the minute details that separate good books from great ones, and they have been a pleasure to work with.

This monumental project never would have gotten off the ground without the enthusiastic support of John Walsh and John Skipper of ESPN. I'm forever grateful to count them as friends and bosses. One of the ways the "worldwide leader in sports" got that way is because everyone pitches in. Proof came from senior vice president and general manager Geoff Reiss, who graciously permitted us to tap ESPN The Magazine's editing, research and production resources to complete the project, and from ESPN The Magazine editor in chief Gary Hoenig, who served as wise counsel throughout, and then freed up key members of his staff for help on the last two years of the project. Jay Lovinger provided his expert editorial input early in the game.

On a more personal note, I'm grateful to my friends in the business, agent Sloan Harris and lawyer Rick Pappas, for their continued guidance. And I want to thank my mother, Lois MacCambridge, as well as Danica Frost, Greg Emas, Brian Hay and Dr. Keith O. Garner for their help and support throughout the project. Mostly, I'm grateful to my children, Miles and Ella, who have spent a lot of time at FedEx Kinko's over the past few years. Someday, I hope they'll both spend a sunny autumn Saturday afternoon in the stands at Ann Arbor or Palo Alto or Lincoln. And then they'll understand what this was all about.

MJM
St. Louis, June 2005

POSTGAME

CONTRIBUTORS

Andrew Bagnato attended his first college football game on Oct 17, 1970. He saw his father's alma mater, Pittsburgh, overcome a 35-8 halftime deficit to defeat archrival West Virginia 36-35 in Pitt Stadium. Not surprisingly, he was immediately hooked on the sport. After graduating from Northwestern University in 1985, Bagnato joined the *Chicago Tribune*, just in time to cover Notre Dame's last national title team in 1988. Bagnato reports on national college football and basketball for *The Arizona Republic*. He lives with his family in Phoenix.

Historian, freelance writer and Bowl Championship Series pollster, **Richard Billingsley** has been ranking college football teams for over 35 years. Since being selected by the BCS in 1999, Billingsley has been instrumental in shaping the formula used to determine the national championship. Currently he serves as the designated representative of the computer group to the BCS.

When **Chuck Culpepper** was 9, his father, mother, uncle and aunt—Virginia Cavaliers fans to the core—took him to see Virginia Tech edge Virginia 6-0 on Nov. 6, 1971, in Charlottesville. Somehow, he managed to surmount that disappointment and become an avid follower of college football, even during his four years at … the University of Virginia. He has written about college football as sports columnist at the Lexington (Kentucky) *Herald-Leader*, sports columnist at *The Oregonian* in Portland, and sportswriter at *Newsday* in New York. Chuck says he particularly loves walking into Times Square at 5:30 a.m. on a Saturday in the fall, hailing a taxi to an airport, and ending up in someplace like Auburn.

Beano Cook, who graduated from the University of Pittsburgh in 1954, has been writing about and commenting on college football for more than 50 years, for ESPN, ABC Sports and the *Football News* among others.

Stu Durando covers college sports for the *St. Louis Post-Dispatch*, where he has worked since 1996. The graduate of Cal State Fullerton previously spent seven years at the *Las Vegas Sun*.

Dan Galvin is a reporter for *ESPN The Magazine*. His father, Jim, two brothers, James and Robert, and sister Kelly gather around the TV on Saturdays to watch their father speak in tongues to the Notre Dame coaching staff. The whole family still believes the Rocket clipping penalty was a bad call.

Derrick Goold covers the St. Louis Cardinals and Major League Baseball for the *St. Louis Post-Dispatch*. For three years, he covered the St. Louis Blues and the National Hockey League for the paper.

Kevin Gleason, columnist for the *Times-Herald Record* in Middletown, New York, has been a sportswriter for 20 years. He's won several awards in column, enterprise and feature writing, and has covered Army football as a beat writer and columnist for 12 years. Gleason lives in Middletown with his wife, Mary Beth, and two young children, Gabrielle and Dillon.

Vahe Gregorian has been with the *St. Louis Post-Dispatch* since 1988 after earning his master's degree at the University of Missouri. He has covered national college football and basketball since the mid 1990s and the Olympics since 1996. The University of Pennsylvania graduate is a four-time first-place writing award winner in the Football Writers Association of America contest and three-time Missouri Sportswriter of the Year. His work was published in *Best American Sportswriting 2001*.

Bob Harig, a graduate of Indiana University, covers college football and golf for the *St. Petersburg Times* and ESPN.com.

Ryan Hockensmith grew up in central Pennsylvania doing what all kids from central Pennsylvania do—root for Penn State. In November 1989, as a present for his 12th birthday, he got to see his first game at Beaver Stadium where the Nittany Lions forced West Virginia Heisman candidate Major Harris into five fumbles and an interception in a 19-9 win. Hockensmith cultivated his love for college football as a PSU student, graduating in 2001 with a degree in journalism. Today he covers college football as an associate editor at *ESPN The Magazine*.

Michael Hurd has written for *USA Today* and the *Austin American-Statesman*, among many publications, and is the

author of *Black College Football, 1892-1992: One Hundred Years of History, Education, and Pride.*

Dan Jenkins is one of America's most acclaimed sportswriters as well as a best-selling novelist, not to mention a native Texan who grew up watching such Southwest Conference football immortals as Sam Baugh, Davey O'Brien, Bobby Layne and Doak Walker.

Todd Jones is a sports columnist for the *Columbus Dispatch* and a former writer for the *Cincinnati Post*. The Associated Press Society of Ohio named him the best sportswriter in Ohio in 2003 and awarded him second place in the competition for best sports columns in 2004. The Cleveland Press Club awarded him first place for sports columns in Ohio in 2004. He is a member of the board of directors for the College Football Writers Association of America. Todd lives in Columbus, Ohio, with his wife and two daughters.

Ed Krzemienski is a professor of history. He has taught at Purdue, the Citadel and Indiana University-Purdue University Indianapolis. He is currently working on a book about college football in the south during the 1960s.

Chris Pepus is a freelance writer in St. Louis. His work has appeared in such publications as *American Theatre* and *St. Louis Magazine.*

Joe Posnanski has been a sports columnist for *The Kansas City Star* since 1996. Prior to joining *The Star*, Posnanski was a columnist in Cincinnati and Augusta, Georgia. He was named the best sports columnist in America by the Associated Press Sports Editors in 2003 and was featured in *Best American Sportswriting 2004.*

Dave Reardon was schooled on numerous playing fields, as well as at Northwestern University and the University of Hawaii. Then he became a sportswriter, working for the *Honolulu Star-Bulletin, Honolulu Advertiser, Gainesville* (Fla.) *Sun* and *Island Scene* magazine the past 25 years. He

is a multiple winner of Hawaii Publishers Association and Society of Professional Journalist awards for general column and sportswriting. But he considers being the occasional target of Steve Spurrier's wit and June Jones' ire his career highlights.

Mike Vaccaro is the lead sports columnist for the *New York Post*, as well as the author of *Emperors and Idiots*, detailing the history of the Yankees-Red Sox rivalry. A graduate of St. Bonaventure University, he lives in Hillsdale, New Jersey

Mark Wangrin is a senior writer with the *San Antonio Express-News* whose work has also appeared in *Sports Illustrated, The New York Times* and on ESPN.com. The Northwestern graduate contributed to *ESPN Sports Century* and co-authored *Raising Cole*. He lives in Austin, Texas, with his wife, Barbara, daughter, Makala, and son, Ben.

Seth Wickersham is a staff writer for *ESPN The Magazine*, where he has worked since graduating from the University of Missouri in 2000. A native of Anchorage, Alaska, he has covered three Super Bowls, two World Series, two Final Fours, the NHL and NBA playoffs and the Athens Games.

Seattle Times writer **Bud Withers** has covered college football and basketball since the early 1970s for three Northwest newspapers. He has written two books on college basketball, including *BraveHearts*, the story of the rise of the Gonzaga program.

Gene Wojciechowski, a senior writer for *ESPN The Magazine*, has written (or co-authored) six books of non-fiction and one novel, all on sports themes. He lives in Wheaton, Illinois.

Bruce Wood has been the beat writer covering Dartmouth College and Ivy League football for *The Valley News* for nearly 20 years. A graduate of Upsala College with a master's degree in journalism from Penn State, Wood also spent five years working in college sports information. He is currently a freelance writer.

Elevens

Try selecting your all-time favorites. Just try. It ain't easy.

MOST OF THE *ESPN COLLEGE FOOTBALL ENCYCLOPEDIA* is designed to settle arguments. This section is meant to start a few. We asked a panel of some of the foremost experts on college football to weigh in with their personal judgments on the best players, games and teams they've seen during their time spent watching college football.

There weren't many hard-and-fast rules. We asked the panel to name the 11 best players they ever saw, either live or on television, selecting one player from each of the main position groups, then adding four more wild-card choices from any position (denoted by an "x"). The other 11 bests and favorites are self-explanatory, entirely subjective, occasionally idiosyncratic and always deeply, passionately felt.

College football, of course, has a long-standing appreciation for the role of fans as the 12th Man, so we left room at the end for you to select your own Best 11 and 11 Best.

FURMAN BISHER

Longtime columnist, The Atlanta Journal-Constitution
North Carolina, 1938; Furman, 1999

Bisher's Best 11

QB	Steve Spurrier, Florida
RB	Charlie Justice, North Carolina
WR	Terry Beasley, Auburn
OL	Moon Pie Wilson, Georgia
DL	Richard Seymour, Georgia
LB	George Morris, Georgia Tech
DB	Terry Kinard, Clemson
x-RB	Jackie Parker, Mississippi State
x-TB	George McAfee, Duke
x-FB	Herschel Walker, Georgia
x-QB	Fran Tarkenton, Georgia

Bisher's 11 Best

Best Team Duke, 1938.

Best Season 1938, when Duke ripped through the season unscored on until the final minute of the Rose Bowl.

Best Game Tennessee 6, Georgia Tech 0, 1956.

Biggest Upset Georgia Tech 41, Virginia 38, 1990.

Best Bowl Game 1964 Sun Bowl: Georgia 7, Texas Tech 0.

Vince Dooley's first UGA team: little talent, lots of heart.

Best Stadium Kenan Stadium, Chapel Hill.

Best Fans Furman University.

Best Uniforms. Any that I can read the numbers on, such as not Tennessee.

Best Book Don't know that I've seen one better than the one I was involved with, titled *The College Game*.

Favorite Coach (Tie) Bobby Dodd and Vince Dooley.

Favorite Player So many of them—Ray Beck, Sam Huff, George Morris, Charlie Justice, Ace Parker, Bob King (Furman, 1937), Hootie Johnson.

BEANO COOK

Writer, historian, commentator, ESPN analyst
Pittsburgh, 1954

Cook's Best 11

QB	Jim Plunkett, Stanford
RB	O.J. Simpson, Southern California
WR	Larry Fitzgerald, Pittsburgh
OL	Orlando Pace, Ohio State
DL	Bruce Clark, Penn State
LB	Chuck Bednarik, Pennsylvania
DB	Johnny Lattner, Notre Dame
x-RB	Tony Dorsett, Pittsburgh
x-TB	Dick Kazmaier, Princeton (single-wing)
x-TB	Doak Walker, SMU (single-wing)
x-QB	Johnny Lujack, Notre Dame (also a super DB)

Cook's 11 Best

Best Team As the 1946 Notre Dame team did, the 1947 Fighting Irish won the national title. And as the 1946 team did, they never trailed once.

Best Season (Tie) 1946 and 1973. Just as there's no such thing as a bad Bogart movie, there's no such thing as a bad football season.

Best Game Nebraska 35, Oklahoma 31, 1971. Oh, what a beautiful game. Great games must mean something on a national level, and something must happen late in the game. This game had both.

Biggest Upset Navy 14, Army 2, 1950. Army lost its first game since 1947—and the national title to Oklahoma.

Best Bowl Game 1973 Sugar Bowl, which featured the first meeting ever between two national giants: Notre Dame 24, Alabama 23.

Best Stadium Ohio State's Ohio Stadium. It's all in the eye of the beholder.

Best Fans Nebraska. They show respect for teams and display sportsmanship, even to hated Oklahoma, in an age in which sportsmanship seems to be lacking more and more, even in Pee Wee football.

Best Uniforms Army. As noted, it's in the eye of the beholder.

Best Book *Saturday's America*, by Dan Jenkins. Nobody captures the color, the passion and the scene in college football better than Jenkins.

Favorite Coach Carmen Cozza, Yale. A class act for 32 years. He still has nightmares about the 29-29 tie with Harvard in 1968. Can you blame him?

Favorite Player Mike Ditka, Pittsburgh. In his senior year, 1960, Mike went 7-for-7 on all-opponent teams. (Three teams didn't vote.) At the conclusion of the Army game, an Army player told Mike as he was getting helped off the field after being injured on the last play of the game, "You, Mike Ditka, are the greatest player I've ever seen."

LEE CORSO

Player, coach, ESPN College GameDay *cohost*
Florida State, 1957

Corso's Best 11

QB	Roger Staubach, Navy
RB	Archie Griffin, Ohio State
WR	Braylon Edwards, Michigan
OL	Tony Boselli, Southern California
DL	Warren Sapp, Miami, Fla.
LB	Tom Jackson, Louisville
DB	Deion Sanders, Florida State
x-RB	Ernie Davis, Syracuse
x-QB	Michael Vick, Virginia Tech
x-QB	Matt Leinart, Southern California
x-TE	Kellen Winslow, Missouri

Corso's 11 Best

Best Team Southern California, 2004. In a big-time game, the Trojans destroyed an excellent Oklahoma team 55-19. They could have scored 70 points that day.

Best Season The 1959 season, highlighted by a dominant Syracuse team, the best defensive team in history.

Best Game Ohio State's win over Miami in the 2003 Fiesta Bowl for the national title.

Biggest Upset Troy 24, Missouri 14, 2004.

Best Bowl Game 1979 Holiday Bowl: Indiana 38, Brigham Young 37. There were eight lead changes in the game.

Best Stadium Neyland Stadium, Tennessee, at night.

Best Fans Nebraska.

Best Uniforms Michigan.

Best Book *Championship Football by 12 Great Coaches*, edited by Tom Ecker and Paul Jones.

Favorite Coach My own coach and mentor, Tom Nugent, one of the fathers of presnap motion in the Straight I. A terrific coach at VMI, Florida State and Maryland.

Favorite Player Roger Staubach, because he single-handedly took the Naval Academy to a shot at the national title in his junior year. Greatest season-long performance I ever saw.

BILL CURRY

Player, coach, ESPN color commentator
Georgia Tech, 1965

Curry's Best 11

QB	Byron Leftwich, Marshall
RB	Bo Jackson, Auburn
WR	Larry Fitzgerald, Pittsburgh
OL	John Davis, Georgia Tech
DL	Derrick Thomas, Alabama
LB	Maxie Baughan, Georgia Tech
DB	Charles Woodson, Michigan
x-LB	Mike Curtis, Duke (also a FB)
x-DL	Pat Swilling, Georgia Tech (also a LB)
x-QB	Peyton Manning, Tennessee
x-WB	Johnny Rodgers, Nebraska (also a KR)

Curry's 11 Best

Best Team Alabama, 1961. They refused to lose. Gritty, lightning quick, near perfect in their fundamentals.

Best Season 1997, my first year as an ESPN analyst, when Michigan and Nebraska were co-national champions. We broadcast four Michigan games, and I got to see Lloyd Carr surface as a big-game coach, Brian Griese become a championship quarterback and Charles Woodson win the Heisman by starring in all three phases of the game.

Best Game Arkansas at Ole Miss, 2001. Arkansas won in seven overtimes, and the score was so big I don't even remember it.

[Ed.'s note: It was Razorbacks 58, Rebels 56, Coach.]

Biggest Upset North Carolina 31, Miami 28, 2004. Going in, Miami was 6–0 and ranked No. 4, while the Tar Heels were 0–37–1 against Top 5 opponents. Now they're 1–37–1.

Best Bowl Game 2001 Rose Bowl: Washington 34, Purdue 24. A perfect Pasadena day. It's the only Rose Bowl I've ever attended. Nothing else in college football matches it. Purdue's Drew Brees and Washington's Marques Tuiasosopo were the marquee players, but the event itself was the star.

Best Stadium Tiger Stadium, Baton Rouge, at night. I first encountered this magical venue in 1961, when I was a Georgia Tech sophomore. I'd never heard a sound like that crowd. I've gone back as coach of two programs and as an analyst. I've only attended night games, and don't wish to be there in the light of day. The spirits would surely vanish.

Best Fans Bobby Bowden told me a story, one echoed by other Nebraska rivals, about a time in the 1980s when he took an upstart Florida State team to Lincoln. Somehow FSU escaped with a win, and Bobby said he worried about getting his players out of the stadium without incident. To his amazement, the people in red stood and escorted the Seminoles off the field to a standing ovation.

Best Uniforms Penn State. Simplicity and tradition. That says what JoePa believes, and what he believes is the truth.

Best Book *Bootlegger's Boy*, by Barry Switzer. No artifice, no self-flagellation, no self-aggrandizement. It's unvarnished truth, and it's compelling. And it explains the basis for Switzer's amazing success at Oklahoma.

Favorite Coach Bobby Dodd, with no close second. My college coach was light-years ahead of his time. In 22 years at Georgia Tech, 92% of his players graduated from one of the country's toughest schools. He won big, but so did his student-athletes. Bear Bryant often said, "Saturday, I'd rather look across the field and see anybody other than that damn Dodd. He can beat you with his brain!"

Favorite Player After my first two years at Georgia Tech, our record was 2–19–1. Two kids I was recruiting, linebackers Ted Roof and Pat Swilling, could have gone almost anywhere. They were persuaded to join us by the idea of building a unique team. Four years later, we were a Top 20 program. That wouldn't have happened without Ted and Pat. Roof's now head coach at Duke. Swilling had a long career in the NFL and later served as a state representative in Louisiana.

CHRIS FOWLER
ESPN College GameDay *cohost*
Colorado, 1985

Fowler's Best 11

QB	Tommie Frazier, Nebraska
RB	Barry Sanders, Oklahoma State
WR	Randy Moss, Marshall
OL	Orlando Pace, Ohio State
DL	Warren Sapp, Miami
LB	Cornelius Bennett, Alabama
DB	Deion Sanders, Florida State
x-RB	Herschel Walker, Georgia
x-LB	Zach Thomas, Texas Tech
x-LB	Pat Tillman, Arizona State
x-RB	Marshall Faulk, San Diego State

Fowler's 11 Best

Best Team Nebraska, 1995. Unbeaten champs who grew more untouchable as the season progressed, destroying Florida 62-24 in the Fiesta Bowl. Scary to watch.

Best Season 1990. A frantic championship chase, with upsets shaking up the polls through November. My alma mater, Colorado, won the AP's piece of the title, despite a loss and a tie, by holding on against Notre Dame in the Orange Bowl. Having been there in the depths of 1–10 seasons, I enjoyed a proud moment, untangling myself from a microphone cord in the postgame chaos and getting the first interview with coach Bill McCartney.

Best Game Ohio State's win over Miami in the 2003 Fiesta Bowl had everything: high stakes, overtime drama, controversy, heartbreak (I witnessed up close the excruciating mangled knee suffered by Willis McGahee) and triumph (the Buckeyes' first post-Woody national title).

Biggest Upset Temple 28, Virginia Tech 24, 1998. The Owls won in Blacksburg as five-touchdown underdogs. Payback was brutal the next year: Virginia Tech 62-7 in Philly.

Best Bowl Game 2003 Fiesta Bowl. (See Best Game, above.)

Best Stadium My favorite is the Rose Bowl, hands down. My favorite on-campus stadium is Florida's Swamp.

Best Fans South Carolina. Unquestioned loyalty and packed houses through thick and thin, mostly thin.

Best Uniforms LSU's home whites, USC's home cardinal and gold.

Best Book *The Junction Boys*, by Jim Dent.

Favorite Coach Steve Spurrier: enigmatic, entertaining, honest, brilliant.

Favorite Player Warren Sapp. A destructive force on the D-line, he was charismatic and very, very quotable.

KIRK HERBSTREIT

Former player, ESPN College GameDay *cohost*
Ohio State, 1993

Herbstreit's Best 11

QB	Michael Vick, Virginia Tech	
RB	Ricky Williams, Texas	
WR	Raghib "Rocket" Ismail, Notre Dame	
OL	Orlando Pace, Ohio State	
DL	Peter Boulware, Florida State	
LB	Micheal Barrow, Miami	
DB	Charles Woodson, Michigan	
x-QB	Art Schlichter, Ohio State	
x-QB	Jamelle Holieway, Oklahoma	
x-QB	Matt Leinart, Southern California	
x-RB	Bo Jackson, Auburn	

Herbstreit's 11 Best

Best Team Southern California, 2005. With the players they have returning, I think Pete Carroll will have one of the most prolific offenses we've ever seen. Combine that with his defensive scheme, and I think it could be one of the best teams ever to play college football.

Best Season 2002. Miami, coming off the national championship, rolled through the regular season again. Meanwhile, Ohio State stumbled, rumbled and fumbled along, needing a bunch of fourth-quarter comebacks to stay undefeated. Then, in a classic national championship game at the Fiesta Bowl, David beat Goliath 31-24.

Best Game Tennessee-Florida, 1998, when Tee Martin led the Vols to a 20-17 win en route to the national title. SEC people know Phillip Fulmer had a mental hump to get over when it came to Florida and Steve Spurrier. That game got the monkey off his back, and it showed Fulmer for what he is—one of the best coaches ever to coach in that conference.

Biggest Upset Alabama 34, Miami 13 in the 1993 Sugar Bowl. The Superdome was turned into Bryant-Denny Stadium, giving Alabama a huge home-field advantage. Miami had more talent on paper, but Alabama was a great team, and after that game, people had to put their defense up with the greatest in the game.

Best Bowl Game Ohio State's 31-24 national title OT thriller over Miami in the 2003 Fiesta Bowl. (See Best Season, above.) What a great thing for college football, to have the national title game go into double-overtime, and to see both teams play at such a high, competitive level.

Best Stadium Florida Field, University of Florida. I've been to just about every stadium in the country, and I think The Swamp is the most impressive because the noise is so deafening. You can be a foot away from someone and not be able to hear a word until the crowd noise dies down.

Best Fans Texas A&M. Doesn't matter how young or old you are, you stand for four quarters, and you go bananas for your Aggies. It starts with a Friday evening yell practice that draws 40,000. The Aggies fans are what I like to refer to as proactive, not reactive, and that's a crucial difference.

Best Uniforms Florida State's garnet pants, white shirts and gold helmets, especially late in the year when they have the decals all over the helmets. Just a great look.

Best Book *A Civil War*, by John Feinstein. A nice job of talking about a great rivalry (Army-Navy) and the meaning behind it, and what college football means to this country.

Favorite Coach Pete Carroll. He's revolutionizing the college game, not just with his skills as a tactical coach and recruiter, but also because of the way he motivates his team.

Favorite Player On offense, Eddie George, Ohio State. He was a talented player, but more important, he was a guy who got the most out of his ability with his work ethic, a guy you had to kick out of the weight room and the film room. And Eddie didn't care whether he had 50 yards or 300 yards; he was all about what the team did. On defense, Ed Reed, Miami. He's gone on to a great pro career, but for me he'll always be No. 20 for the Hurricanes. After some hard times his freshman and sophomore seasons, he capped his career with a national championship. A great leader; all he cared about was representing the U on the side of his helmet.

KEITH JACKSON

The Voice of College Football
Washington State University, 1954

Jackson's Best 11

QB	John Elway, Stanford	
RB	Earl Campbell, Texas	
WR	Larry Fitzgerald, Pittsburgh	
OL	Dave Rimington, Nebraska	
DL	Hugh Green, Pittsburgh	
LB	Jerry Robinson, UCLA	
DB	Charles Woodson, Michigan	
x-B	Doak Walker, SMU	
x-QB	Doug Flutie, Boston College	
x-RB	Archie Griffin, Ohio State	
x-LB	Les Richter, California (also a C)	

Jackson's 11 Best

Best Team Southern California, 1972. A remarkable group

of athletes. Never threatened in an unbeaten national championship season.

Best Season Has to be 2000, when 14 teams won 10 or more games. Oklahoma ran the table (13–0).

Best Game USC 21, UCLA 20, 1967. National championship, conference championship, Rose Bowl, Heisman Trophy—all decided in this one game.

Biggest Upset Penn State 14, Miami 10, 1987 Fiesta Bowl.

Best Bowl Game The 1979 Sugar Bowl: Alabama 14, Penn State 7. No. 2 beats No. 1, plus a hundred other story lines in this one, and a helluva goal-line stand by the Tide.

Best Stadium Rose Bowl.

Best Fans Nebraska.

Best Uniforms Michigan. Coach Crisler's winged helmets make it so, but he sure did mess up the kitchen when he designed the first one.

Best Book I still like Dan Jenkins' *Saturday's America*. And I'm glad it was written then, not now.

Favorite Coach Paul Bryant. Lots of sides to Bear. Brilliant at marketing his product.

Favorite Player Don McKeta, RB, Washington, 1958-60. Two Rose Bowl wins. Short on physical talent, but incredibly tough and willing. That one-eyed QB, Bob Schloredt, wasn't bad either. They played together on the same teams.

MICHAEL MacCAMBRIDGE

Editor, ESPN College Football Encyclopedia
Creighton, 1985; Northwestern, 1986

MacCambridge's Best 11

QB	John Elway, Stanford
RB	Tony Dorsett, Pittsburgh
WR	Johnny Rodgers, Nebraska
OL	Anthony Muñoz, Southern California
DL	Lee Roy Selmon, Oklahoma
LB	Al Wilson, Tennessee
DB	Roy Williams, Oklahoma
x-QB	Chuck Ealey, Toledo
x-RB	Billy Sims, Oklahoma
x-DL	Derrick Thomas, Alabama
x-DB	Deion Sanders, Florida State

MacCambridge's 11 Best

Best Team Southern California, 1972. Every year, someone gripes that they were robbed, or deserved a shot at No. 1. But after USC tore through its schedule and dismantled Ohio State in the Rose Bowl, no one complained. The Trojans were that good.

Best Season The underrated 1970 season, which opened with Stanford upsetting Arkansas on the road, gave us Elmo Wright's touchdown dance and marked the dawn of Oklahoma's lethal version of the wishbone. It concluded with a New Year's Day trifecta: Notre Dame knocking off unbeaten Texas in the Cotton, Stanford upsetting unbeaten Ohio State in the Rose and then Nebraska—courtesy of Jerry Tagge's outstretched arms on a fourth-quarter quarterback sneak—shading LSU 17-12 in the Orange Bowl for the national title.

Best Game The true game of the century: Nebraska 35, Oklahoma 31, 1971. The quality of play—and the severity of the pressure—is still palpable on repeat viewings.

Biggest Upset Northwestern's shocker against Notre Dame to open the 1995 season is a personal favorite. But the score that most defied belief was Kansas 23, Oklahoma 3 in 1975, snapping the Sooners' 28-game winning streak.

Best Bowl Game 1984 Orange Bowl: Miami 31, Nebraska 30. In front of a raucous Orange Bowl crowd, the Hurricanes knocked off the Cornhuskers. And Tom Osborne became a folk hero in defeat.

Best Stadium LSU's Tiger Stadium, at night.

Best Fans Texas A&M in a tight race over Nebraska and Arkansas. Standing throughout the game earns extra credit.

Best Uniforms UCLA's home unis, Michigan's road gear, Florida State's helmet. For a matchless combination, try the gorgeous day of Sept. 25, 1982, when Penn State in blue and Nebraska in red battled on Beaver Stadium's sun-drenched natural green grass in Happy Valley.

Best Book *Saturday's America,* by Dan Jenkins.

Favorite Coach The inimitable Jake Gaither at Florida A&M, who uttered these classic words: "I want my boys to be agile, mobile and hostile."

Favorite Player Masterful option quarterback Turner Gill, one of the great underrated leaders of his era, who posted a 28–2 record as a three-year starter at Nebraska. Gill was the first full-time black starting QB at Nebraska, and a cerebral, commanding figure who exuded an otherworldly presence and authority on the field. At a time when Nebraska's Scoring Explosion offense was making headlines, Gill was a bigger star within the state than any of his more celebrated teammates, such as Heisman winner Mike Rozier and top draft choices Dean Steinkuhler and Irving Fryar.

EDWIN POPE

Longtime columnist, The Miami Herald
Georgia, 1948

Pope's Best 11

QB	Sam Baugh, TCU
RB	Charley Trippi, Georgia
WR	Johnny Rodgers, Nebraska
OL	John Hannah, Alabama
DL	Bill Stanfill, Georgia
LB	Dan Morgan, Miami
DB	Doak Walker, SMU
x-QB	Johnny Rauch, Georgia
x-LB	Tommy Nobis, Texas
x-RB	Tony Dorsett, Pittsburgh
x-TB	Frank Sinkwich, Georgia

Pope's 11 Best

Best Team Miami, 2001. This team had everything: great quarterbacking with Ken Dorsey, a great defense led by Ed Reed. No wonder the Canes routed Nebraska in the Rose Bowl to win the national title.

Best Season I've never seen a bad one.

Best Game and Best Bowl Game 1984 Orange Bowl: Miami 31, Nebraska 30. Tom Osborne could have settled for a tie and the national championship, but he did the courageous thing—he tried a two-point conversion, and it failed.

Biggest Upset Navy 14, Army 2, 1950. Army's first loss since 1947 gave Oklahoma the national title.

Best Stadium University of Georgia, Between the Hedges. I was born there (well, a mile away) and I'd gladly die there.

Best Fans Nebraska. Most sportsmanlike. I wish they could bottle that stuff and bring it east.

Best Uniforms Michigan, of course, especially the helmet.

Best Book *American Football*, by Walter Camp. Published in 1891, it was (to my knowledge) the first book on college football. Amazingly, almost all of the principles Camp set forth still apply. Second place, and first for the "modern" era, goes to Dan Jenkins' *Saturday's America*. Just for research purposes, I shamelessly favor my own book, *Football's Greatest Coaches,* which by dint of copious TV plugs from Ed Sullivan, Red Barber and others enabled me financially to flee Atlanta for *The Miami Herald,* at least for the next 50-odd years.

Favorite Coach Tie between Wallace Butts, my second father in Athens, and, surprisingly, Bobby Dodd, the arch-enemy in Atlanta. Totally different and wonderful men.

Favorite Player Charley Trippi did everything for Georgia.

Brilliant runner with fantastic vision and instincts. Terrific passer. Fine punter. Good defender. The best player I ever saw. In fact, I never saw a better athlete than Trippi in *any* sport. A good guy to boot. As they say, you don't hardly get them kind no more.

BLACKIE SHERROD

Longtime columnist, The Dallas Times-Herald *and* The Dallas Morning News
Howard Payne University, 1941

Sherrod's Best 11

QB	Sam Baugh, TCU
RB	Doak Walker, SMU
WR	Johnny Rodgers, Nebraska
OL	Jim Weatherall, Oklahoma
DL	Dick Modzelewski, Maryland
LB	Tommy Nobis, Texas
DB	Johnny Lujack, Notre Dame
x-OB	Johnny Majors, Tennessee (also a DB)
x-OB	Billy Cannon, LSU (also a DB)
x-RB	Jim Brown, Syracuse
x-QB	Roger Staubach, Navy

Sherrod's 11 Best

Best Team Southern California, 1972.

Best Season 1969 was the best season I ever personally witnessed. Penn State, Texas and Arkansas competing for perfect records and the national championship, with everything coming down to Texas-Arkansas on Dec. 6. Before the season began, ABC—as a result of Beano Cook's foresight and urging—persuaded the two schools to move their game to a late date, after everything else was over. Beano looked like a genius when the Longhorns nipped the Razorbacks 15-14 before a huge TV audience, then capped the season by beating Notre Dame in the Cotton Bowl.

Best Game Texas 15, Arkansas 14, 1969.

Biggest Upset Notre Dame 7, Oklahoma 0, 1957.

Best Bowl Game 1970 Cotton Bowl: Texas 21, Notre Dame 17.

Best Stadium Ohio State's Ohio Stadium.

Best Fans Yale.

Best Uniforms SMU, 1935.

Best Book *Football's Greatest Coaches,* by Edwin Pope.

Favorite Coach Darrell Royal.

Favorite Player Doak Walker.

DAN JENKINS

Longtime writer, Sports Illustrated; *best-selling novelist*
TCU, 1953

Jenkins' Best 11

QB	Sam Baugh, TCU
RB	Tom Harmon, Michigan
WR	Johnny Rodgers, Nebraska
OL	Jim Weatherall, Oklahoma
DL	DeWitt Coulter, Army
LB	Tommy Nobis, Texas
DB	Doak Walker, SMU
x-RB	O.J. Simpson, Southern California
x-QB	Johnny Lujack, Notre Dame
x-DB	Charley Trippi, Georgia
x-WR	Michael Irvin, Miami

Jenkins' 11 Best

Best Team Southern California, 1972. John McKay's 12–0 Trojans destroyed every opponent, and why? They had Anthony Davis, Sam "Bam" Cunningham, Lynn Swann, Mike Rae, Charles Young and Richard "Batman" Wood, plus a couple of subs named Pat Haden and J.K. McKay. They scored more than 40 points against seven teams, including humiliations of Notre Dame (45-23) and Ohio State (42-17 in the Rose Bowl).

Best Season Two for me. The 1938 season has special meaning for the obvious reason that my old alma mater, TCU (10–0), led by Heisman winner Davey O'Brien, the nation's passing and total offense leader, won the national championship in a poll race with Tennessee (10–0), Oklahoma (10–0), Duke (9–0), Notre Dame (8–1), Cal (10–1), Carnegie Tech (7–1) and Pittsburgh (8–2). Don't laugh: Carnegie Tech was a power in the 1930s, as were the Horned Frogs. Today, when I think of TCU outpolling Oklahoma, Tennessee and Notre Dame, I wake up screaming.

Then there's 1947. The No. 1 race was another thriller involving Michigan (9–0), Notre Dame (9–0), Penn State (9–0), SMU (9–0–1), Kansas (8–0–2) and Texas (9–1). Never have so many legends spread so many heroics over so many fields in a single year. Among the stars: SMU's Doak Walker, Texas' Bobby Layne, Notre Dame's Johnny Lujack, Michigan's Bob Chappuis, Kansas' Ray Evans, Mississippi's Charlie Conerly, Arkansas' Clyde "Smackover" Scott, North Carolina's Charlie "Choo Choo" Justice and Alabama's Harry Gilmer.

Best Game Has to be a Poll Bowl between unbeatens with a big buildup, in which both teams play well. That means Nebraska 35, Oklahoma 31, Johnny Rodgers vs. Jack Mildren,

on Thanksgiving Day 1971 is still the boss of bosses.

Runners-up: Miami 26, Florida State 25 in 1987 (Irvin vs. Deion); SMU 14, Texas 13 in 1947 (Doak vs. Bobby); Notre Dame 0, Army 0 in New York in 1946 (Lujack vs. Davis and Blanchard).

Biggest Upset Nov. 16, 1957, in Norman, Okla., when the lowly Golden Domers (2–8 the previous year) stunned Oklahoma 7-0, ending the Sooners' 47-game winning streak.

Best Bowl Game It should mean something, and the 1970 Cotton Bowl did. National champion Texas 21, Notre Dame 17, decided on a Longhorns drive in the last moments, with Texas' James Street edging Joe Theismann in a quarterback duel. (Close second, 1975 Rose Bowl: USC 18, Ohio State 17. Pat Haden tops Archie Griffin.)

Best Stadium Rose Bowl, no contest. Michigan's Big House comes in second.

Best Fans Nebraska, hands down. Friendly, good sports, happy to have you in town, even if they lose, which is rare.

Best Uniforms Michigan. Especially in the dark jerseys. Simple. Reliable. And you can't go up against those Fritz Crisler helmets.

Best Book I like Beano's choice.

Favorite Coach Darrell Royal at Texas. Sharp, original, great at pregame, great at postgame, nobody smarter during the game. All-time most quotable.

Favorite Player Doak Walker, SMU. Merely the greatest player who ever lived, and one of the nicest. Ran, passed, caught, returned, blocked, tackled, intercepted, punted, place-kicked. A miracle man, dazzling in the open field. Won the Heisman in 1948, but should have won it in 1947, as well. Averaged 57 minutes a game in a platoon era. I've said it before: If Red Grange or Chic Harley were poetry in motion, the only people you could put in the backfield with Doak would be Byron, Shelley and Keats.

MY ELEVENS
(*Okay, now it's your turn…*)

Name_____

School, Year_____

QB_____

RB_____

WR_____

OL_____

DL_____

LB_____

DB_____

x-_____

x-_____

x-_____

x-_____

Best Team _____

_____

Best Season_____

_____

Best Game_____

_____

Biggest Upset _____

_____

Best Bowl Game _____

_____

Best Stadium _____

_____

Best Fans_____

_____

Best Uniforms _____

_____

Best Book _____

_____

Favorite Coach _____

_____

Favorite Player _____

_____

Care to share? Pick your own Best 11 and 11 Best. Make your case with a couple of lines. Log on to espn.com. Click on College Football. Then search for us with the keyword: CFE. We'll post the Top 10 Best 11s and 11 Bests each week. As noted at the top, this section is intended to *start* arguments, so let's hear from you.

ALABAMA/AUBURN
MICHIGAN/OHIO STATE
UCLA/USC

FEEL THE HATE.